Fiction,
Folklore,
Fantasy &
Poetry
for Children,
1876-1985

Fiction, Folklore, Fantasy & Poetry for Children, 1876–1985 was prepared by the R.R. Bowker Company's Database Publishing Group.

Senior staff of the Database Publishing Group:

Beverley Lamar, Managing Editor

Mike Gold, Manager, Systems Development
Antonio Penuela, Programmer Analyst

Peter Simon, Vice President, Database Publishing

Fiction, Folklore, Fantasy & Poetry for Children, 1876-1985

AUTHOR INDEX

ILLUSTRATOR INDEX

TITLE INDEX

AWARDS INDEX

R. R. BOWKER COMPANY
New York

Published by R.R. Bowker Company, a division of Reed Publishing USA
245 West Seventeenth Street, New York, N.Y. 10011
Copyright © 1986 by Reed Publishing USA,
a division of Reed Holdings, Inc.

International Standard Book Number (set) 0-8352-1831-7
International Standard Book Number (Vol. 1) 0-8352-2272-1
International Standard Book Number (Vol. 2) 0-8352-2271-3

Printed on acid free paper and
bound in the United States of America

Library of Congress Cataloging in Publication Data
Main entry under title:
Fiction, Folklore, Fantasy & Poetry for Children, 1876–1985
 "Prepared by the R.R. Bowker Company's Database
Publishing Division in collaboration with the Publications
Systems Department"—
Includes index.
1. Children's Stories. 2. Children's
 Stories—Bibliography—Indexes
I. R.R. Bowker Company. Dept. of Bibliography.
II. R.R. Bowker. Publications Systems Dept.
Z1037.A2C54 1986   [PN1009]   016.8080′8   84-20474
ISBN 0-8352-1831-7
ISBN 0-8352-2271-3
ISBN 0-8352-2272-1

Contents

Foreword

Out of recognition of the need for a comprehensive, single reference source covering children's literature, the R. R. Bowker Company began work on a bibliography of fictional work of children's literature in late 1983. As the activities of producing such a bibliography got under way, we realized that this task was monumental and decided to expand the scope of fictional works to include works we felt were akin to that category—folklore, fantasy and poetry. Covering the period of time from 1876-1985, a bibliography with over 133,000 entries was developed.

In tracing the history of cataloging information relating to children's literature, we realized that in order to publish a comprehensive reference work of this nature, we had to go beyond our immediate available sources of the AMERICAN BOOK PUBLISHING RECORD, and BOOKS IN PRINT Database, both of which collectively have approximately 3,000,000 titles. It was most difficult to locate one or two sources we felt would sufficiently supplement our existing databases. Because of this, we went to the source that basically reported all titles published by those publishers included—the PUBLISHER'S TRADE LIST ANNUAL for the years 1873-1975. A manual review of hundreds of these volumes was undertaken, and information for entries developed in the process. Additionally, for quality control checks and verification, we have used TWENTIETH CENTURY AMERICAN WRITERS, St. Martin's Press, 1978; BEST BOOKS FOR CHILDREN, 3rd edition, R. R. Bowker Company, 1985; BOOKS FOR BOYS AND GIRLS, 4th edition, Ryerson Press, 1966; CONTEMPORARY AUTHORS, Gale Research Publishing Company, 1962-1984; a microfiche of the LIBRARY OF CONGRESS SHELFLIST, Library of Congress Classification numbers PZ5-10.

To further enhance the value of this publication, we have also included information on twenty (20) children's book awards, honor books, and special merits of distinction given by the Award Society.

These awards and honors are among some of the most prestigious given to children's literature. The Awards and their codes are: American Book Award, ABA; American Library Association Notable Books for Children, ALA; Hans Christian Andersen, HCAM; Mildred L. Batchelder Award, MLB; Boston Globe-Horn Book Award, BGH; Randolph Caldecott Medal, RCM; Canada Council Children's Literature Prizes, CCCL; Canadian Library Association Book of the Year, CLA; Carnegie Medal, CMA; Kate Greenaway Medal, KGM; Amelia Frances Howard-Gibbon, AFH; International Board on Books for Young People, IBBY; International Reading Association Children's Book Award, IRA; Coretta Scott King Award, CSKA; National Book Award, NBA; National Council of Teachers of English, NCT; New York Times Choice of Best Illustrated Books for Children, NYT; John Newbery Medal, JNM; Scott O'Dell Award for Historical Fiction, SOA; and Laura Ingalls Wilder Award, LIW. Codes representing these awards are designated by us and are appended to specific editions of works that received them, (for example, if an award was given to a book published in 1937 by Harper and Row, the award code(s) will be appended to the entry for that specific edition only and not reprints, new editions etc.). Because this publication includes only titles published or distributed in the United States, listings for titles which originated in foreign countries will be incomplete.

Selection of Entries

The selection of data from the Library of Congress cataloging information was based primarily on the Library of Congress Classification numbers PZ5-10. For the categories of poetry, plays, legends, and songs we also used the content of subject tracings to identify works for children. Selecting entries from the PUBLISHER'S TRADE LIST ANNUAL proved, to say the least, to be a most formidable task. While some publishers had indicators as to whether or not titles were juvenile fiction, folklore, poetry, etc. others did not.

For such publishers, the selection was done subjectively based upon several contributing factors. The criterions used included, whether or not the author wrote prolifically for children and key words in titles such as stories, tales, rhymes, etc. While this could have resulted in some incorrect selection of titles, it was the best approach to select these titles because of the sparsity of entry information. At times, it was especially difficult to clarify the border between titles for children and young adults. Classical works retold for children were also selected. Entries selected for the early years of the PUBLISHER'S TRADE LIST ANNUAL are sometimes very sparse but, we have made every effort, through extensive research, to decrease the number of such entries. Although the title of this publication cites the years of titles included as 1876-1985, you will find approximately 3,889 dated titles included which were published prior to 1876. Mass markets publications are not included, as well as import titles that were not identified as being distributed in the United States.

Entry Information

Entries included list all of the following elements whenever they are available: Author/Editor(s), Primary Author Dates, Pseudonyms, Illustrators, Primary Illustrator Dates, variant form of author name, Title, Sub-Title, Series, Pagination entries with the notation p.c.m. are Cataloging in Publication entries (CIP) and do not have pagination, Size, Publication Date, Grade Levels, edition information, Library of Congress card number, ISBN Number, and Publisher. Author data

information preceded by four zeros (0000) signifies that birth dates for these authors could not be found. Special Award(s) notations are appended only to the editions that received award(s) (see list). Entries for which we could not locate publication dates will be annotated with "N.D.", in the place where dates should have been located.

Entries cataloged by the Library of Congress have not been modified and reflect cataloging rules for that period in which they were issued. We have, however, made every effort to standardize the authors' names, using as our source of authority CONTEMPORARY AUTHORS and the NATIONAL UNION CATALOG. To eliminate duplicate entries appearing under both pseudonyms and real names, we opt to use the form of name used most frequently by the Library of Congress, if titles were duplicated under both. Cross-references are made from real names to pseudonyms, and pseudonyms to real names as well as from joint authors, and variant forms of author names. Whenever possible, if a pseudonym was used by more than one author, the pseudonym will be cross-referenced to the real name when they are primary authors. In some instances, however, a common pseudonym cannot be uniquely identified with the appropriate work, therefore, the cross-reference is omitted. A primary example is the pseudonym Kathryn Kenny used by several authors who write books in the "Trixie Belden" Series.

Another group of writers with which we had great difficulty in appropriately crediting the authorship of specific works are the "ghost writers" of the Stratemeyer Syndicate. For clarification and authenticity of authors and their works affiliated with this syndicate, we used STRATEMEYER PSEUDONYM AND SERIES BOOKS, compiled and edited by Deidre Johnson, Greenwood Press, 1982. To date, the Stratemeyer Syndicate has produced over 1,300 books written under more than 100 pseudonyms. In some cases these pseudonyms belong to specific individual writers. Far more frequently, though, the pseudonyms were creations of the Stratemeyer Syndicate, itself, and the books produced under a certain pseudonym may have been the work of several ghost writers. Often times, there is little or no way to verify which ghost writer was responsible for which book. It was not unusual for a single book to be the product of several collaborating writers.

In cases where a verifiable source credits all books written under a recognized Stratemeyer Syndicate pseudonym to a single ghost writer, the titles will be listed under the pseudonym with a cross-reference given to the author's real name. The true author when identified as such is thereby accredited the sole authorship of those books.

In cases where a pseudonym is known only as a Stratemeyer Syndicate house name and has been used by more than one ghost writer, the books are listed under the pseudonym with a cross-reference given to the Stratemeyer Syndicate. The Stratemeyer Syndicate, as a corporate body, is thereby accredited the authorship of those books. In addition, when a verifiable source indicates that a specific ghost writer contributed to a specific book under a Stratemeyer Syndicate house pseudonym, that information will be included within the entry for that book.

The reader should understand that the Stratemeyer Syndicate is a collaborative organization and that any book published under its auspices may be the work of more than one writer. The Syndicate was, and still is, so incredibly prolific that there are simply no sources available to offer complete, uncontested, bibliographical information for every book it produced.

Format

There are four indexes, Author, Title, Illustrator and Awards.

Author Index

The Author Index includes all available information stated in the entry information. The alphabetical sequence of entries is: author or author information, editor, etc., title and publisher. Real names are cross-referenced to pseudonyms and pseudonyms to real names when used as primary author information. For example Norton, Alice Mary see Norton, André. Titles that have received an award(s) have a code(s) appended after the entry information. If the title has received more than one award, the codes representing the awards are separated by a semi-colon. Entries with and without publication dates without additonal authorship information, e.g. illustrator, will file at the beginning of their pertinent alphabetical sequence in order of publisher. Entries with and without publication dates which have additional authorship information will follow in order of the authorship information and then by publisher. Publishers are filed by the first letter of their names, e.g. J. B. Lippincott will file under J. The example of filing sequence is as follows:

> Author—Aesop
> Titles—Aesop's Fables
>   N.D.Leavitt
>   —Aesop's Fables N.D.
>   T. Y. Crowell
>   —Aesop's Fables. Chadwick,
>   Mara Louise Pratt, Mrs.,
>   ed. N. D. McKay
>   —Aesop's Fables. Conde,
>   J. M. Illus N. D. D Appleton.

Entries are filed according to these criterions: Author names are filed up to 35 characters and include author related information, for example, birth dates. An ampersand (&) used in a corporate author is converted to "and", Mc is changed to Mac, Dr. to Doctor, St. to Saint and Mr. to Mister. In cases where there are joint authors, as much of the second author's last name will be included to the maximum of 35 characters.

Titles are sorted under their respective authors for up to 40 characters including both the title and subtitle, however, the abbreviations Dr., St., and Mr. are not sorted when they are found in the titles.

Title Index

The Title Index includes all available information stated in the entry information. The alphabetical sequence of entries is: title, author, author related information, editor, etc., and publisher. Titles that have received an award have a code(s) appended after the entry information. If the title has received more than one award, the codes representing the awards are separated by a semi-colon. Titles having 40 characters sort to include their subtitle to 36 characters plus the first characters of the next four words. The filing sequence of titles in this index is the same as in the Author Index.

Illustrator's Index

The entries in this index are abbreviated. The main entry is the illustrator. Elements of entry included are: title (sorting parameters are as indicated in the author index), author related information, publisher and publication dates. Award code(s) is appended after the entry information.

Joint illustrators are listed collectively with cross-references. Titles are cross-referenced to the full Author Index entry by page number references.

Award Index

This index is in alphabetical sequence according to the name of the award. If a title has received more than one award it will appear under each of them. Titles will be listed under their respective award(s) in ascending order by publication dates. In any instance where the publication date is missing, the Library of Congress card number was used to generate this information.

As this goes to press, titles for the 1967 and 1974 ALA Awards have not yet been supplied to us. We are, therefore, unable to include them in this edition.

The entries are abbreviated. Elements of entry information included are: author, author related information, editor, etc., title, publisher and publication dates. Titles are cross-referenced to the Author Index by page number references.

Awards that are people awards cannot be appended to a specific entry, e.g. the Laura Ingalls Wilder Award, therefore, a listing for these awards will be found at the end of the alphabetical sequence of the Award Index. Unlike the other award(s), the dates for these listings indicate receipt dates of the awards.

Presented here is a brief description of the awards appended to the entries in this publication.

American Book Awards

This award was established in 1980 by the Association of American Publishers. It is an annual award and replaces the discontinued National Book Award. Two of its four purposes is "to recognize and reward books of literary and artistic merit" and to "generate the public awareness of books". Seventeen categories are represented, four of which pertain directly to children's literature and are children's fiction hardcovers and paperbacks (2) and non-fiction hardcovers and paperbacks (2). "There are also six categories which pertain specifically to graphics in which children's books are considered". The recipient must be a U.S. citizen who has written, translated or designed the book during the preceding year. A Louise Nevelson wall sculpture for graphic works and $1,000 for literary works are given as prizes.

American Library Association Notable Books for Children

This award is given by The Association for Library Service to Children (ALSC), a division of the American Library Association. Some of the criterions used by the committee in selecting books are "outstanding literary merit" and the likelihood of acceptance by children.

Hans Christian Andersen

This award is said to be the most distinguished international prize in children's literature. It was established in 1956 by the International Board on Books for young people and is given biennially. Originally given to an author since 1956, and an illustrator since 1966 (at least one author must be living). The recipient must have made an important contribution to children's literature internationally. The prize is a gold medal and a diploma.

Mildred L. Batchelder Award

This award honors Mildred L. Batchelder and was established by the Children's Services Division (now Association for Library Services to Children) of the American Library Association. Its purpose is to "encourage international exchange of quality children's books by recognizing U.S. publishers of such books, in translation." "It is presented annually to an American publisher for the most outstanding English translation of a children's book originally published in a foreign language in a foreign country during the preceding year." The winning publisher receives a citation.

Boston Globe-Horn Book Award

The Boston Globe and the Horn Book Magazine are co-sponsors of this award which was established in 1967. Initially, awards were given for text and illustration, however, these categories were changed in 1976 to outstanding fiction and non-fiction as well as illustration. Among some of the prizes the winners receive are "$200 and an engraved pewter bowl." The recipients of this award do not have to be American citizens but the books must be published here.

Randolph Caldecott Medal

The Randolph Caldecott Medal is an award given to an illustrator(s) of the most distinguished picture book. The late Frederic G. Melcher established this award in 1937, because he thought Randolph Caldecott (1846-1886) to be one of the most distinguished English illustrators. Awarded annually to books published in the United States during the preceding year by the awards committee of the America Library Association Children's Services Division, of the American Library Association, the recipient must be a citizen or a resident of the U.S.

Canada Council Children's Literature Prizes

This award is bilingual in nature because it is given to both French and English language authors and/or illustrators. Established in 1976 by the Canadian Council it is given annually to a Canadian or a "landed" immigrant with five years residence. "The book must be published during the preceding year, either in Canada or abroad". The award is monetary in the sum $2,500.

Canadian Library Association Book of the Year for Children Award

This award was established by the Canadian Association of Children's Librarians of the Canadian Library Association in 1946, and was first presented in 1947. It is an annual award given to a children's book of outstanding literary merit. The recipient must be a citizen or resident of Canada, and receives a bronze medal "bearing Albert Laliberte's figure of Marie Rollet Herbert reading with her children." Starting 1954-1973 a bronze medal was given to "the most outstanding French-Canadian Publication for children."

Carnegie Medal

This award is given to books published in the United Kingdom. It has been awarded annually since 1937 by the British Library Association and was created to mark the centenary of Andrew Carnegie's birth. The award is given to an outstand-

ing children's book written in English and first published the previous year in the United Kingdom.

Kate Greenaway Medal

This award is presented annually to an illustrator who has produced the most distinguished work in illustration of a children's book published during the preceding year. Administered by the British Library Association since 1955, it is given to children's books first published in the United Kingdom during the preceding year.

Amelia Frances Howard-Gibbon – Illustrator's Award

Amelia Frances Howard-Gibbon, after whom this award was named, was born in 1826 and died in 1874. This award was established in 1969 by the Canadian Association of Children's Literature; is given annually, and is presented to the most outstanding Canadian illustrator, for a work published in Canada. Included are picture books, fiction and non-fiction. Recipients must be Canadian born, or currently residing there. Nominations are made by members of the CACL. However, final selections are made by a five-member committee composed entirely of children's librarians. The recipient of this award is given a "monetary prize", as well as a citation and a medal designed by James Houston, a Canadian author and illustrator.

International Board on Books for Young People (IBBY) Honor List

Books for excellence in writing, illustration and translation, chosen by the same jury that selects the Hans Christian Andersen Awards, are recognized. This award has been established since 1956 and is given biennially. Works representing the best literature for children internationally are awarded.

International Reading Association Children's Book Award

This award is given to an author's first or second title for juvenile audience. The categories are fiction and non-fiction, as well as young adult titles written in any language. The author receives for his/her prize a plaque and $1,000. This is an annual award.

Coretta Scott King

The Coretta Scott King award was established in 1969. It is not only to commemorate the life and works of the late Dr. Martin Luther King, but also to honor Mrs. King. It is presented annually at the Ameican Library Association convention.

National Book Award

Established in 1950 by the Association of American Publishers, it did not include a children's category until 1969. This award recognizes the most distinguished book published during the preceding year. The recipient is given a $1,000 prize citation, and must be a U.S. citizen.

National Council of Teachers of English Award for Excellence in Poetry for Children

Presented by the National Council of Teachers of English, in the fall of 1977, it is given to a living American poet in recognition of his/her cumulated works in poetry.

New York Times Choice of Best Illustrated Books for Children

This award honors the highest quality illustrations in children's books published in the U.S. It was first awarded in 1952 and is given to books published in the U.S. during the year.

John Newberry Award

The late Frederic G. Melcher donated and named this award to honor John Newberry (1713-1767), whom it is said was the first publisher of children's books. Its original intent was to encourage "original and creative work in the field of books for children". Since 1922 and every year since, the Newberry Medal has been presented by an award committee of the Children's Services Division of the American Library Association. It is given to the author of the most distinguished contribution to literature for children published in the U.S. during the preceding year. The recipient must be a citizen of the U.S. or a resident, and receives a medal donated by the Melcher family.

Scott O'Dell Award for Historical Fiction

This award was established in 1981, by Scott O'Dell. The book content must be historical fiction set in the New World and have literary merit. It must have been published in the previous year by a United States publisher. It is given primarily to juvenile literature, but includes young adults also. This award is administered by the Advisory Committee of the Bulletin of the Center for Children's Books.

Laura Ingalls Wilder Award

This award is presented to authors and or illustrators who have indelibly and substantially over a period of years, contributed to children's literature. It was established in 1954 to honor the creator of the "Little House," Laura Ingalls Wilder books. From 1954 to 1960 it was given quinquennially. Since 1980 the award is presented every three years.

Acknowledgments

The R. R. Bowker Company extends great appreciation to Beverley Lamar, Managing Editor, the American Book Publishing Record Database, who supervised this project, and Janet Nelson-Henry, Editorial Coordinator. Ava Chevannes, Robert Davis, Judith Facey, Nancy Goldstein and Barbara Goldman, were Assistant Editors.

It would be impossible to conclude without mentioning the interest displayed, and the ideas contributed by Tess Carey of the Marketing Development Department; Michael Gold, Director, Systems Department and Tony Penuela, Systems Analysts who worked on the technical aspects of this project; and to Paul Fasana, Chief of Technical Services, of the New York Public Library, who was kind enough to let us use retrospective volumes of PUBLISHERS TRADE LIST ANNUAL.

1. Children's Literature Awards and Winners: a Directory of Prizes, Authors, and Illustrators 1st edition, Detroit, Neal-Schuman Publishers in association with Gale.

Introduction

It is truly an ambitious task to attempt identifying children's books earlier than a century ago, since books for children never attained the popularity accorded them today and toward the latter part of the nineteenth century. In the early years, prior to the eighteenth century, reading materials intended for children were intentionally didactic, moralistic or served merely as means of instruction. Books produced for children were designed to divert what was seen as their natural human instincts or tendencies to evil, and were meant to instill goodness in behavior and intellect.

The *Gesta Romanorum*, written about the fourteenth century, was perhaps one of the earliest books shared with children that contained stories of adventure and daring. Malory's King Arthur stories, *Aesop's Fables* and the *Reynard* tales were available later and widely known to people of letters although initially they were definitely not intended for children. These works were for the privileged adults, while children who had access to reading materials, were expected to read about proper deportment or exemplary ways of accepting death. The latter were often detailed in doggerel.

John Locke has been hailed as one of the first champions of children because of the ideas in his book, *Some Thoughts Concerning Education*, published in 1693. Locke implied that learning could be fun: "There may be Dice and Playthings with the letters on them . . . some easy pleasant Book Suited to His Capacity should be put into his Hands, where in the Entertainment that he finds might draw him on . . ." He even advised the reading of *Aesop's Fables* and *Reynard the Fox*, but warned against frightening stories about goblins and other creatures of the dark, and fairy tales which were not considered to have utilitarian values.

Early American books were usually based on books originally published in England, but by the latter part of the nineteenth century, the beginning dates for this bibliography, narrative fiction for children became the province of the children's magazines of the time. "Fiction" as Gillian Klein in a recent article in *Children's Literature in Education* (Vol. 17, no. 1: 58) states: "Can be crucial in the extension of understanding of imaginative experience of values and attitudes and of real learning for all children." Certainly the Horatio Alger stories which regularly appeared in *St. Nicholas* magazine may be said to have inspired a peculiarly American ethic. The road to success and riches was paved with hard work, honesty and discipline of the most rigorous order. Here, the moral issues revolved around integrity, stability and controlled use of one's inner resources.

Some of the magazines of the period were *The Riverside Magazine For Young People*, *Harper's Young People*, and *St. Nicholas Magazine*. Their significance lay in the fact that many of their authors of fiction were later represented in books written for children: writers such as Mark Twain, Frances Hodgson Burnett, Lucretia P. Hale, or Louisa May Alcott. They provided fare which became popular with children. Improvements in bookmaking, and the fine art of photoengraving meant there were better designed books as well. Artist, Howard Pyle and others associated with the Howard Pyle school of art: Maxfield Parrish, Jessie Wilcox Smith, and, notably, N.C. Wyeth were instrumental in illustrating books which were later to be received as classics in the field of children's literature. Books by Samuel G. Goodrich, *Peter Parley's Tales About America*, retained some elements of didacticism and were a popular series about history, geography and natural history, in the nineteenth century. Jacob Abbott's *Rollo* series also continued the instructional mode of the *Peter Parley* books with information presented in a palatable fashion for the young reader.

Books then, other than the Sunday school texts, etiquette manuals, and instructional hornbooks, became an acceptable medium for children by the end of the nineteenth century in America. Poetry, fiction, and fantasy themes formed a large part of their content. The Elsie Dinsmore books, which comprised a sizable series of twenty-six books, and the Horatio Alger books with over one hundred titles, the Susan C. Woolsey books about *Katy*, and the *Little Pepper* series by Harriet M. Lothrop, who wrote under the pseudonym of Margaret Sidney, captured the imagination and reading interests and appetites of children. *Treasure Island*, the adventurous tale about piracy, first appeared in serial form in the magazine, *Our Young Folks* in 1882, and Daniel Defoe's *Robinson Crusoe* was also a product of the nineteenth century.

With this brief glance at the early development of children's book publication it becomes apparent that trying to document by comprehensive listing those books written or published in this country for children is indeed a monumental undertaking.

1) The publication of children's books in this country has experienced phenomenal growth from the late nineteenth century to the present, declining only briefly during the years of World War II. In fact, the period between 1925 to 1940 has been referred to as the "Golden Age of Children's Bookmaking in America." Since then, approximately 2,000 children's books are published annually in this country.

2) The proliferation of *series* books poses a dilemma for selection or criteria for inclusion in any bibliography striving for comprehensive coverage.

3) There are books by popular authors, which have been "continued" and written by someone other than the original writer. The *Miss Pickerell* science series, the

famous Nancy Drew or Carolyn Keene mysteries now in the hands of the Stratemeyer syndicate, and the ever popular *Oz* books are good examples.

4) There are several editions of well-known 'classics' and landmarks in children's literature—some abridged, or adapted, many first issued in limited editions. One need only compare editions of *Arabian Nights, Aesop's Fables, Alice in Wonderland* to mention a few, many of which may be found with different illustrators, variations in texts and varying degrees of departure from the original contents of the first editions.

5) Books such as Defoe's *Robinson Crusoe* are part of a genre of books "adopted" by children but were not initially intended for children. Sources of reference may include such a title in adult fiction and may not include the title for juvenile use. Also interesting is a book like *Watership Down*, by Richard Adams which was published for both the adult and juvenile market. J.R.R. Tolkien's *Hobbit* and *Ring* stories are enjoyed by both children and adults.

7) Changing views and attitudes about children and the emergence of the teenage novel have confused the parameters of what constitutes a children's book today. Children's authors who may have several children's books to their credit may also write adult and young adult titles. Judy Blume comes to mind with her definitely identifiable younger books and faithful young audience who want to read everything after *Are You There God? Its Me Margaret*, and ask for *Forever*.

The penchant for looking for 'another good book' like the one read before probably explains the popularity of series among children. Many books in series do not always indicate their relationship to previous books and thus are difficult to identify. The Tolkien books are a case in point: *The Fellowship of the Ring, The Two Towers* and *The Return of the King*; or Mildred Taylor's trilogy, *Song of the Trees, Roll of Thunder Hear My Cry*, and *Let the Circle Be Unbroken*, all published by the Dial Press.

If the purpose of a comprehensive bibliography is to record for historical reasons the publications for children, it lessens the task somewhat. Many references are available, including The Library of Congress Catalog, listings of special collections such as the updated 1982 edition of Carolyn Field's *Special Collections in Children's Literature*, existing bibliographies from libraries or library organizations, booksellers' catalogs, standard library bibliographic aids, or other references. What compounds the difficulty in the compilation of such a work as this is the abundance of material which must be sifted through before selections can be made.

Some of the same frustrations confront the librarians engaged in a retrospective or cumulative compilation of children's books for public use. The greatest hazard, if it is to be a viable tool from which members of the public will seek out information or locate specific titles, is in finding that copies of some books are unavailable anywhere. Less challenging, however, than this comprehensive bibliography being published by Bowker, is the scope of work for a particular collection. In a library situation, it is possible to establish criteria that limit the scope and narrowly define the focus of the bibliography. Of course the scope is defined in this comprehensive bibliography, too, since it will only encompass children's books of fiction and related subjects such as folklore and poetry.

Considerations for one Library bibliography included a recognition of the favorable reception by children of certain books, the continuing availability of some titles on library shelves through the years, and use by librarians in their work with children. The timeless quality of the books and provision of a list that would serve the needs of students of children's literature and librarians were added criteria for inclusion. Unlike this Bowker bibliography, the library listing did not attempt complete inclusion of award-winning books, but reflected those titles that have withstood the test of time in child appeal. Librarians working with children on a daily basis not only consulted reliable reference sources, but also relied on their face to face contacts with children, judging their readers' reactions by their frequent requests for specific titles and subjects.

Selecting from the many editions which may have been published is a problem common to any bibliographer. For a smaller library list, however, it is easier to control and describe the purpose and intent of the list and the needs of the intended audience. While the library bibliography encompassed fiction, including picture books, non-fiction and reference materials, the intention was to present an overview within the framework of the different decades of time (1911-1986), and to indicate the changing attitudes, perceptions and everyday shifts in social and economic conditions which affected themes, formats and even the quantities of books published for children.

The advent of well-illustrated books by contemporary artists of the time, Beatrix Potter, and E. Boyd Smith, is duly noted in the mid-1900's. When in 1922, *The Story of Mankind* by Hendrik Van Loon was awarded the first Newbery medal, it signified the recognition and acknowledgement of the merits of good writing and a need for standards of excellence in books written for children. The 1920's still reflected the taste for books published abroad, especially those from England. There were Walter De La Mare's poetry anthology, Leslie Brooke's drawings for the nursery rhymes in *Ring O' Roses* and Eleanor Farjeon's original tales of fancy in her book, *Italian Peep Show...*, and A.A. Milne's *Winnie-the-Pooh*, with the Ernest Shepard illustrations. The reference books cited reflect the preoccupation with critical evaluation of the time: *The Three Owls* by Anne Carroll Moore (Macmillan), and *Realms of Gold*, compiled by Bertha E. Mahony and Elinor Whitney, (Doubleday).

Although series books were popular in the latter part of the nineteenth century, they appear on the library's bibliography with a listing of the popular titles from the 1930's: Jean de Brunhoff's *Babar* stories, P.L. Travers, *Mary Poppins* books and Laura Ingalls Wilder's American Saga as presented in *The Little House* books. The library followed its policy of careful evaluation of series books avoiding, as much as possible, automatically including all the works of one author. Each title in a series, therefore, that is included in a bibliography is evaluated singly on its own merit. The ones included have not only withstood the test of time, but the of individual evaluation.

In the selection of series titles for a comprehensive bibliography the real spectre to be faced is the multiple titles from the prolific pens of some authors. For example, Thornton Burgess' popular *Old Mother West Wind* stories was only the first of an eight volume series! The other problem is tracing authorship which was mentioned earlier in connection with different authors from the original. There is the inclination of some authors to write several books under different pseu-

donyms. Tracing pseudonymous authors may well complicate the indentification of a book by a specific author.

The children's book scene in this country during the 1950's and '60's was indicative of changes in the social and political climate of the time. While ethnic literature was always a part of the literature for children, it generally had its origins in Europe and was rooted in the European heritage or backgrounds of America's early immigrants at the turn of the century. Minority concerns and people who were not always represented by authors and illustrators from their own group, began to attain a noticeable visibility now. By the late 1960's, new Black authors and illustrators were first published and were to leave their imprint on the literature. Gwendolyn Brooks, the only Black to be awarded the Pulitzer prize for poetry, published her one book for children, *Bronzeville Boys and Girls* (Harper) in 1956. *To be a Slave*, by Julius Lester, illustrated by black artist, Tom Feelings, was cited as a Newbery Honor book. Virginia Hamilton's *House of Dies Drear* appeared in the 1950's and she was later to win a Newbery medal for her *M.C. Higgins the Great*. Ezra Jack Keats, though not a member of a minority group, pictured his protagonist, Peter, as a small black child in the book, *The Snowy Day* which was awarded the Caldecott medal. *Harriet the Spy,* by Louise Fitzhugh, though neither ethnic in theme nor character, brought a sophisticated look at modern lifestyles among the American middle class, in a children's book.

Picture books from the 1950's through the 1960's were plentiful and distinguished for their illustrations. There were books by Ungerer, Suess, Lionni, Taro Yashima, Wildsmith, Munari, and a black teenager, named John Steptoe. Maurice Sendak's *Where the Wild Things Are* brought a new insight to childhood and his book won the Caldecott award. It was also the time to bury easy readers like *Fun With Dick and Jane* and substitute in their place, Dr. Seuss' *Cat in the Hat*, and others inspired by his example, *Little Bear*, by Else Minarik with the Sendak drawings, and the first of a series by Peggy Parish, *Amelia Bedelia*.

Since the greater control can be exercised in a small bibliography, such as the one designed and based on an existing collection in a library, it is easier to readily discern those changes in attitudes about children and their books through the years. Should some books published in the early part of the century be retained on a retrospective bibliography if they fail to meet today's standards on stereotyping and sexist terminology and concepts? Should the only criteria for inclusion be sensitivity to the diversity of ideologies, people, and mores, that we presently find acceptable? These were the questions the librarians engaged in a library compilation have to answer. One device to justify inclusion of a questionable title is to note the problems in a carefully worded annotation of the book. On the one hand, if a book scores high on quality of writing, illustrations and theme or plot, and has been beloved by generations of children, it is at least historically a worthy candidate for inclusion. In a less comprehensive bibliography, the dilemma for the librarian is how to weigh various factors such as literary quality, child appeal, and readability when consulting numbers of children's books.

Some feel the need to classify books by subject; some bibliographies are graded. Then, the task is to match reading ability to subject matter. The difficulty with a graded bibliography is the tendency to overlook the fact that some children have abilities far beyond their grade assignment and others have interest beyond their reading skills. The danger here, too, is

that a parent or teacher may accept the assigned grade rating as dogma and fail to venture or explore other titles for the child's sake, because a book is supposedly a difficult book to read.

Today, even the category "picture book" is dubious as a classification intended for the very young. There is a vast difference between *Masquerade* and *Curious George* as a genre in picture books. There are also the wordless picture books, the pop-up books, and a range of reading difficulty may even be found among *ABC* books.

Recent changes in the publishing market have probably had the greatest impact on what is available in children's books. Any compiler of lists or extensive bibliography cannot fail to notice the number of books that are now out of print. If a bibliography is intended as a purchasing guide, the out of print status of a book is most discouraging to the potential buyer. As a reference tool however, a bibliography geared to a comprehensive listing will certainly include out of print titles to demonstrate the breadth of publications for children within designated periods of time. It is here that smaller library initiated bibliographies find the work frustrating, for out of print books may exist only on the shelves of some libraries and a new generation of children may be missing some latter day favorite that no modern book can quite duplicate in content and quality of presentation.

In a retrospective listing it becomes obvious that fairy tales, folk tales or hero tales are the most consistent and traditional of books present in children's literature since they represent a record often based on the oral traditions of various people and cultures. A study of some folk stories such as *Cinderella*, for example, may be found in variants as far distant as China and again in Europe. The folktale often confirms the kinship of people and the universality of the human experience in matters of traditional values. An extensive bibliography may include tales common to many cultures as well as the output of modern imaginative stories by creators such as Howard Pyle, Oscar Wilde, Hans Christian Andersen who based some of his stories on folk tales, Frank R. Stockton, Rudyard Kipling, or in recent times, Jane Yolen. More frequently, the listings may reveal the various retellings, and translations from many countries, based on the original sources, but adapted with new illustrations, or new formats, for different generations of children.

In the 1880's, Sidney Lanier's *The Boy's King Arthur,* was published. It was retold from Malory's *Morte d' Arthur*. A retelling of the Norse legend by James Baldwin, *The Story of Siegfried*, and Howard Pyle's, *Merry Adventures of Robin Hood of Great Renown in Nottinghamshire* appeared in the same decade. About the same time also, Pyle's collection of folk-like stories, *Pepper and Salt* was published. The original stories of Oscar Wilde, *The Happy Prince and other Tales* were published in New York while, by 1898, the first of the 'color' fairy books by Andrew Lang, *The Blue Fairy Book*, made its debut in the literature.

By the turn of the century, certain retellings were distinguished by illustrations in certain editions. There were the popular Arthur Rackham illustrations for perennial favorites like *Aesop's Fables*, for *Grimm's Fairy Tales* and Lewis Carroll's, *Alice in Wonderland*. The end of the nineteenth century and the early years of the twentieth was a favorable period for the publication of narrative fiction, fairy tales, fantasy and poetry.

With the influx of new immigrants to America in the early 1900's and the concept of a free public education system for children, (although children of the poor still had to work long hours), books became a visible part of children's leisure time entertainment. The children's magazines which flourished in the United States during the nineteenth century, as noted, contained a wealth of fiction by competent authors. Interspersed with the narrative fiction, were historical sketches and informational pieces, and poetry was also an important feature. Poets of the time included Robert Louis Stevenson whose *A Child's Garden of Verses* was first published in England. One American edition in 1905 was notable for its illustrations by Jessie Wilcox Smith. James Whitcomb Riley wrote a book of verse, in dialect, *Rhymes of Childhood*, the most popular of its poems probably being "Little Orphan Annie." A few years earlier in 1874, John Greenleaf Whittier's, *Child Life, A Collection of Poems*, included poets, Edward Lear, James Russell Lowell, and Elizabeth Barrett Browning in the anthology. *St. Nicholas Magazine* also initiated through its St. Nicholas League, in 1898, a contest for children who were awarded silver and gold badges if the prose or poetry they submitted was published in the magazine. Among these young contributors were poets, Rosemary and Stephen Benet, and others who were to become well-known essayists, novelists or journalists: Bennett Cerf, Edmund Wilson, Ring Lardner and Cornelia Otis Skinner.

Another memorable period for poets of children's verses occurred in the thirties and 1950's. There were the Benéts, Carl Sandburg, Laura E. Richards, and Robert Frost. Anthologists, Arnold Adoff and Lee Bennett Hopkins were responsible for the publication of works of contemporary poets among them many minority poets. Black poets, Arna Bontemps, Langston Hughes, Gwendolyn Brooks and in the 1960's, Nikki Giovani, and Lucille Clifton, were being represented in single volumes or in anthologies. Even a cursory study of the fiction and poetry section through the years may reveal the trends in children's literature.

The success of children's book publishing in this country during the 1920's brought with it a consideration for the quality of books being produced for children. The establishment of juvenile book departments, and the awarding of the Newbery Medal also had an impact on the type of books written and illustrated for children. Some publishing houses were known for their fine juvenile book departments. Macmillan had Louise Seaman as its children's book editor, and Doubleday, May Massee. Their names became synonymous with the discoveries of talented writers and illustrators for children's books. Added to the rise of interest in children's books, was the appearance of the *Horn Book Magazine* with its literary reviews devoted to children's books, and the critical appraisals and monitoring by Anne Carroll Moore from the time that she first worked at the Pratt Institute Free Library in Brooklyn and later at the New York Public Library. Miss Moore believed that "to miss the joy of reading and rereading outstanding books of the first class in childhood means irreparable loss, for no grown-up ever brings to story or poem what a child brings to his first reading." Her critical reviews were frank and direct. Even in her time, she spoke of developments in book-making which were making it possible to better reproduce illustrations in children's books, and she bemoaned, even then, what she called the "provokingly out of print" books she wished to place on her lists for children.

Years of economic decline, war, and experimentation in the educational field, have all affected books for children. Most significant perhaps were the changing views about children and childhood. Recognition of the child's interests at different stages of development, brought changes in educational thinking. Theories about child-rearing, though varied, were brought to the attention of parents, and ideas about the innate predilection of children to evil, were dismissed as the basis for moral teachings and training.

Even greater impact on books and the reading of children has been the evolution of new technology. In the printing of books, it has meant the 'streamlining' of processes for printing and the reproduction of illustrations for children's books. With new methods, however, costs have risen, the mass produced book has become more prevalent, while the complaint about the declining reading abilities of children has surfaced. The latter fact has affected the quality and degree of difficulty in the use of language in books for children today. Television has been blamed for the diminishing interst in books and reading. To meet the challenge, several creators of books for the juvenile market have produced stories that strive to capture the limited attention span of potential readers. Narrative fiction may be more episodic. The advent of the high interest, low reading level book for 'reluctant readers' is a modern phenomenon. Books for younger readers rely more on visual characteristics. There has been a reemergence of toy books in this century. There are trick books and pop-up books, and wordless books have become more evident.

High costs of paper for printing and financial restrictions on publishers' book lists have meant that in the 1980's, buyers of children's books are once more faced with the problem of the "provokingly out of print" titles. This is the omnipresent problem of the librarian in the '80's. The picture is not completely dismal, however. The concerns about children's education and methods of child-rearing, plus the alarming rate of reading failures in the schools, has brought a resurgence of interest in reading. Parents and educators speak of going "back to the basics" which includes Reading. Once educationists can be convinced that *the method* is not necessarily the message, books will come into their own once again.

Tim Trelease, in his *Read-Aloud Handbook*, in attempting to explain to parents, teachers and librarians, the reasons for reading aloud, has written that the purpose is: "to reassure, to entertain, to inform or explain, to arouse curiosity, and to inspire.... All those experiences create or strengthen a positive attitude about reading..." As Alice Jordan in an article on "Children's Classics", in the Horn Book Magazine (February 1947), noted, "Foundation for the growth of discriminating literary taste lies within the covers of...famous books, which open shyly the door of imagination, enchant by their poetry and humor... or simply give visions of unguessed worlds of adventure and friendship." These award-winning books, singled out as 'classics' of their time, along with recognized favorites, may be found in an extensive bibliography.

The absence of a single database of children's literature makes a comprehensive bibliography all the more desirable as a reference tool. By starting with fiction, folklore, fantasy, and poetry, it will be possible to examine the literature which has been created for children over the past century. Changing lifestyles, shifts in political thought, economic upheavals and new educational theories, and of course, technological discoveries are all reflected in the literature for children.

Good books for children particularly, engage the adult intellect as well as the child's. Each can bring a measure of appreciation, separated only by a depth of experience, to the reading of a good children's book. The more comprehensive the bibliography, the better the chance for the student of children's literature, the librarian, or interested parent, to see the breadth of publications in the field. It would be a good time to see whether the values expounded in the books for the young were truly different in the nineteenth century from the books in the twentieth century. Is there truth to the contention that today's children's books are as didactic, with perhaps more subtle meanings which still definitely attempt to teach the child reader? It would be interesting to make comparisons between the centuries of fiction books or books of fantasy to see whether fewer modern books are powerful enough to arouse the imagination and spark the emotional responses of children to books because of the instant action to which television exposes them. This bibliography should prove to be a valuable reference source and basis for study of children and their reading.

Barbara Rollock
Coordinator of Children's Services
New York Public Library

Children's Book Information:
R. R. Bowker Company's Service Tradition

The R. R. Bowker Company has been on its way to the production and publication of this monumental, retrospective list of books for children for over a century.

I am very glad that this company decided to pursue this project for these reasons:

- it provides part of the book publishing record that was never kept accurately.
- it will be of inestimable value to scholars, librarians, publishers, rare book dealers and their clientele.
- its existence means that never again will a member of R. R. Bowker Company's staff have to answer the question, "Why doesn't your company try to do something about an historic record of the children's books published in the United States?"

At last something—quite something!—has been done by R. R. Bowker Company about recording this country's steady growth in the numbers of books published for children. Recognize that it could be done because of relatively recent technological advances in information storage methods. And, remember that the R. R. Bowker Company has a long history of providing information, bibliographies and selection aids in support of the booksellers and librarians who work with reading materials intended for the young.

This tradition at R. R. Bowker Company was fostered for nearly 100 years by the first four men who successively lead the company from the last quarter of the 19th century to just past the middle of the 20th century—Frederick Leypoldt, Richard Rogers Bowker, Frederic G. Melcher and Daniel Melcher—1872-1968—a century during which the R. R. Bowker Company's commitment to children's book publishing concerns, children's bookselling problems and children's library service expansion goals provided a pattern for the corporations that purchased the company—Xerox in 1967 and Reed Publishing, U.S.A. in 1985.

* * *

Frederick Leypoldt (1835-1884)

The late Daniel Melcher, president of the R. R. Bowker Company from 1963 to 1968 once said, "A great variety of new Bowker publications could be developed (and many have been) from those that Frederick Leypoldt proposed or tried out, along with those which have been published continuously since he began them." This retrospective compilation of fiction, drama and poetry for children is just the latest example in support of Dan's contention. At long last, the new technology has made it possible to retrieve an essential part of the record of children's book publishing in the United States. In his day, it constituted a small fraction of Leypoldt's awesome resolution to provide the primary record of each year's total publishing output in his adopted country—a task he set himself in the 1860's.

Frederick Leypoldt is not as well known to booksellers and librarians today as other leaders of the R. R. Bowker Company—Richard Rogers Bowker himself or Frederick G. and Daniel Melcher. Certainly, his role in promoting children's book publishing and library services for children tends to be scanted in the slender collection of biographical essays on Leypoldt and overshadowed by his accomplishments as the founding editor of R. R. Bowker Company's *Publishers Weekly* and its *Publishers' Trade List Annual*. However, it is a fact that Leypoldt was a leader among the American publishers of the 19th century in his attention to books for children.

Leypoldt began publishing in Philadelphia in 1863 and among the 20 titles on the first list he issued were three that were widely used with children: *The Ice-Maiden and Other Tales* by Hans Christian Andersen, translated by Fanny Fuller; *The Sleeping Beauty in the Wood* (with 6 photographs of illustrations by Gustave Dore) by Charles Perrault; and the first American edition of *Landmarks of History* by Charlotte Mary Yonge.

Leypoldt continued to publish from Philadelphia until 1865. He continued to publish legends and he brought out American

editions of German and French renditions of *Mother Goose*. When he formed a partnership with Henry Holt in New York City in 1866, the lists took on a textbook emphasis, but some of Leypoldt's earlier selections for younger readers continued to be reissued.

After Leypoldt sold *Publishers Weekly* to Richard Rogers Bowker in 1879, this tireless organizer of the American publishing record continued to edit the magazine and start new projects of importance to the history of children's books and library services. Chief among these were *Books for the Young; a Guide for Parents and Children* in 1882 by Caroline M. Hewins and *Libraries and Schools*; papers selected by Samuel Swett Green issued in 1883, both landmark documents in the advancement of publishing and library services for the young. Neither title was expected to do much more than return costs to the publisher, but both exist as evidence of the company's founders commitment to promotion of the goals of our pioneer librarians. Hewins' guide sold steadily in quantity for many years.

Leypoldt, with Richard Rogers Bowker and Melville Dewey, were founding members of the American Library Association (ALA) in 1876 the same year that the R. R. Bowker Company with Dewey as editor began to issue *The American Library Journal*. Caroline M. Hewins was by 1882 well known for the missionary zeal she brought to work with children at what is now Hartford (Connecticut) Public Library. She was the first woman ever to address ALA's Council and regularly rose to lead its programs on work with the young. She maintained a heated correspondence in the letters columns of leading New England newspapers decrying the dearth of worthwhile books for children and the oversupply of dime novels, series and melodramas. When she was invited to publish *Books for the Young*, she was ready with an annotated list of over 100 titles that she had winkled from the undifferentiated by-age lists of American publishers as books worth the reading time of children. Hewins revised her list for R. R. Bowker Company in 1884 and this continued to sell very well until 1896. Hewins' list reappeared as one of the American Library Association's earliest publications in 1897 under the title *Books for Boys and Girls: A Selected List*, which was revised and reissued by ALA in two more editions in 1904 and 1915.

Frederick Leypoldt died at 49 years of age in 1884. There is a story handed down about him here at the R. R. Bowker Company. Nobody now living can swear it is true, but like all good stories that ought to be true, this one continues to get told. The legend has it that Leypoldt had a string that went from his desk chair to the wall behind it on which he dried out the handkerchiefs that he'd soaked with his tears, to which he was easily moved. Foremost among the many things that could move him to tears was the frequent, frustrating thought that he could never realize his dream of providing a completely accurate bibliographic record of each year of publishing in the United States. This was certainly true of the record of children's books published in his time. The publishers seldom identified, on their lists or in their advertising those books that might be of special interest to younger readers. We like to imagine that one of Leypoldt's hankies was always wet because of this oversight.

Richard Rogers Bowker (1848-1933)

I once asked Daniel Melcher to assess Richard Rogers Bowker's leadership of the R. R. Bowker Company after the death of Frederick Leypoldt. Dan chewed that question over for a week before he answered me. "He led by delegation," Dan

said. "You have to remember two things about R. R.," Dan said. "He was blind from 1902 on and the R. R. Bowker Company was only one of his enthusiasms. He led it by delegation, but make no mistake about it, R. R. set the tone."

R. R. Bowker: Militant Liberal (University of Oklahoma Press, 1952) by E. McClung Fleming is the best full portrait we have of the man who gave his name to this company over a century ago. A careful study of this carefully worded biography shows that even in his most active years, the R. R. Bowker Company took up less than 25% of R. R.'s working or thinking time. He was not driven by Leypoldt's resolves to produce general and specialized bibliographies—nor to drive his delegates to do so. Richard Rogers Bowker, however, continued to support and promote books and library services for children through the columns and coverage of his magazines, *Publishers Weekly* and *Library Journal* until he died.

Personally, I think the fact of R. R. Bowker's blindness prevented him from leading his staff to capture a specialized bibliographic record of children's book publishing after the start in 1919 of children's book departments in established publishing houses. By then, he was leading through delegation a staff of editors whose interests were directed to scholarly bibliography.

However, one can only speculate on whether or not a sighted Richard Rogers Bowker would have noticed children's books required a more accurate record than their own publishers gave them in supplying less than complete information on their children's books for *Publishers' Trade List Annual*.

What today's librarians can be most grateful for to Richard Rogers Bowker is his unflagging support for library services to the young, a concept he promoted with skill and vigor in his speeches and in his writings at every opportunity from 1876 forward.

Frederic Gershon Melcher (1879-1963)

Richard Rogers Bowker delegated well. He had a talent for identifying, attracting and keeping a superior team at his company. In 1918, he brought in Frederic G. Melcher as a vice president and general manager, who had 23 years experience as a bookseller behind him—18 years at Lauriat's bookstore in Boston and 5 years as manager of Stewart's bookstore in Indianapolis. During those years, F.G. Melcher had developed a deep and abiding love for children's books.

Frederic G. Melcher had a central role in the establishment of Children's Book Week (1919) and is best known now as the original sponsor of the John Newbery Medal (1922) and the Randolph Caldecott Medal (1937), the world's most successful literary prizes for children's books administered, selected and celebrated each year by ALA's Association for Library Service to Children. The Medals continue to be donated by F.G. Melcher's family.

Frederic G. Melcher was an artist at promoting his enthusiasms and a determined proselytizer for good books for children in the pages of *Publishers Weekly*. To his extensive acquaintanceship among book publishers and booksellers, both here and abroad, he added a numberless following among children's public and school librarians, who often turned to him for help in publicizing and promoting their projects and were never turned away.

In his years as R. R. Bowker Company's president, Frederic G. Melcher presided over the start of children's book reviews in both *Publishers Weekly* and *Library Journal* and the annual provision of selected lists of new books for children. What surprised me when I joined the R. R. Bowker Company in 1966

was that Frederic G. Melcher had never attempted to tighten up the reporting of available children's books through the *Publishers' Trade List Annual* or to mount an effort to retrieve the lost record. This did not rhyme with his demonstrated devotion to children's books.

As usual, I brought my question to his son, Daniel Melcher, who started off by telling me he didn't know why his father had not started this project. I suggested that perhaps the Great Depression followed by World War II might have made such an extensive bibliography for this underfunded, understaffed specialty in library services financially unfeasable. Dan said he didn't think that was the reason. I then suggested that no leading librarians of the '30's, '40's or '50's had asked his father for such a record. Dan said, "That's probably it."

It probably is. Frederic G. Melcher was responsive as a publisher to the indicated needs of the market for R. R. Bowker Company publications. During the 1930's, the 1940's and the 1950's, library specialists in work with children and young people were emphasizing such immediate practical needs as sufficient numbers of children's book reviews, topical selection aids, and more periodical and journal attention to and information on the library management problems associated with library work with the young.

It was also a period in children's library services when selectivity in library collections for younger readers was insistently promoted by public and school librarians as their mission. Leaders in this field spared very little attention to and raised few concerns about the missing paraphernalia of scholarship, of a history deliberately lost to the record by children's book publishers themselves who continued to fail to list all the children's books they kept in print in the catalogs they submitted for the *Publishers' Trade List Annual.*

If there had been a concerned audience among children's book publishers or librarians for an historic record of children's books published in the United States, Frederic G. Melcher would probably have tried to do something about it. He really cared about the history of publishing, particularly children's book publishing in this country and most particularly about R. R. Bowker Company's part in it. For instance, when in 1947 the New England Library Association decided to establish an honor lecture on children's books and library services, he rushed to propose himself as the donor of the honorarium for the lecture, which was named for Caroline M. Hewins. He was especially pleased to do this because of her connection with the R. R. Bowker Company through its first publication of her *Books for the Young* in 1882.

In 1947 Frederic G. Melcher hired his son Daniel Melcher, who became the firm's next president in 1963. Some months after Dan resigned as R. R. Bowker Company's chairman in 1969, I tried to pay him a great compliment. We were talking about his father and Dan asked me what I thought his father's greatest contribution to the company had been. He said he had his own ideas on this, but he was checking to see if other Bowkerites agreed. Dan Melcher was about as graceful in taking a compliment as a "hog on ice." After 3½ years of working with him I knew it, but I decided to try anyway. I said, "Your father's greatest gift to the R. R. Bowker Company was his son." He was very severe. He said, "I asked you a *serious* question." Well, I told him then and I mean it now—he got my serious answer.

Daniel Melcher (1912-1985)

When Daniel Melcher joined R. R. Bowker Company in 1947, the effect was like that of a stone flung in a calm pond. Over the following 20 years, one new project after another rippled out. Only those that had an impact on children's books and library services will be described here.

In the process of returning *Library Journal* to the cutting edge among library periodicals, Dan recognized the need for a similar publication for libraries serving children and youth. Against sustained opposition from his fellow officers, he founded *Junior Libraries* in 1954. The name was changed to *School Library Journal (SLJ)* in 1961 and the magazine flourished under his guidance. He perceived its Book Review services as *SLJ*'s center and presided over the decisions that led to the expansion of *SLJ* Book Review's mission to the coverage of all new children's general trade books issued each year.

By the middle of the 1960's, Dan was on his way toward adding the first edition of *Children's Books In Print* to R. R. Bowker Company's... *In Print* series, made possible when Dan devised methods and machines to index *Publishers' Trade List Annual.*

The expansion of *SLJ's Book Review* to total coverage of children's general trade book output brought a steady submission of the over 2,500 new children's books that were being issued each year. This resource, wedded to the 20,000 children's titles cataloged for *LJ* card kits formed a basis from which to plan *Children's Books In Print.* Dan had established a subsidiary of R. R. Bowker Company in 1966 to produce catalog card kits but had confined its first efforts to cataloging only those children's books issued in library bindings. Once again, this eventually very successful project had not appealed to the company's directors, but Dan had foreseen the demand for shelf-ready books that would arise as soon as the five-year flow of federal funds for books reached the nation's school libraries.

Dan Melcher helped secure the cooperation of the Children's Book Council, Inc., whose members agreed to supply copies of all of their backlist titles in trade bindings. This was combined with the *LJ Card Kits* records of children's book titles in library bindings, which enabled us to publish the first edition of *Children's Books In Print* in late 1969 and its companion volume, *Subject Guide to Children's* in early 1970, a great step toward control of the bibliographic record of children's books published in the United States.

It was an exciting time to be working closely with Daniel Melcher, who respected Frederick Leypoldt's genius, but whose own genius, vision and energy transcended that of the R. R. Bowker Company's founder.

As the plans for the first edition of *Children's Books In Print* moved forward, Dan alluded to the possibility of retrieving a closer record of the children's books of the past.

*   *   *

R. R. Bowker Company had over a century of leaders with an unusual regard for children's books and the people who work with them. It is the natural place to begin the Sisyphus task of finding, recording and making available this country's widely unrecognized contribution to the world of books—the children's books of yesterday and today.

Lillian N. Gerhardt
Editor-in-Chief
School Library Journal

September, 1986

Authors Index

A. C. D.
--Sylvia and Janet, 1 of 23 Vols. (Illus.). (Warne's Golden Links Ser.: No. 23). N.D. Scribner & Welford.
--Sylvia and Janet. (Warne's Star Ser.). N.D. Scribner & Welford.
--Sylvia and Janet: Or, Too Quickly Judged. N.D. Scribner, Welford & Armstrong.
--Sylvia and Janet. Too Quickly Judged. (Home Sunshine Library). N.D. R. Worthington & Co.

A. C. W.
--Aunt Rebecca's Charge. N.D. Bradkey & Woodruff's.

A. E. D.
--A Chance Acquaintance: Or, Susan's Lesson (Pub. by Society for Promoting Christian Knowledge). N.D. E. & J. B. Young & Co.
--Helen's Probation. N.D. E. & J. B. Young & Co.
--Vanity and Vexation (Pub. by Society for Promoting Christian Knowledge). N.D. E. & J. B. Young & Co.

A. E. H.
--Little Miss Duck. Willis, Bess Goe, illus. LC 30-195008. 56 p., 1 l. incl. col. front., col. illus. 15 cm. (Altemus' wee books for wee folks). c.1930. Henry Altemus Company.

A. E. W., pseud.
--Newlyn House: The Home of the Davenports. Mason, Alfred Edward Woodley. (Noble Aim Series for Girls). 1873. Leavitt & Allen Bros.

A Friend to Youth
--Love Triumphant: Or, Constancy Rewarded: in a Series of Familiar Letter, for the Amusement & Instruction of Youth, in Language Suited to Their Capacities. To Which Is Added, a Poetical Appendix. 122 p. front. 13 cm. 1797. Printed by Luther Pratt & Co.

A Lady
--Lights of Education: Or, Mr. Hope and His Family: a Narrative for Young Persons. LC 36-15509. iv, 9-179 p. 15 cm. 1825. E. J. Coale.

A. M. M.
--Katie Johnstone's Cross. (Illus.). N.D. Methodist Bk Concern.

A. R. W.
--Carrie Williams & Her Scholars, 1 of 20 vols. (Illus.). 197p. (Selected Bks for Sunday School: No. 23). N.D. Set. Methodist Bk Concern.

A. W. C.
--Sybil's Way. (Fern Glen Ser.). N.D. D. Lothrop Co.

Aanrud, Hans (1863-)
--Lisbeth Longfrock. Holmboe, Othar, illus. Poulsson, Laura Elizabeth (1851-), tr. LC 7-213627. ix, 149 p. front., 5 pl. 17 1/2 cm. 1907. Ginn & Company.

--Sidsel Longskirt and Solve Suntrap, Two Children of Norway. D'Aulaire, Ingri Mortenson & D'Aulaire, Edgar Parin (1898-), illus. Mortenson, Dagny & Bianco, Margery Williams, Mrs. (1880-), trs. LC 35-12195. 22cm. 257p. 1935. The John C. Winston company.
--Sidsel Longskirt, Girl of Norway. N.D. John C. Winston.
--Solve Suntrap: A Boy of Norway. D'Aulaire, Ingri Mortenson (1904-1980) & D'Aulaire, Edgar Parin (1898-), illus. Mortenson, Dagny & Bianco, Margery Williams, Mrs. (1881-1944), trs. vii, 128 p. col. front., illus., col. plates. 22 cm. c.1935. The John C. Winston Company.

Aardema, Verna (1911-)
--Behind the Back of the Mountains: Black Folktales from Southern Africa. Dillon, Leo (1933-) & Dillon, Diane (1933-), illus. LC 72-7602. (Illus.). 85 p. 24cm. 1973. Dial Press. **Award: (ALA).**
--Bimwili & the Zimwi: A Tale from Zanzibar. Meddaugh, Susan (1944-), illus. LC 85-4449. (Illus.). 32 p. 1985. (ISBN 0-8037-0212-4). (ISBN 0-8037-0213-2). Dial Books for Young Readers.
--Ji-Nongo-Nongo Means Riddles. Pinkney, Jerry (1939-), illus. LC 78-4038. (Illus.). 33 p. 26cm. c.1978. (ISBN 0-590-07474-1). Four Winds Press.
--More Tales from the Story Hat. Fax, Elton Clay (1909-), illus. LC 66-131372. 72 p. illus. 27 cm. 1966. (ISBN 0-698-30241-9). Coward-McCann.
--The Na of Wa. Fax, Elton Clay (1909-), illus. LC 60-12477. 1960. Coward-McCann Inc.
--Oh, Kojo! How Could You!. An Ashanti Tale. Brown, Marc Tolon (1946-), illus. LC 84-1710. (Illus.). 32 p. 28cm. 1984. (ISBN 0-8037-0006-7) (ISBN 0-8037-0007-5). Dial Books for Young Readers.
--Otwe. Fax, Elton Clay (1909-), illus. LC 60-12476. unpaged. illus. 23cm. 1960. Coward-McCann.
--The Sky-God Stories. Fax, Elton Clay (1909-), illus. LC 60-12475. unpaged. illus. 23cm. 1960. Coward-McCann.
--Tales for the Third Ear: From Equatorial Africa. Ohlsson, Ib (1935-), illus. LC 69-20308. (Illus.). 96 p. 24cm. 1969. Dutton.
--Tales from the Story Hat. Fax, Elton Clay (1909-), illus. Baker, Augusta, intro. by. LC 60-6852. 72p. illus. 27cm. 1960. (ISBN 0-698-30348-2). Coward-McCann.
--Tales from the Story Hat. Fax, Elton Clay (1909-), illus. (Illus.). (gr. 3-5). 1960. (ISBN 0-698-30348-2, Coward). Putnam Pub Group.
--What's So Funny, Ketu?. Brown, Marc Tolon (1946-), illus. LC 81-68776. p. cm. c.1982. (ISBN 0-8037-9364-2). (ISBN 0-8037-9370-7). Dial Press.

--Who's in Rabbit's House?. Dillon, Leo (1933-) & Dillon, Diane (1933-), illus. LC 77-71514. p. cm. c.1977. (ISBN 0-8037-9550-5). (ISBN 0-8037-9551-3). Dial Press.
--Who's in Rabbit's House?. A Masai Tale. Dillon, Leo (1933-) & Dillon, Diane (1933-), illus. LC 77-71514. (Illus.). 32p. (ps-3). 1979. (Pied Piper Book). Dial Bks Young.

Aardema, Verna (1911-), retold by.
--Bringing the Rain to Kapiti Plain. Vidal, Beatriz, illus. LC 80-25886. (Illus.). 30 p. c.1981. (ISBN 0-8037-0809-2). (ISBN 0-8037-0807-6). Dial Press.
--Half-a-Ball-of-Kenki: An Ashanti Tale. Zuromskis, Diane (1943-), illus. LC 78-16135. (Illus.). 31 p. 21cm. c.1979. (ISBN 0-7232-6158-X). F. Warne.
--The Riddle of the Drum: A Tale from Tizapan, Mexico. Chen, Tony (1929-), illus. LC 78-23791. (Illus.). 32p. (gr. k-3). 1979. (ISBN 0-590-07489-X, Four Winds). Scholastic Inc.
--Why Mosquitoes Buzz in People's Ears. Dillon, Leo (1933-) & Dillon, Diane (1933-), illus. LC 74-2886. p. cm. 1975. (ISBN 0-8037-6089-2). (ISBN 0-8037-6087-6). Dial Press. **Awards: (RCM); (ALA).**
--Why Mosquitoes Buzz in People's Ears: A West African Tale. Dillon, Leo (1933-) & Dillon, Diane (1933-), illus. LC 77-71514. (ps-3). 1978. (Pied Piper Bk). Dial Bks Young.

Aarle, Thomas Van
--Don't Put Your Cart Before the Horse Race. (gr. k-3). 1980. (ISBN 0-395-29095-3). HM.

Aaron, Chester (1923-)
--An American Ghost. 1st Ed. ed. Lemon, David Gwynne, illus. LC 72-88166. (Illus.). 189 p. 21cm. 1973. (ISBN 0-15-203050-6). Harcourt Brace Jovanovich.
--Better Than Laughter. 1st Ed. ed. LC 73-181536. 154 p. 22cm. 1972. (ISBN 0-15-206950-X). Harcourt Brace Jovanovich.
--Catch Calico!. 1st Ed. ed. LC 78-12319. 148 p. 22cm. c.1979. (ISBN 0-525-27551-7). Dutton.
--Duchess. 1st ed. LC 81-47755. 182 p. 21cm. c.1982. (ISBN 0-397-31947-9). (ISBN 0-397-31948-7). J B Lippincott Jr. Books.
--Gideon. 11 x 12 1/2. 200p. Repr. of 1982 ed (Pub. by Lippincott). (17 pt.). (gr. 7-10). N.D. Am Printing Hse.
--Gideon. LC 80-12779. p. cm. c.1980. (ISBN 0-525-30548-3). E. P. Dutton.
--Gideon. LC 81-48066. p. cm. c.1982. (ISBN 0-397-31947-9). (ISBN 0-397-31948-7). Lippincott.
--Hello to Bodega. LC 74-18176. 22cm. 183p. 1975. (ISBN 0-689-50015-7). Atheneum Publishers.
--Out of Sight, Out of Mind. LC 84-48356. 184 p. 21cm. c.1985. (ISBN 0-397-32100-7). (ISBN 0-397-32101-5). Lippincott.
--Spill. LC 76-28467. 214 p. 22cm. 1977. (ISBN 0-689-50069-6). Atheneum.

Aaron, Samuel Francis, jt. auth. see Whipple, Wayne.

Aasen, Helen B.
--Lilliput. (Illus.). (gr. 2-5). 1960. (ISBN 0-682-40001-7). Exposition.

Aaseng, Nate see Aaseng, Nathan.

Aaseng, Nathan (1953-)
--Batting Ninth for the Braves. 132p. (Orig.). (Pennypincher Bks.). (gr. 3-6). 1982. (ISBN 0-89191-708-X). Cook.
--Forty-Two Red on Four. LC 83-70902. c.1983. (ISBN 0-89191-754-3). Chariot Books.

Abbe, Elfriede Martha (1919-), illus.
--Seven Irish Tales. LC 57-48123. 44 p. 29 cm. 1957. Cornell University Press.

Abbe, George
Mr. Quill's Crusade. N.D. Island Press Cooperative, Inc.

Abbot, Alice Balch
--The Frigate's Namesake. 204p. N.D. Century Co.

Abbot, Anne Wales
--Good Boys' Annual: A Christmas and New Year's Gift. LC 15-21832. 3 p. l., 3-279 p. front., illus., plates 17 1/2 cm. N.D. Allen Brothers.

Abbot, Julia Wade, jt. auth. see Hallock, Grace Taber.

Abbot, Willis John (1863-)
--Philip Derby, Reporter. LC 22-18650. 4 p. l., 232 p. col. front. 19 1/2 cm. 1922. Dodd, Mead and Company.

Abbott, Charles Edward see Old Harlo, pseud.

Abbott, Charles Edward (1811-1880)
--Down the Hill: Or, The History of Samuel Woden. Old Harlo, pseud. LC 17-22992. 136 p. incl. front., plates. 14 1/2 cm. 1834. Crocker and Brewster.

Abbott, Edward
--Long Look House. Hinds, Helen Maria, illus. (The Long Look Ser.). N.D. Noyes, Snow and Company.
--Out Doors at Long Look. Hinds, Helen Maria, illus. (The Long Look Ser.). N.D. Noyes, Snow and Company.

Abbott, Elenore Plaisted, ed. see Grimm, Jakob Ludwig Karl (1785-1863) & Grimm, Wilhelm Karl.

Abbott, Ethelyn, jt. auth. see Cowles, Julia Darrow, Mrs.

Abbott, Frederick
--The Lollipop Tree. N.D. Bruce Humphries.

Abbott, Jacob, jt. auth. see Edgeworth, Maria.

Abbott, Jacob (1803-1879)
--Abbott. (The Rollo Story Bks.). N.D. Sheldon & Co.
--Abbott's Franconia Stories: Malleville, Mary bell, Ellen Linn, Wallace, Beechnut, Stuyvasent, Agnes, Mary Erskine, Rodolphus, Caroline, 5 vols; 2 in 1. (Orig.). N.D. Sets. Harper & Brothers Trade-List.
--Adventures of a Country Boy. Johnson, Clifton (1865-), ed. LC 16-1890. 270 p. incl. front., illus. 19 cm. c.1916. American Book Company.

--Agnes, 1 of 10 vols. (Illus.). (Franconia Stories: Vol. 10). 1882. Harper's Trade-List.

--The Alcove. LC 48-32259. (Illus.). 17 cm. 100p. (Harper's Story Bks.: No. 28). 1884. Harper & brothers.

--The Alcove: Containing Some Further Account of Timboo, Mark, and Fanny. LC 44-27168. xii, 13-160 p. incl. front., illus. 17 1/2 x 14 1/2 cm. (Half-title: Harper's story books. No. 23). 1856. Harper & Brothers.

--Apple Gathering. (The Rollo Story Bks.). N.D. Sheldon & Co.

--August and Elvie. (The August Ser.). N.D. Dodd & Mead Co.

--August and Elvie, 1 of 4 Vols. (August Ser.). N.D. Set. Thomas Y. Crowell & Co.

--August Stories, 4 Vols. N.D. Thomas Y. Crowell & Co.

--Beechnut, 1 of 10 vols. (Illus.). (Franconia Stories: Vol. 5). 1882. Harper.

--Beechnut: A Franconia Story. LC 75-280372. (Illus.). vi, 211 p. 17cm. 1850. Harper.

--Blueberrying. (The Rollo Story Bks.). N.D. Sheldon & Co.

--A Boy on a Farm: At Work and at Play. Johnson, Clifton (1865-), ed. LC 3-3874. 182 p. illus. 19 cm. (Lettered on cover: Eclectic school readings). c.1903. American Book Company.

--Bruno: Or, Lessons of Fidelity, Patience, and Self-Denial Taught by a Dog. LC 44-27169. viii p., 2 l., 13-160 p. incl. front., illus. 17 1/2 x 14 cm. (Half-title: Harper's story books. A series of narratives, dialogues, biographies, and tales, for the instruction and entertainment of the young. By Jacob Abbott. No. 1). 1854. Harper & Brothers.

--Caleb in the Country, 1 of 6 Vols. (Illus.). (The Jonas Bks.). N.D. Set. Clark & Maynard.

--Caleb in the Country, 1 of 6 Vols. (Jonas Ser.). N.D. Set. Thomas Y. Crowell & Co.

--Caleb in the Country. A Story for Children. LC 21-12212. 180 p. front. 16 cm. 1839. Crocker & Brewster.

--Caleb in Town, 1 of 6 Vols. (Illus.). (The Jonas Bks.). N.D. Set. Clark & Maynard.

--Caleb in Town, 1 of 6 Vols. N.D. Set. Thomas Y. Crowell & Co.

--Carl and Jocko: Or, The Adventures of the Little Italian Boy and His Monkey. LC 44-27170. 160 p. incl. front., illus. 17 1/2 x 14 cm. (Half-title: Harper's story books. A series of narratives, dialogues, biographies, and tales, for the instruction and entertainment of the young. By Jacob Abbott. No. 28). 1857. Harper & Brothers.

--Caroline, 1 of 10 vols. (Illus.). (Franconia Stories). 1882. Harper.

--Causey Building. (The Rollo Story Bks.). N.D. Sheldon & Co.

--Congo: Or, Jasper's Experience in Command. LC 44-27092. 160 p. incl. front., illus. 17 1/2 x 14 1/2 cm. (Half-title: Harper's story books. A series of narratives, dialogues, biographies, and tales, for the instruction and entertainment of the young. By Jacob Abbott. No. 34). 1857. Harper & Brothers.

--The Corner Stone, 1 of 4 vols. (Illus.). (Young Christian Ser.). 1882. Harper.

--Cousin Lucy Among the Mountains. new, rev. ed. LC 21-12214. 180 p. incl. plates front., illus. 15 1/2 cm. (Added t.-p.: The Lucy books). 1870. Clark & Maynard.

--Cousin Lucy at Play. LC 21-12213. 180 p. incl. front., plates. 16 cm. 1842. B. B. Mussey.

--Cousin Lucy at Play, 1 of 6 Vols. (Illus.). (The Lucy Bks.). N.D. Set. Clark & Maynard.

--Cousin Lucy on the Seashore. new, rev. ed. LC 21-12213. 1 p. l., 180 p. incl. front., illus., plates 15 1/2 cm. (Added t.-p.: The Lucy books.). 1870. Clark and Maynard.

--Cousin Lucy's Conversations. LC 21-12216. 180 p. incl. front., illus., plates. 16 cm. 1842. B.B. Mussey.

--Cousin Lucy's Stories, 1 of 6 Vols. (Illus.). (The Lucy Bks.). N.D. Set. Clark & Maynard.

--Cousin Lucy's Studies, 1 of 6 Vols. (Illus.). (The Lucy Bks.). N.D. Set. Clark & Maynard.

--Elfred: Or, The Blind Boy and His Pictures. LC 25-7524. 160 p. incl. front., illus. 18 cm. 1856. Harper & Brothers.

--Ellen Linn, 1of 10 vols. LC 1-3301. (Illus.). 16cm. 215p. (Franconia Stories: Vol. 7). 1852. Harper & brothers.

--Ellen Linn, 1 of 10 vols. (Illus.). (Franconia Stories: Vol. 7). 1882. Harper.

--The Engineer: Or, How to Travel in the Woods. LC 44-33361. 160 p. incl. front., illus. 17 1/2 x 14 cm. (Half-title: Harper's story books. A series of narratives, dialogues, biographies, and tales, for the instruction and entertainment of the young. By Jacob Abbott. No. 19). 1856. Harper & Brothers.

--The English Channel, 1 of 6 Vols. (The Florence Stories: Vol. 4). N.D. D. Lothrop Co.

--The English Channel. (The Florence Stories). N.D. Sheldon & Co.

--Florence and John, 1 of 6 Vols. (The Florence Stories: Vol. 1). N.D. D. Lothrop Co.

--Florence and John. (The Florence Stories). N.D. Sheldon & Co.

--The Florence Stories, 6 Vols. (Illus.). N.D. De Wolfe, Fiske, & Co.

--The Florence Stories. LC 23-24506. 4 v. fronts., plates. 17 cm. 1859. Sheldon & Company.

--The Florence Stories: Containing: "Florence and John" "The Orkney Island" "The English Channel" " Grimkie" "The Isle of Wight" "Florence's Return". N.D. D. Lothrop Co.

--Florence's Return. (The Florence Stories). N.D. Sheldon & Co.

--The Franconia Stories. LC 17-13033. 10 v. fronts., illus. 17 1/2 cm. 1850. Harper & Brothers.

--Franconia Stories. LC 21-12962. 10 v. fronts., illus. 17 1/2 cm. 1878. Harper & Brothers.

--Franconia Stories, 10 vols. (Illus.). 1882. Harper.

--The Franconia Stories. LC 4-17806. 17 1/2cm. 1904. Harper Brothers.

--Franconia Stories. Armstrong, Margaret Neilson (1867-), ed. Armstrong, Helen Maitland (1869-), illus. LC 23-127161. ix, 321 p. col. front., plates. 21 cm. 1923. G. P. Putnam's Sons.

--The Franconia Stories. Moynihan, Ruth Barnes, pref. by. LC 75-32164. 2 v. ill. 19 cm. (Classics of Children's Literature, 1621-1932). 1976, c.1850. (ISBN 0-8240-2277-7). Garland Pub.

--The French Flower. (The Harlie Stories). N.D. Sheldon & Co.

--The Freshet. (The Rollo Story Bks.). N.D. Sheldon & Co.

--Friskie, the Pony. (The Harlie Stories). N.D. Sheldon & Co.

--Georgie. (The Rollo Story Bks.). N.D. Sheldon & Co.

--The Gibraltar Gallery: Being an Account of Various Things Both Curious and Useful. LC 44-333629. xii, 13-160 p. incl. front., illus. 17 1/2 x 14 cm. (Half-title: Harper's story books. A series of narratives, dialogues, biographies, and tales, for the instruction and entertainment of the young. By Jacob Abbott. No. 22). 1856. Harper & Brothers.

--Granville Valley. LC 42-47442. 346 p. front., plates. 17 1/2 cm. (The August stories, v. 4). 1872. Dodd & Mead.

--Granville Valley. (Crowell's Library For Young People). N.D. Thomas Y. Crowell & Co.'s Catalogue.

--Granville Valley, 1 of 4 Vols. (August Stories). N.D. Set. Thomas Y. Crowell & Co.

--Grimkie, 1 of 6 vols. (Florence Stories: Vol. 2). N.D. Set. D. Lothrop Co.

--Grimkie. (The Florence Stories). N.D. Sheldon & Co.

--Handie, 1 of 5 vols. (Illus.). (Rainbow and Lucky Ser.). 1882. Harper.

--Harlie Stories. Gilbert, John Clitherae, illus. N.D. Worthington Company.

--Harlie's Letter. Gilbert, John Clitherae, illus. (Illus.). (The Harlie Stories). N.D. Sheldon & Co.

--Harper's Story Books: Containing: Bruno, Willie and the Mortgage and The Strait Gate, 12 Vols, Vol I. (Illus.). (The Harper Story Books Ser). N.D. Harper & Brothers.

--Harper's Story Books: Containing: Carl and Jocko, Lapstone, and Orkney the Peacemaker, 12 Vols, 3 bks. per Vol. (Illus.). (The Harper Story Book Ser). N.D. Harper & Brothers.

--Harper's Story Books: Containing: Congo, Viola, and Little Paul, 12 Vols., 3 bks. per vol, Vol. 12. (Illus.). (The Harper Story Books Ser). N.D. Harper & Brothers.

--Harper's Story Books: Containing: Elfred, The Museum, The Engineer, 1 of 12 vols. (Illus.). (Vol. 6). N.D. Set. Harper & Brothers.

--Harper's Story Books: Containing: John True, Elfred, and The Museum, 12 Vols., 3 bks. per vol, Vol. 6. (Illus.). (The Harper Story Books Ser). N.D. Harper & Brothers.

--Harper's Story Books: Containing: Judge Justin, Minigo, and Jasper, 12 vols, 3 bks. per vol, Vol. 11. (Illus.). (The Harper Story Books Ser). N.D. Harper & Brothers.

--Harper's Story Books: Containing: Prank, Emma, and Virginia, 12 vols, Vol. II. (Illus.). (The Harper Story Books Ser). N.D. Harper & Brothers.

--Harper's Story Books: Containing: The Engineer, Rambles Among the Alpes, and The Three Gold Dollars, 12 Vols., 3 bks per vol, Vol. 7. (Illus.). (The Harper Story Book Ser). N.D. Harper & Brothers.

--Harper's Story Books: Containing: The Great Elm, Aunt Margaret, and Vernon, 12 Vols. 3 bks. per Vol, Vol. 9. (Illus.). (The Harper Story Book Ser). N.D. Harper & Brothers.

--Harper's Story Books: Containing: The Gibraltar Gallery, The Alcove, and Dialogues, 12 Vols., 3 bks. per vol, Vol. 8. (Illus.). (The Harper Story Books Ser). N.D. Harper & Brothers.

--Harper's Story Books: Containing: The Harper Establishment, Franklin, and The Studio, 12 vols., 3 bks per vol, Vol. 4. (Illus.). (The Harper Story Book Ser). N.D. Harper & Brothers.

--Harper's Story Books: Containing: The Little Louvre, Prank, Emma, 12 Vols, Vol. 2. (Illus.). N.D. Set. Harper & Brothers.

--Harper's Story Books: Containing: Virginia, Timboo and Joliba and Timboo and Fanny, 12 vols., 3 bks. per vol, Vol. 3. (Illus.). N.D. Vols I-XII. Harper & Brothers.

--Hoaryhead and M'Donner. LC 23-14545. xii p. 1 l., 15-402 p. illus. 20 cm. (Added t.-p., Jacob Abbott's Young Christian series ... iv). 1855. Harper & Brothers.

--Hoaryhead and M'Donner. LC 23-454845. xii p., 1 l., 15-402 p. illus. 20 cm. (Added t.-P.: Jacob Abbott's Young Christian series ... iv). 1870. Harper & Brothers.

--Hoaryhead & M'Donner, 1 of 4 vols. (Illus.). (Young Christian Ser.). 1882. Harper.

--Hubert. LC 20-19842. 308 p. front., plates. 17 cm. (Added t.-p.: The Juno stories. v. 4). 1870. Dodd & Mead.

--Hubert. (Crowell's Library For Young People). N.D. Thomas Y. Crowell & Co.'s Catalogue.

--Hunter and Tom. (The August Ser.). N.D. Dodd & Mead Co.

--Hunter and Tom. (Crowell's Library For Young People). N.D. Thomas Y. Crowell & Co.'s Catalogue.

--Hunter and Tom, 1 of 4 Vols. (August Stories). N.D. Set. Thomas Y. Crowell & Co.

--The Isle of Wight. (The Florence Stories). N.D. Sheldon & Co.

--Jasper: Or, The Spoiled Child Recovered. LC 44-27091. 160 p. incl. front., illus. 17 1/2 x 14 cm. (Half-title: Harper's story books. A series of narratives, dialogues, biographies, and tales, for the instruction and entertainment of the young. By Jacob Abbott. No. 33). 1857. Harper & Brothers.

--John Gay Series, 4 Vols. N.D. N. Tibbals & Sons.

--John Gay Series: Including: Work for Summer, Winter, Spring, & Autumn, 4 Vols. N.D. Ward & Drummond.

--John Gay: Work for Boys, 4. Herrick, H. W., illus. N.D. Hurd & Houghton.

--Jonas A Judge, 1 of 6 Vols. (Illus.). (The Jonas Bks.). N.D. Set. Clark & Maynard.

--Jonas a Judge, 1 of 6 Vols. (Jonas Ser.: Vol. 4). N.D. Set. Thomas Y. Crowell & Co.

--Jonas Books, 6 Vols. N.D. Thomas Y. Crowell & Co.'s Catalogue.

--Jonas on a Farm in Summer, 1 of 6 Vols. (Illus.). (The Jonas Bks.: Vol. 2). N.D. Set. Clark & Maynard.

--Jonas on a Farm in Summer, 1 of 6 Vols. (Jonas Ser.: Vol. 2). N.D. Set. Thomas Y. Crowell & Co.

--Jonas on a Farm in Winter, 1 of 6 Vols. (Illus.). (The Jonas Bks.: Vol. 3). N.D. Set. Clark & Maynard.

--Jonas on a Farm in Winter, 1 of 6 Vols. (Jonas Ser.: Vol. 3). N.D. Set. Thomas Y. Crowell & Co.

--Jonas' Stories, 1 of 6 Vols. (Illus.). (The Jonas Bks.). N.D. Set. Clark & Maynard.

--Jonas Stories, 1 of 6 Vols. N.D. Thomas Y. Crowell & Co.

--Judge Justin: Or, The Little Court of Morningdale. LC 44-27089. 160 p. incl front., illus. 17 1/2 x 14 cm. (Half-title: Harper's story books. A series of narratives, dialogues, biographies, and tales, for the instruction and entertainment of the young. By Jacob Abbott. No. 31). 1857. Harper & Brothers.

--Juno and Georgie. LC 20-193432. 312 p. plates. 17 cm. 1870. Dodd & Mead.

--Juno and Georgie. (The Juno Stories). N.D. Dodd & Mead.

--Juno and Georgie. (Crowell's Library For Young People). N.D. Thomas Y. Crowell & Co.

--Juno and Georgie, 1 of 4 Vols. (Juno Stories: Vol. 2). N.D. Set. Thomas Y. Crowell & Co.

--Juno on a Journey. LC 20-19344. 300 p. front., plates. 17 1/2 cm. (Added t.-p.: The Juno stories. v. 3). 1870. Dodd & Mead.

--Labor Lost. (The Rollo Story Bks.). N.D. Sheldon & Co.

--Lapstone: Or, The Sailor Turned Shoemaker. LC 44-27087. 160 p. incl. front., illus. 18 x 14 cm. (Half-title: Harper's story books. A series of narratives, dialogues, biographies, and tales, for the instruction and entertainment of the young. By Jacob Abbott. No. 29). 1857. Harper & Brothers.

--The Little Louvre: Or, The Boys' and Girls' Gallery of Pictures. LC 48-30439. (Illus.). 18cm. 160p. (Harper's Story Bks.: No. 4). 1855. Harper & brothers.

--Little Paul: Or, How to Be Patient in Sickness and Pain. LC 44-27438. 160 p. incl. front., illus. 17 1/2 x 14 cm. (Half-title: Harper's story books. A series of narratives, dialogues, biographies, and tales, for the instruction and entertainment of the young. By Jacob Abbott. No. 36). 1857. Harper & Brothers.

--Lucy Among The Mountains, 1 of 6 Vols. (The Lucy Ser.). N.D. Set. Thomas Y. Crowell & Co.

--Lucy at Play, 1 of 6 Vols. (The Lucy Ser.). N.D. Set. Thomas Y. Crowell & Co.

--Lucy at Study, 1 of 6 Vols. (The Lucy Ser.). N.D. Set. Thomas Y. Crowell & Co.

--Lucy on the Sea-Shore, 1 of 6 Vols. (The Lucy Ser.). N.D. Set. Thomas Y. Crowell & Co.

--The Lucy Series, 6 Vols. N.D. Thomas Y. Crowell & Co.

--Lucy's Conversations, 1 of 6 Vols. (The Lucy Ser.). N.D. Set. Thomas Y. Crowell & Co.

--Lucy's Visit. (The Rollo Story Bks.). N.D. Sheldon & Co.

--Madame Roland, a Heroine of the French Revolution. (Illus.). (Young People's Lib). N.D. Henry Altemus Co.

--Malleville, 1 of 10 vols. (Illus.). (Franconia Stories). 1882. Harper.

--Marco Paul's Voyages & Travels, Maine. LC 22-17361. 4 p. l., 11-191 p. illus. 16 1/2 cm. (His Marco Paul's voyages & travels. vol. III). 1852. Harper & Brothers.

--Mary Bell, 1 of 10 vols. (Illus.). (Franconia Stories). 1882. Harper.

--Mary Erskine, 1 of 10 vols. (Illus.). (Franconia Stories). 1882. Harper.

--Mary Gay Series, 4 Vols. N.D. N. Tibbals & Sons.

--Mary Gay: Work for Girls, 4. Herrick, H. W., illus. N.D. HUrd & HOughton.

--Mary Osborne. LC 20-19345. 3 p. l., 9-301 p. front., plates. 17 cm. (The Juno Stories. v. 2). 1870. Dodd & Mead.

--Mary Osborne, 1 of 4 Vols. (Illus.). (Juno Stories). N.D (Set.). Thomas Y. Crowell & Co.

--Minigo: Or, The Fairy of Cairnstone Abbey. LC 44-270901. 160 p. incl. front., illus. 17 1/2 x 14 cm. (Half-title: Harper's story books. A series of narratives, dialogues, biographies, and tales, for the instruction and entertainment of the young. By Jacob Abbot. No. 32). 1857. Harper & Brothers.

--The New Shoes. Gilbert, John Clitherae, illus. (Illus.). (The Harlie Stories). N.D. Sheldon & Co.

--The Orkney Islands. (The Florence Stories). N.D. D. Lothrop Co.

--The Orkney Islands. (The Florence Stories). N.D. Sheldon & Co.

--Orkney the Peacemaker: Or, The Various Ways of Settling Disputes. LC 44-27088. 160 p. incl. front., illus. 17 1/2 x 14 cm. (Half-title: Harper's story books. A series of narratives, dialogues, biographies, and tales, for the instruction and entertainment of the young. By Jacob Abbott. No. 30). 1857. Harper & Brothers.

--Rainbow and Lucky Series, 5 vols. (Illus.). 1882. Harper.

--Rainbow's Journey, 1 of 5 vols. (Illus.). (Rainbow and Lucky Ser.). 1882. Harper.

--Rodolphus, 1 of 10 vols. (Illus.). (Franconia Stories: Vol. 6). 1882. Harper.

--Rodolphus: A Franconia Story. LC 77-353267. (Illus.). p. 433-448, 577-592, 721-736. 26cm. 1852. Harper & Bros.

--The Rollo and Lucy Books of Poetry, 3. N.D. Dodd & Mead.

--Rollo at Play. New, Rev. ed. LC 41-40972. 191 p. incl. front., illus. 15 1/2 cm. (His Rollo series). N.D. Phillips, Sampson, and Company.

--Rollo at Play. (The Rollo Bks.). N.D. Sheldon & Co.

--Rollo at Play, 1 of 24 vols. (Illus.). (Children's Favorite Classics). 1900. T. Y. Crowell & Co.

--Rollo at Play. (Illus.). Repr. (Children's Favorite Classics). 1915. Thomas Y Crowell.

--Rollo at Play. Copeland, Charles, illus. LC 12-30004. (Illus.). 191. 17cm. 1897. T.Y. Crowell & Company.

--Rollo at School ... New, Rev. ed. LC 41-40973. 4 p. l., 7-197 (l. e. 180) p. illus., plates. 17 1/2 cm. (His The Rollo series). 1855. Phillips, Sampson, and Company.

--Rollo at School. new, rev. ed. LC 43-26661. 2 p. l., 7-197 (i.e. 189) p. 1 illus., plates. 16 cm. (His The Rollo series). 1863. Sheldon & Company.

--Rollo at Work. new, rev. ed. LC 41-409752. 4 p. l., 7-191 p. illus., plates. 17 1/2 cm. (His Rollo series). N.D. Phillips, Sampson, and Company.

--Rollo at Work. new, rev. ed. LC 21-139577. 159 p. illus., plates. 15 1/2 cm. (Rollo series). 1865. Sheldon & Company.

--Rollo at Work, 1 of 24 vols. (Illus.). (Children's Favorite Classics). 1900. T. Y. Crowell & Co.

--Rollo at Work. (Illus.). Repr. (Children's Favorite Classics). 1915. Thomas Crowell.

--Rollo at Work. Copeland, Charles, illus. LC 12-30003. 4 p. l., 7-191 p. col. front., illus., plates. 17 cm. c.1897. T. Y. Crowell & Company.

--Rollo at Work, and Rollo at Play. Rhys, Ernest, ed. Crump, Lucy, intro. by. (Illus.). 18cm. 298p. (Everyman's Library). 1908. E .P Dutton & Co.

--The Rollo Books, 7 Vols; 2 Vols in 1. (Illus.). N.D. T. Y. Crowell & Co.

Abells, Chana
--The Children We Remember. LC 82-23377. (Illus.). 48p. (gr. 4-8). 1983. (ISBN 0-930494-20-2). (ISBN 0-930494-21-0). Kar Ben.
Abels, Harriette Sheffer see Sheffer, H. R., pseud.
Abels, Harriette Sheffer
--Call Me Clown. Lamb, Jim, illus. LC 76-43328. (Illus.). 47 p. 24cm. (Jobs for Juniors). c.1977. (ISBN 0-516-03205-4). Childrens Press.
--The Circus Detectives. Jeffers, Susan, illus. LC 73-125136. (Illus.). 63 p. 21cm. (Magic circle book: reading 360). 1971. Ginn.
--The Creature of Saxony Woods. Daley, Joann, illus. LC 78-11305. (Illus.). 47 p. 21cm. c.1979. (ISBN 0-516-03447-2). Childrens Press.
--Emmy, Beware!. Wahl, Richard (1939-), illus. LC 80-28458. p. cm. (Prime time adventures). 1981. (ISBN 0-516-02105-2). Childrens Press.
--A Forgotten World. LC 79-4633. (Galaxy). 1979. (ISBN 0-89686-032-9). Crestwood House.
--Green Invasion. Schroeder, Howard, ed. Furan, Rodney & Furan, Barbara Howell, illus. LC 79-4639. (Illus.). 47 p. 23cm. (Galaxy). c.1979. (ISBN 0-89686-030-2). Crestwood House.
--The Haunted Cottage. Dunnington, Tom, illus. LC 77-16619. p. cm. 1978. (ISBN 0-516-03486-3). Childrens Press.
--The Haunted Motorcycle Shop. Daley, Joann, illus. LC 78-6617. p. cm. 1978. (ISBN 0-516-03488-X). Childrens Press.
--The Last Meet. Schroeder, Howard, ed. Vista III Design, illus. LC 80-28766. (Illus.). 47 p. 23cm. (Her Teammates). c.1981. (ISBN 0-89686-113-9). (ISBN 0-89686-103-1). Crestwood House.
--Medical Emergency. LC 79-9823. p. cm. (Galaxy). 1979. (ISBN 0-89686-029-9). Crestwood House.
--Meteor from the Moon. LC 79-4650. p. cm. (Galaxy). 1979. (ISBN 0-89686-025-6). Crestwood House.
--Motocross Monkey. Schroeder, Howard, ed. Vista III Design, illus. LC 80-28762. (Illus.). 47 p. 23cm. (Team-Mates). c.1981. (ISBN 0-89686-106-6). (ISBN 0-89686-116-3). Crestwood House.
--Mystery on Mars. LC 79-9923. p. cm. (Galaxy). 1979. (ISBN 0-89686-024-8). Crestwood House.
--Mystery on the Delta. LC 72-168448. 186 p. 21cm. 1971. (ISBN 0-8313-0001-9). Lantern Press.
--Partners on Wheels. Schroeder, Howard, ed. Vista III Design, illus. LC 80-28428. (Illus.). 46 p. 23cm. (Team-Mates). c.1981. (ISBN 0-89686-105-8). (ISBN 0-89686-115-5). Crestwood House.
--Planet of Ice. LC 79-9920. p. cm. (Galaxy). 1979. (ISBN 0-89686-026-4). Crestwood House.
--September Storm. Gustafson, Scott, illus. LC 80-28430. p. cm. (Prime time adventures). 1981. (ISBN 0-516-02110-9). Childrens Press.
--The Silent Invaders. LC 79-4644. p. cm. (Galaxy). 1979. (ISBN 0-89686-031-0). Crestwood House.
--Strangers on NMA-6. Schroeder, Howard, ed. Furan, Rodney & Furan, Barbara Howell, illus. LC 79-4627. (Illus.). 47 p. 23cm. (Galaxy). c.1979. (ISBN 0-89686-027-2). Crestwood House.
--Street-Hockey Lady. Schroeder, Howard, ed. Vista III Design, illus. LC 80-29531. (Illus.). 47 p. 23cm. (Team-Mates). c.1981. (ISBN 0-89686-102-3). (ISBN 0-89686-112-0). Crestwood House.
--Unwanted Visitors. LC 79-9922. p. cm. (Galaxy). 1979. (ISBN 0-89686-028-0). Crestwood House.
--Winner on the Court. Schroeder, Howard, ed. Vista III Design, illus. LC 80-28451. (Illus.). 47 p. 23cm. (Team-Mates). c.1981. (ISBN 0-89686-107-4). (ISBN 0-89686-117-1). Crestwood House.
Abelson, Danny (1950-)
--If I Were King of the Universe. Di Fiori, Lawrence, illus. LC 83-22708. (Illus.). 32. 21cm. c.1984. (ISBN 0-03-071087-1). Holt, Rinehart, and Winston.
Abenheim, Peter
--Captain Impossible at Sea. Abenheim, Peter, illus. LC 59-12513. unpaged. illus. 29cm. 1959. Spindrift Books.
--A Horse with a Horn a-Head. Abenheim, Peter, illus. LC 59-15885. 71p. illus. 24 x 26cm. c.1959. Hesperian House.
Abercrombie, Barbara
--Amanda and Heather, and Company. St. John, Mimi, illus. LC 78-72117. (Illus.). 31 p. 23cm. 1979. (ISBN 0-89799-086-2). (ISBN 0-89799-017-X). Dandelion Press.
--Cat-Man's Daughter. LC 79-2676. p. cm. c.1981. (ISBN 0-06-020030-8). (ISBN 0-06-020031-6). Harper & Row.
--The Other Side of a Poem. Bertschmann, Harry, illus. LC 76-21394. (Illus.). (gr. 3-9). 1977. (ISBN 0-06-020028-6, HarpJ). (ISBN 0-06-020029-4). Har-Row.
Abernethy, Francis E.
--How the Critters Created Texas. Sargent, Ben, illus. LC 82-80440. (Illus.). 40p. 1982. (ISBN 0-936650-01-X). E C Temple.
Aberson, Helen, jt. auth. see Disney, Walt, Productions.
Abisch, Roslyn Kroop see Roche, A. K, pseud.
Abisch, Roslyn Kroop see Abisch, Roz.
Abisch, Roz (1927-)
--Anywhere in the World. Kaplan, Boche (1926-), illus. LC 66-20644. 1v. (unpaged) col. illus. 24cm. c.1966. (ISBN 0-679-25018-2). McKay.
--Around the House That Jack Built. Kaplan, Boche (1926-), illus. LC 70-174606. (Illus.). 32 p. 27cm. 1972. (ISBN 0-8193-0553-7). (ISBN 0-8193-0554-5). Parents' Magazine Press.
--Do you Know what Time it is. Kaplan, Boche (1926-), illus. 1969. Prentice-Hall.
--Mai-Ling and the Mirror. Kaplan, Boche (1926-), illus. LC 69-13717. (Illus.). 32 p. 26cm. 1969. Prentice-Hall.
--The Make-It, Play-It, Show-Time Book. Kaplan, Boche (1926-), illus. LC 76-57067. (gr. 2-6). 1977. (ISBN 0-8027-6287-5). (ISBN 0-8027-6288-3). Walker & Co.
--Open Your Eyes. Kaplan, Boche (1926-), illus. LC 64-19765. (Illus.). 1 v. (unpaged. 26cm. 1964. Parents' Magazine Press.
--The Shoe for Your Left Foot Won't Fit on Your Right. Kaplan, Boche (1926-), illus. LC 75-113735. (Illus.). 32 p. 27cm. 1970. (ISBN 0-8415-2008-9). McCall Pub. Co.
--Stories from Miss A. Perle, Ruth Lerner, ed. Kaplan, Boche (1926-), illus. (Illus.). (Alpha Vowel Books). (gr. k-1). 1977. (ISBN 0-89796-850-6). Arista Corp NDE.
--Stories from Miss I. Perle, Ruth L., ed. Kaplan, Boche (1926-), illus. (Illus.). (Alpha Vowel Books). (gr. k-1). 1977. (ISBN 0-89796-852-2). Arista Corp NDE.
--Stories from Miss O. Perle, Ruth L., ed. Kaplan, Boche (1926-), illus. (Illus.). (Alpha Vowel Books). (gr. k-1). 1977. (ISBN 0-89796-853-0). Arista Corp NDE.
--T'was in the Moon of Wintertime. Kaplan, Boche (1926-), illus. LC 69-12825. (Illus.). 32 four color ils. 32p. (ps-3). 1969. (ISBN 0-13-933358-4). P-H.
Abisch, Roz (1927-), adapted by.
--Sweet Betsy from Pike. Kaplan, Boche (1926-), illus. LC 75-104127. (Illus.). 31 p. 23cm. 1970. (ISBN 0-8415-2006-2). McCall Pub. Co.
Abkoude, Christiaan van
--Brown Sails and Silver Guilders:. Jack Snoek of Volendam. Rinke, Jan, illus. LC 36-22339. (Illus.). 204 p. 21cm. 1936. B. Mussey.
Abolafia, Yossi
--My Three Uncles. LC 84-4195. (Illus.). 9 7/8 x 8. 32p. (16 pt.). (gr. k-3). 1985. (ISBN 0-688-04024-1). (ISBN 0-688-04025-X). Greenwillow.
Abott, Kenyon Taylor
--Thirteen. Breed, Gertude, illus. LC 30-3063. 28p. incl. front., illus. 19 1/2cm. c.1929. Private Print.
About, Edmond
--The King of the Mountains: Le Roi des Montagnes. Crewe-Jones, Florence & Avison, George F. (1885-), illus. N.D. Cupples & Leon Co.
--The Man with the Broken Ear. (Leisure Hour Ser.). N.D. Henry Holt & Co.
--The Notary's Nose. (Leisure Hour Ser.). N.D. Henry Holt & Co.
Abraham, Jean-Pierre
--Lec the Invisible. LeScanff, Jacques, illus. LC 72-141535. (Illus.). 32p. (Harlin Quist Bks). (gr. 3 up). 1973. (ISBN 0-8252-0053-9). (ISBN 0-8252-0054-7). Dial.
--Pigeon Man. Cober, Alan Edwin (1935-), illus. (Illus.). (gr. 4 up). N.D. (ISBN 0-531-04015-1). (ISBN 0-531-05015-7). Quist.
Abraham, Norma J.
--Erik of the Dragon Ships. Bordner, Ellen P., ed. Steiner, Pat, illus. (Illus.). 163p. (Orig.). 1983. (ISBN 0-912661-00-3). Woodsong Graph.
Abrahams, Anthony
--Polonius Penguin and the Flying Doctor. Abrahams, Hilary Ruth (1938-), illus. LC 65-10778. 33 p. illus. (part col.) 28 cm. 1966. F. Watts.
--Polonius Penguin Learns to Swim. Abrahams, Hilary Ruth (1938-), illus. LC 63-18595. (Illus.). 1 v. (unpaged. 28cm. 1963. F. Watts.
Abrahams, Robert David (1905-)
--The Bonus of Redonda. Bramley, Peter, illus. LC 69-11292. (Illus.). 136 p. 21cm. 1968, c.1969. Macmillan.
--Humphrey's Ride. Brown, Dennis, illus. LC 65-17632. 127p. illus. 19cm. 1965, c.1964. Crowell.
--Mr. Benjamin's Sword. Levit, Herschel (1912-), illus. LC 48-3441. (Illus.). 19cm. 183p. (Covenant Ser.). (gr. 6-10). 1948. Jewish Pubn.
--Sound of Bow Bells: The Story of Sir David Salomons. LC 62-12320. 148p. illus. 22cm. (Covenant bks., 14). c.1962. Farrar.
--The Uncommon Soldier: Major Alfred Mordecai. Garchik, Morton, illus. LC 59-5578. 178p. illus. 22cm. (Convenant books, 5). 1959. Farrar, Straus & Cudahy.
Abrahams, Roger D. (1933-), ed.
--Jump-Rope Rhymes. 228p. 1969. (ISBN 0-292-78400-7). University of Texas Press.
Abramovitz, Anita Zeltner Brooks see Brooks, Anita, pseud.
Abrams, Lawrence
--Throw it out of Sight. (Illus.). 100p. (Doing & Learning Bks.). (gr. 5 up). 1984. (ISBN 0-87518-247-X). Dillon.
Abrams, Michael D, adapted by see Lorenzini, Carlo.
Abranz, Alfred & Knight, John, eds.
--Woody Woodpecker's Pogo Stick Adventures. authorized. Walter Lantz Studio, illus. LC 54-35679. (Original Author: Walter Lantz). unpaged. illus. 17cm. (Tell-a-tale Books). c.1954. Whitman Pub. Co.
Abrashkin, Raymond, jt. auth. see Williams, Jay.
Abrons, Mary Goldwater
--For Alice, a Palace. 48p. (gr. k-2). 1966. (ISBN 0-201-09189-5, A-W Childrens). A-W.
--For Alice, a Palace: A Story in Verse. Barrer-Russell, Gertrude (1921-), illus. LC 66-11408. 1v. (unpaged) col. illus. 26cm. (Young Scott bk.). c.1966. Scott.
Absolon, K. B., ed. see Absolon, Karel B.
Absolon, Karel B.
--The Tale of the Bad Macocha & the Fable of the Underground Punkva River. Absolon, K. B., ed. Absolon, K. B., illus. (Illus.). 40p. (Orig.). 1st U.S. edition. (Moravian Tales, Legends, Myths Ser.). (gr. 4). 1984. (ISBN 0-930329-02-3). KABEL Pubs.
Acacio, Arsenio B. & Galang, Ricardo C.
--Work and Play in the Philippines. Bird, Esther Brock, illus. LC 45-1952. 80 p. incl. col. front., illus. (part col.) 21 1/2 cm. (Half-title: New world neighbors). c.1944. D. C. Heath and Company.
Achard, Emile
--The History of My Friends. 1875. G. P. Putnam's Sons.
Achebe, Chinua (1930-)
--Chike and the River. Theobalds, Pruce, illus. LC 66-10087. 63 p. illus. 19 cm. 1966. University Press.
Achebe, Chinua (1930-) & Iroaganachi, John
--How the Leopard Got His Claws. Christiansen, Per, illus. LC 72-93382. (Illus.). 35 p. 26cm. 1973. (ISBN 0-89388-056-6). Third Press.
Acher, Don (1917-)
--Puddgin and Twidget: How the Squirrels Got Their Tails. Brody, Marc, illus. LC 48-7974. 27 p. illus. 19 x 26 cm. c.1948. Story Book House.
Acheson, Judy
--Judy in Constantinople. Peck, Anne Merriman (1884-), illus. LC 30-243404. x p. 3 l., 200 p. col. front., illus. 20 1/2 cm. 1930. Frederick A. Stokes Company.
Acheson, Nora
--Up the Steps: A Tale of Old Aldeburgh. Acheson, Nora, illus. Padfield, Peter LC 75-316300. (Illus.). 176 p. 21cm. 1974. (ISBN 0-904570-00-2). Anglian Cards Ltd.
Acker, Helen
--Lee Nationi: Young Navajo. Kennedy, Richard (1910-), illus. LC 58-680722. 136p. illus. 21cm. 1958. Abelard- Schuman.
--School Train. (Illus.). (gr. 3-5). 1953. (ISBN 0-8382-0725-1). Hale.
--The School Train. Smalley, Janet (1893-), illus. LC 53-6803. 118p. illus. 22cm. (gr. 3-7). 1953. Abelard Press.
--Three Boys of Old Russia. N.D. Nelson Bks.
Ackerman, Eugene Francis (1888-1974)
--Jeb and the Bank Robbers. Kinstler, Everett Raymond (1926-), illus. LC 58-12913. 187p. illus. 21cm. 1958. Bobbs-Merrill.
--Tonk and Tonka. Burger, Carl Victor (1888-1967), illus. LC 62-749459. (Illus.). 47 p. 23cm. 1962. Dutton.
Ackerman, Irene R
--Singing Thro' the Year,". A Book for Little Children to Sing and Play. LC 46-28303. 3 p. l., 30 p. 30 1/2 cm. 1940. Irene R. Ackerman.
Ackley, Edith Flack, Mrs. (1877-)
--Please. LC 41-21172. 11p. col. illus. 15 1/2 x 13cm. c.1941. Frederick A. Stokes.
Ackworth, Robert Charles (1923-)
--Surprise at East High. LC 60-6280. 202 p. 21cm. 1960. Chilton Co., Book Division.
Acland, A. H. D., Mrs.
--The Queer Beasts. N.D. Henry Holt.
Acland, Eric
--Adventure Westward. (gr. 7 up). 1967. Nelson.
Ada, Alma Flor, tr. see Garcia, Maria.
Ada, Alma Flor, tr. see Rohmer, Harriet.
Adair, Aldon, pseud., see Meigs, Cornelia Lynde.
Adair, Aldon, pseud. (1884-1973)
--At the Sign of the Two Heroes. Meigs, Cornelia Lynde. Smyth, S. Gordon, illus. LC 20-16500. 5 p. l., 3-270 p. front., plates. 20 cm. 1920. The Century Co.
--Helga & the White Peacock: A Play. Meigs, Cornelia Lynde. Browne, Margaret, photos by. Bingham, Ruth, designed by. 1922. Macmillan.
--The Hill of Adventure. Meigs, Cornelia Lynde. Shepherd, J. Clinton, illus. LC 22-181009. 4 p. l., 3-281 p. front., plates. 20 cm. 1922. The Century Co.
--The Island of Appledore. Meigs, Cornelia Lynde. Rev. ed. King, W. B., illus. LC 17-28795. 4 p. l., 211 p. front., plates. 20 cm. 1917. The Macmillan Company.
Adair, Gilbert, ed.
--Alice Through the Needle's Eye. Thorne, Jenny, illus. 1985. Dutton.
Adair, James R., ed.
--Tom Skinner: Top Man of the Lords & Other Stories. (gr. 6-10). N.D. Baker Bk.
Adair, Margaret Weeks (0000-1971)
--A Far Voice Calling. LC 64-16236. 190 p. 22 cm. 1964. Doubleday.
Adair, Margaret Weeks (0000-1971) & Patapoff, Elizabeth
--Folk Puppet Plays for the Social Studies. LC 79-89325. (Illus.). color photos. black & white drawings. 96p. (gr. 2-5). 1972. (ISBN 0-381-97001-9, JD-J). Har-Row.
--Folk Puppet Plays For The Social Studies. 1970. John Day.
Adam, Barbara
--The Big Big Box. 1st ed. LC 60-713248. unpaged. illus. 25cm. c.1960. Doubleday.
--Who's Jenny?. Adam, Barbara, illus. LC 63-9743. (Illus.). 32 p. 1963. Doubleday.
Adam, Eustace Lane (1891-)
--The Runaway Airship. LC 29-28181. iv, 220 p. front. 19 1/2 cm. (An Andy Lane story). c.1929. Grosset & Dunlap.
Adam, Graeme Mercer (1839-1912), abridged by see Kingsley, Charles.
Adam, Robert J. (1919-)
--Two Years Under Arms: A Novel of Life in a Military School. 1st ed. LC 53-7663. 175p. 21cm. 1953. Exposition Press.
Adam, Ruth C.
--Personality Tails. 1981. (ISBN 0-8062-1830-4). Carlton.
Adam, Ruth, Mrs.
--War on Saturday Week. LC 37-13864. 310 p. 21 cm. c.1937. J. B. Lippincott Company.
Adams, Adrienne, jt. auth. see Gordon, Patricia.
Adams, Adrienne (1906-)
--The Christmas Party. Adams, Adrienne (1906-), illus. LC 78-16230. 26cm. 227p. 1978. (ISBN 0-684-15930-9). Scribner.
--The Easter Egg Artists. LC 75-39301. (Illus.). 32 p. 27cm. c.1976. (ISBN 0-684-14652-5). Scribner.
--The Great Valentine's Day Balloon Race. LC 80-19527. p. cm. 1980. (ISBN 0-684-16640-2). Scribner.
--A Halloween Happening. LC 81-8969. p. cm. 1981. (ISBN 0-684-17166-X). Scribner.
--A Woggle of Witches. LC 70-161536. (Illus.). 32 p. 27cm. 1971. (ISBN 0-684-12506-4). Scribner.
Adams, Adrienne (1906-), ed.
--Bring a Torch, Jeannette, Isabella. Adams, Adrienne (1906-), illus. (Illus.). (ps-3). 1963. (ISBN 0-684-13444-6). Scribner. **Award: (ALA).**
--Poetry of Earth & Sky. Adams, Adrienne (1906-), illus. LC 70-39577. (Illus.). 48p. (gr. 1-4). 1972. (ISBN 0-684-13012-2, ScribJ). Scribner.
Adams, Alice W.
--Rhymes for Little Readers. Adams, Alice W., illus. LC 15-265. illus. (part col. 221/2cm. c.1890. D. Lothrop Co.
Adams, Alicen
--The Christmas Unicorn. (Illus.). 112p. 1983. (ISBN 0-682-40141-2). Exposition.
Adams, Andy, pseud., see Gibson, Walter Brown.
Adams, Andy, pseud. (1897-)
--African Ivory Mystery. Gibson, Walter Brown. LC 62-2454. 175p. illus. 20cm. (His A Biff Brewster mystery adventure, 5). c.1961. Grosset & Dunlap.
--Alaska Ghost Glacier Mystery. Gibson, Walter Brown. LC 62-2453. 175p. illus. 20cm. (His A Biff Brewster mystery adventure, 6). c.1961. Grosset & Dunlap.
--Brazilian Gold Mine Mystery. Gibson, Walter Brown. LC 60-514612. 182p. illus. 20cm. (His A Biff Brewster mystery adventure). 1960. Grosset & Dunlap.
--British Spy Ring Mystery. Gibson, Walter Brown. LC 64-2161. 175 p. illus. 20 cm. (His A Biff Brewster mystery adventure, 11). 1964. Grosset & Dunlap.
--Cattle Brands. Gibson, Walter Brown. N.D. Houghton Mifflin.
--Egyptian Scarab Mystery. Gibson, Walter Brown. LC 63-1131. 170 p. illus. 20 cm. (His A Biff Brewster mystery adventure, 9). 1963. Grosset & Dunlap.

--Hawaiian Sea Hunt Mystery. Gibson, Walter Brown. LC 60-517695. 182p. illus. 20cm. (His A Biff Brewster mystery adventure, 3). 1960. Grosset & Dunlap.
--Mystery of the Alpine Pass. Gibson, Walter Brown. LC 65-13771. 170p. illus. 20cm. (His Biff Brewster mystery adventure, no. 13). c.1965. Grosset.
--Mystery of the Ambush in India. Gibson, Walter Brown. LC 62-260653. 170p. illus. 20cm. (His A Biff Brewster mystery adventure). 1962. Grosset & Dunlap.
--Mystery of the Arabian Stallion. Gibson, Walter Brown. LC 65-185. 176p. illus. 20cm. (Biff Brewster mystery adventure). c.1964. Grosset.
--Mystery of the Caribbean Pearls. Gibson, Walter Brown. LC 62-5961. 172p. illus. 20cm. (His A Biff Brewster mystery adventure, 8). 1962. Grosset & Dunlap.
--Mystery of the Chinese Ring. Gibson, Walter Brown. LC 60-517689. 182p. illus. 20cm. (His A Biff Brewster mystery adventure, 2). 1960. Grosset & Dunlap.
--Mystery of the Mexican Treasure. Gibson, Walter Brown. LC 61-301161. 182p. illus. 20cm. (His A Biff Brewster mystery adventure). 1961. Grosset & Dunlap.
--Mystery of the Tibetan Caravan. Gibson, Walter Brown. LC 63-1036. 174 p. illus. 20 cm. (His a Biff Brewster mystery adventure, 10). 1963. Grosset & Dunlap.
--Wells Brothers: The Young Cattle Kings. Gibson, Walter Brown. (Riverside Library for Boys & Girls). N.D. Houghton Mifflin.

Adams, Audrey
--Karankawa Boy. LC 65-259251. xiii, 70p. illus. 20cm. c.1965. Naylor.

Adams, Carolyn H.
--Try Me, Teacher. (gr. 1-3). N.D. Carlton.

Adams, Charlotte
--Ben Howard: or, Truth and Honesty. N.D. George Routledge & Sons.
--Boys at Home. Gilbert, John Clitherae, illus. N.D. George Routledge & Sons.
--Edgar Clifton: or, Right and Wrong. N.D. George Routledge & Sons.
--The Errand Boy: Or, Your Time is Your Employer's. (Illus.). N.D. E. & J. B. Young & Co.
--John Hartley, and How he Got on in Life. N.D. George Routledge & Sons.
--Laura and Lucy: A Tale for Girls. (Illus.). N.D. Scribner, Welford & Armstrong.
--Matilda Lonsdale. N.D. George Routledge & Sons.

Adams, Cornelia
--The Make-it-up Story Book. N.D. Robert M. McBride.

Adams, Darwin James (1898-)
--The Adventures of Monte and Molly. Van Zelm, L. Franklin, illus. LC 38-194055. 5 p. l., 152 p. col. front., illus., plates (part col.) 26 cm. N.D. The Macaulay Company.

Adams, Edith, pseud., see Shine, Deborah.

Adams, Edith, pseud. (1932-)
--The Charmkins Discover Big World. Shine, Deborah. Fleming, Denise, illus. LC 83-4457. p. cm. 1983. (ISBN 0-394-86115-9). Random House.
--My Little Pony & The New Friends. Shine, Deborah. Beylon, Catherine M., illus. LC 84-60331. (Illus.). 32p. (My Little Pony Mini-Storybooks Ser.). (ps-3). 1984. (ISBN 0-394-86810-2, Pub. by BYR). Random.
--The Noisy Book: Starring Yakety Yak. Shine, Deborah. Hefter, Richard (1942-), illus. LC 82-50431. c.1983. (ISBN 0-394-85544-2). Random House.

Adams, Edward B., ed.
--Blindman's Daughter. Choi, Dong Ho, illus. (Illus.). 32p. (Korean Folk Story for Children Ser.: Bk. 1). (gr. 3). 1981. (ISBN 0-8048-1472-4, Pub. by Seoul Intl Publishing House). C E Tuttle.
--Herdboy & Weaver. Choi, Dong-Ho, illus. (Illus.). 32p. (Korean Folk Story for Children Ser.). (gr. 3). 1981. (ISBN 0-8048-1470-8, Pub by Seoul Intl Publishing House). C E Tuttle.
--Korean Cinderella. Choi, Dong Ho, illus. (Illus.). 32p. (Korean Folk Story for Children Ser.: Bk. 4). (gr. 3). 1982. (ISBN 0-8048-1473-2, Pub. by Seoul Intl Publishing House). C E Tuttle.
--Two Brothers & Their Magic Gourds. Dong-Ho, Choi, illus. (Illus.). 32p. (Korean Folk Stories for Children Ser.). (gr. 3). 1981. (ISBN 0-8048-1474-0, Pub. by Seoul Intl Tourist Korea). C E Tuttle.
--Woodcutter & Nymph. Choi, Dong-Ho, illus. (Illus.). 32p. (Korean Folk Story for Children Ser.). (gr. 3). 1982. (ISBN 0-8048-1471-6, Pub by Seoul Intl Publishing House). C E Tuttle.

Adams, Ellen
--The Scaredy Book. Hefter, Richard (1942-), illus. LC 82-50426. (Illus.). 32p. (Sweet Pickles Mini-Storybooks). (ps-k). 1983. (ISBN 0-394-85542-6). Random.

Adams, Ellinor Davenport
--A Girl of To-Day. (The Rugby Series for Boys and Girls). N.D. A. L. Burt Company.
--A Girl of To-Day. (Illus.). (The Wellesley Series for Girls). N.D. A. L. Burt.
--A Girl of To-Day. (Illus.). (Scribner-Blackie Series of books for young people). N.D. Charles Scribner's Sons.
--Little Miss Conceit. (Illus.). 112p. N.D. A. I. Bradley & Co.'s Pubs.
--Robin's Ride. (Illus.). (The Little Men Ser.). N.D. A. L. Burt's Pubs.
--Robin's Ride. Stacey, W. S., illus. (Illus.). (Wanted--A King Ser.). N.D. Cassell & Co.'s Pubs.
--Robin's Ride: A Story for Children. (Illus.). (The Rugby Series For Boys). 1915. A L Burt & Co.

Adams, Emily
--Six Months at Mrs. Prior's, 1 of 20 vols. New ed. (Illus.). 350p. (Sunday-School Lib: No. 13). 1895. Set. Lothrop Pub Co.

Adams, Estella
--Pioneer Life for Little Children. Fisher, Harrison, illus. c.1916. Bobbs-Merrill Co.

Adams, Eustace Lane (1891-)
--Across the Top of the World. LC 31-22656. 20cm. 243p. (The Andy Lane Ser.). c.1931. Grosset & Dunlap.
--The Adventures of the Boy Gliders. LC 31-25048. 223. 20cm. 1931. Warren & Putnam.
Doomed Demons. LC 35-7572. v, 210 p. 19cm. 1935. Grosset & Dunlop.
--Fifteen Days in the Air. LC 28-19958. 20cm. 194p. (The ANdy Lane Ser.). (The Andy Lane Ser.). c.1928. Grosset & Dunlap.
--The Flying Windmill. LC 30-11608. v. 211 p. front. 19 1/2 cm. (The Andy Lane Ser.). c.1930. Grosset & Dunlap.
--The Mysterious Monoplane. LC 30-2680. v. 192 p. front. 19 1/2 cm. (The Andy Lane Ser.). c.1930. Grosset & Dunlap.
--On the Wings of Flame. LC 29-16921. 3 p.l., 199 p. front. 19 1/2 cm. (The Andy Lane Ser.). c.1929. Grosset & Dunlap.
--Over the Polar Ice. LC 28-20220. 20cm. 208p. (The Andy Lane Ser.). (The Andy Lane Ser.). c.1928. Grosset & Dunlap.
--Pirates of the Air. LC 29-10964. 3 p. l., 213 p. front. 19 1/2 cm. c.1929. Grosset & Dunlap.
--The Plane Without a Pilot. LC 30-27773. v. 216 p. front. 19 1/2 cm. (The Andy Lane Ser.). c.1930. Grosset & Dunlap.
--Prisoners of the Clouds. LC 32-2024. v. 238 p. front. 19 1/2 cm. (The Andy Lane Ser.). c.1932. Grosset & Dunlap.
--Racing Around the World. LC 28-213751. iii, 210 p. front. 19 1/2 cm. (The Andy Lane Ser.). c.1928. Grosset & Dunlap.
--War Wings. (The Air Combat Ser.). N.D. Grosset & Dunlap.
--War Wings. Gretter, J. Clemens, illus. LC 38-1043. iii, 216 p. front. 19 1/2 cm. c.1937. Grosset & Dunlap.
--Wings of Adventure. LC 31-12975. v. 246 p. front. 19 1/2 cm. (The Andy Lane Ser.). c.1931. Grosset & Dunlap.
--Wings of the Navy. (The Air Combat Ser.). N.D. Grosset & Dunlap.
--Wings of the Navy. Gretter, J. Clemens, illus. LC 36-41960. iii, 211 p. front., plates 19 1/2 cm. c.1936. Grosset & Dunlap.

Adams, Florence
--Mushy Eggs. Hirsh, Marilyn (1944-), illus. LC 73-77420. (Illus.). 32 p. 22cm. 1973. (ISBN 0-399-20365-6). (ISBN 0-399-20365-6). Putnam.

Adams, Florence & McCarrick, Elizabeth
--Highdays & Holidays. Brock, Emma Lillian (1886-1974), illus. (Illus.). (gr. 3-7). 1927. (ISBN 0-525-31962-X). Dutton.

Adams, Frank, illus.
--The Beautiful Book of Nursery Rhymes. 5 pt. in 1 v. illus., plates (part col.) 27 1/2 cm. N.D. The Dodge Publishing Company.
--The Frog Who Would a Wooing Go. (Little Tot Library: Vol. 2). N.D. Dodge.
--Sam the Sportsman. (Little Tot Library). N.D. Dodge.
--Simple Simon. (Little Tot Library: Vol. 1). N.D. Dodge.
--Three Jolly Anglers. (Little Tot Library). N.D. Dodge.

Adams, George A
--First Things: A Picture Book in Natural Color Photos. Henning, Paul, photos by. LC 48-16662. 52 p. col. illus. 18 x 19 cm. 1947. Platt & Munk Co.
--What Goes with What: A New Playbook in Color Photography. LC 46-8410. 31 p. col. illus. 21 x 17 1/4 cm. (On cover: A Lothrop color book). c.1946. Lothrop, Lee & Shepard Co., Inc.

Adams, Guy, jt. auth. see Adams, Ruth Joyce.

Adams, H. I. (1822-1896), tr. see Segur, Sophie Rostopchine, Mrs.

Adams, Harriet Stratemeyer see Appleton, Victor, pseud.

Adams, Harriet Stratemeyer see Keene, Carolyn, pseud.

Adams, Harriet Stratemeyer see Sheldon, Ann, pseud.

Adams, Harriet Stratemeyer (1894-1982), rev. by see Dixon, Franklin W.

Adams, Harriet Stratemeyer (1894-1982), rev. by see Hope, Laura Lee.

Adams, Harrison, pseud., see Rathborne, St. George.

Adams, Harrison, pseud. (1854-1928)
--The Pioneer Boys of Kansas: Or, A Prairie Home in Buffalo Land. Rathborne, St. George. Merrill, Frank Thayer (1848-), illus. LC 28-25466. x p., 1 l., 301 p. front., illus., plates. 20 cm. (The Young Pioneer Ser.: Vol. 8). 1928. L. C. Page & Company.
--The Pioneer Boys of the Colorado: Or, Braving the Perils of the Grand Canyon Country. Rathborne, St. George. Merrill, Frank Thayer (1848-), illus. 20 cm. 321p. (The Young Pioneers Ser.: Vol. 7). c.1926. L. C. Page & Company.
--The Pioneer Boys of the Columbia: Or, In the Wilderness of the Great Northwest. Rathborne, St. George. Rogers, Walter S., illus. LC 16-14051. viii, 2, 345 p. front., illus., plates. 20 cm. (The Young Pioneer Ser.: Vol. 6). 1916. L. C. Page & Company.
--The Pioneer Boys of the Mississippi: Or, The Homestead in the Wilderness. Rathborne, St. George. Boehm, H. Richard, illus. LC 13-15267. viii, 2, 345 p. front., illus., plates. 20 cm. (The Young Pioneer Ser.: Vol. 3). 1913. L. C. Page & Company.
--The Pioneer Boys of the Missouri: Or, In the Country of the Sioux. Rathborne, St. George. Rogers, Walter S., illus. LC 14-6566. viii, 2, 358 p. front., illus., plates. 20 cm. (The Young Pioneer Ser.: Vol. 4). 1914. L. C. Page & Company.
--The Pioneer Boys of the Ohio: Or, Clearing the Wilderness. Rathborne, St. George. Bull, Charles Livingston (1874-1932), illus. LC 12-17660. viii, 2, 331 p. front., illus., plates. 20 cm. (The Young Pioneer Ser.: Vol. 1). 1912. L. C. Page & Company.
--The Pioneer Boys of the Yellowstone: Or, Lost in the Land of Wonders. Rathborne, St. George. Rogers, Walter S., illus. LC 15-13558. vii, 5, 346 p. front., illus., plates. 20 cm. (The Young Pioneer Ser.: Vol. 5). 1915. L. C. Page & Company.
--The Pioneer Boys on the Great Lakes: Or, On the Trail of the Iroquois. Rathborne, St. George. Bull, Charles Livingston (1874-1932), illus. LC 12-22566. viii, 2, 345 p. front., illus., plates. 20 cm. (The Young Pioneer Ser.: Vol. 2). 1912. L. C. Page & Company.

Adams, Helen Simmons see Barnes, Nancy, pseud.

Adams, Helen Simmons (1897-)
--The Wonderful Year. Barnes, Nancy, pseud. Seredy, Kate (1899-1975), illus. LC 46-6103. 4 l., 3-185 p. illus. 22 cm. 1946. J. Messner.

Adams, Henry Cadwallader (1817-1899)
--Balderscourt: Or, Holiday Tales. N.D. George Routledge & Sons.
--Barford Bridge: Or, School-Boy Trials. N.D. George Routledge & Sons.
--The Boy Cavaliers: Or, the Siege of Clidesford. N.D. George Routledge & Sons.
--The Boys of Westonbury. (Illus.). (Routledge's Welcome Series of Boys's Books). N.D. George Routledge & Sons.
--Charlie Lucken, 1 of 11 vols. (Popular Bks for Boys). 1900. Set. J B Lippincott.
--Charlie Lucken at School & College. (Illus.). 1900. J B Lippincott.
--Charlton School, 1 of 3 Vols. (Illus.). (The Schoolboy Stories Library). N.D. Set. George Routledge & Sons.
--The Cherry Stones. (Illus.). (Sixty-Cent Juvenile Library). N.D. George Routhledge & Sons.
--The Cherry Stones: Or, the Force of Conscience. Absolon, illus. N.D. George Routledge & Sons.
--The Chief of the School: Or, School-Boy Ambition. N.D. George Routledge & Sons.
--College Days at Oxford. (Illus.). N.D. E. P. Dutton & Co.
--The Doctor's Birthday: Or, the Force of Example. N.D. George Routledge & Sons.
--The Falcon Family; Meta and Willie. (Home Sunshine Ser.). N.D. R. Worthington & Co.
--Falcon Family: Or, Meta and Willie. 1875. Scribner, Welford, & Armstrong.
--Falconhurst: Or, Birthday Tales. N.D. E. P. Dutton.
--Falconhurst: Or, Birthday Tales. (Illus.). N.D. Scribner, Welford & Armstrong.
--The First of June. (Illus.). (Sixty-Cent Juvenile Library). N.D. George Routledge & Sons.
--The First of June: or, School-Boy Rivalry. Absolon, illus. N.D. George Routledge & Sons.
--Friend or Foe: A Tale of Sedgmoor. N.D. George Routledge & Sons.
--Gannet Island. (Illus.). (Warne's Home Circle Ser.). N.D. Scribner & Welford.
--Gannet Island: Or, Willie's Birthday. (Illus.). N.D. Scribner, Welford & Armstrong.
--Hair-Breadth Escapes: Or, The Adventures of Three Boys in South Africa. (Illus.). N.D. E & J B Young.
--Hair-Breadth Escapes: Or, The Adventures of Three Boys in South Africa. (Author of "Schoolboy Honor" and "Tales of Charlton School."). N.D. E P Dutton.
--The Indian Boy. N.D. George Routledge & Sons.
--The Lost Life. 1875. George Routledge & Sons.
--The Lost Rifle. N.D. George Routledge & Sons.
--Mystery of Beechy Grange: Or, The Missing Host. (Illus.). N.D. E. P. Dutton.
--Schoolboy Honor, 1 of 3 Vols. (Illus.). (The Schoolboy Stories Library). N.D. Set. George Routledge & Sons.
--Stories of the Prophets, 1 of 22 Vols. (Illus.). (Warne's Home Circle Ser.). N.D. Scribner & Welford.
--Tales of Charlton School. Absolon, illus. N.D. George Routledge & Sons.
--Tales of Charlton School. New Ed. ed. Fraser, F. A., illus. N.D. George Routledge.
--Tales of Nethercourt: A New Book for Boys. (Illus.). N.D. George Routledge.
--Tales of the Civil War. N.D. George Routledge & Sons.
--Walter's Friend: Or, Big Boys and Little Boys. N.D. George Routledge & Sons.
--Walter's School-Days, 1 of 3 Vols. (Illus.). (The Schoolboy Stories Library). N.D. Set. George Routledge & Sons.
--The Weaver Boy Who Became a Missionary. N.D. Thomas Whittaker.
--The White Brunswickers: Or, Reminiscences of Schoolboy Life. LC 42-27118. vii, l. 416 p. front., plates. 18 1/2 cm. 1865. Routledge, Warne, & Routledge.
--Who Did It?. Or, Holmwood Priory. (Illus.). N.D. E P Dutton.
--Winborough Boys. N.D. George Routledge & Sons.
--The Wonder Book of Traveler's Tales. N.D. Liveright Publications.
--The Woodleigh Stories: Or, Tales for Sunday Readings. N.D. Scribner, Welford & Armstrong.
--The Woodleigh Stories: Tales for Sunday Readings. (Home Sunshine Library). N.D. R. Worthington & Co.

Adams, Herbert
--Caroline Ormesby's Crime. LC 29-6668. 391 p. 29 cm. 1929. J. B. Lippincott Company.
--The Secret of Bogey House. 1925. J.B.Lippincott.

Adams, J. A., illus.
--The Fairy-Book. LC 44-35371. (Illus.). 2 p. l., iii-iv, xvi, 17-301 p. front., illus. 18 cm. 1836. Harper and Brothers.

Adams, J. C.
--The Encombe Stories, 1 of 8 Vols. (Illus.). (Warne's Home Sunshine Library). N.D. Scribner & Welford.

Adams, James Donald (1891-1968), ed. see Emerson, Ralph Waldo.

Adams, James Douglas (1875-)
--Cap'n Ezra, Privateer. LC 40-4720. viii, 248 p. incl. front., plates. 22 cm. 1940. Harcourt, Brace and Company.
--Skinny. Rodgers, Richard H. (1876-1953), illus. LC 38-312871. 4 p. l., 3-197 p. incl. front., illus., plates. 22 1/2 cm. c.1938. Harcourt, Brace and Company.

Adams, Jean, jt. auth. see Kimball, Margaret.

Adams, Julia Davis (1900-)
--Mountains Are Free. Nadejen, Theodore, illus. LC 30-22749. x p., 2 l., 3-250 p. incl. front., illus., plates. 21 cm. c.1930. E. P. Dutton & Co., Inc. **Award: (JNM).**
--Vaino, a Boy of New Finland. Ostman, Lempi (1899-), illus. LC 29-20673. xiii, 273 p. front., illus., plates. 23 cm. c.1929. E. P. Dutton & Co., Inc. **Award: (JNM).**

Adams, Julia Davis (1900-), retold by.
--Swords of the Vikings. Lassen, Suzanne, illus. LC 28-18231. (Stories from the works of Saxo Grammaticus). 23cm. 225p. 1928. E P Dutton.

Adams, Katharine
--Blackthorn. N.D. Grosset & Dunlap.
--Blackthorn. Dobias, Frank (1902-), illus. LC 31-25215. (Illus.). 20cm. 218p. 1931. Macmillan Co.
--Grey Eyes, a Mystery of the Riviera. De Angeli, Marguerite Lofft, Mrs. (1889-), illus. LC 34-5290. (Illus.). 19cm. 267p. 1934. Macmillan Co.
--Mehitable. N.D. Grosset & Dunlap.
--Mehitable. LC 20-21185. 5 p. l., 2-278 p. front., plates. 19 1/2 cm. 1920. The Macmillan Company.
--Midsummer. N.D. Grosset & Dunlap.
--Midsummer: A Story for Boys and Girls. LC 21-19197. 8 p. l., 241 p. front., plates. 19 1/2 cm. 1921. The Macmillan Company.
--Midwinter. N.D. Grosset & Dunlap.
--Midwinter. Pape, Eric (1870-), illus. LC 27-22487. 4 p. l., 228 p. col. front. 19 1/2 cm. 1927. The Macmillan Company.

--Prince of Paris: And Thirty-Nine Other Stories Around the World. LC 48-6351. 332 p. illus. 21 cm. 1947. Hinds, Hayden & Eldredge.
--Red Caps and Lilies. Van Everen, Jay, illus. LC 24-9269. ix p., 1 l., 351 p. front., plates. 19 1/2 cm. 1924. The Macmillan Company.
--Scarlet Sheath. Merwin, Decie (1894-1961), illus. LC 36-19264. 20cm. 262p. 1936. The Macmillan Company.
--The Silver Tarn. N.D. Grosset & Dunlap.
--The Silver Tarn. Williamson, Ada Clendenin, illus. LC 24-249456. 20cm. 249p. 1924. The Macmillan Company.
--Stork's Nest: A Story of Alsacs. Ayer, Margaret (0000-1981), illus. LC 35-4806. 5 p. l., 296 p. illus. 19 1/2 cm. 1935. The Macmillan Company.
--Thistle Inn. Richards, George Mather (1880-), illus. LC 30-28634. 4 p. l., 307 p. front., illus. 19 1/2 cm. 1930. The Macmillan Company.
--Toto and the Gift. Pape, Eric (1870-), illus. LC 26-113164. 5 p. l., 235 p. col. front. 19 1/2 cm. 1926. The Macmillan Company.
--Wisp: A Girl of Dublin. N.D. Grosset & Dunlap.
--Wisp: A Girl of Dublin. Van Everen, Jay, illus. LC 22-194783. viii, 309 p. front., illus. 19 1/2 cm. 1922. The Macmillan Company.

Adams, Kathleen & Bacon, Frances Elizabeth Atchinson, Mrs. (1903-), eds.
--A Book of Enchantment. Lenski, Lois (1893-1974), illus. LC 28-22791. 7 p. l., 230 p. 1 l. col. front., illus., col. plates. 24 1/2 cm. 1928. Dodd, Mead & Company.
--A Book of Giant Stories. Lahr, Robert W., illus. LC 26-180950. viii p., 3 l., 205 p. front., plates. 20 1/2 cm. c.1926. Dodd, Mead and Company.
--A Book of Princess Stories. Lenski, Lois (1893-1974), illus. LC 27-21416. 6 p. l., 223 p. col. front., illus., col. plates. 24 cm. 1927. (ISBN 0-396-04184-1). Dodd, Mead & Company.
--There Were Giants. Lenski, Lois (1893-1974), illus. LC 29-18479. 7 p. l., 234 p. front., illus., plates. 21 cm. 1929. Dodd, Mead & Company.

Adams, Laurie & Coudert, Allison (1941-)
--Alice and the Boa Constrictor. McCully, Emily Arnold (1939-), illus. LC 82-15769. p. cm. 1983. (ISBN 0-395-33068-8). Houghton Mifflin.

Adams, Lawrence Stowell see Miles, Sande, pseud.

Adams, Lawrence Stowell (1875-)
--Three Pals on the Desert. Miles, Sande, pseud. Nesslage, Kent, illus. LC 46-8582. 248 p. illus. 21 1/2 cm. 1946. R. M. McBride & Company.

Adams, Leith, pseud., see Laffan, Bertha Jane.

Adams, Leith, Mrs., pseud. (0000-1912)
--Aunt Hepsy's Foundling. Laffan, Bertha Jane. (Illus.). N.D. J. B. Lippincott.

Adams, Leta Zoe
--Island of the Red God. Sperry, Armstrong W. (1897-1976), illus. LC 39-30338. 6 p. l., 15-304 p. incl. illus., double map. 21 cm. c.1939. Rand McNally & Company.

Adams, Mary Hall Barrett, Mrs. (1816-1860), ed.
--The Rainbow: And Other Stories. LC 49-387848. 172 p. illus. 17 cm. 1848. J. M. Usher.
--The Sabbath School Annual for 1846. 4th ed. LC 15-17152. viii, 9-168 p. col. front., illus., plates. 15 1/2 cm. 1846. J. M. Usher.

Adams, Mary Scott, pseud., see Willis, Priscilla D.

Adams, Mildred, jt. auth. see Fenton, Carroll Lane.

Adams, Oscar Fay
--Dear Old Story Tellers. 1889. Lothrop,Lee & Shapard.

Adams, Pam, ed.
--Number Rhymes. Adams, Pam, illus. (Illus.). color ils. 48p. (gr. k-3). 1971. (ISBN 0-531-01978-0). Watts.

Adams, Pam, illus.
--The Gingerbread Man. (Illus.). 24p. 1981. (ISBN 0-85953-107-4, Pub. by Child's Play England). Playspaces.
--The House That Jack Built. (Illus.). 16p. (Books with Holes Ser.). 1978. (ISBN 0-85953-076-0, Pub. by Child's Play England). Playspaces.
--If I Weren't Me. (Illus.). 24p. 1981. (ISBN 0-85953-108-2, Pub. by Child's Play England). Playspaces.
--Mrs. Honey's Hat. (Illus.). 24p. 1980. (ISBN 0-85953-099-X, Pub. by Child's Play England). Playspaces.
--Oh, Soldier! Soldier!. (Illus.). 16p. (Books with Holes Ser.). 1978. (ISBN 0-85953-093-0, Pub. by Child's Play England). Playspaces.
--Old MacDonald. (Illus.). 16p. (Books with Holes Ser.). 1978. (ISBN 0-85953-054-X, Pub. by Child's Play England). Playspaces.
--Old Macdonald Had a Farm. LC 76-6817. (Illus.). unpaged. 30cm. 1976, c.1975. (ISBN 0-448-12579-X). (ISBN 0-448-13375-X). Grosset & Dunlap.
--Shopping Day. (Illus.). 24p. (Pre-Reading Ser.). 1974. (ISBN 0-85953-033-7, Pub. by Child's Play England). Playspaces.
--There Was an Old Lady. (Illus.). 16p. (ps-3). 1975. (ISBN 0-448-11910-2). G&D.
--There Was an Old Lady Who Swallowed a Fly. (Illus.). 16p. (Books with Holes Ser.). 1973. (ISBN 0-85953-018-3, Pub. by Child's Play England). Playspaces.
--This Is the House That Jack Built. 16p. (Orig.). (Books with Holes Ser.). 1977. (ISBN 0-85953-075-2, Pub. by Child's Play England). Playspaces.
--This Old Man. (Illus.). 16p. (ps-3). 1975. (ISBN 0-448-11911-0). G&D.
--This Old Man. (Illus.). 16p. (Orig.). (Books with Holes Ser.). N.D. (ISBN 0-85953-026-4, Pub. by Childs Play England). Playspaces.

Adams, Pam & Jones, Ceri, illus.
--A Book of Ghosts. (Illus.). 32p. (Orig.). (Imagination Ser.). 1974. (ISBN 0-85953-073-6, Pub. by Child's Play England). (ISBN 0-85953-028-0). Playspaces.

Adams, Phylliss, et al.
--Pippin at the Gym. (Illus.). 32p. (Double Scoop Ser.). (gr. k-3). 1983. (ISBN 0-695-41681-2, Dist. by Caroline Hse). (ISBN 0-695-31681-8). Modern Curr.
--Pippin Cleans Up. (Illus.). 32p. (Double Scoop Ser.). (gr. k-3). 1983. (ISBN 0-695-41680-4, Dist. by Caroline Hse). (ISBN 0-695-31680-X). Modern Curr.
--Pippin Eats Out. (Illus.). 32p. (Double Scoop Ser.). (gr. k-3). 1983. (ISBN 0-695-41679-0, Dist. by Caroline Hse). (ISBN 0-695-31679-6). Modern Curr.
--Pippin's Lucky Penny. Connelly, Gwen, illus. LC 82-82451. (Illus.). 32 p. 23cm. (Follett double scoop books). (The Adventures of Pippin). c.1983. (ISBN 0-695-41682-0). Follett Pub. Co.
--Stop the Bed. Sandford, John, illus. (Illus.). 32p. (Double Scoop Ser.). (gr. k-3). 1982. (ISBN 0-695-41644-8, Dist. by Caroline Hse). (ISBN 0-695-31644-3). Modern Curr.

Adams, Phylliss & Hartson, Eleanore
--A Dog Is Not a Troll. Hockerman, Dennis, illus. LC 81-17409. p. cm. (Follett double scoop books). (The Troll Family Stories). c.1982. (ISBN 0-695-41612-X). Follett.
--Etta Can Get It!. Hockerman, Dennis, illus. LC 81-17410. p. cm. (Follett double scoop books). (The Troll Family Stories). c.1982. (ISBN 0-695-41616-2). (ISBN 0-695-31616-8). Follett.
--Go, Wendall, Go!. Hockerman, Dennis, illus. LC 81-17415. (Illus.). 32 p. 23cm. (Follett double scoop books). (The Troll Family Stories). 1982. (ISBN 0-695-41614-6). (ISBN 0-695-31614-1). Follett.
--Good Show. Sandford, John, illus. 32p. (Double Scoop Bks.). (gr. k-3). 1982. (ISBN 0-695-41648-0, Dist. by Caroline Hse). (ISBN 0-695-31648-6). Modern Curr.
--Hi, Dog!. Hockerman, Dennis, illus. LC 81-17414. (Illus.). 32 p. 23cm. (Follett double scoop books). (The Troll Family Stories). c.1982. (ISBN 0-695-41611-1). (ISBN 0-695-31611-7). Follett.
--I Love Wheels. Hockerman, Dennis, illus. LC 81-17413. p. cm. (Follett double scoop books). (The Troll Family Stories). c.1982. (ISBN 0-695-41615-4). (ISBN 0-695-31615-X). Follett.
--Jump In! Now!. Sandford, John, illus. (Illus.). 32p. (Double Scoop Ser.). (gr. k-3). 1982. (ISBN 0-695-41645-6, Dist. by Caroline Hse). (ISBN 0-695-31645-1). Modern Curr.
--Pippin at the Gym. Connelly, Gwen, illus. LC 82-82454. c.1983. (ISBN 0-695-41681-2). Follett Pub. Co.
--Pippin at the Gym: Group III. (Illus.). 32p. (Double Scoop Bks.). (gr. k-2). 1983. (ISBN 0-516-09723-7). Childrens.
--Pippin Cleans Up: Group III. (Illus.). 32p. (Double Scoop Bks). (gr. k-2). 1983. (ISBN 0-516-09725-3). Childrens.
--Pippin Eats Out: Group III. (Illus.). 32p. (Double Scoop Bks.). (gr. k-2). 1983. (ISBN 0-516-09724-5). Childrens.
--Pippin Goes to Work. Connelly, Gwen, illus. LC 82-82456. (Illus.). 32 p. 23cm. (Follett double scoop books). (The Adventures of Pippin). c.1983. (ISBN 0-695-41678-2). (ISBN 0-695-31678-8). Follett Pub. Co.
--Pippin Learns a Lot. Connelly, Gwen, illus. LC 82-82453. c.1983. (ISBN 0-695-41679-0). (ISBN 0-695-31679-6). Follett Pub. Co.
--Pippin Learns a Lot: Group III. (Illus.). 32p. (Double Scoop Bks.). (gr. k-2). 1983. (ISBN 0-516-09727-X). Childrens.
--Pippin's Lucky Penny: Group III. (Illus.). 32p. (Double Scoop Bks.). (gr. k-2). 1983. (ISBN 0-516-09728-8). Childrens.
--This Way Down. Sandford, John, illus. (Illus.). 32p. (Double Scoop Ser.). (gr. k-3). 1982. (ISBN 0-695-41647-2, Dist. by Caroline Hse). (ISBN 0-695-31647-8). Modern Curr.
--Time Out!. Sandford, John, illus. (Illus.). 32p. (Double Scoop Ser.). (gr. k-3). 1982. (ISBN 0-695-41643-X, Dist. by Caroline Hse). (ISBN 0-695-31643-5). Modern Curr.
--A Troll, a Truck, and a Cookie. Hockerman, Dennis, illus. LC 81-17412. p. cm. (Follett double scoop books). (The Troll Family Stories). 1982. (ISBN 0-695-41617-0). Follett Pub. Co.
--Where Is Here?. Sandford, John, illus. (Illus.). 32p. (Double Scoop Ser.). (gr. k-3). 1982. (ISBN 0-695-41646-4, Dist. by Caroline Hse). (ISBN 0-695-31646-X). Modern Curr.

Adams, Richard George (1920-)
--The Tyger Voyage. Bayley, Nicola (1935-), illus. LC 76-368435. (Illus.). 30 p. 26cm. 1976. (ISBN 0-224-01237-1). J. Cape.
--The Tyger Voyage. Bayley, Nicola (1935-), illus. LC 76-3972. (Illus.). 30 p., 1 leaf of plates. 26cm. 1976. (ISBN 0-394-40796-2). Knopf.
--Watership Down. 1972. Macmillan. **Award: (CMA).**
--Watership Down. LC 73-6044. (Illus.). ix, 429 p. 24cm. 1974, c.1972. (ISBN 0-02-700030-3). Macmillan.

Adams, Richard George (1920-) & Aldridge, Alan
--The Ship's Cat. LC 77-6121. p. cm. c.1977. (ISBN 0-394-42334-8). Knopf : Distributed by Random House.

Adams, Robert
--Abysmal Gloom. (Illus.). 32p. 1984. (ISBN 0-584-62073-X, Pub. by Salem Hse Ltd). Merrimack Pub Cir.

Adams, Robert J., tr. see Seki, Keigo.

Adams, Ruth
--Fidelia. LC 74-116340. (Illus.). color ils. 32p. 24cm. (gr. 1-4). 1970. (ISBN 0-688-51120-1). Lothrop.

Adams, Ruth Cady
--Sky High in Bolivia. Knight, Katharine, illus. LC 42-10029. 63, 1 p. incl. col. front., illus. (part col.) 21 1/2 cm. (Half-title: New world neighbors). c.1942. Etc., D. C. Heath and Company.

Adams, Ruth Joyce
--Mr. Picklepaw's Popcorn. Werth, Kurt (1896-), illus. LC 65-13392. 34p. illus. (pt. col.) 25cm. c.1965. Lothrop.

Adams, Ruth Joyce & Adams, Guy (1919-)
--Mr. Picklepaw's Puppy. Werth, Kurt (1896-), illus. LC 77-97819. (Illus.). 32 p. 26cm. 1970. (ISBN 0-688-51381-6). Lothrop, Lee & Shepard Co.

Adams, St. Clair, jt. ed. see Morris, Joseph.

Adams, Samuel, jt. auth. see White, Stewart Edward.

Adams, Samuel Hopkins (1871-)
--Chingo Smith of the Erie Canal. Vosburgh, Leonard W. (1912-), illus. LC 58-6197. 275p. illus. 21cm. 1958. Random Houe.
--The Harvey Girls. N.D. World Publishing.
--The Pony Express. Ames, Lee Judah (1921-), illus. LC 50-10533. 185 p. col. illus. 22 cm. (Landmark books 7). 1950. Random House.
--The Santa Fe Trail. Ames, Lee Judah (1921-), illus. LC 51-14138. 181 p. illus. 22 cm. (Landmark books, 13). 1951. Random House.
--The Secret of Lonesome Cave. Schoonover, Frank Earle (1877-1972), illus. c.1912. Bobbs-Merrill Co.
--Wagons to the Wilderness: A Story of Westward Expansion. Rudolph, Norman Guthrie (1896-1983), illus. LC 54-5066. 182p. illus. 22cm. (Winston adventure books). 1954. Winston.

Adams, Sarah B.
--Amy and Marion's Voyage Around the World. N.D. D. Lothrop Co.

Adams, Sherred Willcox
--Five Little Friends. Petersham, Maud Sylvia Fuller, Mrs. (1890-1971) & Petersham, Miska (1888-1960), illus. LC 23-10101. 2 p., l., 139 p. col. illus. 19 cm. 1922. The Macmillan Company.

Adams, Susi, illus.
--Miss Mouse. (Illus.). 26p. (Look Again Bks.). (ps). 1984. (ISBN 0-590-33160-4). Scholastic Inc.
--Mr. Rabbit. (Illus.). 26p. (Look Again Bks.). (ps). 1984. (ISBN 0-590-33161-2). Scholastic Inc.
--Mr. Squirrel. (Illus.). 26p. (Look Again Bks.). (ps). 1984. (ISBN 0-590-33162-0). Scholastic Inc.
--Mrs. Hedgehog. (Illus.). 26p. (Look Again Bks.). (ps). 1984. (ISBN 0-590-33163-9). Scholastic Inc.

Adams, Veotta McKinley
--Captain Joe and the Eskimo. LC 43-51287. 25cm. 40p. 1943. William R. Scott Inc.

Adams, Will, ed. see Stevenson, Robert Louis.

Adams, William, compiled by.
--Fables and Rhymes: AEsop and Mother Goose. LC 12-30051. 18 1/2cm. 96p. (Lakeside literature series: Book 1.). 1898. Western Publishing House.
--Myths of Old Greece in Story and Song. LC 1-29152. 256 p. illus. 18 1/2 cm. (Lakeside literature series. Book III). 1900. Western Publishing House.

Adams, William Henry Davenport (1828-1891)
--The Golden Book of English Song. N.D. Thomas Nelson & Sons.
--The Land of the Incas. (Illus.). (The Boy's Own Authors Ser.). N.D. Dana Estes & Co.
--Page, Squire and Knight. (Or, The Days Of Chivalry). N.D. Estes & Lauriat.

Adams, William Henry Davenport (1828-1891), adapted by.
--The Days of Chivalry. (Illus.). (The Boy's Own Authors Ser.). N.D. Dana Estes & Co.
--The Days of Chivalry. (Illus.). N.D. Estes & Lauriat's.
--The Days of Chivalry: Or, How Aimery the Bright-of-Face Became Page, Squire, and Knight. Strang, Ray C., illus. LC 25-9616. (Original Author. Mme. Josephine Blanche Bouchet Colomb). 2 p. l., iii-viii p., 1 l., 313 p. col. front., plates. 20 1/2 cm. 1925. L.C. Page & Company C.

Adams, William Taylor see McCormick, Brooks, pseud.

Adams, William Taylor see Optic, Oliver, pseud.

Adams, William Taylor see Winterton, Gayle, pseud.

Adams, William Taylor (1822-1897), ed. see Defoe, Daniel.

Adams, William Taylor (1822-1897), ed. see Adams, William Taylor (1822-1897) & Kellogg, Elijah.

Adams, William Taylor (1822-1897)
--Across India: Or, Live Boys in the Far East. Optic, Oliver, pseud. (All-Over-the-World-Series). N.D. Lothrop,Lee & Shepard.
--All Aboard: Or, Life on the Lake. Optic, Oliver, pseud. (Oliver Optic Series.). 1915. A L Burt & Co.
--All Aboard: Or, Life on the Lake. Optic, Oliver, pseud. (The Rugby Series for Boys and Girls). N.D. A. L. Burt Company.
--All Aboard: Or, Life on the Lake. Optic, Oliver, pseud. Empire ed. 1905. American News Co.
--All Aboard: Or, Life on the Lake. Optic, Oliver, pseud. (Illus.). (The Young Folks Library). N.D. Caldwell.
--All Aboard: Or, Life on the Lake. Optic, Oliver, pseud. (Illus.). (The Alcazar Classics). N.D. Caldwell.
--All Aboard: Or, Life on the Lake. Optic, Oliver, pseud. (Famous Boat-Club Ser.). N.D. Colby and Rich.
--All Aboard: Or, Life on the Lake. Optic, Oliver, pseud, 1 of 6 vols. New ed. (Illus.). (Boat Club Ser.). 1900. Set. H. M. Caldwell.
--All Aboard: Or, Life on the Lake. Optic, Oliver, pseud, 39 vols. (Illus.). (Famous Books for Boys Ser.: No. 1). 1905. Set. H M Caldwell Co.
--All Aboard: Or, Life on the Lake. Optic, Oliver, pseud, 1 of 64 vols. (Young America Library: No. 4). 1900. Set. Hurst & Co.
--All Aboard: Or, Life on the Lake. Optic, Oliver, pseud, 1 of 103 vols. (The Pearl Library: No. 2). 1900. Hurst & Co.
--All Aboard: Or, Life on the Lake. Optic, Oliver, pseud, 1 of 5 vols. (Standard Ser.). 1900. Set. Hurst & Co.
--All Aboard: Or, Life on the Lake. Optic, Oliver, pseud. (Illus.). 256p. 1874. Lee & Shepard.
--All Aboard: Or, Life on the Lake. Optic, Oliver, pseud, 1 of 6 vols. (Illus.). (Famous "Boat-Club" Ser.). 1882. Set. Lee & Shepard.
--All Aboard: Or, Life on the Lake. Optic, Oliver, pseud, 1 of 60 vols. (American Boys' Ser.: No. 2). 1900. Set. Lee & Shepard.
--All Aboard: Or, Life on the Lake. Optic, Oliver, pseud. LC 42-26188. 18 cm. 256p. (Oliver Optic's Best Club Ser.). 1874. Lee,Shepard & Dillingham.
--All Aboard: or, Life on the Lake. Optic, Oliver, pseud. (Illus.). (Oliver Optic Ser.). N.D. Lothrop Lee & Shepard.
--All Aboard: Or, Life on the Lake. Optic, Oliver, pseud. rev ed. LC 4648. 194p. front., plates. 16cm. 1900. W. B. Conkey.
--All Abroad: Or, Life on the Lake. Optic, Oliver, pseud. (Oliver Optic Ser.). 1910. Hurst & Co.
--All Adrift: Or, The Gold Wing Club. Optic, Oliver, pseud. (Illus.). (The Boatbuilder Ser.). 1882. Lee & Shepard.
--All Adrift: Or, The Gold Wing Club. Optic, Oliver, pseud. (Illus.). (Oliver Optic Series.). N.D. Lothrop Lee & Shepard.
--All Adrift: Or, The Goldwing Club. Optic, Oliver, pseud. (Boat Builders Ser.). N.D. Lothrop, Lee & Shepard.

--Freaks of Fortune: Or, Half Round the World. Optic, Oliver, pseud. (Starry Flag Ser.). N.D. Colby and Rich.
--Freaks of Fortune: Or, Half Round the World. Optic, Oliver, pseud, 1 of 6 vols. (Illus.). (Starry Flag Ser.). 1882. Set. Lee & Shepard.
--Freaks of Fortune: Or, Half Round the World. Optic, Oliver, pseud. LC 12-37393. 3 p. l., 5-303 p. front., plates. 17 1/2 cm. (Added t.-p.: Oliver Optic's starry flag series. II). c.1896. Lee and Shepard.
--Freaks of Fortune: Or, Half Round the World. Optic, Oliver, pseud. (Illus.). (Oliver Optic Ser.). N.D. Lothrop Lee & Shepard.
--Going South: Or, Yachting on the Atlantic Coast. Optic, Oliver, pseud, 1 of 6 vols. (Illus.). (Great Western Ser.). 1882. Set. Lee & Shepard.
--Going South: Or, Yachting on the Atlantic Coast. Optic, Oliver, pseud. LC 7-42465. xi, 13-333 p. front., plates. 19 cm. (His The great western series v. 4). c.1907. Lothrop, Lee & Shepard Co.
--Going West: Or, The Perils of a Poor Boy. Optic, Oliver, pseud, 1 of 6 vols. (Illus.). (Great Western Ser.). 1882. Set. Lee & Shepard.
--Going West: Or, The Perils of a Poor Boy. Optic, Oliver, pseud. LC 3-17943. 350 p. front., plates. 19 cm. (His The great western series. I). 1903. Lee and Shepard.
--Going West: Or, The Perils of a Poor Boy. Optic, Oliver, pseud. (Illus.). (Oliver Optic Ser.). 1910. Lothrop Lee & Shepard.
--The Gold Thimble. Optic, Oliver, pseud. (Flora Lee Story Books). N.D. Colby and Rich.
--The Gold Thimble. Optic, Oliver, pseud, 1 of 12 vols. New ed. (Illus.). (Riverdale Story Books). 1882. Lee & Shepard.
--The Gold Thimble. Optic, Oliver, pseud, 1 of 6 vols. (Illus.). (Flora Lee Library). N.D. Set. Lee & Shepard.
--The Gold Thimble: A Story for Little Folks. Optic, Oliver, pseud. LC 12-373947. 92 p. incl. front., illus., plates. pl. 16 1/2 cm. (Half-title: Riverdale stories...By Oliver Optic. v. 11). 1890. Lee and Shepard.
--The Great Western Series. Optic, Oliver, pseud, 6 vols. 1882. Set. Lee & Shepard.
--Half Round the World. Optic, Oliver, pseud. (All-Over-the-World Library, Third Ser). N.D. Lee and Shepard.
--Haste and Waste: Or, The Young Pilot of Lake Champlain. Optic, Oliver, pseud. (Woodville Stories). N.D. Colby and Rich.
--Haste and Waste: Or, The Young Pilot of Lake Champlain. Optic, Oliver, pseud, 1 of 6 vols. (Illus.). (Woodville Stories). 1882. Lee & Shepard.
--Haste & Waste: Or, The Young Pilot of Lake Champlain. Optic, Oliver, pseud, 1 of 60 vols. (Illus.). (American Boys' Ser.: No. 21). 1900. Lee & Shepard.
--Haste and Waste: Or, The Young Pilot of Lake Champlain. Optic, Oliver, pseud. (Oliver Optic Ser.). N.D. Lothrop Lee & Shepard.
--Haste and Waste: Or, The Young Pilot of Lake Champlain, a Story for Young People. Optic, Oliver, pseud. LC 12-37395. 2 p. l., 3-313 p. front., 2 pl. 17 cm. (Added t.-p.: Woodville stories by Oliver Optic. v. 6). 1867. Lee and Shepard.
--Haste and Waste: Or, Young Pilot of Lake Champlain. Optic, Oliver, pseud. (Oliver Optic Ser.). 1910. Hurst & Co.
--Hope and Have: Or, Fanny Grant Among the Indians. Optic, Oliver, pseud. (Woodville Stories). N.D. Colby and Rich.
--Hope and Have: Or, Fanny Grant Among the Indians. Optic, Oliver, pseud. (Oliver Optic Ser.). 1910. Hurst & Co.
--Hope and Have: Or, Fanny Grant Among the Indians. Optic, Oliver, pseud. (Illus.). 1893. Lee & Shepard.
--Hope & Have: Or, Fanny Grant Among the Indians. Optic, Oliver, pseud, 1 of 60 vols. (Illus.). (American Boys' Ser.: No. 22). N.D. Lee & Shepard.
--Hope and Have: Or, Fanny Grant Among the Indians. Optic, Oliver, pseud. (Woodville Stories). N.D. Lothrop, Lee & Shepard.
--Hope and Have: Or, Fanny Grant Among the Indians. Optic, Oliver, pseud. (Illus.). (Oliver Optic Ser.). N.D. Lothrop Lee & Shepard.
--Hope and Have: Or, Fanny Grant Among the Indians, a Story for Young People. Optic, Oliver, pseud. LC 12-37396. 3 p. l., 5-283 p. front., 2 pl. 17 1/2 cm. (Added t.-p.: Woodville stories by Oliver Optic. v. 5). 1893. Lee and Shepard.
--In Doors and Out: Or, Views from the Chimney Corner. Optic, Oliver, pseud. LC 3-18313. (Illus.). 19 1/2cm. 381p. (The Household Library: V. 1). 1903. Lee and Shepard.
--In School and Out. Optic, Oliver, pseud. (The Rugby Series for Boys and Girls). N.D. A. L. Burt Company.
--In School and Out: Or, The Conquest of Richard Grant. Optic, Oliver, pseud. (Illus.). (Oliver Optic Series.). 1915. A L Burt & Co.
--In School and Out: Or, The Conquest of Richard Grant. Optic, Oliver, pseud. (Woodville Stories). N.D. Colby and Rich.
--In School and Out: Or, The Conquest of Richard Grant. Optic, Oliver, pseud. (Oliver Optic Ser.). 1910. Hurst & Co.
--In School and Out: Or, The Conquest of Richard Grant. Optic, Oliver, pseud, 1 of 6 vols. (Illus.). (Woodville Stories). 1882. Lee & Shepard.
--In School & Out: Or, The Conquest of Richard Grant. Optic, Oliver, pseud, 1 of 60 vols. (Illus.). (American Boys' Ser.: No. 23). 1900. Lee & Shepard.
--In School and Out: Or, The Conquest of Richard Grant. Optic, Oliver, pseud. 286p. N.D. Lee & Shepard.
--In School and Out: Or, The Conquest of Richard Grant, a Story for Young People. Optic, Oliver, pseud. LC 12-37397. 3 p. l., 5-286 p. front., 2 pl. 17 1/2 cm. (Added t.-p.: Woodville stories by Oliver Optic. v. 2). 1893. Lee and Shepard.
--In the Saddle. Optic, Oliver, pseud. (The Blue and the Gray On Land). N.D. Lothrop, Lee & Shepard.
--Isles of the Sea: Or, Young America Homeward Bound, a Story of Travel and Adventure. Optic, Oliver, pseud. LC 42-436182. 3 p. l., 5-374 p. front., plates. 17 1/2 cm. (Young America abroad. By Oliver Optic. 2d ser. VI). 1877. Lee and Shepard.
--Isles of the Sea: Or, Young America Homeward Bound, a Story of Travel and Adventure. Optic, Oliver, pseud. LC 5-33625. 374 p. front., plates. 19 cm. (On cover: Young America abroad. 2d series). c.1905. Lothrop, Lee & Shepard Co.
--Isles of the Sea: Or, Young America Homeward Bound. Optic, Oliver, pseud, 1 of 12 vols. Nast & Stevens, illus. (Young America Abroad Ser. (Second Ser.)). 1882. Lee & Shepard.
--Just His Luck. Optic, Oliver, pseud. (Illus.). (Famous Books for Boys). N.D. H. M. Caldwell Co.
--Just His Luck. Optic, Oliver, pseud, 1 of 60 vols. (Illus.). (American Boys's Ser.: No. 25). 1900. Lee & Shepard.
--Just his Luck. Optic, Oliver, pseud. LC 5-33624. 19cm. 335p. (On cover: American boys series: No. 25). 1905. Lothrop, Lee & Shepard.
--Just His Luck. Optic, Oliver, pseud. (Illus.). (Oliver Optic Series.). 1910. Lothrop Lee & Shepard.
--Lake Breezes: Or, The Cruise of the Sylvania. Optic, Oliver, pseud, 1 of 6 vols. (Illus.). (Great Western Ser.). 1882. Set. Lee & Shepard.
--Lake Breezes: Or, The Cruise of the Sylvania. Optic, Oliver, pseud, 1 of 6 vols. (Great Western Ser.). 1900. Set. Lee & Shepard.
--Lake Breezes: Or, The Cruise of the Sylvania. Optic, Oliver, pseud. LC 6-348095. xi, 13-325 p. front., plates. 19 1/2 cm. (His The great western series v. 3). c.1906. Lothrop, Lee & Shepard Co.
--Lake Shore Series. Optic, Oliver, pseud, 6 vols. (Illus.). 1882. Set. Lee & Shepard.
--A Lieutenant at Eighteen. Optic, Oliver, pseud. LC 12-373996. 483 p. front., plates. 19 cm. (Half-title: The blue and the gray on land, by Oliver Optic. v. 3). 1896. Lee and Shepard.
--Lighting Express: Or, The Rival Academies. Optic, Oliver, pseud, 1 of 6 vols. (Illus.). (Lake Shore Ser.). 1882. Set. Lee & Shepard.
--Lightning Express: Or, The Rival Academies. Optic, Oliver, pseud. (Lake Shore Ser.). N.D. Colby and Rich.
--Lightning Express: Or, The Rival Academies. Optic, Oliver, pseud. LC 12-37550. 4 p. l., 7-312 p. front., plates. 19 cm. (Added t.-p.: Lake shore series By Oliver Optic v. 2). c.1897. Lee and Shepard.
--Lightning Express: Or, The Rival Academies. Optic, Oliver, pseud. (Illus.). 312p. 1897. Lee & Shepard.
--Lightning Express: Or, The Rival Academies. Optic, Oliver, pseud. (Illus.). (Oliver Optic: Series.). N.D. Lothrop Lee & Shepard.
--Little Bobtail: Or, The Wreck of the Penobscot. Optic, Oliver, pseud. (Yacht Club Ser.). N.D. Colby and Rich.
--Little Bobtail: Or, The Wreck of the Penobscot. Optic, Oliver, pseud, 1 of 6 vols. (Illus.). 356p. (Yacht Club Ser.). 1900. Lee & Shepard.
--Little Bobtail: Or, The Wreck of the Penobscot. Optic, Oliver, pseud. (Illus.). (Oliver Optic Ser.). 1910. Lothrop Lee Shepard.
--Little Bobtail: Or, The Wreck of the Penobscot. Optic, Oliver, pseud. (Yacht Club Ser.). N.D. Lothrop, Lee & Shepard.
--Little by Little: Or, The Cruise of the Flyaway. Optic, Oliver, pseud, 98 vols. (The Rugby Ser.). 1905. Set. A L Burt Co.
--Little by Little: Or, The Cruise of the Flyaway. Optic, Oliver, pseud. (Illus.). (Oliver Optic Series). 1915. A L Burt & Co.
--Little by Little: Or, The Cruise of the Flyaway. Optic, Oliver, pseud. Empire ed. 1905. American News Co.
--Little by Little: Or, The Cruise of the Flyaway. Optic, Oliver, pseud. (Famous Boat-Club Ser.). N.D. Colby and Rich.
--Little by Little: Or, The Cruise of the Flyaway. Optic, Oliver, pseud, 1 of 6 vols. New ed. (Illus.). (Boat Club Ser.). 1900. Set. H. M. Caldwell Co.
--Little by Little: Or, The Cruise of the Flyaway. Optic, Oliver, pseud. (Illus.). (Famous Books for Boys). N.D. H. M. Caldwell Co.
--Little by little: Or, The Cruise of the Flayaway. Optic, Oliver, pseud. (Oliver Optic Ser.). 1910. Hurst & Co.
--Little by Little: Or, The Cruise of the Flyaway. Optic, Oliver, pseud, 1 of 6 vols. (Illus.). (Famous "Boat-Club" Ser.). 1882. Set. Lee & Shepard.
--Little by Little: Or, The Cruise of the Flyaway. Optic, Oliver, pseud, 1 of 60 vols. (Illus.). (American Boys' Ser.: No. 27). 1900. Lee & Shepard.
--Little by Little: Or, The Cruise of the Flyaway. Optic, Oliver, pseud. (Illus.). 280p. N.D. Lee & Shepard.
--Little by Little: or, The Cruise of the Flyaway. Optic, Oliver, pseud. (Illus.). (Oliver Optic Series.). N.D. Lothrop Lee & Shepard.
--Little by Little: Or, The Cruise of the Flyaway. Optic, Oliver, pseud. LC 47-36814. 1 p. l., 5-233 p. 19 cm. N.D. W. B. Conkey Company.
--Little by Little: Or, The Cruise of the Flyaway; a Story for Young Folks. Optic, Oliver, pseud. LC 12-37539. 3 p. l., 5-280 p. front. 17 1/2 cm. (On cover: Boat club series by Oliver Optic, v. 6). c.1888. Lee and Shepard.
--Little Merchant. Optic, Oliver, pseud. (Riverdale Story Books). N.D. Colby and Rich.
--Little Merchant. Optic, Oliver, pseud, 1 of 12 vols. New ed. (Illus.). (Riverdale Story Books). 1882. Set. Lee & Shepard.
--Little Merchant. Optic, Oliver, pseud. (Illus.). 96p. 1890. Lee & Shepard.
--Little Merchant: A Story for Little Folks. Optic, Oliver, pseud. (Oliver Optic Ser.). 1910. Hurst & Co.
--The Little Merchant: A Story for Little Folks. Optic, Oliver, pseud. LC 12-374005. 94 p. incl. front., illus., plates. pl. 16 1/2 cm. (Half-title: Riverdale stories...By Oliver Optic v. 1). 1890. Lee and Shepard.
--Living Too Fast: Or, the Confessions of a Bank Officer. Optic, Oliver, pseud. (Illus.). N.D. Lee & Shepard.
--Make or Break: Or, The Rich Man's Daughter. Optic, Oliver, pseud. (Starry Flag Ser.). N.D. Colby and Rich.
--Make or Break: Or, The Rich Man's Daughter. Optic, Oliver, pseud. LC 12-37401. 3 p. l., 5-328 p. front., plates. 17 1/2 cm. (Added t.-p.: Oliver Optic's starry flag series. v). c.1896. Lee and Shepard.
--Make or Break: Or, The Rich Man's Daughter. Optic, Oliver, pseud, 1 of 6 vols. (Illus.). (Starry Flag Ser.). N.D. Set. Lee & Shepard.
--Make or Break: Or, The Rich Man's Daughter. Optic, Oliver, pseud. (Starry Flag Ser.). N.D. Lothrop, Lee & Shepard.
--Make or Break: or, The Rich Man's Daughter. Optic, Oliver, pseud. (Illus.). (Oliver Optic Ser.). N.D. Lothrop Lee & Shepard.
--A Millionaire at Sixteen: Or, The Cruise of the Guardian Mother. Optic, Oliver, pseud. (All-Over-the-World-Series). N.D. Lothrop, Lee & Shepard.
--A Millionaire at Sixteen: Or, The Cruise of the Guardian Mother. Optic, Oliver, pseud. (Illus.). (Oliver Optic Ser.). N.D. Lothrop Lee & Shepard.
--A Missing Million: Or, The Adventures of Louis Belgrave. Optic, Oliver, pseud. LC 12-37541. xii, 327 p. front., plates. 19 cm. (His All-over-the-world series. v. 1). 1892. Lee and Shepard.
--A Missing Million: Or, The Adventures of Louis Belgrave. Optic, Oliver, pseud. (All-Over-The-World Library: 1). N.D. Lee & Shepard.
--A Missing Million: or, The Adventures of Louis Belgrave. Optic, Oliver, pseud. (Illus.). (Oliver Optic Series.). N.D. Lothrop Lee & Shepard.
--Money Maker: Or, The Victory of the Basilisk. Optic, Oliver, pseud. 1873. Lee & Shepard.
--Money-Maker: Or, The Victory of the Basilisk. Optic, Oliver, pseud, 1 of 6 vols. (Illus.). (Yacht Club Ser.). 1882. Lee & Shepard.
--Money Maker: Or, The Victory of the Basilisk. Optic, Oliver, pseud. LC 2-11141. 19cm. 361p. (The Yacht Club Ser.). 1901. Lee and Shepard.
--Nature's Young Nobleman. McCormick, Brooks, pseud. LC 5-42962000003. 16cm. 224p. (Munsey's Popular Ser.). 1888. F. A. Munsey.
--Never or Never: The Adventures of Bobby Bright. Optic, Oliver, pseud. (Illus.). (Oliver Optic Series.). 1915. A L Burt & Co.
--Northern Lands: or, Young America in Russia and Prussia. Optic, Oliver, pseud. (Oliver Optic Series.). N.D. Lothrop Lee & Shepard.
--Northern Lands: Or, Young America in Russia and Prussia. Optic, Oliver, pseud, 1 of 12 vols. Nast & Stevens, illus. (Young America Abroad Ser. (Second Ser.)). 1882. Lee & Shepard.
--Northern Lands: Or, Young America in Russia and Prussia, A Story of Travel and Adventure. Optic, Oliver, pseud. LC 1-22053. 360 p. front., plates. 17 cm. (Added t.-p.: Young America abroad. 2d ser. II). 1872. Lee & Shepard.
--Northern Lands: Or, Young America in Russia and Prussia. A Story of Travel and Adventure. Optic, Oliver, pseud. LC 41-28206. 17cm. 300p. (Young America Abroad). 1874. Lee and Shepard.
--Northern Lands: Or, Young America in Russia and Prussia, a Story of Travel and Adventure. Optic, Oliver, pseud. LC 2774. 360 p. incl. front. plates. 19 cm. (His Young America abroad--Second ser. v. 2). c.1900. Lee and Shepard.
--Now or Never: Or, The Adventures of Bobby Bright, a Story for Young Folks. Optic, Oliver, pseud. LC 12-37402. 3 p. l., 5-263 p. front. 17 1/2 cm. (On cover: Boat club series by Oliver Optic. v. 3). c.1884. Lee and Shepard.
--Now or Never: Or, The Adventures of Bobby Bright. Optic, Oliver, pseud. (Oliver Optic Ser.). N.D. A. L. Burt.
--Now or Never: Or, The Adventures of Bobby Bright. Optic, Oliver, pseud. Empire ed. 1905. American News Co.
--Now or Never: Or, The Adventures of Bobby Bright. Optic, Oliver, pseud. (Illus.). (The Young Folks Library). N.D. Caldwell.
--Now or Never: Or, The Adventures of Bobby Bright. Optic, Oliver, pseud. (Famous Boat-Club Ser.). N.D. Colby and Rich.
--Now or Never: Or, The Adventures of Bobby Bright. Optic, Oliver, pseud, 1 of 6 vols. New ed. (Illus.). (Boat Club Ser.). 1900. Set. H. M. Caldwell Co.
--Now or Never: Or, The Adventures of Bobby Bright. Optic, Oliver, pseud. (Illus.). (Famous Books for Boys). N.D. H. M. Caldwell Co.
--Now or Never: Or, The Adventures of Bobby Bright. Optic, Oliver, pseud, 1 of 64 vols. (Young America Library: No. 29). 1900. Set. Hurst & Co.
--Now or Never: Or, The Adventures of Bobby Bright. Optic, Oliver, pseud, 1 of 103 vols. (The Pearl Library: No. 68). 1900. Set. Hurst & Co.
--Now or Never: Or, The Adventures of Bobby Bright. Optic, Oliver, pseud, 1 of 5 vols. (Standard Ser.). 1900. Hurst & Co.
--Now or Never: Or, The Adventures of Bobby Bright. Optic, Oliver, pseud. (Oliver Optic Ser.). 1910. Hurst & Co.
--Now or Never: Or, The Adventures of Bobby Bright. Optic, Oliver, pseud, 1 of 6 vols. (Illus.). (Famous "Boat-Club" Ser.). 1882. Set. Lee & Shepard.
--Now or Never: Or, The Adventures of Bobby Bright. Optic, Oliver, pseud. (Illus.). 263p. 1884. Lee & Shepard.
--Now or Never: Or, The Adventures of Bobby Bright. Optic, Oliver, pseud, 1 of 60 vols. (Illus.). (American Boys' Ser.: No. 31). 1900. Lee & Shepard.
--Now or Never: Or, The Adventures of Bobby Bright. Optic, Oliver, pseud. (Oliver Optic Series.). 1910. Lothrop Lee & Shepard.
--Now or Never: Or, The Adventures of Bobby Bright. Optic, Oliver, pseud. LC 4541. 206 p. front. (port.) plates. 16 cm. 1900. W.B. Conkey Company.
--Now or Never: The Adventures of Bobby Bright. Optic, Oliver, pseud. (The Rugby Series for Boys and Girls). N.D. A. L. Burt Company.
--Ocean-Born: Or, The Cruise of the Clubs. Optic, Oliver, pseud. LC 3-15220. 368 p. front., plates. 19 cm. (Added t.-p.: Oliver Optic's yacht club series. 6). 1903. Lee and Shepard.
--Ocean Born: Or, The Cruise of the Clubs. Optic, Oliver, pseud, 1 of 6 vols. (Illus.). (Yacht Club Ser.). 1882. Lothrop,Lee & Shepard.
--Oliver Optic's Magazine: Containing four Serial Stories, Sketches, etc. Optic, Oliver, pseud, 2 vols. in 1, Vols. 3-4. (Illus.). 822p. 1868. Lee & Shepard.
--Oliver Optic's Magazine: Containing four Serial Stories, Sketches, etc. Optic, Oliver, pseud, 2 vols. in 1, Vols. 5-6. (Illus.). 832p. 1870. Lee & Shepard.
--Oliver Optic's Magazine: Containing three Serial Stories, sketches, etc. Optic, Oliver, pseud, 2 vols. in 1, Vols. 1-2. (Illus.). 832p. 1867. Lee & Shepard.
--Oliver Optic's New Story Book. Optic, Oliver, pseud. (Illus.). (The St. Nicholas Ser.). N.D. Hurst and Company.
--Oliver Optic's New Story Book. Optic, Oliver, pseud. (Illus.). (Fireside Ser.). N.D. Hurst and Company.
--Oliver Optic's The Boat Club. Optic, Oliver, pseud. rev. ed. O'Shea, James P., ed. LC 75-17659. 173 p. 21cm. (Geneva book). 1968. Carlton Press.

AUTHOR INDEX ADAMS, WILLIAM

--On the Blockade. Optic, Oliver, pseud. (The Blue & Gray Afloat). N.D. Lothrop, Lee & Shepard.
--On the Staff. Optic, Oliver, pseud. LC 12-37360. 4 p. l., 7-474 p. front. plates. 18 1/2 cm. (Half-title: The blue and the gray series, by Oliver Optic). 1897. Lee and Shepard.
--On Time: Or, The Young Captain of the Ucayga Steamer. Optic, Oliver, pseud. (Lake Shore Ser.). N.D. Colby and Rich.
--On Time: Or, The Young Captain of the Ucayga Steamer. Optic, Oliver, pseud, 1 of 6 vols. 282p. (Lake Shore Ser.). 1882. Lee & Shepard.
--The Onward and Upward Series. Optic, Oliver, pseud, 6 vols. (Illus.). 1882. Lee & Shepard.
--Our Boys and Girls Companion: Containing:"Lightning Express", "On Time",etc. Optic, Oliver, pseud. Adams, William Taylor (1822-1897), ed. Optic, Oliver, pseud. N.D. Colby and Rich.
--Our Boys and Girls Companion: Containing Serial Stories, Sketches, etc. Optic, Oliver, pseud. Adams, William Taylor (1822-1897), ed. Optic, Oliver, pseud. (Illus.). N.D. Lee &
--Our Boys and Girls Favorite: Containing:"The Starry Flag", etc. Optic, Oliver, pseud. Adams, William Taylor (1822-1897), ed. Optic, Oliver, pseud. N.D. Colby and Rich.
--Our Boys and Girls Favorite: Containing "The Starry Flag", Tales of Wonder, etc. Optic, Oliver, pseud. Adams, William Taylor (1822-1897), ed. Optic, Oliver, pseud. (Illus.). N.D. Lee & Shepard.
--Our Boys and Girls Keepsake: Containing Stories, Wonder Tales,etc. Optic, Oliver, pseud. Adams, William Taylor (1822-1897), ed. Optic, Oliver, pseud. (Illus.). N.D. Lee & Shepard.
Our Boys and Girls Offering. Containing Stories, Tales of Wonder, etc. Optic, Oliver, pseud. (Illus.). N.D. Lee & Shepard.
--Our Boys and Girls Repository: Containing:"Bear & Forbear", "Field & Forest",etc. Optic, Oliver, pseud. N.D. Colby and Rich.
--Our Boys and Girls Repository: Containing Stories, Tales, etc. Optic, Oliver, pseud. Adams, William Taylor (1822-1897), ed. Optic, Oliver, pseud. (Illus.). N.D. Lee & Shepard.
--Our Boys and Girls Souvenir: Containing Stories, Tales, etc. Optic, Oliver, pseud. Adams, William Taylor (1822-1897), ed. Optic, Oliver, pseud. (Illus.). N.D. Lee & Shepard.
--Our Boys and Girls Story Teller: Containing Stories of the Sea, Tales of Wonder, etc. Optic, Oliver, pseud. Adams, William Taylor (1822-1897), ed. Optic, Oliver, pseud. (Illus.). N.D. Lee & Shepard.
--Our Boys and Girls Treasure: Containing Stories, Tales of Wonder, etc. Optic, Oliver, pseud. Adams, William Taylor (1822-1897), ed. Optic, Oliver, pseud. (Illus.). N.D. Lee & Shepard.
--Our Boys and Girls Treasure: Containing:"Brake Up", "Switch Off", etc. Optic, Oliver, pseud. Adams, William Taylor (1822-1897), ed. Optic, Oliver, pseud. N.D. Colby and Rich.
--Out West: Or, Roughing It on the Great Lakes. Optic, Oliver, pseud. (Great Western Ser.). N.D. Lothrop,Lee & Shepard.
--Outward Bound: Or, Young America Afloat; A Story of Travel and Adventure. Optic, Oliver, pseud. LC 41-28297. 3 p. l., 5-336 p. front. plates. 17 1/2 cm. (Young America abroad. By Oliver Optic...1st ser.1). 1873. Lee and Shepard.
--Outward Bound: Or, Young America Afloat. Optic, Oliver, pseud, 1 of 60 vols. (Illus.). (American Boys' Ser.: No. 52). 1900. Lee & Shepard.
--Outward Bound: Or, Young American Afloat. A Story of Travel and Adventure. Optic, Oliver, pseud. LC 12-37542. 17cm. 336p. 1894. Lee and Shepard.
--Outward Bound: Or, Young American Afloat. Optic, Oliver, pseud. (Oliver Optic Ser.). 1910. Hurst & Co.
--Outward Bound: Or, Young Americans Afloat. Optic, Oliver, pseud. (Young America Abroad Ser.). N.D. Colby and Rich.
--Pacific Shores: Or, Adventures in Eastern Seas. Optic, Oliver, pseud. LC 12-37361. xii p. 1 l., 392 p. front., plates. 19 cm. (All-over-the-world library by Oliver Optic v. 4 of 3d ser.). 1898. Lee and Shepard.
--Palace and Cottage: Or, Young America in France and Switzerland. Optic, Oliver, pseud. (Young America Abroad Ser.). N.D. Colby and Rich.
--Palace and Cottage: Or, Young America in France and Switzerland, a Story of Travel and Adventure. Optic, Oliver, pseud. LC 41-267068. 3 p. l., 5-348 p. front., 2 pl 17 1/2 cm. (Added t.-p: Young America abroad, by Oliver Optic 1st ser, v). 1869. Lee and Shepard.
--Palace and Cottage: Or, Young America in France and Switzerland, a Story of Travel and Adventure. Optic, Oliver, pseud. LC 41-28208. 3 p. l., 5-348 p. front., plates. 17 1/2 cm. (Young America abroad. By Oliver Optic...1st ser. v). 1872. Lee and Shepard.
--Palace and Cottage: Or, Young America in France and Switzerland. Optic, Oliver, pseud, 1 of 12 vols. Nast & Stevens, illus. (Young America Abroad Ser. (First Ser.)). 1882. Lee & Shepard.
--The Picnic Party. Optic, Oliver, pseud. (Flora Lee Story Books). N.D. Colby and Rich.
--The Picnic Party. Optic, Oliver, pseud. N.D. E. P. Dutton & Co.
--The Picnic Party. Optic, Oliver, pseud, 1 of 12 vols. New ed. (Illus.). (Riverdale Story Books). 1882. Set. Lee & Shepard.
--The Picnic Party: A Story for Little Folks. Optic, Oliver, pseud. LC 12-37363. 60 p. incl. front., plates. 3 pl. 16 1/2 cm. (Half-title: Riverdale stories..By Oliver Optic. v. 10). 1890. Lee and Shepard.
--Plane and Plank: Or, The Mishaps of a Mechanic. Optic, Oliver, pseud. (Onward and Upward Ser.). N.D. Colby and Rich.
--Plane and Plank: Or, The Mishaps of a Mechanic. Optic, Oliver, pseud, 1 of 6 vols. (Illus.). 315p. (Onward and Upward Ser.). 1898. Lee & Shepard.
--Poor & Proud: Or, Fortunes of Katy Redburn. Optic, Oliver, pseud, 1 of 64 vols. (Young America Library: No. 33). 1900. Set. Hurst & Co.
--Poor and Proud: Or, The Fortunes of Katy Redburn, a Story for Young Folks. Optic, Oliver, pseud. LC 12-37364. 3 p. l., 5-274 p. front. 17 1/2 cm. (On cover: Boat club series by Oliver Optic. v. 5). c.1886. Lee and Shepard.
--Poor and Proud: Or, The Fortunes of Katy Redburn. Optic, Oliver, pseud. (Illus.). (Oliver Optic Series.). 1915. A L Burt & Co.
--Poor and Proud: Or, The Fortunes of Katy Redburn. Optic, Oliver, pseud. (Illus.). (The Rugby Ser.). N.D. A. L. Burt.
--Poor and Proud: Or, The Fortunes of Katy Redburn. Optic, Oliver, pseud. Empire ed. 1905. American News Co.
--Poor and Proud: Or, The Fortunes of Katy Redburn. Optic, Oliver, pseud. (Famous Boat-Club Ser.). N.D. Colby and Rich.
--Poor and Proud: Or, The Fortunes of Katy Redburn. Optic, Oliver, pseud, 1 of 6 vols. New ed. (Illus.). (The Boat Club Ser.). 1900. Set. H. M. Caldwell Co.
--Poor & Proud: Or, The Fortunes of Katy Redburn. Optic, Oliver, pseud, 1 of 103 vols. (The Pearl Library: No. 73). 1900. Set. Hurst & Co.
--Poor & Proud: Or, The Fortunes of Katy Redburn. Optic, Oliver, pseud, 1 of 5 vols. (Standard Ser.). 1900. Hurst & Co.
--Poor and Proud: Or, The Fortunes of Katy Redburn. Optic, Oliver, pseud. (Oliver Optic Ser.). 1910. Hurst & Co.
--Poor and Proud: Or, The Fortunes of Katy Redburn. Optic, Oliver, pseud, 1 of 6 vols. (Illus.). (Famous "Boat-Club" Ser.). 1882. Set. Lee & Shepard.
--Poor and Proud: or, The Fortunes of Katy Redburn. Optic, Oliver, pseud. (Illus.). 274p. 1898. Lee & Shepard.
--Poor & Proud: Or, The Fortunes of Katy Redburn. Optic, Oliver, pseud, 1 of 60 vols. (Illus.). (American Boys' Ser.: No. 32). 1900. Lee & Shepard.
--Poor and Proud: Or, The Fortunes of Katy Redburn. Optic, Oliver, pseud. (Illus.). (Oliver Optic Series.). N.D. Lothrop Lee & Shepard.
--Poor and Proud: Or, The Fortunes of Katy Redburn a. Optic, Oliver, pseud. LC 63-57442. 19 cm. 305p. 1858. Mershon Co.
--Proud and Lazy. Optic, Oliver, pseud. (Riverdale Story Books). N.D. Colby and Rich.
--Proud and Lazy. Optic, Oliver, pseud, 1 of 12 vols. New ed. (Illus.). (Riverdale Story Books). 1882. Set. Lee & Shepard.
--Proud and Lazy. Optic, Oliver, pseud. (Illus.). 96p. 1890. Lee & Shepard.
--Proud and Lazy: A Story for Little Folks. Optic, Oliver, pseud. LC 12-373582. 91 p. incl. front., 1 illus., plates. 2 pl. 16 1/2 cm. (Half-title: Riverdale stories...By Oliver Optic, v. 7). 1890. Lee and Shepard.
--Proud and Lazy: Or, A Story for Little Folks. Optic, Oliver, pseud. (Oliver Optic Ser.). 1910. Hurst & Co.
--Ready About: Or, Sailing the Boat. Optic, Oliver, pseud. (Illus.). N.D. Lee and Shepard.
--Ready About: Or, Sailing the Boat. Optic, Oliver, pseud. (Boat Builders Ser.). N.D. Lothrop, Lee & Shepard.
--Red Cross: or, Young America England Wales. Optic, Oliver, pseud. (Illus.). (Oliver Optic Ser.). N.D. Lothrop Lee & Shepard.
--Red Cross: Or, Young America in England and Wales; A Story of Travel and Adventure. Optic, Oliver, pseud. LC 41-26707. 8 p. l., 5-336 p. front. 2 pl. 17 1/2 cm. (Added t.-p.: Young America abroad, by Oliver Optic 1st ser., iii). 1868. Lee and Shepard.
--Red Cross: Or, Young America in England and Wales. Optic, Oliver, pseud. (Young America Abroad Ser.). N.D. Colby and Rich.
--Red Cross: Or, Young America in England and Wales. Optic, Oliver, pseud. LC 12-37365. 3 p. l., 5-336p. front., 2 pl. 17 1/2cm. (First Ser.: 111). c.1895. Lee & Shepard.
--Red Cross: Or, Young America in England and Wales. Optic, Oliver, pseud, 1 of 12 vols. Nast & Stevens, illus. (Young America Abroad Ser. (First Ser.)). 1882. Lee & Shepard.
--Rich and Humble: A Story for Young People. Optic, Oliver, pseud. LC 49-40499. 150 p. illus. 19 cm. 1911. New York Book Co.
--Rich and Humble: Or, The Mission of Bertha Grant. Optic, Oliver, pseud. (Illus.). (The Rugby Ser.). N.D. A. L. Burt.
--Rich and Humble: Or, The Mission of Bertha Grant. Optic, Oliver, pseud. (Oliver Optic Ser.). N.D. A. L. Burt.
--Rich and Humble: Or, The Mission of Bertha Grant. Optic, Oliver, pseud. (Woodville Stories). N.D. Colby and Rich.
--Rich and Humble: Or, The Mission of Bertha Grant. Optic, Oliver, pseud. (Oliver Optic Ser.). 1910. Hurst & Co.
--Rich and Humble: Or, The Mission of Bertha Grant. Optic, Oliver, pseud, 1 of 6 vols. (Woodville Stories). 1882. Lee & Shepard.
--Rich & Humble: Or, The Mission of Bertha Grant. Optic, Oliver, pseud, 1 of 60 vols. (Illus.). (American Boys' Ser.: No. 33). 1900. Lee & Shepard.
--Rich and Humble: Or, The Mission of Bertha Grant. Optic, Oliver, pseud. 296p. N.D. Lee & Shepard.
--Rich and Humble: Or, The Mission of Bertha Grant. Optic, Oliver, pseud. (Illus.). (Oliver Optic Series.). N.D. Lothrop Lee & Shepard.
--The Rival Battalions. McCormick, Brooks, pseud. LC 1-5109. 300 p. incl. front. plates. 19 cm. (On cover: Leather-clad tales. no 29). c.1891. United States Book Company.
--Riverdale Story Books. Optic, Oliver, pseud, 12 vols. New ed. 1882. Set. Lee & Shepard.
--Robinson Crusoe Jr. Optic, Oliver, pseud. (Riverdale Story Books). N.D. Colby and Rich.
--Robinson Crusoe, Jr. Optic, Oliver, pseud, 1 of 12 vols. New ed. (Illus.). 96p. (Riverdale Story Books). 1890. Lee & Shepard.
--Robinson Crusoe, Jr. A Story for Little Folks. Optic, Oliver, pseud. LC 12-37367. 92 p. incl. front., illus., plates. 2 pl. 16 1/2 cm. (Half-title: Riverdale stories...By Oliver Optic v. 9). 1890. Lee and Shepard.
--The Sailor Boy. Optic, Oliver, pseud. (Army and Navy Stories). N.D. Colby and Rich.
--The Sailor Boy: Or, Jack Somers in the Navy. Optic, Oliver, pseud. (Illus.). (Oliver Optic Series.). 1915. A L Burt & Co.
--The Sailor Boy: Or, Jack Somers in the Navy. Optic, Oliver, pseud. (Sailor Boy Ser.). N.D. Colby and Rich.
--Sailor Boy: Or, Jack Somers in the Navy. Optic, Oliver, pseud. (Oliver Optic Ser.). 1910. Hurst & Co.
--The Sailor Boy: Or, Jack Somers in the Navy. Optic, Oliver, pseud, 1 of 3 Vols. (Illus.). 333p. (The Sailor Boy Ser.). 1865. Lee & Shepard.
--The Sailor Boy: Or, Jack Somers in the Navy. Optic, Oliver, pseud. (Army & Navy Stories). N.D. Lothrop,Lee & Shepard.
--The Sailor Boy: or, Jack Somers in the Navy. Optic, Oliver, pseud. (Illus.). (Oliver Optic Ser.). N.D. Lothrop Lee & Shepard.
--The Sailor Boy: Or, Jack Sommers in the Navy. Optic, Oliver, pseud. 18cm. 336p. 1865. Lee & Shepard.
--Sea and Shore: Or, The Tramps of a Traveller. Optic, Oliver, pseud. (Onward and Upward Ser.). N.D. Colby and Rich.
--Sea and Shore: Or, The Tramps of a Traveller. Optic, Oliver, pseud. LC 1-22952. (Illus.). 3 p. l., 5-350 p. front., plates. 17 1/2 cm. (Added t.-p., illus.: Onward and upward series. v. 6). 1872. Lee and Shepard.
--Sea and Shore: Or, The Tramps of a Traveller. Optic, Oliver, pseud, 1 of 6 vols. (Illus.). (Onward And Upward Ser.). 1882. Set. Lee & Shepard.
--Sea and shore: Or, The Tramps of a Traveller. Optic, Oliver, pseud. 12cm. 350p. (The Upward and Onward Ser.: Vol. 6). 1900. Lee & Shepard.
--Sea and Shore: Or, The Tramps of a Traveller. Optic, Oliver, pseud. LC 4. 12cm. 350p. (The Upward and Onward Ser.). 1900. Lee & Shepard.
--Seek and Find: Or, The Adventures of a Smart Boy. Optic, Oliver, pseud. (Starry Flag Ser.). N.D. Colby and Rich.
--Seek and Find: Or, The Adventures of a Smart Boy. Optic, Oliver, pseud. LC 41-42137. 5 p. l., 5-304 p. front., plates. 17 1/2 cm. (Added t.-p.: Oliver Optic's Starry flag series. Iv). 1868. Lee and Shepard.
--Seek and Find: Or, The Adventures of a Smart Boy. Optic, Oliver, pseud, 1 of 6 vols. (Illus.). (The Starry Flag Ser.). 1882. Lee & Shepard.
--Seek and Find: Or, The Adventures of a Smart Boy. Optic, Oliver, pseud. LC 12-373684. 3 p. l., 5-304 p. front., plates. 17 1/2 cm. (Added to.-p.: Oliver Optic's starry flag series. iv). c.1895. Lee and Shepard.
--Seek and Find: Or, The Adventures of a Smart Boy. Optic, Oliver, pseud. (Illus.). (Oliver Optic Ser.). N.D. Lothrop Lee & Shepard.
--Shamrock and Thistle: Or, Young America in Ireland and Scotland. Optic, Oliver, pseud. (Young America Abroad Ser.). N.D. Colby and Rich.
--Shamrock and Thistle: Or, Young America in Ireland and Scotland; A Story of Travel and Adventure. Optic, Oliver, pseud. LC 14-22450. 1 p. l., 343 p. front., pl. 17 1/2 cm. (=added t.-p.: Young America abroad). c.1895. Lee and Shepard.
--Shamrock and Thistle: Or, Young America in Ireland and Scotland. Optic, Oliver, pseud. (Illus.). (Oliver Optic Series.). N.D. Lothrop Lee & Shepard.
--Shamrock and Thistle: Or, Young America in Ireland and Scotland. Optic, Oliver, pseud, 1 of 11 vols. Nast & Stevens, illus. (Illus.). 343p. (Young America Abroad Ser. (First Ser.)). 1868. Lee & Shepard.
--Snug Harbor: Or, The Champlain Mechanics. Optic, Oliver, pseud. LC 4-31646. 18cm. 343p. (The Boat-Builder Ser.; Vol. 2). 1884. Lee & Shepard.
--Snug Harbor: Or, The Champlain Mechanics. Optic, Oliver, pseud. (Boat Builders Ser.). N.D. Lothrop, Lee & Shepard.
--The Soldier Boy: Or, Tom Somers in the Army, a Story of the Great Rebellion. Optic, Oliver, pseud. LC 8-2134. 3 p. l., 5-333 p. front., plates. 17 cm. N.D. Lee and Shepard.
--The Soldier Boy: Or, Tom Somers in the Army. Optic, Oliver, pseud. (Illus.). (Oliver Optic Series.). 1915. A L Burt & Co.
--The Soldier Boy: Or, Tom Somers in the Army. Optic, Oliver, pseud. (Illus.). (The Rugby Ser.). N.D. A. L. Burt.
--The Soldier Boy: Or, Tom Somers in the Army. Optic, Oliver, pseud. (Soldier Boy Ser.). N.D. Colby and Rich.
--Soldier Boy: Or, Tom Somers in the Army. Optic, Oliver, pseud. (Oliver Optic Ser.). 1910. Hurst & Co.
--The Soldier Boy: Or, Tom Somers in the Army. Optic, Oliver, pseud, 1 of 6 vols. (Illus.). (Army and Navy Stories). 1882. Set. Lee & Shepard.
--The Soldier Boy: Or, Tom Somers in the Army. Optic, Oliver, pseud, 1 of 60 vols. (Illus.). (American Boys' Ser.: No. 53). 1900. Lee & Shepard.
--The Soldier Boy: Or, Tom Somers in the Army. Optic, Oliver, pseud, 1 of 3 Vols. (The Soldier Boy Ser.). N.D. Lee & Shepard.
--The Soldier Boy: Or, Tom Somers in the Army. Optic, Oliver, pseud. (Illus.). (Army and Navy Stories). N.D. Lee and Shepard.
--Square and Compasses: Or, Building the House. Optic, Oliver, pseud. LC 12-37370. 3 p. l., v-x, 9-314 p. front., 2 pl. 18 cm. (Added t.-p.: Oliver Optic's Boat-builder series. iii). 1885. Lee and Shepard.
--Stand by the Union. Optic, Oliver, pseud. (The Blue & Gray Ser.). N.D. Lothrop,Lee & Shepard.
--The Starry Flag: Or, The Young Fisherman of Cape Ann. Optic, Oliver, pseud. (Starry Flag Ser.). N.D. Colby and Rich.
--The Starry Flag: Or, The Young Fisherman of Cape Ann. Optic, Oliver, pseud, 1 of 6 vols. LC 12-37372. 3 p. l., 5-312 p. front, plates. 17 1/2 cm. (Added t.-p.: Oliver Optic's starry flag series. 1). c.1895. Lee and Shepard.
--The Starry Flag: Or, The Young Fisherman of Cape Ann. Optic, Oliver, pseud, 1 of 60 vols. (Illus.). (American Boys' Ser.: No. 54). 1900. Lee & Shepard.
--The Starry Flag: Or, The Young Fisherman of Cape Ann. Optic, Oliver, pseud. (Illus.). (Oliver Optic Series.). N.D. Lothrop Lee & Shepard.
--The Starry Flag Series. Optic, Oliver, pseud, 6 vols. (Illus.). 1882. Set. Lee & Shepard.
--Stem and Stern: Or, Building the Boat. Optic, Oliver, pseud. (Boat Builders Ser.). N.D. Lothrop, Lee & Shepard.
--Strange Sights Abroad: Or, Adventures in European Waters. Optic, Oliver, pseud. (All-Over-the-World-Series). N.D. Lothrop,Lee & Shepard.
--Strange Sights Abroad: Or, Adventures in European Waters. Optic, Oliver, pseud. (Illus.). (Oliver Optic Series.). N.D. Lothrop Lee & Shepard.

--Sunny Shores: Or, Young America in Italy and Austria. Optic, Oliver, pseud. LC 2-22400. 19cm. 409p. (Young America abroad, Second Ser.: Vol. 4). 1902. Lee & Shepard.
--Sunny Shores: Or, Young America in Italy and Austia. Optic, Oliver, pseud. (Illus.). (Oliver Optic Ser.). 1873. Lothrop Lee & Shepard.
--Sunny Shores: Or, Young America in Italy and Austria. Optic, Oliver, pseud, 1 of 12 vols. Nast & Stevens, illus. (Illus.). (Young America Abroad Ser. (Second Ser.)). 1882. Lee & Shepard.
--Switch off: Or, The War of the Students. Optic, Oliver, pseud. (Lake Shore Ser.). N.D. Colby and Rich.
--Switch Off: Or, The War of the Students. Optic, Oliver, pseud, 1 of 6 vols. (Illus.). (Lake Shore Ser.). 1882. Set. Lee & Shepard.
--Switch Off: Or, The War of the Students. Optic, Oliver, pseud. (Illus.). 288p. 1894. Lee & Shepard.
--Switch off: Or, The War of the Students. Optic, Oliver, pseud. LC 12-37375. 3 p. l., 5-288 p. front., plates. 19 cm. (Added t.-p.: Lake shore series. By Oliver Optic v. 4). c.1897. Lee and Shepard.
--Swith Off: Or, The War of the Students. Optic, Oliver, pseud. (Illus.). (Oliver Optic Ser.). N.D. Lothrop Lee & Shepard.
--Taken by the Enemy. Optic, Oliver, pseud. (Illus.). 18cm. 344p. (The Blue and Gray Ser.). 1888. Lothrop, Lee & Shepard.
--Taken by the Enemy. Optic, Oliver, pseud. (The Blue & Gray Afloat). N.D. Lothrop, Lee & Shepard.
--The Yacht Club: Or, The Young Boatbuilders. Optic, Oliver, pseud, 1 of 6 vols. (Illus.). (Yacht Club Ser.). 1901. Lee & Shepard.
--Three Millions!. Or, The Way of the World. Optic, Oliver, pseud. LC 12-37404. 464 p. front., plates. 19 cm. 1891. Lee and Shepard.
--Through by Daylight: Or, The Young Engineer of the Lake Shore Railroad. Optic, Oliver, pseud. (Lake Shore Ser.). N.D. Colby and Rich.
--Through by Daylight: Or, The Young Engineer of the Lake Shore Railroad. Optic, Oliver, pseud, 1 of 6 vols. (Illus.). (Lake Shore Ser.). 1882. Set. Lee & Shepard.
--Through by Daylight: Or, The Young Engineer of the Lake Shore Railroad. Optic, Oliver, pseud. LC 12-37376. 3 p. l., 5-300 p. front., plates. 19 cm. (Added t.-p.: Lake shore series. By Oliver Optic v. 1). c.1897. Lee and Shepard.
--Through by Daylight: Or, The Young Engineer of the Lake Shore Railroad. Optic, Oliver, pseud, 1 of 60 vols. (Illus.). (American Boys' Ser.: No. 55). 1900. Lee & Shepard.
--Through by Daylight: Or, The Young Engineer of the Lake Shore Railroad. Optic, Oliver, pseud. (Illus.). (Oliver Optic Ser.). N.D. Lothrop Lee & Shepard.
--Try Again: Or, The Trials and Triumphs of Harry West. Optic, Oliver, pseud, 98 vols. (The Rugby Ser.). 1905. Set. A L Burt Co.
--Try Again: Or, The Trials and Triumphs of Harry West. Optic, Oliver, pseud. (Illus.). (Oliver Optic Series.). 1915. A L Burt & Co.
--Try Again: Or, The Trials and Triumphs of Harry West. Optic, Oliver, pseud. Empire ed. 1905. American News Co.
--Try Again: Or, The Trials and Triumphs of Harry West. Optic, Oliver, pseud. (Famous Boat-Club Ser.). N.D. Colby and Rich.
--Try Again: Or, The Trials and Triumphs of Harry West. Optic, Oliver, pseud, 1 of 6 vols. New ed. (Illus.). (The Boat Club Ser.). 1900. Set. H. M. Caldwell Co.
--Try Again: Or, The Trials & Triumphs of Harry West. Optic, Oliver, pseud, 1 of 64 vols. (Young America Library: No. 49). 1900. Set. Hurst & Co.
--Try Again: Or, The Trials & Triumphs of Harry West. Optic, Oliver, pseud, 1 of 103 vols. (The Pearl Library: No. 97). 1900. Hurst & Co.
--Try Again: Or, The Trials and Triumphs of Harry West. Optic, Oliver, pseud, 1 of 5 vols. (Standard Ser.). 1900. Hurst & Co.
--Try Again: Or, The Trials and Triumphs of Harry West. Optic, Oliver, pseud. (Oliver Optic Ser.). 1910. Hurst & Co.
--Try Again: Or, The Trials and Triumphs of Harry West. Optic, Oliver, pseud, 1 of 6 vols. (Illus.). (Famous "Boat-Club Ser.). 1882. Set. Lee & Shepard.
--Try Again: Or, The Trials & Triumphs of Harry West. Optic, Oliver, pseud, 1 of 60 vols. (Illus.). (American Boys' Ser.: No. 40). 1900. Lee & Shepard.
--Try Again: Or, The Trials and Triumphs of Harry West. Optic, Oliver, pseud. (Oliver Optic Series.). N.D. Lothrop Lee & Shepard.
--Try Again: Or, The Trials and Triumphs of Harry West, A Story for Young Folks. Optic, Oliver, pseud. LC 20-23158. 3 p. l., 5-281 p. front. 17 1/2 cm. (Oliver Optic's Boat club series). 1874. Lee and Shepard.
--Try Again: Or, The Trials and Triumphs of Harry West, a Story for Young Folks. Optic, Oliver, pseud. LC 12-37377. 3 p. l., 5-281 p. front. 17 1/2 cm. (On cover: Boat club series by Oliver Optic v. 4). c.1885. Lee and Shepard.
--Try Again: Or, The Trials and Triumphs of Harry West, a Story for Young Folks. Optic, Oliver, pseud. LC 2-23158. 3 p. l., 5-281 p. front. 17 1/2 cm. 1859. Phillips, Sampson & Company.
--Try Again: Or, The Trials and Triumphs of Harry West, A Story for Young Folks. Optic, Oliver, pseud. N.D (Standard Books). The American News Co.
--Uncle Ben. Optic, Oliver, pseud. (Flora Lee Story Books). N.D. Colby and Rich.
--Uncle Ben. Optic, Oliver, pseud, 1 of 12 vols. New ed. (Illus.). (Riverdale Story Books). 1882. Set. Lee & Shepard.
--Uncle Ben: A Story for Little Folks. Optic, Oliver, pseud. LC 12-37349. 95 p. incl. front., illus., plates. 16 1/2 cm. (Half-title: Riverdale stories ... by Oliver Optic v. 5). 1890. Lee and Shepard.
--Up and Down the Nile: Or, Young Adventurers in Africa. Optic, Oliver, pseud. LC 12-37350. 2 p. l., vii-xiii p., 1 l., 352 p. front., plates. 19 cm. (All-over-the-world series by Oliver Optic. 2d ser., v. 3). 1894. Lee and Shepard.
--Up the Baltic: or, Young America in Norway. Optic, Oliver, pseud. (Illus.). (Oliver Optic Ser.). N.D. Lothrop Lee & Shepard.
--Up the Baltic: Or, Young America in Norway, Sweden, and Denmark. Optic, Oliver, pseud, 1 of 12 vols. Nast & Stevens, illus. (Young America Abroad Ser. (Second Ser.)). 1882. Lee & Shepard.
--Up the Baltic: Or, Young America in Norway, Sweden, and Denmark, a Story of Travel and Adventure. Optic, Oliver, pseud. LC 17-130143. 4 p. l., 7-368 p. front., 2 pl. 17 1/2 cm. (Young America abroad--Second series. v. 1). 1871. Lee and Shepard.
--Up the Baltic: Or, Young America in Norway, Sweden, and Denmark, a Story of Travel and Adventure. Optic, Oliver, pseud. LC 99-1921. 368 p. front., 2 pl. 19 cm. (Young America abroad--Second series. v. 1). 1899. Lee and Shepard.
--Up the River: Or, Yachting on the Mississippi. Optic, Oliver, pseud, 1 of 6 vols. (Great Western Ser.). 1900. Set. Lee & Shepard.
--A Victorious Union. Optic, Oliver, pseud, 1 of 6 vols. (Illus.). (The Blue & the Gray - Afloat Ser.). 1900. Set. Lee & Shepard.
--A Victorious Union. Optic, Oliver, pseud. (The Blue and Gray Afloat). N.D. Lothrop, Lee & Shepard.
--Vine and Olive: Or, Young America in Spain and Portugal. Optic, Oliver, pseud. 19cm. 412p. (Young America Abroad, Second Ser.: Vol. 5). 1904. Lee & Shepard.
--Vine and Olive: Or, Young America in Spain and Portugal. Optic, Oliver, pseud. (Illus.). (Oliver Optic Ser.). N.D. Lothrop Lee & Shepard.
--Vine and Olive: Or, Young America in Spain and Portugal. Optic, Oliver, pseud, 1 of 12 vols. Nast & Stevens, illus. (Illus.). (Young America Abroad Ser. (Second Ser.)). 1882. Lee & Shepard.
--Watch and Wait. Optic, Oliver, pseud. (The Rugby Series for Boys and Girls). N.D. A. L. Burt Company.
--Watch and Wait: Or, The Young Fugitives, a Story for Young People. Optic, Oliver, pseud. LC 12-37352. 3 p. l., 5-276 p. front., 2 pl. 17 1/2 cm. (Added t.-p.: Woodville stories by Oliver Optic. v. 3). 1893. Lee and Shepard.
--Watch and Wait: Or, The Young Fugitives. Optic, Oliver, pseud. (Illus.). (Oliver Optic Series.). 1915. A L Burt & Co.
--Watch and Wait: Or, The Young Fugitives. Optic, Oliver, pseud. (Woodville Stories). N.D. Colby and Rich.
--Watch and Wait: Or, The Young Fugitives. Optic, Oliver, pseud. (Oliver Optic Ser.). 1910. Hurst & Co.
--Watch and Wait: Or, The Young Fugitives. Optic, Oliver, pseud, 1 of 6 vols. (Illus.). 276p. (Woodville Stories). 1882. Lee & Shepard.
--Watch & Wait: Or, The Young Fugitives. Optic, Oliver, pseud, 1 of 60 vols. (Illus.). (American Boys' Ser.: No. 43). 1900. Lee & Shepard.
--Way of the World. Optic, Oliver, pseud. N.D. Colby and Rich.
--The Way of the World. Optic, Oliver, pseud, 1 of 6 vols. (Illus.). (Household Library). N.D. Set. Lee & Shepard.
--Within the Enemy's Lines. Optic, Oliver, pseud. LC 12-37552. 349 p. front., plates. 19 1/2 cm. (Half-title: The blue and the gray series, by Oliver Optic v. 2). 1890. Lee and Shepard.
--Within the Enemy's Lines. Optic, Oliver, pseud, 1 of 6 vols. (Illus.). (The Blue & the Gray - Afloat Ser.). 1900. Set. Lee & Shepard.
--Wolf Run: Or, The Boys of the Wilderness. Optic, Oliver, pseud, 1 of 60 vols. (Illus.). (American Boys' Ser.: No. 46). 1900. Lee & Shepard.
--Woodville Stories. Optic, Oliver, pseud, 6 vols. (Illus.). 1882. Set. Lee & Shepard.
--Work and Win: Or, Noddy Newman on a Cruise, a Story for Young People. Optic, Oliver, pseud. LC 12-37353. 3 p. l., 5-288 p. front., 2 pl. 17 1/2 cm. (Added t.-p.: Woodville stories by Oliver Optic v. 4). 1893. Lee and Shepard.
--Work and Win: Or, Noddy Newman on a Cruise. Optic, Oliver, pseud. (Illus.). (Oliver Optic Series). 1916. A L Burt & Co.
--Work and Win: Or, Noddy Newman on a Cruise. Optic, Oliver, pseud. (The Rugby Series for Boys and Girls). N.D. A. L. Burt Company.
--Work and Win: Or, Noddy Newman on a Cruise. Optic, Oliver, pseud. (Woodville Stories). N.D. Colby and Rich.
--Work and Win: Or, Noddy Newman on a Cruise. Optic, Oliver, pseud. (Oliver Optic Ser.). 1910. Hurst & Co.
--Work and Win: Or, Noddy Newman on a Cruise. Optic, Oliver, pseud, 1 of 6 vols. (Illus.). 288p. (Woodville Stories). 1882. Lee & Shepard.
--Work and Win: Or, Noddy Newman on a Cruise. Optic, Oliver, pseud, 1 of 60 vols. (Illus.). (American Boys' Ser.: No. 47). 1900. Lee & Shepard.
--Work and Win: Or, Noddy Newman on a Cruise. Optic, Oliver, pseud. (Illus.). (Oliver Optic Ser.). N.D. Lothrop Lee & Shepard.
--The Yacht Club: Or, The Young Boat-Builder. Optic, Oliver, pseud. LC 2-11147. (Illus.). 340 p. front., plates. 19 cm. (yacht club series. v. 2). 1901. Lee and Shepard.
--The Yacht Club: Or, The Young Boat Builders. Optic, Oliver, pseud. (Yacht Club Ser.). N.D. Colby and Rich.
--Yacht Club Series. Optic, Oliver, pseud, 6 vols. (Illus.). 1882. Set. Lee & Shepard.
--The Yankee Middy. Optic, Oliver, pseud. (Illus.). (Oliver Optic Series.). 1915. A L Burt & Co.
--The Yankee Middy. Optic, Oliver, pseud. (Army and Navy Stories). N.D. Colby and Rich.
--The Yankee Middy: Or, Adventures of a Naval Officer. Optic, Oliver, pseud. (Sailor Boy Ser.). N.D. Colby and Rich.
--The Yankee Middy: Or, Adventures of a Naval Officer. Optic, Oliver, pseud, 1 of 3 Vols. (The Sailor Boy Ser.). N.D. Lee & Shepard.
--The Yankee Middy: Or, Adventures of a Naval Officer. Optic, Oliver, pseud. (Oliver Optic Ser.). N.D. Lothrop Lee & Shepard.
--The Yankee Middy: Or, Adventures of a Navel Officer. Optic, Oliver, pseud. (The Rugby Series for Boys and Girls). N.D. A. L. Burt Company.
--The Yankee Middy: Or, The/Adventures of a Naval Officer. Optic, Oliver, pseud. (Illus.). 332p. N.D. Lee & Shepard.
--The Yankee Middy: Or, The Adventures of a Naval Officer, a Story of the Great Rebellion. Optic, Oliver, pseud. LC 20-231677. 332 p. front., plates. 17 1/2 cm. (On cover: Army and navy series). 1892. Lee and Shepard.
--The Yankee Middy: Or, The Adventures of a Naval Officer, a Story of the Great Rebellion. Optic, Oliver, pseud. LC 6-26731. 332 p. 18 cm. (On cover: Army and navy series). c.1893. Lee and Shepard.
--The Yankee Middy: Or, The Adventures of an Navy Officer. Optic, Oliver, pseud, 1 of 6 vols. (Illus.). (Army & Navy Stories). 1882. Set. Lee & Shepard.
--The Yankee Middy: Or, The Adventures of Naval Officer. Optic, Oliver, pseud. (Oliver Optic Ser.). 1910. Hurst & Co.
--The Young Actor: Or, The Solution of a Mystery. Winterton, Gayle, pseud. LC 5-42964. 19cm. 202p. (On cover: Leather-clad tales, no. 27). c.1891. United States Book Co.
--Young America Abroad Series. Optic, Oliver, pseud, 12 vols. Nast & Stevens, illus. (First & Second Ser.). 1882. Two sets. Lee & Shepard.
--A Young Knight-Errant: Or, Cruising in the West Indies. Optic, Oliver, pseud. LC 12-37354. x, 329 p. plates. 29 cm. (All-over-the-world series by Oliver Optic. 1st ser., v. 3). 1893. Lee and Shepard.
--A Young Knight Errant: Or, Cruising in the West Indies. Optic, Oliver, pseud. (Oliver Optic Ser.). N.D. Lothrop Lee & Shepard.
--A Young Knight Errant: Or, Crusing in the West Indies. Optic, Oliver, pseud. (All-Over-The-World Library: 1). N.D. Lee & Shepard.
--Young Lieutenant. Optic, Oliver, pseud. (The Rugby Series for Boys and Girls). N.D. A. L. Burt Company.
--The Young Lieutenant. Optic, Oliver, pseud. (Army and Navy Stories). N.D. Colby and Rich.
--The Young Lieutenant: Or, Adventures of an Army Officer. Optic, Oliver, pseud. (Illus.). (Oliver Optic Series.). N.D. Lothrop Lee & Shepard.
--The Young Lieutenant: Or, The Adventures of an Army Officer. Optic, Oliver, pseud. (Illus.). (Oliver Optic Series). 1915. A L Burt & Co.
--The Young Lieutenant: Or, The Adventures of an Army Officer. Optic, Oliver, pseud. (Soldier Boy Ser.). N.D. Colby and Rich.
--The Young Lieutenant: Or, The Adventures of an Army Officer. Optic, Oliver, pseud, 1 of 6 vols. (Illus.). 1882cm. (Army And Navy Stories). N.D. Set. Lee & Shepard.
--The Young Lieutenant: Or, The Adventures of and Army Officer. Optic, Oliver, pseud, 1 of 3 Vols. (The Soldier Boys Ser.). N.D. Lee & Shepard.
--The Young Lieutenant: Or, The Adventures of an Army Officer; a Story of the Great Rebellion. Optic, Oliver, pseud. LC 12-37355. 3 p. l., 5-373 p. front., plates. 17 1/2 cm. (On cover: Army and navy series by Oliver Optic. v. 3). 1893. Lee and Shepard.
--Young Lieutenant: Or, The Adventures of Army Officer. Optic, Oliver, pseud. (Oliver Optic Ser.). N.D. Hurst & Co.
--The Young Navigators: Or, The Foreign Cruise of the Maud. Optic, Oliver, pseud. LC 12-37348. xii p. 1 l., 344 p. front., plates. 19 cm. (All-over-the-world series by Oliver Optic 2d ser., v. 2). 1894. Lee and Shepard.
--The Young Navigators: Or, The Foreign Cruise of the Maud. Optic, Oliver, pseud. (All-Over-The-World Library, Second Ser). N.D. Lee and Shephard.
--The Young Voyagers. Optic, Oliver, pseud. (Riverdale Story Books). N.D. Colby and Rich.
--The Young Voyagers. Optic, Oliver, pseud, 1 of 12 vols. New ed. (Illus.). 96p. (Riverdale Story Books). 1890. Lee & Shepard.
--The Young Voyagers: A Story for Little Folks. Optic, Oliver, pseud. LC 12-37356. 92 p. incl. front., plates. 2 pl. 16 1/2 cm. (Half-title: Riverdale stories... By Oliver Optic. v. 2). 1890. Lee and Shepard.

Adams, William Taylor (1822-1897), ed.
--Folk Story and Verse. Optic, Oliver, pseud. rev. ed. LC 99-1509. (Illus.). 18 1/2cm. 176p. (Lakeside Literature Ser.: Bk. 11). 1899. Western Pub House.
--Oliver Optic's Annual, 1891. Optic, Oliver, pseud. N.D. Estes & Lauriat.
--Our Boys and Girls Keepsake: Containing:"Desk & Debit","Plane & Plank",etc. Optic, Oliver, pseud. N.D. Colby and Rich.
--Our Little Ones Annual. Optic, Oliver, pseud. (Vol. 10). N.D. Estes & Lauriat.
--Our Little Ones' Annual Eighteen Ninety-Five. Optic, Oliver, pseud. (Illus.). N.D. Estes & Lauriat's.

Adams, William Taylor (1822-1897) & Kellogg, Elijah (1813-1901)
--Oliver Optic's Magazine. Optic, Oliver, pseud, 2 vols. in 1, Vols. 17-18. (Containing Serial Stories, Sketches, etc.). (Illus.). 832p. 1875. Lee & Shepard.
--Oliver Optic's Magazine: Containing Serial Stories, Sketches, etc. Optic, Oliver, pseud, 2 vols. in 1, Vol. 9-10. May, Sophie, pseud. (Illus.). 832p. 1871. Lee & Shepard.
--Oliver Optic's Magazine: Containing Serial Stories, Sketches, etc. Optic, Oliver, pseud, 2 vols. in 1, Vol. 11-12. May, Sophie, pseud. (Illus.). 832p. 1872. Lee & Shepard.
--Oliver Optic's Magazine: Containing Serial Stories, Sketches, etc. Optic, Oliver, pseud, 2 vols. in 1, Vols. 13-14. (Illus.). 832p. 1873. Lee & Shepard.
--Oliver Optic's Magazine: Containing Serial Stories, Sketches, etc. Optic, Oliver, pseud, 2 vols. in 1, Vols. 15-16. (Illus.). 832p. 1874. Lee & Shepard.
--Our Boys and Girls Album: Containing Stories, Poems, Sketches, etc. Optic, Oliver, pseud. Adams, William Taylor (1822-1897), ed. Optic, Oiver, pseud. (Illus.). N.D. Lee & Shepard.
--Our Boys and Girls Cabinet: Containing Stories, Poems, Sketches, etc. Optic, Oliver, pseud. Adams, William Taylor (1822-1897), ed. Optic, Oliver, pseud. (Illus.). N.D. Lee & Shepard.
--Our Boys and Girls Mirror: Containing Stories, Poems and Sketches. Optic, Oliver, pseud. Adams, William Taylor (1822-1897), ed. Optic, Oliver, pseud. (Illus.). N.D. Lee & Shepard.
--Our Boys and Girls Museum: Containing Stories, Poems, Sketches, etc. Optic, Oliver, pseud. Adams, William Taylor (1822-1897), ed. Optic, Oliver, pseud. (Illus.). N.D. Lee & Shepard.

Adams, William Taylor (1822-1897) & Stratemeyer, Edward L. (1862-1930)
--An Undivided Union. Optic, Oliver, pseud. 12cm. 432p. (The Blue and Gray Ser.: Vol. 6). 1899. Lee & Shepard.

AUTHOR INDEX ADLER, DAVID

--An Undivided Union. Optic, Oliver, pseud. (The Blue and the Gray--On Land: No. 6). N.D. Lothrop, Lee & Shepard.

Adams, William (1814-1848)

--Allegories: Containing: The Distant Hills, Shadow of the Cross, Old Man's Home, King's Messenger. 1888. Thomas Whittaker.

--Allegories: Includes "The Distant Hills," "The King's Messengers," "The Old Man's Home," and "The Shadow of the Cross.". N.D. E P Dutton.

--The King's Messengers: An Allegorical Tale. 6th american ed. Howland, William, illus. Weir, designed by. LC 42-28866. 3 p.l., 5-141 p. front., plates. 15 cm. 1849. General Prot. Episcopal S. S. Union, D. Dana, Jr. Agent.

Adamson, Douglas

--Charles Bear and the Mystery of the Forest. Adamson, Douglas, illus. LC 77-2805. p. cm. 20cm. 85p. 1977. (ISBN 0-395-25841-3). Houghton Mifflin.

Adamson, Gareth, jt. auth. see Adamson, Jean.

Adamson, Gareth (1925-1982)

--Harold, the Happy Handyman. american ed. Adamson, Gareth (1925-1982), illus. LC 68-14149. (Illus.). 43 p. 25cm. 1968. Harvey House.

--Mr. Budge Builds a House. LC 68-21155. (Illus.). 31 p. 24cm. 1968, c.1963. Chilton Book Co.

--Mr. Budge Buys a Car. (Illus.). 32 p. 25cm. 1968, c.1965. Chilton Book Co.

--Old Man up a Tree. Adamson, Gareth (1925-1982), illus. LC 63-7060. 1 v. (unpaged) col. illus. 27 cm. 1963. Abelard-Schuman.

--Three Discontented Clowns. Adamson, Gareth (1925-1982), illus. LC 66-118905. 1 v. (unpaged) col. illus. 27cm. 1966. Abelard.

Adamson, George

--A Finding Alphabet. LC 66-2165. 1v. (unpaged) col. illus. 19x25cm. 1966, c.1964. Faber & Faber.

Adamson, Jean

--Hop Like Me. Adamson, Gareth (1925-1982), illus. LC 72-79799. (Illus.). 32p. (gr. k-3). 1972. (ISBN 0-8075-3363-7). A Whitman.

Adamson, Jean & Adamson, Gareth (1925-1982)

--Family Tree. LC 68-22187. (Illus.). 32 p. 24cm. 1968. A. Whitman.

--Topsy & Tim Cross the Channel. (gr. k-3). 1977. (ISBN 0-8277-5338-1). British Bk Ctr.

--Topsy & Tim Go Sailing. (gr. k-3). 1977. (ISBN 0-8277-5339-X). British Bk Ctr.

--Topsy & Tim Visit the Dentist. (gr. k-3). 1977. (ISBN 0-8277-5340-3). British Bk Ctr.

--Topsy & Tim Visit the Doctor. (gr. k-3). 1977. (ISBN 0-8277-5336-5). British Bk Ctr.

--Topsy & Tim's New Brother. (gr. k-3). 1977. (ISBN 0-8277-5335-7). British Bk Ctr.

--Topsy & Tim's Snowy Day. (gr. k-3). 1977. (ISBN 0-8277-5337-3). British Bk Ctr.

Adamson, Joy Friederike Victoria (1910-1980)

--Elsa. 1963. Pantheon Books.

--Elsa & Her Cubs. LC 65-23973. (Illus.). (gr. 5 up). 1965. (ISBN 0-15-225471-4). HarBraceJ.

--Pippa: The Cheetah and Her Cubs. (Illus.). 48p. 1970. H B J.

Adcock, Marion St. John see Webb, Marion St. John Adcock, Mrs.

Addams, Charles Samuel (1912-)

--The Chas. Addams Mother Goose. 1977. (Windmill). Dutton.

--Chas. Addams Mother Goose. Addams, Charles Samuel (1912-), illus. (gr. 1-6). 1967. (ISBN 0-06-020018-9, HarpJ). (ISBN 0-06-020019-7). Har-Row.

Addams, Charles Samuel (1912-) & Gwynne, Frederick Hubbard

--A Treasury of Windmill Books. Addams, Charles Samuel (1912-) & Aruego, Jose, illus. (Illus.). 64p. (gr. 1 up). N.D. (ISBN 0-671-44406-9). Windmill Bks.

Addie

--The Silly Book of Animals. Drawson, Blair (1943-), illus. LC 73-80371. (Illus.). 28 p. 33cm. 1973. Golden Press.

Addington, Luther Foster (1899-)

--The Little Fiddler of Laurel Cove. Gotlieb, Jules, illus. LC 60-6941. 159p. illus. 22cm. 1960. Bobbs-Merrill.

--Sugar in the Gourd. Gotlieb, Jules, illus. LC 61-79217. 128p. illus. 22cm. 1961. Bobbs-Merrill.

--Tip-off to Win. Aloise, Frank E., illus. LC 62-19334. 155p. illus. 22cm. 1962. Bobbs-Merrill.

--Tipoff to Win. Gotlieb, Jules, illus. (Illus.). (gr. 2-6). 1962. (ISBN 0-672-50539-8). Bobbs.

Addington, Sarah (1891-)

--The Boy Who Lived in Pudding Lane: Being a True Account, If Only You Believe It, of the Life and Ways of Santa, Oldest Son of Mr. and Mrs. Claus. Kay, Gertrude Alice (1884-1939), illus. LC 22-22058. viii p., 1 l., 93 p. col. front., col. plates. 21 1/2 cm. c.1922. The Atlantic Monthly Press.

--The Great Adventures of Mrs. Santa Claus. Kay, Gertrude Alice, illus. 1923. Little,Brown & Co.

--The Great Adventures of Mrs. Santa Claus. Kay, Gertrude Alice (1884-1939), illus. 1923. J.B. Lippincott.

--Hound of Heaven. LC 35-14233. 3 p. l., 50 p. 19 1/2 cm. 1935. D. Appleton-Century Company, Incorporated.

--Jerry Juddikins. Kay, Gertrude Alice (1884-1939), illus. LC 27-1233. 3 p. l., 65 p. col. front., col. plates. 20 1/2 cm. c.1926. David McKay Company.

--The Pied Piper in Pudding Lane: Being the Truth About the Pied Piper, As Santa, Oldest Son of Mr. and Mrs. Claus, Discovered It Before Ever He Left Pudding Lane. Kay, Gertrude Alice (1884-1939), illus. LC 23-13422. vii p. 1 l., 97 p. col. front., col. plates. 21 1/2 cm. c.1923. The Atlantic Monthly Press.

--Pudding Lane People. Scott, Janet Laura, illus. LC 26-17756. 4 p. l., 103 p. col. front., col. plates. 22 1/2 cm. 1926. Little, Brown, and Company.

--Round the Year in Pudding Lane. Kay, Gertrude Alice (1884-1939), illus. LC 24-210502. 4 p. l., 231 p. front., plates. 22 1/2 cm. 1924. Little, Brown, and Company.

Addis, Marguerite Lynch

--George the Rooster. Rader, Jack, illus. LC 45-10700. 3 p. l., 3-38, 1 p. illus. 21 1/2 cm. 1945. W. Hebberd.

Addison, Harry Wayne

--Write That Down for Me Daddy. Schendle, Kathy Addison, illus. LC 78-9028. (Illus.). 60 p. 20cm. N.D. (ISBN 0-88289-116-2). Pelican Pub. Co.

Addison, Robert B.

--Children's Voices. Bennett, Harriet M., illus. N.D. Publications of E. P. Dutton & Co.

Additon, Elizabeth

--A Candle for Santa Claus. (Illus.). (gr. k-3). N.D. Vantage.

Addy, Sharon

--We Didn't Mean to. Blair, Jay, illus. LC 80-24976. p. cm. c.1981. (ISBN 0-8172-1370-8). Raintree Childrens Books.

Ade, George (1866-1944)

--Fables in Slang: A Book of Moral Stories. N.D. Duffield.

--The Girl Proposition: A Bunch of He and She Fables. LC 2-24481. xii, 192 p. incl. front., illus. 17 1/2 cm. 1902. R.H. Russell.

--Hand-Made Fables. McCutcheon, John T., illus. 1920. Doubleday Page & Co.

--The Slim Princess. Kerr, George F., illus. 1907. Bobbs-Merrill Co.

Adelberg, Doris, pseud., see Orgel, Doris.

Adelberg, Doris, pseud. (1929-)

--Grandma's Holidays. Orgel, Doris. Kennedy, Paul Edward (1929-), illus. LC 63-16421. (Illus.). (gr. k-3). 1963. (ISBN 0-8037-3019-5). (ISBN 0-8037-3020-9). Dial.

--Lizzie's Twins. Orgel, Doris. Bodecker, Niels Mogens (1922-), illus. LC 64-12292. 32 p. illus. 18 cm. 1964. Dial Press.

Adelborg, Ottilia (1855-)

--Clean Peter and the Children of Grubbylea. Wallas, Ada Radford, Mrs. (1959-), tr. LC 4-16244. 24 numb. l. col. illus. 20 1/2 x 28 1/2 cm. 1901. Longmans, Green, and Co.

Adelman, Bor & Hall, Susan

--Us & Them. (Illus.). 64p. (gr. 3-7). 1971. World Pub.

Adelson, Leone, jt. auth. see Moore, Lilian.

Adelson, Leone (1908-)

--All Ready for School. Elgin, Kathleen (1923-), illus. LC 57-7639. unpaged. illus. 27cm. c.1957. (ISBN 0-679-25008-5). D. McKay Co.

--All Ready for Summer. Elgin, Kathleen (1923-), illus. LC 56-5381. (Illus.). unpaged. 27cm. c.1956. D. McKay Co.

--All Ready for Summer. Elgin, Kathleen (1923-), illus. 1956. (ISBN 0-8382-0025-7, Cadmus Books). E. M. Hale and Company.

--All Ready for Winter. Elgin, Kathleen (1923-), illus. LC 52-13321. unpaged. illus. 26cm. c.1952. (ISBN 0-679-25010-7). D. McKay Co.

--The Blowaway Hat. Wagstaff, Dorothy, illus. (gr. 2). N.D. David McKay Co.

--The Blowaway Hat. Wagstaff, Dorothy, illus. LC 46-7969. 32 p. col. illus. 26 1/2 x 19 1/2 cm. 1946. Reynal & Hitchcock.

--Fly Away at the Air Show. Golbin, Andree, illus. (Illus.). (Easy Readers Ser). (gr. k-3). N.D. Wonder.

--The House with Red Sails. Wiese, Kurt (1887-1974), illus. LC 51-10586. 185 p. illus. 21 cm. 1951. D. McKay Co.

--Please Pass the Grass. Duvoisin, Roger Antoine (1904-1980), illus. LC 60-5153. (Illus.). (gr. 1-3). 1960. (ISBN 0-679-25111-1). McKay.

--Red Sails on the James. Koering, Ursula (1921-), illus. LC 53-7547. 181p. illus. 21cm. 1953. D. McKay Co.

--Who Blew That Whistle?. Fabres, Oscar (1900-), illus. LC 46-119009. 2 p. l., 9-45 p. col. illus. 24 1/2 cm. 1946. W. R. Scott, Inc.

Adelson, Leone (1908-) & Moore, Lillian

--Mister Twitmeyer & the Poodle. Shortall, Leonard W., illus. (Illus.). 24cm. 83p. (The Random House easy to read library). (Gateway Ser: No. 29). (gr. 3-5). 1963. (ISBN 0-394-90129-0, BYR). Random.

--Old Rosie. 1952. Random House, Inc.

--Old Rosie, the Horse Nobody Understood. (Illus.). (Gateway Ser.: No. 38). (gr. 3-7). 1959. (ISBN 0-394-90108-8, BYR). Random.

--The Terrible Mr. Twitmeyer. LC 52-7220. (Gateway Ser.: No. 5). (gr. 3-7). 1952. (ISBN 0-394-90105-3). Random.

Adeney, jt. ed. see Bennett.

Adeney, W. F. & Bennett, W. H.

--Bible Stories Retold. (Every Boy's and Every Girl's Ser.). 1900. Macmillan Co.

Adis, Dorothy Kelley (1896-)

--Is Anybody Hungry?. Marokvia, Artur F. (1909-), illus. LC 64-10080. 63 p. illus. 22 cm. 1964. Putnam.

Adkins, Jan (1944-)

--Luther Tarbox. LC 77-6711. (Illus.). 32 p. 20cm. c.1977. (ISBN 0-684-14931-1). Scribner.

--Moving on: Stories of Four Travelers. Adkins, Jan (1944-), illus. LC 78-1041. (Encore Edition). (gr. 5 up). 1978. (ISBN 0-684-17730-7, ScribJ). Scribner.

--Moving on: Stories of Four Travelers. Adkins, Jan (1944-), illus. LC 78-1041. (Illus.). 96 p. 21cm. c.1978. (ISBN 0-684-14931-1). Scribner.

--Small Garden, Big Surprise. Adkins, Jan (1944-), illus. LC 73-81583. (Illus.). 16 p. 20cm. (Magic circle book). 1974. (ISBN 0-663-25445-0). Ginn.

--A Storm Without Rain. 1st ed. LC 82-20342. p. cm. c.1982. (ISBN 0-316-01084-7). Little, Brown. **Award: (ALA)**

Adler, Bill

--Boys Are Very Funny People. Gantz, David, illus. 126p. illus. 18cm. (40-125). 1963, c.1962. McFadden.

--Boys Are Very Funny People. Gantz, David, illus. LC 62-19724. 128p. illus. 20cm. c.1962. Morrow.

--Dear Pastor. Beach, Bettye Rene, illus. LC 80-24088. (Illus.). ca. 100 p. 16cm. c.1980. (ISBN 0-8407-5218-0). T. Nelson Publishers.

--The World's Worst Jokes. LC 76-6819. (Illus.). 128p. (gr. 3-8). 1976. (ISBN 0-685-66553-4). G&D.

--World's Worst Riddles and Jokes. Malsberg, Edward, illus. LC 76-6819. (Illus.). 110 p. 28cm. c.1976. (ISBN 0-448-12586-2). (ISBN 0-448-13382-2). Grosset & Dunlap.

Adler, Bill, ed.

--Letters to Smokey Bear. Perl, Susan (1922-1983), illus. LC 66-14302. (Illus.). 48 p. 22cm. (Laugh books). 1966. Wonder Books.

Adler, Bill, jt. auth. see Carter, Amy.

Adler, Carole Schwerdtfeger (1932-)

--Binding Ties. LC 84-15580. 183 p. 22cm. c.1985. (ISBN 0-385-29293-7). Delacorte Press.

--The Cat That Was Left Behind. LC 80-28123. p. cm. c.1981. (ISBN 0-395-31020-2). Houghton Mifflin/Clarion Books.

--Down by the River. LC 81-685. 206 p. 22cm. c.1981. (ISBN 0-698-20532-4). Coward, McCann & Geoghegan.

--The Evidence That Wasn't There. LC 82-1194. p. cm. c.1982. (ISBN 0-89919-117-7). Clarion Books.

--Fly Free. LC 83-16599. 159 p. 22cm. c.1984. (ISBN 0-698-20606-1). Coward-McCann.

--Footsteps on the Stairs: A Novel. LC 81-15146. 151 p. 22cm. c.1982. Delacorte Press.

--Get Lost, Little Brother. LC 82-9579. p. cm. 1983, c.1982. (ISBN 0-89919-154-1). Clarion Books.

--Goodbye, Pink Pig. LC 85-6329. p. cm. 1985. (ISBN 0-399-21282-5). Putnam.

--In Our House Scott Is My Brother. LC 79-20693. 139 p. 22cm. c.1980. (ISBN 0-02-700140-7). Macmillan.

--The Magic of the Glits. Forberg, Ati, pseud. (1925-), illus. Forberg, Beate Gropius. LC 78-12149. (Illus.). 112 p. 22cm. c.1979. (ISBN 0-02-700120-2). Macmillan.

--The Once in a While Hero. LC 82-1511. 111 p. 22cm. c.1982. (ISBN 0-698-20553-7). Coward, McCann & Geoghegan.

--Roadside Valentine. LC 83-9394. 180p. (gr. 7 up). 1983. (ISBN 0-02-700350-7). Macmillan.

--Shadows on Little Reef Bay. LC 83-15207. 180p. (gr. 6 up). 1984. (ISBN 0-89919-217-3, Clarion). HM.

--The Shell Lady's Daughter. LC 82-19801. 140 p. 23cm. c.1983. (ISBN 0-698-20580-4). Coward-McCann.

--Shelter on Blue Barns Road. LC 80-24715. 133 p. 22cm. c.1981. (ISBN 0-02-700280-2). Macmillan Pub. Co.

--The Silver Coach. LC 79-10430. 122 p. 22cm. c.1979. (ISBN 0-698-20504-9). Coward, McCann & Geoghegan.

--Some Other Summer. LC 82-7161. 126 p. 22cm. c.1982. (ISBN 0-02-700290-X). Macmillan Pub. Co.

--With Westie and the Tin Man. LC 84-20154. 194 p. 22cm. c.1985. (ISBN 0-02-700360-4). Macmillan.

Adler, David A. (1947-)

--Bible Fun Book: Puzzles, Riddles, Magic, & More. (Illus., Orig.). (A Bonim Fun-to-Do Bk.). (gr. 1-5). 1979. (ISBN 0-88482-769-0). Hebrew Pub.

--Bunny Rabbit Rebus. Linden, Madelaine Gill, illus. (gr. 1-3). 1983. Harper & Row.

--Bunny Rabbit Rebus. 1st ed. Linden, Madelaine Gill, illus. LC 82-45574. (Illus.). 38 p. 18cm. c.1983. (ISBN 0-690-04196-9). (ISBN 0-690-04197-7). T.Y. Crowell.

--Cam Jansen & Mystery Carnival Prize. Natti, Susanna (1948-), illus. LC 84-3617. (Illus.). 22cm. 64p. (Cam Jansen Adventure Ser.: No. 9). (gr. 2-5). 1984. (ISBN 0-670-20034-4, Viking Kestrel). Viking.

--Cam Jansen and the Mystery at the Monkey House. Natti, Susanna (1948-), illus. LC 85-40443. (Illus.). 56 p. 22cm. (Cam Jansen Adventure ; 10). 1985. (ISBN 0-670-80782-6). Viking Kestrel.

--Cam Jansen & the Mystery Monster Movie. Natti, Susanna (1948-), illus. LC 83-16693. (Illus.). 64p. (Cam Jansen Mystery Adventure Ser.). (gr. 2-5). 1984. (ISBN 0-670-20035-2, Viking Kestrel). Viking.

--Cam Jansen & the Mystery of the Babe Ruth Baseball. Natti, Susanna (1948-), illus. LC 81-71902. (Illus.). 64p. (Cam Jansen Ser.: No. 6). (gr. 2-5). 1982. (ISBN 0-670-20037-9). Viking Pr.

--Cam Jansen and the Mystery of the Circus Clown. Natti, Susanna (1948-), illus. LC 82-50363. p. cm. (The Cam Jansen Adventure Ser.: 7). 1983. (ISBN 0-670-20036-0). Viking Press.

--Cam Jansen and the Mystery of the Dinosaur Bones. Natti, Susanna (1948-), illus. LC 80-25132. (Illus.). 56 p. 22cm. (A Cam Jensen Adventure). 1981. (ISBN 0-670-20040-9). Viking Press.

--Cam Jansen and the Mystery of the Gold Coins. Natti, Susanna (1948-), illus. LC 81-16158. (Illus.). 57 p. 22cm. (Cam Jansen Adventure Ser.: 5). 1982. (ISBN 0-670-20038-7). Viking Press.

--Cam Jansen and the Mystery of the Stolen Diamonds. Natti, Susanna (1948-), illus. LC 79-20695. (Illus.). 58 p. 22cm. (Cam Jansen Adventure Ser.: 1). 1980. (ISBN 0-670-20039-5). Viking Press.

--Cam Jansen and the Mystery of the Television Dog. Natti, Susanna (1948-), illus. LC 81-2207. p. cm. (Cam Jansen Adventure Ser.: 4). 1981. (ISBN 0-670-20040-9). Viking.

--Cam Jansen and the Mystery of the U.F.O. Natti, Susanna (1948-), illus. LC 80-15580. p. cm. (Cam Jansen Adventure Series: 2). 1980. (ISBN 0-670-20041-7). Viking Press.

--The Carsick Zebra & Other Animal Riddles. De Paola, Tomie, pseud. (1934-), illus. De Paola, Thomas Anthony. LC 82-48750. (Illus.). 64p. (gr. 1-4). 1983. (ISBN 0-8234-0479-X). Holiday.

--The Children of Chelm. Friedman, Arthur (1935-), illus. LC 79-20617. (Illus.). 30 p. 24cm. c.1979. (ISBN 0-88482-773-9). Bonim Books.

--Eaton Stanley and the Mind Control Experiment. Drescher, Joan E. LC 84-21135. (Illus.). 88 p. 21cm. (Eaton Stanley adventure). ((Series: Adler, David A.). (Eaton Stanley adventure.). c.1985. (ISBN 0-525-44117-4). Dutton.

--The Fourth Floor Twins and the Fish Snitch Mystery. Trivas, Irene, illus. LC 85-43408. p. cm. 1986, c.1985. (ISBN 0-14-032082-2). Puffin Books.

--The Fourth Floor Twins and the Fish Snitch Mystery. Trivas, Irene, illus. LC 84-25713. (Illus.). 58 p. 22cm. (Fourth Floor Twins Series ; #1). 1985. (ISBN 0-670-80087-2). Viking Kestrel.

--The Fourth Floor Twins and the Fortune Cookie Chase. Trivas, Irene, illus. LC 85-43407. p. cm. (1947-). 1986, c.1985. (ISBN 0-14-032083-0). Puffin Books.

--The Fourth Floor Twins and the Fortune Cookie Chase. Trivas, Irene, illus. LC 84-21924. (Illus.). 58 p. 22cm. (Fourth floor twins ; 2). 1985. (ISBN 0-670-80641-2). Viking Kestrel.

--Hanukkah Fun Book: Puzzles, Riddles, Magic, and More. LC 76-47459. (Illus.). 47 p. 28cm. c.1976. (ISBN 0-88482-754-2). Bonim Books.

--The House on the Roof. Hirsh, Marilyn, illus. LC 84-12555. (Illus.). 32p. (gr. 4). N.D. (ISBN 0-930494-34-2). (ISBN 0-930494-28-8). Kar-Ben.

--The House on the Roof: A Sukkot Story. Hirsh, Marilyn (1944-), illus. LC 84-12555. (Illus.). 30 p. 26cm. 1984. (ISBN 0-930494-34-2). (ISBN 0-930494-35-0). Kar-Ben Copies.

--The House on the Roof: A Sukkot Story. Hirsh, Marilyn (1944-), illus. LC 84-12555. (Illus.). 32p. (gr. 4). 84. . (ISBN 0-930494-34-2). (ISBN 0-930494-28-8). Kar-Ben.

--The House on the Roof: A Sukkoth Story. 1976. Hebrew.
--Jeffrey's Ghost and the Fifth-Grade Dragon. Jenkins, Jean, illus. LC 85-886. (Illus.). 52 p. 22cm. c.1985. Holt, Rinehart, and Winston.
--Jeffrey's Ghost and the Leftover Baseball Team. Jenkins, Jean, illus. LC 83-22662. 58p. (gr. 3-6). 1984. (ISBN 0-03-069282-2). HR&W.
--A Little at a Time. Bodecker, Niels Mogens (1922-), illus. LC 75-8068. p. cm. 1975. (ISBN 0-394-82533-0). (ISBN 0-394-92533-5). Random House.
--My Dog and the Key. Barton, Byron (1930-), illus. LC 82-2790. (Byron Barton is the legal name change of Byron Vartanian.). p. cm. (An Easy-Read Story Book). 1982. (ISBN 0-531-03555-7). (ISBN 0-531-04449-1). F. Watts.
--My Dog and the knock Knock Mystery. Winborn, Marsha, illus. LC 84-19213. (Illus.). 32p. (First Mystery Book). (ps-1). c.1985. (ISBN 0-8234-0551-6). Holiday.
--Passover Fun Book: Puzzles, Riddles, Magic, and More. LC 77-27422. (Illus.). 48 p. 28cm. (Bonim fun-to-do book). c.1978. (ISBN 0-88482-759-3). Bonim Books.
--The Twisted Witch and Other Spooky Riddles. Chess, Victoria (1939-), illus. LC 85-909. (Illus.). 62 p. 22cm. c.1985. (ISBN 0-8234-0571-0). Holiday House.
--You Think It's Fun to Be a Clown!. Cruz, Raymond (1933-), illus. LC 79-7594. (Illus.). 32 p. 29cm. c.1980. (ISBN 0-385-14459-8). (ISBN 0-385-14460-1). Doubleday.

Adler, Irving (1913-)
--The Adler Book of Puzzles & Riddles: Or, Sam Loyd Up-To-Date. Adler, Peggy, illus. LC 62-14898. (Illus.). (gr. 3-6). 1962. (ISBN 0-381-99977-7, JD-J). Har-Row.
--Second Adler Book of Puzzles & Riddles. LC 63-15912. (Illus.). (gr. 3-6). 1963. (ISBN 0-381-99946-7, JD-J). Har-Row.

Adler, James B., ed.
--In Praise of Babies. Fry, Rosalind, illus. LC 68-14049. (Illus.). 1 v. (unpaged. 21cm. 1968. Doubleday.

Adler, Samuel, et al.
--Songs for Children. Spiro, J. D., intro. by. (gr. k-5). 1970. UAHC.

Adler, Warren
--Banquet Before Dawn. LC 75-31651. 256p. 1976. (ISBN 0-399-11642-7). Putnam Pub Group.
--The Henderson Equation. LC 76-13040. 1976. (ISBN 0-399-11755-5). Putnam Pub Group.

Adoff, Arnold (1935-)
--All the Colors of the Race. Steptoe, John Lewis (1950-), illus. LC 81-11777. (Illus.). 56p. (gr. 5 up). 1982. (ISBN 0-688-00879-8). (ISBN 0-688-00880-1). Lothrop. **Award: (ALA).**
--Big Sister Tells Me That I'm Black. Lynch, Lorenzo (1932-), illus. LC 75-32249. c.1976. (ISBN 0-03-014546-5). Holt, Rinehart and Winston.
--Birds. Howell, Troy, illus. LC 81-47753. (Illus.). 48p. (gr. k-5). 1982. (ISBN 0-397-31949-5, JBL-J). (ISBN 0-397-31950-9). Har-Row.
--Birds: Poems. Howell, Troy, illus. LC 81-47753. (Illus.). 64 p. 22cm. c.1982. (ISBN 0-397-31973-8). (ISBN 0-397-31974-6). Lippincott.
--Black Is Brown Is Tan. McCully, Emily Arnold (1939-), illus. LC 72-9855. (Illus.). 31 p. 22cm. 1973. (ISBN 0-06-020083-9). (ISBN 0-06-020083-9). Harper & Row.
--The Cabbages Are Chasing the Rabbits. Stevens, Janet, illus. LC 85-893. (Illus.). 32 p. 1985. (ISBN 0-15-213875-7). Harcourt Brace Jovanovich.
--Eats: Poems. Russo, Susan (1947-), illus. LC 79-11300. p. cm. c.1979. (ISBN 0-688-51901-6). Lothrop, Lee & Shepard. **Award: (ALA).**
--Friend Dog. Howell, Troy, illus. 1980. Harper.
--Friend Dog. Howell, Troy, illus. LC 80-7773. p. cm. c.1980. (ISBN 0-397-31911-8). (ISBN 0-397-31912-6). Lippincott.
--I Am the Running Girl. Himler, Ronald Norbert (1937-), illus. LC 78-14083. (Illus.). 40 p. 24cm. c.1979. (ISBN 0-06-020094-4). (ISBN 0-06-020095-2). Harper & Row.
--MA nDA LA. McCully, Emily Arnold (1939-), illus. LC 76-146000. (Illus.). 25 p. 24cm. 1971. (ISBN 0-06-020085-5). Harper & Row. **Award: (ALA).**
--Make a Circle, Keep Us in: Poems for a Good Day. Himler, Ronald Norbert (1937-), illus. LC 74-22162. (Illus.). 32 p. 1975. (ISBN 0-440-05908-9). (ISBN 0-440-05909-7). Delacorte Press.
--Outside Inside Poems. 1st ed. Steptoe, John Lewis (1950-), illus. LC 79-22168. p. cm. c.1980. (ISBN 0-688-41942-9). (ISBN 0-688-51942-3). Lothrop, Lee & Shepard Books.
--Today We Are Brother & Sister. Coalson, Glo (1946-), illus. LC 80-16075. (Illus.). 32p. (gr. 2-6). 1981. (ISBN 0-688-41973-9). (ISBN 0-688-51973-3). Lothrop.
--Tornado! Poems. Himler, Ronald Norbert (1937-), illus. LC 76-47241. (Illus.). 48 p. c.1977. (ISBN 0-440-08964-6). (ISBN 0-440-08965-4). Delacorte Press.
--Under the Early Morning Trees: Poems. Himler, Ronald Norbert (1937-), illus. LC 78-5561. (Illus.). 48 p. c.1978. Dutton.
--Where Wild Willie. McCully, Emily Arnold (1939-), illus. LC 76-21390. (Illus.). 31 p. 24cm. c.1978. (ISBN 0-06-020092-8). (ISBN 0-06-020093-6). Harper & Row.

Adoff, Arnold (1935-), ed.
--Black Out Loud. Hollingsworth, Alvin C., illus. 1970. Macmillan.
--Brothers & Sisters. LC 76-102961. 256p. (Modern Stories by Black Americans Ser). (gr. 7 up). 1970. (ISBN 0-02-700130-X). Macmillan.
--Celebrations: A New Anthology of Black American Poetry. LC 76-19888. (gr. 6 up). 1977. (ISBN 0-695-80699-8). (ISBN 0-695-40699-X). Follett.
--City in All Directions: An Anthology of Modern Poems. Carrick, Donald (1929-), illus. LC 70-78073. (Illus.). xv, 128 p. 22cm. 1969. Macmillan.
--I Am the Darker Brother: An Anthology of Modern Poems by Black Americans. 160p. (gr. 6 up). 1970. (ISBN 0-02-041120-0, Collier). Macmillan.
--I Am the Darker Brother: An Anthology of Modern Poems by Negro Americans. Andrews, Benny (1930-), illus. LC 68-12077. frontispiece & 6 full-page pen & ink drawings.160p. (gr. 7 up). 1968. (ISBN 0-02-700080-X). (ISBN 0-02-296520-3). Macmillan. **Award: (ALA).**
--It Is the Poem Singing into Your Eyes: Anthology of New Young Poets. LC 79-157898. 128p. (gr. 7 up). 1971. (ISBN 0-06-020088-X, HarpJ). Har-Row.
--My Black Me: A Beginning Book of Black Poetry. LC 73-16445. xii, 83 p. 24cm. 1974. (ISBN 0-525-35460-3). Dutton.
--The Poetry of Black America: Anthology of the Twentieth Century. Brooks, Gwendolyn (1917-), intro. by. LC 72-76518. 576p. (gr. 7 up). 1973. (ISBN 0-06-020089-8, HarpJ). (ISBN 0-06-020090-1). Har-Row.

Adorjan, Carol Madden (1934-)
--The Cat Sitter Mystery. Krush, Beth (1918-) & Krush, Joe (1918-), illus. LC 72-12652. (Illus.). 110 p. 24cm. 1973. (ISBN 0-87955-205-0). (ISBN 0-87955-205-0). J. P. O'Hara.
--The Electric Man. Dunnington, Tom, illus. LC 80-27107. (Illus.). 59 p. 22cm. (Prime time adventures). c.1981. (ISBN 0-516-02104-4). Children's Press.
--Jonathan Bloom's Room. Kock, Carl, illus. LC 78-186883. (Illus.). 32 p. 23cm. (Lead-off book). 1972. (ISBN 0-87955-102-X). (ISBN 0-87955-702-8). J. P. O'Hara.
--Pig Party. Meents, Len W, illus. LC 80-27654. p. cm. (Prime time adventures). 1981. (ISBN 0-516-02108-7). Childrens Press.
--Someone I Know. Keyser, Corinne, illus. LC 68-23664. (Illus.). 28 p. 23cm. (Random House early bird book). 1968. Random House.

Adrian, Mary, pseud., see Jorgenson, Mary Venn.
Adrian, Mary, pseud., see Venn, Mary Eleanor.

Adrian, Mary, pseud. (1908-)
--American Alligator. Jorgenson, Mary Venn. Vaughan-Jackson, Genevieve (1913-), illus. (Illus.). 64p. (gr. 2-5). N.D. (ISBN 0-8038-0310-9). Hastings.
--Fiddler Crab. Jorgensen, Mary Venn. 1953. (ISBN 0-8382-0249-7, Cadmus Books). E. M. Hale and Company.
--The Fireball Mystery. Jorgenson, Mary Venn. Lonette, Reisie Dominee (1924-), illus. LC 77-17151. 22cm. 111p. c.1977. (ISBN 0-8038-2325-8). Hastings House.
--Firehouse Mystery. Jorgenson, Mary Venn. (Illus.). (gr. 4-6). 1950. (ISBN 0-395-06536-4). HM.
--Fox Hollow Mystery. Jorgenson, Mary Venn. (gr. 4-6). 1959. (ISBN 0-8038-2252-9). Hastings.
--Ghost Town Mystery. Jorgenson, Mary Venn. Lonette, Reisie Dominee (1924-), illus. (Illus.). 8 line drawings. 129p. (Adrian Nature Mysteries Ser). (gr. 4-6). 1971. (ISBN 0-8038-2645-1). Hastings.
--Indian Horse Mystery. Jorgenson, Mary Venn. Coe, Lloyd (1899-1976), illus. (Illus.). (gr. 4-6). 1966. (ISBN 0-8038-3349-0). Hastings.
--Jonathan Crow, Detective. Jorgenson, Mary Venn. N.D. E. M. Hale and Co.
--Jonathan Crow, Detective. Jorgenson, Mary Venn. Nichols, Marie C. (1905-), illus. LC 58-11202. 126 p. illus. 22 cm. 1958. Hastings House.
--Kite Mystery. Jorgenson, Mary Venn. Coe, Lloyd (1899-1976), illus. LC 67-25609. (Illus.). 8 line drawings. 128p. (gr. 4-6). 1968. (ISBN 0-8038-3937-5). (ISBN 0-8038-3938-3). Hastings.
--The Lightship Mystery. Jorgenson, Mary Venn. Tolford, Joshua (1909-), illus. LC 69-15052. (Illus.). 8 drawings. 128p. 22cm. (Double H Keep Reading Bk.). (gr. 4-6). 1969. (ISBN 0-8038-4264-3). (ISBN 0-8038-4263-5). Hastings.
--Mystery of the Dinosaur Bones. Jorgenson, Mary Venn. Coe, Lloyd (1899-1976), illus. (Illus.). (1908-). (gr. 4-6). 1967. (ISBN 0-8038-4644-4). Hastings.
--The Mystery of the Dinosaur Graveyard. Jorgenson, Mary Venn. Hannans, Nancy, illus. (Illus.). 128p. (gr. 4-7). 1982. (ISBN 0-8038-4738-6). Hastings.
--Mystery of the Night Explorers. Jorgenson, Mary Venn. Coe, Lloyd (1899-1976), illus. (Illus.). (gr. 4-6). 1962. (ISBN 0-8038-4645-2). Hastings.
--Rare Stamp Mystery. Jorgenson, Mary Venn. Coe, Lloyd (1899-1976), illus. (Illus.). (gr. 4-6). 1960. (ISBN 0-8038-6294-6). Hastings.
--Skin Diving Mystery. Jorgenson, Mary Venn. 1978. (ISBN 0-8038-6719-0). Hastings.
--Skin Diving Mystery. Jorgenson, Mary Venn. Coe, Lloyd (1899-1976), illus. (Illus.). (gr. 4-6). 1964. (ISBN 0-8038-6657-7). Hastings.
--Tugboat Mystery. Jorgenson, Mary Venn. (Illus.). (gr. 4-6). 1952. (ISBN 0-8382-0902-5). Hale.
--Uranium Mystery. Jorgenson, Mary Venn. Coe, Lloyd (1899-1976), illus. (Illus.). (gr. 4-6). 1956. (ISBN 0-8038-7494-4). Hastings.

Adshead, Gladys Lucy (1896-)
--Brownies--Hurry. Ilsley, Velma Elizabeth (1918-), illus. LC 59-5539. (Illus.). (gr. k-3). 1959. (ISBN 0-8098-1057-3). Walck.
--Brownies--Hush!. Jones, Elizabeth Orton (1910-), illus. LC 59-12740. unpaged. illus. 15 x 19cm. 1959, c.1938. H. Z. Walck.
--Brownies--Hush!. Jones, Elizabeth Orton (1910-), illus. LC 88-27579. 64 p. illus. 14 1/2 x 19 cm. c.1938. Oxford University Press.
--Brownies, Hurry. (Illus.). (gr. k-2). 1959. (ISBN 0-8382-0120-2). Hale.
--Brownies-Hush. 1938. David McKay Company.
--Brownies: Hush. Jones, Elizabeth Orton (1910-), illus. 1939. Henry Z. Walck Inc.
--Brownies: Its Christmas. 1955. (ISBN 0-8098-1041-7). David McKay Company.
--Brownies: It's Christmas. (Illus.). (gr. k-2). 1955. (ISBN 0-8382-0122-9). Hale.
--Brownies Its Christmas. Ilsley, Velma Elizabeth (1918-), illus. LC 62-17862. 72p. 1955. Henry Z. Walck, Inc., Publishers.
--Brownies They're Moving. 1970. (ISBN 0-8098-1163-4). David McKay Company.
--Brownies, They're Moving. Lebenson, Richard, illus. LC 71-100703. (Illus.). 62 p. 1970. H. Z. Walck.
--Casco. Bostlemann, Else, illus. LC 43-5898. 63 p. col. illus. 21 1/2 cm. 1943. Oxford University Press.
--Smallest Brownie and the Flying Squirrel. Lebenson, Richard, illus. LC 72-3202. (Illus.). 56 p. 1972. (ISBN 0-8098-1195-2). H. Z. Walck.
--Smallest Brownie's Fearful Adventure. Ilsley, Velma Elizabeth (1918-), illus. (Illus.). (gr. k-3). 1961. (ISBN 0-8098-1069-7). Walck.
--Something Surprising. Rinald, H., illus. 80p. 1939. Oxford University Press.
--What Miranda Knew. Jones, Elizabeth Orton (1910-), illus. LC 44-9775. 48 p. col. illus. 17 x 15 1/2 cm. 1944. Oxford University Press.
--Where Is Smallest Brownie?. Lebenson, Richard, illus. LC 73-142448. (Illus.). 44 p. 1971. (ISBN 0-8098-1178-2). H. Z. Walck.

Adshead, Gladys Lucy (1896-) & Duff, Annis
--Inheritance of Poetry. Unwin, Nora Spicer (1907-), illus. (Illus.). (gr. 7-9). 1948. (ISBN 0-395-06537-2). HM.

Adshead, Gladys Lucy (1896-) & Shapiro, G. H.
--Seventeen to Sing. Merwin, Decie (1894-1961), illus. 39p. 1946. Oxford University Press.

Adshead, Mary, jt. auth. see Bone, Stephen.

Aebersold, Maria
--The Lost Islands. (gr. 4-6). 1973 (Starline). Schol Bk Serv.

Aebersold, Maria, jt. auth. see Grieder, Walter.

Aenis, Marie E
--Oh, What a Busy Day. Kaula, Edna Mason (1906-), illus. LC 47-58751. 58 p. illus. (part col.) 26 cm. (Saalfield treasure book). 1947. Saalfield Pub. Co.
--Sally's a Big Girl. De Frehn, Sarah, illus. LC 47-15859. 56 p. illus. (part col.) 17 cm. (Little treasure series). 1946. The Saalfield Publishing Company.

Aesop, Abraham, pseud., see Newberg, John.

Aesop, Abraham, pseud. (1713-1767)
--The Wolf, and the Fox in the Well. Newberg, John. (Aesop's Fables). N.D. McLoughlin Bros.

Aesopus
--Aesop: A Hundred Fables of Aesop. L'Estrange, Sir Roger (1616-1704), intro. by. Billinghurst, Percy J. (1859-1932), illus. N.D. John Lane Company.
--Aesop & Hyssop. Leonard, William Ellery, ed. (Fables Adapted & Original, in a Variety of Verse Forms Picturesque, Lively, & Humorous in Phrasing). xxii, 158p. N.D. Open Court.
--Aesop: Fables. Jacobs, Joseph (1854-1916), ed. 1900. Macmillan Co.
--Aesop for Children. Winter, Milo Kendall (1888-1956), illus. LC 19-14083. 2 p. 1., 7-112 p. col. illus. 30 1/2 cm. 1919. Rand McNally & Co.
--The Aesop for Children. Winter, Milo Kendall (1888-1956), illus. LC 84-60664. (Illus.). 96p. (gr. 2 up). 1984. (ISBN 0-528-82134-2). Rand.
--Aesop in Verse. (Library of Fables). 1873. Leavitt & Allen.
--Aesop's Fable. LC 14-7957. (English Classic Ser.: No. 133). 1894. Maynard, Merrill & Co.
--Aesop's Fables. N.D. A. L. Burt Co.
--Aesop's Fables. (The Oxford Ser.). N.D. A. L. Burt Company.
--Aesop's Fables. (The Manhattan Ser.). N.D. A. L. Burt's Pubs.
--Aesop's Fables. (Illus.). (Burt's Young Folks' Library). N.D. A. L. Burt's Pubs.
--Aesop's Fables, No. 2. (The Cornell Ser.). N.D. A. L. Burt's Pubs.
--Aesop's Fables. Empire ed. 1905. American News Co.
--Aesop's Fables, 1 Vol. (The Excelsior Edition). N.D. American News Company.
--Aesop's Fables. (Illus.). (Popular Standard Editions). N.D. Belford, Clarke & Co.
--Aesop's Fables. (Illus.). (Caxton Edition). N.D. Belford, Clarke & Co.
--Aesop's Fables. 400p. (Royal Octavo Edition). N.D. Cassell, Petter, Galpin.
--Aesop's Fables. N.D. Claxton,Remsen & Haffelfinger.
--Aesop's Fables. (Illus.). (Chandos Classics). N.D. Frederick Warne & Co.
--Aesop's Fables. (Illus.). (Young People's Library). N.D. George Routledge & Sons.
--Aesop's Fables. (The Good Value Books). N.D. Grosset & Dunlap.
--Aesop's Fables, 12 vols. (Illus.). 376p. (Juvenile Classics Ser.). 1905. Set. H M Caldwell Co.
--Aesop's Fables. (Illus.). (Caldwell's Illustrated Library of Famous Books and Famous Authors). N.D. H. M. Caldwell Co.
--Aesop's Fables. (Illus.). (Berkeley Lib.). N.D. H. M. Caldwell Co.
--Aesop's Fables. (Illus.). (Juvenile Classics). N.D. H. M. Caldwell Co.
--Aesop's Fables. (Illus.). (The Empyreal Lib). N.D. H. M. Caldwell Co.
--Aesop's Fables. (Illus.). (The Young Folks Lib.). N.D. H. M. Caldwell Co.
--Aesop's Fables. (Illus.). 1905. Henry Altemus Co.
--Aesop's Fables. (Altemus' New Illustrated Young People's Library). N.D. Henry Altemus Company.
--Aesop's Fables. (Illus.). (Young People Lib.). N.D. Henry Atemus Co.
--Aesop's Fables. (Illus.). (One-Syllable Ser.). N.D. Henry Altemus Co.
--Aesop's Fables, 1 of 6 vols. (One Syllable Ser.). 1900. Set. Hurst & Co.
--Aesop's Fables. Library ed. (Illus.). (Hurst's Fairy Tale Ser.). 1900. Hurst and Company.
--Aesop's Fables. (Illus.). (Young American Library). N.D. Hurst & Co.
--Aesop's Fables. (Illus.). (Hurst's Half Leather Classics). N.D. Hurst and Company.
--Aesop's Fables. (Illus.). (The Cambridge Classics). N.D. Hurst and Company.
--Aesop's Fables. (Illus.). (The Laurelhurst Ser.). N.D. Hurst and Company.
--Aesop's Fables. (Illus.). (The New Argyle Ser.). N.D. Hurst and Company.
--Aesop's Fables. (Illus.). (Arlington Edition). N.D. Hurst and Company.
--Aesop's Fables. (Illus.). 196p. (St. Nicholas Ser.). N.D. Hurst & Co.
--Aesop's Fables. (New Aldine Ser). N.D. International Book Co.
--Aesop's Fables. (Illus.). N.D. J. B. Lippincott & Co.
--Aesop's Fables. (Illus.). 64p. (Ogilvie's Books for Boys and Girls). N.D. J. S. Ogilvie.
--Aesop's Fables. (Library of Fables). 1873. Leavitt & Allen Bros.
--Aesop's Fables, 4. (The Children's Favorites). N.D. Leavitt & Allen Bros.
--Aesop's Fables. N.D. Lovell, Coryell & Co.
--Aesop's Fables. (Illus.). (Children's Classics). N.D. Penn Publishing Co.
--Aesop's Fables, 3 Vols. (Illus.). (Entertaining Library). N.D. Porter & Coates.
--Aesop's Fables, 1 of 163 Vols. (Illus.). (The Cottage Library Ser.). N.D. R. Worthington.
--Aesop's Fables. N.D. Rand McNally & Co.
--Aesop's Fables. (The Advance Library Ser.: Vol. 4). N.D. Rand, McNally & Co.
--Aesop's Fables. (Illus.). (The Independent Library Ser.: Vol. 4). N.D. Rand, McNally & Co.
--Aesop's Fables. (Illus.). (The Junior Library Ser.: Vol. 1). N.D. Rand, McNally & Co.

--The Herford Esop: Fifty Fables in Verse. Herford, Oliver (1863-1935), ed. Herford, Oliver (1863-1935), illus. LC 21-10246. viii, 90 p col. front., illus. 19 cm. c.1921. Ginn and Company.
--A Hundred Fables of Aesop. Billinghurst, Percy J. (1859-1932), illus. L'Estrange, Roger, Sir (1616-1704), tr. Grahame, Kenneth (1859-1932), intro. by. 2 p. l., xv, 201 p. front., illus. 24 cm. 1910. J. Lane.
--A Hundred Fables of Aesop. L'Estrange, Robert, tr. N.D. Dodd, Mead & Co.
--Jack Kent's Fables of Aesop. Kent, Jack, pseud. (1920-), ed. Kent, John Wellington. LC 76-181498. (Illus.). 55 p. 20cm. 1972. (ISBN 0-8193-0540-5). (ISBN 0-8193-0541-3). Parents' Magazine Press.
--The Lion & the Mouse. Dole, Bob, illus. LC 80-28154. (Illus.). 32p. (gr. k-2). 1981. (ISBN 0-89375-466-8). (ISBN 0-89375-467-6). Troll Assocs.
--The Lion and the Mouse. Dole, Bob, illus. LC 80-28154. p. cm. c.1981. (ISBN 0-89375-466-8). (ISBN 0-89375-467-6). Troll Associates.
--The Lion & the Mouse. Young, Ed (1931-), illus. LC 79-1863. (Illus.). (gr. 1-3). 1980. Doubleday.
--Lions and Lobsters and Foxes and Frogs: Fables from Aesop. Rees, Ennis Samuel, Jr. (1925-), ed. Gorey, Edward St. John (1925-), illus. LC 75-155912. (Illus.). 48 p. 22cm. 1971. (ISBN 0-201-09246-8). Young Scott Books.
--The Man, his Son, and his Ass. (Aesop's Fables). 1873. McLoughlin Bros.
--The Miller, His Son, and Their Donkey. Duvoisin, Roger Antoine (1904-1980), illus. LC 62-9987. 26cm. 30p. 1962. Whittlesey Hose.
--The Miller, His Son, and Their Donkey: A Fable from Aesop. Sopko, Eugen, illus. LC 85-7198. (Illus.). 24 p. 30cm. (North-South picture book). 1985. North-South Books : Distributed in the U.S. by Holt, Rinehart, and Winston.
--More Fables of Aesop. Kent, Jack, pseud. (1920-), ed. Kent, John Wellington. LC 73-13635. (Illus.). 55 p. 20cm. 1974. (ISBN 0-8193-0750-5). (ISBN 0-8193-0750-5). Parents' Magazine Press.
--My Book of Aesop's Fables. Nardini, Sandro, illus. LC 62-17744. unpaged. illus. 33cm. 1962. Maxton Pub. Corp.
--Never-Grow Old Stories. Grover, Edwin Osgood (1870-), retold by. Billinghurst, Percy J. (1859-1932), illus. LC 25-20622. (Illus.). 19cm. 144p. 1925. Lyons & Carnahan.
--Never-Grow-Old Stories: Retold from AEsop's Fables. Grover, Edwin Osgood (1870-), ed. Billinghurst, Percy J. (1859-1932), illus. LC 25-20622. 144 p. incl. col. front., col. illus. 19 1/2 cm. c.1925. Lyons & Carnahan.
--Once in a Wood: Ten Tales from Aesop. 1st ed. Rice, Eve Hart (1951-), adapted by. Rice, Eve Hart (1951-), illus. LC 78-16294. (Illus.). 64 p. 22cm. (Greenwillow read-alone). c.1979. (ISBN 0-688-80191-9). (ISBN 0-688-84191-0). Greenwillow Books.
--Some of Aesop's Fables. Caldecott, Randolph (1846-1886), designed by. N.D. MacMillan.
--The Stag in the Ox's Stall. (Aesop's Fables). N.D. McLoughlin Bros.
--Stone Broth. (Aesop's Fables). 1873. McLoughlin Bros.
--Tales from Aesop. Miller, John Parr (1913-), ed. LC 74-2539. (Illus.). 32 p. 21cm. (Random House pictureback). c.1976. (ISBN 0-394-82812-7). Random House.
--Three Aesop Fox Fables. Galdone, Paul (1914-), retold by. Galdone, Paul (1914-), illus. LC 79-133061. (Illus.). 32 p. 30cm. 1971. Seabury Press.
--The Town Mouse & the Country Mouse. Galdone, Paul (1914-), ed. Galdone, Paul (1914-), illus. LC 75-141296. (Illus.). 32 p. 1971. (ISBN 0-07-022694-6). McGraw-Hill.
--Town Mouse & the Country Mouse. new ed. Garcia, T. R., illus. LC 78-18062. (Illus.). 32p. (gr. k-4). 1979. (ISBN 0-89375-131-6). (ISBN 0-89375-109-X). Troll Assocs.
--Twelve Tales from Aesop. Carle, Eric (1929-), retold by. Carle, Eric (1929-), illus. LC 80-17824. (Illus.) 29 p. 29cm. 1st U.S. edition. 1980. (ISBN 0-399-20753-8). (ISBN 0-399-61163-0). Philomel Books.
--The Wolf, and the Fox in the Well. (Aesop's Fables). 1873. McLoughlin Bros.
--The Word-Picture Fable Books: Or, Old Aesop in a New Dress. (Illus.). N.D. Thomas Nelson & Sons.

Aesopus, et al.
--Aesop's Fables. Weir, Harrison William (1824-1906), illus. N.D. Belford, Clarke.
Aesopus, jt. auth. see Day, Thomas.
Aesopus, jt. auth. see Dodsley, Robert.
Aesopus, jt. auth. see Harwood, Stefanie.
Aesopus, jt. auth. see La Fontaine, Jean De.
Aesopus, jt. auth. see Stobbs, William.
Aesopus, Clodius
--Aesop's Fables. N.D. J. B. Lippincott.
--Aesop's Fables. N.D. Porter & Coates.
--Aesop's Fables. New ed. Griset, Ernest, illus. N.D. Cassell, Petter & Galpin.

Aesopus & Garcia, T. R
--The Town Mouse and the Country Mouse: An Aesop Fable. LC 78-18062. (Illus.). 32 p. 24cm. c.1979. (ISBN 0-89375-131-6). Troll Associates.

Aesopus & James, Thomas
--Aesop's Fables. Jennie, J., illus. N.D. D. Lothrop Co.

Aesopus & La Fontaine, Jean De (1621-1695)
--A Child's Version of AEsop's Fables: With a Supplement Containing Fables from La Fontaine and Krilof. Lansing, M Jenny H, Mrs. (1840-), ed. LC 13-30197. xvii, 204 p. incl. front., illus. 18 cm. (On cover: Classics for children, v. 8). 1886. Ginn & Company.
--The Fables of Aesop. Dash, Josephine Eugene, illus. Croxall, Samuel (0000-1732), tr. LC 26-4921. 254, 1 p. incl. col. front., illus. (part col.) 23 1/2 cm. (World-wide edition of a just right book). 1925. A. Whitman & Co.

Aesopus & Stuart, Marie
--Aesop's Fables. Ayton, Robert, illus. LC 76-52370. p. cm. c.1975. (ISBN 0-8467-0306-8). Two Continents Pub. Group.

Aesopus & Wescott, Glenway (1901-)
--Twelve Fables of Aesop. Limited. Frasconi, Antonio (1919-), illus. LC 54-12967. 33 p. illus. 23cm. 1954. Museum of Modern Art.
--Twelve Fables of Aesop. Frasconi, Antonio (1919-), illus. LC 64-57301. 32 p. illus. 22 cm. 1964, c.1954. Museum of Modern Art.

Aesopus & White, Anne Terry
--Aesop's Fables. Siegl, Helen (1924-), illus. LC 63-11948. (Illus.). 77 p. 24cm. 1964. Random House.

Aesopus & Young, Ed
--The Lion and the Mouse: An Aesop Fable. LC 79-1863. (Illus.). 32 p. 22cm. c.1979. (ISBN 0-385-15462-3). (ISBN 0-385-15463-1). Doubleday.

Afanasev, Aleksandr Nikolaevich (1826-1871), ed.
--Foma the Terrible: A Russian Folktale. Gobbato, Imero (1923-), illus. Daniels, Guy (1919-), tr. LC 78-103440. 38p. 1970. (ISBN 0-440-02655-5). Delacorte Press.
--Ivan Korovavich: The Son of the Cow. Lesch, Christiane, illus. (Illus.). 28p. (gr. 1-2). 1982. (ISBN 0-903540-57-6, Pub. by Floris Books Scotland). St George Bk Serv.
--Russian Fairy Tales. Alexeieff, Alexander A. (1901-), illus. Guterman, Norbert (1900-1984), tr. from Rus. Jakobson, Roman, commentary by. LC 45-37884. (Illus.). 664p. Repr. of 1945 ed. 1975. (ISBN 0-394-49914-X). Pantheon.
--Russian Folk Tales. Bilibin, Ivan Iakovlevich (1876-1942), illus. Chandler, Robert (1953-), tr. LC 80-50746. p. cm. 1980. (ISBN 0-394-51353-3). Shambhala.
--Russian Folk Tales. Hart, Dick (1920-), illus. Duddington, Nataliia Aleksandrovna Ertel, tr. LC 69-12152. (Illus.). 144 p. 21cm. 1969, c.1967. Funk & Wagnalls.

After School Club of America, jt. auth. see University Society, New York.
After School Club of America, jt. ed. see University Society, New York.
Agard, John
--Dig Away Two Hole Tim. 32p. N.D. (ISBN 0-370-30421-7, Pub. by Chatto-Bodley-Jonathan). Merrimack Pub Cir.

Agassiz, Laura, Mrs.
--Tessie: A Story of My Life. LC 28-19458. 18 1/2cm. 120p. 1928. Laura Agassiz.

Agay, Denes & Gilbert Van Poznak, Joan
--Unicef Book of Children's Songs. Kaufman, William I., photos by. Incl. Unicef Book of Children's Prayers. Kaufman, Rosamond V. & Gilbert Van Poznak, Joan, eds. Kaufman, William I., photos by. (Illus.). 96p. (gr. 5 up, 5102); Unicef Book of Children's Legends. Kaufman, Rosamond V., adapted by. Kaufman, William I., photos by. (Illus.). 96p. (gr. 5 up, 5101); Unicef Book of Children's Poems. Gilbert Van Poznak, Joan, ed. Kaufman, William I., photos by. (Illus.). 96p. (gr. 5 up, 5104). (Illus.). 96p. (gr. 5 up). N.D (5103). US Comm UNICEF.

Agee, Helene Barret
--Little Davie. 1st ed. LC 53-12758. (Illus.). 21cm. 44p. 1953. Pageant Press.

Agee, Jon
--Ellsworth. Agee, Jon, illus. LC 83-2325. p. cm. (gr. k-2). 1983. (ISBN 0-394-95995-7). Pantheon.
--If Snow Falls: A Story for December. LC 82-6549. (Illus.). 32 p. 15cm. c.1982. (ISBN 0-394-85520-5). (ISBN 0-394-95520-X). Pantheon Books.
--Moon Valley. Agee, Jon, illus. LC 83-26198. p. cm. 1984. (ISBN 0-394-86260-0). (ISBN 0-394-96260-5). Pantheon Books.

Ager, Trygve Martinus, tr. see Bojer, Johan.
Ageton, Arthur Ainsley (1900-)
--Mary Jo and Little Liu. Bailey, Olive, illus. LC 45-37892. (Illus.). 26cm. 52p. 1945. Whittlesey House.

Agle, Nan Hayden (1905-)
--Baney's Lake. Mars, Witold Tadeusz J. (1912-), illus. LC 72-77526. (Illus.). 127 p. 22cm. 1972. (ISBN 0-8164-3089-6). Seabury Press.
--Constance the Honeybee. Yardley, Richard Q. (1903-1979), illus. LC 59-5084. 21cm. 38p. 1959. Holt, Rinehart and Winston.
--Joe Bean. Ilsley, Velma Elizabeth (1918-), illus. LC 66-31695. 126p. illus. 21cm. c.1967. Seabury.
--Joe Bean. Ilsley, Velma Elizabeth (1918-), illus. LC 66-10882. (Illus.). (gr. 3-6). 1967. (ISBN 0-8164-3032-2, Clarion Bk). Seabury.
--K Mouse and Bo Bixby. Berson, Harold (1926-), illus. LC 77-171863. (Illus.). 96 p. 20cm. 1972. Seabury Press.
--Kate and the Apple Tree. Ilsley, Velma Elizabeth (1918-), illus. LC 65-18709. 96p. illus. 21cm. c.1965. Seabury.
--Kish's Colt. Eitzen, Allan (1928-), illus. LC 68-14083. (Illus.). 63 p. 21cm. 1968. Seabury Press.
--The Lords Baltimore. 1962. Holt, Rinehart and Winston.
--Makon and the Dauphin. Frankenberg, Robert Clinton (1911-), illus. LC 61-13608. 126p. c.1961. Scribners.
--Maple Street. Prince, Leonora E., illus. LC 78-97034. (Illus.). 126 p. 21cm. 1970. Seabury Press.
--My Animals and Me. Hayden, Emily, photos by. 1970. Seabury.
--Princess Mary of Maryland. Sopher, Aaron (1905-), illus. N.D. Gale Reprints.
--Princess Mary of Maryland. Sopher, Aaron (1905-), illus. LC 56-9285. 108p. illus. 21cm. 1956. Scribner.
--Princess Mary of Maryland. Sopher, Aaron (1905-), illus. LC 70-12561. (Illus.). 108 p. 21cm. 1967, c.1956. Tradition Press.
--Susan & Sereena & the Cat's Place. Robinson, Charles (1931-), illus. (gr. 4-6). 1976. (ISBN 0-590-09830-6, Schol Trade Pap). Schol Bk Serv.
--Susan's Magic. Robinson, Charles (1931-), illus. LC 73-7124. (Illus.). 140 p. 21cm. 1973. Seabury Press.
--Tarr of Belway Smith. Seuling, Barbara (1937-), illus. LC 69-13441. (Illus.). 93 p. 22cm. 1969. Seabury Press.

Agle, Nan Hayden (1905-) & Wilson, Ellen Janet Cameron (0000-1976)
--Three Boys & a Helicopter. Honigman, Marian, illus. LC 58-5973. (Illus.). (gr. 2-6). 1958. (ISBN 0-684-12357-6). Scribner.
--Three Boys and a Lighthouse. Honigman, Marian, illus. LC 51-10329. (Illus.). 100 p. 20cm. 1951. Scribner.
--Three Boys and a Mine. Honigman, Marian, illus. LC 54-8782. 122p. illus. 20 cm. 1954. Scribner.
--Three Boys and a Train. Honigman, Marian, illus. LC 56-5659. 116p. illus. 20cm. 1956. Scribner.
--Three Boys and a Tugboat. Honigman, Marian, illus. LC 53-7785. 121p. illus. 20cm. 1953. Scribner.
--Three Boys and as Lighthouse. 1951. Trade Publications.
--Three boys and H20. 1968. Trade Publication.
--Three Boys and H20. Honigman, Marian, illus. LC 68-12513. (Illus.). 156 p. 20cm. 1968. Scribner.
--Three Boys and Space. Honigman, Marian, illus. LC 62-9080. (Illus.). 159 p. 20cm. 1962. Scribner.
--Three Boys and the Remarkable Cow. 1962. Trade Publication.
--Three Boys and the Remarkable Cow. Honigman, Marian, illus. LC 52-9129. 127 p. illus. 20 cm. 1952. Scribner.

Agnew, Edith, jt. auth. see Jump, Margaret.
Agnew, Edith J (1897-)
--The Gray Eyes Family. Martinez, Jean, illus. LC 52-10586. 127 p. illus. 21 cm. 1952. Friendship Press.
--Larry. Turkle, Brinton Cassaday (1915-), illus. LC 60-7448. 125 p. illus. 21cm. 1960. Friendship Press.
--Leo of Alaska. Turkle, Brinton Cassaday (1915-), illus. LC 58-7041. 114p. illus. 21cm. 1958. Friendship Press.
--Nezbah's Lamb. Martinez, Jean, illus. LC 54-6956. (Illus.). 21cm. 32p. (Little Playmate Series). (ps). 1954. (ISBN 0-377-68821-5). Friend Pr.
--People of the Way. large type ed. Troyer, Johannes (1902-), illus. (Illus.). (gr. 1-3). 1960. (ISBN 0-664-46232-4). Westminster.
--Sandy and Mr. Jalopy. Carol, Elayne, illus. LC 49-48972. 127 p. illus. 21 cm. 1949. Friendship Press.
--The Three Henrys and Mrs. Hornicle. Carol, Elayne, illus. LC 50-12375. 126 p. illus. 21 cm. 1950. Friendship Press.
--Treasure For Toma's. Turkle, Brinton Cassaday (1915-), illus. LC 64-11006. 21cm. 126p. 1964. Friendship Press.

Agnew, Georgette
--Let's Pretend: Poems. Shepard, Ernest Howard (1879-1976), illus. LC 27-20240. 63 1 p. illus. 21 cm. 1927. G. P. Putnam's Sons.

Agnew, John Holmes (1804-1865), tr. see Krummacher, Friedrich Adolf.
Agnew, Seth M.
--The Giant Sandwich. Byfield, Barbara Ninde (1930-), illus. LC 70-94673. (Illus.). 41 p. 22cm. 1970. Doubleday.

Agostinelli, Maria Enrica (1929-)
--I Know Something You Don't Know. Agostinelli, Maria Enrica (1929-), illus. LC 79-104030. (Illus.). (gr. k-3). 1970. (ISBN 0-531-01920-9). Watts.

Agree, Rose H (1913-), ed.
--How to Eat a Poem & Other Morsels: Food Poems for Children. Wilson, Peggy, illus. LC 67-14230. (Illus.). 87 p. 24cm. 1967. (ISBN 0-394-91622-0). Pantheon Books.

Aguilar, Grace
--Days of Bruce. Jackson, Alice F., retold by. (Illus.). (Classics Retold to Children). 1915. George W. Jacobs & Co.

Aguilar, Grace & Aulnoy, Marie Catherine Jumelle de Bernville (1650-1705)
--Every Girl's Story. (Illus.). N.D. George Routledge & Sons.

Ahern, Denise
--Bread & the Wine, No. Sixteen. (Illus.). (Arch Bk.). 1979. (ISBN 0-570-06127-X). Concordia.

Ahl, Vivian J., jt. auth. see Macdonald, Zillah Katherine.
Ahlberg, Allan
--Master Salt the Sailor's Son. Amstutz, Andre, illus. LC 81-84176. (Illus.). 24 p. 20cm. (Wacky Family Bks.: No. 8). 1982, c.1980. (ISBN 0-307-31708-0). (ISBN 0-307-61708-4). Golden Press.
--Miss Brick, the Builder's Baby. McNaughton, Colin, illus. LC 81-84174. (Illus.). 24 p. 21cm. (Wacky families). 1982, c.1981. (ISBN 0-307-31702-1). (ISBN 0-307-61702-5). Golden Press.
--Mr. & Mrs. Hay the Horse. McNaughton, Colin, illus. LC 81-84173. (Illus.). 24 p. 21cm. (Wacky Family Bks.: No. 4). 1982, c.1981. (ISBN 0-307-31704-8). (ISBN 0-307-61704-1). Golden Press.
--Mr. Biff the Boxer. Ahlberg, Janet, illus. LC 81-84170. (Illus.). 24 p. 21cm. (Wacky Family Bks.: No. 1). 1982, c.1980. (ISBN 0-307-61701-7). (ISBN 0-307-31701-3). Golden Press.
--Mr. Buzz the Beeman. Jaques, Faith (1923-), illus. LC 81-84172. (Illus.). 24 p. 20cm. (Wacky Family Bks.: No. 3). 1982, c.1981. (ISBN 0-307-31703-X). Golden Press.
--Mrs. Lather's Laundry. Amstutz, Andre, illus. LC 81-84152. (Illus.). 24 p. 21cm. (Wacky Family Bks.: No. 5). 1982, c.1981. (ISBN 0-307-31705-6). (ISBN 0-307-61705-X). Golden Press.
--Mrs. Plug the Plumber. Wright, Joe, illus. LC 81-84171. (Illus.). 24 p. 20cm. (Wacky Family Bks.: No. 6). 1982, c.1980. (ISBN 0-307-31706-4). (ISBN 0-307-61706-8). Golden Press.
--The Vanishment of Thomas Tull. Ahlberg, Janet, illus. LC 78-15662. p. cm. 1978. (ISBN 0-684-15968-6). Scribner.

Ahlberg, Allan, jt. auth. see Ahlberg, Janet.
Ahlberg, Janet & Ahlberg, Allan
--The Baby's Catalogue. LC 82-9928. (Illus.). 22 cm. 32p. 1st U.S. edition. c.1982. (ISBN 0-316-02037-0, Atlantic Monthly Press). Little, Brown. **Award: (ALA).**
--Burglar Bill. LC 76-40339. (Illus.). 32 p. 21cm. c.1977. (ISBN 0-688-80078-5). (ISBN 0-688-84078-7). Greenwillow Books.
--Burglar Bill. (Illus.). 1977. Penguin.
--Burglar Bill. LC 78-17989. p. cm. 1979, c.1977. (ISBN 0-14-050301-3). Puffin Books.
--Cops and Robbers. LC 78-5354. (Illus.). 32 p. 21cm. 1979, c.1978. (ISBN 0-688-80178-1). Greenwillow Books.
--Each Peach Pear Plum. Ahlberg, Janet & Ahlberg, Allan, illus. (Illus.). 32p. (ps-3). 1981. (ISBN 0-590-31621-4). Scholastic Inc.
--Each Peach Pear Plum: An "I Spy" Story. LC 78-16726. (Illus.). 32 p. (I-spy-book). 1979, c.1978. (ISBN 0-670-28705-9). Viking Press. **Award: (ALA).**
--Funnybones. Ahlberg, Janet & Ahlberg, Allan, illus. LC 79-24872. (Illus.). 32 p. 26cm. 1981. (ISBN 0-688-80238-9). (ISBN 0-688-84238-0). Greenwillow Books.
--Jeremiah in the Dark Woods. LC 77-6641. p. cm. 23cm. 47p. 1978. (ISBN 0-670-40637-6). Viking Press.
--The Little Worm Book. LC 79-22289. p. cm. 1980, c.1979. (ISBN 0-670-43438-8). Viking Press.
--Peek-a-Boo!. LC 81-1925. p. cm. 1981. (ISBN 0-670-54598-8). Viking Press. **Award: (ALA).**
--Playmates. Ahlberg, Janet, illus. LC 84-40123. (Illus.). 16 p. 23cm. 1985, c.1984. (ISBN 0-670-55988-1). Viking Kestrel.
--Yum Yum. LC 84-40124. p. cm. 1985. (ISBN 0-670-79620-4). Viking Kestrel.

Aitken, Amy (1952-)
--Kate & Mona in the Jungle. LC 80-15110. (Illus.). 32p. 1st U.S. edition. (ps-2). 1981. (ISBN 0-02-700320-5). Bradbury Pr.
--Kate and Mona in the Jungle. Aitken, Amy (1952-), illus. LC 80-15110. p. cm. 1980. (ISBN 0-87888-167-0). Bradbury Press.
--Ruby!. Aitken, Amy (1952-), illus. LC 78-21283. (Illus.). 32 p. 24cm. c.1979. (ISBN 0-87888-144-1). Bradbury Press.
--Ruby, the Red Knight. Aitken, Amy (1952-), illus. LC 82-9590. p. cm. 1982. (ISBN 0-87888-208-1). Bradbury Press.
--Ruby the Red Knight. Aitken, Amy (1952-), illus. LC 82-9590. (Illus.). 1st U.S. edition. (gr. k-2). 1983. (ISBN 0-02-700340-X). Bradbury Pr.
--Wanda's Circus. Aitken, Amy (1952-), illus. LC 84-20488. p. cm. 1985. Bradbury Press.

Aitken, Dorothy Lockwood (1916-)
--Cherry on Top. Converse, James, illus. LC 77-188538. (Illus.). 128 p. 21cm. (Penguin series). 1973. Review and Herald Pub. Association.
--The Hard Way. LC 70-79130. 96 p. 22cm. 1969. Southern Pub. Association.
--Suzie and the Secret of Effingham House. Van Dolson, Bobbie Jane, ed. Crews, Terry (1950-), illus. LC 79-22515. (Illus.). 128 p. 21cm. (Penguin series). 1980. Review and Herald Pub. Assoc.
--Timmi-Ti and Other Stories from Far Away. LC 76-16217. (Illus.). 128 p. 21cm. (Penguin series). 1978. Review and Herald Pub. Association.

Aitmatov, Chingiz
--Cranes Fly Early. 91p. 1983. (ISBN 0-8285-2639-7, Pub. by Raduga Pubs USSR). Imported Pubns.
--The White Ship. 1st ed. Ginsburg, Mirra, tr. from Rus. LC 76-185095. 23cm. xiii, 160p. (gr. 9 up). 1972. (ISBN 0-517-50074-4). Crown.

Ajo
--Doll-Land. N.D. Knopf.
--Jack, Jake and Jim. Ajo, illus. (The Dinky Tile Books). N.D. Dodge.
--Monkey-Land. N.D. Knopf.
--Nell and the China Twins. Ajo, illus. (The Dinky Tile Books). N.D. Dodge.
--Polly and Her Dollies. Ajo, illus. (The Dinky Tile Books). N.D. Dodge.
--Tommy and Sarita. Ajo, illus. (The Dinky Tile Books). N.D. Dodge.

A K C , pseud., see Crichton, Antoinette K..

Akeley, Carl & Akeley, Mary L. Jobe
--Adventures in the African Jungle. N.D. Dodd Mead and Co.

Akeley, Mary L. Jobe, jt. auth. see Akeley, Carl.

Aken, Helen Van see Van Aken, Helen.

Aken, Rosamond Jordan
--Tiger Goes on TV. Aken, Dolly, illus. LC 56-8102. unpaged. illus. 22x28cm. 1957. Bruce Humphries.

Akerly, Fredrika G (1898-)
--Rhymes for Curly Heads. Didd, Kay T., illus. LC 50-1110. 104 p. illus. 21 cm. c.1949. Decker Press.

Akers, Dwight
--The King's Mule. Illingworth, L. G., illus. LC 83-31765. 5 p. l., 3-173 p. front., illus. 20 1/2 cm. c.1933. Minton, Balch & Company.
--Sleepy Tom. Ball, Robert (1890-), illus. LC 39-24731. vi, 217 1 p. illus. 21 cm. 1939. G. P. Putnam's Sons.
--Young Turkey. Chaplin, Christine, illus. LC 47-4018. xi, 208 p., 1 l. illus. 22 1/2 cm. 1947. G. P. Putnam's Sons.

Akers, Floyd, pseud., see Baum, Lyman Frank.

Akers, Floyd, pseud. (1856-1919)
--The Boy Fortune Hunters in Alaska. Baum, Lyman Frank. LC 8-22799. 271 p. incl. front., pl. pl. 19 1/2 cm. c.1908. The Reilly & Britton Co.
--The Boy Fortune Hunters in China. Baum, Lyman Frank. LC 9-17584. (Illus.). 19.5 cm. 324p. (The Boy Fortune Hunters Ser.). 1909. Reilly & Britton Co.
--The Boy Fortune Hunters in Egypt. Baum, Lyman Frank. LC 9-20660. 291 p. incl. front. plates. 19 1/2 cm. c.1908. The Reilly & Britton Co.
--The Boy Fortune Hunters in Panama. Baum, Lyman Frank. LC 8-20659. 310 p. incl. col. front., illus. (map) col. plates. 19 1/2 cm. c.1908. The Reilly & Britton Co.
--The Boy Fortune Hunters in the South Seas. Baum, Lyman Frank. LC 11-24134. 20cm. 263p. (The Boy Fortune Hunters Ser.). 1911. Reilly & Britton Co.
--The Boy Fortune Hunters in Yucatan. Baum, Lyman Frank. LC 11-7741. (Illus.). 19.5 cm. 343p. (The Boy Fortune Hunters Ser.). 1910. Reilly & Britton Co.

Akim, Y.
--Desmanado. (Illus.). 15p. 1978. (ISBN 0-8285-1291-4, Pub. by Progress Pubs USSR). Imported Pubns.
--Helpless Can't Do. 16p. 1977. (ISBN 0-686-86117-5, Pub. by Progress Pubs USSR). Imported Pubns.

Akin, Florence
--Opera Stories from Wagner. N.D. Houghton Mifflin.

Akina, Allen, jt. auth. see Mower, Nancy Alpert.

Akooy, Philip Van
--Fishfeather's Quest. Fluit, Jansie, illus. (gr. 4-7). 1976. (ISBN 0-8277-4743-8). British Bk Ctr.

Aks, Patricia
--Junior Prom. 176p. (Orig.). (gr. 7 up). 1982. (ISBN 0-590-32003-3, Wildfire). Scholastic Inc.
--The Two Worlds of Jill. 192p. (Orig.). (gr. 7 up). 1981. (ISBN 0-590-31801-2, Wishing Star). Scholastic Inc.
--Who Needs a Stepsister?. 176p. (Orig.). (gr. 7 up). 1982. (ISBN 0-590-32358-X, Wishing Star). Scholastic Inc.
--You Don't Have to Be a Perfect Girl. 192p. (Orig.). (gr. 7-12). 1981. (ISBN 0-590-31397-5). Scholastic Inc.

Aksakov, Sergei Timofeevich (1791-1859)
--The Little Scarlet Flower. 30p. 1976. (ISBN 0-8285-1192-6, Pub. by Progress Pubs USSR). Imported Pubns.

Alabado, Ceres S.
--Dog, What Do You Say?. (gr. k-6). 1975. (ISBN 0-686-09525-1). Cellar.
--Kangkong, 1896. N.D. Cellar.
--The Rattan Gatherer. (Illus.). (gr. k-6). 1975. (ISBN 0-686-09526-X). Cellar.
--Tasaday. (Illus.). (gr. k-6). 1975. (ISBN 0-686-09527-8). Cellar.
--The Terrible Devil. (Illus.). (ps-3). N.D. (ISBN 0-686-09528-6). Cellar.
--What Is Christmas?. (Illus.). (ps-3). 1975. (ISBN 0-686-09529-4). Cellar.
--What Is Red & What Is Blue & What Is Yellow?, 3 vols. (Illus.). (ps). 1975. (ISBN 0-686-09530-8). Cellar.

Alabama Centennial Commission, jt. auth. see Owen, Marie Bankhead, Mrs.

Aladdin
--Aladdin and His Wonderful Lamp. Serkin, Amalia, illus. LC 45-9190. 34, 2 p. incl. col. front., col. illus. 19 1/2 x 17 1/2 cm. (On cover: A Lothrop color storybook). 1945. Lothrop, Lee & Shepard Co., Inc.
--Aladdin and His Wonderful Lamp: From the Arabian Nights' Entertainment. Harwood, John, illus. LC 49-7417. 48 p. illus. (part col.) 23 cm. (Porpoise books). 1947. Penguin Books.
--Aladdin and the Wonderful Lamp. N.D. E. P. Dutton & Co.
--Aladdin and the Wonderful Lamp. Illuminated with Ten Pictures. LC 44-39870. 1 p. l., 32 p. illus. 17 1/2 cm. (On cover: Hewet's illuminated household stories, for little folks ...). c.1855. H. W. Hewet.
--Aladdin: Or, The Wonderful Lamp. LC 5-23029. 40 p. col. front., illus. 17 x 13 cm. (Altemus' Banbury Cross series). c.1905. Henry Altemus Company.
--Aladdin: Or, The Wonderful Lamp, and Other Stories. LC 3-14866. 2 p. l., 155p. col. front., illus. 24cm. 1903. McLoughlin Bros.
--The Story of Aladdin and the Wonderful Lamp. Kettelwell, John, ed. Kettelwell, John, illus. Walpole, Hugh, pref. by. LC 29-9624. vii, 1 109, 1 p., 1 l. incl. front., illus., plates. 26 cm. 1928. A. A. Knopf.
--The Story of Aladdin and the Wonderful Lamp: From "The Arabian Nights". Stead, William Thomas (1849-), ed. LC 8-23090. 63 p. illus. 18 1/2 cm. 1908. The Penn Publishing Company.

Aladdin & Carruth, Jane
--My Book of Aladdin and His Wonderful Lamp. LC 64-21582. 28 p. col. illus. 32 cm. (Giant Maxton book). 1964. Follett Pub. Co.

Aladdin & Latham, Jean Lee (1902-)
--Aladdin. Ramirez, Pablo, illus. LC 61-7621. unpaged. illus. 24cm. c.1961. Bobbs-Merrill.

Aladdin & Miller, Doris R, pseud.
--Aladdin. Mosesson, Gloria Rubin. Mosesson, Gloria Rubin. Matamoros, Concha, illus. LC 65-24747. 1 v. (unpaged) col. illus. 24 cm. (Holly story book library). 1965. World Pub. Co.

Aladdin & White, Anne Terry
--Aladdin and the Wonderful Lamp. Bock, Vera, illus. LC 59-766520. 52p. illus. 22cm. (Legacy books, Y-5). 1959. Random House.

Alain, pseud., see Brustlein, Daniel.

Alan, Frances, jt. auth. see Yates, Patty M.

Alan, Sandy (1909-)
--The Plaid Peacock. Oechsli, Kelly (1918-), illus. LC 65-20650. 1 v. (unpaged) col. illus. 20 x 26 cm. 1965. Pantheon Books.

Alban, Harold
--Visit to the White Farm. Montefiore, E. B. S., illus. N.D. Dutton.

Albano, John
--Pac-Man & the Ghost Diggers. Costanza, John, illus. (Illus.). 24p. (Golden Look-Look Bks.). (ps-2). 1983. (ISBN 0-307-11790-1, Golden Pr). Western Pub.

Albeck, Pat
--Ben & His Toys. (Illus.). color ils. 16p. 1st U.S. edition. (Ben Bks.). (ps). 1971. World Pub.
--Ben at the Shop. (Illus.). color ils. 16p. 1st U.S. edition. (Ben Bks.). (ps). 1971. World Pub.
--Ben in the Garden. (Illus.). color ils. 16p. 1st U.S. edition. (Ben Bks.). 1971. World Pub.
--Ben in the Kitchen. (Illus.). color ils. 16p. 1st U.S. edition. (Ben Bks.). (ps). 1971. World Pub.

Albee, George Sumner
--Three young Kings. Keats, Jack Ezra (1916-1983), illus. LC 56-5849. (Illus.). 28cm. 47p. 1956. Franklin Watts, Inc.

Albers, Edna, jt. ed. see Wunsch, Robert.

Albert, Edna
--Little Pilgrim to Penn's Woods. Brann, Esther, illus. LC 30-18561. xiii p., 1 l., 300 p. incl. front., illus., plates. 19 1/2 cm. 1930. Longmans, Green and Co.

Albert, Louise (1928-)
--But I'm Ready to Go. LC 76-9949. 22cm. 230p. (gr. 6-9). 1976. (ISBN 0-87888-107-7). Bradbury Pr.

Albert, Marvin H.
--The Gargoyle Conspiracy. LC 74-18777. 288p. 1975. (ISBN 0-385-08562-1). Doubleday.

Albert, Mary
--Wandering Blindfold: A Boy's Trouble. (Illus.). N.D. E P Dutton.

Alberti, Trude
--The Animals' Lullaby. Nakatani, Chiyoko (1930-), illus. LC 67-23339. (Illus.). 21 x 23cm. 22p. 1967. World Pub. Co.

Alberts, Frances Jacobs (1907-)
--A Gift for Genghis Khan. Busoni, Rafaello (1900-1962), illus. LC 61-7575. 112p. illus. 21cm. 1961. Whittlesey House.

Albes, William, as told to see Kanguk.

Albion-Meek, Peggy
--The Great Adventurer. 1958. St Martin's Press.

Alborough, Jez
--Bare Bear. Alborough, Jez, illus. LC 83-25119. (Illus.). 28 p. c.1984. (ISBN 0-394-96808-5). (ISBN 0-394-86808-0). Knopf : Distributed by Random.
--Running Bear. Alborough, Jez, illus. LC 85-12681. p. cm. 1st U.S. edition. c.1985. (ISBN 0-394-87963-5). (ISBN 0-394-97963-X). Knopf : Distributed by Random House.

Albrecht, Lillie Vanderveer (1894-)
--Deborah Remembers. Newton, Rita, illus. LC 59-10844. 111p. illus. 22cm. 1959. Hastings House.
--The Grist Mill Secret. Coe, Lloyd (1899-1976), illus. LC 62-16192. (Illus.). 126 p. 22cm. 1962. Hastings House.
--Hannah's Hessian. Williams, Berkeley, Jr., illus. LC 58-9009. 101p. illus. 22cm. 1958. Hastings House.
--Spinning Wheel Secret. Payne, Joan Balfour (1923-1973), illus. LC 64-8124. (Illus.). 22cm. 124p. (gr. 4-6). 1965. (ISBN 0-8038-6668-2). Hastings.
--Susanna's Candlestick. Woehr, Lois, illus. LC 77-126422. (Illus.). 128 p. 22cm. 1970. (ISBN 0-8038-6691-7). Hastings House.

Albright, Nancy T.
--Do Tell!. Holiday Draw & Tell Stories. (Draw & Tell Stories). (ps-4). 1981. (ISBN 0-913545-02-3). Moonlight FL.

Albright, Nancy T., illus.
--I Know an Old Lady Who Swallowed a Fly. (Illus., Orig.). (Flannel Board Ser.). (ps-5). N.D. (ISBN 0-913545-10-4). Moonlight FL.

Albus, Harry James (1920-)
--The Boy from Northfield. N.D. Wm. B. Eerdmans Publishing Co.
--Deep River Girl. N.D. Wm. B. Eerdmans Publishing Co.
--One Hundred and Forty Stories for the Children's Hour. 3 p. l., 9-90 p. 20 cm. 1946. Zondervan Publishing House.
--The Peanut Man. N.D. Wm. B. Eerdmans Publishing Co.
--Two Hundred and Twenty-Five Stories for the Children's Hour. LC 58-193151. 120p. 20cm. c.1957. Zondervan Pub. House.

Alcanter de Brahm, Jeanne Ichard see Rosmer, Jean, pseud.

Alcock, Gudrun
--Dooley's Lion. LC 85-9957. p. cm. c.1985. (ISBN 0-88045-066-5). Stemmer House.
--Duffy. Clayton, Robert (1941-), illus. LC 72-1085. (Illus.). 192 p. 22cm. 1972. (ISBN 0-688-40009-4). (ISBN 0-688-40009-4). Lothrop, Lee & Shepard Co.
--Run, Westy, Run. Mars, Witold Tadeusz J. (1912-), illus. LC 66-14612. (Illus.). 22cm. 158p. (gr. 4-7). 1966. (ISBN 0-688-51058-2). Lothrop.
--Turn the Next Corner. LC 69-14321. 160 p. 22cm. 1969. Lothrop, Lee & Shepard.

Alcock, Vivien (1924-)
--The Haunting of Cassie Palmer. LC 81-15230. 149 p. 22cm. 1982, c.1980. (ISBN 0-440-03538-4). Delacorte Press.
--The Stonewalkers: A Novel. LC 82-13956. p. cm. 1983, c.1981. (ISBN 0-440-08321-4). Delacorte Press.
--The Sylvia Game. LC 84-3279. 192p. (gr. 4-6). 1984. (ISBN 0-385-29341-0). Delacorte.
--Travelers by Night. LC 85-1663. 182 p. 22cm. 1985, c.1983. (ISBN 0-385-29406-9). Delacorte Press. **Award: (ALA).**

Alcott, Frances Jenkins (1872-1963), ed.
--The Arabian Nights Entertainments. Orr, Munro Scott (1874-), illus. Lane, Edward William (1801-1876), tr. LC 13-222068. (Based on a Translation from the Arabic). xi, 294 p. col. front., col. plates. 22 cm. 1913. H. Holt and Company.

Alcott, Louisa May, et al. (1832-1888)
--The Horn of Plenty of Home Poems and Pictures. New & Enlarged. (Illus.). N.D. R. Worthington.
--Meadow Blossoms. (Illus.). 160p. 1879. T. Y. Crowell.
--Sparkles for Bright Eyes. (Illus.). 320p. N.D. Thomas Y. Crowell.
--Water Cresses. (Illus.). 160p. 1879. T. Y. Crowell.

Alcott, Louisa May (1832-1888)
--An Old-Fashioned Girl. (Illus.). (Little Women Ser.). 1882. Roberts Brothers.
--An Old-Fashioned Girl. Smith, Jessie Willcox (1863-1935), illus. (Little Women Ser.). N.D. Little Brown & Co.
--An Old-Fashioned Thanksgiving. N.D. Set. Robert Brothers.
--Aunt Jo's Scrap-Bag. N.D. Grosset & Dunlap.
--Aunt Jo's Scrap-Bag. LC 1-26201. v. fronts., plates. 17 cm. 1899. Little, Brown, and Company.
--Aunt Jo's Scrap-Bag. LC 4-17519. 6 v. fronts., illus., plates. 17 1/2 cm. 1900. Little, Brown and Company.
--Aunt Jo's Scrap-Bag. LC 6996. 6 v. fronts., illus., plates. 16 cm. 1872. Roberts Brothers.
--Aunt Jo's Scrap-Bag. LC 45-26346. v. fronts. 16 1/2 cm. 1889. Roberts Brothers.
--Aunt Jo's Scrap-Bag. Stevens, Beatrice (1876-), illus. Martin, Helen (1889-), intro. by. LC 29-22679. ix p., 4 l., 3-354 p. col. front., illus. 21 1/2 cm. 1929. Little, Brown, and Company.
--Becky's Christmas Dream. 188p. (Christmas Ser.). N.D. W. B. Conkey Company.
--Behind a Mask: The Unknown Thrillers of Louisa May Alcott. Stern, Madeleine Bettina (1912-), ed. LC 74-31046. (Illus.). 320p. 1st U.S. edition. 1975. (ISBN 0-688-00338-9). Morrow.
--Candy Country. (Illus.). 1 p 1, 52p front, pl 12. (The Children's Friend Ser.). 1900. Little, Brown and Company.
--A Christmas Dream. (Illus.). (The Children's Friend Ser.). 1901. Little, Brown and Company.
--Chronicle of the March Family. Blaisdell, Elinore (1904-), illus. 1946. Little, Brown & Co.
--Cupid and Chow Chow. N.D. Set 6.00. Robert Brothers.
--The Doll's Journey. LC 2-19104. 20cm. 72p. (The Children's Friend Ser.). 1902. Little, Brown & Co.
--Eight Cousins. (Famous Bk. for Young Americans). N.D. A. L. Burt Co.
--Eight Cousins. 278 p. 22 cm. 1961, c.1927. Grosset & Dunlap.
--Eight Cousins. (The Children's Favorite Series). N.D. Grosset & Dunlap.
--Eight Cousins. (The Winston Clear-Type Popular Classics). N.D. John C. Winston.
--Eight Cousins. Repr. of 1874 ed. (Orchard House Edition). 1934. Little, Brown & Co.
--Eight Cousins. (Classic Ser.). N.D. World Publishing Co.
--Eight Cousins. Burd, Clara Miller, illus. (The Children's Bookshelf). N.D. John C. Winston.
--Eight Cousins. Falls, Charles Buckles (1874-1960), illus. Becker, May Lamberton, Mrs. (1873-1958), intro. by. LC 48-11257. 252 p. illus. (part col.) 22 cm. (Rainbow Classics). 1948. World Pub. Co.
--Eight Cousins. unabridged. Lonette, Reisie Dominee (1924-), illus. LC 65-11916. 254p. col. illus. 22cm. (Whitman classics lib.). c.1965. Whitman Pub.
--Eight Cousins. Richards, Harriet Roosevelt, illus. (Little Women Ser.). N.D. Little Brown & Co.
--Eight Cousins: Or, The Ant-Hill. Doremus, Robert (1913-), illus. LC 55-39148. (Illus.). 21cm. 284p. (Whitman Famous Classics). 1955. Whitman.
--Eight Cousins: Or, The Aunt-Hill. N.D. A L Burt Co.
--Eight Cousins: Or, The Aunt-Hill. LC 47-23564. 3 p. l., 243 p. col. front. 19 cm. (Newbery classics). 1947. David McKay Company.
--Eight Cousins: Or, The Aunt-Hill. LC 3-25163. (Illus.). 17cm. 291p. 1902. Little, Brown and Company.

--Little Women. Van Stockum, Hilda Gerarda (1908-), illus. 320p. 1947. The World Publishing Co.
--Little Women and Eight Cousins. N.D. World Publishing Co.
--Little Women & Good Wives. N.D. Norton & Co.
--Little Women & Good Wives. (Illus.). N.D. William Collins Sons & Company.
--Little Women & Good Wives. Rhys, Ernest, ed. Rhys, Grace, intro. by. 17cm. 451p. (Everyman's Library). 1911. E. P. Dutton & Co.
--Little Women: Good Wives. Rhys, Grace, intro. by. LC 76-377259. (Illus.). 19cm. xvi, 448p. (Everyman's Library). 1970. (ISBN 0-460-00248-1). Dutton.
--Little Women: Or, Meg, Jo, Beth, and Amy. complete authorized. LC 35-28559. viii p., 1 l., 424p. incl. col. front. plates. 21cm. 1932. A. L. Burt.
--Little Women: Or, Meg, Jo, Beth and Amy. LC 47-23563. 2 p. l., 271 p., 2 l., 295 p. col. front. 19 cm. (Newbery classics). 1947. David McKay Company.
--Little Women: Or, Meg, Jo, Beth and Amy. LC 2-8868. 532 p. 1 l. front., plates. 17 1/2 cm. 1901. Little, Brown, and Company.
--Little Women: Or, Meg, Jo, Beth, and Amy. Players' ed. LC 12-20797. viii p., 1 l., 617 p. front., plates. 20 cm. 1912. Little, Brown, and Company.
--Little Women: Or, Meg, Jo, Beth, and Amy. LC 16-7735. 532 l) p. front., plates. 17 1/2 cm. 1915. Little, Brown, And Company.
--Little Women: Or, Meg, Jo, Beth and Amy. LC 20-123491. 532 p. front. 17 1/2 cm. 1919. Little, Brown, and Company.
--Little Women: Or, Meg, Jo, Beth and Amy. LC 34-27039. Repr. of 1868 ed. (Orchard House Edition). 1934. Little, Brown and Co.
--Little Women: or, Meg, Jo, Beth and Amy. (Fiction). (MacMillan Bks. for Boys & Girls). (gr. 7-9). N.D. MacMillan Bks.
--Little Women: Or, Meg, Jo, Beth and Amy. LC 12-10052. xvi, 586 p. front. (port.) illus., plates. 21 1/2 cm. c.1880. Roberts Brothers.
--Little Women: Or, Meg, Jo, Beth, and Amy, 2 Vols. (Illus.). 1882. Robert Brothers.
--Little Women: Or, Meg, Jo, Beth, and Amy. Cooney, Barbara (1917-), illus. LC 55-7329. 554p. illus. 23cm. 1955. Crowell.
--Little Women: Or, Meg, Jo, Beth, and Amy. Lonette, Reisie Dominee (1924-), illus. LC 50-14748. 376 p. illus. (part col.) 22 cm. 1950. Literary Guild of America.
--Little Women; or, Meg, Jo, Beth and Amy. McIntyre, Kevin, illus. LC 62-201978. 543p. illus. 18cm. (Collier books, AS457). 1962. Collier Books.
--Little Women: Or, Meg, Jo, Beth, and Amy. Merrill, Frank Thayer (1848-), illus. Garrett, Edmund H., photos by. LC 9-35178. xvi, 586 p. incl. front., illus. plates. 21 cm. 1908. Little, Brown, and Company.
--Little Women: Or, Meg, Jo, Beth, and Amy. Morse, Katherine, intro. by. LC 26-14233. xvi, 535 p. 19 1/2 cm. (Modern readers series). 1926. The Macmillan Company.
--Little Women: Or, Meg, Jo, Beth, and Amy. Rowland, Albert Lindsay (1882-), ed. Burd, Clara Miller, illus. LC 26-118505. xiii, 496 p. col. front., illus., col. plates. 21 cm. (Winston clear-type popular classics). c.1926. The John C. Winston Company.
--Little Women: Or, Meg, Jo, Beth and Amy. Smith, Jessie Willcox (1863-1935), illus. LC 15-19810. viii p., 1 l., 617 p. col. front., col. plates. 21 cm. $2.5. 1915. Little, Brown, and Company.
--Little Women: Or, Meg, Jo, Beth, and Amy. Smith, Jessie Willcox (1863-1935), illus. viii p., 1 l., 397 p. col. front., col. plates. 22 1/2 cm. 1922. Little, Brown, and Company.
--Little Women: Or, Meg, Jo, Beth, and Amy. Smith, Jessie Willcox (1863-1935), illus. LC 24-26905. viii p., 1 l., 397 p. col. front., col. plates. 22 1/2 cm. (Beacon Hill bookshelf). 1924. Little, Brown, and Company.
--Little Women: Or, Meg, Jo, Beth, and Amy. Smith, Jessie Willcox (1863-1935), illus. LC 34-27039. viii p., 1 l., 524 p. col. front., col. plates. 21 cm. 1934. Little, Brown, and Company.
--Little Women: Or, Meg, Jo, Beth, and Amy. centennial ed. Smith, Jessie Willcox (1863-1935), illus. Meigs, Cornelia (1884-1973), intro. by. LC 68-21171. (Illus.). xvii, 444 p. 24cm. 1968. Little, Brown.
--Little Women: Or, Meg, Jo, Beth and Amy. Stephens, Alice Barber (1858-1932), illus. LC 2-23996. viii p., 1 l., 617 p. front., plates. 20 1/2 cm. 1902. Little, Brown, and Company.
--Little Women: Or, Meg, Jo, Beth, and Amy. Van Stockum, Hilda Gerarda (1908-), illus. Becker, May Lamberton, Mrs. (1873-1958), intro. by. LC 46-6847. 537 p., 1 l. col. front., illus., col. plates. 22 cm. (Half-title: Rainbow classics). 1946. The World Publishing Company.
--Little Women: Or, Meg, Jo, Beth, and Amy. Warner, Frances Lester (1888-), ed. LC 28-17387. xviii, 611 p. incl. front. (port.) illus. 19 cm. (Standard English classics). c.1928. Ginn and Company.
--The Little Women Play. (Illus.). (The Children's Friend Ser.). N.D. Little, Brown and Company.
--The "Little Women" Play. Gould, Elizabeth Lincoln (0000-1914), adapted by. Birch, Reginald Bathurst (1856-1943), illus. LC 1-30074. 20 cm. 101p. 1900. Little, Brown.
--The Louisa Alcott Reader. N.D. Little, Brown & Co.
--The Louisa Alcott Story Book. Coe, Fanny E., ed. LC 19-18650. xix, 202 p. front. 17 1/2 cm. 1910. Little, Brown, and Company.
--Louisa Alcott's People. Becker, Lamberton, Mrs. (1873-1958), ed. Fogarty, Thomas (1873-), illus. LC 36-244010. ix 1 p., 2 l., 3-211 p. incl. illus., plates, color front., col. plates. 24 cm. 1936. C. Scribner's Sons.
--Louisa M. Alcott's Eight Cousins: Or, The Aunt-Hill. Lowe, Viola Ruth (1908-), ed. Taylor, Ethel Bonney, illus. LC 40-845340. 1 p. l., 5-94 p. illus. (part. col.) 17 x 13 1/2 cm. c.1940. Whitman Publishing Co.
--Louisa's Wonder Book: An Unknown Alcott Juvenile. Stern, Madeleine Bettina (1912-), ed. 1975. Clarke Historical Library.
--Lulu's Library. N.D. Grosset & Dunlap.
--Lulu's Library. LC 11-8220. 3 v. illus. 17 cm. 1886. Roberts Brothers.
--Lulu's Library. Kay, Gertrude Alice (1884-1939), illus. Leslie, Eva G., frwd. by. LC 30-20593. xix p. 3 l., 3)-229 . col. front., col. plates. 21 1/2 cm. 1930. Little, Brown, and Company.
--Marjorie's Three Gifts. (Illus.). (The Children's Friend Ser.). 1899. Little, Brown and Company.
--May Flowers. LC 99-4860. 1 p. l., 56 p. front., plates. 19 cm. c.1899. Little, Brown, and Company.
--May Flowers. (Illus.). (The Children's Friend Ser.). N.D. Little, Brown and Company.
--A Modern Cinderella. (Illus.). (The Alcazar Classics). N.D. Caldwell.
--A Modern Cinderella. (Alcott and Whitney Ser.). N.D. Hurst & Co.
--A Modern Cinderella, 1 of 12 vols. Lukens, Winfield S., illus. (Illus.). (Illustrated Holly-Tree Ser.: No. 3). 1905. Henry Altemus Co.
--Moods. 359p. N.D. Little, Brown.
--Moods. LC 22-15156. (Illus.). 17cm. 297p. 1864. Loring.
--Morning Glories. N.D. G. W. Carlton & Co.
--Morning-Glories: And Other Stories. LC 17-13048. 195 p. front., plates. 18 cm. 1868. H. B. Fuller.
--Morning-Glories and Queen Aster. LC 4-17220. 1 p. l., 41 p. front., pl. 19 1/2 cm. (The Children's Friend Ser.). 1904. Little, Brown, and Company.
--Mountain-Laurel and Maiden-Hair. LC 3-17531. 1 p. l., 48 p. 1 l. front., plates. 19 1/2 cm. (The Children's Friend Ser.). 1903. Little, Brown, and Company.
--My Boys. (Illus.). (The Boys' and Girls' Books). N.D. Little, Brown and Company.
--My Boys. N.D. Roberts Bros.
--My Girls. 229p. N.D. Little, Brown.
--My Girls. (Illus.). (The Boys' and Girls' Books). N.D. Little, Brown and Company.
--My Girls. (Illus.). N.D. Set 6.00. Robert Brothers.
--An Old-Fashioned Girl. LC 47-23201. 4 p. l., 340 p. col. front. 19 cm. (Newbery classics). 1947. David McKay Company.
--An Old-Fashioned Girl. (The Children's Favorite Ser.). N.D. Grosset & Dunlap.
--An Old-Fashioned Girl. N.D. Grosset & Dunlap.
--An Old-Fashioned Girl. Repr. of 1869 ed. (Orchard House Edition). 1934. Little, Brown & Co.
--An Old-Fashioned Girl. LC 20-23156. 4 p. 1 l., 378 p. front., 3 pl. 17 cm. 1870. Roberts Brothers.
--An Old-Fashioned Girl. LC 12-31403. 4 2, 378 p. front., plates. 17 1/2 cm. 1897. Roberts Brothers.
--An Old-Fashioned Girl. Abbott, Elenore Plaisted, illus. LC 20-27446. 5 p. l., 328 p. col. front., col. plates. 22 1/2 cm. (Beacon Hill bookshelf). 1926. Little, Brown, and Company.
--An Old-Fashioned Girl. Abbott, Elenore Plaisted, illus. LC 34-271914. vi p., 2 l., 371 p. col. front., col. plates. 21 cm. 1934. Little, Brown, and Company.
--An Old-Fashioned Girl. Brundage, Frances, illus. LC 26-12881. 401 p. incl. front., illus., plates. 19 1/2 cm. (Half-title: Every child's library). c.1928. The Saalfield Publishing Company.
--An Old-Fashioned Girl. Brundage, Frances, illus. LC 28-15155. 4 p. l., 13-401 p. incl. plates, illus., col. front. 23 cm. (Lettered on cover: Companion series). c.1928. The Saalfield Publishing Company.
--An Old-Fashioned Girl. Burd, Clara Miller, illus. (The Children's Bookshelf). N.D. John C. Winston.
--An Old-Fashioned Girl. Burd, Clara Miller, illus. LC 29-3487. ix, 342 p. col. front., illus., col. plates. 21 cm. (On cover: The Winston clear-type popular classics). c.1928. The John C. Winston Company.
--An Old-Fashioned Girl. Smith, Jessie Willcox (1863-1935), illus. N.D. A. L. Burt Co.
--An Old-Fashioned Girl. Smith, Jessie Willcox (1863-1935), illus. LC 2-23997. vi p. 2 l., 371 p. front., plates. 20 1/2 cm. 1902. Little, Brown, and Company.
--An Old-Fashioned Girl. Weber, Nettie, illus. Becker, May Lamberton, Mrs. (1873-1958), intro. by. LC 47-30356. 319 p. illus., col. plates. 22 cm. (Rainbow classics). 1947. World Pub. Co.
--An Old-Fashioned Thanksgiving. 234p. N.D. Little, Brown.
--An Old-Fashioned Thanksgiving. N.D. Robert Brothers.
--An Old-Fashioned Thanksgiving. Johnson, Holly, illus. LC 73-15698. (Illus.). 73 p. 21cm. 1974. (ISBN 0-397-31515-5). Lippincott.
--Pansies and Water-Lilies. LC 2-19103. (Illus.). 19.5 cm. 76p. (The Children's Friend Ser.). 1902. Little, Brown and Company.
--Poppies and Wheat. LC 5880. 1 p. l., 54 p. front., 2 pl. 19 cm. 54cm. 19p. 1900. Little, Brown, and Company.
--Poppies and Wheat. (Illus.). (The Children's Friend Ser.). N.D. Little, Brown and Company.
--Proverb Stories. New revised. 1882. Robert Brothers.
--Proverb Stories. Brown, Ethel Pennewill, illus. LC 8-25994. 5 p. l., 334 p. 1 l. front., 7 p. 20 1/2 cm. (Her The spinning wheel series). 1908. Little, Brown, and Company.
--Rose in Bloom. (Famous Bks. for Young Americans). N.D. A. L. Burt Co.
--Rose in Bloom. LC 47-23210. 319 p. incl. col. front., plates. 19 1/2 cm. (Newbery classics). 1947. David McKay Company.
--Rose in Bloom. (The Children's Favorite Ser.). N.D. Grosset & Dunlap.
--Rose in Bloom. (The Winston Clear-Type Popular Classics). N.D. John C. Winston.
--Rose in Bloom. Repr. of 1876 ed. (Orchard House Edition). 1934. Little, Brown & Co.
--Rose in Bloom. LC 17-13049. (A Sequel to "Eight Cousins"). viii, 375 p. incl. front. (port.) 17 1/2 cm. 1876. Roberts Brothers.
--Rose in Bloom. (Classic Ser.). N.D. World Publishing Co.
--Rose in Bloom. Burd, Clara Miller, illus. LC 33-31888. 1 p. l., v-viii, 320 p. col. front., illus., col. plates. 22 cm. c.1933. The John C. Winston Company.
--Rose in Bloom. Modern Abridged. Fleur, Anne Elizabeth (1901-), illus. Sari, pseud. LC 52-4604. 236 p. illus. 21 cm. (Whitman classic). 1952. Whitman Pub. Co.
--Rose in Bloom. Richards, Harriet Roosevelt, illus. (Little Women Ser.). N.D. Little Brown & Co.
--Rose in Bloom: A Sequel to "Eight Cousins". LC 7-740. viii, 375 p. incl. front. 17 1/2 cm. 1900. Little, Brown, and Company.
--Rose in Bloom: A Sequel to "Eight Cousins". LC 4-29787. viii, 375 p. incl. front. plates. 18 cm. 1904. Little, Brown, and Company.
--Rose in Bloom: A Sequel to "Eight Cousins". LC 20-155942. 4 p. l., 344 p. front. 17 1/2 cm. 1919. Little, Brown, and Company.
--Rose in Bloom: A Sequel to "Eight Cousins". LC 26-859442. 4 p. l., 344 p. front. 17 1/2 cm. 1924. Little, Brown, and Company.
--Rose in Bloom: A Sequel to "Eight Cousins". (Illus.). (Little Women Ser.). 1882. Roberts Brothers.
--Rose in Bloom: A Sequel to "Eight Cousins". Price, Harriet Longstreet (1891-), illus. LC 27-19313. 5 p. l., 322 p. col. front., col. plates. 22 1/2 cm. (Beacon Hill bookshelf). 1927. Little, Brown, and Company.
--Rose in Bloom: A Sequel to "Eight Cousins". Price, Harriet Longstreet (1891-), illus. LC 34-27192. 5 p. l., 344 p. col. front., col. plates. 21 cm. 1934. Little, Brown, and Company.
--Rose in Bloom: A Sequel to "Eight Cousins". Richards, Harriet Roosevelt, illus. LC 4-24563. 5 p. l., 344 p. 1 l. front., 7 pl. 20 cm. 1904. Little, Brown, and Company.
--A Round Dozen. Eaton, Anne Thaxter (1881-1971), ed. Tudor, Tasha (1915-), illus. (Illus.). (gr. 6-9). 1963. (ISBN 0-670-60878-5). Viking Pr.
--A Round Dozen: Stories. Tudor, Tasha (1915-), illus. Eaton, Anne Thaxter, frwd. by. LC 63-18366. 256 p. illus. 22 cm. 1963. Viking Press.
--Shawl-Straps. (Illus.). N.D. Robert Brothers.
--Silver Pitchers. N.D. Grosset & Dunlap.
--Silver Pitchers, and Independence, a Centennial Love. Kennedy, J. W. Ferguson, illus. LC 8-25992. 20 1/2cm. 365p. (The Spinning Wheel Ser.). 1908. Little Brown.
--Silver Pitchers, and Independence: A Centennial Love Story. LC 4-12217. 2 p. l., 307 p. 17 1/2 cm. 1903. Little, Brown, and Company.
--Spinning Wheel Stories. N.D. Grosset & Dunlap.
--Spinning Wheel Stories. LC 4-18682. 2 p. l., 276 p. 1 l. 17 cm. 1902. Little, Brown, and Company.
--Spinning-Wheel Stories. (Illus.). (The Boys' and Girls' Books). N.D. Little, Brown and Company.
--Spinning-Wheel Stories. 1884. Robert Brothers.
--Spinning Wheel Stories. McCullough, William A., illus. LC 3-25991. 4 p. l., 304 p., 1 l. front., 7 pl. 20 cm. (Her The spinning wheel series). 1908. Little, Brown, and Company.
--Three Proverb Stories: Kitty's class-day; Aunt Kipp; Psyche's Art. Hoppin, Augustus (1828-1896), illus. LC 62-57450. 18cm. 148p. 1868. Loring.
--Trudel's Siege. Skardinski, Stanley, illus. LC 76-3405. (Illus.). p. cm. 21cm. 55p. (gr. 4-6). 1976. (ISBN 0-07-057791-9). McGraw-Hill.
--Under the Lilacs. (Famous Bks. for Young Americans). N.D. A. L. Burt Co.
--Under the Lilacs. LC 47-23209. 250 p. col. front. 19 1/2 cm. (Newbery classics). 1947. David McKay Company.
--Under the Lilacs. N.D. Grosset & Dunlap.
--Under the Lilacs. (The Winston Clear-Type Popular Classics). N.D. John C. Winston.
--Under the Lilacs. LC 2-8246. 4 p. l., 305 p. front., plates. 17 cm. 1901. Little, Brown, and Company.
--Under the Lilacs. LC 5-27399. 4 p. l., 305 p. front., plates. 18 cm. 1904. Little, Brown, and Company.
--Under the Lilacs. Repr. of 1877 ed. (Orchard House Edition). 1934. Little, Brown & Co.
--Under the Lilacs. LC 17-130523. 4 p. l., 305 p. front., plates 27 cm. 1878. Roberts Brothers.
--Under the Lilacs. (Illus.). (Little Women Ser.). 1882. Roberts Brothers.
--Under the Lilacs. Davis, Marguerite (1889-), illus. LC 28-19008. 6 p. l., 3-284 p. col. front., col. plates. 22 1/2 cm. (Beacon Hill bookshelf). 1928. Little, Brown, and Company.
--Under the Lilacs. Davis, Marguerite (1889-), illus. LC 34-27198. 5 p. l., 302 p. col. front., col. plates. 21 cm. 1934. Little, Brown, and Company.
--Under the Lilacs. Ives, Ruth, illus. LC 55-537. 316p. illus. 22cm. c.1955. Junior Deluxe Editions.
--Under the Lilacs. Lawson, George, illus. LC 35-16589. 348 p. incl. col. front., illus. 21 cm. c.1935. The Saalfield Publishing Company.
--Under the Lilacs. Murray, Irene (1935-), illus. LC 62-19970. 317 p. illus. 18 cm. 1962. Collier Books.
--Under the Lilacs. Stephens, Alice Barber (1858-1932), illus. LC 5-30270. 5 p. l., 302 p. 1 l. front., 7 pl. 20 cm. 1905. Little, Brown, and Company.
--Under the Lilacs. Stephenson, Eunice Holmes, illus. LC 34-23272. vi, 282 p. col. front., illus., col. plates. 22 cm. c.1934. The John C. Winston Company.
--Work: A Story of Experience. LC 1-30218. 3 p. l., 443 p. illus. 17 1/2 cm. 1900. Little, Brown, and Company.
--Work: A Story of Experience. LC 17-13050. 3 p. l., 443 p. illus. 18 cm. 1873. Roberts Brothers.
--Work: A Story of Experience. Eytinge, Sol, illus. 443p. N.D. Little, Brown.

Alcott, Louisa May (1832-1888), contrib. by.

--Christmas Plum Pudding. Thorne, Olive, contrib. by. (Illus.). N.D. T. Y. Crowell.

Alcott, Louisa May (1832-1888) & Trowbridge, John Townsend (1827-1916)

--Happy Days: A Story and Picture Book for Boys and Girls. (Illus.). N.D. Porter and Coates.

Alcott, Virginia

--World Friendship Plays for Young People. Egan, Florence, illus. LC 29-8848. xiii, 276 p. col. front., illus., col. plates. 20 cm. 1929. Dodd, Mead and Company.

Alda, Arlene (1933-)

--Matthew and His Dad. Alda, Arlene (1933-), photos by. LC 83-9423. (Illus.). 44 p. 27cm. c.1983. (ISBN 0-671-45158-8). (ISBN 0-671-46814-6). Little Simon.
--Sonya's Mommy Works. Alda, Arlene (1933-), photos by. LC 82-12448. 48. 1982. (ISBN 0-671-46167-2). J. Messner.
--Sonya's Mommy Works. Alda, Arlene (1933-), photos by. LC 82-6550. p. cm. c.1982. (ISBN 0-671-45157-X). Little Simon.

Aldan, Daisy (1923-), ed.
--Poems from India. Low, Joseph (1911-), illus. LC 72-78253. (Illus.). halftone drawings. index. 202p. (Poems of the World). (gr. 7 up). 1969. (ISBN 0-690-63862-0, TYC-J). Har-Row.

Aldeberg, Doris
--Grandma's Holiday. 1963. The Dial Press, Inc.

Alden, Albert
--A Present for Good Children. LC 64-20505. (Illus.). 13cm. 17p. 1964. Barre.
--A Present for Good Children. LC 65-59800. (Illus.). 13cm. 16p. 1965. Barre Publishers.
--Pretty Scenes for Children. Alden, Albert, illus. LC 65-20506. (Illus.). 13cm. 17p. 1964. Barre.

Alden, Alice Gordon
--Elizabeth Benton. N.D. Harper & Bros.
--Schoolmistress. N.D. Harper & Bros.

Alden, Alice Wight, Jt. auth. see Drama League of America.

Alden, Carella, pseud., see Remington, Ella-Carrie.

Alden, Carella, pseud. (1914-)
--Royal Persia: Tales & Art of Iran. Remington, Ella-Carrie. LC 72-1818. (Illus.). index. 64p. (Art Tells a Story Ser.). (gr. 4-6). 1972. (ISBN 0-8193-0610-X). (ISBN 0-8193-0611-8). Parents.

Alden, Cynthia May Westover, Mrs. (1862-)
--Bushy: A Romance Founded on Fact. Walker, J. A., illus. LC 21-20578. vi, 318 p. front., plates. 19 cm. 1896. The Morse Company.

Alden, Gustavus R.
--Glimpses of Boyhood. 19cm. 80p. 1892. D. Lothrop Company.

Alden, Isabella Macdonald see Pansy, pseud.

Alden, Isabella Macdonald (1841-1930)
--Agatha's Unknown Way: A Story of Missionary Guidance. Pansy, pseud. LC 96-115. 2 p. l., 3-58 p. front. 18 1/2 cm. (The looking upward booklets). c.1898. Fleming H. Revell Company.
--Alexander the Great. Pansy, pseud, 1 of 12 vols. (Illus.). (Pansy Primary Lib: No. 4). N.D. Set. Lothrop Pub. Co.
--Amy Robb. Pansy, pseud, 1 of 20 vols. (Illus.). (Pansy Primary Lib: No. 2). N.D. Set. Lothrop Pub Co.
--An Hour with Miss Streator. Pansy, pseud. LC 25-7195. 14cm. 40p. 1884. D. Lothrop.
--An April Walk. Pansy, pseud, 1 of 12 vols. (Illus.). (Pansy Primary Lib: No. 4). N.D. Set. Lothrop Pub Co.
--At Home and Abroad. Pansy, pseud. (The Pansy Books). N.D. Lothrop.
--Aunt Hannah, and Martha, and John. Pansy, pseud. N.D. D. Lothrop Co.
--Bargaining. Pansy, pseud, 1 of 12 vols. (Illus.). (Mother's Boys and Girls' Library). 1882. D Lothrop.
--Ben Hadad's First Christmas. Pansy, pseud, 1 of 12 vols. (Illus.). (Pansy Primary Lib: No. 4). N.D. Set. Lothrop Pub. Co.
--Bernie's White Chicken. Pansy, pseud. (Illus.). (The Pansy Books). N.D. Lothrop Pub. Co.
--Better than Gold. Pansy, pseud, 1 of 36 vols. (Select Primary Lib). N.D. Set. Lothrop Pub. Co.
--Bobby's Wolf and Other Stories. Pansy, pseud. (Illus.). N.D. Lothrop.
--Boys of Algeria. Pansy, pseud, 1 of 20 vols. (Illus.). (Pansy Primary Lib: No. 2). N.D. Set. Lothrop Pub. Co.
--Brave Tommy. Pansy, pseud, 1 of 12 vols. (Illus.). (Mother's Boys and Girls' Library). 1882. D Lothrop.
--The Browning Boys. Pansy, pseud. (Pansy Intermediate Library). N.D. D. Lothrop Co.
--By Moonlight. Pansy, pseud, 1 of 12 vols. (Illus.). (Pansy Primary Lib: No. 3). N.D. Set. Lothrop Pub. Co.
--Carrie's Experiment. Pansy, pseud, 1 of 20 vols. (Illus.). (Pansy Primary Lib: No. 2). N.D. Set. Lothrop Pub. Co.
--The Chautauqua Girls at Home. Pansy, pseud, 1 of 5 vols. (Illus.). (Chautauqua Girls Library). N.D. D. Lothrop Co.
--The Chautauqua Girls at Home. Pansy, pseud. LC 5-33617. 406 p. front., pl. 19 1/2 cm. c.1905. Lothrop, Lee & Shepard Co.
--Chautauqua Girls at Home. Pansy, pseud. (Illus.). (The Pansy Books). N.D. Lothrop.
--Chop Sticks. Pansy, pseud, 1 of 30 vols. (Illus.). (Pansy Primary Library: No. 1). N.D. Set. Lothrop Pub Co.
--Christie's Christmas. Pansy, pseud. (Illus.). (The Pansy Books). N.D. Lothrop Pub.
--A Christmas Time. Pansy, pseud. (Illus.). N.D. D. Lothrop & Co.
--Claire's Bewilderment. Pansy, pseud, 1 of 12 vols. (Illus.). (Pansy Primary Lib: No. 4). N.D. Set. Lothrop Pub. Co.
--Cloud and Cliff. Pansy, pseud. N.D. Lothrop Pub. Co.
--Company Try. Pansy, pseud, 1 of 30 vols. (Illus.). (Pansy Primary Library: No. 1). N.D. Set. Lothrop Publishing Co.
--Cunning Workman. Pansy, pseud, 1 of 6 vols. (Illus.). (Cunning Workman Ser.). N.D. D Lothrop.
--Daisy and Grandpa. Pansy, pseud, 1 of 4 Vols. (Illus.). 190p. (Pansy Picture Library). 1876. Set. D Lothrop & Co.
--Danger Cliff. Pansy, pseud, 1 of 20 vols. (Illus.). (Pansy Primary Lib: No. 2). N.D. Set. Lothrop Pub. Co.
--David Ransom's Watch. Pansy, pseud. Fosbery, Ernest, illus. (Illus.). (The Pansy Books). N.D. Lothrop Lee & Shepard Co.
--Day in the Country. Pansy, pseud, 1 of 20 vols. (Illus.). (Pansy Primary Lib: No. 2). N.D. Set. Lothrop Pub. Co.
--Docia's Journal: Or, God Is Love. Pansy, pseud, 1 of 4 vols. (Illus.). (Pansy Ser.). N.D. D. Lothrop Co.
--Doris Farrand's Vocation. Pansy, pseud. Fosbery, Ernest, illus. (Illus.). [illegible]p. (The Pansy Books). 1904. Lothrop Lee & Shepard & Co.
--Dorrie's Day. Pansy, pseud, 1 of 30 vols. (Illus.). (Pansy Primary Library: No. 1). N.D. Set. Lothrop Pub. Co.
--A Dozen of Them. Pansy, pseud. (Pansy Intermediate Library). N.D. D. Lothrop Co.
--A Dozen of Them. Pansy, pseud. (Illus.). (The Pansy Books). N.D. Lothrop Pub.
--Echoing and Re-echoing. Pansy, pseud, 1 of 6 vols. (Illus.). (Household Library). N.D. D Lothrop.
--Eighty-Seven. Pansy, pseud. N.D. D. Lothrop Co.
--Emma's Ambition. Pansy, pseud, 1 of 30 vols. (Illus.). (Pansy Primary Library: No. 1). N.D. Set. Lothrop Pub. Co.
--An Endless Chain. Pansy, pseud. N.D. D. Lothrop Co.
--Enlisted. Pansy, pseud, 1 of 30 vols. (Illus.). (Pansy Primary Library: No. 1). N.D. Set. Lothrop Pub. Co.
--The Esselstynes. Pansy, pseud, 1 of 12 vols. (Illus.). (Mother's Boys and Girls' Library). 1882. D Lothrop.
--Ester Ried. Pansy, pseud. (Illus.). N.D. D. Lothrop Co.
--Ester Ried: Asleep and Awake. Pansy, pseud. LC 20-19327. iv, 5-346 p. front., pl. 18 1/2 cm. 1870. Western Tract and Book Society.
--Ester Ried Yet Speaking. Pansy, pseud. (Illus.). N.D. D. Lothrop Co.
--Ester Ried's Namesake. Pansy, pseud. Fosbery, Ernest, illus. LC 6-34818. v, 429 p. front., 3 pl. 19 1/2 cm. 1906. Lothrop, Lee & Shepard Co.
--The Exact Truth. Pansy, pseud. (The Pansy Books). N.D. Lothrop.
--Five Friends. Pansy, pseud, 1 of 5 vols. (Illus.). (Young Heroine Library). 1882. D Lothrop.
--Five Friends. Pansy, pseud. (Illus.). N.D. D. Lothrop Co.
--Flossie's Triumph. Pansy, pseud, 1 of 20 vols. (Illus.). (Pansy Primary Lib: No. 2). N.D. Set. Lothrop Pub. Co.
--The Fortunate Calamity. Pansy, pseud. Norcross, Grace, illus. LC 27-18380. 272 p. col. front., plates. 19 1/2 cm. 1927. J. B. Lippincott Company.
--Four Girls at Chautauqua. Pansy, pseud. 474p. 1876. Lothrop.
--Four Girls at Chautauqua. Pansy, pseud. LC 4-18898. 474 p. front. pl. 19 1/2 cm. c.1904. Lothrop Publishing Company.
--Fred's House. Pansy, pseud, 1 of 30 vols. (Illus.). (Pansy's Primary Lib: No. 1). N.D. Set. Lothrop Pub. Co.
--Fred's Puzzle. Pansy, pseud, 1 of 20 vols. (Illus.). (Pansy Primary Lib: No. 2). N.D. Set. Lothrop Pub. Co.
--Friend in Need. Pansy, pseud, 1 of 12 vols. (Illus.). (Pansy Primary Lib: No. 3). N.D. Set. Lothrop Pub. Co.
--From Different Standpoints. Pansy, pseud. (Illus.). N.D. D. Lothrop Co.
--From Different Standpoints. Pansy, pseud, 1 of 5 vols. (Illus.). (Chautauqua Girls Library). N.D. D Lothrop.
--Gertrude's Diary. Pansy, pseud. N.D. D. Lothrop Co.
--Getting Ahead. Pansy, pseud. (Pansy-Also known as Alden/Mrs. G. R.). (Illus.). N.D. D. Lothrop Co.
--Getting Ahead. Pansy, pseud. LC 6-12562. (Illus.). 18cm. 92p. Repr. of 1877 ed. 1906. Lothrop Publishing Co.
--Getting Ahead. Pansy, pseud. (Mrs. Isabella Alden also Known as "Mrs. G. R. Alden"). (Illus.). (The Pansy Books). N.D. Lothrop Pub.
--A Girl's Money. Pansy, pseud. (Illus.). N.D. D. Lothrop & Co.
--Going Halves. Pansy, pseud, 1 of 30 vols. (Isabella Alden also Known as Mrs. G. R. Alden). (Illus.). (Pansy Primary Library: No. 1). N.D. Set. Lothrop Pub. Co.
--Going Halves. Pansy, pseud, 1 of 10 vols. (Illus.). (Little Pansy Ser.). N.D. Set. Lothrop Publishing Co.
--A Golden Thought. Pansy, pseud, 1 of 12 vols. (Illus.). (Mother's Boys and Girls' Library). 1882. D Lothrop.
--At Grandpa Bogart's. Pansy, pseud, 1 of 12 vols. (Illus.). (Pansy Primary Lib: No. 3). N.D. Set. Lothrop Pub. Co.
--Grandpa's Darlings. Pansy, pseud. LC 20-19320. v, 7-323 p. front., 2 pl. 18 1/2 cm. 1875. D. Lothrop & Co.
--Grandpa's Darlings. Pansy, pseud. (Illus.). N.D. D. Lothrop Co.
--Grandpa's Darlings. Pansy, pseud, 1 of 6 vols. (Illus.). (Cunning Workman Ser.). N.D. D Lothrop.
--Grandpa's Darlings. Pansy, pseud. (The Pansy Books). N.D. Lothrop.
--Hall in the Grove. Pansy, pseud. N.D. D. Lothrop Co.
--Happy Summer. Pansy, pseud, 1 of 20 vols. (Illus.). (Pansy Primary Lib: No. 2). N.D. Set. Lothrop Pub Co.
--The Harrisville Young Ladies Band. Pansy, pseud. (Illus.). N.D. D. Lothrop & Co.
--Harry's Invention. Pansy, pseud, 1 of 12 vols. (Illus.). (Pansy Primary Lib: No. 3). N.D. Set. Lothrop Pub. Co.
--Hedge Fence. Pansy, pseud, 1 of 3 Vols. (Illus.). (Side By Side Library: No. 2). N.D. D. Lothrop & Co.
--A Hedge Fence. Pansy, pseud. (Pansy Intermediate Library). N.D. D. Lothrop Co.
--A Hedge Fence. Pansy, pseud. (Illus.). (The Pansy Books). N.D. Lothrop.
--Helen Lester. Pansy, pseud, 1 of 4 vols. (Illus.). (Pansy Ser.). N.D. D. Lothrop & Co.
--Helen Lester: To Which is Added Nannie's Experiment. Pansy, pseud. (Illus.). N.D. Lothrop Publishing Co.
--Helen the Historian. Pansy, pseud. (Illus.). (The Pansy Books). N.D. Lothrop.
--Hester's Experience. Pansy, pseud, 1 of 12 vols. (Illus.). (Pansy Primary Lib: No. 4). N.D. Set. Lothrop Pub. Co.
--Horace Brooks. Pansy, pseud, 1 of 30 vols. (Illus.). (Pansy Primary Library: No. 1). N.D. Set. Lothrop Pub. Co.
--How He Escaped. Pansy, pseud, 1 of 12 vols. (Illus.). (Pansy Primary Lib: No. 3). N.D. Set. Lothrop Pub. Co.
--In Vacation. Pansy, pseud, 1 of 20 vols. (Illus.). (Pansy Primary Lib: No. 2). N.D. Set. Lothrop Pub Co.
--Jessie Wells. Pansy, pseud, 1 of 4 vols. (Illus.). (Pansy Ser.). N.D. D Lothrop.
--John and Mary. Pansy, pseud, 1 of 30 vols. (Illus.). (Pansy Primary Library: No. 1). N.D. Set. Lothrop Pub. Co.
--Judge Burnham's Daughter. Pansy, pseud. (Pansy Books). N.D. Lothrop, Lee & Shepard.
--Judge Burnham's Daughters. Pansy, pseud. LC 21-16865. 3 p. l., 339 p. front. 18 cm. c.1888. D. Lothrop Company.
--Julia Reid. Pansy, pseud. (Illus.). N.D. D. Lothrop & Co.
--Julia Reid. Pansy, pseud. (Illus.). (The Pansy Books). N.D. Lothrop.
--Julia Reid. Pansy, pseud. 372p. (The Pansy Bks.). N.D. Western Tract Society.
--The King's Daughter. Pansy, pseud. LC 1-34558. iv, 5-305 p. front. 19 1/2 cm. c.1901. Lothrop Pub. Co.
--Laura's Plan. Pansy, pseud, 1 of 30 vols. (Illus.). (Pansy Primary Library). N.D. Lothrop Pub. Co.
--Laura's Promise. Pansy, pseud, 1 of 30 vols. (Illus.). (Pansy Primary Lib: No. 1). N.D. Set. Lothrop Pub. Co.
--Leafy Fern. Pansy, pseud, 1 of 30 vols. (Illus.). (Pansy Primary Library: No. 1). N.D. Set. Lothrop.
--Leafy Fern. Pansy, pseud, 1 of 10 vols. (Illus.). (Little Pansy Ser.). N.D. Set. Lothrop Publishing Co.
--Leonard's April Fool. Pansy, pseud, 1 of 30 vols. (Illus.). (Pansy Primary Library: No. 1). N.D. Set. Lothrop Pub. Co.
--Leonard's April Fool. Pansy, pseud, 1 of 10 vols. (Illus.). (Little Pansy Ser.). N.D. Set. Lothrop Publishing Co.
--Light from Persia. Pansy, pseud, 1 of 20 vols. (Illus.). (Pansy Primary Lib: No. 2). N.D. Set. Lothrop Pub. Co.
--Links in Rebecca's Life. Pansy, pseud, 1 of 5 vols. (Illus.). (Chautauqua Girls Library). N.D. D. Lothrop & Co.
--Links in Rebecca's Life. Pansy, pseud. LC 6-17876. vi, 7-422 p. incl. front. 19 1/2 cm. c.1906. Lothrop, Lee & Shepard Co.
--Links in Rebecca's Life. Pansy, pseud. (Illus.). 19cm. 422p. Repr. of 1848 ed. (The Pansy Books). 1906. Lothrop Pub.
--Little by Little. Pansy, pseud, 1 of 30 vols. (Illus.). (Pansy Primary Library: No. 1). N.D. Set. Lothrop Pub. Co.
--Little by Little. Pansy, pseud, 1 of 10 vols. (Illus.). (Little Pansy Ser.). N.D. Set. Lothrop Publishing Co.
--The Little Card. Pansy, pseud. N.D. Lothrop Publishing Co.
--Little Fishers and Their Nets. Pansy, pseud. (Illus.). (The Pansy Books). N.D. Lothrop.
--Little Hands. Pansy, pseud. LC 20-16490. (Illus.). 16cm. 47p. 1879. D. Lothrop and Company.
--Little Hands. Pansy, pseud, 1 of 30 vols. (Illus.). (Pansy Primary Library: No. 1). N.D. Set. Lothrop Pub. Co.
--Little Hands. Pansy, pseud, 1 of 10 vols. (Illus.). (Little Pansy Ser.). N.D. Set. Lothrop Publishing Co.
--Little Minnie. Pansy, pseud, 1 of 4 Vols. (Illus.). (Pansy Picture Library). N.D. Set. D Lothrop & Co.
--Little Missionary. Pansy, pseud, 1 of 30 vols. (Illus.). (Pansy Primary Lib: No. 1). N.D. Set. Lothrop Pub. Co.
--Little People in Picture and Story. LC 21-16864. 1 p. l., 7-190 p. front., illus. 21 cm. c.1877. D. Lothrop & Co.
--Little Sara's Wisdom. Pansy, pseud, 1 of 12 vols. (Illus.). (Pansy Primary Lib. No. 4). N.D. Set. Lothrop Pub. Co.
--Lost Nellie. Pansy, pseud, 1 of 12 vols. (Illus.). (Mother's Boys and Girls' Library). 1882. D Lothrop.
--Mag and Margaret. Pansy, pseud. Emerson, C. chase, illus. (The Pansy Books). N.D. Lothrop Lee & Shepard & Co.
--The Man of the House. Pansy, pseud. (Illus.). (The Pansy Books). N.D. Lothrop.
--The Man of the House. Pansy, pseud. Lewis, Robert, illus. N.D. D. Lothrop Co.
--Mara. Pansy, pseud. (Illus.). (The Pansy Books). N.D. Lothrop Lee & Shepard & Co.
--Marjory. Pansy, pseud, 1 of 30 vols. (Illus.). (Pansy Primary Library: No. 1). N.D. Set. Lothrop Pub. Co.
--Mary Burton Abroad. Pansy, pseud. N.D. D. Lothrop Co.
--Mary's Prizes. Pansy, pseud, 1 of 30 vols. (Illus.). (Pansy Primary Library: No. 1). N.D. Set. Lothrop Pub. Co.
--Miss Dee Dunmore Bryant. Pansy, pseud. N.D. Lothrop Publishing Co.
--Miss Dr. Bellby. Pansy, pseud, 1 of 12 vols. (Illus.). (Pansy Primary Lib: No. 3). N.D. Set. Lothrop Pub. Co.
--Miss Priscilla Hunter. Pansy, pseud, 1 of 7 vols. (Illus.). (Idle Hour Ser.). N.D. D Lothrop.
--Miss Priscilla Hunter and My Daughter Susan. Pansy, pseud, 1 of 6 vols. (Illus.). (Cunning Workman Ser.). N.D. D Lothrop.
--Miss Priscilla Hunter: And My Daughter Susan. Pansy, pseud. LC 7-23529. 1 p. l., 7-135, 2, 7-146 p. incl. plates. front. 19 cm. c.1907. Lothrop, Lee & Shepard Co.
--Missent: Or, The Story of a Letter. Pansy, pseud. LC 1219. 175, 1 p. front. 19 cm. 1900. Lothrop Publishing Company.
--Mission of a Gray Sock. Pansy, pseud, 1 of 12 vols. (Illus.). (Pansy Primary Lib: No. 3). N.D. Set. Lothrop Pub. Co.
--A Modern Sacrifice: A Story of Kissie Gordon's Experiment. Pansy, pseud. (Illus.). N.D. Lothrop Publishing Co.
--Monteagle. Pansy, pseud. (Illus.). (The Pansy Books). N.D. Lothrop.
--Morning Ride. Pansy, pseud, 1 of 20 vols. (Illus.). (Pansy Primary Lib: No. 2). N.D. Set. Lothrop Pub. Co.
--Mother's Boys and Girls' Library. Pansy, pseud, 12 vols. (Illus.). 1882. Set. D Lothrop.
--Mrs. Dunlap. Pansy, pseud, 1 of 30 vols. (Illus.). (Pansy Primary Lib: No. 1). N.D. Set. Lothrop Pub. Co.
--Mrs. Harry Harper's Awakening. Pansy, pseud, 1 of 5 vols. (Illus.). (Young Heroine Library). 1882. D Lothrop.
--Mrs. Harry Harper's Awakening. Pansy, pseud. (Illus.). N.D. D. Lothrop Co.
--Mrs. Solomon Smith Looking On. Pansy, pseud. (Illus.). N.D. D. Lothrop Co.
--My Daughter Susan. Pansy, pseud. (Illus.). (Idle Hour Ser.). N.D. D. Lothrop & Co.
--Nellie's Light. Pansy, pseud, 1 of 30 vols. (Illus.). (Pansy Primary Library: No. 1). N.D. Lothrop Pub. Co.
--Nettie in the Kitchen. Pansy, pseud, 1 of 12 vols. (Illus.). (Mother's Boys and Girls' Library). 1882. D Lothrop.
--A New Graft on the Family Tree. Pansy, pseud. (Illus.). (The Pansy Books). N.D. Lothrop.
--New Year's Tangles. Pansy, pseud. (Illus.). N.D. D. Lothrop Co.
--Next Things. Pansy, pseud, 1 of 5 vols. (Illus.). (Young Heroine Library). 1882. D Lothrop.
--Old Soldier's Story. Pansy, pseud, 1 of 20 vols. (Illus.). (Pansy Primary Lib: No. 2). N.D. Set. Lothrop Pub. Co.
--The Older Brother: A Story of Self-Denials. Pansy, pseud. (Illus.). N.D. Lothrop Publishing Co.
--One Commonplace day. Pansy, pseud. (Illus.). N.D. D. Lothrop & Co.
--Only a Spark. Pansy, pseud, 1 of 30 vols. (Illus.). (Pansy Primary Library: No. 1). N.D. Set. Lothrop Pub. Co.
--Only Ten Cents. Pansy, pseud. N.D. Lothrop Publishing Co.

--Opportunity. Pansy, pseud, 1 of 12 vols. (Illus.). (Pansy Primary Lib: No. 4). N.D. Set. Lothrop Pub. Co.
--Our Hero. Pansy, pseud, 1 of 30 vols. (Illus.). (Pansy Primary Lib: No. 2). N.D. Set. Lothrop Pub Co.
--Our Little Figure. Pansy, pseud, 1 of 12 vols. (Illus.). (Mother's Boys and Girls' Library). 1882. D Lothrop.
--Overruled. Pansy, pseud. (Illus.). N.D. Lothrop Publishing Co.
--Package for Rose. Pansy, pseud, 1 of 12 vols. (Illus.). (Pansy Primary Lib: No. 3). N.D. Set. Lothrop Pub. Co.
--Pansies. Pansy, pseud. N.D. D. Lothrop Co.
--Pansy. Pansy, pseud. (Illus.). (The Brookside Library For Girls). N.D. Set. Cheap Sunday-School Library.
--The Pansy. Pansy, pseud. (Illus.). (The Pansy Books). N.D. Lothrop.
--The Pansy Fairy Book. Pansy, pseud. (Illus.). (Little Fairy Envelope Books). N.D. Dodd Mead & Co.
--A Pansy Society. Pansy, pseud, 1 of 12 vols. (Illus.). (Pansy Primary Lib: No. 4). N.D. Set. Lothrop Pub. Co.
--Pansy Stories. Alden, Isabella Macdonald. Pansy, pseud, 1 of 25 vols. (Illus.). (Intermediate, Primary and Infant Libs.). N.D. A. I. Bradley & Co.'s Pubs.
--Pansy's Boys' and Girls' Library: Containing: Nettie in the Kitchen, What Keeping Still, All About April, Lost Nellie, Quarrel, Brave Tommy, Our Little Figure, Wise Alice, Bargaining, Esselstynes, Workers, Golden Thought. Pansy, pseud. (Illus.). N.D. Set=12 Vols. Lothrop Pub. Co.
--Pansy's Home Story Book. Pansy, pseud. LC 15-19181. 298 p. front., illus., plates. 28 1/2 cm. c.1883. D. Lothrop & Company.
--Pansy's Picture Book. Pansy pseud. N.D. D. Lothrop Co.
--Pansy's Scrap Book. Pansy, pseud, 1 of 5 vols. (Illus.). (Young Heroine Library). 1882. D Lothrop.
--Pansy's Scrap Book: Or, The Teacher's Helper. Pansy, pseud. (Illus.). N.D. D. Lothrop Co.
--Pansy's Story Book. Pansy, pseud. (Illus.). (The Pansy Books). N.D. Lothrop.
--Pansy's Sunday Book. Pansy, pseud. N.D. D. Lothrop Co.
--Pictures from Bobby's Life. Pansy, pseud, 1 of 4 Vols. (Illus.). (Pansy Picture Library). N.D. Set. D Lothrop & Co.
--The Pocket Measure. Pansy, pseud. N.D. D. Lothrop Co.
--Pretty Soon. Pansy, pseud, 1 of 30 vols. (Illus.). (Pansy Primary Lib). N.D. Set. Lothrop Pub. Co.
--Pretty Soon. Pansy, pseud, 1 of 10 vols. (Illus.). (Little Pansy Ser.). N.D. Set. Lothrop Publishing Co.
--A Quarrel. Pansy, pseud, 1 of 12 vols. (Illus.). (Mother's Boys and Girls' Library). 1882. D Lothrop.
--Railroad Building. Pansy, pseud, 1 of 12 vols. (Illus.). (Pansy Primary Lib: No. 3). N.D. Set. Lothrop Pub Co.
--Ralph's Wolves. Pansy, pseud, 1 of 20 vols. (Illus.). (Pansy Primary Lib: No. 2). N.D. Set. Lothrop Pub. Co.
--The Randolphs. Pansy, pseud. (Illus.). (The Pansy Books). N.D. Lothrop.
--Red Ribbon. Pansy, pseud, 1 of 30 vols. (Illus.). (Pansy Primary Lib: No. 1). N.D. Set. Lothrop Pub. Co.
--Red Ribbon. Pansy, pseud, 1 of 10 vols. (Illus.). (Little Pansy Ser.). N.D. Set. Lothrop Publishing Co.
--Reuben's Hindrances: A Story for Boys. Pansy, pseud. (Illus.). N.D. Lothrop Publishing Co.
--Ringing Words. Pansy, pseud, 1 of 20 vols. (Illus.). (Pansy Primary Lib: No. 2). N.D. Set. Lothrop Pub. Co.
--Robbie and the Stars. Pansy, pseud, 1 of 4 Vols. (Illus.). (Pansy Picture Library). N.D. Set. D Lothrop & Co.
--Ruth Erskine's Crosses. Pansy, pseud, 1 of 5 vols. (Illus.). (Chautauqua Girls Library). N.D. D. Lothrop & Co.
--Ruth Erskine's Crosses. Pansy, pseud. LC 8-273. 434 p. front., pl. 19 1/2 cm. c.1907. Lothrop, Lee & Shepard Co.
--Sadie's Victory. Pansy, pseud, 1 of 20 vols. (Illus.). (Pansy Primary Lib: No. 1). N.D. Set. Lothrob Pub Co.
--A Sevenfold Trouble. Pansy, pseud. (Illus.). N.D. D. Lothrop Co.
--Side By Side. Pansy, pseud, 1 of 3 Vols. (Illus.). (Side By Side Library). N.D. D. Lothrop & Co.
--Side by Side. Pansy, pseud. (Pansy Intermediate Library). N.D. D. Lothrop Co.
--Sidney Martin's Christmas. Pansy, pseud, 1 of 3 vols. LC 20-19322. (Illus.). 18cm. 610p. (Picture Story Book Ser.). 1879. D. Lothrop Co.
--Sidney Martin's Christmas. Pansy, pseud. (Illus.). 19cm. 486p. Repr. of 1878 ed. 1907. D. Lothrop & Co.
--Sidney Martin's Christmas. Pansy, pseud. LC 7-7198. 486 p. front., illus., plates. 19 1/2 cm. c.1907. Lothrop, Lee & Shepard Co.
--Six Little Girls. Pansy, pseud. (Illus.). N.D. D. Lothrop Co.
--Six Little Girls. Pansy, pseud. LC 7-7192. 1 p. l., 7-158 p. incl. plates. front. 19 cm. c.1907. Lothrop, Lee & Shepard Co.
--Six Little Girls. Pansy, pseud. (Illus.). (The Pansy Books). N.D. Lothrop Pub. Co.
--Six O'Clock in the Evening. Pansy, pseud. (Pansy Intermediate Library). N.D. D. Lothrop Co.
--Six O'Clock in the Evening. Pansy, pseud. (Illus.). (The Pansy Books). N.D. Lothrop Pub. Co.
--Sketches and Stories. Pansy, pseud, 1 of 12 vols. (Illus.). (Pansy Primary Lib: No. 3). N.D. Set. Lothrop Pub. Co.
--Some Boys and Girls. Pansy, pseud. (Illus.). N.D. D. Lothrop & Co.
--Some Young Heroines. Pansy, pseud, 1 of 5 vols. (Illus.). (Young Heroine Library). 1882. D Lothrop.
--Some Young Heroines. Pansy, pseud. (Illus.). N.D. D. Lothrop Co.
--Some Young Heroines. Pansy, pseud. (Illus.). (The Pansy Books). N.D. Lothrop.
--Sowing Seeds. Pansy, pseud, 1 of 30 vols. (Illus.). (Pansy Primary Lib: No. 1). N.D. Set. Lothrop Pub. Co.
--Spun From Fact. Pansy, pseud. N.D. D. Lothrop Co.
--Spun from Fact. Pansy, pseud. (Illus.). (The Pansy Books). N.D. Lothrop.
--Stella at Home. Pansy, pseud, 1 of 30 vols. (Illus.). (Pansy Primary Lib: No. 1). N.D. Set. Lothrop Pub. Co.
--Stephen Mitchell's Journey. Pansy, pseud. LC 21-205987. 2 p. l., 347 p. front. plates. 20 1/2 cm. 1893. D. Lothrop Company.
--Stitch in Time. Pansy, pseud, 1 of 20 vols. (Illus.). (Pansy Primary Lib: No. 2). N.D. Set. Lothrop Pub. Co.
--Stories and Pictures from the Life of Jesus. Pansy, pseud. (Illus.). N.D. D. Lothrop Co.
--Stories of Remarkable Women. Pansy, pseud. (Pansy Intermediate Library). N.D. D. Lothrop Co.
--Stories Told for a Purpose. Pansy, pseud. (The Pansy Books). N.D. Lothrop.
--Story of Puff. Pansy, pseud. (Pansy Intermediate Library). N.D. D. Lothrop Co.
--Sunday Chat. Pansy, pseud. (Illus.). N.D. D. Lothrop Co.
--Sunshine Factory. Pansy, pseud, 1 of 30 vols. (Illus.). (Pansy Primary Lib: No. 1). N.D. Set. Lothrop Pub. Co.
--Sunshine Factory. Pansy, pseud, 1 of 10 vols. (Illus.). (Little Pansy Ser.). N.D. Set. Lothrop Publishing Co.
--Talking it up. Pansy, pseud, 1 of 12 vols. (Illus.). (Pansy Primary Lib: No. 3). N.D. Set. Lothrop Pub. Co.
--Thanksgiving. Pansy, pseud, 1 of 20 vols. (Illus.). (Pansy Primary Lib: No. 2). N.D. Set. Lothrop Pub Co.
--Thanksgiving Dinner. Pansy, pseud, 1 of 12 vols. (Illus.). (Pansy Primary Lib: No. 2). N.D. Set. Lothrop Pub Co.
--The Pansy. Pansy, pseud. N.D. D. Lothrop Co.
--Those Boys. Pansy, pseud, 1 of 5 vols. (Illus.). (Household Library). N.D. D Lothrop.
--A Thoughtful Daughter. Pansy, pseud, 1 of 12 vols. (Illus.). (Pansy Primary Lib: No. 4). N.D. Set. Lothrop Pub. Co.
--Three People. Pansy, pseud. LC 99-3223. 412 p. pl. 12 cm. 1899. Lothrop Pub. Co.
--Three Times Three. Pansy, pseud. LC 99-3318. (Illus.). 123 illus. 20. 1899. Fleming H. Revell.
--Three Times Three. Pansy, pseud. N.D. Rand, McNally & Co's.
--Through the Woods. Pansy, pseud, 1 of 12 vols. (Illus.). (Pansy Primary Lib: No. 4). N.D. Set. Lothrop Pub Co.
--Tiny Making Up. Pansy, pseud, 1 of 30 vols. (Illus.). (Pansy Primary Lib: No. 1). N.D. Set. Lothrop Pub. Co.
--Tiny Making Up. Pansy, pseud, 1 of 10 vols. (Illus.). (Little Pansy Ser.). N.D. Set. Lothrop Publishing Co.
--Tip Lewis. Pansy, pseud, 6 Vols. (Illus.). (The Kitty Kent Library). N.D. Ward & Drummond.
--Tip Lewis and His Lamp. Pansy, pseud. (Illus.). (The Pansy Books). N.D. Lothrop Pub. Co.
--Tony Keating's Surprises. Pansy, pseud. LC 14-4262. 205 p. incl. front. plates. 19 1/2 cm. $0.7. c.1914. M. A. Donohue & Co.
--Their Treasures. Pansy, pseud, 1 of 30 vols. (Illus.). (Pansy Primary Lib: No. 1). N.D. Set. Lothrop Pub. Co.
--Turning the Mill-Wheel. Pansy, pseud, 1 of 20 vols. (Illus.). (Pansy Primary Lib: No. 2). N.D. Set. Lothrop Pub Co.
--Twenty Minutes Late. Pansy, pseud. (The Pansy Bks.). N.D. Lothrop.
--Two Boys. Pansy, pseud. LC 6-13420. 98 p. front., illus., plates. 19 cm. c.1906. Lothrop, Lee & Shepard Co.
--Two Boys. Pansy, pseud. (Illus.). (The Pansy Books). N.D. Lothrop Pub. Co.
--Two Singers. Pansy, pseud, 1 of 30 vols. (Illus.). (Pansy Primary Lib: No. 1). N.D. Set. Lothrop Pub. Co.
--Wanted. Pansy, pseud. (The Pansy Books). N.D. Lothrop.
--We Twelve Girls. Pansy, pseud. (Illus.). (The Pansy Books). N.D. Lothrop Pub. Co,.
--What Keeping Still Did. Pansy, pseud, 1 of 12 vols. (Illus.). (Mother's Boys and Girls' Library). 1882. D Lothrop.
--What She Said. Pansy, pseud, 1 of 6 vols. (Illus.). (Cunning Workman Ser.). N.D. D Lothrop.
--What She Said: What She Said; And What She Meant, and People Who Haven't Time And Can't Afford It. Pansy, pseud. LC 12-19576. (Illus.). 1880. D. Lothrop Co.
--Where I Went. Pansy, pseud, 1 of 12 vols. (Illus.). (Pansy Primary Lib: No. 4). N.D. Set. Lothrop Pub. Co.
--Whisk and Frisk. Pansy, pseud, 1 of 12 vols. (Illus.). (Pansy Primary Lib: No. 4). N.D. Set. Lothrop Pub. Co.
--Who Did It. Pansy, pseud, 1 of 20 vols. (Illus.). (Pansy Primary Lib: No. 2). N.D. Set. Lothrop Pub Co.
--Wise Alice. Pansy, pseud, 1 of 12 vols. (Illus.). (Mother's Boys and Girls'). 1882. D Lothrop.
--Wise and Otherwise. Pansy, pseud. LC 2-20822. 388 p. front., plates. 19 1/2 cm. (Lettered on cover: The Pansy books). c.1901. Lothrop Publishing Company.
--The Workers. Pansy, pseud, 1 of 12 vols. (Illus.). (Mother's Boys and Girls' Library). 1882. D Lothrop.
--A World of Little People. Pansy, pseud. (Pansy Intermediate Library). N.D. D. Lothrop Co.
--Worth Having. Pansy, pseud. (Illus.). N.D. Lothrop Pub. Co.
--Young Folks' Stories of American History and Home Life. Pansy, pseud. N.D. D. Lothrop & Co.
--Young Folks' Stories of Foreign Lands. Pansy, pseud. (Illus.). N.D. D. Lothrop & Co.
--Young Folks Worth Knowing. Pansy, pseud. (Illus.). N.D. Lothrop Pub. Co.
--Young Tommy. Pansy, pseud, 1 of 30 vols. (Illus.). (Pansy Primary Lib: No. 1). N.D. Set. Lothrop Pub. Co.

Alden, Isabella Macdonald (1841-1930) & Foster, Theodosia Maria Toll, Mrs. (1838-)
--Modern Prophets and other sketches. Pansy, pseud, 1 of 5 vols. Huntington, Faye, pseud. LC 2-21995. (Illus.). 20cm. 354p. (Household Library). 1902. D Lothrop.

Alden, Isabella Macdonald (1841-1930) & Huntington, Faye
--Dr. Deane's Way, and Other Stories. Pansy, pseud, 1 of 6 vols. (Cunning Workman Ser.). N.D. Lothrop Pub. Co.
--Getting Ahead Library: Containing: "Getting Ahead" "Six Little Girls" "Two Boys" "That Boy Bob" "Pansie" "Mary Burton" "Monteagle" "Couldn't be Bought". Pansy, pseud. (Illus.). N.D. D. Lothrop Co.
--Modern Prohets. Pansy, pseud. (Illus.). N.D. Lothrop Pub Co.
--That Boy Bob. Pansy, pseud. (Illus.). N.D. Lothrop.

Alden, Isabella Macdonald (1841-1930) & Livingston, C. M., Mrs.
--Divers Women. Pansy, pseud. (Illus.). N.D. D. Lothrop Co.
--Profiles. Pansy, pseud. (Illus.). N.D. D. Lothrop Co.

Alden, Jack
--Cocky: The Little Helicopter. Biers, Clarence, illus. N.D. G. P. Putnam & Co.

Alden, John, jt. auth. see Brooks, Elbridge Streeter.

Alden, John B, ed.
--What Next?. Favorite Poems, for Boys and Girls. LC 16-10116. iv, 12 p. 25 cm. 1873. J. B. Alden.

Alden, John Carver
--Chuckles, This Idiocy. Hilliam, B. C., illus. 1920. Marshall Jones.

Alden, Joseph (1807-1885)
--Alice Gordon. (Harper's Fireside Library). N.D. Harper & Brothers'.
--The Cardinal Flower, 1 of 4. (Alden Ser.). N.D. Colby and Rich.
--The Cardinal Flower, 1 of 4 vols. (Illus.). (Alden Ser.). 1882. Lee & Shepard.
--The Cardinal Flower. N.D. Lee & Shepard.
--The Dying Robin: And Other Stories. (Harper's Fireside Library). N.D. Harper & Brothers'.
--Dying Robin and Other Tales. N.D. Harper & Bros.
--Henry Ashton, 1 of 4. (Alden Ser.). N.D. Colby and Rich.
--Henry Ashton, 1 of 4 vols. (Illus.). (Alden Ser.). 1882. Lee & Shepard.
--Lawyer's Daughter. N.D. Harper & Bros.
--Lawyer's Daughter. (Harper's Fireside Library). N.D. Harper & Brothers'.
--The Light-Hearted Girl, 1 of 4. (Alden Ser.). N.D. Colby and Rich.
--The Light-Hearted Girl, 1 of 4 vols. (Illus.). (Alden Ser.). 1882. Lee & Shepard.
--The Lighthearted Girl. N.D. Lee & Shepard.
--The Lost Lamb, 1 of 4. (Alden Ser.). N.D. Colby and Rich.
--The Lost Lamb, 1 of 4 vols. (Illus.). (Alden Ser.). 1882. Lee & Shepard.
--The Old Revolutionary Soldier. LC 20-19826. vi, 7-152 p. front., 4 pl. 15 cm. 1848. Gates & Stedman.
--The Sleigh-Ride. LC 22-58557. 64 p. incl. plates. 15 cm. c.1847. Gates & Stedman.
--Young Schoolmistress. (Harper's Fireside Library). N.D. Harper & Brothers'.

Alden, Laura (1955-)
--I Read about God's Care: Grade 2. rev. ed. (Illus.). 128p. (Basic Bible Readers). (gr. 2). 1983. (ISBN 0-87239-662-2). Standard Pub.
--Learning About Fairies. Stasiak, Krystyna, illus. LC 81-15502. p. cm. (The Learning About Series). c.1982. (ISBN 0-516-06532-7). Childrens Press.
--Learning About Unicorns. Stasiak, Krystyna, illus. LC 85-9926. p. cm. (The Learning About Series). 1985. (ISBN 0-516-06539-4). Childrens Press.

Alden, Miriam
--Bashie's Service: or, Where's a Will, There's A Way. 224p. (Crowell's Sunday-School Library No. 6). N.D. T. Y. Crowell.
--Bashie's Service: Or, Where's A Will, There's A Way. (Illus.). N.D. Thomas Y. Crowell & Co.
--Marjorie's Good Year. 246p. N.D. American Tract Society.

Alden, Mrs G. R. see Alden, Isabella Macdonald.

Alden, Raymond Macdonald (1873-1924)
--The Boy Who Found the King: A Tournament of Stories. Lohse, William R., illus. LC 22-18959. 3 p. l., 154 p. front., illus. (incl. music) plates. 23 cm. c.1922. The Bobbs-Merrill Company.
--The Christmas Tree Forest. N.D. E. M. Hale & Co.
--The Christmas Tree Forest. Busoni, Rafaello (1900-1962), illus. LC 58-12914. (Illus.). 32 p. 26cm. c.1958. Bobbs-Merrill.
--The Forest Full of Friends. Speakman, Harold, illus. LC 15-16007. 54 p. illus. 19 cm. $0.5. c.1915. The Bobbs-Merrill Company.
--The Hunt for the Beautiful. Fletcher, Sydney E. & Samuels, George H., illus. LC 15-16011. 19cm. 48p. 1915. Bobbs-Merrill Co.
--The Knights of the Silver Shield. Greenland, Katherine Hayward, illus. 1906. Bobbs-Merrill Co.
--The Knights of the Silver Shield. Lohse, William R., illus. LC 23-17988. (Illus.). 19cm. 44p. 1923. Bobbs-Merrill.
--Once There Was a King: A Tournament of Stories. Alden, Raymond MacDonald (1873-1924), illus. LC 46-7366. 176 p. col. front., illus. (incl. music) col. plates. 24 cm. 1946. The Bobbs-Merrill Company.
--Palace Made by Music. Bunker, Mayo, illus. 1910. Bobbs-Merrill Co.
--Why The Chimes Rang. N.D. E. M. Hale & Co.
--Why the Chimes Rang. Busoni, Rafaello (1900-1962), illus. LC 54-11943. (Illus.). 28 p. 27cm. c.1954. Bobbs-Merrill.
--Why the Chimes Rang. Greenland, Katherine Hayward, illus. LC 8-231018. 5 p. l., 148 p. 1 l. front., illus., plates. 23 1/2 cm. 1908. The Bobbs-Merrill Company.
--Why the Chimes Rang. Race, Martha, adapted by. N.D. Pilgrim Press.
--Why the Chimes Rang: An Old Christmas Legend. LC 75-308265. (Illus.). 14 p. 16cm. 1924. G. F. Trenholm.
--Why the Chimes Rang & Other Stories. Copelman, Evelyn, illus. (Illus.). (gr. 2-6). N.D. (ISBN 0-672-50581-9). Bobbs.
--Why the Chimes Rang: And Other Stories. Copelman, Evelyn, illus. LC 45-10261. 146 p. col. front., illus., col. plates. 24 cm. 1945. The Bobbs-Merrill Company.
--Why the Chimes Rang: And Other Stories. Sturges, Katharine, illus. LC 24-22822. 5 p. l., 148, 1 p. col. front., illus., col. plates 23 cm. c.1924. The Bobbs-Merrill Company.
--A World of Little People. LC 21-182942. 2 p. l., 76 p. incl. illus., plates. 18 1/2 cm. c.1888. D. Lothrop Company.

Alden, Richard & San Francisco. Public Library. Friends
--Prize Poems, 1965-1967. LC 73-11491. 30 p. 37cm. 1967. Friends of the San Francisco Public Library.

Alden, William Livingston (1837-1908)
--The Adventures of Jimmy Brown. LC 4-23564. vi, 5-236 p. incl. plates. front. 16 1/2 cm. 1885. Harper & Brothers.
--Adventures of Jimmy Brown. (Harper's Young People Ser.). N.D. Harper & Bros.
--The Cruise of the Canoe Club. N.D. Grosset & Dunlap.

AUTHOR INDEX ALEGRIA, RICARDO

--The Cruise of the Canoe Club. LC 12-30170. 2 p. l., 7-166 p. front., plates. 16 1/2 cm. 1883. Harper & Brothers.
--Cruise of the Canoe Club. (Harper's Young People Ser.). N.D. Harper & Bros.
--The Cruise of the "Ghost". LC 13-9388. 210 p. incl. front., illus., plates. 16 1/2 cm. 1882. Harper & Brothers.
--The Cruise of the "Ghost". (Harper's Young People Ser.). N.D. Harper & Brothers.
--Jimmy Brown in Europe. N.D. Harper & Brothers.
--Jimmy Brown Trying to Find Europe. N.D. Harper & Bros.
--The Loss of the Swansea: A Story of the Florida Coast. Small, Frank O., illus. LC 74-180994. (Illus.). 193 p. 19cm. c.1889. Lothrop Pub. Co.
--The Moral Pirates. LC 11-10502. 148 p. incl. front. plates. 16 1/2 cm. 1881. Harper & Brothers.
--The Moral Pirates. LC 54-49951. (Illus.). 18cm. 148p. 1901. Harper.
--The Moral Pirates. LC 4-18927. 148 p. incl. front. plates. 18 cm. (Harper's young people series). 1904. Harper & Brothers.
--The Moral Pirates. LC 8-22797. 148 p. incl. front. 14 pl. 17 1/2 cm. (On verse of t.-p.: Harper's young people series). c.1908. Harper & Brothers.
--A New Robinson Crusoe. LC 12-30170. 8 p. l., 147 p. front., plates. 16 1/2 cm. (Harper's young people series). 1888. Harper & Brothers.
Alderman, Clifford Lindsey (1902-)
--Gathering Storm: The Story of the Green Mountain Boys. LC 71-123179. (Illus.). 4 photos. bibl. index. 192p. (Milestones in History Ser). (gr. 7-12). 1970. (ISBN 0-671-32311-3). (ISBN 0-671-32312-1). Messner.
--Joseph Brant: Chief of the Six Nations. LC 58-109258. 192p. 22cm. 1958. Messner.
--The Vengeance of Abel Wright. LC 64-11709. 22cm. 191p. 1964. Doubleday.
--The Way of the Eagles. LC 65-19941. ix, 200p. maps. 22cm. c.1965. Doubleday.
Alderson, Brian W., compiled by.
--A Book of Bosh: Lyrics & Prose of Edward Lear. 224p. (gr. 5 up). 1975. (ISBN 0-14-030665-X, Puffin). Penguin.
--Cakes and Custard: Children's Rhymes. Oxenbury, Helen (1938-), illus. LC 75-24523. (Illus.). 156 p. 25cm. 1975, c.1974. (ISBN 0-688-22050-9). (ISBN 0-688-32050-3). W. Morrow. **Award: (ALA).**
Alderson, Brian W., jt. ed. see Lang, Andrew.
Alderson, Brian W, tr. see Grimm, Jakob Ludwig Karl (1785-1863) & Grimm, Wilhelm Karl.
Alderson, Dorothy
--Little Creek Giggling. (gr. 2-4). 1970. Vantage.
Alderson, Sue Ann
--The Adventures of Prince Paul. Wolsak, Jane (1942-), illus. LC 79-322698. (Illus.). 31 p. 22cm. (Karpet series). 1977. (ISBN 0-88976-016-0). Ftorbez Enterprises.
Aldin, Cecil Charles Windsor (1870-1935)
--The Black Puppy Book. Aldin, Cecil Charles Windsor (1870-1935), illus. (Illus.). N.D. George H. Doran.
--A Conceited Puppy. N.D. E P Dutton.
--Doggie and His Ways. Aldin, Cecil Charles Windsor (1870-1935), illus. (Illus.). N.D. George H. Doran.
--The Doggy Book. N.D. E P Dutton.
--Farm Babies: A Day in the Life of a Venturesome Duckling. Aldin, Cecil Charles Windsor (1870-1935), illus. (Illus.). N.D. George H. Doran.
--Farm Yard Folks and Their Ways. Aldin, Cecil Charles Windsor (1870-1935), illus. (Illus.). N.D. George H. Doran.
--Farm Yard Puppies. LC 36-6036. 52 p. illus. (part col.) 23 1/2 x 21 1/2 cm. c.1935. Oxford University Press.
--Jock and Some Others. N.D. E P Dutton.
--Mac. (Illus.). N.D. George H Doran.
--Mrs. Tickler's Caravan: A Story for Children. Aldin, Cecil Charles Windsor (1870-1935), illus. LC 83-311582. 4 p. l., 11-91 p. col. ullus. 24 1/2 cm. 1931. C. Scribner's Sons.
--Pickles: A Day in the Life of a Naughty Puppy. Aldin, Cecil Charles Windsor (1870-1935), illus. (Illus.). N.D. George H. Doran.
--Puppy Tails. N.D. E P Dutton.
--Pussy and Her Ways. Aldin, Cecil Charles Windsor (1870-1935), illus. (Illus.). N.D. George H. Doran.
--Rough and Tumble: How They Tried to Keep Out of Mischief and Failed. N.D. George H Doran.
--The Twins: The Adventures of Two Puppies. N.D. George H Doran & Co.
--The Twins: The Adventures of Two Troublesome Puppies. Aldin, Cecil Charles Windsor (1870-1935), illus. (Illus.). N.D. George H. Doran.
--The White Kitten Book: The Story of a Kitten Told by Herself. Aldin, Cecil Charles Windsor (1870-1935), illus. (Illus.). N.D. George H. Doran.
--The White Puppy Book. LC 29-19912. 51 p. illus. (part col.) 23 1/2 cm. 1929. Oxford University Press.
--The White Puppy Book. Aldin, Cecil Charles Windsor (1870-1935), illus. LC 29-19912. (Illus.). 1929. George H. Doran.
--The Young Folks' Birthday Book. (Illus.). N.D. Frederick A. Stokes Co.
--Zoo Babies. Aldin, Cecil Charles Windsor (1870-1935), illus. (Illus.). N.D. George H. Doran.
Aldis, Dorothy Keeley, Mrs. (1896-1966)
--All Together: A Child's Treasury of Verse, Including Selections from Everything and Anything, Here, There, and Everywhere, Hop, Skip, and Jump, Before Things Happen, with Poems Previously Unpublished in Book Form. Jameson, Helen D. & Flack, Marjorie (1897-1958), illus. LC 52-9826. (With Poems Previously Unpublished in Book Form.). 192 p. illus. 22 cm. 1952. Putnam.
--All Together: A Child's Treasury of Verse. Jameson, Helen D. & Flack, Marjorie (1897-1958), illus. (Illus.). (gr. 1-4). 1952. (ISBN 0-399-20006-1). Putnam Pub Group.
--Before Things Happen. LC 39-30695. viii, 85 p. illus. 19 1/2 cm. c.1939. G. P. Putnam's Sons.
--The Boy Who Cared. Geer, Charles Hand (1922-), illus. LC 57-12204. 64p. illus. 23cm. 1950. Putnam.
--Cindy. Bacon, Peggy, pseud. (1895-), illus. Bacon, Margaret Frances. LC 42-588. 61 p. illus. 21 x 16 cm. 1942. G. P. Putnam's Sons.
--Cindy. rev. ed. Bolian, Polly (1925-), illus. LC 59-7196. 64p. illus. 21cm. 1959. Putnam.
--Dark Summer. LC 47-18541. 4 p. l., 3-186 p. 19 1/2 cm. 1947. G. P. Putnam's Sons.
--Dumb Stupid David. Miller, Jane Judith (1925-), illus. LC 65-20669. 46p. illus. 23cm. c.1965. (ISBN 0-399-60141-4). Putnam.
--Everything and Anything. LC 27-26439. x, 99 p. illus. 19 1/2 cm. 1927. Minton, Balch & Company.
--Favorite Poems of Dorothy Aldis. Lerman, Jack, illus. LC 75-110323. (Illus.). 64 p. 23cm. 1970. Putnam.
--Hello Day. Elson, Susan, illus. 64p. illus. 22cm. 1959. Putnam.
--Here, There and Everywhere. Flack, Marjorie (1897-1958), illus. LC 28-218066. x, 99 p. illus. 19 1/2 cm. 1928. Minton, Balch & Company.
--Hop, Skip and Jump. LC 34-4343. xii p., 2 l., 8-95 p. incl. front., illus. 19 1/2 cm. c.1934. Minton, Balch and Company.
--Is Anybody Hungry: A Book of Verse. Marokvia, Artur F. (1909-), illus. LC 64-18028. (Illus.). (gr. 1-5). 1964. (ISBN 0-399-60304-2). Putnam.
--Jane's Father. LC 29-19256. 5 p. l., 3-142 p. illus. 19 1/2 cm. 1929. Minton, Balch and Company.
--Jane's Father. Stevens, Mary E. (1920-1966), illus. LC 54-98567. 126p. illus. 20cm. 1954. Putnam.
--Lucky Year. McKee, John Dukes, illus. LC 51-13748. 175 p. illus. 21 cm. 1951. Rand McNally.
--The Magic City. Freeman, Margaret (1893-), illus. 95p. (gr. 3). N.D. G P Putnam's Sons.
--Miss Quinn's Secret. Fry, Rowena, illus. LC 49-2339. vi. 164 p. illus. 20 cm. 1949. G. P. Putnam's Sons.
--Poor Susan. LC 42-24102. 204 p. 19 1/2 cm. 1942. G. P. Putnam's Sons.
--Quick As a Wink. Westphal, Peggy, illus. LC 60-6854. 63p. illus. 22cm. 1960. (ISBN 0-399-60527-4). Putnam.
--Ride the Wild Waves: A True Story of Adventure. LC 57-10262. 182p. illus. 22cm. 1957. Putnam.
--The Secret Place. Cole, Olivia H. H., illus. LC 62-532501. 48 p. illus (part col.) 16 x 21 cm. 1962. Scholastic Book Services.
--Seven to Seven. Freeman, Margaret (1893-), illus. LC 31-10515. 32 p. col. illus. 18 x 23 1/2 cm. 1931. Minton, Balch and Company.
--Squiggles: Or, The Little Red Cape. Freeman, Margaret (1893-), illus. LC 29-19255. 6 p. l., 3-140 p. incl. front., illus., plates. 20 cm. 1930. Minton, Balch & Company.
--Their Own Apartment. LC 35-6957. 240 p. 20 cm. c.1935. G. P. Putnam's Sons.
--We're Going to Town. 1st ed. Gehr, Mary, illus. LC 52-10700. 56 p. illus. 26 cm. 1952. Bobbs-Merrill.
Aldis, Dorothy Keeley, Mrs. (1896-1966) & Belloc, Hilaire (1870-1953)
--The Hundred Best Poems for Boys and Girls. Barrows, Ruth Marjorie (1892-1983), ed. Good, Paula Rees, illus. LC 30-317426. 1 p. l., 7-123, 2 p. illus. 19 cm. c.1930. Whitman Publishing Company.
Aldis, Mary
--The Princess Jack. LC 15-26978. 89 p. incl. front. 22 1/c cm. $1.00. 1915. A. C. McClurg & Co.
Aldiss, Brian Wilson, jt. ed. see Harrison, Harry Max.
Aldiss, Brian Wilson (1925-) & Harrison, Harry Max (1925-)
--Decade, the 1950s. LC 76-376544. 219 p. 21cm. 1976. (ISBN 0-333-19001-7). Macmillan.
Aldon, Adair, pseud., see Meigs, Cornelia Lynde.
Aldous, Allan
--Bushfire. Acs, Laszlo Bela (1931-), illus. LC 68-15235. (Illus.). 144 p. 22cm. 1968, c.1967. Criterion Books.
--Doctor with Wings. Payne, Roger, illus. LC 61-12800. (Illus.). 126 p. 22cm. (Criterion book for young people). 1961, c.1960. Criterion Books.
Aldredge, Edna & McKee, Jessie Fulton
--Apron Springs and Rowdy. Miller, Edward (1905-1974), illus. LC 48-3845. 120 p. col. illus. 21 cm. 1948. Beckley-Cardy Co.
--The Timbertoes. Gee, John, illus. LC 43-12119. 3 p. l., 5-123, 1 p. col. illus. 20 cm. 1943. Beckley-Cardy Company.
--The Timbertoes. Gee, John, illus. LC 32-29909. 119 1 p. col. illus. 23 cm. c.1932. The Harter Publishing Company.
Aldrich, Andy, jt. auth. see McDermott, Caroline.
Aldrich, Anna Morrison
--The Travels of Three Insects. Morrison, Mary A., illus. LC 21-18290. 20cm. 27p. 1892. R. Clarke & Co.
Aldrich, Bess Streeter
--Journey into Christmas and Other Stories. N.D. Appleton-Century-Crofts.
--A Lantern in Her Hand. 1928. Appleton-Century-Crofts.
--A Lantern in Her Hand. (Illus.). (gr. 9 up). 1928. (ISBN 0-696-67973-6). Hawthorn.
--A Lantern in Her Hand. 318p. (gr. 7-12). 1968 (Schol Trade Pap). Schol Bk Serv.
--The Rim of the Prairie. 1925. A L Burt Co.
Aldrich, Mary M
--Too Many Pets. Cooney, Barbara (1917-), illus. LC 52-8556. 66 p. 21 cm. 1952. Macmillan.
Aldrich, Thomas Bailey (1836-1907), tr. see Bedolliere, Emile Gigault De La.
Aldrich, Thomas Bailey (1836-1907)
--Marjorie Daw and Other People. 1873. James R. Osgood.
--An Old Town by the Sea. N.D. Houghton, Mifflin & Company.
--The Story of a Bad Boy. N.D. A L Burt Co.
--The Story of a Bad Boy. LC 48-32255. 261 p. ilus. 19 cm. 1870. Fields, Osgood.
--The Story of a Bad Boy. LC 75-32173. p. cm. (Classics of Children's Literature, 1621-1932). 1976. (ISBN 0-8240-2285-8). Garland Pub.
--The Story of a Bad Boy. (The Children's Favorite Ser.). N.D. Grosset & Dunlap.
--The Story of a Bad Boy. 47th ed. LC 4-16117. iv p., 1 l., 7-261 p. front., illus., pl. 20 1/2 cm. 1897. Houghton, Mifflin and Company.
The Story of a Bad Boy, 1 of 4 vols. (B. B. B. Ser.). 1900. Set. Houghton Mifflin & Co.
--The Story of a Bad Boy. LC 24-222229. 261 p. front., illus., plates. 18 1/2 cm. c.1911. Houghton Mifflin Company.
The Story of a Bad Boy. Jubilee ed. (Illus.). N.D. Houghton, Osgood & Co.
--The Story of a Bad Boy. N.D. James R. Osgood.
--The Story of a Bad Boy. (The Winston Clear-Type Popular Classics). N.D. John C. Winston.
--The Story of a Bad Boy. Anderson, Charles Joseph, ed. LC 28-184. xviii p. 1 l., 298 p. illus., plates. 18 1/2 cm. (Riverside literature series)). c.1927. Houghton Mifflin Company.
--The Story of a Bad Boy. Breet, Harold M. (1880-), illus. LC 23-15255. iv p., 1 l., 279 p. col. front., illus., col. plates. 22 cm. (Riverside bookshelf). 1923. Houghton Mifflin Company.
--The Story of a Bad Boy. Chittick, Victor Lovitt Oakes, intro. by. LC 30-14665. xxii p., 1 l., 238 p. 18 1/2 cm. (modern readers series)). 1930. The Macmillan Company.
--The Story of a Bad Boy. Frost, Arthur Burdett (1851-1928), illus. LC 13-12929. xiii, 286 p. incl. plates. front., illus. 20 cm. 1895. Houghton, Mifflin and Company.
--The Story of a Bad Boy. Frost, Arthur Burdett (1851-1928), illus. LC 54-49953. xiii, 286p. illus. 20cm. c.1911. Houghton Mifflin.
--The Story of a Bad Boy. New ed. Kiefer, Henry C., illus. LC 29-1565. vi p., 1 l., 245 p. front., plates. 21 1/2 cm. (father and son library). c.1928. J. H. Sears & Company, Inc.
--The Story of a Bad Boy. Marsh, Reginald (1898-1954), illus. LC 51-13435. (Illus.). 232 p. 22cm. 1951. Pantheon Books.
--The Story of a Bad Boy. Moynihan, Roberta, illus. LC 56-145675. 221p. illus. 22cm. 1956. Junior Deluxe Editions.
--The Story of a Bad Boy. visitors' ed.). Olcott, Charles S., illus. LC 14-120742. xvii, 278 p. 1 l., front., illus., plates. 20 cm. 1914. Houghton Mifflin Company.
--The Story of a Bad Boy. Prittie, Edwin John, illus. (The Children's Bookshelf). N.D. John C. Winston.
--The Story of a Bad Boy. Prittie, Edwin John, illus. LC 28-6925. vii, 253 p. col front., illus., col. plates. 22 cm. c.1927. The John C. Winston Company.
--The Story of a Bad Boy. Turner, Leslie & Akron, O., illus. LC 36-13304. 255 p. incl. col. front., illus. 21 cm. c.1936. The Saalfield Publishing Company.
--The Story of Bad Boy. Beattie, Ann (1947-), pref. by. LC 75-32173. iv, 261p. ill. 19cm. 1976. (ISBN 0-8240-2285-8). Garland Pub.
--Tom Bailey's Adventures: Or, The Story of Bad Boy. LC 6-502. (Illus.). 261p. 1877. J. R. Osgood.
--Two Bites at Cherry: With Other Tales. N.D. Houghton, Mifflin & Company.
Aldridge, Adele (1934-)
--Once I Was a Square: A Visual Fable for Children, Adults & Others. LC [illegible] (Illus.). 63 p. 22cm. 1974. (ISBN 0-913660-05-1). Magic Circle Press; Distributed by J. P. O'Hara, Chicago.
Aldridge, Alan, jt. auth. see Adams, Richard George.
Aldridge, Alan (1943-) & Plomer, William Charles Franklin (1903-1973)
--Butterfly Ball & the Grasshapper's Feast. Aldridge, Alan (1943-), illus. (Illus.). 74p. (gr. 2-5). 1980. (ISBN 0-224-00808-0, Pub. by Chatto, Bodley Head & Jonathan). Merrimack Pub Cir.
--The Butterfly Ball and the Grasshopper's Feast. Atkins, Edward G., ed. Aldridge, Alan (1943-), illus. LC 75-19329. p. cm. 1975. (ISBN 0-670-19786-6). Grossman Publishers
Aldridge, Alan (1943-) & Walker, Ted (1934-)
--The Lion's Cavalcade. Aldridge, Alan (1943-) & Willock, Harry, illus. (Illus.). 32p. 1st U.S. edition. (gr. 3 up). 1981. (ISBN 0-224-01701-2, Pub. by Chatto-Bodley-Jonathan). Merrimack Pub Cir.
Aldridge, James
--The Broken Saddle. 128p. (Julia MacRae Ser.). (gr. 5 up). 1983. (ISBN 0-531-04579-X, MacRae). Watts.
--The Marvelous Mongolian. LC 73-20234. (Illus.). 22cm. 183p. 1974. (ISBN 0-316-03120-8). Little, Brown.
Aldridge, Janet
--The Meadow-Brook Girls Across Country: The Young Pathfinders on a Summer Hike. (The Meadow-Brook Girls). N.D. Henry Altemus Co.
--The Meadow-Brook Girls Afloat: The Stormy Cruise of the Red Rover. (The Meadow-Brook Girls Ser.). N.D. Henry Altemus Co.
--The Meadow-Brook Girls by the Sea: Or, The Loss of the Lonesome Bar. (The Meadow-Brook Girls Ser.). N.D. Henry Altemus Co.
--The Meadow-Brook Girls in the Hills: The Missing Pilot of the White Mountains. (The Meadow-Brook Girls Ser.). N.D. Henry Altemus Co.
--The Meadow-Brook Girls on the Tennis Courts: Or, Winning Out in the Big Tournament. (The Meadow-Brook Girls Ser.). N.D. Henry Altemus Co.
--The Meadow-Brook Girls under Canvas: Or, Fun and Frolic in the Summer Camp. (The Meadow-Brook Girls Ser.). N.D. Henry Altemus Co.
Aldridge, Josephine Haskell
--The Best of Friends. Peterson, Betty Ferguson (1917-), illus. LC 63-18901. 1 v. (unpaged) col. illus. 19 cm. c.1963. Parnassus Press.
--Fisherman's Luck. Robbins, Ruth (1917-), illus. LC 67-1894. (Illus.). 1 v. (unpaged. 25cm. 1966. Parnassus Press.
--A Penny and a Periwinkle. Robbins, Ruth (1917-), illus. LC 60-15035. (Illus.). unpaged. 26cm. 1961. Parnassus Press.
Aldridge, Josephine Haskell & Aldridge, Richard Boughton (1930-)
--Reasons and Raisins. Larrecq, John Maurice (1926-1980), illus. LC 72-156875. (Illus.). 34 p. 21cm. 1972. (ISBN 0-87466-002-5). Parnassus Press.
Aldridge, Melanie & Tester, Sylvia Root (1939-)
--Paula's Feeling Angry. rev. ed. Haag, Peg Roth, illus. LC 79-10773. (Illus.). 32 p. 25cm. (A Values Series). c.1979. (ISBN 0-89565-076-2). Child's World.
Aldridge, Richard Boughton, jt. auth. see Aldridge, Josephine Haskell.
Alegria, Fernando (1918-)
--Lautaro. Goetz, Delia, tr. LC 44-751754. x, 176 p. incl. illus., plates. 19 1/2 cm. 1944. Farrar & Rinehart, Inc.
Alegria, Ricardo E. (1921-), ed.
--The Three Wishes. Homar, Lorenzo (1913-), illus. 128p. 1968. H B J.
--The Three Wishes: A Collection of Puerto Rican Folktales. Homar, Lorenzo (1913-), illus. LC 69-13770. (Illus.). 128 p. 21cm. 1969. Harcourt, Brace & World.

Alehin, Alexander Fedor (1891-)
--The First Sin: And Other One Act Plays. LC 27-18920. 95 p. front. 21 cm. (On cover: Drama series, vol. II). c.1927. Expression Company.
Aleichem, Sholem, pseud., see Rabinovitch, Sholem.
Aleichem, Sholem, pseud. (1859-1916)
--Hanukkah Money. Rabinovitch, Sholem. Shulevitz, Uri (1935-), illus. 1978. Greenwillow.
--Holiday Tales of Sholem Aleichem. Rabinovitch, Sholem. 1979. Scribner.
Aleksin, Anatolii Georgievich (1924-)
--Alik, the Detective. LC 77-24121. 192 p. 22cm. 1977. (ISBN 0-688-22117-3). (ISBN 0-688-32117-8). W. Morrow.
--A Late-Born Child. Robinson, Charles (1931-), illus. Polushkin, Maria, tr. LC 71-162571. (Illus.). 75 p. 22cm. 1971. World Pub.
--My Brother Plays the Clarinet: Two Stories. Brown, Judith Gwyn (1933-), illus. Glagoleva, Fainna, tr. LC 74-19708. (Illus.). 114 p. 22cm. 1975. (ISBN 0-8098-3123-6). H. Z. Walck.
Alemany, Norah, tr. see Maury, Inez.
Alessios, Alison Baigrie, Mrs.
--Buffo and Petro. Kalab, Theresa, illus. LC 38-29628. 24cm. 30p. c.1938. Longmans Green & Co.
--Round the Mulberry Hill. Froderstrom, Alma Wentzel, illus. 21cm. 4p. 1939. Longmans Green & Co.
--The Singing Shoemaker. Vasiliu, Mircea (1920-), illus. LC 57-8492. 132p. illus. 21cm. 1957. Scribner.
--The Spear of Ulysses. Busoni, Rafaello (1900-1962), illus. LC 41-14043. v, 213p. illus. 21cm. 1941. Longmans, Green & Co.
Alewyn, Veronica, tr. see Coleno, Alice.
Alex, Marlee, tr. see Andersen, Hans Christian.
Alexander, Anne Barbara Cooke see Cooke, Barbara, pseud.
Alexander, Anne Barbara Cooke (1913-)
--ABC of Cars & Trucks. (ps-k). 1971. Doubleday.
--ABC of Cars and Trucks. 1st ed. Ninon, pseud. (1908-), illus. MacKnight, Ninon. LC 56-576232. unpaged. illus. 22x27cm. c.1956. Doubleday.
--Connie. Owens, Gail, illus. LC 76-4477. (Illus.). 179 p. 22cm. 1976. (ISBN 0-689-30534-6). Atheneum.
--I Want to Whistle. Graboff, Abner (1919-), illus. LC 58-8935. unpaged. illus. 27cm. c.1958. Abelard-Schuman.
--I Want to Whistle. Graboff, Abner (1919-), illus. (Illus.). (gr. k-2). 1958. (ISBN 0-8382-0361-2). Hale.
--Linda. 1st. ed. LC 64-16235. 192 p. /22 cm. 1964. Doubleday.
--Little Foreign Devil. Nebel, Gustave E., illus. LC 70-98605. (Illus.). 232 p. 22cm. 1970. Atheneum.
--Noise in the Night. Graboff, Abner (1919-), illus. LC 59-8288. (Illus.). 1 v. (unpaged. 26cm. c.1960. Rand McNally.
--The Pink Dress. LC 59-12611. 214 p. 22cm. 1959. Doubleday.
--To Live a Lie. Ilsley, Velma Elizabeth (1918-), illus. LC 75-6837. (Illus.). 165 p. 22cm. 1975. (ISBN 0-689-30470-6). Atheneum.
--Trouble on Treat Street. Jones, John Ralph (1935-), illus. LC 74-75552. p. cm. 22cm. 116p. 1974. (ISBN 0-689-30401-3). Atheneum.
Alexander, Barbara (1940-)
--A Furnace for Castle Thistlewart. Alexander, Barbara (1940-), illus. LC 85-21384. p. cm. (Make believe and me series). c.1985. (ISBN 0-86679-018-7). Oak Tree Publications.
--A Little Bigalow Story. Alexander, Barbara (1940-), illus. LC 85-21391. p. cm. (Make believe & me Ser.). c.1985. (ISBN 0-86679-021-7). Oak Tree Publications.
--Muddle-Mole and His Exploding Birthday Party. Alexander, Barbara (1940-), illus. LC 85-21427. (Illus.). 32 p. 27cm. (Make Believe & Me Ser.). c.1985. (ISBN 0-86679-020-9). Oak Tree Publications.
--The Mysterious Disappearance of Ragsby. Alexander, Barbara (1940-), illus. LC 85-21377. (Illus.). 32 p. 27cm. (Make Believe & Me Ser.). c.1985. (ISBN 0-86679-019-5). Oak Tree Publications.
Alexander, Beatrice
--The Story of Jesus. Lerch, Steffie E. (1908-), illus. (Little Golden Book). 1946. Golden Press.
Alexander, Cecil Frances Humphreys, Mrs. (1818-1895)
--All Things Bright and Beautiful: A Hymn. Politi, Leo (1908-), illus. LC 62-17588. unpaged. illus. 26cm. c.1962. (ISBN 0-684-13474-8). Scribner.
--Baron's Little Daughter, and Other Tales. 1888. Thomas Whittaker.
--The Baron's Little Daughter, and Other Tales. 1891. Thomas Whittaker.
--Baron's Little Daughter, and other Tales in Prose and Verse. (Illus.). N.D. E. P. Dutton & Co.
Alexander, Cecil Frances Humphreys, Mrs. (1818-1895), ed.
--The Sunday Book of Poetry. (Golden Treasury Ser.). N.D. Macmillan & Co.
--The Sunday Book of Poetry for the Young. New & Cheaper Ed. ed. (Golden Treasury Ser.). N.D. Set. MacMillan.
Alexander, Cecil Frances, Mrs.
--Hymns for Little Children. N.D. E. P. Dutton.
Alexander, Charles (1897-1962)
--Bobbie: A Great Collie. LC 26-9759. 3 p. l., 5-114 p. front., plates 19 1/2 cm. 1926. Dodd, Mead and Company.
--Bobbie: A Great Collie. Tamer, Salem, illus. LC 66-23220. 113 p. illus. 21 cm. 1966. Dodd, Mead.
--Bobbie, a Great Collie. rev. ed. Tamer, Salem, illus. (Adapted for disadvantaged readers). (Illus.). (gr. 8 up). 1966. (ISBN 0-396-05370-X). Dodd.
--The Fang in the Forest. Bransom, Paul (1885-), illus. LC 23-152962. 5 p. l., 244 p. front., plates. 19 1/2 cm. $2.0. 1923. Dodd, Mead and Company.
Alexander, David (1907-1973)
--The Red Coat Mystery: A Jack Barton Adventure. LC 66-25283. 144 p. 22cm. 1966. Bobbs-Merrill.
Alexander, Edward Porter (1835-)
--Catterel Ratterel Doggerel. Ficklen, Bessie Alexander, Mrs., illus. LC 15-16825. 39p. incl. front. illus. 18 x 26cm. 1890. G. P. Putman & Sons.
Alexander, Elsie M
--Adventures of Tudie: The Story of the Field Mouse. LC 28-105187. 4 p. l., 119 p. col. front., col. plates 19 1/2 cm. (Her Sunnybrook series). c.1928. A. L. Burt Comapny.
--Buff and Duff: The Story of the Children of Mrs. White-Hen. LC 28-130268. 4 p. l., 120 p. col. front., col. plates 19 1/2 cm. (Her Sunnybrook series). c.1928. A. L. Burt Company.
--Buster Rabbit, the Explorer: The Story of the Bunny Rabbit Family. LC 28-12193. 4 p. l., 120 p. col. front., col plates. 19 1/2 cm. (Her Sunnybrook series). c.1928. A. L. Burt Company.
--Daffy, the Polecat: The Story of Mrs. Polecat's Journey. LC 29-127151. 4 p. l., 120 p. col. front., col. plates. 19 1/2 cm. (Her Sunnybrook series). c.1929. A. L. Burt Coampny.
--The Happy Family of Beechnut Grove: The Story of Peter Gray Squirrel and Family. LC 28-12194. 4 p. l., 120 p. col. front., col. plates. 19 1/2 cm.(her sunnybrook series. c.1928. A. L. Burt Company.
--Roody and His Underground Palace: The Story of Mr. Woodchuck in His Happy Home. LC 28-121934. 4 p. l., 120 p. col. front., col. plates 19 1/2 cm. (her sunnybrook series. c.1928. A. L. Burt Company.
--Speedy, the Fox: The Story of the Fox Family. LC 29-12714. 4 p. l., 120 p. col. front., col. plates 19 1/2 cm. (her sunnybrook series. c.1929. A. L. Burt Company.
--Tabitha Dingle: The Story of the Famous Cat of Sunnybrook Meadow. LC 28-10519. 4 p. l., 120 p. col. front., col. plates. 19 1/2 cm. (Her Sunnybrook series). c.1928. A. L. Burt Company.
Alexander, Esther Frances see Alexander, Francesca, pseud.
Alexander, Florence Bibo
--The Big Game Hunter. Read, Isobel, illus. LC 47-5588. 32 p. col. illus. 17 cm. (Tell-a-tale books). c.1947. Whitman Pub. Co.
--Nancy and Jane. Sturtevant, Harriet, illus. LC 45-4377. 45 p. incl. col. illus., 14 col. pl. 18 x 22 cm. 1945. Howell, Soskin.
Alexander, Frances Laura (1888-), ed.
--Mother Goose on the Rio Grande. (Illus.). 96p. 1983. (ISBN 0-8442-7641-3, Passport Bks). Natl Textbk.
--Mother Goose on the Rio Grande: Mexican Folklore. Baker, Charlotte (1910-), illus. Alexander, Frances Laura (1888-), tr. LC 61-4065. 101p. illus. 23cm. 1960. B. Upshaw.
--Pebbles from a Broken Jar: Fables and Hero Stories from Old China. LC 69-13728. (Illus.). 24cm. 29p. 1967. Bobbs-Merrill.
Alexander, Frances Laura (1888-) & Hunnicutt, Helen Mar, eds.
--Mother Goose on the Rio Grande: Mexican Folklore. Baker, Charlotte (1910-), illus. LC 44-1332. 3 p. l. 9-101p. 1 p. illus. (part. col) 22cm. 1944. B. Upshaw and Company.
Alexander, Francesca, pseud., see Alexander, Esther Frances.
Alexander, Francesca, pseud. (1837-1917)
--The Hidden Servants, and Other very Old Stories. Alexander, Esther Frances. 1900. Little Brown & Co.
Alexander, Frank, ed. see Johnson, Walter Ryerson.
Alexander, Georgia, jt. ed. see Blake, Katherine Devereux.
Alexander, Grace
--Judith. Wright, George, illus. N.D. Bobbs-Merrill Co.
--Prince Cinderella. King, W. B., illus. N.D. Bobbs-Merrill Co.
Alexander, James W.
--The Candy Girl: or, Maria Cheeseman. 158p. N.D. Presbyterian Committee of Publication.
--Charles Clifford: The Children at River Bank. N.D. American Sunday-School Union.
--Short Stories for the Little Ones at Home. 180p. N.D. American Sunday-School Union.
--The Silver Rifler the Little Ones at Home. N.D. American News Co.
--Uncle Austin and His Nephews. N.D. American Sunday-School Union.
Alexander, Janet see McNeill, Janet.
Alexander, Jean
--The Adventures of the Elfins. 1965. Vantage Press, Inc.
Alexander, Jocelyn Anne Arundel see Arundel, Jocelyn, pseud.
Alexander, Judy, adapted by.
--The James Bond Storybook of the Movie, A View to a Kill. LC 85-5631. (From the Original Screenplay by Richard Maibaum and Mildred G. Wilson). (Illus.). 60 p. 29cm. c.1985. (ISBN 0-448-18972-0). Grosset & Dunlap.
Alexander, Judy & Bellisario, Donald P
--Tales of the Gold Monkey Storybook. LC 83-3299. (Illus.). 58 p. 29cm. 1983. (ISBN 0-399-20990-5). G.P. Putnam's Sons.
Alexander, Linda (1935-)
--A Job Well Done. Petie, Haris, pseud. (1915-), illus. Petty, Roberta. LC 67-19631. (Illus.). 32 p. 24cm. 1967. Lantern Press.
Alexander, Liza
--Ernie Gets Lost. Cooke, Tom, illus. LC 84-81593. (Illus.). 25 p. 22cm. (A Growing-up Book). c.1985. (ISBN 0-307-12015-5). (ISBN 0-307-62115-4). Western Pub. Co. in Conjunction with Children's Television Workshop.
Alexander, Lloyd Chudley (1924-)
--Beggar Queen. 224p. (gr. 6up). 1984. (ISBN 0-525-44103-4). Dutton.
--The Black Cauldron. LC 65-13868. (Illus.). 224 p. 24cm. 1965. Holt, Rinehart and Winston. **Awards: (ALA); (JNM).**
--The Book of Three. LC 64-18250. (Illus.). 217 p. 24cm. 1964. Holt, Rinehart and Winston. **Award: (ALA).**
--Border Hawk: August Bondi. Krigstein, Bernard (1919-), illus. LC 57-112267. 182p. illus. 22cm. (Convenant books, 2). 1958. Straus and Cudahy.
--The Castle of Llyr. LC 66-13461. (Illus.). 201 p. 24cm. 1966. Holt, Rinehart and Winston. **Award: (ALA).**
--The Cat Who Wished to Be a Man. LC 73-77447. viii, 107 p. 24cm. 1973. Dutton. **Awards: (ALA); (BGH).**
--The Cat Who Wished to Be a Man. 10p. 20cm. (Anytime Books). 1977, c.1973. (ISBN 0-525-45034-3). Dutton.
--Coll and His White Pig. Ness, Evaline Michelow, Mrs. (1911-), illus. LC 65-21540. (Illus.). 32 p. 1965. Holt, Rinehart and Winston.
--The First Two Lives of Lukas-Kasha. LC 77-26699. 213 p. 24cm. c.1978. (ISBN 0-525-29748-0). Dutton.
--The Flagship Hope: Aaron Lopez. Krigstein, Bernard (1919-), illus. LC 60-12282. 179p. illus. (Covenant books, 12). c.1960. Jewish Publication Society Dist. New York, Farrar, Strauss and Cudahy.
--The Foundling, and Other Tales of Prydain. Zemach, Margot (1931-), illus. LC 73-5964. (Illus.). vii, 87 p. 25cm. 1973. (ISBN 0-03-007431-2). Holt, Rinehart and Winston. **Award: (ALA).**
--The Four Donkeys. Abrams, Lester, illus. LC 70-150029. (Illus.). 40 p. 25cm. 1972. (ISBN 0-03-080213-X). (ISBN 0-03-080213-X). Holt, Rinehart and Winston. **Award: (ALA).**
--The High King. LC 68-11833. (Illus.). 285 p. 24cm. 1968. Holt, Rinehart and Winston. **Awards: (JNM); (ALA).**
--The Kestrel. LC 81-15290. (Illus.). 244 p. 22cm. c.1982. Dutton. **Award: (ALA).**
--The King's Fountain. Keats, Ezra Jack (1916-1983), illus. LC 72-133109. (Illus.). 34 p. 1971. (ISBN 0-525-33240-5). Dutton.
--Marvelous Misadventures of Sebastian. LC 70-166879. 24cm. 204p. (gr. 4 up). 1970. Dutton. **Award: (NBA).**
--The Marvelous Misadventures of Sebastian: Grand Extravaganza, Including a Performance. LC 70-116879. x, 204 p. 20cm. (Dutton anytime books, AB01). 1973, c.1970. (ISBN 0-525-45009-2). E. P. Dutton.
--Taran Wanderer. LC 67-2847. (Illus.). 256 p. 24cm. 1967. Holt, Rinehart and Winston.
--Time Cat: The Remarkable Journeys of Jason and Gareth. 1963. Dutton.
--Time Cat: The Remarkable Journeys of Jason and Gareth. Sokol, Bill, pseud. (1925-), illus. Sokol, William. LC 63-9451. 191 p. illus. 22 cm. 1963. Holt, Rinehart and Winston.
--The Town Cats and Other Tales. Kubinyi, Laszlo (1937-), illus. LC 76-13647. p. cm. 1977. (ISBN 0-525-41430-4). Dutton.
--The Truthful Harp. Ness, Evaline Michelow, Mrs. (1911-), illus. LC 67-19058. (Illus.). 32 p. 22cm. 1967. Holt, Rinehart and Winston.
--Westmark. LC 80-22242. 184 p. 22cm. c.1981. (ISBN 0-525-42335-4). Dutton. **Awards: (ABA); (ALA).**
--The Wizard in the Tree. Kubinyi, Laszlo (1937-), illus. LC 74-23760. (Illus.). 137 p. 24cm. 1975. (ISBN 0-525-43128-4). Dutton.
Alexander, Lura V. Smith (1873-)
--A Garden of Children. LC 50-12795. 62 p illus. port. 22 cm. 1950. Murray & Gee.
Alexander, Marge, pseud., see Edwards, Roselyn.
Alexander, Marge, pseud. (1929-)
--The Merry-Go Bush: Stories for Boys and Girls. Edwards, Roselyn. LC 72-77018. (Illus.). 127 p. 21cm. (Penguin series). 1972. Review and Herald Pub. Association.
Alexander, Martha G (1920-)
--And My Mean Old Mother Will Be Sorry, Blackboard Bear. Alexander, Martha G. (1920-), illus. LC 72-707. (Illus.). 32 p. 19cm. 1972. Dial Press.
--And My Mean Old Mother Will Be Sorry, Blackboard Bear. Alexander, Martha G. (1920-), illus. LC 80-66814. (Illus.). 32 p. 1981. (ISBN 0-8037-2756-9). Dial Press.
--Babies Are Like That. Alexander, Martha G. (1920-), illus. (Illus.). 1967. (ISBN 0-307-40160-X, Golden Pr). Western Pub.
--Blackboard Bear. Alexander, Martha G. (1920-), illus. LC 69-17975. (Illus.). 32 p. 19cm. 1969. Dial Press.
--Blackboard Bear. Alexander, Martha G. (1920-), illus. LC 80-66812. (Illus.). 32 p. 1981. (ISBN 0-8037-2756-9). Dial Press.
--Bobo's Dream. Alexander, Martha G. (1920-), illus. LC 73-102825. 32 p. of col. illus. 20cm. 1970. Dial Press.
--Even That Moose Won't Listen to Me. Alexander, Martha G. (1920-), illus. LC 85-4338. p. cm. 1985. (ISBN 0-8037-0187-X). (ISBN 0-8037-0188-8). Dial Books for Young Readers.
--How My Library Grew, By Dinah. Alexander, Martha G. (1920-), illus. LC 82-20204. (Illus.). 32p. 1983. (ISBN 0-8242-0679-7). (ISBN 0-8242-0670-3). Wilson.
--I Sure Am Glad to See You, Blackboard Bear. Alexander, Martha G. (1920-), illus. LC 76-2280. (Illus.). 32 p. 19cm. 32p. c.1976. (ISBN 0-8037-4002-6). (ISBN 0-8037-4003-4). Dial Press.
--I Sure Am Glad to See You, Blackboard Bear. Alexander, Martha G. (1920-), illus. LC 76-2280. (Illus.). 1979. (Pied Piper Book). Dial Bks Young.
--I Sure Am Glad to See You, Blackboard Bear. Alexander, Martha G. (1920-), illus. LC 80-66813. (Illus.). 32 p. 1981. (ISBN 0-8037-2756-9). Dial Press.
--I'll Be the Horse If You'll Play with Me. Alexander, Martha G. (1920-), illus. LC 75-9207. (Illus.). 31 p. 16cm. 31p. 1975. (ISBN 0-8037-5458-2). (ISBN 0-8037-5511-2). Dial Press.
--I'll Protect You from the Jungle Beasts. LC 73-6015. (Illus.). 32 p. 18cm. 1973. Dial Press.
--Maggie's Moon. LC 82-1575. (Illus.). 24 p. 18cm. c.1982. (ISBN 0-8037-5708-5). (ISBN 0-8037-5721-2). Dial Press.
--Marty McGee's Space Lab, No Girls Allowed. Alexander, Martha G. (1920-), illus. LC 81-2497. p. cm. c.1981. (ISBN 0-8037-5156-7). (ISBN 0-8037-5157-5). Dial Press.
--Maybe a Monster. LC 68-28732. (Illus.). 31 p. 24cm. 1968. Dial Press.
--Move Over, Twerp. Alexander, Martha G. (1920-), illus. LC 80-21405. (Illus.). 32 p. c.1981. (ISBN 0-8037-6139-2). (ISBN 0-8037-6140-6). Dial Press.
--No Ducks in Our Bathtub. Alexander, Martha G. (1920-), illus. LC 72-7598. (Illus.). 31 p. 20cm. 1973. Dial Press.
--Nobody Asked Me If I Wanted a Baby Sister. Alexander, Martha G. (1920-), illus. LC 78-153731. (Illus.). 32 p. 1971. Dial Press.
--Out! Out! Out!. LC 68-15251. 1 v. of illus. 16cm. 1968. Dial Press.
--Pigs Say Oink. Alexander, Martha G. (1920-), illus. (Illus.). 32p. (ps-3). 1981. (ISBN 0-394-93838-0). (ISBN 0-394-83838-6). Random.
--Sabrina. Alexander, Martha G. (1920-), illus. LC 72-134855. (Illus.). 32 p. 16cm. 1971. Dial Press.
--The Story Grandmother Told. Alexander, Martha G. (1920-), illus. LC 79-85543. (Illus.). 31 p. 20cm. 1969. Dial Press.
--We Never Get to Do Anything. Alexander, Martha G. (1920-), illus. LC 78-121575. (Illus.). 32 p. 19p. 1970. Dial Press.

--We're in Big Trouble, Blackboard Bear. LC 79-20631. (Illus.). 32 p. c.1980. (ISBN 0-8037-9741-9). (ISBN 0-8037-9742-7). Dial Press.
--We're in Big Trouble, Blackboard Bear. Alexander, Martha G. (1920-), illus. LC 80-66815. (Illus.). 32 p. 1981. (ISBN 0-8037-2756-9). Dial Press.
--When the New Baby Comes, I'm Moving Out. Alexander, Martha G. (1920-), illus. LC 79-4275. (Illus.). 32 p. 16cm. c.1979. (ISBN 0-8037-9557-2). (ISBN 0-8037-9558-0). Dial Press.

Alexander, Martha G. (1920-), ed.
--Poems and Prayers for the Very Young. Alexander, Martha G. (1920-), illus. LC 73-2449. (Illus.). 32 p. 21cm. 1973. (ISBN 0-394-82705-8). Random House.

Alexander, Mrs.
--Ralph Wilton's Weird. (The Leisure Hour Ser.). N.D. Henry Holt.
--Ralph Wilton's Weird. (Sunset Ser.). N.D. J. S. Ogilvie.

Alexander, Myra
--Purple Stripe-a-Dots and No Spots: Featuring Ididit Bugs. Alexander, Myra, illus. LC 77-154836. (Illus.). 42 p. 29cm. c.1977. Eglantine.

Alexander, Pat (1937-)
--The Nelson Children's Bible: Stories from the Old and New Testaments. Evans, Lyndon, illus. LC 81-82690. (Illus.). 256 p. 22cm. c.1981. (ISBN 0-8407-5238-5). T. Nelson Publishers.

Alexander, Scott
--Rhinoceros Success. 16th ed. Smallwood, Laurie, illus. LC 80-51648. (Illus.). 123p. (Orig.) 1980. (ISBN 0-937382-00-0). Rhinos Pr.

Alexander, Shirley
--William. Coe, Lloyd (1899-1976), illus. LC 41-17577. 4 p. l., 184 p. incl. illus., plates. 21 cm. c.1941. Lothrop, Lee & Shepard Co.

Alexander, Sue (1933-)
--Dear Phoebe. Christelow, Eileen (1943-), illus. LC 83-23856. (Illus.). 32p. (ps-3). 1984. (ISBN 0-316-03132-1). Little.
--Marc the Magnificent. De Paola, Tomie, pseud. (1934-), illus. De Paola, Thomas Anthony. LC 78-3285. p. cm. 22cm. 32p. 1978. (ISBN 0-394-83728-2). (ISBN 0-394-93728-7). Pantheon.
--More Witch, Goblin, and Sometimes Ghost. Winter, Jeanette, illus. LC 78-5329. p. cm. 24cm. 60p. (Read alone book). 1978. (ISBN 0-394-83933-1). (ISBN 0-394-93933-6). Pantheon Books.
--Nadia the Willful. Bloom, Lloyd, illus. LC 82-12602. p. cm. 1983. (ISBN 0-394-85265-6). Pantheon Books.
--Peacocks Are Very Special. Chess, Victoria (1939-), illus. LC 74-31309. (Illus.). 24 p. 20cm. c.1976. (ISBN 0-385-01939-4). Doubleday.
--Seymour the Prince. Hoban, Lillian (1925-), illus. LC 78-31406. (Illus.). 46 p. 24cm. (I am reading book). c.1979. (ISBN 0-394-94141-1). (ISBN 0-394-84141-7). Pantheon Books.
--Small Plays for Special Days. Huffman, Tom, illus. 1977. Houghton.
--Small Plays for Special Days. Huffman, Tom, illus. LC 76-28424. (Illus.). 64 p. 27cm. c.1977. (ISBN 0-8164-3184-1). Seabury Press.
--Small Plays for You and a Friend. Cole, Olivia H. H., illus. LC 74-4019. (Illus.). 48 p. 18cm. 1974, c.1973. (ISBN 0-8164-3125-6). Seabury Press.
--Whatever Happened to Uncle Albert?. And Other Puzzling Plays. Huffman, Tom, illus. LC 80-15075. (Illus.). xii, 94 p. 21cm. c.1980. (ISBN 0-395-29104-6). Houghton Mifflin/Clarion Books.
--Witch, Goblin, and Ghost Are Back: Five I Am Reading Stories. Winter, Jeanette, illus. LC 83-22157. (Illus.). 62 p. 24cm. (I Am Reading Bk.). c.1985. (ISBN 0-394-86296-1). (ISBN 0-394-96296-6). Pantheon Books.
--Witch, Goblin, and Ghost in the Haunted Woods: Five I Am Reading Stories. Winter, Jeanette, illus. LC 80-20863. (Illus.). 60 p. 24cm. (I am reading books). c.1981. (ISBN 0-394-84443-2). (ISBN 0-394-94443-7). Pantheon Books.
--Witch, Goblin, and Sometimes Ghost!. Six Read-Alone Stories. Winter, Jeanette, illus. LC 76-8657. (Illus.). 59 p. 24cm. c.1976. (ISBN 0-394-83216-7). Pantheon Books.
--World Famous Muriel. Demarest, Christopher Lynn (1951-), illus. LC 82-17186. (Illus.). (ps-3). 1984. (ISBN 0-316-03131-3). Little.
--World Famous Muriel and the Scary Dragon. Demarest, Christopher Lynn (1951-), illus. LC 85-6806. p. cm. c.1985. (ISBN 0-316-03134-8). Little, Brown.

Alexander, William Prindle, jt. auth. see Cormack, Maribelle B.

Alexander, William Prindle (1881-) & Cormack, Maribelle
--Bruce and Marcia: Woodsmen. Hartwell, Marjorie, illus. LC 39-7443. 4 p. l., 221 p. front., illus. (incl. map) 19 1/2 cm. c.1939. American Book Company.

Alexenberg, Melvin L.
--Sound Science. De Paola, Tomie, pseud. (1934-), illus. De Paola, Thomas Anthony. (Illus.). 48 p. 26cm. 1968. Prentice-Hall.
--What Is a Human. LC 63-21332. 46 p. col. illus. 21 cm. (What is it series). 1964. Benefic Press.

Alexeyev, S.
--My First Book. 26p. 1982. (ISBN 0-8285-2490-4, Pub. by Progress Pubs. USSR). Imported Pubns.

Alexiera, Marguerite, ed. see Karaliichev, Angel.

Alfau, Felipe
--Old Tales from Spain. Wells, Rhea (1891-), illus. LC 29-17951. xii p., 1 l., 207, 1 p. incl. front., illus., plates 21 cm. 1929. Doubleday, Doran & Company, Inc.

Alford, Gene
--Busy litte fingers. Figh, Mary, illus. LC 48-3050. 83p. illus. 22cm. 1948, c.1947. Van Nort Press.
--Busy little feet: Verse for children. Snowden, Chester, illus. LC 39-19910. 87p. incl. front. illus. 22cm. c.1939. Van Nort & Co.

Alford, Sarah C., Mrs.
--Thrills on a Texas Ranch. LC 38-38066. 21cm. 263p. 1938. Naylor Co.

Alger
--World's Choice Fables. (Classics for Children). N.D. Ginn and Company.

Alger, Edwin
--Phil Hardy's Greatest Test. Schaeffer, Phil, illus. LC 30-13876. vii, 206 p. front. 19 1/2 cm. (His Bound to win series). c.1930. Grosset & Dunlap.
--Phil Hardy's Struggle. Townsend, Ernest N., illus. LC 30-13101. ix. 196 p. front., plates. 19 1/2 cm. (His Bound to win series). c.1930. Grosset & Dunlap.
--Phil Hardy's Triumph. Townsend, Ernest N., illus. LC 30-13100. vii, 232 p. front., plates. 19 1/2 cm. (His Bound to win series). c.1930. Grosset & Dunlap.

Alger, Horatio see Putnam, Arthur Lee, pseud.
Alger, Horatio see Putnam, Arthur Lee, pseud.
Alger, Horatio, pseud., see Stratemeyer, Edward L..

Alger, Horatio, Jr. (1832-1899)
--Adrift in New York, (The Rugby Ser.). 1905. Set. A L Burt Co.
--Adrift in New York. N.D. Consolidated Retail Booksellers.
--Adrift in New York. (Alger Ser.). N.D. World Publishing Co.
--Adrift in New York: Or, Tom and Florence Braving the World. LC 41-42138. 19cm. 266p. N.D. A. L. Burt Company.
--Adrift in New York: Or, Tom and Florence Braving the World. LC 38-1827. 19cm. 274p. (Alger Ser.). N.D. Hurst & Co.
--Adrift in the City. (Illus.). (Eclipse Ser.). N.D. John C. Winston.
--Adrift in the City: Or, Oliver Conrad's Plucky Fight. (Illus.). (Victory Ser.). N.D. Set. Henry T. Coates & Co.
--Adrift in the City: Or, Oliver Conrad's Plucky Fight, 1 of 3 Vols. (Victory Ser.). N.D. Set. John C. Winston co.
--Adrift in the City: Paul Conrad Plucky Fight. (Illus.). N.D. New Books.
--Adventures of a Telegraph Boy. (The Boys Own Library). N.D. David McKay.
--Adventures of a Telegraph Boy, (Illus.). (Famous Books for Boys Ser.: No. 2). 1905. H M Caldwell Co.
--Andy Gordon. (Illus.). (The Chimney Corner Ser.). N.D. A. L. Burt.
--Andy Gordon. LC 58-200042. iv. (Unpaged) front. 20cm.). N.D. Goldsmith Pub. Co. N. D.
--Andy Gordon. (Alger Ser.). N.D. World Publishing Co.
--Andy Gordon: Or, Fortunes of a Young Janitor. (Alger Ser.). N.D. Hurst & Co.
--Andy Grant's Pluck, (The Chimney Corner Ser.). 1905. Set. A L Burt Co.
--Andy Grant's Pluck. LC 2-18087. 19cm. iv, 335p. 1902. H. T. Coates & Co.
--Andy Grant's Pluck: And How He Won it, 98 vols. (The Rugby Ser.). 1905. Set. A L Burt Co.
--Andy Grant's Pluck: And How He Won It. (Alger Ser.). N.D. Hurst & Co.
--Andy Grant's Pluck: And How He Won it. (Illus.). (The Winston Ser.). N.D. John C. Winston.
--Andy Grant's Pluck: And How He Won it. (Illus.). (Eclipse Ser.). N.D. John C. Winston.
--The Backwoods Boy. (The Boys' Own Library). N.D. David McKay.
--Ben Bruce. (Illus.). (The Chimney Corner Ser.). N.D. A. L. Burt.
--Ben Bruce: Or, Only a Bowery Newsboy. LC 61-55555. 19cm. 315p. (New Medal Library). 1908, c.1901. Street and Smith.
--Ben Bruce: Or, The Life of Bowery Newsboy. (Illus.). (Alger Ser.). N.D. Hurst & Co.
--Ben Logan 's Triumph. (Alert Ser.). N.D. Grosset & Dunlap.
--Ben, the Luggage Boy. (Ragged Dick Ser.). N.D. John C. Winston.
--Ben the Luggage Boy. (Illus.). (Ragged Dick Ser.). 1888. Porter & Coates.
--Ben the Luggage Boy, 1 of 6 vols. (Ragged Dick Ser.). 1891. Set. Porter & Coates.
--Ben, The Luggage Boy: or, Among the Wharves, 5 of 6, Vol. 5. (Horatio Alger's Books for Boys). (Ragged Dick Ser.). N.D. Loring.
--Ben the Luggage Boy: Or, Among the Wharves, 1 of 6 Vols. (Illus.). (Ragged Dick Ser.). N.D. Set. Porter & Coates.
--Ben's Nugget, 1 of 4 Vols. (Roundabout Library). (Pacific Ser.). N.D. Set. John C. Winston Co.
--Ben's Nugget. (Illus.). (Winston Ser.). N.D. John C. Winston.
--Ben's Nugget. (Eclipse Ser.). N.D. John C. Winston.
--Ben's Nugget, 1 of 4 vols. (Pacific Ser.). 1891. Set. Porter & Coates.
--Ben's Nugget: or, A Boy's Search for Fortune. (Illus.). (Pacific Ser.). 1888. Porter & Coates.
--Bernard Brooks Adventures: or, The Experience of a Plucky Boy. (Illus.). (Alger Ser.). N.D. Hurst & Co.
--Bernard Brook's Adventures: The Experiences of a Plucky Boy. (The Chimney Corner Ser.). N.D. A. L. Burt
--Bernard Brook's Adventures: The/Story of a Brave Boy's Trials. Davis, J. Watson, illus. LC 3-11669. 19cm. 306p. 1903. A. L. Burt Company.
--Bertha's Christmas Vision. N.D. Hurst & Co.
--Bob Burton. (Illus.). (The Chimney Corner Ser.). N.D. A. L. Burt.
--Bob Burton, 1 of 4 Vols. (Roundabout Library). (Way to Success Ser.). N.D. Set. John C. Winston Co.
--Bob Burton. (Illus.). (Winston Ser.). N.D. John C. Winston.
--Bob Burton. (Eclipse Ser.). N.D. John C. Winston.
--Bob Burton, 1 of 4 vols. (Way to Success Ser.). 1891. Set. Porter & Coates.
--Bob Burton. (Alger Ser.). N.D. World Publishing Co.
--Bob Burton: Or, The Young Ranchman of the Missouri. LC 41-40532. 19cm. vi, 330p. 1888. C. Winston Co.
--Bob Burton: Or, The Young Ranchman of the Missouri, 1 of 4 vols. (Illus.). (Roundabout Lib.). (Way To Success Ser.). N.D. Set. Henry T. Coates & Co.
--Bob Burton: Or, The Young Ranchman of the Missouri. (Alger Ser.). N.D. Hurst & Co.
--Bob Burton: Or, The Young Ranchman of the Missouri. (Illus.). (Atlantic Ser.). 1888. Porter & Coates.
--Bound To Rise. (Illus.). 1905. John C. Winston & Co.
--Bound to Rise. (Alger Ser.). N.D. World Publishing Co.
--Bound to Rise: Books for Boys, (The Chimney Corner Ser.). 1905. Set. A L Burt Co.
--Bound to Rise: Or, How Harry Walton Rose in the World, vols (The Rugby Ser.). 1905. Set. A L Burt Co.
--Bound to Rise: Or, How Harry Walton Rose in the World. (Illus.). (The Chimney Corner Ser.). N.D. A. L. Burt.
--Bound to Rise: Or, How Harry Walton Rose in the World. Empire ed. 1905. American News Co.
--Bound to Rise: Or, How Harry Walton Rose in the World. (Boys' Select Library). N.D. Consolidated Retail Booksellers.
--Bound to Rise: Or, How Harry Walton Rose in the World, 1 of 4 Vols. (Luck and Pluck Second Ser.). N.D. Set. John C. Winston Co.
--Bound to Rise: Or, How Harry Walton Rose in the World. (Illus.). (Winston Ser.). N.D. John C. Winston.
--Bound to Rise: Or, How Harry Walton Rose in the World. (Eclipse Ser.). N.D. John C. Winston.
--Bound to Rise: Or, How Harry Walton Rose in the World. (Illus.). (Luck Pluck Second Ser.). 1888. Porter & Caotes.
--Bound to Rise: Or, How Harry Walton Rose in the World, 1 of 4 vols. (Luck & Pluck Ser.: Second Ser.). 1891. Set. Porter & Coates.
--Bound to Rise: Or, Up the Ladder. (Alger Ser.). N.D. Hurst & Co.
--A Boy's Fortune: Or, The Strange Adventures of Ben Baker, 1 of 3 vols. (Illus.). 20cm. iv, 325p. (Good Fortune Ser.). 1898. Set. Henry T. Coates & Co.
--A Boy's Fortune: Or, the Strange Adventures of Ben Barker, 1 of 3 vols. (Good Fortune Library Ser.). N.D. Set. John C. Winston Co.
--A Boy's Fortune: Or, The Strange Adventures of Ben Baker. (Illus.). (Winston Ser.). N.D. John C. Winston.
--A Boy's Fortune: Or, The Strange Adventures of Ben Baker. (Illus.). (Eclipse Ser.). N.D. John C. Winston.
--Brave and Bold. (Alger Ser.). N.D. World Publishing Co.
--Brave and Bold: Books for Boys, (The Chimney Corner Ser.). 1905. Set. A L Burt Co.
--Brave and Bold: or, The Fortunes of Robert Rushton. (Alger Ser.). N.D. Hurst & Co.
--Brave and Bold: Or, the Story of a Factory Boy, (The Rugby Ser.). 1905. Set. A L Burt Co.
--Brave and Bold: Or, the Story of a Factory Boy. (Illus.). (The Chimney Corner Ser.). N.D. A. L. Burt.
--Brave and Bold: Or, the Story of a Factory Boy. Empire ed. 1905. American News Co.
--Brave and Bold: Or, the Story of a Factory Boy. (Boys' Select Library of Famous Alger Books). N.D. Consolidated Retail Booksellers.
--Brave and Bold: Or, the Story of a Factory Boy, 1 of 4 vols. (Brave and Bold Ser.). N.D. Set. John C. Winston Co.
--Brave and Bold: Or, the Story of a Factory Boy. (Illus.). (Winston Ser.). N.D. John C. Winston
--Brave and Bold: Or, the Story of a Factory Boy. (Illus.). (Eclipse Ser.). N.D. John C. Winston.
--Brave and Bold: Or, the Story of a Factory Boy, 1 of 4 Vols. (Illus.). (Brave and Bold Ser.). 1888. Porter & Caotes.
--Brave & Bold: Or, The Story of a Factory Boy, 1 of 4 vols. (Brave & Bold Ser.). 1891. Set. Porter & Coates.
--Canal Boy to President. (Famous Books for Boys). N.D. H. M. Caldwell Co.
--The Cash Boy. LC 42-47437. 1 p. l. 254 p. 19 cm. (Alger series for boys). N.D. Hurst & Company.
--The Cash Boy. LC 44-15714. 247 p. 19 cm. (Alger series for boys). N.D. M. A. Donohue & Company.
--The Cash Boy. LC 52-56512. 294 p. 20 cm. 1906. M.A. Donohue.
--The Cash-Boy. LC 41-418491. (Published in 1887 under the title: Frank Fowler, the cash boy). 19cm. 294p. N.D. Mershon Company.
--Cash Boy. (Alger Ser.). N.D. World Publishing Co.
--Cash Boy: Or, Frank Fowler's Early Struggles. Empire ed. 1905. American News Co.
--Cash Boy: Or, Frank Fowler's Early Struggles. (Boys' Select Library of Famous Alger Books For Boys). N.D. Consolidated Retail Booksellers.
--Cash Boy: or, Frank Fowler's Early Struggles. (Alger Ser.). N.D. Hurst & Co.
--Charlie Codman's Cruise. (Illus.). (The Chimney Corner Ser.). N.D. A. L. Burt.
--Charlie Codman's Cruise, 1 of 3 Vols. (Campaign Ser.). N.D. Set. John C. Winston Co.
--Charlie Codman's Cruise. (Illus.). (Winston Ser.). N.D. John C. Winston.
--Charlie Codman's Cruise. (Illus.). (Eclipse Ser.). N.D. John C. Winston.
--Charlie Codman's Cruise. (Illus.). (Campaign Ser.). 1888. Porter & Caotes.
--Charlie Codman's Cruise, 1 of 3 vols. (Campaign Ser.). 1891. Set. Porter & Coates.
--Charlie Codman's Cruise: A Story for Boys. (Alger Ser.). N.D. Hurst & Co.
--Chester Rand, (The Rugby Ser.). 1905. Set. A L Burt Co.
--Chester Rand. (The Chimney Corner Ser.). N.D. A. L. Burt.
--Chester Rand. (Illus.). (Winston Ser.). N.D. John C. Winston.
--Chester Rand. (Illus.). (Eclipse Ser.). N.D. John C. Winston.
--Chester Rand: Books for Boys, (The Chimney Corner Ser.). 1905. Set. A L Burt Co.
--Chester Rand: Or, A New Path to Fortune. LC 3-21289. iv, 383 p. front., plates. 19 cm. 1903. H. T. Coates & Co.
--Chester Rand: Or, A New Path to Fortune. N.D. John C. Winston Co.
--Chester Rand: Or, The New Path to Fortune. LC 38-12755. 19cm. 328p. N.D. A. L. Burt Company.
--Chester Rand: Or, the New Path to Fortune. (Alger Ser.). N.D. Hurst & Co.
--Chester Rand: Or, The New Path to Fortune. LC 62-55513. 250. 18cm. (Medal Library). 1905. Street & Smith.
--A Cousin's Conspiracy. (Illus.). (The Chimney Corner Ser.). N.D. A. L. Burt.
--A Cousin's Conspiracy: Or, A Boy's Struggle from Inheritance. (Alger Ser.). N.D. Hurst & Co.
--Dan the Newsboy. LC 58-53857. 19cm. 296p. (Wide Awake Boys Ser.). 1893. A. L. Burt.
--Dan, The Newsboy. (Illus.). (The Alger Series for Boys). N.D. A. L. Burt's Pubs.
--Dean Dunham. (The Boys Own Library). N.D. David Mckay.

--Dean Dunham, (Illus.). (Famous Books for Boys Ser.: No. 6). 1905. Set. H M Caldwell Co.
--Dean Dunham: Or, The Waterford Mystery. LC 73-89612. (Illus.). iii, 275 p., 4 leaves of plates. 23cm. 1975, c.1900. (ISBN 0-88411-801-0). Aeonian Press.
--Dean Dunham: The Waterford Mystery. 12cm. 275p. (Medal Library: No. 50). 1900. Street & Smith.
--A Debt of Honor. (Illus.). (The Alger Series for Boys). N.D. A. L. Burt's Pubs.
--A Debt of Honor: Or, Gerald Lane's Success. (Illus.). N.D. Hurst & Co.
--A Debt of Honor: The Story of Gerald Lane's Success in the Far West. Davis, J. Watson, illus. LC 3790. iv, 202 p. front., plates. 19 cm. 1900. A. L. Burt.
--A Debt of Honor: The Story of Gerald Lane's Success in the West. (Illus.). (The Chimney Corner Ser.). N.D. A. L. Burt.
--Digging for Gold, 1 of 3 vols. (New World Ser.). N.D. Set. John C. Winston Co.
--Digging for Gold. (Eclipse Ser.). N.D. John C. Winston.
--Digging for Gold: A Story of California, 1 of 3 vols. LC 51-52455. iv. 352 p. illus. 20 cm. (New World Ser.). c.1892. Porter & Coates.
--Digging for Gold: A Story of California. Seelye, John, intro. by. LC 68-12712. xx, 201 p. 19 cm. xx, 201p. 1968. Collier Books.
--Do and Dare. (Illus.). (Eclipse Ser.). N.D. John C. Winston.
--Do and Dare. (Alger Ser.). N.D. World Publishing Co.
--Do and Dare: Books for Boys, (The Chimney Corner Ser.). 1905. Set. A L Burt Co.
--Do and Dare: Or, A Brave Boy's Fight for Fortune. (The Rugby Ser.). 1905. Set. A L Burt Co.
--Do and Dare: Or, A Brave Boy's Fight for Fortune. (Illus.). (The Chimney Corner Ser.). N.D. A. L. Burt.
--Do and Dare: Or, A Brave Boy's Fight for Fortune. (Boys' Select Library of Famous Alger Books). N.D. Consolidated Retail Booksellers.
--Do and Dare: Or, A Brave Boy's Fight for Fortune, 1 of 4 vols. (Illus.). (Roundabout Lib.). (Atlantic Ser.). N.D. Henry T. Coates & Co.
--Do and Dare: Or, A Brave Boy's Fight for Fortune. LC 38-12753. 1 p. l, 245 p. 19 cm. 1905. Hurst & Company.
--Do and Dare: Or, A Brave Boy's Fight for Fortune. (Illus.). (The Cambridge Classics). N.D. Hurst and Company.
--Do and Dare: or, A Brave Boy's Fight for Fortune. (Alger Ser.). N.D. Hurst & Co.
--Do and Dare: Or, A Brave Boy's Fight for Fortune, 1 of 4 vols. (Roundabout Library). (Atlantic Ser.). N.D. Set. John C. Winston Co.
--Do & Dare: Or, A Brave Boys's Fight for Fortune, 1 of 4 vols. (Atlantic Ser.). 1891. Set. Porter & Coates.
--Driven from Home, (The Rugby Ser.). 1905. Set. A L Burt Co.
--Driven from Home. (The Chimney Corner Ser.). N.D. A. L. Burt.
--Driven From Home. (Boys' Select Library of Famous Alger Books). N.D. Consolidated Retail Booksellers.
--Driven from Home: Or, Carl Crawford's Experience. (The Chimney Corner Ser.). 1905. Set. A L Burt Co.
--Driven from Home: Or, Carl Crawford's Experience. LC 52-56511. 245 p. 20 cm. 1906. M. A. Donohue.
--The Erie Train Boy. (Illus.). (The Chimney Corner Ser.). N.D. A. L. Burt.
--The Erie Train Boy. (Illus.). (The Young Folks Library). N.D. Caldwell.
--Erie Train Boy. (Boys' Select Library of Famous Alger Books). N.D. Consolidated Retail Booksellers.
--The Erie Train Boy. (The Boys Own Library). N.D. David McKay.
--Erie Train Boy, (Illus.). (Famous Books for Boys Ser.: No. 7). 1905. Set. H M Caldwell Co.
--The Erie Train Boy, 1 of 64 vols. (Young America Library: No. 17). 1900. Set. Hurst & Co.
--The Erie Train Boy. (Alger Ser.). 1900. Hurst & Co.
--The Erie Train Boy. 12cm. 270p. (Medal Library: No. 61). 1900. Street & Smith.
--The Erie Train Boy. Gardner, Ralph D., intro. by. LC 73-89613. (Illus.). vii, 271 p. 23cm. 1975. (ISBN 0-88411-802-9). Aeonian Press.
--The Errand Boy: How Phil Bert Won Success. (Illus.). (The Boys' Home Ser.). N.D. A. L. Burt.
--The Errand Boy: How Phil Bert Won Success. (Illus.). (The Alger Series for Boys). N.D. A. L. Burt's Pubs.
--The Errand Boy: How Phil Bert Won Success, 1 of 3 vols. (Illus.). (The Errand Boy Ser.). N.D. Set. A. L. Burt's Pubs.
--The Errand Boy: How Phil Bert Won Success. (Illus.). (Alger Ser.). N.D. Hurst & Co.
--The Errand Boy: How Phil Brent Won Success. (Illus.). (The Chimney Corner Ser.). N.D. A. L. Burt.
--The Errand Boy: Or, How Phil Brent Won Success. LC 38-350608. 281 p. front. 19 cm. c.1888. A. L. Burt.
--Facing the World, (The Chimney Corner Ser.). 1905. Set. A L Burt Co.
--Facing the World. (Alger Ser.). N.D. World Publishing Co.
--Facing the World: Or, The Haps and Mishaps of Harry Vane. (The Rugby Ser.). 1905. Set. A L Burt Co.
--Facing the World: Or, The Haps and Mishaps of Harry Vane. (Boys' Select Library of Famous Alger Books). N.D. Consolidated Retail Booksellers.
--Facing the World: Or, The Haps and Mishaps of Harry Vane, 1 of 3 vols. (Illus.). (New World Ser.). N.D. Set. Henry T. Coates & Co.
--Facing the World: or, The Haps and Mishaps of Harry Vane. (Alger Ser.). N.D. Hurst & Co.
--Facing the World: Or, The Haps and Mishaps of Harry Vane, 1 of 3 Vols. (New World Ser.). N.D. Set. John C. Winston Co.
--Facing the World: or, The Haps and Mishaps of Harry Vane. (Illus.). (Winston Ser.). N.D. John C. Winston.
--Facing the World: Or, The Haps and Mishaps of Harry Vane. (Illus.). (Eclipse Ser.). N.D. John C. Winston.
--Fame and Fortune. (Ragged Dick Ser.). N.D. John C. Winston.
--Fame and Fortune: or, The Progress of Richard Hunter, 2 of 6, Vol. 2. (Horatio Alger's Books for Boys). (Ragged Dick Ser.). N.D. Loring.
--Fame and Fortune: Or, The Progress of Richard Hunter, 1 of 6 Vols. (Illus.). (Ragged Dick Ser.). 1888. Set. Porter & Coates.
--Fame & Fortune: Or, The Progress of Richard Hunter, 1 of 6 vols. (Ragged Dick Ser.). 1891. Set. Porter & Coates.
--Finding a Fortune. (Illus.). (The Little People's Ser.). N.D. Penn Publishing Co.
--Finding a Fortune. Lukens, Winfield S., illus. LC 4-10932. 19cm. 364p. 1904. Penn Publishing Co.
--Finding a Fortune. Lukens, Winfield S., illus. (Adventure Stories Ser.). N.D. Penn Publishing Co.
--The Five Hundred Dollar Check. (The Boys Own Library). N.D. David McKay.
--The Five Hundred Dollar Check, 39 vols. (Famous Books for Boys Ser.: No. 9). 1905. Set. H M Caldwell Co.
--The Five-Hundred Dollar Check. (Illus.). N.D. International Book Co.
--The Five Hundred Dollar Check. LC 1-30449. 1 p. l., 304 p. 18 cm. (Medical library, no. 87). c.1901. Street & Smith.
--The Five Hundred Dollar Check: Or, Jacob Marlowe's Secret. (Alger Ser.). N.D. Hurst & Co.
--Forging Ahead. (Illus.). (The Little People's Ser.). N.D. Penn Publishing Co.
--Forging Ahead. 4 p., 1 l., 5-369 p. front., 6 pl. 19 cm. (Adventure Stories Ser.). 1903. The Penn Publishing Company.
--Frank and Fearless. (Illus.). (Eclipse Ser.). N.D. John C. Winston.
--Frank and Fearless: Or, The Fortunes of Jasper Kent. LC 73-89616. (Illus.). iii, 322 p., 1 leaf of plates. 23cm. 1975, c.1897. (ISBN 0-88411-803-7). Aeonian Press.
--Frank and Fearless: Or, The Fortunes of Jasper Kent. LC 13-23603. iv, 322 p. front., plates. 19 cm. 1897. H. T. Coates & Co.
--Frank and Fearless: Or, The Fortunes of Jasper Kent, 1 of 3 vols. (Illus.). (Frank and Fearless Ser.). N.D. Set. Henry T. Coates & Co.
--Frank and Fearless: Or, The Fortunes of Jasper Kent, 1 of 3 Vols. (Frank and Fearless Ser.). N.D. Set. John C. Winston Co.
--Frank Fowler, the Cash Boy. (The Rugby Ser.). 1905. Set. A L Burt Co.
--Frank Fowler, the Cash Boy. (Illus.). (The Boys' Home Ser.). N.D. A. L. Burt.
--Frank Fowler, the Cash Boy. (Illus.). (The Alger Series for Boys). N.D. A. L. Burt's Pubs.
--Frank Fowler, the Cash Boy, 1 of 3 vols. (Illus.). (The Errand Boy Ser.). N.D. Set. A. L. Burt's Pubs.
--Frank Fowler, the Cash Boy: Books for Boys, 30 vols. (The Chimney Corner Ser.). 1905. Set. A L Burt Co.
--Frank Hunter's Peril. LC 11-822895. iv, 5-335 p. front., plates. 19 1/2 cm. c.1896. H. T. Coates & Co.
--Frank Hunter's Peril, 1 of 3 vols. (Illus.). (Frank and Fearless Ser.). N.D. Set. Henry T. Coates & Co.
--Frank Hunter's Peril, 1 of 3 Vols. (Frank and Fearless Ser.). N.D. Set. John C. Winston Co.
--Frank Hunter's Peril. (Illus.). (Winston Ser.). N.D. John C. Winston.
--Frank Hunter's Peril. (Illus.). (Eclipse Ser.). N.D. John C. Winston.
--Frank Hunter's Peril. LC 41-38138. iv, 5-335 p. col. front., col. plates. 19 cm. c.1896. The John C. Winston Co.
--Frank's Campaign, 1 of 3 Vols. (Campaign Ser.). N.D. Set. John C. Winston Co.
--Frank's Campaign. (Illus.). (Winston Ser.). N.D. John C. Winston.
--Frank's Campaign. (Illus.). (Eclipse Ser.). N.D. John C. Winston.
--Frank's Campaign, 1 of 3 vols. (Campaign Ser.). 1891. Set. Porter & Coates.
--Frank's Campaign. (Alger Ser.). N.D. World Publishing Co.
--Frank's Campaign: Or, The Farm and the Camp. (Alger Ser.). N.D. Hurst & Co.
--Frank's Campaign: Or, The Farm and the Camp. (Illus.). (Campaign Ser.). 1888. Porter & Coates.
--From Canal Boy to President. (The Boys Own Library). N.D. David McKay.
--From Canal Boy to President, (Illus.). (Famous Books for Boys Ser.: No. 10). 1905. Set. H M Caldwell Co.
--From Farm Boy to Senator. (The Boys' Own Library). N.D. David McKay.
--Grand'ther Baldwin's Thanksgiving with other ballads and poems. LC 7-2793. 18cm. 125p. 1879. Loring.
--Grit: Or, The Young Boatman of Pine Hill. LC 62-55508. 19cm. 288p. (Alger Ser.). 1907. Hurst & Co.
--Grit, the Young Boatman of the Pine Point. (Illus.). (The Chimney Corner Ser.). N.D. A. L. Burt.
--Hector's Inheritance. (The Chimney Corner Ser.). 1905. Set. A L Burt Co.
--Hector's Inheritance. (The Rugby Ser.). 1905. Set. A L Burt Co.
--Hector's Inheritance. (Boys' Select Library of Famous Alger Books). N.D. Consolidated Retail Booksellers.
--Hector's Inheritance, 1 of 4 Vols. (Roundabout Library). (Atlantic Ser.). N.D. Set. John C. Wilson Co.
--Hector's Inheritance. (Illus.). (Winston Ser.). N.D. John C. Winston.
--Hector's Inheritance. (Illus.). (Eclipse Ser.). N.D. John C. Winston.
--Hector's Inheritance. (Illus.). (Atlantic Ser.). 1888. Porter & Coates.
--Hector's Inheritance, 1 of 4 vols. (Atlantic Ser.). 1891. Set. Porter & Coates.
--Hector's Inheritance: Or, The Boys of Smith's Institute, 1 of 4 vols. (Illus.). (Roundabout Lib.). (Atlantic Ser.). N.D. Set. Henry T. Coates & Co.
--Hector's Inheritance: or, The Boys of Smith Institute. (Alger Ser.). N.D. Hurst & Co.
--Helen Ford. (Illus.). (Alger Ser.). N.D. Hurst & Co.
--Helen Ford. (Illus.). 1905. John C. Winston & Co.
--Helen Ford. (Illus.). (Winston Ser.). N.D. John C. Winston.
--Helen Ford. (Illus.). (Eclipse Ser.). N.D. John C. Winston.
--Helen Ford. LC 12-19578. 19cm. 297p. 1866. Loring.
--Helping Himself. (Illus.). (The Chimney Corner Ser.). N.D. A. L. Burt.
--Helping Himself, 1 of 4 Vols. (Roundabout Library). (Atlantic Ser.). N.D. Set. John C. Winston Co.
--Helping Himself. (Illus.). (Winston Ser.). N.D. John C. Winston.
--Helping Himself. (Illus.). (Eclipse Ser.). N.D. John C. Winston.
--Helping Himself, 1 of 4 vols. (Atlantic Ser.). 1891. Set. Porter & Coates.
--Helping Himself. (Alger Ser.). N.D. World Publishing Co.
--Helping Himself: Or, Grant Thornton's Ambition, 1 of 4 vols. (Illus.). (Roundabout Lib.). (Atlantic Ser.). N.D. Set. Henry T. Coates & Co.
--Helping Himself: Or Grant Thornton's Ambition. LC 37-219671. 230 p. incl. front. plates 19 1/2 cm. N.D. The John C. Winston Co.
--Helping Himself: Or, Grant Thornton's Ambition. LC 44-15713. 1 p. l. 258 p. 17 cm. (On cover: The Alger series, no. 8). N.D. The Superior Printing Co.
--Helping Himself: or, Grant Thornton's Rapid Rise in New York. (Illus.). (Alger Ser.). N.D. Hurst & Co.
--Herbert Carter's Legacy, (The Chimney Corner Ser.). 1905. Set. A L Burt Co.
--Herbert Carter's Legacy, (The Rugby Ser.). 1905. Set. A L Burt Co.
--Herbert Carter's Legacy. (Boys' Select Library of Famous Alger Books). N.D. Consolidated Retail Booksellers.
--Herbert Carter's Legacy, 1 of 4 Vols. (Luck and Pluck, Second Ser.). N.D. Set. John C. Winston Co.
--Herbert Carter's Legacy. (Illus.). (Winston Ser.). N.D. John C. Winston.
--Herbert Carter's Legacy. (Illus.). (Eclipse Ser.). N.D. John C. Winston.
--Herbert Carter's Legacy. LC 44-15715. 1 p. l. 247 p. 19 cm. (Alger series for boys). N.D. M. A. Donohue & Company.
--Herbert Carter's Legacy, 1 of 4 vols. (Luck & Pluck Second Ser.). 1891. Set. Porter & Coates.
--Herbert Carter's Legacy: or, The Inventor's Son. (Alger Ser.). N.D. Hurst & Co.
--Herbert Carter's Legacy: Or, The Inventor's Son, 1 of 4 vols. (Illus.). (Luck and Pluck Second Ser.). 1888. Porter & Coates.
--In a New World, (The Chimney Corner Ser.). 1905. Set. A L Burt Co.
--In a New World, 98 vols. (The Rugby Ser.). 1905. Set. A L Burt Co.
--In a New World. (Boys' Select Library of Famous Alger Books for Boys). N.D. Consolidated Retail Booksellers.
--In a New World, 1 of 3 Vols. LC 58-51514. 19cm. 323p. (New World Ser.). 1893. Set. John C. Winston Co.
--In a New World. (Illus.). (Eclipse Ser.). N.D. John C. Winston.
--In a New World: Or, Among the Gold Fields of Australia. LC 53-53026. 289p. 20cm. N.D. A. L. Burt N.D.
--In a New World: Or, Among the Gold Fields of Australia. LC 63-57444. 19cm. 263p. (Alger Series for Boys). 1905. Hurst & Co.
--In a New World: Or, the Goldfields of Australia. LC 72-78979. 22cm. 217p. (It's a Real Horatio Alger Story). (gr. 6up). 1972. (ISBN 0-912064-05-6). Media.
--In Search of Treasure. (Illus.). (The Chimney Corner Ser.). N.D. A. L. Burt.
--In Search of Treasure. (Illus.). (Alger Ser.). N.D. Hurst & Co.
--In Search of Treasure: The Story of Guy's Eventful Voyage. Davis, J. Watson, illus. LC 7-11212. 19 1/2cm. 301p. c.1907. A. L. Burt Company.
--Jack's Ward, (The Rugby Sr.). 1905. Set. A L Burt Co.
--Jack's Ward. (The Chimney Corner Ser.). N.D. A. L. Burt.
--Jack's Ward. (Boys' Select Library of Famous Alger Books). N.D. Consolidated Retail Booksellers.
--Jack's Ward, 1 of 4 Vols. LC 9-19670. 20cm. 331p. (Brave and Bold Ser.). 1875. Set. John C. Winston Co.
--Jack's Ward. (Illus.). (Winston Ser.). N.D. John C. Winston.
--Jack's Ward. (Illus.). (Eclipse Ser.). N.D. John C. Winston.
--Jack's Ward, 1 of 4 vols. (Brave & Bold Ser.). 1891. Set. Porter & Coates.
--Jack's Ward: Books for Boys. (The Chimney Corner Ser.). 1905. Set. A L Burt Co.
--Jack's Ward: or, The Boy Guardian. (Illus.). (Alger Ser.). N.D. Hurst & Co.
--Jack's Ward: Or, The Boy Guardian. LC 43-26892. 331 p. front., plates. 19 cm. (Added t.-p. Brave and bold series v. 2). c.1875. Loring.
--Jack's Ward: Or, The Boy Guardian. LC 4-31658. 20cm. 331p. (Brave & Bold Ser.: Vol. 2). 1875. Porter & Coates.
--Jack's Ward: Or, The Boy Guardian, 1 of 4 Vols. (Illus.). (Brave and Bold Ser.). 1888. Porter & Coates.
--Jack's Ward: Or, The Boy Guardian. 331 p. front., 2 pl. 19 1/2 cm. (Added t.-p.: Brave & bold series v. 2). c.1875. The J. C. Winston Co.
--Jacob Marlowe's Secret. (Illus.). (The Chimney Corner Ser.). N.D. A. L. Burt.
--Jed, the Poorhouse Boy. (Illus.). (The Chimney Corner Ser.). N.D. A. L. Burt.
--Jed, the Poorhouse Boy. 12cm. 363p. 1900. H. T. Coates & Co.
--Jed, the Poorhouse boy. New ed. (Illus.). N.D. Henry T. Coates & Co.
--Jed, the Poorhouse Boy. LC 9-22005. (Illus.). 19cm. 368p. (Winston Ser.). 1899. John C. Winston.
--Jed, the Poorhouse Boy, 1 of 3 Vols. (How to Rise Library Ser.). N.D. Set. John C. Winston Co.
--Jed, the Poorhouse Boy. (Illus.). (Eclipse Ser.). N.D. John C. Winston.
--Jed, the Poorhouse Boy. LC 9-220059. iv, 363 p. front., plates. 19 cm. c.1899. The John C. Winston Co.
--Jed, the Poorhouse Boy: or, From Poverty to Title. (Alger Ser.). N.D. Hurst & Co.
--Joe's Luck. (Illus.). (The Boys' Home Ser.). N.D. A. L. Burt.
--Joe's Luck. (Illus.). (The Alger Series for Boys). N.D. A. L. Burt's Pubs.
--Joe's Luck, 1 of 3 vols. (Illus.). (The Train Boy Ser.). N.D. Set. A. L. Burt's Pubs.
--Joe's Luck. (Illus.). (The Chimney Corner Ser.). N.D. A. L. Burt.
--Joe's Luck. (Alger Ser.). N.D. World Publishing Co.
--Joe's Luck: Or, Always Wide Awake. (Alger Ser.). N.D. Hurst & Co.
--Julius. (Illus.). 1905. John C. Winston & Co.

--Sink or Swim: Or, Harry Raymond's Resolve. LC 49-404952. 314 p. 20 cm. N.D. A.L. Burt Co.
--Sink or Swim: Or, Harry Raymond's Resolve. (Alger Ser.). N.D. Hurst & Co.
--Sink or Swim: Or, Harry Raymond's Resolve, 1 of 4 Vols. (Illus.). (Luck and Pluck Ser.: No. 1). 1888. Porter & Coates.
--Slow and Sure. (The Rugby Ser.). 1905. Set. A L Burt Co.
--Slow and Sure. (The Chimney Corner Ser.). N.D. A. L. Burt.
--Slow and Sure. Empire ed. 1905. American News Co.
--Slow and Sure. (Boys' Select Library of Famous Alger Books). N.D. Consolidated Retail Booksellers.
--Slow and Sure. (Illus.). 1905. John C. Winston & Co.
--Slow and Sure, 1 of 4 vols. (Tattered Tom Ser.). N.D. Set. John C. Winston Co.
--Slow and Sure. (Illus.). (Eclipse Ser.). N.D. John C. Winston.
--Slow & Sure, 1 of 4 vols. (Tattered Tom Ser.: First Ser.). 1891. Set. Porter & Coates.
--Slow and Sure. (Illus.). N.D. Thompson & Thomas.
--Slow and Sure: Books for Boys, (The Chimney Corner Ser.). 1905. Set. A L Burt Co.
--Slow and Sure: Or, From the Sidewalk to the Shop. (Alger Ser.). N.D. Hurst & Co.
--Slow and Sure: or, From the Sidewalk to the Shop, 4 of 4, Vol. 4. (Horatio Alger's Books for Boys). (Tattered Tom Ser.: No. 1). N.D. Loring.
--Slow and Sure: Or, From the Sidewalk to the Shop, 1 of 4 Vols. (Illus.). (Tattered Tom Ser.: No. 1). N.D. Porter & Coates.
--Slow and Sure: Or, From the Street to the Shop. LC 25-23756. 1 p. l., iv, 7-244 p. 19 cm. (Lettered on cover: Fireside series for boys. no. 60). 1872. W. L. Allison Company.
--Slow and Sure: Or, The Sidewalk to the Shop. (Illus.). (Tattered Tom Ser.). 1888. Porter & Caotes.
--Slow and Sure: The Story of Paul Hoffman, the Young Street-Merchant. LC 52-56519. 280 p. front. 20 cm. 1907. Burt.
--Store Boy. Empire ed. 1905. American News Co.
--The Store Boy: Books for Boys. (The Chimney Corner Ser.). 1905. Set. A L Burt Co.
--The Store Boy: Or, the Fortunes of Ben Barclay. (The Rugby Ser.). 1905. Set. A L Burt Co.
--The Store Boy: Or, the Fortunes of Ben Barclay. (Illus.). (The Chimney Corner Ser.). N.D. A. L. Burt.
--The Store Boy: Or, the Fortunes of Ben Barclay. (Boys' Select Library of Famous Alger Books for Boys). N.D. Consolidated Retail Booksellers.
--The Store Boy: Or, The Fortunes of Ben Barclay, 1 of 4 vols. (Illus.). (Roundabout Lib.). (Way To Success Ser.). N.D. Set. Henry T. Coates & Co.
--Store Boy: Or, The Fortunes of Ben Barclay. (Alger Ser.). N.D. Hurst & Co.
--The Store Boy: Or, the Fortunes of Ben Barclay, 1 of 4 vols. (Roundabout Library). (Way to Success Ser.). N.D. Set. John C. Winston Co.
--Store Boy: Or, the Fortunes of Ben Barclay. (Illus.). (Eclipse Ser.). N.D. John C. Winston.
--The Store Boy: Or, the Fortunes of Ben Barclay, 1 of 4 vols. (Way to Success Ser.). 1891. Set. Porter & Coates.
--The Store Boy: Or, the Fortunes of Ben Barclay. (Illus.). (Atlantic Ser.). N.D. Porter & Coates.
--The Storm's Gift. (Illus.). N.D. Thomas Nelson & Sons.
--Strive and Succeed. (Illus.). 1905. John C. Winston & Co.
--Strive and Succeed. (Illus.). (Luck and Pluck First Ser.). 1888. Porter & Coates.
--Strive and Succeed: Books for Boys. (The Chimney Corner Ser.). 1905. Set. A L Burt Co.
--Strive and Succeed: Julius: Or, The Street Boy Out West and The Store Boy; or, The Fortunes of Ben Barclay. LC 67-12645. 146, 173 p. 22cm. 1967. Holt, Rinehart and Winston.
--Strive and Succeed: Or, the Progress of Walter Conrad. (The Rugby Ser.). 1905. Set. A L Burt Co.
--Strive and Succeed: Or, the Progress of Walter Conrad. Empire ed. 1905. American News Co.
--Strive and Succeed: Or, the Progress of Walter Conrad. (Boys' Select Library of Famous Alger Books). N.D. Consolidated Retail Booksellers.
--Strive and Succeed: Or, The Progress of Walter Conrad, 1 of 4 vols. (Illus.). (Luck and Pluck Ser.: No. 1). N.D. Set. Henry T. Coates & Co.
--Strive and Succeed: or, The Progress of Walter Conrad. (Alger Ser.). N.D. Hurst & Co.
--Strive and Succeed: Or, the Progress of Walter Conrad, 1 of 4 Vols. (Luck and Pluck Ser.). N.D. Set. John C. Winston Co.
--Strive and Succeed: Or, the Progress of Walter Conrad. (Illus.). (Eclipse Ser.). N.D. John C. Winston.
--Strive and Succeed: Or, The Progress of Walter Conrad, 4 of 4, Vol. 4. (Luck and Pluck Ser.: No. 1). N.D. Loring.
--Strive and Succeed: Or, The Progress of Walter Conrad. LC 72-78977. 215 p. 22cm. 1972. (ISBN 0-912064-04-8). Media Books.
--Strive & Succeed: Or, the Progress of Walter Conrad, 1 of 4 vols. (Luck & Pluck Ser.: No. 1). 1891. Set. Porter & Coates.
--Strive and Suceed: Or, The Progress of Walter Conrad, 4 of 4 Vols. (Illus.). (Luck and Pluck Ser.). N.D. Porter & Coates.
--Strong and Steady. N.D. Consolidated Retail Booksellers.
--Strong and Steady. (Illus.). 1905. John C. Winston & Co.
--Strong and Steady: Books for Boys, 30 vols. (The Chimney Corner Ser.). 1905. Set. A L Burt Co.
--Strong and Steady: Or, Paddle Your Own Canoe. (The Rugby Ser.). 1905. Set. A L Burt Co.
--Strong and Steady: Or, Paddle Your Own Canoe. (The Chimney Corner Ser.). N.D. A. L. Burt.
--Strong and Steady: Or, Paddle Your Own Canoe. Empire ed. 1905. American News Co.
--Strong and Steady: or, Paddle Your own Canoe. (Alger Series for Boys.). N.D. Hurst & Co.
--Strong and Steady: Or, Paddle Your Own Canoe. LC 52-565161. 362 p. front. 20 cm. 1911, c.1871. J.C. Winston Co.
--Strong and Steady: Or, Paddle Your Own Canoe, 1 of 4 Vols. (Luck and Pluck ser.). N.D. Set. John C. Winston Co.
--Strong and Steady: Or, Paddle Your Own Canoe. (Illus.). (Winston Ser.). N.D. John C. Winston.
--Strong and Steady: Or, Paddle Your Own Canoe. (Illus.). (Eclipse Ser.). N.D. John C. Winston.
--Strong and Steady: or, Paddle Your Own Canoe, 1 of 4 Vols. (Illus.). (Luck and Pluck First Ser.: No. 1). 1888. Porter & Coates.
--Strong & Steady: Or, Paddle Your Own Canoe, 1 of 4 vols. (Luck & Pluck Ser.: No. 1). 1891. Set. Porter & Coates.
--Strong and Steady: The Story of a Successful Boy. LC 52-565133. 371 p. front. 20 cm. 1907. Burt.
--Struggling Upward: Or, Luke Larkin's Luck. (Illus.). (The Chimney Corner Ser.). N.D. A. L. Burt.
--Struggling Upward: Or, Luke Larkin's Luck. LC 84-7977. 1984. (ISBN 0-486-24737-6). Dover Publications.
--Struggling Upward: Or, Luke Larkin's Luck, 1 of 4 vols. (Illus.). (Roundabout Lib.). (Way To Success Ser.). N.D. Set. Henry T. Coates & Co.
--Struggling Upward: or, Luke Larkin's Luck. (Alger Ser.). N.D. Hurst & Co.
--Struggling Upward: Or, Luke Larkin's Luck, 1 of 4 vols. (Roundabout Library). (Way to Success Ser.). N.D. Set. John C. Winston Co.
--Struggling Upward: Or, Luke Larkin's Luck. (Illus.). (Eclipse Ser.). N.D. John C. Winston.
--Struggling Upward: Or, Luke Larkin's Luck. a nautilus facsim. 1st ed. LC 72-158557. (Illus.). 333, 2 p. 19cm. 1971, c.1890. (ISBN 0-87874-005-8). Nautilus Books.
--Struggling Upward: Or, Luke Larkin's Luck, 1 of 4 vols. (Way to Success Ser.). 1891. Set. Porter & Coates.
--Tattered Tom: Or, the Story of a Street Arab, 1 of 4 Vols. (Tattered Tom Ser.). N.D. Set. John C. Winston Co.
--Tattered Tom: or, The Story of a Street Arab, 1 of 4, Vol. 1. (Horatio Alger's Books for Boys). (Tattered Tom Ser.: No. 1). N.D. Loring.
--Tattered Tom: or, The Story of a Street Arab. (Illus.). (Tattered Tom Series.). 1888. Porter & Coates.
--Tattered Tom: Or, the Story of a Street Arab, 1 of 4 vols. (Tattered Tom First Ser.). 1891. Set. Porter & Coates.
--The Telegraph Boy: Or, Making His Way in New York. (Illus.). (The Chimney Corner Ser.). N.D. A. L. Burt.
--The Telegraph Boy: Or, Making His Way in New York. (Alger Series for Boys). N.D. Hurst & Co.
--The Telegraph Boy: Or, Making His Way in New York. (Illus.). (Eclipse Ser.). N.D. John c. Winston.
--The Telegraph Boy: Or, Making His Way in New York. (Illus.). (Tattered Tom Second Ser.). 1888. Porter & Coates.
--The Telegraph Boy: Or, Making His Way in New York, 1 of 4 vols. (Tattered Tom Second Ser.). 1891. Set. Porter & Coates.
--The Tin Box, and What it contained. (Illus.). (The Chimney Corner Ser.). N.D. A. L. Burt.
--Tin Box, and What it Contained. (Alger Series for Boys). N.D. Hurst & Co.
--Tom Brace, (Illus.). (Famous Books for Boys Ser.: No. 26). 1950. Set. H M Caldwell Co.
--Tom Brace. LC 4-34566. 18cm. 254p. (Medal Library: No. 122). 1901. Street & Smith.
--Tom Temple's Career. (Illus.). (The Boys' Home Ser.). N.D. A. L. Burt.
--Tom Temple's Career. (Illus.). (The Alger Series for Boys). N.D. A. L. Burt's Pubs.
--Tom Temple's Career, 1 of 3 vols. (Illus.). (The Errand Boy Ser.). N.D. Set. A. L. Burt's Pubs.
--Tom Temple's Career. (Illus.). (The Chimney Corner Ser.). N.D. A. L. Burt.
--Tom Temple's Career. (Illus.). (Alger Ser.). N.D. Hurst & Co.
--Tom Thatcher's Fortune. LC 24-22205. (277 p. incl. front., illus. 19 cm.). c.1888. A. L. Burt.
--Tom Thatcher's Fortune. (Illus.). (The Boys' Home Ser.). N.D. A. L. Burt.
--Tom Thatcher's Fortune. (Illus.). (The Alger Series for Boys). N.D. A. L. Burt's Pubs.
--Tom Thatcher's Fortune, 1 of 3 vols. (Illus.). (The Train Boy Ser.). N.D. Set. A. L. Burt's Pubs.
--Tom Thatcher's Fortune. (Illus.). (The Chimney Corner Ser.). N.D. A. L. Burt.
--Tom Thatcher's Fortune. (Illus.). (Alger Ser.). N.D. Hurst & Co.
--Tom, the Bootblack: Books for Boys, (The Chimney Corner Ser.). 1905. Set. A L Burt Co.
--Tom, the Bootblack: Or, A Western Boy's Success. (The Rugby Ser.). 1905. Set. A L Burt Co.
--Tom, the Bootblack: Or, A Western Boy's Success, 1 of 3 vols. (Illus.). (The Newsboy Ser.). N.D. Set. A. L. Burt's Pubs.
--Tom, the Bootblack: Or, A Western Boy's Success. (Boys' Select Library of Famous Alger Books). N.D. Consolidated Retail Booksellers.
--Tom, the Bootblack: Or, A Western Boy's Success. (Alger Series for Boys). N.D. Hurst & Co.
--Tom, the Bootblack: Or, The Road to Success. (Illus.). (The Alger Series for Boys). N.D. A. L. Burt's Pubs.
--Tom, the Hero. (Illus.). (The Alger Series for Boys). N.D. A. L. Burt's Pubs.
--Tom Tracy, 39 vols. (Illus.). (Famous Books for Boys Ser.: No. 27). 1905. Set. H M Caldwell Co.
--Tom Tracy: Or, The Trials of a New York Newsboy. Putnam, Arthur Lee, pseud. 12cm. 208p. (Medal Library: No. 51). 1900. Street & Smith.
--Tom Turner's Legacy. (Illus.). (The Chimney Corner Ser.). N.D. A. L. Burt.
--Tom Turner's Legacy. (Alger Ser.). N.D. Hurst & Co.
--Tom Turner's Legacy. Davis, J. Watson, illus. LC 2-17549. 20cm. 316p. 1902. A. L. Burt Company.
--Tony, the Hero: A Brave Boy's Adventures With a Tramp, 1 0f 3 vols. (Illus.). 19p. (The Newboy Ser.). 1890. Set. A. L. Burt's Pubs.
--Tony, the Tramp: or, Right Might. (Alger Ser.). N.D. Hurst & Co.
--The Train Boy, 1 of 3 vols. (Illus.). (The Train Boy Ser.). N.D. Set. A. L. Burt's Pubs.
--The Train Boy. LC 13-177514. 298 p. incl. front. 19 cm. 1883. G. W. Carleton & Co.
--The Train Boy. Gardner, Ralph D., illus. LC 73-89619. (Illus.). 298 p., 6 leaves of plates. 23cm. 1975, c.1883. (ISBN 0-88411-807-X). Aeonian Press.
--The Treasure-Finders. (Illus.). (The Alger Series for Boys). N.D. A. Burt's Pubs.
--Try and Trust, (The Rugby Ser.). 1905. Set. A L Burt Co.
--Try and Trust. (Boys' Select Library of Famous Alger Books). N.D. Consolidated Retail Booksellers.
--Try and Trust. (Illus.). 1905. John C. Winston & Co.
--Try and Trust, 1 of 4 Vols. (Luck and Pluck Second Ser.). N.D. Set. John C. Winston Co.
--Try and Trust. (Illus.). (Eclipse Ser.). N.D. John C. Winston.
--Try & Trust, 1 of 4 vols. (Luck & Pluck Ser.: Second Ser.). 1891. Set. Porter & Coates.
--Try and Trust: or, Abner Holden's Bound Boy. (Alger Ser.). N.D. Hurst & Co.
--Try and Trust: Or, The Story of a Bound Boy, Books for Boys, (The Chimney Corner Ser.). 1905. Set. A L Burt Co.
--Try and Trust: or, the Story of a Bound Boy. (Illus.). (Luck Pluck Second Ser.). 1888. Porter & Coates.
--Victor Vane: Or, The Young Secretary. (Illus.). (Victory Ser.). N.D. Henry T. Coates & Co.
--Victor Vane: Or, The Young Secretary, 1 of 3 vols. (Victory Ser.). N.D. Set. John C. Winston Co.
--Wait and Hope. (Illus.). (The Chimney Corner Ser.). N.D. A. L. Burt.
--Wait and Hope, 1 of 4 Vols. (Brave and Bold Ser.). N.D. Set. John C. Winston Co.
--Wait and Hope. (Illus.). (Winston Ser.). N.D. John C. Winston.
--Wait and Hope. (Eclipse Ser.). N.D. John C. Winston.
--Wait & Hope, 1 of 4 vols. (Brave & Bold Ser.). 1891. Set. Porter & Coates.
--Wait and Hope: or, A Plucky Boy's Luck. (Alger Ser.). N.D. Hurst & Co.
--Wait and Hope: or, Ben Bradford's Motto, 1 of 4 Vols. (Illus.). (Brave and Bold Ser.). 1888. Porter & Coates.
--Wait and Win. (Illus.). (The Chimney Corner Ser.). N.D. A. L. Burt.
--Wait and Win; the Story of Jack Drummond's Pluck. Davis, J. Watson, illus. LC 8-5581. i p. l., 279 p. front., plates. 19 1/2 cm. c.1908. A. L. Burt Company.
--Walter Griffith: Or, The Adventures of a Young Street Salesman. LC 1-26279. 19cm. 253p. 1901. Sreet & Smith.
--Walter Sherwood's Probation. (Illus.). (The Chimney Corner Ser.). N.D. A. L. Burt.
--Walter Sherwood's Probation. LC 37-18316. iv, 351 p. front., plates. 19 1/2 cm. 1897. H. T. Coates & Co.
--Walter Sherwood's Probation. (Good Fortune Ser.). N.D. Henry T. Coates & Co.
--Walter Sherwood's Probation, 1 of 3 vols. (Good Fortune Library Ser.). N.D. Set. John C. Winston Co.
--Walter Sherwood's Probation. (Illus.). (Winston Ser.). N.D. John C. Winston.
--Walter Sherwood's Probation. (Illus.). (Eclipse Ser). N.D. John C. Winston.
--Walter Sherwood's Probation: Or, Cool Head Warm Heart. (Illus.). (Alger Ser.). N.D. Hurst & Co.
--The Western Boy: Or, The Road to Success. N.D. American News Co.
--The Western Boy: Or, Tom the Bootblack. (Illus.). N.D. Thompson & Thomas.
--The World Before Him. (Illus.). 19cm. 383p. (The Little People's Ser.). 1902. Penn Publishing Co.
--The World Before Him. Mason, Robert L., illus. (Adventure Stories Ser.). N.D. Penn Publishing Co.
--The Young Acrobat. (Illus.). (The Chimney Corner Ser.). N.D. A. L. Burt.
--The Young Acrobat. (Boys' Select Library of Famous Alger Books). N.D. Consolidated Retail Booksellers.
--The Young Acrobat. N.D. David McKay.
--The Young Acrobat, (Illus.). (Famous Books for Boys Ser.: No. 33). 1905. Set. H M Caldwell Co.
--The Young Acrobat, 1 of 64 vols. (Young America Library: No. 60). 1900. Set. Hurst & Co.
--The Young Acrobat, of the Great North American Circus. LC 62-55511. (Illus.). 19cm. 192p. (Alger Ser.). N.D. Hurst & Co.
--The Young Acrobat of the Great North American Circus. 12cm. 208p. (Medal Library: No. 42). 1900. Street & Smith.
--The Young Adventurer. (Illus.). (The Chimney Corner Ser.). N.D. A. L. Burt.
--The Young Adventurer, 1 of 4 Vols. (Roundabout Library). (Pacific Ser.). N.D. Set. John C. Winston Co.
--The Young Adventurer. (Illus.). (Eclipse Ser.). N.D. John C. Winston.
--The Young Adventurer. (Illus.). (Pacific Ser.). 1888. Porter & Coates.
--The Young Adventurer, 1 of 4 vols. (Pacific Ser.). 1891. Set. Porter & Coates.
--The Young Adventurer: Or, Tom's Trip Across the Plains, 1 of 4 Vols. (Illus.). (Pacific Ser.). N.D. Porter & Coates.
--The Young Bank Messenger. 12cm. 325p. 1898. H. T. Coates & Co.
--The Young Bank Messenger, 1 of 3 vols. (Illus.). (Good Fortune Ser.). N.D. Set. Henry T. Coates & Co.
--The Young Bank Messenger, 1 of 3 Vols. (Good Fortune Library Ser.). N.D. Set. John C. Winston Co.
--The Young Bank Messenger. (Illus.). (Winston Ser.). N.D. John C. Winston.
--The Young Bank Messenger. (Illus.). (Eclipse Ser.). N.D. John C. Winston.
--The Young Bank Messenger. LC 42-44505. iv, 325 p. col. front., col. plates. 19 cm. c.1898. The John C. Winston Co.
--The Young Boatman. (Illus.). (Adventure Stories Ser.). N.D. Penn Publishing Co.
--The Young Boatman. (Illus.). (The Little People's Ser.). N.D. Penn Publishing Co.
--The Young Circus Rider, 1 of 4 Vols. (Roundabout Library). (Atlantic Ser.). N.D. Set. John C. Winston Co.
--The Young Circus Rider, 1 of 4 vols. (Atlantic Ser.). 1891. Set. Porter & Coates.
--The Young Circus Rider: Or, The Mystery of Robert Rudd, 1 of 4 vols. (Illus.). (Roundabout Lib.). (Atlantic Ser.). N.D. Set. Henry T. Coates & Co.
--The Young Circus Rider: or, The Mystery of Robert Rudd. (Illus.). (Atlantic Ser.). 1888. Porter & Coates.
--The Young Explorer. (Illus.). (The Chimney Corner Ser.). N.D. A. L. Burt.

--The Young Explorer. (Illus.). (Eclipse Ser.). N.D. John C. Winston.
--The Young Explorer: or, Among the Sierras, 1 of 4 Vols. (Illus.). (Pacific Ser.). 1888. Porter & Coates.
--The Young Explorer: Or, Among the Sierras. (Illus.). N.D. Porter & Coates.
--Young Explorer: Or, Claiming His Fortune. (Alger Ser.). N.D. Hurst & Co.
--The Young Explorers, 1 of 4 Vols. (Roundabout Library). (Pacific Ser.). N.D. Set. John C. Winston co.
--The Young Explorers, 1 of 4 vols. (Pacific Ser.). 1891. Set. Porter & Coates.
--The Young Miner. (Illus.). (The Chimney Corner Ser.). N.D. A. L. Burt.
--The Young Miner, 1 of 4 Vols. (Roundabout Library). (Pacific Ser.). N.D. Set. John C. Winston Co.
--The Young Miner. (Illus.). (Eclipse Ser.). N.D. John C. Winston.
--The Young Miner, 1 of 4 vols. (Pacific Ser.). 1891. Set. Porter & Coates.
--The Young Miner: or, Tom Nelson in California, 1 of 4 Vols. (Illus.). (Pacific Ser.). 1888. Porter & Coates.
--The Young Miner: Or, Tom Nelson Out West. (Alger Ser.). N.D. Hurst & Co.
--The Young Musician. (Illus.). (The Chimney Corner Ser.). N.D. A. L. Burt.
--The Young Musician. (Illus.). (The Little People's Ser.). N.D. Penn Publishing Co.
--The Young Musician. Deland, Clyde O., illus. LC 6-11304. 341 p. front., 6 pl. 19 1/2 cm. (The Alger Bks.). 1906. The Penn Publishing Company.
--The Young Musician: or, Fighting His Way. (Alger Ser.). N.D. Hurst & Co.
--The Young Outlaw, (The Chimney Corner Ser.). 1905. Set. A L Burt Co.
--The Young Outlaw, (The Rugby Ser.). 1905. Set. A L Burt Co.
--The Young Outlaw. (Illus.). (The Chimney Corner Ser.). N.D. A. L. Burt.
--The Young Outlaw. Empire ed. 1905. American News Co.
--The Young Outlaw. (Boys' Select Library of Famous Alger Books). N.D. Consolidated Retail Booksellers.
--The Young Outlaw. (Illus.). 1905. John C. Winston & Co.
--The Young Outlaw, 1 of 4 Vols. (Tattered Tom Second Ser.). N.D. Set. John C. Winston Co.
--The Young Outlaw. (Illus.). (Winston Ser.). N.D. John C. Winston.
--The Young Outlaw. (Illus.). (Eclipse Ser.). N.D. John C. Winston.
--Young Outlaw: or, Adrift in the Streets. (Alger Ser.). N.D. Hurst & Co.
--The Young Outlaw: Or, Adrift in the Streets, 1 of 4 vols. (Tattered Tom Ser.: No. 2). 1891. Set. Porter & Coates.
--The Young Outlaw: or, Adrift in the World, 2 of 4, Vol. 2. (Horatio Alger's Books for Boys). (Tattered Tom Ser.: No. 2). N.D. Loring.
--The Young Outlaw: Or, Adrift in the World, 1 of 4 Vols. (Illus.). (Tattered Tom Ser.: No. 2). N.D. Porter & Coates.
--Young Salesman. (The Chimney Corner Ser.). 1905. Set. A L Burt Co.
--The Young Salesman, (The Rugby Ser.). 1905. Set. A L Burt Co.
--The Young Salesman, 1 of 3 vols. (Illus.). (Frank and Fearless Ser.). N.D. Set. Henry T. Coates & Co.
--The Young Salesman, 1 of 3 Vols. (Frank and Fearless Ser.). N.D. Set. John C. Winston Co.
--The Young Salesman. (Illus.). (Eclipse Ser.). N.D. John C. Winston.
--Young Salesman: or, Scott Walton's Early Struggles. (Illus.). (Alger Ser.). N.D. Hurst & Co.

Alger, Horatio, Jr., pseud. (1862-1930)
--Ben Logan's Triumph: Or, the Boys of Boxwood Academy. Stratemeyer, Edward L.. (Written by Edward L. Stratemeyer, 1862-1930, under the pseudonym, Horatio Alger, Jr.). (Illus.). (Rise in Life Ser.). 1908. Cupples & Leon.
--Ben Logan's Triumph: Or, The Boys of Boxwood Academy. Stratemeyer, Edward L.. (Written by Edward L. Stratemeyer, 1862-1930, under the pseudonym, Horatio Alger, Jr.). Repr. of 1908 ed (Pub. by Cupples & Leon Co). (Rise in Life Ser.: Vol. 11). N.D. Grosset & Dunlap.
--Ben Logan's Triumph: Or, The Boys of Boxwood Academy. Stratemeyer, Edward L.. (Written by Edward L. Stratemeyer, 1862-1930, under the pseudonym, Horatio Alger, Jr.). Repr. of 1908 ed (Pub. by Cupples & Leon Co). (The Alger Ser.: No. 96). 1919. Street & Smith.
--From Farm to Fortune: Or, Nat Nason's Strange Experience. Stratemeyer, Edward L.. (Written by Edward L. Stratemeyer, 1862-1930, under the pseudonym, Horatio Alger, Jr.). (Illus.). Repr. of 1905 ed (Pub. by Stitt Publishing Co). (Rise in Life Ser.: Vol. 2). N.D. Grosset & Dunlap.
--From Farm to Fortune: Or, Nat Nason's Strange Experience. Stratemeyer, Edward L., 1 of 8 vols. LC 5-32734. (Written by Edward L. Stratemeyer, 1862-1930, under the pseudonym, Horatio Alger, Jr.). 19cm. 248p. (Rise in Life Ser.). 1905. Stitt Publishing.
--From Farm to Fortune: Or, Nat Nason's Strange Experience. Stratemeyer, Edward L.. (Written by Edward L. Stratemeyer, 1862-1930, under the pseudonym, Horatio Alger, Jr.). Repr. of 1905 ed (Pub. by Stitt Publishing Co). (The Alger Ser.: No. 88). 1919. Street & Smith.
--From Farm to Fortune: Or, Nat Nasson's Strange Experience. Stratemeyer, Edward L., 1 of 9 vols. (Written by Edward L. Stratemeyer, 1862-1930, under the pseudonym, Horatio Alger, Jr.). Repr. of 1905 ed (Pub. by Stitt Publishing Co). (Rise in Life Ser.). 1906. Chatterton-Peck Co.
--Jerry the Backwoods Boy: Or, The Parkhurst Teasure. Stratemeyer, Edward L., 1 0f 9 vols. (Written by Edward L. Stratemeyer, 1862-1930, under the pseudonym, Horatio Alger, Jr.). Repr. of 1904 ed (Pub. by Mershon Co). (Rise in Life Ser.). 1906. Chatterton-Peck Co.
--Jerry, the Backwoods Boy: Or, the Parkhurst Treasure. Stratemeyer, Edward L.. (Written by Edward L. Stratemeyer, 1862-1930, under the pseudonym, Horatio Alger, Jr.). (Illus.). Repr. of 1904 ed (Pub. by Mershon Co). (Rise in Life Ser.: Vol. 8). N.D. Grosset & Dunlap.
--Jerry, the Backwoods Boy: Or, The Parkhurst Treasure. Stratemeyer, Edward L., 1 of 6 vols. LC 4-29184. (Written by Edward L. Stratemeyer, 1862-1930, under the pseudonym, Horatio Alger, Jr.). 19cm. 248p. (Rise in Life Ser.). 1904. Mershon Company.
--Jerry the Backwoods Boy: Or, The Parkhurst Treasure. Stratemeyer, Edward L., 1 of 8 vols. (Written by Edward L. Stratemeyer, 1862-1930, under the pseudonym, Horatio Alger, Jr.). Repr. of 1904 ed (Pub. by Mershon Co). (Rise in Life Ser.). 1905. Stitt Publishing Co.
--Jerry the Backwoods Boy: Or, The Parkhurst Treasure. Stratemeyer, Edward L.. (Written by Edward L. Stratemeyer, 1862-1930, under the pseudonym, Horatio Alger, Jr.). Repr. of 1904 ed (Pub. by Mershon Co). (The Alger Ser.: No. 95). 1919. Street & Smith.
--Joe the Hotel Boy: Or, Winning Out by Pluck. Stratemeyer, Edward L.. LC 6-25693. (Written by Edward L. Stratemeyer, 1862-1930, under the pseudonym, Horatio Alger, Jr.). 3 p. l. 268 p. front., plates 19 1/2 cm. (Rise in Life Ser.). 1906. Cupples & Leon.
--Joe the Hotel Boy: Or, Winning Out by Pluck. Stratemeyer, Edward L.. (Written by Edward L. Stratemeyer, 1862-1930, under the pseudonym, Horatio Alger, Jr.). Repr. of 1906 ed (Pub. by Cupples & Leon Co). (Rise in Life Ser.: Vol. 10). N.D. Grosset & Dunlap.
--Joe, the Hotel Boy: Or, Winning out by Pluck. Stratemeyer, Edward L.. (Written by Edward L. Stratemeyer, 1862-1930, under the pseudonym, Horatio Alger, Jr.). Repr. of 1906 ed (Pub. by Cupples & Leon Co). (The Alger Ser.: No. 90). 1919. Street & Smith.
--Lost at Sea: Or, Robert Roscoe's Strange Cruise. Stratemeyer, Edward L., 1 of 9 vols. (Written by Edward L. Stratemeyer, 1862-1930, under the pseudonym, Horatio Alger, Jr.). Repr. of 1904 ed (Pub. by Mershon Co). (Rise in Life Ser.). 1906. Chatterton-Peck Co.
--Lost at Sea: Or, Robert Roscoe's Strange Cruise. Stratemeyer, Edward L.. (Written by Edward L. Stratemeyer, 1862-1930, under the pseudonym, Horatio Alger, Jr.). (Illus.). Repr. of 1904 ed (Pub. by Mershon Co). (Rise in Life Ser.: Vol. 7). N.D. Grosset & Dunlap.
--Lost at Sea: Or, Robert Roscoe's Strange Cruise. Stratemeyer, Edward L., 1 of 6 vols. LC 4-28955. (Written by Edward L. Stratemeyer, 1862-1930, under the pseudonym, Horatio Alger, Jr.). 19cm. 250p. (Rise in Life Ser.). 1904. Mershon Company.
--Lost at Sea: Or, Robert Roscoe's Strange Cruise. Stratemeyer, Edward L., 1 of 8 vols. (Written by Edward L. Stratemeyer, 1862-1930, under the pseudonym, Horatio Alger, Jr.). Repr. of 1904 ed (Pub. by Mershon Co). (Rise in Life Ser.). 1905. Stitt Publishing Co.
--Lost at Sea: Or, Robert Roscoe's Strange Cruise. Stratemeyer, Edward L.. (Written by Edward L. Stratemeyer, 1862-1930, under the pseudonym, Horatio Alger, Jr.). Repr. of 1904 ed (Pub. by Mershon Co). (The Alger Ser.: No. 87). 1919. Street & Smith.
--Randy of the River: Or, The Adventures of a Young Deckhand. Stratemeyer, Edward L., 1 of 9 vols. LC 6-42425. (Written by Edward L. Stratemeyer, 1862-1930, under the pseudonym, Horatio Alger, Jr.). vi, 7-274 p. front., plates. 19 cm. (Rise in Life Ser.). c.1906. Chatterton-Peck Company.
--Randy of the River: Or, the Adventures of a Young Deckhand. Stratemeyer, Edward L.. (Written by Edward L. Stratemeyer, 1862-1930, under the pseudonym, Horatio Alger, Jr.). (Illus.). Repr. of 1906 ed (Pub. by Chatterton-Peck Co). (Rise in Life Ser.: Vol. 9). N.D. Grosset & Dunlap.
--Randy of the River: Or, The Adventures of a Young Deckhand. Stratemeyer, Edward L.. (Written by Edward L. Stratemeyer, 1862-1930, under the pseudonym, Horatio Alger, Jr.). Repr. of 1906 ed (Pub. by Chatterton-Peck Co). (The Alger Ser.: No. 94). 1919. Street & Smith.
--The Young Book Agent: Or, Frank Hardy's Road to Success. Stratemeyer, Edward L., 1 of 9 vols. (Written by Edward L. Stratemeyer, 1862-1930, under the pseudonym, Horatio Alger, Jr.). Repr. of 1905 ed (Pub. by Stitt Publishing Co). (Rise in Life Ser.). 1906. Chatterton-Peck Co.
--The Young Book Agent: Or, Frank Hardy's Road to Success. Stratemeyer, Edward L.. (Written by Edward L. Stratemeyer, 1862-1930, under the pseudonym, Horatio Alger, Jr.). (Illus.). Repr. of 1905 ed (Pub. by Stitt Publishing Co). (Rise in Life Ser: Vol. 1). N.D. Grosset & Dunlap.
--The Young Book Agent: Or, Frank Hardy's Road to Success. Stratemeyer, Edward L., 1 of 8 vols. LC 5-32388. (Written by Edward L. Stratemeyer, 1862-1930, under the pseudonym, Horatio Alger, Jr.). 19cm. 272p. (Rise in Life Ser.). 1905. Stitt Publishing Company.
--The Young Book Agent: Or, Frank Hardy's Road to Success. Stratemeyer, Edward L.. (Written by Edward L. Stratemeyer, 1862-1930, under the pseudonym, Horatio Alger, Jr.). Repr. of 1905 ed (Pub. by Stitt Publishing Co). (The Alger Ser.: No. 97). 1919. Street & Smith.

Alger, Horatio, Jr. (1832-1899) & Chenay, Olive Augusta Alger (1833-)
--Seeking His Fortune. (Illus.). N.D. Ward & Drummond.
--Seeking His Fortune and Other Dialogues. (Plucky Fellows Library). N.D. George Routledge & Sons.

Alger, Horatio, Jr. (1832-1899) & Ellis, Edward Sylvester (1840-1916)
--Tom Temple's Career: Including "Over and Under" & "A Strange Craft. 277 p. incl. front., illus. 19 cm. N.D. A. L. Burt C.

Alger, Horatio, Jr. (1832-1899) & Winfield, Arthur M., pseud. (1862-1930)
--Falling in with Fortune: Or, Experiences of a Young Secretary. Stratemeyer, Edward L.. (Arthur M. Winfield is a pseudonym of Edward L. Stratemeyer, 1862-1930). (Illus.). Repr. of 1900 ed (Pub. by Mershon Co). (Rise in Life Ser.: Vol. 4). N.D. Grosset & Dunlap.
--Falling in with Fortune: Or, The Experiences of a Young Secretary, 1 of 9 vols. Stratemeyer, Edward L.. (Arthur M. Winfield is a pseudonym of Edward L. Stratemeyer, 1862-1930). Repr. of 1900 ed (Pub. by Mershon Co). (Rise in Life Ser.). 1906. Chatterton-Peck Co.
--Falling in with Fortune: Or, The Experiences of a Young Secretary. Stratemeyer, Edward L.. (Arthur M. Winfield is a pseudonym of Edward L. Stratemeyer, 1862-1930). 12cm. 282p. (Rise in Life Ser.: Vol. 2). 1900. Mershon Co.
--Falling in with Fortune: Or, The Experiences of a Young Secretary, 1 of 8 vols. Stratemeyer, Edward L.. (Arthur M. Winfield is a pseudonym of Edward L. Stratemeyer, 1862-1930). Repr. of 1900 ed (Pub. by Mershon Co). (Rise in Life Ser.). 1905. Stitt Publishing Co.
--Falling in with Fortune: Or, The Experiences of a Young Secretary. Stratemeyer, Edward L.. (Arthur M. Winfield is a pseudonym of Edward L. Stratemeyer, 1862-1930). Repr. of 1900 ed (Pub. by Mershon Co). (The Alger Ser.: No. 92). 1919. Street & Smith.
--Nelson the Newsboy: Or, Afloat in New York, 1 of 9 vols. Stratemeyer, Edward L.. (Arthur M. Winfield is a pseudonym of Edward L. Stratemeyer, 1862-1930). Repr. of 1901 ed (Pub. by Mershon Co). (Rise in Life Ser.). 1906. Chatterton-Peck Co.
--Nelson, the Newsboy: Or, Afloat in New York. Stratemeyer, Edward L.. (Arthur M. Winfield is a pseudonym of Edward L. Stratemeyer, 1862-1930). (Illus.). Repr. of 1901 ed (Pub. by Mershon Co). (Rise in Life Ser.: Vol. 6). N.D. Grosset & Dunlap.
--Nelson the Newsboy: Or, Afloat in New York, 1 of 8 vols. Stratemeyer, Edward L.. (Arthur M. Winfield is a pseudonym of Edward L. Stratemeyer, 1862-1930). Repr. of 1901 ed (Pub. by Mershon Co). (Rise in Life Ser.). 1905. Stitt Publishing Co.
--Nelson the Newsboy: Or, Afloat in New York. Stratemeyer, Edward L.. (Arthur M. Winfield is a pseudonym of Edward L. Stratemeyer, 1862-1930). Repr. of 1901 ed (Pub. by Mershon Co). (The Alger Ser.: No. 93). 1919. Street & Smith.
--Nelson the Newsboy: Or, Afloat in New York. Stratemeyer, Edward L.. LC 1-26044. (Arthur M. Winfield is a pseudonym of Edward L. Stratemeyer, 1862-1930). vi, 276 p. front., pl. 19 cm. (Rise in Life Ser.: Vol. 4). 1901. The Mershon Co.
--Out for Business: Or, Robert Frost's Strange Career, 1 of 9 vols. Stratemeyer, Edward L.. (Arthur M. Winfield is a pseudonym of Edward L. Stratemeyer, 1862-1930). Repr. of 1900 ed (Pub. by Mershon Co). (Rise in Life Ser.). 1906. Chatterton-Peck Co.
--Out for Business: Or, Robert Frost's Strange Career. Stratemeyer, Edward L.. (Arthur M. Winfield is a pseudonym of Edward L. Stratemeyer, 1862-1930). (Illus.). Repr. of 1900 ed (Pub. by Mershon Co). (Rise in Life Ser.: Vol. 3). N.D. Grosset & Dunlap.
--Out for Business: Or, Robert Frost's Strange Career. Stratemeyer, Edward L.. LC 4955. (Arthur M. Winfield is a pseudonym of Edward L. Stratemeyer, 1862-1930). 12cm. 267p. (Rise in Life Ser.: Vol. 1). 1900. Mershon Company.
--Out for Business: Or, Robert Frost's Strange Career, 1 of 8 vols. Stratemeyer, Edward L.. (Arthur M. Winfield is a pseudonym of Edward L. Stratemeyer, 1862-1930). Repr. of 1900 ed (Pub. by Mershon Co). (Rise in Life Ser.). 1905. Stitt Publishing Co.
--Out for Business: Or, Robert Frost's Strange Career. Stratemeyer, Edward L.. (Arthur M. Winfield is a pseudonym of Edward L. Stratemeyer, 1862-1930). Repr. of 1900 ed (Pub. by Mershon Co). (The Alger Ser.: No. 91). 1919. Street & Smith.
--Young Captain Jack: Or, The Son of a Soldier. Stratemeyer, Edward L.. LC 73-89620. (Arthur M. Winfield is a pseudonym of Edward L. Stratemeyer, 1862-1930). (Illus.). v, 262 p., 4 leaves of plates. 23cm. 1975, c.1901. (ISBN 0-88411-808-8). Aeonian Press.
--Young Captain Jack: Or, The Son of a Soldier, 1 of 9 vols. Stratemeyer, Edward L.. (Arthur M. Winfield is a pseudonym of Edward L. Stratemeyer, 1862-1930). Repr. of 1901 ed (Pub. by Mershon Co). (Rise in Life Ser.). 1906. Chatterton-Peck Co.
--Young Captain Jack: Or, the Son of a Soldier. Stratemeyer, Edward L.. (Arthur M. Winfield is a pseudonym Of Edward L. Stratemeyer, 1862-1930). (Illus.). Repr. of 1901 ed (Pub. by Mershon Co). (Rise in Life Ser.: Vol. 5). N.D. Grosset & Dunlap.
--Young Captain Jack: Or, The Son of a Soldier, 1 of 8 vols. Stratemeyer, Edward L.. (Arthur M. Winfield is a pseudonym of Edward L. Stratemeyer, 1862-1930). Repr. of 1901 ed (Pub. by Mershon Co). (Rise in Life Ser.). 1905. Stitt Publishing Co.
--Young Captain Jack: Or, The Son of a Soldier. Stratemeyer, Edward L.. (Arthur M. Winfield is a pseudonym of Edward L. Stratemeyer, 1862-1930). Repr. of 1901 ed (Pub. by Mershon Co.). (The Alger Ser.: No. 89). 1919. Street & Smith.
--Young Captain Jack: Or, The Son of a Soldier. Stratemeyer, Edward L.. LC 1-20296. (Arthur M. Winfield is a pseudonym of Edward L. Stratemeyer, 1862-1930). v, 1, 262 p. front., pl. 19 cm. (Rise in Life Ser.: Vol. 3). 1901. The Mershon Company.

Alger, Joseph, jt. auth. see June, Larry.

Alger, Joseph & Nash, Ogden (1902-1971)
--The Cricket of Carador. Rule, Christopher, illus. LC 25-90477. ix, p. 1 l., 165 p. col. front., illus., plates. 20 cm. 1925. Doubleday, Page & Co.

Alger, Leclaire Gowans see Nic Leodhas, Sorche, pseud.

Ali Baba
--Ali Baba and the Forty Thieves. N.D. E. P. Dutton & Co.
--Ali Baba and the Forty Thieves. LC 5-23030. 47, 1 p. col. front., illus. 17 x 18 cm. (Altemus' Banbury Cross series). c.1905. Henry Altemus Company.
--Ali Baba and the Forty Thieves. (Illus.). (National Fairy Tales). N.D. John E Potter & Co.
--Ali Baba and the Forty Thieves. Anderson, Anne, illus. LC 28-8652. 40 p. incl. col. front, col. illus. 19 cm. 1928. T. Nelson and Sons.
--Ali Baba and the Forty Thieves. Williams, Alexander (1939-), adapted by. Frame, Paul (1913-), illus. LC 79-115139. (Illus.). 31 p. 24cm. 1979. (ISBN 0-89799-085-4). (ISBN 0-89799-056-0). Dandelion Press.
--Ali Baba and the Forty Thieves, and Other Stories, (Illus.). (St. Nicholas Ser.). 1905. Set. A L Burt Co.

--Ali Baba: Or, The Forty Thieves. LC 44-38244. 12 p. illus. (part col.) 28 1/2 cm. (Wonder-story series). c.1889. McLoughlin Bros.
--Ali Baba: Or, The Forty Thieves. LC 44-38245. 16 p. col. illus. 27 x 28 1/2 cm. c.1898. McLoughlin Bros.

Ali-El, Yusuf
--Once Upon a Ryme Tyme for Growing Minds. Pride, Alexis & Bey, Sarah K., illus. LC 83-90101. (Illus.). 90p. (gr. k-5). 1983. (ISBN 0-912475-09-9). Natl Res Unltd.

Alice, Epstein, jt. auth. see Fenton, Carroll Lane.

Alice, Ritchie
--The Treasure of Li-Po and Other Stories. 1948. Dufour.

Alicia, Mary, tr. see Geyser, Alfons, Sr.

Alicia, Mary, tr. see Schupp, Ambrose.

Aliki, pseud., see Brandenberg, Aliki Liacouras.

Aliki, pseud. (1929-)
--At Mary Bloom's. Brandenberg, Aliki Liacouras. Aliki, pseud. (1929-), illus. Brandenberg, Aliki Liacouras. LC 75-45482. (Illus.). 32 p. 26cm. c.1976. (ISBN 0-688-80048-3). (ISBN 0-688-84048-5). Greenwillow Books.
--At Mary Bloom's. Brandenberg, Aliki Liacouras. Aliki, pseud. (1929-), illus. Brandenberg, Aliki Liacouras. LC 75-45482. (Illus.). 8 x 9 7/8. 32p. (28). (gr. k-3). 1983. (ISBN 0-688-02480-7). (ISBN 0-688-02481-5). Greenwillow.
--At Mary Bloom's. Brandenberg, Aliki Liacouras. Aliki, pseud. (1929-), illus. Brandenberg, Aliki Liacouras. LC 77-17971. (Illus.). 32 p. 23cm. (Picture puffin). 1978, c.1976. (ISBN 0-14-050278-5). Puffin Books.
--The Eggs: A Greek Folk Tale. Brandenberg, Aliki Liacouras. Aliki, pseud. (1929-), illus. Brandenberg, Aliki Liacouras. LC 69-13452. (Illus.). 32 p. 27cm. (gr. k-3). 1969. (ISBN 0-394-81091-0). Pantheon Books.
--George & the Cherry Tree. Brandenberg, Aliki Liacouras. Aliki, pseud. (1929-), illus. Brandenberg, Aliki Liacouras. LC 64-12290. (Illus.). 22cm. 32p. (gr. k-3). 1964. Dial.
--Hush Little Baby. Brandenberg, Aliki Liacouras. Aliki, pseud. (1929-), illus. Brandenberg, Aliki Liacouras. LC 68-12194. (Illus.). 24cm. 32p. (ps-1). 1968. (ISBN 0-13-448167-4, Pub. by Treehouse). (ISBN 0-13-448175-5). P-H.
--Jack & Jake. Brandenberg, Aliki Liacouras. Aliki, pseud. (1929-), illus. Brandenberg, Aliki Liacouras. LC 85-9911. (Illus.). 9 7/8 x 8. 32p. (14 pt.). (ps-3). 1986. (ISBN 0-688-06099-4). (ISBN 0-688-06100-1). Greenwillow.
--June Seven. Brandenberg, Aliki Liacouras. Aliki, pseud. (1929-), illus. Brandenberg, Aliki Liacouras. LC 72-75347. (Illus.). 32 p. (gr. 1-5). 1972. (ISBN 0-02-700400-7). Macmillan.
--Keep Your Mouth Closed, Dear. Brandenberg, Aliki Liacouras. Aliki, pseud. (1929-), illus. Brandenberg, Aliki Liacouras. LC 66-19310. (Illus.). iv. illus. pt. col 24cm. (gr. k-3). 1966. Dial Bks Young.
--Keep Your Mouth Closed, Dear. Brandenberg, Aliki Liacouras. Aliki, pseud. (1929-), illus. Brandenberg, Aliki Liacouras. LC 66-19310. (Illus.). 48p. Repr. of 1966 ed. (ps-2). 1980. (Pied Piper Bk.). Dial Bks Young.
--Keep Your Mouth Closed, Dear. Brandenberg, Aliki Liacouras. Aliki, pseud. (1929-), illus. Brandenberg, Aliki Liacouras. (Illus.). (gr. 1-3). 1966. (ISBN 0-8382-1020-1). Hale.
--My Visit to the Dinosaurs. Brandenberg, Aliki Liacouras. Aliki, pseud. (1929-), illus. Brandenberg, Aliki Liacouras. LC 70-78255. (Illus.). 3 color. 40p. (A Let's-Read-&-Find-Out Science Bk). (gr. k-3). 1969. (ISBN 0-690-57401-0, TYC-J). (ISBN 0-690-57402-9, TYC-J). (ISBN 0-690-57403-7, TYC-J). Har-Row.
--Story of Johnny Appleseed. Brandenberg, Aliki Liacouras. Aliki, pseud. (1929-), illus. Brandenberg, Aliki Liacouras. (Illus.). (ps-2). 1963. (ISBN 0-13-850800-3). (ISBN 0-13-850818-6). P-H.
--The Story of Johnny Appleseed. Brandenberg, Aliki Liacouras. library ed. Aliki, pseud. (1929-), illus. Brandenberg, Aliki Liacouras. LC 63-8507. (Illus.). 32 p. 24cm. 1963. Prentice-Hall.
--The Story of William Penn. Brandenberg, Aliki Liacouras. Aliki, pseud. (1929-), illus. Brandenberg, Aliki Liacouras. LC 64-14025. (Illus.). 32 p. 24cm. 1964. Prentice-Hall.
--The Story of William Tell. Brandenberg, Aliki Liacouras. Aliki, pseud. (1929-), illus. Brandenberg, Aliki Liacouras. LC 61-65113. unpaged. illus. 25cm. (Wonderful world book). 1961. Barnes.
--Three Gold Pieces: A Greek Folk Tale. Brandenberg, Aliki Liacouras. Brandenberg, Aliki Liacouras. LC 67-14228. (Illus.). 31 p. 27cm. 1967. Pantheon Books.
--The Twelve Months: A Greek Folktale. Brandenberg, Aliki Liacouras. Aliki, pseud. (1929-), illus. Brandenberg, Aliki Liacouras. LC 78-3554. p. cm. 1978. (ISBN 0-688-80164-1). Greenwillow Books.
--The Two of Them. Brandenberg, Aliki Liacouras. Aliki, pseud. (1929-), illus. Brandenberg, Aliki Liacouras. LC 79-10161. (Illus.). 30 p. 26cm. c.1979. (ISBN 0-688-80225-7). (ISBN 0-688-84225-9). Greenwillow Books.
--Use Your Head, Dear. Brandenberg, Aliki Liacouras. Aliki, pseud. (1929-), illus. Brandenberg, Aliki Liacouras. LC 82-11911. (Illus.). 7 1/2 x 9 1/2 cm. 48p. (14 pt.). (gr. k-3). 1983. (ISBN 0-688-01811-4). (ISBN 0-688-01812-2). Greenwillow.
--We Are Best Friends. Brandenberg, Aliki Liacouras. Aliki, pseud. (1929-), illus. Brandenberg, Aliki Liacouras. LC 81-6549. (Illus.). 34 p. 26cm. c.1982. (ISBN 0-688-00822-4). (ISBN 0-688-00823-2). Greenwillow Books.
--A Weed Is a Flower: The Life of George Washington Carver. Brandenberg, Aliki Liacouras. Aliki, pseud. (1929-), illus. Brandenberg, Aliki Liacouras. LC 65-25223. iv. (unpaged) col. illus. 24cm. c.1965. Prentice.
--The Wish Workers. Brandenberg, Aliki Liacouras. Aliki, pseud. (1929-), illus. Brandenberg, Aliki Liacouras. LC 62-15392. unpaged. illus. 20x26cm. 1962. Dial Press.

Aliki, pseud. (1929-), illus.
--Go Tell Aunt Rhody. Brandenberg, Aliki Liacouras. LC 74-681. lv. (chiefly illus.). 26cm. 1974. (ISBN 0-02-711920-3). MacMillan.

Alington, Cyril Argentine (1872-)
--Shrewsbury Fables. 19.5 cm. 84p. 1917. Longmans, Green & Co.

Alison, Annie H., jt. auth. see Lide, Alice Alison, Mrs.

Alkin, Lucy, jt. auth. see Defoe, Daniel.

Allamand, Pascale (1942-)
--The Animals Who Changed Their Colors. LC 79-196. (Illus.). 32 p. 1979. (ISBN 0-688-41900-3). (ISBN 0-688-51900-8). Lothrop, Lee & Shepard.
--The Camel Who Left the Zoo. LC 76-19372. (English Version by Michael Bullock). (Illus.). 32 p. 1977, c.1976. (ISBN 0-684-14824-2). Scribner.
--The Little Goat in the Mountains. LC 77-78094. (English Version by Michael Bullock). (Illus.). 32 p. c.1977. (ISBN 0-7232-6149-0). F. Warne.
--The Pop Rooster. LC 75-4030. (English Version by Michael Bullock). (Illus.). 32 p. c.1975. Scribner.

Allan, E. P., Mrs.
--Foxwood Boys at School, 1 of 50 vols. 267p. (Library of Best Authors). 1905. American Tract Society.
--Vacation Days at Foxwood. 224p. N.D. American Tract Society.

Allan, Mabel Esther see Estoril, Jean, pseud.

Allan, Mabel Esther see Hagon, Priscilla, pseud.

Allan, Mabel Esther see Pilgrim, Anne, pseud.

Allan, Mabel Esther (1915-)
--The Ballet Family. Whitear, A. R., illus. LC 66-15166. 190p. illus. 22cm. c.1966. Criterion.
--Ballet for Drina. Estoril, Jean, pseud. LC 58-9223. 192 p. 22cm. 1958. (ISBN 0-8149-0299-5). Vanguard Press.
--Black Forest Summer. LC 59-939495. 207p. 21cm. c.1959. Vanguard Press.
--Bridge of Friendship. LC 76-53432. 149 p. 21cm. 1977, c.1975. (ISBN 0-396-07431-6). Dodd, Mead.
--Catrin in Wales. LC 61-9009. 204p. 21cm. 1961. Vanguard Press.
--A Chill in the Lane. LC 74-733. 157 p. 22cm. 1974. (ISBN 0-8407-6384-0). Nelson.
--Clare Goes to Holland. Pilgrim, Anne, pseud. LC 62-24168. 191. 21cm. 1962. Abelard Schuman.
--Crow's Nest. Dennis, Peter (1950-), illus. (gr. 2-5). 1976. (ISBN 0-8277-4734-9). British Bk Ctr.
--Cruising to Danger. Hagon, Priscilla, pseud. Plummer, William Kirtman, illus. LC 66-139035. 192p. illus. 21cm. c.1966. World.
--The Dancing Garlands. Whitear, A. R., illus. LC 67-23455. (Illus.). 22cm. 192p. Orig. Title: The Ballet Family Again. 1968. Criterion Bks.
--Dancing to Danger. Hogan, Priscilla, pseud. Suba, Susanne (1913-), illus. LC 67-23354. (Illus.). 160 p. 21cm. 1967. World Pub. Co.
--A Dream of Hunger Moss. LC 83-14036. p. cm. 1983. (ISBN 0-396-08224-6). Dodd, Mead.
--The Flash Children. Rowe, Gavin, illus. LC 75-11445. 21cm. 119p. 1975. (ISBN 0-396-07229-1). Dodd, Mead.
--A Formidable Enemy. (gr. 7-12). 1977. (ISBN 0-590-09093-3). Scholastic Inc.
--A Formidable Enemy. LC 75-1198. 154 p. 21cm. 1975. (ISBN 0-8407-6443-X). T. Nelson.
--Hilary's Summer on Her Own. LC 61-607560. 201p. 21cm. 1961, c.1960. F. Watts.
--Home to the Island. LC 66-169781. 159p. 22cm. c.1966. Vanguard.
--The Horns of Danger. LC 81-43230. p. cm. 1981. (ISBN 0-396-07987-3). Dodd, Mead.
--An Island in a Green Sea. Robinson, Charles (1931-), illus. LC 72-75263. (Illus.). 200 p. 25cm. 1972. (ISBN 0-689-30044-1). Atheneum. **Award: (BGH).**
--Kraymer Mystery. LC 68-31715. 176p. (gr. 5-9). 1969. (ISBN 0-200-71994-7, AbS-J). Har-Row.
--A Lovely Tomorrow. LC 79-6642. 190 p. 22cm. 1980, c.1979. (ISBN 0-396-07813-3). Dodd, Mead.
--The May Day Mystery. LC 70-134561. 191 p. 22cm. 1971. (ISBN 0-200-71789-8). Criterion Books.
--The Mills Down Below. LC 80-2782. 205 p. 22cm. 1981, c.1980. (ISBN 0-396-07926-1). Dodd, Mead.
--Mystery at Saint-Hilaire. Hagon, Priscilla, pseud. Plummer, William Kirtman, illus. LC 68-26971. (Illus.). 160. 21cm. 1968. World Pub. Co.
--Mystery at the Villa Bianca. Hagon, Priscilla, pseud. Plummer, William Kirtman, illus. LC 78-81639. (Illus.). 159 p. 21cm. 1969. World Pub. Co.
--The Mystery Began in Madeira. LC 67-15256. 174 p. 22cm. 1967. Criterion Books.
--Mystery in Arles. LC 64-23321. 170 p. 22cm. 1964. Vanguard Press.
--Mystery in Manhattan. Hagon, Priscilla, pseud. Wetherbee, Margaret, illus. LC 68-28342. (Illus.). 173 p. 22cm. 1968, c.1967. Vanguard Press.
--Mystery in Rome. LC 72-90477. 191 p. 21cm. (gr. 7 up). c.1974. (ISBN 0-8149-0726-1). Vanguard Press.
--Mystery in Wales. LC 79-89664. 163 p. 21cm. 1971, c.1970. (ISBN 0-8149-0664-8). Vanguard Press.
--The Mystery of the Secret Square. Hagon, Priscilla, pseud. Abel, Raymond (1911-), illus. LC 72-89500. (Illus.). 128 p. 19cm. 1970. World Pub.
--Mystery of the Ski Slopes. LC 66-22772. 159 p. 22cm. 1966. Criterion Books.
--Mystery on the Fourteenth Floor. (Illus.). (gr. 6-9). 1965. (ISBN 0-8382-0577-1). Hale.
--Mystery on the Fourteenth Floor. Hughes, Shirley (1929-), illus. LC 65-15259. 186p. illus. 21cm. 1965, c.1964. Criterion.
--Mystery on the Fourteenth Floor. Hughes, Shirley (1929-), illus. LC 65-15259. (Illus.). (gr. 7 up). 1965. (ISBN 0-200-00088-8, AbS-J). Har-Row.
--New York for Nicola. LC 63-13791. 192 p. 22 cm. 1963. Vanguard Press.
--The Night Wind. Robinson, Charles (1931-), illus. LC 73-84819. (Illus.). 212 p. 25cm. 1974. (ISBN 0-689-30127-8). Atheneum.
--On Stage, Flory!. LC 61-6551. 185p. 21cm. 1961, c.1959. F. Watts.
--The Rising Tide. LC 76-383393. 136 p. 23cm. 1976. (ISBN 0-434-92696-5). Heinemann.
--The Rising Tide. LC 77-14653. 135 p. 22cm. 1978, c.1976. (ISBN 0-8027-6317-0). Walker.
--Romance in Italy. LC 62-11214. 192 p. 21 cm. 1962. Vanguard Press.
--Romansgrove. Owens, Gail, illus. LC 75-9628. (Illus.). 217 p. 22cm. 1975. (ISBN 0-689-30471-4). Atheneum.
--Selina's New Family. Pilgrim, Anne, pseud. Byfield, Graham, illus. LC 67-13610. (Illus.). 191. 22cm. 1967. Abelard-Schuman.
--Ship of Danger. LC 74-8986. 153 p. 22cm. 1974. (ISBN 0-200-00143-4). Criterion Books.
--The Sign of the Unicorn. Hughes, Shirley (1929-), illus. LC 63-19080. 155 p. illus. 22 cm. (Criterion book for young people). 1963. Criterion Books.
--Signpost to Switzerland. LC 64-12003. 189 p. 21cm. 1964, c.1962. Criterion Books.
--A Strange Enchantment. LC 82-5049. 191 p. 22cm. 1982, c.1981. (ISBN 0-396-08044-8). Dodd, Mead.
--Strangers in New York. Pilgrim, Anne, pseud. LC 64-22348. 192. 21cm. 1964. Abelard-Schuman.
--Strangers in Skye. LC 58-6446. 223p. 22cm. (Criterion book for young people). 1958. Criterion Books.
--A Summer in Provence. Pilgrim, Anne, pseud. LC 63-16223. 190. 21cm. 1963. Abelard-Schuman.
--Summer of Decision. Whittam, Geoffrey William (1916-), illus. LC 57-9179. 192p. illus. 21cm. 1957. Abelard-Schuman.
--Swiss Holiday. LC 57-122651. 222p. 22cm. 1957. Vanguard Press.
--Time to Go Back. LC 72-39323. 160p. 1st U.S. edition. (gr. 7 up). N.D. (ISBN 0-200-71876-2). Criterion Bks.
--The View Beyond My Father. LC 78-7736. 22cm. 192p. 1978. (ISBN 0-396-07612-2). Dodd, Mead.
--We Danced in Bloomsbury Square. Estoril, Jean, pseud. Wood, Muriel, illus. LC 78-88865. 181 p. 23cm. 1970, c.1967. (ISBN 0-8149-0253-7). (ISBN 0-695-80083-3). Follett Pub. Co.
--Wood Street Secret. Hughes, Shirley (1929-), illus. LC 70-95141. (Illus.). drawings. 128p. 1st U.S. edition. (gr. 3 up). 1970. (ISBN 0-200-72006-6). Abelard.

Allan, Marguerite Buller
--The Rhyme Garden. Allan, Marguerite Buller, illus. LC 18-2498. 64 p. col. front., illus., col. plates. 25 cm. 1917. John Lane.

Allard, Harry
--Bumps in the Night. Marshall, James (1942-), illus. LC 78-22301. (Illus.). 32 p. 27cm. c.1979. (ISBN 0-385-12942-4). (ISBN 0-385-12943-2). Doubleday.
--Crash Helmet. Suares, Jean-Claude, illus. LC 76-54738. 22cm. 32p. c.1977. (ISBN 0-13-188961-3). Prentice-Hall.
--I Will Not Go to Market Today. Marshall, James (1942-), illus. LC 78-72474. (Illus.). 32 p. 22cm. c.1979. (ISBN 0-8037-4019-0). (ISBN 0-8037-4020-4). Dial Press.
--It's So Nice to Have a Wolf Around the House. Marshall, James (1942-), illus. LC 76-48836. (Illus.). 32 p. 22cm. c.1977. (ISBN 0-385-11300-5). (ISBN 0-385-11301-3). Doubleday.
--May I Stay?. Fitzgerald, F. A, illus. LC 77-3024. p. cm. 1978, c.1977. (ISBN 0-13-566323-7). Prentice-Hall.
--Miss Nelson Is Back. Marshall, James (1942-), illus. LC 82-9357. p. cm. 1982. (ISBN 0-395-32956-6). Houghton Mifflin Co.
--Miss Nelson Is Missing!. Marshall, James (1942-), illus. LC 76-55918. (Illus.). 32 p. 28cm. 1977. (ISBN 0-395-25296-2). Houghton Mifflin.
--The Stupids Die. Marshall, James (1942-), illus. LC 80-27103. (Illus.). 30 p. 1981. (ISBN 0-395-30532-2). Houghton Mifflin.
--The Stupids Have a Ball. Marshall, James (1942-), illus. LC 77-27660. (Illus.). 30 p. 26cm. 1978. (ISBN 0-395-26497-9). Houghton Mifflin.
--The Stupids Step Out. Marshall, James (1942-), illus. LC 73-21698. (Illus.). 30 p. 26p. 1974. (ISBN 0-395-18513-0). Houghton Mifflin.
--There's a Party at Mona's Tonight. Marshall, James (1942-), illus. LC 79-7319. (Illus.). 32 p. 26cm. c.1981. (ISBN 0-385-15187-X). (ISBN 0-385-15186-1). Doubleday.
--Tutti-Frutti Case: Starring the Four Doctors of Goodge. Marshall, James (1942-), illus. LC 74-20912. (Illus.). 32p. (ps-2). 1975. (ISBN 0-13-933200-6). (ISBN 0-13-933218-9). P-H. **Award: (NYT).**

Allard, Harry, jt. auth. see Waechter, Friedrich Karl.

Allbright, Viv
--Ten Go Hopping. LC 85-13010. p. cm. c.1985. (ISBN 0-571-13473-4). Faber and Faber.

Allee, Marjorie Hill, Mrs. (1890-1945)
--Ann's Surprising Summer. De Gogorza, Maitland, illus. LC 33-29644. 6 p. l., 198, 1 p. front., illus., plates. 20 cm. 1933. Houghton Mifflin Company.
--The Camp at Westlands. Best, Allena Champlin, Mrs. (1892-1974), illus. Berry, Erick, pseud. LC 41-5680. 5 p. l., 241, 1 p. illus. 21 cm. 1941. Houghton Mifflin Company.
--The Great Tradition. Baldridge, Cyrus LeRoy (1889-), illus. LC 37-16378. 5 p. l., 205 p. col. front, col. plates. 22 cm. 1937. Houghton Mifflin Company.
--The House. Blair, Helen (1910-), illus. LC 44-8096. 3 p. l. 181 p. front., plates.21 1/2 cm. 1944. Houghton Mifflin Company.
--A House of Her Own. Lee, Manning de Villeneuve (1894-1980), illus. LC 34-25919. 4 p. l., 239 p. front., plates. 20 1/2 cm. 1934. Houghton Mifflin Company.
--Jane's Island. De Gogorza, Maitland, illus. LC 31-112754. vii, 1 p., 2 l., 285, 1 p. front., plates. 20 1/2 cm. 1931. Houghton Mifflin Company. **Award: (JNM).**
--Judith Lankester. Price, Harriet Longstreet (1891-), illus. LC 30-268911. 6 p. l., 241 p. front., plates. 20 1/2 cm. 1930. Houghton Mifflin Company.
--The Little American Girl. Quinn, Paul, illus. LC 38-183891. 6 p. l., 237 p. front., illlus., plates. 21 1/2 cm. 1938. Houghton Mifflin Company.
--Off to Philadelphia!. Hendrickson, David (1896-), illus. LC 36-285078. xii p., 1 l., 214 p. col. front., illus., col. plates. 20 1/2 cm. 1936. Houghton Mifflin Company.
--The Road to Carolina. Lee, Manning De Villeneuve (1894-1980), illus. LC 32-219031. 6 p. l., 240, 1 p. front., plates. 20 cm. 1932. Houghton Mifflin Company.
--Runaway Linda. Hendrickson, David (1896-), illus. LC 39-27841. (Illus.). x, 220 p. 21cm. 1939. Houghton Mifflin.
--Smoke Jumper. Lee, Manning De Villeneuve (1894-1980), illus. LC 45-7578. 4 p. l. 160 p. plates 20 cm. 1945. Houghton Mifflin Company.
--Susanna and Tristram. Price, Harriet Longstreet (1891-), illus. LC 29-192575. 5 p. l., 220 p. front., plates. 20 1/2 cm. 1929. Houghton Mifflin Company.

Allen, Jay Winthrop
--The Trail Boys of the Plains: Or, The Hunt for the Big Buffalo. 350p. 1921. George Sully & Co.
--The Trail Boys of the Plains: Or, The Hunt for the Big Buffalo. Rogers, Walter S., illus. LC 15-19626. 5 p. l., 339 p. front., plates. 19 1/2 cm. c.1915. Dodd, Mead and Company.
Allen, Jeffrey
--Bonzini!. The Tattooed Man. Marshall, James (1942-), illus. LC 76-16537. (Illus.). 40 p. c.1976. (ISBN 0-316-03427-4). Little, Brown.
--Mary Alice, Operator Number Nine. Marshall, James (1942-), illus. (Illus.). 32p. (gr. 1-3). 1976. (ISBN 0-316-03425-8). Little.
--Mary Alice, Operator Number Nine. Marshall, James (1942-), illus. (Illus.). (gr. 2-8). 1978. (ISBN 0-14-050265-3, Puffin). Penguin.
--Mary Alice, Operator Number 9. Marshall, James (1942-), illus. LC 75-12513. (Illus.). 31 p. 24cm. 1975. (ISBN 0-316-03425-8). Little, Brown.
--Mary Alice, Operator Number 9. Marshall, James (1942-), illus. LC 77-10924. (Illus.). 34 p. 23cm. (Picture puffin). 1978, c.1975. (ISBN 0-14-050265-3). Little, Brown.
--Nosey Mrs. Rat. Marshall, James (1942-), illus. LC 84-19618. (Illus.). 32 p. 27cm. 1985. (ISBN 0-670-51622-8). Viking Kestrel.
--The Secret Life of Mr. Weird. LC 81-8400. p. cm. 1982. (ISBN 0-316-03428-2). Little, Brown.
Allen, Jennifer, jt. auth. see Anderson, Robin.
Allen, Jerry (1941-)
--The Adventures of Jimmy Poole. Koechel, David, illus. LC 75-43586. (Illus.). 176 p. 22cm. c.1976. (ISBN 0-87518-114-7). Dillon Press.
Allen, Joan, illus.
--Ask a Silly Question. N.D. Golden Press.
--Tiny Bear and His New Sled. (A Golden Beginning Reader Bk.). N.D. Golden Press.
Allen, John
--Animals on the Farm. Becker, Victor G., illus. LC 42-43718. 26 1/2 x 23 1/2cm. 16p. c.1939. Saalfield Pub, Co.
Allen, Jonathan
--A Bad Case of Animal Nonsense. Allen, Jonathan, illus. LC 81-47137. (Illus.). (ps up). 1981. (ISBN 0-87923-398-2). Godine.
Allen, Judy
--The Lord of the Dance. LC 76-51438. 124 p. 22cm. 1977, c.1976. (ISBN 0-525-34163-3). Dutton.
--The Spring on the Mountain. LC 73-82694. 153 p. 21cm. 1973. (ISBN 0-374-37148-2). Farrar, Strauss and Giroux.
Allen, Junius Mordecai
--Rhymes, Tales, and Rhymed Tales. LC 6-34708. 20cm. 153p. 1906. Crane & Company.
Allen, Kenneth
--One Day in Tutankhamen's Egypt. LC 73-21096. (Illus.). bibl. index. 48p. (Day Book Ser). (gr. 3 up). 1974. (ISBN 0-200-00136-1). Abelard.
Allen, Laura Jean
--A Fresh Look at Flowers. LC 63-16348. 45 p. col. illus. 22 cm. 1963. F. Watts.
--Mr. Jolly's Sidewalk Market. LC 63-9571. 26p. col. illus. 17 x 24cm. 1963. Holt, Rinehart & Winston.
--Mr. Jolly's Sidewalk Market. LC 65-26802. 1 v. (unpaged) col. illus. 17 x 24 cm. (Little owl book, LC17). 1965, c.1963. Holt, Rinehart and Winston.
--Ottie & the Star. Allen, Laura Jean, illus. LC 78-22485. (Illus.). 5 7/8 x 8 1/2. 32p. (18 pt.). (Early I Can Read Bks.). (ps-3). 1979. (ISBN 0-06-020107-X). (ISBN 0-06-020108-8). Har-Row.
--Rollo and Tweedy and the Case of the Missing Cheese. 1st ed. LC 82-47731. p. cm. c.1983. (ISBN 0-06-020096-0). (ISBN 0-06-020097-9). Harper & Row.
Allen, Lee
--The Hot Stove League. N.D. A. S. Barnes & Co.
Allen, LeRoy (1913-)
--Shawnee Lance. LC 72-103444. 151 p. 21cm. 1970. Delacorte Press.
Allen, Linda (1925-)
--Lionel and the Spy Next Door. Apple, Margot, illus. LC 79-23275. (Illus.). 94 p. 21cm. 1980. (ISBN 0-688-22225-0). (ISBN 0-688-32225-5). W. Morrow.
--Mr. Simkin's Grandma. Lustig, Loretta, illus. LC 78-20917. (Illus.). 32 p. 21cm. 1979. (ISBN 0-688-22191-2). (ISBN 0-688-32191-7). Morrow.
--Mrs. Simkin's Bed. Lustig, Loretta, illus. LC 80-12262. (Illus.). 32 p. 21cm. 1980, c.1976. (ISBN 0-688-22233-1). (ISBN 0-688-32233-6). Morrow.
Allen, Linda (1925-), ed.
--Stepping Stones, 1 of 50 bks. (Illus.). (New Primary Lib.). N.D. American Tract Society.
Allen, Lois
--Bear for Alice. Allen, Lois, illus. LC 73-75191. (Illus.). line drawings. 25cm. 32p. (gr. 1-4). 1970. Hawthorn Books.
--Mystery of the Blue Nets. Fiammenghi, Gioia (1929-), illus. LC 57-12194. 191p. illus. 20cm. 1957. Coward-McCann.
--Venturesome Voyage. LC 66-7050. 22cm. 208p. (gr. 4-6). 1966. (ISBN 0-03-059885-0). (ISBN 0-03-059890-7). HR&W.
Allen, Lorenzo
--Fifer for the Union. Wildsmith, Brian Lawrence (1930-), illus. LC 64-12040. 256 p. illus. 22 cm. 1964. Morrow.
Allen, M. P.
--The Spirit of the Eagle. N.D. Longmans, Green & Co.
Allen, M. R, Mrs.
--Stories for Children. LC 12-9569. 106 p. 19 cm. 1912. The Cosmopolitan Press.
Allen, Mabel Esther see Estoril, Jean, pseud.
Allen, Margaret Buell
--What Is It? Said the Dog. Goodwin, Judy Sue, illus. LC 73-81586. (Illus.). 16 p. (Magic circle book). 1974. (ISBN 0-663-25463-9). Ginn.
Allen, Marie Louise
--Pocketful of Poems. Greenwald, Sheila, pseud. (1934-), illus. Green, Sheila Ellen. (Illus.). (gr. k-3). 1957. (ISBN 0-06-020016-2). Har-Row.
--A Pocketful of Rhymes. 1st ed. Allen, Marie Louise, illus. LC 39-6844. 47p. col. illus. 22cm. 1939. Harper & Bros.
Allen, Marjorie N., jt. auth. see Schick, Alice.
Allen, Marjorie N. (1931-)
--One, Two, Three-Ah-Choo!. Gackenbach, Dick, illus. LC 79-11489. (Illus.). 62 p. 22cm. (Break-of-day book). c.1980. (ISBN 0-698-30718-6). Coward, McCann & Geoghegan.
Allen, Marjorie N (1931-) & Allen, Carl (1961-)
--Farley, Are You for Real?. Schick, Joel (1945-), illus. LC 76-15628. 23cm. 62p. (Break-of-day book). c.1976. (ISBN 0-698-30633-3). Coward, McCann & Geoghegan.
--The Marble Cake Cat. Hafner, Marylin (1925-), illus. LC 76-46992. (Illus.). 47 p. 20cm. 1977. (ISBN 0-698-20401-8). Coward, McCann & Geoghegan.
Allen, Mathews F., Jr., jt. auth. see Rhodes, Daniel D.
Allen, Maurice
--Our Invisible Friends. N.D. Liveright Publications.
Allen, Merritt Parmelee, et al. (1892-1954)
--Teen-Age Humorous Stories. Furman, Abraham Loew (1902-), ed. Vaughn, Frank E., illus. LC 57-8907. (Illus.). 254 p. 21cm. 1957. Lantern Press.
Allen, Merritt Parmelee (1892-1954)
--Battle Lanterns. Ray, Ralph (1920-1952), illus. LC 49-756751. 278 p. illus. 22 cm. 1949. Longmans, Green.
--Black Rain. MacDonald, James, illus. LC 39-22048. vii p., 1 l., 213 p. illus. 20 cm. 1939. Longmans, Green and Co.
--Blow, Bugles, Blow. 1st ed. Moyler, Alan, illus. LC 56-104929. 217p. illus. 21cm. 1956. Longmans, Green.
--Blow, Bugles, Blow. Moyler, Alan, illus. (gr. 6-9). 1956. (ISBN 0-679-25023-9). McKay.
--Drake's Sword. Pitz, Henry Clarence (1895-1976), illus. LC 34-310721. 3 p. l., 226 p. front., illus. 19 1/2 cm. 1934. D. Appleton-Century Company, Incorporated.
--East of Astoria. 1st ed. McGee, Millard, illus. LC 56-7064. 250p. illus. 21cm. 1956. Longmans, Green.
--East of Astoria. McGee, Millard, illus. (gr. 6-9). 1956. (ISBN 0-679-20044-4). McKay.
--The Flicker's Feather. 1st ed. O'Sullivan, Tom, illus. LC 52-12698. 220p. 21cm. 1953. Longmans, Green.
--The Flicker's Feather. O'Sullivan, Tom, illus. (Illus.). (gr. 6-9). N.D. McKay.
--The Ghost of the Glimmerglass. Hall, T. Victor, illus. LC 28-193906. 4 p. l., 246 p. front., plates. 19 1/2 cm. 1928. Harper & Brothers.
--The Green Cockade. Gillette, Henry Sampson (1915-), illus. LC 42-235561. 3 p. l. 199 p. illus. 21 cm. 1942. Longmans, Green & Co.
--The Hermit of Honey Hill: A Mystery Story for Boys. Lee, Manning De Villeneuve (1894-1980), illus. xi, 265 p. incl. front., illus. 19 1/2 cm. c.1931. The Century Co.
--Johnny Reb. 1st ed. Ray, Ralph (1920-1952), illus. LC 52-5635. 250 p. illus. 21 cm. 1952. Longmans, Green.
--Johnny Reb. Ray, Ralph (1920-1952), illus. (gr. 6-9). 1952. (ISBN 0-679-20083-5). (ISBN 0-679-25071-9). McKay.
--Make Way for the Brave. Collins, Kreigh (1908-), illus. (gr. 6-9). 1950. (ISBN 0-679-50263-7). McKay.
--Make Way for the Brave: The Oregon Quest. 1st ed. Collins, Kreigh (1908-), illus. LC 50-8478. 236 p. illus. 21 cm. 1950. Longmans, Green.
--The Mudhen. Voorhies, Stephen J., illus. LC 45-8459. 3 p. l. 201 p. illus. 21 cm. 1945. Longmans, Green and Co., Inc.
--The Mudhen Acts Naturally. 1st ed. Voorhies, Stephen J., illus. LC 55-672429. 184p. illus. 22cm. 1955. Longmans, Green.
--The Mudhen and the Walrus. 1st ed. Voorhies, Stephen J., illus. LC 50-5686. 216 p. 21 cm. 1950. Longmans, Green.
--Out of a Clear Sky. LC 38-27615. vii, 225 p. illus. 20 1/2 cm. 1938. Longmans, Green and Company.
--Raiders' Hoard. LC 36-16926. 3 p. l., 262 p. illus. 19 1/2 cm. 1936. Longmans, Green and Co.
--Red Heritage. Ray, Ralph (1920-1952), illus. LC 46-6030. 4 p. l. 3-314 p. illus. 21 cm. 1946. Longmans, Green and Co., Inc.
--The Silver Wolf. 1st ed. Thomas, Allan (1901-), illus. LC 51-9332. 216 p. 22 cm. 1951. Longmans, Green.
--Silver Wolf. Thomas, Allan (1901-), illus. (gr. 6-9). 1951. (ISBN 0-679-25138-3). McKay.
--The Sun Trail. LC 43-140849. viii p. 1 l. 198 p. illus. 21 cm. 1943. Longmans, Green and Co.
--Tied in the Ninth. Lassell, Charles, illus. LC 30-10608. ix, 251 p. front., plates. 19 1/2 cm. c.1930. The Century Co.
--Western Star: A Story of Jim Bridger. LC 41-518879. 3 p. l., 186 p. illus. 22 cm. 1941. Longmans, Green and Co.
--The White Feather. Falls, Charles Buckles (1874-1960), illus. LC 44-60350. 3 p. l. 196 p. 21 1/2 cm. 1944. Longmans, Green and Co.
--Wilderness Diamonds. Lee, Manning De Villeneuve (1894-1980), illus. LC 32-7607. ix, 245 p. illus. 19 1/2 cm. c.1932. The Century Co.
--Wilderness Way. 1954. E M Hale.
--The Wilderness Way. Toschik, Larry, illus. LC 54-6159. (Illus.). 246 p. 21cm. 1954. Longmans, Green.
Allen, Olive, retold by.
--Holiday House. (Illus.). N.D. E P Dutton & Co.
Allen, Pamela
--Bertie and the Bear. LC 83-19044. (Illus.). 32 p. 20cm. 1984. (ISBN 0-698-20600-2). (ISBN 0-698-20607-X). Coward-McCann.
--Bertie & the Bear. Allen, Pamela, illus. (Illus.). 32p. (gr. k-3). 1984. (ISBN 0-698-20600-2, Coward). (ISBN 0-698-20607-X, Coward). Putnam Pub Group.
--A Lion in the Night. LC 85-12346. p. cm. 1986, c.1985. (ISBN 0-399-21203-5). Putnam.
--Mr. Archimedes' Bath. LC 79-19881. (Illus.). (gr. k-3). 1980. (ISBN 0-688-41919-4). (ISBN 0-688-51919-9). Lothrop.
--Who Sank the Boat?. LC 82-19832. p. cm. 1983. (ISBN 0-698-20576-6). Coward, McCann.
Allen, Pat M
--Love Is Easy-Love Is Hard, and Other Stories. Halford, Stephen K., illus. LC 80-70858. (Illus.). 24 p. 28cm. c.1981. (ISBN 0-88494-421-2). Bookcraft.
Allen, Philip Schuyler (1871-), ed. see Malory, Thomas, Sir.
Allen, Philip Schuyler (1871-), tr. see Malot, Hector Henri.
Allen, Philip Schuyler (1871-), tr. see Spyri, Johanna Heusser.
Allen, Philip Schuyler (1871-), tr. see Verne, Jules.
Allen, Philip Schuyler (1871-)
--The Begging Bear. Moe, Louis Maria Niels Peder Halling (1858-), illus. LC 32-29689. 1 p. l., 9-60 p. col. front., illus. (part col.) col. pl. 25 x 31 cm. c.1932. Reilly & Lee Company.
--Robin Hood: Earl of Huntington. LC 30-5147. 62 p. incl. front., plates. 17 1/2 cm. 1930. The Torch Castle.
Allen, Philip Schuyler (1871-), ed.
--King Arthur & His Knights. Schaeffer, Mead (1898-1980), illus. (Windermere Ser.). N.D. Rand McNally.
Allen, Phillippa & Heal, Edith (1903-), eds.
--Junior Story-Teller's House. LC 31-34142. v. front., plates. 24 cm. N.D. Thomas S. Rockwell Company.
--The Story-Teller's House. LC 32-7127. v. front., plates. 23 1/2 cm. N.D. Thomas S. Rockwell Company.
Allen, Phoebe
--Jack and Jill's Journeys. N.D. E. P. Dutton & Co.
--Two Little Victims. (Illus.). N.D. E & J B Young.
Allen, Phoebe, tr. see Harry, Myriam.
Allen, Robert, pseud., see Garfinkel, Bernard Max.
Allen, Robert
--Jamie and the Leopard. Sugita, Yutaka (1930-), illus. LC 69-20247. (Illus.). 26 p. 25cm. 1967. Platt & Munk.
--Jamie & the Leopard. Sugita, Yutaka (1930-), illus. LC 69-20247. (Illus.). 24 color ils. 24p. (gr. k-3). 1969. Platt.
--This Is Yellow & This Is Red. Witt, Edith, illus. LC 72-78044. (Illus.). 32p. (ps-3). 1969. Platt.
Allen, Robert Thomas
--The Mystery of the Missing Emerald. Hammond, Arthur, ed. Collins, Gordon, illus. LC 64-10556. (Illus.). 160 p. 20cm. (The Secret Circle Mysteries). 1964, c.1963. Little, Brown.
--The Violin. Pastic, George, illus. (Illus.). (gr. 3-6). 1977. (ISBN 0-07-082620-X, GB). McGraw.
--The Violin: From the Story by George Pastic & Andrew Welsh. LC 76-374450. (Illus.). 78 p. c.1976. (ISBN 0-07-082300-6). McGraw-Hill Ryerson.
Allen, Stanton P.
--The Boy Trooper with Sheridan. (Illus.). 8cm. 216p. 1899. Lothrop Publishing Co.
Allen, Steve (1921-)
--Princess Snip Snip and the Puppy-Kittens. Gantz, David, illus. LC 72-97789. (Illus.). 48 p. 24cm. 1973. Platt & Munk.
--Steve Allen's Bop Fables. 1955. Simon & Schuster, Inc.
Allen, Sybil & Tomelty, Roma
--Lissamor's Child. LC 74-31432. 127 p. 21cm. 1975. (ISBN 0-8407-6437-5). T. Nelson.
Allen, Sydney Earl, Jr. (1929-)
--The Electric Grass Company. LC 74-84612. 89 p. 21cm. (Crown book). 1974. (ISBN 0-8127-0086-4). Southern Pub. Association.
Allen, T. D., pseud., see Allen, Terril Diener.
Allen, T. D., pseud. (1908-) & Allen, Don B.
--Doctor in Buckskin. Allen, Terril Diener. LC 51-12098. (T. D. Allen is the joint pseud. of Terril Diener Allen, (1908-) and Don B. Allen). 1951. (ISBN 0-06-010096-6, HarpT). Har-Row.
--Doctor, Lawyer: Merchant, Chief. Allen, Terril Diener. LC 65-11381. (T. D. Allen is a joint pseud. of Terril Diener Allen (1908-) and Don B. Allen). 208 p. 21 cm. 1965. Westminster Press.
--Miss Alice and the Cunning Comanche. Allen, Terril Diener. (T. D. Allen is the joint pseud. of Terril Diener Allen (1908-) and Don B. Allen). 1960. Friendship Press.
--More Playettes. Allen, Terril Diener. (T. D. Allen is the joint pseud. of Terril Diener Allen (1908-) and Don B. Allen). 1959. Friendship Press.
--Prisoners of the Polar Ice. Allen, Terril Diener. LC 62-17384. (T. D. Allen is the joint pseud. of Terril Diener Allen (1908-) and Don B. Allen). 172p. 1962. Westminster Press.
--Tall As Great Standing Rock. Allen, Terril Diener. LC 63-13353. (T. D. Allen is the joint pseud. of Terril Diener Allen (1908-) and Don B. Allen.). 160 p. 21 cm. 1963. Westminster Press.
Allen, Ted
--Willie the Squowse. Blake, Quentin (1932-), illus. LC 78-1716. 24cm. 57p. 1978. (ISBN 0-8038-8086-3). Hastings House.
Allen, Terril Diener see Allen, T. D., pseud.
Allen, Terril Diener see Allen, Terry D., pseud.
Allen, Terry D., pseud., see Allen, Terril Diener.
Allen, Terry D., pseud. (1908-), ed.
--Arrows Four: Prose and Poetry by Young American Indians. Allen, Terril Diener. (Illus.). 175 p. 18cm. (washington Square Press book). 1974, c.1972. (ISBN 0-671-47835-4). Pocket Books.
Allen, Virginia F., ed. see Smith, Betty Wehner.
Allen, W. S., ed.
--Longman Structural Readers: Stage 1, Scoops, 5 bks. Incl. The Ghost of Granby Hall. (ISBN 0-582-53039-3); The Gold Divers. (ISBN 0-582-53040-7); Jane Saves the Jet. (ISBN 0-582-53036-9); A Lucky Escape. (ISBN 0-582-53038-5); Oil Rig in Danger. (ISBN 0-582-53037-7). (English As a Second Language Bk.). 1965. (ISBN 0-582-53113-6). (ISBN 0-582-53699-5). Longman.
Allen, William Harvey, jt. auth. see Salsbury, Rebecca.
Allen, Willis Boyd (1855-1938)
--The Boyhood of John Kent. 368p. N.D. Pilgrim Press.
--The Boyhood of John Kent. 368p. N.D. Sunday-School Library.
--Camp and Tramp Series: Containing: Lost in Umbagog, The Mammoth Hunters. N.D. Lothrop Pub. Co.
--Christmas at Surf Point. 168p. N.D. Pilgrims Press.
--Cleared for Action. N.D. E P Duttonb.
--Cloud and Cliff: Or, Summer Days at the White Mountains. LC 21-16877. 227 p. front., plates. 18 1/2 cm. (His Pine cone stories. v). 1889. D. Lothrop Company.
--The Great Island, or Cast Away on New Guinea. (Illus.). N.D. Lothrop Publishing.
--Gulf and Glacier: Or, The Percivals in Alaska. LC 14-1795. 243 p. front., plates. 18 1/2 cm. (pine cone stories, v. 6). c.1992. D. Lothrop Company.
--John Brownlow's Folks. N.D. Lothrop Pub. Co.
--Kelp. 242p. N.D. Pilgrim Press.
--Kelp: A Story of the Isles of Shoals. LC 21-16876. 342 p. front., illus. 18 1/2 cm. (His Pine cone stories, iv). 1888. D. Lothrop Company.
--Lost on Umbagog. (Illus.). N.D. Lothrop Publishing Co.
--Mountaineer Series, 5 vols. (Illus.). N.D. Pilgrims Press.

--Mountaineer Series, 5 Vols. N.D. Sunday-School Library.
--The Mountainers. LC 58-51507. 18cm. 45p. (His Mountaineer Ser.: No. 1). 1887. Congregational Sunday-School and Pub. Society.
--The Northern Cross. LC 12-10048. (Illus.). 19cm. 224p. (Pine Cone Stories). 1887. Lothrop.
--Pine Cone Series. (Including: Pine Covers, Silver Rags, Nothern Cross, Cloud and Cliff, Kelp, Gulf and Glacier). N.D. Lothrop.
--Pine Cones. LC 12-10049. (Illus.). 19cm. 224p. 1885. D. Lothrop & Co.
--Pine Cones. 224p. N.D. Pilgrim Press.
--The Pineboro Quartette. (Illus.). (Every Boy's Library). N.D. Caldwell.
--Pineboro Quartette. (Illus.). (Every Boy's Library). N.D. Dodge Publishing Co.
--The Pineboro Quartette, 1 of 13 Vols. Stephens, Alice Barber (1858-1932), illus. (The Young of Heart Ser.). N.D. Set. Dana Estes & Co.
--Play Away. Bridgman, Lewis Jesse (1857-1931), illus. LC 2-15999. (Illus.). 19cm. 171p. 1902. Dana Estes and Company.
--Prince's Pine. LC 22-4768. 53 p. front., plates. 17 1/2 cm. (forest home series, no. 1). c.1889. Congregational Sunday-School and Publishing Society.
--Prince's Pine. LC 22-4768. 58 p. 17cm. (The Forest Home Ser.). 1889. Congregational Sunday-School and Publishing Society.
--The Red Mountain of Alaska. LC 14-1794. 346 p. incl. front., plates. 22 1/2 cm. 1889. Estes and Lauriat.
--Silver Rags. LC 21-168731. 224 p. front., plates. 18 1/2 cm. (His Pine cone stories, v. 2)). 1886. D. Lothrop and Company
--Snowed In. (Illus.). 192p. N.D. Pilgrims Press.

Allert, Kathy
--My Animal Friends. (Illus.). (ps). 1979. (Gingerbread). Dutton.

Allert, Kathy, illus.
--The Get Along Gang on the Go. (Illus.). 12p. (Orig.). (Get Along Gang Ser.). (gr. 2-4). 1984. (ISBN 0-590-33198-1). Scholastic Inc.
--Meet the Get Along Gang. (Illus.). 12p. (Orig.). (The Get Along Gang Ser.). (gr. 2-4). 1984. (ISBN 0-590-33197-3). Scholastic Inc.

Alley, R. W
--The Silly Riddle Book. LC 80-84788. (Illus.). 24 p. 21cm. (Golden look-look book). c.1981. (ISBN 0-307-11860-6). Golden Press.

Alley-Rice, Myrtle
--Friends of Fur and Feather. LC 27-1312. 3 p. l., 3-120 p. incl. front., illus. 19 1/2 cm. c.1926. Pacific Press Publishing Association.

Alley, Robert (1955-)
--The Ghost in Dobbs Diner. Alley, Robert (1955-), illus. LC 81-4864. (Illus.). 48p. (ps-3). 1981. (ISBN 0-8193-1055-7). (ISBN 0-8193-1056-5). Parents.

Alleyne, Margaret, pseud., see Burrell, Kathleen Joan.

Alleyne, Margaret
--Story of Mister Prettimouse. (Illus.). (gr. k-3). 1946. (ISBN 0-7232-0971-5). Warne.
--The Story of Mr. Prettimouse. Robinson, Mary B., illus. N.D. Frederick Warne & Co.
--Story of Sammy Sticklepin. (Illus.). (gr. 1-3). 1948. (ISBN 0-7232-0435-7). Warne.
--Story of Timothy Twitter. (Illus.). (gr. 1-3). 1946. (ISBN 0-7232-0434-9). Warne.

Allfrey, Katherine
--Golden Island. Kaufmann, John (1931-), illus. Bruehl, Edelgard von Heydekampf, tr. LC 66-10444. 190 p. illus. 25 cm. 1966. Doubleday.

Allin, John
--Circus Life. (Illus.). 48p. (ps-5). 1983. (ISBN 0-7207-1344-7, Pub. by Michael Joseph). Merrimack Pub Cir.

Allingham, William (1824-1889)
--The Dirty Old Man: A Lay of Leadenhall. Blegvad, Erik (1923-), illus. LC 65-11030. (Illus.). 1 v. (unpaged. 18cm. 1965. (ISBN 0-13-215608-3). Prentice-Hall.
--In Fairyland: A Series of Pictures from the Elf-World. Doyle, Richard (1824-1883), illus. LC 79-4837. (Illus.). 64 p. 29cm. (Studio book). 1979. (ISBN 0-670-39505-6). Viking Press.
--Rhymes for the Young Folk. Allingham, Helen Paterson (1848-1926) & Greenaway, Kate (1846-1901), illus. LC 24-30912. 75, 1 p. incl. col. front., illus. (incl. music) plates (part col.) 22 cm. 1887. Cassell and Company, Limited.
--Rhymes for the Young Folks. Allingham, Helen Paterson (1848-1926) & Greenaway, Kate (1846-1901), illus. N.D. Frederick Warne & Co.
--Robin Redbreast, and Other Verses. Allingham, Helen Paterson (1848-1926), illus. LC 78-74507. (Illus.). xi, 113 p. 20cm. 1979. (ISBN 0-8486-0007-X). Core Collection Books.
--Robin Redbreast, and Other Verses. Allingham, Helen Paterson (1848-1926) & Greenaway, Kate (1846-1901), illus. LC 36-168878. xi, 113 p. incl. illus., plates. col. front. 16 1/2 cm. (On cover: The Little library). 1930. The Macmillan Company.

Allington, Richard L & Krull, Kathleen (1952-)
--Stories. Coganchery, Helen, illus. LC 82-10208. p. cm. (Beginning to Learn About). c.1982. (ISBN 0-8172-1386-4). Raintree Childrens Books.
--Time. Miyake, Yoshi, illus. (Illus.). 32p. (Beginning to Learn about). (gr. 1-2). 1983. (ISBN 0-8172-1388-0). Raintree Pubs.

Allinson, Alec A. & Allinson, Beverley Lynn Rouse (1936-)
--Mediamind. LC 74-3881. (Illus.). 132 p. 25cm. 1974. (ISBN 0-8372-1035-6). Bowmar.

Allinson, Beverley Lynn Rouse, jt. auth. see Allinson, Alec A.

Allinson, Beverley Lynn Rouse (1936-)
--The Dog Power Tower. Daniel, Alan (1939-), illus. LC 78-105194. (Illus.). 34 p. (Mr. Dressup book). 1978, c.1977. (ISBN 0-458-93060-1). Methuen.
--Mitzi's Magic Garden. Buckett, George (1936-), illus. LC 77-155567. (Illus.). 40 p. 24cm. 1971. (ISBN 0-8116-6702-2). Garrard Pub. Co.

Allison, Anne C. E.
--Children of the Way. N.D. Harcourt Brace & Co.

Allison, Bob & Hill, Frank Ernest (1888-1969)
--Kid Who Batted One Thousand. 1951. (ISBN 0-385-07354-2). Doubleday.
--The Kid Who Batted One Thousand (Pub. by Doubleday). (gr. 7-12). 1972. (ISBN 0-590-03112-0, Schol Trade Pap). Schol Bk Serv.

Allison, Joy, pseud., see Cragin, Mary A..

Allison, Joy, pseud.
--Billow Prairie. Cragin, Mary A.. (Illus.). (The Wellesley Series for Girls). N.D. A. L. Burt.
--Billow Prairie: A Story of Life in The Great West. Cragin, Mary A.. (The Girl Chums Ser.). N.D. A. L. Burt Company.
--Kate Jameson and Her Friends. Cragin, Mary A.. 308p. 1886. Congregational Sunday-School and Publishing Society.

Allison, Samuel Buell, ed. see Defoe, Daniel.

Allison, Samuel Buell (1861-), adapted by.
--An American Robinson Crusoe for American Boys and Girls. LC 19-4447. 171p. 1918. Educational Publilshing Co.

Allison, William
--A Secret of the Sea. N.D. Doubleday Page & Co.
--The Turnstile of Night. N.D. Doubleday Page & Co.

Allred, Gordon Thatcher (1930-)
--Dori the Mallard. (gr. 4-6). 1970. G&D.
--Dori the Mallard. Brown, Margery, illus. 128p. 1968. (ISBN 0-8392-3052-4). Astor Books.
--Lonesome Coyote. LC 70-90756. 150 p. 22cm. 1969. Lantern Press.
--Old Crackfoot. (gr. 5 up). N.D. G&D.
--Old Crackfoot. Brown, Margery, illus. (Illus.). (gr. 5 up). 1965. (ISBN 0-8392-3051-6). Astor-Honor.
--Old Crackfoot. Brown, Margery, illus. LC 65-17970. 22cm. 116p. (An Astor Book). 1965. I. Obolensky.
--Old Crackfoot. Brown, Margery, illus. LC 65-17970. 116p. illus. 22cm. (Astor bk.). N.D. (ISBN 0-8392-3051-6). World.
--Starfire. LC 81-67182. 190 p. 24cm. 1981. (ISBN 0-87747-871-6). Deseret Book Co.

Allred, Mary
--Grandmother Poppy & the Children's Tea Party. Behrens, Paul R., illus. LC 84-4933. (Illus.). (gr. k-3). 1984. (ISBN 0-8054-4292-8). Broadman.
--Grandmother Poppy and the Funny-Looking Bird. Behrens, Paul R., illus. LC 81-65832. (Illus.). 32 p. 24cm. c.1981. (ISBN 0-8054-4269-3). Broadman Press.
--The Move to a New House. Behrens, Paul R, illus. LC 78-113092. (Illus.). 32 p. 24cm. c.1978. (ISBN 0-8054-1186-0). Broadman Press.

Allsburg, Chris Van see Van Allsburg, Chris.

Allshouse, Mary
--They Named Me Christopher Noel. LC 76-46225. N.D. (ISBN 0-913182-78-8). Grossmont Pr.

Allsop, Kenneth (1920-1973)
--Last Voyages of the Mayflower: A Story of the Pilgrims' Ship. 1st ed. Rudolph, Norman Guthrie (1896-1983), illus. LC 55-5056. 179p. illus. 23cm. (Winston adventure books). 1955. Winston.

Allston, Emma F, ed.
--The Jewel: A Holiday Gift for Boys and Girls. LC 15-16815. vi, 7-160 p. front., plates. 14 cm. 1844. J. Winchester.

Allstrom, Elizabeth C.
--Here & There With The Bible. 128p. 1960. Friendship Press.
--The Round Window. Wong, Jeanyee (1920-), illus. LC 53-9263. 127p. illus. 22cm. 1953. Friendship Press.
--The Round Window. Wong, Jeanyee, illus. LC 53-9263. 22cm. 127p. 1953. Friendship Press.
--The Singing Secret. 128p. 1955. Friendship Press.
--Songs Along the Way. Silverman, Melvin Frank (1931-1966), illus. (Illus.). (gr. 3-9). 1960. (ISBN 0-687-39103-2). Abingdon.

Allum, Faith T.
--Respite. Allum, Lois Saarinen, illus. (Illus.). 48p. (Orig.). 1st U.S. edition. 1985. (ISBN 0-9613349-2-4). F T Allum.

Allum, Tom
--Boy Beyond the Moon. 1st ed. Russell, Jack, illus. LC 60-7172. (Illus.). 255p. illus. 22cm. (gr. 4-8). 1960. Bobbs-Merrill.

Allyn, Rose, ed.
--Fairy Tales. Burd, Clara Miller & Higgins, Violet Moore, illus. LC 19-14228. 126 p. front., illus., plates 23 1/2 cm. c.1918. Stanton and Van Vliet Co.

Allyn, Rose, ed. see Mother Goose.

Almack, John Conrad (1883-)
--The Painted Pony. Sichel, Harold M. (1881-), illus. LC 44-6841. 2 p. l. 9-161 p. illus. 21 1/2 cm. 1944. W. Hebberd.

Almedingen, E. M., pseud., see Almedingen, Martha Edith von.

Almedingen, Martha Edith von see Almedingen, E. M., pseud.

Almedingen, Martha Edith von (1898-1971)
--Anna. Almedingen, E. M., pseud. Micklewright, Robert (1923-), illus. LC 72-171080. (Illus.). x, 131 p. 23cm. 1972. (ISBN 0-19-271337-X). Oxford University Press.
--Anna (Anna Khlebnikova De Poltoratzky, 1770-1840). Almedingen, E. M., pseud. LC 71-175823. 180 p. 21cm. 1972. (ISBN 0-374-30361-1). Farrar, Straus & Giroux.
--A Candle at Dusk. Almedingen, E. M., pseud. Roberts, Doreen (1922-), illus. LC 69-14972. vi, 182 p. 22cm. 1969. Farrar, Straus & Giroux.
--The Crimson Oak. Almedingen, E. M., pseud. LC 82-12556. 112 p. 22cm. 1st U.S. edition. 1983, c.1981. (ISBN 0-698-20569-3). Coward, McCann.
--Ellen. 272p. 1970. (ISBN 0-374-32105-1). Farrar, Straus and Giroux.
--Fanny. Almedingen, E. M., pseud. Ribbons, Ian (1924-), illus. (gr. 6-9). 1970. (ISBN 0-374-32277-5). FS&G.
--Frossia: A Novel of Russia. Almedingen, E. M., pseud. (gr. 6 up). 1969. Hawthorn.
--Katia. Almedingen, E. M., pseud. Ambrus, Victor G., pseud. (1935-), illus. Ambrus, Gyozo Laszlo. LC 67-5078. (Illus.). ix, 207 p. 21cm. (Ariel book). 1967, c.1966. Farrar, Straus & Giroux.
--The Knights of the Golden Table. Almedingen, E. M., pseud. Keeping, Charles William James (1924-), illus. LC 64-20627. 190p. illus. 22cm. 1964, c.1963. Lippincott.
--Little Katia. Almedingen, E. M., pseud. Ambrus, Victor G., pseud. (1935-), illus. Ambrus, Gyozo Laszlo. LC 66-73858. 192 p. front., illus. 22 cm. 16/. 1966. Oxford U. P.
--One Little Tree. Almedingen, E. M., pseud. Brown, Denise, illus. (gr. 4-6). N.D. (ISBN 0-448-26093-X). G&D.
--One Little Tree: A Christmas Card of a Finnish Landscape. Almedingen, E. M., pseud. Brown, Denise, illus. LC 68-22716. 94p. illus. 22cm. 1968, c.1963. Norton.
--Russian Fairy Tales. 305p. 1957. Dufour.
--Russian Fairy Tales. Almedingen, E. M., pseud. Cook, Hazel, illus. 1963. Putnam.
--The Scarlet Goose. Almedingen, E. M., pseud. LC 74-98913. 306 p. 22cm. 1970, c.1957. Holt, Rinehart and Winston.
--Stephen's Light. LC 76-80313. viii, 290 p. 22cm. 1969, c.1956. (ISBN 0-03-081489-8). Holt, Rinehart and Winston.
--The Story of Gudrun: Based on the Third Part of the Epic of Gudrun. Almedingen, E. M., pseud. 1st ed. Arno, Enrico (1913-1981), illus. Gudrun LC 67-18670. 123p. illus. 24cm. 1967. Norton.
--Too Early Lilac. N.D. (ISBN 0-8149-0694-X). The Vanganguard Press.
--The Treasure of Siegfried. Almedingen, E. M., pseud. Keeping, Charles William James (1924-), illus. LC 65-216532. 159p. illus. 22cm. 1st U.S. edition. 1965, c.1964. Lippincott.
--Young Mark. Almedingen, E. M., pseud. Ambrus, Victor G., pseud. (1935-), illus. Ambrus, Gyozo Laszlo. LC 68-13675. (Illus.). 22 drawings. 192p. (gr. 7 up). 1968. (ISBN 0-374-38745-1). FS&G. **Awards: (ALA); (BGH).**
--Young Mark: The Story of a Venture. Almedingen, E. M., pseud. Ambrus, Victor G., pseud. (1935-), illus. Ambrus, Gyozo Laszlo. LC 67-104139. 146 p. illus. 22 1/3 cm. 1967. Oxford U.P.
--The Young Pavlova. Almedingen, E. M., pseud. Brown, Denise, illus. 1961. Roy.

Almer, Alvin T (1898-)
--North to St. Paul: Adventures of a Boy and Girl in the Early Days in Minnesota. LC 49-7488. 80 p. illus. 20 cm. 1948. Augustana Book Concern.

Almond, Linda Stevens
--Little Glad Heart. Withington, Elizabeth R., illus. LC 22-16971. 4 p. l., 317 p. front., plates. 20 cm. 1922. The Page Company.
--Mary Redding Takes Charge. Whittemore, Constance, illus. LC 26-7020. 310 p. col. front., col. plates. 20 1/2 cm. c.1926. Thomas Y. Crowell Company.
--Peter Rabbit and the Little Girl. Willis, Bess Goe, illus. 58 p. 1 l. incl. col. front., col. illus. 14 cm. (Altemus' Peter Rabbit series). c.1930. Henry Altemus Company.

Almond, Linda Stevens, jt. auth. see Potter, Helen Beatrix

Almquist, Bertil
--The Stone Age Kids Discover America. Bothmer, Gerry, tr. from Swedish. LC 62-21315. unpaged. illus. 28cm. 1st U.S. edition. 1962. Macmillan.
--The Vasa Saga. 21x25cm. 24p. (gr. 6 up). 1966. Vanous.

A. L. O. E. , pseud., see Parker, Charlotte Maria

Alofsin, Dorothy (1898-)
--Happiness for Sale: Stories of Jewish Life. Knoring, Shirley, illus. LC 47-83. vii, 168 p. illus. 23 1/2 cm. 1946. Bloch Publishing Company.
--The Nightingale's Song. N.D. Harlem Book Co.

Alois, Bro.
--Frontier Priest and Congressman: Father Gabriel Richard, S.S. Dougherty, Charles L., illus. LC 58-131180. 176p. illus. 22cm. (Banner books). 1958. Benziger Bros.

Alsen, Joseph (1807-1885)
--Adventures of Jimmy Brown. (Illus.). N.D. Harper & Brothers'.
--Moral Pirates. (Illus.). N.D. Harper & Brothers'.
--The New Robinson Crusoe. (Illus.). N.D. Harper & Brothers'.

Alsop, Mary O'Hara see O'Hara, Mary.

Alsop, Reese Fell
--George and His Horse, Bill. Brown, Paul (1893-1958), illus. LC 48-104274. xi. 164 p. illus. 21 cm. 1948. Dodd, Mead.
--George and His Horse Go West. Brown, Paul (1893-1958), illus. LC 52-7210. 160 p. illus. 21 cm. 1952. Dodd, Mead.

Altamirano, Ignacio Manuel (1834-1893)
--Christmas in the Mountains. Johnson, Harvey L., tr. N.D. University Of Florida Press.

Altemeier, Edna Wyss
--Herbie and His God. Baxendell, Julia, illus. LC 76-356239. (Illus.). v, 22 p. 19cm. 1975. Whimsie Press.

Altemus, Howard Eyre (1860-1933)
--The Children of France: A Book of Stories of the Heroism and Self-sacrifice of Youthful Patriots of France During the Great War. LC 18-20123. 187p. col. front., 17cm. c.1918. Henry Altemus Co.
--Piffle's ABC book of funny animals. LC 52-50342. 57p. illus. 15cm. c.1919. Altemus Co.

Alter, Judith MacBain (1938-)
--After Pa Was Shot. LC 78-1019. 189 p. 22cm. 1978. (ISBN 0-688-22136-X). (ISBN 0-688-32136-4). Morrow.
--Luke and the Van Zandt County War: A Novel. LC 84-101. (Illus.). 131 p. 24cm. c.1984. (ISBN 0-912646-88-8). Texas Christian University Press.

Alter, Robert Edmond (1925-1965)
--The Dark Keep. Orbaan, Albert F. (1913-), illus. LC 62-14407. 190p. illus. 21cm. 1962. Putnam.
--The Day of the Arkansas. Orbaan, Albert F. (1913-), illus. LC 65-10861. 204p. illus. 21cm. (gr. 5-9). c.1965. (ISBN 0-399-20039-8). Putnam.
--High Spy. Orbaan, Albert F. (1913-), illus. LC 67-8894. (Illus.). 222 p. 22cm. 1967. Putnam.
--Listen, the Drum!. A Novel of Washington's First Command. LC 63-96863. 189p. illus. 21cm. (gr. 5 up). c.1963. Putnam.
--Rabble on a Hill. Orbaan, Albert F. (1913-), illus. LC 64-18024. 224 p. illus. 21 cm. 1964. Putnam.
--Red Water. Savage, Steele (1900-), illus. LC 68-15037. (Illus.). 223 p. 22cm. 1968. Putnam.
--Shovel Nose and the Gator Grabbers. Eldridge, Harold, illus. LC 63-17086. 191 p. illus. 21 cm. 1963. Putnam.
--Time of the Tomahawk. (Illus.). (gr. 6 up). 1964. (ISBN 0-8382-0873-8). Hale.
--Time of the Tomahawk. Gringhuis, Richard H. (1918-1974), illus. Gringhuis, Dirk, pseud. LC 63-15555. (Illus.). (gr. 5 up). 1964. (ISBN 0-399-20218-8). Putnam.
--The Treasure of Tenakertom. Aloise, Frank E., illus. LC 64-10409. 191 p. illus. 21 cm. 1964. Putnam.

--Two Sieges of the Alamo. Orbaan, Albert F. (1913-), illus. LC 65-20668. 192p. illus., map. 21cm. (gr. 6-10). c.1965. (ISBN 0-399-20222-6). Putnam.

Althea, pseud., see Braithwaite, Althea.

Altman, Addie Richman, Mrs.

--The Jewish Child's Bible Stories. Babin, Resa, illus. 1959. Bloch Pub Co.

--The Jewish Child's Bible Stories. Babin, Resa, illus. 138p. 1960. (ISBN 0-8197-0196-3). Bloch Publishing Company.

Altman, Frances (1937-)

--Reggie the Goat. Lindberg, Howard E., illus. LC 67-14446. (Illus.). 29 p. 29cm. 1967. T. S. Denison.

--The Something Egg. Kleitz, Mary, illus. LC 76-83717. (Illus.). 48 p. 29cm. 1969. T. S. Denison.

Altman, Margery

--Jaws 2 - Shark Tales. Duenewald, Doris, ed. LC 78-58462. (Illus.). (Inkpot Books Ser.). (gr. 3-7). 1978. (ISBN 0-448-16337-3). G&D.

--Jaws 2 - Sharks: All That's Good & Bad About Them. Duenewald, Doris, ed. LC 78-58461. (Illus.). (Inkpot Ser.). (gr. 3-7). 1978. (ISBN 0-448-16336-5, Treasure Books). G&D.

Altman, Millys N.

--Racing in Her Blood. 1980. Harper.

--Racing in Her Blood. LC 79-3018. 117 p. 21cm. c.1980. (ISBN 0-397-31854-5). (ISBN 0-397-31895-2). Lippincott.

Alton, Everett E

--Gridiron Courage. Meyers, Robert William (1919-), illus. LC 49-48413. 236 p. illus. 21 cm. 1949. Wilcox & Follett Co.

Alton, Margaret

--The Rise of Richard. Robinson, Jessie Berkowitz, illus. LC 43-13639. 4 p. l., 210 p. illus. 21 1/2 cm. 1943. Harper & Brothers.

Altsheler, Joseph Alexander (1862-1919)

--Apache Gold. (Miscellaneous Indian Stories). N.D. D. Appleton and Company.

--Apache Gold. (Illus.). (gr. 7-10). 1952. (ISBN 0-696-51588-1). Hawthorn.

--The Border Watch: A Story of the Great Chief's Last Stand. LC 12-11159. 5 p. l., 370 1 p. col. front., col. plates 20 cm. 1912. D. Appleton and Company.

--The Candidate. N.D. D.Appleton-Century, Inc.

--Eyes of the Woods. (Illus.). (Young Trailers Ser.). (gr. 7-10). N.D. (ISBN 0-696-59476-5). Hawthorn.

--The Eyes of the Woods: A Story of the Ancient Wilderness. Hutchison, D. C., illus. LC 17-8584. 5 p. l., 318, 1 p. col. front., col. plates. 20 cm. (His The young trailers series). 1917. D. Appleton and Company.

--The Forest of Swords: A Story of Paris and the Marne. Wrenn, Charles L., illus. LC 15-9700. 5 p. l., 316, 1 p. col. front., col. plates. 19 1/2 cm. (His World war series). 1915. D. Appleton and Company.

--The Forest Runners: A Story of the Great War Trail in Early Kentucky. LC 8-27801. 5 p. l., 362 p., 1 l. col. front., 3 col. pl. 20 1/2 cm. 1908. D. Appleton and Company.

--Free Rangers. (Illus.). (Young Trailers Ser.). (gr. 7-10). 1950. (ISBN 0-696-61071-X). Hawthorn.

--The Free Rangers: A Story of Early Days Along the Mississippi. LC 9-25641. 5 p. l., 364 p. 1 l. col. front., 3 col. pl. 20 1/2 cm. 1909. D. Appleton and Company.

--The Great Sioux Trail: A Story of Mountain and Plain. Wrenn, Charles L., illus. LC 18-41571. 5 p. l., 340, 1 p. col. front., col. plates. 19 1/2 cm. 1918. D. Appleton and Company.

--The Guns of Bull Run: A Story of the Civil War's Eve. LC 14-4303. 4 p. l., 347, 1 p. col. front., col. plates. 20 cm. 1914. D. Appleton and Company.

--The Guns of Europe. N.D. D. Appleleton-Century Co., Inc.

--The Guns of Shiloh: A Story of the Great Western Campaign. LC 14-4304. 5 p. l., 335 1 p. col. front., col. plates. 20 cm. 1914. D. Appleton and Company.

--The Horseman of the Plains. (Every Boy's Library). N.D. Grosset & Dunlap.

--Horsemen of the Plains. (Thrushwood Bks.). N.D. Grosset & Dunlap.

--The Horsemen of the Plains. (Illus.). (gr. 7 up). 1967. (ISBN 0-02-700650-6). Macmillan.

--The Hosts of the Air. N.D. D. Appleton-Century, Inc.

--The Hunters of the Hills: A Story of the Great French and Indian War. 1944. Appleton.

--The Hunters of the Hills: A Story of the Great French and Indian War. Hutchison, D. C., illus. 20cm. 359p. 1916. D. Appleton and Company.

--The Keepers of the Trail. (The Young Trailers Ser.). N.D. D. Appleton & Co.

--The Keepers of the Trail: A Story of the Great Woods. Hutchison, D. C., illus. (Illus.). (gr. 7-10). 1922. (ISBN 0-696-67393-2). Hawthorn.

--The Last of the Chiefs. (Every Boy's Library). N.D. Grosset & Dunlap.

--The Last of the Chiefs. (Illus.). (gr. 7-10). 1952. (ISBN 0-696-68002-5). Hawthorn.

--The Last of the Chiefs: A Story of the Great Sioux War. 1937. Appleton.

--The Last of the Chiefs: A Story of the Great Sioux War. LC 9-25637. vii, 336 p., 1 l. col. front., 8 col. pl. 20 1/2 cm. 1909. D. Appleton and Company.

--The Lords of the Wild: A Story of the Old New York Border. Wrenn, Charles L., illus. LC 19-4445. 5 p. l., 297, 1 p. col front., col. plates 19 1/2 cm. (His The French and Indian war series). 1919. D. Appleton and Company.

--The Lost Hunters. (The Great West Ser.). N.D. D. Appleton & Co.

--The Lost Hunters. (Illus.). (Great West Ser). (gr. 7-10). 1952. (ISBN 0-696-69220-1). Hawthorn.

--The Lost Hunters: A Story of Wild Man and Great Beasts. Wrenn, Charles L., illus. LC 18-18892. ix, 341, 1 p. col front., col. plates 19 1/2 cm. (His The great West series v. 2). 1918. D. Appleton and Company.

--The Masters of the Peaks: A Story of the Great North Woods. LC 18-18958. 5 p. l., 310, 1 p. col. front., col. plates. 19 1/2 cm. (His The French and Indian war series. v. 4). 1918. D. Appleton and Company.

--Quest of the Four. (Illus.). (gr. 7-10). N.D. (ISBN 0-696-76354-0). Hawthorn.

--The Quest of the Four: A Story of the Comanches & Buena Vista. 1911. D. Appleton and Company.

--Riflemen of the Ohio. (Illus.). (Young Trailers Ser.). (gr. 9 up). 1950. Hawthorn.

--The Riflemen of the Ohio: A Story of Early Days Along "the Beautiful River". LC 10-20851. vii. 1 p. 1 l., 254 p. 1 l. col. front., col. plates. 20 cm. 1910. D. Appleton and Company.

--The Rock of Chickamauga. N.D. D. Appleton-Century Co. Inc.

--The Rulers of the Lakes. (French and Indian War Ser.). N.D. Appleton-Century-Crofts, Inc.

--The Scouts of Stonewall. (Civil War Ser.). (gr. 7-11). 1951. (ISBN 0-696-78326-6). Hawthorn.

--The Scouts of Stonewall: The Story of the Great Valley Campaign. Wrenn, Charles L., illus. LC 14-16480. 5 p. l., 351, 1 p., col. front., col. plates. 20 cm. (His Civil war series). 1914. D. Appleton and Company.

--The Scouts of the Valley. (The Young Trailers Ser.). N.D. D. Appleton & Co.

--The Scouts of the Valley. (Young Trailers Ser.). (gr. 9 up). 1950. (ISBN 0-696-78355-X). Hawthorn.

--The Shades of the Wilderness. (Illus.). (Civil War Ser.). (gr. 7-11). 1951. (ISBN 0-696-79254-0). Hawthorn.

--The Shades of the Wilderness: A Story of Lee's Great Stand. Wrenn, Charles L., illus. LC 16-5192. 5 p. l., 311, 1 p. col. front., col. plates. 20 cm. (His The Civil war series). 1916. D. Appleton and Company.

--The Shadow of the North. (Illus.). (French & Indian War Ser.). (gr. 7-11). 1952. (ISBN 0-696-79225-7). Hawthorn.

--The Shadow of the North: A Story of Old New York and a Lost Campaign. Wrenn, Charles L., illus. LC 17-8585. 5 p. l., 357, 1 p. col. front., col. plates. 19 cm. (His The French and Indian war series). 1917. D. Appleton and Company.

--The Star of Gettysburg. N.D. D. Appleton-Century Co., Inc.

--The Star of Gettysburg. Wrenn, Charles L., illus. (Illus.). (Civil War Ser.). (gr. 7 up). N.D. (ISBN 0-696-80936-2). Hawthorn.

--The Sun of Quebec. (Illus.). (French & Indian War Ser.). (gr. 6-10). 1952. (ISBN 0-696-82067-6). Hawthorn.

--The Sun of Quebec: A Story of a Great Crisis. Wrenn, Charles L., illus. LC 19-14352. 6 p. l., 333 1 p. col. front., col. plates. 19 1/2 cm. 1919. D. Appleton and Company.

--The Sword of Antietam. (Illus.). (Civil War Ser.). (gr. 7-11). 1951. (ISBN 0-696-82241-5). Hawthorn.

--The Sword of Antietam: A Story of the Nation's Crisis. Wrenn, Charles L., illus. LC 14-16479. 5 p. l., 335, 1 p. col. front., col. plates. 20 cm. (His Civil war series). 1914. D. Appleton and Company.

--The Texan Scouts. (The Texan Ser.). 1913. D. Appleton and Company.

--The Texan Star. (The Texan Ser.). N.D. D. Appleton and Company.

--The Texan Triumph. (The Texan Ser.). N.D. D. Appleton and Company.

--The Texan Triumph. (Illus.). (Texan Ser). (gr. 7 up). 1952. (ISBN 0-696-82734-4). Hawthorn.

--The Tree of Appomattox. (Illus.). (Civil War Ser.). (gr. 7-11). 1951. (ISBN 0-696-84619-5). Hawthorn.

--The Tree of Appomattox: A Story of the Civil War's Close. Wrenn, Charles L., illus. LC 16-194225. ix p., 2 l., 321 p. col. front., col. plates 20 cm. (His The Civil war series). 1916. D. Appleton and Company.

--The Young Trailers: A Story of Early Kentucky. LC 7-29578. ix 331 p. col. front., 3 col. pl. 20 1/2 cm. 1907. D. Appleton and Company.

Alvarez, Juan & Kwapil, Marie J.

--Five Stories: Cinco Cuentos. (gr. k-4). 1972. (ISBN 0-685-32664-0). Leslie Pr.

Alvaro, Albert M., ed. see Santos, Elsie S.

Alvera

--The Tiny Little Tow Truck. (Illus.). 1980. (ISBN 0-682-49542-5). Exposition.

Alverson, Charles E

--Bears Don't Cry. Ohlsson, Ib (1935-), illus. LC 69-17134. (Illus.). 60 p. 1969. Norton.

Alyeshmerni, Mansoor, tr. see Bahar, Mehrdad.

Amarant, Julius

--Tall Baseball Stories. N.D. Association Press.

Amazing Life Games

--Good Cents. LC 74-9378. (Illus.). 128p. (gr. 4-6). 1974. (ISBN 0-395-19500-4). HM.

Ambler, Beth (1961-)

--Don't Hog up the Lily Pad. Ambler, Beth, illus. LC 74-81563. (Illus.). 32 p. 21cm. c.1974. (ISBN 0-87133-024-5). Franklin Pub. Co.

Ambler, Christopher Gifford (1886-)

--Ten Little Foxhounds. LC 73-159667. (Illus.). 30 p. 24cm. 1968. Childrens Press.

--Ten Little Foxhounds. N.D. Grosset & Dunlap.

Ambler, Eric (1909-)

--Intrigue. Repr. of 1960 ed. (gr. 9 up). N.D. (ISBN 0-394-41234-6). Knopf.

Ambler, Sara Ellmaker

--The Dear Old Home. McIlvaine, Thomas, illus. LC 6-34046. 4 p. l., 290 p. 1 l., front., 7 pl. 20 1/2 cm. 1906. Little Brown, and Company.

Ambrose, Blanche Ashley

--Old Grumoy Porcupine. Harding, Madge, illus. LC 45-111523. 4 p. l., 3-42 p. illus. 21 1/2 cm. 1945. W. Hebbard.

Ambrose, Kenneth (1919-)

--The Story of Peter Cronheim. 1st ed. Grant, Elisabeth, illus. LC 62-15476. 159p. illus. 21cm. 1962. Duell, Sloan and Pearce.

Ambrose, Mary N

--What Can I Do with a Paper Bag?. Herrero, Lowell, illus. LC 68-54979. (Illus.). 24 p. 29cm. (Carousel book). 1969. L. W. Singer Co.

Ambrosi, Marietta

--Italian Child-Life: Or, Marietta's Good Times. LC 22-11356. 18 1/2cm. 182p. c.1892. D. Lothrop & Co.

--When I Was a Girl in Italy. LC 6-27991. 162 p. front., plates, ports. 18 1/2 cm. c.1906. Lothrop, Lee & Shepard Co.

Ambrus, Gyozo Laszlo see Ambrus, Victor G., pseud.

Ambrus, Victor G, pseud., see Ambrus, Gyozo Laszlo.

Ambrus, Victor G., pseud. (1935-)

--Blackbeard the Pirate. Ambrus, Gyozo Laszlo. (Illus.). 32p. (gr. 2-9). 1983. (ISBN 0-19-279771-9, Pub by Oxford U Pr Childrens). Merrimack Pub Cir.

--The Brave Soldier Janosh. Ambrus, Gyozo Laszlo. (Illus.). 36p. (ps-3). 1979. (ISBN 0-19-272108-9). Oxford U Pr.

--Brave Soldier Janosh. Ambrus, Gyozo Laszlo. Ambrus, Victor G., pseud. (1935-), illus. Ambrus, Gyozo Laszlo. LC 67-8387. 27cm. (gr. k-3). 1967. (ISBN 0-15-211990-6, HJ). HarBraceJ.

--A Country Wedding. Ambrus, Gyozo Laszlo. LC 74-8814. (Illus.). 25 p. 29cm. 1975. (ISBN 0-201-00197-7). Addison-Wesley.

--Dracula: Everything You Always Wanted to Know But Were Too Afraid to Ask. Ambrus, Gyozo Laszlo. Ambrus, Victor G., pseud. (1935-), illus. Ambrus, Gyozo Laszlo. (Illus.). 32p. (gr. 2-9). 1983. (ISBN 0-19-279746-8, Pub by Oxford U Pr Childrens). (ISBN 0-19-272121-6). Merrimack Pub Cir.

--Dracula's Bedtime Storybook: Tales to Keep you Awake at Night. Ambrus, Gyozo Laszlo. (Illus.). 32p. 1982. (ISBN 0-19-279762-X, Pub. by Oxford U Pr Childrens). (ISBN 0-19-272130-5). Merrimack Pub Cir.

--Grandma, Felix, and Mustapha Biscuit. Ambrus, Gyozo Laszlo. Ambrus, Victor G., pseud. (1935-), illus. Ambrus, Gyozo Laszlo. LC 82-2133. (Illus.). 24 p. 26cm. 1982. (ISBN 0-688-01285-X). (ISBN 0-688-01287-6). W. Morrow.

--The Little Cockerel. Ambrus, Gyozo Laszlo. LC 68-7855. (Illus.). 26cm. 24p. 1968. Harcourt, Brace & World.

--The Little Cockerel. Ambrus, Gyozo Laszlo. 24 p. (chiefly col. illus.). 26cm. 1968. Oxford U.P.

--Mishka. Ambrus, Gyozo Laszlo. LC 77-84602. (Illus.). 24 p. 29cm. 1978, c.1975. (ISBN 0-7232-6150-4). F. Warne.

--The Seven Skinny Goats. Ambrus, Gyozo Laszlo. Ambrus, Victor G., pseud. LC 78-468636. (Illus.). 26cm. 24p. 1969. Oxford University Press.

--The Seven Skinny Goats. Ambrus, Gyozo Laszlo. Ambrus, Victor G., pseud. (1935-), illus. Ambrus, Gyozo Laszlo. LC 70-11257. 24 p. (chiefly col. illus. 26cm. 1970, c.1969. (ISBN 0-15-272926-7). Harcourt, Brace & World.

--The Sultan's Bath. Ambrus, Gyozo Laszlo. LC 72-193392. (Illus.). 24 p. 26cm. 1972. (ISBN 0-15-282400-6). Harcourt Brace Jovanovich.

--Under the Double Eagle. Ambrus, Gyozo Laszlo. (Illus.). 48p. 1982. (ISBN 0-19-279722-0, Pub. by Oxford U Pr Childrens). Merrimack Pub Cir.

--The Valiant Little Tailor. Ambrus, Gyozo Laszlo. LC 80-516527. (Illus.). 24 p. 31cm. 1980. (ISBN 0-19-279727-1). Oxford University Press.

Ambrus, Victor G., pseud. (1935-), retold by

--Three Poor Tailors. Ambrus, Gyozo Laszlo. Ambrus, Victor G., pseud. (1935-), illus. Ambrus, Gyozo Laszlo. LC 66-11196. (Illus.). (gr. k-3). 1966. (ISBN 0-15-286847-X, HJ). HarBraceJ. **Awards: (ALA); (KGM).**

Amdur, Nikki

--One of Us. Sanderson, Ruth, illus. LC 81-65847. p. cm. 1981. (ISBN 0-8037-6742-0). (ISBN 0-8037-6743-9). Dial Press.

Amend, Ottilie

--Jolly Jungle Jingles. Barte, Eleanore, illus. 32p. N.D. P. F. Volland Co.

Amerel

--The Child's Story Book: A Holiday Gift. LC 42-48364. 98 p. front., illus., plates. 15 x 12 cm. 1850. D. Appleton and Co.

The, American Boy

--American Boy Adventure Stories: Selected Stories from "The American Boy". LC 37-22607. viii p., 1 l., 408 p. inci. front. 21 cm. (Young moderns bookshelf). 1937. The Sun Dial Press, Inc.

--American Boy Adventure Stories: Selected Stories from "The American Boy". Ellis, Griffith Ogden (1869-), ed. LC 28-23671. viii p., 1 l., 406 p. ioncl. col. front. 21 cm. 1928. Double-Day, Doran & Company, Inc.

--The American Boy Anthology. Reck, Franklin Mering (1896-1965), ed. Geary, Clifford N. (1916-), illus. LC 51-12894. 488 p. illus. 21 cm. 1951. Crowell.

--American Boy Sea Stories. Ellis, Griffith Ogden (1869-), ed. LC 47-2980. 5 p. l., 390 p. 20 1/2 cm. (Young moderns). N.D. Doubleday & Company Inc.

--American Boy Sea Stories: Selected Stories from "The American Boy". Ellis, Griffith Ogden (1869-), ed. LC 27-24891. 5 p. l., 390 p. col. front. 21 cm. 1927. Doubleday, Page & Company.

--American Boy Sea Stories: Selected Stories from "the American Boy". Ellis, Griffith Ogden (1869-), ed. LC 31-11733. 5 p. l., 390 p. front. 21 cm. (windmill books). 1931. Doubleday, Doran & Company, Inc.

--American Boy Sports Stories. Ellis, Griffith Ogden (1869-), ed. LC 46-7627. 6 p. l., 366 p. 20 1/2 cm. (Young moderns). 1946. Doubleday & Co., Inc.

--American Boy Sports Stories: Selected Stories from "The American Boy". Ellis, Griffith Ogden (1869-), ed. LC 29-17996. v p., 3 l., 366 p. front. 21 cm. 1929. Doubleday, Doran & Company,Inc.

--American Boy Stories: Selected Stories from "The American Boy". Ellis, Griffith Ogden (1869-), ed. LC 26-19347. 6 p. l., 331 p. col. front. 20 cm. 1926. Doubleday, Page & Company.

--American Boy Stories: Selected Stories from "The American Boy". Ellis, Griffith Ogden (1869-), ed. LC 37-22236. 6 p. l., 351 p. 21 cm. (Young moderns bookshelf). 1937. The Sun Dial Press, Inc.

The, American Girl

--The American Girl Book of Sports Stories. LC 65-14991. 183 p. illus. 22 cm. (American girl library, 8). 1965. Random House.

--Christmas All Year 'round: Twenty-Five Christmas Stories from the American Girl. Vetter, Marjorie Meyn, ed. LC 52-14792. 320p. 23cm. 1952. Abelard Press.

--On My Honor: Twenty Stories from "The American Girl". Vetter, Marjorie Meyn, ed. LC 51-6803. 229 p. 22 cm. 1951. Longmans, Green.

--Stories to Live by: A Treasury of Fiction from "The American Girl". Vetter, Marjorie Meyn, ed. LC 60-116255. 280p. 22cm. 1960. Platt & Munk.

--When Girls Meet Boys: Stories of Romance from the American Girl Magazine. LC 65-19725. 181 p. illus. 22 cm. (American girl library, 10). 1965. Random House.

American Girl Magazine Staff, ed.

--American Girl Book of Dog Stories. Kocsis, James C. (1936-), illus. Paul, James, pseud. LC 65-14990. (Illus.). 185p. (gr. 5-9). 1965. (ISBN 0-394-81085-6). (ISBN 0-394-91085-0). Random.

--The American Girl Book of First Date Stories. Karlin, Eugene (1918-), illus. LC 63-18284. 182p. illus. 22cm. (American girl lib., 2). c.1963. Random.

--American Girl Book of First Date Stories. Karlin, Eugene (1918-), illus. (Illus.). (gr. 5-9). 1963. (ISBN 0-394-90901-1). Random.

--American Girl Book of Horse Stories. (Illus.). (gr. 5-9). 1963. (ISBN 0-394-90899-6, BYR). Random.

--Touch Me Not!. (Illus.). 20p. (gr. 2 up). 1983. (ISBN 0-937836-09-5). Precious Res.

An Observer

--City Cries: Or, A Peep at Scenes in Town. Croome, William H., illus. LC 24-6303. 1 p. l., vi, 9-102 p. incl. plates. pl. 14 1/2 x 12 cm. 1851. G. S. Appleton.

Anand, Mulk R.

--Maya of Mohenjo-Daro. 3rd ed. Biswas, Pulak, illus. (Illus.). 24p. (Orig.). (gr. k-3). 1980. (ISBN 0-89744-214-8, Pub. by Children's Bk Trust India). Auromere.

Anastasio, Dina (1941-)

--Crazy Freddy's in Trouble Again & His Parents Are Going to ... !!. (Illus.). 48p. (Write-It-Yourself Bks.). N.D. (ISBN 0-8431-0280-2). Price Stern.

--Dear Priscilla, I Am Sending You a Pet... for Your Birthday. (Illus.). 48p. (Write-It-Yourself Bks.). 1980. (ISBN 0-8431-0283-7). Price Stern.

--Everybody's Invited to Dudley's Party Except ... !!. (Illus.). 48p. (Write-It-Yourself Bks.). 1980. (ISBN 0-8431-0277-2). Price Stern.

--Georgina's Too ... for Her Own Good, & Someday She's Going to Be Very Sorry!!. (Illus.). 48p. (Write-It-Yourself Bks.). N.D. (ISBN 0-8431-0276-4). Price Stern.

--My Wish Book. 48p. (My Book Ser.). 1981. (ISBN 0-8431-0698-0). Price Stern.

--A Question of Time. Payson, Dale (1943-), illus. LC 78-4916. (Illus.). 90 p. 23cm. c.1978. Dutton.

--Somebody Kidnapped the Mayor & Hid Her in ... !!. (Illus.). 48p. (Write-It-Yourself Bks.). 1980. (ISBN 0-8431-0279-9). Price Stern.

--Watch It Sarah!! the ... Is Right Behind You!!. (Illus.). 48p. (Write-It-Yourself Bks.). 1980. (ISBN 0-8431-0278-0). Price Stern.

Anatole, France

--Honey Bee: A Fairy Story for Children. Lane, John, Mrs. & Lundborg, Florence, illus. N.D. Dodd Mead & Co.

Anchondo, Mary, jt. ed. see Rohmer, Harriet.

Anckarsvard, C. M., tr. see Anckarsvard, Karin Inez Maria.

Anckarsvard, Karin Inez Maria (1915-1969)

--Aunt Vinnie's Invasion. Hutchinson, William Miller (1916-), illus. MacMillan, Annabelle, pseud. (1922-), tr. from Swedish. Quick, Annabelle. LC 62-170393. 128p. illus. 21cm. 1st U.S. edition. 1962. (ISBN 0-15-204621-6). Harcourt, Brace & World.

--Aunt Vinnie's Victorious Six. Hutchinson, William Miller (1916-), illus. MacMillan, Annabelle, pseud. (1922-), tr. from Swedish. Quick, Annabelle. LC 64-12505. 155 p. illus. 21 cm. 1st U.S. edition. (gr. 5-9). 1964. (ISBN 0-15-204635-6). Harcourt, Brace & World.

--Bonifacius and Little Bonnie. Rosell, Ingrid, illus. Anckarsvard, C. M. & Beales, K. H., trs. LC 63-10514. 94 p. illus. 21 cm. 1963. Abelard-Schuman.

--Bonifacius the Green. Rosell, Ingrid, illus. Anckarsvard, C. M. & Beales, K. H., trs. LC 61-5587. 95 p. illus. 21 cm. 1962. Abelard-Schuman.

--Doctor's Boy. Rocker, Fermin (1907-), illus. MacMillan, Annabelle, pseud. (1922-), tr. from Swedish. Quick, Annabelle. LC 65-12330. 156p. illus. 21cm. 1st U.S. edition. N.D. Harcourt.

--Madcap Mystery. Galdone, Paul (1914-), illus. MacMillan, Annabelle, pseud. (1922-), tr. from Swedish. Quick, Annabelle. LC 62-8343. 189 p. illus. 21 cm. 1962. Harcourt, Brace & World.

--The Madcap Mystery. Galdone, Paul (1914-), illus. 1970. Harcourt.

--The Mysterious Schoolmaster. Galdone, Paul (1914-), illus. MacMillan, Annabelle, pseud. (1922-), tr. from Swedish. Quick, Annabelle. LC 59-10170. 190 p. illus. 22 cm. 1st U.S. edition. 1959. Harcourt, Brace.

--The Riddle of the Ring. Hampshire, Michael Allen, illus. MacMillan, Annabelle, pseud. (1922-), tr. from Swedish. Quick, Annabelle. LC 66-12586. 188 p. illus. 21 cm. 1st U.S. edition. 1966. (ISBN 0-15-266905-1). Harcourt, Brace & World.

--Rider by Night. MacMillan, Annabelle, pseud. (1922-), tr. from Swedish. Quick, Annabelle. LC 60-11249. 192 p. illus. 21 cm. 1st U.S. edition. 1960. Harcourt, Brace.

--The Robber Ghost. Galdone, Paul (1914-), illus. MacMillan, Annabelle, pseud. (1922-), tr. from Swedish. Quick, Annabelle. LC 61-6307. (Illus.). 188 p. 21cm. 1st U.S. edition. 1961. (ISBN 0-15-267804-2). Harcourt, Brace & World.

--Springtime for Eva. MacMillan, Annabelle, pseud. (1922-), tr. from Swedish. Quick, Annabelle. LC 61-12340. 157 p. 21 cm. 1st U.S. edition. 1961. Harcourt, Brace.

--Struggle at Soltuna. Rocker, Fermin (1907-), illus. MacMillan, Annabelle, pseud. (1922-), tr. from Swedish. Quick, Annabelle. LC 68-14110. (Illus.). 156 p. 21cm. 1st U.S. edition. 1968. (ISBN 0-15-281822-7). Harcourt, Brace & World.

Ancona, George (1929-)

--Bananas: From Manolo to Margie. Ancona, George (1929-), illus. (Illus.). 48p. (gr. 3-6). 1982. (ISBN 0-89919-100-2, Clarion). HM.

--Sheep Dog. LC 84-20100. (Illus.). 64p. (gr. 5 up). 1985. (ISBN 0-688-04118-3). (ISBN 0-688-04119-1). Lothrop. **Award: (ALA).**

Anders, Rebecca

--Clover the Calf. Hammarberg, Dyan, tr. from Fr. LC 76-29448. (Illus.). (Animal Friends Books). (gr. k-4). 1977. (ISBN 0-87614-073-8). Carolrhoda Bks.

--Lorito the Parrot. Hammarberg, Dyan, tr. from Fr. LC 76-1208. (Illus.). 24p. (The Animal Friends Bks). (gr. k-4). 1976. (ISBN 0-87614-068-1). Carolrhoda Bks.

--Whiskers the Rabbit. Hammarberg, Dyan, tr. from Fr. LC 76-1236. (Illus.). 24p. (The Animal Friends Bks). (gr. k-4). 1976. (ISBN 0-87614-070-3). Carolrhoda Bks.

--Winslow the Hamster. Hammarberg, Dyan, tr. from Fr. LC 76-40966. (Illus.). (Animal Friends Books). (gr. k-4). 1977. (ISBN 0-87614-078-9). Carolrhoda Bks.

Anders, Rebecca & Pajot, Anne Marie

--Ali the Desert Fox. LC 76-29469. (Illus.). 24 p. 23cm. (Animal friends books). 1977. (ISBN 0-87614-076-2). Carolrhoda Books.

--Dolly the Donkey. LC 76-1283. (Illus.). 24 p. 23cm. (Animal friends books). 1976. (ISBN 0-87614-062-2). Carolrhoda Books.

Andersdatter, Karla Margaret see Margaret, Karla, pseud.

Andersdatter, Karla Margaret (1938-)

--Follow the Blue Butterfly. Koff, Deborah, illus. (Illus.). (gr. 4-8). 1980. (ISBN 0-935430-00-8). In Between.

--Witches and Whimsies. Margaret, Karla, pseud. Meyers, Diane, illus. LC 75-32851. (Illus.). 20cm. 102p. 1975. In-Between Pub. Co.

Andersen, Benny E

--Let's Start a Puppet Theatre. LC 73-3940. (Illus.). 91 p. 23cm. c.1973. (ISBN 0-442-29986-9). Van Nostrand Reinhold Co.

Andersen, Doris

--Blood Brothers. Craig, David, illus. LC 67-17800. (Illus.). 136 p. 22cm. 1967. St. Martin's Press.

Andersen, Gerda M., tr. see Andersen, Hans Christian.

Andersen, Hans Christian, et al. (1805-1875)

--Stories I Like. (Treasure Books Ser.). N.D. Steck Co.

Andersen, Hans Christian, jt. auth. see Brown, Marcia.

Andersen, Hans Christian, jt. auth. see Disney, Walt, Productions.

Andersen, Hans Christian, jt. auth. see Friskey, Margaret Richards.

Andersen, Hans Christian, jt. auth. see Short, Robin.

Andersen, Hans Christian, jt. auth. see Sleeping Beauty.

Andersen, Hans Christian (1805-1875)

--The Andersen Fairy Book: The Tales of Hans Andersen. Choate, Florence & Curtis, Elizabeth, illus. LC 21-151063. vi p., 1 l., 416 p. col. front., plates (part col.) 25 cm. c.1921. Frederick A. Stokes Company.

--Andersen Fairy Tales. New and Revised. (Illus.). N.D. Worthington's Sons.

--Andersen's Best Fairy Tales. Henderson, William P., illus. Henderson, Alice Corbin, tr. LC 11-31694. 20cm. 200p. 1911. Rand, McNally & Co.

--Andersen's Danish Story Book. (German Popular Tales). 1873. Leavitt & Allen Bros.

--Andersen's Fairy Library: Containing "Dream of Little Tuk", "Little Ellie", "Little Match Girl", etc, 6 vols. (Illus.). N.D. James Miller.

--Andersen's Fairy Tales. (Illus.). (The Cornell Series). 1915. A L Burt & Co.

--Andersen's Fairy Tales. (The Fairy Library). N.D. A. L. Burt Co.

--Andersen's Fairy Tales. (The Manhattan Ser.). N.D. A. L. Burt's Pubs.

--Andersen's Fairy Tales. (Illus.). (Burt's Young Folks' Library). N.D. A. L. Burt's Pubs.

--Andersen's Fairy Tales. Empire ed. 1905. American News Co.

--Andersen's Fairy Tales. (The Caxton Edition). N.D. Belford, Clarke.

--Andersen's Fairy Tales. Popular ed. N.D. Belford, Clarke & Co.

--Andersen's Fairy Tales. N.D. (ISBN 0-516-04211-4). Childrens Press.

--Andersen's Fairy Tales. 450 p. incl. col. front., 7 col. pl. 20 cm. (golden books for children). 1918. D. McKay.

--Andersen's Fairy Tales. (Illus.). (The Favorite Lib.). N.D. DeWolfe, Fiske & Co.

--Andersen's Fairy Tales. N.D. Estes & Lauriat.

--Andersen's Fairy Tales. Popular ed. N.D. Fairbanks & Palmer.

--Andersen's Fairy Tales. (Washington Square Classics Ser.). N.D. George W Jacobs.

--Andersen's Fairy Tales, 1 of 3 Vols. (Illus.). (The Fairy Library). N.D. Set. George Routledge & Sons.

--Andersen's Fairy Tales. (Illus.). 512p. (Colored Classics). N.D. George Routledge & Sons.

--Andersen's Fairy Tales. (Illus.). (Young People's Library). N.D. George Routledge & Sons.

--Andersen's Fairy Tales. (Illus.). (The Children's Favorite). N.D. George W. Jacobs & Co.

--Andersen's Fairy Tales. (The Good Value Books). N.D. Grosset & Dunlap.

--Andersen's Fairy Tales. (G&D Fairy Bks.). N.D. Grosset & Dunlap.

--Andersen's Fairy Tales, 12 vols. (Illus.). 512p. (Juvenile Classics Ser.). 1905. Set. H M Caldwell Co.

--Andersen's Fairy Tales. (Illus.). (Caldwell's Illustrated Library of Famous Books by Famous Authors). N.D. H. M. Caldwell Co.

--Andersen's Fairy Tales. (Illus.). (Berkeley Lib.). N.D. H. M. Caldwell Co.

--Andersen's Fairy Tales. (Illus.). 1905. Henry Altemus Co.

--Andersen's Fairy Tales. (Altemus' New Illustrated Young People's Library). N.D. Henry Altemus Company.

--Andersen's Fairy Tales. (Illus.). (Children's Gift Ser.). N.D. Henry Altemus Company Publications.

--Andersen's Fairy Tales. (Illus.). (Boys and Girls' Classics). N.D. Henry Altemus.

--Andersen's Fairy Tales, 1 of 10 vols. (Mother Goose Ser.). 1900. Set. Hurst & Co.

--Andersen's Fairy Tales, 1 of 64 vols. (Young American Library: No. 5). 1900. Set. Hurst & Co.

--Andersen's Fairy Tales. (Argyle Ser). N.D. Hurst & Company.

--Andersen's Fairy Tales. (Illus.). (Hurst's Presentation Ser). N.D. Hurst & Company.

--Andersen's Fairy Tales. (Illus.). (Home Ser.). N.D. Hurst and Company.

--Andersen's Fairy Tales. (Illus.). (The Cosmos Ser.). N.D. Hurst and Company.

--Andersen's Fairy Tales. (Illus.). (Hurst's Family Tale Ser.). N.D. Hurst and Company.

--Andersen's Fairy Tales. (Illus.). (Arlington Edition). N.D. Hurst and Company.

--Andersen's Fairy Tales. (Illus.). (The St. Nicholas Ser.). N.D. Hurst and Company.

--Andersen's Fairy Tales. (Illus.). (Fireside Ser.). N.D. Hurst and Company.

--Andersen's Fairy Tales. (New Red Letter Ser). N.D. International Book Company.

--Andersen's Fairy Tales. (New Aldine Ser). N.D. International Book Co.

--Andersen's Fairy Tales. (Victoria Edition). 1882. J B Lippincott.

--Andersen's Fairy Tales. LC 17-15095. 1 p. l., 5-390 p. 19 cm. (On cover: Lovell's library. v. 8, no. 419). 1884. J. W. Lovell Company.

--Andersen's Fairy Tales, 1 of 5 Vols. (Illus.). (Enchanting Library). N.D. Set. James Miller.

--Andersen's Fairy Tales. (Sears Juvenile Classics). N.D. J.H.Sears & Co.

--Andersen's Fairy Tales. (The Young People's Library). 1905. John C. Winston.

--Andersen's Fairy Tales. New ed. (Illus.). N.D. John Wiley & Sons.

--Andersen's Fairy Tales. (New Acorn Library). N.D. John C. Winston Co.

--Andersen's Fairy Tales. (German Popular Tales). 1873. Leavitt & Allen Bros.

--Andersen's Fairy Tales. (New Fairy Library). 1873. Leavitt & Allen Bros.

--Andersen's Fairy Tales, 1 of 2 vols. (New Oxford Ser: No. 15). N.D. Set. Lovell, Coryell & Co.

--Andersen's Fairy Tales. (The Washington Square Classics). N.D. Macrae Smith.

--Andersen's Fairy Tales. N.D. Oxford University Press--American Branch.

--Andersen's Fairy Tales. (Illus.). (Young People's Classics). N.D. R. F. Fenno & Co.

--Andersen's Fairy Tales, 1 of 74 Vols. (The Chandos Classics Ser.). N.D. R. Worthington.

--Andersen's Fairy Tales, 1 of 14 Vols. (Warne's Poets and Fiction Ser.). N.D. R. Worthington.

--Andersen's Fairy Tales. (The Junior Library: Vol.2). 1910. Rand McNally & Co.

--Andersen's Fairy tales. (Illus.). 1958. Random House Incorporation.

--Andersen's Fairy Tales. (Twentieth Century Ser.). N.D. Rand, McNally & Co.'s.

--Andersen's Fairy Tales. (New Alpha Library). N.D. Rand, McNally & Co.'s.

--Andersen's Fairy Tales. (The Advance Library Ser.: Vol. 10). N.D. Rand, McNally & Co.

--Andersen's Fairy Tales. (Illus.). (The Independent Library Ser.: Vol. 10). N.D. Rand, McNally & Co.

--Andersen's Fairy Tales, 1 of 24 vols. (Illus.). (Children's Favorite Classics). 1900. T. Y. Crowell & Co.

--Andersen's Fairy Tales. (Illus.). (Crowell's Home Library). 1915. T Y Crowell.

--Andersen's Fairy Tales. (Illus.). (The Waldorf Lib.). N.D. T. Y. Crowell & Co.

--Andersen's Fairy Tales. LC 17-15099. 32 p. 23 cm. c.1909. The O. Brewer Publishing Co.

--Andersen's Fairy Tales. (The Forward Ser.). 1905. William Collins Co.

--Andersen's Fairy Tales. (Classic Ser.). N.D. World Publishing Co.

--Andersen's Fairy Tales. Brundage, Frances, illus. LC 25-15968. 310 p. col. front., illus. 23 cm. (Lettered on cover: Companion series). c.1925. The Saalfield Publishing Company.

--Andersen's Fairy Tales. Bryan, Brigitte, illus. LC 71-110034. (Illus.). 192 p. 29cm. 1970, c.1969. Childrens Press.

--Andersen's Fairy Tales. Comstock, Harriet Theresa, Mrs. (1860-), retold by. (Illus.). (Burt's Series on One Syllable Bks.). N.D. A. L. Burt's Pubs.

--Andersen's Fairy Tales. Day, Lillian (1893-), ed. Taylor, John Peter (1920-), illus. LC 46-5785. 56 p. incl. col. front., illus. (part col.) 28 cm. 1946. The Hyperion Press and Duell, Sloan and Pearce.

--Andersen's Fairy Tales. Dobbs, Rose, ed. Hjortlund, Gustav, illus. Frank, Josette (1893-) (Illus.). 63 p. 29cm. c.1958. Random House.

--Andersen's Fairy Tales. Frasee, Laura, ed. Richardson, Frederick (1862-1937), illus. LC 36-11775. viii, 276 p. col. front., illus., col. plates. 21 cm. (The Winston cleartype popular classics). c.1992. The John C. Winston Company.

--Andersen's Fairy Tales. Kredel, Fritz (1900-1973), illus. Hersholt, Jean (1886-), tr. LC 44-40084. 3 p. l., ix-xx, 2, 297 p. col. illus. 23 cm. 1943. The Heritage Press.

--Andersen's Fairy Tales. New Ed. ed. Linson, Corwin Knapp, illus. N.D. Frederick A. Stokes Co.

--Andersen's Fairy Tales. MacKinstry, Elizabeth (0000-1956), illus. Moore, Anne Carroll (1871-1961), intro. by. LC 33-272875. 255, 1 p. incl. col. front., illus., col. plates. 29 cm. c.1933. Coward-McCann.

--Andersens' Fairy Tales. Neill, John Rea (1878-1943) & Owen, Robert Emmett (1879-), illus. 192p. N.D. Cupples & Leon Co.

--Andersen's Fairy Tales. Osborne, Margherita Osborne Cassino, Mrs. (1878-), ed. Kutcher, Ben (1895-), illus. LC 30-28866. 367 p. col. front., illus., col. plates. 25 cm. c.1930. The Penn Publishing Company.

--Andersen's Fairy Tales. Paull, Mrs., ed. (Illus.). (Warne's Lansdowne Fairy Library). N.D. Scribner & Welford.

--Andersen's Fairy Tales. Paull, H. B., tr. (Illus.). (The Excelsior Edition). N.D. American News Company.

--Andersen's Fairy Tales. Paull, Henry H. B., Mrs., tr. from Ger. N.D. Frederick Warne & Co.

--Andersen's Fairy Tales. Rackham, Arthur (1867-1939), illus. N.D. David McKay Co.

--Andersen's Fairy Tales. Rich, Edwin Gile (1879-), ed. Robinson, William Heath (1872-1944), illus. LC 37-1447. 2 p. l., 355 p. col. front., col. illus 24 cm. 1931. Houghton Mifflin Company.

--Andersen's Fairy Tales. Rich, Edwin Gile (1879-), ed. LC 22-21117. 3 p. l., 355 p. col. front., col. plates. 24 cm. 1922. Small, Maynare & Company.

--Andersen's Fairy Tales. Richardson, Frederick (1862-1937), illus. Atwood, William T., intro. by. LC 57-12796. 278p. illus. 22cm. (Children's classics). 1957. Winston.

--Andersen's Fairy Tales. Szyk, Arthur (1894-1951), illus. Lucas, Alice & Paull, Henry H. B., Mrs., trs. LC 46-5786. 4 p. l., 327 p. col. front., illus., col. plates. 24 cm. (Illustrated junior library). 1945. Grossett & Dunlap.

--Andersen's Fairy Tales. Thorndike, Edward Lee (1874-), ed. Tenggren, Gustaf (1896-1970), illus. LC 35-2780. viii, 224 p. incl. front., illus 20 cm. (Thorndike library). c.1935. D. Appleton-Century Company Incorporated.

--Andersen's Fairy Tales. Weisgard, Leonard Joseph (1916-), illus. N.D. Doubleday.

--Andersen's Fairy Tales and Stories. Good Value ed. N.D. Grosset & Dunlap.

--Andersen's Fairy Tales: Classics for the Young. (Illus.). 1888. R Worthington.

--Andersen's Fairy Tales: First Series. Stickney, Jennie H. (1840-), ed. (Classics for Children). N.D. Ginn and Company.

--Andersen's Fairy Tales: Retold in Words of One Syllable. Comstock, Harriet Theresa Smith, Mrs. (1860-), ed. LC 3795. 2 p. l., 97 p. 10 pl. (incl. front.) 21 cm. 1900. A. L. Burt.

--Andersen's Fairy Tales: Second Series. Stickney, Jennie H. (1840-), ed. (Classics for Children). N.D. Ginn and Company.

--Andersen's Fairy Tales: The/Roxburghe Classics. N.D. Estes & Lauriat's.

--Andersen's Famous Tales. (German Popular Tales). 1873. Leavitt & Allen Bros.

--Andersen's German Fairy Tales. (The World-Renowned Ser.). N.D. Leavitt & Allen Bros.

--Andersen's Story Book, 1 of 5 Vols. (Illus.). (Enchanting Library). N.D. Set. James Miller.

--Andersen's Story Book. (German Popular Tales). 1873. Leavitt & Allen Bros.

--The Fir Tree. Otto, Svend (1916-), illus. LC 70-141643. (Illus.). 30 p. 1971. Van Nostrand Reinhold.
--The Fir Tree. Schlesinger, Alice, illus. LC 47-6905. 24 p. illus. (part col.) 28 cm. 1947. Grosset & Dunlap.
--First Book of Hans Christian Andersen Stories. Cloke, Rene, illus. LC 79-52798. (Illus.). 183 p. 34cm. (Derrydale fun time library). 1979, c.1975. (ISBN 0-517-29264-5). Derrydale Books.
--The Flower Maiden and Other Stories. Abbott, Elenore Plaisted & Shenton, Edward (1895-), illus. LC 23-6925. 118 p. col. front., plates (part col) 20 cm. c.1922. G. W. Jacobs & Company.
--The Flying Trunk ... Twenty-Four Stories. Goetz, Renate, illus. Jensen, Lyda, tr. LC 51-6317. 317 p. illus. 22 cm. N.D. Scott, Foresman.
--Forty-Two Fairy Tales. Jacques, Robin (1920-), illus. James, M. R., tr. LC 68-124000. 346p. 1968. (ISBN 0-498-08493-0). A. S. Barens & Company.
--Forty-Two Stories. Jacques, Robin (1920-), illus. James, Montague Rhodes (1862-1936), tr. LC 59-12802. 346p. illus. 22cm. (Wonderful world book). 1959. A. S. Barnes.
--Four Tales from Hans Andersen: A New Version of the First Four. Keigwin, R. P., ed. Raverat, Gwendolen Mary (1885-1957), illus. LC 36-27064. xiii, 76, 2 p. col. front., illus. 19 cm. 1935. The University Press.
--The Goloshes of Fortune. (Hans C. Andersen's Fairy Library for the Young). N.D. George Routledge & Sons.
--The Goloshes of Fortune, 1 of 5 Vols. (Illus.). (Little Red Shoes Library). N.D. Set. George Routledge & Sons.
--Good Humor, 1 of 6 Vols. (Illus.). (Andersen Library). N.D. George Routledge & Sons.
--Good Wishes for the Children. LC 17-151052. 2 p. l., 41 p. 36 pl. 21 cm. 1873. Printed at the Riverside Press.
--Great Claus & Little Claus. Schreiter, Rick (1936-), illus. LC 68-8857. (Illus.). 32p. (ps-3). 1968. Grove.
--Hans Andersen. New ed. Ipsen, L. S., designed by. (Illus.). 466p. N.D. Estes & Lauriat's.
--Hans Andersen Fairy Tales. Baumhauer, Hans (1913-), illus. (Children's Illustrated Classics). N.D. E. P. Dutton & Co.
--Hans Andersen Favorites: Four Well-Known Stories Retold After Hans Christian Andersen. LC 49-1917. 52 p. col. illus. 27 cm. (Chanticleer junior book). c.1948. Chanticleer Press.
--Hans Andersen, His Classic Fairy Tales. Foreman, Michael (1938-), illus. Haugaard, Erik Christian (1923-), tr. LC 78-107654. (Illus.). 185 p. 26cm. c.1974. (ISBN 0-385-13364-2). Doubleday.
--Hans Andersen's Best Stories. N.D. Thomas Nelson & Sons.
--Hans Andersen's Best Stories. (Standard Literature Ser.: No. 52). N.D. University Publishing Co.
--Hans Andersen's Fairy Stories. (Illus.). 64p. (Ogilvie's Books for Boys and Girls). N.D. J. S. Ogilvie.
--Hans Andersen's Fairy Tales. 1962. (ISBN 0-8098-2354-3). David McKay Company.
--Hans Andersen's Fairy Tales. Baumhauer, Hans (1913-), illus. (Children's Illustrated Classics). N.D. E. P. Dutton & Co.
--Hans Andersen's Fairy Tales. Clarke, Harry (1890-), illus. N.D. Brentano's.
--Hans Andersen's Fairy Tales. Kirk, Maria Louise (1860-) & Lehman, E. A., illus. LC 11-26006. 4 p. l., 219 p. incl. illus., plates (part col.) col. front., col.. plates. 21 cm. 1911. J. B. Lippincott Company.
--Hans Andersen's Fairy Tales. Lansing, Jenny H. Stickney, Mrs. (1840-), ed. Pedersen, Thomas Vilhelm (1820-1859), illus. LC 17-15998. 2 v. illus. 18 cm. (On cover: Classics for children. v. 10, 15). 1886. Ginn & Company.
--Hans Andersen's Fairy Tales. Lansing, Jenny H. Stickney, Mrs. (1840-), ed. Hart, Edna F., illus. LC 15-6136. 2 v. illus. 18 cm. c.1915. Ginn and Company.
--Hans Andersen's Fairy Tales. Mora, Joseph Jacinto (1876-), illus. Siewers, Carl, tr. LC 2-19886. 4 p. l., 188 p. front., illus., plates. 25 cm. 1902. D. Estes & Company.
--Hans Andersen's Fairy Tales, 1 of 6 Vols. Paull, Mrs., ed. (Illus.). (Warne's Lansdowne Fairy Library Ser.). N.D. R. Worthington.
--Hans Andersen's Fairy Tales. Roberton, E. Jean, ed. Hughes, Shirley (1929-), illus. Peachey, Caroline, tr. LC 79-64120. (Illus.). 264 p. 21cm. 1979. (ISBN 0-8052-3719-4). (ISBN 0-8052-0632-9). Schocken Books.
--Hans Andersen's Fairy Tales. Robinson, William Heath (1872-1944), illus. LC 25-1042. 310. 1 p. incl. col. front. illus., col. plates. 24 cm. 1924. George H. Doran Company.
--Hans Andersen's Fairy Tales. Shepard, Ernest Howard (1879-1976), illus. N.D. Henry Z. Walck Inc.
--Hans Andersen's Fairy Tales. Siewers, Carl, retold by. McCracken, James & Mora, J. J., illus. 256p. (The World Wide Library). N.D. A. Whitman & Co.
--Hans Andersen's Fairy Tales. Sumiko, illus. LC 79-20407. (Illus.). 94 p. 27cm. 1979. (ISBN 0-8052-3732-1). (ISBN 0-8052-3719-4). Schocken Books.
--Hans Andersen's Fairy Tales. Winter, Milo Kendall (1888-1956), illus. Paulsen, Valdemar Edward (1882-), tr. LC 21-881226. 286 p. col. front., col. plates. 24 cm. (Windermere series). c.1916. Rand McNally & Company.
--Hans Andersen's Fairy Tales: A Selection. Lewis, Naomi, intro. by. Pedersen, Thomas Vilhelm (1820-1859) & Frolich, Lorenz (1820-1903), illus. Kingsland, Leslie William (1912-), tr. from Danish. LC 84-7120. (Illus.). xxiv, 349 p. 19cm. (World's classics). 1984. (ISBN 0-19-281699-3). Oxford University Press.
--Hans Andersen's Fairy Tales and Wonder Stories. Rhead, Louis John (1857-1926), illus. Howells, W. D., intro. by. LC 14-18122. xii, 1, 442, 1 p. incl. front. (port.) illus., plates. 22 cm. 1914. Harper & Brother.
--Hans Andersen's Stories. Scudder, Horace Elisha (1838-1902), tr. LC 17-15103. xii, 13-205 p., 1 l. 18 cm. (On cover: Riverside literature series. no. 49-50). 1891. Houghton Mifflin and Company.
--Hans Andersen's Stories: In two Parts. 96p. (Nos. 49-50). N.D. Houghton, Mifflin and Company.
--Hans Andersen's Stories, Newly Translated: In Two Parts. Scudder, Horace Elisha (1838-1902), tr. LC 17-151045. 2 v. in 1. 18 cm. (On cover: Riverside literature series. nos. 49-50). 1891. Houghton, Mifflin Company.
--Hans Andersen's Story Book. Howitt, Mary Botham, Mrs. (1799-1888), illus. LC 35-28571. vi p., 1 l., 9-152 p. front. 18 cm. 1860. C. S. Francis and Company.
--Hans Andersen's Wonder Tales. Turpin, Edna Henry Lee (1867-), ed. 280 p. illus. 19 cm. (Graded classics series). c.1917. B. F. Johnson Publishing Company.
--Hans Anderson's Fairy Tales. Sumiko, illus. 1980. Schocken.
--Hans Christian Andersen's Danish Fairy Tales. 1900. Maynard Merrill & Co.
--Hans Christian Andersen's Fairy Tales. (Illus.). N.D. Estes & Lauriat.
--Hans Christian Andersen's Fairy Tales. Caraway, James, illus. N.D (Wonder Books). Grosset & Dunlap.
--Hans Christian Andersen's Fairy Tales. Mora, Joseph Jacinto (1876-), illus. (Illus.). N.D. Dana Estes and Company.
--Hans Christian Andersen's Fairy Tales. Stretton, Helen, illus. N.D. Dodge Publishing Co.
--Hans Christian Andersen's Fairy Tales. Tegner, Hans Christian Harald (1853-1970), illus. Braekstad, Hans Lien (1845-1915), tr. Gosse, Edmund, intro. by. LC 78-11706. p. cm. 1979. Beekman House.
--Hans Christian Andersen's Fairy-Tales. Tegner, Hans Christian Harald (1853-1970), illus. Braekstad, Hans Lien (1845-1915), tr. 500p. (New Books for Boys and Girls). 1900. The Century Co.
--Hans Christian Andersen's Fairy Tales & Stories. 1960. (ISBN 0-460-00004-7, Evman). Dutton.
--Hans Christian Andersen's Favorite Fairy Tales. Durand, Paul, illus. 144p. (ps-k). 1974. (ISBN 0-307-16814-X, Golden Pr). (ISBN 0-307-66814-2). Western Pub.
--Hans Christian Andersen's Stories for the Household. LC 17-15097. iv, 316 p. col. front., illus. 17 cm. c.1893. McLoughlin Brothers.
--Hans Christian Andersen's "The Steadfast Tin Soldier". Di Grazia, Thomas (0000-1983), illus. LC 81-11968. (Illus.). 32 p. 29cm. c.1981. (ISBN 0-13-846295-X). Prentice-Hall.
--Hans Christian Andersen's Wonder Book. N.D. Estes & Lauriat's.
--Hans Clodhopper. Shtainmets, Leon, retold by. LC 74-23674. (gr. k-3). 1975. (ISBN 0-397-31614-3, JBL-J). Har-Row.
--Hans Clodhopper. 1st ed. Shtainmets, Leon, retold by. Shtainmets, Leon, illus. LC 74-23674. (Illus.). 32 p. 26cm. 1975. (ISBN 0-397-31614-3). Lippincott.
--The Hardy Tin Soldier, 1 of 5 Vols. (Illus.). (Ice Maiden Library). N.D. Set. George Routledge & Sons.
--Household Stories. Dulcken, H. W., tr. N.D. E P Dutton.
--The Ice Maiden. (Hans C. Andersen's Fairy Library for the Young). N.D. George Routledge & Sons.
--The Ice Maiden, 1 of 5 Vols. (Illus.). (Ice Maiden Library). N.D. Set. George Routledge & Sons.
--Ice Maiden, and Other Stories. (Illus.). N.D. E P Dutton.
--The Ice-Maiden, and Other Tales. Fuller, Fanny, tr. LC 17-15094. 4 p. l., 7-189 p. 15 cm. 1863. F. Leypoldt; Etc., Etc.
--The Improvisatore. (Cambridge Classics Ser.). N.D. Houghton Mifflin.
--In Sweden, 1 of 5 Vols. (Illus.). (Ice Maiden Library). N.D. Set. George Routledge & Sons.
--It's Absolutely True. 28p. (Hans Christian Andersen Story Bks.). (gr. 3-6). 1985. (ISBN 0-87239-861-7). Standard Pub.
--It's Perfectly True: And Other Stories. Bennett, Richard Michael (1899-), illus. Leyssac, Paul, tr. LC 38-27263. x, 305 p. incl. illus., plates. 28 cm. c.1938. Harcourt, Brace and Company.
--Kate Greenaway's Original Drawings for "The Snow Queen". Greenaway, Kate (1846-1901), illus. Boner, Charles, tr. LC 81-46406. p. cm. 1981. (ISBN 0-8052-3776-3). Schocken Books.
--Little Claus and Big Claus. Bregnhi, Palle, illus. LC 74-141644. (Illus.). 27 p. 1971. Van Nostrand Reinhold Co.
--Little Ellie, 1 of 6 Vols. (Andersen's Fairy Library). N.D. Set. James Miller.
--Little Ellie. (Fairy Library). 1873. Leavitt & Allen Bros.
--Little Ellie. (Story Teller Ser.). 1873. Leavitt & Allen Bros.
--Little Ellie and Other Stories. (Illus.). N.D. James Miller.
--Little Fairy Shut-Eye: An Andersen Fairy Tale. 1925. Duffield.
--Little Fairy Sleepy-Eyes. N.D. Duffield.
--The Little Lead Soldier. Wright, Adele J., ed. Ramirez, Pablo, illus. LC 66-14057. 1 v. (unpaged) col. illus. 24 cm. (Holly story book library). 1966. World Pub. Co.
--The Little Match-Girl. (Hans C. Andersen Fairy Library for the Young). N.D. George Routledge & Sons.
--The Little Match Girl, 1 of 5 Vols. (Illus.). (Will-o'-Wisp Library). N.D. Set. George Routledge & Sons.
--Little Match Girl, 1 of 6 Vols. (Andersen's Fairy Library). N.D. Set. James Miller.
--The Little Match Girl. Lent, Blair (1930-), illus. LC 68-28050. (Illus.). 43 p. 28cm. 1968. Houghton Mifflin.
--The Little Match Girl. Tenggren, Gustaf (1896-1970), illus. LC 44-8800. 28 p. incl. col. front., illus. (part col.) 28 x 22 cm. 1944. Grosset & Dunlap.
--Little Match Girl, and Other Stories. (Illus.). N.D. James Miller.
--The Little Mermaid. 1 v. (unpaged) illus. (pt. col.) 27cm. 1966. Golden.
--The Little Mermaid. Bianco, Pamela (1906-), illus. James, Montague Rhodes (1862-1936), tr. LC 35-27383. 55, 1 p. illus. 20 cm. 1935. Holiday House.
--The Little Mermaid. Duffy, Marguerite R., retold by. Correas, Jose, illus. LC 66-14049. 1 v. (unpaged) col. illus. 24 cm. (Holly story book library). 1966, c.1963. World Pub. Co.
--The Little Mermaid. 1st ed. Frascino, Edward, illus. Le Gallienne, Eva (1899-), tr. LC 72-157899. (Illus.). 50 p. 24cm. 1971. (ISBN 0-06-023783-X). Harper & Row.
--The Little Mermaid. Iwasaki, Chihiro (1918-1974), illus. 1984. Neuberger.
--The Little Mermaid. Iwasaki, Chihiro (1918-1974), illus. LC 84-9490. c.1984. (ISBN 0-907234-59-3). Picture Book Studio USA: Dist. by Alphabet Press.
--The Little Mermaid. Lathrop, Dorothy Pulis (1891-1980), illus. LC 39-81198. 48 p. illus. (part col.) 26 cm. 1939. The Macmillan Company.
--The Little Mermaid. Thamer, Katie, illus. LC 83-48519. p. cm. c.1984. (ISBN 0-87923-490-3). D.R. Godine.
--The Little Mermaid, and Other Fairy Tales. heirloom ed. Hjortlund, Gustav, illus. Keigwin, R. P., tr. LC 63-14250. (Illus.). 122 p. 28cm. 1963. Platt & Munk.
--Little Mermaid and Other Tales. (Illus.). N.D. Putnam's Trade List.
--Little Ones' Hans Andersen. Towers, Alton, ed. (Illus.). (The Little Ones' Library Ser.). N.D. Frederick A. Stokes Co.
--Little Rudy. (Fairy Library). 1873. Leavitt & Allen Bros.
--Little Rudy. (Little Rudy Story Bks.). 1873. Leavitt & Allen Bros.
--The Little Sea Maid, 1 of 6 Vols. (Andersen Library). N.D. Set. George Routledge & Sons.
--The Little Tin Soldier. LC 66-6702. 1v. (unpaged) illus. (pt. col.) 27cm. 1966. Golden.
--Little Tulk, 1 of 6 Vols. N.D. Set. George Routledge & Sons.
--The Marsh King's Daughter. (Hans C. Andersen Fairy Library for the Young). N.D. George Routledge & Sons.
--The Marsh King's Daughter, 1 of 5 Vols. (Illus.). (Little Red Shoes Library). N.D. Set. George Routledge & Sons.
--The Mermaid and other Fairy Tales. Tilney, Frederick Colin, ed. Lucas, Edgar, Mrs., tr. 19cm. 127p. (Tales for Children from Many Lands). N.D. E. P. Dutton & Co.
--Michael Hague's Favorite Hans Christian Andersen Fairy Tales. Hague, Michael R., ed. Hague, Michael R., illus. LC 81-47455. p. cm. c.1981. (ISBN 0-03-059528-2). Holt, Rinehart, and Winston.
--More Fairy Tales. Rhys, Ernest, ed. Peachey, Caroline, intro. by. (Illus.). 18cm. 234p. (Everyman's Library: No. 822). 1928. E. P. Dutton & Co.
--Mud King's Daughter. (Fairy Library). 1873. Leavitt & Allen Bros.
--Mud King's Daughter. (Little Rudy Story Bks.). 1873. Leavitt & Allen Bros.
--My Book of the Little Tin Soldier. Nardini, Sandro, illus. LC 61-66504. unpaged. illus. 33cm. (Giant Maxton book). c.1960. Maxton Pub. Corp.
--New Tales, Eighteen Forty-Three. Incl. The Angel; The Nightingale; Sweethearts; The Ugly Duckling. 1973. (ISBN 8-7142-7349-7, D743). Vanous.
--The Nightingale. LC 35-27246. 32 p. illus. 19 cm. 1934. Helen & B. Gentry.
--The Nightingale. N.D. R. H. Russell.
--The Nightingale. Berson, Harold (1926-), illus. (Illus.). 1962. Lippincott.
--The Nightingale. Bier, Anna, adapted by. Demi, pseud. (1942-), illus. Hitz, Demi. LC 85-2765. (Illus.). 30 p. 28cm. c.1985. Harcourt Brace Jovanovich. **Award: (NYT).**
--The Nightingale. Burkert, Nancy Ekholm (1933-), illus. Le Gallienne, Eva (1899-), tr. LC 64-18574. 32p. illus. (pt. col.) 28cm. c.1965. Harper. **Award: (ALA).**
--The Nightingale. Grozat, Francois, illus. Alex, Marlee, tr. LC 85-19926. p. cm. (Scandinavia Fairy Tales). 1985, c.1984. (ISBN 0-8120-5710-4). Barron's Educational Series.
--The Nightingale. Marine, Edmund, illus. LC 37-211398. 1 p. l., 20 p., 1 l. col. front., col. illus. 20 cm. 1937. Harper & Brothers.
--The Nightingale. Milnazik, Kim, illus. LC 78-317337. (Illus.). 38 p. 53cm. c.1976. Moonlight Express.
--The Nightingale. Newill, Mary J., illus. Dulcken, Henry William, Dr. (1832-1894), tr. LC 17-9135. 4 p. l., 16, 4 l. incl. 3 blank l. illus. 23 cm. 1896. B. Updike.
--The Nightingale. Pelgrave, E. J. (1805-1875), adapted by. Testa, Fulvio, illus. LC 73-17648. (Illus.). 24 p. 30cm. 1974. (ISBN 0-200-00133-7). Abelard-Schuman.
--The Nightingale. Zwerger, Lisbeth, illus. 1984. Neugebauer.
--The Nightingale. Zwerger, Lisbeth, illus. Bell, Anthea, tr. LC 84-9492. (Illus.). 24 p. c.1984. (ISBN 0-907234-68-2). Picture Book Studio USA : Distributed by Alphabet Press.
--The Nightingale: And Other Stories from Hans Andersen. Dulac, Edmund (1882-1953), illus. LC 43-58305. 7 p. l., 3-125, 1 p., 1 l. incl. mounted col. plates. 24 cm. N.D. Hodder and Toughton.
--The Nightingale and the Emperor. Jauss, Anne Marie (1907-), illus. LC 74-89782. (Illus.). 37 p. 26cm. 1970. (ISBN 0-8178-4582-8). (ISBN 0-8178-4581-X). Harvey House.
--The Old Church-Bell. (Hans C. Andersen's Fairy Library for the Young). N.D. George Routledge & Sons.
--The Old Church Bell, 1 of 5 Vols. (Illus.). (Snow Queen Library). N.D. Set. George Routledge & Sons.
--The Old Man Is Always Right: Adapted from Hans Christian Andersen. Rojankovsky, Feodor Stepanovich (1891-1970), illus. LC 40-2479. 28 p. incl. col. front., illus. (part col.) 24 x 22 cm. c.1940. Harper & Brothers.
--Only a Fiddler. (First Complete Edition in English). N.D. Houghton, Mifflin and Company.
--Out of the Heart, Spoken to the Little Ones. (Illus.). N.D. George Routledge & Sons.
--Picture Book without Pictures. (Fairy Library). 1873. Leavitt & Allen Bros.
--Picture Book without Pictures. (Little Rudy Story Bks.). 1873. Leavitt & Allen Bros.
--Poultry Meg's Family. (Hans C. Andersen's Fairy Library for the Young). N.D. George Routledge & Sons.
--Poultry Meg's Family, 1 of 5 Vols. (Illus.). (Snow Queen Library). N.D. Set. George Routledge & Sons.
--The Princess and the Pea. Duntze, Dorothee, illus. LC 85-7199. (Illus.). 24 p. 32cm. 1985. North-South Books : Distributed in the U.S. by Holt, Rinehart, and Winston.
--The Princess and the Pea. Gackenbach, Dick, illus. LC 82-17954. p. cm. c.1983. (ISBN 0-02-735800-3). Macmillan.
--The Princess and the Pea. Galdone, Paul (1914-), illus. 1978. Houghton.
--The Princess and the Pea. Galdone, Paul (1914-), illus. LC 77-12707. (Illus.). 32 p. 26cm. c.1978. (ISBN 0-8164-3202-3). Seabury Press.
--The Princess and the Pea. Stevens, Janet, adapted by. Stevens, Janet, illus. LC 81-13395. p. cm. c.1982. (ISBN 0-8234-0442-0). Holiday House.

--The Ugly Duckling: And Other Fairy Tales. Armfield, Maxwell (1881-), illus. Lucas, Alice, tr. 127 p. col. front., col. plates. 18 cm. (Half-title: Tales for children from many lands, ed. by F. C. Tilney). 1914. J. M. Dent & Sons, Limited.
--The Ugly Duckling & Two Other Stories. Moore, Lilian, ed. Hyman, Trina Schart (1939-), illus. (Illus.). (gr. k-3). 1973. (ISBN 0-590-08764-9, Schol Pap). Schol Bk Serv.
--Ugly Duckling: In Friskey, Margaret 1901- Farm Friends. LC 51-7127. 1951. Childrens Press.
--Under the Willow-Tree. (Hans C. Andersen's Fairy Library for the Young). N.D. George Routledge & Sons.
--Under the Willow Tree, 1 of 5 Vols. (Illus.). (Snow Queen Library). N.D. Set. George Routledge & Sons.
--Walt Disney Productions Presents the Emperor's New Clothes. LC 74-34485. p. cm. (Disney's wonderful world of reading ; 29). 1975. (ISBN 0-394-92568-8). (ISBN 0-394-82568-3). Random House.
--Walt Disney's The Ugly Duckling: Adapted from Hans Christian Andersen. Walt Disney, Productions, Ltd., ed. 40 p. illus. (part col.) 21 x 27 cm. c.1939. J. B. Lippincott Company.
--What the Good Man Does Is Always Right. Schreiter, Rick (1936-), illus. LC 68-28734. (Illus.). 32 p. 29cm. 1968. Dial Press.
--What the Moon Saw, and other Tales. Bayes, Alfred Walter, illus. (Illus.). N.D. George Routledge & Sons.
--The Wild Swans. (Hans C. Andersen Fairy Library for the Young). N.D. George Routledge & Sons.
--The Wild Swans, 1 of 5 Vols. (Illus.). (Little Red Shoes Library). N.D. Set. George Routledge & Sons.
--The Wild Swans, 1 of 6 Vols. (Illus.). (Andersen Library). N.D. George Routledge & Sons.
--The Wild Swans. LC 66-6696. 1 v. (unpaged) illus. (part col.) 27 cm. 1966. Golden Press.
--The Wild Swans. Barrett, Angela, illus. 1984. Harper.
--The Wild Swans. Brown, Marcia (1918-), illus. James, Montague Rhodes (1862-1936), tr. LC 63-18748. 80 p. illus. (part col.) 26 cm. 1963. Scribner. **Award: (ALA).**
--The Wild Swans. Milone, Karen, illus. LC 80-27685. p. cm. c.1981. (ISBN 0-89375-480-3). (ISBN 0-89375-481-1). Troll Associates.
--The Wild Swans and Other Stories. Abbott, Elenore Plaisted & Shenton, Edward (1895-), illus. LC 23-6924. 117 p. col. front., plates (part col.) 20 cm. c.1922. G. W. Jacobs & Company.
--The Wild Swans, and Other Tales from Andersen. (Illus.). (Stories Old and New Ser.). N.D. Caldwell.
--Will-o'-the-Wisp, 1 of 5 Vols. (Illus.). (Will-o'-Wisp Library). N.D. Set. George Routledge & Sons.
--The Will-o'-the-Wisps are in Town, and Other Stories. (Illus.). N.D. George Routledge & Sons.
--The Will o'the Wisp. (Hans C. Andersen's Fairy Library for the Young). N.D. George Routledge & Sons.
--Wonder Stories told for Children. (Illus.). N.D. Houghton, Mifflin.
--Wonder Stories Told for Children. author's ed. Pedersen, Thomas Vilhelm (1820-1859) & Stone, M. L., illus. LC 26-15766. 2 p. l., 555 p. incl. illus., plates. front. 20 cm. N.D. Houghton Mifflin Company.
--Wonderful Tales. N.D. D. Lothrop Co.
--Wonderful Tales, 1 of 6 Vols. (Illus.). (Andersen's Wonderful Library). N.D. Set. James Miller.
--Wonderful Tales: German Popular Tales. (Illus.). N.D. James Miller.

Andersen, Hans Christian (1805-1875) & Bayes, A. W.
--Fairy Tales. Weir, Harrison William (1824-1906) & Padersen, V., illus. (New Alta Lib.). N.D. Henry T. Coates & Co.

Andersen, Hans Christian (1805-1875) & Dulac, Edmund (1882-1953)
--Dulac's The Snow Queen, and Other Stories from Hans Andersen. LC 76-7308. (Illus.). 143 p. 24cm. 1976. (ISBN 0-385-11677-2). Doubleday.

Andersen, Hans Christian (1805-1875) & Grimm, Jakob Ludwig Karl (1785-1863)
--Enchanting Library: Contains "Andersen's Fairy Tales", "Andersen's Story Book" and "Grimm's Home Fairy Tales" etc, 5 vols. N.D. James Miller.

Andersen, Hans Christian (1805-1875) & Grimm, Wilhelm Karl (1786-1859)
--Stories That Never Grow Old: The Emperor's New Clothes, The Valiant Little Tailor, Rapunzel. Brackett, Esther M. (1920-), illus. Tingle, Dolli, pseud. LC 67-814. 1 v. (unpaged) col. illus. 20 cm. 1966. Random House.

Andersen, Hans Christian (1805-1875) & James, Montague Rhodes (1862-1936)
--The Little Mermaid. Palecek, Josef, illus. James, Montague Rhodes (1862-1936), tr. LC 82-670021. (Illus.). 42 p. 32cm. 1981. (ISBN 0-571-11847-X). Faber and Faber.

Andersen, Hans Christian (1805-1875) & Lewis, Naomi
--The Wild Swans. Barrett, Angela, illus. LC 83-15805. (Illus.). 34 p. 1984. (ISBN 0-911745-36-X). P. Bedrick Books.

Andersen, Hans Christian (1805-1875) & Nielsen, Kay Rasmus (1886-1957)
--Fairy Tales. LC 81-43012. p. cm. (Studio book). 1981. (ISBN 0-670-30557-X). Viking Press.

Andersen, Hans Christian (1805-1875) & Owens, Lily
--The Complete Hans Christian Andersen Fairy Tales. avenel 1981 ed. LC 81-942. p. cm. 1981. (ISBN 0-517-33632-4). Avenel Books : Distributed by Crown Publishers.
--The Complete Hans Christian Andersen Fairy Tales. LC 84-14200. (Illus.). xii, 803 p. 24cm. 1984, c.1981. (ISBN 0-517-45375-4). Chatham River Press : Distributed by Crown Publishers.

Andersen, Hans Christian (1805-1875) & Richards, George M
--The Steadfast Tin Soldier. LC 76-361259. (Illus.). 41 p. 15cm. (happy hour books). 1934, c.1927. Macmillan.

Andersen, Karen Born
--What's the Matter, Sylvie, Can't You Ride?. Andersen, Karen Born, illus. LC 80-12514. (Illus.). 32 p. c.1981. (ISBN 0-440-79613-X). (ISBN 0-440-79621-0). Dial Press.

Andersen, Karen Born, jt. auth. see Yorinks, Arthur.

Andersen Press & Hutchinson Publishing Group, eds.
--Biminy in Danger. Ash, Jutta, illus. (Illus.). 128p. 1981. (ISBN 0-905478-60-6, Pub. by Andersen-Hutchinson England). State Mutual Bk.
--The Doomsday Experiment. 144p. 1981. (ISBN 0-905478-93-2, Pub. by Andersen-Hutchinson England). State Mutual Bk.
--A Nag Called Wednesday. (Illus.). 96p. 1981. (ISBN 0-905478-13-4, Pub. by Andersen-Hutchinson England). State Mutual Bk.

Andersen, Robert
--Jack Champney: A Story for Boys. LC 2-27424. 306 p. front., pl. 21 cm. (Pastime & Adventure Ser.). 1902. G. W. Jacobs & Co.

Anderson
--The Doctor's Return. N.D. Zondervan Publishing House.

Anderson, Ada Woodruff
--The Heart of the Red Firs. N.D. Little Brown & Co.
--The Strain of White. 300p. N.D. Little Brown & Co.

Anderson, Alexander (1775-1870), illus.
--Fables of Pilpay. N.D. Hurd & Houghton.
--The Happy Family: Or Winter Evenings' Employment. by a friend of youth. with cuts by anderson ... ed. A Friend of Youth & More, Hannah (1745-1833) LC 22-5876. 1 p. l., v-vi, 7-106 p. front., illus. 14 cm. 1807. From Sidney's Press, for Increase Cooke and Co.
--The House of the Thief: Or, The Eighth Commandment Practically Illustrated. LC 21-175940. 171 p. incl. front. 15 cm. N.D. The Gen. Protestant Episcopal Sunday School Union.

Anderson, Anita Melva (1906-)
--Friday, the Arapaho Indian. Betts, Emmett A., ed. Merryweather, Jack, illus. LC 51-8307. 172 p. illus. 19 cm. (American adventure series). 1951. Wheeler Pub. Co.
--Fur Trappers of the Old West. Merryweather, Jack, illus. LC 46-1876. 2 p. l., 252 p. illus. 19 cm. (American adventure series). 1946. Wheeler Publishing Company.
--Grant Marsh: Steamboat Captain. Betts, Emmett A., ed. Merryweather, Jack & Anderson, Carl A., illus. LC 59-1891. 220p. illus. 20cm. (American adventure series). 1959. Wheeler Pub. Co.
--Portugee Phillips and the Fighting Sioux. Betts, Emmett A., ed. Merryweather, Jack, illus. LC 57-135399. 172p. illus. 20cm. (American adventure series). 1956. Wheeler Pub. Co.
--Squanto and the Pilgrims. Betts, Emmett A., ed. Osebold, John, illus. 156p. (The American Adventure Ser.). (gr. 2). 1949. Franklin Watts, Inc.
--Squanto and the Pilgrims. Betts, Emmett A., ed. Osebold, John, illus. LC 49-4826. 156 p. illus. 19 cm. (American adventure series). 1949. Wheeler Pub. Co.
--Wild Bill Hickok. Betts, Emmett A., ed. Merryweather, Jack, illus. LC 48-2354. 19cm. 252p. (The American Adventure Ser.). 1947. Wheeler Pub. Co.

Anderson, Anita Melva (1906-) & Johnson, Robert Elliott (1907-)
--Pilot Jack Knight. Betts, Emmett A., ed. Merryweather, Jack, illus. LC 50-4465. 188 p. illus. 19 cm. (American adventure series). 1950. Wheeler Pub. Co.

Anderson, Anita Melva (1906-) & Keogh, Myles Walter (1840-1876)
--Comanche and His Captain. Betts, Emmett A., ed. Merryweather, Jack & Hazelrigg, Paul, illus. LC 65-413118. 224p. illus., maps. 20cm. (Amer. adventure ser.). c.1965. Harper.

Anderson, Anita Melva (1906-) & Regli, Adolph Casper
--Alec Majors. Betts, Emmett A., ed. Merryweather, Jack, illus. LC 53-2143. 204p. illus. 19cm. (American adventure series). 1953. Wheeler Pub. Co.

Anderson, Anne
--The Anne Anderson Fairy-Tale Book. Anderson, Anne, illus. LC 26-27486. 190 p. col. front., illus., col. plates. 29 1/2 cm. 1926. T. Nelson and Sons.
--The Sleeping Beauty. Anderson, Anne, illus. LC 23-5955. 40 p. incl. col. front., col. illus. 18 cm. 1928. T. Nelson and Sons.

Anderson, Anne, ed.
--Aladdin And The Wonderful Lamp. Anderson, Anne, illus. (Anne Anderson Beauty Bks.). N.D. Thomas Nelson & Sons.
--Anne Anderson's Fairy Tales. Anderson, Anne, illus. 20 p. illus. (part col.) 32 cm. c.1935. Whitman Publishing Company.
--Hop O' My Thumb. Anderson, Anne, illus. (Anne Anderson Beauty Bks.). N.D. Thomas Nelson & Sons.
--Old Mother Goose. Anderson, Anne, illus. N.D. Thomas Nelson & Sons.
--Red Shoes. Anderson, Anne, illus. (Anne Anderson Beauty Bks.). N.D. Thomas Nelson & Sons.
--Snowdrop and the Seven Dwarfs. Anderson, Anne, illus. LC 28-8656. 18cm. 35p. (Anne Anderson Beauty Bks.). 1928. Thomas Nelson & Sons.

Anderson, Barbara Tunnell, Mrs.
--The Days Grow Cold. LC 41-15922. 5 p. l., 3-277 p. 21 cm. 1941. The Macmillan Company.

Anderson, Bernice Goudy (1894-)
--Indian Sleep Man Tales. Anderson, Bernice Goudy & Sears, Frank, illus. N.D. Caxton Printers.
--Indian Sleep Man Tales. Anderson, Bernice Goudy (1894-) & Frank, Sears, illus. 145p. N.D. Reilly & Lee Co.
--Topsy Turvy and the Tin Clown. Friend, Esther, illus. LC 32-127550. 78 p. illus. (part col.) 24 cm. c.1932. Rand, McNally & Company.
--Topsy Turvy's Pigtails. Friend, Esther, illus. LC 30-22871. 2 p. l., 7-81 p. illus. (part col.) 24 cm. c.1930. Rand McNally & Company.

Anderson, Bertha Christiana (1887-)
--The Baffling Bluejays. Whittam, Geoffrey William (1916-), illus. LC 58-11862. 144p. 1958. Obelard-Schumann.
--Eric Duffy, American. 1st ed. Coe, Lloyd (1899-1976), illus. LC 55-8090. 177p. illus. 21cm. 1955. Little, Brown.
--Tinker's Tim and the Witches. 1st ed. Coe, Lloyd (1899-1976), illus. LC 53-7303. 147p. illus. 21cm. 1953. Little, Brown.

Anderson, Betty Baxter
--Adventures in 4-H. LC 38-17716. viii, 308 p. front. 20 cm. 1938. Cupples & Leon Company.
--Alabama Raider. 1st ed. Stein, Harve (1904-), illus. LC 57-10193. 115p. illus. 24cm. 1957. Winston.
--Ann Porter, Nurse: A Career Story for Older Girls. Paflin, Roberta, pseud. (1903-), illus. Petty, Roberta Harris Plaflin. LC 42-21001. 21cm. 246p. 1942. Cupples & Leon Co.
--Connie Benton, Reporter: A Career Story for Older Girls. Paflin, Roberta, pseud. (1903-), illus. Petty, Roberta Harris Pfafflin. LC 41-12910. vi, 247 p. front. 21 cm. c.1941. Cupples & Leon Company.
--Curtain Call for Connie. 1954. Thomas Nelson & Sons.
--Curtain Call for Connie. Genia, pseud. (1930-), illus. Wennerstrom, Genia Katherine. LC 53-724421. 192p. 22cm. 1953. T. Nelson.
--Four Girls and a Radio: A Career Story for Older Girls. LC 45-1434. iii, 243 p. front. 21 cm. c.1944. Cupples & Leon Company.
--Holly Saunders, Designer: A Career Story for Older Girls. LC 48-6289. iv. 243 p. front. 21 cm. 1947. Cupples & Leon Co.
--Julia Brent of the WAAC: A Career Story for Older Girls. Paflin, Roberta, pseud. (1903-), illus. Petty, Roberta Harris Pfafflin. LC 43-165487. vi, 248 p. front. 22 cm. 1943. Cupples & Leon Company.
--Nancy Blake, Copywriter: A Career Story for Older Girls. Paflin, Roberta, pseud. (1903-), illus. Petty, Roberta Harris Pfafflin. LC 42-21056. vi, 248 p. front., plates. 22 cm. 1942. Cupples & Leon Company.
--Peggy Wayne, Sky Girl: A Career Story for Older Girls. Paflin, Roberta, pseud. (1903-), illus. Petty, Roberta Harris Pfafflin. LC 41-128175. vi. 246 p. front. plates. 21 cm. c.1941. Cupples & Leon Company.
--Powder Monkey. Maps by Raphael Palacios. LC 62-190533. (Illus.). 196p. illus. 21cm. 1962. New York Graphic Society.
--Secret of the Old Books. Galdone, Paul (1914-), illus. LC 52-10881. 158 p. 21 cm. 1952. T. Nelson.

Anderson, Bradley Jay (1924-) & Leeming, Dorothy
--Marmaduke. (Illus.). (gr. 5 up). 1968. (ISBN 0-590-08071-7). Scholastic Inc.
--Marmaduke Rides Again (Pub. by Toni Mendez). (gr. 5-8). 1972. (ISBN 0-590-08072-5). Scholastic Inc.

Anderson, Carl Thomas (1865-)
--Henry in Lollipop Land. N.D (Wonder Books). Grosset & Dunlap.
--Henry in Lollipop Land. LC 54-16670. unpaged. illus. 21cm. (Treasure books, 871). 1953. Treasure Books.

Anderson, Carter
--Doctor Monkey and His Jungle Friends. LC 54-10228. 55p. illus. 23cm. c.1954. Vantage Press.

Anderson, Catherine Corley (1909-)
--Officer O'Malley on the Job. Maltman, Chauncey, illus. LC 54-9941. 64p. illus. 24cm. 1954. A. Whitman.
--Sister Beatrice and the Mission Mystery. Anderson, Catherine Corley (1909-), illus. LC 63-20696. v. 136 p. illus. 22 cm. 1963. Bruce Pub. Co.
--Sister Beatrice Goes to Bat. LC 58-12163. 136p. illus. 22cm. 1958. Bruce Pub. Co.
--Sister Beatrice Goes West. Anderson, Catherine Corley (1909-), illus. LC 61-10740. 154p. illus. 22cm. 1961. Bruce Pub. Co.

Anderson, Cay M.
--Here Comes Jonathan. LC 82-81067. (Illus.). 36p. (ps-1). 1982. (ISBN 0-941478-04-1). Paraclete Pr.

Anderson, Charles Joseph, ed. see Aldrich, Thomas Bailey.

Anderson, Clarence William see Hutchins, Pat, et al.

Anderson, Clarence William (1891-1971)
--Afraid to Ride. LC 57-10011. 89p. illus. 24cm. 1957. Macmillan.
--Another Man O' War. Anderson, Clarence William (1891-1971), illus. LC 66-7263. (Illus.). (gr. 4-6). 1966. (ISBN 0-02-701610-2). Macmillan.
--Before the Bugle. 1968. Macmillan Company.
--Big Red. N.D. Macmillan.
--Billy and Blaze. LC 62-14797. (Illus.). 46 p. 23cm. 1973, c.1964. Collier Books.
--Billy and Blaze. 1936. (ISBN 0-8382-0082-6, Cadmus Books). E. M. Hale and Company.
--Billy and Blaze. LC 36-8200. 56 p. illus. 26 cm. 1936. The Macmillan Company.
--Billy & Blaze Book Bag, 3 bks. Anderson, Clarence William (1891-1971), illus. Incl. Billy & Blaze. 48p. (ISBN 0-02-041420-X); Blaze Finds the Trail. 48p. (ISBN 0-02-041430-7); Blaze & the Forest Fire. 48p. (ISBN 0-02-041410-2). (Illus.). (gr. k-3). 1973. Set. (ISBN 0-02-041450-1, Collier). Macmillan.
--Blaze and the Forest Fire. LC 62-14796. (Illus.). 1 v. (unpaged. 23cm. 1972, c.1938. Collier Books.
--Blaze and the Forest Fire. LC 62-14796. 48 p illus. 26 cm. (Macmillan easy-to-read books). 1962, c.1938. Macmillan.
--Blaze and the Forest Fire. LC 38-27768. 55 p. illus. 28 cm. 1938. The Macmillan Company.
--Blaze and the Forest Fire. Anderson, Clarence William (1891-1971), illus. 1969. Macmillan.
--Blaze and the Gray Spotted Pony. Anderson, Clarence William (1891-1971), illus. LC 68-10997. (Illus.). 46 p. 23cm. (His Billy and Blaze books). 1974, c.1968. Collier Books.
--Blaze and the Gray Spotted Pony. Anderson, Clarence William (1891-1971), illus. LC 68-10097. (Illus.). 46 p. 25cm. (His Billy and Blaze books). c.1968. Macmillan.
--Blaze and the Gypsies. LC 37-4888. (Illus.). 26cm. 56p. 1937. Macmillan Co.
--Blaze and the Gypsies. LC 62-14795. 48 p. illus. 26 cm. (Billy and Blaze books). 1962. Macmillan.
--Blaze and the Indian Cave. Anderson, Clarence William (1891-1971), illus. LC 64-14529. (Illus.). 47 p. 25cm. (His Billy and Blaze books). 1964. Macmillan.
--Blaze and the Lost Quarry. Anderson, Clarence William (1891-1971), illus. LC 66-10356. (Illus.). 46 p. 23cm. 1973, c.1966. Collier Books.
--Blaze and the Lost Quarry. Anderson, Clarence William (1891-1971), illus. LC 66-10356. 46 p. illus. 25 cm. (His Billy and Blaze books). c.1966. Macmillan.
--Blaze and the Mountain Lion. LC 59-11293. 26cm. 46p. 1959. Macmillan.
--Blaze & the Mountain Lion. (gr. 1-3). 1969. (ISBN 0-02-702630-2). Macmillan.

--To Nowhere and Back. LC 74-16335. 141 p. 22cm. 1975. (ISBN 0-394-83036-9). (ISBN 0-394-93036-3). Knopf : Distributed by Random House.

Anderson, Margaret Johnson (1909-)

--The Mists of Time. LC 83-19555. 192p. (gr. 4 up). c.1984. (ISBN 0-394-96573-6). (ISBN 0-394-86573-1). Knopf.

Anderson, Marjorie

--That's Why, Bimi. Converse, James, illus. LC 62-19056. 98p. illus. 23cm. 1962. Pacific Press Pub. Association.

Anderson, Mary, jt. auth. see Campbell, Hope.

Anderson, Mary Eleanor Roberts, Mrs. (1840-1916)

--New Songs for Little People. Humphrey, Lizzie B., illus. 1873. Lee & Shepard.

--New Songs for Little People. Humphrey, Lizzie B., illus. LC 15-241. viii. 9-119 p. front., illus. 17 cm. 1874. Lee & Shepard.

--New Songs for Little People, 1 of 3 vols. Humphrey, Lizzie B., illus. (Illus.). (Baby Ballads Ser.). 1882. Lee & Shepard.

Anderson, Mary Gooch

--Stories of the Golden Age. LC 14-18125. 18cm. 231p. (Everychild's Ser.). 1914. Macmillan.

Anderson, Mary (1939-)

--Catch Me, I'm Falling in Love. LC 85-3774. 134 p. 22cm. c.1985. (ISBN 0-385-29409-3). Delacorte.

--The Catnapping Caper. LC 83-15655. 128p. (Escapade Ser.). (gr. 4-6). N.D. (ISBN 0-689-31378-0). Atheneum.

--Emma's Search for Something. Parnall, Peter (1936-), illus. LC 73-76313. (Illus.). 163 p. 22cm. 1973. (ISBN 0-689-30104-9). Atheneum.

--Forever Ahbra. LC 81-1926. p. cm. 1981. (ISBN 0-689-30839-6). Atheneum.

--FTC and Company. Sibley, Don (1922-), illus. LC 78-12097. (Illus.). 195 p. 22cm. 1979. (ISBN 0-689-30673-3). Atheneum.

--FTC Superstar. Owens, Gail, illus. LC 75-30565. (Illus.). 156 p. 22cm. 1976. (ISBN 0-689-30497-8). Atheneum.

--I'm Nobody! Who Are You?. LC 73-84818. 215 p. 22cm. 1974. (ISBN 0-689-30128-6). Atheneum.

--Just the Two of Them. Anderson, Carl (1931-), illus. LC 74-75554. (Illus.). 178 p. 22cm. 1974. (ISBN 0-689-30402-1). Atheneum.

--Matilda Investigates. Anderson, Carl (1931-), illus. LC 72-86924. (Illus.). 166 p. 22cm. 1973. Atheneum.

--Matilda's Masterpiece. Murdocca, Salvatore, illus. LC 76-40981. (Illus.). 168 p. 22cm. 1977. (ISBN 0-689-30565-6). Atheneum.

--Mystery of the Missing Painting. (gr. 4-6). 1977. (ISBN 0-590-11883-8, Schol Pap). Scholastic Inc.

--The Mystery of the Missing Painting. 208p. (Cat's Eye Mysteries Ser.). (gr. 3-6). 1983. (ISBN 0-590-32783-6). Scholastic Inc.

--The Rise and Fall of a Teen-Age Wacko. LC 80-12396. p. cm. 1980. (ISBN 0-689-30767-5). Atheneum.

--R.I.S.K. LC 83-6428. p. cm. (Escapade). 1983. (ISBN 0-689-31371-3). Atheneum.

--Step on a Crack. LC 77-22767. 180 p. 22cm. 1978. (ISBN 0-689-30610-5). Atheneum.

--That's Not My Style. LC 82-13772. p. cm. 1983. (ISBN 0-689-30968-6). Atheneum.

--Tune in Tomorrow. LC 83-15656. 192p. (gr. 5 up). 1984. (ISBN 0-689-31009-9). Atheneum.

--You Can't Get There from Here. LC 81-10813. xvii, 194 p. 22cm. 1982. (ISBN 0-689-30903-1). Atheneum.

Anderson, Mildred D. see Dykes, Rochelle, pseud.

Anderson, Mildred Napier

--A Gift for Merimond. Paget-Fredericks, Joseph E. P. Rous Marten (1903-1963), illus. LC 53-7261. 84p. illus. 23cm. (EOxford books for boys and girls). 1953. Oxford University Press.

--Sandra and the Right Prince. Paget-Fredericks, Joseph E. P. Rous-Marten (1903-1963), illus. LC 51-2312. 70 p. illus. 24 cm. 1951. Oxford University Press.

Anderson, Mildred Travers

--Cinderella's Cousin: A Story for Girls. LC 38-32416. 20cm. 150p. 1938. Dorrance and Co.

--The House with the Closed Shutters: A Mystery Story for Young People. LC 39-21568. 210 p. 20 cm. c.1939. Dorrance and Company.

Anderson, Nancy Mae

--Swede Homestead. 188p. 1942. Caxton Printers.

Anderson, Neil, pseud., see Beim, Jerrold.

Anderson, Neil

--Freckle Face. (Illus.). (gr. 1-4). 1957. (ISBN 0-8382-0268-3). Hale.

--Freckle Face. Cooney, Barbara (1917-), illus. (Illus.). (gr. k-4). 1957. (ISBN 0-690-31698-4). T Y Crowell.

--Tina and the Too-Big Doll. Wiggins, Mary Katherine, illus. 44p. 1956. Thomas Y. Crowell Co.

Anderson, Nephi

--The Boys of Springtown: With Special Reference to William Wallace Jones and Ned Fisher. Tillotson, C. E., illus. LC 21-279. 160 p. front., illus. 19 cm. 1920. Zion's Printing and Publishing Company.

Anderson, Norma Randolph

--An Elfindale Story. LC 81-5977. p. cm. 1981. (ISBN 0-913504-64-5). Lowell Press.

Anderson, Norman Dean (1928-) & Brown, Walter R.

--Ferris Wheels. LC 83-3959. (Illus.). 64p. (gr. 3-7). 1983. (ISBN 0-394-85460-8). (ISBN 0-394-95460-2). Pantheon.

Anderson, Paul Lewis (1880-1956)

--The Cub Arrives. LC 27-17789. 4 p. l., 233, 1 p. front., 1 illuis. 19 cm. 1927. D. Appleton and Company.

--For Freedom and for Gaul. Painter-Duhring, M., illus. LC 57-9449. (Illus.). 294 p. 21cm. (Roman life and times series, v. 3). 1957, c.1931. Biblo and Tannen.

--For Freedom and Gaul. Painter-Duhring, M., illus. LC 31-24139. vii, 1 p., 1 l., 294, 1 p. front., illus. (incl. maps) 20 cm. 1931. D. Appleton and Company.

--Half-Pint Shannon. LC 28-8590. 4 p. l., 284, 1 p. front., illus. 20 cm. 1928. D. Appleton and Company.

--The Knights of St. John. Painter-Duhring, M., illus. LC 32-11374. 5 p. l., 269, 1 p. front., illus. (incl. maps) 20 cm. 1932. D. Appleton and Company.

--Pugnax the Gladiator. Pitz, Henry Clarence (1895-1976), illus. LC 61-1111. (Illus.). 296 p. 21cm. (Roman life and times series, v. 5). 1959, c.1939. Biblo and Tannen.

--Pugnax the Gladiator. Pitz, Henry Clarence (1895-1976), illus. LC 39-403. xiv p., 1 l., 296 p. incl. front., plates. 20 cm. 1939. D. Appleton-Century Company, Incorporated.

--A Slave of Catiline. Roberts, Norman L., illus. LC 57-944659. 254p. illus. 21cm. (His Roman life and times services, v. 2). c.1930. Biblo and Tannen,.

--A Slave of Catiline. Roberts, Norman L., illus. LC 30-227483. 5 p. l., 254, 1 p. front., illus. (incl. maps) 20 cm. 1930. D. Appleton and Company.

--The Sword of Sergestus. Modder, Montague F., illus. LC 32-4547. 32 p. illus. (incl. port.) 29 cm. c.1932. Scholastic Corporation.

--Swords in the North. LC 57-9448. 270p. (gr. 7-11). 1935. (ISBN 0-8196-0103-9). Biblo.

--Swords in the North. LC 35-16481. 1935. D. Appleton-Century, Inc.

--With the Eagles. LC 57-9447. vii, 279p. illus. 21cm. (His Roman life and times series, v. 1). 1957, c.1929. Biblo and Tannen.

--With the Eagles. LC 29-6796. vii p., 1 l., 279, 1 p. front., illus. (maps. plan) 20 cm. 1929. D. Appleton and Company.

Anderson, Paul Seward (1913-1975)

--Boy & the Blind Storyteller. (Illus.). (gr. 3-5). 1964. (ISBN 0-8382-1009-0). Hale.

--The Boy & the Blind Storyteller. Yong Hwan Kim, illus. (Illus.). (Cadmus Bks). (gr. 1-4). 1964. (ISBN 0-8382-0109-1). Hale.

--The Boy and the Blind Storyteller. Yong Hwan Kim, illus. LC 64-13580. 22cm. 91p. (Young Scott Books). 1964. W. R. Scott.

--Pan Chao: A Girl of Old China. LC 53-9444. 34p. illus. 23cm. 1954, c.1953. Comet Press.

--Red Fox & the Hungry Tiger. 48p. (gr. k-3). 1962. (ISBN 0-201-09327-8, A-W Childrens). A-W.

--Red Fox & the Hungry Tiger: A Tale. Kraus, Robert (1925-), illus. LC 62-516423. unpaged. illus. 22 x 25cm. (Young Scott books). c.1962. W. R. Scott.

--Yong Kee of Korea: A Story. Yong Hwan Kim, illus. LC 58-9559. 90p. illus. 22cm. (Young Scott books). 1959. W. R. Scott.

Anderson, Penny S

--The Big Storm. Fleishman, Seymour (1918-), illus. LC 82-19928. p. cm. (Making Choices). 1983. Dandelion House.

--The Operation. Karch, Paul, illus. LC 79-16202. (Handling Difficult Times). c.1979. Child's World.

--A Pretty Good Team. Wahl, Richard (1939-), illus. LC 79-15928. p. cm. (Handling Difficult Times). 1979. (ISBN 0-89565-097-5). Child's World.

--The Sound of the Bell. Halverson, Lydia, illus. LC 83-7453. (Illus.). 32p. (gr. 3-4). 1983. (ISBN 0-89693-217-6). Dandelion Hse.

Anderson, Poul William (1926-), ed. see Molbech, Christian.

Anderson, Poul William (1926-)

--The Broken Sword. 1954. Abelard-Schuman, Inc.

--Ensign Flandry. 1967. Lancer.

--Vault of the Ages. LC 79-4324. xiii, 210 p. 21cm. (Gregg Press science fiction series). 1979, c.1952. (ISBN 0-8398-2521-8). Gregg Press.

--Vault of the Ages. LC 52-8971. 210 p. 22cm. (Science fiction novel). 1952. Winston.

Anderson, Poul William (1926-) & Dickson, Gordon Rupert (1923-)

--Star Prince Charlie. 189 p. 18cm. (Berkley Medallion Book). 1976, c.1975. (ISBN 0-425-03078-4). Berkley Publishing Corp.

--Star Prince Charlie. LC 74-21078. 190 p. 22cm. 1975. (ISBN 0-399-20443-1). Putnam.

Anderson, Poul William (1926-) & Klass, Philipl William, eds.

--Children of Wonder: Twenty-One Remarkable and Fantastic Tales. Tenn, William, pseud. LC 53-8490. 336p. 21cm. 1953. Simon and Schuster.

Anderson, R. L., Jr.

--The Abominable Spaceman. Anderson, R. L., Jr., illus. LC 79-90732. (Illus.). 182 p. 22cm. c.1979. (ISBN 0-935138-00-5). Hobby Horse Pub.

Anderson, Rachel (1943-)

--Little Angel Comes to Stay. (Illus.). 64p. (An Eagle Bk.). (gr. 3-7). 1984. (ISBN 0-19-271472-4, Pub. by Oxford U Pr Childrens). Merrimack Pub Cir.

--Moffat's Road. (Illus.). 256p. (gr. 3-6). 1980. (ISBN 0-224-01381-5, Pub. by Chatto Bodley Jonathan). Merrimack Pub Cir.

--The Poacher's Son. (Illus.). 137p. 1983. (ISBN 0-19-271468-6, Pub. by Oxford U Pr Childrens). Merrimack Pub Cir.

Anderson, Rasmus Bjorn (1846-1936)

--The Younger Edda: Also Called Snorre's Edda, or the Prose Edda. index. notes. vocab. N.D. S. C. Griggs and Company.

--Viking Tales of the North. 3rd ed. Stephens, George, tr. N.D. S. C. Griggs and company.

Anderson, Rasmus Bjorn (1846-1936), ed.

--Norse Mythology: Or, The Religion of our Forefathers. 5th ed. Anderson, Rasmus Bjorn index. vocab. N.D. S. C. Griggs and Company.

Anderson, Robert Gordon (1881-)

--Eight O'clock Stories. Smith, Dorothy Hope, illus. LC 23-17470. viii p., 1 l., 269 p. col. front., col. plates. 24 cm. c.1923. G. P. Putnam's Sons.

--Half-Past Seven Stories. Smith, Dorothy Hope, illus. LC 22-24685. viii p., 1 l., 251 p. col. front., illus., col. plates. 24 cm. c.1922. G. P. Putnam's Sons.

--Over the Hill Stories. Jordan, Nina Ralston, illus. LC 25-223802. 140 p., 1 l. col. front., illus. 24 cm. 1925. G. P. Putnam's Sons.

--Seven O'clock Stories. Smith, Elmer Boyd (1860-1943), illus. LC 20-20944. vii p., 1 l., 180 p. col. front., col. plates. 24 cm. c.1920. G. P. Putnam's Sons.

Anderson, Robert L. & Bradford, John

--House That Jack Built & Other Favorite Jingles. (Illus.). (gr. k up). 1967. (ISBN 0-531-04037-2). (ISBN 0-531-05037-8). Quist.

Anderson, Robin & Allen, Jennifer

--Sinabouda Lily: A Folk Tale from Papua New Guinea. LC 80-486987. (Illus.). 24 p. 26cm. (ps-2). 1979. (ISBN 0-19-554201-0). Oxford University Press.

Anderson, Ruth L.

--Lost Hill. (Illus.). (gr. 4-6). 1976. (ISBN 0-933892-06-3). Child Focus Co.

Anderson, Scarvia Bateman (1926-) & Katz, Martin (1929-)

--Meeting the Test. (Illus.). 192p. 1965. Four Winds Press.

Anderson, Susan

--May Perry of Africa. 1967. Broadman Press.

Anderson, Virginia McLean

--From Spring to Fall With Jane and Andy. LC 39-21569. 68 p. illus., 14 x 17 cm. 1939. Rand McNally & Company.

--Jane and Andy. N.D. Rand McNally & Co.

Anderson, W. H., Dr.

--The Catholic Crusoe: Or, The Adventures of Owen Evans. N.D. International Book Co.

Anderson, Walter Inglis (1903-1965)

--Robinson, the Pleasant History of an Unusual Cat. Anderson, Walter Inglis (1903-1965), illus. LC 82-10868. (Illus.). 70 p. 23cm. c.1982. (ISBN 0-87805-170-8). University Press of Mississippi.

Anderson, Walter W.

--Indian and Famous Scout Plays. 166p. N.D. T. S. Denison & Co Inc.

Anderson, Wayne, jt. auth. see Logue, Christopher.

Anderson, Wayne (1946-)

--A Mouse's Tale. LC 83-48170. (Illus.). 32p. (gr. 1-4). 1984. (ISBN 0-06-020109-6, HarpJ). (ISBN 0-06-020110-X). Har-Row.

Anderson, William Charles (1920-)

--Penelope: The Damp Detective. LC 73-91506. 224p. 1974. (ISBN 0-517-51481-8). Crown.

Andersson, Stig

--The Boy Who Made an Elephant. 32p. (gr. k-3). N.D. (ISBN 0-89191-190-1). Cook.

Andes, Dorothy P.

--Blocks. (gr. 4-7). N.D. Carlton.

Andler, Kenneth

--Mission to Fort No. 4. Kaufmann, Max R. (1905-), illus. LC 75-43447. (Illus.). 64 p. 22cm. (Bicentennial historiettes series). 1975. (ISBN 0-915892-04-9). Regional Center for Educational Training.

--The Signal Net. 1st ed. Hartman, C. L., illus. LC 53-7092. 183p. illus. 22cm. 1953. Ariel Books.

--The Stolen Spruce: A Mystery Adventure in the Maine Woods. 1st ed. Hartman, C. L., illus. LC 52-8448. 168 p. illus. 22 cm. 1952. Ariel Books.

Andre, Evelyn Marie (1924-)

--Places I Like to Be. LC 79-23964. (Illus.). 28 p. 26cm. c.1980. (ISBN 0-687-31540-9). Abingdon.

--Things We Like to Do. (Illus.). 28 p. 27cm. 1968. Abingdon Press.

Andre, Richard

--Ada's Birthday. 32p. (The Oak Leaf Library). 1882. A. C. Armstrong.

--Animated Tea Service. 32p. (The Oak Leaf Library). 1882. A. C. Armstrong.

--Dame Durden's Cooper Kettle, 1 of 6 Vols. (Illus.). (Tiny Shoes Ser.). N.D. E. & J. B. Young & Co.

--Dollie's Big Bath. 32p. (The Oak Leaf Library). 1882. A. C. Armstrong.

--Ebb and Flow. (The Gordon Library). N.D. Frederick Warne & Co.

--George's Money-Box. 32p. (The Oak Leaf Library). 1882. A. C. Armstrong & Son.

--Grandmother's Thimble. 32p. (The Oak Leaf Library). 1882. A. C. Armstrong & Son.

--Jack's Slate. 32p. (The Oak Leaf Library). 1882. A. C. Armstrong.

--Little Blossom: A Book of Child Fancies. (Illus.). 1884. E. J. B. & Co.

--The Magic Ring, 1 of 6 Vols. (Illus.). (Tiny Shoes Ser.). 1884. E. & J. B. Young & Co.

--Make Believe and Reality, 1 of 6 Vols. (Illus.). (Tiny Shoes Ser.). 1884. E. & J. B. Young & Co.

--May's Muff, 1 of 6 Vols. (Illus.). (Tiny Shoes Ser.). 1884. E. & J. B. Young & Co.

--The Outpost. (The Gordon Library). N.D. Frederick Warne & Co.

--Uncle Jim, 1 of 6 Vols. (Illus.). (Tiny Shoes Ser.). 1884. E. & J. B. Young & Co.

Andre, Richard, illus.

--The Babes in the Wood: Children in the Wood Ballad. LC 75-330204. 14p. col. ill. 21cm. (Little Folks Ser.). c.1888. McLoughlin Bros.

--Tiny Shoes, 1 of 6 Vols. (Illus.). (Tiny Shoes Ser.). 1884. E. & J. B. & Co.

Andreas, Evelyn, retold by.

--The Big Treasure Book of Fairy Tales. Seiden, Art, illus. LC 55-19. unpaged. illus. 34 cm. (Big treasure books). c.1954. Grossett & Dunlap.

--The Big Treasure Book of Nursery Tales. Weisgard, Leonard Joseph (1916-), illus. LC 54-4402. unpaged. illus. 34cm. (Big treasure books). c.1954. Grosset & Dunlap.

--Cinderella. Ives, Ruth, illus. (Illus.). (ps). 1964. (ISBN 0-448-04208-8). G&D.

--Cinderella. Ives, Ruth, illus. LC 55-20. unpaged. illus. 34 cm. (Big treasure books). c.1954. Grosset & Dunlap.

--Cinderella. Ives, Ruth, illus. LC 54-4893. unpaged. illus. 21 cm. (Treasure books. 879). 1954. Treasure Books.

--The Cub Scout Book of Cowboys and Indians. Hayes, William Dimitt (1913-), photos by. LC 54-37749. 21cm. 64p. (Wonder Books Ser.). 1954. Wonder Books.

--Fairy Tale. N.D. (ISBN 0-448-00323-6). Grosset & Dunlap.

--Fairy Tales. Seiden, Art, illus. (Illus.). color ils. 32p. (Silver Dollar Library Ser.). (gr. k-7). 1962. (ISBN 0-448-00323-6, G&D). Putnam Pub Group.

--Snow White and the Seven Dwarfs. N.D (Wonder Books). Grosset & Dunlap.

Andreas, Evelyn, adapted by see Lorenzini, Carlo.

Andreas, Evelyn, retold by see Sleeping Beauty.

Andreus, Hans

--Mr. Bumblemoose & the Glad Dog. Van Wely, Babs, illus. (gr. 2-5). 1975. (ISBN 0-8277-4493-5). British Bk Ctr.

Andrew, Mabel

--Dorothy's Adventure in Bedroom Land. 50p. N.D. Century Co.

Andrew, Margaret Hamer see Browne, Maggie, pseud.

Andrew, Prudence Hastings (1924-)

--Close Within My Own Circle. LC 79-78148. (gr. 7 up). 1980. (ISBN 0-525-66650-8). Lodestar Bks.

--The Constant Star. Orig. Title: The Earthworm. 1964. Putnam.

--Dog!. Stubley, Trevor Hugh (1932-), illus. LC 72-12920. (Illus.). 122 p. 22cm. 1973. (ISBN 0-8407-6272-0). (ISBN 0-8407-6272-0). T. Nelson.

--The Hooded Falcon. 1961. Putnam.

--Mister O'Brien. LC 73-7796. 161 p. 22cm. 1973. (ISBN 0-8407-6334-4). T. Nelson.

--A New Creature. 1968. G P Putman's Sons.

--Ordeal by Silence: A Story of Medieval Times. 1961. Putnam.

--A Question of Choice. 1962. Putnam.

--Una and the Heaven Baby. LC 75-16190. 142 p. 21cm. 1975, c.1972. (ISBN 0-8407-6421-9). T. Nelson.

Andrews, Addison Fletcher, et al.

--Tiny Tunes for Tiny People. Van Schaick, S. W, illus. 1900. Dodge Publishing Co.

Andrews, Anna

--Peggy and Michael of the Coffee Plantation. LC 31-14345. 20cm. 205p. (Peggy Lee Ser.). N.D. Cupples & Leon Co.

--Peggy Lee and the Mysterious Islands. LC 31-14349. 2 p. l., 212 p. front. 19 1/2 cm. (Her Plantation series). c.1931. Cupples & Leon Company.

--Peggy Lee of the Golden Thistle Plantation. LC 31-14347. 3 p. l., 210 p. front. 19 1/2 cm. (Her Plantation series). c.1931. Cupples & Leon Company.

--Peggy Lee, Sophomore. LC 32-137835. 3 p. l., 207 p. front. 19 1/2 cm. (Her Plantation series). c.1932. Cupples & Leon Company.

--Peggy Lee Stories for Girls. N.D. Cupples & Leon.

Andrews, Arthur (1923-)

--A Dog-eared book. 1st ed. Friss, Patricia, illus. LC 73-83475. 63p. ill. 29cm. c.1974. (ISBN 0-87949-015-2). Ashley Books.

Andrews, Charlton (1878-)

--The Butterfly Murder. LC 32-241326. 5p. 1., 233 p. 19 1/2 cm. c.1932. Sears Publishing Company.

Andrews, Clarence A., tr. see Gravel, Fern.

Andrews, Dorothy Westlake

--Boy with a Song. (Illus.). (gr. k). 1965. (ISBN 0-8042-2726-8). John Knox.

--Davie Decides. Marsh, Lucille Patterson, illus. LC 48-856520. 45 p. col. illus. 21 cm. (Children's hour library). 1948. Westminister Press.

--Flaco. Hutchinson, William Miller (1916-), illus. LC 58-7042. 122p. illus. 20cm. 1958. Friendship Press.

--God's World & Johhny. 1983. (ISBN 0-318-01335-5). Rod & Staff.

--Holiday for Helpers. Smalley, Janet (1893-), illus. LC 49-10816. 48 p. illus. (part col.) 21 cm. (Children's hour library). 1949. Westminister Press.

Andrews, Dorothy Westlake & Scott, Louise Binder

--The Secret Suitcase. Baldridge, Cyrus LeRoy (1889-), illus. LC 53-9535. 125p. illus. 21cm. 1953. Friendship Press.

Andrews, Elinor

--The Little People of Wood and Stream. Andrews, Elinor, illus. LC 41-104673. 72 p. illus. 21 1/2 cm. c.1941. House of Field, Inc.

--Monkey Shines. LC 40-82429. 21cm. 24p. N.D. Platt & Munk.

Andrews, Frances King

--Fairest Lord Jesus. White, John, illus. 1958. Broadman Press.

Andrews, Frank

--Cinderella Wore a Mini. (Illus.). (gr. 1-6). N.D. Vantage.

Andrews, Frank Emerson (1902-1978)

--For Charlemagne. Karov, Joseph, illus. LC 49-115675. 207 p. front. 21 cm. 1949. Harper.

--The Gingerbread House. Paflin, Roberta, pseud. (1903-), illus. Petty, Roberta Harris Pfafflin. LC 43-16589. 48 p. col. illus. 22 x 20 cm. 1943. Oxford University Press.

--Knights and Daze: A Family Fun Book. Hawes, Charles, illus. LC 66-104612. 48p. col. illus. 25cm. c.1966. Putnam.

--Nobody Comes to Dinner. Dabcovich, Lydia, illus. LC 76-3533. (Illus.). 32 p. 17x22cm. c.1976. (ISBN 0-316-04221-8). Little, Brown.

--Numbers, Please. Watson, Aldren Auld (1917-), illus. 1961. Little, Brown and Company.

--Upside-Down Town. Slobodkin, Louis (1903-1975), illus. LC 58-5171. (Illus.). (gr. 2-6). 1958. (ISBN 0-316-04188-2). (ISBN 0-316-04189-0). Little.

Andrews, Freida

--The Night the Sky Lit Up. Verdick, Mary, ed. Wenzel, David, illus. (Illus., Orig.). (Pal Paperbacks - Pal Skills I Ser.). (gr. 7-12). 1978. (ISBN 0-8374-3530-7). Xerox Ed Pubns.

Andrews, Glenn, jt. auth. see Sobol, Donald J.

Andrews, H. P.

--Six Steps to Honor: Or, Great Truths, 1 of 20 vols. (Illus.). 213p. (Selected Bks for Sunday School: No. 22). N.D. Set. Methodist Bk Concern.

Andrews, J. S

--The Bell of Nendrum. LC 85-21419. (Reprint of 1969 Bodley Head Edition). p. cm. 1985. (ISBN 0-85640-353-9). (ISBN 0-85640-341-5). Blackstaff Press.

--Cargo for a King. LC 72-89834. 173 p. 22cm. 1973, c.1972. (ISBN 0-525-27460-X). E. P. Dutton.

--The Green Hill of Nendrum. LC 70-102414. (Illus.). 214 p. 21cm. 1970. Hawthorn Books.

--Man from the Sea. LC 70-157948. 22cm. 154p. (gr. 4-7). 1971. (ISBN 0-525-34530-2). Dutton.

Andrews, Jan

--Ella: An Elephant-Unelephant. Bonn, Pat, illus. (Illus.). (Mini Books for Mini Hands Ser.). (gr. k-3). 1977. (ISBN 0-912766-24-7). (ISBN 0-686-86798-X). Tundra Bks.

Andrews, Jane (1833-1887)

--Agoonack and the Others. N.D. Lee & Shephard.

--Each and All. N.D. Ginn and Company.

--Each and All: Or, How the Seven Little Sisters Prove their Sisterhood. (A sequel to "The Seven Little Sisters."). (Illus.). 1882. Lee & Shepard.

--Each and All: Or, the Seven Little Sisters Prove Their Sisterhood. (Illus.). 142p. N.D. Dana Estes and Company.

--Geographical Plays. Complete ed. N.D. Ginn and Company.

--Geographical Plays. LC 12-22104. 6v. 18 1/2 cm. 1881. Lee and Shepard.

--Only a Year, and What it Brought. (Illus.). (The Seven Little Sisters Lib). N.D. Lee & Shepard.

--Only a Year, and what it Brought. (Illus.). (Our Girls' Prize Library Ser.). N.D. Lee & Shepard.

--Only a Year and What It Brought. N.D. Lothrop.

--Seven Little Sisters. N.D. Ginn and Company.

--Seven Little Sisters. (Illus.). N.D. Lee & Shepard.

--The Seven Little Sisters Who Live on the Round Ball that Floats in the Air. (Illus.). 121p. N.D. Dana Estes and Company.

--The Seven Little Sisters Who Live on the Round Ball That Floats in the Air. LC 4-16118. 1 p. l., 143 p. illus., plates. 18 cm. (On cover: Classics for home and school). 1893. Ginn and Company.

--The Seven Little Sisters Who Live on the Round Ball that Floats in the Air. (Illus.). (Seven Little Sisters Lib.). 1882. Lee & Shepard.

--The Seven Little Sisters Who Live on the Round Ball that Floats in the Air. LC 76-35460. 18cm. 127p. 1864, c.1860. Ticknor and Flields.

--The Seven Little Sisters Who Live on the Round Ball That Floats in the Air. Hopkins, Louisa Parsons Stone (1834-1895), ed. LC 42-44990. 4 p. l., vii-xxiv, 121 p. col. plates. 20 cm. 1902. Ginn & Company.

--The Seven Little Sisters Who Live on the Round Ball that Floats in the Air. Hopkins, Louisa Parsons, intro. by. LC 42-44990. 20cm. 121p. 1902. Ginn & Co.

--The Seven Little Sisters Who Live on the Round Ball that Floats in the Air. Hopkins, Louisa Parsons Stone, ed. LC 21-8710. 4 p. l., 7-142 p. plates. 17 1/2 cm. 17cm. 142p. (On cover: Classics for home and school). 1888. Lee and Shepard.

--The Stories Mother Nature told her Children. (Illus.). 131p. N.D. Dana Estes and Company.

--Stories Mother Nature Told her Children. N.D. Ginn & Co.

--The Stories Mother Nature Told Her Children. (Illus.). (The Seven Little Sisters Lib). 1895. Lee & Shepard.

--Stories of My Four Friends. (Illus.). 100p. N.D. Dana Estes and Company.

--Stories of my Four Friends. N.D. Ginn & Co.

--Ten Boys who Lived on the Road from Long Ago to Now. LC 13-9332. (Illus.). 18cm. 243p. (Classics for Home and School). 1893. Ginn & Company.

--Ten Boys Who Lived on the Road from Long Ago to Now. new ed. LC 24-21428. ix, 248 p. incl. front., illus. 19 1/2 cm. c.1924. Ginn and Company.

--Ten Boys Who Lived on the Road from Long Ago to Now. 3 p. l., 3-240 p. front. illus., plates. 18 cm. 1886. Lee and Shepard.

--The Ten Little Boys who Lived on the Road from Long Ago to Now. (Illus.). (The Seven Little Sisters Lib). N.D. Lee & Shepard.

Andrews, Julie see Edwards, Julie.

Andrews, Julie (1935-)

--The Last of the Really Great Whangdoodles. Kubinyi, Laszlo (1937-), illus. LC 73-5482. (gr. 3-7). 1974. (ISBN 0-06-021805-3, HarpJ). (ISBN 0-06-021805-3). Har-Row.

--Mandy. 1st ed. Brown, Judith Gwyn (1933-), illus. LC 76-157901. (Illus.). 188 p. 24cm. 1971. (ISBN 0-06-021803-7). Harper & Row.

Andrews, Leonora De Lima

--Do You Believe in Fairies?. LC 24-689448. 78 p. 19 1/2 cm. c.1924. Literary Commodities.

--This Way to the Farm: A Collection of Old and New Stories. Becker, Victor G., illus. LC 39-237596. 64 p. incl. col. front., illus. (part col.) 30 1/2 cm. c.1939. McLoughlin Bros., Inc.

Andrews, Leonora de Lima, ed. see Swift, Jonathan.

Andrews, Lillian E

--How Dan McRae Won Out. LC 25-10300. 62 p. 18 cm. c.1925. The Bible Institute Colportage Ass'n.

Andrews, Martin & Pucci, Mario

--Wild Animals. Nemo, illus. LC 75-111339. (Illus.). 26 p. 33cm. (Beginning nature books). 1970. Platt & Munk.

Andrews, Mary Evans

--Bugie: A Puppy in Old Yorktown. Lee, Manning de Villeneuve (1894-1980), illus. LC 58-7057. 23cm. (Tip Top Elf Books). 1958. Rand McNally.

--Hostage to Aledander. Decorations by Avery Johnson. 1st Ed. LC 61-9716. 244p. illus. 22cm. 1961. Longmans, Green.

--Hostage to Alexander. (gr. 6-9). 1961. McKay.

--Lanterns Aloft. 1st ed. Harper, Arthur, illus. LC 55-672595. 212p. illus. 21cm. 1955. Longmans, Green.

--Lanterns Aloft. Harper, Arthur, illus. (gr. 6-9). 1955. McKay.

--Messenger by Night. 1st ed. Johnson, Avery Fischer (1906-), illus. LC 52-13046. 206p. illus. 22cm. 1953. Longmans, Green.

Andrews, Mary Raymond Shipman, Mrs.

--The Better Treasure. Bunker, H. M., illus. N.D. Bobbs-Merrill Co.

--The Enchanted Forest, and Other Stories. Smith, Elmer Boyd (1860-1943), illus. LC 9-26471. 7 p. l., 11-235 p. col. front., 5 pl. 21 cm. c.1909. E. P. Dutton and Company.

--The Marshal. N.D. Bobbs-Merrill Co.

--Passing the Torch. LC 24-25742. 3 p. l., 84 p. front. 19 cm. 1924. C. Scribner's Sons.

Andrews, Ned

--Cowdog. LC 46-18719. 222 p. 21 cm. 1946. W. Morrow and Company.

--Jerky: The Story of Two Boys in the Old West. Tousey, Thomas Sanford, illus. LC 36-19225. 6 p. l., 3-295 p. incl. illus., plates. col. front. 21 cm. c.1936. W. Morrow & Company.

--Little Stranger: The Story of a Western Pony. Andrews, Ned, illus. LC 41-15459. 5 p. l., 3-248 p. front., plates. 21 cm. 1941. W. Morrow & Co.

--The Lost "Chicken Henry". LC 37-22645. 3 p. l., 3-276 p. incl. front., illus. 21 cm. 1937. W. Morrow & Co.

Andrews, Robert (1903-)

--Windfall: A Novel About Ten Million Dollars. LC 31-215391. 4 p. l., 3-280 p., 1 l. 19 1/2 cm. c.1931. The John Day Company.

Andrews, Roy C.

--Quest in the Desert. Wiese, Kurt (1887-1974), illus. (Illus.). (gr. 7-11). 1950. (ISBN 0-670-58461-4). Viking Pr.

--Quest of the Snow Leopard. Wiese, Kurt (1887-1974), illus. (Illus.). (gr. 7 up). 1955. (ISBN 0-670-58480-0). Viking Pr.

Andrews, Siri, tr. see Beskow, Elsa Maartman.

Andrews, Siri, tr. see Christensen, Haaken.

Andrews, Siri, tr. see Fitinghoff, Laura Matilda Bernhardina Runsten.

Andrews, Siri, tr. see Lindberg, Maja.

Andrews, Siri, tr. see Palm, Amy.

Andrews, Siri, tr. see Schram, Constance Wiel Nygaard.

Andrews, Tailer, ed.

--Animal Stories for Children, Collected. Kirmse, Marguerite (1885-1954), illus. LC 27-22445. viii, 241 p. col. front., illus. 25 cm. (Sears illustrated juveniles). c.1927. J. H. Sears & Company, Inc.

Andrews, Theodore

--Andy Breaks Trail. N.D. Macmillan.

--Angel in the Woods. N.D. Macmillan.

Andrews, Virginia Cleo

--Heaven. LC 85-16890. p. cm. c.1985. (ISBN 0-671-60536-4). Poseidon Press.

--High Up in a Penthouse. Andrews, Virginia Cleo, photos by. 24cm. 38p. 1938. Harper & Brothers.

Andrews, Wayne (1906-), tr. see Grimm, Jakob Ludwig Karl (1785-1863) & Grimm, Wilhelm Karl.

Andrews, Wendy

--The Supergirl Storybook. LC 84-3320. (Illus.). 64p. 1984. (ISBN 0-399-21075-X, Putnam). (ISBN 0-399-21077-6). Putnam Pub Group.

--The Supergirl Storybook: Based on the Motion Picture Supergirl. LC 84-3320. (Illus.). 60 p. 29cm. c.1984. (ISBN 0-399-21075-X). Putnam.

--Vacation Fever!. LC 84-3235. 1984. (ISBN 0-399-21084-9). Pacer Books.

--Vacation Fever!. 160p. (gr. 7 up). 1984. (ISBN 0-399-21084-9, Putnam). (ISBN 0-399-21083-0, Putnam). Putnam Pub Group.

Andreyev, L

--The Little Angel. N.D. Knopf.

Andros, Guy

--Freddie the Owl. MacKenzie, Garry (1921-), illus. LC 47-18373. 32 p. illus. 18 x 18 cm. 1947. Oxford University Press.

Andru, Ross & Orlando, Joe, illus.

--Superman Mix or Match Storybook. LC 79-84525. (ps-3). 1979. (ISBN 0-394-84211-1, BYR). Random.

Andrus, Vera (1895-)

--Black River: A Wisconsin Story. Burns, Irene, illus. LC 67-2655. 133 p. illus. 21 cm. 1967. Little, Brown.

--Sea-Bird Island. Andrus, Vera (1895-), illus. LC 39-21150. 24cm. 142p. N.D. Harcourt Brace & Co.

Andruss, Bessie Edmond

--Bible Stories as told to very Little Children. 156p. N.D. Coward-McCann.

--Rarely told Bible Stories for Bigger Children. Pointer, Priscilla, illus. 192p. N.D. Coward-McCann.

Anelay, Henry, illus.

--The Mother's Picture Alphabet. Stockham, Peter, intro. by. LC 74-75846. (Illus.). 64 p. 29cm. 1974. (ISBN 0-486-23089-9). Dover Publications.

Angel, Marie

--The Ark. LC 73-5475. (Illus.). 1 v. 1973. (ISBN 0-06-020139-8). Harper & Row.

Angeles, Peter

--Pouf: A Moth and Mite. Aramaya, illus. (Illus.). (Mini Books for Mini Hands Ser.). (gr. k-3). 1977. (ISBN 0-912766-25-5). (ISBN 0-686-86800-5). Tundra Bks.

Angeli, Arthur C. De see De Angeli, Arthur Craig.

Angeli, Arthur C. De see De Angeli, Arthur Craig & De Angeli, Marguerite Lofft, Mrs.

Angeli, Marguerite Lofft de see De Angeli, Arthur Craig & De Angeli, Marguerite Lofft, Mrs.

Angeli, Marguerite Lofft de see De Angeli, Marguerite Lofft, Mrs.

Angeli, Marguerite Lofft de see De Angeli, Marguerite Lofft, Mrs.

Angelico, Bernice Randall, Mrs.

--In Song Land: Rote Songs for Kindergarten and Primary Grades. LC 32-1787. 4 p. l., 72 p. 1 illus. 19 1/2 x 25 1/2 cm. 1932. The University Publishing Company.

Angelis, Nancy de, pseud., see Angelo, Nancy Carolyn Harrison.

Angell, Judie (1937-)

--The Buffalo Nickel Blues Band. LC 81-18075. 183 p. 22cm. c.1982. (ISBN 0-87888-195-6). Bradbury Press.

--Dear Lola: Or, How to Build Your Own Family : a Tale. LC 80-15111. p. cm. (gr. 4-6). 1980. (ISBN 0-87888-170-0). Bradbury Press.

--First the Good News. LC 83-6074. p. cm. 1983. (ISBN 0-02-705820-4). Bradbury Press.

--A Home Is to Share...& Share..& Share... LC 83-21356. 144p. (gr. 5-6). 1984. (ISBN 0-02-705830-1). Bradbury Pr.

--In Summertime It's Tuffy. LC 76-57810. 230 p. 23cm. c.1977. (ISBN 0-87888-117-4). Bradbury Press.

--One-Way to Ansonia. LC 85-5652. p. cm. 1985. (ISBN 0-02-705860-3). Bradbury Press.

--Ronnie and Rosey. LC 77-75362. 283 p. 22cm. c.1977. (ISBN 0-87888-124-7). Bradbury Press.

--Secret Selves. LC 79-12710. p. cm. 1979. (ISBN 0-87888-158-1). Bradbury Press.

--Suds, a New Daytime Drama. LC 82-22732. 167 p. 22cm. c.1983. (ISBN 0-87888-213-8). Bradbury Press.

--Tina Gogo. LC 77-16439. 196 p. 22cm. c.1978. (ISBN 0-87888-132-8). Bradbury Press.

--What's Best for You. LC 80-27425. p. cm. 1981. (ISBN 0-87888-181-6). Bradbury Press.

--A Word from Our Sponsor: Or, My Friend Alfred. LC 78-25716. 140 p. 22cm. c.1979. (ISBN 0-87888-142-5). Bradbury Press.

Angell, Polly

--Andy Jackson: Long Journey to the White House. 1st ed. Vosburgh, Leonard W. (1912-), illus. LC 56-5479. 192p. illus. 21cm. (American heritage series). 1956. Aladdin Books.

--Pat and the Iron Horse: New Americans in the 1840's. 1st ed. Schule, Clifford H., illus. LC 55-587818. 192p. illus. 21cm. (American heritage series). 1955. Aladdin Books.

Angelo

--The Dancing Imps of the Wine: Or, Stories and Fables. (Illus.). N.D. Hurst & Co.

Angelo, Nancy Carolyn Harrison see Angelis, Nancy de, pseud.

Angelo, Nancy Carolyn Harrison (1928-)

--Camembert. Angelis, Nancy de, pseud. LC 57-12079. (Illus.). 21cm. 28p. 1958. Houghton Mifflin.

Angelo, Ruth V

--The Sea Gulls. Richards, R. D., illus. 37 p. illus. 21 cm. c.1964. Vantage Press.

Angelo, Valenti (1897-)

--Acorn Tree. (Illus.). (gr. 1-3). 1958. (ISBN 0-8382-0010-9). Hale.

--Acorn Tree. Angelo, Valenti (1897-), illus. LC 58-14711. (Illus.). (gr. k-3). 1958. (ISBN 0-670-10233-4). (ISBN 0-670-10234-2). Viking Pr.

--Angelino and the Barefoot Saint. LC 61-13668. (Illus.). 62 p. 26cm. 1961. Viking Press.

--A Battle in Washington Square. Angelo, Valenti (1897-), illus. 1942. Golden Cross Press.

--The Bells of Bleecker Street. Angelo, Valenti (1897-), illus. LC 49-8136. 185 p. illus. 22 cm. 1949. Viking Press.

--Big Little Island. Angelo, Valenti (1897-), illus. LC 55-14875. 190p. illus. 22cm. 1955. Viking Press.
--The Candy Basket. Angelo, Valenti (1897-), illus. N.D. E . M. Hale and Co.
--The Candy Basket. Angelo, Valenti (1897-), illus. LC 60-4372. (Illus.). 26cm. 40p. 1960. Viking Press.
--Golden Gate. LC 74-17918. p. cm. (The Italian American Experience). 1975, c.1939. (ISBN 0-405-06391-1). Arno Press.
--Golden Gate. Angelo, Valenti (1897-), illus. N.D. Viking Press.
--Hill of Little Miracles. Angelo, Valenti (1897-), illus. LC 42-36294. 200 p. illus. 24 cm. 1942. The Viking Press.
--The Honey Boat. Angelo, Valenti (1897-), illus. LC 59-4690. (Illus.). 160 p. 22cm. 1959. Viking Press.
--Look Out Yonder. Angelo, Valenti (1897-), illus. LC 43-51251. 197 p. incl. front., illus. 22 cm. 1943. The Viking Press.
--The Marble Fountain. Angelo, Valenti (1897-), illus. LC 51-12128. 223 p. illus. 22 cm. 1951. Viking Press.
--The Merry Marcos. Angelo, Valenti (1897-), illus. LC 63-18370. 141 p. illus. 22 cm. 1963. Viking Press.
--Nino. Angelo, Valenti (1897-), illus. (Illus.). (gr. 4-7). 1938. (ISBN 0-670-51397-0). (ISBN 0-670-51398-9). Viking Pr. **Award: (JNM).**
--Paradise Valley. Angelo, Valenti (1897-), illus. LC 40-32147. 230 p. col illus. 23 cm. 1940. The Viking Press.
--The Rooster Club. Angelo, Valenti (1897-), illus. LC 44-7664. 150 p. incl. front., illus. 22 cm. 1944. The Viking Press.
--The Tale of a Donkey. Angelo, Valenti (1897-), illus. LC 66-119157. 110p. illus. 22cm. (gr. 3-6). c.1966. (ISBN 0-670-69150-X). Viking.

Angelo, Valenti (1897-), illus.
--The Arabian Nights. Burton, Richard (1897-), tr. N.D. Heritage Press.
--Persian Fairy Tales. LC 42-23229. 3 p. l., 9-104 p., 1 l. 23 1/2 x 12 1/2 cm. 1939. The Peter Pauper Press.

Angier, Bradford, jt. auth. see Dixon, Jeanne.

Angier, Bradford & Corcoran, Barbara
--Ask for Love and They Give You Rice Pudding. LC 77-354. 151 p. 22cm. 1977. (ISBN 0-395-25300-4). Houghton Mifflin.

Anglund, Joan Walsh, jt. auth. see Mother Goose.

Anglund, Joan Walsh (1926-)
--A is for Always: An ABC Book. LC 68-15423. 11cm. 32p. 1968. (ISBN 0-15-200670-2). Harcourt Brace Jovanovich.
--Baby Brother. LC 84-15121. (Illus.). 34 p. 23cm. c.1985. (ISBN 0-394-86837-4). (ISBN 0-394-96837-9). Random House.
--The Brave Cowboy. LC 59-5627. (Illus.). unpaged. 19cm. 1959. Harcourt, Brace.
--The Brave Cowboy. LC 76-15638. p. cm. (Voyager book ; AVB 104). 1976, c.1959. Harcourt Brace Jovanovich.
--Childhood Is a Time of Innocence. LC 64-20974. 1 v. (unpaged) illus. (part col.) 18 cm. 1964. Harcourt, Brace & World.
--A Child's Book of Old Nursery Rhymes. LC 73-75429. (Illus.). 30 p. 17cm. 1973. Atheneum.
--A Christmas Book. LC 83-3384. (Illus.). 48p. (gr. k-3). 1983. (ISBN 0-394-85551-5). (ISBN 0-394-95551-X). Random.
--Christmas Candy Book. (Illus.). 1983. Determined Prods.
--Christmas is a Time for Giving. Anglund, Joan Walsh (1926-), illus. LC 61-10106. 32p. 1961. Harcourt Brace Jovanovich.
--Christmas Joys. (Illus.). 1982. Determined Prods.
--Cowboy and His Friend. LC 61-6110. (Illus.). 1 v. (unpaged. 19cm. 1961. Harcourt, Brace & World.
--Cowboy and His Friend. LC 76-16112. p. cm. (Voyager book ; AVB 105). 1976, c.1961. (ISBN 0-15-622715-0). Harcourt Brace Jovanovich.
--The Cowboy's Christmas. LC 70-190551. (Illus.). 40 p. 19cm. 1972. Atheneum.
--Cowboy's Secret Life. LC 63-16029. unpaged. illus. 19 cm. 1963. Harcourt, Brace & World.
--Do You Love Someone?. LC 76-152692. (Illus.). 32 p. 18cm. 1971. (ISBN 0-15-224190-6). Harcourt Brace Jovanovich.
--Emily & Adam, 3 bks. Anglund, Joan Walsh (1926-), illus. Incl. The Emily Book. LC 78-20719; The Adam Book. LC 78-20720; The Emily & Adam Book of Opposites. LC 78-20722. (Illus.). (ps-1). 1979. Boxed Set. (ISBN 0-394-84254-5, BYR). Random.
--A Friend Is Someone Who Likes You. 1st ed. LC 58-8624. unpaged. illus. 18cm. 1958. Harcourt, Brace. **Award: (NYT).**
--In a Pumpkin Shell. Anglund, Joan Walsh (1926-), illus. LC 60-10243. (Illus.). (ps-2). 1977. (ISBN 0-15-644425-9, VoyB). HarBraceJ.
--The Joan Walsh Anglund Storybook. Anglund, Joan Walsh (1926-), illus. LC 78-55913. p. cm. 1978. (ISBN 0-394-83803-3). (ISBN 0-394-93803-8). Random House.
--Little Bookshelf. Anglund, Joan Walsh (1926-), illus. (Illus.). (gr. 3 up). 1970. Set. (ISBN 0-15-245615-5). HarBraceJ.
--Look Out the Window. LC 59-9271. (Illus.). 35 p. 21cm. 1959. Harcourt, Brace.
--Love Is a Special Way of Feeling. Silver Anniversary ed. Anglund, Joan Walsh (1926-), illus. LC 60-6224. (Illus.). 1 v. (unpaged. 18cm. 1985, c.1960. Harcourt, Brace.
--Love Is a Special Way of Feeling. silver anniversary ed. Anglund, Joan Walsh (1926-), illus. LC 84-19296. (Illus.). 32 p. 18cm. 1985, c.1960. (ISBN 0-15-249724-2). Harcourt Brace Jovanovich.
--Morning Is a Little Child. Anglund, Joan Walsh (1926-), illus. LC 69-11592. (Illus.). 32p. col. illus. 25cm. (gr. 4-6). 1969. (ISBN 0-15-255652-4, HJ). HarBraceJ.
--Nibble Nibble Mousekin: A Tale of Hansel and Gretel. 1st Ed. LC 62-144221. unpaged. illus. 25cm. 1962. Harcourt, Brace & World.
--Nibble Nibble Mousekin: A Tale of Hansel and Gretel. LC 76-41386. (Original Authors: The Grimm Brothers.). (Illus.). 32 p. 23cm. (Voyager book ; AVB 110). 1977, c.1962. (ISBN 0-15-665588-8). Harcourt Brace Jovanovich.
--A Pocketful of Proverbs. LC 64-12373. 32 p. illus. (part col.) 11 cm. 1964. Harcourt, Brace & World.
--See the Year. Anglund, Joan Walsh (1926-), illus. LC 84-60248. (Illus.). 28p. (Chunky Bks.). (ps). 1984. (ISBN 0-394-86641-X, Pub. by BYR). Random.
--Slice of Snow: A Book of Poems. Anglund, Joan Walsh (1926-), illus. LC 70-11830. (gr. 1-5). 1970. (ISBN 0-15-183015-0, HJ). HarBraceJ.
--Spring Is a New Beginning. LC 63-7892. unpaged. illus. 18 cm. 1963. Harcourt, Brace & World.
--What Color Is Love?. LC 66-13795. 1v. (unpaged) illus. (pt. col.) 18cm. c.1966. Harcourt.
--A Year Is Round. Anglund, Joan Walsh (1926-), illus. LC 66-8496. (Illus.). (ps-6). 1966. (ISBN 0-15-299810-1). HarBraceJ.

Anglund, Joan Walsh (1926-), illus.
--Golden Treasury of Poetry. N.D. Golden Books.

Angress, Therese, jt. auth. see Boiko, Claire.

Angrist, Stanley Wolff (1933-)
--Other Worlds, Other Beings. (Illus.). 1973. (ISBN 0-690-60205-7). Thomas Y Crowell.

Angulo, Jaime De see De Angulo, Jaime.

Angus, David, ed.
--Roses and Thorns: Scottish Teenage Verse. LC 73-155536. (Illus.). 12, 105, 16 p. 19cm. 1972. Club Leabhar.

Anker, Charlotte (1934-)
--Last Night I Saw Andromeda. Fetz, Ingrid (1915-), illus. LC 74-19709. (Illus.). 126 p. 22cm. 1975. (ISBN 0-8098-2427-2). H. Z. Walck.

Ann, Fay, ed. see Corey, Dorothy.

Annabel, Russell
--Alaskan Tales. N.D. A. S. Barnes & Co.

Anna Louise (1873-)
--Poetry for Junior Students: With Suggestive Studies. LC 29-5266. xiv, 152 p. illus. 19 cm. c.1929. Ginn and Company.

Anna St. John, pseud., see Baker, Virginia.

Annen, Sharon, tr. see Desnos, Robert.

Annett, Cora, pseud., see Scott, Cora Annett Pipitone.

Annett, Cora, pseud. (1931-)
--Cora Annett's Homerhenry. Scott, Cora Annette Pipitone. Pinkney, Jerry (1939-), illus. LC 75-88690. (Illus.). 32 p. 27cm. 1970. Addison-Wesley.
--Dog Who Thought He Was a Boy. Scott, Cora Annett Pipitone. Lorraine, Walter Henry (1929-), illus. (Illus.). (gr. k-3). 1965. (ISBN 0-395-18471-1). HM.
--The Dog Who Thought He Was a Boy. Scott, Cora Annett Pipitone. Lorraine, Walter Henry (1929-), illus. (Illus.). 48p. (gr. k-3). 1974. (ISBN 0-395-18564-5, Sandpiper). HM.
--The Dog Who Thought He Was a Boy. Scott, Cora Annette Pipitone. Lorraine, Walter Henry (1929-), illus. LC 65-11352. 48p. col. illus. 26cm. c.1965. (ISBN 0-395-18471-1). Houghton.
--How the Witch Got Alf. Scott, Cora Annett Pipitone. Kellogg, Steven (1941-), illus. LC 74-8808. (Illus.). 47 p. 23cm. 1975. (ISBN 0-531-02791-0). F. Watts.
--When the Porcupine Moved in. Scott, Cora Annett Pipitone. Parnall, Peter (1936-), illus. LC 71-131152. (Illus.). 40 p. 26cm. 1971. (ISBN 0-531-01987-X). F. Watts.

Annixter, Jane, pseud., see Sturtzel, Jane Levington Comfort.

Annixter, Jane, pseud. (1903-)
--The Devil of the Woods: A Collection of Thirteen Animal Stories. Sturtzel, Jane Levington Comfort. LC 58-13214. 175 p. 21cm. 1958. Hill and Wang.

Annixter, Jane, pseud. (1903-) & Annixter, Paul, pseud. (1894-)
--Buffalo Chief. Sturtzel, Jane Levington Comfort. Sturtzel, Howard Allison. LC 58-3776. (Illus.). 219 p. 22cm. 1958. Holiday House.
--The Great White. Sturtzel, Jane Levington Comfort. Sturtzel, Howard Allison. LC 66-8846. 158 p. 22cm. 1966. Holiday House.
--The Last Monster. Sturtzel, Jane Levington Comfort. Sturtzel, Howard Allison. LC 80-7978. p. cm. c.1980. (ISBN 0-15-243614-6). Harcourt Brace Jovanovich.
--The Phantom Stallion: A Penny of Paintrock Story. Sturtzel, Jane Levington Comfort. Sturtzel, Howard Allison. Schultz, Robert, illus. LC 61-16936. 188 p. illus. 20 cm. 1961. Golden Press.
--The Runner. Sturtzel, Jane Levington Comfort. Sturtzel, Howard Allison. LC 56-13885. 220 p. illus. 22 cm. 1956. Holiday House.
--Trouble at Paintrock: A Penny of Paintrock Story. Sturtzel, Jane Levington Comfort. Sturtzel, Howard Allison. Micale, Albert (1913-), illus. LC 62-15849. 188p. illus. 20cm. 1962. Golden Press.
--Trumpeter: The Story of a Swan. Sturtzel, Jane Levington Comfort. Sturtzel, Howard Allison. LC 73-76796. (Illus.). (gr. 4 up). 1973. (ISBN 0-8234-0227-4). Holiday.
--Vikan the Mighty. Sturtzel, Jane Levington Comfort. Sturtzel, Howard Allison. LC 77-3949. 192 p. 22cm. 1969. Holiday House.
--Wagon Scout. Sturtzel, Jane Levington Comfort. Sturtzel, Howard Allison. 204p. (gr. 7 up). 1965. (ISBN 0-8234-0128-6). Holiday.
--Wagon Scout. Sturtzel, Jane Levington Comfort. Sturtzel, Howard Allison. LC 65-7563. 204p. 22cm. c.1965. (ISBN 0-8234-0128-6). Holiday House.
--Wapootin. Sturtzel, Jane Levington Comfort. Sturtzel, Howard Allison. LC 75-10676. (Illus.). 63 p. 24cm. c.1976. (ISBN 0-698-20353-4). Coward, McCann & Geoghegan.
--White Shell Horse. Sturtzel, Jane Levington Comfort. Sturtzel, Howard Allison. LC 70-151751. (Illus.). 188 p. 22cm. 1971. (ISBN 0-8234-0187-1). Holiday House.
--Windigo. Sturtzel, Jane Levington Comfort. Sturtzel, Howard Allison. LC 63-3018. 196 p. 22 cm. 1963. Holiday House.
--The Year of the She-Grizzly. Sturtzel, Jane Levington Comfort. Sturtzel, Howard Allison. Riswold, Gilbert, illus. LC 77-26724. (Illus.). (gr. 3-5). 1978. (ISBN 0-698-20456-5, Coward). Putnam Pub Group.

Annixter, Paul, pseud., see Sturtzel, Howard Allison.

Annixter, Paul, jt. auth. see Annixter, Jane.

Annixter, Paul, pseud. (1894-)
--The Best Nature Stories of Paul Annixter. Sturtzel, Howard Allison. LC 74-9347. xii, 181 p. 22cm. 1974. (ISBN 0-88208-043-1). L. Hill.
--The Best Nature Stories of Paul Annixter. Sturtzel, Howard Allison. Robinson, Ruth, intro. by. N.D. Lawrence Hill & Co Inc.
--The Cat That Clumped. Sturtzel, Howard Allison. Turkle, Brinton Cassaday (1915-), illus. LC 66-3351. (Illus.). 36p. (gr. k-3). 1966. (ISBN 0-8234-0025-5). Holiday.
--The Devil of the Woods: A Collection of Thirteen Animal Stories. Sturtzel, Howard Allison. LC 70-81259. ix, 175 p. 21cm. (Short story index reprint series). 1969, c.1958. Books for Libraries Press.
--The Devil of the Woods: A Collection of Thirteen Animal Stories. Sturtzel, Howard Allison. LC 58-13214. 175 p. 21 cm. 1958. Hill and Wang.
--Horns of Plenty. Sturtzel, Howard Allison. Annixter, Jane, pseud. (1903-) Sturtzel, Jane Levington Comfort. LC 60-50960. 203 p. llus. 22 cm. 1960. Holiday House.
--The Hunting Horn and Other Dog Stories. Sturtzel, Howard Allison. 1957. Hill & Wang.
--Pride of Lions. Sturtzel, Howard Allison. 192p. (gr. 7-12). 1960. (ISBN 0-8090-7885-6). Hill & Wang.
--Pride of Lions: And Other Stories. Sturtzel, Howard Allison. LC 60-7319. 177p. 21cm. 1960. Hill and Wang.
--Puck of the Dusk. Sturtzel, Howard Allison. Riswold, Gilbert, illus. LC 71-103634. (Illus.). 32 p. 24cm. 1970. Scribner.
--Swiftwater. Sturtzel, Howard Allison. (gr. 7 up). 1950. (ISBN 0-8090-9080-5). Hill & Wang.
--Swiftwater. Sturtzel, Howard Allison. (gr. 7-9). N.D. (ISBN 0-590-02903-7, Schol Pap). Scholastic Inc.
--Swiftwater. Sturtzel, Howard Allison. (Keith Jennison Large Type Bks). (gr. 6 up). N.D. (ISBN 0-531-00287-X). Watts.
--Teen-Age Wild Animal Stories. Sturtzel, Howard Allison. Furman, Abraham Loew (1902-), ed. LC 66-5582. 192p. 21cm. 1966. Lantern.
--Wilderness Ways. Sturtzel, Howard Allison. Bull, Charles Livingston (1874-1932), illus. N.D. Penn Publishing Co.

Anno, Mitsumasa (1926-)
--Anno's Alphabet: An Adventure in Imagination. Anno, Mitsumasa (1926-), illus. LC 73-21652. 64 p. (chiefly col. illus.). 26cm. 1975, c.1974. (ISBN 0-690-00540-7). (ISBN 0-690-00540-7). Crowell. **Awards: (NYT); (BGH); (ALA).**
--Anno's Animals. LC 79-11721. p. cm. 1979, c.1977. (ISBN 0-529-05545-7). (ISBN 0-529-05546-5). Collins.
--Anno's Britain. Anno, Mitsumasa (1926-), illus. LC 81-21058. (Illus.). 48 p. 26cm. 1982, c.1981. (ISBN 0-399-20861-5). Philomel Books. **Award: (NYT).**
--Anno's Counting Book. Anno, Mitsumasa (1926-), illus. LC 76-28977. (Illus.). 28 p. 1977, c.1975. (ISBN 0-690-01287-X). (ISBN 0-690-01288-8). Crowell. **Award: (BGH).**
--Anno's Counting House. (Illus.). 48p. 1982. (ISBN 0-399-20896-8, Philomel). Putnam Pub Group. **Award: (ALA).**
--Anno's Flea Market. Anno, Mitsumasa (1926-), illus. LC 83-21954. (Illus.). 44p. (gr. k-3). 1984. (ISBN 0-399-21031-8, Philomel). Putnam Pub Group.
--Anno's Italy. LC 79-17649. (Illus.). 48 p. 25cm. 1980, c.1978. (ISBN 0-529-05559-7). (ISBN 0-529-05560-0). Collins.
--Anno's Italy. LC 83-17439. 1984, c.1978. (ISBN 0-399-20770-8). Philomel Books.
--Anno's Journey. Anno, Mitsumasa (1926-), illus. LC 77-16336. (Illus.). 47 p. 26cm. 1978, c.1977. (ISBN 0-529-05418-3). (ISBN 0-529-05419-1). Collins-World. **Awards: (BGH); (ALA).**
--Anno's Magical ABC: An Anamorphic Alphabet. Anno, Mitsumasa (1926-), illus. 1981. Philomel.
--Anno's Medieval World. Anno, Mitsumasa (1926-), illus. LC 79-28367. 32p. 1st U.S. edition. (gr. 3 up). 1980. (ISBN 0-399-20742-2, Philomel). (ISBN 0-399-61153-3). Putnam Pub Group. **Award: (ALA).**
--Anno's USA. LC 83-13107. p. cm. 1983. Philomel Books.
--Bigger Is Better. Beneduce, Ann K., ed. (Illus.). (ps-2). N.D. (ISBN 0-686-24408-7). (ISBN 0-686-24409-5). Collins Pubs.
--Dr. Anno's Magical Midnight Circus. LC 72-78598. 28 p. (chiefly col. illus. 28cm. 1972. (ISBN 0-8348-2011-0). Weatherhill.
--The King's Flower. Anno, Mitsumasa (1926-), illus. LC 78-9596. (Illus.). 30 p. 29cm. 1979, c.1976. (ISBN 0-529-05458-2). (ISBN 0-529-05459-0). Collins.
--The King's Flower. Anno, Mitsumasa (1926-), illus. LC 78-9596. (Illus.). 32p. (ps-3). 1979. (ISBN 0-399-20764-3, Philomel). (ISBN 0-399-61167-3). Putnam Pub Group. **Award: (ALA).**
--Topsy-Turvies: Pictures to Stretch the Imagination. Anno, Mitsumasa (1926-), illus. LC 71-96054. (Illus.). 28p. (gr. k-5). 1970. (ISBN 0-8348-2004-8). Weatherhill. **Award: (NYT).**
--Upside-Downers: More Pictures to Stretch the Imagination. LC 71-157269. (Illus.). 27 p. 28cm. 1971. (ISBN 0-8348-2005-6). Walker/Weatherhill I.E. J. Weatherhill; Distributed by Walker.

A. Nobody
--A. Nobody's Nonsense for Somebody, Anybody, or Everybody, Particularly the Baby Body. (Illus.). N.D. DeWolfe, Wiske & Co.

Anrooy, Frans Van
--The Bird Tree. Tol, Jaap, illus. LC 67-558271. 1 v. (unpaged) col. illus. 29cm. 1st U.S. edition. 1967. Harcourt.
--The Lady of the Sea. Tol, Jaap, illus. LC 79-108013. (Illus.). 24 p. 29cm. 1971. (ISBN 0-87614-027-4). Carolrhoda Books.
--The Sea Horse. Tol, Jaap, illus. LC 68-136916. 1 v. (unpaged) col. illus. 29cm. 1st U.S. edition. 1968, c.1967. Harcourt.

Ansell, Jack (1925-1976)
--Giants. 260p. 1975. (ISBN 0-87795-111-X). Arbor House Publishing Company.
--Jelly. 244p. 1971. (ISBN 0-87795-018-0). Arbor House Publishing Company.

Ansell, Mary
--The Happy Garden. Dawson, Charles E., illus. N.D. Funk & Wagnalls.
--Happy Houses. N.D. Funk & Wagnalls.

Ansley, Gladys Piatt (1906-)
--Will It Bite? Can I Eat It?. Converse, James, illus. LC 61-15590. 61p. illus. 24cm. 1961. Pacific Press Pub. Association.

Anson, Alice
--The Dormitory Mystery. LC 37-9477. iii, 208 p. front. 20 cm. c.1937. Cupples & Leon Company.
--Escape by Night. LC 41-129119. vii 106 p. front. 20 cm. c.1941. Cupples and Leon Company.

Anson, Brian (1935-)
--Gus and Gilly. Anson, Brian (1935-), illus. LC 72-102735. (Illus.). 1970. E.P. Dutton & Co.
--Gus and Gilly: The Winter Journey. LC 76-102736. (Illus.). 27 p. 16cm. 1970. E. P. Dutton.

--The Movie Boys' First Showhouse: Or, Fighting for a Foothold in Fairlands. Stratemeyer Syndicate. LC 27-731073. 1 p. l., 206 p. 18 1/2 cm. Repr. of 1931 ed (Pub. by Grosset & Dunlap). (The Movie Boys Ser.: No. 11). Orig. Title: The Motion Picture Chums' First Venture; Or, Opening a Photo Playhouse in Fairlands. 1926. Garden City Publishing Company, Inc.

--The Movie Boys in Earthquake Land: Or, Filming Pictures Amid Strange Perils. Stratemeyer Syndicate. 1 p. l., 214 p. 18 1/2 cm. Repr. of 1913 ed (Pub. by Grosset & Dunlap). (The Movie Boys Ser.: No. 5). Orig. Title: The Moving Picture Boys in Earthquake Land; Or, Working Amid Many Perils. 1926. Garden City Publishing Company, Inc.

--The Movie Boys in Peril: Or, Strenuous Days Along the Panama Canal. Stratemeyer Syndicate. LC 26-22317. 1 p. l., 218 p. 19 cm. Repr. of 1915 ed (Pub. by Grosset & Dunlap). (The Movie Boys Ser.: No. 7). Orig. Title: The Moving Picture Boys at Panama; Or, Stirring Adventures Along the Great Canal. 1926. Garden City Publishing Co., Inc.

--The Movie Boys in the Jungle: Or, Lively Times Among the Wild Beasts. Stratemeyer Syndicate. LC 26-128326. 1 p. l., 211 p. 18 1/2 cm. Repr. of 1913 ed (Pub. by Grosset & Dunlap). (The Movie Boys Ser.: No. 4). Orig. Title: The Moving Picture Boys in the Jungle; Or, Stirring Times Among the Wild Animals. 1926. Garden City Publishing Company, Inc.

--The Movie Boys in the Wild West: Or, Stirring Days Among the Cowboys and Indians. Stratemeyer Syndicate. LC 26-602973. 1 p. l., 212 p. 19 cm. Repr. of 1913 ed (Pub. by Grosset & Dunlap). (The Movie Boys Ser.: No. 2). Orig. Title: The Moving Picture Boys in the West; Or, Taking Scenes Among the Cowboys and Indians. 1926. Garden City Publishing Company, Inc.

--The Movie Boys' New Idea: Or, Getting the Best of Their Enemies. Stratemeyer Syndicate. 1 p. l., 213 p. 18 1/2 cm. Repr. of 1914 ed (Pub. by Grosset & Dunlap). (The Movie Boys Ser.: No. 15). Orig. Title: The Motion Picture Chums' New Idea; Or, The First Educational Photo Playhouse. 1926. Garden City Publishing Company, Inc.

--The Movie Boys on Broadway: Or, The Mystery of the Missing Cash Box. Stratemeyer Syndicate. LC 27-73218. 1 p. l., 218 p. 19 cm. Repr. of 1913 ed (Pub. by Grosset & Dunlap). (The Movie Boys Ser.: No. 13). Orig. Title: The Motion Picture Chums on Broadway; Or, The Mystery of the Missing Cash Box. 1926. Garden City Publishing Company, Inc.

--The Movie Boys on Call: Or, Filming the Perils of a Great City. Stratemeyer Syndicate. LC 26-6032. 1 p. l., 206 p. 18 1/2 cm. Repr. of 1913 ed (Pub. by Grosset & Dunlap). (The Movie Boys Ser.: No. 1). Orig. Title: The Moving Picture Boys; Or, The Perils of a Great City Depicted. 1926. Garden City Publishing Company, Inc.

--The Movie Boys' Outdoor Exhibition: Or, The Film that Solved a Mystery. Stratemeyer Syndicate. Repr. of 1914 ed (Pub. by Grosset & Dunlap). (The Movie Boys Ser.: No. 14). Orig. Title: The Motion Picture Chums' Outdoor Exhibition; Or, The Film that Solved a Mystery. 1927. Garden City Publishing Company, Inc.

--The Movie Boys Under Fire: Or, The Search for the Stolen Film. Stratemeyer Syndicate. LC 26-22315. 1 p. l., 213 p. 19 cm. Repr. of 1918 ed (Pub. by Grosset & Dunlap). (The Movie Boys Ser.: No. 9). Orig. Title: The Moving Picture Boys on the War Front; Or, The Hunt for the Stolen Army Film. 1926. Garden City Publishing Company, Inc.

--The Movie Boys Under the Sea: Or, The Treasure of the Lost Ship. Stratemeyer Syndicate. LC 26-22316. 1 p. l., 214 p. 19 cm. Repr. of 1916 ed (Pub. by Grosset & Dunlap). (The Movie Boys Ser.: No. 8). Orig. Title: The Moving Picture Boys Under the Sea; Or, The Treasure of the Lost Ship. 1926. Garden City Publishing Co., Inc.

--The Movie Boys Under Uncle Sam: Or, Taking Pictures for the Army. Stratemeyer Syndicate. LC 26-22323. 1 p. l., 212 p. 19 cm. Repr. of 1919 ed (Pub. by Grosset & Dunlap). (The Movie Boys Ser.: No. 10). Orig. Title: The Moving Picture Boys on French Battlefields; Or, Taking Pictures for the U. S. Army. 1926. Garden City Publishing Company, Inc.

--The Movie Boys' War Spectacle: Or, The Film That Won the Prize. Stratemeyer Syndicate. LC 27-12673. 1 p. l., 210 p. 18 1/2 cm. Repr. of 1916 ed (Pub. by Grosset & Dunlap). (The Movie Boys Ser.: No. 17). Orig. Title: The Motion Picture Chums' War Spectacle; Or, The Film That Won the Prize. 1927. Garden City Publishing Company, Inc.

--The Moving Picture Boys and the Flood: Or, Perilous Days on the Mississippi. Stratemeyer Syndicate. Rogers, Walter S., illus. (The Moving Picture Boys Ser.: No. 6). 1914. Grosset & Dunlap.

--The Moving Picture Boys at Panama: Or, Stirring Adventures Along the Great Canal. Stratemeyer Syndicate. Rogers, Walter S., illus. (The Moving Picture Boys Ser.: No. 7). 1915. Grosset & Dunlap.

--The Moving Picture Boys at Seaside Park: Or, The Rival Photo Theatres of the Boardwalk. Stratemeyer Syndicate. Richards, Dick, illus. Reissue of 1913 ed. (The Moving Picture Boys Ser.: No. 12). Orig. Title: The Motion Picture Chums at Seaside Park; Or, The Rival Photo Theatres of the Boardwalk. 1921. Grosset & Dunlap.

--The Moving Picture Boys' First Showhouse: Or, Opening up for Business in Fairlands. Stratemeyer Syndicate. Richards, Dick, illus. Reissue of 1913 ed. (The Moving Picture Boys Ser.: No. 11). Orig. Title: The Motion Picture Chums' First Venture; Or, Opening a Photo Playhouse in Fairlands. 1921. Grosset & Dunlap.

--The Moving Picture Boys in Earthquake Land: Or, Working Amid Many Perils. Stratemeyer Syndicate. Rogers, Walter S., illus. (The Moving Picture Boys Ser.: No. 5). 1913. Grosset & Dunlap.

--The Moving Picture Boys in the Jungle: Or, Stirring Times Among the Wild Animals. Stratemeyer Syndicate. Rogers, Walter S., illus. (The Moving Picture Boys Ser.: No. 4). 1913. Grosset & Dunlap.

--The Moving Picture Boys in the West: Or, Taking Scenes Among the Cowboys and Indians. Stratemeyer Syndicate. Rogers, Walter S., illus. (The Moving Picture Boys Ser.: No. 2). 1913. Grosset & Dunlap.

--The Moving Picture Boys' New Idea. Stratemeyer Syndicate. Rogers, Walter S., illus. Reissue of 1914 ed. (The Moving Picture Boys Ser.: No. 15). Orig. Title: The Motion Picture Chums' New Idea; Or, The First Educational Photo Playhouse. 1922. Grosset & Dunlap.

--The Moving Picture Boys on Broadway: Or, The Mystery of the Missing Cash Box. Stratemeyer Syndicate. Richards, Dick, illus. Reissue of 1914 ed. (The Moving Picture Boys Ser.: No. 13). Orig. Title: The Motion Picture Chums on Broadway; Or, The Mystery of the Missing Cash Box. 1921. Grosset & Dunlap.

--The Moving Picture Boys on French Battlefields: Or, Taking Pictures for the U. S. Army. Stratemeyer Syndicate. Owen, Robert Emmett (1878-), illus. (The Moving Picture Boys Ser.: No. 10). 1919. Grosset & Dunlap.

--The Moving Picture Boys on the Coast: Or, Showing the Perils of the Deep. Stratemeyer Syndicate. Rogers, Walter S., illus. (The Moving Picture Boys Ser.: No. 3). 1913. Grosset & Dunlap.

--The Moving Picture Boys on the War Front: Or, The Hunt for the Stolen Army Film. Stratemeyer Syndicate. Owen, Robert Emmett (1878-), illus. (The Moving Picture Boys Ser.: No. 9). 1918. Grosset & Dunlap.

--The Moving Picture Boys: Or, The Perils of a Great City Depicted. Stratemeyer Syndicate. Rogers, Walter S., illus. (The Moving Picture Boys Ser.: No. 1). 1913. Grosset & Dunlap.

--The Moving Picture Boys' Outdoor Exhibition: Or, The Film That Solved a Mystery. Stratemeyer Syndicate. Rogers, Walter S., illus. Reissue of 1914 ed. (The Moving Picture Boys Ser.: No. 14). Orig. Title: The Motion Picture Chums' Outdoor Exhibition; Or, The Film That Solved a Mystery. 1922. Grosset & Dunlap.

--The Moving Picture Boys Under the Sea: Or, The Treasure of the Lost Ship. Stratemeyer Syndicate. Rogers, Walter S., illus. (The Moving Picture Boys Ser.: No. 8). 1916. Grosset & Dunlap.

--Tom Swift Among the Diamond Makers: Or, The Secret of Phantom Mountain. Stratemeyer Syndicate. Boehm, H. Richard, illus. LC 13-16338. iv, 216 p. front. 19 1/2 cm. (The Tom Swift Ser.: No. 7). c.1911. Gorsset & Dunlap.

--Tom Swift Among the Fire Fighters: Or, Battling with the Flames from the Air. Stratemeyer Syndicate. Rogers, Walter S., illus. (The Tom Swift Ser.: No. 24). 1921. Grosset & Dunlap.

--Tom Swift and His Aerial Warship: Or, the Naval Terror of the Seas. Stratemeyer Syndicate. Rogers, Walter S., illus. (The Tom Swift Ser.: No. 18). 1915. Grosset & Dunlap.

--Tom Swift and His Air Glider: Or, Seeking the Platinum Treasure. Stratemeyer Syndicate. Boehm, H. Richard, illus. LC 12-139428. iv, 209 p. front. 19 1/2 cm. (The Tom Swift Ser.: No. 12). c.1912. Grosset & Dunlap.

--Tom Swift and His Air Scout: Or, Uncle Sam's Mastery of the Sky. Stratemeyer Syndicate. (The Tom Swift Ser.: No. 22). 1919. Grosset & Dunlap.

--Tom Swift and His Airline Express: Or, From Ocean to Ocean by Daylight. Stratemeyer Syndicate. Rogers, Walter S., illus. (The Tom Swift Ser.: No. 29). N.D. Grosset & Dunlap.

--Tom Swift and His Airline Express: Or, From Ocean to Ocean by Daylight. Stratemeyer Syndicate. Rogers, Walter S., illus. Repr. of 1926 ed (Pub. by Grosset & Dunlap). (The Tom Swift Ser.: Vol. 6). N.D. Whitman Publishing Co.

--Tom Swift and His Airship: Or, The Stirring Cruise of the Red Cloud. Stratemeyer Syndicate. Mencl, Rudolf, illus. LC 12-16334. iv, 216 p. front. 19 1/2 cm. (The Tom Swift Ser.: No. 3). c.1910. Grosset & Dunlap.

--Tom Swift and His Big Dirigible: Or, Adventures Over the Forest of Fire. Stratemeyer Syndicate. Rogers, Walter S., illus. LC 30-2683. 3 p. l., 214 p. front. 19 1/2 cm. (The Tom Swift Ser.: No. 33). c.1930. Grosset & Dunlap.

--Tom Swift and His Big Dirigible: Or, Adventures Over the Forest of Fire. Stratemeyer Syndicate. Rogers, Walter S., illus. Repr. of 1930 ed (Pub. by Grosset & Dunlap). (The Tom Swift Ser.: Vol. 8). N.D. Whitman Publishing Co.

--Tom Swift and His Big Tunnel: Or, The Hidden City of the Andes. Stratemeyer Syndicate. Rogers, Walter S., illus. LC 17-29727. iv, 218 p. front. 19 1/2 cm. (The Tom Swift Ser.: No. 19). 1916. Grosset & Dunlap.

--Tom Swift and His Chest of Secrets: Or, Tracing the Stolen Inventions. Stratemeyer Syndicate. Rogers, Walter S., illus. 2 p. l., 216 p. front. 19 1/2 cm. (The Tom Swift Ser.: No. 28). c.1925. Grosset & Dunlap.

--Tom Swift and His Electric Locomotive: Or, Two Miles a Minute on the Rails. Stratemeyer Syndicate. Rogers, Walter S., illus. (The Tom Swift Ser.: No. 25). 1922. Grosset & Dunlap.

--Tom Swift and His Electric Rifle: Or, Daring Adventures in Elephant Land. Stratemeyer Syndicate. Boehm, H. Richard, illus. iv, 212 p. front. 19 1/2 cm. (The Tom Swift Ser.: No. 10). c.1911. Grosset & Dunlap.

--Tom Swift and His Electric Runabout: Or, The Speediest Car on the Road. Stratemeyer Syndicate. Mencl, Rudolf, illus. LC 12-163323. iv, 216 p. front. 19 1/2 cm. (The Tom Swift Ser.: No. 5). c.1910. Grosset & Dunlap.

--Tom Swift and His Flying Boat: Or, The Castaways of the Giant Iceberg. Stratemeyer Syndicate. Rogers, Walter S., illus. (The Tom Swift Ser.: No. 26). 1923. Grosset & Dunlap.

--Tom Swift and His Giant Cannon: Or, the Longest Shots on Record. Stratemeyer Syndicate. Boehm, H. Richard, illus. (The Tom Swift Ser.: No. 16). 1913. Grosset & Dunlap.

--Tom Swift and His Giant Magnet: Or, Bringing up the Lost Submarine. Stratemeyer Syndicate. Falk, Nat, illus. LC 32-212870. 3 p. l., 216 p. front. 19 1/2 cm. (The Tom Swift Ser.: No. 35). c.1932. Grosset & Dunlap.

--Tom Swift and His Giant Magnet: Or, Bringing up the Lost Submarine. Stratemeyer Syndicate. Falk, Nat, illus. Repr. of 1932 ed (Pub. by Grosset & Dunlap). (The Tom Swift Ser.: Vol. 9). N.D. Whitman Publishing Co.

--Tom Swift and His Giant Telescope. Stratemeyer Syndicate. (Written for the Stratemeyer Syndicate by Harriet Stratemeyer Adams, 1894-1982, under the pseudonym, Victor Appleton). (The Tom Swift Ser.: No. 39). 1939. Whitman Publishing Co.

--Tom Swift and His Great Oil Gusher: Or, The Treasure of Goby Farm. Stratemeyer Syndicate. Rogers, Walter S., illus. (The Tom Swift Ser.: No. 27). 1924. Grosset & Dunlap.

--Tom Swift and His Great Searchlight: Or, On the Border for Uncle Sam. Stratemeyer Syndicate. Boehm, H. Richard, illus. LC 12-139457. iv, 214 p. front. 19 1/2 cm. (The Tom Swift Ser.: No. 15). c.1912. Grosset & Dunlap.

--Tom Swift and His House on Wheels: Or, A Trip to the Mountain of Mystery. Stratemeyer Syndicate. Rogers, Walter S., illus. LC 29-281768. 2 p. l., 216 p. front. 19 1/2 cm. (The Tom Swift Ser.: No. 32). c.1929. Grosset & Dunlap.

--Tom Swift and His House on Wheels: Or, A Trip to the Mountain of Mystery. Stratemeyer Syndicate. Rogers, Walter S., illus. Repr. of 1929 ed (Pub. by Grosset & Dunlap). (The Tom Swift Ser.: Vol. 2). N.D. Whitman Publishing Co.

--Tom Swift and His Magnetic Silencer. Stratemeyer Syndicate. White, H. R., illus. (Written for the Stratemeyer Syndicate by Harriet Stratemeyer Adams, 1894-1982, under the pseudonym, Victor Appleton). (The Tom Swift Ser.: No. 40). 1941. Whitman Publishing Co.

--Tom Swift and His Motor-Boat: Or, The Rivals of Lake Carlopa. Stratemeyer Syndicate. Mencl, Rudolf, illus. LC 12-16330. iv, 212 p. front. 19 1/2 cm. (The Tom Swift Ser.: No. 2). c.1910. Grosset & Dunlap.

--Tom Swift and His Motor-Cycle: Or, Fun and Adventure on the Road. Stratemeyer Syndicate. Mencl, Rudolf, illus. LC 12-163312. iv, 206 p. front. 19 1/2 cm. (The Tom Swift Ser.: No. 1). c.1910. Grosset & Dunlap.

--Tom Swift and His Ocean Airport: Or, Foiling the Haargolanders. Stratemeyer Syndicate. Falk, Nat, illus. 2 p. l., 214 p. front. 19 1/2 cm. (The Tom Swift Ser.: No. 37). c.1934. Grosset & Dunlap.

--Tom Swift and His Ocean Airport: Or, Foiling the Haargolanders. Stratemeyer Syndicate. Falk, Nat, illus. Repr. of 1934 ed (Pub. by Grosset & Dunlap). (The Tom Swift Ser.: Vol. 5). N.D. Whitman Publishing Co.

--Tom Swift and His Photo Telephone: Or, The Picture That Saved a Fortune. Stratemeyer Syndicate. Rogers, Walter S., illus. LC 14-6989. 2 p. l., 216 p. front. 19 1/2 cm. (The Tom Swift Ser.: No. 17). c.1914. Grosset & Dunlap.

--Tom Swift and His Planet Stone: Or, Discovering the Secret of Another World. Stratemeyer Syndicate. Falk, Nat, illus. LC 35-182965. (Written for the Stratemeyer Syndicate by Harriet Stratemeyer Adams, 1894-1982, under the pseudonym, Victor Appleton). 2 p. l., 203 p. front. 19 1/2 cm. (The Tom Swift Ser.: No. 38). c.1935. Grosset & Dunlap.

--Tom Swift and His Planet Stone: Or, Discovering the Secret of Another World. Stratemeyer Syndicate. Falk, Nat, illus. Repr. of 1935 ed (Pub. by Grosset & Dunlap). (The Tom Swift Ser.). N.D. Whitman Publishing Co.

--Tom Swift and His Sky Racer: Or, The Quickest Flight on Record. Stratemeyer Syndicate. Boehm, H. Richard, illus. LC 13-16344. iv, 207 p. front. 19 1/2 cm. (The Tom Swift Ser.: No. 9). c.1911. Grosset & Dunlap.

--Tom Swift and His Sky Train: Or, Overland Through the Clouds. Stratemeyer Syndicate. Rogers, Walter S., illus. LC 31-2173. 2 p. l., 218 p. front. 19 1/2 cm. (The Tom Swift Ser.: No. 34). c.1931. Grosset & Dunlap.

--Tom Swift and His Sky Train: Or, Overland Through the Clouds. Stratemeyer Syndicate. Rogers, Walter S., illus. Repr. of 1931 ed (Pub. by Grosset & Dunlap). (The Tom Swift Ser.: Vol. 3). N.D. Whitman Publishing Co.

--Tom Swift and His Submarine Boat: Or, Under the Ocean for Sunken Treasure. Stratemeyer Syndicate. Mencl, Rudolf, illus. LC 12-16333. iv, 216 p. front. 19 1/2 cm. (The Tom Swift Ser.: No. 4). c.1910. Grosset & Dunlap.

--Tom Swift and His Talking Pictures: Or, The Greatest Invention on Record. Stratemeyer Syndicate. Rogers, Walter S., illus. LC 28-5407. 2 p. l., 216 p. front. 19 1/2 cm. (The Tom Swift Ser.: No. 31). c.1928. Grosset & Dunlap.

--Tom Swift and His Talking Pictures: Or, The Greatest Invention on Record. Stratemeyer Syndicate. Rogers, Walter S., illus. Repr. of 1928 ed (Pub. by Grosset & Dunlap). (The Tom Swift Ser.: Vol. 7). N.D. Whitman Publishing Co.

--Tom Swift and His Television Detector: Or, Trailing the Secret Plotters. Stratemeyer Syndicate. Falk, Nat, illus. LC 33-125365. 2 p. l., 217 p. front. 19 1/2 cm. (The Tom Swift Ser.: No. 36). c.1933. Grosset & Dunlap.

--Tom Swift and His Television Detector: Or, Trailing the Secret Plotters. Stratemeyer Syndicate. Falk, Nat, illus. Repr. of 1933 ed (Pub. by Grosset & Dunlap). (The Tom Swift Ser.: Vol. 1). N.D. Whitman Publishing Co.

--Tom Swift and His Undersea Search: Or, The Treasure on the Floor of the Atlantic. Stratemeyer Syndicate. (The Tom Swift Ser.: No. 23). 1920. Grosset & Dunlap.

--Tom Swift and His War Tank: Or, Doing His Bit for Uncle Sam. Stratemeyer Syndicate. (The Tom Swift Ser.: No. 21). 1918. Grosset & Dunlap.

--Tom Swift and His Wireless Message: Or, The Castaways of Earthquake Island. Stratemeyer Syndicate. Boehm, H. Richard, illus. (The Tom Swift Ser.: No. 6). 1911. Grosset & Dunlap.

--Tom Swift and His Wizard Camera: Or, Thrilling Adventures While Taking Moving Pictures. Stratemeyer Syndicate. Boehm, H. Richard, illus. LC 12-139435. iv, 210 p. front. 19 1/2 cm. (The Tom Swift Ser.: No. 14). c.1912. Grosset & Dunlap.

--Tom Swift Circling the Globe: Or, The Daring Cruise of the Air Monarch. Stratemeyer Syndicate. Rogers, Walter S., illus. (The Tom Swift Ser.: No. 30). 1927. Grosset & Dunlap.

--Tom Swift Circling the Globe: Or, The Daring Cruise of the Air Monarch. Stratemeyer Syndicate. Rogers, Walter S., illus. Repr. of 1927 ed (Pub. by Grosset & Dunalp). (The Tom Swift Ser.: Vol. 4). N.D. Whitman Publishing Co.
--Tom Swift in Captivity: Or, A Daring Escape by Airship. Stratemeyer Syndicate. Boehm, H. Richard, illus. LC 12-13946. iv, 218 p. front. 19 1/2 cm. (The Tom Swift Ser.: No. 13). c.1912. Grosset & Dunlap.
--Tom Swift in the Caves of Ice: Or, The Wreck of the Airship. Stratemeyer Syndicate. Boehm, H. Richard, illus. LC 13-163371. iv, 214 p. front. 19 cm. (The Tom Swift Ser.: No. 8). c.1911. Grosset & Dunlap.
--Tom Swift in the City of Gold: Or, Marvelous Adventures Underground. Stratemeyer Syndicate. Boehm, H. Richard, illus. LC [illegible]. iv, 216 p. front. 19 1/2 cm. (The Tom Swift Ser.: No. 11). c.1912. Grosset & Dunlap.
--Tom Swift in the Land of Wonders: or, The Underground Search for the Idol of Gold. Stratemeyer Syndicate. Rogers, Walter S., illus. (The Tom Swift Ser.: No. 20). 1917. Grosset & Dunlap.

Appleton, Victor, II, pseud. (1894-1982)
--Chaos on Earth. Adams, Harriet Stratemeyer. (The Tom Swift, Jr. Ser.: No. 12). (gr. 2-7). 1984. (ISBN 0-671-53230-8). Wanderer Bks.
--Crater of Mystery. Adams, Harriet Stratemeyer. LC 82-13479. (The Tom Swift, Jr. Ser.: No. 8). N.D. (ISBN 0-671-43954-5). (ISBN 0-671-43955-3). Wanderer Books.
--Gateway to Doom. Adams, Harriet Stratemeyer. LC 82-20238. (The Tom Swift, Jr. Ser.: No. 9). c.1983. (ISBN 0-671-43956-1). Wanderer Books.
--The Invisible Force. Adams, Harriet Stratemeyer. LC 83-4721. 190 p. (The Tom Swift. Jr. Ser.: No. 10). N.D. (ISBN 0-671-43958-8). Simon & Schuster.
--The Invisible Force. Adams, Harriet Stratemeyer. Barish, Wendy, ed. 192p. (Orig.). (The Tom Swift, Jr. Ser.: No. 10). (gr. 3-8). 1983. (ISBN 0-671-43959-6). Wanderer Bks.
--Planet of Nightmares. Adams, Harriet Stratemeyer. Schwartz, Betty, ed. LC 83-19770. 176p. (The Tom Swift, Jr. Ser.: No. 11). (gr. 3-7). 1984. (ISBN 0-671-49924-6). Wanderer Bks.
--Tom Swift and His Aquatomic Tracker. Adams, Harriet Stratemeyer. Moritz, Edward, illus. LC 64-2159. (Illus.). 178 p. 20cm. (The Tom Swift, Jr. Ser.: Vol. 23). 1964. Grosset & Dunlap.
--Tom Swift and His Atomic Earth Blaster. Adams, Harriet Stratemeyer. Kaye, Graham, illus. LC 55-1155. 210p. illus. 20cm. (The Tom Swift, Jr. Ser.: Vol. 5). 1954. Grosset & Dunlap.
--Tom Swift and His Cosmotron Express. Adams, Harriet Stratemeyer. Johnson, Ray (1900-), illus. LC 74-100117. (Illus.). 180 p. 20cm. (The Tom Swift, Jr. Ser.: Vol. 32). 1970. Grosset and Dunlap.
--Tom Swift and His Deep-Sea Hydrodome. Adams, Harriet Stratemeyer. Kaye, Graham, illus. LC 58-14649. 184p. illus. 20cm. (The Tom Swift, Jr. Ser.: Vol. 11). 1958. Grosset & Dunlap.
--Tom Swift and His Diving Seacopter. Adams, Harriet Stratemeyer. Kaye, Graham, illus. LC 56-23972. 214p. illus. 20cm. (The Tom Swift, Jr. Ser.: Vol. 7). 1956. Grosset & Dunlap.
--Tom Swift and His Dyna-4 Capsule. Adams, Harriet Stratemeyer. Johnson, Ray (1900-), illus. LC 69-12165. (Illus.). 175 p. 20cm. (The Tom Swift, Jr. Ser.: Vol. 31). 1969. Grosset and Dunlap.
--Tom Swift and His Electronic Retroscope. Adams, Harriet Stratemeyer. Kaye, Graham, illus. LC 59-16337. (Illus.). 184 p. 20cm. (The Tom Swift, Jr. Ser.: Vol. 14). 1959. Grosset & Dunlap.
--Tom Swift and His Flying Lab. Adams, Harriet Stratemeyer. Kaye, Graham, illus. LC 54-408. (Illus.). 208 p. 20cm. (The Tom Swift, Jr. Ser.: Vol. 1). 1954. Grosset & Dunlap.
--Tom Swift and His G-Force Inverter. Adams, Harriet Stratemeyer. Johnson, Ray (1900-), illus. (Illus.). 175 p. 19cm. (The Tom Swift, Jr. Ser.: Vol. 30). 1968. Grosset and Dunlap.
--Tom Swift and His Giant Robot. Adams, Harriet Stratemeyer. Kaye, Graham, illus. LC 54-132625. 211p. illus. 20cm. (The Tom Swift, Jr. Ser.: Vol. 4). 1954. Grosset & Dunlap.
--Tom Swift and His Jetmarine. Adams, Harriet Stratemeyer. Kaye, Graham, illus. LC 54-372132. 208p. illus. 20cm. (The Tom Swift, Jr. Ser.: Vol. 2). 1954. Grosset & Dunlap.
--Tom Swift and His Megascope Space Prober. Adams, Harriet Stratemeyer. Brey, Charles, illus. LC 62-52098. 176p. illus. 20cm. (The Tom Swift, Jr. Ser.: Vol. 20). 1962. Grosset & Dunlap.
--Tom Swift and His Outpost in Space. Adams, Harriet Stratemeyer. Kaye, Graham, illus. LC 56-197195. 210p. illus. 20cm. (The Tom Swift, Jr. Ser.: Vol. 6). 1955. Grosset & Dunlap.
--Tom Swift and His Polar-Ray Dynasphere. Adams, Harriet Stratemeyer. Moritz, Edward, illus. LC 65-13776. 177p. illus. 20cm. (The Tom Swift, Jr. Ser.: Vol. 25). c.1965. Grosset.
--Tom Swift and His Repelatron Skyway. Adams, Harriet Stratemeyer. Moritz, Edward, illus. LC 63-18956. 179 p. illus. 20 cm. (The Tom Swift, Jr. Ser.: Vol. 22). 1965. Grosset & Dunlap.
--Tom Swift and His Rocket Ship. Adams, Harriet Stratemeyer. Kaye, Graham, illus. LC 54-373. (Illus.). 208 p. 20cm. (The Tom Swift, Jr. Ser.: Vol. 3). 1954. Grosset & Dunlap.
--Tom Swift and His Sonic Boom Trap. Adams, Harriet Stratemeyer. Moritz, Edward, illus. LC 65-18451. 178p. illus. 20cm. (The Tom Swift Jr. Ser.: Vol. 26). 1965. Grosset.
--Tom Swift and His Space Solartron. Adams, Harriet Stratemeyer. Kaye, Graham, illus. LC 59-160117. 183p. illus. 20cm. (The Tom Swift, Jr. Ser.: Vol. 13). 1959, c.1958. Grosset & Dunlap.
--Tom Swift and His Spectromarine Selector. Adams, Harriet Stratemeyer. Kaye, Graham, illus. LC 60-32698. 184p. illus. 20cm. (The Tome Swift, Jr. Ser.: Vol. 15). 1960. Grosset & Dunlap.
--Tom Swift and His Subocean Geotron. Adams, Harriet Stratemeyer. Moritz, Edward, illus. LC 66-10712. 178p. illus. 20cm. (The Tom Swift, Jr. Ser.: Vol. 27). c.1966. Grosset.
--Tom Swift and His Triphibian Atomicar. Adams, Harriet Stratemeyer. Brey, Charles, illus. LC 62-2601. 188p. illus. 29cm. (The Tom Swift, Jr. Ser.: Vol. 19). 1962. Grosset Dunlap.
--Tom Swift and His Ultrasonic Cycloplane. Adams, Harriet Stratemeyer. Kaye, Graham, illus. LC 57-48437. 182p. illus. 20cm. (The Tom Swift, Jr. Ser.: Vol. 10). 1957. Grosset & Dunlap.
--Tom Swift and His 3-D Telejector. Adams, Harriet Stratemeyer. Moritz, Edward, illus. LC 64-55928. 177 p. illus. 20 cm. (The Tom Swift, Jr. Ser.: Vol. 24). 1964. Grosset & Dunlap.
--Tom Swift and the Asteroid Pirates. Adams, Harriet Stratemeyer. Brey, Charles, illus. LC 63-1035. 178 p. illus. 20 cm. (The Tom Swift, Jr. Ser.: Vol. 21). 1963. Grosset & Dunlap.
--Tom Swift and the Captive Planetoid. Adams, Harriet Stratemeyer. Johnson, Ray (1900-), illus. (The Tom Swift, Jr. Ser.: Vol. 29). 1967. Grosset & Dunlap.
--Tom Swift and the Cosmic Astronauts. Adams, Harriet Stratemeyer. Kaye, Graham, illus. LC 60-519922. 184p. illus. 20cm. (The Tom Swift, Jr. Ser.: Vol. 16). 1960. Grosset & Dunlap.
--Tom Swift and the Electronic Hydrolung. Adams, Harriet Stratemeyer. Brey, Charles, illus. LC 62-13362. 188p. illus. 20cm. (The Tom Swift, Jr. Ser.: Vol. 18). c.1961. Grosset & Dunlap.
--Tom Swift and the Galaxy Ghosts. Adams, Harriet Stratemeyer. Dolwick, Bill, illus. LC 74-130338. (Illus.). 180 p. 20cm. (The Tom Swift, Jr. Ser.: Vol. 33). 1971. (ISBN 0-448-09133-X). Grosset and Dunlap.
--Tom Swift and the Mystery Comet. Adams, Harriet Stratemeyer. Johnson, Ray (1900-), illus. LC 67-6408. (Illus.). 178 p. 20cm. (The Tom Swift, Jr. Ser.: Vol. 28). 1966. Grosset and Dunlap.
--Tom Swift and the Visitor from Planet X. Adams, Harriet Stratemeyer. Kaye, Graham, illus. LC 61-163113. 184p. illus. 20cm. (The Tom Swift, Jr. Ser.: Vol. 17). 1961. Grosset & Dunlap.
--Tom Swift: Ark Two. Adams, Harriet Stratemeyer. (Illus.). 192p. (The Tom Swift, Jr. Ser.: No. 7). (gr. 3-7). 1982. (ISBN 0-671-43952-9). (ISBN 0-671-43953-7). Wanderer Bks.
--Tom Swift: Crater of Mystery. Adams, Harriet Stratemeyer. Barish, Wendy, ed. 192p. (The Tom Swift, Jr. Ser.: No. 8). (gr. 3-7). 1983. (ISBN 0-671-43954-5). (ISBN 0-671-43955-3). Wanderer Bks.
--Tom Swift: Gateway to Doom. Adams, Harriet Stratemeyer. Barish, Wendy, ed. 192p. (The Tom Swift, Jr. Ser.: No. 9). (gr. 8-10). 1983. (ISBN 0-671-43956-1). (ISBN 0-671-43957-X). Wanderer Bks.
--Tom Swift in the Caves of Nuclear Fire. Adams, Harriet Stratemeyer. Kaye, Graham, illus. LC 56-4977. 214p. illus. 20cm. (The Tom Swift, Jr. Ser.: Vol. 8). 1956. Grosset & Dunlap.
--Tom Swift in the Race to the Moon. Adams, Harriet Stratemeyer. Kaye, Graham, illus. LC 58-148693. 180p. illus. 20cm. (The Tom Swift, Jr. Ser.: Vol. 12). 1958. Grosset & Dunlap.
--Tom Swift on the Phantom Satellite. Adams, Harriet Stratemeyer. Kaye, Graham, illus. LC 57-136092. 214p. illus. 20cm. (The Tom Swift, Jr. Ser.: Vol. 9). 1957, c.1956. Grosset & Dunlap.
--Tom Swift: Terror on the Moons of Jupiter. Adams, Harriet Stratemeyer. LC 80-26446. 192p. (The Tom Swift, Jr. Ser.: No. 2). (gr. 3-7). 1981. (ISBN 0-671-41182-9). (ISBN 0-671-41183-7). Wanderer Bks.
--Tom Swift: The Alien Probe. Adams, Harriet Stratemeyer. LC 80-28768. 192p. (Orig.). (The Tom Swift, Jr. Ser.: No. 3). (gr. 3-7). 1981. (ISBN 0-671-42538-2). (ISBN 0-671-42578-1). Wanderer Bks.
--Tom Swift: The City in the Stars. Adams, Harriet Stratemeyer. LC 80-27001. 192p. (Orig.). (The Tom Swift, Jr. Ser.: No. 1). (gr. 3-7). 1981. (ISBN 0-671-41120-9). (ISBN 0-671-41115-2). Wanderer Bks.
--Tom Swift: The Rescue Mission. Adams, Harriet Stratemeyer. 192p. (The Tom Swift, Jr. Ser.: No. 6). (gr. 3-7). 1981. (ISBN 0-671-43370-9). (ISBN 0-671-43386-5). Wanderer Bks.
--Tom Swift: The Space Fortress. Adams, Harriet Stratemeyer. 192p. (The Tom Swift, Jr. Ser.: No. 5). (gr. 3-7). 1981. (ISBN 0-671-43369-5). (ISBN 0-671-43385-7). Wanderer Bks.
--Tom Swift: The War in Outer Space. Adams, Harriet Stratemeyer. 192p. (Orig.). (The Tom Swift, Jr. Ser.: No. 4). (gr. 3-7). 1981. (ISBN 0-671-42539-0). (ISBN 0-671-42579-X). Wanderer Bks.

April, Steve
--Route Thirteen. 224p. N.D. Funk & Wagnalls.

Arabian Nights
--Ali Baba and Other Stories: From The Arabian Nights. Housman, Laurence (1865-1959), ed. Dulac, Edmund (1882-1953), illus. LC 12-20331. 77 p. col. front., col. plates. 21 cm. 1911. Hodder and Stoughton.
--The Arabian Nights. LC 45-30232. 536 p. front., illus. 20 cm. c.1879. Claxton, Remsen & Haffelfinger.
--The Arabian Nights. Goodenow, Earle (1913-), illus. LC 46-22695. 4 p. l., 3-327 p. col. front., illus., col. plates 24 cm. (Illustrated junior library). 1946. Grosset & Dunlap.
--Arabian Nights. Lang, Andrew (1844-1912), ed. Bock, Vera, illus. Davis, Mary Gould, intro. by. LC 46-3909. xiii p., 1 l., 303 p. incl. front., illus. 22 cm. 1946. Longmans, Green and Co.
--The Arabian Nights. Lowe, Orton, intro. by. LC 57-12794. 276p. illus. 22cm. (Children's classics). 1957. Winston.
--The Arabian Nights. Saroyan, William (1908-1981), intro. by. Lummer, W. K., illus. LC 66-12292. 319 p. illus. 24 cm. (Cricket book). 1966. Platt & Munk.
--Arabian Nights. Williams-Ellis, Amabel (1894-), ed. Baynes, Pauline Diana (1922-), illus. LC 58-962736. 348p. illus. (part col.) 23cm. 1958, c.1957. Criterion Books.
--The Arabian Nights. A Selection of Stories from Alif Laila Wa Laila, the Arabian Nights Entertainment. Hale, Edward Everett (1822-1909), ed. Lane, Edward William (1801-1876), tr. LC 45-30231. xii, 366 p. incl. plates. front., illus. 18 cm. (On cover: Classics for children v. 19). 1888. Ginn & Company.
--Arabian Nights: Aladdin, or the Wonderful Lamp. 1900. Maynard Merrill & Co.
--Arabian Nights' Entertainment. (Illus.). N.D. Edson C Eastman.
--The Arabian Nights Entertainment. (Illus.). (Young People's Classics). N.D. R. F. Fenno & Co.
--Arabian Nights' Entertainments. Empire ed. 1905. American News Co.
--The Arabian Nights' Entertainments. Eliot, Samuel (1821-1898), ed. Scott, Jonathan (1754-1829), tr. LC 45-30233. 210 p. front., illus. 20 cm. 1880. Lee and Shepard.
--The Arabian Nights Entertainments. Lang, Andrew (1844-1912), ed. Ford, Henry Justice (1860-1941), illus. LC 67-26991. xvi, 424 p. 66 illus. 21 cm. 1967. Schocken Books.
--The Arabian Nights' Entertainments: Arranged for the Perusal of Youthful Readers. Sugden, Marianne Cookson, Mrs. (0000-1908), ed. vii, 501 p. front., plates. 18 cm. 1863. G. Routledge and Sons.
--The Arabian Night's Entertainments. With 10 Illustrations. LC 45-32783. 271 p. incl. col. front., illus. 16 x 12 cm. (Altemus' Young people's library). 1897. H. Altemus.
--The Arabian Nights Picture Book. 1st ed. Watson, Nancy Dingman, ed. Burton, Richard Francis, Sir, tr. Watson, Aldren Auld (1917-), illus. LC 58-9663. 88p. col. illus. 32cm. 1959. Garden City Books.
--The Arabian Nights: Tales of Wonder and Magnificence. Colum, Padraic (1881-1972), ed. Ward, Lynd Kendall (1905-1985), illus. LC 53-8479. xiii, 344p. col. illus. 22cm. (New children's classics). 1953. Macmillan.
--Fairy Tales from the Arabian Nights. Dixon, E., ed. LC 52-14427. 333p. illus. 21cm. (Children's illustrated classics). 1951. Dutton.
--Golden Tales from the Arabian Nights: The Most Famous Stories from the Great Classic A Thousand and One Nights. Soifer, Margaret K & Shapiro, Irwin (1911-), eds. Tenggren, Gustaf (1896-1970), illus. LC 57-14043. 96p. illus. 34cm. (Giant golden book, 755). 1957. Simon and Schuster.
--The Lion and the Carpenter, and Other Tales from the Arabian Nights. Stafford, Jean (1915-1979), ed. Nardini, Sandro, illus. LC 64-956139. 43 p. illus. 34 cm. 1962, c.1959. Macmillan.
--Stories from the Arabian Nights. Housman, Laurence (1865-), ed. Goodenow, Girard, illus. 191p. illus. 22cm. 1955. Julior Deluxe Editions.
--Stories from the Arabian Nights: With an Introductory Note ... LC 45-32782. 2 v. 18 cm. (Riverside literature series. No. 117-118). 1897. Houghton, Mifflin and Company.
--Tales from the Arabian Nights. Gille, Elisabeth, illus. Haas, Merle S. (1896-1985), tr. LC 63-14751. 36 p. col. illus. 83 cm. 1964. Random House.
--Tales from the Arabian Nights. Goulden, Shirley, retold by. Benvenuti, G., illus. LC 57-4883. 60p. illus. 35cm. 1957. Grosset & Dunlap.
--Tales from the Arabian Nights. Smola, Hedwig, ed. Dixon, Charlotte, tr. Grabianski, Janusz (1928-1976), illus. LC 64-54833. 319 p. col. illus. 25 cm. (Splendor book). 1964. Duell, Sloan and Pearce.

Aragon, Claude, jt. auth. see Cathey, Wallace.

Aragon, Hilda, illus.
--My First Nursery Rhyme Book. 28p. (Orig.). 1st U.S. edition. (ps-7). 1981. (ISBN 0-915347-07-5). Pueblo Acoma Pr.

Aragon, Louis (1897-1982) & Chevalier, Haakon M., Tr
--Residential Quarter. LC 39-39008. x p., 2 l., 3-505 p. 21 cm. c.1938. Harcourt, Brace and Company.

Aragon, Macine De see De Aragon, Maximo.

Aragon, Ray John De see De Aragon, Ray John.

Arason, Steingrimur
--Golden Hair. LC 45-10156. 21cm. 223p. 1945. Macmillan.
--Smokey Bay. Howe, Gertrude Herrick (1902-), illus. (Illus.). (gr. 4-6). 1966. (ISBN 0-02-705610-4). Macmillan.

Aratari, Anthony
--Jingle Pennies. Swift, Don, illus. LC 78-72943. (Illus.). 64p. 1978. (ISBN 0-87793-166-6). Ave Maria.

Arbeit, Eleanor Werner (1915-)
--Mrs. Cat Hides Something. Arbeit, Eleanor Werner (1915-), illus. LC 85-8291. p. cm. 1985. (ISBN 0-87905-205-8). Gibbs M. Smith, Inc.

Arbore, Lily
--The Princess and the Unicorn. Chagnon, Mary, illus. LC 70-171068. (Illus.). 32 p. 27cm. 1972. (ISBN 0-87614-028-2). Carolrhoda Books.

Arbuckle, Dorothy Fry (1910-1982)
--The After-Harvest Festival: The Story of a Girl of the Old Kankakee. Whitman, Maurice, illus. LC 55-6375. 248p. illus. 21cm. 1955. Dodd, Mead.
--Andy's Dan'l Boone Rifle. Arbuckle, Dorothy Fry (1910-1982), illus. LC 67-5909. 221 p. illus., map. 22 cm. 1966. The Villager.

Arbuthnot, May Hill (1884-1969), ed.
--The Arbuthnot Anthology of Children's Literature. 3d ed. Bennett, Rainey (1907-), illus. LC 73-154794. (Illus.). xxiv, 1271 p. 27cm. 1971. Scott, Foresman.
--The Arbuthnot Anthology of Children's Literature. Paul, Arthur, illus. Kearney, Hal, designed by. LC 53-12449. (Single Volume Edition of Time for Poetry, Time for Fairy Tales and Time for True Tales). 196, 391, 418p. illus. 27cm. 1953. Scott, Foresman.
--The Arbuthnot Anthology of Children's Literature. rev. ed. Paul, Arthur, illus. LC 61-5727. (Single Volume Edition of Time for Fairy Tales and Time for True Tales). (Illus.). 207, 418, 459 p. 27cm. 1961. Scott, Foresman.
--Time For Fairy Tales. N.D. Albert Whitman & Company.
--Time for Fairy Tales. 1952. Scott, Foresman & Co.
--Time for Fairy Tales Old and New. Averill, John, et al., illus. Kearney, Hal, designed by. LC 52-2804. (A Representative Collection of Folk Tales, Myths, Epics, Fables, and Modern Fanciful Tales for Children, to be used in the Classroom, Home, or Camp.). 403 p. illus. 27 cm. 1952. Scott, Foresman.
--Time for Fairy Tales, Old and New. rev. ed. Averill, John, et al., illus. LC 61-5726. (Illus.). 431 p. 27cm. 1961. Scott, Foresman.
--Time for Poetry. N.D. Albert Whitman & Co.
--Time for Poetry. Bahnc, Salcia, illus. LC 51-2431. (Illus.). 438 p. 22cm. (Curriculum foundation series). 1951. Scott, Foresman.

--Time for Poetry: A Representative Collection of Poetry for Children. General ed. Paul, Arthur, illus. Kearney, Hal, designed by. LC 52-2070. (To be Used in the Classroom, Home, or Camp). 213 p. illus. 27 cm. 1952. Scott, Foresman.
--Time for Poetry; a Representative Collection of Poetry for Children: To Be Used in the Classroom, Home, or Camp; Especially Planned for College Classes in Children's Literature; with an Introd. for Teachers and Parents on Reading Poetry to Children and Using Poetry in Verse Choirs. general ed. rev. Paul, Arthur, illus. LC 61-5724. (Illus.). 227 p. 27cm. 1961. Scott, Foresman.
--Time for True Tales and Almost True: A Representative Collection of Realistic Stories for Children,. Bennett, Rainey (1907-), illus. Kearney, Hal, designed by. LC 53-2061. (To Be Used in the Classroom, Home, or Camp). 396p. illus. 27cm. 1953. Scott, Foresman.
--Time for True Tales and Almost True: A Representative Collection of Realistic Stories for Children. Rev. ed. Bennett, Rainey (1907-), illus. Kearney, Hal, designed by. LC 61-5725. (To Be Used in the Classroom, Home, or Camp). 435p. illus. 27cm. 1961. Scott, Foresman.

Arbuthnot, May Hill (1884-1969) & Broderick, Dorothy M. (1925-), eds.
--The Arbuthnot Anthology of Children's Literature. 4th ed. / rev. by zena sutherland. Bennett, Rainey (1907-), illus. LC 75-29998. (Illus.). xxii, 1088 p., 4 leaves of plates. 27cm. 1976. (ISBN 0-688-41725-6). Lothrop, Lee & Shepard.
--The Arbuthnot Anthology of Children's Literature. 4th ed. / rev. by zena sutherland. Bennett, Rainey, et al. (1907-), illus. LC 75-29030. (Illus.). xxii, 1088 p., 4 leaves of plates. 27cm. c.1976. Scott, Foresman.
--Time for Stories of the Past and Present. Bennett, Rainey (1907-), illus. LC 68-31566. (Illus.). x, 259 p. 27cm. 1968. Scott, Foresman.

Arbuthnot, May Hill (1884-1969) & Gray, William Scott (1885-), eds.
--Time for Poetry. Rev. ed. Bennett, Rainey (1907-), illus. LC 59-111735. 512p. illus. 22cm. 1959. Scott, Foresman.

Arbuthnot, May Hill (1884-1969) & Root, Shelton L., eds.
--Time for Poetry: A Representative Collection of Poetry for Children,. 3d general ed. Paul, Arthur, illus. LC 67-22022. (To be Used in the Classroom, Home, or Camp). (Illus.). xvi, 277 p. 27cm. 1967, c.1968. Scott, Foresman.

Arbuthnot, May Hill (1884-1969) & Taylor, Mark, eds.
--Time for New Magic. Averill, John, et al., illus. LC 78-151536. (Illus.). viii, 300 p. 28cm. 1971. Scott, Foresman.
--Time for Old Magic. Averill, John, et al., illus. LC 73-91952. (Illus.). ix, 389 p. 27cm. 1970. Scott, Foresman.

Arc, Kathleen
--The Big Cat. Alesch, Joann L., illus. LC 56-806. (Illus.). 20p. (Windings & Purrs & Tails Ser.). (gr. 3-6). 1981. (ISBN 0-9607074-0-9). ANURA Pub.

Arceneaux, Marc, illus.
--The Little Big Rig. (Illus.). 14p. (Beep Beep Board Bks.). 1983. (ISBN 0-671-47339-5, Little Simon). S&S.
--The Little Cement Mixer. (Illus.). 14p. (Beep Beep Board Bks.). 1983. (ISBN 0-671-47340-9, Little Simon). S&S.
--The Little Fire Engine. (Illus.). 14p. (Beep Beep Board Bks.). 1983. (ISBN 0-671-47338-7, Little Simon). S&S.
--The Little Garbage Truck. (Illus.). 14p. (Beep Beep Board Bks.). 1983. (ISBN 0-671-47341-7, Little Simon). S&S.

Archambault, John, jt. auth. see Martin, William Ivan, Jr.

Archer, Gleason Leonard (1880-)
--The Gaint of Eagle Mountain. N.D. Pageant Press INC.
--Robert, Duke of Kragcastle. 1st ed. Chapman, Billie, illus. LC 62-710. 262p. illus. 21cm. c.1961. Pageant Press.

Archer, Jay, jt. auth. see Olgin, Joseph.

Archer, Jeffrey Howard (1940-)
--Willie Visits the Square World. Matthews, Derek, illus. (Illus.). 48p. (gr. 5 up). N.D. (ISBN 0-7064-1200-1, Rutledge Pr). Smith Pubs.

Archer, Lane, pseud., see Hauck, Louise Platt.

Archer, Lucie Agens, tr. see Schmid, Christoph Von.

Archer, Marion Fuller (1917-)
--Keys for Signe. Cunningham, David (1938-), illus. LC 65-15100. 160 p. illus. 22 cm. 1965. A. Whitman.
--Nine Lives of Moses on the Oregon Trail. Armstrong, George Douglas (1927-), illus. LC 68-22188. (Illus.). 160 p. 22cm. 1968. A. Whitman.
--Sarah Jane. Nelson, Jane E., illus. LC 73-165816. (Illus.). line drawings. 192p. (gr. 5-8). 1971. (ISBN 0-8075-7241-1). A Whitman.
--There Is a Happy Land. Cunningham, David (1938-), illus. LC 63-13327. (Illus.). (gr. 5-7). 1963. (ISBN 0-8075-7861-4). A Whitman.

Archer, Myrtle Lily (1926-)
--The Young Boys Gone. LC 77-78983. 218 p. 22cm. c.1978. (ISBN 0-8027-6304-9). Walker.

Archer, Peggy
--One of the Family. Sanderson, Ruth, illus. LC 82-82289. (Illus.). 24p. (Little Golden Bk.). 1983. (ISBN 0-307-02082-7, Golden Pr). (ISBN 0-307-02082-7). Western Pub.

Archer, Peter & Loew's Incorporated
--M G M's Tom and Jerry's Merry Christmas. MGM Cartoons, illus. Eisenberg, Harvey & Armstrong, Samuel, eds. LC 54-14443. unpaged. illus. 21cm. (Little golden book, 197). 1954. Simon and Schuster.
--M-G-M's Tom and Jerry's Merry Christmas. Eisenberg, Harvey & Armstrong, Samuel, illus. (Little Golden Book). 1954. Golden Press.
--The Stagecoach Robbery. Krush, Joe (1918-) & Krush, Beth (1918-), illus. LC 49-491914. 124 p. col. illus. 18 cm. (Golden story books, 5). 1949. Simon and Schuster.

Archer, Peter, ed.
--Gergely's Golden Circus. Gergely, Tibor (1900-1978), illus. LC 54-12822. unpaged. illus. 28cm. (Big golden book, 485). 1954. Simon and Schuster.
--Nursery Tales. Medvey, Steven, illus. LC 52-3307. unpaged. illus. 21 cm. (See-saw books, 5). 1952. Simon and Schuster.

Archer, Peter, ed. see Baum, Lyman Frank.

Archer, Thomas & Atkinson, J. C.
--Every Boy's Stories. (Illus.). 501p. N.D. George Routledge & Sons.

Archibald, George, pseud., see Palmer, Anna Campbell.

Archibald, George, Mrs., pseud. (1854-1928)
--A Dozen Good Times. Palmer, Anna Campbell. (Illus.). (Lady Gay Ser.). N.D. Lothrop Lee & Shepard Co.
--Lady Gay. Palmer, Anna Campbell. (Illus.). (LAdy Gay Ser.). N.D. Lothrop Lee & Shepard Co.
--A Little Brown Seed. Palmer, Anna Campbell. (Illus.). N.D. Methodist Bk Concern.
--Summerville Prize: A Story for Girls. Palmer, Anna Campbell. N.D. Publications of the Methodist Book Concern.

Archibald, Joseph, jt. auth. see Innis, Pauline B. Coleman.

Archibald, Joseph Stopford (1898-)
--Aviation Cadet. (gr. 9 up). 1955. McKay.
--Aviation Cadet. 1st Ed. LC 55-8305. 167p. 22cm. 1955. Longmans, Green.
--Backcourt Commando. LC 77-108862. 192 p. 21cm. 1970. Macrea Smith Co.
--Backfield Twins. LC 60-14038. 192 p. 22cm. 1960. Macrae Smith Co.
--Big League Busher. LC 63-12441. 187 p. 22cm. 1963. Macrae-Smith.
--Block That Kick. LC 53-788855. 223p. 22cm. 1953. Macrae Smith Co.
--Bonus Kid. LC 59-8238. 189p. 22cm. 1959. Macrae Smith.
--Catcher's Choice. LC 58-8728. 188 p. 22cm. 1958. Macrae Smith.
--Centerfield Rival. LC 74-4487. 153 p. 22cm. 1974. (ISBN 0-8255-1434-7). (ISBN 0-8255-1434-7). Macrae Smith.
--Circus Catch. LC 57-6641. 199p. illus. 22cm. 1957. Macrae Smith.
--Crazy Legs McBain. LC 61-14960. (Illus.). 187 p. 22cm. 1961. Macrae Smith.
--Double Play Rookie. LC 55-644785. 208p. 22cm. 1955. Macrae Smith.
--The Easy Out. LC 65-16328. 187p. 22cm. c.1965. Macrae.
--Falcons to the Fight. LC 59-13258. 191p. 22cm. 1959. Macrae Smith Co.
--Fast Break Fury. LC 68-31144. 176 p. 21cm. 1968. Macrae Smith.
--The Fifth Base. LC 73-523. 176 p. 22cm. 1973. (ISBN 0-8255-1430-4). (ISBN 0-8255-1430-4). Macrae Smith.
--Fight, Team, Fight: A Sports Novel. LC 58-12067. 190 p. 22cm. 1958. Macrae Smith.
--Fighting Coach. LC 54-103644. 192p. 22cm. 1954. Macrae Smith.
--First Base Hustler. LC 60-9186. 190p. 22cm. 1960. Macrae Smith.
--Full Count. LC 56-6183. 204p. 21cm. 1956. Macrae Smith.
--Fullback Fury. LC 55-107364. 192p. 21cm. 1955. Macrae Smith.
--Go Navy, Go. LC 56-104392. 192p. illus. 22cm. 1956. Macrae Smith Co.
--Hard Nosed Halfback. LC 63-20495. 22cm. 187p. 1963. Macrae.
--Hold That Line!. LC 50-9794. 220 p. 22 cm. 1950. Macrae Smith Co.
--Inside Tackle. LC 51-13999. 208 p. 22 cm. 1951. Macrae Smith.
--Jet Flier. 1960. McKay.
--Jet Flier. Junker, Bruno, illus. LC 60-11343. (Illus.). 182 p. 21cm. 1960. Longmans, Green.
--The Long Pass. LC 66-9624. 191 p. 22cm. 1966. Macrae Smith.
--Mitt Maverick. LC 68-18808. 186 p. 21cm. 1968. Macrae Smith.
--Mr. Slingshot. LC 57-12003. 183p. 22cm. 1957. Macrae Smith.
--Old Iron Glove. LC 64-16326. (Illus.). 187 p. 22cm. 1964. Macrae Smith Co.
--Outfield Orphan. LC 61-8302. 208 p. 22cm. 1961. Macrae Smith.
--Payoff Pitch. LC 74-150676. 192 p. 21cm. 1971. (ISBN 0-8255-1407-X). Macrae Smith Co.
--Phantom Blitz. LC 72-4377. 176 p. 22cm. 1972. (ISBN 0-8255-1428-2). Macrae Smith Co.
--Powerback. LC 79-127425. (Illus.). 189 p. 21cm. 1970. Macrae Smith.
--Pro Coach. LC 75-87981. 188 p. 21cm. 1969. Macrae Smith.
--Quarterback & Son. LC 64-23919. 22cm. 190p. 1964. Macrae Smith Co.
--Rebel Halfback. LC 47-31441. 192 p. 22 cm. 1947. Westminister Press.
--Red-Dog Center. LC 62-19161. 189p. 22cm. 1962. Macrae Smith Co.
--Right Field Rookie. LC 67-15810. 179 p. 21cm. 1967. Macrae Smith Co.
--Right Field Runt. LC 72-38961. 188 p. 22cm. 1972. (ISBN 0-8255-1417-7). (ISBN 0-8255-1418-5). Macrae Smith.
--The Scrambler. LC 67-26977. 184 p. 22cm. 1967. Macrae Smith.
--Shortstop on Wheels. LC 62-11719. 205 p. 22cm. 1962. Macrae Smith.
--The Smoke Eaters. Tashiro, Yukio, illus. LC 65-14130. 206p. illus. 21cm. c.1965. (ISBN 0-679-20185-8). McKay.
--Southpaw Speed. LC 66-17879. 173p. 22cm. 1966, c.1965. Macrae.
--Special Forces Trooper. LC 67-26862. 186 p. 21cm. 1967. D. McKay Co.
--Three-Point Hero. LC 73-12936. 158 p. 22cm. 1973. (ISBN 0-8255-1432-0). (ISBN 0-8255-1433-9). Macrae Smith.
--Touchdown Glory. N.D. The Westminster Press.
--Two Time Rookie. LC 69-18899. 170 p. 21cm. 1969. Macrae Smith.
--West Point Wingback. LC 65-24906. 189p. 22cm. c.1965. Macrae.
--Windmill Pilot. Voorhies, Stephen J., illus. LC 63-13177. (Illus.). 234 p. 21cm. 1963. D. McKay Co.

Archibald, Leon
--Animal Babies at the Zoo. Yokoi, Daisuke, illus. LC 85-175812. (Illus.). 44 p. 14cm. (A Super Chubby). c.1985. (ISBN 0-671-54736-4). Simon & Schuster.
--Things I Like to Do. Fujita, Miho, illus. LC 85-175806. (Illus.). 44 p. 14cm. (A Super Chubby). c.1985. (ISBN 0-671-54735-6). Simon & Schuster.

Archibald, Leon, jt. ed. see Schwartz, Betty Ann.

Archibald, William (1924-1970)
--A Day in the Life of a Clown. Archibald, William (1924-1970), illus. LC 63-20059. 1 v. (chiefly illus.) 34 cm. 1963. Stein and Day.
--The Magic Blot. Archibald, William (1924-1970), illus. LC 63-18381. unpaged. illus. 34 cm. 1963. Stein and Day.

Arden, Barbi, pseud., see Stoutenberg, Adrien Pearl.

Arden, Barbi, pseud. (1916-)
--Remembered Island. Stoutenberg, Adrien Pearl. 1st ed. LC 56-6222. 224p. 21cm. 1956. Holt.

Arden, John & D'Arcy, Margaretta
--The Business of Good Government: A Christmas Play. 2nd ed. 54p. 1984. (ISBN 0-413-53460-X, Pub. by Eyre Methuen England). Methuen Inc.

Arden, William, pseud., see Lynds, Dennis.

Arden, William, pseud. (1924-) & Arthur, Robert, pseud. (1909-1969)
--Alfred Hitchcock & the Three Investigators in the Mystery of the Shrinking House. Lynds, Dennis. Feder, Robert Arthur. LC 72-1588. (Based on Characters created by Robert Arthur Feder, 1909-1969). (Illus.). (Three Investigators Ser.: No. 18). (gr. 4-7). 1972. (ISBN 0-394-82482-2, BYR). (ISBN 0-394-92482-7). (ISBN 0-394-83777-0). Random.
--Alfred Hitchcock and the Three Investigators in The Mystery of the Dead Man's Riddle. Lynds, Dennis. Feder, Robert Arthur. LC 79-3519. (Based on characters created by Robert Arthur Feder, 1909-1969). viii, 145 p. 20cm. (Alfred Hitchcock and the Three Investigators Series). 1980, c.1974. (ISBN 0-394-84451-3). Random House.
--Alfred Hitchcock and the Three Investigators in the Mystery of the Deadly Double. Lynds, Dennis. Feder, Robert Arthur. LC 79-29638. (Based on characters by Robert Arthur Feder, 1909-1969). 160p. (Alfred Hitchcock & the Three Investigators Ser.). (gr. 4-7). 1981. (ISBN 0-394-84491-2). Random.
--Alfred Hitchcock and the Three Investigators in The Mystery of the Deadly Double. Lynds, Dennis. Feder, Robert Arthur. LC 79-27778. (Based on characters created by Robert Arthur Feder, 1909-1969). p. cm. 1981. (ISBN 0-394-82927-1). (ISBN 0-394-84451-3). (ISBN 0-394-92927-6). (ISBN 0-394-92927-6). Random House.
--Alfred Hitchcock and the Three Investigators in The Mystery of the Dancing Devil. Lynds, Dennis. Feder, Robert Arthur. LC 80-29350. (Based on characters created by Robert Arthur Feder, 1909-1969). p. cm. (Alfred Hitchcock and the three investigators series ; 25). 1981, c.1976. (ISBN 0-394-84862-4). Random House.
--Alfred Hitchcock and the Three Investigators in The Mystery of the Headless Horse. Lynds, Dennis. Feder, Robert Arthur. LC 80-29259. (Based on characters created by Robert Arthur Feder, 1909-1969). p. cm. (Alfred Hitchcock and the three investigators series ; 26). 1981, c.1977. (ISBN 0-394-84861-6). Random House.
--Alfred Hitchcock and the Three Investigators in The Mystery of the Dancing Devil. Lynds, Dennis. Feder, Robert Arthur. Hearne, Jack, illus. LC 76-8134. (Based on the characters created by Robert Arthur Feder, 1909-1969). (Illus.). viii, 141 p. 22cm. (Alfred Hitchcock Mystery Ser.: No. 25). c.1976. (ISBN 0-394-83289-2). (ISBN 0-394-93289-7). Random House.
--Alfred Hitchcock and the Three Investigators in The Mystery of the Headless Horse. Lynds, Dennis. Feder, Robert Arthur. Hearne, Jack, illus. LC 77-74458. (Based on characters created by Robert Arthur Feder, 1909-1969). p. cm. (Alfred Hitchcock Mystery Ser.: No. 26). 1977. (ISBN 0-394-83569-7). (ISBN 0-394-93569-1). Random House.
--Alfred Hitchcock and the Three Investigators in The Mystery of the Shrinking House. Lynds, Dennis. Feder, Robert Arthur. Hearne, Jack, illus. LC 77-29210. (Based on Characters created by Robert Arthur Feder, 1909-1969). (Illus.). 153 p. 20cm. 1978, c.1972. (ISBN 0-394-83777-0). Random House.
--Alfred Hitchcock & the Three Investigators in the Mystery of the Dead Man's Riddle. Lynds, Dennis. Feder, Robert Arthur. Hearne, William, illus. LC 74-4934. (Based on Characters created by Robert Arthur Feder, 1909-1969). (Illus.). 160p. (Three Investigators Ser.: No. 22). (gr. 4-7). 1974. (ISBN 0-394-82927-1, BYR). (ISBN 0-394-92927-6). (ISBN 0-394-84451-3). Random.
--Alfred Hitchcock and the Three Investigators in The Mystery of the Moaning Cave. Lynds, Dennis. Feder, Robert Arthur. Kane, Harry, illus. LC 68-23677. (Based on characters created by Robert Arthur Feder, 1909-1969). (Illus.). 176 p. 22cm. (Alfred Hitchcock Mystery Series, 10). 1968. Random House.
--Alfred Hitchcock and the Three Investigators in The Mystery of the Laughing Shadow. Lynds, Dennis. Feder, Robert Arthur. Kane, Harry, illus. LC 78-75885. (Based on Characters created by Robert Arthur Feder, 1909-1969). (Illus.). 178 p. 22cm. (Alfred Hitchcock Mystery Ser.: No. 12). 1969. Random House.
--Alfred Hitchcock and the Three Investigators in The Mystery of the Moaning Cave. Lynds, Dennis. Feder, Robert Arthur. Kane, Harry, illus. LC 77-28731. (Based on characters created by Robert Arthur Feder, 1909-1969). (Illus.). 176 p. 20cm. 1978, c.1968. (ISBN 0-394-83773-8). Random House.
--Alfred Hitchcock and the Three Investigators in The Mystery of the Laughing Shadow. Lynds, Dennis. Feder, Robert Arthur. Kane, Harry, illus. LC 77-28725. (Based on characters created by Robert Arthur Feder, 1909-1969). (Illus.). 178 p. 20cm. 1978, c.1969. (ISBN 0-394-83775-4). (ISBN 0-394-91492-9). Random House.
--Alfred Hitchcock and the Three Investigators in The Mystery of the Deadly Double. Lynds, Dennis. Feder, Robert Arthur. Mott, Herb, illus. LC 78-55960. (Based on characters created by Robert Arthur Feder, 1909-1969). (Illus.). x, 147 p. 22cm. (Alfred Hitchcock Mystery Ser.: No. 28). c.1978. (ISBN 0-394-83902-1). (ISBN 0-394-93902-6). Random House.
--Alfred Hitchcock and the Three Investigators in The Secret of Phantom Lake. Lynds, Dennis. Feder, Robert Arthur. LC 79-10234. (Based on characters created by Robert Arthur Feder, 1909-1969). p. cm. 1979, c.1973. (ISBN 0-394-84257-X). (ISBN 0-394-92651-X). Random House.
--Alfred Hitchcock and the Three Investigators in The Secret of Shark Reef. Lynds, Dennis. Feder, Robert Arthur. LC 79-9925. (Based on characters created by Robert Arthur Feder, 1909-1969). p. cm. (Alfred Hitchcock Mystery Series ; No. 30). 1979. (ISBN 0-394-84249-9). (ISBN 0-394-94249-3). Random House.

AUTHOR INDEX ARMFIELD, ANNE

--Alfred Hitchcock and the Three Investigators in The Secret of Phantom Lake. Lynds, Dennis. Feder, Robert Arthur. Hearne, Jack, illus. LC 73-4035. (Based on characters created by Robert Arthur Feder, 1909-1969). (Illus.). viii, 148 p. 22cm. (Alfred Hitchcock Mystery Ser.: No. 19). 1973. (ISBN 0-394-82651-5). (ISBN 0-394-82651-5). (ISBN 0-394-84257-X). Random House.
--Alfred Hitchcock and the Three Investigators in The Secret of the Crooked Cat. Lynds, Dennis. Feder, Robert Arthur. Kane, Harry, illus. LC 70-117537. (Based on characters created by Robert Arthur Feder, 1909-1969). (Illus.). vii, 182 p. 22cm. (Alfred Hitchcock Mystery Series, 13). 1970. (ISBN 0-394-81188-7). (ISBN 0-394-91188-1). Random House.
--The Secret of Phantom Lake. Lynds, Dennis. Feder, Robert Arthur. LC 84-15968. (Based on Characters created by Robert Arthur Feder, 1909-1969). p. cm. 1984. (ISBN 0-394-86419-0). Random House.
--The Three Investigators in The Mystery of the Dancing Devil. Lynds, Dennis. rev. ed. Feder, Robert Arthur. LC 83-23082. (Based on Characters Created by Robert Arthur Feder, 1909-1969). viii, 134 p. 20cm. (The Three Investigators Mystery Ser.: No. 25). 1984, c.1976. (ISBN 0-394-86425-5). Random House.
--The Three Investigators in The Mystery of the Deadly Double. Lynds, Dennis. rev. ed. Feder, Robert Arthur. LC 83-26940. (Based on Characters Created by Robert Arthur Feder, 1909-1969). x, 140 p. 20cm. (The Three Investigators Mystery Ser.: No. 28). 1985, c.1978. (ISBN 0-394-86428-X). Random House.
--The Three Investigators in The Mystery of the Headless Horse. Lynds, Dennis. rev. ed. Feder, Robert Arthur. LC 83-27052. (Based on Characters created by Robert Arthur Feder, 1909-1969). x, 144 p. 20cm. (The Three Investigators Mystery Ser.: No. 26). 1985, c.1977. (ISBN 0-394-86426-3). Random House.
--The Three Investigators in The Mystery of the Laughing Shadow. Lynds, Dennis. rev. ed. Feder, Robert Arthur. LC 83-23081. (Based on characters created by Robert Arthur Feder, 1909-1969). x, 157 p. 20cm. (The Three Investigators Mystery Series: No. 12). 1985, c.1969. (ISBN 0-394-86412-3). Random House.
--The Three Investigators in The Mystery of the Moaning Cave. Lynds, Dennis. rev. ed. Feder, Robert Arthur. LC 83-26985. (Based on Characters created by Robert Arthur Feder, 1909-1969). x, 160 p. 20cm. (The Three Investigators Mystery Ser.: No. 10). 1985, c.1968. (ISBN 0 394 86410 7). Random House.
--The Three Investigators in the Mystery of the Purple Pirate. Lynds, Dennis. Feder, Robert Arthur. LC 82-372. (Based on Characters created by Robert Arthur Feder, 1909-1969). p. cm. (The Three Investigators Mystery Ser.: No. 33). 1982. (ISBN 0-394-94951-X). (ISBN 0-394-84951-5). Random House.
--The Three Investigators In The Mystery of the Smashing Glass. Lynds, Dennis. Feder, Robert Arthur. LC 83-26984. (Based on Characters Created by Robert Arthur Feder, 1909-1969). viii, 165 p. 22cm. (The Three Investigators Mystery Series: No. 38). c.1984. (ISBN 0-394-96550-7). (ISBN 0-394-86550-2). Random House.
--The Three Investigators in The Mystery of the Shrinking House. Lynds, Dennis. rev. ed. Feder, Robert Arthur. LC 83-26938. (Based on Characters Created by Robert Arthur Feder, 1909-1969). vii, 145 p. 20cm. (The Three Investigators Mystery Series: No. 18). 1984, c.1972. (ISBN 0-394-86418-2). Random House.
--The Three Investigators in The Secret of Shark Reef. Lynds, Dennis. rev. ed. Feder, Robert Arthur. LC 83-26981. (Based on characters created by Robert Arthur Feder, 1909-1969). viii, 181 p. 20cm. (The Three Investigators Mystery Ser.: No. 30). 1985, c.1979. (ISBN 0-394-86430-1). Random House.
--The Three Investigators in The Secret of the Crooked Cat. Lynds, Dennis. rev. ed. Feder, Robert Arthur. LC 83-23086. (Based on Characters Created by Robert Arthur Feder, 1909-1969). viii, 168 p. 20cm. (The Three Investigators Mystery Series: No. 13). 1984, c.1970. (ISBN 0-394-86413-1). Random House.

Ardizzone, Aingelda
--The Night Ride. 1st ed. Ardizzone, Edward Jeffrey Irving (1900-1978), illus. LC 75-6743. (Illus.). 32 p. 1975, c.1973. (ISBN 0-525-61535-0). Windmill Books.

Ardizzone, Aingelda, jt. auth. see Ardizzone, Edward Jeffrey Irving.

Ardizzone, Edward Jeffrey Irving (1900-1979), ed. see Andersen, Hans Christian.

Ardizzone, Edward Jeffrey Irving (1900-1979)
--Diana and Her Rhinoceros. Ardizzone, Edward Jeffrey Irving (1900-1979), illus. LC 64-22549. 32 p. illus. (part col.) 22 x 27 cm. 1964. H. Z. Walck.
--Diana and Her Rhinoceros. Ardizzone, Edward Jeffrey Irving (1900-1979), illus. LC 79-2367. (Illus.). 32 p. 1979, c.1964. (ISBN 0-19-520172-8). Oxford University Press.
--Diana & Her Rhinocerous. Ardizzone, Edward Jeffrey Irving (1900-1979), illus. (Illus.). Repr (Pub. by Bodley Head). (ps-3). 1979. (ISBN 0-19-520172-8). Oxford U Pr.
--Johnny the Clockmaker. LC 60-9373. unpaged. illus. 27cm. 1960. H. Z. Walck.
--Little Tim & Brave Sea Captain. Ardizzone, Edward Jeffrey Irving (1900-1979), illus. (Illus.). 48p. (ps-3). 1983. (ISBN 0-14-050175-4, Puffin). Penguin.
--Little Tim and the Brave Sea Captain. 2nd ed. Ardizzone, Edward Jeffrey Irving (1900-1979), illus. unpaged. illus. 26cm. 1961. H. Z. Walck.
--Little Tim & the Brave Sea Captain. Ardizzone, Edward Jeffrey Irving (1900-1979), illus. LC 36-22341. (Illus.). 33 1/2cm. 32p. Repr. of 1936 ed. (ps-3). 1978. (ISBN 0-19-279542-2). Oxford U Pr.
--Little Tim & the Brave Sea Captain. Ardizzone, Edward Jeffrey Irving (1900-1979), illus. LC 62-230. (Illus.). (gr. k-3). 1955. (ISBN 0-8098-1042-5). Walck.
--Little Tim and the Brave Sea Captain: Completely Redrawn and with Additional Text. 2nd ed. Ardizzone, Edward Jeffrey Irving (1900-1979), illus. LC 55-13631. unpaged. illus. 27cm. 1955. Oxford University Press.
--Lucy Brown and Mr. Grimes. Ardizzone, Edward Jeffrey Irving (1900-1979), illus. LC 78-133294. (Illus.). 48 p. 27cm. 1971, c.1970. (ISBN 0-8098-1179-0). H. Z. Walck.
--Lucy Brown and Mr. Grimes. Ardizzone, Edward Jeffrey Irving (1900-1979), illus. 32p. 1937. Oxford University Press.
--Lucy Brown and Mr. Grimes. Ardizzone, Edward Jeffrey Irving (1900-1979), illus. 1971. Walck.
--Nicholas and the Fast-Moving Diesel. Ardizzone, Edward Jeffrey Irving (1900-1979), illus. LC 59-5540. unpaged. illus. 27cm. 1959. H. Z. Walck.
--Paul, the Hero of the Fire. Ardizzone, Edward Jeffrey Irving (1900-1979), illus. LC 63-7321. unpaged. illus. 26 cm. 1st U.S. edition. 1963, c.1962. H. Z. Walck.
--Paul, the Hero of the Fire. Ardizzone, Edward Jeffrey Irving (1900-1979), illus. 1949. Houghton Mifflin Co.
--Paul, the Hero of the Fire. Ardizzone, Edward Jeffrey Irving (1900-1979), illus. LC 49-7874. 40 p. col illus. 23 cm. (Porpoise books). 1948. Penguin Books.
--Peter the Wanderer. Ardizzone, Edward Jeffrey Irving (1900-1979), illus. 1963. E M Hale.
--Peter the Wanderer. Ardizzone, Edward Jeffrey Irving (1900-1979), illus. LC 64-13129. (Illus.). 48 p. 26cm. 1964, c.1963. H. Z. Walck.
--Sarah and Simon and No Red Paint. Ardizzone, Edward Jeffrey Irving (1900-1979), illus. LC 66-8647. 48p. col. illus. 25cm. p2.7. 1st U.S. edition. 1966, c.1965. Delacorte.
--Ship's Cook Ginger. Ardizzone, Edward Jeffrey Irving (1900-1979), illus. LC 78-7518. (Illus.). (gr. 1-4). 1978. (ISBN 0-02-705680-5). Macmillan.
--Tim All Alone. Ardizzone, Edward Jeffrey Irving (1900-1979), illus. 1975. (ISBN 0-8098-1048-4). David McKay Company Inc.
--Tim All Alone. Ardizzone, Edward Jeffrey Irving (1900-1979), illus. unpaged. illus. 27cm. 1961. H. Z. Walck.
--Tim All Alone. Ardizzone, Edward Jeffrey Irving (1900-1979), illus. LC 57-132519. unpaged. illus. 27cm. 1957. Oxford University Press. **Award: (KGM).**
--Tim All Alone. Ardizzone, Edward Jeffrey Irving (1900-1979), illus. 48p. (gr. 1-3). 1957. Walck.
--Tim and Charlotte. Ardizzone, Edward Jeffrey Irving (1900-1979), illus. LC 51-13196. (Illus.). unpaged. 26cm. 1951. Oxford University Press.
--Tim and Ginger. Ardizzone, Edward Jeffrey Irving (1900-1979), illus. LC 65-23250. (Illus.). 1 v. (unpaged. 27cm. 1965. H. Z. Walck.
--Tim & Lucy Go to Sea. Ardizzone, Edward Jeffrey Irving (1900-1979), illus. LC 58-14989. unpaged. illus. 26cm. 1958. H. Z. Walck.
--Tim and Lucy Go to Sea. Ardizzone, Edward Jeffrey Irving (1900-1979), illus. 64p. 1938. Oxford University Press.
--Tim in Danger. Ardizzone, Edward Jeffrey Irving (1900-1979), illus. LC 66-17041. i v. illus. (part col.) 26 cm. 48p. N.D. H. Z. Walck.
--Tim In Danger. Ardizzone, Edward Jeffrey Irving (1900-1979), illus. 1955. (ISBN 0-8098-1032-8). McGraw Hill.
--Tim in Danger. Ardizzone, Edward Jeffrey Irving (1900-1979), illus. LC 53-121039. 1v. (unpaged) illus. (part col.) 27cm. 1953. Oxford University Press.
--Tim to the Lighthouse. Ardizzone, Edward Jeffrey Irving (1900-1979), illus. LC 68-29028. (Illus.). 1 v. (unpaged. 27cm. 1968. (ISBN 0-8098-1133-2). H. Z. Walck.
--Tim to the Lighthouse. Ardizzone, Edward Jeffrey Irving (1900-1979), illus. LC 68-116114. (Illus.). 48 p. 26cm. 1968. Oxford U.P.
--Tim To The Rescue. Ardizzone, Edward Jeffrey Irving (1900-1979), illus. 1949. (ISBN 0-8098-1019-0). David Mckay Company.
--Tim to the Rescue. Ardizzone, Edward Jeffrey Irving (1900-1979), illus. LC 66-17042. N.D. H. Z. Walck.
--Tim to the rescue. Ardizzone, Edward Jeffrey Irving (1900-1979), illus. 40p. 1949. Henry Z. Walck, Inc.,Publishers.
--Tim to the Rescue. Ardizzone, Edward Jeffrey Irving (1900-1979), illus. LC 49-48087. 32p. (gr. k-2). 1949. Oxford University Press.
--Tim's Friend Towser. Ardizzone, Edward Jeffrey Irving (1900-1979), illus. 1962. E M Hale.
--Tim's Friend Towser. Ardizzone, Edward Jeffrey Irving (1900-1979), illus. LC 62-17811. unpaged. illus. 27cm. 1962. H. Z. Walck.
--Tim's Last Voyage. Ardizzone, Edward Jeffrey Irving (1900-1979), illus. LC 72-10112. (Illus.). 47 p. 27cm. 1973, c.1972. (ISBN 0-8098-1200-2). Walck. **Award: (NYT).**
--Waterless Mountain. Ardizzone, Edward Jeffrey Irving (1900-1979), illus. 1931. (ISBN 0 679 20233-1). David McKay Company.
--The Wrong Side of the Bed. Ardizzone, Edward Jeffrey Irving (1900-1979), illus. LC 79-80132. 32 p. of illus. 20cm. 1970. Doubleday.

Ardizzone, Edward Jeffrey Irving (1900-1979), illus.
--The Old Ballad of the Babes in the Wood. LC 72-3209. (Illus.). 28 p. 24cm. (Walck fairy tales with historical notes). 1972. (ISBN 0-8098-1197-9). H. Z. Walck.

Ardizzone, Edward Jeffrey Irving (1900-1979) & Ardizzone, Aingelda
--The Little Girl and the Tiny Doll. Ardizzone, Edward Jeffrey Irving (1900-1979), illus. LC 67-19770. (Illus.). 1 v. (unpaged. 24cm. 1967, c.1966. Delacorte Press.
--The Little Girl and the Tiny Doll. Ardizzone, Edward Jeffrey Irving (1900-1979), illus. 1980. Penguin.

Ardley, Neil
--Fact or Fantasy?. (Illus.). 1982. Watts.
--Out into Space. (Illus.). 40p. (The World of Tomorrow Ser.). (gr. 4 up). 1981. (ISBN 0-531-04345-2). Watts.

Arenstein, Misha, jt. ed. see Hopkins, Lee Bennett.

Aresty, Esther B
--The Grand Venture. LC 63-19006. 190 p. 22 cm. 1963. Bobbs-Merrill.

Argent, Kerry, jt. auth. see Trinca, Rod.

Argonauts' Club (1925-)
--The Gravity Stealers: Written by Boys and Girls of Australia. Gunn, John, ed. LC 66-3216. 64 p. illus. (part col.) 26 cm. 1965. Lansdowne Press.

Argyle, C. S.
--Nursery Verses. (gr. k-3). 1970. Vantage.

Ariana
--Sleeping Beauty Retold: For Those Who Can't Wait 100 Years for a Happy Ending. Carleton, Marci, illus. (Illus.). 22p. (Orig.). (Faerytales Retold Ser.). (gr. 1-6). 1983. (ISBN 0-916549-00-3). Ariana Prods.

Arico, Diane, ed. see Dixon, Franklin W.

Arico, Diane, ed. see Hope, Laura Lee.

Arico, Diane, ed. see Keene, Carolyn.

Arico, Diane, ed. see Milton, Hilary Herbert.

Arico, Diane, ed. see Rotsler, William.

Ariga, Shinobu
--Who Has the Yellow Hat?. Ariga, Shinobu, illus. 22p. (Surprise Bks.). 1982. (ISBN 0-8431-0638-7). Price Stern.

Aristophanes
--Five Comedies. Matulay, Laszlo (1912-), illus. 288p. 1948. The World Publishing Co.
--Four Major Plays. new ed. Teitel, N. R., intro. by. Incl. The Acharnians; The Birds; The Clouds; Lysistrata. (Classics Ser.). (gr. 11 up). 1968. (ISBN 0-8049-0189-9, CL-189). Airmont.

Arkhurst, Joyce Cooper (1921-)
--The Adventures of Spider. Pinkney, Jerry (1939-), illus. LC 64-13975. (Illus.). (Six tales of a favorite West African character). (gr. 2-6). 1964. (ISBN 0-316-05106-3). Little.

Arkin, Alan Wolf (1934-)
--The Lemming Condition. Sandin, Joan (1942-), illus. LC 75-6296. (Illus.). 57 p. 21cm. c.1976. (ISBN 0-06-020133-9). (ISBN 0-06-020134-7). Harper & Row.
--Tony's Hard Work Day. Stevenson, James Walker (1929-), illus. LC 76-183161. (Illus.). 32 p. 28cm. 1972. (ISBN 0-06-020137-1). (ISBN 0-06-020138-X). Harper & Row.

Arkin, David (1906-)
--Black and White. Arkin, David (1906-), illus. LC 66-265165. (A Song That is a Story About Freedom to Go to School Together.). 1v. (unpaged) illus. (pt. col.) 25cm. 1966. Ritchie.

Arkin, David (1906-) & Robinson, Earl (1910-)
--Black and White. (A song That is a Story About Freedom to Go to School Together.). (Illus.). 36 p. 25cm. 1966. (ISBN 0-378-68013-7). W. Ritchie Press.

Arkle, Phyllis
--Magic at Midnight. Williams, Ferelith Eccles (1920-), illus. LC 68-26417. (Illus.). 80 p. 1968, c.1967. Funk & Wagnalls.

Arkwright, Ruth
--Brownikins. (Illus.). N.D. Frederick A. Stokes Co.

Arlen, Al, pseud., see Pannullo, Aldo Joseph.

Arlen, Michael J, (1930-)
--Passage to Ararat. 293p. 1975. (ISBN 0-374-22989-9). FS&G.

Armand, Frances Ullman De see DeArmand, Frances Ullmann.

Armando, Baez
--The Fleas of the Panther: Las Pulgas De la Pantera. Prieto, Mariana Beeching (1912-), compiled by. LC 75-11622. p. cm. 1975. (ISBN 0-13-322297-7). Prentice-Hall.

Armando, Jeanne & Cleary, Ruth
--Rolito. Patterson, Russell (1894-), illus. LC 41-24409. cover-title, 63, 1 p. illus. 30 1/2 x 23 cm. c.1941. Pan-American Music Company, Incorporated.

Armas, Linda M., ed. see Martin, Patricia Miles.

Armengol, illus.
--Spanish Fairy Stories. 2d ed. enl. Woolsey, Gamel, tr. LC 51-6061. 103 p. illus. 19 cm. 1946. Transatlantic Arts.

Armeno, Christoforo
--Serendipity Tales. Hodges, Elizabeth Jamison, adapted by. LC 66-12847. (Illus.). 179 p. 24cm. 1966. Atheneum.
--The Three Princes of Serendip. Hodges, Elizabeth Jamison, ed. Berg, Joan, pseud. (1942-), illus. Victor, Joan Berg. LC 64-11887. 158 p. illus. 24 cm. 1964. Antheneum.

Armer, Alberta Roller (1904-)
--Cherry House. Madison, Winifred, illus. LC 58-6244. (Illus.). 23cm. 1958. Beacon Press.
--Hark, the Herald Angel. Madison, Winifred, illus. LC 59-6238. unpaged. illus. 24cm. 1959. Arlington Books.
--Hi, the Story of a Giraffe. Armer, Elinor, illus. LC 64-8301. (Illus.). 27cm. 1964. Simmons Pub. Co.
--Runaway Girl. Guzzi, George, illus. LC 70-101851. (Illus.). 190 p. 21cm. 1970. World Pub. Co.
--Screwball. Mars, Witold Tadeusz J (1912-), illus. LC 81-7365. p. cm. 1981, c.1963. (ISBN 0-399-20837-2). Philomel Books.
--Screwball. Mars, Witold Tadeusz J. (1912-), illus. LC 63-8914. (Illus.). 202 p. 21cm. 1963. World Pub. Co.
--Steve & the Guide Dogs. Kocsis, James C. (1936-), illus. Paul, James, pseud. LC 65-22153. (Illus.). (gr. 7-9). 1965. (ISBN 0-529-03927-3). World Pub.
--Troublemaker. Kocsis, James C. (1936-), illus. Paul, James, pseud. LC 66-8281. (Illus.). 191 p. 21cm. 1966. World Pub. Co.
--The Two Worlds of Molly O'. Wilde, Carol (1938-), illus. LC 62-15077. (Illus.). unpaged. 22cm. (Wonderful world book). 1962. A. S. Barnes.
--The View from Stevenson House. Gold, Ethel, illus. (Illus.). 157 p. 21cm. 1967. World Pub. Co.

Armer, Laura Adams, Mrs. (1874-1963)
--Dark Circle of Branches. Armer, Sidney (1871-), illus. LC 33-27246. ix, 212 p. front., plates. 23 1/2 cm. 1933. Longmans, Green and Co.
--Farthest West. Armer, Sidney (1871-), illus. LC 39-22047. ix, 190 p. front., plates. 23 1/2 cm. 1939. Longmans, Green and Co.
--The Forest Pool. 1st ed. Armer, Laura Adams, Mrs. (1874-1963), illus. LC 38-27619. (Illus.). 26 1/2 cm. 40p. c.1938. Longmans, Green and Co. **Award: (RCM).**
--The Traders' Children. Armer, Laura Adams, Mrs. (1874-1963) & Armer, Sidney (1871-), illus. LC 37-18109. ix p., 1 l., 241 p. front., plates. 22 cm. 1937. Longmans, Green and Co.
--Waterless Mountain. Armer, Laura Adams, Mrs. (1874-1963) & Armer, Sidney (1871-), illus. LC 31-28005. xi, 212 p. front., plates. 23 1/2 cm. 1931. Longmans, Green and Co. **Award: (JNM).**
--Waterless Mountain. Armer, Laura Adams, Mrs. (1874-1963) & Armer, Sidney (1871-), illus. LC 34-18325. xi, 212 p. front., plates. 23 cm. 1933. Longmans, Green and Co.

Armfield, Anne Constance Smedley see Smedley, Constance, pseud.

Armfield, Anne Constance Smedley, Mrs.
--Sylvia's Travels. Armfield, Maxwell (1881-), illus. 21cm. 255p. 1911. E. P. Dutton & Co.

--Tales from Timbuktu. LC 24-15200. xi, 179, 1 p. incl. illus., plates. col. front. 22 1/2 cm. 1924. Bracet and Company.
--The Wizards of Ryetown. MacGregor, Augustine, illus. LC 5-37580. v, 273 p. incl. front., illus. 19 cm. 1905. H. Holt and Company.
--Wonder Tales of the World. Armfield, Maxwell (1881-), illus. LC 20-18948. 6 p. l., 3-271 p. incl. illus., plates col. front., col. plates. 21 cm. 1920. Harcourt, Brace and Howe.

Armin, Jule
--Animated Northwest Stories. Armin, Jule, illus. LC 37-10636. 6 p. l., 194 p. illus. 20 cm. 1935. Perry Eldredge Publishing Co.

Armistead, Charles
--In Search of the Golden Rainbow. Van Dolson, Bobbie Jane, ed. (gr. 5-9). 1981. (ISBN 0-8280-0086-7). Review & Herald.

Armitage, David, jt. auth. see Armitage, Ronda.

Armitage, Frank, ed. see Disney, Walter Elias (1901-1966) & Bedford, Annie North.

Armitage, Marie Teresa & Dykema, Peter William (1873-), eds.
--Merry Music. Setchell, Martha Powell, illus. LC 39-21120. 176 p. col. illus. 22 x 17 1/2 cm. 1939. C. C. Birchard and Company.
--We Sing. Setchell, Martha Powell, illus. LC 40-29663. 192 p. illus. (part col.) 22 cm. c.1940. C. C. Birchard.
--We Sing. Pitcher, Gladys (1890-), illus. LC 42-145832. 244 p. 27 1/2 x 21 cm. c.1942. C. C. Birchard and Company.

Armitage, Marie Teresa & Scholastica, Mary, eds.
--Song Wings: Teachers' Manual and Accompaniments. LC 42-4472. 83 p. illus. (music) 28 cm. c.1941. C. C. Birchard and Company.

Armitage, Ronda
--The Bossing of Josie. Armitage, David (1943-), illus. 1980. Dutton.
--Ice Creams for Rosie. Armitage, David (1943-), illus. (Illus.). 32p. (ps-2). 1982. (ISBN 0-233-97361-3). Andre Deutsch.
--Lighthouse Keeper's Lunch. Armitage, David (1943-), illus. (Illus.). (ps-2). 1979. (ISBN 0-233-96868-7). Andre Deutsch.
--One Moonlit Night. Armitage, David (1943-), illus. (Illus.). 32p. (ps-2). 1983. (ISBN 0-233-97540-3). Andre Deutsch.

Armitage, Ronda & Armitage, David (1943-)
--The Bossing of Josie. LC 79-8656. (Illus.). 32 p. 26cm. 1980. (ISBN 0-233-97231-5). A. Deutsch.
--Don't Forget, Matilda!. Armitage, Ronda & Armitage, David (1943-), illus. LC 78-74473. (Illus.). 32 p. 23cm. 1979. (ISBN 0-233-97075-4). A. Deutsch.
--Grandma Goes Shopping. (Illus.). 32p. (ps-2). N.D. (ISBN 0-233-97627-2). Andre Deutsch.

Armitage, Taylor
--Bob Spencer the Life Saver: Or, Guarding the Coast for Uncle Sam. LC 14-7574. viii p., 1 l., 308 p. front., plates. 19 1/2 cm. (His Uncle Sam's service series) $1.00.). c.1914. Sully and Kleinteich.

Armothy, Christine
--I Am Fifteen - & I Don't Want to Die. 128p. (gr. 7 up). 1974. (ISBN 0-590-02528-7). Scholastic Inc.

Armour, Anobel (1908-)
--Little Shepherd. Martin, Barry, illus. (Winston Tell-Well Story Bks.). 1954. John C. Winston Co.
--Little Shepherd. Martin, Bill & Martin, Bernard Herman (1912-), illus. LC 51-8588. unpaged. illus. 28 cm. N.D. Tell-Well Press.

Armour, R. C.
--North American Indian Fairy Tales, Folklore and Legends. Armour, R. C., illus. viii p., 1 l., 192 p. front., plates. 19 cm. 1905. J. B. Lippincott.

Armour, Richard Willard (1906-)
--The Adventures of Egbert the Easter Egg. Galdone, Paul (1914-), illus. LC 64-66014. (Illus.). 32 p. 26cm. 1965. McGraw-Hill.
--All Sizes and Shapes of Monkeys and Apes. Galdone, Paul (1914-), illus. LC 75-115137. 37 illus. (part col.) 27. 1970. McGraw.
--Animals on the Ceiling. Galdone, Paul (1914-), illus. LC 65-28231. (Illus.). (ps-3). 1966. (ISBN 0-07-002230-5). McGraw.
--A Dozen Dinosaurs. Galdone, Paul (1914-), illus. LC 67-21593. (Illus.). 32 p. 26cm. 1967. McGraw-Hill.
--Have You Ever Wished You Were Something Else?. Gustafson, Scott, illus. LC 82-17102. (Illus.). 48p. (gr. k-3). 1983. (ISBN 0-516-03475-8). Childrens.
--Odd Old Mammals: Animals After the Dinosaurs. Galdone, Paul (1914-), illus. LC 68-24338. 36p. (gr. k-3). 1968. (ISBN 0-07-002262-3). McGraw.
--Sea full of Whales. N.D. (ISBN 0-07-002279-8). McGraw Hill.
--The Strange Dreams of Rover Jones. Gurney, J. Eric (1910-), illus. LC 72-8784. (Illus.). 40 p. 25cm. 1973. (ISBN 0-07-002268-2). (ISBN 0-07-002268-2). McGraw-Hill.
--Strange Monsters of the Sea. Galdone, Paul (1914-), illus. 1979. McGraw.
--Who's in Holes?. Galdone, Paul (1914-), illus. LC 71-159318. (Illus.). 38 p. 27cm. 1971. McGraw-Hill.
--The Year Santa Went Modern. Galdone, Paul (1914-), illus. LC 64-19501. (Illus.). 32 p. 28cm. 1964. McGraw-Hill.

Armstron, Jessie
--My Friend Anne: A Story of the Time of Henry VIII. (The Albion Library). N.D. Frederick Warne & Co.

Armstrong, Annie E.
--Marian and Dorothy, 36 vols. (Illus.). (St. Nicholas Ser.). 1905. Set. A L Burt Co.
--Marian and Dorothy. (Illus.). (The Wellesley Series for Girls). N.D. A. L. Burt.
--Marian and Dorothy: A Book for Girls. (The Rugby Ser.). N.D. A. L. Burt Company.
--Mona St. Clair. (Warne's Adventure Library). N.D. Frederick Warne & Co.
--My Ladies Three. (Illus.). 1910. Frederick Warne & Co.
--My Ladies Three. (The Albion Library). N.D. Frederick Warne & Co.
--Three Bright Girls. (Illus.). (Fireside Ser. for Girls). N.D. A. L. Burt's Publications.
--Three Bright Girls. (Illus.). (The Wellesley Series for Girls). N.D. A. L. Burt's Pubs.
--Three Bright Girls. (Illus.). (The Meade Series for Girls). N.D. A. L. Burt.
--Three Bright Girls. (Illus.). (Scribner-Blackie Series of Books for young people). N.D. Charles Scribner's Sons.
--Three Bright Girls. (Illus.). (Famous Books for Girls). N.D. Dodge Publishing Co.
--Three Bright Girls, 31 vols, No. 22. (Illus.). (Famous Books for Girls Ser.). 1905. Set. H M Caldwell Co.
--Three Bright Girls: A Story for Girls. (The Rugby Ser.). N.D. A. L. Burt Company.
--Three Bright Girls: A Story of Chance and Mischance. Perkinson, W., illus. N.D. Charles Scribner.
--A Very Odd Girl. (Illus.). (Scribner-Blackie Series of books for young people). N.D. Charles Scribner's Sons.
--A Very Odd Girl: Or, Life at the Gabled Farm. (Illus.). (The Meade Series for Girls). N.D. A. L. Burt.
--A Very Odd Girl: Or, Life at the Gabled Farm. (Illus.). (The Wellesley Series for Girls). N.D. A. L. Burt.
--A Very Odd Little Girl: Or, Life at the Gabled Farm. (The Rugby Ser.). N.D. A. L. Burt Company.
--Violet Vereker's Vanity. (Illus.). (Scribner-Blackie Series of books for young lpeople). N.D. Charles Scribner's Sons.

Armstrong, April Oursler
--Ben and the Green Corduroy Angel. 1957. Bruce Pub Co.
--Stories From the Life of Jesus. Gotlieb, Jules, illus. N.D. Doubleday.

Armstrong, Audrey I
--Harness in the Parlour: A Book of Early Canadian Fact and Folklore. LC 75-308723. (Illus.). 90 p. 21cm. 1974. (ISBN 0-7737-1005-1). Musson Book Co.

Armstrong, Beverly
--Dinosaur Detective. Armstrong, Beverly, illus. (Illus.). 32p. (Skill Builder Ser.). (gr. k-3). 1979. (ISBN 0-88160-075-X). Learning Wks.

Armstrong, Beverly, jt. auth. see Renfro, Nancy.

Armstrong, Charlotte
--The Girl With a Secret. N.D. Fawcett Pub Inc.

Armstrong, Edith Mason
--Kitty Landon's Girlhood. (Home Series for Girls). N.D. Hurst & Co.
--The Lost Teddy Bear: And Other Stories. Walker, Ora, illus. LC 43-2343. 2 p. l., 7-64 p. illus. (part col.) 17 x 13 cm. c.1942. Rand McNally & Company.
--The Mason Children. Carsey, Alice & Foster, Genevieve Stump (1893-1979), illus. LC 32-16260. 202 p. incl. front., illus. 20 cm. c.1932. Rand, McNally & Company.

Armstrong, F. C.
--The Young Middy, 1 of 50 vols. (Illus.). (The Norwood Ser.: No. 2). 1900. Lee & Shepard.

Armstrong, Frances
--Changed Lots: Or, Nobody Cares. Ferm, Annie S., illus. N.D. Brentano's Publications.
--A Fair Claimant. (Illus.). (Scribner-Blackie Series of books for young people). N.D. Charles Scribner's Sons.
--A Girl's Loyalty. (Illus.). (Scribner-Blackie Series of books for young people). N.D. Charles Scribner's Sons.

Armstrong, George Douglas, jt. auth. see Armstrong, Gerry Breen.

Armstrong, Gerry Breen (1929-) & Armstrong, George Douglas (1927-)
--Boat on the Hill. Armstrong, George Douglas (1927-), illus. LC 67-17413. (Illus.). (gr. 2-4). 1967. (ISBN 0-8075-0815-2). A Whitman.
--The Fairy Thorn. LC 75-79547. (Illus.). 40 p. 24cm. 1969. A. Whitman.
--The Magic Bagpipe. (Illus.). 38 p. 24cm. 1964. A. Whitman.

Armstrong, H. A, jt. auth. see Newbury, Norman Frederick.

Armstrong, Harry & Armstrong, Louise
--Let's Write a Story. N.D. Reilly & Lee.

Armstrong, Jessie
--Dan's Little Girl. (Maple Leaf Ser.). N.D. Fleming H. Revell Co.
--Kitty Landon's Girlhood, 1 of 32 vols, Vol. 12. (Illus.). (Famous Books for Girls). N.D. H. M. Caldwell Co.
--Mark Marksen's Secret: A Tale. (Illus.). N.D. Thomas Nelson & Sons.
--My Friend Anne. (Illus.). (Warne's Adventure Library). 1910. Frederick Warne & Co.
--The Shadow on the Threshold: Or, A Little Leaven, 1 of 12 Vols. (Illus.). 244p. N.D. Fleming H Revell.

Armstrong, Louise
--Arthur Gets What He Spills. Hoff, Sydney (1912-), illus. LC 78-32029. p. cm. (Let me read book). 1979. (ISBN 0-15-204106-0). (ISBN 0-15-607945-3). Harcourt Brace Jovanovich.
--The Thump, Blam, Bump Mystery. Cruz, Raymond (1933-), illus. LC 74-24582. (Illus.). 32 p. 29cm. 1975. (ISBN 0-8027-6208-5). (ISBN 0-8027-6207-7). Walker.

Armstrong, Louise, jt. auth. see Armstrong, Harry.

Armstrong, Louise & Hearne, Jack
--Saving the Big-Deal Baby. LC 79-22838. (Illus.). 42 p. 22cm. (Skinny book). c.1980. (ISBN 0-525-38805-2). (ISBN 0-525-45050-5). Dutton.

Armstrong, Margaret Neilson (1867-), ed. see Abbott, Jacob.

Armstrong, Matt
--Turtle River Filly. 1st ed. Wilson, Charles Banks (1918-), illus. LC 50-9385. 213 p. illus. 22 cm. 1950. Doubleday.

Armstrong, Mel, adapted by see Disney, Walt, Productions & Bedford, Annie North.

Armstrong, Nancy
--Navajo Long Walk. (gr. 4-9). 1983. (ISBN 0-89992-083-7). MT Coun Indian.

Armstrong, Nancy M., jt. auth. see Wood, Jean.

Armstrong, Richard see Renton, Cam, pseud.

Armstrong, Richard (1903-)
--The Albatross. Humphreys, Graham (1945-), illus. LC 73-107095. 186 p. 21cm. 1970. D. McKay.
--The Big Sea. Dodds, Andrew (1927-), illus. LC 65-19277. 154 p. 21cm. 1965, c.1964. D. McKay Co.
--Cold Hazard. Carey, Robert V., ed. Hodges, Cyril Walter (1909-), illus. (Illus.). viii, 199 p. 22cm. (Riverside reading series). 1968. Houghton Mifflin.
--Cold Hazard. Hodges, Cyril Walter (1909-), illus. LC 56-5544. (Illus.). 180 p. 22cm. 1956, c.1955. Houghton Mifflin.
--Fight for Freedom: An Adventure of World War II. Lambo, Donald W. (1903-1966), illus. LC 66-22208. 150p. illus. 21cm. 1st U.S. edition. 1966, c.1963. McKay.
--Horseshoe Reef. Valentine, Donald Graham (1929-), illus. LC 61-14126. 1961. Duell sloan & Pearce.
--The Lost Ship: A Caribbean Adventure. LC 57-12712. 192 p. 21cm. 1958, c.1956. J. Day Co.
--The Mutineers. Floyd, Gareth (1940-), illus. 181 p. 21cm. 1968. D. McKay Co.
--No Time for Tankers. LC 58-10608. 192p. 21cm. 1st U.S. edition. 1959, c.1958. J. Day Co.
--The Secret Sea. Payne, Roger, illus. LC 66-12678. (Illus.). 150 p. 21cm. 1966. D. McKay Co.
--Ship Afire!. 1959. E M Hale.
--Ship Afire!. A Story of Adventure at Sea. LC 60-8697. 188 p. 21cm. 1961, c.1959. John Day Co.
--Trial Trip. 1963. E M Hale.
--Trial Trip. Valentine, Donald Graham (1929-), illus. LC 63-12459. 181 p. illus. 22 cm. 1st U.S. edition. 1963, c.1962. Criterion Books.

Armstrong, Richard (1903-), ed.
--Treasure & Treasure Hunters. 1st U.S. edition. (gr. 7 up). 1969. D White.

Armstrong, Rodolfo L (1918-)
--Desperate Voyage. 1st ed. Orbaan, Albert F. (1913-), illus. LC 53-6083. 184p. illus. 21cm. 1953. Dutton.

Armstrong, Sam, jt. ed. see Thomson, Riley.

Armstrong, Samuel, ed. see Archer, Peter & Loew's Incorporated.

Armstrong, Samuel, ed. see Disney, Walt, Productions.

Armstrong, Samuel, ed. see Lantz, Walter.

Armstrong, Velma
--The Banana Horse. LC 85-51966. p. cm. c.1985. (ISBN 0-938232-98-3). Winston-Derek.

Armstrong, Warren
--Last Voyage. 256p. 1958. John Day & Co.
--Sea Pantoms. 224p. 1961. John Day & Co.

Armstrong, William Howard (1914-), ed. see Doskocilova, Hana.

Armstrong, William Howard (1914-)
--The Angels Must Have Smiled. 2nd ed. Hargrave, Art, illus. Bishop, Jim, pref. by. LC 70-101346. (Illus.). 144p. (Orig.). 1969. (ISBN 0-913452-01-7). Jesuit Bks.
--Hadassah: Esther, the Orphan Queen. LC 72-76114. (Illus.). N.D. (ISBN 0-385-08832-9). (ISBN 0-385-08843-4). Doubleday & Company.
--Joanna's Miracle. LC 77-89708. (Illus.). 127 p. 20cm. c.1977. (ISBN 0-8054-6921-4). Broadman Press.
--The MacLeod Place. Keith, Eros, illus. LC 72-83601. 188 p. 22cm. 1972. (ISBN 0-698-20193-0). (ISBN 0-698-20193-0). Coward, McCann & Geoghegan.
--The Mills of God. Armstrong, David (1947-), illus. LC 72-95712. (Illus.). 115 p. 22cm. 1973. (ISBN 0-385-00344-7). (ISBN 0-385-00344-7). Doubleday.
--My Animals. Hanak, Mirko, illus. LC 73-81411. (Illus.). 32 p. 27cm. 1974. (ISBN 0-385-02836-9). (ISBN 0-385-02836-9). Doubleday.
--Sounder. Barkley, James Edward (1941-), illus. LC 70-85030. (Illus.). 116 p. 22cm. 1969. Harper & Row. **Awards: (JNM); (ALA).**
--Sour Land. Armstrong, David (1947-), illus. LC 70-135783. 116 p. 22cm. 1971. (ISBN 0-06-020141-X). Harper & Row.
--The Tale of Tawny and Dingo. Mikolaycak, Charles (1937-), illus. LC 78-19486. p. cm. c.1979. (ISBN 0-06-020113-4). (ISBN 0-06-020114-2). Harper & Row.

Arnaout, Nancy, jt. auth. see Greenvale School.

Arndt, Walter W. (1916-), retold by see Busch, Wilhelm.

Arneson, Don Jon (1935-)
--A Friend Indeed: True Tales of Dog Heroism. LC 80-23062. (Illus.). 91 p. 22cm. 1981. (ISBN 0-531-04257-X). Watts.
--Jokes and Riddles Roundup. Kersell, Jim, illus. LC 72-83533. (Illus.). 63 p. 18cm. 1972. Xerox Education Publications.
--The Most Famous Ghost of All and Other Ghost Stories. LC 78-14772. p. cm. 1978, c.1971. (ISBN 0-671-32974-X). Wanderer Books.
--Secret Places. 1st ed. Arnold, Peter (1934-), photos by. LC 77-141007. (Illus.). 40 p. 1971. (ISBN 0-03-086225-6). Holt, Rinehart and Winston.
--Sometimes in the Dead of Night. LC 82-10514. 124 p. 19cm. c.1983. (ISBN 0-671-45593-1). Simon & Schuster.

Arneson, Donald (1932-)
--Arnie, Knight of the Day. Schneider, Carol (1938-), illus. LC 79-18491. p. cm. c.1979. (ISBN 0-934778-01-9). Bookmaker Pub.
--Doing Something Nice, Inc. & Other Short Plays for Kids. Schneider, Carol (1938-), illus. (Illus.). 72p. (Orig.). (gr. 3-6). 1978. (ISBN 0-934778-00-0). Bookmaker.

Arnett, Anna Williams
--The Brother Bears And Other Stories. Ludwig & Regina, illus. LC 28-325. 125 p. col. illus. 19 1/2 cm. c.1927. Beckley-Cardy Company.

Arnin, Mary A.
--April Baby's Book of Tunes. N.D. MacMillan.

Arno, Ed, illus.
--The Gingerbread Man. Repr. (Starbright Editions). (gr. k-3). 1973. Schol Bk Serv.

Arno, Peter (1904-1968)
--Peter Arno's Circus. N.D. Liveright Publishing.
--Peter Arno's Hullabaloo. N.D. Liveright Publishing.
--Peter Arno's Parade. N.D. Liveright Publishing.

Arnold, Adelaide Wilson
--A Son of the First People. Barton, Loren, illus. LC 40-32629. 4p.1., 248 p. illus. 21 cm. 1940. The Macmillan Company.
--Traveler's Moon. 1st ed. Lantz, Paul (1908-), illus. LC 62-11375. 228p. illus. 22cm. 1962. Doubleday.

Arnold, Arnold Ferdinand (1921-), compiled by.
--The Big Book of Tongue Twisters & Double Talk. Arnold, Arnold Ferdinand (1921-), illus. LC 63-20110. 62 p. illus. (part col.) 29 cm. N.D. Random House.
--Pictures and Stories from Forgotten Children's Books. LC 77-86640. (Illus.). viii, 170 p. (Dover pictorial archive series). 1969. (ISBN 0-486-22041-9). Dover Publications.
--Pictures and Stories From Forgotten Children's Books. (Illus.). N.D. (ISBN 0-8446-0459-3). Peter Smith Publisher, Inc.

Arnold, Caroline & Nicklaus, Carol
--My Friend from Outer Space. LC 80-22045. (Illus.). 32 p. 22cm. (Easy-read story book). 1981. (ISBN 0-531-02473-3). F. Watts.

Arnold, Charlotte Vimont
--The Black and White Book. Arnold, Charlotte Vimont, illus. LC 35-19379. 32p. illus. 17 x 22cm. c.1915. Gibson & Perin.

Arnold, Clara, ed.
--The Juvenile Keepsake: A Gift Book for Young People. LC 15-18373. 4 p. l., 13-148 p. front., plates. 19 cm. c.1851. Phillips, Sampson & Company.

AUTHOR INDEX ARTHUR, ROBERT

Arnold, Edgar (1856-)
--The Young Refugees: The Adventures of Two Lads from Old Virginia. LC 12-29475. 305 p. front. (port.) plates. 20 cm. $1.0. 1912. The Hermitage Press.
Arnold, Edwin, Sir (1832-1904), ed.
--Oriental Fairy Tales. Cramer, Rie, illus. LC 24-27637. 4 p. l., viii, 1 p., 1 l., 5-627 p. mounted col. front., mounted col. plates. 23 cm. 1923. Duffield & Company.
--Oriental Fairy Tales. Stevens, Beatrice (1876-), illus. LC 3-17905. 2 p. l., ix, 627 p. col. front., col. pl. 21 cm. (Added t.-p.,: Library for young people ... vol. v). 1903. P. F. Collier & Son.
Arnold, Elliott (1912-1980)
--Brave Jimmy Stone. 1st ed. Goldstein, Leslie, illus. (Illus.). 119p. (gr. 7 up). 1962. (ISBN 0-394-80982-3). (ISBN 0-394-90982-8). Knopf.
--Brave Jimmy Stone. Shortall, Leonard W., illus. (Illus.). (gr. 4-6). 1975. (ISBN 0-590-09093-4, Schol Pap). Scholastic Inc.
--Broken Arrow. Nicholas, Frank, illus. LC 54-5128. (Illus.). 246 p. 21cm. 1954. Duell, Sloan and Pearce.
--Broken Arrow. Nicholas, Frank, illus. 1954. Little, Brown & Co.
--A Kind of Secret Weapon. LC 69-12598. 191 p. 22cm. 1969. Scribner.
--The Spirit of Cochise. LC 72-494. 183 p. 22cm. 1972. (ISBN 0-684-12989-2). Scribner.
--White Falcon. 1st ed. Chapman, Frederick Trench (1887-), illus. LC 55-8952. 246p. illus. 22cm. 1955. (ISBN 0-394-81815-6). Knopf.
Arnold, Emily see McCully, Emily Arnold.
Arnold, Esther Watkins
--I Don't Want To: A Play for Children in three Acts. 11p. 1929. Elridge Entertainment House.
--King Quarrel and the Beggar: A Christmas Play in One Act. 7p. 1927. Elridge Entertainment House.
--The Magic Pills: A Fairy Play for Children in Two Acts. 16p. 1931. Elridge Entertainment House.
--The Witch and the Christmas Story: One Act Play for Children. 12p. 1983. Elridge Entertainment House.
Arnold, Francena Harriet Long (1888-)
--Straight Down a Crooked Lane. (gr. 9-12). 1959. (ISBN 0-8024-0041-8). Moody.
Arnold, Hannah Winifred (1874-)
--Little Merry Christmas. LC 14-16201. 91 p. front., plates. 19 1/2 cm. $0.6. c.1914. Fleming H. Revell Company.
--Little Merry Christmas, 1 of 12 Vols. (Illus.). (The "Dew-Drop" Ser.). N.D. Set. Thomas Nelson & Sons.
--Miss Emeline's Kith and Kin. LC 19-182981. 224 p. incl. front. 19 1/2 cm. c.1919. Fleming H. Revell Company.
--The Twins "Pro" and "Con". Relyea, Charles M., illus. LC 17-86. 269 p. incl. front. plates. 20 1/2 cm. c.1916. Fleming H. Revell Company.
Arnold, Henry H. (1886-)
--Bill Bruce and the Pioneer Aviators. LC 28-99925. 250 p. front. 19 cm. (His Aviator series). c.1928. A. L. Burt Company.
--Bill Bruce Becomes an Ace. LC 28-9991. 227 p. front. 19 cm. (His Aviator series). c.1928. A. L. Burt Company.
--Bill Bruce in the Trans-Continental Race. LC 28-14231. 246 p. front. 19 1/2 cm. (His Aviator series). c.1928. A. L. Burt Company.
--Bill Bruce on Border Patrol. LC 28-119752. 232 p., 1 l. front. 19 1/2 cm. (His Aviator series no. 4). c.1928. A. L. Burt Company.
--Bill Bruce on Forest Patrol. LC 28-14119. 255 p. front. 19 1/2 cm. (His Aviator series). c.1928. A. L. Burt Company.
--Bill Bruce: The Flying Cadet. LC 28-99914. 241 p. front. 19 cm. (His Aviator series). c.1928. A. L. Burt Company.
--Bill Bruce, the Flying Cadet. (The Bill Bruce Air Pilot Ser.). N.D. A L Burt Co.
Arnold, Joanne M.
--Man-Killer. McCarthy, Patricia, ed. Rich, Harry, illus. (Illus., Orig.). (Pal Paperbacks Ser., Kit A). 1974. (ISBN 0-8374-3476-9). Xerox Ed Pubns.
Arnold, Katrin
--Anna Joins in. Seeling, Renate, illus. 28p. (gr. 6 up). 1983. (ISBN 0-687-01530-8). Abingdon.
Arnold, Lattye Eunice
--Aunt Malissa's Memory Jug: Original Folk Stories. 1st ed. LC 62-51122. 141p. 21cm. (Exposition-Lochinvar book). 1962. Exposition Press.
--When the Birds came to Bethlehem. 1963. Exposition Press Inc.
Arnold, Lydia W
--Little Green Pickles and Other Stories,. LC 27-288093. 5p. 1., 3-99p. 1927. The Baker & Taylor Co.
Arnold, Lydia W. Felbach & Vigilans and Sequus
--Little Green Pickles and Other Stories. Strackey, John St. Loe (1860-), illus. LC 27-23859. 5 p. l., 3-99 p. 19 1/2 cm. 1927. The Baker & Taylor Co.
Arnold, Margaret Gordon
--Folk Tales Retold. Beem, Frances M., illus. LC 26-758027. 93 p. col. illus. 20 cm. 1926. The Bruce Publishing Company.
Arnold, Marti (1928-)
--Alaska, Uncle Jim, and Me. 1st ed. Dessereau, April & Present, David, illus. LC 83-80267. p. cm. c.1983. (ISBN 0-912683-00-7). Fireweed Press.
Arnold, Mary Ellicott
--In the Land of the Grasshopper Song. Reed, Mabel, illus. N.D. Vantage Press.
Arnold, Nason Henry (1874-)
--Rusty: The Adventures of a Little Dog. Tyng, Griswold, illus. LC 30-24233. 272 p. col. front., illus. 19 1/2 cm. c.1930. Lothrop, Lee & Shepard Co.
--Rusty's Travels. A Little Dog's Part in a Vacation. Tyng, Griswold, illus. LC 31-24063. 272 p. front., illus. 20 1/2 cm. c.1931. Lothrop, Lee & Shepard Co.
--Tinker of Stone Bluff. Sutterlin, Charles E., illus. LC 36-19163. 5 p. l., 318 p. incl. front., illus. 20 1/2 cm. 1936. Doubleday, Doran & Company, Inc.
Arnold, Oren (1900-)
--Are We All Here?. Making the Scene in Europe, [illegible] 211 p. illus. 22 cm. 1964. Grosset & Dunlap.
--The Chili Pepper Children. Critchfield, Carol, illus. LC 60-5189. 114p. illus. 21cm. 1960. Broadman Press.
--Cowboy in Europe. Molnar, Agnes, illus. LC 72-105256. (Illus.). 191 p. 22cm. 1970. (ISBN 0-200-71671-9). Abelard-Schuman.
--The Great Sleepy Gun Animal Hunt. Unada, pseud. (1927-), illus. Gliewe, Unada Grace. LC 68-9260. (Illus.). 184 p. 22cm. 1968. F. Fell.
--Hidden in the Hills. Eitzen, Allan (1928-), illus. LC 67-10094. (Illus.). viii, 144 p. 21cm. 1967. Broadman Press.
--Hidden Treasure in the Wild West. With Photo Supplement. Grifalconi, Ann (1929-), illus. LC 66-141192. 160p. illus., maps, ports. 22cm. 1967, c.1966. Abelard.
--Mystery of Superstition Mountain. Ihms, Jimmie, illus. LC 76-185060. (Illus.). 191 p. 22cm. 1972. (ISBN 0-8178-4871-1). (ISBN 0-8178-4871-1). Harvey House.
--Pieces of the Sky. Rice, Elizabeth (1913-), illus. LC 73-93520. (Illus.). 42 p. 1973. (ISBN 0-8178-4981-5). Harvey House.
--Rancho M'lee. LC 67-14977. 192p. 22cm. 1967. Abelard.
--The Sky Y Train. Toschik, Larry (1922-), illus. LC 61-5062. 157p. illus. 21cm. 1961. Broadman Press.
--White Danger. 1962. E M Hale.
--White Danger. LC 62-686321. 192p. illus. 22cm. 1962. Holiday House.
Arnold, Paul & Steele, Marshall
--Nursery Rhymes and Music. N.D. Funk & Wagnalls.
Arnold, Rist
--I Like Birds. LC 76-58705. (Illus.). 28 p. c.1977. (ISBN 0-912766-45-X). Tundra Books.
Arnold, Rollo (1926-)
--Bracken Block. Jenks, W., illus. LC 66-191590. 143p. illus. 20cm. 1966. Angus &Robertson.
Arnold, Wesley F.
--Fun with Next to Nothing. Cardy, Wayne C., illus. 1962. (ISBN 0-06-020145-2). Harper and Row.
Arnosky, Jim (1946-)
--I Was Born in a Tree & Raised by Bees. LC 76-12632. (Illus.). (gr. k-4). 1977. (ISBN 0-399-61018-9). Putnam Pub Group.
--Mouse Numbers & Letters. LC 81-13305. (Illus.). 48 p. 21cm. c.1982. (ISBN 0-15-256022-X). Harcourt Brace Jovanovich.
--Mouse Writing. LC 83-4298. (Illus.). 48 p. 22cm. 1983. (ISBN 0-15-256028-9). Harcourt Brace Jovanovich.
--Mudtime & More: Nathaniel Stories. LC 78-10864. (Illus.). (gr. k-3). 1979. (ISBN 0-201-00173-X, A-W Childrens). A-W.
--Nathaniel. LC 77-13505. (Illus.). 48 p. 19cm. c.1978. (ISBN 0-201-00171-3). Addison-Wesley.
--Watching Foxes. LC 84-20157. (Illus.). 24p. (ps-3). 1984. (ISBN 0-688-04260-0). (ISBN 0-688-04259-7). Lothrop.
Arnot, William
--A Friend Shut Out, 1 of 6 bks. (Illus.). (Lessons in Life Ser.: No. 4). N.D. Set. Thos Nelson & Sons.
--He Careth for Thee, 1 of 6 bks. (Illus.). (Lessons in Life Ser.: No. 3). N.D. Set. Thos Nelson & Sons.
--An Incident of Travel, 1 of 6 bks. (Illus.). (Lessons in Life Ser.: No. 2). N.D. Set. Thos Nelson & Sons.
--The Man at the Wheel, 1 of 6 bks. (Illus.). (Lessons in Life Ser.: No. 1). N.D. Set. Thos Nelson & Sons.
--The Parables of Our Lord. N.D. Thomas Nelson & Sons.
Arnott, Kathleen, ed. see Davis, Bette.
Arnott, Kathleen (1914-), ed.
--African Fairy Tales. (gr. 1-4). 1971. (ISBN 0-584-62351-8). Transatlantic.
--African Myths & Legends. Kiddell-Monroe, Joan (1908-) & Jegede, Taiwo, illus. (Illus.). Repr. of 1962 ed. (Oxford Myths & Legends Ser.). (gr. 6-12). 1978. (ISBN 0-19-274115-2). Oxford U Pr.
--African Myths & Legends. Kiddell-Monroe, Joan (1908-), illus. LC 63-7590. (Illus.). (gr. 4-7). 1963. (ISBN 0-8098-2362-4). Walck.
--Animal Folk Tales Around the World. Watts, Anna Bernadette (1942-), illus. LC 71-133295. (Illus.). 18, 252 p. 23cm. 1971, c.1970. (ISBN 0-8098-2415-9). H. Z. Walck.
--Dragons, Ogres, and Scary Things: Two African Folktales. Cary, Louis Favreau (1915-), illus. Cary, pseud. LC 74-9876. (Illus.). 64 p. 23cm. 1974. (ISBN 0-8116-6978-5). Garrard Pub. Co.
--Tales of Temba: Traditional African Stories. Feelings, Thomas (1933-), illus. LC 68-23880. (Illus.). 144 p. 22cm. 1969. (ISBN 0-8098-2409-4). H. Z. Walck.
Arnov, Boris, Jr. (1926-)
--Bally the Blue Whale: Life Story of the Largest Living Mammal. 1st ed. Mack, John, illus. LC 64-15315. 96 p. illus. 22 cm. 1964. Criterion Books.
Arnow, Harriette Louisa Simpson (1908-)
--The Dollmaker. 1962. (ISBN 0-02-016310-X, Collier). Macmillan.
--Kentucky Trace: A Novel of the American Revolution. 1974. (ISBN 0-394-48990-X). Knopf.
Arnstein, Helene Solomon (1915-)
--Billy and Our New Baby. LC 73-7951. (Illus.). 35 p. 24cm. 1973. (ISBN 0-87705-093-7). Behavioral Publications.
Arntson, Herbert Edward (1911-)
--Adam Gray: Stowaway: A Story of the China Trade. Gillette, Henry Sampson (1915-), illus. LC 61-11884. (Illus.). 195 p. 21cm. 1961. F. Watts.
--Caravan to Oregon. LC 57-132078. 194p. illus. 28cm. c.1957. Binfords & Mort.
--Frontier Boy: A Story of Oregon. Ferguson, William, illus. LC 67-13346. 112p. illus. 21cm. 1967. Washburn.
--Mountain Boy in Oregon. LC 67-30937. (Illus.). 138 p. 21cm. 1968. I. Washburn.
--River Boy. Ferguson, William, illus. LC 69-12911. (Illus.). 153 p. 21cm. 1969. Washburn.
--Two Guns in Old Oregon. Gillette, Henry Sampson (1915-), illus. LC 64-12126. 151p. illus. 22cm. 1964. F. Watts.
Aron, Bill, jt. auth. see White, Wallace.
Aronin, Ben (1904-1980)
--Jolly Jingles for the Jewish Child. LC 48-1186. 62 p. illus. 26 cm. 1947. Behrman House.
--The New Mother Goose Rhymes. Johnson, Fridolf (1905-), illus. LC 44-27714. 128 p. incl. col. front., illus. (part col.) 29 cm. c.1943. Pub. for Remington-Morse by Consolidated Book Publishers, Inc.
--Remington-Morse Mother Goose and Father Gander. Johnson, Fridolf (1905-), illus. LC 45-9992. 128 p. incl. col. front., illus. (part col.) 29 cm. c.1945. Pub. by Lexington Press.
--Remington-Morse New Mother Goose Book. Johnson, Fridolf (1905-), illus. LC 44-47727. 128 p. incl. col. front., col. illus. 29 cm. c.1944. Consolidated Book Publishers.
--The Secret of the Sabbath Fish. Rieger, Shay (1929-), illus. LC 78-63437. (Illus.). 52 p. 29cm. 1980. (ISBN 0-8276-0110-7). Jewish Publication Society of America.
Aronoff, Daisy F.
--A. B. C. Bible and Holiday Stories. Danciger, Leila Nash, illus. N.D. Bloch Publishing Co.
Aronow, Sara
--Seven Days of Creation. Seligson, Judith, illus. (Illus.). 32p. (Bible Stories in Rhymes Ser.: Vol. 1). (ps-2). 1985. (ISBN 0-87203-119-5). Hermon.
Arora, Shirley Lease (1930-)
--The Left-Handed Chank. LC 66-16936. 256 p. 23cm. 1966. Follett Pub. Co.
--What Then, Raman?. Guggenheim, Hans (1924-), illus. LC 60-133571. 176p. illus. 24cm. (gr. 4-6). 1960. (ISBN 0-695-49275-6). Follett Pub. Co.
Arouet De Voltaire, Francois Marie see Voltaire, Francois Marie Arouet De.
Arr, Marjory
--Tiny Tales from Happywood. N.D. (ISBN 0-533-05659-4). Vantage.
Arre, John, pseud., see Holt, John Robert.
Arre, John, pseud. (1926-)
--Message to My Daughter. Holt, John Robert. (Orig.). (gr. 7-12). 1975. (ISBN 0-515-03603-X). Pyramid Pubns.
Arrick, Fran
--Chernowitz!. A Novel. LC 81-7712. p. cm. 1981. (ISBN 0-87888-190-5). Bradbury Press.
--God's Radar. LC 83-2666. p. cm. 1983. (ISBN 0-02-705710-0). Bradbury Press.
--Nice Girl from Good Home. LC 84-11002. 199 p. 22cm. c.1984. (ISBN 0-02-705840-9). Bradbury Press.
--Steffie Can't Come Out to Play. LC 78-4423. 196 p. 22cm. c.1978. (ISBN 0-87888-135-2). Bradbury Press.
--Tunnel Vision. LC 79-25939. 167 p. 22cm. c.1980. (ISBN 0-87888-163-8). Bradbury Press.
Arrighi, Mel
--Freak Out. 1968. G P Putman's Sons.
Arriola, Gus, ed.
--Gordo's Cat. Arriola, Gus, illus. LC 81-9563. (Illus.). 128p. (Orig.). 1st U.S. edition. 1981. (ISBN 0-916392-84-8). Oak Tree Pubns.
Arrowsmith, Donald Pogue & Rhodes, Nelson
--The Princess's Birthday Party: A Story. LC 76-364057. (Illus.). 47 p. 22cm. (gr. 2-4). [illegible]
Arroyo, Anita
--El Grillo Grunon: Cuentos Para Chicos y Grandes. 1a ed. Oliva Robain, Armando, illus. LC 84-13199. (Illus.). 122 p. 28cm. 1984. (ISBN 0-8477-3527-3). Editorial De la Universidad De Puerto Rico.
Ars Edition Staff
--Ida Bohatta Picture Diary. Bohatta, Ida (1900-), illus. (Illus.). 120p. (Stationery Bks.). 1984. (ISBN 0-86724-124-1). Ars Edition.
Ars Sacra
--The Hummel. Ars Edition Staff, ed. Hummel, Berta, illus. (Illus.). 78p. 1st U.S. edition. 1981. (ISBN 0-86724-031-8). Ars Edition.
Ars Edition Staff, jt. auth. see Keussen, Gudrun.
Ars Edition Staff, ed. see Ars Sacra.
Arsenyev, Vladimir
--With Dersu the Hunter. White, Anne Terry, adapted by. LC 65-25971. (Juv.). (gr. 6-9). 1965. (ISBN 0-8076-0325-2). Braziller.
Arth, Michael E.
--Palms: Anatomy of a Passion. (Illus.). 104p. (gr. 6-12). 1984. (ISBN 0-912467-02-9). (ISBN 0-912467-03-7). Linnaea.
Arthur, Catherine & Talbot, Nathan
--My Sister's Silent World. LC 78-13140. p. cm. 1979. (ISBN 0-516-02022-6). Childrens Press.
Arthur, Clara M.
--Etchings from Two Lands, 1 of 50 vols. (Illus.). 350p. (Sunday-School Lib: No. 14). N.D. Set. Lothrop Pub. Co.
Arthur, Ella Bentley, Mrs.
--Sonny Boy's Day at the Zoo. Arthur, Stanley Clisby, photos by. 25 cm. 75p. 1913. The Century Co.
Arthur, Mildred H
--God, Why Am I So Miserable?. LC 79-12307. p. cm. c.1979. (ISBN 0-570-03623-2). Concordia Pub. House.
--Holidays of Legend: From New Year's to Christmas. Pelkey, Sofia, illus. LC 73-148110. (Illus.). 112p. (gr. 4-7). 1971. (ISBN 0-8178-4842-8). Harvey.
Arthur, Pat
--Calvin Crocker in a Very Busy Day. (Illus.). 22p. (ps-3). 1983. (ISBN 0-89954-212-3). Antioch Pub Co.
--Dracula's Castle. Rudegeair, Jean, illus. (Illus.). 12p. (ps-4). 1982. (ISBN 0-89954-204-2). Antioch Pub Co.
Arthur, Robert, pseud., see Feder, Robert Arthur.
Arthur, Robert, jt. auth. see Arden, William.
Arthur, Robert, jt. auth. see Brandel, Marc.
Arthur, Robert, jt. auth. see Carey, Mary Virginia.
Arthur, Robert, jt. auth. see West, Nick.
Arthur, Robert, pseud. (1909-1969)
--Alfred Hitchcock & the Three Investigators in the Mystery of the Stuttering Parrot. Feder, Robert Arthur. (Illus.). 1964. Random House Inc.
--Alfred Hitchcock and the Three Investigators in The Mystery of the Green Ghost. Feder, Robert Arthur. LC 79-12324. p. cm. (Alfred Hitchcock & the Three Investigators Ser.). 1979, c.1965. (ISBN 0-394-84258-8). (ISBN 0-394-91228-4). Random House.
--Alfred Hitchcock and the Three Investigators in The Mystery of the Vanishing Treasure. Feder, Robert Arthur. LC 79-3520. 152 p. 20cm. (Alfred Hitchcock and the Three Investigators Ser.). 1980, c.1966. (ISBN 0-394-84452-1). (ISBN 0-394-81550-5). (ISBN 0-394-91550-X). Random House.
--Alfred Hitchcock and the Three Investigators in The Mystery of the Green Ghost. Feder, Robert Arthur. Kane, Harry, illus. LC 65-222164. x, 181p. illus. 22cm. (Alfred Hitchcock mystery ser., 4). (Alfred Hitchcock Mystery Ser.: No. 4). c.1965. Random.
--Alfred Hitchcock and the Three Investigators in the Mystery of the Whispering Mummy. Feder, Robert Arthur. Kane, Harry, illus. LC 65-17278. (Illus.). 185 p. 22cm. (Alfred Hitchcock Mystery Ser.: No. 3). 1965. Random House.

--Alfred Hitchcock and the Three Investigators in The Mystery of the Vanishing Treasure. Feder, Robert Arthur. Kane, Harry, illus. LC 66-9093. (Illus.). 159 p. 22cm. (Alfred Hitchcock Mystery Ser.: No. 5). 1966. Random House.

--Alfred Hitchcock and the Three Investigators in The Mystery of the Fiery Eye. Feder, Robert Arthur. Kane, Harry, illus. LC 67-20382. (Illus.). viii, 180 p. 22cm. (Alfred Hitchcock Mystery Ser.: No. 7). 1967. Random House.

--Alfred Hitchcock and the Three Investigators in The Mystery of the Silver Spider. Feder, Robert Arthur. Kane, Harry, illus. LC 67-20383. (Illus.). 184 p. 22cm. (Alfred Hitchcock Mystery Ser.: No. 8). 1967. Random House.

--Alfred Hitchcock and the Three Investigators in the Mystery of the Screaming Clock. Feder, Robert Arthur. Kane, Harry, illus. (Illus.). viii, 184 p. 22cm. (Alfred Hitchcock mystery series, 9). (Alfred Hitchcock Mystery Ser.: No. 9). 1968. Random House.

--Alfred Hitchcock and the Three Investigators in The Mystery of the Talking Skull. Feder, Robert Arthur. Kane, Harry, illus. LC 69-20274. (Illus.). viii, 179 p. 22cm. (Alfred Hitchcock mystery Ser., 11). (Alfred Hitchcock Mystery Ser.: No. 11). 1969. Random House.

--Alfred Hitchcock and the Three Investigators in The Mystery of the Stuttering Parrot. Feder, Robert Arthur. Kane, Harry, illus. LC 73-176517. (Illus.). ix, 182 p. 21cm. (Windward book 23). 1973, c.1964. (ISBN 0-394-82200-5). Random House.

--Alfred Hitchcock and the Three Investigators in The Mystery of the Fiery Eye. Feder, Robert Arthur. Kane, Harry, illus. LC 77-28860. (Illus.). viii, 180 p. 20cm. 1978, c.1967. (ISBN 0-394-83770-3). Random House.

--Alfred Hitchcock and the Three Investigators in The Mystery of the Stuttering Parrot. Feder, Robert Arthur. Kane, Harry, illus. LC 77-28870. (Illus.). ix, 182 p. 20cm. 1978, c.1964. (ISBN 0-394-83767-3). Random House.

--Alfred Hitchcock and the Three Investigators in The Mystery of the Talking Skull. Feder, Robert Arthur. Kane, Harry, illus. LC 77-28877. (Illus.). viii, 179 p. 20cm. 1978, c.1969. (ISBN 0-394-83774-6). Random House.

--Alfred Hitchcock and the Three Investigators in The Mystery of the Screaming Clock. Feder, Robert Arthur. Kane, Harry, illus. LC 77-28720. (Illus.). viii, 184 p. 20cm. 1978, c.1968. (ISBN 0-394-83772-X). Random House.

--Alfred Hitchcock and the Three Investigators in The Mystery of the Whispering Mummy. Feder, Robert Arthur. Kane, Harry, illus. LC 77-28737. (Illus.). 185 p. 20cm. 1978, c.1965. (ISBN 0-394-83768-1). Random House.

--Alfred Hitchcock and the Three Investigators in The Mystery of the Silver Spider. Feder, Robert Arthur. Kane, Harry, illus. LC 78-23. (Illus.). 184 p. 20cm. 1978, c.1967. (ISBN 0-394-83771-1). Random House.

--Alfred Hitchcock and the Three Investigators in The Secret of Terror Castle. Feder, Robert Arthur. Kane, Harry, illus. LC 64-19642. (Illus.). ix, 179 p. 22cm. (Alfred Hitchcock Mystery Ser.: No. 1). 1964. Random House.

--Alfred Hitchcock and the Three Investigators in The Secret of Skeleton Island. Feder, Robert Arthur. Kane, Harry, illus. LC 66-9779. (Illus.). 158 p. 22cm. (Alfred Hitchcock Mystery Ser.: No. 6). 1966. Random House.

--Alfred Hitchcock and the Three Investigators in The Secret of Terror Castle. Feder, Robert Arthur. Kane, Harry, illus. LC 77-29129. (Illus.). ix, 179 p. 20cm. 1978, c.1964. (ISBN 0-394-83766-5). Random House.

--Alfred Hitchcock and the Three Investigators in The Secret of Skeleton Island. Feder, Robert Arthur. Kane, Harry, illus. LC 77-28741. (Illus.). 158 p. 20cm. 1978, c.1966. (ISBN 0-394-83769-X). Random House.

--Ghosts and More Ghosts. Feder, Robert Arthur. LC 63-9033. (Illus.). 211 p. 25cm. 1963. Random House.

--Mystery and More Mystery. Feder, Robert Arthur. Lambert, Saul (1928-), illus. LC 66-9539. (Illus.). 234 p. 24cm. 1966. Random House.

--Mystery of the Screaming Clock. Feder, Robert Arthur. (gr. 5-6). N.D. (ISBN 0-590-30330-9, Schol Pap). Scholastic Inc.

--The Three Investigators in The Mystery of the Fiery Eye. Feder, Robert Arthur. Rev. ed. LC 83-22991. viii, 164 p. 20cm. (The Three Investigators Mystery Ser.: No. 7). 1984, c.1967. (ISBN 0-394-86407-7). Random House.

--The Three Investigators in The Mystery of the Green Ghost. Feder, Robert Arthur. rev. ed. LC 83-26933. ix, 179 p. 20cm. (The Three Investigators Mystery Ser.: No. 4). 1985, c.1965. Random House.

--The Three Investigators in the Mystery of the Screaming Clock. Feder, Robert Arthur. rev. ed. LC 83-24484. (The Three Investigators Mystery Ser.: No. 9). 1984, c.1968. (ISBN 0-394-86409-3). Random House.

--The Three Investigators in The Mystery of the Stuttering Parrot. Feder, Robert Arthur. rev. ed. LC 83-26983. (Based on Characters Created by Robert Arthur). viii, 174 p. 20cm. (The Three Investigators Mystery Ser: No. 2). 1985, c.1964. (ISBN 0-394-86402-6). Random House.

--The Three Investigators in The Mystery of the Silver Spider. Feder, Robert Arthur. rev. ed. LC 83-26982. vii, 168 p. 20cm. (The Three Investigators Mystery Ser.: No. 8). 1985. (ISBN 0-394-86408-5). Random House.

--The Three Investigators in The Mystery of the Talking Skull. Feder, Robert Arthur. rev. ed. LC 83-23010. viii, 164 p. 20cm. (The Three Investigators Mystery Ser.: No. 11). 1984, c.1969. (ISBN 0-394-86411-5). Random House.

--The Three Investigators in The Mystery of the Vanishing Treasure. Feder, Robert Arthur. rev. ed. LC 83-27030. 152 p. 20cm. (The Three Investigators Mystery Ser.: No. 5). 1985, c.1966. (ISBN 0-394-86405-0). Random House.

--The Three Investigators in The Mystery of the Whispering Mummy. Feder, Robert Arthur. rev. ed. LC 83-27027. x, 180 p. 20cm. (The Three Investigators Mystery Ser.: No. 3). 1985, c.1965. (ISBN 0-394-86403-4). Random House.

--The Three Investigators in The Secret of Skeleton Island. Feder, Robert Arthur. rev. ed. LC 83-26939. viii, 152 p. 20cm. (The Three Investigators Mystery Ser.: No. 6). 1985. (ISBN 0-394-86406-9). Random House.

--The Three Investigators in The Secret of Terror Castle. Feder, Robert Arthur. rev. ed. Kane, Harry, illus. LC 83-26987. (Based on Characters Created by Robert Arthur). ix, 165 p. 20cm. (The Three Investigators Mystery Ser.: No. 1). 1985. (ISBN 0-394-86401-8). Random House.

Arthur, Robert, pseud. (1909-1969), ed.

--Davy Jones' Haunted Locker: Great Ghost Stories of the Sea. Feder, Robert Arthur. Cellini, Joseph (1924-), illus. LC 65-18168. 204p. col. illus. 27cm. 1965. (ISBN 0-394-81081-3). Random.

--Spies & More Spies. Feder, Robert Arthur. Lambert, Saul (1928-), illus. (gr. 7-11). 1967. (ISBN 0-394-91673-5, BYR). (ISBN 0-394-82190-4). Random.

--Thrillers and More Thrillers. Feder, Robert Arthur. Lambert, Saul (1928-), illus. LC 68-23653. (Illus.). 208 p. 24cm. 1968. Random House.

Arthur, Ruth Mabel (1905-1979)

--After Candlemas. Gill, Margery Jean (1925-), illus. LC 73-84820. (Illus.). 121 p. 22cm. 1974. Atheneum.

--The Autumn People. Gill, Margery Jean (1925-), illus. LC 72-86925. (Illus.). 166 p. 22cm. 1973. Atheneum.

--A Candle in Her Room. Gill, Margery Jean (1925-), illus. LC 66-12854. (Illus.). 212 p. 22cm. 1966. Atheneum.

--A Candle in Her Room. Gill, Margery Jean (1925-), illus. 1972. Delacorte.

--Dragon Summer. Gill, Margery Jean (1925-), illus. (Illus.). (gr. 5 up). 1963. (ISBN 0-689-20012-9). Atheneum.

--The Little Dark Thorn. Gill, Margery Jean (1925-), illus. LC 74-154746. (Illus.). 195 p. 22cm. 1971. Atheneum.

--Miss Ghost. LC 79-63117. 119 p. 22cm. 1979. (ISBN 0-689-30702-0). Atheneum.

--My Daughter, Nicola. Rocker, Fermin (1907-), illus. LC 65-21721. 122p. illus. 22cm. c.1965. Atheneum.

--An Old Magic. Gill, Margery Jean (1925-), illus. LC 77-8335. (Illus.). 175 p. 22cm. 1977. (ISBN 0-689-30577-X). Atheneum.

--On the Wasteland. Gill, Margery Jean (1925-), illus. LC 75-328451. (Illus.). 159 p. 22cm. 1975. (ISBN 0-689-30473-0). Atheneum.

--Portrait of Margarita. Gill, Margery Jean (1925-), illus. LC 68-12230. (Illus.). 185 p. 22cm. (1905-1979). 1968. Atheneum.

--Requiem for a Princess. Gill, Margery Jean (1925-), illus. LC 67-2667. (Illus.). 182 p. 22cm. 1967. Atheneum.

--The Saracen Lamp. Gill, Margery Jean (1925-), illus. LC 73-98606. (Illus.). 210 p. 22cm. 1970. Atheneum.

--The Whistling Boy. Gill, Margery Jean (1925-), illus. LC 69-13531. (Illus.). 200 p. 22cm. 1969. Atheneum.

Arthur, Timothy Shay see Uncle Herbert, pseud.

Arthur, Timothy Shay (1809-1885)

--After a Shadow. Uncle Herbert, pseud. (Home Stories). N.D. Sheldon & Co.

--All for the Best. Uncle Herbert, pseud. N.D. Nichols & Hall.

--All For The Best: Or, The Old Peppermint Man. (Illus.). N.D. James Miller.

--Fireside Angel. Uncle Herbert, pseud. (Illus.). N.D. D. Lothrop & Co.

--The Fireside Angel. LC 42-49308. 64 p. incl. front. 12 cm. 1858. G. G. Evans.

--The Fireside Angel. LC 42-49807. 64 p. incl. front. 12 cm. 1856. J. W. Bradley.

--Hidden Wings. (Home Stories). N.D. Sheldon & Co.

--Idle Hands, and Other Stories. Uncle Herbert, pseud. N.D. Porter & Coates.

--Not Anything for Peace. (Home Stories). N.D. Sheldon & Co.

--The Peace-Maker. (Home Stories). N.D. Sheldon & Co.

--The Pitcher of Cool Water. Uncle Herbert, pseud, 1 of 6 Vols. (Broken Rock Ser.). N.D. National Temperance Society.

--The Poor Woodcutter and Other Stories. Croome, William H., illus. LC 41-31398. 151 (i.e. 149) p. incl. plates. front., pl. 16 cm. 1860. J. B. Lippincott & Co.

--Sowing the Wind. (Home Stories). N.D. Sheldon & Co.

--Sunshine at Home. (Home Stories). N.D. Sheldon & Co.

--Ten Nights in a Bar Room. Uncle Herbert, pseud. (Illus.). (The Rugby Series for Boys). 1905. A. L. Burt's Pubs.

--Ten Nights in a Bar Room. (Illus.). (The Empyreal Library of Handy Volume). N.D. H. M. Caldwell Co.

--Ten Nights in a Bar-room. Uncle Herbert, pseud. (Illus.). (Boys' and Girls' Classics). N.D. Henry Altemus Co.

--Wreaths of Friendship: A Gift for the Young. Woodworth, Francis Channing (1812-1859), illus. LC 15-23122. 2 p. l., vii-xii, 13-240 p. front., illus. 19 cm. 1849. Baker & Scribner.

Arthur, W.

--The Successful Merchant, 1 of 15 vols. (Selected Bks for Sunday School: The/Ludlow Library). N.D. Set. Methodist Bk Concern.

Artis, Vicki Kimmel (1945-)

--Brown Mouse and Vole. Hughes, Jan, illus. LC 74-14387. (Illus.). 47 p. 23cm. 1975. (ISBN 0-399-60922-9). Putnam.

--Gray Duck Catches a Friend. Maestro, Giulio (1942-), illus. LC 73-86475. (Illus.). 46 p. 23cm. (See and read storybook). 1974. (ISBN 0-399-60871-0). (ISBN 0-399-20381-8). (ISBN 0-399-20381-8). Putnam.

Artis, Vicki Kimmel (1945-) & McCully, Emily Arnold (1939-)

--Pajama Walking. LC 80-22658. (Illus.). 32 p. 1981. (ISBN 0-395-30343-5). Houghton Mifflin.

Artists and Writers Guild

--The Tall Book of Nursery Tales. Rojankovsky, Feodor Stepanovich (1891-1970), ed. Rojankovsky, Feodor Stepanovich (1891-1970), illus. LC 44-3881. 120 p. incl. col. front., illus. (part col.) 30 1/2 x 13 cm. 1944. Artists and Writers Guild, Inc., Harper and Brothers, Distributors.

Artists and Writers Guild, jt. auth. see Wyckoff, Marjorie Elaine Morrison.

Artists and Writers Guild, jt. ed. see Watson, Jane Werner.

Artley, Stern, jt. auth. see Monroe, Marion.

Artzybasheff, Boris Mikhailovich (1899-1965), ed. see Aesopus.

Artzybasheff, Boris Mikhailovich (1899-1965)

--Poor Shaydullah. N.D. MacMillan.

--Seven Simeons: A Russian Tale. Artzybasheff, Boris Mikhailovich (1899-1965), illus. 1937. Viking Press. **Award: (RCM).**

--Seven Simeons: Russian Tale. Artzybasheff, Boris Mikhailovich (1899-1965), illus. (Illus.). (gr. 4-8). 1961. (ISBN 0-670-63574-X). Viking Pr.

Artzybasheff, Boris Mikhailovich (1899-1965), ed.

--Aesop's Fables. 1933. Viking.

Artzybasheff, Boris Mikhailovich (1899-1965), illus.

--The Fairy Shoemaker and Other Fairy Poems. LC 28-256526. 114 p. 1 l. incl. front., illus., plates. 23 cm. 1928. The Macmillan Company.

Aruego, Ariane see Kraus, Robert (1925-) & Dewey, Ariane.

Aruego, Jose (1932-)

--Juan and the Asuangs: A Tale of Philippine Ghosts and Spirits. LC 72-99008. (Illus.). 32 p. 27cm. 1970. Scribner.

--The King and His Friends. LC 75-85270. (Illus.). 40 p. 1969. Scribner.

--Look What I Can Do. Aruego, Jose (1932-), illus. LC 73-158880. (Illus.). 32 p. 27cm. (gr. k-2). 1971. (ISBN 0-684-12493-9). Scribner. **Award: (NYT).**

--Pilyo the Piranha. Aruego, Jose (1932-), illus. LC 77-123132. (Illus.). color ils. 32p. (gr. k-3). 1971. (ISBN 0-02-705690-2). Macmillan.

Aruego, Jose (1932-) & Dewey, Ariane (1937-)

--A Crocodile's Tale. LC 75-37185. (Illus.). 32 p. 1972. (ISBN 0-684-12806-3). Scribner.

--A Crocodile's Tale: A Philippine Folk Story. (gr. k-2). 1976. Scholastic.

--We Hide, You Seek. LC 78-13638. (Illus.). 32 p. 26cm. c.1979. (ISBN 0-688-80201-X). (ISBN 0-688-84201-1). Greenwillow Books. **Award: (ALA).**

Arundel, Honor (1919-1973)

--The Amazing Mr. Prothero. Paton, Jane Elizabeth (1934-), illus. LC 70-181673. (Illus.). 80 p. 22cm. 1972. (ISBN 0-8407-6210-0). T. Nelson.

--The Blanket Word. LC 73-1128. 138 p. 22cm. 1973. (ISBN 0-8407-6306-9). T. Nelson.

--Emma in Love. LC 70-180290. 159 p. 23cm. 1972. (ISBN 0-8407-6204-6). T. Nelson.

--Emma's Island. LC 72-102412. 149 p. 21cm. 1970, c.1968. Hawthorn Books.

--A Family Failing. LC 72-3231. 160 p. 23cm. 1972. (ISBN 0-8407-6256-9). T. Nelson.

--The Girl in the Opposite Bed. LC 70-140083. 122 p. 21cm. 1971. (ISBN 0-8407-6128-7). T. Nelson.

--Green Street. Armitage, Eileen, illus. LC 77-102416. (Illus.). 154 p. 21cm. 1970. Hawthorn Books.

--The High House. Armitage, Eileen, illus. LC 68-11911. 126 p. illus. 22 cm. 1968, c.1967. Meredith Press.

--The Longest Weekend. LC 70-123114. 159 p. 21cm. 1970. T. Nelson.

--Love Is a Blanket Word. (gr. 7-12). 1976. (ISBN 0-590-05183-0). Scholastic Inc.

--The Terrible Temptation. LC 74-160149. 173 p. 23cm. 1971. (ISBN 0-8407-6160-0). T. Nelson.

--The Two Sisters. LC 69-16299. 156 p. 21cm. 1969, c.1968. Meredith Press.

Arundel, Jocelyn, pseud., see Alexander, Jocelyn Anne Arundel.

Arundel, Jocelyn, pseud. (1930-)

--Dugan & the Hobo. Alexander, Jocelyn Anne Arundel. 1st ed. Dennis, Wesley (1903-1966), illus. LC 60-14611. 24cm. 121p. (gr. 4-6). 1960. (ISBN 0-07-002371-9). (ISBN 0-07-002370-0). McGraw.

--Dugan and the Hobo. Alexander, Jocelyn Anne Arundel. 1st ed. Dennis, Wesley (1903-1966), illus. LC 60-14611. 121p. illus. 24cm. 1960. Whittlesey House.

--Jingo: Wild Horse of Abaco. Alexander, Jocelyn Anne Arundel. Dennis, Wesley (1903-1966), illus. (Illus.). 1977. Durrell.

--Jingo, Wild Horse of Abaco. Alexander, Jocelyn Anne Arundel. 1st ed. Dennis, Wesley (1903-1966), illus. LC 59-14437. 137p. illus. 24cm. 1959. Whittlesey House.

--Little Stripe. Alexander, Jocelyn Anne Arundel. Kaufmann, John (1931-), illus. (gr. 2-4). 1967. (ISBN 0-8038-4245-7). Hastings.

--Little Stripe: An African Zebra. Alexander, Jocelyn Anne Arundel. Kaufmann, John (1931-), illus. LC 67-16252. 58p. illus. 24cm. (Preserve our wildlife ser.). c.1967. (ISBN 0-8038-4245-7). Hastings.

--Mighty Mo: The Story of an African Elephant. Alexander, Jocelyn Anne Arundel. 1st ed. Dennis, Wesley (1903-1966), illus. LC 61-143516. 24cm. (Young Pioneer Books). (gr. 4-6). 1961. (ISBN 0-07-078061-7). McGraw.

--Mighty Mo: The Story of an African Elephant. Alexander, Jocelyn Anne Arundel. Dennis, Wesley (1903-1966), illus. 124p. illus. 19cm. (Young Pioneer bk.). 1967, c.1961. McGraw.

--Mighty Mo: The Story of an African Elephant. Alexander, Jocelyn Anne Arundel. 1st ed. Dennis, Wesley (1903-1966), illus. LC 61-143516. 124p. illus. 24cm. 1961. Whittlesey House.

--Shoes for Punch. Alexander, Jocelyn Anne Arundel. LC 64-21626. 26cm. 32p. (gr. k-3). 1964. (ISBN 0-07-002375-1). (ISBN 0-07-002376-X). McGraw.

--Simba of the White Mane. Alexander, Jocelyn Anne Arundel. 1st ed. Dennis, Wesley (1903-1966), illus. LC 58-984744. 127p. illus. 24cm. 1958. (ISBN 0-07-002366-2). Whittlesey House.

--Whitecap's Song. Alexander, Jocelyn Anne Arundel. Dennis, Wesley (1903-1966), illus. LC 62-19641. (Illus.). 123 p. 24cm. 1962. Whittlesey House.

Arundel, Louis

--Motor Boat Boys Mississippi Cruise: Or, The Dash for Dixie. LC 12-10753. 237 p. incl. front. 20 cm. c.1912. M. A. Donohue & Co.

--Motor Boat Boys on the Great Lakes: Or, Exploring the Mystic Isle of Mackinac. LC 13-31619. 227 p. incl. front. 19 1/2 cm. $0.5. c.1912. M. A. Donohue & Co.

--Motor Boat Boys on the St. Lawrence: Or, Solving the Mystery of the Thousand Islands. LC 12-10754. 238 p. incl. front. 19 1/2 cm. c.1912. M. A. Donohue & Co.

--Motor Boat Boys' River Chase: Or, Six Chums Afloat and Ashore. LC 14-10731. 257 p. incl. front. 19 1/2 cm. $0.5. c.1914. M. A. Donohue & Company.

Arvin, Newton, ed. see Melville, Herman.

Asantewa, Doris

--Two Make a Team. Seville, Michele, illus. LC 76-20192. (Illus.). 39 p. 1976. (ISBN 0-917336-01-1). Pambili Books.

AUTHOR INDEX ASHER, INEZ

Asbjornsen, Peter Christen (1812-1885)
--Cat on the Dovrefell: A Christmas Tale. De Paola, Tomie, pseud. (1934-), illus. De Paola, Thomas Anthony. 1979. Putnam.
--East of the Sun and West of the Moon. Collin, Hedvig, illus. LC 53-8476. (Illus.). 22cm. 141p. (New Children's Classics). N.D. Macmillan.
--East of the Sun and West of the Moon. D'Aulaire, Ingri Mortenson (1904-1980) & D'Aulaire, Edgar Parin (1898-), eds. D'Aulaire, Ingri Mortenson (1904-1980) & D'Aulaire, Edgar Parin (1898-), illus. N.D. Viking Press.
--East of the Sun and West of the Moon: Old Tales from the North. Nielsen, Kay Rasmus (1886-1957), illus. Dasent, George Webbe, Sir (1817-1896), tr. LC 32-21560. 5 p. l., 9-204 p. col. front., col. plates. 22 1/2 cm. N.D. Garden City Publishing Company, Inc.
--The Fairy Tales from Far North. (The Fairy Library). N.D. A. L. Burt.
--Fairy Tales from the Far North. N.D. Grosset & Dunlap.
--Fairy Tales from the Far North. Braekstad, Hans Lien (1845-1915), tr. LC 38-27690. vi, 285 p. col. front., illus., plates. 21 cm. (Famous books for young Americans). N.D. Blue Ribbon Books, Inc.
--The Fairy World. Braekstad, Hans Lien (1845-1915), tr. (Illus.). 325p. N.D. DeWolfe, Fiske & Co.
--Favorite Fairy Tales Told in Norway. 1st ed. Haviland, Virginia (1911-), retold by. Weisgard, Leonard Joseph (1916-), illus. LC 61-9283. (Illus.). 88 p. 24cm. (gr. 2-6). 1961. (ISBN 0-316-35053-2). Little, Brown.
--Folks and Fairy Tales. Braekstad, Hans Lien (1845-1915), tr. Gosse, Edmund W., intro. by. (Illus.). 1882. A. C. Armstrong & Son.
--The Man Who Was Going to Mind the House. McKee, David (1935-), retold by. McKee, David (1935-), illus. LC 72-6104. (Illus.). 28 p. 1973, c.1972. (ISBN 0-200-71893-2). (ISBN 0-200-71893-2). Abelard-Schumann.
--A New Book of Folk and Fairy Tales. Tenth ed. Braekstad, Hans Lien (1845-1915), tr. 1888. A. C. Armstrong & Son's.
--Round the Yule Log: Christmas in Norway. Bridgman, Lewis Jesse (1857-1931), illus. Broekstad, H. L., tr. (Christmas in Many Lands Ser.). 1895. Dana Estes and Company.
--Round the Yule-Log: Christmas in Norway. Norwegian Folk and Fairy Tales. Bridgman, Lewis Jesse (1857-1931), illus. Braekstad, H. L., tr. LC 13-12205. 32 p. incl. front., illus., plates 19 1/2 cm. (Christmas in Many Lands' Ser). 1895. Estes & Lauriat's.
--Round the Yule Log: Norwegian Folk and Fairy Tales. N.D. J. B. Lippincott Co.
--Tales from the Field. Smith, John Moyr, illus. Dasent, George Webbe, Sir (1817-1896), tr. LC 69-13232. (Illus.). xx, 403 p. 21cm. 1970. Blom.
--Tales from the Field: A Series of Popular Tales from the Norse. new ed. Smith, John Moyr, illus. Dasent, George Webbe, Sir (1817-1896), tr. xx, 403 p. incl. front., illus. 19 1/2 cm. 1908. G. P. Putnam's Sons.
--Three Billy Goats Gruff. Ames, Lee Judah (1921-), illus. LC 55-1600. unpaged. illus. 17cm. (Tell-a-tale books). c.1954. Whitman Pub. Co.
--The Three Billy Goats Gruff. Galdone, Paul (1914-), illus. LC 72-85338. (Illus.). 32 p. 30cm. 1973. (ISBN 0-8164-3080-2). Seabury Press.
--The Three Billy Goats Gruff. Maxey, Dale (1927-), illus. LC 67-6174. (Illus.). 32cm. 26p. (Whitman Giant Tell-a Tale Book). 1966. Whitman Pub. Co.
--The Three Billy Goats Gruff. Neebe, William, illus. O'Grady, Alice & Throop, Frances (1868-), trs. LC 57-8252. unpaged. illus. 21cm. (Rand McNally elf book, 583). c.1957. Rand McNally.
--The Three Billy Goats Gruff. O'Grady, Alice & Throop, Frances (1868-), eds. Brice, Tony, illus. LC 40-7925. 48 p. illus. (part col.) 17 x 14 cm. c.1940. Rand McNally & Company.
--The Three Billy Goats Gruff. Parker, Edward, illus. LC 78-18068. (Illus.). 32 p. 24cm. c.1979. (ISBN 0-89375-121-9). Troll Associates.
--The Three Billy-Goats Gruff: A Norwegian Folktale. Blair, Susan B., illus. LC 63-8842. unpaged. illus. 17 x 24 cm. (Little owl book). 1963. Holt, Rinehart and Winston.

Asbjornsen, Peter Christen (1812-1885) & Grimm, Jakob Ludwig Karl (1785-1863)
--Three Billy Goats Gruff and the Wolf and the Kids. Scarry, Richard McClure (1919-), illus. LC 53-3218. unpaged. illus. 21cm. (Little Golden library, 173). 1953. Simon and Schuster.

Asbjornsen, Peter Christen (1812-1885) & Moe, Jorgen Engebretsen (1813-1882)
--The Boy Who Tried to Cheat Death. 1st ed. Mikolaycak, Charles (1937-) & Kismaric, Carole (1942-), eds. Mikolaycak, Charles (1937-), illus. LC 79-138506. (Illus.). 32 p. 29cm. 1971. Doubleday.
--Doodle Doo" the Rooster Who Fell into the Pea Soup: Also the Story of "The Three Billy Goats Gruff" Adapted for Children from Old Norwegian Fairy Tales. LC 29-7655. 26 p. illus. (part col.) 20 1/2 cm. 1929. C. E. Graham & Co.
--East O' the Sun and West O' the Moon. Dasent, George Webbe, Sir (1817-1896), tr. 8p.1., 11-289 p. col. front., col. pl. 20 c. (golden books for children). c.1921. D. McKay.
--East O' the Sun and West O' the Moon. Taylor, Alta Lucretia (1885-), ed. Brundage, Frances, illus. LC 25-6878. 248 p. incl. col. front., illus. 24 cm. (Lettered on cover: Mayflower series). c.1924. The Saalfield Publishing Co.
--East O' the Sun and West O' the Moon and Other Norse Fairy Tales. Dasent, George Webbe, Sir (1817-1896), tr. LC 17-11576. v, 308 p. front., plates. 20 1/2 cm. 1917. G. P. Putnam's Sons.
--East O' the Sun and West O' the Moon: Fifty-Nine Norwegian Folk Tales from the Collection of Peter Christen Asbjornsen and Jorgen Moe. Dasent, George Webbe, Sir (1817-1896), tr. LC 70-97214. (Illus.). xiv, 418 p. 22cm. 1970. Dover Publications.
--East O' the Sun and West O' the Moon: Norwegian Folk Tales. Seaton, Walter, illus. LC 57-1324. 288p. illus. 22cm. 1957. Junior Deluxe Editions.
--East O' the Sun and West O' the Moon With Other Norwegian Folk Tales. Rasmussen, Inger Margrete, Mrs., retold by. Higgins, Violet Moore, illus. Rassussen, Inger Margrete, Mrs., tr. LC 24-21429. 192 p. incl. col. front., col. illus. 23 1/2 cm. (Just right book). c.1924. A. Whitman & Company.
--East O' the Sun and West O' the Moon: With Other Norwegian Folk Tales. Thorne-Thomsen, Gudrun, Mrs. (1873-), retold by. Richardson, Frederick (1862-1937), illus. Thorne-Thomsen, Gudrun, retold by. LC 12-185491. 218 p. incl. col. plates. 18 1/2 cm. c.1912. Row, Peterson & Company.
--East O' the Sun and West O' the Moon: With Other Norwegian Folk Tales. Thorne-Thomsen, Gudrun, Mrs. (1873-), retold by. Richardson, Frederick (1862-1937), illus. LC 46-18417. 144 p., 1 l. illus. (part col.) 21 x 19 cm. 1946. Row, Peterson and Company.
--East of the Sun & West of the Moon. 1963. MacMillan.
--East of the Sun & West of the Moon. Collin, Hedvig, illus. LC 28-14163. 5 p. l., 198 p. incl. illus., plates. col. front., col. plates. 19 1/2 cm. (Macmillan children's classics). 1928. The Macmillan Company.
--East of the Sun & West of the Moon. Nielsen, Kay Rasmus (1886-1957), illus. (gr. 1 up). 1977. Doubleday.
--East of the Sun & West of the Moon & Other Tales. (Illus.). (gr. k-3). 1953. (ISBN 0-02-705740-2). Macmillan.
--East of the Sun and West of the Moon, and Other Tales. Vroman, Tom, illus. 1965. Macmillan.
--East of the Sun and West of the Moon: Old Tales from the North. Nielsen, Kay Rasmus (1886-1957), illus. LC 77-74791. (Illus.). 108 p. 26cm. 1977. (ISBN 0-385-13213-1). (ISBN 0-385-13214-X). Doubleday.
--East of the Sun and West of the Moon: Old Tales from the North. Nielsen, Kay Rasmus (1886-1957), illus. Dasent, George Webbe, Sir (1817-1896), tr. 5 p. l., 9-204 p. col. front., illus., col. pl. 23 1/2 cm. 1922. G. H. Doran Company.
--East of the Sun and West of the Moon: Old Tales from the North. Nielsen, Kay Rasmus (1886-1957), illus. Dasent, George Webbe, Sir (1817-1896), tr. LC 42-27492. 5 p. l., 9-205 (i.e. 204) p. col. mounted front., illus., col. mounted plates. 25 cm. N.D. George H. Doran Company.
--East of the Sun and West of the Moon: Twenty-One Norwegian Folk Tales. D'Aulaire, Ingri Mortenson (1904-1980) & D'Aulaire, Edgar Parin (1898-), eds. D'Aulaire, Ingri Mortenson (1904-1980) & D'Aulaire, Edgar Parin (1898-), illus. Dasent, George Webbe, Sir (1817-1896), tr. LC 38-28936. 188 p. illus. 29 1/2 cm. 1938. The Viking Press.
--East of the Sun and West of the Moon: Twenty-One Norwegian Folk Tales. D'Aulaire, Ingri Mortenson (1904-1980) & D'Aulaire, Edgar Parin (1898-), eds. D'Aulaire, Ingri Mortenson (1904-1980) & D'Aulaire, Edgar Parin (1898-), illus. Dasent, George Webbe, Sir (1817-1896), tr. LC 75-3978. (Illus.). 224 p. 25cm. 1969. Viking Press.
--Norse Fairy Tales. Simmons, F. J., adapted by. Knowles, Reginald L. & Knowles, Horace J., illus. Dasent, George Webbe, Sir (1817-1896), tr. 20cm. 463p. 1910. J. B. Lippincott.
--Norwegian Fairy Tales. Gade, Hellen Rebecca, Mrs. (1845-) & Gade, John Allyne (1875-), illus. LC 25-26115. 5 p. l., ix-xv p., 1 l., 250, 1 p. front., illus. 19 cm. (Half-title: Scandinavian classics. vol. XXIV). 1924. The American-Scandinavian Foundation: Etc., Etc.
--Norwegian Folk Tales. Kittelsen, Theodor & Werenskiold, Erik, illus. Iversen, Pat Shaw & Norman, Carl, trs. (Illus.). (gr. 5 up). 1961. (ISBN 0-670-51609-0). Viking Pr.
--Norwegian Folk Tales. Werenskiold, Erik & Kittelsen, Theodor, illus. Iversen, Pat Shaw & Norman, Carl, trs. 1960. Viking.
--Popular Tales from the Norse. Dasent, George Webbe, Sir (1817-1896), tr. LC 18-1670. lxix p., 1 l., 379 p. 19 1/2 cm. 1859. D. Appleton and Company.
--Popular Tales from the Norse. new ed. Dasent, George Webbe, Sir (1817-1896), tr. Dasent, Arthur Irwin (1859-), memoir by. clxxvii, 2, 443 p. 21 cm. 1908. G. P. Putnam's Sons.
--The Sheep and the Pig Who Went into the Woods to Live by Themselves. Adapted for Children from an Old Norwegian Tale. LC 29-7654. 26 p. illus. (part col.) 20 1/2 cm. c.1929. C. E. Graham & Co.
--The Squire's Bride. Sewall, Marcia (1935-), illus. 1975. Atheneum.
--The Three Billy Goats Gruff. 1st ed. Brown, Marcia (1918-), illus. Dasent, George Webbe, Sir (1817-1896), tr. LC 57-5265. unpaged. illus. 26cm. 1957. Harcourt, Brace. **Award: (ALA).**
--The Three Billy Goats Gruff. Rudin, Ellen (1812-1885), retold by. Obligado, Lilian Isabel (1931-), illus. LC 81-83362. (Illus.). 24 p. 16cm. (First little golden book). c.1982. (ISBN 0-307-10117-7). (ISBN 0-307-68117-3). Golden Press.
--The Three Billy Goats Gruff: A Picture Book. Stobbs, William (1914-), illus. LC 68-15742. (Illus.). 32 p. 1968, c.1967. McGraw-Hill.

Asch, Frank (1946-)
--Bear Shadow. LC 84-18250. (Illus.). 32 p. 22cm. c.1985. (ISBN 0-13-071580-8). Prentice-Hall.
--Bear's Bargain. LC 85-6355. p. cm. c.1985. (ISBN 0-13-071606-5). Prentice-Hall.
--The Blue Balloon. LC 76-160704. 46 p. (chiefly col. illus. 26cm. 1971. McGraw-Hill.
--Bread and Honey. Asch, Frank (1946-), illus. LC 81-16893. (Illus.). 39 p. 23cm. (A Frank Asch Bear Story). c.1981. (ISBN 0-8193-1077-8). (ISBN 0-8193-1078-6). Parents Magazine Press.
--City Sandwich: Poems. LC 77-18902. (Illus.). 48 p. 24cm. c.1978. (ISBN 0-688-80156-0). (ISBN 0-688-84156-2). Greenwillow Books.
--Country Pie. LC 78-14837. (Illus.). 32 p. 24cm. c.1979. (ISBN 0-688-80188-9). (ISBN 0-688-84188-0). Greenwillow Books.
--Elvira Everything. LC 78-104752. (Illus.). 48 p. 1970. Harper & Row.
--George's Store. LC 69-16249. (Illus.). 46 p. 1969. McGraw-Hill.
--George's Store. Wiseman, Bernard (1922-), illus. LC 82-22298. (Illus.). 46 p. 23cm. c.1983. (ISBN 0-8193-1101-4). (ISBN 0-8193-1102-2). Parents Magazine Press.
--Gia and the One Hundred Dollars Worth of Bubble Gum. LC 73-17437. p. 1974. McGraw-Hill.
--Good Lemonade. Zimmerman, Marie, illus. LC 72-1361. 32p. (gr. k-3). 1976. (ISBN 0-531-01093-7). Watts.
--Goodbye House. LC 85-19263. p. cm. c.1985. (ISBN 0-13-360272-9). Prentice-Hall.
--Goodnight Horsey. Asch, Frank (1946-), illus. LC 81-7332. p. cm. c.1981. (ISBN 0-13-360461-6). Prentice-Hall.
--Happy Birthday, Moon. Asch, Frank (1946-), illus. LC 81-19210. p. cm. (ps-1). c.1982. (ISBN 0-13-383687-8). Prentice-Hall.
--I Can Roar. LC 85-24347. p. cm. c.1985. (ISBN 0-517-56120-4). Crown.
--I Met a Penguin. LC 72-1600. (Illus.). 47 p. 1972. (ISBN 0-07-002400-6). (ISBN 0-07-002401-4). McGraw-Hill.
--In the Eye of the Teddy. LC 73-5156. (Illus.). 48 p. 1973. (ISBN 0-06-020151-7). (ISBN 0-06-020151-7). Harper & Row.
--Just Like Daddy. Asch, Frank (1946-), illus. LC 80-26000. (Illus.). 30 p. 24cm. (ps-1). c.1981. (ISBN 0-13-514042-0). Prentice-Hall.
--The Last Puppy. Asch, Frank (1946-), illus. LC 80-215. (Illus.). 30 p. c.1980. (ISBN 0-13-524058-1). Prentice-Hall.
--Linda. LC 73-88321. (Illus.). 46 p. 1969. McGraw-Hill.
--Little Devil's One Two Three. Asch, Frank (1946-), illus. LC 79-11867. (Illus.). (Encore Edition). (ps-1). 1979. (ISBN 0-684-17352-2, ScribJ). Scribner.
--MacGooses' Grocery. Marshall, James (1942-), illus. LC 77-86270. (Illus.). 32 p. (ps-2). c.1978. (ISBN 0-8037-5237-7). (ISBN 0-8037-5231-8). Dial Press.
--Milk and Cookies. LC 82-7962. p. cm. (Bear story.). (A Frank Asch Bear Story). 1982. (ISBN 0-8193-1087-5). (ISBN 0-8193-1088-3). Parents Magazine Press.
--Monkey Face. Asch, Frank (1946-), illus. LC 76-18101. (Illus.). 33 p. 27cm. c.1977. (ISBN 0-8193-0862-5). (ISBN 0-8193-0863-3). Parents' Magazine Press.
--Moon Bear. Asch, Frank (1946-), illus. LC 78-4444. (Illus.). 32 p. 26cm. (ps-k). c.1978. (ISBN 0-684-15810-8). Scribner. **Award: (ALA).**
--Moon Cloud. LC 84-4897. p. cm. c.1984. (ISBN 0-13-600552-7). Prentice-Hall.
--Mooncake. LC 82-21449. (Illus.). 32 p. 21cm. c.1983. (ISBN 0-13-601013-X). Prentice-Hall.
--Moongame. Asch, Frank (1946-), illus. LC 84-8405. (Illus.). 32p. (gr. k-3). 1984. (ISBN 0-13-600503-9). (ISBN 0-13-600503-9). P-H.
--Pearl's Promise. Asch, Frank (1946-), illus. LC 83-17153. (Illus.). 160p. (gr. 4-6). 1984. (ISBN 0-385-29325-9). (ISBN 0-385-29321-6). Delacorte.
--Popcorn. Asch, Frank (1946-), illus. LC 79-216. p. cm. 1979, c.1978. (ISBN 0-8193-1001-8). (ISBN 0-8193-0988-5). Parent's Magazine Press.
--Rebecka. LC 72-76522. (Illus.). 32 p. 1972. (ISBN 0-06-020149-5). Harper & Row.
--Sand Cake. LC 78-11183. (Illus.). 33 p. 24cm. (A Frank Asch Bear Story). c.1978. (ISBN 0-8193-0985-0). (ISBN 0-8193-0986-9). Parents' Magazine Press.
--Sand Cake. Asch, Frank (1946-), illus. LC 78-11183. (Illus.). 48p. (ps-3). 1979. (ISBN 0-686-86571-5). (ISBN 0-8193-0986-9). Parents.
--Skyfire. LC 83-16165. (Illus.). 32p. 1984. (ISBN 0-13-812389-6). (ISBN 0-13-812389-6). P-H.
--Starbaby. LC 79-24309. (Illus.). 32 p. 26cm. c.1980. (ISBN 0-684-16490-6). Scribner.
--Turtle Tale. (Illus.). (gr. 3). N.D. (ISBN 0-590-30386-4, Schol Pap). Scholastic Inc.
--Turtle Tale. Asch, Frank (1946-), illus. LC 78-51328. (Illus.). (ps-2). 1978. Dial Bks Young.
--Turtle Tale. Asch, Frank (1946-), illus. LC 78-51328. (Illus.). 32p. (gr. 3-7). 1980. (Pied Piper Bks). Dial Bks Young.
--Yellow Yellow. Stamaty, Mark Alan (1947-), illus. LC 77-140251. (Illus.). 45 p. 1970, c.1971. McGraw-Hill.

Asch, Sholem (1880-1957)
--In the Beginning. Klemm, Eleanor M., illus. 120p. (gr. 4). N.D. G P Putnam's Sons.
--In the Beginning: Stories from the Bible. Cunningham, Caroline, tr. LC 66-24907. (Illus.). 120 p. 21cm. 1966, c.1935. Schocken Books.
--In the Beginning: Stories from the Bible. Klemm, Eleanor M., illus. 1979. Schocken.

Aschmann, Helen Tann
--Connie Bell, M. D. LC 63-16268. 301 p. 21cm. 1963. Dodd, Mead.

Asendorf, James C
--The Bear Seeds. Fetz, Ingrid (1915-), illus. LC 69-10651. (Illus.). 74 p. 21cm. 1969. Little, Brown.

Ash, Enid S
--Funny Folks' Farm. LC 36-12816. 51, 1 p. col. illus. 19 x 23 cm. 1935. F. Warne & Co., Ltd.

Ashabranner, Brent Kenneth, jt. auth. see Davis, Russell Gerard.

Ashabranner, Brent Kenneth (1921-)
--Gavriel & Jamal: Two Boys of Jerusalem. Conklin, Paul S., photos by. LC 84-8135. (Illus.). 96p. (gr. 4-7). 1984. (ISBN 0-396-08455-9). Dodd. **Award: (ALA).**

Ashcraft, Phyllis
--ABC Bible Rhymes. Greene, Tom, illus. (Illus.). (gr. 2-5). 1976. (ISBN 0-87239-244-9). Standard Pub.

Ashe, Geoffrey (1925-)
--King Arthur in Fact & Legend. LC 70-145922. (Illus.). 71 photos. app. bibl. index. photo index. 1st U.S. edition. (gr. 6 up). 1971. (ISBN 0-8407-6136-8). Nelson.

Ashe, Marjorie Dugdale
--The Princess & the Enchanted Wood & Other Fairy Tales. (Illus.). 80p. 1982. (ISBN 0-682-49842-4). Exposition.
--The Princess and the Enchanted Wood: And Other Fairy Tales. Neden, Vivienne Dugdale, illus. LC 52-6155. 80 p. illus. 23 cm. 1951. Exposition Press.

Asher, Inez
--Look at Me!. A See-Yourself Book for Girls. Verses by Inez Asher. Ravinsky, Alice, illus. LC 51-6841. unpaged. illus. 17 c. 1951. Garden City Books.

Asher, Sandy Fenichel (1942-)

--Daughters of the Law. LC 80-20400. 157 p. 22cm. c.1980. (ISBN 0-8253-0006-1). Beaufort Books.

--Just Like Jenny. LC 82-70436. 148 p. 22cm. c.1982. (ISBN 0-440-04299-2). Delacorte Press.

--Missing Pieces. LC 83-14381. 144p. (gr. 7 up). 1984. (ISBN 0-385-29318-6). Delacorte.

--Summer Begins. LC 80-12321. 173 p. 21cm. c.1980. (ISBN 0-525-66696-6). Elsevier/Nelson Books.

--Summer Begins. 1980. Lodestar.

--Things Are Seldom What They Seem. LC 82-72819. 134 p. 22cm. c.1983. (ISBN 0-440-08932-8). Delacorte Press.

Asheron, Sara

--Fraidy Cat. Huehnergarth, John, illus. LC 77-86703. (Illus.). 60 p. 22cm. (Easy reader). 1970. Grosset & Dunlap.

--Funny Face at the Window. Tallarico, Tony, illus. LC 71-131022. (Illus.). 61 p. 22cm. (Easy reader). 1970. Grosset & Dunlap.

--How to Find a Friend. Perl, Susan (1922-1983), illus. (Illus.). (Easy Readers Ser.). (gr. k-3). N.D. Wonder.

--Laurie & the Yellow Curtains. Dawson, Isabel, illus. (Illus.). (Easy Readers Ser.). (gr. k-3). N.D. Wonder.

--Little Gray Mouse and the Train. LC 64-9925. (Illus.). 61 p. 22cm. 1964. Grosset & Dunlap.

--Little Gray Mouse Goes Sailing. Nankivel, Claudine, illus. LC 65-14756. (Illus.). 60 p. 22cm. (Wonder Books easy reader). (gr. k-3). 1965. Wonder Books.

--Little Popcorn. (Easy Readers Ser.). (gr. k-4). N.D. (ISBN 0-448-04250-9). (ISBN 0-448-05949-5). Wonder.

--The Surprise in the Story Book. LC 64-9029. 1963. Grosset & Dunlap.

--Surprise in the Tree. 61 p. illus. 22 cm. c.1962. Grosset & Dunlap.

--Three Coats of Benny Bunny. (Easy Readers Ser.). (gr. k-3). N.D. (ISBN 0-448-04253-3). Wonder.

--Will You Come to My Party?. Suba, Susanne (1913-), illus. (Illus.). (Easy Readers Ser.). (gr. k-3). N.D. (ISBN 0-448-05901-0). Wonder.

Ashford, Ann

--If I Found a Wistful Unicorn. Drath, Bill, illus. LC 78-59094. (Illus.). 39 p. 28cm. c.1978. (ISBN 0-931948-00-2). Peachtree Publishers.

Ashford, Jeffrey, pseud., see Jeffries, Roderic Graeme.

Ashford, Jeffrey, pseud. (1926-)

--Dick Knox at Le Mans. Jeffries, Roderic Graeme. 160p. (Putnam Sports Shelf). (gr. 5 up). 1974. (ISBN 0-399-60893-1). Putnam Pub Group.

--Grand Prix Britain. Jeffries, Roderic Graeme. new ed. 160p. (Putnam Sports Shelf). (gr. 6 up). 1973. (ISBN 0-399-60821-4). Putnam Pub Group.

--Grand Prix Germany. Jeffries, Roderic Graeme. (Putnam Sports Shelf Ser.). (gr. 6 up). 1970. (ISBN 0-399-60202-X). Putnam.

--Grand Prix Monaco. Jeffries, Roderic Graeme. LC 68-24499. (Illus.). 127 p. illus. 22cm. 1968. (ISBN 0-399-60203-8). Putnam.

Ashlee, Ted

--Voyage into Danger: Adventure in the Queen Charlotte Islands. Daniel, Alan (1939-), illus. (Illus.). glossary. 138p. (gr. 7-10). 1971. (ISBN 0-03-923308-1). HR&W.

Ashley, Audrey Zinger

--Biggest House. Ashley, Audrey Zinger, illus. (Illus.). (gr. k-3). 1961. (ISBN 0-8114-7504-2). Steck-V.

--Some Do & Some Don't. Ashley, Audrey Zinger, illus. LC 31-31365. (Illus.). 21cm. 40p. (gr. k-3). 1960. (ISBN 0-8114-7561-1). Steck-V.

Ashley, Barnas Freeman (1833-)

--Air Castle Don: Or, From Dreamland to Hardpan. LC 21-12981. 340 p. front., plates. 20 cm. (Young America ser.). c.1896. Laird & Lee.

--Air Castle Don: Or, From Dreamland to Hardpan, 1 of 5 vols. (Illus.). (Sterling Stories for Boys & Girls Ser.). 1901. Set. Laird & Lee.

--Dick and Jack's Adventures on Sable Island. LC 21-12979. 312 p. incl. illus., plates, map. front. 20 cm. (Young America series). c.1895. Laird & Lee.

--Dick & Jack's Adventures on Sable Island, 1 of 5 vols. LC 21-12979. (Illus.). (Sterling Stories for Boys & Girls). 1901. Set. Laird & Lee.

--A Tan Pile Jim: Or, A Yankee Waif Among the Bluenoses. LC 29-253061. 259p. front., illus. 29 cm. 1894. Laird & Lee.

--Tan Pile Jim: Or, A Yankee Waif Among the Bluenoses, 1 of 5 vols. (Illus.). (Sterling Stories for Boys & Girls Ser.). 1901. Set. Laird & Lee.

Ashley, Bernard (1935-)

--All My Men. LC 78-12683. p. cm. 1978, c.1977. S. G. Phillips.

--Break in the Sun: A Novel. Keeping, Charles William James (1924-), illus. LC 80-21407. (Illus.). 185 p. 22cm. (gr. 6 up). 1980. (ISBN 0-87599-230-7). S. G. Phillips.

--Dinner Ladies Don't Count. LC 80-83008. (Illus.). (Julia MacRae Bks.). (gr. k-3). 1981. (ISBN 0-531-04281-2). Watts.

--High Pavement Blues. (Illus.). 176p. (Julia Macrae Bks.). (gr. 6up). N.D. (ISBN 0-531-04607-9). Watts.

--A Kind of Wild Justice. Keepling, William James (1924-), illus. LC 78-40281. p. cm. 1979, c.1978. (ISBN 0-19-271417-1). Oxford University Press. **Award: (CMA).**

--A Kind of Wild Justice: A Novel. Keeping, Charles William James (1924-), illus. LC 78-10899. (Illus.). 182 p. 22cm. (gr. 7 up). 1979, c.1978. (ISBN 0-87599-229-3). S. G. Phillips.

--Linda's Lie. Duchesne, Janet (1930-), illus. LC 82-18792. (Illus.). 44 p. 21cm. (Blackbird Books). 1982. (ISBN 0-86203-099-4). Julia McRae.

--Terry on the Fence. Keeping, Charles William James (1924-), illus. LC 76-39898. (Illus.). 196 p. 22cm. 1977, c.1975. (ISBN 0-87599-222-6). S. G. Phillips.

--Your Guess Is as Good as Mine. Cain, Steven, illus. 48p. (Redwing Bks.). (gr. 7-11). 1984. (ISBN 0-531-03765-7, Macrae). Watts.

Ashley, C. B.

--Gilbert the Boy Trapper. (The Boys Own Library). N.D. David McKay.

--Gilbert the Boy Trapper. (Illus.). (St. Nicholas Series for Boys). N.D. International Book Co.

--Gilbert the Trapper: Or, The Heir in Buckskin. 18cm. 224p. (Medal Library: No. 58). 1900. Street & Smith.

Ashley, Doris

--Children's Stories from French Fairy Tales. Attwell, Mabel Lucie (1879-1964), illus. (Raphael House Library). N.D. David McKay.

--Children's Stories from Scott. Earnshaw, Harold C, illus. (Raphael House Library). N.D. David McKay.

--King Arthur & the Knights of the Round Table. Dixon, Arthur A., illus. (Raphael House Library). N.D. David McKay.

Ashley, Mabel Pierce

--The Other Crowd. LC 20-200137. 4 p. l., 3-231 p. col. front. 19 1/2 cm. c.1929. Harcourt, Brace and Company.

Ashley, Meg (1948-)

--Danger on the Quarry Path. LC 85-1966. 139 p. 21cm. (Boarding House Adventure ; 4). (gr. 6-9). c.1985. (ISBN 0-8307-1034-5). Regal Books.

--The Deserted Rooms. LC 84-11493. p. cm. (A Boarding House Adventure). (gr. 6-9). c.1984. (ISBN 0-8307-0973-8). Regal Books.

--Lights in the Lake. LC 83-10980. (Illus.). 149 p. 21cm. (Regal galaxy book). (A Boarding House Adventure: 2). c.1983. (ISBN 0-8307-0846-4). Regal Books.

--The Secret of the Old House. LC 82-13158. p. cm. c.1982. (ISBN 0-8307-0845-6). Regal Books.

Ashley, Robert Paul, Jr. (1915-)

--Rebel Raiders: A Story of the St. Albans Raid. 1st ed. Torbert, Floyd James (1922-), illus. LC 55-5016. 176p. illus. 22cm. (Winston adventure books). 1956. Winston.

--The Stolen Train: A Story of the Andrews Raiders. 1st ed. Torbert, Floyd James (1922-), illus. LC 53-73350. 182p. illus. 22cm. (Winston adventure books). 1953. Winston.

Ashley, Zinser

--Some Do and Some Don't: Little Animal's adventure. 1960. The Steck Company.

Ashman, Howard

--Flash Gordon Puzzlers. (Flash Gordon Puzzles Ser.). (gr. 3-6). 1979. (ISBN 0-448-15999-6, Cinnamon Hse). G&D.

Ashmore, Annie, pseud., see Simpson, J. M..

Ashmore, Annie, pseud.

--The Smuggler's Cave. Simpson, J. M.. (Boys Own Library). N.D. David McKay.

--The Smuggler's Cave: Or, Who shall be the Heir?. Simpson, J. M.. 18cm. 215p. (Medal Library: No. 68). 1900. Street & Smith.

Ashmore, Marion

--Lost Stolen or Strayed. Aldin, Cecil Charles Windsor (1870-1935), illus. (Illus.). (Home Circle Series for Girls). N.D. American Tract Society.

--Lost, Stolen, or Strayed: The Adventures of an Aberdeen Terrier. Aldin, Cecil Charles Windsor (1870-1935), illus. LC 31-31365. 96 p. incl. col. front., illus. 21 cm. 1931. C. Scribner's Sons.

Ashmun, M.

--The Singing Swan. N.D. Yale University Press.

Ashmun, Margaret Eliza

--Brenda Stays at Home. LC 26-20629. 4 p. l., 279 p. col. front. 19 cm. 1926. The Macmillan Company.

--David and the Bear Man. Crowther, Robert, illus. LC 29-197986. 5p.1., 236 p. col. front., plates. 20 cm. 1929. The Macmillan Company.

--The Heart of Isabel Carleton. Caswell, Edward C., illus. LC 17-25745. 6 p. l., 3-286 p. front., plates, 20 cm. $1.2. 1917. The Macmillan Company.

--Including Mother. LC 22-186468. 4 p. l., 211 p. front. 19 1/2 cm. 1922. The Macmillan Company.

--Isabel Carleton at Home. LC 20-19502. 4 p. l., 262 p. front. 19 1/2 cm. 1920. The Macmillan Company.

--Isabel Carleton in the West. LC 19-15683. 4 p. l., 277 p. front. 20 cm. 1919. The Macmillan Company.

--Isabel Carleton's Friends. Caswell, Edward C., illus. LC 18-18544. 5 p. l., 299 p. front., plates. 20 cm. 1918. The Macmillan Company.

--Isabel Carleton's Year. LC 16-18333. 5 p. l., 291 p. front., plates. 20 cm. 1916. The Macmillan Company.

--Marian Frear's Summer. LC 20-107296. 4 p. l., 239 p. front. 19 1/2 cm. 1920. The Macmillan Company.

--Mother's Away. Bachellor, Clarence Daniel (1887-1977), illus. LC 27-224864. 5 p. l., 259 p. incl. plates, col. front. 19 1/2 cm. 1927. The Macmillan Company.

--No School To-Morrow. LC 25-191091. 6 p. l., 215 p. front., plates. 19 1/2 cm. 1925. The Macmillan Company.

--Pa. (MacMillan Bks. for Boys & Girls). (gr. 7-9). N.D. MacMillan Bks.

--School Keeps To-Day. LC 26-9916. 6 p. l., 235 p. front. 19 1/2 cm. 1926. The Macmillan Company.

--Stephen's Last Chance. Caswell, Edward C., illus. LC 18-6523. 5p.l., 250 p. front., plates 20 cm. 1918. The Macmillan Company.

--Susie Sugarbeet. Barney, Maginel Wright, Mrs. (1881-1966), illus. LC 30-29017. 5p.l., 224, 1 p. front., plates. 21 cm. 1930. Houghton, Mifflin Company.

Ashton, Dudley & Schmidt, Anna M.

--Characteristic Rhythms for Children. N.D. A. S. Barnes & Co.

Ashton, Leila M.

--It's Sabbath. (Illus.). (My Church Teaches Ser.). 1978. (ISBN 0-8127-0177-1). Review & Herald.

--Today Is Friday. (Illus.). (My Church Teaches Ser.). (ps-1). 1978. (ISBN 0-8127-0176-3). Review & Herald.

Ashton, Leonora Sill

--The Pursuit of Happiness: A Story of New York Young People in the Time of the Revolution. Merrill, Frank Thayer (1848-), illus. LC 32-235710. 251 p. front., plates. 20 1/2 cm. c.1932. Lothrop, Lea & Shepard Co.

Ashton, Myriel Cluff, jt. auth. see Dalton, Alene.

Ashton, S. G., Mrs.

--Fifty Pictures and Stories for the Little Ones. 203p. N.D. T. Y. Crowell.

--Fifty Pictures and Stories, for the Little Ones. N.D. Warren & Wyman.

Ashworth, Alice

--Just a Little Boy: Stories About Willie. Zeigler, Lee Woodward, illus. LC 12-30398. 5 p. l., 50 p. front., plates. 21 1/2 cm. c.1897. F. Warne & Co.

--Just a Little Girl: Stories About Gracie. Palin, Ethel, illus. LC 7-40800. 61 p. incl. 4 pl. front. 21 1/2 x 17 1/2 cm. 1907. F. Warne & Co.

Ashworth, Mae Hurley

--Dark Places. (gr. 9 up). 1957. Friend Pr.

--Six Times True. Eitzen, Allan (1928-), illus. LC 72-13597. (Illus.). 47 p. 22cm. 1973. Friendship Press.

--Ten Pairs of Shoes. Turkle, Brinton Cassaday (1915-), illus. LC 58-7040. 126p. illus. 20cm. 1958. Friendship Press.

Ashworth, Rala, jt. auth. see Potter, Bronson.

Asian Cultural Centre for Unesco, ed.

--Folk Tales from Asia for Children Everywhere, Bk. 3. (Illus.). (gr. 2-5). 1975. Weatherhill.

--Stories from Asia Today: A Collection for Young Readers. LC 79-19059. (Illus.). v. 24cm. (Asian copublication programme series four ; book 1-). N.D. (ISBN 0-8348-1038-7). Weatherhill/Heibonsha.

Asimov, Isaac see French, Paul, pseud.

Asimov, Isaac, et al. (1920-), eds.

--After the End. Vaccarello, Paul (1945-), illus. LC 81-8520. p. cm. c.1981. (ISBN 0-8172-1729-0). Raintree.

--Bug Awful. Ersland, William (1948-), illus. LC 83-21309. (Illus.). 48p. (Science Fiction Shorts Ser.). (gr. 4-12). 1984. (ISBN 0-8172-1739-8). (ISBN 0-8172-1739-8). Raintree Pubs.

--Caught in the Organ Draft: Biology in Science Fiction. LC 82-15756. p. cm. 1982. (ISBN 0-374-31228-1). Farrar, Straus, Giroux.

--Children of the Future. VanSeveren, Joe, illus. LC 83-21316. (Illus.). 48p. (Science Fiction Shorts Ser.). (gr. 4-12). 1984. (ISBN 0-8172-1740-1). Raintree Pubs.

--Earth Invaded. Miyake, Yoshi, illus. LC 81-19170. (Illus.). 46 p. 25cm. (Science Fiction Shorts). c.1982. (ISBN 0-8172-1732-0). Raintree Publishers.

--Fantastic Creatures: An Anthology of Fantasy and Science Fiction. LC 81-10412. 155 p. 24cm. 1981. (ISBN 0-531-04342-8). Watts.

--The Immortals. Naprstek, Joel Langhorne, illus. LC 83-21315. (Illus.). 48p. (Science Fiction Shorts Ser.). (gr. 4-12). 1984. (ISBN 0-8172-1741-X). (ISBN 0-8172-1741-X). Raintree Pubs.

--Mutants. Ersland, William (1948-), illus. LC 81-17738. (Illus.). 46 p. 25cm. c.1982. (ISBN 0-8172-1734-7). Raintree Publishers.

--Thinking Machines. Bond, Bruce, illus. LC 81-8662. p. cm. c.1981. (ISBN 0-8172-1727-4). Raintree Publishers.

--Time Warps. Nass, Rikard & Nass, Rhonda, illus. LC 83-22888. (Illus.). 48p. (Science Fiction Shorts Ser.). (gr. 4-12). 1984. (ISBN 0-8172-1742-8). (ISBN 0-8172-1742-8). Raintree Pubs.

--Young Monsters. LC 84-48352. 224p. (gr. 6-9). 1985. (ISBN 0-06-020170-3). (ISBN 0-06-020169-X). HarpJ.

Asimov, Isaac, jt. auth. see Asimov, Janet.

Asimov, Isaac, ed. see Berry, James R.

Asimov, Isaac (1920-)

--The Best New Thing. Shimin, Symeon (1902-), illus. LC 70-128520. (Illus.). 26 p. 1971. World Pub. Co.

--The Disappearing Man and Other Mysteries. Miyake, Yoshi, illus. LC 84-2934. 64p. (gr. 3-5). 1985. (ISBN 0-8027-6578-5). (ISBN 0-8027-6602-1). Walker & Co.

--Fantastic Voyage. (gr. 8 up). 1966. (ISBN 0-395-07352-9). HM.

--Fifty Short Science Fiction Tales. 1963. MacMillan Publishing Company.

--The Heavenly Host. Colonna, Bernard, illus. LC 78-4553. p. cm. 1978, c.1975. (ISBN 0-14-031117-3). Puffin Books.

--The Heavenly Host. Colonna, Bernard, illus. LC 75-16515. (Illus.). 79 p. 22cm. c.1975. (ISBN 0-8027-6226-3). Walker.

--I, Robot. LC 63-6943. N.D. Doubleday.

--Isaac Asimov's Limericks for Children. Neibart, Wally, illus. LC 83-23987. (Illus.). 48p. 1984. (ISBN 0-89845-239-2). (ISBN 0-89845-240-6). Caedmon.

--The Key Word and Other Mysteries. Burke, Rod, illus. LC 77-4597. (Illus.). 54 p. 22cm. 1977. (ISBN 0-8027-6302-2). (ISBN 0-8027-6303-0). Walker.

--Kingdom Of The Sun. 1963. (ISBN 0-8382-0406-6, Cadmus Books). E. M. Hale And Company.

--The Kite That Won the Revolution. (Illus.). 1963. Houghton Mifflin company.

--Lucky Starr and the Rings of Saturn. LC 58-9653. 179 p. 22cm. 1958. Doubleday.

--Lucky Starr and the Rings of Saturn. LC 78-12246. p. cm. (The Lucky Starr Ser.). 1978, c.1958. (ISBN 0-8398-2491-2). Gregg Press.

--Mars. Herrick, Herb, illus. (Illus.). 29 p. 21cm. (Follett beginning science books). 1967. Follett Pub. Co.

--The Rest of the Robots. (gr. 7 up). N.D. Pyramid Pubns.

--Satellites in Outer Space. rev. ed. Polgreen, John, illus. LC 63-20664. 61 p. col. illus. 24 cm. (Easy to read series, R-16). 1964. Random House.

--Sattelites in Outer Space. Polgreen, John, illus. LC 60-9424. 79p. illus. 24cm. 1960. Random House.

--The Story of Ruth. LC 72-83137. (Illus.). N.D. (ISBN 0-385-08594-X). (ISBN 0-385-05208-1). Doubleday & Company.

--The Stars, Like Dust. 1951. Doubleday & Co.

--Words from the Myths. Barss, William (1916-), illus. (Illus.). (gr. 5-10). 1961. (ISBN 0-395-06568-2). HM.

Asimov, Isaac (1920-), ed.

--Tomorrow's Children. Schongut, Emanuel, illus. LC 66-10376. (Illus.). (gr. 7-9). 1966. (ISBN 0-385-00923-2). Doubleday.

Asimov, Isaac (1920-) & Greenberg, Martin Harry (1941-), eds.

--Mad Scientists. Naprstek, Joel Langhorne, illus. LC 81-17739. (Illus.). 48 p. 25cm. c.1982. (ISBN 0-8172-1733-9). Raintree Publishers.

--Those Amazing Electronic Thinking Machines!. An Anthology of Robot and Computer Stories. LC 83-5956. 1983. (ISBN 0-531-04667-2). F. Watts.

--Tomorrow's TV. Hargreaves, Greg, illus. LC 81-17737. (Illus.). 48 p. 25cm. c.1982. (ISBN 0-8172-1735-5). Raintree.

--Travels Through Time. Leonard, Thomas (1955-), illus. LC 81-8521. p. cm. c.1981. (ISBN 0-8172-1726-6). Raintree Publishers.

--Wild Inventions. Ersland, William (1948-), illus. LC 81-8511. p. cm. (Science-fiction readers). c.1981. (ISBN 0-8172-1728-2). Raintree Publishers.

--Young Extraterrestrials. LC 83-49489. xiv, 240 p. 21cm. 1984. (ISBN 0-06-020167-3). (ISBN 0-06-020168-1). Harper & Row.

--Young Ghosts. LC 85-42644. xiv, 210 p. 22cm. c.1985. (ISBN 0-06-020171-1). (ISBN 0-06-020172-X). Harper & Row.

Attwell, Lucie
--Lucie Attwell's Goodnight Stories. LC 84-28689. p. cm. 1985. (ISBN 0-517-46903-0). Derrydale Books.
Attwood, Frederic
--Vavache, the Cow Who Painted Pictures. 1st ed. Duvoisin, Roger Antoine (1904-1980), illus. LC 50-7585. ix, 77 p. illus. (part col.) 20 cm. 1950. Aladdin Books.
--Vavache: The Cow Who Painted Pictures. Duvoisin, Roger Antoine (1904-1980), illus. N.D. E. P. Dutton & Co.
Attwood, Mary Shaw
--The Adventures of Six Little Pussy-Cats Told by Sandy: A Kindness Story. LC 15-25495. 63 p. front., plates. 18 cm. 1915. The Murray Press.
Attwood, William (1919-)
--The Fairly Scary Adventure Book. Bugg, Bob, illus. LC 75-89986. (Illus.). 96 p. 25cm. 1969. (ISBN 0-06-020158-4). Harper & Row.
Atwater, Claire Nelson
--Manoel. Kalab, Theresa, illus. LC 40-13524. 2 p. l., 67, 1 p. incl. front., illus. 24 x 19 cm. c.1940. Longmans, Green and Co.
Atwater, Emily Paret (1873-)
--How Sammy Went to Coral-Land. LC 2-19169. (Illus.). 112 p. front., plates. 19 1/2. 1902. George W. Jacobs & Co.
--In Ocean Land. Fisher, Elizabeth M., illus. LC 27-16836. 5 p. l., 13-112 p. incl. col. front., col. illus. col. plates. 19 cm. c.1927. A. Whitman & Company.
--Tommy's Adventures. Betts, John Henderson, illus. LC 1-29005. 4 p. l., 7-110 p. front., pl. 19 1/2 cm. (Lad & Lassie Ser.). 1900. G. W. Jacobs & Co.
--Trixsey's Travels. LC 5-28190. 19cm. 138p. 1905. G. W. Jacobs & Co.
Atwater, Florence Hasseltine Carroll, Mrs., jt. auth. see Atwater, Richard Tupper.
Atwater, George Parkin (1874-)
--The Young Crusaders at Washington. LC 12-228707. 5 p. l., 303 p. front., plates. 20 cm. (His The young crusaders series). 1912. Little, Brown, and Company.
--The Young Crusaders: The Story of a Boys' Camp. LC 19-18896. 5 p. l., 5-304 p. front., illus., plates. 20 cm. 1911. Parish Publishers.
Atwater, Montgomery Meigs (1904-)
--Avalanche Patrol. LC 51-9983. 247 p. illus. 21 cm. 1951. Random House.
--Cattle Dog. LC 54-7015. 245p. 21cm. 1954. Random House.
--Flaming Forest. Elwell, R. Farrington, illus. LC 41-19196. vii, 211 1 p. incl. illus., plates. front. 21 cm. 1941. Little, Brown and Company.
--Government Hunter. LC 40-4228. 6 p. l., 158 p. illus. 22 cm. 1940. The Macmillan Company.
--Hank Winton, Smokechaser. Dreany, E. Joseph, illus. LC 47-4722. 6 l., 3-210 p. illus. 21 cm. 1947. Random House.
--Rustlers on the High Range. (gr. 7-9). 1952. (ISBN 0-394-81573-4). (ISBN 0-394-91573-9). Random.
--The Ski Lodge Mystery. LC 59-5516. 184p. illus. 21cm. 1959. Random House.
--Ski Patrol. LC 43-5782. 5 p. l., 3-237 p. incl. illus., map. 20 1/2 cm. 1943. Random House.
--Smoke Patrol. LC 49-10417. 214 p. 21 cm. 1949. Random House.
--Snow Rangers of the Andes. LC 67-20605. 215 p. 22cm. 1967. Random House.
--The Trouble Hunters. LC 56-9468. 214p. illus. 21cm. 1956. Random House.
Atwater, Richard Tupper (1892-1948)
--Doris and the Trolls. Gee, John, illus. LC 31-16581. 124 p. illus., col. pl. 22 cm. c.1931. Rand, McNally & Company.
Atwater, Richard Tupper (1892-1948) & Atwater, Florence Hasseltine Carroll, Mrs.
--Mr. Popper's Penguins. Lawson, Robert (1892-1957), illus. LC 38-27840. 5 p. l., 3-138, 1 p. incl. col. front., illus. col. plates. 22 cm. 1938. Little, Brown and Company. **Award: (JNM).**
Atwell, Ruth
--The Blue and the Jungle. Martin, Philip L., illus. LC 42-28979. 296 p. col. front., illus. 21 cm. 1942. W. A. Wilde Company.
Atwood, Ann Margaret (1913-)
--Fly with the Wind, Flow with the Water. Atwood, Ann Margaret (1913-), photos by. (Illus.). 32p. (gr. 1-5). 1979. (ISBN 0-684-16103-6, ScribJ). Scribner.
--Haiku: The Mood of the Earth. Atwood, Ann Margaret (1913-), photos by. LC 70-162737. (Illus.). color photos. 32p. (gr. 3 up). 1971. (ISBN 0-684-12494-7, ScribJ). (ISBN 0-684-16214-8, ScribJ). Scribner.
--The Little Circle. Atwood, Ann Margaret (1913-), photos by. LC 67-24045. (Illus.). 32 p. 27cm. 1967. Scribner.
--My Own Rhythm: An Approach to Haiku. LC 67-24045. (Illus.). 32p. (gr. 3 up). 1973. (ISBN 0-684-13248-6, ScribJ). Scribner.
--New Moon Cove. Atwood, Ann Margaret (1913-), photos by. 1969. Scribner. **Award: (BGH).**
--Wild Young Desert. LC 73-106536. (Illus.). photos. (gr. 6 up). 1970. (ISBN 0-684-12625-7, ScribJ). Scribner.
Atwood, Richard A., jt. ed. see Amsbary, George S.
Aubery-Fletcher, Henry Lancelot (1887-)
--The Duke of York's Steps. LC 29-269004. 350 p., 1 l. 20 cm. c.1929. Payson & Clarke Ltd.
Aubry, Claude (1914-)
--Agouhanna. Brinckloe, Julie Lorraine (1950-), illus. Swados, Harvey (1920-1972), tr. LC 72-76209. (Illus.). 96p. (gr. 6up). 1972. (ISBN 0-385-04786-X). (ISBN 0-385-04338-4). Doubleday.
--The King of the Thousand Islands. Cohoe, Grey (1944-), illus. Swados, Harvey (1920-1972), tr. LC 70-144303. (Illus.). 64 p. 22cm. 1971. Doubleday.
Aubry, Lynn, tr. see Held, Kurt.
Aubry, Lynn, tr. see Hocker, Karla.
Aubry, Lynn, tr. see Klaber, Kurt.
Auclair, Marcelle
--The Little Friends of Jesus. 1954. Henry Regnery Co.
Aucutt, John W
--Rancho San Jacinto. LC 43-5526. 229 p. 21 cm. 1943. Wetzel Publishing Co. Inc.
Auden, W. H. (1907-1973)
--Collected Shorter Poems, 1927-1957: 1927 to 1957. 352p. N.D. (ISBN 0-394-40333-9, Vin). (ISBN 0-394-72015-6). Random.
Audubon, Harriet B., as told by.
--Aladdin and His Wonderful Lamp and Whittington and His Cat, 1 of 8 vols. (Told in Words of One Syllable.). (Famous Fairy Tales). N.D. J B Lippincott.
--Beauty and the Beast and Children in the Wood, 1 of 8 Vols. (Famous Fairy Tales Ser.). N.D. J. B. Lippincott & Co.
--Blue Beard and Jack and the Bean Stalk, 1 of 8 Vols. (Famous Fairy Tales Ser.). N.D. J. B. Lippincott & Co.
--Cinderella and The Fair One with Golden Locks, 1 of 8 Vols. (Famous Fairy Tales Ser.). N.D. J. B. Lippincott & Co.
--Famous Fairy Tales, 8 vols. (Told in words of One Syllable.). N.D. Set. J B Lippincott.
--Goody Two Shoes and Tom Thumb, 1 of 8 Vols. (Famous Fairy Tales Ser.). N.D. J. B. Lippincott & Co.
--Gulliver in Liliput Land and Puss in Boots, 1 of 8 Vols. (Famous Fairy Tales). N.D. J. B. Lippincott & Co.
--Popular Fairy Tales. 1873. Leavitt & Allen Bros.
--Robin Hood and Hop-o'my-Thumb, 1 of 8 Vols. (Famous Fairy Tales Ser.). N.D. J. B. Lippincott & Co.
--Treasury of Fairy Tales, in Words of One Syllable. LC 44-31059. 838 p. incl. front., plates. 19 cm. 1881. J. B. Lippincott & Co.
--Valentine and Orson an Little Red Riding Hood, 1 of 8 Vols. (Famous Fairy Tales Ser.). N.D. J. B. Lippincott & Co.
Audubon, Hattie
--The Favorite Fairy Tales. 832p. N.D. World Publishing House.
Audubon Society of Portland, Oregon see Horsfall, Carra Elisabeth Hunting.
Auerbach, Berthold (1812-1882)
--Black Forest Village Stories. (Leisure Hour Ser.). N.D. Henry Holt & Co.
--Edelweiss. (Leisure Hour Ser.). N.D. Henry Holt & co.
--German Tales. (Leisure Hour Ser.). N.D. Henry Holt & Co.
--Joseph in the Snow. (Leisure Hour Ser.). N.D. Henry Holt & Co.
--Little Barefoot. (Leisure Hour Ser.). 1875. Henry Holt & Co.
--Little Barefoot. (Illus.). (St. Nicholas Series for Girls). N.D. International Book Co.
--On the Heights. Bunnett, Fanny Elizabeth, tr. LC 4-16856. 1 p. l., 692 p. front. 19 cm. (On cover: The home library). N.D. A. L. Burt Company.
Auerbach, Marjorie
--King Lavra and the Barber. (Illus.). 40 p. 1964. Knopf.
--Seven Uncles Come to Dinner. Auerbach, Marjorie Hoffberg (1932-), illus. LC 63-9099. (Illus.). (gr. 5 up). 1963. (ISBN 0-394-91606-9). Knopf.
Auerbach, Stevanne (1938-)
--The Alphabet Tree. Patch, Lila, illus. LC 85-51922. p. cm. c.1985. (ISBN 0-932433-15-4). Windswept House.
Auffenberg, Elinor, jt. auth. see Auffenberg, Walter.
Auffenberg, Walter & Auffenberg, Elinor
--Komodo Island of Dragons. 1976. MacMillan Publishing Company.
Augarde, Steve (1950-)
--Barnaby Shrew, Black Dan, and the Mighty Wedgwood. LC 79-53140. (Illus.). 32 p. 26cm. 1979. (ISBN 0-233-97104-1). Deutsch.
--Barnaby Shrew Goes to Sea. LC 78-311718. (Illus.). 32 p. 25cm. 1979. (ISBN 0-233-96957-8). Deutsch.
--Mr. Mick. Augarde, Steve (1950-), illus. LC 80-65660. (Illus.). 32 p. 26cm. 1980. (ISBN 0-233-97254-4). A. Deutsch.
--Pig. LC 76-9943. (Illus.). 26 p. 28cm. 1977, c.1975. (ISBN 0-87888-099-2). Bradbury Press.
Augsburger, Myron S. (1929-)
--The Broken Chalice. Wallace, Edwin B., illus. LC 70-160721. (Illus.). 136 p. 21cm. 1971. (ISBN 0-8361-1651-8). Herald Press.
Aulaire, Edgar Parin d' see Asbjornsen, Peter Christen (1812-1885) & Moe, Jorgen Engebretsen.
Aulaire, Edgar Parin d' see D'Aulaire, Edgar Parin (1898-) & D'Aulaire, Ingri Mortenson.
Aulaire, Edgar Parin d' see D'Aulaire, Ingri Mortenson (1904-1980) & D'Aulaire, Edgar Parin.
Aulaire, Ingri Mortenson d' see Asbjornsen, Peter Christen.
Aulaire, Ingri Mortenson d' see Asbjornsen, Peter Christen (1812-1885) & Moe, Jorgen Engebretsen.
Aulaire, Ingri Mortenson d' see D'Aulaire, Edgar Parin (1898-) & D'Aulaire, Ingri Mortenson.
Aulaire, Ingri Mortenson d' see D'Aulaire, Ingri Mortenson (1904-1980) & D'Aulaire, Edgar Parin.
Aulaire, Ingri Mortenson d' see Zwilgmeyer, Dikken (1859-1913) & D'Aulaire, Ingri Mortenson.
Aulick, Will Wroth (1873-), ed. see Mathewson, Christopher.
Aulnoy, Marie Catherine Jumelle de Berneville, jt. auth. see Perrault, Charles.
Aulnoy, Marie Catherine Jumelle de Berneville, jt. auth. see Aguilar, Grace.
Aulnoy, Marie Catherine Jumelle De Berneville (1650-1705)
--Aulnoy Marie Catheherine Jumelle de Berneville. N.D. George Routledge & Sons.
--Beauty & the Beast. Delessert, Etienne (1941-), illus. 48p. (Collection of Fairy Tales Ser.). 1983. (ISBN 0-87191-946-X). Childrens Bk Co.
--The Blue Bird. Ducornet, Erica (1650-1705), adapted by. Ducornet, Erica (1943-), illus. LC 78-97775. (Illus.). 60 p. 24cm. 1970. Knopf.
--The Children's Fairy-Land: Translated and Adapted from the Fairy Tales of the Countess D' Aulnoy. Olcott, Harriet Mead, illus. LC 19-14010. 5 p. l., 3-189 p. front., illus. 21 cm. 1919. H. Holt and Company.
--D'Aulnoy's Fairy Tales. (The Children's Favorites). N.D. George W. Jacobs & Co.
--D'Aulnoy's Fairy Tales. Browne, Gordon Frederick (1858-1932) & Emmet, Lydia F., illus. Planche, James Robison (1796-1880), tr. xii, 468 p. front., illus., plates. 22 x 18 cm. N.D. D. McKay.
--D'Aulnoy's Fairy Tales. Tenggren, Gustaf (1896-1970), illus. xii. 457 p. col. front., illus., col. plates. 25 cm. 1923. David McKay Company.
--Fairy Tales. N.D. Taplinger.
--Fairy Tales. Browne, Gordon Frederick (1858-1932), illus. Planche, James Robison (1796-1880), tr. N.D. George Routledge & Sons.
--Fairy Tales. Planche, James Robison (1796-1880), tr. (Illus.). N.D. Putnam's Sons.
--Jack & the Beanstalk. Francois, Andre (1915-), illus. 32p. (Collection of Fairy Tales Ser.). 1983. (ISBN 0-87191-947-8). Childrens Bk Co.
--The Old, Old Fairy Tales. (Illus.). (Warne's Fairy Library). 1910. Frederick Warne & Co.
--The Tales of the Fairies in Three Parts, Compleat: Extracted from the Second Edition in English of the Diverting Works of the Countess D'Anois, London, 1715. Hearn, Michael Patrick, pref. by. LC 75-32137. (Illus.). xiv p., p. 369-648, 6 leaves of plates. 22cm. (Classics of Children's Literature, 1621-1932). 1977. (ISBN 0-8240-2254-8). Garland Pub.
--The White Cat. Lubin, Leonard B., adapted by. Lubin, Leonard B., illus. LC 77-5845. (Illus.). 48 p. c.1978. (ISBN 0-316-53490-0). Little, Brown.
--The White Cat: And Other Old French Fairy Tales. Field, Rachel Lyman (1894-1942), ed. MacKinstry, Elizabeth (0000-1956), illus. LC 29-2702. ix p., 3 l., 150 p. incl. illus., plates (part col.) 29 cm. 1928. The Macmillan Company.
--White Cat & Other Old French Fairy Tales. MacKinstry, Elizabeth (0000-1956), illus. Field, Rachel Lyman (1894-1942), tr. (Illus.). (gr. 1-6). 1967. (ISBN 0-02-726250-2). Macmillan.
Aulnoy, Marie Catherine Jumelle de Berneville (0000-1705) & Field, Rachel Lyman (1894-1942), eds.
--White Cat and Other Old French Fairy Tales. MacKinstry, Elizabeth (0000-1956), illus. (Folk Lore and Fairy Tales). (gr. 4-6). N.D. MacMillan Bks.
Ault, Lena, jt. auth. see Ault, Norman.
Ault, Norman (1880-)
--Dreamland Shores: A Book of Verse for Children and Others. LC 21-14802. ix, 11-83 p. col. front., illus., col. plates. 25 cm. 1920. Dodd, Mead and Company.
Ault, Norman (1880-) & Ault, Lena
--The Rhyme Book. (Illus.). (Warne's Nursery Literature). 1910. Frederick Warne & Co.
Ault, Phil, pseud., see Ault, Phillip Halliday.
Ault, Phil, pseud. (1914-)
--Whistles Round the Bend: Travel on America's Waterways. Ault, Phillip Halliday. (Illus.). 192p. (gr. 7 up). 1982. Dodd.
Ault, Phillip Halliday see Ault, Phil, pseud.
Aumerle, Richard
--Between Friends. N.D. Benziger Bros.
--Brownie and D. N.D. Benziger Bros.
Aung, Maung Htin see Htin Aung, U (1909-) & Trager, Helen Gibson.
Aunt, Fanny, pseud., see Barrow, Frances Elizabeth Mease.
Aunt Callie, pseud., see Miller, Harriet.
Aunt Carrie, pseud., see Shillaber, Carrie Wheeler.
Aunt Edith
--The Little Housekeeper. (Illus.). N.D. E. & J. B. Young & Co.
Aunt Fanny, pseud., see Barrow, Frances Elizabeth Mease.
Aunt Friendly, pseud., see Baker, Sarah Schoonmaker Tuthill.
Aunt Funny, jt. auth. see Holly, S. B., Mrs.
Aunt Hattie
--Little Princess: And Other Stories. N.D. Methodist Book concern.

Aunt Julia
--Brandy Drops & Temperance Boys, 1 of 25 vols. (Illus.). (Selected Bks for Sunday School: No. 21). N.D. Set. Methodist Bk Concern.

Aunt Laura
--Bird Stories. LC 42-43989. 64 p. 48 x 38 cm. 1863. Breed, Butler & Co.
--The Bunch of Grapes. LC 43-31962. 64 p. 4 x 3 cm. 1863. Breed, Butler & Co.
--Carl's Visit to the Child Island. LC 16-1218. 61 p. 47 x 37 cm. 1863. Breed, Butler & Co.
--The Doll's Surprise Party. LC 16-121916. 64 p. 48 x 37 cm. 1863. Breed, Butler & Co.
--Grandma's Story of the Vain Little Girl. LC 43-319634. 61 p. 5 x 4 cm. 1863. Breed, Butler & Co.
--Old Testament Stories. LC 16-122112. 64 p. 54 x 40 cm. 1862. Breed, Butler & Co.
--The Silver Medal. 64 p. 42 x 33 cm. 1863. Breed, Butler & Co.

Aunt Louisa
--Book of Animal Stories. (Warne's Nursery Literature). N.D. Frederick Warne and Co.
--Book of Favorite Simple Fairy Tales. (Warne's Nursery Literature). 1910. Frederick Warne & Co.
--Book of Nursery Rhymes. (Warne's Nursery Literature). N.D. Frederick Warne & Co.
--Books of Fairy Stories and Wonder Tales, Second Coll. N.D. Frederick Warne & Co.
--Golden Gift. (Aunt Louisa's Gift Books For Children). 1882. J B Lippincott.
--Home Favorite Book. (Aunt Louisa's Gift Books for Children). 1882. J B Lippincott.
--Nursery Favorite, 1 of 12 Vols. (Illus.). (Aunt Louisa's London Toy Books Ser. 2: Vol. 2). N.D. R. Worthington.
--Nursery Favorite, 1 of 19 Vols. (Illus.). (Aunt Louisa's Choice Books Ser.: Vol. 6). N.D. Scribner & Welford.
--Nursery Favorite, 1 of 4 Vols. (Illus.). (Aunt Friendly's Picture Books Ser.: Vol. 4). N.D. Scribner & Welford.
--Punch and Judy, 1 of 64 Vols. (Illus.). (Aunt Louisa's London Toy Books Ser). N.D. Scribner & Welford.
--Red Riding Hood, 1 of 64 Vols. (Illus.). (Aunt Louisa's London Toy Books Ser.). N.D. Scribner & Welford.
--Uncle's Farmyard, 1 of 64 vols. (Illus.). (Aunt Louisa's London Toy Books Ser.: No. 16). N.D. Scribner & Welford.
Aunt Margie
--Roundabout Tales: Told for Children. (Illus.). N.D. George Routledge & Sons.
Aunt Martha
--Little Sylvia of Hartford and Her Indian Boy. LC 77-254042. (Illus.). 19cm. 56p. 1890. American Pub. Co.
Aunt Mattie
--Laughing Kittie and Purring Kittie, with Other Little Folks at Robinwood. (Illus.). 151p. N.D. American Tract Society.
Aunt Mavor
--Aladdin: or, The Wonderful Lamp. (Illus.). N.D. George Routledge.
--The Babes in the Wood. (Illus.). N.D. George Routledge.
--The Cat's Tea-Party. (Illus.). N.D. Geroge Routledge.
--The Cherry Orchard. (Illus.). (Aunt Mavor's Picture Bks.). N.D. George Routledge.

AUTHOR INDEX

AUSTIN, STELLA

--THe Dog's Dinner Party. (Illus.). (Aunt Mavor Picture Bks). N.D. George Routledge.
--The Fancy Dress Ball. (Illus.). (Aunt Mavor's Picture Bks.). N.D. George Routledge.
--History of Tom Thumb. (Illus.). N.D. George Routledge.
--Hop O' My Thumb. (Illus.). (Aunt Mavor Picture Bks). N.D. George Routledge.
--The House that Jack Built. (Illus.). (Aunt Mavor Picture Bks.). N.D. George Routledge.
--Jack the Giant-Killer. (Illus.). (Aunt Mavor Picture Books). N.D. George Routledge.
--The Juvenile Party. (Illus.). (Aunt Mavor's Picture Bks.). N.D. George Routledge.
--King Grisley Beard. (Illus.). (Aunt Mavor's Picture Bks.). N.D. George Routledge.
--Little Hunchback. (Illus.). (Aunt Mavor Picture Books). N.D. George Routledge.
--Old King Cole. (Illus.). (Aunt Mavor's Picture Books). N.D. George Routledge.
--Old King Cole. New ed. (Aunt Mavor's Ser.). N.D. McLoughlin Bros.
--Our Puss and her Kittens. (Illus.). (Aunt Mavor Picture Bks.). N.D. George Routledge.
--Punch and Judy. (Illus.). (Aunt Mavor Picture Bks). N.D. George Routledge.
--Rumpelstilskin. (Illus.). (Aunt Mavor's Picture Bks.). N.D. George Routledge.
--Tom Thumb's Alphabet. N.D. George Routledge.
--The White Cat. (Illus.). (Aunt Mavor's Picture Bks.). N.D. George Routldege.

Aunt Naomi, pseud., see Landa, Gertrude.

Auntie Bee
--Rosabella: A Doll's Christmas Story. White, D. T., illus. (Illus.). N.D. George Routledge.

Aurelio, John
--The Beggars' Christmas. Skardinski, Stanley, illus. LC 79-65893. (Illus.). 66 p. 21cm. c.1979. (ISBN 0-8091-2221-0). Paulist Press.
--The Boy Who Stole the Christmas Star. Skardinski, Stanley, illus. LC 81-9714. p. cm. 1981. (ISBN 0-8245-0079-2). Crossroad.
--Gather Round: Christian Fairy Tales for All Ages. LC 81-84389. (Illus.). 159 p. 21cm. c.1982. (ISBN 0-8091-2444-0). Paulist Press.
--Story Sunday: Christian Fairy Tales for Young and Old Alike. Johnson, Lonnie Sue, illus. LC 78-51587. (Illus.). v, 93 p. 21cm. c.1978. (ISBN 0-8091-2115-8). Paulist Press.

Aurell, Kathrine, ed. see Lagerlof, Selma Ottiliana Lovisa.

Aurell, Tage, ed. see Lagerlof, Selma Ottiliana Lovisa.

Aurembou, Renee
--Snowbound!. Bisset, Douglas, illus. Bell, Anthea, tr. LC 66-10085. 127p. illus. 23cm. 1966, c.1965. Abelard.

Auringer, O. C.
--Scythe and Sword. N.D. D. Lothrop Co.

Aurora Productions, jt. auth. see Reit, Seymour.

Auroy, J., jt. auth. see Isserlis, H.

Auslander, Joseph, jt. auth. see Hill, Frank Ernest.

Auslander, Joseph & Hill, Frank Ernest (1888-1916), eds.
--Winged Horse Anthology. Honore, Paul (1885-), illus. (Illus.). (gr. 7-9). 1949. (ISBN 0-385-07566-9). Doubleday.

Auslander, Joseph & Wurdemann, A.
--My Uncle Jan. N.D. Longmans, Green & Co.

Austell, Jan
--What's in a Play. Austell, Jan, illus. 160p. N.D. Harcourt Brace Jovanovich Inc.

Austen, Frances Vescelius
--Elfie and the Katydid. Austen, Edward J., illus. LC 27-13674. 80 p. incl. front., illus. plates. 22 cm. c.1895. The Merriam Company.
--Elfie's Visit to Cloudland and the Moon: Or, The Tricks of E-Ma-Ji-Na-Shun. Austen, Edward J., illus. LC 44-149997. 84 p. incl. front., illus., pl. 28 cm. c.1891. Estes &

Austen, Jane (1775-1817)
--Emma. N.D. George Routledge & Sons.
--Emma. N.D. James R. Osgood.
--Emma. (The Nelson Classics). N.D. Nelson Bks.
--Emma. 488p. N.D. Oxford University Press.
--Emma. (gr. 7-12). 1972 (Starline). Schol Bk Serv.
--Emma. 605p. (Franklin Watts Classics). (gr. 7 up). 1971. (ISBN 0-531-00434-1). Watts.
--Emma. Brock, Charles Edmond (1870-1938), illus. (Everyman's Library). 1908. E P Dutton.
--Emma. Brock, Charles Edmond (1870-1938) & Brock, Henry Matthew (1875-1960), illus. (The Rittenhouse Classics). 1925. Macrae Smith.
--Emma. Dobson, Austin, intro. by. N.D. St. Martin's Press.
--Emma. Gough, Philip (1908-), illus. (The Macdonald Illustrated Classic). N.D. Coward-McCann.
--Mansfield Park. (The People's Library). N.D. Funk & Wagnalls Co.
--Mansfield Park. (Magnum Easy Eye Classic Ser.). (gr. 8-12). N.D. Lancer.
--Mansfield Park. N.D. Patheon Bks.
--Mansfield Park. (Franklin Watts Classics). (gr. 7 up). 1971. (ISBN 0-531-00435-X). Watts.
--Mansfield Park. Brock, Charles Edmond (1870-1938), illus. (Everyman's Library). 1906. E P Dutton.
--Mansfield Park. Brock, Charles Edmond (1870-1938), illus. (The Rittenhouse Classics). N.D. Macrae Smith Co.
--Mansfield Park. Dobson, Austin N.D. St. Martin's Press.
--Mansfield Park. Swinnerton, Frank, intro. by. N.D. Dodd Mead and Co.
--Northange Abbey and Persuasion. Dobson, Austin N.D. St. Martin's Press.
--Northanger Abbey. (Magnum Easy Eye Classic Ser.). (gr. 8-12). N.D. Lancer.
--Northanger Abbey. Boas, F. S., Mrs., ed. Thomson, Hugh (1860-1920), illus. (Scholar's Library). N.D. St. Martin's Press.
--Northanger Abbey. Brock, Charles Edmond (1870-1938), illus. (Everyman's Library). N.D. E P Dutton.
--Persuasion. (Magnum Easy Eye Classic Ser.). (gr. 8-12). N.D. Lancer.
--Persuasion. 312p. (Franklin Watts Classics). (gr. 7 up). 1971. (ISBN 0-531-00437-6). Watts.
--Persuasion. Brock, Charles Edmond (1870-1938), illus. (Everyman's Library). N.D. E P Dutton.
--Pride and Prejudice. (Burt's Home Library). N.D. A L Burt Co.
--Pride and Prejudice. 1950. Dutton.
--Pride and Prejudice. N.D. George Routledge & Sons.
--Pride and Prejudice. N.D. James R. Osgood.
--Pride & Prejudice. (Magnum Easy Eye Classic Ser.). (gr. 8-12). N.D. Lancer.
--Pride & Prejudice. (gr. 7-12). 1972 (Starline). Schol Bk Serv.
--Pride and Prejudice, 1 of 2 vols. Somerset ed. (Illus.). N.D. Set. T. Y. Crowell & Co.
--Pride & Prejudice. (Franklin Watts Classics). (gr. 7 up). 1969. (ISBN 0-531-00406-6). Watts.
--Pride & Prejudice. (Keith Jennison Large Type Bks). (gr. 7 up). N.D. (ISBN 0-531-00268-3). Watts.
--Pride and Prejudice. Becker, May Lamberton, intro. by. (Great Illustrated Classics). (gr. 9 up). N.D. Dodd Mead & Co.
--Pride and Prejudice. Binyon, Helen, illus. N.D. Penguin Books.
--Pride & Prejudice. Brock, Charles Edmond (1870-1938), illus. (Everyman's Library). 1902. E P Dutton.
--Pride and Prejudice. Brock, Charles Edmond (1870-1938), illus. (The Rittenhouse Classics). N.D. Macrae Smith Co.
--Pride & Prejudice. Brock, Henry Matthew (1875-1960), illus. (The Rittenhouse Classics). N.D. Macrae Smith.
--Pride and Prejudice. Bryson, Bernarda (1905-1977), illus. (Illus.). (gr. 9 up). 1962. (ISBN 0-02-707710-1). Macmillan.
--Pride & Prejudice. Cogancherry, Helen, illus. Stewart, Diana, adapted by. LC 81-5215. (Illus.). 48p. (Raintree Short Classics). (gr. 4 up). 1981. (ISBN 0-8172-1673-1). Raintree Pubs.
--Pride and Prejudice. Daniel, Robert, ed. 367p. 1949. Rinehart & Co.
--Pride and Prejudice. Dobson, Austin, intro. by. N.D. St. Martin's Press.
--Pride and Prejudice. Howells, William Dean, intro. by. N.D. Charles Scribner's Sons.
--Pride and Prejudice. Kronenberger, Louis, intro. by. (Harper's Modern Classics). N.D. Harper & Brothers.
--Pride and Prejudice. Newbolt, Henry, Sir, ed. (The Nelson Classics). N.D. Thomas Nelson & Sons.
--Pride and Prejudice. Pritchett, V. S., intro. by. (Collins New Classics). N.D. William Collins Sons & Co.
--Pride and Prejudice. Sewell, Helen Moore (1896-1957), illus. N.D. Heritage Press.
--Pride & Prejudice. Stewart, Diana, adapted by. Cogancherry, Helen, illus. LC 81-5215. (Illus.). 48p. (Raintree Short Classics). (gr. 4-12). 1983. (ISBN 0-8172-2018-6). Raintree Pubs.
--Pride & Prejudice. New ed. Willoughby, Vera, illus. (1775-1817). 1930. Frederick A. Stokes Co.
--Pride and Prejudice and Sense and Sensibility. N.D. The Modern Library.
--Sense and Sensibility. (Burt's Home Library). N.D. A L Burt Co.
--Sense and Sensibility. (The People's Library). N.D. Funk & Wagnalls Co.
--Sense and Sensibility. N.D. George Routledge & Sons.
--Sense & Sensibility. (Magnum Easy Eye Classic Ser.). (gr. 8-12). N.D. Lancer.
--Sense & Sensibility. 458p. (Franklin Watts Classics). (gr. 7 up). 1971. (ISBN 0-531-00438-4). Watts.
--Sense and Sensibility. Boas, F. S., Mrs., abridged by. (English Literature Ser.). N.D. St. Martin's Press.
--Sense & Sensibility. Brock, Charles Edmond (1870-1938), illus. (Everyman's Library). 1908. E P Dutton.
--Sense and Sensibility. Brock, Charles Edmond (1870-1938), illus. (The Rittenhouse Classics). N.D. Macrae Smith Co.
--Sense and Sensibility. Davenport, Basil, intro. by. (Illus.). (Great Illustrated Classics). (gr. 9 up). N.D. Dodd Mead & Co.
--Sense and Sensibility. Dobson, Austin, intro. by. N.D. St. Martin's Press.
--The Works of Jane Austen: Vol. 1-Sense and Sensibility. Bailey, John, intro. by. (Georgian Edition). N.D. Dodd Mead & Co.
--The Works of Jane AUsten: Vol. 2-Pride and Prejudice. Bailey, John, intro. by. (Georgian Edition). N.D. Dodd Mead & Co.
--The Works of Jane Austen: Vol. 3-Mansfield Park. Bailey, John, intro. by. (Georgian Edition). N.D. Dodd Mead & Co.
--The Works of Jane Austen: Vol. 4-Emma & Northanger Abbey. Bailey, John, intro. by. (Georgian Edition). N.D. Dodd Mead & Co.
--The Works of Jane Austen: Vol. 5-Persuasion, Lady Susan, and The Watsons. Bailey, John, intro. by. (Georgian Edition). N.D. Dodd Mead & Co.

Austen, John, illus.
--David Copperfield. 832p. N.D. Heritage Press.

Austen, Nancy Virginia, jt. auth. see Sugimoto, Etsu Inagaki.

Austin, ed. see Crane, Stephen Townley.

Austin, Caroline
--Cousin Geoffrey and I. (Illus.). (The Wellesley Series for Girls). N.D. A. L. Burt.
--Cousin Geoffrey and I. (Illus.). (Scribner-Blackie series of books for young people). N.D. Charles Scribner's Sons.
--Cousin Geoffrey and I: A Story for Girls. (The Rugby Series for Boys and Girls). N.D. A. L. Burt Company.
--Hugh Herbert's Inheritance. (Scribner-Blackie series of books for young people). N.D. Charles Scribner's Sons.

Austin, Clare
--The Bells of Freiburg: A Christmas Tale. Bensel, Gottfried, narrated by. (Illus.). N.D. E & J B Young.
--Crooked S. Leighton, John, illus. N.D. Brentano's Publications.
--In the Garden of Eden: An Old Story Retold to Children. N.D. E. J. B. Young & Co.

Austin, Ellen Lake
--School Playhouse. (gr. 3 up). 1934. (ISBN 0-8283-1156-0). Branden.
--The School Playhouse. N.D. Howell Soskin Publishers.

Austin, Ethel L.
--A Babe in the Woods. N.D. Vantage press.

Austin, G. Jane
--Moonfolk. (Moonfolk Ser.). N.D. G. P. Putman Sons.

Austin, Grace Jewett (1872-1948)
--Poems for a Child Under a Big Tree. LC 48-28260. 44 p. 20 cm. 1948. Story Book Press.

Austin, Isabella, jt. auth. see Blaisdell, S. Lillian.

Austin, Jane Goodwin
--Dora Darling: The Daughter of a Regiment. N.D. Lothrop,Lee & Shepard.

Austin, Lou
--My Secret Power. (gr. 1-6). N.D. (ISBN 0-934538-22-0). (ISBN 0-934538-27-1). Partnership Foundation.

Austin, Margot, Mrs.
--Archie Angel. Austin, Margot, Mrs., illus. LC 57-8975. 26cm. 45p. 1957. E. P. Dutton & Co.
--Barney's Adventure. (Illus.). (gr. k-3). 1973. (ISBN 0-590-01573-7, Schol Pap). Schol Bk Serv.
--Barney's Adventure. Austin, Margot, Mrs., illus. LC 46-306. (Illus.). 26cm. 42p. (gr. k-2). 1941. Dutton.
--Brave John Henry. Austin, Margot, Mrs., illus. LC 55-11079. 26cm. 43p. 1955. E. P. Dutton & Co.
--Churchmouse Stories: A Collection of Peter Churchmouse, and Other Children's Favorites. Austin, Margot, Mrs., illus. LC 56-8291. 171p. illus. 23cm. 1956. Dutton.
--Cousin's Treasure. Austin, Margot, Mrs., illus. LC 60-11866. (Illus.). 26cm. 45p. (ps-2). 1960. (ISBN 0-525-28357-9). Dutton.
--Cousin's Treasure. Austin, Margot, Mrs., illus. 1964. E.P. Dutton & Co.
--Effelli. Austin, Margot, Mrs., illus. LC 42-155727. 56 p. illus. 28 cm. 1942. E. P. Dutton and Company, Inc.
--First Prize for Danny. Austin, Margot, Mrs., illus. LC 52-8253. 26cm. 43p. 1952. E. P. Dutton & Co.
--Gabriel Churchkitten. Austin, Margot, Mrs., illus. LC 42-16714. (Illus.). 25cm. 36p. (gr. k-2). 1942. Dutton.
--Gabriel Churchkitten and the Moths. Austin, Margot, Mrs., illus. LC 48-8252. 41 p. illus. 26 cm. 1948. E. P. Dutton.
--Growl Bear. Austin, Margot, Mrs., illus. LC 51-12668. (Illus.). 26cm. 42p. (gr. k-2). 1951. (ISBN 0-525-31055-X). Dutton.
--Lutie. Austin, Margot, Mrs., illus. LC 44-6370. 25cm. 40p. 1944. E. P. Dutton & Co.
--Manuel's Kite String: And Other Stories, Told and Pictured. Austin, Margaret, illus. LC 43-36608. 4 p. l., 3-112 p., 1 l. illus. (part col.) 20 cm. 1943. C. Scribner's Sons.
--Margot Austin's Churchmouse Stories. Austin, Margot, Mrs., illus. LC 56-8291. N.D. E. P. Dutton & Co.
--Moxie and Hanty and Bunty. Austin, Margot, Mrs., illus. LC 39-30547. 44p. 1939. Charles Scribner's Sons.
--Once Upon a Springtime. Austin, Margot, Mrs., illus. LC 40-6899. 43p. 1940. Charles Scribner's Sons.
--Peter Churchmouse. Austin, Margot, Mrs., illus. LC 41-9382. 25 1/2 x 22 1/2cm. (ps-2). 1941. Dutton.
--Poppet. Austin, Margot, Mrs., illus. LC 49-10283. 40 p. illus. 26 cm. 1949. E. P. Dutton.
--The Three Silly Kittens. Austin, Margot, Mrs., illus. LC 50-9935. 26cm. 44p. 1950. E. P. Dutton & Co.
--Trumpet. Austin, Margot, Mrs., illus. LC 43-10685. 40 p. illus. 25 1/2 x 23 cm. 1943. E. P. Dutton & Company, Inc.
--Tumble Bear. Austin, Margot, Mrs., illus. LC 40-30719. 44p. 1940. Charles Scribner Sons.
--The Very Young Mother Goose. Austin, Margot, Mrs., illus. (Illus.). 92 p. 32cm. 1963. Platt & Munk.
--Williamette Way. LC 41-5101. 44p. 1941. Charles Scribner's Sons.
--William's Shadow. Austin, Margot, Mrs., illus. LC 54-9308. 26cm. 43p. 1954. E. P. Dutton & Co.

Austin, Mary Carrington, jt. ed. see Sheldon, William Denley.

Austin, Mary Carrington (1915-) & Mills, Queenie Beatrice (1911-), eds.
--The Sound of Poetry. LC 63-2504. (Illus.). xxvii, 420 p. 22cm. 1963. Allyn and Bacon.

Austin, Mary Hunter, Mrs. (1868-1934)
--The American Rhythm. 1930. Houghton Mifflin Co.
--The Arrow Maker. Rev. ed. 1915. Houghton Mifflin Co.
--The Basket Woman. N.D. Houghton Mifflin Co.
--The Basket Woman: A Book of Fanciful Tales for Children. LC 73-97885. vii, 220 p. 23cm. 1969. AMS Press.
--The Children Sing in the Far West. Cassidy, Gerald, illus. 1928. Houghton Mifflin Co.
--Earth Horizon. Smith, Elmer Boyd (1860-1943), illus. 1906. Houghton Mifflin Co.
--The Flock. N.D. Houghton Mifflin Co.
--The Land of Little Rain. New Ed. ed. 1903. Houghton Mifflin Co.
--The Lands of the Sun. 1927. Houghton Mifflin Co.
--One-Smoke Stories. 1934. Houghton Mifflin Co.
--Starry Adventure. 1931. Houghton Mifflin Co.
--The Trail Book. Winter, Milo Kendall (1888-1956), illus. LC 18-21685. xi, 304, 2 p. col. front., illus., col. plates. 21 cm. 1918. Houghton Mifflin Company.

Austin, Oscar Phelps (1848-1933)
--Uncle Sam's Boy at War: An American Boy Sees the European War; a Sequel to "Uncle Sam's Soldier's". LC 17-29728. xi, 253 p. front., illus. 19 cm. 1917. D. Appleton and Company.
--Uncle Sam's Children. N.D. D. Appleton and Company.
--Uncle Sam's Secrets. Harris, William T., ed. (Appletons' Home-Reading Bks.). N.D. D. Appleton & Co.
--Uncle Sam's Soldiers: A Story of the War with Spain. LC 99-2868. xxii, 346 p. col. front., illus. 19 cm. (Half-title: Appletons' home reading books. Division 3 Social science). 1899. D. Appleton and Company.

Austin, Paul Britten, tr. see Gripe, Maria Kristina.

Austin, Robert, jt. auth. see Harrison, Ada M.

Austin, Sarah Taylor, Mrs. (1793-1867), tr. see Carove, Friedrich Wilhelm.

Austin, Stella
--Ben Cramer: A Tale for Boys and Girls. (Illus.). N.D. E. P. Dutton & Co.
--Ben Cramer, Working Jeweler: A Tale for Boys and Girls. N.D. E & J B Young.
--Ben Cramer, Working Jeweller. (Illus.). 1888. Thomas Whittater.
--A Faithful Heart. (Illus.). (Two Stories of Two: Part II). N.D. E. P. Dutton.
--For Old Sake's Sake (Pub. by Society for Promoting Christian Knowledge). N.D. E. & J. B. Young & Co.
--For Old Sake's Sake. N.D. E. P.Dutton.
--For Old Sake's Sake. (Illus.). 1888. Thomas Whittaker.
--Grandmother's Darlings: Two Stories. (Illus.). (Part I). N.D. E. P. Dutton & Co.
--Great Grandmother's Shoes. N.D. E. & J. B Young & Co.
--Great Grandmother's Shoes. 1891. Thomas Whittaker.
--Great Grandmother's Shoes: A Story for Children. (Illus.). N.D. E. P. Dutton & Co.
--Kenneth's Children. (Illus.). N.D. E. P. Dutton & Co.
--Kenneth's Children. (Illus.). 1888. Thomas Whittaker.
--Little Princess Angel. N.D. E. P. Dutton & Co.

--Mother Bunch. (Illus.). N.D. E. P. Dutton.
--Mother Bunch: A Story for Boys and Girls. (Illus.). 1888. E & J B Young.
--Not a Bit Like Mother. (Illus.). N.D. E & J B Young.
--Not a Bit Like Mother. N.D. E. P. Dutton & Co.
--Not a Bit Like Mother. (Illus.). 1888. Thomas Whittaker.
--Other People. (Illus.). N.D. E. P. Dutton & Co.
--Other People: A tale of Modern Chivalry. 1888. Thomas Whittaker.
--Our Next Door Neighbor. N.D. E & J B Young.
--Our Next Door Neighbor. N.D. E P Dutton.
--Our Next-Door Neighbor. (Illus.). N.D. Thomas Whittaker.
--Pat. (A story for Boys and Girls.). (Illus.). N.D. E P Dutton.
--Pat: A Story for Boys. (Illus.). N.D. E. P. Dutton.
--Pat: A Story for Boys. (Illus.). 1888. Thomas Whittaker.
--Rags and Tatters. N.D. E. P. Dutton.
--Rags and Tatters. (Illus.). 1888. Thomas Whittaker.
--Rags and Tatters: A Story for Boys and Girls. (Illus.). N.D. E & J B Young.
--Somebody. (Illus.). N.D. E & J B Young.
--Somebody. N.D. E. P. Dutton.
--Somebody. (Illus.). 1888. Thomsas Whittaker.
--Stumps. N.D. E. P. Dutton.
--Stumps: A Story for Children. (Illus.). 1888. E & J B Young.
--Stumps: A Story for children. (Illus.). N.D. E. P. Dutton & Co.
--Tib and Sib. N.D. Thomas Whittaker.
--Tom the Hero (Pub. by Society for Promoting Christian Knowledge). N.D. E. & J. B. Young & Co.
--Tom the Hero. N.D. E. P. Dutton & Co.
--Tom the Hero. (Illus.). 1888. Thomas Whittaker.
--Two Stories of Two, Part 1 & 2. (Illus.). N.D. Publications of E.P. Dutton & Co.
--Uncle Philip. (Illus.). N.D. E P Dutton.
--Uncle Philip. (Illus.). 1888. Thomas Whittaker.

Australia. Broadcasting Commission, jt. auth. see Kindergarten of the Air (Radio Program).

Ausubel, Nathan, ed.
--Treasury of Jewish Folklore. 741p. N.D. Crown Pub Inc.

Author of Allie Moore's Lesson
--The Troublesome Secret and What It Cost. LC 12-39587. vi, 7-335 p. front., plates. 17 cm. c.1870. American Sunday-School Union.

Author of "Aunt Hattie's Library"
--Bertie and His Sisters. (Happy Home Stories for Boys). N.D. Henry A. Young.
--Cousin Willie. (Happy Stories for Boys). N.D. Henry A. Young.
--Diligent Dick: Happy Home Stories for Boys. N.D. Henry A. Young.
--Fleda's Childhood. (Happy Home Stories for Girls). N.D. Henry A. Young.
--Lazy Robert. (Happy Home Stories for Boys). N.D. Henry A. Young.
--Little Flyaway. (Happy Home Stories for Girls). N.D. Henry A. Young.
--Little Fritz. (Happy Home Series for Boys). N.D. Henry A. Young.
--Molly and the Wineglass. (Happy Home Stories for Girls). N.D. Henry A. Young.
--The New Buggy. (Happy Home Stories for Boys). N.D. Henry A. Young.
--The Singing Girl. (Happy Home Stories for Girls). N.D. Henry A. Young.
--The Spoiled Picture. (Happy Home Stories for Girls). N.D. Henry A. Young.
--The Twins. (Happy Home Stories for Girls). N.D. Henry A. Young.

Author of, Bertha Weisser's Wish
--Ned Grant's Quest. 195p. N.D. E. P. Dutton.

Author of, Bessie Hartwell
--The Good Fight of Faith: or, How Libby Won the Victory. 276p. N.D. T. Y. Crowell.

Author of "Child-Nature" & Other Poems for Young People
--The Village School. 96 p. illus. 25 cm. 1876. J. B. Lippincott & Co.

Author of Copsley Annals
--Susie Grant: or, the Lost Property Office. N.D. E. P.Dutton.

Author of, Flower in the Prison
--Little People Whom the Lord Loved. 251p. N.D. T. Y. Crowell.

Author of, Grace Houghton's Story
--Redesdale. N.D. E. P. Dutton.

Author of "Janet Thorne"
--Big Bruce and Little Moss. 144p. N.D. T. Y. Crowell.

Author of, Laura Linwood
--The White Cross and the Dove of Pearls. 500p. 1877. T. Y. Crowell.

Author of, Little Rosy's Travels
--Little Mother. N.D. American Sunday-School Union.

Author of "Mary Matheson"
--Witless Willie: The ID OT Boy. 1873. Leavitt & Allen.

Author of My Little Geography, jt. auth. see Baker, Sarah Schoonmaker Tuthill, Mrs.

Author of, Neighbor's House
--Margaret's Old Home: A Tale of Christian Love. 364p. (Crowell's Sunday-School Library No. 6). N.D. T. Y. Crowell.

Author of, Pond Lily Stories
--Sunday All the Week. N.D. American Sunday-School Union.

Author of, Rosa Lindsay
--Violet and Daisy: or, the Picture With Two Sides. 235p. N.D. T. Y Crowell.

Author of Rose and Her Lamb
--The Little Child's Friend. LC 43-27888. iv, 3, 7-120 p. incl. plates. 15 cm. 1851. Ticknor, Reed, and Fields.

Author of, Ruby Adams
--Del Dunstan's Childhood. N.D. American Sunday-School Union.

Author of "Ruth Derwent"
--Bessie Hartwell: Or, Charity. (The Ollie Library). N.D. Warren & Wyman.

Author of "The Child's First Book", jt. auth. see Berquin, Arnaud.

Author of Village Boys
--Life in the West: Or, The Moreton Family. LC 12-36204. 100 p., 1 l., 105-258 p. incl. front., illus., pl. 16 cm. c.1851. American Sunday-School Union.

Autry, Ewart A (1900-)
--Ghost Hound of Thunder Valley. Savitt, Sam (1917-), illus. LC 65-11474. 177p. illus. 24cm. c.1965. Dodd.

Autry, Gene (1907-)
--Gene Autry and the Lost Dogie. Authorized. Armstrong, Samuel, illus. LC 54-21569. unpaged. illus. 17cm. (Tell-a-tales. 932). c.1953. Whitman Pub. Co.
--Gene Autry Goes to the Circus. Ushler, John, illus. LC 51-16236. (Illus.). 17cm. 28p. (Tell-a Tale Books). 1950. Whitman Pub. Co.

Autry, Raz (1929-)
--The Adventures of ... Bad Sam. Golden, Ardyss L., illus. LC 85-15748. (Illus.). 104 p. 22cm. c.1985. (ISBN 0-934145-00-8). Airborne Press : Distributed by Leigh-Newcomb Co.

Auvinen, Jewell S.
--Ringer the Kitten Learns to Read. Albright, Christy, illus. (Illus.). 22p. (ps-3). 1982. (ISBN 0-9610158-0-2). J S Auvinen.

Avallone, Michael Angelo Jr. see Stanton, Vance, pseud.

Avallone, Michael Angelo, Jr. (1924-)
--Five-Minute Mysteries: Cases from Files of Ed Noon. (gr. 7 up). 1978. (ISBN 0-590-05368-X). Scholastic Inc.
--The Haunted Hall. (The Partridge Family Ser.: No. 2). (gr. 4-12). 1970. Curtis.
--Partridge Family, No. 3. ca. 120p. (gr. 6-12). 1970. Curtis.
--Son of Name That Movie. (gr. 7-12). 1979. (ISBN 0-590-05772-3, Schol Pap). Scholastic Inc.
--Where Monsters Walk. (gr. 7 up). 1978. (ISBN 0-590-11914-1). Scholastic Inc.

Avary, M. L.
--A Virginia Girl in the Civil War. N.D. D. Appleton and Company.

Avdeenko, Aleksandr Evstigneevich
--I Love: A Novel. Wixley, Anthony, tr. from Russ. LC 36-9864. 283 p. front. (port.) 19 cm. 1935. International Publishers.

Ave Maria
--Tales for Eventide: A Collection of Stories for the Young Folks. Reprinted from the "Ave Maria.". LC 12-39347. 248 p. 15 cm. c.1887. The Ave Maria.

Avelot, Henri (1873-)
--Philibert's Bright Ideas. Avelot, Henri (1873-), illus. Owen, Helen Hammett, tr. LC 37-886. vii p., 1 l., 84 p. col. front., illus., col. plates. 25 cm. c.1932. F. Warne & Co., Inc.

Aven, Del
--Anna's Tree Swing. Aven, Debra, illus. LC 81-65799. (Illus.). 30 p. 24cm. c.1981. (ISBN 0-8054-4268-5). Broadman Press.
--God Has Special Places. (Illus.). (gr. k-3). 1979. (ISBN 0-8054-4253-7). Broadman.

Avent, Sue
--Spells, Chants, & Potions. LC 77-22779. (Illus.). (Myth, Magic & Superstition). (gr. 4-5). 1977. (ISBN 0-8172-1035-0). Raintree Pubs.

Averill, Esther, tr. see Mariotti, Jean.

Averill, Esther Holden (1902-)
--The Adventures of Jack Ninepins. Averill, Esther Holden (1902-), illus. LC 44-87235. 63, 1 p. col. illus. 22 cm. 1944. Harper & Brothers.
--Captains of the City Streets: A Story of the Cat Club. Averill, Esther Holden (1902-), illus. LC 72-76500. (Illus.). 147 p. 20cm. 1972. (ISBN 0-06-020176-2). (ISBN 0-06-020176-2). Harper & Row.
--Carter Sails the St. Lawrence. Rojankovsky, Feodor Stepanovich (1891-1970), illus. 1956. Harper & Brothers.
--The Cat Club: Or, The Life and Times of Jenny Linsky. Averill, Esther Holden (1902-), illus. LC 44-3239. 31, 1 p. illus. (part col.) 19 1/2 cm. (gr. k-3). c.1944. Harper & Brothers.
--Daniel Boone. Rojankovsky, Feodor Stepanovich (1891-1970), illus. 1946. Harper & Brothers.
--The Fire Cat. Averill, Esther Holden (1902-), illus. LC 60-10234. (Illus.). 5 7/8 x 8 1/2. 64p. (18 pt.). (I Can Read Bks.). (gr. k-3). 1960. (ISBN 0-06-020196-7). (ISBN 0-06-444038-9). Har-Row.
--The Hotel Cat. Averill, Esther Holden (1902-), illus. LC 74-77941. (Illus.). 161 p. 20cm. 1969. Harper & Row.
--How the Brothers Joined the Cat Club. Averill, Esther Holden (1902-), illus. LC 53-7592. (Illus.). 32 p. illus. 20 cm. (gr. k-3). 1953. (ISBN 0-06-020211-4, HarpJ). Har-Row.
--Jenny and the Cat Club: A Collection of Favorite Stories About Jenny Linsky. Averill, Esther Holden (1902-), illus. LC 72-9862. (Illus.). 1 v. (various pagings). 20cm. 1973. (ISBN 0-06-020222-X). (ISBN 0-06-020222-X). Harper & Row.
--Jenny Goes to Sea. Averill, Esther Holden (1902-), illus. LC 57-9261. 126p. illus. 20cm. (gr. k-3). 1957. (ISBN 0-06-020220-3). Harper.
--Jenny's Adopted Brothers. Averill, Esther Holden (1902-), illus. LC 52-7849. (Illus.). 32 p. 20cm. 1952. Harper.
--Jenny's Bedside Book. Averill, Esther Holden (1902-), illus. LC 59-8963. unpaged. illus. 19x26cm. c.1959. Harper.
--Jenny's Birthday Book. N.D. E. M. Hale & Co.
--Jenny's Birthday Book. Averill, Esther Holden (1902-), illus. LC 54-6589. (Illus.). 1 v. (unpaged. c.1954. Harper. **Award: (NYT).**
--Jenny's First Party. Averill, Esther Holden (1902-), illus. LC 48-5694. 31 p. col. illus. 19 cm. 1948. Harper.
--Jenny's Moonlight Adventure. Averill, Esther Holden (1902-), illus. LC 49-8288. 31 p. col. illus. 20 cm. 1949. Harper.
--King Philip the Indian Chief. Belsky, Vera, illus. 1950. Harper & Brothers.
--The School for Cats. Averill, Esther Holden (1902-), illus. LC 47-30683. 31 p. illus. (part col.) 19 cm. 1947. Harper.
--When Jenny Lost Her Scarf. Averill, Esther Holden (1902-), illus. LC 51-11654. (Illus.). 30 p. 20cm. 1951. Harper.

Averill, Esther Holden (1902-) & Stanley, Lila (1902-)
--Flash: The Story of a Horse, a Coach-Dog and the Gypsies. Rojankovsky, Feodor Stepanovich (1891-1970), illus. 1934. Harrison Smith & Robert Haas, Inc.
--Flash: The Story of a Horse, a Coach-Dog and the Gypsies. Rojankovsky, Feodor Stepanovich (1891-1970), illus. N.D. Random House.
--Powder: The Story of a Colt, a Duchess and the Circus. Rojankovsky, Feodor Stepanovich (1891-1970), illus. LC 33-27356. 29, 3 p. col. illus. 27 cm. 1933. H. Smith and R. Haas.
--Powder: The Story of a Colt, a Duchess, and the Circus. Rojankovsky, Feodor Stepanovich (1891-1970), illus. N.D. Random House.

Averill, Naomi
--Choochee. N.D. Grosset & Dunlap.
--Whistling-Two-Teeth. LC 39-19161. 24cm. 24p. 1939. Grosset & Dunlap.

Avernikov, Y.
--Whose Is the Sun?. 16p. 1973. (ISBN 0-8285-1270-1, Pub. by Progress Pubs USSR). Imported Pubns.

Avery, Al, pseud., see Montgomery, Rutherford George.

Avery, Al, pseud. (1894-)
--A Yankee Flier with the R. A. F. Montgomery, Rutherford George. Laune, Paul Sidney (1899-) & Knight, Clayton (1891-1969), illus. LC 41-14773. v p., 1 l., 214 p. incl. front. 20 cm. c.1941. Grosset & Dunlap.

Avery, Gillian Elise, et al. (1926-)
--Authors' Choice. Turska, Krystyna Zofia (1933-), illus. LC 76-126978. (Illus.). appendix. 240p. (gr. 7 up). 1971. (ISBN 0-690-11141-X, TYC-J). T Y Crowell.

Avery, Gillian Elise (1926-)
--Call of the Valley. LC 68-11837. (Illus.). 229 p. 22cm. 1968, c.1966. Holt, Rinehart and Winston.
--The Echoing Green: Memories of Victorian Youth. (Illus.). 256p. (gr. 7 up). 1974. (ISBN 0-670-28837-3). Viking Pr.
--The Elephant War. Verney, John, Sir (1913-), illus. LC 71-146713. (Illus.). 256 p. 22cm. 1971, c.1960. (ISBN 0-03-086307-4). Holt, Rinehart and Winston.
--Ellen and the Queen. Turska, Krystyna Zofia (1933-), illus. (gr. 3-5). 1975. Lodestar.
--Ellen and the Queen. Turska, Krystyna Zofia (1933-), illus. LC 74-18080. p. cm. 1974. (ISBN 0-8407-6415-4). T. Nelson.
--The Hole in the Wall, and Other Stories. Roberts, Doreen (1922-), illus. LC 68-102923. xi, 161 p. illus. 22 cm. 15/. (SBN 19 271281 0) (b 68-05519). 1968. Oxford U. P.
--The Italian Spring. Verney, John, Sir (1913-), illus. LC 72-82148. (Illus.). 256 p. 20cm. 1st U.S. edition. 1972, c.1964. (ISBN 0-03-002931-7). (ISBN 0-03-002931-7). Holt, Rinehart and Winston.
--A Likely Lad. Jaques, Faith (1923-), illus. LC 77-155871. (Illus.). 222 p. 22cm. 1971. (ISBN 0-03-080291-1). Holt, Rinehart and Winston. **Award: (CMA).**
--To Tame a Sister. Verney, John, Sir (1913-), illus. LC 64-25987. (Illus.). 255 p. 20cm. 1964, c.1961. Van Nostrand.
--To Tame a Sister. Verney, John, Sir (1913-), illus. LC 74-811. p. 1st U.S. edition. 1973, c.1961. (ISBN 0-670-71777-0). Viking Press.
--The Warden's Niece. Hart, Dick (1920-), illus. LC 64-1011. 205 p. illus. 19 cm. (Puffin books, PS202). 1963, c.1957. Penguin Books.

Avery, Gillian Elise (1926-), ed.
--In the Window-Seat: A Selection of Victorian Stories. Einzig, Susan (1922-), illus. LC 65-17042. xii, 259p. illus. 23cm. c.1965. Van Nostrand.
--Victorian Doll Stories. LC 69-14797. (Illus.). 141 p. 21cm. (Victorian revivals). 1969. Schocken Books.

Avery, Harold (1867-1943)
--An Old Boy's Yarns. (Illus.). (Story Books for Boys). N.D. Cassell & Co.'s Pubs.
--The Dormitory Flag: A School Story. (Illus.). N.D. Thomas Nelson & Sons.
--Frank's First Term. (Illus.). N.D. Thomas Nelson & Sons.
--Mobsley's Mohicans: A Tale of Two Terms. Bacon, John H., illus. LC 5-18490. (Illus.). viii p., 1 l., 9-318 p. front., 5 pl. 19 1/2 cm. 1900. Thomas Nelson & Sons.
--The Orderly Officer. N.D. E. & J. B Young & Co.
--Stolen or Strayed: A School Story. (Illus.). N.D. Thomas Nelson & Sons.

Avery, Karen, illus.
--Beauty & the Beast. (Illus.). 10p. (Carousel Bks.). (ps-2). N.D. (ISBN 0-8431-0902-5). Price Stern.
--Puss in Boots. (Illus.). (Carousel Bks.). (ps-2). N.D. (ISBN 0-8431-0900-9). Price Stern.

Avery, Kay (1915-)
--All for a Friend. Watson, Aldren Auld (1917-), illus. LC 56-9795. 183p. illus. 21cm. 1956. Crowell.
--All for a Ghost. Watson, Aldren Auld (1917-), illus. LC 57-924695. 149p. illus. 21cm. 1957. Crowell.
--All for a Horse. Watson, Aldren Auld (1917-), illus. LC 55-9202. 165p. illus. 21cm. 1955. Crowell.
--Goodbye Blue Jeans. Lewis, Richard William (1933-1966), illus. LC 63-12152. 174 p. illus. 21 cm. 1963. I. Washburn.
--Saltwater Sam. Maclain, Scott, illus. LC 62-10748. 146p. illus. 21cm. (gr. 4-6). 1962. Washburn.
--Wee Willow Whistle. Bromhall, Winifred, illus. LC 47-30144. 31 p. col. illus. 26 x 21 cm. 1947. A. A. Knopf.

Avery, Lynn, pseud., see Cole, Lois Dwight.

Avery, Lynn, pseud. (1903-1979)
--Cappy and the River. Cole, Lois Dwight. Orbaan, Albert F. (1913-), illus. LC 60-12840. (Illus.). 21cm. 132p. 1960. Duell, Sloan and Pearce Pub.
--The Mystery of the Vanishing Horses. Cole, Lois Dwight. LC 63-10356. 149 p. illus. 21 cm. 1963. Duell, Sloan and Pearce.
--Mystery of the Vanishing Horses. Cole, Lois Dwight. (gr. 3-7). 1963. (ISBN 0-696-72526-6). Hawthorn.

Avi, pseud., see Wortis, Avi.

Avi, pseud. (1937-)
--Bright Shadow. Wortis, Avi. LC 85-5719. p. cm. 1985. (ISBN 0-02-707750-0). Bradbury Press.
--Captain Grey. Wortis, Avi. Mikolaycak, Charles (1937-), illus. LC 76-41182. (Illus.). 141 p. 22cm. c.1977. (ISBN 0-394-83484-4). (ISBN 0-394-93484-9). Pantheon Books.
--Devil's Race. Wortis, Avi. LC 84-47636. 160p. (A Lippincott Page-Turner). (gr. 7 up). 1984. (ISBN 0-397-32094-9). (ISBN 0-397-32095-7). Lipp Jr Bks.
--Emily Upham's Revenge: Or, How Deadwood Dick Saved the Banker's Niece : a Massachusetts Adventure. Wortis, Avi. Zelinsky, Paul O., illus. LC 77-13739. (gr. 5-8). 1978. (ISBN 0-394-83506-9). (ISBN 0-394-93506-3). Pantheon.
--Encounter at Easton. Wortis, Avi. LC 79-9439. 138 p. 22cm. c.1980. (ISBN 0-394-84342-8). (ISBN 0-394-94342-2). Pantheon Books.
--The Fighting Ground. Wortis, Avi. Thompson, Ellen M., illus. LC 82-47719. (Illus.). 160p. (gr. 5 up). 1984. (ISBN 0-397-32073-6, JBL-J). (ISBN 0-397-32074-4). Har-Row. **Awards: (ALA); (SOA).**
--The History of Helpless Harry: To Which is Added a Variety of Amusing and Entertaining Adventures. Wortis, Avi. Zelinsky, Paul O., illus. 1980. Pantheon.
--Man from the Sky. Wortis, Avi. LC 79-26909. p. cm. (Capers). c.1980. (ISBN 0-394-84468-8). (ISBN 0-394-94468-2). Knopf.
--Night Journeys. Wortis, Avi. LC 78-10151. 143 p. 22cm. c.1979. (ISBN 0-394-84116-6). (ISBN 0-394-94116-0). Pantheon Books.

--No More Magic. Wortis, Avi. LC 74-15299. 138 p. 22cm. 1975. (ISBN 0-394-83084-9). (ISBN 0-394-93084-3). Pantheon Books.
--A Place Called Ugly. Wortis, Avi. Adams, Jeanette, illus. LC 80-23326. (Illus.). 224p. (gr. 7-9). 1981. (ISBN 0-394-84755-5). (ISBN 0-394-94755-X). Pantheon.
--Shadrach's Crossing. Wortis, Avi. LC 82-19008. p. cm. 1983. (ISBN 0-394-85816-6). Pantheon Books.
--Snail Tale: The Adventures of a Rather Small Snail. Wortis, Avi. Kindron, Tom, illus. LC 72-1307. (Illus.). 48 p. 24cm. 1972. Pantheon Books.
--Sometimes I Think I Hear My Name: A Novel. Wortis, Avi. LC 81-38421. 144 p. 22cm. c.1982. (ISBN 0-394-85048-3). (ISBN 0-394-95048-8). Pantheon Books.
--S.O.R. Losers. Wortis, Avi. LC 84-11022. 112p. (gr. 5-7). 1984. (ISBN 0-02-793410-1). Bradbury Pr.
--S.O.R. Losers. Wortis, Avi. 1984. Macmillan.
--Things That Sometimes Happen. Wortis, Avi. Robbin, Jodi, illus. LC 78-116183. (Illus.). 78 p. 27cm. 1970. Doubleday.
--Who Stole the Wizard of Oz?. Wortis, Avi. James, Derek, illus. LC 81-884. (Illus.). 116 p. 20cm. c.1981. (ISBN 0-394-84644-3). (ISBN 0-394-94644-8). Knopf : Distributed by Random House.
Avis, Peter, tr. see Novy, Karel.
Avison, George F., jt. auth. see Nadig, Henry Davis.
Avlu, Atya, tr. see Zemach, Margot.
Avlu, Atya, tr. see Zeman, Kamil.
Avlu, Iv T., tr. see Zeman, Kamil.
Avrett, Robert (1901-)
--The Timid Pup. Petie, Haris, pseud. (1915-), illus. Petty, Roberta. LC 64-13173. (Illus.). 24cm. 62p. (gr. 1-3). 1964. (ISBN 0-8313-0004-3). Lantern.
Awasthy, Rajendra
--Stories of Valour. Roy, Sharadindu Sen, illus. (Illus.). (Nehru Library for Children). (gr. 1-9). 1979. (ISBN 0-89744-182-6). Auromere.
Awdry, Wilbert Vere (1911-)
--Branch Line Engines. rev. ed. (Illus.). (ps-3). 1965. Verry.
--Duck and the Diesel Engine. 64p. (Railway Series). 1958. British Book Centre Inc.
--Duck & the Diesel Engine. rev. ed. (Illus.). (ps-3). 1965. Verry.
--Edward the Blue Engine. 64p. N.D. British Book Centre Inc.
--Four Little Engines. 64p. (Railway Series). N.D. British Book Center Inc.
--Four Little Engines. rev. ed. (Illus.). 64p. (Railway Ser.). 1964. Lawrence Verry Inc.
--Gallant Old Engine. rev. ed. (ps-3). 1966. Verry.
--Gallant Old Engine. Kennedy, John T., illus. LC 53-32230. 56p. col. plates. 17x15cm. (Railway ser., no. 17). 1966, c.1962. Edward Ward.
--Gordon the Big Engine. 64p. (Railway Series). N.D. British Book Centre Inc.
--Gordon the Big Engine. rev. ed. (Illus.). (ps-3). 1960. Verry.
--Henry the Green Engine. 64p. (Railway Series). N.D. British Book Centre Inc.
--James the Red Engine. 64p. (Railway Series). N.D. British Book Centre Inc.
--James the Red Engine. rev. ed. (Illus.). (ps-3). 1965. Verry.
--Main Line Engines. (Illus.). (ps-3). 1966. Verry.
--Mountain Engines. (Illus.). (ps-3). 1964. Verry.
--Percy the Small Engine. 64p. (Railway Series). N.D. British Book Centre Inc.
--Percy the Small Engine. rev. ed. (Illus.). (ps-3). 1965. Verry.
--Tank Engine Thomas Again. 64p. (Railway Series). N.D. British Book Centre Inc.
--Tank Engine Thomas Again. rev. ed. (Illus.). (ps-3). 1966. Verry.
--Three Railway Engines. 64p. (Railway Series). N.D. British Book Centre Inc.
--Three Railway Engines. rev. ed. (Illus.). (ps-3). 1963. Verry.
--Toby the Tram Engine. 64p. (Railway Series). N.D. British Book Centre Inc.
--Toby the Tram Engine. rev. ed. (Illus.). (ps-3). 1966. Verry.
--Troublesome Engines. 64p. (Railway Series). N.D. British Book Centre Inc.
--Troublesome Engines. rev. ed. (Illus.). (ps-3). 1964. Verry.
--Very Old Engines. (Illus.). (ps-3). 1965. Verry.
Awiaka, Marilou (1936-)
--Rising Fawn & the Fire Mystery. Bringle, Beverly, illus. LC 83-13824. (Illus.). 27cm. 48p. (Orig.). (A Child's Christmas in Memphis Ser.: Vol. 1). (gr. 5 up). 1983. (ISBN 0-918518-29-6). St Luke TN.
Axford, Michael D.
--The Stick People & The Family Help A Wounded Deer. 1984. (ISBN 0-8062-2306-5). Carlton.
Axmann, Hanne, jt. auth. see Zimnik, Reiner.
Axtell, Frances Elizabeth (1901-)
--The Adventures of Pidgee Mouse. LC 31-8954. 54 p. illus. 29 cm. c.1931. The Union Pacific Magazine.
Axworthy, Ann, jt. auth. see Brandreth, Gyles Daubeney.
Ayal, Ora
--Ugbu. Nakao, Naomi Low, tr. LC 79-1716. (Illus.). 31 p. 25cm. 1979, c.1977. (ISBN 0-06-020307-2). (ISBN 0-06-020308-0). Harper & Row.
Ayal, Ora & Nakao, Naomi Low
--The Adventures of Chester the Chest. Ayal, Ora, illus. LC 81-48642. (Illus.). 32 p. 21cm. c.1982. (ISBN 0-06-020304-8). (ISBN 0-06-020306-4). Harper & Row.
Ayars, James Sterling, jt. auth. see Caudill, Rebecca.
Ayars, James Sterling (1898-)
--Another Kind of Puppy. Donald, Elizabeth, illus. LC 65-12120. 60 p. col. illus. 22 cm. 1965. Abellard-Schuman.
--Basketball Comes to Lonesome Point. Cypher, Bob, illus. LC 52-13702. 192 p. illus. 21 cm. 1952. Viking Press.
--Caboose On The Roof. N.D. E. M. Hale & Co.
--Caboose on the Roof. Hodgell, Bob, illus. LC 56-10387. 75p. illus. 22cm. 1956. Abelard-Schuman.
--Happy Birthday, Mom. 1963. (ISBN 0-8382-0316-7, Cadmus Books). E. M. Hale and Company.
--Happy Birthday, Mom!. Donald, Elizabeth, illus. LC 63-8636. 61 p. illus. 22 cm. 1963. Abelard-Schuman.
--Pet Parade. Donald, Elizabeth, illus. LC 60-13920. (Illus.). 60 p. 22cm. 1961, c.1960. Abelard-Schuman.
--Track Comes to Lonesome Point. LC 73-77455. 141 p. 22cm. 1973. (ISBN 0-525-41440-1). Dutton.
Ayd, Joseph D
--Tomorrow's Memories. LC 51-14139. 247 p. 21cm. 1951. Dodd, Mead.
Aydelotte, Dora
--Green Gravel. N.D. D. Appleton-Century Co.
Aydt, Deborah
--How Can We Talk?. 144p. (Orig.). (gr. 7 up). 1982. (ISBN 0-590-32282-6, Wishing Star). Scholastic Inc.
--I Don't Want to Be Your Shadow. 144p. (Orig.). (gr. 7 up). 1981. (ISBN 0-590-31719-9, Wishing Star). Scholastic Inc.
--Secrets. 160p. (Orig.). (gr. 7 up). 1981. (ISBN 0-590-32518-3, Wishing Star). Scholastic Inc.
Aye, Olive
--Freddie and Santa Claus in Circus Land. (Illus.). N.D. Laird & Lee.
--Santa Claus' Candy Circus. (Illus.). 32p. N.D. Laird & Lee's Publications.
Ayer, Jacqueline (1930-)
--Little Silk. LC 78-115754. (Illus.). 32 p. 1970. Harcourt Brace Jovanovich.
--Nu Dang and His Kite. 1975. Harcourt.
--Nu Dang & His Kite. Ayer, Jacqueline (1930-), illus. LC 59-6561. (Illus.). (gr. k-3). 1959. (ISBN 0-15-257601-0). (ISBN 0-15-257603-7). HarBraceJ.
--Paper-Flower Tree: A Tale from Thailand. Ayer, Jacqueline (1930-), illus. LC 62-7726. (Illus.). (gr. k-3). 1962. (ISBN 0-15-259470-1). HarBraceJ.
--A Wish for Little Sister. LC 60-7032. (Illus.). unpaged. 1960. Harcourt Brace.
Ayer, Jean Y.
--Donald Duck and His Friends. Disney, Walt, Studio, illus. LC 39-20472. 3 p. l., 102 p. col. illus. 21 1/2 cm. (On cover: Walt Disney story books). 1939. D. C. Heath and Company.
Ayer, Jean Y., jt. auth. see Disney, Walt, Productions.
Ayer, Margaret (0000-1981)
--The Wish That Went Wild. Ayer, Margaret (0000-1981), illus. LC 52-13322. 96 p. illus. 21 cm. 1952. Abelard Press.
Ayers, Minny Maud Hanff
--The Quest of the Golden Key. LC 19-18167. (Illus.). 19cm. 24p. 1919. Art, Book and Crafts Shop.
Ayers, Peggy Griffin
--The Little Jeep. LC 43-977. 55, 9 p. illus. 16 x 23 cm. c.1942. Griffin-Patterson Publishing Co.
Ayers, Raymond Fuller
--The King of Kinkiddie and Other Fairy Tales of Now. Bobbett, Walter, illus. LC 4-25108. v. 262 p. front., illus., 14 pl. 20 cm. 1904. E. P. Dutton & Company.
Aylesworth, Jim (1943-)
--Hush up!. Rounds, Glen Harold (1906-), illus. LC 79-21237. (Illus.). 31 p. (gr. k-2). c.1980. (ISBN 0-03-054841-1). Holt, Rinehart and Winston.
--Mary's Mirror. Egielski, Richard (1952-), illus. LC 81-6917. (Illus.). 32 p. 25cm. c.1982. (ISBN 0-03-060392-7). Holt, Rinehart and Winston.
--Siren in the Night. Centola, Tom, illus. LC 83-3654. p. cm. (Self-Starter Books). 1983. (ISBN 0-8075-7374-4). A. Whitman.
Aylesworth, Jim (1943-) & Friedman, Judi (1935-)
--The Bad Dream. LC 85-685. p. cm. 1985. (ISBN 0-8075-0506-4). A. Whitman.
Aylesworth, Jim (1943-) & Wallner, John C (1945-)
--Tonight's the Night. LC 81-103. (Illus.). 32 p. 19cm. (gr. k-2). c.1981. (ISBN 0-8075-8020-1). A. Whitman.
Aylesworth, Thomas Gibbons (1927-)
--Animal Superstitions. LC 80-21389. (Illus.). 24cm. 120p. c.1981. McGraw-Hill.
--Monsters From the Movies. (Illus.). 1972. J. B. Lippincott Company.
--Servants of the Devil. LC 73-118996. 22 ils. index. 128p. 1st U.S. edition. (gr. 8-12). 1970. (ISBN 0-201-00145-4, A-W Childrens). A-W.
--The Story of Dragons and Other Monsters. LC 79-21550. (Illus.). 90 p. 23cm. c.1980. (ISBN 0-07-002646-7). McGraw-Hill.
--The Story of Vampires. (Illus.). (gr. 4-6). 1977. (ISBN 0-07-002647-5, GB). McGraw.
--The Story of Werewolves. LC 78 8136. (Illus.). vi, 90 p. 22cm. c.1978. (ISBN 0-07-002645-9). McGraw-Hill.
--Vampires & Other Ghosts. LC 76-392966. (Illus.). bibl. index. 128p. 1st U.S. edition. (gr. 6 up). 1972. (ISBN 0-201-00157-8, A-W Childrens). A-W.
--Werewolves and Other Monsters. LC 72-12885. (Illus.). vii, 131 p. 25cm. 1973, c.1971. (ISBN 0-8161-6071-6). G. K. Hall.
Ayling, Keith
--Semper Fidelis. N.D. Houghton Mifflin Co.
Aylmer, J. E., Mrs.
--Distant Homes: Or, The Graham Family in New Zealand, 1 of 6 vols. (Birthday Library). N.D. E P Dutton.
Aymar, Gordon Christian, jt. auth. see Aymar, Peggy.
Aymar, Gordon Christian (1893-)
--Start 'em Sailing. N.D. A. S. Barnes & Co.
--A Treasury of Sea Stories. N.D. A. S. Barnes & Co.
Aymar, Peggy & Aymar, Gordon Christian (1893-)
--Michael Sails the Mud Hen: A Story Guide for Beginning Sailors. Smith, Robert, illus. (Illus.). (gr. 1-4). 1961. (ISBN 0-8038-4620-7). Hastings.
Ayme, Marcel (1902-1967)
--The Magic Pictures: More About the Wonderful Farm. 1st ed. Sendak, Maurice Bernard (1928-), illus. Norman, Denny (1901-), tr. LC 54-6336. 117p. illus. 22cm. 1954. Harper.
--Wonderful Farm. Sendak, Maurice Bernard, illus. Denny, Norman (1928-), tr. from Fr. LC 51-13662. (Illus.). (gr. 3-7). 1951. (ISBN 0-06-020311-0, HarpJ). Har-Row.
--The Wonderful Farm. Sendak, Maurice Bernard (1928-), illus. 1959. Harper & Row Publishers.
Ayr, Landis, Mrs.
A Priest and a Woman. LC 1-29631. 8 p. l., 11-268 p. 8. 1900. The Abbey Press.
Ayre, Robert Hugh (1900-)
--Sketco the Raven: Folk tales of Canadian Indians. Surrey, Phillip, illus. (Illus.). 1962. St Martin's Press.
--Sketko the Raven. (gr. 4-9). 1974. (ISBN 0-590-08801-7, Schol Trade Pap). Schol Bk Serv.
Ayres, Ruby Mildred (1883-)
--Afterglow. LC 36-7900. 5 p. l., 303 p. 20 cm. 1936. Doubleday, Doran & Co., Inc.
Ayrton, Matilda Chaplin, Mrs. (1946-1883) & Griffis, William Elliot (1843-1928), eds.
--Child-Life in Japan and Japanese Child Stories. LC 1-31816. xiv, 70 p. incl. front., illus. 20 cm. (Heath's home and school classics). 1901. D. C. Heath and Co.
Ayscough, Florence Wheelock, Mrs. (1878-)
--The Autobiography of a Chinese Dog: Edited by His Missuss. Douglass, Lucille, illus. LC 26-20543. xiv, 105 p. front., illus., plates. 20 cm. 1926. Houghton Mifflin Company.
--Firecracker Land. Douglass, Lucille, illus. 1932. Houghton Mifflin Co.
Azaad, Meyer
--Half for You. Haghighat, Nahid, illus. LC 78-128813. (Illus.). (gr. k-5). 1971. (ISBN 0-87614-016-9). Carolrhoda Bks.
--The Tale of Ringy. Haghighat, Nahid, illus. Ghanoonparvar, Mohammad R. & Wilcox, Diane L., trs. (Illus.). 24p. (Orig.). 1st U.S. edition (Pub. by Lerner Publications). Orig. Title: Persian. (gr. 3 up). 1983. (ISBN 0-686-43078-6). Mazda Pubs.
Azaad, Meyer, jt. auth. see Farjam, Faridah.
Azad, Musrif M.
--Poems for Children. (Illus.). (gr. 10-12). 1972. (ISBN 0-685-82865-4). Intl Bk Ctr.
Azar, Florence
--Adventures of Flossie & Dewey: Safety Lessons Clubhouse, 4 vols, Vol. 1. (Illus.). 18p. (gr. 2-6). 1981. (ISBN 0-86649-005-1). Twentieth Century.
--Adventures of Flossie & Dewey Storybooks, 10 vols. Azar, Florence, illus. (Illus.). 32p. (Orig.). (gr. 2-8). N.D. (ISBN 0-86649-010-8). Twentieth Century.
Azarian, Mary
--John Barleycorn, or, From Barley to Beer: A Traditional English Tale. Azarian, Mary, illus. LC 82-3130. p. cm. 1982. (ISBN 0-87923-446-6). (ISBN 0-87923-447-4). D.R. Godine.
Azmon, Edward
--Encounter on the High Seas: Chim Cham, Bobo, Wally & Emile. Azmon, Edward, illus. LC 74-127393. (Illus.). 40p. (Roundi Doundi Gang Ser.). (ps). 1971. (ISBN 0-87460-232-7). (ISBN 0-87460-233-5). Lion Bks.
--A Hunt in the Jungle: Chim Cham & Bobo. Azmon, Edward, illus. LC 70-127342. (Illus.). 40p. (The Roundi Doundi Gang Ser). (ps). 1971. (ISBN 0-87460-230-0). (ISBN 0-87460-231-9). Lion.
--Wally & Emile. full color throughout. (Roundi Doundi Gang Ser.). (gr. k-3). N.D. (ISBN 0-87460-232-7). (ISBN 0-87460-233-5). Lion.
Azmon, Edward & Azmon, Xenia
--The Roundi Doundi Gang Featuring Chim Cham and Bobo in A Hunt in the Jungle. Azmon, Edward, illus. LC 70-127392. (Illus.). 44 p. 22cm. 1971. (ISBN 0-87460-230-0). (ISBN 0-87460-231-9). Lion Books.
--The Roundi Doundi Gang Featuring Chim Cham, Bobo, Wally, and Emile in Encounter on the High Seas. Azmon, Edward, illus. LC 74-127393. (Illus.). 45 p. 22cm. 1971. (ISBN 0-87460-232-7). (ISBN 0-87460-233-5). Lion Books.
Azmon, Xenia, jt. auth. see Azmon, Edward.
B., A. A, jt. auth. see Andersen, Hans Christian.
B & W Associates, ed.
--Double Play Reading Series, 5 kits. Irwin, Bud, illus. Incl. Kit 1. The Thief Who Liked Baseball, Showdown!. (ISBN 0-8372-2542-6); Kit 2. The Golden Puma, Grunk's Fantastic Basketball Team. (ISBN 0-8372-2543-4); Kit 3. Fire on 7th Street, King Toop's Revenge. (ISBN 0-8372-2544-2); Kit 4. Ten Speed Thieves, the Visitors. (ISBN 0-8372-2545-0); Kit 5. Juan's Story, the Millville Lions. (ISBN 0-8372-2546-9). (Illus.). 1977. (ISBN 0-8372-2559-0). Bowmar-Noble.
B. B.
--The Monster Fish. D'Andrea, Bernard, illus. (Illus.). Orig. Title: The Whopper. (gr. 4-6). 1972. (ISBN 0-590-09255-3, Schol Pap). Schol Bk Serv.
Baastad, Babbis Friis (1921-1970)
--Wanted! A Horse!. Robinson, Charles (1870-1937), illus. McKinnon, Lise Somme, tr. LC 72-153952. (Illus.). 188 p. 21cm. 1972. (ISBN 0-15-294750-7). Harcourt Brace Jovanovich.
Baba, Noburo
--Eleven Hungry Cats. LC 79-93858. (Illus.). 39 p. 26cm. 1970. Parents' Magazine Press.
--Eleven Hungry Cats. Baba, Noburo, illus. Tresselt, Alvin R. (1916-), tr. LC 79-93858. (Illus.). japanese. color ils. Orig. Title: Eleven Pikino Neko. (gr. k-3). 1970. (ISBN 0-8193-0384-4, Four Winds). (ISBN 0-8193-0385-2). Scholastic Inc.
Baba Hari Dass
Mystic Monkey. Kelley, Elizabeth A., illus. LC 81-51051. (Illus.). 64p. (Orig.). (gr. 4-8). 1984. (ISBN 0-918100-05-4). Sri Rama.
Baba-Iaga see Small, Ernest.
Babbit, Ellen C., retold by see Jakatas.
Babbitt, Adeline, jt. ed. see Hubbard, Alice.
Babbitt, Ellen C., retold by.
--The Animals Own Story Book. Stocking, Margery, illus. Farrand, Livingston, intro. by. LC 30-28805. 21cm. 132p. 1930. The Century Co.
Babbitt, Ellen C., retold by see Jatakas.
Babbitt, Lorraine
--Pink Like the Geranium. Dobrin, Arnold (1928-), illus. LC 73-17247. (Illus.). 32 p. 24cm. 1974. (ISBN 0-516-08841-6). Childrens Press.
Babbitt, Natalie (1932-)
--The Devil's Storybook. Babbitt, Natalie (1932-), illus. LC 74-5488. (Illus.). 101 p. 22cm. 1974. (ISBN 0-374-31770-4). Farrar, Straus, Giroux.
--Dick Foote and the Shark. Babbitt, Natalie (1932-), illus. LC 67-5555. (Illus.). 25 p. 27cm. (Ariel book). 1967. Farrar, Straus and Giroux.
--The Eyes of the Amaryllis. LC 77-11862. p. cm. 1977. (ISBN 0-374-32241-4). Farrar, Straus and Giroux.
--Goody Hall. Babbitt, Natalie (1932-), illus. LC 73-149221. (Illus.). 176 p. 22cm. 1971. (ISBN 0-374-32745-9). Farrar, Straus & Giroux.
--Herbert Rowbarge. LC 82-18274. p. cm. 1982. (ISBN 0-374-32959-1). (ISBN 0-374-51852-1). Farrar, Straus, Giroux.
--Kneeknock Rise. Babbitt, Natalie (1932-), illus. LC 79-105622. 21cm. 117p. 1970. (ISBN 0-374-34257-1). (ISBN 0-374-44260-6). Farrar and Straus. **Award: (JNM).**
--Phoebe's Revolt. Babbitt, Natalie (1932-), illus. LC 68-13679. (Illus.). 1 v. (unpaged. 1968. Farrar, Straus and Giroux.
--The Search for Delicious. LC 69-20374. (Illus.). 167 p. 19cm. 1974, c.1969. Camelot Books.

--The Search For Delicious. Babbitt, Natalie (1932-), illus. 1969. Farrar, Straus And Giroux.
--The Something. Babbitt, Natalie (1932-), illus. LC 70-125143. (Illus.). 39 p. 19cm. 1970. Farrar, Straus and Giroux.
--Tuck Everlasting. Babbitt, Natalie (1932-), illus. LC 75-33306. 139 p. 22cm. 1975. Farrar, Straus, Giroux. **Awards: (IBBY); (ALA).**

Babbitt, Robert, pseud., see Bangs, Robert Babbitt.

Babbitt, Robert, pseud. (1914-)
--The Adventures of Bumpy. Bangs, Robert Babbitt. 1st ed. Berger, Charles J., illus. 96 p. 21cm. 1974. (ISBN 0-682-47830-X). Exposition Press.

Babbitt, Samuel F
--The Forty-Ninth Magician. Babbitt, Natalie (1932-), illus. LC 66-12458. 1v. (unpaged) illus. 26cm. c.1966. Pantheon.

Babcock, Bernie Smade, Mrs. (1868-)
--Lighthorse Harry's Boy: The Boyhood of Robert E. Lee. Pyle, Walter, illus. LC 31-30501. 256 p. col. front., plates. 20 cm. 1931. J. B. Lippincott Company.
--Little Abe Lincoln. Wolf, W. H., illus. LC 26-21892. 272 p. col. front., plates. 20 cm. 1926. J. B. Lippincott Company.

Babcock, Elisabeth S Thompson
--The Expandable Pig. LC 49-10268. 114 p. illus. 20 cm. 1949. C. Scribner's Sons.

Baber, Frank
--Frank Baber's Mother Goose Nursery Rhymes. Baber, Frank, illus. LC 79-88462. p. cm. 1979, c.1976. Derrydale Books.
--Frank Baber's Mother Goose Nursery Rhymes. Spriggs, Ruth, ed. Baber, Frank, illus. LC 76-24878. p. cm. 1976. (ISBN 0-517-52819-3). Crown Publishers.

Baber, Frank see Lorenzini, Carlo.

Babin, Maria Teresa & Steiner, Stan
--Borinquen: An Anthology of Puerto Rican Literature. 1974. Borzoi Books.

Babson, Susan
--Jimmy's Christmas, an Old-Fashioned Story. Wonson, Mildred, illus. LC 32-326. 16cm. 46p. 1931. F. S. & A. H. McKenzie.

Baby Rue
--Her Adventures and Misadventures, Her Friends and Her Enemies. N.D. Messrs. Roberts Brothers.

Bach, Alice Hendricks (1942-)
--The Day After Christmas. Chalmers, Mary Eileen (1927-), illus. LC 74-9073. (Illus.). 31 p. 24cm. c.1975. (ISBN 0-06-020313-7). (ISBN 0-06-020314-5). Harper & Row.
--A Father Every Few Years. LC 76-24303. p. cm. c.1977. (ISBN 0-06-020342-0). (ISBN 0-06-020343-9). Harper & Row.
--Grouchy Uncle Otto. Kellogg, Steven (1941-), illus. LC 76-24304. (Illus.). 36 p. 24cm. c.1977. (ISBN 0-06-020344-7). (ISBN 0-06-020345-5). Harper and Row.
--He Will Not Walk with Me. LC 85-4570. 182 p. 22cm. c.1985. (ISBN 0-385-29410-7). Delacorte Press.
--The Meat in the Sandwich. LC 75-6302. 182 p. 22cm. c.1975. (ISBN 0-06-020336-6). (ISBN 0-06-020337-4). Harper & Row.
--Millicent the Magnificent. 1st ed. Kellogg, Steven (1941-), illus. LC 77-11840. (Illus.). 43 p. 23cm. c.1978. (ISBN 0-06-020309-9). (ISBN 0-06-020312-9). Harper and Row.
--Mollie Make-Believe. LC 73-14334. 147 p. 22cm. 1974. (ISBN 0-06-020315-3). (ISBN 0-06-020315-3). Harper & Row.
--The Most Delicious Camping Trip Ever. Kellogg, Steven (1941-), illus. LC 76-2956. p. cm. c.1976. (ISBN 0-06-020338-2). (ISBN 0-06-020339-0). Harper & Row.
--The Smartest Bear and His Brother Oliver. Kellogg, Steven (1941-), illus. LC 74-29348. (Illus.). 20, 10 p., 2 leaves of plates. 23cm. 1975. (ISBN 0-06-020334-X). (ISBN 0-06-020335-8). Harper & Row.
--They'll Never Make a Movie Starring Me. LC 72-12240. 194 p. 22cm. 1973. (ISBN 0-06-020322-6). (ISBN 0-06-020322-6). Harper & Row.
--Waiting for Johnny Miracle. LC 79-2813. p. cm. c.1980. (ISBN 0-06-020348-X). (ISBN 0-06-020349-8). Harper & Row.
--Warren Weasel's Worse Than Measles. Knight, Hilary (1926-), illus. LC 78-22491. (Illus.). 97 p. 23cm. c.1980. (ISBN 0-06-020324-2). (ISBN 0-06-020327-7). Harper & Row.
--When the Sky Began to Roar. LC 84-12901. 176p. (gr. 7 up). 1984. (ISBN 0-395-36071-4). HM.

Bach, Margaret Frieda (1925-)
--Journey to Freedom. LC 53-13164. 117p. 21cm. 1953. W.B. Eerdmans Pub. Co.

Bach, Othello, jt. auth. see D'Addio, Janie.

Bach, Othello (1941-)
--Funny Bone Poems. Huffaker, Sandy (1943-), illus. LC 85-24286. p. cm. c.1985. Caedmon.
--Hector McSnector & the Mail Order Christmas Witch. LC 84-740001. (Illus.). 40p. (ps-4). 1985. (ISBN 0-89845-264-3). Caedmon.
--Hector McSnector and the Mail-Order Christmas Witch. Hildebrandt, Tim (1939-), illus. LC 83-26353. p. cm. c.1984. (ISBN 0-89845-263-5). Caedmon.
--Lilly, Willy & the Mail-Order Witch. Hildebrandt, Tim (1939-), illus. LC 83-7422. (Illus.). 36p. (ps-4). 1983. (ISBN 0-89845-048-9). (ISBN 0-89845-161-2). Caedmon.
--Whoever Heard of a Fird?. Dorman, Michelle, illus. LC 83-23985. c.1984. (ISBN 0-89845-276-7). Caedmon.

Bach, Richard David (1936-)
--Jonathan Livingston Seagull. Munson, Russell, photos by. LC 75-119617. (Illus.). 93 p. 22cm. 1970. Macmillan.

Bache, Anna, Mrs.
--Legends of Fairy Land. LC 44-36617. ix, 11-172 p. front., plates. 16 1/2 cm. 1885. Cassell & Company, Limited.
--Legends of Fairy Land. N.D. Claxton, Remsen, & haffelfinger.

Bache, Richard Meade
--The Young Wrecker. (Roundabout Library). N.D. John C. Winston Co.
--The Young Wrecker of the Florida Reef: or, the Trials and Adventures of Fred Ransom. N.D. Claxton, Remsen, & Haffelfinger.
--The Young Wrecker of the Florida Reef: Or, The Trials and Adventures of Fred Ransom. 6th ed. LC 12-30653. viii, 9-381 p. front., plates. 18 cm. (On cover: Our boys prize library). c.1893. Lee and Shepard.

Bachelin, Anita
--Pepe. Bachelin, Franz, illus. LC 62-16366. (Illus.). 28cm. 48p. 1962. Golden, Gate Junior Books.

Bachelis, Faren, ed. see Neff, Carolyn & Verett, Dotty.

Bacheller, Irving (1859-1950)
--A Boy for the Ages. Child, Charles Jesse (1901-), illus. N.D. Farrar & Rinehart.
--Keeping up with William. 1918. Bobbs-Merrill Co.
--The Light in the Clearing. (Growing Literature Ser.). N.D. Grosset & Dunlap.
--The Light in the Clearing. Keller, Arthur I., illus. 1917. Bobbs-Merrill Co.

Bachelor, Joseph Morris (1889-1947), ed.
--The Book of Baby Verse. LC 23-10839. ix, 214 p. col. front. (port.) 20 cm. 1923. G. Sully & Company.

Bacher, William A (1922-), ed.
--Radio Minstrel Tales. LC 31-14061. 143 p. illus. 24 cm. c.1931. Fleming H. Revell Company.

Bachman, Fred (1949-)
--Hang in at the Plate. Berson, Harold (1926-), illus. LC 73-19249. (Illus.). 104 p. 21cm. 1974. (ISBN 0-8098-2426-4). H. Z. Walck.

Bachmann, Evelyn Trent
--Black-Eyed Susan. Obligado, Lilian Isabel (1931-), illus. LC 68-18122. (Illus.). 159 p. 22cm. 1968. (ISBN 0-670-17158-1). Viking Press.
--Tressa. Bjorklund, Lorence F. (1913-1978), illus. LC 66-14416. (Illus.). (gr. 4-7). 1966. (ISBN 0-670-73008-4). (ISBN 0-670-73009-2). Viking Pr.

Bachmann, Frieda, tr. see Lebermann, Norbert.

Bachmann, Mary Lee, jt. auth. see Guillaume, Jeanette G. Fliert.

Bacigalupa, Andrea (1923-)
--A Good & Perfect Gift. Pear, Jeannie, illus. LC 78-60727. (Illus.). 42 p. 24cm. (OSV read-along book). c.1978. (ISBN 0-87973-352-7). Our Sunday Visitor.

Bacigalupa, Drew (1923-)
--Franco and Pirata. Marelli, Angelo, illus. LC 85-25822. p. cm. 1985. (ISBN 0-915138-80-8). Pickwick Publications.
--The Song of Guadalupana. Pear, Jeannie, illus. LC 79-88028. (Illus.). 48 p. 23cm. c.1979. (ISBN 0-87973-357-8). Our Sunday Visitor.

Backer, Alice, tr. see Hofman, Ota.

Backer, Marjory Esther
--Lonely Chico. Wind, Betty, illus. LC 58-3373. unpaged. illus. 22cm. 1958. Concordia Pub. House.

Backman, Helen Lawrence
--The Adventures of Calico Cotton. Langelier, Joyce, illus. LC 68-4541. 195 p. illus. (part col.) 25 cm. 1967. Rolton House.

Bacmeister, Rhoda Warner, Mrs. (1893-)
--Jet: The True Story of a Talking Crow. Downer, Marion (1892-1971), illus. LC 38-19403. 89 p. illus. 21 cm. 1938. E. P. Dutton & Company, Inc.
--People Downstairs & Other City Stories. Galdone, Paul (1914-), illus. (Illus.). (gr. k-3). 1964. (ISBN 0-698-30415-2, Coward). Putnam Pub Group.
--Stories to Begin on. Maley, Thomas, illus. LC 40-12417. 134 p. incl. front., illus., plates. 21 cm. 1940. E. P. Dutton & Co., Inc.
--Voices in the Night. Grifalconi, Ann (1929-), illus. LC 65-17707. 117p. illus. 23cm. c.1965. Bobbs.

Bacon, Albion Fellows, jt. auth. see Johnston, Annie Fellows, Mrs.

Bacon, Albion Fellows, Mrs. (1865-)
--The Charm String. Chapman, Billie, illus. LC 29-18664. ix p., 2 l., 204 p. col. front., col. plates. 23 cm. c.1929. L. C. Page & Company.

Bacon, Antoinette Montgomery Frissell (1907-), illus.
--Toni Frissell's Mother Goose. LC 48-11000. 94 p. illus. 28 cm. 1948. Harper.

Bacon, Dolores, ed.
--Operas Every Child Should Know. Ostertag, Blanche, illus. (Illus.). (The Every Child Should Know Bks.). N.D. Doubleday, Page & Co.
--Songs Every Child Should Know. (Every Child Should Know Ser.). N.D. Grosset & Dunlap.
--Songs Every Child Should Know. Ostertag, Blanche, illus. (Illus.). (The Every Child Should Know Bks.). N.D. Doubleday, Page & Co.

Bacon, Elizabeth see Morrow, Betty, pseud.

Bacon, Elizabeth (1914-)
--Great Miracle: The Story of Hanukkah. Morrow, Betty, pseud. Simon, Howard (1903-1979), illus. LC 68-22984. (Illus.). 48p. of ils. 48p. (gr. 3-6). 1968. (ISBN 0-8178-4332-9). Harvey.
--See up the Mountain. Morrow, Betty, pseud. (Illus.). (gr. 3-6). N.D. (ISBN 0-06-024326-0, HarpJ). Har-Row.
--See Up the Mountain. Morrow, Betty, pseud. Lubell, Winifred A. Milius (1914-), illus. 1958. Harper & Brothers.

Bacon, Frances Elizabeth Atchinson, Mrs., jt. ed. see Adams, Kathleen.

Bacon, Frances Elizabeth Atchinson (1903-)
--Kitty Come Down. Wilkin, Eloise Burns (1904-), illus. LC 44-8751. 30, 2 p. illus. 18 1/2 x 18 cm. 1944. Oxford University Press.
--Turkey Tale. Paull, Grace A. (1898-), illus. LC 35-27263. 19cm. 48p. 1935. Oxford University Press.

Bacon, Henry
--Dumb Betty Lamp. N.D. D. Lothrop Co.

Bacon, Jo A.
--Don't Die Baby. McCarthy, Patricia, ed. Morrell, Dave, illus. (Illus., Orig.). (Pal Paperbacks Ser., Kit A). (gr. 7-12). 1974. (ISBN 0-8374-3471-8). Xerox Ed Pubns.

Bacon, Joan
--Pussycat Tiger. Obligado, Lilian Isabel (1931-), illus. (Illus.). 24p. (ps-4). 1972. (ISBN 0-307-60362-8, Golden Pr). Western Pub.

Bacon, Josephine, tr. see Biber, Yehoash.

Bacon, Josephine Dodge Daskam, Mrs. (1876-1961)
--Cassie-on-the-Job. Stivers, harley Ennis, illus. LC 37-2754. 20cm. 250p. 1937. D. Appleton-Century Co.
--The Door in the Closet. LC 40-141942. 246 p. 22 cm. 1940. The Viking Press.
--Fables For The Fair. N.D. Charles Scribner's Sons.
--The Girl at the Window. Peck, Clara Elsene, illus. LC 34-3725. 4 p. l., 278 p. front., illus. 20 cm. 1934. D. Appleton-Century Company, Incorporated.
--Girl Wanted!. A Mystery Story. Peck, Clara Elsene, illus. LC 30-4987. 4 p. l., 254 p. incl. front., illus. 20 cm. 1936. D. Appleton-Century Company, Incorporated.
--The House by the Road. Stein, Harve (1904-), illus. LC 37-184413. 5 p. l., 274 p. incl. front., illus. 20 cm. 1937. D. Appleton-Century Company, Incorporated.
--The Imp and the Angel. Rosenmeyer, Bernard J., illus. LC 74-81260. (Illus.). 168 p. 21cm. (Short story index reprint series). 1969. Books for Libraries Press.
--The Imp and the Angel. Rosenmeyer, Bernard J., illus. LC 7-29579. 6 p. l., 3-191 p. front., 7 pl. 20 cm. 1907. C. Scribner's Sons.
--Kathy. Esley, Joan, illus. LC 34-29556. ix p., 1 l., 835 p. incl. front., illus. 20 cm. 1934. Longmans, Green and Co.
--Luck of Lowry. Esley, Joan, illus. LC 31-20607. ix p., 1 l., 303 p. incl. front., illus., plates. 20 cm. 1931. Longmans, Green and Co.
--On Our Hill. Bevans, T. M. & Bevans, M. T., illus. LC 18-18743. xii, 336, 1 p. incl. illus., plates. col. front., col. plates. 22 cm. 1918. C. Scribner's Sons.
--The Room on the Roof: A Mystery Novel for Girls. Peck, Clara Elsene, illus. LC 35-2724. 4 p. l., 275 p. incl. front., illus. 20 cm. 1935. D. Appleton-Century Company, Incorporated.
--The Root and the Flower. N.D. D. Appleton-Century Co.
--Sister's Vocation and Other Girl's Stories. N.D. Charles Scribner's Sons.
--Smith College Stories. N.D. Charles Scribner's Sons.
--Stunt Poems for Little People. 47 p. 19 cm. c.1936. Ivan Bloom Hardin Company.
--While Caroline Was Growing. N.D. Macmillan.
--The World in His Heart. N.D. D. Appleton-Century Co.

Bacon, M.
--Songs That Every Child Should Know. (ps-6). N.D. (ISBN 0-8490-1086-1). Gordon Pr.

Bacon, Margaret Frances see Bacon, Peggy, pseud.

Bacon, Margaret Hope (1921-)
--Rebellion at Christiana. 224p. 1974. (ISBN 0-517-51576-8). Crown.

Bacon, Martha Sherman (1917-1981)
--In the Company of Clowns. LC 72-12893. (Illus.). 176p. (gr. 7 up). 1973. (ISBN 0-316-07510-8, Pub. by Atlantic Monthly Pr). Little.
--Moth Manor: A Gothic Tale. 1st ed. Burroughs, Gail, illus. LC 78-59680. (Illus.). (gr. 3-7). 1978. (ISBN 0-316-07511-6, Pub. by Atlantic Monthly Pr). Little.
--Sophia Scrooby Preserved. White, David Omar (1927-), illus. LC 68-21167. (Illus.). 227 p. 22cm. 1968. Little, Brown.
--The Third Road. Jacques, Robin (1920-), illus. LC 70-129906. (Illus.). 188 p. 22cm. 1971. Little, Brown.

Bacon, Peggy, pseud., see Bacon, Margaret Frances.

Bacon, Peggy (1895-)
--The Ballad of Tangle Street. 4 p.l., 22p. front., illus 23 x 30cm. (Poetry, Music And Art). 1929. Macmillan.
--The Forty-Ninth Magician. Bacon, Margaret Frances. Bacon, Peggy, pseud. (1895-), illus. Bacon, Margaret Frances. 1966. Pantheon Books.
--The Ghost of Opalina: Or, Nine Lives. Bacon, Margaret Frances. Bacon, Peggy, pseud. (1895-), illus. Bacon, Margaret Frances. (Illus.). (A cat whose spirit haunts a two-hundred-year-old house tells about the children who have lived in it throughout the years). (gr. 5-7). 1967. (ISBN 0-316-07502-7). Little.
--Good American Witch. 1957. (ISBN 0-8382-0298-5, Cadmus Books). E. M. Hale and Company.
--The Good American Witch. LC 57-7542. 222p. illus. 22cm. 1957. F. Watts.
--The Lion-Hearted Kitten and Other Stories. Bacon, Margaret Frances. Bacon, Peggy, pseud. (1895-), illus. Bacon, Margaret Frances. LC 27-18472. 6 p. l., 3-102 p. incl. illus., plates. front., plates. 23 cm. 1927. The Macmillan Company.
--The Magic Touch. Bacon, Margaret Frances. Bacon, Peggy, pseud. (1895-), illus. Bacon, Margaret Frances. LC 68-15385. (Illus.). 112 p. 21cm. 1968. Little, Brown.
--Mercy and the Mouse and Other Stories. Bacon, Margaret Frances. Bacon, Peggy, pseud. (1895-), illus. Bacon, Margaret Frances. LC 26-25503. xi p., 1 l., 85 p. incl. front., illus. plates 23 cm. 1928. The Macmillan Company.
--Mischief in Mayfield: A Sequel to The Terrible Nuisance. Bacon, Margaret Frances. Bacon, Peggy, pseud. (1895-), illus. Bacon, Margaret Frances. LC 33-27247. xii, 177 p. incl. front., illus., plates. 23 cm. N.D. Harcourt, Brace and Company.
--The Mystery at East Hatchett: Or, Eric the Pink. Bacon, Margaret Frances. Bacon, Peggy, pseud. (1895-), illus. Bacon, Margaret Frances. LC 39-25328. 170 p. incl. illus., plates. 22 cm. 1939. The Viking Press.
--The Oddity. LC 62-51926. 70p. illus. 23cm. 1962. Pantheon.
--The Terrible Nuisance and Other Tales. Bacon, Margaret Frances. Bacon, Peggy, pseud. (1895-), illus. Bacon, Margaret Frances. LC 31-2166. 6 p. l., 3-142. 1 p. incl. front., illus., plates. 23 cm. c.1931. Harcourt, Brace and Company.
--The True Philosopher and Other Cat Tales. Bacon, Margaret Frances. Bacon, Peggy, pseud. (1895-), illus. Bacon, Margaret Frances. LC 19-15977. 6 p. l., 9-55 p. front., plates. 20 cm. 1919. The Four Seas Company.

Bacon, Ronald Leonard (1924-)
--Again the Bugles Blow. 1976. (ISBN 0-8002-0453-0). Intl Pubns Serv.
--Boy & the Taniwha. Matchitt, Para, illus. (Illus.). 30 color ils. 30p. (gr. 2-5). 1971. Tri-Ocean.
--Rua & the Sea People. (gr. 5up). 1976. (ISBN 0-8002-0480-8). Intl Pubns Serv.
--Rua & the Sea People. Matchitt, Para, illus. (Illus.). 30 color ils. 30p. (gr. 2-6). 1971. Tri-Ocean.

Bacon, Ronald Leonard (1924-) & Matchitt, Para
--The Boy and the Taniwha. (Illus.). 1969. Tri-Ocean Books.

Bacon, Susie Lee
--A Siren's Son. 1895. Charles H. Kerr & Co.

Badcock, Jack Clement
--The Truants. Wetherbee, Margaret, illus. LC 53-9943. 123p. illus. 22cm. 1953. Pantheon Books.

Bade, Jane (1932-)
--Nine on a String. Jungles, Dorothy, illus. LC 70-166453. (Illus.). 16 p. 24cm. (Magic circle book). 1972. (ISBN 0-663-22964-2). Ginn.

Badenoch, Nena Frances Wilson (1889-)
--Go Home, Puppy. Young, Elsa Goldy, illus. LC 38-21546. (Illus.). 20cm. 37p. 1938. Saalfield Pub. Co.

--Everyday Stories. Knowles, Frederick, illus. LC 19-11560. 157 p. incl. front. plates. 20 cm. (For the children's hour series). 1919. Milton Bradley Company.
--Finnegan Two: His Nine Lives. Seredy, Kate (1899-1975), illus. LC 53-12890. (Illus.). (gr. 3-7). 1953. (ISBN 0-670-31508-7). Viking Pr. **Award: (ALA).**
--Flickertail. MacKenzie, Garry (1921-), illus. LC 62-10060. (Illus.). 90 p. 23cm. 1962. H. Z. Walck.
--Flint: The Story of a Trail. Lassell, Charles, illus. LC 22-12894. 2 p. l., 315 p. front., plates. 20 cm. c.1922. Milton Bradley Company.
--Folk Stories and Fables. Nagler, Frederick A., illus. LC 20-168. 2 p. l., 7-120 p. illus. 20 cm. (For the children's hour series). 1919. Milton Bradley Company.
--For the Children's Hour. (Treasure Book Ser.). N.D. Platt & Munk Co.
--For the Story Teller: Story Telling and Stories to Tell. LC 74-23576. viii, 261 p. 22cm. 1975, c.1913. (ISBN 0-8103-3802-5). Gale Research Co.
--For the Story Teller: Story Telling and Stories to Tell. LC 78-174005. viii, 261 p. 22cm. 1971. Gryphon Books.
--For the Story Teller: Story Telling and Stories to Tell. LC 13-194291. viii, 261 p. 20 cm. 1913. Milton Bradley Company.
--Friendly Tales: A Community Story Book. LC 23-957652. 7 p. l., 377 p. 20 cm. c.1923. Milton Bradley Company.
--Hero Stories. Knowles, Frederick, illus. LC 19-11561. 182 p., 1 l. incl. front. plates. 20 cm. (For the children's hour series). 1919. Milton Bradley Company.
--Homespun Playdays. Paull, Grace A. (1898-), illus. 216p. N.D. Viking Press.
--The Jingle Primer: A First Book in Reading Based on Mother Goose Rhymes and Folk Tales. 1905. American Book Company.
--Li'l' Hannibal. LC 38-29631. 21cm. 24p. (Never Grow Old Ser.). 1938. Platt & Munk.
--Lincoln Time Stories. LC 25-2142. 110 p. incl. col. front., illus. (part col.) 19 cm. (Just right books). c.1924. Albert Whitman Company.
--Little Men and Women Stories. LC 25-214151. 107 p. incl. col. front., illus. (part col.) 19 cm. (Just right book). c.1924. Albert Whitman Company.
--Little Men and Women Stories. LC 37-1750. 125 p. incl. col. front., illus. (part col.) 18 cm. (Just right books). c.1926. Albert Whitman Company.
--The Little Rabbit Who Wanted Red Wings. Grider, Dorothy (1915-), illus. LC 48-3300. 32 p. (on double leaves) col. illus. 20 cm. 1945. Platt & Munk Co.
--The Little Rabbit Who Wanted Red Wings. Grider, Dorothy (1915-), illus. LC 61-11467. (Illus.). 1 v. (unpaged). 20cm. 1961, c.1945. Platt & Munk.
--Little Red SchoolHouse. N.D. E . M. Hale and Co.
--The Little Red Schoolhouse. Morse, Dorothy Bayley (1906-1979), illus. LC 57-2347. 134p. illus. 22cm. 1957. Viking Press.
--Merry Christmas Book. Smith, Eunice Young, illus. LC 49-318. 95 p. illus. (part col.) 21 cm. 1948. A. Whiteman.
--Miss Hickory. Gannett, Ruth Chrisman Arens (1896-1979), illus. LC 46-7275. 120p. 3p illus. 23cm. 1946. The Viking Press. **Award: (JNM).**
--Old Man Rabbit's Dinner Party. Robinson, illus. LC 49-11783. 32 p. (on double leaves) col. illus. 20 cm. 1949. Platt & Munk Co.
--Once Upon a Time Animal Stories. LC 16-179215. v. 145 p. col. front., illus. 20 cm. 1918. Milton Bradley Company.
--The Outdoor Story Book. LC 18-14990. ix, 222 p. 19 cm. c.1918. The Pilgrim Press.
--The Peter Newell Mother Goose: The Old Rhymes Reproduced in Connection with Their Veracious History. Newell, Peter (1862-1924), illus. LC 5-36120. viii p., 1 l., 265 p. incl. 21 pl. 20 cm. 1905. H. Holt and Company.
--Pioneer Art in America. Paull, Grace A. (1898-), illus. LC 44-9352. 221 p. illus. 23 cm. 1944. The Viking Press.
--Plays for the Children's Hour. LC 31-15444. 2 p. l., 3-257 p. 22 cm. c.1931. Milton Bradley Company.
--Plays for the Children's Hour: An American Childhood Presentation. LC 77-94332. 257 p. 20cm. 1978. (ISBN 0-8486-2032-1). Core Collection Books.
--Rabbit Who Wanted Red Wings. Grider, Dorothy (1915-), illus. (Illus.). (Children's Hour Ser). (ps-3). 1970. (ISBN 0-8228-0513-8). Platt.
--Read Aloud Stories. Lupprian, Hildegard (1897-), illus. LC 20-14209. 4 p. l., 215 p. col. front., col. plates. 20 cm. c.1929. Milton Bradley Company.
--Reading Time Stories. iii p. incl. col. front., illus (part col.) 19 cm. ("A Just Right Book"). 1923. Albert Whitman Company.
--Stories and Rhymes for a Child. Wright, Christine, illus. viii p., 2 l., 194 p. col. front., 5 pl. 21 cm. 1909. M. Bradley Company.
--Stories for Any Day. LC 17-28851. 6 p. l., 3-163 p. 18 cm. c.1917. The Pilgrim Press.
--Stories for Every Holiday. LC 73-20149. 277 p. 18cm. 1974. Gale Research Co.
--Stories for Every Holiday. LC 18-16896. 277 p. 20 cm. c.1918. The Abingdon Press.
--Stories for Sunday Telling. 1916. Pilgrim Press.
--Stories From An Indian Cave: The Cherokee Cave Builders. Dash, Josephine Eugene, illus. 256p. (The World Wide Library). 1924. A. Whitman & Co.
--Tell Me a Birthday Story. Ayer, Margaret (0000-1981), illus. N.D. Frederick A. Stokes.
--Tell Me a Birthday Story. Ayer, Margaret (0000-1981), illus. 1935. J. B. Lippincott Co.
--This Way to Animal Land. (With Ditzy Baker). 1936. Saalfield.
--Tops and Whistles: True Stories of Early American Toys and Children. Paull, Grace A. (1898-), illus. LC 37-31484. 6 p. l., 3-196 p. illus. 28 cm. 1937. The Viking Press.
--The Torch of Courage, and Other Stories. LC 21-6167. iii, 112 p. front. 19 cm. 1921. Milton Bradley Company.
--When Grandfather Was a Boy. Whitney, George Gillett, illus. LC 28-5560. x, 164 p. incl. front., illus. 19 cm. c.1928. Ginn and Company.
--When Grandfather Was a Boy: Stories to Read to Children. LC 26-14631. 6 p. l., 3-163 p. 19 cm. c.1923. The Pilgrim Press.
--Wonder Stories. N.D. Grosset & Dunlap.
--Wonder Stories: The Best Myths for Boys and Girls. Burd, Clara Miller, illus. LC 20-12815. 344 p. col. front., col. plates. 22 cm. 1920. Milton Bradley Company.
--The Wonderful Days. New ed. Falls, Charles Buckles (1874-1960) & Dash, Joseph Eugene, illus. (The World Wide Library). 1930. A. Whitman & Co.
--The Wonderful Tree and Golden Day Stories. Dash, Josephine Eugene, illus. LC 26-182611. 254 p. incl. col. front., illus. (part col.) 24 cm. ("A just right book"). c.1925. A. Whitman & Co.
--The Wonderful Window and Other Stories. Wireman, Katharine Richardson, illus. LC 26-12718. 64 p. illus., col. plates. 31 cm. (Cokesbury character series for boys and girls). c.1926. Cokesbury Press.

Bailey, Carolyn Sherwin (1875-1961), retold by.
--Firelight Stories: Folk Tales Retold for Kindergarten, School and Home. Horne, Diantha W., illus. LC 7-23711. 192 p. front., plates. 20 cm. 1907. M. Bradley Company.
--For the Children's Hour. Chase, Rhoda Campbell, illus. LC 26-13343. 336 p. col. front. col. plates. 20 cm. 1926. Milton Bradley Company.
--For the Children's Hour. Chase, Rhoda Campbell, illus. LC 41-5149. x p., 1 l., 326 p. incl. col. front. col. plates. 21 cm. c.1939. Milton Bradley Company.
--For the Children's Hour. Chase, Rhoda Campbell, illus. LC 44-337. x p., 1 l., 326 p. col. front., col. plates. 20 1/2 cm. 1943. The Platt & Munk Co. Inc.
--For the Children's Hour. Nagler, Frederick A., illus. 1916. Milton Bradley Co.
--In the Animal World. LC 24-22051. x, 472 p. 20 cm. 1924. Milton Bradley Company.
--Merry Tales for Children: Best Stories of Humor for Boys and Girls. LC 21-10256. 5 p. l., 374 p. 20 cm. c.1921. Milton Bradley Company.
--Merry Tales for Children: Best Stories of Humor for Boys and Girls. LC 44-330. 5 p. l., 374 p. col. front. 20 1/2 cm. 1943. The Platt & Munk Co., Inc.
--Stories Children Need. LC 16-10878. xxiv, 364 p. 20 cm. 1916. Milton Bradley Company.
--Stories Children Want. Perkins, Jack, illus. LC 31-24663. 4 p. l., 298 p. front., illus., plates. 20 cm. c.1931. Milton Bradley Co.
--Stories Children Want. Perkins, Jack, illus. LC 44-331. 4 p. l., 298 p. col. front., illus., plates. 20 1/2 cm. 1943. The Platt & Munk Co. Inc.
--Stories of Great Adventures. Burd, Clara Miller, illus. LC 19-7098. 222 p. col. front. 20 cm. (For the Children Hour Ser.). c.1919. Milton Bradley Company.
--The Story-Telling Hour. N.D. Gale Reprint.
--The Story-Telling Hour: Edited for the New York Story League. New York Story League LC 34-570086. x p., 1 l., 252 p. 20 cm. gincludes stories and bibliographies of children's literature. 1934. Dodd, Mead & Company.
--Tell Me Another Story: The Book of Story Programs. LC 18-9291. xii, 335 p. 20 cm. 1918. Milton Bradley Company.
--Tell Me Another Story: The Book of Story Programs. LC 44-332. xii, 335 p. col. front. 20 1/2 cm. 1943. The Platt & Munk Co., Inc.

Bailey, Carolyn Sherwin (1875-1961) & Ehrmann, Mary B.
--Songs of Happiness: The/"Blue Bird" Song Book. 128p. 1912. Milton Bradley Co.

Bailey, Carolyn Sherwin (1875-1961) & Gannett, Ruth Chrisman Arens (1896-1979)
--Miss Hickory. LC 77-1997. p. cm. 1977. (ISBN 0-14-030956-X). Puffin Books.

Bailey, Carolyn Sherwin (1875-1961) & Lewis, Clara M., eds.
--Favorite Stories for the Children's Hour. Rutherford, Bonnie & Rutherford, Bill, illus. Lewis, Claudia LC 65-15195. 384 p. illus. 22 cm. 1965. (ISBN 0-448-40083-9). Platt & Munk.
--For the Children's Hour. Breck, G. William, illus. LC 73-20186. (Illus.). 336 p. 18cm. 1974. Gale Research Co.
--For the Children's Hour. Breck, G. William, illus. LC 6-21388. 336 p. illus., 8 pl. 21 cm. 1906. M. Bradley Company.

Bailey, Carolyn Sherwin (1875-1961) & Szekeres, Cyndy (1933-)
--A Christmas Party: Poem. LC 75-2543. (Illus.). 26 p. 1975. (ISBN 0-394-83094-6). (ISBN 0-394-93094-0). Pantheon.

Bailey, Charles W., jt. auth. see Knebel, Fletcher.

Bailey, Charles William, et al. (1864-)
--The Quest of The Golden Fleece and other plays from epic Poetry. 1929. Thomas Nelson & Sons.

Bailey, Edith
--What a Wonderful World. Boyer, Irv, illus. 87p. illus. 24cm. 1955. Creative Enterprises.

Bailey, Esther
--A House for James. LC 65-23307. 17 p. illus. 23 cm. 1965. Beacon Press.
--When Brucie Came to Play And Other Stories. LC 67-24898. 72p. illus. 24cm. (ps). 1967. (ISBN 0-8070-1916-X). Beacon.
--Won't You Miss Me?. LC 65-23306. 18 p. illus. 23 cm. 1965. Beacon Press.

Bailey, Faith Coxe
--Tales for Teens. 128p. 1955. Moody.
--Young Rebel in Bristol. 159p. 1958. Moody Press.

Bailey, Flora L
--Between the Four Mountains. Ray, Ralph (1920-1952), illus. LC 49-115960. 197 p. 22 cm. 1949. Macmillan.
--Summer at Yellow Singer's. Ray, Ralph (1920-1952), illus. LC 48-7187. 199 p. illus. 22 cm. 1948. Macmillan Co.

Bailey, Gertrude B.
--Two Stories for Little Folk: I Love That School Bus & Guess What Flew in the Window. (gr. k-4). 1977. (ISBN 0-682-48684-1). Exposition.

Bailey, Guy Andrew, jt. auth. see Carpenter, Harry Allen.

Bailey, H. C.
--The Best of Mr. Fortune Stories. N.D. Pocket Bks. Inc.
--Colonel Greatheart. Ralph, Lester, illus. N.D. Bobbs-Merrill Co.

Bailey, H. W., et al. (1919-)
--Danger on the Alaskan Trail: Plus the Mysterious Camel of India & the Israeli Oil Well Mystery. LC 77-75906. 117p. (gr. 3-7). 1977. (ISBN 0-88207-478-4). Victor Bks.

Bailey, H. W. (1919-)
--Jim Kent and the Air Bandits. LC 54-44363. 80p. 21cm. 1954. Scripture Press.
--Jim Kent's Dangerous Mission: Alaskan Dogtrain Stories from the Land of Ice and Snow. LC 54-44362. 77p. illus. 21cm. 1954. Scripture Press.

Bailey, James M.
--Life in Danbury. New ed. 1874. Henry L. Shepard & Co.

Bailey, Jane Horton (1916-)
--The Sea Otter Struggle. (Illus.). (gr. 4 up). 1979. (ISBN 0-9602484-1-2). El Moro.

Bailey, Janey C.
--The Wooden Bicycle. Francis, R. D., illus. LC 65-6412. 21cm. 47p. 1965. Vantage Press.

Bailey, Jean (1917-)
--Cherokee Bill, Oklahoma Pacer. Crowell, Pers (1910-), illus. LC 52-11646. (Illus.). 190 p. 22cm. 1952. Abingdon-Cokesbury Press.
--Cherokee Bill, Oklahoma Pacer. Crowell, Pers (1910-), illus. LC 70-112359. (Illus.). 190 p. 22cm. (Merit books). 1970, c.1952. Houghton Mifflin.
--Rod's Dog. Quinn, Sidney, illus. LC 54-3332. 191p. illus. 22cm. 1954. Abingdon Press.

Bailey, Jean (1917-) & Lamb, Elizabeth Searle (1917-)
--The Pelican Tree, and Other Panama Adventures. Beaudry, Jeanne Stauffer, illus. LC 54-2425. 95p. illus. 25cm. 1953. North River Press.

Bailey, Joseph A., jt. auth. see Stone, Jon.

Bailey, Margery (1891-)
--The Little Man with One Shoe. Preston, Alice Bolam (1889-), illus. N.D. Little Brown & Co.
--The Little Man with One Shoe: This Book Concerns Him, the Six Tales He Told Me and the Six Songs of Simple Pattern with Which I Had to Bargain for the Same. LC 21-130135. 5 p. l., 3-227, 1 p. front. illus. (incl. music) 21 cm. 1921. Little, Brown, and Company.
--Seven Peas in the Pod. Preston, Alice Bolam (1889-), illus. N.D. Little Brown & Co.
--Whistle for Good Fortune: In Which It Is Shown How Six from Six Makes Six and One to Carry, with Other Riddles Here and There Along the Way. Preston, Alice Bolam (1889-), illus. LC 40-3669. 6 p. l., 3-237 p. incl. front., illus., plates. 21 cm. 1940. Little, Brown and Company.

Bailey, Martin J.
--Windbreaks. 128p. 1959. Friendship Press.

Bailey, Matilda, pseud., see Radford, Ruby Lorraine.

Bailey, Pearl (1918-)
--Duey's Tale. LC 74-22278. (Illus.). 59 p. 21cm. 1975. (ISBN 0-15-126576-3). Harcourt Brace Jovanovich. **Award: (CSKA).**

Bailey, Peter
--Forts & Castles. LC 80-52515. (Starters Ser.). N.D. (ISBN 0-382-06490-9). Silver.

Bailey, Ralph Edgar (1893-)
--Argosies of Empire: The Adventures of Great Sea Captains of Trade, 1200 B.C.-1500 A.D. MacDonald, James, illus. LC 47-31328. 263 p. illus., map. 21 cm. 1947. E. P. Dutton.
--Sea Hawks of Empire: Eastward to the Indies for Trade and Treasure, 1500-1700. MacDonald, James, illus. LC 48-4524. 256 p. illus. 21 cm. 1948. E. P. Dutton.
--Tim's Fight for the Valley. 1st ed. LC 51-11427. 246 p. front. 21 cm. 1951. Dutton.
--Tony Sees It Through. 1st ed. LC 53-606632. 224p. illus. 22cm. 1953. Dutton.
--Wagons Westward: The Story of Alexander Majors. (Illus.). 1969. (ISBN 0-688-21423-1). William Morrow and Company.

Bailey, Roy Rutherford
--Sure Pop and the Safety Scouts. LC 15-17319. vi, 129 p. illus. (part col.) 19 cm. 1915. World Book Company.

Bailey, Temple
--Contrary Mary. Carson, Charles S., illus. 1914. Penn Pub. Co.
--Judy. N.D. Grosset & Dunlap.
--Judy. Kennedy, J. W. Ferguson, illus. LC 7-30439. viii p., 1 l., 317 p. front., 5 pl. 19 cm. 1907. Little, Brown, and Company.
--Judy. Pilsbry, Elizabeth, illus. LC 23-141114. viii p., 1 l., 317 p. frotn., plates. 19 cm. 1923. The Penn Publishing Company.
--So This Is Christmas? And Other Christmas Stories. LC 31-29023. 188 p. col. front., illus. 22 cm. 1931. The Penn Publishing Company.
--The Tin Soldier. 1921. Grosset & Dunlap.

Bailey, Una Locke, pseud., see Bailey, Urania Locke.

Bailey, Urania Locke see Bailey, Una Locke, pseud.

Bailey, Urania Locke, et al. (1820-1882)
--Rose and Millie Library: Containg "Mabel Livingstone," "Dr. Plassid's Patients," "Rose and Millie" and "The Robinsons". Bailey, Una Locke, pseud, 4 vols. N.D. Set. D. Lothrop & Co.

Bailey, Urania Locke (1820-1882)
--Dr. Plassid's Patients. Bailey, Una Locke, pseud. (Fern Glen Ser.). N.D. D. Lothrop Co.

Bailey, Urania Locke (1820-1882) & Yorke, Zaida
--The Fourth of July in New England and the Fifth of November in Old England. Bailey, Una Locke, pseud. LC 42-35046. 159 p. incl. front., plates. 16 1/2 cm. (High days and holidays in old England and New England). c.1870. Carlton & Lanahan.

Bain, tr. see Kunos, Ignacz.

Bain, Archibald Watson, ed.
--A Poetry Book for Children. LC 28-24763. xiv, 1, 103, 1 p. 20 cm. 1927. The University Press.

Bain, Robert Nisbet (1854-1909), ed.
--Cossack Fairy Tales and Folk-Tales. Mitchell, E. W., illus. LC 34-326908. 1 p. l., viii, 356 p. front., illus., pl. 19 cm. 1894. A. L. Burt Company.
--Cossack Fairy Tales and Folk-Tales. Mitchell, E. W., illus. LC 44-316451. viii (i.e. x), 356 p. front., illus., plates. 19 cm. N.D. A. L. Burt.
--Cossack Fairy Tales and Folk-Tales. Mitchell, E. W., illus. LC 76-9882. (Illus.). viii, 356 p., 24 leaves of plates. 20cm. (Children's literature reprint series). 1976. (ISBN 0-8486-0200-5). Core Collection Books.
--Cossack Fairy Tales and Folk Tales. Nisbet, Noel Laura (1887-), illus. LC 74-22131. (Illus.). 287 p. 25cm. 1975. (ISBN 0-527-04404-0). Kraus Reprint Co.
--Russian Fairy Tales. (The Fairy Library). N.D. A. L. Burt Co.
--Russian Fairy Tales. (Illus.). N.D. Charles Sscribner's Sons.
--Russian Fairy Tales. (Fairy Ser.). N.D. Frederick A. Stokes.
--Turkish Fairy Tales. (The Fairy Library). N.D. A. L. Burt Co.
--Turkish Fairy Tales and Folk Tales. 275p. N.D. (ISBN 0-486-22344-2). Dover Books.

Baines, Minnie Willis (1845-)
--His Cousin the Doctor, 1 of 25 vols. 198p. (Selected Bks for Sunday School: The/Clifton Library). N.D. Set. Methodist Bk Concern.

Baker, Elmer Le Roy

--Jack Stanton's Christmas. LC 27-18542. 54 p. 21 cm. c.1927. The Christopher Publishing House.

Baker, Elsa Gorham

--The Christmas Package And Other Stories for Children. LC 29-11674. 96 p. 18 cm. c.1929. Augustana Book Concern.

--Jerry: Contains: Jerry, Willing Workers, and The Stonewall Corner Garden. 96p. N.D. Augustana Book Concern.

--Tony, And Other Stories for Juniors. LC 42-221685. 94 p. 18 cm. 1942. The Wartburg Press.

Baker, Emilie Kip, ed.

--The Children's First-Third Book of Poetry. LC 15-7788. 3 v. illus. 19 cm. c.1915. American Book Company.

--Out of the Northland: Stories from the Northern Myths. ix, 165 p. front. 15 cm. (Macmillan's pocket American and English classics). 1904. The Macmillan Company.

--Stories from Northern Myths. LC 14-16569. ix, 276 p. plates. 20 cm. 1914. The Macmillan Company.

--Stories of Old Greece and Rome. LC 13-18733. (Illus.). xii p., 1 l., 382 p. front., plates. 1913. The Macmillan Company.

Baker, Ethel Mary (1895-)

--The Shadow of Half-Moon Pass. Arrows, Russell, illus. LC 38-6008. 5 p. l., 13-213, 1 p. incl. illus., plates. 21 cm. c.1936. Suttonhouse, Ltd.

--Tower House. LC 44-571921. 298 p. col. front., illus. 22 cm. 1944. The Caxton Printers, Ltd.

Baker, Etta Iva Anthony, Mrs.

--The Captain of the "S. I. G.'s,". Burgess, H., illus. LC 11-11821. x p. 2 l., 323 p. incl. front. plates 20 cm. (Staten Island giants series). 1911. Little, Brown, and Company.

--Fairmount Girls in School and Camp. Tousey, Maud, illus. LC 11-28743. 6 p. l., 371 p. front., plates. 20 cm. (Her The Fairmount girls series). 1911. Little, Brown, and Company.

--Fairmount's Quartette. Relyea, Charles M., illus. LC 14-170966. viii p., 3 l., 358 p., 1 l. front., plates. 20 cm. (Her The Fairmount girls series). 1914. Little, Brown, and Company.

--Frolics at Fairmount. Tousey, Maud, illus. LC 10-21598. xiv p., 408 p. front., 3 pl. 20 cm. (Fairmount girls series). 1910. Little, Brown, and Company.

--The Girls of Fairmount. Tousey, Maud, illus. LC 9-25809. 6 p. l., 295 p. front., 3 pl. 20 cm. 1909. Little, Brown, and Company.

--The Youngsters of Centerville. Day, Francis, illus. LC 7-30441. ix, 340 p. front., 3 pl. 20 cm. 1907. H. Holt and Company.

Baker, Eugene H

--About a Bicycle for Linda. Herrington, Roger, illus. LC 68-31400. (Illus.). 46 p. 22cm. (Melmont look, read, learn). 1968. Melmont Publishers.

--At the Scene of the Crime. (Illus.). 32p. (Junior Detective Bks.). (gr. 2-6). 1980. (ISBN 0-516-06470-3). Childrens.

--At the Scene of the Crime. Axeman, Lois, illus. LC 80-14091. (Illus.). 32p. (Junior Detective Ser.). (gr. 2-5). 1980. (ISBN 0-89565-151-3). Childs World.

--I Want to Be a Bank Teller. Temple, James G., illus. LC 75-178491. (Illus.). 31 p. 25cm. 1972. (ISBN 0-516-01788-8). Childrens Press.

--I Want to Be a Basketball Player. Wahl, Richard (1939-), illus. LC 70-182385. (Illus.). 31 p. 25cm. 1972. (ISBN 0-516-01789-6). Childrens Press.

--I Want to Be a Beauty Operator. Morey, Jean W., illus. LC 77-79577. (Illus.). 30 p. 25cm. 1969. Childrens Press.

--I Want to Be a Forester. Wiskur, Darrell D., illus. LC 70-79578. (Illus.). 30 p. 25cm. 1969. Childrens Press.

--I Want to Be a Service Station Attendant. Fickle, Richard, illus. LC 70-178495. (Illus.). 31 p. 25cm. 1972. (ISBN 0-516-01797-7). Childrens Press.

--I Want to Be a Taxi Driver. O'Malley, Robert, illus. LC 73-79576. (Illus.). 32 p. 25cm. 1969. Childrens Press.

--I Want to Be a Waitress. Mlodock, Richard, illus. LC 72-178493. (Illus.). 32 p. 1972. Childrens Press.

--I Want to Be a Weatherman. Wiskur, Darrell D., illus. LC 76-178494. (Illus.). 31 p. 25cm. 1972. (ISBN 0-516-01799-3). Childrens Press.

--I Want to Be an Architect. Palm, Felix, illus. LC 70-79575. (Illus.). 32 p. 25cm. 1969. Childrens Press.

--In the Detective's Lab. LC 80-17787. (Illus.). 32p. (Junior Detective Bks.). (gr. 2-6). 1980. (ISBN 0-516-06471-1). Childrens.

--In the Detective's Lab. Axeman, Linda, illus. LC 80-17787. (Illus.). 32p. (The Junior Detective Ser.). (gr. 2-5). 1980. (ISBN 0-89565-154-8). Childs World.

--Master of Disguise. LC 80-11297. (Illus.). 32p. (Junior Detective Bks.). (gr. 2-6). 1980. (ISBN 0-516-06472-X). Childrens.

--Master of Disguise. Axeman, Lois, illus. LC 80-11297. (Illus.). 32p. (The Junior Detective Ser.). (gr. 2-5). 1980. (ISBN 0-89565-149-1). Childs World.

--Secret Writing-Codes & Messages. Axeman, Lois, illus. LC 80-11416. (Illus.). 32p. (The Junior Detective Ser.). (gr. 2-5). 1980. (ISBN 0-89565-150-5). Childs World.

--Shadowing the Suspect. LC 80-13982. (Illus.). 32p. (Junior Detective Bks.). (gr. 2-6). 1980. (ISBN 0-516-06474-6). Childrens.

--What's Right?. Buerger, Jane, ed. LC 80-17552. (Illus.). 112p. 1980. (ISBN 0-89565-175-0). Standard Pub.

--Your Manners Are Showing. Buerger, Jane, ed. (Illus.). 112p. 1980. (ISBN 0-89565-178-5). Standard Pub.

Baker, Eugene H. & Downing, Joan

--Workers Long Ago. Dumler, Doris, illus. LC 68-9775. (Illus.). 32p. (Easy Reading Picture Story Books Series). Orig. Title: Busy People. (gr. 1-5). 1968. (ISBN 0-516-03669-6). Childrens Press.

Baker, Franklin T., ed. see Dickens, Charles John Huffam.

Baker, Franklin T. & Jones, Richard, eds.

--Addison and Steele's The Sir Roger de Coverley Papers. N.D. D. Appleton-Century, Inc.

Baker, Fred, et al.

--Galactic Adventures. Skilleter, Andrew, et al., illus. LC 80-80321. (Illus.). 192p. 1st U.S. edition. (gr. 3-7). 1980. (ISBN 0-528-82374-4). Rand.

Baker, G. Cornelius, ed.

--When Men Were Boys: A Collection of Poetry About Boys, Written by Noted Poets. LC 26-15739. xviii, 211 p. front., plates. 20 cm. 1926. Association Press.

Baker, George Edward (1902-)

--Lionheart: The Story of Richard Coeur-De-Lion. LC 56-5025. 151p. illus. 21cm. 1955. Roy Publishers.

--The New Sad Sack. 1946. Simon and Schuster.

--Press Of A Switch. N.D. Transatlantic Arts.

Baker, George Melville see Uno, pseud.

Baker, George Melville (1832-1890)

--Amateur Dramas, 1 of 3. (Amateur Drama Ser.). N.D. Colby & Rich.

--Baby Ballads. Pletsch, Oscar (1830-1888), illus. LC 15-1592. 80 p. incl. front., illus. 18 cm. 1877. Lee and Shepard.

--Running to Waste: The Story of a Tomboy. LC 2-22403. 245 p. front., plates. 19 cm. (On cover: American girl's series. v. 32). 1902. Lee and Shepard.

--Running to Waste: The Story of a Tomboy. (The Maidenhood Ser.). N.D. Lee & Shepard.

Baker, Harriette Newell Woods see Leslie, Madeline, pseud.

Baker, Harriette Newell Woods, Mrs. (1815-1893)

--Annie and the Bears. Leslie, Madeline, pseud, 1 of 25 vols. (Illus.). (New Primary Lib.: No. 15). N.D. Set. A. I. Bradley & Co.'s Pubs.

--Annie and the Bears. Leslie, Madeline, pseud, 1 of 6. (Daisy Dale Library). N.D. Andrew F. Graves.

--Annie and the Bears. Leslie, Madeline, pseud. N.D. Bradley & Woodruff.

--Art and Artlessness. Leslie, Madeline, pseud. LC 74-151668. (Illus.). 256 p. 18cm. (Her Little Agnes' library). (Mrs. Leslie's juvenile series.). 1864. Lee and Shepard.

--Art and Artlessness. Leslie, Madeline, pseud. (Illus.). 256p. (Little Agnes' Library For Girls). N.D. Ward & Drummond.

--The Bear. Leslie, Madeline, pseud. (Georgey's Menagerie). N.D. Andrew F. Graves.

--The Bear. Leslie, Madeline, pseud, 1 of 6 Vols. (Illus.). (Georgey's Menagerie). N.D. Set. Thomas Y. Crowell & Co.

--Behind the Curtain: Lelinau the Indian Girl. Leslie, Madeline, pseud. (Golden Spring Ser.). N.D. Andrew F. Graves.

--Bertie and the Carpenters. Leslie, Madeline, pseud. (Woodlawn Ser.). N.D. Henry A. Young.

--Bertie and the Carpenters: Or, The Way to Be Happy. Leslie, Madeline, pseud. LC 43-27309. 4 p. l., vii-ix, 11-163 p. front., 1 illus., pl. 15 1/2 cm. (Her The Woodlawn series. II). c.1868. Woolworth, Ainsworth & Company.

--Bertie and the Gardeners. Leslie, Madeline, pseud. (Woodlawn Ser.). N.D. Henry A. Young.

--Bertie and the Masons. Leslie, Madeline, pseud. (Woodlawn Ser.). N.D. Henry A. Young.

--Bertie and the Masons: Or, The Way to Be Happy. Leslie, Madeline, pseud. LC 43-273103. 4 p. l., vii-ix, 11-161 p. front., 1 illus. pl. 15 1/2 cm. (Her The Woodlawn series. III). c.1868. Woolworth, Ainsworth & Company.

--Bertie and the Painters. Leslie, Madeline, pseud. (Woodlawn Ser.). N.D. Henry A. Young.

--Bertie and the Painters: Or, The Way to Be Happy. Leslie, Madeline, pseud. LC 43-27311. 2 p. l., 3-5, vii-ix, 11-161, p. front., 1 illus. pl. 15 1/2 cm. (Her The Woodlawn series. v). c.1868. A. S. Barnes & Company.

--Bertie and the Plumbers. Leslie, Madeline, pseud. (Woodlawn Ser.). N.D. Henry A. Young.

--Bertie's Home. Leslie, Madeline, pseud. (Woodlawn Ser.). N.D. Henry A. Young.

--Bessie and the Squirrels. Leslie, Madeline, pseud. (Corwin's Nest Ser.). N.D. Andrew F. Graves.

--Birthday Party. Leslie, Madeline, pseud. (Corwin's Nest Ser.). N.D. Andrew F. Graves.

--The Bound Boy. Leslie, Madeline, pseud, 1 of 36 vols. (Illus.). (Primary Lib.: No. 8). N.D. Set. A. I. Bradley & Co.'s Pubs.

--The Bound Boy. Leslie, Madeline, pseud. (The Do Good Library). N.D. Henry Hoyt.

--The Bound Girl. Leslie, Madeline, pseud. (The Do Good Library). N.D. Henry Hoyt.

--Breach of Trust. Leslie, Madeline, pseud. (Golden Spring Ser.). N.D. Andrew F. Graves.

--Breach of Trust. Leslie, Madeline, pseud. N.D. D. Lothrop Co.

--The Camel. Leslie, Madeline, pseud. (Georgey's Menagerie). N.D. Andrew F. Graves.

--The Camel. Leslie, Madeline, pseud, 1 of 6 Vols. (Georgey's Menagerie). N.D. Set. Thomas Y. Crowell & Co.

--Children at Play. Leslie, Madeline, pseud. (Corwin's Nest Ser.). N.D. Andrew F. Graves.

--Cora and the Doctor: Or, The Revelations of a Physician's Wife. Leslie, Madeline, pseud. (Home Life Ser.). N.D. Colby and Rich.

--The Courtesies of Wedded Life. Leslie, Madeline, pseud. (Home Life Ser.). N.D. Colby and Rich.

--Daisy Dale Library: Containing: Little Daisy's Letter, Papa's Present, Ida and the Beggars, Annie and the Bears, The New Society, The Twins. Leslie, Madeline, pseud. (Illus.). 382p. N.D. Ira Bradley & Co's.

--The Deer. Leslie, Madeline, pseud. (Georgey's Menagerie). N.D. Andrew F. Graves.

--The Deer. Leslie, Madeline, pseud, 1 of 6 Vols. (Illus.). (Georgey's Menagerie). N.D. Set. Thomas Y. Crowell & Co.

--Earning and Spending: Or, The Two Homes. Leslie, Madeline, pseud, 1 of 5. (The Leslie Stories). N.D. Henry A. Young.

--The Elephant. Leslie, Madeline, pseud. (Georgey's Menagerie). N.D. Andrew F. Graves.

--The Elephant. Leslie, Madeline, pseud, 1 of 6 Vols. (Illus.). (Georgey's Menagerie). N.D. Set. Thomas Y. Crowell & Co.

--Every Day Duties. Leslie, Madeline, pseud. (Select Library). N.D. Henry Hoyt.

--Georgey's Menagerie. Leslie, Madeline, pseud, 6 Vols. (Illus.). N.D. Thomas Y. Crowell & Co.

--The Governer's Garden. Leslie, Madeline, pseud. N.D. D. Lothrop Co.

--Helps and Hindrances at the Cross. Leslie, Madeline, pseud. (Golden Spring Ser.). N.D. Andrew F. Graves.

--The Household Angel in Disguise. Leslie, Madeline, pseud. (Home Life Ser.). N.D. Colby and Rich.

--Howard and His Teacher. Leslie, Madeline, pseud, 1 of 4 Vols. (Illus.). (Play and Study Series for Boys and Girls). N.D. Lee & Shepard.

--Howard and His Teacher. Leslie, Madeline, pseud. (Illus.). 244p. (Play and Study For Boys and Girls). N.D. Ward & Drummond.

--Ida and the Beggar. Leslie, Madeline, pseud, 1 of 6 Vols. (Daisy Dale Library). N.D. Andrew F. Graves.

--Ida and the Beggar. Leslie, Madeline, pseud. (Illus.). 63p. N.D. Ira Bradley & Co's.

--I'll Try. Leslie, Madeline, pseud. N.D. Lee & Shepard.

--I'll Try. Leslie, Madeline, pseud. (Illus.). 232p. (Little Agnes' Library For Girls). N.D. Ward & Drummond.

--Ingleside. Leslie, Madeline, pseud, 1 of 6 vols. (Leslie Library). N.D. Set. Bradley & Woodruff.

--Jack and the Chimney-Sweeper. Leslie, Madeline, pseud, 1 of 4 Vols. (Illus.). 245p. (Play and Study For Boys and Girls). N.D. Ward & Drummond.

--Jamie and His Pony. Leslie, Madeline, pseud. (Corwin's Nest Ser.). N.D. Andrew F. Graves.

--Leslie Stories for Boys. Leslie, Madeline, pseud, 4 Vols. 1884. A Sumner & Co.

--Light and Shade. Leslie, Madeline, pseud. (Select Library). N.D. Henry Hoyt.

--The Lion. Leslie, Madeline, pseud. (Georgey's Menagerie). N.D. Andrew F. Graves.

--The Lion. Leslie, Madeline, pseud, 1 of 6 Vols. (Illus.). (Georgey's Menagerie). N.D. Set. Thomas Y. Crowell & Co.

--Little Agnes. Leslie, Madeline, pseud. N.D. Lee & Shepard.

--Little Agnes. Leslie, Madeline, pseud. (Illus.). 271p. (Little Agnes' Library For Girls). N.D. Ward & Drummond.

--Little Daisy's Letter. Leslie, Madeline, pseud, 1 of 25 Vols. (Illus.). (New Primary Lib.: No. 15). N.D. Set. A. I. Bradey & Co.'s Pubs.

--Little Daisy's Letter. Leslie, Madeline, pseud, 1 of 6 Vols. (Daisy Dale Library). N.D. Andrew F. Graves.

--Little Daisy's Letter. Leslie, Madeline, pseud. N.D. Bradley & Woodruff.

--Little Frankie and His Cousins. Leslie, Madeline, pseud. (The Little Frankie Ser.). N.D. Henry L. Shepard & Co.

--Little Frankie and His Father. Leslie, Madeline, pseud. (The Little Frankie Ser.). N.D. Henry L. Shepard & Co.

--Little Frankie and His Mother. Leslie, Madeline, pseud. (The Little Frankie Ser.). N.D. Henry L. Shepard & Co.

--Little Frankie at His Plays. Leslie, Madeline, pseud. (The Little Frankie Ser.). N.D. Henry L. Shepard & Co.

--Little Frankie at School. Leslie, Madeline, pseud. (The Little Frankie Ser.). N.D. Henry L. Shepard & Co.

--Little Frankie on a Journey. Leslie, Madeline, pseud. LC 38-12746. 1 p. l., 7-104 p. front, 1 illus. 15 cm. (Her Little Frankie series). 1860. Crosby and Nichols.

--Little Frankie on a Journey. Leslie, Madeline, pseud. (The Little Frankie Ser.). N.D. Henry L. Shepard & Co.

--Little Frankie Stories. Leslie, Madeline, pseud. N.D. Set. Nichols & Hall.

--Little Rag-Pickers. Leslie, Madeline, pseud. (The Do Good Library). N.D. Henry Hoyt.

--The Little Rag-Pickers. Leslie, Madeline, pseud. (Illus.). 176p. N.D. Ira Bradley & Co's.

--Little Robins' Friends. Leslie, Madeline, pseud. (The Robin Redbreast Ser.). N.D. Henry L. Shepard & Co.

--Little Robins in the Nest. Leslie, Madeline, pseud. (The Robin Redbreast Ser.). N.D. Henry L. Shepard & Co.

--Little Robins in Trouble. Leslie, Madeline, pseud. (The Robin Redbreast Ser.). N.D. Henry L. Shepard & Co.

--Little Robins Learning to Fly. Leslie, Madeline, pseud. (The Robin Redbreast Ser.). N.D. Henry L. Shepard & Co.

--Little Robins' Love One to Another. Leslie, Madeline, pseud. LC 68-52400. 104 p. illus. 16 cm. (mrs. leslie's books for little children. (Robin Redbreast Series). 1860. Crosby and Nichols.

--Little Robins' Love One to Another. Leslie, Madeline, pseud. (The Robin Redbreast Ser.). N.D. Henry L. Shepard & Co.

--Live and Learn. Leslie, Madeline, pseud. (Fern Glen Ser.). N.D. D. Lothrop Co.

--Minnie and Her Pets. Leslie, Madeline, pseud, 1 of 6 vols. (Illus.). 1882. Lee & Shepard.

--Minnie's Pet Cat. Leslie, Madeline, pseud. (Minnie and Her Pets). N.D. Colby and Rich.

--Minnie's Pet Cat. Leslie, Madeline, pseud, 1 of 6 vols. (Illus.). (Minnie and Her Pets Ser.). 1882. Lee & Shepard.

--Minnie's Pet Cat. Leslie, Madeline, pseud. (Illus.). 144p. (Minnie and Her Pets). N.D. Ward & Drummond.

--Minnie's Pet Dog. Leslie, Madeline, pseud. (Minnie and Her Pets). N.D. Colby and Rich.

--Minnie's Pet Dog. Leslie, Madeline, pseud, 1 of 6 vols. (Illus.). (Minnie and Her Pets Ser.). 1882. Lee & Shepard.

--Minnie's Pet Dog. Leslie, Madeline, pseud. (Illus.). 152p. (Minnie and Her Pets). N.D. Ward & Drummond.

--Minnie's Pet Lamb. Leslie, Madeline, pseud. (Minnie and Her Pets). N.D. Colby and Rich.

--Minnie's Pet Lamb. Leslie, Madeline, pseud, 1 of 6 vols. (Illus.). (Minnie and Her Pets Ser.). 1882. Lee & Shepard.

--Minnie's Pet Lamb. Leslie, Madeline, pseud. (Illus.). 168p. (Minnie and Her Pets). N.D. Ward & Drummond.

--Minnie's Pet Monkey. Leslie, Madeline, pseud. (Minnie and Her Pets). N.D. Colby and Rich.

--Minnie's Pet Monkey. Leslie, Madeline, pseud, 1 of 6 vols. (Minnie and Her Pets Ser.). 1882. Lee & Shepard.

--Minnie's Pet Monkey. Leslie, Madeline, pseud. (Illus.). 152p. (Minnie and Her Pets). N.D. Ward & Drummond.

--Minnie's Pet Parrot. Leslie, Madeline, pseud. (Minnie and Her Pets). N.D. Colby and Rich.

--Minnie's Pet Parrot. Leslie, Madeline, pseud, 1 of 6 vols. (Illus.). (Minnie and Her Pets Ser.). 1882. Lee & Shepard.

--Minnie's Pet Parrot. Leslie, Madeline, pseud, 6 Vols. (Illus.). 144p. (Minnie and Her Pets). N.D. Ward & Drummond.

--Minnie's Pet Pony. Leslie, Madeline, pseud. (Minnie and Her Pets). N.D. Colby and Rich.

--Minnie's Pet Pony. Leslie, Madeline, pseud. (Minnie and Her Pets Ser.). N.D. Lee & Shepard.

--Minnie's Pet Pony. Leslie, Madeline, pseud. (Illus.). 160p. (Minnie and Her Pets). N.D. Ward & Drummond.

--The Motherless Children. Leslie, Madeline, pseud, 1 of 4. (Illus.). (Play and Study Series for Boys and Girls). N.D. Lee & Shepard.

Baker, Nina Brown, Mrs. (1888-1957)
--Amerigo Vespucci. 1st ed. Valentino, Paul, illus. LC 56-5272. 143p. illus. 22cm. 1956. Knopf.
--A Boy for a Man's Job: The Story of the Founding of St. Louis. 1st ed. Cortese, Edward F., illus. LC 52-5484. 179 p. illus. 22 cm. (Winston adventure books). 1952. Winston.
--The Chinese Riddle: A Mystery Story for Girls. Gretter, J. Clemens, illus. LC 32-23428. 222 p. incl. front., plates. 21 cm. c.1932. Lothrop, Lee & Shepard Co.
--The Cinderella Secret. LC 38-18758. 5 p. l., 13-211 p. 21 cm. 1938. Lothrop, Lee & Shepard Company.
--Henry Hudson. 1st ed. Fulton, George, illus. LC 58-5356. 142p. illus. 22cm. 1958. Knopf.
--Inca Gold. LC 38-34555. 320 p. incl. front. 21 cm. c.1938. W. A. Wilde Company.
--Inca Gold. N.D. Wilcox & Follett Co.
--Juan Ponce De Leon. 1st ed. Doremus, Robert (1913-), illus. LC 57-7082. 145p. illus. 21cm. 1957. Knopf.
--The Luck of the Salabars. LC 37-24575. 319 p. front. 21 cm. c.1937. W. A. Wilde Company.
--Luck of the Salabars. N.D. Wilcox & Follett Co.
--Mystery at Four Chimneys. King, Ruth, illus. LC 39-24729. 269 p. front., illus. 21 cm. 1939. Lothrop, Lee & Shepard Company.
--Nelly Bly. Fulton, George, illus. 1956. Holt, Rineheart and Winston.
--The Ranee's Ruby. Best, Allena Champlin, Mrs. (1892-1974), illus. Berry, Erick, pseud. LC 35-196874. xi, 225 p. incl. front., plates. 21 cm. 1935. Lothrop, Lee and Shepard Company.
--The Secret of Hallam House: A Mystery Story for Girls. Buttera, F. J., illus. LC 31-23962. 214 p. front., illus., plates. 21 cm. c.1931. Lothrop, Lee & Shepard Co.
--The Story of Abraham Lincoln. Baumgartner, Warren, illus. LC 52-11073. 176 p. illus. 22 cm. (Signature books). 1952. Grosset & Dunlap.
--The Story of Christopher Columbus. Hendrickson, David (1896-), illus. LC 52-11066. 179 p. illus. 22 cm. (Signature books). 1952. Grosset & Dunlap.

Baker, Olaf
--Bengey and the Beast. Dowling, Victor J. (1906-), illus. LC 47-2100. vi, 2, 243 p. illus. 21 cm. 1947. Dodd, Mead & Company.
--Buffalo Barty. Schuyler, Remington (1884-1955), illus. 21cm. 267p. 1932. Dodd, Mead & Co.
--Dusty Star. Bransom, Paul (1885-), illus. LC 22-21352. 5 p. l., 3-302 p. front., plates. 21 cm. 1922. Dodd, Mead and Company.
--Panther Magic. Wiese, Kurt (1887-1974), illus. LC 28-27613. 4 p. l., 312 p. col. front., illus., col. plates. 21 cm. 1928. Dodd, Mead & Company.
--Peter in Process. LC 25-19830. 4 p. l., 300 p. 20 cm. 1925. Dodd, Mead and Company.
--Shasta and Gimmery. Savitt, Sam (1917-), illus. LC 58-13209. 210p. illus. 21cm. 1958. Dodd, Mead.
--Shasta of the Wolves. Bull, Charles Livingston (1874-1932), illus. 1919. Dodd Mead & Co.
--Thunder Boy. Bransom, Paul (1885-), illus. LC 24-26941. 6 p. l., 3-288 p. front., plates (part double) 21 cm. 1924. Dodd, Mead and Company.
--Where the Buffaloes Begin. Gammell, Stephen, illus. LC 80-23319. (Illus.). 48 p. 26cm. 1981. (ISBN 0-7232-6195-4). F. Warne. **Awards: (NYT); (ALA); (BGH); (RCM).**
--Where the Buffaloes Begin. Gammell, Stephen, illus. LC 85-5682. (Illus.). 44 p. 26cm. 1985, c.1981. (ISBN 0-14-050560-1). Puffin Books.

Baker, P.
--The Wild Bunch at Robbers Roost. (Illus.). 1971. (ISBN 0-200-71782-0). Abelard-Schuman.

Baker, R. Ray
--The Red Brother and Other Indian Stories. LC 27-249528. 7 p. l., 17-155 p. incl. front., illus., plates. 21 cm. c.1927. G. Wahr.

Baker, Rachel Mininberg (1904-1978)
--Americas First Trained Nurse: Linda Richards; Born: July 27, 1841; Died: April 16, 1930. LC 59-7008. 192p. 22cm. 1959. Messner.
--Mr. Turkey Gobbler, and Other Stories. 1st ed. LC 54-13362. 91p. illus. 24cm. 1954. Pageant Press.

Baker, Richard, ed. see Keller, Charles.

Baker, Richard St. Barbe, Dr. (1889-1982)
--Kamiti. Nkrumah, Kwame, frwd. by. 1960. Duell, Sloan and Pearce Pub.

Baker, Robin
--Land Rovers. Bateman, Robert, as told to (Pub. by Constable). (gr. 7-12). 1972 (Starline). Schol Bk Serv.

Baker, Rosalie & Baker, Charles, III, eds.
--Classical Calliope: 1981 Cumulative Edition, Vol. 1. (Illus.). 160p. (Orig.). 1st U.S. edition. (gr. 7-12). 1983. (ISBN 0-9607638-1-3). Cobblestone Pub.
--Classical Calliope: 1982 Cumulative Edition, Vol. 2. (Illus.). 160p. (Orig.). 1st U.S. edition. (gr. 7-12). 1983. (ISBN 0-9607638-2-1). Cobblestone Pub.

Baker, Russell (1925-)
--The Upside-Down Man. Wilson, Gahan (1930-), illus. LC 77-6272. (Illus.). 43 p. 26cm. c.1977. (ISBN 0-07-003356-0). (ISBN 0-07-003357-9). McGraw-Hill.

Baker, St. Barbe Richard, Dr. (1889-1982)
--Kamiti. N.D. E . M. Hale and Co.

Baker, Samuel White, Sir (1821-1893)
--Boys' Adventures: Containing: Eight Years' Wanderings in Ceylon, and Rifle and Hound in Ceylon, 2 vols. (Illus.). N.D. International Book Co.
--Cast Up By the Sea. (The Rugby Ser.). 1905. Set. A L Burt Co.
--Cast Up by the Sea, No. 20. (The Cornell Ser.). N.D. A. L. Burt's Pbs.
--Cast Up By The Sea. N.D. American News Company.
--Cast Up by the Sea. LC 6-6874. (Illus.). 29cm. 61p. (Franklin Square Library: 137). 1880. Harper & Brothers.
--Cast Up By the Sea. LC 16-14094. 15-410. 18cm. (Lovell's Library: No. 206). 1883. J. W. Lovell Company.
--Cast Up By The Sea. (Illus.). (The Junior Library Ser.: Vol. 5). N.D. Rand, McNally & Co.
--Cast Up by the Sea. Huard, illus. N.D. J B Lippincott.
--Cast up by the Sea: A Boy's Story. xxiii, 336 p. 18 cm. (Half-title: Everyman's library, ed. by Ernest Rhys. For young people no. 539). 1911. J. M. Dent & Sons, Ltd.
--Rifle and Hound in Ceylon. (Illus.). (St. Nicholas Books for Boys). N.D. International Book Co.

Baker, Sarah Schoonmaker Tuthill see Aunt Friendly, pseud.

Baker, Sarah Schoonmaker Tuthill, Mrs. (1824-1906)
--Amy and Her Brothers. Aunt Friendly, pseud. 149p. N.D. American Tract Society.
--Aunt Friendly's Nursery Keepsake. Aunt Friendly, pseud, 1 of 9 Vols. (Illus.). (Little Folks' Library Ser.). N.D. Scribner & Welford.
--The Babes in the Basket. Aunt Friendly, pseud. N.D. A. D. F. Randolph.
--Babes in the Basket: Or, Daph and Her Charge. Aunt Friendly, pseud. (Illus.). 1888. Thomas Whittkaker.
--Barton Todd. Aunt Friendly, pseud. N.D. A. D. F. Randolph Co.
--The Blue Flag. Aunt Friendly, pseud. 200p. 1905. American Tract Society.
--Bound Out. Aunt Friendly, pseud. 1859. A. D. F. Randolph.
--Bound Out: Or, Abby at the Farm. Aunt Friendly, pseud. LC 41-40535. 80 p. front. 16 cm. 1859. A. D. F. Randolph.
--Christmas at Sea. Aunt Friendly, pseud, 1 of 6 Vols. (Aunt Friendly Library). N.D. Set. T Whittaker.
--Christmas Eve. Aunt Friendly, pseud, 1 of 6 Vols. (Aunt Friendly Library). N.D. Set. T Whittaker.
--Coming to the Light. Aunt Friendly, pseud. N.D. A. D. F. Randolph.
--Emily And Uncle Hans. Aunt Friendly, pseud. N.D. American Tract Society.
--Fisherman's Boy. Aunt Friendly, pseud. (Illus.). (The Star Lib.). N.D. Set. American Tract Society.
--Hannah's Path. Aunt Friendly, pseud. (Illus.). 118p. 1905. American Tract Society.
--Hatty and Marcus. Aunt Friendly, pseud. (Aunt Friendly's Library). N.D. A. D. F. Randolph.
--Heart and Hand. Aunt Friendly, pseud. N.D. A. D. F. Randolph.
--The Jewish Twins. Aunt Friendly, pseud, 1 of 103 vols. (The Pearl Library: No. 42). 1900. Set. Hurst & Co.
--Kate Darley. Aunt Friendly, pseud. (Aunt Friendly's Library). N.D. A. D. F. Randolph.
--The Little Musicians. Aunt Friendly, pseud. (Aunt Friendly's Library). N.D. A. D. F. Randolph.
--Mary Burns. Aunt Friendly, pseud. N.D. A. D. F. Randolph.
--Meggie of the Pines. Aunt Friendly, pseud. N.D. A. D. F. Randolph.
--Meggie of the Pines. Aunt Friendly, pseud. (Illus.). N.D. Set. Cheap Sunday-School Library.
--Nono, the Golden House. Aunt Friendly, pseud. (Illus.). N.D. Thomas Nelson & Sons.
--Nursery Gift. Aunt Friendly, pseud, 1 of 4 Vols. (Illus.). (Aunt Friendly's Picture Books Ser.: Vol. 3). N.D. Scribner & Welford.
--The Orange Seed. Aunt Friendly, pseud. LC 41-40526. iii, 5-106 p. front. 18 cm. 1859. A. D. F. Randolph.
--Poor Little Joe. Aunt Friendly, pseud. LC 35-28591. 108 p. front. 16 cm. 1869. A. D. F. Randolph & Co.
--The Swedish Twins: A Tale for the Young. Aunt Friendly, pseud. (Illus.). N.D. Thomas Nelson & Sons.
--Timid Lucy. Aunt Friendly, pseud. 3rd ed. Robbett & Edmonds, illus. LC 80-467629. (Illus.). 238, 4 leaves of plates. 16cm. 1852. General Prot. Episcopal Sunday School Union : D. Dana, Jr., Agent.
--Timid Lucy. Aunt Friendly, pseud. Bobbett & Edmonds, illus. LC 80-467630. (Illus.). 238 p., 4 leaves of plates. 18cm. 1851. General Prot. Episcopal Sunday School Union : D. Dana, Jr., Agent.
--Under the Pear Tree. Aunt Friendly, pseud. N.D. A. D. F. Randolph.

Baker, Tim & Heath, Tim
--The Dragons at Marshmouldings. (Illus.). 72p. 1984. (ISBN 0-8052-8196-7, Pub. by Allison & Busby England). Schocken.

Baker, Vern, jt. auth. see Stanford, Donald Kent.

Baker, Virginia see Anna St. John, pseud.

Baker, Virginia (1914-)
--Crusaders on Wheels. LC 39-5778. 92 p. illus. 18 cm. c.1938. The Bible Institute Colportage Association.
--Hope House. Anna St. John, pseud. LC 39-83446. 94 p. incl. front., illus. 18 cm. c.1939. The Bible Institute Colportage Ass'n.
--Tuckers at Gateshead. LC 46-20184. 128 p. incl. front., illus. 19 1/2 cm. 1946. Moody Press.
--Tuckers Turn Out. LC 44-212278. 125 p. incl. front., illus. 19 1/2 cm. 1944. Moody Press.

Baker, Will
--Chip. LC 79-87510. +002. c.1979. (ISBN 0-15-217526-1). Harcourt Brace Jovanovich.

Baker, Willard F.
--Bob Dexter and the Aeroplane Mystery: Or, The Secret of the Jint San. LC 30-13348. 2 p. l., 212 p. front. 20 cm. (His Bob Dexter mystery series). c.1930. Cupple & Leon Company.
--Bob Dexter and the Beacon Beach Mystery: Or, the Wreck of the Sea Hawk. (The Bob Dexter Ser.). N.D. Cupples & Leon Co.
--Bob Dexter and the Club House Mystery: Or, The Missing Golden Eagle. LC 25-11512. 2 p. l., 248 p. col. front., plates 20 cm. (His Bob Dexter mystery series). c.1925. Cupples & Leon Company.
--Bob Dexter and the Radio Mystery: Or, The Secret of the Counterfeiters. LC 33-9286. 2 p. l., 211 p. front. 20 cm. (His Bob Dexter mystery series). c.1933. Cupples & Leon Company.
--Bob Dexter and the Red Auto Mystery: Or, The Secret of the Flying Car. LC 32-13683. 2 p. l., 206 p. front. 20 cm. (His Bob Dexter mystery series). c.1932. Cupples & Leon Company.
--Bob Dexter and the Seaplane Mystery: Or, The Secret of the White Stones. LC 31-14186. 2 p. l., 206 p. front. 20 cm. (His Bob Dexter mystery series). c.1931. Cupples & Leon Company.
--Bob Dexter and the Storm Mountain Mystery: Or, the Secret of the Log Cabin. (The Bob Dexter Ser.). N.D. Cupples & Leon Co.
--The Boy Ranchers Among the Indians: Or, Trailing the Yaquis. (The Boy Rancher Ser.). N.D. Cupples & Leon Co.
--The Boy Ranchers at Spur Creek: Or, Fighting the Sheep Herders. (The Boy Rancher Ser.). N.D. Cupples & Leon Co.
--The Boy Ranchers in Camp: Or, the Water Fight at Diamond X. (The Boy Ranchers Ser.). N.D. Cupples & Leon Company.
--The Boy Ranchers in Death Valley: Or, Diamond X and the Poison Mystery. LC 28-157861. 2 p. l., 210 p. front. 20 cm. (His Boy ranchers series). c.1928. Cupples & Leon Company.
--The Boy Ranchers in Terror Canyon: Or, Diamond X Winning Out. LC 30-16896. 2 p. l., 212 p. front. 20 cm. (His Boy ranches series). c.1930. Cupples & Leon Company.
--The Boy Ranchers in the Desert: Or, Diamond X and the Lost Mine. LC 24-150676. iv. 208 p. front. 20 cm. (His Boy ranchers series). c.1924. Cupples & Leon Company.
--The Boy Ranchers on Roaring River: Diamond X and the Chinese Smugglers. (The Boy Ranchers Ser.). N.D. Cupples & Leon Co.
--The Boy Ranchers on the Trail: Or, The Diamond X After Cattle Rustlers. (The Boy Rancher Ser.). N.D. Cupples & Leon Company.
--The Boy Ranchers: Or, Solving the Mystery at Diamond X. (The Boy Ranchers Ser.). N.D. Cupples & Leon Company.
--Western Stories for Boys, 4 Bks. in 1 Vol. LC 34-6274. 3 p. l., 210 p. 2 l., 206 p., 2 l., 206 p., 2 l., 206 p. front. 22 cm. c.1934. Cupples & Leon Co.

Baker, William Arthur Howard see Ballinger, W. A., pseud.

Baker, Woods
--Little Tora, the Swedish Schoolmistress: And, Other Stories. (Illus.). N.D. Thomas Nelson & Sons.
--The Swedish Foster-Brothers. (Illus.). N.D. Thomas Nelson & Sons.

Bakewell, Mary Ella (1868-)
--True Fairy Stories. LC 2-27246. 152 p. illus. 19 cm. (Eclectic school readings). 1902. American Book Company.

Bakken, Harold (1935-)
--The Special String. LC 81-7333. p. cm. c.1981. (ISBN 0-13-826370-1). Prentice-Hall.

Bala, Nimet
--The Story of Tiny the Snail Hunter. Lyons, Dave, illus. LC 53-841. 21cm. 47p. 1952. Pageant Press, Inc.

Balanchine, George
--The Steadfast Tin Soldier. Caras, Steven, illus. Wentink, Andrew Mark & New York City Ballet LC 81-67059. (Illus.). 77 p. 23cm. c.1981. (ISBN 0-87127-125-7). Dance Horizons.

Balch, Annie G.
--Good Times at Grandpa's. 160p. N.D. Newson & Co.

Balch, Ernest
--Amateur Circus Life. N.D. Macmillan.

Balch, Glenn (1902-)
--The Brave Riders. Keats, Ezra Jack (1916-1983), illus. LC 59-11387. (Illus.). 191 p. 21cm. 1959. Crowell.
--Buck, Wild. Sanderson, Ruth, illus. LC 75-44168. (Illus.). 136 p. 21cm. c.1976. Crowell.
--Buck, Wild. Sanderson, Ruth, illus. LC 75-44168. (Illus.). 21cm. 136p. (gr. 5 up). 1976. (ISBN 0-690-01055-9, TYC-J). Har-Row.
--Christmas Horse. (Illus.). N.D. (ISBN 0-8446-0019-9). Peter Smith Publisher, Inc.
--Christmas Horse. Crowell, Pers (1910-), illus. LC 49-111952. 246 p. illus. 21 cm. 1949. Crowell Co.
--The Flaxy Mare. Bjorklund, Lorence F. (1913-1978), illus. LC 67-6649. (Illus.). 142 p. 21cm. 1967. Crowell.
--Hide-Rack Kidnapped. Mason, George Frederick (1904-), illus. LC 39-25709. 3 p. l., 302 p. double plates. 21 cm. 1933. Thomas Y. Crowell Company.
--Horse in Danger. Ames, Lee Judah (1921-), illus. LC 60-624953. (Illus.). (gr. 5-9). 1960. (ISBN 0-690-40289-9). T Y Crowell.
--Horse of Two Colors. Bjorklund, Lorence F. (1913-1978), illus. LC 69-11079. (Illus.). 170 p. 21cm. 1969. Crowell.
--Indian Fur. Frankenberg, Robert Clinton (1911-), illus. LC 51-6448. 248 p. illus. 21 cm. 1951. Crowell.
--Indian Paint. (gr. 7-9). 1972. (ISBN 0-590-02179-6, Schol Trade Pap). Schol Bk Serv.
--Indian Paint. Hogner, Nils (1893-1970), illus. (Illus.). (gr. 4-6). N.D. (ISBN 0-448-02279-6). G&D.
--Indian Paint, the Story of an Indian Pony. 4 p. l., 244 p. illus. 21 cm. 1942. Thomas Y. Crowell Company.
--Indian Paint: The story of an Indian Pony. Hogner, Nils (1893-1970), illus. 256p (Pub. by T Y Crowell). (gr. 5-9). 1970. (ISBN 0-8152-0503-1, AE-J). Apollo Eds.
--Indian Paint: The Story of an Indian Pony. Hogner, Nils (1893-1970), illus. LC 70-112628. (Illus.). 244 p. 21cm. (Apollo editions, J-503). 1970, c.1942. Crowell.
--Indian Saddle-Up. (Illus.). N.D. (ISBN 0-8446-0018-0). Peter Smith Publisher, Inc.
--Indian Saddle-up. Frankenberg, Robert Clinton (1911-), illus. LC 53-8407. (Illus.). 216 p. 21cm. 1953. Crowell.
--Keeping Horse. Cellini, Joseph (1924-), illus. LC 66-7404. (Illus.). (gr. 4-7). 1966. (ISBN 0-690-47105-X). T Y Crowell.
--Little Hawk and the Free Horses. Keats, Ezra Jack (1916-1983), illus. LC 57-9247. (Illus.). 180 p. 21cm. 1957. Crowell.
--Lost Horse. Crowell, Pers (1910-), illus. LC 50-8507. (Illus.). 246 p. 22cm. 1950. Crowell.
--Lost Horse. Crowell, Pers (1910-), illus. 246 p. illus. 22 cm. 1961. Grosset & Dunlap.
--Midnight Colt. Crowell, Pers (1910-), illus. (Illus.). 208p (Pub. by T Y Crowell). (Junior Bks). (gr. 8-12). 1970. (ISBN 0-8152-0511-2, AE-J). Apollo Eds.
--The Midnight Colt. Crowell, Pers (1910-), illus. LC 52-7857. 194 p. illus. 21 cm. 1952. Crowell.
--The Midnight Colt. Crowell, Pers (1910-), illus. N.D. (ISBN 0-8446-0020-2). Peter Smith Publisher, Inc.
--Riders of the Rio Grande. Elwell, R. Farrington, illus. 300p. N.D. Thomas Y. Crowell Co.
--The Runaways. LC 63-12883. 192 p. 22cm. 1963. Doubleday.
--Spotted Horse. Bjorklund, Lorence F. (1913-1978), illus. LC 61-104841. 176p. illus. c.1961. Crowell.
--Squaw Boy. Valentino, Paul, illus. LC 52-7041. (Illus.). 180 p. 21cm. 1952. Crowell.
--The Stallion King. Paull, Grace A. (1898-), illus. LC 60-6250. (Illus.). 118 p. 23cm. 1960. Crowell.

AUTHOR INDEX BALIAN, LORNA

--Stallion's Foe. Bjorklund, Lorence F. (1913-1978), illus. LC 63-9207. 179 p. illus. 21 cm. 1963. Crowell.
--Tiger Roan. Townsend, Lee (1895-), illus. LC 38-75763. 2 p. l., 296 p. 1 illus., double plates 21 cm. c.1938. Thomas Y. Crowell Company.
--Viking Dog. LC 49-8497. 147 p. 21 cm. 1949. T. Y. Crowell Co.
--White Ruff. LC 59-161832. 235p. illus. 22cm. (Famous dog stories). 1959, c.1958. Grosset & Dunlap.
--Wild Horse. Crowell, Pers (1910-), illus. LC 76-112627. (Illus.). 338 p. 21cm. (Apollo editions, J-502). 1970, c.1947. Crowell.
--Wild Horse. Crowell, Pers (1910-), illus. LC 48-6620. 338 p. illus. 21 cm. 1947. T. Y. Crowell Co.
--Wild Horse Tamer. Quigley, E. B., illus. LC 54-9929. (Illus.). 179 p. 21cm. 1955. Crowell.
--Winter Horse. LC 51-5637. 177 p. 21cm. 1951. Crowell.
Balch, Mickey
--Word-a-Day. (gr. 7-9). 1972. (ISBN 0-590-08118-7, Schol Trade Pap). Schol Bk Serv.
Balcombe, Donna
--Year of Janie's Diary. LC 65-13925. (gr. 7 up). 1965. (ISBN 0-8019-5010-4). Chilton.
Baldwin, Margaret
--When Jays Fly to Barbmo. Ambrus, Victor G, pseud. (1935-), illus. Ambrus, Gyozo Laszlo. LC 79-17970. (Illus.). 238 p. 21cm. (Gregg Press Children's Literature Series). 1980, c.1968. (ISBN 0-8398-2601-X). Gregg Press.
--When Jays Fly to Barbmo. Ambrus, Victor G., pseud. (1935-), illus. Ambrus, Gyozo Laszlo. LC 74-81638. (Illus.). 239 p. 21cm. 1st U.S. edition. 1969, c.1968. World Pub. Co. **Award: (ALA).**
Baldick, Jaqueline, tr. see Verne, Jules.
Baldick, Robert, ed. see Verne, Jules.
Baldick, Robert, tr. see Verne, Jules.
Baldner, Gaby
--Joba and the Wild Boar. Joba und das Wildschwein. Oberlander, Gerhard, illus. LC 61-661900. unpaged. illus. 21x30cm. c.1961. Constable.
--Penguins of Penguin Town. Oberlander, Gerhard, illus. LC 64-11467. (Illus.). 32 p. col. illus. 31 cm. (gr. k-3). 1962. (ISBN 0-668-01174-2). (ISBN 0-668-01175-0). Arco.
Baldridge, Cyrus Le Roy, jt. auth. see Singer, Caroline.
Baldridge, Dorothy A.
--Operation Knapsacks. LC 54-10105. 192 p. 23 cm. 1954. Follett Pub. Co.
Baldrige, Cyrus LeRoy, jt. auth. see Singer, Caroline.
Balducci, Carolyn Feleppa (1946-)
--Earwax. LC 72-12922. 189 p. 25cm. 1973, c.1972. (ISBN 0-8161-6077-5). G. K. Hall.
--Earwax. LC 72-2760. 151 p. 21cm. 1972. (ISBN 0-395-14328-4). Houghton Mifflin.
--Is There a Life After Graduation, Henry Birnbaum?. LC 78-163168. 140 p. 22cm. (gr. 7 up). 1971. (ISBN 0-395-12749-1). Houghton Mifflin.
Baldwin, Alfred, Mrs.
--The Pedlar's Pack. Pears, Charles (1873-1958), illus. LC 26-1831. 6 p. l., 11-397, 1 p. col. front., illus., col. plates. 21 cm. N.D. W. & R. Chambers, Limited.
Baldwin, Anne Norris (1938-)
--A Friend in the Park. Forberg, Ati, pseud. (1925-), illus. Forberg, Beate Gropius. LC 73-77538. (Illus.). 38 p. 25cm. 1973. Four Winds Press.
--Jenny's Revenge. McCully, Emily Arnold (1939-), illus. LC 73-88071. (Illus.). 38 p. 23cm. 1974. Four Winds Press.
--A Little Time. LC 77-27764. 119 p. 22cm. 1978. (ISBN 0-670-43392-6). Viking Press.
--The Sometimes Island. 1st ed. Robinson, Charles (1931-), illus. LC 68-9491. (Illus.). 36 p. 27cm. 1969. Norton.
--Sunflowers for Tina. Grifalconi, Ann (1929-), illus. LC 75-81701. (Illus.). 45 p. 27cm. 1970. Four Winds Press.
--Sunlight Valley. LC 70-161020. 253 p. 22cm. 1971. Four Winds Press.
Baldwin, Arthur H.
--Sou'wester Goes North. Grant, Gordon H. (1875-1962), illus. LC 38-15486. ix p. 1 l., 13-310 p. incl. front., illus. plates. 21 cm. c.1938. Random House.
--Sou'wester Sails. Grant, Gordon H. (1875-1962), illus. LC 36-9699. 262, 1 p. incl. front., illus., plates. 21 cm. 1936. Random House.
--Sou'wester Victorious. Grant, Gordon H. (1875-1962), illus. LC 39-185068. 5 p. l., 3-276 p. incl. illus., plates. front. 21 cm. c.1939. Random House.
Baldwin, Clara
--Cotton for Jim. Fax, Elton Clay (1909-), illus. LC 54-11963. 159 p. illus. 22 cm. 1954. Abingdon Press.
--The Hermit of Crab Island. Campbell, Ray Scott, illus. LC 58-3108. 176p. illus. 22cm. (gr. 4-7). 1958. (ISBN 0-687-16918-6). Abingdon Press.
--Little Tuck. Galdone, Paul (1914-), illus. (Illus.). 95 p. 25cm. 1959. Doubleday.
--Timber from Terry Forks. Leamon, Tom, illus. LC 56-3903. 159 p. illus. 22 cm. 1956. Abingdon Press.
Baldwin, Dorothy Arno
--The May Party Mystery And Other Stories. Foster, Imogene Watson, illus. LC 26-11853. 68 p. illus., col. plates. 31 cm. (Cokesbury character series for boys and girls). c.1926. Cokesbury Press.
Baldwin, E., selected by.
--Baldwin's Fables. N.D. Collins Brother's Publications.
--The Book of Fables. (Selections from Aesop and Other Authors). (Illus.). N.D. Collins & Brother.
Baldwin, Faith
--Babs. (The Divine Corners Ser.). N.D. Grosset & Dunlap.
--The Girls of Divine Corners: Containing, "Judy," "Babs," "Mary Lou," and "Myra". N.D. Farrar & Rinehart.
--Judy. (The Divine Corners Ser.). N.D. Grosset & Dunlap.
--Judy, A Story of Divine Corners. N.D. Dodd Mead & Co.
--Mary Lou. (The Divine Corner Ser.). N.D. Grosset & Dunlap.
--Myra. (The Divine Corners Ser.). N.D. Grosset & Dunlap.
Baldwin, Henry, jt. auth. see Richards, Laura Elizabeth Howe, Mrs.
Baldwin, James (1841-1925), ed. see Defoe, Daniel.
Baldwin, James (1841-1925)
--Another Fairy Reader. 1907. American Book Company.
--The Devil Finds Work. 1976. Dial.
--Don Quixote for Young People. N.D. American Book Company.
--The Fairy Reader. 1905. American Book Company.
--Fairy Stories and Fables. 1895. American Book Company.
--Favorite Tales of Long Ago. Rethi, Lili (1894-), illus. LC 55-6311. (Illus.). 150 p. 20cm. 1955. Aladdin Books.
--Favorite Tales of Long Ago. Rethi, Lili (1894-), illus. N.D. E. P. Dutton & Co.
--Fifty Famous People. A Book of Short Stories. LC 12-21617. 19cm. 190p. c.1912. American Book Company.
--Fifty Famous Rides and Riders. LC 16-17492. 306 p. incl. col. front., illus. 19 cm. c.1916. American Book Company.
--Fifty Famous Stories. LC 4-17302. 172 p. illus. 19 cm. (On cover: Eclectic school readings). 1896. American Book Company.
--The Golden Fleece: More Old Greek Stories. LC 6-1902. 288 p. illus. 19 cm. (On cover: Eclectic readings). c.1905. American Book Company.
--Gulliver's Travels Retold. N.D. American Book Company.
--Hero Tales Told in School. LC 4-10921. 19cm. 183p. 1904. Charles Scribner's Sons.
--Heroes of the Olden Time. Hurd, Peter (1904-1984), illus. N.D. Charles Scribner's Sons.
--The Horse Fair. (Illus.). 420p. 1905. Century Co.
--Horse Fair. LC 76-9890. (Illus.). (Children's Literature Reprint Ser). (gr. 5-6). 1976. (ISBN 0-8486-0201-3). Core Collection.
--John Bunyan's Dream Story. N.D. American Book Company.
--Old Greek Stories. (Eclectic School Readings). N.D. American Book Company.
--Old Stories of the East. (Eclectic School Readings). N.D. American Book Co.
--Robinson Crusoe. N.D. American Book Company.
--The Sampo: A Wonder Tale of the Old North. Wyeth, Newell Convers (1882-1945), illus. viii p., 1 l., 368 p. col. front., ccol. plates. 20 cm. (His Heroes of the olden time). 1917. C. Scribner's Sons.
--The Sampo: Hero Adventures from the Finnish Kalevala. Wyeth, Newell Convers (1882-1945), illus. LC 12-23922. viii p., 1 l., 368 p. col. front., col. plates. 22 cm. 1912. C. Scribner's Sons.
--Second Fairy Reader. N.D. American Book Company.
--The Story of Roland. Birch, Reginald Bathurst (1856-1943), illus. LC 14-183119. xiii p., 1 l., 415 p. front., plates. 20 cm. 1883. C. Scribner's Sons.
--The Story of Roland. Birch, Reginald Bathurst (1856-1943), illus. 1 p. l., xiii, 415 p. 16 pl. (incl. front.) 19 cm. (His Heroes of the olden time). 1888. C. Scribner's Sons.
--The Story of Roland. Hurd, Peter (1904-1984), illus. LC 30-26892. xiv, 347 p. col. plates. 24 cm. c.1930. C. Scribner's Sons.
--The Story of Siegfried. Hurd, Peter (1904-1984), illus. LC 31-86113. xiv p., 2 l., 8-279 p. col. plates. 24 cm. c.1931. C. Scribner's Sons.
--The Story of Siegfried. Pyle, Howard (1853-1911), illus. LC 44-49394. xvi p., 2 l., 306 p. front., plates. 19 cm. 1882. C. Scribner's Sons.
--The Story of Siegfried. Pyle, Howard (1853-1911), illus. LC 14-1823. xiv p., 2 l., 306 p. front., plates. 19 cm. (His Heroes of the olden time). 1888. C. Scribner's Sons.
--The Story of Siegfried. Pyle, Howard (1853-1911), illus. xvi p., 2 l., 306 p. front., 5 pl. 20 cm. (His Heroes of the olden time). 1904. C. Scribner's Sons.
--A Story of the Golden Age. Pyle, Howard (1853-1911), illus. LC 14-1832. xii p., 2 l., 286 p. incl. front. plates. 2 maps (1 fold.) 19 cm. 1887. C. Scribner's Sons.
--A Story of the Golden Age. Pyle, Howard (1853-1911), illus. LC 16-25490. xii p., 1 l., 286 p. front., plates, maps (1 fold.) 19 cm. (His Heroes of the olden time). 1897. C. Scribner's Sons.
--A Story of the Golden Age. Pyle, Howard (1853-1911), illus. LC 4-42011. xii p. 2 l., 286 p. incl. front. 11 pl., 2 maps (1 double) 20 cm. (His Heroes of the olden time). 1902. C. Scribner's Sons.
--Thirty More Famous Stories. LC 5-40804. 235 p. illus. 19 cm. (On cover: Eclectic readings). c.1905. American Book Company.
--Thirty More Famous Stories. LC 77-89716. (Illus.). 235 p. 20cm. (Children's Literature Reprint Series). 1977. (ISBN 0-8486-0213-7). Core Collection Books.
Baldwin, Jeanne & Baldwin, Victor
--The Outcast Kitten. Baldwin, Jeanne & Baldwin, Victor, illus. LC 70-97825. (Illus.). 32 p. 24cm. 1970. Golden-Gate Junior Books.
Baldwin, Josephine L
--Nancy Comes to the Scratch and Other Stories for Boys and Girls. LC 31-880640. 217 p. illus. 20 cm. c.1931. The Abingdon Press.
Baldwin, Margaret
--Kisses of Death: A Great Escape Story of World War II. (Illus.). 64p. (Jem - High Interest-Low Reading Level Ser.). (gr. 7-9). 1983. (ISBN 0-671-43850-6). Messner.
Baldwin, Mary
--The Cottage in the Woods. N.D. Macmillan.
--The House of Mystery. N.D. Macmillan.
Baldwin, May
--Barbara Bellamy. (The Girls' Own Library). N.D. David McKay.
--Barbara Bellamy. N.D. E P Dutton.
--The Brilliant Girls of the School. Rainey, William R. I. (1852-1936), illus. LC 26-12533. 2 p. l., 9-343 p. front., plates. 20 cm. 1925. J. B. Lippincott Company.
--Corah's School Chums. N.D. J. B. Lippincott.
--Dora: A High School Girl. (Illus.). N.D. J B Lippincott.
--Follies of Fifi. (Illus.). N.D. J B Lippincott.
--The Girls' Eton. N.D. E P Dutton.
--The Girls of St Gabriel's. (Illus.). N.D. J B Lippincott.
Golden Square High School. (Illus.). N.D. J B Lippincott.
--Holly House and Ridges Row. (Illus.). N.D. J B Lippincott.
--Irene to the Rescue. N.D. E P Dutton.
--Jean and the Boys. N.D. J. B. Lippincott.
--Miss Peter. N.D. J. B. Lippincott.
--Moll Meredyth Madcap. N.D. J. B. Lippincott Co.
--Mrs. Manning's Wards. N.D. J. B. Lippincott.
--Muriel. (Illus.). N.D. J B Lippincott.
--Mysie: A Highland Lassie. (Illus.). N.D. J B Lippincott.
--A New School Story. (Illus.). N.D. J. B. Lippincott.
--Only Pat. N.D. J.B. Lippincott.
--Peg's Adventures in Paris. N.D. E P Dutton.
--A Plucky Girl. (The Girls' Own Library). N.D. David McKay.
--A Plucky Girl. (Illus.). N.D. J B Lippincott.
--A Popular Girl. (The Girls' Own Library). N.D. David McKay.
--A Popular Girl. N.D. J. P. Lippincott.
--A Riotous Term at St. Norbert's. 382p. N.D. J. B. Lippincott.
--A Ripping Girl. N.D. J. B. Lippincott.
--Sarah's School Friend. Tarrant, Percy, illus. 19cm. 287p. N.D. J. B. Lippincott Co.
--The School in the Wilds. Brisley, Nina K., illus. LC 27-279263. 2 p. l., 9-320 p. front., plates. 20 cm. 1928. W. & R. Chambers, Limited.
--A Schoolgirl of Moscow. Rainey, William R. I. (1852-1936), illus. LC 12-39029. 4 p. l., 378 p., 1 l., col. front., col. plates. 20 cm. 1911. E. P. Dutton & Company.
--A Schoolgirl's Dairy. N.D. J. B. Lippincott.
--Sibyl. (Illus.). N.D. J B Lippincott.
--Sibyl: Or, Old School Friends. (The Girls' Own Library). N.D. David McKay.
--Sunset Rock. N.D. E P Dutton.
--Teddy's and Lily's Adventures. (Illus.). 317p. N.D. J. B. Lippincott Co.
--That Awful Little Brother. (Illus.). N.D. J B Lippincott.
--That Little Limb. Attwell, Mabel Lucie (1879-1964), illus. LC 6-37924. 250 p. front., 3 pl. 19 cm. 1906. G. W. Jacobs & Co.
--Two Schoolgirls of Florence. Earnshaw, Harold C., illus. 19cm. 320p. 1910. E. P. Dutton & Co.
Baldwin, Michael (1930-), ed.
--Poems By Children. Foreman, Michael (1938-), illus. 123p. 1962. Dufour Editions.
--Poems by Children, 1950-1961. LC 64-976282. xiv, 123p. illus. 21cm. 1962. Routledge & K Paul Dist. Chester Springs, Pa., Dufour.
Baldwin, Myra
--Nancy's Easter Gift. LC 2-12111. (Illus.). 20cm. 10p. 1902. The Abbey Press.
Baldwin, Ruth M.
One Hundred Nineteenth-Century Rhyming Alphabets in English. (Illus.). 320p. 1972. (ISBN 0-8093-0509-7). Southern Illinois Universety Press.
Baldwin, Sidney, compiled by see Molesworth, Mary Louisa Stewart, Mrs.
Baldwin, Sidney (1885-)
--Ben of Old Monhegan: A Boy's Life Among the Fisher Folk off the Coast of Maine. LC 33-270751. 263 p. incl. illus. pl. map 19 cm. c.1933. Row, Peterson and Company.
--Five Plays and Five Pantomines. Donovan, Mary Rose, illus. LC 22-23315. 6 p. l., 128 p. 10 pl., diagrs. 23 cm. 1922. The Penn Publishing Company.
--Princess Hildegarde. Chamberlin, Helen, illus. LC 35-943. 304 p. illus. 19 cm. c.1935. Row, Peterson and Company.
--Robin Rides Away. Chamberlin, Helen, illus. LC 34-105194. 256 p. illus 19 cm. c.1934. Row, Peterson and Company.
--Young Prince Hubert. Compton, Nell Hukle, illus. LC 31-252704. 230 p. col. illus. 19 cm. 1931. Row, Peterson and Company.
Baldwin, Victor, jt. auth. see Baldwin, Jeanne.
Bales, Carol Ann (1940-)
--Kevin Cloud: Chippewa Boy in the City. LC 79-183833. (Illus.). 32p. (gr. k-3). 1972. (ISBN 0-8092-8673-4). (ISBN 0-685-23699-4). Contemp Bks.
Balet, Jan Bernard (1913-)
--Amos and the Moon. (Illus.). 25 p. 27cm. 1959, c.1948. H. Z. Walck.
--Amos and the Moon. LC 48-9819. 26 p. col. illus. 27 cm. 1948. Oxford Univ. Press.
--The Fence: A Mexican Tale. Balet, Jan Bernard (1913-), illus. LC 77-85757. (Illus.). 26 p. 27cm. 1969. Delacorte Press.
--The Five Rollatinis. Balet, Jan Bernard (1913-), illus. LC 59-12352. unpaged. illus. 27cm. 1959. Lippincott.
--The Gift: A Portuguese Christmas Tale. Balet, Jan Bernard (1913-), illus. LC 67-24091. (Illus.). 1 v. (unpaged). 1967. Delacorte Press.
--Joanjo, a Portuguese Tale. Balet, Jan Bernard (1913-), illus. LC 67-10705. (Illus.). (ps-2). 1967. (Sey Lawr). (Sey Lawr). Delacorte.
--The King & the Broom Maker. Balet, Jan Bernard (1913-), illus. LC 68-28672. (Illus.). 4 color ils. (gr. k-3). 1969. (Sey Lawr). (Sey Lawr). Delacorte.
--Ladismouse: Or, The Advantages of Higher Education. LC 77-142449. (Illus.). 22 p. 23cm. 1971. (ISBN 0-8098-1180-4). H. Z. Walck.
--Ned and Ed and the Lion. LC 49-11386. 26 p. col. illus. 26 cm. (Oxford books for boys and girls). 1949. Oxford University Press.
Balfour, C. L., Mrs.
--Cousin Bessie. (Young Folk Series, Number Three). N.D. Fleming H Revell Co.
--The Family Honor, 1 of 4 vols. (Illus.). (The School Girl's Library). N.D. Cassell, Petter, Galpin.
--One By Herself. N.D. Thomas Nelson & Sons.
Balian, Lorna (1929-)
--An Elephant. Balian, Lorna (1929-), illus. LC 64-10147. (Illus.). (gr. k-3). 1964. (ISBN 0-687-01515-4). Abingdon.
--The Animal. LC 74-186614. (Illus.). 48 p. 27cm. 1972. (ISBN 0-687-01267-8). Abingdon Press.
--Bah! Humbug?. LC 76-50625. (Illus.). 32 p. 29cm. 1977. (ISBN 0-687-02345-9). Abingdon.
--A Garden for a Ground Hog. LC 84-28233. p. cm. 1985. (ISBN 0-687-14009-9). Abingdon Press.
--Humbug Potion: An A-B-Cipher. LC 83-15808. 1984. (ISBN 0-687-18021-X). Abingdon Press.
--Humbug Rabbit. LC 73-9555. (Illus.). 32 p. 29cm. 1974. (ISBN 0-687-18046-5). Abingdon Press.
--Humbug Witch. LC 65-14089. 1v. (unpaged) col. illus. 21cm. c.1965. Abingdon.
--I Love You Mary Jane. LC 67-7216. 1 v. (chiefly illus. 24cm. 1967. Abingdon Press.
--Leprechauns Never Lie. Balian, Lorna (1929-), illus. LC 79-25950. (Illus.). 32 p. 21cm. c.1980. (ISBN 0-687-21371-1). Abingdon.
--Mother's Mother's Day. LC 81-10988. (Illus.). 32 p. 18cm. c.1982. (ISBN 0-687-27253-X). Abingdon.

--Sometimes It's Turkey, Sometimes It's Feathers. LC 72-3867. (Illus.). 32 p. 24cm. 1973. (ISBN 0-687-39074-5). Abingdon Press.

--The Sweet Touch. LC 74-34217. (Illus.). 40 p. c.1976. (ISBN 0-687-40773-7). Abingdon Press.

--A Sweetheart for Valentine. LC 79-9924. p. cm. c.1979. (ISBN 0-687-40771-0). Abingdon.

--Where in the World Is Henry?. LC 72-80737. (Illus.). 32 p. 19cm. 1972. (ISBN 0-87888-049-6). Bradbury Press.

--Where in the World Is Henry?. Balian, Lorna (1929-), illus. LC 79-10391. (Illus.). Repr (Pub. by Bradbury Press). (gr. k-11). 1980, c.1972. (ISBN 0-687-45092-6). Abingdon.

Balika, Susan S.

--Jesus Is My Special Friend. N.D. Standard Pub.

Balinska, Irena

--The Secret Camp. Rajchman, Marthe, illus. LC 47-3260. 5 p. l., 245 p. illus., maps, diagrs. 21 cm. (Morrow junior books). 1947. V. Morrow and Company.

Balis, Andrea F. (1948-)

--P.J. Reiser, Robert, illus. LC 83-26475. 150 p. 22cm. 1984. (ISBN 0-395-36006-4). Houghton Mifflin.

Balk, Eliza

--Ride 'Em Peggy. N.D. Houghton Mifflin Co.

Balkoff-Drowne, Tatiana, tr. see Prishvin, Mikhail Mikhailovich.

Ball, Anne W

--Guess Who?. Axeman, Lois, illus. LC 70-178487. (Illus.). 31 p. 25cm. 1972. (ISBN 0-516-03663-7). Childrens Press.

Ball, Brian

--Princess Priscella. James, Lisa, illus. (gr. 4-7). 1976. (ISBN 0-8277-4744-6). British Bk Ctr.

Ball, Dorothy Whitney

--Don't Drive up a Dirt Road. LC 73-112653. 160p. (gr. 5-9). 1969. (ISBN 0-87460-144-4). Lion Bks.

--Hurricane: The Story of a Friendship. LC 64-25310. 147p. 22cm. 1965. Bobbs.

--Hurricane: The Story of Friendship. N.D. (ISBN 0-448-04836-1, . Grosset & Dunlap Pub.

Ball, Eileen

--Tales from the End Cottage. (gr. 5-7). 1974. (ISBN 0-14-030431-2, Puffin). Penguin.

Ball, Elsie

--Perilous Voyage. Ray, Ralph (1920-1952), illus. LC 51-12142. 127 p. illus. 21 cm. 1951. Abingdon-Cokesbury Press.

--The Story Peter Told. N.D. Henry Holt & Co.

--Ten Days till Harvest. Werth, Kurt (1896-), illus. LC 49-981710. 127 p. illus. 21 cm. 1949. Abingdon-Cokesbury Press.

--The Greatest Name. N.D. Abingdon-Cokesbury Press.

Ball, Francis Kingsley (1833-), ed. see Kingsley, Charles.

Ball, Francis Kingsley, jt. ed. see Lamb, Charles.

Ball, John Dudley, Jr. (1911-)

--Arctic Showdown: An Alaskan Adventure. LC 66-13484. (Illus.). 147 p. 22cm. 1966. Duell, Sloan and Pearce.

--Judo Boy. LC 63-16838. xii, 148 p. 21cm. 1964. Duell, Sloan and Pearce.

--Operation Springboard. 1958. Duell, Sloan and Pearce Pub.

--Rescue Mission. LC 66-13854. 211 p. 22cm. 1966. Harper & Row.

--Spacemaster I. 1st ed. LC 60-12841. 148p. 21cm. 1960. Duell, Sloan and Pearce.

Ball, Lola M.

--A Bathtub for Two. 32p. (gr. 1-3). 1984. (ISBN 0-89962-409-X). Todd & Honeywell.

Ball, Marion W.

--Thomasina Travels. (Illus.). (gr. k-3). N.D. Vantage.

Ball, Martha Jane

--Timothy Crunchit the Calico Bunny. Woodring, Gaye, illus. LC 30-25180. 127 p. illus., col. plates. 26 cm. c.1930. Laidlaw Brothers.

Ball, Robert Stawell

--Star Land. (Illus.). 402p. N.D. Ginn and Co. Trade Department.

Ball, Robert (1890-), ed.

--Good Housekeeping's Best Book of Animal Stories. 1st ed. Ball, Robert (1890-), illus. LC 57-12952. (Illus.). 21cm. 384p. 1957. Good Housekeeping Magazine: Dist. by Prentice-Hall.

Ball, Sara

--Croguphant. LC 83-15738. p. cm. 1984. (ISBN 0-911745-25-4). P. Bedrick Books : Blackie.

Ball, Sherry De Volld

--Wildcat. Hansen, Roy, illus. LC 52-16433. unpaged. illus. 27 cm. 1951. Erle Press.

Ball, Walter Savage (1875-)

--Carmella Commands. Steele, Frederic Dorr, illus. LC 29-206531. vii p. 1 l., 277 p. incl. plates. col. front. 21 1/2 cm. 1929. Harper & Brothers.

Ball, Zachary, pseud., see Janas, Frankie-Lee.

Ball, Zachary, pseud., see Masters, Kelly Ray.

Ball, Zachary, pseud. (1897-)

--Bristle Face. Masters, Kelly Ray. LC 62-2219. (Illus.). 206 p. 22cm. 1962. Holiday House. **Award: (ALA).**

--Joe Panther. Masters, Kelly Ray. Means, Elliott, illus. LC 50-10209. (Illus.). 21 cm. 241p. 1950. Holiday House.

--Keelboat Journey. Masters, Kelly Ray. Helweg, Hans H. (1917-), illus. LC 58-9568. (Illus.). 21cm. 190p. N.D. Dutton.

--Kep. Masters, Kelly Ray. 1961. (ISBN 0-8382-0403-1, Cadmus Books). E. M. Hale And Company.

--Salvage Diver. Masters, Kelly Ray. (Illus.). (gr. 6-10). 1961. (ISBN 0-8382-0718-9). Hale.

--Skin Diver. Masters, Kelly Ray. 1956. E M Hale.

--Skin Diver. Masters, Kelly Ray. LC 56-14156. 251 p. 21cm. 1956. Holiday House.

--Sky Diver. Masters, Kelly Ray. LC 67-1937. 213 p. 22 cm. 1967. Holiday House.

--Sputters. Masters, Kelly Ray. LC 63-6534. 220p. (gr. 7 up). 1963. (ISBN 0-8234-0109-X). Holiday.

--Swamp Chief. Masters, Kelly Ray. LC 52-9567. 212 p. 21cm. 1952. Holiday House.

--Tent Show. Masters, Kelly Ray. LC 64-7315. (Illus.). 186 p. 22cm. 1964. Holiday House.

--Wilderness Teacher. Masters, Kelly Ray. 1956. E M Hale.

--Young Mike Fink. Masters, Kelly Ray. N.D. E . M. Hale and Co.

Ball, Zachary, pseud. (1908-)

--Piney. Janas, Frankie-Lee. 1st ed. LC 50-7647. 273. 20cm. 1950. Little, Brown.

Ball, Zachary, pseud. (1897-) & Fowler, Myra

--Wilderness Teacher. Masters, Kelly Ray. Vosburgh, Leonard W. (1912-), illus. LC 56-6052. (Illus.). 224 p. 22cm. 1956. Rand McNally.

Balland, Todhunter

--Gold in California!. N.D. Doubleday & Co.

Ballantine, William Gay (1848-)

--Peggy in the Park: Verses. Tufts, Alice Barri, Mrs. (1870-), illus. LC 33-33953. 49 p. illus. 26 cm. c.1933. Milton Bradley Company.

Ballantyne, H. M.

--Fire Brigade: Fighting the Flames. N.D. Porter & Coates.

--The Floating Light on the Goodwin Sands. N.D. Portr & Coates.

Ballantyne, Lereine Hoffman, Mrs. (1891-1962)

--The Scout Who Led an Army. Clifton, Lee, illus. LC 64-10240. 106p. illus., map. 20cm. (Buckskin bks. 8). c.1963. St. Martin's.

--Spirit Fire: A Story of the Petun Indians. LC 32-6102. 188 p. 19 1/2 cm. c.1932. Fleming H. Revell Company.

Ballantyne, Randall H.

--Mabel Grant. N.D. Robert Carter & Brothers.

Ballantyne, Robert Michael, jt. auth. see Wilder, Ira.

Ballantyne, Robert Michael (1825-1894)

--Away in the Wilderness, 1 of 4 vols. (Boys' Miscellany of Travel and Adventure Ser.). N.D. Set. John C. Winston Co.

--Away in the Wilderness: Life among the Red Indians & Fur Traders of North America, 1 of 4 Vols. (Illus.). (Boy's Miscellany of Travel and Adventure). N.D. Porter & Coates.

--Away in the Wilderness: Or, Life Among the Red Indians and Fur-Traders of North America. LC 52-560098. 144 p. illus. 17 cm. 1876. Porter & Coates.

--Ballantyne Library of Story: Containing: "Fire Brigade", "Erling the Bold", "Deep Down in the Mines", 3 Vols. (Illus.). N.D. J B Lippincott & Co.

--The Battery & the Boiler: Or, Adventures in the Laying of Submarine Electric Cables. (Illus.). N.D. Thomas Nelson & Sons.

--The Big Otter: A Tale of the Great Nor'west. 1887. Routledge.

--Black Ivory: A Tale of Adventure Among the Slavers of East Africa. LC 79-99338. (Illus.). vi, 416 p. 22cm. 1969. Afro-Am Press.

--Black Ivory: A Tale of Adventure among the Slavers of East Africa, 1 of 5 vols. (Illus.). (Life Boat Ser.). 1873. Set. Thomas Nelson & sons.

--Blown to Bits: Or, The Lonely Man of Rakata. (Illus.). N.D. Thomas Nelson & Sons.

--Boys' Stories: Containing: The Fire Brigade, The Red Eric, and Erling the Bold, 3 vols. (Illus.). N.D. International Book Co.

--The Buffalo Runners: A Tale of the Red River Plains. Ballantyne, Robert Michael (1825-1894), illus. (Illus.). 1891. Thomas Nelson & Sons.

--Charlie to the Rescue. (Illus.). N.D. Thos Nelson & Sons.

--Chasing the Sun, 1 of 4 Vols. (Boys' Miscellany of Travel and Adveture Ser.). N.D. Set. John C. Winston Co.

--Chasing the Sun: Or, Rambles in Norway., 1 of 4 Vols. (Illus.). (Boys' Miscellany of Travel and Adventure). N.D. Set. Porter & Coates.

--The Coral Island. (The Magnet Library). N.D. Frederick Warne & Co.

--The Coral Island. LC 75-32167. (Illus.). xxi, 438 p., 6 leaves of plates. 19cm. (Classics of Children's Literature, 1621-1932 Ser.). 1977. (ISBN 0-8240-2280-7). Garland Pub.

--Coral Island. N.D. Longmans Green & Co.

--The Coral Island. (The R. M. Ballantyne Books for Boys). 1927. Nelson.

--Coral Island. (Illus.). N.D. William Collins Sons & Company Ltd.

--The Coral Island. Bates, Leo, illus. (Children's Illustrated Classics). 1949. E. P. Dutton & Co.

--The Coral Island. Strang, Herbert, ed. (Illus.). (Herbert Strang's Library). N.D. George H. Doran.

--The Coral Island: A Tale of the Pacific, 1 of 4 vols. (Illus.). (Martin Rattler Ser.). N.D. Set. Thomas Nelson & Sons.

--The Coral Island: A Tale of the Pacific Ocean. new ed. LC 28-26215. 336 p. col. front., col. plates. 21 cm. (Honor books). 1927. T. Nelson and Sons.

--Coral Island: A Tale of the Pacific Ocean. More, B., ed. LC 23-13885. ix, 334 p. front., pl. 19 1/2 cm. (On verso of half-title: World adventure books for boys and girls). 1923. The Cornhill Publishing Company.

--The Crew of the Water Wagtail. N.D. Thomas Whittaker.

--Deep Down, 1 of 4 Vols. (Illus.). (Light House Ser.). N.D. Set. Thomas Nelson & Sons.

--Deep Down: A Tale of the Cornish Mines. N.D. J B Lippincott & Co.

--Deep Down in the Mines. cover-title, 420 p. 18 1/2 cm. (Cover-title: Lovell's library, v. 5. no. 241). c.1883. J. W. Lovell Co.

--The Dog Crusoe. (Illus.). 1st U.S. edition. Repr. of 1966 ed. (Childrens Illustrated Classics Ser.). 1972. (ISBN 0-460-05070-2, Pub. by J. M. Dent England). Biblio Dist.

--The Dog Crusoe. (Roundabout Lib.). N.D. Henry T. Coates & Co.

--The Dog Crusoe, 1 of 3 vols. Juv ed. (Roundabout Library). (Land Stories). N.D. John C. Winston Co.

--The Dog Crusoe. (The R. M. Ballantyne Books for Boys). N.D. Nelson.

--The Dog Crusoe, 1 of 4 Vols. (Illus.). (The Famous Ballantyne Bks. (Land Stories)). N.D. Set. Porter & Coates.

--The Dog Crusoe. Ambrus, Victor G., pseud. (1935-), illus. Ambrus, Gyozo Laszlo. LC 66-75027. vii. 246p. col. front., illus., 3 col. plates. 22cm. (Children's illus. classics no. 70). 1966. Dent.

--Dog Crusoe. Green, Roger Lancelyn (1918-), ed. Ambrus, Victor G., pseud. (1935-), illus. Ambrus, Gyozo Laszlo. (Illus.). (gr. 5-9). 1966. (ISBN 0-525-28808-2). Dutton.

--The Dog Crusoe: A Tale of the Western Prairies. Alta ed. (Illus.). 1888. Porter & Coates.

--The Dog Crusoe and His Master: A Story of Adventure in the Western Prairies. Brock, Henry Matthew (1875-1960), illus. LC 9-18722. 320 p. incl. front. 7 pl. 20 1/2 cm. (Bowman's illustrated library of world-favorite books). 1909. C. L. Bowman & Co.

--The Dog Crusoe and His Master: A Story of Adventures on the Western Prairies, 1 of 3 Vols. (Illus.). (Gorilla Hunter Ser.). N.D. Set. Thomas Nelson & Sons.

--Dusty Diamonds Cut and Polished: A Tale of City-Arab Life and Adventure. 1883. Nelson.

--Erling, the Bold. 184 p. 18 1/2 cm. (On cover: Seaside library. Pocket ed. no. 96). c.1883. G. Munro.

--Erling the Bold. (Illus.). (St. Nicholas Series for Boys). N.D. International Book Company.

--Erling, the Bold. cover-title, 4 437 p. 18 1/2 cm. (On cover: Lovell's library. v. 5, no. 239). c.1883. J. W. Lovell Co.

--Erling the Bold. (The R.M. Ballantyne Books for Boys). N.D. Nelson.

--Erling the Bold. Strang, Ray C., illus. LC 27-18559. vi p., 3 l., 306 p. col. front., plates. 20 1/2 cm. c.1927. L. C. Page & Company.

--Erling, the Bold: A Tale of the Norse Sea Kings, 98 vols. (The Rugby Ser.). 1905. Set. A L Burt Co.

--Erling the Bold: A Tale of the Norse Sea-Kings. Ballantyne, Robert Michael (1825-1894), illus. LC 41-32453. vi p., 1 l., 437 p. front., plates. 19 1/2 cm. 1874. J. B. Lippincott & Co.

--Fast in the Ice: Adventures in the Polar Regions. N.D. Porter & Coates.

--Fast in the Ice: Dr. Rambles in Norway, 1 of 4 Vols. (Boys' Miscellany of Travel and Adventure Ser.). N.D. Set. John C. Winston Co.

--Fast in the Ice: Or, Rambles in Norway, 1 of 4 Vols. (Illus.). (Boy's Miscellany of Travel and Adventure). N.D. Porter & Coates.

--Fighting the Whales, 1 of 4 Vols. (Boys' Miscellany of Travel and Adventure Ser.). N.D. Set. John C. Winston Co.

--Fighting the Whales: Or, Doings and Dangers of a Fishing Cruise, 1 of 4 Vols. (Illus.). (Boy's Miscellany of Travel and Adventure). N.D. Porter & Coates.

--The Fire Brigade. (Illus.). (St. Nicholas Series for Boys). N.D. International Book Co.

--The Fire Brigade: Or, Fighting the Flames. N.D. J B Lippincott & Co.

--The Fire Brigade: Or, Fighting the Flames, 1 of 4 Vols. (Illus.). (Famous Ballantyne Bks.). (Land Stories). N.D. Set. Porter & Coates.

--The Fire Brigade: Or, Fighting the Flames, a Tale. 170 p. 18 1/2 cm. (On cover: Seaside library. Pocket ed. no. 95). c.1883. G. Munro.

--The Fire Brigade: Or, Fighting the Flames, a Tale. 1 p. l., 420 p. 18 1/2 cm. (On cover: Lovell's library, v. 5. no. 226). c.1883. J. W. Lovell Company.

--The Floating Light of the Goodwin Sands. N.D. Claxton, Remsen, & Haffelfinger.

--The Floating Light of the Goodwin Sands. (Roundabout Lib.). N.D. Henry T. Coates & Co.

--Floating Light of The Goodwin Sands. Juv ed. (Roundabout Library). (Sea Stories). N.D. John C. Winston Co.

--The Floating Light of the Goodwin Sands, 1 of 4 Vols. (Illus.). (Famous Ballantyne Bks.). (Sea Stories). N.D. Set. Porter & Coates.

--Floating Light of the Goodwin Sands. (Illus.). N.D. Thomas Nelson & Sons.

--Freaks on the Fells: Or, Three Months' Rustication and, Why I Did Not Become a Sailor. (Illus.). (Ballantyne's Library of Sporting Adventure). N.D. George Routledge & Sons.

--Freaks on the Fells: Or, Three Months' Rustication, and Why I did not Become a Sailor. (Roundabout Lib.). N.D. Henry T. Coates & Co.

--Freaks on The Fells: Or, Three Months' Rustication and, Why I Did Not Become a Sailor. (Roundabout Library). (Sea Stories). N.D. John C. Winston Co.

--Freaks on the Fells: Or, Three Months' Rustication, And Why I Did Not Become a Sailor. 379 p. front., plates. 17 1/2 cm. c.1865. Porter & Coates.

--The Fugitives: Or, The Tyrant Queen of Madagascar. (Illus.). 1887. Thomas Nelson & Sons.

--Gascoyne: The Sandal Wood Trader, 1 of 6. (Ballantyne's Library of Adventure). N.D. Claxton, Remsen, & Haffelfinger.

--Gascoyne, the Sandal-Wood Trader, 1 of 4 Vols. (Illus.). (Famous Ballantyne Bks.). (Sea Stories). N.D. Set. Porter & Coates.

--Gascoyne, the Sandal-Wood Trader. LC 23-9848. 5 p. l., 3-343 p. col. front., plates. 19 1/2 cm. 1923. The Cornhill Publishing Company.

--Gascoyne, the Sandal-Wood Trader: A Tale of the Pacific. 1 p. l., 5-259 p. 18 1/2 cm. (On cover: Seaside library. Pocket ed. no. 772). c.1886. G. Munro.

--Gascoyne, the Sandalwood Trader, 98 vols. (The Rugby Ser.). 1905. Set. A L Burt Co.

--Gascoyne the Sandalwood Trader. (Illus.). (The Round Table Ser.). N.D. A. L. Burt's Pubs.

--Gascoyne, the Sandalwood Trader. (Roundabout Lib.). N.D. Henry T. Coates & Co.

--Gascoyne, The Sandalwood Trader. Juv ed. (Roundabout Library). (Sea Stories). N.D. John C. Winston Co.

--The Giant of the North: Or, Poking Around the Pole. 1881. Nelson.

--The Golden Dream, 1 of 4 Vols. (Illus.). (Light House Ser.). N.D. Set. Thomas Nelson & Sons.

--The Gorilla Hunter, 98 vols. (The Rugby Ser.). 1905. Set. A L Burt Co.

--The Gorilla Hunters. (Illus.). (The Round Table Ser.). N.D. A. L. Burt's Pubs.

--The Gorilla Hunters. (Illus.). (The Rugby Series for Boys). N.D. A. L. Burt's Pubs.

--The Gorilla Hunters, 1 of 6. (Ballantyne's Library of Adventure). N.D. Claxton, Remsen, & Haffelfinger.

--The Gorilla Hunters. (Roundabout Lib.). N.D. Henry T. Coates & Co.

--The Gorilla Hunters, 1 of 3 vols. Juv ed. (Roundabout Library). (Land Stories). N.D. John C. Winston Co.

--The Gorilla Hunters. (The R.M. Ballantyne Books for Boys). N.D. Nelson.

--The Gorilla Hunters, 1 of 4 Vols. (Illus.). (Famous Ballantyne Bks.). (Land Stories). N.D. Set. Porter & Coates.

--The Gorilla Hunters, 1 of 3 Vols. (Illus.). (Gorilla Hunters Ser.). N.D. Set. Thomas Nelson & Sons.

--Gorilla Hunters. (The Forward Ser.). N.D. William Collins Co.

--The Gorilla Hunters: A Tale of the Wilds of Africa. LC 22-24783. 406 p. front., plates. 17 1/2 cm. 1865. Crosby and Ainsworth.

--The Gorilla Hunters: A Tale of the Wilds of Africa. alta ed. LC 49-40698. 408 p. illus. 20 cm. N.D. Porter & Coates.

--Gorrilla Hunter Series, 3 Vols. (Illus.). N.D. Thomas Nelson & Sons.

--The Hot Swamp: A Romance of Old Albion. 1892. Nelson.

--Hudson's Bay: Or, Every-Day Life in the Wilds of North America. (Illus.). N.D. Thos Nelson & Sons.

--Hunted and Harried: A Tale of the Scottish Covenanters. 1893. Bradley.

--Hunting the Lions, 1 of 6 Vols. (Illus.). (Ballantyne's Tales for Boys). N.D. Set. Thomas Nelson and Sons.
--In the Track of the Troops, 1 of 4 Vols. (Illus.). (Light House Ser.). N.D. Set. Thomas Nelson & Sons.
--Jarwin and Cuffy. (Illus.). (Warne's Home Circle Library). N.D. Frederick Warne & Co.
--Jarwin and Cuffy. (Illus.). (The Home and Enterprise Library Ser.). N.D. Frederick Warne & Co.
--Jarwin and Cuffy, 1 of 16 Vols. (Illus.). (Warne's incident and Adventure Library). N.D. Scribner & Welford.
--The Life Boat. (Illus.). (Famous Books for Boys). N.D. H. M. Caldwell Co.
--The Life Boat, 1 of 50 vols. (Illus.). (The Norwood Ser.: No. 4). 1900. Lee & Shepard.
--The Life Boat. (Illus.). (Life-Boat Ser). N.D. Lee & Shepard.
--The Life Boat, 1 of 5 Vols. (Illus.). (Life Boat Ser.). N.D. Set. Thomas Nelson & Sons.
--Life in the Red Brigade. (Illus.). 1873. George Routledge & Sons.
--The Light House, 1 of 4 Vols. (Illus.). (Light House Ser.). N.D. Set. Thomas Nelson & Sons.
--Light House Series, 4 Vols. (Illus.). N.D. Thomas Nelson & Sons.
--The Lighthouse. (The R.M. Ballantyne Books for Boys). N.D. Nelson.
--The Lonely Island: Or, The Refuge of the Mutineers. (Illus.). 1880. Thomas Nelson & Sons.
--Lost in the Forest, 1 of 6 Vols. (Illus.). (Ballantyne's Tales for Boys). N.D. Set. Thomas Nelson and Sons.
--Mabel Grant. (Carters' Fireside Library). N.D. Robert Carter & Brothers.
--Martin Rattler. (The R.M. Ballantyne Books for Boys). N.D. Nelson.
--Martin Rattler. (The Forward Ser.). N.D. William Collins Co.
--Martin Rattler: Or, A Boy's Adventures in Brazil, 1 of 4 Vols. (Illus.). (Martin Rattler Ser.). N.D. Set. Thomas Nelson & Sons.
--The Norseman, 1 of 5 Vols. (Illus.). (Life Boat Ser.). N.D. Set. Thomas Nelson & sons.
--The Pioneers, 1 of 6 Vols. (Illus.). (Ballantyne's Tales For Boys). N.D. Set. Thomas Nelson and Sons.
--The Pirate City: An Algerian Tale, 1 of 5 vols. (Illus.). (Life Boat Ser.). 1874. Set. Thomas Nelson & Sons.
--Post Haste: A Tale of Her Majesty's Mails. 1880. Nelson.
--The Red Eric, 98 vols. (The Rugby Ser.). 1905. Set. A L Burt Co.
--Red Eric. (The R.M. Ballantyne Books for Boys). N.D. Nelson.
--The Red Eric: Or, The Whaler's Last Cruise. 178 p. 18 1/2 cm. (On cover: Seaside library. Pocket ed. no. 89). c.1883. G. Munro.
--The Red Eric: Or, The Whaler's Last Cruise. 1 p. l., 7-420 p. 18 1/2 cm. (Lovell's library, v. 5. no. 215). c.1883. J. W. Lovell Company.
--The Red Eric: or, the Whaler's Last Cruise. Coleman, illus. N.D. George Routledge & Sons.
--The Red Eric: Or, The Whale's Last Cruise. (Illus.). (St. Nicholas Series for Boys). N.D. International Book Co.
--The Red Eric: Or, The Whale's Last Cruise, 1 of 5 Vols. (Land and Ocean Adventure Library). N.D. Set. J B Lippincott.
--Red Rooney: Or, The Last of the Crew. 1886. Nelson.
--Rivers of Ice, 1 of 5 vols. (Illus.). (Life Boat Ser.). N.D. Set. Thomas Nelson & Sons.
--The Rover of the Andes: A Tale of Adventure in South America. 1885. Nelson.
--The Settler and the Savage: A Tale of Peace and War in South Africa. 1887. Nelson.
--Shifting Winds, 1 of 6. (Ballantyne's Library of Adventure). N.D. Claxton, Remsen, & Haffelfinger.
--Shifting Winds. (Roundabout Lib.). N.D. Henry T. Coates & Co.
--Shifting Winds. Juv ed. (Roundabout Library). (Sea Stories). N.D. John C. Winston Co.
--Shifting Winds: A Story of the Sea, 1 of 4 Vols. (Illus.). (The Famous Ballantyne Bks. (Sea Stories)). N.D. Set. Porter & Coates.
--Silver Lake. (The Star Library). N.D. Frederick Warne & Co.
--The Silver Lake. (The Bradford Library). N.D. Frederick Warne.
--The Silver Lake. (Illus.). (The Home and Enterprise Library Ser.). N.D. Frederick Warne & Co.
--The Silver Lake. (Illus.). N.D. Scribner, Welford & Armstrong.
--The Silver Lake: Or, Lost in the Snow. (Illus.). (Warne's Home Circle Library). N.D. Frederick Warne & Co.
--Silver Lake: Or, Lost in the Snow. LC 6-8389. vii, 110 p. front., plates. 18 cm. 1868. J. B. Lippincott & Co.
--Snowflakes and Sunbeams: Or, The Young Fur Traders. A Tale of the Far North. LC 6-8390. 2 p. l., vi, 429 p. front., plates. 18 1/2 cm. 1856. T. Nelson and Sons.
--Story of the Rock, 1 of 6 Vols. (Illus.). (Ballantyne's Tales for Boys). N.D. Set. Thomas Nelson and Sons.
--Sunk at Sea, 1 of 6 Vols. (Illus.). (Ballantyne's Tales for Boys). N.D. Set. Thomas Nelson and Sons.
--Three Months' Rustication, 1 of 6. (Ballantyne's Library of Adventure). N.D. Claxton, Remsen, & Haffelfinger.
--Under the Waves. (Illus.). N.D. Thomas Nelson & Sons.
--Ungava: A Tale of Esquimaux land. (The R.M. Ballantyne Books for Boys). N.D. Nelson.
--Ungava, a Tale of Esquimaux Land, 1 of 3 Vols. (Illus.). (Gorilla Hunter Ser.). N.D. Set Thomas Nelson & Sons.
--The Walrus Hunters:. A Romance of the Realms of Ice. LC 76-253775. (Illus.). vi, 410. 20cm. 1893. Nelson.
--The Wild Man of the West, 1 of 6. (Ballantyne's Library of Adventure). N.D. Claxton, Remsen, & Haffelfinger.
--The Wild Man of the West. (Roundabout Lib.). N.D. Henry T. Coates & Co.
--The Wild Man of the West. (The R.M. Ballantyne Books for Boys). N.D. Nelson.
--The Wild Man of the West, 1 of 4 Vols. (Illus.). (Famous Ballantyne Bks.). (Land Stories). N.D. Set. Porter & Coates.
--The Wild Man of the West. Zwecker, illus. N.D. George Routledge & Sons.
--Wild Men of the West, 1 of 3 vols. Juv ed. (Land Stories). N.D. John C. Winston Co.
--The World of Ice. (The R.M. Ballantyne Books for Boys). N.D. Nelson.
--The world of Ice: Or, Adventures in the Polar Regions, 1 of 4 Vols. (Illus.). (Martin Rattler Ser.). N.D. Set. Thomas Nelson & Sons.
--Wrecked Not Ruined, 1 of 6 Vols. (Illus.). (Ballantyne's Tales for Boys). N.D. Set. Thomas Nelson and Sons.
--The Young Fur Traders. (The R.M. Ballantyne Books for Boys). N.D. Nelson.
--The Young Fur Traders, 1 of 4 vols. (Illus.). (Martin Rattler Ser.). N.D. Set. Thomas Nelson & Sons.

Ballantyne, William
--Adventures Among the Glaciers of the Alps. 1875. Pott, Young, & Co.
--Tales of Adventure by Flood, Field, and Mountain, 1 of 4 Vols. (Illus.). (Tales of Adventure). N.D. Set. Pott, Young & Co.
--Tales of Adventure on the Coast, 1 of 4 Vols. (Illus.). (Tales of Adventure). N.D. Set. Pott, Young & Co.
--Tales of Adventure on the Sea, 1 of 4 Vols. (Illus.). (Tales of Adventure). N.D. Set. Pott, Young & Co.
--Tales of Adventure: Or, Wild Work in Strange Places, 1 of 4 Vols. (Illus.). (Tales of Adventure). N.D. Set. Pott, Young & Co.

Ballard, Charles Martin (1929-)
--Benjie's Portion. Phillips, Douglas, illus. LC 76-82779. (Illus.). 208 p. 21cm. 1969. World Pub. Co.
--Dockie. LC 73-5476. 214 p. 22cm. 1973. (ISBN 0-06-020400-1). (ISBN 0-06-020400-1). Harper & Row.
--Dockie. 1st American ed. LC 73-5476. 22cm. 214p. 1973. (ISBN 0-06-020400-1). Harper & Row.
--Emir's Son. Floyd, Gareth (1940-), illus. (gr. k-4). 1967. World Pub.
--The Monarch of Juan Fernandez. Whitear, A. R., illus. 1968. Scribner.
--Sea Port City. Floyd, Gareth (1940-), illus. (Illus.). 208p. 1966. Lawrence Verry.

Ballard, Joan Kadey
--A Child Asks: Who? Why? and Where?. Schaeffer, Peg, photos by. LC 64-15554. 1 v. (unpaged) illus. 29 cm. 1964. Zondervan Pub. House.

Ballard, Julia Perkins, Mrs.
--Caught and Fettered. (Illus.). 267p. N.D. National Temperance Society.
--The Hole in the Bag and Other Stories. (Illus.). 255p. N.D. National Temperance Society.
--Lift a Little: Or, the Old Quilt. 80p. (Missing Boat Stories). N.D. Lockwood, Brooks, & Co. for American Tract Society.
--The Little Gold Keys. 151p. N.D. American Tract Society.
--Little Life. 112p. N.D. T. Y. Crowell.
--A Little Life. N.D. Warren & Wyman.

Ballard, Juliet B., ed.
--East of the Sun. 48p. (gr. 1-7). 1972. (ISBN 0-87604-057-1). ARE Pr.

Ballard, Kadey
--I Saw a Mother Chicken. 20p. 1963. Moody.

Ballard, Mignon Franklin
--Aunt Matilda's Ghost. LC 77-91932. 162 p. 22cm. c.1978. (ISBN 0-87695-210-4). Aurora Publishers.

Ballard, Susan
--Fairy Tales from Far Japan. (Illus.). N.D. Fleming H. Revell Co.

Ballas, Shimon (1930-)
--The Shoes of Tanboury. Eitan, Ora (1940-), illus. LC 79-82698. (Illus.). 39 p. 28cm. 1970. (ISBN 0-87631-016-1). Sabra Books.

Baller, Albert
--Hoppie the Hopper. Corwin, Eleanor, illus. LC 51-4226. 23cm. 28p. (An In action book). 1951. Rand McNally & Co.
--Pop-in, The Bunny. Corwin, Eleanor & Brice, Tony, illus. LC 52-31433. unpaged. illus. 23 cm. (In action book). N.D. Rand McNally.
--Robbie, the Little Lost Robin. Bendel, Ruth, illus. LC 56-37141. unpaged. illus. 22 cm. (In action book). 1955. Rand McNally and Phillips Publishers.

Ballew, Charles
--One Crazy Cowboy. N.D. A L Burt Co.

Balley, Bernadine Freeman, ed. see Dalgliesh, Alice

Balliet, Thomas Minard (1852-), ed. see Ewing, Juliana Horatia Gatty, Mrs.

Ballinger, W. A., pseud., see Baker, William Arthur Howard.

Ballinger, W. A., pseud. (1925-)
--The Carrion Eaters. Baker, William Arthur Howard. 1971. (ISBN 0-399-10121-7). G.P. Putnam's Sons.

Ballou, Arthur W (1915-)
--Bound for Mars. LC 78-108167. 218 p. 22cm. 1970. Little, Brown.
--Marooned in Orbit. (gr. 7 up). 1968. (ISBN 0-316-07975-8). Little.

Ballowe, Hewitt L.
--Creole Folk Tales: Stories of the Lousiana Marsh Country. 1948. Kennikat Press.

Balmer, Edwin
--Ruth of the U.S.A. Betts, Harold H., illus. N.D. Grosset & Dunlap.

Balmer, Edwin & Wylie, Philip (1902-1971)
--When Worlds Collide. Bd. with After Worlds Collide. 1950. (ISBN 0-397-00023-5). Lippincott.

Balmes, Pat
--Danger at the Flying Y. LC 81-22857. (Illus.). 44 p. 18cm. (Perspectives book). c.1982. (ISBN 0-87879-299-6). Academic Therapy Publications.

Balow, Tom, jt. auth. see Carpenter, John Allan.

Balterman, Marci Ridlon see Ridlon, Marci, pseud.

Baltermants, Dmitrii Nikolaevich & Levin, Deana
--Nikolai Lives in Moscow. Baltermants, Dmitri, photos by. (Illus.). 48 p. 22cm. (Children everywhere series). 1968, c.1966. Hastings House.

Balys, Jonas, jt. ed. see Thompson, Stith.

Balzac, Honore de (1799-1850)
--Cousin Bette. Wormeley, Katharine Prescott (1830-1908), tr. (Beacon Library of Fiction Classics). 1928. Little Brown & Co.
--Golden Tales from Balzac. Saintsbury, George, intro. by. N.D. Dodd Mead & Co.
--The Magic Skin. N.D. Robert Brothers.
--The Magic Skin. Arvil, P., illus. Woreley, Katharine Prescott (1830-1908), tr. (Beacon Library of Fiction Classics). 1915. Little Brown & Co.
--A Passion in the Desert. Arnosky, Jim (1946-), illus. LC 83-71790. c.1983. (ISBN 0-87191-965-6). Creative Education.
--Pere Goriot. Sedgwick, Jane M., tr. Klots, Allen, Jr., intro. by. (Great Illustrated Classics). N.D. Dodd Mead & Co.
--Tales from Balzac. (The Lotus Library of Continental Masterpieces). N.D. Brentano's.

Balzano, Jeanne Koppel see Bell, Gina, pseud.

Balzano, Jeanne Koppel see Bell-Zano, Gina, pseud.

Balzano, Jeanne Koppel (1912-)
--Andy and Mr. Wagner. Wilde, George A., illus. LC 57-13926. 30 p. illus. (part col.) 21 cm. 1957. Abingdon Press.
--Good for Nothing. Bell, Gina, pseud. Wilde, George A., illus. LC 61-7041. (Illus.). 31 p. 21cm. (gr. k-3). 1961. (ISBN 0-687-15492-8). Abingdon Press.
--Presents for Johnny Jerome. Bell-Zano, Gina, pseud. Polseno, Jo, illus. LC 66-10717. (Illus.). 31. 24cm. 1966. Ginn.
--Three Boys and a Dog. Wilde, George A., illus. LC 63-7968. 30 p. illus. (part col.) 21 cm. 1963. Abingdon.
--Wanted ... a Brother. Wilde, George A., illus. LC 59-7503. 31 p. illus. (part col.) 21 cm. 1959. Abingdon Press.
--The Wee Moose. Bell-Zano, Gina, pseud. Arno, Enrico (1913-1981), illus. LC 64-19767. (Illus.). 26cm. 1964. Magazine Press.
--What Makes Siggy Smart?. Kurek, Sarah C., illus. (Illus.). 37 p. 21cm. (An Easy-to-read book). 1967. Abingdon Press.
--Who Wants Willy Wells?. Tamburine, Jean (1930-), illus. LC 65-10719. 37 p. illus. (part col.) 21 cm. (Easy-to-read book). 1965. Abingdon Press.

Bambara, Toni Cade (1939-), ed.
--Tales and Stories for Black Folks. LC 79-144248. 164 p. 22cm. (Zenith anthologies). 1971. Zenith Books.

Bamberger, Helen R., Mrs. (1888-)
--Mystery of World's End. Sanchez, Carlos M. (1908-), illus. LC 30-197237. viii p., 1 l., 226 p. incl. front., 1 illus. 21 cm. 1930. Longmans, Green and Co.
--Nobody's Joan. Rodgers, Richard H. (1876-1953), illus. LC 31-33551. 314 p. incl. front. plates. 20 cm. c.1931. Newark, N.J. Barse & Co.

Bamberger, Richard G.
--My First Big Story-Book. (Illus.). 220p. 1967. (ISBN 0-8178-3972-0). (ISBN 0-8178-3971-2). Harvey House.
--My First Big Story-Book. Wallenta, Emanuela, illus. Thin, James, tr. LC 67-19640. 219 p. illus. (part col.) 24 cm. c.1965. Harvey House.
--My First Big Story-Book. Wallenta, Emanuela, illus. Thin, James, tr. (Illus.). 185 p. 20cm. (Young puffin Books). 1972, c.1965. (ISBN 0-14-030405-3). Penguin.
--My Second Big Story-Book. Wallenta, Emanuela, illus. Thin, James, tr. LC 69-13652. (Illus.). 50 ils, 13 color. 224p. 1st U.S. edition. (gr. 2-5). 1969. (ISBN 0-8178-4442-2). Harvey.
--My Second Big Story-Book. Wallenta, Emanuela, illus. LC 66-66273. (Illus.). 224 p. 24cm. 1966. Oliver & Boyd.

Bambote, Pierre
--Daba's Travels from Ouadda to Bangui. Buchanan-Brown, John, tr. from Fr. LC 76-117457. (Illus.). 170 p. 22cm. 1970. (ISBN 0-394-92050-3). Pantheon Books.

Bamford, Mary Ellen
--The Denby Children at the Fair. 64 p. illus. 17 1/2 cm. 1904. D.C. Cook Publishing Company.
--Eleanor and I. (Illus.). (The Pilgrim Endeavor Library). N.D. Pilgrims Press.
--Father Lambert's Family: A Story of Oldtime France, 1 of 25 vols. 128p. (Selected Bks for Sunday School: No. 24). N.D. Set. Methodist Bk Concern.
--Her Twenty Heathen and Other Missionary Stories. N.D. Pilgrim Press.
--Jessie's Three Resolutions. 192p. N.D. Sunday-School Publications.
--Look-About Club. (Illus.). N.D. Lothrop.
--Number one, or Number Two?. N.D. Methodist Book Concern.
--A Piece of Kitty Hunter's Life. N.D. Methodist Bk Concern.
--The Second Year of the Look-About Club. (Illus.). N.D. Lothrop Publishing Company.
--Three Roman Girls: A Tale of the Catacombs. 252p. N.D. Sunday-School Publications.
--Up and Down the Brooks. (Illus.). (The Riverside Library). N.D. Houghton, Mifflin & Co.

Bamman, Henry A., et al. (1918-)
--Bone People. Herrington, Roger, illus. LC 79-103285. (Illus.). 72 p. 24cm. (Space science fiction series). 1970. Benefic Press.
--Ice Men of Rime. Rohrer, George, illus. LC 76-103287. (Illus.). 72 p. 24cm. (Space science fiction series). 1970. Benefic Press.
--Inviso Man. Herrington, Roger, illus. LC 72-103286. (Illus.). 72 p. 24cm. (Space science fiction series). 1970. Benefic Press.
--Milky Way. Herrington, Roger, illus. LC 75-103284. (Illus.). 71 p. 24cm. (Space science fiction series). 1970. Benefic Press.
--Mystery Adventure. Herrington, Roger & Rohrer, George, illus. LC 68-56127. (Illus.). v. 24cm. 1969. Benefic Press.
--Planet of the Whistlers. Rohrer, George, illus. LC 79-101394. (Illus.). 72 p. 24cm. (Space science fiction series). 1970. Benefic Press.
--Space Pirate. Herrington, Roger, illus. LC 71-103283. (Illus.). 72 p. 24cm. (Space science fiction series). 1970. Benefic Press.

Bamman, Henry A. (1918-) & Kennedy, Leonard
--Mystery Adventure at Longcliff Inn. Herrington, Roger, illus. LC 69-19640. (Illus.). 96. 24cm. (Mystery Adventure Ser.). 1969. Benefic Press.

Bamman, Henry A. (1918-) & Whitehead, Robert John (1928-)
--Hunting Grizzly Bears. Lackey, William, illus. LC 63-15508. 72 p. illus. 24 cm. (World of adventures series). c.1963. Benefic Press.

Banai, Margalit see Russcol, Margalit, pseud.

Banai, Margalit (1928-)
--Achmed, Boy of the Negev. Russcol, Margalit, pseud. LC 64-257592. 63p. illus. 21cm. c.1965. Putnam.
--Yael and the Queen of Goats. Friedel, illus. Reznik, Ruth, tr. (Illus.). 63 p. 25cm. (Sabra book). 1968. Funk and Wagnalls.

Banbery, Fred, jt. auth. see Bond, Thomas Michael.

Bancks, G. W.
--World Beneath the Waters: Or, Merman's Country. N.D. Cassell & Co.

Bancroft, Alberta (1873-)
--The Goblins of Haubeck. Sichel, Harold M. (1881-), illus. LC 25-233605. 6 p. l. 3-117 p. incl. illus., plates. 19 1/2 cm. 1923. R. M. McBride & Company.

--Lost Village. Barney, Maginel Wright, Mrs. (1881-1966), illus. LC 27-19560. 3 p. l., 9-130 p. col. front., illus., col. plates (1 double) 21 cm. c.1927. George H. Doran Company.
--Royal Rogues. Betta, L., illus. 1901. G.P. Putnam's Sons.

Bancroft, Edith
--Jane Allen: Center. Gooch, Thelma, illus. LC 21-7719. 4 p. l., 310 p. front., plates. 20 1/2 cm. (Her Jane Allen series). c.1920. Cupples & Leon Company.
--Jane Allen: Junior. Gooch, Thelma, illus. LC 21-130627. 5 p. l., 300 p. front., plates. 20 cm. (Her Jane Allen series). c.1921. Cupples & Leon Company.
--Jane Allen of the Sub-Team. Willams, Roy L., illus. LC 17-279018. vi p., 1 l., 338 p. front., plates. 20 cm. c.1917. Cupples & Leon Company.
--Jane Allen: Right Guard. Owen, Robert Emmett (1878-), illus. LC 19-861. vi p., 1 l., 310 p. front., plates. 20 cm. (Her Jane Allen series). c.1918. Cupples & Leon Company.
--Jane Allen: Senior. Gooch, Thelma, illus. LC 22-9666. 5 p. l., 310 p. front., plates. 20 cm. (Her Jane Allen series). c.1922. Cupples & Leon Company.

Bancroft, Griffing (1907-)
--Snowy: The Story of an Egret. Hunter, Mel (1927-), illus. (gr. 7 up). 1970. (ISBN 0-525-39560-1). Dutton.
--Snowy: The Story of an Egret. Hunter, Mel (1927-), illus. LC 71-113734. (Illus.). viii, 149 p. 21cm. 1970. (ISBN 0-8415-2007-0). McCall.
--Vanishing Wings: A Tale of Three Birds of Prey. LC 77-182289. (Illus.). 160p. (gr. 9 up). 1972. (ISBN 0-531-02041-X). Watts.
--The White Cardinal. Frace, Charles, illus. LC 72-89756. (Illus.). 124 p. 22cm. 1973. Coward, McCann & Geoghegan.

Bancroft, John
--Borodin Affair. (gr. 9 up). 1966. (ISBN 0-685-20972-5). Verry.

Bancroft, Laura, pseud., see Baum, Lyman Frank.

Bancroft, Laura, pseud. (1856-1919)
--Bandit Jim Crow. Baum, Lyman Frank. Enright, Maginel Wright, illus. LC 6-28218. 62, 1 p. col. illus. 17 1/2 cm. (Her The Twinkle tales). c.1906. The Reilly & Britton Co.
--Mr. Woodchuck. Baum, Lyman Frank. Enright, Maginel Wright, illus. LC 6-26070. 62 p., 1 l. col. illus. 17 1/2 cm. (Her The Twinkle tales). c.1906. The Reilly & Britton Co.
--Policeman Bluejay. Baum, Lyman Frank. LC 81-9044. Repr. of 1907 ed. 1981. (ISBN 0-8201-1367-0). Schol Facsimiles.
--Policeman Bluejay. Baum, Lyman Frank. Enright, Maginel Wright, illus. LC 7-241867. 115, 1 p. col. front., illus., 7 col. pl. 24 cm. c.1907. The Reilly & Britton Co.
--Prairie Dog Town. Baum, Lyman Frank. Enright, Maginel Wright, illus. (Twinkle Tales). 1906. Reilly & Lee.
--Prairie-Dog Town. Baum, Lyman Frank. Enright, Maginel Wright, illus. LC 6-26071. 61 p., 1 l. col. illus. 17 1/2 cm. (Her The Twinkle tales). c.1906. The Reilly & Britton Co.
--Prince Mud Turtle. Baum, Lyman Frank. Enright, Maginel Wright, illus. (Twinkle Tales). 1906. Reilly & Lee.
--Prince Mud-Turtle. Baum, Lyman Frank. Enright, Maginel Wright, illus. LC 6-27993. 61 p. col. illus. 17 1/2 cm. (Her The Twinkle tales). c.1906. The Reilly & Britton Co.
--Sugar Loaf Mountain. Baum, Lyman Frank. Enright, Maginel Wright, illus. (Twinkle Tales). 1906. Reilly & Lee.
--Sugar-Loaf Mountain. Baum, Lyman Frank. Enright, Maginel Wright, illus. 64 p. col. illus. 18 cm. (Her The Twinkle tales). c.1906. The Reilly & Britton Co.
--Twinkle and Chubbins. Baum, Lyman Frank. Enright, Maginel Wright, illus. Orig. Title: Twinkle Tales. 1911. Reilly and Britton.
--Twinkle's Enchantment. Baum, Lyman Frank. Enright, Maginel Wright, illus. LC 6-27990. 64 p. col. illus. 17 1/2 cm. (Her The Twinkle tales). c.1906. The Reilly & Britton Co.

Band, Edward A.
--The Fifer Boy of the Boston Siege. (Bks. for Boy Scouts). N.D. Abingdon Press.
--Ship Ashore. (Bks. for Boy Scouts). N.D. Abingdon Press.

Bandel, Betty (1912-), compiled by.
--Walk into My Parlor. LC 76-158783. (gr. 6 up). 1972. (ISBN 0-8048-0920-8). C E Tuttle.

Bandelier, Adolf Francis Alphonse (1840-1914)
--Delight Makers. (Illus.). (gr. 9 up). N.D. (ISBN 0-396-00087-8). Dodd.

Banel, Joseph (1943-)
--Lee Wong, Boy Detective. Malsberg, Edward, illus. LC 72-1923. (Illus.). 62 p. 23cm. 1972. (ISBN 0-8116-6967-X). Garrard Pub. Co.

Baner, Skulda Vanadis (1897-1964)
--First Parting. LC 60-9877. 211 p. 21cm. 1960. Longmans, Green.
--Pims: Adventurea of a Dala Horse. Bock, Vera, illus. (Illus.). 148 p. 19cm. (gr. 3-7). 1964. D. McKay Co.
--Voice of the Lute. 1959. McKay.

Banerjea, S. B.
--Tales of Bengal. Skrine, Francis Henry, ed. 1910. Longmans, Green.

Banet, Doris Beatrice Robinson (1925-)
--Flicker, the Discontented Firefly. Spiegel, Lawrence M., illus. (Illus.). (Nature & Science Bk.). (gr. k-6). N.D. Denison.
--Flicker, the Discontented Firefly. Spiegel, Lawrence M., illus. LC 60-15144. unpaged. illus. 29cm. 1960. T. S. Denison.
--Tiny, the Teeny Turtle. Lindberg, Howard E., illus. LC 60-12621. unpaged. illus. 29cm. (gr. 3-4). 1960. T. S. Denison.

Banfield, Beryle, jt. ed. see Meyers, Ruth S.

Bang, Betsy (1912-), ed. see Chen, Tony.

Bang, Betsy (1912-), adapted by.
--The Old Woman & the Red Pumpkin. Bang, Molly Garrett (1943-), illus. LC 74-13057. (Illus.). 32p. (gr. k-3). 1975. (ISBN 0-02-708360-8). Macmillan.

Bang, Garrett, see Bang, Molly Garrett.

Bang, Garrett, (1943-), ed.
--Men from the Village Deep in the Mountains and Other Japanese Folk Tales. Bang, Molly Garrett. Bang, Garrett, pseud. (1943-), illus. Bang, Molly Garrett. LC 72-92431. (Illus.). 84 p. 23cm. 1973. (ISBN 0-02-708350-0). Macmillan.

Bang, Kirsten
--Yougga Finds Mother Teresa: The Adventures of a Beggar Boy in India. Svensson, Kamma, illus. LC 83-4267. (Illus.). 165 p. 22cm. 1983. (ISBN 0-8164-2469-1). Seabury Press.

Bang, Molly Garrett see Bang, Garrett,

Bang, Molly Garrett (1943-)
--Dawn. LC 83-886. (gr. 4-7). 1983. (ISBN 0-688-02400-9). (ISBN 0-688-02404-1). Morrow.
--The Grey Lady and the Strawberry Snatcher. LC 85-29224. p. cm. 1985, c.1980. (ISBN 0-02-708140-0). Four Winds Press.
--The Grey Lady and the Strawberry Snatcher. Bang, Molly Garrett (1943-), illus. LC 79-21243. (Illus.). 48 p. c.1980. (ISBN 0-590-07547-0). Four Winds Press. **Awards: (ALA); (BGH); (RCM).**
--The Paper Crane. Bang, Molly Garrett (1943-), illus. LC 84-13546. (Illus.). 32 p. c.1985. (ISBN 0-688-04108-6). (ISBN 0-688-04109-4). Greenwillow Books.
--Ten, Nine, Eight. Bang, Molly Garrett (1943-), illus. LC 81-20106. (Illus.). 8 x 7. 24p. (28 pt.). (ps-1). 1983. (ISBN 0-688-00906-9). (ISBN 0-688-00907-7). Greenwillow. **Awards: (ALA); (RCM).**
--Ten, Nine, Eight. Bang, Molly Garrett (1943-), illus. LC 84-3321. (Illus.). 24 p. (Picture puffins). 1985, c.1983. (ISBN 0-14-050481-8). Puffin Books.
--Tye May and the Magic Brush. LC 80-16488. (Illus.). 55 p. 22cm. (Greenwillow read-alone). c.1981. (ISBN 0-688-80290-7). (ISBN 0-688-84290-9). Greenwillow Books.

Bang, Molly Garrett (1943-), ed.
--The Buried Moon and other Stories. Bang, Molly Garrett (1943-), illus. LC 76-58328. 21 cm. 63p. 1977. Scribner.
--The Goblins Giggle, and Other Stories. Bang, Molly Garrett (1943-), illus. LC 72-9033. (Illus.). 57 p. 23cm. 1973. (ISBN 0-684-13226-5). Scribners.
--Wiley and the Hairy Man: Adapted from an American Folktale. Bang, Molly Garrett (1943-), illus. LC 75-35581. (Illus.). 64 p. 23cm. (Ready-to-read). c.1976. (ISBN 0-02-708370-5). Macmillan. **Award: (ALA).**

Bang, Molly Garrett (1943-), illus.
--The Demons of Rajpur: Five Tales from Bengal. Bang, Betsy (1912-), tr. LC 80-10467. p. cm. 1980. (ISBN 0-688-80263-X). (ISBN 0-688-84263-1). Greenwillow Books.
--The Old Woman and the Rice Thief. Bang, Betsy (1912-), tr. LC 76-30671. (Illus.). 32 p. 26cm. c.1978. (ISBN 0-688-80098-X). (ISBN 0-688-84098-1). Greenwillow Books.
--Tuntuni, the Tailor Bird. LC 78-2274. (Illus.). 63 p. 22cm. (Greenwillow read-alone). c.1978. (ISBN 0-688-80167-6). (ISBN 0-688-84167-8). Greenwillow Books.

Bangert, Ethel Elizabeth (1912-)
--Polly Perry, T.V. Cook. LC 59-11413. 185. 1959. Putnam.

Bangs, Edward (1756-1818)
--Steven Kellogg's Yankee Doodle. Kellogg, Steven (1941-), illus. LC 75-19190. (Illus.). 38 p. c.1976. (ISBN 0-8193-0833-1). (ISBN 0-8193-0834-X). Parents' Magazine Press. **Award: (ALA).**
--Yankee Doodle. Kellogg, Steven (1941-), illus. LC 80-17024. p. cm. 1980, c.1976. (ISBN 0-590-07782-1). Four Winds Press.

Bangs, Ella Matthews
--At the House on the Ground: A Story for Girls. LC 13-23412. 5 p. l., 3-307 p. front., plates. 20 cm. $1.2. c.1913. The Pilgrim Press.

Bangs, John Kendrick (1862-1922)
--Andiron Tales. Dwiggins, Clare Victor (1874-), illus. LC 7-2057. 101, 1 p. incl. col. front., illus. col. plates 24 1/2 cm. c.1906. The J. C. Winston Co.
--Bikey the Skicycle. (Illus.). N.D. Harper & Brothers Trade-List.
--Bikey the Skicycle: & Other Tales of Jimmieboy. Newell, Peter (1862-1924), illus. LC 2-214822. 321 p. incl. col. front. plates. 20 cm. 1902. Riggs Publishing Company.
--Half Hours with Jimmieboy. N.D. R. H. Russell.
--Half-Hours with Jimmieboy. VerBeck, Frank (1858-1933) & Johnson, Charles Howard, illus. 112p. N.D. De Witt Publishing House.
--Houseboat on the Styx. N.D. Harper & Bros.
--In Camp With a Tin Soldier. New ed. N.D. R. H. Russell.
--In Camp With a Tin Tales: A Sequel to the Tiddledywink Tales. Ashe, E. M., illus. 236p. N.D. De Witt Publishing House.
--Jack and the Check Book. Levering, Albert, illus. 4 p. l., 235, 1 p. incl. illus., plates. front. 18 1/2 cm. 1911. Harper & Brothers.
--The Mantal-Piece Minstrels and Other Stories. LC 78-85689. (Illus.). 9-84 p. 21cm. (Short story index reprint series). 1969. Books for Libraries Press.
--Mantelpiece Minstrels. New ed. N.D. R. H. Russell.
--Mollie and the Unwiseman Abroad. Wiederseim, Grace G., illus. LC 10-21602. 261, 1 p. col. front., col. plates. 21 cm. 1910. J. B. Lippincott Company.
--Molly and the Unwiseman. Levering, Albert & Dwiggins, Clare Victor, illus. N.D. John C. Winston.
--Molly and the Unwiseman: A Humorous Story for Children. N.D. John C. Winston.
--Pursuit of the Houseboat. N.D. Harper & Bros.
--Tiddledywink Tales. N.D. R. H. Russell.
--Tiddledywink Tales. Johnson, Charles Howard, illus. 236p. N.D. De Witt Publishing House.
--The Tiddledywink's Poetry Book. Johnson, Charles Howard, illus. 30p. N.D. De Witt Publishing House.
--The Tiddledywink's Poetry Book. Johnson, Charles Howard, illus. LC 14-22733. 64 p. illus. 19 1/2 cm. 1892. R. H. Russell & Son.

Bangs, John Kendrick (1862-1922) & Macauley, Charles Raymond
--Emblemland. LC 3-170. (Illus.). 164. 21cm. 1902. R. H. Russell.

Bangs, Robert Babbitt see Babbitt, Robert, pseud.

Banigan, Kippy & Stearns, Sharon (1912-), illus.
--So Big Book of Mother Goose. N.D. Garden City Publishing Co.

Banigan, Sharon Church
--Nineteen Little Rabbits. LC 51-27546. 28p. col. illus. 32cm. 1951. John Martin House.

Banigan, Sharon Church see Stearns, Sharon.

Banigan, Sharon Stearns (1912-)
--Circus Magic: Verses. Maillard, Katharina, illus. LC 59-3882. unpaged. illus. 30cm. 1959, c.1958. Dutton.

Banish, Roslyn
--I Want to Tell You About My Baby. Banish, Roslyn, illus. 1982. Wingbow Press.

Bank Street College of Education
--Voyage of the Mimi. (Illus.). 160p. (gr. 4-7). 1984. (ISBN 0-03-000753-4). (ISBN 0-03-000943-X). HR&W.

Bankart, Henry Reginald (1913-)
--Bolivar. Bankart, Henry Reginald (1913-), illus. LC 41-19429. (Illus.). 25cm. 39p. 1941. Smith & Durrell.

Banker, Harriet
--Jobie and Jake. LC 56-12113. (Illus.). 57 p. 22cm. (A Pan Press Young-Folks Book). 1956. Pan Press.

Banks
--Children's Summer, 1 of 50 vols. (The Golden Rod Lib.). N.D. Set. American Tract Society.

Banks, Ann (1943-) & Evans, Nancy (1950-)
--Goodbye, House. (Illus.). 64p. 1980. (Harmony). Crown.

Banks, Charles Eugene (1852-)
--A Child of the Sun. Betts, Louis, illus. 3 p. l., 166 p. 1 l. col. front., col. plates. 22 cm. 1900. H. S. Stone & Company.

Banks, Elizabeth
--Dik: A/Dog of Belgium and His Allies. LC 16-2134. 18cm. 31p. 1916. James Kempster Printing Company.

Banks, Eulalie M. see Eulalie, pseud.

Banks, G. Linnaeus, Mrs.
--Miss Pringle's Pearls. N.D. Thomas Whittaker.

Banks, Helen Ward
--The Boynton Pluck. (The Vacation Ser.). N.D. Penn.
--The Boynton Pluck. (Sunbeam Ser. for Young People). N.D. Penn.
--The Boynton Pluck. Deland, Clyde O., illus. LC 5-20916. 20cm. 193p. 1905. Penn Publishing Co.
--The House of the Lions. Rosenmeyer, Bernard J., illus. LC 24-20564. 6 p. l., 3-249 p. front., plates. 19 1/2 cm. c.1924. The Century Co.
--Polly's Garden. Pogany, Willy (1882-1955), illus. LC 18-8162. ix, 96 p. col. front., col. plates. 19 1/2 cm. (Half-title: The opening door series). 1918. The Macmillan Company.

Banks, Louis Albert (1855-)
--Live Boys in Oregon: Orm AN Oregan Boyhood. LC 1-29263. 19cm. 173p. 1900. Lothrop, Lee & Shepard.
--An Oregon Boyhood. LC 1-5148. 2 p. l., 173 p. front., plates. 19 cm. 1898. Lee and Shepard.

Banks, Lynne Reid (1929-)
--The Adventures of King Midas. (Illus.). 1976. (ISBN 0-460-06752-4, Pub. by J. M. Dent England). Biblio Dist.
--The Farthest-Away Mountain. Ambrus, Victor G., pseud. (1935-), illus. Ambrus, Gyozo Laszlo. LC 77-355295. (Illus.). 5, 140 p. 21cm. 1976. (ISBN 0-200-72461-4). Abelard-Schuman.
--The Farthest-Away Mountain. Ambrus, Victor G., pseud. (1935-), illus. Ambrus, Gyozo Laszlo. LC 77-72412. (Illus.). 140 p. 22cm. N.D. (ISBN 0-385-12875-4). Doubleday.
--My Darling Villain. LC 76-58718. 237 p. 21cm. c.1977. (ISBN 0-06-020392-7). (ISBN 0-06-020393-5). Harper & Row.
--One More River. LC 72-93971. 288 p. 22cm. 1973. (ISBN 0-671-65205-2). Simon and Schuster.
--Sarah and After: Five Women Who Founded a Nation. LC 76-16250. 183 p. 22cm. c.1975. (ISBN 0-385-11456-7). (ISBN 0-385-11455-9). Doubleday.
--The Writing on the Wall. LC 81-47796. p. cm. c.1981. (ISBN 0-06-020388-9). (ISBN 0-06-020389-7). Harper & Row.

Banks, Lynne Reid (1929-) & Cole, Brock
--The Indian in the Cupboard. LC 79-6533. (Illus.). 181 p. 22cm. 1981. (ISBN 0-385-17051-3). (ISBN 0-385-17060-2). Doubleday.

Banks, Martha Burr
--Castle Daffodil. 209p. N.D. Pilgrims Press.
--The Children's Summer. (Illus.). 440p. N.D. Merrill & Baker.
--The Children's Summer. N.D. Robert Carter & Brothers.
--A Galahad of Nowadays. (Illus.). N.D. Methodist Bk Concern.
--Little Comrade Mine, 1 of 50 vols. 271p. (Library of Best Authors). 1905. American Tract Society.
--Little Comrade Mine. (Illus.). N.D. Merril & Baker.
--Princess Dandelion's Secret, 1 of 50 vols. (Illus.). 238p. (Library of Best Authors). 1905. American Tract Society.
--Princess Dandelion's Secret. (Illus.). N.D. Merrill & Baker.
--Richard and Robin, 1 of 50 vols. (The Golden Rody Lib.). 1905. Set. American Tract Society.
--Richard and Robin. Mueller, Rose, illus. 408p. N.D. Merrill & Baker.

Banks, Richard
--The Beaver Hunters. Kane, Harry, illus. LC 64-10144. 213 p. illus. 21 cm. 1964. St Martin's Press.
--The Mysterious Leaf. 1st ed. Haas, Irene (1929-), illus. LC 54-8527. 54 p. illus. 22 cm. 1954. Harcourt, Brace.

Banks, Stockton Voorhees (1908-1980)
--Washington Adventure. Pitz, Henry Clarence (1895-1976), illus. LC 50-10734. 191 p. illus. 22 cm. 1950. Whittlesey House.

Bank Street College of Education-New York, jt. auth. see Black, Irma Simonton, Mrs.

Banner, Angela, pseud., see Maddison, Angela Mary.

Banner, Angela, pseud. (1923-)
--Ant & Bee. Maddison, Angela Mary. LC 63-20113. (Illus.). (Ant & Bee Bks). (gr. k-3). 1958. (ISBN 0-531-01155-0). Watts.
--Ant & Bee & Kind Dog. Maddison, Angela Mary. (Illus.). (Ant & Bee Bks). (gr. k-3). 1964. Watts.
--Ant and Bee, and Kind Dog. Maddison, Angela Mary. Ward, Bryan, illus. LC 63-20114. 110p. col. illus. 10 x 13cm. 1963. F. Watts.
--Ant and Bee and the A B C. Maddison, Angela Mary. Ward, Bryan, illus. LC 66-16692. (Illus.). 94 p. 1966. F. Watts.
--Ant & Bee & the Doctor. Maddison, Angela Mary. Banner, Angela, pseud. (1923-), illus. Maddison, Angela Mary. LC 77-152853. (Illus.). color ils. 92p. (Ant & Bee Ser). (gr. k-3). 1971. (ISBN 0-531-01167-4). Watts.
--Ant and Bee and the Rainbow: A Story about Colours. Maddison, Angela Mary. Ward, Bryan, illus. LC 62-17671. 11 x 13cm. 89p. 1962. Watts.
--Ant and Bee and the Secret. Maddison, Angela Mary. Banner, Angela, pseud. (1923-), illus. Maddison, Angela Mary. LC 74-97837. (Illus.). 77 p. 1970. F. Watts.

AUTHOR INDEX

BARBATO, JULI

--Ant & Bee Go Shopping. Maddison, Angela Mary. Banner, Angela, pseud. (1923-), illus. Maddison, Angela Mary. LC 74-185921. (Illus.). 80p. 1st U.S. edition. (Ant & Bee Bks.). (gr. k-3). 1972. (ISBN 0-531-01168-2). Watts.
--Ant and Bee Time. Maddison, Angela Mary. Banner, Angela, pseud. (1923-), illus. Maddison, Angela Mary. LC 69-12354. (Illus.). 95 p. (incl. cover). 1969. F. Watts.
--Around the World with Ant and Bee. Maddison, Angela Mary. Ward, Bryan, illus. LC 61-63053. 93p. (incl. cover) col. illus. 11x31cm. 1963, c.1958. Watts.
--Happy Birthday with Ant and Bee. Maddison, Angela Mary. Ward, Bryan, illus. LC 64-19107. (Illus.). 95 p. 1964. F. Watts.
--More & More Ant & Bee. Maddison, Angela Mary. (Ant & Bee Bks). (gr. k-3). 1970. (ISBN 0-531-01164-X). Watts.
--More and More Ant and Bee: Another Alphabetical Story. Maddison, Angela Mary. Ward, Bryan, illus. LC 62-17672. (Illus.). 110. 10 x 13cm. 1962. F. Watts.
--More Ant & Bee. Maddison, Angela Mary. (Ant & Bee Bks). (gr. k-3). 1958. (ISBN 0-531-01161-5). Watts.
--One, Two, Three with Ant and Bee: A Counting Story. Maddison, Angela Mary. Ward, Bryan, illus. LC 59-13687. 91p. illus. 11 x 13cm. c.1958. F. Watts.

Bannerman, Helen Brodie Cowan Watson, Mrs. (1863-1946)
--The Jumbo Sambo. LC 42-186611. 223, 1 p. col. illus. 22 cm. 1942. Frederick A. Stokes Company.
--The Jumbo Sambo. N.D. J. B. Lippincott Co.
--Little Black Sambo. LC 26-2808. 63 p. incl. col. front., col. illus. 23 1/2 cm. ("A just right book"). c.1925. A. Whitman & Co.
--Little Black Sambo. cover-title, 12 p. illus. (part col.) 31 cm. 1933. The Platt & Munk Co., Inc.
--Little Black Sambo. Jordan, Nina Ralston, illus. LC 36-7005. 42 p. illus. (part col.) 17 cm. c.1934. Whitman Publishing Co.
--Little Black Sambo. Moore, Robert J., illus. LC 42-182835. 22 p. incl. col. front., illus. (part col.) 24 x 21 cm. 1942. Grosset & Dunlap.
--Little Black Sambo. Peat, Fern Bisel, Mrs. (1893-), illus. 20 p. illus. (part col.) 23 cm. (Lettered on cover: Calico classics). c.1932. The Saalfield Publishing Company.
--Little Black Sambo. Rutherford, Bonnie & Rutherford, Bill, illus. LC 76-3986. (Illus.). 21 p. 32cm. (Golden Book)). 1976, c.1971. (ISBN 0-307-10503-2). Golden Press/Western Pub. Co.
--Little Black Sambo. Tenggren, Gustaf (1896-1970), illus. LC 49-9407. 42 p. illus. (part col.) 20 cm. (Little golden library, 57). 1948. Simon and Schuster.
--Little Black Sambo. Ward, Keith, illus. LC 35-20109. 16 p. illus. 34 cm. c.1935. Whitman Publishing Co.
--Little Black Sambo. Wehr, Julian, illus. LC 45-1342. 18 p. col. illus. 22 x 17 1/2 cm. c.1943. Duenewald Printing Corporation.
--Little Black Sambo. Wehr, Julian, illus. LC 49-941. 18 p. col. illus. 22 cm. 1949. Duenewald Print. Corp.
--Little Black Sambo. Wehr, Julian, illus. LC 43-133357. 24 p. col. illus. 22 x 17 cm. 1943. E. P. Dutton & Co., Inc.
--The Little Black Sambo Story Book. Bannerman, Helen Brodie Cowan Watson (1863-1946) & Ver Beck, Frank (1858-1933), illus. LC 30-30716. 63, 1 p. incl. col. front., col. illus. 24 1/2 cm. c.1930. Henry Altemus Company.
--The Little Black Sambo Story Book: With the original story. Bannerman, Helen Brodie Cowan Watson (1863-1946) & Ver Beck, Frank (1858-), illus. LC 62-13188. 63p. illus. 25cm. (Platt & Munk classic, 117). 1962. Platt & Munk.
--The Little Red Hen, Black Sambo and Peter Rabbit. Miloche, Hilda & Kane, Wilma, illus. LC 45-1079. 64 p. col. illus. 28 1/2 cm. c.1944. Whitman Publishing Company.
--Pat and the Spider: The Biter Bit. 142 1 incl. col. front., col. plates. 14 cm. c.1905. F. A. Stokes Company.
--Rama and the Tigers. Chorpenning, Charlotte Lee Barrows (1872-1955), adapted by. Orig. Title: Little Black Sambo and the Tigers. 1954. Coach House Press.
--Sambo and the Twins. Bannerman, Helen Brodie Cowan Watson, Mrs. (1863-1946), illus. 1936. J. B. Lippincott Co.
--Sambo and the Twins: A New Adventure of Little Black Sambo. LC 36-20371. 2 p. l., 90, 1 p. col. illus. 16 cm. 1936. Frederick A. Stokes Company.
--Sambo and the Twins, a New Adventure of Little Black Sambo. Bannerman, Helen Brodie Cowan Watson, Mrs. (1863-1946), illus. N.D. J. P. Lippincott Co.
--Sambo and the Twins Other Tales. Bannerman, Helen Brodie Cowan Watson, Mrs. (1863-1946), illus. 1936. J. B. Lippincott.
--The Story of Little Black Bobtail. LC 33-27621. 63 p. incl. col. front., col. illus. 15 cm. c.1937. Frederick A. Stokes Company.
--The Story of Little Black Bobtail. Bannerman, Helen Brodie Cowan Watson, Mrs. (1863-1946), illus. N.D. J. B. Lippincott Co.
--Story of Little Black Mingo. (Illus.). (Dumpy Books). N.D. Frederick A. Stokes Co.
--The Story of Little Black Mingo. N.D. J. B. Lippincott.
--The Story of Little Black Mingo. Bannerman, Helen Brodie Cowan Watson, Mrs. (1863-1946), illus. 1902. Frederick A. Stokes Co.
--The Story of Little Black Quibba. LC 12-30679. 142, 2 p. incl. col. front., col. plates. 14 cm. 1903. F. A. Stokes Company.
--The Story of Little Black Sambo. N.D. David McKay Co.
--The Story of Little Black Sambo. LC 23-26581. ii-iv, 1, 56 p. col. front., col. illus. 14 1/2 cm. N.D. Frederick A. Stokes Company.
--The Story of Little Black Sambo. 1923. J. B. Lippincott.
--The Story of Little Black Sambo. LC 51-14665. 56 p. illus. 14 cm. 1st U.S. edition. N.D. Lippincott.
--The Story of Little Black Sambo. Baum, Lyman Frank, intro. by. LC 5-16888. 5 p. l., 56 p., 1 l. col. front., col. plates. 10 1/2 cm. (Christmas stocking series). 1905. The Reilly & Britton, Co.
--The Story of Little Black Sambo. Cloud, Claude Carey (1899-), illus. 1 p. l., 5-60 (i.e. 62) p. illus. (1 col.) 13 cm. (On cover: The midget pop-up books). c.1934. Blue Ribbon Press.
--The Story of Little Kettle-Head: An Awful Warning to Bad Babas. LC 4-17218. 142 p., 1 l. incl. col. front., col. plates, 14 cm. 1904. Frederick A. Stokes Company.
--The Story of the Little Black Bobtail. 14cm. 115p. 1909. Frederick A. Stokes Co.
--The Story of the Teasing Monkey. LC 7-26460. 142 p. 1 l., incl. col. front., col. plates. 14 cm. c.1907. F. A. Stokes Company.

Bannerman, Helen Brodie Cowan Watson, Mrs. (1863-1946), illus.
--The Teasing Monkey. N.D. J. B. Lippincott Co.

Banning, George Hugh
--Wheels of Empire. Voorhies, Stephen J., illus. LC 35-4226. viii p., 2 l., 13-68 p. incl. front., illus. 19 1/2 cm. (Half-title: Our changing world ... editor: R. G. Reynolds). 1935. T. Nelson and Sons.

Banning, Kendall
--Submarine! the Story of Undersea Fighters. N.D. Random House Inc.

Banning, Nina Lloyd
--Pit Pony. Collett, Farrell R., illus. LC 47-31031. 4 l., 3-167 p. illus. 21 cm. 1947. A. A. Knopf.

Bannon, Laura May (0000-1963)
--Baby Roo. Bannon, Laura May (0000-1963), illus. LC 47-30787. 28 p. illus. 24 cm. 1947. Houghton Mifflin Co.
--The Best House in the World. Bannon, Laura May (0000-1963), illus. (Illus.). 31 p. 24cm. 1952. Houghton Mifflin.
--Big Brother. Bannon, Laura May (0000-1963), illus. LC 50-7815. (Illus.). 48 p. 27cm. 1950. Whitman.
--Billy and the Bear. Bannon, Laura May (0000-1963), illus. LC 49-8137. 47 p. illus. (part col.) col. map. 28 cm. N.D. Houghton Miffin Co.,.
--Burro Boy and His Big Trouble. Bannon, Laura May (0000-1963), illus. LC 55-1946. 21cm. 46p. 1955. Abingdon Press.
--The Contented Horse Trader. (Illus.). 96 p. 21cm. 1963. A. Whitman.
--The Famous Baby-Sitter. 47 p. 24cm. 1960. A. Whitman.
--The Gift of Hawaii. Bannon, Laura May (0000-1963), illus. LC 61-14608. unpaged. illus. 24cm. 1961. A. Whitman.
--Gregorio and the White Llama. Bannon, Laura May (0000-1963), illus. LC 44-9332. 44, 3 p. illus. (part col.) 24 x 21 cm. 1944. A. Whitman & Co.
--Hat for a Hero, a Tarascan Boy of Mexico. Bannon, Laura May (0000-1963), illus. LC 54-9939. unpaged. illus. 26cm. 1954. A. Whitman.
--Hawaiian Coffee Picker. Bannon, Laura May (0000-1963), illus. LC 62-7534. (Illus.). 48 p. 25cm. 1962. Houghton Mifflin.
--Hop-High the Goat. N.D. E . M. Hale and Co.
--Hop-High, the Goat. 1st ed. Bannon, Laura May (0000-1963), illus. LC 60-6939. 64p. illus. 23cm. 1960. Bobbs-Merrill.
--Horse on a Houseboat. Bannon, Laura May (0000-1963), illus. LC 51-13919. (Illus.). 94 p. 22cm. 1951. Whitman.
--Jo-Jo The Talking Crow. N.D. E. M. Hale & Co.
--Jo-Jo, the Talking Crow. Bannon, Laura May (0000-1963), illus. (Illus.). 47 p. 25cm. 1958. Houghton Mifflin.
--Katy Comes Next. Bannon, Laura May (0000-1963), illus. (Illus.). 47 p. 24cm. 1959. A. Whitman.
--Little People of the Night. Bannon, Laura May (0000-1963), illus. (Illus.). 31 p. 21cm. c.1963. Houghton Mifflin.
--The Little Sister Doll. Bannon, Laura May (0000-1963), illus. (Illus.). 30 p. 24cm. 1955. A. Whitman.
--Make Room for Rags. Guthrie, Vee, illus. LC 64-19381. 64 p. illus. 21 cm. 1964. Houghton Mifflin.
--Manuela's Birthday. new ed. LC 74-188426. (Illus.). 32 p. 1972. (ISBN 0-8075-4973-8). A. Whitman.
--Manuela's Birthday in Old Mexico. LC 39-23303. (Illus.). 46 p. 24 x 21cm. (Junior Press Bks.). 1939. A. Whitman & Co.
--Nemo Meets the Emperor. Evans, Katherine Floyd (1901-1964), illus. (Illus.). 45 p. 24cm. 1957. A. Whitman.
--The Other Side of the World. Bannon, Laura May (0000-1963), illus. LC 60-5252. (Illus.). 48 p. 26cm. 1960. Houghton Mifflin.
--Patty Paints a Picture. Bannon, Laura, illus. LC 47-36632. 48 p. illus. (part col.) 24 x 21 cm. 1946. A. Whitman & Company.
--Red Mittens. Bannon, Laura May (0000-1963), illus. (Illus.). (gr. 1-3). 1946. (ISBN 0-8382-0694-8). Hale.
--Red Mittens. Bannon, Laura May (0000-1963), illus. LC 47-669. 32 p. illus. (part col.) 20 x 17 1/2 cm. 1946. (ISBN 0-395-19863-1). Houghton Mifflin Company.
--The Scary Thing. Bannon, Laura May (0000-1963), illus. LC 56-9597. (Illus.). 21cm. 28p. 1956. Houghton Mifflin.
--The Tide Won't Wait: A Nova Scotia Story. Bannon, Laura May (0000-1963), illus. (Illus.). 64 p. 25cm. 1957. A. Whitman.
--Toby's Friends. Bannon, Laura May (0000-1963), illus. LC 63-8864. (Illus.). 32 p. 24cm. 1963. A Whitman.
--Twirlup on the Moon. Gordon, Will & Bannon, Laura May (0000-1963), illus. LC 64-7720. (Illus.). 63 p. 21cm. 1964. A. Whitman.
--Watchdog. Bannon, Laura May (0000-1963), illus. LC 48-65181. 48 p. illus. (part co.) 27cm. 1948. A. Whitman.
--When the Moon Is New. Bannon, Laura May (0000-1963), illus. LC 53-7925. (Illus.). (gr. 3-5). 1953. (ISBN 0-8075-8896-2). A Whitman.
--Whistle for a Pilot. Bannon, Laura May (0000-1963), illus. LC 59-5188. (Illus.). 24cm. 48p. (gr. 4-6). 1959. HM.
--Who Walks the Attic?. Bannon, Laura May (0000-1963), illus. (Illus.). 126 p. 21cm. 1962. A. Whitman.
--The Wonderful Fashion Doll. Bannon, Laura May (0000-1963), illus. LC 53-6210. 86p. illus. 22cm. N.D. Houghton Mifflin,.

Banta-Benson, Alpha, adapted by.
--Daffydowndilly and the Golden Touch. Dulin, James Harvey, illus. LC 24-683. (Illus.). 32. 18cm. (The Little Classic Ser.). 1923. A. Flanagan.
--The Pied Piper And Other Stories. LC 44-480946. 59 p. 20 cm. c.1896. A. Flanagan.
--Really Truly Fairy Tales. Dulin, James Harvey, illus. LC 23-105939. 128 p. col. illus. 19 cm. 1923. A. Flanagan Company.

Banta-Benson, Alpha & Banta, Nathaniel Moore (1867-)
--The Brownies and the Goblins. (The Children's Hour Bks). N.D. Grosset & Dunlap.
--Ten Little Brownie Men. (The Children's Hour Bks). N.D. Grosset & Dunlap.

Banta, Milt, ed. see Disney, Walt, Productions.

Banta, Nathaniel Moore, jt. auth. see Banta-Benson, Alpha.

Banta, Nathaniel Moore (1867-)
--The Bluebird Book. LC 24-239. (Illus.). 32 p. 18cm. (The Little Classic Ser.). 1923. A. Flanagan Company.
--Brownies in the Greenwood. Dulin, Dorothy, illus. 20cm. 128p. 1927. A. Flanagan Co.
--Busy Little Brownies. (The Children's Hour Bks). N.D. Grosset & Dunlap.
--Fairies of the Nine Hills. Dulin, Dorothy, illus. LC 23-4365. 128 p. col. illus. 18 1/2 cm. 1923. A. Flanagan Company.
--Old Tales of the East. Dulin, Dorothy, illus. LC 24-22146. 128 p. col. illus. 18 1/2 cm. 1924. A. Flanagan Company.
--The Robin Redbreast Book. LC 24-246. (Illus.). 32 p. 18cm. (The Little Classic Ser.). 1922. A. Flanagan Company.
--The Second Brownie Book. Wagner, Frank U., illus. LC 12-187902. 128 p. col. illus. 20 cm. c.1911. A. Flanagan Company.

Banta, Nathaniel Moore (1867-), adapted by.
--Bluest of Bluebirds. LC 24-238. (Illus.). 31. 18cm. 1923. A. Flanagan Company.
--Drakestail and Choosing a King. LC 24-240. (Illus.). 32 p. 18cm. (The Little Classic Ser.). 1923. A. Flanagan.
--Little Black Sambo, and Other Stories. LC 24-241. 32 p. 18cm. (The Little Classic Ser.). 1922. A. Flannagan Company.
--The Little Brown Pitcher. LC 24-243. (Illus.). 32 p. 18cm. (The Little Classic Ser.). 1923. A. Flanagan Company.
--Little Goody Two Shoes. LC 24-245. (Illus.). 31 p. 18cm. (The Little Classic Ser.). 1922. A. Flannagan Company.
--Spring and Summer Festivals: A Collection of Plays, Drills, Dialogues, Exercises, Carnivals, Festivals, Pageants, Songs, Quotations, Stories, Readings, and Recitations for Spring and Summer Holidays. LC 24-28795. 192 p. illus. (incl. music) 18 cm. 1924. A. Flanagan Company.
--The Stories of Robin Hood. LC 24-246. 32 p. 18cm. (The Little Classic Ser.). 1922. A. Flanagan Co.

Banta, Nathaniel Moore (1867-) & Banta-Benson, Alpha
--The Brownies and the Goblins. (Illus.). 20cm. 128p. 1915. A. Flanagan Co.
--Ten Little Brownie Men. LC 21-19405. 127, 1 p. col. illus. 20 cm. 1920. A. Flanagan Company.
--Ten Little Brownie Men. LC 22-7463. 128 p. incl. col. front., col. illus. 20 cm. 1922. A. Flanagan Company.

Banta, Nathaniel Moore (1867-) & Cowles, Julia Darrow, Mrs. (1862-1919)
--Once Upon a Time Stories. Dulin, Dorothy, illus. LC 23-7498. 128 p. incl. col. front., col. illus. 18 1/2 cm. 1922. A. Flanagan Company.

Banta-Benson, Alpha, jt. auth. see Banta, Nathaniel Moore.

Banta-Benson, Alpha, ed. see Grimm, Jakob Ludwig Karl (1785-1863) & Grimm, Wilhelm Karl.

Bantock, Granville, Sir (1868-) & Coburn, Alvin Langdon (1882-)
--Fairy Gold. LC 45-47810. (A play for children). 25cm. 87p. 1938. C. C. Birchard Co.

Bantock, Myrrha
--Tales of Elfintown. N.D. E P Dutton.

Banvard, J.
--Heads and Feet: Stories About Heads and Feet. (Illus.). 90p. N.D. Sunday-School Publications.
--Wonderful Stories About Little Things. (Illus.). 90p. N.D. Sunday-School Publications.

Bar, Le Mary Evelyn (1910-)
--One Hundred Four Short True-to-Life Stories for Fours & Fives. 104p. (ps-k). 1960. (ISBN 0-88207-253-6). Victor Bks.

Bar, Mary Evelyne Le see Bar, Le Mary Evelyn.

Barak, Michael
--The Secret List of Heinrich Roehm. new ed. LC 75-28316. 228p. 1976. (ISBN 0-688-02991-4). Morrow.

Baraldi, Severino & Guerra, Aldo, illus.
--Sleeping Beauty, and, The Soldier and the Six Giants. LC 84-18657. p. cm. c.1985. (ISBN 0-88110-255-5). Educational Development Corp.

Baram, Robert
--The Shiny Penny. N.D. (ISBN 0-8283-1197-8). Branden Press.

Baranauskas, Albinas, tr. see Tamulaitis, Vytas.

Bararee, Charlotte
--The Jumbled Gymnast. 1982. (ISBN 0-570-08406-7). Concordia.

Barash, Asher (1889-1952), retold by.
--A Golden Treasury of Jewish Tales. Roston, Murray, tr. from Hebrew. LC 66-21271. (Illus.). 166 p. 27cm. 1966, c.1965. Dodd, Mead.

Barath, Betty
--Little Lion That Couldn't Roar. 1980. (ISBN 0-8062-1299-3). Carlton.

Baratinsky, Viacheslav
--My Pupils and I: Memories of a Teacher. 1st ed. Lisousky, M. & Shreter, G., illus. LC 55-11745. 78p. illus. 22cm. 1955. Comet Press Books.

Barbary, James, pseud., see Baumann, Amy Brown Beeching.

Barbary, James, pseud. (1922-)
--The Engine and the Gun. Baumann, Amy Brown Beeching. McLaren, William, illus. LC 67-266134. 159p. illus. 21cm. 1st U.S. edition. 1967, c.1963. Meredith.
--Fort in the Wilderness. Baumann, Amy Brown Beeching. (gr. 5-8). N.D. G&D.
--The Fort in the Wilderness: An Adventure in History. Baumann, Amy Brown Beeching. McLaren, William, illus. (Illus.). 144 p. 21cm. 1965, c.1962. Norton.
--The Student Buccaneer. Baumann, Amy Brown Beeching. McLaren, William, illus. LC 65-11693. 140p. illus. 21cm. 1965, c.1963. Roy.
--Ten Thousand Heroes. Baumann, Amy Brown Beeching. McLaren, William, illus. LC 65-116923. 140p. illus. 21cm. 1965, c.1963. Roy.

Barbato, Juli
--From Bed to Bus. Schatell, Brian, illus. LC 84-20159. (Illus.). 30 p. c.1985. (ISBN 0-02-708380-2). Macmillan.
--Mom's Night Out. Schatell, Brian, illus. LC 85-3096. (Illus.). 32 p. c.1985. (ISBN 0-02-708480-9). Macmillan.

Barbauld, Anna Letitia Aikin, jt. auth. see Aikin, John.

Barbauld, Anna Letitia Aikin, Mrs., jt. auth. see Aikin, John.

Barbauld, Anna Letitia Aikin, Mrs., jt. auth. see Aikin, John.

Barbauld, Anna Letitia Aikin, Mrs. (1743-1825)

--Hymns in Prose for Children. LC 39-17472. 15 x 12cm. 71p. 1818. C. Harris.

--Lessons for Children. LC 12-1005. 14 x 11cm. 1825. Wells and Lilly.

--Lessons for Children. Pike, S. & Anderson, Dr., illus. LC 21-2668. 15cm. 102p. 1818. Benjamin Warner.

--Lessons for Children from Four to Five Years Old. LC 6-25820. 10cm. 67p. 1801. P. Brynberg.

--Lessons for Children from Four to Five Years Old. LC 25-24337. 107 p. 9 1/2 x 8 1/2 cm. 1788. Printed by B.F. Bache.

--Mrs. Barbauld's Hymns. (Half Hours with the Bible: 2nd). N.D. McLoughlin Bros.

--Poetic Gift. Elliott, Mary Belson, compiled by. Belson, Mary, pseud. LC 66-58807. (Illus.). 15cm. 24p. N.D. S. Babcock.

--Tales, Poems, and Essays. LC 18-4742. 18cm. 199p. 1884. Roberts Brothers.

--Things by their Right Names. Hale, Sarah Josepha Buell, Mrs. (1789-1879), ed. LC 18-4743. 16cm. 263p. 1840. Marsh, Capen, Lyon, and Webb.

Barbauld, Anna Letitia Aikin, Mrs. (1743-1825) & More, Hannah (1745-1833)

--Hymns in Prose for Children. LC 75-32144. (Illus.). ca. 350 p. in various pagings. 18cm. (Classics of Children's Literature Ser., 1621-1932). 1977. (ISBN 0-8240-2259-9). Garland Pub.

Barbe, Waitman

--Pippa Passes and the Parable of the Sower. 1925. Hinds, Hayden & Eldredge.

Barbe, Walter Burke (1926-), ed.

--Fables and Folktales from Many Lands. LC 72-188146. (Illus.). 33 p. 29cm. (Highlights handbook). 1972. (ISBN 0-87534-147-0). Highlights for Children.

Barbeau, Charles Marius (1883-1969) & Hornyansky, Michael, eds.

--The Golden Phoenix. Price, Arthur, illus. (Illus.). 20cm. 128p. 1965. Scholastic.

--The Golden Phoenix, and Other French-Canadian Fairy Tales. Price, Arthur, illus. (Illus.). 144 p. 22cm. 1958. H. Z. Walck. **Awards: (ALA); (CLA).**

Barbeau, Marius (1883-1969)

--The Magic Tree & Other Stories. Hornyansky, Michael, retold by. Price, Arthur, illus. (Illus., Pub. by Walck). Orig. Title: The Golden Phoenix. (gr. 4-6). 1972 (Starline). Schol Bk Serv.

Barbee, Lindsey (1876-)

--Cinderella and Five Other Fairy Plays. Tarbell, Harlan, illus. LC 22-22064. 146 p. incl. illus,. diagrs. front 18 1/2 cm. c.1922. T.S. Denison & Company.

--Fanciful Plays for Children. 160p. N.D. T. S. Denison & Co Inc.

--Hands Up!. A Comedy in Two Acts for High Schools. 45p. 1933. T. S. Denison & Co.

--Let's Pretend: A Book of Children's Plays. Nendick, Buckton, illus. 160 p. front., illus., diagrs. 19 1/2 cm. c.1917. T.S. Denison & Company.

--Sally Pulls the Strings. 48p. N.D. T. S. Denison & Co.

--Take off Your Mask. 36p. N.D. T. S. Denison & Co.

--Thunder in the Air. 63p. N.D. T. S. Denison & Co.

Barber, Alice Margaret

--Carlos and His Friends. Barber, Alice Margaret, illus. LC 40-347374. 53, 5 p. col. front., col. illus. 25 1/2 cm. c.1940. Library Book Supply Co.

Barber, Antonia, pseud., see Anthony, Barbara.

Barber, Antonia, pseud. (1932-)

--The Affair of the Rockerbye Baby. Anthony, Barbara. Seuling, Barbara (1937-), illus. LC 75-102000. (Illus.). 205 p. 22cm. 1st U.S. edition. 1970, c.1966. Delacorte Press.

--The Ghosts. Anthony, Barbara. LC 73-85362. 189 p. 21cm. 1969. Farrar, Straus & Giroux.

Barber, Bulah & Dysinger, Mabel

--Cubby and Stubby. Cleveland, J. K., illus. LC 39-2927. 1 p. l., 7-45 p. illus. 28 cm. 1938. The Harter Publishing Company.

--Stubby Alone. Cleveland, J. K., illus. LC 39-2926. 2 p. l., 7-45 p. illus. 23 cm. 1938. The Harter Publishing Company.

Barber, Dulan F. see Fletcher, David, pseud.

Barber, Elsie Marion (1914-)

--Trembling Years. (gr. 7 up). 1949. (ISBN 0-02-506850-4). Macmillan.

Barber, Harriet Boomer see Templeton, Faith, pseud.

Barber, Harriett Scott

--Tony Tompkins, the Lion Tamer. Newman, Clyde J., illus. LC 6-27356. (Illus.). 7-44 p. 22cm. 1906. The Reilly & Britton Co.

Barber, Janet

--The Voyage of Jim. Wegner, Fritz (1924-), illus. LC 72-7663. (Illus.). 32 p. 1973. (ISBN 0-87614-041-X). Carolrhoda Books.

Barber, Martha (1920-)

--The Funny Old Man and the Funny Old Woman. unpaged. illus. 27 cm. (a tell-well book. 1962. Winston.

--The Funny Old Man and the Funny Old Woman. Barber, Martha (1920-), illus. (Tell-Well Story Books). 1954. Holt, Rinehart and Winston.

--The Funny Old Man and the Funny Old Woman. Barber, Martha (1920-), illus. LC 52-68112. unpaged. illus. 29cm. c.1952. Tell-Well Press.

--The Funny Old Man and the Funny Old Woman. Renfro, Ed, illus. LC 63-12418. 1 v. (unpaged) col. illus. 24 cm. (Young owl book). 1964, c.1963. Holt, Rinehart and Winston.

Barber, Phyllis

--Smiley Snake's Adventure. Jordan, Alton, ed. (Illus.). (Buppet Series). (gr. k-3). 1981. (ISBN 0-89868-098-0, Read Res). (ISBN 0-89868-109-X). ARO Pub.

Barber, Richard

--A Companion to World Mythology. Baynes, Pauline Diana (1922-), illus. LC 79-16843. (Illus.). (gr. 4 up). 1980. Delacorte.

Barber, Ruth

--Teddy Bears Go Everywhere. Wilson-Heaney, Katherine, illus. (Illus.). 24p. (Teddy Bears Are Ser.). (gr. 1-6). 1984. (ISBN 0-89954-279-4). Antioch Pub Co.

Barber, Sadie Pike

--Beverly Butterfly: The Story of a Butterfly's Adventures. Still, Jack, illus. LC 55-12196. unpaged. illus. 22cm. 1955. Comet Press Books.

Barberis, Franco (1905-)

--Would You Like a Parrot?. (Illus.). 28 p. 21cm. 1967, c.1964. Scroll Press.

Barbour, Harriot Buston, retold by.

--Old English Tales. Thomson, Rodney, illus. LC 25-201. ix. 245 p. illus. 20 1/2 cm. 1924. The Macmillian Company.

Barbour, Mary A.

--Spotty. LC 39-6106. (Illus.). 18cm. 28p. 1939. Mary A. Barbour.

Barbour, Ralph Henry (1870-1944)

--Adventure: A Ralph Henry Barbour Omnibus Containing, Pirates of the Shoals, The Crew of the "Casco", Peril in the Swamp. LC 35-9852. 5 p. l. 3-250 p., 21., 3-277 p., 2 l., 3-272 p. illus. 20 cm. c.1935. Farrar & Rinehart, Incorporated.

--The Adventure Club Afloat. Caswell, Edward C., illus. LC 17-247037. 6 p. l., 302 p. front., plates. 20 1/2 cm. c.1917. Dodd, Mead and Company.

--The Adventure Club with the Fleet. Caswell, Edward C., illus. LC 18-18535. 4 p. l., 296 p. front., plates. 20 1/2 cm. c.1918. Dodd, Mead and Company.

--Adventures of Tom Marvel. Peck, A. Gladys, illus. LC 26-5400. 4 p. l., 162, 1 p. front., illus. 19 1/2 cm. 1928. D. Appleton and Company.

--All Hands Stand By!. Lee, Manning de Villeneuve (1894-1980), illus. LC 42-117113. vii p., 1 l., 261 p. illus. 20 cm. 1942. D. Appleton-Century Company, Incorporated.

--Around the End. (Yardley Hall Ser.). N.D. D. Appleton & Co.

--The Arrival of Jimpson: And Other Stories for Boys about Boys. LC 4-23880. 6 p. l., 253 p. front., 5 pl. 20 cm. 1904. D. Appleton and Company.

--Barclay Back. Hazelton, Isaac Brewster, illus. LC 42-19167. vii p., 1 l., 255 p. illus. 20 cm. 1942. D. Appleton-Century Company, Incorporated.

--Barry Locke, Half-Back. Relyea, Charles M., illus. LC 25-17697. vii, 335 p. front., plates. 19 1/2 cm. c.1925. The Century Co.

--Bases Full!. LC 25-5964. 3 p. l. 276, 1 p. front. 19 1/2 cm. 1925. D. Appleton and Company.

--Beaton Runs the Mile. O'Keeffe, Neil, illus. LC 33-45487. 4 p. l., 291, 1 p. front., illus. 20 cm. 1933. D. Appleton and Company.

--Behind the Line: A Story of College Life and Football. Relyea, Charles M., illus. LC 9-22905. xi, 258 p. col. front., plates, diagrs. 20 cm. 1902. D. Appleton and Company.

--Benton's Venture. LC 14-4305. 5 p. l., 312, 1 p. col. front., col. plates. 20 cm. 1914. D. Appleton and Company.

--The Brother of a Hero. Relyea, Charles M., illus. LC 14-16197. 5 p. l., 301 1 p. front., plates. 19 1/2 cm. 1914. D. Appleton and Company.

--Candidate for the Line. Scott, Arthur O., illus. LC 30-213334. v, 1 p., 1 l., 272, 1 p. front., plates. 20 cm. 1930. D. Appleton and Company.

--Captain Chub. Relyea, Charles M., illus. LC 9-36149. ix, 413 p. incl. 22 pl. front 20 cm. 1909. The Century Co.

--Captain of the Crew. Relyea, Charles M., illus. LC 1-229782. ix, 279 p. front., 5 pl. 20 cm. 1901. D. Appleton and Company.

--Center Rush Rowland. (The Ralph Henry Barbour Books for Boys). N.D. Grosset & Dunlap.

--Center Rush Rowland. Caswell, Edward C., illus. LC 17-25858. 4 p. l., 312 p. front., plates. 20 cm. 1917. Dodd, Mead and Company.

--Change Signals: A Story of the New Football. LC 12-217639. 5 p. l., 330, 1 p. col. front., col. plates. 20 cm. 1912. D. Appleton and Company.

--Comrades of the Key. LC 28-5641. ix, 248 p. front., plates. 19 1/2 cm. c.1928. The Century Co.

--Coxswain of the Eight. LC 22-17944. 3 p. l, 258. 1 p. col. front. 19 1/2 cm. 1922. D. Appleton and Company.

--The Crew of the "Casco". An Adventure of the Maine Coast. LC 33-28405. v. 277 p. front. 19 1/2 cm. c.1933. Farrar & Rinehart, Incorporated.

--The Crimson Sweater. Relyea, Charles M., illus. LC 6-34684. x, 367 p. incl. 27 pl. front. 20 cm. 1906. The Century Co.

--Crofton Chums. Relyea, Charles M., illus. LC 12-225608. ix, 338 p. incl. plates. front. 20 cm. 1912. The Century Co.

--The Cub Battery. Avison, George F. (1885-), illus. LC 32-50367. vi p. 1 l., 275, 1 p. front., illus. 19 1/2 cm. 1932. D. Appleton and Company.

--Danby's Error. LC 31-6791. 4 p. l., 239 p. front. 19 1/2 cm. 1931. Cosmopolitan Book Corporation.

--Danforth Plays the Game: Stories for Boys Little and Big. Coughlin, John A., illus. LC 15-1902. 5 p. l., 3-333 1 p. col. front., col. plates. 19 1/2 cm. 1915. D. Appleton and Company.

--Danger Ahead: More Automobile Adventures. LC 20-214833. 265 p. front., plates. 19 1/2 cm. c.1928. Fleming H. Revell Company.

--Double Play: A Story of School and Baseball. LC 9-25638. 5 p. l., 314 p., 1 l. col. front., 3 col. pl. 20 1/2 cm. 1909. D. Appleton and Company.

--Fighting Guard. Graef, Robert A., illus. LC 38-215506. vii p., 2 l., 304 p. incl. front., illus. 20 cm. 1938. D. Appleton-Century Company, Incorporated.

--The Fighting Scrub. LC 24-23287. 3 p. l., 277. 1 p. front. 19 1/2 cm. 1924. D. Appleton and Company.

--Finkler's Field: A Story of School and Baseball. LC 11-254393. vii, 226, 1 p. col. front., col. plates. 20 cm. 1911. D. Appleton and Company.

--The Five-Dollar Dog. Caswell, Edward C., illus. LC 25-164744. ix, 244 p. incl. front., illus. 20 cm. 1935. D. Appleton-Century Company, Incorporated.

--Five Points Service. Caswell, Edward C., illus. LC 35-459293. ix, 275 p. incl. front., illus. 19 1/2 cm. 1935. D. Appleton-Century Company, Incorporated.

--Flashing Oars. LC 30-52445. 3 p. l., 272. 1 p. front. 19 1/2 cm. 1930. D. Appleton and Company.

--Follow the Ball. LC 24-20563. vi p. 1 l., 251 1 p. front. 19 1/2 cm. 1924. D. Appleton and Company.

--For the Freedom of the Seas. Wrenn, Charles L., illus. LC 18-18956. 5 p. l., 290, 1 p. col. front., col. plates. 19 1/2 cm. 1918. D. Appleton and Company.

--For the Good of the Team. LC 23-12866. v, 287, 1 p. front. 19 1/2 cm. 1923. D. Appleton and Company.

--For the Honor of the School. (Every Boy's Library). N.D. Grosset & Dunlap.

--For the Honor of the School: A Story of School Life and Interscholastic Sport. Relyea, Charles M., illus. ix, 253 p. front., 5 pl., map. 19 1/2 cm. 1900. D. Appleton and Company.

--For Yardley: A Story of Track and Field. (Yardley Hall Ser.). 1911. D. Appleton & Co.

--Foreword Pass: A Story of the "New Football". LC 2-20082. vii, 1 p. 1 l., 340 p., 7 l. col. front., 8 col. pl. 20 cm. 1908. D. Appleton and Company.

--The Fortunes of the Team. LC 28-82000. 4 p. l., 279 p. front., plates. 19 1/2 cm. 1928. Houghton Mifflin Company.

--Fortunes of War. Relyea, Charles M., illus. LC 19-14013. 5 p. l., 3-352 p. front., plates. 19 1/2 cm. 1919. The Century Co.

--Forward Pass. (Yardley Hall Ser.). N.D. D. Appleton-Century Co.

--Four Afloat: Being the Adventures of the Big Four on the Water. LC 7-29577. ix, 275 p. col. front., 3 col. pl. 20 1/2 cm. 1907. D. Appleton and Company.

--Four Afoot: Being the Adventures of the Big Four on the Highway. x p., 1 l., 285 p. col. front., 3 col. pl. 20 1/2 cm. 1906. D. Appleton and Company.

--Four in Camp: A Story of Summer Adventures in the New Hampshire Woods. LC 5-30269. viii p., 1 l., 249 p. front., 4 pl., plan. 20 1/2 cm. 1905. D. Appleton and Company.

--Fourth Down!. LC 20-17530. v, 316, 1 p. front. 19 1/2 cm. 1920. D. Appleton and Company.

--Foward Pass: A Story of New Football. (Yardley Hall Ser.). 1908. D. Appleton & Co.

--Full-Back Foster. Caswell, Edward C., illus. LC 19-15681. vi p., 1 l., 326 p. front., plates. 20 1/2 cm. 1919. Dodd, Mead and Company.

--Fullback Foster. (The Ralph Henry Barbour Books for Boys). N.D. Grosset & Dunlap.

--The Fumbled Pass. Avison, George F. (1885-), illus. LC 31-21309. v, 1 p., 1 l., 287, 1 p. front., illus. 19 1/2 cm. 1931. D. Appleton and Company.

--Giles of the Mayflower. Scott, Arthur O., illus. LC 29-17281. 4 p. l., 158, 1 p. illus. 19 1/2 cm. 1929. D. Appleton and Company.

--The Glendale Five. LC 85-145677. 4 p. l., 3-278 p. front. 19 1/2 cm. c.1935. Farrar & Rinehart, Incorporated.

--Goal-to-Go. O'Keeffe, Neil, illus. (Hillfields). 1933. Appleton Century Co.

--The Golden Heart. O'Keeffe, Neil, illus. LC 33-21520. vii, 1 p., 1 l., 277, 1 p. front., illus. 19 1/2 cm. 1938. D. Appleton-Century Company, Incorporated.

--Grantham Gets On. LC 29-4414. 3 p. l., 249, 1 p. front. 19 1/2 cm. 1929. D. Appleton and Company.

--Guarding His Goal. Avison, George F (1885-), illus. LC 19-14351. 4 p. l., 321, 1 p. col. front., col. plates. 19 1/2 cm. 1919. D. Appleton and Company.

--The Half-Back. (Thrushwood Bks.). N.D. Grosset & Dunlap.

--The Half-Back: A Story of School, Football, and Golf. Clinedinst, B. West, illus. LC 99-4151. v p., 1 l., 267 p. front. illus. (plan) plates, diagrs. 19 1/2 cm. 1899. D. Appleton and Company.

--The Halfback. (Every Boy's Library). N.D. Grosset & Dunlap.

--Harry's Island. Relyea, Charles M., illus. 5 p. l., 3-306 p. incl. illus. (map) 19 pl. front. 20 cm. 1908. The Century Co.

--Heading North: Automobile Adventures. LC 27-12388. 4 p. l., 7-336 p. front., plates. 19 1/2 cm. c.1927. Fleming H. Reveill Company.

--Hero of the Camp. Meilink, William, illus. LC 82-20781. ix, 265, 1 p. front., illus. 20 cm. N.D. D. Appleton and Company,.

--Hitting the Line. Rockwell, Norman Percevel (1894-1978), illus. LC 17-24165. 4 p. l., 332, 1 p. col. front., col. plates. 19 1/2 cm. (His The Grafton series). 1917. D. Appleton and Company.

--Hold 'em, Wyndham!. LC 25-15638. 4 p. l., 269, 1 front. 19 1/2 cm. 1925. D. Appleton and Company.

--Holly. Bayha, Edwin F., illus. 1910. J B Lippincott.

--Hunt Holds the Center. (Highwood Ser.). 1925. D. Appleton & Co.

--Hunt Holds the Center. LC 28-204658. 3 p. l., 247 p. front. 10 1/2 cm. 1928. D. Appleton and Company.

--Hurricane Sands. Reid, James (1907-), illus. LC 40-30582. viii p., 2 l., 255 p. incl. front., illus. 20 cm. 1940. D. Appleton-Century Company, Incorporated.

--Infield Rivals. LC 24-7315. v, 257, 1 p. col. front. 19 1/2 cm. 1924. D. Appleton and Company.

--The Infield Twins. Robison, Robert S., illus. LC 41-43757. viii p., 2 l., 273 p. incl. front., illus. 20 cm. 1941. D Appleton-Century Company, Incorporated.

--The Junior Trophy. 1913. D. Appleton and Company.

--Keeping His Course. Louderback, Walt, illus. LC 18-5747. 4 p. l., 285 p., 1 p. col. front., col. plates. 19 1/2 cm. 1918. D. Appleton & Company,.

--Kick Formation. LC 21-15189. 3 p. l., 265, 1 p. front. 19 1/2 cm. 1921. D. Appleton and Company.

--Kingsford, Quarter. Relyea, Charles M., illus. LC 10-216344. 6 p. l., 3-326 p. incl. plates. front. 20 cm. 1910. The Century Co.

--The Last Play. LC 26-149150. 3 p. l., 273, 1 p. front. 19 1/2 cm. 1926. D. Appleton and Company.

--The Last Quarter. Earle, Edwin (1887-1974), illus. LC 89-907984. viii p., 2 l., 276 p. incl. front., illus. 20 cm. 1939. D. Appleton-Century Company, Incorporated.

--Left End Edwards. (The Ralph Henry Barbour Books for Boys). N.D. Grosset & Dunlap.

--Left End Edwards. Relyea, Charles M., illus. LC 14-182482. 5 p. l., 3-365 p. front., plates. 20 1/2 cm. 1914. Dodd, Mead and Company.

--Left Guard Gilbert. (The Ralph Henry Barbour Books for Boys). N.D. Grosset & Dunlap.

--Left Guard Gilbert. Caswell, Edward C., illus. LC 16-19457. 5 p. l., 310 p. front., plates. 20 1/2 cm. c.1916. Dodd, Mead and Company.

--Left Half Harmon. Crump, Leslie (1894-), illus. LC 21-157161. 4 p. l., 312 p. front., plates. 19 1/2 cm. (His the football eleven books). 1921. Dodd, Mead and Company.

--Left Tackle Thayer. (The Ralph Henry Barbour Books for Boys). N.D. Grosset & Dunlap.

--Left Tackle Thayer. Relyea, Charles M., illus. LC 15-188267. 5 p. l., 3-338 p. front., plates. 20 1/2 cm. 1915. Dodd, Mead and Company.
--The Lilac Girl. Underwood, Clarence F. & Holloway, Edward Stratton, illus. LC 9-28246. 236 p., 1 l. col. front., illus. 4 col. pl. 21 1/2 cm. 1909. J. B. Lippincott Company.
--The Long Pass. LC 27-17799. 3 p. l., 200, 1 p. front. 19 1/2 cm. 1927. D. Appleton and Company.
--The Lost Dirigible. LC 20-8037. v, 276, 1 p. col. front. 19 1/2 cm. 1920. D. Appleton and Company.
--Lovell Leads off. LC 26-2674. 3 p. l, 236 p. front. 19 1/2 cm. 1928. D. Appleton and Company.
--The Lucky Seventh. Rockwell, Norman Percevel (1894-1978), illus. (Purple Pennant Ser.). 1915. D. Appleton & Co.
--A Maid in Arcady. Von Rapp, Frederic J., illus. 213, 1 p. incl. col. front, illus 8 col. pl. 21 1/2 cm. 1906. J. B. Lippincott Company.
--Merritt Leads the Nine. Richards, George Mather (1880-), illus. LC 36-4986. ix p., 1 l., 256 p. incl. front., illus. plates. 20 cm. 1936. D. Appleton-Century Company, Incorporated.
--Metipom's Hostage: Being a Narrative of Certain Surprising Adventures Befalling One David Lindall in the First Year of King Philip's War. LC 21-8386. 4 p. l., 289, 1 p. front., plates. 19 1/2 cm. 1921. Houghton Mifflin Company.
--Mystery Island. Whiting, John Downes (1884-), illus. LC 31-5121. vii, 301 p. front., illus. (plan) plates. 19 1/2 cm. c.1931. The Century Co.
--The Mystery of the Rubber Boat. Caswell, Edward C., illus. LC 43-3661. ix p., 1 l., 260 p. incl. front., illus. 19 cm. 1943. D. Appleton-Century Company, Incorporated.
--Mystery on the Bayou. McGowen, Thomas (1927-), illus. LC 43-14570. 6 p. l., 237, 1 p. front., illus. 19 1/2 cm. 1943. D. Appleton-Century Company, Incorporated.
--The New Boy at Hilltop: And Other Stories. LC 10-21600. 5 p. l., 269, 1 p. col. front., 3 col. pl. 20 cm. 1910. D. Appleton and Company.
--Nid and Nod. Relyea, Charles M., illus. LC 23-124007. 5 p. l., 3-360 p. front., plates. 19 1/2 cm. 1923. The Century Co.
--Ninth Inning Rally. Graf, Robert A., illus. LC 40-471800. 5 p. l., 3-265 p. front., illus. 20 cm. 1940. D. Appleton-Century Company, Incorporated.
--On Your Mark!. A Story of College Life and Athletics. Relyea, Charles M., illus. LC 4-25098. 5 p. l., 267 p. col. front., 3 col. pl. 20 cm. 1904. D. Appleton and Company.
--An Orchard Princess. (Illus.). 1910. J B Lippincott.
--Over Two Seas. LC 22-4436. 3 p. l., 264, 1 p. front. 19 1/2 cm. 1922. D. Appleton and Company.
--Partners Three. Relyea, Charles M., illus. LC 13-167864. 2 p. l., 330 p. col. front., illus. (map) col. plates. 19 1/2 cm. c.1913. M. A. Donohue & Co.
--Peril in the Swamp. LC 34-82218. 4 p. l., 3-272 p. front. 19 1/2 cm. c.1934. Farrar & Rinehart, Inc.
--Pirates of the Shoals. LC 32-8071. v, 250 p. incl front. 21 1/2 cm. c.1932. Farrar & Rinehart.
--The Play That Won. LC 19-143300. vii. 240, 1 p. col. front., col. plates. 19 1/2 cm. 1919. D. Appleton and Company.
--Pud Pringle, Pirate. LC 26-613050. 3 p. l., 296 p. front. 19 1/2 cm. 1926. Houghton Miffin Company.
--The Purple Pennant. Rockwell, Norman Percevel (1894-1978), illus. LC 16-749819. 4 p. l., 322, l p. col. front., col. plates. 19 1/2 cm. (His The purple pennant series). 1916. D. Appleton and Company.
--Quarter-Back Bates. Rigney, Francis Joseph (1882-), illus. LC 20-18679. 3 p. l., 294 p. front., plates. 191 cm. 1920. Dodd, Mead and Company.
--Quarter-Back Gates. (Ralph Henry Barbour Bks). N.D. Grosset & Dunlap.
--The Relief Pitcher. LC 27-4063. 3 p. l., 266, 1 p. front. 19cm. 1927. D. Appleton and Company.
--Right End Emerson. Crump, Leslie (1894-), illus. LC 22-17731. vi p., 2 l., 270 p. front., plates. 19cm. (His The football eleven books). 1922. Dodd, Mead and Company.
--Right Guard Grant. Crump, Leslie (1894-), illus. LC 23-12867. 4 p. l., 288 p. front., plates. 19 1/2cm. 1923. Dodd, Mead and Company.
--Right Half Hollins. (Ralph Henry Barbour Bks.). N.D. Grosset & Dunlap.
--Right Half Hollins. Crump, Leslie (1894-), illus. LC 25-17413. 4 p. l., 288 p. front., plates. 19 1/2cm. 1925. Dodd, Mead and Company.
--Right Tackle Todd. (Ralph Henry Barbour Bks.). N.D. Grosset & Dunlap.
--Right Tackle Todd. Crump, Leslie (1894-), illus. LC 24-20558. v p., 1 l., 291 p. front., plates. 19 1/2 cm. 1924. Dodd Mead and Company.
--Rivals for the Team: A Story of School Life and Football. Relyea, Charles M., illus. LC 16-194277. 4 p. l., 336, 1 p. col. front., col. plates. 19 1/2 cm. 1916. D. Appleton and Company.
--Rivals on the Mound. Czap, Charles, illus. LC 38-57541. viii p., 2 l., 303 p. incl. front., illus., plates. 20cm. 1938. D. Appleton-Century Company, Incorporated.
--The School That Didn't Care. Smith, Inglewood, illus. LC 37-18440. ix, 278 p. incl. front., illus. 20cm. 1937. D. Appleton-Century Company, Incorporated.
--The Score Is Tied. Graef, Robert A., illus. ix, 277 p. incl. front, illus., plates. 19 1/2cm. 1937. D. Appleton-Century Company, Incorporated.
--The Scoring Play. O'Keeffe, Neil, illus. LC 34-295538. vi p., 1 l., 281 p. front., illus. 19 1/2cm. 1934. D. Appleton-Century Company, Incorporated.
--The Secret Play. Rockwell, Norman Percevel (1894-1978), illus. LC 15-188256. 4 p. l., 334 1 p. col. front., col. plates. 19 1/2cm. (His purple pennant series). 1915. D. Appleton and Company.
--Skate, Glendale!. LC 32-23138. 4 p. l., 3-249 p. front. 21 1/2cm. c.1932. Farrar & Rinehart, Incorporated.
--Southworth Scores. O'Keeffe, Neil, illus. LC 34-3726. 4 p. l., 269 p. front., illus. 19 1/2cm. 1934. D. Appleton-Century Company, Incorporated.
--Spaniard's Cave. Relyea, Charles M., illus. LC 24-20562. 5 p. l., 3-324 p. front., plates. 19 1/2cm. c.1924. The Century Co.
--The Spirit of the School. LC 7-20576. ix, 272 p. front., 7 pl. 20 cm. 1907. D. Appleton and Company.
--Squeeze Play. Avison, George F. (1885-), illus. LC 31-5068. 4 p. l., 251 1 p. front., illus. 19 1/2cm. 1931. D. Appleton and Company.
--The Story My Doggie Told to Me. Rae, John (1882-1963), illus. LC 14-18905. 6 p. l., 3-182 p. front., illus., plates. 19 1/2cm. 1914. Dodd, Mead and Company.
--Substitute Jimmy. Lassell, Charles, illus. LC 28-22460. vii, 321 p. front., plates. 19 1/2cm. 1928. The Century Co.
--The Target Pass. O'Keeffe, Neil, illus. LC 41-145464. xi p., 1 l., 280 p. incl. front., illus. 20 cm. 1941. D. Appleton-Century Company, Incorporated.
--Team-Mates. Relyea, Charles M., illus. LC 11-24128. vi p., 2 l., 3-381 p. incl. plates. front. 20 cm. 1911. The Century Co.
--Thad and the G-Man. O'Keeffe, Neil, illus. LC 42-280218. viii p., 2 l., 257 p. incl. front., illus. 20cm. 1942. D. Appleton-Century Comnapy, Incorporated.
--Three-Base Benson. LC 21-9440. 3 p. l., 285, 1 p. col. front. 19 1/2cm. 1921. D. Appleton and Company.
--The Three-Cornered Dog. Brinkerhoff, Robert Moore (1880-), illus. LC 39-4409. ix p. 1 l., 273 p. incl. front., illus. 20cm. 1939. D. Appleton-Century Company, Incorporated.
--Three in a Trailer. Caswell, Edward C., illus. LC 37-197472. ix p., 1 l., 258 p. incl. front., illus., plates. 20 1/2cm. 1937. D. Appleton-Century Company, Incorporated.
--Tod Hale at Camp. (The Tod Hale Ser.). N.D. Grosset & Dunlap.
--Tod Hale at Camp. Crump, Leslie (1894-), illus. LC 27-183200. v p., 1 l., 280 p. col. front., col. plates. 19 1/2cm. 1927. Dodd, Mead and Company.
--Tod Hale on the Nine. Crump, Leslie (1894-), illus. LC 29-201195. 4 p. l., 280 p. front., plates. 10 1/2cm. (Memoirs of the Museum of comparative zoology at Harvard). 1929. Dodd, Mead and Company.
--Tod Hale on the Scrub. (The Tod Hale Ser.). N.D. Grosset & Dunlap.
--Tod Hale on the Scrub. Crump, Leslie (1894-), illus. LC 28-20608. 4 p. l., 312 p. front., plates. 19 1/2cm. 1928. Dodd, Mead and Company.
--Tod Hale with the Crew. LC 26-15370. 5 p. l., 307 p. front., plates. 19 1/2cm. 1926. Dodd, Mead and Company.
--Tod Hale With the Crew. (The Tod Hale Ser.). N.D. Grosset & Dunlap.
--Tom, Dick, and Harriet. Relyea, Charles M., illus. LC 7-321588. 5 p. l., 3-384 p. incl. 16 pl. front. 20cm. 1907. The Century Co.
--The Turner Twins. Relyea, Charles M., illus. LC 22-177241. 5 p. l., 3-280 p. front., plates. 19 1/2cm. 1922. The Century Co.
--Under the Yankee Ensign. 5 p. l., 3-335, 1 p. col. front., col. plates. 19cm. 1919. D. Appleton and Company.
--Watch That Pass!. Richards, George Mather (1880-), illus. LC 36-185682. ix, 261 p. incl. front., illus., plates. 19 1/2cm. 1936. D. Appleton-Century Company, Incorporated.
--Weatherby's Inning: A Story of College Life and Baseball. Relyea, Charles M., illus. LC 3-22513. ix, 249 p. col. front., 5 col. pl. 20 1/2 cm. 1903. D. Appleton and Company.
--Winning His Game. Louderback, Walt, illus. v, 1 p., 1 l., 307, 1 p. col. front., col. plates. 19 1/2 cm. (His The Grafton series). 1917. D. Appleton and Company.
--Winning His "Y". A Story of School Athletics. LC 10-208503. vii, 1 p., 1 l., 286 p., 1 l. col. front., col. plates. 20cm. 1910. D. Appleton and Company.
--The Winning Year. LC 26-5382. 3 p. l., 251, 1 p. front. 19 1/2cm. 1926. D. Appleton and Company.

Barbour, Ralph Henry (1870-1944), ed.
--The Year's Best Stories for Boys. LC 26-19103. 2 v. 19 1/2cm. N.D. Dodd Mead & Co.

Barbour, Ralph Henry (1870-1944) & Holt, H. P.
--Lost Island. Relyea, Charles M., illus. 1918. Appleton Century Co.
--The Mystery of the Sea-Lark. Relyea, Charles M., illus. LC 20-14289. 5 p. l., 3-321 p. front., illus. (map) plates. 19 1/2 cm. 1920. The Century Co.

Barbour, Ralph Henry (1870-1944) & Kelland, Clarence Budington
--American Boy Action Stories. (Young Moderns Edition). 1949. Doubleday & Co.

Barce, Elmore
--Little Bear: A Kickapoo Boy of the Wabash. LC 26-18280. 106 p. col. front. 20 1/2cm. c.1926. The Christopher Publishing House.

Barchas, Sarah
--I Was Walking Down the Road. Kent, Jack, pseud. (1920-), illus. Kent, John Wellington. (Illus.). (gr. k-3). 1976. (ISBN 0-590-10137-4, Schol Pap). Schol Bk Serv.
--Janie and the Giant. Kent, Jack, pseud. (1920-), illus. Kent, John Wellington. LC 78-310177. (Illus.). 32 p. 21cm. (Read it yourself book). c.1977. (ISBN 0-590-11865-X). Scholastic Book Services.

Barchilon, Jacques, ed. see Perrault, Charles.

Barclay, Gail
--The Little Brown Gazelle. Komoda, Kiyoaki (1937-), illus. LC 68-15252. (Illus.). 24cm. 32p. 1968. Dial Press.

Barclay, McKee, jt. auth. see Stevens, William Oliver.

Barclay, Rhoda S.
--Girl of Yesterday. LC 45-8593. 119 p. 20 cm. 1945. House of Field-Doubleday, Inc.

Barclay, Vera Charlesworth (1893-)
--Danny Again: Further Adventures of "Danny the Detective". LC 20-12601. vii p., 1 l., 135 p. front., plates. 19 1/2 cm. 1920. G. P. Putnam's Sons.
--Danny the Detective. LC 18-22168. vi p., 1 l., 143 p. front., plates. 19 1/2cm. 1918. G. P. Putnam's Sons.
--The Mysterious Tramp. LC 21-1893. 2 p. l., iii-v, 175 p. front., plates. 19 1/2cm. 1921. G. P. Putnam's Sons.
--Saints by Fire Light: Stories for Guides and Rangers. LC 32-14931. xi p., 2 l., 17-206 p. 19 cm. 1931. The Macmillan Company.

Barcynska, Countess, pseud., see Evans, Marguerite Florence Helene Jervis.

Barcynska, Helene
--The Honey Pot. N.D. E P Dutton.
--If Wishes Were Horses. N.D. E P Dutton.

Bard, Lori
--Hello World. 124p. 1970. (ISBN 0-87787-001-2). Mara Books Inc.

Bard, Mary
--Best Friends. 1st ed. Elgin, Jill, illus. LC 55-5648. 182p. illus. 21cm. c.1955. Lippincott.
--Best Friends at School. Morse, Dorothy Bayley (1906-1979), illus. LC 61-7981. (Illus.). 192 p. 21cm. 1961. Lippincott.
--Best Friends in Summer. LC 60-5716. (Illus.). 185 p. 21cm. 1960. Lippincott.
--Just Be Yourself. LC 56-11676. 255 p. 21cm. 1956. Lippincott.

Bardach, John
--Downstream. N.D. (ISBN 0-448-00197-7). Grosset & Dunlap.

Bardeen, Charles William (1847-)
--Tom and Tom Tit and Other Stories about Schools. LC 11-29353. 286 p. 19 1/2 cm. (School bulletin publications)). 1911. C. W. Bardeen.

Bardin, John Franklin (1916-1981)
--Christmas Comes But Once a Year. LC 54-5913. 241 p. 20cm. 1954. Scribner.

Bardon, Minna
--His Best Girl. LC 49-9886. 255 p. 20 cm. 1949. Arcadia House.

Bardwell, Harrison, pseud., see Craine, Edith Janice.

Bare, Arnold Edwin (1920-)
--Maui's Summer. (Illus.). 48 p. 29cm. 1952. Houghton Mifflin.

Bare, Colleen Stanley
--Ground Squirrels. LC 80-13649. (Illus.). 64p. (A Skylight Bk.). (gr. 2-5). 1980. Dodd.

Bare, Margaret Ann
--John Deere, Blacksmith Boy. Doremus, Robert (1913-), illus. (Illus.). 200 p. 20cm. (Childhood of famous Americans). 1964. Bobbs-Merrill.
--John Deere, Blacksmith Boy. Doremus, Robert (1913-), illus. LC 64-24808. 200p. col. illus. 20cm. (Childhood of famous Americans) Bibl.). 1965, c.1964. Bobbs.

Barendrecht, C., tr. see Van Der Land, Sipke.

Barfield, Owen (1898-)
--The Silver Trumpet. Beeby, Betty (1923-), illus. LC 68-28847. (Illus.). 147 p. 27cm. 1968. W. B. Eerdmans Pub. Co.

Barford, Carol (1931-)
--Let Me Hear the Music. LC 78-23966. 124 p. 22cm. c.1979. (ISBN 0-8164-3224-4). Seabury Press.

Bargar, Gary W.
--Life Is Not Fair. LC 83-15299. c.1984. (ISBN 0-89919-218-1). Clarion Books.
--Life is Not Fair. 1984. Houghton.
--What Happened to Mr. Forster?. LC 80-28259. [illegible] c.1981. (ISBN [illegible]). Houghton Mifflin/Clarion Books.

Barham, Richard Harris see Ingoldsby, Thomas, pseud.

Baring-Gould, Sabine (1834-1924)
--The Crock of Gold. Bedford, Francis Donkin (1864-1950), illus. (Books For Young People Ser.). N.D. L. C. Page & Co.
--Fairy Tales. N.D. J. B. Lippincott.
--Grettir the Outlaw. (Illus.). (The Round Table Ser.). N.D. A. L. Burt's Pubs.
--Grettir the Outlaw. (Illus.). (Scribner-Blackie Series of books for young people). N.D. Charles Scribner's Sons.
--Grettir, the Outlaw: A Story of Iceland. (The Rugby Series for Boys and Girls). 1905. A. L. Burt Company.
--My Birthday Present. (Illus.). 1888. E & J B Young.

Baring-Gould, Sabine (1834-1924), ed.
--A Book of Nursery Songs and Rhymes. LC 8-31507. xvi, 159, 1 p. incl. front. 21 cm. 1st U.S. edition. 1907. A. C. McClurg & Co.; Etc., Etc.
--Book of Nursery Songs and Rhymes. (Illus.). N.D. J. B. Lippincott.
--A Book of Nursery Songs and Rhymes. LC 74-163419. (Illus.). xvi, 159 p. 22cm. 1895. Methuen.
--A Book of Nursery Songs and Rhymes. LC 68-23135. (Illus.). xvi, 159 p. 23cm. 1969. Singing Tree Press.
--A Book of Nursery Songs and Rhymes. Birmingham Art School, illus. LC 68-23135. 159p. Repr. of 1895 ed. 1969 (Gale Reprints). Methuen: Distributed by Singing Tree Press.
--Old English Fairy Tales. (The Fairy Library). N.D. A. L. Burt Co.

Baring-Gould, Ceil, ed. see Mother Goose.
Baring-Gould, Ceil see Mother Goose.
Baring-Gould, Sabine (1834-1924), suppls. by see Henderson, William James.
Baring-Gould, William Stuart, ed. see Mother Goose.
Baring-Gould, William Stuarty see Mother Goose.
Barish, Wendy, jt. auth. see Lawson, Don.
Barish, Wendy, ed. see Appleton, Victor, II.
Barish, Wendy, ed. see Dixon, Franklin W.
Barish, Wendy, ed. see Grimm, Jakob Ludwig Karl (1785-1863) & Grimm, Wilhelm Karl.
Barish, Wendy, ed. see Hope, Laura Lee.
Barish, Wendy, ed. see Keene, Carolyn, pseud. (1894-1982) & Dixon, Franklin W.
Barish, Wendy, ed. see Packard, Mary.
Barish, Wendy, ed. see Rotsler, William.
Barish, Wendy, ed. see Sheldon, Ann.

Barkan, Stanley H.
--The Blacklines Scrawl. Barkan, Bebe, illus. (Poetry Ser.). 1976. (ISBN 0-686-77309-8). (ISBN 0-89304-017-7). (ISBN 0-89304-010-X). pap. 3.00 signed ltd. ed. o.p.). Crestwood Hse. 1977. (ISBN 0-913940-55-0). Crestwood Hse. ward). Putnam Pub Group. 89191-285-1); The Rich Man. (ISBN 0-89191-287-8). Cross Cult.

Barke, Jas, ed. see Burns, Robert.

Barker, Carol Minturn (1938-)
--Arjun and His Village in India. Barker, Carol Minturn (1938-), illus. LC 79-40574. (Illus.). 32 p. 31cm. 1979. (ISBN 0-19-279734-4). Oxford University Press.
--The Boy and the Lion on the Wall. Barker, Carol, illus. LC 69-15920. (Illus.). 37 p. 29cm. 1969. Watts.
--King Midas and the Golden Touch. Barker, Carol Minturn (1938-), illus. LC 74-169355. 2-55 p. chiefly col. illus. 1972. (ISBN 0-85166-114-9). F. Watts. **Award: (KGM).**
--An Oba of Benin. LC 75-45370. (Illus.). 35 p. 27cm. (Carol Barker's Worlds of yesterday). 1977. (ISBN 0-201-00423-2). Addison-Wesley.
--A Prince of Islam. LC 75-45479. (Illus.). 35 p. 27cm. (Carol Barker's Worlds of yesterday). 1977, c.1976. (ISBN 0-201-00424-0). Addison-Wesley.
--A Prince of Islam. Barker, Carol Minturn (1938-), illus. LC 76-373211. (Illus.). 38 p. 28cm. (Carol Barker's Worlds of yesterday). 1976. (ISBN 0-356-08178-8). Macdonald and Jane's.

--Worlds of Yesterday: An Oba of Benin. LC 75-45370. (gr. k-3). 1977 (A-W Childrens). A-W.

Barker, Cicely Mary

--Autumn Songs with Music. Barker, Cicely Mary, illus. (Songs of the Seasons). N.D. Dodge.

--Blossom Flower Fairies: Poems and Pictures. LC 81-1727. (Illus.). 16 p. 11cm. 1981. (ISBN 0-399-20823-2). Philomel Books.

--The Children's Book of Hymns. N.D. Fleming H. Revell Co.

--Fairy's Gift. Barker, Cicely Mary, illus. (Illus.). 1st U.S. edition. (Cicely Mary Barker Storybooks). 1977. (ISBN 0-685-78524-6, Pub. by Two Continents). Hippocrene Bks.

--A Flower Fairies Alphabet: Poems and Pictures. LC 85-70557. p. cm. c.1985. (ISBN 0-87226-023-2). Bedrick/Blackie.

--The Flower Fairies Miniature ABC. (Illus.). 48p. (Flower Fairies Ser.). 1984. (ISBN 0-911745-75-0, Bedrick Blackie). P Bedrick Bks.

--Flower Fairies Miniature Library. LC 81-5180. p. cm. 1981. (ISBN 0-399-20823-2). Philomel Books.

--Flower Fairies of the Autumn. (Poetry, Music And Art). (MacMillan Books For Boys And Girls). N.D. MacMillan Bks.

--Flower Fairies of the Autumn: With the Nuts and Berries They Bring : Poems and Pictures. LC 84-45890. (Illus.). 41 p. 16cm. 1985. (ISBN 0-911745-92-0). Bedrick.

--Flower Fairies of the Garden: Poems. Barker, Cicely Mary, illus. LC 85-70559. p. cm. 1985. (ISBN 0-87226-021-6). P. Bedrick Books.

--Flower Fairies of the Seasons. Barker, Cicely Mary, illus. LC 83-73462. (Illus.). 96p. 1st U.S. edition. (Flower Fairies Ser.). 1984. (ISBN 0-911745-48-3). P Bedrick Bks.

--Flower Fairies of the Spring. Barker, Cicely Mary, illus. (Illus.). (gr. 3 up). N.D. (ISBN 0-685-24605-1). Merry Thoughts.

--Flower Fairies of the Spring: Poems. Barker, Cicely Mary, illus. LC 84-85877. p. cm. 1985. (ISBN 0-911745-90-4). P. Bedrick.

--Flower Fairies of the Summer. (Poetry, Music And Art). (MacMillan Bks. For Boys And Girls). N.D. MacMillan Bks.

--Flower Fairies of the Summer: Poems and Pictures. LC 84-45889. (Illus.). 41 p. 16cm. 1985. (ISBN 0-911745-91-2). Bedrick.

--Flower Fairies of the Trees: Poems. Barker, Cicely Mary, illus. LC 85-70558. p. cm. 1985. (ISBN 0-87226-022-4). P. Bedrick Books.

--Flower Fairies of the Wayside: Poems. Barker, Cicely Mary, illus. LC 85-70560. p. cm. 1985. (ISBN 0-87226-020-8). P. Bedrick Books.

--Flower Fairy: A Little Book of Old Rhymes. Barker, Cicely Mary, illus. (Illus.). 1st U.S. edition. (Cicely Mary Barker Storybooks). (gr. k-4). 1977. (ISBN 0-8467-0257-6, Pub. by Two Continents). Hippocrene Bks.

--Flower Songs of the Seasons. Barker, Cicely Mary, illus. (Songs of the Seasons). N.D. Dodge.

--The Lord of Rushie River. Barker, Cicely Mary, illus. (Illus.). 1st U.S. edition. (Cicely Mary Barker Storybooks). (gr. k-4). 1977. (ISBN 0-8467-0258-4, Pub. by Two Continents). Hippocrene Bks.

--The Rhyming Rainbow. Barker, Cicely Mary, illus. (Illus.). (Cicely Mary Barker Storybooks). (gr. k-4). 1977. (ISBN 0-8467-0259-2, Pub. by Two Continents). Hippocrene Bks.

--Spring Songs with Music. Barker, Cicely Mary, illus. (Songs of the Season). N.D. Dodge.

--Summer Songs with Music. Barker, Cicely Mary, illus. (Songs of the Seasons). N.D. Dodge.

Barker, Cicely Mary, ed.

--Old Rhymes for All Times. Barker, Cicely Mary, illus. 64 p. col. front., illus., col. plates. 26 cm. N.D. The Dodge Publishing Company.

Barker, Cicely Mary & Kovar, Edith May (1905-), eds.

--Old Rhymes for All Times. Windsor, Mary, pseud. Barker, Cicely Mary, illus. LC 36-6325. 3 p. l., 11-76 p. col. front., illus., col. plates. 25 cm. c.1935. Artists and Writers Guild, Inc.

--Rhymes New and Old. Windsor, Mary, pseud. Barker, Cicely Mary, illus. 3 p. l., 11-76 p. col. front., illus., col. plates. 25 cm. c.1935. Artists and Writers Guild, Inc.

Barker, Elliott S.

--Beatty's Cabin. (Illus.). N.D. University of New Mexico Press.

Barker, Elsa, Mrs.

--Stories from the New Testament for Children. Moore, Herbert, illus. N.D. Duffield & CO.

Barker, Else Inga-Lill (1925-) & Barker, George

--Why Teddy Bears Are Brown. LC 48-3614. 32 p. col. illus. 18 x 20 cm. N.D. T. Y. Crowell.

Barker, Frank Granville (1923-)

--The Flying Dutchman. LC 80-52507. (Masterworks of Opera Ser.). N.D. (ISBN 0-382-06430-5). Silver.

Barker, George, jt. auth. see Barker, Else Inga-Lill.

Barker, Gracie Z.

--Wee Tall Tales. N.D. Pageant Press INC.

Barker, Jane Valentine, jt. auth. see Downing, Sybil.

Barker, Jane Valentine (1930-) & Downing, Sybil

--Adventures in the West. Wilson, Robert Franklin (1937-), illus. LC 79-52142. (Illus.). 40 p. 23cm. (Colorado Heritage Series: Book 5). c.1979. (ISBN 0-87108-220-9). Pruett Pub. Co.

--Building Up. 1st ed. Wilson, Robert Franklin (1937-), illus. LC 79-90624. (Illus.). 44 p. 23cm. (Colorado Heritage Series: Book 7). c.1979. (ISBN 0-87108-228-4). Pruett Pub. Co.,.

--Trappers and Traders. Wilson, Robert Franklin (1937-), illus. LC 79-83745. (Illus.). 36 p., 1 leaf of plates. 22cm. (Colorado Heritage Series: Book 3). c.1979. Pruett Pub. Co.

--Wagons and Rails. 1st ed. Wilson, Robert Franklin (1937-), illus. LC 79-91986. (Illus.). 23cm. 44p. (Colorado Heritage Ser.: Book 9). c.1980. Pruett Pub. Co.

Barker, Kathleen Frances

--Himself. Barker, Kathleen Frances (1901-1973), illus. LC 37-362. vi p., 1 l., 9-96 p. front., illus., plates. 25 cm. 1935. Scribner's sons.

Barker, Lady

--The Christmas Cake cut into Four Quarters: A Story Book for Children. N.D. Frederick Warne.

--A Christmas Cake in Four Quarters. (Series of Books for the Young). N.D. Macmillan & Co.

--Ribbon Stories. (Illus.). (Golden Links Ser.). N.D. Frederick Warne & Co.

--Ribbon Stories. (Series of Books for the Young). N.D. Macmillan & Co.

--Sybil's Book. (Series of Books for the Young). N.D. Macmillan & Co.

--The White Rat and Other Stories. (Illus.). N.D. Macmillan & Co.

Barker, Lucy Davis (1841-), contrib. by see Greenaway, Kate.

Barker, Lucy Davis, Mrs. (1841-)

--Kate Greenaway's Birthday Book. derrydale 1980 ed. Greenaway, Kate (1846-1901), illus. LC 79-28520. (Illus.). 126 p. 15cm. 1980. (ISBN 0-517-31005-8). Derrydale Books.

--Kate Greenaway's Birthday Book for Children. Greenaway, Kate (1846-1901), illus. LC 12-32656. 126, 2 p. col. front., illus., col. plates. 10 x 10 cm. 1880. G. Routledge and Sons.

Barker, Mary Libal

--Milenka's Happy Summer. Lantz, Paul (1908-), illus. LC 61-81780. 187p. illus. 24cm. 1961. Dodd, Mead.

Barker, Melvern J. (1907-)

--Country Fair. N.D. E. M. Hale & Co.

--Country Fair. (Illus.). 32 p. 27cm. (Oxford books for boys and girls). 1955. Oxford University Press.

--Different Twins. 1957. (ISBN 0-8382-0204-7, Cadmus Books). E. M. Hale and Company.

--The Different Twins. (Illus.). 32 p. 26cm. 1957. Lippincott.

--How Little Boats Grow. LC 55-7980. 32 p. 26cm. 1955. Lippincott.

--The Little Island Star. 1954. (ISBN 0-8382-0456-2, Cadmus Books). E. M. Hale And Company.

--Little Island Star. (Illus.). 32 p. 27cm. (Oxford books for boys and girls). 1954. Oxford University Press.

--Little Sea Legs. LC 51-6973. (Illus.). unpaged. 26cm. 1951. Oxford University Press.

--Shipshape Boy. (Illus.). 32 p. 26cm. 1961. Scribner.

--Six O'clock Rooster. LC 53-7262. unpaged. illus. 26cm. (Oxford books for boys and girls). 1953. Oxford University Press.

Barker, Reginald Charles

--Gentleman Grizzly. N.D. A L Burt Co.

--The Hair Trigger Brand. N.D. A L Burt Co.

Barker, Sale, Mrs.

--Lily's Home. (Illus.). 1875. George Routledge & Sons.

--Lily's Magic Lantern. (Illus.). N.D. George Routledge.

--Lily's Scrap Book. (Illus.). N.D. George Routledge & Sons.

--Lily's Screen. (Illus.). N.D. George Routledge & Sons.

--Lily's Visit to Grandmamma. (Illus.). N.D. George Routledge.

--Little Lily's library, 4 Vols. (Illus.). N.D. George Routledge.

--Little Wide-Awake Poetry Book. (Illus.). N.D. George Routledge.

--Only a Little Child. Blood, Laura, illus. (Illus.). N.D. George Routledge.

--Picture Story Album for Girls. (Illus.). N.D. George Routledge & Sons.

--Puff the Pomeranian and Other Tales. Cooper, Alfred W., illus. N.D. George Routledge & Sons.

--Some of My Little Friends. (Illus.). 1882. Robert Brothers.

--Some of My Little Friends. Kronheim & Co., illus. (Illus.). N.D. George Routledge.

--Those Boys. (Illus.). N.D. George Routledge.

--With a Stout Heart. N.D. George Routledge & Sons.

Barker, Sale, Mrs. & Edgeworth, Maria (1767-1849)

--Every Child's Story. (Illus.). N.D. George Routledge & Sons.

Barker, Shirley Frances (1911-1965)

--The Road to Bunker Hill. 1st ed. LC 62-12175. 181p. 21cm. 1962. Duell, Sloan and Pearce.

--The Trojan Horse. Kredel, Fritz (1900-1973), illus. LC 59-6139. 56p. illus. 22cm. (Legacy books, Y-3). 1959. Random House.

Barker, William Henry (1882-1929) & Sinclair, Cecelia

--West African Folk-Tales. Sinclair, Cecilia, illus. Roberts, Hermese, frwd. by. LC 72-99339. (Illus.). 183 p. 23cm. 1972. (ISBN 0-8411-0010-1). Metro Books.

Barkin, Carol & James, Elizabeth

--Are We Still Best Friends?. Kluetmeier, Heinz, photos by. LC 75-19482. (Illus.). 32p. (Moods & Emotions Ser.). (gr. k-3). 1975. (ISBN 0-8172-0032-0). Raintree Pubs.

--Doing Things Together. Kluetmeier, Heinz, photos by. LC 75-20083. (Illus.). 32p. (Moods & Emotions Ser.). (gr. k-2). 1975. (ISBN 0-8172-0036-3). Raintree Pubs.

--I'd Rather Stay Home. Kluetmeier, Heinz, photos by. LC 75-19481. (Illus.). 32p. (Moods & Emotions). (gr. k-2). 1975. (ISBN 0-8172-0030-4). Raintree Pubs.

--Sometimes I Hate School. Kluetmeier, Heinz, photos by. LC 75-20143. (Illus.). 32p. (Moods & Emotions Ser.). (gr. k-2). 1975. (ISBN 0-8172-0034-7). Raintree Pubs.

Barkins, Evelyn (1919-)

--The Magic Pod. N.D. Island Press Cooperative, Inc.

Barklem, Jill

--Autumn Story. Barklem, Jill, illus. LC 80-15433. (Illus.). 32p. 1st U.S. edition. (The Brambly Hedge Bks.). (gr. 1 up). 1980. (ISBN 0-399-20745-7, Philomel). (ISBN 0-399-61155-X). Putnam Pub Group.

--The Big Book of Brambly Hedge. LC 81-8829. p. cm. 1981. (ISBN 0-399-20833-X). Philomel Books.

--Spring Story. LC 80-15300. (Illus.). 31 p. 18cm. (Brambly Hedge). ((Series: Barklem, Jill.). (Brambly Hedge.). 1980. (ISBN 0-529-05607-0). Philomel Books.

--Spring Story. Barklem, Jill, illus. LC 80-15300. (Illus.). 32p. 1st U.S. edition. (The Brambly Hedge Bks.). (gr. 1 up). 1980. (ISBN 0-399-20746-5, Philomel). (ISBN 0-399-61156-8). Putnam Pub Group.

--Summer Story. Barklem, Jill, illus. LC 80-15423. (Illus.). 32p. (The Brambly Hedge Bks.). (gr. 1 up). 1980. (ISBN 0-399-20747-3, Philomel). (ISBN 0-399-61157-6). Putnam Pub Group.

--Winter Story. Barklem, Jill, illus. LC 80-15422. (Illus.). 32p. (The Brambly Hedge Bks.). (gr. 1 up). 1980. (ISBN 0-399-20748-1, Philomel). (ISBN 0-399-61158-4). Putnam Pub Group.

Barklem, Jill, illus.

--The Secret Staircase. LC 83-6270. p. cm. (Brambly Hedge). 1983. (ISBN 0-399-20994-8). Philomel Books.

Barkley, Henry C.

--My Boyhood: A Story for Boys. (Illus.). 320p. N.D. E. P. Dutton & Co.

Barkowski, Renee

--My Home. Fry, R. O., illus. (Illus.). (ps-4). 1971. (ISBN 0-307-60115-3, Golden Pr). Western Pub.

Barks, Carl, illus.

--Uncle Scrooge & the Secret of Old Castle. (Illus.). 36p. 1981. (ISBN 0-89659-180-8). Abbeville Pr.

Barksdale, Lena

--Daring Riders: And Other Tales of Young America. Nicholas, Frank, illus. LC 46-727445. 6 p. l., 3-86 p. illus. (part col.) 20 cm. 1946. A. A. Knopf.

--The First Thanksgiving. Lenski, Lois (1893-1974), illus. LC 42-213062. 4 p. l., 3-57 p. col. front., illus., col. plates (1 double) 19 1/2 cm. 1942. A. A. Knopf.

--Milly and Her Dogs. Steiner, Charlotte, illus. LC 42-16022. 31 p. illus. (part col.) 21 x 26 cm. 1942. Doubleday, Doran & Company, Inc.

Barksdale, Lena, ed.

--The Treasure Bag. Stories and Poems. Brevannes, Maurice (1904-), illus. LC 47-31032. 139 p. illus. (part col.) 28 cm. (Bermel books for young people). 1947. A. A. Knopf.

Barksdale, Lena E.

--The Chickens of Fowl Farm. Barksdale, Lena E., illus. 35p. 1898. Allen, Lane, & Scott.

Barlee, E., Miss

--Three Paths in Life: A Story for Girls, 1 of 4 Vols. (Treasure Library). N.D. Set. Pott, Young & Co.

Barlef, Adi, tr. see Rabinowitz, Shalom.

Barlett, Frederick Orin (1876-)

--Mistress Dorothy. Noble-Ives, Sarah, illus. (Illus.). 12cm. 37p. 1901. E. P. Dutton & Co.

Barlettani, Elvio

--Lampo, the Traveling Dog. (Illus.). (gr. 5 up). 1963. (ISBN 0-394-81313-8). Pantheon.

Barlow, Genevieve (1910-), ed.

--Latin American Tales: From the Pampas to the Pyramids of Mexico. Hutchinson, William Miller (1916-), illus. LC 66-845542. (Illus.). 144 p. 22cm. 1966. (ISBN 0-528-80088-4). Rand McNally.

Barlow, Roger, pseud., see Leckie, Robert Hugh.

Barlow, Roger, pseud. (1920-)

--Black Treasure. Leckie, Robert Hugh. LC 63-14104. 159 p. illus. 18 cm. (His Sandy Steele adventures). 1963. Grosset & Dunlap.

--Black Treasure. Leckie, Robert Hugh. LC 59-13882. 192p. illus. 20cm. (His Sandy Steele adventures, 1). 1959. Simon and Schuster.

--Danger at Mormon crossing. Leckie, Robert Hugh. LC 59-16727. 20cm. 191p. (The Sandy Steele Adventure Series). 1959. Simon and Schuster.

--Fire at Red Lake. Leckie, Robert Hugh. LC 59-16718. 20cm. 160p. (The Sandy Steele Adventure Series). 1959. Simon and Schuster.

--Secret Mission to Alaska. Leckie, Robert Hugh. LC 59-16715. 188p. illus. 20cm. (His Sandy Steele adventures, 5). 1959. Simon and Schuster.

--Stormy Voyage. Leckie, Robert Hugh. LC 59-16716. 187p. illus. 20cm. (His Sandy Steele adventures, 3). 1959. Simon and Schuster.

--Troubled Waters. Leckie, Robert Hugh. N.D. (ISBN 0-448-04825-6). Grosset & Dunlap Pub.

--Troubled Waters. Leckie, Robert Hugh. LC 59-16717. (Illus.). 20cm. 186p. (His Sandy Steele Adventures, 6.). 1959. Simon and Schuster.

Barlow, Ruth C. (1898-)

--Fun at Happy Acres. Martinson, Melvin (1889-), illus. LC 35-8580. d4,1 p. illus. 23 1/2 x 23 1/2 cm. 1935. Thomas Y. Crowell Company.

--Lisbeth Holly. La Riviere, Rodolphe, illus. LC 47-31033. viii, 209 p. illus. 21 cm. 1947. Dodd, Mead.

Barlowe, Wayne Douglas, illus.

--Star Wars: A Pop-up Book. Penick, Ib, contrib. by. LC 77-90464. (Illus.). 16 p. 24cm. c.1978. (ISBN 0-394-83754-1). Random House.

Barmby, James (1822-1899)

--Barmby's Plays for Young People. (Illus.). 201p. N.D. Dick & Fitzgerald.

--Plays for Young People: With Songs and Choruses, Suitable for Private Theatricals. Rogers, Thomas (1839-), contrib. by. LC 13-20356. iv p. 2 l., 9 -201 p. 17 cm. 1879. Happy Hours Company.

Barnaby, Horace Thomas (1870-)

--The Long Eared Bat. Peat, Fern Bisel, Mrs. (1893-), illus. LC 29-10196. 60 p. col. front., illus., col. plates. 28 cm. c.1929. The Saalfield Publishing Co.

Barnard, Charles, jt. auth. see De Mille, William Churchill.

Barnard, Charles (1838-)

--The Door in the Book. Lathbury, Mary Artemisia (1841-1913), illus. LC 3-26373. 1903. Fleming H. Revell Co.

Barnard, Elizabeth H.

--Chipper Gets Liberated. (Mini-Bk.). (gr. 1-4). 1972. (ISBN 0-912472-11-1). Miller Bks.

Barnard, Eveline

--The Brothers Are Walking. LC 77-353006. 136 p. 21cm. 1976. (ISBN 0-234-77577-7). Dobson.

Barnard, Helen Pearson

--The Boys of North Parish. N.D. Pilgrim Press.

--The Boys of North Parish. 320p. N.D. Sunday-School Library.

--Patty's Grand Uncle. 425p. N.D. Pilgrim Press.

Barnard, Patricia

--The Contemporary Mouse: A Fable for Art Lovers. Dowling, Constance Jean, illus. Moore, Edward J., photos by. LC 54-10139. (Illus.). 47 p. 24cm. 1954. Coward-McCann.

Barnard, Philip

--Don't Tickle the Elephant Tree: Sensitive Plants. (Illus.). 64p. (gr. 4-6). 1982. (ISBN 0-671-41625-1). Messner.

Barnard, Simon

--The Dragon of St. Pancras. (Illus.). 1976. (ISBN 0-685-86594-0). State Mutual Bk.

Barnard, Winifred E.

--Kembo: A Little Girl of Africa. 64p. 1951. Friendship Press.

--Kembo: A Little Girl of Africa. Wood, Elsie Anna, illus. LC 35-8472. 60, 1 p. col. illus. 14 cm. the nursery series. 1928. Friendship Press.

--Mitsu, a Little Girl of Japan. Jacobs, Helen M., illus. LC 35-8471. 1 p. l., 58, 1 p. col. illus. 14 cm. the nursery series. c.1930. Friendship Press.

Barnard & La Clair

--Dragon, Dragon. N.D. Carlton.

Barne, Kitty, pseud., see Barne, Marion Catherine.

Barne, Kitty, pseud. (1883-1957)
--The Amber Gate. Barne, Marion Catherine. Gervis, Ruth S. (1894-), illus. N.D. Thomas Nelson & Sons.
--Barbie. Barne, Marion Catherine. Foster, Marcia Lane (1897-), illus. LC 69-11779. 257 p. 21cm. 1969. Little, Brown.
--Dog Stars. Barne, Marion Catherine. Molony, Alice, illus. LC 51-2811. 238 p. illus. 21 cm. 1951. Dodd, Mead.
--Family Footlights. Barne, Marion Catherine. Gervis, Ruth S. (1894-), illus. LC 40-271805. vii, 244 p., 1 l., incl. front., illus. 20 1/2 cm. 1939. Dodd, Mead & Company.
--In the Same Boat. Barne, Marion Catherine. Gervis, Ruth S. (1894-), illus. LC 45-10647. 5 p. l., 208 p. illus. 19 cm. 1945. Dodd, Mead & Company.
--May I Keep Dogs!. Barne, Marion Catherine. Johnston, Arnold Bamiiza (1893-), illus. LC 43-161365. 294, 1 p. incl. front., illus. 20 1/2 cm. 1942. Dodd, Mead & Company.
--Rosina Copper, the Mystery Mare. Barne, Marion Catherine. Purtscher, Alfons, illus. 1956. Dutton.
--Secret of the Sand Hills. Barne, Marion Catherine. LC 49-7830. 245. p. 21 cm. (Junior Red badge mysteries). 1949. Dodd, Mead.
--She Shall Have Music. Barne, Marion Catherine. Gervis, Ruth S. (1894-), illus. x, 261, 1 p. incl. front., illus. 20 1/2 cm. 1939. Dodd, Mead & Company.
--Three and a Pigeon. Barne, Marion Catherine. Tresilian, Cecil Stuart (1891-), illus. LC 44-235631. 4 p. l., 206 p. incl. plates. 21 cm. 1944. Dodd, Mead & Company.
--Visitors from London. Barne, Marion Catherine. Gervis, Ruth S. (1894-), illus. vii, 262 p., 1 l., incl. front., illus. 20 cm. 1940. Dodd, Mead & Company. **Award: (CMA).**
--We'll Meet in England. Barne, Marion Catherine. Spurrier, Arnrid, illus. N.D. Dodd Mead & Co.
--The Windmill Mystery. Barne, Marion Catherine. Foster, Marcia Lane (1897-), illus. LC 50-6187. 248 p. illus. 21 cm. 1950. Dodd, Mead.

Barne, Marion Catherine see Barne, Kitty, pseud.

Barner, Bob (1947-)
--The Elephant's Visit. LC 75-12605. (Illus.). 32 p. 20cm. 1975. (ISBN 0-316-56315-3). Little, Brown.

Barner, Skuldavanadis
--Pims: Adventures of Dala Horse. Bock, Vera, illus. LC 64-19405. (Illus.). 1964. McKay.

Barnes, Annie Maria (1857-)
--An American Girl in Korea. (The Vacation Ser.). N.D. Penn.
--An American Girl in Korea. Strehlan, Carl A., illus. LC 5-13203. 19cm. 392p. (Keystone Ser.). N.D. Penn Publishing Co.
--Carmio: The Little Mexican-Indian Captive. LC 28-4855. 104 p. col. front., illus. 19 cm. c.1897. American Baptist Publication Society.
--The Ferry Maid of the Chattahoochee. Waugh, Ida, illus. (Keystone Ser.). 1899. Penn Publishing Co.
--The Ferry Maid of the Chattahoochee: A Story for Girls. Waugh, Ida, illus. LC 99-3325. 343 p. pl. 19 cm. (Vacation Ser.). 1899. The Penn. Pub. Co.
--The House of Grass. LC 6-8657. 336 p. 19 cm. 1892. Methodist Episcopal Church.
--How A-Chon-Ho-Ah Found the Light. LC 6-865861. 266 p. 19 1/2 cm. 1894. Presbyterian Committee of Publication.
--Izilda: A Story of Brazil. 195 p. front., pl. 19 1/2 cm. c.1896. Presbyterian Committee of Publication.
--A Lass of Dorchester. Merrill, Frank Thayer (1848-), illus. LC 4-21721. 5 p. l., 341 p. front., 3 pl. 20 1/2 cm. 1904. Lee and Shepard.
--The Laurel Token: A Story of Yamassee Uprising. Picknell, George W., illus. viii p., 1 l., 347 p. front., 5 pl. 19 1/2 cm. 1904. Lee and Shepard.
--Little Betty Blew. Merrill, Frank Thayer (1848-), illus. LC 3-13622. N.D. Lothrop, Lee & Shepard.
--A Little Lady at the Fall of Quebec. (Historical Stories for Girls Ser.). N.D. Penn.
--The Little Lady of the Fort. N.D. Grosset & Dunlap.
--The Little Lady of the Fort. (Historical Stories for Girls). N.D. Penn.
--The Little Lady of the Fort. (The Outdoor Bks.). N.D. Penn Publishing Co.
--The Little Lady of the Fort. Wood, Helene, illus. (Keystone Ser.). 1903. Penn Publishing Co.
--The Lost Treasure of Umdilla. LC 25-93382. 224 p. front., pl. 19 1/2 cm. c.1925. Fleming H. Revell Company.
--Marti: A Story of the Cuban War. LC 99-5373. 96 p. illus. 21 cm. (New Sabbath library, v. 2, no. 8). 1899. D.C. Cook Pub. Co.
--Matouchon: A Story of Indian Child Life. LC 6-8656. 316 p. incl. front. plates. 19 1/2 cm. 1895. The American Sunday-School Union.
--Mistress Moppet. Winner, Margaret F., illus. LC 4-10931. 3 p., 1 l., 5-197 p. front., 4 pl. 20 cm. (Sunbeam Ser. for Young People). 1904. The Penn Publishing Company.
--Mistress Moppett. (The Vacation Ser.). N.D. Penn.

Barnes, Annie Maria (1857-) & Griggs, William Charles (1867-), eds.
--The Red Miriok: Shan Folk-Lore Stories. Newman, George A., illus. LC 3-2037. 1 p. 1., 127, vii, 1, 9-108 p., 1 l. illus., plates. 19 cm. 1903. American Baptist Publication Society.

Barnes, Djuna (1892-1982)
--Creatures in an Alphabet. LC 82-5086. ill. 21cm. 64p. c.1982. (ISBN 0-385-27797-0). (ISBN 0-385-27806-3). Dial Press.
--A Night Among the Horses, and other Stories. N.D. Liveright Publishing.
--Ryder. N.D. Liveright Publishing.

Barnes, E. J.
--Silver Beach: Or, The Mother's Legacy. N.D. Methodist Bk Concern.

Barnes, Elmer Tracey, pseud., see Stratemeyer Syndicate.

Barnes, Elmer Tracey, pseud.
--The Motion Picture Comrades Aboard a Submarine: Or, Searching for Treasure Under the Sea. Stratemeyer Syndicate. Lester, illus. (The Motion Picture Comrades Ser.: Vol. 4). 1917. New York Book Co.
--The Motion Picture Comrades Aboard a Submarine: Or, Searching for Treasure Under the Sea. Stratemeyer Syndicate. Lester, illus. Repr. of 1917 ed (Pub. by New York Book Co). (The Motion Picture Comrades Ser.: Vol. 4). N.D. Saalfield Publishing Co.
--The Motion Picture Comrades Along the Orinoco: Or, Facing Perils in the Tropics. Stratemeyer Syndicate. Lester, illus. (The Motion Picture Comrades Ser.: Vol. 3). 1917. New York Book Co.
--The Motion Picture Comrades along the Orinoco: Or, Facing Perils in the Tropics. Stratemeyer Syndicate. Lester, illus. Repr. of 1917 ed (Pub. by New York Book Co). (The Motion Picture Comrades Ser.: Vol. 3). N.D. Saalfield Publishing Co.
--The Motion Picture Comrade's Great Venture: Or, On the Road with the Big Round-Top. Stratemeyer Syndicate. Lester, illus. (The Motion Picture Comrades Ser.: Vol. 1). 1917. New York Book Co.
--The Motion Picture Comrades' Great Venture: Or, On the Road with the Big Round-Top. Stratemeyer Syndicate. Lester, illus. Repr. of 1917 ed (Pub. by New York Book Co). (The Motion Picture Comrades Ser.: Vol. 1). N.D. Saalfield Publishing Co.
--The Motion Picture Comrades in African Jungles: Or, The Camera Boys in Wild Animal Land. Stratemeyer Syndicate. Lester, illus. (The Motion Picture Comrades Ser.: Vol. 2). 1917. New York Book Co.
--The Motion Picture Comrades Producing a Success: Or, Featuring a Sensation. Stratemeyer Syndicate. Lester, illus. (The Motion Picture Comrades Ser.: Vol. 5). 1917. New York Book Co.
--The Motion Picture Comrades Producing a Success: Or, Featuring a Sensation. Stratemeyer Syndicate. Lester, illus. Repr. of 1917 ed (Pub. by New York Book Co). (The Motion Picture Comrades Ser.: Vol. 5). N.D. Saalfield Publishing Co.
--The Motion Picture Comrades through African Jungles: Or, The Camera Boys in Wild Animal Land. Stratemeyer Syndicate. Lester, illus. Repr. of 1917 ed (Pub. by New York Book Co). (The Motion Picture Comrades Ser.: Vol. 2). Orig. Title: The Motion Picture Comrades in African Jungles; Or, The Camera Boys in Wild Animal Land. N.D. Saalfield Publishing Co.

Barnes, Emily Ann & Young, Bess Margaret, eds.
--Plays: Dramatizations by Sixth Grade Children. LC 32-10060. xxvi, 218 p. incl. illus., plates. col. front. 22 cm. (Half-title: Lincoln school of Teachers college. Columbia university ... Children's series). 1932. Pub. by Bureau of Publications of Teachers College, Columbia University, for Lincoln School of Teachers College.

Barnes, George Foster, illus.
--Four Doll Mammas. (Pussy Willow Ser.). N.D. D Lothrop.
--Little Chief. (Pussy Willow Ser.). N.D. D Lothrop.
--One Winter's Day. (Pussy Willow Ser.). N.D. D Lothrop.
--Pussy Willow. (Pussy Willow Ser.). N.D. D Lothrop.
--Rover's Fun. (Pussy Willow Ser.). N.D. D Lothrop.
--Trotry's Pocket. (Pussy Willow Ser.). N.D. D Lothrop.

Barnes, George Foster, jt. auth. see Smithson, Isabel.

Barnes, Gregory Allen (1934-)
--Wind of Change. (gr. 7 up). 1968. (ISBN 0-688-51009-4). Lothrop.

Barnes-Grundy, Mabel
--Hilary on Her Own. (Illus.). N.D. Baker & Taylor Co.

Barnes, James, jt. auth. see Seawell, Molly Elliott.

Barnes, James (1866-1936)
--The Blockaders and Other Stories. LC 5-6280. 2 p. l., 202, 1 p. front. 17 1/2 cm. 1905. Harper & Brothers.
--Commodore Bainbridge: From the Gunroom to the Quaterdeck. Gibbs, George, et al., illus. (Young Heroes of Our Navy Ser.). 1897. D. Appleton & Co.
--Drake and His Yeomen: A True Accounting of the Character and Adventures of Sir Francis Drake. Chapman, Carlton T., illus. Maunsell, Mathew, Sir, as told by. LC 224. xiii, 415 p. col. front., 7 pl. 20 1/2 cm. 1899. The Macmillan Company.
--For King or Country: A Story of the American Revolution. LC 4-16120. iv p., 1 l., 269 p. front., 20 pl. 19 cm. 1896. Harper & Brothers.
--Giant of Three Wars. N.D. Appleton Century Co.
--The Hero of Erie: Commodore Perry. (Young Heroes of Our Navy Ser.). 1898. D. Appleton & Co.
--Light-Horse Harry. (Illus.). (Harper's Young People Series.). N.D. Harper Brothers.
--A Loyal Traitor. (Illus.). (Select Juvenile Ser.). N.D. Harper & Brothers.
--A Loyal Traitor. (Harper's Young People Ser.). N.D. Harper & Brothers Trade-List.
--A Loyal Traitor: A Story of the War of 1812. Keller, A. J., illus. LC 4-16121. x, 306 p. front, 20 pl. 19 cm. 1897. Harper & Brothers.
--Midshipman Farragut. Chapman, Carlton T., et al., illus. (Young Heroes of Our Navy Ser.). 1896. D. Appleton & Co.
--A Princetonian: A Story of Undergraduate Life at the College of New Jersey. LC 5-2454. xiii p., 1 l., 431 p. front., 2 pl. 18 cm. 1896. G. P. Putnam's Sons.
--Rifle and Caravan: Or, Two Boys in East Africa. LC 12-23716. 5 p. l., 325, 1 p. col. front., 1 illus., col. plates. 20 cm. 1912. D. Appleton and Company.
--The Son of Light Horse Harry. Mears, W. E., illus. LC 4-12973. 3 p. l., 242, 1 p. front., 7 pl. 19 cm. 1904. Harper & Brothers.
--With the Flag in the Channel: Or, The Adventures of Captain Gustavus Conyngham. Chapman, Carlton T., illus. LC 2-228561. vii, 158 p. front., 5 pl., 2 facsim. 20 cm. (On cover: Young heroes of our navy). 1902. D. Appleton and Company.
--Yankee Ships and Yankee Sailors: --Tales of 1812. Zogbaum, R. F. & Chapman, Carlton T., illus. LC 4-28566. ix p., 3 l., 3-281 p. front., 12 pl. 20 cm. 1897. The Macmillan Company.

Barnes, Joseph Fels (1907-1970), tr. see Frolov, Vadim.

Barnes, Josiah
--Wonderful Adventures by Land and Sea. (Illus.). (St. Nicholas Series for Boys). N.D. International Book Co.

Barnes, Kate, jt. ed. see Coatsworth, Elizabeth Jane.

Barnes, Lyle J.
--Sand Man Stories. LC 44-511059. 84 p. 20 1/2 cm. 1944. Wetzel Publishing Co., Inc.

Barnes-Murphy, Rowan
--Old MacDonald Had a Farm. LC 85-15607. p. cm. (Flap-up book). 1985. (ISBN 0-8120-5693-0). Barron's Educational Series.

Barnes, Nancy, pseud., see Adams, Helen Simmons.

Barnes, Nancy
--Wonderful Year. Seredy, Kate (1899-1975), illus. (Illus.). (gr. 4 up). 1946. (ISBN 0-671-32060-2). Messner. **Award: (JNM).**

Barnes, Ruth A.
--I Hear America Singing. Lawson, Robert (1892-1957), illus. Van Doren, Carl, intro. by. N.D. John C. Winston.

Barnes, Samuel Gill (1913-)
--Ready, Wrestle!. LC 65-11789. xx, 171p. 22cm. N.D. Ariel Bks.

Barness, Richard (1917-)
--Listen to Me!. LC 74-11901. 95 p. 23cm. 1975, c.1976. (ISBN 0-8225-0758-7). Lerner Publications Co.

Barnetson, John
--Critter Chronicles: Fables for Here and Now. Tanner, Suzy-Jane, illus. LC 80-66262. p. cm. 1982. (ISBN 0-89087-291-0). Celestial Arts.

Barnett, Belle McFall (1884-)
--From Knee-High to So-High: Twenty-One Tales for Children. 1st ed. Pomerantz, Norman, illus. LC 59-12921. 63p. illus. 23cm. 1959. Greenwich Book Publishers.

Barnett, Donald R.
--A Cross of Gold. LC 39-13887. 258 p. 20 cm. c.1939. Dorrance and Company.

Barnett, Evelyn Scott Snead, Mrs.
--Jerry's Reward. Barry, Etheldred Breeze (1870-), illus. LC 2-15354. 76 p. incl. front., illus., plates. 19 cm. (Cosy corner series). 1903. L. C. Page & Company.
--Jerry's Reward. Barry, Etheldred Breeze (1870-), illus. (Illus.). (Goldenrod Library Ser.). 1903. L. C. Page & Co.

Barnett, Grace Treleven (1899-) & Barnett, Olive Elizabeth (1911-)
--Beaded Buckskin. Barnett, Grace Treleven (1899-) & Barnett, Olive Elizabeth (1911-), illus. LC 40-324302. 149 p. col. front., illus., col. plates. 22 cm. c.1940. Oxford University Press.
--The Cock that Crowed at Two. Barnett, Grace Treleven (1899-) & Barnett, Olive Elizabeth (1911-), illus. LC 37-14736. 21cm. 35p. N.D Lothrop Lee & Shepard.
--Dark Island Mystery. LC 49-8187. 181 p. illus. 21 cm. 1949. Oxford Univ. Press.
--Fire Beads. Barnett, Grace Treleven (1899-) & Barnett, Olive Elizabeth (1911-), illus. LC 42-196486. vii, 1, 9-160 p. incl. front., illus. 21 x 16 cm. 1942. Oxford University Press.
--Ghost Town Mystery. LC 53-11729. 221 p. illus. 21 cm. (Oxford books for boys and girls). 1953. Oxford University Press
--Grasshopper Gold. Barnett, Grace Treleven (1899-) & Barnett, Olive Elizabeth (1911-), illus. LC 39-27711. 89 p. col. front., illus. 22 cm. c.1939. Oxford University Press.
--Homesteaders' Horses. Barnett, Grace Treleven (1899-) & Barnett, Olive Elizabeth (1911-), illus. LC 41-17943. 141 p. incl. front., illus., plates 21 x 16 cm. c.1941. Oxford University Press.
--The Little Duck Said Quack, Quack, Quack. Kendrick, Alcy, illus. LC 55-37194. 21cm. (Wonder books,: 636). 1955. Wonder Books.
--The Mystery at Yogo Creek. Barnett, Grace Treleven & Barnett, Olive Elizabeth, illus. LC 44-209666. 160 p. illus. 20 1/2 cm. 1944. Oxford University Press.
--The Mystery in Mission Valley. LC 47-31183. 171 p. illus. 21 cm. 1947. Oxford University Press.
--The Mystery of the Missing Wallet. LC 46-80620. 188 p. illus. 21 cm. 1946. Oxford University Press.
--Silver in the Teapot. Barnett, Grace Treleven (1899-) & Barnett, Olive Elizabeth (1911-), illus. N.D. Lothrop Lee & Shepard.
--They Hunted High and Low. Barnett, Grace Treleven (1899-) & Barnett, Olive Elizabeth (1911-), illus. N.D. Lothrop Lee & Shepard Co.

Barnett, Lincoln
--The World We Live In, Life's. Watson, Jane Werner, adapted by. (A Deluxe Golden Book). 1956. Golden Press.

Barnett, Marguerite, tr. see Golon, Sergeanne.

Barnett, Maybelle Fuller, Mrs.
--A Child's Garden: A Fantasy. Ilyin, Gleb, illus. LC 42-2900. xii p., 1 l., 15-64 p. incl. illus., col. port. on 1 l. 27 cm. 1941. Margent Press.

Barnett, Moneta
--First Pink Light. (gr. k-3). 1979. (ISBN 0-590-12083-2, Schol Pap). Scholastic Inc.

Barnett, Naomi
--I Know a Dentist. Boehm, Linda, illus. LC 77-24968. (Illus.). (Community Helper Bks.). (gr. k-4). 1978. (ISBN 0-399-61097-9). Putnam Pub Group.

Barnett, Naomi see Buchheimer, Naomi Barnett.

Barnett, Olive Elizabeth, jt. auth. see Barnett, Grace Treleven.

Barnett, Regina R.
--Let Out the Sunshine. 144p. (Orig.). 1981. (ISBN 0-697-01762-1). Wm C Brown.

Barney, Maginel Wright, jt. auth. see Baum, Lyman Frank.

Barnhart, Nancy (1889-), ed.
--The Lord is My Shepherd: Stories from the Bible Pictured in Bible Lands. 1949. (ISBN 0-684-20734-6). Scribner.

Barnhart, Peter
--The Wounded Duck. Adams, Adrienne (1906-), illus. LC 79-88022. (Illus.). 32 p. 27cm. c.1979. (ISBN 0-684-16255-5). Scribner.

Barnicle
--Pehe Nu-e. (Illus.). N.D. D. Lothrop Co.

Barnitz, Elizabeth Downing, Mrs.
--Bippy. LC 40-326390. 57 p. front., illus. 22 x 20 cm. 1940. T. Nelson and Sons.
--Bippy Rides Again: Story and Pictures. LC 43-14772. 64 p. incl. col. front., illus. (part col.) 20 1/2 cm. 1943. The John Day Company.

Barnitz, Wirt
--The Adventures of Tom Tiller. LC 54-13135. 167 p. 23 cm. 1955. Vantage Press.

Barnouw, Victor (1915-)
--Dream of the Blue Heron. Ward, Lynd Kendall (1905-1985), illus. LC 66-20995. (Illus.). (gr. 4-6). 1966. (Sey Lawr). Delacorte.

Barnstone, Aliki (1956-)
--Real Tin Flower: Poems about the World at Nine. Giovanopoulos, Paul Arthur (1939-), illus. LC 68-22122. (Illus.). 11 ils. index. 64p. 1968. (ISBN 0-02-708430-2, CCPr). Macmillan. **Award:** (NYT).
Barnstone, Willis (1927-), tr. see Lewis, Richard.
Barnstone, Willis (1927-)
--A Day in the Country. 1st ed. Knotts, Howard Clayton, Jr. (1922-), illus. LC 75-135771. (Illus.). 30 p. 29cm. 1971. (ISBN 0-06-020408-7). Harper & Row.
Barnum, Frances Courtenay Baylor, Mrs. (1848-1920)
--A Georgian Bungalow. LC 496443. (Illus.). iv p., 1 l., 121, 1 p. front., & pl. 1900. Houghton, Mifflin and Company.
--Juan and Juanita. new ed. Molloy, Anne G., ed. Tenggren, Gustaf (1896-1970), illus. LC 30-3874. v, 306 p. front., plates. 19 cm. (Riverside literature series). c.1930. Houghton Mifflin Company.
--Juan and Juanita. Sandham, Henry, illus. LC 4-16452. 276 p. incl. illus., plates. front. 22 cm. 1888. Ticknor and Company.
--Juan and Juanita. Tenggren, Gustaf (1896-1970), illus. LC 26-15955. 5 p. l., 300 p. col. front., col. plates. 22 cm. (Riverside bookshelf). 1926. Houghton Mifflin Company.
--Miss Nina Barrow. LC 6-8655. 4 p. l., 243 p. front. 19 cm. 1897. The Century Co.
Barnum, Jay Hyde (1888-1962)
--Little Old Truck. (Illus.). (gr. 1-3). 1953. (ISBN 0-8382-0463-5). Hale.
--The Little Old Truck. Barnum, Jay Hyde (1888-1962), illus. LC 52-12112. 22cm. 46p. 1953. Morrow.
--Motorcycle Dog. 1958. E M Hale.
--Motorcycle Dog. Barnum, Jay Hyde (1888-1962), illus. (Illus.). (gr. k-3). 1958. Morrow.
--The New Fire Engine. Barnum, Jay Hyde (1888-1962), illus. LC 52-5008. (Illus.). 47 p. 23cm. 1952. Morrow.
Barnum, Madalene Demarest
--Little Plays. N.D. Harper & Brothers.
--School Plays for all Occasions. N.D. Barse & Hopkins.
Barnum, Madalene Demarest, jt. auth. see Johnston, Emma Louisa.
Barnum, Phineas Taylor (1810-1891)
--Animal Stories: An Account of the Author's Famous Expedition in Search of Wild Animals for the Circus, Presenting Natural History from a New Standpoint. Williams, Florence White, illus. LC 27-894. 8 p. l., 13-239 p. front., illus. 20 cm. (Half-title: Every child's library). c.1926. The Saalfield Publishing Company.
--Dick Broadhead: A Tale of Perilous Adventures. LC 13-23601. 312 p. front., plates. 19 cm. 1888. G. W. Dillingham.
--Funny Stories. 1890. George Routledge.
--Jack in the Jungle. N.D. G. W. Dillingham Co.
--Jack in the Jungle: A Tale of Land and Sea ... LC 13-33877. 363 p. front., plates. 19 cm. 1880. G. W. Carleton & Co.
--Lion Jack. N.D. G. W. Dillingham Co.
Barnum, Phoebe TY.
--Tellus Stories. N.D. Pageant Press INC.
Barnum, Richard, pseud., see Stratemeyer Syndicate.
Barnum, Richard, pseud.
--Blackie, a Lost Cat: Her Many Adventures. Stratemeyer Syndicate. Rogers, Walter S., illus. (Vol. 7). 1916. Barse & Hopkins.
--Chunky, the Happy Hippo. Stratemeyer Syndicate. (The Kneetime Animal Stories: Vol. 11). 1918. Barse & Hopkins.
--Dido, the Dancing Bear: His Many Adventures. Stratemeyer Syndicate. (The Kneetime Animal Stories: Vol. 6). 1916. Barse & Hopkins.
--Don, a Runaway Dog. Stratemeyer Syndicate. (The Kneetime Animal Stories: Vol. 5). 1915. Barse & Hopkins.
--Flop Ear, the Funny Rabbit. Stratemeyer Syndicate. Rogers, Walter S., illus. (The Kneetime Animal Stories: Vol. 8). 1916. Barse & Hopkins.
--Light Foot, the Leaping Goat: His Many Adventures. Stratemeyer Syndicate. Rogers, Walter S., illus. (The Kneetime Animal Stories: Vol. 10). 1917. Barse & Hopkins.
--Mappo, the Merry Monkey: His Many Adventures. Stratemeyer Syndicate. Tooker, Harriet H., illus. LC 15-9963. 126 p. incl. plates. front. 21 cm. (The Kneetime Animal Stories: Vol. 3). 1915. Barse & Hopkins.
--Nero, the Circus Lion: His Many Adventures. Stratemeyer Syndicate. (The Kneetime Animal Stories: Vol. 13). 1919. Barse & Hopkins.
--Shaggo, the Mighty Buffalo: His Many Adventures. Stratemeyer Syndicate. Rogers, Walter S., illus. (The Kneetime Animal Stories: Vol. 16). 1921. Barse & Hopkins.
--Sharp Eyes, the Silver Fox: His Many Adventures. Stratemeyer Syndicate. (The Kneetime Animal Stories: Vol. 12). 1918. Barse & Hopkins.

--Slicko, the Jumping Squirrel: Her Many Adventures. Stratemeyer Syndicate. Tooker, Harriet H., illus. LC 15-9962. 126 p. incl. plates. front. 21 cm. (The Kneetime Animal Stories: Vol. 2). 1915. Barse & Hopkins.
--Squinty the Comical Pig: His Many Adventures. Stratemeyer Syndicate. Tooker, Harriet H., illus. LC 15-996199. 126 p. incl. plates. front. 21 cm. (The Kneetime Animal Stories: Vol. 1). 1915. Barse & Hopkins.
--Tamba, the Tame Tiger. Stratemeyer Syndicate. (The Kneetime Animal Stories: Vol. 14). 1919. Barse & Hopkins.
--Tinkle, the Trick Pony. Stratemeyer Syndicate. Rogers, Walter S., illus. (The Kneetime Animal Stories: Vol. 9). 1917. Barse & Hopkins.
--Toto, the Bustling Beaver: His Many Adventures. Stratemeyer Syndicate. Rogers, Walter S., illus. (The Kneetime Animal Stories: Vol. 15). 1920. Barse & Hopkins.
--Tum Tum, the Jolly Elephant. Stratemeyer Syndicate. (The Kneetime Animal Stories: Vol. 4). 1915. Barse & Hopkins.
--Winkie, the Wily Woodchuck. Stratemeyer Syndicate. (Illus.). (The Kneetime Animal Stories: Vol. 17). 1922. Barse & Hopkins.
Barnum, Vance, pseud., see Stratemeyer Syndicate.
Barnum, Vance, pseud.
--Frank and Andy Afloat: Or, The Cave on the Island. Stratemeyer Syndicate. (Original title published under the pseudonym, Clarence Young). (Illus.). Repr. of 1912 ed (Pub. by Cupples & Leon). (The Frank and Andy Ser.: Vol. 1). Orig. Title: The Racer Boys; Or, The Mystery of the Wreck. 1921. George Sully & Co.
--Frank and Andy Afloat: Or, The Cave on the Island. Stratemeyer Syndicate. (Original title published under the pseudonym, Clarence Young). Repr. of 1912 ed (Pub. by Cupples & Leon). (The Frank and Andy Ser.: Vol. 1). Orig. Title: The Racer Boys: Or, The Mystery of the Wreck. N.D. Whitman Publishing Co.
--Frank and Andy at Boarding School: Or, Rivals for Many Honors. Stratemeyer Syndicate. (Original title published under the pseudonym, Clarence Young). (Illus.). Repr. of 1912 ed (Pub. by Cupples & Leon). (The Frank and Andy Ser.: Vol. 2). Orig. Title: The Racer Boys at Boarding School; Or, Striving for the Championship. 1921. George Sully & Co.
--Frank and Andy at Boarding School: Or, Rivals for Many Honors. Stratemeyer Syndicate. (Original title published under the pseudonym, Clarence Young). Repr. of 1912 ed (Pub. by Cupples & Leon). (The Frank and Andy Ser.: Vol. 2). Orig. Title: The Racer Boys at Boarding School; Or, Striving for the Championship. N.D. Whitman Publishing Co.
--Frank and Andy in a Winter Camp: Or, The Young Hunters' Strange Discovery. Stratemeyer Syndicate. (Original title published under the pseudonym, Clarence Young). (Illus.). Repr. of 1912 ed (Pub. by Cupples & Leon). (The Frank and Andy Ser.: Vol. 3). Orig. Title: The Racer Boys to the Rescue; Or, Stirring Days in a Winter Camp. 1921. George Sully & Co.
--Frank and Andy in a Winter Camp: Or, The Young Hunter's Strange Discovery. Stratemeyer Syndicate. (Original title published under the pseudonym, Clarence Young). Repr. of 1912 ed (Pub. by Cupples & Leon). (The Frank and Andy Ser.: Vol. 3). Orig. Title: The Racer Boys to the Rescue; Or, Stirring Days in a Winter Camp. N.D. Whitman Publishing Co.
--Joe Strong and His Box of Mystery: Or, The Ten Thousand Dollar Prize Trick. Stratemeyer Syndicate. Hess, Erwin L., illus. Repr. of 1916 ed. (Joe Strong Ser.: Vol. 6). N.D. Whitman Publishing Co.
--Joe Strong and His Box of Mystery: Or, The Ten Thousand Dollar Prize Trick. Stratemeyer Syndicate. Kroeger, Jerome L., illus. (Joe Strong Ser.: Vol. 6). 1916. Hearst's International Library Co.
--Joe Strong and His Box of Mystery: Or, The Ten Thousand Dollar Prize Trick. Stratemeyer Syndicate. Rogers, Walter S., illus. (Joe Strong Ser.: Vol. 6). 1916. George Sully & Co.
--Joe Strong and His Wings of Steel: Or, A Young Acrobat in the Clouds. Stratemeyer Syndicate. Hess, Erwin L., illus. Repr. of 1916 ed. (Joe Strong Ser.: Vol. 5). N.D. Whitman Publishing Co.
--Joe Strong and His Wings of Steel: Or, A Young Acrobat in the Clouds. Stratemeyer Syndicate. Kroeger, Jerome L., illus. (Joe Strong Ser.: Vol. 5). 1916. Hearst's International Library Co.
--Joe Strong and His Wings of Steel: Or, A Young Acrobat in the Clouds. Stratemeyer Syndicate. Rogers, Walter S., illus. (Joe Strong Ser.: Vol. 5). 1916. George Sully & Co.

--Joe Strong on the High Wire: Or, Motorcycle Perils of the Air. Stratemeyer Syndicate. Hess, Erwin L., illus. Repr. of 1916 ed. (Joe Strong Ser.: Vol. 4). N.D. Whitman Publishing Co.
--Joe Strong on the High Wire: Or, Motorcycle Perils of the Air. Stratemeyer Syndicate. Kroeger, Jerome L., illus. (Joe Strong Ser.: Vol. 4). 1916. Hearst's International Library Co.
--Joe Strong on the High Wire: Or, Motorcycle Perils of the Air. Stratemeyer Syndicate. Rogers, Walter S., illus. (Joe Strong Ser.: Vol 4). 1916. George Sully & Co.
--Joe Strong on the Trapeze: Or, The Daring Feats of a Young Circus Performer. Stratemeyer Syndicate. Hess, Erwin L., illus. Repr. of 1916 ed. (Joe Strong Ser.: Vol. 2). N.D. Whitman Publishing Co.
--Joe Strong on the Trapeze: Or, The Daring Feats of a Young Circus Performer. Stratemeyer Syndicate. Kroeger, Jerome L., illus. (Joe Strong Ser.: Vol. 2). 1916. Hearst's International Library Co.
--Joe Strong on the Trapeze: Or, The Daring Feats of a Young Circus Performer. Stratemeyer Syndicate. Rogers, Walter S., illus. (Joe Strong Ser.: Vol. 2). 1916. George Sully & Co.
--Joe Strong, the Boy Fire-Eater: Or, The Most Dangerous Performance on Record. Stratemeyer Syndicate. Hess, Erwin L., illus. Repr. of 1916 ed. (Joe Strong Ser.: Vol. 7). N.D. Whitman Publishing Co.
--Joe Strong, the Boy Fire-Eater: Or, The Most Dangerous Performance on Record. Stratemeyer Syndicate. Kroeger, Jerome L., illus. (Joe Strong Ser.: Vol. 7). 1916. Hearst's International Library Co.
--Joe Strong, the Boy Fire-Eater: Or, The Most Dangerous Performance on Record. Stratemeyer Syndicate. Rogers, Walter S., illus. (Joe Strong Ser.: Vol. 7). 1916. George Sully & Co.
--Joe Strong, the Boy Fish: Or, Marvellous Doings in a Big Tank. Stratemeyer Syndicate. Rogers, Walter S., illus. (Joe Strong Ser.: Vol. 3). 1916. George Sully & Co.
--Joe Strong, the Boy Fish: Or, Marvelous Doings in a Big Tank. Stratemeyer Syndicate. Hess, Erwin L., illus. Repr. of 1916 ed. (Joe Strong Ser.: Vol. 3). N.D. Whitman Publishing Co.
--Joe Strong, the Boy Fish: Or, Marvelous Doings in a Big Tank. Stratemeyer Syndicate. Kroeger, Jerome L., illus. (Joe Strong Ser.: Vol. 3). 1916. Hearst's International Library Co.
--Joe Strong, the Boy Wizard: Or, The Mysteries of Magic Exposed. Stratemeyer Syndicate. Hess, Erwin L., illus. Repr. of 1916 ed. (Joe Strong Ser.: Vol. 1). N.D. Whitman Publishing Co.
--Joe Strong, the Boy Wizard: Or, The Mysteries of Magic Exposed. Stratemeyer Syndicate. Kroeger, Jerome L., illus. (Joe Strong Ser.: Vol. 1). 1916. Hearst's International Library Co.
--Joe Strong, the Boy Wizard: Or, The Mysteries of Magic Exposed. Stratemeyer Syndicate. Rogers, Walter S., illus. (Joe Strong Ser.: Vol. 1). 1916. George Sully & Co.
Barnwell, D. Robinson (1915-)
--Head into the Wind. Johnson, Avery Fischer (1906-), illus. LC 65-20929. 247p. 21cm. c.1965. McKay.
--Head into the Wind. Johnson, Avery Fischer (1906-), illus. (gr. 9 up). 1966. McKay.
--Shadow on the Water. 216 p. 21cm. 1967. D. McKay Co.
Barnwell, Mildred Telford (1891-)
--Cindy for Short: The/Saga of a Favorite Cat. LC 50-5397. (Illus.). 24cm. 10p. 1949. William-Frederick Press.
Barofsky, Seymour, tr. see Sendak, Philip.
Baron, A. L.
--The X-Bodies & the Answer. (gr. 7 up). 1970. (ISBN 0-529-00810-6). Collins-World.
Baron, Henry James
--I Am Waiting. LC 76-150043. (Illus.). xiv, 161 p. 23cm. (Soundings Ser.). c.1976. (ISBN 0-87463-433-4). Curriculum Dept., National Union of Christian Schools.
--The Nest. LC 76-150030. (Illus.). xvi, 229 p. 23cm. (Soundings Ser.). c.1976. (ISBN 0-87463-431-8). Curriculum Dept., National Union of Christian Schools.
--Nothing Ever Happens. LC 76-150035. (Illus.). xii, 196 p. 23cm. (Soundings Ser.). c.1976. (ISBN 0-87463-435-0). Curriculum Dept., National Union of Christian Schools.
--Voyage. LC 77-355678. (Illus.). xviii, 317 p. 23cm. (Soundings Ser.). c.1976. (ISBN 0-87463-437-7). Curriculum Dept., National Union of Christian Schools.
Baron, Henry James, et al., eds.
--A Smiling Hippopotamus. LC 76-150034. (Illus.). xvi, 168 p. 23cm. (Soundings Ser.). c.1976. (ISBN 0-87463-429-6). Curriculum Dept., National Union of Christian Schools.

Baron, Lindamichelle
--The Sun Is On. rev. ed. Elam, Keith, illus. Dee, Ruby, intro. by. (Illus.). 48p. (gr. 1-6). 1982. (ISBN 0-940938-02-2). Harlin Jacque.
Baron, Nancy
--Tuesday's Child. LC 84-2944. 120p. (gr. 4-6). 1984. (ISBN 0-689-31042-0). Atheneum.
Baron, Virginia Olsen (1931-), ed.
--Here I Am: An Anthology of Poems. McCully, Emily Arnold (1939-), illus. LC 73-81714. (Written by young people in some America's minority groups). (Illus.). 159 p. 22cm. 1969. (ISBN 0-525-31708-2). Dutton.
--The Seasons of Time: Tanka Poetry of Ancient Japan. Kobashi, Yasuhide, illus. LC 68-15225. (Illus.). 26ils. index. 64p. (gr. 7 up). 1968. (ISBN 0-8037-7785-X). Dial. **Award:** (ALA).
--Sunset in a Spider Web. Park, Chung S., tr. from Korean. LC 73-14657. (Illus.). (gr. 2 up). 1974. (ISBN 0-03-012071-3). HR&W.
Barons, Philip B., illus.
--Little Animal Stories. LC 42-19759. 60 p. incl. col. front., illus. (part col.) 17 1/2 x 13 1/2 cm. (On cover: The Little color classics ... 812). 1942. McLoughlin Bros., Inc.
Barow, John, pseud., see Carlin, Steve.
Barquist, Grace
--Farm Girl. Smalley, Janet (1893-), illus. LC 55-14812. (Illus.). 22cm. 47p. 1955. Abingdon Press.
Barr, Amelia Edith Huddleston, Mrs. (1831-1919)
--The Belle of Bowling Green. N.D. Dodd, Mead & Co.
--The Bow of Orange Ribbon. N.D. Dodd, Mead & Co.
--The House on Cherry Street. N.D. Dodd, Mead & Co.
--The Maid of Maiden Lane. N.D. Dodd, Mead & Co.
--A Maid of Old New York. N.D. Dodd, Mead & Co.
--Remember the Alamo. (Phenix Ser.). N.D. Dodd Mead & Co.
--Sheila Vedder. Fisher, Harrison, illus. N.D. Dodd, Mead & Co.
--A Song of a Single Note. N.D. Dodd, Mead & Co.
--The Strawberry Handkerchief. N.D. Dodd, Mead & Co.
--Trinity Bells. N.D. Dodd, Mead & Co.
--The Young People of Shakespeare's Dramas. Gilbert, John Clitherae, illus. LC 13-14792. 19cm. 257p. 1882. D. Appleton & Co.
Barr, Beryl
--Wonders, Warriors, & Beasts Abounding. Hoving, Thomas P., frwd by. LC 66-10499. (gr. 5-9). 1967. (ISBN 0-385-06067-X). Doubleday.
Barr, Carolyn
--Six Plays for Six Grades. LC 30-80904. 100 p. 20 cm. 1930. The Penn Publishing Company.
Barr, Catherine, jt. auth. see Preston, Hall.
Barr, Cathrine
--All About Bird. LC 74-5450. (Illus.). 32 p. 24cm. 1974. (ISBN 0-8098-1223-1). H. Z. Walck.
--Bears in Bears Out. (Illus.). 32 p. 24cm. 1967. H. Z. Walck.
--Bobo and Mozart. (Illus.). 32 p. 24cm. 1964. H. Z. Walck.
--Dan & Sandy. Barr, Cathrine, illus. (Illus.). (gr. k-3). 1959. (ISBN 0-8098-1059-X). Walck.
--Gingercat's Catch. LC 70-124111. (Illus.). 32 p. 24cm. 1970. H. Z. Walck.
--A Horse for Sherry. (Illus.). 32 p. 24cm. 1963. H. Z. Walck.
--Hound Dog's Bone. (Illus.). 32 p. 24cm. 1961. H. Z. Walck.
--Jeff and the Fourteen Eyes. (Illus.). 32 p. 24cm. 1958. H. Z. Walck.
--Jingle and Sox. LC 72-3203. (Illus.). 32 p. 23cm. 1972. (ISBN 0-8098-1196-0). H. Z. Walck.
--Little Ben. (Illus.). 32 p. 24cm. 1960. H. Z. Walck.
--Mister Black's Secret. Barr, Cathrine, illus. LC 65-14368. (Illus.). (gr. k-3). 1965. (ISBN 0-8098-1106-5). (ISBN 0-8098-1107-3). Walck.
--Mr. Black's Secret. N.D. (ISBN 0-8098-1106-5) David McKay Company.
--Mr. Black's Secret. 32p. 1965. Henry Z. Walck, Inc., Publishers.
--Ninety-Nine Ducks Plus One. LC 79-82671. (Illus.). 31 p. 24cm. 1969. H. Z. Walck.
--On with the Chase. LC 58-13201. (Illus.). 32 p. 24cm. 1958, c.1957. H. Z. Walck.
--On with the chase. LC 57-5975. 32p. illus. 24cm. N.D. Oxford University Press.
--Peppy of Portugal. 1971. David McKay Company.
--Peppy of Portugal. LC 72-158861. (Illus.). 32 p. 24cm. 1971. (ISBN 0-8098-1182-0). H. Z. Walck.
--Raffie. LC 68-23881. (Illus.). 32 p. 24cm. 1968. H. Z. Walck.
--The Runaway Chimps. 1954. (ISBN 0-8098-1038-7). David McKay company.
--The Runaway Chimps. (Illus.). 32 p. 29cm. 1964, c.1954. H. Z. Walck.

--The Runaway Chimps. LC 54-11997. unpaged (chiefly illus.) 26 cm. 1954. Oxford University Press.
--Sammy Seal of the Circus. LC 64-8137. (Illus.). 32 p. 27cm. 1955. H. Z. Walck.
--Sammy Seal of the Circus. LC 55-10427. unpaged. illus. 26 cm. (Oxford books for boys and girls). 1955. Oxford University Press.
--Seven Chicks Missing. (Illus.). 32 p. 24cm. c.1962. H. Z. Walck.
--Whoo Whoo.". LC 66-13950. 1 v. (unpaged) col. illus. 24 cm. 1966. H. Z. Walck.

Barr, Donald (1921-)
--Arithmetic for Billy Goats. 1st ed. Madden, Donald B. (1927-), illus. LC 66-216082. 108p. illus. 21cm. (Curriculum-related bks.). 1966. Harcourt.

Barr, Elizabeth K.
--Willy & Nilly & the Silly Silly Cat. 24p. (gr. k-3). 1976. (ISBN 0-685-62384-X). Valkyrie Hse.

Barr, Gene
--Conard the Clock. N.D. Wilcox & Follett Co.

Barr, George (1907-)
--Young Scientist and the Fire Department. Waltrip, Mildred, illus. LC 66-15830. 143p. illus. 21cm. c.1966. McGraw.
--Young Scientist Takes a Ride: Guide to Outdoor Observations from a Car Window. Hayes, William Dimitt (1913-), illus. LC 60-882355. 160p. illus. 21cm. 1960. Whittlesay House.

Barr, Gladys Hutchison (1904-1976)
--Cross, Sword, and Arrow. LC 55-5559. 233 p. 23 cm. 1955. Abingdon Press.

Barr, Henrietta C. & Drew, Mina P.
--The Nest. N.D. Marshall Jones Co.

Barr, Jene (1900-)
--Baker Bill. Maltman, Chauncey, illus. LC 53-13326. unpaged. illus. 21 cm. 1953. A. Whitman.
--Ben's Busy Service Station. Maltman, Chauncey, illus. LC 56-10685. unpaged. illus. 21cm. c.1956. A. Whitman.
--Conrad the Clock. Wittert, Elaine, illus. LC 44-9402. (Illus.). 26 1/2cm. 1944. Wilcox & Follett.
--Dan, the Weatherman. Hoff, P. J., illus. LC 58-9951. unpaged. illus. 21cm. 1958. A. Whitman.
--Fast Trains! Busy Trains!. Maltman, Chauncey, illus. LC 56-7752. (Illus.). unpaged. 22cm. 1956. A. Whitman.
--Fire Snorkel Number 7. Rogers, Joe, illus. LC 65-15101. 1v. (unpaged) illus. (pt. col.) 21cm. (Community helpers series). c.1965. A. Whitman.
--Fireman Fred. Maltman, Chauncey, illus. LC 52-2582. (Illus.). unpaged. 21cm. 1952. Whitman.
--Good Morning, Teacher. Hawkinson, Lucy Ozone (1924-1971) & Hawkinson, John Samuel (1912-), illus. LC 57-77548. unpaged. illus. 21cm. 1957. A. Whitman.
--Little Circus Dog: A Read-It-Yourself Story. Wiese, Kurt (1887-1974), illus. LC 49-11547. 32 p. illus. (part col.) 21 cm. 1949. A. Whitman.
--Little Prairie Dog: A Read-It-Yourself Story. Wiese, Kurt (1887-1974), illus. LC 49-11546. 32 p. illus. (part col.) 21 cm. 1949. A. Whitman.
--Mike the Milkman. Maltman, Chauncey, illus. LC 53-13327. unpaged. illus. 21 cm. 1953. A. Whitman.
--Miss Terry at the Library. (The Community Helpers Series). N.D. Albert Whitman &Company.
--Mister Zip & U. S. Mail. Fulkerson, Helen, illus. LC 64-16364. (Illus.). (Career Awareness-Community Helpers Ser.). (gr. k-2). 1964. (ISBN 0-8075-5180-5). A Whitman.
--Mr. Mailman. Maltman, Chauncey, illus. LC 54-3054. (Illus.). unpaged. 21cm. 1954. Whitman.
--Policeman Paul. Maltman, Chauncey, illus. LC 52-14395. (Illus.). 32 p. 21cm. 1952. A. Whitman.
--Surprise for Nancy. Benoit, Margie, illus. LC 51-287. (Illus.). 32 p. 21cm. (Read it yourself story). 1950. A. Whitman.
--Texas Pete. Maltman, Chauncey, illus. (Illus.). (gr. k-2). 1952. (ISBN 0-8075-7814-2). A Whitman.
--Texas Pete, Little Cowboy. Maltman, Chauncey, illus. LC 51-285. (Illus.). 32 p. 21cm. (Read it yourself story). 1950. A. Whitman.

Barr, Jene (1900-) & Chapin, Cynthia
--What Will the Weather Be?. Hoff, P. J., illus. (Illus.). 32 p. 21cm. (Community helpers series). 1965. A. Whitman.

Barr, Ken, illus.
--The Lone Ranger. Penick, Ib, contrib. by. LC 80-52868. (Illus.). 14 p. 24cm. c.1981. (ISBN 0-394-84691-5). Random House.

Barr, Lloyd Stanley
--Buddy. LC 51-12191. 104 p. 23 cm. 1951. Vantage Press.

Barr, Nina
--The Little Red Hen. N.D. Carlton Press Inc.

Barr, Robert
--Little Chuff-Chuff and Big Streamliner. Barr, Cathrine, illus. LC 51-18919. (Illus.). 32 p. 17cm. (Tell-a-Tale Bks.). 1950. Whitman.

Barr, Stephen (1904-)
--Puzzlequiz: Wit Twisters, Brain Teasers, Riddles, Puzzles & Tough Questions. LC 77-2647. (Illus.). (gr. 4 up). 1978. (ISBN 0-690-01355-8, TYC-J). (ISBN 0-690-01294-2). Har-Row.

Barr, Stringfellow (1897-1982)
--Copydog in India. Wiese, Kurt (1887-1974), illus. LC 55-14950. 127 p. illus. 25 cm. 1955. Viking Press.

Barrack, George M.
--Louis and the Fabulous Car. N.D. Vantage Press INc.

Barrault, Jean-Louis
--Barred Road. N.D. Macmillan.

Barret, Ethel Barrett
--Muffy & the Mystery of the Stolen Eggs. (Stories to Grow on Ser.). (gr. 2-6). 1980. (ISBN 0-8307-0689-5). Regal.

Barret, Leighton, adapted by see Cervantes Saavedra, Miguel de.

Barrett, A, notes by see Goldsmith, Oliver.

Barrett, Anna Pearl
--The Middlebatchers Throw a Party for the Marriage of Hetty Wish & Lester Leg. LC 84-10068. p. cm. (Middlebatcher series ; v. 1) 1984. (ISBN 0-89896-105-X). Larksdale.

Barrett, Anne Mainwaring (1911-)
--The Journey of Johnny Rew. 1st U.S. ed. Hughes, Shirley (1929-), illus. LC 55-7536. 250 p. 22 cm. 1st U.S. edition. 1955. Bobbs-Merrill.
--Midway. Gill, Margery Jean (1925-), illus. LC 68-14314. 254 p. 21 cm. 1968, c.1967. Coward-McCann.
--Songberd's Grove. Bodecker, Niels Mogens (1922-), illus. LC 57-12852. 247p. illus. 22cm. 1957. Bobbs-Merrill. **Award: (CMA).**
--Stolen Summer. Robison, John, illus. LC 52-141122. 236 p. 21 cm. 1953. Dodd, Mead.

Barrett, Charles Leslie (1879-) & Shead, Isobel Ann
--Kooborr the Koala. Kiddell-Monroe, Joan (1908-), illus. LC 43-7757. (Illus.). 26cm. 48p. 1942. Oxford University Press.

Barrett, Ethel
--Abraham. LC 82-12330. p. cm. (Great Heroes of the Bible Series). c.1982. (ISBN 0-8307-0769-7). Regal Books.
--Blister Lamb. (ps-1). 1978. (ISBN 0-8307-0420-5). Regal.
--Buzz Bee. (Stories to Grow on Ser.). (ps-1). 1978. (ISBN 0-8307-0419-1). Regal.
--Cracker, the Horse Who Lost His Temper: Communicating Christian Values to Children. (Stories to Grow on Ser.). (gr. 2-6). 1979. (ISBN 0-8307-0687-9). Regal.
--David the Gaintslayer. LC 82-80009. 128p. (Bible Biography Ser.). (gr. 3). 1982. (ISBN 0-8307-0770-0). Regal.
--Ethel Barrett Tells Favorite Bible Stories. LC 77-93051. 128p. (Bible Biography Ser.). 1978. (ISBN 0-8307-0615-1). Regal.
--God & a Boy Named Joe. LC 74-16957. (Illus.). 144p. (Orig.). (Venture Stories Ser.). (gr. 4-8). 1975. (ISBN 0-8307-0324-1). Regal.
--Gregory the Grub. (ps-1). 1978. (ISBN 0-8307-0421-3). Regal.
--Ice, Water & Snow. (Stories to Grow on Ser.). (gr. 2-6). 1980. (ISBN 0-8307-0690-9). Regal.
--If I Had a Wish. LC 74-83139. 144p. (Orig.). (gr. 4-8). 1975. (ISBN 0-8307-0314-4). Regal.
--Moses: Mission Impossible!. LC 82-16521. (Bible Biographies Ser.). 1982. (ISBN 0-8307-0772-7). Regal.
--Quacky & Wacky. (ps-1). 1978. (ISBN 0-8307-0418-3). Regal.
--The Strangest Thing Happened. LC 76-84599. (Illus.). 137 p. 20cm. (Regal venture book). 1970, c.1969. G/L Regal Books.
--Sylvester the Three-Spined Stickleback. 24p. (Stories to Grow on Ser.). (gr. 2-6). 1980. (ISBN 0-8307-0688-7). Regal.
--Which Way to Nineveh?. LC 79-96703. (Illus.). 135 p. 20cm. 1969. G/L Regal Books.

Barrett, Ethel Cook
--Betty Jane of the Cheer Shop. Greene, Julia, illus. LC 27-191800. 302 p. front., plates. 20 cm. c.1927. Lothrop, Lee & Shepard Co.
--Betty Jane of the "House of Smiles". N.D. Lothrop,Lee & Shepard.

Barrett, John
--The Bear Who Slept Through Christmas. LC 75-37678. (Illus.). 32p. (Bear Bks.). (gr. k-4). 1976. (ISBN 0-516-09480-7). Childrens.
--The Bears Find Thanksgiving. (Illus.). 32p. (Bear Bks). (gr. k-4). 1981. (ISBN 0-516-09192-1). Childrens.
--The Bears Find Thanksgiving. Reinert, Rick, illus. 32p. (gr. k-6). 1981. (ISBN 0-8249-8019-0). Ideals.
--Christmas Comes to Monster Mountain. (Illus.). 32p. (Bear Bks). (gr. k-4). 1981. (ISBN 0-516-09181-6). Childrens.
--Christmas Comes to Monster Mountain. 32p. (gr. k-6). 1981. (ISBN 0-8249-8024-7). Ideals.
--The Easter Bear. (Illus.). 32p. (gr. k-4). 1981. (ISBN 0-516-09190-5). Childrens.
--The Easter Bear. Reinert, Rick, illus. 32p. (gr. k-6). 1981. (ISBN 0-8249-8007-7). Ideals.
--The Great Bear Scare. (Illus.). 32p. (Bear Bks). (gr. k-4). 1981. (ISBN 0-516-09191-3). Childrens.
--The Great Bear Scare. Reinert, Rick, illus. 32p. (gr. k-6). 1981. (ISBN 0-8249-8018-2). Ideals.

Barrett, John, jt. auth. see Duncan, Glenn.

Barrett, John E. & View-Master International, photos by
--Big Bird's Mother Goose. LC 83-63404. (Illus.). 28p. (Chunky Bks). (ps). 1984. (ISBN 0-394-86745-9, Pub. by BYR). Random.

Barrett, John M
--Daniel Discovers Daniel. Servello, Joe (1932-), illus. LC 79-17897. p. cm. 1979. Human Sciences Press.
--The Day Toys Came to Silver Dollar City. Ruth, Rod (1912-), illus. LC 78-112285. (Illus.). 32 p. 22cm. 1978. (ISBN 0-686-22891-X). Silver Dollar City.
--The Littlest Mule. Baer, Jane & Baer, Dale, illus. (Illus.). (Silver Dollar City Stories). (ps-5). 1977. (ISBN 0-686-19125-0). Silver Dollar.
--No Time for Me: Learning to Live with Busy Parents. Servello, Joe (1932-), illus. LC 78-21257. 32p. 1979. (ISBN 0-87705-385-5). (ISBN 0-89885-183-1). Human Sci Pr.
--Zeke Hatfield and the Ghost Named Rocky. Ruth, Rod (1912-), illus. LC 78-112668. (Illus.). 32 p. 22cm. c.1978. Silver Dollar City.

Barrett, John M & Servello, Joe (1932-)
--Oscar the Selfish Octopus. LC 78-18760. (Illus.). 32 p. 24cm. c.1978. (ISBN 0-87705-335-9). Human Sciences Press.

Barrett, Judi see Barrett, Judith.

Barrett, Judith (1941-)
--Animals Should Definitely Not Act Like People. Barrett, Ron (1937-), illus. LC 80-13364. (Illus.). 31 p. 24cm. 1980. (ISBN 0-689-30768-3). Atheneum.
--Animals Should Definitely Not Wear Clothing. 1st ed. Barrett, Ron (1937-), illus. LC 70-115078. (Illus.). 32 p. 24cm. 1970. (ISBN 0-689-20568-6). Atheneum.
--An Apple a Day. Lewis, Tim, illus. LC 73-76315. (Illus.). 32 p. 14cm. 1973. (ISBN 0-689-30105-7). Atheneum.
--Benjamin's Three Hundred Sixty-Five Birthdays. Barrett, Ron (1937-), illus. LC 72-86926. (Illus.). 40p. (gr. k-2). 1974. (ISBN 0-689-30130-8). Atheneum.
--Benjamin's Three Hundred Sixty Five Birthdays. Barrett, Ron (1937-), illus. (Illus.). 1978. (ISBN 0-689-70443-7, Aladdin). Atheneum.
--Cloudy with a Chance of Meatballs. Barrett, Ron (1937-), illus. LC 78-2945. (Illus.). 32 p. 1978. (ISBN 0-689-30647-1). Atheneum. **Award: (NYT).**
--I Hate to Go to Bed. Cruz, Raymond (1933-), illus. LC 77-1583. (Illus.). 31 p. 15cm. c.1977. (ISBN 0-590-07472-5). Four Winds Press.
--I Hate to Go to Bed. Cruz, Raymond (1933-), illus. (gr. k-3). 1977. Scholastic.
--I Hate to Take a Bath. Slackman, Charles B. (1934-), illus. LC 74-19356. p. cm. 1975. Atheneum Publishers.
--I Hate to Take a Bath. Slackman, Charles B. (1934-), illus. LC 75-6955. (Illus.). 30 p. 1975. (ISBN 0-590-07429-6). Four Winds Press.
--I'm Too Small, You're Too Big. 1st ed. Rose, David S. (1947-), illus. LC 80-23883. (Illus.). 31 p. 23cm. (ps-1). 1981. (ISBN 0-689-30800-0). Atheneum.
--Old Mac Donald Had an Apartment House. Barrett, Ron (1937-), illus. LC 69-18970. (Illus.). 32 p. 26cm. 1969. (ISBN 0-689-20030-7). Atheneum.
--Old McDonald Had a Apartment House. Barrett, Ron (1937-), illus. (Illus.). (ps-3). N.D. (ISBN 0-689-70401-1, Aladdin). Atheneum.
--Peter's Pocket. Noonan, Julia (1946-), illus. LC 74-75555. (Illus.). 31 p. 1974. (ISBN 0-689-30403-X). Atheneum.
--A Snake Is Totally Tail. Johnson, Lonnie Sue, illus. LC 83-2657. (Illus.). 32p. (ps). 1983. (ISBN 0-689-30979-1). Atheneum.

Barrett, Judith (1941-) & Dawson, Diane
--The Wind Thief. LC 76-40407. (Illus.). 32 p. 29cm. 1977. (ISBN 0-689-30564-8). Atheneum.

Barrett, Katharine Ruth Ellis, Mrs. (1879-)
--Girls in the High Sierras: A Tale of the Sierra Nevada with Himalayan Echoes. Miles, Harold W., illus. LC 25-1963. xii p. 3 l., 335 p. front., illus., plates. 21 cm. 1924. Doubleday, Page & Company.
--Katy of the Eighties: Sing Song Rhymes. LC 36-17322. 83 p. front. (port.) 21 cm. c.1936. The Torch Press.
--Red Shoes: Thoughts by Carlisle Ellis. Ordell, Dorothy Fuller, illus. LC 31-523. viii p., 2 l., 3-77 p. 25 cm. 1930. The Woman Press.
--The Wide Awake Girls. Gallagher, Sears (1869-1955), illus. LC 8-32649. 5 p. l., 3-317 p. front., 5 pl. 20 cm. 1908. Little, Brown, and Company.
--The Wide Awake Girls at College. Gallagher, Sears (1869-1955), illus. LC 10-21590. 7 p. l., 3-294 p., 1 l., front. 4 pl. 20 cm. (Wide awake girl series). 1910. Little, Brown, and Company.
--The Wide Awake Girls in Winsted. Gallagher, Sears (1869-1935), illus. LC 9-25975. 7 p. l., 3-293 p. front., 4 pl. 20 cm. (Her The Wide awake girls series). 1909. Little, Brown, and Company.

Barrett, Lawrence Louis (1897-)
--Twinkle, the Baby Colt. Barrett, Lawrence Louis (1897-), illus. LC 45-4228. (Illus.). 17 x 22 1/2cm. 48p. (gr. k-3). 1945. (ISBN 0-394-91780-4). Knopf.

Barrett, Leila
--Pirate Prey. Barsis, Max (1894-1973), illus. LC 59-6022. 208p. illus. 21cm. 1959. Dodd, Mead.

Barrett, Leone
--Buffin. Gaug, Margaret A., illus. LC 35-16000051. (Illus.). 32 p. 24 1/2cm. 1935. A. Whitman & Co.

Barrett, Mary
--Our Summer at Hillside Farm. (Illus.). 256p. N.D. American Tract Society.
--Steps in the Upward Way. 279p. N.D. Hurd & Houghton for American Tract Society.
--Steps In the Upward Way. 279p. N.D. Lockwood, Brooks, & Co. for American Tract Society.
--Summer at Hillside Farm. 256p. N.D. Hurd & Houghton for American Tract Society.
--Summer at Hillside Farm. 256p. (The Prairie Library). N.D. Lockwood, Brooks, & Co. for American Tract Society.

Barrett, Michael
--Antarctic Secret. Tresilian, Cecil Stuart (1891-), illus. (Illus.). (gr. 6 up). 1966. Roy.

Barrett, Oliver
--Little Benny Wanted a Pony. Scarry, Richard McClure (1919-), illus. (Little Golden Book). 1950. Golden Press.
--Little Benny Wanted a Pony. Scarry, Richard McClure (1919-), illus. LC 50-11910. 42p. col. illus. 21cm. (Little Golden Library). 1950. Simon & Schuster.

Barrett, Peter & Barrett, Susan
--The Circle Sarah Drew. Barrett, Peter & Barrett, Susan, illus. Incl. The Line Sophie Drew. LC 76-174716. (ISBN 0-87592-029-2); The Square Ben Drew. (ISBN 0-87592-049-7). LC 72-89449. (Illus.). 32p. (ps-2). 1973. (ISBN 0-87592-012-8). Scroll Pr.

Barrett, Philip
--The Deaf Shoemaker, and Other Stories. N.D. Dodd, Mead & Co.

Barrett, Ron (1937-)
--The Daily Blab. LC 81-2618. p. cm. 1981. (ISBN 0-394-84811-X). Random House.
--Hi-Yo Fido!. Barrett, Ron (1937-), illus. LC 83-15110. (Illus.). 32p. (gr. 2-5). 1984. (ISBN 0-517-55215-9). Crown.

Barrett, Sarah Louise
--A Leaf of Gold. LC 52-3151. 238 p. 21 cm. 1952. Dodd, Mead.
--Silver Blades. LC 50-12351. 250 p. 21 cm. 1950. Dodd, Mead.

Barrett, Stephen Melvil (1865-)
--Bob, The Pioneer. LC 39-23869. ix p., 1 l., 186 p. incl. front. plates. 20 cm. 1938. Harlow Publishing Corporation.
--Joe, the Cherokee. LC 44-595426. 4 p. l., 13-124 p. front., illus. 20 1/2 cm. 1944. Burton Publishing Company.

Barrett, Susan, jt. auth. see Barrett, Peter.

Barrett, William Edmund (1900-)
--Lilies of the Field. Silverman, Burton Philip (1928-), illus. LC 62-8085. (Illus.). (gr. 7 up). 1962. (Image). Doubleday.

Barretto, Larry, pseud., see Barretto, Laurence Brevoort.

Barretto, Larry, pseud. (1890-1971)
--Three Roads from Paradise. Barretto, Laurence Brevoort. LC 83-221626. 5 p. l., 3-305 p. 20 cm. c.1933. Farrar & Rinehart, Incorporated.
--To Babylon. Barretto, Laurence Brevoort. LC 25-354421. 5 p. l., 3-822 p. 20 cm. 1925. Little, Brown, and Company.

Barretto, Laurence Brevoort see Barretto, Larry, pseud.

Barretto, Laurence Brevoort (1890-1971) & Cooper, Bryant
--Hawaiian Holiday. Barretto, Larry, pseud. Barretto, Ann, illus. LC 38-27247. 246p. 21cm. 1938. Dodd Mead & Co.

Barrie, Donald Conway (1905-)
--Phoebe and the MacFairlie Mystery. Fligg, Kathryn L., illus. LC 63-11667. 176 p. illus. 22 cm. 1963. Lothrop, Lee & Shepard.

Barrie, James Matthew, Sir, jt. auth. see Carey, Mary Virginia.

Barrie, James Matthew, Sir, jt. auth. see Disney, Walt, Productions.

Barrie, James Matthew, Sir, jt. auth. see Owen, Robert.

Barrie, James Matthew, Sir (1860-1937)
--Alice Sit-by-the-Fire. 1920. Charles Scribner's Son .

--Alice Sit-by-the-Fire. LC 19-13628. 19cm. 139p. (The Uniform Edition of the Plays of J. M. Barrie). 1919. Hodder & Stoughton.
--J. M. Barrie's Peter Pan & Wendy. Byron, May Clarissa Gillington, Mrs., ed. Attwell, Mabel Lucie (1879-1964), illus. LC 26-16118. viii, 9-134, 1 p. col. front., illus., col. plates. 22 cm. 1926. C. Scribner's Sons.
--J. M. Barrie's Peter Pan in Kensington Gardens. Byron, May Clarissa Gillington, Mrs., ed. Rackham, Arthur (1867-1939), illus. LC 30-621017. vi p., 1 l., 9-123 p. incl. illus., plates. col. front., col. plates. 21 cm. 1930. C. Scribner's Sons.
--A Kiss for Cinderella. 1921. Charles Scribner's Sons'.
--The Little Minister. (Burt's Home Library). N.D. A L Burt Co.
--The Little Minister. 232p. Repr. 1981. (ISBN 0-89966-329-X). Buccaneer Bks.
--The Little Minister. N.D. Charles Scribner's Sons.
--The Little Minister. (Green Room Edition). N.D. Dodge.
--The Little Minister. 1921. Funk & Wagnalls.
--Little Minister. N.D. Grosset & Dunlap.
--The Little Minister. (Illus.). N.D. H. M. Caldwell Co.
--The Little Minister, 2 Vols, Vols. I & II. (Illus.). (The Calumet Ser.: No. 26). N.D. H. M. Caldwell Co.
--The Little Minister, 2 vols, Vol. 1. (Illus.). (Empyreal Library of Handy Volume Classics). N.D. H. M. Caldwell Co.
--The Little Minister. 300p. Repr. 1980. (ISBN 0-89967-007-5). Harmony & Co.
--The Little Minister. (Classic Ser.). N.D. World Publishing Co.
--The Little Minister. Ritchie, G. W., designed by. (Illus.). N.D. H. M. Caldwell Co.
--Mary Rose. N.D. Charles Scribner's Sons.
--Peter and Wendy. Bedford, Francis Donkin (1864-1950), illus. LC 11-26958. vii p., 1 l., 267 p. front., plates 22 cm. 1911. C. Scribner's Sons.
--Peter and Wendy. Bedford, Francis Donkin, illus. N.D. Grosset & Dunlap.
--Peter and Wendy. Bedford, Francis Donkin (1864-1950), illus. 1911. Hodder and Stoughton.
--Peter Pan. Best, Roy, illus. N.D. Grosset & Dunlap.
--Peter Pan. Frank, Josette (1893-), ed. Chanslor, Marjorie Torrey Hood (1899-), illus. Torrey, Marjorie, pseud. LC 57-7525. 64 p. illus. (part col.) 31 cm. 1957. Random House.
--Peter Pan. Goode, Diane (1949-), illus. 1983. Random.
--Peter Pan. Hyman, Trina Schart (1939-), illus. LC 80-14510. p. cm. 1980. (ISBN 0-684-16611-9). Scribner.
--Peter Pan. Unwin, Nora Spicer (1907-), illus. LC 50-9328. (Illus.). 242 p. 21cm. 1950. Scribner.
--Peter Pan. Wilson, Phoebe, adapted by. Wood, Ruth, illus. LC 56-58682. 69p. illus. 29cm. 1956. Grosset & Dunlap.
--Peter Pan and Wendy. Attwell, Mabel Lucie (1879-1964), illus. LC 21-19156. viii, 185 p. col. front., illus., col plates. 20 cm. 1921. C. Scribner's Sons.
--Peter Pan and Wendy. Attwell, Mabel Lucie (1879-1964), illus. (The Scribner Illustrated Classics). N.D. Charles Scribner's Sons.
--Peter Pan and Wendy. Blampied, Edmund, illus. 1926. Charles Scribner.
--Peter Pan and Wendy. Byron, May Clarissa Gillington, Mrs., retold by. Attwell, Lucie Mabel (1879-1964), illus. N.D. Charles Scribner's Sons.
--Peter Pan and Wendy. Byron, May Clarissa Gillington, Mrs., retold by. Adams, Kathleen, illus. N.D. Charles Scribner's Sons.
--Peter Pan and Wendy for Boys and Girls. Rackham, Arthur (1867-1939), illus. Byron, May, retold by. N.D. Charles Scribner's Sons.
--Peter Pan and Wendy for Little People. Rackham, Arthur (1867-1939), illus. Bryon, May, retold by. N.D. Charles Scribner's Sons.
--Peter Pan: Disney Classic. Hazen, Barbara Shook (1930-), ed. 1976. (ISBN 0-515-04106-8). BJ Pub Group.
--Peter Pan in Kensington Gardens. 175p. Repr. 1981. (ISBN 0-89966-328-1). Buccaneer Bks.
--Peter Pan in Kensington Gardens. 150p. Repr. 1980. (ISBN 0-89967-006-7). Harmony & Co.
--Peter Pan in Kensington Gardens. 1906. Scribner.
--Peter Pan in Kensington gardens. Byron, May Clarissa Gillington, Mrs., ed. Rackham, Arthur (1867-1939), illus. 1930. Charles Scribner's Sons.
--Peter Pan in Kensington Gardens. Byron, May Clarissa Gillington, Mrs., ed. Rackham, Arthur (1867-1939), illus. (Illus.). (gr. k-2). 1957. (ISBN 0-684-20738-9). Scribner.
--Peter Pan: Or,The boy who would not grow up. 1928. Charles Scribner's Sons'.
--The Peter Pan Picture Book. Best, Roy, illus. 89 p. col. illus. 33 x 25 cm. c.1931. Whitman Publishing Company.
--The Peter Pan Picture Book. derrydale 1980 ed. O'Connor, Daniel Stephen (1880-), ed. Woodward, Alice Bolingbroke (1862-), illus. LC 79-24213. (Illus.). 96 p. 21cm. c.1980. (ISBN 0-517-30944-0). Derrydale Books.
--The Peter Pan Picture Book: The Story Simplified from Sir J. M. Barrie's Play. O'Connor, Daniel Stephen (1880-), ed. Woodward, Alice Bolingbroke (1862-), illus. LC 24-26824. 4 p. l., 96 p. incl. illus. (music) 12 pl. col. front., 8 col. pl. 17 cm. (On verso of half-title: The Little library). 1923. The Macmillan Company.
--Peter Pan: The Boy Who Would Never Grow up to Be a Man, Retold from Sir James M. Barrie's Famous Play. Perkins, Frederick Orville, ed. Woodward, Alice Bolingbroke (1862-), illus. LC 16-14841. xii p., 1 l., 73 (t. e. 70) p. col. front, illus. (music) plates. 20 x 17 cm. c.1916. Silver, Burdett & Company.
--Peter Pan: The Story of Peter & Wendy. (Illus.). ca. 250p. (Thrushwood Bks.). (gr. 5-11). 1970. (ISBN 0-448-02525-6). G&D.
--Peter Pan: The Story of the Play. Graham, Eleanor (1896-), ed. Ardizzone, Edward Jeffrey Irving (1900-1979), illus. LC 63-14737. 175 p. illus. (part col.) 24 cm. 1962. Scribner.
--The Story of Peter Pan. LC 30-10005. 95. 1 p. incl. col. front., col. ilus. 14 cm. (Altemus' wee books for wee folks). c.1930. Henry Altemus Company.
--The Story of Peter Pan. O'Connor, Daniel, retold by. N.D. Macmillan.
--Tommy and Grizel. 1900. Charles Scribner's Sons.
--The Wonderful Story of Peter Pan. Lowe, Edith May Kovar (1905-), retold by. Windsor, Mary, pseud. Pollard, Nancy D. (1925-), illus. LC 66-15391. 29 p. col. illus. 29 x 14 cm. (Read aloud book). 1966. Follett.

Barringer, Daniel Moreau (1900-)
--And the Waters Prevailed. Hutchison, P. A., illus. LC 56-8310. (Illus.). 188 p. 22cm. 1956. Dutton. **Award: (ALA).**

Barringer, Marie
--The Four and Lena. Petersham, Maud Sylvia Fuller, Mrs. (1890-1971) & Petersham, Miska (1889-1960), illus. LC 38-345397. 216 p. incl. col. front., illus. (part col.) 21 cm. 1938. Doubleday, Doran & Company, Inc.
--Martin the Goose Boy. Petersham, Maud Sylvia Fuller, Mrs. (1890-1971) & Petersham, Miska (1889-1960), illus. LC 32-21197. x p., 1 l., 188 p. incl. illus., plates. col. front., col. plates. 21 cm. N.D. Doubleday, Doran & Company, Inc.,.

Barrington, G. W. (1903-)
--Jan, the Dutch Barge Dog. 1st ed. Barrington, G. W. (1903-), illus. LC 53-6055. (Illus.). 148 p. 21cm. 1953. Longmans, Green.
--Wind Runner: The Story of an African Antelope. Barrington, G. W. (1903-), illus. LC 51-9728. (Illus.). 160 p. 22cm. 1951. Longmans, Green.

Barris, Anna Andrews, Mrs.
--The Mystery of the Jade Idol. LC 43-9097. 2 p. l., 208 p. front. 20 cm. 1943. Cupples & Leon Company.
--Red Tassels for Huki in Peru. Johnson, Iris Beatty, illus. LC 39-29731. 62 1 p. incl. front., illus. 24 cm. 1939. A. Whitman & Co.

Barritt, Leon, ed.
--All the World Over: By Rail, Sail, Saddle, Paddle, and on Foot. LC 22-17366. 206 p. front., illus., plates. 19 cm. c.1892. D. Lothrop and Company.

Barron, Elwyn A.
--Deeds of Heroism and Bravery. N.D. Harper & Brothers.

Barron, John N
--Howdy Doody's Clarabell Clown and the Merry-Go-Round. Authorized. Crawford, Mel (1925-), illus. LC 55-565163. (Featuring the famous Star of the Television Show, Howdy Doody.). unpaged. illus. 17cm. (Tell-a-tale books, 2558). c.1955. Whitman Pub. Co.

Barrow, Frances Elizabeth Mease see Aunt, Fanny, pseud.

Barrow, Frances Elizabeth Mease see Aunt Fanny, pseud.

Barrow, Frances Elizabeth Mease, pseud. (1822-1894)
--All Sorts of Pop-Guns. Barrow, Frances Elizabeth Mease. Aunt Fanny, pseud, 6 Vols, Vol. III. (Orig.). (Pop-Gun Ser). N.D. Vols. I-VI. Estes & Lauriat's.
--All Sorts of Pop-guns. Aunt Fanny, pseud, 1 of 6 Vols. (Pop-guns Stories: Vol. 111). N.D. G P Putman & Sons.
--All Sorts of Pop-Guns. Aunt Fanny, pseud, 1 of 6 Vols. (Illus.). (The Pop-Gun Stories). N.D. Set. Sheldon & Co.
--Aunt Fanny's New Stories: Containing: Mittens, Little Mittens, More Mittens, The Two Story Mittens New Little Mittens, The Orphan's Home Mittens. Aunt, Fanny, pseud, 6 Vols. (Illus.). N.D. Set. D. Appleton & Co.
--Baby Night Caps. Barrow, Frances Elizabeth Mease. Aunt Fanny, pseud, 6 Vols, Vol. III. New ed. (Illus.). (Nightcap Ser). N.D. Vols. I-VI. Estes & Lauriat's.
--Baby Night-caps. Aunt Fanny, pseud, 1 0f 6 Vols. (Night-cap Stories: Vol. III). N.D. G P Putman & Sons.
--Big Night Caps. Aunt Fanny, pseud, 1 of 6 Vols, Vol. V. New ed. (Illus.). (Nightcap Set.). N.D. Vols. I-VI. Estes & Lauriat's.
--Big Night-caps. Aunt Fanny, pseud, 1 of 6 Vols. (Night-caps Stories: Vol. V). N.D. G P Putman & Sons.
--Fairy Night Caps. Aunt Fanny, pseud, 1 of 6 Vols, Vol. VI. New ed. (Illus.). (Nightcap Ser). N.D. Estes & Lauriat's.
--Fairy Night-caps. Aunt Fanny, pseud, 1 of 6 Vols. (Night-caps Stories: Vol. VI). N.D. G P Putman & Sons.
--Funny Pop-Guns. Aunt Fanny, pseud, 6 Vols, Vol. IV. (Illus.). (Pop-Gun Ser). N.D. Vols. I-VI. Estes & Lauriat's.
--Funny Pop-Guns. Aunt Fanny, pseud, 1 of 6 Vols. (Illus.). (Pop-Gun Ser.). N.D. Set. G. P. Putnam's Sons.
--Funny Pop-guns. Aunt Fanny, pseud, 1 of 6 Vols. (Pop-guns Stories: Vol. IV). N.D. Set. G P Putman.
--Funny Pop-Guns. Aunt Fanny, pseud, 1 of 6 Vols. (Illus.). (The Pop-Gun Stories). N.D. Set. Sheldon & Co.
--Good Little Hearts. Aunt Fanny, pseud, 4 Vols. N.D. Hurd & Houghton.
--Grasshopper Pop-Guns. Aunt Fanny, pseud, 6 Vols, Vol. V. (Illus.). (Pop-Gun Ser). N.D. Vols I-VI. Estes & Lauriat's.
--Grasshopper Pop-guns. Aunt Fanny, pseud, 1 of 6 Vols. (Pop-guns Stories: Vol. V). N.D. G P Putman & Sons.
--Grasshopper Pop-Guns. Aunt Fanny, pseud, 1 of 6 Vols. (Illus.). (The Pop-Gun Stories). N.D. Set. Sheldon & Co.
--Little Night Caps. Aunt Fanny, pseud, 6 Vols, Vol. IV. New ed. (Illus.). (Nightcap Ser). N.D. Vols. I-VI. Estes & Lauriat's.
--Little Night-caps. Aunt Fanny, pseud, 1 of 6 Vols. (Night-cap Stories: Vol. 1V). N.D. G P Putman & Sons.
--Little Pet Books. Aunt Fanny, pseud, 3 vols. N.D. Hurd & Houghton.
--New Night Caps. Aunt Fanny, pseud, 6 Vols, Vol. II. New ed. (Illus.). (NightCap Ser). N.D. Vols. I-VI. Estes & Lauriat's.
--New Night-caps. Aunt Fanny, pseud, 1 of 6 Vols. (Night-cap Stories: Vol. 11). N.D. G P Putman & Sons.
--Night Caps. Aunt Fanny, pseud, 6 Vols, Vol. I. New ed. (Illus.). (Nightcap Ser). N.D. Vols. I-VI. Estes & Lauriat's.
--Night-caps. Aunt Fanny, pseud, 1 of 6 Vols. (Night-cap Stories: Vol. 1). N.D. G P Putman & Sons.
--Nightcap Stories. Aunt Fanny, pseud, 6 Vols. N.D. G P Putman's Sons.
--One Big Pop-Gun. Aunt Fanny, pseud, 1 of 6 Vols. (Illus.). (The Pop-Gun Stories). N.D. Set. Sheldon & Co.
--Our Big Pop-Guns. Aunt Fanny, pseud, 6 Vols, Vol. II. (Pop-Gun Ser). N.D. Vols. I-VI. Estes & Lauriat's.
--Our Big Pop-Guns. Aunt Fanny, pseud. (Illus.). (Pop-Gun Ser.). N.D. Set. G. P. Putnam's Sons.
--Our Pop-guns. Aunt Fanny, pseud, 1 of 6 Vols. (Pop-guns Stories: Vol.11). N.D. G P Putmans.
--Pop-Gun Stories. Aunt Fanny, pseud, 6 Vols. (Illus.). N.D. G. P. Putnam's Sons.
--Pop-Guns. Aunt Fanny, pseud, 6 Vols, Vol. 1. (Illus.). (Pop-Gun Ser). N.D. Vols. I-VI. Estes & Lauriat's.
--Pop-guns. Aunt Fanny, pseud, 1 of 6 Vols. (Illus.). (Pop-gun Stories: Vol. 1). N.D. G P Putman.
--Pop-Guns. Aunt Fanny, pseud, 1 of 6 Vols. (Illus.). (The Pop-Gun Stories). N.D. Set. Sheldon & Co.
--Pop-Guns. One Serious and One Funny. Being the First Book of the Series. Aunt Fanny, pseud. LC 28-4849. 157 p. front., illus., plates. 18 cm. (Pop-gun series. 1). 1864. Sheldon & Co.
--Post Office Pop-Guns. Aunt Fanny, pseud, 6 Vols, Vol. VI. (Illus.). (Pop-Gun Ser). N.D. Vols. I-VI. Estes & Lauriat's.
--Post-Office Pop-Guns. Aunt Fanny, pseud, 1 of 6 Vols. (Illus.). (Pop-Gun Ser.). N.D. Set. G. P. Porter & Sons.
--Post Office Pop-guns. Aunt Fanny, pseud, 1 of 6 Vols. (Pop-guns Stories: Vol. V1). N.D. G P Putman & Sons.
--Post Office Pop-Guns, 1 of 6 Vols. (Illus.). (The Pop-Gun Stories). N.D. Set. Sheldon & Co.

Barrows, Fannie
--Baby is King. N.D. D. Lothrop Co.

Barrows, John Stewart
--A Son of Old Ironsides: The Story of a boy on the United States Frigate Constitution during the War of 1812. Merrill, Frank Thayer (1848-), illus. LC 31-10083. 346p. front., pl. 22 1/2cm. c.1931. Lothrop Lee & Shephard.

Barrows, Marjorie see Barrows, Ruth Marjorie.

Barrows, Marjorie see Treasure Trails.

Barrows, Marjorie see Barrows, Ruth Marjorie.

Barrows, Ruth Majorie p, ed. see Child Life.

Barrows, Ruth Marjorie see Dixon, Ruth, pseud.

Barrows, Ruth Marjorie see Graham, Hugh, pseud.

Barrows, Ruth Marjorie (1892-1983), ed. see Aldis, Dorothy Keeley, Mrs. (1896-1966) & Belloc, Hilaire.

Barrows, Ruth Marjorie, ed. see Child Life.

Barrows, Ruth Marjorie (1892-1983), ed. see Treasure Trails.

Barrows, Ruth Marjorie (1892-1983)
--Bartholomew the Beaver. Pierce, Alice, illus. LC 56-8662. unpaged. illus. 33cm. (Rand McNally giant book). 1956, c.1952. Rand McNally.
--The Child Life Mystery-Adventure Book: A Collection of Favorite Stories for Boys and Girls. Cavanah, Frances, ed. LC 36-32110. 96 p. illus. (part col.) 22 cm. c.1936. Rand, McNally & Company.
--Ezra the Elephant. Smock, Nell Stolp, illus. LC 34-34017. 21 1/2 x 20cm. 41p. 1934. Grosset & Dunlap.
--Four Little Kittens: A Real Live Animal Book. Frees, Harry Whittier, photos by. LC 57-9056. (Illus.). unpaged. illus. 21cm. (Rand McNally elf book, 566). c.1957. Rand McNally.
--Four Little Puppies: A Real Live Animal Book. Dixon, Ruth, pseud. Frees, Harry Whittier, photos by. LC 57-9057. (Illus.). unpaged. illus. 21cm. (Rand McNally elf book, 578). c.1957. Rand McNally.
--Fraidy Cat. Maynard, Barbara, illus. LC 42-21064. 29 x 17cm. 28p. 1942. Rand McNally & Co.
--The Frances Tipton Hunter Picture Book. Hunter, Frances Tipton, illus. LC 35-21950. 2 p. l., 9-61 p. illus. (part col.) 33 cm. c.1935. Whitman Publishing Company.
--Hoppity. N.D. Rand McNally & Co.
--Johnny Giraffe. Smock, Nell Stolp, illus. LC 35-10037. 21 1/2 x 20cm. 40p. 1935. Grosset & Dunlap.
--JoJo. Biers, Clarence, illus. LC 44-9335. 19 1/2 x 17cm. 26p. 1944. Rand McNally & Co.
--Lancelot. N.D. Rand McNally & Co.
--Let's Fly to Bermuda. Maynard, Barbara, illus. LC 42-25182. 64 illus. (part col.) 19 x 24. N.D. Albert Whitman & Co.
--Little Duck. Myers, Marie Hondre, illus. LC 35-10038. 22cm. 48p. 1935. Grosset & Dunlap.
--Little Friends, Kittens, Puppies, Bunnies,. Dixon, Ruth, pseud. Gaddis, Rie, photos by. LC 52-18385. (Illus.). unpaged. illus. 21 cm. (Rand McNally book-elf book, 455). 1951. Rand McNally.
--The Magic Umbrella. McKee, John Dukes, illus. LC 39-1746. 28p. incl. front., illus. 14 x 20cm. c.1937. Follett Publishing Co.
--The Magic Umbrella Abroad. McKee, John Dukes, illus. LC 30-28266. 26p. illus. 18 1/2cm. 1930. Thomas S. Rockwell Co.
--Muggins Becomes a Hero. 1965. (ISBN 0-8382-0556-9, Hale Giant Books). E. M. Hale and Company.
--Muggins Becomes a Hero. Leaf, Anne Sellers, illus. LC 68-21697. (Illus.). 22 p. (incl. lining papers. 33cm. (Rand McNally giant book). 1968, c.1965. Rand McNally.
--Muggins' Big Balloon. (Illus.). (gr. k-2). 1964. (ISBN 0-8382-0557-7). Hale.
--Muggins' Big Balloon. Leaf, Anne Sellers, illus. LC 65-18939. 1v. (unpaged) col. illus. 33cm. (Rand McNally Giant bk.). 1967, c.1964. (ISBN 0-528-88898-6). Rand McNally.
--Muggins Mouse. 1964. (ISBN 0-8382-0558-5, Hale Giant Books). E. M. Hale and Company.
--Muggins Mouse. Leaf, Anne Sellers, illus. LC 65-15342. (Illus.). 1 v. (unpaged. 32cm. 1965, c.1964. Rand McNally.
--Muggins Mouse. Ward, Keith, illus. LC 32-296880. 1 p. l., 7-60 p. col. front., illus. (part col.) col. pl. 33 cm. c.1932. Reilly and Lee Co.
--Muggins Takes off. 1964. (ISBN 0-8382-0559-3, Hale Giant Books). E. M. Hale and Company.
--Muggins Takes off. Leaf, Anne Sellers, illus. LC 65-18938. 1 v. (unpaged) col. illus. 33 cm. (Rand McNally giant book). 1964. Rand McNally.
--Nursery Tales. LC 50-32759. 30p. col. illus. 20cm. (A Friendly book). 1950. John Martin's House.
--The Pirate of Pooh,and Other Plays for Children. LC 36-15412. 192 p. illus. 20 cm. c.1936. Rand, McNally & Company.
--Pudgy the Little Bear. Tamburine, Jean (1930-), illus. (Illus.). (gr. 1 up). 1972. (ISBN 0-528-88814-5). Rand.

AUTHOR INDEX BARTLETT, HELMRATH

--Pudgy, the Little Black Bear. LC 48-3912. 26 p. col. illus. 20 cm. ("Glowing-eye" book). c.1948. Rand McNally.
--The Rand McNally Book of Favorite Muggins Mouse Stories. Leaf, Anne Sellers, illus. LC 65-18932. 95p. col. illus. 32cm. 1965. Rand McNally.
--Scalawag,the Monkey. Dixon, Ruth, pseud. Gaddis, Rie, photos by. LC 53-31780. unpaged. illus. 21cm. (Rand McNally book-elf book. 477). c.1953. Rand McNally.
--Scamper. Biers, Clarence, illus. LC 49-8324. 26 p. col. illus., 20 cm. ("Glowing-eye" book). c.1949. Rand McNally.
--Scamper. Tamburine, Jean (1930-), illus. LC 70-118336. (Illus.). 22 p. 33cm. (Rand McNally giant book). c.1959. Rand McNally.
--Snuggles. N.D. G.P. Putnam's Sons.
--Snuggles. Frees, Harry Whittier, photos by. LC 33-33661. 21 x 19cm. 33p. 1933. Rand McNally & Co.
--Snuggles. Dixon, Ruth, pseud. Frees, Harry Whittier, photos by. LC 58-6560. unpaged. illus. 21cm. (Tip-top elf book, 1005). c.1958. Rand McNally.
--Sukey, You Shall Be My Wife, and Other Stories from Mother Goose. Elizabeth, Anne, pseud. (1901-), illus. Fleur, Anne Elizabeth. LC 45-132889. 32 p. col. illus. 28 1/2 cm. c.1944. Samuel Lowe Company.
--Three Little Bunnies. Dixon, Ruth, pseud. Brooks, Dale, photos by. LC 56-6746. unpaged. illus. 32cm. (Rand McNally giant book, 816). 1956, c.1950. Rand McNally.
--Three Little Bunnies. Dixon, Ruth, pseud. Rooks, Dale, photos by. LC 50-10071. (Illus.). 21cm. 36p. (A Rand McNally Book-Elf Bk.). 1950. Rand McNally.
--Timothy Tiger. Keith, Ward, illus. LC 43-15293. 19 1/2 x 17cm. 28p. 1943. Rand McNally & Co.
--Tut! tut! tales. Graham, Hugh, pseud. Biers, Clarence, illus. LC 50-11911. 41p. illus. 31cm. 1950. Garden City Pub. Co.
--Waggles. Biers, Clarence, illus. N.D. Rand McNally & Co.
--Whiskers. Frees, Harry Whittier, photos by. LC 37-5404. 20 1/2 x 19cm. 33p. 1937. Rand McNally & Co.
--Who's Who in the Zoo: Descriptive Stories of Animal Life. Winter, Milo Kendall (1888-1956), illus. LC 32-29687. 2 p. l., 9-60 p. incl. front., illus. (part col.) col. pl. 33 cm. N.D. The Reilly & Lee Co.
--Yip and Yap, a Real Live Animal Book. Dixon, Ruth, pseud. LC 58-8222. unpaged. illus. 21cm. (Tip-top elf book, 1022). c.1958. Rand McNally.

Barrows, Ruth Marjorie (1892-1983), ed.
--The Children's Treasury. Wuerfel, Lillian B., illus. LC 48-2021. v. illus. (part col.) 22 cm. N.D. Consolidated Book Publishers.
--One Hundred Best Poems for Boys and Girls. Good, Paula Rees, illus. LC 76-9891. (Illus.). 123 p. 20cm. 1976. (ISBN 0-8486-0000-2). Core Collection Books.
--One hundred best poems for boys and girls. Good, Paula Rees, illus. LC 30 31742. 1 p. l., 7-123p. illus. 19cm. c.1930. Whitman Publishing Co.
--The Organ Grinders' Garden: Poems Younger Children Love. Evers, Helen Dean Bryant & Evers, Alf (1905-), illus. LC 38-29524. 64 p. col. illus. 26 cm. c.1938. Rand, McNally & Company.
--The Picture Book of Poetry. LC 32-30924. 78 p. col. illus. 32 cm. c.1932. Rand, McNally & Company.
--Read-Aloud Poems Every Young Child Should Know. Cooper, Marjorie (1910-), illus. LC 57-10602. 72p. illus. 27cm. (gr. k-2). 1957. (ISBN 0-528-82345-0). Rand McNally.
--Two Hundered best poems for boys and girls. Scott, Janet Laura & Good, Paula Rees, illus. LC 39-25043. 253p. ill. 18 1/2cm. c.1938. Whitman Publishing Co.

Barrows, Ruth Marjorie (1892-1983) & Schirmer, Mathilda, eds.
--The Children's Hour. LC 74-76542. (Illus.). 16 v. 24cm. 1969. (ISBN 0-7172-1350-1). Grolier.
--The Children's Hours. LC 65-21839. 16 v. illus. (part col.) 24 cm. 1966. Grolier Incorporated.

Barrows, Sarah Tracy (1870-) & Hall, Katharine Hedges
--Jack-in-the-Box. Gregg, Harold, illus. LC 39-10641. 21p. illus. 18 x 17cm. 1942. Expression Co.

Barrows, William
--Twelve Nights in a Hunter's Camp, 1 of 50 vols. (Illus.). (The Norwood Ser.: No. 3). 1900. Lee & Shepard.
--Twelve Nights in the Hunter's Camp. (Illus.). (Frontier Camp Ser). N.D. Lee & Shepard.

Barry, Alfred Scott
--The Little Girl Who Couldn't Get Over it. N.D. E P Dutton.

Barry, Etheldred Breeze (1870-)
--Bilberry Boys and Girls: Their Adventures and Misadventures, Their Trials and Triumphs. Barry, Etheldred Breeze (1870-), illus. N.D. Lothrop Lee & Shepard Co.
--The Countess of the Tenements. (Illus.). (Editha Ser.). N.D. Caldwell.
--The Countess of the Tenements, 1 of 25 vols. (Illus.). N.D. Set. Dana Estes & Co.
--Little Dick's Christmas. (Young Hearts Ser.: No. 37). N.D. Dana Estes and Company.
--Little Dick's Christmas. (Illus.). (Every Boy's Library). N.D. Caldwell.
--Little Dick's Christmas. Barry, Etheldred Breeze (1870-), illus. LC 3-18937. 19cm. 66p. 1903. D. Estes & Co.
--Miss De Peyster's Boy. (Illus.). (The Sunshine Library for Young People). N.D. Thomas Y. Crowell.
--Miss De Peyster's Boy. Barry, Etheldred Breeze (1870-), illus. LC 2-20823. 20 cm. 82p. (The Golden Hour Ser.). 1904. Thomas Y. Crowell & Co.
--Little Tong's Mission. (Illus.). (Every Boy's Library). N.D. Caldwell.
--Little Tong's Mission, 1 of 25 vols. LC 99-5038. (The Young of Heart Ser.: No. 15). 1899. Set. Dana Estes & Co.
--What Paul Did. (Illus.). (Every Boy's Library). N.D. Caldwell.
--What Paul Did. Barry, Etheldred Breeze (1870-), illus. LC 4-17227. 19 cm. 79p. 1904. Dana Estes and Company.

Barry, Fanny
--Soap Bubbles Stories. Cox, Palmer (1840-1924), illus. N.D. James Pott & Co.'s.

Barry, Florence V.
--A Century of Children's Books. 1923. George H Doran.

Barry, John
--South Sea Shipmates. N.D. Macmillan.

Barry, Katharina
--A is for Anything: An ABC Book of Pictures and Rhymes. 1st. ed. LC 61-10107. 18cm. 56p. 1961. Harcourt, Brace & World.
--A Bug to Hug. 1st ed. LC 64-11488. (Illus.). 40 p. col. illus. 17 x 18 cm. 1964. Harcourt, Brace & World.

Barry, Lucy
--Stagestruck Secretary. LC 66-12085. 192 p. 21cm. 1966. W. Morrow.

Barry, Margaret N
--The Little Dame and the Wild Animals: A Story. LC 51-54220. 18 p. illus. 18 cm. 1880. Printed by H. Barry.

Barry, Margaret Stuart (1927-)
--Simon and the Witch. Birch, Linda, illus. LC 76-377642. (Illus.). 78 p. 24cm. 1976. (ISBN 0-00-184749-X). Collins.

Barry, Mary E. & Hanna, Paul R.
--Wonder Flights of Long Ago. N.D. Appleton Century Co.

Barry, Robert Everett (1931-)
--Animals Around the World. LC 67-16297. (Illus.). 32 p. 26cm. 1967. McGraw-Hill.
--Boo. LC 59-7479. (Illus.). 15 x 18cm. 40p. (gr. k-3). 1959. (ISBN 0-395-06610-7). HM.
--Faint George. N.D. E. M. Hale & Co.
--Faint George. Barry, Robert Everett (1931-), illus. LC 37-3884. (Illus.). 28cm. 32p. (gr. k-3). 1957. (ISBN 0-395-06612-3). HM. **Award: (NYT).**
--Just Pepper. LC 58-10170. (Illus.). 25cm. 37p. 1958. Houghton Mifflin.
--Mr. Willowby's Christmas Tree. Galdone, Paul (1914-), illus. LC 63-17084. (Illus.). 32p. illus. 26 cm. (gr. k-3). 1963. (ISBN 0-07-003877-5, GB). McGraw.
--The Musical Palm Tree: A Story of Puerto Rico. (Illus.). 32 p. 26cm. 1965. McGraw-Hill.
--Next Please. (Illus.). 40 p. 17cm. 1961. Houghton Mifflin.
--Ramon and the Pirate Gull: A Story of Puerto Rico. LC 77-144766. (Illus.). 40 p. 26cm. 1971. (ISBN 0-07-003833-3). McGraw-Hill.
--The Riddle of Castle Hill. LC 68-27504. (Illus.). 40 p. 26cm. 1968. McGraw-Hill.

Barry, Robert Everett (1931-) & Frascino, Edward
--Snowman's Secret. LC 75-15801. (Illus.). 32 p. 26cm. 1975. (ISBN 0-02-708390-X). Macmillan.

Barry F. Smith and Associates, ed. see Burow, Daniel R.

Barson, Robert Gale
--Bill's Mistake. 1921. Harr Wagner Publishing Co.

Barstad, Anvor, tr. see Scott, Gabriel.

Barstad, Glenna & Thomsen, Halvard J.
--Ahmed, Boy of Jerusalem. Padgett, Jim, illus. LC 64-23324. 167p. illus. 21cm. c.1965. Southern Pub.

Barstow, Charles H.
--Angels Unawares. (The Welcome Library). N.D. Frederick Warne & Co.
--Natty's Violin. (Illus.). (The Home and Enterprise Library Ser.). N.D. Frederick Warne & Co.
--Through Deep Waters. (Illus.). (The Home and Enterprise Library Ser.). N.D. Frederick Warne & Co.

Barstow, Montagu, illus.
--Old Hungarian Fairy Tales. Orczy, Emma Magdelena Rosalia Maria Josefa Barbara (1865-1947), tr. LC 69-17095. (Illus.). drawings. 95p (Pub. by Dean & Son Ltd, London). (gr. k-6). 1969. (ISBN 0-486-22293-4). Dover.

Bart, Lionel, jt. auth. see Hastings, Mary.

Barte, Eleanore
--John Hoe: Or, "A Penny Saved". Barte, Eleanore, illus. LC 38-32016. (Illus.). 21cm. 86p. N.D. Frederick A. Stokes Co.

Bartelme, Elizabeth
--Simon Brute and the Western Adventure. N.D. P. J. Kennedy & Sons.

Bartels, Lambert
--Arrows in the Jungle. Benson, Andrew, illus. Louws, Cornelius, tr. LC 55-7858. 184p. illus. [illegible] Bruce Pub. Co.

Barth, C. A.
--Defeat and Victory: A Story for Young People. LC 26-17612. 130 p. front., pl. 18 cm. c.1926. Augustann Book Concern.

Barth, Charles G.
--Poor Henry: Or, The Pilgrim's Hut on the Weissenstein. (A Story For the Young). N.D. American Sunday-School Union.
--The Raven's Feather. N.D. American Sunday-School Union.
--Setma, the Turkish Maiden: A Story for the Young. N.D. American Sunday-School Union.

Barth, Claire H., ed. see Wingeier, Carol.

Barth, Edna (1914-1980)
--A Christmas Feast: An Anthology of Poems, Sayings, Greetings, and Wishes. Arndt, Ursula, illus. LC 79-13282. p. cm. c.1979. (ISBN 0-8164-3235-X). Seabury Press.
--A Christmas Feast: Poems, Sayings, Greetings, & Wishes. Arndt, Ursula, illus. (Illus.). 176p. (gr. 3-6). 1979. (ISBN 0-395-28965-3, Clarion). HM.
--Cupid and Psyche. Forberg, Ati, pseud. (1925-), illus. Forberg, Beate Gropius. LC 76-8821. p. cm. c.1976. (ISBN 0-8164-3174-4). Seabury Press.
--Cupid & Psyche: A Love Story. Forberg, Ati, pseud. (1925-), illus. Forberg, Beate Gropius. LC 76-8821. (Illus.). 64p. (gr. 3-6). 1976. (ISBN 0-395-28840-1, Clarion). HM.
--The Day Luis Was Lost. 1st ed. Obligado, Lilian Isabel (1931-), illus. LC 76-117020. (Illus.). 58 p. 25cm. 1971. Little, Brown.
--Jack-O-Lantern. Galdone, Paul (1914-), illus. 1974. Houghton.
--Jack-O'-Lantern. Galdone, Paul (1914-), illus. LC 73-20194. (Illus.). 46 p. 26cm. 1974. (ISBN 0-8164-3120-5). Seabury Press.
--Lilies, Rabbits & Painted Eggs: The Story of the Easter Symbols. Arndt, Ursula, illus. (Illus.). 64p. (gr. 3-6). 1981. (ISBN 0-395-30550-0, Clarion). HM.
--Witches, Pumpkins, and Grinning Ghosts: The Story of Halloween Symbols. Arndt, Ursula, illus. LC 72-75705. (Illus.). 95 p. 27cm. 1972. (ISBN 0-8164-3087-X). Seabury Press.

Barth, Edna (1914-1980) & Cuffari, Richard (1925-1978)
--Balder and the Mistletoe: A Story for the Winter Holidays. LC 78-4523. p. cm. 1979, c.1978. (ISBN 0-8164-3215-5). Seabury Press.

Barth, G. G
--Bible Stories for the Young, 2 Vols in 1. (Illus.). 421p. N.D. United Presbyterian.

Barth, John
--The End of the Road. N.D. (ISBN 0-448-00240-X). Grosset & Dunlap.

Barthelme, Donald (1931-)
--The Slightly Irregular Fire Engine: Or the Hithering Thithering Djinn. Barthelme, Donald (1931-), illus. LC 70-162793. (Illus.). 32p. (ps-3). 1971. (ISBN 0-374-37038-9). FS&G. **Award: (NBA).**

Barthold, Helga, tr. see Freyhold, K. F. E. Von (1878-) & Morgenstern, Christian.

Bartholic, Edward L.
--Cricket & Sparrow. Rader, Laura, illus. LC 78-13141. (Illus.). 48p. (ps-3). 1979. (ISBN 0-529-05512-0, Philomel). (ISBN 0-529-05513-9). Putnam Pub Group.
--Cricket and Sparrow: Four Stories. Rader, Laura, illus. LC 78-13141. (Illus.). 58 p. 21cm. c.1979. (ISBN 0-529-05513-9). (ISBN 0-529-05512-0). Collins.

Bartholomen, Edith, tr. see Bartholomew, Edith.

Bartholomew
--Bad Mouth Christopher. Bartholomew, illus. LC 79-27658. (Illus.). 32 p. 26cm. c.1980. (ISBN 0-570-03482-5). Concordia Pub. House.
--Jimmy and the White Lie. Bartholomew, illus. LC 75-45231. (Illus.). 32 p. 27cm. c.1976. (ISBN 0-570-03460-4). Concordia Pub. House.

Bartholomew, Barbara (1941-)
--Flight into the Unknown. (Orig.). (Making Choices Ser.: No. 2). (gr. 3-8). 1982. (ISBN 0-89191-561-3). Cook.
--Flight into the Unknown: Starring You. LC 82-71335. p. cm. (A Making Choices Book). c.1982. (ISBN 0-89191-561-3). Chariot Books.
--The Great Gradepoint Mystery. Salzman, Yuri, illus. LC 83-61239. p. cm. (A Microkid Mystery). 1983. (ISBN 0-02-708510-4). Macmillan.

Bartholomew, Edith, ed.
--The Queen of the Dolls: As Told by the Dolls Themselves. Duruy, illus. Bartholomen, Edith, tr. LC 65-4806. 54 p. illus., col. plates. 29 cm. 1965. Calico Print Shop.

Bartholomew, Martin Luther
--The Parson of Roulin Ridge. LC 56-12339. 122p. 21cm. (A Nobel Book). 1956. Comet Press Books.

Bartholomew, Ralph L.
--Gopher Hole Treasure Hunt. Mlodock, Richard, illus. LC 77-80443. (Illus.). 120 p. 20cm. (Winner book). c.1977. (ISBN 0-88207-479-2). Victor Books.

Bartlett, Alice Wiles
--Montana Meadow Star. Padgett, Jim, illus. LC 65-10247. 198 p. illus. 21 cm. 1965. Southern Pub. Association.

Bartlett, Arthur Charles, jt. auth. see Waldo, Fullerton Leonard.

Bartlett, Arthur Charles (1901-)
--Four H Cowboy. LC 38-34553. 301 p. front. 21 cm. c.1938. W. A. Wilde Company.
--Game-Legs: The Biography of a Horse with a Heart. Cue, Harold, illus. LC 29-4467. 2 p. l., 3-292 p. col. front. 20 cm. 20cm. c.1928. W. A. Wilde Company.
--General Jim: The Story of a Horse. LC 32-421932. 292 p. front. 20 cm. c.1931. W. A. Wilde Company.
--Gumpy--Son of Spunk: The Story of a Little Sled Dog with a Big Heart. Cue, Harold, illus. LC 80-31174. 304 p. front. 20 cm. N.D. C.
--Hustler, the Farm Dog. LC 37 31571. 306 p. front. 21 cm. c.1937. W. A. Wilde Company.
--Pal, the Story of a Dog Who Lived up to His Name. Cue, Harold, illus. LC 33-491. 301 p. front. 20 cm. c.1932. W. A. Wilde Company.
--Pilgrim and Pluck: Dogs of the Mayflower. Cue, Harold, illus. LC 37-290. 303 p. front. 20 cm. c.1936. W. A. Wilde Company.
--The Runaway Dog Team. Cue, Harold, illus. LC 30-9226. 303 p. front. 20 cm. c.1929. W. A. Wilde Company.
--The Sea Dog. (Junior Books for Boys and Girls). N.D. Cupples & Leon.
--The Sea Dog. Cue, Harold, illus. LC 27-37396. 299 p. col. front. 20 cm. c.1927. W. A. Wilde Company.
--Sergeant Squiffy: Army Dog. LC 42-198. 2 p. l., 3-299 p. incl. front. 21 cm. c.1941. W. A. Wilde Company.
--Skipper: The Guide Dog. Cue, Harold, illus. LC 34-2351. 315 p. front. 20 cm. c.1933. W. A. Wilde Co.
--A Son of the Wild Pack. LC 35-1207. 312 p. front. 20 cm. c.1934. W. A. Wilde Company.
--Spunk Leader of the Dog Team: Being the Story of a Dog Who Won His Place at the Head of the Dog Team and a Hermit's Son Who Might Have Been What He Became, Had It Not Been for "Spunk". Martin, P. L., illus. LC 26-21297. 311 p. front. 19 cm. c.1926. W. A. Wilde Company.
--Yankee Doodle: The Story of a Pioneer Boy and His Dog. Cue, Harold, illus. LC 36-72. 318 p. front. 20 cm. c.1935. W. A. Wilde Company.

Bartlett, Carol, jt. auth. see Bartlett, David.

Bartlett, Charles Henry (1853-)
--Tales of Kankakee Land. Vawter, Will, illus. 1904. Charles Scribner's Sons.

Bartlett, David
--Life of Joan of Arc , Maid of Orleans. (Illus.). 1905. John C. Winston & Co.

Bartlett, David & Bartlett, Carol
--Adam's New Friend, and Other Stories from the Bible. Stapleton, Scott, illus. LC 80-279. (Illus.). 95 p. 24cm. c.1980. (ISBN 0-8170-0882-9). Judson Press.

Bartlett, Frances
--Christmas in Austria: Or, Fritzl's Friends. Hoxie, Bertha Davidson, illus. LC 10-25676. 30p. incl. col. front. col. ill. 19 1/2cm. c.1910. D. Estes & Co.

Bartlett, Frederick Orin (1876-)
--The Forest Castaways. Varian, George, illus. LC 11-24131. 6 p. l., 3-302 p. incl. plates. front. 20 cm. 1911. The Century Co.
--The Lady of the Lane. Caswell, Edward C., illus. LC 12-22559. 6 p. l., 3-336 p. incl. plates. front. 20 cm. 1912. The Century Co.
--The Web of the Golden Spider. Fisher, Harrison & Relyea, Charles M., illus. N.D. Small, Maynard & Co.

Bartlett, George B.
--Picnic Days, 1 of 6 vols. (Illus.). (Firelight Stories). 1882. D Lothrop.

Bartlett, Helmrath
--Bobby Bear Finds Maple Sugar. 32p. N.D. Oddo Publishing Inc.
--Bobby Bear's Rocket Ride. 32p. N.D. Oddo Publishing Inc.
--Bobby Bera's Halloween. 32p. N.D. Oddo Publishing Inc.

Bartlett, Janet La Spiza, jt. auth. see Helmrath, Marilyn Olear.

Bartlett, Janet La Spiza, jt. auth. see Hemrath, Marilyn Olear.

Bartlett, Margaret Farrington, jt. auth. see Bassett, Preston R.

Bartlett, Margaret Farrington (1896-)

--Joy Money. Oechsli, Kelly (1918-), illus. LC 65-23019. 96p. illus. 22cm. N.D. Duell.

--Rock All Around. Kaufmann, John (1931-), illus. LC 79-106934. (Illus.). 43 p. 22cm. 1970. Coward-McCann.

--Where the Brook Begins. Watson, Aldren Auld (1917-), illus. (Illus.). 38 p. (Let's read and find out). 1961. Crowell.

Bartlett, Mary C.

--Little Figures: And Other Stories. N.D. Lockwood, Brooks, and Co.

--Real Boys and Girls. N.D. Worthington Company.

Bartlett, Myrth

--By the Bridge of a Thousand Ages: The Adventure of Lingsan. Bartlett, Alice Marie & Roberts, Arthur D., illus. LC 40-32431. 3 p. l., 9-232 p. illus. 20 cm. c.1940. Willing Publishing Company.

Bartlett, N. Gray, Mrs., photos by.

--Mother Goose of '93. LC 15-246. 24 1/2cm. 10p. 1893. J. Knight company.

Bartlett, Philip A., pseud., see Stratemeyer Syndicate.

Bartlett, Philip A., pseud.

--The Cliff Island Mystery. Stratemeyer Syndicate. Foster, John M., illus. LC 30-219320. 248 p. front. 20 cm. (The Roy Stover Stories: Vol. 3). 1930. Barse & Co.

--The Cliff Island Mystery. Stratemeyer Syndicate. Foster, John M., illus. Repr. of 1930 ed (Pub. by Barse & Co.). (The Roy Stover Stories: Vol. 3). N.D. Grosset & Dunlap.

--The Lakeport Bank Mystery. Stratemeyer Syndicate. Foster, John M., illus. LC 29-21549. iv p., 1 l., 7-246 p. front., plates. 20 cm. (The Roy Stover Stories: Vol. 1). 1929. Barse & Co.

--The Mystery of the Snowbound Express. Stratemeyer Syndicate. Foster, John M., illus. LC 29-21548. 243 p. front., plates. 20 cm. (The Roy Stover Stories: Vol. 2). 1929. Barse & Co.

--The Mystery of the Snowbound Express. Stratemeyer Syndicate. Foster, John M., illus. Repr. of 1929 ed (Pub. by Barse & Co.). (The Roy Stover Stories: Vol. 2). N.D. Grosset & Dunlap.

--The Mystety of the Circle of Fire. Stratemeyer Syndicate. Foster, John M., illus. (The Roy Stover Stories: Vol. 4). 1934. Grosset & Dunlap.

Bartlett, Robert Merrill (1898-)

--Thanksgiving Day. Mars, Witold Tadeusz J. (1912-), illus. LC 65-16178. lv. (unpaged) col. illus. 22cm. (Holiday bk.). c.1965. Crowell.

Bartlett, Ruth

--The Miracle of the Talking Jungle. Lent, Blair (1930-), illus. (Illus.). xiii, 96 p. 24cm. 1965. Van Nostrand.

Bartlett, Stephen see Slade, Gurney, pseud.

Bartlett, Stephen (0000-1956)

--Captain Quid. Slade, Gurney, pseud. Mills, Reginald, illus. LC 41-38941. 256 p. col. front. 20 cm. 1937. F. Warne & Co., Ltd.

--In Lawrence's Bodyguard. Slade, Gurney, pseud. Siegel, William (1905-), illus. LC 30-24344. ix p., 2 l., 267 p. incl. front., illus. 20 cm. 1930. Frederick A. Stokes Company.

--Lawrence in the Blue. Slade, Gurney, pseud. LC 36-177122. 288 p. col. front., illus. (map) plates. 20 cm. 1936. F. Warne and Co., Ltd.

--Lawrence in the Blue. Slade, Gurney, pseud. LC 36-19447. vii, 1, 269 p. front., illus. (map) plates. 20 cm. 1936. Frederick A. Stokes Company.

Bartman, J. Werner Illus. by see Homan, Beulah.

Bartman, Mark

--Yank in Africa. Thorne, Diana (1895-), illus. LC 44-5455. (Illus.). 21 x 19cm. 30p. 1944. A. Whitman & Company.

--Yank in France. Thorne, Diana (1894-), illus. LC 46-3776. 24 x 18 1/2cm. 30p. 1946. Albert Whitman & Co.

--Yank in Sicily. Thorne, Diana (1894-), illus. LC 45-1419. 24 x 19cm. 32p. 1944. Albert Whitman & Co.

Barto, A.

--Mashenka. 14p. 1976. (ISBN 0-8285-1204-3, Pub. by Progress Pubs USSR). Imported Pubns.

Barto, E.

--Chubby Bear. N.D. Longmans Green & Co.

Barto, Emily Newton (1886-), ed. see Mother Goose.

Barto, Renzo, illus.

--Annie & Her Dog Friends. LC 82-80386. (Illus.). 24p. (Shape Bks.). (ps-1). 1982. (ISBN 0-394-85439-X). Random.

Bartoli, Jennifer

--In a Meadow, Two Hares Hide. Ishida, Takeo (1922-), illus. LC 78-15221. p. cm. (International Picture Books). 1978. (ISBN 0-8075-3628-8). A. Whitman.

--The Story of the Grateful Crane: A Japanese Folktale. Shimizu, Kozo (1925-), illus. LC 77-3969. (Illus.). 24 p. 29cm. 1977. (ISBN 0-8075-7630-1). A. Whitman.

Bartoli, Jennifer & Drescher, Joan Elizabeth (1939-)

--Nonna. Drescher, Joan Elizabeth (1939-), illus. LC 74-25423. (Illus.). 48 p. 24cm. c.1975. (ISBN 0-8178-5212-3). Harvey House.

Bartoli, Jennifer & Herring, Ann King

--Snow on Bear's Nose: A Story of a Japanese Moon Bear Cub. Ishida, Takeo (1922-), illus. LC 76-40261. 24 p. 30 cm. 1976. (ISBN 0-8075-7520-8). A. Whitman.

Barton, A., Mrs.

--Stories from Waverley for Children. (Macmillian School Library). N.D. MacMillian & Co.

Barton, Amsel

--Chummy Chipmunk's First Family. Stubenhaus, Joanne, illus. (gr. k-5). 1976. (ISBN 0-682-48451-2). Exposition.

Barton, Betty F.

--Jeannie. Templin, Laura Schiel, illus. LC 66-554. 1 v. (unpaged) illus. 18 cm. 1965. Banner Press.

Barton, Blake

--Merchant Adventurers: The Story of Sea Commerce. Mayer, Fred A., illus. LC 36-3998. vi, 7-68 p. incl. front., illus. 20 cm. (Our changing world). 1936. T. Nelson and Sons.

Barton, Bob

--Old Covered Wagon Show Days. Thomas, George Ernest, as told to. Simon, Howard (1903-1979), illus. LC 39-225877. 238 p. incl. front., illus. 21 cm. c.1939. E. P. Dutton & Co., Inc.

--Trixie: Stories of the Circus. Thomas, George Ernest, as told to. Hodges, Cyril Walter (1909-), illus. LC 37-28570. 183 p. incl. front., illus. 22 cm. 1937. E. P. Dutton & Co., Inc.

Barton, Byron (1930-)

--Applebet Story. LC 72-91395. (Illus.). 32 p. 1973. (ISBN 0-670-12964-X). Viking Press.

--Applebet Story. (Illus.). 32. (Viking Seafarer B00k). 1975, c.1973. (ISBN 0-670-05099-7). Viking Press.

--Buzz, Buzz, Buzz. LC 73-1965. (Illus.). 31 p. 1973. (ISBN 0-02-708450-7). Macmillan.

--Buzz, Buzz, Buzz. LC 78-18391. (Illus.). 32 p. (Picture puffin). 1979, c.1973. (ISBN 0-14-050307-2). Puffin Books.

--Elephant. LC 74-154301. 32 p. of col. illus. 15cm. 1971. Seabury Press.

--Harry Is a Scaredy-Cat. LC 73-6039. (Illus.). 32 p. 21cm. 1974. (ISBN 0-02-708440-X). Macmillan.

--Hester. LC 75-9668. (Illus.). 32 p. 1975. (ISBN 0-688-80009-2). (ISBN 0-688-84009-4). Greenwillow Books.

--Hester. LC 78-3658. (Illus.). 32 p. (Picture puffin). 1978, c.1975. (ISBN 0-14-050281-5). Puffin Books.

--Jack and Fred. LC 74-6205. (Illus.). 32 p. 1974. Macmillan.

--Where's Al?. Barton, Byron (1930-), illus. LC 78-171866. (Illus.). 32 p. 1972. (ISBN 0-8164-3088-8). Seabury Press. **Award: (NYT).**

Barton, Byron (1930-) & Pomerantz, Charlotte (1930-)

--Where's the Bear?. Barton, Byron (1930-), illus. LC 84-17928. (Illus.). 32. c.1984. (ISBN 0-14-050514-8). Puffin Books.

Barton, Dunbar Plunkett & Benham, Charles

--The Story of the Inns of Court. N.D. Houghton Mifflin.

Barton, George (1866-)

--Barry Wynn: Or,the Advertures of a Page Boy in the U.S. Congress. Huybers, John, illus. N.D. Small, Maynard & c.

--The Bell Haven Eight. Gray, Charles Paxson, illus. LC 14-17165. 318 p. front., plates. 20 cm. (His The Bell Haven series). c.1914. The John C. Winston Company.

--The Bell Haven Eleven. Gray, Charles Paxson, illus. LC 15-18101. 296 p. front., plates. 19 cm. (His The Bell Haven series). c.1915. The John C. Winston Company.

--The Bell Haven Five. Gray, Charles Paxson, illus. LC 15-181020. 315 p. front., plates. 19 cm. (His The Bell Haven series). c.1915. The John C. Winston Company.

--The Bell Haven Nine. Gray, Charles Paxson, illus. LC 14-15175. 328 p. front., plates. 20 cm. (Half-title: The Bell Haven series). c.1914. The John C. Winston Company.

--In Quest of the Golden Chest: A Story of Adventure. N.D. Benziger Brothers.

--The Mystery of Cleverly: A Story for Boys. LC 7-19594. 232 p. 20 cm. 1907. Benziger Brothers.

Barton, May Hollis, pseud., see Stratemeyer Syndicate.

Barton, May Hollis, pseud.

--Charlotte Cross and Aunt Deb: Or, The Queerest Trip on Record. Stratemeyer Syndicate. Tandy, Russell H., illus. LC 31-14187. (Written for the Stratemeyer Syndicate by Harriet Stratemeyer Adams, 1894-1982, under the pseudonym, May Hollis Barton). 2 p. l., 205 p. front. 20 cm. (Barton Books for Girls: Vol. 14). 1931. Cupples & Leon Co.

--Favorite Stories for Girls. Stratemeyer Syndicate. (Includes: Kate Martin's Problem; Charlotte Cross and Aunt Deb; The Girl from the Country; Hazel Hood's Strange Discovery). (Barton Books for Girls). 1937. Cupples & Leon Co.

--Four Little Women of Roxby: Or, The Queer Old Lady Who Lost Her Way. Stratemeyer Syndicate. (Illus.). (Barton Books for Girls: Vol. 4). 1926. Cupples & Leon Co.

--The Girl From the Country: Or, Laura Mayford's City Experiences. Stratemeyer Syndicate. (Illus.). (Barton Books for Girls: Vol. 1). 1926. Cupples & Leon Co.

--The Girl in the Top Flat: Or, The Daughter of an Artist. Stratemeyer Syndicate. Hait, illus. 2 p. l., 204 p. front. 20 cm. (Barton Books for Girls: Vol. 11). 1930. Cupples & Leon Co.

--The Girls of Lighthouse Island: Or, The Strange Sea Chest. Stratemeyer Syndicate. LC 29-112874. (Illus.). 2 p. l., 204 p. front. 20 cm. (Barton Books for Girls: Vol. 9). 1929. Cupples & Leon Co.

--Hazel Hood's Strange Discovery: Or, The Old Scientist's Treasure Box. Stratemeyer Syndicate. LC 28-16618. (Illus.). 2 p. l., 208 p. front. 20 cm. (Barton Books for Girls: Vol. 7). 1928. Cupples & Leon Co.

--Kate Martin's Problem: Or, Facing the Wide World. Stratemeyer Syndicate. Tandy, Russell H., illus. LC 29-11286. 2 p. l., 264 p. front. 20 cm. (Barton Books for Girls: Vol. 10). 1929. Cupples & Leon Co.

--Little Miss Sunshine: Or, The Old Bachelor's Ward. Stratemeyer Syndicate. LC 28-16179. (Illus.). 2 p. l., 206 p. front. 20 cm. (Barton Books for Girls: Vol. 6). 1928. Cupples & Leon Co.

--Nell Grayson's Ranching Days: Or, A City Girl in the Great West. Stratemeyer Syndicate. Rogers, Walter S., illus. (Barton Books for Girls: Vol. 3). 1926. Cupples & Leon Co.

--Plain Jane and Pretty Betty: Or, The Girl Who Won Out. Stratemeyer Syndicate. (Illus.). (Barton Books for Girls: Vol. 5). 1926. Cupples & Leon Co.

--Sallie's Test of Skill: Or, Winning the Trophy. Stratemeyer Syndicate. Tandy, Russell H., illus. LC 31-141888. (Written for the Stratemeyer Syndicate by Harriet Stratemeyer Adams, 1894-1982, under the pseudonym, May Hollis Barton). 2 p. l., 212 p. front. 20 cm. (Barton Books for Girls: Vol. 13). 1931. Cupples & Leon Co.

--The Search for Peggy Ann: Or, A Mystery of the Flood. Stratemeyer Syndicate. Tandy, Russell H., illus. LC 30-168951. 2 p. l., 206 p. 20 cm. (Barton Books for Girls: Vol. 12). 1930. Cupples & Leon Co.

--Three Girl Chums at Laurel Hall: Or, The Mystery of the School by the Lake. Stratemeyer Syndicate. (Illus.). (Barton Books for Girls: Vol. 2). 1926. Cupples & Leon Co.

--Two Girls and a Mystery: Or, The Old House in the Glen. Stratemeyer Syndicate. Townsend, Ernest N., illus. LC 28-161785. 2 p. l., 204 p. front. 20 cm. (Barton Books for Girls: Vol. 8). 1928. Cupples & Leon Co.

--Virginia's Venture: Or, Strange Business at the Tea House. Stratemeyer Syndicate. LC 32-13682. (Written for the Stratemeyer Syndicate by Harriet Stratemeyer Adams, 1894-1982, under the pseudonym, May Hollis Barton). 2 p. l., 208 p. front. 20 cm. (Barton Books for Girls: Vol. 15). 1932. Cupples & Leon Co.

Barton, Olive Roberts

--Cloud Boat Stories. Winter, Milo Kendall (1888-1956), illus. LC 17-24982. viii, 138 p., 1 l. col. front., illus., col. plates. 23 cm. 1917. Houghton Mifflin Company.

--Nancy and Nick in Helter-Skelter-Land. N.D. George H Doran.

--Nancy and Nick in Helter-Skelter-Land. Higgins, Edward Roberts, illus. (The Nancy and Nick Books). N.D. A. L. Burt Co.

--Nancy and Nick in Scrub-Up-Land. N.D. George H Doran.

--Nancy and Nick in Scrub-up-Land. Higgins, Edward Roberts, illus. (The Nancy and Nick Books). N.D. A. L. Burt Co.

--Nancy and Nick in the Land-of-Dear-Knows-Where. N.D. George H Doran.

--Nancy and Nick in the-Land-of-Dear-Knows-Where. Higgins, Edward Roberts, illus. (The Nancy and Nick Books). N.D. A. L. Hunt Co.

--Nancy and Nick in the Land-of-Near-By. N.D. George H Doran.

--Nancy and Nick in the Land of-Near-by. Higgins, Edward Roberts, illus. (The Nancy and Nick Books). N.D. A. L. Burt Co.

--Nancy and Nick in Topsy-Turvy-Land. Higgins, Edward Roberts, illus. (The Nancy and Nick Books). N.D. A. L. Burt Co.

--Nancy and Nick in Topsy-Turvy-Land. N.D. George H Doran.

--The Wonderful Land of Up. McCoy, Neely, illus. LC 18-20044. viii p., 1 l., 11-146 p. incl. col. front. illus. col. plates. 22 cm. c.1918. George H. Doran Company.

Barton, Thomas Frank (1905-)

--John Smith: Jamestown Boy. Morrow, Gray, illus. LC 66-24115. (Illus.). 200 p. 20cm. (Childhood of famous Americans). 1966. Bobbs-Merrill.

--Patrick Henry, Boy Spokesman. Bolden, Melvin Reed (1919-), illus. (Illus.). 192 p. 20cm. (Childhood of famous Americans). 1960. Bobbs-Merrill.

Barton, William Eleazer (1861-1930)

--The Pairie Schooner. N.D. W. A. Wilde Co.

--The Story of a Pumpkin Pie: Told in Verses. Willard, Archibald M. (1836-1918), illus. LC 41-35164. 50 p. front., illus. 26 cm. 1898. The Pilgrim Press.

--When Boston Braved The King. N.D. W. A. Wilde Co.

Bartos-Hoppner, Barbara (1923-)

--Avalanche Dog. 1st ed. Bell, Anthea, tr. LC 67-2907. 159 p. 21cm. 1967, c.1966. H. Z. Walck.

--The Conquering Ships. Bell, Anthea, tr. (Illus.). 216p. 1981. (ISBN 0-905478-23-1, Pub. by Andersen-Hutchinson England). State Mutual Bk.

--The Cossacks. Ambrus, Victor G., pseud. (1935-), illus. Ambrus, Gyozo Laszlo. Humphries, Stella, tr. (Illus.). 295 p. 23cm. 1st U.S. edition. 1963, c.1962. H. Z. Walck. **Award: (ALA).**

--Hunters of Siberia. Bell, Anthea, tr. LC 72-82672. viii, 242 p. 22cm. 1969. H. Z. Walck.

--Save the Khan. Ambrus, Victor G., pseud. (1935-), illus. Ambrus, Gyozo Laszlo. Humphries, Stella, tr. LC 64-150804. 240p. illus., map. 23cm. 1964, c.1961. Walck.

--Storm Over the Caucasus. Bell, Anthea, tr. LC 68-11226. (gr. 8 up). 1968. (ISBN 0-8098-3070-1). Walck.

Bartosh, Julia Ann

--Kenny Visits the Hospital. 1st. ed. Sweeney, J. Shirley, frwd. by. LC 56-955770. (A Story in PIctures). 62p. (chiefly illus.) 21cm. (Banner book). 1956. (ISBN 0-682-40008-4). Exposition Press.

Bartosiak, Janet

--A Dog for Ramon. Frankenberg, Robert Clinton (1911-), illus. LC 67-583. (Illus.). 44 p. 24cm. 1966. Dial Press.

Bartow, Annie Key

--The Holly and the Rose. N.D. Thomas Whittaker.

--The Sign of the North Star. N.D. Thomas Whittaker.

Bartrug, Carey Milton (1892-)

--Blacky. Bracker, Charles Eugene (1895-), illus. LC 39-13757. 61 p. incl. col. front., illus. (part col.) 18 cm. (On cover: The little color classics). c.1939. McLoughlin Brothers, Inc.

--Blacky. Bracker, Charles Eugene (1895-), illus. LC 41-721. 61 p. incl. col. front., col. illus. 17 cm. (On cover: The little color classics). c.1940. McLoughlin Brothers, Inc.

--Mother Goose Etiquette Rhymes. Peters, Marjorie, illus. LC 41-22366. 32p. illus. 17 1/2 x 21cm. 1941. Whitman & Co.

--Mother Goose Health Rhymes. Peters, Marjorie, illus. LC 42-15598. 32p. illus. 17 1/2 x 21cm. 1942. Whitman & Co.

--Mother Goose Safety Rhymes. Peters, Marjorie, illus. LC 40-9522. 32p. illus. 17 x 20 1/2cm. 1940. A. Whitman & Co.

Bartusis, Constance

--Shades of Difference. LC 68-25182. 180 p. 22cm. 1968. St. Martin's Press.

Baruch, Dorothy Walter, jt. auth. see Disney, Walt, Productions.

Baruch, Dorothy Walter, Mrs. (1899-1962), ed. see Lorenzini, Carlo.

Baruch, Dorothy Walter, Mrs., jt. ed. see Morse, Mary Lincoln.

Baruch, Dorothy Walter, Mrs. (1899-1962)

--Baby Goes Riding. (gr. 1-3). N.D. Lothrop Bks.

--Big Fellow at Work. Hader, Berta Hoerner (1890-1976) & Hader, Elmer Stanley (1889-1973), illus. LC 30-23551. 7 p. l., 106 p. incl. illus., plates. front. 20 cm. (Nursery Ser.). 1930. Harper & Brothers.

--Big Fellow, the Story of a Road-Making Machine. Van Everen, Jay, illus. LC 29-18028. 7 p. l., 131, 1 p. incl. illus., plates. col. front. 20 cm. 1929. Harper & Brothers.

--Blimps and Such. (Nursery Ser.). 1932. Harper & Bros.

--Who Built the Dam: A Picture Story. Bate, Norman Arthur (1916-), illus. (Illus.). (gr. k-5). 1958. (ISBN 0-684-81975-9). Scribner.
--Who Built the Highway?. A Picture Story. (Illus.). 56 p. 28cm. 1953. Scribner.
--Who Fishes for Oil?. A Picture Story. (Illus.). 46 p. 28cm. 1955. Scribner.

Bate, W. J., ed. see Johnson, Samuel.

Bateman, Anya

--Big Ben Is Back. LC 83-72684. c.1983. (ISBN 0-88494-504-9). Bookcraft.

Bateman, Doris I.

--The Secret of Allenby Acres. LC 46-18716. 224 p. 21 cm. 1946. The Westminster Press.

Bateman, Robert Moyes Carruthers (1922-1973)

--Archie Abroad. (gr. 6 up). 1963. (ISBN 0-685-20933-4). Verry.
--Archie & the Missing Stamps. (gr. 6 up). 1965. Verry.
--Archie, Young Detective. (gr. 6 up). 1963. (ISBN 0-685-20934-2). Verry.
--Archie's Italian Adventure. (Illus.). (gr. 6 up). 1966. (ISBN 0-685-20935-0). Verry.
--Mystery for Archie. (gr. 6 up). 1963. Verry.
--Race Against the U-Boats. (gr. 7-11). 1966. Verry.
--Rough Passage. Kesteven, Peter, illus. (Illus.). 114 p. 21cm. 1966, c.1965. Duell, Sloan and Pearce.

Baten, Helen, jt. auth. see Martin, William Ivan, Jr.

Bates, Arlo, jt. auth. see Putnam, Eleanor.

Bates, Barbara Snedeker (1919-)

--The Happy Birthday Present. Scott, Marguerite K., illus. LC 51-35509. unpaged. illus. 21 cm. (Wonder books, 564). 1951. Wonder Books.
--Hoppy the Puppy. N.D. Grosset & Dunlap.
--New Boy Next Door. Eitzen, Allan (1928-), illus. LC 65-106903. 48p. col. illus. 23cm. (gr. 1-2). c.1965. (ISBN 0-8054-4214-6). Broadman.
--The Roly Poly Puppy. Berthold, Leon, illus. N.D. Grosset & Dunlap.
--The Roly-Poly Puppy. Berthold, Leon, illus. LC 51-15791. 41 p. col. illus. 21cm. 1950. Wonder Books.
--Trudy Philips: Headline Year. Grider, Dorothy (1915-), illus. LC 55-2240. 282p. illus. 21cm. 1955, c.1954. Whitman Pub. Co.
--Trudy Phillips, New Girl. Grider, Dorothy (1915-), illus. LC 54-304982. 282p. illus. 20cm. 1954, c.1953. Whitman Pub. Co.

Bates, Betty, pseud., see Bates, Elizabeth.

Bates, Betty, pseud. (1921-)

--Bugs in Your Ears. Bates, Elizabeth. LC 77-3821. p. cm. c.1977. (ISBN 0-8234-0304-1). Holiday House.
--Call Me Friday the Thirteenth. Bates, Elizabeth. Edwards, Linda Strauss, illus. LC 83-6146. p. cm. c.1983. (ISBN 0-8234-0498-6). Holiday House.
--Herbert and Hortense. Bates, Elizabeth. Wallner, John C. (1945-), illus. LC 84-2387. 1984. (ISBN 0-8075-3222-3). A. Whitman.
--It Must've Been the Fish Sticks. Bates, Elizabeth. LC 81-85091. viii, 136 p. 21cm. c.1982. (ISBN 0-8234-0446-3). Holiday House.
--Love Is Like Peanuts. Bates, Elizabeth. LC 79-21686. 125 p. 22cm. c.1980. (ISBN 0-8234-0402-1). Holiday House.
--My Mom, the Money Nut. Bates, Elizabeth. LC 78-24213. 158 p. 21cm. c.1979. (ISBN 0-8234-0347-5). Holiday House.
--Picking up the Pieces. Bates, Elizabeth. LC 80-8811. 157 p. 21cm. c.1981. (ISBN 0-8234-0390-4). Holiday House.
--Say Cheese. Bates, Elizabeth. Spence, Jim, illus. LC 84-47837. (Illus.). 112p. (gr. 3-6). 1984. (ISBN 0-8234-0540-0). (ISBN 0-8234-0540-0). Holiday.
--Stories from the Moorland. Bates, Elizabeth. 236p. N.D. Hurd & Houghton for American tract Society.
--That's What T.J. Says. Bates, Elizabeth. LC 82-80815. p. cm. c.1982. (ISBN 0-8234-0465-X). Holiday House.
--The Ups and Downs of Jorie Jenkins. Bates, Elizabeth. LC 77-16698. 126 p. 21cm. c.1978. (ISBN 0-8234-0321-1). Holiday House.
--Westbrooke. Bates, Elizabeth. 256p. (Golden Sheaves Library). N.D. Lockwood, Brooks, & Co. for American Tract Society.

Bates, Clara Doty, Mrs., et al., eds. see Aesopus.

Bates, Clara Doty, Mrs. (1838-1895), retold by.

--Baby Classic Ser. Containing "Silver Locks and the Bears", "Puss in Boots", "Little Red Riding-Hood", "Cinderella", etc. N.D. D. Lothrop & Co.
--Beggar king: Goody Two Shoes. LC 15-256. 14p. front. col. ill. 25cm. c.1885. Lothrop & Co.
--Blind Jakey. (Illus.). N.D. D. Lothrop Co.
--Child Lore. Humphrey, Lizzie B. & Curtis, Jessie, illus. (Illus.). 1879. Lothrop.
--Classics of Babyland. (Illus.). N.D. D. Lothrop & Co.
--Classics of Babyland: For the Little Ones at Home. LC 15-239. 72 p. front., illus., 12 pl. 26 cm. c.1891. D. Lothrop Company.
--Doll Rosy's days. Hassam, F. Childe, illus. LC 15-251. 28p. incl. col. front. 15cm. c.1884. D. Lothrop & Co.
--Goody Two Shoes and other Nursery Ballads. (Illus.). N.D. D. Lothrop Co.
--Grandpa's Guests. Childhood Poems. Lawson, Lizzie, illus. LC 15-252. 60 p. front., illus. 18 cm. 1884. D. Lothrop and Company.
--Little Bo Beep; Wee Willie Winkie; Sleeping princes. LC 15-255. 14p. front. illus. 25cm. 1884. D. Lothrop & Co.
--More Classics of Babyland. (Illus.). N.D. D. Lothrop & Co.
--Nursery Jingles. LC 15-2600. 1 p. l., 7-92 p. illus., plates. 17 cm. c.1879. D. Lothrop & Co.
--Nursery tiles: The boys and girls painting book. Barnes, George Foster, illus. LC 15-249. 30p. col. front., illus. 13 x 20cm. c.1880. D. Lothrop & Co.
--Old Time Jingles. Boz, illus. LC 15-257. (Collected and arranged by Clara Doty Bates). (Illus.). 32p. front., illus., 7pl. 24cm. 1881. D. Lothrop & Co.
--On the Tree-Top: Children's Favorite Stories, Versified. by clara doty bates and others. illustrations by frank t. merrill, edmund h. garrett, and other well known artists. Merrill, Frank Thayer (1848-) & Garrett, Edmund Henry (1853-1929), illus. LC 15-20725. 90 p. front., illus., plates. 26 cm. c.1891. D. Lothrop Company.
--On The Way to Wonderland. N.D. D. Lothrop Co.
--Songs for Gold Locks. Finley, Charlotte Doty, illus. LC 14-22734. 22p. front., illus. 1877. E. B. Smith & Co.
--Ted, Goldlocks, and others. Lawson, Lizzie, illus. LC 14-22735. 26p. front. illus. 3pl. 24cm. c.1883. D. Lothrop & Co.

Bates, Daisy, jt. auth. see Ker Wilson, Barbara.

Bates, Elizabeth see Bates, Betty, pseud.

Bates, Ellen Arnott

--High-Up House. 1st ed. LC 56-128289. 142p. illus. 24cm. 1957, c.1956. Pageant Press.

Bates, Esther Willard (1887-)

--Marilda and the Bird of Time. Schrotter, Gustav, illus. LC 60-13337. 184p. illus. 21cm. 1960. D. McKay.
--Marilda and the Witness Tree. Schrotter, Gustav, illus. LC 57-10507. 180p. illus. 21cm. c.1957. D. McKay Co.
--Marilda's House. Schrotter, Gustav, illus. 213p. illus. 21cm. 1956. D. McKay Co.

Bates, Gordon

--The Khaki Boys Along the Rhine: Or, Winning the Honors of War. (The Khaki Boys Ser.). N.D. Cupples & Leon Co.
--The Khaki Boys at Camp Sterling: Or, Training for the Big Fight in France. (The Khaki Boys Ser.). N.D. Cupples & Leon Co.
--The Khaki Boys at the Front: Or, Shoulder to Shoulder in the Trenches. (The Khaki Boys Ser.). N.D. Cupples & Leon Co.
--The Khaki Boys Fighting to Win: Or, Smashing the German Lines. (The Khaki Boys Ser.). N.D. Cupples & Leon Co.
--The Khaki Boys on the Way: Or, Doing Their Bit on Sea and Land. (The Khaki Boys Ser.). N.D. Cupples & Leon Co.
--The Khaki Boys Over the Top: Or, Doing and Daring for Uncle Sam. (The Khaki Boys Ser.). N.D. Cupples & Leon Co.

Bates, Harriet Leonora Vose see Putnam, Eleanor, pseud.

Bates, Harriet Leonora Vose. (1856-1886)

--Prince Vance: The Story of a Prince with a Court in His Box. Myrick, Frank (1850-1918), illus. LC 11-10646. 153 p. incl. front., illus., plates. 20 cm. 1888. Roberts Brothers.

Bates, Helen Dixon

--Betsy Ross. LC 36-25288. 6 p. l., 3-127 p. front., illus. 21 cm.f gillustrated lining-papers. c.1936. Whittlesey House, McGraw-Hill Book Company, Inc.

Bates, Herbert Ernest (1905-1974)

--Achilles and Diana. Barker, Carol Minturn (1938-), illus. (Illus.). 41 p. 30cm. 1963. F. Watts.
--Achilles and the Twins. Barker, Carol Minturn (1938-), illus. LC 65-10088. 1v. (unpaged) col. illus. 30cm. 1965, c.1964. Watts.
--Achilles the Donkey. 1963. (ISBN 0-8382-0009-5, Cadmus Books). E. M. Hall and Company.
--Achilles the Donkey. Barker, Carol Minturn (1938-), illus. LC 63-7341. unpaged. illus. 30 cm. 1963. D. Dobson.

Bates, Katharine Lee, ed. see Edda Snorra Sturlusonar.

Bates, Katharine Lee (1859-1929), ed. see Ruskin, John.

Bates, Katharine Lee (1859-1929), ed.

--Cinderella. Endres, Helen & Neebe, William, illus. LC 56-115694. unpaged. illus. 22cm. (Rand McNally elf book, 551). c.1956. Rand McNally.
--Cinderella. Price, Margaret Evans, Mrs. (1888-1973) & Snow, Dorothea Johnston (1909-), illus. N.D. Rand McNally & Co.
--Fairy Gold: Poems. 1916. E P Dutton.
--Hermit Island. N.D. Lothrop.
--In Sunny Spain with Pilarica and Rafael. LC 13-227605. xvi, 2 p., 1 l., 300 p. col. front., plates. 20 cm. (On verso of half-title: Little schoolmate series, ed. by F. Converse). c.1913. E. P. Dutton & Company.
--Jack and the Beanstalk: Also, Toads and Diamonds; and The Frog Prince. Price, Margaret Evans, Mrs. (1888-1973) & Harman, Joan, illus. LC 37-17661. 64 p. illus. (part col.) 17 cm. c.1937. Rand McNally & Company.
--Jack the Giant-Killer: Also Rumpel-Stilt-Skin. Price, Margaret Evans, Mrs. (1888-1973), illus. LC 37-17662. 3 p. l., 9-63 p. illus. (part col.) 17 cm. (gr. 1-2). c.1937. Rand, McNally & Company.
--Little Red Riding-Hood. Price, Margaret Evans, Mrs. (1888-1973), illus. 32p. (Once Upon A Time Ser.). (gr. 1-2). N.D. Rand McNally & Co.
--Little Robin Stay-Behind, And Other Plays in Verse for Children. LC 23-17717. 4 p. l., 3-229 p. 20 cm. 1923. The Womans Press.
--Once Upon a Time: A Book of Old-Time Fairy Tales. Price, Evans Margaret, illus. LC 21-17818. 128 p. col. illus. 31 cm. c.1921. Rand, McNally & Company.
--The Retinue and Other Poems. 1918. E P Dutton.
--Rose and Thorn. LC 20-16485. 361 p. front., plates. 20 cm. (Pilgrim prize series. v. 1). c.1889. Congregational Sunday-School and Publishing Society.
--Rose and Thorn. 361p. (Prize Ser.). N.D. Pilgrim Press.
--Santa Claus Riddle. (Illus.). N.D. D. Lothrop Co.
--Sigurd Our Golden Collie, and Other Comrades of the Road. 1919. E P Dutton.
--The Sleeping Beauty. Price, Margaret Evans, Mrs. (1888-1973), illus. 32p. (Once Upon A Time Ser.). (gr. 1-2). N.D. Rand McNally & Co.
--Tom Thumb, And Other Old-Time Fairy Tales. 32 p. col. front., col. illus. 31 cm. (Once upon a time series). c.1926. Rand, McNally & Company.

Bates, L., Miss

--Anchored. (Illus.). (Sunday-Hour Lib.). N.D. American Tract Society.
--Beginning. (Illus.). N.D. James A. Moore.
--The Boy of Newkirk's. (Fern Glen Ser.). N.D. D. Lothrop Co.
--The Builders. (Illus.). N.D. James A. Moore.
--The Climbers. (Illus.). (Sunday-Hour Lib.). N.D. American Tract Society.
--Drawn Together: A Story of the Green Mountains. (Illus.). 313p. N.D. Sunday-School Publications.
--Drierstock. (Illus.). 193p. 1905. American Tract Society.
--Eric the Scandinavian: Or, Life With the Norsemen of the West. (Illus.). 314p. N.D. Sunday-School Publications.
--John Brent's Field: Or, Life on the Frontier. 285p. N.D. Sunday-School Publications.
--The Last of the Line. (Illus.). 318p. N.D. Sunday-School Publications.
--The Miner's Daughter. 320p. N.D. American Baptist Publishing Society.
--The Miner's Daughter. 320p. N.D. Sunday-School Publications.
--Stories of the Flowers. 192p. N.D. American Tract Society.
--That Boy of Newkirk's. (Fern Glen Ser.). N.D. D. Lothrop Co.
--That Boy of Newkirk's, 1 of 20 vols. New ed. (Illus.). 350p. (Sunday-School Lib: No. 13). 1895. Set. Lothrop Pub. Co.
--The True Boy. 55p. N.D. American Tract Society.
--Villanova-Solaro: A Story of the Vaudois. (Illus.). 317p. N.D. Sunday-School Publications.

Bates, L., Miss, et al.

--Golden Rule Library: Containing "The Builders", "Woodcliff Children", "Sword and Shield" and "Three Rules", 4 vols. (Illus.). N.D. James A. Moore.

Bates, L., Miss, jt. auth. see Hosmer, Margaret Kerr, Mrs.

Bates, L., Mrs., jt. auth. see Huntington, Faye.

Bates, Lila Curtis

--Frankie in Froggy-Land. LC 40-81946. 15p. incl front., illus. 25cm. c.1940. House of Field.

Bates, Lizzie

--Battle Worth Fighting, 1 of 103 vols. (The Pearl Library: No. 5). 1900. Hurst & Co.
--Had You been in His Place. N.D. Robert Carter & Bros.
--That Boy of Newkirk's. LC 58-52811. 247 p. illus. 19cm. 1878. D. Lothrop.

Bates, Lois, jt. ed. see Heller, Mrs.

Bates, Margret Holmes

--Shylock's Daughter. (Illus.). N.D. Charles H. Kerr & Co.

Bates, Stephen, ed. see Harris, Joel Chandler.

Bates, Zelda M

--Roses Are Blue. LC 62-10293. 203p. 21cm. 1962. Westminster Press.

Batey, Tom see Tomkins, Jasper, pseud.

Batherman, Muriel (1926-)

--Some Things You Should Know About My Dog. Batherman, Muriel (1926-), illus. LC 76-10172. p. cm. c.1976. (ISBN 0-13-822544-3). Prentice-Hall.

Batherman, Muriel (1926-) & Garten, Jan

--The Alphabet Tale. 1964. Random House Incorporation.

Bathgate, Olive M.

--Ducky, Snowy, and Tige. LC 42-16179. 127 p. incl. front., illus. 21 cm. 1942. Pacific Press Publishing Association.

Batko, Susan

--The Red Book of Wordplay Stories. Batko, Susan, illus. LC 77-70444. (Illus.). 127 p. 29cm. c.1977. (ISBN 0-918468-02-7). Vocab.
--The Yellow Book of Wordplay Stories. Batko, Susan, illus. LC 77-70443. (Illus.). 128 p. 29cm. c.1977. (ISBN 0-918468-01-9). Vocab.

Batley, Dorothea Sibella

--Chand's Little Sisters. N.D. Macmillan.

Bato, Joseph (1888-)

--The Sorcerer. Donnelly, Katherine Fair, ed. LC 76-12230. p. cm. 1976. (ISBN 0-679-20363-X). D. McKay Co.

Battaglia, Aurelius (1910-), illus.

--Baby's Mother Goose. (Re-issue of Little Golden Book "Pat-A-Cake"). (Little Golden Book). 1957. Golden Press.
--Captain Kangaroo's Read-Aloud Book. LC 62-18149. unpaged. illus. 33cm. 1962. Random House.
--Captain Kangaroo's Sleepytime Book. LC 63-9909. unpaged. col. illus. 33cm. c.1963. Random.
--Captain Kangaroo's Storybook. LC 63-81166. (Illus.). 92 p. 33cm. 1963. Random House.
--Little Brown Bear. (Illus.). (A Teddy Board Book). (ps). 1977. (ISBN 0-448-40869-4). Platt.
--Mother Goose. LC 73-2447. (Illus.). 32 p. 21cm. 1973. (ISBN 0-394-82661-2). Random House.
--My First Mother Goose Book. LC 80-50140. (Illus.). 21 p. 24cm. (Golden storytime book). c.1980. (ISBN 0-307-11987-4). Golden Press.
--Stories to Read to the Very Young. LC 66-31284. (Illus.). 1 v. (unpaged. 32cm. 1966. Random House.
--Three Little Pigs. LC 76-24170. (Illus.). 32 p. 21cm. (Random House pictureback). (Best book club ever). c.1977. (ISBN 0-394-83459-3). Random House.
--Three Little Pigs. LC 76-24170. (Illus.). 32p. (Picturebacks Ser.). (ps-2). 1982. (ISBN 0-394-93459-8). (ISBN 0-394-83459-3). Random.

Batten, Harry Mortimer (1888-1958)

--Ray of the Rainbows. Stokes, Vernon, illus. LC 55-9142. 177p. illus. 22cm. N.D. Roy Publishers.
--The Singing Forest. Wilson, Maurice Charles John (1914-), illus. LC 64-14106. viii, 214 p. illus. 21 cm. 1964. Farrar, Straus.

Batten, John Dickson (1860-1932)

--Indian Fairy Tales. Jacobs, Joseph (1854-1916), ed. LC 76-9897. (Illus.). x, 314 p., 8 leaves of plates. 20cm. 1976. (ISBN 0-8486-0205-6). Core Collection Books.

Batten, Mortimer J.

--Many Trails. N.D. Henry Holt.

Batterberry, Ariane Ruskin

--The Pantheon Story of Art for Young People. rev. ed. LC 74-24717. p. cm. 1975. (ISBN 0-394-83107-1). Pantheon Books.

Battis, George

--Barnaby Bear and the Black Forest. Cochran, Georgia Lee, illus. LC 66-30765. 25 p. col. illus. 22 cm. ("Mother read to me" book). 1966. Marlbee Press.

Battle, Edith Kent Childe (1877-)

--Boys and Girls who knew Jesus. Cooper, Marjorie (1910-), illus. LC 56-6741. 44 p.. illus.24cm. 1956. Rand McNally.

Battle, Gerald Nichols (1914-)

--Armed with Love: Stories of the Disciples. Cox, Charles T. (1937-), illus. LC 73-626. (Illus.). 224p. (gr. 5 up). 1973. (ISBN 0-687-01741-6). Abingdon.
--Gideon: The Boy Who Learned to Lead. Teichman, Dorothy, illus. LC 78-144367. (Illus.). 124 p. 24cm. 1971. Word Books.
--Luke: The Boy Who Wanted to Make People Well. Teichman, Dorothy, illus. LC 72-84152. (Illus.). 144 p. 24cm. 1972. Word Books.
--Simon Peter: The Boy Who Became a Fisherman. Teichman, Dorothy, illus. LC 75-135353. (Illus.). 128 p. 23cm. 1970. Word Books.

Battle, Gerald Nichols (1914-) & Dunn, Theo

--The Littlest Fiddler at the Opry. LC 75-126940. (Illus.). 75 p. 19cm. 1970. Word Books.

Battles, Edith (1921-)

--Eddie Couldn't Find the Elephants. Funk, Thompson (1911-), illus. LC 74-13997. (Illus.). 32 p. 19cm. 1974. A. Whitman.

--The Marvelous Land of Oz: A Sequal to the Wizard of Oz. LC 4-17928. 287 p. col. front., illus., col. plates. 24 cm. 1904. The Reilly & Britton Co.

--The Master Key. Cory, Fanny Young, illus. N.D. Bobbs-Merrill Co.

--The Master Key. Cory, Fanny Young, illus. LC 1-24123. 21cm. 245p. 1901. Bowen-Merrill Co.

--The Master Key: An Electrical Fairy Tale. Cory, Fanny Young, illus. LC 76-12893. (Illus.). 245 p., 12 leaves of plates. 21cm. 1976. (ISBN 0-486-23382-0). Dover Publications.

--The Master Key: An Electrical Fairy Tale. Cory, Fanny Young, illus. LC 73-13247. (Illus.). 245 p. 23cm. (Classics of science fiction). 1974. (ISBN 0-88355-103-9). (ISBN 0-88355-103-9). Hyperion Press.

--Mother Goose in Prose. Parrish, Frederick Maxfield (1870-1966), illus. LC 8-2950. 25cm. 265p. 1901. G. M. Hill Co.

--Mother Goose in Prose. Parrish, Frederick Maxfield (1870-1966), illus. LC 5-27131. 265 p. front., 11 pl. 24 cm. c.1905. The Bobbs-Merrill Company.

--Mother Goose in Prose. Parrish, Frederick Maxfield (1870-1966), illus. LC 14-6555. 5 p. l., 9-265 p., 1 l., 12 pl. (incl. fron.) 29 x 24 cm. 1897. Way and William.

--The Navy Alphabet: Verse. Kennedy, Harry Otis & Costello, Charles Jerome, illus. LC 3-3283. 29 l. col. illus. 32 cm. 1900. G. M. Hill Company.

--The New Wizard of Oz. Copelman, Evelyn & Denslow, William Wallace (1856-1916), illus. LC 44-47006. 4 p. l., 209 p. illus., plates (part col.) 24 1/2 cm. 1944. The Bobbs-Merrill Company.

--The New Wizard of Oz. Denslow, William Wallace (1856-1915), illus. LC 20-19398. 259 p., 1 l., col. illus., col. plates, port. 29 cm. c.1903. The Bobbs-Merrill Company.

--The New Wizard of Oz. Weisgard, Leonard Joseph (1916-), illus. LC 55-288427. 192p. illus. 22cm. 1955. Junior Deluxe Editions.

--A New Wonderland. Verbeck, Frank (1858-1933), illus. (Illus.). 1900. R. H. Russell.

--Off to See the Wizard. Naden, C. J., ed. LC 78-84171. 32p. (gr. 2-5). 1980. (ISBN 0-89375-194-4). (ISBN 0-89375-190-1). Troll Assocs.

--Once Upon a Time. (Oz-Man Tales). N.D. Reilly & Lee.

--Over the Rainbow. Naden, C. J., ed. Morrison, Bill (1935-), illus. LC 79-84151. (Illus.). 32p. (gr. 2-5). 1980. (ISBN 0-89375-197-9). (ISBN 0-89375-193-6). Troll Assocs.

--Oz-Man Tales, 6 Vols. Neill, John Rea (1878-1943), illus. Orig. Title: The Snuggle Tales. 1920. Reilly and Britton.

--Ozma of Oz. Kellogg, Jean Defrees (1916-1978), ed. Martin, Dick (1927-), illus. (Illus.). 61 p. 31cm. 1961. Reilly & Lee Co.

--Ozma of Oz. Neill, John Rea (1878-1943), illus. LC 84-18768. (Illus.). 270 p. 21cm. 1985. (ISBN 0-486-24779-1). Dover.

--Ozma of Oz. Neill, John Rea (1878-1943), illus. LC 72-27639. (Illus.). 258 p. 24cm. 1971, c.1907. Rand McNally.

--Ozma of Oz. Neill, John Rea (1878-1943), illus. N.D. Reilly & Lee Co.

--Ozma of Oz ... Neill, John Rea (1878-1943), illus. LC 7-24773. 270 p. incl. col. front., illus. (port. col.) 24 cm. c.1907. The Reilly & Britton Co.

--The Patchwork Girl of Oz. Neill, John Rea (1878-1943), illus. LC 73-156344. (Illus.). 340 p. 24cm. (His The famous Oz books). 1972, c.1913. (ISBN 0-528-82702-2). Rand McNally.

--The Patchwork Girl of Oz. Neill, John Rea (1878-1943), illus. LC 13-15522. 4 p. l., 15-340 p. 1 l. col. front. illus. (part col.) 24 cm. c.1913. The Reilly, & Britton Co.

--Phoebe Daring. Nuyttens, Joseph Pierre, illus. 1912. The Reilly & Britton Co.

--The Pop-up Wizard of Oz. Avery, Karen, illus. (Illus.). 12p. (Windmill Pop-up Bks.). (ps-2). 1982. (ISBN 0-671-44433-6). Windmill Bks.

--The Purple Dragon, and Other Fantasies. Kirk, Tim, illus. LC 76-44600. (Illus.). 201 p. 23cm. 1976. Fictioneer Books.

--Queen Zixi of Ix: Or, The Story of the Magic Cloak. (Illus.). N.D. (ISBN 0-8446-0026-1). Peter Smith Publisher, Inc.

--Queen Zixi of Ix, or the Story of the Magic Cloak. Richardson, Frederick (1862-1937), illus. Gardner, Martin, intro. by. LC 72-142287. (Pub. by Century). (gr. 1-3). 1971. Dover.

--Queen Zixi of Ix: Or, The Story of the Magic Cloak. Richardson, Frederick (1862-1937), illus. LC 5-281852. 5 p. l., 3-303 p. incl. col. illus., col. plates. col. front. 24 cm. 1905. The Century Co.

--Queen Zixi of Ix: Or, The Story of the Magic Cloak. Richardson, Frederick (1862-1937), illus. LC 27-134373. 6 p. l., 3-303 p. incl. front. illus., plates. 23 cm. 1922. The Century Co.

--Rinkitink in Oz. Neill, John Rea (1878-1943), illus. N.D. Rand McNally & Co.

--Rinkitink in Oz. Neill, John Rea (1878-1943), illus. LC 16-14719. 6 p. l., 17-314, 1 p. col. front., illus. col. plates. 24 cm. c.1916. The Reilly & Britton Co.

--The Road to Oz. Archer, Peter, adapted by. McNaught, Harry, illus. (Little Golden Book). 1951. Golden Press.

--The Road to Oz. Archer, Peter, ed. McNaught, Harry, illus. LC 52-6566. unpaged. illus. 21 cm. (Little golden book, 144). 1951. Simon and Schuster.

--The Road to Oz. Neill, John Rea (1878-1943), illus. LC 75-27870. (Illus.). 268 p. 24cm. 1971, c.1909. Rand McNally.

--The Road to Oz. Neill, John Rea (1878-1943), illus. LC 77-375863. (Illus.). 268 p. 24cm. (His Famous Oz books). 1977, c.1909. Reilly & Lee Co.

--The Road to Oz. Neill, John Rea (1878-1943), illus. LC 9-19332. 261 p. incl. front., illus. 24 cm. c.1909. The Reilly & Britton Co.

--The Road to Oz. Neill, John Rea (1878-1943), illus. LC 28-14646. 261 p. incl. front., illus. 23 1/2 cm. 1927. The Reilly & Lee Co.

--The Royal Book of Oz. Neill, John Rea (1878-1943), illus. 1921p. N.D. Reilly & Lee.

--The Scarecrow and the Tin Woodman of Oz. Neill, John Rea (1878-1943), illus. N.D. Rand McNally & Co.

--The Scarecrow of Oz. Neill, John Rea (1878-1943), illus. LC 73-156345. (Illus.). 288 p. 24cm. (His The famous Oz books). 1972, c.1915. (ISBN 0-528-82703-0). Rand McNally.

--The Scarecrow of Oz. Neill, John Rea (1878-1943), illus. LC 15-2568. 288p. 1915. Reilly & Lee Company.

--The Scarecrow of Oz. Neill, John Rea (1878-1943), illus. LC 36-29650. 288 p. col. front., illus. col. plates. 24 cm. N.D. The Reilly & Lee Co.

--Sea Fairies. Neill, John Rea (1878-1943), illus. (Illus.). 342p. (gr. 1 up). 1969. (ISBN 0-8092-8576-2). Contemp Bks.

--The Sea Fairies. Neill, John Rea (1878-1943), illus. 239, 1 p. col. front. illus., col. plates. 24 cm. c.1911. The Reilly & Britton Co.

--Sky Island. Neill, John Rea (1878-1943), illus. LC 78-125373. 288p. Repr. (gr. 2-4). 1970. Contemp Bks.

--Sky Island. Neill, John Rea (1878-1943), illus. LC 78-125373. (Illus.). 287 p. 24cm. 1970, c.1912. Reilly & Lee Co.

--Sky Island. Neill, John Rea (1878-1943), illus. LC 12-20311. 287, 1 p. col. front., illus., 11 col. pl. 24 x 18 cm. c.1912. The Reilly & Britton Co.

--Songs of Father Goose. N.D. Bobbs-merrill Co.

--The Songs of Father Goose. Denslow, William Wallace (1856-1915), illus. (Music by Alberta N. Hall). 1900. George M. Hill.

--The Surprising Adventures of the Magical Monarch of Mo and His People. 5 p. l., 236 p., 1 l. col. front. illus., col. plates. 24 cm. 1903. The Bobbs-Merrill Company.

--The Surprising Adventures of the Magical Monarch of Mo and His People. Copelman, Evelyn, illus. LC 47-31282. 187 p. illus. (part col.) 25 cm. 1947. Bobbs-Merrill Co.

--The Surprising Adventures of the Magical Monarch of Mo and His People. VerBeck, Frank (1858-1933), illus. LC 68-19550. (Illus.). xi, 236 p. 21cm. 1968. Dover Publications.

--The Wizard of Oz & the Land of Oz. 1960. Random House.

--Tik-Tok of Oz. Neill, John Rea (1878-1943), illus. LC 14-12287. 271, 1 p. col. front., illus. col. plates, 24 cm. c.1914. The Reilly & Britton Co.

--Tik-Tok of Oz. Neill, John Rea (1878-1943), illus. LC 36-29649. 271, 1 p. illus. 24 cm. N.D. The Reilly & Lee Co.

--The Tin Woodman. (Illus.). (gr. k-6). 1918. Rand.

--The Tin Woodman of Oz. Archer, Peter, ed. McNaught, Harry, illus. (Illus.). 28 p. 21cm. (Little golden library, 159). 1952. Simon and Schuster.

--The Tin Woodman of Oz. Neill, John Rea (1878-1943), illus. LC 77-27691. (Illus.). 287 p. 24cm. 1971, c.1918. Rand McNally.

--The Tin Woodman of Oz. Neill, John Rea (1878-1943), illus. N.D. Reilly & Lee Co.

--The Tin Woodman of Oz. Neill, John Rea (1878-1943), illus. LC 18-12622. 287. 1 p. col. front., illus. col. plates. 24 cm. c.1918. The Reilly & Britton Co.

--The Visitors from Oz. Martin, Dick (1927-), illus. LC 60-120085. 93p. illus. 29cm. 1960. Reilly & Lee Co.

--The Wizard. Baum, Lyman Frank (1856-1919), adapted by. (A Play. Music by Paul Tietjens.). 1902. Chicago.

--The Wizard of Oz. N.D. Bobbs - Merrill Co.

--The Wizard of Oz. (Illus.). (Classics Illus. Ser.). N.D. (ISBN 0-685-74099-4). Guild Bks.

--Wizard of Oz. (Illus.). color ils. 32p. (Grosset Picture Bks.). (ps). 1970. (ISBN 0-448-16305-5, G&D). Putnam Pub Group.

--Wizard of Oz. (Illus.). 224p. (Illustrated Junior Library). 1981. (ISBN 0-448-11026-1, G&D). Putnam Pub Group.

--The Wizard of OZ. (Illus.). 244p. 1964. Reilly & Lee Company.

--Wizard of Oz. (gr. k-3). N.D. (ISBN 0-448-00543-3). Wonder.

--The Wizard of Oz. Atkinson, Allen, illus. LC 85-18215. p. cm. c.1985. (ISBN 0-671-60509-7). Little Simon.

--The Wizard of Oz. Bryan, Brigitte, illus. LC 79-79990. (Illus.). 192 p. 29cm. 1969. Childrens Press.

--The Wizard of Oz. Chaffee, Allen, ed. Loeb, Anton, illus. Frank, Josette, produced by. LC 50-10602. 63 p. illus. (part col.) 29 cm. 1950. Random House.

--The Wizard of Oz. Copelman, Evelyn & Denslow, William Wallace (1856-1915), illus. LC 56-14198. 204p. illus. 21cm. (Illustrated junior library). 1956. Grosset & Dunlap.

--The Wizard of Oz. Denslow, William Wallace (1856-1915), illus. 208p. 1960. Dover Pub Inc.

--The Wizard of Oz. Denslow, William Wallace (1856-1915), illus. Fadiman, Clifton, afterword by. LC 62-18386. 244p. illus. 24cm. (Macmillan classics, 5). 1962. Macmillan.

--The Wizard of Oz. Denslow, William Wallace (1856-1915), illus. LC 72-27872. (Illus.). 236 p. 24cm. 1971, c.1956. Rand McNally.

--The Wizard of Oz. Hague, Michael R., illus. LC 82-1109. (Illus.). ix, 219 p. 26cm. 1982. (ISBN 0-03-061661-1). Holt, Rinehart and Winston.

--The Wizard of Oz. Hildebrandt, Greg (1939-), illus. LC 85-8479. p. cm. c.1985. (ISBN 0-88101-018-9). Unicorn Pub. House.

--The Wizard of Oz. Hockerman, Dennis, illus. LC 85-14824. p. cm. c.1985. (ISBN 0-671-60504-6). Little Simon.

--The Wizard of Oz. Lebeck, Oskar, illus. LC 30-21140. (Based on the Original and Complete Wizard of Oz.). 56 p. incl. col. front., illus. (part col.) 18 x 24 cm. c.1939. Grosset & Dunlap.

--The Wizard of Oz. Magagna, Anna Marie, illus. (Illus.). vi, 185 p. 20cm. (Companion library). 1963. Grosset & Dunlap.

--The Wizard of Oz. Maraja, Libico, illus. Maraja, pseud. LC 58-4557. 120p. illus. 34cm. 1958. Grosset & Dunlap.

--The Wizard of Oz. Wehr, Julian, illus. LC 44-9095. 24 p. col. illus. 22 1/2 cm. 1944. The Saalfield Publishing Company.

--The Wizard of Oz. Adapted for Younger Children. Kellogg, Jean Defrees (1916-1978), ed. Martin, Dick (1927-), illus. LC 61-12108. unpaged. illus. 31cm. 1961. Reilly & Lee Co.

--Wizard of Oz & the Land of Oz. (Illus.). (Looking Glass Library: No. 16). (gr. 3 up). 1960. (ISBN 0-394-80466-X). (ISBN 0-394-90466-4). Random.

--The Wizard of Oz & The Land of Oz. Fava, Rita (1932-), illus. LC 60-11938. 415p. illus. 20cm. (Looking glass library, 16). 1960. Distributed by Random House.

--The Wizard of Oz & Who He Was. Nye, Russel Blaine (1913-) & Gardner, Martin (1914-), eds. LC 56-802285. 208p. illus. 25cm. c.1957. Michigan State University Press.

--Wizard of Oz to Read Aloud. (Read-Aloud Bks.). (gr. k-3). N.D. (ISBN 0-448-02038-6). Wonder.

--The Wizard of Oz Waddle Book. LC 35-8414. 4 p. l., 210. 1 p. illus. (part col.) col. plates. 23 cm. c.1934. Blue Ribbon Books, Inc.

--Wizards. (Story Bks.). N.D (Usborne-Hayes). EDC.

--The Woggle-Bug Book. Morgan, Ike, illus. 1905. Reilly and Britton.

--The Woggle-Bug Book. Morgan, Ike & Greene, Douglas G., illus. LC 78-6887. (Illus.). xvii, 48 p., 1 leaf of plates. 23cm. 1978, c.1905. (ISBN 0-8201-1308-5). Scholars' Facsimiles & Reprints.

--The Wonderful Wizard of Oz. Biro, Val, pseud. (1921-), illus. Biro, Balint Stephen. (Children's Illustrated Classics). 1966. E.P. Dutton & Co.

--The Wonderful Wizard of Oz. Biro, Val, pseud. (1921-), illus. Biro, Balint Stephen. LC 66-1639. xii, 147 p. illus. (part col.) 22 cm. (Illustrated classics for older readers, no. 68). 1965. J. M. Dent.

--The Wonderful Wizard of Oz. Denslow, William Wallace (1856-1915), illus. LC 85-11668. p. cm. 1985. Children's Classics : Distributed by Crown Publishers.

--The Wonderful Wizard of Oz. Denslow, William Wallace (1856-1915), illus. Gardner, Martin, intro. by. LC 61-428. 268p. illus. 21cm. c.1960. Dover Publications.

--The Wonderful Wizard of Oz. Denslow, William Wallace (1856-1915), illus. 1900. George M Hill Co.

--The Wonderful Wizard of Oz. Denslow, William Wallace (1856-1915), illus. N.D. (ISBN 0-8446-1610-9). Peter Smith Publisher, Inc.

--Wonderful Wizard of Oz. Hazen, Barbara Shook (1930-), ed. Mill, Eleanor, illus. (Illus.). (Kids Paperbacks). (ps-4). 1977. (ISBN 0-307-62361-0, Golden Pr). (ISBN 0-307-12361-8). Western Pub.

--The Wonderful Wizard of Oz. Hildebrandt, Greg (1939-), illus. LC 85-4281. p. cm. 1985. (ISBN 0-394-87207-X). (ISBN 0-394-97207-4). Knopf.

--The Wonderful Wizard of Oz, and the Marvelous Land of Oz. Denslow, William Wallace (1856-1915), illus. Neill, John Rea (1878-1943), photos by. LC 64-15712. 392p. 1964. Parent's Magazine Press.

--Wonderland of Oz. N.D. Dover Pub Inc.

--The Yellow Hen. (Oz-Man Tales). N.D. Reilly & Lee.

Baum, Lyman Frank (1856-1919), ed.

--Cinderella & Sleeping Beauty. LC 5-17279. 119 p. 1 l. incl. col. front., illus. (part col.) 10 1/2 cm. (Christmas Stocking Series). 1905. Reilly & Britton Co.

Baum, Lyman Frank (1856-1919) & Barney, Maginel Wright (1877-)

--Policemen Bluejay. LC 81-9044. (Illus.). xiv, 115 p. 22cm. 1981. (ISBN 0-8201-1367-0). Scholars' Facsimilies & Reprints.

Baum, Lyman Frank (1856-1919) & Hall, Alberta (1856-1915)

--Songs of Father Goose. Denslow, William Wallace (1856-1915), illus. N.D. Bobbs-Merrill Co.

Baum, Lyman Frank (1856-1919) & Hearn, Michael Patrick

--The Annotated Wizard of Oz: The Wonderful Wizard of Oz. LC 72-80842. (Illus.). 384 p. 1973. (ISBN 0-517-50086-8). C. N. Potter.

Baum, Lyman Frank (1856-1919) & Leydenfrost, Robert J. (1925-)

--The Wizard of Oz. Leydenfrost, Robert J. (1925-), illus. LC 78-60468. (Illus.). x, 153 p., 10 leaves of plates. 22cm. c.1978. Nelson Doubleday.

Baum, Lyman Frank (1856-1919) & Miller, Albert Griffith (1905-1982)

--The Wizard of Oz. Chambers, Dave & Spencer, John, illus. LC 70-3971. (Illus.). 24 p. 25cm. (Pop-up classic, 1). 1968. Random House.

Baum, Max Z.

--Battle for Earth. Joyce, Brad & Edelman, Roberta, illus. LC 85-199336. (Illus.). 45 p. 29cm. (The Transformers). c.1985. (ISBN 0-87135-062-9). Hasbro Bradley.

Baum, Roger S.

--Long Ears & Tailspin in Candy Land: A Faraway Adventure. (Illus.). (gr. k-3). 1968. (ISBN 0-682-46759-6). Exposition.

Baum, Thomas (1940-)

--The Blue Grass Special. (Orig.). 1976. (ISBN 0-515-04215-3). Pyramid Pubns.

--Hugo the Hippo. 1st. ed. LC 76-14354. (Illus.). 63 p. c.1976. Harcourt Brace Jovanovich.

--It Looks Alive to Me!. LC 75-25401. 168 p. 21cm. c.1976. (ISBN 0-06-020403-6). (ISBN 0-06-020404-4). Harper & Row.

--It Looks Alive to Me!. 169p. 20cm. (Harpy Trophy Book). 1977, c.1976. (ISBN 0-06-440086-7). Harper & Row.

Baum, Willi (1931-)

--Birds of a Feather. LC 76-88685. 33 p. (chiefly col. illus. 23cm. 1969. Addison-Wesley.

--The Expedition. LC 77-85227. (Illus.). (Barron's Juvenile Books). (gr. k-6). 1978. (ISBN 0-8120-5199-8). Barron.

Baum, Willi (1931-) & Ekker, Ernst Alfred

--The Golden Mountain. LC 77-85677. (Illus.). 32 p. 21cm. (Best book club ever). c.1978. (ISBN 0-394-83756-8). Random House.

Bauman, Elizabeth Hershberger (1924-)

--Coals of Fire, 1 of 25 vols. (Illus.). (Infant Lib.: No. 9). N.D. Set. A. I. Bradley & Co.'s Pubs.

--Coals of Fire. LC 53-12197. (Illus.). (Christian Peace Shelf Ser.). (gr. 5-9). 1954. (ISBN 0-8361-1957-6). Herald Pr.

Bauman, Kurt, jt. auth. see Wilkon, Jozef.

Baumann, Amy Brown Beeching see Barbary, James, pseud.

Baumann, Amy Brown Beeching see Brown, Alexis, pseud.

Baumann, Amy Brown Beeching (1922-)

--Treasure in Devils' Bay. Brown, Alexis, pseud. Chapman, Gaynor (1935-), illus. LC 64-66041. 144p. illus. 21cm. 1965, c.1962. McGraw.

Baumann, Elwood D.

--The Devil's Triangle. LC 75-22020. (Illus.). bibl. index. 160p. (gr. 7 up). 1976. (ISBN 0-531-01094-5). Watts.

--They Came from Space. LC 76-44435. (Illus.). (gr. 6 up). 1977. (ISBN 0-531-00388-4). Watts.

--Vampires. N.D. (ISBN 0-531-00128-8). Watts.

Baumann, Hans (1914-)

--Alexander's Great March. 144p. 1968. Henry Z. Walck Inc.

--Angelina and the Birds. Schramm, Ulrik (1912-), illus. Potts, Katherine, tr. LC 59-13688. 63p. illus. 25cm. 1959. F. Watts.

--The Barque of the Brothers: A Tale of the Days of Henry the Navigator. Schramm, Ulrik (1912-), illus. McHugh, Isabel & McHugh, Florence, trs. (Illus.). 245 p. 23cm. 1958. (ISBN 0-8098-3019-1). H. Z. Walck.
--Caspar and His Friends: A Collection of Puppet Plays. Lebenson, Richard, illus. Emerson, Joyce, tr. Speaight, George, frwd. by. LC 68-23883. (Illus.). 117 p. 24cm. 1969, c.1967. H. Z. Walck.
--The Caves of the Great Hunters. McHugh, Isabel & McHugh, Florence, trs. LC 54-7066. (Illus.). 158 p. 22cm. 1954. Pantheon Books.
--Chip Has Many Brothers. Carle, Eric (1929-), illus. LC 85-3671. (Illus.). 25 p. 29cm. c.1985. (ISBN 0-399-21283-3). Philomel Books.
--Dimitri and the False Tsars. 1972. (ISBN 0-8098-3106-6). David McKay.
--Fenny, the Desert Fox. Schmid, Eleonore (1939-), illus. Carle, J. J., tr. LC 79-77421. (Illus.). 23 p. 1970. Pantheon Books.
--Gatalop the Wonderful Ball. Eckert, Horst (1931-), illus. Wilkin, Refna (1931-), tr. LC 73-119567. (Illus.). 24 p. 29cm. 1971. (ISBN 0-8098-1168-5). H. Z. Walck.
--The Hare's Race. Boratynski, Anthoni, illus. Crawford, Elizabeth D., tr. LC 75-37913. (Illus.). 25 p. 23cm. 1976. (ISBN 0-688-22067-3). (ISBN 0-688-32067-8). Morrow.
--I Marched with Hannibal. Schramm, Ulrik (1912-), illus. Potts, Katherine, tr. LC 62-16055. 226p. 1962, c.1960. Walck. **Award: (ALA).**
--Jackie the Pit Pony. Schramm, Ulrik (1912-), illus. LC 71-7180. (Illus.). 52 p. 24cm. 1958. F. Watts.
--Lion Gate and Labyrinth. (Illus.). 1967. Pantheon Books.
--Mischa & His Brothers. Michl, Reinhard, illus. Neumeyer, Peter, tr. from Ger. (Illus.). 32p. (gr. 1 up). 1985. (ISBN 0-88138-051-2, Star & Elephant Bks.). Green Tiger Pr.
--Son of Columbus. Stobbs, William (1914-), illus. 256p. 1957. Henry Z Walck, Inc.
--Son of Columbus. 1st London ed. Stobbs, William (1914-), illus. McHugh, Isabel & McHugh, Florence, trs. LC 57-14052. 248p. illus. 24cm. 1957. Oxford University Press.
--Sons of the Steppe. Rothfuchs, Heiner, illus. McHugh, Isabel & McHugh, Florence, trs. LC 58-783. (Illus.). (gr. 8 up). 1958. (ISBN 0-8098-3020-5). Walck. **Award: (ALA).**
--Sons of the Steppe: The Story of How the Conqueror Genghis Khan Was Overcome. (Illus.). 273 p. 23cm. 1961, c.1957. H. Z. Walck.
--The Stolen Fire. Holzing, Herbert, illus. Humphries, Stella, tr. LC 73-15107. (Illus.). 150 p. 24cm. 1974, c.1972. (ISBN 0-394-82675-2). (ISBN 0-394-92675-7). Pantheon Books.
--The Stolen Fire: Legends of Heroes & Rebels from Around the World. Holzing, Herbert, illus. LC 73-5107. (Illus.). 176p. (gr. 5 up). 1973. (ISBN 0-394-92675-7). Pantheon.
--The World of the Pharaohs. Renner, Hans Peter, illus. Burges, Albert, photos by. Winston, Richard & Winston, Clara, trs. (Illus.). 255 p. 22cm. 1960. Pantheon Books.

Baumann, John
--Idaho Sprout: The Story of a Western Boyhood. Townsend, Lee (1895-), illus. (Based on Old Man Crow's Boy). 250p. (gr. 7). 1950. William Morrow & Co.

Baumann, Kurt, jt. auth. see Testa, Fulvio.

Baumann, Kurt (1909-), adapted by see Perrault, Charles.

Baumann, Kurt (1909-)
--Joseph, the Border Guard. McKee, David (1935-), illus. LC 70-178743. (Illus.). 32 p. 30cm. 1972, c.1971. (ISBN 0-8193-0548-0). (ISBN 0-8193-0549-9). Parents' Magazine Press.
--Joseph, the Border Guard. McKee, David (1935-), illus. LC 70-178743. 1st U.S. edition. (gr. k-3). 1972. (ISBN 0-8193-0548-0, Four Winds). (ISBN 0-8193-0549-9). Scholastic Inc.
--The Pied Piper of Hamelin. Claverie, Jean (1946-), illus. LC 78-62168. (Illus.). 32 p. 30cm. c.1978. (ISBN 0-458-93800-9). Methuen.
--Piro and the Fire Brigade. Bernard, Jiri, contrib. by. LC 82-670023. (Illus.). 24 p. 29cm. 1981. (ISBN 0-571-11843-7). Faber and Faber.

Baumann, Lotte, tr. see Ranke, Kurt.

Baumbach, Rudolf (1840-1905)
--Baumbach's Tales, 1 of 88 vols. popular ed. (Handy Volume Classics). N.D. T. Y. Crowell & Co.
--Summer Legends. Dole, Helen B., tr. from Ger. 1888. Thomas Y. Crowell.
--Tales from the Swiss Alps. Papadopoulos, Electra, illus. Mitchell, Harley W., tr. LC 30-208317. xiii p., 1 l., 17-192 p. incl. illus., col. plates. 23 1/2 cm. 1930. Thomas S. Rockwell Company.
--Tales from Wonderland. Silber, William S. M., ed. Dole, Helen B., tr. LC 3-14708. iv p., 1 l., 122 p. 19 cm. 1903. A. Lovell & Company.
--Wonderful Wonderland Tales. Stradling, J. M., ed. Dole, Helen B., tr. LC 3-24828. 17cm. 146p. 1903. J. M. Stradling & Co.

B.A.V, jt. auth. see Bumgartner, Alexander.

Bava, Domenick
--Favorite Stories for Boys & Girls. 160p. (gr. k-6). 1980. (ISBN 0-89962-023-X). Todd & Honeywell.

Bavier, Robert N., Jr.
--The Forest of the Railway. Bavier, Robert N., Jr., illus. N.D. Dodd, Mead & Co.

Baw, Cindy & Brownlow, Paul C.
--Children of the Bible: Twenty-Six Exciting Stories about Children of the Bible. (Illus.). 1984. (ISBN 0-915720-19-1). Brownlow Pub Co.

Bawden, Nina, pseud., see Kark, Nina Mary Mabey.

Bawden, Nina, pseud. (1925-)
--Carrie's War. Kark, Nina Mary Mabey. LC 76-198. 235 p. 25cm. 1976, c.1973. (ISBN 0-8161-6355-3). G. K. Hall.
--Carrie's War. Kark, Nina Mary Mabey. LC 72-13253. (Illus.). 159 p. 20cm. 1973. (ISBN 0-397-31450-7). Lippincott. **Award: (ALA).**
--Carrie's War. Kark, Nina Mary Mabey. (gr. 4-6). 1973. Penguin.
--Carrie's War. Kark, Nina Mary Mabey. Jaques, Faith (1923-), illus. LC 79-28221. 141 p. 18cm. 1980, c.1973. (ISBN 0-14-005581-9). Penguin Books.
--Devil By the Sea. Kark, Nina Mary Mabey. 1976. Harper.
--Devil by the Sea. Kark, Nina Mary Mabey. 1957. Lippincott.
--Devil by the Sea. Kark, Nina Mary Mabey. LC 76-13177. 228 p. 21cm. c.1976. (ISBN 0-397-31683-6). Lippincott.
--The Finding. Kark, Nina Mary Mabey. LC 84-25069. 160p. (gr. 3 up). 1985. (ISBN 0-688-04979-6). Lothrop.
--A Handful of Thieves. Kark, Nina Mary Mabey. LC 67-19264. 189 p. 22cm. 1967. Lippincott.
--The House of Secrets. Kark, Nina Mary Mabey. Worth, Wendy, illus. LC 64-11448. (Illus.). 190 p. 21cm. 1964. Lippincott.
--Kept in the Dark. Kark, Nina Mary Mabey. LC 81-20765. 170 p. 22cm. c.1982. (ISBN 0-688-00900-X). Lothrop, Lee & Shepard Books. **Award: (ALA).**
--The Peppermint Pig. Kark, Nina Mary Mabey. Lilly, Charles, illus. LC 74-26922. 191 p. 21cm. 1st U.S. edition. 1975. (ISBN 0-397-31618-6). Lippincott.
--Rebel on a Rock. Kark, Nina Mary. LC 77-10686. 158 p. 21cm. c.1978. (ISBN 0-397-31772-7). Lippincott.
--The Robbers. Kark, Nina Mary Mabey. LC 79-1152. 155 p. 22cm. c.1979. (ISBN 0-688-41902-X). (ISBN 0-688-51902-4). Lothrop, Lee & Shepard. **Award: (ALA).**
--Runaway Summer. Kark, Nina Mary Mabey. 1969. Harper.
--The Runaway Summer. Kark, Nina Mary Mabey. LC 77-82408. 185 p. 22cm. 1969. Lippincott.
--Squib. Kark, Nina Mary Mabey. LC 79-151468. 143 p. 21cm. 1971. Lippincott. **Award: (ALA).**
--Squib. Kark, Nina Mary Mabey. Blaustein, Hank, illus. LC 82-75. (Illus.). 159 p. 22cm. 1982, c.1971. (ISBN 0-688-01299-X). Lothrop, Lee & Shepard.
--Squib. Kark, Nina Mary Mabey. Hughes, Shirley (1929-), illus. LC 76-351505. (Illus.). 109 p. 18cm. (Puffin books). 1971. (ISBN 0-14-030581-5). Penguin Books.
--Three on the Run. Kark, Nina Mary Mabey. Worth, Wendy, illus. LC 65-13430. (Illus.). 224 p. 21cm. 1st U.S. edition. (gr. 4-6). 1965, c.1964. (ISBN 0-397-30836-1). Lippincott.
--The White Horse Gang. Kark, Nina Mary Mabey. Longtemps, Kenneth (1933-), illus. LC 66-10893. (Illus.). 188 p. 21cm. 1st U.S. edition. 1966. Lippincott.
--William Tell. Kark, Nina Mary Mabey. Allamand, Pascale (1942-), illus. LC 80-24786. (Illus.). 32 p. 27cm. 1st U.S. edition. c.1981. (ISBN 0-688-41985-2). (ISBN 0-688-51985-7). Lothrop, Lee & Shepard Books.
--The Witch's Daughter. Kark, Nina Mary Mabey. 1966. Harper.
--The Witch's Daughter. Kark, Nina Mary Mabey. LC 66-7115. 181 p. 22cm. 1966. Lippincott.

Bax, Clifford (1886-)
--Old King Cole: A Play for Children, in Three Acts. 63 p. 18 1/2 cm. (On cover: French's plays for juvenile performers, no. 30). c.1935. S. French, Ltd.

Baxendale, Esther M.
--Fairy: The Autobiography of a Real Dog. Barry, Etheldred Breeze (1870-), illus. LC 9-30321. 6 p. l., 310, 4 p. incl. illus., plates. front. 20 1/2 cm. (Princess series). 1907. L. C. Page & Company.

Baxendale, Jean
--First Bible Lessons: A Course for Two and Three-Year-Olds. rev. ed. Arthur, Lorraine, illus. LC 81-53021. (Illus.). 144p. 1982. (ISBN 0-87239-486-7). Standard Pub.

Baxendale, Leo
--The Willy the Kid, Bk. 1. (Illus.). 1976. (ISBN 0-7156-1090-2, Pub. by Duckworth England). Biblio Dist.
--The Willy the Kid, Bk. 2. (Illus.). 1977. (ISBN 0-686-11819-7, Pub. by Duckworth England). Biblio Dist.

Baxley, Claude
--Comrades. LC 99-4719. iv, 7-287 p. 12 cm. (Neely's universal library, no. 64). 1899. F. T. Neely.

Baxter, Betty
--Becky Bryans's Secret. LC 37-5828. 4 p. l., 15-246p. 19 1/2cm. c.1937. Goldsmith Pub.
--Daughter of the Coast Guard. LC 38-3426. 4 p. l., 15-252 p. 19 1/2 cm. c.1938. The Goldsmith Publishing Company.
--The Unseen Enemy. LC 38-3425. 4 p. l., 15-250 p. 19 1/2 cm. c.1938. The Goldsmith Publishing Company.

Baxter, Caroline (1956-)
--The Stolen Telesm. LC 76-17307. 192 p. 21cm. c.1975. (ISBN 0-397-31686-0). Lippincott.

Baxter, Gillian
--Horses & Heather. (Illus.). (gr. 4-7). 1956. (ISBN 0-7232-0393-8). Warne.

Baxter, Lorna
--The Eggchild. LC 79-16223. 157 p. 22cm. 1979, c.1978. (ISBN 0-525-29155-5). Dutton.
--The Eggchild. LC 78-314986. (Illus.). 157 p. 21cm. 1978. (ISBN 0-571-11205-6). Faber and Faber.
--The White Rose and the Black. LC 81-126770. 147 p. 21cm. 1979. (ISBN 0-571-11413-X). Fabar and Faber.

Baxter, Lucy W. (1834-1925), tr. see Monniot, Victorine.

Baxter, Ruth H.
--A Norwegian Birthday Party. LC 78-63421. (Illus.). 25p. N.D. (ISBN 0-533-03978-9). Vantage.

Baxter, W.
--Pea Ridge & Prairie Grove, 1 of 15 vols. (Selected Bks for Sunday School: The/Ludlow Library). N.D. Set. Methodist Bk Concern.

Bay, Andre
--The Snow Queen, and Other Tales: A Selection of Traditional Russian Fairy Tales. Segur, Adrienne, illus. Ponsot, Marie (1922-), tr. LC 61-8489. 136 p. illus. 34 cm. (Deluxe golden book). 1961. Golden Press.

Bay, Jens Christian, jt. ed. see Hatch, Mary Cottam.

Bay, Jens Christian (1871-), tr. see Hatch, Mary Cottam.

Bay, Jens Christian (1871-), ed.
--Danish Fairy & Folk Tales: A Collection of Popular Stories and Fairy Tales. Grundtvig, Svend Hersleb, 1824-1883 & Kristensen, Evald Tang, 1843-1929 LC 99-1643. 7 p. l., 296 p. front., plates. 19 cm. 1899. Harper & Brothers.
--Danish Fairy Tales. (Twilight Ser.). N.D. Harper & Bros.

Bay, Timothy
--Fake Giants and Other Great Hoaxes. special ed. LC 80-21132. p. cm. c.1980. (ISBN 0-88436-766-5). EMC Corp.

Bay, W. Bu see DuBay, W.

Bayard, Emile & Griset, E., illus.
--Captain Wolf. N.D. D. Appleton & Co.

Bayer, Eleanor Rosenfeld & Bayer, Leo G.
--Dirty Hands Across the Sea. 1st ed. O'Sickey, Joseph B., illus. LC 52-103251. unpaged. illus. 23cm. 1952. World Pub. Co.

Bayer, Jane
--A, My Name is Alice. Kellogg, Steven (1941-), illus. LC 84-7059. (Illus.). (gr. k-3). 1984. (ISBN 0-8037-0123-3). (ISBN 0-8037-0124-1). Dial Bks for Young Readers.

Bayer, Leo G., jt. auth. see Bayer, Eleanor Rosenfeld.

Bayes, A. W., jt. auth. see Andersen, Hans Christian.

Bayha, Anne
--Song of the Weeping Willow. 1st ed. LC 61-6724. 205p. 21cm. 1961. Chilton Co., Book Division.

Bayley, Frederic William Naylor (1808-1853)
--Blue Beard. LC 45-42402. 64 p. incl. illus., plates. 19 cm. (With Smith, A. R. Beauty and the beast. New York 187). N.D. Manhattan Publishing Company.
--Blue Beard. Crowquill, Alfred, pseud. (1804-1872), illus. Forrester, Alfred Henry. LC 16-5958. 64 p. incl. col. front., col. illus. 14 1/2 cm. 1845. Burgess, Stringer, & Co.
--Blue Beard. Forrester, Alfred Henry (1804-1872), illus. LC 22-5862. 64 p. incl. front., illus. 2 pl. 14 1/2 cm. 1855. Leavitt & Allen.
--Jack the Giant Killer. Leech, John (1817-1864), illus. LC 16-5960. 96 p. incl. col. front., col. illus., col. plates. 14 1/2 cm. 1845. Burgess, Stringer, & Co.
--Jack the Giant Killer. Leech, John (1817-1864), illus. LC 45-42401. 96 p. incl. illus., plates. 19 cm. (With Smith, A. R. Beauty and the beast. New York 187-). N.D. Manhattan Publishing Company.
--Little Red Riding Hood. LC 16-5959. 64 p. incl. col. front., col. illus., col. plates. 14 1/2 cm. 1845. Burgess, Stringer & Co.
--Little Red Riding Hood. LC 45-42400. 64 p. incl. illus., plates. 19 cm. (With Smith, A. R. Beauty and the beast. New York 187-). N.D. Manhattan Publishing Company.
--Little Red Riding Hood. LC 42-44504. 1 p. l., 5-60, 1 p. incl. illus., plates. 14 1/2 cm. 1844. Wilson & Company.

Bayley, Monica & Schulz, Charles Monroe (1922-)
--Snoopy Omnibus. LC 82-71285. (Illus.). 1983. Determined Prods.

Bayley, Nicola (1935-)
--As I Was Going up and Down, and Other Nonsense Rhymes. Bayley, Nicola (1935-), illus. LC 84-27693. p. cm. 1985. (ISBN 0-394-87490-0). (ISBN 0-394-97490-5). Random House.
--Crab Cat. Bayley, Nicola (1935-), illus. LC 84-773. (Illus.). 24p. (Copycats Ser.). (gr. k up). N.D. (ISBN 0-394-86499-9). Knopf.
--Elephant Cat. Bayley, Nicola (1935-), illus. LC 84-774. (Illus.). 18 p. 15cm. (Copycats). c.1984. (ISBN 0-394-86497-2). Knopf : Distributed by Random House.
--Nicola Bayley's Book of Nursery Rhymes. LC 76-57923. (Illus.). 32 p. 26cm. 1977, c.1975. (ISBN 0-394-83561-1). (ISBN 0-394-93561-6). Knopf.
--One Old Oxford Ox. Bayley, Nicola (1935-), illus. LC 77-77866. p. cm. 1977. (ISBN 0-689-30608-3). Atheneum.
--Parrot Cat. Bayley, Nicola (1935-), illus. LC 83-23749. (Illus.). 24p. (Copycats Ser.). (gr. k up). c.1984. (ISBN 0-394-86496-4). Knopf.
--Polar Bear Cat. Bayley, Nicola (1935-), illus. LC 83-23744. (Illus.). 24p. (Copycats). (gr. k up). c.1984. (ISBN 0-394-86501-4). Knopf.
--Spider Cat. Bayley, Nicola (1935-), illus. LC 84-772. (Illus.). 20 p. 15cm. (Copycats). c.1984. (ISBN 0-394-86500-6). Distributed by Random House.

Bayley, Verna Hills
--All Aboard for the Beach. Tolford, Joshua (1909-), illus. LC 54-5207. 143p. illus. 22cm. 1954. Ariel Books.
--Here Comes Peter. Maden, Eleanora, illus. LC 35-16898. 64 p. illus. (part col.) 20 cm. 1935. Lothrop, Lee & Shepard Company.
--Here, Suzy!. Downer, Marion (1892-1971) & Ingersoll, W. King, illus. LC 48-3989. 123 p. illus. 24 cm. 1948. Lothrop, Lee & Shepard Co.
--Martin and Judy. Rev. ed. Breed, Lydia N., illus. LC 59-7381. 3v. illus. 24cm. 1959. Beacon Press.
--Martin & Judy in Sunshine & Rain. rev. ed. (ps). 1959. (ISBN 0-8070-1910-0). Beacon Pr.
--Martin & Judy Playing & Learning. rev. ed. (ps). 1959. (ISBN 0-8070-1912-7). Beacon Pr.

Bayley, Viola Powles (1911-)
--Jersey Adventure. (Illus.). 1st U.S. edition. 1969. (ISBN 0-460-05264-0, Pub. by J. M. Dent England). Biblio Dist.

Bayliss, Alfred Edward MacDuff, ed.
--Invitation to Verse: An Anthology. LC 72-167475. 224 p. 21cm. (Granger index reprint series). 1971. (ISBN 0-8369-6280-X). Books for Libraries Press.

Bayliss, Blanche
--The Long Road. N.D. Augustana Book.

Bayliss, Clara Kern, Mrs. (1848-)
--The Little Cliff Dweller: A Story of Lolami, for the Little Folk. LC 9-20909. 114, viii p. front., illus. 18 cm. c.1908. The Public School Publishing Co.
--Lolami, in Tusayan. LC 3-6968. 244 p. incl. front. (map) illus. 18 cm. 1903. Public School Publishing Co.
--Lolami: The Little Cliff-Dweller. LC 1-31820. 188 p. incl. front. (map) 17 1/2 cm. 1901. Public School Publishing Company.
--Old Man Coyote. (Illus.). (Crowell's Every Land Series For Children). 1915. T Y Crowell.
--Old Man Coyote. Blaisdell, E. Warde, illus. LC 8-24867. (Illus.). 20cm. 1908. T. Y. Crowell & Co.
--A Treasury of Eskimo Tales. Carlson, George L., illus. (The Treasury Series for Children). 1922. Thomas Y. Crowell Co.
--A Treasury of Indians Tales. (The Treasury Series for Children). 1921. Thomas Y. Crowell Co.
--Two Little Algonkin Lads. LC 9-22949. 204 p. illus., plates, fold. map. 19 cm. N.D. Educational Publishing Company,.

Baylor, Adelaide S.
--Adventures of Miss Tabby Gray. Bruce, Josephine, illus. N.D. W. A. Wilde.

Baylor, Byrd see Scheitzer, Byrd Baylor, pseud.

Baylor, Byrd see Schweitzer, Byrd Baylor, pseud.

Baylor, Byrd (1924-)
--Before You Came This Way. Bahti, Tom, illus. LC 74-81709. (Illus.). 32 p. 26cm. 1969. Dutton.
--The Best Town in the World. Himler, Ronald Norbert (1937-), illus. LC 83-9033. p. cm. 1983. (ISBN 0-684-18035-9). Scribner.
--Coyote Cry. Shimin, Symeon (1902-), illus. LC 74-138553. (Illus.). 39 p. 26cm. 1972. Lothrop, Lee & Shepard Co.
--The Derser Is Theirs. Parnall, Peter (1936-), illus. 1984. Scribner's.
--Desert Voices. Parnall, Peter, illus. LC 80-17061. p. cm. 1980. (ISBN 0-684-16712-3). Scribner. **Award: (ALA).**
--Everybody Needs a Rock. Parnall, Peter (1936-), illus. LC 74-9163. 32 p. col. ill. 21 x 27cm. 1974. Scribner's.
--A God on Every Mountain Top: Stories of Southwest Indian Sacred Mountains. Brown, Carol (1937-), illus. LC 80-24984. (Illus.). 64 p. 24cm. (gr. 3-7). 1981. (ISBN 0-684-16758-1). Scribner.
--Guess Who My Favorite Person Is. Parker, Robert Andrew (1927-), illus. LC 77-7151. p. cm. 1977. (ISBN 0-684-15197-9). Scribner.
--Hawk, I'm Your Brother. Parnall, Peter (1936-), illus. LC 75-39296. (Illus.). 48 p. 26cm. c.1976. (ISBN 0-684-14571-5). Scribner. **Awards: (ALA); (RCM).**
--If You Are a Hunter of Fossils. Parnall, Peter (1936-), illus. LC 79-17926. p. cm. 1979. (ISBN 0-684-16419-1). Scribner.
--Moon Song. Himler, Ronald Norbert (1937-), illus. LC 81-18427. (Illus.). 24 p. 24cm. c.1982. (ISBN 0-684-17463-4). Scribner.
--The Other Way to Listen. Parnall, Peter (1936-), illus. LC 78-23430. (Illus.). (gr. 1-4). 1978. (ISBN 0-684-16017-X, ScribJ). Scribner.
--Plink, Plink, Plink. Marshall, James (1942-), illus. LC 76-155556. (Illus.). 46 p. 23cm. 1971. (ISBN 0-395-12751-3). Houghton Mifflin.
--Sometimes I Dance Mountains. Longtemps, Kenneth, illus. Sears, Bill, photos by. LC 73-1330. (Illus.). 44 p. 27cm. 1973. Scribner.
--They Put on Masks. Ingram, Jerry, illus. LC 73-19557. (Illus.). 48p. (gr. 1-4). 1974. (ISBN 0-684-13767-4, ScribJ). Scribner.
--The Way to Start a Day. Parnall, Peter (1936-), illus. 1978. Scribner.
--We Walk in Sandy Places. Schweitzer, Marilyn, photos by. LC 75-8341. (Illus.). 40 p. c.1976. (ISBN 0-684-14526-X). Scribner.
--When Clay Sings. Bahti, Tom, illus. LC 70-180758. (Illus.). (gr. 1-5). 1972. (ISBN 0-684-12807-1, ScribJ). (ISBN 0-689-70482-8). Scribner. **Awards: (ALA); (RCM).**
--Yes Is Better Than No. LC 76-57705. 187 p. 22cm. c.1977. (ISBN 0-684-14897-8). Scribner.
--Your Own Best Secret Place. Parnall, Peter, illus. LC 78-21243. (Illus.). 32 p. 26cm. c.1979. (ISBN 0-684-16111-7). Scribner.

Baylor, Byrd (1924-), ed.
--And It Is Still That Way: Legends. LC 76-42242. p. cm. 1976. (ISBN 0-684-14676-2). Scribner.

Baylor, Edith Miriam Hedges, Mrs. (1870-)
--A Little Prospector. x, 236 p. front, 23 pl. 19 1/2 cm. c.1907. Lothrop, Lee & Shepard Co.

Baylor, Frances Courtenay
--Juan and Juanita. (Illustrated Quarto Juveniles). N.D. Houghton, Mifflin and Company.

Bayly, Ada Ellen see Lyall, Edna, pseud.

Bayly, Ada Ellen (1857-1903)
--The Burges Letters: A Record of Child Life in the Sixties. Lyall, Edna, pseud. Stacey, W. S., illus. LC 2-24719. 4 p. 1., 142 p. col. front., plates. 19 1/2 cm. 1902. Longmans, Green, and Co.
--Donovan. Lyall, Edna, pseud, 1 of 32 vols, Vol. 4. (Illus.). (Famous Books for Girls). N.D. H. M. Caldwell Co.
--How the Children Raised the Wind. Lyall, Edna, pseud. LC 12-36329. 64. 1 p. incl. front., plates. 19 1/2 cm. 1896. Fleming H. Revell Company.
--How the Children Raised the Wind. Lyall, Edna, pseud. Lathbury, Mary Artemisia (1841-1913), illus. N.D. Rand, McNally & Co's.
--In the Golden Days. Lyall, Edna, pseud. (Illus.). (The Wellesley Series for Girls). N.D. A. L. Burt's Pubs.
--In the Golden Days. Lyall, Edna, pseud. (Illus.). (Caldwell's Illustrated Library of Famous Books by Famous Authors). N.D. H. M. Caldwell Co.
--In the Golden Days. Lyall, Edna, pseud, 1 of 32 vols, Vol. 8. (Illus.). (Famous Books for Girls). N.D. H. M. Caldwell Co.
--The Knight Errant. Lyall, Edna, pseud. (Illus.). (Caldwell's Illustrated Library of Famous Books by Famous Authors). N.D. A. L. Burt' Pubs.
--The Knight Errant. Lyall, Edna, pseud, 1 of 32 vols, Vol. 13. (Illus.). (Famous Books For Girls). N.D. H. M. Caldwell Co.

Bayly, Joseph Tate (1920-)
--The Gospel Blimp & Other Stories. 1983. (ISBN 0-89191-731-4). Cook.

Bayne, Charles S.
--My Book of Best Fairy Tales. Bayne, Charles S., selected by. Rountree, Harry (1878-1950), illus. N.D. Funk & Wagnalls.

Bayne, Marie
--Fairy Tales From Far Away. (Fireside Library). N.D. Thomas Nelson & Sons.
--Old Mother Grunter. (Fireside Library). N.D. Thomas Nelson & Sons.

Baynes, Ernest Harold (1868-1925)
--Jimmie: The Story of a Black Bear Cub. N.D. MacMillan.
--Jimmy: The Story of a Black Bear Cub. Baynes, Ernest Harold (1868-1925) & Baynes, Louise Birt, illus. 1923. Macmillan.
--Polaris: The Story of an Eskimo Dog. Baynes, Ernest Harold (1868-1925) & Baynes, Louise Birt, illus. LC 22-201208. xiv p., 2 1., 137 p. incl. front., illus. plates. 21 cm. 1922. The Macmillan Company.
--The Sprite: The Story of a Red Fox. Baynes, Ernest Harold (1868-1925) & Baynes, Louise Birt, illus. LC 24-24369. xvii, p., 2 1., 134. 2 incl front., illus. plates. 21 cm. 1924. The Macmillan Company.
--War Whoop and Tomahawk: The Story of Two Buffalo Calves. (MacMillan Bks. for Boys & Girls). (gr. 7-9). N.D. MacMillan Bks.

Baynes, Pauline Diana (1922-)
--How Dog Began. LC 85-30601. p. cm. 1st U.S. edition. 1986, c.1985. Holt, Rinehart and Winston.

Baynes, Richard
--The Happy Shepherd. Karch, Pat, illus. (Illus.). 24p. (Orig.). (gr. k-3). 1979. (ISBN 0-87239-305-4). Standard Pub.
--Jesus Loves Me. Hook, Frances Arnold (1912-), illus. (Illus.). 24p. (Orig.). (gr. k-3). 1979. (ISBN 0-87239-306-2). Standard Pub.

Baynton, Martin
--The Three Little Pigs. LC 81-83719. (Illus.). 24p. (ps up). 1982. (ISBN 0-688-01028-8). Lothrop.

Baynton, Martin, illus.
--Goldilocks & the Three Bears. LC 81-83721. (Illus.). 24p. (ps up). 1982. (ISBN 0-688-01039-3). Lothrop.
--Hansel & Gretel. LC 81-83722. (Illus.). 24p. (ps up). 1982. (ISBN 0-688-01030-X). Lothrop.

Bazin, Rene (1853-1932)
--Juniper Farm: "Il Etait Quatre Petits Enfants". Bianco, Margery Williams, Mrs. (1881-1944), tr. LC 28-223122. vii, p., 1 l., 180 p. incl. illus., plates. col. front., col. plates. 19 1/2 cm. (The Macmillan children's classics). 1928. The Macmillan Company.

BB, pseud., see Watkins-Pitchford, Denys James.

Beach, Alfred see Oldfellow, Alfred, pseud.

Beach, Charles A.
--Too Good for Anything. (Incident and Adventure Library). N.D. Scribner, Welford & Armstrong.
--Waifs of the World: Adventures Afloat and Ashore. (Hopeful Enterprise Library). N.D. Scribner, Welford & Armstrong.
--The Way to Win. (Incident and Adventure Library). N.D. Scribner, Welford & Armstrong.

Beach, Charles Amory, pseud., see Stratemeyer Syndicate.

Beach, Charles Amory, pseud.
--Air Service Boys Flying for France: Or, The Young Heroes of the Lafayette Escadrille. Stratemeyer Syndicate. Repr. of 1918 ed (Pub. by George Sully & Co). (Air Service Boys Ser.: No. 1). N.D. Goldsmith Publishing Co.
--Air Service Boys Flying for France: Or, The Young Heroes of the Lafayette Escadrille. Stratemeyer Syndicate. Repr. of 1918 ed (Pub. by George Sully & Co). (Air Service Boys Ser.: No. 1). N.D. Saalfield Publishing Co.
--Air Service Boys Flying for France: Or, The Young Heroes of the Lafayette Escadrille. Stratemeyer Syndicate. Herbert, Robert Gaston, illus. LC 18-10273. iv, 218 p. front. 19 1/2 cm. (Air Service Boys Ser.: No. 1). 1918. George Sully & Co.
--Air Service Boys Flying for France: Or, The Young Heroes of the Lafayette Escadrille. Stratemeyer Syndicate. Herbert, Robert Gaston, illus. Repr. of 1918 ed (Pub. by George Sully & Co). (Air Service Boys Ser.: No. 1). N.D. World Syndicate Publishing Co.
--Air Service Boys Flying for Victory: Or, Bombing the Last German Stronghold. Stratemeyer Syndicate. Repr. of 1919 ed (Pub. by George Sully & Co). (Air Service Boys Ser.: No. 5). N.D. Goldsmith Publishing Co.
--Air Service Boys Flying for Victory: Or, Bombing the Last German Stronghold. Stratemeyer Syndicate. Rogers, Walter S., illus. (Air Service Boys Ser.: No. 5). 1919. George Sully & Co.
--Air Service Boys Flying for Victory: Or, Bombing the Last German Stronghold. Stratemeyer Syndicate. Rogers, Walter S., illus. Repr. of 1919 ed (Pub. by George Sully & Co). (Air Service Boys Ser.: No. 5). N.D. World Syndicate Publishing Co.
--Air Service Boys in the Big Battle: Or, Silencing the Big Guns. Stratemeyer Syndicate. Repr. of 1919 ed (Pub. by George Sully & Co). (Air Service Boys Ser.: No. 4). N.D. Saalfield Publishing Co.
--Air Service Boys in the Big Battle: Or, Silencing the Big Guns. Stratemeyer Syndicate. Angell, Clare, illus. (Air Service Boys Ser.: No. 4). 1919. George Sully & Co.
--Air Service Boys in the Big Battle: Or, Silencing the Big Guns. Stratemeyer Syndicate. Angell, Clare, illus. Repr. of 1919 ed (Pub. by George Sully & Co). (Air Service Boys Ser.: No. 4). N.D. World Syndicate Publishing Co.
--Air Service Boys Over the Atlantic: Or, The Longest Flight on Record. Stratemeyer Syndicate. Repr. of 1920 ed (Pub. by George Sully & Co). (Air Service Boys Ser.: No. 6). N.D. Goldsmith Publishing Co.
--Air Service Boys Over the Atlantic: Or, The Longest Flight on Record. Stratemeyer Syndicate. Repr. of 1920 ed (Pub. by George Sully Co). (Air Service Boys Ser.: No. 6). N.D. Saalfield Publishing Co.
--Air Service Boys Over the Atlantic: Or, The Longest Flight on Record. Stratemeyer Syndicate. Cress, illus. (Air Service Boys Ser.: No. 6). 1918. George Sully & Co.
--Air Service Boys Over the Atlantic: Or, The Longest Flight on Record. Stratemeyer Syndicate. Cress, illus. Repr. of 1920 ed (Pub. by George Sully & Co). (Air Service Boys Ser.: No. 6). N.D. World Syndicate Publishing Co.
--Air Service Boys Over the Enemy's Lines: Or, The German Spy's Secret. Stratemeyer Syndicate. Herbert, Robert Gaston, illus. (Air Service Boys Ser.: No. 2). 1918. George Sully & Co.
--Air Service Boys Over the Enemy's Lines: Or, The German Spy's Secret. Stratemeyer Syndicate. Herbert, Robert Gaston, illus. Repr. of 1918 ed (Pub. by George Sully & Co). (Air Service Boys Ser.: No. 2). N.D. World Syndicate Publishing Co.
--Air Service Boys Over the Rhine: Or, Fighting Above the Clouds. Stratemeyer Syndicate. Repr. of 1918 ed (Pub. by George Sully & Co). (Air Service Boys Ser.: No. 3). N.D. Goldsmith Publishing Co.
--Air Service Boys Over the Rhine: Or, Fighting Above the Clouds. Stratemeyer Syndicate. Herbert, Robert Gaston, illus. LC 19-9537. iv, 218 p. front. 19 1/2 cm. (Air Service Boys Ser.: No. 3). 1918. George Sully & Co.
--Air Service Boys Over the Rhine: Or, Fighting Above the Clouds. Stratemeyer Syndicate. Herbert, Robert Gaston, illus. Repr. of 1918 ed (Pub. by George Sully & Co). (Air Service Boys Ser.: No. 3). N.D. World Syndicate Publishing Co.

Beach, Edward Latimer (1918-)
--An Annapolis First Classman. Merrill, Frank Thayer (1848-), illus. LC 10-10699. 367 p. front., plates. 19 1/2 cm. 1910. The Penn Publishing Company.
--An Annapolis First Classman. Merrill, Frank Thayer (1848-), illus. LC 38-6985. 367 p. front. 19 cm. c.1938. The Penn Publishing Company.
--An Annapolis Plebe. Merrill, Frank Thayer (1848-), illus. LC 7-32841. 435 p. front., 6 pl. 19 1/2 cm. (Annapolis Ser.). 1907. The Penn Publishing Company.
--An Annapolis Plebe. Merrill, Frank Thayer (1848-), illus. LC 35-286767. 435, 1 p. front., plates. 19 cm. 1929. The Penn Publishing Company.
--An Annapolis Second Classman. Merrill, Frank Thayer (1848-), illus. LC 38-12748. 380, 1 p. front., plates. 19 cm. 1929. The Penn Publishing Company.
--An Annapolis Youngster. Merrill, Frank Thayer (1848-), illus. LC 8-16468. 386 p. front., 6 pl. 19 1/2 cm. 1908. The Penn Publishing Company.
--An Annapolis Youngster. Merrill, Frank Thayer (1848-), illus. LC 36-106831. 4, 7-386 p. front. 19 cm. 1936. The Penn Publishing Company.
--Dan Quin of the Navy. LC 22-21108. viii, 383 p. front. 19 1/2 cm. 1922. The Macmillan Company.
--Ensign Ralph Osborn: The Story of His Trials and Triumps in a Battleship's Engine Room. Merrill, Frank Thayer (1848-), illus. LC 11-296651. 338 p. front., plates. 20 cm. c.1911. W. A. Wilde Company.
--Lieutenant Ralph Osborn Aboard a Torpedo Boat Destroyer: Being the Story of How Ralph Osborn Became a Lieutenant and of His Cruises in an American Torpedo Boat Destroyer in West Indian Waters. Merrill, Frank Thayer (1848-), illus. LC 12-21319. 342 p. front., plates. 20 cm. c.1912. W. A. Wilde Company.
--Midshipman Ralph Osborn at Sea: A Story of the U.S. Navy. Merrill, Frank Thayer (1848-), illus. LC 10-38166. 20cm. 330p. N.D. W. A. Wilde.
--Ralph Osborn--Midshipman at Annapolis: A Story of Life at the U.S. Naval Academy. Merrill, Frank Thayer (1848-), illus. LC 9-25972. 366 p. front., 4 pl. 20 cm. c.1909. W. A. Wilde Company.
--Ralph Osborn--Midshipman at Annapolis. LC 2-25972. 20cm. 366p. N.D. W. A. Wilde.
--Roger Paulding: Apprentice Seaman. Merrill, Frank Thayer (1848-), illus. LC 11-22021. 355 p. front., plates. 20 cm. 1911. The Penn Publishing Company.
--Roger Paulding, Ensign. Merrill, Frank Thayer (1848-), illus. LC 14-6282. (The Roger Paulding Ser.). 1914. Penn Publishing Co.
--Roger Paulding, Gunner. Merrill, Frank Thayer (1848-), illus. LC 13-15264. 351 p. col. front., illus., plates. 20 cm. (Roger Paulding Stories). 1913. The Penn Publishing Company.
--Roger Paulding, Gunner's Mate. Merrill, Frank Thayer (1848-), illus. LC 12-141151. 349 p. front., plates. 20 cm. 1912. The Penn Publishing Company.
--Run Silent, Run Deep. (gr. 9 up). 1955. (ISBN 0-03-026645-9). HR&W.

Beach, Lewis (1891-)
--A Square Peg: A Play in Three Acts. 1924. Little, Brown & Co.

Beach, Mary & York, Carol Beach (1928-)
--One Summer. Meryman, Hope, illus. LC 63-10168. 125 p. illus. 30 cm. 1963. Coward-McCann.

Beach, Milo Cleveland, adapted by.
--The Adventures of Rama. (Illus.). 64p. (Orig.). 1983. (ISBN 0-934686-51-3). Freer.
--The Adventures of Rama. (Illus.). (gr. 4-6). 1983. Smithsonian Institution.

Beach, Ransford
--Ginger Snaps. Dannenbaum, Marta, contrib. by. LC 56-11549. 47p. illus. 24cm. 1956. Dorrance.
--Playmates in America. Hartman, Elsa Alison, illus. LC 26-8958. x, 141 p. illus 26 cm. c.1926. H. Holt and Company.

Beach, Rex Ellingwood (1877-)
--The Goose Woman and Other Stories. N.D. A L Burt Co.

Beach, Stewart Taft (1899-1979)
--Good Morning, Sun's up!. Sugita, Yutaka (1930-), illus. LC 79-108178. (Illus.). 27 p. 26cm. 1970. Scroll Press.
--Racing Start. N.D. Little, Brown & Co.

Beach, Sunny
--Stan Goes on Safari. 1981. (ISBN 0-533-04641-6). Vantage.

Beachcroft, Nina (1931-)
--Well Met by Witchlight. LC 73-75430. 137 p. 22cm. 1973, c.1972. (ISBN 0-689-30414-5). Atheneum.
--The Wishing People. LC 81-15289. 183 p. 22cm. 1982, c.1980. (ISBN 0-525-45112-9). E.P. Dutton.

Beachy, J. Wayne
--A Bird of Peace is Born in Petersburg. Hawkins, Beverly, illus. (Illus., Orig.). (gr. 5). 1981. (ISBN 0-9608084-0-X). B Hawkins Studio.
--The Extraordinary Ordinary Christmas Matoaca, 1870. Hawkins, Beverly, illus. (Illus.). 20p. (Orig.). (gr. 5). 1984. (ISBN 0-9608084-2-6). B Hawkins Studio.
--The Ghost of Rat Castle: A Story of Old Petersburg. Hawkins, Beverly, illus. (Illus.). 24p. (gr. 5). 1983. (ISBN 0-9608084-1-8). B Hawkins Studio.

Beadle, Jeremy, jt. auth. see Winn, Chris.

Beagle, Peter Soyer, jt. auth. see Derby, Pat.

Beagle, Rebecca S., tr. see Soyer, Abraham.

Beais, Frank L., ed.
--Moby Dick. (Illus.). 184p. (Famous Story Ser.). N.D. (ISBN 0-8111-0245-9). The Naylor Company.

Beal, Mary Barnes
--The Boys of Clovernook: The Story of Five Boys on a Farm. Barry, Etheldred Breeze (1870-), illus. N.D. Lothrop Lee & Shepard Co.

Bealby, John Thomas (1858-), tr. see Hoffmann, Ernst Theodor Amadeus.

Beale, Anne
--Glady's the Reaper. (Illus.). (The Girl's Own Favorite Ser.). N.D. E. P. Dutton & Co.
--The Heiress of Courtleroy. (Scribner-Blackie Series of books for young people). N.D. Charles Scribner's Sons.
--Simplicity and Fascination. (Illus.). (The Girls' Own Favorite Ser.). N.D. E. P. Dutton & Co.

Beale, Harriet Stanwood Blaine, Mrs.
--Stories from the Old Testament for Children. Shrader, Roscoe E. & Moore, Herbert, illus. (Illus.). 1907. Duffield & Co.
Beale, John, pseud., see Kalbaugh, Osborne Beale.
Beale, Will
--Binky. Bobri, V., pseud. (1898-), illus. Bobritsky, Vladimir V.. LC 53-6753. 125p. illus. 24cm. 1954. Lothrop, Lee & Shepard.
--Seapiece: The Story of a Maine Boy. Handlen, Frank, illus. LC 66-197745. xi, 147p. illus. 22cm. 1966. Wheelwright.
Bealer, Alex Winkler (1921-1980)
--Only The Names Remain: The Cherokees and The Trail of Tears. 1972. Little Brown and Company.
--The Picture-skin story. N.D. E. M. Hale and Co.
--The Picture-Skin Story. Bealer, Alex Winkler (1921-1980), illus. LC 57-1452. unpaged. illus. 21cm. 1957. Holiday House.
Beales, K. H., tr. see Anckarsvard, Karin Inez Maria.
Beall, Pamela
--Wee Sing Campfire Songs. Nipp, Susan, illus. (Illus.). 64p. (Orig.). 1982. (ISBN 0-8431-0311-6). Price Stern.
--Wee Sing Silly Songs. Nipp, Susan, illus. (Illus.). 64p. (Orig.). 1982. (ISBN 0-8431-0310-8). Price Stern.
--Wee Sing Silly Songs Book & Cassette. Nipp, Susan, illus. (Wee Sing Ser.). (ps-6). 1983. (ISBN 0-8431-0741-3). Price Stern.
Beall, Pamela & Nipp, Susan
--Wee Sing. 1982. (ISBN 0-8431-0676-X). Price Stern.
--Wee Sing & Play. (Illus.). 64p. (Orig.). 1981. (ISBN 0-8431-0391-4). Price Stern.
--Wee Sing & Play Book & Cassette. (Wee Sing Ser.). (ps-6). 1983. (ISBN 0-8431-0743-X). Price Stern.
--Wee Sing Around the Campfire Book & Cassette. (Wee Sing Ser.). (ps-6). 1983. (ISBN 0-8431-0742-1). Price Stern.
Beals, Carleton (1893-1973)
--Adventure of the Western Sea. Landau, Jacob (1917-), illus. 1956. Holt, Rinehart and Winston.
Beals, Carleton (1893-1979)
--Stories Told by the Aztecs Before the Spaniards Came. Pickard, Charles, illus. LC 77-95140. (Illus.). drawings. bibl. index. 224p. (gr. 7 up). 1970. (ISBN 0-200-71636-0, AbS-J). Har-Row.
Beals, Frank Lee
--The Prince & the Pauper. (Illus.). (Famous Story Ser.). N.D. Naylor.
Beals, Frank Lee (1881-1972), adapted by see Dana, Richard Henry.
Beals, Frank Lee (1881-1972), ed. see Dana, Richard Henry, Jr.
Beals, Frank Lee (1881-1972), adapted by see Dumas, Alexandre.
Beals, Frank Lee (1881-1972), adapted by see Melville, Herman.
Beals, Frank Lee (1881-1872), adapted by.
--The Story of Robinson Crusoe. King, E. E., illus. LC 46-5653. 21cm. 86p. (Famous Story Ser.). 1946. B. H. Sanborn & Co.
Beals, Frank Lee (1881-1972)
--Chief Black Hawk. rev. ed. Merryweather, Jack, illus. LC 60-1634. (Illus.). 252 p. 20cm. (American adventure series). 1960. Wheeler Pub. Co.
--Famous Story Series. N.D. Naylor Company.
--The Rush for Gold. Merryweather, Jack, illus. LC 47-15512. 19cm. 252p. (The American Adventure Ser.). 1946. Wheeler Publishing Co.
Beals, Frank Lee (1881-1972), retold by.
--Deerslayer. LC 65-23685. ix, 150p. illus. 22cm. (Famour story ser.). c.1965. Naylor.
--Lemuel Gulliver in Lilliput Land. Beals, Frank Lee, retold by. (Illus.). (Famous Story Ser.). N.D. Naylor.
--Moby Dick. N.D. Naylor Company.
--Robinson Crusoe. LC 65-23686. ix. 86 p. illus. 22 cm. (Famous story series). 1965. Naylor.
--Robinson Crusoe. LC 65-23686. ix, 86p. illus. 22cm. (Famous story ser.). N.D. Tex.
--The Story of Lemuel Gulliver in Lilliput Land. King, E. E., illus. LC 46-6295. 21x16cm. 102p. (Famous Story Ser.). 1946. B. H. Sanborn & Co.
--The Story of the Prince and the Pauper. King, E. E., illus. LC 53-3897. 152p. illus. 21cm. (Famous story Ser.). 1953. B. H. Sanborn.
--Treasure Island. LC 65-23690. (Original Author: Robert Louis Stevenson, 1850-1894). 108 p. illus. 22 cm. (Famous story series). 1965. Naylor Co.
Beals, Frank Lee (1881-1872) & Bailey, Bernadine, eds.
--The Story of the Treasure Island. King, E. E., illus. LC 47-24778. 21cm. 108p. (A Famous Story Ser.). 1947. B. H. Sanborn.
Beals, Katherine McMillan, Mrs.
--Flower Lore & Legend. 1917. Henry Holt.
Beaman, Joyce Proctor (1931-)
--All for the Love of Cassie. LC 73-86471. 102 p. 23cm. c.1973. (ISBN 0-87716-046-5). Moore Pub. Co.
--Broken Acres. Goslen, Mary, illus. LC 72-156457. (Illus.). 145 p. 21cm. 1971. (ISBN 0-910244-60-X). J. F. Blair.
Beaman, S. G. Hulme, retold by.
--The Seven Voyages of Sinbad the Sailor. Beaman, S. G. Hulme, illus. LC 27-6239. ix. p., 1 l., 71 p. incl. col. front., illus. col. plates. 25 1/2 cm. 1926. R.M. McBride and Company.
Beaman, Sallie Louise, tr. see Robitaillie, Henriette.
Beame, Rona (1934-)
--Calling Car Twenty-Four Frank: A Day with the Police. LC 70-180530. (Illus.). b&w photos. 64p. 64p. (gr. 3-6). 1972. (ISBN 0-671-32507-8). Messner.
Beamer, Charles
--Joshua Wiggins & the King's Kids. Dyrud, Chris W., illus. LC 81-10162. 143p. (Orig.). (gr. 2-7). 1981. (ISBN 0-87123-268-5). Bethany Hse.
--Lightning in the Bottle. Francis, Philip, pseud. (1927-) & Beach, Bettye, illus. Lockyer, Roger. LC 81-1690. (Illus.). 317 p. 21cm. (The Legends of Eorthe: Bk. 2). c.1981. (ISBN 0-8407-5233-4). T. Nelson Publishers.
--Magician's Bane. Pallarito, Don, illus. LC 79-28151. (Illus.). 203 p. 22cm. (The Legends of Eorthe: Bk. 1). c.1980. T. Nelson Publishers.
Beamer, Nona
--Talking Story with Nona Beamer. LC 83-70357. (Illus.). 128p. (gr. 6-9). 1983. (ISBN 0-935848-20-7). Bess Pr.
Bean, F
--Pudney and Walp. (Warldorf Series). N.D. Merriam Co.
Bear, Carolyn D.
--Digby: The Biggest Dog in the World. Hills, Gillian, illus. LC 74-9678. (Illus.). (gr. 5 up). 1974. (ISBN 0-200-00145-0, AbS-J). Har-Row.
Bear, Constance De see Burger, Isabel & DeBear, Constance.
Beard, Adelia Belle, jt. auth. see Beard, Lina.
Beard, Alice
--The Magic String Book: Being the Thrilling Adventures of the Stringum Family with the String on Which the Thrills Are Strung. Beard, Alice, illus. LC 83-461541. (Illus.). 78 p. 26cm. c.1916. F.A. Stokes.
--Mother Goose Movies. N.D. Frederick A. Stokes.
Beard, Alice, jt. auth. see Rogers, Frances.
Beard, Daniel Carter (1859-1941)
--The American Boys' Book of Birds and Brownies of the Woods. Beard, Daniel Carter (1859-1941), illus. xi p., 3 l., 3 242 p. front., illus. 21 cm. (Woodcraft series). 1923. J. B. Lippincott Company.
--The Black Wolf Pack. LC 22-20347. viii p., 1 l., 220 p. front., plates. 19 1/2 cm. 1922. C. Scribner's Sons.
--Dan Beard's Animal Book, and Camp-fire Stories. Beard, Daniel Carter (1859-1941), illus. (Illus.). 1907. Moffat, Yard & Co.
Beard, Frederica
--Wonder Stories from the Gospels. 80p. 1903. Winona Publishing Co.
Beard, Isobel R.
--Puzzles & Riddles. (Activity Fun Bks). (ps-3). N.D. (ISBN 0-695-90643-7, Dist. by Caroline Hse). Follett.
Beard, James Carter (1837-)
--Billy Possum. Barnes, Culmer, illus. LC 9-28043. 7 p. l., 81 p. incl. illus., 12 pl. col. front., xi col. pl. 24 1/2 cm. $1.00. 1909. F. A. Stokes Company.
Beard, Lina & Beard, Adelia Belle (1857-1920)
--Mother Nature's Toy Shop. Beard, Lina (0000-1933) & Beard, Adelia Belle (1857-1920), illus. 1918. Charles Scribner's Sons.
--On the Trail. Beard, Lina (0000-1933) & Beard, Adelia Belle (1857-1920), illus. 1915. Charles Scribner's Sons.
Beard, Patten
--Acting Plays for Boys and Girls. LC 28-936. 114 p. incl. front. 19 cm. (Educational play-book series). c.1927. Beckley-Cardy Company.
--Billy Cory: Adventurer. Young, Eleanor Mussey, illus. LC 36-29598. 196 p. incl. col. front., illus. 22 1/2 cm. 1936. A. Whitman & Co.
--The Bluebird's Garden. LC 16-2602. 7 p. l., 3-164 p. col. front., illus., col. pl. 20 1/2 cm. c.1915. The Pilgrim Press.
--The Jolly Year. Hull, Arthur Gibson, illus. LC 16-24922. 7 p. l., 3-159 p. col. front., illus., col. pl. 20 1/2 cm. c.1916. The Pilgrim Press.
--Marjorie's Literary Dolls. Beard, Patten, illus. LC 17-7815. 5 p. l., 114 p., 1 l. front., illus. 26 1/2 cm. c.1916. Frederick A. Stokes Company.
--Marjorie's Little Doll School. LC 17-29138. x p., 1 l., 13-208 p. front., plates. 23 1/2 cm. c.1917. George H. Doran Company.
--The Pantalette Doll. Hubbard, Eleanore Mineah, illus. LC 31-21184. (Illus.). 160p. Repr. of 1931 ed. (Pub. by A Whitman & Co.). 1981. Doll Works.
--The Pantalette Doll from the Metropolitan Museum. Hubbard, Eleanore Mineah, illus. LC 81-21184. 160 p. col. front., illus., col. plates. 23 1/2 cm. c.1931. A Whitman & Co.
--Pillow-Time Tales. Eger, Ruth Caroline, illus. LC 27-21121. 96 p. illus. (part col.) 24 cm. c.1927. Rand, McNally & Company.
--The Surprise Book. Beard, Alice, illus. LC 18-19302. xiii, 210 p. col. front., 1 illus. 19 1/2 cm. c.1918. The Pilgrim Press.
--Tucked In Tales. Biers, Clarence, illus. N.D. Rand McNally.
--Twilight Tales. Eger, Ruth Caroline, illus. LC 29-25603. 96 p. illus. (part col.) 23 1/2 cm. c.1929. Rand, McNally & Company.
--What Happened After. Higgins, Violet Moore, illus. (Young Heart Bks.). N.D. A. Whitman & Co.
Beard, Patten, ed. see Mother Goose.
Bearden, Donna
--Monica the Computer Mouse. Foster, Brad W., illus. (Illus.). 64p. (gr. k-3). 1984. (ISBN 0-89588-214-0). SYBEX.
Beardmore, George (1908-1978)
--The Treasure of Spanish Bay. LC 76-41181. p. cm. 1976, c.1975. (ISBN 0-8407-6510-X). T. Nelson.
Beardsley, Alice
--The Turn Around Book. LC 16-6074. 3p. l. 26pl. 221/2cm. 1914. Bobbs-Merrill Co.
Beardsley, Samuel B.
--The First Night of Christmas. Jarvis, Margaret, illus. LC 67-29315. (Illus.). 1 v. (unpaged. 19cm. 1968. C. R. Gibson Co.
--Night Before Christmas, And Annie and Willie's Prayer. (Illus.). N.D. E. P. Dutton & Company.
Beardwoman, Helen, ed. see Budapest, Zsuzsanna.
Beare, Cornelia, ed. see Lorenzini, Carlo.
Bearman, Jane Ruth (1917-)
--David. Bearman, Jane Ruth (1917-), illus. LC 65-21753. (Illus.). (gr. 3 up). 1965. (ISBN 0-8246-0085-1). Jonathan David.
--Good Shabos. (Illus.). (gr. k-2). 1950. UAHC.
--Shalom!. Bearman, Jane Ruth (1917-), illus. LC 58-42605. 49p. 1958. Jonathan David Co.
--Shovuos Time. (Illus.). (gr. k-2). 1947. UAHC.
Bearne, Catherine, Mrs.
--The Cross of Pearls. N.D. Macmillan.
--In Perilous Days: A Tale of the French Revolution. N.D. Macmillan.
Bearne, David
--Charlie Chittywick. LC 6-32674. 205 p. 19 1/2 cm. 1906. Cincinnati Etc. Benziger Brothers.
--The Guild Boys at Ridingdale. N.D. Benziger Brothers.
--Jack South, and Some Other Jacks. LC 9-4964. 2 p. l., 266 p. 20 1/2 cm. 1909. B. Herder.
--Melor of the Silver Hand, and other Stories of the Bright Ages. LC 7-27161. 176 p. 19 1/2 cm. 1907. Benziger Brothers.
--New Boys at Ridingdale. N.D. Benziger Brothers.
--Our Lady's Lutenist, and other Stories of the Bright Ages. 1910. Benziger Brothers.
--Ridingdale Flower Show. Baines, T., illus. 183 p. illus. 20 1/2 cm. 1907. Benziger Brothers.
--The Romance of the Silver Shoon: A Story of the Sixteenth Century. LC 9-30117. 195 p. 19 1/2 cm. 1909. Benziger Brothers.
--Sheer Pluck. 179p. 1908. Benziger Brothers.
--The Witch of Ridingdale. Baines, T., illus. 195 p. illus. 20 1/2 cm. 1907. Benziger Brothers.
Beaton-Jones, Cynon (1921-)
--Adventures of So Hi. Ward, John (1917-), illus. (Illus.). (gr. 1-3). 1955. (ISBN 0-8149-0270-7). Vanguard.
--The Adventures of So Hi. Ward, John (1917-), illus. LC 56-78892. 178p. illus. 22cm. 1956. Vanguard Press.
--So Hi and the White Horse. Ward, John (1917-), illus. LC 57-12260. 120p. illus. 22cm. N.D. (ISBN 0-8149-0271-5). Vanguard Press.
Beattie, Ann (1947-), pref. by see Aldrich, Thomas Bailey.
Beattie, Ann (1947-)
--Spectacles. Pels, Winslow (1947-), illus. LC 85-15088. p. cm. (Goblin Tales). 1985. (ISBN 0-89480-926-1). Ariel Books : Workman.
Beattie, Frank, Jr.
--Hey! That's My Donkey. (Orig.). 1981. (ISBN 0-937172-16-2). JLJ Pubs.
--In the Dark of Night. (Orig.). 1981. (ISBN 0-937172-18-9). JLJ Pubs.
Beattie, Janet
--Good for Scuffles. Kirmse, Marguerite (1885-1954), illus. N.D. Houghton Mifflin Co.
--Good for Scuffles!. Kirmse, Marguerite (1885-1954), illus. LC 44-47008. (Illus.). 26cm. 41p. 1944. Howell, Soskin.
--In Came Horace. Jauss, Anne Marie (1907-), illus. LC 54-5590. (Illus.). 32 p. 1954. Lippincott.
--The Little Woman Who Forgot Everything. Ware, Kay & Sutherland, Lucille, eds. Rapp, Rita, illus. LC 61-66452. unpaged. illus. 23cm. (Read for fun series). c.1961. Webster Pub. Co.
--Mr. Bunny. N.D. Houghton Mifflin Co.
--Mr. Bunny. Hopkins, Hildegarde L., illus. LC 44-3446. (Illus.). 26cm. 40p. 1944. Howell, Soskin.
--Never Mixed up Again. Edmunds, Filby, illus. LC 56-5707. 61p. illus. 24cm. 1956. Lippincott.
--Poof Poof. Borja, Robert (1923-), illus. Borja, Robert, designed by. LC 62-11074. unpaged. illus. 25cm. 1962. A. Whitman.
Beattie, Sara Smith
--School on a Raft. Laite, Gordon (1925-), illus. LC 73-123880. (Illus.). 45 p. 23cm. (Magic circle book. Reading 360). 1971. Ginn.
Beatty, Hetty Burlingame (1907-1971)
--Blitz. (Illus.). (gr. 4-6). 1961. (ISBN 0-8382-0099-0). Hale.
--Blitz. Tolford, Joshua (1909-), illus. (Illus.). 144p. (gr. 3-6). 1974. (ISBN 0-395-18565-3, Sandpiper). HM.
--Blitz. Tolford, Joshua (1909-), illus. LC 61-5134. 118p. illus. 22cm. 1961. (ISBN 0-395-06615-8). Houghton Mifflin
--Bronto. Beatty, Hetty Burlingame (1907-1971), illus. LC 52-9862. (Illus.). 136 p. 21cm. 1952. Doubleday.
--Bryn. LC 65-22506. (Illus.). 250 p. 21cm. 1965. Houghton Mifflin.
--Bucking Horse. LC 57-7199. (Illus.). 37 p. 26cm. 1957. Houghton Mifflin.
--Droopy. N.D. E. M. Hale & Co.
--Droopy. LC 53-10991. (Illus.). 26 p. 26cm. 1954. Houghton Mifflin.
--The Little Owl Indian. 1951. (ISBN 0-8382-0464-3, Cadmus Books). E. M. Hale And Company.
--Little Owl Indian. Beatty, Hetty Burlingame (1907-1971), illus. LC 51-1376. (Illus.). 32 p. 26cm. c.1951. Houghton Mifflin.
--Little Wild Horse. Beatty, Hetty Burlingame (1907-1971), illus. LC 49-7540. 31 p. col. illus. 27 cm. 1949. Houghton Mifflin Co.
--Moorland Pony. Beatty, Hetty Burlingame (1907-1971), illus. LC 61-10625. (Illus.). 40 p. 26cm. 1961. Houghton Mifflin.
--Rebel, the Reluctant Racehorse. LC 68-28053. (Illus.). 30 p. 26cm. 1968. Houghton Mifflin.
--Saint Francis and the Wolf. (Illus.). 1953. Houghton Mifflin.
--Thumps. LC 55-8219. 26cm. 29p. 1955. Houghton Mifflin Co.
--Topsy. N.D. Houghton Mifflin Co.
--Trumper. Tolford, Joshua (1909-), illus. LC 63-15274. (Illus.). 165 p. 22cm. 1963. Houghton Mifflin.
--Voyage of the Sea Wind. (Illus.). 37 p. 26cm. 1959. Houghton Mifflin.
Beatty, Jane
--Davey's adventures with the Clyde Beatty Circus. Pinchot, Ann, ed. 160p. 1965. Abelard-Schumann.
Beatty, Jerome, Jr. (1918-)
--Blockade. Verrier, Suzanne, illus. LC 79-157575. (Illus.). 12 halftones. 128p. (gr. 5). 1971. (ISBN 0-385-06507-8). (ISBN 0-385-02490-8). Doubleday.
--Bob Fulton's Amazing Soda-Pop Stretcher: An International Spy Story. Wilson, Gahan (1930-), illus. (Illus.). 239 p. 23cm. (Young Scott books). 1963. W. R. Scott.
--Bob Fulton's Amazing Soda-Pop Stretcher. Wilson, Gahan (1930-), illus. 240p. (gr. 4-9). 1963. (ISBN 0-201-09125-9, A-W Childrens). A-W.
--From New Bedford to Siberia: A Yankee Whaleman in the Frozen North. 1st ed. Keith, Eros, illus. LC 76-23748. (Illus.). xii, 143 p. 22cm. c.1977. (ISBN 0-385-03206-4). (ISBN 0-385-03207-2). Doubleday.
--Matthew Looney and the Space Pirates. Wilson, Gahan (1930-), illus. LC 73-179371. (Illus.). 158 p. 23cm. 1972. (ISBN 0-201-09282-4). Young Scott Books.
--Matthew Looney and the Space Pirates: A Space Story. Wilson, Gahan (1930-), illus. LC 84-40767. p. cm. 1985, c.1972. (ISBN 0-201-09282-4). Lippincott.
--Matthew Looney in the Outback. Wilson, Gahan (1930-), illus. (Illus.). 224p. (gr. 4-8). 1969. (ISBN 0-201-09275-1, Young Scott Bks). A-W.
--Matthew Looney in the Outback: A Space Story. Wilson, Gahan (1930-), illus. LC 69-14567. (Illus.). 223 p. 23cm. 1969. W. R. Scott.
--Matthew Looney's Invasion of the Earth: A Space Story. Wilson, Gahan (1930-), illus. LC 84-40768. p. cm. (Young Scott Books). 1985, c.1965. (ISBN 0-201-09273-5). J.B. Lippincott.
--Matthew Looney's Invasion of the Earth: A Space Story. Wilson, Gahan (1930-), illus. LC 65-12582. (Illus.). 155 p. 23cm. 1965. W. R. Scott.

--Matthew Looney's Invasion of the Earth. LC 65-12582. (Illus.). 160p. (gr. 3-8). 1965. (ISBN 0-201-09273-5, A-W Childrens). A-W.
--Matthew Looney's Voyage to the Earth. (Illus.). 144p. (gr. 3-8). 1961. (ISBN 0-201-09279-4, A-W Childrens). A-W.
--Matthew Looney's Voyage to the Earth. Wilson, Gahan (1930-), illus. (Illus.). (Cadmus Bks). (gr. 3-5). 1961. (ISBN 0-8382-0509-7). Hale.
--Matthew Looney's Voyage to the Earth: A Space Story. Wilson, Gahan (1930-), illus. (Illus.). 131 p. 23cm. (Young Scott books). 1961. W. R. Scott.
--Sheriff Stonehead and the Teen-Age Termites. Holtan, Gene, illus. LC 72-106052. (Illus.). 220 p. 21cm. 1970. Young Scott Books.
--Sheriff Stonehead And The Teenage Termites. 244p. 1970. (ISBN 0-201-09345-6). Addison Wesley Publishing.

Beatty, John Louis (1922-1975)
--Pirate Royal. LC 69-16209. (Illus.). 209 p. 21cm. 1969. Macmillan.

Beatty, John Louis (1922-1975) & Beatty, Patricia Robbins (1922-)
--At the Seven Stars. LC 62-17330. (Illus.). 273 p. 22cm. 1963. Macmillan.
--At the Seven Stars. 1967. MacMillan Publishing company.
--Campion Towers. LC 65-13594. 293p. 22cm. c.1965. Macmillan.
--A Donkey for the King. Siberell, Anne, illus. LC 66-18200. (Illus.). (gr. 4-6). 1966. (ISBN 0-02-708560-0). (ISBN 0-02-708570-8). Macmillan.
--Holdfast. LC 75-187902. bibl. 224p. (gr. 7-9). 1972. (ISBN 0-688-31434-1). Morrow.
--King's Knight's Pawn. LC 78-155988. 224 p. 23cm. 1971. Morrow.
--King's Knight's Pawn. 1975. (ISBN 0-688-31432-5). William Morrow and Company.
--Master Rosalind. LC 74-5050. 221 p. 22cm. 1974. (ISBN 0-688-21819-9). (ISBN 0-688-21819-9). Morrow.
--The Queen's Wizard. LC 67-17206. 246 p. 21cm. 1967. Macmillan.
--The Royal Dirk. Altschuler, Franz (1923-), illus. LC 66-11233. 22cm. 256p. (gr. 7 up). 1966. (ISBN 0-688-21431-2). Morrow.
--Who Comes to King's Mountain?. LC 75-11997. 287 p. 22cm. 1975. (ISBN 0-688-22041-X). (ISBN 0-688-32041-4). Morrow.
--Witch Dog. Altschuler, Franz (1923-), illus. (Illus.). 254 p. 22cm. 1968. Morrow.

Beatty, Patricia Robbins, jt. auth. see Beatty, John Louis.

Beatty, Patricia Robbins (1922-)
--The Bad Bell of San Salvador. LC 73-4921. (Illus.). 253 p. 22cm. 1973. Morrow.
--Billy Bedamned, Long Gone by. LC 76-55386. 223 p. 22cm. 1977. (ISBN 0-688-22101-7). Morrow.
--Blue Stars Watching. LC 76-82649. 191 p. 22cm. 1969. W. Morrow.
--Bonanza Girl. Dauber, Elizabeth, illus. LC 62-7736. (Illus.). 224 p. 22cm. 1962. Morrow.
--By Crumbs, It's Mine!. Eutemey, Loring, contrib. by. LC 75-31574. (Illus.). 254 p. 22cm. 1976. (ISBN 0-688-22062-2). (ISBN 0-688-32062-7). Morrow.
--The Coach That Never Came. LC 85-15213. 164 p. 22cm. c.1985. (ISBN 0-688-05477-3). Morrow.
--Eight Mules from Monterey. LC 81-22284. p. cm. 1982. (ISBN 0-688-01047-4). Morrow.
--Hail Columbia. Dauber, Elizabeth, illus. LC 72-105319. (Illus.). 251 p. 22cm. 1970. Morrow.
--How Many Miles to Sundown. Quackenbush, Robert Mead (1929-), illus. LC 73-14583. (Illus.). 222 p. 22cm. 1974. Morrow.
--I Want My Sunday, Stranger!. LC 77-23789. 254 p. 22cm. 1977. (ISBN 0-688-22118-1). (ISBN 0-688-32118-6). Morrow.
--Indian Canoe-Maker. Beaudreau, Barbara, illus. LC 59-548755. 194p. illus. (part col.) 22cm. c.1960. Idaho, Caxton Printers.
--Indian Canoe- Maker. Beaudreau, Barbara, illus. LC 59-5487. 194p. illus. 22cm. N.D. JUV.
--Jonathan Down Under. LC 82-8245. 219 p. 22cm. 1982. (ISBN 0-688-01467-4). Morrow.
--Just Some Weeds from the Wilderness. LC 77-28433. 254 p. 22cm. 1978. (ISBN 0-688-22137-8). Morrow.
--Lacy Makes a Match. LC 79-9813. 222 p. 22cm. 1979. (ISBN 0-688-32183-6). Morrow.
--The Lady from Black Hawk. Frankenberg, Robert Clinton (1911-), illus. LC 67-2668. (Illus.). 189 p. 21cm. 1967. McGraw-Hill.
--A Long Way to Whiskey Creek. Altschuler, Franz, contrib. by. LC 75-134486. (Illus.). 224 p. 22cm. 1971. Morrow.
--Lupita Manana. LC 81-505. 192 p. 22cm. 1981. (ISBN 0-688-00358-3). (ISBN 0-688-00359-1). Morrow.
--Me, California Perkins. Dauber, Elizabeth, illus. LC 68-19142. (Illus.). 253 p. 22cm. 1968. Morrow.
--Melinda Takes a Hand. LC 83-7971. 1983. (ISBN 0-688-02422-X). Morrow.
--The Nickel-Plated Beauty. Dauber, Elizabeth, illus. LC 64-16443. (Illus.). 255 p. 22cm. 1964. Morrow.
--O the Red Rose Tree. Dauber, Elizabeth, illus. LC 77-168468. (Illus.). 222 p. 22cm. 1972. (ISBN 0-688-21429-0). Morrow.
--The Queen's Own Grove. Dauber, Elizabeth, illus. LC 66-18740. (Illus.). 221 p. 22cm. 1966. Morrow.
--Red Rock Over the River. LC 72-5883. (Illus.). 253 p. 22cm. 1973. (ISBN 0-688-20065-6). (ISBN 0-688-20065-6). W. Morrow.
--Rufus, Red Rufus. Lewin, Ted (1935-), illus. LC 74-26981. (Illus.). 190 p. 22cm. 1975. (ISBN 0-688-22021-5). (ISBN 0-688-32021-X). W. Morrow.
--The Sea Pair. Altschuler, Franz (1923-), illus. LC 76-113178. (Illus.). 224 p. 22cm. 1970. Morrow.
--Something to Shout About. LC 76-22185. p. cm. 1976. (ISBN 0-688-22078-9). (ISBN 0-688-32078-3). W. Morrow.
--Squaw Dog. Altschuler, Franz (1923-), illus. LC 65-185071. (Illus.). 188 p. 22cm. 1965. W. Morrow.
--The Staffordshire Terror. LC 79-21787. 223 p. 22cm. 1979. (ISBN 0-688-22201-3). (ISBN 0-688-32201-8). Morrow.
--That's One Ornery Orphan. LC 80-10200. 222 p. 22cm. 1980. (ISBN 0-688-22227-7). (ISBN 0-688-32227-1). W. Morrow.
--Turn Homeward, Hannalee. LC 84-8960. 193 p. 22cm. 1984 (Morrow Junior Bks.). (ISBN 0-688-03871-9). W. Morrow.
--Wait for Me, Watch for Me, Eula Bee. LC 78-12782. p. cm. 1978. (ISBN 0-688-22151-3). Morrow.

Beatty, R. C., ed. see Crane, Stephen Townley.
Beatty, R. C., ed. see Twain, Mark.
Beatty, Richmond Croom, ed. see Hawthorne, Nathaniel.
Beatty, Willard W., ed. see Clark, Ann Nolan, Mrs.
Beatty, Williard W., ed. see Clark, Ann Nolan, Mrs.

Beaty, Janice Janowski (1930-)
--Nufu & the Turkeyfish. Funai, Mamoru R. (1932-), illus. LC 78-77429. (Illus.). ca. 27 ils. 128p. (gr. 3-6). 1969. (ISBN 0-394-80808-8). (ISBN 0-394-90808-2). Pantheon.

Beaty, John Yocum (1884-)
--The Baby Whale, Sharp Ears. Carter, Helene (1887-1960), illus. LC 38-28937. 106, 1 p. col. illus. (incl. map) 21 1/2 x 22 cm. c.1938. J. B. Lippincott Company.
--Billy Berk: The Story of a Berkshire Pig. Nelson, Don, illus. LC 30-28314. 64 p. incl. front., illus. 20 1/2 cm. 1930. Thomas S. Rockwell Company.
--Farm Pets. Allen, J. C., photos by. LC 35-4110. 60 p. illus. 14 x 17 cm. c.1935. Rand, McNally & Company.
--Fun on the Farm: A Children's Picture and Story Book of Farm Scenes. Allen, J. C., photos by. LC 37-18320. 41 p. incl. front., illus. 31 cm. c.1933. M. A. Donohue & Company.
--Jolly Outdoor Life: A Children's Picture Book of Farm and Animal Life. Allen, J. C., photos by. 89 p. incl. front., illus. 31 1/2 cm. c.1933. M. A. Donohue & Co.
--Just Dogs: A Children's Picture Book of Dogs and Stories About Them. Allen, J. C., photos by. LC 33-18899. 41 p. incl. front., illus. 31 1/2 cm. c.1933. M. A. Donohue & Co.
--Old Abe: The Story of a Lincoln Sheep. Nelson, Don, illus. LC 31-14967. 64 p. incl. front., illus., plates. 20 1/2 cm. 1931. Thomas S. Rockwell Company.
--Spotty: The Story of a Holstein Cow. Nelson, Don, illus. LC 31-14346. 64 p. incl. front., illus. 20 1/2 cm. 1931. Thomas S. Rockwell Company.
--Sunshine Rose: The Story of a Shetland Pony. Nelson, Don, illus. LC 31-15562. 64 p. incl. front., illus., plates. 20 1/2 cm. 1931. Thomas S. Rockwell Company.
--Vacation Days: A Children's Picture Book of Vacation Days on the Farm. Allen, J. C., photos by. LC 33-18900. 41 p. incl. front., illus. 31 1/2 cm. c.1933. M. A. Donohue & Co.

Beaty, Richard Edward
--The Blue Ridge Boys: Narrations of Early, Actual Mountain Experiences and Humorous Anecdotes of the Shenandoah National Park Section. LC 39-15200. 4 p. l., 134 p. front (port.) plates. 17 cm. c.1938. R. E. Beaty.

Beaudry, Evien G.
--Puppy Stories. Thorne, Diana (1894-), illus. LC 34-33277. 3 p. l., 11-92 p. col. front., col. plates. 30 1/2 cm. c.1934. The Saalfield Publishing Company.
--Stories of Farmyard Animals. Thorne, Diana (1894-), illus. LC 34-24859. 3 p. l., 9-90 p. col. front., col. plates. 31 cm. c.1934. The Saalfield Publishing Company.

Beaudry, Jo & Ketchum, Lynne
--Carla Goes to Court. Hamilton, Jack (1941-), photos by. LC 82-2854. p. cm. c.1982. (ISBN 0-89885-088-6). Human Sciences Press.

Beaufoy-Lane, H. J. & Burroughs, Polly
--The Tail of the Dragon. Beef, illus. LC 66-31383. (Illus.). 1 v. (unpaged. 1966. Barre Publishers.

Beaumont, Cyril William (1891-1976)
--The Mysterious Toyshop: A Fairy Tale. Payne, Wyndham, illus. LC 85-11555. (Illus.). 32 p. 23cm. 1985. (ISBN 0-87099-429-8). Metropolitan Museum of Art and Holt, Rinehart and Winston.

Beaumont, Grace
--Aunt Judith. N.D. Thos Nelson & Sons.

Beaumont, Marie see De Beaumont, Marie.

Beausay, Florence Edith (1911-)
--Bold White Stranger. LC 58-39438. 152p. 21cm. 1958. Zondervan Pub. House.
--The Clouded Sky. LC 63-1536. 148 p. 21 cm. c.1962. Zondervan Pub. House.
--Moccasin Steps. LC 60-519073. 115p. 20cm. 1960. Zondervan Pub. House.

Beautyman, Joan
--The Adventures of Arfa the Ape. LC 82-90317. 1983. (ISBN 0-533-05412-5). Vantage.

Beauvais, John H
--Mister Raccoon. LC 66-21132. 60 p. illus. 27 cm. 1966. H. A. Doyle.

Beaver, Edmund
--Travel Games. (gr. 4 up). 1974. (ISBN 0-910208-01-8). Beavers.

Beaver, Harold Lothar (1929-), ed. see Melville, Herman.

Beaver, Robert Pierce (1906-)
--Below the Great Wall: Chinese Folk Tales for Children. Minton, Harold, illus. LC 47-11059. 63 p. illus. 23 cm. 1947. Christian Education Press.

Bebenroth, Charlotta M. (1890-)
--Meriwether Lewis, Boy Explorer. Caswell, Edward C., illus. LC 53-705. 182p. illus. 20cm. (Childhood of famous Americans series). 1953. Bobbs-Merrill.
--Meriwether Lewis, Boy Explorer. Caswell, Edward C., illus. LC 46-6707. 182 p. illus. 20 cm. (The Childhood of famous Americans series) "First edition."). 1946. The Bobbs-Merrill Company.
--Meriwether Lewis, Boy Explorer. Fiorentino, Al, illus. LC 62-12700. 200p. illus. 20cm. (Childhood of famous Americans). 1962. Bobbs-Merrill.

Be Berus, Virginia
--Montana Jones. 1st. ed. LC 57-969019. 75p. 21cm. 1957. Vantage Press.

Bebey, Francis (1929-)
--The Ashanti Doll. Hutchinson, Joyce A., tr. LC 76-58396. 179 p. 22cm. 1st U.S. edition. 1977. (ISBN 0-88208-075-X). L. Hill.

Bechdolt, Jack, pseud., see Bechdolt, John Ernest.

Bechdolt, Jack see Bechdolt, John Ernest.
Bechdolt, John Ernest see Bechdolt, Jack, pseud.

Bechdolt, John Ernest (1884-)
--Fairy Kittens. Merwin, Decie (1894-1961), illus. LC 47-2897. 39, 1 p. incl. col. front., col. illus. 19 x 15 1/2 cm. 1947. Oxford University Press.
--Footlights for Mary. LC 53-8250. (Illus.). 181 p. 21cm. 1953. Dutton.
--Frozen Treasure. Bechdolt, Jack, pseud. LC 31-11382. viii, 238 p. 19cm. (The Barrow Brothers Ser.). 1931. Cosmopolitan Book Corporation.
--Greg Sheridan, Reporter. Merwin, Decie (1894-1961), illus. N.D. E. P. Dutton & Co.
--Hidden Waters. Bechdolt, Jack, pseud. LC 31-11276. viii, 271 p. 19cm. (The Barrow Brothers Ser.). 1931. Cosmopolitan Book Corporation.
--Horse Stories. DeWitt, Cornelius Hugh (1905-), illus. (Golden Story Book). 1949. Golden Press.
--Horse Stories. De Witt, Cornelius Hugh (1905-), illus. LC 50-8333. 126 p. col. illus. 19 cm. (Golden story book. 14). 1950. Simon and Schuster.
--Jungle Diamonds. Bechdolt, Jack, pseud. LC 31-31122. x, 254 p. 19cm. (Barrow Brothers Ser.). 1931. Cosmopolitan Book Corporation.
--Junior Air Raid Wardens. Floethe, Richard (1901-), illus. LC 42-221466. 175 p. incl. front., illus. 21 cm. 1942. J. B. Lippincott Company.
--Little Boy With a Big Horn. Battaglia, Aurelius (1910-), illus. (Little Golden Book). 1951. Golden Press.
--Mystery at Hurricane Hill. 1st ed. LC 51-5105. 189 p. 21 cm. 1951. Dutton.
--Oliver Becomes a Weatherman. Ramstad, Ralph, illus. LC 53-10494. 63p. illus. 22cm. (Everyday science stories). 1953. J. Messner.
--Oliver Sounds off!. Ramstad, Ralph, illus. LC 53-8276. 63p. illus. 22cm. (Everyday science stories). 1953. J. Messner.
--On the Air: A Story of Television. 1st ed. LC 50-14493. 192 p. 21 cm. 1950. Dutton.
--The Race of the Rails. Bechdolt, Jack, pseud. LC 31-11386. viii, 261 p. 19cm. (The Barrow Brothers Ser.). 1931. Cosmopolitan Book Corporation.
--Roscoe. Merwin, Decie (1894-1961), illus. LC 39-5856. 19cm. 54p. 1939. Oxford University Press.
--Runaway from Riches. Front. by Woodi Ishmael. 1st Ed. LC 52-8250. 191 p. illus. 21 cm. 1952. Dutton.
--Saturday Magic. Merwin, Decie (1894-1961), illus. LC 40-81797. 20cm. 92p. 1940. Oxford University Press.
--Trusty, the Story of a Police Horse. 1st ed. Merwin, Decie (1894-1961), illus. LC 47-5700. 191 p. illus. 21 cm. 1947. E. P. Dutton.
--The Vanishing Hounds. Merwin, Decie (1894-1961), illus. LC 41-18121. 21cm. 154p. 1941. Oxford University Press.

Bechdolt, John Ernest (1884-) & De Witt, Cornelius Hugh (1905-)
--Crazy about Horses and other Horse Stories. (Golden Story Bks.). 1949. Simon & Schuster.

Bechdolt, John Ernest (1884-) & Garfield, Robert, pseud.
--The Golden Treasure Book. Jackson, Kathryn. (Robert Garfield is the joint pseudonym of Kathryn Jackson and Byron Jackson). (Big Golden Book: 560). 1951. Simon and Schuster.
--The Golden Treasure Book. Jackson, Kathryn. Battaglia, Aurelius, et al. (1910-), illus. (Robert Garfield is the joint pseudonym of Kathryn Jackson and Byron Jackson). (Big Golden Book). 1951. Golden Press.

Bechdolt, John Ernest (1884-) & Merwin, Decie (1894-1961)
--Bandmaster's Holiday. LC 38-7732. 71, 1, p. incl. front., illus. 19 cm. 72p. 1938. Oxford University Press.
--Dulcie and Her Donkey. LC 44-6372. 68, 3 p. incl. col. front., col. illus. 18 1/2 x 17 cm. 1944. E. P. Dutton & Co., Inc.
--Dulcie and the Gypsies. LC 48-8134. 63 p. illus. 19 cm. 1948. E. P. Dutton.
--Dulcie: Or, Half-a-Yard of Linsey-Woolsey. LC 43-3847. 71, 1 p. incl. col. front., col. illus. 18 1/2 x 17 cm. 1943. E. P. Dutton & Co., Inc.
--Dulcie Sews A Sampler. LC 45-160. 19cm. 70p. N.D. E. P. Dutton & Co.
--John's Dragon. LC 37-5563. 19cm. 47p. 1937. Oxford University Press.

Bechstein, Ludwig (1801-1860)
--Fairy Tales. Schreiber, Irene, illus. Bell, Anthea, tr. LC 67-19419. (Illus.). 205 p. 24cm. 1967. Abelard-Schuman.
--The Rabbit Catcher, and Other Fairy Tales. Fontana, Ugo, illus. Jarrell, Randall, tr. LC 64-4550. 32 p. illus. 34 cm. 1962, c.1961. Macmillan.

Bechtel, Beverley
--Lancelot the Ocelot. Horvat, Laurel, illus. LC 78-186859. (Illus.). 32 p. 27cm. 1972. (ISBN 0-87614-031-2). Carolrhoda Books.

Bechtel, John (1899-)
--The Chicken Devil Mystery. N.D. E. P. Dutton & Co.
--The Chicken Devil Mystery. LC 44-470117. 102 p. illus. 20 cm. 1944. Wm. B. Eerdmans Publishing Company.
--The Dragon Boat Mystery. N.D. E. P. Dutton & Co.
--The Harrison Road Mystery. LC 41-6800. 104 p. 20 cm. 1941. Wm. B. Eerdmans Publishing Company.
--The Mystery Ship. LC 58-7174. 126p. illus. 20cm. 1953, c.1952. Van Kampen Press.
--Perla of the Walled City. LC 46-7382. 119 p. illus. (plan) 20 cm. 1946. Wm. B. Eerdmans Publihsing Company.
--The Pig's Birthday. LC 42-247713. 248 p. 20 cm. 1942. The Moody Press.
--The Shanghai Mystery. LC 45-391471. 88 p. illus. 20 cm. 1945. Wm. B. Eerdmans Publishing Company.

Bechtel, Louise Seaman (1894-)
--Mr. Peck's Pets. Hader, Berta Hoerner (1890-1976) & Hader, Elmer Stanley (1889-1973), illus. LC 47-30651. 96 p. illus. 23 cm. 1947. Macmillan Co.

Bechtel, Mary
--Choice Books and Records for Children: Recommended Expressly for Christian Families. 63 p. 1963. Christian Life Publications.

Bechtle, Raymond
--Every Day Is a World. Chalmers, Mary Eileen (1927-), illus. LC 57-713420. 63p. illus. 21cm. 1957. Harper.

Bechtold, Gans Grace
--Great Short Stories. 192p. 1962. Hart Publishing Co., Inc.

Beck, Billy De see De Beck, Billy.

Beck, Christopher
--Strong Hand Saxon. N.D. J. B. Lippincott.

Beck, Christopher see Bridges, Thomas Charles.

Beck, Ethel Fyles
--Lummi Indian How Stories. 124p. 1955. Caxton Printers.

Bedford-Atkins, Gladys
--The Luck of the House: The Story of a Family and a Sword. Orioff, Gregory, illus. LC 38-31619. 8 p. 1., 19-303 p. incl. front., illus., plates. 23 cm. 1938. A. Whitman & Co.

Bedford, Francis Donkin (1864-1950)
--A Night of Wonders: A Christmas Fairy Story. N.D. Frederick A. Stokes.

Bedford, Francis Donkin (1864-1950), illus.
--The Battle of the Frogs and Mice. Barlow, Jane. C, tr. N.D. Frederick A Stokes Co.

Bedford, H. Louise, jt. auth. see Everett-Green, Evelyn.

Bedford, Louisa H.
--Miss Chilcott's Legacy (Pub. by Society for Promoting Christian Knowledge). N.D. E. & J. B. Young & Co.
--Ralph Rodney's Mother. N.D. E. & J. B. Young & Co.
--The Village by the River. N.D. E J B Young.

Bedford, R. M.
--Rosycheeks and Goldenhead. (Illus.). N.D. Frederick A. Stokes Co.

Bedford, Stewart
--Instant Replay. (Illus.). N.D. (ISBN 0-686-36816-9). Inst Rational-Emotive.

Bedier, Julie, pseud., see Bedier, Mary Juliana.

Bedier, Mary Juliana see Bedier, Julie, pseud.

Bedier, Mary Juliana (1896-)
--A Horse for Christmas. Bedier, Julie, pseud. Trevisan, Louise, illus. LC 43-15134. 32 p. illus. (part col.) 18 1/2 x 20 cm. 1913. Longmans, Green and Co.
--The Important Pig. Bedier, Julie, pseud. Trevisan, Louise, illus. LC 42-50421. 32 p. illus. (part col.) 18 1/2 x 20 1/2 cm. 1942. Longmans, Green and Co.
--Little Miss Moses. Bedier, Julie, pseud. Trevisan, Louise, illus. LC 43-5945. 31 p. illus. (part col.) 18 1/2 x 20 cm. 1943. Longmans, Green and Co.
--The Long Road to Lo-Ting. Bedier, Julie, pseud. Trevisan, Louise, illus. LC 41-10148. 31 p. illus. (part col.) 19 x 20 cm. 1941. Longmans, Green and Co.
--Lots of Brothers and Sisters. Bedier, Julie, pseud. Trevisan, Louise, illus. N.D. Macmillan.
--Margaret. Sax, Robert M., illus. LC 58-14455. unpaged. illus. 21cm. (Patron saint book). 1959. Sheed & Ward.
--Pattern for Tomorrow. LC 43-17135. vii, 128 p. 20 1/2 cm. 1943. The Bruce Publishing Company.
--Thomas the Good Thief. Bedier, Julie, pseud. Trevisan, Louise, illus. LC 42-7636. 31 p. illus. (part col.) 19 x 21 1/2 cm. 1942. Longmans, Green and Co.

Bedini, Silvio A. (1917-)
--The Spotted Stones: A Story About the Game of Dominoes. Erdoes, Richard (1912-), illus. LC 78-3283. (Illus.). (gr. 3-6). 1978. (ISBN 0-394-83573-5). (ISBN 0-394-93573-X). Pantheon.

Bednar, Kamil & Tchaikovsky, Peter Ilyich (1840-1893)
--Swan Lake: The Story of Prince Siegfried and the Swan Queen. Jirincova, Ludmila, illus. Layton, Jean, tr. LC 68-10471. (Illus.). 63 p. 29cm. (Curtain-raiser book). 1968. F. Watts.

Bednarik, Rosi & Bond, Susan McDonald (1937-)
--Elefish. Bednarik, Rosi, illus. LC 70-130220. (Illus.). 33 p. 26cm. 1971, c.1969. Scroll Press.

Bedolliere, Emile Gigault De La see La Bedolliere, Emile Gigault De.

Bedolliere, Emile Gigault De La (1812-1883)
--Mother Michel and Her Cat. Fuller, Fanny, tr. from Fr. LC 20-19317. 4 p. l., 11-104 p. front. 17 cm. 1865. F. Leypoldt; Etc., Etc.
--Mother Michel and Her Cat. Fuller, Fanny, tr. N.D. Hurd & Houghton.
--Story of a Bad Boy. Aldrich, Thomas Bailey (1836-1907), tr. from Fr. (Illus.). N.D. Houghton Mifflin.
--The Story of a Cat. Aldrich, Thomas Bailey (1836-1907), tr. from Fr. LC 12-36049. 2 p. l., v, 7-100 p. illus. 21 cm. 1879. Houghton, Osgood and Company.
--The Story of a Cat. Aldrich, Thomas Bailey (1836-1907), tr. LC 6-376028. 2 p. l., v. 7-100 p. illus. 21 cm. c.1906. Houghton, Mifflin and Company.

Bee, Clair Francis (1900-)
--Backboard Fever. LC 53-1370. 210p. illus. 20cm. (His chip Hilton sports series 10). 1953. Grosset &Dunlap.
--Backcourt Ace. LC 61-65226. 182p. illus. 20cm. (His Chip Hilton sports series 19). 1961. Grosset & Dunlap.
--Buzzer Basket. LC 62-4128. 175p. illus. 20cm. (His A Chip Hilton sports stories, 20). 1962. Grosset & Dunlap.
--Championship Ball. LC 48-395002. 210 p. illus. 20 cm. (His Chip Hilton sports series 2). 1948. Grosset & Dunlap.
--Clutch Hitter. LC 49-677539. 206 p. illus. 20 cm. (His Chip Hilton sports series 4). 1949. Grosset & Dunlap.
--Comeback Cagers. LC 63-18958. 170 p. illus. 20 cm. (His Chip Hilton sports series, 21). 1963. Grosset & Dunlap.
--Dugout Jinx. LC 52-8135. 210 p. illus. 20 cm. (His Chip Hilton sports series 8). 1952. Grosset & Dunlap.
--Fence Busters. 208p. illus. 20cm. (His Chip Hilton sports series 11). 1953. Grosset &Dunlap.
--Fourth Down Showdown. LC 56-31267. 213p. illus. 20cm. (His A Chip Hilton sports story 13). 1956. Grosset & Dunlap.
--Freshman Quarterback. LC 52-13022. 212 p. illus. 20 cm. (His Chip Hilton sports series 9). 1952. Grosset & Dunlap.
--Hardcourt Upset. LC 58-14554. 181p. illus. 20cm. (His Chip Hilton sports series 15). 1958, c.1957. Grosset & Dunlap.
--Home Run Feud. LC 64-14828. 176 p. illus. 20 cm. (His A Chip Hilton sports story, 22). 1964. Grosset & Dunlap.
--Hoop Crazy. LC 50-5622. 215 p. illus. 20 cm. (His Chip Hilton sports series 5). 1950. Grosset & Dunlap.
--Hungry Hurler. LC 64-21267. (Illus.). 184 p. 29cm. (His A Chip Hilton sports story). 1966. Grosset & Dunlap.
--No-Hitter. LC 59-16410. 182p. illus. 20cm. (His Chip Hilton sports series 17). 1959. Grosset & Dunlap.
--A Pass and a Prayer. LC 51-6064. 216 p. illus. 20 cm. (His Chip Hilton sports series 7). 1951. Grosset & Dunlap.
--Pay-off Pitch. LC 59-718. 182p. illus. 20cm. (His Chip Hilton sports series 16). 1958. Grosset & Dunlap.
--Pitchers' Duel. LC 50-12306. 212 p. illus. 20 cm. (His Chip Hilton sports series 6). 1950. Grosset & Dunlap.
--Strike Three. LC 49-145353. 212 p. illus. 20 cm. (His Chip Hilton sports series 3). 1949. Grosset & Dunlap.
--Ten Seconds to Play!. LC 55-12575. 213p. illus. 20cm. (His Chip Hilton sports series 12). 1955. Grosset & Dunlap.
--Touchdown Pass. LC 48-371453. 212 p. illus. 20 cm. (His Chip Hilton sports series). 1948. Grosset and Dunlap.
--Tournament Crisis. LC 57-136104. 214p. illus. 20 cm. (His A Chip Hilton sports story 14). 1957. Grosset & Dunlap.
--Triple-Threat Trouble. LC 60-160875. 182p. illus. 20cm. (His Chip Hilton sports series 18). 1960. Grosset & Dunlap.

Bee, Martha
--The Adventures of Barney Bean. Nair, Christina, illus. (Illus.). 1977. (ISBN 0-533-02890-6). Vantage.

Beebe, B. F. see Johnson, Burdetta Faye Beebe.

Beebe, Burdetta Faye (1920-)
--Appalachian Elk. Johnson, James Ralph (1922-), illus. LC 62-157726. 152p. illus. 21cm. 1962. D. McKay Co.
--Coyote, Come Home. Toschik, Larry (1922-), illus. (Illus.). (gr. 7-9). 1963. McKay.
--Run, Light Buck, Run. Toschik, Larry (1922-), illus. (Illus.). (gr. 6-10). 1962. McKay.

Beebe, Catherine (1898-)
--ABCs for Catholic boys and girls. 1st ed. Bebbe, Robb, illus. LC 38-30382. 32p. illus. 21 1/2cm. c.1938. Longmans Green & Co.
--Bible Story. (Vision Book). 1957. Farrar, Straus and Cudahy, Inc.
--Bob's Bike. Beebe, Robb (1891-), illus. LC 42-7637. 48 p. illus. (part col.) 21 x 16 cm. 1942. Oxford University Press.
--The Calendar. Beebe, Robb (1891-), illus. LC 40-31798. 21cm. 63p. 1940. Oxford University Press.
--Christmas--This Way!. Beebe, Robb (1891-), illus. LC 43-10499. 53, 3 p. illus. (part col.) 21 x 16 1/2 cm. 1943. Oxford University Pres.
--Do You Like to Open Packages?. Beebe, Robb (1891-), illus. LC 37-10496. 48 p. illus. (part col.) 21 1/2 x 19 cm. c.1937. T. Nelson & Sons.
--Dominic and the Rosary. 1955 ed. (Vision Book). N.D. Farrar, Straus and Caudahy, Inc.
--Happily Ever After. Beebe, Robb (1891-), illus. LC 38-17085. 93 p. illus. (part col.) 21 1/2 x 19 cm. c.1938. T. Nelson & Sons.
--Just Around the Corner. Beebe, Robb (1891-), illus. LC 39-27107. 78, 1 p. illus. 21 cm. c.1939. Oxford University Press.
--The Pet Show. Beebe, Robb (1891-), illus. LC 46-6987. 46, 1 p. col. illus. 20 1/2 x 16 cm. 1946. Oxford University Press.
--Saint Dominic and the Rosary. Beebe, Robb (1891-), illus. LC 56-7280. 188p. illus. 22cm. (Vision books, 11). 1956. Vision Books.
--St. John Bosco and the Children's Saint: Dominic Savio. Beebe, Robb (1891-), illus. LC 55-9793. 191p. illus. 22cm. (Vision books, 1). 1955. Vision Books.
--The Story of Jesus for Boys and Girls. Beebe, Robb (1891-), illus. 1945. Bruce Publishing Co.
--The Story of Mary, the Mother of Jesus. Beebe, Robb (1891-), illus. 1950. Bruce Publishing Co.
--A Wish for Timothy. Beebe, Robb (1891-), illus. LC 38-25344. 48 p. illus. (part col.) 22 cm. c.1938. Oxford University Press.

Beeby, Betty
--Just Josie. LC 60-7655. (Illus.). 32p. illus. 21cm. 1960. Reily & Lee and Company.

Beecham, Tom, illus.
--The Lone Ranger. (Illus.). (Rocking Bks.). (ps-3). N.D. (ISBN 0-394-84690-7). Random.

Beecher, Elizabeth
--Gene Autry and Red Shirt. Marsh, Jesse, illus. LC 52-16456. 78 p. illus. 19 cm. (Young readers' library). 1951. Simon and Schuster.
--Gene Autry Makes a New Friend. Authorized. Case, Richard, illus. unpaged. illus. 17cm. (Tell-a-tale books). c.1952. Whitman Pub. Co.
--Hopalong Cassidy and the Bar 20 Cowboy, Starring William Boyd: Based on Characters Created by Clarence E. Mulford. Sahula-Dycke, illus. LC 52-9881. unpaged. illus. 21 cm. (Little golden library. 147). 1952. Simon and Schuster.
--Hopalong Cassidy and the Two Young Cowboys. Authorized. Higgs, John, illus. LC 52-21712. unpaged. illus. 21 cm. (Cozy corner book). N.D. Whitman Pub. Co.
--Little Beaver. Based on the Famous Newspaper Strip, 'Red Ryder' by Fred Herman. Authorized. LC 54-33169. unpaged. illus. 17cm. (Tell-a-tale books, 935). c.1954. Whitman Pub. Co.
--Roy Rogers and Cowboy Toby. Crawford, Mel (1925-), illus. LC 54-3676. unpaged. illus. 21cm. (Little golden book, 195). 1954. Simon and Schuster.
--Roy Rogers and the Sure'nough Cowpoke. Steffen, Randy, illus. LC 52-65922. (Illus.). unpaged. 17cm. (Tell-a-tale books). N.D. Whitman Pub. Co.
--Roy Rogers' Bullet and Trigger: Wild Horse Roundup. Lenox, August, illus. LC 53-37577. unpaged. illus. 21cm. (Cozy corner book). c.1953. Whitman Pub. Co.
--Roy Rogers on the Double-R Ranch. Nordly, Ernest, illus. LC 52-16449. 77 p. illus. 19 cm. (Sandpiper books). 1951. Simon and Schuster.
--Roy Rogers,King of the Cowboys. Alvarado, Peter, illus. LC 53-35264. 112p. illus. 28cm. (Big golden book, 575). 1953. Simon and Schuster.

Beecher, Elizabeth, adapted by.
--Bugs Bunny's Birthday. Dempster, Al & Heimdahl, Ralph, illus. (Little Golden Book). 1950. Golden Press.

Beecher, Elizabeth, jt. auth. see Westrate, Edwin Victor.

Beecher, Elizabeth, adapted by see Disney, Walter Elias.

Beecher, Elizabeth, adapted by see Disney, Walter Elias (1901-1966) & Porter, Eleanor Hodgman.

Beecher, Elizabeth, retold by see Disney, Walt, Productions.

Beecher, H. W., ed.
--Two Families: and, Two Aims in Life. (Father Merrill Ser.). N.D. Warren and Wyman.

Beecher, Julia H.
--Aim, Fire, Bang Stories. (Illus.). 1882. Lee & Shepard.

Beecher, Thomas Kinnicut (1824-1900)
--In Time with the Stars: Stories for Children. LC 1-26535. v, 165 p. front., port. 18 cm. 1901. H. H. Billings.

Beechick, Ruth (1925-)
--The Donkey That Talked & Other Bible Stories. (Illus.). (gr. 1-3). 1976. (ISBN 0-916406-24-5). Accent Bks.
--The Man Who Was Reading & Other Bible Stories. (Illus.). (gr. 1-3). 1976. (ISBN 0-916406-23-7). Accent Bks.
--The Story of David & Other Bible Stories. Cheyney, Jeanne S., illus. (Illus.). (gr. 1-3). 1976. (ISBN 0-916406-25-3). Accent Bks.

Beeching, H. C., ed.
--A Book of Christmas Verse. Crane, Walter (1845-1915), illus. Crane, Walter, designed by. (out of print). N.D. Dodd, Mead & Co.

Beechwood
--Jerry and His Dog (Pub. by Society for Promoting Christian Knowledge). N.D. E. & J. B. Young & Co.

Beecroft, John William Richard (1902-1966), ed. see Kipling, Joseph Rudyard.

Beecroft, John William Richard (1902-1966)
--Rocco Came in. Wiese, Kurt (1887-1974), illus. LC 59-9620. unpaged. illus. 26cm. 1959. Dodd, Mead.
--What?,Another Cat!. Wiese, Kurt (1887-1974), illus. LC 60-9153. unpaged. illus. 27cm. 1960. Dodd, Mead.

Beecroft, John William Richard (1902-1966) & Haycraft, Howard, eds.
--Treasury of Great Mysteries. 1957. Simon and Schuster.

Beeks, Graydon (1919-)
--Hosea Globe and the Fantastical Peg-Legged Chu. 1st ed. Nicklaus, Carol, illus. LC 74-19269. (Illus.). 170 p. 22cm. 1975. (ISBN 0-689-30464-1). Atheneum.

Beem, Frances
--The Three Little Pigs. N.D. Rand McNally.

Beem, Thelma
--Carters of Bear Pen Cove. (gr. 1-5). 1969. (ISBN 0-8127-0021-X). Southern Pub.

Beer, Kathleen Costello (1926-)
--Bumble and Me. Gellert, Judith (1925-), photos by. LC 68-54834. (Illus.). 62 p. 26cm. 1968. Van Nostrand.

Beer, Lisl
--Great is Kush. N.D. (ISBN 0-8283-1258-3). Branden Press.
--Horns of the Moon. N.D. (ISBN 0-8283-1252-4). Branden Press.
--Jonah and the Whale. N.D. (ISBN 0-8283-1255-9). Branden Press.
--Mister Vinegar. N.D. (ISBN 0-8283-1250-8). Branden Press.
--The Prince and the Mermaid. N.D. (ISBN 0-8283-1247-8). Branden Press.
--Second Shepherd's Play. N.D. (ISBN 0-8283-1246-X). Branden Press.
--Sir Eglamore and the Dragon. N.D. (ISBN 0-8283-1245-1). Branden Press.
--Somebody-Nothing. N.D. (ISBN 0-8283-1253-2). Branden Press.
--This is My Land. N.D. (ISBN 0-8283-1103-X). Branden Press.

Beer, Lisl, ed.
--Punch and Judy. N.D. (ISBN 0-8283-1244-3). Branden Press.

Beerbohm, Henry Maximillian (1872-1956)
--The Happy Hypocrite. DeHoff, George, illus. LC 85-70301. (Illus.). 54p. 1985. (ISBN 0-88138-038-5, Star & Elephant Bks.). Green Tiger Pr.
--The Happy Hypocrite: A Fairy Tale for Tired Men, 1 of 6 vols. (The Bodley Booklets Ser.: No. 1). 1900. Set. John Lane.

Beerbohm, Julius
--Among the Ostrich Hunters. (Illus.). (The Rugby Ser.). 1905. Set. A L Burt Co.

Beerman, Miriam, ed.
--The Enduring Beast. LC 70-173649. (Illus.). 64p. (gr. 5up). 1972. (ISBN 0-385-08392-0). (ISBN 0-385-03546-2). Doubleday.

Beers, Lorna Doone (1897-)
--Book of Hugh Flower. Mill, Eleanor, illus. (Illus.). (gr. 7 up). 1952. (ISBN 0-06-020420-6, HarpJ). Har-Row.
--The Book of Hugh Flower. 1st ed. Mill, Eleanor, illus. LC 52-9758. 186 p. illus. 22 cm. 1952. Harper.
--The Crystal Cornerstone. 1st Ed. ed. LC 53-853357. 218p. (gr. 7 up). 1953. (ISBN 0-06-020425-7, HarpJ). Har-Row.

Beers, Ronald A., jt. auth. see Beers, Victor Gilbert.

Beers, Victor Gilbert (1928-)
--Along Thimblelane Trails. LC 81-14197. p. cm. c.1981. (ISBN 0-8024-0298-4). Moody Press.
--Around the World with My Red Balloon. Krisvoy, Juel, illus. LC 72-13628. (Illus.). 26 p. 1973. (ISBN 0-8024-0303-4). Moody Press.
--Captain Maxi's Secret Island. 96p. (Muffin Family Ser.: No. 11). 1983. (ISBN 0-8024-9573-7). Moody.
--A Child's Treasury of Bible Stories. LC 78-31399. (Illus.). 4 v. 27cm. c.1970. Parent and Child Institute.
--Coco's Candy Shop. 32p. (gr. 3-6). 1973. (ISBN 0-8024-1586-5). Moody.
--Do You Know My Friend?. Jones, Jan M. (1949-), illus. LC 76-20329. (Illus.). 96 p. 23cm. (Learning to read from the Bible ; primer 2). 1977, c.1976. (ISBN 0-310-20830-0). Zondervan Pub. House.
--Do You Love Me?. Jones, Jan M. (1949-), illus. LC 76-20328. (Illus.). 96 p. 23cm. (Learning to read from the Bible ; primer 3). c.1976. Zondervan Pub. House.
--From Castles in the Clouds. Endres, Helen Elise, illus. LC 82-153067. (Illus.). 96 p. 27cm. (Muffin family picture Bible / V. Gilbert Beers). ((Series: Beers, V. Gilbert (Victor Gilbert), 1928-). (Muffin family picture Bible.). c.1980. (ISBN 0-8024-2879-7). Moody Press.
--A Gaggle of Green Geese. Krisvoy, Juel, illus. LC 73-20885. (Illus.). 26 p. 1974. (ISBN 0-8024-2911-4). Moody Press.
--God Is My Friend. Boehmer, Robert, illus. LC 72-85562. (Illus.). 96 p. 24cm. (His Learning to read from the Bible series). 1973. Zondervan Pub. House.
--God Is My Helper. Boehmer, Robert, illus. LC 72-85561. (Illus.). 96 p. 23cm. (His Learning to read from the Bible series). 1973. Zondervan Pub. House.
--Honeyphants and Elebees. Krisvoy, Juel, illus. LC 73-20886. (Illus.). 26 p. 1974. (ISBN 0-8024-3612-9). Moody Press.
--The House in the Hole in the Side of the Tree. Jones, Jan M. (1949-), illus. LC 72-13629. (Illus.). 26 p. 20 x 26cm. 1973. (ISBN 0-8024-3599-8). Moody Press.
--The Magic Merry-Go-Round. Carlton, Suzanne, illus. LC 72-94874. (Illus.). 26 p. 1973. (ISBN 0-8024-5138-1). Moody Press.

AUTHOR INDEX BEIMES, CHARLOTTE

--May I Help You?. Jones, Jan M. (1949-), illus. LC 76-20330. (Illus.). 96 p. 23cm. (Learning to read from the Bible ; primer 1). 1977, c.1976. (ISBN 0-310-20820-3). Zondervan Pub. House.
--Muffkins on Parade. Endres, Helen Elise, illus. LC 82-6338. (Illus.). 96 p. 26cm. (Muffin family picture Bible). c.1982. Moody Press.
--Out of the Treasure Chest. Endres, Helen Elise, illus. LC 81-1601. p. cm. 1981. (ISBN 0-8024-6099-2). Moody Press.
--Over Buttonwood Bridge. Endres, Helen Elise, illus. LC 78-13103. p. cm. (Muffin family picture Bible). 1978. (ISBN 0-8024-6266-9). Moody Press.
--Through Golden Windows. Endres, Helen Elise, illus. LC 75-25535. (Illus.). 144 p. 26cm. (Muffin family picture Bible). 1975. (ISBN 0-8024-8753-X). Moody Press.
--Toyland Tales. Endres, Helen Elise, illus. LC 83-23802. (Muffin Family Ser.). (ps). c.1984. (ISBN 0-8024-9574-5). (ISBN 0-8024-9574-5). Moody.
--Treehouse Tales. Endres, Helen Elise & Axeman, Lois, illus. LC 81-19011. (Illus.). 96 p. 26cm. (The Muffin Family Picture Bible). c.1982. (ISBN 0-8024-9571-0). Moody Press.
--Under the Tagalong Tree. Endres, Helen Elise, illus. LC 76-22173. p. cm. c.1976. (ISBN 0-8024-9021-2). Moody Press.
--Will You Come with Me?. Jones, Jan M. (1949-), illus. LC 76-20390. (Illus.). 96 p. 23cm. (Learning to read from the Bible ; primer 4). 1977, c.1976. (ISBN 0-310-20850-5). Zondervan Pub. House.
--With Maxi and Mini in Muffkinland. Endres, Helen Elise, illus. LC 80-39767. (Illus.). 96 p. 26cm. (Muffin family picture bible). c.1981. (ISBN 0-8024-4063-0). Moody Press.
--With Sails to the Wind. LC 77-24955. p. cm. c.1977. (ISBN 0-8024-9570-2). Moody Press.

Beers, Victor Gilbert (1928-) & Beers, Ronald A.
--Bible Stories To Live By. De Jonge, Reint, illus. 192p. (gr. 3-6). 1983. (ISBN 0-89840-044-9). Heres Life.
--Walking with Jesus. De Jonge, Reint, illus. 192p. (gr. 1-6). 1984. (ISBN 0-89840-069-4). Heres Life.

Beeson, Ernest, tr. see Grimm, Jakob Ludwig Karl (1785-1863) & Grimm, Wilhelm Karl.

Beeson, Harold, jt. auth. see Maddox, Bill.

Beeson, Helen K.
--Little Firemen. Newton, Ruth E., et al., illus. LC 37-345. 34x31cm. 28p. 1936. Whitman Publishing co.
--Little Storekeepers. Newton, Ruth E., et al., illus. LC 44-12297. 24x30cm. 28p. 1937. Whitman Publishing co.
--Puppy Dogs and Pussy Cats. Newton, Ruth E. & Horn, Mabel G., illus. LC 37-347. 32p. col. illus. 33 1/2cm. c.1936. Whitman.

Beetschen, Louis
--Ragbag Treasure. N.D. Transatlantic Inc.
--The Treasure Series. N.D. Taplinger.

Begbie, Joan (1903-)
--Freelance, the Pony. Grey, Frank R., illus. LC 52-9255. 205 p. illus. 21 cm. 1952. Dodd, Mead.

Begg, John
--Two Little Tigers and How They Flew. 32p. (gr. k-1). 1947. Oxford University Press.

Beggs, Robert Henry (1844-1914), ed. see Hawthorne, Nathaniel.

Begley, Evelyn M
--Duck in the Park, Duck in the Dark. Provest, Jon, illus. LC 73-76835. (Illus.). 16 p. (Magic circle book). 1974. (ISBN 0-663-25453-1). Ginn.
--The Little Red Hen. Hauge, Carl & Hauge, Mary, illus. LC 67-2673. (Illus.). 1 v. (unpaged). 22cm. (Whitman big tell-a-tale). 1966. Whitman Pub. Co.
--Rory, the Red. Danska, Herbert (1928-), illus. LC 68-54835. (Illus.). 190 p. 22cm. 1968. Van Nostrand.

Behm, Bill (1922-)
--The Night Jesus Was Born. LC 63-23438. 1v. (unpaged) illus. (pt. col.) 27cm. c.1964. Concordia.

Behman, Marguerite
--Lindenwood Tales. Meyer, H. C., illus. LC 55-45816. 27cm. 68p. 1921. Wilder & Buell.

Behn, Harry (1898-1973)
--All Kinds of Time. 1st ed. Behn, Harry (1898-1973), illus. LC 50-9110. 61 p. col. illus. 19 cm. 1950. Harcourt, Brace.
--Chrysalis: Concerning Children and Poetry. 99p. N.D. (ISBN 0-15-217920-8). Harcourt Brace Jovanovich.
--Crickets & Bullfrogs & Whispers of Thunder: Poems & Pictures. Hopkins, Lee B. (1938-), selected by. Behn, Harry (1898-1973), illus. LC 83-18347. (Illus.). 96p. (ps-3). 1984. (ISBN 0-15-220885-2, HJ). (ISBN 0-15-220885-2). HarBraceJ.
--The Faraway Lurs. 192p. 1963. (ISBN 0-529-03750-5). (ISBN 0-529-03751-3). Collins & World. **Award: (ALA).**
--The Faraway Lurs. LC 80-24712. p. cm. (Gregg Press Children's Literature Series). 1981, c.1963. (ISBN 0-8398-2722-9). Gregg Press.
--The Faraway Lurs. LC 81-15676. 190 p. 21cm. 1982. (ISBN 0-399-20860-7). Philomel Books.
--The Golden Hive: Poems and Pictures. Behn, Harry (1898-1973), illus. LC 66-12587. (Illus.). (gr. 3 up). 1966. (ISBN 0-15-231200-5, HJ). HarBraceJ. **Award: (ALA).**
--The House Beyond the Meadow. LC 55-5544. unpaged. illus. 23cm. 1955. Pantheon.
--The Little Hill: Poems and Pictures. 1st ed. Behn, Harry (1898-1973), illus. LC 49-101989. 58 p. illus. 19 cm. 1949. Harcourt, Brace.
--Omen of the Birds. Behn, Harry (1898-1973), illus. LC 64-20961. 157 p. illus. 21 cm. 1964. World Pub. Co.
--The Painted Cave. N.D. E. M. Hale & Co.
--The Painted Cave. 1st. ed. Behn, Harry (1898-1973), illus. LC 57-8584. (Illus.). 63 p. 23cm. 1957. Harcourt, Brace.
--Roderick. 1st ed. Silverman, Melvin Frank (1931-1966), illus. LC 61-6111. 63p. illus. 24cm. 1961. Harcourt, Brace.
--The Wizard in the Well. Behn, Harry (1898-1973), illus. LC 56-5232. (Illus.). (gr. k-3). 1959. (ISBN 0-15-298929-3, HJ). HarBraceJ.
--Timmy's Search. Cooney, Barbara (1917-), illus. LC 58-9200. 93p. illus. 21cm. (Seabury series, R- -1B). 1958. Seabury Press.
--The Two Uncles of Pablo. Silverman, Melvin Frank (1931-1966), illus. LC 59-8949. (Illus.). 96 p. 22cm. 1959. Harcourt, Brace.
--What a Beautiful Noise. Berson, Harold (1926-), illus. LC 75-128519. (Illus.). 32 p. 1970. World Pub. Co.
--Windy Morning: Poems, and Pictures. Behn, Harry (1898-1973), illus. LC 52-11965. (Illus.). 61 p. 19cm. 1953. (ISBN 0-15-297676-0). Harcourt, Brace.
--The Wizard in the Well: Poems and Pictures. Behn, Harry (1898-1973), illus. LC 56-5232. (Illus.). (gr. k-3). 1959. (ISBN 0-15-298929-3, HJ). HarBraceJ.
--The Wizard in the Well: Poems and Pictures. 1st ed. Behn, Harry (1898-1973), illus. LC 56-5232. 62p. illus. 19cm. c.1956. Harcourt, Brace.

Behn, Harry (1898-1973), tr.
--More Cricket Songs: Japanese Haiku. LC 77-137755. (Photos). (Illus.). (gr. 4 up). 1971. (ISBN 0-15-255440-8, HJ). HarBraceJ.

Behnke, Frances L.
--What We Find When We Look Under Rocks. Zallinger, Jean Day (1918-), illus. LC 71-91677. (Illus.). 34 p. 26cm. (What we find when we look series). 1971. (ISBN 0-07-004276-4). McGraw-Hill.

Behnke, John (1945-)
--Stories from Creation to Samson Retold in Everyday Language for Today's Children. LC 83-82022. (Orig.). (gr. k up). 1984. (ISBN 0-8091-6552-X). Paulist Pr.

Behrangi, Samad
--The Little Black Fish. Mesghali, Farsheed, illus. LC 74-128812. (Illus.). 24 p. 20cm. 1971. (ISBN 0-87614-013-4). Carolrhoda Books.
--The Little Black Fish and Other Modern Persian Stories. LC 77-370941. xxvii, 133 p. 23cm. c.1976. (ISBN 0-914478-21-4). (ISBN 0-914478-22-2). Three Continents Press.

Behrens, Bertha see Heimburg, W., pseud.

Behrens, Gerda Frederiksen, tr. see With, Karl Henrik.

Behrens, June York (1925-)
--Christmas-Magic Wagon. Burgeson, Marjorie, illus. LC 75-14007. (Illus.). 32p. (Holiday Play Books). (gr. k-4). 1975. (ISBN 0-516-08880-7, Golden Gate). Childrens.
--Fiesta!. Taylor, Scott, illus. 1978. Children's Press.
--Looking at Beasties. LC 77-6331. (Illus.). (Adventures in Art Ser.). (gr. k-4). 1978. (ISBN 0-516-08823-8, Golden Gate). Childrens.
--My Favorite Thing. Streano, Vince (1945-), illus. LC 77-359654. (Illus.). 32 p. c.1975. (ISBN 0-914844-09-1). J. Alden Publishers.
--Soo Ling Finds a Way. Yashima, Taro, pseud. (1908-), illus. Iwamatsu, Jun Atsushi. LC 63-9155. (Illus.). (gr. k-3). 1965. (ISBN 0-516-08739-8, Golden Gate). Childrens.
--Together. 1975. (ISBN 0-516-07634-5). Childrens Press.
--A Walk in the Neighborhood. Gindraux, Jim, illus. LC 68-8270. (Illus.). 48 p. 1968. Elk Grove Press.
--What I hear in my school. Grimm, Michele & Grimm, Tom, photos by LC 76-9099. p. cm. 1976. (ISBN 0-516-08745-2). Childrens Press.
--Who Am I?. Ambraziunas, Ray, photos by. LC 68-54691. (Illus.). 41 p. 1968. Elk Grove Press.

Behrens, June York (1925-) & Brower, Pauline (1929-)
--Canal Boats West. LC 77-17138. (Illus.). 31 p. 25cm. (Living heritage series). c.1978. (ISBN 0-516-07468-7). Childrens Press.
--Death Valley. LC 79-23325. (Illus.). 32p. (Living Heritage Ser.). (gr. 1-4). 1980. (ISBN 0-516-08714-2, Golden Gate). Childrens.

Behrman, Carol Helen (1925-)
--Catch a Dancing Star. Rieniets, Judy King, illus. LC 74-28120. (Illus.). 94 p. 23cm. 1975. (ISBN 0-87518-113-9). Dillon Press.

Beichner, Paul E.
--Once Upon a Parable: Fables for the Present. (Illus.). 240p. 1975. (ISBN 0-8362-0603-7). Sheed & Ward, Inc.

Beier, Ulli (1922-)
--The Stolen Images. LC 77-364513. (Illus.). 55 p. 22cm. 1976. (ISBN 0-521-20901-3). Cambridge University Press.

Beiler, Edna (1923-)
--Adventures with the Buttonwoods. Sondern, Ferd A., illus. LC 60-14464. (Illus.). (gr. 3-7). 1960. (ISBN 0-8361-1301-2). Herald Pr.
--Mattie Mae. Graber, Esther Rose, illus. LC 67-24800. (Illus.). 109 p. 22cm. 1967. Herald Press.
--Mitsy Buttonwood. Sondern, Ferd A., illus. LC 63-20202. 91 p. illus., port. 22 cm. c.1963. Herald Press.
--Ten of a Kind. 1956. Eerdmans.
--Ten of a Kind. Stage, Ruth, illus. LC 53-12198. 106p. illus. 21cm. 1953. Herald Press.
--White Elephant for Sale. Gretzer, John, illus. LC 66-11121. 125 p. illus. 19 cm. (gr. 4-6). 1966. (ISBN 0-377-06601-X). Friendship Press.

Beim, Jerrold see Anderson, Neil, pseud.

Beim, Jerrold, jt. auth. see Beim, Lorraine Levey.

Beim, Jerrold (1910-1957)
--Across the Bridge. 1st ed. Maley, Thomas, illus. LC 51-9575. 183 p. illus. 21 cm. 1951. Harcourt, Brace.
--Andy & the School Bus. Shortall, Leonard W., illus. LC 47-30835. (Illus.). 22cm. 48p. (gr. k-3). 1947. (ISBN 0-688-31022-2). Morrow.
--Beach Boy. 1st ed. Freedgood, Lillian (1911-), illus. LC 52-6457. 206 p. illus. 22 cm. 1952. Harcourt, Brace.
--The Boy on Lincoln's Lap. Sugarman, Tracy (1921-), illus. LC 55-5436. (Illus.). 46 p. 22cm. (Morrow junior books). 1955. Morrow.
--The Boy on Lincoln's Lap. Sugarman, Tracy (1921-), illus. 1955. William Morrow & Co.
--Buzz Wants a Boat. Anderson, Neil, pseud. Dillon, Corinne Boyd, illus. LC 56-6783. 158p. illus. 21cm. 1956. Messner.
--Country Fireman. Shortall, Leonard W., illus. LC 48-4143. 48 p. illus. (part col.) 22 cm. (Morrow junior Books). 1948. W. Morrow.
--Country Garage. Darling, Louis, Jr. (1916-1970), illus. LC 52-5065. (Illus.). 48 p. 22cm. 1952. Morrow.
--Country Mailman. Shortall, Leonard W., illus. (Illus.). 48 p. 22cm. 1958. Morrow.
--Country School. Darling, Louis, Jr. (1916-1970), illus. LC 54-6540. (Illus.). 47 p. 22cm. (Morrow junior books). 1955. Morrow.
--Country Train. Shortall, Leonard W., illus. LC 50-8414. (Illus.). 48 p. 22cm. (Morrow junior books). (gr. k-5). 1950. (ISBN 0-688-31195-4). Morrow.
--Danny and the Dog Doctor. Levy, Edgar, illus. LC 50-5486. (Illus.). 48 p. 22cm. (Morrow junior books). 1950. Morrow.
--Eric on the Desert. Darling, Louis, Jr. (1916-1970), illus. LC 52-12113. (Illus.). 44 p. 22cm. (Morrow Junior Bk.). 1953. Morrow.
--Flood Waters. 1st ed. Sibley, Don (1922-), illus. LC 56-107372. 115p. illus. 22cm. 1956. Harcourt, Brace.
--Jay's Big Job. Sugarman, Tracy (1921-), illus. (Illus.). (Morrow Junior Books). (gr. 1-5). 1957. Morrow.
--Kid Brother. Sugarman, Tracy (1921-), illus. LC 52-5926. (Illus.). 46 p. 22cm. (Morrow junior books). 1952. Morrow.
--The Lost and Found Ball. Ware, Kay (1916-) & Sutherland, Lucille, eds. Kallstrom, Ylva, illus. LC 61-663836. unpaged. illus. 23cm. (Read for fun series). c.1961. Webster Pub. Co.
--Meet Sandy Smith. Anderson, Neil, pseud. (Illus.). (gr. 3-5). 1954. (ISBN 0-8382-0513-5). Hale.
--Meet Sandy Smith. Anderson, Neil, pseud. Stevens, Mary E. (1920-1966), illus. LC 54-6761. (Illus.). 160 p. 22cm. 1954. J. Messner.
--Mister Boss. Sugarman, Tracy (1921-), illus. LC 54-5187. (Illus.). 42 p. 22cm. 1954. Morrow.
--Rocky's Road. 1st ed. Galdone, Paul (1914-), illus. LC 53-7861. 150p. illus. 21cm. 1953. Harcourt, Brace.
--Shoeshine Boy. Darling, Louis, Jr. (1916-1970), illus. LC 53-9758. (Illus.). 48 p. 22cm. (Morrow junior books). 1954. Morrow.
--The Smallest Boy in the Class. Wohlberg, Meg (1905-), illus. LC 49-9991. 47 p. illus. (part col.) 22 cm. (Morrow junior books). 1949. W. Morrow.
--Swimming Hole. Darling, Louis, Jr. (1916-1970), illus. LC 51-9337. (Illus.). 45 p. 22cm. (Morrow junior books). 1950, c.1951. Morrow.
--The Taming of Toby. Sugarman, Tracy (1921-), illus. LC 53-6663. (Illus.). 47 p. 22cm. (Morrow junior-books). 1953. Morrow.
--Thin Ice. Darling, Louis, Jr. (1916-1970), illus. LC 56-5179. (Illus.). 46 p. 22cm. (Morrow junior books). 1956. Morrow.
--Tim and the Tool Chest. Sugarman, Tracy (1921-), illus. LC 51-4409. (Illus.). 48 p. 22cm. (Morrow junior books). 1951. Morrow.
--Time for Gym. Darling, Louis, Jr. (1916-1970), illus. LC 57-5074. unpaged. illus. 22cm. 1957. Morrow.
--Time for Gym. Quinn, Tom, illus. (Illus.). 22cm. 48p. (Merit bk.). 1968, c.1957. Houghton.
--Tina and the too-big Doll. Anderson, Neil, pseud. LC 56-5698. 44p. 1956. Crowell.
--Too Many Sisters. Dodge, Dick (1918-1974), illus. LC 56-7383. (Illus.). 43 p. 22cm. (Morrow junior books). 1956. Morrow.
--Trouble After School. Sibley, Don (1922-), illus. LC 57-9738. (Illus.). (gr. 5-9). 1957. (ISBN 0-15-290695-9, HJ). HarBraceJ.
--A Vote for Dick. 1st ed. Sibley, Don (1922-), illus. LC 55-8670. 117p. illus. 22cm. 1955. (ISBN 0-15-294275-0). Harcourt, Brace.
--Who's Who in Your Family. Stevens, Mary E. (1920-1966), illus. LC 54-5951. 56p. illus. 23cm. 1954. F. Watts.
--With Dad Alone. 1st ed. Sibley, Don (1922-), illus. LC 54-85670. 145p. illus. 21cm. 1954. (ISBN 0-15-298750-9). Harcourt, Brace.

Beim, Jerrold (1910-1957) & Crichlow, Ernest (1914-)
--Twelve O'clock Whistle. LC 46-20646. 61 p. illus. (part col.) 21 x 17 cm. 1946. W. Morrow and Company.

Beim, Jerrold (1910-1957) & Sugarman, Tracy (1921-)
--Sir Halloween. LC 59-5000. (Illus.). 48 p. 22cm. (Morrow junior books). 1959. Morrow.

Beim, Lorraine Levey (1909-1951)
--Alice's Family. La Mont, Violet, illus. LC 48-8366. v. 120 p. illus. 23 cm. 1948. Harcourt, Brace.
--Benjamin Busybody. La Mont, Violet, illus. LC 47-30208. 61 p. col. illus. 21 1/2 x 17 cm. 1947. Harcourt, Brace and Company.
--Burro That Had A Name. 1962. (ISBN 0-8382-0135-0, Cadmus Books). E. M. Hale and company.
--Carol's Side of the Street. Malman, illus. LC 51-13195. (Illus.). (gr. 3-6). 1951. (ISBN 0-15-214641-5, HJ). HarBraceJ.
--Hurry Back. Levy, Edgar, illus. LC 49-10964. 200 p. illus. 21 cm. 1949. Harcourt, Brace.
--Just Plain Maggie. 1st ed. Cooney, Barbara (1917-), illus. LC 50-9617. 185 p. illus. 21 cm. 1950. Harcourt, Brace.
--Sugar and Spice. LC 47-31310. 3 l., 3-215 p. 21 cm. 1947. Harcourt, Brace.
--Triumph Clear. LC 46-3638. 4 p. l., 3-200 p. 20 1/2 cm. 1946. Harcourt, Brace and Company.
--Triumph Clear. 20cm. 200p. (Voyager bk.: AVB35). 1966, c.1946. Harcourt.

Beim, Lorraine Levey (1909-1951) & Beim, Jerrold (1910-1957)
--Blue Jeans. Hazelton, Isaac Brewster, illus. LC 41-3682. viii, 239 p. incl. front., plates. 21 cm. 1941. Harcourt, Brace and Company.
--The Burrow That Had a Name. LC 39-27628. 63 p. illus. 21 1/2 cm. c.1939. Harcourt, Brace and Company.
--Gregori's Lamb. Busoni, Rafaello (1900-1962), illus. LC 48-4444. 92 p. illus. (part col.) 22 cm. (Saalfield treasure book). c.1948. Saalfield Pub. Co.
--The Little Igloo. Simon, Howard (1903-1979), illus. LC 41-15460. 72 p. col. illus. 21 1/2 x 18 cm. 1941. Harcourt, Brace and Company.
--Lucky Pierre. N.D. E. M. Hale & Co.
--Lucky Pierre. LC 40-32630. 61 p. col. illus. 21 1/2 c 18 cm. 1940. Harcourt, Brace and Company.
--Sasha and the Samovar. Busoni, Rafaello (1900-1962), illus. LC 44-40173. 68 p. illus. 21 1/2 x 17 1/2 cm. 1944. Harocurt, Brace and Company.
--Snow Hill. Panesis, Nicholas (1913-), illus. LC 42-5826. 5 p. l., 3-230 p. incl. illus., plates. front. 21 cm. 1942. Harcourt, Brace and Company.
--Spotlight for Danny. Malvern, Corinne (1905-1956), illus. LC 43-3407. 3 p. l., 3-198 p. incl. plates. front. 21 cm. 1943. Harcourt, Brace and Company.
--Sunshine and Shadow. 1st ed. LC 52-6910. 182 p. 21 cm. 1952. Harcourt, Brace.
--Two is a Team. Crichlow, Ernest T. (1914-), illus. LC 45-86003. 61 p. illus. (part. col.) 21 x 17 1/2 cm. 1945. Harcourt, Brace and Company.
--Two is a Team. Crichlow, Ernest T. (1914-), illus. LC 73-12939. (Illus.). 61 p. 22cm. (Voyager book, AVB 86). 1974, c.1945. (ISBN 0-15-692050-6). Harcourt Brace Jovanovich.

Beimdieck, John F. see Junior, B., pseud.

Beimes, Charlotte Reger
--Naughty Frisky. Gilmour, Marie E., illus. LC 37-24116. 1 p. l., 6 p. col. illus. 26 cm. c.1937. H. A. Beimes.

Beiner, Stan J.
--Sedra Scenes: Skits for Every Torah Portion. 225p. (Orig.). (gr. 6-12). 1982. (ISBN 0-86705-032-2). AIRE.
Beisert, Heide Helene
--Poor Fish. Beisert, Heide Helene, illus. LC 82-11822. p. cm. 1982. (ISBN 0-571-12514-X). Faber and Faber in Association with Nord-Sud Verlag.
Beisner, Monika
--An Address Book: With Riddles, Rhymes, Tales, & Tongue Twisters. (Illus.). 1979. (ISBN 0-374-30053-4). FS&G.
--The Birthday Box of Dreams. Beisner, Monika, illus. LC 74-18130. (Illus.). 32p. (Picture Bk). (ps-1). 1975. (ISBN 0-695-80532-0). (ISBN 0-695-40532-2). Follett.
--A Book of Riddles. Beisner, Monika, illus. LC 83-81529. (Illus.). 32p. (gr. 1 up). 1983. (ISBN 0-374-30866-7). (ISBN 0-374-30866-7). FS&G.
--Fantastic Toys. LC 74-79249. (Illus.). 24 p. 28cm. 1975, c.1973. (ISBN 0-695-80504-5). (ISBN 0-695-40504-7). Follett.
Beistle, Aldarilla S., Mrs.
--I Spy,". Beistle, Mary Alice, illus. LC 44-75921. 17 p. col. illus. 23 x 18 1/2 cm. 1944. David McKay Company.
--Just Puggy. Beistle, Mary Alice, illus. LC 39-25700. 63 1 p. illus. 21 cm. c.1939. David McKay Company.
--Mr. Heinie. Beistle, Mary Alice, illus. LC 38-86981. 32 p. illus. (part col.) 16 x 23 cm. c.1938. David McKay Company.
--Mr. Heinie and Scroot. 1st ed. Beistle, Mary Alice, illus. LC 39-7588. 36 p. col. illus. 16 x 23 cm. c.1939. David McKay Company.
--Open Daily. Beistle, Mary Alice, illus. LC 42-13307. 90, 2 p. illus. (part col.) 25 x 19 cm. 1942. The David McKay Company.
Beith, Norton, ed.
--World Over. An Illustrated Anthology for Jewish Youth. LC 52-7053. 538 p. illus. 22 cm. 1952. Bloch Pub. Co.
Bejna, Barbara, jt. auth. see Zelonky, Joy.
Belacee, pseud., see Lacy, Barnet W..
Belair, Richard L.
--Double Take. LC 79-17056. 192p. (gr. 7-9). 1979. (ISBN 0-688-22202-1). (ISBN 0-688-32202-6). Morrow.
Belaney, Archibald Stansfield see Grey Owl, pseud.
Belasco, David (1859-1931)
--Girl from the Golden West. N.D. Grosset & Dunlap.
Belasco, David (1859-1931) & Byrne, C.
--A Book of Fairy Tales. (Illus.). N.D. Baker & Taylor Co.
Belden, Shirley
--Sand in My Castle. LC 58-9741. (Illus.). 174 p. 22cm. 1958. Longmans, Green.
--Star Dust. 1st. ed. LC 56-9213. 214p. illus. 21cm. 1956. Longmans, Green.
Belden, Wilanne Schneider (1925-)
--Mind-Call. LC 80-18488. 252p. (gr. 5-9). 1981. (ISBN 0-689-30796-9, Argo). Atheneum.
--The Rescue of Ranor. LC 82-13806. p. cm. 1983. (ISBN 0-689-30951-1). Atheneum.
Belew, M. Wendell (1922-)
--The Dark's A-Creepin'. Fields, Don, illus. LC 77-94678. Repr. of 1964 ed (Pub. by Home Mission Board). (gr. k-6). 1979. (ISBN 0-8054-4416-5). Broadman.
Bel Geddes, Barbara
--I Like to Be Me. Bel Geddes, Barbara, illus. LC 63-8531. (Illus.). 34cm. 32p. (ps-1). 1963. (ISBN 0-670-39059-3). Viking Pr.
--So do I. LC 72-79617. 18cm. 31p. c.1972. Arbor House.
--So Do I. Duenewald, Doris, ed. Bel Geddes, Barbara, illus. (Illus.). 36p. (ps-2). 1972. G&D.
Belger, Mary Josita, Sr.
--Sing a Song of Holy Things. Malopolski, M. Maxine, Sr., illus. LC 46-948. 6 p. l., 111 p. incl. col. front., illus. (part col.) 21 1/2 cm. 1945. The Tower Press.
Belina, Tom
--Flight to Fear. (Illus.). (Pacesetters Ser.). (gr. 4 up). 1978. (ISBN 0-516-02155-9). Childrens.
Beling, Mabel Ashe, Mrs.
--The Wicked Goldsmith: Tales of Ancient India. LC 41-4809. 7 p. l., 144 p. front., illus., plates. 22 cm. c.1941. Harper & Brothers.
Belisle, D. W.
--The American Family Robinson: Adventures of a Family Lost in the Great Desert of the West. N.D. Porter & Coates.
Bell, Adelaide Fuller
--Clare's Problem: Or, Was it her Duty. N.D. American Baptist Society.
--The King's Rubies: A Story for Boys and Girls. N.D. John C. Winson Co.
Bell, Adrian Hanbury (1901-1980)
--Apple Acre. rev ed. Kennedy, Richard (1910-), illus. (Illus.). (gr. 7 up). 1964. (ISBN 0-685-20932-6). Verry.
--A Young Man's Fancy. 1956. Abelard-Schuman.
Bell, Alexander Graham (1847-1922)
--The Sanders Reader. LC 74-15016. (Illus.). 20 l. 21cm. 1969. Alexander Graham.

Bell, Anna & Hastings, H. L.
--Bible Rhymes and Bible Lessons. 80p. N.D. Publications of H. L. Hastings.
Bell, Anthea
--The Great Menagerie. 1980. Viking.
--Stories of the Arabian Nights. Giannini, Jean, illus. LC 83-71485. p. cm. 1983. (ISBN 0-911745-02-5). P. Bedrick Books.
Bell, Anthea, adapted by see Grimm, Jakob Ludwig Karl (1785-1863) & Grimm, Wilhelm Karl.
Bell, Anthea, adapted by see Hoffmann, Ernst Theodor Amadeus.
Bell, Anthea, adapted by see Strahl, Rudi.
Bell, Anthea, tr. see Andersen, Hans Christian.
Bell, Anthea, tr. see Aurembou, Renee.
Bell, Anthea, tr. see Bartos-Hoppner, Barbara.
Bell, Anthea, tr. see Bechstein, Ludwig.
Bell, Anthea, tr. see Donnelly, Elfie.
Bell, Anthea, tr. see Fahrmann, Willi.
Bell, Anthea, tr. see Fehse, Willi Richard (1906-) & Petis De la Croix, Francois.
Bell, Anthea, tr. see Goscinny, Rene.
Bell, Anthea, tr. see Grimm, Jakob Ludwig Karl (1785-1863) & Grimm, Wilhelm Karl.
Bell, Anthea, tr. see Haertling, Peter.
Bell, Anthea, tr. see Hauff, Wilhelm.
Bell, Anthea, tr. see Hoffmann, Ernst Theodor Amadeus.
Bell, Anthea, tr. see Hurlimann, Ruth.
Bell, Anthea, tr. see Koenig, Alma Johanna.
Bell, Anthea, tr. see Korinetz, Yuri Iosifovich.
Bell, Anthea, tr. see Nostlinger, Christine.
Bell, Anthea, tr. see Pesek, Ludek.
Bell, Anthea, tr. see Peyo.
Bell, Anthea, tr. see Peyo, pseud. & Delporte, Yvan.
Bell, Anthea, tr. see Preussler, Otfried.
Bell, Anthea, tr. see Schirmann, Lilli.
Bell, Anthea, tr. see Schmid, Eleonore.
Bell, Anthea, tr. see Shirmann, Lilli.
Bell, Anthea, tr. see Strahl, Rudi.
Bell, Anthea, tr. see Tluchor, Alois.
Bell, Anthea, tr. see Tom Thumb & Grimm, Jakob Ludwig Karl.
Bell, Anthea, tr. see Voltaire, Francois Marie Arouet De.
Bell, Anthea, tr. see Wilkon, Jozef (1930-) & Bauman, Kurt.
Bell, Anthea, tr. see Wolfel, Ursula.
Bell, Anthea & Rogers, Anne
--More Favourite Tales From Grimm. Otto, Svend (1916-), illus. (Illus.). 112p. (gr. k-3). 1984. (ISBN 0-7207-1486-9). Merrimack Pub Cir.

Bell, Beth Hamilton
--Lord Ham. Pollard, Ann Carter, illus. LC 60-15717. (Illus.). (gr. 5 up). 1960. (ISBN 0-910244-20-0). Blair.

Bell, Bill
--Saxophone Boy. (Illus.). 24p. (gr. 4 up). 1980. (ISBN 0-912766-98-0). Tundra Bks.

Bell, Bob & Bell, Elise
--Television and Teamwork. LC 61-15983. 240 p. 21 cm. (Dodd, Mead career books). 1962. Dodd, Mead.

Bell, Carl Irving (1912-)
--Christmas in Old New England. LC 80-69858. (Illus.). 45 p. 22cm. c.1981. (ISBN 0-917780-02-7). April Hill Publishers.

Bell, Catherine Douglas (0000-1861)

--Allen and Harry. (Birthday Ser.). N.D. R. Worthington & Co.
--Allen and Harry: Or, Set About it at Once. (Illus.). N.D. Scribner, Welford & Armstrong.
--Arnold Lee. (Birthday Ser.). N.D. R. Worthington & Co.
--Arnold Lee: Or, Rich and Poor Boys. (Illus.). N.D. Scribner, Welford & Armstrong.
--Aunt Ailie: Or, Patience and Its Reward. N.D. Scribner, Welford & Armstrong.
--Aunt Allie. (Home Sunshine Library). N.D. R. Worthington & Co.
--An Autumn at Karnford. (Birthday Ser.). N.D. R. Worthington & Co.
--Autumn at Karnford. (Illus.). N.D. Scribner, Welford & Armstrong.
--The Douglas Family. (Birthday Ser.). N.D. R. Worthington & Co.
--The Douglas Family: Or, Friendship. (Illus.). N.D. Scribner, Welford & Armstrong.
--Ella and Marian. (Home Sunshine Library). N.D. R. Worthington & Co.
--Ella and Marian: Or, Rest and Unrest. N.D. Scribner, Welford & Armstrong.
--Every Saturday. (Illus.). N.D. Scribner, Welford & Armstrong.
--Georgie and Lizzie. (Birthday Ser.). N.D. R. Worthington & Co.
--Georgie and Lizzie: Or, Self-Denial. (Illus.). N.D. Scribner, Welford & Armstrong.
--The Grahams. (Home Sunshine Library). N.D. R. Worthington & Co.
--The Grahams: Or, Home Life. N.D. Scribner, Welford & Armstrong.
--Home Sunshine: Or, The Gordons. N.D. Scribner, Welford & Armstrong.
--Home Sunshine: The Gordons. (Home Sunshine Library). N.D. R. Worthington & Co.
--Hope Campbell. (Home Sunshine Library). N.D. R. Worthington & Co.
--Hope Campbell: Or, Know Thyself. N.D. Scribner, Welford & Armstrong.
--Horace and May. (Home Sunshine Library). N.D. R. Worthington & Co.
--Horace and May: Or, Unconscious Influence. N.D. Scribner, Welford & Armstrong.
--The Huguenot Family. (Golden Link Ser.). N.D. R. Worthington & Co.
--Jane Thorne: Or,The Head and the Heart. N.D. Henry Hoyt.
--Jennie Carter: Or,Trust in God. N.D. Henry Hoyt.
--Kenneth and Hugh. (Home Sunshine Library). N.D. R. Worthington & Co.
--Lilly Gordon: Or, The Young Housekeeper. (Cousin Kate Library). N.D. Frederick Warne & Co.
--Lily Gordon, 1 of 33 Vols. (Illus.). (Warne's Golden Links Ser.: No.3). N.D. Scribner & Welford.
--Margaret Cedil. (Home Sunshine Library). N.D. R. Worthington & Co.
--Mary Elliot, 1 of 22 Vols. (Illus.). (Warne's Home Circle Ser.: No.3). N.D. Scribner & Welford.
--Mary Elliott. (Warne's Star Ser.). N.D. Scribner & Welford.
--Rosa's Wish. (Home Sunshine Library). N.D. R. Worthington & Co.
--Trust In God. 64p. (Moss-Rose Stories). N.D. Lockwood, Brooks, & Co. for American Tract Society.
Bell, Clare
--Clan Ground. LC 84-6289. 276p. (gr. 7 up). 1984. (ISBN 0-689-50304-0, Argo). Atheneum.
--Ratha's Creature. LC 82-13875. 259 p. 22cm. 1983. (ISBN 0-689-50262-1). Atheneum. **Award: (IRA).**
Bell, Corydon, frwd. by see Moore, Clement Clarke.
Bell, Corydon Whitten (1894-)
--John Rattling-Gourd of Big Cave: A Collection of Cherokee Legends. N.D. Macmillan.
Bell, Currer, ed. see Bronte, Charlotte.
Bell, Eileen (1907-)
--Tales from the End Cottage. Seward, Prudence, illus. LC 75-19645. (Illus.). 20cm. 125p. (A Young Puffin original). 1970. Penguin.
Bell, Elise, jt. auth. see Bell, Bob.
Bell, Elizabeth Rose (1912-)
--Magic-Go-Round. Slater, Cher, illus. LC 73-12098. (Illus.). 64 p. 25cm. 1974. (ISBN 0-516-07626-4). Childrens Press.
Bell, Emerson, pseud., see Stratemeyer, Edward L..
Bell, Emerson, pseud. (1862-1930)
--The Electric Wizard: Or, Through Air and Water to the Pole. Stratemeyer, Edward L.. (Brave and Bold Ser.: No. 198). 1906. Street & Smith.
Bell, Esther
--At Grips with the Dragon: A Novel of Old China and the New World. LC 42-204. 282 p. 20 cm. c.1941. Zondervan Publishing House.
Bell, Florence Eveleen Eleanore Oliffe, Lady (1851-1930)
--Fairy Tale Plays. N.D. Longmans,Green & Co.
Bell, Florence Eveleen Eleanore Olliffe, Lady (1851-1930)
--The Cat and Fiddle Book: Eight Dramatised Nursery Rhymes for Nursery Performers. Richmond, Florence Elsa Bell, Lady, contrib. by. LC 26-26052. 47 p. illus. (music) 19 cm. 1922. Longmans, Green and Co.
Bell, Frederic
--Jenny's Corner. Onyshkewych, Zenowij, illus. LC 73-18741. (Illus.). 58 p. 22cm. 1974. (ISBN 0-394-82741-4). (ISBN 0-394-82741-4). Random House.
Bell, Gail Winther (1936-)
--In the Strange, Strange Wood. Magleby, McRay, illus. LC 76-190286. (Illus.). 29 p. 27cm. (Magic with words series). 1972. (ISBN 0-8425-0445-1). Brigham Young University Publications.
Bell, George H., tr. see Guillot, Rene.
Bell, Gertrude Wood (1911-)
--First Crop. Hood, Susan, illus. LC 72-89608. (Illus.). 164 p. 21cm. 1973. (ISBN 0-8309-0082-9). Independence Press.
--A Ladder for Silvanus. Livesay, John, illus. LC 74-82509. (Illus.). 47 p. 24cm. 1975. (ISBN 0-8309-0126-4). Independence Press.
--Posse of Two. 1964. E M Hale.
--Posse of Two. Kidwell, Carl (1910-), illus. LC 64-23455. 160 p. illus. 22 cm. (Criterion book for young people). 1964. Criterion Books.
--Roundabout Road. Ritchie, Judith, illus. LC 72-4574. (Illus.). 173 p. 21cm. 1972. (ISBN 0-8309-0074-8). Independence Press.
--Where Runs the River. LC 76-4918. p. cm. c.1976. (ISBN 0-8309-0118-3). Independence Press.
Bell, Gina, pseud., see Balzano, Jeanne Koppel.
Bell, Gina, pseud. (1912-)
--Andy & Mr. Wagner. Balzano, Jeanne Koppel. N.D. E. M. Hale & Co.
--Andy & Mr. Wagner. Balzano, Jeanne Koppel. Wilde, George A., illus. (Illus.). (gr. k-3). 1957. (ISBN 0-687-01490-5). Abingdon.
--Three Boys & a Dog. Balzano, Jeanne Koppel. Wilde, George A., illus. (Illus.). (gr. k-3). N.D. (ISBN 0-687-41929-8). Abingdon.
--Wanted-a Brother. Balzano, Jeanne Koppel. Wilde, George A., illus. (Illus.). (gr. k-3). 1959. (ISBN 0-687-43998-1). Abingdon.
--What Makes Siggy Smart. Balzano, Jeanne Koppel. Kurek, Sarah C., illus. (Illus.). (gr. k-3). 1967. (ISBN 0-687-44824-7). Abingdon.
--Who Wants Willy Wells. Balzano, Jeanne Koppel. (Illus.). (gr. 1-3). 1965. (ISBN 0-8382-0951-3). Hale.
--Who Wants Willy Wells. Balzano, Jeanne Koppel. Tamburine, Jean (1930-), illus. (Illus.). (gr. k-3). N.D. (ISBN 0-687-45324-0). Abingdon.
Bell, H.
--Nursery Comedies. N.D. Longmans Green & Co.
Bell, Jack Mackintosh, jt. auth. see Brown, Abbie Farwell.
Bell, Janet, pseud., see Clymer, Eleanor Lowenton.
Bell, Janet, pseud. (1906-)
--The Monday-Tuesday-Wednesday Book. Clymer, Eleanor Lowenton. Stevens, Mary E. (1920-1966), illus. LC 47-361. 32 p. illus. (part col.) 23 1/2 x 19 1/2 cm. 1946. R. M. McBride & Company.
--Sunday in the Park. Clymer, Eleanor Lowenton. Appel, Aline, illus. LC 48-3617. 25cm. 26p. 1946. McBride.
Bell, Jessica Hedrick (1884-)
--The Dish Boat. LC 43-17661. 94 p. 18 cm. 1943. The Wartburg Press.
--Joe and Jennie. LC 47-11913. 64 p. 18 cm. 1947. Wartburg Press.
Bell, John Jay (1871-)
--Kiddies. 19cm. 278p. 1917. F. A. Stokes Co.
--Later Adventures of Wee Macgreegor. N.D. Harper & Brothers Trade-List.
--Mr. Pennycook's Boy. LC 5-11898. 18cm. 271p. 1905. Harper & Brothers.
--Wee MAcGreegor. (The Good Value Books). N.D. Grosset & Dunlap.
--Wee MacGreegor. (Sunset Set.). N.D. J. S. Ogilvie.
--Wee Macgregor. 1903. Harper & Bros.
Bell, Kensil (1907-)
--Coast Guard Cadet. U. S. Coast Guard, photos by. LC 41-22367. viii p., 1 l., 232 p. plates. 21 cm. (Career books). 1941. Dodd, Mead & Company.
--Danger on the Jersey Shore. LC 59-10108. 243p. illus. 21cm. 1959. Dodd, Mead.
--Ice Patrol: Jim Steele's Adventures with the U. S. Coast Guard. Beaudouin, Frank, illus. U. S. Coast Guard, photos by. LC 37-23637. ix p., 2 l., 262 p. front., illus., plates. 21 cm. 1937. Dodd, Mead & Company.
--Jersey Rebel. LC 51-13073. 248 p. 21 cm. 1951. Dodd, Mead.
--Secret Mission for Valley Forge. LC 55-5212. 246 p. 21cm. 1955. Dodd, Mead.
Bell, Lettice
--Go-to-Bed Stories. N.D. George H Doran.
--Go-to-Bed Stories. LC 9-17651. 22cm. 170p. 1909. Gospel Publishing House.
--G0-To-Bed Stories. N.D. Loizeaux Bros.
--The Tuck-Me-Up Book: Bed-time Stories. N.D. George H Doran.
Bell, Lilian Lida (1867-)
--Hope Loring. Merrill, Frank Thayer (1848-), illus. N.D. Page Co.
--Land of Don't Want-To. Winter, Milo Kendall (1888-1956), illus. N.D. Rand McNally.
--The Runaway Equator: And the Strange Adventures of a Little Boy in Pursuit of It. Newell, Peter (1862-1924), illus. LC 11-22133. ix, 118 p. front., plates. 22 cm. 1911. Frederick A. Stokes Company.
Bell, Louise Price, Mrs.
--Grimpo & Grumpy. Koehne, John, illus. (gr. k-4). 1964. (ISBN 0-8272-1211-9). Bethany Pr.
--Pedro. Baerg, Harry John (1909-), illus. LC 61-119763. 59p. illus. 24cm. 1961. Review and Herald Pub. Association.
--Sick-a-Bed Sally. Phares, Margaret, illus. LC 32-22196. 96 p. incl. front., illus. 22 cm. N.D. Thomas Y. Crowell Company.C.
--What did Tommy Say?. Dunn, Dorothy, illus. LC 60-7185. 23cm. 1960. Warner Press.
Bell, Lucille
--Dog Goes to Nursery School. Eugenie, illus. (Illus.). 24p. (First Little Golden Bks.). (ps). 1982. (ISBN 0-307-10134-7, Golden Pr). Western Pub.

--Summer's Coming in. Adams, Adrienne (1906-), illus. LC 74-98921. (Illus.). 48 p. 1970. (ISBN 0-03-084250-6). Holt, Rinehart and Winston.

--The Sun is a Golden Earring. 1st ed. Bryson, Bernarda (1905-1977), illus. LC 62-14216. (Illus.). 48 p. 1962. Holt, Rinehart and Winston. **Awards: (ALA); (RCM).**

--The Sun Is a Golden Earring. Bryson, Bernarda (1905-1977), illus. (Illus.). 1 v. (Holt owlet Book, H0234). 1973, c.1962. (ISBN 0-03-088503-5). Holt.

--Three Apples Fell from Heaven: Unfamiliar Legends of the Trees. 1st ed. Jauss, Anne Marie (1907-), illus. LC 53-887717. 158p. illus. 23cm. 1953. Bobbs-Merrill.

--Verity Mullens & the Indian. Fisher, Leonard Everett (1924-), illus. LC 60-13072. (Illus.). 32p. (gr. k-4). 1960. (ISBN 0-03-032785-7). HR&W.

--Winter's Eve. Cober, Alan Edwin (1935-), illus. LC 73-85425. (Illus.). 48 p. 27cm. 1969. (ISBN 0-03-082931-3). Holt, Rinehart, and Winston. **Award: (NYT).**

Belting, Natalia Maree (1915-), compiled by.

--Our Fathers Had Powerful Songs. Kubinyi, Laszlo (1937-), illus. LC 73-13968. (Illus.). 32p. (gr. 2-6). 1974. Dutton.

--Whirlwind is a Ghost Dancing. Dutton, Leo (1933-) & Dutton, Diane (1933-), illus. 1974. Dutton.

Beltramelli, Antonio (1874-)

--Piccolo Pomi. Ongley, Leo, tr. LC 25-12735. vi p., 1 l., 254 p. illus. 20 cm. c.1925. E. P. Dutton & Company.

Beltz, George W

--Bull-Bull, the Indian Boy. Pickel, Charlotte, illus. LC 65-2135. 1 v. (unpaged) illus. 21 cm. 1965. Bethany Press.

Beman, Delmar W., Sr. (1888-)

--And I Learn About People: Chapters in a Dog's Life, by "Sincerely Yours, D. W.,". 1st ed. Mitchell, Jo Ann, illus. LC 52-10676. 75 p. illus. 21 cm. 1952. Exposition Press.

Bemelmans, Ludwig (1898-1962)

--The Castle Number Nine. Bemelmans, Ludwig (1898-1962), illus. LC 37-286805. 48 p. illus. (part col.) 25 cm. 1937. The Viking Press.

--Fifi. Bemelmans, Ludwig (1898-1962), illus. LC 40-298780. 46 p. col. illus. 31 x 24 cm. c.1940. Simon and Schuster.

--Fifi. Bemelmans, Ludwig (1898-1962), illus. LC 76-366657. (Illus.). 46 p. 31cm. 1976, c.1940. Simon and Schuster.

--The Golden Basket. LC 36-19451. 95, 1 illus. (part col.) 26 cm. 1936. The Viking Press. **Award: (JNM).**

--Hansi. 1962. Viking.

--Hansi. Bemelmans, Ludwig (1898-1962), illus. LC 34-33475. 64 p. illus. (port col.) 31 cm. 1934. The Viking Press.

--The Happy Place. Bemelmans, Ludwig (1898-1962), illus. LC 52-8338. (Illus.). 58 p. 21cm. 1952. Little, Brown. **Award: (NYT).**

--The High World. Bemelmans, Ludwig (1898-1962), illus. LC 54-8936. (Illus.). 113 p. 24cm. 1954. Harper.

--Madeline. new ed. 1960. Viking.

--Madeline. (Illus.). 48 p. 32cm. 1963. Viking Press.

--Madeline. Bemelmans, Ludwig (1898-1962), illus. (Little Golden Book). 1954. Golden Press.

--Madeline. Bemelmans, Ludwig (1898-1962), illus. LC 76-50664. p. cm. 1977, c.1939. (ISBN 0-14-050198-3). Puffin Books.

--Madeline. Bemelmans, Luwig (1898-1962), illus. LC 39-21791. 48 p. illus. (port col.) 31 cm. 1939. Simon and Schuster.

--Madeline. Bemelmans, Ludwig (1898-1962), illus. LC 54-2640. unpaged. illus. 21cm. (Little golden books, 196). c.1954. Simon and Schuster.

--Madeline. Bemelmans, Ludwig (1898-1962), illus. (Illus.). (gr. k-3). 1939. (ISBN 0-670-44580-0). Viking Pr. **Award: (RCM).**

--Madeline. Bemelmans, Ludwig (1898-1962), illus. LC 64-55753. 1 v. (unpaged) col. illus 32cm. 1963. Viking Press.

--Madeline and the Bad Hat. Bemelmans, Ludwig (1898-1962), illus. LC 77-1976. p. cm. 1977, c.1956. (ISBN 0-14-050207-6). Puffin Books.

--Madeline and the Bad Hat. 1st ed. Bemelmans, Ludwig (1898-1962), illus. LC 57-62. 54p. col. illus. 32cm. 1956. Viking Press.

--Madeline & the Bad Hat. Bemelmans, Ludwig (1898-1962), illus. (Illus.). (gr. k-3). 1957. (ISBN 0-670-44614-9). Viking Pr.

--Madeline and the Gypsies. LC 77-23792. p. cm. 1977. (ISBN 0-14-050261-0). Puffin Books.

--Madeline & the Gypsies. Bemelmans, Ludwig (1898-1962), illus. LC 59-16391. (Illus.). (gr. k-3). 1959. (ISBN 0-670-44682-3). Viking Pr.

--Madeline in London. LC 76-54807. p. cm. 1977, c.1961. (ISBN 0-14-050199-1). Puffin Books.

--Madeline in London. Bemelmans, Ludwig (1898-1962), illus. LC 61-11672. (Illus.). (gr. k-3). 1961. (ISBN 0-670-44648-3). Viking Pr.

--Madeline's Christmas Tree in Texas. Bemelmans, Ludwig (1898-1962), illus. 1955. Nieman, Marcus.

--Madeline's Rescue. (Illus.). 48p. (gr. k-3). 1969 (StarLine). Schol Bk Serv.

--Madeline's Rescue. Bemelmans, Ludwig (1898-1962), illus. LC 77-2573. p. cm. 1977, c.1953. (ISBN 0-14-050207-6). Puffin Books.

--Madeline's Rescue. Bemelmans, Ludwig (1898-1962), illus. LC 53-8709. 56p. illus. 31cm. (gr. k-3). 1953. (ISBN 0-670-44716-1). Viking Press. **Awards: (RCM); (NYT); (ALA).**

--Marina. LC 62-133262. unpaged. illus. 26x33cm. 1962. Harper Row.

--Parsley. Bemelmans, Ludwig (1898-1962), illus. LC 55-7682. (Illus.). 46 p. 1955. Harper. **Award: (NYT).**

--Quito Express. Bemelmans, Ludwig (1898-1962), illus. 1938. Viking.

--Quito Express. Bemelmans, Ludwig (1898-1962), illus. LC 38-31285. 47p. illus. 29x24cm. 1965, c.1938. (ISBN 0-670-58570-X). Viking.

--Rosebud. LC 42-24489. 32 p. col. illus. 26 x 21 cm. 1942. Random House.

--Sunshine, a story about the city of New York. Bemelmans, Ludwig (1898-1962), illus. LC 50-7955. 1950. Simon & Schuster.

--A Tale of Two Glimps. LC 48-153. 50 p. illus. (part col.) 20 cm. 1947. Columbia Broadcasting System.

--Welcome Home!. After a Poem by Beverley Bogert. LC 60-9447. unpaged. illus. 26x32cm. 1960. (ISBN 0-06-020465-6). Harper.

Beming, Howe

--One Girl's Way Out. (The Girl CHums Ser.). N.D. A. L. Burt Company.

Bemis, Katharine Isabel, jt. ed. see Van Buren, Maud.

Bemister, Margaret

--Golden Caravel. LC 62-19600. 22cm. 153p. (Catholic Treasury Books). 1962. Bruce Publishing Company.

--Indian Legends. (Everychild's Ser.). N.D. Macmillan.

Ben-Ami, pseud., see Scharfstein, Ben-Ami.

Ben-Israel, Shelomo

--The Strange Adventures of Danny Noor. Brazelton, Julian, illus. LC 47-397907. 4 p. l., 3-142, 1 p. illus. 23 1/2 cm. 1945. Behrman House.

Ben-Moring, Alvin Lester (1931-)

--Balthazar, the Black and Shining Prince: A Christmas Legend. Gretzer, John, illus. LC 74-8177. (Illus.). 124 p. 24cm. 1974. (ISBN 0-664-32554-8). Westminster Press.

--Quadrus and Goliath. Malik, George A., illus. LC 75-43633. 159 p. 21cm. c.1976. Westminster Press.

Benabo, Brian

--Moonlight Kingdom. Jupp, Michael, illus. LC 75-29608. (Illus.). 92 p. 24cm. 1976, c.1972. St. Martin's Press.

Benarde, Anita

--The Pumpkin Smasher. Benarde, Anita, illus. LC 76-189792. (Illus.). 32 p. 1972. (ISBN 0-8027-6109-7). Walker.

Benardete, Jane Johnson (1930-) & Moe, Phyllis, eds.

--Companions of Our Youth: Stories by Women for Young People's Magazines, 1865-1900. LC 80-5339. (Illus.). 1980. (ISBN 0-8044-2043-2). (ISBN 0-8044-6047-7). Ungar.

Benary-Isbert, Margot (1889-1979)

--The Ark. Winston, Richard & Winston, Clara, trs. LC 52-13677. 246 p. 21cm. 1953. Harcourt, Brace. **Award: (ALA).**

--Blue Mystery. Arno, Enrico (1913-1981), illus. Winston, Richard & Winston, Clara, trs. from Ger. LC 57-6558. 190p. (gr. 4-7). 1957. (ISBN 0-15-209092-4, HJ). HarBraceJ.

--Blue Mystery. Arno, Enrico (1913-1981), illus. LC 57-6558. (Illus.). (gr. 4-7). 1965. (ISBN 0-15-613225-7, VoyB). HarBraceJ.

--Castle on the Border. 1st. ed. Arno, Enrico (1913-1981), illus. Winston, Clara & Winston, Richard (1917-1979), trs. from Ger. LC 56-5871. (gr. 10 up). 1956. (ISBN 0-15-214999-6, HJ). HarBraceJ. **Award: (ALA).**

--Dangerous Spring. Kirup, James, tr. from German. LC 61-8192. 252 p. 21cm. 1961. Harcourt, Brace & World.

--The Long Way Home. Winston, Clara & Winston, Richard (1917-1979), trs. from Ger (Pub. by Harcourt). (gr. 7-12). 1972 (Starline). Schol Bk Serv.

--The Long Way Home. Winston, Richard & Winston, Clara, trs. from Ger. LC 59-7519. 280 p. 21cm. 1959. Harcourt, Brace.

--Rowan Farm. Winston, Clara & Winston, Richard (1917-1979), trs. from Ger. LC 54-8568. (gr. 7-9). 1954. (ISBN 0-15-269236-3). HarBraceJ. **Award: (ALA).**

--The Shooting Star. Liebman, Oscar (1919-), illus. Winston, Richard (1917-1979) & Winston, Clara, trs. from Ger. LC 54-5150. (Illus.). 118 p. 20cm. 1954. Harcourt, Brace.

--A Time to Love. Benary-Isbert, Margot (1889-1979) & Emerson, Joyce, trs. from Ger. LC 62-15626. 256 p. 21cm. 1962. Harcourt, Brace & World.

--The Wicked Enchantment. Arno, Enrico (1913-1981), illus. Winston, Richard (1917-1979) & Winston, Clara, trs. from Ger. LC 55-8671. (Illus.). 181 p. 21cm. 1955. Harcourt, Brace. **Award: (ALA).**

Benary-Isbert, Margot (1889-1979), ed.

--Under a Changing Moon. Ockenden, Rosaleen & Benary-Isbert, Margot, trs. from German LC 64-17084. 285 p. 21 cm. 1964. Harcourt, Brace & World.

Benary-Isbert, Margot, tr. see Benary-Isbert, Margot.

Benbow, Harriet Beecher

--My Little Arbutus Flower: A Tale from the Great Pinetree Regions. Rosenkrans, Beth & Lyon, Mildred, illus. LC 21-14291. 64 p. incl. front., illus. 19 cm. ("Just right books"). c.1921. Albert Whitman Company.

Bence, William

--People of the Bison. 1st ed. LC 66-9211. 186 p. 21cm. 1966. Duell, Sloan and Pearce.

Benchley, Belle

--Shirley Visits the Zoo. Kirkpatrick, G. E., illus. 1946. J. B. Lippincott.

Benchley, Nathaniel Goddard (1915-1981), retold by see Sindbad the Sailor.

Benchley, Nathaniel Goddard (1915-1981)

--Beyond the Mists. LC 75-9389. 160p. (gr. 7 up). 1975. (ISBN 0-06-020459-1, HarpJ). (ISBN 0-06-020460-5). Har-Row.

--Bright Candles: A Novel of the Danish Resistance. LC 73-5477. 256 p. 22cm. 1974. (ISBN 0-06-020461-3). (ISBN 0-06-020461-3). Harper Row.

--The Deep Dives of Stanley Whale. Richter, Mischa (1910-), illus. LC 72-11241. (Illus.). 31 p. 24cm. 1973. (ISBN 0-06-020463-X). (ISBN 0-06-020463-X). Harper & Row.

--Demo and the Dolphin. Gammell, Stephen, illus. LC 80-8434. p. cm. c.1981. (ISBN 0-06-020509-1). (ISBN 0-06-020510-5). Harper & Row.

--Feldman Fieldmouse. Knight, Hilary (1926-), illus. LC 72-135773. (Illus.). 96p. (gr. 4-7). 1971. (ISBN 0-06-440032-8, Trophy). Har-Row.

--Feldman Fieldmouse: A Fable. Knight, Hilary (1926-), illus. 1970. Harper.

--Feldman Fieldmouse: A Fable. Knight, Hilary (1926-), illus. LC 72-135773. (Illus.). 96 p. 20cm. (Trophy Book, J32). 1973, c.1971. (ISBN 0-06-440032-8). Harper.

--The Flying Lesson of Gerald Pelican. Funai, Mamoru R. (1932-), illus. LC 70-105478. (Illus.). 31 p. 24cm. 1970. Harper & Row.

--George the Drummer Boy. Bolognese, Donald Alan (1934-), illus. LC 76-18398. (Illus.). 5 7/8 x 8 1/2. 64p. (18 pt.). (I Can Read History Bks.). (gr. k-3). 1977. (ISBN 0-06-020500-8) (ISBN 0-06-020501-6) Har-Row.

--A Ghost Named Fred. Shecter, Ben (1935-), illus. LC 68-24322. (Illus.). 5 7/8 x 8 1/2. 64p. (18 pt.) (I Can Read Mysteries Ser.). (gr. k-3). 1968. (ISBN 0-06-020474-5) (ISBN 0-06-444022-2) Har-Row.

--Gone & Back. LC 73-145998. (gr. 7 up). 1971. (ISBN 0-06-440016-6, Trophy). Har-Row.

--Kilroy and the Gull. Schoenherr, John Carl (1935-), illus. LC 76-24309. (Illus.). 118 p. 21cm. c.1977. (ISBN 0-06-020502-4). Harper and Row.

--The Magic Sled. Furukawa, Mel, illus. LC 74-183166. (Illus.). 44 p. 24cm. (Harpercrest). 1972. (ISBN 0-06-020489-3). (ISBN 0-06-020490-7). Harper & Row.

--A Necessary End: A Novel of World War II. LC 75-37105. xi, 193 p. 22cm. c.1976. (ISBN 0-06-020498-2). (ISBN 0-06-020499-0). Harper & Row.

--Only Earth and Sky Last Forever. LC 73-12626. 264 p. 25cm. 1973, c.1972. (ISBN 0-8161-6149-6). G. K. Hall.

--Only Earth and Sky Last Forever. LC 72-82891. 191 p. 22cm. 1972. (ISBN 0-06-020493-1). (ISBN 0-06-020493-1). Harper & Row.

--Oscar Otter. Lobel, Arnold, illus. LC 66-11499. (Illus.). 5 7/8 x 8 1/2. 64p. (18 pt.). (I Can Read Bks.). (gr. k-3). 1966. (ISBN 0-06-020472-9). (ISBN 0-06-444025-7). Har-Row.

--Oscar Otter. Lobel, Arnold Stark (1933-), illus. LC 66-11499. (Illus.). 64p. (I Can Read Bk.). (gr. k-3). 1980. (ISBN 0-06-444025-7, Trophy). Har-Row.

--Red Fox & His Canoe. Lobel, Arnold Stark (1933-), illus. LC 64-16650. (Illus.). 5 7/8 x 8 1/2. 64p. (18 pt.). (I Can Read Bks.). (gr. k-3). 1964. (ISBN 0-06-020476-1). Har-Row.

--Running Owl the Hunter. Funai, Mamoru R. (1932-), illus. LC 78-22156. (Illus.). 5 7/8 x 8 1/2. 64p. (18 pt.). (I Can Read Bks.). (gr. k-3). 1979. (ISBN 0-06-020453-2). (ISBN 0-06-020454-0). Har-Row.

--Sam the Minuteman. Lobel, Arnold Stark (1933-), illus. LC 68-10211. (Illus.). 5 7/8 x 8 1/2. 64p. (18 pt.). (I Can Read History Bks.). (gr. k-3). 1969. (ISBN 0-06-020479-6) (ISBN 0-06-020480-X) Har-Row.

--The Several Tricks of Edgar Dolphin. Funai, Mamoru R. (1932-), illus. LC 79-85038. (Illus.). 5 7/8 x 8 1/2. 64p. (18 pt.). (I Can Read Bks.). (gr. k-3). 1970. (ISBN 0-06-020468-0). Har-Row.

--Sinbad the Sailor. O'Sullivan, Tom, illus. LC 60-10166. (Illus.). 23cm. 53p. (Legacy books, Y-14: No. 14). (gr. 4-7). 1960. (ISBN 0-394-80164-4). Random.

--Small Wolf. Sandin, Joan, illus. LC 70-183170. (Illus.). 5 7/8 x 8 1/2. 64p. (18 pt.). (I Can Read History Bks.). (gr. k-3). 1972. (ISBN 0-06-020492-3) Har-Row.

--Snip. Trivas, Irene, illus. LC 80-696. (Illus.). 63 p. 22cm. c.1981. (ISBN 0-385-15997-8). Doubleday.

--Snorri & the Strangers. Bolognese, Donald Alan, illus. LC 76-3290. (Illus.). 5 7/8 x 8 1/2. 64p. (18 pt.). (I Can Read History Bks.). (gr. k-3). 1976. (ISBN 0-06-020457-5) Har-Row.

--The Strange Disappearance of Arthur Cluck. Lobel, Arnold Stark (1933-), illus. LC 67-4151. (Illus.). 5 7/8 x 8 1/2cm. 64p. (18 pt.). (I Can Read Mysteries Ser.). (gr. k-3). 1967. (ISBN 0-06-020478-8) (ISBN 0-06-444024-9) Har-Row.

--Walter, the Homing Pigeon. Darrow, Whitney, Jr. (1909-), illus. LC 79-2696. (Illus.). 26 p. 24cm. c.1981. (ISBN 0-06-020508-3). (ISBN 0-06-020507-5). Harper & Row.

Benchley, Peter Bradford (1940-)

--Jonathan Visits the White House. Bergere, Richard, illus. LC 63-22427. 32 p. illus. (part col.) 26 cm. 1964. McGraw-Hill.

Benchley, Robert, jt. ed. see Becker, May Lamberton, Mrs.

Bendel, Ruth, illus.

--Three Little Pigs. LC 56-8344. unpaged. illus. 17 cm. (Rand McNally junior elf book, 695). c.1956. Rand McNally.

Bender, Anne Kendrick

--Flying Saucers and the Three Men. N.D. Wehman Brothers.

Bender, Eric J.

--I Never Knew That Before. Scott, Janet Laura, illus. LC 38-21860. 2 p. l., 11-123 p. col. front., illus. (part col.) 26 cm. c.1938. The Saalfield Publishing Company.

Bender, Lucy Ellen (1942-)

--The Outside World. Moon, Ivan, illus. LC 69-13138. (Illus.). 112 p. 22cm. 1969. Herald Press.

Bender, Millicent Schwab, Mrs. (1878-), tr. from Ger.

--Great Opera Stories. 186p. (Poetry, Music & Art). (Everychild's Ser.). (gr. 4-6). N.D. MacMillan Bks.

Bendick, Jeanne, jt. auth. see Simon, Leonard.

Bendick, Jeanne (1919-)

--The Blonk From Beneath The Sea. N.D. E. M. Hale & Co.

--The Blonk from Beneath the Sea. Bendick, Jeanne (1919-), illus. LC 58-6909. (Illus.). 55 p. 1958. Watts.

--A Fresh Look at Night. LC 63-16347. (Illus.). 40 p. 23cm. 1963. F. Watts.

--The Good Knight Ghost. Bendick, Jeanne (1919-), illus. LC 56-9543. 51p. illus. 26cm. 1956. F. Watts.

--Have a Happy Measle, Have Merry Mumps, & Cheery Chicken Pox. (Illus.). (gr. k-3). 1958. (ISBN 0-07-004472-4). McGraw.

--Lightning. Bendick, Jeanne (1919-), illus. LC 61-6841. 61p. illus. 24cm. c.1961. Rand McNally.

--Measuring. Bendick, Jeanne (1919-), illus. LC 76-150734. (Illus.). 71 p. 23cm. (Science experiences). 1971. (ISBN 0-531-01435-5). Watts.

--Scare a Ghost, Tame a Monster. 1st ed. Bendick, Jeanne (1919-), illus. LC 82-23696. (Illus.). 120 p. 23cm. c.1983. (ISBN 0-664-32701-X). Westminster Press.

--Sea So Big, Ship So Small. (Illus.). 80 p. 24cm. 1963. Rand McNally.

--Shapes. Bendick, Jeanne (1919-), illus. LC 68-11889. 70 p. col. illus. 23 cm. (Science experiences). 1967, c.1968. F. Watts.

--Why Can't I?. Bendick, Jeanne (1919-), illus. LC 73-77555. (Illus.). 48 p. 26cm. 1969. McGraw-Hill.

Bendick, Karen (1948-)

--A Horse Named Summer. LC 65-10755. (Illus.). 127 p. 22cm. 1965. Rand McNally.

Benedek, Elissa P.

--The Secret Worry. Rosamilia, Patricia, illus. LC 83-8366. (Illus.). 32 p. 24cm. c.1984. (ISBN 0-89885-133-5). Human Sciences Press.

Benedetti, Mario, ed.

--Unstill Life: An Introduction to the Spanish Poetry of Latin America. Frasconi, Antonio (1919-), illus. LC 69-17114. (Illus.). woodcuts. 128p. (gr. 9 up). 1969. (ISBN 0-15-292856-1). HarBraceJ.

AUTHOR INDEX BENNETT, JAY

Benedict, Anne Kendrick, Mrs. (1851-)
--Centa-The Child Violinist. 192p. N.D. Sunday-School Publications.
--The Fisherman's Daughter. (Illus.). 219p. N.D. American Baptist Pub. Society.
--An Island Story. (Illus.). 200p. N.D. American Baptist Pub. Co.
--My Wonder Story. N.D. D. Lothrop Co.
Benedict, Dorothy Potter, Mrs. (1889-1979)
--Bandoleer. Papin, Joseph (1914-), illus. LC 63-8503. 219 p. illus. 22 cm. 1963. Pantheon Books.
--Fabulous. Papin, Joseph (1914-), illus. LC 61-14776. (Illus.). (gr. 5-8). 1961. (ISBN 0-394-91137-7). Pantheon.
--Pagan the Black. Groth, John (1908-), illus. LC 60-11487. 188p. illus. 22cm. 1960. (ISBN 0-394-91476-7). Pantheon Books.
Benedict, Emma Lee
--The Gregory Guards. Merrill, Frank Thayer (1848-), illus. 1905. Lee and Shepard Company.
Benedict, F. L.
--Miss Dorothy's Charge. N.D. Harper & Bros.
--Miss Van Kortland. N.D. Harper & Bros.
--Mr. Vaughan's Heir. N.D. Harper & Bros.
--My Daughter Elinor. N.D. Harper & Bros.
--St. Simon's Niece. N.D. Harper & Bros.
Benedict, Lois Trimble
--Canalboat Mystery. 1st. ed. Allen, Thomas Burt (1928-), illus. LC 63-10369. 116 p. illus. 22 cm. 1963. Atheneum.
Benedict, Ralph L
--The Golden Gate and Other Stories. LC 31-14965. 112 p. 21 cm. c.1931. Dorrance & Company, Inc.
Benedict, Rex Arthur (1920-)
--The Ballad of Cactus Jack. LC 74-15301. 136 p. 22cm. 1975. (ISBN 0-394-83085-7). (ISBN 0-394-93085-1). Pantheon Books.
--Good Luck Arizona Man. LC 72-445. 168 p. 22cm. 1972. (ISBN 0-394-82441-5). (ISBN 0-394-92441-X). Pantheon Books.
--Goodbye to the Purple Sage: The Last Great Ride of the Sheriff of Medicine Creek. LC 72-7622. 120 p. 22cm. 1973. (ISBN 0-394-82547-0). (ISBN 0-394-82547-0). Pantheon Books.
--Last Stand at Goodbye Gulch. LC 74-12443. 134 p. 22cm. 1974. (ISBN 0-394-83016-4). (ISBN 0-394-83016-4). Pantheon Books.
--Oh.. Brother Juniper. Berg, Joan, pseud. (1942-), illus. Victor, Joan Berg. 1963. Pantheon Books.
Benedict, Steve (1899-)
--Bill Shaw, Fruit Tramp. Stevens, Mary, illus. LC 57-13927. (Illus.). 191 p. 22cm. 1957. Abingdon Press.
--Gabee of the Delta. Collins, Fred, illus. LC 53-2572. 160p. illus. 22cm. 1953. Abingdon-Cokesbury Press.
--The Little House on Wheels. Solem, Dan, illus. LC 53-8778. unpaged. illus. 29cm. N.D. C.
Benedictus, Roger
--Fifty Million Sausages. Mahood, Kenneth (1930-), illus. LC 79-64182. (Illus.). 26 p. 26cm. 1975. (ISBN 0-233-96692-7). A. Deutsch.
Beneduce, Ann K., ed. see Anno, Mitsumasa.
Benet, Laura (1884-1979)
--Barnum's First Circus: And Other Stories. LC 49-3885. viii, 230 p. 21 cm. 1949. Dodd, Mead.
--Caleb's Luck. Credle, Ellis (1902-), illus. LC 42-255583. 28 p. incl. col. front., illus. (part col.) 24 1/2 x 21 cm. (Story parade picture book). c.1942. Grosset & Dunlap.
--Enchanting Jenny Lind. Whitney, George Gillett, illus. N.D. Dodd Mead & Co.
--Fairy Bread. 1921. Thomas Seltzer.
--Famous American Humorists. (Illus.). photos. (gr. 7-9). 1959. (ISBN 0-396-04167-1). Dodd.
--The Hidden Valley. Wiese, Kurt (1887-1974), illus. LC 38-746012. ix, 207 p. incl. illus., plates. 23 cm. 1938. Dodd, Mead and Company.
--Horseshoes Nail. Kidder, Harvey, illus. LC 65-14152. 24cm. 55p. (A Wise Owl Book). 1965, c.1943. Holt, Rinehart and Winston.
--Roxana Rampant. Sawyer, Helen, illus. LC 40-33628. 5 p. l., 221 p. 21 cm. 1940. Dodd, Mead & Company.
--Washington Irving, Explorer of American Legend. Stein, Harve (1904-), illus. LC 44-9705. (Illus.). 21cm. viii, 293p. N.D. Dodd, Mead and Co.
Benet, Rosemary Carr, Mrs., jt. auth. see Benet, Stephen Vincent.
Benet, Rosemary Carr, Mrs., tr. see Maurois, Andre.
Benet, Stephen Vincent (1898-1943)
--The Ballad of William Sycamore, 1790-1871. Turkle, Brinton Cassaday (1915-), illus. LC 75-170170. (Illus.). 32 p. 24cm. 1972, c.1959. Little, Brown.
--The Devil and Daniel Webster. Denison, Harold, illus. N.D. Farrar & Rinehart.
--The Devil & Daniel Webster. LC 38-5407. (Illus.). (gr. 9 up). 1937. (ISBN 0-03-028550-X). HR&W.
--John Brown's Body. 1928. Doubleday Doran & Co.
Benet, Stephen Vincent (1898-1943) & Benet, Rosemary Carr, Mrs.
--A Book of Americans. Rev. ed. Child, Charles Jesse (1901-), illus. 1952. Holt.
Benet, Sula, jt. ed. see Withers, Carl A.
Benet, William Rose, jt. auth. see Flack, Marjorie.
Benet, William Rose, jt. ed. see Gillis, Adolph.
Benet, William Rose (1886-), ed. see Mother Goose.
Benet, William Rose (1886-1950)
--Adolphus the Adopted Dolphin. N.D. Houghton Mifflin Co.
--The Flying King of Kurio: A Story for Children. Smalley, Janet (1893-), illus. LC 26-16416. viii p., 3 l., 15-289 p. col. front., illus., col. plates. 21 cm. c.1926. George H. Doran Company.
--Timothy's Angels: Verse. Alajalov, Constantin (1900-), illus. LC 47-11765. (Illus.). 26cm. 24p. N.D. T. Y. Crowell.
--With Wings as Eagles. N.D. Dodd, Mead & Co,.
Benet, William Rose (1886-1950), ed.
--Golden Fleece, A Collection of Poems and Ballads, Old and New. N.D. Dodd, Mead & Co.
--Poems for Youth. (gr. 7 up). 1923. (ISBN 0-525-37234-2). Dutton.
--Poems for Youth. 1925. Dutton.
Benezra, Barbara Beardsley (1921-)
--Fire Dragon. Roggeri, Franc & Roggeri, Constance, illus. LC 76-117989. (Illus.). 223 p. 22cm. 1970. Criterion Books.
--Gold Dust and Petticoats. LC 64-253112. 1965, c.1964. Bobbs.
--Nuggets in My Pocket. LC 66-25286. 176 p. 22cm. 1966. Bobbs-Merrill
Benford, Gregory Albert (1941-)
--Jupiter Project. LC 75-17913. 175p. (gr. 6 up). 1975. (ISBN 0-525-66456-4). Elsevier-Nelson.
Benford, Gregory Albert (1941-) & Simak, Clifford Donald (1904-)
--Threads of Time: Three Original Novellas of Science Fiction. Silverberg, Robert, ed. LC 74-10279. 224p. 1974. (ISBN 0-8407-6402-2). Elsevier-Nelson.
Bengescu, Carmen Sylva see Elisabeth, Queen Consort Of Charles I King Of Rumania, pseud.
Benham, Charles, jt. auth. see Barton, Dunbar Plunkett.
Benham, Leslie (1922-) & Benham, Lois (1924-)
--The Heroine of Long Point. Mould, Vernon, illus. LC 63-13664. 113 p. illus. 20 cm. (Buckskin books, 4). 1963. St Martin's Press.
Benham, Lois, jt. auth. see Benham, Leslie.
Benig, Irving, ed.
--The Children: Poems and Prose from Bedford-Stuyvesant. LC 76-158357. xiii, 112 p. 18cm. (Evergreen black cat book, B-317-N). 1971. Grove Press.
Benignus, Wilhelm
--Ringelringel: Kinderlieder Fur Tanz und Spiel. Ringelringel; Children's Songs for Dance and Game. LC 16-24928. 2 p. l., 3-34 p. illus. 24 cm. c.1916. Rosswaag's Stuyvesant Press.
Benjamin, Alan
--A Change of Plans. Kellogg, Steven (1941-), illus. LC 82-1521. (Illus.). 32 p. 24cm. c.1982. (ISBN 0-590-07730-9). Four Winds Press.
--One Thousand Monsters. Murdocca, Salvatore, illus. LC 79-10682. (Illus.). 10 p. c.1979. (ISBN 0-590-07636-1). Four Winds Press.
--One Thousand Monsters. Murdocca, Salvatore, illus. LC 79-55339. (Illus.). 22 p. (Fun to flip). 1981, c.1980. (ISBN 0-590-07667-1). Four Winds Press.
--One Thousand Space Monsters--(Have Landed). Murdocca, Salvatore, illus. LC 79-55339. (Illus.). 10p. (ps-2). 1980. (ISBN 0-590-07667-1, Four Winds). Scholastic Inc.
--Ribtickle Town. Schweninger, Ann (1951-), illus. LC 82-9934. (Illus.). (ps-2). 1983. (ISBN 0-590-07880-1, Four Winds). (ISBN 0-517-54633-7). Scholastic Inc.
Benjamin, Alan, retold by.
--The Nightingale. Montresor, Beni (1926-), illus. LC 83-23956. (Original Author: Hans Christian Andersen, 1805-1875). (Illus.). 30 p. c.1985. (ISBN 0-517-55211-6). Crown.
Benjamin, Bezaleel Solomon (1938-) & Howell, Alvin
--Susan Altencroft. Howell, Alvin, illus. LC 75-38234. (Illus.). 104 p. 22cm. c.1976. Ashnorjen Bezaleel Pub. Co.
Benjamin, Carol Lea
--Mary of Mile Eighteen. Benjamin, Carol Lea, illus. 1978. Tundra.
--Nobody's Baby Now. LC 83-18714. viii, 157 p. 22cm. c.1984. (ISBN 0-02-708850-2). Macmillan.
--The Wicked Stepdog. LC 81-43322. (Illus.). 119 p. 21cm. c.1982. (ISBN 0-690-04170-5). (ISBN 0-690-04171-3). Crowell.
Benjamin, E. Bedell, Mrs.
--Brightside, 1 of 103 vols. (The Pearl Library: No. 12). 1900. Set. Hurst & Co.
--Brightside. 1873. Robert Carter & Bros.
Benjamin, Nora Gottheil (1899-)
--Fathom Five: A Story of Bermuda. Benjamin, Nora Gottheil (1899-), illus. LC 39-16519. 241 p. col. plates, col. maps (on lining papers) 22 cm. 1939. Random House.
--Hard Alee!. Benjamin, Nora Gottheil (1899-), illus. LC 36-18544. (Illus.). 211p. 21cm. 1936. Random House.
--Joel: A Novel of Young America. LC 52-7881. 207p. 22cm. 1952. (ISBN 0-06-023471-7). Harper.
--King Solomon's Navy. 1st ed. Benjamin, Nora Gottheil (1899-), illus. LC 54-8979. (Illus.). 181 p. 22cm. 1954. Harper.
--Make Way for a Sailor. Stein, Harve (1904-), illus. LC 48-2110. 161 p. illus. (part col.) 21 cm. 1946. Reynal & Hitchcock.
--Remember the Valley. (Starlight Novels). N.D. Grosset & Dunlap.
--Remember the Valley. 1st ed. LC 51-13578. 216 p. 22 cm. 1951. Harper.
--Roving All the Day. Benjamin, Nora Gottheil (1899-), illus. LC 37-17020. 220 p. col. plates, col. map (on lining papers) 22 cm. 1937. Random House.
Benjamin, Robert Spiers
--Call to Adventure. N.D. World Publishing Co.
Benner, Judith Ann (1942-)
--Lone Star Rebel. Dance, Robert B., illus. LC 70-179906. (Illus.). 232 p. 22cm. 1971. (ISBN 0-910244-62-6). J. F. Blair.
Bennet, Ethel Hume
--Judy's Perfect Year. N.D. Houghton Mifflin Co.
Bennet, Virginia
--The Duck Tale, 1 of 4 vols. Stewart, E., illus. (Old Farm Story Box). N.D. Dutton.
--The Field-Mouse Tale, 1 of 4 vols. Hardy, E. Stuart, illus. (Old Farm Story Box). N.D. Dutton.
--The Pigeon Tale, 1 of 4 vols. Hardy, E. Stuart, illus. (Old Farm Story Box). N.D. Dutton.
--The Windmill Tale, 1 of 4 vols. Heatley, E., illus. (Old Farm Story Box). N.D. Dutton.
Bennett
--When all is Young. (Illus.). N.D. Publications of E. P. Dutton & Co.
Bennett, A. Y.
--Picture Dictionary, ABCs, Telling Time, Counting Rhymes, Riddles & Finger Plays. (Illus.). color ils. 160p. (gr. k-3). 1970. (ISBN 0-448-02813-1, G&D). Putnam Pub Group.
Bennett, Anna Elizabeth (1914-)
--Little Witch. (Illus., Orig.). (gr. 3-5). N.D. (ISBN 0-590-08066-0, Schol Pap). Scholastic Inc.
--Little Witch. Stone, Helen (1904-), illus. LC 52-1374. (Illus.). (gr. 4-6). 1953. (ISBN 0-397-30261-4, JBL-J). Har-Row.
--Little Witch. Stone, Helen (1904-), illus. (Illus.). 128p. (gr. 2-5). 1981. (ISBN 0-06-440119-7, Trophy). Har Row.
--Little Witch. 1st ed. Stone, Helen (1904-), illus. LC 52-13721. (Illus.). 127 p. 22cm. 1953. Lippincott.
Bennett, Arthur S.
--The Most Beautiful Gingerbread House. (gr. 4-7). N.D. Carlton.
Bennett, Billy L.
--Danger Trails North. LC 37-9476. vi, 204 p. front. 20 cm. c.1937. Cupples & Leon Company.
Bennett, Charles Henry (1829-1867), ed.
--Chimes, Rhymes, and Jingles. Bennett, Charles Henry (1829-1867), illus. N.D. James Miller.
--Chimes, Rhymes, Jingles: Containing the Remainder of Mother Goose's Songs. Bennett, Charles Henry (1829-1867), illus. (Illus.). N.D. Thomas R. Knox & Co.
--Old Nurse's Book of Rhymes, Jingles and Ditties. Bennett, Charles Henry (1829-1867), illus. N.D. James Miller.
--Rhymes Without Reason. Bennett, Charles Henry (1829-1867), illus. N.D. Hurd & Houghton.
Bennett, Charles Moon (1899-)
--A Buccaneer's Log. LC 29-14872. 287 p. front., plates. 20 cm. N.D. E. P. Dutton & Co., Inc. C.
--Mutiny Island. LC 28-19757. 303 p. front., plates. 20 cm. c.1928. E. P. Dutton & Company.
--Pedro of the Black Death. LC 26-165359. vii p., 1 l., 349 p. front., plates. 20 cm. c.1926. E. P. Dutton & Company.
--Red Pete the Ruthless. LC 33-6256. 285 p. front. 20 cm. c.1933. E. P. Dutton & Co., Inc.
--Tim Kane's Treasure. N.D. E. P. Dutton & Co.
--With Morgan on the Main. N.D. E. P. Dutton & Co.
Bennett, Christine, pseud., see Newbauer, William Arthur.
Bennett, Christine, pseud. (1916-)
--Wind in the Sage. Newbauer, William Arthur. 224 p. 20 cm. (Arcadia teen-age romance, 8). 1962. Arcadia House.
Bennett, Cleo, jt. auth. see Dalgliesh, Alice.
Bennett, Deborah
--Jean's Black Diamond. (Teen Fiction Ser.). (gr. 7-10). 1970. (ISBN 0-87508-684-5). Chr Lit.
--Jean's Black Diamond. 1951. Christian Lit.
--Son of Diamond. (Teen Fiction Ser). (gr. 7-10). 1970. (ISBN 0-87508-759-0). Chr Lit.
--Son of Diamond. 1954. Christian Lit.
Bennett, Dorothea, pseud., see Young, Dorothea Bennett.
Bennett, Dorothea, pseud. (1924-)
--The Jigsaw Man. Young, Dorothea Bennett. 256p. 1976. (ISBN 0-698-10729-2, Coward). Putnam Pub Group.
Bennett, Dorothy Agnes (1909-)
--The Golden Almanac. Stern, Marie Simchow (1909-), illus. Masha, pseud. LC 44-40136. 2 p. l., 9-94, 2 p. illus. (part col.) 28 1/2 x 23 cm. 1944. Simon and Schuster.
--The Golden Encylopedia. DeWitt, Cornelius Hugh (1905-), illus. 1946. Golden Press.
--The New Golden Encyclopedia. Watson, Jane Werner, ill. by DeWitt, Cornelius Hugh (1905-), illus. (A Giant Golden Book). 1963. Golden Press.
--Sold to the Ladies. 259p. N.D. George W. Stewart.
Bennett, Dorothy Agnes (1909-), ed.
--The Golden Mother Goose. Provensen, Alice (1918-) & Provensen, Martin (1916-), illus. (Illus.). 1976. (ISBN 0-307-13766-X, Golden Pr). (ISBN 0-307-63766-2). Western Pub.
Bennett, Edyth M.
--In the Land of Make-Believe. N.D. Carlton Press Inc.
Bennett, Ethel Hume Patterson, Mrs. (1881-)
--Camp Conqueror. LC 28-9157. 5 p. l., 281 p. front., illus., plates. 20 cm. 1928. Houghton Miffin Company.
--Camp Ken - Jockety. LC 23-173402. 4 p. l., 311 p. front., plates. 20 cm. 1923. Houghton Mifflin Company.
--Judy of York Hill. Cue, Harold, illus. LC 22-19043. 4 p. l., 3-281 p. front., plates. 20 cm. 1922. Houghton Miffin Company.
--Judy's Prefect Year. LC 25-19436. 3 p. l., 288 p. front. 20 cm. 1925. Houghton Mifflin Company.
--A Treasure Ship of Old Quebec. Boswell, Hazel (1882-), illus. LC 36-30323. 4 p. l., 266 p. incl. front. illus. plates. 21 cm. 1936. Dodd, Mead & Company.
Bennett, Eve
--April Wedding. LC 60-7047. 190 p. 22cm. 1960, c.1959. Messner.
--Concerning Casey. LC 58-7259. 100 p. 22cm. 1958. Messner.
I, Judy. LC 57-6585. 192p. 22cm. 1957. Messner.
--Little Bit. LC 61-7997. 189 p. 22cm. 1961. J. Messner.
--Walk in the Moonlight. LC 59-7010. 190 p. 22cm. 1959. Messner.
Bennett, Gertrude
--Juan, Carmela & the Pirates. Valla, Victor, illus. (Illus.). 1978. (ISBN 0-533-03108-7). Vantage.
Bennett, Grace Irene
--Diddle Daddle Duckling. O'D, Pat, illus. LC 35-167. (Illus.). 22cm. 36p. 1934. Whitman Publishing Co.
Bennett, Harriet M.
--Queen of the Meadow. (Illus.). 64p. N.D. Publications of E. P. Dutton & Co.
Bennett, Harriet M. & Mack, Robert Ellis
--All Around the Clock. N.D. Publications of E. P. Dutton & Co.
Bennett, Harve
--Star Trek III, the Search for Spock: Storybook. Weinberg, Larry, adapted by. LC 85-132884. (Illus.). 57 p. 29cm. c.1984. (ISBN 0-671-47662-9). Little Simon.
Bennett, J.
--A Packet of Poems. Mounter, Paddy, illus. (Illus.). 112p. 1983. (ISBN 0-19-276049-1, Pub by Oxford U Pr Childrens). Merrimack Pub Cir.
Bennett, Jack (1934-)
--The Voyage of the Lucky Dragon. LC 81-19267. 149 p. 22cm. 1982, c.1981. (ISBN 0-13-944165-4). Prentice-Hall.
Bennett, James
--I Chose Prison. 1970. Borzoi Books.
Bennett, Jay (1912-)
--The Birthday Murderer: A Mystery. LC 76-47239. 150 p. 21cm. c.1977. (ISBN 0-440-00584-1). Delacorte Press.
--The Dangling Witness: A Mystery. LC 74-5502. 160p. (gr. 7 up). 1974. Delacorte.
--Deadly Gift. (gr. 7 up). 1969. (ISBN 0-8015-1968-3). Dutton.
--The Deadly Gift: A Novel. LC 70-93837. 135 p. 22cm. 1969. Meredith Press.
--Deathman, Do Not Follow Me. (gr. 7 up). 1968. Dutton.
--Deathman, Do Not Follow Me (Pub. by Meredith). (gr. 7-12). 1972. (ISBN 0-590-02963-0). Scholastic Inc.
--The Killing Tree. LC 76-189567. 128p. (gr. 7-12). 1972. (ISBN 0-531-02559-4). Watts.
--The Long Black Coat: A Mystery. LC 73-7217. 116 p. 22cm. 1973. Delacorte Press.
--Masks: A Love Story. LC 79-147396. 121 p. 22cm. 1971. (ISBN 0-531-01979-9). Watts.

--The Pigeon. LC 79-26270. 147 p. 22cm. c.1980. (ISBN 0-416-30631-4). Methuen.
--Say Hello to the Hit Man. LC 75-32919. 160p. 1976. Delacorte.
--Shadows Offstage. LC 74-675. 160p. (gr. 6 up). 1974. (ISBN 0-8407-6385-9). Nelson.
--To Be a Killer. LC 84-20281. 153 p. 18cm. c.1985. (ISBN 0-590-33208-2). Scholastic Inc.

Bennett, Jill, jt. ed. see Oxenbury, Helen.

Bennett, Jill (1947-)
--Days Are Where We Live and Other Poems. Bennett, Jill, ed. Roffey, Maureen (1936-), illus. LC 81-8353. (Illus.). 41 p. 22cm. 1982. (ISBN 0-688-00852-6). Lothrop, Lee & Shepard Books.

Bennett, Jill (1947-), retold by.
--Jack & the Robbers. Biro, Val, pseud. (1921-), illus. Biro, Balint Stephen. (Illus.). 32p. (An Umbrella Bk.). (gr. k-3). 1984. (ISBN 0-19-278204-5, Pub. by Oxford U Pr Childrens). Merrimack Pub Cir.
--Roger Was a Razor Fish, and Other Poems. Roffey, Maureen (1936-), illus. LC 80-17166. (Illus.). 43 p. 22cm. c.1980. (ISBN 0-688-41986-0). Lothrop, Lee & Shepard Books.
--Tiny Tim: Verses for Children. Oxenbury, Helen (1938-), illus. 1982. Delacorte.

Bennett, John (1865-1956)
--Barnaby Lee. De Land, Clyde O., illus. LC 2-22477. x, 454 p. incl. plates. front. 20 cm. 1902. The Century Co.
--Master Skylark. N.D. E . M. Hale and Co.
--Master Skylark. Mahoney, Kathryn F. & Preble, Laura E., eds. Landrigan, Mary F., illus. LC 53-1000. 292p. illus. 21cm. 1953. Globe Book Co.
--Master Skylark. Pitz, Henry Clarence (1895-1976), illus. LC 22-18237. viii p., 2 l., 3-322 p. col. front., illus. (incl. music) col. plates. 24 cm. 1922. The Century Co.
--Master Skylark: A Story of Shakespeare's Time. Birch, Reginald Bathurst (1856-1943), illus. LC 76-365097. (Illus.). 302 p., 5 leaves of plates. 20cm. c.1924. Grosset & Dunlap.
--Master Skylark: A Story of Shakespeare's Time. Birch, Reginald Bathurst (1856-1943), illus. LC 19-2908. xi p., 1 l., 380 p. incl. plates. front. 19 cm. 1897. The Century Co.
--Master Skylark: A Story of Shakespeare's Time. Birch, Reginald Bathurst (1856-1943), illus. LC 4-17522. xi p., i l., 380 p. incl. 39 pl. front. 19 cm. 1898. The Century Co.
--Pigtail of Ah Lee Ben Loo. N.D. Liveright Publishing.
--Pigtail of Ah Lee Ben Loo. 1928. Longmans. **Award: (JNM).**
--The Treasure of Peyre Gaillard. (Illus.). 370p. N.D. Century Co.

Bennett, Judith K.
--The Ahae Gang Meets Melvin. 112p. 1984. (ISBN 0-533-05677-2). Vantage.

Bennett, Kay Curley (1922-) & Bennett, Russ
--A Navajo Saga. LC 68-56028. (Illus.). xii, 239 p. 22cm. 1969. Naylor Co.

Bennett, Mabel R.
--The Hidden Garden. Voute, Kathleen (1892-), illus. LC 55-5934. 191p. illus. 21cm. 1955. J. Day.

Bennett, Margaret
--Dr. Owl's Problem. 1st ed. Efting, Barbara, illus. LC 68-26121. (Illus.). 32 p. 23cm. 1968. Hawthorn Books.

Bennett, Marian
--Baby Jesus. Svensson, Borje, illus. (Illus.). 12p. (Mini Pop-Ups Ser.). (gr. k-2). 1979. (ISBN 0-87239-368-2). Standard Pub.
--Bible Numbers. (Illus.). 24p. (Orig.). (Little Happy Day Bks.). (gr. k-3). 1983. (ISBN 0-87239-653-3). Standard Pub.
--Daniel in the Lions Den. Svensson, Borje, illus. (Illus.). (Mini Pop-up Books). (gr. k-2). 1978. (ISBN 0-87239-222-8). Standard Pub.
--David & Goliath. Svensson, Borje, illus. (Illus.). (Mini Pop-up Books). (gr. k-2). 1978. (ISBN 0-87239-223-6). Standard Pub.
--David, the Shepherd. Wahl, Richard (1939-), illus. (Illus.). 24p. (Happy Day Bible Stories Bks.). (ps-2). 1984. (ISBN 0-87239-763-7). Standard Pub.
--God Made Kittens. Sparks, Judith, ed. (Illus.). 24p. (A Happy Day Book). (ps). 1980. (ISBN 0-87239-404-2). Standard Pub.
--The Good Samaritan. Svensson, Borje, illus. (Illus.). (Mini Pop-up Books). (gr. k-2). 1978. (ISBN 0-87239-224-4). Standard Pub.
--Little Lamb. Svensson, Borje, illus. (Illus.). 12p. (Mini Pop-Ups Ser.). (gr. k-2). 1979. (ISBN 0-87239-369-0). Standard Pub.
--My Book of Special Days. Hook, Frances Arnold (1912-), illus. (Illus.). (gr. 4-8). 1977. (ISBN 0-87239-156-6). Standard Pub.
--My First Valentine's Day Book. Peltier, Pam, illus. LC 84-21511. (Illus.). 31 p. 25cm. c.1985. (ISBN 0-516-02906-1). Childrens Press.
--The Story of Moses. Svensson, Borje, illus. (Illus.). 12p. (Mini Pop-up Bks). (gr. k-2). 1979. (ISBN 0-87239-367-4). Standard Pub.
--The Story of Noah. Svensson, Borje, illus. (Illus.). 12p. (Mini Pop-Ups). (gr. k-2). 1979. (ISBN 0-87239-366-6). Standard Pub.

Bennett, Marian, compiled by.
--Bible Memory Verses. (Illus.). 24p. (Orig.). (Little Happy Day Bks.). (gr. k-3). 1983. (ISBN 0-87239-652-5). Standard Pub.

Bennett, Marian, ed. see Rabens, Neil W.

Bennett, Mary E.
--Six Boys. 339p. N.D. American Tract Society.

Bennett, Olivia
--A Farm in the City. (Illus.). (gr. k-2). 1984. (ISBN 0-241-11202-8, Pub. by Hamish Hamilton England). David & Charles.
--A Turkish Afternoon. Cormack, Christopher, illus. (Illus.). 32p. (gr. 2-5). 1983. (ISBN 0-241-11033-5, Pub. by Hamish Hamilton England). David & Charles.

Bennett, Paul A. (1897-)
--Peter Piper's Practical Principles of Plain & Perfect Pronunciation. Lydemberg, Harry Miller (1874-), intro. by. LC 38-38716. 99 p. illus. (part col.) 21 cm. 1936. Mergenthaler Linotype Company.

Bennett, Paul Lewis (1921-)
--Robbery on the Highway. LC 61-13323. 191p. 21cm. 1961. Abelard-Schuman.

Bennett, Rainey (1907-)
--After the Sun Goes Down. 1st ed. Bennett, Rainey (1907-), illus. unpaged. illus. 23x27cm. 1961. World Pub. Co.
--The Secret Hiding Place. 1st ed. Bennett, Rainey (1907-), illus. LC 60-7206. (Illus.). unpaged. 1960. World Pub. Co. **Award: (ALA).**
--What Do You Think?. 1st. ed. Bennett, Rainey (1907-), illus. LC 58-5781. unpaged. illus. 19cm. 1958. World Pub. Co.

Bennett, Richard Michael (1899-)
--Hannah Marie. LC 39-276290. 3 p l., 70 p. incl. front., illus. 26 cm. 1939. Doubleday, Doran & Co., Inc.
--Little Dermot and the Thirsty Stones, And Other Irish Folk Tales. Bennett, Richard Michael (1899-), illus. LC 53-5228. 91p. illus. 22cm. 1953. Coward-McCann.
--Mick and Mack and Mary Jane. LC 48-8545. 42 p. illus. 25 cm. (Junior books). 1948. Doubleday.
--Mister Ole. LC 40-332763. 3 p. l., 60 p. col. front., illus. (par col.) col. pl. 28 x 22 cm. 1940. Doubleday, Doran & Co., Inc.
--Not a Teeny Weeny Wink. 1st ed. Bennett, Richard Michael (1899-), illus. LC 59-5894. 56p. illus. 27cm. c.1959. Doubleday.
--Shawneen & the Gander. Bennett, Richard Michael (1899-), illus. LC 61-5182. (Illus.). (ps-4). 1960. (ISBN 0-385-06395-4). Doubleday.
--Shawneen and the Garden. LC 37-6385. (Illus.). 24 x 22cm. 56p. N.D. Doubleday, Doran and Co.
--Skookum and Sandy. LC 35-273004. 71 p. incl. front., illus., plates. 25 cm. 1935. Doubleday, Doran & Company, Inc.

Bennett, Rowena Bastin, Mrs. (1896-)
--Around a Toadstool Table: A Child's Book of Verse. Holling, Lucille Webster, Mrs. (1900-), illus. LC 30-5148. 109 p. illus. 21 cm. 1920. Thomas S. Rockwell Company.
--Day Is Dancing & Other Poems. Bennett, Rainey (1907-), illus. LC 68-10478. (Illus.). 96p. (gr. k-3). 1968. (ISBN 0-695-81896-1). (ISBN 0-695-41896-3). Follett.
--Happy Hour Stories. De Frehn, Sarah, illus. LC 46-17841. 382 p. illus. (part. col.) 26 1/2 cm. 1946. Whitman Publishing Company.
--Holiday Plays for Little People. LC 41-31248. 62 p. 19 c. N.D. The Dramatic Publishing Companyc.
--Runner for the King. Mastri, Fiore, illus. LC 45-1215. 2 p. l., 46, 2 p. incl. col. front., col. illus. 24 1/2 x 21 cm. c.1944. Follett Publishing Company.
--Songs from Around a Toadstool Table. Fraser, Betty M., pseud. (1928-), illus. Fraser, Elizabeth Marr. LC 67-156181. 60p. illus. 20cm. 1967. Follett.
--Songs from around a Toadstool Table: A Child's Book of Verse. Holling, Lucille Webster, Mrs. (1900-), illus. LC 38-2973. 63p. illus. 21cm. 1937. Follett Pub. Co.
--Story-Teller Poems. Cooke, Donald Ewin (1916-), illus. Benet, William Rose, frwd. by. LC 48-5621. xv. 76 p. illus. 21 cm. 1948. J. C. Winston Co.

Bennett, Russ, jt. auth. see Bennett, Kay Curley.

Bennett, Russell, ed. see McLenighan, Valjean.

Bennett, Russell, ed. see McReynolds, Ginny.

Bennett, Russell, ed. see Wilson, Lionel.

Bennett, Susan
--The Underground Cats. LC 73-18360. (Illus.). 32 p. 22cm. 1974. (ISBN 0-02-709100-7). Macmillan.

Bennett, W. H., jt. auth. see Adeney, W. F.

Bennett & Adeney, eds.
--The Bible Story Retold for Young People. 1900. Macmillan Co.

Benning, Howe, pseud., see Henry, Mary H..

Benning, Howe, pseud.
--Grace Courtney: or, Seeking the Shepherd. Henry, Mary H.. vi, 7-225 p. front., plates. 18 cm. c.1871. I. P. Warren.
--Grace Courtney: or, Seeking the Shepherd. Henry, Mary H.. 224p. (Crowell's Sunday-School Library No. 6). N.D. T. Y. Crowell.
--Nix's Offerings. Henry, Mary H.. 1 p. l., 400 p. front., plates. 17 1/2 cm. (Added t.-p.: $500 prize series of illustrated books). c.1873. Warren and Wyman.

Benoit, Clement F. (1833-1937), ed.
--Children's Poems That Never Grow Old. LC 22-13224. Repr. of 1922 ed (Pub. by Reilly). (Granger Poetry Library). (gr. k-6). 1976. (ISBN 0-89609-004-3). Granger Bk.
--Children's Poems That Never Grow Old: For Little Folks from Six to Twelve Years Old. Neill, John Rea (1878-1943), illus. LC 22-13554. xxi, 298 p. col. ront., col. plates. 20 cm. c.1922. The Reilly & Lee Co.

Benscoter, Grace A, ed. see Dickens, Charles John Huffam.

Bensel, Gottfried, narrated by see Austin, Clare.

Bensel, James Berry
--In the King's Garden. N.D. D. Lothrop Co.

Benson, Alpha Banta, ed. see Grimm, Jakob Ludwig Karl (1785-1863) & Grimm, Wilhelm Karl.

Benson, Edward Frederic (1867-1940)
--All About Lucia. LC 36-28500. 1235 p. 20 cm. 1936. Doubleday, Doran & Company, Inc.
--David Blaize. 1916. Doubleday Doran & Co.
--David Blaize and the Blue Door. Ford, Henry Justice (1860-1941), illus. LC 19-27584. viii, 9-217 p. incl. front., illus. 20 cm. 1919. George H. Doran Company.

Benson, Ellen
--Philip's Little Sister. Davis, Rachael, illus. LC 78-12627. p. cm. 1979. Childrens Press.

Benson, Ethel Mitchell, jt. auth. see Ramstad, Josie Winship.

Benson, Ginny, pseud., see Benson, Virginia.

Benson, Ginny, pseud. (1923-)
--According to Amos. Benson, Virginia. Williams-McKenna, Barbara, illus. LC 81-10775. (Illus.). iii, 134 p. 26cm. c.1981. (ISBN 0-86550-026-6). A & P Books.

Benson, Hilda Marie
--Little Seekers. N.D. Augustana Book Concern.

Benson, John Prentiss (1865-)
--The Woozlebeasts. Benson, John Prentiss (1865-), illus. (Illus.). 135p. illus. 20 x 22cm. 1905. Moffat, Yard & Co.

Benson, Kathleen, jt. auth. see Haskins, James.

Benson, Kathleen (1947-)
--Joseph on the Subway Trains. McCully, Emily Arnold (1939-), illus. Arnold, Emily, pseud. LC 81-3437. p. cm. c.1981. (ISBN 0-201-03996-6). Addison-Wesley.
--Joseph on the Subway Trains. McCully, Emily Arnold (1939-), illus. Arnold, Emily, pseud. LC 84-46022. p. cm. 1985, c.1981. (ISBN 0-201-03996-6). Crowell.

Benson, Mildred W. (1905-)
--Dangerous Deadline. LC 57-11670. 209p. 21cm. 1957. Dodd, Mead.
--Quarry Ghost. LC 59-6515. 183 p. 21cm. 1959. Dodd, Mead.

Benson, Murray & Ladd, Fred
--Famous Fairy Tales. Duenewald, Doris, ed. LC 78-53666. (Illus.). 26cm. 128p. (gr. k-5). 1978. (ISBN 0-448-14728-9, G&D). Putnam Pub Group.

Benson, Nora, pseud., see Mendelsohn, Zora.

Benson, Patrick, ed.
--The Twelve Days of Christmas. LC 84-7798. p. cm. 1984. (ISBN 0-399-21168-3). Philomel Books.

Benson, Sally, Mrs. (1900-1972), ed. see Bulfinch, Thomas.

Benson, Sally, Mrs. (1900-1972)
--Junior Miss. (gr. 7 up). 1947. (ISBN 0-385-07349-6). Doubleday.

Benson, Therese
--The Unknown Daughter. LC 29-926. 4 p. l., 323 p. 20 cm. 1929. Dodd, Mead & Company.

Benson, Virginia see Benson, Ginny, pseud.

Benstead, Vivienne, adapted by see Three Little Pigs.

Bentel, Pearl Bucklen (1901-)
--Coed off Campus. Abel, Raymond (1911-), illus. LC 65-14133. 182 p. illus. 21 cm. 1965. D. McKay Co.
--Freshman at Large. 1959. McKay.
--Freshman at Large. Troger, Johannes, contrib. by. LC 59-12746. (Illus.). 186 p. 21cm. 1959. Longman's Green.
--I'll Know my Love. 1955. McKay.
--Program for Christine. 1st. ed. Tucker, Orell Zell, illus. LC 52-12697. (Illus.). 249 p. 21cm. 1953. Longmans, Green.

Bentham, Edwards M.
--Pearla. N.D. Thomas Whittaker.

Bentinck, Henry
--The Avenue of Flutes. Bartlett, Maurice, illus. LC 67-85742. 5, 136 p. illus. 20 1/2 cm. 15/. (B66-22315). 1966. Chatto & Windus.

Bentley, Anne & Bentley, Roy
--The Groggs' Day Out. LC 80-2689. (Illus.). 32 p. 26cm. 1981. (ISBN 0-233-97348-6). Andre Deutsch.
--The Groggs Have a Wonderful Summer. LC 80-498846. (Illus.). 32 p. 27cm. 1980. (ISBN 0-233-97199-8). Deutsch.

Bentley, J. M., jt. auth. see Elliott, James William.

Bentley, Nicolas Clerihew (1907-1978), ed. see Belloc, Joseph Hilaire Pierre.

Bentley, Phyllis Eleanor (1894-1977)
--The Adventures of Tom Leigh. Silverman, Burton Philip (1928-), illus. LC 66-12175. (Illus.). 187 p. 22cm. 1966, c.1964. Doubleday.
--Forgery!. LC 68-11787. (Illus.). 188 p. 22cm. 1968. Doubleday.
--Oath of Silence. Silverman, Burton Philip (1928-), illus. LC 67-11180. (Illus.). 214 p. 22cm. 1967. Doubleday.

Bentley, Roy, jt. auth. see Bentley, Anne.

Bently, James
--Simon & Schuster Children's Bible. Maclean, Colin & Maclean, Moira, illus. (Illus.). 240p. (Children's Illustrated Bible Ser.). (gr. 2-5). 1983. (ISBN 0-671-47089-2, Little Simon). S&S.

Benton-Banai, Edward (1934-)
--The Mishomis Book: The Voice of the Ojibway. LC 80-138057. (Illus.). v, 114 p. 21cm. c.1979. Indian Country Press.

Benton, Caroline French
--Saturday Mornings: Or, How Margaret Learned to Keep House. N.D. Dana Estes & Co.

Benton, Caroline Rita (1881-)
--The Elf of Discontent, and Other Plays. LC 79-50017. (Illus.). 350 p., 7 leaves of plates. 20cm. (One-Act Plays in Reprint). 1979. (ISBN 0-8486-2041-0). Core Collection Books.
--The Elf of Discontent, and Other Plays. LC 27-19556. xii p., 3 l., 19-350 p. front., plates. 20 cm. c.1927. George H. Doran Company.

Benton, John (1933-)
--Carmen. 192p. (Orig.). (gr. 7-12). 1974. (ISBN 0-8007-8159-7, New Hope Bks). Revell.
--Julie. 192p. (Orig.). (gr. 7-12). 1981. (ISBN 0-8007-8399-9, New Hope Bks). Revell.
--Lefty. 192p. (Orig.). (gr. 7-12). 1981. (ISBN 0-8007-8401-4, New Hope Bks). Revell.
--Lori. 160p. (Orig.). (gr. 7-12). 1980. (ISBN 0-8007-8385-9, New Hope Bks). Revell.
--Marji. (Orig.). (gr. 7-12). 1980. (ISBN 0-8007-8378-6, New Hope Bks). Revell.
--Marji & the Gangland Wars. 192p. (Orig.). (gr. 7-12). 1981. (ISBN 0-8007-8407-3, New Hope Bks). Revell.
--Sheila. 192p. (gr. 7-12). 1982. (ISBN 0-8007-8419-7, New Hope Bks.). Revell.
--Sherri. 192p. (gr. 7-12). 1980. (ISBN 0-8007-8390-5, New Hope Bks). Revell.
--Valarie. 192p. (Orig.). (gr. 7-12). 1982. (ISBN 0-8007-8430-8, New Hope Bks.). Revell.

Benton, Maude M. (0000-1948)
--Animal Bones and Waterfalls: Verse. LC 48-8123. 65 p. 23 cm. 1947, c.1948. Exposition Press.

Benton, Patricia (1907-)
--Barkie the Dog. Simon, A. Christopher, illus. LC 64-23450. 1 v. (unpaged) col. illus. 16 x 24 cm. 1964. F. Fell.
--Merry-Go-Sounds at the Zoo. Millman, Ike, illus. LC 61-2647. unpaged. illus. 23cm. N.D. F. Fell.

Benton, Rita (1881-)
--The Star-Child and Other Plays. LC 21-14214. 143, 1 p. front., illus., plates. 20 cm. c.1921. The Writers Publishing Co., Inc.

Benton, Robert Douglass (1932-)
--Don't Ever Wish for a 7-Foot Bear. 1st ed. Benton, Sally, illus. LC 73-39594. (Illus.). 32 p. 27cm. (gr. k-3). 1972. (ISBN 0-394-82399-0). (ISBN 0-394-92399-5). Knopf.
--Little Brother, No More. Benton, Robert Douglass (1932-), illus. LC 60-5509. (Illus.). (ps-2). 1960. (ISBN 0-394-91343-4). Knopf.

Benvenuti, G., illus.
--Bremen Town Musicians. LC 78-31726. (Illus.). (Goodnight Bks.). (ps-2). 1979. (ISBN 0-394-84188-3). Knopf.
--The Enchanted Princess & Other Fairy Tales. King, Leon, tr. Seward, Anna. 1961. Golden Press.
--Golden Book of Grimm's Fairy Tales. 1977. (ISBN 0-307-16543-4, Golden Pr). (ISBN 0-307-66543-7). Western Pub.
--The House That Jack Built. LC 79-634. (Illus.). 21 p. 17cm. (Goodnight book). c.1978. (ISBN 0-394-84240-5). Knopf : Distributed by Random House.
--Japanese Fairy Tales. Marmur, Mildred (1930-), tr. LC 61-16298. (Illus.). 64 p. 37cm. (Giant golden book). 1960. Golden Press.
--Paddy the Bear Cub. (Illus.). 12p. (Bedtime Bks). (ps). 1972. (ISBN 0-307-11264-0, Golden Pr). Western Pub.
--Puss in Boots. LC 78-31286. (Illus.). (Goodnight Bks.). (ps-1). 1979. (ISBN 0-394-84189-1). Knopf.

--Traveling Twins. Smalley, Janet (1893-), illus. Carroll, John & Kelly, Donald, created by. LC 53-20878. unpaged. illus. 21cm. (Wonder books, 596). c.1953. Wonder Books.
--Wee Little Man. Geer, Charles Hand (1922-), illus. (Illus.). (Beginning-to Read Ser.). (gr. 1-3). 1963. (ISBN 0-695-89220-7). (ISBN 0-695-49220-9). Follett.
--What Harry Found When He Lost Archie. Massey, Cal, illus. LC 70-115097. (Illus.). 112 p. 24cm. 1970. (ISBN 0-664-32476-2). Westminster Press.

Berg, Jean Horton (1913-), ed.
--The Little Red Hen. Pekarsky, Mel, illus. LC 63-7661. (Illus.). 26 p. 21cm. (Follett beginning-to-read series). 1963. Follett Pub. Co.

Berg, Leila Rita (1917-)
--A Box for Benny. Willett, Jillian, illus. LC 61-15546. (Illus.). 94 p. 24cm. 1961. Bobbs-Merrill.
--Folk Tales for Reading and Telling. Him, George (1900-1982), illus. LC 66-9540. (Illus.). 122 p. 23cm. 1966. World Pub. Co.
--Fourteen What-Do-You-Know Stories. Jackson, Stanley, illus. LC 59-15311. 107p. illus. 22cm. 1959, c.1948. Roy Publishers.
--The Little Car. Rose, Gerald Hembdon Seymour (1935-), illus. LC 74-186928. (Illus.). 92 p. 20cm. (young puffin). 1974. (ISBN 0-14-030682-X). Puffin Books.
--Little Pete Stories. Garland, Henrietta, illus. LC 61-39910. 93p. illus. 18cm. (Puffin books, PS124). 1959. Penguin Books.
--Little Pete Stories. Garland, Henrietta, illus. (Illus.). (gr. 1-3). 1964. (ISBN 0-685-21308-0). Verry.

Berg, Olive S.
--I've Got Your Number, John. Strimban, Robert & Strimban, Jack, illus. LC 65-14140. (Illus.). 1 v. (unpaged). 29cm. (wise owl book, WA15). c.1965. Holt, Rinehart and Winston.

Bergaust, Erik (1925-1978)
--Mars, Planet for Conquest. LC 67-24138. (Illus.). 95 p. 24cm. 1968, c.1967. Putnam.

Bergendahl, Suzanne H., tr. see Hopp, Zinken.

Bergengren, Ralph Wilhelm (1871-)
--David the Dreamer: His Book of Dreams. Freud, Tom, illus. LC 22-19553. 22x27cm. 67p. 1922. Atlantic Monthly Press.
--Jane, Joseph & John: Their Book of Verses. Day, Maurice (1892-) & Hapgood, T. B., illus. LC 18-19506. 62 p., 1 l. col. illus. 30 cm. c.1918. The Atlantic Monthly Press.
--Jane, Joseph & John: Their Book of Verses. Day, Maurice (1892-) & Hapgood, T. B., illus. LC 21-19957. 67, 1 p. col. illus. 30 cm. c.1921. The Atlantic Monthly Press.
--Jane, Joseph and John: Their Books of Veres. Day, Maurice (1892-), illus. 1918. Little, Brown & Co.
--Susan and the Butterbees. Vaughan, Anne (1913-), illus. LC 47-1966. 6 p. l., 175, 1 p. incl. illus., plates. 21 cm. 1947. Longmans, Green and Co.

Berger, Barbara
--The Donkey's Dream. LC 84-18905. p. cm. 1985. (ISBN 0-399-21233-7). Philomel Books.
--Grandfather Twilight. Berger, Barbara, illus. LC 83-19490. (Illus.). 32p. (ps-3). 1984. (ISBN 0-399-20996-4, Philomel). Putnam Pub Group.

Berger, Donald Paul
--Folk Songs of Japanese Children. N.D. (ISBN 0-8048-0193-2). Charles E. Tuttle Co.

Berger, Fredericka
--Nuisance. LC 82-20848. 272p. (gr. 4 up). 1983. (ISBN 0-688-01738-X). Morrow.

Berger, Gilda & Berger, Melvin
--Bizarre Murders. (Illus.). 128p. (gr. 9-12). 1983. (ISBN 0-671-45583-4). Messner.

Berger, Helen
--Nobody's Joan. N.D. Grosset & Dunlap.

Berger, Josef (1903-1971), tr. see Voronkova, Liubov Fedorovna.

Berger, Josef (1903-1971)
--Captain Bib. Evers, Helen Baker, illus. LC 29-18334. 4 p. l., 108 p. illus. 24 cm. c.1929. H. Holt and Company.
--Come Along. Thomas, Dorothy Gay, illus. LC 30-28395. 3 p. l., 120, 1 p. col. front., illus., col. plates. 22 cm. 1930. Houghton Mifflin Company.
--Copy Boy. LC 38-32850. 3 p. l., 9-268 p. plates. 21 cm. c.1938. Macrae Smith Company.
--Counterspy Jim. Coggins, Jack Banham (1914-), illus. LC 46-56554. xii, 308 p. front., plates 20 1/2 cm. 1946. Little, Brown and Company.
--Operation Underground. Berger, David, illus. LC 47-305765. 5 p. l., 3-300 p. front. illus., plates. 20 1/2 cm. 1947. Little, Brown and Company.
--Pogo: The Circus Horse. Reid, James (1907-), illus. LC 34-41987. 4 p. l., 213 p. front., illus. 21 cm. c.1934. Coward, McCann, Inc.
--Sleepy Steve. Thomas, Dorothy Gay, illus. LC 31-8207. 2 p. l., 200 p. front., illus. 21 cm. c.1931. Minton, Blach & Company.
--Subchaser Jim. Coggins, Jack Banham (1914-), illus. LC 43-12359. 5 p. l., 3-302 p. front., plates. 20 1/2 cm. 1943. Little, Brown and Company.
--Swordfisherman Jim. Ashley, Clifford Warren (1881-), illus. LC 39-31053. 6 p. l., 3-296 p. incl. plates. front. 22 cm. 1939. Little, Brown and Company.

Berger, Judith & Landau, Terry
--Butterflies & Rainbows. Lowhar, Carmen F., illus. LC 82-71932. (Illus.). 48p. (ps-2). 1982. (ISBN 0-943760-00-3). Bande Hse Pub.

Berger, Knute, et al.
--A Visit to the Doctor. Givan, Thurman B., intro. by. LC 60-16090. 69p. illus. 25cm. 1960. Grosset & Dunlap.

Berger, Melvin, jt. auth. see Berger, Gilda.

Berger, Melvin (1927-)
--The Funny Side of Science. Handelsman, J. B., illus. (Illus.). 1973. Harper.
--Mad Scientists in Fact & Fiction. (gr. 5 up). 1980. (ISBN 0-531-04153-0). Watts.
--Why I Cough, Sneeze, Shiver, Hiccup, & Yawn. Keller, Holly, illus. LC 82-45587. (Illus.). 40p. (A Let's-Read-&-Find-Out Science Bk.). (gr. k-3). 1983. (ISBN 0-690-04253-1, TYC-J). (ISBN 0-690-04254-X). Har-Row.

Berger, Terry (1933-)
--Being Alone, Being Together. Kluetmeier, Heinz, photos by. LC 74-17092. (Illus.). 31 p. 25cm. 1974. (ISBN 0-516-03005-1). Advanced Learning Concepts; Distributed by Childrens Press, Chicago.
--Ben's ABC Day. Kandell, Alice S., photos by. LC 81-13754. (Illus.). 32 p. c.1982. (ISBN 0-688-00881-X). Lothrop, Lee & Shepard.
--Big Sister, Little Brother. Kluetmeier, Heinz, photos by. LC 75-19467. (Illus.). 32p. Repr. of 1974 ed. (Identity II Ser.). (gr. k-3). 1975. (ISBN 0-8172-0049-5). Raintree Pubs.
--Black Fairy Tales. White, David Omar (1927-), illus. Bourhill, E. J., adapted by. LC 70-75517. (Illus.). 137 p. 25cm. 1969. (ISBN 0-689-20036-6). Atheneum.
--I Have Feelings. Spivak, I. Howard, illus. LC 70-147123. (Illus.). 41 p. 24cm. (Children's series on psychologically relevant themes). 1971. Behavioral Publications.
--Lucky. LC 73-16817. 48p. 1st U.S. edition. (Lead-off Bks). (ps-3). 1975. (ISBN 0-87955-110-0). (ISBN 0-87955-710-9). O'Hara.
--Lucky: A Lead of Book. Wiskur, Darrell D., illus. 1974. J. Philip O'Hara Inc.
--A New Baby. Kluetmeier, Heinz, photos by. LC 75-19415. (Illus.). 32p. Repr. of 1974 ed. (Moods & Emotions Ser.). (gr. k-3). 1975. (ISBN 0-8172-0053-3). Raintree Pubs.
--Special Friends. (Illus.). 1979. Messner.
--Stepchild. Hechtliinger, David, photos by. LC 79-28100. (Illus.). 64p. (gr. 3-5). 1980. (ISBN 0-671-33008-X). Messner.
--The Turtles' Picnic and Other Nonsense Stories. Alanen, Erkki, illus. LC 77-3309. p. cm. c.1977. (ISBN 0-517-52998-X). Crown Publishers.

Bergere, Thea
--Jean and Jacqueline: Paris in the Rain. Bergere, Richard, illus. LC 63-14326. 26cm. 32p. 1963. McGraw-Hill Book Co.

Bergeret, Annie. & Tenaille, Marie
--Tales from China. Boudignon, Francoise, illus. LC 80-52513. (Illus.). 139 p. 25cm. (The World Folktale Library). 1981, c.1977. Silver Burdett Co.

Bergeron, Victor Jules, Jr. (1902-)
--The Menehunes. Told by Trader Vic. Walworth, Jane Armstrong, illus. LC 70-165388. (Illus.). 32 p. 20cm. 1972. Doubleday.

Bergey, Alyce Mae (1934-)
--Beggar's Greatest Wish. (Arch Bks: No. 6). (gr. 4-6). 1969. (ISBN 0-570-06040-0). Concordia.
--The Beggars Greatest Wish. 1969. Lutheran Publications.
--The Boy Who Saved His Family: Genesis 37-50 for Children. Wind, Betty, illus. (Illus.). unpaged. 21cm. (Arch bks.: Set 3, No. 59-1126). c.1966. Concordia.
--The Boy Who was Lost. (Illus.). 32p. (Arch Bks: Set 9). (ps-4). 1972. (ISBN 0-570-06065-6). Concordia.
--The First Rainbow. Brophy, Ruth, illus. LC 64-770510. 1 v. (unpaged) col. illus. 29 cm. N.D. T. S. Denison.
--The Great Promise: Genesis 12: 1-21: 3 for Children. Wind, Betty, illus. (Illus.). 32 p. 21cm. (Arch books). 1968. Concordia Pub. House.
--Rocky: The Rocket Mouse. Spiegel, Lawrence M., illus. LC 61-180910. unpaged. illus. 29cm. 1961. T. S. Denison.

Bergh, Haakon, jt. auth. see Grenzeback, Joe.

Bergman, David, ed. see La Fontaine, Jean De.

Bergmann, Ann (1911-)
--Blueberry. 1st ed. Bergmann, Ann (1911-), illus. LC 57-114602. unpaged. illus. 22x27cm. c.1957. Pageant Press.

Bergman Sucksdorff, Astrid
--Chendru: The Boy and the Tiger. Sacksdorff, Arne & Bergman Sacksdorff, Astrid, photos by Sanson, William, tr. from Fr. LC 60-2381. 56p. (chiefly illus.) 30 cm. 1960. Harcourt, Brace. **Award: (ALA).**
--Micky, the Baby Fox. 1959. MacMillan Co.
--The Roe Deer. Bergman Sucksdorff, Astrid, photos by. Tapsell, Alan, tr. from Swedish. LC 70-1820. (Illus.). 48p. (gr. 3 up). 1969. (ISBN 0-15-268365-8, HJ). HarBraceJ.
--Tooni, the Elephant Boy. Bergman Sucksdorff, Astrid, photos by. LC 73-137762. (Illus.). 48p. (gr. 3 up). 1971. (ISBN 0-15-289426-8, HJ). HarBraceJ.

Bergse, Vilhelm, jt. auth. see Jensen, Virginia Allen.

Bergsma, Stuart (1900-)
--See that Holy Child: The story of the twelve-year-old Christ. LC 68-55389. (A fictional account of twelve-year-old Jesus encounter with the wise men in the teimple.). 80p. ill. col. 20cm. c.1968. Baker Book House.

Bergstrom, Corinne
--Losing Your Best Friend. Rosamilia, Patricia, illus. LC 79-20622. p. cm. 1980. (ISBN 0-87705-471-1). Human Sciences Press.

Bergstrom, Richard (1828-1893) & Tappan, Eva March (1854-1930), eds.
--The Prince from Nowhere and Other Tales. LC 28-212145. 5 p. l., 206, 1 p. col. front., col. plates. 20 1/2 cm. 1928. Houghton Mifflin Company.

Bergvall, S.
--The Little Elves of Elf Nook. (Illus.). 32x25cm. 32p. (gr. 2-6). 1966. Vanous.

Beris, Sandra
--The Pink Panther & the Fancy Party. Baker, Darrell, illus. LC 82-82613. 24p. (Golden Look-Look Bk.). (gr. 4-8). 1983. (ISBN 0-307-11887-8, Golden Pr). (ISBN 0-307-11887-8). Western Pub.
--Poochie & Fastball. Gantz, David, illus. (Illus.). 16p. (Golden Fuzzy Shape Bks.). (ps). 1983. (ISBN 0-307-25792-4, Golden Pr). Western Pub.
--Poochie-Flower Power. Gantz, David, illus. (Illus.). 16p. (Golden Fuzzy Shape Bks.). (ps). 1983. (ISBN 0-307-25790-8, Golden Pr). Western Pub.

Beris, Sandra, adapted by see Seguin-Fontes, Martha.

Beris, Sandra, tr. see Seguin-Fontes, Martha.

Berk, Lucile
--Proverb Stories of Many Lands. LC 24-20615. 4 p. l., 3-250 p. front., plates. 20 cm. c.1924. The Century Co.

Berk, Phyllis
--The Duke's Command. Petie, Haris, pseud. (1915-), illus. Petty, Roberta. (Illus.). 1966. (ISBN 0-8313-0005-1). Lantern Press Inc Publishers.

Berke, Helen
--Dick Tracy and the Mad Killer: Story Based on the Famous Newspaper Strip by Chester Gould. Gould, Chester (1900-1985), illus. LC 48-16133. 286 p. illus. 12 cm. (The Better Little Book: No. 1436). c.1947. Whitman Pub. Co.
--Little Orphan Annie and the Gooneyville Mystery. Gray, Harold Lincoln (1894-1968), illus. LC 48-16134. (Story based on the Famous Newspaper Strip by Harold Gray). 286 p. illus. 12 cm. (The Better Little Book: No. 1436). c.1947. Whitman Pub. C.
--Winnie Winkle and the Diamond Heirlooms: An Original Story Based on Martin Branner's Famous Newspaper Strip "Winnie Winkle". authorized. Branner, Martin Michael (1888-1970), illus. LC 46-8187. 2 p. l., 9-248 p. illus. 20 1/2 cm. 1946. Whitman Publishing Co.

Berke, Sally
--Monster at Loch Ness. LC 77-24715. (Illus.). 48p. (Great Unsolved Mysteries Ser.). (gr. 4up). 1983. (ISBN 0-8172-2160-3). Raintree Pubs.

Berkebile, Fred Donovan (1900-1978)
--Captured!. LC 74-32602. (Illus.). 176p. (Orig.). (gr. 4-9). 1975. (ISBN 0-912692-59-6). Cook.
--The Magic City. Peterson, Harold, illus. LC 54-9100. 100p. illus. 22cm. 1954. Caxton Printers.
--Moroccan Adventure. McCann, Gerald (1916-), illus. (Illus.). (Young Readers Bookshelf). (gr. 4-7). N.D. (ISBN 0-8313-0006-X). Lantern.
--Young Readers Moroccan Adventure. McCann, Gerald (1916-), illus. LC 59-133715. 191p. illus. 21cm. 1960. Lantern Press.

Berkeley, E. Geraldine
--Fun with the Fairies. N.D. Small,Maynard & Co.

Berkeley, M.
--A Naval Alphabet. Hartley, J. H., illus. N.D. Macmillan.

Berkey, Barry, jt. auth. see Berkey, Velma.

Berkey, Ben B.
--Hopi Holiday: A Story of the Hopi Indians. Berkey, Ben B., illus. LC 67-30007. 1 v. (unpaged) illus. 29cm. c.1967. Denison.
--Jumbo: The Elephant. 64p. (Children's Picture Bks.). N.D. T. S. Denison & Co.
--Liberty Hill. Berkey, Ben B., illus. LC 58-13803. 77p. illus. 25cm. (Upper Grade Book). (gr. 4-6). 1959. Denison.
--Oscar: The Curious Ostrich. Berkey, Ben B., illus. LC 59-14408. unpaged. illus. 29cm. (Third Grade Book). (gr. 3-4). 1959. T. S. Denison.

Berkey, Helen Lamar, Mrs. (1898-)
--Aunty Pinau's Banyan. Lanterman, Raymond E. (1916-), illus. 1965. Charles E. Turtle Co.,Inc.
--Aunty Pinau's Banyan Tree. Lanterman, Raymond E. (1916-), illus. LC 65-20616. (Illus.). 27cm. 61p. 1967. C. E. Tuttle Co.
--Aunty Pinau's Banyan Tree. Lanterman, Raymond E. (1916-), illus. 1966. (ISBN 0-8048-0046-4). Charles E. Tuttle Co.
--The Secret Cave of Kamanawa. Lanterman, Raymond E. (1916-), illus. LC 68-18606. (Illus.). 100 p. 27cm. 1968. C. E. Tuttle Co.

Berkey, Velma & Berkey, Barry (1935-)
--Robbers, Bones & Mean Dogs. Hafner, Marylin (1925-), illus. LC 77-10727. (Illus.). 1978. (ISBN 0-201-00570-0, A-W Childrens). A-W.

Berkness, Hazelle M.
--Pick a Bunch of Stars. N.D. Vantage Press.
--Pick a Bunch of Stars. Bromhall, Winifred, illus. LC 44-47150. 4 p. l., 64 p. illus. 21 1/2 cm. 1944. The Paebar Company.

Berkowitz, Henry Joseph (1894-)
--The Fire Eater. LC 41-11285. vii, 394 p., 1 l. plates. 19 cm. 1941. The Jewish Publication Society of America.

Berlin, Isaiah (1909-)
--The Hedgehog and the Fox. 1953. Simon and Schuster.

Berliner, Franz (1930-)
--The Lake People. Bering, Claus, illus. Thygesen-Blecher, Lone, tr. LC 72-94271. (Illus.). 124 p. 21cm. 1973. (ISBN 0-399-20347-8). (ISBN 0-399-20347-8). Putnam.

Berlitz, Charles, ed. see Berlitz Schools Of Languages.

Berlitz Schools Of Languages
--French for Children: The Three Bears and Little Red Riding Hood. Berlitz, Charles (1914-) & Strumpen-Darrie, Robert (1912-), eds. Wilson, Dagmar (1916-), illus. (Illus.). (gr. 4-6). 1959. (ISBN 0-448-01440-8). G&D.

Berlitz Schools Of Languages (1914-)
--German for Children: Three Bears and Little Red Riding Hood. Berlitz, Charles (1916-) & Strumpen-Darrie, Robert (1912-), eds. Wilson, Dagmar (1916-), illus. (Illus.). (gr. 4-6). 1960. (ISBN 0-448-01443-2). G&D.
--Italian for Children: The Three Bears and Little Red Riding Hood. Berlitz, Charles (1912-) & Strumpen-Darrie, Robert, eds. Wilson, Dagmar (1916-), illus. (Illus.). (gr. 4-6). N.D. (ISBN 0-448-01441-6). G&D.
--Spanish for Children: The Three Bears and Little Red Riding Hood. Berlitz, Charles (1912-) & Strumpen-Darrie, Robert, eds. Wilson, Dagmar (1916-), illus. (Illus.). (gr. 4-6). 1959. (ISBN 0-448-01442-4). G&D.

Berlitz Institute, tr. see Brown, Joel.

Berman, A.
--Folktale Reader. 1976. Macmillan Publishing company.

Berman, Linda (1948-)
--The Goodbye Painting. Hannon, Mark, illus. LC 81-20217. p. cm. 1982. Human Sciences Press.

Berman, Paul
--The Make-Believe Empire. Berman, Paul, illus. LC 81-10847. (Illus.). 96p. (ps). 1982. (ISBN 0-689-30909-0). Atheneum.

Berman, Rhoda A.
--When You Were a Little Baby. Foster, Marian Curtis (1909-1978), illus. Mariana, pseud. LC 53-6727. unpaged. illus. 26cm. 1954. Lothrop, Lee & Shepard.

Berman, Sadye A
--Plays for the Schoolroom: Safety. Character. Holiday. LC 37-29633. 136 p. 19 cm. c.1936. S. French.

Berman, Sam
--Dinosaur Joke Book. LC 69-17282. (Illus.). 41 p. 29cm. 1969. Grosset & Dunlap.

Berman, Sam & O'Mellish, Phineas
--Pixie Pete's Christmas Party. N.D. Modern Age Books.

Bermont, Hubert Ingram, jt. auth. see Langston, Shelley.

Berna, Paul (1910-)
--The Clue of the Black Cat. Seward, Prudence, illus. Buchanan-Brown, John (1929-), tr. from Fr. LC 65-20652. 170p. illus. 22cm. 1965, c.1964. (ISBN 0-394-91038-9). Pantheon.
--Continent in the Sky. Duchesne, Janet (1930-), illus. Buchanan-Brown, John (1929-), tr. from Fr. LC 63-8232. 192 p. illus. 21 cm. 1963. Abelard-Schuman.
--Flood Warning. Keeping, Charles William James (1924-), illus. Buchanan-Brown, John (1929-), tr. from Fr. LC 63-15477. 22cm. 157p. 1963. Pantheon Books.
--The Horse Without a Head. Kennedy, Richard (1910-), illus. Buchanan-Brown, John (1929-), tr. from Fr. LC 58-13488. (Illus.). 180 p. 22cm. 1959, c.1958. Pantheon Books. **Award: (ALA).**

AUTHOR INDEX BERRY, JOY

--The Knights of King Midas. Wildsmith, Brian Lawrence (1930-), illus. LC 61-14778. (Illus.). 187 p. 22cm. 1961. Pantheon Books. **Award: (ALA).**
--The Mule on the Expressway. Floyd, Gareth (1940-), illus. Buchanan-Brown, John (1929-), tr. from Fr. LC 68-24562. (Illus.). 169 p. 22cm. 1968, c.1967. Pantheon Books.
--Mystery of Saint Salgue. Broomfield, Robert (1930-), illus. Buchanan-Brown, John, tr. from Fr. LC 64-18315. (Illus.). (gr. 5-9). 1964. (ISBN 0-394-91437-6). Pantheon.
--The Secret of the Missing Boat. Wilkinson, Barry, illus. Buchanan-Brown, John (1929-), tr. from Fr. LC 67-142332. 150p. illus. 22cm. 1967, c.1966. Pantheon.
--They Didn't Come Back. Buchanan-Brown, John (1929-), tr. from Fr. LC 73-117459. 22cm. 212p. 1970. (ISBN 0-394-[illegible]) Pantheon Bks.
--Threshold of the Stars. 1960. E M Hale.
--Threshold of the Stars. Spence, Geraldine (1931-), illus. Buchanan-Brown, John (1929-), tr. LC 60-13913. 21cm. 176p. 1960. Abelard-Schuman.
--Truckload of Rice. Seward, Prudence, illus. LC 78-101182. (Illus.). 15 line drawings. 160p. 22cm. 153p. (gr. 5 up). 1968. (ISBN 0-394-[illegible]). Pantheon.

Bernadette, pseud., see Watts, Anna Bernadette.

Bernadine, Cook
--Looking For Susie. N.D. E . M. Hale and Co.

Bernal, jt. auth. see Ludwig.

Bernanos, Geroges
--Joy. 1946. Pantheon Books Inc.

Bernanos, Michel
--The Other Side of the Mountain. N.D. Norman S. Berg Pub.

Bernard, Christine
--A Host of Ghosts. LC 77-9054. 256 p. 22cm. c.1976. (ISBN 0-397-31756-5). Lippincott.

Bernard, Florence Scott
--Diana of Briarcliffe. Hubon, Edna F. Hart, illus. LC 23-12399. 269 p. front., plates. 20 cm. c.1923. Lothrop, Lee & Shepard Co.
--Through the Cloud Mountain with Jan and the Storybook Fold We Love. Kay, Gertrude Alice (1884-1939), illus. LC 22-17975. 215 p. col. front., col. plates. 24 cm. 1922. J. B. Lippincott Company.

Bernard, Jack, ed. see Hartmann, Sven & Hartner, Thomas.

Bernard, Jack, tr. see Held, Jacqueline.

Bernard, Jack F. (1930-), ed. see Hartmann, Sven & Hartner, Thomas.

Bernard, Joseph, ed. see Marryat, Frederick.

Bernardin, Claude Augustus James
--The Shoemaker of Kish. Macgregor, Sheila, illus. LC 55-1453. 80p. illus. 22cm. 1954. F. Warne.

Bernath, Stefen, jt. auth. see Yolen, Jane Hyatt.

Bernays, Anne (1930-)
--Growing Up Rich. 352p. 1975. (ISBN 0-316-09185-5). Little.

Berndt, Walter (1900-1979)
--Smitty. 86p. (The Smitty Ser.: The Famous Sixty Cents Quarto Comics). N.D. Cupples & Leon Co.
--Smitty at the Ball Game. 86p. (The Smitty Ser.: The Famous Sixty Cents Quarto Comics). N.D. Cupples & Leon Co.
--Smitty in Military School. (The Smitty Ser.). N.D. Cupples & Leon Co.
--Smitty in the North Woods. (The Smitty Ser.). N.D. Cupples & Leon Co.
--Smitty the Flying Office Boy. 86p. (The Smitty Ser.: The/Famous Sixty Cents Quarto Comics). N.D. Cupples & Leon Co.
--Smitty the Jockey. (The Smitty Ser.). N.D. Cupples & Leon Co.

Berne, Eric Leonard (1910-1970)
--The Happy Valley. Selig, Sylvie (1942-), illus. LC 68-17720. (Illus.). 63 p. 27cm. 1968. Grove Press.

Bernede, Arthur (1871-)
--The Mystery of the Louvre. LC 31-35207. 1 p. l., 7-139 p. 17 cm. N.D. World Wide Publishing Co., Inc.

Bernhard, Josephine. Butkowska, Mrs., tr. see Lorentowicz, Irena.

Bernhard, Josephine Butkowska, Mrs., tr. see Le Valley, Elisabeth Frances.

Bernhard, Josephine Butkowska, Mrs., tr. see Porazinska, Janina.

Bernhard, Josephine Butkowski, Mrs.
--The Master Wizard. 1934. A. A. Knopf.

Bernhard, Marcelle
--Jamie's Magic Bullet. LC 68-11081. (Illus.). 52 p. 22cm. 1968. C. E. Tuttle Co.

Bernhardsen, Einar Christian Rosenvinge (1923-)
--Fight in the Mountains. Sinding, Franey, tr. from Danish. LC 68-28800. 128 p. 21cm. 1968. Harcourt, Brace & World.

Bernhardt, Melvin
--The Pied Piper of Hamelin. (Children's Theatre Playscript Ser.). 1963. (ISBN 0-88020-043-X). Coach Hse.

Bernheim, Evelyne, jt. auth. see Bernheim, Marc.

Bernheim, Marc (1924-) & Bernheim, Evelyne (1935-)
--The Drums Speak: The Story of Kofi a Boy of West Africa. Bernheim, Marc (1924-) & Bernheim, Evelyne (1935-), illus. N.D. Harcourt Brace Jovanovich.

Bernikow, Louise, ed.
--The World Split Open: Four Centuries of Women Poets in England & America, 1552-1950. Rukeyser, Muriel (1913-1980), pref. by. LC 74-8582. 1974. (ISBN 0-394-71072-X, Vin). Random.

Bernsen, Paul S.
--Bugle of the Elk. Amundsen, Richard E., illus. LC 75-43033. viii, 82 p. ill. 26 cm. c.1977. (ISBN 0-679-20313-3). D. McKay Co.
--The Goose That Went to Hollywood. Amundsen, Richard E., illus. LC 75-[illegible] (Illus.). 90 p. 26cm. c.1976. D. McKay Co.

Bernstein, Anna Ruth Epstein see Todd, Ann, pseud.

Bernstein, Anna Ruth Epstein, Mrs. (1893-)
--No Time for Funnies. Todd, Ann, pseud. Slocum, Rosalie (1906-), illus. LC 42-18439. 54, 2 p. incl. col. front., illus. (part col.) 20 x 16 cm. 1942. Oxford University Press.
--A Time for Swapping. Todd, Ann, pseud. Slocum, Rosalie (1906-), illus. LC [illegible], 1 p. col. illus. 19 1/2 x 15 1/2 cm. 1944. Oxford University Press.
--Timothy Came Instead. Todd, Ann, pseud. Slocum, Rosalie (1906-), illus. LC 42-16143. 20cm. 46p. 1941. Oxford University Press.
--The Umbrella That Got Wet. Todd, Ann, pseud. Slocum, Rosalie (1906-), illus. LC 38-27676. 55, 1 p. incl. col. front., illus. (part col.) col. plates, 20 cm. c.1938. Oxford University Press.

Bernstein, Joanne Eckstein, et al. (1943-)
--Un-Frog-Getable Riddles. Fay, Ann, ed. LC 81-11548. 32p. (gr. 1-5). 1981. (ISBN 0-8075-8322-7). A Whitman.

Bernstein, Joanne Eckstein (1943-) & Bernstein, Michael J
--Dmitry: A Young Soviet Immigrant's. LC 81-2251. p. cm. c.1981. (ISBN 0-89919-034-0). Clarion Books.

Bernstein, Joanne Eckstein (1943-) & Cohen, Paul (1945-)
--Happy Holiday Riddles to You!. Seltzer, Meyer, illus. LC 85-717. (Illus.). 32 p. 21cm. 1985. (ISBN 0-8075-3154-5). A. Whitman.
--More Unidentified Flying Riddles. Seltzer, Meyer, illus. LC 85-15537. p. cm. 1985. (ISBN 0-8075-5279-8). A. Whitman.
--Unidentified Flying Riddles. Seltzer, Meyer, illus. LC 83-17097. p. cm. 1983. (ISBN 0-8075-8329-4). A. Whitman.

Bernstein, Ken
--The Senator's Ransom. (gr. 7 up). 1971. (ISBN 0-698-10331-9). Coward.

Bernstein, Margery, jt. auth. see Kobrin, Janet.

Bernstein, Margery (1933-) & Kobrin, Janet (1942-)
--Coyote Goes Hunting for Fire: A California Indian Myth. Heffernan, Ed, illus. LC 73-19361. (Illus.). 38 p. 1974. (ISBN 0-684-13768-2). Scribner.
--Earth Namer. Heffernan, Ed, illus. (Illus.). (Encore Edition). (gr. k-3). 1974. (ISBN 0-684-15829-9, ScribT). Scribner.
--Earth Namer: A California Indian Myth. Heffernan, Ed, illus. LC 73-19362. (Illus.). 40 p. 24cm. 1974. Scribner.
--The First Morning: An African Myth. Romanek, Enid Warner, illus. LC 75-27705. (Illus.). 48 p. 24cm. c.1976. (ISBN 0-684-14533-2). Scribner.
--How the Sun Made a Promise and Kept It: A Canadian Indian Myth. Heffernan, Ed, illus. LC 73-19363. (Illus.). 40 p. 24cm. 1974. (ISBN 0-684-13770-4). Scribner.
--The Summermaker: An Ojibway Indian Myth. Burgess, Anne (1942-), illus. LC 76-14875. 48p. (Encore Edition: Myths You Can Read by Yourself). (gr. 1-3). 1977. (ISBN 0-684-17356-5, ScribJ). Scribner.

Bernstein, Michael J, jt. auth. see Bernstein, Joanne Eckstein.

Berquin, Arnaud (1749-1791) & Author of "The Child's First Book"
--The Beauties of The Children's Friend: Being a Selection of Interesting Pieces from ... M. Berquin, Intended to Promote a Love of Truth and Virtue. For the Use of Schools. LC 77-353792. 312 p. 18cm. 1808. Manning & Loring, and L. Blake.
--The Blossoms of Morality: Intended for the Amusement and Instruction of Young Ladies and Gentlemen. Anderson, Alexander (1775-1870), illus. LC 10-4177. 3 p. l., 196 p. illus. (part col.) 18 m. 1807. Published by Evert Duyckinck, Bookesllr & Stationer. McFarlane and Long, Printers.
--The Child's Friend. LC 1-6. (Illus.). 252 p. 16cm. 1840. Marsh, Capen, Lyon & Webb.
--Child's Friend. (Harper's Massachusetts School Library, Juvenile Ser.). N.D. Harper & Bros.
--The Friend of Youth. LC 6-11323. 2 v. 18 x 11 cm. N.D. Printed by John Mycall, for the Proprietor of the Boston Book Store, N , Cornhill, Boson.
--The Friend of Youth. LC 6-11323. 18 x 10cm. Orig. Title: Fr. 1800. John Mycall.
--Looking-Glass for the Mind, 1 of 18 Vols. (Illus.). (Happy Child's Library). N.D. D. Appleton & Co.
--The Looking Glass For the Mind: Or, Intellectual Mirror. LC 72-87845. (Illus.). 18cm. xi, 271p. Repr. of 1794 ed. (Early Children's Bks.). 1969. Johnson Reprint Corp.
--The Looking-Glass for the Mind: Or, Intellectual Mirror. Anderson, Alexander (1775-1870), illus. Cooper, Mr., tr. LC 21-7611. (Being an Elegant Collection of the Most Delightful Little Stories and Interesting Tales, Chiefly Tr. from That Much Admired Work L'Ami Des Enfans). iv, 5-216 p. illus. 15 cm. 1832. A. Towar, Hogan & Thompson.
--The Looking-Glass for the Mind: Or, Intellectual Mirror. new ed. Anderson, Alexander (1775-1870), illus. Cooper, Mr., tr. LC 16-16966. (Being an Elegant Collection of the Most Delightful Little Stories and Interesting Tales, Chiefly Translated from That Much Admired Work, L'Ami Des Enfans.). 4 p. l., 252 p. front., illus. 17 cm. 1794. By Carter And Wilkinson, and Sold at Their Book and Stationary Store.
--The Looking-Glass for the Mind: Or, Intellectual Mirror; Being an Elegant Collection of the Most Delightful Little Stories, and Interesting Tales, Chiefly Tr. from That Much Admired Work L'Ami Des Enfans. Anderson, Alexander (1775-1870), illus. Cooper, Mr., tr. LC 21-17582. iv, 203 p. illus. 18 cm. 1807. Printed by McFarlane and Long, No. Broadway.
--The Looking-Glass for the Mind: Or, The Intellectual Mirror; Being an Elegant Collection of the Most Delightful Little Stories, and Interesting Tales, Chiefly Translated from That Much Admired Work L'Ami Des Enfans. Anderson, Alexander (1775-1870), illus. Cooper, Mr., tr. LC 87-82801. (The Translation is ascribed to a "Rev. Mr. Cooper" variously given as Samuel W. D. and J.). iv, 203 p. illus. 19 cm. 1818. E. Duyckinck.
--The Looking-Glass for the Mind: Or The Juvenile Friend, Being a Valuable Collection of Interesting and Miscellaneous Incidents, Calculated to Exhibit to Young Minds the Happy Effects of Youthful Innocence and Filial Affection; in Prose and Verse; Designed to Amuse and Improve the Rising Generation; Embellished with an Elegant Frontispiece, and Seventy-Three Cuts. Cooper, Mr., tr. LC 16-1223. 192 p. front., illus. 18 cm. 1824. Printed by J. Bioren.
--The Looking-Glass for the Mind: Or, The Juvenile Friend. Cooper, Mr., tr. (Being a Valuable Collection of Interesting and Miscellaneous Incidents, Calculated to Exhibit to Young Minds the Happy Effects of Youthful Innocence, and Filial Affection; in Prose and Verse: Designed to Improve and Amuse the Rising Generation; Embellished with an Elegant Frontspiece, and Seventy-Three Cuts.). iv. 271 p. front. 18 cm. 1815. Printed and Sold by John Bioren, No. , Chestnut Street.
--The Looking-Glass for the Mind: Or, The Juvenile Friend, No. 88. Cooper, Mr., tr. LC 38-35069. (Being a Valuable Collection of Interesting and Miscellaneous Incidents, Calculated to Exhibit to Young Minds the Happy Effects of Youthful Innocence, and Filial Affection; in Prose and Verse: Designed to Improve and Amuse the Rising Generation). iv, 271 p. front., illus. 19 cm. 1819. Printed and Published by John Bioren, No. , Chestnut Street.

Berquist, Grace
--Boy Who Couldn't Roar. Van Sciver, Ruth (1915-), illus. LC 60-6818. (Illus.). 22cm. 31p. (gr. k-3). 1960. (ISBN 0-687-03964-9). Abingdon.
--Speckles Goes to School. Elgin, Kathleen (1923-), illus. LC 52-2951. (Illus.). 21cm. 46p. (gr. k-3). 1952. (ISBN 0-687-39153-9). Abingdon.
--Speckles Goes to School. Elgin, Kathleen (1923-), illus. N.D. Arlington Press.

Berra, Lawrence Peter (1925-) & Ferdenzi, Til
--Behind the Plate. LC 62-14091. 190p. 21cm. 1962. Argonaut Books.

Berri, Claude
--The Rooster Who Laid Eggs. Fox, Robin, ed. (Illus.). (gr. 2-6). 1967. (ISBN 0-87460-031-6). (ISBN 0-87460-044-8). Lion.

Berridge, Celia
--Wet-Day Witches. LC 76-383971. (Illus.). 32 p. 27cm. 1976. (ISBN 0-233-96778-8). Deutsch.

Berrien, Edith Heal see Heal, Edith.

Berrien, Edith Heal (1903-)
--The Downy Duck. Maclay, Tony, illus. LC 46-8463. 16 p. col. illus. 23 cm. 1946. J. Messner.
--The Golden Bowl. Cannon, Marian, illus. LC 47-30152. 21cm. 72p. 1947. Lothrop, Lee and Shepard.
--Mr. Pink and the HOuse on the Roof. Ferry, Cay, illus. LC 41-22369. 26cm. 56p. 1941. J. Messner.
--Robin Hood. Allen, Phillippa, intro. by. LC 28-25083. 24cm. 626p. (The Windermere Ser.). 1923. Rand, McNally.
--Siegfried. Winter, Milo Kendall (1888-1956), illus. LC 30-25663. 24cm. 368p. 1930. T. S. Rockwell.
--Tim Trains His Terrier. Opitz, Marge, illus. LC [illegible] p. illus. 23 cm. 195[illegible]. A. Whitman.
--The Topaz Seal. Stempel, Marjorie, illus. LC 29-7398. 20cm. 291p. (Young American Ser.). 1928. Laidlaw Bros.
--What Happened to Jenny. Giventer, Abbi, illus. LC 62-10248. 62 p. illus. 21 cm. 1962. Atheneum.

Berrigan, Darrell
--The Forbidden Forest. Dominis, John, illus. LC 49-10330. 90 p. illus. 23 cm. 1949. J. Day Co

Berrill, Jacquelyn Batsel (1905-)
--River Girl. Loh, George, illus. LC 68-26155. (Illus.). x, 180 p. 22cm. 1968. Dodd, Mead.

Berrill, Margaret, retold by.
--The Three Musketeers. LC 85-12469. (Original Author: Alexandre Dumas, 1802-1870). p. cm. 1985. (ISBN 0-8172-2500-5). (ISBN 0-8172-2508-0). Raintree Childrens Books.

Berrisford, Judith Mary, pseud., see Lewis, Judith Mary.

Berrisford, Judith Mary, pseud. (1921-)
--Colt in the Family. Lewis, Judith Mary. Gordon, Anne, illus. (Illus.). (gr. 5 up). 1962. Verry.
--Jackie Won a Pony. Lewis, Judith Mary. Whittam, Geoffrey William (1916-), illus. (Illus.). (gr. 3-6). 1958. (ISBN 0-685-21260-2). Verry.
--Jackie's Pony Patrol. Lewis, Judith Mary. Whittam, Geoffrey William (1916-), illus. (Illus.). (gr. 3-6). 1961. Verry.
--The Ponies Next Door. Lewis, Judith Mary. Whittam, Geoffrey William (1916-), illus. LC 55-52331. 175p. illus. 21cm. 1955, c.1954. Dodd, Mead.
--A Pony in the Family. Lewis, Judith Mary. Gordon, Anne, illus. LC 62-750414. 124p. illus. 22cm. 1962. Reilly & Lee.
--Red Rocket, Mystery Horse. Lewis, Judith Mary. Atkinson, Leslie, illus. LC 53-6132. 146p. illus. 21cm. 1953, c.1952. Dodd, Mead.
--Show Jumper in the Family. Lewis, Judith Mary. Gordon, Anne, illus. (Illus.). (gr. 5 up). 1964. Verry.
--Sue's Circus Horse. Lewis, Judith Mary. Atkinson, Leslie, illus. LC 52-7332. 180 p. illus. 21 cm. 1952. Dodd, Mead.

Berry, Barbara J. (1937-)
--His Majesty's Mark. Hopper, John Edgar, illus. LC 76-11631. (gr. 4 up). 1976. (ISBN 0-672-52182-2). Bobbs.
--Just Don't Bug Me. De Velasco, Joe E., illus. LC 72-118926. (Illus.). 125 p. 23cm. 1970. (ISBN 0-695-80142-2). Follett.
--A Look of Eagles. Mars, Witold Tadeusz J. (1912-), illus. LC 72-75890. (Illus.). 112 p. 22cm. 1973. Bobbs-Merrill.
--Shannon. Ambrus, Victor G., pseud. (1935-), illus. Ambrus, Gyozo Laszlo. LC 68-13795. (Illus.). 191 p. 23cm. 1968. Follett Pub. Co.

Berry, Barbara J (1937-) & Hopper, John Edgar (1921-)
--His Majesty's Mark. Hopper, John Edgar (1921-), illus. LC 78-3651. (Illus.). 130 p. 22cm. 1977, c.1976. (ISBN 0-672-52182-2). Bobbs-Merrill.

Berry, Claude Perrin (1877-)
--Ruth Jane Talks with the Animals. Blair, Virginia, illus. LC 42-8780. 106 p. illus. 24 cm. c.1941. Dorrance and Company.

Berry, E. M., Mrs.
--Crooked and Straight. N.D. Colby and Rich.
--The Hard Knot. 264p. (Golden Sheaves Library). N.D. Lockwood, Brooks, & Co. for American Tract Society.

Berry, Erick, pseud., see Best, Allena Champlin.

Berry, James R.
--Dar Tellum. Longtemps, Kenneth (1933-), illus. (Illus.). (gr. 4-6). 1974. (ISBN 0-590-00009-8, Schol Trade Pap). Schol Bk Serv.
--Dar Tellum: Stranger from a Distant Planet. Asimov, Isaac, ed. Scull, Enrico, illus. LC 72-95780. (Illus.). 64 p. 25cm. 1973. Walker.
--Kids on the Run: The Stories of Seven Teen-Age Runaways. LC 77-15845. 112p. (gr. 7 up). 1978. (ISBN 0-590-07507-1, Four Winds). Scholastic Inc.

Berry, Joy Wilt
--Being Destructive. Costanza, John, illus. 1984. Children's Press.

--What to Do When Your Mom or Dad Says: "Be Careful!". Kelley, Orly, ed. Bartholomew, illus. LC 83-80837. (Illus.). 48p. (Survival Series for Kids). (gr. k-6). N.D. (ISBN 0-941510-12-3). Living Skills.

Berry, Linda

--Christmas Plays for Older Children. (gr. 5-7). 1981. (ISBN 0-8054-9733-1). Broadman.

Berry, Liz

--Easy Connections. LC 83-16675. 180p. (gr. 7-9). 1984. (ISBN 0-670-28694-X, Viking Kestrel). Viking.

Berry, Martha E., Mrs.

--Band of Six. N.D. American Tract Co.

--Carolina. (Fern Glen Ser.). N.D. D. Lothrop Co.

--Carolina, the Hotel-Keeper's Daughter. N.D. D. Lothrop & Co.

--Carolina, the Hotel-Keeper's Daughter. (Sunday School Bks.). N.D. Hurd & Houghton for American Tract Society.

--Carolina, the Hotel-Keeper's Daughter. 297p. N.D. Lockwood, Brooks, & Co. for American Tract Society.

--Celesta, 1 of 3 vols. (Illus.). (The Celesta Stories). 1882. Lee & Shepard.

--Celesta, 1 of 25 vols. (Illus.). (Mayflower Ser. for Girls: No. 4). 1900. Lee & Shepard.

--Celesta: A Girl's Book. N.D. Colby and Rich.

--The Crook Straightened, 1 of 3 vols. (Illus.). (The Celesta Stories). 1882. Lee & Shepard.

--Crook Straightened, 1 of 25 vols. (Illus.). (Pilgrim Ser. for Boys: No. 5). 1900. Lee & Shepard.

--Crooked and Straight, 1 of 3 vols. (Illus.). (The Celesta Stories). 1882. Lee & Shepard.

--Crooked & Straight, 1 of 25 vols. (Illus.). (Pilgrim Ser. for Boys: No. 6). 1900. Lee & Shepard.

--The Hard Knot. 264p. N.D. Hurd & Houghton for American Tract Society.

--The Hard Knot. 264p. N.D. Lockwood, Brooks, & Co. for American Tract Society.

--Lottie Lane. 440p. N.D. American Tract Society.

Berry, Martha E., Mrs., et al.

--Pro and Con Ser. Containing ""Pro and Con," "Tried in the Fire," "Carolina," and "Edith Prescott", 1 of 4 vols. N.D. D. Lothrop & Co.

Berry, Paulette, jt. auth. see Warner, Laverne.

Berry, Rex, pseud., see Walburg, Simon C..

Berry, Rex, pseud.

--The Secret of Cranberry Creek: Or, Tim and Sal's Stamp Mystery,. Walburg, Simon C.. LC 49-9168. 89 p. 21 cm. 1949. W. B. Eerdmans Pub. Co.

Berry, Roland, jt. auth. see Maynard, Christopher.

Berry, Rotha McClain

--Swift Deer, the Navajo. LC 53-9094. (Illus.). 22cm. 101p. 1953. Naylor.

Berry, Ruth Eugenie

--The Cheerful Chimps. Mulliken, Barbara, illus. LC 41-9383. 185 p. incl. front., illus. 23 cm. c.1940. The Falcon Press.

Berry, Ruth Eugenie & Mulliken, Barbara

--The Cheerful Chimps. Comstock, Enos B, pref. by. LC 42-17883. 185 p. incl. front., illus. 23 cm. c.1941. Gotham House, Inc.

Berry, William David (1926-)

--Deneki: An Alaskan Moose. Berry, William David (1926-), illus. LC 65-165645. 1v. (unpaged) illus. (pt. col.) 27cm. c.1965. Macmillan.

Bersier

--Micheline. Brock, Carey, Mrs., tr. N.D. E. P. Dutton.

Bersier, Mrs.

--Changes and Chances. Brock, Carey, Mrs., tr. from Fr. (Illus.). N.D. E. P. Dutton.

--Children at Home. Brock, Carey, Mrs., tr. from Fr. 320p. N.D. E. P. Dutton.

--Margaret's Secret, And it's Success. Brock, Carey, Mrs., tr. from Fr. N.D. E. P. Dutton & Co.

Berson, Barbara

--What's Going to Happen to Me?. LC 75-39300. 22cm. 192p. (gr. 7-10). 1976. (ISBN 0-684-17755-2, ScribJ). Scribner.

Berson, Harold, jt. auth. see Mirkovic, Irene.

Berson, Harold, jt. auth. see Walden, Daniel.

Berson, Harold (1926-)

--Barrels to the Moon. Berson, Harold (1926-), illus. LC 81-5520. (Illus.). 32 p. c.1982. (ISBN 0-698-20551-0). Coward, McCann & Geoghegan.

--The Boy, the Baker, the Miller, and More. 1st ed. Berson, Harold (1926-), illus. LC 72-96413. (Illus.). 32 p. 1974. (ISBN 0-517-50326-3). Crown Publishers.

--Charles and Claudine. LC 79-23693. (Illus.). 32 p. c.1980. (ISBN 0-02-709230-5). Macmillan.

--Joseph and the Snake. LC 78-12317. (Illus.). 32 p. c.1979. (ISBN 0-02-709200-3). Macmillan.

--Larbi and Leila: A Tale of Two Mice. LC 73-12378. (Illus.). 32 p. 1974. (ISBN 0-8164-3113-2). Seabury Press.

--A Moose Is Not a Mouse. LC 74-16552. (Illus.). 32 p. 29cm. 1975. (ISBN 0-517-51869-4). Crown Publishers.

--The Rats Who Lived in the Delicatessen. Berson, Harold (1926-), illus. LC 76-2458. (Illus.). 32 p. c.1976. (ISBN 0-517-52604-2). Crown Publishers.

--The Thief Who Hugged a Moonbeam. Berson, Harold (1926-), illus. LC 70-190382. (Illus.). 32 p. 1972. (ISBN 0-8164-3084-5). Seabury Press.

--Truffles for Lunch. Berson, Harold (1926-), illus. LC 80-13367. p. cm. (gr. k-3). 1980. (ISBN 0-02-709800-1). Macmillan.

--Why the Jackal Won't Speak to the Hedgehog. Berson, Harold (1926-), illus. LC 69-13439. (Illus.). color ils. 32p. (ps-3). 1969. (ISBN 0-395-28768-5, Clarion). HM.

Berson, Harold (1926-), adapted by.

--Balarin's Goat. Berson, Harold (1926-), illus. LC 72-79795. (Illus.). 32 p. 20cm. 1972. (ISBN 0-517-50068-X). (ISBN 0-517-50068-X). Crown Publishers.

--Henry Possum. Berson, Harold (1926-), illus. LC 72-94563. (Illus.). 32 p. (gr. k-2). 1973. (ISBN 0-517-50297-6). Crown Publishers.

--How the Devil Gets His Due. Berson, Harold (1926-), illus. LC 79-185085. (Illus.). 30 p. 1972. Crown Publishers. **Award: (ALA).**

--I'm Bored, Ma!. Berson, Harold (1926-), illus. LC 75-31940. (Illus.). 32 p. 20cm. c.1976. (ISBN 0-517-52508-9). Crown Publishers.

--Kassim's Shoes. Berson, Harold (1926-), illus. LC 77-4688. p. cm. c.1977. (ISBN 0-517-53063-5). Crown Publishers.

--Pop Goes the Turnip. Berson, Harold (1926-), illus. LC 66-711835. 1v. (unpaged) col. illus. 24cm. 1966. Grosset.

--Raminagrobis and the Mice. Berson, Harold (1926-), illus. LC 65-18708. 1v. (unpaged) illus. 20cm. c.1965. Seabury.

Berson, Harold (1926-), illus.

--Treasury of Mother Goose. (gr. k-3). 1967. (ISBN 0-448-02994-4). G&D.

Bertail, Inez

--Billy and His Steam Roller. N.D. Wonder Books.

--Complete Nursery Song Book. rev. ed. Kelly, Walter Crawford (1913-1973), illus. (Illus.). (gr. k up). 1954. Lothrop.

--Goody, a Mother Cat Story. Leaf, Anne Sellers, illus. LC 53-18606. unpaged. illus. 21cm. (Rand McNally book-elf book, 470). 1953, c.1952. Rand McNally.

--Lullabies From Every Land. Larch, Steffie E., illus. N.D. Garden City Publishing Co.

--Summer and Winter. Davis, Rosemary, illus. LC 48-3615. 32 p. illus. (part col.) 19 x 26 cm. c.1945. Veritas Press.

--Time for Bed. MacKnight, Ninon (1908-), illus. Ninon, pseud. N.D. Doubleday & Co.

Bertail, Inez, ed.

--A Child's Book of Christmas Carols. N.D. Random House.

Bertail, Inez & McAnulla, Jan

--The Complete Book of Nursery Songs. N.D. Lothrop Lee & Shepard.

Bertelli, Luigi see Vamba, pseud.

Bertelli, Luigi (1858-1920)

--The Emperor of the Ants. Vamba, pseud. Di Pietro, Nicola, tr. LC 35-18069. (Illus.). 21.5 cm. 239p. 1935. Thomas Y. Crowell Co.

--The Prince and His Ants: (Ciondolino). Vamba, pseud. Kellogg, Vernon Lyman (1867-1937), ed. Woodruff, Sarah Frances (1848-), tr. from Ital. (Illus.). 19 1/2 cm. 275p. N.D. Henry Holt.

Berthiaume, Augusta

--Happy Days With Jackie. Lindberg, Howard E., illus. LC 59-14413. 29cm. 48p. (Children's Picture Bks.). 1959. T. S. Denison & Co.

Bertol, Roland

--Charles Drew. 1970. (ISBN 0-690-18597-9). (ISBN 0-690-18598-7). Thomas Y. Crowell Company.

--The Two Hats: A Story of Portugal. Eitzen, Allan (1928-), illus. LC 69-11080. (Illus.). 56 p. 23cm. (Stories from many lands). 1969. Crowell.

Bertol, Roland, retold by.

--Sundiata: The Epic of the Lion King. Prestopino, Gregorio, illus. LC 75-81945. (Illus.). x, 81 p. 23cm. 1970. T. Y. Crowell Co.

Berton, Pierre (1920-)

--Drifting Home. 1974. Borzoi Books.

--The Secret World of Og. Winter, William, illus. LC 62-802875. 116p. illus. 23cm. 1962. Little, Brown.

--Stampede for Gold: The Story of the Klondike. Macpherson, Duncan, illus. 1955. Borzoi.

Berton, Shirley L.

--A Barrel of Clams. De Gogorza, Maitland, illus. N.D. Harcourt Brace & Co.

Bertram, Florence Baker, jt. auth. see Bond, Gladys Baker.

Bertram, Harry

--Johnny Venture: A Story of an Exciting Journey. (Illus.). N.D. Thomas Nelson & Sons.

Bertram, Rosamund

--Ann Thorne comes to America. Woerner, K. S., illus. 40p. 1941. William Morrow & Co.

Bertsch, Lory

--Willie Visits Tulip Time. Brolin, Ed, illus. (Illus.). 40p. 1983. (ISBN 0-682-49980-3). Exposition.

Bertz, E.

--French Prisoners: A Story for Boys. 234p. 1884. Macmillan.

Berwick, Douglas R

--Five Plays for Chilren. 53 p. 19 cm. (On cover: French's plays for children, no. 34). c.1935. S. French, Ltd.

Berwick, Jean Shepherd (1929-)

--Arthur and the Golden Guinea. Berwick, Jean Shepherd (1929-), illus. LC 63-7535. unpaged. illus. 24 x 25cm. 1963. Golden Gate Junior Books.

Berzins, Helga, tr. see Knutsson, Gosta Lars August.

Besancon-Flot, Jeannette

--Princess Kalina and the Hedgehog. Duntze, Dorothee, illus. LC 82-670024. (Illus.). 16 p. 29cm. 1981. (ISBN 0-571-11844-5). Faber and Faber.

Besant, Walter

--Uncle Jack. (The Crown Ser.). N.D. The American News Co.

--Uncle Jack and Other Stories. N.D. Harper & Brothers' Trade-List.

Besier, Rudolph

--The Barretts of Wimpole Street. N.D. Little, Brown & Co.

Beskin, Linda, ed.

--Seventh Grade Visions. Beskin, Linda C, intro. by. LC 81-51737. 64p. (Orig.). (gr. 7). 1981. (ISBN 0-932238-11-4). Avant Bks.

Beskow, Elizabeth Maria see Runa, pseud.

Beskow, Elizabeth Maria (1870-1928)

--The Castaway, A Story for the Young. Runa, pseud. LC 18-17355. 136p. 18cm. 1918. Augustana Book Concern.

--A Christmas Home-Coming: And Other Stories for Children. Runa, pseud. LC 21-11922. 100, 1 p. front., pl. 18 cm. c.1920. Augustana Book Concern.

--The Royal Page and Other Stories for Children. Runa, pseud. 128 p. plates. 18 cm. c.1920. Augustana Book Concern.

--Twilight Hours. Runa, pseud. LC 27-23638. 17cm. 133p. 1927. Augustana Book Concern.

Beskow, Elsa Maartman (1874-1953)

--The Adventures of Peter and Lotta. Beskow, Elsa Maartman (1874-1953), illus. LC 31-28008. 32cm. 31p. 1931. Harper & Bros.

--Aunt Brown's Birthday. N.D. Harper & Bros.

--Aunt Green, Aunt Brown, Aunt Lavender. Beskow, Elsa Maartman (1874-1953), illus. LC 28-26940. 25cm. 15p. 1928. Harper & Bros.

--Buddy's Adventures in the Blueberry Patch. Beskow, Elsa Maartman (1874-1953), illus. Andrews, Siri, tr. from Swedish. LC 31-28427. 32cm. 17p. 1931. Harper & Bros.

--Children of the Forest. Beskow, Elsa Maartman (1874-1953), illus. Smith, William Jay (1918-), tr. from Swedish. LC 69-18439. (Illus.). 32 p. 1970, c.1969. Delacorte Press.

--Elf Children of the Woods. N.D. Harper & Bros.

--Hat House: A Story in verse with the last word in each couplet left bland for the children to fill in the rhyme. Beskow, Zita, tr. from Swedish. LC 33-1110. 171p. col. illus 20 x 20cm. 1931. Harper & Bros.

--Olle's Ski Trip. Beskow, Elsa Maartman (1874-1953), illus. Andrews, Siri, tr. from Swedish. LC 28-20044. 21cm. 29p. 1928. Harper & Bros.

--Pelle's New Suit. Beskow, Elsa Maartman (1874-1953), illus. 1929. Harper & Bros.

--Pelle's New Suit. Nestrick, Nova, ed. Frost, Bruno, illus. LC 62-12643. (Illus.). 28 p. 24cm. (Early fun-to-read classic). 1962. Platt & Munk.

--Pelle's New Suit: Picture Book. Woodburn, Marion Letcher, tr. unpaged. illus. 23 x 33 cm. 1961. Harper.

--Peter in Blueberry Land. (Illus.). 34p. 1984. (ISBN 0-510-00129-7, Pub. By Salem Hse Ltd). Merrimack Pub Cir.

--Peter's Voyage. Beskow, Elsa Maartman (1874-1953), illus. LC 31-28009. 14p. col. illus. 26 1/2cm. 1931. Knopf.

--The Sun-Egg. 1933. Harper & Bros.

--The Tale of the Wee Little Old Woman. Beskow, Elsa Maartman (1874-1953), illus. Woodburn, Marion Letcher, tr. LC 31-20027. 27cm. 1930. Harper & Bros.

Beskow, Katja

--The Astonishing Adventures of Patrick the Mouse. LC 67-5969. 84 p. illus. 22 cm. 1967. Delacorte Press.

Beskow, Zita, tr. see Beskow, Elsa Maartman.

Besnon, Mary, jt. auth. see Marshal, Emma.

Bess, Clayton

--Big Man and the Burn-Out. LC 85-11822. p. cm. 1985. (ISBN 0-395-36173-7). Houghton Mifflin.

--Story for a Black Night. LC 81-13396. 84 p. 22cm. 1982. (ISBN 0-395-31857-2). Parnassus Press.

--The Truth About the Moon. Hoffman, Rosekrans (1926-), illus. LC 83-247. . cm. 1983. (ISBN 0-395-34551-0). Houghton Mifflin.

Besser, Marianne

--The Cat Book. Stirnweis, Shannon (1931-), illus. (Illus.). 91 p. 23cm. 1967. Holiday House.

Bessett, Jane M., Mrs.

--The Black Princess. N.D. George Routledge & Sons.

--Memoirs of a Doll. N.D. George Routledge & Sons.

Best, Allena Champlin see Berry, Erick, pseud.

Best, Allena Champlin, jt. auth. see Knox, Eva.

Best, Allena Champlin, Mrs., jt. auth. see Best, Herbert.

Best, Allena Champlin, Mrs., jt. auth. see Evans, E. K.

Best, Allena Champlin, Mrs. (1892-1974), ed. see Lundy, Jo Evalin.

Best, Allena Champlin, Mrs. (1892-1974)

--Beckoning Landfall: A Novel. Berry, Erick, pseud. LC 59-6281. 192p. illus. 21cm. (Your fair land series). 1959. J. Day Co.

--Careers of Cynthia. Berry, erick, pseud. King, Ruth, illus. 230p. (gr. 7-11). N.D. Harcourt, Brace & Co.

--Cynthia Steps Out. Berry, Erick, pseud. Best, Allena Champlin, Mrs. (1892-1974), illus. Berry, Erick, pseud. LC 37-5834. 3 p. l., 11-253 p. 20 cm. c.1937. The Goldsmith Publishing Company.

--Forty-Seven Keys. Berry, Erick, pseud. LC 49-7990. 200 p. 22 cm. 1949. Macmillan Co.

--Go and Find Wind. Berry, Erick, pseud. Best, Allena Champlin (1892-1974), illus. Berry, Erick, pseud. 251p. 1939. Oxford University Press.

--Green Door to the Sea. Berry, Erick, pseud. Best, Allena Champlin, Mrs. (1892-1974), illus. Berry, Erick, pseud. LC 55-1379. 192p. illus. 22cm. 1955. Viking Press.

--Harvest of the Hudson. Berry, Erick, pseud. Best, Allena Champlin, Mrs. (1892-1974), illus. Berry, Erick, pseud. LC 45-8647. xi p., 1 l., 230 p. illus. 22 cm. 1945. The Macmillan Company.

--Hay-Foot, Straw-Foot. Berry, Erick, pseud. Best, Allena Champlin, Mrs. (1892-1974), illus. Berry, Erick, pseud. LC 54-8230. (Illus.). (gr. 5-9). 1954. (ISBN 0-670-36430-4). Viking Pr.

--Hearthstone in the Wilderness. Berry, Erick, pseud. Best, Allena Champlin, Mrs. (1892-1974), illus. Berry, Erick, pseud. LC 44-5434. 242 p. incl. front., illus. 22 cm. 1944. The Macmillan Company.

--Honey of the Nile. Berry, Erick, pseud. Best, Allena Champlin, Mrs. (1892-1974), illus. Berry, Erick, pseud. 224 p., 2 l. incl. front. illus., plates. 23 cm. c.1938. Oxford University Press.

--Honey of the Nile. Berry, Erick, pseud. rev. ed. Best, Allena Champlin, Mrs. (1892-1974), illus. Berry, Erick, pseud. LC 63-8529. 192 p. illus. 22 cm. 1963. (ISBN 0-670-37815-1). Viking Press.

--Horses for the General. Berry, Erick, pseud. LC 56-11571. 191p. 21cm. 1956. Macmillan.

--Horses for the General. Berry, Erick, pseud. (gr. 7 up). 1963. (ISBN 0-02-041550-8, Acorn). Macmillan.

--The House That Jack Built. Berry, Erick, pseud. Best, Allena Champlin, Mrs. (1892-1974), illus. Berry, Erick, pseud. LC 34-28615. 3 p. l., 3-253, 1 p. front., illus. 22 cm. 1934. Dodd, Mead & Company.

--Hudson Frontier. Berry, Erick, pseud. Best, Allena Champlin (1892-1974), illus. Berry, Erick, pseud. LC 42-17834. 239 p. incl. front., illus., plates. 23 cm. 1942. Oxford University Press.

--Humbo the Hippo. Berry, Erick, pseud. LC 38-185264. 18 p. col. illus. 23 cm. c.1938. Grosset & Dunlap.

--Illustrations of Cynthia: A Story of Art School. Berry, Erick, pseud. King, Ruth, illus. LC 31-22236. c.1931. Harcourt, Brace and Company.

--Juma of the Hills: A Story of West Africa. Berry, Erick, pseud. Best, Allena Champlin, Mrs. (1892-1974), illus. Berry, Erick, pseud. LC 32-21904. xi, 260 p. incl. front., illus., plates. 21 cm. c.1932. Harcourt, Brace and Company.

--The King's Jewel. Berry, Erick, pseud. Chapman, Frederick Trench (1887-), illus. LC 57-140449. 189p. illus. 21cm. 1957. Viking Press.

--The Little Farm in the Big City. Berry, Erick, pseud. Best, Allena Champlin, Mrs. (1892-1974), illus. Berry, Erick, pseud. LC 47-2388. N.D. Viking Press.

--Lock Her Through. Berry, Erick, pseud. Best, Allena Champlin, Mrs. (1892-1974), illus. Berry, Erick, pseud. LC 40-27634. 246 p. front., plates, 21 cm. c.1940. Oxford University Press.

--Magic Banana & Other Polynesian Tales. Berry, Erick, pseud. Amorosi, Nicholas, illus. LC 68-11158. (Illus.). 12 b&w drawings. 128p. (gr. 3 up). 1968. (ISBN 0-381-99938-6). John Day.

--Mom Du Jos: The Story of a Little Black Doll. Berry, Erick, pseud. Best, Allena Champlin, Mrs. (1892-1974), illus. Berry, Erick, pseud. LC 31-22906. 6 p. l., 116 p. incl. illus., plates. col. front., double col. pl. 21 cm. 1931. Doubleday, Doran & Company, Inc.

--Nancy Herself. Berry, Erick, pseud. LC 36-34271. 4 p. l., 15-249 p. 19 cm. c.1947. The Goldsmith Publishing Company.

--One-String Fiddle. Berry, Erick, pseud. Webster, Lillian, contrib. by. LC 39-27630. 64 p. illus. (part col., incl. music) 24 x 18 cm. c.1939. The John C. Winston Company.

--Penny-Whistle. Berry, Erick, pseud. Best, Allena Champlin (1892-1974), illus. LC 30-14130. 1930. MacMillan.

--A Pretty Little Doll. Berry, Erick, pseud. LC 46-7185. 30 p. col. illus. 19 1/2 x 18 1/2 cm. 1946. Oxford University Press.

--The Road Runs Both Ways. Berry, Erick, pseud. LC 50-10360. 196 p. 22 cm. 1950. MacMillan.

--Seven Beaver Skins: A Story of the Dutch in New Amsterdam. Berry, Erick, pseud. Best, Allena Champlin, Mrs. (1892-1974), illus. Berry, Erick, pseud. LC 10 10808. xi, 273 p. illus., map. 22 cm. (Land of the Free Series). 1948. J. C. Winston Co.

--The Springing of the Rice: A Story of Thailand. Berry, Erick, pseud. Kaufmann, John (1931-), illus. LC 66-10762. 89p. illus. 22cm. c.1966. Macmillan.

--Stars in My Pocket. A Novel Based on Events in the Life of Maria Mitchell, America's First Woman Astronomer. Berry, Erick, pseud. LC 60-11297. 190p. illus. 21cm. (Daughters of valor series). 1960. John Day Co.

--Strings to Adventure. Berry, Erick, pseud. Best, Allena Champlin, Mrs. (1892-1974), illus. Berry, Erick, pseud. LC 35-21567. x p., 1 l., 13-221 p. incl. front., plates. pl. 21 cm. 1935. Lothrop, Lee and Shepard Company.

--Sunhelmet Sue. Berry, Erick, pseud. LC 36-16931. 239 p. incl. front., illus., plates. 21 cm. 1936. Lothrop, Lee & Shepard Company.

--Sybil Ludington's Ride. Berry, Erick, pseud. Best, Allena Champlin, Mrs. (1892-1974), illus. Berry, Erick, pseud. LC 52-8188. 128 p. illus. 24 cm. 1952. Viking Press.

--There Is the Land. Berry, Erick, pseud. LC 43-13159. 240 p. illus. 21 cm. 1943. Oxford University Press.

--The Tinmaker Man of New Amsterdam. Berry, Erick, pseud. Sprackling, Nelson, illus. LC 41-244057. 63 p. illus. (part col., incl. music) 24 x 16 cm. c.1941. The John C. Winston Company.

--The Valiant Little Potter. Berry, Erick, pseud. Haghighat, Nahid, illus. LC 72-77630. (Illus.). 32 p. 23cm. (Magic circle book). c.1973. (ISBN 0-663-25501-5). Ginn.

--The Wavering Flame: Connecticut, 1776. Berry, Erick, pseud. Best, Allena Champlin, Mrs. (1892-1974), illus. Berry, Erick, pseud. LC 53-12261. 266p. illus. 21cm. (Strength of the Union). 1953. Scribner.

--Whistle Round the Bend. Berry, Erick, pseud. Best, Allena Champlin (1892-1974), illus. Berry, Erick, pseud. LC 41-17944. 266, 1 p. front., plates. 21 cm. c.1941. Oxford University Press.

--The Winged Girl of Knossos. Berry, Erick, pseud. Best, Allena Champlin, Mrs. (1892-1974), illus. Berry, Erick, pseud. LC 33-32924. xiii, 253 p. incl. front., illus., illus. 22 cm. 1933. D. Appleton-Century Company, Inc. **Award: (JNM).**

Best, Allena Champlin, Mrs. (1892-1974), ed.
--Black Folk Tales: Retold from the Haussa of Northern Nigeria, West Africa. Berry, Erick, pseud. Best, Allena Champlin, Mrs. (1892-1974), illus. Berry, Erick, pseud. LC 28-22488. x, 80 p. illus. 22 cm. 1928. Harper & Brothers.

Best, Allena Champlin (1892-1974)
--Homespun. Berry, Erick, pseud. Von Schmidt, Harold (1896-1982), illus. LC 37-22502. 21cm. 308p. 1937. Lothrop Lee & Shepard.

--Humbo the Hippo and little-boy-Bumbo. Berry, Erick, pseud. Best, Allena Champlin (1892-1974), illus. Berry, Erick, pseud. LC 32-22562. 41p. col. ill. 21 1/2cm. 1932. Harper & Brothers.

--Sojo, the Story of Little Lazy-bones. Berry, Erick, pseud. LC 34-19671. 23cm. 40p. 1934. Harter Publishing Co.

Best, G. A.
--The Home of Santa Claus. (Illus.). N.D. Cassell & Co.

Best, Herbert (1894-)
--Border Iron. Best, Allena Champlin, Mrs. (1892-1974), illus. Berry, Erick, pseud. LC 45-35170. 219 p. illus. 21 cm. 1945. The Viking Press.

--Bright Hunter of the Skies. Bryson, Bernarda (1905-1977), illus. LC 61-11097. 164p. illus. c.1961. Macmillan.

--Carolina Gold. LC 61-5639. 192p. 22cm. (Daughters of Valor series). 1961. John Day Co.

--Desmond and Dog Friday. Mars, Witold Tadeusz J. (1912-), illus. LC 68-27569. (Illus.). 126 p. 21cm. 1968. Viking Press.

--Desmond & the Peppermint Ghost. Obligado, Lilian Isabel (1931-), illus. LC 65-13355. (Illus.). 93p. (gr. 4-7). 1968. (ISBN 0-670-05005-9, Puffin). Penguin.

--Desmond and the Peppermint Ghost: The Dog Detective's Third Case. Obligado, Lilian Isabel (1931-), illus. LC 65-13355. (Illus.). 93 p. 22cm. 1965. Viking Press.

--Desmond the Dog Detective. Obligado, Lilian Isabel (1931-), illus. LC 62-9626. 96p. (gr. 4-6). 1969. (ISBN 0-670-05029-6, Seafarer). Viking Pr.

--Desmond the Dog Detective: The Case of the Lone Stranger. Obligado, Lilian Isabel (1931-), illus. LC 62-9626. (Illus.). 96 p. 22cm. 1962. Viking Press.

--Desmond's First Case. Keats, Ezra Jack (1916-1983), illus. LC 61-7695. (Illus.). (gr. 4-7). 1961. (ISBN 0-670-27060-1). Viking Pr.

--Flag of the Desert. Best, Allena Champlin, Mrs. (1892-1974), illus. Berry, Erick, pseud. LC 36-18199. viii p., 1 l., 242 p. incl. front. 21 cm. 1936. The Viking Press.

--Garram the Chief: The Story of the Hill Tribes. Best, Allena Champlin, Mrs. (1892-1974), illus. Berry, Erick, pseud. LC 32-268624. viii p., 2 l., 261 p. incl. illus., plates. front. 21 cm. 1932. Doubleday, Doran & Company, Inc.

--Garram the Hunter: A Boy of the Hill Tribes. Best, Allena Champlin, Mrs. (1892-1974), illus. Berry, Erick, pseud. LC 30-9209. viii p., 2 l., 3-332 p. incl. illus., plates. front. 21 cm. 1930. Doubleday, Doran & Company, Inc. **Award: (JNM).**

--Gunsmith's Boy. Best, Allena Champlin, Mrs. (1892-1974), illus. Berry, Erick, pseud. LC 42-22455. 3 p. l., v-ix, 220 p. col. front., illus. 23 1/2 cm. 1942. The John C. Winston Company.

--The Long Portage: A Story of Ticonderoga and Lord Howe. Best, Allena Champlin, Mrs. (1892-1974), illus. Berry, Erick, pseud. LC 48-4724. v, 250 p. illus. 22 cm. 1948. Viking Press.

--Not Without Danger: A Story of the Colony of Jamaica in Revolutionary Days. Best, Allena Champlin, Mrs. (1892-1974), illus. Berry, Erick, pseud. LC 51-14074. 286 p. 21cm. 1951. Viking Press.

--Ranger's ransom: A Story of Ticonderoga. 1st ed. Best, Allena Champlin (1892-1974), illus. Berry, Erick, pseud. LC 53-12166. 21cm. 192p. (American Heritage). 1953. Aladdin Books.

--The Sea Warriors. LC 59-12337. 176p. 22cm. 1959. Macmillan.

--Son of the Whiteman. Best, Allena Champlin, Mrs. (1892-1974), illus. Berry, Erick, pseud. LC 31-21751. x, 318 p. incl. illus., plates. front. 21 cm. 1931. Doubleday, Doran & Company, Inc.

--Son of the Whiteman. Best, Allena Champlin, Mrs. (1892-1974), illus. Berry, Erick, pseud. LC 31-21751. x, 318 p. incl. front., illus., plates. 21 cm. (Young moderns books). 1936. Doubleday, Doran & Company, Inc.

--Tal of the Four Tribes. Best, Allena Champlin, Mrs. (1892-1974), illus. Berry, Erick, pseud. LC 33-12955. viii p. 1 l., 295 p. incl. front., illus. 21 cm. 1938. Doubleday, Doran & Co., Inc.

--Watergate: A Story of the Irish on the Erie Canal. 1st ed. Best, Allena Champlin, Mrs. (1892-1974), illus. Berry, Erick, pseud. LC 51-10428. xv, 240 p. illus. 22 cm. (Land of the Free series). 1951. Winston.

Best, Herbert (1894-) & Best, Allena Champlin, Mrs. (1892-1974)
--The Polynesian Triangle. Berry, Erick, pseud. (Illus.). (Young Reader's Book Ser.). 1968. (ISBN 0-308-80224-1). Funk & Wagnalls.

Best, Signe Ellison, Mrs.
--Whys and Otherwise. Best, Catherine, illus. LC 29-12706. 3 p. l., 86 p. illus. 21 cm. c.1929. The Golden Press.

Best, Stan
--Hidden City of the Amazon. 128p. (Teen Books Ser). (gr. 7 up). 1970. (ISBN 0-8024-6355-X). Moody.

Best, Susie M., retold by see Reynard the Fox. English.

Best, Susie Montgomery
--Egypt and her Neighbors. LC 18-2982. 19cm. 185p. (Her World famous stories in historic settings, v.1.). 1918. Macmillan Co.

--Glorious Greece and Imperial Rome. LC 18-2981. xi, 225 p. illus., maps. 19 cm. (Her World famous stories in historic settings, v. 2). 1918. Macmillan Co.

--Merry England. LC 18-4708. 19cm. 185p. (Her World famous stories in historic settings, v. 4.). 1918. Macmillan.

Bestall, Alfred
--Rupert Annual. (Illus.). (Rupert Daily Express Annual Ser.). (gr. 4-6). 1975. (ISBN 0-685-56545-9). Scholium Intl.

Bester, John, tr. see Miyazawa, Kenji.

Bester, Roger
--Fireman Jim. (Illus.). 32p. 1981. Crown.
--Guess What?. LC 79-24945. (Illus.). 32p. (ps-1). 1980. Crown.

Besterman, Catherine (1908-)
--The Extraordinary Education of Johnny Longfoot in His Search for the Magic Hat. 1st ed. Chappell, Warren (1904-), illus. LC 49-114434. 158 p. illus. 23 cm. 1949. Bobbs-Merrill Co.

--The Quaint and Curious Quest of Johnny Longfoot, the Shoe King's Son. 1st ed. Chappell, Warren (1904-), illus. LC 47-11161. 147 p. illus. 23 cm. 1947. Bobbs-Merrill Co. **Award: (JNM).**

Beston, Henry B., pseud., see Sheahan, Henry Beston.

Beston, Henry B. pseud. (1888-1968)
--Chimney Farm Bedtime Stories. Coatsworth, Elizabeth Jane (1893-), ed. The, Christian Science Monitor Deny, Maurice (1892-), illus. LC 66-31608. 79 p. illus. 22 cm. 1966. Holt, Rinehart and Winston.

--Fairy Tales. Kredel, Fritz (1900-1973), illus. LC 52-12601. (Illus.). 353 p. 21cm. 1952. Aladdin Books.

--The Firelight Fairy Book, 8. N.D. Little, Brown & Co.

--The Sons of Kai: The Story the Indian Told. LC 26-20426. 16cm. 55p. (The Little Library). 1926. The Macmillan Co.

--The Starlight Wonder Book, 8. N.D. Little, Brown & Co.

--The Tree That Ran Away. Eichenberg, Fritz (1901-), illus. LC 41-5505. 69, 1 p. illus. 20 cm. 1941. The Macmillan Company.

Beswick, Ethel
--Jataka Tales. 1956. Grove Press.

Beta
--Enchanted Closet. Beta, illus. LC 67-18488. (Illus.). (gr. k-2). 1967. (ISBN 0-87460-117-7). Lion Bks.

Betancourt, Jeanne (1941-)
--The Edge. LC 84-20286. 154 p. 18cm. (Point). c.1985. (ISBN 0-590-33259-7). Scholastic Inc.

Betenson, E. W.
--Tale of Two Collies. Lowen, Lucien L., illus. LC 53-791. 121p. illus. 20cm. 1953, c.1949. Parkwood Press.

Bethancourt, T. Ernesto, pseud., see Paisley, Tom.

Bethancourt, T. Ernesto, pseud. (1932-)
--The Dog Days of Arthur Cane. Paisley, Tom. LC 76-15033. 160 p. 22cm. c.1976. (ISBN 0-8234-0286-X). Holiday House.

--Doris Fein, Dead Heat at Long Beach. Paisley, Tom. LC 82-48754. p. cm. c.1983. (ISBN 0-8234-0485-4). Holiday House.

--Doris Fein: Deadly Aphrodite. Paisley, Tom. LC 81-85093. 160p. 1982. (ISBN 0-8234-0445-5). Holiday.

--Doris Fein: Legacy of Terror. Paisley, Tom. LC 83-18497. 144p. 1984. (ISBN 0-8234-0506-0). (ISBN 0-8234-0506-0). Holiday House.

--Doris Fein, Murder Is No Joke. Paisley, Tom. LC 82-80817. p. cm. c.1982. (ISBN 0-8234-0468-4). Holiday House.

--Doris Fein-Phantom of the Casino. Paisley, Tom. LC 80-8814. 160 p. 22cm. c.1981. (ISBN 0-8234-0391-2). Holiday House.

--Doris Fein, Quartz Boyar. Paisley, Tom. LC 80-15920. 187 p. 22cm. c.1980. (ISBN 0-8234-0378-5). Holiday House.

--Doris Fein: Quartz Boyar. Paisley, Tom. 176p. (Doris Fein Mystery Ser.). (gr. 7 up). 1982. (ISBN 0-590-32383-0). Scholastic Inc.

--Doris Fein, Superspy. Paisley, Tom. LC 79-23339. 155 p. 22cm. c.1980. (ISBN 0-8234-0408-0). Holiday House.

--Doris Fein: Superspy. Paisley, Tom. 144p. (Doris Fein Mystery Ser.). (gr. 7 up). 1982. (ISBN 0-590-32382-2). Scholastic Inc.

--Doris Fein: The Mad Samurai. Paisley, Tom. LC 81-4041. 128p. 1981. (ISBN 0-8234-0431-5). Holiday.

--Doris Fein: Legacy of Terror. Paisley, Tom. 144p. 1983. (ISBN 0-8234-0506-0). Holiday.

--Dr. Doom, Superstar. Paisley, Tom. LC 78-6151. 160 p. 22cm. c.1978. (ISBN 0-8234-0333-5). Holiday House.

--The Great Computer Dating Caper. Paisley, Tom. LC 83-20971. 160p. (gr. 7 up). 1984. (ISBN 0-517-55213-2). Crown.

--Instruments of Darkness. Paisley, Tom. LC 78-11133. 159 p. 22cm. c.1979. (ISBN 0-8234-0346-7). Holiday House.

--The Mad Samurai. Paisley, Tom. 128p. (Doris Fein Mystery Ser.). (gr. 7 up). 1983. (ISBN 0-590-32385-7). Scholastic Inc.

--The Me Inside of Me: A Novel. Paisley, Tom. LC 85-10292. p. cm. c.1985. (ISBN 0-8225-0728-5). Lerner Publications Co.

--The Mortal Instruments. Paisley, Tom. LC 76-50526. 157 p. 22cm. c.1977. (ISBN 0-8234-0298-3). Holiday House.

--New York City, Too Far from Tampa Blues. Paisley, Tom. LC 74-24692. 190 p. 22cm. 1975. (ISBN 0-8234-0256-8). Holiday House.

--Nightmare Town. Paisley, Tom. LC 79-2091. 158 p. 22cm. c.1979. (ISBN 0-8234-0366-1). Holiday House.

--T.H.U.M.B.B. Paisley, Tom. 1st ed. LC 83-6119. p. cm. c.1983. (ISBN 0-8234-0494-3). Holiday House.

--The Tomorrow Connection. Paisley, Tom. LC 84-47836. 144p. 1984. (ISBN 0-8234-0543-5). Holiday.

--Tune in Yesterday. Paisley, Tom. LC 77-15640. 156 p. 22cm. c.1978. (ISBN 0-8234-0316-5). Holiday House.

--Where the Deer and the Cantaloupe Play: A Novel. Paisley, Tom. LC 80-27110. x, 132 p. 24cm. c.1981. (ISBN 0-916392-69-4). Oak Tree Publications.

Bethell, Augusta
--Maud Latimer: Or, Patience and Impatience, 1 of 36 Vols. (Illus.). (Wane's Gift Book Ser.). N.D. Scribner & Welford.

--Millicent and Her Cousins. (Illus.). (The Girl's Own Favorite Ser.). H.B. E. P. Dutton & Co.

--Millicent and her Cousins. (Illus.). 246p. N.D. Publications of E. P. Dutton & Co.

Bethell, Jean Frankenberry (1922-)
--Barbie Goes to a Party. LC 64-57311. 61 p. (p. 61 advertisement) col. illus. 22 cm. (Easy readers, 5946). 1964. Grosset & Dunlap.

--Barney Beagle. LC 63-6667. 61 p. illus. 22 cm. (Easy readers). c.1962. Grosset & Dunlap.

--Barney Beagle and the Cat. Wood, Ruth, illus. LC 65-20011. (Illus.). 60 p. 22cm. (Wonder books easy reader). 1965. Grosset & Dunlap.

--Barney Beagle and the Cat. Wood, Ruth, illus. LC 65-20011. (Illus.). 22cm. 60p. (Wonder bks. easy reader). 1965. Grosset.

--Barney Beagle & the Cat. Wood, Ruth, illus. (Illus.). (Easy Readers Ser.). (gr. k-3). N.D. Wonder.

--Barney Beagle Goes Camping. Wood, Ruth, illus. LC 70-86704. (Illus.). 60 p. 22cm. (Easy reader). 1970. Grosset & Dunlap.

--Barney Beagle Plays Baseball. LC 64-9028. 60 p. col. illus. 22 cm. c.1963. Grosset & Dunlap.

--Bathtime. LC 78-14092. (Illus.). (gr. k-1). 1979. (ISBN 0-03-044636-8). HR&W.

--The Clumsy Cowboy. LC 63-18948. 61 p. col. illus. 22 cm. c.1963. Grosset & Dunlap.

--Hooray for Henry. Wood, Ruth, illus. (Illus.). (Easy Readers Ser.). (gr. k-3). N.D. Wonder.

--Look Who's Taking a Bath. (Illus.). 32p. Repr (Pub. by Holt, Rhinehart & Winston). 1980. (ISBN 0-590-30150-0). Scholastic Inc.

--The Monkey in the Rocket. 61 p. illus. 22 cm. c.1962. Grosset & Dunlap.

--Petey, the Peanut Man. Wood, Ruth, illus. (Illus.). (Easy Readers Ser). (gr. k-3). N.D. Wonder.

--Playmates. Bethell, Jean (1922-), photos by. LC 80-20542. 32p. (gr. k-2). 1981. (ISBN 0-03-053821-1). HR&W.

--Raggedy Ann and Andy and the Absent Minded Magician. LC 81-18194. (Illus.). 28 p. 23cm. c.1982. (ISBN 0-672-52721-9). Bobbs-Merrill.

--Three Cheers for Mother Jones. Garry-McCord, Kathleen, illus. LC 79-28655. (Illus.). 48p. (gr. 2-4). 1980. (ISBN 0-03-054831-4). HR&W.

--Walt Disney Productions' Pete's Dragon: Based on Walt Disney Productions' Full-Length Cartoon Feature Film. LC 77-91860. (Illus.). 91 p. 21cm. 1978. (ISBN 0-448-16101-X). Wonder Books.

--When I Grow Up. Wood, Ruth, illus. LC 65-14755. (Illus.). 22cm. 60p. (Wonder bks. easy reader: No. 5937). 1965. Grosset.

--When I Grow Up. Wood, Ruth, illus. LC 65-14755. (Illus.). 60p. (Easy Readers Ser.). (gr. k-3). 1965. (ISBN 0-448-05937-1). Wonder.

Bethers, Ray (1902-)
--Islands of Adventure. Bethers, Ray (1902-), illus. LC 59-16442. 26cm. 47p. N.D. Hastings House.

--Ports of Adventure. Bethers, Ray (1902-), illus. LC 62-18649. 46 p. illus. 26 cm. 1963. Hastings House.

--Rivers of Adventure. Bethers, Ray (1902-), illus. LC 60-11314. 26cm. 47p. N.D. Hastings House.

--Ships of Adventure. Bethers, Ray (1902-), illus. LC 62-1227. 47p. col. illus. 26cm. 1961. Hastings.

--This is Our World. Bethers, Ray (1902-), illus. LC 64-10616. (Illus.). 47. 26cm. (The Our World Ser.). 1964. St. Martin's Press.

--What Happens in the Sea?. LC 63-1848. 45 p. illus. 26 cm. (Our world series). 1962. Macmillan.

Bettelheim, Bruno (1903-)
--The Uses of Enchantment: The Meaning and Importance of Fairy Tales. LC 75-36795. vi, 328, xi p. 24cm. 1976. (ISBN 0-394-49771-6). Knopf : Distributed by Random House.

--The Uses of Enchantment: The Meaning and Importance of Fairy Tales. LC 76-41020. 328, xi p. 21cm. 1977, c.1976. (ISBN 0-394-72265-5). Vintage Books.

Betten, N.
--The Doll in the Window. 1952. (ISBN 0-8098-1033-6). David McKay.

Better Homes & Gardens Books, ed.
--Better Homes & Gardens Story Book. rev. ed. LC 50-9504. (Illus.). (gr. k-3). 1970. (ISBN 0-696-00030-X). BH&G.

Bettina, pseud., see Ehrlich, Bettina Bauer.

Bettina, pseud. (1903-)
--Trovato. Ehrlich, Bettina Bauer. (Illus.). (gr. 1-4). 1959. (ISBN 0-374-37821-5). FS&G.

Bettinger, Craig
--Follow Me, Everybody. Hollander, Edward S., photos by. LC 68-14012. (Illus.). 93 p. 1968. Doubleday.

Bettison, W. J.
--Basil Grey: Or, Tried and True. (Illus.). N.D. Thomas Nelson & Sons.
--Dorothy Fisher: Or, The Guiding Hand (Pub. by Society for Promoting Christian Knowledge). N.D. E. & J. B Young & Co.

Betts, Emmett A., ed. see Coombs, Charles Ira.

Betts, Emmett A., ed. see Anderson, Anita Melva.

Betts, Emmett A., ed. see Anderson, Anita Melva (1906-) & Johnson, Robert Elliott.

Betts, Emmett A., ed. see Anderson, Anita Melva (1906-) & Keogh, Myles Walter.

Betts, Emmett A., ed. see Anderson, Anita Melva (1906-) & Regli, Adolph Casper.

Betts, Emmett A., ed. see Coombs, Charles Ira.

Betts, Emmett Albert (1903-), ed. see Coombs, Charles Ira.

Betts, Ethel Franklin
--The Complete Mother Goose. Betts, Ethel Franklin, illus. N.D. Frederick A. Stokes Co.
--Fairy Tales From Grimm. Mabie, Hamilton Wright (1845-1916), intro. by. (Illus.). 132p. N.D. Barse and Hopkins.
--Familiar Nursery Jingles. Betts, Ethel Franklin, illus. N.D. Frederick A. Stokes Co.

Betts, Ethel Franklin, illus.
--Humpty Dumpty. (Illus.). N.D. Dodd, Mead & Company.

Betts, Miriam Parker
--Tomboy Teacher. LC 61-6364. 190p. 21cm. (Career romance for young moderns). 1961. Messner.

Betz, Eva Kelly (1897-1968)
--The Amazing John Tabb. Poppert, Robert V., illus. LC 58-10486. 22cm. 155p. 1958. Bruce Pub Co.
--Blessed Sebastian & the Oxen. (gr. 1-4). 1961. St Anthony.
--Desperate Drums. Driscoll, June, illus. LC 51-8259. 213 p. illus. 21 cm. 1951. St. Anthony Guild Press.
--Freedom Drums. 1st ed. Driscoll, June, illus. LC 50-58263. 172 p. illus. 21 cm. N.D. Abelard Press.
--Freedom Drums. 2nd ed. Driscoll, June, illus. LC 53-13467. 188p. illus. 21cm. 1953. St. Anthony Guild Press.
--Knight of Molokai. 1956. St. Anthony Guild Press.
--Man Who Fought the Devil. 1958. St. Anthony Guild Press.
--Priest on Horseback: Father Farmer, 1720-1786. Polseno, Jo, illus. LC 58-10558. 160p. illus. 21cm. 1958. Sheed & Ward.
--Priest on Horseback: Father Farmer, 1720-1786. Polseno, Jo, illus. LC 66-1263. 160p. illus. 22cm. 1966, c.1958. St. Anthony's Guild.
--The Quiet Flame: Mother Marianne of Molokai. Ostendorf, Arthur Lloyd, Jr. (1921-), illus. LC 63-20155. vii, 150p. illus. 22cm. (Catholic Treasury Bks.). 1963. Bruce.
--St. Brigid & the Cows. (gr. 1-3). 1964. St Anthony.
--St. Colum & the Crane. (gr. 1-3). 1961. St Anthony.
--St. Germaine & the Sheep. (gr. 1-4). 1961. St Anthony.
--To far Places: The Story of Francis Xavier Ford. Landa, Peter, illus. LC 62-16229. 192p. N.D. Hawthorn Books, Inc.
--Victory Drums. Driscoll, June, illus. LC 55-13755. (Illus.). 21cm. 235p. (gr. 7 up). 1955. St Anthony.
--The Web Begun. Vukovich, Charles B., illus. LC 61-11597. 148p. illus. 22cm. 1961. Bruce Pub. Co.
--Yankee at Molokai. 1960. St. Anthony Guild Press.
--Young Eagles. (Illus.). (gr. 5-9). 1952. St Anthony.
--Young Eagles. Driscoll, June, illus. LC 47-6657. 190 p. illus. 21 cm. 1947. D. X. McMullen Co.

Beulah
--Tatters, 1 of 30 vols. (American Girls' Ser.: No. 23). 1900. Set. Lee & Shepard.

Beust, Nora Ernestine, jt. ed. see Hale, Jeanne.

Beutter, Carl, jt. auth. see Disney, Walter Elias.

Bevans, Margaret Van Doren see Van Doren, Margaret.

Bevans, Margaret Van Doren (1917-), ed.
--I Wonder Why?" Thought the Owl: An Old World Tale Retold. Weil, Lisl (1910-), illus. LC 65-20711. 47 p. col. illus. 29 cm. 1965. Putnam.
--McCall's Read Me a Story Book. Weisgard, Leonard Joseph (1916-), illus. LC 60-12519. 256p. col. illus. 26cm. c.1961. Putnam.

Bevans, Tom Torre (1868-1930)
--Where,oh Where?. Bevans, Tom Torre (1868-1930), illus. LC 39-23531. 22cm. 48p. 1939. Viking Press.

Beven, Annette & Gellek, Nazli
--The Spade Sage. Hall, Diane Andrews, illus. LC 81-473414. (Illus.). 24 p. 29cm. c.1976. (ISBN 0-913546-24-0). Dharma Pub.

Bever, Nellie Maude Hull, Mrs.
--Little Wolf-Lights-the-Pipe. LC 39-1037. 20cm. 41p. 1938. Dorrance & Co.

Beveridge, Nancy, tr. see Fedorov, Vadim Dmitrievich.

Beverly, David
--The Tale of the Wise Little Sea Turtle. 1982. (ISBN 0-533-05506-7). Vantage.

Beverly, E. A.
--Magic Brushes & Other Children's Stories. N.D. Carlton.

Bevis, Donald L.
--Little Dog, Go Home. (gr. 2-4). 1970. Vantage.

Bevis, Katherine
--God's flowers, and other Stories for Children. LC 56-7179. 35p. 1956. Bruce Humphries.

Bewick, Thomas (1753-1828), illus.
--Bewick's Select Fables. N.D. George Routledge & Sons.

Beyer, Audrey White (1916-)
--Capture at Sea. 1st ed. Hall, H. Tom, illus. LC 59-7367. (Illus.). 148 p. 21cm. 1959. Knopf.
--Dark Venture. Dillon, Leo (1933-) & Dillon, Diane (1933-), illus. LC 67-15805. 205 p. illus. 24 cm. 1968. Knopf. **Award: (BGH).**
--Katharine Leslie. 1st ed. Bolian, Polly (1925-), illus. LC 63-9110. 1963. Knopf.
--The Sapphire Pendant. Jacques, Robin (1920-), illus. LC 61-6058. (Illus.). 178 p. 22cm. 1961. Knopf.

Beyer, Ernestine Cobern (1893-)
--Aesop with a smile. Guthrie, Vee, illus. LC 60-12000. 46p. illus. 22cm. 1960. Reilly & Lee.
--Happy Animal Families: Poems. unpaged. col. illus. 34 cm. (Nursery treasure bk.). 1962, c.1952. Grosset.
--Happy Animal Families: Poems. Pike, John, illus. LC 52-13548. unpaged. illus. 34 cm. (Big treasure books). N.D. Grosset & Dunlap.
--Story of Lengthwise. Madden, Donald B. (1927-), illus. LC 67-17285. (Illus.). 23cm. 31p. (ps-3). 1967. (ISBN 0-695-88360-7). (ISBN 0-695-48360-9). Follett.
--The Story of Little Big. Guthrie, Vee, illus. LC 62-7501. 21cm. 47p. 1962. Reilly & Lee Company.

Beyer, Evelyn M. (1907-)
--Who Likes Dinner?. Cunningham, Dellwyn, illus. unpaged. illus. 21cm. (Wonder books. 598). c.1953. Wonder Books.

Beyl, Judith
--Sunshine, Rainbows & Friends. Sydlik, Danilea & Campbell, Elisa L., illus. LC 80-50828. (Illus.). 83p. (Orig.). (ps-k). 1980. (ISBN 0-933308-01-9). West Village.

Beyrich, Clementine Helm see Helm, Clementine.

Beyrich, Clementine Helm (1825-1896)
--Cecily (Elf Goldihair). Kay, Gertrude Alice (1884-1939), illus. Stork, Elisabeth Pansinger, Mrs., tr. LC 24-21350. 298 p. col. front., col. plates. 25 cm. c.1924. J. B. Lippincott Company.

Bezdekova, Zdenka
--They Called Me Leni. LC 77-175227. 1973. (ISBN 0-672-51331-5). Bobbs.

Bhativedanta, A. C. (1896-)
--Prahlad: A Story for Children from the Ancient Vedas of India. Das, Goursundar & Govinda Devi Dasi, illus. LC 75-319632. (Illus.). 32 p. 28cm. c.1973. Iskcon Children's Press.

Bial, Morrison David (1917-)
--The Hanukkah Story. N.D. Behrman House Inc.
--Jeremy and Judy Say The Sh'ma. N.D. Behrman House Inc.
--Jeremy and the Torah. N.D. Behrman House Inc.
--Jeremy Learns About God. N.D. Behrman House Inc.
--Jeremy's A B C Book. N.D. Behrman House Inc.
--Jeremy's And Judy's Book Of Blessings. N.D. Behrman House Inc.
--Jeremy's And Judy's Hanukah. N.D. Behrman House Inc.
--The Passover Story. N.D. Behrman House Inc.

Bialik, Hayyim Nahman (1873-1934)
--Far Over the Sea: Poems and Jingles for Children. Sampter, Jessie Ethel (1883-1938), tr. Union of American Hebrew Congregations Kabrin, Louis, illus. LC 40-263107. xiv, 99 p. illus. 24 cm. 1939. The Union of American Hebrew Congregations.

Bialk, Elisa (1912-)
--The Colt of Cripple Creek. 1st ed. Shenton, Edward (1895-), illus. LC 52-13240. (Illus.). 180 p. 21cm. 1953. World Pub. Co.
--Giant of the Rockies: A Story About John Colter. 1st ed. LC 55-52887. 211p. illus. 21cm. 1955. World Pub. Co.
--The Horse Called Pete. Moyers, William (1916-), illus. LC 48-6068. 80 p. illus. 25 cm. 1948. Houghton Mifflin Co.
--Jill's Victory. 1st ed. Shenton, Edward (1895-), illus. LC 52-5181. 184 p. illus. 21 cm. 1952. World Pub. Co.
--Marty. LC 53-6644. 221 p. 21cm. 1953. World Pub. Co.
--Marty Goes to Hollywood. (gr. 5-6). N.D. Pyramid Pubns.
--Marty Goes to Hollywood. 1st Ed. LC 54-8175. 221p. illus. 21cm. 1954. World Pub. Co.
--Marty on the Campus (Pub. by World). (gr. 7-12). 1972 (Starline). Schol Bk Serv.
--Marty on the Campus. 1st Ed. LC 56-5314. 223p. 21cm. 1956. World Pub. Co.
--Orville Mouse at the Opera House. Gordon, Will, illus. LC 67-26514. (Illus.). 96 p. 21cm. 1967. A. Whitman.
--Passport Summer. 1st ed. LC 59-121163. 216p. 21cm. 1959. World Pub. Co.
--Ride 'em, Peggy!. Brown, Paul (1893-1958), illus. LC 50-6556. 196 p. illus. 22 cm. 1950. Houghton Mifflin.
--The Silver Purse. 1st ed. Galdone, Paul (1914-), illus. LC 52-8426. 169 p. illus. 21 cm. 1952. World Pub. Co.
--Taffy's Foal. Moyers, William (1916-), illus. LC 49-7506. 179 p. illus. 25 cm. 1949. Houghton Mifflin Co.
--Tizz. Mutchler, Dwight (1903-), illus. LC 55-3180. (Illus.). 95 p. 24cm. 1955. Childrens Press.
--Tizz & Company. Mutchler, Keith, illus. LC 58-3283. 95p. illus. 24cm. 1958. Childrens Press.
--Tizz at the Fiesta. Lehmann, Hildegard, illus. LC 73-102789. (Illus.). 95 p. 24cm. 1970. Childrens Press.
--Tizz at the Stampede. Lehmann, Hildegard, illus. LC 68-24376. (Illus.). 94 p. 24cm. 1968. Childrens Press.
--Tizz in Cactus Country. Lehmann, Hildegard, illus. LC 64-11108. (Illus.). 94 p. 24cm. 1964. Childrens Press.
--Tizz in Texas. Lehmann, Hildegard, illus. (Illus.). (Tizz Bks.). (gr. 2-4). 1966. (ISBN 0-516-03109-0). Childrens.
--Tizz in the Canadian Rockies. Lehmann, Hildegard, illus. LC 68-24377. (Illus.). 92 p. 24cm. 1968. Childrens Press.
--Tizz Is a Cow Pony. Suba, Susanne (1913-), illus. LC 61-10098. (Illus.). 93 p. 24cm. 1961. Childrens Press.
--Tizz on a Horse Farm. Lehmann, Hildegard, illus. LC 64-11109. (Illus.). 95 p. 24cm. 1964. Childrens Press.
--Tizz on a Pack Trip. Suba, Susanne (1913-), illus. LC 61-100992. 94p. illus. 24cm. 1961. Childrens Press.
--Tizz on a Trail Ride. Lehmann, Hildegard, illus. LC 66-11617. 94p. illus. 24cm. (gr. 2-4). c.1966. Childrens.
--Tizz Plays Santa Claus. Mutchler, Dwight (1903-), illus. LC 57-3195. (Illus.). 96 p. 24cm. 1957. Childrens Press.
--Tizz South of the Border. Lehmann, Hildegard, illus. LC 76-148588. (Illus.). 94 p. 24cm. 1971. Childrens Press.
--Tizz Takes a Trip. Mutchler, Dwight (1903-), illus. LC 56-4238. 96p. illus. 24cm. 1956. Childrens Press.
--Tizz Takes a Trip. Mutchler, Dwight (1903-), illus. (Illus.). (Tizz Bks.). (gr. 2-4). 1956. (ISBN 0-516-03105-8). Childrens.
--Wild Horse Island. Brown, Paul (1893-1958), illus. LC 51-9242. (Illus.). 201 p. 22cm. 1951. Houghton Mifflin.

Bianco, Margery Williams, jt. auth. see Bowman, James Cloyd.

Bianco, Margery Williams, Mrs., tr. see Aanrud, Hans.

Bianco, Margery Williams, Mrs. (1881-1944), tr. see Bazin, Rene.

Bianco, Margery Williams, Mrs. (1881-1944), tr. see Cendrars, Blaise.

Bianco, Margery Williams, Mrs. (1881-1944)
--The Adventures of Andy. Underwood, Leon (1890-), illus. LC 27-19562. 5 p. l., 13-227 p. col. front., illus., col. plates. 24 cm. c.1927. George H. Doran Company.
--The Apple Tree. Artzybasheff, Boris Mikhailovich (1899-1965), illus. LC 26-8493. 21cm. 47p. 1926. Doubleday Doran & Co.
--Bright Morning. Platt, Margaret, illus. LC 42-20810. 145 p. illus. 21 cm. 1942. Viking Press.
--The Candlestick. Rodo, Ludovic, illus. LC 29-22916. 3 p. l., 46, 3 p. incl. illus., plates. col. front., col. plates. 21 cm. 1929. Doubleday, Doran.
--Forward, Commandos!. Busoni, Rafaello (1900-1962), illus. LC 44-7724. 184 p. incl. illus., col. plates. 20 1/2 cm. 1944. Viking Press.
--The Good Friends. Paull, Grace A. (1898-), illus. LC 34-24144. 142, 1 p. illus. 23 cm. 1934. The Viking Press.
--Herbert's Zoo and Other Favorite Stories. Julian, illus. LC 50-6258. 124 p. col. illus. 18cm. (Golden story books, 1). c.1949. Simon and Schuster.
--House That Grew Smaller. Field, Rachel Lyman (1894-1942), illus. LC 31-22144. 1931. MacMillan.
--The Hurdy-Gurdy Man. Lawson, Robert (1892-1957), illus. LC 79-18020. p. cm. (Gregg Press Children's Literature Series). 1979, c.1933. (ISBN 0-8398-2603-6). Gregg Press.
--The Hurdy-Gurdy Man. Lawson, Robert (1892-1957), illus. LC 33-24727. 55. 1 p. incl. front., illus. 19 cm. c.1933. Oxford University Press.
--The Little Wooden Doll. Bianco, Pamela (1906-), illus. LC 25-18186. 6 p. l., 3-65 p. col. front., illus., plates (part col.) 17 cm. the little library. 1925. The Macmillan Company.
--The Little Wooden Doll House. Bianco, Pamela (1906-), illus. 1967. MacMillan Publishing Company.
--Other People's Houses. LC 39-278441. 3 p. l., 201 p. pl. 22 cm. 1939. The Viking Press.
--Other People's Houses. 1930. Viking Press.
--Penny and the White Horse. Collison, Marjory, illus. LC 42-23866. 1942. Julian Messner.
--Poor Cecco: The Wonderful Story of a Wonderful Wooden Dog Who Was the Jolliest Toy in the House Until He Went Out to Explore the World. Rackham, Arthur (1867-1939), illus. LC 23-21158. x p., 2 l., 15-175, 1 p. incl. mounted col. front., illus., mounted col. plates. 25 cm. c.1925. George H. Doran Company.
--The Skin Horse. Bianco, Pamela (1906-), illus. 1927. Doubleday Doran & Co.
--The Skin Horse. Bianco, Pamela (1906-), illus. (Illus.). 1978. (ISBN 0-914676-24-5, Star & Eleph Bks). (ISBN 0-914676-25-3). Green Tiger Pr.
--A Street of Little Shops. Baker, Augusta (1911-), intro. by. LC 81-4272. p. cm. (Gregg Press Children's Literature Series). 1981, c.1932. (ISBN 0-8398-2725-3). Gregg Press.
--A Street of Little Shops. Paull, Grace A. (1898-), illus. LC 32-24547. 6 p. l., 3-111 p., 1 l. incl. illus., col. plates. col. front. 21 cm. 1932. Doubleday, Doran & Company, Inc.
--The Velveteen Rabbit. Atkinson, Allen, illus. (Illus.). N.D. (ISBN 0-394-53221-X). Knopf.
--The Velveteen Rabbit. Jorgenson, David, illus. LC 85-4257. (Illus.). 40 p. c.1985. (ISBN 0-394-87711-X). (ISBN 0-394-87712-8). Knopf : Distributed by Random House.
--Velveteen Rabbit. Klimo, Kate, ed. Ho, Tien, illus. (Illus.). 48p. 1983. (ISBN 0-671-44498-0, Little Simon). S&S.
--The Velveteen Rabbit: Or, How Toys Became Real. Nicholson, William Newman Prior, Sir (1872-1949), illus. LC 79-8427. (Illus.). 44 p. 25cm. N.D. Doubleday.
--The Velveteen Rabbit, or, How Toys Become Real: , HOw Toys Become Real. Ho, Tien, illus. LC 82-42887. (Illus.). 37 p. 29cm. c.1983. (ISBN 0-671-46784-0). (ISBN 0-671-44498-0). Little Simon.
--The Velveteen Rabbit: Or, How Toys Become Real. Angel, Marie (1923-), illus. LC 75-314681. (Illus.). 37 p. 20cm. 1974. A. Colish Press.
--The Velveteen Rabbit: Or, How Toys Become Real. Green, Michael (1943-), illus. LC 81-1454. p. cm. c.1981. (ISBN 0-89471-128-8). (ISBN 0-89471-127-X). Running Press.
--The Velveteen Rabbit: Or, How Toys Become Real. Green, Michael (1943-), illus. LC 84-6975. c.1984. (ISBN 0-89471-266-7). Running Press Book Publishers.
--The Velveteen Rabbit: Or, How Toys Become Real. Nicholson, William Newman Prior, Sir (1872-1949), illus. 4 p. l., 19. 1 p. col. plates (part double) 26 cm. 1922. Doubleday, Doran.
--Velveteen Rabbit: Or, How Toys Become Real. Nicholson, William Newman Prior, Sir (1872-1949), illus. (Illus.). (gr. 3-5). 1958. Doubleday.
--The Velveteen Rabbit: Or, How Toys Become Real. Plume, Ilse, illus. LC 82-3148. (Illus.). 48p. (ps-4). 1983. (ISBN 0-87923-444-X). (ISBN 0-87923-465-2). Godine.
--The Velveteen Rabbit, or, How Toys Become Real: Or, How Toys Become Real. Hague, Michael R., illus. LC 82-15606. (Illus.). 33 p. 26cm. 1983. (ISBN 0-03-063517-9). Holt, Rinehart and Winston.
--Winterbound. Seredy, Kate (1899-1975), illus. v. 234 p. plates. 22 cm. 1936. The Viking Press. **Award: (JNM).**

--Stories of Mother Goose Village. Brison, Ella S., illus. LC 3-10937. 196 p. col. illus. 20 x 16 cm. 1903. Rand, McNally & Company.
--The Wishing Fairies. LC 15-21453. 5 p. l., 37 p. col. front., col. plates. 21 cm. 1915. Dodd, Mead and Company.
--Within the Silver Moon. Otis, Elizabeth, illus. LC 11-27458. 20cm. 249p. 1911. Little, Brown, & Co.

Bignell, Effie Molt, Mrs. (1855-)
--Mr. Chupes and Miss Jenny. (Illus.). N.D. Baker & Taylor.
--A Quintette of Graycoats. (Illus.). N.D. Baker & Taylor.

Bigot, Marie Healy (1843-)
--Little Peter's Task. Sylvester, Margo, illus. Magurie, Hortenmse G., tr. LC 31-18739. vii, 96p. illus. 19cm. c.1931. Heath & Co.

Bigot, Mme. Charles see Bigot, Marie Healy.

Bijur, Hilda & Smith, Nancy
--Jason the Lobsterman. Bijur, Hilda, illus. LC 78-58577. 1978. (ISBN 0-932384-00-5). Tashmoo.

Bileck, Marvin, jt. auth. see De Regniers, Beatrice Schenk Freedman.

Bileck, Marvin, jt. auth. see Scheer, Julian Weisel.

Bilhuber, Valeeta Nellie (1921-)
--Hubba-hubba Tales: A Royal Rhyme Book. Szepelak, Helen Lucy (1919-), illus. LC 49-5069. 32p. col. illus. 27cm. 1949. Hollywood Pub. Co.

Bilibin, Ivan Iakovlevich (1876-1942)
--The Frog Princess. Bilibin, Ivan Iakovlevich (1876-1942), illus. (Illus.). 12p. 1979. (ISBN 0-8285-1147-0, Pub. by Goznak Pubs USSR). Imported Pubns.

Bill, Alfred Hoyt (1879-1964)
--The Red Prior's Legacy: The Story of the Adventures of an American Boy in the French Revolution. Pitz, Henry Clarence (1895-1976), illus. LC 29-13782. 21cm. 256p. 1929. Longmans, Green & Co.
--The Ring of Danger: A Tale of Elizabethan England. Chapman, Frederick Trench (1887-), illus. LC 48-8740. 259 p. illus. 23 cm. 1948. A. A. Knopf.

Bill, Helen E.
--The Shoes Fit For A King. N.D. E. M. Hale & Co.
--The Shoes Fit for a King. Slobodkin, Louis (1903-1975), illus. LC 56-5848. (Illus.). unpaged. 28cm. 1956. Watts.

Billam, Rosemary
--Fuzzy Rabbit. Julian-Ottie, Vanessa, et al., illus. LC 83-17637. (Illus.). 32p. (Picturebacks Ser.). (ps-3). 1984. (ISBN 0-394-86346-1, BYR). (ISBN 0-394-96346-6). Random.

Billard, Miss, tr. see Billard, Susan.

Billard, Susan
--Fairy Tales From Far Japan. Billard, Miss, tr. N.D. Fleming H. Revell.

Billerbeck-Gentz, F., tr. see May, Karl Friedrich.

Bill Hart's Pinto Pony, pseud., see Hart, William Shakespeare.

Bill Hart's Pinto Pony, pseud.
--Told Under a White Oak Tree. Hart, William Shakespeare. Flagg, James Montgomery (1877-), illus. N.D. Houghton Mifflin Co.

Billinghurst, Percy J. (1859-1932), ed.
--Fables from Aesop. (Illus.). N.D. Frederick A. Stokes.
--A Hundred Anecdotes of Animals. N.D. John Lane.

Billings, Augusta (1917-) & Billings, Henry (1901-)
--Gilbert: The Gay Poodle. LC 49-10517. 32 p. col. illus. 26 cm. 1949. Viking Press.

Billings, Charlene Winterer (1941-)
--Salamanders. LC 80-21838. p. cm. (Skylight book). 1981. (ISBN 0-396-07913-X). Dodd, Mead.

Billings, Edna
--Buttons and Bo. LC 40-6444. 32 p. illus. 31 cm. c.1940. Random House.

Billings, Edward Everett
--A Redman of Quality. LC 2-21490. 259 p. incl. front., plates. 19 cm. 1902. The Saalfield Publishing Company.

Billings, Henry, jt. auth. see Billings, Augusta.

Billings, Peggy
--The Waiting People. 128p. 1962. Friendship Press.

Billingsley, Sue Black
--Little Woolly Jumbo. LC 51-11274. 78 p. illus. 23 cm. 1951. Vantage Press.

Billington, Elizabeth Thain
--Getting to Know Me: A Novel. LC 81-15952. 147 p. 22cm. c.1982. (ISBN 0-7232-6206-3). F. Warne.
--The Move. LC 82-21568. 128p. (gr. 5-9). N.D. (ISBN 0-7232-6259-4). (ISBN 0-7232-6259-4). Warne.
--Part-Time Boy. DeGroat, Diane (1947-), illus. LC 79-23273. (Illus.). 87 p. 22cm. 1980. (ISBN 0-7232-6175-X). F. Warne.

Billout, Guy Rene (1941-)
--The Number Twenty-Four. Billout, Guy Rene (1941-), illus. LC 73-80927. (Illus.). 32p. (Harlin Quist Bks). (gr. 2-5). 1973. (ISBN 0-8252-0094-6). Dial. **Award: (NYT).**
--Thunderbolt & Rainbow: A Look at Greek Mythology. Billout, Guy Rene (1941-), illus. LC 80-18359. (Illus.). 31 p. 29cm. c.1981. (ISBN 0-13-608778-7). Prentice-Hall.

Bilyk, Ivan (1845-1905)
--Ivanko and the Dragon: An Old Ukrainian Folk Tale from the Original Collection of Ivan Rudchenko. Yaroslava, pseud. (1925-), illus. Mills, Yaroslava Surmach. Bloch, Marie Halun (1910-), tr. LC 69-18958. (Illus.). 46 p. 1969. Atheneum.

Binder, Eando, pseud., see Binder, Otto Oscar.

Binder, Eando, pseud. (1911-1974)
--The Mind from Outer Space. Binder, Otto Oscar (Pub. by Scott Meredith). (gr. 8 up). 1971. Curtis.

Binder, Eando, pseud. (1911-1974) & O'Donnell, K. M., pseud. (1939-)
--Missing World & Other Stories. Binder, Otto Oscar. Maltzberg, Barry N.. Elwood, Roger, ed. Groenjes, Kathleen, illus. LC 73-21481. 48p. (Science Fiction Bks). (gr. 4-8). 1974. (ISBN 0-8225-0955-5). Lerner Pubns.

Binder, Otto, ed. see Wells, Herbert George.

Binder, Otto Oscar see Binder, Eando, pseud.

Binder, Otto Oscar see Giles, Gordon, pseud.

Binder, Otto Oscar (1911-1974), ed. see Shelley, Mary Wollstonecraft Godwin.

Binder, Otto Oscar (1911-1974)
--Riddles of Astronomy. (Illus.). (gr. 6 up). 1964. (ISBN 0-8382-0702-2). Hale.

Bindloss, Harold (1866-)
--The Boy Ranchers of Puget Sound. Megargee, Edwin, illus. LC 10-163884. 5 p. l., 326 p. front., plates. 20 cm. 1910. Frederick A. Stokes Company.
--The Boys of Wildcat Ranch. LC 24-21816. 4 p. l., 242, 1 p. col. front. 20 cm. 1924. Frederick A. Stokes Company.
--The Young Traders: The Adventures of Two Boys in Western Africa. LC 7-26590. 5 p. l., 308 p. front., 5 pl. 20 cm. 1907. F. A. Stokes Company.

Bindrum, Elsie Spaney (1906-)
--The Ant and the Grasshopper Go to Sea. N.D. Lothrop Lee & Shepard.
--The Ant and the Grasshopper Sail Away. Bindrum, Elsie Spaney (1906-), illus. LC 41-5702. 47p. illus. 21 x 19 1/2cm. 1941. Lothrop, Lee & Shepard.
--The Little Covered Bridge. Bindrum, Elsie Spaney (1906-), illus. LC 42-24607. 47p. illus. 21 1/2 x 18cm. 1942. Lothrop Lee & Shepard.
--Meg and Moe. Bindrum, Elsie Spaney (1906-), illus. LC 38-19837. (Illus.). 45p. 1938. Lothrop Lee & Shepard.
--Needles: The Wobbling Pincushion. N.D. Lothrop Lee & Shepard.

Binfield, A. D.
--Eda May: or, the Twin Roses. N.D. Thomas Nelson & Sons.

Binger, Carl
--The Dollar. 1945. Norton Company.

Bingham, Clifton, jt. auth. see Molesworth, Olive.

Bingham, Clifton, jt. auth. see Nister, Ernest.

Bingham, Clifton, jt. auth. see Wain, Louis.

Bingham, Evangeline Marquerite Ladys Elliot see Elliot, Geraldine, pseud.

Bingham, Graham Clifton (1859-1913)
--Fairies' Playtime. N.D. E. P. Dutton & Co.
--Fun and Frolic. N.D. E. P. Dutton & Co.
--Jingles and Jokes and Funny Folks. Wain, Louis, illus. (Illus.). N.D. E. P. Dutton and Co.

Bingham, Graham Clifton (1859-1913) & Myrtoun, Hope
--See Saw Pictures: A Book of Changing Scenes. LC 55-54075. 16p. illus. (part col.) 25cm. 1955, c.1897. E. P. Dutton.

Bingham, Mildred
--It's a Mystery: Stories of Suspense. Kling, Wendell & Stine, Al, illus. LC 65-23326. (Illus.). 22cm. 156p. (Whitman Teen-age bk.). 1965. Whitman Pub.

Bingley, Barbara
--The Story of Tit Be & His Friend Mouffette. Gill, Margery Jean (1925-), illus. LC 62-10144. 153p. illus. 21cm. 1962. Abelard-Schuman.
--Vicky and the Monkey People. Acs, Laszlo Bela (1931-), illus. LC 67-76079. (Illus.). 192 p. 22cm. 1966. Abelard-Schuman.

Binkley, Daisy R.
--The Isolation of Lupe. (Illus.). N.D. (ISBN 0-8111-0556-3). The Naylor Company.

Binney, Ida (1912-)
--Boppet, Please Stop It. LC 48-597819. 48 p. illus. (part col.) 23 cm. (Young Scott books). 1948. W. R. Scott.

Binns, Archie Fred (1899-)
--The Enchanted Islands. 1st ed. Meitzler, Neil, illus. LC 56-95821. 239p. illus. 21cm. 1956. Duell, Sloan and Pearce.
--Here, Buster (Pub. by Duell, Sloan). Orig. Title: The Sea Pup. (gr. 4-6). 1972 (Starline). Schol Bk Serv.
--The Radio Imp. 1st ed. Busoni, Rafaello (1900-1962), illus. LC 50-6011. 216 p. illus. 22 cm. 1950. Winston.
--Sea Pup. (Illus.). (gr. 5-7). 1954. (ISBN 0-8382-0729-4). Hale.
--Sea Pup. 1st ed. Candy, Robert (1920-), illus. LC 54-5113. 215p. illus. 21cm. 1954. Duell, Sloan and Pearce.
--Sea Pup. Candy, Robert (1920-), illus. (Illus.). (gr. 5-8). 1954. (ISBN 0-696-78500-5). Hawthorn.
--Sea Pup. Candy, Robert (1920-), illus. 1954. Little, Brown & Co.
--Sea Pup Again. LC 65-14406. 156p. 22cm. c.1965. Duell Dist. Meredith.
--Secret of the Sleeping River. 1st ed. Busoni, Rafaello (1900-1962), illus. LC 52-5483. 213 p. illus. 22 cm. 1952. Winston.

Binyon, Helen
--The Children Next Door. Binyon, Helen, illus. LC 49-11834. 47 p. illus. (part col.) 23 cm. 1949. Aladdin Books.

Binzen, Bill
--Alfred Goes Flying. Binzen, Bill, illus. LC 75-38573. (Illus.). 32 p. 27cm. 1976. (ISBN 0-385-08610-5). Doubleday.
--Alfred Goes House Hunting. Binzen, Bill, illus. LC 73-81425. (Illus.). 32 p. 27cm. 1974. (ISBN 0-385-04820-3). (ISBN 0-385-04820-3). Doubleday.
--Alfred, the Little Bear. Binzen, Bill, illus. LC 78-99465. (Illus.). 47 p. 20cm. 1970. Doubleday.
--Carmen. Binzen, Bill, illus. LC 71-85288. (Illus.). 47 p. 26cm. 1970, c.1969. Coward-McCann.
--First Day in School. Binzen, Bill, illus. LC 73-183147. (Illus.). 33 p. 1972. Doubleday.
--Little Will, The Buggle Boy. Binzen, Bill, illus. 1963. E M Hale.
--Little Will, the Bugle Boy. Binzen, Bill, illus. LC 63-16217. 42 p. col. illus. 26 cm. (gr. k-3). 1963. Abelard-Schuman.
--Little Will the Bugle Boy. Binzen, Bill, illus. (Illus.). (gr. 1-3). 1963. (ISBN 0-8382-0475-9). Hale.
--Miguel's Mountain. Binzen, Bill, illus. LC 68-13018. (Illus.). 1 v. (unpaged. 26cm. 1968. Coward-McCann.
--Punch and Jonathan. Binzen, Bill, illus. LC 70-77416. (Illus.). 40 p. 1969. Pantheon Books.
--Rooftop Hogi. Binzen, Bill, illus. LC 76-179388. (Illus.). 32 p. 1972. Doubleday.
--The Rory Story. Binzen, Bill, illus. LC 73-9011. (Illus.). 32 p. 1974. (ISBN 0-385-08752-7). (ISBN 0-385-08752-7). (ISBN 0-385-08752-7). Doubleday.
--The Walk. Binzen, Bill, illus. LC 76-180912. (Illus.). 47 p. 27cm. 1972. Coward, McCann & Geoghegan.

Binzen, William see Binzen, Bill.

Bios, Gaylord Du see Du Bois, Gaylord.

Birch, Austin E.
--The Boys' Brigade. (gr. 7 up). N.D. Soccer.

Birch, Cyril (1925-)
--Chinese Myths and Fantasies. Kiddell-Monroe, Joan (1908-), illus. LC 61-858150. (Illus.). 200 p. 23cm. (Oxford myths and legends). 1961. H. Z. Walck.
--Chinese Myths and Fantasies. Kiddell-Monroe, Joan (1908-), illus. (Myths and Legends Ser.). N.D. Henry Z. Walck Inc.

Birch, Reginald Bathurst (1856-1943)
--Piccino and other Child Stories. Birch, Reginald Bathurst (1856-1943), illus. N.D. Charles Scribner's Sons.

Birch, Reginald Bathurst (1856-1943), illus.
--Sara Crewe Little Saint Elizabeth and Other Stories. N.D. Charles Scribner's Sons.

Birch, Robert, tr. see Mathiesen, Egon.

Birch, White
--Apache Gold. N.D. Grosset & Dunlap.

Bird, Bettina
--Crash Landing. Adam, John, illus. LC 68-16546. (Illus.). 98 p. 18cm. (Trend books). 1968. Cheshire.
--A Real Hero. Mason, Heather, illus. LC 68-16543. (Illus.). 67 p. 18cm. (Trend books). 1969. Cheshire.

Bird, Bettina & Scanlon, Tony
--A Fabulous Day in the Life of Professor Mortimer G. Mugwump. Haem, Hans, illus. LC 78-81190. (Illus.). 18cm. 88p. (Trend bk.). 1969. Cheshire.

Bird, Dr.
--Calavar: The Knight of the Conquest. Darley, Felix Octavius Carr (1822-1888), illus. N.D. W J Widdleton.

Bird, Dorothy Maywood (1899-)
--The Black Opal. LC 49-11322. 202 p. 22 cm. 1949. Macmillan Co.
--The Black Opal. LC 64-9562. 190 p. 21 cm. (Acora books). 1963, c.1949. Macmillan.
--Granite Harbor. Howe, Gertrude Herrick (1902-), illus. LC 44-7511. 3 p. l., 211 p. illus. 22 cm. 1944. The Macmillan Company.
--Mystery at Laughing Water. LC 64-9592. 177 p. 21 cm. (Acorn books, AB3). 1963, c.1946. Macmillan.
--Mystery at Laughing Water. Howe, Gertrude Herrick (1902-), illus. LC 46-3810. 3 p. l., 203 p. illus. 22 cm. 1946. The Macmillan Company.

Bird, E. J.
--Ten Tall Tales. Bird, E. J., illus. LC 84-12086. (Illus.). 96p. (Carolrhoda Good Time Library). (gr. 2-6). c.1984. (ISBN 0-87614-267-6). Carolrhoda Bks.

Bird, Harriet & Freed, Margaret M.
--The Warm Fuzzy Song Book. Dick, JoAnn, illus. LC 79-90080. (Illus., Orig.). (Transactional Analysis for Everybody Ser.). (gr. k-6). 1980. (ISBN 0-915190-14-1). Jalmar Pr.

Bird, Laurice
--Maxie Mongoose, and Other Animal Stories. 1st ed. Dunlop, D. G., illus. Lewis, C. Bernard, frwd. by. LC 51-18362. 93 p. illus. 19 cm. 1950. Pioneer Press.

Bird, M., jt. auth. see Lingstrom, F.

Bird, Malcolm
--The Sticky Child. LC 81-4071. (Illus.). 32 p. 22cm. c.1981. (ISBN 0-15-280338-6). Harcourt Brace Jovanovich.

Bird, Maria
--Andy Pandy & the Gingerbread Man. Wright, Matvyn, illus. LC 74-168177. (Illus.). 1st U.S. edition. (Andy Pandy Bks.). (ps-1). 1973. (ISBN 0-87955-014-7, Potato Pr). O'Hara.
--Andy Pandy & the Hedgehog. Wright, Matvyn, illus. LC 74-170440. (Illus.). 1st U.S. edition. (Andy Pandy Bks.). (ps-1). 1973. (ISBN 0-87955-012-0, Potato Pr). O'Hara.
--Andy Pandy Paints His House. Wright, Matvyn, illus. (Illus.). 20p. 1st U.S. edition. (Andy Pandy Bks.). (ps-2). 1972. (ISBN 0-87955-003-1). O'Hara.
--Andy Pandy's Kite. Wright, Matvyn, illus. (Illus.). 20p. 1st U.S. edition. (Andy Pandy Bks.). (ps-2). 1972. (ISBN 0-87955-000-7). O'Hara.
--Andy Pandy's New Pet. Wright, Matvyn, illus. LC 74-170441. (Illus.). (Andy Pandy Bks.). (ps-1). 1973. (ISBN 0-87955-013-9, Potato Pr). O'Hara.
--Andy Pandy's Puppy. Wright, Matvyn, illus. (Illus.). 20p. 1st U.S. edition. (Andy Pandy Bks.). (ps-2). 1972. (ISBN 0-87955-002-3). O'Hara.
--Andy Pandy's Shop. Wright, Matvyn, illus. (Illus.). 20p. 1st U.S. edition. (Andy Pandy Bks.). (ps-2). 1972. (ISBN 0-87955-001-5). O'Hara.
--Andy Pandy's Weather House. Wright, Matvyn, illus. LC 74-170867. (Illus.). 1st U.S. edition. (Andy Pandy Bks.). (ps-1). 1973. (ISBN 0-87955-015-5, Potato Pr). O'Hara.

Bird, Mary Herrick
--How the Indian Suit Ran Away. Claghorn, Joseph C, illus. (Illus.). 87p. (The Toyland Ser.). N.D. Edward Stern & Co.
--The Snowman's Christmas. Claghorn, Joseph C, illus. (Illus.). (The Toyland Ser.). N.D. Edward Stern & Co.
--The Wreck of the Nursery Flyer. Claghorn, Joseph C, illus. 87p. (The Toyland Ser.). N.D. Edward Stern & Co.

Bird, Robert
--Uncle Elephant's Adventures. Cowell, Cyril (1888-), illus. N.D. Frederick Warne & Co.

Bird, Robert Montgomery
--Nick of the Woods. McClintock, Marshall, adapted by. N.D. Vanguard Press.
--One Hundred Bible Stories. (Illus.). N.D. Thomas Nelson & Sons.

Bird, S. M.
--In the Sky Garden. N.D. Yale University Press.

Bird, Theodocia Walton
--Bristles. Strothmann, F., illus. LC 30-235938. 5 p. l., 3-147 p. col. front., illus. 22 cm. 1930. Little, Brown, and Company.

Bird, Zenobia, pseud., see Le Fevre, Laura Zenobia.

Bird, Zenobia, pseud.
--Muffy: The Tale of a Muskrat. Le Fevre, Laura Zenobia. Wiese, Kurt (1887-1974), illus. LC 41-9384. 46, 2 p. incl., col. front., illus. (part col) 24 x 19 cm. 1941. A. Whitman & Company.
--Sally Jo. N.D. Fleming H. Revell Co.

Birdsall, Katharine Newbold, jt. ed. see Burnett, Frances Hodgson, Mrs.

Birdsall, Katharine Newbold (1877-)
--Jacks of All Trades and What They Did: A Story. Russell, Walter Bowman (1871-) & Truman, E. S., illus. LC 2-22179. ix, 236 p. col. front., illus., 5 col. pl. 21 cm. 1902. D. A. Appleton and Company.

Birdsall, Lawrence E
--Animal Pictures and Rhymes: Photographs and Statements in Verse Approved by the Academy of Natural Sciences of Philadelphia ... LC 34-10715. 32 p. illus. 31 cm. c.1934. E. Stern & Company, Incorporated.

--The Ductild Duck. Weaver, Albert Buraley (1898-), illus. LC 31-38338. 94p. illus. (part col). 22cm. 1931. Gollifox Press.

Birdsell, Ella S.

--Phil Preston: Or, Into the Light. N.D. Methodist Bk Concern.

Birenbaum, Barbara (1941-)

--The Gooblins' Night. Birenbaum, Barbara (1941-), illus. LC 85-62585. (Illus.). 37 p. 22cm. 1985. (ISBN 0-935343-31-8). Peartree.

--Light After Light. Birenbaum, Barbara (1941-), illus. LC 85-21810. p. cm. 1985. (ISBN 0-935343-14-8). Peartree.

Birkeland, Thoger

--Lemonade Murder. 128p. (gr. 3-7). 1971. (ISBN 0-698-20079-9). Coward.

--The Lemonade Murder. Jensen, Virginia Allen, tr. LC 76-132598. 126 p. 22cm. 1971. Coward, McCann & Geoghegan.

--When the Cock Crows. Shortall, Leonard W., illus. Jensen, Virginia Allen (1927-), tr. from Swedish. LC 68-23876. (Illus.). 159 p. 22cm. 1968. Coward-McCann.

Birla, Lakshminiwas L. (1909-)

--Folk Tales from Rajasthan. Bhushan, Phani, illus. viii, 60 p. col. illus. 25 cm. 1964. Asia Pub. House.

Birley, Caroline

--Jessamine and Her Lesson-Books: And How She Missed the Gypsy Tea. (Illus.). N.D. E & J B Young.

--Linen Room Window. N.D. Pott & Co.

--We are Seven. N.D. Pott & Co.

Birnbaum, Abe (1899-)

--Green Eyes. Birnbaum, Abe (1899-), illus. LC 53-12576. (Illus.). unpaged. 28cm. 1953. Capitol Pub. Co. **Awards: (NYT); (RCM).**

Birner, William B., ed.

--Twenty Plays for Young People: A Collection of Plays for Children. LC 67-751819. (Illus.). xxi, 1154 p. 23cm. 1967. Anchorage Press.

Birney, Hoffman (1891-)

--Ay-Chee, Son of the Desert. Ha-so-de, illus. LC 35-253828. 112 p. incl. illus., plates. col. plates. 19 x 25 cm. c.1955. The Penn Publishing Company.

--Kudlu, the Eskimo Boy. Macdonald, Jean, illus. LC 32-28972. vii p., 1 l., 11-247 p. col. front., illlus. 19 cm. c.1932. The Penn Publishing Company.

--Mountain Chief: An Indian Legend for Children. LC 38-33567. 82 p. incl. col. illus., col. plates. col. front. 23 1/2 cm. c.1938. The Penn Publishing Company.

--The Pinto Pony. N.D. Grosset & Dunlap.

--The Pinto Pony: A Real Horse. LC 30-29345. 5 p. l., 13-266 p. col. front., illus., plates. 19 1/2 cm. c.1930. The Penn Publishing Company.

--Steeldust: The Story of a Horse. N.D. Grosset & Dunlap.

--Steeldust, the Story of a Horse. LC 28-29071. 294 p. col. front., illlus., plates. 19 1/2 cm. c.1928. The Penn Publishing Company.

--Tu'kwi of the Peaceful People. Macdonald, Jean, illus. LC 33-30723. xii p., 1 l., 15-240 p. col. front., illus. 19 cm. c.1933. The Penn Publishing Company.

--Two Little Navajos: A Tale of the Children of the Painted Desert. Macdonald, Jean, illus. LC 31-31743. 279 p. col. front., illus. 19 cm. c.1931. The Penn Publishing Company.

Birney, Theodore W., Mrs.

--Childhood. N.D. Frederick A. Stokes Co.

Birnhack, Sarah

--Happy Is the Heart: A Year in the Life of a Jewish Girl. Birnhack, Sarah, illus. (Illus.). (gr. 5-8). 1976. (ISBN 0-87306-131-4). Feldheim.

Biro, Balint Stephen see Biro, Val, pseud.

Biro, Gyuri

--The Money Hat and Other Hungarian. N.D. Westminster Press.

Biro, Val, pseud., see Biro, Balint Stephen.

Biro, Val, pseud. (1921-)

--Bumpy's Holiday. Biro, Balint Stephen. Biro, Val, pseud. (1921-), illus. Biro, Balint Stephen. 1945. Transatlantic Arts.

--Gumdrop. Biro, Balint Stephen. Biro, Val, pseud. (1921-), illus. Biro, Balint Stephen. (Illus.). (ps-3). 1967. (ISBN 0-695-83618-8). (ISBN 0-695-43618-X). Follett.

--Gumdrop and the Farmer's Friend. Biro, Balint Stephen. Biro, Val, pseud. (1921-), illus. Biro, Balint Stephen. LC 68-13803. (Illus.). 27 p. 25cm. 1968, c.1967. Follett Pub. Co.

--Gumdrop and the Farmyard Caper. Biro, Balint Stephen. LC 85-12687. p. cm. 1985. (ISBN 0-918831-11-3). G. Stevens.

--Gumdrop and the Great Sausage Caper. Biro, Balint Stephen. LC 85-12690. p. cm. (Gumdrop Quickstart Readers). 1985. (ISBN 0-918831-13-X). G. Stevens.

--Gumdrop & the Secret Switches. Biro, Balint Stephen. LC 82-14786. 32p. (Gumdrop Ser.). 1982. (ISBN 0-89813-051-4). Childrens Bk Co.

--Gumdrop and the Steamroller. Biro, Balint Stephen. LC 76-50025. (Illus.). 24 p. 21cm. (Stepping stones). 1977, c.1976. (ISBN 0-516-03597-5). Childrens Press.

--Gumdrop at the Rally. Biro, Balint Stephen. Biro, Val, pseud. (1921-), illus. Biro, Balint Stephen. LC 69-10802. (Illus.). 29 p. 25cm. 1969, c.1968. Follett Pub. Co.

--Gumdrop at the Zoo. Biro, Balint Stephen. LC 85-12685. p. cm. (The Gumdrop Quickstart Readers). 1985. (ISBN 0-918831-10-5). G. Stevens.

--Gumdrop Catches a Cold. Biro, Balint Stephen. LC 85-12689. p. cm. (Gumdrop Quickstart Readers). 1985. (ISBN 0-918831-14-8). G. Stevens.

--Gumdrop Finds a Ghost. Biro, Balint Stephen. LC 82-17686. 32p. (Gumdrop Ser.). 1982. (ISBN 0-89813-050-6). Childrens Bk Co.

--Gumdrop Floats Away. Biro, Balint Stephen. LC 85-12688. p. cm. (Gumdrop Quickstart Readers). 1985. (ISBN 0-918831-53-9). (ISBN 0-918831-09-1). G. Stevens.

--Gumdrop Gets His Wings. Biro, Balint Stephen. LC 82-17716. 32p. (Gumdrop Ser.). 1982. (ISBN 0-89813-053-0). Childrens Bk Co.

--Gumdrop Goes to London. Biro, Val, pseud. (1921-), illus. Biro, Balint Stephen. LC 71-168884. (Illus.). 32p. 1st U.S. edition. (gr. k-3). 1972. (ISBN 0-87955-100-3). O'Hara.

--Gumdrop Has a Birthday. Biro, Balint Stephen. LC 82-17770. 32p. (Gumdrop Ser.). 1982. (ISBN 0-89813-055-7). Childrens Bk Co.

--Gumdrop in Double Trouble. Biro, Balint Stephen. LC 82-17687. 32p. (Gumdrop Ser.). 1982. (ISBN 0-89813-054-9). Childrens Bk Co.

--Gumdrop Is the Best Car. Biro, Balint Stephen. LC 85-12686. p. cm. (Gumdrop Quickstart Readers). 1985. (ISBN 0-918831-12-1). G. Stevens.

--Gumdrop on the Move. Biro, Balint Stephen. LC 79-118925. (Illus.). 30 p. 25cm. 1970, c.1969. Follett.

--Gumdrop Posts a Letter. Biro, Balint Stephen. LC 76-50584. (Illus.). 24 p. 21cm. (Stepping stones). 1977, c.1976. (ISBN 0-516-03596-7). Childrens Press.

--Gumdrop: The Adventures of a Vintage Car. Biro, Balint Stephen. Biro, Val, pseud. (1921-), illus. Biro, Balint Stephen. LC 67-3601. (Illus.). 29 p. 25cm. 1967, c.1966. Follett Pub. Co.

--The Honest Thief: A Hungarian Folktale. Biro, Balint Stephen. Biro, Val, pseud. (1921-), illus. Biro, Balint Stephen. LC 72-92577. 1 v. (chiefly illus.). 26cm. 1973, c.1972. (ISBN 0-8234-0222-3). Holiday House.

--The Magic Doctor. Biro, Balint Stephen. (Illus.). 32p. 1982. (ISBN 0-19-279752-2, Pub. by Oxford U Pr Childrens). Merrimack Pub Cir.

--The Pied Piper of Hamelin. Biro, Balint Stephen. LC 84-52469. (Illus.). 32 p. 29cm. 1985. (ISBN 0-382-09014-4). Silver Burdett.

Birrer, Cynthia & Birrer, William

--The Shoemaker & the Elves. LC 83-1145. 32p. (gr. k-3). 1983. (ISBN 0-688-01988-9). (ISBN 0-688-01989-7). Lothrop.

Birrer, William, jt. auth. see Birrer, Cynthia.

Bisbee, Mariana M.

--Tent V. Chautauqua, 1 of 20 vols. New ed. (Illus.). 350p. (Sunday-School Lib: No. 13). 1895. Set. Lothrop Pub. Co.

Bisbee, Susie A., Mrs.

--Ben Gilbert's Victory, 1 of 30 vols. (Illus.). (Morning Glory Ser). N.D. Lothrop Pub. Co.

--Daisy Green Stories, 1 of 30 vols. (Illus.). (Morning Glory Ser). N.D. Lothrop Pub. Co.

--Milly's Little Wanderer, 1 of 20 vols. New ed. (Illus.). 350p. (Sunday-School Lib: No. 13). 1895. Set. Lothrop Pub. Co.

--Milly's Little Wanderer: Author of "Daisy Green Stories". N.D. D. Lothrop & Co.

Bischel, Leonard

--A Merry-Go-Round. Bishel, Arlynn, illus. (Illus.). 72p. (Orig.). (gr. 1-5). 1980. (ISBN 0-935110-01-1). Blackjack Ent.

Bischoff, Alesia

--The Beautiful Puppy. (Illus.). (Little Book Ser). (gr. k-6). 1976. (ISBN 0-89409-008-9). Childrens Art.

Bischoff, David Frederick (1951-)

--The Phantom of the Opera. (gr. 7 up). 1977. (ISBN 0-590-10312-1, Schol Pap). Scholastic Inc.

Bischoff, David Frederick (1951-) & Westermann, Paul

--Quest. LC 76-44815. (Illus.). 64 p. 23cm. c.1977. (ISBN 0-8172-0528-4). (ISBN 0-8172-0527-6). Raintree Editions.

--Strange Encounters. LC 76-45662. (Illus.). 64 p. 23cm. c.1977. (ISBN 0-8172-0526-8). Raintree Editions.

Bischoff, Helmut, jt. auth. see Winter, Klaus.

Bischoff, Helmut & Winter, Klaus (1928-)

--The Happy Owls. Edelberg, Linda R., adapted by. LC 67-27696. (Illus.). 31 p. 31cm. 1967. Lion Press.

--Hoopla Hoppla Farmerman. (gr. k-3). 1966. (ISBN 0-516-03470-7). Childrens.

Bischoff, Ilse Marthe, jt. auth. see Vinall, Emilie.

Bischoff, Ilse Marthe (1903-)

--Painter's Coach. 1st ed. Williams, Berkeley (1904-), illus. LC 43-51357. (Illus.). vi, 186. 21cm. 1943. Longmans, Green and Co.

--The Wonderful Poodle. LC 49-6318. 79 p. illus. 24 cm. 1949. T. Y. Crowell Co.

Bischoff, Julia Bristol (1909-1970)

--A Dog for David. 112p. (gr. 3-6). 1966 (A-W Childrens). A-W.

--A Dog for David. Moriarty, Jerome B., illus. LC 66-17572. (Illus.). 110 p. 22cm. 1966. W. R. Scott.

--Great-Great-Uncle Henry's Cats. 64p. (gr. 1-3). 1965. (ISBN 0-201-09205-0, Young Scott Bks). A-W.

--Great-Great Uncle Henry's Cats. Woodward, Hildegard (1898-), illus. LC 65-208287. 62p. illus. 23cm. (Young Scott bk.). c.1965. Scott

--Mystery on the Rancho Grande. Charlot, Martin, illus. LC 77-82266. (Illus.). 224 p. 22cm. 1969. Young Scott Books.

--Paddy's Preposterous Promises. Fetz, Ingrid (1915-), illus. LC 68-27027. (Illus.). 159 p. 22cm. 1968. Young Scott Books.

Biscoe, Ellen L.

--Katharine's Experience. 378p. N.D. Lockwood, Brooks, & Co. for American Tract Society.

Biscoe, Ellen L. see Hollis, Ellen L. Biscoe

Bisconti, Patrick R & Fox, Martin A.

--Gypsy Wizard: Adventures in Realityland. unlimited. LC 76-45054. (Illus.). v. 28cm. N.D. Madjic Books.

Bishop, Ann

--Annie O'Kay's Riddle Roundup. Warshaw, Jerry (1929-), illus. LC 80-27115. p. cm. 1981. (ISBN 0-525-66729-6). Elsevier/Nelson Books.

--Chicken Riddle. Warshaw, Jerry (1929-), illus. LC 72-83681. (Illus.). 40 p. 21cm. 1972. (ISBN 0-8075-1140-4). A. Whitman.

--Cleo Catra's Riddle Book. Warshaw, Jerry (1929-), illus. LC 80-17104. p. cm. 1980. (ISBN 0-525-66706-7). Elsevier/Nelson Books.

--The Ella Fannie Elephant Riddle Book. Warshaw, Jerry (1929-), illus. LC 74-14931. (Illus.). 40 p. 21cm. 1974. (ISBN 0-8075-1966-9). A. Whitman.

--Hello, Mr. Chipps!. Warshaw, Jerry (1929-), illus. 1982. Lodestar.

--Hey Riddle Riddle!. Warshaw, Jerry (1929-), illus. LC 68-22189. (Illus.). 1 v. (unpaged. 21cm. 1968. A. Whitman.

--Merry-Go-Riddle. Warshaw, Jerry (1929-), illus. LC 73-7321. (Illus.). 38 p. 21cm. 1973. (ISBN 0-8075-5072-8). A. Whitman.

--Noah Riddle?. Warshaw, Jerry (1929-), illus. LC 71-115893. (Illus.). 40 p. 22cm. 1970. A. Whitman.

--Oh, Riddlesticks!. Rubin, Caroline, ed. Warshaw, Jerry (1929-), illus. LC 76-41418. (Illus.). (Riddle Bk.). (gr. 2-6). 1976. (ISBN 0-8075-5916-4). A Whitman.

--Riddle Ages. Warshaw, Jerry (1929-), illus. LC 77-12828. p. cm. 1977. (ISBN 0-8075-6965-8). A. Whitman.

--Riddle Raddle, Fiddle Faddle. Mathews, Roy, illus. LC 68-22189. (Illus.). (Riddle Bk.). (gr. 2-4). 1966. (ISBN 0-8075-6974-7). A Whitman.

--Riddle Red Riddle Book. Warshaw, Jerry (1929-), illus. LC 72-79549. (Illus.). 40 p. 21cm. 1969. A. Whitman.

--Wild Bill Hiccup's Riddle Book. Warshaw, Jerry (1929-), illus. LC 75-33161. (Illus.). 40 p. 22cm. 1975. (ISBN 0-8075-9097-5). A. Whitman.

Bishop, Austin

--Bob Thorpe, Sky Fighter in Italy. N.D. Harcourt Brace.

--Bob Thorpe: Sky Fighter in Italy. Neill, John Rea (1878-1943), illus. LC 20-16156. 3 p. l., 275 p., 1 l., incl. illus. plates, map. front. 19 1/2 cm. 1920. Harcourt, Brace and Howe.

--Bob Thorpe, Sky Fighter in the Lafayette Flying Corps. N.D. Harcourt Brace.

--Bob Thorpe: Sky Fighter in the Lafayette Flying Corps. Neill, John Rea (1878-1943), illus. LC 19-19055. 4 p. l., 3-276 p. front., illus. 19 1/2 cm. 1919. Harcourt, Brace and Howe.

--Tom of the Raiders. Dennis, Morgan (1891-1960), illus. LC 21-147075. 5 p. l., 3-260 p. front., plates. 19 1/2 cm. 1921. Harcourt, Brace and Company.

Bishop, Bonnie (1943-)

--No One Noticed Ralph. LC 78-18555. (gr. k-3). 1979. Doubleday.

--Ralph Rides Away. Kent, Jack, pseud. (1920-), illus. Kent, John Wellington. LC 78-20710. (Illus.). 63 p. 25cm. (Reading on my own book). c.1979. (ISBN 0-385-14213-7). (ISBN 0-385-14214-5). Doubleday.

Bishop, Claire Huchet, Mrs.

--All Alone. Rojankovsky, Feodor Stepanovich (1891-1970), illus. LC 53-8168. 90p. illus. 26cm. 1953. (ISBN 0-670-11336-0). Viking Press. **Award: (JNM).**

--Augustus. Paull, Grace A. (1898-), illus. LC 46-8468. (Illus.). 32p. 1945. Viking Press.

--Bernard and His Dogs. Brevannes, Maurice (1904-), illus. LC 52-7143. 70 p. illus. 24 cm. 1952. Houghton Mifflin.

--The Big Loop. Fontsere, Carles, illus. LC 55-13649. 221 p. illus. 22cm. 1955. Viking Press.

--Blue Spring Farm. LC 48-202923. 183 p. 21 cm. 1948. Viking Press.

--Christopher the Giant. 1950. Houghton Mifflin Co.

--The Ferryman. Wiese, Kurt (1887-1974), illus. LC 41-24254. 64 p. col. illlus. 17 x 25 1/2 cm. c.1941. Coward-McCann, Inc.

--The Five Chinese Brothers. N.D. E. M. Hale & Co.

--The Five Chinese Brothers. Wiese, Kurt (1887-1974), illus. LC 38-27908. 50 p. illus. 17 x 25 1/2 cm. c.1938. Coward-McCann, Inc.

--Georgette. Landshoff, Ursula (1908-), illus. LC 72-94140. (Illus.). 60 p. 22cm. (Break-of-day book). 1973. (ISBN 0-698-20260-0). (ISBN 0-698-20260-0). Coward, McCann & Geoghegan.

--The Kings' Day. Spiegel, Doris (1901-), illus. LC 40-27750. 47 p. illus. 25 1/2 cm. 1940. Coward-McCann, Inc.

--The Man Who Lost His Head. McCloskey, John Robert (1914-1969), illus. LC 42-25584. 53 p. illus. 18 1/2 x 24 cm. 1942. Viking Press.

--The Man Who Lost His Head. McCloskey, John Robert (1914-1969), illus. (Illus.). 1 v. u.p. (Viking Seafarer Book). 1974, c.1970. (ISBN 0-670-05094-6). Viking.

--Pancakes-Paris. Schreiber, Georges (1904-1977), illus. LC 47-2541. (Illus.). 62, 1 p. 26cm. 1947. The Viking Press. **Award: (JNM).**

--A Present from Petros. Davis, Dimitris (1905-), illus. LC 61-11678. (Illus.). 84 p. 24cm. 1961. Viking Press.

--Toto's Triumph. N.D. E . M. Hale and Co.

--Toto's Triumph. Ponsot, Claude, illus. LC 57-137947. 127p. illus. 22cm. 1957. Viking Press.

--The Truffle Pig. Wiese, Kurt (1887-1974), illus. LC 70-132619. (Illus.). 48 p. 23cm. (Break-of-day book). 1971. Coward, McCann & Geoghegan.

--Twenty and Ten. Du Bois, William Sherman Pene (1916-), illus. (gr. 4-6). 1984. Peter Smith.

--Twenty and Ten. Du Bois, William Sherman Pene (1916-), illus. LC 52-12483. (Illus.). 76 p. 24cm. 1952. Viking Press.

--Twenty and Ten. Joly, Janet, Mrs., ed. Du Bois, William Sherman Pene (1916-), illus. LC 77-12730. (Illus.). 76 p. 20cm. 1978, c.1952. (ISBN 0-14-031076-2). Puffin Books.

--Twenty-Two Bears. Wiese, Kurt (1887-1974), illus. LC 64-12636. 31 p. col. illus. 19 x 26 cm. 1964. Viking Press.

--Yeshu, Called Jesus. Bolognese, Donald Alan (1934-), illus. 1966. Farrar, Straus And Giroux.

Bishop, Claire Huchet, Mrs., ed.

--Happy Christmas: Tales for Boys & Girls. Raskin, Ellen (1928-1984), illus. LC 56-13330. (Illus.). (gr. 1-8). 1956. (ISBN 0-8044-5111-7, Pub. by Stephen Daye Pr). Ungar.

Bishop, Curtis Kent see Carroll, Curt, pseud.

Bishop, Curtis Kent (1912-1967)

--Banjo Hitter. LC 51-10662. 204 p. 22 cm. 1951. Steck Co.

--The Big Game. LC 63-13044. 156 p. 22cm. 1963. Steck Co.

--Dribble up. LC 56-100522. 191p. 22cm. 1956. Steck Co.

--Fast Break. LC 67-19265. 185 p. 21cm. 1967. Lippincott.

--Field Goal. LC 64-19049. 187 p. 21 cm. 1964. Lippincott.

--Fighting Quarterback. LC 54-12513. 208p. 22cm. 1954. Steck Co.

--Goal to Go. LC 55-9888. 202 p. 22cm. 1955. Steck Co.

--Gridiron Glory. LC 66-8494. 175 p. 22cm. 1966. Lippincott.

--Hackberry Jones, Split End. LC 68-24425. 174 p. 21cm. 1968. Lippincott.

--Half-Time Hero. LC 56-10049. 183p. 22cm. 1956. Steck Co.

--Hero at Halfback. LC 53-126521. 187p. 22cm. 1953. Steck Co.

--Lank of the Little League. 1st ed. LC 58-101377. 190p. 21cm. 1958. Lippincott.

--Larry Comes Home. LC 55-7876. 202 p. 22cm. 1955. Steck Co.

--Larry Leads off. LC 54-6831. 149 p. 22cm. 1954. Steck Co.

--Larry of Little League. LC 53-5658. 161p. 22cm. 1953. Steck Co.

--The Last Outlaw. 144 p. 21cm. 1967. Broadman Press.

--Little League Amigo. LC 64-13809. 187 p. 21 cm. 1964. Lippincott.

--Little League Double Play. 1st Ed. LC 62-933437. 189p. 21cm. 1962. (ISBN 0-397-30614-8). Lippincott.

--Little League Heroes. LC 60-6758. 190 p. 21cm. 1960. Lippincott.

--Little League Little Brother. LC 68-10778. 185 p. 21cm. 1968. Lippincott.
--Little League Stepson. LC 65-13432. 154 p. 21cm. 1965. Lippincott.
--Little League Victory. LC 67-3796. 187 p. 21cm. 1967. Lippincott.
--Little League Visitor. LC 66-10894. 192 p. 21 cm. 1966. Lippincott.
--The Little League Way. LC 57-6487. 159p. 22cm. 1957. Steck Co.
--Little Leaguer. 172p. 22cm. c.1956. Steck Co.
--Lonesome End. LC 63-18501. 188 p. 21 cm. 1963. Lippincott.
--The Lost Eleven. N.D. Steck Co.
--The Playmaker. LC 60-116640. 200p. 22cm. 1960. Steck Co.
--Rebound. LC 62-15515. 157 p. 21cm. 1962. Lippincott.
--San Jacinto. Carroll, Curt, pseud. Rice, Elizabeth (1913-), illus. LC 57-5115. 185p. illus. 22cm. 1957. (ISBN 0-8114-7640-5). Steck Co.
--Saturday Heroes. 1951. Steck-Vaughn Company.
--Sideline Pass. LC 65-21661. 190p. 21cm. c.1965. Lippincott.
--Sideline Quarterback. LC 60-12914. 191 p. 20cm. 1960. Lippincott.
--Teamwork. Rice, Elizabeth (1913-), illus. LC 42-18437. 5 p. l., 326 p. incl. front., illlus. 21 1/2 cm. 1942. The Steck Company.

Bishop, Curtis Kent (1912-1967) & Bishop, Grace
--Stout Rider. Davis, M. J., illus. LC 53-5660. 104p. illus. 21cm. 1953. (ISBN 0-8114-7643-X). Steck Co.

Bishop, Dorothy Sword.
--The Lion and the Mouse. LC 72-80085. (Illus.). 66 p. 23cm. (Her Fables bilingues). (Bilingual series). c.1978. National Textbook Co.
--The Lion and the Mouse: Der Lowe und Die Maus. LC 73-12067. (Illus.). 63 p. 23cm. (Her Fabeln in zwei Sprachen). (The Bilingual Ser.). c.1972. National Textbook Co.
--The Tortoise and the Hare: La Tortue et le Lievre. LC 73-11470. (Illus.). 71 p. 23cm. (Her Fables bilingues). (The Bilingual Ser.). c.1972. National Textbook Co.

Bishop, Elizabeth (1911-1979)
--The Ballad of the Burglar of Babylon. Grifalconi, Ann (1929-), illus. LC 68-13681. (Illus.). 1 v. (unpaged). 1968. Farrar, Straus & Giroux.

Bishop, Farnham (1886-1930)
--The Black Bloodhound. LC 27-3099. 5 p. l., 3-296 p. 19 1/2 cm. 1927. Little, Brown, and Company.

Bishop, Farnham (1886-1930) & Brodeur, Arthur Gilchrist (1888-)
--The Altar of the Legion. Pitz, Henry Clarence (1895-1976), illus. LC 26-4302. xv, 316 p. front., plates. 19 1/2 cm. 1926. Little, Brown, and Company.

Bishop, Gavin
--Mrs. McGinty & the Bizarre Plant. Bishop, Gavin (1946-), illus. (Illus.). 32p. (ps) 1983. (ISBN 0-19-558074-5, Pub by Oxford U Pr Childrens). Merrimack Pub Cir.

Bishop, Gavin (1946-), adapted by.
--Mr. Fox. Bishop, Gavin (1946-), illus. LC 83-670230. (Illus.). 32p. (ps-1). 1983. (ISBN 0-19-558089-3). (ISBN 0-19-558089-3). Oxford U Pr.

Bishop, Giles, Jr.
--Captain Comstock, U.S.M.C. Humphreys, Donald S., illus. LC 23-12442. 358 p. front., illlus. (incl. maps) plates. 19 1/2 cm. 1923. The Penn Publishing Company.
--Lieutenant Comstock: U.S. Marine. Humphreys, Donald S., illus. LC 22-191651. 363 p. front., illlus. plates. 19 1/2 cm. 1922. The Penn Publishing Company.
--The Marines Have Advanced. Humphreys, Donald S., illus. 393 p. front., illlus., plates. 19 1/2 cm. 1922. The Penn Publishing Company.
--The Marines have Landed. Humphreys, Donald S., illus. LC 20-21478. (Illus.). 356p. N.D. Penn Publishing Co.

Bishop, Grace
--Prissy Misses. Warren, Betsy, pseud. (1916-), illus. Warren, Elizabeth Avery. LC 56-6374. unpaged. illus. 24cm. c.1956. Steck Co.
--Prissy Missy. 1956. Steck Company.

Bishop, Grace, jt. auth. see Bishop, Curtis Kent.

Bishop, Jim
--The Golden Ham. 1956. Simon and Schuster.

Bishop, Jim, jt. auth. see Bishop, Virginia Lee.

Bishop, Julia Truitt
--The Great Round World: Natural History Stories A Series of True Stories. LC 22-14784. 2 v. illus. 19 cm. 1897. W. B. Harrison.

Bishop, Kay
--Chris. Setchell, Martha Powell, illus. LC 46-3132. 22cm. 32p. 1946. Oxford University Press.

Bishop, R. F.
--Camerton Slope. (Illus.). N.D. Methodist Bk Concern.

Bishop, Richard
--From Kite to Kitty Hawk. 1960. (ISBN 0-8382-0272-1, Cadmus Books). E. M. Hale and Company.

Bishop, Ruth M., illus.
--The Mermaid's Message and Other Stories. LC 20-1286. 3 p. l., 5-179 p. front., plates. 20 cm. 1919. Milton Bradley Company.

Bishop, Virginia Lee & Bishop, Jim
--Fighting Father Duffy. 1956. Farrar, Straus and Cudahy, Inc.

Bishop, W. H., et al.
--The Forbes-Doolan Affair, 1 of 4 vols. (Illus.). 190p. (Out of School Ser.). N.D. D Lothrop.

Bishop, William Avery (1894-) & Stuart-Wortley, Rothesay
--The Flying Squad. (Windmill Bks.). N.D. Doubleday Doran & Co.
--The Flying Squad. LC 27-19774. 209 p. col. front., illlus., plates. 19 1/2 cm. c.1927. George H. Duran Company.
--The Flying Squad. Hearlin, C., illus. LC 39-17656. 200 p. 20 1/2 cm. (Young moderns bookshelf). 1938. The Sun Dial Press, Inc.

Bispham, H. C.
--Papa's Book of Animals, Wild and Tame. N.D. Porter & Coates.

Biss, Roderick
--Gambit Book of Children's Songs. Mitchell, Donald Charles Peter (1925-), ed. Le Cain, Errol John (1941-), illus. LC 74-118215. (Illus.). 1970. (ISBN 0-87645-023-0). Gambit.

Bissell, LeClair & Watherwax, Richard
--The Cat Who Drank Too Much. (Illus.). 48p. (gr. 4 up). 1982. (ISBN 0-911153-00-4). Spanish ed. (ISBN 0-911153-01-2). Bibulophile Pr.

Bissell, Mary L.
--The Robinsons. N.D. D. Lothrop & Co.
--The Robinsons. (Fern Glen Ser.). N.D. D. Lothrop Co.

Bissell, Richard Pike (1913-1977)
--Julia Harrington, Winnebago, Iowa, 1913. LC 70-86617. (Illus.). 84 p. 29cm. 1969. Little, Brown.

Bisset, Donald (1910-)
--Hazy Mountain. Hughes, Shirley (1929-), illus. (Illus.). 32p. (Picture Bks. - Puffin Easy Readers). (gr. 1-3). 1975. (ISBN 0-14-050143-6, Puffin). Penguin.

Bissett, Donald John (1930-)
--Poems and Verse about the City. LC 79-2640. 127p. 21cm. c.1968. Chandler Pub. Co.
--Poems and Verses About Animals. 96 p. 21cm. (Poetry and verse for urban children, book 2). 1967. Chandler Pub. Co.
--Poems and Verses to Begin On. LC 76-2772. 104p. 21cm. c.1967. Chandler Pub. Co.

Bisson, Thomas A.
--Bixxy and the Secret Message. N.D. Macmillan.

Bitney, Mayme R
--Pageants and Plays: For Holidays. LC 26-17810. 161 p. illus., diagrs. 18 cm. c.1926. Paine Publishing Company.

Bittel, Tobi C.
--Jungle Baby. N.D. Vantage Press INc.

Bittleston, Adam, tr. see Von Goethe, Johann W. & Steiner, Rudolf.

Bixby, William A.
--The Impossible Journey of Sir Ernest Shackleton. 1960. Little, Brown and Company.

Bixler, William A.
--Light on the Child's Path. 128p. N.D. Gospel Trumpet Company.

Bizet, Alexandre Cesar Leopold Geroges see Merimee, Prosper (1803-1870) & Bizet, Georges.

Bizet, Georges, jt. auth. see Merimee, Prosper.

Bjerke, Odd & Moston, Meredith
--The Search for Trollhaven. Wood, Marvin, illus. LC 77-77794. (Illus.). 172 p. 21cm. c.1977. (ISBN 0-916238-06-7). Beatty Books.

Bjoernson, Bjoernstjerne Martinius (1832-1910)
--Arne: The Happy Boy. N.D. John Allyn.
--The Fisher Maiden: A Norwegian Story. Niles, M. E., tr. (Leisure Hour Ser.). N.D. Henry Holt & Co.
--The Fishing Girl. N.D. Cassell, Petter, & Galpin.
--Happy Boy. N.D. Macmillan.
--The Railroad and Churchyard. N.D. John Allyn.

Bjoland, Esther M., ed.
--Parade of Stories. LC 68-303. (Illus.). 192 p. 26cm. (Child horizons). 1967, c.1965. Standard Education Society.
--Stories of Childhood. Armstrong, George Douglas, et al. (1927-), illus. Wing, Helen LC 74-12319. p. cm. (The Child's World). 1974, c.1971. Standard Educational Corp.
--The Story Hour. LC 53-12354. 192p. illus. 26cm. 1953. Standard Education Society.
--The Story Parade. LC 54-1630. 192p. illus. 26cm. (Child horizons). 1954. Standard Education Society.

Bjork, Elizabeth C.
--A Purple Pig for Pedro. Holmer, Edvin K., illus. LC 43-18433. 80 p. col. illus. 28 1/2 x 22 cm. 1943. The Wartburg Press.

Bjorkman, Nancy Roth
--Wilma and the Water Pistol That Wouldn't Shoot Straight. Stahl, Ben F., illus. LC 75-4444. (Illus.). 30 p. 29cm. c.1976. Golden Press.

Bjorn, T. F.
--Papa's Wife. 1955. Holt Rinehart and Winston.

Bjornson, Magnus F.
--Dan Patch And Other Stories of Pioneering in the West. Daniel, Alan (1939-), illus. LC 78-304590. (Illus.). 110 p. 19cm. 1975. Scholastic-Tab Publications.

Black, Algernon David (1900-)
--The Woman of the Wood: A Tale from Old Russia. Ness, Evaline Michelow, Mrs. (1911-), illus. LC 72-91649. (Illus.). 32 p. 25cm. 1973. Holt, Rinehart and Winston.
--The Young Citizens. 416p. N.D. Frederick Ungar Publishing Co Inc.

Black, Dorothy
--The Magic Egg: A Story for Children. N.D. Macmillan.

Black, Elizabeth Griswold & Moore, Mamie Wiser
--Twelve Button Shoes. Moore, Mamie Wiser, illus. LC 79-114718. (Illus.). 86 p. 24cm. c.1979. Black.

Black, Elsie A.
--Dog Days. N.D. Carlton Press.

Black, Floyd & Nicklaus, Carol
--Alphabet Cat. LC 79-1911. (Illus.). 20 p. 32cm. c.1979. (ISBN 0-525-69008-5). (ISBN 0-525-69009-3). Gingerbread House.

Black, George (1920-)
--Alloys in Cooperland. Lionhill Studios, illus. LC 52-21718. unpaged. illus. 24 cm. N.D. Cooper Alloy Foundry Co.

Black, Harry G.
--The Lost Dutchman Mine: A Short Story of a Tall Tale. N.D. (ISBN 0-8283-1613-9). Branden Press.

Black, Helen (1890-), tr. see Radlov, Nikolal Ernestovich.

Black, Irma Simonton, jt. auth. see Mitchell, Lucy Sprague, Mrs.

Black, Irma Simonton, jt. ed. see Mitchell, Lucy Sprague, Mrs.

Black, Irma Simonton, Mrs. (1906-1972)
--Barbara's Birthday. Takis, Nicholas (1903-), illus. LC 46-794394. 2 p. l., 7-44 p. col. illus. 22 1/2 c 18 1/2 cm. c.1946. W. R. Scott, Inc.
--Big Puppy and Little Puppy. Sherman, Theresa (1916-), illus. LC 60-509618. unpaged. illus. 23cm. 1960. Holiday House.
--Big Puppy & Little Puppy. Sherman, Theresa (1916-), illus. (Illus.). 36p. (gr. 1-3). 1960. (ISBN 0-8234-0006-9). Holiday.
--Busy Water. Castle, Jane, illus. LC 58-1356. unpaged. illus. 24cm. c.1958. Holiday House.
--Doctor Proctor and Mrs. Merriwether. Weisgard, Leonard Joseph (1916-), illus. LC 78-150800. (Illus.). 32 p. 24cm. 1971. (ISBN 0-8075-1654-6). A. Whitman.
--The Dog Doctor: A Comedy Short Starring Patsy and Chipper. Fischetti, John R. (1916-1980), illus. LC 47-30808. (Illus.). 40. 19 x 25cm. (Young Scott Bks.). 1947. W.R. Scott.
--Dusty and His Friends. Latham, Barbara (1896-), illus. LC 50-10210. 56 p. illus. 20 cm. 1950. Holiday House.
--Flipper: A Sea-Lion. Rounds, Glen Harold (1906-), illus. LC 40-27720. 50 p. col. front., col. illus., col. plates. 21 x 16 cm. c.1940. Holiday House.
--Hamlet: A Cocker Spaniel. Wiese, Kurt (1887-1974), illus. LC 38-27984. 72 p. illus. 19 1/2 cm. c.1938. Holiday House.
--Is This My Dinner?. Fry, Rosalind, illus. LC 72-83682. (Illus.). 32 p. 18cm. 1972. (ISBN 0-8075-3665-2). A. Whitman.
--Kip, a Young Rooster. Wiese, Kurt (1887-1974), illus. LC 39-33741. 68 p. illus. 19 1/2 cm. c.1939. Holiday House.
--The Little Old Man Who Cooked and Cleaned. Fleishman, Seymour (1918-), illus. LC 72-126437. (Illus.). 32 p. 24cm. 1970. (ISBN 0-8075-4619-4). A. Whitman.
--The Little Old Man Who Could Not Read. Fleishman, Seymour (1918-), illus. LC 68-9115. (Illus.). 1 v. (unpaged. 24cm. 1968. A. Whitman.
--Maggie: A Mischievous Magpie. Latham, Barbara, illus. LC 49-11747. 61 p. illus. 20 cm. 1949. Holiday House.
--Monsters and Wild Creatures. LC 78-60563. (Illus.). 47 p. 24cm. (Houghton Mifflin reading series). c.1979. Houghton Mifflin.
--Night Cap. N.D. E. M. Hale & Co.
--Night Cat. Galdone, Paul (1914-), illus. LC 57-13989. unpaged. illus. 17x25cm. c.1957. Holiday House.
--Pete: The Parakeet. Werth, Kurt (1896-), illus. LC 54-128155. 97p. illus. 20cm. 1954. Holiday House.
--Pete the Parakete. N.D. E. M. Hale and Co.
--Pudge: A Summertime Mixup. Bacon, Peggy, pseud. (1895-), illus. Bacon, Margaret Frances. LC 53-263588. 182p. illus. 20cm. 1953. Holiday House.
--Spoodles: The Puppy Who Learned. Fischetti, John R. (1916-1980), illus. LC 48-5936. 48 p. illus. 18 x 22 cm. (Young Scott books). 1948. W. R. Scott.
--Toby: A Curious Cat. LC 48-5936. 63 p. illus 20 cm. N.D. C.
--Toby, a Curious Cat. Gay, Zhenya (1906-1978), illus. LC 48-7295. 20cm. 63p. 1948. Holiday House.
--The Troublemaker. 1st ed. Fava, Rita (1932-), illus. LC 59-100239. 90p. illus. 21cm. 1959. (ISBN 0-394-81776-1). Knopf.

Black, Irma Simonton, Mrs. (1906-1972), adapted by.
--This is Bread that Betsy ate: Adapted from "Mother Goose". 32p. N.D. William R. Scott Inc.

Black, James M.
--New Junior Songs. N.D. Abingdon-Cokesbury Press.

Black, Jane
--Mythology for Young People. N.D. Charles Scribner's Sons'.

Black, Margaret Katherine (1921-)
--Three Brothers and a Lady. 64p. N.D. British Book Centre.
--Two Young Explorers: The Adventures of Ulf and Bryn. N.D. British Book Centre.

Black, Marian
--Child Life Stories. LC 45-122284. 64 p. incl. front., illus. 23 1/2 cm. 1944. The Wartburg Press.
--Childhood's Golden Dawn. LC 45-12227. 88, 2 p., 1 l. incl. col. front., illus. (part col.) 23 1/2 cm. 1944. The Wartburg Press.
--The Child's Story Garden. LC 45-10238. 92 p. incl. col. front., illus. (part col.) 23 cm. 1945. The Wartburg Press.
--Precious Moments with Children: Stories, Verses, and Pictures for Children. LC 42-22169. 64 p. illus. 23 1/2 cm. 1942. The Wartburg Press.
--Sunbeams for Children. LC 43-18240. 92 p. incl. col. front., illus. (part col.) 23 1/2 cm. 1943. The Wartburg Press.
--Sunny Side Stories for Children. LC 45-10237. 64 p. incl. front., illus. 23 cm. 1945. The Wartburg Press.

Black, Mary Martin
--Summerfield Farm. Dennis, Wesley (1903-1966), illus. LC 51-10170. (Illus.). 143 p. 26cm. 1951. Viking Press.

Black, Millard H., jt. auth. see McClellan, Jack.

Black, Millard H., jt. ed. see Granite, Harvey R.

Black, Sonia
--The Get Along Gang & the New Neighbor. Gantz, David, illus. (Illus.). 32p. (Orig.). (Get Along Gang Ser.). (ps-2). 1984. (ISBN 0-590-33190-6). Scholastic Inc.
--The Get Along Gang & the Tattletale. Allert, Kathy, illus. (Illus.). 32p. (Orig.). (The Get Along Gang Ser.). (ps-2). 1984. (ISBN 0-590-33279-1). Scholastic Inc.

Black, Susan Adams (1953-)
--Crash in the Wilderness. Strobel, Tom, illus. LC 79-21852. (Illus.). 47 p. 24cm. c.1980. (ISBN 0-8172-1553-0). Raintree Pub.

Black, William (1841-1898)
--The Four Macnicols. (Author of "A Princess of Thule."). (Illus.). (Harper's Young People Ser.). 1882. Harper & Brothers.
--The Four Macnicols and "An Adventure in Thule". LC 4-17534. 217 p. incl. plates. front. 17 1/2 cm. (Harper's young people series, new ed.). 1900. Harper & Brothers.

Blackall, Christopher Rubey (1830-1924) & Blackall, Emily Lucas, Mrs.
--Bible Lore. The Child Jesus; Three Bible Stories from "Stories About Jesus". LC 34-39873. 28 p. incl. col. front., illus. (incl. map) 28 1/2 cm. 1891. American Baptist Publication Society.

Blackall, Emily Lucas, Mrs., jt. auth. see Blackall, Christopher Rubey.

Blackburn, Casper
--Annapolis Ahoy!. LC 45-106404. 287 p. col. front. 20 cm. 1945. Macrae-Smith-Company.

Blackburn, Edith H
--The Bells of Carmel: Mission Days in California. 1st ed. Nicholas, Frank, illus. LC 54-6084. 191p. illus. 22cm. (American heritage series). 1954. Aladdin Books.
--The Golden Promise. Anderson, Rus, illus. LC 56-10124. 160p. illus. 22cm. 1956. Abelard-Schuman.
--Land of the Silver Spruce: A Story of the Colorado Rockies. LC 56-5906. 173p. illus. 22cm. 1956. Abelard-Schuman.
--Mystery of the Glory Hole Mine. Nicholas, Frank, illus. LC 56-7708. 155p. illus. 21cm. 1956. Sterling Pub. Co.
--One Bit of Land: A Story of Imperial Valley. 1st ed. Nicholas, Frank, illus. LC 55-587971. 192p. illus. 21 cm. (American heritage series). 1955. Aladdin Books.

Blackburn, Francis, et al., eds. see White, Terence Hanbury.

Blackburn, Joyce Knight (1920-)
--The Bloody Summer of Seventeen Forty-Two: A Colonial Boy's Journal. Graham, Critt, illus. (Illus.). 64p. (gr. 5-8). 1985. (ISBN 0-930803-00-0). Fort Frederica.
--Suki & the Invisible Peacock. LC 64-8841. (Illus.). 56p. (ps-3). 1968. (ISBN 0-87680-885-2). Word Bks.

--Suki and the Invisible Peacock. Clayton, Stephanie, illus. LC 64-8841. 1 v. (unpaged) illus. (pt. col.) 26cm. c.1965. Zondervan.
--Suki and the Magic Sand Dollar. Clayton, Stephanie, illus. LC 69-20230. (Illus.). 68 p. 26cm. 1969. Word Books.
--Suki and the Old Umbrella. Clayton, Stephanie, illus. LC 66-18943. (Illus.). 1 v. (unpaged. 26cm. 1966. Zondervan Pub. House.
--Suki and the Wonder Star. Clayton, Stephanie, illus. LC 73-160292. (Illus.). 66 p. 26cm. 1971. Word Books.
Blackburn, Lorraine A., jt. ed. see Brewton, John Edmund.
Blackburn, Paul, tr. see Jimenez-Landi, Antonio.
Blackerby, Alva W. (1909-) & Forrest, Linn Argyle (1905-)
--Tale of an Alaska Whale. LC 55-43676. (Illus.). 30 p. 15cm. 1955. Binfords & Mort.
Blackfeet Heritage Program, jt. auth. see Rides At The Door.
Blackford, Charles Minor, III (1898-)
--Deep Treasure: A Story of the Greek Sponge Fishers of Florida. Key, Alexander Hill (1904-1979), illus. LC 54-5069. (Illus.). 243 p. 22cm. (Land of the free series). 1954. Winston.
Blackley, R. H., tr. see Lory, Marie Joseph.
Blackman, Marilyn
--Hokulea. Momoa, Joseph Namakaeha, illus. LC 76-1785. (Illus.). 39 p. 28cm. (Na puke huakai kamalii = Books for children on sea voyaging ; book 4). (Na Puke Huakai Kamalii Ser.: Book 4). 1976. Polynesian Voyaging Society.
Blackmore
--Cripps the Carrier. (Burt's Home Lib.). N.D. A. L. Burt's Pubs.
Blackmore, Anauta Ford
--Wild Like the Foxes; the True Story of an Eskimo Girl: By Anauta; Pseud. LC 56-5975. 192p. illus. 21cm. 1956. J. Day Co.
Blackmore, Richard Doddridge (1825-1900)
--Kit and Kitty: A Novel. LC 6-13860. 227 p. 21 1/2 cm. (On cover: Harper's Franklin square library, no. 663). 1889. Harper & Brothers.
--Lorna Doone. N.D. A. L. Burt Co.
--Lorna Doone. (The International Classics). N.D. Dodd Mead & Co.
--Lorna Doone. N.D. Ginn & Co.
--Lorna Doone. N.D. Grosset & Dunlap.
--Lorna Doone, 2 vols, Vol. II. (Illus.). (Empyreal Library of Handy Volume Classics). N.D. H. M. Caldwell Co.
--Lorna Doone. N.D. Harper & Bros.
--Lorna Doone. N.D. J.B. Lippincott.
--Lorna Doone. (The Rittenhouse Classics). N.D. Macrae Smith.
--Lorna Doone. 686p. N.D. Oxford University Press.
--Lorna Doone. (Crowell's Pocket Library). N.D. Thomas Y. Crowell Company.
--Lorna Doone. N.D. Thomas Nelson & Sons.
--Lorna Doone. Austen, John (1886-), illus. 566p. N.D. Heritage Press.
--Lorna Doone. Bailey, Carolyn Sherwin (1875-1961), abridged by. Brett, Harold Matthews (1880-), illus. N.D. Milton Bradley Co.
--Lorna Doone. Cann, Y. W., abridged by. (English Literature Ser.). N.D. St. Martin's Press.
--Lorna Doone. Davenport, Basil, intro. by. (Great Illustrated Classics). N.D. Dodd Mead & Co.
--Lorna Doone. Edwards, Lionel Dalhousie Robertson (1878-), illus. (Children's Illus. Classics). 1951. Dutton.
--Lorna Doone. Jones, Olive, ed. Baynes, Pauline Diana (1922-), illus. LC 77-106510. (Illus.). 215 p. 23cm. (Lifetime library). 1970. American Education Publications.
--Lorna Doone. Key, Alexander Hill (1904-1979), illus. N.D. Scott Foresman & Co.
--Lorna Doone. Lynne, Broom, illus. (The Macdonald Illustrated Ser.). N.D. Coward-McCann.
--Lorna Doone. Strong, L. A. G., intro. by. (Collins New Classics). N.D. William Collins Sons & Co.
--Lorna Doone: A Romance of Exmoor. N.D. G.P. Putnam's Sons.
--Lorna Doone: A Romance of Exmoor. 454p (Pub. by George Munro). (gr. 8-12). 1981. (ISBN 0-86649-036-1). Twentieth Century.
Blackmore, Vivian, retold by.
--Why Corn Is Golden: Stories about Plants. Martinez-Ostos, Susana LC 82-17280. (Illus.). (gr. k-3). 1984. (ISBN 0-316-54820-0). Little.
Blackstock, C.
--Foggy, Foggy Dew and Dewey Death. 220p. 1959. British Book Centre Inc.
Blackstock, Josephine
--Island on the Beam. LC 44-1341. 4 p. l., 3-221 p. incl. front., illus. 21 cm. 1944. G. P. Putnam's Sons.
--Rue Plays the Game: A Story for Young People. LC 48-5398. 215 p. 20 cm. 1948. G. P. Putnam's Sons.
--Songs for Sixpence: A Story About John Newbery. Bower, Maurice L., illus. LC 55-7507. (Illus.). 158 p. 25cm. 1955. Follett Pub. Co.
--Wings for Nikias: A Story of the Greece of Today. Busoni, Rafaello (1900-1962), illus. Diamontopoulos, Cimon, frwd. by. LC 42-23977. 181 front., illus. 23c. 1942. G. P. Putnam's Sons.
Blackwell, Bunyan
--Tales From the Brush Country. N.D. Naylor Company.
Blackwell, Etta M, ed.
--A Child's Verses for the Seasons: An Anthology of Verse Written by Elementary Grade Students. 41 p. illus. 21 cm. c.1964. Carlton Press.
Blackwell, Muriel Fontenot (1929-)
--The Dream Lives On. LC 83-73865. c.1984. (ISBN 0-8054-4808-X). Broadman Press.
--Peter, the Prince of Apostles. Karch, Paul, illus. LC 76-382762. (Illus.). 48 p. 24cm. (Biblearn series). c.1976. (ISBN 0-8054-4227-8). Broadman Press.
--The Secret Dream. Hester, Ronald, illus. LC 80-70406. (Illus.). 127 p. 20cm. c.1981. (ISBN 0-8054-4804-7). Broadman Press.
Blackwood, Algernon, et al. (1869-1951)
--Spine-Chillers: Unforgettable Tales of Terror. Elwood, Roger (1943-) & Goldsmith, Howard (1943-), eds. LC 77-16887. viii, 396 p. 22cm. c.1978. (ISBN 0-385-09720-4). (ISBN 0-385-09722-0). Doubleday.
Blackwood, Algernon (1869-1951)
--Best Ghost Stories. Bleiler, E. F., intro. by. N.D. (ISBN 0-8446-5006-4). Peter Smith Publisher, Inc.
--Best Ghost Stories of Algernon Blackwood. Bleiler, E. F., intro. by. 366p. 1974. (ISBN 0-486-22977-7). Dover Books.
--The Education of Uncle Paul. N.D. Henry Holt.
--The Education of Uncle Paul. (Folk Lore and Fairy Tales). (MacMillan Bks. For Boys And Girls). (gr. 4-6). N.D. MacMillan Bks.
--Pan's Garden. (Fiction). (MacMillan Bks. for Boys & Girls). (gr. 7-9). N.D. MacMillan Bks.
--A Prisoner in Fairyland: The Book That "Uncle Paul" Wrote. LC 13-15686. 5 p. l., 506 p 20 cm. 1913. The Macmillan Company.
--Sambo and Snitch. Teago, Audrey, illus. LC 27-27965. 89, l p. inci. col. mounted front., illus. 25 cm. 1927. D. Appleton and Company.
Blackwood, E. J., ed.
--To Mexico with Scott. N.D. Harvard University Press.
Blackwood, Gladys Rourke
--Whistle for Cindy. Blackwood, Gladys Rourke, illus. LC 52-14746. unpaged. illus. 24 cm. 1952. A. Whitman.
Bladen, Elizabeth S.
--Water Waif. N.D. Claxton, Remsen, & Haffelfinger.
Blades, Ann Sager, jt. auth. see Waterton, Betty Marie.
Blades, Ann Sager (1947-)
--A Boy of Tache. (Illus.). 1977. Tundra.
--A Boy of Tache. Blades, Ann Sager (1947-), illus. LC 74-77407. (Illus.). 19 p. 1973. (ISBN 0-912766-10-7). Tundra Books.
--Mary of Mile Eighteen. Blades, Ann Sager (1947-), illus. LC 79-179430. (Illus.). 40 p. 22cm. 1971. (ISBN 0-912766-01-8). Tundra Books. **Award: (CLA).**
Bladow, Suzanne Wilson (1937-)
--The Midnight Flight of Moose, Mops, and Marvin. Mathieu, Joseph (1945-), illus. LC 75-8972. (Illus.). 40 p. 22cm. 1975. (ISBN 0-07-005535-1). (ISBN 0-07-005536-X). McGraw-Hill.
Blagden, Ola Gates
--Happyland. N.D. Christopher Publishing House.
Blain, Mary E, adapted by see Sewell, Anna.
Blaine, John, pseud., see Goodwin, Harold Leland.
Blaine, John, pseud. (1914-)
--The Blue Ghost Mystery. Goodwin, Harold Leland. Harkins, Peter J.. LC 60-327. 181p. illus. 20cm. (His A Rick Brant science-adventure story 15). 1960. Grosset & Dunlap.
--The Boy Scouts on a Submarine. Goodwin, Harold Leland. Harkins, Peter J.. LC 19-4518. 2 p. l., 3-235 p. front. 19 cm. c.1918. The Saalfield Publishing Company.
--Caves of Fear. Goodwin, Harold Leland. Harkins, Peter J.. (gr. 6-10). N.D. (ISBN 0-448-08808-8). G&D.
--Danger Below!. Goodwin, Harold Leland. Harkins, Peter J.. LC 68-26152. (Illus.). 178 p. 19cm. (His A Rick Brant science-adventure story, 23). 1968. Grosset & Dunlap.
--Deadly Dutchman. Goodwin, Harold Leland. Harkins, Peter J.. (Rick Brant Ser). (gr. 4-8). 1967. (ISBN 0-448-08822-3). G&D.
--The Egyptian Cat Mystery. Goodwin, Harold Leland. Harkins, Peter J.. LC 61-11957. 182p. illus. 20cm. (Rick Brant science-adventure story 16). 1961. Grosset & Dunlap.
--The Electronic Mind Reader. Goodwin, Harold Leland. Harkins, Peter J.. LC 57-136117. 214p. illus. 20 cm. (Rick Brant science-adventure story 12). 1957. Grosset & Dunlap.
--The Flaming Mountain. Goodwin, Harold Leland. Harkins, Peter J.. LC 62-13355. 172p. illus. 20cm. (His A Rick Brant science-adventure story. 17). 1962. Grosset & Dunlap.
--The Flying Stingaree. Goodwin, Harold Leland. Harkins, Peter J.. LC 63-1034. 176 p. illus. 20 cm. (A Rick Brant science-adventure story, 18). 1963. Grosset & Dunlap.
--The Golden Skull. Goodwin, Harold Leland. Harkins, Peter J.. LC 54-103935. 214p. illus. 20cm. (Rick Brant science-adventure story 10). 1954. Grosset & Dunlap.
--The Lost City. Goodwin, Harold Leland. Harkins, Peter J.. LC 47-1072. vi p., 1 l., 209 p. incl. front. 19 1/2 cm. 1947. Grosset & Dunlap.
--One Hundred Fathoms Under. Goodwin, Harold Leland. Harkins, Peter J.. LC 47-11158. vi, 209 p. maps. 20 cm. 1947. Grosset & Dunlap.
--The Phantom Shark. Goodwin, Harold Leland. Harkins, Peter J.. LC 49-2094. viii, 206 p. illus. 20 cm. (Rick Brant science-adventure story). 1949. Grosset & Dunlap.
--The Pirates of Shan. Goodwin, Harold Leland. Harkins, Peter J.. LC 59-16078. 181p. illus. 20cm. (A Rick Brant science-adventure story 14). 1959, c.1958. Grosset & Dunlap.
--Rocket Jumper. Goodwin, Harold Leland. Harkins, Peter J.. LC 66-11319. 177p. illus. 20cm. (His A Rick Brant sci.-adventure story; 8821). c.1966. Grosset.
--The Rocket's Shadow. Goodwin, Harold Leland. Harkins, Peter J.. LC 47-1071. vi p., 1 l., 209 p. incl. front. 19 1/2 cm. 1947. Grosset & Dunlap.
--The Ruby Ray Mystery. Goodwin, Harold Leland. Harkins, Peter J.. LC 64-2158. 176 p. illus. 20 cm. (His A Rick Brant science-adventure story, 19). 1964. Brosset & Dunlap.
--The Scarlet Lake Mystery. Goodwin, Harold Leland. Harkins, Peter J.. LC 58-146501. 184p. illus. 20cm. (Rick Brant science-adventure story 13). 1958. Grosset & Dunlap.
--Sea Gold. Goodwin, Harold Leland. Harkins, Peter J.. LC 47-3785. vi, 2, 214 p. incl. front., illus. (plan) 19 1/2 cm. (gr. 6-10). 1947. (ISBN 0-448-08803-7). Grosset & Dunlap.
--Smugglers' Reef. Goodwin, Harold Leland. Harkins, Peter J.. LC 51-90. vii, 211 p. front. 20 cm. (Rick Brant science-adventure story). (gr. 7-11). 1950. Grosset & Dunlap.
--Stairway to Danger. Goodwin, Harold Leland. Harkins, Peter J.. LC 52-10237. 210 p. illus. 20 cm. (Rick Brant Science-Adventure Story ;9). 1952. Grosset & Dunlap.
--The Veiled Raiders. Goodwin, Harold Leland. Harkins, Peter J.. LC 65-13777. 178p. illus. 20cm. (His Rick Brant sci.-adventure story, 20). c.1965. Grosset.
--The Wailing Octopus. Goodwin, Harold Leland. Harkins, Peter J.. LC 56-136344. 209p. illus. 20cm. (Rick Brant science-adventure story 11). 1956. Grosset & Dunlap.
--The Whispering Box Mystery. Goodwin, Harold Leland. Harkins, Peter J.. LC 48-6950. vi, 216 p. illus. 20 cm. (Rick Brant Science-Adventure Story). 1948. Grosset & Dunlap.
Blaine, Margery Kay (1937-)
--Dvora's Journey. Lisowski, Gabriel (1946-), illus. LC 78-26349. (Illus.). 126 p. 22cm. c.1976. (ISBN 0-03-048306-9). Holt, Rinehart, and Winston.
--The Terrible Thing That Happened at Our House. Wallner, John C. (1945-), illus. LC 80-15280. p. cm. 1980, c.1975. (ISBN 0-590-07780-5). Four Winds Press.
--The Terrible Thing That Happened at Our House. Wallner, John C. (1945-), illus. LC 74-12288. (Illus.). 33 p. 26cm. 1975. (ISBN 0-8193-0781-5). (ISBN 0-8193-0781-5). Parents' Magazine Press. **Award: (ALA).**
Blair, Al
--Moosewhopper: A Juicy, Moosey Min-Min-Minnesota Burger Tale. 3rd ed. McMurray, Chuck, illus. LC 83-61092. (Illus.). 32p. 1983. (ISBN 0-930366-04-2). Northcountry Pub.
Blair, Alan, tr. see Hogstrand, Olle.
Blair, Anne Denton
--Arthur, the White House Mouse. 1st ed. Spandorf, Lily, illus. LC 75-27472. (Illus.). 25 p. 24cm. c.1975. Media/America.
--Hurrah for Arthur!. A Mount Vernon Birthday Party. 1st ed. Watson, Carol Stuart, illus. LC 82-10636. (Illus.). 56 p. 25cm. c.1982. (ISBN 0-932020-15-1). Seven Locks Press.
--Where's Rachel?. Another Adventure of Arthur, the White House Mouse. Watson, Carol Stuart, illus. LC 78-12953. p. cm. 1978. (ISBN 0-87491-264-4). Acropolis Books.
Blair, Bruce Van
--Eli and the Tiger. N.D. Vantage Press Inc.
Blair, Dorothea W
--Roger: a Most Unusual Rabbit. Knight, Hilary (1926-), illus. LC 58-5614. 63p. illus. 21cm. 1958. Lippincott.
Blair, Eric Hugh see Orwell, George, pseud.
Blair, Irene
--Bill's Birthday Surprise. Hoecker, Hazel, illus. LC 55-17931. unpaged. illus. 17 cm. (Tell-a-tale books. 966). c.1954. Whitman Pub. Co.
Blair, Mary Robinson (1911-)
--Up & Down. Blair, Mary Robinson (1911-), illus. LC 64-9792. 1 v. chiefly col. illus. 31cm. (A Happy Book). 1964. Golden Press.
Blair, Matilda, compiled by.
--The Golden Glow Speaker: Little Verses for Little Boys. LC 7-29734. 20cm. 96p. 1906. McLoughlin Brothers.
--Little Plays For Little Players, Ed. 152 p. col. front., col. plates, diagr. 19 1/2 cm. c.1907. McLoughlin Brothers.
--McLoughlin's Christmas Annual for Young People (and Some Older Ones). Containing Christmas in Story and Song, As Well As Indoor Amusements for the Christmas Tide and Winter Evenings. Christmas Annual LC 5-35417. 192 p. col. front., illus. (part col.) 26 1/2 x 22 cm. c.1905. McLoughlin Brothers.
--The Pansy Speaker. LC 7-29735. 20cm. 96p. (Little Verses for Little Girls). 1906. McLoughlin Brothers.
Blair, Olive Tinker (1892-)
--What Next Gerty. Grace, Helen, illus. LC 56-12936. 48p. col. illus. 24cm. 1956. Comet Press Books.
Blair, Perry
--The Easter Rainbow. Reed, Susan, illus. (Illus.). 24p. (Orig.). 1st U.S. edition. (gr. k-6). 1981. (ISBN 0-9607782-0-9). Blair Pub.
Blair, Peter Hunter
--The Coming of Pout. Hyman, Trina Schart (1939-), illus. LC 69-10652. (Illus.). 158 p. 22cm. 1969. Little, Brown.
Blair, Ruth Van Ness (1912-)
--A Bear Can Hibernate-Why Can't I?. Foster, Celeste K., illus. LC 76-156809. (Illus.). 32 p. 29cm. 1972. (ISBN 0-513-01155-2). Denison.
--Mary's Monster. Cuffari, Richard (1925-1978), illus. LC 74-16651. (Illus.). 66p. (A Science Discovery Book). (gr. 2-6). 1975. (ISBN 0-698-20304-6, Coward). Putnam Pub Group.
--Puddle Duck. Rice, Elizabeth (1913-), illus. LC 66-12936. 48p. col. illus. 24cm. (gr. k-3). 1966. (ISBN 0-8114-7551-4). Steck.
--Willa-Willa, the Wishful Witch. Talarczyk, June, illus. LC 72-81189. (Illus.). 56 p. 1972. (ISBN 0-513-01224-9). Denison.
Blair, Susie
--Easter Pony. LC 63-9071. unpaged. illus. 21 x 24 cm. 1963. Ariel Books.
--Show Ring: Easter Pony Grows Up. (Illus.). (gr. 1-4). 1965. FS&G.
--The Show Ring: Easter Pony Grows up. Kohara, Tommy T, photos by. LC 65-193357. 1v. (unpaged) illus. 21x24cm. (Ariel bks.). c.1965. Farrar.
Blair, Walter (1900-)
--Davy Crockett: Frontier Hero. Wiese, Kurt (1887-1974), illus. N.D. Coward-McCann Inc.
--Mark Twain And Huck Finn. 1960. University Of California Press.
--Tall Tale America. Rounds, Glen Harold (1906-), illus. (Illus.). (gr. 4-9). 1944. (ISBN 0-698-30350-4, Coward). Putnam Pub Group.
Blaisdell, Albert Franklin
--Stories of the Civil War. N.D. Lothrop Lee & Shepard Co.
Blaisdell, E. Warde
--The Animals at the Fair. LC 2-23860. 47p. col. illus. 22 1/2 x 30 1/2cm. 1902. R. H. Russell.
Blaisdell, Elinore (1904-)
--Falcon, Fly Back. Blaisdell, Elinore (1904-), illus. LC 39-29486. 5 p. l., 13-177, 1 p. illus., plates (1 double) 24 cm. c.1939. J. Messner, Inc.
Blaisdell, Mary Frances, jt. auth. see McDonald, Etta Austin Blaisdell, Mrs.
Blaisdell, Mary Frances (1874-)
--Bunny Rabbit's Diary. Rev. ed. Jauss, Anne Marie (1907-), illus. LC 59-15821. 91p. illus. 21cm. 1960. Little, Brown.
--Bunny Rabbit's Diary. Kerr, George F., illus. 19cm. 103p. 1915. Little, Brown, & Co.
--Cherry Tree Children. Jauss, Anne Marie (1907-), illus. LC 57-841921. (Illus.). Repr. of 1912 ed. (gr. k-3). 1957. (ISBN 0-316-09922-8). Little.
--Pine Tree Playmates. LC 25-8017. (Illus.). 19cm. 126p. 1925. B. H. Sanborn & Co.
--Pretty Polly Flinders. Wireman, Eugenie M., illus. LC 15-5296. x. 188 p. col. front., illus., col. plates. 19 x 15 1/2 cm. 1914. Little, Brown, and Company.
--Tommy Tinker's Book. Nosworthy, Florence England, illus. LC 11-35889. 19cm. 177p. 1911. Little, Brown, & Co.
--Twilight Town. Adams, Henrietta S., illus. 19cm. 173p. 1913. Little, Brown, & Co.

Blaisdell, Mary Frances (1874-) & McDonald, Etta Austin Blaisdell, Mrs. (1872-)
--Mother Goose Children. LC 16-269918. 111 p. incl. col. front., col. illus. 19 cm. 1916. Little, Brown, and Company.
Blaisdell, S. Lillian (1869-) & Austin, Isabella
--Story Friends. LC 3-24264. (Illus.). 19cm. 134p. (The Hawthorne Readers). 1903. Globe School Book Co.
Blake, Emily Calvin
--Marcia of the Little Home. LC 11-23061. 5 p. l., 268, 1 p. front., plates. 19 1/2 cm. 1911. D. Appleton and Company.
Blake, Emma Turner
--The King of the Trail. Salg, Bert N., illus. LC 28-104239. 4 p. l., 285 p. incl. illus., plates. front. 19 1/2 cm. 1928. I. Washburn.
Blake, Forrester
--Riding the Mustang Trail. N.D. Charles Scribner's Sons.
Blake, George (1893-)
--David and Joanna. LC 36-22619. 3 p. l., 345 p. 19 1/2 cm. c.1936. H. Holt and Company.
Blake, Gladys
--At Bow View. LC 26-14920. 251 P. 19cm. 1926. D. Appleton and Company.
--Belinda in Old New Orleans. Stein, Harve (1904-), illus. vi. p., 1 l., 295, 1 p. front., illus. 19 1/2 cm. 1932. D. Appleton and Company.
--Cornelia's Colony. Doane, Pelagie (1906-1966), illus. LC 31-506952. 4 p. l., 257, 1 p. front., illus. 19 1/2 cm. 1931. D. Appleton and Company.
--Deborah's Discovery: A Mystery Tale of Old Virginia. Beebe, Robb (1891-), illus. LC 33-4545. 4 p. l., 280, 1 p. front., illus. 20 cm. 1933. D. Appleton and Company.
--Dona Isabella's Adventures. LC 28-19624. 3 p. l., 222, 1 p. front. 19 1/2 cm. 1928. D. Appleton and Company.
--Doris Decides. LC 27-21889. 3 p. l., 245, 1 p. front. 19 1/2 cm. 1927. D. Appleton and Company.
--Even Sara. LC 30-5248. 3 p. l., 230, 1 p. front. 19 1/2 cm. 1930. D. Appleton & Company.
--The Faraway Mystery. Stein, Harve (1904-), illus. LC 35-131692. ix. 274 p. incl. front., illus. 20 cm. 1935. D. Appleton-Century Company, Incorporated.
--The Fortunate Shipwreck. Price, Norman Mills (1877-1951), illus. LC 36-5254. x p., 1 l., 256 p. incl. front., illus. 20 cm. 1936. D. Appleton-Century Company, Incorporated.
--Henrietta and the Governor. Sherman, Theresa (1916-), illus. LC 64-18995. 126 p. illus. 24 cm. 1964. Morrow.
--The Mysterious Tutor. LC 25-4853. 3 p. l., 253, 1 p. front. 19 1/2 cm. 1925. D. Appleton and Company.
--A Mystery for Margery: In the Home of Andrew Jackson. Parks, Elise, illus. LC 40-30533. viii p., 1 l., 266 p. incl. front., illus. 20 cm. 1940. D. Appleton-Century Company, Incorporated.
--The Mystery of the Silver Chain. Birch, Reginald Bathurst (1856-1943), illus. LC 39-4498. viii p., 2 l., 266 p. incl. front., illus., plates. 20 cm. 1939. D. Appleton-Century Company, Incorporated.
--The Old King's Treasure. LC 26-5383. 3 p. l., 252, 1 p. front. 19 1/2 cm. 1926. D. Appleton and Company.
--The Poindexter Pride. 3 p. l., 269, 1 p. front. 19 1/2 cm. 1929. D. Appleton & Company.
--Sally Goes to Court. Stein, Harve (1904-), illus. LC 37-19879. 5 p. l., 270 p. incl. front., illus 20 cm. 1937. D. Appleton-Century Company, Incorporated.
--The Scratches on the Glass. LC 27-3941. 3 p. l., 246, 1 p. front. 19 cm. 1927. D. Appleton and Company.
Blake, Isabel M
--Fez and Turban Tales. LC 20-13701. viii. 9-115 p. incl. front. plates. 19 1/2 cm. c.1920. Interchurch Press.
Blake, James Vila (1842-)
--Legends from Storyland. (Illus.). 94p. N.D. Charles H. Kerr & Co.
Blake, Katherine, pseud., see Walter, Dorothy Blake.
Blake, Katherine Devereux (1858-) & Alexander, Georgia, eds.
--Graded Poetry Readers. 1st-8th Years. LC 6-14536. 7 v. 17 1/2 cm. 1905. Maynard, Merrill, & Co.
Blake, Katherine, pseud. (1908-)
--My Sister my Friend. Walter, Dorothy Blake. 1965. Reynal & Company Inc.
Blake, Louisa Dumaresque
--Children's Thoughts: In Song and Story. De Meza, Wilson, illus. LC 14-6560. 60 p. illus. 24 1/2 cm. 1883. Cassell & Company, Limited.
Blake, M. M.
--When the Century was Young. (Illus.). N.D. Dana Estes & Co.
Blake, Mrs.
--Cecile Raye. N.D. George Routledge & Sons.
Blake, Olive
--The Grape Jelly Mystery. Goodman, Joan E., illus. LC 78-18040. (Illus.). 46 p. 23cm. (Troll easy-to-read mystery). c.1979. (ISBN 0-89375-096-4). Troll Associates.
--Mystery of the Lost Letter. Kossin, Sandy (1926-), illus. LC 78-18037. (Illus.). 48 p. 23cm. (Troll easy-to-read mystery). c.1979. (ISBN 0-89375-093-X). Troll Associates.
--Mystery of the Lost Pearl. Parker, Edward, illus. LC 78-60121. (Illus.). 48 p. 23cm. (Troll easy-to-read mystery). c.1979. (ISBN 0-89375-086-7). Troll Associates.
Blake, Pamela
--Peep-Show: A Book of Rhymes. Blake, Pamela, illus. LC 72-80750. (Illus.). 32p. (ps-3). 1973. (ISBN 0-02-710700-0). Macmillan.
Blake, Paul
--Expelled: A Story of Eastcote School. (The Gordon Library). N.D. Frederick Warne & Co.
Blake, Quentin, jt. auth. see Yeoman, John.
Blake, Quentin (1932-), ed. see Nash, Frederic Ogden.
Blake, Quentin (1932-)
--Mister Magnolia. Blake, Quentin (1932-), illus. 32p. (gr. k-3). 1980. (ISBN 0-224-01612-1, Pub. by Chatto Bodley Jonathan). Merrimack Pub Cir. **Award: (KGM).**
--Patrick. Blake, Quentin (1932-), illus. LC 69-17911. (Illus.). 32 p. 27cm. 1969, c.1968. H. Z. Walck.
--Quentin Blake's Nursery Rhyme Book. Blake, Quentin (1932-), illus. (Illus.). 32p. (gr. k-3). 1984. (ISBN 0-06-020533-4, HarpJ). (ISBN 0-06-020532-6). Har-Row.
--Snuff. Blake, Quentin (1932-), illus. LC 73-5954. (Illus.). 32 p. 28cm. 1973. (ISBN 0-397-31469-8). Lippincott.
--The Story of the Dancing Frog. Blake, Quentin (1932-), illus. LC 84-12222. (Illus.). 32p. (ps-3). 1985. (ISBN 0-394-97033-0). (ISBN 0-394-87033-6). Knopf.
Blake, Quentin (1932-) & Yeoman, John, eds.
--The Improbable Book of Records. Blake, Quentin (1932-), illus. LC 76-4466. p. cm. 1976. (ISBN 0-689-30535-4). Atheneum.
Blake, Vinton E.
--The Dalzells of Daisydown. N.D. D. Lothrop Co.
Blake, Vivienne see Vivienne, pseud.
Blake, Vivienne
--Hop, Skippy and Jump. Vivienne, pseud. LC 47-5589. 32 p. col. illus. 17 cm. (Tell-a-tale books). c.1947. Whitman Pub. Co.
--Mrs. Duck's Lovely Day. Blake, Vivienne, illus. LC 55-8200. unpaged. illus. 17cm. (Rand McNally junior elf book, 691). c.1955. Rand McNally.
Blake, W. H., tr. see Hemon, Louis.
Blake, William James (1894-1968)
--The Painter and Lady. 1939. Simon and Schuster.
Blake, William (1757-1827)
--Grain of Sand. Manning, Rosemary (1911-), ed. Blake, William (1757-1827), illus. (Illus.). (gr. 4-6). N.D. (ISBN 0-531-01683-8). Watts.
--Land of Dreams. Bianco, Pamela (1906-), ed. Bianco, Pamela (1906-), illus. (MacMillan Bks. for Boys & Girls). (gr. 4-6). N.D. MacMillan Bks.
--Poems of William Blake. Munson, Amelia H., selected by. 1964. Crowell.
--Songs of Innocence. Jones, Harold (1904-), illus. 1961. Barnes.
Blakeley, Peggy, tr. see Iguchi, Bunshu.
Blakely, Elizabeth Seal
--Children of the Swamp. Bliss, Madge Deveneau, illus. LC 35-5118. 143 p. incl. col. front., plates. 19 1/2 cm. c.1934. Pioneer Publishing Co.
--Fairy Starlight and the Dolls. Perkins, Lucy Fitch, Mrs. (1865-1937), illus. LC 44-29956. 213 p. incl. illus., plates, front. 19 cm. 1896. A. C. McClurg and Company.
Blakely, Peggy, tr. see Aichinger, Helga.
Blaker, Richard
--The Jefferson Secret: A Mystery with Love and Without a Murder. LC 29-14757. 3 p. l., 274 p. 19 1/2 cm. 1929. Doubleday, Doran & Company, Inc.
--The Needle-Watcher. LC 32-21194. 6 p. l., 3-501 p. 20 1/2 cm. 1932. Doubleday, Doran & Company, Inc.
Blakey, Madge Beattie & Collver, Carol
--Calypso Island. Fiorentino, Al, illus. LC 70-96697. (Illus.). 112 p. 24cm. 1970. (ISBN 0-664-32463-0). Westminster Press.
Blanc, Lucille Le see Le Blanc, Lucille.
Blance, Ellen, et al. (1931-)
--Monster Books: Set 1, 12 bks. Reynolds, Quentin, illus. Incl. Monster Comes to the City. (ISBN 0-8372-0826-2); Monster Looks for a House. (ISBN 0-8372-0827-0); Monster Cleans His House. (ISBN 0-8372-0828-9); Monster Looks for a Friend. (ISBN 0-8372-0829-7); Monster on the Bus. (ISBN 0-8372-0830-0); Monster Meets Lady Monster. (ISBN 0-8372-0831-9); Monster Goes to the Museum. (ISBN 0-8372-0832-7); Monster Goes to School. (ISBN 0-8372-0833-5); Monster at School. (ISBN 0-8372-0834-3); Monster & the Magic Umbrella. (ISBN 0-8372-0835-1); Monster Has a Party. (ISBN 0-8372-0836-X); Monster Goes to the Zoo. (ISBN 0-8372-0837-8); Monster & the Toy Sale. (ISBN 0-8372-2133-1). (Avail. in Spanish). (Illus.). (ps-3). 1973. (ISBN 0-8372-0300-7, 300). (ISBN 0-8372-0301-5, 301). Bowmar-Noble.
Blance, Ellen (1931-) & Cook, Ann (1940-)
--Lady Monster Has a Plan. LC 76-3908. (Illus.). 37 p. 23cm. (Monster book). c.1976. (ISBN 0-8372-2135-8). Bowmar.
Blanchard, Amy Ella (1856-1926)
--An Independant Daughter. N.D. J.B. Lippincott.
--The Awakening of Martha: A Story. Merrill, Frank Thayer (1848-), illus. LC 23-183713. 306 p. incl. front. 19 1/2 cm. c.1923. W. A. Wilde Company.
--Baby Blossom. Waugh, Ida, illus. (No. 2). 1888. R Worthington.
--Because of Conscience: Being a Novel Relating to the Adventures of Certain Huguenots in Old New York. LC 1-25694. 355 p. incl. front 20 cm. 1901. J. B. Lippincott Company.
--Becky, 1 of 25 vols. (Illus.). (New Primary Lib.: No. 15). N.D. Set. A. I. Bradley & Co.'s Pubs.
--Becky: A Story. Merrill, Frank Thayer (1848-), illus. LC 23-2470. 304 p. front. 19 1/2 cm. c.1922. W. A. Wilde Company.
--Betty of Wye. LC 6-14902. 258 p. front., plates. 19 cm. 1897. J. B. Lippincott Company.
--Betty of Wye, 1 of 11 vols. (Illus.). (Popular Bks for Girls). 1900. Set. J B Lippincott.
--Bonnie Bairns. Waugh, Ida, illus. (Illus.). 48p. (No. 1). 1888. R Worthington.
--Bonny Lesley of the Border. 331p. (The Pioneer Ser.). 1910. W. A. Wilde Co.
--Bonny Lesley: Of the Border. Stecher, William Frederick (1864-), illus. LC 4-24574. 331 p. front., 4 pl. 20 cm. (On cover: The pioneer series). 1904. W. A. Wilde Company.
--The Camp Fire Girls of Brightwood. Merrill, Frank Thayer (1848-), illus. 20cm. 309p. 1915. W. A. Wilde Co.
--A Daughter of Freedom. New ed. 312p. (Revolutionary Ser.). 1910. W. A. Wilde Co.
--A Daughter of Freedom: A Story of the Latter Period of the War for Independence. Waugh, Ida, illus. LC 4973. 312 p. front., plated 19 cm. 1900. W. A. Wilde Company.
--A Dear Little Girl. (Dear Little Girl Ser.). N.D. George W Jacobs.
--A Dear Little Girl. N.D. George W Jacobs.
--A Dear Little Girl. (Illus.). (Little Maid Ser.). N.D. Hurst and Company.
--A Dear Little Girl at School. LC 10-30734. 4 p. l., 248 p. col. front., col. plates. 20 cm. 1910. G. W. Jacobs & Company.
--A Dear Little Girl's Summer Holidays. LC 11-22023. 4 p. l., 283 p. col. front., col. plates. 20 cm. 1911. G. W. Jacobs & Company.
--A Dear Little Girl's Thanksgiving Holidays. LC 12-17661. 246 p. col. front., col. plates. 20 cm. (Her The "dear little girl" series). 1912. G. W. Jacobs & Company.
--Dimple Dallas. (Little Maid Ser.). N.D. George W Jacobs.
--Dimple Dallas. (Illus.). (Little Maid Ser.). N.D. Hurst and Company.
--Dimple Dallas. (The Vacation Bks.). (gr. 2-7). N.D. Penn Publishing Co.
--Dimple Dallas. Waugh, Ida, illus. LC 1-29012. 12cm. 194p. 1900. G. W. Jacobs & Co.
--Elizabeth, Betsy and Bess. (Illus.). 284p. N.D. W. A. Wilde Co.
--Elizabeth, Betsy, and Bess. Kennedy, J. W. Ferguson, illus. LC 13-26566. 284 p. incl. col. front. 19 1/2 cm. c.1913. W. A. Wilde Company.
--Elizabeth, Betsy, and Bess--Schoolmates. Merrill, Frank Thayer (1848-), illus. LC 15-12827. 306 p. col. front. 19 1/2 cm. c.1914. W. A. Wilde Company.
--Elizabeth, Betsy and Bess: Schoolmates. (Illus.). 320p. N.D. W. A. Wilde Co.
--An Everyday Girl: A Story. Merrill, Frank Thayer (1848-), illus. LC 24-27649. 5, 9-320 p. front. 19 1/2 cm. c.1924. W. A. Wilde Company.
--Fagots and Flames. 306p. N.D. W. A. Wilde.
--The Four Corners. LC 6-35454. 387 p. front., 4 pl. 20 1/2 cm. (Corner series). 1906. G. W. Jacobs & Company.
--The Four Corners. (The Outdoor Bks.). N.D. Penn Publishing Co.
--The Four Corners Abroad. LC 9-22943. 417 p. front., plates 20 cm. (Corner series). 1909. G. W. Jacobs & Company.
--The Four Corners Abroad. (The Outdoor Bks.). N.D. Penn Publishing Co.
--The Four Corners at College. LC 11-24974. 352 p. front., plates. 20 1/2 cm. 1911. G. W. Jacobs & Company.
--The Four Corners at College. (The Outdoor Bks.). N.D. Penn Publishing Co.
--The Four Corners at School. LC 8-346069. 410 p. front., 4 pl. 20 1/2 cm. (Corner series). 1906. G. W. Jacobs & Company.
--The Four Corners at School. (The Outdoor Bks.). N.D. Penn Publishing Co.
--The Four Corners in California. LC 7-30993. 341 p. front., 4 pl. 20 1/2 cm. (Corner series). 1907. G. W. Jacobs & Company.
--The Four Corners in California. (The Outdoor Bks.). N.D. Penn Publishing Co.
--The Four Corners in Camp. LC 10-22724. 379 p. 5 pl. 20 1/2 cm. (Corner series). 1910. G. W. Jacobs & Company.
--The Four Corners in Camp. (The Outdoor Bks.). N.D. Penn Publishing Co.
--The Four Corners in Egypt. N.D. George W Jacobs.
--The Four Corners in Egypt. (The Outdoor Bks.). N.D. Penn Publishing Co.
--The Four Corners in Japan. LC 12-21732. 377 p. front., plates. 20 cm. (Corner series). 1912. G. W. Jacobs & Company.
--The Four Corners in Japan. (The Outdoor Bks.). N.D. Penn Publishing Co.
--From Tenderfoot to Golden Eaglet: A Girl Scout Story. Merrill, Frank Thayer (1848-), illus. LC 22-652361. 7, 11-317 p. front. 20 cm. c.1921. W. A. Wilde Company.
--A Frontier Knight. Stecher, William Frederick (1864-), illus. LC 5-32867. 20cm. 339p. (The Pioneer Ser.). 1905. W. A. Wilde Co.
--A Frontier Knight: A Story of Early Texan Border Life. 339p. (The Pioneer Ser.). 1910. W. A. Wilde & Co.
--A Gentle Pioneer: Being the Story of the Early Days in the New West. Waugh, Ida, illus. LC 3-22814. 320 p. front., 4 pl. 20 cm. 1903. W. A. Wilde Company.
--A Gentle Power. (Illus.). 339p. (The Pioneer Ser). 1910. W. A. Wilde Co.
--The Girl Lady: The Amy E. Blanchard Ser. N.D. A. L. Burt Company.
--A Girl of Seventy-Six. N.D. Frederick Warne & Co.
--A Girl of Seventy-Six. (Revolutionary Ser.). 1910. W. A. Wilde Co.
--A Girl of Seventy-Six. Waugh, Ida, illus. 331 p. front., plates 20 cm. c.1898. W. A. Wilde & Company.
--A Girl Scout of Red Rose Troop. Copeland, Charles, illus. LC 19-7918. 7, 11-323 p. incl. col. front., plates 19 1/2 cm. c.1918. W. A. Wilde Company.
--Girls Together, 1 of 11 vols. (Illus.). (Popular Bks for Girls). 1900. Set. J B Lippincott.
--Girls Together. Waugh, Ida, illus. LC 6-149012. 4 p. l., 7-259 p. front., plates. 18 1/2 cm. 1896. J. B. Lippincott Company.
--The Glad Lady. LC 10-14938. 297 p. front., plates. 21 cm. c.1910. D. Eates & Company.
--Her Very Best. Winner, Margaret F., illus. 271 p. front., plates. 19 cm. 1901. J. B. Lippincott Company.
--A Heroine of Eighteen-Twelve: A Maryland Romance. 335p. (Revolutionary Ser.). 1910. W. A. Wilde co.
--A Heroine of Eighteen-Twelve: A Maryland Romance. Waugh, Ida, illus. LC 1-23644. 335 p. front., plates 19 1/2 cm. c.1901. W. A. Wilde Company.
--The House that Jack Built. N.D. W A Wilde Co.
--Ida Waugh's Alphabet Book for Little Ones: Who, If They Look, Will Find Their Letters in This Book. Waugh, Ida, illus. LC 15-250. 28 l. illus. 27 1/2 cm. 1888. J. B. Lippincott Company.
--In Camp with the Muscoday Campfire Girls. N.D. W. A. Wilde Co.
--In Camp with the Muskoday Camp Fire Girls. Merrill, Frank Thayer (1848-), illus. LC 18-1874. 317 p. col. front. 19 1/2 cm. c.1917. W. A. Wilde Company.
--An Independent Daughter. Stephens, Alice Barber (1858-1932), illus. 1900. J B Lippincott.
--Janet's College Career. LC 4-25101. 365 p. front., 4 pl. 20 1/2 cm. 1904. G. W. Jacobs & Co.
--A Journey of Joy. (The Amy E. Blanchard Ser.). N.D. A. L. Burt Company.
--A Journey of Joy. Bridgman, Lewis Jesse (1857-1931), illus. LC 8-16948. 306 p. front., 6 pl. 21 1/2 cm. c.1908. D. Estes & Company.
--June Duncan: A Story. Tulloch, Avis, illus. LC 26-212902. 320 p. col. front. 19 cm. c.1926. W. A. Wilde Company.
--Kittyboy's Christmas. (Lad and Lassie Series.). 1915. George W Jacobs.

--Kittyboy's Christmas. Waugh, Ida, illus. LC
98-122. 2 p. l., 7-74 p. front., plates 19 1/2
cm. 1898. G. W. Jacobs & Co.

--Little Grandmother. (Little Maid Ser.). N.D.
George W. Jacobs.

--Little Grandmother Jo. LC 5-31868. (Illus.).
20cm. 235p. 1905. G. W. Jacobs & Co.

--Little Grandmother Jo. (Illus.). (Little Maid
Ser.). N.D. Hurst and Company.

--Little Grandmother Jo. (The Vacation Bks.). (gr.
2-7). N.D. Penn Publishing Co.

--Little Maid Marian. LC 8-37359. 20cm. 235p.
1908. G. W. Jacobs & Co.

--Little Maid Marian. N.D.
George W. Jacobs.

--Little Maid Marian. (The Vacation Bks.). (gr.
2-7). N.D. Penn Publishing Co.

--A Little Maid of Picardy. Merrill, Frank Thayer
(1848-), illus. LC 20-7297. 220 p. incl. col.
front., plates. 19 1/2 cm. c1919. W. A. Wilde
Company.

--Little Miss Mouse. LC 6-37601. 230 p. col.
front., 4 col. pl. 19 1/2 cm. 1906. G. W.
Jacobs & Company.

--Little Miss Mouse. (Little Maid Ser.). N.D.
George W. Jacobs.

--Little Miss Mouse. (The Vacation Bks.). (gr.
2-7). N.D. Penn Publishing Co.

--Little Miss Oddity. (Little Maid Ser.). N.D.
George W. Jacobs.

--Little Miss Oddity. (Illus.). (Little Maid Ser.).
N.D. Hurst and Company.

--Little Miss Oddity. (The Vacation Bks.). (gr.
2-7). N.D. Penn Publishing Co.

--Little Miss Oddity. Waugh, Ida, illus. LC
2-20031. 225 p. incl. pl. front. 19 1/2 cm.
1902. G. W. Jacobs & Co.

--Little Sister Anne. LC 4-17221. 234 p. front., 4
pl. 19 1/2 cm. 1904. G. W. Jacobs &
Company.

--Little Sister Anne. (Little Maid Ser.). N.D.
George W. Jacobs.

--Little Sister Anne. (Illus.). (Little Maid Ser.).
N.D. Hurst and Company.

--Little Sister Anne. (The Vacation Bks.). (gr.
2-7). N.D. Penn Publishing Co.

--A Little Tomboy. LC 3-17234. 220 p. front., 4
pl. 19 cm. 1903. G. W. Jacobs & Company.

--A Little Tomboy. (Illus.). (Little Maid Ser.).
N.D. Hurst and Company.

--A Little Tomboy. (The Vacation Bks.). (gr. 2-7).
N.D. Penn Publishing Co.

--A Loyal Lass: A Story of the Niagara Campaign
of 1814. (Illus.). 319p. (Revolutionary Ser.).
1910. W. A. Wilde Co.

--A Loyal Lass: A Story of the Niagara Campaign
of 1814. Merrill, Frank Thayer (1848-), illus.
LC 2-20084. 319 p. front., pl. 20 cm. 1902. W.
A. Wilde Company.

--Lucky Penny of Thistle Troop: A Girl Scout
Story. Merrill, Frank Thayer (1848-), illus. LC
21-4507. 7, 11-312 p. col. front. 19 1/2 cm.
c.1920. W. A. Wilde Company.

--Mabel's Mishap. LC 1-29013. 111 p. front.,
plates 19 cm. c.1900. G. W. Jacobs & Co.

--Mabel's Mishap. 1915. George W Jacobs.

--Miss Blanchard's Library for Girls: Consisting of
Two Girls and Girls Together. N.D. J. B.
Lippincott.

--Miss Vanity. Goe, Bess, illus. 278 p. front.,
plates 19 cm. 1900. J. B. Lippincott Company.

--Mistress May. (Little Maid Ser.). N.D. George
W. Jacobs.

--Mistress May. (Illus.). (Little Maid Ser.). N.D.
Hurst and Company.

--Mistress May. (The Vacation Bks.). (gr. 2-7).
N.D. Penn Publishing Co.

--Mistress May. Waugh, Ida, illus. LC 1-24968.
231 p. front., plates 19 1/2 cm. 1901. G. W.
Jacobs & Co.

--Nancy First and Last. Stecher, William
Frederick (1864-), illus. LC 17-28760. 304 p.
col. front., plates. 20 cm. 1917. J. B.
Lippincott Company.

--On the Lawn. N.D. E P Dutton.

--Playmate Polly. LC 9-18022. 218 p. col. front.,
4 col. pl. 19 1/2 cm. 1909. G. W. Jacobs &
Company.

--Playmate Polly. (The Vacation Bks.). (gr. 2-7).
N.D. Penn Publishing Co.

--A Revolutionary Maid. 321p. (Revolutionary
Ser.). 1910. W. A. Wilde Co.

--A Revolutionary Maid: A Story of the Middle
Period of the War for Independence. Waugh,
Ida, illus. LC 99-4624. 321 p. front., plates 19
1/2 cm. c.1899. W. A. Wilde Company.

--A Sweet Little Maid. N.D. George W Jacobs.

--A Sweet Little Maid. (Illus.). (Little Maid Ser.).
N.D. Hurst and Company.

--A Sweet Little Maid. (The Vacation Bks.). (gr.
2-7). N.D. Penn Publishing Co.

--A Sweet Little Maid. Waugh, Ida, illus. LC
99-4876. 215 p. front., plates. 19 1/2 cm.
c.1899. G. W. Jacobs & Co.

--Taking a Stand. (Pastime and Adventure Ser.).
N.D. George W Jacobs.

--Taking a Stand. Waugh, Ida, illus. LC 6-14899.
4 p. l., 7-202 p. front., plates 19 1/2 cm. 1896.
G. W. Jacobs & Co.

--Talbot's Angles. (The Amy E. Blanchard Ser.).
N.D. A. L. Burt Company.

--Tangles and Curls: Or, Little Boys and Girls.
Waugh, Ida, illus. (No. 4). 1888. R
Worthington.

--Tell Me A Story. Waugh, Ida, illus. (Illus.).
(NO. 3). 1888. R Worthington.

--Three Little Cousins. LC 7-28974. 222 p. col.
front., 4 col. pl. 19 1/2 cm. 1907. G. W.
Jacobs & Company.

--Three Little Cousins. (Little Maid Ser.). N.D.
George W. Jacobs.

--Three Pretty Maids. Stephens, Alice Barber
(1858-1932), illus. LC 6-14900. 4 p. l., 7-243
p. front., plates 19 cm. 1897. J. B. Lippincott
Company.

--Thy Friend Dorothy. N.D. George W Jacobs.

--Thy Friend Dorothy. Waugh, Ida, illus. LC
Nm177. 319 p. front., plates 19 1/2 cm. 1888
G. W. Jacobs & Co.

--Twenty Little MAidens. N.D J. B. Lippincott.

--Twenty Little Maidens. Waugh, Ida, illus.
(Illus.). N.D. J. B. Lippincott.

--Two Girls, 1 of 11 vols. (Illus.). (Popular Bks for
Girls). 1900. Set. J B Lippincott.

--Two Girls. N.D. J.B. Lippincott.

--Two Girls. Waugh, Ida, illus. LC 12-31114.
20cm. 256p. 1894. J. B. Lippincott.

--Two Girls and Girls Together. 2 vols in 1.
Waugh, Ida, illus. N.D. J. B. Lippincott.

--Two Maryland Girls. LC 3-24219. 3 p. l., 367 p.
front., 4 pl. 20 1/2 cm. 1903. G. W. Jacobs &
Co.

--Wee Babies: Printed in Colours from Original
Designs. Waugh, Ida, illus. LC 15-243. 48 p.
col. front., col. illus. 27 cm. c.1882. E. P.
Dutton & Co.; Etc.; Etc.

--When Mother Was a Little Girl. Waugh, Ida,
illus. N.D. Dutton.

--Wit's End. (The Amy E. Blanchard Ser.). N.D.
A. L. Company.

--Wit's End. Bridgman, Lewis Jesse (1857-1931),
illus. LC 9-22944. 368 p. incl. front., plates. 21
1/2 cm. 1909. D. Estes & Company.

--The Wonderful Fan. LC 44-29964. 96 p. incl.
front., illus. 21 cm. 1882. E. P. Dutton &
Company.

--Worth His While. LC 1-24606. 106 p. front.,
plates. 19 1/2 cm. c.1901. G. W. Jacobs & Co.

--Worth His While. LC 1-24606. 20cm. 106p.
1901. G. W. Jacobs & Co.

--Worth His While. (Lad and Lassie Series.).
1915. Geroge W Jacobs.

Blanchard, Arlene

--The Dump Truck. Wells, Tony, illus. LC
85-1791. p. cm. 1985. (ISBN 0-394-87494-3).
(ISBN 0-394-97494-8). Random House.

Blanchard, Grace

--Phil's Happy Girlhood. (Illus.). 1910. W. A.
Wilde Co.

**Blanchard, Lucy Mansfield Blanchard, Mrs.
(1870-)**

--Carita: And How She Became a Patriotic
American. Goss, John, illus. LC 18-19577. 3 p
l., 303 p. front. plates. 20 cm. 1918. The Page
Company.

--Carita's New World. Goss, John, illus. LC
19-15731. 5 p. l., 342 p. front, plates. 20 cm.
1919. The Page Company.

--Chico: The Story of a Homing Pigeon.
(Riverside Literature Ser.). N.D. Houghton
Mifflin.

--Chico: The Story of a Homing Pigeon. Healey,
Katherine G., illus. LC 22-168811. 4 p. l., 141,
1 p. col. front., illus. 20 cm. c.1922. Houghton
Mifflin Company.

--Chico: The Story of a Homing Pigeon. New ed.
Rogers, Frances (1888-1974), illus. LC
29-14913. xxii, 164 p. front., illus., plates. 19
1/2 cm. (The Riverside Literature Series).
c.1929. Houghton Mifflin Company.

--A Little-Singing Bird. Healey, Katherine G.,
illus. LC 23-13724. 3 p. l., 122 p. col. front., 1
illus. 20 cm. c.1923. Houghton Mifflin
Company.

**Blanchard, Lucy Mansfield, Mrs., jt. auth. see
Jacobs, Caroline Elliott Hoogs, Mrs.**

Blanchette, Zelda Beth & Martin, Clyde Inez

--Around Our Village. Klapp, Bill, illus. LC
58-20194. 192p. illus. 22cm. 1958. W. S.
Benson.

Blanck, Jacob Nathaniel (1906-1974)

--Jonathan and the Rainbow. N.D. E. M. Hale
and Co.

--Jonathan and the Rainbow. Slobodkin, Louis
(1903-1975), illus. LC 48-8473. 47 p. col. illus.
27 cm. 1948. Houghton Mifflin Co.

--The King and the Noble Blacksmith. Slobodkin,
Louis (1903-1975), illus. LC 50-8842. 1950.
Houghton Mifflin Co.

Blancke, Cecil Trout

--Verses for Children. Blancke, Cecil Trout, illus.
LC 23-13307. 80 p. col. front., illus. 23 1/2
cm. 1922. The Westminster Press.

Blancke, Wendell W.

--Juarez of Mexico. LC 75-143964. (Illus.). 10 ils.
bibl. index. 128p. (Young Readers Ser). (gr. 9
up). 1971. Praeger.

Blanco, Tomas & Delano, Jack

--The Child's Gift: A Twelfth Night Tale. Delano,
Irene (1919-), illus. LC 75-46530. (Illus.). 32p.
1976. (ISBN 0-664-32595-5). Westminster.

--Los Aguinaldos Del Infante: Glosa De Epifania
The Child's Gifts : a Twelfth Night Tale.
Delano, Irene (1919-), illus. LC 75-46530.
(Illus.). 33 p. 29cm. 1976. (ISBN
0-664-32595-5). Westminster Press.

Bland, Edith Nesbit see Nesbit, E., pseud.

Bland, Edith Nesbit, Mrs. (1858-1924)

--The Bastable Children: Containing The Treasure
Seekers, The Wouldbegoods, The New
Treasure Seekers. LC 41-32449. xviii, 296 p.
illus. 21 1/2 cm. 1929. Coward-McCann, Inc.

--The Bastables: The Story of the Treasure
Seekers. Ardizzone, Edward (1900-) & Streatfeild,
Noel, illus. 368p. illus. 25cm. (Nonesuch
cygnet). 1966, c.1965. Watts.

--The Book of Dragons. Nesbit, E., pseud. Millar,
Harold Robert (1869-1939), illus. 1900.
Harper & Brothers.

--Bunny Tales, 1 of 4 Vols. (Little People's
Natural History Box). N.D. Dodge.

--Bunny Tales, 1 of 4 Vols. (Little People's
Natural History Box). N.D. Dutton.

--Cat Tales. Nesbit, E., pseud. Watkin, Isabel,
illus. (Illus.). 1904. E. P. Dutton & Co.

--The Children's Shakespeare, 1 of 15 vols.
(Original Author: William Shakespeare,
1564-1616). (Illus.). (Dainty Ser. of Choice
Gift Bks: No. 3). 1905. Set. Henry Altemus
Co.

--Children's Shakespeare. Nesbit, E., pseud.
(Illus.). (gr. 4-7). 1938. (ISBN 0-394-91014-1)
Random.

--The Cocka Toucan. 1967. (ISBN 0-88302-349-0,
Peter Possum). Mulberry Pr.

--The Complete Book of Dragons. Blegvad, Erik
(1923-), illus. LC 72-165245. (Illus.). 198 p.
25cm. 1973, c.1972. Macmillan.

--The Conscience Pudding. Blegvad, Erik (1923-),
illus. LC 70-120095. (Illus.). 45 p. 23cm. 1970.
Coward-McCann.

--The Deliverers of Their Country. Nesbit, E.,
pseud. Zwerger, Lisbeth, illus. LC 85-9389.
(Illus.). 25 p. 30cm. c.1985. (ISBN
0-88708-005-7). Picture Book Studio USA :
Distributed by Alphabet Press.

--The Enchanted Castle. Nesbit, E., pseud. 239p.
Repr. of 1964 ed. (Childrens Illustrated
Classics Ser.). 1968. (ISBN 0-460-05080-X,
Pub. by J. M. Dent England). Biblio Dist.

--Enchanted Castle. Nesbit, E., pseud. Repr. (gr.
4-7). 1974. (ISBN 0-8277-2139-0). British Bk
Ctr.

--Enchanted Castle. Nesbit, E., pseud. 1981. (ISBN
0-8398-2730-X, Gregg). G K Hall.

--Enchanted Castle. Nesbit, E., pseud. 231p. Repr.
1981. (ISBN 0-89966-361-3). Buccaneer Bks.

--Enchanted Castle. Nesbit, E., pseud. 179p. Repr.
1981. (ISBN 0-89967-035-0). Harmony & Co.

--The Enchanted Castle. Nesbit, E., pseud. LC
8-15327. 296p. 1908. Harper & Brothers.

--The Enchanted Castle. Fraser, Betty M., pseud.
(1928-). Fraser, Elizabeth Marr. LC
66-13596. 275 p. illus. 24 cm. (Platt & Munk
cricket book). 1966. Platt & Munk.

--Enchanted Castle. Nesbit, E., pseud. Fraser,
Betty M., pseud. (1928-), illus. Fraser,
Elizabeth Marr. (Illus.). (Cricket Book). (gr.
4-7). 1966. Platt.

--Enchanted Castle. Nesbit, E., pseud. Leslie,
Cecil, illus. (Illus.). (Children's Illustrated
Classics). (gr. 4-7). 1964. (ISBN
0-525-29290-X). Dutton.

--The Enchanted Castle. Millar, Harold Robert
(1869-1939), illus. Becker, May Lamberton,
pref. by. LC 33-27289. c.1933.
Coward-McCann, Inc.

--Five Children & It. Nesbit, E., pseud. Repr. (gr.
3 up). 1974. (ISBN 0-8277-2137-4). British Bk
Ctr.

--Five Children & It. Nesbit, E., pseud. 188p.
Repr. 1981. (ISBN 0-89966-362-1). Buccaneer
Bks.

--Five Children & It. Nesbit, E., pseud. 182p.
Repr. 1981. (ISBN 0-89967-036-9). Harmony
& Co.

--Five Children & It. Nesbit, E., pseud. (Illus.).
(Looking Glass Library). (gr. 3 up). 1959.
(ISBN 0-394-80451-1). Random.

--Five Children and It. Goodall, John Strickland
(1908-), illus. LC 49-8802. 275 p. illus. 20 cm.
N.D. Coward-McCann.

--Five Children and It. Nesbit, E., pseud. Millar,
Harold Robert (1869-1939), illus. 1957.
Coward.

--Five Children and It. Nesbit, E., pseud. Millar,
Harold Robert (1869-1939), illus. 1905. Dodd, Mead & Company.

--Five Children & It. Nesbit, E., pseud. Millar,
Harold Robert (1869-1939), illus. (gr.
3-4). 1957. (ISBN 0-486-21492-3). Dover.

--Five Children & It. Nesbit, E., pseud. Millar,
Harold Robert (1869-1939), illus. (gr. 4-7).
1959. (ISBN 0-14-030128-3, Puffin). Penguin.

--Five Children and It. Millar, Harold Robert
(1869-1939), illus. LC 67-110654. (Illus.).
18cm. 215p. (Puffin Books: Nos. 3-6). N.D.
Penguin Books.

--The Five Children: Containing Five Children
and It; The Phoenix and the Carpet; The Story
of the Amulet. LC 81-26629. xi, 212, 200, 306
p. incl. illus., pl. col. front. 21 1/2 cm. 1930.
Coward-McCann, Inc.

--The Five Children: Contains: "Five Children and
It", "The Phoenix and the Carpet", and "The
Story of the Amulet". Nesbit, E., pseud. (gr.
5-7). 1930. Coward-McCann, Inc.

--Five of Us--and Madeline. Unwin, Nora Spicer
(1907-), illus. LC 32-26335. 310 pl incl. pl.
col. front., plates 19 cm. 1932. Greenberg.

--Five of Us- and Madeline. Nesbit, E., pseud.
Freeman, Peter, illus. 1958. Coward.

--Five of Us and Madeline. Nesbit, E., pseud.
Freeman, Peter, illus. 1960. Coward-McCann
Inc.

--Harding's Luck. Nesbit, E., pseud. (gr. 3-4).
1974. (ISBN 0-8277-2145-5). British Bk Ctr.

--Harding's Luck. Nesbit, E., pseud. Millar,
Harold Robert (1869-1939), illus. 1961.
Coward.

--Harding's Luck. Nesbit, E., pseud. Millar,
Harold Robert (1869-1939), illus. (Illus.). (gr.
3-4). 1961. (ISBN 0-486-21491-X). Dover.

--Harding's Luck. Nesbit, E., pseud. Millar,
Harold Robert (1869-1939), illus. LC
10-18659. 6 p. l., 308 p. front., plates 19 1/2
cm. 1910. Frederick A. Stokes Company.

--Harding's Luck. Nesbit, E., pseud. Walduck,
Desmond, illus. 1960. Coward-McCann Inc.

--The House of Arden. Nesbit, E., pseud. N.D.
British Book Centre.

--The House of Arden. LC 68-892942. ix, 244p
illus., col. plates. 22cm. (Children's illus.
classics, no. 76). 1967. Dent.

--House of Arden. Nesbit, E., pseud. Hutton,
Clarke (1898-), illus. (gr. 4-8). 1968. Dutton.

--House of Arden. Nesbit, E., pseud. Millar,
Harold Robert (1869-1939), illus. 1960.
Coward-McCann Inc.

--The House of Arden. Nesbit, E., pseud. Millar,
Harold Robert (1869-1939), illus. 1909.
Dutton.

--The Last of the Dragons. Nesbit, E., pseud.
Firmin, Peter (1928-), illus. LC 79-28584.
(Illus.). 32p. (gr. k-4). 1980. (ISBN
0-07-046285-2). McGraw.

--The Last of the Dragons and Some Others.
Nebit, E., pseud. LC 85-42967. p. cm. 1985.
(ISBN 0-14-035069-1). Puffin Books.

--Long Ago When I Was Young. Ardizzone,
Edward Jeffrey Irving (1900-1979), illus.
Streatfeild, Noel (1897-), intro. by. LC
66-63703. 127p. illus. 22cm. 1966. Watts.

--The Magic City. Nesbit, E., pseud. 1981. (ISBN
0-8398-2730-X, Gregg). G K Hall.

--The Magic City. LC 81-292. p. cm. (Gregg
Press Children's Literature Series). 1981.
(ISBN 0-8398-2730-X). Gregg Press.

--Magic City. Nesbit, E., pseud. Millar, Harold
Robert (1869-1939), illus. 1960.
Coward-McCann Inc.

--Magic City. Nesbit, E., pseud. Millar, Harold
Robert (1869-1939), illus. (Illus.). (gr. 3-4).
1958. (ISBN 0-486-21496-6). Dover.

--Magic World. Nesbit, E., pseud. Repr. (gr. 3-6).
1974. (ISBN 0-8277-2140-4). British Bk Ctr.

--The Magic World. Nesbit, E., pseud. Millar,
Harold Robert (1869-1939) & Pryse, Gerald
Spencer (1882-), illus. 1959. Coward.

--The Magic World. Nesbit, E., pseud. Millar,
Harold Robert (1869-1939), illus. 1960.
Coward-McCann Inc.

--Magic World. Nesbit, E., pseud. Millar, Harold
Robert (1869-1939) & Pryse, Gerald Spencer
(1882-). illus. (Illus.). (gr. 3-4). 1959. (ISBN
0-486-21497-4). Dover.

--The Magic World. Millar, Harold Robert
(1869-1939) & Pryse, Gerald Spencer (1882-),
illus. LC 60-2238. 280p. illus. 21cm. 1959. E.
Benn.

--The Magic World. Nesbit, E., pseud. Millar,
Harold Robert (1869-1939) & Pryse, Gerald
Spencer (1882-), illus. 1912. Macmillan.

--The Magic World. Millar, Harold Robert
(1869-1939) & Pryse, Gerald Spencer (1882-),
illus. LC 80-23782. p. cm. (Facsmile Classics
Series). 1980. (ISBN 0-8317-5738-8).
Mayflower Books.

--The New Treasure Seekers. Nesbit, E., pseud.
Repr. (gr. 3-6). 1974. (ISBN 0-8277-2135-8).
British Bk Ctr.

--The New Treasure Seekers. LC 31-26709. 10 p.
l., 5-203 p. illus. 19 1/2 cm. 1931.
Coward-McCann, Inc.

--New Treasure Seekers. Nesbit, E., pseud. 1962.
Coward.

--New Treasure Seekers. Nesbit, E., pseud.
Browne, Gordon Frederick (1858-1932) &
Baumer, Lewis (1870-), illus. (Illus.). (gr. 3-4).
1962. (ISBN 0-486-21498-2). Dover.

--New Treasure Seekers. Nesbit, E., pseud.
Browne, Gordon Frederick (1858-1932) &
Baumer, Lewis (1870-), illus. 1904. Frederick
A. Stokes.

--The New Treasure Seekers. Nesbit, E., pseud. Hodges, Cyril Walter (1909-), illus. (gr. 5-7). 1948. Coward-McCann, Inc.
--Nine Unlikely Tales. Nesbit, E., pseud. (Illus.). 1961. Coward-McCann, Inc.
--Nine Unlikely Tales. Nesbit, E., pseud. Millar, Harold Robert (1869-1939) & Shepperson, Claude A., illus. (Illus.). (gr. 3-4). 1960. (ISBN 0-486-21499-0). Dover.
--Nine Unlikely Tales for Children. Nesbit, E., pseud. Millar, Harold Robert (1869-1939), illus. 1901. Dutton.
--Old Nursery Stories. Nesbit, E., pseud. Margetson, W. H., illus. (Illus.). (The Children's Bookcase). N.D. George H. Doran.
--Oswald Bastable & Others. Nesbit, E., pseud. Repr. (gr. 3-6). 1974. (ISBN 0-8277-0167-5). British Bk Ctr.
--Oswald Bastable and Others. Brock, Charles Edmond (1870-1938) & Millar, Harold Robert (1869-1939), illus. 1960. Coward McCann.
--Oswald Bastable & Others. Nesbit, E., pseud. Brock, Charles Edmond (1870-1938) & Millar, Harold Robert (1869-1939), illus. (Illus.). (gr. 3-4). 1960. (ISBN 0-486-21500-8). Dover.
--Oswald Bastable and Others. Brock, Charles Edmond (1870-1938) & Millar, Harold Robert (1869-1939), illus. 369 p. illus. 21 cm. 1960. E. Benn.
--Our New Story Book. Nesbit, E., pseud. Wood, Elsie Anna & Wain, Louis (1861-1939), illus. 1913. Dutton.
--Phoenix & the Carpet. Nesbit, E., pseud. Repr. (gr. 3 up). 1974. (ISBN 0-8277-2144-7). British Bk Ctr.
--The Phoenix and the Carpet. Nesbit, E., pseud. 1956. Coward.
--Phoenix and the Carpet. Nesnit, E., pseud. N.D. Penguin Bks.
--Phoenix & the Carpet. Nesbit, E., pseud. (Illus.). (Looking Glass Library). (gr. 3 up). 1960. (ISBN 0-394-80461-9). Random.
--The Phoenix and the Carpet. Bland, Edith Nesbit. Nesbit, E., pseud. (Every Boy's and Every Girl's Ser.). N.D. The Macmillan Co.
--The Phoenix and the Carpet. Goodall, John Strickland (1908-), illus. LC 49-8325. 328 p. illus. 20 cm. N.D. Coward-McCann.
--The Phoenix and the Carpet. Goodall, John Strickland (1908-), illus. LC 60-2219. (Illus.). 285 p. 20cm. (Looking glass library, 11). 1960. Looking Glass Library; Distributed by Random House.
--Phoenix & the Carpet. Nesbit, E., pseud. Millar, Harold Robert (1869-1939), illus. (Illus.). (gr. 3-4). 1956. (ISBN 0-486-21501-6). Dover.
--Phoenix & the Carpet. Nesbit, E., pseud. Millar, Harold Robert (1869-1939), illus. (gr. 4-7). 1959. (ISBN 0-14-030129-1, Puffin). Penguin.
--The Phoenix and the Carpet. Millar, Harold Robert (1869-1939), illus. LC 4-26868. vii, 257 p. front., 7 pl. 20 cm. 1904. The Macmillan Company.
--The Princess & the Cat. Nesbit, E., pseud. Pollard, Michael, illus. (gr. 1-4). 1977. (ISBN 0-8277-5394-2). (ISBN 0-8277-5393-4). British Bk Ctr.
--Pug Peter. Nesbit, E., pseud. (Illus.). N.D. Frederick A. Stokes.
--Pussy Tales and Doggy Tales. Nesbit, E., pseud. Kemp-Welch, Lucy, illus. N.D. E. P. Dutton & Co.
--Railway Children. Nesbit, E., pseud. Repr. (gr. 3-6). 1974. (ISBN 0-8277-2136-6). British Bk Ctr.
--The Railway Children. Nesbit, E., pseud. 1975. Penguin.
--The Railway Children. Nesbit, E., pseud. 240p. (Puffin Classics Ser.). (gr. 3-7). 1983. (ISBN 0-14-035005-5, Puffin). Penguin.
--Railway Children. Nesbit, E., pseud. Brock, Charles Edmond (1870-1938), illus. (gr. 2-5). 1961. (ISBN 0-14-030147-X, Puffin). Penguin.
--The Railway Children. Brock, Charles Edmond (1870-1938), illus. LC 67-9685. 239 p. illus. 19 cm. (Puffin books, PS147). 1965. Penguin Books.
--The Railway Children. Nesbit, E., pseud. Brock, Charles Edmond (1870-1938), illus. LC 6-34371. ix, 309 p. front., 19 pl. 20 cm. 1906. The Macmillan Company.
--The Railway Children. Nesbit, E., pseud. Lamb, Lynton Harold (1907-1977), illus. 1958. Coward-McCann Inc.
--Railway Children. Nesbit, E., pseud. Lamb, Lynton Harold (1907-1977), illus. (Illus.). (gr. 3-4). 1957. (ISBN 0-486-21502-4). Dover.
--The Railway Children. Nesbit, E., pseud. Mozley, Charles (1915-), illus. (Illus.). (Children's Illustrated Classics). 1975. E.P. Dutton & Co.
--Revolt of the Toys, and What Comes from Quarrelling. Nesbit, E., pseud. Dudley, Ambrose, illus. (The Rosebud Ser.). 1902. E. P. Dutton & Co.
--Story of the Amulet. Nesbit, E., pseud. (gr. 3-6). 1974. (ISBN 0-8277-2138-2). British Bk Ctr.
--The Story of the Amulet. Nesbit, E., pseud. 1957. Coward.
--Story of the Amulet. Nesbit, E., pseud. N.D. Penguin Bk.
--The Story of the Amulet. Goodall, John Strickland (1908-), illus. LC 49-102285. 367 p. illus. 21 cm. N.D. Coward-McCann.
--Story of the Amulet. Nesbit, E., pseud. Goodall, John Strickland (1908-), illus. (Illus.). (Looking Glass Library). (gr. 3 up). 1960. (ISBN 0-394-80468-6). Random.
--Story of the Amulet. Nesbit, E., pseud. Millar, Harold Robert (1869-1939), illus. (Illus.). (gr. 3-4). 1957. (ISBN 0-486-21503-2). Dover.
--The Story of the Amulet. Millar, Harold Robert (1869-1939), illus. 2 p. l., 9-374 p., 1 l. front., illus. 21 cm. 1907. E. P. Dutton and Company.
--Story of the Amulet. Nesbit, E., pseud. Millar, Harold Robert (1869-1939), illus. 288p. (gr. 4 up). 1959. (ISBN 0-14-030130-5, Puffin). Penguin.
--The Story of the Amulet. Millar, Harold Robert (1869-1939), illus. LC 67-9717. 281 p. illus. 18 cm. (Puffin books, PS130). 1965, c.1901. Penguin Books.
--Story of the Treasure Seekers. Nesbit, E., pseud. Repr. (gr. 3-6). 1974. (ISBN 0-8277-0168-3). British Bk Ctr.
--The Story of the Treasure Seekers. Nesbit, E., pseud. Browne, Gordon Frederick (1858-1932), illus. 1958. Coward.
--Story of the Treasure Seekers. Nesbit, E., pseud. Browne, Gordon Frederick (1858-1932), illus. (Illus.). (gr. 3-4). 1958. (ISBN 0-486-21504-0). Dover.
--Story of the Treasure Seekers. Nesbit, E., pseud. Leslie, Cecil, illus. (gr. 3-6). 1959. (ISBN 0-14-030116-X, Puffin). Penguin.
--The Story of the Treasure Seekers: Being the Adventures of the Bastable Children in Search of a Fortune. Browne, Gordon Frederick (1858-1932) & Baumer, Lewis, illus. LC 2204. vii, 296 p. front., plates. 19 cm. c.1899. Frederick A. Stokes Company.
--The Story of the Treasure Seekers: Being the Adventures of the Bastable Children in Search of a Fortune. Hodges, Cyril Walter (1909-), illus. LC 48-601750. 275 p. illus. 21 cm. 1948. Coward-McCann.
--The Treasure Seekers. Nesbit, E., pseud. LC 31-26708. 9 p. l., 5-209 p. illus. 19 1/2 cm. 1931. Coward-McCann, Inc.
--The Treasure Seekers. Nesbit, E., pseud. (Illus.). (Library for Boys and Girls Ser.). N.D. Frederick A. Stokes Co.
--The Treasure Seekers. Nesbit, E., pseud. Browne, Gordon Frederick (1858-1932), illus. N.D. Frederick A. Stokes.
--The Treasure Seekers. Nesbit, E., pseud. Hodges, Cyril Walter (1909-), illus. (gr. 5-7). 1948. Coward-McCann, Inc.
--Wet Magic. LC 38-4098. 244 p. incl. plages col. front. 211/2 cm. 1937. Coward-McCann, Inc.
--Wet Magic. Nesbit, E., pseud. Millar, Harold Robert (1869-1939), illus. 1958. Coward.
--Wet Magic. Nesbit, E., pseud. Millar, Harold Robert (1869-1939), illus. (Illus.). (gr. 3-4). 1958. (ISBN 0-486-21505-9). Dover.
--Wonderful Garden. Nesbit, E., pseud. (gr. 3-4). 1974. (ISBN 0-8277-2142-0). British Bk Ctr.
--The Wonderful Garden. Nesbit, E., pseud. Millar, Harold Robert (1869-1939), illus. 1959. Coward.
--Wonderful Garden. Nesbit, E., pseud. Millar, Harold Robert (1869-1939), illus. (Illus.). (gr. 3-4). 1959. (ISBN 0-486-21506-7). Dover.
--The Wonderful Garden: Or, The Three C's. illustrated by h. r. millar. Millar, Harold Robert (1869-1939), illus. LC 35-27386. xvi p. 1 l., 298 p. incl. front., illus. 21 1/2 cm. c.1935. Coward-McCann, Inc.
--The Would-Be-Goods. Nesbit, E., pseud. Hodges, Cyril Walter (1909-), illus. 384p. 1948. Coward-McCann.
--Wouldbegoods. Nesbit, E., pseud. Repr. (gr. 3-6). 1974. (ISBN 0-8277-2143-9). British Bk Ctr.
--The Wouldbegoods. Nesbit, E., pseud. LC 31-26764. 9 p. l., 5-309 p. illus. 19 1/2 cm. 1931. Coward-McCann,Inc.
--The Wouldbegoods. Nesbit, E., pseud. 1958. Coward.
--The Wouldbegoods. Nesbit, E., pseud. (gr. 3-6). 1974. (ISBN 0-14-030122-4, Puffin). Penguin.
--The Wouldbegoods. Nesbit, E., pseud. Birch, Reginald Bathurst (1856-1943), illus. LC 1-229638. 5 p. l., 312 1 p. front., plates. 19 1/2 cm. 1901. Harper & Brothers.
--Wouldbegoods. Nesbit, E., pseud. Buckland, Arthur H. & Hassall, John (1868-1948), illus. (Illus.). (gr. 3-4). 1965. (ISBN 0-486-21507-5). Dover.
--The Wouldbegoods: Being the Further Adventures of the Treasure Seekers. Hodges, Cyril Walter (1909-), illus. LC 48-8250. 383 p. illus. 20 cm. 1947. Coward-McCann.

Bland, Edith nesbit, Mrs. (1858-1924) & Furnivall, F J
--Children's Stories from Shakespeare. Nesbit, E., pseud. Bacon, John H, illus. (Raphael House Library). N.D. David McKay.

Bland, Edith Nesbit, Mrs. (1858-1924) & Weedon, L. L.
--Little People's Book of Fun. Nesbit, E., pseud. Playne, Alfred C., ed. (Illus.). N.D. E. P. Dutton & Co.

Blanding, Don (1894-)
--Stowaways in Paradise: Two Boy Adventurers in Hawaii. Blanding, Don (1894-), illus. LC 31-29816. 5 p. l., 233 p. col. front. illus. 24 cm. 1931. Cosmopolitan Book Corporation.

Blane, Gertrude see Blumenthal, Gertrude.

Blaney, Charles E.
--Josie the Little Madcap. N.D. J. S. Ogilvie Co.

Blank, Clair
--The Adventure Girls: At Happiness House. LC 36-9844. 4 p. l., 7-241 p. front. 20 1/2 cm. (Her Adventure girls series). c.1936. A. L. Burt Company.
--The Adventure Girls: At K Bar O. LC 36-9345. 4 p. l., 7-248 p. front. 20 1/2 cm. (Her Adventure girls series). c.1936. A. L. Burt Company.
--The Adventure Girls in the Air. LC 36-9348. 255 p. front. 20 1/2 cm. (Her Adventure girls series). c.1936. A. L. Burt Company.
--Beverly Gray at the World's Fair. LC 35-8285. 250 p. front. 20 1/2 cm. (Her The Beverly Gray college mystery series). c.1935. A. L. Burt Company.
--Beverly Gray, Freshman. LC 34-14764. 254 p. front. 20 1/2 cm. (Her The Beverly Gray college mystery series). c.1934. A. L. Burt Company.
--Beverly Gray, Freshman. (The Beverly Gray College Mystery Ser.). (gr. 7-10). N.D. Grosset & Dunlap.
--Beverly Gray in the Orient. LC 57-5306. vi p., 1 l., 9-251 p. front. 21 cm. (Her Beverly Gray college mystery series). 1937. A. Burt Company.
--Beverly Gray in the Orient. (The Beverly Gray College Mystery Stories). N.D. Grosset & Dunlap.
--Beverly Gray, Junior. LC 34-14766. 254 p. front.20 1/2 cm. (Her The Beverly Gray college mystery series). c.1934. A. L. Burt Company.
--Beverly Gray, Junior. (Beverly Gray College Mystery Ser.). N.D. Grosset & Dunlap.
--Beverly Gray on a Treasure Hunt. LC 38-320218. 4 p. l., 243 p. front. 20 1/2 cm. (Her The Beverly Gray college mystery series). c.1938. Grosset & Dunlap.
--Beverly Gray on a World Cruise. LC 36-9346. vi, 7-251 p. front 20 1/2 cm. (Her The Beverly Gray college mystery series). c.1936. A. L. Burt Company.
--Beverly Gray on a World Cruise. (The Beverly Gray College Mystery Stories). N.D. Grosset & Dunlap.
--Beverly Gray, Reporter. LC 40-6550. v p., 1 l., 9-239 p. front 20 1/2 cm. (Her The Beverly Gray college mystery series). c.1940. Grosset & Dunlap.
--Beverly Gray, Senior. LC 34-14767. 253 p. front. 20 1/2 cm. (Her The Beverly Gray college mystery series). c.1934. A. L. Burt Company.
--Beverly Gray, Senior. (Beverly Gray College Mystery Ser.). N.D. Grosset & Dunlap.
--Beverly Gray Sophomore. LC 34-14765. 256 p. front. 20 1/2 cm. (Her The Beverly Gray college mystery series). c.1934. A. L. Burt Company.
--Beverly Gray. Sophomore. (The Beverly Gray College Mystery Ser.). N.D. Grosset & Dunlap.
--Beverly Gray's Adventure. LC 44-20101. 4 p. l., 213 p. incl. front. 19 cm. (Her The Beverly Gray college mystery series). 1944. Grosset & Dunlap.
--Beverly Gray's Assignment. LC 47-230590. v p. 1 l., 212 p. incl. front. 19 1/2 cm. (Her The Beverly Gray mystery series). 1947. Grosset & Dunlap.
--Beverly Gray's Career. 254 p. front. 20 1/2 cm. (Her The Beverly Gray college mystery series). c.1935. A. L. Burt Company.
--Beverly Gray's Career. (Beverly Gray College Mystery Ser.). (gr. 7-10). N.D. Grosset & Dunlap.
--Beverly Gray's Challenge. LC 45-214405. v p., 1 l., 207 p. incl. front. 19 cm. (Her Beverly Gray college mystery series). 1945. Grosset & Dunlap.
--Beverly Gray's Discovery. LC 53-8381. 183 p. front. 20 cm. (Her The Beverly Gray mystery series). 1953. Grosset & Dunlap.
--Beverly Gray's Fortune. LC 50-6594. vii. 207 p. front. 20 cm. (Her The Beverly Gray mystery series). 1950. Grosset & Dunlap.
--Beverly Gray's Island Mystery. LC 52-10223. (Illus.). 179 p. 20cm. (The Beverly Gray Mystery Ser.). 1952. Grosset & Dunlop.
--Beverly Gray's Journey. LC 46-20645. vii p., 1 l., 209 p. incl. front. 19 1/2 cm. (Her The Beverly Gray college mystery series). 1946. Grosset & Dunlap.
--Beverly Gray's Mystery. LC 48-400194. vii. 207 p. front. 20 cm. (Her The Beverly Gray mystery series). 1948. Grosset & Dunlap.
--Beverly Gray's Problem. LC 43-6168. 4 p. l., 214 p. incl. front. 19 1/2 cm. (Her The Beverly Gray college mystery series). 1943. Grosset & Dunlap.
--Beverly Gray's Quest. LC 42-28930. 220 p. incl. front 19 1/2 cm. (Her The Beverly Gray college mystery series). c.1942. Grosset & Dunlap.
--Beverly Gray's Return. LC 39-107650. v p., 1 l., 9-251 p. front. 20 1/2 cm. (Her Beverly Gray college mystery series). c.1939. Grosset & Dunlap.
--Beverly Gray's Romance. LC 41-807. 250 p. incl. front. 20 cm. (Her Beverly Gray college mystery series). c.1941. Grosset & Dunlap.
--Beverly Gray's Scoop. LC 54-8463. (Illus.). 184 p. 20cm. (The Beverly Gray Mystery Ser.). 1954. Grosset & Dunlop.
--Beverly Gray's Secret. LC 51-2313. vii, 212 p. 20cm. (The Beverly Gray Mystery Ser.). 1951. Grosset & Dunlop.
--Beverly Gray's Vacation. LC 49-546047. vii. 212 p. front. 20 cm. (Her The Beverly Gray mystery series). 1949. Grosset & Dunlap.
--Beverly Grey on a World Cruise. (Beverly Gray College Mystery Ser.). N.D. Grosset & Dunlap.

Blankenship, George H.
--Tootsie Toots. N:D. Carlton Press Inc.

Blankenship, Judy (1944-)
--Teddy Beddy Bear's Bedtime Songs & Poems. Blankenship, Judy (1944-), illus. LC 84-4837. (Illus.). 32p. (Picturebacks Ser.). (ps). 1984. (ISBN 0-394-86826-9, Pub. by BYR). (ISBN 0-394-86826-9). Random.

Blankenship, William Douglas (1934-)
--Tiger Ten. LC 75-29531. 256p. 1976. (ISBN 0-399-11679-6). Putnam.

Blankfort, Henry
--Henry, The Smiling Dog. Aragones, Sergio, illus. (Illus.). (gr. 2-4). 1966. (ISBN 0-399-60237-2). Putnam.
--Henry, the Smiling Dog. Aragones, Sergio, illus. LC 67-446. 48p. illus. 19x24cm. 1967, c.1966. Putnam.

Blanton, Catherine (1907-)
--The Gold Penny. Orbaan, Albert F. (1913-), illus. LC 57-9719. 187 p. illus. 21 cm. 1957. J. Day Co.
--Hold Fast to Your Dreams. LC 55-6922. 185 p. 22cm. 1955. J. Messner.
--Pedro's Choice. Price, Harold L. (1912-), illus. LC 48-8764. 64 p. illus. 24 cm. 1948. Whittlesey House.
--The Three Miracles. Politi, Leo (1908-), illus. LC 46-7571. 23cm. 47p. (gr. 3-7). 1946. John Day Bks.
--Trouble on Old Smoky. Peck, Anne Merriman (1884-), illus. LC 51-13296. 142 p. illus. 21 cm. 1951. Whittlesey House.
--What a Break!. Hutchison, William Miller (1916-), illus. LC 62-78530. 144p. illus. 21cm. 1962. Friendship Press.

Blanton, Mary T.
--Knock on a Door. Connelly, Gwen, illus. LC 84-7027. (Illus.). 32p. (ps-k). 1984. Dandelion Hse.

Blanton, Rosa A
--The Mesquite. LC 47-3208. 3 p. l., 135 p. plates, ports. 21 1/2 cm. 1947. The Hobson Book Press.

Blasco-Ibanez, Vicente (1867-1928)
--The Last Lion and Other Stories. N.D. (ISBN 0-8283-1444-6). Branden Press.
--The Last Lion and Other Stories. N.D. Publications of Bruce Humphries.

Blashfield, Jean
--Star Rangers & the Spy. LC 83-91422. 80p. (Fantasy Forest Adventures Ser.). (gr. 2-5). 1984. (ISBN 0-394-72457-7). Random.

Blashfield, Jean, ed. see Gilbert, William Schwenck, Sir (1836-1911) & Sullivan, Arthur Seymour, Sir.

Blassingame, Wyatt Rainey (1909-)
--Bowleg Bill: Seagoing Cowboy. Vestal, Herman B., illus. LC 75-22230. (Illus.). 48p. (American Folktales Ser.). (gr. 2-5). 1976. (ISBN 0-8116-4044-2). Garrard.
--How Davy Crockett Got a Bearskin Coat. Korach, Mimi (1922-), illus. LC 74-180783. (Illus.). 34 p. 23cm. 1972. (ISBN 0-8116-4035-3). Garrard Pub. Co.
--John Henry and Paul Bunyan Play Baseball. Burns, Raymond Howard (1924-), illus. LC 72-151138. (Illus.). 39 p. 23cm. 1971. (ISBN 0-8116-4027-2). Garrard Pub. Co.
--Paul Bunyan Fights the Monster Plants. Vestal, Herman B., illus. LC 73-16032. (Illus.). 40 p. 22cm. 1974. (ISBN 0-8116-4039-6). Garrard Pub. Co.

AUTHOR INDEX BLOOM, PAULINE

--Pecos Bill and the Wonderful Clothesline Snake. Vestal, Herman B., illus. LC 77-17972. (Illus.). 40 p. 23cm. c.1978. (ISBN 0-8116-4046-9). Garrard Pub. Co.
--Pecos Bill Catches a Hidebehind. Vestal, Herman B., illus. LC 76-23336. (Illus.). 40 p. 23cm. c.1977. (ISBN 0-8116-4045-0). Garrard Pub. Co.
--Pecos Bill Rides a Tornado. Schroeder, Ted (1931-1973), illus. LC 73-5894. (Illus.). 30 p. 23cm. 1973. Garrard Pub. Co.
--Underwater Warriors. LC 81-787. (Illus.). 160p. (Landmark Paperback: No. 11). (gr. 3-8). 1982. (ISBN 0-394-84884-5). Random.

Blatchford, Claire H
--All Alone (Except for My Dog Friday). LC 83-70903. 124 p. 18cm. c.1983. (ISBN 0-89191-755-1). Chariot Books.

Blatchford, Mary [illegible]
--Polly and the Aunt, by the Aunt. LC 6-35947. 64p. front. 19 1/2cm. 1906. Houghton Mifflin & Co.
--The Story of Little Jane and Me. LC 98-1016. 20cm. 100p. 1898. Houghton Mifflin Co.

Blatter, Dorothy Gertrude (1901-)
--Cap and Candle. LC 61-6765. 190 p. 21cm. 1961. Westminster Press.
--The Thirsty Village. Blatter, Dorothy Gertrude (1901-), illus. LC 50-[illegible]. 1[illegible]p. illus. 21cm. 1950. Friendship Press.
--Uncle Ali's Secret: A/Story of New Turkey. Blatter, Dorothy Gertrude (1901-), illus. LC 39-16744. (Illus.). 32 p. 24cm. (Junior Press Bks.). 1939. A. Whitman & Co.

Blau, Judith Hope
--The Bagel Baker of Mulliner Lane. LC 76-2526. (Illus.). 40 p. 26cm. c.1976. (ISBN 0 07 005882 2). (ISBN 0 07 005883 0). McGraw-Hill.

Blau, Melinda
--Killer Bees. LC 77-10010. (Illus.). (Great Unsolved Mysteries). (gr. 4-5). 1977. (ISBN 0-8172-1055-5). Raintree Pubs.

Blaustein, Muriel
--Baby Mabu and Auntie Moose. LC 82-21034. p. cm. c.1983. (ISBN 0-590-07874-7). Four Winds Press.

Blayer, Florence
--A Thousand Faces. N.D. (ISBN 0-8283-1339-3). Branden Press.

Blech, Dietlind
--Hello Irina. Karsunke, Yaak (1934-), tr. LC 70-113451. (Illus.). 36 p. 1971, c.1970. (ISBN 0-03-084252-2). Holt, Rinehart & Winston.

Blecher, George, tr. see Kullman, Harry.
Blecher, George, tr. see Lagercrantz, Rose Elsa.
Blecher, George, tr. see Rydberg, Viktor.
Blecher, Lone Thygesen, tr. see Kullman, Harry.
Blecher, Lone Thygesen, tr. see Rydberg, Viktor.
Blecher, Wilfried
--Blue Rooster. Blecher, Wilfried, illus. Wolff, Angelika, tr. LC 79-86977. (Illus.). ger. 32 color ils. 32p. 1st U.S. edition. (ps-2). 1969. (ISBN 0-87460-050-2). (ISBN 0-87460-116-9). Lion.
--No End of Nonsense: Humorous Verses. 1st ed. Blecher, Wilfried, illus. Prelutsky, Jack, tr. from German. LC 68-17512. (Illus.). 24 p. 31cm. 1968. Macmillan.
--Where Is Willie?. LC 67-18640. (Illus.). 1 v. (unpaged. 1967. McGraw-Hill.

Bledsoe
--Dear Uncle Bramwell. N.D. The Swallow Press.

Bleecker, Mary Noel, ed.
--Big Music Or, Twenty Merry Tales to Tell. Glanzman, Louis S. (1922-), illus. LC 46-1912. 256 p. incl. illus., plates. 22 cm. 1946. The Viking Press.

Bleeker, Sonia, pseud., see Zim, Sonia Bleeker.
Bleeker, Sonia, pseud. (1909-1971)
--The Crow Indians: Hunters of the Northern Plains. Zim, Sonia Bleeker. Karr, Althea, illus. LC 52-121147. 156p. illus. 20cm. (Morrow junior books). 1953. Morrow.
--Horsemen of the Western Plateus: The Nez Perce Indians. Zim, Sonia Bleeker. Bodell, Patricia, illus. 1957. William Morrow & Co.
--The Navajo: Herders, Weavers, and Silversmiths. Zim, Sonia Bleeker. Boodell, Patricia, illus. LC 58-5025. (Illus.). 159 p. 20cm. (Morrow junior books). 1958. Morrow.

Blegvad, Erik, jt. auth. see Blegvad, Lenore.
Blegvad, Erik (1923-), tr. see Andersen, Hans Christian.
Blegvad, Erik (1923-)
--Burnie's Hill: A Traditional Rhyme. Blegvad, Erik (1923-), illus. LC 76-28512. (Illus.). 28 p. 21cm. 1977. (ISBN 0-689-50070-X). Atheneum.

Blegvad, Erik (1923-), illus.
--Rare Treasures from Grimm: Fifteen Little Known Tales. Manheim, Ralph (1907-), tr. (Illus.). 112p. 1981. Doubleday.
--The Three Little Pigs. LC 80-10410. p. cm. 1980. (ISBN 0-689-50139-0). Atheneum.

Blegvad, Lenore (1926-)
--Anna Banana and Me. Blegvad, Erik (1923-), illus. LC 84-457. (Illus.). 32 p. 1985. (ISBN 0-689-50274-5). Atheneum.
--Mister Jensen & Cat. Blegvad, Erik (1923-), illus. LC 65-17987. (Illus.). (gr. 1-3). 1965. (ISBN 0-15-256214-1, HJ). HarBraceJ.
--Moon-Watch Summer. 1st ed. Blegvad, Erik (1923-), illus. LC 74-187855. (Illus.). 62 p. 21cm. 1972. (ISBN 0-15-255350-9). Harcourt Brace Jovanovich.

Blegvad, Lenore (1926-), compiled by.
--Hark! Hark! the Dogs Do Bark: And Other Rhymes About Dogs. Blegvad, Erik (1923-), illus. LC 75-9788. (Illus.). 21cm. 32p. 1st U.S. edition. (ps-3). 1976. (ISBN 0-690-50035-1, McElderry Bk). Atheneum.
--Mittens for Kittens, And Other Rhymes About Cats. Blegvad, Erik (1923-), illus. LC 74-76269. (Illus.). 32p. (ps-3). 1974. (ISBN 0-689-50003-3, McElderry Bk). Atheneum.
--The Parrot in the Garret and Other Rhymes About Dwellings. Blegvad, Erik (1923-), illus. LC 81-10859. p. cm. 1982. (ISBN 0-689-50217-6). Atheneum.
--This Little Pig-A-Wig and Other Rhymes about Pigs. Blegvad, Erik (1923-), illus. LC 78-7015. (Illus.). 32p. (ps-3). 1978. (ISBN 0-689-50110-2, McElderry Bk). Atheneum. **Award: (NYT).**

Blegvad, Lenore (1926-) & Blegvad, Erik (1923-)
--The Great Hamster Hunt. LC 69-13780. (Illus.). 32 p. 21cm. 1969. Harcourt, Brace & World.
--One Is for the Sun. 1st ed. LC 67-17151. 32p. illus. (pt. col.) 17x22cm. 1968. Harcourt.

Bleiler, E. F., ed. see LeFanu, Joseph Sheridan.
Bleiler, Everett Franklin (1920-), ed.
--Marmaduke Multiply's Merry Method of Making Minor Mathematicians. LC 70-170394. (Illus.). 103 p. 16cm. 1971. (ISBN 0-486-20171-6). (ISBN 0-486-22773-1). Dover Publications.
--Mother Goose's Melodies. LC 77-108034. (Illus.). xxiii, 116 p. 16cm. 1970. Dover Publications.

Bleitreu, J. N.
--The Parable of the Beast. 1967. Macmillan Company.

Bleneau, Adele
--The Nurse's Story. Bracker, M. Leone, illus. N.D. Bobbs-Merrill Co.

Blesh, Rudi & Geldmacher, Horst
--O Susanna. (Illus.). 1960. Grove Press.

Blessing, Richard Allen
--A Passing Season. LC 82-12740. 201 p. 21cm. c.1982. (ISBN 0-316-09957-0). Little, Brown & Co.

Bley, Edgar S.
--Best Singing Games for Children of All Ages. rev. ed. Willen, Patt, illus. LC 57-1014. (Illus.). (gr. k-6). 1959. (ISBN 0-8069-4450-1). (ISBN 0-8069-4451-X). Sterling.

Blish, James Benjamin (1921-1975)
--A Life for the Stars. LC 62-14388. 188 p. 21cm. (His Cities in flight, 2). 1962. Putnam.
--Mission to the Heart Stars. LC 65-13318. 158 p. 21cm. 1965. Putnam.
--The Star Dwellers. LC 61-127261. 192p. 21cm. 1961. Putnam.
--Star Trek 9. LC 73-8532. viii, 183 p. 18cm. (Bantam pathfinder editions). 1973. Bantam Books.
--Vanished Jet. LC 68-10256. (gr. 7-11). N.D. Weybright.
--Welcome to Mars. LC 67-24141. 159 p. 21cm. 1968. Putnam.

Blish, James Benjamin (1921-1975) & Roddenberry, Gene (1921-)
--Star Trek Eight. LC 72-7375. 170 p. 18cm. (Bantam pathfinder editions). 1972. Bantam Books.
--The Star Trek Reader. LC 76-20260. 422 p. 22cm. 1976. (ISBN 0-8415-0467-9). Dutton.
--The Star Trek Reader IV. LC 78-102307. 472 p. 22cm. 1978. (ISBN 0-525-20962-X). E. P. Dutton.
--Star Trek Seven. LC 72-1559. 155 p. 18cm. 1972. Bantam Books.

Blishen, Edward, jt. auth. see Garfield, Leon.
Blishen, Edward (1920-), ed.
--Miscellany One. LC 65-10736. 202p. illus., col. plates. 24cm. 1965, c.1964. Watts.
--Miscellany Three. LC 67-10996. v. illus. (pt. col.) 24cm. 1967. Watts.
--Miscellany Two. LC 65-22598. 196p. illus. (pt. col.) 25cm. 1st U.S. edition. 1966, c.1965. Watts.
--Oxford Book of Poetry for Children. Wildsmith, Brian Lawrence (1930-), illus. LC 63-19891. (Illus.). 167 p. 26cm. 1964, c.1963. F. Watts. **Award: (ALA).**
--Oxford Book of Poetry for Children. Wildsmith, Brian Lawrence (1930-), illus. LC 83-21500. p. cm. 1984. (ISBN 0-911745-34-3). P. Bedrick Books.
--Robin Hood. 80p. (Jackanory Ser.). (gr. 1-3). N.D. (ISBN 0-563-08462-6). BBC.

Bliss, Austin, jt. auth. see Bliss, Corinne Demas.
Bliss, Corinne Demas (1947-) & Bliss, Austin
--That Dog Melly!. LC 80-36701. (Illus.). 32 p. 23cm. c.1981. (ISBN 0-8038-7217-8). Hastings House.

Bliss, Helen Cory, Mrs.
--Honorable Goat. Watson, Aldren Auld (1917-), illus. LC 40-30720. 4 p. l., 168 p. incl. front., illus. 21 1/2 cm. 1940. Thomas Y. Crowell Company.

Bliss, Ida E
--Mother Gosse up to Date. LC 40-3579. 32 p. 20 1/2 cm. 1940. Priv. Print. Country Life Press.
--Says the Aeroplane!. The Lemon Tree, and Other Stories. James, Elizabeth S., illus. LC 38-6979. 95 p. illus. (part col.) 23 1/2 cm. 1938. Priv. Print. Country Life Press.

Bliss, Ronald Gene (1942-)
--Eagle Trap. Herman, R. C, illus. Davenport, May, intro. by. LC 82-71045. (Illus.). 108p. (gr. 3-5). 1982. (ISBN 0-943864-06-2). (ISBN 0-943864-05-4). Davenport.
--Indian Softball Summer. LC 73-15378. (gr. 3-7). 1974. [illegible]
--Indian Softball Summer: Or, Kickapoos Never Say Good-Bye. Moyers, William (1916-), illus. LC 73-15378. (Illus.). 126 p. 21cm. 1974. Dodd, Mead.

Blitch, Fleming Lee, pseud., see Lee, Fleming.
Blitch, Fleming Lee, pseud. (1933-)
--The Amazing Adventures of Peter Grunt, Gentleman Pig of Yatapalachee County, Florida: His Thrilling Adventures, His Daring Ideas, His Narrow Escapes. Lee, Fleming. Shortall, Leonard W., illus. LC 63-14265. 120 p. illus. 22 cm. 1963. Lippincott.
--The Last Dragon. Lee, Fleming. Zemach, Margot (1931-), illus. LC 64-19051. (Illus.). 1 v. (unpaged). 24cm. 1964. Lippincott.

Blizard, Marie
--Daughter of a Star. LC 54-5272. 174p. 21cm. 1954. Westminster Press.
--The Ghost at Kimball Hill. LC 56-5169. 187p. illus. 21cm. 1956. Westminster Press.

Bloch, Bertram
--The Little Laundress and the Fearful Knight. 1st ed. Shanks, George, illus. LC 54-10776. 122p. illus. 22cm. 1954. Doubleday.

Bloch, Marguerite
--Favorite Dog Stories. Doremus, Robert (1913-), illus. N.D. World Publishing Co.

Bloch, Marie Halun (1910-), tr. see Bilyk, Ivan.
Bloch, Marie Halun (1910-), tr. see Rudchenko, Ivan & Lukiyanenko, Maria.
Bloch, Marie Halun (1910-)
--Aunt America. Berg, Joan, pseud. (1942-), illus. Victor, Joan Berg. LC 63-7265. 148 p. illus. 21 cm. 1963. Atheneum. **Award: (ALA).**
--Aunt America. Berg, Joan, pseud. (1942-), illus. Victor, Joan Berg. (gr. 4-7). 1972. Atheneum.
--Bern, Son of Mikula. 1st ed. Kozak, Edward (1902-), illus. LC 73-175549. (Illus.). 177 p. 24cm. 1972. Atheneum.
--Big Steve, the Double Quick Tunnelman. Nicolas, pseud. (1911-1973), illus. Mordvinoff, Nicolas. LC 52-4220. 71 p. illus. 23 cm. 1952. Coward-McCann.
--Danny Doffer. Robinson, Jessie Berkowitz, illus. LC 46-7805. viii p., 1 l., 103 p. incl. front., illus. 21 1/2 cm. 1946. Harper & Brothers.
--Displaced Person. Davis, Allen, illus. LC 78-13083. 191 p. 22cm. c.1978. (ISBN 0-688-41860-0). Lothrop, Lee & Shepard.
--Displaced Person. Davis, Allen, illus. 1978. Morrow.
--The Dollhouse Story. Erhard, Walter (1920-), illus. LC 61-15207. 63p. illus. 21cm. 1961. H. Z. Walck.
--Herbert: The Electrical Mouse. McGee, Millard, illus. LC 53-10497. 63p. illus. 22cm. (Everyday science stories). 1953. J. Messner.
--Herbert, the Electrical Mouse. McGee, Millard, illus. LC 53-10497. 63p. illus. 22cm. 1953. Messner.
--The House on Third High. Walker, Charles W., illus. LC 62-13077. 85p. 21cm. 1962. Coward-McCann.
--Marya of Clark Avenue. Suba, Susanne (1913-), illus. LC 57-6961. (Illus.). 190 p. 21cm. 1957. Coward-McCann.
--Tony of the Ghost Towns. Marino, Dorothy Bronson (1912-), illus. LC 56-7137. 155p. illus. 22cm. c.1956. Coward- McCann.
--The Two Worlds of Damyan. Quackenbush, Robert Mead (1929-), illus. LC 66-5955. 169 p. illus. 22 cm. 1966. (ISBN 0-689-10045-0). Atheneum.

Blocher, Arlo
--Folk. new ed. LC 75-39815. (Illus.). 32p. (gr. 5-10). 1976. (ISBN 0-89375-013-1). (ISBN 0-89375-029-8). Troll Assocs.

Block, Irvin (1917-)
--George and the Ferocious Ferblundget. Jacks, Flo, illus. (Illus.). 1961. A. S. Barnes & Co, Inc.
--The Real Book About Christopher Columbus. Anderson, Rus, illus. LC 53-7205. (Illus.). 190 p. 21cm. (Real books R40). 1953. Garden City Books, by Arrangement with F. Watts New York.

Block, Jean Libman
--Linda Jordan: Lawyer. LC 53-7426. 173p. 21cm. (Romance for young moderns). 1953. J. Messner.

Blockinger, Peggy O'More see O'More, Peggy.
Blocklinger, Betty, pseud., see O'More, Peggy.
Blocksma, Mary
--Apple Tree! Apple Tree!. Kalthoff, Sandra Cox, illus. LC 82-19852. p. cm. (Just one more). 1983. (ISBN 0-516-01584-2). (ISBN 0-516-41584-0). Childrens Press.
--The Best Dressed Bear. Kalthoff, Sandra Cox, illus. LC 84-9565. (Illus.). 24 p. 22cm. (A Just One More Book Just for You). c.1984. (ISBN 0-516-01585-0). (ISBN 0-516-41585-9). Childrens Press.
--Did You Hear That?. Kalthoff, Sandra Cox, illus. LC 82-19877. (Illus.). 24p. (A Just One More Book Just for You). (ps-2). 1983. (ISBN 0-516-01581-8). (ISBN 0-516-41581-6). Childrens.
--Grandma Dragon's Birthday. Kalthoff, Sandra Cox, illus. LC 82-19851. p. cm. (Just one more). 1983. (ISBN 0-516-01582-6). Childrens Press.
--The Pup Went up. Kalthoff, Sandra Cox, illus. LC 82-19862. p. cm. (Just one more). 1983. (ISBN 0-516-01583-4). Childrens Press.
--Rub-a-Dub-Dub: What's in the Tub?. Kalthoff, Sandra Cox, illus. Hampton-Brown Company LC 84-12139. (Illus.). 24 p. 21cm. (A Just One More Book Just for You). c.1984. (ISBN 0-516-01586-9). Childrens Press.
--Where's That Duck!. Kalthoff, Sandra Cox, illus. Hampton-Brown Company LC 85-15001. p. cm. (A Just Onc More Book Just for You). 1985. (ISBN 0-516-01587-7). Children's Press.

Blocksma, Mary & Long, Sherry
--Bears in the Basement. Dyer, Jane, illus. (Illus.). 32p. (Sticker Stories Ser.). (gr. 1-8). 1983. (ISBN 0-89586-203-4). H P Bks.
--Spin Around the Birthday Planet. Dyer, Jane, illus. (Illus.). 32p. (Sticker Stories Ser.). (gr. 1-8). 1983. (ISBN 0-89586-202-6). H P Bks.

Blodgett, Harriet F
--Songs of the Days and the Year: For Children Old and Young. LC 1-27363. x, 163 p. 16 1/2 cm. 1901. The Grafton Press.

Blodgett, Mabel Fuller, Mrs. (1869-)
--The Giant's Ruby and other Fairy Tales. Pyle, Katharine D. (0000-1938), illus. LC 3-24223. (Illus.). 20.5 cm. 292p. 1903. Little Brown & Co.
--The Magic Slippers. Blodgett, Mabel Fuller, Mrs. (1869-), illus. LC 17-24076. 4 p. l., 90, 1 p. col. front., illus., col. plates. 19 cm. 1917. Little, Brown, and Company.
--Pensblossom: The Adventures of the Pine Tree Fairy and Others. Blodgett, Mabel Fuller, Mrs. (1869-), illus. LC 17-29188. ix p., 1 l., 13-177 p. col. front., illus., col. plates 21 cm. c.1917. George H. Doran Company.
--The Strange Story of Mr. Dog and Mr. Bear. Bridgman, Lewis Jesse (1857-1931), illus. LC 15-19216. 7 p. l., 3-178 p. incl. front., illus., plates. 20 x 16 cm. 1915. The Century Co.
--When Christmas Came Too Early. McCleean, Ralph, illus. LC 12-219521. 4 p. l., 107 p. col. front., illus., col. plates. 1915. Little, Brown, and Company.

Blomquist, David
--Daddy is Home. Grossman, Larry, contrib. by. Aliki, pseud. (1929-), illus. Brandenberg, Aliki Liacouras. LC 63-16417. (Illus.). 175 p. 24cm. (A Little Owl Bk.). 1963. Holt, Rinehart and Winston.

Blondell, Richard, ed.
--Keepsakes: Stories. Neville, Vera (1900-1978), illus. LC 36-30868. xiv, 96 p. incl. illus, plates. 21 cm. 1936. T. Nelson and Sons.

Blood, Charles Lewis (1929-) & Link, Martin A. (1934-), eds.
--The Goat in the Rug. Parker, Nancy Winslow (1930-), illus. LC 80-17315. p. cm. 1980, c.1976. (ISBN 0-590-07763-5). Four Winds Press.
--The Goat in the Rug. Parker, Nancy Winslow (1930-), illus. LC 75-19192. (Illus.). 38 p. 26cm. c.1976. (ISBN 0-8193-0828-5). (ISBN 0-8193-0827-7). Parents' Magazine Press.

Bloom, Freddy (1914-)
--The Boy Who Couldn't Hear. Charlton, Michael Alan (1923-), illus. 30p. 1979. (ISBN 0-370-01811-7, Pub. by Chatto Bodley Jonathan). Merrimack Pub Cir.

Bloom, Harold (1930-) & Hollander, John (1929-), eds.
--Wind & the Rain. (gr. 7 up). N.D. Doubleday.

Bloom, Margaret (1893-), tr. see Sand, George.
Bloom, Margaret (1893-)
--Black Hawk's Trail. Beck, Peggy Paver, illus. LC 31-33895. 6 p. l. 233 p. incl. illus., col. plates. col. front. 20 cm. (Young American Series). 1931. Laidlaw Brothers.
--Down the Ohio. Coons, Gaye Woodring, illus. LC 38-16225. 7 p. l., 17-201 p. incl. col. front, illus., plates (part col.) 21 1/2 cm. (Young America books). 1938. A. Whitman & Co.

Bloom, Patti A.
--Eric. Raven, Gertrude, illus. 1980. (ISBN 0-533-03738-7). Vantage.

Bloom, Pauline
--Toby, Law Stenographer. LC 59-7132. 191 p. 21cm. (Romance for young moderns). 1959. Messner.

Bloome, Enid P. (1925-)
--Dogs Don't Belong on Beds. Sommerschield, Rose, illus. LC 79-139337. (Illus.). 32 p. 1971. Doubleday.
Bloomfield, Frena
--The Dragon Paths. (gr. 5 up). 1973. (ISBN 0-85468-197-3). David & Charles.
Bloomfield, Howard Van Lieu
--Last Cruise of the Nightwatch. LC 56-8156. (Illus.). 213 p. 22cm. (Lodestar book). 1956. Prentice-Hall.
Bloomfield, Julia K.
--Glenwood. N.D. Methodist Book Concern.
Bloomfield, Robert (1766-1823)
--Little Davy's New Hat. N.D. George Routledge.
Bloomgarden, Lee
--Skinny Joins the Circus. Creekmore, Raymond (1905-), illus. LC 53-827910. 63p. illus. 22cm. (Everyday science stories). 1953. J. Messner.
Blos, Joan Winsor, jt. auth. see Miles, Betty.
Blos, Joan Winsor (1928-)
--Brothers of the Heart: A Story of the Old Northwest, 1837-1838. LC 85-40293. p. cm. 1985. (ISBN 0-684-18452-4). Scribner.
--A Gathering of Days: A New England Girl's Journal, 1830-32. LC 79-16898. (gr. 6-8). 1979. (ISBN 0-684-16340-3, ScribJ). (ISBN 0-689-70750-9). Scribner. **Awards: (ABA); (JNM); (ALA).**
--It's Spring," She Said. Maas, Julie, illus. LC 68-11168. (Illus.). 1 v. (unpaged. 22cm. 1968. Knopf.
--Martin's Hats. Simont, Marc (1915-), illus. LC 83-13389. (Illus.). 32 p. 1984. (ISBN 0-688-02027-5). (ISBN 0-688-02033-X). Morrow.
Blossom, Frederick Augustus (1913-), tr. see Colette, Sidonie Gabrielle (1873-1954) & Gauthier, Villare Henry.
Blotner, Joseph Leo (1923-), ed. see Faulkner, William Cuthbert.
Blotnick, Elihu (1939-)
--Blue Turtle Moon Queen. Robinson, Barbara, illus. (Illus.). 120p. 1st U.S. edition. (gr. 8-12). 1980. (ISBN 0-915090-20-1). Calif Street.
Blough, Dorris Murdock (1927-)
--Tied to a Leopard. LC 82-1188. p. cm. 1982. (ISBN 0-87178-845-4). Brethren Press.
Blough, Glenn Orlando (1907-)
--After the Sun goes Down: The Story of Animals at Night. Rendick, Jeanne, illus. LC 56-9623. 48p. illus. 26cm. c.1956. Whittlesey House.
--Beno: The Riverburg Mayor. De Cuir, John F., illus. LC 48-5581. 73 p. illus. 25 cm. 1948. H. Holt.
--Bird Watchers and Bird Feeders. LC 63-161942. 48 p. illus. 26 cm. 1963. Whittlesey House.
--Discovering Dinosaurs. Schrotter, Gustav, illus. LC 60-8020. 48p. illus. 28cm. c.1960. Whittlesey House.
--Lookout for the Forest. N.D. Whittlesey House.
--The Monkey with a Notion. De Cuir, John F., illus. LC 46-7095. 3 p. l., 88 p. illus. 24 cm. 1946. H. Holt and Company.
--Not Only for Ducks: The Story of Rain. Bendick, Jeanne (1919-), illus. LC 53-900984. unpaged. illus. 26cm. c.1954. Whittlesey House.
--Soon After September. Bendick, Jeanne (1919-), illus. LC 59-8549. 48p. illus. 26cm. 1959. Whittlesey House.
--Tree on the Road to Turntown. (Illus.). (gr. 1-4). 1953. (ISBN 0-07-006156-4). McGraw.
--The Tree on the Road to Turntown. Bendick, Jeanne (1919-), illus. LC 52-13018. 26cm. 48p. (gr. 3-5). 1953. Whittlesey House.
--Wait for the Sunshine: The Seasons and growing Things. Bendick, Jeanne (1919-), illus. LC 54-8812. c.1954. Whittlesey House.
--Who Lives in This House?. A Story of Animal Families. LC 57-9414. (Illus.). 48 p. 26cm. 1957. Whittlesey House.
Blount, Melesina Mary, Mrs.
--Hylton's Wife. LC 29-4422. 1929. Benziger Brothers.
Blow, Susan Elizabeth (1843-1816), ed. see Froebel, Friedrich Wilhelm August.
Blue, Rose (1931-)
--Bed-Stuy Beat: Sonny's Song. James, Harold Laymont (1929-), illus. LC 75-117182. (Illus.). 48 p. 27cm. 1971, c.1970. (ISBN 0-531-01940-3). F. Watts.
--Bed-Stuy Beat: Sonny's song. James, Harold Laymont (1929-), illus. LC 75-117178. (Illus.). 48p. illus. 27cm. (gr. 4-6). 1970. (ISBN 0-531-01940-3). Watts.
--Black, Black, Beautiful Black. Wigglesworth, Emmett (1939-), illus. LC 73-77240. (Illus.). 43 p. 27cm. 1969. F. Watts.
--Cold Rain on the Water. LC 78-23633. 123 p. 21cm. c.1979. (ISBN 0-07-006168-8). McGraw-Hill.
--Einstein and Me: Breaking Through the Reading Barrier. LC 79-11387. p. cm. 1979. (ISBN 0-87705-388-X). Human Sciences Press.
--Grandma Didn't Wave Back. Lewin, Ted (1935-), illus. LC 70-189568. (Illus.). 62 p. 21cm. 1972. (ISBN 0-531-02557-8). Watts.
--How Many Blocks Is the World?. James, Harold Laymont (1929-), illus. LC 77-77241. (Illus.). 48 p. 27cm. 1970. F. Watts.
--I Am Here, Yo Estoy Aqui. Barnett, Moneta (1922-1976), illus. LC 79-117183. (Illus.). 48 p. 27cm. 1971. (ISBN 0-531-01943-8). Watts.
--A Month of Sundays. Lewin, Ted (1935-), illus. LC 72-182293. (Illus.). 59 p. 22cm. 1972. (ISBN 0-531-02037-1). F. Watts.
--My Mother, the Witch. Lewin, Ted (1935-), illus. LC 79-23950. p. cm. c.1980. (ISBN 0-07-006169-6). McGraw-Hill.
--Nikki 108. Lewin, Ted (1935-), illus. LC 72-6071. (Illus.). 51 p. 21cm. 1972, c.1973. (ISBN 0-531-02602-7). F. Watts.
--The Preacher's Kid. Lewin, Ted (1935-), illus. LC 74-19154. (Illus.). 52 p. 21cm. 1975. (ISBN 0-531-02804-6). Watts.
--A Quiet Place. Feelings, Thomas (1933-), illus. LC 69-11223. (Illus.). 57 p. 22cm. 1969. F. Watts.
--Seven Years from Home. Erickson, Barbara, illus. LC 75-42105. (Illus.). (Fiction). (gr. 5 up). 1976. (ISBN 0-8172-0076-2). Raintree Pubs.
--The Thirteenth Year: A Bar Mitzvah Story. LC 76-54273. (Illus.). 85 p. 22cm. (gr. 5 up). 1977. (ISBN 0-531-00382-5). Watts.
--We Are Chicano. Alcorn, Bob, illus. LC 73-4693. (Illus.). 58 p. 21cm. 1973. (ISBN 0-531-02633-7). Watts.
--Wishful Lying. LC 79-21806. p. cm. 1980. (ISBN 0-87705-473-8). Human Sciences Press.
--The Yo-Yo Kid. Ericksen, Barbara M., illus. LC 76-17623. (Illus.). 64p. (Fiction). (gr. 5 up). 1976. (ISBN 0-8172-0077-0). (ISBN 0-8172-0078-9). Raintree Pubs.
Blue, Wallace, pseud., see Kraenzel, Margaret Powell.
Blue, Wallace, pseud. (1899-)
--The Mouse-Gray Stallion. Kraenzel, Margaret Powell. 1st ed. Moyers, William (1916-), illus. LC 57-9351. 142p. illus. 21cm. 1957. Bobbs-Merrill Co.
Bluestein, Bill & Bluestein, Enid
--Mom, How Come I'm Not Thin?. Kennedy, Susan, illus. LC 81-102326. (Illus.). 34 p. 29cm. c.1981. (ISBN 0-89638-044-0). CompCare Publications.
--The Year Santa Got Thin. Pearson, Joe (1934-), illus. (Illus.). 48p. (gr. k-4). 1981. (ISBN 0-89638-045-9). CompCare.
Bluestein, Enid, jt. auth. see Bluestein, Bill.
Bluhm, Ina R., tr. see Neumann, Rudolf.
Blum, John Morton (1921-), selected by see Our Young Folks.
Blum, Lisa Marie (1911-)
--The Mysterious Merry-Go-Round. Blum, Lisa Marie (1911-), illus. Strachan, Geoffrey, tr. from Ger. LC 62-9731. (Illus.). 127 p. 21cm. 1962. Abelard-Schuman.
Blumberg, Fannie Louise Burgheim see Burgheim, Fanny Louise, pseud.
Blumberg, Fannie Louise Burgheim, Mrs. (1894-)
--The First Circus. Burgheim, Fanny Louise, pseud. LC 41-35155. (Illus.). 24 p. 21cm. (Never Grow Old Stories). 1930. The Platt & Munk Co. Inc.
--Rowena, Teena, Tot and the Blackberries. Grosjean, Mary, illus. LC 34-19031. 32 p. illus. (part col.) 24 cm. c.1934. A. Whitman & Co.
--Rowena, Teena, Tot and the Runaway Turkey. Grosjean, Mary, illus. LC 36-29597. (Illus.). 30 p. 24cm. (Junior Press Bks.). 1936. A. Whitman & Co.
Blumberg, Rhoda (1917-)
--Backyard Bestiary. Tinkelman, Murray (1933-), illus. LC 78-6755. (Illus.). 31 p. c.1979. (ISBN 0-698-20444-1). Coward, McCann & Geoghegan.
--The First Travel Guide to the Moon: What to Pack, How to Go, & What to See When You Get There. Doty, Roy (1922-), illus. LC 80-66244. (Illus.). 96p. (gr. 3-7). 1980. (ISBN 0-590-07663-9, Four Winds). Scholastic Inc.
Blume, Judy Sussman Kitchens (1938-)
--Are You There God? It's Me, Margaret. LC 79-122741. 149 p. 22cm. 1970. Bradbury Press.
--Are You There God? It's Me, Margaret. 5 3/8 x 8 13/16. (16-18 pt.). N.D (Pub. by Lythway Lg Print Bks). G K Hall.
--Blubber. LC 73-94116. 153 p. 22cm. 1974. (ISBN 0-87888-072-0). Bradbury Press.
--Deenie. LC 73-80197. 159 p. 22cm. 1973. (ISBN 0-87888-061-5). Bradbury Press.
--Forever. 1975. Bradbury Press.
--Freckle Juice. Lisker, Sonia O. (1933-), illus. 1971. Four Winds.
--Freckle Juice. Lisker, Sonia O. (1933-), illus. LC 85-280. p. cm. 1985, c.1971. (ISBN 0-02-711690-5). Four Winds Press.
--Iggie's House. LC 70-104340. 117 p. 22cm. 1970. Bradbury Press.
--Iggie's House. N.D. Prentice-Hall.
--It's Not the End of the World. LC 70-181739. 169 p. 22cm. 1972. (ISBN 0-87888-042-9). Bradbury Press.
--The One in the Middle Is the Green Kangaroo. Aitken, Amy (1952-), illus. LC 80-29664. p. cm. 1981, c.1969. (ISBN 0-87888-182-4). Bradbury Press.
--The One in the Middle Is the Green Kangaroo. Axeman, Lois, illus. LC 74-88718. (Illus.). 32 p. 24cm. 1969. Reilly & Lee Books.
--Otherwise Known As Sheila the Great. LC 72-78082. 118 p. 22cm. 1972. (ISBN 0-525-36455-2). E. P. Dutton.
--The Pain and the Great One. Trivas, Irene, illus. LC 84-11009. (Illus.). 32p. (gr. k-3). 1984. (ISBN 0-02-711100-8). Bradbury Pr.
--Starring Sally J. Freedman As Herself. LC 76-57805. 298 p. 22cm. c.1977. (ISBN 0-87888-113-1). Bradbury Press.
--Superfudge. LC 80-10439. 166 p. 22cm. c.1980. Dutton.
--Tales of a Fourth Grade Nothing. Doty, Roy (1922-), illus. LC 70-179050. 120 p. 20cm. (Dutton anytime books). 1973. (ISBN 0-525-45012-2). E. P. Dutton & Co.
--Then Again, Maybe I Won't. LC 77-156548. 160p. 176p. (gr. 5-7). 1971. (ISBN 0-02-711090-7). Bradbury Pr.
--Then Again, Maybe I Won't: A Novel. LC 77-156548. 164 p. 22cm. 1971. (ISBN 0-87888-035-6). Bradbury Press.
--Tiger Eyes. LC 81-6152. 256p. (gr. 7 up). 1981. (ISBN 0-02-711080-X). Bradbury Pr.
Blumenfeld, Lenore
--Plays Around the World: Folk Tales Adapted for the Stage. LC 73-87070. (Illus.). 80 p. 21cm. c.1973. Xerox Education Publications.
Blumenfeld, Simon
--The Iron Garden. LC 36-783. 4 p. l., 310 p. 19 1/2 cm. 1936. Doubleday, Doran & Company, Inc.
Blumenthal, Gertrude see Gertrude, Blane, pseud.
Blumenthal, Gertrude (1907-1971)
--Changeable Charlie. Becker, Charlotte (1906-), illus. LC 42-19680. 48 p. illus. 23 x 22 cm. 1942. Oxford University Press.
--Flower Box Mystery. New ed. Wyler, Rose, ed. Zansky, Louis, illus. LC 65-13674. 62p. col. illus. 22cm. (New everyday sci. story). 1965, c.1953. Melmont.
--Flower Box Surprise. Gertrude, Blane, pseud. Zansky, Louis, illus. LC 53-8278. 62p. illus. 22cm. (Everyday science stories). 1953. J. Messner.
--Louise's Adventure: Her Ride in the Subway. Becker, Charlotte (1906-), illus. LC 41-5299. (32) p. illus. (part col.) 22 1/2 x 27 cm. 1941. Doubleday, Doran & Company, Incorporated.
--Tales About Timothy. Malvern, Corinne (1905-1956), illus. LC 46-3145. 2 p. l., 9-66, 2 p. col. illus. 28 1/2 cm. 1945. Whitman Publishing Company.
--Tit for Tat Tommy. Becker, Charlotte (1906-), illus. LC 44-7481. 47 p. illus. 21 x 25 1/2 cm. 1944. Oxford University Press.
Blumenthal, Judith Louise Teitler see Ellis, Judy, pseud.
Blumenthal, Judith Louise Teitler (1931-)
--The Treasure of Greenbar Island. Ellis, Judy, pseud. Zansky, Louis, illus. LC 53-10501. 63p. illus. 22cm. (Everyday science stories). 1953. J. Messner.
Blundell, Agnes
--The Living Voice. LC 31-31935. 280 p. 19 cm. 1931. Benzinger Brothers.
Bluntzer, Helen
--Peter Pratt Stories. 1978. (ISBN 0-533-03431-0). Vantage.
Blustein, Ellen, jt. auth. see Glasser, Barbara.
Bluth, Brad
--The Buddies in a Day for Knights. Bluth, Toby, illus. LC 84-147717. (Illus.). 44 p. 29cm. c.1984. (ISBN 0-8249-8062-X). Ideals Pub. Corp.
--Siegfried's Silent Night. Keller, Dick, illus. (Illus.). 32p. (Christmas Bks.). (gr. k-4). 1983. (ISBN 0-516-09159-X). Childrens.
Bluth Brothers
--A Day for Knights. Bluth, Brad & Bluth, Toby, illus. (Illus.). 48p. (Buddies Ser.). (gr. k-6). 1984. (ISBN 0-8249-8062-X). Ideals.
--Somebody's Hero. Bluth, Brad & Bluth, Toby, illus. (Illus.). 48p. (Buddies Ser.). (gr. k-6). 1984. (ISBN 0-8249-8063-8). Ideals.
Bly, Robert W. (1926-)
--Ronald's Dumb Computer. Soileau, Hodges, illus. LC 84-124348. (Illus.). 79 p., 1 leaf of plates. 22cm. c.1983. (ISBN 0-440-07486-X). Miles Standish Press.
Bly, Stephen A.
--The President Is Stuck in the Mud. (Orig.). (Making Choices Ser.: No. 4). (gr. 3-8). 1982. (ISBN 0-89191-661-X). Cook.
--Trouble in Quartz Mountain Tunnel. VanSeveren, Joe, illus. (Illus.). 124p. (Making Choices Ser.). (gr. 4-8). 1985. (ISBN 0-89191-979-1, Chariot Bks). Cook.
Blyth, Alan (1929-)
--Cinderella: The Story of Rossini's Opera. Luzzati, Emanuele (1921-), illus. (Illus.). 32p. (gr. 2-4). 1982. (ISBN 0-531-04061-5, MacRae). Watts.
--Lohengrin: The Story of Wagner's Opera. Gambaro, Maria A., illus. (Illus.). 32p. (gr. 2-4). 1982. (ISBN 0-531-04064-X, MacRae). Watts.
Blyth, Hugh Featherstone, jt. auth. see Faizi, Abul-Oasim.
Blythe, LeGette (1900-)
--The Stableboy Who Stayed at Bethlehem: A Fantasy of the First Christmas. Zepeda, Barbara Allen, illus. LC 74-13174. (Illus.). 36 p. 21cm. 1974. (ISBN 0-914998-01-3). Charlotte Pub.
Blythe, Richard
--Dragons & Other Fabulous Beasts. French, Fiona (1944-) & Troughton, Joann, illus. LC 79-51211. (Illus.). (gr. 3-7). 1980. (ISBN 0-448-16561-9, G&D). (ISBN 0-448-13611-2). Putnam Pub Group.
Blyton, Carey (1932-)
--Bananas in Pyjamas. Baring, Tom, illus. N.D. Taplinger.
--Bananas in Pyjamas: A Book of Nonsense. Barling, Tom, illus. 32p. (Orig.). (ps-5). 1976. (ISBN 0-571-10671-4). Faber & Faber.
Blyton, Enid Mary (1897-1968)
--The Astonishing ladder and other stories. N.D. St Martin's Press.
--Be Brave, Little Noddy!. Van Der Beek, Harmsen, illus. Repr. of 1949 ed. (ps-2). 1974. (ISBN 0-8277-3413-1). British Bk Ctr.
--The Blue Story Book. N.D. The Parkwood Press.
--The Boy with the Loaves And Fishes. Walker, Elsie, illus. LC 58-7787. 64p. illus. 19cm. N.D. Roy Publishers.
--The Castle of Adventure. Tresilian, Cecil Stuart (1891-), illus. LC 46-18356. 4 p. l., 251 p. front., illus. 21 cm. 1946. The Macmillan Company.
--Cheer up, Little Noddy!. Van Der Beek, Harmsen, illus. Repr. of 1949 ed. (ps-2). 1974. (ISBN 0-8277-3420-4). British Bk Ctr.
--The Circus of Adventure. Tresilian, Cecil Stuart (1891-), illus. LC 52-147053. 316p. illus. 21cm. (gr. 4-8). 1953. (ISBN 0-312-13930-6). St. Martin's Press.
--The Conjuring Wizard and other stories. (Illus.). N.D. St Martin's Press.
--Do Look Out, Noddy!. Van Der Beek, Harmsen, illus. Repr. of 1949 ed. (ps-2). 1974. (ISBN 0-8277-3415-8). British Bk Ctr.
--The Enid Blyton Story Book. 1962. Golden Press.
--The Famous Jimmy. LC 37-21145. 3 p. l., 11-56, l p. incl. front., illus. 29 1/2 cm. 1937. E. P. Dutton & Co., Inc.
--Five Caught in a Treacherous Plot. Maxey, Betty, illus. LC 72-194735. (Illus.). 188 p. 21cm. (Atheneum. An Aladdin book, B7). 1972. Atheneum.
--Five Fall into Adventure. Maxey, Betty, illus. LC 72-195658. (Illus.). 188 p. 21cm. (Atheneum, B8. An Aladdin book). 1972. Atheneum.
--Five Find a Secret Way. 1972. (ISBN 0-689-70320-1, Aladdin). Atheneum.
--Five Go Adventuring Again. 5 3/8 x 8 13/16. (16-18 pt.). 1986 (Pub. by Lythway Lg Print Bks). G K Hall.
--Five Go Adventuring Again. Neville, Vera (1900-1978), illus. LC 51-1165. 207 p. illus. 21 cm. 1951. Crowell.
--Five Go Down to the Sea. Aloise, Frank E., illus. LC 61-12109. 204p. illus. 21cm. 1961. Reilly & Lee.
--Five Go to Demon's Rocks. Maxey, Betty, illus. LC 80-127000. (Illus.). 184 p. 21cm. (Aladdin book). 1980, c.1972. (ISBN 0-689-70478-X). Atheneum.
--Five Go to Mystery Moor. Aloise, Frank E., illus. LC 63-10907. 181 p. illus. 21 cm. (adventure of the famous five). 1963. Reilly & Lee.
--Five Go to Smuggler's Top. 1972. (ISBN 0-689-70323-6, Aladdin). Atheneum.
--Five Go to Smuggler's Top: Another Adventure of the Four Children And Timmy the Dog. Soper, Eileen Alice (1905-), illus. LC 60-842360. 192p. illus. 19cm. 1960. Reilly & Lee.
--Five Guard a Hidden Discovery. 1972. (ISBN 0-689-70324-4, Aladdin). Atheneum.
--Five on a Secret Trail. Maxey, Betty, illus. LC 80-126998. (Illus.). 184 p. 21cm. (Atheneum ; B8). (Aladdin book). 1980, c.1972. (ISBN 0-689-70477-1). Atheneum.
--Five on a Treasure Island. 1972. (ISBN 0-689-70319-8, Aladdin). Atheneum.
--Five on a Treasure Island. 5 3/8 x 8 13/16. (16-18 pt.). N.D (Pub. by Lythway Lg Print Bks). G K Hall.
--Five on a Treasure Island. Neville, Vera (1900-1978), illus. LC 50-7729. 209 p. illus. 21 cm. 1950. Crowell.
--Five on the Track of a Spook Train. Soper, Eileen Alice (1905-), illus. LC 72-195660. (Illus.). 188 p. 21cm. (Atheneum, B8. An Aladdin book). 1972. Atheneum.
--Five Run Away to Danger. 1972. (ISBN 0-689-70322-8, Aladdin). Atheneum.

--Five Run Away Together: The Third Story of the Adventures of the Four Children and Their Dog. Soper, Eileen Alice (1905-), illus. LC 60-8424. 192p. illus. 19cm. 1960. Reilly & Lee Co.
--The Green Story Book. N.D. The Parkwood Press.
--Here Comes Noddy Again. Van Der Beek, Harmsen, illus. Repr. of 1949 ed. (ps-2). 1974. (ISBN 0-8277-3404-2). British Bk Ctr.
--Hurrah for Little Noddy. Van Der Beek, Harmsen, illus. Repr. of 1949 ed. (ps-2). 1974. (ISBN 0-8277-3402-6). British Bk Ctr.
--I'll tell you another story. N.D. St Martin's Press.
--Just Time for a Story. N.D. Macmillan.
--The Laughing Kitten. Kaye, Paul, photos by. LC 55-600808. unpaged. illus. 22cm. N.D. Roy Publishers.
--Let's Have a Party. Kaye, Paul, photos by. LC 57-5966. unpaged. illus. 22cm. 1957. Roy Publishers.
--The Little Girl at Capernaum. Walker, Elsie, illus. LC 58-7788. 64p. illus. 19cm. N.D. Roy Publishers.
--Mischief Again!. Kaye, Paul, photos by. LC 55-9186. unpaged. illus. 22cm. N.D. Roy Publishers.
--The Mountain of Adventure. Tresilian, Cecil Stuart (1891-), illus. LC 49-10383. ix. p. illus. 21 cm. 1949. Macmillan Co.
--Mr. Plod & Little Noddy. Van Der Beek, Harmsen, illus. Repr. of 1949 ed. (ps-2). 1974. (ISBN 0-8277-3422-0). British Bk Ctr.
--Mr. Tumpy and His Caravan. Wheeler, Dorothy M., illus. LC 51-6515. unpaged. illus. 26 cm. 1951. W. L. McNaughton.
--Mystery Island. LC 64-9579. 207p. Repr. of 1944 ed. 1963. Macmillan Company.
--Mystery Island. Tresilian, Cecil Stuart (1891-), illus. LC 64-9579. 207 p. 21 cm. (Acorn books, AB4). 1963, c.1945. Macmillan.
--Mystery Island. Tresilian, Cecil Stuart (1891-), illus. LC 45-1955. vi, 266 p. incl. front., illus. 21 cm. 1945. The Macmillan Company.
--Mystery of a Strange Message. (Illus.). N.D. British Book Centre.
--The Mystery of Banshee Towers. Chapple, Jenny, tr. Repr. (gr. 3-6). 1974. (ISBN 0-8277-3303-8). British Bk Ctr.
--The Mystery of Holly Lane. 2nd ed. Repr. (gr. 3-6). 1976. (ISBN 0-8277-4474-9). British Bk Ctr.
--Mystery of Strange Messages. Repr. (gr. 3-6). 1975. (ISBN 0-8277-3448-4). British Bk Ctr.
--Mystery of Tally-Ho Cottage. Repr. (gr. 3-6). 1975. (ISBN 0-8277-3447-6). British Bk Ctr.
--The Mystery of the Burnt Cottage. 2nd ed. 166p. Repr. (gr. 4-6). 1973. (ISBN 0-8277-0189-6). British Bk Ctr.
--The Mystery of the Burnt Cottage: The First Adventure of the Five Find-Outers and Dog. Abbey, J., illus. 3 p. l., 160 p. incl. front., illus. 19 1/2 cm. 1946. W. L. McNaughton, Inc.
--The Mystery of the Disappearing Cat. 2nd ed. 179p. Repr. (gr. 4-6). 1973. (ISBN 0-8277-0190-X). British Bk Ctr.
--The Mystery of the Disappearing Cat. The Second Adventure of the Five Find-Outers and Dog. Abbey, J., illus. LC 48-7828. 170 p. illus. 20 cm. 1948. W. L. McHaughton.
--The Mystery of the Hidden House. 2nd ed. 176p. Repr. (gr. 4-6). 1973. (ISBN 0-8277-0191-8). British Bk Ctr.
--The Mystery of the Hidden House. N.D. The Parkwood Press.
--The Mystery of the Invisible Thief. 2nd ed. 176p. Repr. (gr. 4-6). 1973. (ISBN 0-8277-4499-4). British Bk Ctr.
--The Mystery of the Missing Man. Buchanan, Lilian, illus. Repr. (gr. 3-6). 1974. (ISBN 0-8277-3449-2). British Bk Ctr.
--The Mystery of the Missing Necklace. Repr. (gr. 3-6). 1975. (ISBN 0-8277-3302-X). British Bk Ctr.
--The Mystery of the Missing Necklace. N.D. The Parkwood Press.
--The Mystery of the Pantomime Cat. 2nd ed. Repr. (gr. 3-6). N.D. (ISBN 0-8277-4473-0). British Bk Ctr.
--The Mystery of the Pantomime Cat. N.D. The Parkwood Press.
--The Mystery of the Secret Room. Repr. (gr. 3-6). 1975. (ISBN 0-8277-3446-8). British Bk Ctr.
--The Mystery of the Secret Room: The Third Adventure of the Five Find-Outers and Dog. Abbey, J., illus. LC 50-3336. 151 p. illus. 20 cm. 1950. Parkwood Press.
--The Mystery of the Spiteful Letters. 2nd ed. Repr. (gr. 3-6). 1976. (ISBN 0-8277-4472-2). British Bk Ctr.
--The Mystery of the Spiteful Letters. N.D. The Parkwood Press.
--The Mystery of the Strange Bundle. Chapple, Jenny, illus. Repr. (gr. 3-6). 1974. (ISBN 0-8277-3301-1). British Bk Ctr.
--The Mystery of the Vanished Prince. Chapple, Jenny, illus. Repr. (gr. 3-6). 1974. (ISBN 0-8277-3300-3). British Bk Ctr.
--Noddy & His Car. Van Der Beek, Harmsen, illus. Repr. of 1949 ed. (ps-2). 1974. (ISBN 0-8277-3403-4). British Bk Ctr.
--Noddy & Tessie Bear. Van Der Beek, Harmsen, illus. Repr. of 1949 ed. (ps-2). 1974. (ISBN 0-8277-3412-3). British Bk Ctr.
--Noddy & the Aeroplane. Van Der Beek, Harmsen, illus. Repr. of 1949 ed. (ps-2). 1974. (ISBN 0-8277-3424-7). British Bk Ctr.
--Noddy & the Bumpy Dog. Van Der Beek, Harmsen, illus. Repr. of 1949 ed. (ps-2). 1974. (ISBN 0-8277-3414-X). British Bk Ctr.
--Noddy & the Bunkey. Van Der Beek, Harmsen, illus. Repr. of 1949 ed. (ps-2). 1974. (ISBN 0-8277-3419-0). British Bk Ctr.
--Noddy & the Magic Rubber. Van Der Beek, Harmsen, illus. Repr. of 1949 ed. (ps-2). 1974. (ISBN 0-8277-3409-3). British Bk Ctr.
--Noddy & the Tootles. Van Der Beek, Harmsen, illus. Repr. of 1949 ed. (ps-2). 1974. (ISBN 0-8277-3423-9). British Bk Ctr.
--Noddy at the Seaside. Van Der Beek, Harmsen, illus. Repr. of 1949 ed. (ps-2). 1974. (ISBN 0-8277-3407-7). British Bk Ctr.
--Noddy Gets into Trouble. Van Der Beek, Harmsen, illus. Repr. of 1949 ed. (ps-2). 1974. (ISBN 0-8277-3408-5). British Bk Ctr.
--Noddy Goes to School. Van Der Beek, Harmsen, illus. Repr. of 1949 ed. (ps-2). 1974. (ISBN 0-8277-3406-9). British Bk Ctr.
--Noddy Goes to Sea. Van Der Beek, Harmsen, illus. Repr. of 1949 ed. (ps-2). 1974. (ISBN 0-8277-3418-2). British Bk Ctr.
--Noddy Goes to the Fair. Van Der Beek, Harmsen, illus. Repr. of 1949 ed. (ps-2). 1974. (ISBN 0-8277-3421-2). British Bk Ctr.
--Noddy Goes to Toyland. Van Der Beek, Harmsen, illus. Repr. of 1949 ed. (ps-2). 1974. (ISBN 0-8277-3401-8). British Bk Ctr.
--Noddy Has an Adventure. Van Der Beek, Harmsen, illus. Repr. of 1949 ed. (ps-2). 1974. (ISBN 0-8277-3417-4). British Bk Ctr.
--Noddy Meets Father Christmas. Van Der Beek, Harmsen, illus. Repr. of 1949 ed. (ps-2). 1974. (ISBN 0-8277-3411-5). British Bk Ctr.
--The Red Story Book. N.D. The Parkwood Press.
--The River of Adventure. Tresilian, Cecil Stuart (1891-), illus. LC 55-10118. 277p. illus. 21cm. 1955. (ISBN 0-312-68495-9). St. Martin's Press.
--The Sea of Adventure. Tresilian, Cecil Stuart (1891-), illus. LC 48-3677. x. 220 p. illus. 21 cm. 1948. Macmillan Co.
--The Secret Seven and the Bonfire Adventure. Rev. ed. Miller, M. Hughes, ed. Dunnington, Tom, illus. LC 75-185506. (Illus.). 126 p. 21cm. 1st U.S. edition. (Her Secret Seven adventures). 1972. (ISBN 0-516-01465-X). Childrens Press.
--The Secret Seven and the Case of the Dog Lover. american rev. ed. Miller, M. Hughes, ed. Dunnington, Tom, illus. LC 72-185508. (Illus.). 126 p. 21cm. (Her Secret Seven adventures). 1972. (ISBN 0-516-01467-6). Childrens Press.
--The Secret Seven and the Case of the Missing Medals. american rev. ed. Miller, M. Hughes, ed. Dunnington, Tom, illus. LC 76-185509. (Illus.). 122 p. 21cm. (Her Secret Seven adventures). 1972. (ISBN 0-516-01468-4). Childrens Press.
--The Secret Seven and the Case of the Music Lover. american rev. ed. Miller, M. Hughes, ed. Dunnington, Tom, illus. LC 71-185505. (Illus.). 125 p. 21cm. (Her Secret Seven adventures). 1972. (ISBN 0-516-01464-1). Childrens Press.
--The Secret Seven and the Case of the Old Horse. american rev. ed. Miller, M. Hughes, ed. Dunnington, Tom, illus. LC 70-185510. (Illus.). 125 p. 21cm. (Her Secret Seven adventures). 1972. (ISBN 0-516-01469-2). Childrens Press.
--The Secret Seven and the Case of the Stolen Car. american rev. ed. Miller, M. Hughes & Dunnington, Tom, illus. LC 77-185501. (Illus.). 121 p. 21cm. (Her Secret Seven adventures). 1972. (ISBN 0-516-01460-9). Childrens Press.
--The Secret Seven and the Circus Adventure. american rev. ed. Miller, M. Hughes, ed. Dunnington, Tom, illus. LC 76-185497. (Illus.). 121 p. 21cm. (Her Secret Seven adventures). 1972. (ISBN 0-516-01456-0). Childrens Press.
--The Secret Seven and the Grim Secret. american rev. ed. Miller, M. Hughes, ed. Dunnington, Tom, illus. LC 74-185503. (Illus.). 123 p. 21cm. (Her Secret Seven adventures). 1972. (ISBN 0-516-01462-5). Childrens Press.
--The Secret Seven and the Hidden Cave Adventure. american rev. ed. Miller, M. Hughes, ed. Dunnington, Tom, illus. LC 70-185502. (Illus.). 121 p. 21cm. (Her Secret Seven adventures). 1972. (ISBN 0-516-01461-7). Childrens Press.
--The Secret Seven and the Missing Girl Mystery. american rev. ed. Miller, M. Hughes & Dunnington, Tom, eds. LC 78-185504. (Illus.). 121 p. 21cm. (Her Secret Seven adventures). 1972. (ISBN 0-516-01463-3). Childrens Press.
--The Secret Seven and the Mystery of the Empty House. american rev. ed. Miller, M. Hughes, ed. Dunnington, Tom, illus. LC 72-185496. (Illus.). 121 p. 21cm. (Her Secret Seven adventures). 1972. (ISBN 0-516-01455-2). Childrens Press.
--The Secret Seven and the Old Fort Adventure. american rev. ed. Miller, M. Hughes, ed. Dunnington, Tom, illus. LC 79-185507. (Illus.). 123 p. 21cm. (Her Secret Seven adventures). 1972. (ISBN 0-516-01466-8). Childrens Press.
--The Secret Seven: And the Railroad Mystery. american rev. ed. Miller, M. Hughes, ed. Dunnington, Tom, illus. LC 73-185499. (Illus.). 122 p. 21cm. (Her Secret Seven adventures). (gr. 4-5). 1972. (ISBN 0-516-01458-7). Childrens Press.
--The Secret Seven and the Tree House Adventure. american rev. ed. Miller, M. Hughes, ed. Dunnington, Tom, illus. LC 70-185498. (Illus.). 121 p. 21cm. (Her Secret Seven adventures). 1972. (ISBN 0-516-01457-0). Childrens Press.
--The Secret Seven Get Their Man. american rev. ed. Miller, M. Hughes, ed. Dunnington, Tom, illus. LC 73-185500. (Illus.). 121 p. 21cm. (Her Secret Seven adventures). 1972. (ISBN 0-516-01459-5). Childrens Press.
--The Ship of Adventure. Tresilian, Cecil Stuart (1891-), illus. LC 50-11578. ix, 230 p. illus. 21 cm. 1950. Macmillan.
--Silver and Gold. Everett, Ethel F., illus. LC 29-7889. 128 p. col. front., illus., col. plates. 23 cm. 1928. T. Nelson & Sons.
--Sunnyside Stories. (gr. k-5). 1977. (ISBN 0-8277-5009-9). British Bk Ctr.
--Twilight Tales. (gr. k-5). 1977. (ISBN 0-8277-5010-2). British Bk Ctr.
--The Valley of Adventure. Tresilian, Cecil Stuart (1891-), illus. LC 47-4138. 4 p. l., 269, 1 p. front., illus. 21 cm. 1947. The Macmillan Company.
--Well Done Noddy!. Van Der Beek, Harmsen, illus. Repr. of 1949 ed. (ps-2). 1974. (ISBN 0-8277-3405-0). British Bk Ctr.
--The Yellow Story Book. N.D. The Parkwood Press.
--You Funny Little Noddy. Van Der Beek, Harmsen, illus. Repr. of 1949 ed. (ps-2). 1974. (ISBN 0-8277-3410-7). British Bk Ctr.
--You're a Good Friend, Noddy!. Van Der Beek, Harmsen, illus. Repr. of 1949 ed. (ps-2). 1974. (ISBN 0-8277-3416-6). British Bk Ctr.

Bo-Peep
--Little Bo-Peep. N.D. E. P. Dutton & Co.

Boal, Bobby Snow
--A Tree for Phyllis and me. Boal, Bobby Snow, illus. LC 57-9709. 45p. illus. 23cm. 1957. Young Scott Books.

Boardman, Fon Wyman, Jr. (1911-)
--Against the Iroquois. (gr. 5-10). 1978. (ISBN 0-8098-0014-4). Walck.
--Castles. LC 57-11638. (Illus.). 24cm. 104p. (Oxford Books for Boys and Girls). 1957. Oxford University Press.

Boardman, Laurel
--Lill By-Golly. Kennedy, Anna Margaret, illus. LC 44-2095. 5 p. l., 13-112 p. illus., col. pl. 23 cm. 1943. Rockwell-Darmay Publications.
--The Search: Adventures at the R-Bar-R Ranch. Poupard, Eileen, illus. LC 51-26061. 28p. col. illus. 28cm. 1951. Savage & Savage.

Boardman, Neta Jean, Mrs.
--Dodo and Billy. LC 27-6039. 7 p. l., 17-157 p. front. (port.) plates, 19 1/2 cm. c.1926. V. Palmer Company.

Boardman, W. E., Mrs.
--Haps and Mishaps of the Brown Family. (The Boardman Library). N.D. Perkinpine & Higgins.
--The Mother-in-Law. (The Boardman Library). N.D. Perkinpine & Higgins.
--Nellie Gates and the Little Missionary. (The Boardman Library). N.D. Perkinpine & Higgins.
--The Sister's Triumph. (The Boardman Library). N.D. Perkinpine & Higgins.

Boas, F., ed. see Stevenson, Robert Louis.

Boas, F. S., Mrs., ed. see Austen, Jane.

Boase, Wendy
--The Castle. King, Pauline, illus. LC 83-62967. (Illus.). 32p. (Early Bird Bks.). (ps-1). 1984. (ISBN 0-394-86659-2, Pub. by BYR). Random.
--The Circus. Ward, Deborah, illus. LC 83-62968. (Illus.). (Early Bird Bks.: Hide & Seek Sub-Ser.). (ps-1). 1984. (ISBN 0-394-86660-6, Pub. by BYR). Random.
--Fairyland. Rodwell, Jenny, illus. LC 83-62969. (Illus.). 32p. (Early Bird Bks.: Hide & Seek Sub-Ser.). (ps-1). 1984. (ISBN 0-394-86661-4, Pub. by BYR). Random.
--Toyland. Trimby, Elisa (1948-), illus. LC 83-62970. (Illus.). 32p. (Early Bird Bks.: Hide & Seek Sub-Ser.). (ps-1). 1984. (ISBN 0-394-86662-2, Pub. by BYR). Random.

Boaz, Frances Coffin, Mrs., ed.
--Colts of Pegasus. LC 37-37834. 12 p. l., 309 p. front. (port.) 19 1/2 cm. 1936. Tardy Publishing Company, Inc.

Bobrow, Ella
--Three Brave Snowflakes. Buettner, Hans J., illus. (Illus.). 24p. (Orig.). 1982. (ISBN 0-88962-204-3, Pub by Mosaic Pr Canada). Flatiron Book Dist.

Bobrowski, Johannes (1917-1965), adapted by.
--The House in the Meadow. Meyer-Rey, Ingeborg, illus. Gillespie, Moya, tr. LC 77-80951. (Original Author: Samuil Jakovlevich Marshak, 1887-1964). (Illus.). 47 p. 26cm. 1st U.S. edition. 1970. Harvey House.

Bocca, Geoffrey
--King Without Thornes. N.D. Dial Press Inc.

Boccaccio, Giovanni (1313-1375)
--Chichibio and the Crane. Luzzati, Emanuele (1921-), adapted by. Luzzati, Emanuele (1921-), illus. LC 61-12614. unpaged, illus. 18 x 25 cm. (Astor book). 1961. (ISBN 0-8392-3004-4). I. Obolensky.

Boccaccio, Shirley (1935-)
--Penelope and the Earth. Boccaccio, Shirley (1935-), illus. LC 75-11766. 24p. ill. 21cm. 1975. Joyful World Press.
--Penelope & the Mussels. Boccaccio, Shirley (1935-), illus. (Illus.). 24p. (Orig.). (gr. 1-6). 1972. Joyful World Pr.
--Penelope Goes to the Farmer's Market. Boccaccio, Shirley (1935-), illus. (Illus.). 24p. (Orig.). (gr. 1-6). 1973. Joyful World Pr.
--Penelope Goes to the Farmer's Market: A Feminist Children's Book Dedicated to the Liberation of Children and Adults. LC 75-322962. (Illus.). 24 p. 28cm. c.1973. Joyful World Press.

Bocci, Jeri
--Detective Thumb and Sergeant Print and the Mysterious Black Tunnel. LC 77-16222. (Illus.). 55 p. 21cm. c.1977. (ISBN 0-89127-026-4). Omni Publishers.

Bockett-Pugh, J., tr. see Caspar, Franz.

Bockoras, Diane, jt. auth. see Madsen, Jane M.

Bodden, Ilona
--When the Moon Shines Brightly on the House. Poppel, Hans, illus. LC 85-3996. p. cm. 1985, c.1984. (ISBN 0-8120-5669-8). Barron's Educational Series.

Bodder, Charles H
--Under Fire with Farragut: The Signal Boy's Story. LC 19-11155. 6 p. l., 210 p. front., plates. 20 cm. 1919. Signal Boy Publications.

Boddy, Elias Manchester
--Chief Brave Heart of the Woodside Tribe. LC 23-133409. 3 p. l., 11-131 p. front., illus. 20 cm. (Jerry Sands series, book 1). 1922. Times-Mirror Printing and Binding House.

Bodecker, Niels Mogens (1922-)
--Carrot Holes and Frisbee Trees. Winters, Nina, illus. LC 83-2799. p. cm. 1983. (ISBN 0-689-50097-1). Atheneum.
--A Dutchman Who Lived in His Breeches and Other Limericks About Odd Living Conditions. Bodecker, Niels Mogens (1922-), illus. LC 83-48744. p. cm. 1984. (ISBN 0-689-50296-6). Atheneum.
--Hurry, Hurry, Mary Dear and Other Nonsense Poems. Bodecker, Niels Mogens (1922-), illus. LC 76-14841. (Illus.). 118p. (gr. k-3). 1976. (ISBN 0-689-50066-1, McElderry Bk). Atheneum.
--Let's Marry, Said the Cherry, and Other Nonsense Poems. 1st ed. Bodecker, Niels Mogens (1922-), illus. LC 74-76271. (Illus.). 79p. ill. 21. cm. 1974. (ISBN 0-689-70434-8, Aladdin). Atheneum.
--Let's Marry Said the Cherry & Other Nonsense Poems. Bodecker, Niels Mogens (1922-), illus. LC 74-76271. (Illus.). 80p. (gr. 4 up). 1974. (ISBN 0-689-50004-1, McElderry Bk). Atheneum.
--Let's Marry Said the Cherry, and Other Nonsense Poems. Bodecker, Niels Mogens (1922-), illus. LC 74-76271. (Illus.). 79 p. 21cm. 1974. (ISBN 0-689-50004-1). Atheneum.
--The Lost String Quartet. LC 81-140681. (Illus.). 32 p. 1981. (ISBN 0-689-50200-1). Atheneum.
--Miss Jaster's Garden. Bodecker, Niels Mogens (1922-), illus. LC 70-182070. (Illus.). 28 p. 33cm. 1971, c.1972. Golden Press. **Award: (NYT).**
--The Mushroom Center Disaster. 1st. ed. Blegvad, Erik (1923-), illus. LC 73-85317. (Illus.). 48 p. 18cm. 1974. (ISBN 0-689-30424-2). Atheneum.
--A Person from Britain Whose Head Was the Shape of a Mitten and Other Limericks. 1st ed. Bodecker, Niels Mogens (1922-), illus. LC 79-22779. (Illus.). 64 p. 21cm. 1980 (McElderry Bk). (ISBN 0-689-50152-8). Atheneum.

--Pigeon Cubes & Other Verse. LC 82-3954. (Illus.). 80p. (gr. 7up). 1982. (ISBN 0-689-50235-4, McElderry). Atheneum.
--Quimble Wood. Starr, Branka, illus. LC 80-24045. (Illus.). 32 p. 24cm. 1981. (ISBN 0-689-50190-0). Atheneum.
--Snowman Sniffles and Other Verse. Bodecker, Niels Mogens (1922-), illus. LC 82-13927. (Illus.). 80p. (gr. 4-7). 1983. (ISBN 0-689-50263-X, McElderry Bk). Atheneum.

Bodecker, Niels Mogens (1922-), compiled by.
--It's Raining, Said John Twaining: Danish Nursery Rhymes. Bodecker, Niels Mogens (1922-), illus. Bodecker, Niels Mogens (1922-), tr. from Danish. LC 72-85912. (Illus.). 32 p. 1973. Atheneum. **Award: (ALA).**
--It's Raining, Said John Twaining: Danish Nursery Rhymes. Bodecker, Niels Mogens (1922-), illus. Bodecker, Niels Mogens (1922-), tr. from Danish. (Illus.). 1977. (ISBN 0-689-70437-2, Aladdin). Atheneum.

Bodelsen, Anders (1937-)
--Operation Cobra. LC 79-16564. p. cm. 1979, c.1976. (ISBN 0-525-66652-4). Elsevier/Nelson Books.

Boden, Alice
--The Field of Buttercups. LC 74-5451. (Illus.). 32 p. 1974. (ISBN 0-8098-1225-8). H. Z. Walck.

Boden, Arthur, jt. auth. see Woodside, John.

Boden, Arthur & Woodside, John
--Boden's Beasts. Boden, Arthur, illus. (Illus.). (gr. 1-5). 1964. (ISBN 0-8392-3045-1). Astor-Honor.

Boden, George Harry, ed. see Herodotus.

Boden, Hilda, pseud., see Bodenham, Hilda Morris.

Boden, Hilda, pseud. (1901-)
--Faraway Farm. Bodenham, Hilda Morris. (Illus.). (gr. 5-8). 1961. (ISBN 0-8382-0243-8). Hale.
--Faraway Farm. Bodenham, Hilda Morris. Koering, Ursula (1921-), illus. LC 61-6492. 135p. illus. 21cm. 1961. D McKay Co.
--Foxes in the Valley. Bodenham, Hilda Morris. Koering, Ursula (1921-), illus. LC 63-12147. (Illus.). 147 p. 21cm. 1963. D. McKay Co.
--Highland Holiday. Bodenham, Hilda Morris. Koering, Ursula (1921-), illus. LC 65-21602. vi, 151 p. 21cm. 1965. D. McKay Co.
--The House by the Sea. Bodenham, Hilda Morris. Koering, Ursula (1921-), illus. LC 62-16716. 146p. illus. 21cm. 1962. McKay.
--Marlowe Wins a Prize. Bodenham, Hilda Morris. Buchanan, Lilian, illus. 1960. David McKay Co.
--Marlows at Castle Cliff. Bodenham, Hilda Morris. Buchanan, Lilian, illus. LC 61-8517. (Illus.). 121 p. 19cm. 1961, c.1960. McKay.
--Marlows in Town. Bodenham, Hilda Morris. Buchanan, Lilian, illus. (Illus.). (gr. 3-6). 1964. (ISBN 0-685-21326-9). Verry.
--The Mystery of Castle Croome. Bodenham, Hilda Morris. LC 66-21373. vi, 184 p. 22cm. 1966. D. McKay Co.
--The Mystery of Island Keep. Bodenham, Hilda Morris. LC 68-26820. 152 p. 21cm. 1968. D. McKay Co.
--Pony Trek. Bodenham, Hilda Morris. 1948. Macmillan.
--The Severnside Mystery. Bodenham, Hilda Morris. LC 74-125652. vi, 152 p. 21cm. 1970. D. McKay Co.
--Storm Over Wales. Bodenham, Hilda Morris. LC 70-81894. vi, 152 p. 21cm. 1969. D. McKay Co.
--Two Lost Emeralds. Bodenham, Hilda Morris. Buchanan, Lilian, illus. LC 58-5791. 140p. illus. 21cm. 1958. Abelard- Schuman.
--Water Wheel, Turn!. A Novel for Young Adults. Bodenham, Hilda Morris. Koering, Ursula (1921-), illus. LC 64-12926. (gr. 9 up). 1964. D. McKay Co.

Bodenham, Hilda Morris see Boden, Hilda, pseud.

Bodger, J.
--A Toy Party. Barks, Dora, illus. N.D. Frederick Warne & Co.

Bodger, Joan (1923-)
--Belinda's Ball. Thurman, Mark, illus. LC 80-18324. p. cm. 1981. (ISBN 0-689-30836-1). Atheneum.
--Clever-Lazy, the Girl Who Invented Herself. LC 79-10484. p. cm. 1979. (ISBN 0-689-30674-1). Atheneum.

Bodha, Daji, ed. see Da Free, John.

Bodie, Idella Fallow (1925-)
--Ghost in the Capitol. 1st ed. Garvin, Mary Arnold, illus. LC 75-32397. (Illus.). 118 p. (p. 117-118 advertisements). 22cm. c.1976. (ISBN 0-87844-028-3). Sandlapper Store.
--The Mystery of the Pirate's Treasure. Yancey, Louise, illus. LC 72-94930. (Illus.). 136 p. 23cm. 1973. (ISBN 0-87844-018-6). Sandlapper Press.
--The Mystery of the Pirate's Treasure. 1st paperbound ed. Yancey, Louise, illus. LC 84-5451. (Illus.). 136 p. 22cm. 1984, c.1973. (ISBN 0-87844-059-3). Sandlapper Pub. Co.
--The Secret of Telfair Inn. Yancy, Louise, illus. LC 79-177909. (Illus.). 982p. (gr. 5-9). 1983. (ISBN 0-87844-050-X). Sandlapper Pub Co.
--Stranded!. Sookikian, Charles J., illus. LC 84-14098. (Illus.). 132p. (Orig.). (gr. 5-9). 1984. (ISBN 0-87844-060-7). Sandlapper Pub Co.

Bodker, Cecil (1927-)
--The Leopard. Poulsen, Gunnar, tr. from Danish. LC 74-19314. 192p. 1st U.S. edition. (gr. 4-6). 1975. (ISBN 0-689-30444-7). Atheneum. **Award: (MLB).**
--Silas & Ben-Godik. La Farge, Sheila, tr. from Danish. LC 78-50459. (gr. 5-9). 1978. (Sey Lawr). Delacorte. **Award: (BGH).**
--Silas and the Black Mare. La Farge, Sheila, tr. from Danish. LC 77-86303. 153 p. 21cm. c.1978. (ISBN 0-440-07921-7). (ISBN 0-440-07922-5). Delacorte Press/S. Lawrence. **Award: (ALA).**
--Silas & the Runaway Coach. La Farge, Sheila, illus. LC 78-50465. (gr. 5-9). 1978. (Sey Lawr). Delacorte.

Bodkin, Matthias (1896-)
--The Treasure of the Mountain. LC 39-4061. 179 p. incl. front. (map) 19 cm. 1937. Stackpole Sons.

Bodkin, Thomas (1887-)
--A Guide to Caper. Eden, Denis William (1878-), illus. LC 25-9519. vii, 89, 1 p. 1 l., incl. plates. 21 cm. 1924. George H. Doran Company.

Bodoczky, Caroline, tr. see Lesznai, Anna.

Bodrero, James
--Bomba. Bodrero, James S., illus. 21cm. 31p. 1939. Random House.

Bodwell, Gaile
--The Long Day of the Giants. Shtainmets, Leon, illus. Bodwell, Gaile, tr. from Rus. LC 74-26583. (Illus.). 40p. (ps-1). 1975. (ISBN 0-07-006356-7). (ISBN 0-07-006357-5). McGraw.

Boegehold, Betty Virginia Doyle (1913-1985)
--Bear Underground. Arnosky, Jim (1946-), illus. LC 79-7683. (Illus.). 32 p. c.1980. (ISBN 0-385-15062-8). (ISBN 0-385-15063-6). Doubleday.
--Chipper's Choices. Arnosky, Jim (1946-), illus. LC 80-13447. p. c. c.1981. (ISBN 0-698-30725-9). Coward, McCann & Geoghegan.
--Here's Pippa Again. Szekeres, Cyndy (1933-), illus. LC 74-15303. (Illus.). 64p. (ps-2). 1975. (ISBN 0-394-83090-3). (ISBN 0-394-93090-8). Knopf.
--Here's Pippa Again!. Six Read-Aloud/Read-Alone Stories. Szekeres, Cyndy (1933-), illus. LC 74-15303. (Illus.). 55 p. 22cm. 1975. (ISBN 0-394-83090-3). (ISBN 0-394-93090-8). Knopf; Distributed by Random House.
--Hurray for Pippa!. Szekeres, Cyndy (1933-), illus. LC 79-19105. (Illus.). 64p. (gr. k-3). 1980. (ISBN 0-394-84067-4). (ISBN 0-394-94067-9). Knopf.
--Hurray for Pippa!. Four Read-Aloud/Read-Alone Stories. Szekeres, Cyndy (1933-), illus. LC 79-19105. (Illus.). 55 p. 22cm. c.1980. (ISBN 0-394-84067-4). (ISBN 0-394-94067-9). Knopf : Distributed by Random House.
--In the Castle of Cats. Brett, Jan (1949-), illus. LC 80-22144. (Illus.). 32 p. 26cm. (Unicorn book). 1981. (ISBN 0-525-32541-7). Dutton.
--Pawpaw's Run. Price, Christine HIlda (1928-1980), illus. LC 68-13417. (Illus.). 1 v. (unpaged). 1968. Dutton.
--Pippa Mouse. Szekeres, Cyndy (1933-), illus. (Illus.). (gr. k-2). 1973. (ISBN 0-394-82671-X). (ISBN 0-394-92671-4). Knopf.
--Pippa Mouse: Six Read-Aloud/Read-Alone Stories. Szekeres, Cyndy (1933-), illus. LC 73-4916. (Illus.). 62 p. 22cm. N.D. (ISBN 0-394-82671-X). (ISBN 0-394-82671-X). Knopf; Distributed by Random House.
--Pippa Pops Out!. Szekeres, Cyndy (1933-), illus. LC 78-12491. (Illus.). 59 p. 22cm. c.1979. (ISBN 0-394-84057-7). (ISBN 0-394-94057-1). Knopf : Distributed by Random House.
--Three to Get Ready. Chalmers, Mary Eileen (1927-), illus. LC 62-8042. (Illus.). 5 7/8 x 8 1/2. 64p. (18 pt.). (I Can Read Bks.). (gr. k-3). 1965. (ISBN 0-06-020551-2). Har-Row.
--What the Wind Told. Schongut, Emanuel, illus. LC 73-22184. (Illus.). 43 p. 22cm. 1974. (ISBN 0-8193-0756-4). (ISBN 0-8193-0756-4). Parents' Magazine Press.

Boegehold, Betty Virginia Doyle (1913-1985) & Chwast, Jacqueline (1932-)
--Small Deer's Magic Tricks. LC 76-52477. (Illus.). 62 p. 23cm. (Break-of-day book). c.1977. (ISBN 0-698-30659-7). Coward, McCann & Geoghegan.

Boehlke, Neal A.
--Man Who Met Jesus at Bethesda. (Arch Bk.). (gr. k-4). 1981. (ISBN 0-570-06143-1). Concordia.

Boehm, Bruce Janet & Winn, Janet (1928-)
--Connecticut Low. LC 80-16858. 113 p. 22cm. 1980. (ISBN 0-395-29518-1). Houghton Mifflin.

Boehm, David Alfred see Masters, Robert V., pseud.

Boehm, David Alfred (1914-) & Reinfeld, Fred (1910-1964)
--Blazer the Bear. Masters, Robert V., pseud. Simon, Howard (1903-1979), illus. LC 53-11392. 60p. illus. 26cm. 1953. Sterling Pub. Co.

Boer, Friedrich, ed.
--Igloos Yurts And Totem Poles. (Illus.). 1975. Pantheon Books.

Boesch, Mark Joseph (1917-)
--Beyond the Muskingum. Connelly, George L., illus. LC 52-14253. (Illus.). 214 p. 22cm. 1953. Winston.
--The Cross in the West. (Vision Book). 1956. Farrar, Straus and Cudahy, Inc.
--Fire Fighter. LC 54-7622. 187p. 21cm. 1954. W. Morrow.
--Kit Carson of the Old West. Tolford, Joshua (1909-), illus. (Vision Book). 1959. Farrar, Straus and Cudahy, Inc.
--The Lawless Land: A Story of the Vigilantes. 1st ed. Bjorklund, Lorence F. (1913-1978), illus. LC 52-13524. 181 p. illus. 22 cm. (Winston adventure books). 1953. Winston.
--The World of Rice. Steinel, William, illus. (Illus.). 160 p. 24cm. 1967. Dutton.

Boesel, Ann Sterling, Mrs.
--Sing and Sing Again: Tone Plays and Songs for the Beginning Singer. LC 38-27558. 72 p. col. illus. 27 x 22 1/2 cm. c.1938. Oxford University Press.
--Singing with Peter and Patsy. Doane, Pelagie (1906-1966), illus. LC 44-40139. 48 p. col. illus. 19 1/2 x 26 cm. 1944. Oxford University Press.

Boesser, Kate
--Silverbow's Basin. limited. Boesser, Kate, illus. LC 79-117994. (Illus.). 50 p. 24cm. c.1979. Homestead Press.

Boethwick, Jane Laurie (1813-1897)
--The Illustrated Book of Songs for Children. LC 34-9704. x, 2, 13-160 p. incl. front., illus. 19 cm. 1863. T. Nelson and Sons.

Boex, J. H. H. see Rosny, J H, pseud.

Bogan, Louise (1897-1970) & Smith, William Jay (1918-), eds.
--The Golden Journey: Poems for Young People. LC 76-11197. (gr. 1 up). 1976. (ISBN 0-8092-7963-0). Contemp Bks.
--The Golden Journey: Poems for Young People. Kredel, Fritz (1900-1973), illus. LC 65-21489. (Illus.). 275 p. 24cm. 1965. Reilly & Lee. **Award: (ALA).**

Bogart, Bonnie
--The Ewoks Join the Fight. De Groat, Diane (1947-), illus. LC 82-62384. p. cm. 1983. (ISBN 0-394-85858-1). (ISBN 0-394-95858-6). Random House.

Bogatsky, C. H. V
--Golden Treasury. 510p. N.D. American Tract Society.
--Golden Treasury for the Children of God. Smith, James, ed. N.D. Thomas Nelson & Sons.

Bogdanovic, Toma (1937-), illus.
--The Fire Bird. LC 72-75676. (Illus.). 32p. (gr. 1-5). 1973. (ISBN 0-87592-017-9). Scroll Pr.

Bogen, M. Arthur
--Barely Undercover: A Burchardt-Decker Mystery. LC 83-17143. p. cm. (Avon/Flare book). c.1983. (ISBN 0-380-85217-9). Avon Books.
--Double Dealing. LC 82-24397. 141 p. 18cm. (Avon/Flare book). c.1983. (ISBN 0-380-83394-8). Avon Books.

Boggan, Louise Ward
--The Stone Amulet. Ward, Emilie A., illus. LC 68-19925. (Illus.). v. 23cm. N.D. Banner Press.

Boggs, Hobert O
--Children's Comedies and Comic Recitations. LC 37-37085. 127 p. diagr. 18 cm. 1929. Beckley-Cardy Company.
--Comic Plays and Dialogues. LC 27-2052. 112 p. 18 cm. c.1926. Beckley-Cardy Company.
--Funny Plays for Happy Days. 126 p. 18 cm. c.1928. Beckley-Cardy Company.

Boggs, Juanita, jt. auth. see Strand, Julie.

Boggs, Mary Field
--Going on Seventeen. LC 78-8491. 155 p. 20cm. 1969. Beacon Hill Press of Kansas City.

Boggs, Ralph Steele, jt. ed. see Jagendorf, Moritz Adolf.

Boggs, Ralph Steele (1901-)
--Spanish Folk Tales. 1936. (ISBN 0-679-20210-2). David McKay Company.

Boggs, Ralph Steele (1901-) & Davis, Mary Gould (1882-)
--Three Golden Oranges and Other Spanish Folk Tales. Brock, Emma Lillian (1886-1974), illus. LC 36-17125. 137 p. incl. front., illus., plates. 21 cm. 1936. Longmans, Green & Co.
--Three Golden Oranges, and Other Spanish Folk Tales. Brock, Emma Lillian (1886-1974), illus. 1936. McKay.

Bograd, Larry (1953-)
--Bad Apple. LC 82-15727. p. cm. 1982. (ISBN 0-374-30472-6). Farrar, Straus, Giroux.
--The Better Angel. LC 85-42613. 182 p. 21cm. c.1985. (ISBN 0-397-32126-0). (ISBN 0-397-32127-9). Lippincott.
--Egon. Zimmer, Dirk, illus. LC 79-23513. (Illus.). 32 p. 23cm. c.1980. (ISBN 0-02-710970-4). Macmillan.
--Felix in the Attic. Zimmer, Dirk, illus. LC 79-100712. (Illus.). 31 p. 25cm. c.1978. (ISBN 0-8178-5917-9). Harvey House.
--The Kolokol Papers. LC 81-15313. p. cm. 1981, c.1982. (ISBN 0-374-34277-6). Farrar, Straus, Giroux.
--Los Alamos Light. LC 83-11638. (gr. 7 up). N.D. (ISBN 0-374-34656-9). (ISBN 0-374-34656-9). FS&G.
--Lost in the Store. Chess, Victoria (1939-), illus. LC 81-4038. p. cm. c.1981. (ISBN 0-02-710980-1). Macmillan.

Bohanon, Paul
--Golden Kate. Howe, Gertrude Herrick (1902-), illus. LC 43-13336. 62, 1 p. illus. 21 x 17 cm. 1943. Oxford University Press.
--The Wind and Arabella. Holland, Janice (1913-1962), illus. LC 47-30920. 69 p. illus. 21 cm. 1947. Oxford Univ. Press.

Bohatta, Ida (1900-)
--All of the Birds. Bohatta, Ida (1900-), illus. Head, June, tr. from Ger. (Illus.). 18p. 1st U.S. edition. (gr. 3-5). 1981. (ISBN 0-86724-012-1). Ars Edition.
--Barli the Ice Bear. Bohatta, Ida (1900-), illus. Theobald, John, tr. LC 81-214878. (Illus.). 18 p. 15cm. c.1981. (ISBN 0-86724-007-5). ARS Edition.
--Bow Wow. Bohatta, Ida (1900-), illus. Head, June, tr. from Ger. (Illus.). 18p. 1st U.S. edition. (gr. 3-5). 1981. (ISBN 0-86724-001-6). Ars Edition.
--The Brown Family. Bohatta, Ida (1900-), illus. Head, June, tr. from Ger. (Illus.). 18p. 1st U.S. edition. (gr. 3-5). 1981. (ISBN 0-86724-011-3). Ars Edition.
--The Busy Savers. Bohatta, Ida (1900-), illus. Theobald, Mary L., tr. from Ger. (Illus.). 18p. (gr. k up). 1981. (ISBN 0-86724-020-2). Ars Edition.
--The Cloud Kitchen. Bohatta, Ida (1900-), illus. Head, June, tr. from Ger. (Illus.). 18p. 1st U.S. edition. (gr. 3-5). 1981. (ISBN 0-86724-009-1). Ars Edition.
--A Day with Heinzel. Bohatta, Ida (1900-), illus. Theobald, John, tr. from Ger. (Illus.). 26p. 1st U.S. edition. (gr. 3-5). 1981. (ISBN 0-86724-008-3). Ars Edition.
--Doctor Allsgood. Bohatta, Ida (1900-), illus. Head, June, tr. from Ger. (Illus.). 18p. 1st U.S. edition. (gr. 3-5). 1981. (ISBN 0-86724-002-4). Ars Edition.
--Flipp & Flirr. Bohatta, Ida (1900-), illus. Theobald, John, tr. from Ger. (Illus.). 18p. (gr. k up). 1981. (ISBN 0-86724-017-2). Ars Edition.
--Heinzel the Innkeeper. Bohatta, Ida (1900-), illus. Head, June, tr. from Ger. (Illus.). 18p. 1st U.S. edition. (gr. 3-5). 1981. (ISBN 0-86724-003-2). Ars Edition.
--Heinzel the Innkeeper. Bohatta, Ida, illus. Head, June, tr. from Ger. LC 82-103201. (Illus.). 18 p. 15cm. c.1981. (ISBN 0-86724-003-2). (ISBN 0-86724-003-2). Ars Edition.
--The Helpful Dwarfs. Bohatta, Ida (1900-), illus. (Illus.). 26p. (gr. k up). 1981. (ISBN 0-86724-015-6). Ars Edition.
--Ice Men. Bohatta, Ida (1900-), illus. Theobald, John, tr. from Ger. (Illus.). 18p. (gr. k up). 1981. (ISBN 0-86724-021-0). Ars Edition.
--Little Men Underground. Bohatta, Ida (1900-), illus. Theobald, John, tr. from Ger. (Illus.). 18p. (gr. k up). 1981. (ISBN 0-86724-019-9). Ars Edition.
--The Merry Hoppers. Bohatta, Ida (1900-), illus. Theobald, John, tr. from Ger. (Illus.). 18p. 1st U.S. edition. (gr. 3-5). 1981. (ISBN 0-86724-004-0). Ars Edition.
--The Misjudged Mushroom. Bohatta, Ida (1900-), illus. Theobald, John, tr. from Ger. (Illus.). 26p. 1st U.S. edition. (gr. 3-5). 1981. (ISBN 0-86724-006-7). Ars Edition.
--Raindrops. Bohatta, Ida (1900-), illus. Theobald, John, tr. from Ger. (Illus.). 18p. (gr. k up). 1981. (ISBN 0-86724-016-4). Ars Edition.
--Shooting Stars. Bohatta, Ida (1900-), illus. Theobald, John, tr. from Ger. (Illus.). 18p. 1st U.S. edition. (gr. 3-5). 1981. (ISBN 0-86724-005-9). Ars Edition.
--Velvet Paws. Bohatta, Ida (1900-), illus. Theobald, Mary L., tr. from Ger. (Illus.). 18p. 1st U.S. edition. (gr. 3-5). 1981. (ISBN 0-86724-010-5). Ars Edition.
--Winter House. Bohatta, Ida (1900-), illus. Theobald, John, tr. from Ger. (Illus.). 18p. (gr. k up). 1981. (ISBN 0-86724-023-7). Ars Edition.
--Wixi the Easter Rabbit. Bohatta, Ida (1900-), illus. Theobald, John, tr. from Ger. (Illus.). 18p. (gr. 2-5). 1981. (ISBN 0-86724-014-8). Ars Edition.

--Wulli & Susi. Bohatta, Ida (1900-), illus. Theobald, John, tr. from Ger. (Illus.). 18p. (gr. k up). 1981. (ISBN 0-86724-013-X). Ars Edition.

Bohdal, Susi (1951-)

--Bird Adalbert. Clements, Andrew (1949-), tr. LC 83-8165. p. cm. (Picture Book Studio USA). c.1983. (ISBN 0-907234-39-9). Neugebauer Press USA ; Distribution by Alphabet Press.

--Selina, the Mouse, and the Giant Cat. LC 82-670151. (Illus.). 24 p. 30cm. 1982. (ISBN 0-571-11855-0). Faber and Faber in Association with Nord-Sud Verlag.

--Tom Cat. LC 77-247. (Illus.). 28 p. 31cm. c.1977. (ISBN 0-385-13272-7). (ISBN 0-385-13612-9). Doubleday.

--Tom Cat. LC 77-577211. (Illus.). 28 p. 31cm. 1977. (ISBN 0-510-09807-X). E. Benn.

Bohme, Franz Magnus (1827-1898), ed.

--Deutsches Kinderlied and Kinderspiel. Volksuberlieferungen Aus Allen Landen Deutscher Zunge, Gessammelt, Geordnet und Mit Angabe der Quellen, Erlauternden Anmerkungen und Den Zugehoriger Melodien Hrsg, Von Franz Magnus Boehme. 1xvi, 756p. 22cm. 1897. Breitkopf und Hartel.

--Deutsches Kinderlied und Kinderspiel: Volksuberlieferungen Aus Allen Landen Deutscher Zunge. Gesammelt, Geordnet und Mit Angabe der Quellen, Erlauternden Anmerkungen und Den Zugehorigen Melodien, Hrsg. Von Franz Magnus Bohme. LC 68-108061. 1xvi, 756p. 24cm. 1897. Breitkopf und Hartel.

Bohn, tr. see Andersen, Hans Christian.

Bohner, Charles H.

--Bold Journey: West with Lewis and Clark. LC 84-19328. p. cm. 1984, c.1985. (ISBN 0-395-36691-7). Houghton Mifflin.

Bohonek, Jan B. & Bohonek, Stan B.

--How Peter Molar Looked for a Smile. Bohonek, Jan & Bohonek, Stan B., illus. Johnsen, David C. LC 83-73507. (Illus.). 32p. 1st U.S. edition. (gr. 1-3). 1984. (ISBN 0-914827-00-6). Adonis Studio.

Bohonek, Stan B., jt. auth. see Bohonek, Jan B.

Bohoy, Johanna

--The Nothing Zoo. Bohoy, Johanna, illus. LC 70-162047. (Illus.). 15 p. 28cm. (Magic circle book). 1972. (ISBN 0-663-22966-9). Ginn.

Bohrer, Walt & Bohrer, Ann, illus.

--Twenty Smiling Eagles. N.D. Vantage Press.

Boie, Mildred Louise

--Better Than Laughter. 68p. 1946. The University Of Minnesota Press.

Boiko, Claire (1925-)

--Children's Plays for Creative Actors: A Collection of Royalty-Free Plays for Boys and Girls. LC 67-21413. vii, 368p. 22cm. 1967. Plays.

--Children's Plays for Creative Actors: A Collection of Royalty-Free Plays for Boys and Girls. LC 74-30540. ix, 368 p. 22cm. 1971. (ISBN 0-8238-0006-7). Plays, Inc.

--Children's Plays for Creative Actors: A Collection of Royalty-Free Plays for Boys and Girls. rev. ed. LC 81-19180. vii, 372 p. 22cm. c.1981. (ISBN 0-8238-0234-X). Plays, Inc.

--Dramatized Parodies of Familiar Stories: Six One-Act, Royalty-Free Scripts, with Original Song Lyrics Set to Well-Known Melodies, for Performance by Young People. LC 79-20728. 172 p. 24cm. c.1980. (ISBN 0-8238-0240-X). Plays, Inc.

--Plays and Programs for Boys and Girls: A Collection of Thirty Royalty-Free, One-Act Plays for Young Players. LC 72-75324. vi, 306 p. 22cm. 1972. (ISBN 0-8238-0134-9). Plays, Inc.

Boiko, Claire (1925-) & Angress, Therese

--Doctor Din's Disaster. Tallarico, Tony, illus. LC 76-40416. (Illus.). (Play Bks.). (gr. k-3). 1977. (ISBN 0-516-08751-7, Golden Gate). Childrens.

--My Hero!. Tallarico, Tony, illus. LC 78-11505. (Illus.). (Play Bks.). (gr. k-3). 1979. (ISBN 0-516-08887-4, Golden Gate). Childrens.

Boiko, Claire (1925-) & Novick, Sandra

--Cry-Baby Princess. Weissman, Sam Q., illus. LC 78-11266. (Illus.). (Play Bks.). (gr. k-3). 1979. (ISBN 0-516-08884-X, Golden Gate). Childrens.

--Here Comes the Circus!. Anagnostura, Monica, illus. LC 78-11447. (Illus.). (Play Bks). (ps-3). 1979. (ISBN 0-516-08886-6, Golden Gate). Childrens.

--Left Over Dragon. Arnold, Dennis M., illus. LC 76-28721. (Illus.). (Play Bks.). (gr. k-3). 1977. (ISBN 0-516-08752-5, Golden Gate). Childrens.

--Who's Afraid of the Big Bad W-H-a-a-T?. A Play. LC 76-40266. (Illus.). 32 p. 25cm. c.1977. (ISBN 0-516-08753-3). Childrens Press.

Bois, Gaylord Du see Du Bois, Gaylord.

Bois, Mary Constance Du see Du Bois, Mary Constance.

Bois, Theodora McCormick see Dubois, Theodora McCormick.

Bois, Theodora McCormick Du see Dubois, Theodora McCormick.

Bois, William Sherman Pene Du see Du Bois, William Sherman Pene.

Boise, Anne C.

--Adventures of a Roving Playhouse. 1981. (ISBN 0-533-04550-9). Vantage.

Bojer, Johan (1872-)

--The House and the Sea. Ager, Trygve Martinus, tr. LC 34-29906. 4 p. 1., 3-300 p. 19 1/2 cm. 1934. D. Appleton-Century Company, Incorporated.

Bokkon, Pauline

--What's My Lion. (gr. 1-7). N.D. Carlton.

Bold, Alan (1943-)

--A Scottish Poetry Book. (Illus.). 128p. (gr. 4-7). N.D. (ISBN 0-19-916030-9). (ISBN 0-19-916029-5). Oxford U Pr.

Boldey, Ella, tr. see Grimm, Jakob Ludwig Karl (1785-1863) & Grimm, Wilhelm Karl.

Boldrini, Giuliana

--The Etruscan Leopards. Kocsis, James C. (1936-), illus. Paul, James, pseud. Quigley, Isabel, tr. (Illus.). 223 p. 22cm. 1st U.S. edition. 1968. Pantheon Books.

Bole, J. Sheridan

--The Church Mice. Piquet, Elise, illus. LC 66-6186. 1 v. (unpaged) illus. 15cm. 1966. Nelson.

Bolenius, Emma Miller, ed. see Mother Goose.

Bolenius, Emma Miller & Kellogg, Marion George

--Mother Goose Book: A Work and Play Book for Silent Reading. Tenggren, Gustaf (1896-1970), illus. LC 29-4345. (Illus.). 128 p. 21cm. 1929. Houghton Mifflin Co.

Boles, Paul Darcy (1916-)

--I Thought You Were a Unicorn: And Other Stories. LC 70-140477. 207 p. 21cm. 1971. Little, Brown.

--A Million Guitars, and Other Stories. 1st ed. LC 68-15386. 282 p. 21cm. 1968, c.1967. Little, Brown.

Bolgiano, Ella Porter

--Ginger's Hundred Dollar Check: And Other Stories. LC 34-370884. 137 p. 19 1/2 cm. c.1934. Dorrance & Company, Inc.

Bolian, Polly, jt. auth. see Schima, Marilyn.

Boll, Helene H., tr. see Spyri, Johanna Heusser.

Bolland, Margaret J. M.

--The Blue Geranium. N.D. Macmillan.

--A Little Pair of Pilgrims. N.D. Macmillan.

Bollen, Marilyn Sadler

--Alistair's Elephant. Bollen, Roger (1942-), illus. LC 82-23091. 1983. (ISBN 0-13-022756-0). Prentice Hall.

Bolliger, Max, jt. auth. see Brunner, Klaus.

Bolliger, Max (1929-)

--Daniel. Schindler, Edith, illus. LC 74-87169. (Illus.). 109 p. 22cm. 1970. Delacorte Press.

--David. Schindler, Edith, illus. Koenig, Marion, tr. 128p. 1967. (ISBN 0-440-01683-5). Delacorte Press.

--Fireflies. Trnka, Jiri (1912-1969), illus. Hoover, Roseanna, tr. LC 77-98615. (Illus.). ger. color paintings. 48p. (ps-2). 1970. (ISBN 0-689-20498-1). Atheneum.

--The Giants' Feast. Laimgruber, Monika (1946-), illus. Willard, Barbara, tr. LC 75-13333. (Illus.). 22 p. 29cm. 1976, c.1975. (ISBN 0-201-00398-8). Addison-Wesley.

--Golden Apple. Piatti, Celestino (1922-), illus. LC 79-115091. (Illus.). (ps-2). 1970. (ISBN 0-689-20577-5). Atheneum.

--Joseph. Schindler, Edith, illus. LC 68-20107. (Illus.). 109 p. 22cm. 1969. Delacorte Press.

--The Lonely Prince. Obrist, Jurg, illus. LC 81-66439. (Illus.). 25 p. 1st U.S. edition. 1982, c.1981. (ISBN 0-689-50215-X). Antheneum.

--The Most Beautiful Song. Capek, Jindra, illus. (Illus.). (ps-3). 1981. (ISBN 0-316-10117-6). Little.

--Noah and the Rainbow. Aichinger, Helga (1937-), illus. Bulla, Clyde Robert, tr. from Ger. LC 72-76361. (Illus.). 25 p. 31cm. 1972. (ISBN 0-690-58448-2). (ISBN 0-690-58448-2). Crowell.

--Noah & the Rainbow: An Ancient Story. Aichinger, Helga (1937-), illus. Bulla, Clyde Robert (1914-), tr. LC 72-76361. (Illus.). (gr. k-3). 1972. (ISBN 0-690-58448-2, TYC-J). (ISBN 0-690-03814-3). Har-Row.

--Sandy at the Children's Zoo. Brunner, Klaus, illus. Gemming, Elisabeth (1932-), tr. LC 67-18395. (Illus.). (gr. k-2). 1967. (ISBN 0-690-71956-6). T Y Crowell.

--The Wooden Man. Bauer, Fred (1934-), illus. LC 74-1141. (Illus.). 22 p. 29cm. 1974. (ISBN 0-8164-3129-9). Seabury Press.

Bolliger-Savelli, Antonella

--The Knitted Cat. LC 72-163240. 21 p. (chiefly col. illus.). 22cm. 1972, c.1971. Macmillan.

--The Mouse and the Knitted Cat. Shub, Elizabeth, adapted by. LC 72-93303. (Illus.). 22 p. 22cm. 1973. (ISBN 0-02-711710-3). Macmillan.

--Mouse & the Knitted Cat. Shub, Elizabeth, adapted by. LC 72-93303. (Illus.). 28p. (ps-2). 1974. (ISBN 0-02-711710-3). Macmillan.

Bolognese, Don see Bolognese, Donald Alan.

Bolognese, Don see Raphael, Elaine, pseud. (1933-) & Bolognese, Donald Alan.

Bolognese, Donald Alan, jt. auth. see Bolognese, Elaine Raphael Chionchio.

Bolognese, Donald Alan, jt. auth. see Raphael, Elaine.

Bolognese, Donald Alan (1934-)

--A New Day. Bolognese, Donald Alan (1934-), illus. LC 78-122773. (Illus.). 32 p. 24cm. 1970. Delacorte Press.

--Once Upon a Mountain. Bolognese, Donald Alan (1934-), illus. LC 67-19275. (Illus.). 34 p. 23cm. 1967. Lippincott.

Bolognese, Donald Alan (1934-) & Fraser, Betty, pseud. (1928-), illus.

--Favorite Stories: A Collection of the Best-Loved Tales of Childhood. Fraser, Elizabeth Marr. Brooks, Walter, designed by. LC 68-11120. (Illus.). 222 p. 26cm. (Whitman library of giant books). 1968. Whitman Pub. Division, Western Pub. Co.

Bolognese, Elaine Raphael Chionchio see Raphael, Elaine, pseud.

Bolognese, Elaine Raphael Chionchio (1933-) & Bolognese, Donald Alan (1934-)

--Reunion in December. 1962. (ISBN 0-688-21736-2). William Morrow and Company.

--The Sleepy Watchdog. LC 64-14437. (Illus.). 1 v. (unpaged. 23cm. 1964. Lothrop, Lee & Shepard.

--The Stage is Set. 1963. (ISBN 0-688-21624-2). William Morrow And Company.

Bolster, Edith Rebecca

--Ethel in Fairyland. Heyer, Herman, illus. LC 3-14262. 141, 1 p. incl. col. front. 5 col. pl. 19 1/2 x 15 1/2 cm. 1903. Lothrop Publishing Company.

Bolton, C. E. Mrs. see Humphrey, Frances A., Mrs. & Bolton, Sarah Knowles, Mrs.

Bolton, Carole (1926-)

--The Callahan Girls. LC 61-8103. 224 p. 21cm. 1961. Morrow.

--Christy. LC 60-5404. 217 p. 21cm. 1960. Morrow.

--The Dark Rosaleen. LC 64-13264. 224 p. 21cm. 1964. Morrow.

--The Good-Bye Year. LC 82-5043. 186 p. 22cm. c.1982. (ISBN 0-525-66787-3). Dutton.

--Little Girl Lost. LC 79-25151. p. cm. c.1979. (ISBN 0-525-66653-2). Elsevier/Nelson Books.

--Never Jam Today. LC 76-134805. 241 p. 22cm. 1971. Atheneum.

--Reunion in December. LC 62-8904. 220p. 21cm. 1962. Morrow.

--The Search of Mary Katherine Mulloy. LC 73-19929. 192 p. 22cm. 1974. (ISBN 0-8407-6392-1). T. Nelson.

--The Stage Is Set. LC 63-11746. 224 p. 21 cm. 1963. Morrow.

Bolton, Elizabeth

--Case of the Wacky Cat. Harvey, Paul (1926-), illus. LC 84-8725. (Illus.). 48p. (gr. 2-4). 1985. (ISBN 0-8167-0400-7). (ISBN 0-8167-0401-5). Troll Assocs.

--Ghost in the House. Burns, Raymond Howard (1924-), illus. LC 84-20530. (Illus.). 48 p. 24cm. (A Troll Easy-to-Read Mystery). c.1985. (ISBN 0-8167-0418-X). (ISBN 0-8167-0419-8). Troll Associates.

--Secret of the Ghost Piano. Fiammenghi, Gioia (1929-), illus. LC 84-8745. (Illus.). 48p. (gr. 2-4). 1985. (ISBN 0-8167-0410-4). (ISBN 0-8167-0411-2). Troll Assocs.

--Secret of the Magic Potion. Sims, Blanche, illus. LC 84-8881. (Illus.). 48 p. 23cm. (A Troll Easy-to-Read Mystery). c.1985. (ISBN 0-8167-0420-1). (ISBN 0-8167-0421-X). Troll Associates.

--The Tree House Detective Club. Schindler, Steven D., illus. LC 84-8762. (Illus.). 48p. (gr. 2-4). 1985. (ISBN 0-8167-0404-X). (ISBN 0-8167-0405-8). Troll Assocs.

Bolton, Evelyn, pseud., see Bunting, Anne Evelyn.

Bolton, Evelyn, pseud. (1928-)

--Dream Dancer. Bunting, Anne Evelyn. Keely, John, illus. LC 74-9571. 39 p. 23 cm. (Her Creative Education horse stories). 1974. (ISBN 0-87191-371-2). Creative Education; Distributed by Childrens Press, Chicago.

--Goodbye, Charlie. Bunting, Anne Evelyn. Keely, John, illus. LC 74-9572. 31 p. 23 cm. (Her Creative Education horse stories). 1974. (ISBN 0-87191-369-0). Creative Education; Distributed by Childrens Press, Chicago.

--Lady's Girl. Bunting, Anne Evelyn. Keely, John, illus. LC 74-9528. 31 23m. (Her Creative Education horse series). 1974. (ISBN 0-87191-372-0). Creative Education; Distributed by Childrens Press, Chicago.

--Ride When You're Ready. Bunting, Anne Evelyn. Keely, John, illus. LC 74-9763. 31 p. 23 cm. (Her Creative Education horse stories). 1974. (ISBN 0-87191-373-9). Creative Education; Distributed by Childrens Press, Chicago.

--Stable of Fear. Bunting, Anne Evelyn. Keely, John, illus. LC 74-9704. 31 p. 23 cm. (Her Creative Education horse stories). 1974. (ISBN 0-87191-370-4). Creative Education; Distributed by Childrens Press, Chicago.

--The Wild Horses. Bunting, Anne Evelyn. Keely, John, illus. LC 74-9530. (Illus.). 32p. (Evelyn Bolton's Horse Stories Ser). (gr. 3-7). 1974. (ISBN 0-87191-374-7). (ISBN 0-89812-126-4). Creative Ed.

Bolton, Frances Sheldon (1863-1936), compiled by.

--Mother Goose in the Kindergarten. N.D. E Steiger & Co.

--Mother Goose in the Kindergarten. LC 51-48709. 80 p. illus. 22 cm. 1893. Kindergarten Literature Co.

Bolton, Ivy May (1879-)

--The King's Minstrel: A Story of Norman England. Ives, Hazel, illus. LC 25-12246. 5 p. l., 3-229 p. front., plates, 19 1/2 cm. c.1925. L. C. Page & Company.

--A Loyal Foe: A Tale of the Rival Roses. Pitz, Henry Clarence (1895-1976), illus. LC 33-27250. 5 p. l., 260 p. incl. front. illus., plates. 20 1/2 cm. 1933. Longmans, Green and Co.

--Luck of Scotland. Dowling, Victor J. (1906-), illus. LC 40-13164. x, 229 1 p. incl. front. illus., plates. 22 cm. 1940. Longmans, Green and Co.

--Raeburn Unafraid. Berger, William Merritt (1872-), illus. LC 42-24106. viii p., 1 l., 213 p. illus. 21 cm. 1942. Longmans, Green and Co.

--Rebels in Bondage. 1st ed. Hogeboom, Amy (1891-), illus. LC 38-27622. (Illus.). ix, 234 p. 20cm. 1938. Longmans, Green and Co.

--Shadow of the Crown; A Story of Malta. 1st ed. Pitz, Henry Clarence (1895-1976), illus. LC 31-25415. (Illus.). xi, 268 p. 20cm. 1931. Longmans, Green and Co.

--Son of the Land. Bjorklund, Lorence F. (1913-1978), illus. LC 46-83987. 6 p. l., 211 p. illus. 19 1/2 cm. 1946. J. Messner.

--Tennessee Outpost. Mansfield, Louise, illus. LC 39-22046. viii p., 2 l., 244 p. illus. 22 cm. 1939. Longmans, Green and Co.

--Wayfaring Lad. Bjorklund, Lorence F. (1913-1978), illus. LC 48-6741. 192 p. illus. 21 cm. 1948. J. Messner.

--The Young Cavaliers: A Story of the Days When Charles Was King. Everhart, Adelaide, illus. LC 24-229401. 5 p. l., 3-242 p. front., plates. 19 1/2 cm. 1924. L. C. Page & Company, Inc.

--The Young Knight: Or, How Michael Faversham Fought Valiantly with the Knights of Saint John Against the Turkish Hordes and Won His Spurs As a Knight of Malta. Everhart, Adelaide, illus. LC 23-14559. xi p., 3 l., 3-233 p. incl. front. plates. 19 1/2 cm. 1923. L. C. Page & Company (Inc.

Bolton, James

--Ancient Crete & Mycenae. Reeves, Marjorie Ethel (1905-), ed. (Illus.). 96p. (Then & There Ser.). (gr. 7-12). 1968. (ISBN 0-582-20415-1). Longman.

Bolton, Mimi Du Bois (1907-)

--Merry-Go-Round Family. Liebman, Oscar (1919-), illus. LC 54-6319. 245p. illus. 22cm. 1954. Coward-McCann.

Bolton, Sarah Knowles, Mrs., jt. auth. see Humphrey, Frances A., Mrs.

Bolton, Sarah Knowles, Mrs. (1841-1916)

--How Success Is Won. (Reading Union Library). N.D. D. Lothrop Co.

Bolton, Shannon

--Prairie Boy. N.D. Vantage Press Books.

Bomans, Godfried Jan Arnold (1913-1971)

--The Wily Witch, and All the Other Fairy Tales and Fables. Hoogendijk, Wouter, illus. Crampton, Patricia, tr. LC 76-54196. p. cm. 1977. (ISBN 0-916144-09-7). Stemmer House Publishers.

--Wily Wizard & the Wicked Witch. Bartelt, Robert (1926-), illus. (Illus.). (gr. 3-5). 1969. (ISBN 0-531-01918-7). Watts.

--The Wily Wizard and the Wicked Witch, and Other Weird Stories. Bartelt, Robert (1926-), illus. Crampton, Patricia, tr. LC 69-14458. (Illus.). x, 180 p. 25cm. 1969. Watts.

Bomar, Frances M.

--A Special Day. Spiegel, Lawrence M., illus. (Illus.). (First Grade Read-to Bks.). (gr. 1-3). N.D. (ISBN 0-513-00413-0). Denison.

Bombard, Alain

--Doctor Bombard Goes to Sea. LC 57-7890. (gr. 7 up). N.D. (ISBN 0-8149-0272-3). Vanguard.

Bond, Alexander Russell (1876-)

--On the Battle Front of Engineering. LC 16-18905. xiii, 331 p. incl., illus., plates, diagrs. front. 20 cm. 1916. The Century Co.

Bond, Ann Sharpless

--Adam & Noah and the Cops. Shortall, Leonard W., illus. LC 82-21181. p. cm. 1983. (ISBN 0-395-33225-7). Houghton Mifflin.

--Saturdays in the City. Shortall, Leonard W, illus. LC 79-11747. (Illus.). 147 p. 22cm. 1979. (ISBN 0-395-28376-0). Houghton Mifflin.

Bond, Belle Bacon

--Drusilla and Her Dolls: A True Story of a Little Girl of Boston in the '60's. Very, Marjorie, illus. Sharp, Dallas Lore, Mrs., frwd. by. LC 22-104623. 57 p. col. front., plates. 19 1/2 cm. c.1921. The Four Seas Company.

Bond, Carrie Jacobs, Mrs. (1862-1946)

--The Little Monkey with the sad Face and other Stories. Wiese, Kurt (1887-1974), illus. LC 30-31927. 3-47 p. col. illus. 22cm. c.1930. The John Day Co.

--Tales of Little Dogs: Verses. Dodge, Katharine Sturges, illus. LC 54-46561. unpaged. illus. 19cm. (Volland "sunny book" ser.). 1953, c.1921. P. F. Volland Co.

Bond, Elizabeth Anne & Rabin, Joan Elaine

--Crunch, the Squirrel. Wiese, Kurt (1887-1974), illus. LC 39-21184. 48 p. illus. 22 1/2 x 26 cm. 1939. Dodd, Mead and Company.

Bond, Felicia

--Christmas in the Chicken Coop. LC 82-45918. (Illus.). 32p. (ps-3). 1983. (ISBN 0-690-04332-5, TYC-J). (ISBN 0-690-04333-3). Harper & Row.

--Four Valentines in a Rainstorm. 1st ed. LC 82-45586. (Illus.). 28 p. 14cm. c.1983. (ISBN 0-690-04307-4). (ISBN 0-690-04306-6). Crowell.

--The Halloween Performance. LC 82-45920. (Illus.). 32p. (ps-3). 1983. (ISBN 0-690-04308-2, TYC-J). (ISBN 0-690-04309-0). Harper & Row.

--Mary Betty Lizzie McNutt's Birthday. 1st ed. LC 82-45585. (Illus.). 28 p. 14cm. c.1983. (ISBN 0-690-04255-8). (ISBN 0-690-04256-6). Crowell.

--Poinsettia & Her Family. Bond, Felicia, illus. LC 81-43035. (Illus.). 32 p. 24cm. (ps-3). c.1981. (ISBN 0-690-04144-6). (ISBN 0-690-04145-4). Crowell.

--Poinsettia & the Firefighters. LC 83-46169. (Illus.). 32p. (ps-3). 1984. (ISBN 0-690-04400-3). (ISBN 0-690-04401-1). Crowell Jr Bks.

Bond, Gladys Baker see Mendel, Jo, pseud.

Bond, Gladys Baker see Walker, Holly Beth, pseud.

Bond, Gladys Baker (1912-)

--Adventures with Hal. Bolian, Polly (1925-), illus. LC 65-21125. (Illus.). 22cm. 156p. (Whitman tween-age bk.). 1965. Whitman Pub.

--Animal Babies, Wild and Free. Harris, Larry, illus. LC 67-23775. (Illus.). 154 p. 22cm. (Whitman tween-age book). 1967. Whitman Pub. Co.

--Blue Chimney. Shortall, Leonard W., illus. LC 59-16481. (Illus.). 164 p. 20cm. 1959. Holiday House.

--Boy in the Middle. Hyman, Trina Schart (1939-), illus. LC 76-166452. (Illus.). 16 p. (Magic circle book). 1972. (ISBN 0-663-22963-4). Ginn.

--Fawn Baby. Lee, Robert J. (1921-), illus. LC 66-638712. (Illus.). 1 v. (unpaged. 22cm. (Whitman big tell-a-tale). 1966. Whitman Pub. Co.

--A Head on her shoulders. Kennedy, Richard (1910-), illus. LC 63-16219. 20cm. 160p. 1963. Obelard-Schumann.

--Little Stories. Sendak, Maurice Bernard (1928-), illus. LC 64-3637. 80 p. illus. 19 cm. 1964. Anti-Defamation League of B'nai B'rith.

--The Magic Friend-Maker. Nagel, Stina (1918-), illus. LC 67-1923. (Illus.). 26 p. 30cm. (Whitman small world library). c.1966. Whitman Pub. Co.

--The Magic Friend-Maker. Nagel, Stina (1918-), illus. LC 67-1923. (Illus.). 26 p. 30cm. (Whitman small world library). c.1966. Whitman Pub. Co.

--On the Stranger's Mountain. Lucas, Derek, illus. LC 69-14244. (Illus.). 159 p. 22cm. 1969. Abelard-Schuman.

Bond, Gladys Baker (1912-) & Bertram, Florence Baker

--The Mystery at Far Reach. Grant, Elisabeth, illus. LC 67-136139. 160p. illus. 22cm. 1967. Abelard.

--The Secret at Rocky Ridge. Kennedy, Richard (1910-), illus. LC 65-23652. 158p illus. 22cm. c.1965. Abelard.

Bond, Guy Loraine, jt. ed. see Theisen, William Walter.

Bond, Jean Carey

--Brown Is a Beautiful Color. Zuber, Barbara, illus. LC 69-11523. (Illus.). 39 p. 27cm. 1969. F. Watts.

Bond, Leona

--As Tall As a Spear. Bond, Leona, illus. LC 79-141664. (Illus.). 123 p. 23cm. 1971. (ISBN 0-201-09120-8). Young Scott Books.

Bond, Mary Fanning Wickham see Porcher, Mary F. Wickham, pseud.

Bond, Michael see Bond, Thomas Michael.

Bond, Nancy Barbara (1945-)

--The Best of Enemies. LC 77-17363. (Illus.). 247 p. 24cm. 1978. (ISBN 0-689-50108-0). Atheneum.

--Country of Broken Stone. LC 79-23271. p. cm. 1980. (ISBN 0-689-50163-3). Atheneum.

--A Place to Come Back To. LC 83-48745. 204p. (gr. 7 up). 1984. (ISBN 0-689-50302-4, McElderly Bk). Atheneum.

--A String in the Harp. Davis, Allen, illus. LC 75-28181. (Illus.). 370 p. 24cm. 1976. (ISBN 0-689-50036-X). Atheneum. **Awards: (IRA); (ALA); (BGH); (JNM).**

--The Voyage Begun. LC 81-3481. p. cm. 1981. (ISBN 0-689-50204-4). Atheneum.

Bond, Nelson

--Lancelot Biggs. (Young Moderns Edition). 1950. Doubleday & Co.

Bond, Raymond T., ed. see Chesterton, Gilbert Keith.

Bond, Raymond Tostevin (1893-1981), ed. see Christie, Agatha Mary Clarissa.

Bond, Raymond Tostevin (1893-1981), pref. by see Doyle, Arthur Conan, Sir.

Bond, Ruskin (1924-)

--Angry River. Stubley, Trevor Hugh (1932-), illus. (Illus.). 94 p. 18cm. (Puffin book). 1974, c.1972. (ISBN 0-14-030648-X). Penguin.

--Flames in the Forest. LC 80-83009. (Julia MacRae Bks.). (gr. k-3). 1981. (ISBN 0-531-04282-0). Watts.

--The Hidden Pool. Das, Arup, illus. (Illus.). 64p. (Orig.). (gr. k-3). 1980. (ISBN 0-89744-211-3, Pub. by Children's Bk Trust India). Auromere.

--Panther's Moon. Feelings, Thomas (1933-), illus. LC 69-13411. (Illus.). 68 p. 24cm. 1969. Random House.

--The Road to the Bazaar. Littlewood, Valerie, illus. LC 80-50284. (Illus.). 153 p. 23cm. 1980. (ISBN 0-531-04181-6). Julia MacRae Books.

--Tales & Legends From India. Scott, Sally, illus. (Illus.). 160p. (Julia MacRae Bks.). (gr. 3). 1982. (ISBN 0-531-04073-9, MacRae). Watts.

--Tales Told at Twilight. 166p. (gr. 4-6). 1970. (ISBN 0-88253-394-0). Ind-US Inc.

--Tigers Forever. Littlewood, Valerie, illus. 48p. (Redwing Bks). 1984. (ISBN 0-531-03764-9, Macrae). Watts.

Bond, Susan McDonald, jt. auth. see Bednarik, Rosi.

Bond, Susan McDonald, jt. auth. see Lemke, Horst.

Bond, Susan McDonald (1937-)

--Eric: The Tale of a Red-Tempered Viking. Trinkle, Sally, illus. LC 68-29452. (Illus.). 48p. (ps-3). 1968. Grove.

--The Manners Zoo. Trinkle, Sally, illus. LC 70-86255. (Illus.). 31 p. 23cm. 1969. Follett.

Bond, Susan (1900-)

--Foozer: A Catham House Book. LC 49-16171. (A Short tale about a l-o-n-g dog; illus, with actual photographic reproductions, self-posed by Foozer). 44p. illus. 21 x 26cm. c.1949. Susan Bond Workshop.

Bond, Thomas Michael, jt. auth. see Bradley, Alfred.

Bond, Thomas Michael (1926-)

--A Bear Called Paddington. (Illus.). (gr. 4-6). 1958. (ISBN 0-8382-0060-5). Hale.

--Bear Called Paddington. Fortnum, Peggy, pseud. (1919-), illus. Nuttall-Smith, Margaret Emily Noel. (Illus.). (gr. 1-5). 1960. (ISBN 0-395-06636-0). HM.

--A Bear Called Paddington. Fortnum, Peggy, pseud. (1919-), illus. Nuttall-Smith, Margaret Emily Noel, LC 60-9096. (Illus.). 128 p. 21cm. 1960. Houghton Mifflin.

--Book of Bears. (Puffin Story Bks.). 1974. (ISBN 0-14-030662-5, Puffin). Penguin.

--The Complete Adventures of Olga Da Polga. Helweg, Hans H. (1917-), illus. LC 82-72753. (Illus.). 511 p. 24cm. 1983. (ISBN 0-440-00981-2). Delacorte Press.

--The Day the Animals Went on Strike. Hodgson, Jim, illus. LC 78-39153. (Illus.). 28 p. 28cm. 1972. (ISBN 0-07-006478-4). (ISBN 0-07-006478-4). American Heritage Press.

--Here Comes Thursday. Rowles, Daphne, illus. LC 67-225949. 126p. illus. 22cm. 1st U.S. edition. 1967, c.1966. (ISBN 0-688-41064-2). Lothrop.

--The Hilarious Adventures of Paddington, 5 bks. Incl. A Bear Called Paddington; More about Paddington; Paddington at Large; Paddington at Work; Paddington Helps Out. (Illus.). N.D. Dell.

--J. D. Polson & the Liberty Head Dime. (Illus.). 48p. 1980. (ISBN 0-7064-1381-4, Mayflower Bks). Smith Pubs.

--More About Paddington. 1959. E M Hale.

--More About Paddington. LC 62-12247. (Illus.). 127 p. 22cm. 1962, c.1959. Houghton Mifflin.

--Olga Carries on: More Tales of Olga Da Polga. Helweg, Hans H. (1917-), illus. LC 77-8710. (Illus.). 127 p. 22cm. 1977. (ISBN 0-8038-5380-7). Hastings House.

--Olga Counts Her Blessings. LC 77-10658. p. cm. (Olga da Polga ; 3). 1977. (ISBN 0-88436-458-5). EMC Corp.

--Olga Makes a Friend. LC 77-10684. p. cm. (Olga da Polga ; 7). 1977. (ISBN 0-88436-462-3). EMC Corp.

--Olga Makes a Wish. LC 77-10683. p. cm. (Olga da Polga ; 1). 1977. (ISBN 0-88436-456-9). EMC Corp.

--Olga Makes Her Mark. LC 77-10713. p. cm. (Olga da Polga ; 4). 1977. (ISBN 0-88436-459-3). EMC Corp.

--Olga Meets Her Match. Helweg, Hans H. (1917-), illus. LC 75-9627. (Illus.). 127 p. 22cm. (gr. 3-6). 1975, c.1973. (ISBN 0-8038-5377-7). Hastings House.

--Olga Meets Her Match. Helweg, Hans H. (1917-), illus. 1975. Penguin.

--Olga Meets Her Match. Helweg, Hans H. (1917-), illus. LC 74-157888. (Illus.). 128 p. 20cm. (Young Puffin original). 1973. (ISBN 0-14-030600-5). Puffin Books.

--Olga Takes a Bite. LC 77-21321. p. cm. (Olga da Polga ; 5). 1977. (ISBN 0-88436-460-7). EMC Corp.

--Olga's New Home. LC 77-10476. p. cm. (Olga da Polga ; 2). 1977. (ISBN 0-88436-457-7). EMC Corp.

--Olga's Second Home. Helweg, Hans H. (1917-), illus. LC 77-10477. (Illus.). (Olga Da Polga Ser.). (gr. k-3). 1977. (ISBN 0-88436-461-5). EMC.

--Olga's Special Day. LC 77-10714. p. cm. (Olga da Polga ; 8). 1977. (ISBN 0-88436-463-1). EMC Corp.

--Paddington Abroad. Fortnum, Peggy, pseud. (1919-), illus. Nuttall-Smith, Margaret Emily Noel. LC 72-2753. (Illus.). 125 p. 21cm. 1972. (ISBN 0-395-14331-4). Houghton Mifflin.

--Paddington and the Knickerbocker Rainbow. McKee, David (1935-), illus. LC 84-11593. 1984. (ISBN 0-399-21202-7). Putnam.

--Paddington at Large. (Illus.). (gr. 4-6). 1962. (ISBN 0-8382-0627-1). Hale.

--Paddington at Large. Fortnum, Peggy, pseud. (1919-), illus. Nuttall-Smith, Margaret Emily Noel. (Illus.). (gr. 1-5). 1963. (ISBN 0-395-06641-7). HM.

--Paddington at the Fair. McKee, David (1935-), illus. LC 85-5683. (Illus.). 28 p. 17cm. 1986, c.1985. (ISBN 0-399-21271-X). Putnam.

--Paddington at the Tower. Banbery, Fred, illus. LC 77-90189. (Illus.). 32 p. 22cm. (His A Paddington picture book). 1978, c.1975. (ISBN 0-394-83802-5). (ISBN 0-394-93802-X). Random House.

--Paddington at the Zoo. McKee, David (1935-), illus. LC 84-11564. (Illus.). 29 p. 16cm. N.D. (ISBN 0-399-21201-9). Putnam.

--Paddington at Work. Fortnum, Peggy, pseud. (1919-), illus. Nuttall-Smith, Margaret Emily Noel. LC 67-20372. (Illus.). 127 p. 21cm. 1967. Houghton Mifflin.

--Paddington Bear. Banbery, Fred, illus. LC 73-65. (Illus.). 32 p. 22cm. (Paddington picture book). 1973, c.1972. (ISBN 0-394-82642-6). (ISBN 0-394-82642-6). Random House.

--Paddington Goes to Town. Fortnum, Peggy, pseud. (1919-), illus. Nuttall-Smith, Margaret Emily Noel. LC 68-28054. (Illus.). 125 p. 21cm. 1968. Houghton Mifflin.

--Paddington Helps Out. Fortnum, Peggy, pseud. (1919-), illus. Nuttall-Smith, Margaret Emily Noel. (Illus.). (gr. 4-6). 1961. (ISBN 0-395-06639-5). HM.

--Paddington Marches On. 1962. E M Hale.

--Paddington Marches On. (Illus.). (gr. 4-6). 1964. (ISBN 0-8382-0629-8). Hale.

--Paddington Marches On. (Illus.). (gr. 4-6). 1965. (ISBN 0-395-06642-5). HM.

--Paddington Marches On. Fortnum, Peggy, pseud. (1919-), illus. Nuttall-Smith, Margaret Emily Noel. LC 65-14925. 127p. illus. 21cm. 1965, c.1964. Houghton.

--Paddington on Screen. Macey, Barry, illus. LC 82-11965. p. cm. 1982. (ISBN 0-395-32950-7). Houghton Mifflin.

--Paddington on Top. Fortnum, Peggy, pseud. (1919-), illus. Nuttall-Smith, Margaret Emily Noel. LC 75-17026. (Illus.). 124 p. 21cm. 1975, c.1974. (ISBN 0-395-21897-7). Houghton Mifflin.

--Paddington Takes the Air. Fortnum, Peggy, pseud. (1919-), illus. Nuttall-Smith, Margaret Emily Noel. LC 78-147902. (Illus.). 126 p. 21cm. 1971, c.1970. (ISBN 0-395-10909-4). Houghton Mifflin.

--Paddington Takes the Test. Fortnum, Peggy, pseud. (1919-), illus. Nuttall-Smith, Margaret Emily Noel. LC 80-16972. (Illus.). 125 p. 21cm. 1980, c.1979. (ISBN 0-395-29519-X). Houghton Mifflin.

--Paddington Takes to TV. Wood, Ivor, illus. LC 74-8202. (Illus.). 124 p. 21cm. 1974. (ISBN 0-395-19881-X). Houghton Mifflin.

--Paddington's Art Exhibition. McKee, David (1935-), illus. LC 85-3618. (Illus.). 28 p. 17cm. 1986, c.1985. (ISBN 0-399-21270-1). Putnam.

--Paddington's Garden. Banbery, Fred, illus. LC 73-72. (Illus.). 32 p. 22cm. 1st U.S. edition. (Paddington picture book). 1973, c.1972. (ISBN 0-394-82643-4). (ISBN 0-394-82643-4). Random House.

--Paddington's Pop Up Book. Wood, Ivor, illus. (Illus.). 12p. (Orig.). (Pop-Up Bks.). (ps-1). 1977. (ISBN 0-8431-0958-0). Price Stern.

--Paddington's Storybook. Fortnum, Peggy, pseud. (1919-), illus. Nuttall-Smith, Margaret Emily Noel. LC 84-12900. (Illus.). 160p. (gr. 1-5). 1984, c.1974. (ISBN 0-395-36667-4). HM.

--The Tales of Olga Da Polga. Helweg, Hans H. (1917-), illus. LC 72-89048. (Illus.). 113 p. 22cm. 1973, c.1971. Macmillan.

--The Tales of Olga Da Polga. Helweg, Hans H. (1917-), illus. LC 72-184153. (Illus.). 126 p. 20cm. (Young Puffin original). 1971. (ISBN 0-14-030500-9). Penguin Books.

--Thursday Ahoy!. Wood, Leslie (1920-), illus. LC 71-116342. (Illus.). 130 p. 22cm. 1st U.S. edition. 1970, c.1969. Lothrop, Lee & Shepard Co.

--Thursday Rides Again. Sanders, Beryl, illus. LC 69-14322. (Illus.). 128 p. 22cm. 1969, c.1968. Lothrop, Lee & Shepard Co.

Bond, Thomas Michael (1926-) & Banbery, Fred

--Paddington at the Circus. LC 74-12267. (Illus.). 32 p. 22cm. 1974, c.1973. (ISBN 0-394-82918-2). (ISBN 0-394-92918-7). Random House.

--Paddington at the Seaside. LC 77-90190. (Illus.). 32 p. 22cm. (Paddington picture book). 1978, c.1975. (ISBN 0-394-83801-7). (ISBN 0-394-93801-1). Random House.

--Paddington's Lucky Day. LC 74-5007. (Illus.). 32 p. 22cm. (Paddington picture book). 1974, c.1973. (ISBN 0-394-82919-0). (ISBN 0-394-82919-0). Random House.

Bond, Thomas Michael (1926-) & Wood, Ivor

--The Great Big Paddington Book. LC 77-77628. (Illus.). 45 p. 33cm. 1977, c.1976. (ISBN 0-529-05374-8). Collins.

Bone, Florence

--Curiosity Kate. Evans, Treyer, illus. LC 12-21920. vii, 315 p. front., plates. 20 cm. 1912. Little, Brown, and Company.

--The Morning & To-day. N.D. Abongdon Press.

--The Other Side of the Rainbow. LC 12-1129. (Illus.). 20cm. 180p. 1910. Eaton & Mains.

Bone, Stephen & Adshead, Mary

--The Little Boy and His House. LC 37-21372. 93 p. illus. (part col.) 24 cm. c.1937. The John C. Winston Company.

--The Little Boys & Their Boats. (Illus.). 1st U.S. edition. Repr. of 1953 ed. 1967. (ISBN 0-460-05536-4, Pub. by J. M. Dent England). Biblio Dist.

Bonehill, Captain Ralph, pseud., see Stratemeyer, Edward L..

Bonehill, Captain Ralph, pseud. (1862-1930)

--The Boy Land Boomer: Or, Dick Arbuckle's Adventures in Oklahoma. Stratemeyer, Edward L.. (Illus.). N.D. Caldwell.

--The Boy Land Boomer: Or, Dick Arbuckle's Adventures in Oklahoma. Stratemeyer, Edward L.. Reissue of 1902 ed. (Popular Authors Ser.). 1919. Saalfield Publishing Co.

--The Boy Land Boomer: Or, Dick Arbuckle's Adventures in Oklahoma. Stratemeyer, Edward L.. (Illus.). Reissue of 1902 ed. (The Adventure Ser.). N.D. Saalfield Publishing Co.

--The Boy Land Boomer: Or, Dick Arbuckle's Adventures in Oklahoma. Stratemeyer, Edward L.. Reissue of 1902 ed. (The Bonehill Ser.: Vol. 1). N.D. Saalfield Publishing Co.

--The Boy Land Boomer: Or, Dick Arbuckle's adventures in Oklahoma. Stratemeyer, Edward L.. Fry, W. H., illus. LC 2-17863. (Illus.). 20cm. 233p. 1902. Saalfield Publishing Co.

--Boys of the Fort: Or, A Young Captain's Pluck. Stratemeyer, Edward L.. (Illus.). Repr. of 1901 ed (Pub. by Mershon Co). (The Flag of Freedom Ser.: Vol. 5). 1906. Chatterton-Peck Co.

--Boys of the Fort: Or, a Young Captain's Pluck. Stratemeyer, Edward L.. (Illus.). Repr. of 1901 ed (Pub. by Mershon Co). (The Flag of Freedom Ser.: Vol. 2). 1908. Grosset & Dunlap.

--Boys of the Fort: Or, A Young Captain's Pluck. Stratemeyer, Edward L.. (Illus.). Repr. of 1901 ed (Pub. by Mershon Co). (The Flag and Frontier Ser.: Vol. 5). 1912. Grosset & Dunlap.

--Boys of the Fort: Or, A Young Captain's Pluck. Stratemeyer, Edward L.. Shute, A. Burnham, illus. LC 1-23089. vi. 250 p. front., plates. 19 cm. (The Flag of Freedom Ser.: Vol. 5). 1901. The Mershon Company.

--For the Liberty of Texas. Stratemeyer, Edward L.. Meynelle, Louis, illus. 298p. (The Mexican War Ser.: Vol. 1). 1900. Dana Estes & Co.

--Four Boy Hunters: Or, the Outing of the Gun Club. Stratemeyer, Edward L.. Nuttall, Charles, illus. LC 6-28760. vi 235 p. front., plates. 19 1/2 cm. (The Boy Hunters Ser.: Vol. 1). c.1906. Cupples & Leon Co.

--Gun and Sled: Or, The Young Hunters of Snowtop Island. Stratemeyer, Edward L.. Repr. (The Young Hunters Ser: Vol. 1). 1900. Donohue Bros.

--Gun and Sled: Or, The Young Hunters of Snowtop Island. Stratemeyer, Edward L.. (The Young Hunters Ser.: Vol. 1). N.D. W. L. Allison Co.

--Mystery in Little Tokyo. 1st ed. Mizumura, Kazue, illus. LC 66-699561. 125p. illus. 21cm. 1966. (ISBN 0-525-35560-X). Dutton.
--Mystery of the Fat Cat. Smith, Alvin (1933-), illus. LC 68-18348. (Illus.). 160 p. 21cm. 1968. Dutton.
--The Mystery of the Red Tide. Turkle, Brinton Cassaday (1915-), illus. LC 66-113796. 127p. illus. 21cm. c.1966. (ISBN 0-525-35617-7). Dutton.
--The Mystery of the Red Tide. Turkle, Brinton Cassaday (1915-), illus. (Illus.). (gr. 4-6). 1972. (ISBN 0-590-09258-8, Schol Pap). Scholastic Inc.
--The Nitty Gritty. 1st ed. Smith, Alvin (1933-), illus. LC 68-24719. (Illus.). 156 p. 21cm. 1968. Dutton.
--Premonitions. LC 84-3844. (gr. 8 up). 1984. (ISBN 0-03-071306-4). HR&W.
--The Rascals from Haskell's Gym. LC 76-56413. viii, 119 p. 22cm. c.1977. Dutton.
--Speedway Contender. LC 64-13912. viii, 214 p. 21cm. 1964. Crowell.
--The Vagabundos. LC 69-13360. 222 p. 22cm. 1969. Dutton.
--Viva Chicano. LC 77-81715. viii, 179 p. 22cm. 1970. E. P. Dutton.
--War Beneath the Sea. 1962. Crowell.

Bonhomme, Bernard & Clareleux, N.
--Fine Feathered Friend of My Very Best Friends. (gr. k up). N.D. (ISBN 0-531-04010-0). (ISBN 0-531-05010-6). Quist.

Boni, Margaret Bradford (1893-1974) & Lloyd, Norman (1909-1980)
--Fireside Book of Favorite American Songs. Battaglia, Aurelius (1910-), illus. N.D. Simon & Schuster.
--Fireside Book of Folk Songs. Provensen, Alice (1918-) & Provensen, Martin (1916-), illus. (New edition with guitar chords). (Illus.). (gr. 5 up). 1966. (ISBN 0-671-25836-2). S&S.
--Fireside Book of Folk Songs. Provensen, Alice (1918-) & Provensen, Martin (1916-), illus. 1947. Simon & Schuster.

Boning, Richard A
--Alone. Schaare, Harry J., illus. LC 74-33583. (Illus.). 47 p. 24cm. (Incredible series). 1975. (ISBN 0-87966-108-9). Dexter & Westbrook.
--Horror Overhead. (Illus.). (The Incredible Ser). (gr. 5-11). 1972. (ISBN 0-87966-103-8). Dexter & Westbrook.
--Joshua James. (Illus.). 48p. (The Incredible Ser.). (gr. 5-11). 1972. (ISBN 0-87966-104-6, Pub. by Dexter & Westbrook). B Loft.
--The Long Search. (Illus.). 48p. (The Incredible Ser). (gr. 5-11). 1972. (ISBN 0-87966-103-8, Pub. by Dexter & Westbrook). B Loft.
--Seventeen Minutes to Live. (Illus.). 48p. (The Incredible Ser). (gr. 5-11). 1973. (ISBN 0-87966-106-2, Pub. by Dexter & Westbrook). B Loft.
--The Tom Thumb Book. (gr. k-3). 1971. (ISBN 0-87966-100-3, Pub. by Dexter & Westbrook). B Loft.

Bonino, Louise
--The Cozy Little Farm. Angela, pseud., illus. Straeter, Angela. LC 46-221224. 42 p. incl. front., illus. (part col.) 25 x 19 cm. 1946. Wonder Books.

Bonne, Rose, jt. auth. see Mills, Alan.

Bonnell, Dorothy (1914-)
--Passport to Freedom. LC 67-21626. 191 p. 22cm. 1967. J. Messner.
--She Wore a Star. LC 64-11365. 191 p. 22cm. 1964. Messner.
--Target, Williamstown. LC 68-27033. 192 p. 22cm. 1968. J. Messner.
--Target: Williamstown. LC 68-27033. 192p. (gr. 7 up). 1968. Messner.
--Why Did You Go to College Linda Warren?. LC 74-83151. 190 p. 22cm. 1969. J. Messner.

Bonner, Ann & Bonner, Roger
--Earlybirds...Earlywords. LC 72-89449. (Illus.). 32p. (ps-2). 1973. (ISBN 0-87592-013-6). Scroll Pr.

Bonner, Jordan, ed. see Campbell, Carolyn.

Bonner, Jordon, ed. see Campbell, Carolyn & Thompson, Pat.

Bonner, Louise
--What's My Name in Hawaii?. Lanterman, Raymond E. (1916-), illus. LC 67-171299. 43p. illus. 21x24cm. 1967. Tuttle.

Bonner, Mary Graham (1890-1974), ed. see McCann, Rebecca.

Bonner, Mary Graham (1890-1974)
--Adventures in Puddle Muddle. Kolliker, William A., illus. LC 35-14239. 16 p. l., 33-244, 1 p. illus. 19 1/2 cm. 1935. E. P. Dutton and Company Inc.
--The Base-Stealer. Meyers, Robert William (1919-), illus. LC 51-9809. (Illus.). (gr. 4-7). 1951. (ISBN 0-394-90935-6). Knopf.
--Daddy's Bedtime Animal Stories. Choate, Florence & Curtis, Elizabeth, illus. LC 16-16156. 4 p. l., 120 p. col. front., illus., col. plates. 19 cm. c.1916. Frederick A. Stokes Company.
--Daddy's Bedtime Bird Stories. Choate, Florence & Curtis, Elizabeth, illus. LC 18-118189. 4 p. l., 120 p. col. front., illus., 3 col. pl. 19 1/2 cm. c.1917. Frederick A. Stokes Company.
--Daddy's Bedtime Fairy Stories. Choate, Florence & Curtis, Elizabeth, illus. LC 16-16256. 4 p. l., 120 p. col. front., illus., col. plates. 19 1/2 cm. c.1916. Frederick A. Stokes Company.
--Danger on the Coast: A Story of Nova Scotia. LC 41-10974. 6 p. l., 3-249, 1 p., 1 l. 20 cm. 1941. A. A. Knopf.
--Dugout Mystery. 1st ed. David, Jonathan, pseud. (1921-), illus. Ames, Lee Judah. LC 52-122171. 209p. illus. 21cm. (Borzol books for young people). 1953. (ISBN 0-394-91098-2). Knopf.
--Haunted Hut: A Winter Mystery. 1st ed. Meyers, Robert William (1919-), illus. LC 50-9111. 182 p. illus. 21 cm. (gr. 4-6). 1950. Knopf.
--Hidden Village Mystery. 1st ed. Meyers, Robert William (1919-), illus. LC 48-7493. 186 p. illus. 21 cm. 1948. A. A. Knopf.
--A Hundred Trips to Storyland. Lupprian, Hildegard (1897-), illus. LC 30-23883. xii p., 2 l., 327 p. col. front., illus., col. plates. 22 cm. c.1930. The Macaulay Company.
--Madam Red Apple. Scott, Janet Laura, illus. LC 29-14297. 21cm. 101p. 1929. Milton Bradley Co.
--The Magic Clock. Price, Luxor, illus. LC 31-20194. 22cm. 187p. 1931. MaCaulay Co.
--Magic Journeys. Price, Luxor, illus. LC 28-23147. 25cm. 280p. 1928. MaCaulay Co.
--The Magic Map. Price, Luxor, illus. N.D. MaCaulay Co.
--The Magic Music Shop. Price, Luxor, illus. N.D. MaCaulay Co.
--The Magic Universe. Price, Luxor, illus. N.D. Macaulay Books.
--Miss Angelina Adorable. LC 28-17283. 102 p. col. front., illus. (part col.) col. plates. 22 cm. c.1928. Milton Bradley Co.
--Miss Angelina Adorable. Scott, Janet Laura, illus. LC 28-17283. (Illus.). 102p. Repr. of 1928 ed. (Pub. by Milton Bradley Co.). 1981. Doll Works.
--Mrs. Cucumber Green. Scott, Janet Laura, illus. LC 27-16470. 108 p. col. front., col. illus., col. plates. 21 1/2 cm. c.1927. Milton Bradley Co.
--The Mysterious Caboose. Meyers, Robert William (1919-), illus. LC 49-10229. 176 p. illus. 21 cm. 1949. A. A. Knopf.
--Mystery at Lake Ashburn. LC 62-18427. 186p. 22cm. 1962. Lantern Press.
--The Open Door to Story Land. LC 39-1390. 80 p. incl col. front., col. illus. 31 cm. c.1938. McLoughlin Bros., Inc.
--Out to Win: A Baseball Story. Butler, Howard, illus. LC 47-3015. 5 p. l., 3-168 p. illus. 20 1/2 cm. (Borzoi books for young people). 1947. A. A. Knopf.
--Sir Noble: The Police Horse. LC 40-82215. 6 p. l., 3-65 1 p. front., plates. 24 x 18 1/2 cm. 1940. A. A. Knopf.
--Something Always Happens. Johnson, Avery Fischer (1906-), illus. LC 46-66235. 4 p. l., 3-136 2 p. illus. 21 cm. 1946. A. A. Knopf.
--Spray Hitter. (Illus.). (gr. 4-7). 1956. (ISBN 0-8313-0011-6). Lantern.
--Spray Hitter. Prezio, Victor, illus. LC 59-7416. 189p. illus. 21cm. 1959. Lantern Press.
--A Story Teller's Holiday. Scott, Janet Laura, illus. LC 39-138721. 64 p. incl. col. front., col. illus. 30 1/2 cm. c.1938. McLoughlin Bros., Inc.
--The Surprise Place. Lenski, Lois (1893-1974), illus. LC 45-698922. 4 p. l., 119 1 p. illus. 21 cm. 1945. A. A. Knopf.
--Two-Way Pitcher. (gr. 4-7). N.D. (ISBN 0-8313-0008-6). Lantern.
--Two-Way Pitcher. Prezio, Victor, illus. LC 58-5873. 191p. illus. 21cm. 1958. Lantern Press.
--Wait and See. 1st ed. Barron, John N., illus. LC 51-13017. 87 p. illus. 21 cm. (Borzoi books for young people). 1952. Knopf.
--Winning Dive, a Camp Story. 1st ed. Meyers, Robert William (1919-), illus. LC 50-6305. viii, 178 p. illus. 21 cm. 1950. Knopf.
--A World of Our Own. Kolliker, William A., illus. LC 36-18141. 119 p. illus. 19 1/2 cm. 1936. E. P. Dutton & Co., Inc.

Bonner, Mary Graham (1890-1974), ed.
--A.B.C. Nursery Rhyme Book. LC 39-136162. 77 p. incl. col. front., illus. (part col.) 31 cm. c.1939. McLoughlin Bros., Inc.
--Every Child's Story Book. LC 39-1388. 79 p. incl. col. front., col. illus. 31 cm. c.1938. McLoughlin Bros., Inc.
--Three Hundred and Sixty-Five Bedtime Stories. Choate, Florence & Curtis, Elizabeth, illus. LC 23-14254. 9 p. l., 302 p. col. front., col. plates. 24 1/2 cm. 1923. Frederick A. Stokes Company.
--Three Hundred Sixty-Five Bedtime Stories. Choate, Florence & Curtis, Elizabeth, illus. N.D. Grosset & Dunlap.

Bonner, Richard
--The Boy Inventors and the Vanishing Gun. Wrenn, Charles L., illus. LC 12-15744. 287 p. front., plates. 19 1/2 cm. c.1912. Hurst & Company.
--The Boy Inventors' Diving Torpedo Boat. Wrenn, Charles L., illus. LC 12-244891. 313 p. front., plates. 19 1/2 cm. c.1912. Hurst & Company.
--The Boy Inventors' Electric Hydroaeroplane. Wrenn, Charles L., illus. LC 14-14263. 292 p. front., plates. 19 1/2 cm. (The Boy Inventor's Ser.). c.1914. Hurst & Company.
--The Boy Inventors' Flying Ship. (Illus.). (The Boy Inventors' Ser.). N.D. Hurst & Co.
--The Boy Inventors' Radio-Telephone. Wrenn, Charles L., illus. LC 16-1482. 303 p. front. 19 1/2 cm. (The Boy Inventor's Ser.). 1915. Hurst & Company.
--The Boy Inventor's Wireless Triumph. LC 12-12135. 293 p. front., plates. 19 1/2 cm. (The Boy Inventor's Ser.). c.1912. Hurst & Company.

Bonner, Roger, jt. auth. see Bonner, Ann.

Bonners, Susan
--Panda. LC 78-50404. (gr. k-3). 1978. Delacorte.
Award: (ALA).

Bonnet, J. Gustave, tr. see Bowen, C E, Mrs.

Bonnet, Leslie, jt. auth. see Young, Ed.

Bonnici, Peter
--The Festival. Kopper, Lisa, illus. LC 84-15597. (Illus.). 32 p. 1985, c.1984. (ISBN 0-87614-229-3). Carolrhoda Books.
--The First Rains. Kopper, Lisa, illus. LC 84-14979. (Illus.). 24p. (Arjuna Bks.). (ps-3). 1985. (ISBN 0-87614-228-5). Carolrhoda Bks.

Bono, Frank J.
--Hamburger Cartons. (Illus., Orig.). (gr. 2-7). 1978. (ISBN 0-8431-0464-3). Price Stern.

Bonsall, Barbara, pseud., see Bonsall, Crosby Barbara Newell.

Bonsall, Crobsy, pseud., see Bonsall, Crosby Barbara Newell.

Bonsall, Crosby, pseud., see Bonsall, Crosby Barbara Newell.

Bonsall, Crosby Barbara Newell see Bonsall, Barbara, pseud.

Bonsall, Crosby Barbara Newell see Bonsall, Crobsy, pseud.

Bonsall, Crosby Barbara Newell see Bonsall, Crosby, pseud.

Bonsall, Crosby Barbara Newell see Newell, Crosby, pseud.

Bonsall, Crosby Barbara Newell, jt. auth. see Bonsall, George.

Bonsall, Crosby Barbara Newell, jt. auth. see Koffler, Camilla.

Bonsall, Crosby Barbara Newell, jt. auth. see Leavens, George.

Bonsall, Crosby Barbara Newell (1921-)
--And I Mean It, Stanley. Bonsall, Crosby, pseud. Bonsall, Crosby Barbara Newell (1921-), illus. Bonsall, Crosby, pseud. LC 73-14324. (Illus.). 23cm. 32p. (18 pt.). (Early I Can Read Bks.). (ps-3). 1974. (ISBN 0-06-020568-7). (ISBN 0-06-020567-9). Har-Row.
--Boswell's Life of Boswell. Leavens, George, illus. Bouchage, Luc, designed by. LC 58-14635. unpaged. illus. 29cm. 1958. Simon and Schuster.
--Captain Kangaroo's Book. Bonsall, Crosby, pseud. Jeffrey, Evan, illus. LC 58-59640. 109p. illus. 26cm. c.1958. Grosset & Dunlap.
--The Case of the Cat's Meow. Bonsall, Crosby, pseud. Bonsall, Crosby Barbara Newell (1921-), illus. Bonsall, Crosby, pseud. LC 65-11451. (Illus.). 64 p. 22cm. (I Can Read Mystery). 1965. (ISBN 0-06-020561-X). (ISBN 0-06-444017-6). Harper & Row.
--The Case of the Double Cross. Bonsall, Crosby, pseud. Bonsall, Crosby Barbara Newell (1921-), illus. Bonsall, Crosby, pseud. LC 80-7768. p. cm. (I can read book). c.1980. (ISBN 0-06-020602-0). (ISBN 0-06-020603-9). Harper & Row.
--The Case of the Dumb Bells. Bonsall, Crosby, pseud. Bonsall, Crosby Barbara Newell (1921-), illus. Bonsall, Crosby, pseud. LC 66-8267. (Illus.). 64 p. 23cm. (I can read mystery). 1966. (ISBN 0-06-020624-1). (ISBN 0-06-444030-3). Harper & Row.
--The Case of the Hungry Stranger. Bonsall, Crosby, pseud. Bonsall, Crosby Barbara Newell (1921-), illus. Bonsall, Crosby, pseud. LC 63-17947. (Illus.). 5 7/8 x 8 1/2 cm. 64p. (18 pt.). (I Can Read Mysteries Ser.). (gr. k-3). 1963. (ISBN 0-06-020571-7) (ISBN 0-06-444026-5) Har-Row.
--The Case of the Hungry Stranger. Bonsall, Crosby, pseud. Bonsall, Crosby Barbara Newell (1921-), illus. Bonsall, Crosby, pseud. LC 63-17947. (Illus.). 64 p. 23cm. (I can read mystery). 1980, c.1963. (ISBN 0-06-444026-5). Harper & Row.
--The Case of the Scaredy Cats. Bonsall, Crosby, pseud. Bonsall, Crosby Barbara Newell (1921-), illus. Bonsall, Crosby, pseud. LC 75-159039. (Illus.). 64 p. 23cm. (I can read mystery). 1971. (ISBN 0-06-020565-2). (ISBN 0-06-020566-0). Harper & Row.
--The Case of the Scaredy Cats: I Can Read Mystery. Bonsall, Crosby, pseud. Bonsall, Crosby Barbara Newell (1921-), illus. Bonsall, Crosby, pseud. 1971. Haprer & Row Pub.
--El Caso del Forastero Hambriento. Bonsall, Crosby, pseud. Bonsall, Crosby Barbara Newell (1921-), illus. Bonsall, Crosby, pseud. Belpre, Pura, tr. LC 69-14449. (Illus.). 23cm. 64p. (18 pt.). (Spanish I Can Read Bks.). (gr. 2-3). 1969. (ISBN 0-06-020574-1). Har-Row.
--Child Life. Bonsall, Crosby, pseud. N.D (Wonder Books). Grosset & Dunlap.
--The Day I Had to Play with My Sister. Bonsall, Crosby, pseud. Bonsall, Crosby Barbara Newell (1921-), illus. Bonsall, Crosby, pseud. LC 72-76507. (Illus.). 23cm. 32p. (18 pt.). (Early I Can Read Bks.). (ps-3). 1972. (ISBN 0-06-020575-X). (ISBN 0-06-020576-8). Har-Row.
--Deputy Dawg. Bonsall, Crosby, pseud. N.D. Grosset & Dunlap.
--Farmer Alfalfa's Farm. N.D (Wonder Books). Grosset & Dunlap.
--The Goodbye Summer. (gr. 4-6). 1978. Greenwillow.
--The Goodbye Summer. LC 78-23245. 148 p. 22cm. c.1979. (ISBN 0-688-80202-8). (ISBN 0-688-84202-X). Greenwillow Books.
--Here's Jellybean Reilly. Newell, Crosby, pseud. Koffler, Camilla (0000-1955), photos by. Ylla, pseud. (Illus.). photos. (gr. k-3). 1967. (ISBN 0-06-026816-6). Har-Row.
--The House Popeye Built. Bonsall, Crosby, pseud. (gr. k-3). N.D. (ISBN 0-448-00750-9). Wonder.
--Hurry Up, Slowpoke. Bonsall, Crosby, pseud. Bonsall, Crosby Barbara Newell (1921-), illus. Bonsall, Crosby, pseud. (Easy Readers Ser). (gr. k-3). N.D. Wonder.
--Hurry up, Slowpoke. Bonsall, Crosby, pseud. Moore, Lilian, ed. Bonsall, Crosby Barbara Newell (1921-), illus. Bonsall, Crosby, pseud. LC 62-5364. 61 p. illus. 22 cm. c.1961. Grosset & Dunlap.
--I'll Show You Cats. Bonsall, Crosby, pseud. Koffler, Camilla (0000-1955), illus. Ylla, pseud. Bouchage, Luc, designed by. LC 64-12805. (Illus.). 30 cm. 32p. (ps-1). 1964. (ISBN 0-06-026750-X, HarpJ). Har-Row.
Award: (NYT).
--It's Mine!. Bonsall, Crosby, pseud. Bonsall, Crosby Barbara Newell (1921-), illus. LC 64-11839. 32 p. col. illus. 16 cm. (Her A greedy book). 1964. Harper & Row.
--Kippy the Koala. Bonsall, Crosby, pseud. Leavens, George, illus. (Illus.). (gr. k-3). 1960. (ISBN 0-06-023771-6). Har-Row.
--Let's Give a Party. Bonsall, Crosby, pseud. (gr. k-3). N.D. Wonder.
--Listen, Listen. Newell, Crosby, pseud. Koffler, Camilla (0000-1955), illus. Ylla, pseud. Bouchage, Luc, designed by. LC 61-5778. (gr. k-3). 1964. (ISBN 0-06-026755-0, HarpJ). (ISBN 0-06-026756-9). Har-Row.
--Look Who's Talking. Newell, Crosby, pseud. Koffler, Camilla (0000-1955), illus. Ylla, pseud. Bouchage, Luc, designed by. LC 62-15793. unpaged. illus. 30cm. (ps-3). c.1962. (ISBN 0-06-026781-X). Harper.
--Mine's the Best. Bonsall, Crosby, pseud. Bonsall, Crosby Barbara Newell (1921-), illus. Bonsall, Crosby, pseud. LC 72-9863. 23cm. 32p. (18 pt.). (Early I Can Read Bks.). (ps-3). 1973. (ISBN 0-06-020577-6). (ISBN 0-06-020578-4). Har-Row.
--Minute and a Half Man. Bonsall, Crosby, pseud. Bonsall, Crosby Barbara Newell (1921-), illus. Bonsall, Crosby, pseud. N.D (Wonder Books). Grosset & Dunlap.
--Piggle. Bonsall, Crosby, pseud. Bonsall, Crosby Barbara Newell (1921-), illus. Bonsall, Crosby, pseud. LC 73-5478. (Illus.). 23cm. 64p. (18 pt.). (I Can Read Bks.). (gr. k-3). 1973. (ISBN 0-06-020579-2). (ISBN 0-06-020580-6). Har-Row.
--Polar Bear Brothers. Koffler, Camilla (0000-1955), illus. Ylla, pseud. Bouchage, Luc, designed by. LC 60-5793. unpaged (chiefly illus.) 29cm. (gr. k-3). 1960. (ISBN 0-06-026791-7). Harper Bros.
--Puppy Stories. Bonsall, Barbara, pseud. Bonsall, Crosby Barbara Newell (1921-), illus. Bonsall, Barbara, pseud. (Illus.). (Read-Aloud Bks.). (gr. k-3). N.D. Wonder.
--The Surprise Party. Bonsall, Crosby, pseud. Bonsall, Crosby Barbara Newell (1921-), illus. Bonsall, Crosby, pseud. LC 55-42209. unpaged. illus. 21 cm. (Wonder Books, 620). 1955. Wonder Books.

--Tell Me Some More. Bonsall, Crosby, pseud. Bonsall, Crosby Barbara Newell (1921-) & Siebel, Fritz (1913-), illus. Bonsall, Crosby, pseud. (Illus.). 22cm. 64p. (18 pt.). (I Can Read Bks.). (gr. k-3). 1961. (ISBN 0-06-020601-2). Har-Row.

--Tom Terrific. Bonsall, Barbara, pseud. N.D (Wonder Books). Grosset & Dunlap.

--Tom Terrific's Adventures. Bonsall, Crosby, pseud. N.D (Wonder Books). Grosset & Dunlap.

--Twelve Bells for Santa. Bonsall, Crosby, pseud. Bonsall, Crosby Barbara Newell (1921-), illus. Bonsall, Crosby, pseud. LC 76-58714. (Illus.). 5 7/8 x 8 1/2. 64p. (18 pt.). (I Can Read Bks.). (gr. k-3). 1977. (ISBN 0-06-020581-4). (ISBN 0-06-020582-2). Har-Row.

--Underwood. Bonsall, Crosby, pseud. Bonsall, Crosby Barbara Newell (1921-), illus. Bonsall, Crosby, pseud. N.D. (ISBN 0-448-02938-3). Grosset & Dunlap Pub.

--What Spot?. Bonsall, Crosby, pseud. Bonsall, Crosby Barbara Newell (1921-), illus. Bonsall, Crosby, pseud. LC 63-8005. (Illus.). 23cm. 64p. (18 pt.). (I Can Read Bks.). (gr. k-3). 1963. (ISBN 0-06-020610-1). (ISBN 0-06-020611-X). (ISBN 0-06-444027-3). Har-Row.

--What's Good for a Six-Year-Old?. Bonsall, Crosby, pseud. Bonsall, Crosby Barbara Newell (1921-), illus. Bonsall, Crosby, pseud. LC 62-13310. (Illus.). 23cm. 64p. (18 pt.). (I Can Read Bks.). (gr. k-3). 1962. (ISBN 0-06-020621-7). Har-Row.

--Who's Afraid of the Dark?. Bonsall, Crosby, pseud. Bonsall, Crosby Barbara Newell (1921-), illus. Bonsall, Crosby, pseud. LC 79-2700. (Illus.). 22cm. 32p. (18 pt.). (Early I Can Read Bks.). (ps-3). 1980. (ISBN 0-06-020598-9). (ISBN 0-06-020599-7). Har-Row.

Bonsall, Crosby Barbara Newell (1921-) & Reed, E.

--Let Papa Sleep. Bonsall, Crosby, pseud. (Easy Readers Ser.). (gr. k-3). N.D. (ISBN 0-448-05925-8). Wonder.

Bonsall, George

--The Big Joke. Bonsall, Crosby Barbara Newell (1921-), illus. Bonsall, Crosby, pseud. LC 55-23674. unpaged. illus. 21cm. (Wonder books, 628). c.1955. Wonder Books.

--The Really Truly Treasure Hunt. Bonsall, Crosby Barbara Newell (1921-), illus. Bonsall, Crosby, pseud. LC 55-161394. unpaged. illus. 21cm. (Treasure book parade, 391). c.1954. Treasure Books.

Bonsall, George & Bonsall, Crosby Barbara Newell (1921-)

--The Helpful Friends. Bonsall, Crosby, pseud. LC 55-35186. unpaged. illus. 21cm. (Wonder books, 631). 1955. Wonder Books.

--What Are You Looking at!. Bonsall, Crosby, pseud. unpaged. illus. 20cm. (Treasure book parade, 395). c.1954. Treasure Books.

Bonsels, Waldemar (1881-)

--The Adventures of Mario. Wiese, Kurt (1887-1974), illus. Chambers, Whittaker (1901-1961), tr. LC 30-11281. 2 p. l., 3-239, 1 p. front., plates. 23 1/2 cm. 1930. A. & C. Boni.

--The Adventures of Maya the Bee. Bock, Vera, illus. Seltzer, Adele Szold, Mrs. (1876-), tr. LC 29-25964. 6 p. l., 224 p. illus., 6 col. double pl. 24 cm. 1929. A. & C. Boni.

--The Adventures of Maya: The Bee. Boss, Homer, illus. Seltzer, Adele Szold, Mrs. (1876-), tr. LC 22-22798. 5 p. l., 224 p. col. front., illus., col. plates. 23 1/2 cm. 1922. T. Seltzer.

--The Adventures of Maya the Bee. Busoni, Rafaello (1900-1962), illus. Seltzer, Adele Szold, tr. LC 51-12220. 191 p. col. illus. 22 cm. 1951. Pellegrini & Cudahy.

--The Adventures of Maya the Bee. Jacoby, John H., illus. Seltzer, Adele Szold, Mrs. (1876-), tr. LC 64-9788. 191 p. illus. 22 cm. 1964. Grosset & Dunlap.

--Heaven Folk. Seltzer, Adele Szold, Mrs. (1876-) & Guiterman, Arthur (1871-), trs. LC 24-6893. 5 p. l., 257 p. 21 1/2 cm. 1924. T. Seltzer.

Bonser, A. E.

--The Buccaneers. Monsell, John Robert (1877-), illus. (Illus.). N.D. Dana Estes & Co.

--Exmoor Star: Or, The Autobiography of a Pony. LC 7-20617. vii, 100 p. col. front., illus., plates (partly col.) 19 cm. c.1906. A. S. Barnes & Company.

Bonsteel, Abbie Benton

--Hidden Pearls. N.D. Broadman Press.

Bonte, George Willard (1873-)

--A Bedtime Book of Sandman Rhymes. N.D. Dodge.

--Christmas Stocking Rhymes. LC 9-7425. 38 p. col. front., col. illus. 28 cm. c.1904. H. M. Caldwell Co.

--Fun and Nonsense. LC 8-31883. 40 p. col. front., col. illus. 28 x 21 1/2 cm. c.1904. H. M. Caldwell Company.

--The Sandman Rhymes. LC 4-22972. 112 p. incl. col. front., col. illus. 28 x 23 1/2 cm. c.1904. H. M. Caldwell Company.

Bontemps, Alex

--Black Comanche Boy. 1st ed. Mercer, Johnny (1947-1976), illus. LC 70-126797. (Illus.). 55 p. 20cm. (Challenger book, Black series). 1970. Hill and Wang Distributed by Random House.

Bontemps, Arna Wendell (1902-1973)

--Chariot in the Sky: A Story of the Jubilee Singers. new ed. LC 73-160162. x, 238 p. 22cm. 1971, c.1951. (ISBN 0-03-080216-4). (ISBN 0-03-080217-2). Holt, Rinehart and Winston.

--Chariot in the Sky: A Story of the Jubilee Singers. 1st ed. Baldridge, Cyrus Leroy (1889-), illus. LC 51-10429. xiii, 234 p. illus. 22 cm. (Land of the Free series). 1951. Winston.

--Fredrick Douglas: Slave---Fighter---Freeman. Johnson, Eugene Harper, illus. 1959. Alfred A Knopf : distributed by Borzoi Books.

--Lonesome Boy. Topolski, Feliks (1907-), illus. LC 54-9044. (Illus.). 28 p. 22cm. 1955. Houghton Mifflin.

--Mister Kelso's Lion. Ebert, Len, illus. (Illus.). drawings. 48p. (gr. k-3). 1970. (ISBN 0-397-31146-X). Lippincott.

--Mr. Kelso's Lion. 1st ed. Ebert, Len, illus. LC 77-124105. (Illus.). 48 p. 23cm. 1970. Lippincott.

--Sad-Faced Boy. Burton, Virginia Lee (1909-1968), illus. LC 37-5361. 4 p. l., 118. 1 p. col. front., plates (part col.) 21 cm. 1937. Houghton Mifflin Company.

--You Can't Pet a Possum. Bischoff, Ilse Marthe (1903-), illus. LC 34-32567. 4 p. l., 120 p. illus., col. plates. 20 1/2 cm. 1934. W. Morrow and Company.

Bontemps, Arna Wendell (1902-1973), ed.

--Golden Slippers: An Anthology of Negro Poetry. (Illus.). 1941. (ISBN 0-06-010395-7, HarpT). Har-Row.

--Hold Fast to Dreams: Poems Old and New. (Poetry Book Ser). (gr. 7 up). 1969. Follett. Award: (ALA).

Bontemps, Arna Wendell (1902-1973) & Conroy, Jack, pseud. (1899-)

--Fast Sooner Hound. Convoy, John Wesley. Van Sautvoord, George & Coolidge, Archibald C., Jr. (1928-), illus. LC 42-21755. (Illus.). (gr. 4-8). 1942. (ISBN 0-395-18657-9). HM.

--Sam Patch: The High, Wide, & Handsome Jumper. Conroy, John Wesley. Brown, Paul (1893-1958), illus. LC 51-247. (Illus.). 39 p. 22cm. 1951. Houghton Mifflin.

--Slappy Hooper. Koering, Ursula (1921-), illus. 24cm. 44p. 1946. Houghton Miffon Co.

Bontemps, Arna Wendell (1902-1973) & Hughes, Langston (1902-1967)

--Popo and Fifina: Children of Haiti. Campbell, E. Simms (1906-1971), illus. LC 32-24066. 5 p. l., 100 p. incl. illus., plates. front. 22 cm. 1932. The Macmillan Company.

Bontly, Thomas John (1939-)

--The Adventures of a Young Outlaw. 1974. (ISBN 0-399-11248-0). G.P. Putnam's Sons.

Bonville, Frank

--The Little Secrets. LC 4-14543. (Illus.). 17cm. 152p. 1904. F. Bonville.

Bonzon, Paul-Jacques (1908-1978)

--Orphans of Simitra. 1962. E M Hale.

--The Orphans of Simitra. Jeruchim, Simon, illus. Niklaus, Thelma Jones (1912-), tr. from Fr. LC 62-8944. (Illus.). 160 p. 22cm. (Criterion book for young people). 1962, c.1957. Criterion Books. Award: (ALA).

--Paquita, the Ballerina from Mallorca. Durand, Paul, illus. LC 58-12532. (Illus.). 224 p. 21cm. 1958. Sterling Pub. Co.

--Pursuit in the French Alps. Gill, Margery Jean (1925-), illus. Niklaus, Thelma Jones (1912-), tr. from Fr. LC 63-11679. 157 p. illus. 22 cm. 1963. (ISBN 0-688-41183-5). Lothrop, Lee & Shepard.

--The Runaway Flying Horse. Du Bois, William Sherman Pene (1916-), illus. Kotta, Susan, tr. from Fr. LC 76-2525. (Illus.). 38 p. 27cm. c.1976. (ISBN 0-8193-0875-7). Parents' Magazine Press.

Boodle, Anne Adelaide

--The Children's Guest. N.D. E & J B Young & Co.

Booher, Dianna Daniels (1948-)

--Not Yet Free. LC 80-69005. 168 p. 20cm. c.1981. (ISBN 0-8054-7315-7). Broadman Press.

Book Of Knowledge, ed.

--Golden Deeds & Stories to Know. (Illus.). (To Know Bks.). (gr. 4-6). 1967. (ISBN 0-531-01523-8). Watts.

--Poetry to Know. (Illus.). (To Know Bks.). (gr. 4-6). 1967. (ISBN 0-531-01524-6). Watts.

Booker, Barbara A.

--Lonka Belle's Vacation. Reedy, Carol, illus. (Illus.). (gr. 7 up). 1977. (ISBN 0-533-02847-7). Vantage.

Booker, Jim

--Trail to Oklahoma. Moyers, William (1916-), illus. LC 59-5865. 184p. illus. 21cm. 1959. Broadman Press.

Bookman, Charlotte

--A Horse for Johnny. N.D (Wonder Books). Grosset & Dunlap.

Boom, Corrie Ten (1892-1983)

--Hiding Place. 219p. 1971. (ISBN 0-912376-01-5). (ISBN 0-912376-05-8). Chosen Bks Pub.

Boon, Emilie

--Belinda's Balloon. Boon, Emilie, illus. LC 84-21771. (Illus.). 32 p. 26cm. c.1985. (ISBN 0-394-87342-4). (ISBN 0-394-97342-9). Knopf : Distributed by Random House.

--Peterkin Meets a Star. LC 84-29810. p. cm. (Random House pictureback). 1985. (ISBN 0-394-87505-2). Random.

--Peterkin Meets a Star. Schulman, Janet (1933-), ed. Boon, Emilie, illus. LC 83-9691. (Illus.). 32p. (gr. k-2). 1984. (ISBN 0-394-86284-8, BYR). (ISBN 0-394-96284-2). Random.

--Peterkin's Wet Walk. Schulman, Janet, ed. Boon, Emilie, illus. LC 83-8937. (Illus.). 32p. (gr. k-2). 1984. (ISBN 0-394-86285-6). (ISBN 0-394-96285-0). Random.

Boone, Donald C., tr. see Matsutani, Miyoko.

Boone, Pat (1934-)

--Dr. Balaam's Talking Mule. 156p. 1974. (ISBN 0-86694-017-0). Omega Pubns OR.

--Pat Boone's Favorite Bible Stories for the Very Young. Wilhelm, Hans (1945-), illus. LC 84-6837. (Illus.). 64p. (ps-3). 1984. (ISBN 0-394-85891-3, Pub. by BYR). (ISBN 0-394-95891-8). Random.

Boone, Silas K.

--Phil Bradley at the Wheel: Or, The Mountain boys Mad Auto Dash. (The Mountain Boys Ser.). N.D. New York Book co.

--Phil Bradley's Mountain Boys Or, The Birch Bark Lodge. (The Mountain Boys Ser.). N.D. New York Book Co.

--Phil Bradley's Shooting Box: or, The Mountain Boys on Currituck Sound. (The Mountain Boys Ser.). N.D. New York Book Co.

--Phil Bradley's Snow-Shoe Trail: or, The Mountain Boys in the Canadian Wilds. N.D. New York Book Co.

Boonin, Harriet

--A Merry Christmas to You ... and a Happy Chanukah, Too!. Skoog, Roberta, illus. LC 72-10319. 30 p. 22cm. 1972. Schmitt, Hall & McCreary.

Boorman, Linda

--The Giant Trunk Mystery. 96p. (gr. 6-12). 1981. (ISBN 0-686-69419-8). Victor Bks.

Booss, Claire, ed.

--Scandinavian Folk & Fairy Tales: Tales from Norway, Sweden, Denmark, Finland, Iceland. LC 84-442. (Illus.). xxii, 666 p. 24cm. 1984. (ISBN 0-517-43620-5). Avenel Books : Distributed by Crown.

Booth, Charles G.

--Gold Bullets. (Detective Stories for Boys). N.D. Grosset & Dunlap.

Booth, Clarice Foster

--Happy Feet, a Book of Verse for Children. Holt, Eunice M., illus. LC 51-11833. 96 p. illus. 23 cm. 1951. Exposition Press.

Booth, Cordia

--The Nubie: A Story. LC 73-85917. (Illus.). 41 p. 28cm. 1973. EUTU Pub. Co.

Booth, Edward C.

--Miss Parkworth and Three Short Stories. N.D. Dodd, Mead & Co.

Booth, Esma Rideout

--Bright Pathways. 128p. 1953. Friendship Press.

--Bright Pathways. 128p. 1955. Friendship Press.

--Chama's Choice. Baldridge, Cyrus Leroy (1889-), illus. LC 52-2045. 136 p. illus. 21 cm. 1952. Friendship Press.

--Kalena. 1st ed. Johnson, Eugene Harper, illus. LC 58-733007. 181p. illus. 21cm. 1958. Longmans, Green.

--Kalena and Sana. Pious, Robert, illus. LC 62-189657. 152p. illus. 21cm. 1962. David McKay Co.

--New Magic. Hutchinson, William Miller (1916-), illus. LC 59-6598. 128p. illus. 20cm. 1959. Friendship Press.

--Nyanga's Two Villages. Smalley, Janet (1893-), illus. 122p. 1942. Friendship Press.

--Nyanga's Two Villages. Smalley, Janet (1893-), illus. LC 45-4770. 126 p., 1 l. illus. 19 1/2 cm. 1945. Friendship Press.

--Village, City: The World. (gr. 10 up). 1966. (ISBN 0-679-20229-3). McKay.

Booth, Eugene (1940-)

--At the Beach. Collard, Derek, illus. LC 77-7659. (Illus.). 21 p. 24cm. (A Raintree Spotlight Bk.). c.1977. (ISBN 0-8393-0111-1). Raintree Children's Books.

--At the Circus. Collard, Derek, illus. LC 77-7946. p. cm. (Raintree spotlight book). c.1977. (ISBN 0-8393-0112-X). Macdonald-Raintree.

--At the Fair. Collard, Derek, illus. LC 77-7961. (Illus.). 21 p. 24cm. (A Raintree Spotlight Bk.). c.1977. (ISBN 0-8393-0114-6). Raintree Children's Books.

--At the Zoo. Collard, Derek, illus. LC 77-7627. (Illus.). (A Raintree Spotlight Book). (gr. k-3). 1977. (ISBN 0-8393-0107-3). Raintree Pubs.

--In the Air. Collard, Derek, illus. LC 77-7984. 24cm. 21p. (A Raintree spotlight book). c.1977. (ISBN 0-8393-0105-7). Raintree Childrens Books.

--In the City. Collard, Derek, illus. LC 77-7949. p. cm. (Raintree spotlight book). c.1977. (ISBN 0-8393-0109-X). Macdonald-Raintree.

--In the Garden. Collard, Derek, illus. LC 77-7628. (Illus.). (A Raintree Spotlight Book). (gr. k-3). 1977. (ISBN 0-8393-0115-4). Raintree Pubs.

--In the Jungle. Collard, Derek, illus. LC 77-7947. 21p. col. ill. 24cm. (A Raintree spotlight book). c.1977. (ISBN 0-8393-0104-9). Raintree Childrens Books.

--In the Park. Collard, Derek, illus. LC 77-7622. (Illus.). 24cm. 21p. (A Raintree Spotlight Book). (gr. k-3). 1977. (ISBN 0-8393-0106-5). Raintree Pubs.

--On the Farm. Collard, Derek, illus. LC 77-7601. 21p. col. ill. 24cm. (A Raintree spotlight book). c.1977. (ISBN 0-8393-0113-8). Raintree Childrens Books.

--Under the Ground: A/Raintree spotlight book. Collard, Derek, illus. LC 77-8037. 21p. col. ill. 24cm. c.1977. (ISBN 0-8393-0110-3). Raintree Childrens Books.

--Under the Ocean. Collard, Derek, illus. LC 77-7983. p. cm. (Raintree spotlight book). c.1977. (ISBN 0-8393-0108-1). Macdonald-Raintree.

Booth, Mary L. (1831-1889), tr. see Laboulaye, Edouard Rene Lefebvre de.

Booth, Mary L., tr. see Mace, Jean.

Booth, Mary Louise (1831-1889), tr. see Laboulaye, Edouard Rene Lefebvre de.

Booth, Maud Ballington Charlesworth, Mrs. (1865-)

--Lights of Child-Land. Farnsworth-Drew, Alice, illus. LC 1-25811. vii, 193 p. incl. illus., plates. col. front. 21cm. 1901. G. P. Putnam's Sons.

--Sleepy-Time Stories. Humphrey, Maud (1868-), illus. Depew, Chauncey M., intro. by. LC 99-4877. x, 177. p incl. illus., plates. front. 21cm. 1899. G. P. Putnam's Sons.

--Twilight Fairy Tales. LC 6-38892. xi, 273 p. col. front., illus., col. plates. 21 cm. 1906. G. P. Putnam's Sons.

Booth, Olive R.

--Dug Up at the Pyramids: Old Nursery Rhymes. Adamson, Stanley L., illus. 1905. H M Caldwell Co.

Boothby, Guy Newell (1867-1905)

--The Beautiful White Devil. LC 6-15064. 8 p. l., 289 p. 18 1/2cm. (Half-title: Appletons' town and country library, no. 215). 1897. D. Appleton and Company.

Boothe-Carter

--Jimmie and the Junior Safety Council. N.D. World Bk. Co.

--Mary Day Stories. N.D. World Bk. Co.

Booz, Elizabeth Benson

--Josephine. Booz, Elizabeth Benson, illus. LC 62-12248. 22cm. 48p. (gr. k-3). 1962. (ISBN 0-395-06647-6). HM.

--The Seal of Jai. Kennedy, Paul Edward (1929-), illus. LC 68-12085. (Illus.). 179 p. 21cm. 179p. 1968. Macmillan.

--A Treat in a Trout. LC 55-5221. 59p. illus. 25cm. 1955. Houghton Mifflin.

Bopp, Joseph B.

--Herbie Capleenies. Myers, Amy, illus. LC 77-10715. (Illus.). 32 p. 24cm. c.1978. (ISBN 0-201-04721-7). Addison-Wesley.

Borack, Barbara (1942-)

--Gooney. McCully, Emily Arnold (1939-), illus. LC 67-18552. (Illus.). 30 p. 26cm. 1968. Harper & Row.

--Grandpa. Shecter, Ben (1935-), illus. LC 67-2764. (Illus.). 32 p. 24cm. 1967. Harper & Row.

--Someone Small. Lobel, Anita Kempler (1934-), illus. LC 68-24332. (Illus.). 32 p. 23cm. 1969. Harper & Row.

Borad-Cadmus Editorial

--Good Times Together. N.D. E. M. Hale & Co.

Boralse, Skipp

--Stirring Tales of Colonial Adventure. (Illus.). (Warne's Adventure Library). N.D. Frederick Warne & Vo.

Borch, Anka

--Torarin: A Historical Novel of 12th Century Norway. Mickelson, Melva, illus. Herberg, Ruth M., tr. LC 68-25797. (Illus.). 142 p. 21cm. 1968. Augsburg Pub. House.

Borchard, Ruth Berendsohn (1910-)

--The Children of the Old House. Wronker, Lili Cassel (1924-), illus. LC 63-12876. (Illus.). 181. 22cm. 1st U.S. edition. 1963. Doubleday.

--Donkeys for Rogador. LC 67-16207. 198p. 21cm. 1967. Dial.

Borchers, Elisabeth

--Dear Sarah. Schlote, Wilhelm, illus. Shub, Elizabeth, tr. from Ger. LC 80-14512. (Illus.). 32 p. 30cm. c.1981. (ISBN 0-688-80277-X). (ISBN 0-688-84277-1). Greenwillow Books.

--The Old Car. Maurer, Werner, illus. Figes, Eva (1932-), tr. from Ger. LC 73-137214. 30 p. (chiefly col. illus. 24cm. 1971. Bobbs-Merrill.

--There Comes a Time. Blech, Dietlind, illus. Deutsch, Babette (1895-1982), tr. LC 69-19172. (Illus.). color paintings. 48p. (ps-3). 1969. (ISBN 0-385-07935-4). (ISBN 0-385-09457-4). Doubleday.

Borchert, Rudolf, jt. auth. see Fante, John Thomas.

Bord, Janet

--Ghosts. LC 74-8282. 1975. (ISBN 0-7153-6632-7). David & Charles.

Borden, Charles A (1912-1968)

--He Sailed with Captain Cook. Hall, H. Tom, illus. LC 68-18807. 203 p. 21cm. 1968. Macrae Smith.

--He Sailed with Captain Cook. Ray, Ralph (1920-1952), illus. LC 52-7042. 248 p. illus. 21 cm. 1952. Crowell.

Borden, Lucille Papin (1873-)

--The Shining Tree: A Christmas Story. LC 42-50210. 5 p. l., 277 p. 22 cm. 1942. The Macmillan Company.

Border, Rosy

--Nuka's Tale. LC 81-52497. (Starters Ser.). N.D. (ISBN 0-382-06510-7). Silver.

Bordner, Bessie F.

--Mr. & Mrs. Raccoon Find Another World. (Illus.). 32p. (gr. 1-4). 1975. (ISBN 0-8059-2204-0). Dorrance.

Bordner, Ellen P., ed. see Abraham, Norma J.

Bordy, Michael (1909-)

--Hector-the-Trotter?. LC 67-25674. (Illus.). 41 p. 20cm. 1967. Dorrance.

Borea, Phyllis (1924-)

--First Thing in the Morning. LC 71-118915. (Illus.). 32p. 21 x 27 cm. (gr. k-4). 1970. (ISBN 0-402-14000-1). Regnery.

Boreman, Thomas

--The Gigantick History of the Two Famous Giants and Other Curiosities in Guildhall, London. Lurie, Alison (1926-) & Schiller, Justin G., eds. LC 75-32140. (Illus.). xii, 268 p. in various pagings. 15cm. (Classics of Children's Literature, 1621-1932). 1979. (ISBN 0-8240-2256-4). Garland Pub.

Borer, Mary Irene Cathcart (1906-)

--Sophie and the countess. Phillips, W. F., illus. LC 60-11180. (Illus.). 21 cm. 207p. 1960. Franklin Watts, Inc.

Boreta, Anne & Cashel, Sue

--Gummy Bear Goes to Camp. LC 82-50668. (Illus.). 48p. (Orig.). 1982. (ISBN 0-89815-075-2). Ten Speed Pr.

Borg, Inga (1925-)

--Bru--the Brown Bear. LC 61-14415. unpaged. illus. 26cm. c.1961. F. Warne.

--Parrak-the White Reindeer. LC 59-11985. (Illus.). unpaged. 1959. Warne.

--Phipp Builds a House. LC 60-14702. (Illus.). unpaged. 27cm. 1960. F. Warne & Co.

--Redcoat, the Fox. LC 65-10561. 1v. (unpaged) col. illus. 25cm. 1965. Warne.

--Tramper, the Elk. LC 62-14919. unpaged. illus. 28 cm. 1962. F. Wayne.

--Whitewings the Swan. LC 63-19184. (Illus.). (gr. k-3). 1963. Warne.

Borg, Selma, tr. see Schwartz.

Borg, Selma & Brown, Marie A., trs.

--Northern Lights, 1 of 3 Vols. (Illus.). (Roundabout Library). (Famous Fairy Library). N.D. Set. Porter & Coates.

Borhegyi, Suzanne Sims De see De Borhegyi, Suzanne Sims.

Borich, Michael (1949-)

--A Different Kind of Love. LC 84-22492. 165 p. 22cm. c.1985. (ISBN 0-03-003249-0). Holt, Rinehart and Winston.

Borie, Lysbeth Boyd, Mrs.

--David Has His Day. Dobias, Frank (1902-), illus. LC 34-33128. 63 p. col. illus. 23 1/2cm. c.1934. J. B. Lippincott Company.

--More Poems for Peter. LC 31-32743. 104, 1 p. incl. front., illus., plates 20cm. 1931. J. B. Lippincott Company.

--Poems for Peter. LC 28-30362. 110 p. 1 l. illus. 20cm. 1928. J. B. Lippincott Company.

Borisoff, Norman

--Bird Seed & Lightning. Heron, Michal, illus. LC 72-75125. (Illus.). 32 p. 24cm. (Adventures in the city). 1972. (ISBN 0-87191-206-6). Creative Educational Society.

--Don't Give up. Heron, Michal, illus. LC 72-75126. (Illus.). 32 p. 24cm. (Adventures in the city). 1972. (ISBN 0-87191-207-4). Creative Educational Society.

--Unknown Avenues. Heron, Michal, illus. LC 72-77224. (Illus.). 32 p. 24cm. (Adventures in the city). 1972. (ISBN 0-87191-205-8). Creative Educational Society.

--Walkie-Talkie Patrol. Heron, Michal, illus. LC 72-75122. (Illus.). 32 p. 24cm. (Adventures in the city). 1972. (ISBN 0-87191-097-7). Creative Educational Society.

--Who's There. Heron, Michal, illus. LC 72-75123. (Illus.). 32 p. 24cm. (Adventures in the city). 1972. (ISBN 0-87191-098-5). Creative Educational Society.

--You Might Even Like It. (gr. 7 up). 1974. (ISBN 0-590-03840-0, Schol Trade Pap). Schol Bk Serv.

Borland, Hal Glen (1900-1978)

--Dog Who Came to Stay. Oughton, Taylor (1925-), illus. (Illus.). (gr. 7-9). 1962. (ISBN 0-397-00210-6). Lippincott.

--King of Squaw Mountain. a new and rev. ed. Pimlott, John, illus. LC 64-19014. 154 p. illus. 21 cm. Orig. Title: Wapiti Pete. 1964. Lippincott.

--Penny; the Story of a Free-Soul Basset Hound. Oughton, Taylor (1925-), illus. LC 74-37927. (Illus.). 191 p. 22cm. 1972. (ISBN 0-397-00864-3). Lippincott.

--Rocky Mountain Tipi Tales. N.D. Doubleday Page & Co.

--Valor: The Story of a Dog. Townsend, Lee (1895-), illus. LC 34-33673. 182 p. illus. 21 cm. c.1934. Farrar and Rinehart.

--Wapiti Pete: The Story of an Elk. Taylor, John Austin, illus. LC 38-27846. 6 p. 1., 3-176 p. incl. front., illus. 19 1/2 cm. c.1938. Farrar & Rinehart, Incorporated.

--When the Legends Die. LC 63-11753. (gr. 10 up). 1963. (ISBN 0-397-00303-X). Har-Row.

--Youngest Shepherd: A Tale of the Nativity. Buchard, Peter, illus. LC 62-16861. (Illus.). (gr. 4-9). 1962. (ISBN 0-397-00255-6). Lippincott.

Borland, Kathryn Kilby see Land, Jane, pseud.

Borland, Kathryn Kilby, jt. auth. see Speicher, Helen Ross Smith.

Borland, Kathryn Kilby (1916-) & Speicher, Helen Ross Smith (1915-)

--Allan Pinkerton, Young Detective. Goldstein, Nathan (1927-), illus. LC 62-12707. 200 p. illus. 20 cm. (childhood of famous americans). 1962. Bobbs-Merrill.

--Eugene Field: Young Poet. Moyers, William (1916-), illus. LC 64-248102. 200p. col. illus. 20cm. (Childhood of famous Americans)). c.1964. Bobbs.

--Everybody Laughed & Laughed. Land, Jane, pseud. Land, Ross, pseud. Lacy, Jacqueline, illus. LC 64-20850. 31p. col. illus. 24cm. 1964. E. C. Seale.

--Good-by to Stony Crick. Hollinger, Deanne, illus. LC 74-11457. (Illus.). 138 p. 21cm. 1974, c.1975. (ISBN 0-07-006531-4). (ISBN 0-07-006532-2). McGraw-Hill.

--Miles and the Big Black Hat. Land, Jane, pseud. Land, Ross, pseud. Kauper, Jean Dorion, illus. LC 63-21747. 32p. col. illus. 27cm. 1963. E. C. Seale.

Born, Franz

--Jules Verne. 1964. (ISBN 0-8382-0394-9, Cadmus Books). E. M. Hale and Company.

Bornstein, Harry

--Bobby Visits the Dentist. 48p. (Signed English Ser.). 1975. (ISBN 0-913580-38-4). Gallaudet Coll.

--Circus Time. 18p. (Signed English Ser.). 1976. (ISBN 0-913580-51-1). Gallaudet Coll.

--Fireman Brown. Tom, Linda C., illus. 18p. (Signed English Ser.). 1976. (ISBN 0-913580-50-3). Gallaudet Coll.

--The Gingerbread Man. 48p. (Signed English Ser.). 1976. (ISBN 0-913580-52-X). Gallaudet Coll.

--Hansel & Gretel. 66p. (Signed English Ser.). 1975. (ISBN 0-913580-08-2). Gallaudet Coll.

--Happy Birthday Carol. Miller, Ralph R., Sr., illus. 48p. (Signed English Ser.). 1973. (ISBN 0-913580-18-X). Gallaudet Coll.

--I Am a Kitten. 18p. (Signed English Ser.). 1975. (ISBN 0-913580-44-9). Gallaudet Coll.

--I Want to Be a Farmer. 48p. (Signed English Ser.). 1975. (ISBN 0-913580-14-7). Gallaudet Coll.

--Jack & the Beanstalk. 64p. (Signed English Ser.). 1975. (ISBN 0-913580-47-3). Gallaudet Coll.

--Julia Goes to School. 48p. (Signed English Ser.). 1974. (ISBN 0-913580-34-1). Gallaudet Coll.

--Little Lost Sally. 40p. (Signed English Ser.). 1975. (ISBN 0-913580-40-6). Gallaudet Coll.

--Little Poems for Little People. 56p. (Signed English Ser.). 1974. (ISBN 0-913580-31-7). Gallaudet Coll.

--Matthew's Accident. 32p. (Signed English Ser.). 1975. (ISBN 0-913580-45-7). Gallaudet Coll.

--Mealtime at the Zoo. Hrivnak, Suzette & Hrivnak, James R., illus. 48p. (Signed English Ser.). 1973. (ISBN 0-913580-11-2). Gallaudet Coll.

--Mouse's Christmas Eve. 44p. (Signed English Ser.). 1974. (ISBN 0-913580-28-7). Gallaudet Coll.

--My Toy Book. 16p. (Signed English Ser.). 1973. (ISBN 0-913580-22-8). Gallaudet Coll.

--The Night Before Christmas. 56p. (Signed English Ser.). 1976. (ISBN 0-913580-15-5). Gallaudet Coll.

--Night-Day, Work-Play. 48p. (Signed English Ser.). 1974. (ISBN 0-913580-23-6). Gallaudet Coll.

--Nursery Rhymes from Mother Goose. 56p. (Signed English Ser.). 1972. (ISBN 0-913580-07-4). Gallaudet Coll.

--Oliver in the City. 56p. (Signed English Ser.). 1975. (ISBN 0-913580-49-X). Gallaudet Coll.

--The Pet Shop. 16p. (Signed English Ser.). 1976. (ISBN 0-913580-54-6). Gallaudet Coll.

--Policeman Jones. 17p. (Signed English Ser.). 1976. (ISBN 0-913580-53-8). Gallaudet Coll.

--Tale of Peter Rabbit. 64p. (Signed English Ser.). 1975. (ISBN 0-913580-39-2). Gallaudet Coll.

--Three Billy Goats Gruff. 56p. (Signed English Ser.). 1976. (ISBN 0-913580-56-2). Gallaudet Coll.

--Three Little Kittens. 32p. (Signed English Ser.). 1974. (ISBN 0-913580-16-3). Gallaudet Coll.

--Three Little Pigs. 44p. (Signed English Ser.). 1972. (ISBN 0-913580-09-0). Gallaudet Coll.

--Tommy's Day. 48p. (Signed English Ser.). 1973. (ISBN 0-913580-10-4). Gallaudet Coll.

--The Ugly Duckling. 48p. (Signed English Ser.). 1974. (ISBN 0-913580-29-5). Gallaudet Coll.

--We're Going to the Doctor. 28p. (Signed English Ser.). 1974. (ISBN 0-913580-26-0). Gallaudet Coll.

--When I Grow up. 46p. (Signed English Ser.). 1974. (ISBN 0-913580-35-X). Gallaudet Coll.

--With My Legs. 18p. (Signed English Ser.). (ps). 1975. (ISBN 0-913580-42-2). Gallaudet Coll.

Bornstein-Lercher, Ruth (1927-)

--Annabelle. Bornstein-Lercher, Ruth (1927-), illus. LC 77-20059. (Illus.). 26 p. 17cm. c.1978. (ISBN 0-690-03804-6). (ISBN 0-690-03810-0). Crowell.

--The Dancing Man. Bornstein-Lercher, Ruth (1927-), illus. LC 77-29124. (Illus.). 32p. (ps-3). 1978. (ISBN 0-395-28770-7, Clarion). HM.

--The Dancing Man. Bornstein-Lercher, Ruth (1927-), illus. LC 77-29124. p. cm. c.1978. (ISBN 0-8164-3214-7). Seabury Press.

--The Dream of Little Elephant. Bornstein-Lercher, Ruth (1927-), illus. LC 76-27748. (Illus.). 32 p. c.1977. (ISBN 0-8164-3180-9). Seabury Press.

--The Dream of the Little Elephant. Bornstein-Lercher, Ruth (1927-), illus. LC 76-27748. (Illus.). 32p. (ps-3). N.D. (ISBN 0-395-28771-5, Clarion). HM.

--I'll Draw a Meadow. Bornstein-Lercher, Ruth (1927-), illus. LC 78-22481. (Illus.). 23 p. 16cm. c.1979. (ISBN 0-06-020612-8). (ISBN 0-06-020613-6). Harper & Row.

--Indian Bunny. Bornstein-Lercher, Ruth (1927-), illus. LC 72-94226. (Illus.). 32 p. 1973. (ISBN 0-516-08723-1). Childrens Press.

--Jim. Bornstein-Lercher, Ruth (1927-), illus. LC 77-12712. (Illus.). 32 p. c.1978. (ISBN 0-8164-3204-X). Seabury Press.

--Little Gorilla. Bornstein-Lercher, Ruth (1927-), illus. (ps). 1976. Houghton Mifflin.

--Little Gorilla. Bornstein-Lercher, Ruth (1927-), illus. LC 75-25508. (Illus.). 32 p. c.1976. (ISBN 0-8164-3158-2). Seabury Press.

--Of Course a Goat. Bornstein-Lercher, Ruth (1927-), illus. LC 79-2015. (Illus.). 24 p. 17cm. c.1980. (ISBN 0-06-020608-X). (ISBN 0-06-020609-8). Harper & Row.

Borough, Mildred

--Tangled Threads: Or, Linda's Awakening. (Illus.). 192p. N.D. Sunday-School Publications.

Borrow, George

--Lavengo. (Riverside Bookshelf). N.D. Houghton Mifflin Co.

Borska, Ilona & Hoffmann, Ernst Theodor Amadeus (1776-1822)

--Coppelia. Mikulova, Milada, illus. Sebestiakov, Yvonne, tr. LC 74-106161. (Illus.). 62 p. 29cm. (Curtain-raiser book). 1971. (ISBN 0-531-01926-8). Watts.

Borski, Lucia Merecka

--Good Sense and Good Fortune: Polish Folk Tales. Gorecka-Egan, Erica, illus. LC 71-97804. 21cm. 83p. 1970. (ISBN 0-679-20064-9). David McKay Company.

--Jolly Tailor. Klepacki, Kazimir, illus. N.D. Longmans, Green & Co.

Borski, Lucia Merecka, tr. see Ficowski, Jerzy.

Borski, Lucia Merecka, pseud., tr. see Porazinska, Janina.

Borski, Lucia Merecka, tr. see Porazinski, Janinna.

Borski, Lucia Merecka, Mrs. & Miller, Kate B.

--Jolly Tailor & Other Fairy Tales. Klepacki, Kazimir, illus. (Illus.). (gr. 3-5). 1957. (ISBN 0-679-20086-X). McKay.

Borten, Helen Jacobson (1930-)

--Copycat. Borten, Helen Jacobson (1930-), illus. LC 62-136281. unpaged. illus. 26cm. c.1962. Abelard-Schuman.

--Do You Go Where I Go. Borten, Helen Jacobson (1930-), illus. LC 70-38423. (Illus.). (gr. k-3). 1972. (ISBN 0-200-71892-4). (ISBN 0-200-71884-3). Abelard.

--Do You Hear What I Hear. Borten, Helen Jacobson (1930-), illus. (Illus.). (Picture Book Ser). (gr. k-3). 1960. (ISBN 0-200-71299-3). (ISBN 0-200-00004-7). Abelard.

--Do You Hear What I Hear. Borten, Helen Jacobson (1930-), illus. 1960. (ISBN 0-8382-0210-1, Cadmus Books). E. M. Hale and Company.

--Do You Know What I Know?. Borten, Helen Jacobson (1930-), illus. LC 73-123517. (Illus.). 64 p. 27cm. 1970. (ISBN 0-200-71695-6). Abelard-Schuman.

--Do You Move as I Do. LC 53-10466. unpaged. illus. 27cm. 1963. Abelard-Schuman.

--Do You See what I See. Borten, Helen Jacobson (1930-), illus. LC 59-5579. unpaged. illus. 26cm. 1959. Abelard-Schuman.

--Do You See What I See. Borten, Helen Jacobson (1930-), illus. LC 50-5579. (Illus.). (gr. k-3). 1959. (ISBN 0-200-71301-9). Har-Row.

--Halloween. Borten, Helen Jacobson (1930-), illus. LC 65-16184. (Illus.). 1 v. (unpaged). 22cm. (Crowell holiday book). 1965. Crowell.

--The Jungle. Borten, Helen Jacobson (1930-), illus. 32p. N.D. Harcourt Brace Jovanovich.

--A Picture Has a Special Look. Borten, Helen Jacobson (1930-), illus. LC 61-15714. unpaged. illus. 26cm. c.1961. Abelard-Schuman.

Borton, Elizabeth see De Trevino, Elizabeth Borton.

Boruch, Behn

--The Coat of Many Colors: The Story of Joseph. Springsteel, Bernard, illus. LC 59-4210. unpaged. illus. 23cm. c.1959. Hebrew Pub. Co.

Borup, George

--A Tenderfoot with Peary. New Ed. ed. Borup, George, illus. (Boys' Edition). 1930. Frederick A. Stokes co.

Bosa, Stera, pseud., see Walton, Bessye E. Bloom.

Bosa, Stera

--Lappy in the Forest. Latimer, Glenna M. (1898-), illus. N.D. E. P. Dutton & Co.

Bosch, Hermann, Mrs.

--Bible Stories Told to Toddles. LC 10-7811. 20cm. 165p. 1910. Longmans, Green & Co.

--The Good Shepard and His Little Lamb. LC 12-11211. 18cm. 137p. 1912. Longmans, Green & Co.

--When Toddles was Seven: A sequel to Bible Stories Told to Toddles. LC 12-1333. 20cm. 231p. 1911. Longmans, Green & Co.

Bosche, Bill, ed. see Disney, Walt, Productions.

Bosco, Henri (1888-1976)

--The Boy and the River. Lamb, Lynton Harold (1907-1977), illus. Hopkins, Gerard, tr. LC 57-11127. (Illus.). 133 p. 21cm. 1956. Pantheon Books.

Bose, Irene Mott, Mrs.

--The Monkey Tree. Ahmed, Enver, illus. LC 56-5764. 153p. illus. 24cm. 1956. Dodd, Mead.

--Totaram: The Story of a Village Boy in India to-Day. Ayer, Margaret (0000-1981), illus. LC 33-22934. xvi p., 1 l., 118 p. incl. front., illus. 22 1/2 cm. 1933. The Macmillan Company.

Boshell, Gordon (1908-)

--The Mendip Money-Makers. LC 77-359810. (Illus.). 6, 132 p. 23cm. (Secret guardians series). 1976. (ISBN 0-561-00287-8). Bailey and Swinfen.

--The Plot Against Buster the Dog. Dypold, Pat, illus. LC 75-186885. (Illus.). 59 p. 23cm. 1972. (ISBN 0-87955-201-8). (ISBN 0-87955-201-8). J. P. O'Hara.

Bosher, Kate L.

--Kitty Canary. N.D. Harper & Bros.

--Miss Gibbie Gault. N.D. Harper & Bros.

Boshinski, Blanche (1922-)

--Aha and the Jewel of Mystery. Pulido, Shirley, illus. LC 68-21087. (Illus.). 158 p. 22cm. 1968. Parents' Magazine Press.

--The Luck of the Blue Stallion. Russon, Mary Georgina (1937-), illus. LC 67-13908. 181 p. illus. 22 cm. 1967. Meridith Press.

Bosley, Jo Ann

--The Strangest Summer. LC 75-140970. 240 p. 21cm. 1970. (ISBN 0-910244-58-8). J. F. Blair.

Bosley, Keith (1937-), ed.

--The Devil's Horse: Tales from the Kalevala. Bosley, Keith (1937-), tr. LC 70-153981. (Illus.). 148 p. 22cm. 1971, c.1966. (ISBN 0-394-82313-3). (ISBN 0-394-92313-8). Pantheon.

Bosnia, Nella, jt. auth. see Turin, Adela.

Bosschere, Jean De see Bosschere, Jean De.

Bosschere, Jean De see De Bosschere, Jean.

Bosschere, Jean de see DeBosschere, Jean (1878-) & Morris, M. C. O.

Bosschere, Jean De (1878-1953), ed. see Cervantes Saavedra, Miguel de.

Bosschere, Jean De (1878-1953)

--The City Curious. Jesse, Fryniwyd Tennyson, tr. LC 20-187550. xii, 178, 2 p. illus., 8 col. pl. (incl. front.) 23 cm. 1920. Dodd, Mead and Company.

Bosschere, Jean De (1878-1953), compiled by.

--Christmas Tales of Flanders. De Bosschere, Jean (1878-), illus. Morris, M. C. O., tr. LC 18-6940. xii, 144, 1 p., 1 l., incl. illus., plates col. front., col. plates. 27 1/2 cm. 1917. Dodd, Mead & Company.

Bosse, Malcolm Joseph (1933-)

--The Barracuda Gang. LC 81-23675. 174 p. 22cm. c.1982. Lodestar Books.

--Cave Beyond Time. LC 79-7818. p. cm. c.1980. (ISBN 0-690-04075-X). (ISBN 0-690-04076-8). Harper & Row.
--Ganesh. LC 80-2453. 185 p. 21cm. c.1981. (ISBN 0-690-04102-0). (ISBN 0-690-04103-9). Crowell.
--The Seventy-Nine Squares. LC 79-7591. (gr. 7 up). 1979. (ISBN 0-690-03999-9, TYC-J). (ISBN 0-690-04000-8). Har-Row. **Award: (ALA).**
--The Seventy-Nine Squares. 1979. Houghton.

Boston, Lucy Maria Wood (1892-)
--Adventures at Green Knowe, 5 vols. Boston, Peter, illus. Incl. The Children of Green Knowe. Boston, Lucy Maria Wood (1892-) Repr. of 1955 ed; Treasure of Green Knowe. Boston, Lucy Maria Wood (1892-) Repr. of 1958 ed; The River at Green Knowe. Repr. of 1959 ed; Stranger at Green Knowe. Boston, Lucy Maria Wood (1892-) Repr. of 1961 ed; An Enemy at Green Knowe. Boston, Lucy Maria Wood (1892-) Repr. of 1964 ed. (Illus.). (gr. 4-7). 1979. Boxed Set. (ISBN 0-15-603246-5, VoyB). HarBraceJ.
--The Castle of Yew. Gill, Margery Jean (1925-), illus. LC 65-17988. 57 p. illus. 22 cm. 1965. Harcourt, Brace & World.
--The Children of Green Knowe. Boston, Peter, illus. LC 55-7808. 157p. illus. 21cm. 1st U.S. edition. 1955. Harcourt. **Awards: (ALA); (CMA).**
--An Enemy at Green Knowe. Boston, Peter, illus. LC 64-11490. (Illus.). i56 p. 21cm. 1964. Harcourt, Brace & World.
--An Enemy at Green Knowe. Boston, Peter, illus. LC 78-71151. (Illus.). 196 p. 21cm. (Voyager/HBJ book). 1979, c.1964. (ISBN 0-15-628792-7). Harcourt Brace Jovanovich.
--The Fossil Snake. Boston, Peter, illus. LC 75-26997. (Illus.). 53 p. 21cm. 1976, c.1975. (ISBN 0-689-50037-8). Atheneum.
--The Fossil Snake. Boston, Peter, illus. LC 78-305531. (Illus.). 53 p. 21cm. 1st U.S. edition. 1975. (ISBN 0-370-10972-4). Bodley Head.
--The Guardians of the House. Boston, Peter, illus. LC 74-18177. (Illus.). 51 p. 22cm. 1975, c.1974. (ISBN 0-689-50016-5). Atheneum Publishers.
--Nothing Said. Boston, Peter, illus. LC 70-137756. (Illus.). 64 p. 21cm. 1971. (ISBN 0-15-257580-4). Harcourt Brace Jovanovich.
--River at Green Knowe. Boston, Peter, illus. LC 59-8950. (Illus.). (gr. 4-7). 1959. (ISBN 0-15-267446-2, HJ). HarBraceJ.
--River at Green Knowe. Boston, Peter, illus. LC 59-8950. (Illus.). (gr. 4-7). 1966. (ISBN 0-15-677701-0, VoyB). HarBraceJ.
--The Sea Egg. 1st ed. Boston, Peter, illus. LC 67-3334. (Illus.). 94 p. 21cm. 1967. Harcourt, Brace & World.
--The Stones of Green Knowe. Boston, Peter, illus. LC 75-44143. (Illus.). 117 p. 22cm. 1976. (ISBN 0-689-50058-0). Atheneum.
--A Stranger at Green Knowe. Boston, Peter, illus. LC 61-10108. (Illus.). 158 p. 21cm. 1961. Harcourt, Brace. **Awards: (ALA); (CMA).**
--A Stranger at Green Knowe. Boston, Peter, illus. LC 78-71150. (Illus.). 158 p. 20cm. (Voyager/HBJ book). 1979, c.1961. (ISBN 0-15-685657-3). Harcourt, Brace, Jovanovich.
--Treasure of Green Knowe. Boston, Peter, illus. LC 58-8731. 185p. illus. 21cm. 1st U.S. edition. 1958. Harcourt, Brace. **Award: (ALA).**
--Treasure of Green Knowe. Boston, Peter, illus. LC 77-16689. (Illus.). 185 p. 20cm. (Voyager/HBT book). 1978, c.1958. (ISBN 0-15-691302-X). Harcourt Brace Jovanovich.

Boston, Lucy Maria (1892-)
--The Children of Green Knowe. Boston, Peter, illus. LC 77-4506. p. cm. (Voyager/HBJ book). 1977, c.1955. (ISBN 0-15-217147-9). Harcourt, Brace, Jovanovich.

Boston Children's Medical Center Staff, jt. auth. see Selzer, Joan G.

Boswell, Hilda, ed.
--Hilda Boswell's Omnibus. Boswell, Hilda, illus. 256p. 1972. (ISBN 0-00-120308-8). Collins & World.
--Treasury of Children's Stories. Boswell, Hilda, illus. 128p. 1971. (ISBN 0-00-120304-5). Collins & World.
--Treasury of Fairy Tales. Boswell, Hilda, illus. (Illus.). (gr. 2-4). N.D. (ISBN 0-00-137101-0). Collins Pubs.
--Treasury of Nursery Rhymes. Boswell, Hilda, illus. (Illus.). (ps-2). N.D. (ISBN 0-00-120302-9). Collins Pubs.
--Treasury of Poetry. Boswell, Hilda, illus. (Illus.). (ps-2). N.D. (ISBN 0-00-137103-7). Collins Pubs.

Bosworth, Allan Rucker (1901-)
--Ladd of the Lone Star. 1st ed. Malik, George A., illus. LC 52-11812. 192 p. illus. 21 cm. (American heritage). 1952. Aladdin Books.
--Sancho of the Long, Long Horns. 1st ed. Frankenberg, Robert Clinton (1911-), illus. LC 47-11122. 206 p. illus. 23 cm. 1947. Doubleday.

Bosworth, Elenora, jt. auth. see Cunningham, Lois Elizabeth Barstow, Mrs.

Bosworth, J. Allan (1925-)
--All the Dark Places. LC 68-10596. (Illus.). 166 p. 22cm. 1968. Doubleday.
--Among Lions. LC 73-79646. 116 p. 22cm. 1973. (ISBN 0-385-01685-9). (ISBN 0-385-01685-9). Doubleday.
--A Bird for Peter. Simon, Howard (1903-1979), illus. LC 63-19083. 160 p. illus. 22 cm. c.1963. Criterion Books.
--A Darkness of Giants. LC 79-180062. (Illus.). 161 p. 22cm. 1972. Doubleday.
--Voices in the Meadow. Schindelman, Joseph (1923-), illus. LC 61-16240. 191 p. illus. 24 cm. 1964. Doubleday.
--White Water, Still Water. Walker, Charles W., illus. LC 66-11729. 160 p. illus. 22 cm. 1966. Doubleday.
--A Wind Named Anne. LC 74-97652. 135 p. 22cm. 1970. Doubleday.

Botel, Morton, jt. auth. see Brothers, Aileen.
Bothmer, Gerry, tr. see Almquist, Bertil.
Bothmer, Gerry, tr. see Burman, Edor.
Bothmer, Gerry, tr. see Gripe, Maria Kristina.
Bothmer, Gerry, tr. see Holmberg, Ake.
Bothmer, Gerry, tr. see Lindgren, Astrid Ericsson.
Bothmer, Gerry, tr. see Wallin, Marie-Louise.

Bothwell, Jean (0000-1977)
--African Herdboy: A Story of the Masai. Owens, Carl, illus. LC 76-117615. (Illus.). 125 p. 21cm. 1970. Harcourt Brace Jovanovich.
--The Borrowed Monkey. Ayer, Margaret (0000-1981), illus. LC 53-10639. unpaged. illus. 27cm. 1953. Abclard Prcss.
--Cal's Birthday Present. Ayer, Margaret (0000-1981), illus. LC 53-9913. unpaged. illus. 27cm. 1955. Abelard-Schuman.
--Dancing Princess. LC 65-18726. 190 p. 21cm. 1965. Harcourt, Brace and World.
--Defiant Bride. LC 69-13771. 159 p. 21cm. 1969. Harcourt, Brace & World.
--The Emerald Clue. LC 61-12341. (Illus.). 191 p. 21cm. 1961. Harcourt, Brace & World.
--The Empty Tower. Ayer, Margaret (0000-1981), illus. LC 48-7800. 160 p. illus. 21 cm. morrow junior books. 1948. W. Morrow.
--Flame in the Sky: A Story of the Days of the Prophet Elijah. LC 54-115266. 160p. illus. 21cm. 1954. Vanguard Press.
--The Hidden Treasure. Van Arnam, Margaret Newton, illus. LC 54-5574. 137p. illus. 21cm. 1954. Friendship Press.
--Holy Man's Secret: A Story of India. Pearson, Clyde, illus. (Illus.). glossary line drawing. (gr. 3-7). 1967. Abelard.
--The Holy Man's Secret: A Story of India. Pearson, Clyde, illus. LC 67-23075. (Illus.). 160 p. 22cm. 1968, c.1967. Abelard-Schuman.
--Lady of Roanoke. LC 65-13867. 254 p. 22 cm. 1965. Holt, Rinehart and Winston.
--Little Boat Boy: A Story of Kashmir. Ayer, Margaret (0000-1981), illus. LC 45-8415. 5 p. l., 3-252 p., 1 l. incl. front., illus., plates. 21 cm. 1945. Harcourt, Brace and Company.
--The Little Flute Player. 1949. (ISBN 0-8382-0448-1, Cadmus Books). E. M. Hale And Company.
--Little Flute Player. Ayer, Margaret (0000-1981), illus. LC 49-9992. 159 p. illus. 21 cm. 1949. W. Morrow.
--Lost Colony: The Mystery of Roanoke Island. Cortese, Edward F., illus. LC 52-12893. (Illus.). 182 p. 22cm. (Winston Adventure Books Ser.). (gr. 5-7). 1953. (ISBN 0-03-063615-9). Winston.
--The Missing Violin. Marokvia, Artur F. (1909-), illus. LC 59-10171. (Illus.). 187 p. 22cm. 1959. Harcourt, Brace.
--Mystery Angel. 1963. E M Hale.
--The Mystery Angel. Jaeger, Elinor, illus. LC 63-10920. 125 p. illus. 21 cm. 1963. Dial Press.
--Mystery at the House-of-the-Fish. LC 68-11497. 192 p. 21cm. 1968. Harcourt, Brace & World.
--The Mystery Box. Shortall, Leonard W., illus. LC 67-16208. 138p. illus. 21cm. 1967. Dial.
--The Mystery Candlestick. Rocker, Fermin (1907-), illus. LC 77-102826. (Illus.). 148 p. 21cm. 1970. Dial Press.
--Mystery Cargo. (Illus.). (gr. 4-6). 1962. (ISBN 0-8382-0567-4). Hale.
--The Mystery Cargo. Tomes, Jacqueline, illus. LC 62-10131. 147p. illus. 21cm. (gr. 4-6). 1962. (ISBN 0-8037-6250-X). Dial Press.
--The Mystery Clock. Shortall, Leonard W., illus. LC 66-12835. 127p. illus. 21cm. c.1966. Dial.
--The Mystery Cup. Greenwald, Sheila, pseud. (1934-), illus. Green, Sheila Ellen. LC 68-15255. (Illus.). 156 p. 21cm. 1968. Dial Press.
--The Mystery Egg. Tomes, Jacqueline, illus. LC 65-15324. (Illus.). 159 p. 21cm. 1965. Dial Press.
--Mystery Gatepost. 1964. E M Hale.
--The Mystery Gatepost. Obligado, Lilian Isabel (1931-), illus. LC 64-12289. 159 p. illus. 20 cm. 1964. Dial Press.
--Mystery Key. 1961. E M Hale.
--The Mystery Key. Shortall, Leonard W., illus. LC 61-648613. 124p. illus. 21cm. (gr. 3-7). 1961. Dial Press.
--The Mystery Tunnel. Robinson, Charles (1931-), illus. LC 69-18230. (Illus.). 159 p. 21cm. 1969. Dial Press.
--Omen for a Princess: The Story of Jahanara, Royal Poet of the Seventeenth Century. LC 62-13630. 192 p. 21 cm. 1963. Abelard-Schuman.
--Omen for the Princess: The Story of Jahanara. 1963. E M Hale.
--Paddy and Sam. Ayer, Margaret (0000-1981), illus. LC 52-2417. unpaged. illus. 28 cm. 1952. Abelard Press.
--The Parsonage Parrot. Baldwin-Ford, Pamela, illus. LC 73-79848. (Illus.). 186 p. 22cm. 1969. F. Watts.
--Peter Holt, P. K. Ayer, Margaret (0000-1981), illus. LC 50-9578. (Illus.). 241 p. 21cm. 1950. Harcourt, Brace.
--The Promise of the Rose. LC 58-9744. 187 p. 21cm. 1958. Harcourt, Brace.
--The Red Barn Club. Ayer, Margaret (0000-1981), illus. LC 54-8569. (Illus.). 245 p. 21cm. 1954. Harcourt, Brace.
--The Red Scarf. LC 62-14423. 189 p. 21cm. 1960. Harcourt, Brace & World.
--Ride Zarina, Ride. LC 66-618996. 160p. 21cm. c.1966. Harcourt.
--Ring of Fate. LC 57-11340. 218 p. 21cm. 1957. Harcourt, Brace.
--River Boy of Kashmir. Ayer, Margaret (0000-1981), illus. LC 46-25242. 5 p. l., 246 p. incl. front., illus., plates. 21 cm. (Morrow junior books). 1946. W. Morrow & Company.
Romany Girl. LC 64-23041. 192 p. 21 cm. 1964. Harcourt, Brace & World.
--Search for a Golden Bird. Lonette, Reisie Dominee (1924-), illus. LC 56-9550. (Illus.). 172 p. 22cm. 1956. Harcourt, Brace.
--The Secret in the Wall. LC 74-141861. 22cm. 173p. 1971. (ISBN 0-200-71758-8). Abelard-Schuman.
--The Silver Mango Tree. LC 60-12308. 190 p. 21cm. 1960. Harcourt, Brace.
--Star of India. Ayer, Margaret (0000-1981), illus. LC 47-30840. 224 p. illus. 21 cm. 1947. W. Morrow.
--Sword of a Warrior. 1st ed. Ayer, Margaret (0000-1981), illus. LC 51-13445. 228 p. illus. 21 cm. 1951. Harcourt, Brace.
--The Thirteenth Stone: A Story of Rajputana. Ayer, Margaret (0000-1981), illus. LC 46-25121. 6 p. l., 3-225 p. incl. front., illus., plates. 20 1/2 cm. 1946. Harcourt, Brace and Company.
--Tree House at Seven Oaks: A Story of the Flat Water Country in 1853. Hodgell, Bob, illus. LC 57-8085. 239p. illus. 22cm. 1957. (ISBN 0-200-00090-X). Abelard-Schuman.
--White Fawn of Phalera. (gr. 7 up). N.D. (ISBN 0-15-295875-4). HarBraceJ.
--The Wishing Apple Tree. 1st ed. Davis, Marshall, illus. LC 53-7862. 214p. illus. 22cm. 1953. Harcourt, Brace.

Bothwell, Jean (0000-1977) & Sowers, Phyllis Ayer, Mrs.
--Golden Letter to Siam. LC 53-10636. (Illus.). 208 p. 22cm. 1953. Abelard Press.
--Ranch of a Thousand Horns. Ayer, Margaret (0000-1981), illus. LC 55-5375. 152p. illus. 22cm. 1955. Abelard-Schuman.

Botkin, Benjamin Albert (1901-1975), ed.
--The American Play-Party Song. LC 63-22456. 406p. N.D. (ISBN 0-8044-5168-0). Frederick Ungar Publishing Co.
--A Treasury of American Folklore. N.D. Crown Publishers.

Botkin, Benjamin Albert (1901-1975) & Withers, Carl A. (1900-1970), eds.
--The Illustrated Book of American Folklore: Stories, Legends, Tall Tales, Riddles, and Rhymes. Docktor, Irv (1918-), illus. LC 58-4111. 99p. illus. 33cm. 1958. Grosset & Dunlap.

Botsford, Amelia Howard
--Child Life Is All Nations: Or, The Earlingtons' Trip Around the World...Profusely Illustrated with Sixteen Full-Page Half-Tones and Over One Hundred Other Engravings, Including Many Colored Pictures, Showing Children in Their Characteristic National Costume. 1 p. l., 278 p. incl. illus, plates. (part col.) 24 1/2 cm. c.1901. American Book and Bible House.

Botsford, Charles Alexander (1871-)
--At the Front. Smyth, S. Gordon, illus. LC 21-15553. 304 p. front, illus, plates. 20 cm. 1921. The Penn Publishing Company.
--Fighting With the U. S. Army. (The Victory Ser.). N.D. Penn.
--Fighting with the U.S. Army. Humphreys, Donald S., illus. LC 19-14012. 320 p. front., illus., plates. 20 cm. 1919. The Penn Publishing Company.
--In the Trenches. LC 20-13545. 307 p. front, illus., plates. 19 1/2 cm. 1920. The Penn Publishing Company.
--Joining the Colors. Boyer, Ralph L. & Coleman, Ralph Pallen, illus. 347 p. front., illus., plates. 20 cm. 1918. The Penn Publishing Company.

Botsford, Florence Hudson Topping, Mrs.
--Picture Tales from the Italian. Gilkison, Grace, Mrs., illus. LC 29-26901. xii p., 1 l., 106 p. incl. front., illus., plates. 14 x 18 1/2 cm. 1929. Frederick A. Stokes Company.
--Picture Tales from the Italian. Gilkison, Grace, Mrs., illus. 1929. J. B. Lippincott Co.

Botsford, Ward, adapted by see Gilbert, William Schwenck, Sir (1836-1911) & Sullivan, Arthur Seymour, Sir.

Botsford, Ward & Gilbert, William Schwenck, Sir (1836-1911)
--The Pirates of Penzance. Sorel, Edward (1929-), illus. LC 81-5173. p. cm. 1981. (ISBN [illegible]). (ISBN [illegible]). Random House.

Bottcher, Cordelia
--Felix Finestitch. (Illus.). 1982. (ISBN 0-903540-52-5, Pub. by Floris Bks). St George Bk Serv.

Bottell, Helen (1914-)
--Helen Help Us. 224p. (Orig.). (gr. 6 up). 1970 (Tempo). G&D.

Botting, T., tr.
Mitten. 31p. (ps-3). 1983. (ISBN [illegible], Pub. by Malysh Pubs USSR). Imported Pubns.

Bottner, Barbara (1943-)
--Big Boss, Little Boss. LC 78-3281. p. cm. (Read alone book). 1978. (ISBN 0-394-83939-0). (ISBN 0-394-93939-5). Pantheon Books.
--Doing the Toledo. Bottner, Barbara (1943-), illus. LC 76-46291. (Illus.). 32 p. 24cm. c.1977. (ISBN 0-590-07470-9). Four Winds Press.
--Dumb Old Casey Is a Fat Tree. LC 78-19474. (Illus.). 42 p. 23cm. c.1979. (ISBN 0-06-020616-0). (ISBN 0-06-020617-9). Harper & Row.
--Fun House. LC 74-8176. (Illus.). 31 p. 19cm. 1974. (ISBN 0-13-345256-5). Prentice-Hall.
--Horrible Hannah. Drescher, Joan Elizabeth (1939-), illus. LC 79-25944. p. cm. c.1980. (ISBN 0-517-53973-X). Crown Publishers.
--Jungle Day. Bottner, Barbara (1943-), illus. LC 77-72645. p. cm. 1977. (ISBN 0-440-04383-2). (ISBN 0-440-04384-0). Delacorte Press.
--Mean Maxine. LC 79-18587. (Illus.). 32 p. c.1980. (ISBN 0-394-84219-7). (ISBN 0-394-94219-1). Pantheon Books.
--Messy. Bottner, Barbara (1943-), illus. LC 78-50420. (Illus.). 32 p. c.1979. (ISBN 0-440-05492-3). (ISBN 0-440-05493-1). Delacorte Press.
--Myra. LC 78-10417. (Illus.). 31 p. c.1979. (ISBN 0-02-785960-6). Macmillan.
--There Was Nobody There. LC 78-2639. (Illus.). 32 p. c.1978. Macmillan.
--What Would You Do with a Giant?. LC 72-187561. (Illus.). 29 p. 27cm. 1972. Putnam.
--The World's Greatest Expert on Absolutely Everything... Is Crying. Bottner, Barbara (1943-), illus. LC 83-49487. (Illus.). 160p. (gr. 3-6). 1984. (ISBN 0-06-020588-1). (ISBN 0-06-020589-X). HarpJ.

Bottom, Raymond (1927-) & Robertson, O. J.
--Hardwood Hero. Reese, Claudia, illus. LC 76-127372. (Illus.). 160 p. 25cm. 1971. (ISBN 0-687-16645-4). Abingdon Press.

Bottomley, Peg
--Clifford: The Clumsy Dragon. Groedel, Burton, illus. LC 62-10184. unpaged. illus. 23cm. (Wonderful world book). 1962. Barnes.

Botton, Jean De see De Botton, Jean.

Botts, Davi
--Hey, Diddle, Diddle & Other Nonsense Rhymes. Botts, Davi, illus. (Illus.). (gr. k-2). 1956. (ISBN 0-8382-0331-0). Hale.
--Hey, Diddle, Diddle, and Other Nonsense Rhymes. Botts, Davi, illus. LC 56-7105. unpaged illus. 22cm. (Rand McNally elf book, 535). c.1956. Rand McNally.
--Hey, Diddle, Diddle, and Other Nonsense Rhymes. Botts, Davi, illus. LC 65-146375. 1v. (unpaged) col. illus. 32cm. 1965, c.1956. Rand McNally.

Botwin, Esther (1923-), ed.
--A Treasury of Songs for Little Children. Urbanowich, Evelyn, illus. 96p. illus. 25cm. c.1952. Hart.
--A Treasury of Songs for Little Children. Urbanowich, Evelyn, illus. LC 62-51970. 96p. col. illus. 25cm. 1962, c.1954. Hart.

Bouchard, Lois Kalb (1938-)
--The Boy Who Wouldn't Talk. Grifalconi, Ann (1929-), illus. LC 69-12189. (Illus.). 74 p. 24cm. 1969. Doubleday.

Boucher, Alan Estcourt (1918-)
--The Hornstranders. Jones, Carol, illus. LC 72-75696. (Illus.). 149 p. 21cm. 1969, c.1966. Meredith Press.
--The King's Men: A Story of St. Olaf of Norway. 1st ed. Weiss, Emil (1896-1965), illus. LC 62-16743. 192p. illus. 22cm. (Clarion book). 1962. Doubleday.

--The Land Seekers. LC 68-29468. (Illus.). 151 p. 22cm. (Ariel book.). 1968, c.1964. Farrar, Straus and Giroux.
--The Path of the Raven. Patten, Toni, illus. LC 60-4031. 192p. illus. 21cm. 1960. Hastings House.
--The Sword of the Raven. Roberts, Doreen (1922-), illus. LC 73-85275. (Illus.). xi, 258 p. 22cm. 1969. Scribner.

Boucher, Sharon
--Teddy Bear of Bumpkin Hollow. Bryant, Dean, illus. LC 48-7982. 40 p. col. illus. 21 cm. (Rand McNally book-elf book). c.1948. Rand McNally.

Boudin, Jean
--Miranda's Music. Webber, Helen & Morrison, Lillian (1917-), illus. LC 68-21596. (Illus.). 69 p. 21cm. 1968. (ISBN 0-690-54348-4). Crowell.

Bougere, Marguerite Bondy, ed.
--Louisiana Stories for Boys and Girls. Padgett, Jim, illus. LC 66-11660. ix, 207 p. illus. 24 cm. 1966. Louisiana State University Press.

Boughton, Willis Arnold (1885-1977)
--Everglades Adventure. LC 48-2902. 246 p. 21 cm. 1948, c.1947. B. Humphries.

Bouhuys, Mies
--The Lady of Stavoren: A Story from Holland. Van Westering, Fracien, illus. Willems-Treeman, Elizabeth, tr. (Illus.). (Puffin Folktales of the World Ser.). (gr. 2-5). 1979. (ISBN 0-14-030802-4, Puffin). Penguin.
--Wise Men from the East. Herrmann, Reinhard, illus. (Ger). (Illus.). 24p. (Children's Bible Picture Books Series, No. 8). (ps-5). 1968. (ISBN 0-8066-9408-4). Augsburg.

Bouhuys, Mies, jt. auth. see Ridge, Antonia Florence.

Bouhuys, Mies & Ridge, Antonia Florence (0000-1981)
--The Little Red Pony. De Wilde, Dick, illus. LC 62-10029. (Illus.). 94 p. 24cm. 1962. Bobbs-Merrill.

Bouhys, Mies see Mies Bouhys.

Boulanger, jt. auth. see Newman.

Boulden, O. J.
--Tom and Jerry. LC 27-10050. 200 p. 19cm. 1927. Dorrance and Company.

Boulle, Pierre Francois Marie-louis (1912-)
--Planet of the Apes. N.D. The Vanguard Press.

Boumphrey, Geoffrey M., jt. auth. see Walker, Kenneth M.

Boumphrey, Geoffrey Maxwell, jt. auth. see Walker, Kenneth Macfarlane.

Bour, Daniele
--The House from Morning to Night. LC 84-21873. (Illus.). 16p. 1st U.S. edition. (ps-3). 1985, c.1978. (ISBN 0-916291-01-4). Kane Miller Bk.

Bourgeois, Florence (1904-)
--Beachcomber Bobbie. LC 35-169. (Illus.). 32 p. 14 x 18cm. (Junior Bks.). 1935. Doubleday, Doran & Company.
--Molly and Michael. Bourgeois, Florence (1904-), illus. (gr. k-2). N.D. Doubleday Bks.
--Molly and Micheal. LC 36-35994. 141 p. illus. (part col.) 14 1/2 x 18 1/2 cm. 1936. Doubleday, Doran & Company, Inc.
--Nathan's Dark House. MacKnight, Ninon (1908-), illus. Ninon, pseud. LC 43-159. 2 p. l., 58 2 p. illus. (part col.) 23 cm. 1942. Doubleday, Doran & Company, Inc.
--Peter, Peter, Pumpkin Grower. LC 37-369251. 64 p. illus. (part col.) 23 1/2 cm. 1937. Doubleday, Doran & Co., Inc.
--Trailer Dog Trix and Nancy. LC 38-341363. 32 p. illus. (part col.) 18 x 23 1/2 cm. 1938. Doubleday, Doran & Company, Inc.

Bourgholtzer, Crawford N.
--The Story of Bobby Coon. Carlson, George L., illus. N.D. Thomas Y. Crowell Company.

Bourhill, E. J, Mrs. & Drake, J. B., Mrs.
--Fairy Tales from South Africa. Holloway, W. Herbert, illus. LC 72-8576. p. (The Black Heritage Library Collection). 1972. (ISBN 0-8369-9183-4). Books for Libraries Press.

Bourjaily, Barbara Webb
--Mother Goose Secrets: As Told by the Story Gnome. King, Joe (1909-1979), illus. LC 25-20435. 7 p. l., 145, 1 p. col. front illus. 23 cm. 1925. Small, Maynard & Co.

Bourke, Linda
--Ethel's Exceptional Egg. LC 77-155450. (Illus.). 29 p. c.1977. (ISBN 0-8178-5622-6). Harvey House.
--Signs of a Friend. Bourke, Linda, illus. LC 81-20541. (Illus., Orig.). 1st U.S. edition. (gr. 1 up). 1982. (ISBN 0-201-10094-0). A-W.

Bourke, Sadie Ten Eyck
--Fables in Feathers. Conde, J. M., illus. LC 7-24036. 3 p. l., 114 p. front., 8 pl. 20 x 16 cm. 1907. T. Y. Crowell & Co.
--Fables in Feathers. Conde, J. M., illus. (Illus.). (Crowell's Every Land Series For Children). 1915. T Y Crowell.

Bourliaguet, Leonce (1895-1965)
--The Giant Who Drank from His Shoe, and Other Stories. Rose, Gerald Hembdon Seymour (1935-), illus. Buchanan-Brown, John (1929-), tr. from Fr. LC 66-10296. 93 p. illus. 23 cm. 1966. Abelard-Schuman.
--The Guns of Valmy. Rose, Gerald Hembdon Seymour (1935-), illus. Buchanan-Brown, John (1929-), tr. LC 69-10300. 159 p. 23cm. 1968. (ISBN 0-200-71571-2). Abelard-Schuman.
--A Sword to Slice Through Mountains. new ed. Rose, Gerald Hembdon Seymour (1935-), illus. Buchanan-Brown, John (1929-), tr. (gr. 2-6). 1975. (ISBN 0-8277-4492-7). British Bk Ctr.
--A Sword to Slice Through Mountains and Other Stories. Rose, Gerald Hembdon Seymour (1935-), illus. Buchanan-Brown, John (1929-), tr. LC 68-10171. (Illus.). 96 p. 22cm. 1968. (ISBN 0-200-71486-4). Abelard-Schuman.
--Sword to Slice Through Mountains & Other Stories. Rose, Gerald Hembdon Seymour (1935-), illus. Buchanan-Brown, John (1929-), tr. from Fr. LC 68-10170. (Illus.). b&w line drawings, 96p. 1st U.S. edition. (gr. 3-7). 1968. Abelard.

Bourne, Benj F.
--Captive in Patagonia: Or, Life Among the Giants. N.D. D. Lothrop Co.

Bourne, Eulalia
--Blue Colt. 1st ed. Fullerton, Pam, illus. LC 78-65925. (Illus.). (gr. 6-9). 1979. (ISBN 0-87358-185-7). (ISBN 0-87358-191-1). Northland.

Bourne, Miriam Anne (1931-)
--Bright Lights to See by. Hafner, Marylin (1925-), illus. LC 76-381498. (Illus.). 47 p. 23cm. (Break-of-day book). c.1975. (ISBN 0-698-20327-5). (ISBN 0-698-30580-9). Coward, McCann & Geoghegan.
--Bright Lights to See by. Hafner, Marylin (1925-), illus. LC 75-2540. (Illus.). 48p. (Break of Day Bk). (gr. k-3). 1975. (ISBN 0-698-30580-9, Coward). Putnam Pub Group.
--Dog Walk. McKissack, Vernon, illus. LC 81-2510. (Illus.). 31 p. 21cm. c.1981. (ISBN 0-695-41623-5). (ISBN 0-695-31623-0). Follett Pub. Co.
--Emilio's Summer Day. Shecter, Ben (1935-), illus. LC 66-7089. (Illus.). 32p. (gr. k-3). 1966. (ISBN 0-06-020626-8, HarpJ). Har-Row.
--Four-Ring Three. Szekeres, Cyndy (1933-), illus. LC 72-85617. (Illus.). 46 p. 23cm. (Break-of-day book). 1973. (ISBN 0-698-20231-7). (ISBN 0-698-20231-7). Coward, McCann & Geoghegan.
--Nabby Adams' Diary. Gammell, Stephen, illus. LC 74-83017. (Illus.). 128 p. 22cm. 1975. (ISBN 0-698-20312-7). Coward, McCann & Geoghegan.
--Nelly Custis' Diary. Palmer, Heidi (1948-), illus. LC 73-88533. (Illus.). 127 p. 18cm. 1974. (ISBN 0-698-20283-X). (ISBN 0-698-20283-X). (ISBN 0-698-20283-X). Coward, McCann & Geoghegan.
--Patsy Jefferson's Diary. Kubinyi, Laszlo (1937-), illus. LC 75-23371. (Illus.). 96 p. 23cm. c.1976. (ISBN 0-698-20352-6). Coward, McCann & Geoghegan.
--Raccoons Are for Loving. Morton, Marian (1918-), illus. LC 68-23660. (Illus.). 44 p. 1968. Random House.
--Second Car in Town. Burns, Raymond Howard (1924-), illus. LC 74-179027. (Illus.). 47 p. 23cm. (Break-of-day book). 1972. Coward, McCann & Geoghegan.
--Tigers in the Woods. Tripp, Wallace Whitney (1940-), illus. LC 76-169131. (Illus.). 44 p. 23cm. (Break-of-day book). 1971. Coward, McCann & Geoghegan.
--Uncle George Washington & Harriot's Guitar. Primavera, Elise, illus. (Illus.). 64p. (gr. 3-6). 1983. (ISBN 0-698-20573-1, Coward). Putnam Pub Group.
--What Is Papa up to Now?. Gackenbach, Dick, illus. LC 76-51272. (Illus.). 62 p. 23cm. (Break-of-day book). c.1977. (ISBN 0-698-20413-1). (ISBN 0-698-30658-9). Coward, McCann & Geoghegan.

Bourne, Russell, ed. see Hay, Keith, et al.

Bourne, Russell, ed. see LaBastille, Anne.

Bourne, William Oland
--Gems from Fable Land: A Collection of Fables Illustrated by Facts. LC 22-656604. xii, 336 p. front., illus. 18 1/2 cm. 1853. C. Scribner.
--Little Silverstring: Or, Tales and Poems for the Young. LC 15-12467. viii, 9-256 p. front., plates 17 1/2 cm. 1853. C. Scribner.

Bourque, Nina
--The Best Trade of All. Urbanovic, Jackie, illus. LC 83-7352. c.1983. (ISBN 0-940742-33-0). Raintree Publishers.

Boursler-Mougenot, A
--Doudou Flies Away. Lehmann-Haupt, Christopher, illus. LC 37-9925. 55 p. col. illus. 32 1/2 cm. 1937. Grosset & Dunlap.

Boussenard, Louis (1847-1910)
--Crusoes of Guiana: Or, The White Tiger. (Illus.). N.D. A. C. Armstrong & Sons.

Boutell, Clarence Burley see Boutell, Clip, pseud.

Boutell, Clarence Burley (1908-1981)
--The Fat Baron. Boutell, Clip, pseud. Lieberman, Frank Joseph (1910-), illus. LC 46-7096. 24cm. 48p. N.D. Houghton Mifflin Co.

Boutell, Clip, pseud., see Boutell, Clarence Burley.

Boutelle, Edith W
--The Astronaut Witch. LC 62-10183. unpaged. illus. 22cm. (Wonderful world book). 1962. Barnes.
--The Fakir of Jinaika. Fellin, Peter, illus. LC 61-13922. unpaged. illus. 22cm. (Wonderful world book). 1961. Barnes.

Boutet De Monvel, Louis Maurice (1850-1913)
--Susanna's Auction. 1957. Macmillan.
--Susanna's Auction. LC 23-26865. 72 p., 1 l. incl. front., illus., plates. 16 1/2 cm. 1923. The Macmillan Company.

Bouth, Jonathan
--The Nuns Go to Africa. LC 72-75886. (Illus.). 32 p. 29cm. 1971. Bobbs-Merrill.

Boutis, Victoria
--Katy Did It. Owens, Gail, illus. LC 81-1034. (Illus.). 88 p. 22cm. (gr. 3-5). c.1982. (ISBN 0-688-00688-4). (ISBN 0-688-00689-2). Greenwillow Books.

Bouton, Elizabeth Gladwin
--Grandmother's Doll. Carter, Helene (1887-1960), illus. LC 31-15292. 4 p. l, 3-106 p. 1 l, illus. (part col.) col. plates 24 1/2 cm. 1931. Duffield and Green.

Bouton, Josephine, ed.
--Favorite Poems for the Children's Hour. Rutherford, Bonnie & Rutherford, Bill, illus. LC 67-4583. (Illus.). xxvi, 358 p. 22cm. 1967. Platt & Munk.
--Poems for the Children's Hour. LC 27-16356. 2 p. l, iii-xxii, 368 p. 20 cm. 1927. Milton Bradley Company.
--Poems for the Children's Hour. LC 62-13185. (More Than Five Hundred Favorite Poems by Famous Authors, with an Index of First LInes.). 363p. 22cm. 1962. Platt & Munk.
--Poems for the Children's Hour. LC 45-78778. xxii, 363 p. col. front. 21 cm. c.1945. The Platt & Munk Co. Inc.

Boutwell, Beth
--The Stick Book. N.D. Dorrance & Co.

Boutwell, Edna (1894-)
--Daughter of Liberty. LC 67-23343. (Illus.). 143 p. 22cm. 1967. World Pub. Co.
--Daughter of Liberty. Watson, Wendy McLeod (1942-), illus. LC 75-22436. p. cm. 1975, c.1967. (ISBN 0-529-03650-9). (ISBN 0-529-03651-7). Collins & World.
--Red Rooster. Garbutt, Bernard (1900-), illus. 48p. (gr. k-5). N.D. Aladdin Bks.
--Red Rooster. Garbutt, Bernard (1900-), illus. (Illus.). 44p. (gr. k-2). 1950. (ISBN 0-525-38196-1). Dutton.
--Sailor Tom. 1st ed. Werth, Kurt (1896-), illus. LC 60-7201. 89, 7p. illus. 26cm. 1960. World Pub. Co.

Bouve, Pauline Carrington Rust, Mrs.
--Lamp-Light Fairy Tales and Other Stories. LC 23-8575. 4 p. l., 321 p. vol. front., illus. 20 1/2 cm. c.1923. Grosset & Dunlap.
--Lamp-light Tales. Hill, Mabel Betsy (1877-), illus. 21cm. 112p. 1922. Grosset & Dunlap.
--Tales of the Mayflower Children. Brownscombe, J & Hill, Mabel Betsy (1877-), illus. LC 27-18966. xiv, 280 p. col. front., plates (1 col.) 20 1/2 cm. c.1927. Marshall Jones Company.

Bouvet, Marguerite (1865-1915)
--Bernardo & Laurette: Being the Story of Two Little People of the Alps. Armstrong, Helen Maitland (1869-), illus. LC 1-27715. 5 p. l., 5-217 p. incl. front., plates. 20 cm. 1901. A. C. McClurg & Co.
--A Child of Tuscany. Hooper, Will Phillips, illus. LC 12-30859. 3 p. l., 9-207 p. incl. illus., plates. 20 1/2 cm. 1895. A.C. McClurg and Company.
--Clotilde. Enright, Maginel Wright, illus. LC 8-28988. 3 p. l., v-vi p., 1 l., 9-216 p. front., 6 pl. 19 1/2 cm. 1908. A.C. McClurg and Company.
--A Little House in Pimlico. Armstrong, Helen Maitland (1869-), illus. LC 12-30860. 245 p. incl. front., illus., plates. 20 1/2 cm. 1897. A.C. McClurg and Company.
--Little Marjorie's Love-Story. Armstrong, Helen Maitland (1869-), illus. LC 12-30861. 124 p. incl. front., illus., plates. 19 cm. 1891. A.C. McClurg and Company.
--My Lady: A Story of Long Ago. Armstrong, Helen Maitland (1869-), illus. 284p. 1900. A C McClurg & Co.
--Pierrette. Hooper, Will Phillips, illus. 203p. 1900. A C McClurg & Co.
--Prince Tip-Top: A Fairy Tale. Armstrong, Helen Maitland (1869-), illus. LC 44-29957. xiv, 15-134 p. incl. illus., plates. 19 cm. 1892. A. C. McClurg and Company.
--Sweet William. Armstrong, Helen Maitland (1869-) & Armstrong, Margaret Neilson (1867-), illus. LC 12-30862. 20cm. 209p. 1891. McClurg.
--Tales of an Old Chateau. Armstrong, Helen Maitland (1869-), illus. 1900. A C McClurg & Co.

Bova, Benjamin William, jt. auth. see Dickson, Gordon Rupert.

Bova, Benjamin William (1932-)
--City of Darkness. LC 75-32054. 160p. (gr. 7-10). 1976. (ISBN 0-684-14557-X, ScribJ). Scribner. **Award: (ALA).**
--The Dueling Machine. LC 72-80312. 247 p. 22cm. 1969. Holt, Rinehart and Winston.
--The Dueling Machine. 176 p. 18cm. (Signet bk., Q5328). 1973, c.1969. New American Lib.
--End of Exile. LC 75-6748. 214 p. 22cm. 1975. (ISBN 0-525-29297-7). Dutton.
--Escape. LC 70-98920. 128p. (Pacesetter Ser). (gr. 7-12). 1970. (ISBN 0-03-019791-0). HR&W.
--Escape. (gr. 5-9). 1975. (ISBN 0-590-01416-1). Scholastic Inc.
--Exiled from Earth. LC 74-133120. (gr. 5-12). 1971. Dutton.
--Flight of Exiles. 1972. Dutton.
--Millennium. 1976. (ISBN 0-394-49421-0). Random.
--Out of the Sun. LC 68-12441. 128p. (Pacesetter Ser). (gr. 7 up). 1968. (ISBN 0-03-068635-0). HR&W.
--The Star Conquerors. 1st ed. LC 59-13109. 215p. 22cm. 1959. Winston.
--Star Watchman. LC 64-20216. 224 p. 22cm. (Winston Science Fiction Ser.). 1964. Holt, Rinehart and Winston.
--The Weathermakers. 249 p. 22cm. 1967. Holt, Rinehart and Winston.
--The Winds of Altair. first ed. LC 72-89836. 135 p. 22cm. 1973. (ISBN 0-525-42945-X). Dutton.

Bova, Benjamin William (1932-), ed.
--The Many Worlds of Science Fiction. LC 75-162276. 234 p. 22cm. 1971. (ISBN 0-525-34550-7). E. P. Dutton.

Bova, Rosa
--Happily, Bumpily, Noisily. Garris, Norma & Garris, Dan, illus. (gr. k-3). N.D. Western Pub.

Bowden, Joan Chase (1925-)
--The Bean Boy. Murdocca, Salvatore, illus. LC 78-12150. (Illus.). 62 p. 23cm. (Ready-to-read). c.1979. (ISBN 0-02-711800-2). Macmillan.
--Bear's Surprise Party. Scott, Jerry (1941-), illus. (Eager Readers Ser). (gr. k-3). 1975. (ISBN 0-307-60809-3, Golden Pr). Western Pub.
--Bouncy Baby Bunny Finds His Bed. Westerberg, Christine (1950-), illus. (Illus.). (gr. k-3). 1977. (ISBN 0-307-60029-7, Golden Pr). Western Pub.
--Little Grey Rabbit. Cauley, Lorinda Bryan (1951-), illus. (Illus.). (Tell-a-Tale Readers). (gr. k-3). 1979. (ISBN 0-307-68651-5, Whitman). Western Pub.
--A New Home for Snow Ball. (Illus.). v. 21cm. (Eager reader). (A Golden Book). 1974. Golden Press.
--Strong John. Murdocca, Salvatore, illus. LC 79-20689. (Illus.). 63 p. 23cm. (Ready-to-read). c.1980. (ISBN 0-02-711790-1). Macmillan.
--Why the Tides Ebb and Flow. Brown, Marc Tolon (1946-), illus. LC 79-12359. (Illus.). 40 p. 27cm. 1979. (ISBN 0-395-28378-7). Houghton Mifflin. **Awards: (ALA); (BGH).**

Bowden, Liz (1928-)
--Mystery Doubles: The Story of Twins. LC 79-19034. p. cm. 1979. (ISBN 0-89547-080-2). C.P.I.

Bowdon, Gussie Cooper
--Jolly Jingles. LC 65-25099. v, 30p. illus. 20cm. N.D. Tex.

Bowen
--Old-Time Stories. N.D. World Book Co.

Bowen, Betty Morgan (1921-)
--For Love of a Donkey. Bowen, Betty Morgan (1921-), illus. LC 62-16717. 197 p. illus. 22 cm. 1963. D. McKay Co.
--Jan's Victory. Bowen, Betty Morgan (1921-), illus. LC 49-414. 169 p. illus. 22 cm. 1949. Longmans, Green.
--Milo's New World. 1st ed. Bowen, Betty Morgan (1921-), illus. LC 47-1623. 21cm. 180p. 1947. Longmans, Green & Co.
--One Against the Sea. Marokvia, Artur F. (1909-), illus. LC 54-6371. (Illus.). 214 p. 22cm. 1954. Longmans, Green.
--Pride of Them All. Bowen, Betty Morgan (1921-), illus. LC 75-191961. (Illus.). 192p. (gr. 4-6). 1970. (ISBN 0-679-20155-6). (ISBN 0-679-25114-6). McKay.

Bowen, C. E., Mrs.
--Alice Neville and Riversdale. N.D. Robert Carter & Brothers.
--Alice Neville: Or, A Little Child Shall Lead Them. (Illus.). N.D. E & J B Young.
--Among the Brigands, and Other Tales of Adventure. (Illus.). (Holiday Tales Library). N.D. E. P. Dutton & Co.
--Battle and Victory. (Illus.). (Happy Home Library). N.D. E. P. Dutton & Co.

AUTHOR INDEX

BOWLES, ELLA

--Ben's Boyhood. (Golden Lily Ser.). N.D. D. Lothrop Co.
--Ben's Boyhood, 1 of 30 vols. (Illus.). (Morning Glory Ser). N.D. Lothrop Pub. Co.
--Cared for: Or, The Orphan Wanderers. N.D. Thomas Whittaker.
--Frisky the Squirrel. LC 17-3764. cover-title, 14 p. incl. illus. (part col.) 28 x 22 cm. (Christmas eve series). c.1889. McLoughlin Bros.
--Grandma's Relics, 1 of 6 vols. (Author of "Among Brigands."). (Illus.). (Julia Maitland Library). N.D. E P Dutton.
--House on the Bridge. (Illus.). N.D. E. P. Dutton & Co.
--How a Farthing Made a Fortune. (The Dolphin Ser.). N.D. Fleming H. Revell Co.
--How Paul's Penny Became a Pound. (Illus.). (The Staincliffe Ser.: Vol. 3). N.D. Fleming H. Revell Co.
--How Paul's Penny Became a Pound. N.D. Thomas Whittaker.
--How Peter's Pound Became a Penny. (Illus.). (The Staincliffe Ser.: Vol. 2). N.D. Fleming H. Revell Co.
--How Peter's Pound Became a Penny. N.D. Thomas Whittaker.
--Jack the Conqueror. (Partridge's Illustrated Juveniles). N.D. George Routledge & Sons.
Jack the Conqueror. N.D. Robert Carter & Brothers.
--Men's Boyhood. (Illus.). (Morning Glory Ser.). N.D. D. Lothrop Co.
--Paul's Penny. N.D. Robert Carter & Brothers.
--Peter's Pound. N.D. Robert Carter & Brothers.
--Peter's Pound and Paul's Penny. N.D. Robert Carter & Brothers
--Potato Roaster and Boy Guardian. N.D. Robert Carter & Brothers.
--The Robin's Christmas Eve. Bonnet, J. Gustave, tr. LC 17-1348. 11 p. 25 cm. (Aunt Louisa's London toy books). 1869. Koppel Brothers, Printers.

Bowen, Canfield
--At Midway. N.D. Grosset & Dunlap.

Bowen, Elizabeth (1899-1973)
--The Death of the Heart. 352p. N.D. (ISBN 0-394-42172-8, Vin). Random.
--The Good Tiger. Nebel, Gustave E., illus. LC 65-21560. 1v. (unpaged) col. illus. 23cm. (Read alone bk.). (gr. k-3). c.1965. (ISBN 0-394-91204-7). Knopf.

Bowen, Irene
--Mystery of Eel Island. Tomes, Jacqueline, illus. LC 61-7982. (Illus.). 160 p. 21cm. 1961. Lippincott.
--The Mystery of the Talking Well. Bolian, Polly (1925-), illus. LC 66-10895. (Illus.). (gr. 4-6). 1966. (ISBN 0-397-30901-5). (ISBN 0-397-30902-3). Lippincott.
--The Stolen Spoon Mystery. Moyler, Alan, illus. LC 58-867701. (Illus.). 124p. (gr. 4-6). 1958. (ISBN 0-397-30435-8). Lippincott.
--Suddenly-a Witch!. Purdy, Susan Gold (1939-), illus. LC 74-117234. (Illus.). 62 p. 23cm. 1970. Lippincott.

Bowen, John Griffith (1924-)
--The Mermaid and the Boy. (Illus.). N.D. A. S. Barnes & Co.
--Pegasus. LC 59-12810. (Illus.). N.D. A. S. Barnes & Co.

Bowen, Marjorie
--Viper of Milan. LC 65-25494. (gr. 4-8). 1965. Dufour.
--The Viper of Milan. (gr. 7 up). N.D (Puffin). Penguin.

Bowen, Olwen, pseud., see Davies, Olwen Bowen.

Bowen, Richard M. (1928-)
--Nails, a Boy at Bunker Hill and Valley Forge. Goldstein, Nathan (1927-), illus. LC 67-145956. 44p. illus. 24cm. (gr. 3-6). 1967. (ISBN 0-8271-6707-5). Barre Pubs.

Bowen, Robert Sidney see Richard, James Robert, pseud.

Bowen, Robert Sidney (1900-1977)
--The Appaloosa Curse. Richard, James Robert, pseud. LC 56-8523. 189p. 21cm. 1956. Lothrop, Lee Shepard Co.
--Ball Hawk. LC 50-6171. 180 p. 21 cm. 1950. Lothrop, Lee & Shepard.
--Bat Boy. LC 62-11064. 192 p. 21cm. 1962. Lothrop, Lee and Shepard Co.
--Behind the Bat. LC 53-82605. 158p. 22cm. 1953. Lothrop, Lee & Shepard.
--The Big Hit. LC 58-7743. 188p. 21cm. 1958. Lothrop, Lee and Shepard.
--The Big Inning. LC 55-8451. 183 p. 21cm. 1955. Lothrop, Lee & Shepard.
--Blocking Back. LC 50-10536. 187 p. 21 cm. 1950. Lothrop, Lee & Shepard.
--Born to Fly. LC 79-134566. 180 p. 22cm. 1971. (ISBN 0-200-71786-3). Criterion Books.
--Canyon Fury. LC 52-12920. 192 p. 21cm. 1952. Lothrop, Lee & Shepard.
--The Club Team: By James Robert Richard; Pseud. Richard, James Robert, pseud. LC 50-9724. 168 p. 22 cm. 1950. Lothrop, Lee & Shepard.
--Dave Dawson at Casablanca. LC 44-3266. ix p., 1 l., 13-250 p. 13 1/2 cm. (His The war adventures series). 1944. Crown Publishers.
--Dave Dawson at Dunkirk. LC 41-8536. vii p., 1 l., 11-251 p. 19 1/2 cm. (war adventure series). c.1941. Crown Publishers.
--Dave Dawson at Singapore. LC 42-9900. 250 p. 19 1/2 cm. (His The War adventure series). 1942. Crown Publishers.
--Dave Dawson at Truk. LC 47-2848. 5 p. l., 13-243 p. 19 1/2 cm. (His The War adventure series). 1946. Crown Publishers.
--Dave Dawson in Libya. LC 41-14547. vii p., 1 l., 11-252 p. 19 1/2 cm. (His The war adventure series). c.1941. Crown Publishers.
--Dave Dawson on Convoy Patrol. LC 41-22777. 247 p. 19 1/2 cm. (His The war adventure series). 1941. Crown Publisher.
--Dave Dawson on Guadalcanal. LC 43-143184. 5 p. l., 13-246 p. 19 cm. (His The war adventure series). 1943. Crown Publishers.
Dave Dawson on the Russian Front. 252 p. 19 cm. (His The war adventure series). 1943. Crown Publishers.
--Dave Dawson with the Air Corps. LC 42-239524. 251 p. 19 1/2 cm. (His The War adventure series). 1942. Crown Publishers.
--Dave Dawson with the Commandos. LC 42-253664. 246 p. 19 1/2 cm. (His The War adventure series). 1942. Crown Publishers.
--Dave Dawson with the Eighth Air Force. LC 43-437432. 252 p. 18 1/2 cm. (His The war adventure series). c.1944. Crown Publishers.
--Davc Dawson with the Flying Tigers. LC 43-853143. 250 p. 19 1/2 cm. (His The war adventure series). 1943. Crown Publishers.
--Dave Dawson with the Pacific Fleet. 249 p. 19 cm. (His The war adventure series). 1942. Crown Publishers.
--Dave Dawson with the R. A. F. LC 41-123181. 252 p. 19 1/2 cm. (His the war adventure series). c.1941. Crown Publishers.
--Dirt Track Danger. Blair, William, illus. LC 63-8723. (Illus.). 141 p. 22cm. (Signal book). 1963. Doubleday.
--Double M for Morgans. Richard, James Robert, pseud. LC 58-11821. 154p. 21cm. 1958. Lothrop, Lee & Shepard.
--Fighting Halfback. Richard, James Robert, pseud. LC 52-12444. 183 p. 21 cm. 1952. Lothrop, Lee & Shepard.
--Flight into Danger. 1st Ed. LC 62-17341. 206p. 21cm. 1962. Chilton Co., Book Division.
--Fourth Down. LC 49-111179. 192 p. 21 cm. 1949. Lothrop, Lee and Shepard Co.
--The Fourth Out. LC 56-669717. 190p. 21cm. 1956. Lothrop, Lee & Shepard Co.
--Hot Corner Blues. LC 64-14444. 181 p. 21 cm. 1964. Lothrop, Lee and Shepard.
--Hot Rod Angels. LC 60-5827. (gr. 7 up). 1960. (ISBN 0-8019-0457-9). Chilton.
--Hot Rod Doom. LC 72-12074. 176 p. 22cm. 1973. (ISBN 0-200-00010-1). (ISBN 0-200-00010-1). Criterion Books.
--Hot Rod Outlaws. 206 p. 21cm. 1968, c.1969. Chilton.
--Hot Rod Patrol. LC 65-23594. 172p. 22cm. c.1966. Criterion.
--Hot Rod Rodeo. LC 64-12004. 158 p. 22 cm. 1964. Criterion Books.
Hot Rod Showdown. LC 67-11914. 156p. 22cm. 1967. Criterion.
--Infield Flash. LC 69-14320. 158 p. 21cm. 1969. Lothrop, Lee & Shepard.
--Infield Spark. LC 54-8599. 187 p. 21cm. 1954. Lothrop, Lee and Shepard.
--Joker, the Polo Pony. Richard, James Robert, pseud. LC 59-13158. 175p. 22cm. 1959. Lothrop, Lee and Shepard.
--The Last White Line. LC 55-11985. 189p. 21cm. 1955. Lothrop, Lee & Shepard Co.
--Lightning Southpaw. LC 67-18032. 160 p. 21 cm. 1967. Lothrop Lee & Shepard.
--Man on First. LC 66-132145. 158p. 21cm. c.1966. Lothrop.
--The Million Dollar Fumble. LC 54-10295. 180 p. 21cm. 1954. Lothrop, Lee & Shepard.
--Million-Dollar Rookie. LC 60-53428. 189p. 21cm. 1961. Lothrop, Lee and Shepard.
--No Hitter. LC 57-10383. 187p. 22cm. 1957. Lothrop, Lee & Shepard.
--Pennant Fever. LC 60-14568. 186 p. 21cm. 1960. Lothrop, Lee and Shepard.
--Perfect Game. LC 63-11680. 190 p. 21 cm. 1963. Lothrop, Lee and Shepard.
--Phantom Mustang. Richard, James Robert, pseud. LC 54-2193. 192p. 21cm. 1954. Lothrop, Lee and Shepard.
--Pitcher of the Year. LC 52-7591. 183 p. 22cm. 1952. Lothrop, Lee & Shepard.
--Player, Manager. LC 49-2153. 187 p. 22 cm. 1949. Lothrop, Lee & Shepard Co.
--The Purple Palomino. Richard, James Robert, pseud. LC 55-10442. 189p. 21cm. 1955. Lothrop, Lee and Shepard.
--Quarterback: All-American,. Richard, James Robert, pseud. LC 53-13184. 183p. 21cm. 1953. Lothrop, Lee & Shepard.
--Rebel Rookie. LC 65-13827. 186p. 21cm. c.1965. Lothrop.
--Red Randall at Pearl Harbor. LC 43-18843. v, 216 p. front. 19 1/2 cm. N.D. Grosset & Dunlap.
--Red Randall in Burma. LC 45-5183. v p., 1 l., 210, 2 p. incl. front. 19 1/2 cm. 1945. Grosset & Dunlap.
--Red Randall in the Aleutians. LC 44-51104. v p., 1 l., 214 p. incl. front. 19 1/2 cm. 1945. Grosset & Dunlap.
--Red Randall on Active Duty. LC 44-742110. v p., 1 l., 211 p. incl. front. 19 1/2 cm. 1944. Grosset & Dunlap.
--Red Randall on New Guinea. LC 44-803311. v p., 1 l., 206 p. incl. front. 19 1/2 cm. 1944. Grosset & Dunlap.
--Red Randall Over Tokyo. LC 44-5018. v, 1 p., 1 l., 208, 2 p. incl. front. 19 1/2 cm. 1944. Grosset & Dunlap.
--Red Randall's One-Man War. LC 46-1845. v p., 1 l., 215 p. incl. front. 19 cm. 1946. Grosset & Dunlap.
--Snow King: The Lippinzan Horse,. Richard, James Robert, pseud. LC 57-14623. 187p. 21cm. 1957. Lothrop, Lee and Shepard.
--Touchdown Kid. LC 51-7313. 188 p. 21 cm. 1951. Lothrop, Lee & Shepard.
--Triple Play. LC 59-8996. 184p. 21cm. 1959. Lothrop, Lee and Shepard.
--Wings for an Eagle. 1st ed. LC 62-7366. 197p. 21cm. 1962. Chilton Co., Book Division.
--The Winning Pitch. LC 48-6409. 208 p. 22 cm. 1948. Lothrop, Lee & Shepard Co.
--Wipcout. LC 68-15233. 160 p. 22cm. 1969, c.1968. Criterion Books.

Bowen, Vernon
--The Emperor's White Horses. Kreis, Hans, illus. LC 56-86023. 147p. illus. 21cm. 1956. D. McKay.
--The Lazy Beaver. Davis, James H., illus. LC 48-9087. 36 p. illus. (part col.) 28 cm. c.1948. D. McKay Co.
--Snow for Christmas, Story. Wiese, Kurt (1887-1974), illus. LC 53-113656. unpaged. illus. 24cm. c.1953. D. McKay Co.
--The Wonderful Adventures of Ting Ling. Wiese, Kurt (1887-1974), illus. LC 52-11260. unpaged. illus. 24cm. c.1952. D. McKay Co.

Bowen, William (1877-)
--The Enchanted Forest. Petersham, Maud Sylvia Fuller, Mrs. (1890-1971) & Petersham, Miska (1889-1960), illus. LC 20-20549. xii p., 2 l., 197 p. incl. col. front., illus., plates. 19 1/2 cm. 1920. The Macmillan Company.
--Merrimeg. Brock, Emma Lillian (1886-1974), illus. LC 23-13190. 6 p. l., 3-166 p. incl. illus., plates. col. front., col. plates. 19 1/2 cm. 1923. The Macmillan Company.
--The Old Tobacco Shop: A True Account of What Befell a Little Boy in Search of Adventure. LC 21-18318. 6 p. l., 236 p. front., illus. 20 cm. 1921. The Macmillan Company. **Award: (JNM).**
--Philip and the Faun. LC 26-15704. 4 p. l., 3-143 p. illus. 20 1/2 cm. 1926. Little, Brown, and Company.
--Solario the Tailor: His Tales of the Magic Doublet. LC 22-186644. xiii p., 1 l., 232 p. col. front., illus., plates (part col.) 19 1/2 cm. 1922. The Macmillan Company.

Bower, B. M., pseud., see Sinclair, Bertha Muzzy.

Bower, B. M., pseud., see Sinclair, Mrs. Bertha Muzzy.

Bower, B. M., pseud. (1874-1940)
--The Dry Ridge Gang. Sinclair, Mrs. Bertha Muzzy. 294p. 1935. Little, Brown & Co.
--Flying U Ranch. Sinclair, Mrs. Bertha Muzzy. Hutchison, D. C., illus. N.D. Grosset & Dunlap.
--The Flying U Strikes. Sinclair, Mrs. Bertha Muzzy. 1934. Little, Brown & Co.
--The Flying U's Last Stand. Sinclair, Mrs. Bertha Muzzy. 1915. Grosset & Dunlap.
--The Happy Family. Sinclair, Mrs. Bertha Muzzy. N.D. Grosset & Dunlap.
--The Heritage of the Sioux. Sinclair, Mrs Bertha Muzzy. 313p. 1916. Little, Brown.
--Trouble Rides the Wind. Sinclair, Bertha Muzzy. 1935. Little, Brown & Co.
--The Whoop-up Trail. Sinclair, Mrs. Bertha Muzzy. 1933. Little, Brown & Co.

Bower, Barbara, pseud., see Todd, Barbara Euphan.

Bower, Barbara Euphan Todd
--Worzel Gummidge the Scarecrow of Scatterbrook Farm. 5 p. l., 3-200 p. incl. front., illus. 19 1/2 cm. 1947. G. P. Putnam's Sons.

Bower, Barbara Euphan Todd see Todd, Barbara Euphan.

Bower, Louise (1900-) & Tigue, Ethel Erkkila (1918-)
--Packy. McClure, Herbert, illus. LC 67-2656. (Illus.). 192 p. 22cm. 1967. Abingdon Press.
--The Secret of Willow Coulee. McClure, Herbert, illus. LC 66-16998. (Illus.). 192 p. 22cm. 1966. Abingdon Press.

Bower, Mary Ruth, jt. auth. see Gibke, Carl H.

Bowers, Fredson Thayer, ed. see Hawthorne, Nathaniel.

Bowers, Gwendolyn
--The Adventures of Philippe: A Story of Old Kebec. Kredel, Fritz (1900-1973), illus. N.D. E. P. Dutton & Co.
--At the Sign of the Globe. LC 66-71145. 186p. 21cm. 1966. Walck.
--Brother to Galahad. Bolognese, Donald Alan (1934-), illus. LC 63-10909. 222 p. illus. 21 cm. 1963. H. Z. Walck.
--A Date with Dave. LC 59-8185. 187p. 21cm. 1959. Morrow.
--Journey for Jemima. LC 60-7360. 179 p. 21cm. 1960. H. Z. Walck.
--The Lost Dragon of Wessex. N.D. E . M. Hale and Co.
--The Lost Dragon of Wessex. Geer, Charles Hand (1922-), illus. LC 63-18378. 188 p. illus. 21 cm. Repr. of 1957 ed. 1963. Henry Z Walck.
--The Lost Dragon of Wessex. Geer, Charles Hand (1922-), illus. LC 57-6481. 188p. illus. 21cm. 1957. Oxford University Press.
--The Wishing Book Doll. Dillon, Corinne Boyd, illus. LC 57-5426. 64p. illus. 22cm. 1957. Morrow.

Bowers, Kathleen Rice
--At This Very Minute. 1st ed. Shute, Linda, illus. LC 82-4712. p cm c1983 (ISBN 0-316-10400-0). Little, Brown.

Bowers, Norm & Bowers, Pat
--Andy Jacks' Adventures in Europe. LC 74-100011. (Illus.). iv, 130 p. 24cm. 1969. Little House Pub. Co.

Bowers, Pat, jt. auth. see Bowers, Norm.

Bowes, Clare
--The Man from Inverness. LC 68-31508. (Illus.). 1 v. (unpaged). 27cm. (Foreign Land Bks). 1968. Lerner Publications Co.

Bowes, Elmore
--The Trials of David Clark. Owens, Joyce, illus. LC 73-126795. (Illus.). 57 p. 20cm. (Challenger book. Black series). 1970. Hill and Wang; Distributed by Random House.

Bowes-Lyon, Sarah (1920-)
--Harum Scarum. Bowes-Lyon, Sarah (1920-), illus. LC 35-566591. 62, 2 p. mounted col. front., illus., mounted col. plates, 25 cm. 1934. J. M. Dent and Sons, Ltd.

Bowie, Jim, pseud., see Stratemeyer, Edward L..

Bowie, Jim, pseud. (1862-1930)
--Dead Shot Dave in Butte: Or, Breaking the Green Cloth Record. Stratemeyer, Edward L.. (New York Five Cent Library: No. 16). 1892. Street & Smith.
--Dead Shot Dave in Chicago. Stratemeyer, Edward L.. (New York Five Cent Library: No. 53). 1893. Street & Smith.
--Dead Shot Dave in Denver: Or, Foiling the Gamblers. Stratemeyer, Edward L.. (New York Five Cent Library: No. 45). 1893. Street & Smith.
--Dead Shot Dave in Kentucky: Or, The Blue Grass Region Horse Thieves. Stratemeyer, Edward L.. (New York Five Cent Library: No. 62). 1893. Street & Smith.
--Dead Shot Dave in Omaha: Or, The Limit of the Red and Black. Stratemeyer, Edward L.. (New York Five Cent Library: No. 57). 1893. Street & Smith.
--Dead Shot Dave in Spokane: Or, A Lone Hand and a High Stake. Stratemeyer, Edward L.. (New York Five Cent Library: No. 24). 1893. Street & Smith.
--Dead Shot Dave in Tacoma: Or, A Fortune at One Throw. Stratemeyer, Edward L.. (New York Five Cent Library: No. 33). 1893. Street & Smith.
--Dead Shot Dave, the Nerviest Sport on Record: Or, The Card Wizard of the Mississippi. Stratemeyer, Edward L.. (New York Five Cent Library: No. 6). 1892. Street & Smith.

Bowie, Walter Russell (1882-1969)
--Bible Story for Boys & Girls: New Testament. Godwin, Stephani & Godwin, Edward Fell (1912-), illus. (Illus.). (gr. 5-9). N.D. (ISBN 0-687-03395-0). Abingdon.
--Bible Story for Boys & Girls: Old Testament. Godwin, Stephani & Godwin, Edward Fell (1912-), illus. (Illus.). (gr. 5-9). N.D. (ISBN 0-687-03420-5). Abingdon.
--The Story of Jesus for Young People. N.D. Charles Scribner's Sons.

Bowker, John Westerdale (1935-)
--Uncle Bolpenny Tries Things Out. Garland, Sarah, illus. (Illus.). (ps-5). N.D. (ISBN 0-571-09973-4, Pub. by Faber & Faber). Merrimack Pub Cir.

Bowlen, Ruth
--Peter's Escape, and Other Stories. LC 52-44815. 64 p. 20 cm. 1952. Moody Press.
--Songs to Sing & Say for Boys and Girls. N.D. (ISBN 0-89107-950-5). Good News.

Bowler, Jan Bret, jt. auth. see Krensky, Stephen Alan.

Bowles, Ella Shannon, Mrs. (1886-1975)
--Children of the Border. (Lippincott Juniors). N.D. J. B. Lippincott.

--Children of the Border: A Story of New Hampshire Pioneers. Rodgers, Richard H. (1876-1953), illus. LC 29-28506. 230, 1 p. incl. illus., col. plates. col. front. 20 cm. 1929. J. B. Lippincott Company.
--Hubert the Happy: A Story of France in the Xiith Century. Justis, Lyle, illus. LC 30-29567. 207, 1 p. col. front., illus., col. plates 20 cm. 1930. J. B. Lippincott Company.

Bowles, Emily, tr.
--Maggie's Rosary and Other Tales. N.D. Catholic Publication Society.

Bowles, Ralph H
--Bob Hanson: Tenderfoot. Smyth, S. Gordon, illus. LC 21-159950. 223 p. front., plates. 20 cm. 1921. The Penn Publishing Company.

Bowley, F. S
--A Boy Lieutenant. Lipman, M. H., illus. LC 6-39762. ix p., 1 l., 13-117 p. incl. front., illus., plates. 19 cm. c.1906. H. Altemus Company.

Bowlin, William R., ed.
--A Book of Historical Poems. N.D. Albert Whitman & Co.
--A Book of Living Poems. N.D. Albert Whitman & Co.
--A Book of Personal Poems. N.D. Albert Whitman & Co.
--A Book of Treasured Poems. N.D. Albert Whitman & Co.

Bowling, David Louis

--Dirty Dingy Daryl. Martz, John, ed. Bowling, Patricia Hendy, illus. LC 81-83120. (Illus.). 24p. 1981. (ISBN 0-939700-00-X). (ISBN 0-939700-01-8). Inka Dinka Ink.

--Dirty Dingy Daryl for President. Bowling, Patricia Hendy, illus. LC 83-82273. (Illus.). 35 p. 21cm. c.1983. (ISBN 0-939700-03-4). (ISBN 0-939700-02-6). Inka Dinka Ink.

Bowman, Anne
--Among the Tartar Tents: Or, the Lost Fathers. 1875. Scribner, Welford, & Armstrong.
--Among the Tartar Tents: Or, The Lost Fathers, 10 of 15 Vols. (Illus.). (Warne's Hopeful Enterprise Library). N.D. Scribner & Welford.
--Amy Carlton: or, First Days at School. N.D. George Routledge & Sons.
--Bear Hunters. Juv ed. (Roundabout Library). (Bear Hunters' Library). N.D. John C. Winston Co.
--The Bear Hunters of the Rocky Mountains, 1 of 3 Vols. (Illus.). (Bowman's Forest Library of Adventure). N.D. Set. George Routledge & Sons Dist. by E. P. Dutton.
--The Bear Hunters of the Rocky Mountains. (Illus.). (Roundabout Lib.). N.D. Henry T. Coates & Co.
--The Bear Hunters of the Rocky Mountains. LC 43-29020. iv, 474 p. front. 19 1/2 cm. N.D. Porter & Coates.
--The Bear Hunters of the Rocky Mountains. Zwecker, illus. (Illus.). N.D. George Routledge & Sons Dist. by E. P. Dutton.
--The Boy Foresters, 1 of 3 Vols. (Illus.). (Bowman's Forest Library of Adventure). N.D. Set. George Routledge & Sons Dist. by E. P. Dutton.
--The Boy Pilgrims. (Illus.). (Routledge's Welcome Series of Boys' Books). N.D. George Routledge & Sons Dist by E. P. Dutton.
--The Boy Voyagers, 1 of 3 Vols. (Illus.). (Bowman's Voyage Library of Adventure). N.D. Set. George Routledge & Sons Dist. by E. P. Dutton.
--The Castaways, 1 of 3 Vols. (Illus.). (Bowman's Voyage Library of Adventure). N.D. Set. George Routledge & Sons; Dist. by E. P. Dutton.
--The Castaways: or, The Adventures of a Family in the Wilds of Africa. Weir, Harrison William (1824-1906), illus. N.D. George Routledge & Sons; Dist. by E. P. Dutton.
--Clarissa: or, the Mervyn Inheritance. Pasquier, J. A., illus. N.D. George Routledge & Sons.
--Clever Jack: And Other Stories. (Illus.). N.D. James Miller.
--Clever Jack and Other Stories: Author of "Castaways", "Kangaroo Hunters", "Young Exiles". (Illus.). N.D. Thomas R. Knox & Co.
--Esperanza: Or, The Home of the Wanderers, 1 of 3 Vols. (Illus.). (Bowman's Hunter's Library of Adventure). N.D. Set. George Routledge & Sons; Dist. by E. P. Dutton.
--Harry and his Homes: or, the Conquest of Pride. N.D. George Routledge & Sons.
--How to Make the Best of It. N.D. George Routledge & Sons.
--Kangaroo Hunters, 1 of 4 vols. Juv ed. (Roundabout Library). (Bear Hunters' Library). N.D. John C. Winston Co.
--Kangaroo Hunters: Adventures in the Bush. N.D. Nichols & Hall.
--The Kangaroo Hunters: or, Adventures in the Bush. N.D. George Routledge & Sons; Dist. by E. P. Dutton.
--The Kangaroo Hunters: Or, Adventures in the Bush. (Roundabout Lib.). N.D. Henry T. Coates & Co.
--The Kangaroo Hunters: Or, Adventures in the Bush. LC 28-1654. xii, 463 p. incl. front. 20 cm. 1858. Porter & Coates.
--Laura Temple. N.D. George Routledge & Sons.
--The Nile Voyagers, 1 of 3 Vols. (Illus.). (Bowman's Hunter's Library of Adventure). N.D. Set. George Routledge & Sons.
--The Rector's Daughter. N.D. George Routledge & Sons.
--Rolando's Adventures. (Illus.). N.D. George Routledge & Sons; Dist. by E. P. Dutton.
--Sunshine and Clouds in the Morning of Life. N.D. George Routledge & Sons.
--Tom and the Crocodiles, 1 of 3 Vols. (Illus.). (Bowman's Hunter's Library of Adventure). N.D. Set. George Routledge & Sons; Dist. by E. P. Dutton.
--The Young Exiles, 1 of 3 Vols. (Illus.). (Bowman's Forest Library of Adventure). N.D. Set. George Routledge & Sons; Dist. by E. P. Dutton.
--The Young Exiles: or, The Wild Tribes of the North. N.D. George Routledge & Sons; Dist. by E. P. Dutton.
--The Young Nile Voyagers. N.D. George Routledge & Sons; Dist. by E. P. Dutton.
--The Young Yachtsmen, 1 of 3 Vols. (Illus.). (Bowman's Voyage Library of Adventure). N.D. Set. George Routledge & Sons; Dist. by E. P. Dutton.
--The Young Yachtsmen: or, the Wreck of the Gypsy. N.D. George Routledge & Sons; Dist. by E. P. Dutton.

Bowman, Clare
--Busy Bodies: The Busy ABCs. Carten, Virginia, illus. LC 59-8289. unpaged. illus. 24cm. 1959. Rand McNally.

Bowman, Earl Wayland
--The Ramblin' Kid. N.D. Bobbs - Merrill Co.
--The Ramblini Kid. N.D. Grosset & Dunlap.

Bowman, Harold, jt. auth. see Bowman, Marcelle.

Bowman, James Cloyd (1880-1961)
--The Adventures of Paul Bunyan. xiii, 286 p. front., illus., plates. 20 cm. c.1927. The Century Co.
--Mike Fink: Snapping Turtle of the O-Hi-O-O, Snag of the Massassip. 1st ed. Fisher, Leonard Everett (1924-), illus. LC 57-5510. 147p. illus. 25cm. (gr. 7 up). 1957. (ISBN 0-316-10410-8). Little, Brown.
--Mystery Mountain. Wallower, Lucille (1910-), illus. LC 40-10778. 7 p. l., 17-293 p. incl. col. front., illus., plates (part col.) 22 cm. 1940. A. Whitman & Co.
--Pecos Bill. 1937. Little, Brown. **Award: (JNM).**
--Pecos Bill. Bannon, Laura May (0000-1963), illus. LC 37-27327. (Illus.). (Folklore Ser). (gr. 5 up). 1964. (ISBN 0-8075-6384-6). A Whitman.
--Seven Silly Wise Men. Faulkner, John Frink (1922-), illus. LC 65-151020. (Illus.). 1 v. (unpaged. 24cm. 1965. A. Whitman.
--Tales from a Finnish Tupa. Bannon, Laura May (0000-1963), illus. Kolehmainen, Aili, tr. LC 36-17727. xi p., 1 l., 273 p. col. front., illus., col. plates. 23 cm. 1936. A. Whitman & Co.
--Winabojo, Master of Life. Sperry, Armstrong W. (1897-1976), illus. LC 41-18054. (Illus.). 296 p. 23cm. 1941. A. Whitman & Company.

Bowman, James Cloyd (1880-1961) & Bianco, Margery Williams (1881-1944)
--Who Was Tricked. Faulkner, John Frink (1922-), illus. LC 66-16075. (Illus.). (gr. k-2). 1966. (ISBN 0-8075-9070-3). A Whitman.

Bowman, John Gabbert (1877-)
--Happy All Day Through. Scott, Janet Laura, illus. LC 18-7435. 32p. col. illus. 24 x 31 1/2cm. c.1917. P. F. Volland Co.
--The World That Was. LC 26-157381. vii, 81 p. 20 cm. 1926. The Macmillan Company.

Bowman, John Stewart (1931-)
--Book of Islands. 360p. (gr. 1-7). 1971. (ISBN 0-385-01064-8). Doubleday.
--On Guard: Living Things Defend Themselves. Berelson, Howard (1940-), illus. LC 69-15186. (Illus.). 63 p. 29cm. (Living things of the world). 1969. Doubleday.
--The Quest for Atlantis. LC 72-139007. (Illus.). N.D. (ISBN 0-385-02017-1). (ISBN 0-385-03035-5). Doubleday & Company.

Bowman, Marcelle (1914-) & Bowman, Harold
--Catproof, Windproof, Rainproof. LC 69-10995. (Illus.). 38 p. 22cm. 1969. Doubleday.

Bowman, Phila Butler, Mrs.
--The Little Brown Bowl: With Other Tales and Verse. Cleveland, Bess Bruce, illus. LC 28-7630. xviii, 311 p. col. front., illus., col. plates. 24 cm. c.1928. T. Nelson and Sons.

Bowman, Ruth, jt. ed. see Vetter, Marjorie Meyn.

Bowman, Sarah & Vardey, Lucinda
--Pigs. LC 81-3757. (Illus.). 144p. 1981. (ISBN 0-02-514140-6). Macmillan.

Bown, Derick
--Robin Hood and His Merrie Men. Bown, Derick, illus. LC 78-4201. p. cm. (Raintree's illustrated classics). 1978. (ISBN 0-8393-6201-3). Raintree Childrens Books.

Bowood, Richard, pseud., see Daniell, David Scott.

Bowood, Richard, pseud. (1906-)
--Red Gaskell's Gold. Daniell, David Scott. Kesteven, Peter, illus. 1966. St. Martin's Press.

Bowring, C.
--The Poodle. Monro, Arthur, illus. 1966. Macmillan Company.

Bowser, Milton
--Follow Me to Yesterday (Re: Bible History), 3 vols. (Illus.). 150p. (Orig.). 1981. Set. (ISBN 0-940178-02-8). Sitare Inc.

Bowskill, Derek (1928-)
--All About Theatre. LC 76-363798. (Illus.). 157 p. 23cm. 1975. (ISBN 0-491-01815-0). W. H. Allen.

Boxer, Devorah
--Twenty-Six Ways to be Somebody Else. Boxer, Devorah, illus. LC 60-4736. (Illus.). 16x23cm. 64p. 1960. Pantheon Books. **Award: (NYT).**

Boy Scouts Of America
--Boy Scout Songbook. 128p. (gr. 6-12). 1970. (ISBN 0-8395-3224-5). BSA.
--Cub Scout Songbook. (Illus.). 144 songs. 96p. 64p. (gr. 3-5). 1969. (ISBN 0-8395-3222-9). BSA.

Boyce, Annie
--Tall Tales from a Ranch. (Illus.). (gr. 11 up). N.D. (ISBN 0-8111-0192-4). Naylor.

Boyce, Benjamin, ed.
--The Adventures Of Lindamira. 167p. 1949. The University Of Minnesota Press.

Boyce, Burke (1901-)
--The Emperor's Arrow. 1st ed. Frame, Paul (1913-), illus. LC 67-4861. (Illus.). 72 p. 22cm. 1967. Lippincott.
--Lions Backward. Weaver, Jack (1925-), illus. LC 69-15176. (Illus.). 48 p. 1970. Doubleday.

Boyce, Ethel Myrtle
--Little Children. (Bible Story Book). N.D. Warner Press.
--More Stories Jesus Told. Campbell, R. G., illus. (Illus.). (gr. k-6). 1969. (ISBN 0-87162-061-8). Warner Pr.
--Sand in My Hand. Palmer, Janice, illus. LC 65-120889. (Illus.). (gr. k-3). 1965. (ISBN 0-8114-7557-3). Steck-V.
--Wonderful Things Jesus Did. (gr. k-6). 1968. (ISBN 0-87162-064-2). Warner Pr.

Boyce, George Arthur (1898-)
--Some People Are Indians. Kimball, Yeffe (1914-), illus. LC 75-190224. (Illus.). x, 165 p. 21cm. 1974. (ISBN 0-8149-0714-8). Vanguard Press.

Boyd, Candy Dawson
--Circle of Gold. 128p. (Orig.). (gr. 4-6). 1948. (ISBN 0-590-32464-0, Apple Paperbacks). Scholastic Inc.
--Forever Friends. LC 85-43424. p. cm. 1986, c.1985. (ISBN 0-14-032077-6). Puffin Books.

Boyd, Catherine
--Falcon of the Forest. Olderen, Edward, illus. (Illus.). (Upper Grades Bk. Ser.). (gr. 4-6). N.D. (ISBN 0-513-00433-5). Denison.

Boyd, E. E., Mrs.
--Captain Charley: And His Little Right Hand. N.D. Henry Hoyt.
--Captain Charlie, And His Little Right Hand. N.D. Bradley & Woodruff.
--Farmer Burt's Seed. (Illus.). N.D. James A. Moore.
--Jack Bryson. (Illus.). N.D. James A. Moore.
--Lily's Looking Glasses. N.D. Alfred Martien.
--Lily's Looking Glasses. (Illus.). N.D. James A. Moore.
--The Little Slate Picker, and Other Stories. N.D. Alfred Martien.
--The Little Slate Picker, and Other Stories. (Illus.). N.D. James A. Moore.
--Mary Morne and Her Friend: Or, The Two Paths. (Illus.). N.D. James A. Moore.
--Mary Morne and her Friend: The Two Paths. N.D. Alfred Martien.
--Our Guy, 1 of 25 vols. (Illus.). 206p. (Intermediate, Primary and Infant Libs.). N.D. A. I. Bradley & Co.'s Pubs.
--Our Guy: or the Elder Brother. N.D. Henry Hoyt.
--Paul Loring: Mounting the Ladder. N.D. Alfred Martien.
--Paul Loring: Or, Mounting the Ladder. (Illus.). N.D. James A. Moore.
--Quaint Folks of Haverly, 1 of 20 vols. (Illus.). 176p. (Selected Bks for Sunday School: No. 22). N.D. Set. Methodist Bk Concern.
--Together: Or, Life on the Circuit. (Illus.). N.D. Methodist Book Concern.

Boyd, E. E., Mrs., jt. auth. see Wynne, Faith.

Boyd, E. E., Mrs. & Huntington, Faye
--Bryson Library: Containing "Jack Bryson", "Paul Loring", "Mary Morne", and "Kitty Farnham", 4 vols. (Illus.). N.D. James A. Moore.

Boyd, E. E., Mrs. & Johnston, Emma M., Miss
--The Children's Speaker and Anniversary Gem. (Illus.). N.D. James A. Moore.

Boyd, E. E., Mrs. & Ray, Rena
--Looking Glass Library: Containing "Lily's Glasses", "Tabitha Todd", "Dainty Maurice", and "Little Jackie". N.D. James A. Moore.

Boyd, Edith L
--Ben Follows Old Trails. LC 75-96264. (Illus.). ix, 141 p. 22cm. 1969. Printed by C. W. Hill.
--Boy Joe Goes to Sea. Fisher, Leonard Everett (1924-), illus. LC 56-10472. 222p. illus. 21cm. 1959. Rand McNally.

Boyd, Elizabeth Mifflin, Mrs.
--All About David. Sarg, Tony (1882-), illus. LC 40-7928. vii, 117 p. illus. 23 cm. c.1940. The John C. Winston Company.

Boyd, Ernest Augustus (1887-), tr. see Lange, Mariluise.

Boyd, Harriet
--The Jolly Twisters. Bailey, Corinne Ringel, illus. LC 29-10389. (Illus.). 96 p. 23cm. 1929. The Saalfield Publishing Company.

Boyd, James
--Old Pines and Other Stories. 160p. 1952. University Of North Carolina.

Boyd, James (1888-1944)
--Drums. Wyeth, Newell Convers (1882-1945), illus. 1928. Charles Scribner's Sons.

Boyd, John, pseud., see Upchurch, Boyd.

Boyd, John, pseud. (1919-)
--Andromeda Gun. Upchurch, Boyd. 1975. (ISBN 0-399-11377-0). G.P. Putnam's Sons.

Boyd, L. M.
--Clancy's Treasure Book for Children. Boyd, L. M., illus. 166p. (Orig.). 1981. (ISBN 0-941620-34-4). H G Carson Ent.

Boyd, Lilyth Watson & Smith, Hessie
--Merrily We Learn and Sing: Varied Units for Kindergarten and Primary Grades with Music and Color Work Sheets; Text and Work Sheets. Bennett, Juanita C., illus. LC 44-11692. vii, 120 p. illus. 27 1/2 cm. 1944. Clayton F. Summy Co.

Boyd, Lorenz
--Cardinals in the Pine. Brown, Cornelia, illus. Boyd, Loreuz, photos by. LC 69-10612. (Illus.). 48 p. 27cm. 1969. Abingdon Press.

Boyd, M. M.
--Silver Wands. N.D. Yale University Press.

Boyd, Mary
--Barby's Shuttle, and What it Wrought. N.D. Alfred Martien.

Boyd, Mary D. R., Mrs.
--Barby's Shuttle and What It Wrought. (Illus.). N.D. James A. Moore.
--Stepping Stones Over the Brook. N.D. Alfred Martien.
--Stepping Stones over the Brook. (Illus.). N.D. James A. Moore.
--The Three Rules. (Illus.). N.D. James A. Moore.

Boyd, Mary D. R., Mrs., et al.
--Young Pilgrim Library: Containing "Bertie and His Friend", "Stepping Stones", and "Through Patience", 3 vols. (Illus.). N.D. James A. Moore.

Boyd, Mary Eloise (1915-)
--Joy. Drescher, Joan Elizabeth (1939-), illus. LC 69-12372. (Illus.). 28 p. 19cm. (Stardust books). 1969. (ISBN 0-8378-1919-9). C. R. Gibson Co.
--What Is Home. Stang, Judy (1921-1977), illus. LC 69-16106. (Illus.). 26 p. 19cm. (Stardust books). 1969. C. R. Gibson Co.

Boyd, Mildred Worthy (1921-)
--Man, Myth & Magic. LC 68-15239. (Illus.). photos. bibl. index. 192p. (gr. 7 up). 1969. (ISBN 0-200-00007-1, AbS-J). Har-Row.

Boyd, Nellie
--Vagabond Rhymes. LC 20-17343. 18cm. 110p. 1892. J. G. Cupples Co.

Boyd, Patricia Ryerson (1935-)
--The Furry Wind. 1st ed. Spring, Grace J., illus. LC 82-15103. (Illus.). 28 p. 22cm. c.1982. (ISBN 0-9603840-4-9). Andrew Mountain Press.

Boyd, Pauline, jt. auth. see Boyd, Selma.

Boyd, Pearle M.
--Bibs and Tuckers. LC 29-5198. 48p. illus. (part col.) 25cm. 1929. T. Nelson & Sons.
--Jumping Jerusha. Ouillarde, illus. LC 29-18318. 7 p. l., 3-104 p. 21 cm. c.1929. H. Holt and Company.
--Mike. Ouillarde, illus. LC 28-23680. 5 p. l., 3-107 p. illus. 22 cm. c.1928. H. Holt and Company.

Boyd, Pliny Steele
--Rex Ringgold's School: Or, The Imperial Club. (Illus.). 399p. N.D. National Temperance Society.
--Up and Down the Merrimac. (Idle Hour Ser.). 1879. D. Lothrop Co.

Boyd, Selma & Boyd, Pauline
--Footprints in the Refrigerator. Nicklaus, Carol, illus. LC 82-7112. p. cm. (An Easy-Read Story Book). 1982. (ISBN 0-531-04450-5). F. Watts.
--The How. Luks, Peggy, illus. LC 80-13513. p. cm. 1980. (ISBN 0-87705-176-3). Human Sciences Press.
--I Met a Polar Bear. Brewster, Patience, illus. LC 82-10103. p. cm. c.1983. (ISBN 0-688-01629-4). Lothrop, Lee & Shepard Books.

Boyde, Richard
--The Last Dodo. Boyde, Richard, illus. (Illus.). 131 p. 22cm. (Ariel book). 1967. Farrar, Straus & Giroux.

--The Last Dodo. Boyde, Richard, illus. LC 67-23989. (Illus.). 131p. (gr. 3-7). 1967. (ISBN 0-374-34357-8). FS&G.

Boyden, Dariel Busch (1895-)

--The Enchanted Garden. 1st ed. LC 53-39522. 89p. illus. 23cm. 1953. Brewster Pub. Co.

Boyden, Emily Maria Blakeslee, Mrs. (1828-)

--Auntie Em's Songs for Children ... 4 v. front., illus. 17 x 23 cm. N.D. The Author.

Boye, Henry

--Joop Joop, Jeep Jeep & Jopamo: Three Visitors from Jupiter. Boye, Henry, illus. LC 76-187215. (Illus.). 44p. illus. 16 x 21cm. (gr. 1-4). 1972. (ISBN 0-912472-13-8). Miller Bks.

Boye, Henry, retold by see Irving, Washington.

Boye, Inger, tr. see Unnerstad, Edith Totterman.

Boyer, Charles C.

--Against Heavy Odds and A Fearless Trio. (The Norseland Ser.). N.D. Charles Scribner's Sons.

--The Modern Vikings. (Scribner's Series for Young People). (The Norseland Ser.). N.D. Charles Scribner's Sons.

Boyer, Joanne

--Rain Don't Go Away. (gr. 2-5). N.D. Carlton.

Boyer, Linda L

--God Made Me. Arthur, Lorraine, illus. LC 81-50677. (Illus.). 24 p. 20cm. (happy day book). c.1981. (ISBN 0-87239-464-6). Standard Pub. Co.

Boyer, Richard G

--The Accident Kids. Furan, Barbara Howell, illus. LC 73-93019. (Illus.). 31 p. 25cm. c.1974. (ISBN 0-87783-119-X). (ISBN 0-87783-120-3). Oddo Pub.

--Lucky Bus. Furan, Barbara Howell, illus. LC 73-87801. (Illus.). 30 p. 25cm. c.1974. (ISBN 0-87783-131-9). (ISBN 0-87783-132-7). Oddo Pub.

--Safety on Wheels. LC 73-87802. (Illus.). (Oddo Safety Ser.). (gr. k-5). 1974. (ISBN 0-87783-133-5). (ISBN 0-87783-134-3). (ISBN 0-87783-199-8). Oddo.

Boyer, Wilbur Sarles (1876-)

--Johnnie Kelly. LC 20-16092. vi p., 1 l., 301, 1 p. incl. front. plates. 20 cm. 1920. Houghton Mifflin Company.

Boyesen, Hjalmar Hjorth (1848-1895)

--Boyhood in Norway. Stories of Boy-Life in the Land of the Midnight Sun. LC 13-177402. 5 p. l., 243 p. front., 7 pl. 19 cm. 1892. C. Scribner's Sons.

--Boyhood in Norway: Stories of Boy-Life in the Land of the Midnight Sun. 9th ed. LC 8-11827. 5 p. l., 243 p. front., 7 pl. 19 cm. (Norseland series). 1907. C. Scribner's Sons.

--The Modern Vikings. N.D. Charles Scribner's Sons.

--Norseland Tales. 5 p. l., 247 p. front., 6 pl. 19 cm. (Norseland series). 1894. C. Scribner's Sons.

Boyett, Rose-Marie

--The Adventures of Tiger. Logan, Marie, illus. (Illus.). 36p. 1982. (ISBN 0-9609566-0-3). Ro-Mar.

Boylan, Grace Duffie see Geldert, Grace, pseud.

Boylan, Grace Duffie, adapted by see Stowe, Harriet Elizabeth Beecher, Mrs.

Boylan, Grace Duffie, Mrs.

--If Tom O'Shanters had a Wheel and other poems and sketches. (Illus.). 222p. 1898. E. R. Herrick & Co.

--John of Joy: A Story for Children and Grownups. Geldert, Grace, pseud. LC 26-9269. 18 p. 18cm. 1926. E. H. Clarke & Brother.

--Kids of Many Colors. Scott, Florence E., intro. by. (Illus.). 1910. Hurst & Co.

--Our Little Canadian Kiddies. Scott, Florence E., intro. by. 1910. Hurst & Co.

--Our Little Cuban Kiddies. Scott, Florence. E, intro. by. (Illus.). 1910. Hurst & Co.

--Our Little Eskimo Kiddies. Scott, Florence. E, intro. by. (Illus.). 1910. Hurst & Co.

--Our Little Hawaiian Kiddies. Scott, Florence. E, intro. by. (Illus.). 1910. Hurst & Co.

--Our Little Indian Kiddies. Scott, Florence. E, intro. by. (Illus.). 1910. Hurst & Co.

--Our Little Philippine Kiddies. Scott, Florence. E, intro. by. 1910. Hurst & Co.

--The Pipes of Clovis: A Fairy Romance of the Twelfth Century. Chamberlin, Emily Hall, illus. LC 13-20583. ix, 258 p. col. front., col. plates. 20 cm. 1913. Little, Brown, and Company.

--The Steps to Nowhere. Morgan, Ike, illus. LC 10-23324. (Illus.). 230p. 1910. Baker & Taylor Co.

Boylan, Grace Duffie, Mrs., adapted by.

--Young Folks Uncle Toms Cabin. (Original Author:Harriet Elizabeth Beecher Stowe,1811-1896). (Illus.). N.D. Hurst & Co.

Boylan, Grace Duffie, Mrs. & Morgan, Ike

--Kids of Many Colors. LC 10-1156. (Illus.). 23cm. 156p. 1909. Hurst & Co.

--Kids of Many Colors: Rhymes for Children. LC 1-26056. (Illus.). 22 x 18cm. 156p. 1901. Jamieson, Higgins Co.

Boylan, Rowena

--Better Than the Rest. Fitch, Winnie, illus. LC 79-85945. 188 p. 23cm. 1970. (ISBN 0-695-80078-7). Follett.

Boyle, Constance

--Little Owl and the Tree House. LC 85-9206. p. cm. 1985. (ISBN 0-8120-5677-9). Barron's Educational Series.

--Little Owl's Favorite Uncle. LC 85-9204. p. cm. 1985. (ISBN 0-8120-5675-2). Barron's Educational Series.

Boyle, Elizabeth

--Scrap Basket Sam. Gregory, Dorothy Lake, illus. N.D. Rand McNally.

Boyle, Emily Joyce (1901-)

--Adventuring with David. Huppi, Vernon, illus. LC 61-5101. 96p. c.1961. Abingdon Press.

--Bobby's Neighbors. Depper, Hertha, illus. LC 59-7496. (Illus.). 96p. (ps-3). 1959. (ISBN 0-687-03628-3). Abingdon.

--Muskoka Holiday. Paton, C. Marion, illus. 1959. St Martin's Press.

--Muskoka Holiday. Whittam, Geoffrey William (1916-), illus. N.D. Macmillan.

--The Stone cottage mystery. 1959. St Martin's Press.

--Susan's Special Summer. Voute, Kathleen (1892-), illus. LC 54-6742. 95p. illus. 22cm. 1954. Abingdon-Cokesbury Press.

--Timothy's Twelve Months. Middlebrook, Georgia, illus. LC 52-11647. 94 p. illus. 22 cm. 1952. Abingdon-Cokesbury Press.

--Try Again Tommy. Plummer, Nancy, illus. LC 56-13768. 96p. illus. 22cm. c.1956. Abingdon Press.

Boyle, Frederick, jt. auth. see Russan, Ashmore.

Boyle, Ida D

--A Seed. Mills, Susan, illus. LC 60-53401. unpaged. illus. 16x24cm. c.1960. Graphic Literary Service.

Boyle, Kay (1903-)

--Pinky in Persia. Obligado, Lilian Isabel (1931-), illus. LC 68-18472. (Illus.). 1 v. (unpaged. 22cm. 1968. Crowell-Collier.

--Pinky in Persia. Obligado, Lilian Isabel (1931-), illus. LC 68-18472. 1968. Macmillan Company.

--Pinky: The Cat Who Liked to Sleep. Obligado, Lilian Isabel (1931-), illus. LC 66-15375. 28p. illus. 22cm. N.D. Crowell-Collier.

--Pinky, the Cat Who Liked to Sleep. Obligado, Lilian Isabel (1931-), illus. (Illus.). (gr. 1-3). 1968. (ISBN 0-02-711770-7, CCPr). Macmillan.

--Youngest Camel. (Illus.). (gr. 4-6). 1959. (ISBN 0-8382-1000-7). Hale.

--The Youngest Camel. Kredel, Fritz (1900-1973), illus. LC 39-20130. 1939. Little, Brown & Co.

--Youngest Camel. Solbert, Ronni, pseud. (1925-), illus. Solbert, Romaine G.. (Illus.). (gr. 2-6). 1959. (ISBN 0-06-020634-9). Har-Row.

--The Youngest Camel: Reconsidered and Rewritten. Solbert, Ronni, pseud. (1925-), illus. Solbert, Romaine G.. LC 58-5286. 94p. illus. 23cm. 1967, c.1959. Harper.

Boyle, Myrl C

--Lookout Mountain. Abel, Raymond (1911-), illus. LC 57-5812. 215p. illus. 21cm. 1957. D. McKay.

Boyle, Neil, ed. see Disney, Walter Elias (1901-1966) & Bedford, Annie North.

Boyle, Neil, ed. see Disney, Walt, Productions.

Boyle, Virginia A.

--ZAS!. (Musical Children's Theatre Playscript Ser.). 1979. (ISBN 0-88020-005-7). Coach Hse.

Boyles, Trudy & MacMartin, Louise

--Popcorn Party. Szepelak, Helen Lucy (1919-), illus. LC 53-18607. unpaged. illus. 21cm. (Rand McNally book-elf book, 468). 1953, c.1952. Rand McNally.

Boylston, Helen Dore, Mrs. (1895-1984)

--Carol Goes Backstage. Wallace, Frederick E., illus. LC 41-21881. 6 p. l., 3-233 p. front., plates. 21 cm. 1941. Little, Brown and Company.

--Carol on Broadway. Felten, Major, illus. LC 44-4724. 6 p. l., 3-221, 1 p. front., plates. 20 cm. 1944. Little, Brown and Company.

--Carol on Tour. Felten, Major, illus. LC 46-709447. 6 p. l., 3-205 p. front., plates. 19 1/2 cm. 1946. Little, Brown and Company.

--Carol Plays Summer Stock. Felten, Major, illus. LC 42-19681. 6 p. l., 3-220 p. front., plates. 20 1/2 cm. 1942. Little, Brown and Company.

--Sue Barton, Neighborhood Nurse. 1949. Little, Brown & Co.

--Sue Barton, Neighborhood Nurse. Orr, Forrest W. & Felton, Major, illus. (Illus.). (Sue Barton Ser). (gr. 7-12). 1940. (ISBN 0-316-10475-2, Pub. by Atlantic Monthly Pr). Little.

--Sue Barton, Rural Nurse. Orr, Forrest W., illus. LC 39-30078. 6 p. l., 3-254 p. front., plates. 22 cm. 1939. Little, Brown and Company.

--Sue Barton, Senior Nurse. Orr, Forrest W., illus. (Illus.). (Sue Barton Ser). (gr. 7 up). 1937. (ISBN 0-316-10477-9, Pub. by Atlantic Monthly Pr). Little.

--Sue Barton, Staff Nurse. Felten, Major, illus. LC 52-6798. (Illus.). 20cm. 204p. 1952. Little, Brown & Co.

--Sue Barton, Student Nurse. Orr, Forrest W. & Felton, Major, illus. LC 36-221849. (Illus.). 22cm. 244p. (Sue Barton Ser). (gr. 7 up). 1936. (ISBN 0-316-10479-5, Pub. by Atlantic Monthly Pr). Little.

--Sue Barton, Superintendent of Nurses. Orr, Forrest W. & Felton, Major, illus. LC 40-32432. (Illus.). 239p. (Sue Barton Ser). (gr. 8-11). 1940. (ISBN 0-316-10481-7, Pub. by Atlantic Monthly Pr). Little.

--Sue Barton, Visiting Nurse. Orr, Forrest W., illus. LC 38-27910. 7 p. l., 3-244 p. front., plates. 22 cm. 1938. Little, Brown and Company.

--Sue Barton, Visiting Nurse. Orr, Forrest W. & Felton, Major, illus. (Illus.). (Sue Barton Ser). (gr. 8-11). 1938. (ISBN 0-316-10482-5, Pub. by Atlantic Monthly Pr). Little.

Boynton, Henry Walcott, ed. see Martineau, Harriet.

Boynton, Julia H.

--Little Johnny Twoboys. 57p. N.D. Pilgrims Press.

--Little Johnny Twoboys. 57p. N.D. Sunday-School Library.

Boynton, Robert W & Mack, Maynard (1909-)

--Introduction to the Short Story. 2d ed. LC 77-28388. 282 p. 23cm. (Hayden series in literature). c.1978. (ISBN 0-8104-5050-X). Hayden Book Co.

--Whodunits, Farces, and Fantasies: Ten Short Plays. LC 75-33829. 181 p. 23cm. (Hayden series in literature). c.1976. (ISBN 0-8104-5503-X). Hayden Book Co.

Boynton, Sandra

--But not the Hippopotamus. Klimo, Kate, ed. Boynton, Sandra, illus. (Illus.). 14p. (Sandra Boynton Board Bks.). (ps-k). 1982. (ISBN 0-671-44904-4, Little Simon). S&S.

--Chloe and Maude. LC 85-161. p. cm. 1985. (ISBN 0-316-10492-2). (ISBN 0-316-10491-4). Little, Brown.

--The Going to Bed Book. Klimo, Kate, ed. Boynton, Sandra, illus. (Illus.). 14p. (Sandra Boynton Board Bks.). (ps-k). 1982. (ISBN 0-671-44902-8, Little Simon). S&S.

--Good Night, Good Night. LC 85-2098. p. cm. c.1985. (ISBN 0-394-87285-1). (ISBN 0-394-97285-6). Random House.

--Hester in the Wild. Boynton, Sandra, illus. LC 78-67026. (Illus.). 32 p. (ps-2). c.1979. (ISBN 0-06-020631-4). (ISBN 0-06-020654-3). Harper & Row.

--Hey! What's That. Boynton, Sandra, illus. LC 84-61557. (Illus.). 14p. (ps). 1985. (ISBN 0-394-87208-8, BYR). Random.

--Hippos Go Berserk. Boynton, Sandra, illus. LC 79-16134. (Illus.). 31 p. 1979, c.1977. (ISBN 0-316-10488-4). (ISBN 0-316-10489-2). Little, Brown.

Boynton, Sandra & McEwan, James

--If at First ... LC 79-24310. (Illus.). 32 p. c.1980. [illegible] Little, Brown.

Boys' Life Magazine Editors

--Best Jokes from Boys' Life. LC 74-104392. (Illus.). cartoons. 160p. (gr. 4 up). 1970. (ISBN 0-399-20014-2). Putnam Pub Group.

--Boys' Life Book of Baseball Stories. (Boys' Life Library: No. 6). (gr. 5-9). 1964. (ISBN 0-394-91017-6, BYR). Random.

--The Boys' Life Book of Basketball Stories. Schaare, Harry J., illus. LC 66-14885. (Illus.). 186 p. 22cm. (Boys' life library, 11). (gr. 5-9). 1966. (ISBN 0-394-81546-7, BYR). Random House.

--Boys' Life Book of Flying Stories. (Illus.). (Boys' Life Library: No. 7). (gr. 5-9). 1964. (ISBN 0-394-81019-8). Random.

--The Boys' Life Book of Football Stories. Sugarman, Tracy (1921-), illus. LC 63-7834. 186 p. illus. 22 cm. (Boys' life library, 3). 1963. (ISBN 0-394-80964-5). Random House.

--The Boys' Life Book of Horse Stories. Savitt, Sam (1917-), illus. LC 63-7837. 182 p. illus. 22 cm. (Boys' life library, 1). (gr. 4-9). 1963. (ISBN 0-394-90966-6). Random House.

--The Boys' Life Book of Mystery Stories. LC 63-7835. 185 p. illus. 22 cm. (Boys' life library, 2). 1963. Random House.

--The Boys' Life Book of Mystery Stories. Shilstone, Arthur, ed. LC 63-783512. (Illus.). 22cm. 185p. (Boys' Life Library: No. 2). (gr. 4-9). 1963. (ISBN 0-394-80970-X). (ISBN 0-394-90970-4). Random.

--Boys' Life Book of Outer Space Stories. (Illus.). (Boys' Life Library: No. 5). (gr. 5-9). 1964. (ISBN 0-394-81015-5, BYR). Random.

--The Boys' Life book of Sports Stories. Miller, Don (1923-), illus. (Boys Life Library: No. 8). 1965. Random House.

--Boys' Life Book of Wild Animal Stories. (Illus.). (Boys' Life Library: No. 9). (gr. 5-9). 1965. (ISBN 0-394-91067-2). Random.

--The Boys' Life Book of World War II Stories. Slonesky, Leonard, illus. LC 65-22656. 183 p. illus. 22 cm. (Boys' life library, 10). (gr. 5-9). 1965. (ISBN 0-394-91077-X). Random House.

--Boys' Life: The Boys' Life Book of Flying Stories. Kane, Harry, illus. LC 63-7836. 186p. illus. 22cm. (Boy's life lib., 7). 1964. Random.

--Boys' Life: The Boys' Life Book of Horse Stories. Savitt, Sam (1917-), illus. LC 63-7837. 182p. illus. 22cm. (Boys' life lib., 1). N.D. Random.

--Boys' Life: The Boys' Life Book of Outer Space Stories. Kane, Harry, illus. LC 63-962651. 182p. illus. 22cm. (Boy's life lib., 5). 1964. Random.

--Dog Stories. Crump, James Irving (1887-1979), ed. LC 49-11224. 160 p. 21 cm. 1949. Nelson.

--Pedro's Tall Tales. Savage, Steele (1900-), illus. LC 67-24145. (Illus.). 191 p. 21cm. (Pedro books). (gr. 5-7). 1967. (ISBN 0-399-20184-X). Putnam.

Boy's Life Magazine Editors & Crump, James Irving (1887-1979), eds.

--Book of Scout Stories. 2nd ed. LC 52-13571. 219p. 21cm. 1953, c.1952. Doubleday.

Boyton, Neil (1884-)

--Circus at Madison Square Garden. Pollard, George, illus. LC 55-7860. 22cm. 136p. 1955. Bruce Publishing Co.

--Cobra Island: A Catholic Scout's Adventures. LC 22-12020. 176 p. front. 19 cm. 1922. Benziger Brothers.

--Ex-Cub Fitzie. LC 50-11579. 22cm. 206p. 1950. Bruce Publishing Co.

--In God's Country. LC 23-17770. 21cm. 403p. 1923. Benziger Bros.

--In Xavier Lands: Short Stories. LC 38-354077. 175 p. 19 cm. 1930. Benziger Brothers.

--Mangled Hands: A Story of the New York Martyrs. LC 26-13992. 192 p. front. 19 cm. 1926. Benziger Brothers.

--Mississippi's Blackrobe: A Story of Father Marquette. LC 27-25923. 192 p. front. 19 cm. 1927. Benziger Brothers.

--The Mystery of St. Regis. LC 27-23235. vii, 9-207 p. front. 19 cm. 1937. Etc. Benziger Brothers.

--Nothing Ever Happens to Me!. LC 51-6840. 141 p. 22 cm. 1951. Bruce.

--On the Sands of Coney. LC 25-18703. 192 p. front. 19 cm. 1925. Benziger Brothers.

--Redrobes. LC 37-177. viii, 301 p. front., pl., map. 19 cm. 1936. Benziger Brothers.

--The Summer Jerry Never Saw. Beebe, Robb (1891-), illus. LC 45-5921. 3 p. l., 186 p. 21 cm. 1945. Longmans, Green and Co., Inc.

--That Silver Fox Patrol. Beebe, Robb (1891-), illus. LC 44-7710. vii p., 1 l., 257 p. 21 cm. 1944. Longmans, Green and Company.

Where Monkeys Swing: An American Boy's Adventures in India. LC 24-25410. 203 p. front. 19 cm. 1924. Benziger Brothers.

--Whoopee!. The Story of a Catholic Summer Camp. LC 23-94857. 203 p. front. 19 cm. 1923. Benziger Brothers.

Boz, pseud., see Dickens, Charles John Huffam.

Bozanich, Tony L

--Captain Flounder: His Sole Brothers and Friends. Isaksen, Lisa A. & Isaksen, Patricia, illus. LC 84-171533. (Illus.). 16p. (ps-4). 1984. (ISBN 0-930655-00-1). Antarctic Pr.

Bozzo, Maxine Zohn

--Toby in the Country, Toby in the City. Modell, Frank, illus. LC 81-7274. p. cm. c.1982. (ISBN 0-688-00916-6). (ISBN 0-688-00917-4). Greenwillow Books.

Brabazon, Francis

--Four & Twenty Blackbirds. Krynski, Sheila, illus. (Illus.). 52p. 1975. (ISBN 0-913078-22-0). Sheriar Pr.

Brabourne, Edward Hugessen Knatchbull-Hugessen (1829-1893)

--Christmas in Switzerland: The Forest Fairy. (Illus.). (Christmas in Many Lands Ser.). N.D. Dana Estes & Co.

--Crackers for Christmas. N.D. E P Dutton.

--Crackers for Christmas. 5th ed. (Illus.). N.D. Macmillan & Co.

--Crackers for Christmas. (Series of Books for the Young). N.D. MacMillan & Co.

--Crackers for Christmas: More Stories for Children. New Ed. with the originial illus. ed. N.D. George Routledge & Sons; Dist. by E. P. Dutton.

--Ferdinand's Adventure: A New Volume of Fairy Tales. Griset, Ernest, illus. 1891. George Routledge & Sons; Dist. by E. P. Dutton.

--The Forest Fairy, 1 of 7 vols. Bridgman, Lewis Jesse (1857-1931), illus. (Christmas in Many Lands Ser.). N.D. Set. Dana Estes & Co.

--Higgledy-Piggledy: Or, Stories for Everybody and Everybody's Children. 377p. 1876. D. Appleton.

--Moonshine. (Series of Books for the Young). N.D. MacMillan & Co.

--Moonshine. Fairy Stories. Brunton, William, illus. LC 44-102502. x, 2, 338 p. front., plates. 18 cm. 1871. Macmillan and Co.

--Mountain Sprite's Kingdom. N.D. E P Dutton.

--Other Stories: A Book for Children. Griset, Ernest, illus. N.D. George Routledge & Sons; Dist. by E. P. Dutton.
--The Princess with the Pea-Green Nose. with illustrations by myra cocks. ed. Cocks, Myra, illus. LC 27-23569. v, 114 p. incl. illus., plates. col. front. 18 cm. 1927. Harper & Brothers.
--Puss-Cat Mew and Other New Fairy Stories. (Illus.). 1882. Harper Brothers.
--Queer Folk. N.D. E P Dutton.
--Queer Folk. (Series of Books for the Young). N.D. MacMillan & Co.
--Queer Folks: Seven Stories for Children. New ed. N.D. George Routledge.
--River Legends. Dore, Louis Christophe Paul Gustave (1832-1883), illus. (Illus.). N.D. George Routledge & Sons.
--Stories for My Children. N.D. Macmillan & Co.
--Stories for My Children: A New Book of Fairy Tales. N.D. George Routledge & Sons; Dist. by E. P. Dutton.
--Tales at Tea-Time. N.D. E P Dutton.
--Uncle Joe's Stories. Griset, Ernest, illus. N.D. George Routledge & Sons; Dist. by E. P. Dutton.
--Whispers from Fairy-Land. N.D. D. Appleton & Co.

Bracey, Doris C.
--The Tale of Two Towns. (Illus.). 64p. 1984. (ISBN 0-682-40168-4). Exposition.

Bracken, Carolyn
--Animal Crackers: A Menagerie of Jokes and Riddles. Bracken, Carolyn, illus. LC 78-68414. (Illus.). 20 p. 32cm. (Cricket book). c.1979. (ISBN 0-448-46531-0). (ISBN 0-448-13071-8). Platt & Munk.
--Little Teddy Bear. McClain, Mary, illus. (Illus.). 12p. (Shaggies Ser.). (ps-2). 1982. (ISBN 0-671-42550-1, Little Simon). S&S.
--Peter Rabbit's Pockets. Bracken, Carolyn, illus. (Illus.). 8p. (ps). 1982. (ISBN 0-671-44528-6, Little Simon). S&S.
--You Can Drive a Fire Engine. Bracken, Carolyn, illus. LC 82-83117. (Illus.). 12p. (A Golden Drive Away Bk.). (ps-2). 1983. (ISBN 0-307-10761-2, Golden Pr). Western Pub.

Bracken, Carolyn, illus.
--Bunny. (Illus.). 6p. (Floppies Ser.). (ps-k). 1981. (ISBN 0-671-42531-5, Little Simon). S&S.
--Santa's Pockets. (Illus.). (ps). N.D. (ISBN 0-671-47660-2, Little Simon). S&S.
--Teddy Bear's Pockets. (Illus.). 8p. (ps). 1983. (ISBN 0-671-46448-5, Little Simon). S&S.
--You Can Drive an Automobile. (Illus.). 12p. (A Golden Drive Away Bk.). 1983. (ISBN 0-307-10762-0, Golden Pr). Western Pub.

Bracken, Dorothy Kendall
--Rodeo. Rice, Elizabeth (1913-), illus. LC 49-49572. 32 p. col. illus. 27 x 35 cm. 1949. Steck Co.

Bracken, Dorothy Kendall & Reichert, Edwin C.
--Happy Ranch. LC 61-6764. (Illus.). 64 p. 21cm. 1961. Lippincott.

Bracken, Grace L.
--The Adventures of the Alley Cats. N.D. Vantage Press inc.
--Adventures of the Tin Man and Rag Doll. N.D. Vantage Press Inc.
--The Alley Cats on Jupiter. N.D. Carlton Press.

Bracker, Charles Eugene (1895-)
--Chester. Bracker, Charles Eugene (1895-), illus. LC 39-12110. 20cm. 48p. 1939. Julian Messner Inc.
--Chester. Bracker, Charles Eugene (1895-), illus. N.D. Veritas Press.
--Rumpus, the Remarkable Kitten. Bracker, Charles Eugene (1895-), illus. LC 53-8036. unpaged. illus. 21cm. (Jolly books, 211). c.1953. Avon Pub. Co.

Brackett, Anna Callender (1836-1911), ed.
--Treasure Book of Verse. (Illus.). N.D. G. P. Putnam's Sons.

Brackett, Esther M see Tingle, Dolli, pseud.

Brackett, Esther M (1920-)
--The Little Apple Tree. Tingle, Dolli, pseud. Brackett, Esther M (1920-), illus. Tingle, Dolli, pseud. LC 68-21793. (Illus.). 1 v. (unpaged. 20cm. (Stardust books). 1968. C. R. Gibson Co.

Brackett, Leigh, jt. auth. see Weinberg, Larry.

Brackett, Leigh Douglass (1915-1978)
--No Good from a Corpse. LC 44-20857. 4 p. l., 3-202 p. 19 1/2 cm. 1944. Coward-McCann, Inc.

Bradburn, E. W.
--Rosa: Or, The Two Castles. (The Young Folks Ser.: No. 4). N.D. Fleming H. Revell Co.

Bradbury, Bianca (1908-)
--The Amethyst Summer. LC 63-12146. 186 p. 21 cm. 1963. I. Washburn.
--Amos Learns to Talk: The Story of a Little Duck. McKinley, Clare, illus. LC 51-9762. 33 p. col. illus. 21cm. (Rand McNally book-elf book, 446). c.1951. Rand McNally.
--Andy's Mountain. MacLean, Robert (1926-), illus. LC 69-19936. (Illus.). 150 p. 22cm. 1969. Houghton Mifflin.
--The Antique Cat. Thorne, Diana (1894-), illus. Moran, Connie LC 45-35242. 64 p. illus. (part col.) 26 x 21 cm. 1945. The John C. Winston Company.
--The Blue Year. LC 67-15531. 165p. 22cm. 1967. Washburn.
--Boy on the Run. LC 74-22486. 126 p. 22cm. 1975. (ISBN 0-8164-3139-6). Seabury Press.
--Brave Firemen. N.D. Wonder Books.
--The Brave Firemen and the Firehouse Cat. Medvey, Steven, illus. LC 51-35508. unpaged. illus. 21 cm. (Wonder books, 563). 1951. Wonder Books.
--Circus Punk. Geer, Charles Hand (1922-), illus. N.D. (ISBN 0-448-04779-9, Tempo). G&D.
--Circus Punk. Geer, Charles Hand (1922-), illus. LC 64-14872. (Illus.). 21cm. 155p. 1964. Macrae Smith Co.
--Dogs and More Dogs. MacLean, Robert (1926-), illus. (Illus.). 162 p. 22cm. 1968. Houghton Mifflin.
--Flight into Spring. LC 65-13130. 187 p. 21cm. 1965. Washburn.
--A Flood in Still River. Keats, Ezra Jack (1916-1983), illus. LC 61-6487. 128p. illus. 22cm. 1961. Dial Press.
--Girl in the Middle. LC 69-14866. 184 p. 21cm. 1969. I. Washburn.
--The Girl Who Wanted Out. 191p. (Orig.). (gr. 7 up). 1981. (ISBN 0-590-32122-6, Wishing Star Bks). Scholastic Inc.
--Goodness and Mercy Jenkins. LC 63-16697. 170 p. 21 cm. 1963. Washburn.
--Happy Acres. Warren, Betsy, pseud. (1916-), illus. Warren, Elizabeth Avery. LC 58-701161. unpaged. illus. 22x26cm. 1958. Steck Co.
--I'm Vinny, I'm Me. Cuffari, Richard (1925-1978), illus. LC 77-23308. (Illus.). 200 p. 22cm. 1977. (ISBN 0-395-25297-0). Houghton Mifflin.
--In Her Father's Footsteps. Cuffari, Richard (1925-1978), illus. LC 75-43891. (Illus.). 172 p. 22cm. 1976. (ISBN 0-395-24381-5). Houghton Mifflin.
--Jim & His Monkey. Guthrie, Vee, illus. LC 59-9724. (Illus.). 22cm. 43p. (gr. 1-4). 1960. (ISBN 0-395-06649-2). HM.
--Laughter in Our House. LC 64-21806. 183 p. 21cm. 1964. I. Washburn.
--Laurie. LC 65-21603. 172 p. 21 cm. 1965. I. Washburn.
--The Loner. Gretzer, John, illus. LC 75-105246. (Illus.). 140 p. 22cm. 1970. Houghton Mifflin.
--Lots of Love, Lucinda. LC 66-22210. 171p. 21cm. 1966. Washburn.
--The Loving Year. 160p. (Orig.). (gr. 7 up). 1982. (ISBN 0-590-32174-9, Wishing Star). Scholastic Inc.
--Mike's Island. Geer, Charles Hand (1922-), illus. LC 58-13306. 128p. illus. 21cm. 1958. Putnam.
--Mixed-up Summer. LC 78-31792. 195 p. 22cm. 1979. (ISBN 0-395-27816-3). Houghton Mifflin.
--Mother Hen and Her Five Baby Chicks. Walker, Ora, illus. LC 44-6664. 62 p. illus. (part col.) 17 cm. 1944. Rand McNally & Company.
--Muggins. Thorne, Diana (1894-), illus. LC 41-6129. 20 1/2cm. 20p. 1944. Houghton Mifflin & Co.
--Mutt. Stevens, Mary E. (1920-1966), illus. (Illus.). (gr. k-3). 1956. HM.
--Mutt. Stevens, Mary E. (1920-1966), illus. LC 56-5552. (Illus.). 29 p. 21cm. (Sandpiper book). 1974, c.1956. (ISBN 0-395-18560-2). Houghton, Mifflin.
--My Pretty Girl. Robinson, Charles (1931-), illus. LC 73-22061. (Illus.). 172 p. 22cm. 1974. (ISBN 0-395-18518-1). Houghton Mifflin.
--Nancy and Her Johnny-O. LC 78-102660. 150 p. 21cm. 1970. I. Washburn.
--A New Penny. LC 71-135135. 188 p. 22cm. 1971. (ISBN 0-395-12363-1). Houghton Mifflin.
--Red Sky at Night. 184 p. 21cm. 1968. I. Washburn.
--Sam & the Colonels. Geer, Charles Hand (1922-), illus. LC 66-16517. (Illus.). (gr. 3-7). 1966. (ISBN 0-8255-1820-2). (ISBN 0-8255-1821-0). Macrae.
--Say Hello, Candy. LC 61-13398. 190p. 21cm. 1961. Coward-McCann.
--Shoes in September. 1964. E M Hale.
--Shoes in September. LC 64-12458. 154 p. 21cm. 1964. I. Washburn.
--Those Traver Kids. Friedman, Marvin (1930-), illus. LC 72-2759. (Illus.). 204 p. 22cm. 1972. (ISBN 0-395-14330-6). Houghton Mifflin.
--The Three Keys. MacLean, Robert (1926-), illus. LC 67-14703. 170p. (gr. 4-6). 1967. (ISBN 0-395-06653-0). HM.
--To a Different Tune. LC 68-259672. 181p. 21cm. 1968. Washburn.
--Tough Guy. N.D. E. M. Hale & Co.
--Tough Guy. Nichols, Marie C. (1905-), illus. (Illus.). 1953. Houghton Mifflin.
--Two on an Island. MacLean, Robert (1926-), illus. LC 65-121756. (Illus.). 139 p. 22cm. 1965. Houghton Mifflin. **Award: (ALA).**
--The Undergrounders. Nielsen, Jon (1912-), illus. LC 66-14236. 120p. illus. 21cm. (gr. 4-6). c.1966. Washburn.
--Where's Jim Now?. LC 78-14832. 174 p. 22cm. 1978. (ISBN 0-395-27160-6). Houghton Mifflin.

Bradbury, Bianca (1908-) & Nichols, Marie C. (1905-)
--One Kitten Too Many. Nichols, Marie C. (1905-), illus. LC 52-7192. (Illus.). 32 p. 21cm. 1952. Houghton Mifflin.

Bradbury, Jack see Clampett, Bob.

Bradbury, Mary Ann Williams, Mrs.
--The Bradbury Stories. Yarnall, John Val, illus. LC 1-28171. 99p. 1900. Independence Publishing Co.

Bradbury, Peggy (1930-)
--The Snake That Couldn't Slither. Hoff, Sydney (1912-), illus. LC 76-3633. p. cm. 1976. (ISBN 0-399-61015-4). Putnam.

Bradbury, Ray Douglas (1920-)
--The Halloween Tree. Mugnaini, Joseph A., illus. LC 72-2433. (Illus.). 145 p. 24cm. 1972. (ISBN 0-394-82409-1). (ISBN 0-394-92409-6). Knopf; Distributed by Random House.
--I Sing the Body Electric. 1969. Borzoi Books.
--The October Country. 1970. Borzoi Books.
--R Is for Rocket. LC 62-15878. 233 p. 22cm. 1962. Doubleday.
--S Is for Space. LC 66-10379. N.D. (ISBN 0-385-06927-8). Doubleday.
--Switch on the Night. Gekiere, Madeleine (1919-), illus. LC 55-5545. (Illus.). unpaged. 22cm. c.1955. Pantheon Books. **Awards: (NYT); (ALA).**
--When Elephants Last in the Dooryard Bloomed. 1973. Borzoi Books.

Bradby, Henry Christopher (1868-), ed. see Hughes, Thomas.

Bradby, Violet
--Matthew and Miller. Millar, Harold Robert (1869-1939), illus. N.D. Dodge Publishing Co.

Braddock, Gordon
--Rex Kingdon at Walcott Hall. (The Rex Kingdon Ser.). N.D. A. L. Burt Co.
--Rex Kingdon at Walcott Hall. (Rex Kingdon Ser.). N.D. Hurst & Co.
--Rex Kingdon Behind the Bat. (The Rex Kingdon Ser.). N.D. A. L. Burt Co.
--Rex Kingdon in the North. (Rex Kingdon Ser.). N.D. Hurst & Co.
--Rex Kingdon in the North Woods. (The Rex Kingdon Ser.). N.D. A. L. Burt Co.
--Rex Kingdon in the North Woods. Wrenn, Charles L., illus. LC 14-14259. 1 p. l., 11-12, iv, 13-302 p. front., plates. 20 cm. c.1914. Hurst & Company.
--Rex Kingdon of Ridgewood High. (The Rex Kingdon Ser.). N.D. A. L. Burt. Co.
--Rex Kingdon of Ridgewood High. (Rex Kingdon Ser.). N.D. Hurst & Co.
--Rex Kingdon on Storm Island. (The Rex Kingdon Ser.). N.D. A. L. Burt Co.

Braddock, Jonathan, adapted by see Disney, Walter Elias.

Braddon, M. E., Miss
--Joshua Haggard's Daughter, Nos.74-75. (Illus.). (Lakeside Library Ser.). N.D. Donnelley, Loyd & Co.
--Under the Red Flag. (New Red Letter Ser). N.D. International Book Co.

Braden, James Andrew (1872-)
--The Auto Boys' Outing. De Bebian, Arthur, illus. 413 p. incl. front. 3 pl. 19 cm. 1909. The Saalfield Publishing Company.
--Captives Three. Elliott, Fred A., illus. LC 4-28949. 353 p. front., 3 pl. 19 1/2 cm. 1904. The Saalfield Publishing Co.
--The Carved Sea Chest: A Tale of Lost Ships, of Buccaneers and of the Nipissing Indians, the "Sorcerers". Fitzgerald, Pitt L., illus. LC 30-8178. x p., 1 l., 226 p. front. 19 cm. 1930. Harper & Brothers.
--Connecticut Boys in the Western Reserve. (Illus.). N.D. Caldwell.
--Connecticut Boys in the Western Reserve. Dunton, W. Herbert, illus. LC 3-28596. 20cm. 440p. 1903. Saalfield Publishing Co.
--Far Past the Frontier. (Illus.). N.D. Caldwell.
--Far Past the Frontier: Or, Two Boy Pioneers. Fry, W H., illus. LC 2-20004. 347 p. front., plates. 20 cm. 1902. The Saalfield Publishing Co.
--Little Brother of the Hudson: A Tale of the Last Eries. Fitzgerald, Pitt L., illus. LC 28-19245. viii p., 2 l., 279, 1 p. front., illus. 20 cm. 1928. Harper & Brothers.
--The Trail of the Seneca. Vosburgh, R G., illus. LC 7-20706. 371 p. incl. front. 3 pl. 19 cm. c.1907. The Saalfield Publishing Company.

Bradfield, Joan & Bradfield, Roger (1924-)
--Who Are You?. Fitch, Winnie, illus. LC 67-1924. (Illus.). 1 v. (unpaged. 30cm. (Whitman small world library book). 1966. Whitman Pub. Co.

Bradfield, Jolly Roger, pseud., see Bradfield, Roger.

Bradfield, Roger see Bradfield, Jolly Roger, pseud.

Bradfield, Roger, jt. auth. see Bradfield, Joan.

Bradfield, Roger (1924-)
--Benjamin Dilley's Lavender Lion. Bradfield, Jolly Roger, pseud. LC 68-29771. (Illus.). 41 p. 28cm. (Jolly Roger book). 1968. Rand McNally.
--Benjamin Dilley's Thirsty Camel. Bradfield, Jolly Roger, pseud. LC 67-21606. (Illus.). 1 v. (unpaged. 28cm. 160p. (His A Jolly Roger book). 1967. Rand McNally.
--The Flying Hockey Stick. Bradfield, Jolly Roger, pseud. LC 66-180996. 1. v. (unpaged) col. illus. 28cm. (His A Jolly Roger bk.). (ps-2). 1966. (ISBN 0-528-87748-8). Rand McNally.
--Flying Hockey Stick. Bradfield, Jolly Roger, pseud. (gr. k-3). N.D. Rand.
--Giants Come in Different Sizes. Bradfield, Jolly Roger, pseud. LC 66-181005. 1. v. (unpaged) col. illus. 28cm. (His A Jolly Roger bk.). 1966. Rand McNally.
--A Good Knight for Dragons. Bradfield, Jolly Roger, pseud. LC 67-4105. (Illus.). 1 v. (unpaged. 28cm. 48p. 1967. Young Scott Books.
--Jolly Roger Bradfield Storybooks. Bradfield, Jolly Roger, pseud. Incl. Flying Hockey Stock. (ISBN 0-528-82415-5); Giants Come in Different Sizes. (ISBN 0-528-82414-7); Benjamin Dilley's Thirsty Camel. (ISBN 0-528-82417-1); Pickle-Chiffon Pie. (ISBN 0-528-82416-3). (Illus.). 64p. (gr. 4-7). N.D. Rand.
--Pickle-Chiffon Pie. LC 67-21607. (Illus.). 1 v. (unpaged. 28cm. 60p. (His A Jolly Roger book). 1967. Rand McNally.
--There's an Elephant in the Bathtub. N.D. Golden Press.
--There's an Elephant in the Bathtub. Bradfield, Roger (1924-), illus. LC 64-5865. 24 p. col. illus. 33 cm. (Whitman giant tell-a-tale book). 1964. Whitman Pub. Co.

Bradford, Ann, jt. auth. see Gezi, Kalil I.

Bradford, Ann & Gezi, Kalil I. (1930-)
--The Mystery at Misty Falls. LC 80-15708. (Illus.). 32p. (The Maple Street Five Ser.). (gr. 3-6). 1980. (ISBN 0-516-06491-6). Childrens.
--The Mystery at the Tree House. McLean, Mina Gow, illus. LC 80-15654. p. cm. (Maple Street five). c.1980. (ISBN 0-89565-148-3). Child's World.
--The Mystery of the Blind Writer. LC 80-12395. (Illus.). 32p. (The Maple Street Five Ser.). (gr. 3-6). 1980. (ISBN 0-516-06493-2). Childrens.
--The Mystery of the Midget Clown. McLean, Mina Gow, illus. LC 80-12513. p. cm. (Maple Street five). c.1980. (ISBN 0-89565-146-7). Child's World.
--The Mystery of the Missing Dogs. LC 80-10436. p. cm. (Maple Street five). c.1980. (ISBN 0-89565-143-2). Child's World.
--The Mystery of the Square Footprints. LC 80-10437. (Illus.). 32p. (The Maple Street Five Ser.). (gr. 3-6). 1980. (ISBN 0-516-06496-7). Childrens.

Bradford, Barbara Taylor (1933-), ed.
--Children's Stories of Jesus from the New Testament. (Illus.). (gr. 3-7). 1960. Lion.
--Children's Stories of the Bible from the Old Testament. (Illus.). (gr. 3-7). 1966. Lion.

Bradford, Barbara Taylor (1933-) & Halas, Frantisek (1901-1949)
--A Garland of Children's Verse. Janecek, Ota, illus. LC 67-29609. (Illus.). 66 p. 29cm. 1968. Lion Press.

Bradford, Ed, jt. auth. see Graves, Clay.

Bradford, Gigi & Moos, Michael, eds.
--Sixteen Toes: Anthology. (Illus.). (gr. 2-7). 1978. (ISBN 0-930970-00-4). O'Neill Pr.

Bradford, Henry
--Clouds. Niizaka, Kazuo (1943-), illus. LC 74-19155. p. cm. 1975. (ISBN 0-201-00574-3). Addison-Wesley.

Bradford, John, jt. auth. see Anderson, Robert L.

Bradford, Lois Jean (1936-)
--Here Come the Racing Ducks!. Vestal, Herman B., illus. LC 74-174501. (Illus.). 64 p. 24cm. 1972. (ISBN 0-8116-4254-2). Garrard Pub Co.

Bradford, S. H., Mrs.
--Lewie: The/Bended Twig. N.D. Hurd & Houghton.
--The Silver Lake Stories, 6. N.D. Hurd & Houghton.
--Tales for Little Convalescents. N.D. Hurd & Houghton.

Bradford, Sarah H.
--The Dominie: Or, Reminisences of a Girl's Life. (Illus.). N.D. Methodist Bk Concern.

Bradish, Sarah Powers
--Old Norse Stories. 19cm. 240p. (American Book Co.). 1900. American Book Co.
--Stories of Country Life. LC 2-476. 170 p. illus. 19 cm. (Eclectic school readings). 1901. American Book Company.

Bradley, Alfred (1925-) & Bond, Thomas Michael (1926-)
--Paddington on Stage. LC 76-62497. (Illus.). 112 p. 21cm. 1977, c.1974. (ISBN 0-395-25155-9). Houghton Mifflin.

Bradley, Arlene, jt. auth. see Igartua, Arturo.

--Mother Goose: A Treasury of Best Loved Rhymes. Piper, Watty, pseud. Hildebrandt, Greg (1939-) & Hildebrandt, Tim (1939-), illus. LC 72-185969. (Illus.). 32cm. 66p. 1972. Platt & Munk.
--The Pony Engine. Garn, Doris, adapted by. Prestopino, Gregorio, illus. LC 58-4349. (Illus.). unpaged. 29cm. 1958. Grosset & Dunlap.
--The Pony Engine. Garn, Doris, adapted by. Prestopino, Gregorio, illus. LC 57-585209. unpaged. illus. 21cm. (Wonder books, 626). 1957. (ISBN 0-448-00626-X). Wonder Books.
Bragg, Michael, jt. auth. see Garfield, Leon.
Bragga, Meg
--What Do You Hear?. 8p. (ps-1). 1975. (ISBN 0-8307-0318-7). Regal.
--What Do You See?. 8p. (ps-1). 1975. (ISBN 0-8307-0320-9). Regal.
--What Helps Me?. 8p. (ps-1). 1975. (ISBN 0-8307-0317-9). Regal.
--What Is Inside?. 8p. (ps-1). 1975. (ISBN 0-8307-0319-5). Regal.
Brahms, Johannes, jt. auth. see Geis, Darlene Stern.
Brailsford, Frances, pseud., see Wosmek, Frances.
Brailsford, Frances, pseud. (1917-)
--In the Space of a Wink. Wosmek, Frances. Forberg, Ati, pseud. (1925-), illus. Forberg, Beate Gropius. LC 69-15976. (Illus.). 94 p. 22cm. 1969. Follett Pub. Co.
Brain
--My Mother Made Me. (gr. 6). 1979. (ISBN 0-590-05801-0, Schol Pap). Scholastic Inc.
Braine, Sheila E.
--The Princess of Hearts. (Illus.). (Scribner-Blackie Series of books for young people). N.D. Charles Scribner's Sons.
--The Princess of Hearts, 11 vols. (Illus.). (Six to Sixteen Ser.: No. 7). 1905. Set. H M Caldwell Co.
--To Tell the King the Sky is falling. (Illus.). (Scribner-Blackie Series of books for young people). N.D. Charles Scribner's Sons.
--The Turkish Automation. (Illus.). (Scribner-Blackie Series of books for young people). N.D. Charles Scribner's Sons.
Brainerd, Edna S
--Millicent in Dreamland. (Illus.). (Editha Series.). N.D. Dodge Publishing Co.
--Millicent in Dreamland, 25 vols. (Illus.). (The Editha Ser.: No. 25). 1905. Set. H M Caldwell.
--Millicent in Dreamland. Barry, Etheldred Breeze (1870-), illus. LC 2-19578. 94 p. front., illus. 18 1/2cm. 1902, c.1903. L. C. Page & Co.
Brainerd, Eleanor Hoyt, Mrs. (1868-)
--For Love of Mary Ellen: A Romance of Childhood. O'Neill, Rose Cecil (1874-), illus. LC 12-21955. 42 p. illus. 19 1/2cm. 1912. Harper & Brothers.
--Our Little Old Lady. 1919. Doubleday Page & Co.
Brainerd, Norman, pseud., see Fuller, Samuel Richard.
Brainerd, Norman
--Winning His Army Blue. (Five Chums Ser.). N.D. Lothrop, Lee & Shepard.
--Winning His Shoulder Straps: Or, Bob Anderson at Chatham Military School. Smith, Frank Vining, illus. (Five Chums Ser.). 1909. Lothrop, Lee & Shepard.
--Winning the Eagle Prize. (Five Chums Ser.). N.D. Lothrop, Lee & Shepard.
--Winning the Junior Cup. (Five Chums Ser.). N.D. Lothrop, Lee & Shepard.
Braithewaite, Walter
--A Book of Songs. Vaughan, Michael, ed. 29p. (gr. 5-7). 1978. (ISBN 0-88010-036-2, Pub. by Steinerbooks). Anthroposophic.
Braithwaite, Althea see Althea, pseud.
Braithwaite, Althea, et al. (1940-)
--The Big Desmond Story Book. Althea, pseud. (Illus.). 48p. 1980 (Pub. by Dinosaur Pubns). (ISBN 0-85122-193-9). Merrimack Pub Cir.
Braithwaite, Althea (1940-)
--A Baby in the Family. Althea, pseud. Rylands, Ljiljana, illus. (Illus.). (Dinosaur Ser.). (gr. 2-5). 1978. (ISBN 0-85122-103-3, Pub. by Dino Pub). Merrimack Pub Cir.
--Castle Life. Althea, pseud. Galvani, Maureen, illus. (Illus.). 1980. (ISBN 0-85122-124-6, Pub. by Dinosaur Pubns). Merrimack Pub Cir.
--Cuthbert & Bimbo. Althea, pseud. (Illus.). 24p. (Dinosaur Ser.). (gr. k-3). 1978. (ISBN 0-85122-088-6, Pub. by Dino Pub). Merrimack Pub Cir.
--David & His Sister Carol. Althea, pseud. Rylands, Ljiljana, illus. (Illus.). (Dinosaur Ser.). (gr. 2-5). 1978. (ISBN 0-85122-116-5, Pub. by Dino Pub). Merrimack Pub Cir.
--Desmond Meets a Stranger. Althea, pseud. Braithwaite, Althea (1940-), illus. Althea, pseud. (Illus.). color ils. 32p. (Tiptoe Tales Ser). (ps-k). 1971. Platt.
--George & the Baby. Althea, pseud. Braithwaite, Althea (1940-), illus. Althea, pseud. (Illus.). (Dinosaur Ser.). (gr. k-3). 1978. (ISBN 0-85122-038-X, Pub. by Dino Pub). Merrimack Pub Cir.
--Gingerbread Band. Althea, pseud. Braithwaite, Althea (1940-), illus. Althea, pseud. (Illus.). (ps-2). 1971. Platt.
--Jeremy Mouse. Althea, pseud. Braithwaite, Althea (1940-), illus. Althea, pseud. (Illus.). (Dinosaur Ser.). (gr. k-3). 1978. (ISBN 0-85122-037-1, Pub. by Dino Pub). Merrimack Pub Cir.
--Jeremy Mouse & Cat. Althea, pseud. (Illus.). 1979. (ISBN 0-85122-201-3, Pub. by Dinosaur Pubns). Merrimack Pub Cir.
--My Babysitter. Althea, pseud. (Illus.). N.D. (ISBN 0-85122-160-2, Pub. by Dinosaur Pubns). Merrimack Pub Cir.
--My Friend Rab. Althea, pseud. (ps-2). 1979. (ISBN 0-85122-177-7, Pub. by Dinosaur Pubns). Merrimack Pub Cir.
--Peter Pig. Althea, pseud. Braithwaite, Althea (1940-), illus. Althea, pseud. (Illus.). (Dinosaur Ser.). (gr. k-3). 1978. (ISBN 0-85122-036-3, Pub. by Dino Pub). Merrimack Pub Cir.
--Smith the Lonely Hedgehog. Althea, pseud. Braithwaite, Althea (1940-), illus. Althea, pseud. (Illus.). (ps-2). 1971. Platt.
--Victoria & the Flowerbed Children. Althea, pseud. Braithwaite, Althea (1940-), illus. Althea, pseud. (Illus.). color ils. 32p. (Tiptoe Tales Ser). (ps-k). 1971. Platt.
Braithwaite, Eustace Edward Ricardo (1920-)
--To Sir with Love. (gr. 7 up). N.D. Pyramid Pubns.
Braithwaite, Max (1911-)
--The Mystery of the Muffled Man. Rosenthal, Joseph J. (1911-), illus. LC 62-20655. 160 p. illus. 20 cm. (Secret circle mysteries, no. 5). c.1962. Little, Brown.
--The Valley of the Vanishing Birds. Hammond, Arthur, ed. Hawgood, Wendy, illus. LC 64-10557. 160p. ill. 20cm. (The Secret Circle Mysteries: No. 8). 1964, c.1963. Little Brown.
Braithwaite, P. A.
--Cumfa Drums Are Calling. Fenty, A. A, adapted by. Bascom, Harold A., illus. LC 77-370708. (Illus.). 23 p. 26cm. 1973. Ministry of Education, Co-Operative Republic of Guyana.
Braithwaite, William Stanley, intro. by see Wynne, Annette.
Braley, Berton (1882-)
--Delia Demonstrates. 349p. N.D. Century Co.
--The Enchanted Flivver. Birch, Reginald Bathurst (1856-1943), illus. LC 26-18090. 5 p. l., 3-255 p. front., illus. 21 cm. c.1926. The Century Co.
Bralliar, Floyd Burton (1875-)
--Knowing Birds Through Stories. 355p. N.D. Funk & Wagnalls Co.
--Knowing Insects Through Stories. LC 18-19795. xxi, 291 p. col. front., illus., plates (part col.) fold. tab. 20 cm. 1918. Funk & Wagnalls Company.
Braly, David
--Mysteries & Legends of Central Oregon. (gr. 7-12). 1982. (ISBN 0-942206-01-0). Mediaor Co.
Bram, Elizabeth (1948-)
--A Dinosaur Is Too Big. Bram, Elizabeth (1948-), illus. LC 76-22669. (Illus.). 32 p. 17cm. c.1977. (ISBN 0-688-80071-8). Greenwillow Books.
--The Door in the Tree. Bram, Elizabeth (1948-), illus. LC 75-28182. p. cm. c.1976. (ISBN 0-688-80029-7). (ISBN 0-688-84029-9). Greenwillow Books.
--I Don't Want to Go to School. Bram, Elizabeth (1948-), illus. LC 76-51274. (Illus.). 32 p. 14x18cm. c.1977. (ISBN 0-688-80095-5). (ISBN 0-688-84095-7). Greenwillow Books.
--The Man on the Unicycle and Other Stories. Bram, Elizabeth (1948-), illus. LC 76-22666. (Illus.). 55 p. 22cm. (Greenwill read-alone books). c.1977. (ISBN 0-688-80059-9). (ISBN 0-688-84059-0). Greenwillow Books.
--One Day I Closed My Eyes and the World Disappeared. Bram, Elizabeth (1948-), illus. LC 77-86271. (Illus.). 32 p. 22cm. c.1978. (ISBN 0-8037-6611-4). (ISBN 0-8037-6613-0). Dial Press.
--Saturday Morning Lasts Forever. Bram, Elizabeth (1948-), illus. LC 78-51318. p. cm. c.1978. (ISBN 0-8037-7627-6). (ISBN 0-8037-7628-4). Dial Press.
--There Is Someone Standing on My Head. Bram, Elizabeth (1948-), illus. LC 78-72196. (Illus.). 32 p. 22cm. c.1979. (ISBN 0-8037-8648-4). (ISBN 0-8037-8649-2). Dial Press.
--Woodruff and the Clocks. Bram, Elizabeth (1948-), illus. LC 79-20400. (Illus.). 63 p. 23cm. (Dial easy-to-read). c.1980. (ISBN 0-8037-9633-1). (ISBN 0-8037-9634-X). Dial Press.
Bramblett, Ella, ed.
--Shoots of Green: Poems for Young Gardeners. Fetz, Ingrid (1915-), illus. LC 68-11057. (Illus.). 117 p. 21cm. 1968. T. Y. Crowell Co.
Brammer, Louella, et al.
--Man Who Didn't Like Dogs & Other Dog Stories. (Illus., Orig.). (Highlights Handbooks Ser). (gr. 2-6). 1966. (ISBN 0-87534-130-6). Highlights.
Bramson, Paul (1855-)
--Brownie: The Engineer of Beaver Brook. Chaffee, Allen, illus. N.D. Milton Bradley Co.
Bramston, M., Miss
--Abby's Discoveries. N.D. Thomas Whittaker.
--Adventures of Denis. N.D. Thomas Whittaker.
--Dangerous Jewels. N.D. Thomas Whittaker.
--Five Victims. N.D. Thomas Whittaker.
--For Faith and Fatherland, 1 of 4 Vols. (Illus.). (Tales of Heroes). N.D. Set. Pott, Young & Co.
--The Heroine of a Basket Van. N.D. Thomas Whittaker.
--Home and School: A Story for School Girls. (A Sequel to "The Snowball Society"). N.D. E. & J. B. Young & Co.
--Lottie Levison. N.D. Thomas Whittaker.
--Miss Carr's Young Ladies (Pub. by Society for Promoting Christian Knowledge). N.D. E. & J. B. Young & Co.
--Missy and Master. (Illus.). N.D. E & J B Young.
--A Pair of Cousins. N.D. Thomas Whittaker.
--Punch, Judy and Toby. N.D. E. & J. B Young & Co.
--Rosamond Ferrars, 1 of 4 Vols. (Illus.). (Rosamond's Book Shelf). N.D. Set. Pott, Young & Co.
--Shaven Crown. N.D. E. & J. B Young & Co.
--Silver Star Valley. N.D. Thomas Whittaker.
--The Snowball Society: A Story for Children. N.D. E. J. B. Young & Co.
--The Story of a Cat and a Cake. N.D. Thomas Whittaker.
--Their Father's Wrong. N.D. Thomas Whittaker.
--Uncle Ivan: Or, Recollections of Thirty Years Back. N.D. Thomas Whittaker.
--A Village Genius. N.D. Thomas Whittaker.
--Winning His Freedom. N.D. Thomas Whittaker.
Bramwell, Barbara & Bramwell, Heather
--Adventure at the Mill. Lytle, William, illus. LC 63-13665. 113 p. illus. 19 cm. (Buckskin books, 5). 1963. St. Martin's Press.
Bramwell, Heather, jt. auth. see Bramwell, Barbara.
Brancato, Robin Fidler (1936-)
--Blinded by the Light. LC 78-4583. 215 p. 22cm. c.1978. (ISBN 0-394-83721-5). Knopf : Distributed by Random House.
--Come Alive at 505. LC 79-19144. 224p. (gr. 7 up). 1980. (ISBN 0-394-84294-4). (ISBN 0-394-94294-9). Knopf.
--Come Alive at 505: A Novel. LC 79-19144. 210 p. 22cm. c.1980. (ISBN 0-394-84294-4). Knopf : Distributed by Random House.
--Dont Sit Under the Apple Tree. 1975. Borzoi Books.
--Don't Sit Under the Apple Tree. LC 74-15305. 163 p. 22cm. 1975. (ISBN 0-394-83034-2). (ISBN 0-394-83034-2). Knopf; Distributed by Random House.
--Facing Up. LC 83-18708. 182 p. 22cm. c.1984. (ISBN 0-394-85488-8). Knopf.
--Something Left to Lose. LC 75-30699. 179 p. 22cm. c.1976. (ISBN 0-394-83183-7). (ISBN 0-394-93183-1). Knopf : Distributed by Random House.
--Sweet Bells Jangled Out of Tune. LC 81-14283. 200 p. 22cm. c.1982. (ISBN 0-394-84809-8). (ISBN 0-394-94809-2). Knopf : Distributed by Random House.
--Winning. LC 77-5632. viii, 213 p. 22cm. c.1977. (ISBN 0-394-83581-6). Knopf.
Branch, Anna Hempstead (1875-)
--The Bubble Flower. Walker, Dugald Stewart (1888-1937), illus. 1925. Adelphi Co.
--The Shoes that Danced & Other Poems. 1905. Houghton Mifflin Co.
--Sonnets from a Lock Box & Other Poems. 1929. Houghton Mifflin Co.
Branch, Mary Lydia Bolles, Mrs. (1840-1922)
--Guld: The Cavern King. LC 17-30125. 4 p. l., 175 p. 21 cm. 1917. Sherman, French & Company.
--Guld, The Cavern King. Petersham, Maud Sylvia Fuller, Mrs. (1890-1971) & Petersham, Miska (1889-1960), illus. N.D. Penn.
--The Kanter Girls. 1925. Henry Altemus Company.
--The Kanter Girls. Armstrong, Helen Maitland (1869-), illus. N.D. Charles Scribner's Sons.
Branch, Mary (1910-)
--Sierra Trails. LC 74-184348. 120 p. 21cm. (Crown book). 1971. (ISBN 0-8127-0050-3). Southern Pub. Association.
--Tell Me a Story. LC 78-53210. (Stories That Win Ser.). 1978. (ISBN 0-8163-0210-3). Pacific Pr Pub Assn.
--Tell Me a Story, Book II. LC 82-2221. (Outreach Ser.). c.1982. (ISBN 0-8163-0477-7). Pacific Press Pub. Association.
--Valiant Journey. LC 66-24170. (Illus.). 181, 3 p. 23cm. 1967, c.1966. Academy Guild Press.
--The Walking River: And Other Stories. Padgett, Jim, illus. LC 74-76849. (Illus.). 126 p. 22cm. 1969. Southern Pub. Association.
Brand, Christianna, pseud., see Lewis, Mary Christianna Milne.
Brand, Max, pseud., see Faust, Frederick Schiller.
Brand, Max, pseud. (1892-1944)
--Dr. Kildare's Search. Faust, Frederick Schiller. N.D. Dodd Mead & Co.
--The Galloping Broncos. Faust, Frederick Schiller. N.D. Dodd, Mead & Co.
--Larramie's Ranch. Faust, Frederick Schiller. (Keith Jennison Large Type Bks). (gr. 6 up). N.D. (ISBN 0-531-00218-7). Watts.
--Silvertip's Round-up. Faust, Frederick Schiller. N.D. Dodd Mead & Co.
--Silvertip's Search. Faust, Frederick Schiller. N.D. Dodd Mead & Co.
--Single Jack. Faust, Frederick Schiller. N.D. Dodd, Mead & Co.
--The Stolen Stallion. Faust, Frederick Schiller. N.D. Dodd Mead & Co.
Brand, Millen (1906-1980)
--This Little Pig Named Curly. Hamberger, John F. (1934-), illus. LC 68-28822. (Illus.). 1 v. (unpaged). 1968. Crown Publishers.
Brand, Oscar (1920-)
--Singing Holidays: The Calendar in Folk Song. Moynihan, Roberta, illus. (Illus.). (gr. 2 up). 1957. Knopf.
Brand, Oscar (1920-) & Burn, Doris (1923-)
--When I First Came to This Land. LC 74-77596. (Illus.). 48 p. 27cm. 1974, c.1965. (ISBN 0-399-20415-6). (ISBN 0-399-60906-7). Putnam.
Brande, Marlie, jt. auth. see Streatfeild, Noel.
Brande, Marlie (1911-)
--Nicholas. Brande, Marlie (1911-), illus. (Picture Books). (ps-1). 1968. (ISBN 0-695-46200-8). Follett.
--Sleepy Nicholas. Streatfeild, Noel, adapted by. LC 70-97194. (Illus.). 29 p. 1970, c.1969. Follett Pub. Co.
Brandeis, Madeline Frank, Mrs. (1897-1937)
--Adventure in Hollywood: A Story of the Movies for Girls. LC 37-3823. (Illus.). 19 cm. 244p. 1937. Coward-McCann, Inc.
--The All Wrong Book. 49 p. illus. 18 x 23 cm. c.1932. Sutton-House.
--Carmen of the Golden Coast. Brandeis, Madeline Frank, Mrs. (1897-1937), illus. LC 35-8246. 160 p. incl. front., illus. 22 cm. 1935. Grosset & Dunlap.
--Jack of the Circus. Church, Howard, illus. LC 31-16244. 1 p. l., 7-281 p. front., illus. 20 cm. c.1931. The Reilly & Lee Co.
--Little Anne of Canada. Brandeis, Madeline Frank, Mrs. (1897-1937), illus. LC 31-227996. 174 p. incl. front., illus. 22 cm. 1931. Grosset & Dunlap.
--Little Anne of Canada. Brandeis, Madeline Frank, Mrs. (1897-1937), illus. (The Children of all Lands Stories). N.D. Grosset & Dunlap.
--Little Carmen of the Golden Coast. Brandeis, Madeline Frank, Mrs. (1897-1937), illus. (Children of America Stories). N.D. Grosset & Dunlap.
--The Little Dutch Tulip Girl. Brandeis, Madeline Frank, Mrs. (1897-1937), illus. LC 29-6676. 192 p. incl. front., illus. 19 cm. 1929. A. Flanagan Company.
--The Little Dutch Tulip Girl. Brandeis, Madeline Frank, Mrs. (1897-1937), illus. (The Children of All Lands Stories). N.D. Grosset & Dunlap.
--Little Erik of Sweden. Brandeis, Madeline Frank, Mrs. (1897-1937), illus. LC 38-3428. 167 p. incl. front., illus. 23 cm. c.1938. Grosset & Dunlap.
--Little Erik of Sweden. Brandeis, Madeline Frank, Mrs. (1897-1937), illus. (The Children of all Lands Stories). N.D. Grosset & Dunlap.
--Little Farmer of the Middle West. Brandeis, Madeline Frank, Mrs. (1897-1937), illus. LC 37-10926. 143 p. incl. front., illus. 22 cm. (On cover: The children of America stories). c.1937. Grosset & Dunlap.
--The Little Indian Weaver. Brandeis, Madeline Frank, Mrs. (1897-1937), illus. LC 28-30068. 134 p. incl. front., illus. 13 1/2 cm. 1928. A. Flanagan Company.
--The Little Indian Weaver. Brandeis, Madeline Frank, Mrs. (1897-1937), illus. (The Children of All Lands Stories). N.D. Grosset & Dunlap.
--Little Jeanne of France. Brandeis, Madeline Frank, Mrs. (1897-1937), illus. LC 29-22334. 190 p., 1 l. incl. front., illus. 19 cm. (Her The child-life travel books). 1929. A. Flanagan Company.
--Little Jeanne of France. Brandeis, Madeline Frank, Mrs. (1897-1937), illus. (The Children of All Lands Stories). N.D. Grosset & Dunlap.
--Little John of New England. Brandeis, Madeline Frank, Mrs. (1897-1937), illus. LC 36-8202. 156 p. incl. front., illus. 22 cm. (On cover: The children of America stories). c.1936. Grosset & Dunlap.

--The Little Mexican Donkey Boy. Brandeis, Madeline Frank, Mrs. (1897-1937), illus. LC 31-12238. 224 p. incl. front., illus. 23 cm. c.1931. Grosset & Dunlap.
--The Little Mexican Donkey Boy. Brandeis, Madeline Frank, Mrs. (1897-1937), illus. (The Children of all Lands Stories). N.D. Grosset & Dunlap.
--Little Philippe of Belgium. Brandeis, Madeline Frank, Mrs. (1897-1937), illus. LC 30-30708. 189, 2 p. incl. front., illus. 19 cm. 1930. A. Flanagan Company.
--Little Phillipe of Belgium. Brandeis, Madeline Frank, Mrs. (1897-1937), illus. (The Children of All Lands Stories). N.D. Grosset & Dunlap.
--Little Rose of the Mesa. Brandeis, Madeline Frank, Mrs. (1897-1937), illus. 5 p. l., 13-155 p. front., illus., pl. 22 cm. c.1935. Grosset & Dunlap.
--Little Rose of the Mesa. Brandeis, Madeline Frank, Mrs. (1897-1937), illus. (The Children of America Stories). N.D. Grosset & Dunlap.
--The Little Spanish Dancer. Brandeis, Madeline Frank, Mrs. (1897-1937), illus. LC 36-22623. 176 p. incl., front., illus. 19 cm. 1936. A. Flanagan Company.
--The Little Spanish Dancer. Brandeis, Madeline Frank, Mrs. (1897-1937), illus. (The Children of all Lands Stories). N.D. Grosset & Dunlap.
--The Little Swiss Wood-Carver. Brandeis, Madeline Frank, Mrs. (1897-1937), illus. LC 29-6675. 160 p. incl. front., illus. 19 cm. 1929. A. Flanagan Company.
--The Little Swiss Wood Carver. Brandeis, Madeline Frank, Mrs. (1897-1937), illus. (The Children of All Lands Stories). N.D. Grosset & Dunlap.
--Little Tom of England. Brandeis, Madeline Frank, Mrs. (1897-1937), illus. 159 p. incl. front., illus. 22 cm. c.1935. Grosset & Dunlap.
--Little Tom of England. Brandeis, Madeline Frank, Mrs. (1897-1937), illus. (The Children of all Lands Stories). N.D. Grosset & Dunlap.
--Little Tony of Italy. Brandeis, Madeline Frank, Mrs. (1897-1937), illus. LC 34-4631. 159 p. incl. front., illus. 23 cm. c.1934. Grosset & Dunlap.
--Little Tony of Italy. Brandeis, Madeline Frank, Mrs. (1897-1937), illus. (The Children of all Lands Stories). N.D. Grosset & Dunlap.
--Mitz and Fritz of Germany. Brandeis, Madeline Frank, Mrs. (1897-1937), illus. LC 33-3747. 160 p. incl. front., illus. 23 cm. c.1933. Grosset & Dunlap.
--Mitz and Fritz of Germany. Brandeis, Madeline Frank, Mrs. (1897-1937), illus. (The Children of all Lands Stories). N.D. Grosset & Dunlap.
--Shaun O'Day of Ireland. Brandeis, Madeline Frank, Mrs. (1897-1937), illus. 191 p. incl. front., illus. 19 cm. (Her The child-life travel books). 1929. A. Flanagan Company.
--Shaun O'Day of Ireland. Brandeis, Madeline Frank, Mrs. (1897-1937), illus. (The Children of All Lands Stories). N.D. Grosset & Dunlap.
--The Wee Scotch Piper. Brandeis, Madeline Frank, Mrs. (1897-1937), illus. LC 29-6674. 159 p. incl. front., illus. 19 cm. 1929. A. Flanagan Company.
--The Wee Scotch Piper. Brandeis, Madeline Frank, Mrs. (1897-1937), illus. (The Children of All Lands Stories). N.D. Grosset & Dunlap.
--Yankee Doodle's Adventures: An American Fairy Tale. Eulalie, pseud. (1896-), illus. Banks, Eulalie M.. LC 33-194872. 2 p. l., 99 p. illus. (1 col.) 20 cm. c.1932. Suttonhouse.

Brandel, Marc, pseud., see Beresford, Marcus.

Brandel, Marc, pseud. (1919-)
--The Mine of Lost Days. Beresford, Marcus. Verling, John, illus. LC 74-8051. (Illus.). 187 p. 23cm. 1974. (ISBN 0-397-31587-2). Lippincott.
--The Mystery of the Two-Toed Pigeon. Beresford, Marcus. Fanelli, Jenny & Zwecher, Deborah, eds. LC 83-21174. (Illus.). 160p. (The Three Investigators Mystery Ser.: No. 37). (gr. 4-7). 1984. (ISBN 0-394-85976-6, BYR). (ISBN 0-394-95976-0). Random.
--The Three Investigators in The Mystery of the Rogues' Reunion. Beresford, Marcus. LC 84-13395. (Based on Characters Created by Robert Arthur). ix, 176 p. 22cm. (The Three Investigators Mystery Series ; 40). c.1985. (ISBN 0-394-86920-6). (ISBN 0-394-96920-0). Random House.

Brandel, Marc, pseud. (1919-) & Arthur, Robert, pseud. (1909-1969)
--The Three Investigators in The Mystery of the Kidnapped Whale. Beresford, Marcus. Feder, Robert Arthur. LC 83-3008. (Based on Characters Created by Robert Arthur Feder). ix, 163 p. 20cm. (The Three Investigators Mystery Ser.: No. 33). c.1983. (ISBN 0-394-95841-1). (ISBN 0-394-85841-7). Random House.
--The Three Investigators in the Mystery of the Two-Toed Pigeon. Beresford, Marcus. Feder, Robert Arthur. LC 83-43115. (The Three Investigators Mystery Ser.: No. 37). 1984. (ISBN 0-394-86513-8). Random House.

Brandenberg, Aliki Liacouras see Aliki, pseud.

Brandenberg, Franz (1932-)
--Aunt Nina and Her Nephews and Nieces. Aliki, pseud. (1929-), illus. Brandenberg, Aliki Liacouras. LC 82-12004. p. cm. c.1983. (ISBN 0-688-01655-3). (ISBN 0-688-01657-X). Greenwillow Books.
--Aunt Nina's Visit. Aliki, pseud. (1929-), illus. Brandenberg, Aliki Liacouras. LC 83-16531. (Illus.). 9 7/8 x 8. 32p. (20 pt.). (gr. k-3). 1984. (ISBN 0-688-01764-9). (ISBN 0-688-01766-5). (ISBN 0-688-02532-3). Greenwillow.
--Everyone Ready?. Aliki, pseud. (1929-), illus. Brandenberg, Aliki Liacouras. LC 78-13744. (Illus.). 55 p. 22cm. (Greenwillow read-alone). c.1979. (ISBN 0-688-80198-6). (ISBN 0-688-84198-8). Greenwillow Books.
--Fresh Cider and Pie. Aliki, pseud. (1929-), illus. Brandenberg, Aliki Liacouras. LC 73-585. (Illus.). 32 p. 27cm. 1973. (ISBN 0-02-711910-6). Macmillan.
--The Hit of the Party. Aliki, pseud. (1929-), illus. Brandenberg, Aliki Liacouras. LC 84-25913. (Illus.). 32 p. 26cm. (gr. k-3). c.1985. (ISBN 0-688-04240-6). (ISBN 0-688-04241-4). Greenwillow Books.
--I Once Knew a Man. Aliki, pseud. (1929-), illus. Brandenberg, Aliki Liacouras. LC 77-110133. (Illus.). 40 p. 23cm. 1970. Macmillan.
--I Wish I Was Sick, Too!. Aliki, pseud. (1929-), illus. Brandenberg, Aliki Liacouras. LC 75-46610. p. cm. c.1976. (ISBN 0-688-80047-5). (ISBN 0-688-84047-7). Greenwillow Books.
--I Wish I Was Sick, Too!. Aliki, pseud. (1929-), illus. Brandenberg, Aliki Liacouras. LC 78-6113. (Illus.). 32 p. 23cm. 1978, c.1976. (ISBN 0-14-050292-0). Puffin Books.
--It's Not My Fault. Aliki, pseud. (1929-), illus. Brandenberg, Aliki Liacouras. LC 79-24157. (Illus.). 63 p. 22cm. (Greenwillow read-alone books). c.1980. (ISBN 0-688-80235-4). (ISBN 0-688-84235-6). Greenwillow Books.
--Leo and Emily. Aliki, pseud. (1929-), illus. Brandenberg, Aliki Liacouras. LC 80-19657. (Illus.). 55 p. 22cm. (Greenwillow read-alone). c.1981. (ISBN 0-688-80292-3). (ISBN 0-688-84292-5). Greenwillow Books.
--Leo & Emily & the Dragon. Aliki, pseud. (1929-), illus. Brandenberg, Aliki Liacouras. LC 83-14091. (Illus.). 6 1/4 x 8 3/8. 56p. (16 pt.). (gr. 1-3). 1984. (ISBN 0-688-02531-5). (ISBN 0-688-02532-3). Greenwillow.
--Leo and Emily's Big Ideas. Aliki, pseud. (1929-), illus. Brandenberg, Aliki Liacouras. LC 81-6424. (Illus.). 55 p. 22cm. (Greenwillow read-alone). c.1982. (ISBN 0-688-00754-6). (ISBN 0-688-00755-4). Greenwillow Books.
--Nice New Neighbors. Aliki, pseud. (1929-), illus. Brandenberg, Aliki Liacouras. LC 77-1651. (Illus.). 56 p. 22cm. (Greenwillow read-alone). c.1977. (ISBN 0-688-80105-6). (ISBN 0-688-84105-8). Greenwillow Books.
--No School Today!. Aliki, pseud. (1929-), illus. Brandenberg, Aliki Liacouras. LC 74-13186. (Illus.). 32 p. 23cm. 1975. (ISBN 0-02-711930-0). Macmillan.
--Otto is Different. Stevenson, James Walker (1929-), illus. LC 84-13654. (Illus.). 7 3/8 x 8. 24p. (18 pt.). (gr. k-3). 1985. (ISBN 0-688-04253-8). (ISBN 0-688-04254-6). Greenwillow.
--A Picnic, Hurrah!. Aliki, pseud. (1929-), illus. Brandenberg, Aliki Liacouras. LC 77-3950. (Illus.). 56 p. 22cm. (Greenwillow read-alone). c.1978. (ISBN 0-688-80115-3). Greenwillow Books.
--A Robber! A Robber!. Aliki, pseud. (1929-), illus. Brandenberg, Aliki Liacouras. LC 75-26999. (Illus.). 32 p. 24cm. c.1976. (ISBN 0-688-80027-0). (ISBN 0-688-84027-2). Greenwillow Books.
--A Secret for Grandmother's Birthday. Aliki, pseud. (1929-), illus. Brandenberg, Aliki Liacouras. LC 75-10606. (Illus.). 32 p. 24cm. 1975. (ISBN 0-688-80012-2). (ISBN 0-688-84012-4). Greenwillow Books.
--A Secret for Grandmother's Birthday. Aliki, pseud. (1929-), illus. Brandenberg, Aliki Liacouras. LC 75-10606. (Illus.). 8 x 9. 32p. (16 pt.). (gr. k-3). 1985. (ISBN 0-688-05781-0). (ISBN 0-688-05782-9). Greenwillow.
--Six New Students. Aliki, pseud. (1929-), illus. Brandenberg, Aliki Liacouras. LC 77-24883. (Illus.). 56 p. 22cm. (Greenwillow read-alone). c.1978. (ISBN 0-688-80124-2). (ISBN 0-688-84124-4). Greenwillow Books.
--What Can You Make of It?. Aliki, pseud. (1929-), illus. Brandenberg, Aliki Liacouras. LC 76-44406. (Illus.). 56 p. 22cm. (Greenwillow read-alone books). c.1977. (ISBN 0-688-80083-1). (ISBN 0-688-84083-3). Greenwillow Books.

Brandenburg, Albert Jacques see Erlande, Albert, pseud.

Brandenburg, Albert Jacques (1878-)
--A Little French Boy. Erlande, Albert, pseud. Harvitt, Helene Josephine (1884-) & Shea, Aileen, trs. LC 34-31641. 4 p. l., 3-162 p., 1 l. illus. 20 cm. 1934. A. A. Knopf.

Brandhorst, Carl Theodore (1898-) & Sylvester, Robert
--Tale of Whitefoot. (Illus.). (gr. 3-7). 1968. (ISBN 0-671-65000-9, Juveniles). (ISBN 0-671-65001-7). S&S.

Brandon, Frances Sweeney (1916-)
--Rosie the Rock Hound. Van Sciver, Ruth (1915-), illus. LC 63-10805. 60 p. illus. 21 cm. 1963. Abingdon Press.

Brandram, S.
--Shapespeare for the Young. N.D. J. B. Lippincott Co.

Brandreth, Gyles Daubeney (1948-)
--The Biggest Tongue-Twister Book in the World. Chin, Alex, illus. LC 78-57784. (Illus.). (gr. 2 up). 1978. (ISBN 0-8069-4594-X). (ISBN 0-8069-4595-8). Sterling.
--Brain-Teasers and Mind-Benders. Axworthy, Ann, illus. 1979. Sterling.
--Joke-a-Day Book. LC 78-66298. (Illus.). (gr. 3 up). 1979. (ISBN 0-8069-4598-2). (ISBN 0-8069-4599-0). Sterling.
--The Super Joke Book. Berringer, Nick, illus. LC [illegible]. p. cm. [illegible]. (ISBN [illegible]). Sterling Pub. Co.

Brandreth, Gyles Daubeney (1948-) & Axworthy, Ann
--The Great Big Funny Book Presents the Funniest Show on Earth - the Tale of Superpuss, Starring Superpuss and a Cast of Thousands in a Feline Extravaganza Extraordinary in 23 Stupendous Scenes, with Special Guest Star Leofric of Limerick, the Lilting Lad Himself. Axworthy, Ann, illus. LC 78-53474. (Illus.). 96 p. 28cm. c.1978. (ISBN 0-88470-079-8). One Strawberry : Distributed by Larousse.

Brandreth, Gyles Daubeney (1948-) & Robinson, Lucy
--Total Nonsense Z to A. LC 80-54349. (Illus.). 96 p. 21cm. c.1981. (ISBN 0-8069-4644-X). Sterling Pub. Co.

Brandt, Carl
--Bob Hazard, Dam Builder. Stoops, Herbert Morton, illus. LC 16 21709. 272 p. front., plates. 20 cm. c.1916. The Reilly & Britton Co.
--Jerry King, Timber Cruiser. Armstrong, Harry W., illus. LC 17-20860. 287 p. front., plates 20 cm. c.1917. The Reilly & Britton Co.
--Tom Wickham, Corn Grower. Arting, Fred J., illus. LC 16-161552. 288 p. front., plates. 20 cm. c.1916. The Reilly & Britton Co.

Brandt, Harry Alonzo (1885-), ed.
--Fun in the North Woods: Especially What Joyce and Haven Saw on a Trip to the North Country. Palmquist, Gordon C., photos by. LC 45-22128. 3 p. l., 3-58 p., 1 l. incl. front., illus. 22 x 18 cm. 1945. The Elgin Press.

Brandt, Heidi
--Doing Things. LC 46-22077. 53 p. illus. (part col.) 21 1/2 cm. 1946. The World Publishing Company.

Brandt, Keith, pseud., see Subin, Louis.

Brandt, Keith, pseud. (1930-)
--Case of the Missing Dinosaur. Subin, Louis. Wallner, John C. (1945-), illus. LC 81-7620. p. cm. (A Troll Easy-to-Read Mystery). c.1982. (ISBN 0-89375-586-9). (ISBN 0-89375-587-7). Troll Associates.

Brandt, Lois
--In a Time Long Past ... Grippo, Robert Lo, illus. LC 79-157445. (Illus.). 24 p. 20cm. (Magic circle book). 1972. Ginn.

Brandt, Lucile Long Strayer see Long, Lucile, pseud.

Brandt, Lucile Long Strayer see Long, Lucile, pseud.

Brandt, Lucile Long Strayer (1900-)
--Anna Elizabeth: Girl of the Plain People. Long, Lucille, pseud. LC 74-29366. (Illus.). 128 p. 18cm. 1975, c.1942. (ISBN 0-87178-040-2). Breathren Press.
--Anna Elizabeth, Seventeen. Long, Lucille, pseud. Goughnour, Inez, illus. LC 78-9747. 208 p. 21cm. c.1978. (ISBN 0-87178-041-0). Brethren Press.

Brandt, Mary Elizabeth, Mrs.
--Spotover. LC 40-101583. 75 p. 21 cm. c.1940. House of Field, Inc.

Brandt, Rose Katherine (1877-), ed. see U. S. Bureau of Indian Affairs & Tubbs, Rhoda.

Brandt, Rose Katherine (1877-) & Navajo Children
--The Colored Land: A Navajo Indian Book, Written by Navajo Children. LC 37-13702. 80 p. illus., col. plates. 17 x 21 cm. c.1937. C. Scribner's Sons.

Brandt, Thomas O
--Andy; or, When I'm Famous. Brandt, Heidi, illus. LC 68-16134. (Illus.). 1 v. (unpaged). 20cm. 1968. Doubleday.

Branfield, John Charles (1931-)
--The Fox in Winter. LC 81-10793. 158 p. 22cm. 1982. (ISBN 0-689-50219-2). Atheneum.
--The Poison Factory. LC 72-83225. 199 p. 21cm. 1972. (ISBN 0-06-020646-2). (ISBN 0-06-020646-2). Harper & Row.
--Why Me?. LC 73-8005. 233 p. 22cm. 1973. (ISBN 0-06-020662-4). (ISBN 0-06-020662-4). Harper & Row.

Brangwyn, Frank, illus.
--The Thousand & One Nights: Or, Arabian Nights' Entertainments. Lane, Edward William (1801-1876), tr. Jacobs, Joseph (1854-1916), intro. by. LC 4-15414. 6 v. fronts., plates. 18 cm. 1896. Gibbings & Company, Limited.

Branley, Franklyn Mansfield (1915-)
--Big Tracks, Little Tracks. LC 60-6251. (Illus.). (A Let's-Read-&-Find-Out Science Bk). (gr. k-3). 1960. (ISBN 0-690-14371-0, TYC-J). Har-Row.
--Big Tracks, Little Tracks. (gr. k-3). 1975. (ISBN 0-590-00506-5). Scholastic Inc.
--Big Tracks, Little Tracks. Kessler, Leonard P. (1921-), illus. LC 60-511468. unpaged. illus. 21x23cm. (Let's read and find out). 1960. Crowell.
--A Book of Astronauts for You. Kessler, Leonard P. (1921-), illus. LC 63-15083. 1 v. (unpaged) illus. (part col.) 21 x 23 cm. 1963. Crowell.
--The Christmas Sky. Lent, Blair (1930-), illus. LC 66-7687. (Illus.). unpaged. 24 cm. 1966. Crowell.
--The Great Moon Hoax. Brown, Richard Eric (1946-), illus. LC 72-77627. (Illus.). 16 p. 22cm. (Magic circle book). c.1973. (ISBN 0-663-25496-5). Ginn.
--Lodestar: Rocket Ship to Mars. LC 51-764. (gr 5-9). 1951. (ISBN 0-690-50443-8, TYC-J). T Y Crowell.
--Mars. Jauss, Anne Marie (1907-), illus. 148p. 1955. Thomas Y. Crowell.
--The Moon: Jack and Jill and Other Legends. Oka, Jane Teiko, illus. LC 71-157443. (Illus.). 22 p. 21cm. (Magic circle book). 1971, c.1972. (ISBN 0-663-22985-5). Ginn.
--North, South, East, and West. Galster, Robert, illus. LC 66-14486. 1v. (unpaged) col. illus. 22cm. (Let's-read-and-find-out bks.). 1966. Crowell.
--Oxygen Keeps You Alive. Madden, Donald B. (1927-), illus. LC 73-139093. (Illus.). 33 p. (Let's-read-and-find-out science books). 1971. (ISBN 0-690-60703-2). Crowell.
--Rain & Hail. Barton, Harriet, illus. LC 83-45058. (Illus.). 40p. (Let's Read-&-Find-Out Science Bk.). (gr. k-3). 1983. (ISBN 0-690-04352-X, TYC-J). (ISBN 0-690-04353-8). Har-Row.
--Timmy and the Tin-Can Telephone. Galdone, Paul (1914-), illus. LC 58-12297. unpaged. illus. 21cm. 1959. Crowell.
--Weight and Weightlessness. Booth, Graham Charles (1935-), illus. LC 70-132292. (Illus.). 33 p. (Let's read and find out science books). 1972, c.1971. (ISBN 0-690-87328-X). (ISBN 0-690-87329-8). Crowell.
--What Makes Day and Night. Borten, Helen Jacobson (1930-), illus. LC 60-8258. unpaged. illus. 21x23cm. (Let's read and find out). 1961. Crowell.

Branley, Franklyn Mansfield (1915-) & Vaughan, Eleanor K.
--Mickey's Magnet. Johnson, Crockett, pseud. (1906-1975), illus. Leisk, David Johnson. LC 56-63278. unpaged. illus. 21cm. 48p. c.1956. Crowell.
--Mickey's Magnet. Johnson, Crockett, pseud. (1906-1975), illus. Leisk, David Johnson. (Illus.). (gr. k-3). N.D. (ISBN 0-590-02334-9). Scholastic Inc.
--Rusty Rings a Bell. Galdone, Paul (1914-), illus. LC 57-7492. (Illus.). (gr. k-3). 1957. (ISBN 0-690-71601-X, TYC-J). (ISBN 0-690-71602-8). Har-Row.
--Timmy & The Tin-Can Telephone. N.D. E. M. Hale & Co.

Brann, Esther
--Another New Year with Bobbie and Donnie. LC 36-21648. 19cm. 42p. 1936. Macmillan.
--Bobbie and Donnie Were Twins. N.D. MacMillan.
--A Book for Baby. LC 45-35176. 39 p. col. illus. 21 cm. 1945. The Macmillan Company.
--Five Puppies for Sale. LC 48-908811. 80 p. illus. 21 cm. 1948. Macmillan Co.
--Lupe Goes to School. Brann, Esther, illus. LC 30-27931. 5 p. l., 126 p., 1 l. incl. illus, plates. 22 cm. 1930. The Macmillan Company.
--Nanette of the Wooden Shoes. Brann, Esther, illus. LC 29-9001. 5 p. l., 124 p. col. front., illus., col. plates. 23 cm. 1929. The Macmillan Company.
--Nicolina: The Story of a Little Girl in Italy. LC 31-29831. 5 p. l., 3-134 p. incl. illus., plates.col. front. 23 cm. 1931. The Macmillan Company.
--Patrick Goes A-Hunting. N.D. Macmillan.
--Patrick Was His Name: By Esther Brann. LC 38-19068. 49 p. illus. 19 x 21 cm. 1938. The Macmillan Company.

BRANNE, BERIT (cont.)
--Round the World with Esther Brann. LC 35-5465. (Illus.). 19 x 21cm. 41p. 1935. The Macmillan Company.
--Yann and His Island. LC 32-31037. 6 p. l., 141 p. incl. illus., plates. col. front. 23 cm. 1932. The Macmillan Company.

Branne, Berit
--Torris, the Boy from Broad Valley. Rud, Borghild, illus. McKinnon, Lise Somme, tr. LC 79-124841. (Illus.). 157 p. 21cm. 1970. Harcourt, Brace, Jovanovich.

Brannen, Ann, tr. see Sato, Satoru.

Branner, B.
--Winnie Winkle. 48p. (C & L Famous Comics in Book Form). N.D. Cupples & Leon Co.

Branner, John Casper (1850-1922)
--How and Why Stories. LC 21-18007. xi, 104 p. front., illus. 22 cm. 1921. H. Holt and Company.

Brannon, William T. (1906-)
--The Con Game and Yellow Kidd Weil. 297p. Orig. Title: Yellow Kid. 1948. (ISBN 0-486-23127-5). Dover Books.

Branscum, Robbie (1937-)
--The Adventures of Johnny May. Howland, Deborah, illus. LC 83-49464. p. cm. 128p. (gr. 4-7). c.1984. (ISBN 0-06-020614-4). (ISBN 0-06-020615-2). Harper & Row.
--Cheater and Flitter Dick. LC 83-5768. p. cm. 1983. (ISBN 0-670-21350-0). Viking Press.
--For Love of Jody. Davis, Allen, illus. LC 79-2436. (Illus.). 111 p. 22cm. c.1979. (ISBN 0-688-41881-3). (ISBN 0-688-51881-8). Lothrop, Lee & Shepard Books.
--Johnny May. Robinson, Charles (1931-), illus. LC 74-3544. (Illus.). 135 p. 22cm. 1975. (ISBN 0-385-03003-7). (ISBN 0-385-09613-5). Doubleday.
--Me and Jim Luke. LC 74-144252. N.D. (ISBN 0-385-08107-3). (ISBN 0-385-00053-7). Doubleday & Company.
--The Murder of Hound Dog Bates: A Novel. LC 82-1911. 90 p. 22cm. (gr. 3-7). 1982. (ISBN 0-670-49521-2). Viking Press.
--The Saving of P. S. Rounds, Glen Harold (1906-), illus. LC 76-2757. (Illus.). 127 p. 19cm. c.1977. (ISBN 0-385-11270-X). (ISBN 0-385-11271-8). Doubleday.
--Spud Tackett and the Angel of Doom. LC 82-11621. 124 p. 22cm. 1983. (ISBN 0-670-66582-7). Viking Press.
--Three Buckets of Daylight. Davis, Allen, illus. LC 77-17502. (Illus.). 125 p. 22cm. c.1978. (ISBN 0-688-41837-6). (ISBN 0-688-51837-0). Lothrop, Lee & Shepard.
--The Three Wars of Billie Joe Treat. LC 75-10917. p. cm. (gr. 7-12). 1975. (ISBN 0-07-007237-X). (ISBN 0-07-007238-8). McGraw-Hill.
--To the Tune of a Hickory Stick. LC 77-12844. 119 p. c.1978. (ISBN 0-385-13037-6). (ISBN 0-385-13038-4). Doubleday.
--Toby Alone. LC 78-22152. 117 p. 19cm. c.1979. (ISBN 0-385-14017-7). (ISBN 0-385-14018-5). Doubleday.
--Toby and Johnny Joe. LC 78-22153. 99 p. 19cm. c.1979. (ISBN 0-385-13035-X). Doubleday.
--Toby, Granny, and George. Rounds, Glen Harold (1906-), illus. LC 75-21211. (Illus.). 104 p. 19cm. c.1976. (ISBN 0-385-11268-8). Doubleday.
--The Ugliest Boy. Eagle, Michael (1942-), illus. LC 78-14388. p. cm. c.1978. (ISBN 0-688-41859-7). (ISBN 0-688-51859-1). Lothrop, Lee & Shepard Co.

Branson, H. C.
--Salisbury Plain. N.D. E. P. Dutton & Co.

Branson, Karen
--The Potato Eaters. Sterrett, Jane, illus. LC 78-24330. (Illus.). 160 p. 24cm. c.1979. (ISBN 0-399-20678-7). Putnam.
--Streets of Gold. LC 81-13963. 176 p. 22cm. c.1981. (ISBN 0-399-20791-0). Putnam.

Branson, Mary Kinney
--It's Not Easy Being Small. Hester, Ronald, illus. LC 81-65823. (Illus.). 32 p. 24cm. c.1981. (ISBN 0-8054-4160-3). Broadman Press.

Branwell, David
--Going Camping. Wells, Tony, illus. LC 84-26269. p. cm. (An Early Bird Book. Word Finder). 1985. (ISBN 0-394-86704-1). Random House.
--The Race. Wells, Tony, illus. LC 84-26270. p. cm. (An Early Bird Book. Word Finder). 1985. (ISBN 0-394-86703-3). Random House.

Brasch, Walter M.
--Jimmy's Fuzzy Friend. Mulliner, Gary, illus. (gr. k-3). 1978. (ISBN 0-685-80796-7). Brasch & Brasch.

Brasher, Rex
--Secret of the Friendly Woods. 220p. N.D. Century Co.

Brasier, Inez
--Daisy. Niswonger, Newall A., illus. LC 51-6442. 166 p. illus. 20 cm. 1951. Southern Pub. Association.

Brass, Denis, tr. see Torga, Miguel.

Brassey, Richard
--The Famous Lion. (Illus.). 32p. (gr. 1-4). 1980. (ISBN 0-224-01688-1, Pub. by Chatto Bodley Jonathan). Merrimack Pub Cir.

Braswell, Lynn, jt. auth. see Phillips, Louis.

Brate, Charlotte (1890-)
--The Pony Tree. Brate, Charlotte (1890-), illus. 301 p. illus. 19 cm. 1928. Frederick A. Stokes Company.

Bratton, Helen (1899-)
--The Amber Flask. Lambo, Donald W. (1903-1966), illus. LC 64-19407. 181 p. illus. 21 cm. 1964. McKay.
--It's Morning Again. LC 64-11510. 215 p. 21 cm. 1964. D. McKay Co.
--Only in Time. (gr. 7-9). 1967. (ISBN 0-679-20139-4). McKay.

Bratton, John
--Teddy Bear's Picnic. Day, Alexandra, illus. (Illus.). 32p. 1983. (ISBN 0-88138-010-5, Star & Eleph Bks). Green Tiger Pr.

Bratton, Karl H (1906-)
--Tales from Once Upon a Time. Thurston, Jack L. (1919-), illus. LC 60-9025. 191p. illus. 22cm. (gr. 1-3). 1960. (ISBN 0-8158-0057-6). Christopher Pub. House.
--Tales of the Magic Mirror. Thurston, Jack L. (1919-), illus. LC 49-119460. 239 p. illus. 24 cm. 1949. Caxton Printers.

Brattstrom, Inger
--Since That Party. (gr. 7-12). 1978. (ISBN 0-590-11899-4). Scholastic Inc.

Braucher, Bettye H.
--Belinda & Me. Turkle, Brinton Cassaday (1915-), illus. (Illus.). (ps-1). 1966. (ISBN 0-670-15558-6). (ISBN 0-670-15559-4). Viking Pr.

Braude, Michael (1936-)
--Andy Learns about Advertising. Lindberg, Howard E., illus. (Illus.). (Career Guidance Ser.). (gr. 3-6). N.D. Denison.
--Andy Learns About Advertising. Lindberg, Howard E, illus. LC 67-24769. 29 p. col. illus. 29cm. c.1967. T. S. Denison.
--Peter Enters the Jet Age. Lindberg, Howard E., illus. (Illus.). (Career Guidance Ser.). (gr. 3-6). N.D. Denison.
--Shelby Goes to Wall Street. Lindberg, Howard E., illus. LC 64-7708. 1v. (unpaged) col. illus. 29cm. c.1965. Denison.
--Shelby Goes to Wall Street. Lindberg, Howard E, illus. (Illus.). (Career Guidance Ser.). (gr. 3-6). N.D. Denison.

Brauer, D. R.
--Harold, the Easter Rat. 1981. (ISBN 0-8062-1631-X). Carlton.

Braumann, Franz
--Gold in the Taiga. Schramm, Ulrik (1912-), illus. Emerson, Joyce, tr. LC 61-10070. 201p. illus. 22cm. c.1961. F. Watts.
--Malik and Amina. Ambrus, Victor G., pseud. (1935-), illus. Ambrus, Gyozo Laszlo. LC 63-19011. 224 p. illus., map. 22 cm. 1963. Bobbs-Merrill.

Braun, Isabella (1851-1886)
--The Little Actors' Theater: Four Plays to Act Out with Three-Dimensional Scenes and Characters That Really Move. Seymour, Peter S, adapted by. Didriksen, Paula, tr. LC 81-8606. (Illus.). 9 p. 30cm. c.1981. (ISBN 0-399-20846-1). Philomel Books.

Braun, J. R. & Braun, Janine
--The Girl the Boys Pretended to Love. Morris, Carrie, illus. (Illus.). 24p. (ps-4). 1980. (ISBN 0-933656-10-6). Trinity Pub Hse.

Braun, Janine, jt. auth. see Braun, J. R.

Braun, Kathy
--Kangaroo & Kangaroo. McMullan, James (1934-), illus. LC 65-19800. (Illus.). (gr. 2-4). 1965. (ISBN 0-385-01062-1). Doubleday.
  Award: (NYT).

Braun, P. C., ed.
--The Big Book of Favorite Horse Stories. Savitt, Sam (1917-), illus. (Illus.). 336p. (gr. 7 up). 1982. (ISBN 0-448-42641-2). Platt.
--The Big Book of Favorite Horse Stories: Twenty-Five Outstanding Stories. Savitt, Sam (1917-), illus. Savitt, Sam, frwd. by. LC 65-15196. 336p. illus. 23cm. (gr. 7 up). c.1965. Platt & Munk.

Braun, Roman, tr. see Gorska, Halina.

Braune, Anna
--Honey Chile. LC 37-286519. 7 p. l., 152. 1 p. incl. col. front., illus., plates. 23 cm. 1937. Doubleday, Doran & Company, Inc.

Brauner, Theodore
--Silent Visitor. (Illus.). 1962. Atheneum.

Braverman, Libbie Levin (1900-)
--Children of the Emek. rev. ed. Gezari, Temina Nimtzowitz, illus. LC 64-19143. vi, 120 p. illus. 22 cm. 1964. Bloch Pub. Co.
--Children of the Emek. Gezari, Temina Nimtzowitz, illus. LC 50-58335. vi, 120 p. illus. 21 cm. 1950. Furrow Press.
--Children of the Emek. Gezari, Temina Nimtzowitz, illus. LC 38-1579. viii, 118, 1 p. illus. (incl map) 20 1/2 cm. c.1937. The Furrow Press.

Brawley, Eleanor Riggins
--Lisa's Spring Baby. Nellist, Betty Gayhart, illus. LC 69-13656. (Illus.). 60 p 24cm. 1969. John Knox Press.

Bray, Alice S.
--The Baby's Journal. (Illus.). N.D. A. Wessels.

Bray, Mrs.
--Silver Linings. (Illus.). (The Girl's Own Favorite Ser.). N.D. E. P. Dutton & Co.

Bray, R. M., jt. auth. see Cummings, M. J.

Bray, R. M., Mrs.
--Petite. N.D. E. P. Dutton.
--Petite: Or, The Story of a Child's Life. (Illus.). N. D. D. Lothrop Co.
--Ten of Them: Or, The Children of Danehurst. N. D. T. Whittaker.

Brazie, Gladys
--Sixes and Sevens: Life Four Feet Tall. LC 63-6817. 57 p. 21 cm. 1961. Pageant Press.

Brazil, Angela (1869-)
--Captain Peggie. (The Angela Brazil Books for Girls). N.D. A L Burt Co.
--Captain Peggie. Wightman, W. E., illus. LC 25-498523. 5 p. l., 306 p. front., plates. 20 cm. 1924. Frederick A. Stokes Company.
--A Harum-Scarum Schoolgirl. Campbell, John F., illus. LC 20-18764. 288 p. front., plates. 20 cm. c.1920. Frederick A. Stokes Company.
--The Head Girl at the Gables. Salmon, Balliol, illus. LC 20-17658. 288 p. front., plates. 20 cm. c.1920. Frederick A. Stokes Company.
--Joan's Best Chum. (The Angela Brazil Books for Girls). N.D. A L Burt Co.
--Joan's Best Chum. Wightman, W, E., illus. LC 27-173620. vi p., 2 l., 308 p. front., plates. 19 cm. 1927. Frederick A. Stokes Company.
--The Jolliest School of All. (The Angela Brazil Books for Girls). N.D. A L Burt Co.
--The Jolliest School of All. Broadhead, W. Smithson, illus. LC 23-3894. 6 p. l., 315 p. front., plates. 20 cm. 1923. Frederick A. Stokes Company.
--The Luckiest Girl in the School. (The Angela Brazil Books for Girls). N.D. A L Burt Co.
--The Luckiest Girl in the School. Salmon, Balliol, illus. LC 22-112944. 5 p. l., 292 p. front., plates. 20 cm. 1922. Frederick A. Stokes Company.
--The Madcap of the School. Salmon, Balliol, illus. LC 22-112952. 5 p. l., 292 p. front., plates. 20 cm. 1922. Frederick A. Stokes Company.
--Marjorie's Best Year. (The Angela Brazil Books for Girls). N.D. A L Burt Co.
--Marjorie's Best Year. Evans, Treyer, illus. 5 p. l., 269 p. front., plates. 20 cm. 1923. Frederick A. Stokes Company.
--A Popular Schoolgirl. (The Angela Brazil Books for Girls). N.D. A L Burt Co.
--A Popular Schoolgirl. Salmon, Balliol, illus. LC 21-151025. v p., 1 l., 296 p. front., plates. 20 cm. 1921. Frederick A. Stokes Company.
--The Princess of the School. (The Angela Brazil Books for Girls). N.D. A L Burt Co.
--The Princess of the School. Wiles, Frank, illus. LC 21-148511. v p., 1 l., 295 p. front., plates. 20 cm. 1921. Frederick A. Stokes Company.
--Schoolgirl Kitty. (The Angela Brazil Books for Girls). N.D. A L Burt Co.
--Schoolgirl Kitty. Wightman, W. E., illus. vi p., 2 l., 302 p. front., plates. 20 cm. 1924. Frederick A. Stokes Company.

Brazos, Waco, pseud., see Jennings, Michael.

Bream, Gerry
--Christmas Book. Steinhauer, Roger, illus. (Illus., Orig.). (See & Hear Books). (ps-3). 1969. Fortress.

Brearley, William Henry (1846-)
--Wanted, a Copyist. LC 6-17931. 2 p. l., 153 p. 18 cm. (Half-title: The "unkown" library v. 33). c.1894. The Cassell Publishing Co.

Breaux, Adele, tr. see Coloane, Francisco.

Brebner, Arthur
--The Shadow of the Ship: or, John Saint. (The Albion Library). N.D. Frederick Warne & Co.

Brebner, Percy see Lys, Christian, pseud.

Brebner, Percy
--The Knight of the Silver Star: or, The Fortress of Yadasara. (The Treasure Library). N.D. Frederick Warne & Co.

Brebner, Winston
--Doubting Thomas. 32p. 1965. Pitman Publishing.

Brecht, Bertolt (1898-1956)
--Uncle Eddie's Moustache: Twelve Poems for Children. Kirchberg, Ursula, illus. Rukeyser, Muriel (1913-1980), tr. LC 74-147. (Illus.). 28 p. 32cm. (gr. 1-2). 1974. (ISBN 0-394-82819-4). (ISBN 0-394-82819-4). Pantheon Books.

Brecht, Edith (1895-1975)
--Ada and the Wild Duck. Erickson, Charlotte, illus. 64p. 1964. Viking Press.
--Benjy's Luck. Dobrin, Arnold (1928-), illus. (Illus.). 55 p. 23cm. 1967. Lippincott.
--The Little Fox. Sandin, Joan (1942-), illus. LC 68-24415. (Illus.). 60 p. 23cm. 1968. Lippincott.

--The Mystery at the Old Forge. Erickson, Charlotte, illus. LC 66-873022. 70p. illus. 25cm. (gr. 2-5). 1966. (ISBN 0-670-50310-X). Viking.
--Timothy's Hawk. Erickson, Charlotte, illus. LC 65-18157. 78p. illus. 24cm. c.1965. Viking.

Breck, H. Jean, jt. auth. see Brown, Ruth Archambault.

Breck, John
--Told at Twilight Stories ... Andrews, William T., illus. 8 v. fronts., plates. 18 cm. 1923. Doubleday, Page & Company.

Breck, Sarah H
--Wankey. Molitor, Ida B., illus. LC 35-1094. 42 p. illus. 19 cm. c.1934. Dorrance & Company, Inc.

Breck, Vivian, pseud., see Breckenfeld, Vivian Gure.

Breck, Vivian, pseud. (1895-)
--High Trail. Breckenfeld, Vivian Gurney. Weisgard, Leonard Joseph (1916-), illus. (Illus.). (gr. 7-9). 1958. (ISBN 0-385-06351-2). Doubleday.
--Hoofbeats on the Trail. Breckenfeld, Vivian Gurney. Buel, Hubert, illus. (Illus.). (gr. 9-12). 1959. (ISBN 0-385-07326-7). Doubleday.
--Kona Summer. Breckenfeld, Vivian Gı. LC 61-12496. 214 p. 22cm. 1961. Doubleday.
--Maggie. Breckenfeld, Vivian Gurney. LC 54-8914. (gr. 7-9). 1954. (ISBN 0-385-07396-8). Doubleday.
--Maggie. Breckenfeld, Vivian Gurney. N.D (Tempo Books). Grosset & Dunlap.
--Two Worlds of Noriko. Breckenfeld, Vivian Gurney. LC 66-17447. (gr. 7-11). N.D. (ISBN 0-385-06305-9). Doubleday.
--White Water. Breckenfeld, Vivian Gurney. LC 58-6631. 192p. illus. 22cm. 1958. Doubleday.

Breckenfeld, Vivian Gurney see Breck, Vivian, pseud.

Breckenridge, Gerald
--The Radio Boys as Soldiers of Fortune. LC 25-9489. 251 p. front. 20 cm. (His Radio Boys Series). c.1925. A. L. Burt Company.
--The Radio Boys in Darkest Africa. (Burt's Radio Boys Ser.). N.D. A L Burt Co.
--The Radio Boys on Secret Service Duty. (Burt's Radio Boys Ser.). N.D. A L Burt Co.
--The Radio Boys on the Mexican Border. LC 22-9476. 2 p. l., viii, 3-231 p. front., illus. 20 cm. (His Radio boys series). c.1922. A. L. Burt Company.
--The Radio Boys Rescue the Lost Alaska Expedition. (Burt's Radio Boys Ser.). N.D. A L Burt Co.
--The Radio Boys Search for the Inca's Treasure. (Burt's Radio Boys Ser.). N.D. A L Burt Co.
--The Radio Boys Seek the Lost Atlantis. LC 23-119272. 1 p. l., iv, 222 p. front. 20 cm. (His The radio boys series). c.1923. A. L. Burt Company.
--The Radio Boys with the Air Patrol. LC 31-129763. 256 p. front. 20 cm. (His The radio boys series). c.1931. A. L. Burt Company.
--The Radio Boys with the Border Patrol. LC 24-17244. 241 p. front. 20 cm. (His Radio boys series). c.1924. A. L. Burt Company.
--The Radio Boys with the Revenue Guards. (Burt's Radio Boys Ser.). N.D. A L Burt Co.

Breckensiek, Marne, as told to.
--Adam's Apple and Other Stories: As Told by Teenagers to Marne Breckensiek. LC 70-151148. (Illus.). 86 p. 19cm. 1970. Liguorian Books.

Breckler, Rosemary (1920-)
--Where Are the Twins? LC 79-10390. 96 p. 21cm. c.1979. (ISBN 0-664-32651-X). Westminster Press.

Breckwoldt, Ann
--Stories for Young and Old. 1st ed. LC 53-12804. 20p. 21cm. 1953. Pageant Press.

Breen, Gertrude
--Indian Captive: The Story of Mary Jemison. (Children's Theatre Playscript Ser.). 1961. (ISBN 0-88020-030-8). Coach Hse.

Breey, Martha E., Mrs.
--The Celesta Stories, 3 vols. (Illus.). 1882. Lee & Shepard.

Bregman, Adolph, jt. auth. see Coleman, Satis Narrona Barton, Mrs.

Bregnhi, Palle
--Cherry Martin. Bregnhi, Palle, illus. LC 74-2923. (Illus.). 32 p. 27cm. 1974. Carolrhoda Books.

Brehat, Alfred De, pseud., see Guezenec, Alfred.

Brehat, Alfred De, pseud. (1823-1866)
--The French Robinson Crusoe. Guezenec, Alfred, 1 of 50 vols. (Illus.). (The Norwood Ser.: No. 5). 1900. Lee & Shepard.

Brehovszky, Vladimir, illus.
--Russian Fairy Tales. (Illus.). (gr. 3 up). 1976. (ISBN 0-600-37557-9). Hamlyn-Amer.

Breihan, Carl William (1916-)
--Younger Brothers. (Illus.). 274p. 1961. Naylor Company.

Breinburg, Petronella (1927-)
--Doctor Shawn. Lloyd, Errol (1943-), illus. LC 74-15265. (Illus.). 26 p. 24cm. 1975, c.1974. (ISBN 0-690-00721-3). (ISBN 0-690-00722-1). Crowell.
--Sally-Ann in the Snow. Murray, Ossie, illus. LC 77-373633. (Illus.). 26 p. 24cm. 1978. (ISBN 0-370-01809-5). Bodley Head.
--Sally-Ann's Umbrella. Murray, Ossie, illus. (Illus.). 28p. 1979. (ISBN 0-370-10752-7, Pub. by Chatto Bodley Jonathan). Merrimack Pub Cir.
--Shawn Goes to School. Lloyd, Errol (1943-), illus. LC 73-8003. (Illus.). 26 p. 24cm. 1974, c.1973. (ISBN 0-690-00276-9). (ISBN 0-690-00276-9). Crowell.
--Shawn Goes to School. Lloyd, Errol (1943-), illus. 1974. Harper
--Shawn's Red Bike. Lloyd, Errol (1943-), illus. LC 75-40362. (Illus.). 26 p. 24cm. 1976, c.1975. (ISBN 0-690-01114-8). Crowell.
Breitmeyer, Lois, jt. auth. see Leithauser, Gladys Garner.
Breitmeyer, Lois & Leithauser, Gladys (1925-)
--The Dinosaur Dilemma. Maloy, Lois (1902-), illus. LC 64-16316. 158 p. illus. 23 cm. 1964. Golden Gate Junior Books.
Breitner, Sue
--The Bookseller's Advice. Chambless-Rigie, Jane, illus. LC 81-2295. p. cm. 1981. (ISBN 0-670-18139-0). Viking Press.
Breitweiser, Alverta
--And God Cares for Me. Brown, Darrell, illus. Breitwetser, Paul, photos by. LC 57-4266. unpaged. illus. 22x28cm. 1957. Warner Press.
Brelis, Nancy Burns (1929-)
--The Mother Market. Schecter, Ben (1935-), illus. (Illus.). 143 p. 22cm. (Harper Trophy book). Orig. Title: The Mummy Market. 1975, c.1966. Harper & Row.
--The Mummy Market. Schecter, Ben (1935-), illus. LC 66-8277. (Illus.). 145 p. 21cm. 1966. Harper & Row.
Brem, M. M.
--The Man Caught By a Fish. 1967. Concordia Publishing House.
--The Man Caught By A Fish. 1967. Lutheran Publications.
Brem, Peter
--Peter and the Bees. Hodges, David, illus. LC 70-107945. (Illus.). 60 p. 25cm. (Merit books). 1970. (ISBN 0-395-01237-6). Houghton Mifflin.
Bremner, Kate F.
--A Book of Song Games and Ball Games. N.D. A. S. Barnes and Company.
Bremner, Kate F., adapted by.
--More Song Games. N.D. A. S. Barnes and Company.
Brenda
--A Saturday's Bairn. N.D. T. Whittaker.
Breneman, Steven Bret (1943-)
--Fly Away Home. Joy, Carol (1957-), illus. LC 84-6252. (Orig.). (gr. 2-6). c.1984. (ISBN 0-87743-183-3). Bellwood Press.
Brenizer, Meredith Marshall, ed. see Wentworth, Ruth Starbuck.
Brennan, Dennis
--Adventures in Courage: The Skymasters. (Illus.). (gr. 6-8). 1968. Reilly & Lee.
Brennan, Gale, jt. auth. see LaFleur, Tom.
Brennan, Gale P.
--Bingo the Bear, Animal Antics. (Illus.). (gr. 1-4). 1981. (ISBN 0-516-09107-7). Childrens.
--Dugan the Duck. (Illus.). (Animal Antics Ser.). 1980. (ISBN 0-516-09101-8). Childrens.
--Earl the Squirrel. Flint, Russ, illus. 16p. (Orig.). (gr. k-6). 1981. (ISBN 0-8249-8003-4). Ideals.
--Earl the Squirrel, Animal Antics. (Illus.). (gr. 1-4). 1981. (ISBN 0-516-09108-5). Childrens.
--Elihu the Elephant. (Illus.). (gr. 1-4). 1980. (ISBN 0-516-09102-6). Childrens.
--Gloomy Gus the Hippopotamus. (Illus.). (gr. 1-4). 1980. (ISBN 0-516-09105-0). Childrens.
--Here Come the Clowns. Bond, Bruce, illus. (Illus.). 32p. (Orig.). (gr. 1-4). 1980. (ISBN 0-89542-931-4). Ideals.
--In the Land of Sniggle-Dee Bloop. (Illus.). 1980. (ISBN 0-516-09172-7). Childrens.
--In the Land of Sniggle-Dee-Bloop. Dillon, Mike, illus. (Illus.). 48p. (Orig.). (ps-3). 1980. (ISBN 0-89542-936-5). Ideals.
--Isadore the Dinosaur, Animal Antics. (Illus.). (gr. 1-4). 1981. (ISBN 0-516-09109-3). Childrens.
--Spunky the Monkey. (Illus.). (Animal Antics Ser.). (gr. 1-4). 1981. (ISBN 0-516-09110-7). Childrens.
--Toulouse the Mouse. (Illus.). (Animal Antics Ser.). (gr. 1-4). 1981. (ISBN 0-516-09111-5). Childrens.
--Toulouse the Mouse. Flint, Russ, illus. 16p. (Orig.). (gr. k-6). 1981. (ISBN 0-8249-8004-2). Ideals.
--Wooly the Wolf. (Illus.). (Animal Antics Ser.). (gr. 1-4). 1981. (ISBN 0-516-09112-3). Childrens.
Brennan, Gale P. & LaFleur, Thomas J.
--Elihu the Elephant. (Illus.). (Brennan Bks.). N.D. (ISBN 0-685-84613-X). Brennan Bks.
--Gloomy Gus the Hippopotamus. (Illus.). (Brennan Bks.). N.D. (ISBN 0-685-84614-8). Brennan Bks.
--Ulysses S. Ant & Robert E. Flea. (Illus.). (Brennan Bks.). N.D. (ISBN 0-685-84617-2). Brennan Bks.
Brennan, Gerald Thomas (1898-)
--Angel City. 1938. Bruce Pub Co.
--Christmas Storybook. 1957. Bruce Pub Co.
--Father Brennan favorite stories. N.D. Bruce Publishing Company.
--Father Brennan's Christmas Storybook. Eby, George, illus. LC 54-135137. unpaged. illus. 21cm. (Christian child's stories, 2). 1954. Bruce Pub. Co.
--Father Brennan's Tales for Tiny Tots. Eby, George, illus. LC 54-13514. unpaged. illus. 21cm. (Christian child's stories, 1). 1954. Bruce Pub. Co.
--Father Brennan's Tip-Top Tales. Pollard, George, illus. LC 55-4519. unpaged. illus. 21cm. (Christian child's stories, 7). 1955. Bruce Pub. Co.
--Father Brennan's Treasure Chest of Stories. Eby, George, illus. LC 54-13515. unpaged. illus. 21cm. (Christian child's stories, 3). 1954. Bruce Pub. Co.
--The Ghost of Kingdom Come. LC 40-34732. 143 p. incl. front. illus. 20 1/2 cm. c.1940. The Bruce Publishing Company.
--God Died at Three O'Clock. 1947. Bruce Publishing Co.
--The Good Bad Boy: The Diary of an Eighth-Grade Boy. LC 42-22613. 128 p. 20 cm. 1942. The Bruce Publishing Company.
--The Man Who Dared a King. 1941. Bruce Pub Co.
--The Man Who Never Died. 1946. Bruce Pub Co.
--My Jesus. 1960. Bruce Pub Co.
--Tip top tales. 1955. Bruce Publishing Company.
--Toby's Shadow. LC 56-111529. 94p. illus. 20cm. 1956. Bruce Pub. Co.
--Toby's Shadow: A Story for Children. LC 45-22785. 96 p. illus. 20 cm. 1944. Catechetical Guild.
--When Jesus Came. 1956. Bruce Pub Co.
Brennan, Joseph Killorin
--Gobo and the River. Hearn, Diane Dawson, illus. LC 84-22369. (Illus.). 44 p. 22cm. c.1985. (ISBN 0-03-004552-5). Holt, Rinehart and Winston.
Brennan, Joseph Lomas see Lomas, Steve, pseud.
Brennan, Joseph Lomas (1903-)
--Call of the Tide. Lomas, Steve, pseud. LC 59-12764. 190p. 22cm. 1959. J. Messner.
--Diamond Head Diver. Lomas, Steve, pseud. LC 63-12151. 161 p. illus. 21 cm. (gr. 6-8). c.1963. Washburn.
--Fishing Fleet Boy. Lomas, Steve, pseud. Kenyon, Norman, illus. LC 62-15949. (Illus.). (A Signal Bk.). (gr. 7-9). 1963. (ISBN 0-385-02582-3). Doubleday.
--Frog-Suited Fighters. LC 64-10641. 182 p. 21 cm. c.1964. Chilton Books.
--Heart of the Sea. LC 58-6224. 243p. 21cm. 1958. Dodd, Mead.
--Hot Rod Thunder. Coggins, Jack Banham (1914-), illus. LC 62-8928. (Illus.). 144 p. 22cm. (Signal book). 1962. Doubleday.
--A Man Grows Tall. Lomas, Steve, pseud. LC 58-114906. 188p. 22cm. 1958. Messner.
--Pacific Blue. Lomas, Steve, pseud. LC 62-18960. (gr. 7-9). 1962. (ISBN 0-679-27048-5). Washburn.
--Thunder on the Beach. 1st ed. LC 61-11602. 175p. 21cm. 1961. Chilton Co., Book Division.
--Tuna Clipper Challenge. LC 57-6035. 209p. 21cm. 1957. Dodd, Mead.
--Waikiki Beachboy. 1st ed. LC 62-151656. 169p. 22cm. 1962. Chilton Co., Book Division.
Brennan, Nicholas Stephen (1948-)
--Jasper and the Giant. Brennan, Nicholas Stephen (1948-), illus. LC 70-122921. (Illus.). 24 p. 27cm. 1970. (ISBN 0-03-085201-3). Holt, Rinehart and Winston.
--Olaf's Incredible Machine. Brennan, Nicholas Stephen (1948-), illus. LC 74-16386. (Illus.). 25 p. 28cm. 1975, c.1973. (ISBN 0-525-61008-1). Windmill Books.
Brennan, Patricia D.
--Hitchety Hatchety up I Go!. Rayevsky, Robert, illus. LC 85-4124. (Illus.). 32 p. 24cm. c.1985. (ISBN 0-02-712300-6). Macmillan.
Brenner, Anita (1905-1974)
--The Boy Who Could Do Anything. Charlot, Jean (1898-1979), illus. 128p. (gr. k-7). 1942. (ISBN 0-201-09133-X, Young Scott Bks). A-W.
--The Boy Who Could Do Anything: & Other Mexican Folk Tales. Charlot, Jean (1898-1979), illus. LC 42-361082. 3 p. l., 11-134, 2 p. illus (part col.) 25 cm. 1942. W. R. Scott, Inc.
--Dumb Juan & the Bandits. Charlot, Jean (1898-1979), illus. LC 57-9710. unpaged. illus. 23cm. 1957. Young Scott Books.
--A Hero by Mistake. Charlot, Jean (1898-1979), illus. LC 52-7273. 48p. (gr. 1-5). 1953. (ISBN 0-201-09223-9, A-W Childrens). A-W. **Award: (NYT).**
--A Hero by Mistake. Charlot, Jean (1898-1979), illus. LC 52-7273. 43p. illus. 23cm. (Young Scott books). 1953. W. R. Scott. **Award: (NYT).**
--I Want to Fly. Bloch, Lucienne (1909-), illus. LC 43-15135. 34 p. col. illus. 24 1/2 x 21 cm. c.1943. W. R. Scott Inc.
--The Timid Ghost. 48p. (gr. 3-6). 1966. (ISBN 0-201-09371-5, A-W Childrens). A-W.
--The Timid Ghost: Or, What Would You Do with a Sackful of Gold?. Charlot, Jean (1898-1979), illus. LC 66-11406. 1v. (unpaged) col. illus. 29cm. (Young Scott bk.). c.1966. Scott.
Brenner, Barbara Johnes (1925-)
--Amy's Doll. Katzoff, Sy, photos by. LC 63-9101. unpaged. illus. 27 cm. 1963. Knopf.
--Baltimore Orioles. Higginbottom, Jeffrey Winslow (1945-), illus. LC 73-14327. (Illus.). 5 7/8 x 8 1/2. 64p. (18 pt.). (Nature I Can Read Bks.). (gr. k-3). 1974. (ISBN 0-06-020665-9) Har-Row.
--Barto Takes the Subway. Katzoff, Sy, photos by. LC 60-13033. (Illus.). (gr. 2-5). 1961. (ISBN 0-394-90933-X). Knopf.
--Beef Stew. Johnson, John Emil (1929-), illus. LC 65-11965. (Illus.). 1 v. (unpaged. 23cm. (A Read alone book). 1965. Knopf.
--A Bird in the Family. LC 62-51664. (Illus.). 59 p. 23cm. (Young Scott books). 1962. W. R. Scott.
--A Bird in the Family. Brenner, Fred (1920-), illus. 64p. (gr. 2-6). 1962. (ISBN 0-201-09117-8). A-W.
--Cunningham's Rooster. Rockwell, Anne F. (1934-), illus. LC 74-12285. (Illus.). 32 p. 27cm. 1975. (ISBN 0-8193-0783-1). (ISBN 0-8193-0783-1). Parents' Magazine Press.
--A Dog I Know. 1st ed. Brenner, Fred (1920-), illus. LC 82-47572. p. cm. c.1983. (ISBN 0-06-020684-5). (ISBN 0-06-020685-3). Harper & Row.
--Faces. Ancona, George (1929-), illus. LC 70-102737. (Illus.). 48 p. 24cm. 1970. E. P. Dutton.
--The Five Pennies. Blegvad, Erik (1923-), illus. LC 63-9115. 1 v. (unpaged) col. illus. 23 cm. c.1964. Knopf.
--The Flying Patchwork Quilt. Brenner, Fred (1920-), illus. 48p. (gr. 1-4). 1965. (ISBN 0-201-09187-9, A-W Childrens). A-W.
--The Flying Patchwork Quilt. Brenner, Fred (1920-), illus. LC 65-12578. 1v. (unpaged) col. illus. 25cm. (Young Scott bk.). c.1965. Scott.
--The Gorilla Signs Love. LC 84-841. 160p. 1st U.S. edition. (gr. 9 up). 1984. (ISBN 0-688-00995-6). Lothrop.
--Hemi: A Mule. Higginbottom, Jeffrey Winslow (1945-), illus. LC 73-5479. (Illus.). 128p. (gr. 3-7). 1973. (ISBN 0-06-020648-9, HarpJ). (ISBN 0-06-020649-7). Har-Row.
--Hemi: A Mule. Higginbottom, Jeffrey Winslow (1945-), illus. (Illus.). 128p. (Harper Trophy Ser.). (gr. 3-7). 1975. (ISBN 0-06-440063-8, Trophy). Har-Row.
--If You Were an Ant. Brenner, Fred (1920-), illus. LC 72-11242. (Illus.). 32p. (ps-3). 1973. (ISBN 0-06-020619-5, HarpJ). Har-Row.
--A Killing Season. LC 80-69993. viii, 182 p. 22cm. c.1981. (ISBN 0-590-07674-4). Four Winds Press.
--Little One Inch. Brenner, Fred (1920-), illus. LC 76-45434. (Illus.). 32 p. 21cm. 1977. (ISBN 0-698-20408-5). Coward, McCann & Geoghegan.
--Lizard Tails & Cactus Spines. LC 75-6297. (Illus.). 112p. (gr. 3-7). 1975. (ISBN 0-06-020667-5, HarpJ). Har-Row.
--Mr. Tall & Mr. Small. LC 66-11407. 32p. (ps-2). 1966. (ISBN 0-201-09281-6, A-W Childrens). A-W.
--Mr. Tall and Mr. Small. Ungerer, Tomi, pseud. (1931-), illus. Ungerer, Jean Thomas. LC 66-11407. 1v. (unpaged)) col. illus. 27cm. (Young Scott easy to read bk.). c.1966. Scott.
--Mystery of the Disappearing Dogs. Sims, Blanche, illus. LC 82-186. (Illus.). 120 p. 20cm. (Capers). c.1982. (ISBN 0-394-95162-X). (ISBN 0-394-85162-5). Knopf.
--Mystery of the Plumed Serpent. Sims, Blanche, illus. LC 80-17316. (Illus.). 118 p. 20cm. (Capers). 1981, c.1972. (ISBN 0-394-84531-5). (ISBN 0-394-94531-X). Knopf : Distributed by Random House.
--Nicky's Sister. Johnson, John Emil (1929-), illus. LC 66-13778. 1 v. (unpaged) col. illus. 23 cm. (Read alone book). 1966. Knopf.
--On the Frontier with Mr. Audubon. (Illus.). (gr. 3-6). 1977. (ISBN 0-698-20385-2, Coward). Putnam Pub Group.
--The Prince & the Pink Blanket. Langner, Nola (1930-), illus. LC 80-10950. (Illus.). 32 p. 28cm. c.1980. (ISBN 0-590-07614-0). Four Winds Press.
--A Snake-Lover's Diary. LC 79-98113. (Illus.). 90, 6 p. 23cm. 1970. Young Scott Books.
--The Snow Parade. O'Keefe, Mary T., illus. LC 83-18999. (Illus.). 32p. (ps-1). 1984. (ISBN 0-517-55210-8). Crown.
--Somebody's Slippers, Somebody's Shoes. Jacobs, Leslie, illus. LC 57-971362. unpaged. illus. 23cm. (Young Scott books). 1957. W. R. Scott.
--Summer of the Houseboat. Brenner, Fred (1920-), illus. LC 67-19482. (Illus.). 14 b&w line drawings. 176p. (gr. 3-7). 1968. (ISBN 0-394-81712-5). (ISBN 0-394-91712-X). Knopf.
--Wagon Wheels. Bolognese, Donald Alan (1934-), illus. LC 76-21391. (Illus.). 64p. (A Trophy I Can Read Book Ser.). (gr. k-3). 1981. (ISBN 0-06-[illegible], Trophy). Har-Row.
--Wagon Wheels. Bolognese, Donald Alan (1934-), illus. LC 76-21391. (Illus.). 64 p. 23cm. (18pt.). (gr. k-3). c.1978. (ISBN 0-06-020668-3). (ISBN 0-06-020669-1). Harper and Row. **Award: (ALA).**
--A Year in the Life of Rosie Bernard. Sandin, Joan (1942-), illus. LC 70-157902. (Illus.). vii, 179 p. 22cm. 1971. (ISBN 0-06-020657-8). Harper & Row.
Brenner, Barbara Johnes (1925-), adapted by.
--Walt Disney's The Penguin That Hated the Cold. LC 72-12600. (Illus.). 24p. (Disney's Wonderful World of Reading Ser.: No. 7). (ps-3). 1973. (ISBN 0-394-82628-0, BYR). (ISBN 0-394-92628-5). Random.
--Walt Disney's Three Little Pigs. LC 72-5132. (Illus.). 41 p. 25cm. (Disney's wonderful world of reading). 1972. (ISBN 0-394-82522-5). (ISBN 0-394-82522-5). Random House.
Brenner, Barbara Johnes (1925-) & Williams, Vera B.
--Ostrich Feathers. LC 77-24284. p. cm. c.1978. (ISBN 0-8193-0921-4). (ISBN 0-8193-0922-2). Parents' Magazine Press.
Brenner, Henry (1881-)
--The House We Live In. (Being the lamentable comedy of Reynard the Fox as it is played on the jungle-stage of today). (Illus.). 20cm. 72p. 1932. The Raven.
Brenner, Peter
--King for One Day. Wyss, Hanspeter, illus. LC 74-151271. (Illus.). 32 p. 30cm. 1971. Scroll Press.
Brent, Joanna
--A Child Likes. Brent, Adalie, illus. LC 72-193091. (Illus.). 83 p. 34cm. c.1971. Louisiana Arts and Science Center.
Brent, Stuart
--Mister Toast & the Secret of Gold Hill. Porter, George, illus. LC 78-117235. (Illus.). drawings. 96p. (gr. 4-6). 1970. (ISBN 0-397-31145-1). Lippincott.
--Mr. Toast and the Woolly Mammoth. Obligado, Lilian Isabel (1931-), illus. LC 66-11912. 94p. illus. 24cm. c.1966. (ISBN 0-670-49381-3). Viking.
--The Strange Disappearance of Mr. Toast. Goldstein, Leslie, illus. LC 64-12640. 62 p. illus. 25 cm. 1964. Viking Press.
Brentano, Clemens Maria (1778-1842)
--Fairy Tales from Brentano. Freiligrath-Kroeker, Kate, Mrs. (1845-1904), tr. LC 26-299. 326 p., 1 l., col. front., plates. 20 1/2 cm. 1925. Frederick A. Stokes Company.
--Fairy Tales From Brentano. Gould, F. Carruthers, illus. Kroeker, Kate F., tr. 1889. A. C. Armstrong & Son's.
--Gockel, Hinkel and Gackeleia: or, The Magic Stone. Dole, Nathan Haskell, Mrs., tr. N.D. Silver Burdett & Co.
--The Legend of the Rose Petal. Zwerger, Lisbeth, illus. LC 84-27386. (Illus.). 25 p. 34cm. c.1985. (ISBN 0-907234-71-2). Picture Book Studio USA : Distributed by Alphabet Press. **Award: (NYT).**
--New Fairy Tales. Gould, F. Carruthers, illus. Kroeker, Kate F., tr. N.D. A. C. Armstrong & Son's.
--Schoolmaster Whackwell's Wonderful Sons: A Fairy Tale. Orgel, Doris (1929-), retold by. Sendak, Maurice Bernard (1928-), illus. LC 62-90025. 86p. illus. 25cm. 1962. (ISBN 0-394-81586-6). Random House.
--The Tale of Gockel Hinkel and Gackeliah. (Illus.). 1961. Random House Inc.
Brereton, Frederick Sadleir (1872-)
--A Gallant Grenadier. (Illus.). N.D. Caldwell.
--The Great Aeroplane. (The Aviation Library). N.D. Dodge.
--The Great Aeroplane: A Tale of Adventures in Mid-Air. Hodgson, Edward S., illus. (Illus.). N.D. Caldwell.
--The Great Airship. (The Aviation Library). N.D. Dodge.
--A Hero of Sedan: A TAle of the Franco-Prussian War. (Illus.). N.D. Caldwell.
--How Canada Was Won: A Tale of Wolfe and Quebec. Rainey, William R. I. (1852-1936), illus. LC 9-22947. vii, 387 p. incl. maps. front., plates. 19 1/2 cm. c.1908. H. M. Caldwell Co.

--Indian and Scout: A Tale of the Gold Rush to California. Rainey, WilliamR. I. (1852-1936), illus. (Illus.). N.D. Caldwell.

--John Bargreave's Gold: The Adventures of a Rhodes Scholarship Boy in the Region of Panama. (Illus.). N.D. Caldwell.

--Jones of the 64th: A Tale of the Battles of Assaye and Laswaree. Rainey, William R. I. (1852-1936), illus. LC 7-301607. 4 p. l., 313 p. front., 5 pl., map, plan. 20 cm. c.1907. Blackie and Son, Limited.

--Jones of the 64th: A Tale of the Battles of Assaye and Laswaree. Rainey, William R. I. (1852-1936), illus. (Illus.). N.D. Caldwell.

--One of the Fighting Scouts. (The Rugby Series for Boys and Girls). N.D. A. L. Burt Company.

--Roger the Bold: A Tale of the Conquest of Mexico. (Illus.). N.D. Caldwell.

--Roger the Bold: A Tale of the Conquest of Mexico. Wood, Stanley L. (1866-1928), illus. LC 6-34636. 411 p. front., illus. (maps) 8 pl. 19 1/2 cm. 1906. Blackie and Son, Limited.

--Roughriders of the Pampas: A Tale of Ranch Life in South America. (Illus.). N.D. Caldwell.

--Under the Star Spangled Banner. (The Rugby Series for Boys and Girls). N.D. A. L. Burt Company.

--With Rifle and Bayonet. (Illus.). (Scribner-Blackie Series of books for young people). N.D. Charles Scribner's Sons.

--With Roberts to Candahar: A Tale of the Third Afghan War. (Illus.). N.D. Caldwell.

--With Roberts to Candahar: A Tale of the Third Afghan War. Rainey, William R. I. (1852-1936), illus. LC 6-34643. 362 p. front., 5 pl. 19 1/2 cm. 1906. Blackie and Son, Limited.

--With Shield and Assegai. (Illus.). (Scribner-Blackie Series of Books for young people). N.D. Charles Scribner's Sons.

--With Wolseley to Kumasi: A Story of the First Ashanti War. (Illus.). N.D. Caldwell.

--With Wolseley to Kumasi: A Tale of the First Ashanti War. Browne, Gordon Frederick (1858-1932), illus. LC 7-30159. 4 p. l., 347 p. front., 7 pl., map. 19 1/2 cm. 1908, c.1907. Blackie and Son, Limited.

Bresier, Mrs.

--Rectory and the Manor. Brock, Carey, Mrs., tr. from Fr. 400p. N.D. E. P. Dutton.

Breslin, Patricia

--Freddie, the Firefly Who Couldn't Light up. Phillippi, Charles, illus. LC 46-1787. 35 p. illus. 28 x 21 1/2 cm. c.1946. Calif., K. Miles.

Bretherton, J. C.

--Emma's Well. 1976. (ISBN 0-685-86595-9). State Mutual Bk.

Bretnall, George H

--Bulo and Lele. LC 54-7720. 208p. 22cm. 1954. Comet Press Books.

Brett, Bernard (1925-)

--Ghosts. LC 82-13373. (Illus.). 126 p. 19cm. (The Chiller Ser.). 1983, c.1981. (ISBN 0-671-46159-1). Wanderer Books/Simon & Schuster.

--Monsters. LC 82-13452. (Illus.). 126 p. 19cm. (The Chiller Ser.). 1983, c.1981. Wanderer Books.

Brett, David

--David Brett's Nurseryland. (Illus.). N.D. Cupples & Leon.

Brett, Dorothy, jt. auth. see Bright, Robert.

Brett, Edna Payson

--Circus Day & Other Adventure Stories. Riley, Garada Clark, illus. N.D. Rand McNally.

--A Merry Scout. Riley, Garada Clark, illus. LC 55-458232. 64p. illus. 20cm. 1922. Rand McNally.

Brett, Grace Neff (1900-1975)

--Hatsy Catsy. Brett, Grace Neff & Brett, George J., photos by LC 76-88066. (Illus.). 29cm. 37p. (Third Grade Bk. Ser.). (gr. 3-4). N.D. (ISBN 0-513-00472-6). Denison.

--The Runaway. Gotlieb, Jules, illus. LC 58-10091. (Illus.). 223 p. 23cm. 1958. Follett Pub. Co.

--Squiffy the Skunk. Brett, Grace Neff & Brett, George J., photos by LC 53-27751. unpaged. illus. 21cm. (Rand McNally book-elf book, 476). c.1953. Rand McNally.

--That Willy and Wally. LC 64-16372. 159 p. illus. 21 cm. 1964. A. Whitman.

Brett, Jan (1949-)

--Annie and the Wild Animals. Brett, Jan (1949-), illus. LC 84-19818. p. cm. 1985. (ISBN 0-395-37800-1). Houghton Mifflin Co.

--Fritz and the Beautiful Horses. Brett, Jan (1949-), illus. LC 80-26915. (Illus.). 31 p. 24cm. 1981. (ISBN 0-395-30850-X). Houghton Mifflin.

Brett, Mary Elizabeth see Brett, Molly, pseud.

Brett, Molly, pseud., see Brett, Mary Elizabeth.

Brett, Molly, pseud.

--The Japanese Garden. Brett, Mary Elizabeth. Brett, Molly, pseud., illus. Brett, Mary Elizabeth. LC 59-11981. (Illus.). 44 p. 22cm. 1959. Warne.

--The Little Garden. Brett, Mary Elizabeth. Brett, Molly, pseud., illus. Brett, Mary Elizabeth. LC 37-27296. 1936. Frederick Warne & Co.

--The Story of a Toy Car. Brett, Mary Elizabeth. Brett, Molly, pseud., illus. Brett, Mary Elizabeth. LC 60-17406. 22cm. 47p. N.D. Frederick Warne & Co.

Brette, Jean De La see De La Brette, Jean.

Brevik, Kristine

--Search for Silver Mountain. (Illus.). (gr. 1-3). 1968. (ISBN 0-8382-0732-4). Hale.

Brewer, Jo

--The Mysterious Treasure of Cloud Rock. Elgin, Jill, illus. LC 52-12960. 118p. illus. 22cm. 1953. Dutton.

Brewer, John Mason (1896-1975)

--Dog Ghosts and Other Texas Negro Folk Tales. (Illus.). 124p. 1958. University Of Texas Press.

Brewer, Kate

--Fanciful Tales From Legends of the Adirondack Indians. N.D. Neale Publishing Co.

Brewerton, Michelle

--How Ryan Learned to Repent. Romney, S. P., illus. LC 85-101702. (Illus.). 24 p. 28cm. c.1984. (ISBN 0-88494-539-1). Bookcraft.

Brewster, Benjamin, pseud., see Folsom, Franklin Brewster.

Brewster, Edith Gilman

--Some Three Hundred Years Ago. LC 22-13417. 144 p. incl. front., illus. 19 cm. c.1922. The W. B. Ranney Company.

Brewster, Frances Stanton (1857-1926)

--When Mother Was a Little Girl. (Little Maid Ser.). N.D. George W. Jacobs.

--When Mother Was a Little Girl. (Illus.). (Little Maid Ser.). N.D. Hurst and Company.

Brewster, Frances Stanton (1857-1926) & Thomas, Emma A., Mrs.

--Song Stories and Songs for Children. LC 98-698. 139 p. 24 x 19 cm. 1898. American Book Company.

Brewster, Patience

--Ellsworth and the Cats from Mars. Bewster, Patience, illus. LC 80-16298. (Illus.). 32 p. 26cm. (gr. 1-5). c.1981. (ISBN 0-395-29612-9). Houghton Mifflin/Clarion Books.

Brewster, Patience, jt. auth. see Brightbill, Steven.

Brewster, Patience, ed. see Ruskin, John (1819-1900) & Pearson, Mrs.

Brewster, Paul G

--Children's Games and Rhymes. LC 75-35063. p. cm. (Studies in Play and Games). 1976, c.1952. (ISBN 0-405-07914-1). Arno Press.

Brewton, John Edmund, jt. ed. see Brewton, Sara Westbrook.

Brewton, John Edmund, jt. ed. see Brewton, Sara Westbrook.

Brewton, John Edmund (1898-), ed.

--Gaily We Parade. 1940. MacMillan Co.

--Gaily We Parade: A Collection of Poems About People Here, There and Everywhere. Lawson, Robert (1892-1957), illus. 1962. Macmillan.

--Under the Tent of the Sky. Lawson, Robert (1892-1957), illus. (Illus.). (gr. 4-6). 1937. (ISBN 0-02-712470-3). Macmillan.

Brewton, John Edmund (1898-) & Blackburn, Lorraine A, eds.

--In the Witch's Kitchen: Poems for Halloween. Barton, Harriet, illus. LC 79-7822. p. cm. c.1980. (ISBN 0-690-04061-X). (ISBN 0-690-04062-8). Crowell.

--In the Witch's Kitchen: Poems for Halloween. Barton, Harriet, illus. 1980. Harper.

--They've Discovered a Head in the Box for the Bread: And Other Laughable Limericks. Krahn, Fernando (1935-), illus. LC 77-26598. (Illus.). 129 p. 21cm. c.1978. (ISBN 0-690-01388-4). Crowell.

--They've Discovered a Head in the Box for the Bread & Other Laughable Limericks. Krahn, Fernando (1935-), illus. LC 77-26598. (Illus.). (gr. 3-7). 1978. (ISBN 0-690-01388-4, TYC-J). (ISBN 0-690-03883-6). Har-Row.

Brewton, Sara Westbrook & Brewton, John Edmund (1898-), eds.

--America Forever New: A Book of Poems. Grifalconi, Ann (1929-), illus. LC 67-23663. (Illus.). b&w ils. indexes of authors, first lines, titles. 246p. (gr. 4 up). 1968. (ISBN 0-690-06988-X, TYC-J). Har-Row.

--America Forever New: A Books of Poems. (Illus.). 1968. (ISBN 0-690-06988-X). Thomas Y Crowell.

--Birthday Candles Burning Bright: A Treasury of Birthday Poetry. Bock, Vera, illus. LC 60-11211. (Illus.). 199 p. 24cm. (gr. 4-6). 1960. (ISBN 0-02-712560-2). Macmillan.

--Bridled with Rainbows: Poems About Many Things of Earth and Sky. Bock, Vera, illus. LC 49-7721. xix. 191 p. illus. 24 cm. (gr. 4-6). 1949. (ISBN 0-02-712680-3). Macmillan Co.

--Christmas Bells Are Ringing. Merwin, Decie (1894-1961), illus. (Illus.). (gr. 4-6). 1964. (ISBN 0-02-712790-7). Macmillan.

--Gaily We Parade. Lawson, Robert (1892-1957), illus. (Illus.). (gr. 4-6). 1967. (ISBN 0-02-712340-5). Macmillan.

--Laughable Limericks. Fetz, Ingrid (1915-), illus. LC 65-16179. (Illus.). (gr. 2 up). 1965. (ISBN 0-690-48667-7, TYC-J). Har-Row.

--My Tang's Tungled and Other Ridiculous Situations. Booth, Graham Charles (1935-), illus. 1973. Harper.

--My Tang's Tungled and Other Ridiculous Situations. Booth, Graham Charles (1935-), illus. LC 73-254. (Illus.). 1973. (ISBN 0-690-57223-9). Thomas Y Crowell.

--My Tangs Tungled and Other Ridiculous Situations: Humorous Poems. Booth, Graham Charles (1935-), illus. LC 73-254. (Illus.). xiii, 111 p. 21cm. 1973. Crowell.

--Of Quarks, Quasars & Other Quirks: Quizzical Poems for the Supersonic Age. Blake, Quentin (1932-), illus. LC 76-54747. (Illus.). (gr. 4 up). 1977. (ISBN 0-690-01286-1, TYC-J). Har-Row.

--Shrieks at Midnight: Macabre Poems, Eerie & Humorous. Raskin, Ellen (1928-1984), illus. LC 69-11824. (Illus.). index. 177p. (gr. 4 up). 1969. (ISBN 0-690-73518-9, TYC-J). Har-Row. **Award: (ALA).**

--Sing a Song of Seasons. Bock, Vera, illus. (Illus.). (gr. 4-6). 1955. (ISBN 0-02-712890-3). Macmillan.

Breyfogle, William A

--Wagon Wheels: A Story of the National Road. 1st ed. Schule, Clifford H., illus. LC 55-119060. 192p. illus. 21cm. (American heritage series). 1956. Aladdin Books.

Brian, Janeen

--Friends Learn Ballet. u.s. ed. Gully, Jim, illus. LC 85-16319. p. cm. (Growing up). 1985. (ISBN 0-918831-42-3). (ISBN 0-918831-18-0). G. Stevens Pub.

Brice, Tony , illus.

--The Bashful Goldfish. Brice, Tony, illus. LC 38-10618. 61 p. illus. 17 1/2 cm. c.1938. Rand, McNally & Company.

--Little Bobo and His Blue Jacket. Brice, Tony, illus. LC 44-3055. 40 p. illus. (part col.) 23 x 20 cm. N.D. Rand McNally & Company.

--Little Hippo. Brice, Tony, illus. N.D. Rand McNally & Co.

--Little Hippo and His Red Bicycle. Brice, Tony, illus. LC 48-3306. 40 p. illus. (part col.) 23 cm. 1945. Rand McNally.

--Mother Goose. N.D. Rand McNally & co.

--So Long. Brice, Tony, illus. LC 37-14274. 32 p. illus. (part col.) 17 cm. c.1937. Rand, McNally & Company.

--The Tony Brice Picture Book: A Group of Nursery Favorites. Brice, Tony, illus. LC 42-21065. 71, 1 p. illus. (part col.) 30 x 24 1/2 cm. 1942. Rand McNally & Company.

Brick, John (1922-1973)

--Ben Bryan, Morgan Rifleman. 1st ed. LC 63-7415. 150 p. 21cm. 1963. Duell, Sloan and Pearce.

--Captives of the Senecas. LC 64-12442. 149 p. 21 cm. 1964. Duell, Sloan and Pearce.

--Captives Of The Senecas. 1964. (ISBN 0-8382-0152-0, Cadmus Books). E. M. Hale and Company.

--Eagle of Niagara: The Story of David Harper and His Indian Captivity. 1st ed. LC 55-5578. 253p. 22cm. (Cavalcade books). 1955. Doubleday.

--On the old Frontier: A Tim Murphy Adventure. LC 67-2705. (Illus.). 21cm. 157p. 1967. G P Putman's Sons.

--The Raid. LC 60-12842. 184p. 21cm. c.1960. Duell, Sloan and Pearce.

--Tomahawk Trail. LC 62-8524. 149 p. 21cm. 1962. Duell, Sloan and Pearce.

--Yankees on the Run. LC 61-14129. 149 p. 21cm. 1961. Duell, Sloan and Pearce.

Brickford, Faith

--Daddy Joe's Fiddle. (Illus.). (Editha Series.). N.D. Dodge Publishing Co.

Brickhill, Paul Chester Jerome (1916-)

--The Great Escape. 1950. Norton Company.

Brickman, M.

--This Little Pigeon went to Market. N.D. Rand McNally Publications.

--The Three Bears. N.D. Rand MCNally Publications.

Bridge, Ann, pseud., see O'Malley, Mary Dolling Sanders.

Bridge, Ann, pseud. (1889-1924)

--The Ginger Griffin. O'Malley, Mary Dolling Sanders. 1934. Little, Brown & Co.

Bridge, Stephanie Marie

--Puritan Fairy Tales. N.D. United Publishers Association.

Bridgeman, Elizabeth, jt. auth. see Kahn, Joan.

Bridgers, Sue Ellen (1942-)

--All Together Now: A Novel. LC 78-12244. 238 p. 22cm. c.1979. (ISBN 0-394-84098-4). (ISBN 0-394-94098-9). Knopf : Distributed by Random House. **Awards: (ALA); (BGH).**

--Home Before Dark. LC 76-8661. 176 p. 22cm. c.1976. (ISBN 0-394-83299-X). Knopf : Distributed by Random House. **Award: (ALA).**

--Notes for Another Life. LC 81-1673. 256p. 1981. (ISBN 0-394-84889-6). (ISBN 0-394-94889-0). Knopf.

Bridges, Christina

--The Hero. Batten, Linda, illus. (Illus.). 29p. (gr. k-6). 1981. (ISBN 0-917002-39-3). Joyce Media.

Bridges, Roy

--Rat's Castle. N.D. Appleton Century Co.

Bridges, Thomas Charles (1868-)

--The Girl from Golden. (Three Star Bks.). N.D. Frederick Warne & Co.

--Jackie Hightree: The Adventures of a Squirrel, from Animal Autobiographies. Fielding, Jane, ed. LC 13-15902. 1 p. l., 9-134 p. incl. 2 pl. col. front. 20 cm. $0.50. c.1913. A. L. Chatterton Co.

--The Life Story of a Squirrel. N.D. Macmillan.

--Luck or Pluck. (The Magnet Library). N.D. Frederick Warne & Co.

--Luck or Pluck. (The Star Library). N.D. Frederick Warne & Co.

--Martin Crusoe: A Boy's Adventure on Wizard Island. Evison, C. Henry, illus. LC 20-16155. 2 p. l., 263 p. col. front., plates. 19 1/2 cm. 1920. Harcourt, Brace and Howe.

--The River Riders. (The Albion Library). N.D. Frederick Warne & Co.

--The Secret of Sevenstones Key. (The Crown Library for Boys & Girls). N.D. Frederick Warne & Co.

--The Secret of Smoking Swamp. (The Crown Library for Boys & Girls). N.D. Frederick Warne & Co.

--Sons of the Air. LC 31-41882. 280 p. col. front., plates. 20 cm. 1929. F. Warne & Co., Ltd.

Bridges, Victor

--The Secret of the Creek. LC 31-263677. 319 p. 19 1/2 cm. 1930. Houghton Mifflin Company.

Bridges, William Andrew (1901-)

--The Golden Book of Zoo Animals. Johnson, Scott, illus. LC 62-19103. (Illus.). 60 p. 31cm. (Giant golden book). 1962. Golden Press.

--Lion Island. Haas, Emmy & Dunton, Samuel Cady (1910-1975), illus. LC 65-114857. 62 p. illus. 29 cm. 1965. Morrow.

--Ookie, the Walrus Who Likes People. (Illus.). (gr. k-3). 1962. Morrow.

--Toco Toucan. Wiese, Kurt (1887-1974), illus. 82 p. incl. col. front., illus. (part col.) 22 x 19 cm. c.1940. Harper & Brothers.

--Walt Disney's Animal Adventures in Lands of Ice and Snow. LC 63-23602. 91 p. col. illus. 24 cm. (Badger books). c.1963. Whitman Pub. Co.

Bridgman, Elizabeth Klei (1915-)

--Lullaby for Eggs: A Poem. Jones, Elizabeth Orton (1910-), illus. LC 55-14355. unpaged. illus. 21cm. 1955. Macmillan.

Bridgman, Elizabeth P. (1921-)

--All the Little Bunnies. Bridgman, Elizabeth P. (1921-), illus. LC 76-28815. 48p. (ps-2). 1977. (ISBN 0-689-50068-8, McElderry Bk). Atheneum.

--All the Little Bunnies: A Counting Book. Bridgman, Elizabeth P. (1921-), illus. LC 76-28815. (Illus.). 47 p. 16cm. 1977. Atheneum.

--How to Travel with Grownups. Hazard, Eleanor Lanahan, illus. LC 79-2775. (Illus.). 32 p. 21cm. c.1980. (ISBN 0-690-04009-1). (ISBN 0-690-04010-5). Crowell.

--If I Were a Horse. Bridgman, Elizabeth P. (1921-), illus. LC 77-6079. (Illus.). (gr. k-1). 1977. Dodd.

--Nanny Bear's Cruise. Bridgman, Elizabeth P. (1921-), illus. LC 80-8438. p. cm. 1981. (ISBN 0-06-020688-8). (ISBN 0-06-020689-6). Harper & Row.

--New Dog Next Door. Bridgman, Elizabeth P. (1921-), illus. LC 77-25667. p. cm. c.1978. (ISBN 0-06-020672-1). (ISBN 0-06-020673-X). Harper & Row.

Bridgman, Ethel Comstock

--Soapsuds' Last Year. Humphreys, Donald S., illus. LC 27-18851. ix, 270 p. front., plates. 19 cm. $1.75. c.1927. The Century Co.

--A Year at Miss Austin's. Relyea, Charles M., illus. LC 26-15792. vii p., 2 l., 3-252 p. front., plates. 19 1/2 cm. $1.75. c.1926. The Century Co.

Bridgman, Lewis Jesse (1857-1931)

--Bridgman's Kewts. LC 2-22188. 94 p. col. front., col. illus. 25 1/2 cm. 1902. H. M. Caldwell Company.

--Bunny's House. Bridgman, Lewis Jesse (1857-1931), illus. LC 9-7424. 28 x 21cm. 40p. 1904. H. M. Caldwell Co.

--Bunny's House and Other Rhymes, 3 vols. Bridgman, Lewis Jesse (1857-1931), illus. 40p. incl. col. front., col. illus. (The Nursery Hour Ser.: No. 1). 1905. Set. H M Caldwell Co.

--The Cottontail Twins. (Illus.). 1915. George W. Jacobs & Co.

--I Like Red. 1st ed. Bright, Robert (1902-), illus. unpaged. illus. 21cm. (Junior books). c.1955. Doubleday.
--Jorgoto (Georgie). (ps-3). 1980. (ISBN 0-590-30048-2, Schol Pap). Scholastic Inc.
--Me and the Bears. Bright, Robert (1902-), illus. LC 51-12472. (Illus.). 1 v. (unpaged. (Junior books). c.1951. Doubleday.
--Mi Paraguas Rojo. Bright, Robert (1902-), illus. LC 68-20836. (Illus.). 32 p. 18cm. 1968. W. Morrow.
--Miss Pattie. Bright, Robert (1902-), illus. LC 54-10110. (Illus.). unpaged. 26cm. (Junior books). c.1954. Doubleday.
--My Hopping Bunny. 1st ed. Bright, Robert (1902-), illus. LC 60-7133. unpaged. illus. 25cm. 1960. Doubleday.
--My Hopping Bunny. Bright, Robert (1902-), illus. (ps-1). 1971. (ISBN 0-385-07864-1). Doubleday.
--My Red Umbrella. Bright, Robert (1902-), illus. 1973. Morrow.
--My Red Umbrella. Bright, Robert (1902-), illus. LC 59-7928. (Illus.). 32 p. 18cm. 1959. W. Morrrow.
--Richard Brown & the Dragon. Bright, Robert (1902-), illus. (Illus.). (gr. 1-4). 1952. (ISBN 0-385-07467-0). Doubleday.
--Round, Round World. Bright, Robert (1902-), illus. LC 60-4084. (Illus.). 30 p. 22cm. (Golden beginning reader, 4007). 1960. Golden Press.
--The Travels of Ching. Bright, Robert (1902-), illus. LC 43-51304. 65 p. illus. (part col.) 14 1/2 x 21 cm. c.1943. W. R. Scott, Inc.
--Which Is Willy?. 1st ed. Bright, Robert (1902-), illus. LC 62-10071. unpaged. illus. 22x26cm. (gr. k-3). c.1962. (ISBN 0-385-03384-2). Doubleday.

Bright, Robert (1902-) & Brett, Dorothy (1883-1977)
--Hurrah for Freddie!. 1st ed. Bright, Robert (1902-), illus. LC 53-5295. (Illus.). unpaged. c.1953. Doubleday.

Bright, Sarah, pseud., see Shine, Deborah.

Bright, Sarah, pseud. (1932-)
--Hello Kitty's Bedtime Search. Shine, Deborah. Sullivan, Scott (1952-), illus. LC 82-3719. (Illus.). 24p. (ps). 1982. (ISBN 0-394-85397-0). Random.
--Hello Kitty's Early Day. Shine, Deborah. Gray, J. M. L., illus. LC 83-63390. (Illus.). 31 p. c.1984. (ISBN 0-394-86759-9). Random House.
--Hello Kitty's Paper Kiss. Shine, Deborah. McGowin, Bruce, illus. LC 82-3734. (Illus.). 24p. (ps). 1982. (ISBN 0-394-85398-9). Random.
--My Melody's Good-Night Book. Shine, Deborah. Gray, J. M. L., illus. LC 81-86383. (Illus.). 28p. (Chunky Bks.). (ps). 1982. (ISBN 0-394-85262-1). Random.

Bright, Velma
--The Story of the Little Round Barn. Schultz, Patty, illus. LC 81-65540. (Illus.). 48p. (Orig.). (gr. 2-3). 1981. (ISBN 0-9605968-2-8). (ISBN 0-9605968-3-6). Bright Bks.

Brightbill, Steven & Brewster, Patience
--Children's Storybook: Spencer's a Little Worried. N.D. (ISBN 0-8359-0754-6). Reston.

Brightman, Alan
--Like Me. LC 76-21235. (Illus.). 48 p. c.1976. (ISBN 0-316-10808-1). (ISBN 0-316-10807-3). Little, Brown.

Brighton, Catherine
--My Hands, My World. Brighton, Catherine, illus. LC 84-9670. (Illus.). 32p. (gr. k-3). 1984. (ISBN 0-02-712900-4). Macmillan.

Brightwell, C. L.
--Palissy, The Huguenot Potter. (Illus.). N.D. Methodist Book Concern.
--Palissy, the Huguenot Potter. (Illus.). N.D. Nelson & Phillips.

Brightwell, Miss
--Above Rubies. (The Treasure Library for Young Ladies). N.D. Thomas Nelson & Sons.

Brill, Edith (1899-)
--The Golden Bird. Pienkowski, Jan (1936-), illus. LC 69-14457. (Illus.). 151 p. 24cm. 1970. F. Watts.

Brill, Ethel Claire (1877-)
--The Boy Who Went to the East. N.D. E P Dutton.
--Copper Country Adventure. Adams, Bruce, illus. LC 49-10319. 213 p. illus. 21 cm. 1949. Whittlesey House.
--The Island of Yellow Sands. Wolf, W. H., illus. LC 25-209778. 1 p. l., 7-308 p. front., plates, 20 1/2 cm. 1925. Macrae Smith Company.
--Madeleine Takes Command. Adams, Bruce, illus. LC 46-11941. xii, p., 1 l., 204 p. incl. front., illus. 21 cm. 1946. Whittlesey House, McGraw-Hill Book Company, Inc.
--Red River Trail. Wolf, W. H., illus. LC 27-206650. 310 p. front, plates. 19 cm. c.1927. Macrae Smith Company.
--Rupahu's Warning: A Story of the Great Sioux Outbreak. Rodgers, Richard H. (1876-1953), illus. LC 31-570694. 286 p. front., illus. 20 cm. c.1931. Macrae Smith Company.
--The Secret Cache. (Mystery and Adventure Bks. for Boys). N.D. Cupples & Leon Co.
--The Secret Cache. Wolf, W. H., illus. LC 26-16709. 304 p. front., plates. 19 cm. c.1926. Macrae Smith Company.
--South From Hudson Bay. (Mystery and Adventure Bks. for Boys). N.D. Cupples & Leon Co.
--South from Hudson Bay. Stewart, Walter, illus. LC 29-21929. 319 p. incl. col. front. plates. 19 1/2 cm. c.1929. Macrae, Smith Company.
--When Lighthouses Are Dark: A Story of a Lake Superior Island. LC 21-21700. v. 292 p. front., plates. 19 1/2 cm. 1921. H. Holt and Company.
--White Brother: A Story of the Pontiac Uprising. LC 32-29683. vi, 250 p. 19 cm. c.1932. H. Holt and Company.

Brill, George Reiter (1867-)
--Little Bobby Bumpkin. Brill, George Reiter (1867-), illus. LC 2-23312. 21cm. 62p. 1902. D. Biddle.
--Rhymes of the Golden Age. Brill, George Reiter (1867-), illus. LC 8-23517. 123 p. col. front., illus., 11 col. pl. 25 cm. 1908. E. Stern & Co., Inc.

Brill, Walter E
--The Monkeyshines of Peoppo: The Peppermint Candystick Puppet. 1st ed. Brill, Walter E., illus. LC 56-127880. 133p. illus. 21cm. 1957. Vantage Press.

Brimblecom, Charles E.
--An Archer with Columbus. (Illus.). N.D. Joseph Knight Co.
--The Young Archer. (Illus.). (Every Boy's Library). N.D. Caldwell.
--The Young Archer. (Illus.). (Every Boy's Library). N.D. Dodge Publishing Co.
--The Young Archer. (Illus.). (Goldenrod Library Ser.). 1905. L. C. Page & Co.
--The Young Archer. (Cosy Corner Ser.). N.D. L. C. Page & Co.

Brims, Bernagh
--Runaway Riders. (gr. 2-6). 1964. (ISBN 0-672-50470-7). Bobbs.
--Runaway Riders. Lonette, Reisie Dominee (1924-), illus. LC 64-25313. vi, 118p. illus. 21cm. 1965, c.1963. Bobbs.

Brin, Ruth Firestone (1921-)
--David and Goliath. 1976. Lerner Publications Company.
--David & Goliath. Hechtkopf, Henry K. (1910-), illus. (Illus.). 32p. (Foreign Lands Bks). (gr. k-5). 1977. (ISBN 0-8225-0365-4). Lerner Pubns.
--The Story of Esther. LC 75-743. 32p. (Outstanding Books from Foreign Lands Ser.). (gr. 1-4). 1976. (ISBN 0-8225-0364-6). Lerner Pubns.

Brinckloe, Julie Lorraine (1950-)
--Fireflies!. Brinckloe, Julie Lorraine (1950-), illus. LC 85-26767. p. cm. 1986, c.1985. (ISBN 0-689-71055-0). Aladdin Books.
--Fireflies!. Brinckloe, Julie Lorraine (1950-), illus. LC 84-20158. (Illus.). 32 p. 24cm. c.1985. (ISBN 0-02-713310-9). Macmillan.
--Gordon Goes Camping. Brinckloe, Julie Lorraine (1950-), illus. LC 74-17260. (Illus.). 25 p. 25cm. 1975. (ISBN 0-385-06913-8). (ISBN 0-385-06913-8). Doubleday.
--Gordon's House. Brinckloe, Julie Lorraine (1950-), illus. LC 75-33189. (Illus.). 45 p. 24cm. c.1976. (ISBN 0-385-06886-7). Doubleday.
--The Spider Web. LC 73-20695. p. 1974. (ISBN 0-385-04829-7). (ISBN 0-385-04829-7). Doubleday.

Brindel, June Rachuy (1919-)
--Luap. Pyk, Jan (1934-), illus. LC 75-156108. (Illus.). 31 p. 29cm. 1971. Bobbs-Merrill.

Brindl, Helen M., ed. see Rice, Alice Caldwell Hegan, Mrs.

Brindze, Ruth (1903-)
--Story of the Totem Pole. Kimball, Yeffe (1914-), illus. (Illus.). (gr. 4-8). 1951. (ISBN 0-8149-0277-4). Vanguard.

Brine, Mary D., jt. auth. see Douglas, Amanda Minnie.

Brine, Mary D., jt. auth. see Freeman, Mary Eleanor Wilkins, Mrs.

Brine, Mary Dow Northam, Mrs.
--Bessie & Bee. (Illus.). N.D. Methodist Bk Concern.
--Bessie, the Cash Girl, 1 of 23. (Illus.). 195p. (Selected Bks for Sunday School: No. 23). N.D. Set. Methodist Bk Concern.
--Bonnie, Little Bonibel" and Her "Day off,". A Story. Plympton, Almira George (1852-1939), illus. LC 44-29772. 63 p. incl. front., illus. 21 cm. 1890. E. P. Dutton and Company.
--Christmas Dreams. LC 15-264. 48 p. incl. front., illus. 28 cm. 1886. Cassell & Company, Limited.
--Christmas Rhymes and New Year's Chimes. LC 15-263. 124 p. incl. front., illus. 20 x 26 cm. 1883. G. W. Harlan and Co.
--Christmas Rhymes and New Year's Chimes. Ledyard, Addie & Shepherd, Jesse C., illus. N.D. Worthington Company.
--Clover Blossoms. LC 14-227367. 48 p. incl. front., illus. 28 cm. c.1886. Cassell & Company, Limited.
--Dan. (Illus.). N.D. E. P. Dutton & Co.
--Ding Dong Bell. LC 15-262. 32 p. incl. front., illus. 28 cm. c.1886. Cassell & Company, Limited.
--The Doings of a Dear Little Couple ... LC 6362. 48 p. incl. front., illus 8. 1900. Altemus Co.
--The Doings of a Dear Little Couple. (Illus.). N.D. E. P. Dutton & Co.
--The Doings of a Dear Little Couple, 1 of 15 vols. (Illus.). (Dainty Ser. of Choice Gift Bks: No. 9). 1905. Set. Henry Altemus Co.
--A Dozen and One: Or, The Boys and Girls of Polly's Ring. (Illus.). N.D. Cassell & Co.
--Echoes from Story Land. (Illus.). N.D. Cassell & Co.
--Effie's Birthday Present, 1 of 4 bks. (Illus.). (Sunny Hour Ser.). 1905. Set. American Tract Society.
--Four Little Friends: Or, Papa's Daughters in Town. Juv ed. (Illus.). N.D. Cassell & Co.
--The Funnyland Boys. LC 3-20678. (Illus.). 21cm. 1903. D. Biddle.
--Good Times For The Little Ones. (Illus.). N.D. Cassell & Co.
--Grandma's Attic Treasures. N.D. E P Dutton.
--Happy Little People. King, P., illus. 23p. 1898. Lothrop Publishing Co.
--Hither and Thither: Or, Good Times for Papa's Little Daughters. Juv ed. (Illus.). 256p. N.D. Cassell & Co.
--How a Dear Little Couple Went Abroad. (Illus.). N.D. E. P. Dutton & Co.
--How "a Dear Little Couple" Went Abroad. LC 3-12070. (Illus.). 22cm. 47p. 1903. H. Altemus Co.
--How a "Dear Little Couple" Went Abroad, 1 of 15 vols. (Illus.). (Dainty Ser. of Choice Gift Bks: No. 15). 1905. Set. Henry Altemus Co.
--Jack: Or, For Mamma's Sake. 182p. N.D. American Tract Society.
--Jingles and Joys for Wee Girls and Boys. LC 15-260. 100 p. incl. front., illus. 27 1/2 cm. c.1883. Cassell & Company, Limited.
--Jingles and Joys for Wee Girls and Boys. 150 p. front., illus. 27 1/2 cm. 1895. The Cassell Publishing Co.
--Lassie and Laddie: A Story for Little Lads and Lassies. LC 2-19293. v. 241 p. front., 11 pl. 20 cm. 1902. E. P. Dutton and Company.
--Little Lad Jamie. (Illus.). N.D. E. P. Dutton & Co.
--Little Miss Prim, and Other Stories. (Illus.). N.D. E. P. Dutton & Co.
--Little Miss Toddledums. Upton, Florence Kate (1873-1922), illus. N.D. E. P. Dutton & Co.
--The Little New Neighbor. (Illus.). N.D. E. P. Dutton & Co.
--The Little Twin Roses: A Story for Little Girls and Boys. LC 44-29786. 64 p. incl. front., illus., plates. 21 1/2 cm. 1892. E. P. Dutton and Company.
--Love, Home and Mother, the Book for Our Darlings. LC 15-247. 160 p. incl. front., illus. 27 cm. 1890. L. Benham & Co.
--Madge the Violet Girl. LC 20-17772. 25cm. 114p. 1881. G. W. Harlan.
--The Merry Go Round. Juv ed. N.D. Cassell & Co.
--A Merry Little Visit with Auntie. 94 p. incl. front., illus. 22 1/2 cm. 1900. American Tract Society.
--Mother's Little Man. (Illus.). N.D. E. P. Dutton & Co.
--Mother's Little Man. (Illus.). (Dainty Ser.). N.D. Henry Altemus Co.
--My Little Margaret. (Illus.). N.D. E. P. Dutton & Co.
--Nellie's Dream and Other Stories, 1 of 4 bks. (Illus.). (Sunny Hour Ser.). N.D. Set. American Tract Society.
--Papa's Little Daughters. (Author of "My Boy and I; or, On the Road to Slumberland," "Grandma's Attic Treasuers."). (Illus.). 256p. N.D. Cassell, Petter, Galpin.
--Poor Sallie and her Christmas: And Other STories. Upton, Florence Kate (1873-1922), illus. 190p. N.D. E. P. Dutton & Co.
--Rhymes and Chimes for Christmas Times. LC 15-259. 1 p. l., 9-158 p. col. front., illus. 27 1/2 cm. c.1890. Cassell Publishing Company.
--Shadow Sunshine--and Jerry, 1 of 4 bks. (Illus.). (Sunny Hour Ser.). N.D. Set. American Tract Society.
--Stories for Children. LC 20-16486. 4 p. l., 11-63 p. 2 l., 11-138, 5-102 p. 2 l., 11-65 p. incl. illus. plates. 21 1/2 cm. 1894. E. P. Dutton and Company.
--Stories Grandma Told. Juv. ed. (Illus.). N.D. Cassell & Co.
--The Story of Tom, 1 of 4 bks. (Illus.). (Sunny Hour Ser.). N.D. Set. American Tract Society.
--Sunny Hours, 1 of 50 vols. (Illus.). 102p. (Model Library No. 4). 1905. Set. American Tract Society.
--Sunshine and other poems. 62p. (The Temple Ser.). 1899. United Society of Christian Endeavor.
--Twilight Fancies. Juv. ed. (Illus.). N.D. Cassell & Co.
--Wee Little Rhymes. LC 15-258. (Illus.). 32 p. 28cm. c.1886. Cassell & Company.
--What Robbie was Good For. LC 21-870865. 69 p. front., pl. 15 1/2 cm. c.1876. American Tract Society.
--What Robbie was Good For, 1 of 50 vols. (Illus.). 69p. (Model Library No. 4). N.D. Set. American Tract Society.

Brine, Mary Dow Northam, Mrs., ed.
--Christmas in Baby-Land. LC 22-17358. 1 p. l., 5-80 p. front., illus. 24 1/2 cm. c.1890. Cassell Publicating Co.

Brinegar, Lou
--Jose the Armadillo. LC 72-89489. (Illus.). 44 p. 22cm. 1973. (ISBN 0-8059-1763-2). Dorrance.

Bringham, Evangeline Marquerite Ladys Elliot see Elliot, Geraldine, pseud.

Bringle, Mary
--Don't Walk Alone. 176p. (Orig.). (gr. 7 up). 1981. (ISBN 0-590-32154-4, Windswept). Scholastic Inc.

Brings, Lawrence Martin (1897-), ed.
--Choice Comedies for Jr. High Schools. 96p. N.D. T. S. Denison & Co.
--Choice Comedies for Junior High Schools: A Collection of One-Act Plays. 96 p. 19 cm. c.1934. The Northwestern Press.
--Christmas Entertainment Book. 96p. N.D. T. S. Denison & Co Inc.

Bringsvaard, T.
--Phantoms & Fairies. (Illus.). (Tanum of Norway Tokens Ser). 1979. (ISBN 82-518-0853-7). Vanous.

Brinhart, Betty, pseud., see Michajluk, Elizabeth Jane.

Brink, Carol Ryrie, Mrs. (1895-1981)
--All Over Town. Morse, Dorothy Bayley (1906-1979), illus. LC 74-15. (Illus.). 291 p. 22cm. 1968, c.1939. Macmillan.
--All Over Town. Morse, Dorothy Bayley (1906-1979), illus. LC 30-22450. x p., 1 l., 291 p. incl. front., illus. 21 cm. 1939. The Macmillan Company.
--Andy Buckram's Tin Men. Mars, Witold Tadeusz J. (1912-), illus. LC 66-11906. 192 p. illus. 21 cm. (gr. 4-7). 1966. (ISBN 0-670-12467-2). Viking Press.
--Anything Can Happen on the River!. Berger, William Merritt (1872-), illus. LC 34-6710. 6 p. l., 234 p. incl. illus., plates. 20 cm. 1934. The Macmillan Company.
--Baby Island. 1966. MacMillan Publishing Company.
--Baby Island. Sewell, Helen Moore (1896-1957), illus. LC 37-22638. 172 p. incl. col. front., col. plates. 20 cm. 1958. The Macmillan Company.
--Bad Times of Irma Baumlein. (gr. 4-6). 1972. Macmillan.
--The Bad Times of Irma Baumlein. Hyman, Trina Schart (1939-), illus. (Illus.). 134 p. 20cm. 1974, c.1972. Collier Books.
--Caddie Woodlawn. 1954. Macmillan.
--Caddie Woodlawn. LC 35-6159. x p., 3 l., 270 p. incl. front., plates. 21 1/2 cm. 1935. The Macmillan Company. **Award: (JNM).**
--Caddie Woodlawn. new ed. Hyman, Trina Schart (1939-), illus. LC 73-588. (Illus.). x, 275 p. 23cm. 1973. (ISBN 0-02-713670-1). Macmillan.
--The Cupboard was Bare. 1928. Eldridge.
--Family Grandstand. Porter, Jean MacDonald (1906-), illus. LC 52-14057. 208 p. illus. 21 cm. (gr. 5-8). 1952. (ISBN 0-670-30633-9). Viking Press.
--Family Sabbatical. Foster, Susan, illus. LC 56-13798. (Illus.). (gr. 4-7). 1956. (ISBN 0-670-30661-4). (ISBN 0-670-30662-2). Viking Pr.
--The Highly Trained Dogs of Professor Petit. Henneberger, Robert G. (1921-), illus. LC 53-12888. 139p. illus. 21cm. 1953. Macmillan.
--Lad with a Whistle. Ball, Robert (1890-), illus. LC 41-14767. 235 p. illus. 21 1/2 cm. 1941. The Macmillan Company.
--Louly. Fetz, Ingrid (1915-), illus. LC 73-21885. (Illus.). 198 p. 21cm. 1974. (ISBN 0-02-713680-9). Macmillan.
--Mademoiselle Misfortune. Seredy, Kate (1899-1975), illus. LC 36-22183. 7 p. l., 267 p. incl. front., plates. 21 1/2 cm. 1936. The Macmillan Company.
--Magical Melons. 1963. MacMillan Co.
--Magical Melons. LC 44-9999. (gr. 4-6). 1972. (ISBN 0-02-041960-0, Collier). Macmillan.
--Magical Melons. Hyman, Trina Schart (1939-), illus. 1944. Macmillan.
--Magical Melons: More Stories about Caddie Woodlawn. Davis, Marguerite (1889-), illus. LC 44-999. (Illus.). 193p. (gr. 5-7). 1944. (ISBN 0-02-714210-8). Macmillan.
--The Pink Motel. Greenwald, Sheila, pseud. (1934-), illus. Green, Sheila Ellen. LC 59-12838. (Illus.). 182 p. 21cm. 1959. Macmillan.
--The Queen of the Dolls. 1928. Eldridge.
--Two Are Better Than One. Rocker, Fermin (1907-), illus. (Illus.). 180 p. 22cm. 1968. Macmillan.

--Winter Cottage. Rocker, Fermin (1907-), illus. (Illus.). 178 p. 20cm. 1974, c.1968. Collier Books.
--Winter Cottage. Rocker, Fermin (1907-), illus. LC 68-12086. (Illus.). 178 p. 21cm. 1968. Macmillan.
Brink, Carol Ryrie, Mrs. (1895-1981) & Leary, Bernice Elizabeth, eds.
--Best Short Stories for Boys and Girls. 1st-Collection ... LC 35-4002. v. illus. 21 cm. c.1935. Row, Peterson and Company.
Brink, Dana Jane
--The Tall Clump of Grass. N.D. Carlton Press.
Brink, Dori
--Spunky. 160p. (Orig.). (gr. 3-7). 1981. (ISBN 0-590-31301-0, Schol Pap). Scholastic Inc.
Brinkerhoff, Robert Moore (1880-)
--Little Mary Mixup in Fairyland. Brinkerhoff, Robert Moore (1880-), illus. LC 26-21642. 6 p. l., 3-112 p. col. front., illus., plates. 21 cm. 1926. Duffield and Company.
Brinkman, Grover (1903-)
--Night of the Blood Moon. LC 76-11030. 149 p. 21cm. c.1976. (ISBN 0-8309-0149-3). Independence Press.
Brinley, Bertrand Russell (1917-)
--The Big Chunk of Ice. LC 74-7665. 176p. (gr. 4 up). N.D. (ISBN 0-8255-1836-9). Macrae
--The Big Kerplop. A Mad Scientists' Club Adventure. LC 73-21730. p. cm. (gr. 4 up). 1974. (ISBN 0-8255-1834-2). Macrae Smith Co.
--Mad Scientist Club. 1965. E M Hale.
--The Mad Scientists' Club. Geer, Charles Hand (1922-), illus. LC 64-23917. (Illus.). 186 p. 22cm. 1965. (ISBN 0-8255-1830-X). Macrae Smith Co.
--New Adventures of the Mad Scientists' Club. 1968. E M Hale.
--The New Adventures of the Mad Scientists' Club. Geer, Charles Hand (1922-), illus. LC 68-31487. (Illus.). 191 p. 22cm. 1968. (ISBN 0-8255-1832-6). MacRae Smith.
Brinnin, John Malcolm (1906-)
--Arthur, the Dolphin Who Didn't See Venice. Francois, Andr'e (1915-), illus. N.D. Little, Brown and Company.
Brinsmead, Hesba Fay (1922-)
--Beat of the City. Papas, William (1927-), illus. 277 p. 21cm. 1968, c.1966. Coward-McCann.
--Beat of the City. Papas, William (1927-), illus. LC 66-68315. 4, 201 p. illus. 22 1/2 cm. 17/. (B 66-21338). 1966. U. P.
--Pastures of the Blue Crane. Macarthur-Onslow, Annette Rosemary (1933-), illus. LC 66-13132. 250p. 22cm. 1966, c.1964. (ISBN 0-698-20107-8). Coward.
--A Sapphire for September. Ambrus, Victor G., pseud. (1935-), illus. Ambrus, Gyozo Laszlo. LC 75-441792. (Illus.). 23cm. iv, 179p. 1967. Oxford Univ. Press.
--Season of the Briar. Papas, William (1927-), illus. 253 p. 22cm. 1967, c.1965. Coward-McCann.
Brinton, Mary
--Magic White Gate. LC 58-13351. (Illus.). 24cm. 80p. 1958. Dorrance & Co Inc.
Brisco, Patty, pseud., see Matthews, Clayton Harley.
Brisco, Patty, pseud. (1918-)
--Raging Rapids. Matthews, Clayton Harley. Matthews, Patricia Anne (1927-) & Davidson, Kevin, illus. LC 78-71859. (Illus.). 56 p. 24cm. c.1978. (ISBN 0-87191-683-5). Creative Education.
Briscoe, Jill Pauline (1935-)
--Harrow Sparrow. Briscoe, Jill Pauline (1935-), illus. LC 85-5097. (Illus.). 143 p. 19cm. c.1985. (ISBN 0-8407-5428-0). T. Nelson.
--The Innkeeper's Daughter. Hockerman, Dennis, illus. (Illus.). 48p. (gr. k-6). 1984. (ISBN 0-8249-8073-5). Ideals.
--Jonah & the Worm. Armstrong, Tom & Davis, Florence, illus. LC 83-6323. 120p. 1983. (ISBN 0-8407-5289-X). Nelson.
Brisley, Joyce Lankester (1896-)
--Bible Bk. N.D. David McKay Co.
--Bunchy. Brisley, Joyce Lankester (1896-), illus. LC 39-10130. 94, 1 p. col. front., illus. 19 cm. 1937. David McKay Company.
--Bunchy. Brisley, Joyce Lankester (1896-), illus. (Illus.). (Girl's Gem Library). N.D. E. P. Dutton & Co.
--The Dawn Shops and Other Stories. Brisley, Joyce Lankester (1896-), illus. (The Milly-Molly-Mandy Bks.). 1933. David McKay Co.
--Further Doings of Milly-Molly-Mandy. Brisley, Joyce Lankester (1896-), illus. LC 76-46223. (Illus.). 95p. (gr. k-3). 1976. (ISBN 0-679-20388-5). McKay.
--Lambs'-Tails and Suchlike: Verses and Sketches. Brisley, Joyce Lankester (1896-), illus. LC 30-20208. 94, 1 p. col. front., illus. 22 cm. c.1930. David McKay Company.
--Milly-Molly-Mandy Again. Brisley, Joyce Lankester (1896-), illus. LC 76-48834. (Illus.). 95 p. 19cm. 1977. (ISBN 0-679-20398-2). D. McKay Co.
--Milly-Molly-Mandy and Billy Blunt. Brisley, Joyce Lankester (1896-), illus. LC 76-48835. (Illus.). 85 p. 19cm. (gr. k-3). c.1967. (ISBN 0-679-20399-0). D. McKay Co.
--Milly-Molly-Mandy Stories. Brisley, Joyce Lankester (1896-), illus. LC 76-46220. (Illus.). 95 p. 19cm. 1976, c.1928. (ISBN 0-679-20386-9). D. McKay Co.
--More of Milly-Molly-Mandy Stories. Brisley, Joyce Lankester (1896-), illus. LC 76-46222. (Illus.). 94 p. 19cm. 1976, c.1929. (ISBN 0-679-20387-7). D. McKay Co.
--More of Milly-Molly-Mandy. Brisley, Joyce Lankester (1896-), illus. N.D. George Sully & Co.
Bristle, Mable C., jt. auth. see Johnston, Louisa.
Bristol, Jane Curtis
--Little Prickly Weed. Gibson, Mary Richards, illus. LC 63-21265. 25 p. col. illus. 31 cm. (gr. k-3). c.1963. (ISBN 0-87167-120-4). Allied Publications.
Bristol, Mary C.
--Alice Sutherland, 1 of 20 vols. New ed. (Illus.). 350p. (Sunday-School Lib: No. 12). 1895. Set. Lothrop Pub. Co.
--Edna Harrington. 311p. 1905. American Tract Society.
Brisville, Jean-Claude
--King Oleg. Bour, Daniele, illus. (Illus.). 24p. (ps-3). 1982. (ISBN 0-575-03074-7, Pub. by Gollancz England). David & Charles.
--Oleg the Snow Leopard. Bour, Daniele, illus. (Illus.). 24p. (ps-3). 1980. (ISBN 0-575-02557-3, Pub. by Gollancz England). David & Charles.
Brisville, Jean-Claude De see De Brisville, Jean-Claude.

Britcher, Phyllis see Gay, Romney, pseud.

Brition, James, ed.
--An Anthology of Verse for Children. 4v. 20cm. 1957. Oxford University Press.
British Broadcasting Corporation see Thomas, Douglas.
Britt, Albert (1874-1969)
--Boys' Own Book of Adventures. N.D. MacMillan.
Britt, Dell (1934-)
--The Emperor's Big Gift. Hogenbyl, Jan, illus. LC 67-15165. (Illus.). 32 p. 1967. Prentice-Hall.
Brittain, Bill
--All the Money in the World. Robinson, Charles (1931-), illus. LC 77-25635. (Illus.). 150 p. 21cm. c.1979. (ISBN 0-06-020675-6). Harper & Row.
--Devil's Donkey. Glass, Andrew, illus. LC 80-7907. (Illus.). vii, 120 p. 21cm. 1981. (ISBN 0-06-020682-9). (ISBN 0-06-020683-7). Harper & Row. **Award: (ALA).**
--Who Knew There'd Be Ghosts?. Chessare, Michele (1921-), illus. LC 84-48496. (Illus.). 128p. (gr. 4-7). c.1985. (ISBN 0-06-020699-3). (ISBN 0-06-020700-0). HarpJ.
--The Wish Giver: Three Tales of Coven Tree. Glass, Andrew, illus. LC 82-48264. (Illus.). 192p. (gr. 3-7). 1983. (ISBN 0-06-020686-1, HarpJ). (ISBN 0-06-020687-X). Har-Row. **Awards: (ALA); (JNM).**
Brittain, Grady (1944-)
--Platy, the Child in Us. McBroom, Linda, illus. Texas Alcohol Narcotics Education, ed. LC 81-6503. (Illus.). 32 p. 21cm. 1981. (ISBN 0-86663-761-3). Ide House.
Brittain, Harriet G.
--Shoshie, the Hindoo Zenna Teacher, 1 of 6 Vols. (Whittaker's Select Bks). 1888. Thomas Whittaker.
Britten, Jane
--House for Willie: A Story About Time. Goldsborough, June (1923-), illus. (Illus.). 20p. (Golden Preschool Learning Book). (ps). 1971. (ISBN 0-307-12174-7, Golden Pr). Western Pub.
Britton, Angela, tr. see Sanchez-Silva, Jose Maria.
Britton, Anna
--Fike's Point. LC 78-11281. 148 p. 22cm. 1979, c.1977. (ISBN 0-698-20474-3). Coward, McCann & Geoghegan.
Britton, Anne
--Blackie. (gr. 7 up). N.D. Soccer.
Britton, Fay Adams
--Shakespearian Fairy Tales: First Steps for Little Folks in Shakespeare. Wilson, Clara Powers, illus. N.D. Reilly & Britton Co.
Britton, Louisa, pseud., see McGuire, Leslie Sarah.
Britton, Louisa, pseud. (1945-)
--The Bible Story Picture Book: Stories from the Old and New Testaments. McGuire, Leslie Sarah. Mojica, Victor Ramon, illus. LC 74-24952. (Illus.). 69 p. 32cm. (Child guidance book). c.1975. (ISBN 0-8228-7101-7). Platt & Munk.
Britton, Mattie Lula Cooper see Cooper, Mattie Lula.
Britts, Mattie Dyer
--Better Than Gold: A Temperance Story. (Illus.). 320p. N.D. Sunday-School Publications.
--Boys and Girls of Deep Glen: Learning the Way. (Illus.). 256p. N.D. Sunday-School Publications.
--Earle Armstrong. (Illus.). 312p. N.D. Sunday-School Publications.
--Halford's Luck: Or, Which is the Better. 256p. N.D. Sunday-School Publications.
--Hannah. 284p. N.D. Sunday-School Publications.
--Nobody's Boy: Or, How Good Goes On. (Illus.). 250p. N.D. American Baptist Publishing Society.
--Nobody's Boy: Or, How Good Goes On. (Illus.). 250p. N.D. Sunday-School Publications.
--Riy Kennedy's Reward: Or, The Way to Win. 250p. N.D. Sunday-School Publications.
--Rushlights. 252p. N.D. Sunday-School Publications.
--To-Day and To-Morrow. 192p. N.D. Sunday-School Publications.
Brixner, Audrey
--Lucy & the Merman. (gr. 4-6). 1977. (ISBN 0-590-11874-9, Schol Pap). Scholastic Inc.
Brlic-Mazuranic, Ivana (1874-1938)
--The Brave Adventures of Lapitch. Berson, Harold (1926-), illus. LC 76-182531. (Illus.). 137 p. 24cm. 1972. (ISBN 0-8098-2420-5). H. Z. Walck.
Bro, Margueritte Harmon (1894-1977)
--The Animal Friends of Peng-U: By Margueritte H. Bro. Moy, Seong (1921-), illus. LC 65-13167. 96 p. illus. 20 cm. (gr. 1-5). 1965. Doubleday.
--How the Mouse Deer Became King. Low, Joseph (1911-), illus. LC 66-123347. 127p. illus. 25cm. (gr. 4-7). c.1966. Doubleday.
--Sarah. LC 49-10405. (gr. 7-11). 1949. (ISBN 0-385-07479-4). Doubleday.
--Sarah. N.D. (ISBN 0-448-04794-2). Grosset & Dunlap.
--Stub: A College Romance. 1st ed. LC 52-6371. 288 p. 21 cm. 1952. Doubleday.
--Stub: A College Romance. (gr. 9-11). 1959. (ISBN 0-385-07507-3). Doubleday.
--Su-Mei's Golden Year. Wiese, Kurt (1887-1974), illus. (Illus.). (gr. 5-7). N.D. (ISBN 0-385-08523-0). Doubleday.
--Su-Mei's Golden Years. 1st ed. Wiese, Kurt (1887-1974), illus. LC 50-9684. 246 p. illus. 22 cm. 1950. Doubleday.
--Three, and Domingo. Weisgard, Leonard Joseph (1916-), illus. LC 53-998788. 127p. illus. 20cm. 1953. Doubleday.
Broad, John
--Coo CCoo Molly. N.D. Vantage Press.
Broadaxe, Benjamin
--The Bad Boy and His Sister. 350p. N.D. J S Olgivie's.
Broadhead, Helen Cross see Cross, Helen Reeder, pseud.
Broadhurst, Jean (1873-), ed. see Brown, Ethel Clare.
Broadhurst, Jean (1873-)
--All Through the Day the Looking Glass Way. LC 27-2197. 80 p. illus. 19 1/2 cm. c.1926. J.B. Lippincott Company.
--All Through the Day the Mother Goose Way. Mother Goose's Children of Long Ago; What Gave Them Pains and Aches and What Made Them Grow. LC 22-783. 72 p. illus. 19 1/2 cm. c.1921. J.B. Lippincott Company.
Broadley, Mae
--Children's Bedtime Book. (Illus.). 160p. 1982. (ISBN 0-89673-156-1). Bookthrift.
Broadley, Mae, retold by see Andersen, Hans Christian.
Broch, Hermann
--Death of Virgil. N.D. (ISBN 0-448-00184-5). Grosset & Dunlap.
--SleepWalkers: A Trilogy. N.D. (ISBN 0-448-00175-6). Grosset & Dunlap.
Brochmann, Elizabeth
--What's the Matter, Girl?. LC 79-2022. 121 p. 21cm. c.1980. (ISBN 0-06-020677-2). (ISBN 0-06-020678-0). Harper & Row.
Brock, Betty (1923-)
--No Flying in the House. Tripp, Wallace Whitney (1940-), illus. LC 79-104755. (Illus.). 139 p. 21cm. 1970. Harper & Row.
--The Shades. De Larrea, Victoria, illus. LC 79-148421. (Illus.). 128 p. 21cm. 1971. (ISBN 0-06-020644-6). Harper & Row.
Brock, Carey, Mrs.
--Children at Home. N.D. Dodd & Mead.
--Clear Shining After Rain: A Guernsey Story. N.D. E & J. B. Young & Co.
--Hattie and Nellie. N.D. Pott, Young & Co.
--Margaret's Secret, and Its Success. (Illus.). N.D. Publication of E. P. Dutton & Co.
Brock, Carey, Mrs., tr. see Bersier.
Brock, Carey, Mrs., tr. see Bersier, Mrs.
Brock, Carey, Mrs., tr. see Bresier, Mrs.
Brock, Emma Lillian (1886-1974)
--At Midsummer Time: A Story of Sweden. LC 40-6807. 5 p. l., 3-80 p. incl. col. front., illus. col. plates. 2/3 1/2 cm. 1940. A.A. Knopf.
--Ballet for Mary. Brock, Emma Lillian (1886-1974), illus. LC 54-7709. (Illus.). 79 p. 21cm. 1954. Knopf.
--Beppo. Brock, Emma Lillian (1886-1974), illus. LC 36-29596. 79, 1 p. illus. (part col.) 26 cm. 1936. A. Whitman & Co.
--The Birds' Christmas Tree. Brock, Emma Lillian (1886-1974), illus. LC 46-685302. 64 p. col. illus. 13 1/3 x 18 cm. 1946. A. A. Knopf.
--Come On-Along, Fish!. Brock, Emma Lillian (1886-1974), illus. LC 57-5254. 1957. Alfred A Knopf : distributed by Borzoi Books.
--Drusilla. Brock, Emma Lillian (1886-1974), illus. LC 37-4881. 6 p. l., 120 p. incl. illus., plates, front. 20 cm. 1937. The Macmillan Company.
--The Greedy Goat. Brock, Emma Lillian (1886-1974), illus. LC 31-181795. 45 p. illus. 20 1/2 x 22 cm. (gr. k-1). 1931. A. A. Knopf.
--Heedless Susan Who Sometimes Forgot to Remember. Brock, Emma Lillian (1886-1974), illus. LC 39-305307. 5 p. l., 3-169 p. 1 l. incl. front., illus. 23 1/2 cm. (gr. 3-7). 1939. (ISBN 0-394-91231-4). A.A. Knopf.
--The Hen That Kept House. LC 33-25673. 40 p. col. illus. 21 x 23 cm. 1933. A.A. Knopf.
--Here Comes Kristie. Brock, Emma Lillian (1886-1974), illus. LC 42-15602. 5 p. l., 3-80, 1 p., 2 l. col. front., illus., col. plates. 21 x 16 cm. 1942. A. A. Knopf.
--Here Comes Kristie. Brock, Emma Lillian (1886-1974), illus. LC 46-7120. 5 p. l., 3-80, 5 p. col. front., illus., col. plates. 21 cm. 1946. A. A. Knopf.
--High in the Mountains: Robi and Hanni in the Swiss Alps. Brock, Emma Lillian (1886-1974), illus. LC 38-27963. 78, 2 p. illus. (part col.) 26 cm. 1938. A. Whitman & Co.
--Kristie and the Colt and the Others. Brock, Emma Lillian (1886-1974), illus. LC 49-10331. 88 p. illus. (part col.) 21 cm. 1949. A. A. Knopf.
--Kristie Goes to the Fair. Brock, Emma Lillian (1886-1974), illus. (Illus.). 84p. (gr. 3-7). 1953. (ISBN 0-394-91311-6). Knopf.
--Kristie's Buttercup. Brock, Emma Lillian (1886-1974), illus. LC 52-6388. 86 p. illus. 21 cm. 1952. Knopf.
--Little Duchess: Anne of Brittany. Brock, Emma Lillian (1886-1974), illus. (gr. 3-7). 1948. A. A. Knoff.
--Little Fat Gretchen. 1st ed. Brock, Emma Lillian (1886-1974), illus. LC 34-31446. 41 p. illus. 21 x 23 cm. 1934. A.A. Knopf.
--Mary Makes a Cake. Brock, Emma Lillian (1886-1974), illus. LC 64-20170. 83 p. illus. 21 cm. (gr. 4-6). 1964. (ISBN 0-394-91388-4). Knopf.
--Mary on Roller Skates. Brock, Emma Lillian (1886-1974), illus. LC 67-18592. (Illus.). 80 p. 22cm. 1967. Knopf.
--Mary's Camera. Brock, Emma Lillian (1886-1974), illus. LC 63-9116. 81 p. illus. 21 cm. 1963. Knopf.
--Mary's Secret. 1st ed. Brock, Emma Lillian (1886-1974), illus. LC 62-14766. 83p. illus. 21cm. 1962. Knopf.
--Mister Wren's House. Brock, Emma Lillian (1886-1974), illus. LC 44-3685. (Illus.). (ps up). 1944. (ISBN 0-394-91428-7). Knopf.
--Nobody's Mouse. Brock, Emma Lillian (1886-1974), illus. LC 38-303834. 40 p. illus. (part col.) 20 1/2 x 22 cm. 1938. A.A. Knopf.
--One Little Indian Boy. Brock, Emma Lillian (1886-1974), illus. LC 32-19045. 44 p. illus. (part col.) 20 1/2 x 22 cm. 1932. A.A. Knopf.
--Pancakes and the Merry-Go-Round. Brock, Emma Lillian (1886-1974), illus. 1960. Alfred A Knopf : distributed by Borzoi Books.
--Pancakes and the Merry-Go-Round. 1st ed. Brock, Emma Lillian (1886-1974), illus. LC 60-13024. 77p. illus. 22cm. 1960. Knopf.
--Patty on Horseback. LC 59-12569. (Illus.). 79 p. 21cm. 1959. Knopf.
--A Pet for Barbie. Brock, Emma Lillian (1886-1974), illus. LC 47-18222. 3 p. l., 3-50 p. incl. front., illus. 19 1/2 cm. 1947. A. A. Knopf.
--Pig with a Front Porch. (gr. k-3). N.D. Knopf.
--The Pig with a Front Porch and the Pig That Lived Under Half a Boat. LC 37-28562. 43 p. col. illus. 20 1/2 x 22 1/2 cm. 1937. A.A. Knopf.
--Plaid Cow. Brock, Emma Lillian (1886-1974), illus. LC 61-15309. (Illus.). (gr. k-3). 1961. (ISBN 0-394-91510-0). Knopf.
--Plug-Horse Derby. Brock, Emma Lillian (1886-1974), illus. LC 55-8947. (Illus.). 121p. (gr. 4-6). 1955. (ISBN 0-394-91511-9). Knopf.
--A Present for Auntie. LC 39-16411. 96 p. illus. 20 1/2 cm. 1939. A.A. Knopf.
--A Present for Auntie and Too Fast for John. N.D. A. A. Knopf.
--The Runaway Sardine. Brock, Emma Lillian (1886-1974), illus. LC 29-14637. 42 p. col. illus. 21 cm. 1929. A.A. Knopf.
--Skipping Island. Brock, Emma Lillian (1886-1974), illus. LC 58-993915. unpaged. illus. 26cm. 1958. Knopf.
--Spooks & Spirits & Shadowy Shapes. Doremus, Robert (1913-), illus. (Illus.). 167p. (gr. 2-5). 1949. (ISBN 0-525-39753-1). Dutton.

--Spooks, and Spirits and Shadowy Shapes. Doremus, Robert (1913-), illus. (Illus.). 1964. E.P. Dutton & Co.
--Surprise Balloon. Brock, Emma Lillian (1886-1974), illus. LC 49-8188. 63 p. col. illus. 14 x 18 cm. (Borzol books for young people). 1949. A. A. Knopf.
--Then Came Adventure. 1941. A. A. Knopf.
--Three Ring Circus. Brock, Emma Lillian (1886-1974), illus. LC 50-9114. (Illus.). 110 p. 21cm. 1950. Knopf.
--Till Potatoes Grow on Trees. Brock, Emma Lillian (1886-1974), illus. (Illus.). (gr. 3-7). 1938. (ISBN 0-394-91750-2). Knopf.
--Till Potatoes Grow on Trees: Nine Fine Retellable Tales. LC 38-27264. 5 p. l., 3-85, 1 p. illus. 23 1/2 cm. 1938. A.A. Knopf.
--To Market to Market. Brock, Emma Lillian (1886-1974), illus. LC 30-18300. (Illus.). (gr. k-3). 1930. (ISBN 0-394-91754-5). Knopf.
--Too Fast for John. LC 40-100781. 95 p. illus. 20 1/2 cm. 1940. A.A. Knopf.
--Too Many Turtles. 1st ed. Brock, Emma Lillian (1886-1974), illus. LC 51-11073. 89 p. illus. 21 cm. (gr. 2-4). 1951. (ISBN 0-394-81758-3). (ISBN 0-394-91758-8). Knopf.
--The Topsy-Turvy Family. Brock, Emma Lillian (1886-1974), illus. LC 43-9802. 4 p. l., 3-86, 4 p. col. front., illus., col. plates. 21 x 16 cm. 1943. A. A. Knopf.
--Topsy-Turvy Family. Brock, Emma Lillian (1886-1974), illus. (gr. 3-7). 1962. (ISBN 0-394-91760-X). Knopf.
--The Umbrella Man. LC 45-3160. 48 p. incl. col. front., col. illus. 17 x 22 1/2 cm. 1945. A. A. Knopf.
--Uncle Bennie Goes Visiting. Brock, Emma Lillian (1886-1974), illus. LC 44-6541. 3 p. l., 3-57, 1 p. col. front., illus., col. plates. 21 1/2 cm. 1944. A. A. Knopf.

Brock, Emma Lillian (1886-1974), illus.
--Johnny Cake. 30p. N.D. G. P. Putnam's Sons.

Brock, Henry Matthew (1875-1960)
--Art Fairy Tales. Brock, Henry Matthew (1875-1960), illus. (Warne's Nursery Literature). N.D. Frederick Warne & Co.
--Ditto, No. 2. N.D. Frederick Warne & Co.
--The Heroes. Kingsley, Charles (1819-1875), ed. LC 79-21470. p. cm. (Facsimile Classics Series). 1980. Mayflower Books.

Brock, Henry Matthew (1875-1960), illus.
--The Old Fairy Tales. LC 16-4884. (Comprising Valentine & Orson, and Jack the Giant-Killer). 32 p. col. front., illus., col. plates. 29 x 23 cm. 1916. F. Warne & Co.

Brock, Para Lee
--Sahani. Roskos, Inez, illus. LC 81-10611. (Illus.). 189 p. 24cm. c.1981. (ISBN 0-931948-19-3). Peachtree Publishers.

Brock, Ray
--Go Fly a Kite. (Illus.). 1976. (ISBN 0-912846-17-8). Bookstore Pr.

Brock, Stanley Edmunde (1936-)
--Jungle Cowboy. N.D. (ISBN 0-8008-4444-0). Taplinger.

Brockett, Eleanor Hall (1913-1967), retold by.
--Burmese and Thai Fairy Tales. Toothill, Harry & Toothill, Ilse, illus. LC 66-33173. x, 198p. illus. 21cm. 1966, c.1965. F. Mulle.
--Burmese and Thai Fairy Tales. Toothill, Harry & Toothill, Ilse, illus. LC 67-5829. x. 198 p. illus. 23 cm. (World fairy tale collections). 1967, c.1965. Follett Pub. Co.
--Old European Fairy Tales. (gr. 1-4). 1971. (ISBN 0-584-62385-2). Transatlantic.
--Persian Fairy Tales. Toothill, Harry, illus. LC 68-10494. (Illus.). 224 p. 23cm. (World fairy tale collections). 1968. Follett Pub. Co.
--Turkish Fairy Tales. Toothill, Harry & Toothill, Ilse, illus. LC 68-13807. 197. 2 p. illus. 23cm. (World fairy tale collections). 1968, c.1963. Follett.

Brockman, Chris, ed. see Trollope, Anthony.

Brockman, Janie
--Bert. N.D. Potts & Co.
--Right Side Up. Pym, T., illus. N.D. Pott & Co.
--Seven O'Clock: A Home Story, 1 of 3 vols. (Illus.). (Warne's Little Books for Little People Ser.). N.D. Scribner & Welford.
--Worth Doing, 3 of 3 Vols. (Illus.). (Warne's Little Books for Little People Ser.). N.D. Scribner & Welford.

Brockway, Edith E. (1914-)
--The Golden Land. Brockway, Edith E. (1914-), illus. LC 68-22580. (Illus.). 160 p. 21cm. 1968. Herald House.
--Land Beyond the Rivers. LC 66-10969. 272 p. 21cm. 1966. Westminster Press.
--Range Doctor. Lavengood, James, illus. LC 63-20348. (Illus.). (gr. 6-8). 1964. (ISBN 0-8075-6829-5). A Whitman.

Brod, Ruth & Brod, Stan
--How Would You Act?. LC 62-12653. unpaged. illus. 26cm. c.1962. Rand McNally.

Brod, Stan, jt. auth. see Brod, Ruth.

Broderick, Dorothy M., jt. ed. see Arbuthnot, May Hill.

Broderick, Dorothy M. (1929-)
--Hank. LC 65-20253. (gr. 7 up). 1966. (ISBN 0-06-020637-3, HarpJ). Har-Row.
--Leete's Island Adventure. LC 62-113646. 128p. 21cm. 1962. Prentice-Hall.

Broderick, Jessica Potter
--Hide-Away Puppy. Dottie, illus. LC 53-16405. unpaged. illus. 21cm. (Rand McNally book-elf book, 466). c.1952. Rand McNally.
--Ten Little Monkeys. Phillips, Katherine L., illus. LC 53-32910. 17cm. (McNally Book Elf Junior,078). 1953. Rand McNally & Co.

Broderick, Robert C (1913-)
--Paul of St Peter's. Broderick, Virginia, illus. LC 47-11916. 111 p. illus. 21 cm. 1947. Bruce. Pub. Co.

Broderip, Mrs.
--My Grandmother Budget of Stories. (Illus.). N.D. Publications of E. P. Dutton & Co.

Brodersen, Lelia
--The Green One. Ogg, Oscar John (1908-1971), illus. LC 36-21829. 160 p. incl. front., illus. 19 1/2cm. 1936. B. Mussey.

Brodeur, Arthur Gilchrist, jt. auth. see Bishop, Farnham.

Brodfuhrer, J. C., tr. see Hoffmann, Franz.

Brodhead, Eva Wilder
--A Prairie Infanta, 1 of 21 vols. (Illus.). (Boys & Girls Booklovers Ser.: No. 13). 1905. Set. Henry Altemus Co.
--A Prairie Infanta. (Illus.). (Illustrated Cherrycroft Ser.). N.D. Henry Altemus Co.

Brodie, Deborah, ed.
--Stories My Grandfather Should Have Told Me. Baron, Carmela Tal, illus. LC 76-48149. (Illus.). xiii, 113 p. 21cm. 1977. (ISBN 0-88482-752-6). Bonim Books.

Brodkin, Sylvia Z. & Pearson, Elizabeth J., eds.
--Science Fiction. LC 75-29830. (Illus.). 256p. Repr. of 1973 ed (Pub. by McDougal-Littell). (gr. 7 up). 1975. (ISBN 0-688-41723-X). (ISBN 0-688-51723-4). Lothrop.

Brodrip, Freeling
--Wee Maggie: Magnet Stories for Boys and Girls. (Illus.). N.D. Warne & Co.

Brodsky, Beverly
--Secret Places. LC 77-16391. p. cm. c.1978. (ISBN 0-397-31790-5). Lippincott.
--Sedna: An Eskimo Myth. LC 75-4979. p. cm. 1975. (ISBN 0-670-63165-5). Viking Press.

Brodsky, Mimi
--The House at Twelve Rose Street. 1966. (ISBN 0-8382-1060-0, Cadmus Books). E. M. Hale and Company.
--The House at Twelve Rose Street. Hodges, David, illus. LC 67-1918. (Illus.). 157 p. 22cm. (gr. 3-7). 1966. Abelard-Schuman.

Brodtkorb, Reidar
--Flying Free. (Illus.). (gr. 7 up). 1965. (ISBN 0-528-80360-3). Rand.
--The Gold Coin. Mars, Witold Tadeusz J. (1912-), illus. Kingsland, L. W., tr. from Norwegian. LC 66-11198. 219p. illus., map. 21cm. 1st U.S. edition. c.1966. Harcourt.

Brody, Alan
--Coming To. 1975. (ISBN 0-399-11479-3). G.P. Putnam's Sons.

Brody, Paula
--Tum Tum From Tearful. Hornberger, Janet, illus. N.D. Hesperian House.

Broeger, Achim see Broger, Achim.

Broekel, Rainer Lothar see Broekel, Ray, pseud.

Broekel, Ray, pseud., see Broekel, Rainer Lothar.

Broekel, Ray, jt. auth. see White, Laurence B.

Broekel, Ray, pseud. (1923-)
--Hugo the Huge. Broekel, Rainer Lothar. Fiammenghi, Gioia (1929-), illus. LC 67-15765. (Illus.). 48 p. 1968. Doubleday.
--I Have a Green Nose!", said Zanzibar. Broekel, Rainer Lothar. N.D. E. C. Seale & Co.
--I Have a Green Nose!" Said Zanzibar. Broekel, Rainer Lothar. Reisner, Joe, illus. LC 63-20790. (Illus.). 63 p. 23cm. 1963. E. C. Seale.
--The Moustache Pickpocket. Broekel, Rainer Lothar. Brandon, David (1942-), illus. LC 79-52410. (Illus.). 32 p. 16cm. (Corolrhoda mini-mystery). c.1980. (ISBN 0-87614-116-5). Carolrhoda Books.
--The Mystery of the Funny Money. Broekel, Rainer Lothar. Brandon, David (1942-), illus. LC 79-52408. (Illus.). 32 p. 16cm. (Carolrhoda mini-mystery). c.1980. (ISBN 0-87614-114-9). Carolrhoda Books.
--The Mystery of the Stolen Base. Broekel, Rainer Lothar. Brandon, David (1942-), illus. LC 79-52405. (Illus.). 32 p. 16cm. (Carolrhoda mini-mystery). c.1980. (ISBN 0-87614-111-4). Carolrhoda Books.
--Pangborn, the Peanut Bear, and His Tummy Drum. Broekel, Rainer Lothar. Reisner, Joe, illus. LC 65-153606. 63p. col. illus. 23cm. c.1965. E. C. Seale.
--The President Jackson Case. Broekel, Rainer Lothar. Brandon, David (1942-), illus. LC 79-52406. (Illus.). (Carolrhoda Mini-Mysteries Ser.). (gr. 1-4). 1980. (ISBN 0-87614-112-2). Carolrhoda Bks.
--Rodney Bounced Too Much on Monday. Broekel, Rainer Lothar. Reisner, Joe, illus. LC 64-15741. (Illus.). 63 p. 24cm. 1964. E. C. Seale.
--The Saga of Sweet Basil. Broekel, Rainer Lothar. Remington, Barbara, illus. LC 69-14375. (Illus.). 48 p. 1970. (ISBN 0-385-06669-4). Doubleday.
--The Shoelace Solution. Broekel, Rainer Lothar. Brandon, David (1942-), illus. LC 79-52409. (Illus.). (Carolrhoda Mini-Mysteries Ser.). (gr. 1-4). 1980. (ISBN 0-87614-115-7). Carolrhoda Bks.
--Tropical Fish. Broekel, Rainer Lothar. LC 82-19738. (Illus.). 48p. (New True Bks.). (gr. k-4). 1983. (ISBN 0-516-01687-3). Childrens.
--The Twist Tie Riddle. Broekel, Rainer Lothar. Brandon, David (1942-), illus. LC 79-52407. (Illus.). 32 p. 16cm. (Carolrhoda mini-mystery). c.1980. (ISBN 0-87614-113-0). Carolrhoda Books.

Broekstad, H. L., tr. see Asbjornsen, Peter Christen.

Brogan, Helen M., jt. ed. see Kelly, William Roswell.

Broger, Achim (1944-)
--Bruno. Himler, Ronald Norbert (1937-), illus. LC 75-15800. (Illus.). 160 p. 22cm. 1975. (ISBN 0-688-22051-7). (ISBN 0-688-32051-1). Morrow.
--Bruno Takes a Trip. Kalow, Gisela (1946-), illus. LC 78-3878. (Illus.). 32 p. 26cm. 1978. (ISBN 0-688-22138-6). Morrow.
--Caterpillar's Story. Brandt, Katrin, illus. LC 72-89359. (Illus.). 24p. (ps-2). 1973. (ISBN 0-87592-009-8). Scroll Pr.
--Francie's Paper Puppy. Sambin, Michele, illus. LC 83-24987. (Illus.). 28p. 1st U.S. edition. (gr. 1 up). 1984. (ISBN 0-907234-56-9). (ISBN 0-907234-56-9). Picture Bk Studio USA.
--Good Morning, Whale. Kalow, Gisela (1946-), illus. LC 74-9762. (Illus.). 28 p. 24cm. 1974. (ISBN 0-02-714460-7). Macmillan.
--Little Harry. Morgan, Judy, illus. LC 78-26028. (Illus.). 189 p. 21cm. 1st U.S. edition. 1979. (ISBN 0-688-22185-8). (ISBN 0-688-32185-2). Morrow.
--Outrageous Kasimir. Jeschke, Susan (1942-), illus. LC 76-40982. p. cm. 1976, c.1975. (ISBN 0-688-22085-1). (ISBN 0-688-32085-6). Morrow.
--Running in Circles. Crampton, Patricia, tr. from Germ. (gr. 7 up). 1977. (ISBN 0-688-22119-X). (ISBN 0-688-32119-4). Morrow.

Brokamp, Marilyn, Sr. (1920-)
--Halfway. (gr. 3-7). 1971. Vantage.
--Skelly, the Sea Horse. LC 73-78091. (Illustrated by Pupils od St. Mary's School). (Illus.). 32 p. 1973. (ISBN 0-88344-460-7). Orbis Books.

Brokering, Herbert F.
--Christmas in Rhythm and Rhymes. 64p. 1969. Augsburg Publishing House.
--Christmas in Rhythm and Rhymes. 64p. 1969. Lutheran Publications.

Bromberg, Andrew
--Computer Overbyte & Other Stories. Kornblum, Mary, illus. LC 82-81248. (Illus.). 48p. (gr. 2-6). 1982. (ISBN 0-688-00943-3). Greenwillow.
--Computer Overbyte: Plus Two More Codebreakers. Kornblum, Mary, illus. 1982. Greenwillow.
--Flute Revenge. Kornblum, Mary, illus. LC 82-81246. (Illus.). 48p. (Hidden Clue Mystery Ser.). (gr. 2-6). 1982. (ISBN 0-688-00942-5). Greenwillow.
--Flute Revenge: Plus Two More Mysteries. Kornblum, Mary, illus. 1982. Greenwillow.
--The House on Blackthorn Hill: A Hidden Clue Mystery. Kornblum, Mary, illus. LC 82-81245. 48p. (Orig.). (gr. 2-6). 1982. (ISBN 0-688-00941-7). Greenwillow.
--The House on Blackthorn Hill: Plus Two More Mysteries. Kornblum, Mary, illus. 1982. Greenwillow.
--Rubik's Ruse & Other Stories. Kornblum, Mary, illus. LC 82-81247. (Illus.). 48p. (Hidden Clue Codebreaker Ser.). (gr. 2-6). 1982. (ISBN 0-688-00944-1). Greenwillow.
--Rubik's Ruse: Plus Two More Codebreakers. Kornblum, Mary, illus. 1982. Greenwillow.

Bromfield, Annette, Mrs.
--Laddie Boy: The Autobiography of a Dog. Woodruff, Claude W., illus. LC 36-20134. 5 p. l., 74 p. col. front., plates. 19 1/2 cm. 1936. Harper & Brothers.

Bromfield, Louis
--Walt Disney's Vansishing Prairie. (Deluxe Edition). 1957. Golden Press.

Bromfield, Mary E.
--Daddy Dick. N.D. Scribner, Welford & Armstrong.
--Trot's Letters to Her Doll. (Illus.). N.D. Thomas Nelson & Sons.

Bromhall, Winifred
--Belinda's New Shoes. Bromhall, Winifred, illus. LC 45-7579. 31 p. col. illus. 19 1/2 x 25 1/2 cm. 1945. A. A. Knopf.
--Bridget's Growing Day. Bromhall, Winifred, illus. LC 57-5264. (Illus.). unpaged. 1957. Knopf.
--The Chipmunk That Went to Church. Bromhall, Winifred, illus. LC 52-6392. (Illus.). 1 v. (unpaged. 26cm. 1952. Knopf.
--Circus Surprise. Bromhall, Winifred, illus. LC 53-7627. unpaged. illus. 26cm. 1954. (ISBN 0-394-81031-7). Knopf.
--Johanna Arrives. Bromhall, Winifred, illus. LC 41-4027. 3 p. l., 3-57. 1 p. incl. col. front., col. illus. 22 k 17 1/2 cm. c.1941. A. A. Knopf.
--Mary Ann's Duck. Bromhall, Winifred, illus. (Illus.). (gr. k-3). 1967. (ISBN 0-394-81639-0). (ISBN 0-394-91639-5). Knopf.
--Mary Ann's First Adventure. Bromhall, Winifred, illus. (gr. k-4). 1948. A. A. Knopf.
--Mary Ann's First Picture. Bromhall, Winifred, illus. LC 48-5570. 32 p. illus. (part col.) 27 cm. (Borzoi books for young people). 1948. A. A. Knopf.
--Middle Matilda. Bromhall, Winifred, illus. LC 61-12435. (Illus.). 34 p. 1962. Knopf.
--Mrs. Polly's Party. Bromhall, Winifred, illus. LC 49-7859. 32 p. illus. 26 cm. 1949. A. A. Knopf.
--Peter's Three Friends. Bromhall, Winifred, illus. LC 63-14612. (Illus.). 33 p. 1964. Knopf.
--The Pony Tail That Grew. Bromhall, Winifred, illus. LC 59-5218. unpaged. illus. 20 x 26cm. 1957. Knopf.
--The Princess and the Woodcutter's Daughter. Bromhall, Winifred, illus. LC 55-8559. illus. 21x26cm. 36p. (gr. k-3). 1955. (ISBN 0-394-90753-1). Knopf.
--Princess & the Woodcutter's Daughter. Bromhall, Winifred, illus. (Illus.). (gr. k-3). 1955. (ISBN 0-394-90753-1). Knopf.

Bromley, Dudley (1948-)
--Bad Moon. LC 78-72330. (Illus.). (Pacesetters Ser.). (gr. 4 up). 1979. (ISBN 0-516-02182-6). Childrens.
--Balloon Spies. LC 80-65914. (Illus.). 18cm. 75p. (A Pacemaker Bk.). (Talespinners). c.1981. (ISBN 0-8224-6730-5). Fearon Education.
--Bedford Fever. LC 81-82039. 80p. (Doomsday Journals). (gr. 6-12). 1982. (ISBN 0-516-02241-5). Childrens.
--Final Warning. LC 81-82037. 80p. (Doomsday Journals). (gr. 6-12). 1982. (ISBN 0-516-02243-1). Childrens.
--Fireball. LC 81-82035. 80p. (Doomsday Journals). (gr. 6-12). 1982. (ISBN 0-516-02244-X). Childrens.
--Lost Valley. LC 81-82036. 80p. (Doomsday Journals). (gr. 6-12). 1982. (ISBN 0-516-02245-8). Childrens.
--North to Oak Island. LC 77-82062. (Illus.). 64p. (Pacesetters Ser.). (gr. 4 up). 1978. (ISBN 0-516-02171-0). Childrens.
--The Seep. LC 81-82038. 80p. (Doomsday Journals). (gr. 6-12). 1982. (ISBN 0-516-02246-6). Childrens.

Brommer, Elizabeth, tr. see Schmeltzer, Kurt.

Bromwell, Alice, jt. auth. see Green, Ivah E.

Bron, Marion le
--Jimmy Shoestring. N.D. Grosset & Dunlap.

Bronetsky, I., ed.
--Stories & Poems for Children. 143p. 1982. (ISBN 0-8285-2361-4, Pub. by Raduga Pubs USSR). Imported Pubns.

Bronin, Andrew (1947-)
--The Cave: What Lives There. Stahl, Ben F., illus. (Illus.). 32p. (What Lives There Ser.). (gr. 3-5). 1972. (ISBN 0-698-30437-3, Coward). Putnam Pub Group.
--Gus and Buster Work Things Out. Szekeres, Cyndy (1933-), illus. LC 74-16391. (Illus.). 61 p. 23cm. 1975. (ISBN 0-698-30561-2). Coward, McCann & Geoghegan.

Bronk, Mitchell
--Manchester Boys. LC 37-23344. 6 p. l., 128 p. front., illus., pl. 21 cm. c.1937. The Judson Press.

Bronson, Lynn, pseud., see Lampman, Evelyn Sibley.

Bronson, Lynn, pseud. (1907-1980)
--Coyote Kid. Lampman, Evelyn Sibley. LC 51-11160. 224 p. 21cm. 1951. Lippincott.
--Darcy's Harvest. Lampman, Evelyn Sibley. 1st ed. Galdone, Paul (1914-), illus. LC 56-9397. 190p. illus. 22cm. 1956. Doubleday.
--Rogue's Valley. Lampman, Evelyn Sibley. LC 52-7464. 214 p. 21cm. 1952. Lippincott.
--The Runaway. Lampman, Evelyn Sibley. LC 53-8907. 209p. 21cm. 1953. Lippincott.
--Timberland Adventure. Lampman, Evelyn Sibley. LC 50-8909. (Illus.). 221 p. 21cm. 1950. Lippincott.

Bronson, Mildred
--The Last Act. LC 18-17642. 51 p. 20 1/2 cm. 1918. Saulsbury Publishing Company.

Bronson, Sophie see Titterington, Sophie Bronson, Mrs.

Bronson, Wilfrid Swancourt (1894-)
--Cats. Bronson, Wilfrid Swancourt (1894-), illus. LC 50-9467. (Illus.). (gr. 4-6). 1950. (ISBN 0-15-215357-8, HJ). HarBraceJ.
--Children of the Sea. Bronson, Wilfrid Swancourt (1894-), illus. LC 40-27684. 4 p. l., 3-264 p. incl. illus., plates. col. front. 23 1/2 cm. c.1940. Harcourt, Brace and Company.

--Hooker's Holiday. Bronson, Wilfrid Swancourt (1894-), illus. LC 44-8167. 64 p. illus. 21 1/2 x 17 1/2 cm. 1944. Harcourt, Brace and Company.
--Paddlewings. Bronson, Wilfrid Swancourt (1894-), illus. N.D. MacMillan.
--Pinto's Journey. Bronson, Wilfrid Swancourt (1894-), illus. LC 48-627478. 55 p. illus. (part col.) 24 cm. c.1948. J. Messner.
--Pollwiggle's Progress. Bronson, Wilfrid Swancourt (1894-), illus. N.D. Macmillan.
--Stooping Hawk and Stranded Whale: Sons of Liberty. Bronson, Wilfrid Swancourt (1894-), illus. LC 42-36268. 4 p. l., 3-225 p. incl. front., illus., plates. 21 cm. 1942. Harcourt, Brace and Company.

Bronstein, Charlotte
--Tales of the Jewish Holidays. LC 59-15811. (Illus.). (gr. k-4). 1959. (ISBN 0-87441-121-1). Behrman.

Bronte, Charlotte (1816-1855)
--Jane Eyre. N.D. A. L. Burt.
--Jane Eyre. (The Manhattan Ser.). N.D. A. L. Burt's Pubs.
--Jane Eyre. (The Lotus Ser.). N.D. A. L. Burt's Pubs.
--Jane Eyre, 1 of 4 vols, Vol. I. (Charlotte Bronte's Works). N.D. Set. A. L. Burt's Pubs.
--Jane Eyre. No. 70. (The Cornell Ser.). N.D. A. L. Burt's Pubs.
--Jane Eyre. Empire ed. 1905. American News Co.
--Jane Eyre. (Popular Standard Editions). N.D. Belford, Clarke & Co.
--Jane Eyre. (Caxton Edition). N.D. Belford, Clarke & Co.
--Jane Eyre. (Little Lib.). N.D. Bowen-Merrill Pub.
--Jane Eyre. N.D. Bruce Humphries.
--Jane Eyre. (Great Illus. Classics). 1941. Dodd.
--Jane Eyre. (Internation Classics). N.D. Dodd Mead & Co.
--Jane Eyre. N.D. Donohue, Henneberry & Co.
--Jane Eyre. (The Roxburghe Classics). N.D. Estes & Lauriat's.
--Jane Eyre. (Warne's Crown Library). N.D. Frederick Warne.
--Jane Eyre. (The Peoples Library). N.D. Funk & Wagnalls Co.
--Jane Eyre. N.D. George Routledge & Sons.
--Jane Eyre. (The Good Value Books). N.D. Grosset & Dunlap.
--Jane Eyre. 1952. Grove Press.
--Jane Eyre. (Illus.). (Caldwell's Illustrated Library of Famous Books by Famous Authors). N.D. H. M. Caldwell Co.
--Jane Eyre, 1 of 32 vols, Vol. 27. (Illus.). (Famous Books for Girls). N.D. H. M. Caldwell Co.
--Jane Eyre. N.D. Harper & Bros.
--Jane Eyre. (New Alta Lib.). N.D. Henry T. Coates & Co.
--Jane Eyre, 1 of 300 vols. (The Hawthorne Library). 1900. Hurst & Co.
--Jane Eyre. (Argyle Ser). N.D. Hurst & Comapany.
--Jane Eyre. N.D. Hurst & Co.
--Jane Eyre. (Illus.). (Almonte Library). N.D. Hurst and Company.
--Jane Eyre. (Illus.). (Arlington Edition). N.D. Hurst and Company.
--Jane Eyre. (New Red Letter Ser). N.D. International Books Co.
--Jane Eyre. (New Aldine Ser). N.D. International Book Co.
--Jane Eyre. (Illus.). N.D. John E. Porter & Co.
--Jane Eyre. N.D. John C. Winston Co.
--Jane Eyre. (The Best Book Ser). N.D. Joseph Knight Co.
--Jane Eyre, 1 of 2 vols. (New Oxford Ser: No. 17). N.D. Set. Lovell, Coryell & Co.
--Jane Eyre. (The New Century Ser). N.D. Lovell, Coryell & Co.
--Jane Eyre. 1970. Macmillan Publishing Company.
--Jane Eyre. N.D. Mason, Baker, & Pratt.
--Jane Eyre. N.D. Modern Library.
--Jane Eyre. (The Nelson Classics). N.D. Nelson Bks.
--Jane Eyre, No.90. (Riverside Library Ser.). N.D. Norman L. Munro.
--Jane Eyre. 1983. Putnam.
--Jane Eyre. (The Advance Library Ser.: Vol. 147). N.D. Rand, McNally & Co.
--Jane Eyre. (Illus.). (The Independent Library Ser.: Vol. 147). N.D. Rand, McNally & Co.
--Jane Eyre. (Illus.). (The Waldorf Lib.). N.D. T. Y. Crowell & Co.
--Jane Eyre. N.D. The American Book Co.
--Jane Eyre. (Illus.). (Luxembourg Illustrated Classics). 1915. Thomas Y Crowell.
--Jane Eyre. N.D. Thomas Nelson & Co.
--Jane Eyre. (Royal Library of Choice Books). N.D. Ward Lock & Bowden.
--Jane Eyre. N.D. William Collins Sons & Co.
--Jane Eyre. Bell, Currer, ed. (Illus.). N.D. Harper & Brothers.
--Jane Eyre. Davis, Joe Lee (1906-1974), illus. 525p. 1950. Rinehart & Co.
--Jane Eyre. Dobree, Bonamy, intro. by. (Collins New Classics). N.D. William Collins Sons & Co.
--Jane Eyre. Dulac, Edmund (1882-1953), illus. (Everyman's Library). N.D. E P Dutton.
--Jane Eyre. Freedman, Barnett (1901-), illus. 454p. N.D. Heritage Press.
--Jane Eyre. Garrett, Edmund Henry (1853-1929), illus. (Illus.). (The Luxembourg Illustrated Library of Standard Fiction). N.D. T. Y. Crowell & Co.
--Jane Eyre. Garrett, Edmund Henry (1853-1929), illus. (2 vols.). N.D. Thomas Y. Crowell & Co.
--Jane Eyre. Garrett, Edmund Henry (1853-1929), illus. N.D. Thomas Y. Crowell & Co.
--Jane Eyre. Jack, Jane & Smith, Margaret, eds. 1969. Oxford University Press.
--Jane Eyre. Kennett, John, retold by. (gr. 3 up). 1977. (ISBN 0-8277-5378-0). British Bk Ctr.
--Jane Eyre. Stewart, Diana, adapted by. Shaw, Charles (1941-), illus. LC 80-14426. (Illus.). 48 p. 24cm. c.1981. (ISBN 0-8172-1661-8). Raintree Publishers.
--Jane Eyre. Thorne, Jenny, illus. LC 78-3388. p. cm. (Raintree's illustrated classics). 1978. (ISBN 0-8393-6202-1). Raintree Childrens Books.
--Jane Eyre. Wimperis, E. M., illus. N.D. Porter & Coates.
--Professor, 1 of 4 vols, Vol. II. (Charlotte Bronte's Works). N.D. Set. A. L. Burt's Pubs.
--Sense and Sensibility: Works of Charlotte Bronte, 1 of 5 Vols. N.D. Set. Frederick A. Stokes.
--Shirley, 1 of 4 vols, Vol. III. (Charlotte Bronte's Works). N.D. Set. A. L. Burt's Pubs.
--Shirley. (Royal Library of Choice Books). N.D. Ward Lock & Bowden.
--Shirley. (Illus.). (The New Standard Library). N.D. William Collins Co.
--Shirley. Bell, Currer, ed. (Illus.). N.D. Harper & Brothers'.
--Shirley: Warne's Crown Library. N.D. Frederick Warne.
--Villette, 1 of 4 vols, Vol. IV. (Charlotte Bronte's Works). N.D. Set. A. L. Burt's Pubs.
--Villette. 1948. Grove Press.

Bronte, Emily Jane (1818-1848)
--Peculiar Music. Lewis, Naomi, ed. index. 96p. (gr. 5 up). 1972. (ISBN 0-02-714750-9). Macmillan.
--Wuthering Heights. (The Borzoi Classics). 1927. Alfred A. Knopf.
--Wuthering Heights. (Illus.). (Great Illus. Classics). 1942. Dodd.
--Wuthering Heights. (International Classics). N.D. Dodd Mead & Co.
--Wuthering Heights. (The People's Library). N.D. Funk & Wagnalls Co.
--Wuthering Heights. N.D. George Routledge & Sons.
--Wuthering Heights. 1956. Houghton.
--Wuthering Heights. (The Travellers' Library Ser.). N.D. Jonathan Cape & Harrison Smith.
--Wuthering Heights. N.D. Modern Library.
--Wuthering Heights. N.D. Thomas Nelson & Sons.
--Wuthering Heights. N.D. Triangle Books.
--Wuthering Heights. Dobree, Bonamy, intro. by. (Collins New Classics). N.D. William Collins Sons & Co.
--Wuthering Heights. Dulac, Edmund (1882-1953), illus. (Everyman's Library). N.D. E P Dutton.
--Wuthering Heights. Freedman, Barnett (1901-), illus. 320p. N.D. Heritage Press.
--Wuthering Heights. McCullough, Bruce, intro. by. (Harper's Modern Classics). N.D. Harper & Brothers.
--Wuthering Heights. Schorer, Mark (1908-1977), ed. 358p. 1950. Rinehart & Co.
--Wuthering Heights. Thorne, Jenny, illus. LC 78-4049. p. cm. (Raintree's illustrated classics). 1978. (ISBN 0-8393-6203-X). Raintree Childrens Books.
--Wuthering Heights. Wright, Betty Ren, retold by. Cogancherry, Helen, illus. LC 81-15786. (Illus.). 48 p. 24cm. c.1982. (ISBN 0-8172-1682-0). Raintree Publishers.

Brook, Arthur Wilkinson (1878-1963)
--Witch's Hollow: Or, The New Babes in the Wood. Folkard, Charles James (1878-1963), illus. LC 22-501559. vii, 211 p. col. front., illus., col. plates. 21 cm. 1921. Frederick A. Stokes Company.
--Witch's Hollow: Or, The New Babes in the Wood. Folkard, Charles James (1878-1963), illus. N.D. Macmillan.

Brook, Judy (1926-)
--Noah's Ark. Brook, Judy (1926-), illus. LC 73-2024. (Illus.). 40 p. 21cm. 1973, c.1972. (ISBN 0-531-02630-2). F. Watts.
--Tim Mouse. Brook, Judy (1926-), illus. LC 68-21066. (Illus.). 40 p. 1968, c.1966. Platts & Munk.
--Tim Mouse and the Major. Brook, Judy (1926-), illus. LC 72-7344. (Illus.). 40 p. 1973, c.1967. Lothrop, Lee & Shepard.
--Tim Mouse Goes Down the Stream. Brook, Judy (1926-), illus. LC 75-7947. (Illus.). 40 p. 1975, c.1969. (ISBN 0-688-41698-5). (ISBN 0-688-51698-X). Lothrop, Lee & Shepard.
--Tim Mouse Visits the Farm. Brook, Judy (1926-), illus. LC 76-55025. (Illus.). 40 p. 1977, c.1968. (ISBN 0-688-41796-5). (ISBN 0-688-51796-X). Lothrop, Lee & Shepard.
--Tim Mouse Visits the Farm. Brook, Judy (1926-), illus. LC 69-19395. (Illus.). 40 p. 1969, c.1968. Platt & Munk.

Brook, Nelsie
--Come Home, Mother, 1 of 6 Vols. (Broken Rock Ser.). N.D. National Temperance society.

Brooke, Jocelyn
--The Dog at Clambercrown. 1965. Vanguard Press.

Brooke, Leonard Leslie (1862-1940)
--Children's Books: Containing: "The Three Bears" "The Golden Goose", Book. 2. Brooke, Leonard Leslie (1862-1940), illus. (Illus.). 32p. 1910. Frederick Warne & Co.
--Children's Books: The Jumblies and Other Nonsense Verses. Brooke, Leonard Leslie (1862-1940), illus. 1910. Frederick Warne & Co.
--Children's Books: The Pelican Chorus, and Other Nonsense Verses. Brooke, Leonard Leslie (1862-1940), illus. 1910. Frederick Warne & Co.
--Golden Goose. (Illus.). (gr. 1-5). 1905. (ISBN 0-7232-0575-2). Warne.
--The Golden Goose. Brooke, Leonard Leslie (1862-1940), illus. (Illus.). (Art Fairy Stories). N.D. Frederick Warne & Co.
--Golden Goose Book. (Illus.). (gr. 1-4). 1905. (ISBN 0-7232-0555-8). Warne.
--The Golden Goose Book. new ed. Brooke, Leonard Leslie (1862-1940), illus. LC 76-2919. (Illus.). (ps-3). 1977. (ISBN 0-7232-1979-6). Warne.
--The Golden Goose Book: Being the Stories of The Golden Goose, The Three Bears, The 3 Little Pigs, Tom Thumb. Brooke, Leonard Leslie (1862-1940), illus. LC 68-5259. 100 p. illus. (part col.) 26 cm. N.D. F. Warne.
--The Golden Goose Book: Being the Stories of The Golden Goose, The Three Bears, The 3 Little Pigs, Tom Thumb. With Numerous Drawings in Colour and Black-and-White. Brooke, Leonard Leslie (1862-1940), illus. LC 68-5259. (Illus.). 100 p. 26cm. N.D. F. Warne.
--The Golden Goose Book: Containing: "Three Little Pigs" "Tom Thumb" "Three Bears" "TheGolden Goose". Brooke, Leonard Leslie (1862-1940), illus. 1910. Frederick Warne & Co.
--History of Tom Thumb. (Illus.). (gr. 1-5). 1905. (ISBN 0-7232-0574-4). Warne.
--The History of Tom Thumb. Brooke, Leonard Leslie (1862-1940), illus. (Illus.). (Art Fairy Stories). N.D. Frederick Warne & Co.
--Johnny Crow's Garden. (Peter Possum Paperbacks Ser). 1967. (ISBN 0-531-05110-2). Watts.
--Johnny Crow's Garden. Brooke, Leonard Leslie (1862-1940), illus. N.D. E . M. Hale and Co.
--Johnny Crow's Garden. Brooke, Leonard Leslie (1862-1940), illus. (Illus.). 1910. Frederick Warne & Co.
--Johnny Crow's Garden. Brooke, Leonard Leslie (1862-1940), illus. (Illus.). (ps-2). 1903. (ISBN 0-7232-0567-1). Warne.
--Johnny Crow's Party. (Illus.). (ps-2). 1907. (ISBN 0-7232-0566-3). Warne.
--Johnny Crow's Party. Brooke, Leonard Leslie (1862-1940), illus. (Illus.). 1900. Frederick Warne & Co.
--Johnny Crow's Party. Brooke, Leonard Leslie, illus. 1967. (ISBN 0-88302-340-7, Peter Possum). Mulberry Pr.
--Leslie Brooke Children's Books: A Nursery Rhyme Picture Bk, 4 of 4, Vol. 4. 32p. (No. 2). N.D. Frederick Warne & Co.
--Leslie Brooke's Children's Books, 1 of 4 Vols, Vol. 1. N.D. Frederick Warne & Co.
--Leslie Brooke's Children's Books, 1 of 4 Vols, Vol. 3. N.D. Frederick Warne & Co.
--Little Bo-Peep: A Nursery Rhyme Picture Book. Brooke, Leonard Leslie (1862-1940), illus. 1 v. (unpaged) illus. (part col.) 27 cm. (Leslie Brooke's Children's Books). (gr. k-4). 1922. (ISBN 0-7232-0579-5). F. Warne.
--Little Bo-Peep and other Nursery Rhymes. (Leslie Brooke's Art Fairy Stories). N.D. Frederick Warne & Co.
--Man in the Moon. (Illus.). (gr. 1-4). 1913. (ISBN 0-7232-0578-7). Warne.
--The Man in the Moon: A Nursery Rhyme Picture Book. Brooke, Leonard Leslie (1862-1940), illus. 1 v. (unpaged) illus. (part col.) 27 cm. (Leslie Brooke's Children's Books). 1914. F. Warne.
--The Man in the Moon, and other Nursery Songs. (Leslie Brooke's Art Fairy Stories). N.D. Frederick Warne & Co.
--A Nursery Rhyme Picture Book, No. 1. (Illus.). Repr. of 1913 ed. (Leslie Brooke's Children's Book Ser: Bk. 3). (gr. 1-5). N.D. (ISBN 0-7232-0562-0). Warne.
--A Nursery Rhyme Picture Book, No. 2. Repr. of 1922 ed. (Leslie Brooke's Children's Book Ser.: Bk. 4). (gr. 1-5). N.D. (ISBN 0-7232-0563-9). Warne.
--A Nursery Rhyme Picture Book: Containing: "Oranges and Lemons" "The Man in the Moon" Etc, Books 1 & 2. Brooke, Leonard Leslie (1862-1940), illus. (Illus.). N.D. Frederick Warne & Co.
--Nursery Rhymes: Tales and Jingles. Brooke, Leonard Leslie (1862-1940), illus. 1916. Warne.
--Oranges and Lemons: A Nursery Rhyme Picture Book. Brooke, Leonard Leslie (1862-1940), illus. LC 64-9267. (Illus.). 1 v. (unpaged. 27cm. (Leslie Brooke's Children's Books). 1913. (ISBN 0-7232-0577-9). F. Warne.
--Oranges and Lemons, and Other Nursery Songs. Brooke, Leonard Leslie (1862-1940), illus. (Illus.). (Art Fairy Stories). N.D. Frederick Warne & Co.
--Ring o' Roses. new ed. Brooke, Leonard Leslie (1862-1940), illus. LC 76-2920. (Illus.). (ps-3). 1977, c.1922. (ISBN 0-7232-1980-X). Warne.
--Ring O'Roses. A Nursery Rhyme Picture Book. Brooke, Leonard Leslie (1862-1940), illus. LC 23-906. (Illus.). 26cm. 60p. (gr. 1-4). 1923. (ISBN 0-7232-0557-4). Warne.
--The Story of the Three Bears. (Illus.). (Art Fairy Stories). N.D. Frederick Warne & Co.
--Story of the Three Bears. (gr. 1-4). 1905. (ISBN 0-7232-0576-0). Warne.
--The Story of the Three Bears. Bd. with The Golden Goose. (Illus.). Repr. of 1905 ed. (Leslie Brooke's Children's Book Ser.: Bk. 2). (gr. 1-5). N.D. (ISBN 0-7232-0561-2). Warne.
--The Story of the Three Little Pigs. Bd. with The History of Tom Thumb. (Osi). (Illus.). Repr. of 1904 ed. (Leslie Brooke's Children's Book Ser., Bk. 1). N.D. (ISBN 0-7232-0560-4). Warne.
--The Story of the Three Little Pigs. Brooke, Leonard Leslie (1862-1940), illus. 24 p. illus. (part col.) 26 cm. (On cover: Leslie Brooke's Children's Books). 1904. F. Warne & Co., Ltd.
--The Story of the Three Little Pigs. Brooke, Leonard Leslie (1862-1940), illus. (Illus.). (Art Fairy Stories). N.D. Frederick Warne & Co.
--The Story of the Three Little Pigs. Brooke, Leonard Leslie (1862-1940), illus. (Illus.). (gr. 1-4). 1905. (ISBN 0-7232-0573-6). Warne.
--The Tailor and The Crow. Brooke, Leonard Leslie (1862-1940), illus. 1911. Frederick Warne & Co.
--This Little Pig Went to Market: A Nursery Rhyme Picture Book. Brooke, Leonard Leslie (1862-1940), illus. 1 v. (unpaged) illus. (part col.) 26 cm. (Leslie Brooke's Children's Books). (gr. 1-4). 1922. (ISBN 0-7232-0581-7). F. Warne.
--Tom Thumb. Brooke, Leonard Leslie (1862-1940), illus. 24 p. illus. (part col.) 26 cm. (On cover: Leslie Brooke's Children's Books). N.D. F. Warne & Co., Ltd.
--Tom Thumb & Other Favorites. Brooke, Leonard Leslie (1862-1940), illus. 1967. (ISBN 0-88302-308-3, Peter Possum). Mulberry Pr.

Brooke, Leonard Leslie (1862-1940), illus.
--Johnny Crow's New Garden. LC 35-19680. (Illus.). 48 p. 22cm. (gr. k-2). 1935. F. Warne & Company.
--Nursery Rhymes: Rhymes and Lullabies. N.D. Frederick Warne & Co.
--Nursery Rhymes: Songs and Ditties. N.D. Frederick Warne & Co.
--Nursry Rhymes: Tales and Jingles. N.D. Frederick Warne & Co.

Brooke, N.
--Charley Franklin: Or, Time Unveils Truth. N.D. Scribner, Welford & Armstrong.

Brooke, Roger
--Santa's Christmas Journey. Miles, Elizabeth, illus. LC 84-9796. (Illus.). 32p. (Raintree Stories Clippers Ser.). (gr. k-4). 1984. (ISBN 0-8172-2116-6). (ISBN 0-8172-2259-6). (ISBN 0-8172-2244-8). incl. cassette 23.95; (ISBN 0-8172-2269-3); cassette 14.00. Raintree Pubs.

Brooker, Margaret Louisa Jones, Mrs. (1869-)
--Half-Past-Five: Children's Poems. LC 38-35042. 63 p. 21 1/2 cm. c.1938. H. Harrison.

Brookes, Amelia
--Through the Ant Hill. Bates, Jacob, illus. LC 41-8954. 157, 1 p. incl. col. front., illus. (part col.) 23 1/2 x 19 cm. c.1941. J.B. Lippincott Company.

Brookins, Dana (1931-)
--Alone in Wolf Hollow. LC 77-13118. 137 p. 22cm. c.1978. (ISBN 0-8164-3208-2). Seabury Press.
--Rico's Cat. Eagle, Michael (1942-), illus. LC 76-8841. p. cm. c.1976. (ISBN 0-8164-3175-2). Seabury Press.
--Who Killed Sack Annie?. LC 82-9655. p. cm. 1983, c.1982. (ISBN 0-89919-137-1). Clarion Books.

Brooklyn. Public School 48 & Brooklyn. Public School 173
--A Book of Poetry by Children: For Children and Adults. Smith, Mary E., ed. LC 35-9058. vi p., 1 l., 144 p. front., plates. 20 1/2cm. c.1935. Mary E. Smith.
Brooklyn. Public School 173, jt. auth. see Brooklyn. Public School 48.
Brookman, Denise Cass (1921-)
--The Look of Love. LC 60-9187. 183p. 22cm. 1960. Macrae Smith Co.
--The Tender Time: A Story of First Love. LC 58-8725. 184 p. 22cm. 1958. Macrae Smith Co.
--The Young in Love. LC 62-11721. 191p. 22cm. 1962. Macrae Smith Co.
Brooks, Amy, et al. (0000-1931), illus.
--Mother's Verses and Home Songs. (Illus.). N.D. Caldwell.
Brooks, Amy (0000-1931)
--At the Sign of the Three Birches. Brooks, Amy (0000-1931), illus. LC 16-17068. 419 p. front. 20 cm. $1.2. 1916. Lothrop, Lee & Shepard Co.
--Dorothy Dainty. Brooks, Amy (0000-1931), illus. v, 203 p. front., pl. 19 1/2cm. 1902. Lee and Shepard.
--Dorothy Dainty at Crestville. Brooks, Amy (0000-1931), illus. 20 cm. 231p. (Dorothy Dainty Ser.). 1915. Lothrop, Lee & Shepard.
--Dorothy Dainty at Foam Ridge. Brooks, Amy (0000-1931), illus. LC 18-17253. 4 p. l., 229 p. front., plates. 20cm. c.1918. Lothrop, Lee & Shepard Co.
--Dorothy Dainty at Gem Island. Brooks, Amy (0000-1931), illus. LC 20-23175. 4 p. l., 228 p. front., plates. 19 1/2cm. c.1920. Lothrop, Lee & Shepard Co.
--Dorothy Dainty at Glenmore. Brooks, Amy (0000-1931), illus. 4 p. l., 235 p. front., plates. 19 1/2cm. 1917. Lothrop, Lee & Shepard Co.
--Dorothy Dainty at Home. Brooks, Amy (0000-1931), illus. 1 p. l., iii p., 1 l., 236 p. front., 5 pl. 20cm. 1907. Lee & Shepard Co.
--Dorothy Dainty at School. Brooks, Amy (0000-1931), illus. v. 239 p. front., 5 pl. 19 1/2cm. 1904. Lee and Shepard.
--Dorothy Dainty at the Mountains. Brooks, Amy (0000-1931), illus. (Dorothy Dainty Ser.). 1911. Lothrop, Lee & Shepard.
--Dorothy Dainty at the Shore. Brooks, Amy (0000-1931), illus. v, 216 p. front., 5 pl. 19 1/2cm. 1905. Lee and Shepard.
--Dorothy Dainty at the Stone House. Brooks, Amy (0000-1931), illus. vii, 229 p. front., plates. 20cm. c.1919. Lothrop, Lee & Shepard Co.
--Dorothy Dainty in the City. Brooks, Amy (0000-1931), illus. LC 6-23155. 1 p. l., iii p., 1 l., 239 p. front., 5 pl. 20cm. 1906. Lothrop, Lee & Shepard Co.
--Dorothy Dainty in the Country. Brooks, Amy (0000-1931), illus. LC 9-17255. 20 cm. 243p. (Dorothy Dainty Ser.). 1909. Lothrop, Lee & Shepard.
--Dorothy Dainty's Castle. Brooks, Amy (0000-1931), illus. (Illus.). 242p. (Dorothy Dainty Ser.). 1923. Lothrop,Lee & Shepard.
--Dorothy Dainty's Gay Times. Brooks, Amy (0000-1931), illus. LC 8-30701. 3 p. l., 241 p. front., 5 pl. 20cm. 1908. Lee & Shepard Co.
--Dorothy Dainty's Holidays. Brooks, Amy (0000-1931), illus. LC 12-175163. 4 p. l., 240 p. front., plates. 20cm. 1912. Lothrop, Lee & Shepard Co.
--Dorothy Dainty's New Friends. Brooks, Amy (0000-1931), illus. LC 16-25097. 3 p. l., 233 p. front., plates. 19 1/2cm. 1916. Lothrop, Lee & Shepard Co.
--Dorothy Dainty's Red Letter Days. Brooks, Amy (0000-1931), illus. LC 21-15998. 4 p. l., 230 p. front., plates. 19 1/2cm. 1921. Lothrop, Lee & Shepard Co.
--Dorothy Dainty's Treasure Chest. Brooks, Amy (0000-1931), illus. LC 22-190442. (Illus.). 244p. (Dorothy Dainty Ser.). 1922. Lothrop,Lee & Shepard.
--Dorothy Dainty's Vacation. Brooks, Amy (0000-1931), illus. LC 13-234164. 4 p. l., 240 p. front., plates. 20cm. $1.0. 1913. Lothrop, Lee & Shepard Co.
--Dorothy Dainty's Visit. Brooks, Amy (0000-1931), illus. LC 14-145754. 4 p. l., 245 p. front., plates. 20cm. $1.0. 1914. Lothrop, Lee & Shepard Co.
--Dorothy Dainty's Winter. Brooks, Amy (0000-1931), illus. (Dorothy Dainty Ser.). 1910. Lothrop, Lee & Shepard.
--Dorothy's Playmates. Brooks, Amy (0000-1931), illus. LC 3-16063. v, 247 p. front., 5 pl. 19 1/2cm. 1903. Lee and Shepard.
--A Jolly Cat Tale. Brooks, Amy (0000-1931), illus. (Dorothy Dainty Ser.). 1905. Lee and Shepard Company.
--A Jolly Cat Tale. Brooks, Amy (0000-1931), illus. 1901. Lothrop, Lee & Shepard.
--Little Sister Prue. Brooks, Amy (0000-1931), illus. 4 p. l., 233 p. front., 5 pl. 20cm. (Her The Prue books). 1908. Lothrop, Lee & Shepard Co.
--Princess Polly. Brooks, Amy (0000-1931), illus. (Princess Polly Series). N.D. A. L. Burt Co.
--Princess Polly. Brooks, Amy (0000-1931), illus. (Princess Polly Ser.). N.D. Nourse.
--Princess Polly at Cliffmore. Brooks, Amy (0000-1931), illus. LC 25-9633. 3 p. l., 9-251 p. front., plates 20cm. (Her Princess Polly series). c.1925. A. L. Burt Company.
--Princess Polly at Play. Brooks, Amy (0000-1931), illus. (Princess Polly Ser.). 1915. A. L. Burt Co.
--Princess Polly at Play. Brooks, Amy (0000-1931), illus. (Princess Polly Ser.). N.D. Nourse.
--Princess Polly at Play. Brooks, Amy (0000-1931), illus. LC 15-168943. 240 p. front., plates. 20cm. p $0.5. c.1915. The Platt & Peck Co.
--Princess Polly at School. Brooks, Amy (0000-1931), illus. (Princess Polly Ser.). N.D. A. L. Burt Co.
--Princess Polly at School. Brooks, Amy (0000-1931), illus. (Princess Polly Ser.). N.D. Nourse.
--Princess Polly at School. Brooks, Amy (0000-1931), illus. LC 12-252041. 256 p. incl. front. plates. 20cm. p $1.0. c.1912. The Platt & Peck Co.
--Princess Polly by the Sea. Brooks, Amy (0000-1931), illus. (Princess Polly Ser.). N.D. A. L. Burt Co.
--Princess Polly by the Sea. Brooks, Amy (0000-1931), illus. (Princess Polly Ser.). N.D. Nourse.
--Princess Polly's Gay Winter. Brooks, Amy (0000-1931), illus. (Princess Polly Ser.). N.D. A. L. Burt Co.
--Princess Polly's Gay Winter. Brooks, Amy (0000-1931), illus. (Princess Polly Ser.). N.D. Nourse.
--Princess Polly's Playmates. Brooks, Amy (0000-1931), illus. (Princess Polly Ser.). N.D. A. L. Burt Co.
--Princess Polly's Playmates. Brooks, Amy (0000-1931), illus. (Princess Polly Ser.). N.D. Nourse.
--Prue at School. Brooks, Amy (0000-1931), illus. (The Prue Bks.). 1909. Lothrop, Lee & Shepard.
--Prue's Jolly Winter. Brooks, Amy (0000-1931), illus. LC 13-8248. 4 p. l., 240 p. front, plates. 20 cm. (Her The Prue books) $1.00). 1913. Lothrop, Lee & Shepard Co.
--Prue's Little Friends. Brooks, Amy (0000-1931), illus. (The Prue Books). 1912. Lothrop, Lee & Shepard.
--Prue's Merry Times. Brooks, Amy (0000-1931), illus. LC 11-30393. 20 cm. 235p. (The Prue Books). 1911. Lothrop Lee & Shepard.
--Prue's Playmates. Brooks, Amy (0000-1931), illus. LC 10-15398. 4 p. l., 239 p. front., plates. 20cm. (Her The Prue books) p $1.00). 1910. Lothrop, Lee & Shepard Co.
--Randy and Her Friends. Brooks, Amy (0000-1931), illus. LC 2-18089. 20 cm. 253p. (The Randy Books). 1902. Lothrop, Lee & Shepard.
--Randy and Prue. Brooks, Amy (0000-1931), illus. LC 3-15224. 251 p. front., 5 pl. 19cm. (Randy books). 1903. Lee and Shepard.
--Randy's Good Times. Brooks, Amy (0000-1931), illus. LC 4-21722. 19 cm. 265p. (The Randy Books). 1904. Lothrop Lee & Shepard.
--Randy's Loyalty. Brooks, Amy (0000-1931), illus. LC 6-24156. 256 p. front., 5 pl. 19cm. (Randy books). 1906. Lothrop, Lee & Shepard Co.
--Randy's Luck. Brooks, Amy (0000-1931), illus. LC 5-207717. 4 p. l., 258 p. front., 5 pl. 19cm. (Randy books). 1905. Lee and Shepard.
--Randy's Prince. Brooks, Amy (0000-1931), illus. 3 p. l., 244 p. front., 5 pl. 19cm. (Randy books). 1907. Lothrop, Lee & Shepard Co.
--Randy's Summer: A Story for Girls. Brooks, Amy (0000-1931), illus. LC 3320. v, 237 p. front., plates. 19cm. 1900. Lee and Shepard.
--Randy's Winter. Brooks, Amy (0000-1931), illus. LC 1-24955. 12 cm. 228p. (The Randy Books). 1901. Lothrop, Lee & Shepard.
--Rosalie Dare. Brooks, Amy (0000-1931), illus. LC 24-28957. vii, 9-247 p. front., plates. 19 1/2cm. c.1924. Lothrop, Lee & Shepard Co.
--Rosalie Dare's Test. Brooks, Amy (0000-1931), illus. LC 25-8414. 251 p. front., plates. 19 1/2cm. c.1925. Lothrop, Lee & Shepard Co.
Brooks, Amy (0000-1931), illus.
--Home Songs and Speeches for Boys and Girls. (Illus.). (Little People's Recitation Ser.). N.D. Caldwell.
--Home Songs for Little Darlings, 10 vols. (Illus.). (Pleasant Street Ser.: No. 2). 1905. Set. H M Caldwell Co.
Brooks, Andrea
--The Guinea Pigs' Adventure. LC 80-14135. (Illus.). 31 p. 21cm. c.1980. (ISBN 0-316-10961-4). Little, Brown.
Brooks, Anita, pseud., see Abramovitz, Anita Zeltner Brooks.
Brooks, Anita, pseud. (1914-)
--The Picture Book of Tea and Coffee. Abramovitz, Anita Zeltner Brooks. LC 61-8270. 96p. illus. 24cm. 1961. John Day Co.
--The Picture Book of Timber. Abramovitz, Anita Zeltner Brooks. (Illus.). 96 p. 24cm. (Picture aids to world geography). 1967. John Day Co.
--A Small Bird Sang. Abramovitz, Anita Zeltner Brooks. Ellis, Deborah, illus. LC 68-11159. (Illus.). 1 v. (unpaged. 24cm. 1968. John Day Co.
--Winifred. Abramovitz, Anita Zeltner Brooks. Dolezal, Carroll, illus. LC 78-141574. 32 p. (chiefly col. illus. 1971. (ISBN 0-8114-7723-1). Steck-Vaughn Co.
Brooks, Anne
--The Black Pup. Van Doren, Margaret (1917-), illus. 4 p. l., 11-62 p. 1 l. illus. (part col. 1938. The Viking Press.
Brooks, Annie Sills, Mrs.
--Everywhere, Everywhere Christmas Tonight. LC 31-30601. 111 p. 20cm. c.1931. The Bethany Press.
Brooks, Bruce
--The Moves Make the Man. LC 83-49476. 280 p. 21cm. c.1984. (ISBN 0-06-020679-9). (ISBN 0-06-020698-5). Harper & Row. **Awards: (BGH); (JNM); (ALA).**
Brooks, Byron Alden (1845-)
--Phil Vernon and His Schoolmasters. (Illus.). N.D. Publications of the Methodist Book Concern.
--Those Children and their Teachers: A Story of to-day. vi, 272 p. 17 1/2cm. 1882. G. P. Putman's.
Brooks, Charles Timothy (1813-1883), tr. see Busch, Wilhelm.
Brooks, Charlotte K., ed.
--The Outnumbered: Stories, Essays and Poems about Minority Groups by America's Leading Writers. 176p. 1969. (ISBN 0-440-06775-8). Delacorte Press.
Brooks, Clara M
--Alf and His Friends: And Other Stories for Boys and Girls. LC 49-413274. 93 p. illus. 21 cm. 1948. Gospel Pub. House.
--The Climber: A Series of Stories for Boys and Girls. LC 52-64335. 159 p. illus. 20 cm. N.D. Gospel Pub. House.
Brooks, Courtaney
--The Case of the Stolen Dinosaur: A Play in Two Versions: Stage & Radio. Way, Merrilee, illus. (Illus.). 26p. (Orig.). (gr. 4 up). 1983. (ISBN 0-941274-02-0). Belnice Bks.
--Eight Steps to Choral Reading. Way, Merrilee, illus. (Orig.). (gr. 1 up). 1983. (ISBN 0-941274-01-2). Belnice Bks.
--Little Red & the Wolf: A Puppet Play. Way, Merrilee, illus. (gr. k up). 1983. (ISBN 0-941274-04-7). Belnice Bks.
--Pardner & Freddie: A Puppet Play. Way, Merrilee, illus. (Illus.). (gr. k up). 1983. (ISBN 0-941274-03-9). Belnice Bks.
Brooks, Cyrus, tr. see Kastner, Erich.
Brooks, Cyrus Harry (1890-), tr. see Kastner, Erich.
Brooks, D.
--Days in the Woods. 1972. (ISBN 0-13-196790-8). Prentice Hall.
Brooks, Dorothy
--Stories of the Red Children. rev. ed. LC 27-24954. 2 p. l., 7-162 p. illus. 19cm. (Young America series). 1927. Educational Publishing Company.
--Stories of the Red Children. rev. ed. Norris, Louise E., illus. LC 8-21920. 2 p. l., 7-162 p. illus. 18cm. (On cover: Choice literature library). c.1908. Educational Publishing Company.
Brooks, Edna
--The Khaki Girls at Windsor Barracks: Or, "Standing To" With the "Trusty Twenty". (The Khaki Girls Ser.). N.D. Cupples & Leon Co.
--The Khaki Girls Behind the Lines: Or, Driving With the Ambulance Corps. (The Khaki Girls Ser.). N.D. Cupples & Leon Co.
--Khaki Girls in Victory: Or, Home With the Heroes. (The Khaki Girls Ser.). N.D. Cupples & Leon Co.
--The Khaki Girls of the Motor Corps: Or, Finding Their Place in the Big War. (The Khaki Girls Ser.). N.D. Cupples & Leon Co.
Brooks, Edward, Dr. (1831-1912)
--The Story of King Arthur and the Knights of the Table Round. Beardsley, Aubrey Vincent (1872-1898), illus. LC 3419. 383 p. front., plates. 19cm. (Classic Stories Ser. for Boys and Girls). 1900. The Penn Publishing Company.
--The Story of the Aeneid. Pinelli, illus. (Classic Stories for Boys). N.D. Penn Publishing Co.
--The Story of Tristram. LC 2-19883. 334 p. front., plates. 19cm. (Classic Stories Ser. for Boys and Girls). 1902. The Penn Publishing Company.
--Wonder Stories From the Norseland. Bowker, A. R., illus. (Classic Stories). N.D. Penn Publishing Co.
Brooks, Edward, Dr. (1831-1912) & Wagner, Richard (1813-1883)
--The Story of Siegfried. LC 3-11159. 391 p. incl. front. plates. 19cm. (Classic Stories Ser. for Boys and Girls). 1903. The Penn Publishing Company.
Brooks, Edward, Dr. (1831-1912), ed. see Mabinogion.
Brooks, Edward, Dr. (1831-1912), ed. see Spenser, Edmund.
Brooks, Elbridge Streeter (1846-1902)
--Barbara's Heritage. 3558p. N.D. W. A. Wilde Co.
--A Boy of the First Empire. Ogden, H. A., illus. LC 4-16454. x p., 1 l., 320 p. incl. front., illus., plates. 19 1/2cm. 1895. The Century Co.
--A Boy of the First Empire. Thorndike, Edward Lee (1874-), ed. LC 36-3140. viii, 292 p. incl. front., illus. 19cm. (Thorndike library). c.1936. D. Appleton-Century Company, Incorporated.
--The Century Books of Young Americans, 3 vols. 250p. N.D. The Century Co.
--Chivalric Days, and the Boys and Girls who Helped to make Them. LC 21-16838. viii, 306p. front. illus. 21cm. 1886. G. P. Putnam's Sons.
--The Godson of Lafayette: Being the Story of Young Joe Harvey, and How He Found the Way to Duty in the Days of Webster and Jackson and the Conspiracy of That American Adventurer, Eleazer Williams, Sometimes Called "The False Dauphin". Merrill, Frank Thayer (1848-), illus. 333 p. front., 4 pl. 19 1/2cm. (On verse of half-title: "Sons of the republic" series). c.1900. W. A. Wilde Company.
--In Blue and White: The Adventure and Misadventures of Humphrey Vandyne, Trooper in Washington's Lifeguard. Merrill, Frank Thayer (1848-), illus. LC 99-5185. 348 p. front., plates. 20 1/2cm. 1899. Lothrop Publishing Company.
--In Defence of the Flag. N.D. Lothrop, Lee & Shepard.
--In Leisler's Times: An Historical Story of Knickerbocker New York. Smedley, William T., illus. LC 4-150685. 4 p. l., 7-299, 1 p. incl. illus., plates. front., 3 pl. 19 1/2cm. 1886. D. Lothrop & Company.
--In No-Man's Land, 1 of 3 vols. (Fun and Fancy Library). N.D. D. Lothrop Co.
--In No-Man's Land: A Wonder Story. LC 10-8165. 2 p. l., 9-304 p. incl. illus., plates. front. 19cm. c.1885. D. Lothrop and Company.
--The Master of the Strong Hearts: A Story of Custer's Last Rally. Cary, William M., illus. LC 98-124189. vii, 314 p. front., plates. 21 1/2cm. 1898. E. P. Dutton and Company.
--On Woodcove Island. (The Outdoor Bks.). N.D. Penn Publishing Co.
--On Woodcove Island. (Vacation Ser.). N.D. Penn Publishing Co.
--On Woodcove Island. Boston, F. J., illus. (Historical Stories for Boys and Girls Ser.). N.D. Penn Publishing Co.
--A Son of the Revolution: Being the Story of Young Tom Edwards, Adventurer ... in the Days of Burr's Conspiracy. Merrill, Frank Thayer (1848-), illus. LC 12-30975. 301 p. front., plates. 20cm. c.1898. W. A. Wilde & Company.
--Storied Holidays. Pyle, Howard (1853-1911), illus. N.D. Lothrop Lee & Shepard Co.
--Under the Allied Flags: A Boy's Adventures in the International War Against the Boxers and China. Stecher, William Frederick (1864-), illus. LC 1-31830. 322 p. incl. front. plates. 19 cm. 1901. Lothrop Publishing Company.
--Under the Tamaracks. (Vacation Ser.). N.D. Penn Publishing Co.
--Under the Tamaracks: Or, A Summer with General Grant at the Thousand Islands. LC 12-30977. 336 p. incl. front. plates. 19 cm. (Historical Stories Ser. for Boys and Girls). 1896. The Penn Publishing Company.
--With Lawton and Roberts: A Boy's Adventures in the Philippines and the Transvaal. Emerson, C. Chase, illus. LC 3631. vii, 318 p. illus. 20 cm. (Young defenders series, v. 1). 1900. Lothrop Pub. Co.
Brooks, Elbridge Streeter (1846-1902) & Alden, John
--The Long Walls: An American Boy's Adventures in Greece; a Story of Digging and Discovery, Temples and Treasure. Barnes, George Foster, illus. iv p., 2 l., 328 p. front., plates. 20cm. 1896. G. P. Putnam's Sons.
Brooks, Ellen W. see Grahame, Kenneth.
Brooks, Eula Lankford
--She Who Hesitated. LC 36-19560. 262 p. 20 1/2 cm. 1936. Meador Publishing Company.
Brooks, Eva Cannon
--Francisco: Our Little Argentine Cousin. Goss, John, illus. LC 10-16150. ix p., 2 l., 152 p. front., plates. 19 1/2 cm. (On verse of half-title: The little cousin series). 1910. L. C. Page & Company.
--Our Little Argentine Cousin. Goss, John, illus. (The Little Cousin Ser.). N.D. Page Co.

--John of the Woods. Smith, Boyd E., illus. LC 9-28265. viii p., 1 l., 189, 1 p. front., 14 pl. 29 cm. 1909. Houghton Mifflin Company.
--Kisington Town. LC 15-19475. N.D. Houghton Mifflin.
--The Lantern, and Other Plays for Children. LC 77-94333. 152 p. 20cm. (One Act Plays in Reprint). 1978. (ISBN 0-8486-2033-X). Core Collection Books.
--The Lantern and Other Plays for Children. LC 28-19973. 4 p., l., 3-152 p. 20 cm. 1928. Houghton Mifflin Company.
--The Lights of Beacon Hill: A Christmas Message. N.D. Houghton Mifflin.
--The Lonesomest Doll. Pollak, E., illus. LC 1-229872. 3 p., l., 76 p., 1 l. front., plates. 19 1/2 cm. 1901. Houghton, Mifflin and Company.
--The Lonesomest Doll. Rackham, Arthur (1867-1939), illus. LC 28-230978. 3 p. l., 80 1 p. col. front., illus., col. plates. 22 cm. c.1928. Houghton Mifflin Co.
--The Lucky Stone. Birch, Reginald Bathurst (1856-1943), illus. LC 14-16943. 6 p., l., 3-218 p., 1 l., incl. plates. front. 20 cm. 1914. The Century Co.
--Our Christmas Tree. N.D. Houghton Mifflin.
--A Pocketful of Posies. Cory, Fanny Young, illus. vii p., 1 l., 162, 4 p. front., plates. 19 cm. 1902. Houghton, Mifflin and Company.
--Round Robin. LC 21-18417. xxi p., 1 l., 310 p. col. front., plates. 19 cm. 1921. E. P. Dutton & Company.
--The Silver Stair. N.D. Houghton Mifflin Co.
--Songs of Sixpence. N.D. Houghton Mifflin.
--The Star Jewels, and Other Wonders. LC 5-24197. 7 p., l., 3-133 1 p., 1 l. incl. illus., plates. front. 20 cm. 1905. Houghton Mifflin and Company.
--Surprise House. LC 17-295157. 5 p. l., 109. 1 p., 1 l. front., plates. 20 1/2 cm. 1917. Houghton Mifflin Company.
--Their City Christmas: A Story for Boys and Girls. Gallagher, Sears (1869-1955), illus. LC 12-23713. 5 p. l., 86, 2 p. front., plates 19 1/2 cm. 1912. Houghton Mifflin Company.
--Under the Rowan Tree. LC 26-18093. 5 p. l., 189 p. col. front., plates 19 1/2 cm. 1926. Houghton Mifflin Company.

Brown, Abbie Farwell (0000-1927) & Bell, Jack Mackintosh (1877-1934)
--Tales of the Red Children. LC 9-26012. 5 p., l., 125 1 p. incl. illus., plates. front. 19 1/2 cm. 1909. D. Appleton & Company.

Brown, Albert M
--A Collection of Boys' Plays. LC 33-19937. 148 p. 19 cm. c.1933. Walter H. Baker Company.
--Jerry Goes to Camp: A Story for Campers and Counselors and Parents. Silverman, Miles M., illus. LC 49-9411. 114 p. illus. 21 cm. 1949. Bloch Pub. Co.
--A Second Collection of Boys' Plays. 109 p. 19 cm. c.1936. Walter H. Baker Company.
--Six New Plays for Boys. LC 38-202715. 104 p. 19 cm. c.1938. S. French.

Brown, Alexander (1905-)
--Dingle Dinosaur's Good Deed. (Illus.). (gr. k-2). 1967. (ISBN 0-8382-0207-1). Hale.

Brown, Alexis, pseud., see Baumann, Amy Brown Beeching.

Brown, Alice (1857-)
--The Merrylinks. Clarke, Louise, illus. LC 3-26912. 1903. McClure, Phillips & Co.
--The One-Footed Fairy: And Other Stories. LC 11-260037. 5 p. l., 182 p. 1 l. front., plates 22 cm. 1911. Houghton Mifflin Company.
--Secret of the Clan: A Story for Girls. Smith, Sarah K., illus. LC 12-23927. 20cm. 314p. 1912. Macmillan.
--Tiverton Tales. N.D. Houghton Mifflin Co.

Brown, Anice (1907-)
--Dreepy and the Wishing Willow Tree. Lyons, Dave, illus. LC 53-8088. unpaged. illus. 24cm. 1953. Pageant Press.

Brown, Annie G.
--Fireside Battles. Luxe ed. Leyendecker, Joseph C., illus. 1901. Laird & Lee.

Brown, Anthony
--Dangerfoot. Giblin, Jeanette, illus. (Illus.). 187 p. 21cm. 1968, c.1966. Meredith Press.

Brown, Beatrice Bradshaw
--A Doll's Day. Brown, Barbara Haven, illus. LC 31-294252. 57 p. illus. (part col.) 19 1/2 x 23 cm. 1931. Little, Brown, and Company.
--A Paris Pair, Their Day's Doings. Brown, Barbara Haven, illus. LC 24-3559. 59 p. incl. col. plates. 16 x 23 cm. c.1923. E. P. Dutton & Company.

Brown, Beth see Retner, Beth A., pseud.

Brown, Beth see Retner, Beth A., pseud.

Brown, Beth (1909-)
--All Cats go to Heaven. N.D. Grosset & Dunlap Pub.
--All Horses Go to Heaven. Vaughn, Frank E., illus. (Illus.). (gr. 7-9). 1963. (ISBN 0-448-01086-0). G&D.
--Blinkie. Martin, Barry, illus. LC 56-6987. 241p. illus. 22cm. 1956. Prentice-Hall.
--The House Without a Home. Hill, Dorothy (1924-), illus. LC 70-112367. (Illus.). 44 p. 27cm. 1970. (ISBN 0-87460-220-3). (ISBN 0-87460-221-1). Lion Press.
--Hurricane. DeOca, Anthony, illus. (Illus.). 159 p. 22cm. 1968. Prentice-Hall.
--Hurricane's Colt. DeOca, Anthony, illus. LC 69-14992. (Illus.). 167 p. 22cm. 1969. Prentice-Hall.
--Little Girl Blue. Retner, Beth A., pseud. Petersham, Maud Sylvia Fuller, Mrs. (1890-1971) & Petersham, Miska (1889-1960), illus. LC 26-22064. 5 p. l., 289 p. col. front. 20 cm. 1926. Doubleday, Page & Company.
--Mr. Jolly's Hotel for Dogs. De Sanctis, Raymond, illus. LC 47-24780. 287 p. illus. 21 cm. 1947. Regent House.
--That's That!. Retner, Beth A., pseud. Snell, Carroll C., illus. LC 25-9021. ix, 156 p., 1 l. col. frotn., illus., plates 20 cm. 1925. Doubleday, Page & Company.
--The Tired Trolley Car. Retner, Beth A., pseud. Millard, C. E., illus. LC 26-15372. 6 p. l., 158 p. col. front., illus., plates (part col.) 20 cm. 1926. Doubleday, Page & Company.

Brown, Beth (1909-), compiled by.
--Fairy Tales of Birds and Beasts. Walworth, Jane Armstrong, illus. LC 75-25966. p. cm. 1976. (ISBN 0-87460-269-6). (ISBN 0-87460-270-X). Lion Books.
--The Wonderful World of Cats. Shortall, Leonard W., illus. LC 61-12096. 208p. illus. 25cm. 1961. Harper.
--Wonderful World of Dogs. Shortall, Leonard W., illus. LC 61-12097. 261p. (gr. 2-6). 1961. (ISBN 0-06-020671-3, HarpJ). Har-Row.
--The Wonderful World of Horses. Shortall, Leonard W., illus. LC 67-4071. (Illus.). xi, 211 p. 25cm. 1967. Harper & Row.

Brown, Beverly Swerdlow
--The Myth-Adventures of Kraken the Sea Monster. Koplan, Carol Louise, illus. LC 78-72493. (Illus.). 32 p. 26cm. c.1978. (ISBN 0-89554-009-6). Brasch and Brasch.

Brown, Bill, pseud., see Brown, William Louis.

Brown, Bill, jt. auth. see Brown, Rosalie Moore.

Brown, Bill, pseud. (1910-1964)
--Rain Forest. Brown, William Louis. LC 62-12034. (Illus.). 96 p. 26cm. 1962. Coward-McCann.
--Roaring River. Brown, William Louis. Burchard, Peter Duncan (1921-), illus. 1953. Coward-McCann, Inc.
--Uncharted Voyage. Brown, William Louis. LC 55-6892. (Illus.). 248 p. 22cm. 1955. Coward-McCann.

Brown, Bill, pseud. (1910-1964) & Brown, Rosalie Moore (1910-)
--Big Pig. Brown, William Louis. N.D. E. M. Hale & Co.
--Big Pig. Brown, William Louis. Burchard, Peter Duncan (1921-), illus. LC 59-523921. unpaged. illus. 23cm. 1959. Coward-McCann.
--The Boy Who Got Mailed. Brown, William Louis. Burchard, Peter Duncan (1921-), illus. LC 57-11717. (Illus.). unpaged. 23cm. 1957. Coward-McCann.
--The Department Store Ghost. Brown, William Louis. Shortall, Leonard W., illus. LC 60-15460. (Illus.). 38 p. 23cm. (gr. 2-4). 1961. Coward-McCann.
--The Forest Firemen. Brown, William Louis. Powers, Richard M. Gorman (1921-), illus. LC 54-871217. unpaged. illus. 23cm. c.1954. Coward-McCann.
--The Hippopotamus That Wanted to Be a Baby. Brown, William Louis. Petie, Haris, pseud. (1915-), illus. Petty, Roberta. LC 63-17986. 1 v. (unpaged) illus. 24 cm. 1963. Lantern Press.
--Tickly and the Fox. Brown, William Louis. Petie, Haris, pseud. (1915-), illus. Petty, Roberta. LC 62-184261. unpaged. illus. 23cm. c.1962. Lantern Press.
--Whistle Punk. Brown, William Louis. Bennett, Richard Michael (1899-), illus. LC 56-9945. (Illus.). unpaged. 23cm. c.1956. Coward-McCann.

Brown, Blanche Van Leuven
--A Story of the Children's Ward. Jackson, William H & Ziegler, Eustace Paul, illus. 6 p. l., (17)-256 p. front., plates. 19 cm. 1906. The R.B. Clark Co.

Brown, Bob
--The Turtle's Darshan for All the Animals. (Illus.). 32p. (gr. 2 up). 1973. (ISBN 0-913078-17-4). Sheriar Pr.
--We Boys. LC 79-239593. 245 p. 17cm. 1876. Roberts Bro.

Brown, C. E.
--Among the Brigands, and Other Tales of Adventure. (Illus.). N.D. E. P. Dutton & Co.

Brown, C. R., ed.
--Girault's Tale of Gargantua and King Arthur. N.D. Harverd University Press.

Brown, Carol Auburn (1892-)
--Peter and the Twin Giants of Umptyville. Devaney, A., photos by. Rowan, Beverley Clarke, designed by. LC 54-13070. unpaged. illus. 26cm. c.1954. Scylla Pub.

Brown, Caroline, pseud., see Krout, Caroline Virginia.

Brown, Carrie L. see Oliver, Marie, pseud.

Brown, Charles Manley (1921-) & Truher, Helen
--Action Now. LC 76-170768. (Illus.). 192 p. 22cm. 1973. Benefic Press.
--Here It Is. Weise, Phillip LC 72-170767. (Illus.). 160 p. 22cm. 1973. Benefic Press.

Brown, Charles Walter (1866-), ed.
--Santa Claus' Visit. LC 51-34826. 80 p. illus. 26 cm. (Fun and frolic series). N.D. M. A. Donohue.

Brown, Cheryl
--Herbert the Snail. Brown, Cheryl, illus. LC 71-147248. (Illus.). 32 p. N.D. Van Nostrand Reinhold Co.

Brown, Christopher
--Mr. T in Pirate's Gold. (Illus.). 24p. (Mr. T Adventure Mysteries Ser.). (gr. 3-7). 1984. (ISBN 0-89954-282-4). Antioch Pub Co.
--Mr. T in the Everglades Adventure. (Illus.). 24p. (Mr. T Adventure Mysteries Ser.). (gr. 3-7). 1983. (ISBN 0-89954-247-6). Antioch Pub Co.
--Mr. T in the Wilderness Adventure. (Illus.). 24p. (Mr. T Adventure Mysteries Ser.). (gr. 3-7). 1984. (ISBN 0-89954-281-6). Antioch Pub Co.
--Whisper & the Secret of Dark Hollow. Wilson-Heaney, Katherine, illus. (Illus.). 24p. (Whisper the Winged Unicorn Ser.). (gr. 3-7). 1985. (ISBN 0-89954-289-1). Antioch Pub Co.
--Whisper the Winged Unicorn in Flying Is Fun. Wilson-Heaney, Katherine, illus. (Illus.). 22p. (Whisper the Winged Unicorn Ser.). (ps-2). 1985. (ISBN 0-89954-327-8). Antioch Pub Co.
--A Wish for Whisper. Wilson-Heaney, Katherine, illus. (Illus.). 24p. (Whisper the Winged Unicorn Ser.). (gr. 2-6). 1984. (ISBN 0-89954-278-6). Antioch Pub Co.

Brown, Christopher, ed.
--Noah's Ark. Rudegeair, Jean, illus. (Illus.). 24p. (gr. 2-6). 1984. (ISBN 0-89954-287-5). Antioch Pub Co.

Brown, Claude (1937-)
--Manchild in the Promised Land. (gr. 8 up). 1965. (ISBN 0-02-517320-0). Macmillan.

Brown, David, pseud., see Myller, Rolf.

Brown, David, pseud. (1926-)
--Someone Always Needs a Policeman. Myller, Rolf. LC 75-179988. (Illus.). 45 p. 21cm. 1972. (ISBN 0-671-65168-4). Simon and Schuster.

Brown, Dee Alexander (1908-)
--The Girl from Fort Wicked. (American Indian Ser.). (gr. 9-12). 1971. Curtis.
--Lonesome Whistle. LC 79-18990. (Illus.). 160p. (gr. 4-8). 1980. (ISBN 0-03-050666-2). HR&W.
--Tales of the Warrior Ants. 128p. (gr. 6 up). 1973. (ISBN 0-399-60804-4). Putnam Pub Group.
--Tepee Tales of the American Indian. Mofsie, Louis B. (1936-), illus. LC 77-28292. (Illus.). (gr. 5 up). 1979. (ISBN 0-03-022761-5). HR&W.

Brown, Demetra Vaka, Mrs. (1877-)
--Delarah. LC 43-7752. 3 p. l., 250 p. 21 cm. 1943. Ziff-Davis Publishing Company.
--Finella in Fairyland. N.D. Houghton Mifflin Co.

Brown, Dodie
--Three Little Girls Who Lived on a Farm. (Illus.). (ps-2). N.D. Vantage.

Brown, Dolores L.
--My Little Friends. 1983. (ISBN 0-8062-2180-1). Carlton.

Brown, Dorothy Lothrop, jt. auth. see Butterfield, Marguerite Antoinette.

Brown, Dorothy Lothrop & Butterfield, Marguerite Antoinette (1900-)
--Bozo the Woodchuck. Ushler, John, illus. LC 33-10093. 116 p. illus. 18 1/2 cm. c.1933. American Book Company.

Brown, Drollene
--Sybil Rides for Independence. Levine, Abby, ed. Apple, Margot, illus. (Illus.). 48p. (gr. 2-5). 1985. (ISBN 0-8075-7684-0). A Whitman.

Brown, Edith, jt. auth. see Brown, Marion Marsh.

Brown, Edna Adelaide (1875-)
--Archer and the "Prophet". Goss, John, illus. LC 16-17066. 388 p. front., plates. 20 1/2 cm. 1916. Lothrop, Lee & Shepard Co.
--Arnold's Little Brother. Goss, John, illus. LC 15-711266. 346 p. front., plates. 20 1/2 cm. 1915. Lothrop, Lee & Shepard Co.
--At the Butterfly House. Goss, John, illus. LC 18-172521. 364 p. front., plates 20 1/2 cm. 1918. Lothrop, Lee Shepard Co.
--The Chinese Kitten. Inglis, Antoinette, illus. LC 22-17559. 230 p. col. front., col. plates. 20 cm. c.1922. Lothrop, Lee Shepard Co.
--Four Gordons. Black, Norman Irving, illus. LC 11-12124. 1911. Lothrop, Lee & Shepard.
--How Many Miles to Babylon!. Ronay, Stephen, illus. LC 41-12316. x, 11-206 p. illus. 21 1/2 x 17 1/2 cm. c.1941. Lothrop, Lee & Shepard Company.
--Journey's End. 1921. Lothrop, Lee & Shepard.
--Polly's Shop. Inglis, Antoinette, illus. LC 31-100865. 237 p. col. front., col. plates. 20 cm. c.1931. Lothrop, Lee & Shepard Co.
--Rainbow Island. Goss, John, illus. LC 19-6770. 286 p. front., plates. 20 1/2 cm. 1919. Lothrop, Lee & Shepard Co.
--Robin Hollow. Goss, John, illus. LC 24-22820. 390 p. front., plates. 20 1/2 cm. c.1924. Lothrop, Lee & Shepard Co.
--The Silver Bear. Inglis, Antoinette, illus. LC 21-26985. 19cm. 166p. 1921. Lothrop, Lee & Shepard.
--The Spanish Chest. Goss, John, illus. LC 17-23755. 335 p. front., plates. 20 1/2 cm. 1917. Lothrop, Lee & Shepard Co.
--That Affair at St. Peter. Goss, John, illus. N.D. Lothrop, Lee & Shepard.
--Three Gates. Inglis, Antoinette, illus. LC 28-107937. 205 p. col. front., col. plates. 19 1/2 cm. c.1928. Lothrop, Lee & Shepard Co.
--Uncle David's Boys. Goss, John, illus. LC 13-174073. 5 p. l., 9-315 p. front., plates. 20 1/2 cm. 1913. Lothrop, Lee & Shepard Co.
--When Max Came. Goss, John, illus. LC 14-6285. 423 p. front., plates 20 1/2 cm. 1914. Lothrop, Lee & Shepard Co.
--Whistling Rock. Inglis, Antoinette, illus. LC 23-12436. 19cm. 218p. 1923. Lothrop,Lee & Shepard.

Brown, Edna B.
--Daisy Girl. N.D. Carlton Press.

Brown, Edna Honeywell
--Weary Willie & Sunny Smile. Maxam, Robert A., illus. LC 42-8270. 44p. col. illus. 17 x 14cm. 1943. R. R. Smith.

Brown, Eleanor Crerar McLaren
--John and Mary and Tommy. Staynes, P. A., illus. LC 32-358046. 87 p. incl. front., illus. 19 1/2 cm. 1932. Oxford University Press, H. Milford.

Brown, Eleanor Frances (1908-)
--The Colt from Horse Heaven Hills. Crowell, Pers (1910-), illus. LC 56-6785. 192p. illus. 22cm. 1956. Messner.
--Golden Lady. Crowell, Pers (1910-), illus. (gr. 4-7). N.D. Lothrop Bks.
--Golden Lady: The Story of an American Show Horse. Crowell, Pers (1910-), illus. LC 47-1880. 252, 2 p. illus. 21 cm. 1946. Howell, Soskin.
--A Horse for Peter. Crowell, Pers (1910-), illus. LC 50-7384. (Illus.). 128 p. 23cm. 1950. Messner.
--Mountain Palomino. Palmer, Patricia, illus. LC 56-9159. 185p. illus. 22cm. 1956. Lothrop, Lee & Shepard.
--Wendy Wanted a Pony. Crowell, Pers (1910-), illus. LC 51-13191. 144 p. illus. 22 cm. 1951. Messner.

Brown, Elinor
--Holidays and Every Days: The Second Little Story Book. Norcross, Grace, illus. LC 42-17631. 30, 1 p. col. illus. 21 cm. 1942. Oxford University Press.
--The Litte Story Book. Norcross, Grace, illus. LC 40-538546. 30, 1 p. col. illus. 21 x 17 cm. c.1940. Oxford University Press.

Brown, Emily, adapted by see Disney, Walt, Productions.

Brown, Emma E.
--The Children's Hour. (Illus.). (Play and Study Ser.). N.D. D. Lothrop Co.
--Easy to Read. (Illus.). N.D. D. Lothrop & Co.
--From Night to Light, 1 of 4vols. (Illus.). (Hartz Boys Library). N.D. D. Lothrop Co.
--From Night to Light, 1 of 50 vols. (Illus.). 350p. (Sunday-School Lib: No. 14). N.D. Set. Lothrop Pub. Co.
--Jack, Jill and Tot. N.D. D. Lothrop Co.
--Once Upon A Time Play Stories. (Illus.). N.D. D. Lothrop & Co.

Brown, Ethel Clare
--The Green Gate to the Sea. Broadhurst, Jean (1873-), ed. LC 24-3789. viii, 166 p. illus., pl. 19 cm. c.1924. Silver, Burdett and Company.
--The Three Gays. Kelley, Grace G., illus. LC 15-15294. 204 p. front., plates 19 1/2 cm. 1915. The Penn Publishing Company.
--The Three Gays at Merryton. Kelley, Grace G., illus. LC 16-22981. 223 p. front., plates 19 1/2 cm. 1916. The Penn Publishing Company.
--The Three Gays at the Old Farm. Kelley, Grace G., illus. LC 18-18884. 224 p. front., plates 19 1/2 cm. 1918. The Penn Publishing Company.
--The Three Gays in Maine. Kelley, Grace G., illus. LC 17-888818. 216 p. front., plates 19 1/2 cm. 1917. The Penn Publishing Company.

Brown, Ethel Poole see Ewell, Gale, pseud.

Brown, Ethel Poole, Mrs. (1882-)
--Chumash Indians: A Story of Adventure for Young People. Ewell, Gale, pseud. Grant, Campbell (1909-) & Peake, Channing, illus. LC 29-15484. iv, 197 p. front., illus., pl. 20 cm. c.1929. Harr Wagner Publishing Co.

Brown, Eugene de Aguero (1875-)
--Thanksgiving and other Rhymes. LC 4-1035. (Illus.). 19cm. 36p. 1903. The Brown Rhymes Publishing House.

Brown, Eva Mills
--The Little Pink House. N.D. Vantage Press Inc.

AUTHOR INDEX BROWN, KATHRYN

Brown, Evelyn M (1911-)
--Kateri Tekakwitha, Mohawk Maid. Fisher, Leonard Everett (1924-), illus. LC 58-684061. 190p. illus. 22cm. (Vision books, 34). 1958. Vision Books.
Brown, F. C.
--Ben's Boyhood. (Young Folks Series, Number Three). N.D. Fleming H Revell Co.
Brown, F. K., pseud., see Franklin, Freida Kenyon.
Brown, F. W. & Waterbury, E. A.
--Nature Story Hours. N.D. Longmans Green & Co.
Brown, Fern G. (1918-)
--Bugs Bunny, Pioneer. Baker, Darrell, illus. (Illus.). (A Young Reader Ser.). (gr. k-3). 1979. (ISBN 0-307-60144-7, Golden Pr). Western Pub.
--Hard Luck Horse. Wiskur, Darrell D., illus. LC 75-31939. (Illus.). 127 p. 21cm. (Leader). 1975. (ISBN 0-8075-3159-6). A. Whitman.
--Jockey-or Else!. Wiskur, Darrell D., illus. LC 78-1715. p. cm. (Pilot books). 1978. (ISBN 0-8075-3944-9). A. Whitman.
--You're Somebody Special on a Horse. Murphy, Frank C, illus. LC 77-7506. (Illus.). 128 p. 21cm. (Albert Whitman pilot books). c.1977. (ISBN 0-8075-9447-4). A. Whitman.
Brown, [illegible] (1922-)
--Street Boy. LC 80-17309. 128 p. 17cm. c.1980. (ISBN 0-8024-8365-8). Moody Press.
--Street Boy Returns. LC 82-8221. 140 p. 17cm. c.1982. (ISBN 0-8024-8366-6). Moody Press.
Brown, Francine Litt
--Light-House Boy, 1 of 50 bks. Lucas, Derek, illus. (Illus.). (New Primary Lib.). N.D. Set. American Tract Society.
--Lighthouse Boy. Lucas, Derek, illus. LC 68-13230. (Illus.). 144 p. 22cm. 1968. (ISBN 0-200-71537-2). Abelard-Schuman.
Brown, Frederic (1906-1972)
--Mitkey Astromouse. Edelmann, Heinz, illus. LC 71-141540. (Illus.). 30 p. 33cm. (Here-and-there book from Harlin Quist). 1971. (ISBN 0-8252-0073-3). (ISBN 0-8252-0074-1). H. Quist.
Brown, Garrett
--American Fairy Tales. LC 11-22011. (Illus.). 24cm. 132p. 1911. James Mulligan Publishing Co.
--How to Beat the Game. Brown, Garrett, Jr. & Grant, Louis F., illus. LC 3-20472. 18 x 11cm. 117p. 1903. G. W. Dillingham Co.
Brown, George Mackay (1921-)
--Pictures in the Cave. MacInnes, Ian, illus. (Illus.). 136p. (gr. 4-7). 1980. (ISBN 0-7011-5081-5, Pub. by Chatto Bodley Jonathan). Merrimack Pub Cir.
--Six Lives of Fankle the Cat. MacInnes, Ian, illus. LC 82-670081. (Illus.). 120 p. 22cm. 1980. (ISBN 0-7011-2534-9). Chatto & Windus.
Brown, George Pliny (1836-1910)
--The King and His Wonderful Castle: A Story for Boys and Girls. LC 4-9271. 2 p. l., 118 p. 18 1/2 cm. 1904. Public-School Publishing Co.
Brown, Gladys Everets
--Tico Bravo: Shark Hunter. Maclain, Scott, illus. LC 54-5135. (Illus.). pen & ink ils. 132p. Repr. (Merit). (gr. 4-6). 1970. HM.
--Tico Bravo, Shark Hunter. 1st ed. Maclain, Scott, illus. LC 54-5135. 132p. illus. 22cm. 1954. Little, Brown.
--Two-Bow Bill. Barnum, Jay Hyde (1888-1962), illus. LC 55-6213. (Illus.). 46 p. 22cm. (Morrow junior books). 1955. Morrow.
Brown, H. F. M.
--Sketches from Nature, for My Juvenile Friends. N.D. Colby and Rich.
Brown, Harry Leslie
--The Bad Brown Boy. LC 30-18556. 3 p. l., 5-227, 1 p. 20 1/2 cm. c.1930. R.L. Polk Printing Co.
Brown, Harvey Q.
--The Enchanted Castle. N.D. Bruce Humphries, Inc.
Brown, Hazel
--Daisy's Friend: Or, The Girls of Oak Grove Seminary. (Illus.). 256p. N.D. Sunday-School Publications.
Brown, Helen Ada (1914-), compiled by.
--Read Together Poems: An Anthology of Verse for Choral Reading in Kindergarten and Primary Grades. Heltman, Harry Joseph (1885-), compiled by. 162p. 21cm. 1961. Row, Peterson.
Brown, Helen Ada (1914-) & Heltman, Harry Joseph. (1885-), eds.
--Let's-Read-Together Poems: An Anthology of Verse Selected and Arranged for Choral Reading in the Third-Grade,. LC 50-12272. v. 23 cm. N.D. Row, Peterson.
Brown, Helen Dawes (1857-)
--A Book of Little Boys. LC 4-237117. 6 p. l., 3-158 p., 1 l. front., 3 pl. 19 1/2 cm. 1904. Houghton, Mifflin and Company.
--Her Sixteenth Year. LC 1-24192. 2 p. l., 191, 1 p. 19 cm. 1901. Houghton, Mifflin and Company.
--How Phoebe Found Herself: Sequel to Her Sixteenth Year. 1912. Houghton Mifflin.
--Little Jean. LC 18-18524. 3 p. l., 133, 1 p. col. front. 20 cm. 1918. Houghton Mifflin Company.
--Little Miss Phoebe Gay. LC 4-16125. 4 p. l., 139 p. front., 2 pl. 19 1/2 cm. 1895. Houghton, Mifflin and Company.
--Mr. Tuckerman's Nieces. LC 7-32838. vi p., 1 l., 266 p., 1 l. front., 3 pl. 19 1/2 cm. 1907. Houghton, Mifflin and Company.
--Snap-Shots of Nancy and Brothers for the Family Scrap-Book: 1932-1935. LC 39-22740. 2 p. l., 80 p. front. (ports.) 20 cm. 1939. Thomas Todd Co., Printers.
--Two College Girls. N.D. Houghton Mifflin Co.
--Two College Girls. LC 5-2450. 325 p. 19 cm. 1886. Ticknor and Company.
Brown, Helen E., Mrs.
--Agnes in Search of Truth. 184p. N.D. American Tract Society.
--Aunt Winnie's Stories. 128p. N.D. Lockwood, Brooks & Co. for American Tract Society.
--Beautiful Hands. (Illus.). (Sunday-Hour Lib.). 1905. American Tract Society.
--The Cry-Baby. (Illus.). (Aunt Winnie's Stories). N.D. American Tract Society.
--The Cry-Baby. 32p. (Aunt Winnie's Stories). N.D. Lockwood, Brooks, & Co. for American Tract Society.
--Jesus Goes to the Synagogue. Hutchinson, William Miller (1916-), illus. 1960. Abingdon Press.
--The Little Lost Kitty. (Illus.). (Aunt Winnie's Stories). N.D. American Tract Society.
--The Little Lost Kitty. 32p. (Aunt Winnie's Stories). N.D. Lockwood, Brooks, & Co. for American Tract Society.
--Lonnie, Our Little Lamb. 110p. N.D. Hurd & Houghton for American Tract Society.
--Lonnie, our Little Lamb. 110p. N.D. Lockwood, Brooks, & Co. for American Tract Society.
--Lottie's Orange. (Illus.). (Aunt Winnie's Stories). N.D. American Tract Society.
--Lottie's Orange. 32p. (Aunt Winnie's Stories). N.D. Lockwood, Brooks, & Co. for American Tract Society.
--The Medicine Shelf. 315p. N.D. Hurd & Houghton for American Tract Society.
--The Medicine Shelf. 315p. (Honor-bright Library). N.D. Lockwood, Brooks, & Co. for American Tract Society.
--The Mother and Her Work. 137p. N.D. American Tract Society.
--Step by Step: Or, Tidy's Way to Freedom. (Illus.). 192p. N.D. American Tract Society.
--Tidy's Way to Freedom. 192p. N.D. Hurd & Houghton for American Tract Society.
--Tidy's Way to Freedom. 192p. N.D. Lockwood, Brooks, & Co. for American Tract Society.
--The Two Sixpence. (Illus.). (Aunt Winnie's Stories). N.D. American Tract Society.
--The Two Sixpences. 32p. (Aunt Winnie's Stories). N.D. Lockwood, Brooks, & Co. for American Tract Society.
--Walter Lightfoot's Pictures. 180p. N.D. Hurd & Houghton for American Tract Society.
--Walter Lightfoot's Pictures. 180p. (Cozy House Stories). N.D. Lockwood, Brooks, & Co. for American Tract Society.
--The Winter School. 204p. N.D. American Tract Society.
Brown, Howard N.
--Sunday Stories. 220p. N.D. Geo H Ellis.
Brown, Irene Bennett (1932-)
--Before the Lark. LC 82-1729. 191 p. 22cm. 1982. (ISBN 0-689-30920-1). Atheneum.
--Just Another Gorgeous Guy. LC 83-17914. 240p. (gr. 7 up). 1984. (ISBN 0-689-31011-0). Atheneum.
--Morning Glory Afternoon. LC 80-18495. 219 p. 22cm. 1981. (ISBN 0-689-30802-7). Atheneum.
--Run from a Scarecrow. Molina, Charles, illus. LC 77-20502. (Illus.). 128 p. 24cm. (Midwestern Memories). c.1978. (ISBN 0-570-07806-7). (ISBN 0-570-07801-6). Concordia Pub. House.
--Skitterbrain. LC 78-18349. p. cm. c.1978. (ISBN 0-8407-6587-8). T. Nelson.
--To Rainbow Valley. LC 73-81895. (Illus.). 134 p. 21cm. 1969. D. McKay Co.
--Willow Whip. LC 79-11725. p. cm. 1979. (ISBN 0-689-30703-9). Atheneum.
Brown, Irving Henry (1888-)
--Romany Road: The Story of Pete Brockhaus Thought to Have Been Kidnapped by Gypsies. Gallagher, M. J., illus. LC 32-22544. 286 p. incl. front., illus., plates. 19 1/2 cm. 1932. H. Smith and R. Haas.
Brown, Jackum
--Fair Game. LC 78-56558. (Illus.). (Breakthrough Ser.). (gr. 5 up). 1978. (ISBN 0-8178-5989-6). Harvey.
Brown, Janet Hendry, jt. auth. see Chase, Edith Newlin.
Brown, Janet (1856-1932)
--Ailie's Prayer. 64p. 1905. American Tract Society.
--Minnie Penton's Wrong-Doing. (Illus.). 64p. 1905. American Tract Society.
Brown, Janet (1856-1932) & Everett-Green, Evelyn
--Conquest Series, 4 Vols. (Illus.). N.D. American Tract Society.
Brown, Jeanette Perkins, Mrs. (1887-)
--Caterpillar, Caterpillar. Kredel, Fritz (1900-1973), illus. LC 39-10244. 25 p. col. illus. 14 1/2 cm. 1939. Harper & Brothers.
--Deedee's Holiday. Escourido, Joseph, illus. LC 56-9248. (Illus.). unpaged. illus. 21cm. (ps). 1956. (ISBN 0-685-11647-6). (ISBN 0-377-68851-7). Friend Pr.
--Friendship Magic. Smalley, Janet (1893-), illus. LC 45-4811. 128 p. illus. 20 1/2 cm. 1945. Friendship Press.
--Joe Lives in the City. Barnes, Ralph Willet (1900-), illus. LC 38-13913. 33 p. illus. 17 1/2 x 17 cm. c.1938. Friendship Press.
--Keiko's Birthday. Martinez, Jean, illus. LC 54-6955. (Illus.). 17 1/2cm. 35p. (Little Playmate Series). (ps). 1954. (ISBN 0-377-68811-8). Friendship Press.
--A Little Book of Bedtime Songs. Merwin, Decie (1894-1961), illus. N.D. Abelard.
--A Little Book of Bedtime Songs. Merwin, Decie (1894-1961), illus. N.D. Abingdon-Cokesbury Press.
--A Little Book of Singing Graces. Dotterer, Lloyd J., illus. N.D. Abingdon-Cokesbury Press.
--Manuel: A Little Boy of Mexico. Martinez, Jean, illus. LC 51-35507. 61 p. illus. 15 cm. (Little Friendship books). 1951. Friendship Press.
--Ronnie's Wish. Martinez, Jean, illus. LC 54-6957. (Illus.). 21cm. 32p. (Little Playmate Series). (ps). 1954. (ISBN 0-377-68831-2). Friend Pr.
--Rosita: A Little Girl of Puerto Rico. Carol, Elayne, illus. LC 48-9135. 60 p. col. illus. 15 c. (Little Friendship books). 1948. Friendship Press.
--Surprise for Robin. Papy, Dorothy, illus. LC 56-925048. unpaged. illus. 21cm. 1956. Friendship Press.
--Wishes Come True. Wireman, Katharine Richardson, illus. LC 48-8061. 128 p. col. illus. 21 cm. 1948. Friendship Press.
Brown, Jeff (1926-)
--Flat Stanley. Ungerer, Tomi, pseud. (1931-), illus. Ungerer, Jean Thomas. LC 63-17525. (Illus.). (gr. 1-5). 1964. (ISBN 0-06-020681-0, HarpJ). Har-Row.
--A Lamp for the Lambchops. 1st ed. Wheeling, Lynn, illus. LC 82-48628. (Illus.). 93 p. 24cm. c.1983. (ISBN 0-06-020693-4). (ISBN 0-06-020694-2). Harper & Row.
Brown, Joe David (1915-1976)
--Paper Moon: Addie Pray. N.D. New American Library.
Brown, Joel
--The Adventures of Coqui & His Friends. Berlitz Institute, tr. from Sp. Brown, Joel & Hussett, Milton, illus. (Illus.). 44p. (gr. k-3). 1980. (ISBN 0-9605994-0-1). New Day NY
Brown, John, Dr. (1810-1882)
--Marjorie Fleming. (Laddie Ser.). N.D. Henry Altemus Co.
--Miss Hitchcock's Wedding Dress, No.52. (Lakeside Library Ser.). N.D. Donnelley, Loyd & Co.
--Rab and His Friends. N.D. Anson D F Randolph & Co.
--Rab and His Friends. (Illus.). (Savoy Ser.). N.D. Barse and Hopkins.
--Rab and His Friends. (Illus.). (New Relyea Classics). N.D. Barse and Hopkins.
--Rab and His Friends. (Illus.). (The Golden Bks.). N.D. Barse & Hopkins.
--Rab and His Friends. (Dagonet Ser.). N.D. Barse & Hopkins.
--Rab and His Friends. (The Elm Ser.). N.D. Barse & Hopkins.
--Rab and His Friends. (Illus.). (The Alcazar Classics). N.D. Caldwell.
--Rab & His Friends. (Heath's Home & School Classics Ser.). N.D. D C Heath.
--Rab and His Friends. (Remarque Edition of Literary Classics). N.D. Dodge.
--Rab and His Friends. (Illus.). (Editha Series.). N.D. Dodge Publishing Co.
--Rab and His Friends, No.53. (Lakeside Library Ser.). N.D. Donnelley, Loyd & Co.
--Rab and His Friends. (Illus.). N.D. FredericK A Stokes.
--Rab and His Friends. (Illus.). (Broadway Booklets). N.D. George Routledge & Sons; Dist. by E. P. Dutton.
--Rab and His Friends, 25 vols. (Illus.). (The Editha Ser.: No. 20). 1905. Set. H M Caldwell Co.
--Rab and His Friends. (Remarque Edition of Literary Masterpieces). N.D. H. M. Caldwell Co.
--Rab and His Friends. (Illus.). (The Empyreal Library of Handy Volume Classics). N.D. H. M. Caldwell Co.
--Rab and His Friends. (Illus.). (The Young Folks Lib.). N.D. H. M. Caldwell Co.
--Rab and His Friends. (Illus.). (The Exquisite Ser.). N.D. H. M. Caldwell Co.
--Rab and His Friends, 1 of 3 vols. (The Lakeside Seires of Handy Volume Classics: No. 6). N.D. Set. H. M. Caldwell Co.
--Rab and His Friends. (Illus.). (The Chateau Series). N.D. H. M. Caldwell Co.
--Rab & His Friends. 1905. Henry Altemus Co.
--Rab and His Friends. (Illus.). (Vademecum Ser.). N.D. Henry Altemus Co.
--Rab and His Friends. (Illus.). (Boys' and Girls' Classics). N.D. Henry Altemus.
--Rab and His Friends. (Illus.). (Beauxarts Ser.). N.D. Henry Altemus Co.
--Rab and His Friends. Handy Volume, Large Type ed. (Illus.). (Petit-Trianon Ser.). N.D. Henry Altemus.
--Rab and His Friends. (Laddie Ser.). N.D. Henry Altemus Co.
--Rab and His Friends. (Modern Classics: No. 9). N.D. Houghton Mifflin Co.
--Rab and his Friends. (Riverside Classics). N.D. Houghton Mifflin & Co.
--Rab and His Friends. (Illus.). (Knickerbocker Classics). N.D. Hurst & Co.
--Rab and His Friends. N.D. James R. Osgood.
--Rab & His Friends. N.D. J.B. Lippincott.
--Rab and His Friends. (Cosy Corner Ser.). N.D. L. C. Page & Co.
--Rab & His Friends. N.D. Methodist Bk Concern.
--Rab & His Friends, 1 of 5 pts, Pt. 1. (Boy's Pocket Library). N.D. Set. Methodist Bk Concern.
--Rab and His Friends. popular ed. Bridgman, Lewis Jesse (1857-1931), illus. (Illus.). N.D. Lothrop.
--Rab and His Friends. Hoskins, Gayle, illus. LC 7-22206. 58, 1 p. col. front., col. plates. 19 1/2 cm. (children's classics, J.B. Lippincott co.). c.1927. J.B. Lippincott Company.
--Rab and His Friends. Sacker, Amy M., illus. (Cosy Corner Ser.). N.D. L.C. Page & Co.
--Rab and His Friends, and Marjorie Fleming. (First Series). N.D. G P Putman's Sons.
--Rab and His Friends and Marjorie Fleming. (Illus.). (The Vest-Pocket Ser.: 13). N.D. James R Osgood & Co.
--Rab and His Friends, and Marjorie Fleming. (Ariel Booklets). N.D. Putman & Sons.
--Rab and his Friends and other Dogs and Men. (Illus.). (Riverside School Library). N.D. Houghton Mifflin Co.
--Rab and His Friends, and Our Dogs. Lang, Andrew, intro. by. 140p. 1905. Century Co.
--The Runaway Bunny. N.D. (ISBN 0-06-020766-3). Harper & Row.
Brown, John S., jt. auth. see Aiken, Joan.
Brown, John Walker (1814-1849)
--The Christmas Bells. LC 21-16620. 18cm. 221p. 1842. D. Appleton & Co.
Brown, John & Dalziel, Edward (1817-1905), illus.
--Old Favorite Fairy Tales. 1882. J B Lippincott.
Brown, Judith Gwyn (1933-)
--Alphabet Dreams. LC 76-12452. p. cm. c.1976. (ISBN 0-13-022806-0). Prentice-Hall.
--The Happy Voyage. Brown, Judith Gwyn (1933-), illus. LC 65-10245. 1v. (unpaged) illus. 25cm. c.1965. Macmillan.
--Max and the Truffle Pig. Brown, Judith Gwyn (1933-), illus. LC 63-10806. 46 p. illus. 21 cm. 1963. Abingdon Press.
--Max and the Truffle Pig. Brown, Judith Gwyn (1933-), illus. 1963. E M Hale.
--Muffin. LC 72-1541. (Illus.). 32 p. 22cm. 1972. (ISBN 0-200-71895-9). (ISBN 0-200-71895-9). Abelard-Schuman.
Brown, Julia
--The Enchanted Peacock: And Other Stories. LC 11-27459. ix p., 1 l., 13-136 p. col. front., illus., col. plates. 23 1/2 cm. c.1911. Rand, McNally & Co.
--The Enchanted Peacock: And Other Stories. LC 25-15383. x p., 1 l., 13-156 p. col. front., illus., col. plates. 23 1/2 cm. c.1925. Rand McNally & Co.
--The Mermaid's Gift: And Other Stories. Enright, Maginel Wright, illus. LC 12-20196. 168 p. col. front., col. plates. 23 1/2 cm. N.D. Rand, McNally & Company.
Brown, Kate Louise (1857-)
--Alice and Tom: Or, The Record of a Happy Year. LC 8-568. viii, 212 p. illus., port. 18 1/2 cm. 1899. D.C. Heath & Co.
Brown, Kate Weldon
--One Summer. LC 13-13539. (Frontispiece by E. H. Killam). 5-44 p. 30cm. 1913. Broadway Pub.
Brown, Katharine Holland
--Philippa at Halcyon. LC 10-13218. vii, 1 p., 2 l., 3-422 p. front., plates. 19 1/2 cm. 1910. C. Scribner's Sons.
Brown, Kathryn M., pseud., see Brown, Lela K..
Brown, Kathryn M., pseud.
--Blossom Hollow. Brown, Lela K.. (ps-5). N.D. (ISBN 0-8062-2511-4). Carlton.

Brown, Kay (1943-), retold by see Grimm, Jakob Ludwig Karl.
Brown, Kay (1943-), retold by see Irving, Washington.
Brown, Kay (1943-), retold by see Lorenzini, Carlo.
Brown, Kay (1943-), ed. see Spyri, Johanna Heusser.
Brown, Kay (1943-), retold by.
--Ali Baba and the Forty Thieves. Embleton, Gerry, illus. LC 79-51393. p. cm. (Derrydale Fairy Tale Library). 1979. (ISBN 0-517-28801-X). Derrydale Books.
--Beauty and the Beast. Embleton, Gerry, illus. LC 79-51394. (Illus.). 28 p. 31cm. (Derrydale Classic Fairy Tale Ser.). c.1978. (ISBN 0-517-28802-8). Derrydale.
--Jack & the Beanstalk. Embleton, Gerry, illus. LC 79-84830. (Illus.). 28 p. 31cm. (Derrydale Classic Fairy Tale Ser.). c.1978. (ISBN 0-517-28804-4). Derrydale Books.
--Red Riding Hood. Embleton, Gerry, illus. LC 79-14943. p. cm. (Derrydale Fairy Tale Library). 1979. (ISBN 0-517-28810-9). Derrydale Books.
--Sleeping Beauty. Embleton, Gerry, illus. LC 79-14038. p. cm. (Derrydale Fairy Tale Library). 1979. (ISBN 0-517-28811-7). Derrydale Books.
--Snow White and the Seven Dwarfs. Embleton, Gerry, illus. LC 79-14040. p. cm. (Derrydale Fairy Tale Library). 1979. (ISBN 0-517-28812-5). Derrydale Books.
Brown, Kenneth (1868-)
--The Duke's Price. Learned, A. G., illus. N.D. Houghton Mifflin.
--Putter Perkins. N.D. Houghton Mifflin.
--Two Boys in a Gyrocar: The Story of a New York to Paris Motor Race. Goldsmith, Wallace, illus. ix p., 1 l., 309, 1 p. front., plates. 19 cm. 1911. Houghton Mifflin Company.
Brown, L. Kate, jt. auth. see Emerson, U. E.
Brown, Laurene Krasny, jt. auth. see Brown, Marc Tolon.
Brown, Lela K. see Brown, Kathryn M., pseud.
Brown, Levant Frederick
--Prince Harold. Witry, Aline, illus. LC 1-16491. 255p. 1902. L. C. Page & Co.
Brown, Lewis Stacy
--Yes, Helen, There Were Dinosaurs: The Story of a Jurassic Time Trip. Brown, Lewis Stacy, illus. LC 82-144370. (Illus.). vi, 143 p. c.1982. L.S. Brown.
Brown, Lisette
--Tales of the Sea Foam. Townsend, Virginia, illus. (Illus.). photos. 2 color photos. 3 b&w photos. 12 b&w illus. 77p. (gr. 6 up). 1969. Naturegraph.
Brown, Louise Lyons (1897-)
--The Adventure of Two Mice. LC 55-27085. unpaged. illus. 15x22cm. 1954. Comet Press Books.

Brown, Lynn
--Fire & Firecrackers. 3rd ed. Walker, Granville, Jr., ed. Jackson, Gregory A., illus. (Illus.). 14p. (Orig.). 1st U.S. edition. (Fun & Safety Ser.). (ps-6). 1982. (ISBN 0-9608466-1-1). Fun Reading.
--Lightning Storm. Walker, Granville, Jr., ed. Jackson, Gregory A., illus. (Illus.). 14p. (Orig.). (Fun & Safety Ser.). (ps-6). 1982. (ISBN 0-9608466-2-X). Fun Reading.
--Ms. Worm. 3rd ed. Walker, Granville, Jr., ed. Jackson, Gregory A., illus. (Illus., Orig.). 1st U.S. edition. (Fun & Safety Ser.). (ps-6). 1982. (ISBN 0-9608466-0-3). Fun Reading.

Brown, Marc Tolon (1946-)
--Arthur Goes to Camp. LC 81-15588. p. cm. c.1982. (ISBN 0-316-11218-6). Little, Brown.
--Arthur's April Fool. LC 82-20368. (Illus.). 32 p. 27cm. c.1983. (ISBN 0-316-11196-1). Little, Brown.
--Arthur's Christmas. Brown, Marc Tolon (1946-), illus. LC 84-4373. (Illus.). (gr. 1-3). c.1984. (ISBN 0-316-11180-5). Little.
--Arthur's Eye. LC 79-11734. p. cm. c.1979. (ISBN 0-316-11063-9). Little, Brown.
--Arthur's Halloween. Brown, Marc Tolon (1946-), illus. LC 82-14286. (Illus.). 32p. (gr. 1-3). 1983. (ISBN 0-316-11059-0, Pub. by Atlantic Monthly Pr). (ISBN 0-316-11116-3). Little.
--Arthur's Nose. LC 75-30610. (Illus.). 32 p. 26cm. c.1976. (ISBN 0-316-11193-7). Little, Brown.
--Arthur's Thanksgiving. LC 83-798. (Illus.). 32 p. 26cm. c.1983. (ISBN 0-316-11060-4). Little, Brown.
--Arthur's Valentine. LC 80-14001. p. cm. c.1980. (ISBN 0-316-11062-0). Little, Brown.
--The Cloud Over Clarence. LC 79-4656. (Illus.). 32 p. 21cm. (Unicorn book). c.1979. (ISBN 0-525-28013-8). Dutton.
--Finger Rhymes. LC 80-10173. (Illus.). 32p. (ps-2). 1980. (Unicorn Bk). Dutton.
--Lenny and Lola. LC 77-16426. (Illus.). 32 p. 27cm. (unicorn book). c.1978. (ISBN 0-525-33465-3). Dutton.
--Marc Brown's Boat Book. Brown, Marc Tolon (1946-), illus. (Illus.). 14p. (Sturdy Shape Bks.). (ps). 1982. (ISBN 0-307-12262-X, Golden Pr). Western Pub.
--Marc Brown's Full House. LC 77-7962. p. cm. c.1977. (ISBN 0-201-00341-4). Addison-Wesley.
--Moose and Goose. LC 78-6822. (Illus.). 32 p. 24cm. (Unicorn book). c.1978. (ISBN 0-525-35175-2). E. P. Dutton.
--One, Two, Three: An Animal Counting Book. LC 76-17826. (Illus.). 31 p. 26cm. c.1976. (ISBN 0-316-11064-7). Little, Brown.
--Pickle Things. LC 80-10540. p. cm. 1980. (ISBN 0-8193-1027-1). (ISBN 0-8193-1028-X). Parents Magazine Press.
--The Silly Tail Book. LC 83-2250. p. cm. c.1983. (ISBN 0-8193-1110-3). Parents Magazine Press.
--Spooky Riddles. LC 83-6051. (I Can Read It All By Myself). c.1983. (ISBN 0-394-86093-4). Beginner Books.
--Spooky Riddles. Brown, Marc Tolon (1946-), illus. 1983. Random.
--There's No Place Like Home. Brown, Marc Tolon (1946-), illus. LC 84-4229. (Illus.). 41 p. 23cm. (A Parents Magazine Read Aloud and Easy Reading Program Original). c.1984. (ISBN 0-8193-1125-1). Parents Magazine Press.
--The True Francine. Brown, Marc Tolon (1946-), illus. LC 80-22375. p. cm. c.1981. (ISBN 0-316-11212-7). Little, Brown.
--What Do You Call a Dumb Bunny? & Other Rabbit Riddles, Games, Jokes & Cartoons. Brown, Marc Tolon (1946-), illus. LC 82-21650. (Illus.). 32p. (gr. 1-3). 1983. (ISBN 0-316-11117-1, Pub. by Atlantic Monthly Pr). (ISBN 0-316-11119-8, Pub. by Atlantic Monthly Pr). (ISBN 0-316-11192-9). Little.
--Wings on Things. LC 81-12095. (Illus.). 28 p. 24cm. (A Bright and Early Book: BE 26). c.1982. (ISBN 0-394-85130-7). Beginner Books.
--Witches Four. Brown, Marc Tolon (1946-), illus. LC 79-5263. (Illus.). 40 p. 24cm. c.1980. (ISBN 0-8193-1013-1). (ISBN 0-8193-1014-X). Parents Magazine Press.
Brown, Marc Tolon (1946-) & Brown, Laurene Krasny
--The Bionic Bunny Show. Brown, Marc Tolon (1946-), illus. LC 83-22211. (Illus.). 20 x 27 cm. 31p. c.1984. Little, Brown. **Award: (ALA).**

Brown, Marc Tolon (1946-) & Krensky, Stephen Alan (1953-)
--Dinosaurs, Beware!. A Safety Guide. Brown, Marc Tolon (1946-) & Krensky, Stephen Alan (1953-), illus. LC 82-15207. (Illus.). 32p. (gr. k-3). 1982. (ISBN 0-316-11228-3, Pub. by Atlantic Pr). Little. **Award: (ALA).**
Brown, Marcia (1918-), ed. see Prince Ahmed.
Brown, Marcia (1918-), tr. see Cendrars, Blaise.
Brown, Marcia (1918-), tr. see Perrault, Charles.
Brown, Marcia (1918-)
--All Butterflies: An ABC. LC 73-19364. 32 chiefly col. illus. 27cm. 1974. (ISBN 0-684-13771-2). Scribner.
--Backbone of the King. (Illus.). 180p. Repr. of 1966 ed (Pub. by Charles Scribner's Sons). (gr. 4-8). 1984. (ISBN 0-8248-0963-7). UH Pr.
--Backbone of the King: The Story Of Paka'a and His Son Ku. Brown, Marcia (1918-), illus. LC 66-18180. (Illus.). (gr. 5-9). 1966. (ISBN 0-684-20747-8). Scribner.
--The Blue Jackal. Brown, Marcia (1918-), illus. LC 76-54845. (Illus.). 32 p. 26cm. c.1977. Scribner.
--Cinderella. Brown, Marcia (1918-), illus. 1954. Charles Scribner's Sons. **Award: (ALA).**
--Dick Whittington and His Cat. Brown, Marcia (1918-), illus. (Illus.). 32 p. 26cm. 1950. Scribner. **Award: (RCM).**
--Felice. Brown, Marcia (1918-), illus. LC 58-11640. (Illus.). unpaged. 26cm. 1958. Scribner. **Award: (ALA).**
--Henry-Fisherman. Brown, Marcia (1918-), illus. LC 49-1026. (Illus.). 32p. (gr. k-3). 1949. (ISBN 0-684-12399-1, ScribJ). Scribner.
--How, Hippo!. Brown, Marcia (1918-), illus. LC 69-17059. (Illus.). 32 p. 25cm. 1969. Scribner. **Award: (ALA).**
--Little Carousel. Brown, Marcia (1918-), illus. (Illus.). (gr. k-2). 1946. (ISBN 0-684-12314-2, ScribJ). Scribner.
--The Neighbors. Brown, Marcia (1918-), illus. LC 67-24046. (Illus.). 1 v. 27cm. 32p. 1967. Scribner.
--Once a Mouse. LC 61-14769. (Illus.). 32p. (gr. k-3). 1982. (ISBN 0-689-70751-7, Aladdin). Atheneum.
--Once a Mouse...a Fable Cut in Wood. Brown, Marcia (1918-), illus. LC 61-14769. (Illus.). (ps-5). 1961. (ISBN 0-684-12662-1, ScribJ). (ISBN 0-689-70751-7). Scribner. **Awards: (NYT); (ALA); (RCM).**
--Peter Piper's Alphabet. LC 59-11849. unpaged. illus. 21x26cm. 1959. (ISBN 0-684-13128-5). Scribner.
--Skipper John's Cook. Brown, Marcia (1918-), illus. LC 51-12874. (Illus.). unpaged. 26cm. 1951. Scribner. **Award: (RCM).**
--Stone Soup. Brown, Marcia (1918-), illus. 1982. Scribner.
--Stone Soup: An Old Tale. LC 47-11630. 48 p. col. illus. 26 cm. 1947. C. Scribner's Sons.
--Tamarindo!. LC 60-13486. unpaged. illus. 26cm. 1960. Scribner.
Brown, Marcia (1918-), retold by.
--The Flying Carpet. Brown, Marcia (1918-), illus. (Illus.). (gr. 1-5). 1956. (ISBN 0-684-12953-1). Scribner. **Award: (ALA).**
Brown, Marcia (1918-), illus.
--The Bun: A Tale from Russia. 1st ed. Brown, Marcia (1918-), tr. LC 75-167832. (Illus.). 32 p. 27cm. c.1972. (ISBN 0-15-213450-6). Harcourt Brace Jovanovich.
Brown, Marcia (1918-) & Andersen, Hans Christian (1805-1875)
--The Snow Queen. LC 72-168499. (Illus.). 96p. (gr. 1-5). 1972. (ISBN 0-684-12611-7, ScribJ). Scribner.
Brown, Margaret B
--Animal Adventures for Children. 1st ed. LC 55-7170. 86p. 23cm. 1955. Vantage Press.
Brown, Margaret Wise see Golden, MacDonald, pseud.
Brown, Margaret Wise see MacDonald, Golden, pseud.
Brown, Margaret Wise, jt. auth. see Crampton, Gertrude.
Brown, Margaret Wise, jt. auth. see Disney, Walt, Productions.
Brown, Margaret Wise, jt. auth. see Harris, Joel Chandler.
Brown, Margaret Wise, jt. auth. see Koffler, Camilla.
Brown, Margaret Wise, jt. auth. see Sage, Juniper.
Brown, Margaret Wise (1910-1952), adapted by see Harris, Joel Chandler.
Brown, Margaret Wise (1910-1952), contrib. by see Hurd, Clement.
Brown, Margaret Wise (1910-), tr. see La Fontaine, Jean de.
Brown, Margaret Wise (1910-1952)
--The Bad Little Duckhunter. Hurd, Clement (1908-), illus. 32 p. col. illus. 20 x 26 cm. 1947. W. R. Scott.
--Big Book of Nursery Tales. Weisgard, Leonard Joseph (1916-), illus. N.D. (ISBN 0-448-04201-0). Grosset & Dunlap.
--The Big Fur Secret. De Veyrac, Robert (1901-), illus. LC 44-9460. 32p. (gr. k-1). 1944. Harper & Bros.
--Big Red Barn. N.D. E. M. Hale & Co.
--Big Red Barn. Hartman, Rosella, illus. LC 56-5404. (Illus.). 1 v. (unpaged. (Young Scott books). c.1956. W. R. Scott.
--Black and White. Shaw, Charles Green (1892-1974), illus. LC 44-5033. 32 p. illus. 27 1/2 x 20 1/2 cm. c.1944. Harper & Brothers.
--Bumble Bugs and Elephants. Hurd, Clement (1908-), illus. 1938. Scott.
--A Child's Good Morning. Charlot, Jean (1898-1979), illus. LC 52-7270. unpaged. illus. 25 cm. (Young Scott books). 1952. W. R. Scott.
--A Child's Good Night Book. Charlot, Jean (1898-1979), illus. LC 43-151373. 24 p. illus. (part col.) 17 x 14 1/2 cm. c.1943. W. R. Scott, Inc.
--A Child's Good Night Book. Charlot, Jean (1898-1979), illus. LC 51-6286. (Illus.). unpaged. 25cm. (Young Scott books). 1951, c.1950. W. R. Scott.
--A Child's Goodnight Book. 40p. 1950. Young Scott Book.
--A Child's Goodnight Book. Charlot, Jean (1898-1979), illus. 40p. (ps-k). 1950. (ISBN 0-201-09155-0). Addison Wesley Publishing.
--A Child's Goodnight Book. Charlot, Jean (1898-1979), illus. 40p. (Young Scott Books). 1950. W. R. Scott, Inc.
--Christmas in the Barn. LC 52-7858. 32p. 1952. (ISBN 0-690-19271-1). (ISBN 0-690-19272-X). Thomas Y. Crowell Company.
--Christmas in the Barn. Cooney, Barbara (1917-), illus. 1952. Harper.
--The City Noisy Book. Weisgard, Leonard Joseph (1916-), illus. LC 39-31264. (Illus.). (ps). 1976. (ISBN 0-06-443001-4, Trophy). Har-Row.
--The Color Kittens. Provensen, Alice (1918-) & Provensen, Martin (1916-), illus. LC 50-5777. 28 p. col. illus. 20 cm. (little golden book). c.1949. Simon and Schuster.
--The Color Kittens: A Child's First Book About Colors. Provensen, Alice (1918-) & Provensen, Martin (1916-), illus. 1 v. (unpaged) col. illus. 32 cm. c.1958. Golden Press.
--Country Noisy Book. Weisgard, Leonard Joseph (1916-), illus. LC 40-32006. (Illus.). (ps-1). 1940. (ISBN 0-06-020811-2, HarpJ). (ISBN 0-06-443002-2, Trophy). Har-Row.
--The Country Noisy Book. Weisgard, Leonard Joseph (1916-), illus. 42p. N.D. William R. Scott Inc.
--The Dark Wood of the Golden Birds. Weisgard, Leonard Joseph (1916-), illus. LC 50-8605. 58 p. col. illus. 22 cm. 1950. Harper.
--David's Little Indian: A Story. Charlip, Remy (1929-), illus. LC 56-10691. unpaged. illus. 16cm. (Young Scott books 528). 1956. W. R. Scott.
--The Dead Bird. 1958. Addison.
--The Dead Bird. 1958. (ISBN 0-8382-0199-7, Cadmus Books). E. M. Hale and Company.
--The Dead Bird. Charlip, Remy (1929-), illus. LC 58-5525. (Illus.). 48 p. (Young Scott books). 1958. W. R. Scott.
--Diggers. Hurd, Clement (1908-), illus. (Illus.). (gr. k-3). 1960. (ISBN 0-06-020690-X, HarpJ). Har-Row.
--Doctor Squash: The Doll Doctor. Miller, John Parr (1913-), illus. LC 52-10797. unpaged. illus. 21 cm. (Little golden library, 157). 1952. Simon and Schuster.
--Don't Frighten the Lion!. Rey, Hans Augusto (1898-1977), illus. (gr. k-3). N.D. Harper & Bros.
--The Dream Book: First Comes the Dream. Floethe, Richard (1901-), illus. 1950. Random House.
--Duck. Koffler, Camilla (0000-1955), illus. Ylla, pseud. LC 52-12995. (Illus.). photos. (ps-3). 1953. (ISBN 0-06-020696-9, HarpJ). Har-Row.
--The First Story. Simont, Marc (1915-), illus. LC 47-307539. 31 p. illus. (part col.) 23 cm. 1947. Harper.
--The Fish with the Deep Sea Smile. Rauch, Roberta, illus. LC 38-10122. 128 p. illus., double col. plates. 28 cm. c.1938. E.P. Dutton & Co., Inc.
--Four Fur Feet. Charlip, Remy (1929-), illus. LC 61-2007. unpaged. illus. 26cm. c.1961. W.R. Scott.
--Fox Eyes. Charlot, Jean (1898-1979), illus. LC 51-14671. unpaged. illus. 22 cm. N.D. Pantheon Books.
--Fox Eyes. William, Garth Montgomery (1912-), illus. LC 76-43086. (Illus.). 36 p. 29cm. 1977, c.1951. (ISBN 0-394-83116-0). (ISBN 0-394-93116-5). Pantheon Books.
--The Friendly Book. Williams, Garth Montgomery (1912-), illus. LC 54-902406. unpaged. illus. 21cm. (Little golden book, 199). 1954. Simon and Schuster.
--The Golden Bunny and Seventeen Other Stories and Poems. Weisgard, Leonard Joseph (1916-), illus. LC 53-8186. unpaged. illus. 34cm. (Big golden book, 573). 1953. Simon and Schuster.
--The Golden Bunny: And 17 Other Stories. Weisgard, Leonard Joseph (1916-), illus. (Illus.). 26 p. 33cm. (Big golden book). 1963, c.1953. Golden Press.
--The Golden Egg Book. Weisgard, Leonard Joseph (1916-), illus. 1947. Golden Press.
--The Golden Egg Book. Weisgard, Leonard Joseph (1916-), illus. (Big Golden Book: 462). 1947. Simon and Schuster.
--The Golden Egg Book. Weisgard, Leonard Joseph (1916-), illus. (Illus.). 32p. (A Big Golden Book). (ps-3). 1972. (ISBN 0-307-10853-8, Golden Pr). Western Pub.
--The Golden Egg Book. Weisgard, Leonard Joseph (1916-), illus. (Illus.). 32p. (ps-1). 1976. (ISBN 0-307-12045-7, Golden Pr). (ISBN 0-307-60462-4). Western Pub.
--The Golden Sleepy Book. Williams, Garth Montgomery (1912-), illus. LC 73-143792. (Illus.). 33 p. 32cm. (Golden book favorite). 1971, c.1948. Golden Press.
--The Golden Sleepy Book. Williams, Garth Montgomery (1912-), illus. LC 48-8169. 42 p. illus. (part col.) 21 cm. (Little golden library, 46). 1948. Simon and Schuster.
--Goodnight Moon. Hurd, Clement (1908-), illus. LC 47-30762. (Illus.). (ps-1). 1947. (ISBN 0-06-020705-1, HarpJ). (ISBN 0-06-020706-X). Har-Row.
--Goodnight Moon. Hurd, Clement (1908-), illus. (Illus.). (Picture Bk.). (ps-2). 1977. (ISBN 0-06-443017-0, Trophy). Har-Row.
--The Hidden House. 1st ed. Fine, Aaron, illus. LC 52-130623. unpaged. illus. 22cm. 1953. Holt.
--Home for a Bunny. Williams, Garth Montgomery (1912-), illus. LC 56-13746. unpaged. illus. 33cm. (Golden book, 446). c.1956. Simon and Schuster.
--Home for a Bunny. Williams, Garth Montgomery (1912-), illus. (Illus.). 24p. (ps-2). 1983. (ISBN 0-307-10446-X, Golden Pr). Western Pub.
--The House of a Hundred Windows. Rousseau, Henri, et al. (1844-1910), illus. LC 45-4227. 32 p. illus. 29 1/2 x 23 cm. c.1945. Harper & Brothers.
--Important Book. Weisgard, Leonard Joseph (1916-), illus. LC 49-9133. (Illus.). (ps-1). 1949. (ISBN 0-06-020720-5, HarpJ). (ISBN 0-06-020721-3). Har-Row.

AUTHOR INDEX BROWN, MYRA

--Indoor Noisy Book. Weisgard, Leonard Joseph (1916-), illus. LC 42-23589. 44 p. col. illus. 22 1/2 x 18 1/2 cm. 1942. W. R. Scott, Inc.
--The Little Brass Band. Hurd, Clement (1908-), illus. LC 55-882013. unpaged. illus. 21x23cm. 1955. Harper.
--Little Chicken. Weisgard, Leonard Joseph (1916-), illus. LC 43-16942. (Illus.). 32p. (gr. k-3). 1982. (ISBN 0-06-020739-6, HarpJ). (ISBN 0-06-020740-X). Har-Row.
--The Little Cowboy. Slobodkina, Esphyr (1908-), illus. LC 49-8121. 34 p. col. illus. 25 cm. (Young Scott books). 1949. W. R. Scott.
--The Little Farmer. Slobodkina, Esphyr (1908-), illus. LC 48-5906. 40p. (gr. k-1). 1948. Young Scott Bks.
--The Little Fir Tree. Cooney, Barbara (1917-), illus. LC 54-[illegible]. (Illus.). unpaged. 1954. Crowell.
--The Little Fireman. Slobodkina, Esphyr (1908-), illus. LC 84-43127. p. cm. (Young Scott Books). 1985, c.1938. (ISBN 0-201-09261-1). Harper & Row.
--The Little Fireman. Slobodkina, Esphyr (1908-), illus. LC 52-7267. unpaged. illus. 25 cm. 1952. W. R. Scott.
--The Little Fireman. Slobodkina, Esphyr (1908-), illus. LC 39-43846. 34 p. col. illus. 20 1/2 cm. c.1938. W.R. Scott.
--The Little Fisherman. Ipcar, Dahlov Zorach (1917-), illus. LC 45-35212. 34 p. col. illus. 25 x 20 1/2 cm. (On cover: Young Scott books). c.1945. W. R. Scott, Inc.
--Little Fur Family. Williams, Garth Montgomery (1912-), illus. LC 51-11657. (Illus.). unpaged. 23cm. 1951, c.1946. Harper.
--Little Indian. Scarry, Richard McClure (1919-), illus. LC 54-367595. unpaged. illus. 21cm. (Little golden book, 202). 1954. Simon and Schuster.
--Margaret Wise Brown's A Child's Good Night Book. Charlot, Jean (1898-1979), illus. LC 84-43123. p. cm. (Young Scott Books). 1985, c.1943. (ISBN 0-201-09155-0). Harper & Row.
--Margaret Wise Brown's Golden Sleepy Book. new ed. Williams, Garth Montgomery (1912-), illus. 36p. 1st U.S. edition. (gr. 3-6). 1971. (ISBN 0-307-12038-4, Golden Pr). Western Pub.
--Margaret Wise Brown's Wonderful Story Book. Miller, John Parr (1913-), illus. (Big Golden Book). 1948. Golden Press.
--Margaret Wise Brown's Wonderful Storybook. Miller, John Parr (1913-), illus. (Illus.). 64p. Repr. of 1974 ed. (gr. 2). 1985. (ISBN 0-307-15777-6, Pub. by Golden Bks.). Western Pub.
--Mister Dog: The Dog Who Belonged to Himself. Williams, Garth Montgomery (1912-), illus. LC 52-13616. unpaged. illus. 21 cm. (Little golden library, 128). 1952. Simon and Schuster.
--The Moon Balloon. Weisgard, Leonard Joseph (1916-), illus. 1952. Harper.
--My World. Hurd, Clement (1908-), illus. LC 49-11069. 34 p. illus. (part col.) 18 x 21 cm. c.1949. Harper.
--Nibble, Nibble. Weisgard, Leonard Joseph (1916-), illus. LC 59-4895. 64p. (gr. k-5). 1959. (ISBN 0-201-09291-3, A-W Childrens). A-W.
--Nibble Nibble: Poems for Children. Weisgard, Leonard Joseph (1916-), illus. LC 84-43128. p. cm. (Young Scott Books). 1985, c.1959. (ISBN 0-201-09291-3). Harper & Row.
--Nibble Nibble: Poems for Children. Weisgard, Leonard Joseph (1916-), illus. LC 59-4895. unpaged. illus. 28cm. (Young Scott books). 1959. W.R. Scott.
--Night and Day. Weisgard, Leonard Joseph (1916-), illus. LC 42-196826. 32 p. illus. (part col.) 26 x 21 1/2 cm. 1942. Harper & Brothers.
--The Noisy Bird Book. Weisgard, Leonard Joseph (1916-) & Audubon, John James (1785-1851), illus. LC 43-3614. 41 p. illus. (part col.) 23 x 18 1/2 cm. c.1943. W. R. Scott, Inc.
--Noisy Book. LC 30-31264. cover-tile, 42 p. illus. (part col.) 23 cm. c.1939. W.R. Scott, Inc.
--Noisy Book (City). Weisgard, Leonard Joseph (1916-), illus. LC 39-31264. (Illus.). Orig. Title: City Noisy Book. (ps-1). 1939. (ISBN 0-06-020830-9, HarpJ). (ISBN 0-06-020831-7). Har-Row.
--The Noon Balloon. Weisgard, Leonard Joseph (1916-), illus. LC 52-5426. (Illus.). 33 p. 26cm. 1952. Harper.
--On Christmas Eve. Montresor, Beni (1926-), illus. LC 84-43129. p. cm. (Young Scott Books). 1985, c.1965. (ISBN 0-201-09297-2). Harper & Row.
--On Christmas Eve. Montresor, Beni (1926-), illus. LC 61-16197. (Illus.). 1 v. 26cm. 1961. Young Scott Books.
--The Peppermint Family. Hurd, Clement (1908-), illus. (gr. k-1). 1950. Harper & Bros.
--The Polite Penguin. Rey, Hans Augusto (1898-1977), illus. LC 41-221506. 31 p. illus. (part col.) 26 1/2 x 24 1/2 cm. c.1941. Harper & Brothers.
--The Poodle and the Sheep. Weisgard, Leonard Joseph (1916-), illus. LC 41-12321. 55 p. col. illus. 17 x 23 1/2 cm. 1941. E.P. Dutton and Company, Inc.
--Pussy Willow. Weisgard, Leonard Joseph (1916-), illus. (Little Golden Book). 1958. Golden Press.
--Pussy Willow. 1972 ed. Weisgard, Leonard Joseph (1916-), illus. LC 72-179660. (Illus.). 32 p. 33cm. 1972, c.1951. Golden Press.
--Pussy Willow. Weisgard, Leonard Joseph (1916-), illus. LC 52-6581. unpaged. illus. 34 cm. (Big golden book, 564). 1952. Simon and Schuster.
--A Pussycat's Christmas. Stone, Helen (1904-), illus. LC 49-50062. 32 p. col. illus. 19 cm. c.1949. Crowell.
--The Quiet Noisy Book. Weisgard, Leonard Joseph (1916-), illus. LC 50-9797. (Illus.). 34 p. 27cm. c.1950. Harper.
--Red Light, Green Light. Weisgard, Leonard Joseph (1916-), illus. LC 44-8554. 40 p. col. illus. 19 1/2 x 26 cm. c.1944. Doubleday, Doran & Company, Inc.
--The Runaway Bunny. Hurd, Clement (1908-), illus. LC 42-66148. 40 p. illus. (part col.) 18 x 21 cm. 1942. Harper & Brothers.
--The Runaway Bunny. Revised. Hurd, Clement (1908-), illus. 1962. Harper.
--The Runaway Bunny. Hurd, Clement (1908-), illus. LC 71-183168. (Illus.). 39 p. 1972, c.1942. (ISBN 0-06-020766-3). Harper & Row.
--The Sailor Dog. Williams, Garth Montgomery (1912-), illus. LC 53-2327. unpaged. illus. 21cm. (Little golden library, 156). 1953. Simon and Schuster.
--The Seashore Noisy Book. Weisgard, Leonard Joseph (1916-), illus. 1941. Harper & Row
--The Seashore Noisy Book. Weisgard, Leonard Joseph (1916-), illus. LC 41-13238. cover-title, 42 p. illus. (part col.) 22 1/2 x 18 1/2 cm. c.1941. W.R. Scott, Inc.
--Seven Stories About a Cat Named Sneakers. Charlot, Jean (1898-1979), illus. LC 55-5096. 144p. illus. 20cm. (Young Scott books). c.1955. W. R. Scott.
--Shhhhhh Bang. De Veyrac, Robert (1901-), illus. LC 43-5352. (Illus.). (ps-1). 1943. (ISBN 0-06-020781-7, HarpJ). Har-Row.
--Shhhhh...Bang. Veyrac, Robert De, illus. 1974. Harper & Row Pub.
--Sleepy ABC. Slobodkina, Esphyr (1908-), illus. LC 53-6672. unpaged. illus. 25cm. c.1953. Lothrop, Lee and Shepard Co.
--Sneakers, Seven Stories About a Cat. Charlot, Jean (1898-1979), illus. LC 55-5096. (Illus.). (gr. k-3). 1979. (ISBN 0-201-00625-1, A-W Childrens). A-W.
--Sneakers: Seven Stories About a Cat. Charlot, Jean (1898-1979), illus. LC 79-15186. (Illus.). 143 p. 19cm. 1979, c.1955. Addison-Wesley.
--Sneakers: Seven Stories About a Cat. Charlot, Jean (1898-1979), illus. LC 84-43137. p. cm. 1985, c.1955. (ISBN 0-201-00625-1). Harper
--The Steamroiler: A Fantasy. Ness, Evaline Michelow, Mrs. (1911-), illus. LC 74-78107. (Illus.). 32 p. 1974. (ISBN 0-8027-6191-7). (ISBN 0-8027-6192-5). Walker.
--The Streamlined Pig. Wiese, Kurt (1887-1974), illus. LC 38-29158. 32 p. incl. col. front., illus. (part col.) 20 1/2 x 28 cm. 1938. Harper & Brothers.
--The Summer Noisy Book. Weisgard, Leonard Joseph (1916-), illus. LC 51-8509. (Illus.). 34 p. 26cm. c.1951. Harper.
--Three Little Animals. Williams, Garth Montgomery (1912-), illus. LC 56-8139. unpaged. illus. 32cm. 1956. Harper.
--The Train to Timbuctoo. Seiden, Art, illus. LC 51-39071. unpaged. illus. 21 cm. (Little golden library, 118). N.D. Simon and Schuster.
--Train to Timbuctoo. Seiden, Art, illus. (Illus.). (A Young Reader Ser.). (gr. k-3). 1979. (ISBN 0-307-60118-8, Golden Pr). Western Pub.
--Two Little Trains. Charlot, Jean (1898-1979), illus. LC 84-43138. p. cm. 1985, c.1949. (ISBN 0-201-09381-2). Harper & Row.
--Two Little Trains. Charlot, Jean (1898-1979), illus. LC 49-10965. 32 p. illus. (part col.) 25. cm. c.1949. W. R. Scott.
--Wait till the Moon Is Full. Williams, Garth Montgomery (1912-), illus. LC 48-927849. 32 p. col. illus. 27 cm. 1948. Harper.
--Wheel on the Chimney. Gergely, Tibor (1900-1978), illus. LC 54-8486. (Illus.). unpaged. 29cm. 1954. Lippincott. **Award: (RCM).**
--When the Wind Blew. Hayes, Geoffrey, illus. LC 76-58734. (Illus.). 30 p. 16cm. 1977, c.1937. (ISBN 0-06-020867-8). (ISBN 0-06-020868-6). Harper & Row. **Award: (NYT).**
--When the Wind Blew. Slocum, Rosalie (1906-), illus. LC 37-21374. 31 p. illus. (part col.) 23 1/2 cm. 1937. Harper & Brothers.
--Where Have You Been?. Cooney, Barbara (1917-), illus. LC 52-6717. unpaged. illus. 13 x 15 cm. N.D. Crowell.
--Where Have You Been?. Cooney, Barbara (1917-), illus. (Illus.). 32p. (ps-1). 1981. (ISBN 0-8038-8018-9). Hastings.
--Whistle for the Train. MacDonald, Golden, pseud. Weisgard, Leonard Joseph (1916-), illus. LC 56-8230. (Illus.). unpaged. c.1956. (ISBN 0-385-07787-4). Doubleday.
--Willie's Adventures. Johnson, Crockett, pseud. (1906-1975), illus. Leisk, David Johnson. LC 54-6793. 72p. (ps-3). 1954. (ISBN 0-201-09415-0, A-W Childrens). A-W.
--Willie's Adventures, Three Stories. LC 54-6793. (Illus.). 68 p. 20cm. (Young Scott books). 1954. W. R. Scott.
--Willie's Adventures: Three Stories. Johnson, Crockett, pseud. (1906-1975), illus. Leisk, David Johnson. LC 84-43141. p. cm. (Young Scott Books). 1985, c.1954. (ISBN 0-201-09415-0). Harper & Row.
--The Winter Noisy Book. Shaw, Charles Green (1892-1974), illus. 1974. Harper & Row Pub.
--The Winter Noisy Book. Shaw, Charles Green (1892-1974), illus. LC 47-30809. 42 p. illus. (part col.) 23 cm. c.1947. W. R. Scott.
--The Wonderful House. Miller, John Parr (1913-), illus. (Little Golden Bk.). 1950. Golden Press.
--The Wonderful House. rev. ed. Miller, John Parr (1913-), illus. LC 60-3233. (Illus.). 31 p. 22cm. (Golden beginning readers, 4006). 1960. Golden Press.
--Wonderful Story Book. Miller, John Parr (1913-), illus. LC 48-675349. 92 p. illus. (part col.) 29 cm. (Big golden book). 1948. Simon and Schuster.
--Wonderful Storybook. Miller, John Parr (1913-), illus. LC 72-91089. (Illus.). 61 p. 31cm. 1974. Golden Press.
--Young Kangaroo. 72p. N.D. Young Scott Books.
--Young Kangaroo. Shimin, Symeon (1902-), illus. LC 55-5097. (Illus.). 42 p. 22cm. (Young Scott books). 1955. W. R. Scott.

Brown, Margaret Wise (1910-1952), adapted by.
--Brer Rabbit: Stories from Uncle Remus. Frost, Arthur Burdett (1851-1928), illus. LC 41-24406. (Illus.). (gr. 1-5). 1941. (ISBN 0-06-020876-7, HarpJ). Har-Row.
--The Children's Year. 1st ed. Rojankovsky, Feodor Stepanovich (1891-1970), illus. Rojan, pseud. LC 37-21953. (Adapted from the French of Lacote). 26p. col. front. col. illus. 17 1/2 x 19cm. 1937. Harper & Brothers.

Brown, Margaret Wise (1910-1952) & Campbell, Rockbridge
--Willie's Walk to Grandmama. Bloch, Lucienne (1909-), illus. LC 44-830165. 26 p. col. illus. 20 x 17 cm. (On cover: Young Scott books). c.1944. W. R. Scott, Inc.

Brown, Margaret Wise (1910-1952) & Hurd, Edith Thacher, Mrs. (1910-)
--Five Little Firemen. Gergely, Tibor (1900-1978), illus. LC 49-7117. 42 p. illus. (part col.) 20 cm. (Little golden library, 64). 1948. Simon and Schuster.
--The Little Fat Policeman. Provensen, Alice (1918-) & Provensen, Martin (1916-), illus. (Little golden book, 91). 1950. Simon & Schuster.
--Seven Little Postmen. Gergely, Tibor (1900-1978), illus. LC 52-8667. unpaged. illus. 21 cm. (Little golden library, 134). N.D. Simon and Schuster.
--Two Little Gardeners. Elliott, Gertrude, illus. LC 51-11257. unpaged. illus. 21 cm. (Little golden library, 108). 1951. Simon and Schuster.
--Two Little Miners. LC 49-9957. 42 p. illus. (part col.) 20 cm. (Little glden library, no. 66). 1949. Simon and Schuster.

Brown, Margaret Wise (1910-1952) & Koffler, Camilla (0000-1955)
--Sleepy Little Lion. Ylla, pseud. LC 47-11482. (Illus.). (gr. k-3). 1947. (ISBN 0-06-020771-X, HarpJ). Har-Row.
--The Sleepy Little Lion. new ed. Ylla, pseud. (Illus.). (ps-3). 1976. (ISBN 0-06-443015-4, Trophy). Har-Row.

Brown, Margaret Wise (1910-1952) & Strugnell, Ann
--Once Upon a Time in a Pigpen and Three Other Margaret Wise Brown Books. LC 77-5077. p. cm. c.1977. (ISBN 0-201-00343-0). Addison-Wesley.

Brown, Margaret Wise (1910-1952) & Watson, Jane Werner
--My Bedtime Book. Williams, Garth Montgomery (1912-), illus. 1964. Golden Press.

Brown, Margery W
--Animals Made by Me. LC 70-110311. (Illus.). 32 p. 27cm. 1970. Putnam.
--The Second Stone. LC 73-76131. (Illus.). 124 p. 21cm. 1974. (ISBN 0-399-60848-6). (ISBN 0-399-20359-1). (ISBN 0-399-20359-1). Putnam.
--That Ruby. Brown, Marjery W., illus. LC 69-17431. (Illus.). 154 p. 22cm. 1969. Reilly & Lee.
--Yesterday I Climbed a Mountain. Brown, Margery W., illus. LC 76-25865. 32p. illus. 26cm. 1976. Putnam.

Brown, Marice C
--Amen, Brother Ben: A Mississippi Collection of Children's Rhymes. LC 78-32017. (Illus.). x, 101 p. 18cm. c.1979. (ISBN 0-87805-094-9). University Press of Mississippi.

Brown, Marie A., jt. tr. see Borg, Selma.
Brown, Marie A., tr. see Schwartz.
Brown, Marie I
--A Child's Treasure Chest. LC 66-82517. 40 p. illus., incl. front. 21 cm. c.1965. Vantage Press.

Brown, Marie Wilson
--Kute Stunts: Songs and Dances for Kiddies. LC 37-32929. 55 p. 19 cm. c.1929. Eldridge Entertainment House, Inc.

Brown, Marion Marsh (1908-)
--Broad Stripes and Bright Stars. Justis, Lyle, illus. LC 54-116286. 208p. illus. 22cm. c.1955. Westminster Press.
--Frontier Beacon. LC 52-11538. 187p. 21cm. 1953. Westminster Press.
--Homeward the Arrow's Flight. LC 80-11957. (Illus.). 176p. (gr. 7 up). 1980. (ISBN 0-687-17300-0). Abingdon.
--Marnie. LC 70-135653. 189 p. 21cm. 1971. (ISBN 0-664-32491-6). Westminster Press.
--Prairie Teacher. LC 57-12668. 223p. 21cm. 1957. Avalon Books.
--Silent Storm. 1963. E M Hale.
--Stuart's Landing: A Story of Pioneer Nebraska. LC 68-15003. 187 p. 21cm. N.D. Westminster Press.
--The Swamp Fox. Kidwell, Carl (1910-), illus. LC 50-10322. 185 p. illus. 22 cm. 1950. Westminster Press.
--Young Nathan. McDonough, Don, illus. LC 49-5835. 191 p. illus. 22 cm. 1949. Westminister Press.

Brown, Marion Marsh (1908-) & Brown, Edith (1887-1974)
--Alexander: The Tale of a Monkey. Wiese, Kurt (1887-1974), illus. LC 34-16716. 6 p. l., 3-193 p. incl. illus., plates. front. 20 1/2 cm. c.1934. The Bobbs-Merrill Company.

Brown, Marion Marsh (1908-) & Crone, Ruth (1919-)
--The Silent Storm. Kredel, Fritz (1900-1973), illus. LC 63-10807. 250 p. illus. 22 cm. 1963. Abingdon Press.

Brown, Marjorie Dowling, ed. see Meader, Stephen Warren.
Brown, Marjorie Webber
--Pueblo Playmates. Nav, Carol, illus. LC 38-32858. 61, 3 p. incl. col. front., illus. (part col.) 24 cm. 1938. A. Whitman & Co.

Brown, Martha Beach
--Never-Go-Out' Light. Norling, Ernest Ralph (1892-), illus. LC 28-19288. vii, 40 p. front., illus. 21 cm. c.1928. The Author.

Brown, Mary Josephine see Brunowe, Marion J., pseud.
Brown, Mary Loretta Therese
--Angela in Public Relations: Angie Begins a Bright Career. LC 64-23046. viii, 243 p. 21 cm. (dodd, mead career books. (gr. 7-11). 1964. (ISBN 0-396-05068-9). Dodd, Mead.
--The Gift. Neilson, Marion, illus. LC 68-56137. (Illus.). 31 p. 24cm. 1968. Dimension Books.

Brown, Mary R.
--Maggie and Her Friends. N.D. A. D. F. Randolph.

Brown, Michael (1920-)
--Baby's Santa Mouse. Iizawa, Tadasu (1909-) & Hijikata, Shigemi (1915-), illus. LC 73-9314. (Illus.). 21 p. 27cm. 1969. Grosset & Dunlap.
--Santa Mouse. DeWitt, Elfrieda, illus. LC 67-6792. (Illus.). 1 v. (unpaged. 29cm. (Nursery treasure books). 1966. Grosset & Dunlap.
--Santa Mouse Meets Marmaduke. De Santis, George, illus. LC 74-92384. (Illus.). 25 p. 29cm. 1969. Grosset & Dunlap.
--Santa Mouse, Where Are You?. DeWitt, Elfrieda, illus. LC 68-8848. (Illus.). 25 p. 29cm. 1968. Grosset & Dunlap.
--A Treasury of Santa Mouse. DeWitt, Elfrieda & De Santis, George, illus. LC 78-116656. (Illus.). 67 p. 31cm. 1970. Grosset & Dunlap.

Brown, Michael (1931-)
--A Cavalcade of Sea Legends. Turska, Krystyna Zofia (1933-), illus. LC 77-175941. (Illus.). viii, 274 p. 26cm. 1972, c.1971. H. Z. Walck.
--Small Boat Adventures. Floyd, Gareth (1940-), illus. LC 68-25732. (Illus.). 220 p. 23cm. (David White collection). 1968. D. White.

Brown, Mik & Offerman, Lynn
--Little Simon Jokes & Riddles. LC 85-126155. (Illus.). 40p. (Animal Fun Jokes & Riddles Ser.). (gr. k-3). 1984. (ISBN 0-671-52814-9, Little Simon). S&S.

Brown, Morna Davis see Ferrars, E. X., pseud.
Brown, Myra Berry (1918-)
--Amy and the New Baby. LC 65-17098. 1 v. (unpaged) illus. 19 x 22 cm. 1965. F. Watts.

--Benjy's Blanket. Marino, Dorothy Bronson (1912-), illus. LC 62-8427. (Illus.). 1 v. (unpaged. 1962. F. Watts.
--Best Friends. Freeman, Don (1908-1978), illus. LC 67-5102. (Illus.). 47 p. 18cm. 1967. Golden Gate Junior Books.
--Best of Luck. Freeman, Don (1908-1978), illus. LC 73-84696. (Illus.). 46 p. 18cm. 1969. Golden Gate Junior Books.
--Birthday Boy. Maclean, Robert (1926-), illus. LC 63-16925. 1 v. (unpaged) illus. 19 x 22 cm. c.1963. F. Watts.
--Casey's Sore-Throat Day. Hurwitz, Harriet, illus. LC 64-18949. 58 p. col. illus. 19 x 22 cm. 1964. F. Watts.
--Company's Coming for Dinner. (Illus.). (gr. k-2). 1959. (ISBN 0-8382-0178-4). Hale.
--Company's Coming for Dinner. Marino, Dorothy Bronson (1912-), illus. LC 59-5669. unpaged. illus. 19x22cm. c.1959. F. Watts.
--First Night Away from Home. Marino, Dorothy Bronson (1912-), illus. LC 60-110149. (Illus.). (gr. k-3). 1960. (ISBN 0-531-01668-4). Watts.
--Flower Girl. Miller, Jane Judith (1925-), illus. LC 61-5592. unpaged. illus. 19 x 22cm. 1961. Watts.
--Ice Cream for Breakfast. Smith, Lawrence Beall (1909-), illus. LC 62-8435. unpaged. illus. 19 x 22 cm. 1963. F. Watts.
--If You Have a Doll. Gaussot, Christine, illus. LC 67-17876. 48 p. col. illus. 19 x 23 cm. N.D. F. Watts,.
--My Daddy's Visiting Our School Today. Bolian, Polly (1925-), illus. LC 61-6070. unpaged. illus. 19x23cm. c.1961. Watts.
--Pip Camps Out. Graham, Phyllis, illus. LC 65-17715. (Illus.). (gr. k-3). 1966. (ISBN 0-516-08735-5, Golden Gate). Childrens.
--Pip Moves Away. Jackson, Pauline (1918-), illus. (Illus.). 48 p. 1967. Golden Gate Junior Books.
--Sandy Signs His Name. 1967. E M Hale.
--Sandy Signs His Name. Fraser, Betty M., pseud. (1928-), illus. Fraser, Elizabeth Marr. LC 67-1462. 1 v. (unpaged) col. illus. 22 cm. 1967. F. Watts.
--Somebody's Pup. LC 61-10064. (Illus.). unpaged. 1961. Watts.
--Where's Jeremy?. Thollander, Earl Gustave (1922-), illus. (Illus.). 48 p. 27cm. 1968. Golden Gate Junior Books.

Brown, Neva Kanaga, Mrs.
--The Uncle Amos Puppet Show. LC 30-29993. 3 p. l., 56, 2 p. col. front., illus. 21 cm. 1930. Doubleday, Doran & Company, Inc.

Brown, Ozni, retold by see Sewell, Anna.

Brown, P. J
--Starting with UNIX. McCue, Lisa, illus. LC 83-11778. (Illus.). xiv, 221 p. 24cm. (Sebastian, super sleuth). ((Series: Christian, Mary Blount.). c.1984. (ISBN 0-201-13233-8). Readin, Mass. : Addison-Wesley.

Brown, Palmer (1919-)
--Beyond the Pawpaw Trees: The Story of Anna Lavinia. Brown, Palmer (1919-), illus. LC 54-8938. (Illus.). (gr. k-5). 1954. (ISBN 0-06-020885-6, HarpJ). Har-Row.
--Cheerful: A Picture Story. Brown, Palmer (1919-), illus. (Illus.). Repr. 1978. (ISBN 0-06-020895-3, HarpJ). Har-Row.
--Cheerful: A Picture Story. Brown, Palmer (1919-), illus. LC 57-5354. (Illus.). 58 p. 16cm. 1957. Harper.
--Hickory. LC 77-11849. (Illus.). 42 p. 23cm. c.1978. (ISBN 0-06-020887-2). (ISBN 0-06-020888-0). Harper & Row. **Award: (ALA).**
--Silver Nutmeg. Brown, Palmer (1919-), illus. (Illus.). 138p. (gr. 1-5). 1956. (ISBN 0-06-020902-X). Har-Row.
--The Silver Nutmeg: The Story of Anna Lavinia and Toby. Brown, Palmer (1919-), illus. LC 55-882164. 137p. illus. 20cm. 1966. Harper.
--Something for Christmas. (Illus.). (gr. k-3). 1958. (ISBN 0-8382-0775-8). Hale.
--Something for Christmas. Brown, Palmer (1919-), illus. (Illus.). (gr. k-3). 1958. (ISBN 0-06-020910-0, HarpJ). Har-Row.

Brown, Pamela Beatrice (1924-)
--The Bridesmaids. Beetles, Peggy, illus. LC 57-105066. 208p. illus. 21cm. 1957. D. McKay Co.
--Family Troupe. Frankenberg, Robert Clinton (1911-), illus. LC 52-11967. (Illus.). 245 p. 21cm. 1953. Harcourt, Brace.
--Harlequin Corner. LC 79-75695. 184 p. 21cm. 1968, c.1967. Meredith Press.
--Louisa. Sax, illus. LC 57-50537. 172p. illus. 21cm. 1955. Crowell.
--The Other Side of the Street. LC 67-21175. (Illus.). 186 p. 23cm. 1967, c.1965. Follett.
--The Swish of the Curtain. Foy, Ottilie, illus. LC 43-10915. ix. 1, 397 p. col. front., illus. 23 cm. 1943. The John C. Winston Co.
--The Windmill Family. Foster, Marcia Lane (1897-), illus. LC 55-939. 223p. illus. 21cm. 1954. T. Nelson.
--The Windmill Family. Weil, Lisl (1910-), illus. LC 55-920655. 262p. illus. 21cm. c.1954. T. Y. Crowell Co.

Brown, Paul (1893-1958)
--Circus School. LC 47-300330. 64 p. col. illus. 27 1/2 x 21 1/2 cm. c.1946. C. Scribner's Sons.
--Crazy Quilt: The Story of a Piebald Pony. LC 34-35885. 120 p. illus. 22 1/2 x 29 cm. 1934. C. Scribner's Sons.
--Daffy Taffy. Brown, Paul (1893-1958), illus. LC 55-14974. unpaged. illus. 27cm. c.1955. Scribner.
--Fire!. The Mascot. LC 39-30767. 96 p. illus. 27 1/2 cm. 1939. C. Scribner's Sons.
--Hi Guy!. Brown, Paul (1893-1958), illus. N.D. Charles Scribner's Sons.
--Hi Guy: The Cinderella Horse. LC 44-8910. 62 p. illus. 24 x 21 cm. 1944. C. Scribner's Sons.
--Merrylegs: The Rocking Pony. Brown, Paul (1893-1958), illus. LC 46-1630. 64 p. illus. (part col.) 20 1/2 x 17 cm. c.1946. C. Scribner's Sons.
--Mick and Mac: The Perkins' Pups. LC 37-239346. 96 p. illus. 27 1/2 cm. 1937. C. Scribner's Sons.
--No Trouble at All. LC 40-31349. 4 p. l., 126 p. illus. 21 cm. 1940. C. Scribner's Sons.
--Piper's Pony: The Story of Patchwork. LC 35-20671. 120 p. illus. 22 x 29 cm. 1935. C. Scribner's Sons.
--Pony Farm. LC 48-8273. 92 p. illus. 21 cm. 1948. C. Scribner's Sons.
--Pony School. LC 50-9847. 93 p. illus. 21 cm. 1950. Scribner.
--Puff Ball. Brown, Paul (1893-1958), illus. LC 42-21070. 1942. Charles Scribner's Sons.
--Silver Heels. LC 51-13703. unpaged. illus. 21 cm. 1951. Scribner.
--Sparkie and Puff Ball. Brown, Paul (1893-1958), illus. LC 54-8784. (Illus.). unpaged. 27cm. c.1954. Scribner.
--Three Rings;. A Circus Book. LC 38-32402. 76 p. illus. (part col.) 27 cm. 1938. C. Scribner's Sons.
--War Paint. Brown, Paul (1893-1958), illus. (Illus.). (gr. 3-7). 1936. (ISBN 0-684-20755-9). Scribner.
--War Paint: An Indian Pony. LC 36-28508. 96 p. illus. 27 cm. 1936. C. Scribner's Sons.
--Your Pony's Trek Around the World. Brown, Paul (1893-1958), illus. LC 56-142665. unpaged. illus. 26cm. c.1956. Scribner.

Brown, Philip
--Uncle Whiskers. Tansley, Eric, illus. (Illus.). 96p. (gr. 7 up). 1975. (ISBN 0-316-11208-9). Little.

Brown, Phoebe Hinsdale, Mrs. (1783-1861)
--The Village School: To Which Is Added Jenny, or The Conversion of a Child, a Narrative. LC 28-179104. 2 p. l., 9-125, 1 p. 15 1/2 cm. 1836. E. Collier.

Brown, Raphael
--Fifty Animals Stories of St. Francis: As Told to His Companions. 1958. Franciscan Herald Press.

Brown, Raymond Bryan (1923-)
--They Talk and Walk. N.D. (ISBN 0-8283-1335-0). Branden Press.

Brown, Regina Margaret
--Little Brother. Bornschlegel, Ruth, illus. (Illus.). (gr. 3-7). 1962. (ISBN 0-8392-3019-2). Astor-Honor.
--Little Brother. Bornschlegel, Ruth, illus. LC 62-10802. 55p. illus. 24cm. (Astor book). 1962. I. Obolensky.
--A Play at Your House. LC 62-187971. 85 p. 24 cm. (Astor book). c.1962. I. Obolensky.

Brown, Reynold & Crump, James Irving (1887-1979), eds.
--Adventure Stories. LC 50-9072. 224 p. front. 22 cm. 1950. Nelson.

Brown, Richard Eric, jt. auth. see Weiss, Ellen.

Brown, Robert Musser
--The Pig and the Pond. O'Sullivan, Tom, illus. LC 73-77778. (Illus.). 133 p. 23cm. 1973. McKay.

Brown, Rosalie Moore, jt. auth. see Brown, Bill.

Brown, Rosalie Moore (1910-)
--Year of the Children: Poems for a Narrative. LC 76-4689. xvi, 101 p. 25cm. 1977. Woolmer/Brotherson.

Brown, Rosalie Moore (1910-) & Brown, Bill
--Whistle Punk. N.D. E. M. Hale & Co.

Brown, Rose Johnston (1883-)
--Amazon Adventures of Two Children. Eshner, Ann, illus. LC 42-21756. 223, 1 p. incl. front., illus. 23 cm. 1942. J. B. Lippincott Company.
--Two Children and Their Jungle Zoo. Eshner, Ann, ilus. LC 44-3472. 11 p., 1 l., 18-220 p. incl. front., illus., plates. 21 cm. 1944. J. B. Lippincott Company.
--Two Children of Brazil. Sperry, Armstrong W. (1897-1976), illus. LC 41-1481. 23cm. 229p. 1940. J. B. Lippincott.

Brown, Roy Frederick (1921-)
--The Battle of Saint Street. Hunt, James, illus. LC 74-152287. (Illus.). 150 p. 21cm. 1971. Macmillan.
--The Big Test. (Illus.). 128p. 1981. (ISBN 0-905478-02-9, Pub. by Andersen-Hutchinson England). State Mutual Bk.
--The Cage. LC 77-1586. p. cm. c.1977. (ISBN 0-8164-3198-1). Seabury Press.
--The Day of the Pigeons. Hunt, James, illus. LC 75-447280. 160p. 1968. Abelard-Schuman.
--Escape the River. LC 76-179440. 160 p. 22cm. 1972, c.1970. (ISBN 0-8164-3079-9). Seabury Press.
--Find Debbie!. A Novel of Suspense. LC 75-25511. 160 p. 22cm. 1976, c.1975. (ISBN 0-8164-3164-7). Seabury Press.
--Flight of Sparrows. LC 72-92432. 151 p. 22cm. 1972. (ISBN 0-02-714860-2). Macmillan.
--No Through Road. LC 74-3484. 158 p. 22cm. 1974, c.1973. (ISBN 0-8164-3128-0). Seabury Press.
--A Saturday in Pudney. Hunt, James, illus. LC 68-91919. (Illus.). 159 p. 23cm. 1966. Abelard-Schuman.
--A Saturday in Pudney. Hunt, James, illus. LC 66-157309. 152p. map. 21cm. 1968, c.1966. Macmillan.
--Shep the Second. Bayly, Clifford, illus. (gr. 2-5). 1976. (ISBN 0-8277-4738-1). British Bk Ctr.
--Suicide Course. LC 80-15097. 118 p. 22cm. c.1980. (ISBN 0-395-29436-3). Houghton Mifflin/Clarion Books.
--The Swing of the Gate. LC 78-6422. p. cm. c.1978. (ISBN 0-8164-3220-1). Seabury Press.
--The Viaduct. Hunt, James, illus. 168 p. 21cm. 1968, c.1967. Macmillan.
--The White Sparrow. LC 74-19352. 160p. (gr. 6 up). 1975. (ISBN 0-395-28897-5, Clarion). HM.
--The White Sparrow: A Novel. LC 74-19352. 158 p. 22cm. 1975, c.1974. (ISBN 0-8164-3141-8). Seabury Press.

Brown, Roy Frederick (1921-), retold by.
--Reynard the Fox. (Based on the version by Joseph Jacobs). (Illus.). 128p. 1969. (ISBN 0-200-71602-6). Abelard-Shuman Press.

Brown, Ruth
--The Big Sneeze. LC 84-23385. p. cm. 1985. (ISBN 0-688-04665-7). (ISBN 0-688-04666-5). Lothrop, Lee & Shepard Books.
--A Dark Dark Tale. Brown, Ruth, illus. LC 81-66798. (Illus.). 32p. (ps-3). 1981. (ISBN 0-8037-1672-9). (ISBN 0-8037-1673-7). Dial Bks Young.
--If at First You Do Not See. LC 82-15527. p. cm. 1983, c.1982. (ISBN 0-03-063521-7). Holt, Rinehart, and Winston.

Brown, Ruth Alberta
--Heart of Gold. Brundage, Frances, illus. LC 15-6450. 285 p. incl. col. front. 19 1/2 cm. p $1.2. c.1915. The Saalfield Publishing Company.
--The Lilac Lady: The Second of the Peace Greenfield Books. Smith, Oliver Willard, illus. LC 14-8473. 312 p. incl. front. plates. 20 cm. p $1.2. c.1914. The Saalfield Publishing Company.
--Tabitha at Ivy Hall. Russell, Alfred, illus. LC 11-20593. 319 p. incl. front. plates. 20 1/2 cm. p $1.25. c.1911. The Saalfield Publishing Company.
--Tabitha's Glory... Russell, Alfred, illus. LC 12-12487. 319 p. incl. front. plates. 20 1/2 cm. (Her Ivy hall series, vol. ii) $1.25). c.1912. The Saalfield Publishing Company.
--Tabitha's Vacation... Smith, Wuanita (1866-), illus. LC 13-184771. 286 p. incl. front. plates. 20 1/2 cm. (Her Ivy hall series, vol. iii) $1.25). c.1913. The Saalfield Publishing Company.

Brown, Ruth Archambault (1896-) & Breck, H. Jean
--Magic Ring: A Collection of Verse for Children. Feringer, Jo Anne Norling, illus. LC 85-15067. (Illus.). xxi, 182 p. 23cm. c.1985. (ISBN 0-87603-082-7). American Camping Association.

Brown, S. G.
--The Song of Narwa. 1984. (ISBN 0-8062-2272-7). Carlton.

Brown, Sarah
--Five Days of Living With the Land. 48p. 1971. (ISBN 0-201-00755-X). Addison-Wesley.

Brown, Selby V. I
--The Adventures of Jacky Frog. Clemens, Ruth, illus. LC 43-7232. 138 p. col. front., col. plates. 21 cm. 1943. B. Humphries, Inc.

Brown, Shirley Berkowich
--Around the World Stories to Tell to Children. Conner, Angela, illus. LC 62-7384. 140p. illus. 21cm. 1962. F. Watts.
--Cinderella. Kincaid, Eric, illus. LC 72-183128. (Illus.). 48 p. 30cm. 1972. CBS Records.
--Cinderella. Markowitz, Henry, illus. LC 68-8910. (Illus.). 42 p. 30cm. 1968. CBS Records.
--Mighty Miko. Chin, Kay (1920-), illus. LC 73-84917. (Illus.). 32 p. 23cm. 1969. Lancelot Press.

Brown, Slater (1896-)
--Ethan Allen & the Green Mountain Boys. (Illus.). (Landmark Ser.: No. 66). (gr. 4-6). 1956. (ISBN 0-394-90366-8). Random.
--Gray Bonnets in the Days of Roger Williams. 1st ed. Kredel, Fritz (1900-1973), illus. LC 54-6317. 192p. illus. 21cm. (American heritage series). 1954. Aladdin Books.
--Spaceward Bound. LC 55-7321. (Illus.). 213 p. 21cm. (Lodestar books). 1955. Prentice-Hall.
--The Talking Skyscraper. Fabres, Oscar (1900-), illus. LC 45-4612. 27cm. 48p. 1945. Duell Sloan & Pearce Publishers.

Brown, Theron
--The Blount Family: Or, A Widow's Toil, Trust, and Triumph. (Illus.). N.D. Lothrop.
--Stories for Sunday. 156p. N.D. American Tract Society.
--Walter Neil's Example. (Illus.). N.D. Lothrop.

Brown, Thomas Kite (1851-1929)
--When Master Thomas Was a Boy. Whitney, George Gillett, illus. LC 30-122909. vii, 97 p. plates, 2 port. (incl. front.) 19 1/2 cm. c.1929. The John C. Winston Company.

Brown, Tricia
--Someone Special Just Like You. (Illus.). 1984. Holt.

Brown, Vera
--Wings of Love: The Love Story of a Girl Aviator. LC 34-25937. vi, 310 p. 19 1/2 cm. c.1934. Grosset & Dunlap.

Brown, Verne B, adapted by see Clemens, Samuel Langhorne.

Brown, Vinson, ed. see Cossi, Olga.

Brown, Vinson (1912-)
--It All Happened Right Here!. A Child's History of Santa Clara County. Le Baudour, Marie, illus. LC 54-7159. 82p. illus. 21cm. 1954. Stanford University Press.

Brown, Vinson (1912-) & Johnson, Phyllis
--Return of the Indian Spirit. Johnson, W. Cameron, illus. LC 81-65887. (Illus.). 61 p. 21cm. 1982, c.1981. (ISBN 0-89087-401-8). Celestial Arts.

Brown, Virginia
--The Hidden Lookout. Lavell, Tom, illus. LC 65-4176. 92p. col. illus. 23cm. (Skyline series, bk. B). c.1965. Webster-McGraw.

Brown, Virginia, et al.
--Who Cares. Cummins, James (1914-), illus. LC 67-2513. (Illus.). 90 p. 23cm. 1965. McGraw-Hill.

Brown, Virginia Pounds & Owens, Laurella
--Southern Indian Myths and Legends. Glick, Nathan Harold (1912-), illus. LC 85-15608. p. cm. 1985. (ISBN 0-912221-02-X). Beechwood Books.

Brown, Virginia Pounds & Wilson, LaNeil
--The Gold Disc of Coosa. LC 75-24616. (Illus.). 121 p. 24cm. c.1975. (ISBN 0-87397-085-3). Strode Publishers.

Brown, Walter R., jt. auth. see Anderson, Norman Dean.

Brown, Wendell (1902-)
--Willie Woodpecker Magoon and His Birds. LC 60-531798. 87p. illus. 23cm. 1960. T. S. Denison.

Brown, William Louis see Brown, Bill, pseud.

Brown, William Perry see Perry, William B., pseud.

Brown, William Perry
--Florida Lads: And For King or Congress. LC 3-23891. 309 p. front., 3 pl. 19 1/2 cm. 1903. The Saalfield Publishing Co.
--Our Jackies with the Fleet. Perry, William B., pseud. Angell, Clare, illus. LC 18-15718. 2 p. l., 9-362 p. front. 19 1/2 cm. c.1918. The Saalfield Publishing Company.
--Ralph Granger's Fortunes. (Illus.). N.D. Caldwell.
--Ralph Granger's Fortunes. Fry, W. H., illus. LC 2-19999. 20cm. 306p. 1902. Saalfield Publishing Co.
--Sea Island Boys. LC 3-23889. 20cm. 320p. 1903. Saalfield Publishing Co.
--Vance Sevier: Or, From the Big Smokies to Okeefenoke. LC 3-23890. 20cm. 342p. 1903. Saalfield Publishing Co.

Brown, William Wells
--Clotelle: a Tale of the Southern States. 104 p. incl. front., plates. 17 1/2 cm. (On cover: Redpath's books for the camp area, no. 2). c.1864. J. Redpath.

Brown & Worcester, illus.
--The Boston, Cries: And the Story of The Little Matchboy. LC 19-289426. 13 p. col. illus. 19 1/2 x 15 1/2 cm. (On cover: Grandmother's new toy books). 1844. J. C. Riker.

Browne, Anthony Edward Tudor (1946-)
--Bear Hunt. LC 79-21964. (Illus.). 24 p. 23cm. 1980, c.1979. (ISBN 0-689-30733-0). Atheneum.
--Gorilla. Browne, Anthony Edward Tudor (1946-), illus. (Illus.). 32p. 1984. (ISBN 0-531-04609-5). Watts. **Awards: (KGM); (NYT).**
--Through the Magic Mirror. LC 77-351308. (Illus.). 32 p. 1976. (ISBN 0-241-89307-0). Hamilton.
--Willy the Champ. LC 85-10053. p. cm. 1st U.S. edition. c.1985. (ISBN 0-394-87907-4). (ISBN 0-394-97907-9). Knopf : Distributed by Random House.
--Willy the Wimp. Browne, Anthony Edward Tudor (1946-), illus. LC 84-14320. (Illus.). 32p. (ps-3). 1985. (ISBN 0-394-97061-6). (ISBN 0-394-87061-1). Knopf.

--Robbie and Nellie in Business. (Illus.). (Helpful Hand Ser.). N.D. Universalist Publishing House.
--Robbie, Nellie and Susie. (Illus.). (Helpful Hand Ser.). N.D. Universalist Publication House.
--Silver Shadow, and other Stories. (Helpful Hand Ser.). N.D. Universalist Publishing House.
--Thousand a Year, 1 of 25 vols. (Illus.). (Mayflower Ser. for Girls: No. 15). 1900. Lee & Shepard.
--A Week of Life. (vols. 1 & 2). N.D. Universalist Publishing House.

Bruce, George
--Navy Blue and Gold. N.D. Grosset & Dunlap.

Bruce, H. Eddington
--Daniel Boone and the Wilderness Road. N.D. MacMillan.

Bruce, H. Turing
--Winning His Knighthood: Or, The Adventures of Rauoulf De Gyssage. Parker, L., illus. LC 42-26193. 5 p. l., 7-256 p. front., plates. 21 cm. 1929. L. C. Page & Company.

Bruce, Joseph C (1906-)
--The Black Sheep. LC 52-1333. 143 p. 20 cm. 1951. Story Book Press.

Bruce, Linda
--Al Phillip Bettle. (gr. k-3). N.D. G&D.
--Al Phillip Bettle. Bruce, Linda, illus. (Illus.). (gr. k-3). 1965. (ISBN 0-8392-3050-8). Astor-Honor.
--Al Phillip Bettle. Bruce, Linda, illus. LC 64-23763. 1 v. (unpaged) col. illus. 19x29cm. (Astor bk). c.1965. World.

Bruce, Marie
--Kris and Kristina. Daugherty, James Henry (1889-1974), illus. LC 28-326. 1 p. l., 60 p. col. front., illus. (part col.) 21 1/2 cm. c.1927. Doubleday, Page & Co.

Bruce, Marjory, ed.
--A Treasury of Tales for Little Folks. Fry, Nora & Appleton, Honor C., illus. LC 27-17805. 284 p. col. front., illus., col. plates. 23 cm. c.1927. Thomas Y. Crowell Company.

Bruce, Mary Grant, Mrs.
--Circus Ring. LC 37-1524. 4 p. l., 240 p. 20 1/2 cm. c.1937. G. P. Putnam's Sons.
--Road to Adventure. LC 33-7847. ix p., 2 l., 3-248 p. 20 cm. 1933. Balch & Company.

Bruce, Mary (1927-)
--The Bear Who Lost His Hair. Rice, Elizabeth (1913-), illus. LC 68-11218. (Illus.). 32 p. 24cm. 1968. Steck-Vaughn Co.

Bruce, Sheilah B
--The Radish Day Jubilee. 1st ed. Di Fiori, Lawrence, illus. LC 83-10805. (Illus.). 44 p. 22cm. c.1983. (ISBN 0-03-068678-4). Muppet Press : Holt, Rinehart, and Winston.

Bruce, Sheilah B & Henson, Jim (1936-)
--Gonzo and the Giant Chicken. Walz, Richard, illus. LC 82-3862. (Illus.). 32 p. 21cm. c.1982. (ISBN 0-394-85411-X). Muppet Press/Random House.

Bruchac, Joseph, III (1942-)
--Iroquois Stories: Heroes and Heroines, Monsters and Magic. LC 85-5705. p. cm. (gr. 3-7). c.1985. (ISBN 0-89594-167-8). Crossing Press.
--Stone Giants and Flying Heads: Adventure Stories from the Iroquois. (Illus.). 1979. Crossing Press.
--Turkey Brother, and Other Tales: Iroquois Folk Stories. Kahonhes, illus. LC 75-35580. (Illus.). 61 p. 21cm. (Crossing Press series of children's stories). c.1975. (ISBN 0-912278-68-4). Crossing Press.

Bruck, Mary T.
--Night Sky. Ayton, Robert, illus. (Illus.). (gr. 5 up). N.D. (ISBN 0-7214-0104-X). Merry Thoughts.

Brucker, Margaretta see Howe, Margaret, pseud.

Brucker, Margaretta
--Big, Brave, and Handsome. LC 56-616781. 184p. 22cm. 1956. Ariel Books.
--The Girl in the White Cap: By Maragret Howe Pseud. LC 57-8723. 221p. 21cm. 1957. Avalon Books.
--New Boy in Town. LC 58-5313. 180p. 22cm. 1958. Ariel Books.
--Nurse Jenny. Howe, Margaret, pseud. LC 58-125082. 220p. 21cm. 1958. Avalon Books.
--The One and Only. LC 55-6004. 187p. 22cm. 1955. Ariel Books.
--Summer Date. 1st ed. LC 53-9453. 192p. 22cm. 1953. Ariel Books.
--Three Boys and a Girl. LC 57-5993. 192p. 22cm. (Her Junior novels for teen-age girls). 1957. Ariel Books.

Bruckner, Karl (1906-)
--The Day of the Bomb. Lobb, Frances, tr. 189p. 21cm. 1963, c.1962. Van Nostrand.
--Day of the Bomb. Lobb, Frances, tr. LC 63-5738. (gr. 7 up). 1963. (ISBN 0-442-01150-4). Van Nos Reinhold.
--The Golden Pharaoh. (Illus.). 1959. Pantheon Books.
--Viva Mexico. Pelch, Adalbert, illus. (Illus.). (gr. 6-10). N.D. Roy.

Bruderhof Communities
--Behold That Star: A Christmas Anthology. Maendel, Maria Arnold, illus. LC 67-25968. (Illus.). xi, 352 p. 24cm. 1967. Plough Pub. House.

Bruderhof Communities & Swinger, Marlys
--Sing Through the Seasons: Ninety-Nine Songs for Children. LC 70-164916. (Illus.). xiv, 127 p. 28cm. 1972. (ISBN 0-87486-006-7). Plough Pub. House.

Brueggeman, Binnie, illus.
--Shirley Temple's favorite poems. authorized. LC 36-7217. 9-93p. front., illus. 19cm. c.1936. Saalfield Pub, Co.

Brueggemann, Doris
--Little Moe. 16p. 1963. Northwestern Publishing House.
--The Tippy-Toe Man. 8p. 1963. Lutheran Publications.
--Treasure Hunt. 8p. 1963. Lutheran Publications.
--Treasure Hunt. LC 63-23244. 1 v. (unpaged) col. illus. 22 cm. c.1963. Northwestern Pub. House.

Bruehl, Edelgard von Heydekampf, tr. see Allfrey, Katherine.

Bruehl, Edelgard von Heydekampf, tr. see Ruck-Pauquet, Gina.

Bruen, Louisa Jay, ed.
--Poems for Young Persons. LC 16-9865. 90 p. 16 1/2 cm. 1894. F. H. Revell Company.

Bruere, Martha S. Bensley, Mrs.
--Sparky-for-Short. Bruere, Martha S. Bensley, illus. LC 30-246353. 4 p. l., 3-35 p. illus. 22 cm. c.1930. Coward-McCann.

Brumbaugh, Florence
--Donald Duck and His Nephews. Disney, Walt, Studio, illus. LC 40-9819. 3 p. l. 66 p. col. illus. 21 1/2 cm. (On cover: Walt Disney story books). 1940. D. C. Heath and Company.

Brumfield, J C
--The Hand of God and Susie. LC 54-15489. 104p. 20cm. (His The adventures of Susie). 1953. Van Kampen Press.
--Nothing Plus God and Susie. LC 53-907889. 96p. 20cm. (His The adventures of Susie). 1953. Van Kampen Press.
--The Other Boy and Johnny. 96p. 21cm. (Susie and Johnny series). 1953. Van Kampen Press.
--Quicksand. LC 55-39143. 87p. 20cm. (Susie and Johnny series). 1955. Van Kampen Press.

Brumley, Mary Cureton
--Stories About Jesus. N.D. Abingdon Press.

Brumpton, Karen B.
--Freeman Earns a Bike. Feldman, Roper, illus. LC 84-60947. (Illus.). 32p. (ps-4). 1984. (ISBN 0-917487-00-1). McVie Pub.

Brun, Noelle
--Famous Animals in History and Legend. Marin, Lise, illus. LC 68-9411. (Illus.). 63 p. 34cm. c.1968. Lion Press.
--Micias, Boy of the Andes. LC 67-15022. (Illus.). photos. 48p. (Children of the World). (gr. 3-5). 1967. (ISBN 0-695-45704-7). Follett.

Bruna, Dick, jt. auth. see Roodkapje.

Bruna, Dick (1927-)
--Animals. (Dick Bruna Bks.). 1984. (ISBN 0-8431-1575-0). Price Stern.
--Another Story to Tell. LC 77-17742. p. cm. 1978. (ISBN 0-458-92680-9). Methuen.
--The Apple. 28p. 1975. (ISBN 0-8467-0088-3). The Two continents Publishing Group Ltd.
--The Apple: A Toy Box Tale. LC 63-17807. (Illus.). 28 p. 17cm. 1963. Follett Pub. Co.
--B is for Bear: An Abc. 2d ed. LC 77-13498. p. cm. 1977. (ISBN 0-458-92870-4). Methuen.
--Christmas. Bruna, Dick (1927-), illus. LC 74-8056. (Illus.). 26 p. 1969. Doubleday.
--Christmas Book. Bruna, Dick (1927-), illus. (Illus.). (Bruna Books). 1976. (ISBN 0-416-24170-0). Methuen Inc.
--Circus. 28p. 1975. (ISBN 0-8467-0078-6). The Two Continents Publishing Group LTD.
--The Circus. Bruna, Dick (1927-), illus. (Illus.). 28p. (Bruna Books). (ps-2). 1963. (ISBN 0-416-30361-7). Methuen Inc.
--The Circus: A Toy Box Tale. Greifenstein, Sandra, tr. from Dutch. LC 63-17809. 28 p. illus. 17 cm. 1963. Follett Pub. Co.
--Dick Bruna's Cinderella. Bruna, Dick (1927-), illus. LC 67-800. (Illus.). 28 p. 17cm. 1966. Follett Pub. Co.
--Dick Bruna's Little Red Riding Hood. Bruna, Dick (1927-), illus. (Illus.). (ps-1). N.D. (ISBN 0-695-45259-2). Follett.
--Dick Bruna's Read-with-Miffy Frieze. LC 81-104322. (Illus.). 4 folded sheets (28 p.) in portfolio. 23cm. 1980. (ISBN 0-416-88670-1). Methuen Children's Books.
--Dick Bruna's Snow White & the Seven Dwarfs. Bruna, Dick (1927-), illus. LC 67-802. (Illus.). 28p. (ps-1). 1966. (ISBN 0-695-48150-9). Follett.
--Dick Bruna's Tom Thumb. Bruna, Dick (1927-), illus. LC 67-803. (Illus.). 17cm. 28p. (ps-1). 1966. (ISBN 0-695-48867-8). Follett.
--The Egg. LC 68-29353. (Illus.). 28 p. 17cm. 1968. Follett Pub. Co.
--The Egg. 28p. 1975. (ISBN 0-8467-0080-8). The Two Continents Publishing.
--Farmer John. (Dick Bruna Bks.). 1984. (ISBN 0-8431-1526-2). Price Stern.
--The Fish. Bruna, Dick (1927-), illus. (Illus.). 28p. (Bruna Books). (ps-2). 1975. (ISBN 0-416-30341-2). Methuen Inc.
--The Fish: A Toy Box Tale. LC 63-17812. (English verse by Sandra Greifenstein). (Illus.). 28 p. 17cm. 1963. Follett Pub. Co.
--I Can Count. 28p. 1975. (ISBN 0-8467-0082-4). The Two Continents Publishing Group Ltd.
--I Can Dress Myself. LC 77-17739. p. cm. 1978. (ISBN 0-458-93270-1). Methuen.
--I Can Read. LC 77-670140. (Illus.). 26 p. 17cm. (Bruna books). 1975, c.1968. (ISBN 0-8467-0086-7). Two Continents.
--I Can Read. Bruna, Dick (1927-), illus. (Illus.). 28p. (Bruna Books). (ps-2). 1975. (ISBN 0-416-30251-3). Methuen Inc.
--I Can Read More. Bruna, Dick (1927-), illus. LC 77-670141. (Illus.). 26 p. 16cm. (Bruna books). 1976, c.1979. (ISBN 0-8467-0167-7). Methuen.
--The King. LC 68-29352. (Illus.). 28 p. 17cm. 1968. Follett Pub. Co.
--The King. 28p. 1975. (ISBN 0-8467-0087-5). The Two Continents Publishing Group Ltd.
--Kitten Nell: A Toy Box Tale. Bruna, Dick (1927-), illus. LC 63-17810. (English verse by Sandra Greifenstein from the Dutch). (Illus.). (ps-1). 1963. (ISBN 0-695-44870-6). Follett.
--Lisa and Lynn. LC 77-670142. (Illus.). 26 p. 17cm. (Bruna books). 1975. (ISBN 0-8467-0092-1). Two Continents.
--The Little Bird. LC 77-670153. (Illus.). 26 p. 17cm. (Bruna books). 1975. (ISBN 0-8467-0077-8). Two Continents.
--The Little Bird. Bruna, Dick (1927-), illus. (Illus.). 28p. (Bruna Books). (ps-2). 1975. (ISBN 0-416-30321-8). Methuen Inc.
--Little Bird Tweet: A Toy Box Tale. LC 63-17811. 28 p. illus. 17 cm. 1963. Follett Pub. Co.
--Lynn & Lisa. (Dick Bruna Bks.). 1984. (ISBN 0-8431-1537-8). Price Stern.
--Miffy. LC 72-93796. (Illus.). 30 p. 17cm. 1970. Follett.
--Miffy. LC 77-670144. (Illus.). 26 p. 17cm. (Bruna books). 1975. (ISBN 0-8467-0085-9). Two Continents.
--Miffy at the Playground. Bruna, Dick (1927-), illus. (Illus.). (Bruna Books). (gr. 3-6). 1979. (ISBN 0-416-30161-4). Methuen Inc.
--Miffy at the Seaside. LC 73-93799. (Illus.). 30 p. 17cm. 1970. Follett.
--Miffy at the Zoo. LC 76-93797. (Illus.). 30 p. 17cm. 1970. Follett.
--Miffy at the Zoo. 28p. 1975. (ISBN 0-8467-0083-2). The Two Continents Publishing Group Ltd.
--Miffy Goes Flying. LC 77-670145. (Illus.). 26 p. 16cm. 1976. (ISBN 0-8467-0169-3). Methuen.
--Miffy Goes Flying. Bruna, Dick (1927-), illus. (Illus.). 1st U.S. edition. (Bruna Books). (gr. 1-3). 1976. (ISBN 0-416-30431-1). Methuen Inc.
--Miffy Goes to School. 32p. (Dick Bruna Bks.). 1984. (ISBN 0-8431-1530-0). Price Stern.
--Miffy in the Hospital. LC 77-17740. p. cm. 1978. (ISBN 0-458-92700-7). Methuen.
--Miffy in the Snow. LC 70-93798. (Illus.). 30 p. 17cm. 1970. Follett.
--Miffy In the Snow. 28p. 1975. (ISBN 0-8467-0084-0). The Two Continents Publishing Group LtD.
--Miffy's Bicycle. 32p. (Dick Bruna Bks.). 1984. (ISBN 0-8431-1527-0). Price Stern.
--Miffy's Birthday. Bruna, Dick (1927-), illus. (Illus.). 1st U.S. edition. (Bruna Books). (gr. 1-3). 1976. (ISBN 0-416-30421-4). Methuen Inc.
--Miffy's Birthday. Bruna, Dick (1927-), illus. LC 77-670146. (Illus.). 26 p. 16cm. (Bruna book). 1976. (ISBN 0-8467-0170-7). Methuen.
--Miffy's Dream. LC 80-490681. (Illus.). 28 p. 17cm. 1979. (ISBN 0-416-88650-7). Methuen.
--My Shirt Is White. LC 77-670147. (Illus.). 26 p. 17cm. (Bruna books). 1975. (ISBN 0-8467-0081-6). Two Continents.
--My Shirt Is White. Bruna, Dick (1927-), illus. (Illus.). 28p. (Bruna Books). (ps-2). 1975. (ISBN 0-416-30291-2). Methuen Inc.
--Poppy Pig Goes to Market. (Illus.). (Bruna Books). (ps-2). 1981. (ISBN 0-416-20890-8). Methuen Inc.
--The Rescue. (Dick Bruna Bks.). 1984. (ISBN 0-8431-1528-9). Price Stern.
--The Sailor. LC 68-29351. (Illus.). 28 p. 17cm. 1968. Follett Pub. Co.
--The School. LC 68-29350. (Illus.). 28 p. 17cm. 1968. Follett Pub. Co.
--Snuffy. LC 77-670148. (Illus.). 26 p. 17cm. (Bruna books). 1975. (ISBN 0-8467-0079-4). Two Continents.
--Snuffy. Bruna, Dick (1927-), illus. (Illus.). 28p. (Bruna Books). (ps-2). 1975. (ISBN 0-416-30451-6). Methuen Inc.
--Snuffy and the Fire. LC 77-670149. (Illus.). 26 p. 17cm. (Bruna books). 1975. (ISBN 0-8467-0091-3). Two Continents.
--Snuffy & the Fire. Bruna, Dick (1927-), illus. (Illus.). 28p. (Bruna Books). (ps-2). 1975. (ISBN 0-416-30461-3). Methuen Inc.
--A Story to Tell. (Illus.). 28p. (Bruna Books). (ps-2). 1975. (ISBN 0-416-30231-9). Methuen Inc.
--A Story to Tell. LC 77-670150. (Illus.). 28 p. 17cm. (Bruna books). 1975, c.1968. (ISBN 0-8467-0090-5). Two Continents.
--Tilly and Tees: A Toy Box Tale. LC 63-17808. 28 p. illus. 17 cm. 1963. Follett Pub. Co.
--Tilly & Tess. Bruna, Dick (1927-), illus. (Illus.). (ps-1). 1963. (ISBN 0-695-88790-4). (ISBN 0-695-48790-6). Follett.
--When I'm Big. (Illus.). (Bruna Bks.). (ps-k). N.D. (ISBN 0-416-20860-6). Methuen Inc.

Bruna, Dick (1927-) & Klugmann, Judith
--The Happy Apple. LC 62-5083. unpaged. illus. 21 cm. c.1959. Hart Pub. Co.

Brundage, Frances, illus.
--Once-Upon-a-Time Tales :. A Collection for Girls and Boys. (Illus.). 108p. 25cm. 1930. The Saalfield Publishing Compay.
--Once-Upon-a-Time Tales: A/Collection for Girls and Boys. LC 30-767. (Illus.). 25cm. 108p. 1930. The Saalfield Publishing Co.
--The Wonderful Story Book: A Collection of Favorite Fairy Tales and Poems of Childhood. LC 25-16204. 336 p. col. front., illus 24 1/2 cm. c.1925. The Saalfield Publishing Company.

Brundage, Frances & Williams, Florence White, illus.
--Story Time: A Collection of Favorite Tales for Girls and Boys. 108 p. illus. 25 cm. 1930. The Saalfield Publishing Company.

Brune, Lillian, ed. see Mueller, Arnold Carl.

Bruner, Herbert Bascom, jt. ed. see Huber, Miriam Blanton, Mrs.

Brunhoff, Jean de (1899-1937)
--A. B. C. de Babar. new ed. 46p. 1978. (ISBN 0-686-54120-0). French & Eur.
--A B C of Babar. LC 36-185417. 60 p. col. illus. 22 cm. c.1936. Random House.
--Babar and Father Christmas. (Illus.). 1940. Random House Inc.
--Babar & Father Christmas. Brunhoff, Jean De (1899-1937), illus. (Illus.). (ps). 1949. (ISBN 0-394-80578-X, BYR). (ISBN 0-394-90578-4). Random.
--Babar and His Children. (Illus.). 1938. Random House Inc.
--Babar & His Children. Haas, Merle S. (1896-1985), tr. (Illus.). (ps). 1954. (ISBN 0-394-80577-1, BYR). (ISBN 0-394-90577-6). Random.
--Babar and the King. (Illus.). 1934. Random House Inc.
--Babar and the Professor. Haas, Merle, tr. (Illus.). Repr. of 1957 ed. 1966. Random House.
--Babar and Zephir. 1937. Random.
--Babar & Zephir. Haas, Merle S. (1896-1985), tr. LC 42-36269. (Illus.). (ps). 1942. (ISBN 0-394-80579-8, BYR). (ISBN 0-394-90579-2). Random.
--Babar the King. N.D. Harrison Smith & Robert Haas, Inc.
--Babar the King. (Illus.). (ps). 1937. (ISBN 0-394-80580-1, BYR). (ISBN 0-394-90580-6). Random.
--Babar's Birthday Surprise. (Illus.). 1970. Random House.
--Babar's Games. (Illus.). 1968. Random House.
--Babar's Moon Trip. (Illus.). 1969. Random House.
--Meet Babar & His Family. (Illus.). (ps-1). 1973. (ISBN 0-394-82682-5, BYR). Random.
--The Story of Babar, the Little Elephant. LC 84-3308. 1984, c.1933. (ISBN 0-394-86823-4). Random House.
--The Story of Babar, the Little Elephant. Brunhoff, Jean de (1899-1937), illus. 1933. Random House.
--The Story of Babar, the Little Elephant. Brunhoff, Jean de (1899-1937), illus. (ps). 1937. (ISBN 0-394-80575-5, BYR). (ISBN 0-394-90575-X). Random.
--The Story of Babar, the Little Elephant. Brunhoff, Jean de (1899-1937), illus. 47 p. illus. 29 cm. c.1960. Random House.
--The Story of Babar: The Little Elephant. Haas, Merle S. (1896-1985), tr. N.D. Harrison Smith & Robert Haas, Inc.
--The Travels of Babar. 1934. Random.
--The Travels of Babar. LC 85-2236. p. cm. 1985, c.1934. (ISBN 0-394-87453-6). Random House.
--Travels of Babar. Brunhoff, Jean de (1899-1937), illus. (Illus.). (ps). 1937. (ISBN 0-394-80576-3, BYR). (ISBN 0-394-90576-8). Random.
--The Travels of Babar. Haas, Merle, tr. LC 34-31074. 37cm. 47p. N.D. Harrison Smith & Robert Haas, Inc.
--Zephir's Holidays. Haas, Merle, tr. from Fr. LC 37-19760. (Illus.). 40. 37cm. 1937. Random House.

Brunhoff, Jean de (1899-1937) & Brunhoff, Laurent de (1925-)
--Babar's Anniversary Album. Brunhoff, Jean de (1899-1937) & Brunhoff, Laurent de (1925-), illus. Sendak, Maurice Bernard (1928-), intro. by. LC 81-5182. (Illus.). 144p. (ps-3). 1981. (ISBN 0-394-84813-6). (ISBN 0-394-94813-0). Random.
--Babar's 50th Birthday Book. LC 81-5840. p. cm. 1981. (ISBN 0-394-84813-6). (ISBN 0-394-94813-0). Random House.
Brunhoff, Laurent see Brunhoff, Laurent de.
Brunhoff, Laurent de, jt. auth. see Brunhoff, Jean de.
Brunhoff, Laurent de (1925-)
--Anatole and His Donkey. Brunhoff, Laurent de (1925-), illus. Howard, Richard, tr. from Fr. LC 63-13131. unpaged. illus. 18 x 27 cm. 1963. Macmillan.
--Babar and the Doctor. LC 72-154629. (Illus.). 24 p. 1971. Random House.
--Babar & the Ghost. Brunhoff, Laurent de (1925-), illus. LC 80-5753. (Illus.). 32p. 1981. (ISBN 0-394-94660-X). (ISBN 0-394-84660-5). Random.
--Babar & the Professor. new ed. (Illus.). (gr. k-2). 1966. (ISBN 0-394-80590-9, BYR). (ISBN 0-394-90590-3). Random.
--Babar and the Professor. Haas, Merle S., tr. from Fr. 1v. (unpaged) col. illus. 29cm. 1966, c.1956. Random.
--Babar & the Wully-Wully. Brunhoff, Laurent de (1925-), illus. LC 75-8069. (Illus.). 36p. (gr. k-3). 1975. (ISBN 0-394-83077-6, BYR). (ISBN 0-394-93077-0). Random.
--Babar & the Wully-Wully. Brunhoff, Laurent de (1925-), illus. (Illus.). (gr. 3). N.D. (ISBN 0-590-30048-6, Schol Pap). Scholastic Inc.
--Babar at the Seashore. Haas, Merle S. (1896-1985), tr. LC 77-84461. (Illus.). 28 p. (His Babar's trunk). (Babar's Ser.). 1969. Random House.
--Babar Comes to America. Craig, M. Jean, tr. from Fr. LC 65-181637. 1v. (unpaged) col. illus. 32cm. (gr. k-2). 1965. (ISBN 0-394-80588-7, BYR). (ISBN 0-394-90588-1). Random.
--Babar Goes on a Picnic. LC 74-84463. (Illus.). 28 p. (His Babar's trunk). 1969. Random House.
--Babar Goes on a Picnic. Brunhoff, Laurent de (1925-), illus. Haas, Merle, tr. (Illus.). 1969. Random House Inc.
--Babar Goes Skiing. Haas, Merle S. (1896-1985), tr. LC 78-84464. (Illus.). 28 p. (His Babar's Trunk). (Babar's Ser.). 1969. Random House.
--Babar Goes Visiting. Jones, O., tr. (Babar's Ser.). 1969. Methuen.
--Babar in New York. (Illus.). (gr. 4-6). N.D. (ISBN 0-685-11024-9). French & Eur.
--Babar Learns to Cook. Brunhoff, Laurent de (1925-), illus. LC 78-11769. (Illus.). (Picturebacks Ser.). (ps-1). 1979. (ISBN 0-394-94108-X, BYR). (ISBN 0-394-84108-5). Random.
--Babar Learns to Drive. Jones, O., tr. from Fr. (Babar's Ser.). 1969. Methuen.
--Babar Loses His Crown. Brunhoff, Laurent de (1925-), illus. LC 67-21918. (gr. k-3). 1967. (ISBN 0-394-80045-1). (ISBN 0-394-90045-6). Beginner.
--Babar Packs His Trunk: A Storybook to Color. (Illus.). (ps-3). 1978. (ISBN 0-394-83960-9, BYR). Random.
--Babar Saves the Day. LC 76-11684. (Illus.). 32 p. 21cm. (Random House Pictureback Ser.). (gr. 3-6). c.1976. (ISBN 0-394-83341-4, BYR). Random House.
--Babar the Artist. LC 75-154627. (Illus.). 24 p. (Babar's Ser.). 1971. Random House.
--Babar the Athlete. LC 79-154628. (Illus.). 24 p. 1971. Random House.
--Babar the Camper. LC 71-154626. (Illus.). 24 p. 1971. Random House.
--Babar the Gardener. Haas, Merle S. (1896-1985), tr. LC 70-84462. (Illus.). 28 p. (His Babar's Trunk). (Babar's Ser.). 1969. Random House.
--Babar the Magician. Brunhoff, Laurent de (1925-), illus. LC 79-65799. (Illus.). 24p. (Shape Bks.). (ps). 1980. (ISBN 0-394-84360-6, BYR). Random.
--Babar Visits Another Planet. Brunhoff, Laurent de (1925-), illus. Haas, Merle S., tr. LC 72-1584. (Illus.). 29 p. 32cm. 1972. (ISBN 0-394-82429-6, BYR). (ISBN 0-394-92429-0). Random House.
--Babar's ABC. LC 83-2987. c.1983. (ISBN 0-394-95920-5). Random House.
--Babar's Birthday Surprise. LC 74-123071. (Illus.). 29 p. 32cm. (gr. 5). 1970. (ISBN 0-394-80591-7, BYR). (ISBN 0-394-90591-1). Random House.
--Babar's Book of Color. LC 84-42737. (Illus.). 32 p. 32cm. c.1984. (ISBN 0-394-86896-X). (ISBN 0-394-96896-4). Random House.
--Babar's Bookmobile. Brunhoff, Laurent de (1925-), illus. LC 73-22775. (Illus.). 24p. (ps-2). 1974. (ISBN 0-394-82660-4, BYR). Random.
--Babar's Castle. Brunhoff, Laurent de (1925-), illus. Haas, Merle S. (1896-1985), tr. LC 62-8994. (Illus.). 32cm. 30p. (ps). 1962. (ISBN 0-394-80586-0, BYR). (ISBN 0-394-90586-5). Random.
--Babar's Cousin. Brunhoff, Laurent de (1925-), illus. Haas, Merle S. (1896-1985), tr. (Illus.). (ps). 1952. (ISBN 0-394-80581-X, BYR). (ISBN 0-394-90581-4). Random.
--Babar's Cousin: That Rascal Arthur. Brunhoff, Laurent de (1925-), illus. Haas, Merle, tr. (Illus.). Repr. of 1948 ed. 1952. Random House Inc.
--Babar's Cousin: That Rascal Arthur. Haas, Merle S. (1896-1985), tr. LC 48-8143. 47 p. col. illus. 37 cm. 1948. Random House.
--Babar's Fair. Haas, Merle S. (1896-1985), tr. (Illus.). (ps). 1961. (ISBN 0-394-80584-4, BYR). (ISBN 0-394-90584-9). Random.
--Babar's Fair Will Be Opened Next Sunday. Brunhoff, Laurent de (1925-), illus. LC 55-8963. unpaged. illus. 29cm. (Babar's Ser.). 1954. Random House. **Award: (NYT).**
--Babar's French Lessons. (Illus.). (ps). 1963. (ISBN 0-394-80587-9, BYR). (ISBN 0-394-90587-3). Random.
--Babar's Games. Brunhoff, Laurent de (1925-), illus. (Illus.). color action pop-ups. 24p. (Pop-up Books Ser.: No. 13). (gr. k-3). 1968. (ISBN 0-394-81527-0). Random.
--Babar's Little Library: Stories About Earth, About Fire, About Air, About Water, 4 bks. (Illus.). (ps-2). 1980. Set. (ISBN 0-394-84365-7). Random.
--Babar's Moon Trip. Brunhoff, Laurent de (1925-), illus. (Illus.). pop-ups. 24p. (Pop-up Books Ser.). (gr. k-3). 1969. (ISBN 0-394-80583-6). Random.
--Babar's Mystery. Brunhoff, Laurent de (1925-), illus. LC 78-55912. (Illus.). (gr. 1-3). 1978. (ISBN 0-394-83920-X, BYR). (ISBN 0-394-93920-4). Random.
--Babar's Other Trunk, 4 vols. Incl. Babar the Camper; Babar the Artist; Babar the Athlete; Babar the Doctor. (Illus.). 1971. Set. (ISBN 0-394-82159-9). Random.
--Babar's Picnic. LC 49-50294. 39 p. col. illus. 37 cm. 1949. Random House.
--Babar's Picnic. Brunhoff, Laurent de (1925-), illus. Haas, Merle S. (1896-1985), tr. (Illus.). (ps). 1958. (ISBN 0-394-80582-8). (ISBN 0-394-90582-2). Random.
--Babar's Spanish Lessons. Las Lecciones Espanoles De Babar. Brunhoff, Laurent De (1925-), illus. LC 65-18164. (Illus.). 1 v. (unpaged). 32cm. (gr. k-3). 1965. (ISBN 0-394-80589-5, BYR). (ISBN 0-394-90589-X). Random House.
--Babar's Trunk, 4 bks. Brunhoff, Laurent de (1925-), illus. Incl. Babar at the Seashore; Babar the Gardener; Babar Goes Skiing; Babar on a Picnic. (Illus.). (ps-2). 1969. Set. (ISBN 0-394-80585-2). Random.
--Babar's Visit to Bird Island. Haas, Merle S. (1896-1985), tr. (Babar's Ser.). 1952. Random.
--Bonhomme. 1966. MacMillan.
--Bonhomme. Brunhoff, Laurent de (1925-), illus. LC 65-10301. (Illus.). (gr. k-3). 1965. (ISBN 0-394-91095-8). Pantheon.
--Bonhomme & the Huge Monster. Brunhoff, Laurent De (1925-), illus. Howard, Richard, tr. from Fr. LC 74-148. (Illus.). 48p. (ps-2). 1974. (ISBN 0-394-82667-1). Pantheon.
--Captain Serafina. Brunhoff, Laurent de (1925-), illus. LC 63-14777. 1 v. (unpaged) col. illus. 29 cm. 1963. World Pub. Co.
--Gregory and Lady Turtle in the Valley of the Music Trees. Brunhoff, Laurent de (1925-), illus. Howard, Richard, tr. from Fr. LC 78-153975. (Illus.). 96 p. 22cm. 1971. (ISBN 0-394-82321-4). Pantheon Books.
--Gregory & the Turtle. Brunhoff, Laurent de (1925-), illus. (gr. 1-5). 1971. (ISBN 0-394-92321-9). Pantheon.
--Meet Babar and His Family. LC 73-2445. (Illus.). 32 p. 21cm. 1973. (ISBN 0-394-82682-5). Random House.
--The One Pig with Horns. Brunhoff, Laurent de (1925-), illus. Howard, Richard (1929-), tr. from Fr. LC 78-4917. (Illus.). (gr. k-3). 1979. (ISBN 0-394-83673-1). (ISBN 0-394-93673-6). Pantheon.
--Serafina the Giraffe. Brunhoff, Laurent de (1925-), illus. LC 61-6652. (Illus.). unpaged. 29cm. 1961. World Pub. Co.
--Serafina's Lucky Find. 1st ed. Brunhoff, Laurent de (1925-), illus. LC 62-16361. unpaged. illus. 29cm. 1962. World Pub. Co.
Brunner, Fritz
--Trouble in Brusada. Brunner, Klaus, illus. Kirkup, James (1927-), tr. (Illus.). (gr. 5-9). 1962. (ISBN 0-685-21628-4). Verry.
Brunner, John Kilian Houston (1934-)
--The Devil's Work. 1970. (ISBN 0-393-08581-3). Norton & Co.
--The One Hunderedth Millenium. N.D. Ace Books.
--The Stone That Never Came Down. LC 73-79652. 216p. 1973. (ISBN 0-385-03716-3). Doubleday.
Brunner, Klaus & Bolliger, Max
--Sandy at the Children's Zoo. Brunner, Klaus, illus. (Illus.). 43 p. 30cm. 1967, c.1966. Crowell.
Brunowe, Marion J., pseud., see Brown, Mary Josephine.
Brunowe, Marion J., pseud. (1875-1912)
--The Madcap Set at St. Anne's. Brown, Mary Josephine. (American Author Ser.). N.D. Benziger Brothers' Pub.
--The New Scholar at St. Anne's. Brown, Mary Josephine. N.D. Benziger Brothers.
--Seven of Us: Or, Stories for Boys and Girls. Brown, Mary Josephine. N.D. P. J. Kennedy.
Bruns, Walter F.
--In the Sunk Lands. (The Boys Own Library). N.D. David McKay.
Brunton, F Carmichael
--The Enchanted Lochan: Stories of Celtic Mythology. Nisbet, Noel Laura (1887-), illus. LC 18-339951. 207, 1 p. col. front., col. plates. 21 x 16 cm. 1917. Thomas Y. Crowell Company.
Brush, Frederic (1871-)
--Seven Round a Mountain. Barreaux, Adolphe, illus. LC 42-58277. 3 p. l., 11-151 p. front., illus. 21 cm. 1941. Pennsylvania Book Service.
Brush, Mary Elizabeth Quakenbush, Mrs. (1857-)
--The Coming of Caroline. LC 8-10626. 20cm. 128p. 1903. American Tract Society.
--Island Patty. LC 1-19462. (Illus.). 12cm. 96p. 1901. American Tract Society.
--The Scarlet Patch. 1905. Lothrop, Lee & Shepard.
Brustlein, Daniel see Alain, pseud.
Brustlein, Daniel
--The Elephant and the Flea. Alain, pseud. LC 56-962195. 32p. illus. 27cm. (Whittlesey House books for young people). 1956. McGraw-Hill Book Co.
--The Magic Stones. Alain, pseud. (Illus.). (gr. 4-6). 1957. (ISBN 0-8382-0494-5). Hale.
--The Magic Stones. Alain, pseud. LC 57-71716. 31p. illus. 26cm. c.1957. Whittlesey House.
--One, Two, Three, Going to Sea: An Adding and Subtracting Book. LC 64-13589. 1 v. (unpaged) illus. (part col.) 22 cm. 1964. Young Scott Books.
Brustlein, Janice Tworkov see Janice, pseud.
Brustlein, Janice Tworkov
--Angelique. Janice, pseud. Duvoisin, Roger Antoine (1904-1980), illus. LC 60-11692. (Illus.). 32 p. 26cm. c.1960. Whittlesey House.
--It's Spring! It's Spring!. Janice, pseud. Alain, pseud. (1904-), illus. Brustlein, Daniel. LC 56-633119. unpaged. illus. 39cm. c.1956. Lothrop, Lee & Shepard Co.
--Little Bear Learns to Read the Cookbook. Janice, pseud. Foster, Marian Curtis (1909-1978), illus. Mariana, pseud. LC 69-14315. (Illus.). 33 p. 24cm. 1969. Lothrop, Lee & Shepard Co.
--Little Bear Marches in the Saint Patrick's Day Parade. Janice, pseud. Foster, Marian Curtis (1909-1978), illus. Mariana, pseud. LC 67-15712. (Illus.). (gr. k-3). N.D. (ISBN 0-688-51075-2). Lothrop.
--Little Bear Marches in the St. Patricks Day Parade. Janice, pseud. Foster, Marian Curtis (1909-1978), illus. Mariana, pseud. 1969. (ISBN 0-688-51075-2). William Morrow and Company.
--Little Bear's Christmas. Janice, pseud. Foster, Marian Curtis (1909-1978), illus. Mariana, pseud. LC 64-21191. (Illus.). (gr. k-3). 1964. (ISBN 0-688-51076-0). Lothrop.
--Little Bear's New Year's Party. Janice, pseud. Foster, Marian Curtis (1909-1978), illus. Mariana, pseud. LC 72-5234. (Illus.). 32 p. 24cm. 1973. (ISBN 0-688-40002-7). Lothrop, Lee & Shepard.
--Little Bear's Pancake Party. Janice, pseud. Foster, Marian Curtis (1909-1978), illus. Mariana, pseud. LC 59-15445. (Illus.). 24cm. 32p. (gr. k-3). 1959. (ISBN 0-688-51077-9). Lothrop.
--Little Bear's Sunday Breakfast. Janice, pseud. (Illus.). (gr. k-2). 1958. (ISBN 0-8382-0444-9). Hale.
--Little Bear's Sunday Breakfast. Janice, pseud. Foster, Marian Curtis (1909-1978), illus. Mariana, pseud. LC 57-600636. unpaged. illus. 25cm. 1958. Lothrop, Lee & Shepard Co.
--Little Bear's Thanksgiving. Janice, pseud. Foster, Marian Curtis (1909-1978), illus. Mariana, pseud. LC 67-22583. (Illus.). 24cm. 32p. (gr. k-3). 1967. (ISBN 0-688-51078-7). Lothrop.
--Little Bear's Thanksgiving. Janice, pseud. Foster, Marian Curtis (1909-1978), illus. Mariana, pseud. 1964. William Morrow and Company.
--The Lonely Little Lady and Her Garden. Janice, pseud. Foster, Marian Curtis (1909-1978), illus. Mariana, pseud. LC 57-599536. 18cm. 32p. 1957. Lothrop, Lee & Shepard.
--Minette. Janice, pseud. (Illus.). (gr. 1-3). 1959. (ISBN 0-8382-0520-8). Hale.
--Minette. Janice, pseud. Brustlein, Daniel, pseud. (1904-), illus. Brustlein, Daniel. Alain, pseud. LC 59-10715. (Illus.). 32p. 26cm. c.1959. Whittlesey House.
--Mr. and Mrs. Button's Wonderful Watchdogs. Janice, pseud. 1st ed. Duvoisin, Roger Antoine (1904-1980), illus. LC 78-8451. (Illus.). 32 p. 26cm. c.1978. (ISBN 0-688-41848-1). (ISBN 0-688-51848-6). Lothrop, Lee & Shepard.
Bruton, W., illus.
--Johnny Headstrong's trip to Coney Island. LC 17-1338. 19p. illus. pt. col. 27 1/2cm. c.1882. McLoughlin Bros.
Bruyn, Monica Jean Grembowicz de see De Bruyn, Monica Jean Grembowicz.
Bryan, Ashley F. (1923-)
--The Adventures of Aku: Or, How It Came About That We Shall Always See Okra the Cat Lying on a Velvet Cushion, While Okraman the Dog Sleeps Among the Ashes. Bryan, Ashley F. (1923-), illus. LC 75-44245. (Illus.). 70 p. 24cm. 1976. (ISBN 0-689-30519-2). Atheneum.
--Beat the Story-Drum, Pum-Pum. Bryan, Ashley F. (1923-), illus. LC 80-12045. (Illus.). 80p. 1980. (ISBN 0-689-30769-1). Atheneum. **Awards: (CSKA); (ALA).**
--I Greet the Dawn: Poems of Paul Laurence Dunbar. Bryan, Ashley F. (1923-), illus. LC 77-21232. (Illus.). (gr. 6 up). 1978. (ISBN 0-689-30613-X). Atheneum.
--The Ox of the Wonderful Horns, and Other African Folktales. Bryan, Ashley F. (1923-), illus. LC 75-154749. (Illus.). 42 p. 29cm. (gr. 1-5). 1971. Atheneum.
--Walk Together Children. LC 73-84821. (Illus.). 64p. (gr. 3 up). 1974. (ISBN 0-689-30131-6). Atheneum.
--Walk Together Children. Bryan, Ashley F. (1923-), illus. (gr. 2 up). N.D. (ISBN 0-689-70485-2, Aladdin). Atheneum.
Bryan, Ashley F. (1923-), retold by.
--The Cat's Purr. Bryan, Ashley F. (1923-), illus. LC 84-21534. (Illus.). 42 p. 19cm. 1985. (ISBN 0-689-31086-2). Atheneum. **Award: (ALA).**
--The Dancing Granny. Bryan, Ashley F. (1923-), illus. LC 76-25847. (Illus.). 62 p. 18cm. 1977. (ISBN 0-689-30548-6). Atheneum.
Bryan, Catherine
--The Cactus Fence. Madden, Mabra Benjamin (1899-), illus. LC 43-17353. 79, 1 p. incl. front., illus. 22 1/2 cm. 1943. The Macmillan Company.
--Pito's House: A Mexican Folk Tale. Madden, Mabra Benjamin (1899-), illus. LC 43-3201. 90 p. illus. (part col.) 28 x 19 cm. 1943. The Macmillan Company.
Bryan, Dorothy & Bryan, Marguerite
--Bobby Wanted a Pony. LC 37-16935. 32 p. illus. (part col.) 23 x 20 cm. 1937. Dodd, Mead and Company.
--Four Puppies Who Wanted a Homee. Frankel, Simon, illus. LC 50-8334. 21cm. 41p. (Wonder Book for Children). (gr. k-3). 1950. Wonder Books.
--Friendly Little Jonathan. LC 39-23642. 32 p. illus. 21 x 24 cm. 1939. Dodd, Mead & Company.
--Frisky Finding a Home. 32 p. illus. 17 cm. 1938. Dodd, Mead and Company.
--Fun with Michael. LC 34-168443. 32 p. illus. (part col.) 21 x 24 cm. 1934. Doubleday, Dorand & Company, Inc.
--Johnny Penguin. LC 31-177273. 32 p. illus. (part col.) 21 x 24 cm. 1931. Doubleday, Doran & Company, Inc.
--Just Tammie!. LC 51-13037. (Illus.). unpaged. 21cm. 1951. Dodd, Mead.
--Michael and Patsy. LC 53-11134. 1v. (unpaged) illus. 18 x 20cm. 1953, c.1932. Dodd, Mead.
--Michael and Patsy on the Golf Links. LC 33-23677. 32 p. illus. (part col.) 21 x 24 cm. 1933. Doubleday, Doran & Company, Inc.
--Michael Who Missed His Train. LC 32-14442. 32 p. illus. (part col.) 21 x 24 cm. 1932. Doubleday, Doran & Company, Inc.
--Tammie and That Puppy. LC 36-17479. 32 p. illus. (part col.) 22 cm. 1936. Dodd, Mead and Company.
--There Was Tammie!. LC 35-12768. 32 p. illus. (part col.) 22 x 19 cm. 1935. Dodd, Mead and Company.
Bryan, Marguerite, jt. auth. see Bryan, Dorothy.
Bryan, Rita
--The Little Bee That Couldn't Buzz. Bryan, Mary, illus. LC 55-123117. 57p. illus. 22cm. c.1958. Fearon Publishers.
Bryan, William J.
--The Chosen One. N.D. Vantage Press Inc.
Bryans, John Kennedy (1872-)
--Shadowkids. Bryans, John Kennedy (1872-), illus. LC 29-7877. 37 p. incl. front., illus. 18 cm. c.1929. The Platt & Munk Co., Inc.
--Shadowkids at Play. Bryans, John Kennedy (1872-), illus. LC 30-10956. 88 p. incl. front., illus. 18 cm. c.1930. The Platt & Munk Co. Inc.

Bryant, Al (1926-)
--The Bible Picture Primer. LC 56-25008. unpaged. illus. 21cm. (Zondervan stori-picture book). 1955. Zondervan Pub. House.
Bryant, Al (1926-), ed.
--Stories from Other Lands for Boys and Girls. Mastri, Fiore, illus. LC 55-157. 189p. illus. 24cm. 1954. Zondervan Pub. House.
--Stories to Tell Boys and Girls. Merizon, Armand, illus. LC 52-14260. 192p. illus. 24cm. 1952. Zondervan Pub. House.
Bryant, Alice Elizabeth Crandell, Mrs. (1876-), ed.
--A Treasury of Hero Tales. LC 20-151759. vi, 7-128 p. front., plates. 20 cm. c.1920. Thomas Y. Crowell Company.
Bryant, Alice M.
--The Poetry of Flowerland. (Illus.). 224p. (School Library: No. 3). N.D. Educational Publishing Company.
Bryant, Anna Burnham, Mrs.
--Bertha's Garden and Other Stories. LC 99-5592. 57 p. illus. 18 cm. (Sunny hour series, v. 1). c.1899. Pilgrim Press.
--A Bird Party and other Stories. (Illus.). 12cm. 77p. (Sunny Hour Ser.: Vol. 4). 1899. Pilgrim Press.
--The Christmas Cat. Brand, Edith Browning, illus. LC 2-39148. 21 x 10 cm. 207p. 1902. Pilgrim Press.
--Holly Berry Series, 6 Vols. (Illus.). N.D. Pilgrim Press.
--A Jolly Jingle Book. LC 13-25326. 9 p. l., 3-125 p. incl. front, plates. 20 cm. c.1913. The Pilgrim Press.
--Papa's Birthday and Other Stories. LC 99-5594. 74 p. illus. 18 cm. (Sunny hour series, v. 5). c.1899. Pilgrim Press.
--Polly Peacemaker: And Other Stories. LC 99-5595. 77 p. illus. 18 cm. (Sunny hour series, v. 3). c.1899. Pilgrim Press.
--The Prettiest Tree and Other Stories. LC 39-5596. 72 p. illus. 18 cm. (Sunny hour series, v. 6). c.1899. Pilgrim Press.
--The Sunny Hour Series, 6 Vols. (Illus.). N.D. Pilgrim Press.
--Two Little Girls and Other Stories. LC 39-5597. 70 p. illus. 18 cm. (Sunny hour series, v. 2). c.1899. Pilgrim Press.
Bryant, Bernice Morgan (1908-)
--Dan Morgan, Boy of the Wilderness. 1st ed. Laune, Paul Sidney (1899-), illus. LC 52-5815. 183 p. illus. 20 cm. (Childhood of famous Americans series). 1952. Bobbs-Merrill.
--Dan Morgan: Wilderness Boy. Goldstein, Nathan (1927-), illus. LC 62-16600. 200p. col. illus. 20cm. (Childhood of famous Amers.). N.D. Bobbs.
--Everybody Likes Butch. Falconer, Rebecca (1919-), illus. Becky, pseud. LC 47-20229. 36 p. illus. (part col.) 20 x 17 cm. (Star-bright book. S-301). 1947. Childrens Press, Inc.
--Fancy Free. Copelman, Evelyn, illus. LC 49-11279. 278 p. illus. 21 cm. 1949. Bobbs-Merrill Co.
--Follow the leader. Bailey-Jones, Beryl (1912-), illus. LC 50-9366. 30p. col. illus. 21cm. 1950. Houghton Mifflin & Co.
--Future Perfect. 1957. Bobbs-Merill.
--George Gershwin: Young Composer,. Goldstein, Nathan (1927-), illus. LC 65-23666. 200p. col. illus. 20cm. (Childhood of famous Amers.) Bibl.). c.1965. Bobbs.
--Let's Be Friends. Falconer, Rebecca (1919-), illus. Becky, pseud. (Illus.). (gr. k-2). 1954. (ISBN 0-516-03530-4). Childrens.
--Pedie and the Twins: A Read-It-Yourself Story. Chisholm, Christine, illus. LC 42-24038. 32 p. illus. (part col.) 24 x 19 cm. 1942. A. Whitman & Company.
--Trudy Terrill: Eighth Grader. Chapman, Frederick Trench (1887-), illus. LC 46-7184. 273 p. illus. 21 cm. 1946. The Bobbs-Merrill Company.
--Trudy Terrill: High-School Freshman. Chapman, Frederick Trench (1887-), illus. LC 48-6572. 280 p. illus. 21 cm. 1948. Bobbs-Merrill Co.
--Yammy Buys a Bicycle. Woodward, Hildegard (1898-), illus. LC 40-321414. 6 p. l., 15-163 p. incl. col. front., illus., plates (part col.) 23 x 17 cm. 1940. A. Whitman & Co.
Bryant, Charlotte Margaret Kruger (1917-)
--The Terry Twins in Alaska. LC 57-46776. 76p. 20cm. 1957. Cowman Publications.
--The Terry Twins in Alaska Find a Treasure. LC 61-427317. 91p. 20cm. 1961. Cowman Publications.
Bryant, Chester
--The Lost Kingdom. Ayer, Margaret (0000-1981), illus. LC 51-12795. (Illus.). 184 p. 22cm. 1951. Messner.
Bryant, Dean, illus.
--See the Bear. (ps-2). 1953. (ISBN 0-528-82796-0). Rand.
Bryant, Gertrude Thomson
--Have a Good Year. Simmons, Ellie, illus. LC 66-11779. (Illus.). 144 p. 24cm. 1966. W. W. Norton.
--Two Is Company. LC 62-15514. (Illus.). 94 p. 20cm. 1962. Lippincott.
Bryant, Laura, ed.
--Songs for Children. N.D. American Book Co.
--Songs for Christmas. Luvaas, Morten John (1896-), contrib. by. LC 41-555141. 3 p. l., 57 p. 1 illus. 21 x 17 cm. c.1940. American Book Company.
Bryant, Lorinda Munson, Mrs. (1855-)
--The Children's Book of Animal Pictures. LC 31-23904. x, 105 p. illus. 25 cm. c.1931. The Century Co.
Bryant, Marguerite
--The Princess Cynthia. Havelka, George R., illus. LC 1-27043. 20cm. 494p. 1901. Funk & Wagnalls Co.
Bryant, Paula, tr. see Tersac, Helene.
Bryant, Sara Cone (1873-), ed. see Ewing, Juliana Horatia Gatty, Mrs.
Bryant, Sara Cone (1873-), ed. see Martineau, Harriet.
Bryant, Sara Cone (1873-)
--Best Stories to Tell to Children. Wilson, Patten, illus. LC 12-237090. xi, 1 p., 1 l., 180, 2 p. col. front., col. plates 22 cm. 1912. Houghton Mifflin Company.
--The Burning Rice Fields. Funai, Mamoru R. (1932-), illus. LC 63-9575. (Illus.). 29cm. (A Young Owl Bk.). 1963. Holt, Rinehart and Winston.
--Epaminondas. Merriam, Eve (1916-), retold by. Hyman, Trina Schart (1939-), illus. LC 68-10476. (Illus.). 32 p. 22cm. 1968. Follett Pub. Co.
--Epaminondas & His Auntie. Hogan, Inez (1895-), illus. LC 38-32021. (Illus.). 21cm. 16p. (gr. k-3). 1938. (ISBN 0-395-17130-X). HM.
--Gordon and His Friends; Stories to Read Yourself. Taylor, Ethel C., illus. LC 26-16340. vii, 1 120 p. illus. 20 cm. c.1924. Houghton Mifflin Company.
--Gordon in the Great Woods. Grilley, Virginia, illus. 19cm. 218p. 1929. Houghton Mifflin Co.
--Gordon: More Stories to Read to Yourself. (Illus.). 19cm. 218p. 1926. Houghton Mifflin Co.
--New Stories to Tell the Children: Stories You Never Have Heard. Pape, Frank Cheyne (1878-), illus. LC 24-277497. 2 p. l., 175 p. illus. 18 cm. c.1924. Houghton Mifflin Company.
--New Stories to Tell to Children: Stories You Never Have Heard. Pape, Frank Cheyne (1878-), illus. LC 23-17843. 4 p. l., 151 p. col. front., illus., col. plates 21 cm. 1923. Houghton Mifflin Company.
--Stories to Tell the Littlest Ones. Pogany, Willy (1882-1955), illus. LC 16-23208. xiii, 1 p., 3-177, 1 p., 1 l. col. front., illus., plates (part col.) 22 cm. 1916. Houghton Mifflin Company.
--Stories to Tell to Children: Fifty-One Stories with Some Suggestions for Telling. LC 7-36089. xivii, 248, 1 p. illus. 19 cm. c.1907. Houghton, Mifflin and Company.
Bryant, Thomas Alton (1926-)
--Pictures Of Jesus. N.D. Zondervan Publishing House.
Bryant, W. E., Mrs.
--Aunt Dolly's School Room Stories. N.D. D. Lothrop Co.
Bryant, William Cullen, et al. (1794-1878)
--Little Lays For Little Folk. (Illus.). N.D. George Routledge & Sons.
Bryant, William Cullen (1794-1878)
--Among the Trees. (Illus.). (The Celluloid Ser). N.D. Estes & Lauriat's.
--The Family Library of Poetry and Songs. Bryant, William Cullen (1794-1878), illus. N.D. Fords, Howards & Hulbert.
--Ulysses Among the Phaeacians: From Translation of Homer's Oddyssey. 96p. (Riverside Literature Ser.: No. 43). N.D. Houghton, Mifflin and Company.
Bryce, Catherine T., jt. auth. see Davidson, Isobel.
Bryce, Catherine Turner, ed. see Page, Thomas Nelson.
Bryce, Catherine Turner (1871-)
--The Child Lore Dramatic Reader. N.D. Charles Scribner's Sons'.
--Fables from Afar. 157p. N.D. Newson & Co.
--Folk Lore from Foreign Lands. Choate, Florence & Curtis, Elizabeth, illus. v, 151 p. col. front., col. illus. 20 cm. (Aldine supplementary readers). c.1913. Newson & Company.
--Robert Louis Stevenson Reader. LC 6-14538. vii, 88 p. col. illus. 20 cm. 1906. C. Scribner's Sons.
--The Safe-Way Club. LC 38-116418. 108, 1 p. illus. (part col) 21 cm. 1938. T. Nelson and Sons.
--Short Stories for Little Folks. LC 11-1730. v, 121 p. col. illus. 20 cm. (On cover: Aldine supplementary readers). c.1910. Newson & Company.
--Story-Land Dramatic Reader. N.D. Charles Scribner's Sons'.
--That's Why Stories. 182p. N.D. Newson & Co.
Bryce, Marion
--Nancy in the Wood. Clausen, K., illus. LC 13-257181. 200 p. 8 col. pl. (incl. front.) illus. 22 cm. 1914. John Lane.
Brychta, Alex
--Wishwhat. (Illus.). 32p. (ps-1). 1984. (ISBN 0-19-279786-7, Pub. by Oxford U Pr Childrens). Merrimack Pub Cir.
Bryna, Stevens
--Deborah Sampson Goes to War. Hill, Florence, illus. LC 83-20950. (Illus.). 48p. (Carolrhoda On My Own Bks.). (gr. k-4). 1984. (ISBN 0-87614-254-4). Carolrhoda Bks.
Brynildsen, Kenneth (1944-)
--School's Out!. LC 81-9737. 152 p. 22cm. c.1982. (ISBN 0-698-20537-5). Coward, McCann & Geoghegan.
Bryson, Bernarda (1905-1977)
--The Twenty Miracles of Saint Nicolas. Bryson, Bernarda (1905-1977), illus. 1960. Little, Brown and Company.
--The Zoo of Zeus: A Handbook of Mythological Beasts and Creatures. Bryson, Bernarda (1905-1977), illus. LC 64-7804. 1 v. (unpaged) col. illus. 27cm. 1964. Grossman.
Bryson, Bernarda (1905-1977), retold by.
--Gilgamesh: Man's First Story. Bryson, Bernarda (1905-1977), illus. LC 66-11420. (Illus.). 112 p. 29cm. 1967. Holt, Rinehart & Winston. **Award: (BGH).**
Bryson, Charles Lee (1868-)
--Double Trouble. LC 44-40265. 3 p. l. 336 p. 21 cm. 1944. Ziff-Davis Publishing Company.
--Tan and Teckle. (Comrade Ser.). N.D. Fleming H. Revell Co.
Bryson, Thomas H.
--Juniors of St. Bede. N.D. Benziger Brothers.
B. T. B., pseud. (1870-1917), ed. see Belloc, Joseph Hilaire Pierre.
Bubley, Esther, photos by.
--How Puppies Grow. 1972. Four Winds.
Buboltz, Ethel
--Under the Firefly Lamp. Koski, Barbara, illus. LC 55-8508. 94p. illus. 23cm. 1955. Comet Press Books.
Buchan, Bryan (1945-)
--Copper Sunrise. (gr. 4-6). 1973. (ISBN 0-590-04215-7, Schol Trade Pap). Schol Bk Serv.
--Dragon Children. (gr. 7-9). 1975. (ISBN 0-590-10293-1). Schol Bk Serv.
Buchan, John (1875-1940)
--Greenmantle. (The Nelson Classics). N.D. Nelson Bks.
--Lake of Gold. N.D. Houghton Mifflin Co.
--The Magic Walking-Stick. LC 75-32205. (Illus.). xi, 215 p. 19cm. (Classics of Children's Literature, 1621-1932). 1976, c.1932. Garland Pub.
--The Magic Walking-Stick. Becher, Arthur E., illus. LC 32-81298. 7 p. l., 3-176 p. front., plates. 21 cm. 1932. Houghton Mifflin Company.
--Prester John. (gr. 9 up). 1938. (ISBN 0-395-06663-8). HM.
--Prester John. (Nelson Classics). (gr. 1-6). N.D. (ISBN 0-8407-4021-2). Nelson.
--The Thirty-Nine Steps. (Illus.). 151p. Repr. of 1964 ed. (Children's Illustrated Classics). 1975. (ISBN 0-460-05064-8, Pub by J M Dent England). Biblio Dist.
--Thirty-Nine Steps. Ardizzone, Edward Jeffrey Irving (1900-1979), illus. (Illus.). (Children's Illustrated Classics). (gr. 7 up). 1964. (ISBN 0-525-41108-9). Dutton.
Buchan, Stuart (1942-)
--Fleeced. 1975. (ISBN 0-399-11423-8). G.P. Putnam's Sons.
--A Space of His Own. LC 79-15745. 197 p. 22cm. c.1979. (ISBN 0-684-16282-2). Scribner.
--When We Lived with Pete. LC 77-16440. 147 p. 22cm. c.1978. (ISBN 0-684-15493-5). Scribner.
Buchan, Susan Grosvenor (1882-)
--Maria Mouse. Levetus, Margaret, illus. LC 43-18840. cover-title, 24 p. illus. (part col.) 29 x 22 1/2 cm. 1943. Transatlantic Arts Ltd.
Buchanan, Edgar Simmons (1872-), ed. see Bunyan, John.
Buchanan, Fannie R
--Sunny Crest Farmyard. Biers, Clarence, illus. LC 25-23300. 104 p. illus. (part col.) 24 cm. c.1925. Rand, McNally & Company.
Buchanan, Gladys
--The Five Little Kids. Friend, Esther, illus. LC 41-160702. 32 p. col. illus. 21 x 19 cm. c.1941. Rand McNally & Company.
--The Five Little Raccoons. Biers, Clarence, illus. LC 36-31575. 32 p. illus. 21 x 19 cm. c.1936. Rand, McNally & Company.
Buchanan, Heather S.
--Emily Mouse Saves the Day. Buchanan, Heather S., illus. LC 84-15583. (Illus.). 28 p. 14cm. 1985. (ISBN 0-8037-0175-6). Dial Books for Young Readers.
--Emily Mouse's First Adventure. Buchanan, Heather S., illus. LC 84-15582. (Illus.). 28 p. 14cm. 1985. (ISBN 0-8037-0174-8). Dial Books for Young Readers.
--George Mouse Learns to Fly. LC 84-15581. (Illus.). 28 p. 14cm. 1985. (ISBN 0-8037-0172-1). Dial Books for Young Readers.
--George Mouse's First Summer. LC 84-15584. (Illus.). 28 p. 14cm. 1985. (ISBN 0-8037-0173-X). Dial Books for Young Readers.
Buchanan, Rosemary
--House of Friendship. Ayer, Margaret (0000-1981), illus. LC 46-3806. vii, 165 p. 21 cm. 1946. Longmans, Green and Co.
Buchanan, William, pseud., see Buck, William Ray.
Buchanan, William, pseud. (1930-)
--Christopher Syn. Buck, William Ray. Thorndike, Russell B., ed. (Illus.). 192p. 1960. Obelard-Schuman.
--Doctor Anger's Island. Buck, William Ray. (gr. 7 up). 1961. (ISBN 0-200-71704-9). Abelard.
--Eagles' Paradise. Buck, William Ray. (gr. 7 up). 1964. Abelard.
--Ghost of Dagger Bay. Buck, William Ray. (gr. 7 up). 1963. Abelard.
Buchanan-Brown, John, tr. see Bambote, Pierre.
Buchanan-Brown, John, tr. see Berna, Paul.
Buchanan-Brown, John (1929-), tr. see Bourliaguet, Leonce.
Buchanan-Brown, John, tr. see Cervon, Jacqueline.
Buchanan-Brown, John (1929-), tr. see Ezo.
Bucher, Otmar
--My Elephant Sahib. Reich, Hanns, ed. Mayer, Fred, illus. LC 72-81294. (Illus.). 40p. (gr. k-3). 1972. (ISBN 0-8090-2148-X, Terra Magica). Hill & Wang.
Bucher-Waldis, Angelika (1933-)
--My Elephant Sahib. Mayer, Fred (1933-), illus. Conrad, L. K., tr. LC 73-161233. (Illus.). 36 p. 24cm. 1973, c.1972. (ISBN 0-8090-2148-X). Hill and Wang.
Buchheim, E. S.
--A Self-Willed Family. (Illus.). N.D. Cassell & Co.
Buchheimer, Naomi Barnett, pseud., see Barnett, Naomi.
Buchheimer, Naomi Barnett, pseud. (1927-)
--I Know a Teacher. Barnett, Naomi. Shortall, Leonard W., illus. LC 67-14789. 45 p. illus. (part col.) 23 cm. (Community helper book). 1967. Putnam.
--Let's Go to a Dentist. Sciver, Ruth Van, illus. LC 58-13308. 45p. illus. 21cm. (Let's Go Ser.). 1959. Putnam.
--Let's Go to a School. Sciver, Ruth Van, illus. LC 58-7442. 41p. illus. 21cm. (Let's Go Ser.). 1958, c.1957. Putnam.
--Let's Go to Candy Factory. Voute, Kathleen (1892-), illus. LC 57-12206. unpaged. illus. 21cm. (Let's Go Ser.). 1957. Putnam.
--Let's go to the Post Office. Sciver, Ruth Van, illus. LC 57-9396. 45p. illus. 21cm. (Let's Go Ser.). 1957. Putnam.
--Let's Go to the Post Office. Sciver, Ruth Van, illus. LC 64-22583. 47p. col. ill. 22cm. (Let's Go Ser.). 1964. Putnam.
--Night Outdoors. Barnett, Naomi. Teichman, Dorothy, illus. LC 60-6862. (Illus.). 23cm. 45p. (See & Read Storybooks). (gr. k-3). 1960. (ISBN 0-399-60491-X). Putnam.
Buchwald, Arthur (1925-)
--The Bollo Caper: A Fable for Children of All Ages. Brinckloe, Julie Lorraine (1950-), illus. LC 73-10857. (Illus.). 56 p. 22cm. (gr. 5-8). 1974. (ISBN 0-385-01025-7). (ISBN 0-385-01025-7). Doubleday.
--The Bollo Caper: A Furry Tail for All Ages. Primavera, Elise, illus. LC 83-4583. (Illus.). (gr. 3 up). 1983. (ISBN 0-399-21003-2, Putnam). (ISBN 0-399-21003-2). Putnam Pub Group.
--Irving's Delight. LC 75-16236. 1975. (ISBN 0-679-50569-5). McKay.
Buchwald, Emilie (1935-)
--Floramel and Esteban. Robinson, Charles (1931-), illus. LC 81-7135. (Illus.). 72 p. 21cm. c.1982. (ISBN 0-15-228678-0). Harcourt Brace Jovanovich. **Award: (ALA).**
--Gildaen: The Heroic Adventures of a Most Unusual Rabbit. Flynn, Barbara (1928-), illus. LC 72-91231. (Illus.). 189 p. 21cm. 1973. (ISBN 0-15-230800-8). Harcourt Brace Jovanovich.
Buck, Alan Michael
--Dermot of the Bright Weapons. Bennett, Richard Michael (1899-), illus. LC 39-23643. 199 p. incl. illus., plates. front. 21 cm. c.1939. Oxford University Press.
--The Harper's Daughter. Bennett, Richard Michael (1899-), illus. LC 40-32772. xiii p., 2 l., 19-229 p. incl. front., illus., plates. 21 cm. c.1940. Oxford University Press.
--The Hound of Culain. Bennett, Richard Michael (1899-), illus. LC 38-15731. xii p., 2 l., 17-241 p. incl. front., illus., plates. 21 cm. c.1938. Lothrop, Lee & Shepard Company.
Buck, Charles Neville
--The Roof Tree. N.D. Doubleday Page & Co.

--A Kiss Is Round: Verses. Bobri, V., pseud. (1898-), illus. Bobritsky, Vladimir V.. LC 54-7884. (Illus.). unpaged. 26cm. c.1954. Lothrop, Lee and Shepard Co. **Award: (NYT).**

Budney, Blossom & Mannheim, Grete Solomon (1909-)
--My Pony, Joker. Mannheim, Grete Solomon (1909-), illus. LC 61-8129. unpaged. illus. 23cm. 1961. Knopf.

Buehr, Walter Franklin (1897-1971)
--The Birth of a Liner. Buehr, Walter Franklin (1897-1971), illus. 1961. Little, Brown and Company.
--Bread, the Staff of Life. Buehr, Walter Franklin (1897-1971), illus. LC 59-5056. 80p. illus. 22cm. (Morrow Junior Books). 1959. Morrow.
--Cargoes in the Sky. Buehr, Walter Franklin (1897-1971), illus. LC 58-10203. (Illus.). 23cm. 64p. 1958. Putnam's Sons.
--Chivalry and the Mailed Knight. Buehr, Walter Franklin (1897-1971), illus. LC 63-7731. (Illus.). 93 p. 23cm. 1963. Putnam.
--Famous Small Boat Voyages. (Illus.). (gr. 4-6). 1966. (ISBN 0-399-60162-7). Putnam.
--Knights and Castles: And Feudal Life. LC 56-102675. 72p. illus. 23cm. 1957. Putnam.
--Railroads, today and yesterday. Buehr, Walter Franklin (1897-1971), illus. LC 57-12207. 72p. illus. 23cm. c.1957. Putnam.
--Sea Monsters. Buehr, Walter Franklin (1897-1971), illus. LC 66-10782. 91p. col. illus. 23cm. c.1966. Norton.
--Sending the Word: The Story of Communication. Buehr, Walter Franklin (1897-1971), illus. LC 59-114189. 95p. illus. 23cm. 1959. Putnam.
--The Story of the Wheel. LC 60-12520. 47p. illus. 21 x 26cm. c.1960. Putnam.
--Strange Craft. Buehr, Walter Franklin (1897-1971), illus. LC 62-19906. 96 p. illus. 23 cm. 1963. Norton.
--Trucks and Trucking. Buehr, Walter Franklin (1897-1971), illus. LC 56-102644. 72p. illus. 23cm. 1957, c.1956. Putnam.

Buell, Ellen Lewis, ed.
--Read Me a Poem: Children's Favorite Poetry. Magagna, Anna Marie, illus. LC 65-20043. 45p. illus. (pt. col.) 29cm. (gr. k-5). c.1965. Grosset.
--A Treasury of Golden Books. 1960. Golden Press.
--A Treasury of Little Golden Books: Forty-Eight of the Best-Loved Stories for the VeryYoung. LC 60-14883. 155p. illus. 31cm. 1960. Golden Press.
--A Treasury of Little Golden Books: Forty-Eight of the Best-LovedStories for the Very Young. LC 72-178994. (Illus.). 155 p. 31cm. 1972. Golden Press.
--A Treasury of Little Golden Books: Thirty Best-Loved Stories. rev. and abidged. LC 82-80361. (Illus.). 91 p. 31cm. (gr. 2). c.1982. (ISBN 0-307-96540-6). Golden Press.

Buell, Marjorie Henderson see Marge, pseud.
Buell, Robert Kingery, jt. auth. see Hallin, Emily Watson.

Buerger, Jane
--Obedience. Endres, Helen Elise, illus. LC 80-14590. (Illus.). 32p. (What Does the Bible Say? Ser.). (ps-2). 1980. (ISBN 0-89565-164-5). Childs World.

Buerger, Jane, ed. see Baker, Eugene H.
Buerger, Jane, ed. see Colina, Tessa Patterson.

Buettner, Carl
--Woody Woodpecker. Eisenberg, Harvey & McGray, Norm, illus. (Little Golden Bk.). 1959. Golden Press.

Buettner, Carl, adapted by see Disney, Walt, Productions.

Bufalari, Giuseppe (1927-)
--The Devil's Boat. Wayne, Gallup, illus. Paige, Douglass, tr. LC 78-113051. (Illus.). 146 p. 24cm. 1971. (ISBN 0-394-82289-7). (ISBN 0-394-92289-1). Knopf.
--The Yellow Boat. Neide, Peter, illus. Marci, Alfeo, tr. LC 68-22244. (Illus.). 88 p. 24cm. 1969. Knopf.

Bufano, Remo
--Magic Strings: Marionette Plays with Production Notes. LC 39-27236. xvi, 182 p. incl. plates. 21 cm. 1939. The Macmillan Company.
--The Show Book of Remo Bufano: Seven Plays for Marionettes & People, One for Every Day. LC 29-23352. xii, 182 p. illus. 22 cm. 1929. The Macmillan Company.

Buff, Conrad, jt. auth. see Buff, Mary Marsh, Mrs.

Buff, Mary Marsh, Mrs. (1890-1970)
--The Apple and the Arrow. Buff, Conrad (1886-1975), illus. LC 51-11816. (Illus.). 74 p. 28cm. 1951. Houghton Mifflin. **Award: (JNM).**
--Dancing Cloud: The Navajo Boy. Buff, Conrad (1886-1975), illus. LC 37-27286. 78, 2 p. illus. (part col.) 23 x 28 cm. 1937. The Viking Press.
--Dancing Cloud, the Navajo Boy. Rev. ed. Buff, Conrad (1886-1975), illus. LC 57-13706. 78p. illus. 28cm. 1957. Viking Press.
--Magic Maize. 1953. E M Hale.

Buff, Mary Marsh, Mrs. (1890-1970) & Buff, Conrad (1886-1975)
--Big Tree. LC 46-7347. 79, 1 illus. 28 cm. 1946. The Viking Press. **Award: (JNM).**
--Dash & Dart. Buff, Mary Marsh, Mrs. (1890-1970) & Buff, Conrad (1886-1975), illus. LC 42-363777. 73, 2 p. incl. col. illus., col. plates (part double) 26 cm. (gr. k-3). 1942. (ISBN 0-670-25729-X). The Viking Press. **Award: (RCM).**
--Elf Owl. LC 58-14628. 72p. illus. 27cm. 1958. Viking Press. **Award: (ALA).**
--Forest Folk. Buff, Conrad (1886-1975), illus. (Illus.). (gr. 1-5). 1962. (ISBN 0-670-32361-6). (ISBN 0-670-32362-4). Viking Pr.
--Hah-Nee. (gr. 4-6). 1965. (ISBN 0-395-15081-7). HM.
--Hah-Nee of the Cliff Dwellers. Buff, Mary Marsh, Mrs. (1890-1970) & Buff, Conrad (1886-1975), illus. LC 56-8268. 68p. illus. 28cm. 1956. Houghton, Mifflin. **Award: (ALA).**
--Hurry, Skurry & Flurry. Buff, Conrad (1886-1975), illus. (Illus.). (gr. k-3). 1954. (ISBN 0-670-38886-6). Viking Pr.
--Kemi: An Indian Boy Before the White Man Came. LC 66-16256. vi, 90p. illus. 26cm. c.1966. Golden Gate.
--Kemi: An Indian Boy Before the White Man Came. (Illus.). (gr. 4-6). 1966. (ISBN 0-378-62023-1). Ritchie.
--Kobi: A Boy of Switzerland. LC 39-32826. 128 p. incl. col. front., illus. (part col.) 26 cm. 1939. The Viking Press.
--Magic Maize. LC 53-6212. (Illus.). 76p. (gr. 4-6). 1953. (ISBN 0-395-06665-4). (ISBN 0-395-06666-2). HM.
--Peter's Pinto: A Story of Utah. LC 49-8143. 95 p. illus. 26 cm. 1949. Viking Press.
--Peter's Pinto: A Story of Utah,. LC 65-24168. 95p. illus. 27cm. 1965, c.1949. Ward Ritchie.
--Trix and Vix. LC 60-9088. 28cm. 21p. 1960. Houghton Mifflin.

Buffalo. Public School 52 see Lopata, Theresa.
Buffet, Guy, jt. auth. see Buffet, Pam.

Buffet, Guy & Buffet, Pam
--Adventures of Kama Pua'a. Tabrah, Ruth (1921-), ed. LC 72-76459. (Illus.). (gr. 1-7). 1972. (ISBN 0-89610-003-0). Island Her.
--Pua Pua Lena Lena. Buffet, Guy & Buffet, Pam, illus. LC 72-76458. (Illus.). 78p. 1st U.S. edition. (gr. 4). 1973. (ISBN 0-8348-3003-5). Weatherhill.
--Pua Pua Lena Lena & the Magic Kiha-Pu. Tabrah, Ruth, ed. LC 72-76458. (Illus.). (gr. 1-6). N.D. (ISBN 0-89610-010-3). Island Her.

Buffet, Pam, jt. auth. see Buffet, Guy.

Buffet, Pam & Buffet, Guy
--Kahala: Where the Rainbow Ends. Tabrah, Ruth, ed. LC 72-76459. (Illus.). (gr. 1-7). 1973. (ISBN 0-89610-006-5). Island Her.

Buffler, Esther
--The Friends. 1951. Simon and Schuster.
--The Friends. Forsyth, Constance, illus. LC 51-13704. 58 p. illus. 27 cm. N.D. Steck Co.
--Mary. Rice, Elizabeth (1913-), illus. LC 50-4415. 47 p. col. illus. 21 cm. 1949. Steck Co.
--Rodrigo and Rosalta. Rice, Elizabeth (1913-), illus. LC 49-8649. 64 p. col. illus. 24 cm. (gr. 1-4). 1949. (ISBN 0-8114-7556-5). Steck Co.

Bugbee, Emma (1888-1981)
--Peggy Covers London. LC 39-29728. xii, 300 p. 21 cm. (Career books). 1939. Dodd, Mead & Company.
--Peggy Covers the Clipper. 1941. Dodd, Mead & Co.
--Peggy Covers the News. LC 36-21686. x p., 2 l., 3-270 p. front. 21 cm. 1936. Dodd, Mead & Company.
--Peggy Covers Washington. LC 37-23532. 5 p. l., 3-297 p. front. 21 cm. 1937. Dodd, Mead & Company.
--Peggy Goes Overseas. LC 45-10645. xii, 276 p. 19 1/2 cm. 1945. Dodd, Mead & Company.

Bugbee, Willis Newton (1870-) see Hoxie, Evelyn.

Bugbee, Willis Newton (1870-)
--Aunt Lucindy Stays. N.D. March Brothers.
--Merry Entertainments. LC 25-374. 157 p. 19 cm. 1924. The Penn Publishing Company.

Buhler, Hope
--Sophie Danforth's School Life: or, Shod with Peace. 349p. N.D. E. P. Dutton.

Buie, Hallie, jt. auth. see Fairfax, Virginia.

Buitelaar, Wilma
--The Wishing Tree. (Illus.). 100p. 1969. Tri-Ocean Books.

Buj, Moira, illus.
--Mother Goose. (Illus.). 12p. 1977. (ISBN 0-85953-080-9, Pub. by Child's Play England). Playspaces.

Bulatkin, I. F., ed.
--Eurasian Folk and Fairy Tales. Simon, Howard (1903-1979), illus. LC 65-15265. (Illus.). 128 p. 21cm. 1965. Criterion.

Bulette, Sara
--The Elf in the Singing Tree. Dunnington, Tom, illus. LC 64-10270. (Illus.). 80 p. 21cm. (Follett beginning-to-read series). 1964. Follett Pub. Co.
--Roly Poly Cookie. Shortall, Leonard W., illus. (Illus.). (gr. 1-3). 1962. (ISBN 0-695-47779-X). Follett.
--Splendid Belt of Mr. Big. Myers, Lou, illus. (Illus.). (gr. 1-3). 1964. (ISBN 0-695-48230-0). Follett.

Bulfinch, Maria H.
--Frank Stirling's Choice. (The Old Corner Library Ser.). N.D. Set. E. P. Dutton & Co.
--Ruth and Aunt Alice: A Story for Children. N.D. E. P. Dutton & Co.

Bulfinch, Thomas (1796-1867)
--The Age of Chivalry. LC 1-16709. 1 p. l., viii, 329 p. front. 16 cm. 1901. T. Y. Crowell & Co.
--Age of Chivalry: Or, King Arthur and His Knights. a new, rev. and enl. ed. Scott, John Loughran (1846-), ed. LC 6180. xvi, 405 p. front., illus., plates. 21 cm. c.1900. D. McKay.
--The Age of Chivalry: Or, Legends of King Arthur. New & Enlarged. Hale, Edward Everett (1822-1909), ed. (Illus.). N.D. DeWolfe, Fiske & Co.
--The Age of Chivalry: Or, Legends of King Arthur. Hale, Edward Everett (1822-1909), ed. N.D. Lothrop, Lee & Shepard.
--Age of Fable. Empire ed. 1905. American News Co.
--Age of Fable. (Illus.). (Caldwell's Illustrated Library of Famous Books by Famous Authors). N.D. H. M. Caldwell Co.
--Age of Fable, 1 of 64 vols. (Young America Library: No. 3). 1900. Set. Hurst & Co.
--The Age of Fable. (Illus.). (Young People's Classics). N.D. R. F. Fenno & Co.
--The Age of Fable. Hale, Edward Everett, rev. by. (Illus.). N.D. DeWolfe, Fiske & Co.
--The Age of Fable. William, Stanley, illus. 384p. N.D. Heritage Press.
--The Age of Fable: Or, Beauties of Mythology. Hale, Edward Everett (1822-1909), ed. N.D. Lothrop, Lee & Shepard.
--The Age of Fable: Or, Beauties of Mythology. Klapp, William H., rev. by. Klapp, William H., notes by. 448p. N.D. Henry Altemus Co.
--Book of Myths: Selections from Bulfinch's Age of Fable. Sewell, Helen Moore (1896-1957), illus. (gr. 5-9). 1942. Macmillan.
--Bulfinch's Mythology: The Age of Fable. (Vol. 1). N.D. New American Library.
--Bulfinch's Mytholoy. Blaisdell, Elinore (1904-), illus. N.D. Crowell.
--The Golden Age of Myth and Legend. Godfrey, George H., ed. N.D. Frederick A. Stokes Co.
--Legends of Charlemagne. Wyeth, Newell Convers (1882-1945), illus. N.D. Cosmopolitan Book Co.
--Legends of Charlemagne: Or, Romance of the Middle Ages. N.D. Lothrop Lee & Shepard Co.
--Stories of the Gods and Heroes. Benson, Sally, Mrs. (1900-1972), ed. Savage, Steele (1900-), illus. LC 40-33522. (Stories Taken from the Age of Fables by Thomas Bulfinch). 256 p. incl. illus., plates. 24 cm. 1940. Dial Press.

Bulfinch, Thomas (1796-1867) & Lee, Edgar
--The Age of Fable. Hawley, Carl Tracey, illus. LC 5-39857. 97 p. front., illus. 22 x 17 cm. c.1905. The Saalfield Publishing Company.

Bull, Angela Mary (1936-)
--The Accidental Twins. Bennett, Jill (1947-), illus. (Illus.). 63p. (gr. 2-4). 1983. (ISBN 0-571-11761-9). Faber & Faber.
--The Friend with a Secret. Lynton, Lamb, illus. LC 66-31716. 256 p. 22cm. 1967, c.1965. Holt, Rinehart and Winston.
--Treasure in the Fog. Worth, Joanna, illus. LC 76-359657. (Illus.). 4, 88 p. 21cm. 1976. (ISBN 0-00-184819-4). Collins.
--Wayland's Keep. Hughes, Shirley (1929-), illus. 198 p. 22cm. 1967, c.1966. Holt, Rinehart and Winston.

Bull, Geoffrey Taylor (1921-)
--I Am a Donkey. (Tell-Tale Books Ser.). 1975. (ISBN 0-87508-875-9). Chr Lit.
--I Am a Fish. (Tell-Tale Books Ser.). 1975. (ISBN 0-87508-876-7). Chr Lit.
--I Am a Lamb. (Tell-Tale Books Ser.). 1975. (ISBN 0-87508-877-5). Chr Lit.
--I Am a Mouse. (Tell-Tale Books Ser.). 1975. (ISBN 0-87508-878-3). Chr Lit.
--I Am a Puppy. (Tell-Tale Books Ser.). 1975. (ISBN 0-87508-879-1). Chr Lit.
--I Am a Sparrow. (Tell-Tale Books Ser.). 1975. (ISBN 0-87508-880-5). Chr Lit.
--I Hid in a Basket. (Hide & Seek Bks). 1975. (ISBN 0-87508-881-3). Chr Lit.
--I Hid in a Boat. (Hide & Seek Books Ser.). 1975. (ISBN 0-87508-882-1). Chr Lit.
--I Hid in a Tree. (Hide & Seek Books Ser.). 1975. (ISBN 0-87508-886-4). Chr Lit.
--I Hid in the Hay. (Hide & Seek Books Ser.). 1975. (ISBN 0-87508-883-X). Chr Lit.
--I Hid in the Reeds. (Hide & Seek Books Ser.). 1975. (ISBN 0-87508-885-6). Chr Lit.
--I Wish I Lived When Daniel Did. (Far-Away Books Ser.). 1977. (ISBN 0-87508-892-9). Chr Lit.
--I Wish I Lived When David Did. (Far-Away Bks). 1975. (ISBN 0-87508-890-2). Chr Lit.
--I Wish I Lived When David Did. (Far-Away Books Ser.). 1977. (ISBN 0-87508-890-2). Chr Lit.
--I Wish I Lived When Esther Did. (Far-Away Books Ser.). 1977. (ISBN 0-87508-891-0). Chr Lit.
--I Wish I Lived When Gideon Did. (Far-Away Books Ser.). 1977. (ISBN 0-87508-889-9). Chr Lit.
--I Wish I Lived When Joseph Did. (Far-Away Books Ser.). 1977. (ISBN 0-87508-888-0). Chr Lit.
--I Wish I Lived When Noah Did. (Far-Away Bk. Ser.). (gr. 1-6). 1975. (ISBN 0-87508-887-2). Chr Lit.

Bull, Inez
--Cross Fork Tales. (Illus.). 1970. (ISBN 0-682-47009-0). Exposition Press.
--The Retarded Child. (Illus.). 1973. (ISBN 0-682-47652-8). Exposition Press.

Bull, Margaret
--Kristie and Bill at the Mysterious Mansion. LC 63-17751. 86 p. 21 cm. c.1964. Zondervan Pub. House.

Bull, Norman John (1916-), retold by.
--One Hundred Bible Stories. Biro, Val, pseud. (1921-), illus. Biro, Balint Stephen. (Illus.). 175p. (gr. 5 up). 1983. (ISBN 0-687-29071-6). Abingdon.
--Stories Jesus Told. Byfield, Graham, illus. LC 76-75402. (Illus.). ca. 100p. (gr. 3-7). 1969. (ISBN 0-8066-0924-9). Augsburg.

Bull, Randolph Cecil, ed.
--Great Tales of Mystery. Pagram, Edward, illus. LC 60-147844. (Illus.). 272 p. 22cm. 1960. Hill and Wang.

Bulla, Clyde Robert, tr. see Bolliger, Max.

Bulla, Clyde Robert (1914-)
--Almost a Hero. Stahl, Ben F., illus. LC 81-2060. p. cm. (Skinny book). c.1981. (ISBN 0-525-25470-6). (ISBN 0-525-25469-2). Dutton.
--The Beast of Lor. Sanderson, Ruth, illus. LC 77-6751. (Illus.). 54 p. 21cm. 1977. (ISBN 0-690-01377-9). Crowell.
--Benito. 1961. (ISBN 0-8382-0067-2, Cadmus Books). E. M. Hale and Company.
--Benito. Angelo, Valenti (1897-), illus. LC 61-7613. (Illus.). 84 p. 23cm. 1961. Crowell.
--The Cardboard Crown. Chessare, Michele (1921-), illus. LC 83-45049. (Illus.). 96p. (gr. 2-5). 1984. (ISBN 0-690-04360-0, TYC-J). (ISBN 0-690-04361-9). Har-Row.
--Charlie's House. 1st ed. Dorros, Arthur, illus. LC 82-45576. (Illus.). 81 p. 23cm. c.1983. (ISBN 0-690-04259-0). (ISBN 0-690-04260-4). Crowell.
--Dandelion Hill. Degen, Bruce, illus. LC 81-15164. (Illus.). 32 p. 26cm. c.1982. E.P. Dutton.
--Daniel's Duck. Sandin, Joan, illus. LC 78-22156. (Illus.). 5 7/8 x 8 1/2. 64p. (18 pt.). (I Can Read Bks.). (gr. k-3). 1979. (ISBN 0-06-020908-9). (ISBN 0-06-020909-7). Har-Row.
--Daniel's Duck. Sandin, Joan (1942-), illus. LC 77-25647. p. cm. (I can read book). c.1978. (ISBN 0-06-020908-9). (ISBN 0-06-020909-7). Harper & Row. **Award: (ALA).**
--Dexter. Coalson, Glo (1946-), illus. LC 73-5595. (Illus.). 68 p. 21cm. 1973. (ISBN 0-690-00121-5). (ISBN 0-690-00121-5). Crowell.
--A Dog Named Penny. Seredy, Kate (1899-1975), illus. (Ginn Book-Length Stories). 1955. Ginn & Co.
--The Donkey Cart. Lenski, Lois (1893-1974), illus. LC 46-6089. 3 p. l. 89 p. illus. 21 x 18 cm. 1946. Thomas Y. Crowell Company.
--Down the Mississippi. Burchard, Peter Duncan (1921-), illus. LC 54-5614. (Illus.). 113 p. 21cm. 1954. Crowell.
--Down the Mississippi. Burchard, Peter Duncan (1921-), illus. 1954. Harper.
--Eagle Feather. Two Arrows, Tom, illus. LC 52-13129. (Illus.). 87 p. 21cm. 1953. Crowell.
--Eagle Feathers. Two Arrows, Tom, illus. (Illus.). 21cm. 79p. 1962, c.1953. Schoalastic Book Service.
--The Ghost of Windy Hill. Bolognese, Donald Alan (1934-), illus. LC 68-11059. (Illus.). 84 p. 23cm. 1968. T. Y. Crowell Co.
--Ghost Town Treasure. 80p. (gr. 4-6). 1970. (ISBN 0-590-02064-1). Scholastic Inc.
--Ghost Town Treasure. Freeman, Don (1908-1978), illus. LC 58-5046. (Illus.). (gr. 2-5). 1958. (ISBN 0-690-32835-4, TYC-J). Har-Row.
--I Went for a Walk: A Read-and-Sing Book. Lenski, Lois (1893-1974), illus. (Illus.). 48 p. 16cm. 1958. H. Z. Walck.
--Indian Hill. Spanfeller, James John (1930-), illus. LC 63-15085. (Illus.). 74 p. 23cm. 1963. Crowell.

--John Billington: Friend of Squanto. Burchard, Peter Duncan (1921-), illus. LC 56-9797. 88p. 21cm. 1956. Crowell.
--Johnny Hong of Chinatown. Kingman, Dong Moy Shu (1911-), illus. LC 52-7859. (Illus.). 69 p. 21cm. 1952. Crowell.
--Jonah and the Great Fish. Aichinger, Helga (1937-), illus. LC 69-13636. (Illus.). 39 p. 27cm. 1970. Crowell.
--Joseph, the Dreamer. Laite, Gordon (1925-), illus. LC 75-94791. (Illus.). 64 p. 27cm. 1971. (ISBN 0-690-46554-8). Crowell.
--Keep Running, Allen!. Ichikawa, Satomi (1939-), illus. LC 77-23311. (Illus.). 32 p. c.1978. (ISBN 0-690-01374-4). (ISBN 0-690-01375-2). Crowell.
--Last Look. McCully, Emily Arnold (1939-), illus. LC 78-22507. (Illus.). 81 p. 24cm. c.1979. (ISBN 0-690-03965-4). (ISBN 0-690-03966-2). Crowell.
--Marco Moonlight. 1976. Harper.
--Marco Moonlight. Noonan, Julia (1946-), illus. LC 75-33203. 18cm. 104p. 1976. Crowell.
--Mika's Apple Tree: A Story of Finland. Asmussen, Des, illus. LC 68-21597. (Illus.). 40 p. 23cm. (Stories from many lands). 1968. Crowell.
--The Moon Singer. Hyman, Trina Schart (1939-), illus. LC 72-81947. (Illus.). 46 p. 21cm. 1969. Crowell.
--More Stories of Favorite Operas. Low, Joseph (1911-), illus. LC 65-18691. (Illus.). (gr. 4 up). 1965. (ISBN 0-690-55910-0, TYC-J). T Y Crowell.
--My Friend the Monster. Chessare, Michele (1921-), illus. LC 79-7826. p. cm. c.1980. (ISBN 0-690-04031-8). (ISBN 0-690-04032-6). Crowell.
--My Friend the Monster. Chessare, Michele (1921-), illus. 1980. Harper.
--New Boy in Dublin: A Story of Ireland. Polseno, Jo, illus. LC 77-78257. (Illus.). 41 p. 23cm. (Stories from many lands). 1969. Crowell.
--Old Charlie. Galdone, Paul (1914-), illus. (gr. k-3). 1972. (ISBN 0-590-01314-9, Schol Pap). Schol Bk Serv.
--Old Charlie. Galdone, Paul (1914-), illus. LC 57-6566. (Illus.). (gr. 2-5). 1957. (ISBN 0-690-59248-5, TYC-J). T Y Crowell.
--Open the Door and See All the People. Watson, Wendy McLeod (1942-), illus. LC 73-184980. (Illus.). 69 p. 22cm. 1972. (ISBN 0-690-60045-3). (ISBN 0-690-60045-3). Crowell.
--Pirate's Promise. N.D. E . M. Hale and Co.
--Pirate's Promise. Burchard, Peter Duncan (1921-), illus. (Illus.). 87 p. 23cm. 1958. Crowell.
--Pocahontas and the Strangers. Burchard, Peter Duncan (1921-), illus. LC 77-139094. (Illus.). 180 p. 22cm. 1971. (ISBN 0-690-62903-6). Crowell.
--Poor Boy, Rich Boy. Sewall, Marcia (1935-), illus. (Illus.). 5 7/8 x 8 1/2. (18 pt.). (I Can Read Bks.). (ps-3). 1982. (ISBN 0-06-020896-1). (ISBN 0-06-020897-X). Har-Row.
--Poor Boy, Rich Boy. Sewall, Marcia (1935-), illus. LC 79-2685. p. cm. (I can read book). c.1981. (ISBN 0-06-020896-1). (ISBN 0-06-020897-X). Harper & Row.
--The Poppy Seeds. Charlot, Jean (1898-1979), illus. LC 55-5835. (Illus.). 37 p. 24cm. 1955. Crowell.
--A Ranch for Danny. Paull, Grace A. (1898-), illus. LC 51-6441. (Illus.). 84 p. 21cm. 1951. Crowell.
--Riding the Pony Express. Paull, Grace A. (1898-), illus. LC 48-8051. 95 p. illus., maps. 21 cm. 1948. T. Y. Crowell Co.
--Ring & the Fire: Stories from Wagner's Nibelung Operas. Ross, Clare Romano (1922-) & Ross, John (1921-), illus. LC 62-7740. (Illus.). (gr. 5 up). 1962. (ISBN 0-690-70252-3). T Y Crowell.
--The Secret Valley. Paull, Grace a. (1898-), illus. LC 49-109171. (Illus.). 21cm. 100p. 1949. T. Y. Crowell Co.
--Shoeshine Girl. Grant, Alice Leigh (1947-), illus. LC 75-8516. (Illus.). 84 p. 24cm. 1975. (ISBN 0-690-00758-2). Crowell.
--Song of St. Francis. Angelo, Valenti (1897-), illus. LC 52-6739. 71 p. illus. 21 cm. 1952. Crowell.
--Songs of Mr. Small. Lenski, Lois (1893-1974), illus. (Illus.). 40 p. 28cm. 1954. H. Z. Walck.
--Squanto, Friend of the White Men. Burchard, Peter Duncan (1921-), illus. LC 54-9145. (Illus.). 106 p. 22cm. 1954. Crowell.
--St. Valentine's Day. (Illus.). (Holiday Books). 1965. (ISBN 0-690-71743-1). (ISBN 0-690-71744-X). Thomas Y Crowell.
--St. Valentine's Day. Valenti, Angelo, illus. 1965. Harper.
--Star of Wild Horse Canyon. Paull, Grace A. (1898-), illus. LC 53-8408. (Illus.). 86 p. 22cm. 1953. Crowell.
--Stories of Favorite Operas. Galster, Robert, illus. LC 59-11389. (Illus.). (gr. 5 up). 1959. (ISBN 0-690-77565-2). T Y Crowell.
--Stories of Gilbert & Sullivan Operas. McCrea, Ruth Pirman (1921-) & McCrea, James Craig, Jr. (1920-), illus. LC 68-24583. (Illus.). 192p. 1st U.S. edition. (gr. 4 up). 1968. (ISBN 0-690-77636-5, TYC-J). Har-Row.
--The Stubborn Old Woman. Rockwell, Anne F. (1934-), illus. LC 78-22506. (Illus.). 48p. (gr. 1-4). 1980. (ISBN 0-690-03945-X, TYC-J). (ISBN 0-690-03946-8). Har-Row.
--The Sugar Pear Tree. N.D. E. M. Hale & Co.
--The Sugar Pear Tree. Yashima, Taro, pseud. (1908-), illus. Iwamatsu, Jun Atsushi. LC 60-5055. (Illus.). 54 p. 24cm. 1961, c.1960. Crowell.
--Surprise for a Cowboy. Paull, Grace A. (1898-), illus. LC 50-8608. (Illus.). 82 p. 21cm. 1950. Crowell.
--The Sword in the Tree. (gr. 4-6). N.D. (ISBN 0-590-08594-8, Schol Trade Pap). Schol Bk Serv.
--Sword in the Tree. Galdone, Paul (1914-), illus. LC 56-5699. (Illus.). (gr. 2-5). 1956. (ISBN 0-690-79908-X, TYC-J). Har-Row.
--Three-Dollar Mule. 1960. E M Hale.
--Three-Dollar Mule. Lantz, Paul (1908-), illus. LC 60-11570. (Illus.). 86 p. 21cm. 1960. Crowell.
--The Valentine Cat. Weisgard, Leonard Joseph (1916-), illus. LC 58-12298. (Illus.). 62 p. 26cm. 1959. Crowell.
--Viking Adventure. Gorsline, Douglas Warner (1913-1985), illus. LC 63-9208. (Illus.). 117 p. 23cm. 1963. Crowell.
--What Makes a Shadow?. Adams, Adrienne (1906-), illus. LC 62-110018. unpaged. illus. 21x23cm. (Let s-read-and-find-out books). 1962. Crowell.
--When I Grow up: A Read-and-Sing Book. Lenski, Lois (1893-1974), illus. 48p. col. illus. 16x19cm. c.1960. H. Z. Walck.
--White Bird. Weisgard, Leonard Joseph (1916-), illus. LC 66-7285. (Illus.). 79 p. 23cm. 1966. Crowell.
--White Sails to China. Henneberger, Robert G. (1921-), illus. LC 55-9207. (Illus.). 84 p. 21cm. 1955. Crowell.
--The Wish at the Top. Conover, Chris (1950-), illus. LC 74-5028. (Illus.). 24 p. 24cm. 1974. (ISBN 0-690-00527-X). (ISBN 0-690-00528-8). Crowell.
Bulla, Clyde Robert (1914-) & Syson, Michael
--Conquista!. Himler, Ronald Norbert (1937-), illus. LC 77-26585. (Illus.). viii, 33 p. 24cm. c.1978. (ISBN 0-690-03871-2). Crowell.
Bullard, Ann S.
--Three Little Elves. (gr. 1-3). 1970. Vantage.
Bullard, Asa (1804-1888)
--The Scholar's Welcome, 1 of 12 vols. (Illus.). (Sunnybank Stories). 1882. Lee & Shepard.
Bullard, Asa (1804-1888), compiled by.
--Aunt Lizzie's Stories, 1 of 12 vols. (Illus.). (Sunnybank Stories). 1882. Lee & Shepard.
--Children's Book for Sabbath Hours. LC 15-12468. (Illus.). vi, 400 p. 23 x 18cm. 1873. W. J. Holland & Co.
--Dog Stories, 1 of 12 vols. (Illus.). (Sunnybank Stories). 1882. Lee & Shepard.
--Going to School. (Shady Dell Stories). N.D. Colby and Rich.
--Going to School, 1 of 12 vols. (Illus.). (Sunnybank Stories). 1882. Lee & Shepard.
--Going to School, 1 of 6 Vols. (Illus.). 64p. (Shady Dell Stories). N.D. Lee & Shepard.
--The Good Scholar. (Shady Dell Stories). N.D. Colby and Rich.
--The Good Scholar, 1 of 12 vols. (Illus.). (Sunnybank Stories). 1882. Lee & Shepard.
--The Good Scholar, 1 of 6 Vols. (Illus.). 64p. (Shady Dell Stories). N.D. Lee & Shepard.
--Grandpa's Stories, 1 of 12 vols. (Illus.). 64p. (Sunnybank Stories). 1882. Lee & Shepard.
--The Lighthouse. (Shady Dell Stories). N.D. Colby and Rich.
--The Lighthouse. (Illus.). (Sunnybank Stories). 1882. Lee & Shepard.
--The Lighthouse, 1 of 6 Vols. (Illus.). 4p. (Shady Dell Stories). N.D. Lee & Shepard.
--Mother's Stories, 1 of 12 vols. (Illus.). 64p. (Sunnybank Stories). 1882. Lee & Shepard.
--My Teacher's Gem. (Shady Dell Stories). N.D. Colby and Rich.
--My Teacher's Gem, 1 of 12 vols. (Illus.). (Sunnybank Stories). 1882. Lee & Shepard.
--My Teacher's Gem, 1 of 6 Vols,. (Illus.). 64p. (Shady Dell Stories Ser.). N.D. Lee & Shepard.
--Reward of Merit. (Shady Dell Stories). N.D. Colby and Rich.
--Reward of Merit, 1 of 12 vols. (Illus.). (Sunnybank Stories). 1882. Lee & Shepard.
--Reward of Merit, 1 of 6 Vols. (Illus.). 64p. (Shady Dell Stories). N.D. Lee & Shepard.
--The Scholar's Welcome. (Shady Dell Stories). N.D. Colby and Rich.
--The Scholar's Welcome, 1 of 6 Vols. (Illus.). 64p. (Shady Dell Stories Ser.). N.D. Lee & Shepard.
--Stories for Alice, 1 of 12 vols. (Illus.). 64p. (Sunnybank Stories). 1882. Lee & Shepard.
--Sunnybank Stories. LC 66-57546. (Illus.). 12cm. 1863. Lee & Shepard.
--Sunnybank Stories, 12 vols. (Illus.). 1882. Set. Lee & Shepard.
--Uncle Henry's Stories, 1 of 12 vols. (Illus.). 64p. (Sunnybank Stories Ser.). 1882. Lee & Shepard.
Bullard, Harvelene
--The Curious Princess & Harry, the Sad Easter Bunny. 1978. (ISBN 0-533-01720-3). Vantage.
Bullard, Lauriston F.
--Tad and His Father. 102p. N.D. Little, Brown.
Bullard, Marion Rorty, Mrs.
--Co-Pilot Trott. Hale, Bruce, illus. LC 44-6673. 133 p. illus. 21 cm. 1944. E. P. Dutton & Co., Inc.
--The Cow Next Door. LC 29-19581. 74 p. incl. col. front., illus. (part col.) plates. 21 cm. c.1929. E. P. Dutton & Company, Inc.
--The Enchanted Button. LC 30-186479. 124, 1 p. incl. front., illus., plates. 22 cm. c.1930. E. P. Dutton & Co., Inc.
--The Hog Goes Downstream. Bullard, Marion Rorty, Mrs., illus. LC 36-202507. 5 p. l., 3-95, 1 p. incl. front., illus., plates. 14 x 20 cm. c.1936. Harcourt, Brace and Company.
--James MacGregor from America. Hale, Bruce, illus. N.D. E. P. Dutton & Co.
--Mr. M'Tavish. LC 33-19078. 110 p. incl. front., illus., pl. 20 cm. c.1933. E. P. Dutton & Co., Inc.
--Robbers in the Garden: A Mystery Story for Children. Bullard, Marion Rorty, Mrs., illus. LC 31-22579. 100 p. incl. col. front., illus., col. plates. 21 cm. c.1931. E. P. Dutton & Company, Inc.
--The Sad Garden Toad and Other Stories. ix, 1, 51 p. col. front., illus. (part col.) 19 x 26 cm. c.1924. E. P. Dutton & Company.
--The Somersaulting Rabbit. N.D. E P Dutton.
--Travels of Sammie the Turtle. LC 28-25505. 76 p. incl. illus., plates. front. 22 cm. c.1928. E. P. Dutton & Company.
Bullaty, Sonja & Lomeo, Angelo
--Black Bear Cub. (Illus.). 24p. (Golden Look-Look Bk.). (gr. 4-8). 1983. (ISBN 0-307-11884-3, Pub. by Golden Pr). Western Pub.
Bullaty, Sonja & Lomeo, Angelo, illus.
--The Little Fawn. (Illus.). 24p. (Golden Look-Look Bks.). (ps-3). 1985. (ISBN 0-307-11894-0, Pub. by Golden Bks). Western Pub.
--The Little Wild Ducklings. (Illus.). 24p. (Golden Look-Look Bks.). (ps-3). 1985. (ISBN 0-307-11899-1, Pub. by Golden Bks). Western Pub.
Bullen, Adelaide K
--Jim Tall and Count Small. Johnson, Gene (1902-), illus. LC 74-29741. (Illus.). 42 p. 27cm. 1975. Kendall Books.
Bullen, Frank Thomas (1857-1915)
--The Cruise of the Cachalot. (Famous Bks. for Young Americans). N.D. A. L. Burt Co.
The Cruise of the Cachalot. (Great Illustrated Classics). N.D. Dodd, Mead & Co.
--The Cruise of the Cachalot. LC 25-23745. 20cm. 379p. (Every Boy's Library). N.D. Grosset & Dunlap.
--The Cruise of the Cachalot. (The Fairmount Classics). N.D. Macrae Smith.
--The Cruise of the Cachalot. Blaine, Mahlon, illus. (The Father & Son Library). N.D. Sears Publishing Co.
--Frank Brown, Sea Apprentice. N.D. E P Dutton.
--Frank Brown: Sea Apprentice. Reid, Stephen (1873-1934), illus. LC 26-27427. 5 p. l., 315 p. col. front., col. plates. 20 cm. (golden books). 1926. D. McKay.
--The Cruise of the Cachalot. Schweikert, H. G., ed. N.D. D. Appleton-Century Co., Inc.
Buller, Jon
--Fanny & May. LC 83-15361. 48p. (ps-2). 1984. (ISBN 0-517-55214-0). Crown.
Bullett, Gerald William (1894-)
--The Happy Mariners. Hodges, Cyril Walter (1909-), illus. LC 39-8243. viii, 247, 1 p. incl. front. illus., plates. 20 cm. 1936. Dodge Publishing Company.
Bullingham, Ann
--Penelope and Curlew. 1958. St Martin's Press.
Bullis, Franklin Howard, jt. auth. see Pearson, Molly Winston, Mrs.
Bullitt, John M., ed. see Johnson, Samuel.
Bullivant, Garland
--Fortune's Foal. Bullen, Anne, illus. N.D. Charles Scribner's Sons.
--Fortune's Foal. Bullen, Anne, illus. LC 39-156088. ix, 1, 107 p. front, illus., plates. 22 cm. 1939. Country Life, Ltd.
Bullock, Michael, tr. see Wicki, Peter & Schroeder, Binette.
Bullock-Willis, Virginia
--Jangling Jingles of Fairies. N.D. Pageant Press INC.
--Jingling of Fairies and Flowers: Children's Poems. 1st ed. 5p. 1., 69p. illus. 24cm. c.1957. Pageant Press.
Bulwer-Lytton, Baron see Lytton, Edward George Earle Lytton Bulwer-Lytton.
Bulychev, Kirill Vsevolodovich
--Alice. Galanin, Igor, illus. Ginsburg, Mirra, tr. Ginsburg, Mirra, adapted by. LC 76-47539. (Illus.). (gr. 3-6). 1977. (ISBN 0-02-736520-4). Macmillan.
--Alice: Some Incidents in the Life of a Little Girl of the Twenty-First Century, Recorded by Her Father on the Eve of Her First Day in School. Galanin, Igor, illus. Ginsburg, Mirra, tr. from Russian. LC 76-47539. (Illus.). 64 p. 24cm. c.1977. (ISBN 0-02-736520-4). Macmillan.
Bumford, Mary E.
--Thoughts on My Dumb Neighbors. N.D. Methodist Bk Concern.
Bumgartner, Alexander (1841-1910) & B.A.V
--Three Indian Tales. Long, Helena, tr. from Ger. LC 22-4753. 124 p. 17 1/2 cm. (Added t.-p.: Tales of foreign lands...vol. VI). 1897. B. Herder.
Bump, Margaret
--The Big, Big Egg. Bump, Margaret, illus. (Illus.). (Nature & Science Bk.). (gr. k-6). N.D. Denison.
Bumpass, F. L., ed. see Hawthorne, Nathaniel (1804-1864) & Harte, Bret.
Bumpass, F. L., ed. see Henry, O.
Bumpass, F. L., ed. see Irving, Washington.
Bumpass, F. L., ed. see Twain, Mark, pseud. (1835-1910) & Henry, O.
Bunbury, Selina
--Fanny the Flower Girl, 1 of 103 vols. (The Pearl Library: No. 23). 1900. Set. Hurst & Co.
--Fanny, the Flower Girl. N.D. Robert Carter & Brothers.
Bunce, Arthur
--The Boy Who Wanted to Fly: And Other Talks to Boys and Girls. Ross, M. T. Penny, illus. LC 28-4540. 5 p. l., 3-200 p. illus. 20 cm. c.1928. Harr Wagner Publishing Company.
Bunce, William Harvey (1903-)
--Chula: Son of the Mound Builders. Hazleton, Isaac Brewster, illus. LC 42-14050. 215 p. incl. plates. 21 cm. 1942. E. P. Dutton and Company, Inc.
--Dragon Prows Westward. Bjorklund, Lorence F. (1913-1978), illus. LC 46-6297. x, 199 p. incl. front., illus., plates. 21 cm. 1946. Harcourt Brace and Company.
--Here Comes the School Train. Bunce, William Harvey (1903-), illus. N.D. E. P. Dutton & Co.
--Horned Snake Medicine, a Story of the Mound Builders. McDonald, James, illus. LC 45-7244. 160 p. illus. 20 cm. 1945. E. P. Dutton & Company, Inc.
--Son of the Iroquois. Quinn, Paul, illus. LC 36-32648. 127, 1 p. incl. front., illus. 22 cm. 1936. MacRae Smith Co.
--Treasure Was Their Quest. Glanzman, Louis S. (1922-), illus. LC 47-11026. ix, 230 p. illus. 21 cm. 1947. Harcourt, Brace.
--War Belts of Pontiac. Hazleton, Isaac Brewster, illus. LC 42-51965. 214 p. incl. plates. 21 cm. 1943. E. P. Dutton and Company.
Bund, Ludwig
--Puck's Nightly Pranks. Brooks, T. C., tr. N.D. Robert Brothers.
Bunin, Catherine (1967-) & Bunin, Sherry (1925-)
--Is That Your Sister?. A True Story of Adoption. Bunin, Catherine (1967-), illus. 1976. NACAC.
Bunin, Ivan Alexeyvich (1870-1953)
--Velga. Reader, Sarah, illus. Daniels, Guy (1919-), tr. from Rus. LC 74-120786. (Illus.). 32p. 1st U.S. edition. (gr. 7 up). 1970. (ISBN 0-87599-177-7). S G Phillips.
Bunin, Sherry, jt. auth. see Bunin, Catherine.
Bunker, Dorothy T Schmidt
--The Boy Jesus. Rev. ed. Hanley, Francis J., illus. LC 51-89. 134 p. illus. 26 cm. 1950. Ave Maria Press.
Bunn, Harriet F
--Circus Boy. Richards, George Mather (1880-), illus. LC 36-7115. 6 p. l., 194 p. illus. 21 cm. 1936. The Macmillan Company.
--Trailer Tracks. Dobias, Frank (1902-), illus. LC 37-382441. vii p., 1 l., 241 p., 1 l. illus. 21 cm. 1937. The Macmillan Company.
Bunn, Iola Finch
--Growing up in Alaska: A Story for Children About Today's Eskimos. Salzman, Frederic, illus. LC 65-3470. (Illus.). 126 p. 21cm. 1965. Exposition Press.
--Woolly the Unclaimed Lamb. (Illus.). (gr. 1-4). 1964. (ISBN 0-682-42018-2). Exposition.
Bunn, Scott
--Just Hold on. LC 82-70316. 151 p. 22cm. c.1982. (ISBN 0-440-04257-7). Delacorte Press.
Bunnell, Clarence Orvel
--Legends of the Klickitats. 82p. 1933. Binfords & Mort.
Bunner, H. C.
--Seven Old Ladies. N.D. Harper & Brothers.

Bunnett, Fanny Elizabeth, tr. see Auerbach, Berthold.

Bunny, pseud., see Schultze, Carl Emil.

Bunny, pseud.

--Aloysius Alligator. Schultze, Carle E. Wheelan, Ed (1888-), illus. LC 66-13160. (Illus.). (gr. k-2). 1974. (ISBN 0-87208-008-0). Island Pr.

--Bunny. Schultze, Carl E. N.D. Frederick A. Stokes Co.

--Foxy Grandpa Up-To-Date. Schultze, Carl E. (Illus.). N.D. Frederick A. Stokes Co.

--Foxy Grandpa's Mother Goose. Schultze, Carl E. (Illus.). N.D. Frederick A. Stokes Co.

--Foxy Grandpa's Surprises. Schultze, Carl F.. (Illus.). N.D. Frederick A. Stokes Co.

--The New Adventures of Foxy Grandpa. Schultze, Carl E. (Illus.). N.D. Frederick A. Stokes Co.

--Tigger. Story of a Mayan Ocalot. Schultze, Carl F.. Bunny, pseud., photos by. Schultze, Carl E. LC 66-127469. 1v. (unpaged) illus. 28cm. c.1966. Island Pr Bahia Ave.

Buntain, Ruth Jaeger

--The Birthday Story. Wilkin, Eloise Burns (1904-), illus. LC 53-12627. (Illus.). unpaged. 20cm. (A "Beginning to read" book). 1953. Holiday House.

--Whose Tail Is It?. A Tale About Tails. Larkin, Howard C., illus. LC 59-15765. unpaged. illus. 22x28cm. c.1959. Pacific Press Pub. Association.

Bunting, Anne Evelyn see Bolton, Evelyn, pseud.

Bunting, Anne Evelyn see Bunting, Eve, pseud.

Bunting, Anne Evelyn (1928-)

--Barney the Beard. Gobbato, Imero (1923-), illus. LC 73-23111. (Illus.). 41 p. 24cm. 1975. (ISBN 0-8193-0728-9). (ISBN 0-8193-0729-7). Parents' Magazine Press.

--The Big Cheese. Murdocca, Salvatore, illus. LC 76-45381. 23cm. 44p. 1977. (ISBN 0-02-715370-3). Macmillan.

--The Big Find. Hutchings, Richard, illus. LC 78-12636. (Illus.). 56 p. 24cm. c.1978. (ISBN 0-87191-681-9). Creative Education.

--Blackbird Singing. Gammell, Stephen, illus. LC 79-23294. (Illus.). 92 p. 32cm. c.1980. (ISBN 0-02-715360-6). Macmillan.

--Box, Fox, Ox, and the Peacock. Morrill, Leslie H., illus. LC 73-76834. (Illus.). 24 p. 20cm. (Magic circle book). 1974. (ISBN 0-663-25470-1). Ginn.

--The Cloverdale Switch. LC 79-2404. 119 p. 21cm. c.1979. (ISBN 0-397-31866-9). (ISBN 0-397-31867-7). J. B. Lippincott Co.

--The Creature of Cranberry Cove. Earle, Scott W, illus. LC 76-18124. p. cm. (No such things ...?). 1976. (ISBN 0-88436-300-7). (ISBN 0-88436-301-5). EMC Corp.

--The Day of the Dinosaur. Leo, Judith, illus. LC 75-19023. (Illus.). 40p. (The Dinosaur Machine Ser.). (gr. 7 up). 1975. (ISBN 0-88436-193-4). (ISBN 0-88436-194-2). EMC.

--Day of the Earthlings. Hendricks, Donald (1932-), illus. LC 77-21713. (Illus.). 25 p. 23cm. (Creative science fiction). c.1978. (ISBN 0-87191-621-5). Creative Education.

--Death of a Dinosaur. Leo, Judith, illus. LC 75-17926. p. cm. (Dinosaur machines). 1975. (ISBN 0-88436-199-3). (ISBN 0-88436-200-0). EMC Corp.

--Demetrius and the Golden Goblet. Hague, Michael R., illus. LC 79-14865. (Illus.). 41 p. 26cm. c.1980. (ISBN 0-15-223186-2). (ISBN 0-15-625282-1). Harcourt Brace Jovanovich.

--The Demon. Earle, Scott W., illus. LC 76-18125. p. cm. (No such things ...?). 1976. (ISBN 0-88436-273-6). (ISBN 0-88436-274-4). EMC Corp.

--The Dinosaur Trap. Leo, Judith, illus. LC 75-17909. p. cm. (Dinosaur machines). 1975. (ISBN 0-88436-197-7). (ISBN 0-88436-198-5). EMC Corp.

--The Empty Window. Clifford, Judy, illus. LC 80-13048. p. cm. 1980. (ISBN 0-7232-6186-5). F. Warne.

--Escape from Tyrannosaurus. Leo, Judith, illus. LC 75-19024. 35 p. 21 cm. (Dinosaur machines). 1975. (ISBN 0-88436-195-0). (ISBN 0-88436-196-9). EMC Corp.

--Fifteen. Gadbois, Robert, illus. LC 77-10835. (Illus.). 30 p. 23cm. (Creative Education young romance books). c.1978. (ISBN 0-87191-632-0). Creative Education.

--The Followers. Hendricks, Donald (1932-), illus. LC 78-4921. (Illus.). 35 p. 23cm. (Creative science fiction). c.1978. (ISBN 0-87191-627-4). Creative Education.

--For Always. Gadbois, Robert, illus. LC 77-13085. (Illus.). 31 p. 23cm. (Creative Education young romance books). c.1978. (ISBN 0-87191-636-3). Creative Education.

--The Ghost. Earle, Scott W., illus. LC 76-18131. p. cm. (No such things ...?). 1976. (ISBN 0-88436-271-X). (ISBN 0-88436-272-8). EMC Corp.

--Ghost of Summer. Mars, Witold Tadeusz J. (1912-), illus. LC 76-45310. (gr. 5 up). 1977. (ISBN 0-7232-6141-5). Warne.

--Ghosts of Departure Point. LC 81-48602. p. cm. c.1982. (ISBN 0-397-31997-5). (ISBN 0-397-31998-3). Lippincott.

--A Gift for Lonny. Quackenbush, Robert Mead (1929-), illus. LC 72-80123. (Illus.). 47 p. 23cm. (Magic circle book). c.1973. (ISBN 0-663-25492-2). Ginn.

--The Girl in the Painting. Gadbois, Robert, ed. LC 77-25250. 31 p. 23 cm. 1978. (ISBN 0-87191-639-8). Creative Education.

--The Happy Funeral. Vo-Dinh, Mai (1933-), illus. LC 81-47719. (Illus.). 38 p. 23cm. c.1982. (ISBN 0-06-020893-7). (ISBN 0-06-020894-5). Harper & Row.

--The Haunting of Kildoran Abbey. LC 77-84601. 159 p. 22cm. c.1978. (ISBN 0-7232-6152-0). F. Warne.

--High Tide for Labrador. Garbutt, Bernard (1900-), illus. LC 74-23080. (Illus.). 77 p. 24cm. 1975. (ISBN 0-516-08819-X). Childrens Press.

--Iceberg!. Orig. Title: High Tides for the Labrador. (gr. 5-6). N.D. (ISBN 0-590-30880-7, Schol Pap). Scholastic Inc.

--In Dinosaur Land. Leo, Judith, illus. LC 75-19023. p. cm. (Dinosaur machines). 1975. (ISBN 0-88436-193-4). (ISBN 0-88436-194-2). EMC Corp.

--The Island of One. Hendricks, Donald (1932-), illus. LC 78-5143. (Illus.). 35 p. 23cm. c.1978. (ISBN 0-87191-626-6). Creative Education.

--Josefina Finds the Prince. Palmer, Janice, illus. LC 76-16063. (Illus.). 64 p. 23cm. (For real book). c.1976. (ISBN 0-8116-4300-X). Garrard Pub. Co.

--Just Like Everyone Else. Gadbois, Robert, illus. LC 77-21691. (Illus.). 31 p. 23cm. (Creative Education young romance books). c.1978. (ISBN 0-87191-630-4). Creative Education.

--Karen Kepplewhite is the World's Best Kisser. LC 83-2066. c.1983. (ISBN 0-89919-182-7). Clarion Books.

--Karen Kepplewhite is the World's Best Kisser. 1983. Houghton.

--Maggie the Freak. Gadbois, Robert, illus. LC 77-10682. (Illus.). 30 p. 23cm. c.1978. (ISBN 0-87191-633-9). Creative Education.

--Magic and the Night River. Say, Allen (1937-), illus. LC 77-3813. (Illus.). 44 p. 22cm. c.1978. (ISBN 0-06-020912-7). (ISBN 0-06-020913-5). Harper & Row.

--The Mask. Hendricks, Donald (1932-), illus. LC 78-5107. (Illus.). 35 p. 23cm. (Creative science fiction). c.1978. (ISBN 0-87191-625-8). Creative Education.

--The Mirror Planet. Hendricks, Donald (1932-), illus. LC 78-4541. (Illus.). 35 p. 23cm. (Creative science fiction). c.1978. (ISBN 0-87191-628-2). Creative Education.

--Nobody Knows but Me. Gadbois, Robert, illus. LC 77-21428. (Illus.). 30 p. 23cm. (Creative Education young romance books). c.1978. (ISBN 0-87191-635-5). Creative Education.

--Oh, Rick. Gadbois, Robert, illus. LC 77-10599. (Illus.). 31 p. 23cm. (Creative Education young romance books). c.1978. (ISBN 0-87191-634-7). Creative Education.

--The Once-a-Year Day. Mars, Witold Tadeusz J. (1912-), illus. LC 73-17246. (Illus.). 44 p. 22cm. 1974. (ISBN 0-516-08839-4). Childrens Press.

--One More Flight. De Groat, Diane (1947-), illus. LC 75-32637. (Illus.). 91 p. 23cm. 1976. (ISBN 0-7232-6129-6). Frederick Warne.

--A Part of the Dream. Gadbois, Robert, illus. LC 77-13022. (Illus.). 32 p. 23cm. (Creative Education young romance books). c.1978. (ISBN 0-87191-638-X). Creative Education.

--Pitcher to Center Field. Freas, Len, illus. LC 73-12034. (Illus.). 64 p. 25cm. 1974. (ISBN 0-516-07625-6). Childrens Press.

--The Robot Birthday. De John, Marie, illus. LC 79-19185. (Illus.). 80 p. 25cm. (Smart Cat Book.). c.1980. (ISBN 0-525-38542-8). Dutton.

--The Robot People. Hendricks, Donald (1932-), illus. LC 77-21714. (Illus.). 25 p. 23cm. (Creative science fiction). c.1978. (ISBN 0-87191-622-3). Creative Education.

--Say It Fast. Kelley, True Adelaide (1946-), illus. LC 73-82002. (Illus.). 16 p. 20cm. (Magic circle book). 1974. (ISBN 0-663-25467-1). Ginn.

--The Skate Patrol. Madden, Donald B. (1927-), illus. LC 80-18640. p. cm. (First Read-Alone Mystery). 1980. (ISBN 0-8075-7393-0). A. Whitman.

--The Skate Patrol Rides Again. Madden, Donald B. (1927-), illus. 1982. Whitman.

--Skateboard Four. Kantz, Phil, illus. LC 76-16115. (Illus.). 63 p. 21cm. (Springboard book). 1976. (ISBN 0-8075-7392-2). A. Whitman.

--Someone Is Hiding on Alcatraz Island. LC 84-5019. 144p. (gr. 5-8). 1984. (ISBN 0-89919-219-X, Clarion). HM.

--The Space People. Hendricks, Donald (1932-), illus. LC 77-22086. (Illus.). 27 p. 23cm. c.1978. (ISBN 0-87191-623-1). Creative Education.

--The Spook Birds. Sims, Blanche, illus. LC 81-686. (Illus.). 38 p. 22cm. c.1981. (ISBN 0-8075-7587-9). A. Whitman.

--Springboard to Summer. Sprattler, Rob, illus. LC 75-6615. (Illus.). 63 p. 25cm. 1975. (ISBN 0-516-07461-X). Childrens Press.

--St. Patrick's Day in the Morning. Brett, Jan (1949-), illus. LC 79-15934. (Illus.). 32p. (ps-3). 1980. (ISBN 0-395-29098-8, Clarion). HM.

--St. Patrick's Day in the Morning. Brett, Jan (1949-), illus. (Illus.). 32p. (gr. 3). 1983. (ISBN 0-89919-162-2, Clarion). HM.

--Surfing Country. King, Dale, illus. LC 74-552. (Illus.). 60 p. 24cm. 1974. (ISBN 0-516-07457-1). Childrens Press.

--Surrogate Sister. LC 83-49483. 192p. (gr. 7 up). 1984. (ISBN 0-397-32098-1). (ISBN 0-397-32099-X). Lippincott Junior Bks.

--Survival Camp!. Gadbois, Robert, illus. LC 77-10681. (Illus.). 31 p. 23cm. (Creative Education young romance books). 1978. (ISBN 0-87191-631-2). Creative Educaton.

--Terrible Things. Gammell, Stephen, illus. LC 79-2692. (Illus.). 26 p. c.1980. (ISBN 0-06-020903-8). (ISBN 0-06-020904-6). Harper & Row.

--The Tongue of the Ocean. Earle, Scott W, illus. LC 76-17624. p. cm. (No such things ...?). 1976. (ISBN 0-88436-302-3). (ISBN 0-88436-303-1). EMC Corp.

--The Traveling Men of Ballycoo. Zemach, Kaethe (1958-), illus. LC 82-15799. p. cm. 1983. (ISBN 0-15-289792-5). Harcourt Brace Jovanovich.

--Two Different Girls. Gadbois, Robert, illus. LC 77-13108. (Illus.). 31 p. 23cm. (Creative Education young romance books). c.1978. (ISBN 0-87191-637-1). Creative Education.

--The Two Giants. Von Schmidt, Eric (1931-), illus. LC 77-153913. (Illus.). 22 p. (Magic circle book). 1971, c.1972. (ISBN 0-663-22989-8). Ginn.

--The Undersea People. Hendricks, Donald (1932-), illus. LC 77-21952. (Illus.). 26 p. 23cm. c.1978. (ISBN 0-87191-624-X). Creative Education.

--The Valentine Bears. Brett, Jan (1949-), illus. LC 82-9577. p. cm. 1983 (Clarion Books). (ISBN 0-89919-138-X). HM.

--The Waiting Game. LC 80-8793. 56 p. 22cm. c.1981. (ISBN 0-397-31942-8). (ISBN 0-397-31941-X). Lippincott.

--We Need a Bigger Zoo!. Barner, Bob (1947-), illus. LC 73-81999. 24 p. (chiefly col. illus. (Magic circle book). 1974. (ISBN 0-663-25446-9). Ginn.

--The Wild Horses. Keely, John, illus. LC 74-9530. (Illus.). 31 p. 23cm. (Her Creative Education horse stories). 1974. (ISBN 0-87191-374-7). Creative Education; Distributed by Childrens Press, Chicago.

--Winter's Coming. Knotts, Howard Clayton, Jr. (1922-), illus. LC 76-28321. (Illus.). (Let Me Read Ser.). (gr. 1-3). 1977. (ISBN 0-15-298037-7, VoyB). HarBraceJ.

--Yesterday's Island. Gammell, Stephen, illus. LC 79-13201. (Illus.). 74 p. 21cm. c.1979. (ISBN 0-7232-6166-0). Frederick Warne.

Bunting, Anne Evelyn (1928-) & Knotts, Howard Clayton, Jr. (1922-)

--The Big Red Barn. LC 78-12186. (Illus.). 31 p. 22cm. (Let me read book). c.1979. (ISBN 0-15-207145-8). (ISBN 0-15-611938-2). Harcourt Brace Jovanovich.

--Goose Dinner. LC 80-39747. (Illus.). 32 p. 22cm. (Let me read book). c.1981. (ISBN 0-15-232225-6). Harcourt, Brace, Jovanovich.

Bunting, Elizabeth O

--When Granny Was a Little Girl. LC 70-188539. (Illus.). 32 p. 19cm. 1972. Review and Herald Pub. Association.

Bunting, Eve, pseud., see Bunting, Anne Evelyn.

Bunting, Eve, pseud. (1928-)

--Clancy's Coat. Bunting, Anne Evelyn. Cauley, Lorinda Bryan (1951-), illus. LC 83-6575. (Illus.). 1984, c.1983. (ISBN 0-7232-6252-7). (ISBN 0-7232-6252-7). F. Warne.

--Face at the Edge of the World. Bunting, Anne Evelyn. LC 85-2684. 158 p. 22cm. c.1985. Clarion Books.

--The Haunting of SafeKeep. Bunting, Anne Evelyn. LC 84-48354. 153 p. 21cm. c.1985. (ISBN 0-397-32112-0). (ISBN 0-397-32113-9). Lippincott.

--If I Asked You, Would You Stay. Bunting, Anne Evelyn. LC 82-49052. p.cm. c.1984. (ISBN 0-397-32065-5). Lippincott.

--Jane Martin, Dog Detective. Bunting, Anne Evelyn. Schwartz, Amy (1954-), illus. LC 84-4497. (Illus.). 48p. (ps-3). 1984. (ISBN 0-15-239586-5, HJ). (ISBN 0-15-239586-5). HarBraceJ.

--The Man Who Could Call Down Owls. Bunting, Anne Evelyn. Mikolaycak, Charles (1937-), illus. LC 83-17568. (Illus.). 32p. (gr. k-3). 1984. (ISBN 0-02-715380-0). Macmillan.

--Monkey in the Middle. Bunting, Anne Evelyn. Munsinger, Lynn (1951-), illus. LC 83-18339. (Illus.). 32p. (ps-2). 1984. (ISBN 0-15-255316-9, HJ). (ISBN 0-15-255316-9). HarBraceJ.

--The Skate Patrol and the Mystery Writer. Bunting, Anne Evelyn. Madden, Donald B. (1927-), illus. LC 82-10843. p. cm. 1982. (ISBN 0-8075-7394-9). A. Whitman.

Buntline, Ned see Judson, Edward Zane Carroll.

Bunyan, John see Watson, Jean.

Bunyan, John (1628-1688)

--A Book for Boys and Girls: Or, Country Rhymes for Children. Buchanan, Edgar Simmons (1872-), ed. LC 29-4012. (Illus.). 21cm. 124p. 1928. American Tract Society.

--A Book for Boys & Girls: Or Country Rhymes for Children. Lurie, Alison (1926-) & Sciller, Justin G. (1943-), eds. Incl. Divine Songs. Watts, Isaac (1628-1688; Moral Songs Composed for the Use of Children. Foxton, Thomas (1628-1688. LC 75-32136. (Classics of Children's Literature Ser., 1621-1932). 1978. (ISBN 0-8240-2253-X). Garland Pub.

--Bunyan's Pilgrim's Progress. N.D. American Sunday-School Union.

--Bunyan's Pilgrims Progress. (Altemus' New Illustrated Young People's Library). N.D. Henry Altemus Company.

--Bunyan's Pilgrim's Progress, 1 of 4 vols. (Illus.). (Every Boy's Library). N.D. Set. Thomas Nelson & Sons.

--The Christian Pilgrim: Containing an Account of the Wonderful Adventures and Miraculous Escapes of a Christian, in His Travels from the Land of Destruction to the New Jerusalem. LC 21-2669. 2 v. in i. front., illus. 11 cm. N.D. Printed by Isaiah Thomas, Jun. Sold Wholesale and Retail at His Bookstore.-.

--Divine Emblems: Or, Temporal Things Spiritualized. Fitted for the Use of Boys and Girls. LC 78-309015. (Illus.). 90 p. 14cm. 1796. M. Carey.

--The Little Christian's Pilgrimage. Miles, Helen, illus. N.D. E & J B Young.

--Pilgrim's Home Library. (Burt's Home Library). N.D. A L Burt Co.

--Pilgrim's Progress. (Illus.). (Burt's Young Folks' Library). N.D. A. L. Burt's Pubs.

--Pilgrim's Progress. N.D. American News Co.

--The Pilgrim's Progress. (Illus.). 232p. (gr. 9 up). 1981. (ISBN 0-89323-016-2). BMA Pr.

--The Pilgrim's Progress. N.D. Brewer & Warren Inc.

--Pilgrim's Progress. N.D. Cassell, Petter, & Galpin.

--Pilgrim's Progress. 306p. (Merrill's English Texts). N.D. Charles E Merrill.

--Pilgrim's Progress. N.D. Claxton, Remsen & Haffelfinger.

--Pilgrim's Progress. N.D. Cokesbury Press.

--Pilgrim's Progress. N.D. Collins & Brother's Publications.

--Pilgrim's Progress. (One-Syllable Books). N.D. D. Appleton & Co.

--The Pilgrim's Progress. (Apple II Plus with 48K & 1 DOS 3.3 drive). N.D. D. Appleton & Co.

--The Pilgrim's Progress. N.D. D. Lothrop & co.

--Pilgrim's Progress. (Illus.). 448p. (Colored Classics). N.D. David McKay.

--The Pilgrim's Progress. N.D. Geo. E. Stevens & Co.

--Pilgrim's Progress. (Illus.). 448p. (Colored Classics). N.D. George Routledge & Sons.

--Pilgrim's Progress. (Classics for Children). N.D. Ginn.

--The Pilgrim's Progress. N.D. Gould & Lincoln's Publications.

--Pilgrim's Progress. (The Good Value Books). N.D. Grosset & Dunlap.

--Pilgrim's Progress, 12 vols. (Illus.). 448p. (Juvenile Classics Ser.). 1905. Set. H M Caldwell Co.

--Pilgrim's Progress. (Illus.). (The Young Folks Lib.). N.D. H. M. Caldwell Co.

--Pilgrim's Progress. N.D. Harper & Bros.

--The Pilgrims' Progress. N.D. Henry Altemus Company.

--Pilgrim's Progress. (English Readings Ser.). N.D. Henry Holt.

--Pilgrim's Progress. (Illus.). (Boys' and Girls' Classics). N.D. Henry Altemus Co.

--The Pilgrim's Progress. (Illus.). (Golden Treasury Ser.). N.D. Henry Altemus Co.

--The Pilgrim's Progress. (Illus.). (Ever New Books For Young People). N.D. Henry Altemus Company Publications.

--Pilgrim's Progress. (Illus.). (One-Syllable Ser.). N.D. Henry Altemus Co.

--The Pilgrim's Progress. (Riverside Literature Ser.). N.D. Houghton Mifflin.

--Pilgrim's Progress. 384p. N.D. Hurd & Houghton for American Tract Society.

--Pilgrim's Progress. (The Cottage Library). N.D. J. B. Lippincott.

--The Pilgrim's Progress. (Sears Juvenile Classics). N.D. J.H.Sears & Co.

--Pilgrim's Progress. (The Young People's Library). N.D. John C. Winston.

--Pilgrim's Progress. 491p. (True Life Ser.). N.D. Lee & Shepard.
--The Pilgrim's Progress. LC 26-9284. 15cm. 158p. 1850. Lindsay & Blakiston.
--Pilgrim's Progress. 384p. N.D. Lockwood, Brooks, & Co. for American Tract Society.
--The Pilgrim's Progress. New & Cheaper Ed. ed. (Golden Treasury Ser.). N.D. Set. MacMillan.
--Pilgrim's Progress. 129p. N.D. Moody.
--Pilgrim's Progress. N.D. National Bible Press.
--The Pilgrim's Progress. (Illus.). (Children's Classic). 1910. Penn Publishing Co.
--The Pilgrim's Progress. (Illus.). (Young People's Classics). N.D. R. F. Fenno & Co.
--The Pilgrim's Progress. 1875. Robert Carter & Brothers.
--Pilgrim's Progress. (Carters' Fireside Library). 1875. Robert Carter & Brothers.
--The Pilgrim's Progress. 256p. (The Lake English Classics). N.D. Scott Foresman & Co.
--The Pilgrim's Progress, 30 of 48 Vols. (Illus.). (Excelsior Toy Books Ser.). N.D. Scribner & Welford.
--The Pilgrim's Progress. 423p. 1973. (ISBN 0-85150-250-4). The Attic Press.
--Pilgrim's Progress. (Honor Bks.). N.D. Thomas Nelson & Sons.
--Pilgrim's Progress. (Illus.). (The Standard Juvenile Library). N.D. Set. Thomas Nelson & Sons.
--Pilgrim's Progress. (Illus.). (Children's Favorite Classics). N.D. Thomas Y. Crowell.
--Pilgrim's Progress. (Illus.). (Collins' Juvenile Ser.). N.D. William Collins Co.
The Pilgrim's Progress. (The Bible Story Ser.). N.D. World Publishing House.
Pilgrim's Progress. Barnard Ed. ed. Barnard, Frederick (1847-1896), illus. 327p. (The Sterling Series for Young People). 1952. John C. Winston.
--The Pilgrim's Progress. Barnard, Frederick (1847-1896), illus. (The Children's Bookshelf). N.D. John C. Winston.
--The Pilgrim's Progress. Bennett, Charles Henry (1829-1867), illus. N.D. E P Dutton.
--The Pilgrim's Progress. Blake, William (1757-1827), illus. N.D. Heritage Press.
--The Pilgrim's Progress. Copping, Harold (1863-1932), illus. N.D. Fleming H. Revell Co.
--The Pilgrim's Progress. Crothers, Samuel McChord, Dr., intro. by. (Modern Students Library). N.D. Charles Scribner's Sons.
--The Pilgrim's Progress. Cruikshank, George (1792-1878), illus. N.D. Oxford University Press--American Branch.
--Pilgrim's Progress. Day, Samuel P., retold by. (Illus.). (Burt's Series of One Syllable Books). N.D. A. L. Burt's Pubs.
--The Pilgrim's Progress. Gilbert, John Clitherae, illus. 1874. Pott, Young, & Co.
--Pilgrim's Progress. Inglis, John, notes by. (The Illuminated Ser.). N.D. The American News Co.
--Pilgrim's Progress. Jepson, R. W., ed. N.D. Longmans Green & Co.
--Pilgrim's Progress. Lawson, Robert (1892-1957), illus. N.D. Frederick A. Stokes.
--Pilgrim's Progress. Lawson, Robert (1892-1957), illus. 1939. J. B. Lippincott.
--The Pilgrim's Progress. Maguire, Robert, notes by. (Royal Illuminated Library). N.D. Lee & Shepard.
--The Pilgrim's Progress. Martz, Louis L., ed. 329p. 1949. Rinehart & Co.
--The Pilgrim's Progress. Matthew, Jean Marian, ed. Ford, Henry Justice (1860-1941), illus. N.D. Macmillan.
--Pilgrim's Progress. Montgomery, ed. (Classics for Children). N.D. Ginn and Company.
--Pilgrim's Progress. Pape, Frank Cheyne (1878-), illus. (Children's Illustrated Classics). N.D. E. P. Dutton & Co.
--Pilgrim's Progress. Philip, R. Rev., notes by. (Illus.). N.D. Worthington Co.
--The Pilgrim's Progress. Rhead, Louis John (1857-1926), illus. Potter, Henry C., intro. by. 240p. N.D. Century Co.
--The Pilgrim's Progress. Smith, Edith Freelove, abridged by. N.D. Little Brown & Co.
--The Pilgrim's Progress. Stothard, Thomas, illus. (The Golden Treasury Ser.). N.D. John Allyn.
--The Pilgrim's Progress. Strong, William, illus. N.D. E P Dutton.
--Pilgrim's Progress. Williamson, Hugh Ross, intro. by. (Collins New Classics). N.D. William Collins Sons & Co.
--Pilgrim's Progress In Words of One Syllable. Godolphin, Mary, retold by. (Illus.). N.D. George Routledge & Sons.

Bura, Doris
--The Tale of Lazy Lizard Canyon. LC 75-42251. 24p. ill. 24cm. 1977. (ISBN 0-399-20522-5). (ISBN 0-399-61012-X). Putnam.

Burack, Abraham Saul (1908-1978), ed. see Clapp, Patricia.

Burack, Abraham Saul (1908-1978), ed. see Plays; the Drama Magazine for Young People.

Burack, Abraham Saul (1908-1978), ed.
--Christmas Plays for Young Actors. LC 50-4774. (A Collection of Royalty-Free Stage and Radio Plays). 308 p. 21cm. 1950. Plays, Inc.
--Christmas Plays for Young Actors. rev. ed. LC 70-86850. (A Collection of Royalty-Free Stage and Radio Plays). 308 p. 21cm. 1969. Plays, Inc.
--Four Star Plays for Boys. Rev. ed. 1969. (ISBN 0-8238-0009-1). Plays, Inc.
--Four-Star Radio Plays for Teenagers. N.D. Plays Inc Pub.
--One Hundred Plays for Children: An Anthology of Non-Royalty One-Act Plays. LC 75-99964. viii, 886 p. 22cm. 1970. Plays, Inc.
--Skits, Comedies and Farces for Teen-Agers: A Collection of Humorous One-Act Royalty-Free Plays for All Occasions. LC 79-110497. vii, 433 p. 22cm. 1970. Plays.
--A Treasury of Holiday Plays for Teenagers. N.D. (ISBN 0-8238-0007-5). Plays, Inc.

Burack, Abraham Saul (1908-1978) & Crossley, B. Alice, eds.
--Popular Plays for Classroom Reading. LC 74-998. xx, 353 p. 24cm. 1974. (ISBN 0-8238-0151-9). Plays, Inc.

Burack, Sylvia K. see Kamerman, Sylvia E., pseud.

Burack, Sylvia K. (1916-), ed.
--Blue-Ribbon Plays for Girls: A Collection of Royalty-Free, One-Act Plays for All-Girl Casts. Kamerman, Sylvia E., pseud. LC 55-79510. 359p. 21cm. 1955. Plays, Inc.
--Blue-Ribbon Plays for Graduation. Kamerman, Sylvia E., pseud. N.D. Plays Inc Pub.
--Children's Plays from Favorite Stories: Royalty-Free Dramatizations of Fables, Fairy Tales, Folk Tales, and Legends. Kamerman, Sylvia E., pseud. LC 59-770416. 583 p. 22cm. 1959. Plays.
--Children's Plays from Favorite Stories: Royalty-Free Dramatizations of Fables, Fairy Tales, Folk Tales, and Legends. Kamerman, Sylvia E., pseud. LC 75-17616. vii, 583 p. 22cm. 1970. Plays, Inc.
--Christmas Play Favorites for Young People. Kamerman, Sylvia E., pseud. (Orig.). (gr. 4-12). 1982. (ISBN 0-8238-0257-4). Plays.
--Fifty Plays for Holidays: A Collection of Royalty-Free, One-Act Children's Plays for Holidays and Special Occasions. Kamerman, Sylvia E., pseud. LC 68-57841. ix, 652 p. 22cm. 1969. Plays, Inc.
--Fifty Plays for Junior Actors: A Collection of Royalty-Free, One Act Plays for Young People. Kamerman, Sylvia E., pseud. LC 66-17944. viii, 676 p. 22cm. 1966. Plays, Inc.
--Holiday Plays Round the Year. Kamerman, Sylvia E., pseud. LC 83-13218. p. cm. c.1983. (ISBN 0-8238-0261-2). Plays, Inc.
--Little Plays for Little Players: Fifty Non-Royalty Plays for Children. Kamerman, Sylvia E., pseud. 335 p. 1952. Plays, Inc.
--Little Plays for Little Players: Fifty Non-Royalty Plays for Children. Kamerman, Sylvia E., pseud. LC 75-97943. 335 p. 21cm. 1969. Plays, Inc.
--On Stage for Christmas: A Collection of Royalty-Free One-Act Christmas Plays for Young People. Kamerman, Sylvia E., pseud. LC 78-15517. 488 p. 21cm. c.1978. (ISBN 0-8238-0226-4). Plays, Inc.
--Treasury of Christmas Plays. Kamerman, Sylvia E., pseud. rev. ed. (gr. 5-12). 1976. (ISBN 0-8238-0203-5). Plays.
--A Treasury of Christmas Plays: One-Act, Royalty-Free Plays for Stage or Microphone Performance and Round-the-Table Reading. Kamerman, Sylvia E., pseud. LC 76-350906. 509 p. 22cm. c.1975. (ISBN 0-8238-0203-5). Plays, Inc.

Buranelli, Vincent (1919-), ed. see Dumas, Alexandre.

Buranelli, Vincent (1919-)
--Josiah Royce. N.D. Grosset & Dunlap.

Buranelli, Vincent (1919-), adapted by.
--Oliver Twist. Fromm, Hieronimus (1802-1870), illus. LC 84-50429. (Original Author: Charles Dickens, 1812-1870). (Illus.). 26 p., 1 leaf of plates. 26cm. (Silver Burdett international library selection). (Classics for Kids). 1984. (ISBN 0-382-06808-4). Silver Burdett Co.

Burba, Linda
--Ben's Blanket & the Baby Jesus. 1980. (ISBN 0-570-06137-7, Arch Bk). Concordia.

Burbank, Addison Bushnell (1895-)
--The Cedar Deer. Burbank, Addison Bushnell (1895-), illus. LC 40-275931. 156, 2 p. col. illus., double col. pl. 23 cm. 1940. Coward-McCann, Inc.

Burbank, Addison Bushnell (1895-) & Newcomb, Covelle (1908-)
--Addison Burbank and Covelle Newcomb Present Narizona's Holiday. Burbank, Addison Bushnell (1895-), illus. LC 46-7723. 5 p. l. 13-155 p. illus. 21 cm. 1946. Longmans, Green & Co.

Burbank, Barbara & Wilson, Olivia Lovell
--Comedies for Young Folks. LC 3-10911. 19cm. 144p. 1902. W. H. Baker & Co.

Burch, Aline, tr. see Svensson, Jon Stefan.

Burch, Arthur Eugene (1904-)
--The Adventures of Put-Put: The Puddle Jumper. LC 48-15311. 2 p. illus. (part col.) 22 cm. (Old Faithful books). 1947. Prang Co. Publishers.

Burch, Florence E.
--Chris Willoughby: Or, Against the Current. N.D. Thomas Nelson & Sons.
--Dick & Harry & Tom: Or, For Our Reaping By-and-By. N.D. Thomas Nelson & Sons.
--Rollo and Tricksy. (Illus.). N.D. Thomas Nelson & Sons.

Burch, Harriette E.
--Jacko: A Story for Young. N.D. Thomas Nelson & Sons.
--Sprats Alive O. (Illus.). 80p. (The Rosebud Ser.). N.D. Fleming H. Revell Co.

Burch, Robert Joseph (1925-)
--Christmas with Ida Early. LC 85-5680. p. cm. 1985. (ISBN 0-14-031930-1). Puffin Books.
--Christmas with Ida Early. LC 83-5792. p. cm. 1983. (ISBN 0-670-22131-7). Viking Press.
--D. J.'s Worst Enemy. Weiss, Emil (1896-1965), illus. LC 65-13356. (Illus.). 142 p. 21cm. 1965. Viking Press.
--Doodle and the Go-Cart. Tiegreen, Alan, illus. LC 73-183932. (Illus.). 124 p. 22cm. 1972. (ISBN 0-670-27979-X). Viking Press.
--Funny Place to Live. Lohse, William R., illus. LC 61-11689. (Illus.). 25cm. 40p. (ps-1). 1962. (ISBN 0-670-33263-1). (ISBN 0-670-33264-X). Viking Pr.
--The Hunting Trip. Suba, Susanne (1913-), illus. LC 74-162738. (Illus.). color ils. 32p. (gr. k-3). 1971. (ISBN 0-684-12495-5, ScribJ). Scribner.
--Hut School and the Wartime Home-Front Heroes. Himler, Ronald Norbert (1937-), illus. LC 73-19865. (Illus.). 140 p. 24cm. 1974. Viking Press.
--Ida Early Comes Over the Mountain. LC 79-20532. p. cm. 1980. (ISBN 0-670-39169-7). Viking Press. **Awards: (ALA); (BGH).**
--Joey's Cat. Freeman, Don (1908-1978), illus. LC 69-13077. (Illus.). color ils. 32p. (ps-2). 1969. (ISBN 0-670-40789-5). (ISBN 0-670-90012-5). (ISBN 0-670-90510-0). Viking Pr.
--Joey's Cat. Freeman, Don (1908-1978), illus. 32p. (ps-2). 1972. (ISBN 0-670-05063-6, Seafarer). Viking Pr.
--The Jolly Witch. Grant, Alice Leigh (1947-), illus. LC 75-5891. (Illus.). 31 p. 23cm. 1975. (ISBN 0-525-32797-5). Dutton.
--Queenie Peavy. Lazare, Gerald John (1927-), illus. LC 66-15649. (Illus.). 159 p. 21cm. 1966. Viking Press. **Award: (ALA).**
--Renfroe's Christmas. Negri, Rocco (1932-), illus. (Illus.). 59 p. 24cm. 1968. Viking Press.
--Simon and the Game of Chance. Rocker, Fermin (1907-), illus. LC 77-125851. (Illus.). 128 p. 22cm. 1970. Viking Press.
--Skinny. Sibley, Don (1922-), illus. LC 64-12638. (Illus.). 21cm. 126p. (gr. 4-7). 1964. (ISBN 0-670-64999-6). Viking Pr.
--Traveling Bird. (gr. k-3). N.D. G&D.
--Traveling Bird. Suba, Susanne (1913-), illus. (gr. 1-4). 1959. (ISBN 0-8392-3038-9). Astor-Honor.
--The Traveling Bird. Suba, Susanne (1913-), illus. LC 59-14079. (Illus.). 42 p. 24cm. (Astor book). c.1959. McDowell, Obolensky.
--Two That Were Tough. Cuffari, Richard (1925-1978), illus. LC 76-12453. p. cm. 1976. (ISBN 0-670-73684-8). Viking Press.
--Tyler, Wilkin, and Skee. Sibley, Don (1922-), illus. LC 63-8521. (Illus.). 156 p. 21cm. 1963. Viking Press.
--The Whitman Kick. LC 77-23384. 116 p. 22cm. 1978, c.1977. (ISBN 0-525-42677-9). Dutton.
--Wilkin's Ghost. Bloom, Lloyd, illus. LC 78-6293. (Illus.). 152 p. 22cm. 1978. (ISBN 0-670-76897-9). Viking Press.

Burch, Viola S
--While the Mock Orange Waits. LC 68-17219. 145 p. 22cm. 1968. Dorrance.

Burchard, Marshall
--Sports Hero: Magic Johnson. (Illus.). 96p. (Sports Hero Ser.). (gr. 2-5). 1981. (ISBN 0-399-61187-8). (ISBN 0-399-20839-9). Putnam Pub Group.

Burchard, Peter Duncan (1921-)
--Barn Burners. Burchard, Peter Duncan (1921-), illus. b&w halftones. 92p. (gr. 3-6). 1972. Coward.
--Bimby. Burchard, Peter Duncan (1921-), illus. LC 68-23866. (Illus.). 91 p. 23cm. 1968. Coward-McCann.
--The Carol Moran. Burchard, Peter Duncan (1921-), illus. LC 58-6727. (Illus.). 40 p. 26cm. 1958. Macmillan.
--Chinwe. LC 78-24401. (Illus.). 127 p. 22cm. c.1979. (ISBN 0-399-20667-1). Putnam.
--Chito. Thomas, Katrina, illus. LC 78-88873. (Illus.). 48 p. 27cm. 1969. Coward-McCann.
--The Deserter: A Spy Story of the Civil War. LC 72-94145. (Illus.). 95 p. 21cm. 1973. (ISBN 0-698-20266-X). (ISBN 0-698-20266-X). Coward, McCann & Geoghegan.
--Digger: A Novel. LC 80-15482. p. cm. (gr. 5-12). c.1980. (ISBN 0-399-20717-1). Putnam.
--First Affair. LC 81-15291. p. cm. 1981. (ISBN 0-374-32336-4). Farrar Straus Giroux.
--Jed. (Illus.). (gr. 5-8). 1960. (ISBN 0-8382-0379-5). Hale.
--Jed: The Story of a Yankee Soldier and a Southern Boy. LC 60-12479. (Illus.). 94 p. 21cm. 1960. Coward-McCann.
--North by Night. LC 62-18609. 191p. illus. 21cm. c.1962. Coward.
--A Quiet Place. LC 72-84840. 94 p. 22cm. 1972. (ISBN 0-698-20191-4). (ISBN 0-698-20191-4). Coward, McCann & Geoghegan.
--Rat Hell. Burchard, Peter Duncan (1921-), illus. LC 77-150272. (Illus.). 61 p. 21cm. 1971. Coward, McCann & Geoghegan.
--The River Queen. Burchard, Peter Duncan (1921-), illus. LC 57-6715. (Illus.). 40 p. 26cm. 1957. Macmillan.
--Sea Change. LC 84-47524. (Illus.). 116p. (gr. 7 up). 1983. (ISBN 0-374-36460-5). (ISBN 0-374-36460-5). FS&G.
--Whaleboat Raid. Burchard, Peter Duncan (1921-), illus. LC 77-355. (Illus.). 96p. (gr. 3-6). 1977. (ISBN 0-698-20412-3, Coward). Putnam Pub Group.

Burchardt, Nellie (1921-)
--Project Cat. Rocker, Fermin (1907-), illus. (gr. 4-6). 1971. (ISBN 0-590-08788-6, Schol Trade Pap). Schol Bk Serv.
--Project Cat. Rocker, Fermin (1907-), illus. LC 66-12142. 66p. col. illus. 21cm. (gr. 4-6). c.1966. (ISBN 0-531-01772-9). Watts.
--Reggie's No-Good Bird. Berson, Harold (1926-), illus. LC 67-275. (Illus.). 140 p. 21cm. 1967. F. Watts.
--A Surprise for Carlotta. Lewin, Ted (1935-), illus. LC 70-150376. (Illus.). 126 p. 22cm. 1971. (ISBN 0-531-02001-0). F. Watts.
--What Are We Going to Do, Michael?. Kramer, Dick, illus. LC 73-5743. (Illus.). 152 p. 21cm. 1973. (ISBN 0-531-02637-X). F. Watts.

Burchell, Kate
--Little Folk's First Book. (Illus.). (gr. k-1). 1964. (ISBN 0-7232-0339-3). Warne.
--Little Folk's Second Book. Cloke, Rene, illus. LC 67-2491. (Illus.). 25cm. 62p. 1967, c.1966. F. Warne.

Burd, Clara Miller, ed. see Yonge, Charlotte Mary.

Burdekin, Harold
--Little Children. N.D. E. P. Dutton & Co.

Burdekin, Katharine, Mrs.
--The Children's Country. LC 29-17259. viii p., 2 l., 3-262 p. col. front., col. plates. 22 1/2 cm. c.1929. W. Morrow & Company.

Burdett
--Arthur Martin. (Harper's Fireside Library). N.D. Harper & Bros.
--Mary Grover. N.D. Harper & Brothers.

Burdette, Myron (1909-)
--The Diary of an Acorn. Souder, Jim, illus. LC 73-93147. (Illus.). 47 p. 22cm. 1974. (ISBN 0-8059-1986-4). Dorrance.

Burdick, Annie Mabelle (1868-)
Scovia; the True Story of a Cat Told by Himself. Cooke, W. C., illus. LC 3-22112. 4 p. l. 76 p. front., illus., 3 pl. 23 cm. 1903. Broadway Publishing Company.

Burdick, Jennie Ellis, ed.
--Children's Own Library, 10 Vols. Welsh, Charles (1850-), intro. by. LC 10-24040. (Contents: v. 1. Nursery Tales--v. 2-3. Fairy Tales--v. 4. Wonderland Tales--v. 5. Legendary Stories--v. 6. Stories from Mythology--v. 7. Stories of Adventure--v. 8. Animal Stories--v. 9. Retold Tales--v. 10. Miscellaneous Tales). (Illus.). 19cm. 1910. National Library Co.

Bures, Ruth A.
--Here Comes Christmas. 40p. (gr. k-8). 1982. (ISBN 0-86704-008-4). Clarus Music.

Burford, Lolah
--MacLyon. LC 73-21292. 384p. 1974. (ISBN 0-02-518190-4). Macmillan.

Burg, Marie
--Salt & Gold: Tales from Czechoslovakia. Stubley, Trevor Hugh (1932-), illus. LC 77-373558. (Illus.). 3-95 p. 24cm. 1976. (ISBN 0-216-90143-X). Blackie.

Burg, Marie, tr. see Macourek, Milos.

Burger, Isabel & DeBear, Constance
--Remi's Secret Locket: Nobody's Boy. (Children's Theatre Playscript Ser.). 1957. (ISBN 0-88020-049-9). Coach Hse.

Burger, John Robert (1942-) & Gardner, Lewis (1943-)
--Children of the Wild. LC 78-4627. (Illus.). 128p. (gr. 7 up). 1978. (ISBN 0-671-32879-4). Messner.

Burger, Otis Kidwell
--The String that Went Up. Berg, Joan, pseud. (1942-), illus. Victor, Joan Berg. LC 63-9425. (Illus.). 24cm. 1963. St Martin's Press.

Burgert, Hans-Joachim
--Samulo and the Giant. LC 74-80318. (Illus.). 32 p. 27cm. 1970. Holt, Rinehart and Winston.

Burgess, Andrew, jt. auth. see Burgess, Constance.

Burgess, Andrew (1897-)
--Lan Ta-Te, Landahl of China. 116p. N.D. Augsburg Publishing House.
--Utemba. 30p. N.D. Augsburg Publishing House.
Burgess, Andrew (1897-) & Burgess, Constance (1897-)
--Little Koto. N.D. Augsburg publishing House.
Burgess, Anthony, pseud., see Wilson, John Anthony Burgess.
Burgess, Anthony, pseud. (1917-)
--A Long Trip to Tea Time. Wilson, John Anthony Burgess. Testa, Fulvio, illus. LC 76-56930. (Illus.). 1976. (ISBN 0-88373-063-4). Stonehill Pub Co.
Burgess, Beverly C.
--Little Red Ridinghood. (Illus.). 32p. (Orig.). (gr. 1-3). 1983. (ISBN 0-89274-289-5). Harrison Hse.
--Three Little Pigs: Build Your House Upon the Rock. 32p. (Orig.). (ps). 1983. (ISBN 0-89274-283-6). Harrison Hse.
Burgess, Constance, jt. auth. see Burgess, Andrew.
Burgess, Constance (1897-) & Burgess, Andrew (1897-)
--Mei-Mei. 32p. N.D. Augsburg Publishing House.
--Mitku: A Little Boy of North Alaska. Konsterlie, Paul, illus. LC 56-117917. unpaged. illus. 14cm. c.1956. Augsburg Pub. House.
--Taro. 30p. 1954. Augsburg Publishing House.
Burgess, Frank Gelett see Burgess, Gelett.
Burgess, Gelett (1866-1951)
--Blue Goops and Red. Burgess, Gelett (1866-1951), illus. N.D. Frederick A. Stokes.
--The Burgess Nonsense Book. (Illus.). N.D. Frederick A. Stokes Co.
--The Goop Directory of Juvenile Offenders Famous for Their Misdeeds: And Serving As a Salutary Example for All Virtous Children. LC 13-187103. 78, 1 p. illus. 17 1/2 cm. (On cover: The little goop books). c.1913. Frederick A. Stokes Company.
--The Goop Encyclopedia. Burgess, Gelett (1866-1951), illus. LC 16-186167. xiv, 254 p. illus. 19 1/2 cm. c.1916. Frederick A. Stokes Company.
--Goop Tales. LC 72-93766. (Illus.). 128p. (gr. 1-6). 1973. Dover.
--Goop Tales. (Illus.). N.D. (ISBN 0-8446-4717-9). Peter Smith Publisher, Inc.
--Goop Tales: Alphabetically Arranged. (Illus.). 128p. 1904. (ISBN 0-486-22914-9). Dover Books.
--Goop Tales Alphabetically Told: A Study of the Behavior of Some Fifty-Two Interesting Individuals, Each of Which While Mainly Virtuous, Yet Has Some One Human & Redeeming Fault; with Numerous Illustrations. LC 4-23766. 3 p. l., 106 p. illus. 26 1/2 cm. 1904. F. A. Stokes Company.
--Goops and How to Be Them. (Illus.). 100 p. 26cm. (Legacy library facsimile). 1967. University Microfilms.
--Goops and How to Be them. Burgess, Gelett (1866-1951), illus. N.D. (ISBN 0-531-05130-7). Franklin Watts.
--Goops, and How to Be Them. Burgess, Gelett (1866-1951), illus. 1903. J. B. Lippincott.
--Goops and How to Be Them: A Manual of Manners for Polite Infants Inculcating Many Juvenile Virtures Both by Precept and Example, with Ninety Drawings. Burgess, Gelett (1866-1951), illus. LC 4551. 96 p. illus. 26 x 20 cm. 1900. Frederick A. Stokes Company.
--The Little Father. Egielski, Richard (1952-), illus. 32p. 1985. Farrar Straus & Giroux.
--The Lively City O'Ligg: A Cycle of Modern Fairy Tales for City Children. Burgess, Gelett (1866-1951), illus. LC 99-5598. 219 p. illus., plates. 21 1/2 cm. (Popular Ser. for Young People). 1899. Frederick A. Stokes Company.
--More Goops & How Not to Be Them. (Peter Possum Paperbacks Ser). 1967. (ISBN 0-531-05138-2). Watts.
--More Goops and How Not to be Them. Burgess, Gelett (1866-1951), illus. 1956. J. B. Lippincott.
--More Goops and How Not to Be Them: A Manual of Manners for Impolite Infants Depicting the Characteristics of Many Naughty and Thoughtless Children, with Instructive Illustrations. LC 3-20886. 96 p. illus. 26 x 20 cm. 1903. Frederick A. Stokes Company.
--Purple Cow & Other Nonsense. Burgess, Gelett (1866-1951), illus. (Illus.). (gr. 4-6). 1901. (ISBN 0-486-20772-2). Dover.
--The Purple Cow and Other Poems. Burgess, Gelett (1866-1951), illus. 14p. 1968. Huntington Library Publications.
--Why Be a Goop?. A Primary School of Deportment and Taste for Children. Burgess, Gelett (1866-1951), illus. LC 21-25327. vi, 1, 8-159 p. illus. 21 1/2 cm. 1924. Frederick A. Stokes Company.
Burgess, J. Tom
--Harry Hope's Holidays: What he Saw, What he Did, and What he Learnt during a Year's Rambles in Country Places. N.D. George Routledge & Sons.
Burgess, Lew
--The Tail of Josephine and the German Horse Fly. Eddy, Frederic Arden, illus. LC 45-55953. 43 p. illus. (part col.) 19 1/2 x 22 cm. 1945. Griffin-Patterson Company.
Burgess, Robert Brettle
--Bob Tales. LC 31-19447. 60p. 1931. Meador Publishing Co.
Burgess, Robert Forrest (1927-)
--The Mystery of Mound Key. Donahue, Vic, illus. LC 66-13904. 187p. illus. 21cm. (gr. 4-6). c.1966. World.
--A Time for Tigers. Donahue, Vic, illus. LC 68-14686. (Illus.). 189 p. 21cm. 1968. World Pub. Co.
--Where Condors Fly. Stone, David Karl (1922-), illus. LC 69-13053. (Illus.). 189 p. 21cm. 1969. World Pub. Co.
Burgess, Thornton Waldo, jt. auth. see Bianco, Margery Williams, Mrs.
Burgess, Thornton Waldo, jt. auth. see Bianco, Margery Williams, Mrs.
Burgess, Thornton Waldo (1874-1965)
--The Adventures of Bob White. Cady, Walter Harrison (1877-1970), illus. (Thornton W. Burgess Books). 1962. (ISBN 0-448-02719-4). Grosset & Dunlap.
--The Adventures of Bob White. Cady, Walter Harrison (1877-1970), illus. LC 19-9556. vi p., 1 l., 117 p. front., plates, 17 1/2 cm. (His The bedtime storybooks). 1919. Little, Brown and Company.
--The Adventures of Bobby Coon. Cady, Walter Harrison (1877-1970), illus. (Thornton W. Burgess Books). 1962. (ISBN 0-448-02717-8). Grosset & Dunlap.
--The Adventures of Bobby Coon. Cady, Walter Harrison (1877-1970), illus. LC 18-9663. 4 p. l., 117 p. front., plates, 17 1/2 cm. (His The bedtime story-books). 1918. Little, Brown, and Company.
--The Adventures of Bobby Coon. Cady, Walter Harrison (1877-1970), illus. LC 44-6314. 4 p. l. 94 p. col. front., col. illus. 21 x 17 1/2 cm. (His The bedtime storybooks). 1944. Little, Brown and Company.
--The Adventures of Buster Bear. Cady, Walter Harrison (1877-1970), illus. (Thornton W. Burgess Books). 1962. (ISBN 0-448-02701-1). Grosset & Dunlap.
--The Adventures of Buster Bear. Cady, Walter Harrison (1877-1970), illus. LC 16-957763. vi, p., 1 l., 120 p. front., plates. 17 cm. (Bedtime story-books). 1916. Little, Brown, and Company.
--The Adventures of Buster Bear. Cady, Walter Harrison (1877-1970), illus. LC 41-21729. 4 p. l., 93 p. col. front., col. illus. 21 x 17 1/2 cm. (His The bedtime story-books). 1941. Little, Brown and Company.
--The Adventures of Chatterer the Red Squirrel. Cady, Walter Harrison (1877-1970), illus. (Thornton W. Burgess Books). 1962. (ISBN 0-448-02702-X). Grosset & Dunlap.
--Adventures of Chatterer the Red Squirrel. Cady, Walter Harrison (1877-1970) & Kerr, George, illus. (Bedtime Story Bks.: Vol. 2). (gr. 2-5). 1949. (ISBN 0-448-02702-X, G&D). Putnam Pub Group.
--The Adventures of Chatterer, the Red Squirrel: The Red Squirrel. Cady, Walter Harrison (1877-1970), illus. LC 15-209682. vi p., 1 l., 120 p. front., plates. 17 cm. (His The bedtime story-books). 1915. Little, Brown, and Company.
--The Adventures of Danny Meadow Mouse. Cady, Walter Harrison (1877-1970), illus. (Thornton W. Burgess Books). 1962. (ISBN 0-448-02703-8). Grosset & Dunlap.
--The Adventures of Danny Meadow Mouse. Cady, Walter Harrison (1877-1970), illus. vi p., 1 l., 119 p. front., plates. 17 cm. (bedtime story-books). 1915. Little, Brown, and Company.
--The Adventures of Danny Meadow Mouse. Cady, Walter Harrison (1877-1970), illus. LC 44-5721. 4 p. l. 94 p. col. front., col. illus. 21 x 17 1/2 cm. (His The bedtime storybooks). 1944. Little, Brown and Company.
--The Adventures of Grandfather Frog. Cady, Walter Harrison (1877-1970), illus. (Thornton W. Burgess Bks.). 1962. (ISBN 0-448-02704-6). Grosset & Dunlap.
--The Adventures of Grandfather Frog. Cady, Walter Harrison (1877-1970), illus. LC 15-3971. vi p., 1 l., 120 p. front., plates. 17 1/2 cm. (bedtime story-books). 1915. Little, Brown and Company.
--The Adventures of Grandfather Frog. Cady, Walter Harrison (1877-1970), illus. LC 44-6313. 3 p. l. 96 p. col. front., col. illus. 21 x 17 1/2 cm. (His The bedtime story-books). 1944. Little, Brown and Company.
--The Adventures of Jerry Muskrat. Cady, Walter Harrison (1877-1970), illus. 179 p. illus. 20 cm. (His Bedtime story-books, 5). 1962, c.1942. (ISBN 0-448-02705-4). Grosset & Dunlap.
--The Adventures of Jerry Muskrat. Cady, Walter Harrison (1877-1970), illus. vi p., 1 l., 120 p. front., plates. 17 1/2 cm. (bedtime story-books). 1914. Little, Brown, and Company.
--The Adventures of Jimmy Skunk. Cady, Walter Harrison (1877-1970), illus. (Thornton W. Burgess Bks.). 1962. (ISBN 0-448-02718-6). Grosset & Dunlap.
--The Adventures of Jimmy Skunk. Cady, Walter Harrison (1877-1970), illus. LC 41-21730. 4 p. l. 94 p. col. front., col. illus. 21 x 17 1/2 cm. (His The bedtime story-books). 1941. Little, Brown and Company.
--The Adventures of Jimmy Skunk. Cady, Walter Harrison (1877-1970), illus. LC 18-9664. 4 p. l., 118 p. front., plates. 17 1/2 cm. (His The bedtime story-books). N.D. Little, Brown and Company,.
--The Adventures of Johnny Chuck. Cady, Walter Harrison (1877-1970), illus. (Thornton W. Burgess Bks.). 1962. (ISBN 0-448-02706-2). Grosset & Dunlap.
--The Adventures of Johnny Chuck. Cady, Walter Harrison (1877-1970), illus. 18cm. 120p. (The Bedtime Story-Books). 1913. Little, Brown & Co.
--The Adventures of Johnny Chuck. Cady, Walter Harrison (1877-1970), illus. LC 44-572244. 3 p. l. 96 p. col. front., col. illus. 21 x 17 1/2 cm. (His The bedtime storybooks). 1944. Little, Brown and Company.
--Adventures of Lightfoot the Deer. (Green Forest Ser.: Vol. 1). (gr. k-3). 1944. (ISBN 0-448-02741-0, G&D). Putnam Pub Group.
--The Adventures of Little Peter Cottontail. Cady, Walter Harrison (1877-1970), illus. (Thornton W. Burgess Bks.). 1970 (Wonder Books). Grosset & Dunlap.
--Adventures of Mr. Mocker. Cady, Walter Harrison (1877-1970) & Kerr, George, illus. (gr. 2-5). N.D. (ISBN 0-448-02707-0). G&D.
--The Adventures of Mr. Mocker. Cady, Walter Harrison (1877-1970), illus. 18cm. 120p. (The Bedtime Story-Books). 1914. Little, Brown & Co.
--The Adventures of Ol' Mistah Buzzard. Cady, Walter Harrison (1877-1970), illus. (Thornton W. Burgess Bks.). 1962. (ISBN 0-448-02720-8). Grosset & Dunlap.
--The Adventures of Ol' Mistah Buzzard. Cady, Walter Harrison (1877-1970), illus. vi p. 1 l., 119 p. front., plates. 17 1/2 cm. (His The bedtime story-books). 1919. Little, Brown and Company.
--Adventures of Old Granny Fox. Cady, Walter Harrison (1877-1970) & Kerr, George, illus. (Green Forest Ser.: Vol. 4). (gr. k-3). 1943. (ISBN 0-448-02784-4, G&D). Putnam Pub Group.
--The Adventures of Old Man Coyote. Cady, Walter Harrison (1877-1970), illus. (His bedtime story-books). 1962, c.1944. (ISBN 0-448-02708-9). Grosset & Dunlap.
--The Adventures of Old Man Coyote. Cady, Walter Harrison (1877-1970), illus. LC 16-222827. vi p. 1 l., 120, p. front., plates. 17 1/2 cm. (His The bedtime story-books). 1916. Little, Brown, and Company.
--The Adventures of Old Mr. Toad. Cady, Walter Harrison (1877-1970), illus. (Thornton W. Burgess Bks.). 1962. (ISBN 0-448-02709-7). Grosset & Dunlap.
--The Adventures of Old Mr. Toad. Cady, Walter Harrison (1877-1970), illus. vi p., 1 l., 120 p. front., plates. 17 1/2 cm. (His The bedtime story-books). 1916. Little, Brown, and Company.
--The Adventures of Paddy the Beaver. LC 17-130713. vi p., 1 l., 118 p. front., plates. 17 1/2 cm. (His The bedtime story-books). 1917. Little, Brown, and Company.
--The Adventures of Paddy the Beaver. Cady, Walter Harrison (1877-1970), illus. (Thornton W. Burgess Bks.). 1962. (ISBN 0-448-02710-0). Grosset & Dunlap.
--The Adventures of Peter Cottontail. Cady, Walter Harrison (1877-1970), illus. (Thornton W. Burgess Bks). 1970. (ISBN 0-448-02711-9). Grosset & Dunlap.
--The Adventures of Peter Cottontail. Cady, Walter Harrison (1877-1970), illus. LC 41-22151. 4 p. l., 94 p. col. front., col. illus. 21 x 17 1/2 cm. (His The bedtime story-books). 1941. Little, Brown, and Company.
--The Adventures of Peter Cottontail. Abridged. Erickson, Phoebe (1907-), illus. LC 58-14719. 68p. illus. 32cm. 1958. Grosset & Dunlap.
--The Adventures of Peter Cottontail. abridged. Erickson, Phoebe (1907-), illus. (Illus.). 41 p. 29cm. 1967, c.1958. Grosset & Dunlap.
--The Adventures of Peter Cottontail. Erickson, Phoebe (1907-), illus. vi p., 1 l., 120 p. front., plates, 17 1/2 cm. (bedtime story-books). 1914. Little, Brown, and Company.
--The Adventures of Poor Mrs. Quack. Cady, Walter Harrison (1877-1970), illus. (Thornton W. Burgess Bks.). 1962. (ISBN 0-448-02712-7). Grosset & Dunlap.
--The Adventures of Poor Mrs. Quack. Cady, Walter Harrison (1877-1970), illus. LC 17-13070. vi p., 1 l., 119 p. front., plates. 17 1/2 cm. (His The bedtime story-books). 1917. Little, Brown, and Company.
--The Adventures of Prickly Porky. Cady, Walter Harrison (1877-1970), illus. (Thornton W. Burgess Bks.). 1962. (ISBN 0-448-02713-5). Grosset & Dunlap.
--The Adventures of Prickly Porky. Cady, Walter Harrison (1877-1970), illus. LC 16-222811. 4 p. l., 116 p. front., plates. 17 1/2 cm. (His The bedtime story-books). 1916. Little, Brown, and Company.
--The Adventures of Reddy Fox. Cady, Walter Harrison (1877-1970), illus. (Thornton W. Burgess Bks.). 1962. (ISBN 0-448-02714-3). Grosset & Dunlap.
--The Adventures of Reddy Fox. Cady, Walter Harrison (1877-1970), illus. 18cm. 120p. (The Bedtime Story-Books). 1913. Little, Brown & Co.
--The Adventures of Reddy Fox. Cady, Walter Harrison (1877-1970), illus. LC 41-22152. 4 p. l., 94 p. col. front., col. illus. 21 x 17 1/2 cm. (His The bedtime story-books). 1941. Little, Brown and Company.
--Adventures of Reddy Fox. Cady, Walter Harrison (1877-1970) & Kerr, George, illus. (Thornton W. Burgess Storybks.). (gr. 2-5). 1950. (ISBN 0-448-02714-3, G&D). (ISBN 0-448-13714-3). Putnam Pub Group.
--The Adventures of Sammy Jay. Cady, Walter Harrison (1877-1970), illus. 191 p. illus. 20 cm. (His bedtime story-books). 1962, c.1945. (ISBN 0-448-02715-1). Grosset & Dunlap.
--The Adventures of Sammy Jay. Cady, Walter Harrison (1877-1970), illus. LC 15-20967. vi p., 1 l., 119 p. front., plates. 17 1/2 cm. (His The Bedtime story-books). 1915. Little, Brown and Company.
--The Adventures of Unc' Billy Possum. Cady, Walter Harrison (1877-1970), illus. (Thornton W. Burgess Bks.). 1962. (ISBN 0-448-02716-X). Grosset & Dunlap.
--The Adventures of Unc' Billy Possum. Cady, Walter Harrison (1877-1970), illus. 18cm. 117p. (The Bedtime Story-Books). 1914. Little, Brown & Co.
--Adventures of Unc' Billy Possum. Cady, Walter Harrison (1877-1970) & Kerr, George, illus. (Bedtime Story Bks.: Vol. 16). (gr. 2-5). 1951. (ISBN 0-448-02716-X, G&D). (ISBN 0-448-13723-2). Putnam Pub Group.
--Adventures of Whitefoot the Woodmouse. Cady, Walter Harrison (1877-1970) & Kerr, George, illus. (Green Forest Ser.: Vol. 3). (gr. k-3). 1944. (ISBN 0-448-02743-7, G&D). Putnam Pub Group.
--Along Laughing Brook: A Book of Nature Stories. Cady, Walter Harrison (1877-1970), illus. LC 49-598502. 150 p. illus. 22 cm. (His The bedtime story-books). 1949. Little, Brown.
--Along Laughing Brook. On the Green Meadows. Cady, Walter Harrison (1877-1970), illus. LC 54-9593. 150, 182p. illus. 22cm. N.D. Little, Brown.
--Animal Stories. Cady, Walter Harrison (1877-1970), illus. LC 42-16452. 96 p. illus. (part col.) 21 x 18 cm. c.1942. The Platt & Munk Co., Inc.
--The Animal World of Thornton Burgess. Cady, Walter Harrison (1877-1970), illus. LC 61-846367. unpaged. illus. 22cm. (ps-3). 1961. Platt & Munk.
--At Paddy the Beaver's Pond: A Book of Nature Stories. 1st ed. Cady, Walter Harrison (1877-1970), illus. LC 50-3339. 146 p. illus. 22 cm. 1950. Little, Brown.
--At the Smiling-Pool,. A Book of Nature Stories. Cady, Walter Harrison (1877-1970), illus. LC 45-40198. 5 p. l. 3-134, 1 p. incl. illus., plates, col. front., col. plates. 21 1/2 x 16 1/2 cm. (His The bed-time story-books). 1945. Little, Brown and Company.
--Aunt Sally's Friends in Fur: Or, The Woodhouse Night Club. 1st ed. Burgess, Thornton Waldo (1874-1965), photos by. LC 54-9593. 146p. illus. 20cm. (His The bedtime story book series). c.1955. Little, Brown.
--Baby Animal Friends. Erickson, Phoebe (1907-), illus. N.D (Wonder Books). Grosset & Dunlap.
--Baby Animal Stories. Erickson, Phoebe (1907-), illus. LC 49-49188. 29 p. illus. (part col.) 29 cm. c.1949. Grossett & Dunlap.
--Baby Possum's Queer Voyage. Cady, Walter Harrison (1877-1970), illus. LC 29-3176. 1 p. l., 5-29 p. col. illus. 21 cm. 1928. Stoll & Edwards Co. Inc.
--Bedtime Stories. Hauge, Carl & Hauge, Mary, illus. LC 59-16401. 105p. illus. 32cm. 1959. Grosset & Dunlap.
--The Big Thornton Burgess Story Book. N.D. Little, Brown & Co.
--Billy Mink. (The Smiling Pool Ser.). N.D. Grosset & Dunlap.

--State Champs. Bolden, Joseph, illus. LC 51-9707. (Illus.). vii, 210 p. 22cm. 1951. Winston.

Burgunder, Rose

--From Summer to Summer. (Illus.). (gr. k-3). 1965. (ISBN 0-670-33152-X). Viking Pr.

Burgwyn, Mebane Holoman (1914-)

--The Crackajack Pony. Payson, Dale (1943-), illus. LC 71-82401. (Illus.). 190 p. 22cm. 1969. Lippincott.

--Hunters' Hideout. 1st ed. Mars, Witold Tadeusz J. (1912-), illus. LC 59-5799. 153p. illus. 21cm. 1959. Lippincott.

--Lucky Mischief. Howe, Gertrude Herrick (1902-), illus. 1949. E M Hale.

--Lucky Mischief. Howe, Gertrude Herrick (1902-), illus. LC 49-10305. 246 p. illus. 21 cm. (Oxford books for boys and girls.). 1949. Oxford Univ. Press.

--Moonflower. 1st ed. LC 54-878155. 186p. 21cm. (gr. 7-9). 1954. Lippincott.

--Penny Rose. LC 59-8644. 223p. 21cm. 1959, c.1952. H. Z. Walck.

--Penny Rose. LC 52-9426. 223 p. 21 cm. 1952. Oxford University Press.

--River Treasure. Ray, Ralph (1920-1952), illus. LC 47-2532. 159 p. incl. front., illus. 21 cm. 1947. Oxford University Press.

--True Love for Jenny. 1st ed. LC 56-99034. 189p. 21cm. (gr. 7-9). 1956. (ISBN 0-397-30349-1). Lippincott.

Burk, Bernadine M.

--Sweet Thang is my bloodhound. 1965. Exposition Press Inc.

Burk, William Herbert

--The Christmas Ship. LC 15-1048. 58 p. front., plates. 16 cm. 1914. Printed by the Times Publishing Co.

Burkart, Betty Lou

--Elmer, the Bucket-Mouthed Pelican. Simon, Iris, illus. (ps-1). 1977. (ISBN 0-682-48824-0). Exposition.

--Tuffy, the Purple-Footed Duck. Blumenthal, Paul, illus. (ps-1). 1976. (ISBN 0-682-48679-5). Exposition.

Burke

--Tales from the Beechy Woods. 32p. 1983. (ISBN 0-88625-044-7). EDC.

Burke, Bridget Ellen, Mrs. (1850-), intro. by see Jordan, Margaret E.

Burke, Carl Francis (1917-)

--The Boy Who Stayed Cool, and Other Stories of Young People in the Bible. LC 73-15685. 125 p. 19cm. 1973. (ISBN 0-8096-1877-X). (ISBN 0-8096-1877-X). Association Press.

--God Is Beautiful, Man. 128p. 1969. (ISBN 0-8096-1713-7, Assn Pr). (ISBN 0-8096-1720-X). Follett.

--God Is for Real, Man. 128p. (gr. 9 up). 1966. (ISBN 0-8096-1609-2, Assn Pr). (ISBN 0-8096-1612-2). Follett.

Burke, Charles O

--Anne in Africa: Stories for Young People. 1st ed. Otteson, Madalene, illus. LC 55-11823. 56p. illus. 21cm. 1955. Exposition Press.

Burke, Dorothy Preisler (1913-)

--Thanks to Letty. Howe, Gertrude Herrick (1902-), illus. LC 52-10414. 271 p. illus. 21 cm. 1952. Rand McNally.

Burke, James Wakefield

--The Golden Lure: Stories of Famous Lost Treasures. Pagram, Edward, illus. LC 64-221507. 192p. illus. 23cm. 1964. Hill & Wang.

Burke, Judy

--Migichi: Son of the Lost Empire. Powers, Richard M. Gorman (1921-), illus. LC 66-31766. 236 p. illus. 21 cm. 1967. Crowell.

Burke, Kathleen (1887-)

--Little Heroes of France. Vervees, Paul, illus. LC 20-176080. xv, 223, 1 p. incl. front., illus. 19 1/2 cm. 1920. Doubleday, Page & Company.

--Young Heroes of Britain and Belgium. Davis, Marguerite (1889-), illus. LC 21-19927. xv, 289 1 p. incl. front., plates. 19 1/2 cm. 1921. Doubleday, Page & Company.

Burke, L., Mrs., tr. see Guizot.

Burke, Rod, jt. auth. see Cooper, Margaret C.

Burke, S. J

--For Mack's Sake, 1 of 20 vols. New ed. (Illus.). 350p. (Sunday-School Lib: No. 13). 1895. Set. Lothrop Pub. Co.

Burke, Sarah J., adapted by.

--Fairy Tales for Little Readers. 133p. N.D. Parker P. Simmons.

Burke, Susan

--The Island Bike Business. (Illus.). 80p. (gr. 3-7). 1983. (ISBN 0-19-554297-5, Pub by Oxford U Pr Childrens). Merrimack Pub Cir.

Burke, Suzanne

--Ollie Owl. Jordan, Alton, ed. Reese, Bob, illus. (Illus.). (Elephant Ser.). (gr. k-3). 1975. (ISBN 0-89868-015-8, Read Res). (ISBN 0-89868-048-4). ARO Pub.

Burke, Trude

--The Wild Stranger. Brown, Paul (1893-1958), illus. LC 52-13063. (Illus.). 129 p. 21cm. 1953. Holt.

Burkes, Joyce M.

--The Word Machine, Bk. 1. Rev. ed. LC 79-67050. (Illus.). (gr. k-1). 1983. (ISBN 0-931218-02-0). Joybug.

Burkhardt, Charles B.

--Fairy Tales and Legends of Many Nations. N.D. James Miller.

--Fairy Tales, and Legends of Many Nations. Burkhardt, Charles B., tr. (Illus.). N.D. Thomas R. Knox & Co.

--Fairy Tales and Legends of Many Nations. Walcutt, W. & Cafferty, J. H., illus. LC 11-29291. 3 p. l., v-xii p., 1 l., 15-277 p. front., plates. 17 cm. 1853. C. Scribner.

Burkhardt, Charles B., tr. see Burkhardt, Charles B.

Burkholder, Mabel

--The Shield of Honor. Houy, Hartke, illus. LC 30-9470. 3-76 p. plates. 19 cm. c.1929. David C. Cook Publishing Company.

Burkholder, Ruth C.

--Mi Jun's Difficult Decision. O'Dwyer, Chung S. & Fwhang, Duk S., illus. LC 83-20494. (Illus.). 14p. (Orig.). (gr. 4-6). 1984. (ISBN 0-377-00139-2). Friend Pr.

Burks, Arthur J., jt. auth. see Butler, Smedley Darlington.

Burks, Arthur J. (1898-)

--Children of the Southern Cross. Shipman, Robert A., illus. LC 68-58846. (Illus.). ix, 132 p. 24cm. 1968. Maryknoll Publications.

Burks, Frances Williston

--Barbara's Philippine Journey. Heyer, Herman & Horter, Earl, illus. LC 15-156. 199 p. illus. 20 cm. 1913. World Book Company.

Burland, Brian Berkely (1931-)

--St. Nicholas and the Tub. Low, Joseph (1911-), illus. LC 64-57392. 1 v. (unpaged) col. illus. 26 cm. (gr. k-3). 1964. Holiday House.

--Surprise. LC 74-1878. 240p. 1975. (ISBN 0-06-010592-5, HarpT). Har-Row.

Burland, Cottie Arthur (1905-) & Forman, Werner

--Feathered Serpent & Smoking Mirror: The Gods & Cultures of Ancient Mexico. LC 75-15075. (Illus.). 128p. 1976. (ISBN 0-399-11609-5). Putnam.

Burleigh, Clare Hoyt

--A Four Leaved Clover, and Wayside Rhymes. LC 21-17416. 18cm. 57p. 1884. G. H. Ellis.

Burleigh, Clarence Blendon (1864-1910)

--All Among the Loggers: Or, Norman Carver's Winter in a Lumber Camp. Edwards, Harry C., illus. LC 8-17833. viii p., 1 l., 398 p. front., 15 pl. 20 1/2 cm. (His Norman Carver series). 1908. Lothrop, Lee & Shepard Co.

--The Camp on Letter K: Or, Two Live Boys in Northern Maine. Bridgman, Lewis Jesse (1857-1931), illus. LC 6-20852. vi p., 1 l., 383 p. front., 7 pl. 20 1/2 cm. (Raymond Benson series). 1906. Lothrop, Lee & Shepard Co.

--The Kenton Pines: Or, Raymond Benson in College. Bridgman, Lewis Jesse (1857-1931), illus. LC 7-28458. vi p., 1 l., 382 p. front., 7 pl. 21 cm. (Raymond Benson series). 1907. Lothrop, Lee & Shepard Co.

--Raymond Benson at Krampton: Or, Two Live Boys at Preparatory School. Bridgman, Lewis Jesse (1857-1931), illus. LC 7-8535. vi p., 1 l., 432 p. front., 7 pl. 20 1/2 cm. (Raymond Benson series). 1907. Lothrop, Lee & Shepard Co.

--With Pickpole and Peavey: Or, Two Live Boys on the East Branch Drive. Edwards, Harry C., illus. viii p., 1 l., 381 p. front., 15 pl. 20 1/2 cm. (His Norman Carver series). 1909. Lothrop, Lee & Shepard Co.

--The Young Guide: Or, Two Live Boys in the Maine Woods. Edwards, Harry C., illus. LC 10-20849. viii p., 1 l., 359 p. front., plates. 20 1/2 cm. (Norman Carver ser.). 1910. Lothrop, Lee & Shepard Co.

Burleigh, David Robert (1907-)

--Arrow Messenger. McCann, Gerald (1916-), illus. LC 62-13558. (Illus.). 21cm. 192p. (gr. 4-6). 1962. (ISBN 0-695-40565-9). Follett.

--Messenger from K'itai. LC 64-20341. 176 p. illus 22 cm. 1964. Follett Pub. Co.

--Piggyback. (Beginning-to-Read Ser.). (gr. k-3). 1962. (ISBN 0-695-87035-1). Follett.

--Shoofly. Abril, Ben, illus. LC 63-17799. 1963. Follett Pub. Co.

Burleson, Adele Steiner

--Toughey: Childhood Adventures on a Texas Ranch. Rice, Elizabeth (1913-), illus. LC 50-3845. 119 p. illus. (part col.) 27 cm. 1950. Steck Co.

Burleson, Elizabeth

--A Man of the Family. Stirnweis, Shannon (1931-), illus. LC 65-24231. 189 p. 23 cm. 1965. Follett Pub. Co.

--Middl'un. Roth, George (1932-), illus. LC 68-13783. (Illus.). 192 p. 23cm. 1968. Follett Pub. Co.

Burleson, Grey, et al.

--Marching Plays. Bridgman, Lewis Jesse (1857-1931), illus. N.D. DeWolfe, Fiske & Co.

Burleson, Grey & Saville, Frank E

--Marching Plays. Designed for Little Children at Home. With Suggestions to Mothers for Their Further Use in Connection with Stories, Pictures, and Drawing Lessons. Bridgman, Lewis Jesse (1857-1931), illus. LC 5-29299. 6 p. l., 17-86 p. front., illus. 25 cm. 1936. Alpha Publishing Company.

Burlingame, Cora

--Lord of London. Richards, George Mather (1880-), illus. LC 44-8725. ix, 291, 1 p. incl. front., illus. 20 cm. 1944. D. Appleton-Century Company, Incorporated.

Burlingame, Eugene Watson (1876-)

--The Grateful Elephant: And Other Stories Translated from the Pali. Lathrop, Dorothy Pulis (1891-1980), illus. LC 23-16075. xxxv, 172 p. col. front., plates. 26 cm. 1923. Yale University Press; Etc., Etc.

Burlingame, Roger (1889-1967)

--General Billy Mitchell: Champion of Air Defense. N.D. Whittlesey House.

--Mosquitoes in the Big Ditch: The Story of the Panama Canal. 1st ed. Tee-Van, Helen Damrosch (1893-1976), illus. LC 52-5486. 177 p. illus. 22 cm. (Winston adventure books). 1952. Winston.

--Whittling Boy: The Story of Eli Whitney. LC 41-51519. viii p., 2 l., 3-370 p. illus. 22 cm. c.1941. Harcourt, Brace and Company.

Burlingame, Virginia Struble

--Larry Two-Feathers. Scott, James A., illus. LC 67-15862. 126 p. illus. 21 cm. 1967. Bethany Press.

Burlingame, Virginia Struble see Struble, Virginia.

Burlingham, Mary, jt. auth. see Steiner, Charlotte.

Burman, Alice Caddy see Govan, Christine Noble, Mrs.

Burman, Ben Lucien (1895-1984)

--Blow a Wild Bugle for Catfish Bend. Caddy, Alice, pseud. (1896-1977), illus. Burman, Alice Caddy. LC 77-14331. p. cm. 1977, c.1967. Puffin Books.

--Blow a Wild Bugle for Catfish Bend. Caddy, Alice, pseud. (1896-1977), illus. Burman, Alice Caddy. LC 67-12429. (Illus.). 120 p. 21cm. 1967. Taplinger Pub. Co.

--Blow a Wild Bugle for Catfish Bend. Caddy, Alice, pseud. (1896-1977), illus. Burman, Alice Caddy. LC 67-12429. (Illus.). 120 p. 21cm. 1967. Taplinger Pub. Co.

--Blow for a Landing. 240 p. 18cm. (Mockingbird book). 1974, c.1965. (ISBN 0-345-24072-3). Ballantine Books.

--Children of Noah. N.D. (ISBN 0-685-02658-2). Taplinger.

--High Treason at Catfish Bend. Caddy, Alice, pseud. (1896-1977), illus. Burman, Alice Caddy. LC 78-59685. (Illus., Pub. by Vanguard). (Puffin Story Bks). (gr. 2-5). 1978. (ISBN 0-14-031130-0, Puffin). Penguin.

--High Water at Catfish Bend. Burman, Alice Caddy. 1963. Macmillan Company.

--High Water at Catfish Bend. Caddy, Alice, pseud. (1896-1977), illus. Burman, Alice Caddy. LC 52-9138. 121 p. illus. 21 cm. 1952. J. Messner.

--High Water at Catfish Bend. Caddy, Alice, pseud. (1896-1977), illus. Burman, Alice Caddy. LC 77-1392000005. (Illus.). 123 p. 20cm. (Puffin book). 1974, c.1952. (ISBN 0-14-030711-7). Penguin.

--High Water at Catfish Bend. Caddy, Alice, pseud., illus. Burman, Alice Caddy. N.D. Taplinger Publishing Company.

--Owl Hoots Twice at Catfish Bend. 1963. Macmillan Company.

--The Owl Hoots Twice at Catfish Bend. Caddy, Alice, pseud. (1896-1977), illus. Burman, Alice Caddy. (Illus.). 117 p. 20cm. (Puffin book). 1974, c.1961. (ISBN 0-14-030397-9). Penguin Books.

--The Owl Hoots Twice at Catfish Bend. Caddy, Alice, pseud. (1896-1977), illus. Burman, Alice Caddy. LC 77-14015. p. cm. 1977, c.1961. Penguin Books.

--The Owl Hoots Twice at Catfish Bend. Caddy, Alice, pseud. (1896-1977), illus. Burman, Alice Caddy. LC 61-6672. (Illus.). 115 p. 21cm. 1961. Taplinger Pub. Co.

--Seven Stars for Catfish Bend. 1963. Macmillan Company.

--Seven Stars for Catfish Bend. Caddy, Alice, pseud. (1896-1977), illus. Burman, Alice Caddy. LC 56-7770. (Illus.). 133 p. 21cm. 1956. Funk & Wagnalls.

--Seven Stars for Catfish Bend. Caddy, Alice, pseud. (1896-1977), illus. Burman, Alice Caddy. LC 77-1432. (Illus.). 134 p. 20cm. 1977, c.1956. Puffin Books.

--Steamboat Round the Bend. 1962. Macmillan Company.

--The Strange Invasion of Catfish Bend. Caddy, Alice, pseud. (1896-1977), illus. Burman, Alice Caddy. LC 79-67487. (Illus.). 153 p. 21cm. c.1980. (ISBN 0-8149-0828-4). Vanguard Press.

--Street of the Laughing Camel. N.D. Taplinger Publishing Company.

--Three from Catfish Bend. Caddy, Alice, pseud. (1896-1977), illus. Burman, Alice Caddy. Incl. High Water at Catfish Bend; Seven Stars for Catfish Bend; The Owl Hoots Twice at Catfish Bend. Burman, Alice. LC 67-12490. (Illus.). (gr. 6 up). N.D. (ISBN 0-8008-7676-8). Taplinger.

--Thunderbolt at Catfish Bend. Caddy, Alice, pseud. (1896-1977), illus. Burman, Alice Caddy. (Illus.). 114p. (Catfish Bend Ser.). 1984. (ISBN 0-914373-00-5, Dist. by Vanguard). (ISBN 0-943436-03-6). Wieser & Wieser.

Burman, Edor (1913-)

--The Bears of Big Stream Valley. Wiberg, Harald Albin (1908-), illus. Bothmer, Gerry, tr. LC 68-14981. (Illus.). 179 p. 22cm. (Seymour Lawrence book.). 1968. Delacorte Press.

--Three Wolverines of Rushing Valley. Wiberg, Harald Albin (1908-), illus. Macmillan, Annabelle, pseud. (1922-), tr. from Swedish. Quick, Annabelle. LC 66-11380. (Illus.). 160 p. 25cm. 1966. Dutton.

Burmeister, Laura E.

--Hulda The Cow of Cordova and Double-Nine. N.D. Pageant Press INC.

Burn, Doris, jt. auth. see Brand, Oscar.

Burn, Doris (1923-)

--Andrew Henry's Meadow. Burn, Doris (1923-), illus. LC 65-20384. (Illus.). 1 v. (unpaged. 27cm. 1965. Coward-McCann.

--The Summerfolk. Burn, Doris (1923-), illus. LC 68-23862. (Illus.). 47 p. 25cm. 1968. Coward-McCann.

Burnelli, Vincent, jt. auth. see Twain, Mark.

Burnett, Carol, ed.

--Dear Carol Burnett: A Collection of Children's Poems Sent to Carol Burnett. LC 71-167519. (Illus.). 1 v. (unpaged. 22cm. 1971. (ISBN 0-8402-1211-9). Nash Pub.

Burnett, Carolyn Judson

--The Blue Grass Seminary Girls in the Mountains: Or, Shirley Willing on a Mission of Peace. (The Blue Grass Seminary Girls Ser.). N.D. A. L. Burt Company.

--The Blue Grass Seminary Girls on the Water: Or, Exciting Adventures on a Summer's Cruise through the Panama Canal. (The Blue Grass Seminary Girls Ser.). N.D. A. L. Burt Company.

--The Blue Grass Seminary Girls' Vacation Adventures: Or, Shirley Willing to the Rescue. (The Blue Grass Seminary Girls Ser.). N.D. A. L. Burt Company.

Burnett, Constance Buel (1893-)

--Let the Best Boat Win. (Illus.). 1957. Houghton Mifflin.

--Lucretia Mott: Girl of Old Nantucket. Goldstein, Nathan (1927-), illus. LC 62-16602. 200p. col. illus. 20cm. (Childhood of famous Amers.). N.D. Bobbs.

--Lucretia Mott, Girl of Old Nantucket. 1st ed. James, Sandra, illus. LC 51-12440. 192 p. illus. 20 cm. (Childhood of famous Americans series). 1951. Bobbs-Merrill.

--The Silver Answer: A Romantic Biography of Elizabeth Barrett Browning. 1955. Alfred A Knopf : distributed by Bonzoi Books.

Burnett, E. L.

--A Missionary Twig, 1 of 25 vols. 199p. (Golden Rod Library). 1905. American Tract Society.

--Missionary Twig, 1 of 50 vols. (The Golden Rod Lib.). N.D. Set. American Tract Society.

Burnett, Elizabeth, jt. auth. see Martin, Florence Marie.

Burnett, Frances Hodgson, Mrs., et al. (1849-1924), eds.

--The Children's Book. Nosworthy, Florence England, illus. 1915. Cupples & Leon Co.

Burnett, Frances Hodgson, Mrs. (1849-1924)

--Barty Crusoe and his Man Saturday. N.D. Dodd Mead & Co.

--Barty Crusoe and His Man Saturday. Sichel, Harold M. (1881-), illus. LC 9-29774. vii p., 1 l., 231 p. incl. pl. col. fro,t., plates (part col.) 21 cm. $1.0. 1909. Moffat, Yard and Company.

--The Cozy Lion: As Told by Queen Crosspatch. LC 22-2949. 104, 1 p. incl. col. front., col. plates. 16 1/2 cm. 1917. The Century Co.

--The Cozy Lion: As Told by Queen Crosspatch. Cady, Walter Harrison (1877-1970), illus. LC 7-29094. 104, 1 p. incl. col. front., col. plates. 16 1/2 cm. 1907. The Century Co.

--The Dawn of To-Morrow. Yohn, F. C., illus. 1906. Charles Scribner's Sons.

--Editha's Burglar, 25 vols. (Illus.). (The Editha Ser.: No. 1). 1905. Set. H M Caldwell Co.

--Editha's Burglar. (Illus.). (The Young Folks Lib.). N.D. H. M. Caldwell Co.

--Editha's Burglar. (Illus.). (The Empyreal Library of Handy Volume Classics). N.D. H. M. Caldwell & Co.

--Editha's Burglar. Baby Peggy ed. LC 25-15123. x, 64 p. front., illus., plates. 23 cm. c.1925. L. C. Page & Company.

--Granpa. Burningham, John Mackintosh (1936-), illus. LC 84-17464. p. cm. 1985, c.1984. (ISBN 0-517-55643-X). Crown. **Award: (NYT).**
--Harquin: The Fox Who Went Down to the Valley. Burningham, John Mackintosh (1936-), illus. LC 68-11884. (Illus.). 32 p. 27cm. 1968, c.1967. Bobbs-Merrill.
--Harquin: The Fox Who Went Down to the Valley. Burningham, John MacKintosh (1936-), illus. 1979. Jonathan Cape.
--Humbert, Mister Firkin & the Lord Mayor of London. Burningham, John Mackintosh (1936-), illus. LC 68-1228. (Illus.). 27cm. 32p. 1st U.S. edition. (gr. k-3). 1967, c.1965. (ISBN 0-672-50322-0). Bobbs-Merrill.
--Humbert, Mister Firkin & the Lord Mayor of London. Burningham, John MackinTosh (1936-), illus. (Illus.). 32 p. 27cm. 1st U.S. edition. 1967, c.1965. Bobbs-Merrill.
--Jungleland. Burningham, John Mackintosh (1936-), illus. N.D. George Braziller, Inc.
--Lionland. Burningham, John Mackintosh (1936-), illus. N.D. George Braziller, Inc.
--Mr. Gumpy's Motor Car. Burningham, John Mackintosh (1936-), illus. LC 75-4582. (Illus.). 32 p. 26cm. 1976, c.1973. (ISBN 0-690-00798-1). Crowell.
--Mr. Gumpy's Motor Car. Burningham, John Mackintosh (1936-), illus. LC 74-20512. p. cm. 1975, c.1973. (ISBN 0-02-716200-1). Macmillan.
--Mr. Gumpy's Motor Carr. Burningham, John Mackintosh (1936-), illus. 1976. Harper.
--Mr. Gumpy's Outing. Burningham, John Mackintosh (1936-), illus. LC 77-159507. (Illus.). 32 p. 26cm. 1971. (ISBN 0-03-086612-X). (ISBN 0-03-086613-8). Holt, Rinehart and Winston. **Awards: (NYT); (BGH); (ALA); (KGM).**
--Mr. Gumpy's Outing. Burningham, John Mackintosh (1936-), illus. (Illus.). (ps). N.D. (ISBN 0-317-13465-5, Puffin). Penguin.
--The Rabbit. Burningham, John Mackintosh (1936-), illus. LC 75-4566. p. cm. 1975. (ISBN 0-690-00906-2). (ISBN 0-690-00907-0). Crowell.
--The School. Burningham, John Mackintosh (1936-), illus. LC 75-4611. p. cm. 1975. (ISBN 0-690-00902-X). (ISBN 0-690-00903-8). Crowell.
--Seasons. Burningham, John Mackintosh (1936-), illus. 1970. Bobbs-Merrill.
--The Shopping Basket. Burningham, John Mackintosh (1936-), illus. LC 80-7987. (Illus.). 32p. (ps-2). 1980. (ISBN 0-690-04082-2, TYC-J). (ISBN 0-690-04083-0). Har-Row.
--The Snow. Burningham, John Mackintosh (1936-), illus. LC 75-2492. (Illus.). 20 p. 17cm. 1975, c.1974. (ISBN 0-690-00904-6). (ISBN 0-690-00905-4). Crowell.
--Storyland. Burningham, John Mackintosh (1936-), illus. N.D. George Braziller Inc.
--Time to Get Out of the Bath, Shirley. Burningham, John Mackintosh (1936-), illus. LC 76-58503. (Illus.). 25 p. c.1978. (ISBN 0-690-01378-7). (ISBN 0-690-01379-5). Crowell.
--Trubloff: The Mouse Who Wanted to Play the Balalaika. Burningham, John Mackintosh (1936-), illus. LC 65-18166. (ps). 1965. (ISBN 0-394-91775-8, BYR). Random.
--Trubloff: The Mouse Who Wanted to Play the Balalaika. Burningham, John Mackintosh (1936-), illus. LC 65-18166. (Illus.). 41 p. 27cm. 1965, c.1964. Random House.
--Wonderland. Burningham, John Mackintosh (1936-), illus. N.D. George Brazziller Inc.
--Would You Rather ... Burningham, John Mackintosh (1936-), illus. LC 78-7088. (Illus.). 32 p. 30cm. c.1978. (ISBN 0-690-03917-4). (ISBN 0-690-03918-2). Crowell.
--Would You Rather. Burningham, John Mackintosh (1936-), illus. (ps-2). 1978. Harper & Row.

Burns, Anna L., ed.
--The Roger Books. 1910. Set. A. W. Wilde.

Burns, Bess Hughes
--Cat Tales. LC 39-271042. 48 p. 20 cm. c.1938. The Story Book Press.

Burns, Catherine
--The Winter Bird. Wong, Pamela Evan, illus. LC 70-148399. (Illus.). 32 p. 24cm. 1971. (ISBN 0-87807-020-6). Windmill Books.

Burns, Colette Marie Wagner, Mrs. (1898-) & Kolsbun, Robert (1897-)
--The Animal Fair. LC 35-19151. 95 p. incl. front., illus. 19 x 19 cm. c.1935. Harcourt, Brace and Company.

Burns, Esther
--Mrs. Peregrine and the Yak. Wilkin, Eloise (1904-), illus. LC 38-32607. 58 p. illus. (part col.) 19 cm. c.1938. Ph. Holt and Company.
--Mrs. Peregrine at the Fair. Wilkin, Eloise (1904-), illus. LC 39-17235. 55 p. col. illus. 19 cm. c.1939. J. Messner, Inc.

Burns, George S
--The Strange Adventures of Roger Ward. Allen, Thomas Burt (1928-), illus. LC 80-16967. (Illus.). 46 p. 26cm. c.1981. (ISBN 0-698-20495-6). Coward, McCann & Geoghegan.

Burns, Marilyn
--The Hink Pink Book, or, What Do You Call a Magician's Extra Bunny?. Weston, Martha, illus. LC 81-13638. (Illus.). 48 p. 20cm. (gr. 1 up). c.1981. (ISBN 0-316-11744-7, Pub. by Atlantic Press). (ISBN 0-316-11744-7). Little, Brown.

Burns, Nora
--Jamie. LC 48-17429. 20cm. 87p. N.D. Wm. B. Eerdmans Publishing Co.

Burns, Robert (1759-1796)
--Hand in Hand We'll Go. Hogrogian, Nonny (1932-), illus. LC 65-18692. (Illus.). 28p. illus. 22cm. (gr. 4 up). 1965. (ISBN 0-690-36668-X). T Y Crowell. **Award: (ALA).**
--Poems and Songs. Barke, Jas, ed. Barke, Jas., intro. by. N.D. William Collins Sons & Co.
--Poems of Robert Burns. (gr. 10 up). N.D. Pyramid Pubns.
--Poems of Robert Burns. Frankenberg, Lloyd, ed. Low, Joseph (1911-), illus. LC 67-18513. (Illus.). (Poets Ser). (gr. 7 up). 1967. (ISBN 0-690-63152-9, TYC-J). T Y Crowell.

Burns, Sheila L.
--A Christmas Carol. LC 78-72141. (Illus.). (gr. 2-5). N.D. Dandelion Pr.

Burns, Tex, pseud., see L'Amour, Louis.

Burns, Tex, pseud. (1908-)
--Hopalong Cassidy and the Rustlers of West Fork. L'Amour, Louis. (Young Moderns Edition). 1951. Doubleday & Co.

Burns, Thomas
--Terrence O'Hara. Birch, Reginald Bathurst (1856-1943), illus. LC 39-27849. (Illus.). 3 p.l., 3-155 p. 24cm. c.1939. Harcourt, Brace and Company.

Burnside
--Only a Doll: Book in the Shape of a Doll. N.D. Raphael Tuck & Sons.

Burnside, H. M.
--A Story of a Birthday. Cooper, Alfred W & Evans, Edmund (1826-1905), illus. (Illus., Pub. by Society for Promoting Christian Knowledge). N.D. E & J B Young.

Burnside, Marion Helen
--Golden Days and Silver Eves. Goodman, Maude & Havers, Alice, illus. (No. 81). N.D. Raphael Tuck & Sons.

Burow, Daniel R. (1931-)
--Plattertales. Incl. Bushy-Tailed Helper. (ISBN 0-570-07021-X, 56-1162); Say & Do Thanks. (ISBN 0-570-07022-8, 56-1163); Conrad the Cobbler. (ISBN 0-570-07025-2, 56-1166); The Valley That Didn't Wake. (ISBN 0-570-07026-0, 56-1167); Little King of All. (ISBN 0-570-07024-4, 56-1165); Lester the Jester. (ISBN 0-570-07023-6, 56-1164). 16p. (ps-3). 1974. Concordia.
--Sound of the Bugle: The Adventures of Hans Schmidt. Barry F. Smith and Associates, ed. LC 72-91152. (Illus.). 215 p. 22cm. (gr. 6-9). 1973. (ISBN 0-570-03145-1). Concordia Pub. House.

Burr, Amelia Josephine
--A Child Garden in India: For Very Little People. Clark, Louise, illus. LC 22-18656. 76 p. 1 l., incl. plates (part col.) 15 1/2 cm. c.1922. Central Committee on the United Study of Foreign Missions.

Burr, Betty J.
--Outer Limits of the Mind. Maccabe, Richard D., illus. (Illus., Orig.). (Pal Paperbacks Kit B Ser.). (gr. 7-12). 1974. (ISBN 0-8374-3513-7). Xerox Ed Pubns.

Burr, E. F.
--Sunday Afternoons. N.D. Nelson & Phillips.
--Sunday Afternoons: A Book for Little People. N.D. Publications of the Methodist Book Concern.
--Thy Voyage: Or, A Song of the Sea and, Other Poems. N.D. Methodist Book Concern.

Burr, Hanford Montrose (1864-)
--Around the Fire. LC 12-8837. 17cm. 238p. N.D. Association Press.
--Calling of Boyman. N.D. Association Press.
--Cave Boys. LC 23-9487. 6 p. l., 3-200 p. illus. 19 1/2 cm. 1923. Association Press.
--Every Boy. N.D. Association Press.
--Tales of Telal. N.D. Association Press.

Burr, M. P.
--The Australian Chicken. N.D. Carlton.

Burr, Sybil
--Highland Fling. LC 57-56110. 224p. 21cm. 1957, c.1956. Westminster Press.
--Night Train to Scotland. LC 56-5108. 208p. 21cm. c.1956. Westminster Press.

Burrage, Charles Dana (1857-)
--Stories for Martha Elizabeth. LC 22-932. 32p. front. 23 1/2cm. c.1921. Rosemary press.

Burrage, Edwin Harcourt (1839-1916)
--The Twin Castaways. (Illus.). 1900. Thomas Nelson & Sons.

Burrell, David De Forest (1876-)
--Three Little Angels. LC 31-34927. 30 p. 19 cm. c.1931. Fleming H. Revell Company.

Burrell, Kathleen Joan see Alleyne, Margaret, pseud.

Burrell, Kathleen Joan (1909-)
--The Pig Who Was Too Thin. Alleyne, Margaret, pseud. Webb, Clifford Cyril (1895-1972), illus. LC 47-30867. 71 p. illus. (part col.) 21 cm. 1947. F. Warne.

Burress, John
--Apple on Pear Tree. Gannett, Lewis, illus. N.D. Vanguard Press.
--Little Mule. N.D. The Vanguard Press.
--The Missouri Traveler. N.D. Vanguard Press.
--Punkin Summer. Moynihan, Roberta, illus. LC 57-7686. 212p. illus. 21cm. (gr. 7up). 1957. (ISBN 0-8149-0285-5). Vanguard Press.

Burrill, Edgar White
--Master Skylark. N.D. Appleton Century Co.

Burris, Jim
--Spotted Pony & the Manitou. (Illus.). 32p. (gr. 3-6). 1985. (ISBN 0-89962-446-4). Todd & Honeywell.

Burriss, Genevieve Thomas (1881-)
--Blossoms on the Straight Ahead Road: A Primer for Democracy. 5th ed. Hartman, Violet Thomas, illus. LC 49-7032. 126p. illus. 19cm. 1949, c.1948. Allan Publication.

Burritt, Edwin C.
--The Boy Scout Crusoes: A Tale of the South Seas. Louderback, Walt, illus. LC 16-22848. 280 p. front., 1 illus., plates. 20 1/2 cm. $1.2. c.1916. Fleming H. Revell Company.
--Cameron Island: Further Adventures in the South Seas. Louderback, Walt, illus. 255 p. front., illus., plates. 20 1/2 c. c.1918. Fleming H. Revell Company.

Burrough, Ruth J
--From Snow to Sun: A Mystery Story for Boys. LC 38-24912. 3 p. l., 227 p. illus. 20 1/2 cm. 1938. Longmans, Green and Co.
--Mystery House. Townsend, Lee (1895-), illus. LC 33-21519. vii p., 1 l., 228 p. incl. front., illus. plates. 19 1/2 cm. 1933. Longmans, Green and Co.
--Smiley Adams. N.D. Grosset & Dunlap.
--Smiley Adams. Avison, George F. (1885-), illus. LC 31-244442. vii p., 1 l., 244 p. incl. front., illus. plates. 20 1/2 cm. 1931. Longmans, Green and Co.

Burroughes, Dorothy Mary Burroughes
--The Amazing Adventures of Little Brown Bear. Burroughes, Dorothy Mary Burroughes, illus. viii, 1-3, 1 p. incl. front., illus. 10 cm. 1930. Harper & Brothers Publisher.
--Jack Rabbit, Detective: Or, The Great Pearl Mystery. Burroughes, Dorothy Mary Burroughes, illus. LC 31-33117. (Illus.). vii, 126, 2 p. 16cm. 1931. Methuen & Co., Ltd.
--The Journeyings of Selina Squirrel and Her Friends. Burroughes, Dorothy Mary Burroughes, illus. LC 31-20193. vii, 126 p. incl. front., illus. 16 cm. 1931. Harper & Brothers.

Burroughs, Dwight
--Jack, the Giant Killer, Jr: Being the Thrilling Adventures, Authentically Told, of a Worthy Son of the Celebrated Jack, the Giant Killer. Knipe, Helen Alden & Abbott, Elenore Plaisted, illus. LC 7-31422. 203 p. col. front., 10 col. pl. 23 cm. 1907. G. W. Jacobs & Company.

Burroughs, Edgar Rice (1875-1950)
--At the Earth's Core. St. John, J. Allen, illus. (Popular Copyright Ser.). 1922. A C McClurg.
--The Beasts of Tarzan. (Tarzar Bks.). N.D. Grosset & Dunlap.
--The Beasts of Tarzan. St. John, J. Allen, illus. 1916. A. C. McClurg.
--The Gods of Mars. N.D. Canveral Press.
--The Gods of Mars. St. John, J. Allen, illus. 1918. A. C. McClurg.
--Jungle Tales of Tarzan. (gr. 7 up). N.D. (ISBN 0-448-02630-9). G&D.
--Jungle Tales of Tarzan. St. John, J. Allen, illus. 1919. A. C. McClurg.
--The Land That Time Forgot. N.D. Canaveral Press.
--The Land that Time Forgot. St. John, J. Allen, illus. (Popular Copyright Ser.). 1924. A C McClurg.
--Mad King. St. JOhn, J. Allen, illus. 1926. A. C. McClurg & Co.
--Master Mind of Mars. 1928. A. C. McClurg & Co.
--Monster Men. 1926. A. C. McClurg & Co.
--Monster Men. N.D. Canaveral Press.
--Moon Maid. 1926. A. C. McClurg & Co.
--The Moon Men Moon Maid. N.D. Canaveral Press.
--The Mucker. N.D. Canaveral Press.
--The Mucker. St. John, J. Allen, illus. 1921. A. C. McClurg.
--Outlaw of Torn. 1927. A. C. McClurg & Co.
--Pellucidar. N.D. Canaveral Press.
--Pellucidar: Sequel to At the Earths Core. St. John, J. Allen, illus. (Popular Copyright Ser.). 1923. A C McClurg.
--A Princess of Mars. Schoonover, Frank Earle (1877-1972), illus. 1917. A. C. McClurg.
--Return of Tarzan. (gr. 7 up). N.D. (ISBN 0-448-02631-7). G&D.
--The Return of Tarzan. St. John, J. Allen, illus. 1915. A. C. McClurg.
--Savage Pellucidar. N.D. Canaveral Press.
--The Son of Tarzan. (The Tarzan Bks.). N.D. Grosset & Dunlap.
--The Son of Tarzan. St. John, J. Allen, illus. 1917. A. C. McClurg.
--Tales of Three Planets. N.D. Canveral Press.
--Tanar of Pellucidar. N.D. Canaveral Press.
--Tarzan & the Ant-Men. (Popular Copyright Ser.). 1924. A C McClurg.
--Tarzan and the Ant Men. (gr. 7 up). N.D. (ISBN 0-448-02632-5). G&D.
--Tarzan and the Castaways. N.D. Canaveral Press.
--Tarzan and the Golden Lion. (gr. 7 up). N.D. (ISBN 0-448-02633-3). G&D.
--Tarzan & the Golden Lion. St. John, J. Allen, illus. (Popular Copyright Ser.). 1923. A C McClurg.
--Tarzan and the Jewels. St. John, J. Allen, illus. 1918. A. C. McClurg.
--Tarzan and the Jewels of Opar. (gr. 7 up). N.D. (ISBN 0-448-02634-1). G&D.
--Tarzan and the Madman. N.D. Canaveral Press.
--Tarzan and the Tarzan Twins. N.D. Canaveral Press.
--Tarzan at The Earth's Core. N.D. Canaveral Press.
--Tarzan, Lord of the Jungle. (gr. 7 up). N.D. (ISBN 0-448-02637-6). G&D.
--Tarzan, Lord of the Jungle. St. John, J. Allen, illus. 1928. A. C. McClurg & Co.
--Tarzan of the Apes. Gaydos, Tim, illus. Woods, Harold (1945-), adapted by. LC 81-19873. (Illus.). 96p. (Step-up Adventures Ser.: No. 4). (gr. 2-5). 1982. (ISBN 0-394-95089-5). (ISBN 0-394-85089-0). Random.
--Tarzan of the Apes. St. John, J. Allen, illus. 1914. A. C. McClurg.
--Tarzan of the Apes. Thorne, Alica (1910-1973), ed. (Tarzan Series). (gr. 6 up). 1968. (ISBN 0-448-02638-4). G&D.
--Tarzan the Terrible. (gr. 7 up). N.D. (ISBN 0-448-02635-X). G&D.
--Tarzan the Terrible. St. John, J. Allen, illus. 1920. A. C. McClurg.
--Tarzan the Untamed. (gr. 7 up). N.D. (ISBN 0-448-02636-8). G&D.
--Tarzan the Untamed. St. John, J. Allen, illus. N.D. A. C. McClurg.
--The Tarzan Twins. Grant, Douglas, illus. LC 27-232811. 126 p. illus. (part col.) 21 1/2 cm. (Lettered on cover: Volland Golden youth series). c.1927. The P. F. Volland Company.
--Thuvia, Maid of Mars. St. JOhn, J. Allen, illus. 1921. A. C. McClurg.
--The War Chief. LC 27-21142. 4 p. l., 382 p. 19 1/2 cm. 1927. A. C. McClurg & Co.
--The Warlord of Mars. St. John, J. Allen, illus. 1919. A. C. McClurg.

Burroughs, John
--Bird Stories from Burroughs. N.D. Hohgton Mifflin Co.

Burroughs, Margaret Taylor see Taylor, Margaret.

Burroughs, Margaret Taylor see Taylor, Margaret.

Burroughs, Margaret Taylor (1917-)
--Jasper, the Drummin' Boy. Rev. Ed. ed. Lewin, Ted (1935-), illus. LC 69-15984. (Illus.). 63 p. 22cm. 1970. Follett Pub. Co.

Burroughs, Margaret Taylor (1917-), ed.
--Did You Feed My Cow. rev. ed. De Velasco, Joe E., illus. LC 69-15980. (Illus.). line drawings. ca. 96p. (ps up). 1969. (ISBN 0-695-81960-7). Follett.

Burroughs, Polly, jt. auth. see Beaufoy-Lane, H. J.

Burroughs, Polly (1925-)
--The Honey Boat. Price, Garrett W. (1896-1979), illus. LC 68-14746. (Illus.). 43 p. 22cm. 1968. Little, Brown.

Burroway, Janet Gay, jt. auth. see Lord, John Vernon.

Burroway, Janet Gay (1936-)
--The Truck on the Track. Lord, John Vernon (1939-), illus. LC 78-142441. (Illus.). 32 p. 1971, c.1970. Bobbs-Merrill.

Burrowes, Elisabeth
--Good Night. Paflin, Roberta, pseud. (1903-), illus. Petty, Roberta Harris Pfafflin. LC 54-37052. unpaged. illus. 17cm. (Fuzzy wuzzy book). c.1954. Whitman Pub. Co.
--Little Thunder. Paflin, Roberta, pseud. (1903-), illus. Petty, Roberta Harris Pfafflin. LC 45-5192. 28 p. col. illus. 24 cm. 1945. E. P. Dutton & Co., Inc.
--A Sleepy Story. Brown, Richard Eric (1946-), illus. LC 81-86499. (Illus.). 24 p. 16cm. (First little Golden book). c.1982. (ISBN 0-307-68135-1). (ISBN 0-307-10135-5). Golden Press.

AUTHOR INDEX

BURTON, HAL

Burrows, Cecille Miller
--Clowns of the World: A Collection of Clowns and Verses. Burrows, Tristram Zachary, illus. LC 80-119873. (Illus.). 41 p. 29cm. 1980, c.1978. (ISBN 0-87359-015-5). Northwood Institute.
Burrows, Denys
--Clipper Ship. (Illus.). 182p. 1965. Tri-Ocean Books.
--Fight for Gold. LC 66-78241. 158p. illus. 23cm. 1966. Educational Pr.
Burrows, Edith Maie, Mrs. (1887-) & Henderson, Gertrude (1888-)
--Cheery Comedies for Christmas: A Collection of Plays, Pantomimes, Tableaux, Readings, Recitations, Illustrated Poems, Etc., Suitable for Use at Christmas. LC 15-20613. 25, 16, 15, 73 p. 18 1/2 cm. 1915. W. H. Baker & Co.
Burrows, Elizabeth
--Irene of Tundra Towers. Daugherty, James Henry (1889-1974), illus. 1928. Doubleday Doran & Co.
--Judy of the Whale Gates: The Strange Happenings That Followed the Stranding of the Yacht Aphoon Among the Volcanic Islands of Alaska. Daugherty, James Henry (1889-1974), illus. LC 30-10976. 5 p. l., 296 p. col. front., illus. 21 cm. N.D. Doubleday Doran & Company, Inc.,.
Burrows, Peggy
--The Bears' Picnic. Carlson, Charlotte, illus. LC 54-31288. unpaged. illus. 17cm. (Rand McNally book-elf junior, 686). c.1954. Rand McNally.
--Bunny Tales. 1956. (ISBN 0-8382-1045-7, Hale Giant Bks.). E. M. Hale and Co.
--Bunny Tales. Endres, Helen Elise & Neebe, William, illus. LC 76-91709. (Illus.). 21 p. 33cm. (Rand McNally giant book). 1956. Rand McNally.
--Bunny Tales. Webbe, Elizabeth, illus. LC 56-11565. unpaged. illus. 22cm. (Rand McNally elf book, 577). c.1956. Rand McNally.
--The Enchanted Egg. Webbe, Elizabeth, illus. LC 56-12102. unpaged. illus. 22cm. (Rand McNally elf book, 577). c.1956. Rand McNally.
--Enchanted Egg. Webbe, Elizabeth, illus. (Storytime Books Ser). (ps-2). 1958. Rand.
--Kittens & Puppies. (Illus.). (gr. k-2). 1955. (ISBN 0-8382-0411-2). Hale.
--Kittens and Puppies: Verses. LC 55-12056. unpaged. illus. 21cm. (Rand NcNally Elf Book). c.1955. Rand McNally.
--Kittens and Puppies: Verses. LC 58-9646. unpaged. illus. 33cm. (Rand McNally giant book). 1960, c.1955. Rand McNally.
Burstall, Tim
--Sebastian and the Sausages. Vandenberg, Gerard, photos by. LC 66-74701. 1 v. (unpaged) illus. 26cm. (gr. 4 up). 1965. (ISBN 0-392-04506-0, ABC). Lansdowne, Stamped on P. : Dist. by Sportshelf.
Burstein, Abraham, tr. see Levin, Ali.
Burstein, Abraham (1893-)
--Adventure on Manhattan Island: The Story of Hillel and His Encounter with Peter Stuyvesant and the Indians. LC 58-1389. 128p. illus. 23cm. c.1957. J. David Co.
--A Jewish Child's Garden of Verses. Eckman, Dorothy, illus. LC 40-13274. x, 106 p. illus. 23 x 14 1/2 cm. 1940. Bloch Publishing Company.
Burstein, Chaya M.
--Hanukkah Cat. Bernstein, Chaya M., illus. LC 85-14760. p. cm. 1985. (ISBN 0-930494-48-2). Kar-Ben Copies, Inc.
--Joseph & Anna's Time Capsule: A Legacy of Old Jewish Prague. Edwards, Nancy, illus. (Illus.). 32p. 1984. (ISBN 0-318-00228-0). Summit Bks.
--Rifka Bangs the Teakettle. Burstein, Chaya M., illus. LC 79-91068. (Illus.). 191 p. 21cm. 1970. Harcourt, Brace & World.
--Rifka Grows up. Burstein, Chaya M., illus. LC 76-41412. p. cm. c.1976. (ISBN 0-88482-906-5). Bonim Books.
Burstein, John (1949-)
--The Get-Well Hotel. Durrell, Julie, illus. Dian, Russell, photos by. LC 80-14912. p. cm. 1980. (ISBN 0-07-009244-3). McGraw-Hill.
--Lucky You!. Durrell, Julie & Kirouac, J. Paul, illus. LC 80-14641. (Illus.). 32p. (ps-3). 1980. (ISBN 0-07-009243-5). McGraw.
Burt, Denise
--I Love My Grandma. North American ed. Bartram, Haworth, photos by. LC 85-16323. p. cm. (Growing up). 1985. (ISBN 0-918831-41-5). (ISBN 0-918831-19-9). Gareth Stevens Pub.
--Meet My Friends. U. S. ed. Bartram, Haworth, photos by. LC 85-17389. p. cm. (Growing up). 1985. (ISBN 0-918831-43-1). (ISBN 0-918831-20-2). G. Stevens.
--Our Family Vacation. North American ed. Bartram, Haworth, photos by. LC 85-17388. p. cm. 1985. (ISBN 0-918831-39-3). (ISBN 0-918831-29-6). G. Stevens.
Burt, Katharine Newlin (1882-)
--Girl on a Broomstick. Cather, Carolyn, illus. LC 67-4050. (Illus.). 124 p. 21cm. 1967. Funk & Wagnalls.
--One Silver Spur. Cather, Carolyn, illus. LC 68-27994. (Illus.). 93 p. 22cm. 1968. Funk & Wagnalls.
--Smarty. Donahue, Vic, illus. LC 65-19338. 126p. illus. 21cm. (gr. 3-7). 1965. (ISBN 0-308-80020-6). Funk & Wagnalls.
Burt, Mary Elizabeth, jt. auth. see Custer, George A., Mrs.
Burt, Mary Elizabeth, ed. see Amicis, Edmondo de.
Burt, Mary Elizabeth, ed. see Cable, George Washington.
Burt, Mary Elizabeth, ed. see Cervantes Saavedra, Miguel de.
Burt, Mary Elizabeth, ed. see Field, Eugene.
Burt, Mary Elizabeth, ed. see Homerus.
Burt, Mary Elizabeth, ed. see Howells, William Dean.
Burt, Mary Elizabeth, ed. see Kipling, Joseph Rudyard.
Burt, Mary Elizabeth (1850-1918), ed. see Lorenzini, Carlo.
Burt, Mary Elizabeth (1850-1918), ed.
--Burt's Stories from Plato. (Classics for Children). N.D. Ginn and Company.
--Howells' Story Book. Howells, illus. (The Scribner Series of School Reading). N.D. Charles Scribner's Sons.
--Poems. (Every Child Should Know Stories). N.D. Grosset & Dunlap.
--Poems Every Child Should Know. (Every Child Should Know Ser.). N.D. Grosset & Dunlap.
--Poems Every Child Should Know. Ostertag, Blanche, illus. (The Every Child Should Know Bks.). N.D. Doubleday, Page & Co.
--Poems That Every Child Should Know: A Selection of the Best Poems of All Times for Young People. 1904. (ISBN 0-8274-3160-0). R West.
--Prose Every Child Should Know. Shutz, Eve Watson, illus. (The Every Child Should Know Bks.). N.D. Doubleday, Page & Co.
Burt, Mary Elizabeth (1850-1918) & Cable, Lucy Leffingwell, eds.
--The Cable Story Book. (The Scribner Series of School Reading). N.D. Charles Scribner's Sons.
Burt, Mary Elizabeth (1850-1918) & Ragozin, Zenaide Alexeievna (1835-1924), eds.
--Herakles, the Hero of Thebes: And Other Heroes of the Myth. LC 4990. ix p., 1 l., xi-xvi, 146 p. front., 5 pl. 18 1/2 cm. (Scribner's series of school reading). 1900. C. Scribner's Sons.
Burt, Olive Frank Woolley (1894-)
--Born to Teach. LC 67-21624. 191 p. 22cm. 1967. J. Messner.
--Camel Express: A Story of the Jeff Davis Experiment. 1st ed. Camana, Joseph C., illus. LC 54-5424. 178p. illus. 22cm. (Winston adventure books). 1954. Winston.
--Canyon Treasure. 1st ed. Mayan, Earl E., illus. LC 50-14654. 269 p. illus. 23 cm. 1950. Bobbs-Merrill.
--The Cave of Shouting Silence. LC 60-6864. 191p. illus. 21cm. (Your Fair Land Series). 1960. J. Day Co.
--Chief Joseph, Boy of the Nez Perce. Moyers, William (1916-), illus. LC 67-26335. (Illus.). 200 p. 20cm. (Childhood of famous Americans). 1967. Bobbs-Merrill.
--Cloud Girl. 1st ed. Lees, Harry Hanson, illus. LC 51-13209. 215 p. illus. 23 cm. 1951. Bobbs-Merrill.
--God Gave Me Eyes. Segner, Ellen, illus. 21 p. col. illus. 23 1/2 x 21 1/2 cm. 1942. S. Gabriel Sons & Company.
--God Gave Me Friends: Verses. Powers, Richard M. Gorman (1921-), illus. LC 52-44816. unpaged. illus. 24 cm. 1952. S. Gabriel Sons.
--I Challenge the Dark Sea: A Novel Based on the Life of Prince Henry the Navigator. LC 62-109380. 188p. illus. 21cm. c.1962. John Day.
--Jayhawker Johnny. Orbaan, Albert F. (1913-), illus. LC 66-7317. 119p. illus. 22cm. (gr. 2-6). 1966. John Day.
--Jed Smith: Young Western Explorer. Ponter, James J., illus. LC 62-16617. 200p. col. illus. 20cm. (Childhood of famous Amers.). 1963. Bobbs.
--Jedediah Smith: Fur Trapper of the Old West. Doremus, Robert (1913-), illus. LC 51-13099. 187 p. illus. 22 cm. 1951. Messner.
--Jim Beckwourth: Crow Chief. LC 57-11498. 192p. 22cm. 1957. J. Messner.
--John Alden, Young Puritan. Dowd, Victor, illus. (Illus.). 200 p. 20cm. (Childhood of famous Americans). 1964. Bobbs-Merrill.
--John Charles Fremont: Trail Marker of the Old West (January 21, 1813-July 13, 1890). Orbaan, Albert F. (1913-), illus. LC 55-6923. 192p. illus. 22cm. 1955. J. Messner.
--John Wanamaker: Boy Merchant. Fiorentino, Al, illus. LC 62-16624. 200p. ill. 22cm. (1894-). c.1962. Bobbs-Merrill.
--John Wanamaker, Boy Merchant. 1st ed. Lees, Harry Hanson, illus. LC 52-10697. 192 p. illus. 20 cm. (Childhood of famous Americans series). 1952. Bobbs-Merrill.
--The Oak's Long Shadow: A Story of the Basque Sheepherders in Idaho. 1# 1st ed. Chapman, Frederick Trench (1887-), illus. LC 52-8968. 240 p. illus. 22 cm. (Land of the Free). 1952. Winston.
--Ouray the Arrow. Harper, illus. LC 53-8578. 184p. illus. 22cm. 1953. J. Messner.
--Peter Turns Sheepman: Illustrated with Photos. 1st ed. LC 52-9040. 108 p. illus. 24 cm. 1952. Holt.
--Peter's Story Goes to Press. LC 43-17455. 6 p. l., 112 p. illus. 24 cm. 1943. H. Holt and Company.
--Peter's Sugar Farm, Illustrated with Photos. 1st ed. LC 54-5734. 96p. illus. 24cm. 1954. Holt.
--Petticoats West. LC 63-16793. 191 p. 21 cm. 1963. J. Messner.
--Prince of the Ranch: The Story of a Collie. Myers, Bob, illus. LC 49-10444. 239 p. illus. 23 cm. 1949. Boobs-Merrill Co.
--The Ringling Brothers: Circus Boys. 1st ed. Burns, Raymond Howard (1924-), illus. LC 58-129090. 192p. illus. 20cm. (Childhood of famous Americans series 107). 1958. Bobbs Merrill.
--The Ringling Brothers: Circus Boys. Fiorentino, Al, illus. LC 62-100408. 200p. illus. 20cm. (Childhood of famous Americans). 1962. Bobbs-Merrill.
--Space Monkey. 64p. 1960. John Day & Co.
--Wind Before the Dawn. LC 64-20702. 191p. 21cm. (Daughters of valor ser.). c.1964. John Day.
--Young Jed Smith, Westering Boy. 1st ed. Lees, Harry Hanson, illus. LC 54-652081. 192p. illus. 20cm. (Childhood of famous Americans series 82). 1954. Bobbs-Merrill.
Burtis, Thomson (1896-)
--Daredevils of the Air. Gretter, J. Clemens, illus. LC 32-2022. 3 p. l., 215 p. front., plates. 19 1/2 cm. c.1932. Grosset & Dunlap.
--Doomed Demons. (Air Combat Ser.). N.D. Grosset & Dunlap.
--Flying Blackbirds. Gretter, J. Clemens, illus. LC 32-35812. v, 242 p. front., plates. 19 1/2 cm. c.1932. Grosset & Dunlap.
--Four Aces. Gretter, J. Clemens, illus. LC 32-2026. 3 p. l., 216 p. front., plates. 19 1/2 cm. c.1932. Grosset & Dunlap.
--Haunted Airways. LC 39-17808. 4 p. l., 3-250 p. col. front. 20 1/2 cm. (Young moderns bookshelf). 1937. The Sun Dial Press, Inc.
--Haunted Airways. Dobias, Frank (1902-), illus. LC 30-23906. v p., 2 l., 3-250 p. col. front., illus. 20 1/2 cm. 1930. Doubleday, Doran & Company, Inc.
--Rex Lee, Ace of the Air Mail. LC 29-10955. 3 p. l., 213 p. front. 19 1/2 cm. (His Rex Lee flying series). c.1929. Grossett & Dunlap.
--Rex Lee, Aerial Acrobat. LC 30-24847. (Illus.). 18 1/2cm. 270p. (His Rex Lee Flying Stories). c.1930. Grossett & Dunlap.
--Rex Lee, Flying Detective. LC 32-2027. 3 p. l., 277 p. front. 19 1/2 cm. c.1932. Grosset & Dunlap.
--Rex Lee, Gypsy Flyer. LC 28-21192. 3 p. l., 248 p. front. 19 1/2 cm. c.1928. Grosset & Dunlap.
--Rex Lee, Night Flyer. LC 29-18705. 239p. front. 19 1/2cm. (His Rex Lee Flying Ser.). c.1929. Grosset & Dunlap.
--Rex Lee on the Border Patrol. LC 28-23878. 3 p. l., 280 p. front. 19 1/2 cm. c.1928. Grosset & Dunlap.
--Rex Lee, Ranger of the Sky. LC 28-238772. v, 212 p. front. 19 1/2 cm. c.1928. Grosset & Dunlap.
--Rex Lee, Rough Rider of the Air. LC 30-121507. v, 218 p. front. 19 1/2 cm. c.1930. Grosset & Dunlap.
--Rex Lee, Serial Acrobat. LC 30-248470. 3 p. l., 279 p. front. 19 1/2 cm. (His Rex Lee flying series). c.1930. Grossett & Dunlap.
--Rex Lee, Sky Trailer. LC 29-52328. v, 244 p. front. 19 1/2 cm. c.1929. Grosset & Dunlap.
--Rex Lee, Trailing Air Bandits. LC 31-1927. 3 p. l., 215 p. front. 19 1/2 cm. c.1931. Gorsset & Dunlap.
--Rex Lee's Mysterious Flight. LC 30-268455. 3 p. l., 247 p. front. 19 1/2 cm. (His Rex Lee flying series). c.1930. Grosset & Dunlap.
--Russ Farrell, Airman. LC 25-76455. 4 p. l., 238 p. front. 19 1/2 cm. 1924. Doubleday, Page & Company.
--Russ Farrell, Border Patrolman: An Air Adventure Story for Boys. LC 27-18963. 4 p. l., 228 p. front. 19 1/2 cm. 1927. Doubleday, Page & Company.
--Russ Farrell, Circus Flyer: An Air Adventure Story for Boys. Crump, Leslie (1894-), illus. LC 27-112133. 4 p. l., 222 p. front. 19 1/2 cm. 1927. Doubleday, Page & Company.
--Russ Farrell Over Mexico. LC 29-17892. 3 p. l., 221 p. front. 19 1/2 cm. 1929. Doubleday, Doran & Company, Inc.
--Russ Farrell, Test Pilot. LC 26-16360. 4 p. l., 253 p. front. 19 1/2 cm. 1926. Doubleday, Page & Company.
--Slim Evans: Air Ranger. LC 31-23581. 3 p. l., 3-222 p. 19 cm. c.1931. H. Holt and Company.
--Slim Evans at Mystery Mountain. LC 32-30513. 4 p. l., 3-210 p. 19 cm. c.1932. H. Holt and Company.
--Straight Shooting: Adventures of a Film Flyer. Dobias, Frank (1902-), illus. LC 31-325547. 4 p. l., 279 p. col. front. 21 cm. 1931. Doubleday, Doran & Company, Inc.
--The War of the Ghosts: A Flying Adventure Story. Dobias, Frank (1902-), illus. LC 32-24673. 4 p. l., 3-262 p. col. front. 20 1/2 cm. 1932. Doubleday, Doran & Company, Inc.
--Wing for Wing. Gretter, J. Clemens, illus. LC [illegible]. 3 p. l., 312 p. front., plates. 19 1/2 cm. c.1932. Grosset & Dunlap.
Burton, Alberta N., jt. auth. see Craine, Edith Janice.
Burton, Ardis Edwards, ed. see Disney, Walt, Productions.
Burton, Ardis Edwards, adapted by see Verne, Jules.
Burton, Charles Pierce (1862-)
--The Bob's Cave Boys: A Sequel to "The Boys of Bob's Hill", Being More About the Doings of the "Band", As Told by the "Secretary". Perard, Victor Semon (1870-1957), illus. LC 9-7040. 4 p. l., 302 p. front., illus., plates. 19 cm. 1909. H. Holt and Company.
--Bob's Hill Boys in the Everglades. LC 32-29690. x, 240 p. incl. front., illus. (incl. map) 19 1/2 cm. c.1932. H. Holt and Company.
--Bob's Hill Boys in Virginia. LC 39-230606. 4 p. l., 245 p. front. 19 1/2 cm. c.1939. H. Holt and Company.
--The Bob's Hill Braves. De Lay, H. S., illus. LC 10-20387. 4 p. l., 311 p. front., 3 pl. 19 1/2 cm. 1910. H. Holt and Company.
--Bob's Hill Meets the Andes: Doings of the "Band" in South America As Told in the "Minutes of the Meetin'". LC 28-21374. 287 p. plates. 19 1/2 cm. c.1928. H. Holt and Company.
--Bob's Hill on the Air: Some Adventures That the Secretary Failed to Record in the "Minutes of the Meeting". LC 34-34015. 5 p. l., 3-257 p. front. 19 1/2 cm. c.1934. H. Holt and Company.
--Bob's Hill Trails. LC 22-6521. vii, 268 p. front., plates. 19 1/2 cm. 1922. H. Holt and Company.
--The Boy Scouts of Bob's Hill. (Every Boy's Library). N.D. Grosset & Dunlap.
--Boy Scouts of Bobs Hill. (Juveniles of Distinction). N.D. Grosset & Dunlap.
--The Boy Scouts of Bob's Hill: A Sequel to "The Bob's Hill Braves". Grant, Gordon H. (1875-1962), illus. LC 12-242055. 4 p. l., 313 p. front., plates. 19 1/2 cm. 1912. H. Holt and Company.
--The Boys of Bob's Hill: Adventures of Tom Chapin and the "Band", As Told by the "Secretary". Williams, George Alfred (1875-), illus. LC 5-5931. 4 p. l., 182 p. front., 3 pl. 19 1/2 cm. 1905. H. Holt and Company.
--Camp Bob's Hill. LC 15-194051. 3 p. l., 313 p. front., illus. (map) plates. 19 1/2 cm. 1915. H. Holt and Company.
--Moving the Earth. 255p. N.D. Henry Holt & Co.
--Raven Patrol of Bob's Hill. Grant, Gordon H. (1875-1962), illus. LC 17-29141. 4 p. l., 324 p. front., plates, map. 19 1/2 cm. 1917. H. Holt and Company.
--The Trail Makers. Grant, Gordon H. (1875-1962), illus. LC 19-140115. 3 p. l., 277 p. front., plates. 19 1/2 cm. 1919. H. Holt and Company.
--Treasure Hunters of Bob's Hill. LC 26-172969. 286 p. front., plates 19 cm. 1926. H. Holt and Company.
Burton, Doris
--The Angel Who Guarded the Toys, and Other Stories. Gehr, Mary, illus. LC 55-13516. 181p. illus. 22cm. 1955. H. Regnery Co.
Burton, Earl (1916-) & Burton, Linette Arny Macan (1916-)
--The Exciting Adventures of Waldo. Stone, Helen (1904-), illus. LC 45-35180. 64 p. col. illus. 16 cm. 1945. Whittlesey House, McGraw-Hill Book Company, Inc.
--Taffy and Joe. Stone, Helen (1904-), illus. LC 47-18671. 60 4 p. double col. front., illus. 26 cm. 1947. Whittlesey House, McGraw-Hill Book Company, Inc.
Burton, Hal, pseud., see Burton, Harold Bernard.
Burton, Hal, pseud. (1908-)
--The Walton Boys and Gold in the Snow. Burton, Harold Bernard. authorized. Doremus, Robert (1913-), illus. LC 49-412. 251 p. illus. 21 cm. 1948. Whitman Pub. Co.
--The Walton Boys and Rapids Ahead. Burton, Harold Bernard. Doremus, Robert (1913-), illus. LC 50-4094. 248 p. illus. 21 cm. 1950. Whitman.

--The Walton Boys in High Country. Burton, Harold Bernard. Doremus, Robert (1913-), illus. LC 52-2288. 250 p. illus. 21 cm. 1952. Whitman Pub. Co.

Burton, Harold Bernard see Burton, Hal, pseud.

Burton, Herbert

--The Adventures of Dixie North. LC 76-373304. c.1976. Gadsden Pub. House.

Burton, Hester Wood-Hill (1913-)

--Beyond the Weir Bridge. Ambrus, Victor G., pseud. (1935-), illus. Ambrus, Gyozo Laszlo. LC 77-109906. (Illus.). x, 221 p. 24cm. 1970, c.1969. Crowell. **Award: (BGH).**

--Castors Away!. Ambrus, Victor G., pseud. (1935-), illus. Ambrus, Gyozo Laszlo. LC 63-11959. (Illus.). 254 p. 21cm. 1963, c.1962. World Pub. Co.

--Day That Went Terribly Wrong. (gr. 7-12). 1976. (ISBN 0-590-09902-7, Schol Pap). Schol Bk Serv.

--Five August Days. 176p. 1982. (ISBN 0-19-271454-6, Pub. by Oxford U Pr Childrens). Merrimack Pub Cir.

--The Flood at Reedsmere. Jacques, Robin (1920-), illus. LC 68-15273. (Illus.). 204 p. 21cm. 1968. World Pub. Co.

--The Great Gale. Kiddell-Monroe, Joan (1908-), illus. LC 68-4909. vii, 207 p. illus. 23 cm. 1963, c.1960. Oxford University Press.

--The Henchmans at Home. Ambrus, Victor G., pseud. (1935-), illus. Ambrus, Gyozo Laszlo. LC 78-171003. (Illus.). 182 p. 24cm. 1972, c.1970. (ISBN 0-690-37706-1). Crowell.

--In Spite of All Terror. Ambrus, Victor G., pseud. (1935-), illus. Ambrus, Gyozo Laszlo. LC 69-13060. (Illus.). 203 p. 21cm. 1969, c.1968. World Pub. Co. **Award: (ALA).**

--Kate Rider. Ambrus, Victor G., pseud. (1935-), illus. Ambrus, Gyozo Laszlo. LC 75-8576. (Illus.). 177 p. 24cm. 1975, c.1974. (ISBN 0-690-00978-X). Crowell.

--Kate Rider. Ambrus, Victor G, pseud. (1935-), illus. Ambrus, Gyozo Laszlo. LC 75-332680. (Illus.). 160 p. 23cm. 1974. (ISBN 0-19-271369-8). Oxford University Press.

--No Beat of Drum. Ambrus, Victor G., pseud. (1935-), illus. Ambrus, Gyozo Laszlo. LC 66-68314. 7, 185 p. illus 22 1/2 cm. 16/. (B 66-21339). 1966. Oxford U. P.

--No Beat of Drum. Ambrus, Victor G., pseud. (1935-), illus. Ambrus, Gyozo Laszlo. LC 67-23351. (Illus.). 190 p. 22cm. 1967, c.1966. World Pub. Co.

--The Rebel. Ambrus, Victor G., pseud. (1935-), illus. Ambrus, Gyozo Laszlo. LC 71-181829. (Illus.). 153 p. 24cm. 1972, c.1971. (ISBN 0-690-69010-X). Crowell. **Award: (ALA).**

--Riders of the Storm. Ambrus, Victor G., pseud. (1935-), illus. Ambrus, Gyozo Laszlo. LC 73-4404. (Illus.). viii, 200 p. 24cm. 1973, c.1972. (ISBN 0-690-70074-1). Crowell.

--Riders of the Storm. Ambrus, Victor G., pseud. (1935-), illus. Ambrus, Gyozo Laszlo. LC 73-168863. 170 p. 23cm. 1972. (ISBN 0-19-271345-0). Oxford University Press.

--Thomas. LC 71-558253. (Illus.). 23cm. vii, 178p. 1969. (ISBN 0-19-271308-6). Oxford Univ. Press.

--Time of Trial. LC 64-13514. (Illus.). (gr. 6 up). 1964. (ISBN 0-529-03886-2). Collins Pubs.

--To Ravensrigg. LC 76-54292. 1977. (ISBN 0-690-01354-X, TYC-J). Har-Row.

Burton, Hester Wood-Hill (1913-), ed.

--A Book of Modern Stories. Lawrence, John (1933-), illus. LC 73-168718. (Illus.). 157 p. 19cm. 1972. (ISBN 0-19-911027-1). Oxford University Press.

--Her First Ball;. Short Stories. Einzig, Susan (1922-), illus. LC 61-34021. 152p. illus. 22cm. 1959. Oxford University Press.

Burton, Jean

--Garibaldi: Knight of Liberty. Hood, Egon, illus. 1945. Alfred A. Knopf.

Burton, Leslie, pseud., see McGuire, Leslie Sarah.

Burton, Leslie, pseud. (1945-)

--Children Here, Children There. McGuire, Leslie Sarah. (Illus.). 10 color photos. 12p. (Changing Picture Bks). (ps-3). 1971. Platt.

Burton, Linette Arny Macan, jt. auth. see Burton, Earl.

Burton, Marilee Robin

--Aaron Awoke. LC 81-48638. (Illus.). 40p. (ps-k). 1982. (ISBN 0-06-020891-0, HarpJ). (ISBN 0-06-020892-9). Har-Row.

--The Elephant's Nest: Four Wordless Stories. Burton, Marilee Robin, illus. LC 78-20263. (Illus.). 48 p. (gr. k-2). c.1979. (ISBN 0-06-020905-4). (ISBN 0-06-020906-2). Harper & Row.

Burton, Marion Sturges

--Miss Fairy Queen. 1965. Exposition Press Inc.

Burton, Philip (1904-)

--The Green Isle. Parker, Robert Andrew (1927-), illus. LC 73-6021. (Illus.). 32 p. 30cm. 1974. (ISBN 0-8037-3204-X). Dial Press.

Burton, Richard Francis, Sir, tr. see Arabian Nights.

Burton, Richard Francis, Sir, tr. see Lubin, Leonard B.

Burton, Richard Francis, Sir (1821-1890)

--Aladdin and His Wonderful Lamp. Lubin, Leonard B., illus. LC 82-70308. (Illus.). 37 p. 28cm. c.1982. (ISBN 0-440-00302-4). (ISBN 0-440-00304-0). Delacorte Press.

Burton, Richard Francis, Sir (1821-1890), tr.

--Vikram and the Vampire: Or, Tales of Hindu Devilry. 1873. D. Appleton & Co.

Burton, Richard, Sir, tr. see Basile, Giovanni Battista.

Burton, Richard, Sir (1821-1890), tr. see Franklyn, Julian.

Burton, Virginia Lee (1909-1968)

--Calico the Wonder Horse. Burton, Virginia Lee (1909-1968), illus. 64p. (gr. k-3). 1970 (Starline). Schol Bk Serv.

--Calico, the Wonder Horse: Or, The Saga of Stewy Slinker;. Burton, Virginia Lee (1909-1968), illus. LC 41-20166. 60 p. illus. 14 x 22 cm. 1941. (ISBN 0-395-18659-5). Houghton Mifflin Co.

--Calico, the Wonder Horse: Or, The Saga of Stewy Stinker. Burton, Virginia Lee (1909-1968), illus. LC 50-9367. 1950. (ISBN 0-395-06671-9). Houghton Mifflin.

--Calico The Wonderful Horse or The Saga of Stewy Stinker. Burton, Virginia Lee (1909-1968), illus. N.D. E. M. Hale & Co.

--Choo Choo: The Story of the Little Engine Who Ran Away. Burton, Virginia Lee (1909-1968), illus. (Illus.). (gr. k-3). 1937. (ISBN 0-395-17684-0). HM.

--Katy and the Big Snow. Burton, Virginia Lee (1909-1968), illus. LC 43-18856. 2 p. l., 32, 4 p. col. illus. 22 1/2 x 25 1/2 cm. 1943. Houghton Mifflin Company.

--Katy and the Big Snow. Burton, Virginia Lee (1909-1968), illus. lv. (chiefly illus. 21cm. (Sandpiper book). 1974, c.1971. (ISBN 0-395-18562-9). Houghton, Mifflin.

--Life Story. LC 62-8118. 67p. illus. 24x26cm. 1962. Houghton Mifflin.

--The Little House. Burton, Virginia Lee (1909-1968), illus. LC 42-24744. 2 p. l., 40 p. col. illus. 23 1/2 x 25 cm. 1942. Houghton Mifflin Co. **Award: (RCM).**

--The Little House. Burton, Virginia Lee (1909-1968), illus. LC 79-302678. (Illus.). 40 p. (Sandpiper books). 1978, c.1942. (ISBN 0-395-18156-9). (ISBN 0-395-25938-X). Houghton Mifflin.

--Maybelle, the Cable Car. Burton, Virginia Lee (1909-1968), illus. LC 52-8729. (Illus.). 42 p. 1952. Houghton Mifflin.

--Mike Mulligan & His Steam Shovel. Burton, Virginia Lee (1909-1968), illus. LC 39-30335. (Illus.). (gr. k-3). 1939. (ISBN 0-395-06681-6). HM.

--Mike Mulligan and His Steam Shovel. Burton, Virginia Lee (1909-1968), illus. LC 77-154507. (Illus.). 48 p. (Sandpiper books). 1977, c.1967. (ISBN 0-395-25939-8). Houghton Mifflin.

Burton, William Frederick Padwick (1886-)

--The Magic Drum: Tales from Central Africa. Thompson, Ralph, illus. LC 62-16843. (Illus.). 127 p. 22cm. (Criterion book for young people). 1962, c.1961. Criterion Books.

Buscaglia, Felice Leonardo see Buscaglia, Leo F., pseud.

Buscaglia, Leo F., pseud., see Buscaglia, Felice Leonardo.

Buscaglia, Leo F., pseud. (1924-)

--Because I Am Human!. Buscaglia, Felice Leonardo. Ferguson, Bruce, photos by. LC 72-92809. (Illus.). 36 l. 24cm. c.1972. C. B. Slack.

--The Fall of Freddie the Leaf. Buscaglia, Felice Leonardo. Short, Steven & Todd-Slack, Misty, photos by (Illus.). 1982. (ISBN 0-03-062424-X). HR&W.

--The Fall of Freddie the Leaf: A Story of Life for All Ages. Buscaglia, Felice Leonardo. LC 81-86645. (Illus.). 32 p. c.1982. (ISBN 0-913590-89-4). (ISBN 0-03-062424-X). C.B. Slack.

Busch, Phyllis S. (1909-)

--Lions in the Grass: The Story of the Dandelion. Strong, Arline, illus. LC 68-14684. (Illus.). (gr. k-3). 1968. (ISBN 0-529-00357-0). (ISBN 0-529-00358-9). World Pub.

--Once There Was a Tree: The Story of the Tree, a Changing Home for Plants and Animals. Strong, Arline, illus. LC 68-14685. (Illus.). 48p. 1968. World Pub. Co.

--Puddles and Ponds: Living Things in Watery Places. Strong, Arline, illus. LC 75-82768. (Illus.). 48 p. 1969. World Pub. Co.

Busch, Wilhelm (1832-1908)

--The Bees: A Fairy Tale. Wiemann, Rudolph, retold by. LC 75-314591. (Illus.). 72 p. 21cm. c.1974. (ISBN 0-533-01215-5). Vantage Press.

--Buzz a Buzz: The Bees. N.D. Henry Holt & Co.

--Max and Maurice: A Juvenile History in Seven Tricks. Brooks, Charles Timothy (1813-1883), tr. LC 76-370149. (Illus.). 56 p. 21cm. 1882, c.1870. Roberts Brothers.

--Max and Moritz. N.D. W. S. Heinman.

--Max and Moritz. Arndt, Walter W. (1916-), retold by. LC 85-1241. (Illus.). 59 p. 20cm. 1985. (ISBN 0-915361-19-1). Adama Books.

--Max & Moritz. Klein, H. Arthur, ed. (Bilingual Eng & Ger). (Orig.). (gr. 3-6). 1962. Dover.

Busch, Wilhelm (1832-1908) & Rogers, W. Harry

--A Bushel of Merrythoughts. LC 70-176352. (Illus.). 60 p. 1971. (ISBN 0-486-22426-0). Dover Publications.

Bush, Bertha Evangeline (1866-)

--A Prairie Rose. Pitz, Henry Clarence (1895-1976), illus. LC 25-156713. 4 p. l., 305 p. col. front., col. plates 22 1/2 cm. (Beacon Hill bookshelf). 1925. Little, Brown and Company.

--A Prairie Rose. Tyng, Griswold, illus. LC 10-22987. 4 p. l., 305 p. front., plates 19 cm. 1910. Little, Brown and Company.

--The Story of Robin Hood. 31p. 18 1/2cm. (Instructor Literature Ser.: No. 212). 1912. F. A. Owen ; Hall & McCreary.

Bush, C. G., illus.

--Daffy Dilly and Her Friends. (Illus.). (The Fairy Library). N.D. Worthington Company.

--The History of A. B. C. and Other Tales. (Illus.). (The Fairy Library). N.D. Set. Worthington Company.

--The Wonderful Bag, and What Was In It. (Illus.). (The Fairy Library). N.D. Set. Worthington Company.

Bush, Christopher (1885-)

--The Case of the Deadly Diamonds. LC 69-10609. 159p. 1969. Macmillan Company.

Bush, Don

--Jack Snake. LC 85-112993. (Illus.). 48 p., 6 p. of plates. 26cm. (Little Brook Series). c.1985. (ISBN 0-943978-01-7). Rolling Hills Press.

Bush, Elizabeth

--The Twins Who Quarrelled: A Storybook With Pictures to Color. Bush, Elizabeth, illus. (Illus.). 1982. (ISBN 0-533-05275-0). Vantage.

Bush, Emma Florence

--Nature and Bird Stories for Children. LC 31-8810. 158 p. 19 1/2 cm. c.1931. Fleming H. Revell Company.

Bush, F. L

--Hero Stuff. LC 45-10545. 63 p. 18 cm. 1945. The Wartburg Press.

Bush, Helen Brandon

--Mary Aming's Treasures. Hutchison, P. A., illus. LC 65-27774. 144p. illus., map. 21cm. 1966, c.1965. (ISBN 0-07-009294-X). McGraw.

Bush, Max

--The Chest of Dreams. (Children's Theatre Playscript Ser.). 1979. (ISBN 0-88020-001-4). Coach Hse.

Bush, Paine L., jt. auth. see Drury, Lola Ross.

Bush, Terri, jt. ed. see Jordan, June Meyer.

Bushe, Mary C.

--Rupert of the Rhine. N.D. Pott, Young & Co.

Bushell

--The Wonderful World of Netsuke. (Illus.). 1964. (ISBN 0-8048-0631-4). Charles E. Tuttle.

Bushnell, Catharine

--Raggedy Ann & Andy & the Pirates of Ingo Outlet. LC 80-69646. 1981. (ISBN 0-672-52689-1). Bobbs.

--Raggedy Ann & Andy and the Pirates of Outgo Inlet. McKissack, Vernon, illus. LC 80-69646. (Illus.). 32 p. 24cm. 1981, c.1980. (ISBN 0-672-52689-1). Bobbs-Merrill Co.

--Raggedy Ann & Andy in the Tunnel of Lost Toys. McKissack, Vernon, illus. LC 79-25675. p. cm. 1980. (ISBN 0-672-52249-7). Bobbs-Merrill Co.

Buss, Nancy

--Rose-Petal's Big Decision. Paris, Pat & Ross-Moore, Sharon, illus. LC 83-23818. (Illus.). 44 p. 28cm. (Rose-Petal Place Ser.). (gr. 3). c.1984. (ISBN 0-910313-52-0). Parker Brothers.

Bussell, Chase

--The Mountain Cabin Mystery. LC 35-20299. 122 p. 19 1/2 cm. c.1935. Dorrance & Company.

Bussey, G. Moir

--Fables. Grandville, Jean Ignace Isidore Gerard (1803-1847), illus. N.D. D. Appleton & Co.

Busvine, Katherine, tr. see Samivel.

Butcher, Julia

--The Sheep & the Rowan Tree. Butcher, Julia, illus. LC 83-26423. (Illus.). (gr. k-3). 1984. (ISBN 0-03-071602-0). HR&W.

Butcher, M. P., tr. see Hoffmann, Franz.

Butcher, M. P., tr. see Prohl, Hedwig Taube.

Butcher, S. H., ed. see Homerus.

Butler, Albert (1923-)

--Fast Flows the River. LC 63-16224. (Illus.). 192 p. 21cm. 1963. Abelard-Schuman.

--Reporter for the Sentinel. LC 61-13322. 191p. 21cm. N.D. Abelard-Schuman.

Butler, Annie E.

--Bible Stories for Children: The Genesis. (Lippincott's Popular Library). N.D. J. B. Lippincott Co.

--Bible Stories for Children: The Gospels. (Lippincott's Popular Lib.). N.D. J. B. Lippincott Co.

Butler, Arthur, jt. auth. see Molloy, William Fillmore.

Butler, Audrey, ed. see Wyss, Johann David Von.

Butler, Beverly Kathleen (1932-)

--Captive Thunder. LC 69-16204. viii, 205 p. 21cm. 1969. Dodd, Mead.

--Feather in the Wind. Forberg, Ati, pseud. (1925-), illus. Forberg, Beate Gropius. LC 65-20912. x, 243 p. 21 cm. 1965. Dodd, Mead.

--The Fur Lodge. Mott, Herb, illus. LC 59-9588. (Illus.). 204 p. 21cm. 1959. Dodd, Mead.

--Ghost Cat. LC 84-10200. 192p. (gr. 6 up). 1984. (ISBN 0-396-08457-5). (ISBN 0-396-08457-5). Dodd.

--Gift of Gold. LC 72-3151. 21cm. 278p. 1972. (ISBN 0-396-06636-4). Dodd, Mead & Company.

--Gift of Gold. LC 72-12842. 383 p. 25cm. 1973, c.1972. (ISBN 0-8161-6076-7). G. K. Hall.

--A Girl Named Wendy. LC 76-12507. 211 p. 22cm. c.1976. (ISBN 0-396-07365-4). Dodd, Mead.

--Light a Single Candle. LC 62-16326. 242 p. 21cm. 1962. Dodd, Mead.

--The Lion and the Otter. LC 57-11548. 275 p. 21cm. 1957. Dodd, Mead.

--My Sister's Keeper. LC 79-6637. 220 p. 22cm. c.1980. (ISBN 0-396-07803-6). Dodd, Mead.

--My Sister's Keeper. LC 79-6637. 220 p. 20cm. 1985. (ISBN 0-396-08744-2). Dodd, Mead.

--The Silver Key. LC 61-6936. (Illus.). 239 p. 21cm. 1961. Dodd, Mead.

--Song of the Voyageur. LC 55-9136. 247p. 21cm. 1955. Dodd, Mead.

--The Wind and Me. Vasiliu, Mircea (1920-), illus. LC 70-162612. (Illus.). 32 p. 24cm. 1971. (ISBN 0-396-06380-2). Dodd, Mead.

Butler, Clifford, Mrs.

--Year with the Everards. 211p. N.D. E. P. Dutton.

Butler, Cynthia

--Michael Hendee. Rosse, Allianora, illus. LC 75-43448. (Illus.). 51 p. 22cm. 1976, c.1975. (ISBN 0-915892-05-7). Regional Center for Educational Training.

Butler, David Jonathan (1946-)

--Cat's Whiskers on Saturday. Brewer, Sally King (1947-), illus. LC 75-17434. (Illus.). 36 p. 24cm. c.1976. (ISBN 0-87614-046-0). Carolrhoda Books.

Butler, Edward Crompton (1853-)

--Our Little Mexican Cousin. LC 5-33967. vii p., 2 l., 100 p. front., plates., 20 cm. (On verso of half-title: The Little cousin series). 1905. L. C. Page & Company.

Butler, Ellis Parker (1869-1937)

--The Behind Legs of the 'Orse And Other Stories. 1927. Houghton Mifflin Co.

--Dorna: Or, The Hillvale Affair. LC 29-18167. 1 p. l., 228 1 p. front., plates. 20 1/2 cm. 1929. Houghton Mifflin Company.

--Ghosts What Ain't. 1923. Houghton Mifflin.

--Goat-Feathers. 1919. Houghton Mifflin Co.

--The Incubator Baby. Preston, Mary Wilson, illus. 1906. Funk & Wagnalls.

--Jibby Jones: A Story of Mississippi River Adventure for Boys. Dove, Arthur Garfield (1880-1946), illus. LC 23-127833. (Title-page gives illustrator as "Arthur G. Dorr"). 5 p. l., 265 1 p. front., 1 illus., plates. 19 1/2 cm. 1923. Houghton Mifflin Company.

--Jibby Jones and the Alligator: The Story of the Young Alligator-Hunters of the Upper Mississippi Valley. Dove, Arthur Garfield (1880-1946), illus. LC 24-22821. vii, 1 p., 1 l., 252, 1 p. front., plates. 19 1/2 cm. 1924. Houghton Mifflin Company.

--Many Happy Returns of the Day. 1925. Houghton Mifflin.

--Philo Gubb, Correspondence School Detective. 1918. Houghton Mifflin.

--Pigs Is Pigs & Other Favorites. (Illus.). N.D. Dover.

--Pups and Pies. 20cm. 312p. 1927. Doubleday, Page & Co.

--Swatty; a Story of Real Boys. LC 20-5587. 5 p. l., 300, 2 p. front., plates. 19 1/2 cm. 1920. Houghton Mifflin Company.

Butler, Ellis Parker (1869-1937) & Kent, Louise Andrews, Mrs. (1806-1969)

--Jo Ann, Tomboy. King, Ruth, illus. LC 33-7953. 4 p. l., 263, 1 p. front., plates. 19 cm. 1933. Houghton Mifflin Company.

Butler, Fanny H., Mrs.

--Grandma's Patience: or, Mrs. James's Christmas Gift. N.D. Chase & Hall.

Butler, Francelia McWilliams (1913-)

--The Skip Rope Book. Haley, Gail Einhart (1939-), illus. LC 63-19935. 1 v. (unpaged) col. illus. 18 cm. 1963. Dial Press.

Butler, Gwendoline Williams (1922-)

--The Vesey Inheritance. LC 75-10475. 288p. 1975. (ISBN 0-698-10689-X). Coward.

Butler, Ira

--The Little Lost Reindeer. Deen, Sue, illus. 1982. (ISBN 0-533-05469-9). Vantage.

Butler, Julia

--Singing Paddles. 278p. N.D. Binfords & Mort.

--Singing Paddles. Cooke, Dorothea, illus. LC 39-1393. 3 p. l., 274 p. illus. 21 cm. c.1937. H. Holt and Company.

--LeRoy and the Old Man. LC 79-6553. 154 p. 22cm. c.1980. (ISBN 0-590-07638-8). Four Winds Press.
--L'il Wildcat. Frame, Paul (1913-), illus. LC 67-13829. (Illus.). 160 p. 21cm. 1967. World Pub. Co.
--Marty and the Micro-Midgets. LC 68-22720. 137 p. 21cm. 1970. Norton.
--Maverick on the Mound. Scholefield, Edmund O., pseud. Frame, Paul (1913-), illus. LC 68-14696. (Illus.). 158 p. 21cm. 1968. World Pub. Co.
--A Member of the Family. LC 82-70403. 172 p. 22cm. c.1982. (ISBN 0-590-07828-3). Four Winds Press.
--Moose, the Thing, and Me. LC 82-11730. 151 p. 22cm. 1982. (ISBN 0-395-32077-1). Houghton Mifflin.
--Moving West on One Twenty-Two. LC 73-113441. 187p. (gr. 7 up). 1970. (ISBN 0-316-11910-5). Little.
--My Father is Quite a Guy. 1971. Little Brown and Company.
--The Narc. LC 72-77814. 187 p. 22cm. 1972. Four Winds Press.
--Next Stop, Earth. Frame, Paul (1913-), illus. LC 77-18346. (Illus.). 80 p. 22cm. 1978. (ISBN 0-8027-6322-7). (ISBN 0-8027-6323-5). Walker.
--Orders to Vietnam: A Novel of Helicopter Warfare. LC 68-15387. 145 p. 21cm. 1968. Little, Brown.
--Race Car Team. LC 72-92924. 155 p. 22cm. 1973. (ISBN 0-448-21446-6). (ISBN 0-448-21446-6). Grosset & Dunlap.
--Racing to Glory. Douglas, James McM., pseud. LC 77-75594. 182 p. 21cm. (Sports shelf fiction). 1969. Putnam.
--Redline 7100. LC 68-16571. 168 p. 21cm. 1968. Norton.
--Return to Daytona. LC 73-19239. 166 p. 20cm. (Flying wheels book). 1974. (ISBN 0-448-11716-9). (ISBN 0-448-11716-9). Grosset & Dunlap.
--Return to Racing. LC 79-153919. 186 p. 21cm. 1971. (ISBN 0-448-21411-3). Grosset & Dunlap.
--Road Racer. (gr. 7 up). N.D. G&D.
--Road Racer. 1st ed. 212 p. 21cm. 1967. Norton.
--The Roper Brothers and Their Magnificent Steam Automobile. LC 75-43631. 218 p. 22cm. c.1976. (ISBN 0-590-17410-X). Four Winds Press.
--Slaughter by Auto. LC 80-66245. 185 p. 22cm. c.1980. (ISBN 0-590-07589-6). Four Winds Press.
--Steve Bellamy: A Novel. LC 70-97143. 150 p. 21cm. (gr. 7 up). 1970. (ISBN 0-316-11909-1). Little, Brown.
--Stock-Car Racer. LC 66-10779. 208 p. 21cm. 1966. Norton.
--Stop and Search: A Novel of Small Boat Warfare off Vietnam. LC 69-10648. 152 p. 21cm. (gr. 7 up). 1969. (ISBN 0-316-11908-3). Little, Brown.
--Susan and Her Classic Convertible. LC 75-105333. 190 p. 22cm. 1970. Four Winds Press.
--Team Racer. LC 77-182010. 187 p. 21cm. 1972. (ISBN 0-448-21435-0). (ISBN 0-448-26202-9). Grosset & Dunlap.
--Under the Influence. LC 78-22127. 247 p. 22cm. c.1979. (ISBN 0-590-07465-2). Four Winds Press.
--Wheel of a Fast Car. LC 69-17138. 214 p. 21cm. 1969. Norton.
--Yankee Boy. Scholefield, Edmund O., pseud. Gordon, Lewis W., illus. LC 74-82781. (Illus.). 156p. (gr. 3 up). 1971. (ISBN 0-529-00538-7). (ISBN 0-529-00540-9). Collins-World.
--The 12-Cylinder Screamer. LC 70-113522. 151 p. 22cm. 1970. G. P. Putnam's Sons.

Buttfield-Campbell, Jill, ed. see Oxenbury, Helen.

Buttinger, Joseph
--Manko of Mankoland, 3 vols. Incl. Vol. 1. The Adventures of Young & Impressionable Manko As He Meets His Jungle Friends. (ISBN 0-682-48898-4); Vol. 2. Further Adventures of Manko-Delights & Frights. (ISBN 0-682-48906-9); Vol. 3. Manko Goes to New York & Becomes Famous. (ISBN 0-682-48907-7). (Illus.). (gr. 1-6). 1977. Exposition.

Buttler, Louise Harvey
--The Magic House. Frazee, Hazel, illus. Pratt, Adelene J., intro. by. 128p. (The Red and Gold Library). N.D. A. Whitman & Co.

Butts, David P & Lee, Addison Earl (1914-)
--Watermelon. Warren, Betsy, pseud. (1916-), illus. Warren, Elizabeth Avery. LC 68-11225. (Illus.). 47 p. 23cm. (Wings books). 1968. Steck-Vaughn Co.

Butts, H. N. Greene, Mrs.
--Eda Darling: or, the Little Flower-Girl. N.D. Colby & Rich.
--Little Susie: Or, The New Year's Gift. N.D. Colby and rich.

Butts, M., ed.
--Misfortunes of Ogier the Dane. Linker, Robert, tr. LC 64-8377. (Illus.). (gr. 5-7). 1964. (ISBN 0-910244-38-3). Blair.

Butts, M. F., Mrs.
--Frolic And Her Friends, 1 of 6 vols. (Frolic Stories). N.D. Set. American Tract Society.
--Frolic At Maple Grove, 1 of 6 vols. (Illus.). 160p. (Frolic Books). 1905. Set. American Tract Society.
--Frolic At Uncle Will's, 1 of 6 vols. (Illus.). 136p. (Frolic Books). 1905. Set. American Tract Society.
--Frolic Books, 6 Vols. (Illus.). N.D. American Tract Society.
--Frolic Left Out, 1 of 25 vols. 229p. (Golden Rod Library). 1905. American Tract Society.
--Frolic Left Out, 1 of 6 vols. (Frolic Books). N.D. Set. American Trade Society.
--Frolic On A Journey, 1 of 6 vols. (Frolic Books). N.D. Set. American Tract Society.
--Grandmother Merwin's Heiress. 308p. (Sunday-Hour Lib.). N.D. American Tract Society.
--Lizzie and Her Friends. 144p. N.D. American Tract Society.
--Lottie. 238p. N.D. Congregational Sunday-School and Publishing Society.
--Nellie's New Home, 1 of 50 vols. 236p. (Model Library Number Three). N.D. Set. American Tract Society.
--Patchy and Hippity-Hop. (Little Wanderer Ser.). N.D. D. Lothrop Co.

Butts, Marie, ed. see Ogier le Danois & De Paris, Raimbert.

Butts, Walter E., Jr.
--Brothers of the Senecas. LC 39-10639. 4 p. 1., 13-252p. 19cm. c.1935. Goldsmith Pub,Co.

Buzzati, Dino
--The Bears' Famous Invasion of Italy. N.D. Pantheon Bks.

Byars, Betsy Cromer (1928-)
--After the Goat Man. Himler, Ronald Norbert (1937-), illus. LC 82-12198. p. cm. 1982, c.1974. (ISBN 0-14-031533-0). Puffin.
--After the Goat Man. Himler, Ronald Norbert (1937-), illus. LC 74-8200. (Illus.). 126 p. 22cm. 1974. (ISBN 0-670-10908-8). The Viking Press.
--The Animal, the Vegetable, and John D Jones. Sanderson, Ruth, illus. LC 81-69665. p. cm. c.1982. (ISBN 0-440-00122-6). Delacorte Press.
--The Cartoonist. Cuffari, Richard (1925-1978), illus. LC 77-12782. (Illus.). 119 p. 22cm. 1978. (ISBN 0-670-20556-7). Viking Press.
--Clementine. Wilton, Charles, illus. LC 62-7535. 70p. illus. 22cm. 1962. (ISBN 0-395-06682-4). Houghton Mifflin.
--The Computer Nut. Byars, Guy, illus. LC 85-43421. p. cm. 1986, c.1984. (ISBN 0-14-032086-5). Puffin Books.
--The Computer Nut. Byars, Guy, illus. LC 84-7239. (Illus.). 23. 144p. (gr. 3-7). 1984. (ISBN 0-670-23548-2, Viking Kestrel). Viking.
--Cracker Jackson. 1985. Viking Kestrel.
--The Cybil War. Owens, Gail, illus. LC 80-26912. (Illus.). x, 126 p. 22cm. 1981. (ISBN 0-670-25248-4). Viking Press. **Award: (ALA).**
--Dancing Camel. Berson, Harold (1926-), illus. LC 65-181482. (Illus.). (gr. 1-4). 1965. (ISBN 0-670-25474-6). (ISBN 0-670-25475-4). Viking Pr.
--The Eighteenth Emergency. Grossman, Robert (1940-), illus. 1973. Penguin.
--The Eighteenth Emergency. Grossman, Robert (1940-), illus. (Puffin Story Bk.). 1981. (ISBN 0-14-031451-2, Puffin). Penguin.
--The Eighteenth Emergency. Grossman, Robert (1940-), illus. LC 72-91399. (Illus.). 126 p. 22cm. (gr. 6 up). 1973. (ISBN 0-670-29055-6). Viking Press.
--The Glory Girl. LC 84-11494. 122 p. 20cm. 1985. (ISBN 0-14-031785-6). Puffin Books.
--The Glory Girl. LC 83-5927. 122 p. 22cm. 1983. (ISBN 0-670-34261-0). Viking Press.
--Go and Hush the Baby. McCully, Emily Arnold (1939-), illus. LC 82-12214. p. cm. 1982, c.1971. (ISBN 0-14-050396-X). Puffin Books.
--Go and Hush the Baby. McCully, Emily Arnold (1939-), illus. LC 72-136825. (Illus.). 32 p. 20cm. 1971. (ISBN 0-670-34270-X). Viking Press.
--The Golly Sisters Go West. Truesdell, Susan G., illus. LC 84-48474. p. cm. (An I Can Read Book). c.1985. (ISBN 0-06-020883-X). (ISBN 0-06-020884-8). Harper & Row.
--Good-Bye, Chicken Little. LC 78-19829. 101 p. 21cm. c.1979. (ISBN 0-06-020907-0). (ISBN 0-06-020911-9). Harper & Row.
--Goodbye, Chicken Little. (gr. 4-6). 1979. Harper & Row.
--The Groober. Byars, Betsy Cromer (1928-), illus. LC 67-2929. (Illus.). 32 p. 1967. Harper & Row.
--The House of Wings. Schwartz, Daniel (1929-), illus. LC 82-607. p. cm. 1982. (ISBN 0-14-031523-3). Penguin.
--The House of Wings. Schwartz, Daniel (1929-), illus. LC 77-183933. (Illus.). 142 p. 22cm. 1972. (ISBN 0-670-38025-3). Viking Press. **Award: (ALA).**
--The Lace Snail. Evars, Betsy, illus. LC 74-32376. (Illus.). 32 p. 1975. (ISBN 0-670-41614-2). Viking Press.
--The Midnight Fox. Grifalconi, Ann (1929-), illus. LC 68-27566. 157p. illus. 22cm. 1968. Viking.
--The Night Swimmers. Howell, Troy, illus. LC 79-53597. (Illus.). 131 p. 22cm. c.1980. (ISBN 0-440-06261-6). (ISBN 0-440-06262-4). Delacorte Press. **Awards: (ABA); (BGH).**
--The Pinballs. 1st ed. LC 76-41518. 21 cm. 136p. 1977. (ISBN 0-06-020917-8). (ISBN 0-06-020918-6). Harper & Row.
--Rama, the Gypsy Cat. Bacon, Peggy, pseud. (1895-), illus. Bacon, Margaret Frances. LC 66-8731. 109p. illus. 21cm. 1966. Viking.
--The Summer of the Swans. CoConis, Ted, pseud., illus. CoConis, Constantinos. LC 80-29187. (Illus.). 142 p. 20cm. c.1981. (ISBN 0-14-031420-2). Puffin Books.
--The Summer of the Swans. CoConis, Ted, pseud., illus. CoConis, Constantinos. LC 72-106919. (Illus.). 142 p. 22cm. 1970. (ISBN 0-670-68190-3). Viking Press. **Award: (JNM).**
--Trouble River. Negri, Rocco (1932-), illus. LC 69-18260. 22cm. 158p. 1969. (ISBN 0-670-73258-3). Viking Press.
--The TV Kid. Cuffari, Richard (1925-1978), illus. LC 75-37944. (Illus.). 123 p. 22cm. c.1976. (ISBN 0-670-73331-8). Viking Press.
--The Two-Thousand-Pound Goldfish. LC 81-48652. p. cm. 1982. (ISBN 0-06-020889-9). (ISBN 0-06-020890-2). Harper & Row. **Award: (ALA).**
--The Winged Colt of Casa Mia. Cuffari, Richard (1925-1978), illus. LC 73-5143. (Illus.). 128 p. 22cm. 1973. (ISBN 0-670-77318-2). Viking Press.

Byer, Carol
--Henny Penny. Byer, Carol, illus. LC 80-28146. p. cm. c.1981. (ISBN 0-89375-490-0). (ISBN 0-89375-491-9). Troll Associates.

Byerly, Dorothea J
--The Adventures of Peter the Piano. LC 47-11804. 52 p. illus. 19 cm. c.1947. O. Ditson Co.; T. Presser Co., Distributors.

Byers, Amy Irene (1906-)
--Mystery at Mappins. Ambrus, Victor G., pseud. (1935-), illus. Ambrus, Gyozo Laszlo. LC 66-18539. 208p. illus. 22cm. 1966, c.1964. (ISBN 0-684-13451-9). Scribners.
--Two on the Trail. (Illus.). (Jet Ser). (gr. 7-11). 1963. Verry.

Byers, Andrew L (1869-), ed.
--Bible Stories and Studies: With Illustrations and More Than Three Hundred Questions and Answers. LC 20-9629. 2 p. l., 7-111 p. illus. 23 cm. c.1920. Gospel Trumpet Company.
--Things That Happened: A Collection of Interesting Anecdotes. LC 19-272. 2 p. l., 7-96 p. illus. 23 cm. c.1918. Gospel Trumpet Company.
--Trips and Adventures: Accounts of Interesting and Varied Experiences. LC 19-271. 2 p. l., 7-95 p. illus. 23 cm. c.1918. Gospel Trumpet Company.

Byers, Charles Alma (1879-)
--The Caves of Capistrano. Landau, Jacob (1917-), illus. LC 38-33206. 240 p. incl. front., illus. 21 cm. c.1938. David McKay Company.
--The Inverness Murders. viii p., 2 l., 13-287 p. illus. (plans) 20 cm. c.1935. The Dial Press.

Byers, Ruth
--Jot Hits a Homer. Original Art from JOT Television Series. LC 70-114369. (Illus.). 32 p. (gr. k-5). 1970. (ISBN 0-8054-4607-9). Broadman Press.
--Jot's Cupcake Chase. LC 72-114367. (Illus.). 32 p. 1970. Broadman Press.
--Toy Sounds for Jot. LC 76-114368. (Illus.). 32 p. 1970. Broadman Press.

Byfield, Barbara Ninde (1930-)
--Andrew and the Alchemist. 1st ed. Hollinger, Deanne, illus. LC 76-7694. (Illus.). 102 p. 22cm. c.1977. (ISBN 0-385-12233-0). (ISBN 0-385-12234-9). Doubleday.
--The Haunted Churchbell. Byfield, Barbara Ninde (1930-), illus. LC 72-137849. (Illus.). 40 p. 1971. Doubleday.
--The Haunted Ghost. Byfield, Barbara Ninde (1930-), illus. LC 72-93395. (Illus.). 44 p. 1973. (ISBN 0-385-01408-2). (ISBN 0-385-01408-2). Doubleday.
--The Haunted Spy. Byfield, Barbara Ninde (1930-), illus. LC 79-78689. (Illus.). 40 p. 1969. Doubleday.
--The Haunted Tower. Byfield, Barbara Ninde (1930-), illus. LC 75-11999. (Illus.). 48 p. 16cm. c.1976. (ISBN 0-385-00450-8). Doubleday.
--The Man Who Made Gold. Hollinger, Deanne, illus. (Illus.). 112p. (gr. 3-7). 1981. (ISBN 0-590-30360-0). Scholastic Inc.

Byhring, Lillian
--A Carrousel of Tales for Boys & Girls. Meyd, Orella S., illus. (Illus.). 40p. (gr. 4-8). 1972. (ISBN 0-682-47422-3). Exposition.

Byington, Eloise
--Doll Land Stories. (The Easy Library). N.D. A. Whitman & Co.
--Mother Goose Fun More Stories in Rhyme. Frantz, Kathleen Stowell, illus. LC 31-19279. 128 p. incl. col. front., col. illus. 21 cm. c.1931. A. Whitman & Co.
--The Pancake Brownies: Twelve Stories in Rhyme. Jones, Marguerite M., illus. LC 28-21404. 96 p. incl. col. front., illus. (part col.) 21 cm. a just right book. c.1928. A. Whitman and Company.
--The Wishbone Children. Frantz, Kathleen Stowell, illus. LC 34-33474. 64 p. col. illus. 22 cm. c.1934. A. Whitman & Co.

Bykov, Vasilii Vladimirovich (1924-)
--Pack of Wolves. Solotaroff, Lynn, tr. from Rus. LC 80-2456. 192p. (gr. 7 up). 1981. (ISBN 0-690-04114-4, TYC-J). (ISBN 0-690-04115-2). Har-Row.

Bynner, Edwin Lassiter
--The Chase of the Meteor and Other Stories. N.D. Houghton Mifflin.

Bynon, Mary A.
--My Boy and Other Poems. N.D. Vantage Press.

Byrd, Ann
--The Animals Go Adventuring. 1st ed. Kilgore, Al, illus. LC 54-8167. (Illus.). 31 p. 24cm. 1954. Pageant Press.
--The Tired Donkey, and Other Stories. 1st ed. Kilgore, Al, illus. LC 54-13217. 63p. illus. 21cm. 1954. Pageant Press.

Byrd, Elizabeth
--I'll Get by: A Novel. LC 80-29471. 196 p. 23cm. (gr. 7 up). c.1981. (ISBN 0-670-39134-4). Viking Press.

Byrd, Ernestine N
--The Black Wolf Savage River; a Story of the Alaskan Wild. A Story of the Alaskan Wild. Robbins, Ruth (1917-), illus. LC 59-7369. 159p. illus. 2icm. c.1959. Parnassus Press.
--Ice King. Miller, Marilyn Jean (1925-), illus. (Illus.). 142 p. 21cm. 1965. Scribner.

Byrd, Mitzi & Martin, Peggy
--The Loneliest Chicken. LC 53-12761. unpaged. illus. 21cm. 1953. Macmillan.
--The Loneliest Chicken. 1955. MacMillan.

Byrd, Robert
--Marcella Was Bored. LC 84-28674. (Illus.). 32 p. 27cm. c.1985. (ISBN 0-525-44156-5). Dutton.

Byrde, Elsie
--The Polish Fairy Bk. N.D. J. B. Lippincott.

Byrne, Bess S
--With Mikko Through Finland: The Land of Flame and Snow. Ostman, Lempi (1899-), illus. LC 82-21671. xiii, 230 p. incl. illus., plates. front., plates. 21 cm. 1932. R. M. McBride & Company.

Byrne, C., jt. auth. see Belasco, David.

Byrne, Joan A., compiled by.
--Modern Greek Fairy Tales. LC 6-42424. (Illus.). 19cm. 167p. 1906. A. Flanagan Co.

Byrne, Mary Agnes
--The Fairy Chaser. Craig, Anna B., illus. LC 6-21384. 150 p. incl. front., 5 pl. 19 x 17 cm. c.1906. The Sealfield Publishing Company.
--Litte Dame Trot. (Color Bks.). N.D. DeWolfe, Fiske & Co.
--Little Dame Trot. Corbett, Bertha L., illus. LC 4-30141. 19 x 17cm. 81p. 1904. Saalfield Publishing Co.
--The Little Woman in the Spout. LC 2-18607. 20 x 17cm. 84p. 1902. Saalfield Publishing Co.
--Peggy-Alone. Craig, Anna B., illus. LC 9-15999. 21cm. 334p. 1909. Saalfield Publishing Co.
--Roy and Rosyrocks. LC 2-18605. 20cm. 83p. 1902. Saalfield Publishing Co.

Byrne, Miriam
--The House of the Red Fox. Upjohn, Anna Milo, illus. LC 7-24158. ix p., 1 l., 116 p. front., 7 pl. 18 cm. 1907. F. A. Stokes Company.
--The Would-be Witch. Upjohn, Anna Milo, illus. LC 6-36358. (Illus.). N.D. Frederick A. Stokes.

Byrnes, Eugene F. see Byrnes, Gene, pseud.

Byrnes, Gene, pseud., see Byrnes, Eugene F..

Byrnes, Gene, pseud. (1890-1974)
--Jimmie Dugan and the Reg'lar Fellers. Byrnes, Eugene F.. N.D. Cupples & Leon Co.
--Reg'lar Fellers. Byrnes, Eugene F.. (The Famous Sixty Cent Quarto Comics). N.D. Cupples & Leon Co.

Byron, Gilbert (1903-)
--Chesapeake Duke. Lewis, Jack (1912-), illus. LC 75-40037. (Illus.). 163 p. 22cm. 1975. (ISBN 0-87033-210-4). Tidewater Publishers.
--Chesapeake Duke. Weiss, Emil (1896-1965), illus. LC 65-107566. 180p. illus. 21cm. c.1965. Rand McNally.

Byron, May Clarissa Gillington, Mrs., ed. see Barrie, James Matthew, Sir.

Byron, May Clarissa Gillington (0000-1936)
--Cat's Cradle. (Illus.). (The Happy Child's Library). N.D. Dodge Publishing Co.

AUTHOR INDEX CALDECOTT, RANDOLPH

--Forager's Hunt Breakfast, 1 of 6 Vols. Aldin, Cecil Charles Windsor (1870-1935), illus. (Cecil Aldin's Merry Party Series.). N.D. George H Doran.
--Friday and Saturday: The Adventures of Two Little Pickles. Hassall, John (1868-1948), illus. (The Little Red Hen Series.). N.D. George H Doran.
--Humpty and Dumpty Give a Fancy Dress Party. Aldin, Cecil Charles Windsor (1870-1935), illus. (Cecil Aldin Merry Party Series.). N.D. George H Doran.
--Hungry Peter. Aldin, Cecil Charles Windsor (1870-1935), illus. (Cecil Aldin's Happy Family Series.). N.D. George H Doran.
--The Land of Nod. Petherick, Rosa C, illus. (The Little Red Hen Series.). N.D. George H Doran.
--The Little Black Bear. (The May Byron Books for Children). N.D. George H Doran.
--The Little Black Bear. N.D. Thomas Nelson & Sons.
--The Little Brown Rooster. (The May Byron Books for Children). N.D. George H Doran.
--The Little Brown Rooster. N.D. Thomas Nelson & Sons.
--Little Robin Hood. Hassall, John (1868-1948), illus. (The Red Hen Series.). N.D. George H Doran.
--The Little Small Red Hen. (Illus.). (The Little Red Hen Ser.). N.D. George H. Doran.
--The Little Small Red Hen. (Illus.). 25cm. 52p. 1911. Hodder & Stoughton.
--The Little Tan Terrier. (The May Byron Books for Children). N.D. George H Doran.
--The Little Tan Terrier. N.D. Thomas Nelson & Sons.
--The Little Yellow Duckling. (The May Byron Books for Children). N.D. George H Doran.
--The Little Yellow Duckling. N.D. Thomas Nelson & Sons.
--The Magic Map Book. (Illus.). (The Red Hen Series.). N.D. George H Doran.
--Master Quack's Water Picnic, 1 of 6 Vols. Aldin, Cecil Charles Windsor (1870-1935), illus. (Cecil Aldin Merry Party Series.). N.D. George H Doran.
--The Peek- A-Boos in Town. Preston, Chloe, illus. N.D. George H Doran.
--The Peek-A-Boos Takes a Vacation. Preston, Chloe, illus. N.D. George H Doran.
--Peter's Dinner Party, 1 of 6 Vols. Aldin, Cecil Charles Windsor (1870-1935), illus. (Cecil Aldin Merry Party Series.). N.D. George H Doran.
--Poor Dear Dollies. Petherick, Rosa C, illus. (The Little Red Hen Series.). N.D. George H Doran.
--Rag's Garden Party, 1 of 6 Vols. Aldin, Cecil Charles Windsor (1870-1935), illus. (Cecil Aldin Merry Party Series.). N.D. George H Doran.
--Rufus. Aldin, Cecil Charles Windsor (1870-1935), illus. (Cecil Aldin's Happy Family Series.). N.D. George H Doran.
--Tabitha's Tea Party. Aldin, Cecil Charles Windsor (1870-1935), illus. (Cecil Aldin Merry Party Series.). N.D. George H Doran.
--Teddy Bear Bearocar. (Illus.). (The Little Red Hen Series.). N.D. George H Doran.
--The Teddy Bear Book. Petherick, Rosa C, illus. (The Little Red Hen Series.). N.D. George H Doran.

Byrum, Isabel Coston (1870-)
--Arabella's Hen, and Other Children's Hour Stories. Norman, Vera Stone, illus. LC 27-14949. 63 p. illus. (part col.) 19 cm. c.1927. Gospel Trumpet Press.
--Cripple Willie and Other Children's Hour Stories. LC 27-14950. 64 p. illus. (part col.) 19 cm. c.1927. Gospel Trumpet Press.
--Harry the Newsboy. (gr. 1-5). N.D. Warner Press.
--Harry the Newsboy, and Other Children's Hour Stories. LC 26-19114. 62 p. illus. (part col.) 19 cm. c.1926. Gospel Trumpet Company.
--How John Became a Man. 64p. N.D. (ISBN 0-686-29118-2). (ISBN 0-686-29119-0). Faith Pub Hse.
--How John Became a Man: Life Story of a Motherless Boy. rev. and enl. ed. LC 17-27751. 96 p. incl. front., illus. 19 cm. c.1917. Gospel Trumpet Company.
--Mr. Noah's ABC Zoo. 32p. N.D. Warne Press.
--The Pilot's Voice: Words of Warning to the Youth and Enlightenment for Parents. LC 16-5620. vii, 9-224 p. incl. front., illus. 19 cm. c.1916. Gospel Trumpet Company.
--Tiny Tots in Story Town. 64p. N.D. Warner Press.

Bytovetzski, Pavel L., jt. auth. see Cormack, Maribelle B.

C, S. C., ed.
--Child's Wreath: Or, Poems for Children. LC 15-171694. 128 p. col. front. 12 cm. 1853. J. Buffum.

Caballero, Ann Mallory (1928-)
--Stranger in the House. LC 65-10880. 189p. 21cm. c.1965. Coward.

Caballero, Fernan, pseud., see De Faber, Cecilia Bohl.

Caballero, Fernan, pseud. (1796-1877)
--Spanish Fairy Tales. De Faber, Cecilia Bohl. (Illus.). (St. Nicholas Series for Boys). N.D. International Book Company.
--Spanish Fairy Tales. De Faber, Cecilia Bohl. Davis, J. Watson, illus. Ingram, John H. (1849-1916), tr. LC 25-4688. 3 p. l., ixxi, 241 p. incl. front., plates, 19 cm. (The Fairy Library). N.D. A. L. Burt Company.

Cabassa, Victoria (1912-)
--Trixie and the Tiger. Obligado, Lilian Isabel (1931-), illus. (Illus.). 1967. (ISBN 0-200-72023-6). Abelard-Schuman.
--Trixie and the Tiger. Obligado, Lilian Isabel (1931-), illus. LC 67-19609. 41 col. illus. 26cm. 1968. (ISBN 0-200-72023-6). Abelard.

Cable, George W., jt. ed. see Field, Eugene

Cable, George Washington (1844-1925)
--The Cable Story Book: Selections for School Reading. Burt, Mary Elizabeth & Cable, Lucy Leffingwell (1875-), eds. LC 99-28405. x p., 2 l., 176 p. incl. front. (port.) plates. 19 cm. (Scribner's series of school reading). 1899. C. Scribner's Sons.

Cable, Harold
--Plays for Modern Teen-Agers. 1971. (ISBN 0-8238-0126-8). Plays, Inc.

Cable, Lucy Leffingwell, jt. ed. see Burt, Mary Elizabeth.

Cable, Lucy Leffingwell, ed. see Cable, George Washington.

Cable, Lucy Leffingwell, ed. see Cervantes Saavedra, Miguel de.

Cabot, Carolyn Sturgis Channing, Mrs. (1846-)
--Football Grandma: An Auto-Baby-Ography As Told by Tony. Higginson, Thomas Wentworth, retold by. LC 5-36117. 5 p. l., 3-79, 1 p. front., illus., plates. 23 x 18 cm. 1905. Small, Maynard & Company.

Cabot, Elise Pumpelly, Mrs. (1875-)
--Balloon Moon. Lathrop, Dorothy Pulis (1891-1980), illus. LC 27-24426. viii, 99 p. col. front., illus. 21 cm. c.1927. H. Holt and Company.

Cabot, Isabel
--Nurse Craig. LC 57-12661. 224p. 21cm. 1957. Avalon Books.
--Private Duty Nurse. LC 58-12502. 224p. 20cm. 1958. Avalon Books.

Cabot, Lucia
--A Merry-Go-Round of Verse: Short Poems for Small People. Thurston, Clara Bell, illus. LC 41-895679. 4 p. l., 11-62 p. illus. 19 x 16 cm. 1941. J. Felsberg, Inc.

Cabral, Olga (1909-)
--The Seven Sneezes. Gergely, Tibor (1900-1978), illus. LC 48-6667. (Little Golden Book: 51). 1948. Simon and Schuster.
--So Proudly She Sailed: Tales of Old Ironsides. LC 81-6465. p. cm. 1981. (ISBN 0-395-31670-7). Houghton Mifflin.

Cachiaras, Dot
--I'm Glad God Thought of Mothers. Arthur, Lorraine, illus. (Illus.). 24p. (Happy Day Bks.). (gr. k-3). 1979. (ISBN 0-87239-360-7). Standard Pub.

Cadby, Carine
--The Brownies in Switzerland: A Children's Winter Sport Holiday. Stephenson, John & Stephenson, Eunice, illus. LC 24-18905. vi p., 2 l., 11-127 p. col. front., col illus., col. plates. 24 cm. c.1924. The Macaulay Company.
--The Dolls' Day. N.D. E P Dutton.
--Puppies and Kittens, and Other Stories. Cadby, Will., photos by. LC 20-2690. x p., 1 l., 201 p. incl. front., plates. 17 cm. c.1920. E. P. Dutton & Company.

Caddell, Cecilia Mary
--Wild Times. N.D. Catholic Publication Society.

Caddell, Miss
--The Miner's Daughter. (The Young People's Library). N.D. D. & J. Sadlier.

Caddell, Mrs.
--Nellie Netterville: One of the Transplanted. N.D. Catholic Publication Society.

Cadell, Violet Elizabeth (1903-)
--Sun in the Morning. McNutt, Mildred Coughlin, illus. LC 50-8509. 280 p. illus. 21 cm. 1950. Morrow.

Cadigan, Robert J.
--September to June. N.D. D. Appleton-Century Co.

Cadmus Editorial Board
--Adventures Here & There. (Illus.). (gr. 4-7). 1958. (ISBN 0-8382-0013-3). Hale.
--Fun & Fantasy. (Illus.). (gr. 3-6). 1958. (ISBN 0-8382-0276-4). Hale.
--Stories of Early America. N.D. E. M. Hale & Co.
--Wide: Wonderful World. N.D. E. M. Hale & Co.
--Wonderful Things Happpen. N.D. E. M. Hale & Co.

Cadogan, Mary Rose (1928-) & Craig, Patricia
--You're a Brick, Angela!. A New Look at Girls' Fiction from 1839 to 1975. LC 76-374162. (Illus.). 397 p. 23cm. 1976. (ISBN 0-575-02061-X). Gollancz.

Cady, Bertha Louise Chapman, Mrs. (1873-)
--Tami: The Story of a Chipmunk. LC 28-280221. 104 p. incl. front., illus. 20 cm. c.1927. The Comstock Publishing Co.

Cady, Mary R & Dewey, Julia M., Mrs.
--Picture Stories from the Great Artists. Bonheur, Rosa, et al. (1822-1899), illus. LC 3-14257. 128 p. illus. 19 cm. (Art reader, no. 1). c.1903. Richardson, Smith & Company.

Cady, Walter Harrison (1877-1970)
--Caleb Cottontail: His Adventures in Search of the Cotton Plant,. Cady, Walter Harrison (1877-1970), illus. LC 21-19083. 127, 1 p. incl. col. illus. 20 cm. 1921. Houghton Mifflin Company.

Caen, Herbert Eugene (1916-)
--The Cable Car and the Dragon. Byfield, Barbara Ninde (1930-), illus. LC 77-157151. (Illus.). 32 p. 1972. Doubleday.

Caffrey, Nancy
--Hanover's Wishing Star. Brown, Paul (1893-1958), illus. Brown, Paul (1893-1958), frwd. by. LC 56-8314. 124p. illus. 21cm. 1956. Dutton.
--House Haven. Brown, Paul (1893-1958), illus. LC 55-9795. 93p. illus. 21cm. 1955. Dutton.
--Mig O' the Moor. Mellin, Jeanne (1929-), illus. LC 53-8248. (Illus.). 158 p. 22cm. 1953. Dutton.
--Penny's Worth. 1st ed. Mellin, Jeanne (1929-), illus. LC 52-8243. 120 p. illus. 22 cm. 1952. Dutton.
--Pony Duet. 1st ed. Mutch, Ronnie, illus. LC 57-11630. 91p. illus. 21cm. 1957. Dutton.
--Scene from the Saddle. 1st. ed. Waintrob, A. I. Budd, photos by. LC 58-7811. 88p. illus. 19 x 24cm. 1958. Dutton.
--Show Pony. 1st ed. Brown, Paul (1893-1958), illus. LC 54-8856. 88p. illus. 21cm. 1954. Dutton.
--Somebody's Pony. 1st ed. Mellin, Jeanne (1929-), illus. LC 51-12809. 72 p. illus. 21 cm. 1951. Dutton.

Caggiano, Rosemary, jt. auth. see Fass, Bernie.

Caggiano, Rosemary, jt. auth. see Young, Roger.

Caggiano, Rosemary & Matrinez, Larry
--The Circus. 48p. (gr. k-6). 1978. (ISBN 0-86704-000-9). Clarus Music.

Cagle, James V.
--The Story of Santa Claus, Junior. Durham, Carol, illus. (Illus.). 1979. (ISBN 0-682-49464-X). Exposition.

Cahn, Julie
--Holiday Romance. LC 82-20003. p. cm. 1983. (ISBN 0-671-46450-7). Wanderer Books.
--Spotlight on Love. (Dream Your Own Romance Ser.: No. 3). (gr. 2-7). 1984. (ISBN 0-671-52625-1). Wanderer Bks.

Cahn, Rhoda, jt. auth. see Cahn, William.

Cahn, William (1912-1976) & Cahn, Rhoda (1922-)
--The Story of Writing, from Cave Art to Computer. Lewis, Anne, illus. LC 63-11283. 128 p. illus. 26 cm. (Story of science series book). 1963. Harvey House.

Caidin, Martin (1927-)
--The Mighty Hercules. LC 64-10684. 183p. illus. 21cm. c.1964. Dutton.

Cain, Elizabeth, jt. auth. see Duttweiler, Helen.

Caines, Jeannette Franklin
--Abby. Kellogg, Steven (1941-), illus. LC 73-5480. (Illus.). 32p. (ps-3). 1973. (ISBN 0-06-020921-6, HarpJ). (ISBN 0-06-020922-4). Har-Row.
--Abby. Kellogg, Steven (1941-), illus. LC 73-5480. (Illus.). 32p. (Trophy Picture Bk). (ps-3). 1984. (ISBN 0-06-443049-9, Trophy). Har-Row.
--Daddy. Himler, Ronald Norbert (1937-), illus. LC 76-21388. (Illus.). 32 p. c.1977. (ISBN 0-06-020923-2). (ISBN 0-06-020924-0). Harper & Row.
--Just Us Women. Cummings, Pat, illus. LC 81-48655. (Illus.). 32p. (A Trophy Picture Book Ser.). (gr. k-3). 1984. (ISBN 0-06-443056-1, Trophy). Har-Row.
--Window Wishing. Brooks, Kevin, illus. LC 79-2698. (Illus.). 18 p. 21cm. c.1980. (ISBN 0-06-020933-X). (ISBN 0-06-020934-8). Harper & Row.

Caines, Marilyn A.
--Boomer, the Three Dollar Dog: A Puppy Tale. (Illus.). 48p. (gr. k-5). 1976. (ISBN 0-682-48501-2). Exposition.

Caire, Helen
--Senor Castillo, Cock of the Island. Price, Christine Hilda (1928-1980), illus. LC 48-5868. 76p. illus. 24cm. 1948. Rinehart.

Cairns, Colleen
--Great Gorme: A Novel of Suspense. 1975. (ISBN 0-679-40125-3, Weybright). McKay.

Cairns, Sylvia
--Uncle Willie Mackenzie's Legends of the Goundirs. (Illus.). 46p. 1967. Tri-Ocean Books.

Calahan, Harold Augustin
--Back to Treasure Island. Grant, Louis F., illus. (Illus.). (gr. 4-9). N.D. (ISBN 0-8149-0286-3). Vanguard.
--Hurrah's Nest. Tomaso, Rico, illus. LC 37-22634. x p., 2 l., 3-244 p. incl. front., illus. 21 cm. 1937. The Vanguard Press.

Caldecott, Moyra (1927-)
--Adventures by Leaf Light. Teeple, Bill & Teeple, Lyn, illus. LC 79-105810. (Illus.). 46p. 1978. (ISBN 0-914676-12-1, Star & Eleph Bks). (ISBN 0-914676-20-2). Green Tiger Pr.
--Weapons of the Wolfhound. (Illus.). 1976. State Mutual Bk.

Caldecott, Randolph (1846-1886)
--Babes in the Wood. Caldecott, Randolph (1846-1886), illus. (Illus.). (Caldecott's Picture Book Ser. No. 3). (gr. k-3). 1879. (ISBN 0-7232-0539-6). Warne.
--Caldecott Picture Book No. 3: The Milkmaid, Hey Diddle Diddle, Baby Bunting, A Frog He Would A-Wooing Go, The Fox Jumps Over The Parson's Gate. (Illus.). (gr. k-3). 1883. (ISBN 0-7232-0526-4). Warne.
--Caldecott Picture Books: Containing: The Three Jovial Huntsmen, The Queen of Hearts, Sing a Song a Sixpence, The Farmer's Boy. Caldecott, Randolph (1846-1886), illus. (No. 2). N.D. George Routledge & Sons.
--Caldecott's First Collection. Caldecott, Randolph (1846-1886), illus. (Containing: The Great Panjandrum Himself, Mrs Mary Blaize, Ride a Cock Horse, Come Lassies and Lads) N.D. George Routledge & Sons.
--Caldecott's First Collection: Containing: The Milk Maid, Baby Bunting Hey Diddle Diddle, The Fox Jumped over the Farmer's Gate, The Frog who Would A-Wooing Go. Caldecott, Randolph (1846-1886), illus. (No. 3). N.D. George Routledge & Sons.
--Caldecott's Picture Books: Containing: "Hey Diddle Diddle" "Baby Bunting" "Ride a Cock Horse" "Where are You Going, My Pretty Maid" "The Frog He Would a-Wooing Go", Book No. 3. Caldecott, Randolph (1846-1886), illus. (Illus.). N.D. Frederick Warne & Co.
--Caldecott's Picture Books: Containing: The House that Jack Built, John Gilpin, Babes in the Wood, Elegy on a Mad Dog. Caldecott, Randolph (1846-1886), illus. (No. 1). N.D. George Routledge & Sons.
--Caldecott's Picture Books: Containing:"Come, Lasses and Lads" "The Fox Jumps over the Parson's Gate" "Mrs. Mary Blaize" "The Great Panjandrum Himself", Book No.4. Caldecott, Randolph (1846-1886), illus. (Illus.). N.D. Frederick Warne & Co.
--Collection of Pictures & Songs, 2 Vols. (Illus.). (gr. k-3). 1881. Warne.
--Come, Lasses & Lads. Caldecott, Randolph (1846-1886), illus. (Illus.). (gr. k-3). 1884. (ISBN 0-7232-0549-3). Warne.
--Come, Lassies and Lads. (Illus.). (Caldecott's Picture Books: No. 13). N.D. Frederick Warne & Co.
--Elegy on a Mad Dog. (Illus.). (Caldecott's Picture Book Ser.: No. 4). N.D. Frederick Warne & Co.
--Elegy on a Mad Dog. Caldecott, Randolph (1846-1886), illus. (Illus.). (gr. k-3). 1879. (ISBN 0-7232-0540-X). Warne.
The Farmer's Boy. (Illus.). (Caldecott's Picture Books Ser.: No. 8). N.D. Frederick Warne & Co.
--Farmer's Boy. Caldecott, Randolph (1846-1886), illus. (Illus.). (gr. k-3). 1881. (ISBN 0-7232-0544-2). Warne.
--The Fox Jumps Over the Parson's Gate. (Illus.). (Caldecott's Picture Books Ser.: No. 12). N.D. Frederick Warne & Co.
--Fox Jumps Over the Parson's Gate. Caldecott, Randolph (1846-1886), illus. (Illus.). (gr. k-3). 1883. (ISBN 0-7232-0548-5). Warne.
--A Frog He Would a-Wooing Go. LC 64-55141. (Illus.). 22p. illus. (part col.). (Caldecott's Picture Books Ser.: No. 11). N.D. Frederick Warne & Co.
--Frog He Would A-Wooing Go. Caldecott, Randolph (1846-1886), illus. LC 64-55141. (Illus.). (Caldecott's Picture Book Ser: No.11). (gr. k-3). 1883. (ISBN 0-7232-0547-7). Warne.
--Great Panjandrum Himself. (Illus.). (gr. k-2). 1885. (ISBN 0-7232-0552-3). Warne.
--Hey Diddle Diddle. (Peter Possum Paperbacks). (gr. k-3). 1975. (ISBN 0-531-05132-3). Watts.
--Hey Diddle Diddle. Caldecott, Randolph (1846-1886), illus. Bd. with Baby Bunting. (Illus.). Repr. of 1882 ed. (gr. k-3). N.D. (ISBN 0-7232-0546-9). Warne.
--Hey Diddle Diddle, and Baby Bunting. (Illus.). (Caldecott's Picture Books Ser.: No. 10). N.D. Frederick Warne & Co.
--The Hey Diddle Diddle Picture Book. LC 4-13891. various pagings. illus. (part col.) 21 x 25 cm. N.D. F. Warne and Co.
--House that Jack Built. (Illus.). (Caldecott's Picture Books Ser.: No.2). N.D. Frederick Warne & Co.
--House That Jack Built. Caldecott, Randolph (1846-1886), illus. (Illus.). (gr. k-3). 1878. (ISBN 0-7232-0538-8). Warne.
--The House That Jack Built. Caldecott, Randolph (1846-1886), illus. (Peter Possum Paperbacks Ser). 1967. (ISBN 0-531-05100-5). Watts.

--John Gilpin. (Illus.). (Caldecott's Picture Books Ser.: No. 1). N.D. Frederick Warne & Co.
--John Gilpin. Caldecott, Randolph (1846-1886), illus. (Illus.). (gr. k-3). 1878. (ISBN 0-7232-0537-X). Warne.
--John Gilpin's Ride. N.D. (ISBN 0-531-05125-0). Franklin Watts.
--The Milkmaid. (Illus.). (Caldecott's Picture Books Ser.: No. 9). N.D. Frederick Warne & Co.
--The Milkmaid. Caldecoot, Randolph (1846-1886), illus. (Illus.). (Caldecott's Picture Book Ser.: No.9). (gr. k-3). 1882. (ISBN 0-7232-0545-0). Warne.
--Mrs. Mary Blaize. Caldecoot, Randolph (1846-1886), illus. (Illus.). (gr. k-3). 1885. (ISBN 0-7232-0551-5). Warne.
--The Owls of Olynn Belfry. Caldecott, Randolph (1846-1886), illus. LC 1-3161. 78p. 1885. Scribner & Welford.
--The Panjandrum Picture Book. LC 4-13892. 98 p. illus. (part col.) 21 x 24 cm. N.D. F. Warne and Co.
--Queen of Hearts. (Illus.). (Caldecott's Picture Books Ser.: No. 7). N.D. Frederick Warne & Co.
--Queen of Hearts. Caldecott, Randolph (1846-1886), illus. (Illus.). (gr. k-3). 1881. (ISBN 0-7232-0543-4). Warne.
--R. Caldecott's First Collection of Pictures and Songs. LC 65-6489. 1 v. (various pagings) illus. (part col.) 24 cm. N.D. F. Warne.
--R. Caldecott's Picture Book. Caldecott, Randolph (1846-1886), illus. LC 7-35043. (Containing The Diverting History of John Gilpin, The Three Jovial Huntsmen, an Elergy on the Death of a Mad Dog). 87, 1 p. incl. col. front., illus. (part col.) 14 x 12 cm. 1906. F. Warne & Co.
--R. Caldecott's Picture Book. Caldecott, Randolph (1846-1886), illus. LC 4-13893. (Containing The Diverting History of John Gilpin, The House that Jack Built, The Babes in the Wood, and an Elergy on the Death of a Mad Dog; all exhibited in beautiful engravings, many of which are printed in colours, by E. Evans). various paging. illus. (part col.) 4 col. pl. 24 x 21 cm. N.D. F. Warne and Co.
--R. Caldecott's Picture Book: Containing The House That Jack Built, Sing a Song for Sixpence, The Queen of Hearts. Caldecott, Randolph (1846-1886), illus. LC 7-85044. 87, 1 p. incl. front., illus. (part col.) 14 x 12 cm. 1906. F. Warne & Co.
--R. Caldecott's Picture Book: Containing The House That Jack Built, Sing a Song for Sixpence, The Queen of Hearts. Caldecott, Randolph (1846-1886), illus. LC 26-27431. 87, 1 p. incl. col. front., illus. (part col.) 14 x 12 cm. (Half-title: R. Caldecott's picture book, no. 2). 1926. F. Warne & Co.
--R. Caldecott's Picture Book (No. 2). Containing The Three Jovial Huntsmen, Sing a Song for Sixpence, The Queen of Hearts The Farmer's Boy; All Exhibited in Beautiful Engravings, Many of Which Are Printed in Colours by E. Evans. Caldecott, Randolph (1846-1886), illus. LC 4-13894. 129 p. illus. (part col.) 24 x 21 cm. N.D. F. Warne and Co.
--R. Caldecott's Second Collection of Pictures and Songs. LC 65-869639. 1 v. (various pagings) illus. (part col.) 21 cm. N.D. F. Warne.
--The Randolph Caldecott Picture Book. Caldecott, Randolph (1846-1886), illus. (gr. k-3). 1977. (ISBN 0-7232-1997-4). Warne.
--Randolph Caldecott's John Gilpin and Other Stories: Containing: The Diverting History of John Gilpin; The House that Jack Built; The Frog He Woulda-Wooing Go; The Milkmaid. Caldecott, Randolph (1846-1886), illus. (gr. k-3). 1977. Warne.
--Randolph Caldecott's John Gilpin & Other Stories. Caldecott, Randolph (1846-1886), illus. LC 77-81562. (Illus.). (ps up). 1978. (ISBN 0-7232-2062-X). Warne.
--Ride a Cock Horse. Caldecott, Randolph (1846-1886), illus. Bd. with A Farmer Went Trotting. (Illus.). Repr. of 1884 ed. (gr. k-3). N.D. (ISBN 0-7232-0550-7). Warne.
--Ride a Cock Horse to Banbury Cross: Or, A Farmer Went Trotting Upon His Gray Mare. 20p. N.D. Routledge & Sons.
--Sing a Song for Sixpence. (Illus.). (Caldecott's Picture Books Ser.: No. 8). N.D. Frederick Warne & Co.
--Sing a Song of Sixpence. N.D. Frederick Warne.
--Sing a Song of Sixpence. Caldecott, Randolph (1846-1886), illus. LC 77-153296. (Illus.). 30 p. 24cm. c.1977. (ISBN 0-8055-0359-5). Hart Pub. Co.
--Three Jovial Huntsmen. (Illus.). (Calecott's Picture Books Ser.: No. 5). N.D. Frederick Warne & Co.
--Three Jovial Huntsmen. Caldecott, Randolph (1846-1886), illus. (Illus.). (gr. k-3). 1880. (ISBN 0-7232-0541-8). Warne.

Caldecott, Randolph (1846-1886) & Goldsmith, Oliver (1728-1774)
--R. Caldecott's Picture Book: Containing The Diverting History of John Gilpin, The Three Jovial Huntsmen, An Elegy on the Death of a Mad Dog. Caldecott, Randolph (1846-1886), illus. LC 27-606. 87, 1 p. incl. col. front., illus. (part col.) 14 x 12 cm. (Half-title: R. Caldecott's picture book, no. 1). 1926. F. Warne & Co. Ltd.

Calder, Alexander, tr. see Davidson, Sandra Calder.

Calder, Lyn
--Rainbow Brite: Happy Birthday, Buddy Blue. LC 84-81573. (Illus.). 44 p. 29cm. c.1984. (ISBN 0-307-16002-5). (ISBN 0-307-66002-8). Western Pub. Co.

Caldero, Gordon
--Deep Sea Silver. Anderson, Rus, illus. LC 58-5172. (Illus.). 223 p. 21cm. 1958. Little, Brown.

Calderon, Ramirez Salvador (1869-)
--Stories for Carmencita. Gahan, Aloysius C., tr. LC 15-699. 4 p. l., 7-174 p. illus., ports. 20 cm. c.1914. Printed by Book and Job Department, Brooklyn Daily Eagle.

Calderone, Mary Steichen see Martin, Mary Steichen, Mrs. (1904-) & Steichen, Edward.

Caldwell, Edward Sabiston (1928-)
--She's Gone!. LC 75-43158. (Illus.). 122 p. 18cm. (Radiant books). c.1976. (ISBN 0-88243-893-X). Gospel Pub. House.

Caldwell, Erskine (1903-)
--The Deer at our House. 1965. MacMillan Co.
--The Deer at Our House. Wohlberg, Ben, illus. LC 66-15377. 30p. illus. 22cm. c.1966. Collier.
--Molly Cottontail. Sharp, William (1900-), illus. 1958. Little, Brown.

Caldwell, Frank
--Wolf, the Storm Leader. N.D. Dodd Mead & Co.

Caldwell, George Walter (1866-)
--Rainbow Stories. Flippen, Jane Jefferson, illus. LC 20-22. 5 p. l., 17-90 p. illus. 20 cm. c.1919. Phillips & Van Orden Co.
--The Wizzywab. LC 20-170. 4 p. l., 15-120 p. front. (port.) illus. 20 cm. c.1919. Phillips & Van Orden Co.

Caldwell, Harry R.
--Blue Tiger. N.D. Abingdon Press.

Caldwell, John (1946-)
--Excuses, Excuses: How to Get Out of Practically Everything. LC 81-43028. (Illus.). 48 p. 21cm. c.1981. (ISBN 0-690-04124-1). (ISBN 0-690-04125-X). Crowell.

Caldwell, Malcolm Jones
--The Big Mouth Bullfrog. LC 74-192128. (Illus.). 1 v. (unpaged. 17cm. 1972. Wofford Library Press.

Caldwell, Mary
--Morning, Rabbit, Morning. Schweninger, Ann (1951-), illus. LC 81-47724. (Illus.). 32p. (ps-1). 1982. (ISBN 0-06-020939-9, HarpJ). (ISBN 0-06-020940-2). Har-Row.

Calhoun, Alfred R. (1844-)
--Lost in the Canyon. (The Rugby Series for Boys and Girls). N.D. A. L. Burt Company.
--Lost in the Canyon: Sam Willett's Adventures on the Great Colorado. (Wide Awake Boys Ser.). N.D. A. L. Burt.

Calhoun, Don Gilmore (1914-)
--The Little President. Calhoun, Don Gilmore (1914-), illus. LC 46-3683. 32 p. col. ill. 26cm. 1946. Thomas Y. Crowell.

Calhoun, Donald
--Dear Kids. N.D. Ziff-Davis Publishing.

Calhoun, Dorothy Donnell
--The Book of Brave Adventures. LC 15-20612. (Illus.). 18cm. 147p. (Everychild series). N.D. Macmillan Company.
--Book of Great Adventures. (Everychild's Ser.). N.D. The Macmillan Co.
--Little Folks from Literature. (Little Folks Ser.). N.D. Abingdon Press.
--Little Folks from Literature. (Illus.). N.D. Methodis Book Concern.
--Little Folks of the Bible. N.D. Methodist Book Concern.
--Princess of Let's Pretend. LC 16-251482. xi p., 1 l., 200 p. front., plates. 20 cm. c.1916. E. P. Dutton & Co.

Calhoun, Frances Boyd
--Miss Minerva and William Green Hill. (The Miss Minerva Bks.). N.D. Reilly & Lee Co.

Calhoun, Horace B.
--Two for the Show. Venning, Sue, illus. LC 82-3725. (Illus.). 32p. (Muppet Press Bks.). (gr. 1-4). 1982. (ISBN 0-394-85409-8). Random.

Calhoun, Mary, pseud., see Wilkins, Mary Huiskamp.

Calhoun, Mary Elizabeth (1866-)
--Dorothy's Rabbit Stories. (Illus.). (Crowell's Every Land Series.). 1915. T Y Crowell.
--Dorothys Rabbit Stories. Blaisdell, E. Warde, illus. LC 7-24584. 4 p. l., 115 p. front., & pl. 20 x 17 cm. 4p. c.1907. T. Y. Crowell & Co.

Calhoun, Mary, pseud. (1926-)
--Audubon Cat. Wilkins, Mary Huiskamp. Bonners, Susan, illus. LC 80-16278. (Illus.). 32 p. 26cm. 1981. (ISBN 0-688-22253-6). (ISBN 0-688-32254-9). Morrow.
--The Battle of Reuben Robin & Kite Uncle John. Wilkins, Mary Huiskamp. McCaffery, Janet, illus. LC 72-12947. (Illus.). 32 p. 27cm. 1973. (ISBN 0-688-20075-3). (ISBN 0-688-20075-3). Morrow.
--Big Sixteen. Wilkins, Mary Huiskamp. Hyman, Trina Schart (1939-), illus. LC 83-1007. (Illus.). (gr. 1-3). 1983. (ISBN 0-688-02350-9). (ISBN 0-688-02351-7). Morrow.
--Camels Are Meaner Than Mules. Wilkins, Mary Huiskamp. Vestal, Herman B., illus. LC 72-141255. (Illus.). 60 p. 24cm. 1971. (ISBN 0-8116-4250-X). Garrard Pub. Co.
--Cowboy Cal & the Outlaw. Wilkins, Mary Huiskamp. Nicholas, Frank, illus. LC 61-5032. (Illus.). 48p. (gr. k-5). 1961. Morrow.
--Cross-Country Cat. Wilkins, Mary Huiskamp. Ingraham, Erick, illus. LC 78-31718. (Illus.). 40 p. 26cm. 1979. (ISBN 0-688-22186-6). (ISBN 0-688-32186-0). Morrow. **Award: (BGH).**
--Daisy, Tell Me!. Wilkins, Mary Huiskamp. McCaffery, Janet, illus. LC 70-151936. (Illus.). 32 p. 26cm. 1971. Morrow.
--Depend on Katie John. Wilkins, Mary Huiskamp. Frame, Paul (1913-), illus. LC 61-7328. (Illus.). 181 p. 21cm. 1961. Harper.
--Euphonia and the Flood. Wilkins, Mary Huiskamp. Taback, Simms, illus. LC 75-19274. (Illus.). 34 p. 21cm. c.1976. (ISBN 0-8193-0836-6). (ISBN 0-8193-0837-4). Parents' Magazine Press.
--The Flower Mother. Wilkins, Mary Huiskamp. McCaffery, Janet, illus. LC 70-168469. (Illus.). 32 p. 27cm. 1972. Morrow.
--The Goblin Under the Stairs. Wilkins, Mary Huiskamp. McCaffery, Janet, illus. LC 68-13001. (Illus.). 1 v. (unpaged. 1968, c.1967. (ISBN 0-688-21352-9). Morrow.
--High Wind for Kansas. Wilkins, Mary Huiskamp. Mars, Witold Tadeusz J. (1912-), illus. LC 65-11776. (Illus.). 45 p. 23cm. 1965. Morrow.
--Honestly, Katie John!. Wilkins, Mary Huiskamp. Frame, Paul (1913-), illus. LC 63-8473. (Illus.). 214 p. 22cm. 1963. Harper & Row.
--The Horse Comes First. Wilkins, Mary Huiskamp. Gretzer, John, illus. LC 73-84822. (Illus.). 188 p. 22cm. 1974. Atheneum.
--Hot-Air Henry. Wilkins, Mary Huiskamp. Ingraham, Erick, illus. LC 84-9082. 1984. (ISBN 0-688-04068-3). Morrow.
--Hot Air Henry. Wilkins, Mary Huiskamp. Ingraham, Erick, illus. LC 80-26189. p. cm. 1981. (ISBN 0-688-00501-2). W. Morrow.
--Houn' Dog. Wilkins, Mary Huiskamp. Duvoisin, Roger Antoine (1904-1980), illus. LC 59-5136. (Illus.). (gr. k-3). 1959. (ISBN 0-688-21406-1). Morrow.
--House For Thirty Cats. Wilkins, Mary Huiskamp. Chalmers, Mary Eileen (1927-), illus. 1965. (ISBN 0-8382-0346-9, Cadmus Books). E. M. Hale and Company.
--The House of Thirty Cats. Wilkins, Mary Huiskamp. Chalmers, Mary Eileen (1927-), illus. LC 65-11454. (Illus.). 218 p. 22cm. 1965. Harper & Row.
--Hungry Leprechaun. Wilkins, Mary Huiskamp. Duvoisin, Roger Antoine (1904-1980), illus. (Illus.). (gr. k-3). 1962. (ISBN 0-688-31713-8). Morrow.
--It's Getting Beautiful Now. Wilkins, Mary Huiskamp. Duvoisin, Roger Antoine (1904-1980), illus. LC 77-135777. 149 p. 22cm. 1971. (ISBN 0-06-020938-0). Harper & Row.
--Jack the Wise and the Cornish Cuckoos. Wilkins, Mary Huiskamp. McCrady, Lady (1951-), illus. LC 77-22714. (Illus.). 32 p. 26cm. 1978. (ISBN 0-688-32132-1). Morrow.
--Katie John. Wilkins, Mary Huiskamp. Frame, Paul (1913-), illus. LC 60-5775. (Illus.). 134 p. 21cm. 1960. Harper.
--Katie John and Heathcliff. Wilkins, Mary Huiskamp. LC 80-7770. p. cm. c.1980. (ISBN 0-06-020931-3). (ISBN 0-06-020932-1). Harper & Row.
--The Last Two Elves in Denmark. Wilkins, Mary Huiskamp. McCaffery, Janet, illus. LC 68-11572. (Illus.). 32 p. 1968. W. Morrow.
--Magic in the Alley. Wilkins, Mary Huiskamp. Watson, Wendy Mcleod (1942-), illus. LC 77-98607. (Illus.). 167 p. 22cm. 1970. (ISBN 0-689-20501-5). Atheneum.
--Making the Mississippi Shout. Wilkins, Mary Huiskamp. Galdone, Paul (1914-), illus. LC 57-5119. 96p. illus. 22cm. (Morrow junior books). 1957. Morrow.
--Mermaid of Storms. Wilkins, Mary Huiskamp. McCaffery, Janet, illus. LC 70-103047. (Illus.). 32 p. 26cm. 1970. Morrow.
--Mrs. Dog's Own House. Wilkins, Mary Huiskamp. McCaffery, Janet, illus. LC 72-180536. (Illus.). 32 p. 26cm. 1972. Morrow.
--The Night the Monster Came. Wilkins, Mary Huiskamp. Morrill, Leslie H., illus. LC 81-18712. (Illus.). 62 p. 21cm. 1982. (ISBN 0-688-01167-5). (ISBN 0-688-01168-3). W. Morrow.
--The Nine Lives of Homer C. Cat. Wilkins, Mary Huiskamp. Duvoisin, Roger Antoine (1904-1980), illus. LC 60-999959. unpaged. illus. 27cm. 1961. Morrow.
--Old Man Whickutt's Donkey. Wilkins, Mary Huiskamp. De Paola, Tomie, pseud. (1934-), illus. De Paola, Thomas Anthony. LC 74-12289. (Illus.). 41 p. 24cm. 1975. (ISBN 0-8193-0787-4). (ISBN 0-8193-0787-4). Parents' Magazine Press.
--Ownself. Wilkins, Mary Huiskamp. LC 74-21531. 149 p. 21cm. 1975. (ISBN 0-06-020927-5). (ISBN 0-06-020928-3). Harper & Row.
--Ownself. Wilkins, Mary Huiskamp. 149p. 20cm. (Harper Trophy Book). 1977. (ISBN 0-06-440087-5). Harper and Row.
--The Pixy and the Lazy Housewife. Wilkins, Mary Huiskamp. McCaffery, Janet, illus. LC 69-10353. (Illus.). 32 p. 1969. Morrow.
--River-Minded Boy. Wilkins, Mary Huiskamp. Lohse, William R., illus. LC 58-5252. 159p. illus. 21cm. 1958. W. Morrow.
--The Runaway Brownie. Wilkins, Mary Huiskamp. McCaffery, Janet, illus. LC 67-6296. (Illus.). 1 v. (unpaged. 1967. W. Morrow.
--The Sweet Patootie Doll. Wilkins, Mary Huiskamp. Duvoisin, Roger Antoine (1904-1980), illus. LC 57-5425. unpaged. illus. 26cm. (Morrow junior books). (gr. k-3). 1957. Morrow.
--The Thieving Dwarfs. Wilkins, Mary Huiskamp. McCaffery, Janet, illus. LC 67-2203. (Illus.). 1 v. (unpaged. 1967. W. Morrow.
--Three Kinds of Stubborn. Wilkins, Mary Huiskamp. Malsberg, Edward, illus. LC 78-152793. (Illus.). 48 p. 23cm. 1972. (ISBN 0-8116-4031-0). Garrard Pub. Co.
--Traveling Ball of String. Wilkins, Mary Huiskamp. McCaffery, Janet, illus. LC 69-15042. (Illus.). 32 p. 27cm. 1969. Morrow.
--White Witch of Kynance. Wilkins, Mary Huiskamp. Gundelfinger, John, illus. LC 76-104757. (gr. 7 up). 1970. (ISBN 0-06-020957-7, HarpJ). (ISBN 0-686-76871-X). Har-Row.
--White Witch of Kynance. Wilkins, Mary Huiskamp. Gundelfinger, John, illus. LC 76-104757. 208p. (Trophy Bks). (gr. 7 up). 1971. (ISBN 0-06-440012-3). Har-Row.
--The Witch of Hissing Hill. Wilkins, Mary Huiskamp. McCaffery, Janet, illus. LC 64-15475. (Illus.). 32 p. 26cm. 1964. W. Morrow.
--The Witch Who Lost Her Shadow. Wilkins, Mary Huiskamp. 1st ed. Noble, Trinka Hakes, illus. LC 78-19489. (Illus.). 30 p. c.1979. (ISBN 0-06-020946-1). (ISBN 0-06-020947-X). Harper & Row.
--Wobble, the Witch Cat. Wilkins, Mary Huiskamp. Duvoisin, Roger Antoine (1904-1980), illus. LC 58-5018. 27cm. (Morrow junior books). 1958. Morrow.

Calhoun, Philo, jt. auth. see Webster, H. T.

Califf, Rowena
--Fuzzy Wuzzy and Other Stories. LC 35-8666. 127 p. col. illus. 20 cm. c.1935. The Bruce Publishing Company.
--Pinkey Dew and Other Stories. LC 29-12705. 64 p. col. illus. 20 cm. c.1929. The Bruce Publishing Company.

Calisch, Edith L., ed.
--Bible Tales For Young People, 2 vols. N.D. Behrman House Inc.
--Fairy Tales From Grandfather's Big Book. N.D. Behrman House Inc.

Calkins, Dick & Nowlan, Philip Frances (1888-1940)
--Buck Rogers in the Dangerous Mission: With "Pop-up" Picture. LC 34-163. 1 p. l., 5-60 (i. e. 62) p. illus. (1 col.) 13 cm. (On cover: The midget pop-up hooks). c.1934. Blue Ribbon Press.
--Buck Rogers 25th Century: Featuring Buddy and Allura in "Strange Adventures in the Spider Ship". LC 35-8413. 17 p. front, illus. 24 cm. c.1935. Pleasure Books, Inc.

Calkins, Erling (1917-)
--Adventure at Beaver Falls. LC 79-15601. 96 p. 21cm. (Crown book). 1979. (ISBN 0-8127-0223-9). Southern Pub. Association.

Call, Cora Pinkley
--The Dream Garden. LC 45-2206. 94 p. 18 cm. 1944. The Wartburg Press.
--Shifting Sands. LC 43-16894. 91 p. incl. illus., pl. 18 cm. 1943. The Wartburg Press.

Call, Dwight M.
--Tales by Paw Paw, Bk. 1. 1978. (ISBN 0-533-03483-3). Vantage.

Call, Hughie Florence (1890-)
--Peter's Moose. MacLean, Robert (1926-), illus. LC 61-7701. (Illus.). (gr. 3-6). 1961. (ISBN 0-670-54977-0). Viking Pr.

Camp, Joe
--Oh Heavenly Dog!. 144p. (Orig.). (gr. 7 up). 1980. (ISBN 0-590-31400-9). Scholastic Inc.
Camp, Joe, jt. auth. see Ingoglia, Gina.
Camp, Lyon Sprague De see De Camp, Lyon Sprague (1907-) & De Camp, Catherine Crook.
Camp, Paul K
--A Handful of Stars. LC 69-19599. 184 p. 21cm. 1969. D. McKay Co.
--Shantyboat Bill. MacDonald, James, illus. LC 67-21632. (Illus.). 184 p. 21cm. 1967. D. McKay Co.
Camp, Rosemary De see De Camp, Rosemary.
Camp, Walter Chauncey (1859-1925)
--Captain Danny. LC 14-16209. 4 p. l., 302 1 p. col. front., col., plages. 19 1/2 cm. 1914. D. Appleton and Company.
--Danny Fists. LC 13-21025. 4 p. l., 285 1 p. col. front., col. plates. 20 1/2 cm. 1913. D. Appleton and Company.
--Danny the Freshman. LC 15-254664. 4 p. l., 268, 1 p. col. front., col. plates. 191/2 cm. 1915. D. Appleton and Company.
--Frank Armstrong, Drop Kicker. Scott, Arthur O., illus. LC 12-17206. (Illus.). 4 p., 1 l., 5-307 p. 21cm. c.1912. Hurst & Company.
--Jack Hall at Yale: A Football Story. LC 9-26146. 5 p. l., 297, 1 p. col. front., 3 col. pl. 20 cm. 1909. D. Appleton and Company.
--Old Ryerson. LC 11-23840. ix, 288 p., 1 l. col. front. col. plates 20 cm. 1911. D. Appleton and Company.
--The Substitute: A Football Story. LC 8-26678. vii p., 1 l., 337 1 p. col. front., 8 col. pl. 20 1/2 cm. (The Yale Ser.). 1908. D. Appleton and Company.
Campana, Manny, illus.
--The Saggy Baggy Elephant's Great Big Counting Book. (Illus.). 24p. (ps). 1983. (ISBN 0-307-10442-7, Golden Pr). Western Pub.
Campbell, A. B.
--Queer Shipmates. (Illus.). (gr. 9 up). N.D. (ISBN 0-392-04313-0, SpS). Sportshelf.
Campbell, Agnes
--Tales My Father Told. Kennedy, Richard (1910-), illus. LC 48-8763. 144 p. illus. 24 cm. 1948. Whittlesey House.
Campbell, Alfred Stuart (1900-)
--Under the Capstone, a Tale of the Channel Islands. Dobias, Frank (1902-), illus. LC 40-33277. ix p., 1 l., 234 p. illus. 20 1/2 cm. 1940. London, D. Appleton-Century Company, Incorporated.
--The Wizard and His Magic Powder:. Tales of the Channel Island. Wiese, Kurt (1887-1974), illus. LC 45-4135. 5 p., l., 114 p., 1 l. illus. (part col.) 21 cm. 1945. A. A. Knopf.
Campbell, Alistair (1925-)
--Happy Summer. 122p. (gr. 3-5). 1976. (ISBN 0-685-67462-2). Intl Pubns Serv.
Campbell, Anabel L.
--Jeannie, a Cocker's Diary. 1981. (ISBN 0-8062-1816-9). Carlton.
Campbell, Barbara Mary see Cam, pseud.
Campbell, Barbara Mary (1913-)
--A Girl Called Bob & a Horse Called Yoki. LC 81-68780. 167 p. 22cm. c.1982. (ISBN 0-8037-3149-3). (ISBN 0-8037-3150-7). Dial Press.
--The Story of Buttercup Fairy. Cam, pseud. Campbell, Barbara Mary (1913-), illus. Cam, pseud. LC 51-14775. unpaged. illus. 25cm. N.D. Roy.

Campbell, Bruce, pseud., see Epstein, Samuel.

Campbell, Bruce, pseud. (1909-)
--Black Thumb Mystery. Epstein, Samuel. (gr. 6-10). N.D. (ISBN 0-448-08603-4). G&D.
--Clue of the Coiled Cobra. Epstein, Samuel. (gr. 6-10). N.D. (ISBN 0-448-08605-0). G&D.
--Clue of the Marked Claw. Epstein, Samuel. (gr. 6-10). N.D. (ISBN 0-448-08604-2). G&D.
--The Clue of the Phantom Car. Epstein, Samuel. LC 53-1371. 214 p. illus. 20 cm. (His The Ken Holt mystery stories, 8). 1953. Grosset & Dunlap.
--Clue of the Silver Scorpion. Epstein, Samuel. LC 61-1197. (Illus.). 20cm. 180p. (His The Ken Holt mystery stories, 16). (gr. 6-10). 1961. (ISBN 0-448-08616-6). G&D.
--Mystery of Gallows Cliff. Epstein, Samuel. (gr. 6-10). N.D. (ISBN 0-448-08615-8). G&D.
--Mystery of the Galloping Horse. Epstein, Samuel. (gr. 6-10). N.D. (ISBN 0-448-08609-3). G&D.
--The Mystery of the Gallows Cliff. Epstein, Samuel. LC 60-1209. 20cm. 184p. (The Ken Holt Mystery Stories). 1960. Grosset & Dunlap.
--The Mystery of the Green Flame. Epstein, Samuel. LC 55-106554. 212 p. illus. 20 cm. (His A Ken Holt Mystery 10). c.1955. Grosset & Dunlap.
--Mystery of the Grinning Tiger. Epstein, Samuel. (gr. 6-10). 1956. (ISBN 0-448-08611-5). G&D.
--The Mystery of the Invisible Enemy. Epstein, Samuel. LC 59-16065. 182 p. illus. 20cm. (The Ken Holt Mystery Stories). 1959. Grosset & Dunlap.
--The Mystery of the Iron Box. Epstein, Samuel. LC 52-13027. 214 p. illus. 20 cm. (His Ken Holt Mystery Stories, 7). 1952. Grosset & Dunlap.
--Mystery of the Plumed Serpent. Epstein, Samuel. (gr. 6-10). N.D. (ISBN 0-448-08617-4). G&D.
--The Mystery of the Shattered Glass. Epstein, Samuel. LC 58-14585. 20cm. 181p. (The Ken Holt Mystery Stories). 1958. Grosset & Dunlap.
--The Mystery of the Sultan's Scimitar. Epstein, Samuel. LC 63-18955. 177 p. illus. 20 cm. (Ken Holt Mystery,18). 1963. Grosset & Dunlap.
--Mystery of the Vanishing Magician. Epstein, Samuel. (Illus.). (gr. 6-10). 1956. (ISBN 0-448-08612-3). G&D.
--Riddle of the Stone Elephant. Epstein, Samuel. (gr. 6-10). N.D. (ISBN 0-448-08602-6). G&D.
--Secret of Hangman's Inn. Epstein, Samuel. (gr. 6-10). N.D. (ISBN 0-448-08606-9). G&D.
--Secret of Skeleton Island. Epstein, Samuel. (gr. 6-10). N.D. (ISBN 0-448-08601-8). G&D.
Campbell, Camilla B. (1905-)
--The Bartletts of Box B. Ranch. Chestnut, Glenn, illus. LC 49-8700. 256 p. illus., map (on lining-papers) 21 cm. 1949. Whittlesey House.
--Coronado and His Captains. Stein, Harve (1904-), illus. LC 58-100908. 176p. illus. 23cm. 1958. Follett Pub. Co.
--Star Mountain and other Legends of Mexico. McKinney, Edna, illus. N.D. McGraw-Hill Book Co.
--Viva la Patria. Santiago, Nilo, illus. LC 70-126789. (Illus.). 57 p. 20cm. (Challenger Book. La Raza Series). 1970. Hill and Wang; Distributed by Random House.
Campbell, Carolyn
--Kids, Inc. Bonner, Jordan, ed. Bullington, Jed, illus. (Illus.). 80p. (Orig.). (Papa Jan Ser.: Bk. 2). (gr. 3 up). 1985. (ISBN 0-914007-04-1). Bonner Pub Co.
Campbell, Carolyn & Thompson, Pat
--On My Own. Bonner, Jordon, ed. Bullington, Jed, illus. (Illus.). 80p. (Papa Jan Ser.: Bk. 4). (gr. 3 up). 1985. (ISBN 0-914007-06-8). Bonner Pub Co.
Campbell, Civardi
--Viking Raiders. (Time Travelers Books). (gr. 4-9). 1977. (ISBN 0-86020-086-8, Usborne-Hayes). (ISBN 0-88110-102-8). (ISBN 0-86020-085-X). EDC.
Campbell, Daisy Rhodes
--The Fiddling Girl. Goss, John, illus. N.D. Page Co.
--The Proving of Virginia. Goss, John, illus. N.D. Page Co.
--The Violin Lady. Goss, John, illus. N.D. Page Co.
Campbell, David, et al.
--Land of the Rainbow Gold. Fowler, Mildred M., ed. Newnham, Jack, illus. (Illus.). 52 ils., 16 in color. glossary. notes. 111p. (gr. 6-10). 1971. Tri-Ocean.
Campbell, Dugald
--In the Heart of Bantuland. N.D. J.B. Lippincott.
Campbell, Elizabeth Anderson
--The Carving on the Tree. 1968. Little,Brown and Company.
--Fins and Tails: A Story of Strange Fish. Weisgard, Leonard Joseph (1916-), illus. LC 63-13456. 58 p. illus. 27 cm. 1963. Little, Brown.
Campbell, Gilbert Sir
--Prince Goldenblade: A Fairy Story. (Prize Library). N.D. Ward Lock & Bowden.
Campbell, Gordon (1886-)
--A Son of the Sea. LC 37-12729. 4 p. l., 248 p. col. front., plates 21 cm. 1936. F. Warne & Co., Ltd.
--Witch of the Wave. LC 37-168079. 288 p. col. front., plates 21 1/2 cm. c.1937. F. Warne & Co., Ltd.
Campbell, H. A.
--The Sleepy Song Book. N.D. Robert M. McBride.
Campbell, Harriet Sefton, Mrs.
--Pyx--B. A. (Just a Dog's Life). LC 28-25484. 110 p. front. plates. 18 1/2 cm. c.1928. Frye & Smith.
Campbell, Harriette Russell, Mrs. (1883-)
--The Little Great Lady. LC 25-197294. 5 p. l., 3-264 p. front., plates. 19 cm. c.1925. Harper & Brothers.
--The Mystery of Saint's Island. LC 27-125124. vii p., 1 l., 223 p. front., plates 19 cm. c.1927. Harper & Brothers.
--The New Curiosity Shop. Holberg, Richard A. (1889-1942), illus. LC 29-8543. vi p., 2 l., 262 p. illus. 19 1/2 cm. 1929. Harper & Brother.
--Patsy's Brother. LC 26-16268. 5 p. l., 3-344 p. front., plates. 19 1/2 cm. c.1926. Harper & Brother.
--The Piper's Lad. Trugo, Lui, illus. LC 31-10565. v p. 1 l., 219 p. col. front., illus. 19 1/2 cm. 1931. Harper & Brothers.
--Red Coats and Blue: A Story of a British Girl in the American Revolution. De Angeli, Marguerite Lofft, Mrs. (1889-), illus. LC 30-7424. vii p., 1 l., 324 p. col. front., plates. 19 1/2 cm. 1930. Harper & Brother.
--The String Glove Mystery. LC 36-482. 5 p. l., 3-288 2. fold. map. 19 1/2 cm. 1936. A. A. Knopf.
Campbell, Helen Mary Le Roy (1850-)
--Little Konrad, the Swiss Boy. N.D. David McKay Co.
--Little Metzu, the Japanese Boy. N.D. David McKay Co.
--Story of Little Jan: The Dutch Boy. LC 6-1028. 100 p. incl. illus., pl., map. 19 1/2 cm. (Children of the world series). 1905. Educational Publishing Company.
--The Story of Little Konrad: The Swiss Boy. LC 4-28965. 1 p. l., 64 p. illus. 19 1/2 cm. 1902. Educational Publishing Company.
--Story of Little Metzu,the Japanese Boy. LC 6-1026. 95 p. incl. illus., pl., map. 19 1/2cm. (Children of the world series). 1905. Educational Publishing Company.
--Wah Sing, Our Little Chinese Cousin. LC 6-1376. 64 p. incl. front., illus. 19 1/2 cm. (Young folk's library of choice literature). c.1904. Educational Publishing Company.
--Wah Sing, Our Little Chinese Friend. N.D. David McKay Co.
--Wewa, the Child of the Pueblos. LC 6-1376. 48 p. incl. illus., pl. 20 cm. (Young folk's library of choice literature). c.1903. Educational Publishing Company.
Campbell, Helen Stuart see Weeks, Helen C., pseud.
Campbell, Helen Stuart see Weeks, Helen C., pseud.
Campbell, Helen Stuart see Wheaton, Campbell, pseud.
Campbell, Helen Stuart, Mrs. (1839-1918)
--Ainslee and His Friends. Weeks, Helen C., pseud, 1 of 4 Vols. (Illus.). (The Ainslee Series). N.D. Set. E. P. Dutton & Co.
--The Ainslee Series. Weeks, Helen C., pseud, 4 Vols. (Illus.). N.D. E. P. Dutton & Co.
--The Ainslee Stories. Weeks, Helen C., pseud. Neely, Keith R. (1943-), illus. LC 6-22826. 3 p. l., 411 p. front., plates 17 c. 1868. Hurd and Houghton Etc.
--Four and What They Did. Weeks, Helen C., pseud, 1 of 4 Vols. (Illus.). (The Ainslee Ser.: vol. 2). N.D. Set. E. P. Dutton & Co.
--Four and What They Did. Weeks, Helen C., pseud. (The Ainslee Ser. for Young People). N.D. Hurd & Houghton.
--Grandpa's House. Weeks, Helen C., pseud, 1 of 4 Vols. (Illus.). (The Ainslee Series: vol. 3). N.D. Set. E. P. Dutton & Co.
--Grandpa's House. Weeks, Helen C., pseud. LC 6-22825. 2 p. l., 239 p. front., plates 17 1/2 cm. 1868. Hurd & Houghton.
--Harry's Winter with the Indians, 1 of 4 Vols. (Illus.). (The Ainslee Ser.: vol. 4). N.D. Set. E. P. Dutton & Co.
--Six Sinners: Or, School Days in Bantam Valley. Wheaton, Campbell, pseud. LC 6-22823. iv, 197 p. 17 1/2 cm. 1877. G. P. Putnam's Sons.
--The What-To-Do Club: A Story for Girls. Weeks, Helen C., pseud. 405p. 1885. Roberts Brothers.
--White and Red: A Narrative of Life Among the Northwest Indians. Weeks, Helen C., pseud. LC 6-22824. 1 p. l., 266 p. front., plates. 18 cm. 1869. Hurd & Houghton Etc.
Campbell, Hope see Hughes, Virginia, pseud.
Campbell, Hope (1925-)
--Home to Hawaii. LC 67-2451. 21cm. 174p. (gr. 5-8). 1967. G&D.
--The Legend of Lost Earth. LC 76-48079. 154 p. 22cm. c.1977. (ISBN 0-590-07397-4). Four Winds Press.
--Liza. LC 65-18037. 186 p. 21cm. 1965. Norton.
--Meanwhile, Back at the Castle. LC 76-127731. (Illus.). x, 244 p. 22cm. 1970. Grosset and Dunlap.
--Mystery at Fire Island. Grant, Alice Leigh (1947-), illus. LC 77-18311. (Illus.). 170 p. 22cm. c.1978. (ISBN 0-590-07536-5). Four Winds Press.
--The Peak Beneath the Moon. LC 78-20427. 133 p. 22cm. c.1979. (ISBN 0-590-07565-9). Four Winds Press.
--Peter's Angel. Pinto, Ralph, illus. 1976. Scholastic.
--Peter's Angel: A Story About Monsters. Obligado, Lillian, illus. LC 75-9517. 22cm. 151p. 1975. (ISBN 0-590-07404-0). Four Winds Press.
--Why Not Join the Giraffes?. LC 67-18685. 223 p. 21cm. 1968. Norton.
Campbell, Hope (1925-) & Anderson, Mary (1939-)
--There's a Pizza Back in Cleveland. LC 72-182112. (gr. 5-9). 1972. (ISBN 0-590-17264-6, Four Winds). Schol Bk Serv.
Campbell, Ignatius Roy Dunnachie (1901-1957)
--The Mamba's Precipice. LC 54-7930. 189p. 21cm. 1st U.S. edition. 1954, c.1953. J. Day Co.
Campbell, Janet
--The House That Biff Built. Cooke, Tom, illus. LC 80-67661. (Illus.). 27cm. 26p. c.1980. (ISBN 0-307-23119-4). Western Pub. Co.: Children's Television Workshop.
--Sesame Stories: The Monster in the Mirror & Other Stories from Sesame Street. Cooke, Tom, illus. LC 78-65068. (Illus.). (Golden Storybks.). (ps-3). 1979. (ISBN 0-307-62080-8, Golden Pr). (ISBN 0-307-12080-5, Golden Pr). Western Pub.
Campbell, Janet & Campbell, Roger
--The Great Alphabet Race. O'Sullivan, Tom, illus. LC 73-160209. (Illus.). 51 p. 31cm. 1972. Golden Press.
Campbell, Jeannette Helen (1895-)
--Leaning on the Wind. Campbell, Jeanette Helen (1895-), illus. LC 43-22707. xi, 1, 13-79 p. incl. col. front., illus. 23 1/2 cm. 1943. Dorrance & Company.
Campbell, John Wood, Jr. (1910-1971)
--Cloak of Aesir. LC 75-10664. 254 p. 22cm. (Classics of science fiction). 1976, c.1952. (ISBN 0-88355-359-7). (ISBN 0-88355-449-6). Hyperion Press.
--Cloak of Aesir. Science-Fiction Stories. LC 52-14603. 255 p. 21cm. 1952. Shasta Publishers.
Campbell, Judith, pseud., see Pares, Marion Stapylton.
Campbell, Judith, pseud. (1914-)
--Four Ponies. Pares, Marion Stapylton. Pares, Susan, illus. LC 59-3182. 159p. illus. 19cm. 1958. F. Muller Stamped: Distributed by Sportshelf, New Rochelle, N. Y.
--Four Ponies. Pares, Marion Stapylton. Pares, Susan, illus. (gr. 7 up). N.D. Soccer.

Campbell, Julie, pseud.

--Mystery at Maypenny's. 236p. (Trixie Belden Mystery Ser.). (gr. 4-6). 1980. (ISBN 0-307-61551-0, Golden Pr). (ISBN 0-307-21552-0). Western Pub.
--Mystery of the Midnight 236p. (Trixie Belden Mystery Ser.). (gr. 4-6). 1980. (ISBN 0-307-61552-9, Golden Pr). (ISBN 0-307-21551-2). Western Pub.
--Mystery of the Missing Millionaire. 216p. (Trixie Belden Mystery Ser.). (gr. 4-6). 1979. (ISBN 0-307-61555-3, Golden Pr). Western Pub.
--Mystery of the Vanishing Victim. 216p. (A Trixie Belden Mystery Ser.). (gr. 4-6). 1979. (ISBN 0-307-61554-5, Golden Pr). Western Pub.
--Mystery of the Velvet Gown. 236p. (Trixie Belden Mystery Ser.). (gr. 4-6). 1980. (ISBN 0-307-61550-2, Golden Pr). (ISBN 0-307-21550-4). Western Pub.
--Mystery of the Whispering Witch. 216p. (A Trixie Belden Mystery Ser.). (gr. 4-6). 1979. (ISBN 0-307-61553-7, Golden Pr). Western Pub.
--Trixie Belden & The Secret of the Mansion. Bowden, Joan Chase. Stevens, Mary E. (1920-1966), illus. 1959. Golden Press.
Campbell, Karel
--Blue Jay & the Monster. Seir, Birte, illus. LC 67-14952. (Illus.). (gr. k-5). 1967. (ISBN 0-8225-0258-5). Lerner Pubns.
Campbell, Karel, tr. see Seir, Birte.
Campbell, Ken
--Skungpoomery. 47p. 1984. (ISBN 0-413-33910-6, Pub. by Eyre Methuen England). Methuen Inc.
Campbell, Lady
--Cabin by the Wayside: A Tale for the Young. Campbell, Lady, illus. (Illus.). N.D. George Routledge & Sons.
--The Monsters' Room. (gr. 3-5). N.D. (ISBN 0-590-02076-5, Schol Pap). Scholastic Inc.
--The Story of an Apple: By Lady Campbell. Gilbert, John Clitherae, illus. (Illus.). N.D. George Routledge & Sons.
Campbell, Lang
--The Dinky Ducklings. LC 28-7549. 40 p. illus. (part col.) 19 cm. (On cover: Volland "Sunny book" series). c.1928. The P. F. Volland Company.
Campbell, Lillian J
--Four Little Friends. LC 39-118. 4 p. l., 111 p. illus. 21 cm. 1938. The Naylor Company.
Campbell, Loomis Joseph (1831-1896), selected by.
--Young Folks' Book of Poetry, 3 parts. N.D. Lee and Shepard's Trade List.
--Young Folk's Book of Poetry. N.D. Lothrop,Lee & Shepard.
Campbell, M. Rudolph, adapted by see Dostoevsky, Fyodor Mikhailovich.
Campbell, Marion (1919-)
--The Wide Blue Road. Grey, Frank R., illus. LC 57-10345. 192p. illus. 21cm. 1957. Dutton.

--The Pueblo Girl,. The Story of Coronado on the Rio Grande. Rush, Olive, illus. LC 29-188790. 4 p. l, 174, 1 p. col. front., illus. plates. 21 cm. 1929. Houghton Mifflin Company.

Cannon, James Leonard

--Hoofbeats, a Picture Book of Horses. LC 38-16538. 4 p. l, 7-48 1 p. col. front., illus. (part. col) 26 cm. 1938. A. Whitman & Co.

Cannon, Marian

--Children of the Fiery Mountain. Cannon, Marian, illus. LC 40-30186. 96 p. col. front., illus. col. plates. 26 cm. 1940. E.P. Dutton and Company, Inc.

--San Bao and His Adventures in Peking. Cannon, Marian, illus. LC 39-6486. 5 p. l, 15-71, 3 p. incl. front., illus. 24 cm. 1939. E. P. Dutton and Company, Inc.

--Twins at Our House: Verses. Cannon, Marian, illus. LC 48-3502. 44 p. col. illus. 20 cm. c.1945. Lothrop, Lee and Shepard C.

Cannon, Marian, jt. auth. see Cannon, Wilma.

Cannon, Ralph

--Grid. 273p. N.D. Reilly & Lee Co.

--Grid Star. 273p. N.D. Reilly & Lee.

--Out of Bounds. N.D. Reilly & Lee.

Cannon, Sarah O., jt. auth. see Pearl, Minnie.

Cannon, Wilma & Cannon, Marian

--Peter Is Sweeter. LC 42-21000. 39p. N.D. Lothrop Lee & Shepard.

Canon, Claudia Von see Von Canon, Claudia.

Canright, David

--Ships & the River. 32p. (gr. 5 up). 1975. (ISBN 0-913344-22-2). Interbk Inc.

Cante, Floris

--Ronnie's Adventures with Old King Cole. (Illus.). (gr. k-3). N.D. Vantage.

Cantieni, Benita

--Little Elephant & Big Mouse. Gachter, Fred, illus. Gadsby, Oliver E., tr. from Ger. LC 82-183307. (Illus.). 30p. 1981. (ISBN 0-907234-09-7, Pub. by Picture Bk Studio USA). Neugebauer Pr.

Canton, William (1845-1926)

--The Bible Story. (Illus.). 24cm. 403p. 1915. Hodder & Stoughton.

--A Child's Book of Saints. Rhys, Ernest, ed. (Illus.). 18cm. 258p. (Everyman's Library for Young People: No. 61). 1906. E. P. Dutton & Co.

--A Child's Book of Warriors. Cole, Herbert, illus. 20cm. 318p. 1912. E. P. Dutton & Co.

--The Invisible Playmate and W.V. Her Book. Brock, Charles Edmond (1870-1938), illus. ix, 226 p. pl. 18 1/2 cm. 1898. Dodd, Mead and Company.

--The Reign of King Herla. N.D. E P Dutton.

--The True Annals of Fairyland in the Reign of King Herla. Rhys, Ernest, ed. Robinson, Charles (1870-1937), illus. 18cm. 365p. (Everyman's Library for Young People). N.D. E. P. Dutton & Co.

--W. V.'s Golden Legend. Robinson, Thomas Heath (1869-1950), illus. 12cm. 309p. 1898. Dodd, Mead & Co.

Cantone, Vic

--Rocky, the Rocket Mouse. Cantone, Vic, illus. (Kindergarten Read-to Bks.). (gr. k-2). N.D. (ISBN 0-513-00465-3). Denison.

--Topo, the Mouse. Cantone, Vic, illus. LC 79-88064. (Illus.). 32 p. 29cm. 1969. Denison.

Cantrell, Hilda M.

--The Woodfolk Stories and The Littlest Christmas Tree. Lyons, Dave, illus. LC 55-10186. 39p. illus 24cm. 1955. Pageant Press, Inc.

Cantwell, Ray, jt. auth. see Zarem, Lewis.

Canty, Mary

--The Green Gate. Bock, Vera, illus. LC 65-20935. 134p. illus. 22cm. (gr. 4-6). c.1965. (ISBN 0-679-25057-3). McKay.

--Join Hands with the Ghosts. Goddard, Ragna Tischler, illus. LC 77-81896. (Illus.). 136 p. 21cm. 1969. D. McKay Co.

Capauna, Luigi (1839-1917)

--Nimble-Legs: A Story for Boys. Hazleton, Isaac Brewster, illus. Cooper, Frederic Taber (1834-1897), tr. LC 27-18538. 191 p. incl., illus., plates. col. front. 19 cm. 1927. Longmans, Green and Co.

Cape, Emily Palmer

--Fairy Surprises for Little Folks. LC 8-5579. (Illus.). 18 x 14cm. 137p. 1908. Architecture Press.

Capek, Josef, jt. auth. see Capek, Karel.

Capek, Josef (1887-1945)

--Harum Scarum. Capek, Josef (1887-1945), illus. Jolly, Stephen, tr. LC 66-117751. 95p. illus. (pt. col.) 19cm. 1967, c.1963. Norton.

Capek, Karel (1890-1938)

--Dashenka: Or, The Life of a Puppy. Weatherall, Marie (1897-) & Weatherall, Robert (1899-), trs. LC 34-2907. 93. 8 p. incl. front., illlus., plates, 28 1/2 cm. 1933. H. Holt and Company.

Capek, Karel (1890-1938) & Capek, Josef (1887-1945)

--Fairy Tales, with One Extra As a Make Weight. Weatherall, Maria (1897-) & Weatherall Robert (1899-), trs. LC 34-4647. 3 p. l., 90288 p. illus. 20 cm. 1933. H. Holt and Company.

Capella, F. De see De Capella, F.

Capizzi, Michael (1941-)

--The Boy Who Came up Quietly. Colton, Keita, illus. LC 71-148202. (Illus.). 27 p. 27cm. 1971. World Pub. Co.

--Getting It All Together. Lewin, Ted (1935-), illus. LC 72-1384. (Illus.). 197 p. 21cm. 1972. Delacorte Press.

Caplan, Lydia

--Pepper. Williams, Ben, illus. LC 56-26466. unpaged. illus. 21cm. (Cozy-corner book, 2444). c.1955. Whitman Pub. Co.

Caple, Kathy

--Inspector Aardvark. Caple, Kathy, illus. LC 79-14668. (Illus.). 32p. (gr. 1-5). 1980. (ISBN 0-671-96108-X). Windmill Bks.

--Inspector Aardvark and the Perfect Cake. Caple, Kathy, illus. LC 79-14668. p. cm. 1979. (ISBN 0-525-61596-2). Windmill Books.

Caples, Robert Cole

--The Potter and His Children. N.D. Carlton Press.

Caplin, Al, pseud., see Caplin, Alfred Gerald.

Caplin, Al, pseud. (1909-1979)

--The Life and Times of the Shmoo. Caplin, Alfred Gerald. LC 49-717570. 90 p. illus. (part col.) 27 cm. 1948. Simon and Schuster.

Caplin, Alfred Gerald see Caplin, Al, pseud.

Caplin, Alfred Gerald see Capp, Al, pseud.

Capon, Paul (1912-1969)

--The End of the Tunnel. 1st ed. LC 59-10205. 240p. illus. 21cm. 1959. Bobbs-Merrill.

--The Kingdom of the Bulls: A Story of Ancient Britain and Crete. Zacks, Lewis, illus. LC 62-16391. 101p. illus. 22cm. 1962. Norton.

--Lost: A Moon. LC 56-11650. 222p. 21cm. c.1955. Bobbs-Merrill.

--Warrior's Moon. Orbaan, Albert F. (1913-), illus. LC 64-18034. (Illus.). 190. 21cm. 1964. Putnam.

Capote, Truman (1924-1984)

--A Christmas Memory. Delessert, Etienne (1941-), illus. 32p. (Christmas Stories Ser.). 1983. (ISBN 0-87191-956-7). Childrens Bk Co.

Capouya, Emil, tr. see Denneborg, Heinrich Maria.

Capouya, Emile, tr. see Denneborg, Heinrich Maria.

Capp, Al, pseud., see Caplin, Alfred Gerald.

Capp, Al, pseud. (1909-1979)

--The World of Li'l Abner. Caplin, Alfred Gerald. Steinbeck, John Ernest (1902-1968), intro. by. LC 53-619. 175p. illus. 19cm. 1953. Farrar, Straus and Young.

Cappaccio, Albert, jt. auth. see Sloan, Annette.

Cappe, Jeanne (1895-), ed. see Grimm, Jakob Ludwig Karl (1785-1863) & Grimm, Wilhelm Karl.

Cappe, Jeanne (1895-), retold by see Perrault, Charles.

Capps, Benjamin (1922-)

--Woman of the People. (gr. 7-9). 1966. Hawthorn.

Caprani, Augustus G., tr. see Lorenzini, Carlo.

Caprio, Annie De see De Caprio, Annie.

Capron, Jean F (1924-)

--The Trouble with Lucy. LC 67-819. 206 p. 21cm. 1967. Dodd, Mead.

Capron, Louis Bishop (1891-)

--The Blue Witch. 1st ed. Gorsline, Douglas Warner (1913-1985), illus. LC 57-5750. 256p. illus. 21cm. (Holt books for young people). 1957. Holt.

--The Gold Arrowhead. LC 48-8460. 226p. (A Junior Mystery League Book). 1948. Howell, Soskin.

--Gold Arrowhead. (gr. 5-9). N.D. Lothrop Bks.

--The Red War Pole. Stone, David Karl (1922-), illus. LC 63-19014. 186p. illus. 22cm. (gr. 5-9). 1963. (ISBN 0-672-50464-2). Bobbs.

--White Moccasins. 1st ed. Gorsline, Douglas Warner (1913-1985), illus. LC 55-588853. 248p. illus. 21cm. 1955. Holt.

Capron, Mary J. see Fell, Archie, pseud.

Capron, Mary J

--Apron Strings, and Which Way They Pulled. Fell, Archie, pseud. LC 17-23021. 279 p. front, plates 18 cm. (Crowell's Sunday-School Library No. 6). 1871. T. Y. Crowell.

--Capron's Books: Containing: Plus and Minus, Gold and Gilt, Maybee's Stepping Stone,Mrs. Thorne's Guests. N.D. Set of 4 vols. D. Lothrop Co.

--Charity Hurlburt. N.D. Bradley & Woodruff's.

--Gold and Gilt: Or, Maybee's Puzzle, 1 of 50 vols. (Illus.). 350p. (Sunday-School Lib: No. 14). N.D. Set. Lothrop Pub. Co.

--Maybee's Stepping Stones, 1 of 50 vols. (Illus.). 350p. (Sunday-School Lib: No. 14). N.D. Set. Lothrop Pub. Co.

--Mrs. Thorne's Guests. Fell, Archie, pseud, 1 of 50 vols. (Illus.). 350p. (Sunday-School Lib.: No. 14). N.D. Set. Lothrop.

--Plus and Minus: Or, The Briar-Edge Problem, 1 of 50 vols. (Illus.). 350p. (Sunday-School Lib: No. 14). N.D. Set. Lothrop Pub. Co.

Captain Kangaroo (Television Program)

--Stories to Read Aloud. Wilde, Irma, illus. LC 58-149501. 160p. illus. 21cm. 1958. Grosset & Dunlap.

Captain Barnacle, pseud., see Newell, Charles Martin.

Captain Barnacle, pseud. (1821-)

--Pehe Nu-e, the Tiger Whale. Newell, Charles Martin. (Illus.). N.D. Lothrop & Co.

Captain Curtis

--Captured by the Navajos. (Adventure Library). N.D. Harper & Bros.

Capuana, Luigi (1839-1917)

--Golden-Feather. Freeman, Margaret (1893-), illus. Emmrich, Dorothy, tr. LC 30-17631. vii, 1 p., 1 l., 11-265 p. incl. col. front., illus., pl. 21 cm. c.1930. E. P. Dutton & Company Inc.

--Italian Fairy Tales. Emmrich, Dorothy, tr. LC 29-17316. v, 1, 209 p. incl. col. front., illus. 21 cm. c.1929. E. P. Dutton & Company, Inc.

Caputo, Nathalie

--The Animals Search for Summer. Muller, Gerda Maria, illus. LC 66-4003. (Illus.). 1 v. (unpaged. 21cm. (Albums of Pere Castor). 1966. Golden Press.

Carabis, Anne

--The Magic Rocking Chair. Carabis, Anne, illus. (Illus.). 28p. (Orig.). (gr. 2-6,RL 3.1). 1980. (ISBN 0-9605802-0-4). Carabis.

Carafoli, Marci

--The Strange Hotel: Five Ghost Stories. Sumichrast, Jozef (1948-), illus. LC 74-83609. (Illus.). 32p. (Beginning-to-Read Bks). (gr. 2-4). 1975. (ISBN 0-695-40517-9). (ISBN 0-695-30517-4). Follett.

Caras, Roger Andrew (1928-)

--Coyote for a Day. Paterson, Diane R. Cole (1946-), illus. (ps-2). 1977. (ISBN 0-525-61543-1, Windmill). Dutton.

--Skunk for a Day. (gr. k-3). 1976. (Windmill). Dutton.

Caraway, Caren

--Beauty & the Beast. Caraway, Caren, illus. (Illus.). (A Stemmer House Story-to-Color Book). (ps up). 1980. (ISBN 0-916144-46-1). Stemmer Hse.

--Cinderella. Caraway, Caren, illus. (Illus.). 32p. (Orig.). (A Stemmer House Story-to-Color Bk.). (ps-4). 1981. (ISBN 0-916144-85-2). Stemmer Hse.

--Dick Whittington & His Cat. Caraway, Caren, illus. (Illus.). 32p. (Story-to Color Books Ser.). (gr. 2 up). 1982. (ISBN 0-916144-99-2). Stemmer Hse.

--Hansel & Gretel. Caraway, Caren, illus. 32p. (ps up). 1982. (ISBN 0-88045-017-7). Stemmer Hse.

--Snow White & the Seven Dwarfs. Caraway, Caren, illus. (Illus.). 32p. (Stemmer House Story-to-Color Bks). (ps up). 1980. (ISBN 0-916144-57-7). Stemmer Hse.

Caraway, Susan G.

--Poems for Children. Caraway, Donald G., illus. LC 71-182850. (Illus.). 29 p. 22cm. 1972. Dorrance.

Carbe, Nino (1909-), illus.

--Come with Me to Storyland. LC 50-308. 86 p. col. illus. 33 cm. c.1949. Garden City Pub. Co.

Carbonnier, Jeanne (1894-1974)

--Congo Explorer. (Illus.). (gr. 5 up). 1960. (ISBN 0-684-20766-4). Scribner.

Carden, Priscilla

--Aldo's Tower. 1st ed. Werth, Kurt (1896-), illus. LC 54-520088. 63p. illus. 25cm. 1954. Ariel Books.

--Boy on the Sheep Trail. Werth, Kurt (1896-), illus. LC 57-100185. 95p. illus. 23cm. 1957. Nelson.

--The Vanilla Village. 1st ed. Barnum, Jay Hyde (1888-1962), illus. LC 52-8341. 58 p. illus. 25 cm. 1952. Ariel Books.

--Young Brave: Algonquin. 1st ed. Reardon, Mary A., illus. LC 56-561917. 147p. illus. 22cm. 1956. Little, Brown.

Cardenas, Leo

--Return to Ramos. Santiago, Nilo, illus. (Illus.). (gr. 5-10). 1970 (Challenger, Challenger). Hill & Wang.

Carder, Michael

--Decision at Sundown. (Bull's-Eye Westerns). N.D. Macrae Smith Co.

--Return of the Outlaw. (Bull's-Eye Westerns). N.D. Macmillan.

Cardew, Margaret, retold by see La Bedolliere, Emile Gigault De.

Cardiff, Sara

--Speaking Stones. LC 75-28035. 224p. 1976. (ISBN 0-698-10701-2). Coward.

Cardinale, Vincent

--Mystery of the Black Stamp. Gaughan, Jack, illus. LC 68-16467. (Illus.). 160. p. 22cm. 1968. Criterion Books.

Cardner, Grace H

--Teacher Tells More Tales. In Prose and Rhyme and Pictures, for the Listener of Five and Six and the Reader of Seven or More. LC 56-5385. 87p. illus. 23cm. 1956. William-Frederick Press.

Cardona, Consuelo M., tr. see Lovato, Rebecca.

Careme, Maurice (1899-)

--Mother Raspberry. Wabbes, Marie, illus. LC 70-78258. (Illus.). 26 p. 27cm. 1969. Crowell.

--The Peace. Felix, Monique, illus. Neumeyer, Helen, tr. (Illus.). 8p. (Orig.). 1982. (ISBN 0-914676-68-7, Pub. by Envelope Bks). Green Tiger Pr.

Carew, Jan (1925-)

--Children of the Sun. Dillon, Leo (1933-) & Dillon, Diane (1933-), illus. (Illus.). 40p. (gr. k up). 1980. (ISBN 0-316-12848-1). Little.

--The Third Gift. Dillon, Leo (1933-) & Dillon, Diane (1933-), illus. LC 73-12061. (Illus.). 32 p. 23cm. 1974. (ISBN 0-316-12847-3). Little, Brown.

Carew, Maud

--Miss Pussie. N.D. Society for Promoting Christian Knowledge.

--Pat. N.D. E. & J. B Young & Co.

--Stupid Chris (Pub. by Society for Promoting Christian Knowledge). N.D. E. & J. B. Young & Co.

--Two Little B's. N.D. E & J B Young.

--Uncle Phil (Pub. by Society for Promoting Christian Knowledge). N.D. E. & J. B. Young & Co.

Carey, Alice

--Clovernook Children. N.D. James R. Osgood.

Carey, Annie

--School Girls: Or, Life at Montague Hall, 1 of 4 vols. (Illus.). (The School Girl's Library). N.D. Cassell, Petter, Galpin.

Carey, Arthur Astor (1857-)

--Boy Scouts at Sea: Or, A Chronicles of the B. S. S. Bright Wing. Cue, Harold, illus. LC 18-15780. xi, 291, 1 p. front., plates. 20 cm. 1918. Little Brown, and Company.

Carey, Bonnie, tr. see McCrady, Lady.

Carey, Bonnie, tr. see Ryss, Evgenii Samoilovich.

Carey, Bonnie (1941-)

--Grasshopper to the Rescue. McCrady, Lady (1951-), illus. Carey, Bonnie, tr. from Rus. (Illus.). (gr. k-3). 1979. (ISBN 0-688-22172-6). (ISBN 0-688-32172-0). Morrow.

Carey, Brock, Mrs.

--Sunday Echoes in Week-Day Hours. (Illus.). 500p. (Fifth Ser.). N.D. E. P. Dutton & Co.

Carey, James Thomas, jt. auth. see Lee, James.

Carey, Mabel Colebrooke (1892-), ed.

--Fairy Tales of Long Ago. (Illus.). 1st U.S. edition. Repr. of 1952 ed. (Childrens Illustrated Classics Ser). 1975. (ISBN 0-460-05017-6, Pub. by J. M. Dent England). Biblio Dist.

--Fairy Tales of Long Ago. Watkins-Pitchford, Denys James (1905-), illus. LC 53-883420. (Illus.). 243p. (Children's Illustrated Classics). (gr. 2-7). 1952. (ISBN 0-525-29602-6). Dutton.

Carey, Martha Ward, Mrs. (1837-), ed.

--Fairy Legends Of the French Provinces. (Handy Volume Classics). N.D. Thomas Y. Crowell & Co.

--Fairy Legends of the French Provinces. Carey, Martha Ward, Mrs. (1837-), tr. Jameson, J. F., intro. by. LC 3-21938. 19cm. 300p. 1887. T. Y Crowell & Co.

--Fairy Legends of the French Provinces. Carey, Martha Ward, Mrs. (1837-), tr. LC 3-19673. 1 p. l., 296 p. front., 8 pl. 17 1/2 cm. c.1903. T. Y. Crowell & Co.

--Fairy Legends of the French Provinces. Carey, Martha Ward (1837-), tr. (Children's Favorite Classics). N.D. Thomas Y. Crowell & Co.'s Catalogue.

--French Fairy Tales. Smith, Elmer Boyd (1860-1943), illus. Carey, Martha Ward, Mrs. (1860-1943), tr. 20cm. 287p. 1903. T. Y. Crowell & Co.

Carey, Mary, jt. auth. see Disney, Walt, Productions.

Carey, Mary Virginia (1925-)

--Alfred Hitchcock and the Three Investigators in The Mystery of the Magic Circle. Hearne, Jack, illus. LC 78-55915. (Illus.). viii, 150 p. 22cm. (Alfred Hitchcock Mystery Series ; 27). c.1978. (ISBN 0-394-83607-3). (ISBN 0-394-93607-8). Random House.

--Alonzo Purr: The Seagoing Cat. Hafner, Marilyn (1925-), illus. (Illus.). (Tell-a-Tale Readers). (gr. k-3). 1978. (ISBN 0-307-68569-1, Whitman). Western Pub.

--Caverns of Fear. McWilliams, Alden, illus. (Illus.). 24p. (Golden Super Adventure Books). (gr. k-3). 1983. (ISBN 0-307-11794-4, Golden Bks). Western Pub.

--The Fox & the Hound. 24p. (Little Golden Bks.). (ps). 1981. (ISBN 0-307-01056-2, Golden Pr). (ISBN 0-307-60156-0). Western Pub.

--The Gremlins Storybook. LC 83-83377. (Illus.). 48p. 1984. (ISBN 0-307-15820-9, Golden Pr). Western Pub.

--Happy, Healthy Pooh Book. Matterson, Sylvia, illus. (Illus.). (Look-Look Ser.). 1977. (ISBN 0-307-61832-3, Golden Pr). (ISBN 0-307-11832-0). Western Pub.

--Mrs. Brisby's Important Package. Williams, A. O., illus. LC 81-84376. (Illus.). 24 p. 21cm. (Golden look-look book). c.1982. (ISBN 0-307-11885-1). (ISBN 0-307-61885-4). Golden Press.
--A Place for Allie. LC 85-16005. 250 p. 22cm. c.1985. (ISBN 0-396-08583-0). Dodd, Mead.
--Tawny Scrawny Lion & Clever Monkey. (ps-3). N.D. (ISBN 0-307-60128-5, Golden Pr). Western Pub.
--The Three Investigators in The Secret of the Haunted Mirror. rev. ed. LC 83-23012. (Based on Characters Created by Robert Arthur). viii, 144 p. 20cm. (The Three Investigators Mystery Series: No. 21). 1984, c.1974. (ISBN 0-394-86421-2). Random House.

Carey, Mary Virginia (1925-), adapted by.
Wizard of Oz. Thomas, Dona M. (1951-), illus. (Illus.). (gr. k-3). 1976. (ISBN 0-307-60119-6, Golden Pr). Western Pub.

Carey, Mary Virginia (1925-) & Arthur, Robert, pseud. (1909-1969)
--Alfred Hitchcock and the Three Investigators in The Mystery of the Flaming Footprints. Feder, Robert Arthur. LC 77-28742. (Based on characters created by Robert Arthur). (Illus.). viii, 182 p. 20cm. 1978, c.1971. (ISBN 0-394-83776-2). Random House.
--Alfred Hitchcock and the Three Investigators in The Mystery of the Sinister Scarecrow. Feder, Robert Arthur. LC 79-10034. (Based on characters created by Robert Arthur). p. cm. (Alfred Hitchcock Mystery Series ; No. 29: No.). 1979. (ISBN 0-394-84182-4). (ISBN 0-394-94182-9). Random House.
Alfred Hitchcock and the Three Investigators in The Mystery of Monster Mountain. Feder, Robert Arthur. LC 79-11372. (Based on characters created by Robert Arthur). p. cm. 1979, c.1973. (ISBN 0-394-84259-6). (ISBN 0-394-92664-1). Random House.
--Alfred Hitchcock and the Three Investigators in The Mystery of the Magic Circle. Feder, Robert Arthur. LC 79-27657. (Based on characters created by Robert Arthur). p. cm. 1980. (ISBN 0-394-93607-8). Random House.
--Alfred Hitchcock and the Three Investigators in The Mystery of the Blazing Cliffs. Feder, Robert Arthur. LC 80-10954. (Based on characters created by Robert Arthur). p. cm. (Alfred Hitchcock Mystery Ser.: No. 31). 1980. (ISBN 0-394-84504-8). (ISBN 0-394-94504-2). Random House.
--Alfred Hitchcock and the Three Investigators in The Mystery of the Invisible Dog. Feder, Robert Arthur. LC 79-27778. (Based on characters created by Robert Arthur). p. cm. 1981. (ISBN 0-394-84492-0). (ISBN 0-394-83105-5). (ISBN 0-394-93105-X). Random House.
--Alfred Hitchcock and the Three Investigators in The Mystery of the Singing Serpent. Feder, Robert Arthur. LC 80-18947. (Based on characters created by Robert Arthur). viii, 146 p. 19cm. (Alfred Hitchcock and the Three Investigators Ser.: No. 17). 1981, c.1972. (ISBN 0-394-84678-8). Random House.
--Alfred Hitchcock and the Three Investigators in The Mystery of Death Trap Mine. Feder, Robert Arthur. LC 79-3516. (Based on characters created by Robert Arthur). vii, 145 p. 20cm. (Alfred Hitchcock and the Three Investigators Series). N.D. (ISBN 0-394-84449-1). (ISBN 0-394-93321-4). (ISBN 0-394-93321-4). (ISBN 0-394-93321-4). Random House.
--Alfred Hitchcock and the Three Investigators in The Mystery of Monster Mountain. Feder, Robert Arthur. Hearne, Jack, illus. LC 73-3693. (Illus.). viii, 149 p. 22cm. (Alfred Hitchcock Mystery Series, 20: No.). 1973. (ISBN 0-394-82664-7). Random House.
--Alfred Hitchcock and the Three Investigators in The Mystery of the Invisible Dog: Based on Characters Created by Robert Arthur. Feder, Robert Arthur. Hearne, Jack, illus. LC 75-8073. p. cm. (Alfred Hitchcock Mystery Series ; 23: No.). 1975. (ISBN 0-394-83105-5). (ISBN 0-394-93105-X). Random House.
--Alfred Hitchcock and the Three Investigators in The Mystery of the Flaming Footprints. Feder, Robert Arthur. Kane, Harry, illus. LC 72-155598. (Based on characters created by Robert Arthur). (Illus.). viii, 182 p. 22cm. (Alfred Hitchcock Mystery Series, 15: No.). 1971. (ISBN 0-394-82296-X). Random House.
--Alfred Hitchcock and the Three Investigators in The Mystery of the Singing Serpent. Feder, Robert Arthur. Vebell, Ed., illus. LC 72-1587. (Based on characters created by Robert Arthur). (Illus.). vii, 152 p. 22cm. (Alfred Hitchcock Mystery Ser.: No. 17). 1972. (ISBN 0-394-82408-3). (ISBN 0-394-92408-8). Random House.
--Alfred Hitchcock and the Three Investigators in The Secret of the Haunted Mirror. Feder, Robert Arthur. LC 79-3517. (Based on characters created by Robert Arthur). viii, 145 p. 20cm. (Alfred Hitchcock and the Three Investigators Series). 1980, c.1974. (ISBN 0-394-84450-5). (ISBN 0-394-82820-8). (ISBN 0-394-92820-2). Random House.
--Alfred Hitchcock and the Three Investigators in The Secret of the Haunted Mirror. Feder, Robert Arthur. Hearne, Jack, illus. LC 74-5750. (Based on characters created by Robert Arthur). p. cm. (Alfred Hitchcock Mystery Series, 21). 1974. (ISBN 0-394-82820-8). (ISBN 0-394-82820-8). Random House.
--The Mystery of the Missing Mermaid. Feder, Robert Arthur. LC 83-3030. (Based on characters created by Robert Arthur). (Illus.). 192p. (The Three Investigators Mystery Ser.: No.36). (gr. 4-7). 1983. (ISBN 0-394-85875-1). (ISBN 0-394-95875-6). Random.
--The Mystery of the Scar-Faced Beggar. Feder, Robert Arthur. LC 81-4040. (Based on characters created by Robert Arthur). 192p. (The Three Investigators Mystery Ser.: No. 31). (gr. 4-7). 1981. (ISBN 0-394-94903-X). (ISBN 0-394-84903-5). Random.
--The Mystery of the Wandering Cave Man. Feder, Robert Arthur. LC 82-3667. (Based characters created by Robert Arthur). (Illus.). 192p. (The Three Investigators Mystery Ser.: No. 34). (gr. 4-7). 1982. (ISBN 0-394-95278-2). (ISBN 0-394-85278-8). Random.
--The Three Investigators in the Mystery of Death Trap Mine. rev. ed. Feder, Robert Arthur. LC 83-22990. (Based on characters created by Robert Arthur). (The Three Investigators Mystery Ser.: No. 24). 1984, c.1976. (ISBN 0-394-86424-7). Random House.
--The Three Investigators in The Mystery of Monster Mountain. rev. ed. Feder, Robert Arthur. LC 83-26999. (Based on characters created by Robert Arthur). x, 142 p. 20cm. (The Three Investigators Mystery Series: No. 20). 1985, c.1973. (ISBN 0-394-86420-4). Random House.
--The Three Investigators in The Mystery of the Creep-Show Crooks. Feder, Robert Arthur. LC 85-2237. (Based on Characters Created by Robert Arthur). viii, 177 p. 20cm. (The Three Investigators Mystery Series: 41). c.1985. (ISBN 0-394-87382-3). (ISBN 0-394-97382-8). Random House.
--The Three Investigators in The Mystery of the Flaming Footprints. rev. ed. Feder, Robert Arthur. LC 83-23011. (Based on Characters Created by Robert Arthur). viii, 175 p. 20cm. (The Three Investigators Mystery Series: No.15). 1984, c.1971. (ISBN 0-394-86415-8). Random House.
--The Three Investigators in The Mystery of the Invisible Dog. rev. ed. Feder, Robert Arthur. LC 83-22989. (Based on Characters Created by Robert Arthur Feder). 148 p. 20cm. (The Three Investigators Mystery Series: No. 23). 1984, c.1975. (ISBN 0-394-86423-9). Random House.
--The Three Investigators in the Mystery of the Magic Circle. rev. ed. Feder, Robert Arthur. LC 83-27080. (Based on characters created by Robert Arthur). x, 143 p. 19cm. (The Three Investigators Mystery Ser.: No. 27). 1985, c.1978. (ISBN 0-394-86427-1). Random House.
--The Three Investigators in the Mystery of the Singing Serpent. rev. ed. Feder, Robert Arthur. LC 83-22988. (Based on characters created by Robert Arthur). (The Three Investigators Mystery Ser.: No. 17). 1984, c.1972. (ISBN 0-394-86417-4). Random House.
--The Three Investigators in The Mystery of the Sinister Scarecrow. rev. ed. Feder, Robert Arthur. LC 83-26934. (Based on characters created by Robert Arthur Feder). viii, 151 p. 20cm. (The Three Investigators Mystery Ser.: No. 29). 1985, c.1979. (ISBN 0-394-86429-8). Random House.
--The Three Investigators in The Mystery of the Trail of Terror. Feder, Robert Arthur. LC 84-1952. (Based on Characters Created by Robert Arthur). 182 p. 22cm. (The Three Investigators Mystery Series: No. 39). c.1984. (ISBN 0-394-96609-0). (ISBN 0-394-86609-6). Random House.

Carey, Mary Virginia (1925-) & Barrie, James Matthew, Sir (1860-1937)
--Walt Disney's Peter Pan and Captain Hook. LC 72-4849. (Illus.). 42 p. 25cm. (Disney's wonderful world of reading, 4). 1972. (ISBN 0-394-82517-9). (ISBN 0-394-82517-9). Random House.

Carey, Mary Virginia (1925-) & Giordano, Joe
--The Owl Who Loved Sunshine. LC 76-52894. (Illus.). 72 p. 26cm. (kid's paperback). c.1977. (ISBN 0-307-13433-4). Golden Press.

Carey, Michael, pseud., see Johnson, Johnile Curry.

Carey, Robert V., ed. see Armstrong, Richard.

Carey, Rosa Nouchette (1840-1909)
--Aunt Diana. (Fireside Ser. for Girls). N.D. A. L. Burt's Publications.
--Aunt Diana. (Illus.). (The Wellesley Series for Girls). N.D. A. L. Burt's Pubs.
--Aunt Diana. (Illus.). (The Meade Series for Girls). N.D. A. L. Burt.
--Aunt Diana. Good Value ed. N.D. Grosset & Dunlap.
--Aunt Diana. (Illus.). (Famous Books for Girls Ser.: No. 4). 1905. Set. H M Caldwell Co.
--Aunt Diana. (Illus.). (Caldwell's Illustrated Library of Famous Books by Famous Authors). N.D. H. M. Caldwell Co.
--Aunt Diana, 1 of 32 vols, Vol. 2. (Illus.). (Famous Books for Girls). N.D. H. M. Caldwell Co.
--Aunt Diana. (Argyle Ser). N.D. Hurst & Company.
--Aunt Diana. (Illus.). (Miss Carey's Stories for Girls). N.D. J. B. Lippincott.
--Averil. (Illus.). (Fireside Ser. for Girls). N.D. A. L. Burt's Publications.
--Averil. (Illus.). (The Meade Series for Girls). N.D. A. L. Burt.
--Averil, No. 13. (The Cornell Ser.). N.D. A. L. Burt's Pubs.
--Averil. (Illus.). (The Wellesley Series for Girls). N.D. A. L.Burt's Pubs.
--Averil. Good Value ed. N.D. Grosset & Dunlap.
--Averil. (Illus.). (Famous Books for Girls Ser.: No. 5). 1905. Set. H M Caldwell Co.
--Averil. (Illus.). (Caldwell's Illustrated Library of Famous Books by Famous Authors). N.D. H. M. Caldwell Co.
--Averil. N.D. Hurst & Co.
--Averil. (Illus.). (St. Nicholas Series for Girls). N.D. International Book Co.
--Averil, 1 of 2 vols. (Favorite Series: No. 3). N.D. International Book Co.
--Averil. (Illus.). (Miss Carey's Stories for Girls). N.D. J. B. Lippincott.
--Barbara Heathcote's Trial. (Burt's Home Lib.). N.D. A. L. Burt's Pubs.
--Barbara Heathcote's Trial. (Rosa N. Carey Ser.). N.D. Hurst & Co.
--Barbara Heathcote's Trial. N.D. J. B. Lippincott.
--Cousin Mona: A Story for Girls. LC 6-23107. 337p. (Miss Carey's Stories for Girls). 1896. Lippincott.
--Dora Thorne, 1 of 2 vols. (Favorite Series: No. 4). N.D. International Book Co.
--Dr. Luttrell's First Patient. (Illus.). 1900. J B Lippincott.
--Ester. (Illus.). (The Wellesley Series for Girls). N.D. A. L. Burt's Pubs.
--Esther. (Illus.). (Fireside Ser. for Girls). N.D. A. L. Burt's Publications.
--Esther. (Illus.). (The Meade Series for Girls). N.D. A. L. Burt.
--Esther. N.D. Hurst & Company.
--Esther: A Book for Girls. LC 5-18483. 255p. (Miss Carey's Stories for Girls). 1887. Lippincott.
--Esther: A Story for Girls. (Illus.). (St. Nicholas Series for Girls). N.D. International Book Co.
--For Lilias. (Rosa N. Carey Ser.). N.D. Hurst & Co.
--For Lilias. N.D. J. B. Lippincott.
--Girls' Stories: Containing: Aunt Diana, Merle's Crusade, Our Bessie, Esther, and Averil, 5 vols. (Illus.). N.D. International Book Co.
--Heriot's Choice. (Burt's Home Lib.). N.D. A. L. Burt's Pubs.
--Heriot's Choice, 1 of 32 vols, Vol. 7. (Illus.). (Famous Books For Girls). N.D. H. M. Caldwell Co.
--Heriot's Choice. (Illus.). (St. Nicholas Series for Girls). N.D. International Book Co.
--Library For Girls: Containing: Merle's Crusade, Aunt Diana, Esther. (Illus.). N.D. Set. J. B. Lippincott Co.
--Little Miss Muffet. LC 6-23105. 328p. (Miss Carey's Stories for Girls). 1893. Lippincott.
--Little Miss Muffett and Cousin Mona. (Illus.). (Miss Carey's Stories for Girls). N.D. J. B. Lippincott.
--Merle Crusade. (Illus.). (Miss Carey's Stories for Girls). N.D. J. B. Lippincott.
--Merle's Crusade. (Illus.). (Fireside Series for Girls). N.D. A. L. Burt's Pubs.
--Merle's Crusade. (Illus.). (The Meade Series for Girls). N.D. A. L. Burt.
--Merle's Crusade. (Illus.). (The Wellesley Series for Girls). N.D. A. L. Burt.
--Merle's Crusade, No. 96. (The Cornell Ser.). N.D. A. L. Burt's Pubs.
--Merle's Crusade. (Illus.). (Caldwell's Illustrated Library of Famous Books by Famous Authors). N.D. H. M. Caldwell Co.
--Merle's Crusade. (Rosa N. Carey Ser.). N.D. Hurst & Co.
--Merle's Crusade. (Illus.). (St. Nicholas Series for Girls). N.D. International Book Co.
--Miss Carey's Libaray for Girls: Consisting of Little Miss Muffet and Cousin Mona, 2 vols. (Illus.). N.D. J. B. Lippincott.
--My Lady Frivol. (Illus.). 1900. J B Lippincott.
--My Little Boy Blue. LC 12-32351. 41p. 1895. Fleming H. Revell.
--My Little Boy Blue. (The New Kingship Ser.). N.D. Fleming H. Revell Co.
--Nellie's Memories. (Rosa N. Carey Ser.). N.D. Hurst & Co.
--Nellie's Memories. N.D. J. B. Lippincott.
--Not Like Other Girls. N.D. A. L. Burt Co.
--Not Like Other Girls. (Illus.). (The Wellesley Series for Girls). N.D. A. L. Burt's Pubs.
--Not Like Other Girls, No. 106. (The Cornell Ser.). N.D. A. L. Burt's Pubs.
--Not Like Other Girls. (The Good Value Books). N.D. Grosset & Dunlap.
--Not Like Other Girls. (Illus.). (Famous Books for Girls Ser.: No. 16). 1905. Set. H M Caldwell Co.
--Not Like Other Girls. (Illus.). (Caldwell's Illustrated Library of Famous Books by Famous Authors). N.D. H. M. Caldwell Co.
--Not Like Other Girls. (Argyle Ser). N.D. Hurst & Company.
--Not Like Other Girls. (Rosa N. Carey Ser.). N.D. Hurst & Co.
--Not Like Other Girls. (Illus.). (St. Nicholas Series for Girls). N.D. International Book Co.
--Not Like Other Girls. N.D. J. B. Lippincott.
Not Like Other Girls. N.D. Lovell, Coryell & Co.
--Not Like Other Girls, and Only the Governess, Vol. (Rosa N. Carey Books: Vol. IV). 1895. International Book Co.
--The Old Old Story. N.D. J. B. Lippincott Co.
--Only the Governess, No. 110. (The Cornell Ser.). N.D. A. L. Burt's Pubs.
--Only the Governess. (Rosa N. Carey Ser.). N.D. Hurst & Co.
--Only the Governess. N.D. J. B. Lippincott.
--Our Bessie. (Illus.). (Fireside Ser. for Girls). N.D. A. L. Burt's Publications.
--Our Bessie. (Illus.). (The Wellesley Series for Girls). N.D. A. L. Burt's Pubs.
--Our Bessie. (Illus.). (The Meade Series for Girls). N.D. A. L. Burt.
--Our Bessie, No. 111. (The Cornell Ser.). N.D. A. L. Burt's Pubs.
--Our Bessie. 1905. American News Co.
--Our Bessie, 1 of 32 Vols. (Illus.). (Famous Books for Girls Ser.: No. 17). 1905. Set. H M Caldwell Co.
--Our Bessie. (Illus.). (Caldwell's Illustrated Library of Famous Books by Famous Authors). N.D. H. M. Caldwell Co.
--Our Bessie. (Argyle Ser). N.D. Hurst & Company.
--Our Bessie. (New Red Letter Ser). N.D. International Book Company.
--Our Bessie. (New Aldine Ser). N.D. International Book Co.
--Our Bessie. (Illus.). (St. Nicholas Series for Girls). N.D. International Book Co.
--Our Bessie. (Favorite Series: No. 3). N.D. International Book Co.
--Queenie's Whim. (Burt's Home Library). N.D. A L Burt Co.
--Queenie's Whim, No. 125. (The Cornell Ser.). N.D. A. L. Burt's Pubs.
--Queenie's Whim. (Rosa N. Carey Ser.). N.D. Hurst & Co.
--Queenie's Whim. N.D. J. B. Lippincott.
--Queenie's Whim. (The Crown Ser.). N.D. The American News Co.
--Sir Godfrey's Granddaughters. N.D. J. B. Lippincott Co.
--Uncle Max. 1905. A L Burt Co.
--Uncle Max. (Rosa N. Carey Ser.). N.D. Hurst & Co.
--Uncle Max. N.D. J. B. Lippincott.
--Uncle Max. (The Crown Ser.). N.D. The American News Co.
--Wee Wifie. 1905. A L Burt Co.
--Wee Wifie. (Rosa N. Carey Ser.). N.D. Hurst & Co.
--Wee Wifie. (New Red Letter Ser). N.D. Internatinal Book Company.
--Wee Wifie. (New Aldine Ser). N.D. International Book Co.
--Wee Wifie. (Illus.). (St. Nicholas Series for Girls). N.D. International Book Co.
--Wee Wifie. (Favorite Series: No. 4). N.D. International Book Co.
--Wee Wifie. N.D. J. B. Lippincott.
--Wee Wifie, and Merle's Crusade. (Rosa N. Carey: Vol.IX). N.D. International Book Co.

Carey, Valerie Scho
--Harriet and William and the Terrible Creature. Cherry, Lynne (1952-), illus. LC 84-13721. (Illus.). 32 p. 27cm. c.1985. (ISBN 0-525-44154-9). Dutton.

Cargas, Harry James (1932-)
--David's Decision: Betrayal? Or Trust?. LC 78-13561. (Illus.). 55 p. 23cm. c.1979. (ISBN 0-570-07978-0). Concordia Pub. House.
--Simon the Crossbearer: A Family Is Affected by Their Father's Chance Meeting with the Savior. LC 78-12731. (Illus.). 56 p. 23cm. (Starlight books). c.1979. (ISBN 0-570-07977-2). Concordia Pub. House.

Carhart, Arthur Hawthorne (1892-)
--Son of the Forest. LC 52-9531. 244 p. 21cm. 1952. Lippincott.
Carigiet, Alois (1902-)
--Anton and Anne. Wilkin, Refna, tr. LC 71-81857. (Illus.). 44 p. 1969. H. Z. Walck.
--Anton the Goatherd. LC 66-18535. (Illus.). 1 v. (unpaged. 1966. H. Z. Walck.
--Pear Tree, the Birch Tree & the Barberry Bush. Carigiet, Alois (1902-), illus. LC 67-5331. (Illus.). 33p. (gr. k-3). 1967. (ISBN 0-8098-1125-1). Walck.
Carini, Edward (1923-)
--Take Another Look. Carini, Edward (1923-), illus. LC 76-88153. (Illus.). 32 p. 1970. Prentice-Hall.
Carja, Ion
--Tom Emperor of the Mountains. Cordoso, Rosemary, illus. 1979. (ISBN 0-533-02389-0). Vantage.
Carkhuff, Robert R. & Friel, Ted
--The Story of Who: How Who Develops His Career. Capolongo, Tom, illus. (Illus.). 62p. (Career Skills Ser.). (gr. 6-8). 1973. (ISBN 0-914234-43-9). Human Res Dev Pr.
--The Story of Who: How Who Finds His First Job. Capolongo, Tom, illus. (Illus.). 48p. (Career Skills Ser.). (gr. 4-6). 1973. (ISBN 0-914234-42-0). Human Res Dev Pr.
Carl, Angela R. (1949-)
--A Matter of Choice. Speirs, John Hastie (1906-), illus. LC 84-7040. (Illus.). 32 p. 25cm. c.1984. (ISBN 0-89693-223-0). Dandelion House.
Carle, Eric (1929-), retold by see Aesopus.
Carle, Eric, retold by see Grimm, Jakob Ludwig Karl (1785-1863) & Grimm, Wilhelm Karl.
Carle, Eric (1929-)
--All About Arthur: An Absolutely Absurd Ape. Carle, Eric (1929-), illus. LC 73-9571. (Illus.). 32 p. 27cm. 1974. (ISBN 0-531-02662-0). Watts.
--Catch the Ball. Carle, Eric (1929-), illus. LC 82-359. p. cm. 1982. (ISBN 0-399-20885-2). Philomel Books.
--Do You Want to Be My Friend?. Carle, Eric (1929-), illus. LC 70-140643. 33 p. (chiefly col. illus. (ps-k). 1971. (ISBN 0-690-24276-X). Crowell. **Award: (ALA).**
--Giant Flower. Carle, Eric (1929-), illus. (gr. k-3). 1970. T Y Crowell.
--The Grouchy Ladybug. Carle, Eric (1929-), illus. LC 77-3170. p. cm. 1977. (ISBN 0-690-01391-4). T.Y. Crowell Co.
--The Honeybee & the Robber: A Moving Picture Book. Carle, Eric (1929-), illus. LC 80-23936. (Illus.). 16p. (gr. 4-8). 1981. (ISBN 0-399-20767-8, Philomel). Putnam Pub Group.
--Have You Seen My Cat?. LC 76-185524. (Illus.). 30 p. 1973. (ISBN 0-531-02552-7). F. Watts.
--I See a Song. Carle, Eric (1929-), illus. LC 72-9249. 28 p. (chiefly col. illus. 29cm. 1973. (ISBN 0-690-43306-9). (ISBN 0-690-43306-9). Crowell.
--Let's Paint a Rainbow. Carle, Eric (1929-), illus. LC 82-451. (Illus.). 11 p. 21cm. (Play-and-read book). 1982. (ISBN 0-399-20881-X). Philomel Books.
--The Mixed-up Chameleon. Carle, Eric (1929-), illus. LC 75-5505. (Illus.). 31 p. 30cm. 1975. (ISBN 0-690-00605-5). (ISBN 0-690-00924-0). Crowell.
--The Mixed-up Chameleon. New ed. Carle, Eric (1929-), illus. LC 83-45950. c.1984. (ISBN 0-690-04396-1). (ISBN 0-690-04397-X). Crowell.
--One, Two, Three, to the Zoo. Carle, Eric (1929-), illus. LC 81-8609. (Illus.). 28 p. 30cm. 1982, c.1968. (ISBN 0-399-20772-4). Philomel Books.
--One, Two, Three to the Zoo. Carle, Eric (1929-), illus. LC 68-26967. 1 v. (chiefly col. illus. 30cm. 1968. World Pub. Co.
--Pancakes, Pancakes!. Carle, Eric (1929-), illus. LC 77-106143. (Illus.). 30 p. 27cm. 1970. (ISBN 0-394-90490-7). Knopf.
--The Rooster Who Set Out to See the World. Carle, Eric (1929-), illus. LC 78-171902. (Illus.). 32p. (gr. k-3). 1972. (ISBN 0-531-02042-8). Watts.
--The Secret Birthday Message. Carle, Eric (1929-), illus. LC 75-168726. (Illus.). 26 p. 30cm. 1972. (ISBN 0-690-72347-4). (ISBN 0-690-72347-4). Crowell.
--The Secret Birthday Message. Carle, Eric (1929-), illus. 1972. Harper.
--The Tiny Seed & the Giant Flower. Carle, Eric (1929-), illus. (gr. 1-3). 1976. (ISBN 0-8277-4662-8). British Bk Ctr.
--The Very Busy Spider. Carle, Eric (1929-), illus. LC 84-5907. (Illus.). 32p. (ps-2). 1984. (ISBN 0-399-21166-7, Philomel). Putnam Pub Group. **Award: (ALA).**
--The Very Hungry Caterpillar. Carle, Eric (1929-), illus. LC 79-13202. p. cm. 1979. (ISBN 0-529-00775-4). (ISBN 0-529-00776-2). Collins Publishers.
--The Very Hungry Caterpillar. Carle, Eric (1929-), illus. 1969. Putnam.
--A Very Long Tail: A Folding Book. Carle, Eric (1929-), illus. LC 72-78161. (Illus.). (ps). 1972. (ISBN 0-690-86006-4, TYC-J). Har-Row.
--The Very Long Train: A Folding Book. Carle, Eric (1929-), illus. LC 72-77939. (Illus.). (ps). 1972. (ISBN 0-690-86007-2, TYC-J). Har-Row.
--Watch Out, a Giant!. Carle, Eric (1929-), illus. LC 78-8244. p. cm. 1978. (ISBN 0-529-05455-8). (ISBN 0-529-05456-6). Collins-World.
--What's for Lunch?. Carle, Eric (1929-), illus. LC 82-453. (Illus.). 10 p. 21cm. (Play-and-read book). 1982. (ISBN 0-399-20897-6). Philomel Books.
Carle, Eric (1929-), retold by.
--Seven Stories by Hans Christian Andersen. Carle, Eric (1929-), illus. LC 78-2302. (Illus.). 92 p. 29cm. 1978. (ISBN 0-531-02919-0). Watts.
--Walter the Baker: An Old Story. Carle, Eric (1929-), illus. LC 78-154546. (Illus.). 32 p. 26cm. 1972. (ISBN 0-394-92133-X). Knopf.
Carleon, A. (1922-)
--The May Spoon. LC 81-6101. p. cm. 1981. (ISBN 0-8253-0059-2). Beaufort Books.
Carless, Miss
--Brave Lisette. N.D. Cassell Petter & Galpin.
Carleton, Ada
--The Swinging Match, 1 of 6 vols. (Illus.). (Firelight Stories). 1882. D Lothrop.
Carleton, Barbee Oliver, et al. (1917-)
--Tale of Napoleon Mouse & Other Stories. (Illus., Orig.). (Highlights Handbooks Ser). (gr. k-2). 1965. (ISBN 0-87534-122-5). Highlights.
Carleton, Barbee Oliver (1917-)
--Benny and the Bear. Wilson, Dagmar (1916-), illus. LC 60-13350. (Illus.). 29 p. 21cm. (Follett beginning-to-read series, level 3). c.1960. Follett Pub. Co.
--Chester Jones. Fiammenghi, Gioia (1929-), illus. LC 63-16312. (Illus.). 174 p. 22cm. 1963. Holt, Rinehart and Winston.
--Secret of Saturday Cove. Geer, Charles Hand (1922-), illus. LC 61-5052. (Illus.). 168p. (gr. 4-6). 1961. (ISBN 0-03-035570-2). HR&W.
--The Witches' Bridge. LC 67-6574. (Illus.). 232 p. 22cm. 1967. Holt, Rinehart and Winston.
--The Wonderful Cat of Cobbie Bean. Landau, Jacob (1917-), illus. 1957. Holt, Rinehart and Winston.
Carleton, Captain Latham C., pseud., see Ellis, Edward Sylvester.
Carleton, Katharine
--Dorothy, the Motor Girl. Relyea, Charles M. & Birch, Reginald Bathurst (1856-1943), illus. LC 11-24127. 6 p. l., 3-386 p. incl. plates. front. 20 cm. 1911. The Century Co.
Carleton, Phillips D. (1898-)
--Hawk, the White Indian: The Captivity of David Aiken. Laune, Paul Sidney (1899-), illus. LC 47-31315. 210 p. illus. 21 cm. 1947. Bobbs-Merrill Co.
Carleton, William (1845-1912)
--Poems for Young Americans. LC 6-36422. 20cm. 130p. 1906. Harper & Brothers.
--Poems for Young People. (Illus.). (Harper's Young People Series). N.D. Harper Brothers.
--Young Folks' Centennial Rhymes. LC 21-19904. (Illus.). 19cm. 123p. 1876. Harper & Brothers.
--Young Folks' Centennial Rhymes. (Illus.). 1882. Harper's Trade-List.
Carley, Royal Van Ness (1906-1976)
--That Lazy Cat. LC 69-10882. (Illus.). 25 p. 19cm. (Stardust book). 1969. (ISBN 0-8378-1920-2). C. R. Gibson Co.
Carley, Wayne
--Alone Is No Fun. Hedin, Don, illus. LC 72-1921. (Illus.). 63 p. 23cm. 1972. (ISBN 0-8116-6966-1). Garrard Pub. Co.
--Charley the Mouse Finds Christmas. Bagshaw, Ruth, illus. LC 72-1770. (Illus.). 64 p. 23cm. 1972. (ISBN 0-8116-6953-X). Garrard Pub. Co.
--Color My World. Davidson, Rosalie (1921-), illus. LC 73-21584. (Illus.). 32 p. 23cm. 1974. (ISBN 0-8116-6056-7). Garrard Pub. Co.
--Here Comes Mirium: The Mixed-up Witch!. Schroeder, Ted (1931-1973), illus. LC 72-1771. (Illus.). 62 p. 24cm. 1972. (ISBN 0-8116-6959-9). Garrard Pub. Co.
--Is Anybody Listening?. Hoffmann, Hilde (1927-), illus. LC 73-157997. (Illus.). 38 p. 24cm. 1971. (ISBN 0-8116-6712-X). Garrard Pub. Co.
--Mixed-up Magic. Stone, David Karl (1922-), illus. LC 70-157999. (Illus.). 40 p. 24cm. 1971. (ISBN 0-8116-6711-1). Garrard Pub. Co.
--Percy the Parrot Passes the Puck. Cumings, Art, illus. LC 72-1925. (Illus.). 60 p. 23cm. 1972. (ISBN 0-8116-6969-6). Garrard Pub. Co.
--Percy the Parrot Strikes Out. Stone, David Karl (1922-), illus. LC 77-157998. (Illus.). 37 p. 23cm. 1971. (ISBN 0-8116-6710-3). Garrard Pub. Co.
--Percy the Parrot Yelled Quiet!. Cumings, Art, illus. LC 73-21585. (Illus.). 32 p. 23cm. 1974. (ISBN 0-8116-6058-3). Garrard Pub. Co.
--Puppy Love. Merkling, Erica, illus. LC 75-161027. (Illus.). 40 p. 24cm. 1971. (ISBN 0-8116-6716-2). Garrard Pub. Co.
--Unlucky Day at Camp How-Ja-Do. Cumings, Art, illus. LC 72-1075. (Illus.). 62 p. 23cm. 1972. (ISBN 0-8116-6955-6). Garrard Pub. Co.
--The Witch Who Forgot. Cunette, Lou, illus. LC 73-21729. (Illus.). 31 p. 23cm. 1974. (ISBN 0-8116-6057-5). Garrard Pub. Co.
Carli, Audrey
--Jimmy's Happy Day. Talarczyk, June, illus. LC 67-2702. (Illus.). 32 p. 29cm. 1967. T. S. Denison.
Carlile, Bess Howell
--Come Play with Us. Reppy, Nell, illus. LC 47-7037. 62 p. col. illus. 27 cm. 1947. Rand McNally.
Carlin, Jerome, ed. see Cooper, James Fenimore.
Carlin, Jerome, ed. see Dumas, Alexandre.
Carlin, Jerome, ed. see Scott, Walter, Sir.
Carlin, Jerome, ed. see Stevenson, Robert Louis.
Carlin, John
--The Scratchsides Family: A Book for Young People. Carlin, John, illus. LC 49-371262. 78 p. illus. 19 cm. 1868. W. L. Stone & J. T. Barron.
Carlin, Madeline
--Summer's Edge: Nursery Rhymes. (ps-1). 1970. Vantage.
Carlin, Steve see Barow, John, pseud.
Carlin, Steve
--Rootie Kazootie and the Pineapple Pies. Barow, John, pseud. Crawford, Mel (1925-), illus. LC 54-34201. unpaged. illus. 17cm. (Tell-a-tale books, 936). 1954, c.1953. Whitman Pub. Co.
--Rootie Kazootie, Baseball Star. Barow, John, pseud. Crawford, Mel (1925-), illus. LC 54-2763. unpaged. illus. 21cm. (Little golden books, 190). 1954. Simon and Schuster.
--Rootie Kazootie, Detective. Barow, John, pseud. Crawford, Mel (1925-), illus. LC 53-2329. unpaged. illus. 21cm. (Little golden library, 150). 1953. Simon and Schuster.
--Rootie Kazootie Joins the Circus. Barow, John, pseud. Crawford, Mel (1925-), illus. LC 55-2054. unpaged. illus. 21cm. (Little golden library, 226). 1955. Simon and Schuster.
--Rootie Kazootie Joins the Circus. Barow, John, pseud. Seiden, Art, illus. (Little Golden Book). 1955. Golden Press.
Carling, James L.
--Wadleigh. Nicoll, Bee, illus. (Illus.). (ps-2). 1980. (Gingerbread). Dutton.
Carlisle, Clark, pseud., see Holding, James Clark Carlisle Jr..
Carlisle, Clark, pseud. (1907-)
--Bugs Bunny's Carrot Machine. Holding, James Clark Carlisle Jr.. Strobl, Anthony & Totten, Bob, illus. (Illus.). 24p. (gr. k-3). 1976. (ISBN 0-307-60127-7, Golden Pr). Western Pub.
Carlisle, Jane
--Balloon. Miller, Jane Judith (1925-), illus. LC 68-10484. (Illus.). 31 p. 23cm. 1968. Follett Pub. Co.
Carlisle, Laura Mae, Mrs., jt. ed. see Huffard, Grace Thompson, Mrs.
Carlon, Patricia
--See Nothing, Say Nothing. LC 68-28976. 192 p. 21cm. 1968, c.1967. Walker.
Carlos
--Albear: The Dog Who Could Talk. (Illus.). 64p. (gr. k-2). 1981. (ISBN 0-682-49748-7). Exposition.
Carlsen, George Robert, jt. ed. see Carlsen, Ruth Christoffer.
Carlsen, George Robert (1917-) & Carlsen, Ruth Christoffer (1918-)
--Perception. Treasury ed. LC 83-19594. (Illus.). 630. (The McGraw-Hill Literature Ser.). 1985. (ISBN 0-07-009805-0). Webster Division,McGraw-Hill.
Carlsen, George Robert (1917-) & Tovatt, Anthony
--Insights. Treasury ed. LC 83-17489. (Illus.). xii, 786. (The McGraw-Hill Literature Ser.). 1985. (ISBN 0-07-009809-3). Webster Division.
Carlsen, Ruth Christoffer, jt. auth. see Carlsen, George Robert.
Carlsen, Ruth Christoffer (1918-)
--Encounters: Themes in Literature. 3d ed. Carlsen, George Robert (1917-), ed. LC 77-28473. (Illus.). xii, 754 p. 25cm. (Themes and writers series). c.1979. (ISBN 0-07-009863-8). Webster Division, McGraw-Hill.
--Half-Past Tomorrow. Gretzer, John, illus. LC 72-13581. (Illus.). 161 p. 22cm. 1973. (ISBN 0-395-16036-7). Houghton Mifflin.
--Henerietta Goes West: Adventures Of An Amazing Car. (Illus.). (gr. 4-7). 1966. (ISBN 0-8382-1016-3, Cadmus Books). E. M. Hale and Company.
--Henrietta Goes West. Tripp, Wallace Whitney (1940-), illus. LC 66-12094. (Illus.). (gr. 4-6). 1966. (ISBN 0-395-06687-5). HM.
--Hildy and the Cuckoo Clock. Tripp, Wallace Whitney (1940-), illus. LC 66-9355. (Illus.). 201 p. 22cm. (gr. 4-6). 1966. (ISBN 0-395-06685-9). Houghton Mifflin.
--Monty and the Tree House. Shortall, Leonard W., illus. LC 67-25310. (Illus.). 183 p. 22cm. 1967. Houghton Mifflin.
--Mr. Pudgins. Bradfield, Margaret, illus. LC 51-6. (Illus.). 103 p. 22cm. 1951. Houghton Mifflin.
--Ride a Wild Horse. Krush, Beth (1918-) & Krush, Joe (1918-), illus. LC 71-122908. (Illus.). 164 p. 22cm. 1970. Houghton Mifflin.
--Sam Bottleby. Tripp, Wallace Whitney (1940-), illus. LC 68-29898. (Illus.). 151 p. 22cm. 1968. Houghton Mifflin.
--Sometimes It's up. Gretzer, John, illus. LC 70-161650. (Illus.). 164 p. 23cm. 1971. (ISBN 0-395-12752-1). Houghton Mifflin.
Carlsen, Ruth Christoffer (1918-) & Carlsen, George Robert (1917-), eds.
--Fifty-Two Miles to Terror. 128p. (gr. 7-12). 1969. (ISBN 0-590-08040-7, Schol Pap). Scholastic Inc.
--Fifty Two Miles to Terror. 128p. Repr. (gr. 5 up). 1974 (Starbright). Schol Bk Serv.
Carlson
--A Christmas Lullaby. 24p. (Arch Bks.). (gr. k-4). 1985. (ISBN 0-570-06195-4). Concordia.
Carlson, Aniel Bick, jt. auth. see Carlson, Dale Bick.
Carlson, Anna L
--The Cookie Looker. Wynne, Diana, illus. LC 80-82182. (Illus.). 17 p. c.1980. Karwyn Enterprises.
--Homer Bear's Secret. 1st. ed. Wynne, Diana, illus. (Illus.). 24p. (Orig.). (gr. k-4). 1983. (ISBN 0-939938-05-7). Karwyn Ent.
--The Mouse Family's Christmas. 1st. ed. (Illus.). 24p. (Orig.). (gr. k-4). 1983. (ISBN 0-939938-04-9). Karwyn Ent.
Carlson, Bernice Wells (1910-)
--Act It Out. Matulay, Laszlo (1912-), illus. LC 56-137693. 160p. illus. 24cm. (gr. 3-7). c.1956. (ISBN 0-687-00713-5). Abingdon Press.
--Do It Yourself: Tricks, Stunts & Skits. Matulay, Laszlo (1912-), illus. (Illus.). (gr. 3-7). 1952. (ISBN 0-687-11007-6). Abingdon.
--Funny-Bone Dramatics. Cox, Charles T. (1937-), illus. LC 73-21515. (Illus.). 96 p. 25cm. 1974. (ISBN 0-687-13867-1). Abingdon Press.
--Let's Find the Big Idea. LC 81-19121. p. cm. c.1982. (ISBN 0-687-44879-4). Abingdon.
--Let's Pretend It Happened to You: A Real-People and Storybook-People Approach to Creative Dramatics. McDonald, Ralph J., illus. LC 73-1488. (Illus.). 110 p. 25cm. 1973. (ISBN 0-687-21503-X). Abingdon Press.
--Listen! and Help Tell the Story. Burris, Burmah, illus. LC 65-14090. (Illus.). 176 p. 25cm. 1965. Abingdon Press.
--Picture That!. Rowland, Dolores Marie, illus. LC 76-25813. (Illus.). 143 p. 25cm. c.1977. (ISBN 0-687-31419-4). Abingdon.
--Play a Part. Scholz, Catherine, illus. LC 72-95198. (Illus.). 240 p. 24cm. 1970. Abingdon Press.
--Quick Wits and Nimble Fingers. Rowland, Dolores Marie, illus. LC 79-10035. (Illus.). 128 p. 25cm. c.1979. (ISBN 0-687-35199-5). Abingdon.
--Right Play for You. Boris, Georgette, illus. (Illus.). (gr. 3-9). 1960. (ISBN 0-687-36376-4). Abingdon.
--You Know What? I Like Animals. Van Sciver, Ruth (1915-), illus. LC 67-7459. (Illus.). 26cm. 32p. 1967. Abingdon Press.
Carlson, Bernice Wells (1910-) & Wigg, Ristiina (1946-)
--We Want Sunshine in Our Houses. Stone, David Karl (1922-), illus. LC 72-889. (Illus.). 32 p. 1973. (ISBN 0-687-44344-X). Abingdon Press.
Carlson, Betty, jt. auth. see Smith, Jane S.
Carlson, Dale Bick (1935-)
--Awful Marshall. Carlson, Albert W. D., illus. LC 73-155077. (Illus.). 30 p. 1971. World Pub. Co.
--Baby Needs Shoes. DeLarrea, Victoria, illus. LC 74-75556. (Illus.). 154 p. 22cm. 1974. (ISBN 0-689-30404-8). Atheneum.
--The Beggar King of China. Gretzer, John, illus. LC 70-154750. (Illus.). 185 p. 24cm. 1971. Atheneum.
--Call Me Amanda. LC 81-2629. p. cm. c.1981. (ISBN 0-525-27355-7). Dutton.
--Charlie the Hero. LC 83-8927. p. cm. c.1983. (ISBN 0-525-44072-0). E.P. Dutton.
--The Frog People. Garland, Michael, illus. LC 81-12659. (Illus.). 75 p. 22cm. (Skinny book). c.1982. (ISBN 0-525-45107-2). E.P. Dutton.
--Good Morning, Danny. Carlson, Albert W. D., illus. LC 72-83061. (Illus.). 32 p. 1972. Atheneum.
--Good Morning, Hannah. Carlson, Albert W. D., illus. LC 72-75265. (Illus.). 32 p. 1972. Atheneum.
--The House of Perkins. Carlson, Albert W. D., illus. LC 65-12057. 95 p. illus. 22 cm. 1965. Doubleday.
--The Human Apes. Carlson, Albert W. D., illus. LC 72-86755. (Illus.). 155 p. 25cm. 1973. Atheneum.
--Miss Maloo. Carlson, Albert W. D., illus. LC 66-117288. 191p. illus. 22cm. c.1966. Doubleday.

Carmer, Elizabeth Black (1904-)
--America Sings: Stories and Songs of our Country's Growing. Carmer, Carl Lamson (1893-1976), as told by. 1942. Alfred A. Knopf.
Carmer, Elizabeth Black (1904-) & Carmer, Carl Lamson (1893-1976)
--Captain Abner and Henry Q. LC 65-100596. 1v. (unpaged) col. illus. 23cm. (Tall tales based on Amer. Folklore). c.1965. Garrard.
--Captain Abner & Henry Q. Schroeder, Ted (1931-1973), illus. LC 65-10059. (American Folktales Ser). (gr. 2-5). 1965. (ISBN 0-8116-4001-9). Garrard.
--Mike Fink & the Big Turkey Shoot. Korach, Mimi (1922-), illus. LC 65-17171. (Illus.). 32p. (American Folktales Ser.). (gr. 2-5). 1965. (ISBN 0-8116-4002-7). Garrard.
--Pecos Bill and the Long Lasso. Korach, Mimi (1922-), illus. LC 68-10693. (Illus.). 31 p. 23cm. (Reading shelf books). 1968. Garrard Pub. Co.
--Tony Beaver, Griddle Skater. Korach, Mimi (1922-), illus. LC 65-10274. (American Folktales Ser.). (gr. 2-5). 1965. (ISBN 0-8116-4003-5). Garrard.
Carmichael, Carrie
--Bigfoot: Man, Monster, or Myth?. LC 77-13297. (Illus.). 48p. (Great Unsolved Mysteries Ser.). (gr. 4up). 1983. (ISBN 0-8172-2154-9). Raintree Pubs.
Carmichael, Harry, pseud., see Ognall, Leopold Horace.
Carmichael, Harry, pseud. (1908-1979)
--The Screaming Rabbit. Ognall, Leopold Horace. 1955. Simon and Schuster.
Carmichael, Mary H.
--Pioneer Days. N.D. Duffield.
Carmichael, Philip
--The Man from the Moon. (Illus.). N.D. Frederick A. Stokes.
Carmichael, William Porter
--Island Voyage: A Story of a Surprise Trip to the Farallon Islands. Porter, Jean Macdonald (1906-), illus. LC 68-17509. (Illus.). 45, 3 p. 24cm. 1968. (ISBN 0-679-25069-7). D. McKay Co.
--Lee Fong and His Toy Junk. (Illus.). 1959. McKay.
--Lee Fong and His Toy Junk. Carmichael, William Porter, illus. LC 55-7069. unpaged. illus. 19x26cm. c.1955. D. McKay Co.
Carmichael, William Porter & Dawson, Alexandra D.
--An A B C of Queer Fish. Carmichael, William Porter, illus. LC 56-8600. unpaged. illus. 17 x 26cm. c.1956. D. McKay Co.
Carnahan, Marjorie R., jt. auth. see McFadden, Dorothy Loa Mausolff.
Carner, Charles
--Tawny. Carrick, Donald (1929-), illus. LC 77-17411. (Illus.). 148 p. 22cm. c.1978. (ISBN 0-02-716700-3). Macmillan.
Carner, Mosco (1904-)
--Madam Butterfly. LC 79-67164. (Masterworks of Opera Ser.). N.D. (ISBN 0-382-06313-9). Silver.
Carnes, Captain
--Little Toss. (Fern Glen Ser.). N.D. D. Lothrop Co.
--Uncle Anthony. N.D. D. Lothrop Co.
Carnes, William F. & Morgan, Appleton, pseud. (1845-)
--A School-Boy's Pleasure-Book. Appleton, James. Rossiter, Edwin. LC 15-12478. 187 p. incl. front., illus., plates, ports. 19 cm. c.1888. D. Lothrop Company.
Carney, Don & Hall, Teddy
--Uncle Don's Song, Game and Paint Book. Herbert, Jean (1907-), ed. La Mothe, Henri, illus. LC 44-28860. 31cm. 279p. 1938. Melrose Music Corp.
Carney, Edward, tr. see Pihl, Herman Gottfrid (1894-) & Beckman, Karin.
Carnot, Maurus
--A Pilgrim from Ireland. Mannix, Mary Ellen (1846-), tr. LC 8-4368. vi, 5-132 p. front. 18 cm. 1908. Benziger Brothers.
Carol, Bill J., pseud., see Knott, Bill.
Carol, Bill J., pseud., see Knott, William Cecil.
Carol, Bill J., jt. auth. see Knott, Bill.
Carol, Bill J., jt. auth. see Knott, Bill, Jr.
Carol, Bill J, pseud. (1927-)
--Backboard Scrambler. Knott, William Cecil Jr.. 202 p. 18cm. (Intext sportbook, 106). 1973, c.1963. (ISBN 0-88444-007-9). Intext Press.
--Backboard Scrambler. Knott, William Cecil. LC 63-20818. 202 p. 23cm. 1963. Steck & Co.
--Circus Catch. Knott, William Cecil Jr.. LC 63-13043. 156 p. 22cm. (Steck sports series). 1963. Steck Co.
--Clutch Single. Knott, William Cecil. LC 64-14875. vii, 132 p. 22cm. 1964. Steck.
--Crazylegs Merrill. Knott, William Cecil Jr.. 155p. (gr. 4-9). 1973. (ISBN 0-88444-002-8). Intext Paperbacks.
--Crazylegs Merrill. LC 79-76609. iv, 155 p. 22cm. 1969. (ISBN 0-8114-7667-7). Steck-Vaughn Co.
--Full-Court Pirate. Knott, William Cecil Jr.. LC 65-12083. 193 p. 22 cm. 1965. Steck-Vaughn.
--Hard Smash to Third. Knott, William Cecil. LC 66-129270. 156p. 22cm. c.1966. Steck.
--Hit Away!. Knott, William Cecil Jr.. LC 65-12082. 156 p. 22cm. 1965. Steck-Vaughn Co.
--Inside the Ten. Knott, William Cecil. LC 67-15878. 160 p. 22cm. 22cm. 1967. Steck-Vaughn Co.
--Lefty Plays First. Knott, William Cecil. Smith, Ben, illus. LC 69-16053. 160p. 22cm. (gr. 4-7). 1969. (ISBN 0-8114-7666-9). Steck-V.
--Linebacker Blitz. Knott, William Cecil. LC 79-151705. 124 p. 22cm. 1971. (ISBN 0-8114-7734-7). Steck Vaughn Co.
--Long Pass. Knott, William Cecil Jr.. LC 66-12933. (gr. 7 up). 1966. (ISBN 0-8114-7623-5). Steck-V.
--Scatback. Knott, William Cecil Jr.. LC 64-14876. 172 p. 22 cm. 1964. Steck Co.
--Squeeze Play. Knott, William Cecil Jr.. LC 75-141576. (gr. 4-7). 1971. (ISBN 0-8114-7725-8). Steck-V.
--Touchdown Duo. Knott, William Cecil Jr.. LC 68-22980. 161 p. 22cm. 1968. Steck-Vaughn Co.
Carol, Lois, pseud., see Winkler, Louis.
Carol, Lois, pseud. & Winkler, Carol Serra
--A Hallowe'en Odyssey. Winkler, Louis. Dart, Eleanor, illus. LC 74-33196. (Lois Carol is the Joint Psued of Louis & Carol Serra Winkler). (Illus.). 30 p. 26cm. 1975. Winkler and Winkler.
Caroll, Evelyn
--Dance, Natasha Dance. LC 47-2538. 29 p. illus. (part col) 26 x 21cm. N.D. Rinehart & Co.

Caroll, M., pseud., see Brooks, Martha.

Caroll, M., pseud.
--How Marjorie Helped. Brooks, Martha. (Illus.). (Stories for our Daughters). 1902. Lee & Shepard.

Caroselli, Remus Francis (1916-)
--Mystery at Long Crescent Marsh. LC 84-15716. 152 p. 22cm. c.1985. (ISBN 0-03-001414-X). Holt, Rinehart and Winston.
--The Mystery Cottage in Left Field. LC 78-24368. 140 p. 22cm. c.1979. (ISBN 0-399-20672-8). Putnam.
Carove, Friedrich Wilhelm (1789-1852)
--Story Without an End. Austin, Sarah Taylor, Mrs. (1793-1867), tr. N.D. Colby and Rich.
--The Story Without an End. Austin, Sarah Taylor, Mrs. (1793-1867), tr. from Ger. E. V. B., illus. Higginson, Wentworth LC 2-30053. x p., 1 l., 57 p. incl. plates. front. 20 cm. 1902. D. C. Heath & Co.
--The Story Without an End. Austin, Sarah Taylor, Mrs. (1793-1867), tr. N.D. Duffield.
--The Story Without an End. Austin, Sarah Taylor, Mrs. (1793-1867), tr. (Illus.). (Illustrated Holly-Tree Ser.). N.D. Henry Altemus Co.
--The Story Without an End. Austin, Sarah Taylor, Mrs. (1793-1867), tr. from Ger. LC 7-3550. 5 p. l., 9-58, 2 p. 14 cm. (The brocade series. v). 1897. T. B. Mosher.
--The Story Without an End. Clifford, Aimee G., illus. Austin, Sarah Taylor, Mrs. (1793-1867), tr. from Ger (Pub. by Society for Promoting Christian Knowledge). N.D. E. & J. B. Young & Co.
--Story Without an End. Clifford, Aimee G., illus. Austin, Sarah Taylor, Mrs. (1793-1867), tr. from Ger. N.D. James Miller.
--The Story Without an End. Wager-Smith, Curtis, illus. Austin, Sarah Taylor, Mrs. (1793-1867), tr. from Ger. Wager-Smith, Curtis, intro. by. LC 4-32323. xii p., 1 l., 15-110 p. incl. 9 pl. col. front. 19 cm. 1904. H. Altemus Company.
Carpenter, Bruce
--The Blossoming Year. N.D. Lothrop, Lee & Shepard.
--The Last Waltz. LC 56-6336. 185p. 22cm. 1956. Lothrop, Lee and Shepard.
Carpenter, Edmund Janes (1845-)
--Hellenic Tales: A Book of Golden Hours with the Old Story-Tellers. LC 6-34080. vi, 306 p. front., plates. 20 cm. 1906. Little, Brown, and Company.
--Long Ago in Greece: A Book of Golden Hours with the Old Story-Tellers. LC 6-29768. viii, 306 p. front., 11 pl. 20 cm. 1906. Little, Brown, and Company.
Carpenter, Edmund Snow (1922-), ed.
--The Story of Comock The Eskimo. 1968. Simon and Schuster.
Carpenter, Evelyn
--Little Flower. (Illus.). 48p. (gr. 5 up). 1975. (ISBN 0-8111-0592-X). Naylor.
Carpenter, Flora Leona (1880-), adapted by.
--Animal Stories We Can Read. Grider, Dorothy (1915-), illus. LC 48-165126. 33 p. col. illus. 17 cm. c.1947. Rand McNally.
Carpenter, Frances Aretta (1890-1972)
--African Wonder Tales. Escourido, Joseph, illus. LC 63-16625. 215 p. illus. 24 cm. 1963. Doubleday.
--The Elephant's Bathtub. Guggenheim, Hans (1924-), illus. 1962. (ISBN 0-8382-0224-1, Cadmus Books). E. M. Hale and Company.
--The Elephant's Bathtub: Wonder Tales from the Far East. 1st ed. Guggenheim, Hans (1924-), illus. LC 62-164995. 219p. illus. 25cm. 1962. Doubleday.
--Holiday in Washington. Fulton, George, illus. 1958. Alfred A Knopf : distributed by Borzoi Books.
--The Mouse Palace. Adams, Adrienne (1906-), illus. LC 63-22428. (Illus.). 60 p. 22cm. 1964. McGraw-Hill.
--People from the Sky: Ainu Tales from Northern Japan. Fraser, Betty M., pseud. (1928-), illus. Fraser, Elizabeth Marr. LC 70-151830. (Illus.). 107 p. 25cm. 1972. Doubleday.
--Pocahontas and Her World. 1st ed. Kihn, W. Langdon, illus. LC 56-8905. 241p. illus. 22cm. 1957. Knopf.
--South American Wonder Tales. Creasman, Ralph, illus. LC 69-10250. (Illus.). (gr. 4 up). 1969. (ISBN 0-695-88214-7). Follett.
--Tales of a Basque Grandmother. Garmendia, Pedro, illus. LC 31-260372. xii, 271 p. col. front., illus., col. plates, 24 cm. 1930. Doubleday, Doran & Company, Inc.
--Tales of a Chinese Grandmother. Hasselriis, Malthe M. (1888-1970), illus. LC 72-77514. (Illus.). xi, 261 p. 19cm. (Tut books. L). 1973. C. E. Tuttle Co.
--Tales of a Chinese Grandmother. Hasselriis, Malthe M. (1888-1970), illus. LC 37-29929. xii, p., 1 l., 261 p. col. front., illus., col. plates. 24 cm. 1937. Doubleday, Doran & Company, Inc.
--Tales of a Korean Grandmother. (gr. 7). 1947. Doubleday Bks.
--Tales of a Korean Grandmother. Hasselriis, Malthe M. (1888-1970), illus. LC 72-77515. (Illus.). 287 p. 19cm. (Tut books. L). 1973. (ISBN 0-8048-1043-5). C. E. Tuttle Co.
--Tales of a Russian Grandmother. Bilidine, I., illus. LC 33-23512. x p., 1 l., 292 p. incl. illus., plates, col. front., col. plates. 24 cm. 1933. Doubleday Doran & Company, Inc.
--Tales of a Swiss Grandmother. Bieler, Ernest (1863-), illus. LC 40-277222. xii p., 1 l., 266 p. col. front., illus., plates. (part col.) 24 cm. 1940. Doubleday, Doran & Company, Inc.
--Wonder Tales of Dogs and Cats. Keats, Ezra Jack (1916-1983), illus. LC 55-9228. 255p. illus. 25cm. (gr. 4-7). 1955. (ISBN 0-385-07590-1). Doubleday.
--Wonder Tales of Horses and Heroes. Hayes, William Dimitt (1913-), illus. LC 52-6361. (Illus.). 238 p. 24cm. 1952. Doubleday.
--Wonder Tales of Seas and Ships. 1st ed. Spier, Peter Edward (1927-), illus. LC 59-12619. 285p. illus. 24cm. 1959. Doubleday.
Carpenter, Harriet Frances
--Mother Play in Story. LC 15-22069. v. 19 cm. c.1915. The Baker & Taylor Co.
Carpenter, Harry Allen (1878-1942) & Bailey, Guy Andrew (1874-)
--Adventures in Science with Doris and Billy. LC 41-9562. vi, 249 p. illus. (part col.) 21 cm. (Rainbow Series. Green. iiii). c.1941. Allyn and Bacon.
--Adventures in Science with Jack and Jill. LC 42-22519. vi, 314 p. illus. (part col.) 20 1/2 x 18 cm. (Rainbow series. Blue. 5). 1942. Allyn and Bacon.
--Adventures in Science with Ruth and Jim. LC 43-17414. vi, 407 p. illus. (part col.) 20 x 15 1/2 cm. (Rainbow series. Violet. 6). 1943. Allyn and Bacon.
Carpenter, Humphrey William Bouverie (1946-)
--The Joshers: Or, London To Birmingham with Albert and Victoria : a Story of the Canals. Wilson, Robert J, illus. LC 78-303564. (Illus.). 120 p. 22cm. 1977. (ISBN 0-04-823142-8). G. Allen & Unwin.
Carpenter, Isabella
--The Magic ABC Book. LC 52-2181. (Illus.). unpaged. 21cm. (Magic talking books, T-5). 1955. Wilson.
Carpenter, John Alden (1876-) & Carpenter, Rue Winterbotham, Mrs.
--When Little Boys Sing. Carpenter, John Alden (1876-) & Carpenter, Rue Winterbotham, Mrs., illus. LC 4-33227. 39 p. illus. (part col.) 28 x 30 cm. 1904. A. C. McClurg & Company.
Carpenter, John Allan (1917-) & Balow, Tom
--Botswana. LC 72-10379. (Illus.). 96p. (Enchantment of Africa Ser.). (gr. 5 up). 1973. (ISBN 0-516-04553-9). Childrens.
Carpenter, John Allan (1917-) & Hughes, James (1934-)
--Congo. LC 77-572. (Illus.). (Enchantment of Africa (er)). (Enchantment of Africa Ser.). (gr. 5 up). 1977. (ISBN 0-516-04558-X). Childrens.
Carpenter, Katherine G., jt. ed. see Kingsley, Charles.
Carpenter, Margaret Haley
--A Gift for the Princess of Springtime. LC 63-7621. (Illus.). 27p. 1964. (ISBN 0-913110-02-7). Pentelic Pr.
Carpenter, Patricia Healy Evans see Evans, Patricia Healy, pseud.
Carpenter, Richard
--Catweazle. (ps-4). 1975. (ISBN 0-14-030465-7, Puffin). Penguin.
Carpenter, Rue Winterbotham, Mrs., jt. auth. see Carpenter, John Alden.
Carpenter, T V W
--The Too Long Tail. Grant, Campbell (1909-), illus. LC 52-11460. 17p. illus. 21cm. 1953. Houghton Mifflin.
Carper, Jean Elinor (1932-) & Dickerson, Grace Leslie (1911-)
--Little Turtle: Miami Chief. LC 59-14392. (Illus.). (gr. 4-7). 1959. (ISBN 0-8075-4682-8). A Whitman.
Carper, L. Dean (1931-)
--A Cry in the Wind. Hood, Garry R., illus. LC 73-80211. (Illus.). 128 p. 21cm. 1973. (ISBN 0-8309-0098-5). Herald Pub. House.
--Gib. LC 85-729. 111 p. 21cm. c.1985. (ISBN 0-8309-0413-1). Herald Pub. House.
--The Sound of Drums. LC 73-87638. 120 p. 21cm. 1975. (ISBN 0-8309-0110-8). Herald Pub. House.
Carr, Albert B
--The Black Box. Brooks, William (1914-), illus. LC 69-19111. (A Science Fable for Children and Some Grown-Ups). (Illus.). 30 p. 24cm. 1969. Prentice-Hall.
--The Black Box. Brooks, William (1914-), illus. (A Science Fable for Children & Some Grown-Ups). 1974. (ISBN 0-13-077446-4). Prentice Hall.
Carr, Albert H. Zolotkoff (1902-1971)
--Finding Maubee. 1971. (ISBN 0-399-10300-7). G.P. Putnam's Sons.
Carr, Alice Vansittart Strettell (1850-)
--The Fairy of the Rhone. Smith, Winifred, illus. LC 1-18521. 4 p. l., 69 p. incl. illus., plates. front. 18 1/2 cm. (Cozy corner series). 1901. L. C. Page & Company.
Carr, Annie Roe, pseud., see Stratemeyer Syndicate.
Carr, Annie Roe, pseud.
--Nan Sherwood at Lake View Hall: Or, The Mystery of the Haunted Boathouse. Stratemeyer Syndicate. (Nan Sherwood Ser.: No. 2). 1916. George Sully & Co.
--Nan Sherwood at Lakeview Hall: Or, The Mystery of the Haunted Boathouse. Stratemeyer Syndicate. Repr. of 1916 ed (Pub. by George Sully & Co). (Nan Sherwood Ser.: No. 2). N.D. World Syndicate Publishing Co.
--Nan Sherwood at Palm Beach: Or, Strange Adventures among the Orange Groves. Stratemeyer Syndicate. (Nan Sherwood Ser.: No. 5). 1921. George Sully & Co.
--Nan Sherwood at Palm Beach: Or, Strange Adventures among the Orange Groves. Stratemeyer Syndicate. Repr. of 1921 ed (Pub. by George Sully & Co). (Nan Sherwood Ser.: No. 5). N.D. World Syndicate Publishing Co.
--Nan Sherwood at Pine Camp: Or, The Old Lumberman's Secret. Stratemeyer Syndicate. (Nan Sherwood Ser.: No. 1). 1916. George Sully & Co.
--Nan Sherwood at Pine Camp: Or, The Old Lumberman's Secret. Stratemeyer Syndicate. Repr. of 1916 ed (Pub. by George Sully & Co). (Nan Sherwood Ser.: No. 1). N.D. Saalfield Publishing Co.
--Nan Sherwood at Rose Ranch: Or, The Old Mexican's Treasure. Stratemeyer Syndicate. LC 19-14624. iv p., 1 l., 246 p. front., plates. 21 cm. (Nan Sherwood Ser.: No. 4). 1919. George Sully & Co.
--Nan Sherwood at Rose Ranch: Or, The Old Mexican's Treasure. Stratemeyer Syndicate. Repr. of 1919 ed (Pub. by George Sully & Co). (Nan Sherwood Ser.: No. 4). N.D. World Syndicate Publishing Co.
--Nan Sherwood on the Mexican Border. Stratemeyer Syndicate. (Nan Sherwood Ser.: No. 7). 1937. World Syndicate Publishing Co.
--Nan Sherwood's Summer Holidays. Stratemeyer Syndicate. (Nan Sherwood Ser.: No. 6). 1922. George Sully & Co.
--Nan Sherwood's Summer Holidays. Stratemeyer Syndicate. Repr. of 1922 ed (Pub. by George Sully & Co). (Nan Sherwood Ser.: No. 6). N.D. World Syndicate Publishing Co.
--Nan Sherwood's Winter Holidays: Or, Rescuing the Runaways. Stratemeyer Syndicate. (Nan Sherwood Ser.: No. 3). 1916. George Sully & Co.
--Nan Sherwood's Winter Holidays: Or, Rescuing the Runaways. Stratemeyer Syndicate. Repr. of 1916 ed (Pub. by George Sully & Co). (Nan Sherwood Ser.: No. 3). N.D. World Syndicate Publishing Co.
Carr, Bettye JoCrisler (1926-)
--Trouble with Tikki. Petie, Haris, pseud. (1915-), illus. Petty, Roberta. LC 71-115459. (Illus.). 29 p. 24cm. 1970. Lantern Press.

AUTHOR INDEX **CARROLL, ALICE**

Carr, Deirdre (1902-) & Parrott, Irene Juanita (1898-)
--Now Daddy's in the Army. Shellhase, George, illus. LC 44-7475. 57 p. col. illus. 13 1/2 x 21 cm. 1944. W. Morrow and Company.
Carr, Eva E.
--A Child's Book of Jesus' Friends. 1981. (ISBN 0-570-08304-4). Concordia.
--A Child's Book of Old Testament Stories. 1981. (ISBN 0-570-08305-2). Concordia.
--A Child's Book of Stories Jesus Told. 1981. (ISBN 0-570-08300-1). Concordia.
Carr, Evangeline H
--Chief Watamett, and Other Stories. Arlo, Geer, illus. LC 51-38464. 123 p. illus. 24 cm. 1951. Review and Herald Pub. Association.
--Montana Flash: And Other Stories. Baerg, Harry John (1909-), illus. LC 62-5473. 207p. illus. 22 cm. 1961. Southern Pub. Association.
--Montana Flash & Other Stories. Baerg, Harry John (1909-), illus. (Illus.). 207p. (Crown Ser). (gr. 6-9). 1969. Southern Pub.
Carr, Harriett Helen (1899-)
--Against the Wind. LC 55-14975. 214p. 22cm. 1955. Macmillan.
--Bold Beginning. Neale, Sidnee, illus. LC 64-19076. (Illus.). 150 p. 22cm. 1964. Hastings House.
--Daughter of Brooklyn. LC 55-6160. 210 p. 22cm. 1955. Ariel Books.
--Confidential Secretary. LC 58-10196. 212p. 22cm. 1958. Macmillan.
--Gravel Gold. 1st ed. Hartman, C. L., illus. LC 53-9454. 186p. illus. 22cm. 1953. Ariel Books.
--Miami Towers. LC 56-729318. 202p. 22cm. 1956. Macmillan.
--The Mystery of Ghost Valley. LC 62-8554. 149 p. 22 cm. 1962. Macmillan.
--The Mystery of the Aztec Idol. LC 59-8222. 193p. 21cm. 1959. Macmillan.
--The Mystery of the Aztec Idol. LC 64-9580. 176 p. 21 cm. (Acorn books, AB7). 1963, c.1959. Macmillan.
--Rod's Girl. LC 63-16166. 190 p. 22 cm. 1963. Hastings House.
--Sharon. Thomson, Arline K. (1912-), illus. LC 56-11311. 207p. illus. 22cm. 1956. Hastings House.
--Valley of Defiance. LC 57-9892. 178p. 22cm. 1957. Macmillan.
--Wheels for Conquest. LC 57-5968. 22cm. 185p. (gr. 6-8). 1957. Macmillan.
--Young Viking of Brooklyn. Morse, Dorothy Bayley (1906-1979), illus. LC 61-11677. 72p. 26cm. c.1961. Viking.
Carr, Inez Storie
--Here Comes Willie. Baerg, Harry John (1909-), illus. LC 68-18489. (Illus.). 77 p. 24cm. 1968. Southern Pub. Association.
Carr, Josephine
--No Regrets. LC 82-70194. 183 p. 22cm. c.1982. (ISBN 0-8037-6721-8). Dial Press.
Carr, Kent
--The Big Row at Ranger's. Harrison, John D., illus. LC 27-18967. 3 p. l., 313 p. front., plates. 20 cm. c.1927. Harcourt, Brace and Company.
Carr, Luella Bender
--A Way to California. 1st ed. Lambo, Donald W. (1903-1966), illus. LC 61-12011. 172p. illus. 22cm. 1961. World Pub. Co.
Carr, Mary Jane (1899-)
--Children of the Covered Wagon. rev. ed. Kuhn, Bob, illus. LC 56-13460. (Illus.). 302p. (gr. 3-7). 1957. (ISBN 0-690-18987-7, TYC-J). Har-Row.
--Children of the Covered Wagon: A Story of the Old Oregon Trail. Brann, Esther, illus. LC 34-20016. 318 p. incl. front., illus., plates. 21 cm. c.1934. Thomas Y. Crowell.
--Children of the Covered Wagon: A Story of the Old Oregon Trail. Kuhn, Bob, illus. LC 44-3413. 318 p. incl. front., illus., plates. 21 cm. 1944. Thomas Y. Crowell Company.
--Peggy and Paul and Laddy. Voute, Kathleen (1892-), illus. LC 36-20137. 207, 1 incl. front., illus. 22 cm. c.1936. Thomas Y. Crowell Company.
--Top of the Morning. Jones, Henrietta, illus. LC 41-18719. 96 p. incl. col. front., illus. (part col.) 16 x 19 cm. c.1941. Thomas Y. Crowell Company.
--Young Mac of Fort Vancouver. Holberg, Richard A. (1889-1942), illus. LC 40-313859. vi, 238 p. col. front., illus., plates (part col., part double) 23 cm. 1940. Thomas Y. Crowell Company. **Award: (JNM).**
Carr, Mike
--Robbers & Robots. LC 83-50049. 160p. (Top Secret Endless Quest Bk.). (gr. 5up). 1983. (ISBN 0-394-72100-4). Random.
Carr, Philippa, pseud., see Hibbert, Eleanor Burford.
Carr, Philippa, pseud. (1906-)
--The Lion Triumphant. Hibbert, Eleanor Burford. 1974. (ISBN 0-399-11135-2). G.P. Putnam's Sons.
--The Miracle at St. Bruno's. Hibbert, Eleanor Burford. 1972. (ISBN 0-399-10977-3). G.P. Putnam's Sons.
--The Witch From the Sea. Hibbert, Eleanor Burford. 1975. (ISBN 0-399-11427-0). G.P. Putnam's Sons.
Carr, Rowen, ed. see Kruss, James.
Carr, Rowen, adapted by see Sussmann, Christel.
Carr, Samuel (1913-), ed.
--Birds, Beasts & Fishes: Animal Verse for Children. (Illus.). 96p. (gr. 1-3). 1982. (ISBN 0-7134-4151-8, Pub. by Batsford England). David & Charles.
Carr, Sarah Pratt, Mrs.
--Billy To-morrow in Camp. De Lay, H. S., illus. LC 11-5193. (Illus.). 263p. (Billy Tomorrow Ser.). 1910. A. C. McClurg & Co.
--Billy To-Morrow Stands the Test. De Lay, H. S., illus. LC 11-283572. 277 p. front., plates. 20 cm. (Her "Billy To-morrow" series). 1911. A. C. McClurg & Co.
--Billy Tomorrow. Relyea, Charles M., illus. LC 9-24957. 244p. (Billy Tomorrow Ser.). 1909. A. C. McClurg & Co.
Carr, Terry Gene (1937-), ed.
--Creatures from Beyond: Nine Stories of Science Fiction & Fantasy. LC 75-16244. 175p. 1st U.S. edition. (gr. 6 up). 1975. (ISBN 0-525-66459-9). Elsevier-Nelson.
--The Infinite Arena: Seven Science Fiction Stories About Sports. LC 76-30758. (gr. 8 up). 1977. (ISBN 0-525-66336-2). Lodestar Bks.
--Into the Unknown: Eleven Tales of Imagination. LC 73-7826. 192 p. 22cm. 1973. (ISBN 0-8407-6342-5). T. Nelson.
--Planets of Wonder: A Treasury of Space Opera. LC 76-22506. (gr. 8 up). 1976. (ISBN 0-8407-6526-6). Elsevier-Nelson.
--To Follow a Star: Nine Science Fiction Stories About Christmas. LC 77-2727. Repr. (Nelson Science Fiction Series). (gr. 7 up). 1977. (ISBN 0-525-66573-0). Lodestar Bks.
--Worlds Near and Far: Nine Stories of Science Fiction and Fantasy. LC 74-10273. 176 p. 21cm. 1974. (ISBN 0-8407-6404-9). Nelson.
Carraud
--Afternoons with Grandma. Kinmont, Mary, tr. from Fr. (Illus.). N.D. Methodist Bk Concern.
Carre, John Le see Le Carre, John.
Carrell, Mark, pseud., see Paine, Lauran Bosworth.
Carrell, Mark, pseud. (1916-)
--A Crack in Time. Paine, Lauran Bosworth. (gr. 6 up). 1971. Roy.
Carrera, Paul, tr. see Keats, Mark.
Carret, Mary B
--The Little Heroes of Matanzas. LC 570. 62 p. front. 17 cm. c.1899. J. H. West Company.
Carrick, Alice Van Leer (1875-)
--Kitty-Cat Tales. Keyes, Homer Eaton & Davidson, Bertha G., illus. LC 7-27609. 3 p. l., 3-237 p. front., illus., 9 pl. 21 cm. 1907. Lothrop, Lee & Shepard Co.
--Kitty-Cat Tales. Keyes, Homer Eaton & Davidson, Bertha G., illus. LC 32-10533. xiv, 3-237 p. col. front., illus., plates 20 cm. c.1932. Lothrop, Lee & Shepard Co.
Carrick, Bruce R., jt. auth. see Brooks, Mary B.
Carrick, Carol (1935-)
--The Accident. Carrick, Donald (1929-), illus. LC 76-25722. (Illus.). 32 p. 24cm. c.1976. (ISBN 0-8164-3172-8). Seabury Press.
--Beach Bird. Carrick, Donald (1929-), illus. LC 72-703. (ps-3). 1978. (Pied Piper). Dial Bks Young.
--Ben and the Porcupine. Carrick, Donald (1929-), illus. LC 80-21402. p. cm. c.1981. (ISBN 0-395-30171-8). Clarion Books.
--The Blue Lobster. Carrick, Donald (1929-), illus. LC 74-18594. (Illus.). 32p. (gr. k-3). 1975. Dial Bks Young.
--The Brook. Carrick, Donald (1929-), illus. LC 67-15534. (Illus.). 32 p. 26cm. 1967. Macmillan.
--The Climb. Carrick, Donald (1929-), illus. LC 80-12965. (Illus.). 32 p. 26cm. c.1980. (ISBN 0-395-29431-2). Houghton Mifflin/Clarion Books.
--The Crocodiles Still Wait. Carrick, Donald (1929-), illus. LC 79-23519. (Illus.). 32p. (gr. 1-4). 1980. (ISBN 0-395-29102-X, Clarion). HM.
--Dark & Full of Secrets. Carrick, Donald (1929-), illus. LC 83-21017. (Illus.). 32p. (ps-4). 1984. (ISBN 0-89919-271-8, Clarion). HM.
--The Dragon of Santa Lalia. Levy, Benjamin, illus. LC 74-137714. (Illus.). 32 p. 1971. Bobbs-Merrill.
--The Empty Squirrel. Carrick, Donald (1929-), illus. LC 80-16475. p. cm. c.1981. (ISBN 0-688-80293-1). (ISBN 0-688-84293-3). Greenwillow Books.
--The Foundling. Carrick, Donald (1929-), illus. LC 77-1587. (Illus.). 32 p. 23cm. c.1977. (ISBN 0-8164-3199-X). Seabury Press.
--The Highest Balloon on the Common. Carrick, Donald (1929-), illus. LC 77-23309. (Illus.). 32 p. c.1977. (ISBN 0-688-84100-7). Greenwillow Books.
--The Longest Float in the Parade. Carrick, Donald (1929-), illus. LC 81-6701. (Illus.). 55 p. 22cm. (Greenwillow read-alone). c.1982. (ISBN 0-688-00918-2). Greenwillow Books.
--Lost in the Storm. Carrick, Donald (1929-), illus. LC 74-1051. (Illus.). 32 p. 1974. (ISBN 0-8164-3124-8). Seabury Press.
--Old Mother Witch. Carrick, Donald (1929-), illus. LC 75-4609. (Illus.). 32 p. 24cm. 1975. (ISBN 0-8164-3148-5). Seabury Press.
--Patrick's Dinosaurs. Carrick, Donald (1929-), illus. LC 83-2049. (Illus.). 32p. (gr. k-3). 1983. (ISBN 0-89919-189-4, Clarion). HM.
--Paul's Christmas Birthday. Carrick, Donald (1929-), illus. LC 77-28408. (Illus.). 32 p. 26cm. c.1978. (ISBN 0-688-80159-5). Greenwillow Books.
--The Pond. Carrick, Donald (1929-), illus. LC 70-89580. (Illus.). 1 v. (unpaged. 26cm. 1970. Macmillan.
--A Rabbit for Easter. Carrick, Donald (1929-), illus. LC 78-15647. (Illus.). 32 p. 26cm. c.1979. (ISBN 0-688-80195-1). (ISBN 0-688-84195-3). Greenwillow Books.
--Sleep Out. Carrick, Donald (1929-), illus. 1973. Houghton.
--Some Friend!. Carrick, Donald (1929-), illus. LC 79-11490. p. cm. c.1979. (ISBN 0-8164-3236-8). Seabury Press.
--Stay Away from Simon!. Carrick, Donald (1929-), illus. LC 84-14289. (Illus.). 63 p. 22cm. c.1985. (ISBN 0-89919-343-9). Clarion Books.
--Swamp Spring. Carrick, Donald (1929-), illus. LC 69-10497. (Illus.). 32 p. 26cm. 1969. Macmillan.
--Two Coyotes. Carrick, Donald (1929-), illus. 1982. Houghton.
--The Washout. Carrick, Donald (1929-), illus. LC 78-8135. (Illus.). 32 p. c.1978. (ISBN 0-8164-3217-1). Seabury Press.
--What a Wimp!. Carrick, Donald (1929-), illus. LC 82-9597. p. cm. 1983, c.1982 (Clarion Bks.). (ISBN 0-89919-139-8). Houghton Mifflin.
Carrick, Carol (1935-) & Carrick, Donald (1929-)
--A Clearing in the Forest. Carrick, Donald (1929-), illus. LC 73-125467. (Illus.). 31 p. 1970. Dial Press.
--The Dirt Road. Carrick, Donald (1929-), illus. LC 73-116758. (Illus.). 29 p. 1970. Macmillan.
--The Old Barn. Carrick, Donald (1929-), illus. LC 66-22668. (Illus.). 1 v. (unpaged. 1966. Bobbs-Merrill.
--Sleep Out. Carrick, Donald (1929-), illus. LC 72-88539. (Illus.). 32 p. 1973. (ISBN 0-8164-3094-2). Seabury Press.
Carrick, Donald, jt. auth. see Carrick, Carol.
Carrick, Donald, jt. auth. see Fox, Siv Cedering.
Carrick, Donald (1929-)
--The Deer in the Pasture. LC 75-23193. (Illus.). 8 x 9 7/8. (18 pt.). (gr. 1-3). 1976. (ISBN 0-688-84023-X). Greenwillow.
--The Deer in the Pasture. Carrick, Donald (1929-), illus. LC 75-23193. (Illus.). 32 p. 26cm. (gr. 1-3). c.1976. (ISBN 0-688-80023-8). (ISBN 0-688-84023-X). Greenwillow Books.
--Drip, Drop. Carrick, Donald (1929-), illus. LC 73-4056. 32 p. of illus. 21cm. 1973. (ISBN 0-02-717340-2). Macmillan.
--Harald and the Giant Knight. Carrick, Donald (1929-), illus. LC 81-10243. (Illus.). 32 p. 29cm. c.1982. (ISBN 0-89919-060-X). Clarion Books.
--Milk. Carrick, Donald (1929-), illus. LC 84-25879. (Illus.). 9 7/8 x 8. 24p. (24 pt.). (ps-1). 1985. (ISBN 0-688-04822-6). (ISBN 0-688-04823-4). Greenwillow.
--Morgan & the Artist. Carrick, Donald (1929-), illus. LC 84-14267. (Illus.). 32p. 1st U.S. edition. (ps-4). 1985. (ISBN 0-89919-300-5, Clarion). HM.
--Tree. Carrick, Donald (1929-), illus. LC 70-133556. (Illus.). color ils. 33p. (gr. k-3). 1971. (ISBN 0-02-717290-2). Macmillan.
Carrick, Malcolm (1945-)
--Happy Jack: A Folktale. Carrick, Malcolm (1945-), illus. LC 78-19476. (Illus.). 5 7/8 x 8 1/2. 64p. (18 pt.). (I Can Read Bks.). (gr. k-3). 1979. (ISBN 0-06-021121-0). (ISBN 0-06-021122-9). Har-Row.
--I Can Squash Elephants: A Masai Tale About Monsters. Carrick, Malcolm (1945-), illus. LC 77-3455. (Illus.). 32 p. 1978. (ISBN 0-670-38983-8). Viking Press.
--I'll Get You!". Carrick, Malcolm (1945-), illus. LC 78-19490. (Illus.). 188 p. 21cm. c.1979. (ISBN 0-06-021123-7). (ISBN 0-06-021124-5). Harper & Row.
--Mr. Tod's Trap. Carrick, Malcolm (1945-), illus. LC 79-2012. 5 7/8 x 8 1/2. 64p. (18 pt.). (I Can Read Bks.). (gr. k-3). 1980. (ISBN 0-06-021113-X). (ISBN 0-06-021114-8). Har-Row.
--Mr. Tod's Trap. Carrick, Malcolm (1945-), illus. LC 79-2012. (Illus.). 64 p. 23cm. (I can read book). c.1980. (ISBN 0-06-021113-X). (ISBN 0-06-021114-8). Harper & Row.
--Today Is Shrew's Day. Carrick, Malcolm (1945-), illus. LC 77-11836. (Illus.). 5 7/8 x 8 1/2. 64p. (18 pt.). (I Can Read Bks.). (gr. k-3). 1978. (ISBN 0-06-021119-9). (ISBN 0-06-021120-2). Har-Row.
--Tramp. Carrick, Malcolm (1945-), illus. LC 76-58723. (Illus.). 48 p. 24cm. c.1977. (ISBN 0-06-021117-2). (ISBN 0-06-021118-0). Harper & Row.
Carrick, Malcolm (1945-), adapted by.
--The Wise Men of Gotham. Carrick, Malcolm (1945-), illus. LC 74-10832. p. cm. 1975, c.1973. Viking Press.
Carrick, Valery see Karrik, Valerian Viliamovich.
Carrie, Christopher
--Adventure at the Pirates' Cave. (Illus.). 48p. (Orig.). (Crayola Activity Storybooks). (gr. k-4). 1980. (ISBN 0-86696-025-2). Binney & Smith.
--Adventure of the Haunted Mansion. (Illus.). 48p. (Orig.). (Crayola Activity Storybooks). (gr. k-4). 1980. (ISBN 0-86696-030-9). Binney & Smith.
--Adventure of the Space Robots. (Illus.). 48p. (Orig.). (Crayola Activity Storybooks). (gr. k-4). 1980. (ISBN 0-86696-027-9). Binney & Smith.
--Amazing Cars. (Illus.). 48p. (Orig.). (Crayola Laugh & Play Bks.). (gr. k-4). 1981. (ISBN 0-86696-033-3). Binney & Smith.
--Exciting Outer Space. (Illus.). 48p. (Orig.). (Crayola Laugh & Play Books). (gr. k-4). 1981. (ISBN 0-86696-036-8). Binney & Smith.
--Fantastic Airplanes. (Illus.). 48p. (Orig.). (Crayola Laugh & Play Bks.). (gr. k-4). 1981. (ISBN 0-86696-035-X). Binney & Smith.
--Friendly Monsters. (Illus.). 48p. (Orig.). (Crayola Laugh & Play Bks.). (gr. k-4). 1981. (ISBN 0-86696-034-1). Binney & Smith.
--Mystery of Dinosaur Island. (Illus.). 48p. (Orig.). (Crayola Activity Storybooks). (gr. k-4). 1980. (ISBN 0-86696-029-5). Binney & Smith.
--Mystery of the Missing Wand. (Illus.). 48p. (Orig.). (Crayola Activity Storybooks). (gr. k-4). 1980. (ISBN 0-86696-028-7). Binney & Smith.
--Mystery of the Stolen Gold. (Illus.). 48p. (Orig.). (Crayola Activity Storybooks). (gr. k-4). 1980. (ISBN 0-86696-026-0). Binney & Smith.
Carrier, Lark (1947-)
--There Was a Hill-. LC 84-25536. (Illus.). 22 p. c.1985. (ISBN 0-907234-70-4). Picture Book Studio USA : Distributed by Alphabet Press.
Carriere, Anne
--Jennifer's Walk. Getz, Arthur, illus. LC 72-89615. (Illus.). 25 p. 33cm. 1973. Golden Press.
Carrigan, Nettie W
--Rhymes and Jingles for the Children's Hour. LC 40-29658. 3 p. l., v-vi p., 1 l., 9-57 p. 19 cm. c.1940. The Christopher Publishing House.
Carrington, Edna
--Five Stars in a Little Pool, 1 of 50 vols. x ed. 405p. (Library of Best Authors). 1905. American Tract Society.
--Five Stars in a Little Pool. (Illus.). N.D. Cassell & Co.
Carrington, Elaine Sterne
--The Gypsy Star. LC 28-78709. 4 p. l., 272 p. front., plates. 20 cm. c.1928. Harper & Brothers.
Carrington, Fitz Roy (1869-1954), ed.
--The Quiet Hour. LC 71-160901. (Illus.). xv, 113 p. 21cm. (Granger index reprint series). 1971. (ISBN 0-8369-6264-8). Books for Libraries Press.
--The Quiet Hour. LC 15-20971. 1915. Houghton Mifflin Company.
Carris, Joan Davenport (1938-)
--Pets, Vets, and Marty Howard. Newsom, Carol, illus. LC 84-47635. (Illus.). 186 p. 21cm. 1984. (ISBN 0-397-32092-2). (ISBN 0-397-32093-0). Lippincott.
--The Revolt of Ten-X. LC 80-7980. (gr. 4-6). 1980. (ISBN 0-15-266462-9, HJ). HarBraceJ.
--Rusty Timmons' First Million. Mulkey, Kim, illus. LC 85-40096. (Illus.). 179 p. 22cm. c.1985. (ISBN 0-397-32154-6). (ISBN 0-397-32155-4). Lippincott.
--When the Boys Ran the House. Newsom, Carol, illus. 1982. Harper.
--When the Boys Ran the House. Newsom, Carol, illus. LC 82-47762. (Illus.). 150 p. 21cm. c.1982. (ISBN 0-397-32019-1). (ISBN 0-397-32020-5). Lippincott.
--Witch-Cat. Peck, Beth, illus. LC 83-48448. (Illus.). 160p. (gr. 5 up). 1984. (ISBN 0-397-32067-1, JBL-J). (ISBN 0-397-32068-X). Har-Row.
Carroll-Abbing, John Patrick (1912-)
--A Chance to Live: The Story of the Lost Children of the War. Della Chiesa, Carol, tr. LC 52-5917. 216 p. illus. 21 cm. 1952. Longmans, Green.
Carroll, Alice Lee
--The Capper Cousins. Britcher, Phyllis, illus. LC 29-16077. xi, 274 p., 1 l. incl. front., illus. 20 cm. c.1929. J. H. Sears & Company, Inc.
--The Capper Cousins at the Fair. Britcher, Phyllis, illus. LC 30-19280. ix p., 1 l., 243 p. incl. front., plates. 20 cm. c.1930. Sears Publishing Company,Inc.

Carroll, Archer Latrobe, jt. auth. see Carroll, Ruth Robinson, Mrs.

Carroll, Consolata (1892-)

--I Hear in My Heart. Cirlin, Edgar, illus. LC 49-945310. x. 338 p. 21 cm. 1949. Farrar, Straus.

Carroll, Curt, pseud., see Bishop, Curtis Kent.

Carroll, Eleanor Elliott

--Chariot of the Sun. LC 38-12849. 306 p. 20 cm. c.1938. The Penn Publishing Company.

Carroll, Elizabeth

--Summer Love. LC 82-20116. 121 p. 19cm. c.1983. (ISBN 0-671-46449-3). Wanderer Books.

Carroll, Elsie Frances Caruana (1927-)

--I'm Happy, Hoppy Bunny. Geis, Bernard & Geis, Darlene, contrib. by. (Music by Sherry Madison and Jimmy Carroll.). (Illus.). 1955. C. Winston Co.

Carroll, Gladys Hasty (1904-)

--As the Earth Turns. (gr. 9 up). 1944. (ISBN 0-02-522110-8). Macmillan.

--Cockatoo. Crowther, Robert, illus. LC 29-16434. ix p., 1 l., 223 p. front., plates. 21 cm. 1929. The Macmillan Company.

--Land Spell. N.D. Macmillan.

Carroll, Jeffrey (1950-)

--Climbing to the Sun. LC 77-8617. 126 p. 22cm. c.1977. (ISBN 0-8164-3201-5). Seabury Press.

Carroll, Jock, jt. auth. see Pak, Chong-Yong.

Carroll, John see Berg, Jean Horton.

Carroll, Kay

--The Ewoks Save the Day. Woodend, James & Barto, Renzo, illus. LC 83-60330. (Illus.). 12p. (Return of the Jedi Ser.). (gr. 1-3). 1983. (ISBN 0-394-86118-3). (ISBN 0-394-86118-3). Random.

--Han Solo's Rescue. Eastman, Bryant, illus. LC 83-60329. (Illus.). 12p. (Return of the Jedi Ser.). (gr. 1-3). 1983. (ISBN 0-394-86112-4). Random.

--Little Pops. 12p. (gr. k-3). 1983. Random.

Carroll, Latrobe, jt. auth. see Carroll, Ruth Robinson, Mrs.

Carroll, Lewis, pseud., see Dodgson, Charels Lutwidge.

Carroll, Lewis, pseud., see Dodgson, Charles Lutwidge.

Carroll, Lewis, jt. auth. see Disney, Walt, Productions.

Carroll, Lewis, jt. auth. see Spyri, Johanna Heusser.

Carroll, Lewis, pseud. (1832-1898)

--Adventures from the Original Alice in Wonderland and Through the Looking Glass. Dodgson, Charles Lutwidge. Levin, Marcia Obrasky (1918-), adapted by. Martin, Marcia, pseud. Matulay, Laszlo (1912-), illus. LC 51-7743. unpaged. illus. 34 cm. (Big treasure books). N.D. Grosset & Dunlap.

--The Alice Birthday Book. Dodgson, Charles Lutwidge. Tenniel, John, Sir (1820-1914), illus. (Illus.). 144p. (gr. 2 up). 1984. (ISBN 0-517-55457-7). Crown.

--Alice in Wonderland. Dodgson, Charles Lutwidge. (The Cornell Series). 1915. A L Burt & Co.

--Alice in Wonderland. Dodgson, Charles Lutwidge. (The Oxford Ser.). N.D. A. L. Burt Company.

--Alice in Wonderland. Dodgson, Charles Lutwidge. (Fireside Ser. for Girls). N.D. A. L. Burt's Publications.

--Alice in Wonderland. Dodgson, Charles Lutwidge. (Illus.). (The Wellesley Series for Girls). N.D. A. L. Burt's Pubs.

--Alice in Wonderland. Dodgson, Charles Lutwidge. (Illus.). (Pleasant Hour Ser.). N.D. Barse and Hopkins.

--Alice in Wonderland. Dodgson, Charles Lutwidge. 1977. (ISBN 0-460-01836-1, Evman). Biblio Dist.

--Alice in Wonderland. Dodgson, Charles Lutwidge. (gr. 2-7). 1977. (ISBN 0-8277-4986-4). British Bk Ctr.

--Alice in Wonderland. Dodgson, Charles Lutwidge. 215p. Repr. 1981. (ISBN 0-89966-345-1). Buccaneer Bks.

--Alice in Wonderland. Dodgson, Charles Lutwidge. (Lambskin Library). N.D. Doubleday Page & Co.

--Alice in Wonderland. Dodgson, Charles Lutwidge. N.D. Educational Publishing Company.

--Alice in Wonderland. Dodgson, Charles Lutwidge. (Classics for Children). N.D. Ginn.

--Alice in Wonderland. Dodgson, Charles Lutwidge. (The Good Value Books). N.D. Grosset & Dunlap.

--Alice in Wonderland. Dodgson, Charles Lutwidge. (Illus.). (The Editha Ser.: No. 19). 1905. Set. H M Caldwell Co.

--Alice in Wonderland. Dodgson, Charles Lutwidge. (Illus.). (The Empyreal Lib of Handy Volume Classics). N.D. H. M. Caldwell Co.

--Alice in Wonderland. Dodgson, Charles Lutwidge, 1 of 3 vols. (The Lakeside Series of Handy Volume Classics: No. 9). N.D. H. M. Caldwell Co.

--Alice in Wonderland. Dodgson, Charles Lutwidge, 1 of 32 vols, Vol. 29. (Illus.). (Famous Books for Girls). N.D. H. M. Caldwell Co.

--Alice in Wonderland. Dodgson, Charles Lutwidge. (Queen's Treasures Ser.). N.D. Harcourt Brace & Co.

--Alice in Wonderland. Dodgson, Charles Lutwidge. 299p. Repr. 1981. (ISBN 0-89967-019-9). Harmony & Co.

--Alice in Wonderland. Dodgson, Charles Lutwidge. (Twilight Ser.). N.D. Harper & Bros.

--Alice in Wonderland. Dodgson, Charles Lutwidge. Library ed. 1900. Hurst & Co.

--Alice in Wonderland. Dodgson, Charles Lutwidge. (Illus.). (Home Ser.). N.D. Hurst and Company.

--Alice in Wonderland. Dodgson, Charles Lutwidge. (Illus.). (Hurst's Half Leather Classics). N.D. Hurst and Company.

--Alice in Wonderland. Dodgson, Charles Lutwidge. (Illus.). (The Cambridge Classics). N.D. Hurst and Company.

--Alice in Wonderland. Dodgson, Charles Lutwidge. (Illus.). (The Laurelhurst Ser.). N.D. Hurst and Company.

--Alice in Wonderland. Dodgson, Charles Lutwidge. (Illus.). (The Cosmos Ser.). N.D. Hurst and Company.

--Alice in Wonderland. Dodgson, Charles Lutwidge. (Illus.). (The New Argyle Ser.). N.D. Hurst and Company.

--Alice in Wonderland. Dodgson, Charles Lutwidge. (Illus.). (The Universal Library). N.D. Hurst and Company.

--Alice in Wonderland. Dodgson, Charles Lutwidge. (Illus.). (Knickerbocker Classics). N.D. Hurst & Co.

--Alice in Wonderland. Dodgson, Charles Lutwidge. (Sears Juvenile Classics). N.D. J.H.Sears & Co.

--Alice in Wonderland. Dodgson, Charles Lutwidge. (Illus.). 240p. (Windermere Classics Ser.). (gr. 3 up). 1944. (ISBN 0-528-87166-8). Rand.

--Alice in Wonderland. Dodgson, Charles Lutwidge. (The Advance Library Ser.: Vol. 7). N.D. Rand, McNally & Co.

--Alice in Wonderland. Dodgson, Charles Lutwidge. (Illus.). (The Independent Library: Vol. 7). N.D. Rand, McNally & Co.

--Alice in Wonderland. Dodgson, Charles Lutwidge. (gr. 7 up). N.D (LTB). Soccer.

--Alice in Wonderland. Dodgson, Charles Lutwidge. (Children's Home Library). 1915. T Y Crowell.

--Alice in Wonderland. Dodgson, Charles Lutwidge. (Illus.). (The Waldorf Lib.). N.D. T. Y. Crowell & Co.

--Alice in Wonderland. Dodgson, Charles Lutwidge. (The New Astor Library of Prose). N.D. T. Y. Crowell & Co.

--Alice in Wonderland. Dodgson, Charles Lutwidge. N.D. The Modern Library.

--Alice in Wonderland. Dodgson, Charles Lutwidge. (gr. 3 up). 1979. (ISBN 0-307-21616-0, Golden Pr). Western Pub.

--Alice in Wonderland. Dodgson, Charles Lutwidge. (Illus.). N.D. William Collins Sons & Co.

--Alice in Wonderland. Dodgson, Charles Lutwidge. (Classic Ser.). N.D. World Publishing Co.

--Alice in Wonderland. Dodgson, Charles Lutwidge. N.D. Worthington Co.

--Alice in Wonderland. Dodgson, Charles Lutwidge. Huehnergarth, John, illus. (Winston Pixie Books). 1952. Holt, Rinehart and Winston.

--Alice in Wonderland. Dodgson, Charles Lutwidge. McMurry, Charles Alexander (1857-1929), ed. (Pocket Classics). N.D. Macmillan.

--Alice in Wonderland. Dodgson, Charles Lutwidge. Maraja, pseud., illus. Maraja, Libico. LC 57-4800. 110p. illus. 35cm. 1957. Grosset & Dunlap.

--Alice in Wonderland. Dodgson, Charles Lutwidge. Martin, Marcia, adapted by. N.D. Wonder Books.

--Alice in Wonderland. Dodgson, Charles Lutwidge. Miller, Albert G., adapted by. Taylor, Paul L., illus. (Illus.). 4-color pop-ups.24p. (Pop-up Classics, No. 3). (gr. k-3). 1968. (ISBN 0-394-80898-3). Random.

--Alice in Wonderland. Dodgson, Charels Lutwidge. Miller, Madge (1918-), adapted by. 1953. Children's Theatre Press.

--Alice in Wonderland. Dodgson, Charles Lutwidge. Newell, Peter (1862-1924), illus. N.D. Harper & Brothers.

--Alice in Wonderland. Dodgson, Charles Lutwidge. Pears, Charles (1873-1958) & Robinson, Thomas Heath (1869-1950), illus. (Collins' Illustrated Pocket Classics). N.D. Collins.

--ALice in Wonderland. Dodgson, Charles Lutwidge. Pogany, Willy (1882-1955), illus. N.D. E. P. Dutton & Co.

--Alice in Wonderland. Dodgson, Charles Lutwidge. Rackham, Arthur (1867-1939), illus. (Illus.). N.D. Doubleday, Page & Co.

--Alice in Wonderland. Dodgson, Charles Lutwidge. Robinson, Charles (1870-1937), illus. (Illus.). N.D. Cassell & Co.

--Alice in Wonderland. Dodgson, Charles Lutwidge. Robinson, Charles (1870-1937), illus. N.D. Funk & Wagnalls.

--Alice in Wonderland. Dodgson, Charles Lutwidge. Sowerby, Millicent, illus. N.D. Duffield.

--Alice in Wonderland. Dodgson, Charles Lutwidge. Tenniel, John, Sir (1820-1914), illus. N.D. Doubleday.

--Alice in Wonderland. Dodgson, Charles Lutwidge. Tenniel, John, Sir (1820-1914), illus. 192p. N.D. Heritage Press.

--Alice in Wonderland. Dodgson, Charles Lutwidge. Tenniel, John, Sir (1820-1914), illus. 192p. 1940. Peter Pauper Press.

--Alice in Wonderland. Dodgson, Charles Lutwidge. Tenniel, John, Sir (1820-1914), illus. (Illus.). (gr. 4-6). 1972. (ISBN 0-590-08503-4). Scholastic Inc.

--Alice in Wonderland. Dodgson, Charles Lutwidge. rev. ed. Tenniel, John, Sir (1820-1914), illus. LC 72-9975. (Illus.). (Rainbow Classics Ser.). (gr. 2-10). 1973. (ISBN 0-529-05031-5). (ISBN 0-529-05030-7). World Pub.

--Alice in Wonderland. Dodgson, Charles Lutwidge. Torret, Maraja, illus. LC 55-6061. 62p. illus. 29cm. c.1955. Random House.

--Alice in Wonderland: A Play. Dodgson, Charles Lutwidge. Delafield, Emily Prime, compiled by. N.D. Dodd, Mead & Co.

--Alice in Wonderland and Through a Looking-Glass. Dodgson, Charles Lutwidge. (Caldwell's Illustrated Library of Famous Books by Famous Authors). N.D. H. M. Caldwell Co.

--Alice in Wonderland, and Through the Looking Glass. Dodgson, Charles Lutwidge. (Burt's Home Lib.). N.D. A. L. Burt's Pubs.

--Alice in Wonderland, and Through the Looking Glass. Dodgson, Charles Lutwidge. (Illus.). (Fireside Series for Girls). N.D. A. L. Burt's Pubs.

--Alice in Wonderland and Through the Looking-Glass. Dodgson, Charles Lutwidge. (Illus.). (The Meade Series for Girls). N.D. A. L. Burt.

--Alice in Wonderland and Through the Looking Glass. Dodgson, Charles Lutwidge. N.D. Chanticleer Bks.

--Alice in Wonderland and Through the Looking Glass. Dodgson, Charles Lutwidge. N.D. (ISBN 0-529-05031-5). (ISBN 0-529-05032-3). Collins & World.

--Alice in Wonderland: And, Through the Looking Glass. Dodgson, Charles Lutwidge. 320p. N.D. Grosset & Dunlap.

--Alice in Wonderland and Through the Looking Glass. Dodgson, Charles Lutwidge. (Illus.). (Berkeley Lib.). N.D. H. M. Caldwell Co.

--Alice in Wonderland and Through the Looking Glass. Dodgson, Charles Lutwidge. (Illus.). (Little Men and Women Ser.). N.D. Henry Altemus & Co.

--Alice in Wonderland and Through the Looking-Glass. Dodgson, Charles Lutwidge. (Illus.). (Hurst's Fairy Tale Ser.). N.D. Hurst and Company.

--Alice in Wonderland, and Through the Looking Glass. Dodgson, Charles Lutwidge. N.D. Lothrop,Lee & Shepard.

--Alice in Wonderland & Through the Looking Glass. Dodgson, Charles Lutwidge. Bryan, Brigitte, illus. LC 72-79983. (Illus.). afterword. 1920p. (Fun-To-Read Classics). (gr. 4 up). 1969. (ISBN 0-516-04239-4). Childrens.

--Alice in Wonderland and Through the Looking Glass. Dodgson, Charles Lutwidge. Tenniel, John, Sir (1820-1914), illus. N.D. Grosset & Dunlap.

--Alice in Wonderland and Through the Looking Glass. Dodgson, Charles Lutwidge. Tenniel, John, Sir (1820-1914), illus. N.D. Henry Altemus Company.

--Alice in Wonderland & Through the Looking Glass. Dodgson, Charles Lutwidge. Tenniel, John, Sir (1820-1914), illus. (Illus.). (gr. 4 up). N.D (Puffin). Penguin.

--Alice in Wonderland & Through the Looking Glass. Dodgson, Charles Lutwidge. Tenniel, John, Sir (1820-1914), illus. (Illus.). (gr. 4-6). 1946. (ISBN 0-448-05454-X, G&D). (ISBN 0-448-05804-9). (ISBN 0-448-06004-3). Putnam Pub Group.

--Alice in Wonderland Giant Illustrated Edition. Dodgson, Charles Lutwidge. (Illus.). 1976. (ISBN 0-312-01855-X). St Martin.

--Alice in Wonderland, Through the Looking Glass and The Hunting of the Snark. Dodgson, Charles Lutwidge. N.D. Liveright Publishing.

--Alice in Wonderland, Through the Looking Glass and The Hunting of the Snark. Dodgson, Charles Lutwidge. N.D. Modern Library.

--Alice in Wonderland: Through the Looking Glass and the Hunting of the Snark. Dodgson, Charles Lutwidge. N.D. William Collins Sons & Company Ltd.

--Alice in Wonderland, Through the Looking Glass and The Hunting of the Snark. Dodgson, Charles Lutwidge. Tenniel, John, Sir (1820-1914), illus. Woollcott, Alexander (1887-1943), intro. by. N.D. Horace Liveright.

--Alice in Wonderland,Through the Looking Glass, & Hunting of the Snark. Dodgson, Charles Lutwidge. Woollcott, Alexander (1887-1943), intro. by. N.D. Modern Library.

--Alice Through the Looking-Glass. Dodgson, Charles Lutwidge. N.D. G. P. Putnam's Sons.

--Alice Through the Looking-Glass. Dodgson, Charles Lutwidge. (Illus.). (Harper's Young People Ser.). N.D. Harper & Brothers Trade-List.

--Alice Through The Looking Glass. Dodgson, Charles Lutwidge. Tenniel, John, Sir (1820-1914), illus. 222p. N.D. A. Whitman & Co.

--Alice's Adventure Under Ground. Dodgson, Charles Lutwidge. N.D. (ISBN 0-07-010151-5). McGraw-Hill Book Company.

--Alice's Adventures. Dodgson, Charles Lutwidge. (Children's Favorite Classics). N.D. Thomas Y. Crowell Company.

--Alice's Adventures in Wonderland. Dodgson, Charles Lutwidge. LC 84-5705. 1984. (ISBN 0-394-53227-9). A. A. Knopf.

--Alice's Adventures in Wonderland. Dodgson, Charles Lutwidge. (Illus.). (The Little Women Ser.). N.D. A. L. Burt's Pubs.

--Alice's Adventures in Wonderland. Dodgson, Charles Lutwidge. (Illus.). (Burt's Young Folks' Library). N.D. A. L. Burt's Pubs.

--Alice's Adventures in Wonderland. Dodgson, Charles Lutwidge. (Illus.). N.D. A. L. Chatterton Co.

--Alice's Adventures in Wonderland. Dodgson, Charles Lutwidge. N.D. (ISBN 0-8283-1423-3). Branden Press.

--Alice's Adventures in Wonderland. Dodgson, Charles Lutwidge. (Illus.). (The Young Folks Library). N.D. Caldwell.

--Alice's Adventures in Wonderland. Dodgson, Charles Lutwidge. (Illus.). (The Alcazar Classics). N.D. Caldwell.

--Alice's Adventures in Wonderland. Dodgson, Charles Lutwidge. (Illus.). (The Favorite Lib.). N.D. DeWolfe, Fiske & Co.

--Alice's Adventures in Wonderland. Dodgson, Charles Lutwidge. (Watered Silk Ser.). N.D. Donohue, Henneberry & Co.

--Alice's Adventures in Wonderland. Dodgson, Charles Lutwidge. Bd. with Through the Looking Glass. Dogson, Charles Lutwidge. (Reader's Request). 1980. (ISBN 0-8161-3070-1, Large Print Bks). G K Hall.

--Alice's Adventures in Wonderland. Dodgson, Charles Lutwidge. (Illus.). (The Young Folks Lib.). N.D. H. M. Caldwell Co.

--Alice's Adventures in Wonderland. Dodgson, Charles Lutwidge. (Illus.). (Harper's Young People Ser.). N.D. Harper & Brothers Trade-List.

--Alice's Adventures in Wonderland. Dodgson, Charles Lutwidge. (Altemus' New Vademecum Ser.). N.D. Henry Altemus Co.

--Alice's Adventures in Wonderland. Dodgson, Charles Lutwidge. New ed. (Illus.). (Altemus' Vademecum Ser.). N.D. Henry Altemus Co.

--Alice's Adventures in Wonderland. Dodgson, Charles Lutwidge. (Illus.). (Boys' and Girls' Classics). N.D. Henry Altemus Co.

--Alice's Adventures in Wonderland. Dodgson, Charles Lutwidge. (Illus.). (Petit-Trainon). N.D. Henry Altemus Co.

--Alice's Adventures in Wonderland. Dodgson, Charles Lutwidge. (Illus.). (Beauxarts Ser.). N.D. Henry Altemus Co.

--Alice's Adventures in Wonderland. Dodgson, Charles Lutwidge. (Illus.). (Children's Gift Ser.). N.D. Henry Altemus Company Publications.

--Alice's Adventures in Wonderland. Dodgson, Charles Lutwidge. (Illus.). (Ever New Books for Young People). N.D. Henry Altemus Company Publications.

--Alice's Adventures in Wonderland. Dodgson, Charles Lutwidge. (Cinderella Ser). N.D. Hurst & Company.

--Alice's Adventures in Wonderland. Dodgson, Charles Lutwidge. (Illus.). (Arlington Edition). N.D. Hurst and Company.

--Alice's Adventures in Wonderland. Dodgson, Charles Lutwidge. (Illus.). (Aunt Virginia Ser.). N.D. Hurst and Company.

--Alice's Adventures in Wonderland. Dodgson, Charles Lutwidge. (Illus.). (St. Nicholas Series for Girls). N.D. International Book Co.

--Alice's Adventures in Wonderland. Dodgson, Charles Lutwidge. N.D. J.B. Lippincott Co.

--Poems of Lewis Carroll. Dodgson, Charles Lutwidge. Livingston, Myra Cohn (1926-), compiled by. Tenniel, John, Sir, et al. (1820-1914), illus. Dodgson, Charles Lutwidge. LC 73-7914. (Illus.). (Poets Ser.). (gr. 6 up). 1973. (ISBN 0-690-00178-9, TYC-J). Har-Row.
--The Rectory Umbrella and Mischmasch. Dodgson, Charles Lutwidge. Carroll, Lewis, pseud. (1832-1898), illus. Dodgson, Charles Lutwidge. Milner, Florence, frwd. by. (Illus.). 193p. 1932. (ISBN 0-486-21345-5). Dover Books.
--Rhyme? & Reason?. Dodgson, Charles Lutwidge. LC 75-32188. (Illus.). Repr. of 1883 ed. (Classics of Children's Literature, 1621-1932: Vol. 51). 1976. (ISBN 0-8240-2300-5). Garland Pub.
--Rhyme and Reason. Dodgson, Charles Lutwidge. (Illus.). (St. Nicholas Series for Girls). N.D. International Book Co.
--Rhyme? & Reason?. Dodgson, Charles Lutwidge. Frost, Arthur Burdett (1851-1928) & Holiday, Henry (1839-1927), illus. LC 43-40023. 19 cm. 214p. 1884. MacMillan.
--Selections from Alice's Adventures in Wonderland. Dodgson, Charles Lutwidge. (gr. 7 up). N.D. Pyramid Pubns.
--Songs from Alice. Dodgson, Charles Lutwidge. Harper, Don, ed. Folkard, Charles James (1878-1963), illus. LC 79-11314. (Illus.). 48p. 1979. (ISBN 0-8234-0358-0). (ISBN 0-8234-0421-8). Holiday.
--The Story of Sylvie & Bruno. Dodgson, Charles Lutwidge. Furniss, Harry (1854-1925), illus. (Illus.). 344p. (Mayflower Facsimilie Classics Ser.). 1980. (ISBN 0-8317-8602-7, Mayflower Bks). Smith Pubs.
--Sylvie & Bruno. Dodgson, Charles Lutwidge. LC 75-32196. (Illus.). Repr. of 1889 ed. (Classics of Children's Literature, 1621-1932: Vol. 58). 1976. (ISBN 0-8240-2307-2). Garland Pub.
--Sylvie & Bruno. Dodgson, Charles Lutwidge. Furniss, Harry (1854-1925), illus. 1898. MacMillan.
--Sylvie and Bruno Concluded. Dodgson, Charles Lutwidge. Furniss, Harry (1854-1925), illus. 1893. Macmillan.
--A Tangled Tale. Dodgson, Charles Lutwidge. (Illus.). Repr. N.D. MacMillan.
--A Tangled Tale. Dodgson, Charles Lutwidge. (Illus.). 1976. (ISBN 0-685-86600-9). State Mutual Bk.
--Three Sunsets and Other Poems. Dodgson, Charles Lutwidge. Thomson, Emily Gertrude, illus. 21cm. 67p. 1898. Macmillan Co.
--Through the Looking Glass. Dodgson, Charles Lutwidge. (The Rugby Series for Boys and Girls). N.D. A. L. Burt Company.
--Through the Looking Glass. Dodgson, Charles Lutwidge. (Illus.). N.D. A. L. Chatterton Co.
--Through The Looking Glass. Dodgson, Charles Lutwidge. N.D. (ISBN 0-8283-1459-4). Branden Press.
--Through the Looking Glass. Dodgson, Charles Lutwidge. (Editha Series.). N.D. Dodge Publishing Co.
--Through the Looking Glass. Dodgson, Charles Lutwidge. (Doubleday Classics). N.D. Garden City Books.
--Through the Looking Glass. Dodgson, Charles Lutwidge. (Illus.). (The Editha Ser.: No. 21). 1905. Set. H M Caldwell Co.
--Through the Looking Glass. Dodgson, Charles Lutwidge. (Illus.). (The Empyreal Library of Country Classics). N.D. H. M. Caldwell Co.
--Through the Looking Glass. Dodgson, Charles Lutwidge. (Illus.). (The Young Folks Lib.). N.D. H. M. Caldwell Co.
--Through the Looking Glass. Dodgson, Charles Lutwidge, 1 of 3 vols. (The Lakeside Series of Handy Volume Classics: No. 9). N.D. Set. H. M. Caldwell Co.
--Through the Looking Glass. Dodgson, Charles Lutwidge. (Twilight Ser.). N.D. Harper & Bros.
--Through the Looking Glass. Dodgson, Charles Lutwidge. (Illus.). (Vademecum Ser.). N.D. Henry Altemus.
--Through the Looking-Glass. Dodgson, Charles Lutwidge. (Illus.). (The New Argyle Ser.). N.D. Hurst and Company.
--Through the Looking Glass. Dodgson, Charles Lutwidge. (Home Series for Girls). N.D. Hurst & Co.
--Through the Looking Glass. Dodgson, Charles Lutwidge. (Illus.). (Alligator Classics). N.D. Hurst & Co.
--Through the Looking Glass. Dodgson, Charles Lutwidge. (Illus.). (St. Nicholas Series for Girls). N.D. International Book Co.
--Through the Looking Glass. Dodgson, Charles Lutwidge. (Stories All Children Love Ser.). N.D. J. B. Lippincott Co.
--Through the Looking Glass. Dodgson, Charles Lutwidge. N.D. McGraw-Hill Book Co.
--Through the Looking Glass. Dodgson, Charles Lutwidge. (Illus.). (Children's Home Library). 1915. T Y Crowell.
--Through the Looking Glass. Dodgson, Charles Lutwidge, 1 of 24 vols. (Illus.). (Children's Favorite Classics). N.D. T. Y. Crowell & Co.
--Through the Looking Glass. Dodgson, Charles Lutwidge. (Illus.). (The Waldorf Lib.). N.D. T. Y. Crowell & Co.
--Through the Looking-Glass. Dodgson, Charles Lutwidge. (The New Astor Library of Prose). N.D. T. Y. Crowell & Co.
--Through the Looking Glass. Dodgson, Charles Lutwidge. N.D. The Peter Pauper Press.
--Through the Looking Glass. Dodgson, Charles Lutwidge. (Every Boy's and Every Gilrl's Ser.). N.D. The Macmillan Co.
--Through the Looking Glass. Dodgson, Charles Lutwidge. (Nelson Classics). N.D. Thomas Nelson & Sons.
--Through the Looking Glass. Dodgson, Charles Lutwidge. Kirk, Maria Louise (1860-), illus. N.D. Frederick A. Stokes.
--Through the Looking Glass. Dodgson, Charles Lutwidge. Pease, Bessie Collins, illus. (Illus.). N.D. Dodge Publishing Company.
--Through the Looking Glass. Dodgson, Charles Lutwidge. Tenniel, John, Sir (1820-1914), illus. 181p. N.D. G P Putnam's Sons.
--Through the Looking Glass. Dodgson, Charles Lutwidge. Tenniel, John, Sir (1820-1914), illus. N.D. Heritage Press.
--Through the Looking-Glass. Dodgson, Charles Lutwidge. Tenniel, John, Sir (1820-1914), illus. (Illus.). (Series of Books for the Young). N.D. Macmillan & Co.
--Through the Looking Glass and What Alice Found There. Dodgson, Charles Lutwidge. LC 84-5707. 1984. (ISBN 0-394-86916-8). A. A. Knopf.
--Through the Looking Glass and What Alice Found There. Dodgson, Charles Lutwidge. (Illus.). (The Wellesley Series for Girls). N.D. A. L. Burt's Pubs.
--Through the Looking Glass and What Alice Found There. Dodgson, Charles Lutwidge. (Illus.). (McKay's Young People's Classics). N.D. David McKay.
--Through the Looking-Glass: And what Alice Found There. Dodgson, Charles Lutwidge. (Illus.). 192p. 1899. G. H. McKibbin.
--Through the Looking Glass & What Alice Found There. Dodgson, Charles Lutwidge. 1905. Henry Altemus Co.
--Through the Looking Glass and What Alice Found There. Dodgson, Charles Lutwidge. (Altemus' New Illustrated Young People's Library). N.D. Henry Altemus Company.
--Through the Looking Glass and What Alice Found there. Dodgson, Charles Lutwidge. (Illus.). (Boys' and Girls' Classics). N.D. Henry Altemus Co.
--Through the Looking-Glass, & What Alice Found There. Dodgson, Charles Lutwidge. Library ed. 1900. Hurst & Co.
--Through the Looking Glass, and What Alice Found There. Dodgson, Charles Lutwidge. (Illus.). 1882. Lee & Shepard.
--Through the Looking Glass and What Alice Found There. Dodgson, Charles Lutwidge. 1910. Putnam.
--Through the Looking Glass and What Alice Found There. Dodgson, Charles Lutwidge. (Illus.). (Young People's Classics). N.D. R. F. Fenno & Co.
--Through the Looking-Glass: And What Alice Found There. Dodgson, Charles Lutwidge. LC 12-31246. (Illus.). 17cm. 230p. 1893. T. Y. Crowell & Co.
--Through the Looking-Glass and What Alice Found There. Dodgson, Charles Lutwidge. Tenniel, John, Sir (1820-1914), illus. 224p. N.D. J. W. Lovell Co.
--Through the Looking-Glass, and what Alice found there. Dodgson, Charles Lutwidge. Tenniel, John, Sir (1820-1914), illus. (Macmillan's Dollar and a Half Series of Books for the Young). N.D. Macmillan & Co.
--Through the Looking Glass & What Alice Found There. Dodgson, Charles Lutwidge. Tenniel, John, Sir (1820-1914), illus. (Illus.). (gr. 4 up). 1927. St Martin.
--Through the Looking Glass: And What Alice Found There. Dodgson, Charles Lutwidge. Tenniel, John, Sir (1820-1914), illus. LC 77-77325. (Illus.). (gr. 4 up). 1977. (ISBN 0-312-80374-5). St Martin.
--The Walrus & the Carpenter. Dodgson, Charles Lutwidge. Cattaneo, Tony, illus. LC 74-81671. (Illus.). 32p. (Stuff & Nonsense Bks). (gr. 1-4). 1975. (ISBN 0-7232-1813-7). Warne.
--Walrus & the Carpenter & Other Poems. Dodgson, Charles Lutwidge. Rose, Gerald Hembdon Seymour (1935-), illus. (Illus.). (gr. 1 up). N.D. (ISBN 0-525-42183-1). Dutton.

Carroll, Lewis, pseud. (1832-1898) & Moser, Barry
--Through the Looking-Glass & What Alice Found There: The California Edition of the Pennyroyal Press Book. Dodgson, Charles Lutwidge. Goodacres, Selwyn H., intro. by. Incl. Deluxe Edition. 198p. (ISBN 0-520-05026-6). LC 83-47520. (Illus.). 198p. 1983. (ISBN 0-520-05039-8). U of Cal Pr.

Carroll, Lillian
--Greek Slave Boy. 1st ed. LC 68-19032. viii, 120 p. 21cm. 1968. Meredith Press.
--Secret of the Covered Bridge. (gr. 5-8). 1967. (ISBN 0-696-78732-6). Hawthorn.
--The Secret of the Covered Bridge. 1st ed. LC 67-13912. 121p. 21cm. 1967. Meredith.

Carroll, M., pseud., see Brooks, Martha.

Carroll, M., pseud.
--How Marjory Helped. Brooks, Martha. LC 2-22407. (Illus.). 1 p., l., 9-315 p. front., plates. 17 1/2 cm. 1902. Lee and Shepard.

Carroll, Patrick Joseph (1876-)
--Patch and Fan. LC 49-13402. 282 p. 21 cm. 1948. Ave Maria Press.
--Patch of Askeaton Days. LC 43-552394. 302 p. 18 1/2 cm. 1943. The Ave Maria Press.
--Patch Scatters Culture. LC 53-910745. 223p. 21cm. 1954, c.1953. Ave Maria Press.

Carroll, Paul Vincent
--Plays for My Children. LC 39-27427. 199 p. 21 cm. c.1939. J. Messner, Inc.

Carroll, Ruth Robinson, Mrs. (1899-)
--The Adventures of Chessie. Carroll, Ruth Robinson, Mrs. (1899-), illus. N.D. Julian Messner Inc.
--Bounce and the Bunnies. 2d ed. LC 59-9663. (Illus.). 48 p. 27cm. 1959. H.Z. Walck.
--Bounce and the Bunnies. Carroll, Ruth Robinson, Mrs. (1899-), illus. N.D. Harcourt Brace & Co.
--Bounce and the Bunnies. Carroll, Ruth Robinson, Mrs. (1899-), illus. LC 34-39749. 48 p. illus. (part col.) 26 cm. 1934. Reynal & Hitchcock, Inc.
--Chessie. LC 36-8267. 48 p. illus. (part col.) 26 cm. c.1936. J. Messner, Inc.
--Chessie. Carroll, Ruth Robinson, Mrs. (1899-), illus. N.D. Veritas Press.
--Chessie and Her Kittens. Carroll, Ruth Robinson, Mrs. (1899-), illus. LC 37-29160. 48 p. illus. (part col.) 26 cm. c.1937. J. Messner, Inc.
--Chessie and Her Kittens. Carroll, Ruth Robinson, Mrs. (1899-), illus. N.D. Veritas Press.
--Chimp and Chump. 1933. Reynal & Hitchcock.
--Chimp & the Clown. Carroll, Ruth Robinsone (1899-), illus. LC 68-29029. color ils. 32p. (gr. k-3). 1968. (ISBN 0-8098-1136-7). Walck.
--The Dolphin & the Mermaid. LC 74-5452. 32p. (ps-2). 1974. (ISBN 0-8098-1219-3). Walck.
--Old Mrs. Billups and the Black Cats. Carroll, Ruth Robinson, Mrs. (1899-), illus. LC 61-12884. (Illus.). 48 p. 23cm. 1961. H. Z. Walck.
--Rolling Down Hill. Carroll, Ruth Robinson, Mrs. (1899-), illus. 1973. (ISBN 0-8098-1201-0). David McKay.
--Rolling Downhill. Carroll, Ruth Robinson, Mrs. (1899-), illus. LC 72-10649. (Illus.). 32 p. 24cm. 1973. (ISBN 0-8098-1201-0). H. Z. Walck.
--What Whiskers Did. Carroll, Ruth Robinson, Mrs. (1899-), illus. 1965. (ISBN 0-8098-1108-1). David McKay company.
--What Whiskers Did. Carroll, Ruth Robinson, Mrs. (1899-), illus. LC 65-19730. (Illus.). 1 v. 24cm. 1965. H. Z. Walck.
--What Whiskers Did: A Story Without Words. Carroll, Ruth Robinson, Mrs. (1899-), illus. LC 32-18361. 39 p. of illus. 25 cm. 1932. The Macmillan Company.
--Where's the Bunny. Carroll, Ruth Robinson, Mrs. (1899-), illus. 1950. (ISBN 0-8098-1023-9). David McKay Company.
--Where's the Bunny?. Carroll, Ruth Robinson, Mrs. (1899-), illus. LC 60-15907. illus. 16 x 24 cm. 28p. c.1950. H. Z. Walck.
--Where's the Bunny?. Carroll, Ruth Robinson, Mrs. (1899-), illus. LC 50-9115. (Illus.). 16 x 24cm. 30p. (Oxford Books for Boys and Girls). 1950. Oxford University Press.
--Where's The Kitty. Carroll, Ruth Robinson, Mrs. (1899-), illus. 1962. (ISBN 0-8098-1080-8). David McKay Company.
--Where's the Kitty?. Carroll, Ruth Robinson, Mrs. (1899-), illus. LC 62-14054. (Illus.). 32 p. 1962. H. Z. Walck.
--The Witch Kitten. Carroll, Ruth Robinson, Mrs. (1899-), illus. LC 73-7391. (Illus.). 32 p. of col. illus. 1973. (ISBN 0-8098-1206-1). H. Z. Walck.

Carroll, Ruth Robinson, Mrs. (1899-) & Carroll, Archer Latrobe (1894-)
--Beanie. Carroll, Ruth Robinson, Mrs. (1899-), illus. LC 60-15906. unpaged. illus. 26 cm. 1953. H. Z. Walck.
--Beanie. Carroll, Ruth Robinson, Mrs. (1899-), illus. LC 53-9184. unpaged. illus. 23cm. 1953. Oxford University Press.
--Bumble Pup. Carroll, Ruth Robinson, Mrs. (1899-), illus. LC 68-11227. (Illus.). 31 p. 27cm. 1968. H. Z. Walck.
--The Christmas Kitten. LC 75-109123. (Illus.). 30. 24cm. 1970. (ISBN 0-8098-1164-2). H. Z Walck.
--Danny & the Poi Pup. Carroll, Ruth Robinson, Mrs. (1899-), illus. LC 65-12643. (Illus.). (gr. 4-7). 1965. (ISBN 0-8098-2032-3). Walck.
--Digby, the Only Dog. Carroll, Ruth Robinson, Mrs. (1899-), illus. LC 59-12742. (Illus.). 47 p. 26cm. 1959. H. Z. Walck.
--Digby, the Only Dog. Carroll, Ruth Robinson, Mrs. (1899-), illus. LC 55-8694. 47p. illus. 26cm. (Oxford books for boys and girls). 1955. Oxford University Press.
--Flight of the Silver Bird. Carroll, Ruth Robinson, Mrs. (1899-), illus. LC 39-29403. 94, 1 p. incl. col. front., illus. (part col.) 25 cm. c.1939. J. Messner, Inc.
--The Flying House. LC 46-8401. 127 p. illus. 21 x 23 1/2 cm. 1946. The Macmillan Company.
--Hullaballoo: The Elephant Dog. Carroll, Ruth Robinson, Mrs. (1899-), illus. LC 75-6017. (gr. k-3). 1975. (ISBN 0-8098-1230-4). Walck.
--Luck of the Roll and Go. Carroll, Ruth Robinson, Mrs. (1899-), illus. LC 35-159093. 5 p. l., 131, 1 p. front., illus. 21 cm. 1935. The Macmillan Company.
--The Managing Hen and the Floppy Hound. Carroll, Ruth Robinson, Mrs. (1899-), illus. LC 70-182532. (Illus.). 48 p. 27cm. 1972. (ISBN 0-8098-1190-1). H. Z. Walck.
--Peanut. Carroll, Ruth Robinson, Mrs. (1899-), illus. LC 64-14150. 45 p. col. illus. 22 cm. 1951. H. Z. Walck.
--Peanut. Carroll, Ruth Robinson, Mrs. (1899-), illus. LC 51-6939. 45 p. illus. 27cm. 1951. Oxford University Press.
--Pet Tale. Carroll, Ruth Robinson, Mrs. (1899-), illus. LC 59-10296. 45p. 1959, c.1949. H. Z. Walck.
--Pet Tale. Carroll, Ruth Robinson, Mrs. (1899-), illus. LC 49-100871. 47 p. illus. 22 cm. 1949. Oxford Univ. Press.
--The Picnic Bear. Carroll, Ruth Robinson, Mrs. (1899-), illus. LC 66-5652. 32p. illus. 26cm. c.1966. Walck.
--Picnic Bear. Carroll, Ruth Robinson, Mrs. (1899-), illus. LC 66-10441. (Illus.). (gr. k-3). 1966. (ISBN 0-8098-1117-0). Walck.
--Runaway Pony, Runaway Dog. Carroll, Ruth Robinson, Mrs. (1899-), illus. LC 63-17188. (Illus.). 80 p. 25cm. 1963. H. Z. Walck.
--Salt and Pepper. Carroll, Ruth Robinson, Mrs. (1899-), illus. LC 63-21517. 30 p. col. illus. 22 cm. 1952. H. Z. Walck.
--Salt and Pepper. Carroll, Ruth Robinson, Mrs. (1899-), illus. LC 52-9427. 30 p. illus. 22cm. 1952. Oxford University Press.
--School in the Sky. Carroll, Ruth Robinson, Mrs. (1899-), illus. LC 45-4769. 136 p. illus. 21 x 23 1/2 cm. 1945. The Macmillan Company.
--Scuffles. Carroll, Ruth Robinson, Mrs. (1899-), illus. (Illus.). 47 p. 22cm. 1963, c.1943. H. Z. Walck.
--Scuffles. Carroll, Ruth Robinson, Mrs. (1899-), illus. LC 43-11947. 47 p. illus. 21 1/2 x 18cm. 1943. Oxford University Press.
--Though Enough and Easy. Carroll, Ruth Robinson, Mrs. (1899-), illus. LC 53-102961. 63p. illus. 26cm. 1958. H. Z. Walok.
--Tough Enough. Carroll, Ruth Robinson, Mrs. (1899-), illus. LC 58-14234. (Illus.). 64 p. 26cm. 1954. H. Z. Walck.
--Tough Enough. Carroll, Ruth Robinson, Mrs. (1899-), illus. LC 54-120739. unpaged. illus. 27cm. (Oxford books for boys and girls). 1954. Oxford University Press.
--Tough Enough & Sassy. N.D. E. M. Hale & Co.
--Tough Enough and Sassy. Carroll, Ruth Robinson, Mrs. (1899-), illus. LC 58-10296. (Illus.). 63 p. 26cm. 1958. H. Z. Walck.
--Tough Enough's Indians. Carroll, Ruth Robinson, Mrs. (1899-), illus. LC 60-937410. 64p. illus. 27cm. 1960. H. Z. Walck.
--Tough Enough's Pony. Carroll, Ruth Robinson, Mrs. (1899-), illus. LC 58-14240. 64p. illus. 26cm. 1957. H. Z. Walck.
--Tough Enough's Pony. Carroll, Ruth Robinson, Mrs. (1899-), illus. LC 57-6483. 64p. illus. 27cm. 1957. Oxford University Press.
--Tough Enough's Trip. Carroll, Ruth Robinson, Mrs. (1899-), illus. LC 64-16390. 1 v. (unpaged) illus. 26 cm. 1956. H. Z. Walck.
--Tough Enough's Trip. Carroll, Ruth Robinson, Mrs. (1899-), illus. LC 56-10887. 64p. illus. 26cm. (Oxford books for boys and girls). 1956. Oxford University Press.

Carroll, Theodus (1928-)
--The Mystery of Body Clocks. LC 79-17622. (Unsolved Mysteries of the World Ser.). N.D. (ISBN 0-89547-078-0). Silver.

Carroll, Theodus (1928-) & Yates, Elizabeth (1905-)
--The Lost Christmas Star. Hutchinson, William Miller (1916-), illus. LC 79-12224. (Illus.). 63 p. 23cm. (Mystery book). c.1979. (ISBN 0-8116-6409-0). Garrard Pub. Co.

Carter, Nellie Page, Mrs.
--Persimmon Creek. Caddy, Alice, pseud. (1896-1977), illus. Burman, Alice Caddy. LC 38-27714. ix, 277 p. incl. front., illus., plates. 20 cm. 1938. Longmans, Green and Co.
Carter, Page
--The Ghost Hollow Mystery. 1st ed. Collins, Fred, illus. LC 51-11161. 156 p. illus. 21 cm. (gr. 4-6). 1951. (ISBN 0-397-30199-5). Lippincott.
--Mystery at Ding-Dong Gulch. Collins, Fred, illus. LC 55-118113. (Illus.). (gr. 4-6). 1956. (ISBN 0-397-30338-6). Lippincott.
--Mystery in Little Breeze Street. LC 67-7051. (Illus.). 128 p. 23cm. (Follett Merit Mystery). 1967. Follett Pub. Co.
Carter, Peter, jt. auth. see Opgenoorth, Winfred.
Carter, Peter, tr. see Grimm, Jakob Ludwig Karl (1785-1863) & Grimm, Wilhelm Karl.
Carter, Peter, tr. see Harranth, Wolf.
Carter, Peter (1929-)
--The Black Lamp. Harris, David, illus. LC 75-19100. 174 p. 22cm. c.1973. (ISBN 0-8407-6468-5). T. Nelson.
--Children of the Book. (Illus.). 270p. (gr. 6 up). 1984. (ISBN 0-19-271456-2, Pub. by Oxford U Pr Childrens). Merrimack Pub Cir.
--The Sentinels. 200p. (gr. 7 up). 1980. (ISBN 0-19-271438-4). Oxford U Pr.
Carter, Phyllis Ann
--The Bands Play On. N.D. Robert M. McBride & Co.
Carter, Robert
--Ralph Gemmel. (Fourth Ser.). (Carters' Fireside Library). N.D. Robert Carter & Bros.
Carter, Roy Cecil, ed. see Webster, Jean.
Carter, Russell Gordon, jt. auth. see Powel, Harford Willing Hare, Jr.
Carter, Russell Gordon (1892-1957)
--Bob Hanson, Eagle Scout. Swisher, Paul D., illus. LC 24-2628. 214 p. front., plates. 20 cm. 1923. The Penn Publishing Company.
--Bob Hanson, First Class Scout. Pitz, Henry Clarence (1895-1976), illus. LC 22-148182. 212 p. front., plates. 20 cm. 1922. The Penn Publishing Co.
--Bob Hanson, Scout. Smith, S. Gordon, illus. LC 21-169462. 224 p. front., plates. 20 cm. 1921. The Penn Publishing Company.
--Brothers of the Frontier. Sperry, Armstrong W. (1897-1976), illus. LC 38-575047. 6 p. l., 295 p. incl. front., illus. 20 cm. 1938. D. Applewton-Century Company, Incorporated.
--City of Adventure. Lee, Manning De Villeneuve (1894-1980), illus. LC 34-390557. 804 p. front., illus., plates. 22 cm. c.1934. The Penn Publishing Company.
--The Crimson Cutlass. Schoonover, Frank Earle (1877-1972), illus. LC 33-35701. 302 p. col. front., illus., plates. 22 cm. c.1933. The Penn Publishing Company.
--The Golden Galleon. Price, Norman Mills (1877-1951), illus. LC 36-20141. vii p., 1 l., 234 p. incl. front., illus., plates. 20 cm. 1936. D. Appleton Century Company, Incorporated.
--Good Luck, Lieutenant!. N.D. Little, Brown & Co.
--His Own Star. Fay, Herman B., Jr., illus. LC 31-29192. 5 p. l., 3-273 p. incl. illus., plates. col. front. 21 cm. 1931. Little, Brown, and Company.
--The King's Spurs. O'Donnell, Leo, illus. LC 30-235503. 6 p. l., 3-312 p., 1 l. col. front. illus., col. plates. 21 cm. 1930. Little, Brown, and Company.
--A Patriot Lad of Old Boston. Pitz, Henry Clarence (1895-1976), illus. LC 23-105540. 217 p. front., 1 illus. (map) plates. 20 cm. 1923. The Penn Publishing Company.
--A Patriot Lad of Old Cape Cod. Pitz, Henry Clarence (1895-1976), illus. LC 75-5092. (Illus.). 220 p., 2 leaves of plates. 20cm. 1975, c.1954. (ISBN 0-88492-007-0). (ISBN 0-88492-008-9). Falmouth Bicentennial Committee.
--A Patriot Lad of Old Cape Cod. Pitz, Henry Clarence (1895-1976), illus. LC 27-17121. 220 p. front., plates. 20 cm. 1927. The Penn Publishing Company.
--A Patriot Lad of Old Connecticut. Hargens, Charles, Jr. (1893-), illus. LC 35-25833. 223 p. front., plates. 20 cm. c.1935. The Penn Publishing Company.
--A Patriot Lad of Old Long Island. Hargens, Charles, Jr. (1893-), illus. LC 28-17385. 223 p. incl. front. plates. 20 cm. 1928. The Penn Publishing Company.
--A Patriot Lad of Old Maine. Hargens, Charles, Jr. (1893-), illus. LC 32-32417. 224 p. front., plates. 20 cm. c.1932. The Penn Publishing Company.
--A Patriot Lad of Old New Hampshire. Hargens, Charles, Jr. (1893-), illus. LC 33-354853. 224 p. front., plates. 20 cm. c.1933. The Penn Publishing Company.
--A Patriot Lad of Old Philadelphia. Pitz, Henry Clarence (1895-1976), illus. 3 p., 1., 9-224 p. front., plates 20 cm. 1924. The Penn Publishing Company.
--A Patriot Lad of Old Rhode Island. Hargens, Charles, Jr. (1893-), illus. LC 30-213322. 223 p. front., plates. 20 cm. c.1930. The Penn Publishing Company.
--A Patriot Lad of Old Salem. Pitz, Henry Clarence (1895-1976), illus. LC 25-15385. 3 p. l., 9-222 p. front., plates. 20 cm. 1925. The Penn Publishing Company.
--A Patriot Lad of Old Saratoga. Hargens, Charles, Jr. (1893-), illus. LC 29-185523. 213 p. incl. front. plates. 20 cm. c.1929. The Penn Publishing Company.
--A Patriot Lad of Old Trenton. Little, Nat, illus. LC 26-14674. 224 p. front., plates. 20 cm. 1926. The Penn Publishing Company.
--A Patriot Lad of Old West Point. Anderson, Frederic A., illus. LC 36-194482. 221 p. front., plates. 20 cm. c.1936. The Penn Publishing Company.
--Red Gilbert's Floating Menagerie. Wolf, W. H., illus. LC 26-147582. 219 p. front., plates. 21 cm. 1926. The Penn Publishing Company.
--Red Gilbert's Flying Circus. Couse, Percy, illus. LC 24-174577. 224 p. front., plates. 20 cm. 1924. The Penn Publishing Company.
--Shaggy, the Horse from Wyoming. N.D. Houghton Mifflin Co.
--Shaggy, the Horse from Wyoming. Bradley, E. R., illus. LC 36-170. 152 p. incl. illus., plates (part col.) 24 cm. c.1935. Suttonhouse, Ltd.
--The Singing Dog, and a Whole Gallery of Barnyard Friends. Watson, Bessie Crawford, Mrs., photos by. LC 31-25420. 127 p. illus. 21 cm. c.1931. The Penn Publishing Company.
--Teen-Age Animal Stories. Osborne, Richard N., illus. LC 49-8921. 252 p. illus. 21 cm. (Teen-age books). 1949. Lantern Press.
--Teen-Age Historical Stories. Cirlin, Edgar, illus. LC 48-7081. 251 p. illus 21 cm. (Teen-age library). N.D. Lantern Press.
--Three Points of Honor. N.D. Grosset & Dunlap.
--Three Points of Honor. Wood, Harrie (1902-), illus. LC 29-11247. xi p., 2 l., 287 p. col. front., illus., plates 21 cm. 1929. Little, Brown, and Company.
--The White Plume of Navarre. Stevens, Beatrice (1876-), illus. LC 28-17484. 192 p. incl. col. front. illus. (part col.) 22 cm. c.1928. The P. E. Volland Company.
--Yellow Jacket, the Story of a Domestic Cat. Prather, Ralph Carlyle, illus. LC 31-209213. 270 p. col. front., illus., plates. 20 cm. c.1931. The Penn Publishing Company.
Carter, Thomas
--Stories from Shakespeare. N.D. Dodd, Mead & Co.
--Stories from Shakespeare. (Told Through the Ages Ser.). N.D. Thomas Y. Crowell Co.
Carter, Thomas Lane
--Out of Africa: A Book of Short Stories. LC 11-18838. 288 p. 19 cm. 1911. The Neale Publishing Company.
Carter, Virginia I, jt. auth. see Whittle, Connie R.
Cartland, Barbara
--Princess to the Rescue. Langmore, Jane, illus. (Illus.). 1984. (ISBN 0-531-03782-7). Watts.
Cartlidge, Michelle (1950-)
--The Bears' Bazaar. LC 79-13368. (Illus.). (ps-2). 1980. (ISBN 0-688-41922-4). (ISBN 0-688-51922-9). Lothrop.
--A Mouse's Diary. LC 80-17060. (Illus.). 32 p. 21cm. c.1981. (ISBN 0-688-41987-9). Lothrop, Lee & Shepard Books.
--Munch & Mixer's Puppet Show. (Illus.). 12p. (gr. k-3). 1983. (ISBN 0-13-605345-9). P-H.
--Pippin and Pod. LC 77-17053. (Illus.). 32 p. c.1978. (ISBN 0-394-93845-3). Pantheon Books.
--Teddy Trucks. LC 81-82508. (Illus.). 32 p. 27cm. c.1981. (ISBN 0-688-00904-2). Lothrop, Lee & Shepard Books.
Carton, Jane
--A Child's Garland. 1942. (ISBN 0-571-05352-1). Faber & Faber.
Carton, Lonnie Caming (1928-)
--Daddies. Jacobs, Leslie, illus. LC 63-8115. (Illus.). 24cm. (ps). 1963. (ISBN 0-394-90724-8, BYR). Random.
--Mommies. Jacobs, Leslie, illus. LC 60-796911. unpaged. illus. 19 x 24cm. (ps). 1960. (ISBN 0-394-90736-1). Random House.
Cartwright, Ann & Cartwright, Reg
--Norah's Ark. (Illus.). 32p. (gr. k-2). 1984. (ISBN 0-671-52540-9). Messner.
--Norah's Ark. 1984. (ISBN 0-671-50763-X, Little Simon). S&S.
Cartwright, Frank Thomas (1884-)
--At Trail's End. LC 39-33261. 4 p. l., 3-184 p. front. 20 cm. c.1939. Friendship Press.
Cartwright, Reg, jt. auth. see Cartwright, Ann.
Cartwright, S. E.
--The Eagle's Nest. (Illus.). (Scribner-Blackie Series of books for young people). N.D. Charles Scribner's Sons.
--Tommy the Adventurous. (Illus.). (Scribner-Blackie Series of books for young people). N.D. Charles Scribner's Sons.
Cartwright, Virginia
--Free Spirit. 1978. (ISBN 0-533-02992-9). Vantage.
Cartwright & Rawson
--Gnomes, Goblins & Fairies. (Story Books). (gr. k-4). 1980. (ISBN 0-86020-385-9, Usborne-Hayes). (ISBN 0-88110-054-4). (ISBN 0-86020-384-0). EDC.
--Princes & Princesses. (Story Books Ser.). (gr. k-4). 1980. (ISBN 0-86020-383-2, Usborne-Hayes). (ISBN 0-88110-053-6). (ISBN 0-86020-382-4). EDC.
--Princes, Wizards & Gnomes. (Story Books). (gr. k-4). 1980. (ISBN 0-86020-508-8, Usborne-Hayes). EDC.
--Wizards. (Story Books). (gr. k-4). 1980. (ISBN 0-86020-381-6, Usborne-Hayes). (ISBN 0-88110-052-8). (ISBN 0-86020-380-8). EDC.
Carus, Helena
--Metten of Tyre. Bock, Vera, illus. LC 30-253779. 7 p. l., 171 p. incl. col. front., illus., plate. 21 cm. 1930. Doubleday, Doran & Company, Inc.
Carus, Marianne, jt. ed. see Fadiman, Clifton Paul.
Caruso, Carla
--Felicia. 1978. (ISBN 0-533-03141-9). Vantage.
Caruso, Dee, jt. auth. see Gardner, Gerald.
Carver, Joyce S.
--Jonny Lincoln & His Three Dogs. Sanz, Juan C., illus. (Illus.). 38p. 1982. (ISBN 0-682-49920-X). Exposition.
Carver, Marjorie Reineman
--Grampa Gomez' Garden. Carver, Marjorie Reineman, illus. Riffel, Maria, tr. from Span. LC 77-92711. (Illus.). 36p. (gr. 1-12). 1977. (ISBN 0-918536-04-9). Margaritas Bks For Brown Eyes.
--Lovely Lana, the Hula Champion. Plunkett, Barbara, illus. (Illus.). 20p. (gr. k-12). 1978. (ISBN 0-918536-06-5). Margaritas Bks for Brown Eyes.
--The Practically Purple Pumpkin. McKenna, Helen, ed. Carver, Marjorie Reineman, illus. LC 77-84046. (Illus.). 16, 16 p. (Flip flop book). c.1977. (ISBN 0-918536-03-0). Margarita's Books for Brown Eyes.
Carver, Robin, ed.
--Anecdotes of Natural History. With One Hundred and Twenty Engravings. LC 4-28305. xii, 13-320 p. incl. front., illus. 18 cm. 1833. Lilly, Wait, Colman and Holden.
Carver, Saxon Rowe (1905-)
--William Colgate, Yeoman of Kent. rev ed. Wiese, Kurt (1887-1974), illus. LC 57-8656. 216p. illus. 21cm. 1957. Broadman Press.
Carveth, Lysle, pseud., see Cunningham, Grace F..
Carwell, L'Ann
--Baby's First Bible Story Book. (Illus.). 1979. (ISBN 0-570-08003-7). Concordia.
Cary, Alice (1820-1871)
--Clovernook Children. (Illus.). (St. Nicholas Series for Girls). N.D. International Book Co.
--Clovernook Tales, 4 vols. (Illus.). N.D. International Book Co.
--Snow-Berries. N.D. James R. Osgood.
--Snow Berries: A Book for Young Folks. (Illus.). N.D. A. C. Armstrong & Sons.
--Snow-berries. A Book for Young Folks. LC 21-18278. 28cm. 206p. 1867. Ticknor & Fields.
--Snowberries. (Illus.). (St. Nicholas Series for Girls). N.D. International Book Co.
Cary, Alice (1820-1871) & Cary, Phoebe (1824-1871)
--Ballads for Little Folk. Ames, Mary Clemmer, Mrs. (1830-1884), ed. LC 73-109136. (Illus.). viii, 189 p. 21cm. (Granger index reprint series). 1970. Books for Libraries Press.
--Ballads for Little Folk. Ames, Mary Clemmer, Mrs. (1830-1884), ed. (Illus.). N.D. Houghton, Osgood & Co.
Cary, Elisabeth Luther (1867-1936), ed. see Aesopus.
Cary, Elisabeth Luther (1867-1936)
--Old Play Days: A Story for Little Girls Who Don't Know How to Play. LC 8-442. 27, 1 p. incl. front. 20 cm. c.1907. Valhal Studio.
Cary, Elisabeth Luther (1867-1936), intro. by.
--The Children's Aesop. Conde, J. M., illus. (Illus.). N.D. Moffat, Yard & Co.
Cary, M.
--French Fairy Tales. Smith, Elmer Boyd (1860-1943), illus. N.D. Thomas Y. Crowell Co.
Cary, M. R.
--Isabel's Difficulties: or, Light on the Daily Path. 256p. N.D. E. P. Dutton.
Cary, Mary
--The Owl Who Loved Sunshine. Giordano, Joe, illus. LC 76-52894. (Illus.). 26cm. 72p. (Kids Paperbacks). 1977. (ISBN 0-307-63433-7, Golden Pr). (ISBN 0-307-13433-4). Western Pub.
Cary, Page (1904-)
--Melinda's Hat. Cary, Page (1904-), illus. LC 41-14548. 2 p. l., 28 p. incl. col. front., col. illus. 18 x 21 cm. c.1941. Harper & Brothers.
Cary, Phoebe, jt. auth. see Cary, Alice.
Caryl, Jean, pseud., see Kaplan, Jean Caryl Korn.
Caryl, Jean, pseud. (1926-)
--Bones and the Black Panther. Kaplan, Jean Caryl Korn. Zemsky, Jessica, illus. LC 63-8856. 118 p. illus. 21 cm. 1963. Funk & Wagnalls.
--Bones and the Pointed House. Kaplan, Jean Caryl Korn. Zemsky, Jessica, illus. LC 68-11902. (Illus.). 127 p. 21cm. 1968. Funk & Wagnalls.
--Bones and the Smiling Mackerel. Kaplan, Jean Caryl Korn. Eltonhead, Frank, illus. LC 64-17426. 151 p. illus. 21 cm. 1964. Funk & Wagnalls.
Casad, Mary B.
--Bluebonnet of the Hill Country. Binder, Pat, illus. (Illus.). (gr. k-4). 1983. (ISBN 0-89015-395-7). Eakin Pubns.
Case, Clarence Marsh (1874-)
--The Banner of the White Horse,. A Tale of the Saxon Conquest. LC 16-18491. xii, 2, 235 p. col. front. 19 cm. 1916. C. Scribner's Sons.
Case, Elinor Rutt (1914-)
--Mission Three Hundred Thirteen. LC 63-7122. 208 p. 22 cm. (gr. 7-10). 1963. (ISBN 0-664-32292-1). Westminster Press.
--Yankee Traitor Rebel Spy. LC 61-5175. 204p. 21cm. 1961. (ISBN 0-664-32244-1). Westminster Press.
Case, John Francis (1876-)
--Banners of Scoutcraft. LC 29-23498. 312 p. col. front., col. plates. 20 cm. 1929. J. B. Lippincott Company.
--Peace Valley Warrior. LC 40-7708. 330 p. 20 cm. c.1940. The Interstate.
--Tom of Peace Valley, Boy Knight of Agriculture. LC 25-6622. 232 p. 20 cm. c.1925. J. B. Lippincott Company.
--Under the Four-H Flag. LC 27-3410. 320 p. front., plates. 20 cm. c.1927. J. B. Lippincott Company.
Case, Lambert J
--Approved Boy Scout Plays. 96 p diagrs. 19 cm. c.1931. Walter H. Baker Company.
Case, Laura B., jt. ed. see Case, Nellie E.
Case, Mabel Hamm (1882-1952)
--Holidays With Hector, the Rabbit. LC 52-13295. 38 p. 23cm. 1953. Vantage Press.
Case, Marshal Taylor (1941-)
--Look What I Found. Herbster, Mary L., illus. Case, Marshal T., photos by. (Illus.). index. 95p. (gr. 4-7). 1971. (ISBN 0-85699-023-X). Chatham Pr.
Case, Nellie E & Case, Laura B., eds.
--In Child-Land: A Collection of Drills, Songs, Finger-Plays, and Recitations for Little Children. LC 99-3902. 81 p. 19 cm. 1899. W. H. Baker & Co.
Case, Patricia
--Tiger! Tiger!. N.D. Macmillan.
Casebier, Dennis G.
--The Battle at Camp Cady. 40p. 1972. (ISBN 0-914224-01-8). Tales of The Mojave Road.
--Carleton's Pah-ute Campaign. 64p. 1972. (ISBN 0-914224-00-X). Tales of the MoJave Road.
Caseley, Judith
--Molly Pink. Caseley, Judith, illus. LC 84-4169. (Illus.). 7 3/8 x 8. 32p. (16 pt.). (gr. k-3). 1985. (ISBN 0-688-04004-7). (ISBN 0-688-04005-5). Greenwillow.
--Molly Pink Goes Hiking. Caseley, Judith, illus. LC 84-25335. (Illus.). 7 3/8 x 8. 32p. (16 pt.). (gr. k-3). 1985. (ISBN 0-688-05699-7). (ISBN 0-688-05700-4). Greenwillow.
Casewit, Curtis Werner (1922-)
--Adventure in Deepmore Cave. Michini, Albert, illus. LC 65-14015. 144 p. illus. 22 cm. (Signal book). 1965. Doubleday.
--Ski Racer. LC 68-27269. 222 p. 21cm. 1968. Four Winds Press.
Casey, Anne, jt. auth. see West, Joy Griffin.
Casey, Beatrice M., jt. auth. see Preston, Effa Estelle.
Casey, Beatrice Marie
--Good Plays for Tiny Players, for the Primary Grades. LC 38-14486. 133 p. 18 cm. 1937. T. S. Denison & Company.
--Good Primary Plays for Children of the First and Second Grades. LC 37-37075. 144 p. 18 cm. 1934. T. S. Denison & Company.
--The Popular Christmas Book. 162p. N.D. T. S. Denison.
Casey, Beatrice Marie, jt. auth. see Preston, Effa Estelle.
Casey, Beatrice Marie & Sawyer, Henry S.
--The Christmas Light. N.D. T. S. Denison.
Casey, Beatrice Marie & Wansborough, Harold
--The Carnival Princess. N.D. T. S. Denison.
--Christmas High Jinks. N.D. T. S. Denison.
--Lucky Star. N.D. T. S. Denison.
Casey, Robert (1856-)
--The Parson's Boys. Cessna, Dorothy, et al., illus. LC 6-45353. 24cm. 388p. 1906. The Parson's Boys Publishing Company.
Casey, Rosemary A
--The Cousinly Cousins. Kinstler, Everett Raymond (1926-), illus. LC 61-8179. 175p. illus. 21cm. 1961. Dodd, Mead.
Casey, Winifred Rosen see Rosen, Winifred.

Casey, Winifred Rosen (1943-)
--Cruisin for a Bruisin. Bacon, Paul (1913-), illus. LC 76-5488. 150p. (gr. 6 up). 1976. (ISBN 0-394-83291-4). Knopf.
--Dragons Hate to Be Discreet: A Story. Koren, Edward (1935-), illus. LC 77-13867. (Illus.). 48 p. 29cm. c.1978. (ISBN 0-394-83577-8). Knopf : Distributed by Random House.
--Henrietta & the Day of the Iguana. Chorao, Ann Mckay Sproat (1936-), illus. LC 77-19047. (Illus.). 32p. (gr. k-3). 1978. (ISBN 0-590-07471-7, Four Winds). Scholastic Inc.
--Henrietta & the Gong from Hong Kong. Chorao, Ann Mckay Sproat (1936-), illus. LC 80-19526. (Illus.). 32p. (gr. k-3). 1981. (ISBN 0-590-07657-4, Four Winds). Scholastic Inc.
--Henrietta, the Wild Woman of Borneo. Chorao, Ann Mckay Sproat (1936-), illus. LC 74-31017. (Illus.). 48 p. 1975. (ISBN 0-590-07390-7). Four Winds Press.
--Hiram Makes Friends. Higginbottom, Jeffrey Winslow (1945-), illus. LC 74-7436. (Illus.). 38 p. 1974. (ISBN 0-590-07373-7). Four Winds Press.
--Marvin's Manhole. Wells, Rosemary, illus. LC 70-102827. (Illus.). 32 p. 27cm. 1970. Dial Press.
--Ralph Proves the Pudding: "the Proof of the Pudding Is in the Eating.", 1st ed. Kalish, Lionel, illus. LC 71-187333. (Illus.). 32 p. 22cm. 1972. (ISBN 0-385-00428-1). Doubleday.
--Three Romances. Zelinsky, Paul O, illus. LC 81-5018. p. cm. c.1981. (ISBN 0-394-84509-9). Knopf : Distributed by Random House.

Cash, Grace Savannah (1915-)
--Lands Away: Rhymes from the Child's Everyday World. LC 57-10369. 61p. 23cm. c.1958. Chapman & Grimes.

Cash, Ida Horton
--The Little Professor. (Illus.). (Editha Ser.). N.D. Caldwell.
--The Little Professor. (Illus.). (Editha Series.). N.D. Dodge Publishing & Co.
--The Little Professor. (Illus.). (Goldenrod Library Ser.). 1905. L. C. Page & Co.

Cash, William E.
--To Market, to Market. McDermott, Mary Ellen, illus. LC 47-24085. (Illus.). 48 p. 1946. The Saalfield Pub. Company.

Cashel, Sue, jt. auth. see Boreta, Anne.
Cashman, Seamus, jt. auth. see Quinn, Bridie.
Cason, Emille Mabel Earp, Mrs. (1892-1965)
--Mary Had Ten Little Lambs. LC 41-308. 61 p. col. illus. 20 x 27 cm. c.1938. Southern Publishing Association.
--Ruggy, the Mountain Buck. Cason, Emille Mabel Earp, Mrs. (1892-1965), illus. LC 50-45. 160 p.illus. 20 cm. 1949. Pacific Press Pub. Association.
--Song of the Trail. Munson, Harold W. (1920-), illus. LC 53-10772. 241p. illus. 20cm. 1953. Pacific Press Pub. Association.
--Spotted Boy and the Comanches. Converse, James, illus. LC 63-21055. vii, 153 p. illus. 23 cm. c.1963. Pacific Press Pub. Association.

Caspar, Franz (1916-)
--Oscar, the Dachshund. Schaad, Hans P., illus. Bockett-Pugh, J., tr. LC 62-10113. 155p. illus. 24cm. 1962. Constable.

Cass-Beggs, Barbara
--Your Baby Needs Music. LC 80-50819. (Illus.). 144 p. 22cm. c.1978. (ISBN 0-312-89767-7). (ISBN 0-312-89768-5). St. Martin's Press.

Cass, De Lysle F.
--The Airship Boys in the Great War: Or, The Rescue of Bob Russell. Kennedy, Harry Otis, illus. LC 16-509. (Illus.). 249 p. 20cm. (The Air-Ship Boys Ser.). 1915. The Reilly & Britton Co.

Cass, Joan Evelyn
--Blossom Finds a Home. Stobbs, William (1914-), illus. LC 64-10283. (Illus.). (gr. k-3). 1963. Abelard.
--The Canal Trip. Stobbs, William (1914-), illus. LC 66-11891. (Illus.). 1 v. (unpaged. 27cm. 1966. Abelard-Schuman.
--The Cat Show. Stobbs, William (1914-), illus. LC 62-8382. unpged. illus. 26cm. 1962. Abelard-Schuman.
--The Cat Thief. Stobbs, William (1914-), illus. LC 61-3403. 48p. 1962. Abelard-Schuman.
--Cats' Adventure with Car Thieves. Stobbs, William (1914-), illus. LC 72-134315. (Illus.). color ils. 48p. (gr. k-3). 1971. (ISBN 0-200-71729-4). Har-Row.
--The Cats Go to Market. Stobbs, William (1914-), illus. (Illus.). 48p. 1970. Abelard-Shuman Press.
--Cats Go to Market. Stobbs, William (1914-), illus. LC 69-10301. (Illus.). 48p. 1st U.S. edition. (gr. k-3). 1970. (ISBN 0-200-71860-6). Har-Row.

Cassady, Constance
--Kitchen Magic. Reid, James (1907-), illus. N.D. Farrar & Rinehart.

Cassan, Christiane, illus.
--Why. (A Little Angel Bk.). N.D. Golden Press.

Cassedy, Sylvia, tr. see Cassedy, Sylvia (1930-) & Okamura, Koson.
Cassedy, Sylvia (1930-)
--Behind the Attic Wall. 1983. Harper.
--Behind the Attic Wall. LC 82-45922. 315 p. 21cm. c.1983. (ISBN 0-690-04336-8). (ISBN 0-690-04337-6). T.Y. Crowell. **Award: (ALA).**
--Little Chameleon. Bennett, Rainey (1907-), illus. LC 66-13897. iv. (unpaged) col. illus. 15 cm. 1966. World Pub. Co.
--Marzipan Day on Bridget Lane. 1st ed. Tomes, Margot Ladd (1917-), illus. LC 67-3136. (Illus.). 64 p. 25cm. 1967. Doubleday.
--Pierino and the Bell. Ness, Evaline Michelow, Mrs. (1911-), illus. LC 66-14865. 47p. col. illus. 27cm. c.1966. Doubleday.

Cassedy, Sylvia (1930-) & Okamura, Koson (1899-), eds.
--Birds, Frogs, and Moonlight. Yu-Dinh, Mai (1933-), illus. Cassedy, Sylvia (1930-) & Suetake, Kunihiro, trs. LC 67-15373. (Illus.). 47 p. 1967. Doubleday.

Casselberry, Austin F
--Flying to Victory: A Super Mystery Model for America's Air Forces. LC 43-16521. vi, 246 p. front. 21 1/2 cm. 1943. Cupples & Leon Company.

Cassell
--Cassell's Poetry for Children, 6 bks. notes. N.D. Set. Cassell & Co.

Cassell, Robert H., jt. auth. see Mack, Jacque.
Cassells, Scout Joe
--The Black Watch. N.D. Doubleday Page & Co.

Casserley, Anne Thomasine
--About Barney. (Illus.). N.D. Transatlantic Arts, Inc.
--Barney the Donkey. Kennedy, Richard (1910-), illus. LC 61-8562. 151p. illus. 21cm. (Wonderful world book). 1961. A. S. Barnes.
--Barney the Donkey. Kennedy, Richard (1910-), illus. LC 38-7459. 6 p. l., 145 p. front., illus., plates. 20 cm. 1938. Harper & Brothers.
--Brian of the Mountain. LC 31-29824. vii p., 1 l., 167 p. illus. 20 cm. 1931. Harper & Brothers.
--Michael and His Friends. Kennedy, Richard (1910-), illus. LC 61-856916. 136p. illus. 21cm. (Wonderful world book). 1961. A. S. Barnes.
--Michael of Ireland. N.D. Harper & Bros.
--Roseen. Casserley, Anne Thomasine, illus. LC 29-21677. 4 p. l., 152 p. illus. 20 cm. 1929. Harper & Brothers.
--The Whins on Knockattan. LC 28-301092. 6 p. l., 178 p., 1 l. illus. 20 cm. 1928. Harper & Brothers.

Casserly, Gordon
--Dwellers in the Jungle. Reynolds, Warwick (1880-), illus. LC 27-27681. xi p., 1 l., 239 p. front., plates. 21 cm. 1927. Frederick A. Stokes Company.

Cassiday, Bruce Bingham (1920-)
--Blast-off!. Orbaan, Albert F. (1913-), illus. LC 64-13821. (Illus.). 142 p. 22cm. (Signal book). 1964. Doubleday.
--Guerrilla Scout. LC 65-131163. 131p. 22cm. c.1965. Macmillan.
--Iggy. (Orig.). (gr. 4-6). 1973. (ISBN 0-515-00710-2). Pyramid Pubns.
--The Wild one. (Hi-Lo Reading Ser). (gr. 7-12,RL 3-4). 1970. Pyramid Pubns.

Cassie, Dyan & Orosz-O'Gara, M
--The Three Bears and Other Plays: Six Easy Plays Especially Written for Educationally Handicapped Children. LC 76-48596. (Illus.). x, 48 p. 23cm. Repr. of 1886 ed. c.1977. (ISBN 0-8134-1886-0). Order from the Interstate Printers & Publishers.

Cassil, R. V.
--Pretty Leslie. 1963. Simon and Schuster.

Castagnetta, Grace, jt. ed. see Van Loon, Hendrik Willem.
Castagnola, Lawrence
--Parables for Little People. Muren, Nancy LaBerge, illus. Quinn, Francis A. (Illus.). 101p. (Orig.). (gr. 4 up). 1982. (ISBN 0-89390-034-6). Resource Pubns.

Castagnoli, Martha
--Sleepy-Time for Everyone. Castagnoli, Martha, illus. LC 54-185575. unpaged. illus. 21cm. (Wonder books, 612). 1954. Wonder Books.

Castaneda, Carlos (1931-)
--Tales of Power. 320p. 1974. (ISBN 0-671-21858-1). S&S.

Castelhun, Dorothea
--Dene Avery's Legacy. Goss, John, illus. LC 30-8784. 4 p. l., 365 p. front., plates. 20 cm. c.1930. L. C. Page and Company.
--The House in the Golden Orchard: A New Tale of Penelope and Her Friends. McNulty, William C., illus. LC 25-4049. 5 p. l., 334 p. front., plates. 20 cm. 1925. L. C. Page & Company (Incorporated.
--Penelope and the Golden Orchard. McNulty, William C., illus. LC 24-3170. 5 p. l., 313 p. front., plates. 20 cm. 1924. L. C. Page & Company (Incorporated.
--Penelope in California. Withington, Elizabeth R., illus. LC 26-9268. 4 p. l., 346 p. front., plates. 20 cm. c.1926. L. C. Page & Company (Incorporated.
--Penelope's Problems. Merrill, Frank Thayer (1848-), illus. LC 22-19299. 5 p. l., 311 p. front., plates. 20 cm. 1922. The Page Company.

Castella, Helen I
--The Sandman: His Fairy Stories; or, Joyce in the Land of Nod. Castella, Helen I. & Grant, Jane, illus. 4 p. l., 224 p., 1 l. front., illus. 20 cm. (On verso of half-title: Sandman Stories). 1922. The Page Company.

Castellain, Lois
--Adolphus the TV Horse. LC 67-3337. (Illus.). 48p. 25cm. 1967, c.1964. Delacorte Press.

Castellanos, Jane Mollie Robinson (1913-)
--A Shell for Sam. Borcio, Vesna, illus. LC 63-12547. 1 v. (unpaged) illus. (part col.) 24 cm. 1963. Golden Gate Junior Books.
--Something New for Taco. Garbutt, Bernard (1900-), illus. LC 65-10357. 1 v. (unpaged) illus. 23cm. (gr. k-3). c.1965. (ISBN 0-87464-082-2). Golden Gate.
--Tomasito and the Golden Llamas. Corey, Robert, illus. LC 68-12896. (Illus.). 157 p. 25cm. 1968. Golden Gate Junior Books.

Caster, Andrew
--Pearl Island. Shinn, Florence Scovel, illus. LC 3-10086. iii, 1 p., 1 l., 266, 1 p. front., plates, maps. 19 cm. 1903. Harper & Brothers.

Castex, Pierre Georges (1915-)
--Nightmare Rally. 1964. E M Hale.
--The Nightmare Rally. Shelley, Hugh, tr. from Fr. LC 65-11385. 202 p. 23cm. 1965, c.1964. Abelard-Schuman.
--The Uranium Pirates. Heron, Michael, tr. LC 69-10063. 159 p. 23cm. 1968. (ISBN 0-200-71523-2). Abelard-Schuman.

Castiglia, Julie
--Jill the Pill. Kellogg, Steven (1941-), illus. LC 79-12305. (Illus.). 30 p. 23cm. 1979. (ISBN 0-689-50105-6). Atheneum.

Castle, Caroline
--The Hare and the Tortoise. Weevers, Peter, illus. LC 84-9569. (Illus.). 26 p. 29cm. 1985. (ISBN 0-8037-0138-1). Dial Books for Young Readers.

Castle, Frances, pseud., see Leader, Evelyn Barbara Blackburn.
Castle, Frances, pseud. (1898-)
--The Sisters' Tale. Leader, Evelyn Barbara Blackburn. LC 73-81887. (Illus.). 249 p. 22cm. 1969, c.1968. Little, Brown.

Castle, Jane
--Peep-Lo. Castle, Jane, illus. 1959. E M Hale.
--Peep-Lo. Castle, Jane, illus. LC 59-16480. (Illus.). unpaged. 23cm. (A Beginning to read book). c.1959. Holiday House.
--Whose Tree House?. Castle, Jane, illus. LC 63-3150. (Illus.). 46 p. 24cm. 1963. Holiday House.

Castlemon, Harry, pseud., see Fosdick, Charles Austin.
Castleton, Paul A
--Son of Robin Hood: A Sequel to the Thrilling Adventures of Robin Hood. Schaare, C. Richard, illus. LC 41-12320. x, 210 p. incl. front., illus. 21 cm. c.1941. Cupples & Leon Company.
--Son of Robin Hood in Nottingham. Wilkinson, H. B., illus. LC 42-21057. x, 205 p. incl. front., illus. 20 cm. 1942. Cupples & Leon Company.

Castor, Gaylord B.
--O'Toole's Obedient Orb and Other Fanciful Tales. 1975. (ISBN 0-682-48249-8). Exposition Press.

Castro, Bridget L.
--Ollie & Petey & the Haunted House. LC 80-51846. (Illus.). 35p. 1981. (ISBN 0-533-04705-6). Vantage.

Caswell, Annie Gray
--Susann of Sandy Point. Peck, Anne Merriman (1884-), illus. LC 30-20077. viii p., 1 l., 229 p. front., 1 illus. 21 cm. 1930. Longmans, Green and Co.

Caswell, Helen Rayburn (1923-)
--A New Song for Christmas. Caswell, Helen Rayburn (1923-), illus. LC 66-27518. vi, 95p. illus. 21cm. 1966. Van Nostrand.
--Shadows from the Singing House: Eskimo Folk Tales. Mayokok, Robert, illus. LC 68-13867. (Illus.). (gr. 2-6). 1968. (ISBN 0-8048-0523-7). C E Tuttle.
--A Wind on the Road. Caswell, Helen Rayburn (1923-), illus. LC 64-17950. viii, 107 p. illus. 21 cm. (Van Nostrand books for young readers). 1964. Van Nostrand.
--You Are More Wonderful. Caswell, Helen Rayburn (1923-), illus. LC 70-91821. (Illus.). 25 p. 19cm. N.D. (ISBN 0-8378-2002-2). C. R. Gibson Co.

Cat, Christopher see Cullen, Countee.
Cat, Christopher (1903-1946) & Cullen, Countee (1903-1946)
--The Lost Zoo. Low, Joseph (1911-), illus. LC 69-15765. (Illus.). 95 p. 24cm. 1969, c.1940. Follett Pub. Co. **Award: (ALA).**

Catchpole, Clive
--Deserts. McIntyre, Brian, illus. LC 83-7757. (Illus.). 32p. (gr. 1-4). 1984. (ISBN 0-8037-0035-0). Dial Bks Young.

Cate, Richard Edward Nelson (1932-)
--Flying Free. Stubley, Trevor Hugh (1932-), illus. LC 76-57722. (Illus.). 94 p. 21cm. 1977, c.1975. (ISBN 0-8407-6530-4). T. Nelson.
--Never Is a Long, Long Time. Stubley, Trevor Hugh (1932-), illus. LC 77-10818. p. cm. c.1976. (ISBN 0-8407-6563-0). Nelson.
--A Nice Day Out?. Stubley, Trevor Hugh (1932-), illus. LC 80-22671. p. cm. 1980, c.1981. Elsevier/Nelson Books.
--Old Dog, New Tricks. Stubley, Trevor Hugh (1932-), illus. LC 80-39858. p. cm. 1981, c.1978. (ISBN 0-525-66730-X). Elsevier/Nelson Books.

Cate, Rikki
--A Cat's Tale. Hughes, Shirley (1929-), illus. LC 81-6997. (Illus.). 34 p. 22cm. c.1982. (ISBN 0-15-215538-4). Harcourt Brace Jovanovich.

Caterina, Sr., ed.
--Little Lord, some thoughts of a Little Red-haired Child. Caterina, Sr., illus. LC 30-33336. 17p. col. illus. 29cm. c.1930. Benziger Brothers.

Cathcart, George Rhett, jt. ed. see Swinton, William.
Cather, Katherine Dunlap, Mrs.
--The Castle of the Hawk. Ashbrook, Paul, illus. LC 27-35167. vii, 228 p. front., plates. 20 cm. c.1927. The Century Co.

Cather, Willa Sibert (1873-1947)
--My Antonia. (Keith Jennison Large Type Bks). (gr. 7 up). N.D. (ISBN 0-531-00242-X). Watts.
--O Pioneers. (Keith Jennison Large Type Bks). (gr. 6 up). N.D. (ISBN 0-531-00256-X). Watts.
--Shadows on the Rock. 1958. Knopf.

Catherall, Arthur see Channel, A. R., pseud.
Catherall, Arthur see Corby, Dan, pseud.
Catherall, Arthur see Hallard, Peter, pseud.
Catherall, Arthur see Hallard, Peter J., pseud.
Catherall, Arthur see Ruthin, Margaret, pseud.
Catherall, Arthur (1906-)
--Antlers of the King Moose. Mortelmans, Edward, illus. LC 70-81716. (Illus.). 126 p. 22cm. 1970. Dutton.
--The Arctic Sealer. LC 61-12801. 160 p. 22cm. 1961, c.1960. Criterion Books.
--Barrier Reef Bandits. Marshall, Hugh, illus. LC 60-141367. 183p. illus. 22cm. (Criterion book for young people). 1960. Criterion Books.
--The Big Tusker. Phillips, Douglas, illus. LC 77-120165. (Illus.). 158 p. 22cm. 1970. Lothrop, Lee and Shepard.
--Boy on a White Giraffe. Hallard, Peter J., pseud. Bewley, Sheila, illus. LC 72-79940. 128 p. 22cm. 1969. Seabury Press.
--Camel Caravan. Papin, Joseph (1914-), illus. LC 68-94733. (Illus.). 143 p. 22cm. 1968. Seabury Press.
--China Sea Jigsaw. Whittam, Geoffrey William (1916-), illus. LC 61-17243. (Illus.). (gr. 6-10). 1962. Roy.
--Coral Reef Castaway. Geer, Terrence, illus. (Illus.). 1960. Criterion Books.
--Dangerous Cargo. Whittam, Geoffrey William (1916-), illus. LC 60-9022. 166p. illus. 20cm. 1961, c.1960. Roy Publishers.
--Death of an Oil Rig. Whittam, Geoffrey William (1916-), illus. LC 70-77310. (Illus.). 189 p. 22cm. 1969. S. G. Phillips.
--Duel in the High Hills. Smith, Stanley, illus. LC 78-81927. 160 p. 22cm. 1969. Lothrop, Lee & Shepard.
--Elli of the Northland. Ruthin, Margaret, pseud. LC 68-13673. 186 p. 21cm. 1968, c.1961. Farrar, Straus & Giroux.
--Freedom for a Cheetah. Varma, Shyam, illus. LC 77-152845. (Illus.). 127 p. 22cm. 1971. Lothrop, Lee & Shepard Co.
--Jamboree Challenge. Brookes, Kenneth (1897-), illus. LC 57-10699. 170p. illus. 20cm. N.D. Roy Publishers.
--Jungle Trap. Hogarth, Paul (1917-), illus. LC 67-10285. (Illus.). 160 p. 20cm. 1967, c.1958. Roy Publishers.
--Kalu and the Wild Boar. Hallard, Peter, pseud. LC 72-8916. (Illus.). 120 p. 21cm. 1973. (ISBN 0-531-02600-0). F. Watts.
--Kalu & the Wild Boar. Mars, Witold Tadeusz J. (1912-), illus. LC 72-8916. (Illus.). 96p. (gr. 2-6). 1973. (ISBN 0-531-02600-0). Watts.
--Kidnapped by Accident. Ambrus, Victor G., pseud. (1935-), illus. Ambrus, Gyozo Laszlo. LC 69-14319. (Illus.). 127 p. 22cm. 1969. Lothrop, Lee & Shepard Co.
--Lapland Outlaw. Jeruchim, Simon, illus. LC 66-13211. (Illus.). 160 p. 22cm. 1966. Lothrop, Lee & Shepard.
--Last Horse on the Sands. Farris, David, illus. LC 72-7343. (Illus.). 128 p. 22cm. 1973, c.1972. (ISBN 0-688-40049-3). (ISBN 0-688-40049-3). Lothrop, Lee & Shepard.
--Lone Seal Pup. 1st ed. Kaufmann, John (1931-), illus. LC 65-21274. (Illus.). 115 p. 21cm. 1965. Dutton.
--Night of the Black Frost. Payne, Roger, illus. LC 68-27706. 160 p. 22cm. 1968. Lothrop, Lee & Shepard.

--Orphan Otter. Sandford, Lloyd, illus. LC 63-7891. 127 p. illus. 21 cm. 1963. Harcourt, Brace & World.

--Prisoners in the Snow. Ambrus, Victor G., pseud. (1935-), illus. Ambrus, Gyozo Laszlo. LC 67-22593. (Illus.). 128 p. 22cm. 1967. Lothrop, Lee & Shepard.

--Puppy Lost in Lapland. Tripp, Wallace Whitney (1940-), illus. LC 74-151890. (Illus.). 128p. (gr. 3-7). 1971. (ISBN 0-531-01998-5). Watts.

--Red Sea Rescue. Ambrus, Victor G., pseud. (1935-), illus. Ambrus, Gyozo Laszlo. LC 78-101470. (Illus.). 127 p. 22cm. 1970, c.1969. Lothrop, Lee & Shepard Co.

--Sea Wolves. Whittam, Geoffrey William (1916-), illus. LC 60-6540. 20cm. 100p. 1959. Roy.

--Sicilian Mystery. LC 67-18033. 160 p. 22 cm. 1967. Lothrop, Lee & Shepard Co.

--The Strange Intruder. LC 65-13393. (Illus.). 160 p. 22cm. 1965. Lothrop, Lee & Shepard.

--Tanker Trap. Whittam, Geoffrey William (1916-), illus. LC 65-25928. 166p. illus. 20cm. 1966, c.1965. Roy.

--Ten Fathoms Deep. N.D. Transatlantic Arts.

--Ten Fathoms Deep. Whittam, Geoffrey William (1916-), illus. LC 67-17484. (Illus.). 189 p. 22cm. 1967, c.1968. Criterion Books.

--Tenderfoot Trapper. Osmond, Edmund, illus. LC 59-12201. (Illus.). 160 p. 22cm. 1st U.S. edition. (Criterion book for young people). 1959. Criterion Books.

--Wings for a Gull. 1951. Warne.

--Yugoslav Mystery. rev. text of American ed. LC 64-14441. (Illus.). 158 p. 22cm. 1964. Lothrop, Lee & Shepard.

--A Zebra Came to Drink. Schoenherr, John Carl (1935-), illus. LC 67-20123. (Illus.). 128 p. 21cm. 1967. Dutton.

Catherwood, Mary Hartwell, Mrs. (1847-1902)

--Bony and Ban: The Story of a Printing Venture. LC 12-312033. 103 p. front. pl. 20 cm. c.1898. Lothrop Publishing Company.

--The Dogberry Bunch. LC 61-55551. 19cm. 310p. (Seal Ser.). 1879. Lothrop, Lee & Shepard.

--Old Caravan Days. (Illus.). 19cm. 306p. 1884. D. Lothrop & Co.

--Rocky Fork, 1 of 4 vols. Merrill, Frank Thayer (1848-), illus. LC 12-19583. 19cm. 332p. (Rocky Fork Library). 1882. D Lothrop.

--Rocky Fork. new ed. Merrill, Frank Thayer (1848-), illus. LC 11-6024. vi p., 1 l., 9-322 p. incl. front. plates. 20 cm. c.1911. Lothrop, Lee & Shepard Co.

--Secrets of Roseladies. Rogers, W. A., illus. 187p. 1888. Lothrop.

Catherwood, Mary Hartwell, Mrs. (1847-1902) & Lewis, Alfred Henry (1842-1914)

--Familiar Stories for Children. LC 15-1700. 4 p. l., 3-189 p. incl. front., illus., plates. 23 cm. c.1914. Hurst & Company.

Cathey, Wallace & Aragon, Claude

--The Shoe Game: A Navajo Legend. Lee, Charles (1926-), illus. LC 74-29612. (Illus.). 47 p. 1971. Dept. of Research and Publications, Independent District No.

Cathon, Laura Elizabeth (1908-)

--Tot Botut & His Little Flute. Lobel, Arnold Stark (1933-), illus. LC 70-102962. (Illus.). color ils. 32p. (gr. k-1). 1970. (ISBN 0-02-717840-4). Macmillan.

Cathon, Laura Elizabeth (1908-) & Schmidt, Thusnelda, eds.

--For Patriot Dream. Kurek, Sarah C., illus. N.D. (ISBN 0-687-13292-4). Abingdon Press.

--Perhaps and Perchance; Tales of Nature. Jauss, Anne Marie (1907-), illus. LC 62-7863. omp. 1962. Abingdon Press.

--Treasured Tales: Great Stories of Courage & Faith. Young, Mary E., illus. LC 60-5322. (Illus.). (gr. 4-6). 1960. (ISBN 0-687-42554-9). Abingdon.

Cathy & Wendy

--A is for Alphabet. Suyeoka, George, illus. LC 68-16351. 54p. illus. 26cm. c.1967 (Lothrop, Lee & Shephard). Scott Foresman.

Catlin, Louise Ensign, Mrs. (1861-)

--Marjory and Her Neighbors ... Barry, Etheldred Breeze (1870-), illus. LC 20-16474. viii, 388 p. front., illus., plates. 21 cm. c.1898. Lothrop Publishing Company.

--My Little Lady-in-Waiting. Pollak, Felix (1909-), illus. LC 5-23025. 283p. 1905. Lothrop, Lee & Shepard.

Catlin, Wynelle (1930-)

--Old Wattles. 1st ed. Kuriloff, Ron, illus. LC 74-26660. (Illus.). 92 p. 25cm. 1975. (ISBN 0-385-05114-X). (ISBN 0-385-05121-2). Doubleday.

Catling, Patrick Skene

--The Chocolate Touch. newly illustrated. Apple, Margot, illus. LC 78-31100. (Illus.). 126 p. 21cm. 1979, c.1952. (ISBN 0-688-22187-4). (ISBN 0-688-32187-9). Morrow.

--The Chocolate Touch. McNutt, Mildred Coughlin, illus. LC 52-5929. 95 p. illus. 21 cm. 1952. Morrow.

Caton, Dorothy Webber

--Come Meet My Friends Who Work at Church. Padgett, Jim, illus. LC 64-14790. 32 p. col. illus. 21cm. 1964. Abingdon Press.

Caton, Marion

--First Christmas Tree on the Moon. (Illus.). (gr. 1-5). 1972. (ISBN 0-682-47427-4). Exposition.

Catrevas, Christina

--That Freshman. LC 10-210252. vii p., 1 l., 322 p., 1 l., col. front., col. plates. 20 cm. 1910. D. Appleton and Company.

Catrevas, Christina, ed.

--Fairy Tales for Little People: Put-Together Book. Becker, Charlotte (1906-) & Deane, Elsie, illus. LC 37-9856. 3 p. l., 243, 1 p. col. front., col. plates. 26 cm. c.1937. S. Gabriel Sons & Company.

--Fairy Tales for Little People: Told for Them. Becker, Charlotte (1906-), illus. LC 27-224464. 3 p. l., 246 p. col. front., illus. 25 cm. (Sears illustrated juveniles). c.1927. J. H. Sears & Company, Inc.

Catrevas, Christina & Wick, Jean

--Pegs, Freshman. N.D. G.P. Putnam's Sons.

--Pegs Freshman. LC 20-21289. 3 p. l., 281 p. col. front., col. plates 20 cm. 1920. The James A. McCann Company.

--Pegs, Sophomore. N.D. G.P. Putnam's Sons.

--Pegs Sophomore. LC 22-203492. vii, 279 p. incl. front. plates. 20 cm. c.1922. The James A. McCann Company.

Catter, Angela

--Moonshadow. (Illus.). 32p. 1st U.S. edition. (ps-1). 1983. (ISBN 0-575-03026-7, Pub. by Gollancz England). David & Charles.

Catton, Bruce (1899-1978), ed. see Miers, Earl Schenck.

Catton, Bruce (1899-1978)

--Banners at Shenandoah. LC 64-401621. 220p. illus., maps, port. 22cm. N.D. Globe.

--Banners at Shenandoah: A Story of Sheridan's Fighting Cavalry. 1st ed. LC 55-5579. 254p. 22cm. (Cavalcade books). 1955. Doubleday.

--Banners at Shenandoah: A Story of Sheridan's Fighting Cavalry. LC 76-40255. p. cm. 1976, c.1955. (ISBN 0-89244-019-8). Queens House.

Catton, Charles Bruce see Miers, Earl Schenck.

Cauch, Lydia A

--The Greatest Fun: A Book of Children's Verse. Gilberg, Robert, illus. LC 43-18002. 119 p. illus 23 1/2 cm. (Contemporary poets of Dorrance. 257). 1943. Dorrance & Company.

Caudill, Rebecca (1899-)

--Barrie & Daughter. Williams, Berkeley, Jr., illus. (Illus.). (gr. 7-11). 1943. (ISBN 0-670-14823-7). (ISBN 0-670-14824-5). Viking Pr.

--The Best-Loved Doll. Gilbert, Elliott (1924-), illus. LC 62-14215. (Illus.). 64 p. 24cm. 1962. Holt, Rinehart and Winston.

--A Certain Small Shepherd. 1st ed. DuBois, William Sherman Pene (1916-), illus. LC 65-17604. (Illus.). 48 p. 22cm. 1965. Holt, Rinehart and Winston. **Award: (ALA).**

--Come Along!. Raskin, Ellen (1928-1984), illus. LC 69-11346. (Illus.). 30 p. 1969. Holt, Rinehart and Winston.

--Did You Carry the Flag Today, Charley?. Grossman, Nancy S. (1940-), illus. LC 66-11422. (Illus.). 94 p. 23cm. 1966. Holt, Rinehart and Winston. **Award: (ALA).**

--The Far-off Land. Turkle, Brinton Cassaday (1915-), illus. LC 64-12642. (Illus.). 287 p. 21cm. 1964. Viking Press.

--Happy Little Family. Merwin, Decie (1894-1961), illus. LC 47-12310. 116 p. illus. 21 cm. 1947. J. C. Winston Co.

--Higgins and the Great Big Scare. Krush, Beth (1918-), illus. LC 60-8415. (Illus.). 87 p. 22cm. 1960. Holt, Rinehart and Winston.

--The House of the Fifers. 1954. McKay.

--The House of the Fifers. Genia, pseud. (1930-), illus. Wennerstrom, Genia Katherine. LC 54-7564. 184 p. 21cm. 1954. Longmans, Green.

--A Pocketful of Cricket. 1971. Holt Rinehart and Winston.

--A Pocketful of Cricket. 1st ed. Ness, Evaline Michelow, Mrs. (1911-), illus. LC 64-12617. (Illus.). 48 p. 28cm. 1964. Holt, Rinehart and Winston. **Awards: (ALA); (RCM).**

--Saturday Cousins. 1st ed. Woltemate, Nancy, illus. LC 53-5120. (Illus.). 120 p. 22cm. 1953. Winston.

--Schoolhouse in the Woods. Merwin, Decie (1894-1961), illus. LC 49-113881. 120 p. illus. 21 cm. 1949. Winston Co.

--Schoolroom in the Parlor. Merwin, Decie (1894-1961), illus. LC 59-5085. (Illus.). 119 p. 21cm. 1959. Winston.

--Somebody Go and Bang a Drum. Hearne, Jack, illus. LC 73-13809. (Illus.). 132 p. 24cm. 1974. (ISBN 0-525-39575-X). Dutton.

--Susan Cornish. Johnson, Eugene Harper, illus. LC 55-1558. (Illus.). 286 p. 23cm. 1955. Viking Press.

--Time for Lissa. (gr. 2-5). 1969. (ISBN 0-8407-6091-4). Nelson.

--Time for Lissa. Ilsley, Velma Elizabeth (1918-), illus. (Illus.). (gr. 4-7). 1959. (ISBN 0-8382-0870-3). Hale.

--Time for Lissa. Ilsley, Velma Elizabeth (1918-), illus. LC 59-10495. 139p. illus. 23cm. 1959. T. Nelson.

--Tree of Freedom. Morse, Dorothy Bayley (1906-1979), illus. LC 49-84297. 279 p. illus. 21 cm. 1949. Viking Press. **Award: (JNM).**

--Up and Down the River. Merwin, Decie (1894-1961), illus. LC 51-10371. (Illus.). 115 p. 21cm. 1951. Winston.

--Wind, Sand, and Sky. Carrick, Donald (1929-), illus. LC 75-34113. (Illus.). 32 p. c.1976. (ISBN 0-525-42899-2). Dutton.

Caudill, Rebecca (1899-) & Ayars, James Sterling (1898-)

--Contrary Jenkins. Rounds, Glen Harold (1906-), illus. LC 69-11345. (Illus.). 40 p. 1969. Holt, Rinehart and Winston.

Caudle, Peggy

--Manon & the Prince. 1979. (ISBN 0-8062-1370-1). Carlton.

Caufield, Donald E & Caufield, Lora Joan

--The Incredible Detectives. Komoda, Kiyoaki (1937-), illus. LC 66-8332. (Illus.). 75 p. 21cm. 1966. Harper & Row.

--London Villains Falling Down. Sommerschield, Rose, illus. LC 69-13028. (Illus.). 96 p. 25cm. 1969. Doubleday.

--Never Steal a Magic Cat. Palmer, Janice, illus. LC 72-135852. (Illus.). 89 p. 22cm. 1971. Doubleday.

Caufield, Lora Joan, jt. auth. see Caufield, Donald E.

Caughey, LaRee

--The Wilderness Is a Book: A Story of Young 49'ers on the Trail. Perceval, Don Louis, illus. LC 66-26518. (Illus.). 110 p. 26cm. 1966. W. Ritchie Press.

Cauldwell, Samuel Milbank (1862-1916)

--Chocolate Cake and Black Sand, and Two Other Plays. LC 79-50021. xi, 150 p. 20cm. (Series: One-Act Plays in Reprint Series.). 1979. (ISBN 0-8486-2045-3). Core Collection Books.

--Chocolate Cake and Black Sand: And Two Other Plays. Brewster, Anna Richards, illus. LC 17-16753. xiv p., 1 l., 150 p. front., plates. 21 cm. 1917. G. P. Putnam's Sons.

Cauley, Lorinda Bryan, jt. auth. see The, Three Bears.

Cauley, Lorinda Bryan (1951-), retold by see Andersen, Hans Christian.

Cauley, Lorinda Bryan (1951-)

--The Animal Kids. Cauley, Lorinda Bryan (1951-), illus. LC 78-23632. (Illus.). 32 p. c.1979. (ISBN 0-399-20677-9). Putnam.

--The Bake-off. Cauley, Lorinda Bryan (1951-), illus. LC 77-24877. (Illus.). 48 p. 23cm. (See and read storybook). c.1978. (ISBN 0-399-61086-3). Putnam.

--The Cock, the Mouse, and the Little Red Hen. Cauley, Lorinda Bryan (1951-), illus. LC 80-15666. p. cm. 1981. (ISBN 0-399-20740-6). Putnam.

--Jack and the Beanstalk. Cauley, Lorinda Bryan (1951-), illus. LC 83-4596. p. cm. 1983. (ISBN 0-399-20901-8). (ISBN 0-399-20902-6). G.P. Putnam.

--The New House. Cauley, Lorinda Bryan (1951-), illus. LC 81-611. (Illus.). 48p. (A Let Me Read Bk.). (gr. 1-5). 1981. (ISBN 0-15-257041-1, VoyB). HarBraceJ.

--The Three Little Kittens. Cauley, Lorinda Bryan (1951-), illus. LC 81-17747. (Illus.). 28 p. 18cm. c.1982. (ISBN 0-399-20855-0). (ISBN 0-399-20856-9). Putnam.

--The Town Mouse and the Country Mouse. Cauley, Lorinda Bryan (1951-), illus. LC 84-11532. (Illus.). 32p. (ps-3). c.1984. (ISBN 0-399-21123-3, Putnam). (ISBN 0-399-21126-8). Putnam Pub Group.

Cauley, Lorinda Bryan (1951-) & Basile, Giovanni Battista (1575-1632)

--The Goose and the Golden Coins. Cauley, Lorinda Bryan (1951-), illus. LC 80-24591. (Illus.). 48 p. 26cm. c.1981. (ISBN 0-15-232206-X). (ISBN 0-15-232207-8). Harcourt Brace Jovanovich.

Caulfield, S. F. A.

--By Land and Sea, 1 of 6 vols. (The Fan Library). N.D. Cassell, Petter, Galpin.

Caunter, L. J.

--Children's Pilgrim Progress. N.D. Moody.

Cauper, Eunice

--The Story of the Pilgrims & Their Indian Friends: A Thanksgiving Story for Children. 3rd ed. Cauper, David, illus. (Illus.). (gr. k). 1984. (ISBN 0-8283-1899-9). Branden Pub Co.

Causey, Beth G

--South Carolina Rivers. Thurston, Janet, illus. LC 74-16214. (Illus.). 71 p. 23cm. c.1969. Hope Pub. Co.

Causey, Lillian

--Little Red Riding Hood and Other Fairy Tales. Causey, Lillian, illus. LC 18-21839. 88 p. col. front., illus., col. pl. 24 cm. 1918. The Penn Publishing Company.

--Little Red Riding Hood, and Other Fairy Tales. Causey, Lillian, illus. LC 18-21839. (Illus.). 88 p. 23cm. 1918. The Penn Publishing Co.

Causley, Charles Stanley (1917-)

--As I Went Down Zig Zag. Astrop, John, illus. LC 74-81669. (Illus.). 26 p. 18cm. (Stuff and nonsense books). 1974. (ISBN 0-7232-1812-9). F. Warne.

--The Batsford Book of Stories in Verse for Children. 1979. (Pub by Batsford England). David & Charles.

--Dawn and Dusk: Poems of Our Time. Wilkinson, Gerald, illus. 1963. Watts.

--Dick Whittington: A Story from England. Maitland, Antony Jasper (1935-), illus. (Illus.). (Puffin Folktales of the World Ser.). (gr. 2-6). 1979. (ISBN 0-14-030801-6, Puffin). Penguin.

--Figgie Hobbin: Poems for Children. Hyman, Trina Schart (1939-), illus. Heins, Ethel L., intro. by. LC 72-87351. 1974. (ISBN 0-8027-6131-3). (ISBN 0-8027-6132-1). Walker & Co.

--The Tail of the Trinosaur: A Story in Rhyme. Gardiner, Jill, illus. LC 74-157246. (Illus.). 1, 121 p. 21cm. 1972. (ISBN 0-340-15948-0). Brockhampton P.

Causley, Charles Stanley (1917-), ed.

--Modern Ballads & Story Poems. Netherwood, Anne (1940-), illus. (Illus.). (gr. 7 up). 1965. (ISBN 0-531-01732-X). Watts.

--Puffin Book of Magic Verse. Swiderska, Barbara, illus. (Illus.). (gr. 1-4). 1974. (ISBN 0-14-030660-9, Puffin). Penguin.

Cavallaro, Ann Abelson (1918-)

--Blimp. LC 82-17259. p. cm. c.1983. (ISBN 0-525-67139-0). Lodestar Books.

Cavally, Frederick L., Jr., adapted by see Mother Goose.

Cavanagh, Helen Carol (1939-)

--The Easiest Way. 160p. (Orig.). 1981. (ISBN 0-590-31352-5, Schol Pap). Scholastic Inc.

--Honey. (Wishing Star Ser.). (gr. 7-12). 1980. (ISBN 0-590-32451-9). Scholastic Inc.

--Just a Summer Girl. 192p. (Orig.). (gr. 7 up). 1982. (ISBN 0-590-31962-0, Wildfire). Scholastic Inc.

--A Place for Me. 160p. (Orig.). (gr. 7 up). 1981. (ISBN 0-590-31765-2, Wildfire). Scholastic Inc.

--Second Best. (gr. 7 up). 1979. (ISBN 0-590-32313-X, Wildfire). Scholastic Inc.

Cavanagh, Mary Ann Pauly

--Hooray for Elfie: A Christmas Story. Selvaggio, Gary, illus. LC 76-151236. (Illus.). 32 p. 28cm. c.1976. Elfie Publications.

Cavanagh, Maura, jt. auth. see Smithies, Richard Hugo Ripman.

Cavanah, Frances, ed. see Barrows, Ruth Marjorie.

Cavanah, Frances, ed. see Child Life.

Cavanah, Frances, jt. ed. see Pannell, Lucile.

Cavanah, Frances (1899-1982)

--Abe Lincoln Gets His Chance. 1959. (ISBN 0-8382-0008-7, Cadmus Books). E. M. Hale and Company.

--Abe Lincoln Gets His Chance. Hutchison, Paula (1905-), illus. LC 59-5789. (Illus.). 92 p. 24cm. 1959. Rand McNally.

--Abe Lincoln Gets His Chance. Sibley, Don (1922-), illus. LC 63-25591. (Illus.). 20cm. 124p. 1963, c.1959. Scholastic.

--Adventure in Courage. (Illus.). (gr. 4-7). 1961. (ISBN 0-8382-0011-7). Hale.

--Benjy of Boston. Jackson, Pauline (1918-), illus. N.D. David McKay Co.

--Benjy of Boston. Jackson, Pauline (1918-), illus. (The City Bks.). (gr. 3-5). N.D. David McKay Co.

--The Busters: The Story of Paganini Smith and Two Canine Gentlemen. Schule, Clifford H., illus. LC 64-23920. (Illus.). 61 p. 23cm. 1964. Macrae Smith.

--Down the Santa Fe Trail. Fletcher, Sydney E., illus. LC 42-14389. (Illus.). 34 p. 22cm. (Basic Social Education Ser.). 1942. Row, Peterson & Co.

--Happy Giraffe, The. Biers, Clarence, illus. LC 44-51325. 22cm. 24p. 1944. Wilcox & Follett Co.

--Jenny Lind and Her Listening Cat. Frame, Paul (1913-), illus. N.D. (ISBN 0-8149-0289-8). The Vanguard Press.

--The Knight of the Funny Bone: And Other Plays for Children. LC 37-37073. iii, 138 p. 19 cm. 1929. Walter H. Baker Company.

--Louis of New Orleans. Weisgard, Leonard Joseph (1916-), illus. LC 41-10778. 24cm. 36p. (gr. 3-7). 1941. David McKay Co.

--Marta & the Nazis. Blickenstaff, Wayne, illus. (Illus.). Orig. Title: Marta Finds the Golden Door. (gr. 4-6). N.D. (ISBN 0-590-09928-0, Schol Pap). Schol Bk Serv.

--Marta finds the Golden Door. Holland, Janice (1913-1962) & Stein, Harve (1904-), illus. LC 41-3872. 5 p., l., 118p. col. front. ill. 21 x 17cm. c.1941. Grosset & Dunlap.

--Our Country's Freedom. 1966. E M Hale.

--A Patriot in Hoops. King, Ruth, illus. LC 32-21442. xi, 331 p. incl. front., plates. 20 cm. 1932. R. M. McBride & Company.

Cecil, Mirabel
--Blue Bear's Race. LC 81-1105. (Illus.). 18p. (gr. 1-3). 1982. (ISBN 0-316-13251-9). Little.
--Cora the Crow 011 A Spring Story. Gascoigne, Christina (1938-), illus. LC 79-22538. (Illus.). (A New Ser. of Nature Bks.). (gr. k-3). 1980. (ISBN 0-07-010320-8). McGraw.
--Ruby the Donkey: A Winter Story. Gascoigne, Christina (1938-), illus. LC 79-26422. (Illus.). 26 p. 22cm. 1980. (ISBN 0-07-010321-6). McGraw-Hill.
--Spiky the Hedgehog: An Autumn Story. Gascoigne, Christina (1938-), illus. LC 79-26358. (Illus.). 28 p. 22cm. (gr. k-3). 1980. (ISBN 0-07-010322-4). McGraw-Hill.
--Zig-Zag the Bee: A Summer Story. Gascoigne, Christina (1938-), illus. LC 79-22532. (Illus.). 25 p. 22cm. c.1980. (ISBN 0-07-010319-4). McGraw-Hill.
Cecil, Patricia
--Kata, Son of Red Fang: Wolf Dog of the North. Pitz, Henry Clarence (1895-1976), illus. LC 54-7731. (Illus.). 181 p. 22cm. 1954. Winston.
Cedarbaum, Sophia N.
--Shavuot, the Birthday of the Torah. (gr. k-1). 1961. (ISBN 0-685-20758-7). UAHC.
--Tu bi-Sh'vot, the New Year's Day for Trees. Ross, Clare Romano (1922-) & Ross, John (1921-), illus. LC 61-9695. (Illus.). 30 p. 20cm. 1961. Union of American Hebrew Congregations.
Ceder, Georgiana Dorcas see Dor, Ana, pseud.
Ceder, Georgiana Dorcas
--Ann of Bethany. Torrey, Helen (1901-), illus. LC 51-9908. 95 p. illus. 23 cm. 1951. Abingdon-Cokesbury Press.
--Ethan, The Shepherd Boy. Torrey, Helen (1901-), illus. N.D. Abelard.
--Ethan, the Shepherd Boy. Torrey, Helen (1901-), illus. LC 48-5824. 23cm. 94p. N.D. Abingdon-Cokesbury Press.
--Joel: The Potter's Son. Torrey, Helen (1901-), illus. LC 54-8446. (Illus.). 95 p. 23cm. 1954. Abingdon Press.
--Little Thunder. Jefferson, Robert Louis (1929-), illus. LC 66-10569. 104p. illus. 21cm. (gr. 3-7). c.1966. (ISBN 0-687-22171-4). Abingdon.
--Reluctant Jane. Korach, Mimi (1922-), illus. LC 66-7933. (Illus.). 126p. (gr. 3-7). 1966. (ISBN 0-308-80028-1). Funk & W.
--Winter Without Salt. Walter, Charles, illus. LC 62-7128. 125p. illus. 25cm. (gr. 3-6). 1962. Morrow.
--Ya-Ya. Dor, Ana, pseud. Carsey, Alice, illus. LC 47-30425. 62 p. illus. (part col.) 22 cm. 1947. Abingdon-Cokesbury Press.
Cederborg, Hazel P.
--Bunny Polka Dot. Krock, Helen L., illus. LC 47-27092. 57 p. illus. (part col.) 26 cm. (Saalfield treasure book). c.1947. Saalfield Pub. Co.
--Little Red Wagon. McKinley, Clare, illus. N.D. Rand McNally & Co.
Cedering Fox, Siv see Fox, Siv Cedering (1939-) & Carrick, Donald.
Celli, Rose.
--Baba Yaga: A Popular Russian Tale. Parain, Nathalie, illus. Hawley, Katharine, tr. (Illus.). 16 p. 32cm. (Pere Castor book). c.1935. Artists and Writers Guild.
Celli, Rose, tr.
--A Ghost, a Witch & a Goblin. (gr. k-3). 1970. (ISBN 0-590-04447-8). Scholastic Inc.
Cellini, Joseph, jt. auth. see Hall, Lynn.
Cenac, Claude
--Four Paws into Adventure. Turkle, Brinton Cassaday (1915-), illus. Gross, Sarah Chokla (1906-1976), tr. LC 65-10067. 159p. illus. 21cm. N.D. Watts.
Cendrars, Blaise, pseud., see Sauser-Hall, Frederic.
Cendrars, Blaise, pseud. (1887-1961)
--Little Black Stories for Little White Children. Sauser-Hall, Frederic. N.D. Brewer & Warren Inc.
--Little Black Stories for Little White Children. Sauser-Hall, Frederic. Pinsard, Pierre, illus. Bianco, Margery Williams, Mrs. (1881-1944), tr. LC 29-298410. 5 p. l., 138 p. col. front., illus., col. plates. 24 cm. 1929. Payson & Clarke, Ltd.
--Shadow. Sauser-Hall, Frederic. Brown, Marcia (1918-), illus. Brown, Marcia (1918-), tr. from Fr. (Illus.). 40p. (gr. 1 up). 1982. (ISBN 0-684-17226-7, ScribJ). Scribner. **Awards: (ALA); (RCM).**
Censoni, Robert
--Cowgirl Kate. Censoni, Robert, illus. LC 77-23312. (Illus.). 32 p. 21cm. c.1977. (ISBN 0-8234-0299-1). Holiday House.
--The Shopping-Bag Lady. Censoni, Robert, illus. LC 76-50654. (Illus.). 32 p. 25cm. c.1977. (ISBN 0-8234-0296-7). Holiday House.
Censoni, Robert, jt. auth. see Quin-Harkin, Janet.
Center, Stella Stewart (1878-), compiled by see Garland, Hannibal Hamlin.
Center, Stella Stewart, ed. see Homerus.
Cerf, Bennet Alfred, jt. auth. see Moriarty, Henry C.
Cerf, Bennett Alfred (1898-1971)
--Bennett Cerf's Book of Animal Riddles. McKie, Roy, illus. LC 64-11246. 23cm. 64p. (gr. 2-3). 1964. (ISBN 0-394-80034-6). (ISBN 0-394-90034-0). Beginner.
--Bennett Cerf's Book of Riddles. Mckie, Roy, illus. LC 60-13492. (Illus.). 24cm. 62p. (gr. 1-2). 1960. (ISBN 0-394-80015-X). (ISBN 0-394-90015-4). Beginner.
--Bennett Cerf's Pop-up Riddle Book. (Illus.). (gr. 1-6). 1965. (ISBN 0-394-81125-9). Random.
--Bennett Cerf's Silliest Pop-up Riddles. (Illus.). (gr. 1-6). 1966. (ISBN 0-394-81594-7, BYR). Random.
--Book of Laughs. Rose, Carl (1903-1971), illus. LC 59-13387. (Illus.). 61 p. 24cm. (Beginner booksB-11). 1959. Beginner Books; Distributed by Random House.
--Houseful of Laughter. Roth, Arnold (1929-) & Kelly, Walter Crawford (1913-1973), illus. LC 63-14748. vii, 182p. illus. 27cm. c.1963. Random.
--More Riddles. LC 61-11727. (Illus.). (gr. k-3). 1961. (ISBN 0-394-80024-9). (ISBN 0-394-90024-3). Beginner.
--Vest Pocket Book of Jokes for All Occasions. 1956. Random House.
Cerf, Bennett Alfred (1898-1971), ed.
--Famous Ghost Stories. N.D. The Modern Library.
--Laughing Stock. Rose, Carl (1903-1971), illus. N.D. Grosset & Dunlap.
Cerf, Christopher Bennett, jt. auth. see Lerner, Sharon Ruth.
Cerf, Christopher Bennett (1941-)
--The Truth Machine. Clarke, Jane (1938-1982), illus. LC 77-70857. p. cm. 1977. (ISBN 0-394-93575-6). Random House.
Cerf, Jonathon, jt. auth. see Cerf, Roseanne.
Cerf, Roseanne & Cerf, Jonathon
--Big Bird's Red Book. Smollin, Michael J., illus. (Illus.). (gr. k-3). 1977. (ISBN 0-307-60157-9, Golden Pr). Western Pub.
Cerny, Vaclav, et al. (1905-)
--Tales of the Uncanny. Notzh, Helen, tr. from Czech. LC 77-369784. (Illus.). 211 p. 29cm. 1976. (ISBN 0-600-38716-X). Hamlyn.
Cerutti, Vera
--Kind Little Joe. Bruna, Dick (1927-), illus. unpaged. illus. 21 cm. c.1959. Hart Pub. Co.
Cervantes, Alex, jt. auth. see Michael Cervantes, Esther De.
Cervantes, Alex, tr. see Michael Cervantes, Esther De & Cervantes, Alex.
Cervantes, Alex & Cervantes, Esther De Michael
--Saturday with Daddy. Waldman, Ellen, illus. LC 78-73527. (Illus.). (gr. k-4). N.D. Dandelion Pr.
--Senora Pepino & Her Bad Luck Cats: Senora Pepino y Sus Gatos de Mala Suerte. LC 76-4818. (Illus.). 1976. (ISBN 0-87917-052-2). Ethridge.
Cervantes, Esther De Michael, jt. auth. see Cervantes, Alex.
Cervantes Saavedra, Miguel de (1547-1616)
--Adventures of Don Quixote. (Illus.). (Great Il. Classics). (gr. 9 up). 1962. (ISBN 0-396-04725-4). Dodd.
--Adventures of Don Quixote. (gr. 7 up). 1969. (ISBN 0-448-02380-6). G&D.
--Adventures of Don Quixote. (The Youth's Cabinet of Popular Standard Bks.). N.D. Pott, Young, & Co.
--Adventures of Don Quixote. (Golden River Ser.). N.D. Thomas Nelson & Sons.
--The Adventures of Don Quixote. Daly, Dominick (1834-1910), ed. Troyer, Johannes (1902-), illus. Daly, Dominick (1834-1910), tr. LC 57-2873. viii, 256p. col. illus. 22cm. (New children's classics). 1957. Macmillan.
--The Adventures of Don Quixote. Gilbert, John Clitherae, illus. Jarvis, Charles, tr. (Globe Library). N.D. George Routledge & Sons.
--Adventures of Don Quixote. Gilbert, John Clitherae, illus. Jarvis, Charles, tr. (Globe Library). N.D. George Routledge.
--The Adventures of Don Quixote. Jones, Olive & Him, George (1900-1982), eds. Cohen, John Michael (1903-), tr. LC 79-23512. p. cm. c.1980. Methuen.
--The Adventures of Don Quixote. Rich, Edwin Gile (1879-), adapted by. Bacharach, Herman Ilfeld (1899-), illus. LC 28-22668. 5 p. l., 3-287 p. col. front., col. plates. 25 cm. 1928. Houghton Mifflin Company.
--Adventures of Don Quixote. Rich, Edwin Gile, ed. N.D. Small,Maynard & Co.
--Adventures of Don Quixote de la Mancha. (Illus.). 660p. (The Excelsior Edition). 1879. American News Co.
--The Adventures of Don Quixote De la Mancha. Barret, Leighton, adapted by. Chappell, Warren (1904-), illus. Motteux, Peter Anthony (1663-1718), tr. LC 46-339524. 4 p. l., 3-307 p., 1 l. col. front., illus., 2 col. pl. (1 double) 22 cm. c.1939. A. A. Knopf.
--The Adventures of Don Quixote De la Mancha. Barret, Leighton, adapted by. Chappell, Warren (1904-), illus. LC 60-9442. (Illus.). 307 p. 22cm. 1960. (ISBN 0-394-90892-9). Knopf.
--Adventures of Don Quixote de la Mancha. Jervas, Charles, tr. (New Alta Lib.). N.D. Henry T. Coates & Co.
--Adventures of Don Quixote de la Mancha. New Ed. ed. Jervas, Charles, tr. N.D. Porter & Coates.
--Don Quixote. (Illus.). (The Cornell Series). 1915. A L Burt & Co.
--Don Quixote. (The Empire Ser.). N.D. A. L. Burt's Pubs.
--Don Quixote. (Illus.). (The Princeton Ser.). N.D. A. L. Burt's Pubs.
--Don Quixote. N.D. American News Co.
--Don Quixote. (The Caxton Edition). N.D. Belford, Clarke.
--Don Quixote. (Popular Standard Editions). N.D. Belford, Clarke & Co.
--Don Quixote. (Caxton Edition). N.D. Belford, Clarke & Co.
--Don Quixote. (Popular Illustrated). N.D. Fairbanks & Palmer.
--Don Quixote. N.D. Ginn and Company.
--Don Quixote. (Illus.). (Caldwell's Illustrated Library of Famous Books by Famous Authors). N.D. H. M. Caldwell Co.
--Don Quixote. (Illus.). (Berkeley Lib.). N.D. H. M. Caldwell Co.
--Don Quixote, 2. (Bohn's Popular Library). N.D. Harcourt Brace & Co.
--Don Quixote. N.D. Harper & Bros.
--Don Quixote, 2 Vols. (Illus.). N.D. Henry C. Lea.
--Don Quixote, 1 of 64 vols. (Young America Library: No. 16). 1900. Set. Hurst & Co.
--Don Quixote. (Argyle Ser). N.D. Hurst & Company.
--Don Quixote. (New International Library). N.D. John C. Winston Co.
--Don Quixote. N.D. Lovell, Coryell & Co.
--Don Quixote, 1 of 4 Vols. (Illus.). (Library of Classic Fiction: No. 2). N.D. Set. Porter& Coates.
--Don Quixote, 1 of 74 Vols. (The Chandos Classics Ser.: No. 17). N.D. R. Worthington.
--Don Quixote, 1 of 163 vols. (Illus.). (The Cottage Library Ser.: No. 52). N.D. R. Worthington.
--Don Quixote, 1 of 26 Vols. (Illus.). (Warne's Popular Poets Ser.: No. 23). N.D. R. Worthington.
--Don Quixote. N.D. (ISBN 0-671-48508-3). Simon & Schuster.
--Don Quixote, 1 of 15 vols. (Illus.). (Star Ser.). N.D. T. Y. Crowell.
--Don Quixote, 2 vols. (Illus.). (Crowell's Illustrated Library). N.D. Set. T. Y. Crowell & Co.
--Don Quixote. (The Popular Library of Notable Books). N.D. T. Y. Crowell & Co.
--Don Quixote. (The New Astor Library of Prose). N.D. Thomas Y. Crowell & Co.
--Don Quixote. Barret, Leighton & Chappel, Warren, eds. 1939. Little Brown & Co.
--Don Quixote. Clark, J. W., ed. 900p. N.D. Crown Publishers.
--Don Quixote. Dore, Louis Christophe Paul Gustave (1832-1883), illus. N.D. Modern Library.
--Don Quixote. Houghton, Archibald Boyd, illus. Jarvis, Charles, tr. from Spanish. N.D. Frederick Warne & Co.
--Don Quixote, 2. Johannot, Tony, illus. N.D. Leavitt & Allen Bros.
--Don Quixote. Abridged. Johnson, Clifton, ed. N.D. Macmillan.
--Don Quixote. Kastner, Erich (1899-1974), retold by. Lemke, Horst (1922-), illus. Winston, Richard & Winston, Clara, trs. LC 57-11506. 70p. illus. 27cm. (His Harlequin books). 1957. J. Messner.
--Don Quixote. Legrand, Edy (1893-), illus. N.D. Heritage Press.
--Don Quixote. Rich, Edwin Gile, adapted by. N.D. Houghton Mifflin Co.
--Don Quixote. Robinson, William Heath (1872-1944), illus. (gr. 6-10). 1954. (ISBN 0-525-28836-8). Dutton.
--Don Quixote. Starkie, Walter, tr. N.D. Signet & Mentor Bks.
--Don Quixote De La Mancha. Empire ed. 1905. American News Co.
--Don Quixote De La Mancha. N.D. D. Appleton & Co.
--Don Quixote De La Mancha. N.D. Pott, Young & Co.
--Don Quixote De La Mancha. Burt, Mary Elizabeth (1850-1918) & Cable, Lucy Leffingwell, eds. Duffield & Shelton, trs. N.D. Charles Scribner's Sons'.
--Don Quixote De La Mancha. Izen, Marshall, adapted by. Gantz, David, illus. LC 68-8914. (Illus.). 100 p. 32cm. 1968, c.1969. CBS Records.
--Don Quixote of La Mancha. Bere, Bagnot de la, illus. 1110p. (Color Edition). N.D. Thomas Y Crowell.
--Don Quixote of la Mancha. Dore, Louis Christophe Paul Gustave (1832-1883), illus. Starkie, Walter, tr. N.D. St. Martin's Press.
--Don Quixote of La Mancha. Wheaton, ed. (Classics for Children). N.D. Ginn and Company.
--Don Quixote of the Mancha. Parry, Judge, ed. Crane, Walter (1845-1915), illus. (Illus.). (gr. 7-9). N.D. (ISBN 0-396-01177-2). Dodd.
--Exploits of Don Quixote. Reeves, James (1909-), retold by. Ardizzone, Edward Jeffrey Irving (1900-1979), illus. LC 60-16286. (Illus.). 219 p. 23cm. 1960, c.1959. H. Z. Walck.
--The History of Don Quixote. Methley, Alice A, ed. Browne, Gordon Frederick (1858-1932), illus. LC 24-11838. 312, 1 p. incl. front., illus., plates. 21 cm. 1921. Frederick A. Stokes Company.
--The History of Don Quixote De la Mancha. Bosschere, Jean De (1878-1953), ed. Shelton, Thomas, tr. LC 76-6691. (Illus.). 367 p. 22cm. 1977. (ISBN 0-8055-1196-2). (ISBN 0-8055-0282-3). Hart Pub. Co.
--The Ingenious Gentleman Don Quixote of La Mancha, 4 vols. N.D. Dodd, Mead & Co.
--The Story of Don Quixote. Paulson, Arvid & Edwards, Clayton, eds. Choate, Florence & Curtis, Elizabeth, illus. LC 22-204261. xiv p., 1 l., 341 p. col. front., col. plates. 24 cm. c.1922. Frederick A. Stokes Company.
--Tales from Don Quixote. (gr. 10 up). 1969. Pyramid Pubns.
Cervon, Jacqueline, pseud., see Moussard, Jacqueline.
Cervon, Jacqueline, pseud. (1924-)
--Castaway from Rhodes. Moussard, Jacqueline. Niklaus, Thelma, tr. LC 73-5680. (Illus.). 150 p. 22cm. 1973, c.1969. (ISBN 0-531-02638-8). F. Watts.
--The Day the Earth Shook. Moussard, Jacqueline. Buchanan-Brown, John, tr. LC 69-12659. (Illus.). 186 p. 21cm. 1969. Coward-McCann.
C. E. S
--Leo and Dick: Or, Seeds of Kindness. (Illus.). N.D. E. P. Dutton & Co.
Cesbron, Gilbert
--The Innocents of Paris. Waldman, Marguerite, tr. LC 46-5000. 5 p. l., 212 p. 21 1/2 cm. 1946. Houghton Mifflin Company.
Cescol, Ferderica De see De Cesco, Federica.
Chaconas, Doris J. (1938-)
--Danger in the Swamp. Petie, Haris, pseud. (1915-), illus. Petty, Roberta. LC 74-143701. (Illus.). 31 p. 24cm. 1971. Lantern Press.
--A Hat for Lilly. Warren, Betsy, pseud. (1916-), illus. Warren, Elizabeth Avery. LC 67-1895. (Illus.). 32 p. 24cm. 1967. Steck-Vaughn Co.
--In a Window on Greenwater Street. Dolezal, Carroll, illus. LC 70-101563. (Illus.). 31 p. 27cm. 1970. (ISBN 0-8114-7699-5). Steck-Vaughn Co.
--The Way the Tiger Walked. Bozzo, Frank, illus. LC 70-101889. (Illus.). 32 p. 1970. Simon and Schuster.
Chad
--Everything for Your Birthday Party. 32p. 1984. (ISBN 0-8431-1725-7). Price Stern.
Chadburn, Mabel
--Fairy Bird and Piggy Wig. N.D. E. P. Dutton & Co.
Chadwick, Alice
--The Rescue of the Princess Sylvia: A Fairy Tale for Children. Napier, L., illus. LC 4-7919. 2 p. l., 30 p. front., illus. 25 cm. 1904. Broadway Publishing Company.
Chadwick, Edward
--My Sister's Welfare (Pub. by Society for Promoting Christian Knowledge). N.D. E. & J. B. Young & Co.
Chadwick, Evelyn M
--Little Orphan Willie-Mouse: A Story and Actual Photographs of a Real Live Woodmouse. Chace, Lynwood M., photos by. LC 38-32848. 2 p. l., 52 p. illus. 22 cm. 1938. Little, Brown and Company.
Chadwick, Francis, Mrs.
--The Luck-Piece. Our Little Phil. 61 p. 16 cm. (Catholic library. v. 23). 1898. C. Wildermann.
--Poor Lady Frivole. Bernard Mallory's Repentance. On Good Soil. Three Short Stories. 62 p. 16 cm. (Catholic library. v. 13). 1898. C. Wildermann.
--Short Stories. LC 5361. 3 v. in 1. 16 cm. (At head of special t.-p.: The Catholic library, v. 33, 43, 53). 1900. C. Wildermann.
Chadwick-Freeman
--The Cat that was Lonesome. N.D. World Book Co.
--The Mouse that Lost Her Tail. N.D. World Book Co.
--The Woman and Her Pig. (Chain Stories and Playlets). N.D. World Book Co.
Chadwick, George B.
--Chuck Blue of Sterling. Relyea, Charles M., illus. LC 27-20756. 20cm. 285p. N.D. Century Co.
Chadwick, Kenneth E.
--A Hear Do'n Sing Book: Little Bitty You Little Bitty Me. Boss, Jackie, illus. (Illus.). (ps). 1979. (ISBN 0-9603698-0-5). Bet-Ken Prods.
Chadwick, Lester, pseud., see Stratemeyer Syndicate.

AUTHOR INDEX CHAIN, BEVERLY

Chadwick, Lester, pseud.
--Baseball Joe Around the World: Or, Pitching on a Grand Tour. Stratemeyer Syndicate. Owen, Robert Emmett (1878-), illus. (The Baseball Joe Ser.: Vol. 8). 1918. Cupples & Leon Co.
--Baseball Joe at Yale: Or, Pitching for the College Championship. Stratemeyer Syndicate. Rogers, Walter S., illus. (The Baseball Joe Ser.: Vol. 3). 1913. Cupples & Leon Co.
--Baseball Joe, Captain of the Team: Or, Bitter Struggles on the Diamond. Stratemeyer Syndicate. Gooch, Thelma, illus. LC 24-12434. 2 p. l., 248 p. front., plates. 20 cm. (The Baseball Joe Ser.: Vol. 11). 1924. Cupples & Leon Co.
--Baseball Joe, Champion of the League: Or, The Record That Was Worth While. Stratemeyer Syndicate. Gooch, Thelma, illus. LC 25-11513. 2 p. l., 246 p. front., plates. 20 cm. (The Baseball Joe Ser.: Vol. 12). 1925. Cupples & Leon Co.
--Baseball Joe, Club Owner: Or, Putting the Home Town on the Map. Stratemeyer Syndicate. Gooch, Thelma, illus. (The Baseball Joe Ser.: Vol. 13). 1926. Cupples & Leon Co.
--Baseball Joe, Home Run King: Or, The Greatest Pitcher and Batter on Record. Stratemeyer Syndicate. Gooch, Thelma, illus. LC 22-0667. 2 p. l., 244 p. front., plates. 20 cm. (The Baseball Joe Ser.: Vol. 9). 1922. Cupples & Leon Co.
--Baseball Joe in the Big League: Or, A Young Pitcher's Hardest Struggles. Stratemeyer Syndicate. Rogers, Walter S., illus. (The Baseball Joe Ser.: Vol. 5). 1915. Cupples & Leon Co.
--Baseball Joe in the Central League: Or, Making Good as a Professional Pitcher. Stratemeyer Syndicate. Rogers, Walter S., illus. (The Baseball Joe Ser.: Vol. 4). 1914. Cupples & Leon Co.
--Baseball Joe in the World Series: Or, Pitching for the Championship. Stratemeyer Syndicate. Owen, Robert Emmett (1878-), illus. LC 17-220092. 2 p. l., 242 p. front., plates. 20 cm. (The Baseball Joe Ser.: Vol. 7). 1917. Cupples & Leon Co.
--Baseball Joe of the Silver Stars: Or, The Rivals of Riverside. Stratemeyer Syndicate. Rogers, Walter S., illus. (The Baseball Joe Ser.: Vol. 1). 1912. Cupples & Leon Co.
--Baseball Joe on the Giants: Or, Making Good as a Twirler in the Metropolis. Stratemeyer Syndicate. (The Baseball Joe Ser.: Vol. 6). 1916. Cupples & Leon Company.
--Baseball Joe on the School Nine: Or, Pitching for the Blue Banner. Stratemeyer Syndicate. Rogers, Walter S., illus. (The Baseball Joe Ser.: Vol. 2). 1912. Cupples & Leon Co.
--Baseball Joe, Pitching Wizard: Or, Triumphs off and on the Diamond. Stratemeyer Syndicate. Gooch, Thelma, illus. LC 28-157874. 2 p. l., 210 p. front. 20 cm. (The Baseball Joe Ser.: Vol. 14). 1928. Cupples & Leon Co.
--Baseball Joe Saving the League: Or, Breaking Up a Great Conspiracy. Stratemeyer Syndicate. Gooch, Thelma, illus. (The Baseball Joe Ser.: Vol. 10). 1923. Cupples & Leon Co.
--Batting to Win: A Story of College Baseball. Stratemeyer Syndicate. Boehm, H. Richard, illus. (The College Sports Ser.: Vol. 3). 1911. Cupples & Leon Co.
--The Eight-Oared Victors: A Story of College Water Sports. Stratemeyer Syndicate. Boehm, H. Richard, illus. (The College Sports Ser.: Vol. 6). 1913. Cupples & Leon Co.
--For the Honor of Randall: A Story of College Athletics. Stratemeyer Syndicate. Boehm, H. Richard, illus. LC 12-17965. 2 p. l., 312 p. front., plates. 19 cm. (The College Sports Ser.: Vol. 5). 1912. Cupples & Leon Co.
--A Quarterback's Pluck: A Story of College Football. Stratemeyer Syndicate. Nuttall, Charles, illus. (The College Sports Ser.: Vol. 2). 1910. Cupples & Leon Co.
--The Rival Pitchers: A Story of College Baseball. Stratemeyer Syndicate. Nuttall, Charles, illus. (The College Sports Ser.: Vol. 1). 1910. Cupples & Leon Co.
--The Winning Touchdown: A Story of College Football. Stratemeyer Syndicate. Boehm, H. Richard, illus. (The College Sports Ser.: Vol. 4). 1910. Cupples & Leon Co.
Chadwick, Mara Louise Pratt see Marshall, Francesca, pseud.
Chadwick, Mara Louise Pratt, Mrs., ed
--Aesop's Fables, Vols. I-II. LC 12-30193. (Illus.). (Young Folks Library of Choice Literature). 1892. Educational Publishing Company.
--Aesop's Fables, Vol. I. (Illus.). 127p. (Primary School Library). N.D. Educational Publishing Company.
--Aesop's Fables. (Illus.). 127p. (Thirty Volume School Library). N.D. Educational Publishing Company.
--Aesop's Fables. Library ed. (The Roxburghe Classics). N.D. Estes & Lauriat's.
--Bow-Wow and Mew-Mew. (Action, Imitation and Fun Ser.). N.D. David McKay Co.
--The Cat School. LC 9-23029. (Illus.). 96 p. 20cm. (Folk Lore books. Folleti linchetti series). 1908. Educational Pub. Co.
--Hop O' My Thumb--Tom Thumb. (Action, Imitation and Fun Ser.). N.D. David McKay Co.
--Jack and the Bean Stalk--Diamonds and Toads--Sleeping Beauty. (Action, Imitation and Fun Ser.). N.D. David McKay Co.
--Jack the Giant Killer. (Action, Imitation and Fun Ser.). N.D. David McKay Co.
--Legends of Norseland. (Illus.). (Primary School Library). N.D. Educational Publising Company.
--Legends of the Red Children: A Supplementary Reader for Fourth and Fifth Grade Pupils. LC 44-31643. 128 p. illus. 19 cm. 1897. Werner School Book Company.
--Little Flower Folks, Vol. I. (Illus.). 138p. (Thirty Volume School Library). N.D. Educational Publishing Company.
--Little Flower Folks, Vol. II. (Illus.). 130p. (Thirty Volume School Library). N.D. Educational Publishing Company.
--Little Flower Folks: Or, Stories from Flower-Land, Vols. I & II. N.D. Educational Publishing Company.
--The Little Red Hen. (Action, Imitation and Fun Ser.). N.D. David McKay Co.
--Myths of Old Greece, Vol.1. LC 6-9292. v. illus. 18 cm. c.1906. Educational Publishing Company.
--Puss in Boots and Reynard the Fox. (Action, Imitation and Fun Ser.). N.D. David McKay Co.
--Red Riding Hood--The Seven Kids. (Action, Imitation and Fun Ser.). N.D. David McKay Co.
--Stories from Old Germany. The Nibelungen Lied--Lohengrin--Beowulf, Vol. 1. LC 17-1441. 2 p. l., 7-153 p. ilus., pl. 18 cm. (On cover: Young folks library of choice literature). c.1895. Educational Publishing Company.
--Stories From Shakespeare, Vol. I. (Illus.). 166p. (Thirty Volume School Library). N.D. Educational Publishing Company.
--Stories From Shakespeare, Vol. II. (Illus.). (Thirty Volume School Library). N.D. Educational Publishing Company.
--Stories Of Colonial Children. (Illus.). (Primary School Library). N.D. Educational Publishing Company.
--Stories of Old Rome. LC 6-10304. 314 p. incl. illus., plan. 18 cm. c.1906. Educational Publishing Company.
--The Story of King Arthur, Vol. 1. LC 2-17056. 171 p. incl. front. plates. 18 cm. (Lettered on cover: Educational Juvenile Series). c.1900. Educational Publishing Company.
--Storyland of Stars. (Illus.). 165p. (Primary School Library). N.D. Educational Publishing Company.
--The Three Bears. (Action, Imitation and Fun Ser.). N.D. David McKay Co.
--Three Little Kittens--Chicken Little. (Action, Imitation and Fun Ser.). N.D. David McKay Co.
--The Three Pigs. (Action, Imitation and Fun Ser.). N.D. David McKay Co.
--Wonder Legends of Norse-Land, Vol. 1. 2 p. l., 7-190, iii p. illus. 21 cm. (Jolly Junior Books). 1931. A. Whitman & Co.
--World History in Myth and Legend. LC 6-9293. (Illus.). 154 p. 18cm. 1906. Educational Pub. Co.
Chadwick, Mara Louise Pratt, Mrs., ed. see Aesopus.
Chadwick, Mara Louise Pratt, Mrs., ed. see Ruskin, John.
Chadwick, Mara Louise Pratt, Mrs. & Lamprey, Louise (1869-1951), eds.
--The Alo Man: Stories from the Congo. Crampton, Rollin, illus. LC 21-10627. 170 p. incl. front., illus., map. 19 cm. (Children of the world). 1921. World Book Company.
Chadwick, Mara Louse Pratt see Marshall, Francesca, pseud.
Chadwick, Roxane
--Don't Shoot. Ryan, Edwin H., illus. LC 78-6101. (Illus.). 38 p. 23cm. c.1978. (ISBN 0-8225-0706-4). Lerner Publications Co.
Chafetz, Henry (1916-1978)
--Chanticleer: The Story of a Proud Rooster. Nadler, Robert (1934-), illus. LC 68-12648. (Illus.). 20 ils 3 color il. (gr. 2-4). 1968. (ISBN 0-394-91007-9). Pantheon.
--The Legend of Befana. N.D. E. M. Hale & Co.
--The Legend of Befana. Solbert, Ronni, pseud. (1925-), illus. Solbert, Romaine G.. LC 58-8164. (Illus.). 36 p. 23cm. 1958. Houghton Mifflin.
--Legend of Befana. Tolford, Joshua (1909-), illus. (Illus.). (gr. 4-6). 1958. (ISBN 0-395-06691-3). HM.
--The Lost Dream. Solbert, Ronni, pseud. (1925-), illus. Solbert, Romaine G.. LC 55-8940. unpaged. illus. 27cm. c.1955. Knopf.
--Thunderbirds & Other Stories. (Illus.). (gr. 3-5). 1964. (ISBN 0-394-91747-2). Pantheon.
Chaffe, Beatrice, jt. auth. see Hovelsrud, Joyce.
Chaffee, Allen
--The Adventures of Fleet Foot and Her Fawns. 128p. 1920. Milton Bradley Co.
--The Adventures of Twinkly Eyes: The Little Black Bear. Da Ru, Peter J., illus. LC 19-7742. 4 p. l., 183 p. front., illus., plates. 20 cm. 1919. Milton Bradley Company.
--Adventures on the High Trail. Lassell, Charles, illus. LC 23-11261. 4 p. l., 213 p. front., plates, fold. map. 19 cm. 1923. Milton Bradley Company.
--Adventures on the High Trail: Norma Blaisdell in the High Sierras. LC 30-11386. 4 p. l., 256 p. front., plates. 20 cm. c.1930. McLoughlin Bros., Inc.
--Bambi's Children. (Illus.). N.D. Random House Inc.
--Brownie Flat Tail Builds a Home. LC 37-22977. vi p., 1 l., 99, 1 p., 4 l., 116 p. front. 25 cm. c.1937. McLoughlin Brothers, Inc.
--Brownie, the Engineer of Beaver Brook. Bransom, Paul (1885-), illus. LC 25-23506. (Illus.). xi, 1-99 p. 24cm. 1925. Milton Bradley Company.
--Chinook: The Cinnamon Cub. Da Ru, Peter J., illus. LC 24-12163. 3 p. l., 133 p. front., plates. 19 cm. c.1924. Milton Bradley Company.
--The Forest Giant. Spencer, Hugh, illus. LC 31-25571. 5 p. l., 251 p. front., illus. 20 cm. c.1931. Milton Bradley Company.
--Fuzzy-Wuzz: A Little Brown Bear of the Sierras. Da Ru, Peter J., illus. LC 22-104907. 4 p. l., 142 p. front., plates. 19 cm. c.1922. Milton Bradley Company.
--Fuzzy Wuzz Meets the Ranger. LC 37-22824. 4 p. l., 142 p., 2 l., 94 p. front. 25 cm. c.1937. McLoughlin Brothers, Inc.
--Honk-a-Tonk Takes a Trip. LC 37-334099. 2 p. l., 108 p., 2 l., 133 p. front. 25 cm. c.1937. McLoughlin Brothers, Inc.
--Linda's El Dorado: A Mystery Adventure Story of Washington Territory in 1852. Nelson, Rosalie, illus. LC 28-197589. 6 p. l., 3-203 p. front., plates. 20 cm. c.1928. The Century Co.
--Lost River: Or, The Adventures of Two Boys in the Big Woods. Da Ru, Peter J., illus. LC 21-2385. 3 p., 6., v-ix, 169 p. col. front., plates. 20 cm. 1920. Milton Bradley Company.
--Lost!. Two Boys Battle with the Elements. LC 30-11385. 3 p. l., v-ix, 233 p. front., plates. 20 cm. c.1930. McLoughlin Bros., Inc.
--Mammie Cottontail Uses Her Wits. LC 37-33410. 2 p. l., 9-112 p., 2 l., 121 p. front., illus. 25 cm. c.1937. McLoughlin Brothers, Inc.
--Mammy Cottontail. N.D. Milton Bradley.
--Penn, the Penguin. Suskind, Henry, illus. LC 31-22275. 4 p. l., 102, 1 p. incl. col. illus., col. plates. col. front. 21 cm. 1931. J. Cape & H. Smith.
--Pinocchio. (Illus.). N.D. Random House Inc.
--Sitka, the Snow Baby. Da Ru, Peter J., illus. LC 23-963731. 4 p. l., 116 p. front., plates. 19 cm. c.1923. Milton Bradley Company.
--Sully Joins the Circus. Carman, Albert, illus. LC 26-15706. ix, 270 p. front., plates. 20 cm. c.1926. The Century Co.
--Tawny Goes Hunting. Bransom, Paul (1885-), illus. LC 37-197599. 76, 3 p. incl. illus., plates. 26 cm. 1937. Random House.
--Tony and the Big Top. Parsons, Priscilla B., illus. LC 25-8783. ix, 235 p. front., plates. 20 cm. c.1925. The Century Co.
--Trail and Tree Top. Da Ru, Peter J., illus. LC 20-5819. 20cm. 202p. (The Best of all Nature Stories). 1920. Milton Bradley Company.
--The Travels of Honk-a-Tonk, and Other Stories. Da Ru, Peter J., illus. LC 21-1699. 3 p. l., 108 p. front., plates. 19 cm. 1921. Milton Bradley Company.
--Trial and Tree Top. Da Ru, Peter J., illus. LC 20-58191. 202 p. col. front., illus., plates. 20 cm. 1920. Milton Bradley Company.
--Twinkly Eyes and the Lone Lake Folk: A True-to-Nature Story. Da Ru, Peter J., illus. LC 21-173833. 121 p. front., plates. 19 cm. 1921. Milton Bradley Company.
--Twinkly Eyes at Valley Farm: The Adventures of a Little Black Bear. Da Ru, Peter J., illus. LC 21-173848. 111 p. front., plates. 19 cm. 1921. Milton Bradley Company.
--Twinkly Eyes Goes Visiting. LC 37-22825. 111 p., 3 l, 9-121 p. front. 25 cm. c.1937. McLoughlin Brothers, Inc.
--Unexplored!. Van Dresser, William, illus. LC 22-19395. 4 p. l., 266 p. front., plates. 19 cm. 1922. Milton Bradley Company.
--Unexplored!. With the Forest Rangers of the Northwest. LC 30-9476. 4 p. l., 266 p. front., plates. 20 cm. c.1930. McLoughlin Bros., Inc.
--Wandy: The Wild Pony. LC 32-225534. x, 179 p., 1 l. illus. 20 cm. c.1932. H. Smith & R. Haas.
--Wandy Wins!. Mays, D. L., illus. LC 39-5854. 20 cm. 192p. 1939. Random House.
--Western Wild Life. Tessin, Louise D. & Fenton, C. L., illus. 205p. N.D. Caxton Printers.
--Wild Folk: Stories of Field and Forest. Bull, Charles Livingston (1874-1932) & Da Ru, Peter J., illus. LC 31-8807. 4 p. l., 121 p., 2 l., 108 p., 2 l., 94 p. col. front., illus., plates 20 cm. c.1930. Milton Bradley Company.
--The Wilderness Trail: The Story of Daniel Boone. Winslow, Earle B. (1884-), illus. LC 36-3909. vi, 7-72 p. incl. front., illus. 20 cm. (Our changing world). 1936. T. Nelson and Sons.
--The Winning Hazard. Jackson, John Edwin, illus. LC 29-17045. 20cm. 220p. 1929. Century Co.
Chaffee, Allen, ed. see Baum, Lyman Frank.
Chaffee, Allen, adapted by see Longfellow, Henry Wadsworth.
Chaffee, Allen, ed. see Lorenzini, Carlo.
Chaffee, Allen, ed. see Salten, Felix.
[illegible]
--Baxter Beaver. Paflin, Roberta, pseud. (1903-), illus. Petty, Roberta Harris Pfafflin. LC 42-11050. 40 p. col. illus. 23 x 20 cm. 1942. David McKay Company.
--Boy Meets Pony. N.D. Houghton Mifflin Co.
--Can You?. Throckmorton, Marian Wiggin (1908-), illus. LC 48-4249. 24 p. col. illus. 18 cm. c.1946. F. Fell.
--Miss Canary, If You Please. Paflin, Roberta, pseud. (1903-), illus. Petty, Roberta Harris Pfafflin. LC 42-210667. 47 p. col. illus. 28 cm. 1942. Cupples and Leon Company.
--Peek a Boo. Paflin, Roberta, pseud. (1903-), illus. Petty, Roberta Harris Pfafflin. LC 42-21433. 16 fold. l. col. illus. 15 1/2 by 15 1/2 cm. c.1942. Cupples & Leon Company.
Chaffin, Glen, jt. auth. see Forrest, Hal.
Chaffin, Lillie Dorton (1925-)
--Bear Weather. Aichinger, Helga (1937-), illus. LC 69-10498. (Illus.). 32 p. 27cm. 1968, c.1969. Macmillan.
--Freeman. LC 78-187793. 152 p. 22cm. 1972. Macmillan.
--A Garden Is Good. Cooper, Marjorie (1910-), illus. LC 64-17036. 1 v. (unpaged) col. illus. 32 cm. (Rand McNally giant books). 1964, c.1963. Rand McNally.
--I Have a Tree. Alexander, Martha G. (1920-), illus. LC 69-18088. (Illus.). 131 p. 23cm. 1969. D. White.
--John Henry McCoy. Schongut, Emanuel, illus. LC 78-134878. (Illus.). 169 p. 21cm. 1971. Macmillan.
--Tommy's Big Problem. Petie, Haris, pseud. (1915-), illus. Petty, Roberta. LC 65-19355. 1v. (unpaged) col. illus. 23cm. (gr. k-2). c.1965. Lantern.
--Tommy's Big Problem. Petie, Haris, pseud. (1915-), illus. Petty, Roberta. (gr. k-2). N.D. (ISBN 0-8313-0016-7). Lantern.
--We Be Warm till Springtime Comes. Bloom, Lloyd, illus. LC 80-12380. (Illus.). 32 p. 26cm. c.1980. (ISBN 0-02-717910-9). Macmillan.
Chagnon, Doe
--Michael Loves. (gr. 4-7). N.D. Carlton.
Chaikin, Miriam (1928-)
--Finders Weepers. Egielski, Richard (1952-), illus. LC 79-9608. p. cm. c.1980. (ISBN 0-06-021176-8). (ISBN 0-06-021177-6). Harper & Row.
--Getting Even. Egielski, Richard (1952-), illus. LC 81-48647. (Illus.). 120 p. 23cm. c.1982. (ISBN 0-06-021164-4). (ISBN 0-06-021165-2). Harper & Row.
--The Happy Pair and Otjher Love Stories. Nebel, Gustave E., illus. LC 76-187136. (Illus.). 59 p. 25cm. 1972. (ISBN 0-399-60771-4). (ISBN 0-399-60771-4). Putnam.
--Hardlucky. Krahn, Fernando (1935-), illus. LC 72-8821. (Illus.). 32 p. 27cm. 1973. Lippincott.
--How Yossi Beat the Evil Urge. 1st ed. Mathers, Petra, illus. LC 82-47705. p. cm. c.1983. (ISBN 0-06-021184-9). (ISBN 0-06-021185-7). Harper & Row.
--I Should Worry, I Should Care. Egielski, Richard (1952-), illus. LC 78-19480. (Illus.). 103 p. 23cm. c.1979. (ISBN 0-06-021174-1). (ISBN 0-06-021175-X). Harper & Row.
--Ittki Pittki. Berson, Harold (1926-), illus. LC 75-137000. (Illus.). 38 p. 1971. (ISBN 0-8193-0464-6). Parents' Magazine Press.
--Joshua in the Promised Land. Frampton, David, illus. (Illus.). (gr. 3-8). 1982. (ISBN 0-89919-120-7, Clarion). HM.
--Lower! Higher! You're a Liar!. Egielski, Richard (1952-), illus. LC 83-48445. c.1984. (ISBN 0-06-021186-5). Harper & Row.
--The Seventh Day: The Story of the Jewish Sabbath. Frampton, David, illus. LC 82-16987. p. cm. 1983, c.1980. (ISBN 0-8052-0736-8). Schocken Books.
--Yossi Asks the Angels for Help. Mathers, Petra, illus. LC 84-48351. (Illus.). 64p. (Charlotte Zolotow Bk.). (gr. 3-5). 1985. (ISBN 0-06-021195-4). (ISBN 0-06-021196-2). HarpJ.
Chaillu, Paul Belloni Du see Du Chaillu, Paul Belloni.
Chain, Beverly
--Days of the Decision. 126p. 1961. Friendship Press.

Chaitanya, Krishna

--Rohanta & Nandriya. Chakravarty, Pranab, illus. (Illus.). (Nehru Library for Children). (gr. 1-9). 1979. (ISBN 0-89744-179-6). Auromere.

Chalk, Gary, jt. auth. see Dever, Joseph.

Chalkley, Guy Aubrey

--The Desert Pool: A Romance of Wildest Africa. Chalkley, Guy Aubrey, photos by. LC 38-16231. xii, 228 p. in. 1937. Longmans, Green and Co.

Chall, Jeanne, jt. ed. see Corcoran, Jean Kennedy.

Chall, Jeanne, ed. see Curren, Polly.

Chall, Jeanne, jt. ed. see Hyndman, Jane Andrews Lee.

Chall, Jeanne, jt. ed. see Newman, Shirlee Petkin.

Challacombe, Jessie

--Jenny and His Friend in Trouble. N.D. E J B Young & Co.

Challans, Mary see Renault, Mary, pseud.

Chalmers, Anna Maria Hickman Otis Mead, Mrs. (1809-1891), ed. see Hughes, Thomas.

Chalmers, Audrey (1899-1957)

--Birthday of Obash. Chalmers, Audrey (1899-1957), illus. LC 37-33908. 79, 1 p. incl. front., illus. 19 cm. c.1937. Oxford University Press.

--Birthday of Obash. Chalmers, Audrey (1899-1957), illus. LC 52-8183. 55 p. illus. 19 x 23 cm. 1952. Viking Press.

--Fancy Be Good. Chalmers, Audrey (1899-1957), illus. LC 41-22671. 46 p. illus. 24 cm. 1941. The Viking Press.

--Hector and Mr. Murfit. Chalmers, Audrey (1899-1957), illus. 48p. 1953. Viking Press.

--High Smoke. Chalmers, Audrey (1899-1957), illus. LC 50-10297. (Illus.). 224 p. 21cm. 1950. Viking Press.

--Hundreds and Hundreds of Pancakes. Chalmers, Audrey (1899-1957), illus. LC 42-18438. (Illus.). 38, 1 p. (ps-3). 1942. (ISBN 0-670-38772-X). The Viking Press.

--I Had a Penny. Chalmers, Audrey (1899-1957), illus. LC 44-7723. 44 p. col. illus. 19 cm. 1944. The Viking Press.

--A Kitten's Tale. Chalmers, Audrey (1899-1957), illus. LC 46-11814. 45 p. illus. 23 1/2 cm. 1946. The Viking Press.

--Lolly. Chalmers, Audrey (1899-1957), illus. LC 38-31284. 105 p., 1 l. incl. front., illus., plates. 22 cm. c.1938. Oxford University Press.

--The Lovely Time. Chalmers, Audrey (1899-1957), illus. N.D. E. M. Hale & Co.

--The Lovely Time. Chalmers, Audrey (1899-1957), illus. LC 55-14103. (Illus.). 46 p. 25cm. 1955. Viking Press.

--Mr. Topple's Wish. Chalmers, Audrey (1899-1957), illus. LC 48-4519. 36 p. illus. 19 x 23 cm. 1948. Viking Press.

--Parade of Obash. Chalmers, Audrey (1899-1957), illus. LC 39-23756. 77, 1 p. illus. 19 cm. c.1939. Oxford University Press.

--Poppadilly. Chalmers, Audrey (1899-1957), illus. LC 45-8413. 40 p. illus. 19 cm. 1945. The Viking Press.

--Stove-Pipe-Man and Sandy. Chalmers, Audrey (1899-1957), illus. LC 28-21406. x p., 1 l., 195 p. incl. front., illus. 20 cm. 1928. W. Morrow & Company.

Chalmers, J.

--Fighting the Matabele. (Illus.). (Scribner-Blackie Series of books for young people). N.D. Charles Scribner's Sons.

Chalmers, James, ed.

--Scott's The Lady of the Lake. N.D. D. Appleton-Century Co., Inc.

Chalmers, Margaret Rebecca Piper see Piper, Margaret Rebecca, pseud.

Chalmers, Margaret Rebecca Piper, Mrs. (1879-)

--Babbie. Goss, John, illus. N.D. L. C. Page.

--The House on the Hill. Withington, Elizabeth R., illus. LC 17-14181. 4 p. l., 325 p. front., plates. 21 cm. 1917. The Page Company.

--Peter's Best Seller. Goss, John, illus. LC 23-12873. 4 p. l., 339 p. front., plates. 20 cm. 1923. L. C. Page & Company.

--Pollyanna Protegee. (The Pollyanna Books). N.D. Grosset & Dunlap.

--Pollyanna's Protegee: The Eleventh Glad bk. Cue, Harold, illus. (The Pollyanna bks.). N.D. L. C. Page.

--Sylvia Arden Decides. Piper, Margaret Rebecca, pseud. N.D. Grosset & Dunlap.

--Sylvia Arden Decides. Piper, Margaret Rebecca, pseud. Coffin, Haskell, illus. LC 17-25587. 3 p. l., 316 p. col. front. 20 cm. 1917. The Page Company.

--Sylvia of the Hill Top. Piper, Margaret Rebecca, pseud. N.D. Grosset & Dunlap.

--Sylvia of the Hill Top. Piper, Margaret Rebecca, pseud. Pressler, Gene, illus. LC 16-10879. 3 p. l., 311 p. col. front. 20 cm. 1916. The Page Company.

--Sylvia's Experiment: The Story of an Unrelated Family. Piper, Margaret Rebecca, pseud. Nikolaki, Z. P., illus. LC 14-15362. 3 p. l., 208 p. col. front. 20 cm. 1914. The Page Company.

--Wild Wings: A Romance of Youth. Goss, John, illus. LC 21-17912. 4 p. l., 420 p. front., plates. 20 cm. 1921. The Page Company.

Chalmers, Mary Eileen, jt. auth. see Lauber, Patricia Grace.

Chalmers, Mary Eileen (1927-)

--Be Good, Harry. Chalmers, Mary Eileen (1927-), illus. LC 67-16230. (Illus.). 32 p. 16cm. 1967. Harper & Row.

--Be Good, Harry. Chalmers, Mary Eileen (1927-), illus. 1982. Harper & Row.

--Boats Finds a House. Chalmers, Mary Eileen (1927-), illus. 1958. Harper & Brothers.

--Cat Who Liked to Pretend. Chalmers, Mary Eileen (1927-), illus. (Illus.). (gr. k-2). 1959. (ISBN 0-06-021181-4). Har-Row.

--A Christmas Story. Chalmers, Mary Eileen (1927-), illus. LC 56-8143. unpaged. illus. 10x11cm. 1956. Harper.

--Come for a Walk with Me. Chalmers, Mary Eileen (1927-), illus. LC 55-5523. (Illus.). (gr. k-3). 1955. (ISBN 0-06-021200-4, HarpJ). Har-Row.

--Come to the Doctor, Harry. Chalmers, Mary Eileen (1927-), illus. LC 80-7910. (Illus.). 32 p. 16cm. c.1981. (ISBN 0-06-021178-4). (ISBN 0-06-021179-2). Harper & Row.

--George Appleton. Chalmers, Mary Eileen (1927-), illus. LC 57-9269. 32p. illus. 16cm. 1957. Harper.

--A Hat for Amy Jean. Chalmers, Mary Eileen (1927-), illus. LC 56-51527. unpaged. illus. 16cm. (ps-1). 1956. (ISBN 0-06-021210-1). Harper.

--Here Comes the Trolley Car. Chalmers, Mary Eileen (1927-), illus. LC 55-8590. unpaged. illus. 19x26cm. 1955. Harper.

--Kevin. Chalmers, Mary Eileen (1927-), illus. (Illus.). (ps-1). 1957. (ISBN 0-06-021216-0). Har-Row.

--Merry Christmas, Harry. Chalmers, Mary Eileen (1927-), illus. LC 76-58715. (Illus.). 32p. (Trophy Picture Bk.). (ps-3). 1981. (ISBN 0-06-443029-4, Trophy). Har-Row.

--Merry Christmas, Harry. Chalmers, Mary Eileen (1927-), illus. LC 76-58715. (Illus.). (ps-2). N.D. (ISBN 0-06-021182-2, HarpJ). (ISBN 0-06-021183-0). Har-Row.

--Merry Christmas, Harry. Chalmers, Mary Eileen (1927-), illus. LC 76-58715. p. cm. c.1977. (ISBN 0-06-021182-2). (ISBN 0-06-021183-0). Harper & Row.

--Mister Cat's Wonderful Surprise. Chalmers, Mary Eileen (1927-), illus. (Illus.). (gr. k-3). 1961. (ISBN 0-06-021231-4, HarpJ). Har-Row.

--Take a Nap Harry. Chalmers, Mary Eileen (1927-), illus. 1964. E M Hale.

--Take a Nap, Harry. Chalmers, Mary Eileen (1927-), illus. LC 64-11838. 32 p. illus. 16 cm. 1964. Harper & Row.

--Take a Nap, Harry. Chalmers, Mary Eileen (1927-), illus. (ps-2). 1981. Harper & Row.

--Throw a Kiss, Harry. Chalmers, Mary Eileen (1927-), illus. (Illus.). (ps-1). 1958. (ISBN 0-06-021246-2). Har-Row.

--Throw a Kiss, Harry. Chalmers, Mary Eileen (1927-), illus. LC 58-5294. (Illus.). 1964. (ISBN 0-06-021246-2, HarpJ). Har-Row.

--Throw a Kiss, Harry. Chalmers, Mary Eileen (1927-), illus. LC 58-5294. (Illus.). 32p. (Trophy Picture Bk.). (ps-3). 1981. (ISBN 0-06-443030-8, Trophy). Har-Row.

Chalmers, Muriel & Entwhistle, Mary

--Baby Moses. Wood, Elsie Anna & Waudby, Roberta F. C., illus. (Stories about Jesus). N.D. Thomas Nelson & Co.

--The Farmer and his Field. Wood, Elsie Anna & Waudby, Roberta F. C., illus. (Stories Jesus Told). N.D. Thomas Nelson & Sons.

--Hosanna to the King. Wood, Elsie Anna & Waudby, Roberta F. C., illus. (Stories about Jesus). N.D. Thomas Nelson & Co.

--Isaac of the Tents. Wood, Elsie Anna & Waudby, Roberta F. C., illus. (Old Testament Stories). N.D. Thomas Nelson & Co.

--Jesus, Friend of Little Children. Wood, Elsie Anna & Waudby, Roberta F. C., illus. (Stories about Jesus). N.D. Thomas Nelson & Co.

--The Lost Coin. Wood, Elsie Anna & Waudby, Roberta F. C., illus. (Stories Jesus Told). N.D. Thomas Nelson & Sons.

--The Nobleman's Son. Wood, Elsie Anna & Waudby, Roberta F. C., illus. (Stories about Jesus). N.D. Thomas Nelson & Co.

--Samuel the Temple Boy. Wood, Elsie Anna & Waudby, Roberta F. C., illus. (Old Testament Stories). N.D. Thomas Nelson & Sons.

--The Shepherd and his Sheep. Wood, Elsie Anna & Waudby, Roberta F. C., illus. (Stories Jesus Told). N.D. Thomas Nelson & Co.

--The Song the Shepherds Heard. Wood, Elsie Anna & Waudby, Roberta F. C., illus. (Stories of the Childhood of Jesus). N.D. Thomas Nelson & Sons.

--The Star of the King. Wood, Elsie Anna & Waudby, Roberta F. C., illus. (Stories of the Childhood of Jesus). N.D. Thomas Nelson & Sons.

--When Jesus was a Boy. Wood, Elsie Anna & Waudby, Roberta F. C., illus. (Stories of the Childhood of Jesus). N.D. Thomas Nelson & Sons.

Chalon, Jon, pseud., see Chaloner, John Seymour.

Chaloner, John Seymour see Chalon, Jon, pseud.

Chaloner, John Seymour (1924-)

--Sir Lance-a-Little & the Knights of the Kitchen Table. Chalon, Jon, pseud. LC 72-172343. 32p. (gr. 2-4). 1972. (ISBN 0-672-51626-8). Bobbs.

--The Voyage of the Floating Bedstead. Chalon, Jon, pseud. LC 72-88764. (Illus.). 32 p. 29cm. 1973. Bobbs-Merrill.

Chamberlain, Anna Content Chase, Mrs. (1861-)

--The Bailey Twins and the Rest of the Family. Dunn, Elizabeth Otis, illus. LC 14-14799. 241 p. front., plates. 19 cm. 1914. Lethrop, Lee & Shepard Co.

Chamberlain, Barbara

--The Prisoners' Sword. Kohn, Arnold, illus. LC 77-87256. (Illus.). 117 p. 18cm. c.1978. (ISBN 0-89191-102-2). D.C. Cook Pub. Co.

--Ride the West Wind. Wahl, Richard (1939-), illus. LC 78-73150. (Illus.). 182 p. 18cm. c.1979. (ISBN 0-89191-133-2). D. C. Cook Pub. Co.

Chamberlain, Basil Hall (1850-1935)

--The Bird's Party. (Aino Fairy Tales: No. 2). N.D. Ticknor & Co.

--The Hunter in Fairy Land. (Aino Fairy Tales: No. 1). N.D. Ticknor & Co.

Chamberlain, Chriss & Chamberlain, Margaret

--The Buttercup Buskers' Rainy Day. (Illus.). 24p. 1st U.S. edition. (ps-1). 1983. (ISBN 0-434-93115-2, Pub. by Heinemann England). David & Charles.

Chamberlain, Elinor (1901-)

--Mystery of the Jungle Airstrip. LC 67-2696. 160 p. 22cm. 1967. Lippincott.

--Mystery of the Moving Island. LC 65-13419. 159 p. 21 cm. 1965. Lippincott.

Chamberlain, Eugene

--Barry at Church. (ps). 1966. Broadman.

Chamberlain, George Agnew (1879-)

--Lord Buff and the Silver Star. Dennis, Wesley (1903-1966), illus. LC 55-6647. 116p. illus. 25cm. 1955. Barnes.

Chamberlain, Margaret, jt. auth. see Chamberlain, Chriss.

Chamberlain, Paithene B., Miss

--Chosen Vessels. (Crowell's Library For Young People). N.D. Thomas Y. Crowell & Co.

--Mistress of the House: Author of "Isa Graeme's World", "Nick at the Tavern". (Crowell's Sunday-School Library: No. 6). N.D. Thomas Y. Crowell & Co.

--Posie. (Crowell's Library For Young People). N.D. Thomas Y. Crowell & Co.'s Catalogue.

--Rare Piece Of Work. (Crowell's Library For Young People). N.D. Thomas Y. Crowell & Co.

--Rob Claxton's Story. (Crowell's Library For Young People). N.D. Thomas Y. Crowell & Co.

--What About Fred. (Crowell's Library For Young People). N.D. Thomas Y. Crowell & Co.

Chamberlain, William Edwin (1903-)

--Combat General. LC 63-10230. 184p. illus. 21cm. c.1963. John Day.

--Matt Quarterhill, Rifleman. (gr. 7-10). 1965. John Day.

--The Mountain. LC 68-11303. 191 p. 21cm. 1968. John Day Co.

--Murphy Higheagle, Paratrooper. Orbaan, Albert F. (1913-), illus. LC 66-8327. (Illus.). (gr. 6-9). 1966. John Day.

--Zone of Sudden Death & Other Stories of Combat (Pub. by John Day). Orig. Title: More Combat Stories of World War Two & Korea. (gr. 7-12). 1972 (Starline). Schol Bk Serv.

Chamberlin, Ethel Clere

--The Amazing Adventures of Kermit: The Hermit Crab. Chamberlin, Ethel Clere, illus. LC 30-17105. 9 p. l., 3-121, 1 p. incl. col. front., illus., plates. 24 cm. c.1930. G. Sully & Company, Inc.

--Omar, the Discontented Cat. 3rd ed. Sturgis, Katharine, illus. LC 25-23504. (Illus.). 39 p. 19cm. 1925. The P.F. Volland Company.

Chamberlin, Roy Bullard (1887-)

--Winners. LC 33-29803. 186 p. 20 cm. c.1933. The Abingdon Press.

Chambers, Aidan (1934-)

--Aidan Chambers' Book of Ghosts and Hauntings. Maitland, Antony Jasper (1935-), illus. LC 73-179364. (Illus.). 144 p. 23cm. 1973. (ISBN 0-582-15210-0). Longman Young Books.

--Aidan Chambers' Book of Ghosts and Hauntings. Maitland, Antony Jasper (1935-), illus. LC 74-161798. (Illus.). viii, 144 p. 22cm. 1973. Puffin Books.

--Breaktime. LC 78-19472. (Illus.). 180 p. 22cm. c.1978. (ISBN 0-06-021256-X). (ISBN 0-06-021257-8). Harper & Row.

--Car. 1967. (ISBN 0-435-23166-9). Heinemann Ed.

--Dance on My Grave. LC 82-48258. p. cm. 1983, c.1982. (ISBN 0-06-021253-5). (ISBN 0-06-021254-3). Harper & Row.

--Out of Time: Stories of the Future. LC 84-112088. 155 p. 20cm. 1984. (ISBN 0-370-30532-9). Bodley Head.

--The Present Takers. LC 83-48470. 160p. (A Charlotte Zolotow Bk.). (gr. 5-7). 1984. (ISBN 0-06-021251-9, HarpJ). (ISBN 0-06-021252-7). Har-Row.

--Seal Secret. LC 80-8456. p. cm. 1981, c.1980. (ISBN 0-06-021258-6). (ISBN 0-06-021259-4). Harper & Row.

Chambers, Aidan (1934-), compiled by.

--Out of Time. 186p. 1985. (ISBN 0-06-021201-2). (ISBN 0-06-021202-0). Harper.

Chambers, Arthur, tr. see Verne, Jules.

Chambers, Catherine E.

--California Gold Rush: Search for Treasure. Eitzen, Allan (1928-), illus. LC 83-18280. (Illus.). 32 p. 24cm. (Adventures in frontier America). (gr. 5-9). c.1984. (ISBN 0-8167-0051-6). (ISBN 0-8167-0052-4). Troll Associates.

--Daniel Boone and the Wilderness Road. Guzzi, George, illus. LC 83-18291. (Illus.). 32 p. 24cm. (Adventures in frontier America). c.1984. (ISBN 0-8167-0037-0). (ISBN 0-8167-0038-9). Troll Associates.

--Flatboats on the Ohio: Westward Bound. Lawn, John, illus. LC 83-18278. (Illus.). 32 p. 24cm. (Adventures in Frontier America). c.1984. (ISBN 0-8167-0049-4). (ISBN 0-8167-0050-8). Troll Associates.

--Frontier Dream: Life on the Great Plains. Smolinski, Dick, illus. LC 83-18282. (Illus.). 32 p. 24cm. (Adventures in Frontier America). c.1984. (ISBN 0-8167-0039-7). (ISBN 0-8167-0040-0). Troll Associates.

--Frontier Farmer: Kansas Adventures. Epstein, Len, illus. LC 83-18279. (Illus.). 32 p. 24cm. (Adventures in Frontier America). c.1984. (ISBN 0-8167-0053-2). (ISBN 0-8167-0054-0). Troll Associates.

--Frontier Village: A Town Is Born. Smolinski, Dick, illus. LC 83-18271. (Illus.). 32 p. 24cm. (Adventures in Frontier America). c.1984. (ISBN 0-8167-0045-1). (ISBN 0-8167-0046-X). Troll Associates.

--Indiana Days: Life in a Frontier Town. Lawn, John, illus. LC 83-18283. (Illus.). 32 p. 24cm. (Adventures in Frontier America). c.1984. (ISBN 0-8167-0055-9). (ISBN 0-8167-0056-7). Troll Associates.

--Log-Cabin Home: Pioneers in the Wilderness. Eitzen, Allan (1928-), illus. LC 83-18277. (Illus.). 32 p. 24cm. (Adventures in Frontier America). c.1984. (ISBN 0-8167-0041-9). (ISBN 0-8167-0042-7). Troll Associates.

--Texas Roundup: Life on the Range. Lawn, John, illus. LC 83-18281. (Illus.). 32 p. 24cm. (Adventures in frontier America.). c.1984. (ISBN 0-8167-0047-8). (ISBN 0-8167-0048-6). Troll Associates.

--Wagons West: Off to Oregon. Smolinski, Dick, illus. LC 83-18276. (Illus.). 32p. (Adventures in Frontier America Ser.). (gr. 5-9). 1984. (ISBN 0-8167-0043-5). (ISBN 0-8167-0044-3). Troll Assocs.

Chambers, David Whitaker (1901-1961), tr. see Salten, Felix.

Chambers, Helena

--George's Rocket. LC 50-9070. 103 p. 20 cm. 1950. Dorrance.

--George's Steam Locomotive. N.D. Vantage Press Inc.

Chambers, John W. (1933-)

--The Colonel and Me. LC 84-20440. viii, 190 p. 22cm. 1985. (ISBN 0-689-31087-0). Atheneum.

--Finder. LC 80-23928. (Illus.). vii, 156 p. 22cm. 1981. (ISBN 0-689-30803-5). Atheneum.

--Fire Island Forfeit. LC 84-5671. 192p. (gr. 4-6). 1984. (ISBN 0-689-31043-9). Atheneum.

--Footlight Summer. LC 83-2628. p. cm. 1983. (ISBN 0-689-30980-5). Atheneum.

--Fritzi's Winter. Kowalchez, Carol, illus. LC 79-14672. p. cm. 1979. (ISBN 0-689-30727-6). Atheneum.

--Showdown at Apple Hill. LC 81-10774. vii, 166 p. 22cm. 1982. (ISBN 0-689-30897-3). Atheneum.

Chambers, M. E., pseud., see Crossen, Kendall Foster.

Chambers, M. E., pseud. (1910-)

--Acid Nightmare. Crossen, Kendall Foster. (Pacesetter Book Ser). (gr. 7 up). 1967. (ISBN 0-03-065600-1). HR&W.

Chambers, Maria Cristina Mena

--Boy Heroes of Chapultepec: A Story of the Mexican War. 1st ed. Krush, Joe (1918-), illus. LC 52-14252. 182p. illus. 22cm. (Winston adventure books). 1953. Winston.

AUTHOR INDEX CHANDLER, EDNA

--The Bullfighter's Son. Ortega, Ignacio, illus. LC 44-8363. 94 p. col. illus. 20 1/2 cm. 1944. Oxford University Press.
--The Three Kings. LC 47-180. 38, 1 p. illus. (part col.) 20 1/2 cm. 1946. Oxford University Press.
--The Two Eagles. LC 43-18555. 176 p. illus. 21 cm. 1943. Oxford University Press.
--The Water-Carrier's Secrets. Weisgard, Leonard Joseph (1916-), illus. LC 42-19649. 157 p. col. illus. 23 cm. 1942. Oxford University Press.
Chambers, Miss
--Away on the Moorland, 1 of 4 Vols. (Illus.). (Rosamond's Book Shelf). N.D. Set. Pott, Young & Co.
Chambers, Nancy
--Stir-About Rhymes to Read from Then and Now. Bull, Carolyn, illus. LC 80-85302. (Illus.). 46 p. 21cm. (Blackbird books). 1981. (ISBN 0-531-04069-0). J. MacRae Books.
Chambers, Robert, jt. auth. see Chambers, William.
Chambers, Robert William (1865-1933)
--Cardigan: A Novel. (Harper Junior Classics Ser.). 1901. Harper & Bros.
--Forest-Land. Knipe, Emilie Benson, Mrs. (1870-1958), illus. 1905. D. Appleton & Co.
--Garden-Land. Cady, Walter Harrison (1877-1970), illus. 1907. D. Appleton and Company.
--Hide and Seek in Forest Land. 1909. D. Appleton & Co.
--Mountain-Land. Richardson, Frederick (1862-1937), illus. 1906. D. Appleton and Company.
--Orchard-Land: A Children's Story. Birch, Reginald Bathurst (1856-1943), illus. LC 3-242213. 4 p. l., 112 p. col. front., illus., 6 col. pl. 25 cm. 1903. Harper & Brothers.
--Outdoor-Land. Birch, Reginald Bathurst (1856-1943) & Green, Elizabeth Shippen, illus. LC 32-10226. 4 p. l., 311, 1 p. col. front., illus., col. plates. 24 cm. 1931. D. Appleton and Company.
--Outdoor-Land: A Story for Children. 6 p. l., 105, 1 p. col. illus., col. pl. 24 cm. 1902. Harper & Brothers.
--River-Land. Green, Elizabeth Shippen, illus. LC 4-25109. 25cm. 91p. 1904. Harper & Brothers.
--With the Band. LC 14-6554. 18cm. 134p. 1896. Stone & Kimball.
Chambers, Robert (1802-1871)
--Popular Rhymes of Scotland. N.D. Gale Reprint.
Chambers, Whitman
--The Coast of Intrigue. N.D. World Publishing Co.
Chambers, Whittaker (1901-1961), tr. see Bonsels, Waldemar.
Chambers, Whittaker, tr. see Disney, Walt, Productions & Salten, Felix.
Chambers, William (1800-1883) & Chambers, Robert (1802-1871)
--Happy Hour Library: Containing "Every Day Book", "Leisure Hour Book", and "The Parlor Book". (Illus.). N.D. James Miller.
--Home Books and Miscellany Ser. Containing "Every Day Book", "Leisure Hour Book", "Parlor Book", etc, 6 vols. (Illus.). N.D. James Miller.
--Library of Instructive Amusement: Containing "Summer Day Book", "Winter Evening Book", and "Young Folks' Companion", 3 vols. (Illus.). N.D. James Miller.
--Young Folks' Historical Tales. (Illus.). (St. Nicholas Series for Boys). N.D. International Book Co.
--Young Folks' Library: Containing: Young Folks' Historical Tales, Young Folks' Scottish Tales, Young Folks' Popular Tales, and Young Folk's Tales of Adventures, 4 vols. (Illus.). N.D. International Book Co.
--Young Folks' Popular Tales. (Illus.). (St. Nicholas Series for Boys). N.D. International Book Co.
--Young Folks' Scottish Tales. (Illus.). (St. Nicholas Series for Boys). N.D. International Book Co.
Chambless-Rigie, Jane
--My First Mother Goose Book. Chambless-Rigie, Jane, illus. 24p. (Golden Storytime Bk. of Learning). (ps). 1980. (ISBN 0-307-11987-4). (ISBN 0-307-61981-8). Western Pub.
--The Real Mother Goose Clock Book. Chambless-Rigie, Jane, illus. (Illus.). N.D. (ISBN 0-528-82329-9). Rand.
Chamoud, Simone (1904-), tr. see Lenotre, Therese.
Chamoud, Simone (1904-)
--Picture Tales from the French. Gilkison, Grace, illus. LC 33-273904. x p., 1 l., 115 p. incl. illus., plates. 14 x 19 cm. 1933. Frederick A. Stokes Company.
--Picture Tales from the French. Gilkison, Grace, Mrs., illus. N.D. J. B. Lippincott Co.
Champion, Hope Loring (1913-)
--Betsy Bobbitt and Other Stories. Champion, Hope Loring (1913-), illus. N.D. Garden City Publishing Co.
--Betsy Bobbitt, and Other Stories. LC 49-15154. 36p. col. illus. 25cm. c.1948. John Martin's House.
--The Kitten Who Would Not Wash His Face. Champion, Hope Loring (1913-), illus. N.D. Garden City Publishing Co.
--Mother Goose Nursery Rhymes. Champion, Hope Loring (1913-), illus. LC 62-16897. (Illus.). 20cm. 36p. (ps-3). 1962. (ISBN 0-695-85925-0). Follett.
--So Big Book of Nursery Tales. Champion, Hope Loring (1913-), illus. LC 50-7942. 32 x 15cm. 24p. (So Big Series). 1950. Garden City Publishing Co.
--The Wee Kitten Who Sucked Her Thumb And Other Stories. Champion, Hope Loring (1913-), illus. LC 49-15629. 36 p. col. illus. 25 cm. c.1948. John Martin's House.
Champlin, John, ed. see Connelly, Tony & Holley, Cindy.
Champney, Elizabeth Williams see Champney, Lizzie W., pseud.
Champney, Elizabeth Williams see Williams, Elizabeth.
Champney, Elizabeth Williams, Mrs. (1850-1922)
All Around a Palette. Champney, Lizzie W., pseud. Champ, pseud. (1843-1903), illus. Champney, James Wells. LC 14-22464. 3 p. l., ix-x, 314 p. front., illus., plates. 19 x 15 cm. 1878. Lockwood, Brooks, and Company.
--The Bubbling Teapot, 3 vols. (Fun and Fancy Library). N.D. D. Lothrop Co.
--Great Grandmother's Girls In New France. Champ, pseud. (1843-1903), illus. Champney, James Wells. N.D. Estes & Lauriat.
--Great Grandmother's Girls In New Mexico. Champ, pseud. (1843-1903), illus. Champney, James Wells. N.D. Estes & Lauriat.
--Howling Wolf and His Trick-Pony. Merrill, Frank Thayer (1848-), illus. N.D. Lothrop.
--In The Sky Garden. Champ, pseud. (1843-1903), illus. Champney, James Wells. (Illus.). N.D. Lothrop.
--Paddy O'Learey and His Learned Pig. Steele, Frederic Dorr, illus. LC 12-31338. 171, 1 p. incl. illus., plates. front. 18 cm. 1895. Dodd, Mead & Company.
--Pierre and His Poodle. Steele, Frederic Dorr, illus. LC 20-18848. 4 p. l., 216 p. front., illus. 19 cm. 1897. Dodd, Mead and Company.
--Six Boys. Merrill, Frank Thayer (1848-), illus. LC 12-31339. 4 p. l., 11-235 p. front., plates. 21 cm. c.1893. Estes and Lauriat.
--Six Boys. Merrill, Frank Thayer (1848-), illus. (The American Boy's Library). N.D. L. C. Page & Co.
--Three Vassar Girls Abroad. Champ, pseud. (1843-1903), illus. Champney, James Wells. (Illus.). (Mrs. Champney's Famous "Three Vassar Girls" Ser.). N.D. Dana Estes and Company.
--Three Vassar Girls Abroad. Champ, pseud. (1843-1903), illus. Champney, James Wells. 1882. Estes & Lauriat's.
--Three Vassar Girls at Home. Champ, pseud. (1843-1903), illus. Champbey, James Wells. (Illus.). (Mrs. Champney's Famous "Three Vassar Girls" Ser.). N.D. Dana Estes and Company.
--Three Vassar Girls in England. Champ, pseud. (1843-1903), illus. Champney, James Wells. (Illus.). (Mrs. Champney's Famous "Three Vassar Girls" Ser.). N.D. Dana Estes and Company.
--Three Vassar Girls in France. Champ, pseud. (1843-1903), illus. Champney, James Wells. (Illus.). (Mrs. Champney's Famous "Three Vassar Girls" Ser.). N.D. Dana Estes and Company.
--Three Vassar Girls in Russia and Turkey. Champ, pseud. (1843-1903), illus. Champney, James Wells. (Illus.). (Mrs. Champney's Famous "Three Vassar Girls" Ser.). N.D. Dana Estes and Company.
--Three Vassar Girls in South America. Champ, pseud. (1843-1903), illus. Champney, James Wells. (Illus.). (Mrs. Champney's Famous "Three Vassar Girls" Ser.). N.D. Dana Estes and Company.
--Three Vassar Girls in Switzerland. Champ, pseud. (1843-1903), illus. Champney, James Wells. (Illus.). (Mrs. Champney's Famous "Three Vassar Girls" Ser.). N.D. Dana Estes and Company.
--Three Vassar Girls in the Holy Land. Champ, pseud. (1843-1903), illus. Champney, James Wells. (Illus.). (Mrs. Champney's Famous "Three Vassar Girls" Ser.). N.D. Dana Estes and Company.
--Three Vassar Girls in the Tyrol. Champ, pseud. (1843-1903), illus. Champney, James Wells. (Illus.). (Mrs. Champney's Famous "Three Vassar Girls" Ser.). N.D. Dana Estes and Company.
--Three Vassar Girls on the Rhine. Champ, pseud. (1843-1903), illus. Champney, James Wells. (Illus.). (Mrs. Champney's Famous "Three Vassar Girls" Ser.). N.D. Dana Estes and Company.
--Witch Winnie. Champ, pseud. (1843-1903), illus. Champney, James Wells. (Phenix Ser.). N.D. Dodd, Mead & Company.
--Witch Winnie. Gibson, Charles Dana, et al. (1867-1944), illus. (The Witch Winnie Bks.). N.D. Dodd, Mead & Co.
--Witch Winnie at Shinnecock: a King's Daughter at Summer Art School. Champ, pseud. (1843-1903), illus. Champney, James Wells. (The Witch Winnie Bks.). N.D. Dodd, Mead & Co.
--Witch Winnie at Versailles. Gibson, Charles Dana, et al. (1867-1944), illus. (The Witch Winnie Ser.). N.D. Dodd, Mead & Co.
--Witch Winnie in Holland. Champ, pseud. (1843-1903), illus. Champney, James Wells. (Illus.). (The Witch Winnie Bks.). N.D. Dodd, Mead & Co.
--Witch Winnie in Paris: Or, King's Daughters Abroad. Champ, pseud. (1843-1903), illus. Champney, James Wells. (The Witch Winnie Bks.). N.D. Dodd, Mead & Co.
--Witch Winnie in Spain. Gibson, Charles Dana, et al. (1867-1944), illus. (The Witch Winnie Bks.). N.D. Dodd, Mead & Co.
--Witch Winnie in Venice. Gibson, Charles Dana, et al. (1867-1944), illus. (The Witch Winnie Bks.). N.D. Dodd, Mead & Co.
--Witch Winnie's Mystery: Or, The Old Oak Cabinet. Gibson, Charles Dana, et al. (1867-1944), illus. (Illus.). (The Witch Winnie Bks.). N.D. Dodd, Mead & Co.
--Witch Winnie's Studio: Or, the King's Daughter's Art Life. Champ, pseud. (1843-1903), illus. Champney, James Wells. (Illus.). N.D. Dodd, Mead & Co.
Champney, Lizzie W., pseud., see Champney, Elizabeth Williams.
Champneys, Adelaide, ed.
--Memorial to George. Reid, James (1907-), illus. LC 29-23771. xiv p., i 1., 17-282 p. front., illus. 20 cm. 1929. The Books-Merrill Company.
Chan, Chih-yi, ed.
--The Good-Luck Horse: Adapted from an Old Chinese Legend. Chan, Plato (1931-), illus. Glick, Carl (1890-), frwd. by. LC 43-15772. (Illus.). 15 1/2 x 22 1/2 cm. 47p. 1943. Whittlesey House, McGraw-Hill Book Co. **Award: (RCM).**
Chan, Christina, ed. see Wu, Ch'Eng-En Ca.
Chan, Plato, ed. see Wu, Ch'Eng-En Ca.
Chance, E. B.
--Just in Time for the King's Birthday. Meyer, Arline, illus. (Illus.). (gr. k-3). 1972. (ISBN 0-590-09183-2, Schol Pap). Schol Bk Serv.
Chance, Lulu Maude
--Little Folks of Many Lands. LC 4-27806. 112 p. col. front., illus., col. plates. 19 cm. c.1904. Ginn & Company.
Chance, Stephen, pseud., see Turner, Philip.
Chance, Stephen, pseud. (1925-)
--Septimus and the Danedyke Mystery. Turner, Philip. LC 73-4475. 137 p. 21cm. 1973. T. Nelson.
--Septimus & the Minster Ghost Mystery. Turner, Philip. LC 73-20355. 137p. (gr. 8 up). 1974. (ISBN 0-525-66394-0). Lodestar Bks.
Chancellor, C. see Verne, Jules.
Chancellor, Louise Beecher, Mrs., ed.
--Jingleland. LC 7-507. (Illus.). 4 p. l, iii. 17-256p. col. front., illus. 21cm. 21cm. 256p. (Juvenile Tales: Vol. 1). 1906. E. B. Holmes.
Chandler, Anna Curtis
--Dragons on Guard: An Imaginative Interpretation of Old China in Stories of Art and History. Ayer, Margaret (0000-1981), illus. LC 44-3834. xv, 191 p. col. front., illus. 21 cm. 1944. J. B. Lippincott Company.
--Magic Pictures of the Long Ago: Stories of the People of Many Lands. LC 18-21382. xiv, 144 p. incl. front., illus., ports. 20 cm. 1918. H. Holt and Company.
--More Magic Pictures of the Long Ago: Stories of the People of Many Lands. LC 20-427936. xiv, 176 p. incl. front., illus. 20 cm. 1920. H. Holt and Company.
--Pan the Piper: & Other Marvelous Tales. LC 23-16066. xxvii, 234 p. front., illus., plates. 24 cm. 1923. Harper & Brothers.
--A Voyage to Treasure Land. Berard, Hazel de, illus. LC 29-18820. xxii, 220 p., 1 l. incl. illus., plates. front. (port.) plates, port. 21 cm. 1929. Harper & Brothers.
Chandler, Caroline Augusta (1906-1979)
--Dr. Kay Winthrop, Intern. LC 47-1727. ix p., 1 l., 195 p. 21 cm. (Career books). 1947. Dodd, Mead & Company.
--Susie Stuart, Home Front Doctor. LC 43-16941. 6 p. l., 137 p. 21 cm. (Career books). 1943. Dodd, Mead & Company.
--Susie Stuart, M. D. A Story of a Young Woman Doctor. Park, Edwards A., frwd. by. LC 41-178771. x p., 1 l., 282 p. 21 cm. 1941. Dodd, Mead & Company.
Chandler, David, jt. ed. see Chandler, Susan.
Chandler, Edna Walker (1908-1982)
--Almost Brothers. Irvin, Fred M. (1914-), illus. LC 77-165817. (Illus.). line drawings. 128p. (Albert Whitman pilot books). (gr. 3-6). 1971. (ISBN 0-8075-0289-8). A Whitman.
--The Boy Who Made Faces. Faulkner, John Frink, illus. LC 64-16365. (Illus.). 1 v. (unpaged). 21cm. 1964. A. Whitman.
--Buffalo Boy. (American Indian Books). 1957. Benefic Press.
--Cattle Cars. Merryweather, Jack, illus. LC 71-94908. (Illus.). 95 p. 23cm. (Tom Logan series). 1970. Benefic Press.
--Cattle Drive. Merryweather, Jack, illus. LC 66-12808. 64 p. col. illus. 23 cm. (Tom Logan stories). 1966. Benefic Press.
--Charley Brave. Boyt, Kevin, illus. LC 62-11073. 1962. A. Whitman.
--Circus Train. Merryweather, Jack, illus. LC 73-126342. (Illus.). 96 p. 23cm. (Tom Logan series). 1971. Benefic Press.
--Cowboy Andy. Kinstler, Everett Raymond (1926-), illus. LC 59-4447. (Illus.). 65 p. 24cm. 1959. Beginner Books; Distributed by Random House.
--Cowboy Sam. Merryweather, Jack, illus. LC 51-2319. (Illus.). 64 p. 21cm. 1951. Beckley-Cardy Co.
--Cowboy Sam. Merryweather, Jack, illus. (Cowboy Sam Series). 1951. Benefic Press.
--Cowboy Sam and Big Bill. Merryweather, Jack, illus. LC 60-8888. (Illus.). 47 p. 23cm. 1960. Benefic Press.
--Cowboy Sam And Flop. Merryweather, Jack, illus. (Cowboy Sam Series). 1958. Benefic Press.
--Cowboy Sam and Freddy. Merryweather, Jack, illus. LC 51-6067. (Illus.). 67 p. 32cm. 67p. 1951. Beckley-Cardy Co.
--Cowboy Sam And Freddy. Merryweather, Jack, illus. (Cowboy Sam Series). 1951. Benefic Press.
--Cowboy Sam and Miss Lily. Merryweather, Jack, illus. LC 58-14715. 61 p. 23cm. 1958. Benefic Press.
--Cowboy Sam and Porky. LC 52-12398. (Illus.). 64 p. 21cm. 1952. Beckley-Cardy Co.
--Cowboy Sam and Porky. Merryweather, Jack, illus. (Cowboy Sam Series). 1952. Benefic Press.
--Cowboy Sam and Sally. Merryweather, Jack, illus. LC 59-883288. (Illus.). 95 p. 23cm. 1959. Benefic Press.
--Cowboy Sam and Shorty. Merryweather, Jack, illus. LC 53-7175. (Illus.). 67 p. 21cm. 1953. Beckley-Cardy Co.
--Cowboy Sam and Shorty. Merryweather, Jack, illus. (Cowboy Sam Series). 1953. Benefic Press.
--Cowboy Sam and The Airplane. Merryweather, Jack, illus. (Cowboy Sam Series). 1959. Benefic Press.
--Cowboy Sam and the Dandy. Merryweather, Jack, illus. (Cowboy Sam Series). 1958. Benefic Press.
--Cowboy Sam and the Fair. Merryweather, Jack, illus. LC 53-13306. (Illus.). 94 p. 21cm. 1953. Beckley-Cardy.
--Cowboy Sam and the Fair. Merryweather, Jack, illus. (Cowboy Sam Series). 1953. Benefic Press.
--Cowboy Sam and the Indians. Merryweather, Jack, illus. LC 54-2125. (Illus.). 127 p. 21cm. 1954. Beckley-Cardy Co.
--Cowboy Sam and the Indians. Merryweather, Jack, illus. (Cowboy Sam Series). 1954. Benefic Press.
--Cowboy Sam and the Rodeo. Merryweather, Jack, illus. LC 51-13189. (Illus.). 95 p. 21cm. 1951. Beckley-Cardy Co.
--Cowboy Sam and the Rodeo. Merryweather, Jack, illus. (Cowboy Sam Series). 1951. Benefic.
--Cowboy Sam and the Rustlers. LC 52-66730. (Illus.). 127 p. 21cm. 1952. Beckley-Cardy Co.
--Cowboy Sam and the Rustlers. Merryweather, Jack, illus. (Cowboy Sam Series). 1952. Benefic Press.
--Crystal Pie. Ferguson, William, illus. LC 65-16272. 122 p. illus. 21 cm. 1965. Duell, Sloan and Pearce.
--Five Cent, Five Cent (Liberia). Stull, Betty, illus. LC 67-17414. (Illus.). (gr. 1-3). 1967. (ISBN 0-8075-2463-8). A Whitman.
--Gold Nugget. Merryweather, Jack, illus. LC 66-27578. (Illus.). 96 p. 23cm. (Tom Logan series). 1967. Benefic Press.
--Gold Train. Merryweather, Jack, illus. LC 78-94907. (Illus.). 64 p. 23cm. (Tom Logan series). 1969. Benefic Press.
--Indian Paintbrush. Fitzgerrell-Smith, Lee, illus. LC 75-29160. p. cm. (Leader book). 1975. (ISBN 0-8075-3639-3). A. Whitman.
--Little Wolf and the Thunder Stick. Merryweather, Jack, illus. (American Indian Books). 1956. Benefic Press.
--The Missing Mitt. (Ginn Book-Lenght Stories). 1955. Ginn & Co.

--The New Red Jacket. Miller, Robert, illus. LC 62-19568. unpaged. illus. 24cm. 1962. A. Whitman.
--Pony Rider. Merryweather, Jack, illus. LC 66-12807. 48p. col. illus. 23cm. (Tom Logan stories). 1966. Benefic.
--Popcorn Patch. Wiskur, Darrell D., illus. LC 77-79550. (Illus.). 128 p. 21cm. (Albert Whitman pilot books). 1969. A. Whitman.
--Secret Tunnel. Merryweather, Jack, illus. LC 66-24291. 64 p. col. illus. 23 cm. (Tom Logan series). 1967. Benefic Press.
--Stagecoach Driver. Merryweather, Jack, illus. LC 68-6693. (Illus.). 96 p. 23cm. (Tom Logan series). 1968. Benefic Press.
--Taka & His Dog. (Our Native Americans Books). (gr. 1). N.D. Benefic.
--Talking Wire. Merryweather, Jack, illus. LC 68-56124. (Illus.). 48 p. 22cm. (Tom Logan series). 1968. Benefic Press.
--Tony and His Friend Jeff. 1965. Childrens Press, Inc.
--Tony and His Friend Jeff. Chandler, Don, illus. LC 63-7573. unpaged. illus. 25 cm. (Tony Storybooks). 1963. Duell, Sloan and Pearce.
--Tony and the Little Blue Car. 1965. Duell,Sloan and Pearce.
--Tony and the Little Blue Car. 1st ed. Chandler, Don, illus. LC 62-15469. unpaged. illus. 25cm. 1962. Duell, Sloan and Pearce.
--Tony and the Tree House. Chandler, Don, illus. LC 63-7572. unpaged, illus. 25 cm. (tony storybooks. 1963. Duell, Sloan and Pearce.
--Water Crazy. 1st ed. LC 62-8529. 154p. 21cm. 1962. Duell, Sloan and Pearce.
--Who's Boss in Tony's Family. 1st ed. Chandler, Don, illus. LC 62-154709. unpaged. illus. 25cm. 1962. Duell, Sloan and Pearce.
--Will You Carry Me (Liberia). Seltzer, Meyer, illus. LC 65-23881. (Illus.). (gr. 1-3). 1965. (ISBN 0-8075-9102-5). A Whitman.
--With Books on Her Head. 1st ed. Keeping, Charles William James (1924-), illus. LC 67-24426. (Illus.). 154 p. 21cm. 1967. Meredith Press.
--Young Hawk. LC 57-59006. (Illus.). 128 p. 21cm. (American Indians). 1957. Benefic Press.
--Young Hawk (Yokut). (Our Native Americans Books). (gr. 3-5). N.D. Benefic.

Chandler, Izora Cecilia (0000-1906)
--Anthe. (Illus.). N.D. Methodist Bk Concern.
--Elvira Hopkins of Tompkins Corners. 196p. N.D. Wilbur B Ketcham.
--Three of Us: Barney, Cossack, Rex. (Illus.). N.D. Methodist Bk Concern.

Chandler, Jean (1927-)
--Crustace, the Crabbed Crab. Chandler, Jean (1927-), illus. LC 54-10826. 21cm. 32p. 1954. Pageant Press, Inc.
--The Poky Little Puppy & the Patchwork Blanket. Chandler, Jean (1927-), illus. (Illus.). 24p. (ps-1). 1983. (ISBN 0-307-11418-X, Golden Pr). Western Pub.
--The Poky Little Puppy's Counting Book. Chandler, Jean (1927-), illus. LC 79-67593. (Illus.). 14 p. 25cm. (Golden sturdy shape book). c.1980. (ISBN 0-307-12252-2). Golden Press.
--The Poky Little Puppy's Wonderful Winter Day. Chandler, Jean (1927-), illus. (Illus.). 24p. (First Little Golden Bks.). (ps). 1982. (ISBN 0-307-10118-5, Golden Pr). (ISBN 0-307-68118-1). Western Pub.

Chandler, Jennifer Westwood see Westwood, Jennifer.

Chandler, John Greene (1815-1879)
--The Remarkable History of Chicken Little. LC 41-6234. 45, 1 p. front. (port.) illus. (incl. facsims.) plates. 18 1/2 cm. c.1941. Priv. Print. at the College Press.

Chandler, Linda Smith (1929-)
--David Asks, "Why?". Behrens, Paul R., illus. LC 80-70519. (Illus.). 32 p. 24cm. c.1981. (ISBN 0-8054-4266-9). Broadman Press.
--Hello, My Church. Behrens, Paul R, illus. LC 80-118686. (Illus.). 32 p. 24cm. c.1980. (ISBN 0-8054-4259-6). Broadman Press.
--Uncle Ike. LC 80-70520. (gr. 1-6). 1981. (ISBN 0-8054-4264-2). Broadman.

Chandler, Robert (1953-), tr. see Afanasev, Aleksandr Nikolaevich.

Chandler, Robert (1953-), retold by.
--The Magic Ring and Other Russian Folktales. Kiff, Ken, illus. LC 79-670145. (Illus.). 90 p. 21cm. 1979. (ISBN 0-571-11338-9). Faber & Faber.
--The Magic Ring and Other Russian Folktales. Kiff, Ken, illus. LC 82-25153. p. cm. 1983. (ISBN 0-571-13006-2). Faber & Faber.

Chandler, Ruth Forbes (1894-1978)
--The Happy Answer. Troth, Joy, illus. LC 57-5490. 206p. illus. 22cm. 1957. Abelard-Schuman.
--Ladder To The Sky. 1959. (ISBN 0-8382-0420-1, Cadmus Books). E. M. Hale And Company.
--Ladder to the Sky. Johnson, Eugene Harper, illus. LC 59-6512. (Illus.). 189 p. 21cm. 1959. Abelard-Schuman.
--Middle Island Mystery. Kennedy, Richard (1910-), illus. LC 61-8931. 160p. illus: 21cm. 1961. Abelard-Schuman.
--Three Trumpets. Kennedy, Richard (1910-) & Keeping, Charles William James (1924-), illus. LC 62-17042. (Illus.). (gr. 3-6). 1962. Abelard.
--Too Many Promises. Campbell, Ray Scott, illus. LC 56-5908. 216p. illus: 22cm. 1956. Abelard-Schuman.
--Triple Test for Trudy. Christensen, Christina F., illus. LC 64-22346. (Illus.). 160 p. 21cm. 1964. Abelard-Schuman.

Chandler, Susan & Chandler, David, eds.
--Favourite Stories from Cambodia. (Favourite Stories Ser.). 1978. (ISBN 0-686-60357-5). Heinemann Ed.

Chandoha, Walter
--A Baby Bunny for You. Chandoha, Walter, photos by. LC 68-13703. (Illus.). 24p. 24cm. 1968. World Pub. Co.
--A Foal for You. Chandoha, Walter, photos by. LC 67-152167. 1 v. (chiefly illus.) 24cm. 1967. World.
--A Kitten for You. Chandoha, Walter, photos by. LC 67-15217. 1 v. (chiefly illus.) 24cm. 1967. World.
--A Puppy for You. Chandoha, Walter, photos by. LC 67-152181. 1 v. (chiefly illus.) 24cm. 1967. World.

Chandon, G & Peron, Rene
--Stories from the Iliad and Odyssey. Whelpton, Barbara, ed. Whelpton, Barbara, tr. from Fr. LC 65-179950. 190p. illus. (pt. col.) 19cm. (Myths and legends; Holly bk.). 1965, c.1962. World.

Chandon, G & Vergilius Maro, Publius
--Stories from the Aeneid. Whelpton, Barbara, ed. Peron, Rene, illus. Whelpton, Barbara, tr. from Fr. LC 65-24731. (Illus.). 190 p. 19cm. (Myths and legends). 1965, c.1964. World Pub. Co.

Chaneles, Sol, jt. auth. see Watson, Jane Werner.

Chaneles, Sol (1926-)
--Santa Makes a Change. Snyder, Jerome (1916-1976), illus. LC 74-117557. (Illus.). 41 p. 27cm. 1970. Parents' Magazine Press.

Chaney, George Leonard (1836-1922)
--F. Grant & Co. or, Partnerships. 1875. Roberts Bros.
--Tom: A Home Story. (Illus.). 1882. Roberts Brothers.

Chaney, Jill (1932-)
--The Buttercup Field. LC 77-355768. 152 p. 21cm. 1976. (ISBN 0-234-77654-4). Dobson.
--Half a Candle. LC 77-75070. 186 p. 22cm. 1969, c.1968. Crown Publishers.
--Woffle, R. A. Leeming, Katherine, illus. LC 76-361083. (Illus.). 148 p. 21cm. 1976. (ISBN 0-234-77185-2). Dobson.

Chaney, Maryel & Chaney, Ronald
--Timothy Tattercoat. Mackenzie, Garry (1921-), illus. LC 57-12087. 181p. illus. 21cm. 1958. Houghton Mifflin.

Chaney, Ronald, jt. auth. see Chaney, Maryel.

Chang, Fa-Shun
--The Sky River. Wong, Jeanyee (1920-), illus. LC 50-8027. 156 p. illus. 22 cm. 1950. Lothrop, Lee & Shepard.

Chang, Florence C., retold by.
--Believe It or Not: An Anthology of Ancient Tales Retold. Chang, Shou-Jen, illus. LC 80-68258. (Illus.). 80p. (Chinese Can Be Fun Bks.: Level 5). (gr. 10-12). 1980. (ISBN 0-936620-02-1). Ginkgo Hut.

Chang, Isabelle Chin (1924-)
--Chinese Fairy Tales. Erickson, Shirley, illus. (Illus.). 74 p. 29cm. 1965. Barre Publishers.
--Tales from Old China. Chen, Tony (1929-), illus. LC 69-13410. (Illus.). 66 p. 24cm. 1969. Random House.

Chang, Kathleen
--The Iron Moonhunter. Chang, Kathleen, illus. LC 77-73783. (Illus.). 24 p. 25cm. (Fifth world tales). c.1977. (ISBN 0-89239-011-5). Children's Book Press/Imprenta De Libros Infantiles.

Chang Tien-Yi
--The Magic Gourd. Wu Wen-Yuan, illus. Yang, Gladys, tr. from Chinese. (Illus.). 198p. (gr. 6-10). 1979. (ISBN 0-8351-0606-3). China Bks.

Chanler, Julie, Mrs., jt. auth. see Sohrab, Mirza Ahmad.

Channel, A. R., pseud., see Catherall, Arthur.

Channel, A. R., pseud. (1906-)
--Jungle Nurse. Catherall, Arthur. 1st American ed. Marshall, Hugh, illus. LC 60-11181. (Illus.). 190 p. 21cm. 1960. F. Watts.
--Jungle Rescue. Catherall, Arthur. Watkins-Pitchford, Denys James (1905-), illus. LC 68-16348. (Illus.). (gr. 4-9). 1968. (ISBN 0-87599-143-2). S G Phillips.
--Red Ivory. Catherall, Arthur. Watkins-Pitchford, Denys James (1905-), illus. LC 64-14873. 191 p. illus. 21 cm. 1964. Macrae Smith.
--Rogue Elephant. Catherall, Arthur. Watkins-Pitchford, Denys James (1905-), illus. x. 1963. Macrae Smith Co.

Channing, Barbara H.
--Sunny Skies: Adventures in Italy. (Child Life Ser.). N.D. D. Lothrop & Co.

Channing, Blanche Mary (1863-1902)
--The Balaster Boys. Merrill, Frank Thayer (1848-), illus. LC 2-20979. 19 cm. 294p. 1902. W. A. Wilde.
--The Balaster Boys: A Story. (Illus.). 294p. 1910. W. A. Wilde Co.
--Lullaby Castle. LC 4-25403. 18cm. 62p. 1904. Little, Brown & Co.
--Winifred West. Emerson, C. Chase, illus. LC 1-22993. 20cm. 271p. 1901. W. A. Wilde.
--Winifred West: A Story. (Illus.). 371p. 1910. W. A. Wilde Co.
--Zodiac Stories. LC 99-3053. vii, 311 p. front., illus. 20 cm. 1899. E. P. Dutton & Company.

Channing, E. P., Miss
--Adventures of a German Toy. N.D. Colby and Rich.
--Adventures of a German Toy. (Illus.). 1882. Lee & Shepard.
--Aunt Zelpeth's Baby. (By the Author of "The Adventures of a German Toy."). (Illus.). 1882. Lee & Shepard.

Channon, Frank Ernest (1870-1920)
--An American Boy at Henley. Burgess, H., illus. LC 10-268191. vi p., 1 l., 296 p. front. plates. 20 cm. (Henley schoolboys series). 1910. Little, Brown, and Company.
--Henley on the Battle Line. 314p. (Henley Schoolboy Ser.). N.D. Little, Brown.
--Henley's American Captain. Kirkpatrick, William, illus. LC 12-28869. vi, p., 1 l., 318 p. 1 l., front., plates 20 cm. (His The Henley school-boys series). 1912. Little, Brown, and Company.
--Jackson and His Henley Friends. Burgess, H., illus. LC 11-23871. vi. p., 1 l., 299 p. front., plates. 20 cm. (His The Henley schoolboys series). 1911. Little, Brown, and Company.

Chanover, Alice, jt. auth. see Chanover, Hyman.

Chanover, Hyman (1920-) & Chanover, Alice
--Happy Hanukah Everybody. Sendak, Maurice Bernard (1928-), illus. LC 54-33675. (Illus.). (Holiday Series of Picture Storybooks). (gr. k-2). 1954. (ISBN 0-8381-0712-5). United Syn Bk.
--Pesah Is Coming. Kessler, Leonard P. (1921-), illus. LC 77-379754. (Illus.). 28 p. 28cm. c.1956. United Synagogue.
--Pesah Is Here. Kessler, Leonard P. (1921-), illus. LC 77-379755. (Illus.). 28 p. 28cm. c.1956. United Synagogue.

Chanslor, Marjorie Torrey Hood see Torrey, Marjorie, pseud.

Chanslor, Marjorie Torrey Hood (1899-)
--Artie and the Princess. Torrey, Marjorie, pseud. Chanslor, Marjorie Torrey Hood (1899-), illus. Torrey, Marjorie, pseud. LC 45-4373. 107 p. incl. illus., plates (part. col.) 26 cm. 1945. Howell, Soskin.
--Artie and the Princess. Torrey, Marjorie, pseud. Chanslor, Marjorie Torrey Hood (1899-), illus. Torrey, Marjorie, pseud. (gr. 1-4). N.D. Lothrop Bks.
--The Merriweathers. Torrey, Marjorie, pseud. Chanslor, Marjorie Torrey Hood (1899-), illus. Torrey, Marjorie, pseud. LC 49-10427. 254 p. illus. 22 cm. 1949. Viking Press.
--Penny. Torrey, Marjorie, pseud. Chanslor, Marjorie Torrey Hood (1899-), illus. Torrey, Marjorie, pseud. LC 44-7493. 4 p. l., 126 p., 1 l, incl. illus., col. plates. 23 1/2 cm. (gr. 2-5). 1944. Howell, Soskin.
--Three Little Chipmunks. Torrey, Marjorie, pseud. Chanslor, Marjorie Torrey Hood (1899-), illus. Torrey, Marjorie, pseud. LC 47-30617. 40 p. illus. (part col.) 29 cm. 1947. Grosset & Dunlap.

Chanson De Roland see Williams, Jay.

Chant, Joy, pseud., see Rutter, Eileen Joyce.

Chant, Joy, pseud. (1945-)
--The Grey Mane of Morning. Rutter, Eileen Joyce. LC 77-366025. 262 p. 23cm. 1977. (ISBN 0-04-823137-1). Allen & Unwin.
--Red Moon and Black Mountain: The End of the House of Kendreth. Rutter, Eileen Joyce. LC 75-37547. 277 p. 22cm. (gr. 5-6). 1976, c.1970. (ISBN 0-525-38193-7). Dutton.

Chao, Fu-Hsing
--Hunting with Grandad. Yang, Yung-Ching, illus. LC 76-28838. (Illus.). 24 p. 1965. Foreign Languages Press; Distributed by Guozi Shudian (China Publications Centre).

Chapel, Beatrice Shaw
--Peggy the Nomad. Moore, Agnes Kay Randall, illus. LC 35-75406. 159, 1 p. col. front., illus., plates. 20 cm. 1935. The Caxton Printers, Ltd.

Chapin, Anna Alice, jt. auth. see MacDonough, Glen.

Chapin, Anna Alice (1880-1920)
--The Everyday Fairy Book. Smith, Jessie Willcox (1863-1935), illus. LC 15-20146. 6 p. l., 159, 1 p. col. front., col. plates. 30 cm. 1915. Dodd, Mead & Company.
--Kitty Love. LC 12-21325. 6 p. l., 285 p. front., plates. 20 cm. 1912. Dodd, Mead and Company.
--Konigskinder. N.D. Harper & Brothers.
--The Now-a-Days Fairy Book. Smith, Jessie Willcox (1863-1935), illus. LC 11-29360. 32cm. 159p. 1911. Dodd, Mead & Co.
--Rhinegold. N.D. Harper & Brothers.
--Tales from Wagner. N.D. Harper & Brothers.
--The Topsy-Turvy Fairy. Peck, Anne Merriman (1884-), illus. LC 14-185238. 5 p. l., 225 p. col. front., illus., plates (part col.) 24 cm. 1914. Dodd, Mead and Company.
--The True Story of Humpty Dumpty: How He was Rescued by Three Mortal Children in Make Believe Land. Betts, Ethel Franklin, illus. LC 5-34511. 7 p, l. 3-205 col. front 5 col. pl. 24cm. 24cm. 205p. 1905. Dodd, Mead & Co.
--Wonder Tales from Wagner. Wagner, Richard (1813-1883), ed. LC 6-11435. 19cm. 189p. 1898. Harper & Bros.
--Wotan, Siegfried & Brunnhilde. (Illus.). N.D. Harper & Brothers.

Chapin, Cynthia
--Dairyman Don. Rogers, Joe, illus. LC 64-7719. (Illus.). (Career Awareness - Community Helpers Ser.). (gr. k-2). 1964. (ISBN 0-8075-1438-1). A Whitman.
--Healthy Is Happy. Daley, Joann, illus. LC 72-126429. (Illus.). 32 p. 21cm. (Community helpers series). 1971. (ISBN 0-8075-3183-9). A. Whitman.
--News Travels; Local Communications. LC 67-2271. (Illus.). 32 p. 22cm. (Community helpers series). 1967. A. Whitman.
--Squad Car 55. Fleming, Dale, illus. LC 66-16077. (Illus.). unpaged. 22cm. (Community helpers series). N.D. A. Whitman.

Chapin, Cynthia, jt. auth. see Barr, Jene.

Chapin, Earl V
--Heavy Water. Hogner, Nils (1893-1970), illus. LC 54-5288. 192p. illus. 22cm. 1954. Abelard-Schuman.

Chapin, Henry (1893-1983)
--Adventures of Johnny Appleseed. N.D. Grosset & Dunlap.
--The Adventures of Johnny Appleseed. Daugherty, James Henry (1889-1974), illus. 244p. N.D. Coward McCann.
--Tigertail, the Game Chicken. 72p. (gr. 3-6). 1965. (ISBN 0-201-09367-7, Young Scott Bks). A-W.
--Tigertail: the Game Chicken. Martin, David Stone (1913-), illus. LC 65-12579. 1965. W. R. Scott.

Chapin, Henry (1893-1983) & Throckmorton, Peter
--Spiro of the Sponge Fleet. Kumlien, Bertil, illus. LC 64-10168. 1964. Little, Brown.

Chapin, Jo Bruce
--The Silver Bird of the Andes: And Other Stories. Bruce, Ada Bromilow, illus. LC 42-147394. 3 p. l., 9-114 p. incl. front., plates. 24 cm. 1942. B. Humphries, Inc.

Chapin, Sallie F., Mrs.
--Fitz-Hugh St. Clair. The South Carolina Rebel Boy: Or, It is No Crime to be Born a Gentleman. N.D. Claxton, Remsen & Haffelfinger.

Chapin, Wallace T., ed. see Kipling, Joseph Rudyard.

Chaplain, Stuart
--Snookums Sneaks Through. Talarczyk, June, illus. LC 67-19660. (Illus.). 1 v. (unpaged. 29cm. 1967. Denison.

Chaplan, Berenice
--Trainload of Fun. LC 80-2042. (Illus.). 128p. (Activity Bks.). 1981. (BFYR). Doubleday.

Chaplan, Lucille
--Elephant for Rent. 1st ed. Sibley, Don (1922-), illus. LC 59-5296. 164p. illus. 22cm. 1959. Little, Brown.

Chaplin, Alethea
--A Treasury of Old Fairy Tales. 129p. (The Treasury Series for Children). N.D. Thomas Y. Crowell Co.

Chaplin, Fannie P. & Humphrey, Frances A.
--Little Folks of Other Lands. N.D. Lothrop Lee & Shepard Co.

Chaplin, Jane Dunbar, Mrs. (1819-1884)
--Aunt Elsie's Posts. 180p. (Sunday School Bks.). N.D. Hurd & Houghton for American Tract Society.
--Aunt Elsie's Posts. 180p. N.D. Lockwood, Brooks & Co. for American Tract Society.
--Black and White: Or, The Heart and Not the Face. 174p. N.D. Lockwood, Brooks, & Co. for American Tract Society.
--Charley Hope's Testament. N.D. Lothrop Publishing.
--Firelight Stories. 96p. N.D. Hurd & Houghton for American Tract Society.
--Gems of the Bog. 400p. N.D. Hurd & Houghton for American Tract Society.
--Little Happy-Heart. 190p. N.D. Hurd & Houghton for American Tract Society.
--Little Happy-Heart. 190p. N.D. Lockwood, Brooks, & Co. for American Tract Society.
--Little Happy Heart. 190p. (Mother's Pearl Ser.). N.D. Lockwood, Brooks, & Co. for American Tract Society.
--Maple Hill: Aunt Lucy's Stories. 110p. N.D. Hurd & Houghton for American Tract Society.

--The Young Storekeeper: Or, A Business Boy's Pluck. Stratemeyer Syndicate. Repr. of 1908 ed (Pub. by Cupples & Leon Co). (The Allen Chapman Ser.: Vol. 4). Orig. Title: A Business Boy; Or, Winning Success. N.D. Goldsmith Publishing Co.
--The Young Storekeeper: Or, A Business Boy's Pluck. Stratemeyer Syndicate. Nuttall, Charles, illus. Reissue of 1908 ed. (Boys' Pocket Library: No. 9). Orig. Title: A Business Boy; Or, Winning Success. 1917. Cupples & Leon Co.

Chapman, Barbara
--Escape from the Nuisances. Dodge, Suzanne C., illus. LC 46-7877. 165 p. incl. front., illus. 21 cm. 1946. Oxford University Press.

Chapman, Bess G.
--White Kitten and Black Puppy. Kilgore, Al, illus. LC 53-20025. 21cm. 14p. 1953. Pageant Press, Inc.

Chapman, Carol
--Barney Bipple's Magic Dandelions. Kellogg, Steven (1941-), illus. LC 77-5747. p. cm. 1977. (ISBN 0-525-26215-6). Dutton.
--Herbie's Troubles. Oechsli, Kelly (1918-), illus. LC 80-21848. (Illus.). 32 p. c.1981. (ISBN 0-525-31645-0). Dutton.
--Ig Lives in a Cave. Degen, Bruce, illus. LC 78-12831. (Illus.). 56 p. 24cm. (A Fat Cat Book). c.1979. (ISBN 0-525-36305-X). Dutton.
--The Tale of Meshka the Kvetch. Lobel, Arnold Stark (1933-), illus. LC 80-11225. (Illus.). 32 p. c.1980. (ISBN 0-525-40745-6). Dutton.

Chapman, Don
--I'm a Jet. Bull, Graham, illus. LC 63-14668. 1 v. (chiefly illus. (part col.)) 21 x 29 cm. 1963. Parents' Magazine Press.

Chapman, Dorothy M
--ABC: A Baby Puffin Book. LC 44-472017. 32 p. illus (part col.) 11 x 18 cm. (Baby Puffin books. 1). 1943. Penguin Books Limited.
--One, Two, Three,. A Baby Puffin Book. LC 44-47202. 32 p. illus. (part col.) 11 x 18 cm. (Baby Puffin books. 2). 1943. Penguin Books Limited.

Chapman, E. O.
--The Arabian Nights Entertainment. (Illus.). N.D. Donohue, Henneberry & Co.

Chapman, E. O., ed. see Thomas, Vernon.

Chapman, Gaynor (1935-)
--The Luck Child. LC 68-18446. (Illus.). 32p. 27cm. 1968 ("Based on a Story of the Brothers Grimm"). Atheneum.

Chapman, George (1550-1634), tr. see Lamb, Charles.

Chapman, Gordon
--Rex Cole, Junior and the Crystal Clue. Rodgers, Richard H. (1876-1953), illus. LC 31-122457. 2 p. l., 9-209 p. front. 20 cm. c.1931. Barse & Co.
--Rex Cole, Junior and the Grinning Ghost. Foster, John M., illus. LC 31-12244. 208 p. front. 20 cm. c.1931. Barse & Co.

Chapman, Iva
--Twelve Legendary Stories of Texas. Hunter, Warren, illus. LC 41-4024. viii p., 1 l., 79 p. illus. 24 cm. 1940. The Naylor Company.

Chapman, Jean
--Cowboy. (Illus.). 1969. Tri-Ocean Books.
--Haunts & Taunts. (Illus.). 160p. (Teacher Reference Bks.). 1983. (ISBN 0-516-08959-5). Childrens.
--Moon-Eyes. Lacis, Astra, illus. LC 79-22088. (Illus.). 48 p. 29cm. 1980, c.1978. (ISBN 0-07-010648-7). McGraw-Hill.
--Pancakes and Painted Eggs: A Book for Easter and All the Days of the Year. Niland, Kilmeny, illus. 1982. Children's Press.
--The Someday Dog. (Illus.). 72p. 1968. Tri-Ocean Books.
--The Sugar-Plum Christmas Book: A Book For Christmas and All the Days of the Year. Niland, Deborah (1951-), illus. 1982. Children's Press.
--Velvet Paws & Whiskers. Niland, Deborah (1951-), illus. (Illus.). 168p. (Teacher Resource Collections Ser.). 1982. (ISBN 0-516-08953-6). Childrens.
--Wombat. (Illus.). 32p. 1969. Tri-Ocean Books.

Chapman, John Jay (1862-1933)
--Four Plays for Children. LC 8-18062. viii, 156 p. 20 cm. 1908. Moffat. Yard & Company.

Chapman, John Stanton Higham see Chapman, Maristan, pseud.

Chapman, John Stanton Higham see Selkirk, Jane, pseud.

Chapman, Katharine Elise
--A Fairy Night's Dream: Or, The Horn of Oberon. Price, Gwynne, illus. 1901. Laird & Lee.
--Sanna's Prayer. LC 16-23587. 107 p. front., plates. 19 cm. 1916. Christian Alliance Publishing Co.

Chapman, Kim Westsmith
--The Magic Hat. 2d ed. Clark, Kitty Riley, illus. LC 76-20842. (Illus.). 47 p. 26cm. c.1976. (ISBN 0-914996-10-X). Lollipop Power.

Chapman, Laura (1935-)
--A Change of Heart. 1976. (ISBN 0-525-07938-6). Dutton.

Chapman, Lora
--Smoky alias Major. 1963. Exposition Press Inc.

Chapman, Lucy, jt. auth. see Chapman, Wendell.

Chapman, Maristan, pseud., see Chapman, John Stanton Higham.

Chapman, Maristan, pseud. (1891-1972) & Chapman, Mary Ilsley
--Clue of the Faded Dress. Chapman, John Stanton Higham. Daugherty, James Henry (1889-1974), illus. LC 38-22820. (Maristan Chapman is the joint pseudonym of John Stanton Higham Chapman, 1891-1972, and Mary Ilsley Chapman.). xii p., 1 l., 237 p. incl. front., illus. 20 cm. 1938. D. Appleton-Century Company, Incorporated.
--Doubloons. Chapman, John Stanton Higham. Herrman, Carl T., illus. LC 60-11985. (Maristan Chapman is the joint pseudonym of John Stanton Higham Chapman, 1891-1972, and Mary Ilsley Chapman.). 206p. illus. 21cm. (Wonderful world book). 1960. Barnes.
--Eagle Cliff. Chapman, John Stanton Higham. Mckell, James C., illus. LC 34-29552. (Maristan Chapman is the joint pseudonym of John Stanton Higham Chapman,1891-1972, and Mary Ilsley Chapman.). ix, 271, 1 p. incl. front., illus., plates. 20 cm. 1934. D. Appleton-Century Company, Incorported.
--Flood in Glen Hazard. Chapman, John Stanton Higham. McKell, James C., illus. LC 39-449713. (Maristan Chapman is the joint pseudonym of John Stanton Higham Chapman, 1891-1972, and Mary Ilsley Chapman.). ix, 1 p., 2 l., 262, 1 p. incl. front., illus. 20 cm. 1939. D. Appleton-Century Company, Incorporated.
--Girls of Glen Hazard. Chapman, John Stanton Higham. Daugherty, James Henry (1889-1974), illus. LC 37-184423. (Maristan Chapman is the joint pseudonym of John Stanton Higham Chapman, 1891-1972, and Mary Ilsley Chapman.). x p., 2 l., 264 p. incl. front., illus. 20 cm. 1937. D. Appleton-Century Company, Incorporated.
--Glen Hazard Cowboys. Chapman, John Stanton Higham. (Maristan Chapman is the joint pseudonym of John Stanton Higham Chapman, 1891-1972, and Mary Ilsley Chapman). N.D. Grosset & Dunlap.
--Glen Hazard Cowboys. Chapman, John Stanton Higham. McKell, James C., illus. LC 40-471949. (Maristan Chapman is the joint pseudonym of John Stanton Higham Chapman, 1891-1972, and Mary Ilsley Chapman.). x p., 2 l., 260 p. incl. front., illus., plates. 20 cm. 1940. D. Appleton-Century Company, Incorporated.
--Gulf Coast Treasure. Chapman, John Stanton Higham. McKell, James C., illus. LC 41-4376. (Maristan Chapman is the joint pseudonym of John Stanton Higham Chapman, 1891-1972, and Mary Ilsley Chapman.). 5 p. l., 276 p. front., illus. 20 cm. 1941. D. Appleton-Century Company, Incorporated.
--Marsh Island Mystery. Chapman, John Stanton Higham. McKell, James C., illus. LC 36-5252. (Maristan Chapman is the joint pseudonym of John Stanton Higham Chapman, 1891-1972, and Mary Ilsley Chapman). ix p., 2 l., 3-278, 1 p. incl. front., illus., plates. 20 cm. 1936. D. Appleton-Century Company, Incorporated.
--Mill Creek Mystery. Chapman, John Stanton Higham. (Maristan Chapman is the joint pseudonym of John Stanton Higham Chapman, 1891-1972, and Mary Ilsley Chapman.). N.D. Grosset & Dunlap.
--Mill Creek Mystery. Chapman, John Stanton Higham. Shenton, Edward (1895-), illus. LC 40-30534. (Maristan Chapman is the joint pseudonym of John Stanton Higham Chapman, 1891-1972, and Mary Ilsley Chapman.). ix p., 2 l., 233 p. incl. front., illus. 20 cm. 1940. D. Appleton-Century Company, Incorporated.
--Mountain Mystery. Chapman, John Stanton Higham. Shenton, Edward (1895-), illus. LC 41-14549. (Maristan Chapman is the joint pseudonym of John Stanton Higham Chapman, 1891-1972, and Mary Ilsley Chapman.). 6 p. l., 243 p. incl. front., illus., plates. 20 cm. 1941. D. Appleton-Century Company, Incorporated.
--The Mystery Dogs of Glen Hazard. Chapman, John Stanton Higham. Wiese, Kurt (1887-1974), illus. LC 41-47192. (Maristan Chapman is the joint pseudonym of John Stanton Higham Chapman, 1891-1972, and Mary Ilsley Chapman.). 3 p. l., 82 p. incl. front., illus. 21 x 16 cm. (story parade adventure book). c.1941. Grosset & Dunlap.
--The Mystery of Burro Bray Canyon. Chapman, John Stanton Higham. 1st ed. Johnson, Iris Beatty, illus. LC 58-8194. (Maristan Chapman is the joint pseudonym of John Stanton Higham Chapman, 1891-1972, and Mary Ilsley Chapman.). 179p. illus. 22cm. 1958. Winston.
--Mystery of the Broken Key. Chapman, John Stanton Higham. McKell, James C., illus. LC 38-5753. (Maristan Chapman is the joint pseudonym of John Stanton Higham Chapman, 1891-1972, and Mary Ilsley Chapman.). x p., 2 l., 286, 1 p. incl. front., illus., plates. 20 cm. 1938. D. Appleton-Century Company, Incorporated.
--Mystery of the Missing Car. Chapman, John Stanton Higham. Caddy, Alice, pseud. (1896-1977), illus. Burman, Alice Caddy. LC 39-20773. (Maristan Chapman is the joint pseudonym of John Stanton Higham Chapman, 1891-1972, and Mary Ilsley Chapman). 7 p. l., 236 p. incl. front., plates. 20 cm. 1939. D. Appleton-Century Company, Incorporated.
--Mystery on the Mississippi. Chapman, John Stanton Higham. McKell, James C., illus. LC 42-24490. (Maristan Chapman is the joint pseudonym of John Stanton Higham Chapman, 1891-1972, and Mary Ilsley Chapman.). 6 p. l., 270 p. front., illus. 20 cm. 1942. D. Appleton-Century Company, Incorporated.
--Rogues on Red Hill. Chapman, John Stanton Higham. McKell, James C., illus. LC 37-582739. (Maristan Chapman is the joint pseudonym of John Stanton Higham Chapman, 1891-1972, and Mary Ilsley Chapman.). 6 p. l., 241, 1 p. front., illus. 20 cm. 1937. D. Appleton-Century Company, Incorporated.
--Secret of Wild Cat Cave. Chapman, John Stanton Higham. McKell, James C., illus. LC 44-3164. (Maristan Chapman is the joint pseudonym of John Stanton Higham Chapman, 1891-1972, and Mary Ilsley Chapman.). 6 p. l., 228 p. front., illus. 19 1/2 cm. 1944. D. Appleton-Century Company, Incorporated.
--The Timber Trail. Chapman, John Stanton Higham. McKell, James C., illus. LC 33-215180. (Maristan Chapman is the joint pseudonym of John Stanton Higham Chapman, 1891-1972, and Mary Ilsley Chapman.). vii p., 1 l., 279, 1 p. front., illus. 20 cm. 1933. D. Appleton-Century Company, Incorporated.
--Trail Beyond the Rockies. Chapman, John Stanton Higham. Moran, Constance Oehler (1898-), illus. LC 43-24674. (Maristan Chapman is the joint pseudonym of John Stanton Higham Chapman, 1891-1972, and Mary Ilsley Chapman.). xi, 282 p. incl. front., illus. 19 1/2 cm. 1943. D. Appleton-Century Company, Incorporated.
--The Treasure Hunters. Chapman, John Stanton Higham. Stevens, Mary E. (1920-1966), illus. LC 45-957374. (Maristan Chapman is the joint pseudonym of John Stanton Higham Chapman, 1891-1972, and Mary Ilsley Chapman.). xi p., 1 l., 175, 1 p. front., plates. 19 cm. 1945. D. Appleton-Century Company, Inc.
--Wild Cat Ridge. Chapman, John Stanton Higham. McKell, James C., illus. LC 32-20867. (Maristan Chapman is the joint pseudonym of John Stanton Higham Chapman, 1891-1972, and Mary Ilsley Chapman.). 5 p. l., 232, 1 p. incl. illus., plates. front. 20 cm. 1932. D. Appleton and Company.

Chapman, Mary Ilsley, jt. auth. see Chapman, Maristan.

Chapman, Mary Ilsley, jt. auth. see Selkirk, Jane.

Chapman, Noralee
--The Story of Barbara. Hull, Helen Schuyler, illus. LC 63-8160. (Illus.). 23 p. 20cm. 1963. John Knox Press.

Chapman, O. E., ed. see Defoe, Daniel.

Chapman, Susan
--The Get Along Gang & the Crybaby. Baker, Darrell, illus. (Illus.). 32p. (Orig.). (The Get Along Gang Ser.). (ps-2). 1984. (ISBN 0-590-33278-3). Scholastic Inc.

Chapman, Wendell & Chapman, Lucy
--Beaver Pioneers. N.D. Charles Scribner's Sons.
--Little Wolf. Chapman, Wendell & Chapman, Lucy, photos by (gr. 3-6). 1969. Review & Herald.
--The Little Wolf: A Story of the Coyote of Our Rocky Mountains. LC 36-239095. xii p., 1 l., 140 p. front., plates. 21 cm. 1936. C. Scribner's Sons.

Chappel, Bernice Marie (1910-)
--Happy Hopper and His Friends. Smith, Doris Millar, illus. LC 54-9556. (Illus.). 15 x 22cm. 39p. 1954. Comet Press.
--Happy Hopper Tales. Smith, Doris Millar, illus. LC 55-8506. 38p. illus. 15 x 23cm. 1955. Comet Press Books.
--Harvey Hopper. Brophy, Ruth, illus. (Illus.). (Nature & Science Bk.). (gr. k-6). N.D. Denison.
--Rudolph the Rooster. Whitson, Jack, illus. LC 79-86157. (Illus.). 40 p. 28cm. 1969. Bethany Press.

Chappel, Warren, jt. auth. see Goodwin, John Lonnen.

Chappel, Warren, ed. see Cervantes Saavedra, Miguel de.

Chappell, Annette Jo, jt. auth. see Dickmeyer, Lowell A.

Chappell, Jennie
--The Moonstone Ring. 118p. 1910. A. W. Wilde.
--My Friend Kathleen. (Illus.). (Scribner-Blackie Series of books for young people). N.D. Charles Scribner's Sons.

Chappell, Warren (1904-), adapted by see Perrault, Charles.

Chappell, Warren (1904-)
--Coppelia: The Girl with Enamel Eyes. Chappell, Warren (1904-), illus. LC 65-21567. (Music by Leo Delibes). (Illus.). (gr. 3 up). 1965. (ISBN 0-394-81061-9). (ISBN 0-394-91061-3). Knopf.
--Hansel & Gretel. Chappell, Warren (1904-), illus. LC 44-9580. (Original Authors:Jakob Ludwig Karl Grimm;1785-1863, and Wilhelm Karl Grimm;1786-1859.). (Illus.). 32p. (gr. 3-5). 1944. (ISBN 0-394-91221-7). Knopf.
--They Say Stories. Chappell, Warren (1904-), illus. LC 59-10027. 79p. illus. 22cm. (gr. 4up). 1960. Knopf.

Chappell, Warren (1904-) & Tchaikovsky, Peter Ilyich (1840-1893)
--The Nutcracker. Chappell, Warren (1904-), illus. LC 58-11075. (Based on the Alexandre Dumas Pere Version of the Story by Ernst Theodor Amadeus Hoffmann). 1 v. (unpaged) illus. (part col.) music. 20 x 26cm. c.1958. A. A. Knopf.
--The Nutcracker: Based on the Alexandre Dumas pere Version of the Story by Ernst Theodor Amadeus Hoffmann. Chappell, Warren (1904-), illus. LC 80-15576. (Illus.). 40p (Pub. by Knopf). (gr. k-6). 1980. (ISBN 0-8052-0660-4). Schocken.
--The Sleeping Beauty. Chappell, Warren (1904-), illus. LC 81-40405. (Original Author:Charles Perrault,1628-1703.). p. cm. 1981, c.1961. (ISBN 0-8052-0683-3). Knopf.

Chapple, Jenny, tr. see Blyton, Enid Mary.

Chard, Maire Brigid (1934-)
--Hidden Journey. (Illus.). 1976. State Mutual Bk.

Chardiet, Bernice Knoll (1927-)
--C is for Circus. Turkle, Brinton Cassaday (1915-), illus. LC 79-126121. 1 v. (unpaged) illus. 24 x 29cm. 1971. (ISBN 0-8027-6082-1). (ISBN 0-8027-6083-X). Walker.
--Monkeys & the Water Monster. Bennett, Rainey (1907-), illus. (Illus.). (gr. k-3). 1976. (ISBN 0-590-09865-9, Schol Trade Pap). Schol Bk Serv.

Chardiet, Bernice Knoll (1927-), retold by.
--Juan Bobo and the Pig: A Puerto Rican Folktale. Meryman, Hope, illus. LC 73-81783. (Illus.). 26 p. 1973. (ISBN 0-8027-6155-0). (ISBN 0-8027-6156-9). Walker.

Chardon, Jeanne
--The Golden Chick and the Magic Frying Pan. Brock, Emma Lillian (1886-1974), illus. Tubby, Ruth Peckham (1906-) & Chardon, Jeanne, trs. LC 35-253843. 148 p. incl. col. front., illus., col. plates. 24 cm. 1935. A. Whitman & Co.

Chardon, Jeanne, tr. see Chardon, Jeanne.

Charette, Beverly R.
--Deluxe Story of Easter for Children. Gnat, Erv, illus. (Illus.). 48p. (gr. k-6). 1985. (ISBN 0-8249-8076-X). Ideals.

Charette, Beverly R., ed.
--Christian Nursery Rhymes. (Illus.). (ps-3). 1982. (ISBN 0-516-09225-1). Childrens.

Charette, Beverly R. & Macari, Mario, Jr.
--Star Rangers Meet the Solar Robot. LC 84-50624. 80p. (Fantasy Forest Adventures Ser.). (gr. 2-5). 1984. (ISBN 0-394-72783-5, Pub. by BYR). Random.

Charims, pseud., see Smith, Charlotte Helen.

Charitas, M., Sr.
--The Man Who Built the Secret Door. N.D. Bruce Publication Co.

Chariton, Ella Mae
--A Gift of Turtles. Wilde, Irma, illus. LC 59-6047. 127p. illus. 21cm. 1959. Friendship Press.

Charity
--Can She Forgive. N.D. E. & J. B. Young & Co.

Charlemagne
--The Merry Pilgrimage. Porter, J. Erwin, illus. Sherwood, Merriam (1892-), tr. LC 78-63455. (Illus.). ix, 122 p. 19cm. 1980. (ISBN 0-404-16377-7). AMS Press.
--The Merry Pilgrimage: How Charlemagne Went on a Pilgrimage to Jerusalem in Order to See Whether Hugo of Constantinople Was a Handsomer Man Than He. Porter, J. Erwin, illus. Sherwood, Merriam (1892-), tr. LC 27-214986. ix p., 1 l., 122 p. incl. illus., double plates. col. front. 17 cm. (The Little library). 1927. The Macmillan Company.

Charles, Andrew, Mrs.
--Schonberg-Cotta Family. (Illus.). (The Wellesley Series for Girls). N.D. A. L. Burt's Pubs.
--Schonberg-Cotta Family, 1 of 32 vols, Vol. 21. (Illus.). (Famous Books for Girls). N.D. H. M. Caldwell Co.

Charles, Carole (1943-)
--The Boston Tea Party: A Narrative Poem. Seible, Bob, illus. LC 75-33156. (Illus.). 31 p. 22cm. (Stories of the Revolution). (gr. 2-6). 1976, c.1975. (ISBN 0-913778-18-4). Child's World.
--General George at Yorktown. Seible, Bob, illus. LC 75-33158. (Illus.). (Stories of the Revolution Ser.). (gr. 2-6). 1975. (ISBN 0-913778-23-0). Childs World.
--John Paul Jones: Victory at Sea : a Narrative Poem. Seible, Bob, illus. LC 75-33157. (Illus.). 32 p. 22cm. (Stories of the Revolution). (gr. 2-6). 1976. (ISBN 0-913778-21-4, Distributed by Childrens Press). Child's World.
--Martha Helps the Rebel: A Narrative Poem. Seible, Bob, illus. LC 75-33126. (Illus.). 32 p. 22cm. (Stories of the Revolution). (gr. 2-6). c.1975. (ISBN 0-913778-22-2). Child's World.
--Paul Revere and the Minutemen: A Narrative Poem. Sieble, Bob, illus. LC 75-33204. p. cm. (Stories of the Revolutionary War). (gr. 2-6). c.1975. (ISBN 0-913778-19-2, Distributed by Childrens Press). The Child's World.
--Survival at Valley Forge: A Narrative Poem. Sieble, Bob, illus. LC 75-33159. p. cm. (Stories of the Revolutionary War). (gr. 2-6). c.1975. (ISBN 0-913778-20-6, Distributed by Childrens Press). Child's World.

Charles, Diana, jt. auth. see Yates, Elizabeth.

Charles, Donald, pseud., see Meighan, Donald Charles.

Charles, Donald, pseud. (1929-)
--Busy Beaver's Day. Meighan, Donald Charles. Charles, Donald, pseud. (1929-), illus. Meighan, Donald Charles. LC 72-1467. (Illus.). 31 p. 25cm. 1972. (ISBN 0-516-03420-0). Childrens Press.
--Calico Cat at School. Meighan, Donald Charles. Charles, Donald, pseud. (1929-), illus. Meighan, Donald Charles. LC 81-6096. p. cm. 1981. (ISBN 0-516-03445-6). (ISBN 0-516-43445-4). Childrens Press.
--Calico Cat at the Zoo. Meighan, Donald Charles. Charles, Donald, pseud. (1929-), illus. Meighan, Donald Charles. LC 80-25380. (Illus.). 32p. (Calico Cat Storybooks). (gr. 3). 1981. (ISBN 0-516-03443-X). (ISBN 0-516-43443-8). Childrens.
--Calico Cat Looks Around. Meighan, Donald Charles. Charles, Donald, pseud. (1929-), illus. Meighan, Donald Charles. LC 75-12947. (Illus.). 31 p. 25cm. 1975. (ISBN 0-516-03436-7). Childrens Press.
--Calico Cat Meets Bookworm. Meighan, Donald Charles. Charles, Donald, pseud. (1929-), illus. Meighan, Donald Charles. LC 78-6557. (Illus.). 32p. (Calico Cat Story Bks.). (gr. 3). 1978. (ISBN 0-516-03441-3). (ISBN 0-516-43441-1). Childrens.
--Calico Cat's Exercise Book. Meighan, Donald Charles. Charles, Donald, pseud. (1929-), illus. Meighan, Donald Charles. LC 82-9640. (Illus.). 32 p. 25cm. c.1982. (ISBN 0-516-03457-X). (ISBN 0-516-43457-8). Childrens Press.
--Calico Cat's Rainbow. Meighan, Donald Charles. Charles, Donald, pseud. (1929-), illus. Meighan, Donald Charles. LC 75-12948. (Illus.). 31 p. 25cm. 1975. (ISBN 0-516-03437-5). Childrens Press.
--Calico Cat's Year. Meighan, Donald Charles. Charles, Donald, pseud. (1929-), illus. Meighan, Donald Charles. LC 83-23160. (Illus.). 32p. (Calico Cat Ser.). (ps-3). 1984. (ISBN 0-516-03461-8). (ISBN 0-516-43461-6). Childrens.
--Count on Calico Cat. Meighan, Donald Charles. Charles, Donald, pseud. (1929-), illus. Meighan, Donald Charles. LC 74-8007. (Illus.). 32p. (Calico Cat Story Bks.). (ps-3). 1974. (ISBN 0-516-03435-9). (ISBN 0-516-43435-7). Childrens.
--Fat, Fat Calico Cat. Meighan, Donald Charles. Charles, Donald, pseud. (1929-), illus. Meighan, Donald Charles. LC 77-7154. p. cm. 1977. (ISBN 0-516-03456-1). Childrens Press.
--The Jolly Pancake. Meighan, Donald Charles. Charles, Donald, pseud. (1929-), illus. Meighan, Donald Charles. LC 79-13304. p. cm. 1979. (ISBN 0-516-03513-4). Childrens Press.
--Letters from Calico Cat. Meighan, Donald Charles. Charles, Donald, pseud. (1929-), illus. Meighan, Donald Charles. LC 74-8181. (Illus.). 32p. (Calico Cat Story Bks.). (ps-3). 1974. (ISBN 0-516-03519-3). (ISBN 0-516-43519-1). Childrens.
--Shaggy Dog's Animal Alphabet. Meighan, Donald Charles. Charles, Donald, pseud. (1929-), illus. Meighan, Donald Charles. LC 78-12904. p. cm. 1978. Childrens Press.
--Shaggy Dog's Christmas. Meighan, Charles Donald. Charles, Donald, pseud. (1929-), illus. Meighan, Charles Donald. LC 85-14972. p. cm. c.1985. (ISBN 0-516-03675-0). Childrens Press.
--Shaggy Dog's Halloween. Meighan, Donald Charles. Charles, Donald, pseud. (1929-), illus. Meighan, Donald Charles. LC 84-5901. (Illus.). 31 p. 25cm. c.1984. (ISBN 0-516-03575-4). (ISBN 0-516-43575-2). Childrens Press.
--Shaggy Dog's Tall Tale. Meighan, Donald Charles. Charles, Donald, pseud. (1929-), illus. Meighan, Donald Charles. LC 79-26493. p. cm. 1980. (ISBN 0-516-03616-5). Childrens Press.

Charles, Freda Shapiro
--The Mystery of Missing Chalah. Goldstein, Lil, illus. 40p. (ps). 1981. (ISBN 0-8246-0264-1). Jonathan David.
--The Mystery of the Missing Chalah. Goldstein, Lil, illus. LC 59-149110. unpaged. illus. 29cm. (ps-4). c.1959. J. David.

Charles, Frederick H.
--Young Sir Richard. (Illus.). 337p. N.D. Ira Bradley & Co.'s.

Charles, Louis, pseud., see Stratemeyer, Louis Charles.

Charles, Louis, pseud. & Stratemeyer, Edward L. (1862-1930)
--Fortune Hunters of the Philippines: Or, The Treasure of the Burning Mountain. Stratemeyer, Louis Charles. (Wide Awake Boys Ser.). N.D. A. L. Burt Company.
--Fortune Hunters of the Philippines: Or, the Treasure of the Burning Mountain. Stratemeyer, Louis Charles. N.D. Chatterton-Peck.
--Fortune Hunters of the Philippines: Or, The Treasure of the Burning Mountain. Stratemeyer, Louis Charles. LC 3431. iii, 214 p. front., plates. 19 cm. 1900. The Mershon Company.
--The Land of Fire: Or, Adventures in Underground Africa. Stratemeyer, Louis Charles. (Wide Awake Boys Ser.). N.D. A. L. Burt.
--The Land of Fire: Or, Adventures in Underground Africa. Stratemeyer, Louis Charles. N.D. Chatterton-Peck.
--The Land of Fire: Or, Adventures in Underground Africa. Stratemeyer, Louis Charles. 1900. The Mershon Co.

Charles, Milton, photos by.
--End of the Game. LC 77-172982. (Illus.). 92 p. 21cm. 1971. World Pub.

Charles, Nicholas, see Kuskin, Karla Seidman.

Charles, Nicholas, pseud. (1932-)
--How Do You Get from Here to There?. (1932-), illus. Kuskin, Karla Seidman. LC 62-173321. unpaged. illus. 17 x 24cm. 1962. Macmillan.
--Jane Anne June Spoon and Her Very Adventurous Search for the Moon. (1932-), illus. Kuskin, Karla Seidman. LC 66-10789. 1v. (unpaged) illus. (pt. col.) 26cm. c.1966. Norton.

Charles, Norma M.
--See You Later, Alligator. Moran, Carol, illus. (Illus.). (gr. k-3). 1975. (ISBN 0-590-10167-6, Starline). Schol Bk Serv.

Charles, Robert Henry
--A Roundabout Turn. Brooke, Leonard Leslie (1862-1940), illus. LC 30-26974. 20cm. 48p. 1930. Frederick Warne & Co.

Charles Prince of Wales (1948-)
--The Old Man of Lochnagar. Casson, Hugh Maxwell, Sir (1910-), illus. LC 80-24716. (Illus.). 46 p. 1980. (ISBN 0-374-35613-0). Farrar, Straus & Giroux.

Charlesworth, Maria Louisa (1819-1880)
--The Broken Looking Glass. (Illus.). 313p. N.D. Merrill.
--Dorothy Cope: The Old Looking Glass & Broken Looking Glass. (Illus.). 582p. N.D. Merrill.
--Ministering Children, 1 of 50 vols. 573p. (Library of Best Authors). 1905. American Tract Society.
--Ministering Children. rev., and slightly abridged, from the 29th London ed. LC 42-43535. 542 p. incl. front. plates. 17 1/2 cm. N.D. Carlton & Porter, Sunday-School Union.
--Ministering Children. N.D. Methodist Book Concern.
--Ministering Children. 542p. 1873. Nelson & Phillips.
--Ministering Children. Collins, Sarah H., pref. by. LC 75-32166. (Illus.). viii, iv, 426 p., 20 leaves of plates. 19cm. (Classics of children's literature, 1621-1932). 1977. (ISBN 0-8240-2279-3). Garland Pub.
--Ministering Children: A Tale Dedicated to Childhood. LC 31-19491. viii, 408 p. front., 1 illus., plates. 20 cm. 1874. R. Carter and Brothers.
--The Old Looking Glass. (Illus.). 269p. N.D. Merrill.
--Oliver of the Mill. 1877. Robert Carter & Bros.
--Ruth and Little Jane. (Illus.). 206p. N.D. American Tract Society.
--Sequel to Ministering Children, 1 of 50 vols. 536p. (Library of Best Authors). 1905. American Tract Society.

Charlesworth, Maud Ballington, Mrs.
--Herbert: or, True Charity. 261p. (Ministering Children Library). N.D. Lockwood, Brooks, & Co. for American Tract Society.
--Herbert: True Charity. 261p. N.D. Hurd & Houghton for American Tract Society.
--Patience: Or,Sunshine of the Heart. 166p. (Ministering Children Library). N.D. Lockwood, Brooks, & Co. for American Tract Society.
--Rose: Little Comforter. 206p. N.D. Hurd & Houghton for American Tract Society.
--Rose: Or,the Little Comforter. 206p. (Ministering Children Library). N.D. Lockwood, Brooks, & Co. for American Tract Society.
--Ruth and Jane. 117p. N.D. Hurd & Houghton for American Tract Society.
--Ruth and Jane. 117p. (Ministering Children Library). N.D. Lockwood, Brooks, & Co. for American Tract Society.

Charlie D., jt. auth. see Mrs E.

Charlier, Jean-Michel, jt. auth. see Giruad, Jean.

Charlieu, Hector De (1838-)
--The Little Florentine. Goss, John, illus. Twitchell, Hannah, Mrs. (1851-), tr. LC 14-12485. 4 p. l., 129 p. front., plates. 20 cm. 1914. The Page Company.

Charlip, Remy (1929-)
--Arm in Arm. Charlip, Remy (1929-), illus. LC 80-18081. p. cm. 1980, c.1969. (ISBN 0-590-07758-9). Four Winds Press.
--Arm in Arm: A Collection of Connections, Endless Tales, Reiterations, and Other Echolalia. Charlip, Remy (1929-), illus. LC 69-12610. (Illus.). 39 p. 27cm. (ps up). 1969. Parents' Magazine Press. **Award: (NYT).**
--Dress Up and Let's Have a Party. Charlip, Remy (1929-), illus. LC 56-5424. unpaged. illus. 15 x 22cm. (Young Scott books). c.1956. W. R. Scott.
--Fortunately. Charlip, Remy (1929-), illus. LC 80-36956. p. cm. 1980, c.1964. (ISBN 0-590-07762-7). Four Winds Press.
--Fortunately. Charlip, Remy (1929-), illus. LC 85-4493. p. cm. 1985, c.1975. (ISBN 0-02-718100-6). Four Winds Press.
--Fortunately. Charlip, Remy (1929-), illus. LC 64-10364. (Illus.). 1 v. (unpaged. 26cm. 1964. Parents' Magazine Press.
--It Looks Like Snow. Charlip, Remy (1929-), illus. LC 81-20106. 24p. 1982. (ISBN 0-688-01542-5). Greenwillow.
--It Looks Like Snow. Charlip, Remy (1929-), illus. 1982. (ISBN 0-688-01542-5). Morrow.
--Where is Everybody. Charlip, Remy (1929-), illus. 48p. 1957. (ISBN 0-201-09403-7). Addison-Wesley.
--Where is Everybody?. Charlip, Remy (1929-), illus. N.D. E. M. Hale & Co.
--Where Is Everybody?. Charlip, Remy (1929-), illus. (Illus.). (gr. k-3). 1970 (StarLine). Schol Bk Serv.

Charlip, Remy (1929-) & Joyner, Jerry (1938-)
--Thirteen. Charlip, Remy (1929-) & Joyner, Jerry (1938-), illus. LC 75-8875. (Illus.). 31 p. 26cm. 1975. (ISBN 0-8193-0807-2). (ISBN 0-8193-0808-0). Parents' Magazine Press. **Awards: (NYT); (BGH); (ALA).**

Charlip, Remy (1929-) & Martin, Judith
--Jumping Beans. Charlip, Remy (1929-), illus. (Illus.). (gr. k-3). 1963. (ISBN 0-394-91294-2). Knopf.

Charlip, Remy (1929-) & Supree, Burton (1941-)
--Harlequin and the Gift of Many Colors. Charlip, Remy (1929-), illus. LC 76-136999. (Illus.). 42 p. 26cm. 1973. (ISBN 0-8193-0494-8). (ISBN 0-8193-0495-6). Parents' Magazine Press. **Award: (ALA).**
--Harlequin and the Gift of Many Colors. Charlip, Remy (1929-), illus. 1973. Scholastic.
--Mother, Mother, I Feel Sick, Send for the Doctor Quick, Quick, Quick. Charlip, Remy (1929-), illus. LC 80-17092. p. cm. 1980, c.1966. (ISBN 0-590-07772-4). Four Winds Press.
--Mother, Mother, I Feel Sick, Send for the Doctor Quick, Quick, Quick: A Picture Book and Shadow Play. Charlip, Remy (1929-), illus. LC 66-13331. (Illus.). 1 v. (unpaged. 1966. Parents' Magazine Press.

Charlot, Martin
--Once Upon a Fishhook. Charlot, Martin, illus. Charlot, Martin, tr. LC 74-152567. (Illus.). (gr. 1-7). 1972. (ISBN 0-89610-019-7). Island Her.
--Sunnyside Up. Charlot, Martin, illus. LC 73-173473. (Illus.). (gr. 1-7). 1972. (ISBN 0-89610-020-0). Island Her.
--Sunnyside Up. new ed. Charlot, Martin, illus. LC 73-173473. (Illus.). 56p. (Island Heritage Bk). (gr. 3-7). 1973. (ISBN 0-8348-3000-0). Weatherhill.

Charlton, Elizabeth (1937-)
--Jeremy and the Ghost. Reisman, Celia, illus. LC 78-72120. (Illus.). 32 p. 1979. (ISBN 0-89799-118-4). (ISBN 0-89799-019-6). Dandelion Press.
--Terrible Tyrannosaurus. 1st ed. Glass, Andrew, illus. LC 80-26318. (Illus.). 32 p. 24cm. c.1981. (ISBN 0-525-66724-5). Elsevier/Nelson Books.

Charlton, Ella Mae
--Bart's Wide World. Depper, Hertha, illus. LC 65-10691. (Illus.). 47p. (Primary Storybook Series). (gr. 1-3). 1965. (ISBN 0-8054-4215-4). Broadman.
--A Gift of Turtles. Wilde, Irma, illus. LC 59-6017. 128p. 1959. Friendship Press.
--Landi of Terrebonne Bayou. LC 60-519014. 170p. illus. 21cm. 1960. Broadman Press.
--Penny in Hawaii. Spilka, Arnold (1917-), illus. LC 64-10148. (gr. 4-7). 1964. (ISBN 0-687-30615-9). Abingdon.

Charlton, Gertrude, illus.
--Excellent Jane and Other Stories. N.D. E. P. Dutton & Co.

Charlton, John Edward (1878-)
--Just One More Story: Six-Minute Talks for Boys and Girls. LC 36-20234. 128 p. 20 cm. c.1936. Fleming H. Revell Company.
--More Six-Minute Stories. LC 34-122692. 154 p. 20 cm. c.1934. Fleming H. Revell Company.
--Six-Minute Story Talks for Children. N.D. Fleming H. Revell Co.

Charlton, Lionel Evelyn Oswald (1879-)
--Near East Adventure. Ratcliff, Ernest, illus. LC 36-14278. vii, 247 p. col. front., illus. 21 cm. (Half-title: The Nelsonian library, edited by John Hampden. no. 27). 1934. T. Nelson and Sons Ltd.

Charlton, Moyra
--Pendellion. N.D. British Book Centre.
--Tally Ho: The Story of an Irish Hunter. Edwards, Lionel Dalhousie Robertson (1878-), illus. LC 31-1523. xi, 82, 2 p. col. front., plates. 21 cm. 1930. G. P. Putnam's Sons.
--Three White Stockings. Holiday, Gilbert, illus. LC 36-18158. xi, 118 p. col. front., plates. 21 cm. 1934. Putnam.

Charlton-Perrin, Geoffrey
--Little Lord Blink and His Ice Cream Castle. Lemoine, Georges, illus. (Illus.). 1971. E.P. Dutton & Co.
--Little Lord Blink & His Ice Cream Castle. Lemoine, Georges, illus. Lubalin, Herb, designed by. LC 74-122618. (Illus.). 32 p. 29cm. 1971. (ISBN 0-8415-2022-4). McCall Pub. Co.

Charlton, Warwick
--The Second Mayflower Adventure. 1957. Little, Brown and Company.

Charmatz, Bill (1925-)
--The Cat's Whiskers. Charmatz, Bill (1925-), illus. LC 75-78085. (Illus.). 32 p. 26cm. 1969. Macmillan.
--The Little Duster. Charmatz, Bill (1925-), illus. LC 67-20683. (Illus.). 32p. 26cm. 1967. Macmillan.
--The Troy St. Bus. Charmatz, Bill (1925-), illus. LC 76-45431. (Illus.). 32 p. c.1977. (ISBN 0-02-718160-X). Macmillan.

Charnas, Suzy McKee (1939-)
--The Bronze King. LC 85-8553. 196 p. 22cm. 1985. (ISBN 0-395-38394-3). Houghton Mifflin.

Charnier, V., jt. auth. see Denis, F.

Charnier, V., jt. auth. see Denis, L.

Charnin, Martin Jay (1934-) & Draper, Kate
--The Giraffe Who Sounded Like Ol' Blue Eyes: A Likely Story. Draper, Kate, illus. LC 76-15210. (Illus.). 48 p. c.1976. (ISBN 0-8415-0443-1). Saturday Review Press.

Charnley, Betty Jo, jt. auth. see Charnley, Nathaniel.

Charnley, Nathaniel & Charnley, Betty Jo
--Martha Ann and the Mother Store. 1st ed. Snyder, Jerome (1916-1976), illus. LC 73-5237. (Illus.). 32 p. 26cm. 1973. (ISBN 0-15-252150-X). Harcourt Brace Jovanovich.

Charnock, Joan Thomson (1903-)
--The Russian Twins. Grant, Elisabeth, illus. LC 65-120455. 155p. illus. 21cm. (Twins Ser.). (gr. 6-9). 1965, c.1963. Dufour.

Charnock, Richard W.
--Cubby Ball's Narrow Escapes. Janecke, Sue, illus. (Illus.). (ps-3). N.D. Vantage.

Charosh, Mannis (1906-)
--Straight Lines, Parallel Lines, Perpendicular Lines. Arno, Enrico (1913-1981), illus. LC 76-106569. (Illus.). 33 p. (Young math books). 1970. Crowell.

Charskaia, Lidiia Alekseevna
--Fledglings: As Told by Lida, Chum of Little Princess Nina. Snell, C. C., illus. Shaw, Hana Muskova, tr. LC 26-9571. v, 277 p. col. front. 20 cm. c.1926. H. Holt and Company.
--Little Princess Nina: The Story of a Russian Girl. Shaw, Hana Muskova, tr. LC 24-26842. v p., 1 l., 288 p. col. front. 20 cm. 1924. H. Holt and Company.
--The Little Siberian. Shaw, Hana Muskova, tr. LC 29-18546. viii, 230 p. 20 cm. c.1929. H. Holt and Company.
--The Tartar Princess: A Sequel to "Little Princess Nina" and "Fledglings". Shaw, Hana Muskova, tr. LC 27-173569. vii, 247 p. col. front. 20 cm. c.1927. H. Holt and Company.

Charteris, Leslie (1907-)
--The Saint & the Fiction Makers (Pub. by Doubleday). (gr. 8 up). 1972. Curtis.
--The Saint in New York. 145p. (gr. 8-12). 1972. Curtis.
--The Saint on T.V (Pub. by Doubleday). (gr. 9 up). 1972. Curtis.
--The Saint Overboard (Pub. by Doubleday). (gr. 7 up). 1972. Curtis.
Charters, Janet (1938-) & Foreman, Michael (1938-)
--The General. LC 61-65486. unpaged. illus. 28cm. 1961. Dutton.
Chartier, Normand, jt. auth. see Foote, Timothy Gilson.
Chartier, Normand, jt. auth. see Mathews, Geda Bradley.
Chartier, Normand, jt. auth. see Van Woerkom, Dorothy O' Brien.
Chartier, Normand (1945-)
--Who Am I?. Chartier, Normand (1945-), illus. LC 78-55065. (Illus.). 24 p. (Golden/Sesame Street sturdy book). 1979, c.1978. (ISBN 0-307-12124-0). Golden Press.
Chartier, Normand (1945-), illus.
--Big Bird's Rhyming Book: Featuring Jim Henson's Muppets. Henson, Jim (1936-), created by. Penick, Ib, illus. Children's Television Workshop LC 78-68790. (Illus.). 16 p. 24cm. (CTW Sesame Street Street pop-up). c.1979. (ISBN 0-394-84140-9). Random House.
Chartier, Sandra
--Time for Bed Sleepy Head. Chartier, Normand (1945-), illus. LC 82-82565. (Illus.). 24p. (Golden Storytime Bk.). 1983. (ISBN 0-307-11964-5, Golden Pr). (ISBN 0-307-61964-8). Western Pub.
Chartoc, Shepard, ed. see Gilbert, William Schwenck, Sir (1836-1911) & Sullivan, Arthur Seymour, Sir.
Charushin, Evgenii Ivanovich (1901-)
--Baby Bears: A True Story. Korff, George, illus. Rudolph, Marguerita, tr. LC 44-4850. 40 p. col. illus. 21 cm. 1944. The Macmillan Company.
--The Little Gray Wolf. Korf, George, illus. Rudolph, Marguerita, tr. from Russian. LC 63-9589. 22cm. 1963. MacMillan Co.
Charvat, William (1905-), ed. see Hawthorne, Nathaniel.
Chase, Annie E.
--Children of the Wigwam. LC 4-24571. 143 p. illus. 18 cm. c.1903. Educational Publishing Company.
--Stories From Animal Land. (Illus.). 179p. (Primary School Library). N.D. Educational Publishing Company.
Chase, B.
--Completed Tales of My Knights and Ladies. N.D. Longmans, Green.
--Tales of My Knights and Ladies. N.D. Longmans, Green.
Chase, Catherine
--An Alphabet Book. Goldsborough, June (1923-), illus. LC 78-72095. (Illus.). 31 p. 23cm. 1979. (ISBN 0-89799-087-0). (ISBN 0-89799-000-5). Dandelion Press.
--Baby Mouse Goes Searching. Elgin, Jill, illus. LC 81-2243. (Illus.). 32p. (ps-3). 1982. (ISBN 0-525-66742-3). Dandelion Pr.
--Baby Mouse Goes Shopping. Elgin, Jill, illus. LC 81-2243. p. cm. 1981. (ISBN 0-525-66742-3). Elsevier/Dutton Books.
--Baby Mouse Learns His ABC's. Elgin, Jill, illus. LC 78-72096. (Illus.). 32 p. 23cm. c.1979. (ISBN 0-89799-001-3). (ISBN 0-89799-299-7). Dandelion Press.
--Duncan McTavish in Switzerland. Moffett, Robin, illus. LC 78-64488. (Illus.). 32 p. 23cm. 1978. (ISBN 0-89799-101-X). (ISBN 0-89799-010-2). Dandelion Press.
--Feet. Reiss, Susan, illus. LC 78-72105. (Illus.). 32 p. 23cm. (Dandelion first reader). c.1979. (ISBN 0-89799-020-X). Dandelion Press.
--The Miracles at Cana. Atkinson, Wayne, illus. LC 78-64117. (Illus.). (gr. k-5). 1979. Dandelion Pr.
--The Mouse in My House. Gibbons, Gail (1944-), illus. LC 78-72103. (Illus.). 32 p. (Dandelion first reader). 1979. (ISBN 0-89799-126-5). (ISBN 0-89799-024-2). Dandelion Press.
--My Balloon. Gibbons, Gail (1944-), illus. LC 78-72102. (Illus.). 32 p. 23cm. (Dandelion first reader). 1979. (ISBN 0-89799-127-3). (ISBN 0-89799-022-6). Dandelion Press.
--The Nightingale and the Fool: An Ancient Tale from India. Cheng, Judith, illus. LC 78-72915. (Illus.). 32 p. 23cm. (gr. 1-4). 1979. (ISBN 0-89799-129-X). (ISBN 0-89799-059-5). Dandelion Press.
--Noah's Ark. Ivenbaum, Elliot, illus. LC 78-64415. (Illus.). 32 p. 1979. (ISBN 0-89799-130-3). (ISBN 0-89799-031-5). Dandelion Press.
--Pete, the Wet Pet. Gibbons, Gail (1944-), illus. LC 81-2203. p. cm. c.1981. (ISBN 0-525-66746-6). Elsevier/Dutton Books.
--See the Fly Fly. Weissman, Bari, illus. LC 78-72104. (Illus.). 32 p. 23cm. (Dandelion first reader). 1979. (ISBN 0-89799-133-8). (ISBN 0-89799-023-4). Dandelion Press.
Chase, Charity
--Peanuts!. And a Cowboy Jimminy. Johnson, Helena Chase, illus. LC 46-25219. 70 p., 1 l. illus. 10 x 12 1/2 cm. 1946. Adventure Trails Publications.
Chase, Edith Newlin & Brown, Janet Hendry
--Small Window Panes: Verses for Children. LC 78-111719. (Illus.). 29 p. 25cm. c.1978. Chase.
Chase, Emily
--Best Friends Forever. 192p. (Orig.). (The Girls of Canby Hall Ser.: No. 6). (gr. 7-12). 1984. (ISBN 0-590-33238-4). Scholastic Inc.
--Four Is a Crowd. 160p. (Orig.). (The Girls of Canby Hall Ser.: No. 7). (gr. 6 up). 1984. (ISBN 0-590-33248-1). Scholastic Inc.
--Keeping Secrets. 176p. (Orig.). (The Girls of Canby Hall Ser.: No. 4). (gr. 7 up). 1984. (ISBN 0-590-32892-1). Scholastic Inc.
--Our Roommate Is Missing. 192p. (Orig.). (Girls of Canby Hall Ser.: No. 2). (gr. 7 up). 1984. (ISBN 0-590-32850-6). Scholastic Inc.
--Roommates. 224p. (Orig.). (Girls of Canby Hall Ser.: No. 1). (gr. 7 up). 1984. (ISBN 0-590-32843-3). Scholastic Inc.
--Summer Blues. 192p. (Orig.). (The Girls of Canby Hall Ser.: No. 5). (gr. 7 up). 1984. (ISBN 0-590-33237-6). Scholastic Inc.
--You're No Friend of Mine. 192p. (Orig.). (The Girls of Canby Hall Ser.). (gr. 7 up). 1984. (ISBN 0-590-32889-1). Scholastic Inc.
Chase, Francine
--A Visit to the Hospital. Bama, James, illus. Dunbar, Flanders, intro. by. LC 57-1658. 68p. illus. 25cm. 1957. Grosset & Dunlap.
Chase, Genevieve (1901-)
--Four Young Teachers. LC 47-5529. 21cm. 300p. (Career Books). 1947. Dodd, Mead and Co.
Chase, Jessie Anderson, Mrs. (1865-)
--A Daughter of the Revolution. LC 10-23127. 128 p. front., plates. 20 cm. 1910. R. G. Badger.
--Mayken: A Child's Story of the Netherlands in the Sixteenth Century. Kinney, Margaret & Kinney, Troy, illus. LC 2-23838. 1 p. l., vi p., 2 l., 11-219 p., 1 l. front., 4 pl. 21 cm. 1902. A. C. McClurg & Co.
--The Story of Paul Revere, Junior: Revolutionary Days in Old Boston. Cue, Harold, illus. LC 33-147. 309 p. front., plates. 20 cm. c.1932. W. A. Wilde Company.
--Three Freshmen. 1900. A C McClurg & Co.
Chase, John Allen (1882-)
--Bahama Treasure. LC 40-34535. 304 p. front. 21 cm. c.1940. W. A. Wilde Company.
--Bahama Treasure. N.D. Wilcox & Follett Co.
Chase, John Terry, jt. ed. see Hannum, Sara.
Chase, Joseph
--Jimmy at Happy House. Olden, Marian, illus. LC 24-18766. 221 p. front. 19 cm. 1924. The Penn Publishing Company.
--Jimmy, John and Junior. Klammer, Mildred Buckley, illus. LC 24-5199. 230 p. incl. front. 19 cm. 1924. The Penn Publishing Company.
--Jimmy, John and Junior, Home Again. Bailey, William J., illus. LC 27-14804. 2 p. l., 7-215 p. front. 20 cm. 1927. The Penn Publishing Company.
--John and the Winner's Club. Bailey, William J., illus. LC 25-19907. 2 p. l., 7-221 p. front. 20 cm. 1925. The Penn Publishing Company.
--Junior at the Beach. Bailey, William J., illus. LC 26-147265. 2 p. l., 7-219 p. front. 20 cm. 1926. The Penn Publishing Company.
Chase, Joseph Cummings
--My Friends Look Good to Me. Chase, Joseph Cummings, illus. N.D. Dodd, Mead & Co.
Chase, Joseph Cummings, illus.
--The Night Before Christmas. (Illus.). (The Little Red Hen Series.). N.D. George H Doran & Co.
Chase, Josephine (0000-1931)
--The Blue Shadow Mystery. Lea, Frank, illus. LC 35-248969. 205 p. front. 19 cm. c.1935. The Penn Publishing Company.
--The Golden Imp. Lee, Manning De Villeneuve (1894-1980), illus. LC 33-354800. 200 p. front. 20 cm. c.1933. The Penn Publishing Company.
--The Green Jade Necklace. LC 31-24654. 203 p. front. 19 cm. c.1931. The Penn Publishing Company.
--The Mark of the Red Diamond. LC 29-209731. 222 p. front. 19 cm. c.1929. The Penn Publishing Company.
Chase, Mary Coyle (1907-1981)
--Loretta Mason Potts. 1st ed. Berson, Harold (1926-), illus. LC 58-101381. 24p. illus. 22cm. 1958. Lippincott.
--The Wicked Pigeon Ladies in the Garden. Bolognese, Donald Alan (1934-), illus. LC 68-15327. (Illus.). 115 p. 24cm. 1968. Knopf.
Chase, Mary Ellen (1887-1973)
--Dolly Moses: The Cat and the Clam Chowder. Kennedy, Paul Edward (1929-), illus. LC 64-16080. 58 p. illus. 20 cm. 1964. W. W. Norton.
--Donald McKay and the Clipper Ships. (Illus.). 1959. Houghton Mifflin.
--The Fishing Fleets of New England. 1961. Houghton Mifflin company.
--The Girl from the Big Horn Country. Elwell, R. Farrington, illus. LC 16-2369. 5 p. l., 320 p. col. front., plates. 20 cm. 1916. The Page Company.
--Mary Christmas. Day, Maurice, contrib. by. LC 26-894838. 5 p. l., 3-142 p. incl. front. 20 cm. 1926. Little, Brown, and Company.
--Richard Mansfield: The Prince of Donkeys. Kennedy, Paul Edward (1929-), illus. LC 64-12565. 65 p. illus. 20 cm. 1964. Norton.
--Sailing the Seven Seas. 1958. Houghton Mifflin.
--Uplands. LC 27-165843. 5 p. l., 3-297 p. 20 cm. 1927. Little, Brown and Company.
--Victoria: A Pig in a Pram. Kennedy, Paul Edward (1929-), illus. LC 63-16661. 58 p. illus. 20 cm. 1963. Norton.
--Virginia of Elk Creek Valley. Elwell, R. Farrington, illus. LC 17-108596. 5 p. l., 297 p. col. front., plates. 20 cm. 1917. The Page Company.
--A Walk On An Iceberg. N.D (W. W. Norton Juveniles For Children). Grosset & Dunlap Pub.
Chase, Mary Jane, pseud., see Zillah, Ellis.
Chase, Mary Jane, illus.
--Little Miss Muffet, and Other Nursery Rhymes. LC 56-11586. (Illus.). 22cm. 28p. (Rand McNally Elf Bk.). 1956. Rand McNally.
--Rock-a-bye Baby, and Other Nursery Rhymes. Zillah, Ellis. LC 56-8345. (Illus.). 17cm. (A Rand McNally Junior Elf Bk.). 1956. Rand McNally.
Chase, Rebecca Whilt
--The Lucky Swallow Family, and Other Stories. Macrae, Ruth K., illus. LC 64-24574. (Illus.). 20cm. 38p. 1961. Dorrance.
Chase, Richard (1904-), ed. see Harris, Joel Chandler.
Chase, Richard (1904-)
--American Folk Tales and Songs. (Illus.). 240p. 1956. (ISBN 0-486-22692-1). Dover Books.
--American Folk Tales and Songs. (Illus.). N.D. (ISBN 0-8446-0057-1). Peter Smith Publisher, Inc.
--American Folk Tales & Songs. N.D. Signet & Mentor Bks.
--Grandfather Tales. Williams, Berkeley, Jr., illus. 1948. (ISBN 0-8382-0302-7, Cadmus Books). E. M. Hale and Company.
--Hullabaloo. N.D. Houghton Mifflin Co.
--Jack and the Three Sillies. Tolford, Joshua (1909-), illus. LC 50-8846. (Illus.). 39 p. 24cm. c.1950. Houghton Mifflin.
--Jack Tales. Williams, Berkeley, Jr., illus. (Illus.). (gr. 4-6). 1943. (ISBN 0-395-06694-8). HM.
--Singing Games & Playparty Games. Tolford, Joshua (1909-), illus. (Illus.). (gr. 1-4). 1949. Dover.
--Wicked John and the Devil. Tolford, Joshua (1909-), illus. LC 51-6293. 39 p. illus. 24 cm. 1951. Houghton Mifdin.
Chase, Richard (1904-), compiled by.
--Billy Boy. Rounds, Glen Harold (1906-), illus. LC 66-10801. 1v. (unpaged) col. illus. 20cm. (Jr. bks.). c.1966. (ISBN 0-516-08803-3). Golden Gate. **Award: (ALA).**
--Grandfather Tales. Williams, Berkeley, Jr., illus. 239p. (gr. 4-7). 1948. Houghton, Mifflin.
--Old Songs and Singing Games. 64p. 1938. (ISBN 0-486-22879-7). Dover Books.
--Old Songs and Singing Games. LC 38-12629. xii, 52 p. 24 cm. c.1938. The University of North Carolina Press.
Chasek, Judith
--Have You Seen Wilhelmina Krumpf?. Murdocca, Salvatore, illus. LC 72-12949. (Illus.). 40 p. 25cm. 1973. (ISBN 0-688-41523-7). (ISBN 0-688-41523-7). Lothrop, Lee & Shepard.
Chastain, Madye Lee (1908-)
--Bright Days. Chastain, Madye Lee (1908-), illus. LC 52-10063. (Illus.). 178 p. 21cm. 1952. Harcourt, Brace.
--Bright Days, 1 of 50 vols. Chastain, Madye Lee (1908-), illus. (Boys' & Girls' Library: No. 5). N.D. Set. Lothrop Publishing Co.
--Dark Treasure. 1st ed. Chastain, Madye Lee (1908-), illus. LC 54-8570. 208p. illus. 22cm. 1954. Harcourt, Brace.
--Emmy Keeps a Promise. Chastain, Madye Lee (1908-), illus. LC 56-9200. (gr. 4-6). 1956. (ISBN 0-15-225739-X, HJ). HarBraceJ.
--Emmy Keeps a Promise. Chastain, Madye Lee (1908-), illus. LC 56-9200. (Illus.). (gr. 4-6). 1966. (ISBN 0-15-225741-1, VoyB). HarBraceJ.
--Fripsey Fun. 1st ed. Chastain, Madye Lee (1908-), illus. LC 55-867257. 198p. illus. 21cm. 1955. Harcourt, Brace.
--Fripsey Summer. 1st ed. Chastain, Madye Lee (1908-), illus. LC 58-7863. 210p. illus. 21cm. 1953. Harcourt, Brace.
--Jerusha's Ghost. 1st ed. Chastain, Madye Lee (1908-), illus. LC 58-10793. 188p. illus. 21 cm. 1957. Harcourt, Brace.
--Leave It to the Fripseys. Chastain, Madye Lee (1908-), illus. LC 57-9739. (Illus.). 187p. (gr. 5-9). 1957. (ISBN 0-15-244534-X). HarBraceJ.
--Let's Play Indian. Chastain, Madye Lee (1908-), illus. LC 50-9286. 21cm. 40p. 1950 (Wonder books). Grosset & Dunlap.
--Loblolly Farm. 1st ed. Chastain, Madye Lee (1908-), illus. LC 50-6438. 227 p. illus. 21 cm. 1950. Harcourt, Brace.
--Magic Island. 1st ed. Chastain, Madye Lee (1908-), illus. LC 64-22271. 189 p. illus. 21 cm. 1964. Harcourt, Brace & World.
--Nellie. Chastain, Madye Lee (1908-), illus. LC 49-13594. 42 p. col. illus. 22 cm. (Cozy-corner book). 1948. Whitman Pub. Co.
--Plippen's Palace. 1st ed. Chastain, Madye Lee (1908-), illus. LC 61-6346. (Illus.). 188 p. 21cm. 1961. Harcourt, Brace & Uorld.
--The Sailboat that Ran Away. Chastain, Madye Lee (1908-), illus. LC 50-4109. 17cm. 32p. (Tell-a-Tale Books). 1950. Whitman.
--Steamboat South. 1st ed. Chastain, Madye Lee (1908-), illus. LC 51-11720. 233 p. illus. 21 cm. 1951. Harcourt, Brace.
--Summer at Hasty Cove. 1st ed. Chastain, Madye Lee (1908-), illus. LC 59-926897. 186p. illus. 22cm. (gr. 4-7). 1959. (ISBN 0-15-282464-2). Harcourt, Brace.
Chatalbash, Ron (1959-)
--Dr. Blackfoot's Carnival Extraordinaire. 1st ed. Chatalbash, Ron (1959-), illus. LC 81-85126. (Illus.). 32 p. 1982. (ISBN 0-87923-426-1). D.R. Godine.
--A Perfect Day for the Movies. 1st ed. Chatalbash, Ron (1959-), illus. LC 82-48702. (Illus.). 32 p. 1983. (ISBN 0-87923-463-6). David R. Godine.
Chatelain, Clara De Pontigny De (1807-1876)
--Tony the Sleepless. An Original Tale. LC 43-39051. 4 p. l., 72 p. incl. illus., plates, front., pl. 21 1/2 cm. (Added t.-p.: Six pleasant companions for spare hours. IV). 1852. Crosby, Nichols and Company.
Chatelain, Heli, ed.
--Folk-Tales of Angola: Fifty Tales. (Folk-Lore Society, Memooirs of the American: Vol. I). N.D. Houghton, Mifflin and Company.
Chatelain, Madame De
--Sir Wilfred's Seven Flights: A Fairy Tale. (Illus.). N.D. George Routldege.
Chater, Melville
--The Bubble Ballads. Kay, Gertrude Alice (1884-1939), illus. LC 14-17312. 5 p. l., 148 p. front., illus., plates. 25 cm. 1914. The Century Co.
Chatfield, Keith
--Issi's Magic Tonic. Standon, Edward Cyril (1926-), illus. LC 76-370825. (Illus.). 143 p. 21cm. 1976. (ISBN 0-434-94239-1). Heinemann.
Chatham, Bill
--Journey to Nazgar's Fortress: A Robo Force Adventure. Gimenez, Juan, illus. LC 84-62071. (Illus.). 32p. (Robo Force Mini-Storybooks). (ps-3). 1985. (ISBN 0-394-87175-8, BYR). Random.
Chatrian, Alexandre, jt. auth. see Erckmann, Emile.
Chatterbox
--The Chatterbox of Wild Animals. Robinson, Anna, ed. Weir, Harrison William (1824-1906), illus. LC 41-38150. 223 p. col. front., illus. 25 cm. c.1909. D. Estes and Company.
Chatterton, Edward Keble (1878-)
--Across the Seven Seas. Cammerota, D., illus. LC 27-21014. 251, 1 p. front., plates. 20 cm. 1927. J. B. Lippincott Company.
--Adventures of the Air. McKinney, Harris D., illus. LC 30-19632. 256 p. col. front., illus., col. plates. 20 cm. 1930. J. B. Lippincott Company.
--In Great Waters. Cammerota, D., illus. LC 29-993021. 282 p. front., plates. 20 cm. 1929. J. B. Lippincott Company.
--The King of the Air. Cammerota, D., illus. LC 28-25847. 244, 1 p. front., plates. 20 cm. 1928. J. B. Lippincott Company.
--On the High Seas. 319p. N.D. J. B. Lippincott.
--The Sky Riders: A Story of High Adventure by Sea and Air. Nelson, D. Earle, illus. LC 30-31190. 248 p. front., plates. 20 cm. 1930. J. B. Lippincott Company.
--Through Sea and Sky. Krakusin, Alfred, illus. LC 20-27795. 259 p. front., plates. 20 cm. c.1929. J. B. Lippincott Company.
Chatty Cheerful
--The Little Doings of Some Little Folks. Juv ed. (Illus.). N.D. Cassell & Co.
--What the Little Ones Saw. Juv. ed. (Illus.). N.D. Cassell & Co.
Chaucer, Geoffrey (1340-1400)
--The Canterbury Tales. Hieatt, Allen Kent (1921-) & Hieatt, Constance Bartlett (1928-), eds. Tenggren, Gustaf (1896-1970), illus. LC 61-9183. (Illus.). 139 p. 29cm. 1961. Golden Press.
--The Canterbury Tales. Hoffman, H. Lawrence, illus. Lumiansky, R. M., tr. 1948. Simon & Schuster.

--The Canterbury Tales. Kent, Rockwell (1882-1971), illus. Van Wyck, William, tr. 620p. N.D. Covici-Friede.
--The Canterbury Tales. Stewart, Diana, adapted by. Hubrich, Dan, illus. LC 80-22141. (Illus.). 45 p. 24cm. c.1981. (ISBN 0-8172-1666-9). Raintree Publishers.
--The Canterbury Tales of Geoffrey Chaucer. MacKaye, Percy Wallace (1875-1956), ed. Clark, Walter Appleton, illus. N.D. Duffield.
--Chanticleer and the Fox. Cooney, Barbara (1917-), adapted by. LC 58-10449. (Illus.). unpaged. 27cm. 1958. Crowell. **Awards: (RCM); (ALA).**
--Chanticleer and the Fox. Cooney, Barbara (1917-), adapted by. Cooney, Barbara (1917-), illus. 1958. Harper.
--Chaucer Tales; Retold for Children. (Illus.). N.D. Little Brown & Co.
--The Knight's Tale. Pollard, A. W., ed. (English Classics). 1962. St Martin's Press.
--The Knight's Tale, and The Nun's Priest's Tale. (Riverside Literature Ser.). N.D. Houghton Mifflin Co.
--Scornful Simkin: Adapted from Chaucer's The Reeve's Tale. Lorenz, Lee, retold by. Lorenz, Lee, illus. LC 80-15785. (Illus.). 32 p. 29cm. c.1980. (ISBN 0-13-796664-4). Prentice-Hall.
The Tales of Chaucer. N.D. Hale, Cushman & Flint.
--Tales of the Canterbury Pilgrims. (Illus.). (Fine Art Juvenile Ser.). N.D. Frederick A. Stokes Co.

Chaucer, Geoffrey (1340-1400) & McSpadden, Joseph Walker (1874-)
--Stories from Chaucer. LC 7-25660. xiv, 234 p. incl. col. front., illus. plates, facsim. 18 cm. c.1907. T. Y. Crowell & Company.

Chaucer, Geoffrey (1340-1400) & Spenser, Edmund (1552-1599)
--Canterbury Tales and Faerie Queene: With Other Poems of Chaucer and Spenser. (Illus.). N.D. Lee & Shepard.

Chaucer, Geoffrey (1340-1400) & Tappan, Eva March (1854-)
--The Chaucer Story Book. LC 8-28994. viii, 215, 1 p. illus., port. 22 cm. 1908. Houghton Mifflin Company.

Chaudhri, Rashid Ahmad (1934-)
--Golden Deeds of Muslims. LC 78-321655. 111 p. 19cm. (Children's series ; no. 3). c.1975. Islamic Publications.

Chauire, Yvette, jt. auth. see Lamaitre, Odon-Jerome.

Chaullu, Paul Belloni Du see Du Chaillu, Paul Belloni.

Chauncy, Nancen Beryl Masterman (1900-1970)
--Devils' Hill. Spence, Geraldine (1931-), illus. LC 60-11170. (Illus.). 159 p. 22cm. 1960, c.1958. F. Watts. **Award: (ALA).**
--A Fortune for the Brave. Horder, Margaret L'Anson (1911-), illus. LC 61-6076. 1961. Watts.
--Half a World Away. (Illus.). (gr. 5-8). 1962. (ISBN 0-8382-0312-4). Hale.
--Half-A-World Away. Macarthur-Onslow, Annette Rosemary (1933-), illus. LC 62-21095. 21cm. 194p. 1963. Franklin Watts.
--High & Haunted Island. (gr. 4-6). N.D. G&D.
--High and Haunted Island. Ambrus, Victor G., pseud. (1935-), illus. Ambrus, Gyozo Laszlo. LC 65-209440. 145p. illus. 22cm. 1965, c.1964. Norton.
--Hunted in Their Own Land. Ambrus, Victor G., pseud. (1935-), illus. Ambrus, Gyozo Laszlo. Bader, Barbara, intro. by. LC 72-86640. (Illus.). 165 p. 24cm. 1973. (ISBN 0-8164-3093-4). Seabury Press.
--The Lighthouse Keeper's Son. Ambrus, Victor G., pseud. (1935-), illus. Ambrus, Gyozo Laszlo. LC 77-529943. (Illus.). 23cm. v, 133p. 1969. (ISBN 0-19-271305-1). Oxford Univ. Press.
--Mathinna's People. Ambrus, Victor G., pseud. (1935-), illus. Ambrus, Gyozo Laszlo. LC 67-94104. (Illus.). 8, 163 p. 22cm. 1967. Oxford U.P.
--The Roaring Forty. Macarthur-Onslow, Annette Rosemary (1933-), illus. LC 63-16927. 161 p. illus., map. 21 cm. 1963. F. Watts.
--The Secret Friends. Wildsmith, Brian Lawrence (1930-), illus. LC 62-8434. 180p. 1962. Franklin Watts.
--Tangara:. 'Let's Set off Again'. 1st ed. Wildsmith, Brian Lawrence (1930-), illus. 180p. illus. 23cm. 1960. Oxford University Press.
--They Found a Cave. Horder, Margaret L'Anson (1911-), illus. LC 61-6078. 21cm. 180p. 1961. Watts.
--Tiger In the Bush. Horder, Margaret L'Anson (1911-), illus. LC 60-11175. 152p. 1960. Franklin Watts.
--World's End Was Home. Hughes, Shirley (1929-), illus. LC 61-6077. 21cm. 181p. 1961. Watts.

Chaundler, Christine (1887-1972)
--Carrot Top and Timothy. Morrow, Albert, illus. N.D. Frederick Warne & Co.
--My Book of Stories from the Poets: Told in Prose. Michael, Arthur C., illus. xvi, 319, 1 p. col. front., illus., 11 col. pl. 25 cm. 1920. Funk and Wagnalls Company.

Chaundler, Christine (1887-1972) & Wood, Eric
--My Book of Beautiful Legends. Michael, Arthur C., illus. LC 17-10876. xvi, 367, 1 p. illus. 12 col. pl. (incl. front.) 24 cm. 1916. Funk and Wagnalls Company.

Chavanne, R. N.
--David Farragut: Or, Midshipman. 244p. N.D. Coward-McCann.

Chaves, Doris, et al., trs. see Williams, Letty.

Cheadle, J. A.
--A Donkey's Life: A Story for Children. Thomas, Toni, illus. LC 80-123421. iii, 88p. (Orig.). (gr. 2-6). 1979. (ISBN 0-9604244-0-7). Heahstan Pr.

Cheatham, Karyn Follis (1943-)
--The Best Way Out. LC 81-47528. 168 p. 21cm. c.1982. (ISBN 0-15-206741-8). Harcourt Brace Jovanovich.
--Bring Home the Ghost. LC 80-7981. p. cm. c.1980. (ISBN 0-15-212485-3). Harcourt Brace Jovanovich.
--Life on a Cool Plastic Ice Floe. LC 78-6430. 180 p. 21cm. c.1978. (ISBN 0-664-32632-3). Westminster Press.
--Spotted Flower and the Ponokomita. LC 77-7253. (Illus.). 94 p. 21cm. c.1977. (ISBN 0-664-32617-X). Westminister Press.

Cheatham, Margaret
--Peter Tuttle & the Great Mr. Paddy. LC 82-90586. 150p. 1983. (ISBN 0-533-05505-9). Vantage.

Cheatham, Val R
--Skits and Spoofs for Young Actors: One-Act, Royalty-Free Plays, Skits, and Spoofs for the Amateur Stage. LC 77-23906. vi, 194 p. 22cm. (gr. 7-12). c.1977. (ISBN 0-8238-0220-5). Plays, Inc.

Cheesman, Lillian
--Peter and His Pals. N.D. David McKay Co.

Cheever, Harriet Anna, Mrs.
--The Adventures of Pony Dexter. Horne, Diantha W., illus. LC 12-20309. 3 p. l., 11-88 p. front., plates. 19 cm. 1911. D. Estes & Company.
--Animal Friends. N.D. Page Co.
--Doctor Robin. Barry, Etheldred Breeze (1870-), illus. (Illus.). N.D. Dana Estes and Company.
--Elmcove. 334p. 1905. American Tract Society.
--The Fairies of Fern Dingle. 250p. N.D. Pilgrim Press.
--The Fairies of Fern Dingle: Little Lessons from the Little Folk. LC 12-31341. 250 p. 2 pl. (incl. front.) 18 cm. c.1896. Congregational Sunday-School and Publishing Society.
--Gipsy Jane. Davidson, Bertha G., illus. LC 3-12821. (Illus.). 19cm. 286p. (The Girls' Own Authors Ser.). 1903. Dana Estes & Co.
--Jacky Lee. 286p. N.D. Pilgrims Press.
--Jacky Lee: His Lessons Out of School. LC 12-31336. 286 p. front., plates. 19 cm. c.1894. Congregational Sunday-School and Publishing Society.
--Josie Bean: Flat Street. Horne, Diantha W., illus. LC 5-20732. (Illus.). 19cm. 298p. 1905. Dana Estes and Company.
--Lady Spider: In the King's House. Horne, Diantha W., illus. LC 4-145545. 110 p. incl. front. 5 pl. 19 cm. c.1904. D. Estes & Company.
--Links of Gold. LC 19-2904. 314 p. front., plates. 20 cm. c.1897. The Pilgrim Press.
--Little Jolliby's Christmas. LC 12-31334. 73 p. front. 20 cm. c.1895. Congregational Sunday-School and Publishing Society.
--Little Jolliby's Christmas. 73p. (The Girls' Bookshelf Library). N.D. Pilgrims Press.
--Little Miss Boston. 301p. N.D. Pilgrims Press.
--Little Miss Boston: A Christmas Story. LC 12-313373. 301 p. incl. front., illus. 2 pl. 18 cm. c.1890. Congregational Sunday-School and Publishing Society.
--Little Mr. Van Vere of China. Barry, Etheldred Breeze (1870-), illus. LC 12-31305. 243 p. incl. front., illus., plates. 20 cm. c.1898. Estes and Lauriat.
--Lord Dolphin. Horne, Diantha W., illus. LC 3-14861. 97 p. incl. front. 5 pl. 19 cm. 1903. D. Estes & Company.
--Lou. Davidson, Bertha G., illus. N.D. Dana Estes and Company.
--Madame Angora. Mora, Joseph Jacinto (1876-), illus. (Illus.). N.D. Dana Estes & Co.
--Maid Sally. LC 2-20037. 279 p. front., pl. 19 cm. 1902. D. Estes & Company.
--Mother Bunny. Horne, Diantha W., illus. LC 3-14706. 97 p. incl. front. 5 pl. 19 cm. 1903. D. Estes & Company.
--The Rock Frog. Horne, Diantha W., illus. (Illus.). N.D. Dana Estes and Company.
--St. Rockwells' Little Brother. 400p. N.D. Pilgrim Press.
--The Strange Adventures of Billy Trill. Barry, Etheldred Breeze (1870-), illus. LC 12-313335. 82 p. incl. illus., plates. front. 19 cm. (Young of Heart Ser.). c.1898. Estes and Lauriat.
--Ted's Little Deer. Barry, Etheldred Breeze (1870-), illus. LC 4169. 106 p. incl. front., illus., pl. 12 cm. 1900. D. Estes & Co.
--Tommy Joyce and Tommy Joy. Davidson, Bertha G., illus. LC 5-17283. 19cm. 309p. 1905. Dana Estes and Company.

Cheifetz, Dan (1926-)
--Washer in the Woods. Cohen, Alix, illus. LC 72-86978. (Illus.). 32 ils. 32p. (ps-2). 1969. (ISBN 0-87460-058-8). (ISBN 0-87460-124-X). Lion.

Chekhov, Anton Pavlovich (1860-1904)
--Kashtanka. 1st American ed. Stobbs, William (1914-), illus. Dowsett, Charles, tr. (Illus.). 48 p. 1961, c.1959. H. Z. Walck. **Award: (KGM).**

Cheley, Frank Hobart (1889-)
--Adventure of a Prodigal Father. 1916. Association Press.
--A Big Brother Investment. LC 17-17522. 6 p. l., 3-101 p. 17 cm. 1917. Association Press.
--Boy Days and Boy Ways. LC 35-14578. 4 p. l., 3-185 p. 20 cm. c.1935. The Judson Press.
--Boy Riders of the Rockies: Or, Camping on Top of the World. Cheley, Frank Hobart (1889-), illus. LC 29-4413. 335 p. front., plates. 21 cm. c.1928. W. A. Wilde Company.
--The Boy Scout Trail Blazers: Or, Scouting for Uncle Sam on the Pike National Forest. Wrenn, Charles L., illus. LC 17-22090. 246 p. front. plates. 20 cm. (On verso of t.-p.: The boy scout life series). c.1917. Barse & Hopkins.
--The Boys' Book of Camp Fires. 1925. W A Wilde Co.
--Buffalo Roost. Cheley, Frank Hobart (1889-), illus. N.D. Abingdon Press.
By Ember Glow: Stories Told By a Campfire. Cheley, Frank Hobart (1889-), illus. LC 37-24837. 271 p. front. 20 cm. c.1937. W. A. Wilde Company.
--Camp-Fire Yarns. Merrill, Frank Thayer (1848-), illus. LC 23-120. 264 p. front., pl. 20 cm. c.1922. W. A. Wilde Company.
--Campfire Stories. LC 42-4722. 6 p. l., 329 p. front., illus., plates. 21 cm. 1942. Greenberg.
--Camping with Henry: Stories for the Camp Fire. LC 18-12614. 4 p. l., 3-137 p. front. 17 cm. 1918. Association Press.
--The Mystery of Chimney Rock: Being a Story of the Search for Gold in the Land of the Ute Indians in "the Days of '49". Merrill, Frank Thayer (1848-), illus. LC 24-27879. 300 p. front. 20 cm. c.1924. W. A. Wilde Company.
--The Three Rivers Kids. Cheley, Frank Hobart (1889-), illus. LC 14-8698. 255 p. front., plates. 20 cm. c.1914. Jennings and Graham.
--Told by the Camp Fire. 1914. Association Press.

Chellis, Mary Dwinell
--Aunt Dinah's Pledge, 1 of 4 Vols. (Chellis Library Ser.). N.D. National Temperance Society.
--Bill Drock's Investment, 1 of 4. (The Standard Series of Temperance Tales). N.D. Henry A. Young.
--Charley Wheeler's Reward. (Illus.). N.D. Henry Hoyt.
--The Children's Nonsense Book. (Illus.). N.D. Lothrop Publishing Co.
--The Children's Wonder Book. (Illus.). N.D. Lothrop Publishing Co.
--Dea. Sim's Prayers. (Chellis Ser.). N.D. Henry A. Young.
--Effie Wingate's Work. (Chellis Ser.). N.D. Henry A. Young.
--Father Merrill. 410p. (Crowell's Library For Young). N.D. Thomas Y. Crowell & Co.'s Catalogue.
--Father Merrill. (Father Merrill Ser.). N.D. Warren & Wyman.
--Good Work, 1 of 50 vols. (Illus.). 350p. (Sunday-School Lib: No. 14). N.D. Set. Lothrop Pub. Co.
--Harold Dorsey's Fortune. LC 6-23412. 379 p. front., plates. 19 cm. c.1881. Congregational Publishing Society.
--Jerould's Promise: Stories for Little People, 1 of 4 Vols. Penney, L., ed. 72p. (The Never-Begin Series). N.D. Per set in box 3.00. National Temperance Society.
--Jimmy's Shoes: Or, Starlight. N.D. Henry Hoyt.
--Molly's Bible. (Chellis Ser.). N.D. Henry A. Young.
--Mystery of the Lodge, 1 of 50 vols. (Illus.). 350p. (Sunday-School Lib: No. 14). N.D. Set. Lothrop Pub. Co.
--The Old Doctor's Son, 1 of 4 vols. (The Standard Series of Temperance Tales: No. 2). N.D. Henry A. Young.
--The Old Mill. LC 6-23403. vi, 7-423 p. front., pl. 18 cm. c.1875. Congregational Publishing Society.
--Old Sunapee. (A Prize Volume). (Illus.). 439p. N.D. A. I. Bradley & Co.'s Pubs.
--Old Sunapee. LC 6-23362. 1 p. l., 439 p. front., plates. 18 cm. (Added t.-p.: The Sunday-school series of juvenile religious works). 1867. H. Hoyt.
--The Old Tavern, and Other Stories. 386p. N.D. National Temperance Society.
--The Temperance Doctor, 1 of 4 Vols. (Chellis Library Ser.). N.D. National Temperance Society.

Chen, Tony (1929-)
--The Cucumber Stem: Adapted from a Bengali Folktale. Bang, Betsy (1912-), ed. LC 78-26227. (Illus.). 55 p. 22cm. (Greenwillow read-alone books). c.1980. (ISBN 0-688-80213-3). (ISBN 0-688-84213-5). Greenwillow Books.
--Run, Zebra, Run. Chen, Tony (1929-), illus. LC 75-177313. (Illus.). 34 p. 26cm. 1972. Lothrop, Lee & Shepard Co.

Chen, Yung-Chen, jt. auth. see Ming, Yang.

Chenault, Nell, pseud., see Smith, Linell Nash.

Chenault, Nell, pseud. (1932-)
--Parsifal Rides the Time Wave. Smith, Linell Nash. LC 62-7104. (Illus.). 84 p. 23cm. 1962. Little, Brown.
--Parsifal the Poddley. Smith, Linell Nash. Guthrie, Vee, illus. LC 60-58817. 83p. illus. 23cm. 1960. Little, Brown.

Chenay, Olive Augusta Alger, jt. auth. see Alger, Horatio, Jr.

Chenery, Janet Dai (1923-)
--Pickles and Jake. 1st ed. Obligado, Lilian Isabel (1931-), illus. LC 76-53682. (Illus.). 56 p. 23cm. 1977, c.1975. (ISBN 0-14-030964-0). Puffin Books.
--Pickles and Jake. Obligado, Lilian Isabel (1931-), illus. LC 74-8780. (Illus.). 24cm. 56p. 1975. Viking Press.
--The Toad Hunt. Shecter, Ben (1935-), illus. LC 66-18653. (Illus.). 5 7/8 x 8 1/2. 64p. (18 pt.). (Nature I Can Read Bks.). (gr. k-3). 1967. (ISBN 0-06-021262-4) (ISBN 0-06-021263-2) Har-Row.
--Wolfle. Simont, Marc (1915-), illus. LC 78-77950. (Illus.). 63 p. 23cm. (Science I can read book). 1969. Harper & Row.

Chenery, Janet Dai (1923-), adapted by.
--The Golden Book of Lost Worlds. (A De Luxe Golden Book). 1963. Golden Press.

Cheney, Cora (1916-)
--The Case of the Iceland Dogs. Michini, Albert, illus. LC 76-53635. (Illus.). 160 p. 22cm. c.1977. (ISBN 0-396-07398-0). Dodd, Mead.
--The Christmas Tree Hessian. Price, Edith Ballinger (1897-), illus. 151p. (gr. 4-6). 1976. (ISBN 0-914378-10-4). Countryman.
--The Christmas Tree Hessian. 1st ed. Price, Edith Ballinger (1897-), illus. LC 57-11680. 151p. illus. 21cm. 1957. Holt.
--The Doll of Lilac Valley. 1st ed. Beech, Carol, illus. LC 59-6408. 112p. illus. 21cm. (gr. 4-6). 1959. (ISBN 0-394-91088-5). Knopf.
--Fortune Hill. 1st ed. Weisman, Jerome, illus. LC 56-6225. 123p. illus. 21cm. 1956. Holt.
--The Girl at Jungle's Edge. 1st ed. Wilde, Carol (1938-), illus. LC 62-14772. (Illus.). 150 p. 21cm. 1962. Knopf.
--The Incredible Deborah. LC 67-23683. (A Story based on the Life of Deborah Sampson). (Illus.). 203 p. 22cm. (gr. 5-9). 1967. (ISBN 0-684-13452-7). Scribner.
--Key of Gold. 1st ed. Galdone, Paul (1914-), illus. LC 55-105622. 127p. illus. 21cm. 1955. Holt.
--The Mystery of the Disappearing Cars. Pfahl, Dick, illus. LC 63-14605. (Illus.). 146 p. 22cm. 1964. Knopf.
--The Peg-Legged Pirate of Sulu. 1st ed. Keats, Ezra Jack (1916-1983), illus. LC 60-860268. 109p. illus. 21cm. (gr. 3-7). 1960. (ISBN 0-394-91491-0). Knopf.
--Plantation Doll. Polseno, Jo, illus. LC 55-5889. (Illus.). 136 p. 21cm. 1955. Holt.
--Rocking Chair Buck. N.D. E . M. Hale and Co.
--The Rocking Chair Buck. Galdone, Paul (1914-), illus. LC 56-10125. (Illus.). 128p. (gr. 4-6). 1956. (ISBN 0-03-066385-7). HR&W.
--Rumpus on Commodore Hill. Stevens, Mary E (1920-1966), illus. LC 57-5744. (Illus.). 125p. (Holt Books for Young People). (gr. 3-6). 1957. (ISBN 0-03-031565-4). HR&W.
--Skeleton Cave. 1st ed. Galdone, Paul (1914-), illus. LC 54-5735. (Illus.). 108 p. 21cm. 1954. Holt.
--Treasures of Lin Li-Ti. Besunder, Marvin, illus. LC 76-79286. (Illus.). 23 halftones. 96p. (gr. 4 up). 1969. Hawthorn.

Cheney, Cora (1916-) & Partridge, Benjamin Waring (1915-)
--China Sea Roundup. Hall, H. Tom, illus. LC 60-5511. (Illus.). 21cm. 111p. (gr. 3-7). 1960. (ISBN 0-394-91018-4). Knopf.
--Rendezvous in Singapore. 1st ed. Galdone, Paul (1914-), illus. LC 61-7124. 111p. illus. 21cm. (gr. 4-6). 1961. (ISBN 0-394-91538-0). Knopf.

Cheney, David MacGregor
--The Golden Goblin: A Fantasy. Russell, J. Donald, illus. LC 24-10860. 3 p. l., 18 p. illus. 15 cm. 1924. The House of the Golden Goblin.
--Son of Minos. LC 64-25838. (gr. 7). N.D. (ISBN 0-8196-0142-X). Biblo.

Cheney, Ednah Dow Littlehale, Mrs. (1824-1904)
--Child of the Tide. 1882. Lee & Shepard.

--The Child of the Tide. LC 3-14848. 212 p. front., plates. 19 cm. (American boys' series, 86). c.1902. Lee and Shepard.
--Faithful to the Light: And Other Tales. LC 15-21849. vi p., 1 l., 9-166 p. plates. 17 1/2 cm. (Added t.-p.: Prize series). 1884. American Unitarian Association.
--Sally Williams: The Mountain Girl. Humphrey, Lizzie B., illus. LC 25-23754. 238 p. front., plates. 16 cm. 1873. Lee and Shepard.
--Sally Williams the Mountain Girl, 1 of 30 vols. Humphrey, Lizzie B., illus. LC 2-30270. 238p. (American Girls' Ser.: No. 30). 1900. Set. Lee & Shepard.

Cheney, Elizabeth H
--The Joyous Adventures of John and Betty. Price, Harriet Longstreet (1891-), illus. LC 21-18890. 302 p. front., plates. 19 cm. 1921. The Penn Publishing Company.

Cheney, Emma C.
--Number Forty-Nine Tinkham Street. 1900. A C McClurg Co.

Cheney, Emma C. & Sanford, D. P.
--Feathers, Furs and Fins: Or, Stories of Animal Life for Children. (Illus.). N.D. Dana Estes & Co.

Cheney, Leila H.
--Boys and Girls from Storyland. N.D. J. B. Lippincott.
--Fairies and Goblins from Storyland. N.D. J.B. Lippincott.
--Tell Me a Story Picture Book. Kirk, Maria Louise (1860-), illus. N.D. J.B. Lippincott.

Cheney, Leila H., ed. see Irving, Washington.

Cheney, Lurlene Romney
--Fun and Finger Plays. Ohlsson, Ib (1935-), illus. LC 44-44658. 3 p. l., 5-96 p. illus. 28 1/2 x 22 cm. 1944. F. S. Ewert.

Cheney, Nina Ehlers
--Pippity, Poppity Popcorn. 1st ed. LC 56-5499. 77p. illus. 21cm. 1956. Vantage Press.

Cheney, Richard E
--Really Eager and the Glorious Watermelon Contest. Ohlsson, Ib (1935-), illus. LC 70-89974. (Illus.). 43 p. 1970. Dutton.

Ch'Eng-En, Wu
--Monkey: A Folk Novel of China. Waley, Arthur, tr. from Chinese. N.D. (ISBN 0-8446-1847-0). Peter Smith Publisher, Inc.

Cheng, Hou-Tien
--Six Chinese Brothers: An Ancient Tale. Cheng, Hou-Tien (1944-), illus. LC 79-1218. (Illus.). 32 p. c.1979. (ISBN 0-03-048311-5). Holt, Rinehart, and Winston.

Cheng'an, Jiang, tr. see Shufen, Li.

Chenoweth, Helen S., ed.
--Pageant of Seasons: A Collection of American Haiku. LC 78-134031. (Illus.). (gr. 9 up). 1970. (ISBN 0-8048-0546-6). C E Tuttle.

Chenoweth, Maurene
--Faraway Song. N.D. Alfred A. Knopf.
--Faraway Song. LC 42-14740. 301 p. front. 21 1/2 cm. 1942. Wm. Penn Publishing Corp.
--Green Jade for Laughter. N.D. Alfred A. Knopf.
--Green Jade for Laughter. Brinkman, Lawrence, illus. LC 40-34733. 292 p. front. 22 cm. c.1940. Penn Publishing Company.

Chermayeff, Ivan (1932-)
--Blind Mice. (Illus.). (ps). 1961. Wittenborn.
--Blind Mice and Other Numbers. Chermayeff, Ivan (1932-), illus. LC 63-3494. 40p. illus. 28cm. c.1961. Colorcraft.

Chernoff, Dorothy A., pseud., see Ernst, Lyman John.

Chernoff, Dorothy A., pseud. (1940-)
--Call Us Americans. Ernst, Lyman John. Wolf, Jack, illus. (Illus.). (gr. 9 up). 1968. (ISBN 0-385-09023-4). Doubleday.

Chernoff, Goldie Taub (1909-)
--Puppet Party. LC 76-186171. N.D. (ISBN 0-8027-6100-3). Walker & Co.

Cherr, Pat, jt. auth. see Keats, Ezra Jack.

Cherry, Jeanne Yates see Dalkeith, Lena, pseud.

Cherry, Jeanne Yates (1879-)
--Stories from Roman History. Dalkeith, Lena, pseud. LC 8-35363. (Illus.). 119 p. 15cm. (Stories from History Ser.). 1908. Dutton.

Cherry, Robert L
--Uncle Billy O'Possum. LC 54-9554. 149p. illus. 23cm. c.1954. Comet Press Books.

Cherryholmes, Anne, pseud., see Price, Olive M..

Cherryholmes, Anne, pseud. (1903-)
--Island of the Voyageurs. Price, Olive M.. Jaeger, Elinor, illus. (Illus.). (gr. 3-6). 1964. (ISBN 0-698-20070-5). Coward.

Cherubini, Eugenio (1876-)
--Pinocchio in Africa. Copeland, Charles, illus. Patri, Angelo (1876-), tr. LC 11-14097. viii, 152 p. incl. front., illus. 17 1/2 cm. c.1911. Ginn and Company.

Cherwinski, Joseph (1915-)
--Don Quixote with a Rake. 1964. Publications of Bruce Humphries.

Chesebro', Caroline (1828-1873)
--Amy Carr: Or, the Fortune-Teller. LC 6-20956. 17cm. 226p. 1864. M. W. Dodd.
--The Beautiful Gate, and Other Tales. LC 6-20955. 233 p. front. 17 cm. 1855. Miller, Orton & Mulligan.
--Blessings in Disguise: Or, Pictures of Some of Miss Haydon's Girls. LC 6-20957. 178 p. incl. front. 15 1/2 cm. c.1863. Carlton & Porter.
--The Little Cross-Bearers. LC 6-20989. 160 p. incl. front. 17 cm. 1854. Derby & Miller.
--Little Cross Bearers. (The Amy Harrison Ser.). N.D. Set. Thomas Nelson & Sons.
--Little Cross-Bearers, 1 of 6 vols. (Stories with a Purpose Ser.). N.D. Set. Thos Nelson & Sons.
--The Sparrow's Fall: Or, Under the Willow and Other Stories. LC 6-20954. 178 p. incl. front 15 1/2 cm. c.1863. Carlton & Porter.

Chesher, Kim (1955-)
--Cuthbert and the Thingamabob. Kimura, Yasuko, illus. LC 76-380466. (Illus.). 32 p. 1976. Evans Bros.

Cheshire, Gifford Paul (1905-)
--River of Gold: Oregon and the Challenge of the Gold Rush. 1st ed. Mastri, Fiore, illus. LC 55-5880. 192p. illus. 21cm. (American heritage series). 1955. Aladdin Books.
--Stronghold (Pub. by Doubleday). (American Indian Ser). (gr. 7 up). 1972. Curtis.
--Thunder on the Mountain. 320p (Pub. by Lippincott). (American Indian Ser.). (gr. 9-12). 1971. Curtis.

Chesnutt, Charles Waddell (1858-1932)
--Conjure Tales. 1st ed. Shepard, Ray Anthony, retold by. Ross, John (1921-) & Ross, Clare Romano (1922-), illus. LC 73-77457. (Illus.). ix, 99 p. 24cm. (gr. 4 up). 1973. (ISBN 0-525-28140-1). Dutton.

Chess, Victoria, jt. auth. see Goldberg, Stan J.

Chess, Victoria (1939-)
--Alfred's Alphabet Walk. Chess, Victoria (1939-), illus. LC 79-1185. (Illus.). 32 p. 26cm. c.1979. (ISBN 0-688-80223-0). Greenwillow Books.
--Poor Esme. Chess, Victoria (1939-), illus. 1982. Holiday.

Chess, Victoria (1939-) & Gorey, Edward St. John (1925-)
--Fletcher and Zenobia. Chess, Victoria (1939-), illus. LC 67-22803. 63p. 1967. Meredith Press.

Chessare, Michele, jt. auth. see Marie, Geraldine.

Chessare, Michele (1921-)
--A Lion to Guard Us. Bulla, Clyde Robert (1914-), illus. LC 80-2455. (Illus.). viii, 117 p. 24cm. c.1981. (ISBN 0-690-04096-2). (ISBN 0-690-04097-0). Crowell.

Chesse, Bruce K., jt. ed. see Sims, Judy.

Chessman, Evelyn
--Sealskin for Silk. Whittam, Geoffrey William (1916-), illus. 1956. Abelard-Schuman.

Chessman, Ruth Green (1910-)
--Bound for Freedom. Linton, Anne, illus. LC 65-12122. 158 p. illus. 21 cm. 1965. Abelard-Schuman.

Chester
--The Knights of the Grail. (Illus.). 154p. (The Golden River Ser.). N.D. Thomas Nelson & Sons.

Chester, Annie M. see Myrtle, Annie, pseud.

Chester, Deborah (1957-)
--The Sign of the Owl. LC 80-69998. 219 p. 22cm. c.1981. (ISBN 0-590-07729-5). Four Winds Press.

Chester, George Randolph (1869-)
--The Wonderful Adventures of Little Prince Toofat. Lawson, Robert (1892-1957), illus. LC 22-17772. 5 p. l., 3-70 p. col. front., illus., col. plates. 31 x 27 cm. c.1922. The James A. McCann Company.

Chester, M. S. A.
--Up the Chimney to Ninny Land: A Fairy Story for Children. (Illus.). N.D. Thomas Nelson & Sons.

Chester, Michael
--The Mystery of the Lost Moon. Geer, Charles Hand (1922-), illus. 127p. illus. 21cm. 1962, c.1961. Putnam.

Chester, Michael, jt. auth. see Nephew, William.

Chester, Michael Arthur (1928-)
--Deep-Sea Dive. LC 75-132406. (Illus.). 30 halftones. 90p. 1st U.S. edition. (gr. 5-7). 1971. (ISBN 0-448-21420-2). (ISBN 0-448-26190-1). G&D.
--Let's Go to the Moon. rev. ed. Micale, Albert, illus. (Illus.). (Let's Go Ser.). (gr. 3-5). 1974. (ISBN 0-399-60802-8). Putnam.
--Water Monsters. LC 72-92925. (Illus.). (gr. 4-7). 1978. (ISBN 0-448-14674-6, G&D). Putnam Pub Group.

Chester, Sally
--Her Little World, 1 of 50 Vols. 392p. (Model Library Number Three). 1877. Set. American Tract Society.
--Ollie and The Boys. (Crowell's Library Fr Young People). N.D. Thomas Y. Crowell & Co.'s Catalogue.
--Ollie and the Boys. 320p. (The Ollie Library). N.D. Warren & Wyman.

Chester, Sarah
--Betty and Her Cousin Harry. N.D. American Tract Society.
--Handsome Harry. 294p. N.D. American Tract Society.
--Her Little World, 1 of 25 vols. 302p. (Golden Rod Library). 1905. American Tract Society.
--Nine Saturdays. (Pet Dayton's Library). N.D. A. D. F. Randolph.
--Proud Little Boy. (Illus.). 211p. 1905. American Tract Society.
--Roly and Poly at Aunt Merciful Graticap's. (The Roly and Poly Library). N.D. A. D. F. Randolph.
--Roly and Poly at Pinkville. (The Roly and Poly Library). N.D. A. D. F. Randolph.
--Roly and Poly in the Nursery. (The Roly and Poly Library). N.D. A. D. F. Randolph.
--Sir Genevieve. 1873. A. D. F. Randolph.
--Sir Genevieve, 1 of 6 Vols. (The Household Library). N.D. Set. A D F Randolph & Co.

Chester, Sarah, et al.
--Dear Jane, 1 of 4 vols. (Illus.). (Winter Sunshine Ser.). N.D. D Lothrop.

Chester, W. L.
--Hawk of the Wilderness. N.D. Grosset & Dunlap.

Chesterman, Evan Rayland (1870-)
--The Lady Dragon of Dancing Point. Armstrong, Harry W., illus. LC 22-214823. 256 p. incl. front. 20 cm. (Half-title: The boys' big game series). c.1922. The Reilly & Lee & Co.

Chesterman, Hugh
--The Odd Spot. (Roundabout Ser.). N.D. D. Appleton & Co.
--Proud Sir Pim. N.D. D. Appleton & Co.

Chesterton, Gilbert Keith, jt. auth. see Doyle, Arthur Conan, Sir.

Chesterton, Gilbert Keith (1874-1936)
--Father Brown Mystery Stories. Bond, Raymond T., ed. LC 62-9450. 246 p. 21cm. 1962. Dodd, Mead.

Chesterton, Rupert
--The Phantom Battleship. (Illus.). N.D. J. B. Lippincott.

Chestnutt, David
--Beauty and the Beast. Chestnutt, David, illus. LC 78-54959. (Illus.). 16 p. 21cm. (Random House pictureback). (best book club ever selected editions). c.1978. (ISBN 0-394-83954-4). Random House.

Cheswright, Patricia
--The Farmyard Book in Color Photography. O'Keefe, Patrie, illus. LC 46-8400. 48 p. illus. (part col.) 18 x 18 cm. (On cover: A Lothrop color book). 1946. Lothrop, Lee & Shepard Co., Inc.

Chetin, Helen (1922-)
--Angel Island Prisoner. Lee, Jan, illus. Harvey, Catherine, tr. LC 82-51170. (Illus.). (gr. 3 up). 1982. New Seed.
--How Far Is Berkeley?. LC 77-76435. 122 p. 21cm. c.1977. (ISBN 0-15-236750-0). Harcourt Brace Jovanovich.
--The Lady of the Strawberries. Kunz, Anita (1956-), illus. LC 83-14703. p. cm. 1984. (ISBN 0-8149-0871-3). Vanguard Press.
--Perihan's Promise, Turkish Relatives, and the Dirty Old Imam. Krush, Beth (1918-) & Krush, Joe (1918-), illus. LC 72-13583. (Illus.). 140 p. 23cm. 1973. (ISBN 0-395-16043-X). Houghton Mifflin.
--Tales from an African Drum. Robinson, Charles (1931-), illus. LC 70-117616. (Illus.). 96 p. 21cm. 1970. Harcourt Brace Jovanovich.

Chettle, M. E.
--Jacks and Jills. Jackson, Helen Maria Fiske Hunt, Mrs. (1831-1885), illus. 40p. (No. 342). N.D. Raphael Tuck & Sons.

Chetwin, Grace
--On All Hallows' Eve. LC 84-4391. 160p. (gr. 6 up). 1984. (ISBN 0-688-03012-2). Lothrop.

Chetwode, R. D.
--The Lord Lowedale. Manton, Grenville, illus. N.D. Dana Estes & Co.
--To the Death. (Illus.). 256p. (The Cross and Crown Ser.). N.D. Cassell & Co.'s Pubs.

Chevalier, Christa (1937-)
--The Little Bear Who Forgot. Tucker, Kathleen, ed. Chevalier, Christa (1937-), illus. (Illus.). 32p. (Just for Fun Bks.). (ps-3). 1984. (ISBN 0-8075-4571-6). A Whitman.
--Little Green Pumpkins. Chevalier, Christa (1937-), illus. LC 81-12999. (Illus.). 32 p. c.1981. (ISBN 0-8075-4593-7). A. Whitman.
--Spence & the Sleepytime Monster. Tucker, Kathleen, ed. Chevalier, Christa (1937-), illus. (Illus.). 32p. (Just for Fun Bks.). (ps-1). 1984. (ISBN 0-8075-7574-7). A Whitman.
--Spence Isn't Spence Anymore. Chevalier, Christa (1937-), illus. LC 84-29195. (Illus.). 30 p. 1985. (ISBN 0-8075-7565-8). A. Whitman.
--Spence Makes Circles. Chevalier, Christa (1937-), illus. LC 82-11017. p. cm. 1982. (ISBN 0-8075-7570-4). A. Whitman.

Chevalier, Haakon M., Tr, jt. auth. see Aragon, Louis.

Chevalier, Julier C
--Noah's Grandchildren. Trout, W. C., illus. LC 29-17891. viii p., 2 l., 201 p. incl. col. front. illus., plates. 20 1/2 cm. 1929. Doubleday, Doran & Company, Inc.

Chevalier, Paul Eugene George (1925-)
--I Can See You But You Can't See Me. LC 67-11306. 21cm. 279p. 1967, c.1966. Lippincott Co.

Chevalier, Ragnhild
--Wandering Monday and Other Days in Old Bergen. McCreery, James L., illus. LC 31-84110. xiv p., 3 l., 122 p. incl. front., illus., plates, map. 20 1/2 cm. 1931. The Macmillan Company.

Chevallier, Micheline
--Yo and the Yak. LC 63-15061. 1 v. (unpaged) col. illus. 28 cm. 1963. Orion Press.

Chew, Nathaniel Durbin
--A Basket of Verses. Niefert, Bessie Potter, illus. LC 41-97756. 92 p. front, illus. 20 cm. (Contemporary poets of Dorrance 216)). c.1941. Dorrance and Company.

Chew, Ruth (1920-)
--Earthstar Magic. Chew, Ruth (1920-), illus. LC 79-17927. p. cm. c.1979. (ISBN 0-8038-1955-2). Hastings House.
--The Hidden Cave. Chew, Ruth (1920-), illus. (gr. 4-6). 1974. (ISBN 0-590-06115-1, Schol Trade Pap). Schol Bk Serv.
--The Magic Cave. Chew, Ruth (1920-), illus. LC 78-12972. p. cm. 1978. (ISBN 0-8038-4711-4). Hastings House Publishers.
--The Magic Coin. Chew, Ruth (1920-), illus. (Illus.). 128p. (Orig.). (gr. 3-5). 1983. (ISBN 0-590-32640-6). Scholastic Inc.
--Magic in the Park. Chew, Ruth (1920-), illus. (Illus.). (gr. 4-6). 1974. (ISBN 0-590-09396-7, Schol Pap). Schol Bk Serv.
--Mostly Magic. Chew, Ruth (1920-), illus. LC 81-85095. (Illus.). 126 p. 20cm. c.1982. (ISBN 0-8234-0450-1). Holiday House.
--No Such Thing As a Witch. Chew, Ruth (1920-), illus. LC 79-18153. (Illus.). 112 p. 22cm. 1980, c.1971. (ISBN 0-8038-5073-5). Hastings House.
--Secondhand Magic. Chew, Ruth (1920-), illus. LC 81-3822. p. cm. c.1981. (ISBN 0-8234-0430-7). Holiday House.
--The Secret Tree House. Chew, Ruth (1920-), illus. (Illus.). (gr. 2-3). 1975. (ISBN 0-590-09945-0, Schol Trade Pap). Schol Bk Serv.
--Summer Magic. Chew, Ruth (1920-), illus. (gr. k-3). 1977. (ISBN 0-590-10421-7). Scholastic Inc.
--The Trouble with Magic. Chew, Ruth (1920-), illus. LC 76-10866. (Illus.). 112 p. 21cm. c.1976. (ISBN 0-396-07364-6). Dodd, Mead.
--The Wednesday Witch. LC 72-75598. (Illus.). 128 p. 21cm. 1972, c.1969. (ISBN 0-8234-0210-X). Holiday House.
--What the Witch Left. Chew, Ruth (1920-), illus. LC 73-13649. (Illus.). 128 p. 22cm. 1973. (ISBN 0-8038-8065-0). Hastings House.
--The Wishing Tree. Chew, Ruth (1920-), illus. LC 80-14922. p. cm. c.1980. (ISBN 0-8038-8099-5). Hastings House.
--Witch in the House. (gr. 2-4). 1976. (ISBN 0-8038-8080-4). Hastings.
--Witch in the House. Chew, Ruth (1920-), illus. (Illus.). (gr. 2-3). 1976. (ISBN 0-590-00093-4). Scholastic Inc.
--Witch's Broom. Chew, Ruth (1920-), illus. LC 77-6090. (Illus.). 128 p. 21cm. c.1977. (ISBN 0-396-07486-3). Dodd, Mead.
--The Witch's Buttons. Chew, Ruth (1920-), illus. LC 74-17070. p. cm. 1974. (ISBN 0-8038-8071-5). Hastings House.
--The Witch's Garden. Chew, Ruth (1920-), illus. LC 78-26939. (Illus.). 112 p. 22cm. 1979, c.1978. (ISBN 0-8038-8093-6). Hastings House.
--The Would-Be Witch. Chew, Ruth (1920-), illus. LC 77-24449. p. cm. 1977. (ISBN 0-8038-8084-7). Hastings House.

Cheyne, Wanda
--Animal Crackers: What's Mooranda up to Now?. Shortall, Leonard W, illus. LC 76-15573. (Illus.). 64 p. 29cm. 1976. (ISBN 0-528-82026-5). (ISBN 0-528-80025-6). Rand McNally.
--Janie's Secret. Cheyne, Wanda, illus. LC 77-164852. (Illus.). 38 p. 29cm. 1973. (ISBN 0-513-01214-1). Denison.
--Nectar the Giraffe: Oolie the Owl. Cheyne, Wanda, illus. LC 46-639284. 30, 1 p. col. illus. 22 x 13 1/2 cm. 1946. Conjure House.

Cheyney, Edward Gheen (1878-)
--Matu, the Iroquois. Berger, William Merritt (1872-), illus. LC 28-11167. 5 p. l., 3-303 p. incl plates. front; 21 cm. 1928. Little, Brown, and Company.
--Scott Burton and the Timber Thieves. LC 22-4528. 3 p. l., 275. 1 p. front. 19 1/2 cm. 1922. D. Appleton and Company.
--Scott Burton, Forester. Rockwell, Norman Percevel (1894-1978), illus. LC 17-11697. 4 p. l., 309 1 p. col. front, col. plates. 19 1/2 cm. 1917. D. Appleton and Company.
--Scott Burton in the Blue Ridge. LC 24-206149. vi p., 1 l., 267, 1 p. front. 19 1/2 cm. 1924. D. Appleton and Company.
--Scott Burton, Logger. LC 23-7523. 4 p. l., 253, 1 p. front. 19 1/2 cm. 1923. D. Appleton and Company.
--Scott Burton on the Range. LC 20-17179. 3 p. l., 308 p. front. 19 1/2 cm. N.D. D. Appleton and Company,.

--The Boy Spies at the Battle of New Orleans: A Story of the Port They Took in Its Defense. (The Boy Spies Ser.). N.D. A. L. Burt Company.
--A Brave Defense. Davis, J. Watson, illus. LC 19-36. (Illus.). 12cm. 254p. (The Young Patriot Ser.). 1900. A. L. Burt's Pubs.
--Budd Boyd's Triumph: Or, The Boy-Firm of Fox Island. LC 12-31526. 1 p. l., 5-256 p. front. illus. 19 cm. (On cover: Boys' home library. no. 22). c.1889. A. L. Burt.
--Budd Boyd's Triumph: Or, The Boy Firm of Fox Island. (The Alger Series for Boys). N.D. A. L. Burt's Pubs.
--In Defense of Liberty: A Story of the Burning of the British Schooner Gaspee in 1772. Davis, J. Watson, illus. LC 8-10281. 2 p. l., 3-280 p. front., 5 pl. 19 1/2 cm. c.1908. A. L. Burt Company.
--In Ship and Prison: A Story of Five Years in the Continental Navy with Captain Samuel Tucker. De Bebian, Arthur, illus. LC 8-19718. 357 p. front. 3 pl. 19 1/2 cm. c.1908. The Sealfield Publishing Co.
--In the Track of the Enemy: A Story of Naval Prowess in 1776, As Told by Midshipman Henry Gardiner. Davis, J. Watson, illus. LC 7-9549. 3 p. l., iii-v, 287 p. front., 5 pl. 19 1/2 cm. c.1907. A. L. Burt Company.
--The Navy Boys' Cruise to the Bahamas: The Adventures of Two Yankee Middies With the First Cruise of an American Squadron in 1775. (The Navy Boys Ser.). N.D. A. L. Burt.
--The Navy Boys' Daring Capture: The Story of How the Navy Boys Helped to Capture the British Cutter "Margaretta" in 1775. (The Navy Boys Ser.). N.D. A. L. Burt Company.
--The Navy Boys in Defense of Liberty: A Story of the Burning of the British Schooner Gaspee in 1772. (The Navy Boys Ser.). N.D. A. L. Burt Company.
--The Navy Boys in the Track of the Enemy: The Story of a Remarkable Cruise With the Sloop of War "Providence.". (The Navy Boys Ser.). N.D. A. L. Burt Company.
--Roy Gilbert's Search. (Illus.). (The Alger Series for Boys). N.D. A. L. Burt's Pubs.
--Roy Gilbert's Search. A Tale of the Great Lakes. LC 12-31332. 277 p. incl. front., illus. 19 1/2 cm. (On cover: Boys' home library, v. 1. no. 20). c.1889. A. L. Burt.
--Roy Gilbert's Search: A Tale of the Great Lakes. (The Rugby Series for Boys and Girls). N.D. A. L. Burt Company.
--Roy Gilbert's Search: A Tale of the Great Lakes. (Wide Awake Boys Ser.). N.D. A. L. Burt.
--A Tory's Revenge: Being Ben. Mathew's Account of the Burning of Falmouth in 1775. Davis, J. Watson, illus. LC 5-23027. 19cm. 261p. 1905. A. L. Burt Co.
--Two Yankee Middies: A Story of the First Cruise of an American Squadron in 1775. Davis, J. Watson, illus. LC 4-10922. 19cm. 300p. 1904. A. L. Burt Co.
--A Yankee Lad's Pluck. (Illus.). (The Alger Series for Boys). N.D. A. L. Burt's Pubs.
--A Yankee Lad's Pluck: How Bert Larkin Saved His Father's Ranch. (The Rugby Series for Boys and Girls). N.D. A. L. Burt Company.
--A Yankee Lad's Pluck: How Bert Larkin Saved His Father's Ranch. (Wide Awake Boys Ser.). N.D. A. L. Burt.
--The Young Minuteman. LC 99-53. (Illus.). 12cm. 312p. (The Young Patriot Ser.). 1899. A. L. Burt's Pubs.

Chipman, William Pendleton (1848-1912) & Chipman, Charles Phillips (1878-)
--An Aerial Runaway: The Balloon Adventures of Rod & Tod in North & South America. McCullough, William A., illus. LC 1-31523. 387 p. front., 3 pl. 19 cm. 1901. Lothrop Publishing Company.

Chipperfield, Joseph Eugene (1912-1980)
--Beyond the Timberland Trail. 1st ed. Gay, Zhenya (1906-1978), illus. LC 52-13683. 245p. illus. 22cm. 1953. Longmans, Green.
--Boru: Dog of the O'Malley. Ambler, Christopher Gifford (1886-), illus. LC 66-8358. (Illus.). 180 p. 21cm. 1966. D. McKay Co.
--Checoba, Stallion of the Comanche. Ambler, Christopher Gifford (1886-), illus. LC 66-176003. 192p. illus. 21cm. (gr. 4-8). 1966, c.1964. Roy.
--Dark Fury: Stallion of the Lost River Valley. Ambler, Christopher Gifford (1886-), illus. LC 57-5965. 218p. illus. 21cm. 1957. Roy Publishers.
--A Dog to Trust: The Saga of a Seeing-Eye Dog. Toschik, Larry (1922-), illus. LC 64-11511. (Illus.). 181 p. 21cm. (gr. 7-12). 1964, c.1963. (ISBN 0-679-25038-7). D. McKay Co.
--Ghost Horse, Stallion of the Oregon Trail. Ambler, Christopher Gifford (1886-), illus. LC 61-17211. 21cm. 190p. 1962. Roy.
--The Gray Dog from Galtymore. Shenton, Edward (1895-), illus. LC 62-11930. (Illus.). 184 p. 21cm. 1962. McKay.
--Greatheart: The Salvation Hunter. Ambler, Christopher Gifford (1886-), illus. LC 53-2524. 208p. illus. 21cm. 1953. Roy.
--Greeka: Eagle of the Hebrides. Toschik, Larry (1922-), illus. LC 54-666653. 236p. illus. 21cm. 1st U.S. edition. 1954. Longmans, Green.
--Greeka: Eagle of the Hebrides. Toschik, Larry (1922-), illus. LC 51-6666. 21cm. 236p. 1954. McKay.
--Grey Chieftain. Ambler, Christopher Gifford (1886-), illus. LC 54-10470. 240p. illus. 21cm. 1954. Roy Publishers.
--Hunter of Harter Fell. Ambrus, Victor G., pseud. (1935-), illus. Ambrus, Gyozo Laszlo. LC 77-351983. (Illus.). 192 p. 21cm. 1976. (ISBN 0-09-127680-2). Hutchinson.
--Petrus: Dog of the Hill Country. 1st ed. Tresilian, Cecil Stuart (1891-), illus. LC 60-13341. 176p. illus. 21cm. (gr. 6-9). 1960. Longmans, Green.
--Rooloo: Stag of Dark Water. Ambler, Christopher Gifford (1886-), illus. LC 62-15488. 192 p. illus. 21 cm. (gr. 4-6). 1963. Roy.
--Sabre of Storm Valley. Ambler, Christopher Gifford (1886-), illus. LC 64-25269. 176p. illus. 21cm. (gr. 4-6). 1965, c.1962. Roy.
--Seokoo of the Black Wind. Ambler, Christopher Gifford (1886-), illus. LC 62-18966. 180p. illus. 22cm. (gr. 7-9). 1962. (ISBN 0-679-20282-X). David McKay Co.
--Silver Star, Stallion of the Echoing Mountain. Ambler, Christopher Gifford (1886-), illus. LC 55-5927. 268p. illus. 21cm. 1955. Roy Publishers.
--Storm of Dancerwood. 1st ed. Torrey, Helen (1901-), illus. LC 49-9995. ix, 308 p. illus. 22 cm. 1949. Longmans, Green.
--Windruff of Links Tor. Torrey, Helen (1901-), illus. LC 51-11603. (Illus.). ix, 305 p. 22cm. 1951. Longmans, Green.
--Wolf of Badenoch: Dog of the Grampian Hills. 1st ed. Ambler, Christopher Gifford (1886-), illus. LC 59-9292. (Illus.). 244 p. 21cm. 1959. Longmans, Green.
--Wolf of Badenoch: Dog of the Grampian Hills. Ambler, Christopher Gifford (1886-), illus. (Illus.). (gr. 6-9). 1959. (ISBN 0-679-20255-2). McKay.

Chisholm, Anne, tr. see Reggiani, Renee.

Chisholm, Edwin
--Chummy Book. N.D. Thomas Nelson & Sons.
--Jolly Book. N.D. Thomas Nelson & Sons.

Chisholm, Louey, ed.
--Celtic Tales: Told to the Children. xi. 115 p. col. front. col. plates (incl. front.) 15 cm. (Half-title: Told to the children series: ed. by Louey Chisholm). 1910. T.C. & C. Jack.
--The Enchanted Land. (Illus.). 8vocm. N.D. G. P. Putnam's Sons.
--The Enchanted Land: Tales Told Again. Cameron, Katharine, illus. (Honor Books). N.D. Nelson.
--The Golden Staircase: Poems and Verses for Children. LC 71-37011. (Illus.). 1 v. (various pagings). 23cm. (Granger index reprint series). 1971. (ISBN 0-8369-6310-5). Books for Libraries Press.
--The Golden Staircase: Poems and Verses for Children. LC 20-26974. xxxi, 361 p. col. front 21 cm. 1920. G. P. Putnam's Sons.
--The Golden Staircase: Poems & Verses for Children. LC 79-51973. (Illus.). Repr. of 1906 ed (Pub. by Putnam). (Granger Poetry Library). (gr. 3-8). 1980. (ISBN 0-89609-182-1). Granger Bk.
--The Golden Staircase: Poems and Verses for Children. Spooner, M. Dibdin, illus. xxxi, 361 p. 16 col. pl. (incl. front.) 24 cm. 1907. G. P. Putnam's Sons.
--Gulliver's Travels. Abridged. N.D. Thomas Nelson & Sons.
--Hop O' My Thumb and the Wolf and Seven Kids. N.D. Dodge.
--In Fairyland. (Honor Bks.). N.D. Thomas Nelson & Sons.
--In Fairyland: Tales Told Again. Cameron, Katharine, illus. N.D. G. P. Putnam's Sons.
--Jack and the Bean Stalk, Little Red Riding Hood, and Cinderella. (I Read Them Myself Ser.). N.D. Dodge.
--King Arthur's Knights. N.D. Thomas Nelson & Sons.
--Nursery Rhymes. LC 8-14826. vii, 118 p. 24 col. pl. (incl. front.) 15 x 12 cm. (Half-title: Told to the children series). 1908. E. P. Dutton & Co.
--Nursery Rhymes. N.D. Nelson.
--Nursery Rhymes. Praegar, S. R. & Orr, Jack, illus. N.D. E. P. Dutton & Co.
--Stories for the Eight Year Old. N.D. Frederick A. Stokes.
--Stories for the Nine Year Old. N.D. Frederick A. Stokes.
--Stories for the Seven Year Old. N.D. Frederick A. Stokes.
--Stories for the Ten Year Old. N.D. Frederick A. Stokes.
--Stories from the Arabian Nights. N.D. Thomas Nelson & Sons.

Chisholm, Louey, ed. see Andersen, Hans Christian.

Chisholm, Louey, ed. see Defoe, Daniel.

Chisholm, Louey, as told by see Edgeworth, Maria.

Chisholm, Louey, ed. see Homerus.

Chisholm, Louey, ed. see Macgregor, Mary.

Chisholm, Louey, ed. see Marshall, Henrietta Elizabeth.

Chisholm, Louey, ed. see Shakespeare, William.

Chisholm, Louey & Steedman, Amy, eds.
--A Staircase of Stories. LC 20-26559. (Illus.). 24cm. vii, 526p. N.D. Putnam.

Chisholn, Louey, ed. see Macgregor, Mary Esther Miller, Mrs.

Chiswell
--The Slave Prince. Cooper, Alfred W., illus. N.D. Brentano's Publications.

Chittenden, Anna G., jt. auth. see Colson, Elizabeth.

Chittenden, Charlotte E
--The Christmas Book. N.D. George W. Jacobs.
--What Two Children Did. (Little Maid Ser.). N.D. George W. Jacobs.
--What Two Children Did. (Illus.). (Little Maid Ser.). N.D. Hurst and Company.
--What Two Children Did. (The Vacation Bks.). (gr. 2-7). N.D. Penn Publishing Co.

Chittenden, Margaret (1935-)
--The Mystery of the Missing Pony. Sanderson, Ruth, illus. LC 79-19084. (Illus.). 64 p. 23cm. (Garrard mystery book). c.1980. (ISBN 0-8116-6411-2). Garrard Pub. Co.
--When the Wild Ducks Come. Darwin, Beatrice, illus. (Illus.). 1972. (ISBN 0-695-80348-4). (ISBN 0-695-40348-6). Follett Co.

Chittick, Victor Lovitt Oakes, intro. by see Aldrich, Thomas Bailey.

Chittle, M. E.
--Tiny Toddlers: Poems and Rhymes. Jackson, Helen Maria Fiske Hunt, Mrs. (1831-1885), illus. 36p. (No. 82). N.D. Raphael Tuck & Sons.

Chittum, Ida (1918-)
--The Cat's Pajamas. Cumings, Art, illus. LC 80-10579. (Illus.). 39 p. 24cm. c.1980. (ISBN 0-8193-1029-8). (ISBN 0-8193-1030-1). Parents Magazine Press.
--Clabber Biscuits. Dolezal, Carroll, illus. LC 72-77. (Illus.). 32 p. 1972. (ISBN 0-8114-7745-2). Steck-Vaughn Co.
--Farmer Hoo and the Baboons. Rounds, Glen Harold (1906-), illus. LC 77-132357. (Illus.). 64 p. 1971. Delacorte Press.
--The Ghost Boy of El Toro. LC 78-1079. 169 p. 21cm. c.1978. (ISBN 0-8309-0201-5). Independence Press.
--The Hermit Boy. Rivkin, Jay, illus. LC 77-180923. (Illus.). 164 p. 22cm. 1972. Delacorte Press.
--A Nutty Business. Gammell, Stephen, illus. LC 72-97313. (Illus.). 32 p. 27cm. 1973. (ISBN 0-399-20353-2). (ISBN 0-399-20353-2). Putnam.
--The Princess Book. LC 74-8383. (Illus.). 60 p. 29cm. 1974. (ISBN 0-528-82095-8). (ISBN 0-528-82096-6). Rand McNally.
--The Secrets of Madam Renee. Brackenbury, Robert, illus. LC 74-82424. (Illus.). 154 p. 21cm. 1975. (ISBN 0-8309-0127-2). Independence Press.
--Tales of Terror: Not for Young Children. Altschuler, Franz (1923-), illus. LC 75-14270. p. cm. 128p. (gr. 7up). 1975. (ISBN 0-528-82166-0). (ISBN 0-528-80145-7). Rand McNally.

Chitwood, Deb
--The Magic Ring. Fraydas, Stan (1918-), illus. LC 82-62432. (Illus.). 32p. (ps-3). 1983. (ISBN 0-942044-01-0). (ISBN 0-942044-01-0). Polestar.

Chlad, Dorothy
--Bicycles are Fun to Ride. Halverson, Lydia, illus. 1984. Childrens Pr.

Choate, Agnes M., illus.
--The History of Little Goody Two Shoes. LC 60-58019. 32p. illus. 19cm. (Instructor Literature Ser.: No. 35). c.1912. F. A. Owen Pub. Co.

Choate, Florence
--Fast Turns. 1st ed. LC 52-9529. 176 p. 21 cm. 1952. Lippincott.

Choate, Florence & Curtis, Elizabeth
--Abby in the Gobi: Or, The Last of the Dinosaurs. Choate, Florence & Curtis, Elizabeth, illus. LC 29-18023. 3 p. l., 3-63 p. illus. (part col.) 22 x 28 cm. c.1929. R. M. McBride & Company.
--Absolute Pitch. Choate, Florence & Curtis, Elizabeth, illus. LC 39-23866. 6 p. l., 3-261 p. incl. front., illus., plates. 21 cm. c.1939. Harcourt, Brace and Company.
--The Crimson Shawl: The Story of a Girl from Acadia. Choate, Florence & Curtis, Elizabeth, illus. LC 41-15924. vii p., 2 l., 211 p. incl. illus., plates. 21 1/2 cm. c.1941. Frederick A. Stokes Company.
--Dance of the Hours. Choate, Florence & Curtis, Elizabeth, illus. LC 34-32404. 6 p. l., 3-242 p. incl. illus., plates. front. 21 cm. c.1934. Harcourt, Brace and Company.
--The Five Gold Sovereigns: A Story of Thomas Jefferson's Time. Choate, Florence & Curtis, Elizabeth, illus. LC 43-138333. vii, 207 p. incl. front., illus. 21 cm. 1943. Frederick A. Stokes Company.
--The Five Gold Sovereigns: A Story of Thomas Jefferson's Times. N.D. J. B. Lippincott.
--Linda Takes Over. Choate, Florence & Curtis, Elizabeth, illus. LC 49-107304. 183 p. illus. 21 cm. 1949. J. B. Lippincott Co.
--Lysbet: A Story of Old New York. Choate, Florence & Curtis, Elizabeth, illus. LC 47-31495. 5 l., 3-220 p. illus. 22 cm. 1947. J. B. Lippincott Co.
--Pinafores and Pantalets. Choate, Florence & Curtis, Elizabeth, illus. LC 31-22895. viii p., 2 l., 3-207 p. front., illus., plates. 21 cm. c.1931. Harcourt, Brace and Company.

Choate, Florence & Curtis, Elizabeth, eds.
--The Little People of the Hills. Choate, Florence & Curtis, Elizabeth, illus. LC 28-22372. 2 p. l., iii-v p., 3 l., 3-234 p. incl. illus., plates. 22 1/2 cm. c.1928. Harcourt, Brace and Company.

Choate, Judith Newkirk (1940-)
--Awful Alexander. 1st ed. Kellogg, Steven (1941-), illus. LC 74-28281. p. cm. 1976. (ISBN 0-385-01725-1). (ISBN 0-385-01819-3). Doubleday.

Choate, Lowell
--The Romance of a Letter, 1 0f 18 vols. (Library of Romance Ser). N.D. Lothrop Pub. co.

Chodzko, Aleksander Borejko (1804-1891)
--The Golden Hand Fairy Book. LC 7-28970. (Contents: The Prince with the Golden hand--Imperishable--The Bird of Fire--The story of the Plentiful Tablecloth, the avenging wand, the sash that becomes a lake, and the terrible helmet--The Spirit of the Steppes, The Sovereign of the Mineral Kingdom). (Illus.). 20cm. 127p. 1906. McLouglin Brothers.
--Slav Tales. Harding, Emily J., illus. Harding, Emily J., tr. N.D. Charles Scribner's Sons.
--Tears of Pearls Fairy Book. LC 7-30435. (Illus.). 20cm. 126p. 1906. McLoughlin Brothers.

Cholmeley, K.
--Margery Kempe. N.D. Longmans, Green & Co.

Chonz, Selina
--A Bell for Ursli. Carigiet, Alois (1902-), illus. LC 67-639. (Illus.). 43p. 1966. H. Z. Walck.
--Florina and the Wild Bird. Carigiet, Alois (1902-), illus. Serrailer, Anne & Serrailer, Ian, trs. LC 67-638. (Illus.). 1 v. (unpaged). 1952. H. Z. Walck. **Award: (NYT).**
--Florina and the Wild Bird. Carigiet, Alois (1902-), illus. Serraillier, Anne & Serraillier, Ian Lucien (1912-), trs. from Ger. LC 67-638. 1 v. (unpaged) col. illus. 25 x 33cm. 1966. H. Z. Walck.
--The Snowstorm. 1966. Henry Z. Walck Inc.
--Snowstorm. Carigiet, Alois (1902-), illus. (Illus.). (gr. k-3). 1958. (ISBN 0-8098-1054-9). Walck.
--The Snowstorm. Rev ed. Carigiet, Alois (1902-), illus. LC 58-3713. unpaged. illus. 25x33cm. 1966. Walck.

Chop, Clark
--Animals in the Barnyard, Set A. 31p. 1962. Pitman Publishing Corporation.
--The Country Mouse and Other Stories, Set A. 31p. 1962. Pitman Publishing Corporation.
--In and out, Set A. 31p. 1962. Pitman Publishing Corporation.
--The Pumkin Moon, Set A. 31p. 1962. Pitman Publishing Corporation.
--Rainbow Stories, Set A. 31p. 1962. Pitman Publishing Corporation.

Chopyak, Josephine
--A Turtle's Pond. 1983. (ISBN 0-533-05471-0). Vantage.

Chorao, Ann Mckay Sproat, jt. auth. see Klein, Norma.

Chorao, Ann Mckay Sproat, jt. auth. see Schweninger, Ann.

Chorao, Ann Mckay Sproat (1936-)
--The Baby's Bedtime Book. Chorao, Ann Mckay Sproat (1936-), illus. LC 84-6067. (Illus.). 64p. (ps). 1984. (ISBN 0-525-44149-2). (ISBN 0-525-44149-2). Dutton.
--The Baby's Lap Book. Chorao, Ann Mckay Sproat (1936-), illus. LC 77-23534. p. cm. c.1977. Dutton.
--Ida Makes a Movie. Chorao, Ann Mckay Sproat (1936-), illus. LC 73-20147. (Illus.). 48 p. 1974. (ISBN 0-8164-3121-3). Seabury Press.
--Kate's Box. Chorao, Ann Mckay Sproat (1936-), illus. LC 82-2403. (Illus.). 24p. (ps). 1982. (ISBN 0-525-44010-0). Dutton.
--Kate's Car. Chorao, Ann Mckay Sproat (1936-), illus. LC 82-2393. (Illus.). 24p. (ps). 1982. (ISBN 0-525-44011-9). Dutton.
--Kate's Quilt. Chorao, Ann Mckay Sproat (1936-), illus. LC 82-2395. (Illus.). 24p. (ps). 1982. (ISBN 0-525-44012-7). Dutton.
--Kate's Snowman. Chorao, Ann Mckay Sproat (1936-), illus. LC 82-2407. (Illus.). 24p. (ps). 1982. (ISBN 0-525-44013-5). Dutton.

--Lemon Moon. Chorao, Ann Mckay Sproat (1936-), illus. LC 83-220. p. cm. c.1983. (ISBN 0-8234-0490-0). Holiday House.
--Lester's Overnight. Chorao, Ann Mckay Sproat (1936-), illus. LC 76-50029. (Illus.). 32 p. 25cm. c.1977. (ISBN 0-525-33480-7). E. P. Dutton.
--A Magic Eye for Ida. Chorao, Ann Mckay Sproat (1936-), illus. LC 72-85337. (Illus.). 48 p. 1973. (ISBN 0-8164-3091-8). Seabury Press.
--Maudie's Umbrella. Chorao, Ann Mckay Sproat (1936-), illus. LC 75-5922. (Illus.). 29 p. 27cm. 1975. (ISBN 0-525-34770-4). Dutton.
--Molly's Lies. Chorao, Ann Mckay Sproat (1936-), illus. 1979. Houghton.
--Molly's Lies. Chorao, Ann Mckay Sproat (1936-), illus. LC 78-12383. (Illus.). 32 p. 27cm. c.1979. (ISBN 0-8164-3225-2). Seabury Press.
--Molly's Moe. Chorao, Ann Mckay Sproat (1936-), illus. LC 76-3526. (Illus.). 32 p. 26cm. c.1976. (ISBN 0-8164-3171-X). Seabury Press.
--Oink & Pearl. Chorao, Ann McKay Sproat (1936-), illus. (Illus.). 5 7/8 x 8 1/2. (18 pt.). (I Can Read Bks.). (ps-3). 1982. (ISBN 0-06-021272-1). (ISBN 0-06-021273-X). Har-Row.
--Ralph and the Queen's Bathtub. Chorao, Ann Mckay Sproat (1936-), illus. LC 73-90517. (Illus.). 61 p. 1974. (ISBN 0-374-36179-7). Farrar, Straus and Giroux.
--The Repair of Uncle Toe. Chorao, Ann Mckay Sproat (1936-), illus. LC 77-184129. (Illus.). 45 p. 27cm. 1972. (ISBN 0-374-36245-9). Farrar, Straus and Giroux.

Chorao, Ann McKay Sproat (1936-), retold by.
--The Baby's Story Book. Chorao, Ann McKay Sproat (1936-), illus. 64p. 1985. (ISBN 0-525-44200-6). Dutton.

Chorao, Kay see Chorao, Ann Mckay Sproat.
Chorao, Kay see Klein, Norma (1938-) & Chorao, Ann Mckay Sproat.
Chorao, Kay see Schweninger, Ann (1951-) & Chorao, Ann Mckay Sproat.
Chorao, Kay see Chorao, Ann McKay Sproat.
Chorley, Henry F., tr. see LaPointe, Savinien.
Chorpenning, Charlotte Lee Barrows (1872-1955), adapted by see Andersen, Hans Christian.
Chorpenning, Charlotte Lee Barrows (1872-1955), adapted by see Bannerman, Helen Brodie Cowan Watson, Mrs.
Chorpenning, Charlotte Lee Barrows, adapted by see Clemens, Samuel Langhorne.
Chorpenning, Charlotte Lee Barrows (1872-1955), adapted by see Defoe, Daniel.
Chorpenning, Charlotte Lee Barrows (1872-1955), adapted by see Dodge, Mary Elizabeth Mapes, Mrs.
Chorpenning, Charlotte Lee Barrows (1872-1955), adapted by see Grimm, Jakob Ludwig Karl (1785-1863) & Grimm, Wilhelm Karl.
Chorpenning, Charlotte Lee Barrows (1872-1955), adapted by see Thurber, James Grover.

Chorpenning, Charlotte Lee Barrows (1872-1955)
--Abe Lincoln: New Salem Days. (Children's Theatre Playscript Ser.). 1954. (ISBN 0-88020-006-5). Coach Hse.
--Flibbertygibbet: (His Last Chance). 1952. Children's Theatre Press.
--The Indian Captive. 1936. Children's Theatre Press.
--Jack and the Beanstalk. 1935. Children's Theatre Press.
--Lincoln's Secret Messenger: Boy Detective to a President. (Children's Theatre Playscript Ser.). 1955. (ISBN 0-88020-036-7). Coach Hse.
--Little Lee Bobo, Chinatown Detective. 1948. Children's Theatre Press.
--Little Red Riding Hood: Or, Grandmother Slyboots. 1946. Children's Theatre Press.
--The Magic Horn: A Story of Roland and Charlamagne. (Children's Theatre Playscript Ser.). 1954. (ISBN 0-88020-040-5). Coach Hse.
--Radio Rescue. (Children's Theatre Playscript Ser.). 1970. (ISBN 0-88020-046-4). Coach Hse.
--Rama & the Tigers. rev. ed. (Children's Theatre Playscript Ser.). 1954. (ISBN 0-88020-047-2). Coach Hse.
--Rhodopis: The First Cinderella. 1934. Coach House Press.
--The Three Little Bears. 1949. Children's Theatre Press.

Chorpenning, Charlotte Lee Barrows (1872-1955), adapted by.
--The Adventures of Tom Sawyer. (Children's Theatre Playscript Ser.). 1956. (ISBN 0-88020-008-1). Coach Hse.
--The Adventures of Tom Sawyer. LC 47-25396. (Dramatized from the story by Samuel Langhorne Clemens (Mark Twain, pseud.), 1835-1910). 86p. 1946. The Dramatic Publishing Co.
--Alice in Wonderland. rev. ed. (Children's Theatre Playscript Ser.). 1959. (ISBN 0-88020-018-9). Coach Hse.
--Alice in Wonderland. LC 47-25628. (Dramatized from the story by Charles Lutwidge Dodgson (Lewis Carroll, pseud.), 1832-1898). 19cm. 68p. 1946. The Dramatic Publishing Co.
--The Elves and the Shoemaker. Tully, Nora, illus. 1946. Children's Theatre Press.
--King Midas and the Golden Touch. 1950. Children's Theatre Press.
--Rip Van Winkle. (Children's Theatre Playscript Ser.). 1954. (ISBN 0-88020-050-2). Coach Hse.
--The Sleeping Beauty. 1947. Children's Theatre Press.

Choudhary, Bani Roy
--The Mahabharata. (Illus.). (gr. 3-10). 1979. (ISBN 0-89744-132-X). Auromere.
--Prince of Dwarka. (gr. 4-6). 1970. (ISBN 0-88253-237-5). InterCulture.
--The Story of Krishna. (Illus.). (gr. 3-10). 1979. (ISBN 0-89744-134-6). Auromere.
--The Story of Ramayan. (Illus.). (gr. 3-10). 1979. (ISBN 0-89744-133-8). Auromere.
--Story of Ramayan: The Epic Tale of India. (gr. 4-6). 1970. (ISBN 0-88253-238-3). InterCulture.

Chowen, Agnes B
--Living Wild: Or, Pioneer Children of Montana. Best, Allena Champlin, Mrs. (1892-1974), illus. Berry, Erick, pseud. LC 29-12531. vi p., 2 l., 3-247 p. incl. front., illus. plates. 21 1/2 cm. 1929. E.P. Dutton & Co., Inc.

Chow-Leung, jt. ed. see Davis, Mary Hayes.

Chrestien, F. H
--Evelyn and the Fish. Chrestien, F. H, illus. LC 45-4611. 48 p. incl. col. front., illus. (part col.) 28 cm. 1945. The Hyperion Press, Distributed by Duell, Sloan and Pearce.

Chrestien De Troyes (1150-1190)
--Erec and Enid. 1st ed. Schiller, Barbara, adapted by. Forberg, Ati, pseud. (1925-), illus. Forberg, Beate Gropius. LC 70-116887. (Illus.). 45 p. 22cm. 1970. (ISBN 0-525-29346-9). Dutton.
--The Knight of the Lion. Hieatt, Constance B., retold by. Low, Joseph (1911-), illus. LC 68-13583. (Illus.). 68 p. 25cm. 1968. Crowell.
--The Knight of the Lion. Hopkins, Annette Brown (1879-), adapted by. LC 16-23962. (Tr. and Adapted From the French of Chrestien De Troyes). ix, 152 p. front., illus. 18 cm. (Everychild's series) $0.40.). 1916. The Macmillan Company.
--The Story of the Grail. Linker, White Robert, tr. 208p. 1960. U.N. C. Press.

Chrisman, Arthur Bowie (1889-1953)
--Shen of the Sea: A Book for Children. Hasselriis, Else, illus. LC 25-153841. (gr. 4-7). 1926. Dutton. **Award: (JNM).**
--Shen of the Sea: A Book for Children. Hasselriis, Else, illus. LC 25-153841. xii p., 1 l., 252 p. illus. 20 cm. N.D. Dutton.
--Shen of the Sea: Chinese Stories for Children. Hasselriis, Else, illus. LC 68-13420. (Illus.). 221 p. 22cm. 1968, c.1953. Dutton.
--Treasures Long Hidden: Old Tales and New Tales of the East. Yap, Weda (1894-), illus. LC 41-15194. 302, 1 p. illus. 21 x 16 cm. 1941. E.P. Dutton & Company, Inc.
--The Wind That Wouldn't Blow: Stories of the Merry Middle Kingdom for Children, and Myself. Hasselriis, Else, illus. LC 27-16469. xii, 355 p. illus. 20 cm. 1927. Dutton.

Christ, Eva M.
--A Handful of Gold. 1978. (ISBN 0-533-03909-6). Vantage.

Christ, Henry I., ed. see Cooper, James Fenimore.
Christ, Henry, I, ed. see Scott, Walter, Sir.
Christ, Henry Irvine, ed. see Dumas, Alexandre.
Christ, Henry Irving, ed. see Stevenson, Robert Louis.

Christ, Henry Irving (1915-), adapted by.
--The Odyssey of Homer. Fraumeni, Thomas G., illus. LC 48-2315. (Illus.). xix. 21cm. 259p. 1948. Globe Book, Co.

Christ, Katherine D
--Boots, the Firemen's Dog. Dobias, Frank (1902-), illus. LC 36-31239. 56 p. illus. 19 1/2 cm. c.1936. American Book Company.
--Willow Brook Farm. LC 48-2984. (Illus.). 24cm. 246p. 1948. D. C. Heath.
--Willow Brook Farm. LC 58-1502. 248p. illus. 24cm. 1958. Heath.

Christal, M
--A Journey Thru Earlyland. (Illus.). 96p. 1982. (ISBN 0-682-49925-0). Exposition.

Christelow, Eileen (1943-)
--Henry & the Dragon. Christelow, Eileen (1943-), illus. LC 83-14405. (Illus.). 32p. (ps-2). 1984. (ISBN 0-89919-220-3, Clarion). HM.
--Henry and the Red Stripes. Christelow, Eileen (1943-), illus. LC 82-71402. p. cm. 32p. (ps-3). c.1982. (ISBN 0-89919-118-5). Clarion Books.
--Henry & the Red Stripes. Christelow, Eileen (1943-), illus. (Illus.). 32p. (ps-3). 1982. (ISBN 0-89919-118-5, Clarion). HM.
--Jerome the Babysitter. LC 84-12738. p. cm. (ps-3). 1985. (ISBN 0-89919-331-5). Clarion Books.
--Mr. Murphy's Marvelous Invention. Christelow, Eileen (1943-), illus. LC 82-9594. p. cm. 1983, c.1982. (ISBN 0-89919-141-X). Clarion Books.

Christensen, Abigail M. H, Mrs.
--Afro-American Folk Lore. LC 71-157364. xiv, 116 p. 23cm. (The Black Heritage Library Collection). 1971, c.1892. (ISBN 0-8369-8802-7). Books for Libraries Press.
--Afro-American Folk Lore: Told Round Cabin Fires on the Sea Islands of South Carolina. LC 14-65569. xiv, 116p. 1892. J. G. Cupples Company.
--Afro-American Folk Lore: Told Round Cabin Fires on the Sea Islands of South Carolina. LC 73-78761. (Illus.). xiv, 116 p. 18cm. 1969. (ISBN 0-8371-1387-3). Negro Universities Press.

Christensen, Anne, ed. see Davis, James Robert.

Christensen, Gardell Dano (1907-)
--Buffalo Horse. Christensen, Gardell Dano (1907-), illus. LC 61-13827. 94p. illus. 23cm. 1961. Nelson.
--Buffalo Kill. Christensen, Gardell Dano (1907-), illus. LC 59-5338. (Illus.). 95 p. 23cm. 1959. Nelson.
--The Buffalo Robe. Christensen, Gardell Dano (1907-), illus. LC 60-11471. (Illus.). 95 p. 23cm. 1960. Nelson.
--Chuck Woodchuck's Secret. Christensen, Gardell Dano (1907-), illus. LC 57-11681. (Illus.). 64p. (gr. k-4). 1957. (ISBN 0-03-031590-5). HR&W.
--Mr. Hare. 1st ed. Christensen, Gardell Dano (1907-), illus. LC 56-10033. 63p. illus. 21cm. 1956. Holt.
--Mrs. Mouse Needs a House. 1st ed. Christensen, Gardell Dano (1907-), illus. LC 58-130687. 63p. illus. 21cm. 1958. Holt.

Christensen, Haaken (1886-)
--Little Bruin. Christensen, Haaken (1886-), illus. Thomsen, Gudrun Thorne, tr. from Norwegian. LC 49-9813. 24 p. col. illus. 19 x 22 cm. 1949. Abingdon-Cokesbury.
--Little Bruin and Per. Christensen, Haaken (1886-), illus. Andrews, Siri, tr. from Norwegian. LC 51-12169. (Illus.). unpaged. 1951. Abingdon-Cokesbury Press.
--Little Bruin Keeps House. Christensen, Haaken (1886-), illus. Andrews, Siri, tr. from Norwegian. LC 59-103632. unpaged. illus. 19x22cm. 1959. Abingdon Press.

Christensen, Hedevig (1899-)
--Stories About Our Holidays Told by Grandpas. Heller, Robin, illus. LC 73-77374. (Illus.). 82 p. 22cm. 1973. (ISBN 0-8059-1852-3). Dorrance.

Christensen, Jack
--The Forgotten Rainbow. Christensen, Lee, illus. 1960. William Morrow & Co.

Christensen, Ruth Koch
--Pinky Pig Sprouts Feathers and Other Stories. Walerstedt, Don, illus. LC 59-14542. unpaged. illus. 19x22cm. 1959. Augustana Press.

Christensen, Vera & Nuhn, Elizabeth
--The Big Cache: Fantasy, Fact, Folklore. Bicentennial ed. Burgon, Lorraine, illus. LC 77-156021. (Illus.). 84 p. 1976. Herald Print. Co.

Christesen, Barbara (1940-)
--Myths of the Orient. LC 77-22199. (Illus.). 48 p. 24cm. c.1977. (ISBN 0-8172-1044-X). Contemporary Perspectives.

Christgau, Alice Erickson (1902-)
--The Laugh Peddler: A Story. LC 68-15340. (Illus.). 156 p. 24cm. (gr. 5-8). 1968. (ISBN 0-201-09251-4). Young Scott Books.
--Rosabel's Secret. Watson, Wendy McLeod (1942-), illus. LC 67-3908. 219 p. illus. 22 cm. 1967. Young Scott Books.
--Runaway to Glory. Summers, Leo, illus. LC 65-208279. 216p. (gr. 5-8). 1965. (ISBN 0-201-09335-9, Young Scott Bks). A-W.

Christian, Dorothy E White
--Pretty Boy and His Friends. Baerg, Harry John (1909-), illus. LC 56-15378. 64p. illus. 26cm. 1955. Review and Herald Pub. Association.

Christian, George, pseud., see Grove, Helen Harriot.

Christian, George
--Patch Pants the Tailor. Christian, George, illus. N.D. Garden City Publishing Co.

Christian, Mary Blount, jt. auth. see Van Woerkom, Dorothy O'Brien.

Christian, Mary Blount (1933-)
--Anna and the Strangers. Cox, Charles T. (1937-), illus. LC 81-243. (Illus.). 30 p. 21cm. c.1981. (ISBN 0-687-01529-4). Abingdon.
--April Fool. Dawson, Diane, illus. LC 81-3782. p. cm. c.1981. (ISBN 0-02-718280-0). Macmillan.
--CB Convoy Caper. (The Goosehill Gang Series). (gr. 2-5). 1981. (ISBN 0-570-07352-9). Concordia.
--Christmas Reflections. Kirchhoff, Art, illus. LC 79-27677. (Illus.). 32 p. 26cm. c.1980. (ISBN 0-570-03494-9). Concordia Pub. House.
--Daniel, Who Dared: Daniel in the Lions' Den for Beginning Readers : Daniel 1: 1-8, 6 for Children. Cunningham, Aline, illus. LC 77-6412. (Illus.). 48 p. 23cm. (I can read a Bible story). c.1977. (ISBN 0-570-07325-1). (ISBN 0-570-07319-7). Concordia Pub. House.
--Dead Man in Catfish Bay. Tucker, Kathleen, ed. Adams, Michael, illus. LC 84-19616. (Illus.). 128p. (High-Low Mysteries Ser.). (gr. 4-9). 1985. (ISBN 0-8075-1522-1). A Whitman.
--Deadline for Danger. De John, Marie, illus. LC 82-17470. p. cm. 1982. (ISBN 0-8075-1518-3). A. Whitman.
--The Devil Take You, Barnabas Beane!. Burgess, Anne (1942-), illus. LC 79-7891. (Illus.). 44 p. c.1980. (ISBN 0-690-03997-2). (ISBN 0-690-03998-0). Crowell.
--David & Goliath. Chartier, Normand (1945-), illus. LC 74-2089. (Illus.). 32 p. 24cm. 1974. (ISBN 0-201-01026-7). Addison-Wesley.
--The Doggone Mystery. Trivas, Irene, illus. LC 80-10448. (Illus.). 30 p. 21cm. (First read-alone mysteries). c.1980. (ISBN 0-8075-1656-2). A. Whitman.
--The Firebug Mystery. Davis, Allen, illus. LC 81-11493. p. cm. 1981. (ISBN 0-8075-2444-1). A. Whitman.
--The First Sign of Winter. Komodo, Beverly (1939-), illus. LC 73-1066. (Illus.). 40 p. 24cm. 1973. (ISBN 0-8193-0671-1). (ISBN 0-8193-0671-1). Parents' Magazine Press.
--Go West, Swamp Monsters!. Brown, Marc Tolon (1946-), illus. LC 84-12686. (Illus.). 48 p. 23cm. (Dial easy-to-read). c.1985. (ISBN 0-8037-0091-1). (ISBN 0-8037-0144-6). Dial Books for Young Readers.
--The Goosehill Gang and the C. B. Convoy Caper. Wind, Betty, illus. LC 77-5766. (Illus.). 32 p. 23cm. c.1977. (ISBN 0-570-07352-9). Concordia Pub. House.
--The Goosehill Gang and the Chocolate Cake Caper. LC 76-3638. p. cm. c.1976. (ISBN 0-570-03606-2). Concordia Pub. House.
--The Goosehill Gang and the Christmas Shoe Thief. Wind, Betty, illus. LC 77-4838. (Illus.). 32 p. 23cm. (gr. 2-5). c.1977. (ISBN 0-570-07351-0). Mo. : Concordia Pub. House.
--The Goosehill Gang and the Disappearing Dues. Wind, Betty, illus. LC 76-3634. p. cm. (gr. 1-4). c.1976. (ISBN 0-570-03607-0). Concordia Pub. House.
--The Goosehill Gang and the Ghost in the Garage. Wind, Betty, illus. LC 78-709. p. cm. c.1978. (ISBN 0-570-07360-X). Concordia Pub. House.
--The Goosehill Gang and the May Basket Mystery. Wind, Betty, illus. LC 78-2443. p. cm. c.1978. (ISBN 0-570-07359-6). Concordia Pub. House.
--The Goosehill Gang and the Mystery of the Runaway House. Wind, Betty, illus. LC 77-5697. (Illus.). 32 p. 23cm. c.1977. (ISBN 0-570-07350-2). Concordia Pub. House.
--The Goosehill Gang and the Pocket Park Problem. Wind, Betty, illus. LC 77-6276. (Illus.). 32 p. 23cm. (gr. 2-5). c.1977. (ISBN 0-570-07353-7). Concordia Pub. House.
--The Goosehill Gang and the Shadow on the Shade Mystery. Wind, Betty, illus. LC 78-1291. (Illus.). 32 p. 23cm. c.1978. (ISBN 0-570-07358-8). Concordia.
--The Goosehill Gang and the Stitch-in-Time Solution. Wind, Betty, illus. LC 78-702. p. cm. c.1978. (ISBN 0-570-07357-X). Concordia Pub. House.
--The Goosehill Gang and the Test Paper Thief. LC 76-3639. p. cm. (gr. 1-4). c.1976. (ISBN 0-570-03608-9). Concordia Pub. House.
--The Goosehill Gang and the Vanishing Sandwich. LC 76-4809. p. cm. (gr. 1-4). c.1976. (ISBN 0-570-03609-7). Concordia Pub. House.
--The Green Thumb Thief. Madden, Donald B. (1927-), illus. LC 81-23989. (Illus.). 32 p. 21cm. (First Read-Alone Mysteries). 1982. (ISBN 0-8075-3040-9). A. Whitman.
--Growin' Pains. LC 85-42796. p. cm. c.1985. (ISBN 0-02-718490-0). Macmillan.
--J. J. Leggett, Secret Agent. Hann, Jacquie (1951-), illus. LC 78-6823. (Illus.). 50 p. 22cm. c.1978. (ISBN 0-688-41864-3). (ISBN 0-688-51864-8). Lothrop, Lee & Shepard.
--Jonah, Go to Nineveh!. Jonah and the Whale for Beginning Readers : the Book of Jonah for Children. Cunningham, Aline, illus. LC 76-15286. (Illus.). 48 p. 23cm. (I can read a Bible story). c.1976. (ISBN 0-570-07307-3). Concordia Pub. House.
--The Lucky Man. Rounds, Glen Harold (1906-), illus. LC 79-11024. (Illus.). 63 p. 23cm. (Ready-to-read). c.1979. (ISBN 0-02-718270-3). Macmillan.
--Mary Blount Christian's "His Brother's Keeper" Plus Nine Other Stories. (Bro-Kee Ser.). (gr. 5-9). 1978. (ISBN 0-570-07765-6). Concordia.
--Mystery at Camp Triumph. Schwark, Mary Beth, illus. LC 85-15378. p. cm. 1986. (ISBN 0-8075-5366-2). A. Whitman.

--The Mystery of the Double, Double Cross. Tucker, Kathleen, ed. LC 82-2575. (Illus.). 128p. (High-Low Pilot Book Ser.). (gr. 5-10). 1982. (ISBN 0-8075-5374-3). A Whitman.
--Mystery of the Runaway House. Wind, Betty, illus. (Goosehill Gang Ser.). (gr. 3-5). 1977. (ISBN 0-570-07350-2). Concordia.
--No Dogs Allowed, Jonathan!. Madden, Donald B. (1927-), illus. LC 74-2128. (Illus.). 32 p. 24cm. 1975. (ISBN 0-201-01028-3). Addison-Wesley.
--Nothing Much Happened Today. Madden, Donald B. (1927-), illus. LC 73-4810. (Illus.). 32 p. 24cm. 1973. (ISBN 0-201-01024-0). Addison-Wesley.
--The Sand Lot. Kendrick, Dennis, illus. LC 77-15894. (Illus.). 28 p. c.1978. (ISBN 0-8178-5827-X). Harvey House.
--Scarabee, the Witch's Cat. McEntire, Sybil, illus. LC 72-5509. (Illus.). 32 p. 1973. (ISBN 0-8114-7750-9). Steck-Vaughn Co.
--Sebastian, Super Sleuth. Axeman, Lois, illus. LC 73-2257. (Illus.). 49 p. 22cm. 1974. (ISBN 0-87955-208-5). (ISBN 0-87955-208-5). J. P. O'Hara.
--Sebastian (Super Sleuth) and the Bone to Pick Mystery. McCue, Lisa, illus. LC 83-5406. (Illus.). 55 p. 22cm. (Sabastian, Super Sleuth). c.1983. (ISBN 0-02-718440-4). Macmillan.
--Sebastian (Super Sleuth) and the Clumsy Cowboy. McCue, Lisa, illus. LC 84-21758. (Illus.). 59 p. 22cm. (Sebastian (super sleuth) Ser.). c.1985. (ISBN 0-02-718480-3). Macmillan.
--Sebastian, Super Sleuth, and the Crummy Yummies Caper. McCue, Lisa, illus. LC 82-20861. p. cm. c.1983. (ISBN 0-02-718260-6). Macmillan.
--Sebastian (Super Sleuth) & the Hair of the Dog Mystery. McCue, Lisa, illus. LC 82-10066. (Illus.). 64p. (Sebastian Super Sleuth Mystery Ser.). (gr. 1-4). N.D. (ISBN 0-02-718260-6). Macmillan.
--Sebastian (Super Sleuth) and the Santa Claus Caper. McCue, Lisa, illus. LC 84-4424. (Illus.). 55 p. 22cm. (Sebastian, Super Sleuth Ser.). c.1984. (ISBN 0-02-718460-9). Macmillan.
--Sebastian (Super Sleuth) & the Secret of the Skewered Skier. McCue, Lisa, illus. (Illus.). 64p. (gr. 2-5). 1984. (ISBN 0-02-718450-1). Macmillan.
--Swamp Monsters. LC 82-1574. p. cm. c.1983. Dial Press.
--The Toady and Dr. Miracle. Ohlsson, Ib (1935-), illus. LC 84-21278. (Illus.). 55 p. 23cm. (Ready-to-Read). c.1985. (ISBN 0-02-718470-6). Macmillan.
--Two-Ton Secret. Madden, Donald B. (1927-), illus. LC 81-346. (Illus.). 32 p. 21cm. (First read-alone mysteries). c.1981. (ISBN 0-8075-8165-8). A. Whitman.
--The Undercover Kids & the Museum Mystery. Fay, Ann, ed. Madden, Donald B. (1927-), illus. LC 83-16682. (Illus.). 32p. (First Read-Alone Mysteries Ser.). (gr. 1-3). 1983. (ISBN 0-8075-8302-2). A Whitman.
--The Vanishing Sandwich. (Illus.). 32p. (Goosehill Gang Ser.). (gr. 1-4). 1976. (ISBN 0-570-03609-7). Concordia.
--The Ventriloquist. Funai, Mamoru R. (1932-), illus. LC 81-7795. (Illus.). 48 p. 23cm. (Break-of-day book). c.1982. (ISBN 0-698-30735-6). Coward, McCann & Geoghegan.

Christian Herald see Shoppell, Robert W.

Christiansen, Reidar, ed.
--Folktales of Norway. Iversen, Pat Shaw, tr. 284p. 1964. The University of Chicago Press.

Christiansen, Ruth
--Dance into My Heart. LC 62-5634. 219 p. 21 cm. 1961. Avalon Books.

Christianson, Nora D
--More Tales from Norway. 1st ed. Williams, Jim, illus. LC 56-9041. 153p. illus. 21cm. 1956. Vantage Press.
--Tales of Norway for Children. 1st ed. Syversen, S. Storm, illus. LC 55-7173. 75p. illus. 21cm. 1955. Vantage Press.

Christie, Agatha Mary Clarissa (1890-1976)
--Surprise! Surprise!. A Collection of Mystery Stories with Unexpected Endings. LC 65-16445. viii, 246p. 21cm. c.1965. Dodd.
--Thirteen Clues for Miss Marple. Bond, Raymond Tostevin (1893-1981), ed. (gr. 9 up). 1966. (ISBN 0-396-05377-7). Dodd.
--Thirteen for Luck. Bond, Raymond Tostevin (1893-1981), ed. LC 61-13216. 21cm. 248p. 1961. Dodd, Mead & Co..

Christie, Ann Philippa Pearce see Pearce, Ann Philippa.

Christie, Ann Phillippa see Fairfax-Lucy, Brian (1898-1974) & Pearce, Ann Philippa.

Christie, Caroline
--Silver Heels: A Story of Blackfeet Indians at Glacier National Park. 1st ed. Wilde, George A., illus. LC 58-567410. 150p. illus. 21cm. 1958. Winston.

Christie, Catherine Allison, Mrs. & Hubbell, Mrs. Rose Strong, Mrs.
--Days of Make-Believe;. A Method of Dramatic Games and Songs for Nursery Schools or Kindergarten and Primary Grades. LC 35-7893. 135 p. illus. 30 1/2 cm. c.1935. Clayton F. Summy Co.

Christie, Don & Hamilton, John Ralph (1923-)
--Apache Boy. LC 68-55432. (Illus.). 79 p. 24cm. 1968. Grosset & Dunlap.

Christie, G. F.
--Dumpy Dimple. (Illus.). N.D. Frederick A. Stokes.

Christin, Pierre & Mezieres, Jean-Claude
--Ambassador of the Shadows. (Illus.). 48p. (Valerian Ser.). N.D. (ISBN 2-205-06949-7). Dargaud Pub.
--Heroes of the Equinox. (Illus.). 48p. (Valerian Ser.). N.D. (ISBN 2-205-06575-0). Dargaud Pub.
--Welcome on Alfloflo. (Illus.). 48p. (Valerian Ser.). N.D. (ISBN 2-205-06951-9). Dargaud Pub.
--World Without Stars. (Illus.). 48p. (Valerian Ser.). N.D. (ISBN 2-205-06573-4). Dargaud Pub.

Christison, Mary Ann
--English Through Poetry. Peterson, Kathleen, illus. (Orig.). (ESL Teacher Reference-Resource Ser.). (gr. 3-6). 1982. (ISBN 0-88084-002-1). Alemany Pr.

Christman, Arthur B.
--Shen of the Sea. N.D. E. P. Dutton & Co.

Christman, Catherine, jt. auth. see Christman, Ernest H.

Christman, Elizabeth (1914-)
--A Nice Italian Girl. LC 75-38357. 128p. (gr. 9 up). 1976. Dodd.

Christman, Ernest H. & Christman, Catherine
--Darby's Stable: Cartoons & Stories Level Two, Progressive Phonics. Christman, Ernest H. & Christman, Catherine, illus. LC 84-50859. (Illus.). 88p. (Orig.). (gr. k-12). 1984. (ISBN 0-912329-04-1). Tutorial Press.

Christmas Annual see Blair, Matilda.

Christopher, Anne
--The Monkey Twins. Hogan, Inez (1895-), illus. LC 35-20668. 33 p. illus. 16 1/2 x 21 1/2 cm. c.1935. Whitman Publishing Co.
--Petunia, Be Keerful. Hogan, Inez (1895-), illus. LC 34-40511. (Illus.). 22cm. 41p. 1934. Whitman Pub. Co.

Christopher, Fanny H.
--Bartholet Milon: A Sequel to Duke Christopher. N.D. Chase & Hall.
--Duke Christopher: A Story of the Reformation. N.D. Chase & Hall.

Christopher, John, pseud., see Youd, Samuel.

Christopher, John
--The Tripods Trilogy, 3 bks. Incl. The White Mountains; the City of Gold & Lead. Youd, Samuel; The Pool of Fire. (gr. 6 up). 1980. Boxed Set (Collier). Macmillan.

Christopher, John, pseud. (1922-)
--Beyond the Burning Lands. Youd, Samuel. 216 p. 18cm. 1974, c.1971. Collier Books.
--Beyond the Burning Lands. Youd, Samuel. LC 78-152288. 170 p. 22cm. 1971. Macmillan.
--The City of Gold and Lead. Youd, Samuel. LC 67-21245. 185 p. 21cm. 1967. Macmillan.
--City of Gold & Lead. Youd, Samuel. 224p. (gr. 5 up). 1970. (ISBN 0-02-042700-X, Collier). Macmillan.
--Dom and Va. Youd, Samuel. LC 72-92434. 154 p. 21cm. 1973. Macmillan.
--Empty World. Youd, Samuel. LC 77-18917. 134 p. 22cm. 1978, c.1977. (ISBN 0-525-29250-0). Dutton.
--Fireball. Youd, Samuel. LC 80-22094. p. cm. c.1981. (ISBN 0-525-29738-3). Dutton.
--Guardians. Youd, Samuel. LC 78-99118. 192p. 22cm. (gr. 6 up). 1970. (ISBN 0-02-718370-X). Macmillan.
--Guardians. Youd, Samuel. LC 78-99118. 224p. (gr. 5-9). 1972. (ISBN 0-02-042680-1, Collier). Macmillan.
--The Long Winter. Youd, Samuel. 1962. Simon and Schuster.
--The Lotus Caves. Youd, Samuel. LC 74-78074. 154 p. 21cm. 1969. Macmillan.
--New Found Land. Youd, Samuel. 1st ed. LC 82-18354. p. cm. 1983. (ISBN 0-525-44049-6). Dutton.
--Pool of Fire. Youd, Samuel. LC 68-23062. 192p. 178p. (gr. 5-7). 1968. (ISBN 0-02-718350-5). Macmillan.
--Pool of Fire. Youd, Samuel. 224p. (gr. 5 up). 1970. (ISBN 0-02-042720-4, Collier). Macmillan.
--The Prince in Waiting. Youd, Samuel. LC 70-119838. 182 p. 21cm. 1970. Macmillan.
--A Scent of White Poppies. Youd, Samuel. 1959. Simon and Schuster.
--Science Fiction Trilogy One: The White Mountains, the City of Lead & Gold, & the Pool of Fire. Youd, Samuel. (gr. 7 up). 1975 (Collier). Macmillan.
--The Sword of the Spirit. Youd, Samuel. 1984. (ISBN 0-8446-6158-9). Peter Smith.
--The Sword of the Spirits. Youd, Samuel. LC 74-20762. p. cm. 1975. (ISBN 0-02-042950-9). Collier Books.
--The Sword of the Spirits. Youd, Samuel. LC 74-176419. 162 p. 21cm. 1972. Macmillan.
--The Sword of the Spirits Trilogy. Youd, Samuel, 3 bks. Incl. Beyond the Burning Lands; The Prince in Waiting; The Sword of the Spirits. (gr. 6 up). 1980. Boxed Set. Macmillan.
--The White Mountains. Youd, Samuel. LC 67-1262. 184 p. 21cm. 1967. Macmillan.
--Wild Jack. Youd, Samuel. LC 77-16437. 147 p. 18cm. 1978, c.1974. (ISBN 0-02-042410-8). Collier Books.
--Wild Jack. Youd, Samuel. LC 74-6428. 147 p. 22cm. 1974. (ISBN 0-02-718300-9). Macmillan.

Christopher, Matthew F. see Martin, Fredric, pseud.

Christopher, Matthew F (1917-)
--Baseball Flyhawk. 1st ed. Caddell, Foster (1921-), illus. LC 63-7678. 127 p. illus. 20 cm. 1963. Little, Brown.
--Baseball Pals. Henneberger, Robert G. (1921-), illus. LC 56-5920. (Illus.). 117p. (gr. 4-6). 1956. (ISBN 0-316-13950-5). Little.
--The Basket Counts. 1st ed. Guzzi, George, illus. LC 68-21168. (Illus.). 125 p. 20cm. 1968. Little, Brown.
--Basketball Sparkplug. 1st ed. Wagner, Kenneth (1911-), illus. LC 57-8038. (Illus.). 124 p. 20cm. 1957. Little, Brown.
--Break for the Basket. 1st ed. Caddell, Foster (1921-), illus. LC 60-934659. 152p. illus. 20cm. 1960. Little, Brown.
--Catch that Pass. Kidder, Harvey, illus. LC 77-77442. (Illus.). 20cm. 130p. 1969. Little, Brown.
--Catcher with a Glass Arm. Caddell, Foster (1921-), illus. LC 64-10169. (Illus.). 137 p. 20cm. 1964. Little, Brown.
--Catcher with a Glass Arm. Caddell, Foster (1921-), illus. LC 85-5206. (Illus.). 137 p. 19cm. 1985, c.1964. (ISBN 0-316-13985-8). Little, Brown.
--Challenge at Second Base. Caddell, Foster (1921-), illus. LC 62-8310. (Illus.). 130 p. 20cm. 1962. Little, Brown.
--Championship Team. Johnson, Larry (1949-), illus. (Illus.). 1977. (ISBN 0-685-74292-X). Little.
--The Counterfeit Tackle. Caddell, Foster (1921-), illus. LC 65-178515. 150p. illus. 20cm. c.1965. Little.
--Crackerjack Halfback. 1st ed. Caddell, Foster (1921-), illus. LC 62-12372. (Illus.). 136 p. 20cm. 1962. Little, Brown.
--Desperate Search. 1st ed. Morrill, Leslie H., illus. LC 73-7741. (Illus.). 116 p. 21cm. 1973. (ISBN 0-316-13959-9). Little, Brown.
--Devil Pony. Bjorklund, Lorence F (1913-1978), illus. LC 76-30478. (Illus.). 103 p. 21cm. c.1977. (ISBN 0-316-13973-4). Little, Brown.
--The Diamond Champs. Johnson, Larry (1949-), illus. LC 76-56153. (Illus.). 120 p. 20cm. c.1977. (ISBN 0-316-13972-6). Little, Brown and Co.
--Dirt Bike Racer. 1st ed. Bomzer, Barry, illus. LC 79-745. (Illus.). 149 p. 21cm. c.1979. (ISBN 0-316-13977-7). Little, Brown.
--Dirt Bike Runaway. 1st ed. LC 83-13538. p. cm. c.1983. (ISBN 0-316-13956-4). Little, Brown.
--The Dog That Called the Signals. Ogden, William, illus. LC 82-15234. (Illus.). 31 p. 22cm. c.1982. (ISBN 0-316-13980-7). Little, Brown and Co.
--The Dog That Stole Football Plays. Ogden, William, illus. LC 79-13266. (Illus.). 44 p. 22cm. c.1980. (ISBN 0-316-13978-5). Little, Brown.
--Drag-Strip Racer. LC 81-19378. 161 p. 21cm. c.1982. (ISBN 0-316-13904-1). Little, Brown.
--Earthquake. 1st ed. Lewin, Ted (1935-), illus. LC 75-22153. p. cm. 1975. (ISBN 0-316-13968-8). Little, Brown.
--Face-off. 1st ed. Kidder, Harvey, illus. LC 78-189258. (Illus.). 131 p. 20cm. 1972. Little, Brown.
--Favor for a Ghost. Flotte, Edmund, illus. LC 83-14493. (Illus.). 108p. (gr. 3-6). 1983. (ISBN 0-664-32708-7). Westminster.
--Football Fugitive. 1st ed. Johnson, Larry (1949-), illus. LC 76-22778. (Illus.). 119 p. 20cm. c.1976. (ISBN 0-316-13971-8). Little, Brown.
--The Fox Steals Home. 1st ed. Johnson, Larry (1949-), illus. LC 78-17526. (Illus.). 178 p. 19cm. c.1978. (ISBN 0-316-13976-9). Little, Brown.
--Front Court Hex. 1st ed. Goto, Byron, illus. LC 74-1143. (Illus.). 132 p. 20cm. 1974. (ISBN 0-316-13920-3). Little, Brown.
--Glue Fingers. 1st ed. Venable, Jim, illus. LC 74-22419. (Illus.). 48 p. 22cm. 1975. (ISBN 0-316-13939-4). Little, Brown.
--The Great Quarterback Switch. Nones, Eric Jon, illus. LC 83-25628. (Illus.). (gr. 4-6). 1984. (ISBN 0-316-13903-3). Little.
--Hard Drive to Short. 1st ed. Guzzi, George, illus. LC 69-10653. (Illus.). 145 p. 20cm. 1969. Little, Brown.
--Ice Magic. 1st ed. Goto, Byron, illus. LC 73-4885. (Illus.). 151 p. 20cm. 1973. Little, Brown.
--Jackrabbit Goalie. Parker, Edward, illus. LC 78-5438. p. cm. c.1978. (ISBN 0-316-13975-0). Little, Brown.
--Jinx Glove. 1st Ed. ed. Chartier, Normand (1945-), illus. LC 73-12836. (Illus.). 47 p. 22cm. 1974. (ISBN 0-316-13965-3). Little, Brown.
--Johnny Long Legs. 1st ed. Kidder, Harvey, illus. LC 78-113437. (Illus.). 133 p. 20cm. 1970. Little, Brown.
--Johnny No Hit. 1st ed. Burns, Raymond Howard (1924-), illus. LC 77-5488. (Illus.). 43 p. 22cm. c.1977. (ISBN 0-316-13974-2). Little, Brown.
--The Kid Who Only Hit Homers. 1st ed. Kidder, Harvey, illus. LC 74-169006. (Illus.). 151 p. 20cm. 1972. Little, Brown.
--Little Lefty. 1st ed. Caddell, Foster (1921-), illus. LC 59-762734. 136p. illus. 20cm. (gr. 4-6). 1959. (ISBN 0-316-14031-7). Little, Brown.
--Long Shot for Paul. LC 66-14906. (Illus.). 151 p. 20cm. 1966. Little, Brown.
--Long Stretch at First Base. 1st ed. Caddell, Foster (1921-), illus. LC 60-5872. (Illus.). 149 p. 20cm. 1960. Little, Brown.
--Look Who's Playing First Base. 1st ed. Kidder, Harvey, illus. LC 74-129907. (Illus.). 131 p. 20cm. 1971. Little, Brown.
--The Lucky Baseball Bat. 1st ed. Henneberger, Robert G. (1921-), illus. LC 54-5141. 123p. illus. 20cm. 1954. Little, Brown.
--Lucky Seven: Sports Stories. 1st ed. Kidder, Harvey, illus. LC 75-108169. (Illus.). viii, 194 p. 21cm. 1970. Little, Brown.
--Miracle at the Plate. 1st ed. Caddell, Foster (1921-), illus. LC 67-2553. (Illus.). 129 p. 20cm. 1967. Little, Brown.
--Mystery Coach. 1st ed. Kidder, Harvey, illus. LC 72-11924. (Illus.). 120 p. 19cm. 1973. (ISBN 0-316-13955-6). Little, Brown.
--No Arm in Left Field. 1st ed. Goto, Byron, illus. LC 73-12296. (Illus.). 131 p. 20cm. 1974. (ISBN 0-316-13964-5). Little, Brown.
--The Pigeon with the Tennis Elbow. 1st ed. Johnson, Larry (1949-), illus. LC 75-19468. (Illus.). 115 p. 20cm. 1975. (ISBN 0-316-13966-1). Little, Brown.
--Power Play. 1st ed. Burns, Raymond Howard (1924-), illus. LC 75-33125. (Illus.). 46 p. 22cm. c.1976. (ISBN 0-316-14015-5). Little, Brown.
--The Reluctant Pitcher. Caddell, Foster (1921-), illus. LC 66-10999. (Illus.). (gr. 2-6). 1966 (ISBN 0-316-14008-2). Little.
--The Return of the Headless Horseman. 1st ed. McLaughlin, James (1948-), illus. LC 81-21936. 95 p. 21cm. c.1982. (ISBN 0-664-32690-0). Westminster Press.
--Run, Billy, Run. 1st ed. LC 79-20627. 145 p. 21cm. c.1980. (ISBN 0-316-14020-1). Little, Brown.
--Shadow Over the Back Court. LC 59-11484. 124 p. 22cm. 1959. Watts.
--Shortstop from Tokyo. 1st ed. Kidder, Harvey, illus. LC 72-97141. (Illus.). 121 p. 20cm. 1970. Little, Brown.
--Sink It, Rusty. 1st ed. Caddell, Foster (1921-), illus. LC 63-13457. (Illus.). 138 p. 20cm. 1963. Little, Brown.
--Slide, Danny, Slide. LC 58-7013. 130p. 22cm. 1958. Steck Co.
--Soccer Halfback. 1st ed. Johnson, Larry (1949-), illus. LC 77-28988. (Illus.). 182 p. 20cm. c.1978. (ISBN 0-316-13946-7). Little, Brown.
--Soccer Halfback. Johnson, Larry (1949-), illus. LC 85-5201. (Illus.). 182 p. 19cm. 1985, c.1978. (ISBN 0-316-13981-5). Little, Brown.
--Stranded. 1st ed. Owens, Gail, illus. LC 74-6365. (Illus.). 116 p. 21cm. 1974. (ISBN 0-316-13935-1). Little, Brown.
--The Submarine Pitch. 1st ed. Johnson, Larry (1949-), illus. LC 75-25790. (Illus.). 137 p. 20cm. c.1976. (ISBN 0-316-13969-6). Little, Brown.
--Supercharged Infield. Downing, Julie, illus. LC 85-95. p. cm. c.1985. (ISBN 0-316-13983-1). Little, Brown.
--Tall Man in the Pivot. 1st ed. Caddell, Foster (1921-), illus. LC 61-10490. (Illus.). 128 p. 20cm. 1961. Little, Brown.
--The Team That Couldn't Lose. 1st ed. Caddell, Foster (1921-), illus. LC 67-17550. (Illus.). 133 p. 20cm. 1967. Little, Brown.
--The Team That Stopped Moving. Goto, Byron, illus. LC 74-26911. (Illus.). 127 p. 20cm. 1975. (ISBN 0-316-13940-8). Little, Brown.
--Tight End. LC 80-39744. 137 p. 21cm. c.1981. (ISBN 0-316-14017-1). Little, Brown.
--Too Hot to Handle. 1st ed. Caddell, Foster (1921-), illus. LC 65-10585. (Illus.). 127 p. 20cm. 1965. Little, Brown.

--Rhymes About the Country. Chute, Marchette Gaylord (1909-), illus. LC 41-4025. 5 p. l., 74, 1 p. illus. 26 cm. 1941. The Macmillan Company.
--Rhymes About Us. 1st ed. Chute, Marchette Gaylord (1909-), illus. LC 74-4272. (Illus.). 53 p. 22cm. 1974. (ISBN 0-525-38220-8). Dutton.
--Stories from Shakespeare. LC 56-9256. (gr. 7 up). 1956. (ISBN 0-529-03491-3). Collins Pubs. **Award: (ALA).**
--Stories From Shakespeare. 1956. E M Hale.
--Stories from Shakespeare. (gr. 7 up). 1979. (ISBN 0-529-05533-3, Philomel). Putnam Pub Group.
--The Wonderful Winter. 1st ed. Golden, Grace, illus. LC 54-8857. (Illus.). 216 p. 22cm. 1954. Dutton.

Chute, Mary, jt. auth. see Johnson, Olive McClintic.

Chute, Verne see Scott, Dustin C., pseud.

Chute, Verne (1917-)
--Mojave Joe. Scott, Dustin C., pseud. 1st ed. Candy, Robert (1920-), illus. LC 50-14495. 185 p. illus. 21 cm. 1950. Knopf.
--The Return of Mojave Joe. Scott, Dustin C., pseud. 1st ed. Geer, Charles Hand (1922-), illus. LC 52-6389. 164 p. illus. 21 cm. 1952. Knopf.

Chwast, Jacqueline, jt. auth. see Boegehold, Betty Virginia Doyle.

Chwast, Jacqueline, jt. auth. see Keller, Beverly Lou.

Chwast, Jacqueline (1932-)
--How Mister Berry Found a Home & Happiness Forever. Chwast, Jacqueline (1932-), illus. LC 68-24032. (Illus.). 3 color ils. 48p. (gr. k-3). 1968. S&S.
--When the Baby-Sitter Didn't Come. 1st ed. Chwast, Jacqueline (1932-), illus. LC 67-1819. (Illus.). 1 v. (unpaged. 1967. Harcourt, Brace & World.

Chwast, Seymour (1931-)
--Bushy Bride: A Norwegin Fairy Tale. Chwast, Seymour (1931-), illus. 32p. (Collection of Fairy Tales Ser.). 1983. (ISBN 0-87191-952-4). Childrens Bk Co.
--Flip-Flap Limerickricks. Chwast, Seymour (1931-), illus. (Illus.). (gr. 1 up). 1972. (ISBN 0-394-82481-4). Random.
--Flip-Flap Mother Goooooose. Chwast, Seymour (1931-), illus. LC 72-535. (Illus.). 22 p. 21cm. (Push-pin book). (gr. 1up). 1972. (ISBN 0-394-82480-6). Random House.
--The House That Jack Built. Chwast, Seymour (1931-), illus. LC 73-1387. (Illus.). 22 p. (incl. p. 2 of cover. 25cm. (Push pin book). (A Surprise Size Book). N.D. (ISBN 0-394-82647-7). Random House.
--Limerickricks. Chwast, Seymour (1931-), illus. LC 72-536. (Illus.). 20 p. 21cm. (Push pin book). 1972. (ISBN 0-394-82481-4). Random House.
--Tall City, Wide Country: A Book to Read Forward and Backward. LC 82-50361. p. cm. 1983. (ISBN 0-670-69236-0). Viking Press.

Chwast, Seymour (1931-) & Moskof, Martin Stephen (1930-)
--Still Another Alphabet Book: ABC ... Chwast, Seymour (1931-), illus. LC 70-80968. 57 p. (chiefly col. illus. 27cm. 1969. McGraw-Hill.
--Still Another Children's Book. Chwast, Seymour (1931-), illus. LC 72-2781. (Illus.). 46 p. 27cm. 1972. McGraw-Hill.
--Still Another Number Book. Chwast, Seymour (1931-) & Moskof, Martin Stephen (1930-), illus. LC 74-141916. (Illus.). 63 p. 27cm. 1971. McGraw-Hill.

Ciancio, June
--Scat Cat Finds a Friend. Ciancio, June, illus. (Illus.). 32p. (Orig.). (Make-a-Bk). (ps-6). 1975. (ISBN 0-8467-0047-6, Pub. by Two Continents). Hippocrene Bks.

Cianos, Elizabeth A. & Cianos, Mary E.
--Peter & the Pyramid. 1977. (ISBN 0-533-03080-3). Vantage.

Cianos, Mary E., jt. auth. see Cianos, Elizabeth A.

Ciardi, John Anthony (1916-)
--Doodle Soup. Nacht, Merle, illus. LC 85-814. 57 pp. 1985. (ISBN 0-395-38395-1). Houghton Mifflin Co.
--I Met a Man. Osborn, Robert Chesley (1904-), illus. LC 60-9094. 74p. illus. 25cm. (gr. 2-4). c.1961. Houghton Mifflin. **Award: (ALA).**
--I Met a Man. new ed. Osborne, Robert, illus. (Illus.). 74p. (gr. k-3). 1973. (ISBN 0-395-17447-3, Sandpiper). HM.
--John J. Plenty and Fiddler Dan: A New Fable of the Grasshopper and the Ant. Gekiere, Madeleine (1919-), illus. LC 63-18893. (Illus.). unpaged. 29cm. (gr. k-3). 1963. (ISBN 0-397-30667-9). (ISBN 0-397-30668-7). Lippincott. **Awards: (NYT); (ALA).**
--The King Who Saved Himself from Being Saved. Gorey, Edward St. John (1925-), illus. LC 65-21670. 1 v. (unpaged) illus. 14x16cm. (gr. k-3). 1965, c.1964. Lippincott.
--Man Who Sang the Sillies. Gorey, Edward St. John (1925-), illus. LC 61-11734. (Illus.). (gr. 4-6). 1961. (ISBN 0-397-30568-0, JBL-J). (ISBN 0-397-30569-9). Har-Row.
--The Man Who Sang the Sillies: Poems. Gorey, Edward St. John (1925-), illus. LC 61-11734. (Illus.). 63 p. 25cm. 1961. Lippincott.
--The Monster Den: Or, Look What Happened at My House - and to It. Gorey, Edward St. John (1925-), illus. LC 66-9156. (Illus.). 62p. (gr. k-3). 1966. (ISBN 0-397-30896-5). (ISBN 0-397-30897-3). Lippincott. **Award: (NYT).**
--The Reason for the Pelican. Gekiere, Madeleine (1919-), illus. LC 59-9223. (Illus.). 63 p. 25cm. 1959. Lippincott. **Award: (NYT).**
--Scrappy, the Pup. Miller, Jane Judith (1925-), illus. LC 60-6755. unpaged. illus. 27cm. (gr. k-3). 1960. (ISBN 0-397-30528-1). Lippincott. **Award: (NYT).**
--Someone Could Win a Polar Bear. Gorey, Edward St. John (1925-), illus. (Illus.). drawings. 64p. (gr. k-3). 1970. (ISBN 0-397-31159-1). (ISBN 0-397-31160-5). Lippincott.
--The Wish Tree. 1962. MacMillan Co.
--The Wish-Tree. Glanzman, Louis S. (1922-), illus. LC 62-21619. unpaged. illus. 30 cm. (a modern masters book for children. 1962. Crowell-Collier Press.
--You Know Who. Gorey, Edward St. John (1925-), illus. LC 64-19057. 63 p. illus. 25 cm. 1964. Lippincott.
--You Read to Me: I'll Read to You. Gorey, Edward St. John (1925-), illus. 1961. Harper.
--You Read to Me Ill Read To You. Gorey, Edward St. John (1925-), illus. 64p. 1964. J B Lippincott Company.
--You Read to Me, I'll Read to You. Gorey, Edward St. John (1925-), illus. LC 62-16296. (Illus.). 64 p. 25cm. 1962. Lippincott.

Ciardi, John Anthony (1916-) & Gaver, Becky
--Fast and Slow: Poems for Advanced Children and Beginning Parents. LC 74-22405. (Illus.). 67 p. 23cm. 1975. (ISBN 0-395-20282-5). Houghton Mifflin.

Cimino, Maria
--Disobedient Eels. Nivola, Claire, illus. LC 72-117456. (Illus.). 64p. (gr. 3-6). 1971. (ISBN 0-394-92024-4). Pantheon.

Cimino, Maria, tr. see Jardin, Luis.

Cincinnatus, Hiner Miller see Miller, Joaquin, pseud.

Cindell, Eva
--Scrub-A-Dub. Sterling, Fred, illus. (Illus.). color ils. 12p. (gr. 1-3). 1971. Platt.

Cinderella
--Cinderella. McKean, Emma C., illus. LC 44-21219. 14 p. col. illus. 22 1/2 x 29 1/2 cm. (Magic fairy tales). c.1943. McLoughlin Bros., Inc.
--Cinderella. Wehr, Julian, illus. LC 45-4720. 18 p. illus. (part col.) 22 1/2 x 18 cm. 1945. S. Days, Inc.
--The Story of Cinderella. LC 45-9193. 34, 2 p.i llus. (part col.) 19 1/2 x 17 1/2 cm. (On cover: A Lothrop color storybook). 1945. Lothrop, Lee & Shepard Co., Inc.

Cioni, Ray & Cioni, Sally
--The Babe & the Lamb: A Droodles Christmas Adventure. Cioni, Ray & Cioni, Sally, illus. (The Droodles Bks.). N.D. (ISBN 0-89191-635-0). Cook.
--The Droodles Storybook of Proverbs. Cioni, Ray & Cioni, Sally, illus. LC 81-67803. (Illus.). 63 p. 27cm. (Chariot books). c.1981. (ISBN 0-89191-472-2). D.C. Cook Pub. Co.
--The Droodles Ten Commandments Storybook. Tiritilli, Jerry, illus. LC 83-71235. (Illus.). 63 p. 27cm. (gr. 1-5). 1983. (ISBN 0-89191-636-9). Chariot Books.

Cioni, Sally, jt. auth. see Cioni, Ray.

Cipolla Grasso, Mary Ellen see Grasso, Mary Ellen Cipolla.

Cipriani, Charlotte Jane & Savonarola, Girolamo Maria Francesco Matteo (1452-1498)
--The Little Captain: A Tale of Savonarola's Florence. Nordfeldt-Olsson, Bror J., illus. LC 6-35451. 3 p. l., v-vii, 4, 257, vii-xi p. incl. front., 11 pl. 22 1/2 cm. c.1906. Rand, McNally & Co.

Cisneros, Sandra
--The House on Mango Street. LC 82-72278. 80p. 1983. (ISBN 0-934770-20-4). Arte Publico.

Civardi
--Clues & Suspects. (Good Detective Guides Ser.). (gr. 2-5). 1979. (ISBN 0-86020-226-7, Usborne-Hayes). (ISBN 0-88110-039-0). (ISBN 0-86020-229-1). EDC.

Clack, Mary H., Mrs.
--Gladys: Or, Life of a Texas Schoolgirl. 1917. Hylton.

Claes, Ernest (1885-1968)
--Whitey. Ambrus, Victor G., pseud. (1935-), illus. Ambrus, Gyozo Laszlo. LC 72-184913. (Illus.). 21cm. v, 186p. 1970. (ISBN 0-19-274520-4). Oxford Univ. Press.

Clagett, John Henry (1916-)
--Gunpowder for Boonesborough. LC 65-21395. 184p. map. 22cm. c.1965. Bobbs.
--Jack Darby: Able Seaman. McCann, Gerald (1916-), illus. LC 63-19008. 191 p. illus. 22 cm. 1963. (ISBN 0-672-50330-1). Bobb-Merrill.
--Surprise Attack!. LC 68-17522. 191 p. 22cm. 191p. 1968. J. Messner.
--Torpedo Run on Iron Bottomed Bay. 1st ed. Fritz, Dennis, illus. LC 75-87090. (Illus.). 168 p. 22cm. 1969. Cowles Book Co.
--Typhoon 1944. LC 74-123177. 191 p. 22cm. 1970. Messner.

Claiborne, William Stirling (1871-)
--Roy in the Mountains. LC 16-14834. 214 p. front., plates. 19 cm. 1916. E.S. Gorham.

Clair, Andree (1916-)
--Bemba: An African Adventure. Johnson, Eugene Harper, illus. Ponsot, Marie, tr. LC 62-13332. (Illus.). (gr. 3-7). 1962. (ISBN 0-15-206580-6). HarBraceJ.
--Bemba: An African Adventure. Johnson, Eugene Harper, illus. Ponsot, Marie, tr. LC 62-13332. (Illus.). 158p. (gr. 4-6). 1966. (ISBN 0-15-206583-0, VoyB). HarBraceJ.

Clair, Bevan
--Run Roadrunner. LC 80-82912. 1980. (ISBN 0-686-30719-4). B A Scott.

Clair, Leonard St. see St. Clair, Leonard.

Claire, Anne
--Andro, Star of Bethlehem. Mahany, Patricia, ed. Rettig, Anne, illus. LC 82-62727. (Illus.). 24p. (Happy Day Bks.). (ps-2). 1983. (ISBN 0-87239-631-2). Standard Pub.
--Andro, the Star of Bethlehem. Rettig, Anne, illus. LC 81-50997. (Illus.). 32p. (Orig.). (gr. k-6). 1981. (ISBN 0-87239-472-7). Standard Pub.

Claire, Malcolm see Uncle Mal, pseud.

Claire, Malcolm, as told by see Sewell, Anna.

Claire, Malcolm (1898-)
--Story Hour with Uncle Mal ... LC 46-21740. 63 p. illus. (part. col.) 28 x 21 1/2 cm. 1946. The American Crayon Company.
--Story Time" with Uncle Mal ... LC 46-21742. 48 p. illus. (part col.) 23 x 21 1/2 cm. 1945. The American Crayon Company.
--Tune-in Again: Uncle Mal's Second Story Book. Bailey, Bernadine Freeman, Mrs., ed. Herric, Pru, illus. LC 40-305353. 6 p. l., 208 p. illus. 24 cm. c.1940. Grosset & Dunlap.
--Tune-in Tales: Uncle Mal's Own Story Book. Bailey, Bernadine Freeman, Mrs., ed. Herric, Pru, illus. LC 39-245773. 5 p. l., 228 p. illus. 28 1/2 cm. c.1939. Grosset & Dunlap.
--Uncle Mal's Always New Tales ... LC 46-22074. 63 p. illus. (part col.) 28 1/2 x 21 1/2 cm. 1946. The American Crayon Company.
--Uncle Mal's Favorite "Tell It Again" Tales ... LC 46-21741. 48 p. illus. (part col.) 23 x 21 1/2 cm. 1946. The American Crayon Company.

Claire, Malcolm (1898-), as told by.
--Little Lord Fauntleroy. Uncle Mal, pseud. Kohs, Marion R., illus. LC 47-17190. 62 p. illus. (part col.) 28 cm. 1946. Prang Company.

Claire, Malcom, jt. auth. see Sewell, Anna.

Claire, Robert de see Zuliani, Vilma.

Clampett, Bob
--Beany: Cecil Captured for the Zoo. Clampett, Bob, illus. Hammer, Barbara & Bradbury, Jack LC 55-22309. unpaged. illus. 17cm. (Tell-a-tale books, 2551). c.1954. Whitman Pub. Co.

Clancy, Cleo Faust Garis see Garis, Cleo Fausta, pseud.

Clancy, Louise Marks Breitenbach, Mrs.
--Alma at Hadley Hall. Goss, John, illus. LC 12-102708. 5 p. l., 331 p. front., plates. 20 1/2 cm. $1.5. 1912. L.C. Page & Company.
--Alma's Junior Year. LC 14-3105. 4 p. l., 376 p. front., plates. 20 1/2 cm. (Her The Hadley Hall Series) $1.50). 1914. The Page Company.
--Alma's Senior Year. Goss, John, illus. LC 15-5418. 4 p. l., 318 p. front., plates. 21 cm. (Her The Hadley hall series). 1915. The Page Company.
--Alma's Sophomore Year: A Sequel to "Alma at Hadley Hall,". Goss, John, illus. LC 13-6332. 4 p. l., 303 p. front., plates. 20 1/2 cm. (Her The Hadley Hall Series) $1.50). 1913. L.C. Page & Company.
--Eleanor of the Houseboat. Meister, Charles E., illus. LC 16-10640. 4 p. l., 300 p. front., plates. 20 1/2 cm. $1.5. 1916. The Page Company.
--You're Young But Once. Withington, Elizabeth R., illus. N.D. Page Co.

Clanton, Bruce
--Family Adventures. LC 80-51060. (ps-6). 1980. (ISBN 0-89390-018-4). Resource Pubns.

Clapesattle, Helen
--Mayo Brothers. 1962. E M Hale.

Clapman, Arnold
--Angel the Pig. Clapman, Arnold, illus. LC 78-162049. (Illus.). 32 p. (Magic circle book). 1972. (ISBN 0-663-22969-3). Ginn.

Clapp, Estelle Barnes
--Laurie. 1st ed. (Illus.). (gr. 4-6). N.D. (ISBN 0-448-02299-0). G&D.
--Laurie. 1 st. ed. Wiese, Kurt (1887-1974), illus. LC 53-5294. 255p. illus. 21cm. 1953. Doubleday.

Clapp, Patricia (1912-)
--Constance: A Story of Early Plymouth. LC 68-14064. (Illus.). 255 p. 22cm. 1968. Lothrop, Lee & Shepard Co.
--The Curley Tale. 1958. Art Craft.
--The Do-Nothing Frog: One Hundred Plays for Children. Burack, Abraham Saul (1908-1978), ed. 1970. Plays Inc.
--Edie-Across-the Street. 1960. Baker.
--The Ghost of a Chance. 1958. Heuer.
--The Girl Out Front. 1958. Dramatic Publishing Company.
--The Girl Whose Fortune Sought Her: Children's Plays from Favorite Stories. Kamerman, Sylvia E., pseud. (1916-), ed. Burack, Sylvia. 1959. Plays Inc.
--Her Kissin' Cousin. 1957. Heuer.
--The Honeysuckle Hedge. 1960. Eldridge.
--If a Body Meets a Body. 1963. Heuer.
--I'm Deborah Sampson: A Soldier in the War of the Revolution. LC 76-51770. 176 p. 22cm. c.1977. (ISBN 0-688-41799-X). (ISBN 0-688-51799-4). Lothrop, Lee & Shepard.
--The Incompleted Pass. 1957. Dramatic Publishing Company.
--Inquire Within. 1959. Row Peterson.
--Jane-Emily. LC 69-14326. 160 p. 22cm. 1969. Lothrop, Lee & Shepard.
--King of the Dollhouse. Brown, Judith Gwyn (1933-), illus. LC 73-21827. (Illus.). 94 p. 22cm. 1974. (ISBN 0-688-41585-7). (ISBN 0-688-41585-7). Lothrop, Lee & Shepard Co.
--The Magic Bookshelf, and The Other Side of the Wall: Fifty Plays for Junior Actors. Kamerman, Sylvia E., pseud. (1916-), ed. Burack, Sylvia. 1966. Plays Inc.
--Never Keep Him Waiting. 1961. Dramatic Publishing Company.
--Now Hear This. 1963. Eldridge.
--Peggy's on the Phone. 1956. Dramatic Publishing Company.
--Red Heels and Roses. 1962. McKay.
--Smart Enough to Be Dumb. 1956. Dramatic Publishing Company.
--Witches' Children: A Story of Salem. LC 81-13678. 160 p. 22cm. c.1982. (ISBN 0-688-00890-9). Lothrop, Lee & Shepard Books.

Clardy, Andrea Fleck (1943-)
--Dusty Was My Friend: Coming to Terms with Loss. Alexander, Eleanor, illus. LC 83-6203. (Illus.). 32 p. 24cm. c.1984. (ISBN 0-89885-141-6). Human Sciences Press.

Clare, Andrea M., adapted by see Dickens, Charles John Huffam.

Clare, Andrea M, adapted by see Verne, Jules.

Clare, Frank M.
--Echoes from Song-Land: Verses for Children. LC 29-6370. 32p. 20cm. c.1928. Wetzel Pub. Co.

Clare, Helen, pseud., see Clarke, Pauline.

Clare, Helen, pseud., see Hunter Blair, Pauline Clarke.

Clare, Helen, pseud. (1921-)
--Cat & the Fiddle & Other Stories. Hunter Blair, Pauline Clarke. Pellei, Ida, illus. LC 68-28512. (Illus.). 30p. of color ils. 64p. 1st U.S. edition. (ps-3). 1968. (ISBN 0-13-120485-8). P-H.
--The Cat and the Fiddle, and Other Stories. Hunter Blair, Pauline Clarke. Pellei, Ida, illus. LC 68-19838. (Illus.). 64 p. 24cm. 1968. Prentice-Hall.
--Five Dolls & the Duke. Hunter Blair, Pauline Clarke. Aliki, pseud. (1929-), illus. Brandenburg, Aliki Liacouras. LC 68-14629. (Illus.). 15 line drawings. 112p. 1st U.S. edition. (gr. 3-7). 1968. (ISBN 0-13-321042-1). P-H.
--Five Dolls & the Monkey. Hunter Blair, Pauline Clarke. Aliki, pseud. (1929-), illus. Brandenburg, Aliki Liacouras. LC 67-11098. (Illus.). 21cm. 127p. (gr. 3-7). 1967. (ISBN 0-13-321018-9). P-H.
--Five Dolls and the Monkey. Hunter Blair, Pauline Clarke. Leslie, Cecil, illus. LC 67-11098. (Illus.). vii, 127 p. 21cm. 1967. Prentice-Hall.
--Five Dolls & Their Friends. Hunter Blair, Pauline Clarke. Aliki, pseud. (1929-), illus. Brandenburg, Aliki Liacouras. LC 68-10650. (Illus.). 21cm. 120p. (gr. 3-7). 1967. (ISBN 0-13-321026-X). P-H.
--Five Dolls and Their Friends. Hunter Blair, Pauline Clarke. Leslie, Cecil, illus. LC 68-10650. (Illus.). 120 p. 21cm. 1968. Prentice-Hall.
--Five Dolls in a House. Hunter Blair, Pauline Clarke. Aliki, pseud. (1929-), illus. Brandenberg, Aliki Liacouras. LC 65-226091. viii, 143p. illus. 21cm. (gr. 3-7). N.D. (ISBN 0-13-320994-6). Prentice.
--Five Dolls in the Snow. Hunter Blair, Pauline Clarke. Aliki, pseud. (1929-), illus. Brandenburg, Aliki Liacouras. LC 67-20680. (Illus.). 21cm. 118p. (gr. 3-7). 1967. (ISBN 0-13-321034-0). P-H.
--Five Dolls in the Snow. Hunter Blair, Pauline Clarke. Leslie, Cecil, illus. (Illus.). ix, 118 p. 21cm. 1965. Prentice-Hall.

AUTHOR INDEX CLARK, JAMES

Clare, John
--Dwellers in the Wood. Goodwin, Harold (1919-), illus. (Illus.). (gr. 5 up). 1967. Macmillan.
--Wood Is Sweet. Powell, David, ed. O'Connor, John, illus. (Illus.). index. 96p. (gr. 4-6). 1968. (ISBN 0-531-01830-X). Watts.
Clareloux, N., jt. auth. see Bonhomme, Bernard.
Claret, Maria & O'Sullivan, Jane
--The Chocolate Rabbit. LC 84-24610. (Illus.). 29 p. 22cm. 1985, c.1984. (ISBN 0-8120-5624-8). Barron's.
Clark
--The Adventures of John Whopper. New ed. (Illus.). (Cosy Corner Ser.). 1905. L. C. Page & Co.
--Lighthouse Boy. 1976. Down East.
Clark, Ada & Kibby, Margaret
--Little Plays for Christmas. 132 p. 18 cm. c.1928. Beckley-Cardy Company.
Clark, Allen P., pseud., see Van Doren, Charles L..
Clark, Allen P, pseud. (1926-)
--Growing up in Colonial America. Van Doren, Charles Lincoln. Papin, Joseph (1914-), illus. LC 61-15732. 96p. illus. (pt. col. 1962, c.1961. Bold Face Bks.; Dist. Sterling.
--Growing up in the Wild West. Van Doren, Charles Lincoln. Papin, Joseph (1914-), illus. LC 61-15733. 96p. illus. (pt. col. 1962, c.1961. Bold Face Bks. Dist. Sterling.
--Growing Up in the Wild West. Van Doren, Charles L.. Papin, Joseph (1914-), illus. (Illus.). (gr. 4-8). 1961. (ISBN 0-8090-5321-7). Hill & Wang.
Clark, Ann Nolan, jt. auth. see Lee, Julian, Mrs.
Clark, Ann Nolan (1896-), as told to see Kha, Dang Manh.
Clark, Ann Nolan, Mrs., jt. auth. see Lee, Julian.
Clark, Ann Nolan, Mrs. (1896-)
--All This Wild Land. LC 76-18106. p. cm. 1976. (ISBN 0-670-11444-8). Viking Press.
--Bear Cub. Frace, Charles, illus. LC 65-18149. 62p. illus. (pt. col.) 26cm. c.1965. Viking.
--Blue Canyon Horse. Houser, Allan C. (1914-), illus. LC 54-12161. 54p. illus. 26cm. (gr. 3-7). 1954. (ISBN 0-670-17456-4). Viking Press. **Award: (ALA).**
--Bringer of the Mystery Dog: A/Story of a Young Boy. Beatty, Williard W., ed. Howe, Oscar, illus. LC 58-52808. (Illus.). 18 x 25cm. 40p. (Indian Life Readers, Sioux Ser.). 1943. Dept. of the Interior, Bureau of Indian Affairs.
--Buffalo Caller: The/Story of a Young Sioux Boy of the Early Seventeen Hundreds. Hulsizer, Marian, illus. LC 42-14380. (Illus.). 22cm. 36p. (Basic Social Education ser.). 1942. Row, Peterson and Company.
--The Desert People. Houser, Allan C. (1914-), illus. 56p. 1962. Viking Press.
--Hoofprint on the Wind. Parker, Robert Andrew (1927-), illus. LC 72-80517. (Illus.). 128 p. 22cm. 1972. (ISBN 0-670-37874-7). Viking Press.
--In My Mother's House. Herrera, Velino (1902-), illus. LC 41-51741. 56 p. illus. (part col.) 26 1/2 x 22 cm. 1941. The Viking Press. **Award: (RCM).**
--In the Land of Small Dragon. Chen, Tony (1929-), illus. LC 78-26233. (Illus.). (gr. k-3). 1979. (ISBN 0-670-39697-4). Viking Pr.
--The Little Indian Basket Maker. Begay, Harrison, illus. N.D. E. M. Hale & Co.
--The Little Indian Basket Maker. Begay, Harrison, illus. 1957. Melmont.
--The Little Indian Pottery Maker. N.D. E. M. Hale & Co.
--Little Indian Pottery Maker. Perceval, Don Louis (1908-), illus. (Illus.). (gr. 1-5). 1955. (ISBN 0-516-08545-X). Melmont.
--Little Navajo Bluebird. Lantz, Paul (1908-), illus. LC 43-3618. 143 p. illus. 23 x 17 1/2 cm. 1943. The Viking Press.
--Little Navajo Herder. Denetsosie, Hoke, illus. LC 53-61095. 149p. illus. 28cm. 1951. U. S. Indian Service, Haskell Institute.
--Looking-for-Something: The Story of a Stray Burro of Ecuador. Politi, Leo (1908-), illus. LC 52-7598. 53 p. illus. 23 cm. (ps-3). 1952. (ISBN 0-670-44001-9). Viking Press.
--Magic Money. Politi, Leo (1908-), illus. LC 50-8847. (Illus.). 121 p. 26cm. 1950. Viking Press.
--Medicine Man's Daughter. Bolognese, Donald Alan (1934-), illus. LC 63-11182. 178 p. illus. 22 cm. (Bell books). 1963. Farrar, Strus.
--Paco's Miracle. (Illus.). (gr. 4-7). 1962. (ISBN 0-8382-0626-3). Hale.
--Paco's Miracle. Tait, Agnes (1897-), illus. LC 62-7326. 159p. illus. 22cm. 1962. (ISBN 0-374-35709-9). Farrar Strauss.
--Santiago. Ward, Lynd Kendall (1905-1985), illus. LC 55-1218. 189p. illus. 22cm. (gr. 7 up). 1955. (ISBN 0-670-61814-4). Viking Press. **Award: (ALA).**
--A Santo for Pasqualita. Villarejo, Mary Holan (1915-), illus. LC 59-1693. 96p. illus. 24cm. 1959. Viking Press.
--Secret of the Andes. Charlot, Jean (1898-1979), illus (Pub. by Viking Pr). (Puffin Story Ser). (gr. 3-7). 1976. (ISBN 0-14-030926-8, Puffin). Penguin.
--Secret of the Andes. Charlot, Jean (1898-1979), illus. LC 52-8075. 130 p. illus. 25 cm. (gr. 4-8). 1952. (ISBN 0-670-62975-8). Viking Press. **Award: (JNM).**
--Summer Is for Growing. Tait, Agnes (1897-), illus. LC 68-13684. (Illus.). 180 p. 22cm. (Bell book). 1968. Farrar, Straus & Giroux.
--Third Monkey. Freeman, Don (1908-1978), illus. LC 56-142025. 44p. illus. 26cm. c.1956. Viking Press.
--This for That. Freeman, Don (1908-1978), illus. (Illus.). 62p. (gr. k-3). 1965. (ISBN 0-516-08867-X, Golden Gate). Childrens.
--Tia Maria's Garden. Keats, Ezra Jack (1916-1983), illus. LC 63-8523. (Illus.). 47 p. 24cm. 1963. Viking Press.
--To Stand Against the Wind. Chen, Tony (1929-), illus. LC 78-5966. p. cm. 1978. (ISBN 0-670-71773-8). Viking Press.
--World Song. Wiese, Kurt (1887-1974), illus. LC 60-2812. 140p. illus. 22cm. 1960. Viking Press.
--Year Walk. LC 74-23565. vii, 197 p. 24cm. 1975. (ISBN 0-670-79367-1). Viking Press.
--Young Hunter of Picuris. El Cazadorcito de Picuris. Beatty, Willard W., ed. Jenkins, Christina M., tr. from Spanish. LC 46-43882. (Illus.). 26cm. 56p. (Pueblo Series: No. 2). 1943. Chilocco Agricultural School.
Clark, Anne (1909-)
--Beast and Bawdy: A Book of Fabulous and Fantastical Beasts. N.D. (ISBN 0-8008-0691-3). Taplinger.
Clark, Barbara R.
--Reflections. Davis, Ruby & Gerstung, Estella, eds. 72p. (Orig.). (gr. 4-12). 1982. (ISBN 0-686-37922-5). Williams Com.
Clark, Barrett Harper (1890-) & Jagendorf, Moritz Adolf (1888-1981), eds.
--A World of Stories for Children: A One-Volume Library of the Great Fairy, Folk Tales and Legends of the World from the Earliest Times to the Late Nineteenth Century, for the Use of Parents, Teachers and Young People; Collected, with Notes, Reading Lists and Bibliographies. LC 40-32980. 844 p. col. double plates. 24 1/2 x 17 cm. c.1940. The Bobbs-Merrill Company.
--A World of Stories for Children: The Great Fairy, Folk Tales and Legends of the World from the Earliest Times to the Late Nineteenth Century. Copelman, Evelyn, illus. LC 47-11642. 820 p. col. plates. 22 cm. 1947. Bobbs-Merrill Co.
Clark, Bertha
--Belle River Friends in Wings and Feathers. Key, Alexander Hill (1904-1979), illus. LC 28-15164. 101. 1 p. col. illus. 19 1/2 cm. c.1928. Lyons and Carnahan.
--Belle River Friends in Wings and Feathers. Key, Alexander Hill (1904-1979), illus. LC 39-11087. 101, 1 p. illus. (part col.) 19 1/2 cm. c.1938. Lyons and Carnahan.
--Belle River Friends in Wings and Feathers. Key, Alexander Hill (1904-1979), illus. LC 52-28535. 104 p. illus. 21 cm. 1952. Lyons and Carnahan.
--The Climbing Twins: And Other Stories. Laite, Blanche Fisher, illus. LC 29-2997. vi, 194 p. col. illus. 19 cm. c.1929. Ginn and Company.
--The House on the Hill. Howe, Gertrude Herrick (1902-), illus. LC 31-30700. 4 p. l., 3-142 p. col. front., illus. 19 1/2 cm. 1931. Little, Brown, and Company.
--Stories of Belle River. Key, Alexander Hill (1904-1979), illus. LC 42-166103. v, 1, 214 p. 1 l. col. illus. 19 1/2 cm. 1942. Lyons and Carnahan.
--Work and Play on Belle River Farm. Key, Alexander Hill (1904-1979), illus. LC 26-15165. 150, 1 p. col. illus. 19 1/2 cm. c.1928. Lyons and Carnahan.
Clark, Bettina & Coleman, Lester L.
--Going to the Hospital. Swartz, Walter, illus. (Illus.). color pop-ups. 24p. (gr. k-3). 1971. (ISBN 0-394-82160-2). Random.
Clark, Billy Curtis (1928-)
--The Champion of Sourwood Mountain. Eldridge, Harold, illus. LC 66-15579. 251 p. illus. 21 cm. 1966. Putnam.
--Goodbye Kate. Eldridge, Harold, illus. LC 64-23087. (Illus.). 247 p. 21cm. 1964. Putnam.
--The Mooneyed Hound. Walker, Nedda, illus. LC 58-10204. 128p. illus. 21cm. 1958. Putnam.
--Riverboy. Fleishman, Seymour (1918-), illus. LC 58-140386. 159p. illus. 21cm. 1959, c.1958. Putnam.
--Sourwood Tales. Eldridge, Harold, illus. (Illus.). (gr. 6-9). 1968. (ISBN 0-399-20265-X). Putnam.
--The Trail of the Hunter's Horn. Reed, Veronica, pseud. (1916-), illus. Sherman, Theresa. LC 57-8094. (Illus.). 95 p. 22cm. 1957. Putnam.
--Useless Dog. LC 61-13401. 125p. 21cm. 1961. Putnam.
Clark, Bobby G.
--A Summer Night. Kneff, K., illus. (Illus.). 32p. (Goldseal Children's Ser.). 1984. (ISBN 0-931437-00-8). Golden Valley Pubns.
Clark Brothers Chewing Gum Company Pittsburgh
--The Adventures of Tommy Teaberry. LC 44-14017. 40 p. col. illus. 26 x 20 cm. 1944. Clark Brothers Chewing Gum Company.
Clark, Capt. Charles
--An Antartic Queen: A Sea Story for Boys. (Boys Presentation Library). 1910. Frederick Warne & Co.
Clark, Catherine Anthony Smith (1892-)
--The Man With Yellow Eyes. Raynor, Gordon, illus. LC 64-10824. (Buckakin Books: No.7). 1963. St Martin's Press.
Clark, Catherine Walden (1915-)
--The Story of Judy, the Little Elephant. Campbell, Floy James, illus. LC 50-4389. 24p. illus. (part. col) 28cm. 1950. Bond Pub. co.
Clark, Charlotte
--Black Cowboy: The Story of Nat Love. N.D. (ISBN 0-8382-1051-1, Hale House Bks.). E. M. Hale and Co.
Clark, Cora & Williams, Texa Bowen, eds.
--Pomo Indian Myths And Some Of Their Sacred Meanings. N.D. Brown Book co.
Clark, David Allen, pseud., see Ernst, Lyman John.
Clark, David Allen, pseud. (1940-)
--Jokes, Puns, and Riddles. Ernst, Lyman John. 1st ed. Kalish, Lionel, illus. LC 67-19070. 288p. illus. 22cm. 1968. Doubleday.
Clark, Denis
--Black Lightning. Ambler, Christopher Gifford (1886-), illus. LC 54-703025. (Illus.). 144p. (gr. 5-9). 1954. (ISBN 0-670-17225-1). Viking Pr.
--Boomer: The Life of a Kangaroo. Ambler, Christopher Gifford (1886-), illus. (Illus.). (gr. 5-9). 1955. (ISBN 0-670-18157-9). Viking Pr.
Clark, Dorothy (1897-)
--Little Joe. Weisgard, Leonard Joseph (1916-), illus. LC 40-34536. (Illus.). 25cm. 31p. 1940. Lothrop, Lee & Shepherd.
--Peter on the Min. Yap, Weda (1894-), illus. LC 42-13906. 170, 1 p. illus. (part col.) 21 1/2 x 17 cm. 1942. Lothrop, Lee & Shepard Co.
--The Potiphar Picnic. Bisson, John A., illus. LC 53-29438. (Illus.). 21cm. 131p. 1953. Cowles Press.
Clark, Edward Brayton
--The Jingle Book of Birds. LC 1-27106. 46p. col. 27 x 21cm. 1901. A. W. Mumferd.
Clark, Eleanor (1913-)
--The Song of Roland. Fisher, Leonard Everett (1924-), illus. LC 60-7396. 53p. illus. 22cm. (Legacy books, Y-12). 1960. Random House.
--The Song of Roland. Yap, Weda (1894-), illus. (Illus.). (gr. 4-7). 1960. Random.
Clark, Electa (1910-)
--The Dagger, the Fish, and Casey McKee. Geary, Clifford N. (1916-), illus. LC 55-7071. 218p. illus. 22cm. 1955. D. McKay Co.
--Osceola: Young Seminole Indian. Doremus, Robert (1913-), illus. LC 65-236684. 200p. col. illus. 20cm. (Childhood of famous Americans) Bibl.). c.1965. Bobbs.
--Pennywink Carnival. 1st ed. Orbaan, Albert F. (1913-), illus. LC 50-9781. 208 p. illus. 23 cm. 1950. Bobbs-Merrill.
--The Pennywinks. 1st ed. Orbaan, Albert F. (1913-), illus. LC 49-10445. 180 p. illus. 22 cm. 1949. Bobbs-Merrill Co.
--The River Showfolks. Schrotter, Gustav, illus. LC 57-6601. 216p. illus. 21cm. 1957. McKay.
--Robert Peary: Boy of the North Pole. Fiorentino, Al, illus. LC 62-166033. 200p. col. illus. 20cm. (Childhood of famous Amers.). 1963, c.1953. Bobbs.
--The Seven Q's. 1st ed. LC 52-5816. 170 p. illus. 23 cm. 1952. Bobbs-Merrill.
--Spanish Gold and Casey McKee. Geary, Clifford N. (1916-), illus. LC 56-5382. 218p. illus. 21cm. 1956. D. McKay Co.
--Tony for Keeps: A Story of a House on Wheels. 1st ed. Weil, Lisl (1910-), illus. LC 55-8724. 186p. illus. 22cm. 1955. Winston.
--Wildcat, the Seminole: The Florida War. 1st ed. Nicholas, Frank, illus. LC 55-11893. 192p. illus. 21cm. (American heritage). 1956. Aladdin Books.
Clark, Ella Elizabeth (1896-)
--Guardian Spirit Quest. (Indian Culture Ser.). (gr. 5-12). 1974. (ISBN 0-89992-045-4). MT Coun Indian.
Clark, Ella Elizabeth (1896-), ed.
--In the Beginning. (gr. 5 up). 1977. (ISBN 0-89992-055-1). MT Coun Indian.
Clark, Ellery Harding (1874-)
--The Camp at Sea Duck Cover. Perkins, Lucy Fitch, Mrs. (1865-1937), illus. LC 12-21772. 5 p. l., 276, 2 p. front., plates. 19 1/2 cm. 1912. Houghton Mifflin Company.
--Dick Randall: The Young Athlete. Biggs, Walter, illus. LC 10-193802. 5 p. l., 266 p. 1 l. front., plates. 19 cm. c.1910. The Bobbs-Merrill Company.
--The Lost Galleon: An Adventure Story. LC 27-166796. 4 p. l., 11-309 p. 20 cm. c.1927. Chelsea House.
Clark, Felicia Buttz
--Beppino. LC 1-25813. 68 p. front., plates. 19 cm. 1901. Eaton & Mains.
--Gigi: The Hero of Sicily. LC 7-33909. 3 p. l., 132 p. front., 5 pl. 19 1/2 cm. c.1907. Eaton & Mains.
Clark, Franklin Stetson
--Cuter Tooter. Miret, Gil, illus. LC 57-6002. (Illustrated with Woodcuts). 183p. illus. 22cm. 1957. Lothrop, Lee & Shepard.
Clark, Frederick Stephen see Dalton, Clive, pseud.
Clark, Frederick Stephen (1908-)
--Malay Schooner. Dalton, Clive, pseud. 1st ed. [illegible] p. illus. 19 cm. N.D. Chilton Books.
Clark, G. Minnie, ed. see Van Kirk, Louise. M.
Clark, G. Orr
--The Moon Babies. Hyde, Helen H., illus. 1900. R. H. Russell.
--Nightmare Land. Goodwin, Caroline L., illus. LC 1-25213. 105p. illus. (part col) 30 1/2cm. 1901. R. H. Russell.
Clark, Genevieve
--It's Fun to Listen. LC 53-6465. 43p. illus. 23cm. 1953. Vantage Press.
Clark, Gertrude
--Turtles will be Turtles. N.D. Pageant Press Inc.
--Valentine Holiday. 1st ed. Lyons, Dave, illus. LC 56-11395. 41p. illus. 21cm. 1956. Pageant Press.
Clark, Ginnie, jt. auth. see Merrick, Donna.
Clark, Graves Greenwood
--Tiny Toilers and Their Works. 225p. 1921. Century Co.
Clark, Harry (1885-)
--The First Story of the Whale. Clark, Harry (1885-), illus. LC 38-39431. 32p. illus. (part. col). 24cm. c.1938. Houghton Mifflin.
Clark, Henry Howard (1845-)
--Boy Life in the United States Navy. LC 5-4152. 1 l, 313 front plates 20. 1885. Lothrop, Lee & Shepard.
--Joe Bently: Naval Cadet. LC 2-190212. 2 p. l., 3-434 p. front., plates. 18 1/2 cm. 1889. D. Lothrop Company.
--Joe Bently, Naval Cadet. 1916. Lothrop, Lee & Shepard.
--Midshipman Stanford. Stevens, W O, illus. LC 16-14049. 379 front., plates 20. 1916. Lothrop,Lee & Shepard.
--The Admiral's Aid: A Story of Life in the New Navy. Hazelton, Isaac Brewster, illus. LC 3-19967. 1902. Lothrop,Lee & Shepard.
Clark, Howard, pseud., see Haskin, Dorothy Clark.
Clark, Howard
--Mark the Sparrow. 320p. 1975. Dial.
Clark, Howard, pseud. (1905-)
--Just For Fellows. Haskin, Dorothy Clark. N.D. Zondervan Publishing House.
Clark, Idena McFadin
--Little Dude. 1st ed. Duncan, Matt, illus. LC 52-8450. 186 p. illus. 21 cm. 1952. Ariel Books.
Clark, Imogen
--Santa Claus' Sweetheart. LC 6-29778. 6 p. l., 3-179, 1 p. col. front., col. pl. 19 cm. c.1906. E. P. Dutton & Company.
--We Four and Two More. LC 9-24964. 4 p. l., 274 p. col. front., 3 col. pl. 20 1/2 cm. c.1909. T. Y. Crowell & Co.
--Will Shakespeare's Little Lad. Birch, Reginald Bathurst (1856-1943), illus. (Scribner's Series for Young People). 1902. Charles Scribner's Sons.
Clark, J. Erskine, ed. see R. Worthington.
Clark, J. M.
--Legends of King Arthur and His Knights. N.D. E P Dutton.
Clark, J. W., ed.
--The Adventures of Robinson Crusoe. Golden Treasury Ed. ed. N.D. MacMillan.
Clark, J. W., ed. see Cervantes Saavedra, Miguel de.
Clark, J. W., ed. see Defoe, Daniel.
Clark, James Bayard (1869-)
--Virginia and the Mason-Bee. Barrett, Robert D., illus. LC 80-88778. 55, 1 p. illus. 19 1/2 cm. c.1930. Duttons, Inc.
Clark, James I.
--Shortcut to Peril. Glessner, Marc, illus. LC 79-22151. (Illus.). (Quest, Adventure, Survival). (gr. 4-9). 1982. (ISBN 0-8172-2070-4). Raintree Pubs.
--Steel Coffin at Forty Fathoms. Antonishak, Tom, illus. LC 79-21052. (Illus.). 46p. (Quest, Adventure, Survival). (gr. 4-9). 1982. (ISBN 0-8172-2071-2). Raintree Pubs.
--Three Years on the Ocean. Van Severen, Joe, illus. LC 79-21873. (Illus.). 46p. (Quest, Adventure, Survival). (gr. 4-8). 1980. (ISBN 0-8172-1572-7). Raintree Pubs.

Clark, Jean
--Practical Primary Plays: A Collection of Easy Plays for the Primary Grades Aimed to Inculcate in Children Good Habits of Thrift, Courtesy, Punctuality, Safety, Cooperation, Cleanliness, Etc. ... LC 40-37452. 92 p. 19 cm. 1940. The Northwestern Press.
--The Young Folk Recitation Book. 96p. N.D. T. S. Denison & Co Inc.

Clark, Joan (1934-)
--Early Rising. (gr. 5-8). 1976. Harper.
--Thomasina and the Trout Tree. Hiscox, Ingeborg, illus. LC 72-179431. (Illus.). 40 p. 21cm. 1971. (ISBN 0-912766-02-6). Tundra Books.

Clark, Joseph Deadrick (1893-)
--Beastly Folklore. 1973. (ISBN 0-8108-0684-3). Scarecrow Press, Inc.

Clark, Julia
--Crab Village. Brett, Bernard (1925-), illus. LC 55-105641. 108p. illus. 19cm. (Holt books for young people). 1955. Holt.

Clark, Kate McCosh
--A Southern Cross Fairy Tale. (Illus.). N.D. Estes & Lauriat's.

Clark, Kate Upson, Mrs. (1851-)
--The Dole Twins: Or, Child Life in New England in 1807. Atwood, Clara E., illus. LC 6-18838. viii p., 2 l., 165 p. incl. illus., plates. front. 18 1/2 cm. (Cosy corner series). 1906. L. C. Page & Company.
--Donald's Good Hen: The Nearly True Story of a Real Hen. McCullough, W. C., illus. LC 9-18592. (Illus.). 18cm. 95p. 1905. S. E. Cassino & Son.
--How Dexter Paid His Way. (Illus.). (The From Nine to Twelve Ser.). 1902. Thomas Y. Crowell & Co.
--How Dexter Paid His Way. (The "Bimbi" Series of Children's Booklets). N.D. Thomas Y. Crowell.
--That Mary Ann: The Story of a Country Summer. Kirk, Maria Louise (1860-), illus. (Illus.). N.D. Lothrop.

Clark, Katherine
--The Story of McDuff. Clark, Katherine, illus. LC 51-28014. 24p. illus. (part. col) 20cm. c.1950. S. Lowe Co.

Clark, Leonard (1906-1981), ed.
--All Things New: An Anthology. Tout, Ann, illus. LC 68-12421. (Illus.). 86 p. 25cm. (gr. 7 up). 1968, c.1965. (ISBN 0-8023-1144-X). Dufour Editions.
--Common Ground: An Anthology for the Young. Eldridge, Mildred E. (1909-), illus. LC 66-1923. 223p. illus. 21cm. 1966, c.1964. Faber & Faber.
--Drums and Trumpets: Poetry for the Youngest. Copley, Heather (1920-), illus. LC 63-14354. 96p. col. illus. 26cm. (gr. 1-6). 1963, c.1962. (ISBN 0-8023-1148-2). Dufour.
--Drums & Trumpets: Poetry for the Youngest. Copley, Heather (1920-), illus. LC 67-69351. (Illus.). 96p. 1st U.S. edition. (ps-3). 1979. (ISBN 0-686-34424-3, Pub. by Chatto Bodley Jonathan). Merrimack Pub Cir.

Clark, Lillian F
--Perry Poppett. Allaben, Anne, illus. LC 48-2017. 32 p. col. illus. 23 cm. (Merry-go-round book). 1947. J. Martin's House.

Clark, M.
--African Holiday. 1954. Christian Lit.

Clark, M. L.
--Bud and Blossom, 1 of 6. (May Flower Ser.). 1872. D. Lothrop & Co.
--Little Blossom, 1 of 6 vols. (May Flower Ser.). N.D. D. Lothrop & Co.

Clark, Margaret Goff (1913-)
--Adirondack Mountain Mystery. Barth, Ernest Kurt, illus. LC 66-12578. 158 p. illus. 21 cm. 1966. Funk & Wagnalls.
--Barney and the UFO. Lewin, Ted (1935-), illus. LC 79-52046. (Illus.). 159 p. 21cm. c.1979. (ISBN 0-396-07711-0). Dodd, Mead.
--Barney in Space. Lewin, Ted (1935-), illus. LC 81-43224. p. cm. 1981. (ISBN 0-396-08001-4). Dodd, Mead.
--Barney on Mars. Lewin, Ted (1935-), illus. LC 83-15353. p. cm. 1983. (ISBN 0-396-08222-X). Dodd, Mead.
--The Boy from the UFO. Lewin, Ted (1935-), illus. 160p. (gr. 3-7). 1981. (ISBN 0-590-31594-3). Scholastic Inc.
--The Boy from the UFO Returns. Lewin, Ted (1935-), illus. (Illus.). 160p. (gr. 3-6). 1983. (ISBN 0-590-32509-4). Scholastic Inc.
--Danger at Niagara. Barth, Ernest Kurt, illus. LC 68-27995. (Illus.). 127 p. 21cm. 1968. Funk & Wagnalls.
--Death at Their Heels. LC 74-25514. (Illus.). 146 p. 21cm. 1975. (ISBN 0-396-07075-2). Dodd, Mead.
--Freedom Crossing. Barth, Ernest Kurt, illus. LC 78-80702. (Illus.). 128 p. 21cm. 1969. Funk & Wagnalls.
--The Latchkey Mystery. LC 84-28616. 128p. (gr. 4 up). 1985. (ISBN 0-396-08639-X). Dodd.
--Mystery at Star Lake. (gr. 3-5). N.D. (ISBN 0-590-11927-3, Schol Pap). Scholastic Inc.
--Mystery at Star Lake. Johnson, Eugene Harper, illus. LC 65-11721. 120p. illus. 21cm. (gr. 5up). c.1965. (ISBN 0-308-80012-5). Funk & Wagnalls.
--Mystery Horse. LC 72-1534. (Illus.). 153 p. 21cm. 1972. (ISBN 0-396-06609-7). Dodd, Mead.
--Mystery in the Flooded Museum. LC 77-16860. 173 p. 21cm. c.1978. (ISBN 0-396-07550-9). Dodd, Mead.
--Mystery of Sebastian Island. LC 76-12502. 159 p. 21cm. c.1976. (ISBN 0-396-07349-2). Dodd, Mead.
--The Mystery of Seneca Hill. Granda, Julio, illus. LC 61-5167. 148p. illus. 21cm. 1961. F. Watts.
--The Mystery of the Buried Indian Mask. Murray, Irene (1935-), illus. LC 62-7383. (Illus.). 184 p. 22cm. 1962. F. Watts.
--Mystery of the Marble Zoo. Beck, Charles, illus. LC 64-11116. 121 p. illus. 21 cm. 1964. Funk & Wagnalls.
--Mystery of the Missing Stamps. Donahue, Vic, illus. LC 67-3881. (Illus.). 157 p. 22cm. 1967. Funk & Wagnalls.
--Who Stole Kathy Young?. LC 80-1013. p. cm. 1980. (ISBN 0-396-07888-5). Dodd, Mead.

Clark, Margery, pseud., see Clark, Mary Elizabeth.

Clark, Margery, pseud.
--The Cook's Surprise. Clark, Mary Elizabeth. Anderson, Madge, illus. LC 23-26926. 25p. col. illus 19cm. N.D. Doubleday Page & Co.

Clark, Margery, pseud. & Quigley, Margery C.
--The Poppy Seed Cakes. Clark, Mary Elizabeth. Petersham, Maud Sylvia Fuller (1890-1971) & Petersham, Miska (1888-1960), illus. LC 24-27351. (Margery Clark is the joint pseudonym of Mary Elizabeth Clark and Margery C. Quigley (1886-)). 124 p. illus., col. plates. 20 cm. 1924. Doubleday, Page.

Clark, Marie Whitbeck
--Sing Me a Song!. 50 p. 1 l., 28 x 21 cm. c.1938. Easton Associates.

Clark, Marion
--Bill, of the Pony Express. LC 67-551778. (Illus.). 25 p. (Children of other times). 1967. Webster Division, McGraw-Hill.

Clark, Martha, jt. auth. see Devine, Eleanore.

Clark, Mary Cowden
--The Iron Cousin: or, Mutual Influence. N.D. George Routledge & Sons.
--A Rambling Story. 1875. Roberts Bros.

Clark, Mary Elizabeth see Clark, Margery, pseud.

Clark, Mary Latham
--Birthday Present. (Illus.). (Play and Study Ser.). N.D. D. Lothrop.
--Daisy's Mission, 1 0f 6. (Illus.). (May Flower Ser.). N.D. Macmillan & Co.
--Happy Hour Series: Includes "Daisy's Mission," "Little White Mice Boy," "Bud and Blossom," "Kitty's Tableaux," "Little Blossom," and "Blue Violet.", 6 vols. (Illus.). N.D. Set. D Lothrop.
--Kitty's Tableaux, 6 vols. (May Flower Ser.). N.D. D. Lothrop & Co.
--Little White Mice Boy, 1 of 6 vol. (May Flower Ser.). N.D. D. Lothrop & co.
--May Flower Ser. Containing "Daisy's Mission," "Little White Mice Boy" "Bud and Blossom," "Kitty's Tableaux," "Little Blossom," and "Blue Violet", 6 vols. (Illus.). N.D. Set. D. Lothrop & Co.

Clark, Mary Latham & Strong, Joseph Dwight
--Spring Blossom Library: Containing "Daisy's Mission," "Little White Mice Boy," "Bud and Blossom," etc, 12 vols. N.D. D. Lothrop & Co.

Clark, Mary Margaret
--Jesus Lives!. Musical Plays for Children (from the New Testament) for Stage, Classroom, Home, Church : a Collection of Short Plays with Optional Songs. LC 77-80800. (Illus.). i, 48 p. 28cm. c.1977. (ISBN 0-8091-2050-X). Paulist Press.

Clark, Mary Senior
--The Lost Legends of the Nursery Songs. N.D. George Routledge & Sons.
--Lost Legends of the Nursery Songs. (Queen's Treasure Ser.). N.D. Harcourt Brace.

Clark, Mavis Thorpe
--Blue Above the Trees. Melrose, Genevieve, illus. LC 76-80277. (Illus.). vii, 248 p. 21cm. 1969, c.1968. Meredith Press.
--The Hundred Islands. LC 77-361854. (Illus.). 133 p. 22cm. 1976. (ISBN 0-340-20715-9). Hodder & Stoughton.
--The Hundred Islands. Lacis, Astra, illus. LC 77-5353. 152 p. 22cm. 1977, c.1976. (ISBN 0-02-718900-7). Macmillan.
--If the Earth Falls in. LC 75-4781. 165 p. 24cm. (A Clarion book). 1975, c.1973. (ISBN 0-8164-3153-1). Seabury Press.
--Iron Mountain. LC 76-152290. vi, 204 p. 21cm. 1971, c.1970. Macmillan.
--The Min-Min. Melrose, Genevieve, illus. 1969. Collier. **Award: (ALA).**
--The Min-Min. Melrose, Genevieve, illus. LC 77-16505. 216 p. 18cm. 1978, c.1969. (ISBN 0-02-042280-6). Collier Books. **Award: (ALA).**
--New Golden Mountain. LC 73-173813. 165 p. 22cm. 1973. (ISBN 0-7018-0356-8). Lansdowne.
--The Sky Is Free. LC 76-15171. 173 p. 22cm. 1976, c.1974. (ISBN 0-02-718910-4). Macmillan.
--Spark of Opal. Melrose, Genevieve, illus. LC 72-81054. 215 p. 22cm. 1973. (ISBN 0-02-718950-3). Macmillan.
--Wildfire. LC 73-19049. vii, 211 p. 22cm. 1974, c.1973. (ISBN 0-02-718970-8). Macmillan.

Clark, Mollie
--The Blue Velvet Cat. N.D. William Collins Sons& Co Ltd.
--Christmas Tree Fairy. N.D. William Collins & Company Ltd.
--Five Magic Marbles. 1965. William Collins Sons & Co Ltd.
--The Friendly Puppy. 1965. William Collins Sons & Co Ltd.
--Hobby Horse. N.D. William Collins Sons & Co Ltd.
--Little Nusiance. N.D. William Collins Sons & company Ltd.
--Tom Cat and the Three Mice. N.D. William Collins Sons & Co Ltd.
--White Elephant. N.D. William Collins Sons & Co Ltd.

Clark, Muriel
--When Jesus Was a Carpenter. LC 28-28046. 104 p. 19 1/2 cm. 1927. The Abingdon Press.

Clark, Natalie Lord Rice, Mrs. (1867-)
--Blake Redding: A Boy of the Day. Button, Albert, illus. LC 3-24295. 19cm. 301p. 1903. Little, Brown, & Co.
--The Green Garnet. LC 20-19337. 390 p. front., plates. 19 cm. 1895. Congregational Sunday-School and Publishing Society.
--The Green Garnet. 390p. N.D. Pilgrim Press.

Clark, Patricia Finrow, jt. auth. see Clark, William L Emmer.

Clark, Patricia Finrow (1929-)
--Jan Ken Pon. 64p. 1961. Moody.

Clark, Rebecca Sophie see Sophie, May, pseud.

Clark, Roger William (1928-)
--Ride the White Tiger. Kim, pseud., illus. Clark, Christopher Kim. LC 59-5278. (Illus.). 207 p. 22cm. 1959. Little, Brown.

Clark, Ron (1940-)
--My Buttons Are Blue, and Other Love Poems: From the Digital Heart of an Electronic Computer. LC 81-22777. (Illus.). 94 p. 22cm. (ARCsoft Color Computer Books: No. 5). 1982. (ISBN 0-86668-011-X). ARCsoft Publishers.

Clark, Ruth
--Because of Batty's Boots. Morton-Sale, Isobel (1904-), illus. N.D. Dodd Mead & Co.

Clark, S. H., Mrs.
--Their Children. (Illus.). N.D. D. Lothrop Co.

Clark, S. R. Graham, Mrs.
--Achor. N.D. Lothrop.
--Go's Goings. N.D. Lothrop.
--Herbert Gardenell, Jr. (Illus.). N.D. Lothrop.
--Herbert Gardenell's Children. N.D. Lothrop.
--Our Street. (Illus.). N.D. Lothrop.
--Tom's Street. N.D. Lothrop.
--Tom's Street. N.D. Pilgrim Press.
--The Triple E. N.D. Lothrop.
--The Triple E. (Illus.). (The Kitty Kent Library). N.D. Set. Ward & Drummond.
--Yensie Walton. (Illus.). N.D. Lothrop.
--Yensie Walton's Womanhood. (Illus.). N.D. Lothrop.

Clark, Sarah Jones (1840-)
--Young Master Kirke. Tsinajinie, Andy, illus. LC 22-517022. 156 p. front. plates. 16 1/2 cm. (Silver gate series. v. 1). c.1895. Lee and Shepard.

Clark, Thomas March (1812-1903)
--John Whooper the Newsboy. LC 35-33166. 1935. Longmans Green & Co.
--John Whopper, The Newsboy. New ed. Sturtevant, Helena, illus. Potter, Henry C., intro. by. LC 5-16633. (Illus.). 18cm. 93p. (The Cosy Corner Series). 1905. The Page Company.

Clark, Van Deusen (1909-)
--Peetie the Pack Rat & Other Desert Stories. Tsinajinie, Andy, illus. LC 59-5482. (Illus.). 108p. (gr. 1-3). 1960. (ISBN 0-87004-027-8). Caxton.

Clark, Virginia, pseud., see Gray, Patricia Clark.

Clark, Virginia, pseud.
--The Mysterious Buckskin. Gray, Patricia Clark. LC 60-11212. 164p. 22cm. 1960. Macmillan.

Clark, William, ed. see Shane, Harold Gray.

Clark, William L Emmer & Clark, Patricia Finrow (1929-)
--Children of the Sun. Brannen, Phyllis, illus. LC 65-152915. 70p. illus. (pt. col) 27cm. c.1965. Tuttle.

Clarke, Amanda
--Growing up in Puritan Times. LC 79-56452. (Illus.). 72p. (Growing up Ser.). (gr. 7 up). 1980. (Pub. by Batsford England). David & Charles.

Clarke, Arthur Charles (1917-)
--Boy Beneath the Sea. Wilson, Mike, illus. LC 58-9782. (Illus.). (gr. 5 up). 1958. (ISBN 0-06-021266-7, HarpJ). Har-Row.
--Dolphin Island. 1968, c.1963. (ISBN 0-425-01495-9). Berkley Publishing Company.
--Dolphin Island: A Story of the People of the Sea. LC 63-8704. 186 p. 22cm. 1963. Holt, Rinehart and Winston.
--Fall of Moondust. LC 61-12345. (gr. 10 up). 1961. (ISBN 0-15-130017-8). HarBraceJ.
--The First Five Fathoms. Wilson, Mike, illus. 1960. Harper & Brothers.
--Imperial Earth. LC 75-30595. 303p. 1976. (ISBN 0-15-144233-9). HarBraceJ.
--Indian Ocean Adventure. Wilson, Mike, illus. 1961. Harper & Row Publishers.
--Islands in the Sky. (Winston Science Fiction Ser.). 1953. Holt, Reinhart and Winston.
--Islands in the Sky. LC 52-8970. 209 p. 22cm. (Science fiction novel). 1952. Winston.
--Islands in the Sky. new ed. Moore, Patrick, intro. by. LC 73-153840. (Illus.). 208 p. 19cm. (Puffin books). 1972. (ISBN 0-14-030535-1). Penguin.
--The Other Side of the Sky. LC 58-5477. (gr. 7 up). 1958. (ISBN 0-15-170451-1). HarBraceJ.
--Tales of Ten Worlds. LC 62-16730. (gr. 10 up). 1962. (ISBN 0-15-187980-X). HarBraceJ.

Clarke, Arthur Charles (1917-) & Wilson, Mike
--Indian Ocean Treasure. 1964. (ISBN 0-8382-0366-3, Cadmus Books). E. M. Hale and Company.

Clarke, Benjamin
--From Tent to Palace. (The Rise and Conquer Library). N.D. Thomas Nelson & Sons.
--Pounceford Hall. N.D. Thomas Nelson & Sons.

Clarke, Cecil
--Elsie Grey: A Tale of Truth. N.D. E. P. Dutton & Co.

Clarke, Covington, pseud., see Venable, Clarke.

Clarke, D. W. C., Mrs.
--Lizzie Maitland. N.D. Kelly, Piet & Co.

Clarke, David (1907-)
--The Down-Going of Orpheus Hawkins: A Children's Play. LC 77-366820. 6, 41 p. 22cm. 1976. (ISBN 0-573-05039-2). French.

Clarke, Derrick Harry (1919-)
--The Blue Water Dream. 1981. (ISBN 0-679-51004-4). McKay.

Clarke, Donald Henderson
--Joe and Jennie. N.D. The Vanguard Press.

Clarke, Frances Elizabeth, ed.
--High-Stepping Horses. (gr. 7 up). 1963 (Collier). Macmillan.
--Valiant Dogs: Great Dog Stories of Our Day. LC 36-23200. 23cm. 336p. 1936. Macmillan Company.

Clarke, Harry, ed.
--The Fairy Tales of Perrault. N.D. Dodge.

Clarke, Henry, Mrs.
--Reuben Thorne's Temptation. N.D. E. & J. B. Young & Co.

Clarke, J. P. Gates
--Butterflies. Zim, Herbert S., ed. Durenceau, Andre (1904-), illus. 1963. Golden Press.

Clarke, Jane
--The Truth Machine. LC 77-70857. (Illus.). (Star Trek Bks.). (gr. 2-5). 1977. (ISBN 0-394-93575-6). Random.

Clarke, Joan B. (1921-)
--Early Rising. Martin, Pauline, illus. LC 76-17874. 252 p. 21cm. 1976, c.1974. (ISBN 0-397-31687-9). Lippincott.
--The Happy Planet. Maitland, Antony Jasper (1935-), illus. LC 65-13390. (Illus.). 254 p. 22cm. 1965. Lothrop, Lee & Shepard.

Clarke, John, pseud., see Laklan, Carli.

Clarke, John, pseud.
--Black Soldier. Laklan, Carli. 1st ed. James, Harold Laymont (1929-), illus. LC 68-17808. (Illus.). 144 p. 22cm. (Doubleday signal books). 1968. Doubleday.
--High School Drop Out. Laklan, Carli. 1st ed. Micale, Albert (1913-), illus. LC 64-19263. 143 p. illus. 22 cm. (A Signal book). 1964. Doubleday.
--Roar of Engines. Laklan, Carli. 1st ed. Friedman, Marvin (1930-), illus. LC 67-17273. 144 p. illus. 22 cm. (Doubleday signal books). 1967. Doubleday.

Clarke, Joyce
--Mystery of the Brenton Fort. Summers, Leo, illus. LC 65-134337. (Illus.). (gr. 4-6). 1965. (ISBN 0-397-30830-2). Lippincott.

Clarke, Katherine
--Twenty Thousand Pounds (Pub. by Society for Promoting Christian Knowledge). N.D. E. & J. B. Young & Co.

Clarke, Mary Cowden, Mrs. (1809-1898)
--Christmas in Russia: Little Paulina. Dana Estes & Co, ed. (Illus.). (Christmas in Many Lands Ser.). N.D. Dana Estes & Co.
--The Girlhood of Shakespeare's Heroines: In a Series of Tales. 1873. G. P. Putnam's Sons.
--Little Paulina: Christmas in Russia. Robinson, Anna, adapted by. LC 6-34799. 32 p. incl. front., illus. 19 1/2 cm. 1906. D. Estes & Company.

AUTHOR INDEX CLARKE, REBECCA

--Portia, and other Tales of Shakespeares Heroines. N.D. G. P. Putnam's Sons.
--Uncle, Peep, and I. (Illus.). (The Boys' and Girls' Books). N.D. Little, Brown and Company.
--Uncle Peep, and I. A Child's Novel. LC 12-31528. 300 p. front. 17 1/2 cm. 1886. Roberts Brothers.
--Yarns of an Old Mariner. (Jutland Ser.). N.D. Colby and Rich.
--Yarns of an Old Mariner, 1 of 50 vols. (Illus.). (The Norwood Ser.: No. 7). 1900. Lee & Shepard.
--Yarns of an Old Mariner, 1 of 4 vols. Cruikshank, George (1792-1878), illus. (Illus.). (Jutland Ser.). 1882. Lee & Shepard.

Clarke, Mary Stetson (1911-)
--Bloomer and Ballots. N.D. (ISBN 0 670 17437 8). Viking Press.
--The Glass Phoenix. LC 69-13083. 271 p. 22cm. 1969. Viking Press.
--The Iron Peacock. MacLean, Robert (1926-), illus. LC 66-11909. (Illus.). 251 p. 22cm. 1966. Viking Press.
--The Limner's Daughter. LC 67-3697. 255 p. 22 cm. 1967. Viking Press.
--Petticoat Rebel. MacLean, Robert (1926-), illus. LC 64-21477. 255 p. illus. 21 cm. 1964. Viking Press.
--Piper to the Clan. LC 71-102925. (Illus.). 239 p. 22cm. 1970. (ISBN 0-670-55660-2). Viking Press.

Clarke, Michael, ed.
--Stories from the Arabian Nights. LC 20-13311. 271 p. illus. 19 cm. (Eclectic school readings). 1897. American Book Company.

Clarke, Michael (1844-1916)
--Arabian Nights. (Eclectic School Readings). 1897. American Book Co.

Clarke, Michael (1844-1916) & Homerus
--The Story of Troy. LC 12-31409. 254 p. incl. front. illus. 19 cm. (Eclectic school readings)). 1897. American Book Company.

Clarke, Mollie (1916-)
--Aldar the Trickster. Belsky, Margaret, illus. LC 67-4379. (Illus.). 32 p. 23cm. 1967. Follett Pub. Co.
--Three Brothers: A Serbian Folk Tale. Stobbs, William (1914-), illus. LC 67-20996. (Illus.). 32p. (ps-3). 1967. (ISBN 0-695-88713-0). (ISBN 0-695-48713-2). Follett.

Clarke, Mollie (1916-), retold by.
--Momotaro: A Japanese Folk Tale. Huxtable, Grace, illus. LC 67-3567. (Illus.). 32 p. 23cm. (ps-3). 1967, c.1963. (ISBN 0-695-45872-8). Follett Pub. Co.
--Silly Simon: An English Folk Tale. Eccles, Charles (1922-), illus. LC 67-4680. (Illus.). 32 p. 23cm. (ps-3). 1967, c.1963. (ISBN 0 695 48002 2). Follett Pub. Co.
--The Three Feathers. Oakley, Graham (1929-), illus. (Illus.). 32 p. 23cm. 1968, c.1963. Follett.

Clarke, Nita
--The Mystery at Rancho Verde. (Illus.). (gr. 1-4). 1981. (ISBN 0-933184-13-1). (ISBN 0-933184-14-X). Flame Intl.
--Timothy & the Blanket Fairy. (gr. k-6). 1981. (ISBN 0-933184-06-9). (ISBN 0-933184-16-6). Flame Intl.

Clarke, Pauline see Clare, Helen, pseud.

Clarke, Pauline, see Hunter Blair, Pauline Clarke.

Clarke, Pauline (1921-)
--Five Dolls in a House. Clare, Helen, pseud. Leslie, Cecil, illus. LC 64-6684. (Illus.). 143 p. 20cm. (Puffin Bks.). N.D. Penguin Books.
--Hidden Gold. Hunter Blair, Pauline Clarke. Leslie, Cecil, illus. LC 57-8084. (Illus.). 192 p. 21cm. 1957. Abelard-Schuman.
--The Return of the Twelves. Hunter Blair, Pauline. LC 80-25300. p. cm. (Gregg Press Children's Literature Series). 1981, c.1962. (ISBN 0-8398-2718-0). Gregg Press.
--The Return of the Twelves. Hunter Blair, Pauline Clarke. Bryson, Bernarda (1905-1977), illus. LC 63-15541. (Illus.). 251 p. 21cm. 1st U.S. edition. 1964, c.1962. Coward-McCann. **Awards: (ALA); (CMA).**
--Silver Bells & Cockle Shells. Hunter Blair, Pauline Clarke. Ducksbury, Sally, illus. LC 62-8383. (Illus.). (gr. k-3). 1962. Abelard.
--Torolv the Fatherless. Hunter Blair, Pauline Clarke. Leslie, Cecil, illus. LC 79-670050. (Illus.). 190 p. 21cm. 1978, c.1958. (ISBN 0-571-03620-1). Faber and Faber.
--The Two Faces of Silenus. Hunter Blair, Pauline Clarke. LC 72-76698. 160 p. 21cm. 1972. (ISBN 0-698-20186-8). Coward, McCann & Geoghegan.
--The White Elephant. Hunter Blair, Pauline Clarke. Kennedy, Richard (1910-), illus. LC 57-5436. 145p. illus. 22cm. 1957. Abelard-Schuman.

Clarke, Rebecca Sophia see May, Sophie, pseud.

Clarke, Rebecca Sophia, jt. auth. see Jeffers, Susan.

Clarke, Rebecca Sophia (1833-1906)
--The Asbury Twins. May, Sophie, pseud. (The Maidenhood Ser.). N.D. Lee & Shepard.
--The Asbury Twins. May, Sophie, pseud. Humphrey, Lizzie B., illus. LC 3-18181. 374 p. front., 7 pl. 19 1/2 cm. (Her Quinnebasset Ser., Vol. 5). 1903. Lee and Shepard.
--Aunt Madge's Story. May, Sophie, pseud. (Little Prudy's Flyaway Ser.). N.D. Colby and Rich.
--Aunt Madge's Story. May, Sophie, pseud, 1 of 6 vols. (Illus.). (Little Prudy's Flyaway Ser.). 1882. Lee & Shepard.
--Aunt Madge's Story. May, Sophie, pseud. LC 626. 1 p. l, 7-214 p. front., plates. 16 1/2 cm. (Little Prudy's Flyaway Ser., Vol. 3). 1899. Lee and Shepard.
--Captain Horace. May, Sophie, pseud. LC 20-16489. 6, 5-183 p. front., plates. 16 cm. (Little Prudy Ser.). 1893. Lee and Shepard.
--Doctor Papa. May, Sophie, pseud, 1 of 6 vols. (Illus.). (Flaxie Frizzle Stories). 1882. Set. Lee & Shepard.
--Doctor Papa. May, Sophie, pseud. LC 5-13287. 17cm. 194p. (Flaxie Frizzle Stories: Vol. 2). 1905. Lee & Shepard.
--The Doctor's Daughter. May, Sophie, pseud. LC 42-26111. 1 p. l, 5-330 p. front., plates. 17 cm. 1872. Lee & Shepard.
--The Doctor's Daughter. May, Sophie, pseud. LC 627. 8 p., 1 l, 9-330 p. incl. front. plates. 19 cm. (Quinnebasset series, v. 1). 1899. Lee and Shepard.
--The Doctor's Daughter. May, Sophie, pseud, 1 of 6 vols. (Illus.). (Girlhood Ser.). N.D. Set. Lee & Shepard.
--Dotty Dimple. May, Sophie, pseud. LC 17-13034. 176 p. front., plates. 15 1/2 cm. (Little Prudy Ser.). 1865. Lee and Shepard.
--Dotty Dimple. May, Sophie, pseud. LC 21-129542. 176 p. plates. 16 cm. (Little Prudy Ser., 4d no. 6 5d). 1894. Lee and Shepard.
--Dotty Dimple at Her Grandmothers. May, Sophie, pseud. (Dotty Dimple Stories). N.D. Colby and Rich.
--Dotty Dimple at Her Grandmother's. May, Sophie, pseud, 1 of 6 vols. (Illus.). 190p. (Dotty Dimple Ser.). 1882. Lee & Shepard.
--Dotty Dimple at Her Grandmother's. May, Sophie, pseud. LC 21-12962. 3 p. l, 5-190 p. front., plates. 16 cm. (Dotty Dimple stories, no.1). 1895. Lee and Shepard.
--Dotty Dimple at Home. May, Sophie, pseud. (Dotty Dimple Ser.). N.D. Colby and Rich.
--Dotty Dimple at Home. May, Sophie, pseud. LC 43-30052. 16cm. 171p. (Dotty Dimple Stories). 1868. Lee, & Shepard.
--Dotty Dimple at Home. May, Sophie, pseud, 1 of 6 vols. (Illus.). 171p. (Dotty Dimple Ser.). 1882. Lee & Shepard.
--Dotty Dimple at Play. (Dotty Dimple Stories). N.D. Colby and Rich.
--Dotty Dimple at Play. May, Sophie, pseud. LC 48-34212. 184 p. plates. 16 cm. (Her Dotty dimple stories). 1875. Lee and Shepard.
--Dotty Dimple at Play, 1 of 6 vols. (Illus.). 184p. (Dotty Dimple Ser.). 1882. Lee & Shepard.
--Dotty Dimple at School. May, Sophie, pseud. (Dotty Dimple Stories). N.D. Colby and Rich.
--Dotty Dimple at School. May, Sophie, pseud, 1 of 6 vols. (Illus.). 168p. (Dotty Dimple Ser.). 1882. Lee & Shepard.
--Dotty Dimple at School. May, Sophie, pseud. LC 21-13939. 3 p. l, 5-168 p. front., plates. 17 cm. (Dotty Dimple stories). 1897. Lee and Shepard.
--Dotty Dimple out West. May, Sophie, pseud. (Dotty Dimple Ser.). N.D. Colby and Rich.
--Dotty Dimple out West. May, Sophie, pseud, 1 of 6 vols. (Illus.). (Dotty Dimple Ser.). 1882. Lee & Shepard.
--Dotty Dimple Out West. May, Sophie, pseud. LC 20-164837. 171 p. front., plates. 16 cm. (Dotty Dimple stories). 1896. Lee and Shepard.
--Dotty Dimple Ser. May, Sophie, pseud, 6 vols. (Illus.). 1882. Set. Lee & Shepard.
--Dotty Dimple's Flyaway. May, Sophie, pseud. (Dotty Dimple Stories). N.D. Colby and Rich.
--Dotty Dimple's Flyaway. May, Sophie, pseud, 1 of 6 vols. (Illus.). 200p. (Dotty Dimple Ser.). 1882. Lee & Shepard.
--Dotty Dimple's Flyaway. May, Sophie, pseud. LC 22-17362. 4 p. l, 7-200 p. front., plates. 17 cm. (Dotty Dimple stories, no.6). 1897. Lee and Shepard.
--Drones' Honey. May, Sophie, pseud. N.D. Lee and Shepard's Trade List.
--Fairy Book. May, Sophie, pseud. LC 17-13035. 3 p. l, 9-178 p. front. plates. 15 1/2 cm. 1865. Lee and Shepard.
--Flaxie Frizzle. May, Sophie, pseud. (Illus.). 182p. (Flaxie Frizzle Stories). 1876. Lee & Shepard.
--Flaxie Frizzle. May, Sophie, pseud. 182 p. incl. front. 1904. Lee and Shepard.
--Flaxie Frizzle and Her Friends. May, Sophie, pseud. (Illus.). N.D. Lee & Shepard.
--Flaxie Frizzle Stories. May, Sophie, pseud, 4 vols. (Illus.). 1882. Set. Lee & Shepard.
--Flaxie Growing Up. May, Sophie, pseud, 1 of 6 vols. (Illus.). 202p. (Flaxie Frizzle Stories). 1884. Set. Lee & Shepard.
--Flaxie's Kittyleen. May, Sophie, pseud. (Flaxie Frizzle Stories). N.D. Lothrop,Lee & Shepard.
--Her Friend's Lover. May, Sophie, pseud, 1 of 30 vols. (American Girls' Ser.: No. 5). 1900. Set. Lee & Shepard.
--In Old Quinnebasset. May, Sophie, pseud. (The Quinnebasset Ser.). N.D. Lothrop,Lee & Shepard.
--Janet, a Poor Heiress. May, Sophie, pseud. (Illus.). (The Quinnebasset Ser.). N.D. Lee and Shepard's Trade List.
--Jimmy Boy. May, Sophie, pseud, 3 vols. (Illus.). (Little Prudy's Children: Vol. 3). N.D. Lee & Shepard.
--Jimmy, Lucy, and All. May, Sophie, pseud. LC 3324. iii p., 1 l, 196 p. front., 3 pl. 17 cm. (Little Prudy's children). 1900. Lee & Shepard.
--Joy Bells. A Quinnebasset Story. May, Sophie, pseud. Merrill, Frank Thayer (1848-), illus. LC 3-152257. ix, p., 1 l, 332 p. front., 5 pl. 19 cm. 1903. Lee and Shepard.
--Kittyleen. May, Sophie, pseud. LC 20-16484. 207 p. front., plates. 16 cm. (Flaxie Frizzle stories. no.5). 1884. Lee and Shepard.
--Kittyleen. May, Sophie, pseud, 1 of 6 vols. (Illus.). (Flaxie Frizzle Stories). N.D. Set. Lee & Shepard.
--Kyzee Dunlee-A Golden Girl. May, Sophie, pseud. (Illus.). N.D. Lee & Shepard.
--Kyzie Dunlee. May, Sophie, pseud. (Little Prudy's Children). N.D. Lothrop, Lee & Shepard.
--Little Folks Astray. May, Sophie, pseud. (Little Prudy's Flyaway Ser.). N.D. Colby and Rich.
--Little Folks Astray. May, Sophie, pseud, 1 of 6 vols. (Illus.). (Little Prudy's Flyaway Series). 1882. Lee & Shepard.
--Little Folks Astray. May, Sophie, pseud. LC 96-330. 3 p. l, 5-203 p. pl. 16 1/2 cm. (Little Prudy's Flyaway series, v.1). 1898. Lee and Shepard.
--Little Grandfather. May, Sophie, pseud. (Little Prudy's Flyaway Ser.). N.D. Colby and Rich.
--Little Grandfather. May, Sophie, pseud. (Little Prudy's Flyaway Ser.). 1873. Lee & Shepard.
--Little Grandfather. May, Sophie, pseud, 1 of 6 vols. (Illus.). (Little Prudy's Flyaway Ser.). 1882. Lee & Shepard.
--Little Grandfather. May, Sophie, pseud. LC 1-20315. 16cm. 221p. (Little Prudy's Flyaway Series: Vol. 5). 1901. Lee & Shepard.
--Little Grandmother. May, Sophie, pseud. (Little Prudy's Flyaway Ser.). N.D. Colby and Rich.
--Little Grandmother. May, Sophie, pseud. LC 2798. 16cm. 202p. (Little Prudy's Flyaway Series: Vol. 4). 1900. Lee & Shepard.
--Little Grandmother. May, Sophie, pseud. 1873p. (Little Prudy's Flyaway Ser.). N.D. Lee & Shepard.
--Little Pitchers. May, Sophie, pseud. LC 6-348000. 196 p. incl. front. plates. 17 cm. (Her Flaxie Frizzle stories, v.3). 1906. Lee and Shepard Co.
--Little Pitchers. May, Sophie, pseud, 1 of 6 vols. (Illus.). (Flaxie Frizzle Stories). N.D. Set. Lee & Shepard.
--Little Prudy. May, Sophie, pseud. (Illus.). (Editha Ser.). N.D. Caldwell.
--Little Prudy. May, Sophie, pseud. (Little Prudy Stories). N.D. Colby and Rich.
--Little Prudy. May, Sophie, pseud. (The Little Prudy Stories). N.D. Cupples & Leon Co.
--Little Prudy. May, Sophie, pseud. (Editha Series.). N.D. Dodge Publishing Co.
--Little Prudy. May, Sophie, pseud. (Little Prudy Series.). N.D. Hurst & Co.
--Little Prudy. May, Sophie, pseud. (Home Series for Girls). N.D. Hurst & Co.
--Little Prudy. May, Sophie, pseud. LC 26-3641. 167 p. front. 15 1/2 cm. 1864. Lee and Shepard.
--Little Prudy. May, Sophie, pseud. 16cm. 176p. (Little Prudy Stories). 1891. Lee & Shepard.
--Little Prudy and Little Prudy's Sister. May, Sophie, pseud. (Illus.). (Little Prudy Ser.: Vol. 1). N.D. Set of 3. Caldwell.
--Little Prudy Stories. May, Sophie, pseud, 6 vols. (Illus.). 1882. Set. Lee & Shepard.
--Little Prudy's Captain Horace. May, Sophie, pseud. (Illus.). (Editha Ser.). N.D. Caldwell.
--Little Prudy's Captain Horace. May, Sophie, pseud. (Little Prudy Stories). N.D. Colby and Rich.
--Little Prudy's Captain Horace. May, Sophie, pseud. (The Little Prudy Stories). N.D. Cupples & Leon Co.
--Little Prudy's Captain Horace. May, Sophie, pseud. (Illus.). (Editha Series.). N.D. Dodge Publishing Co.
--Little Prudy's Captain Horace. May, Sophie, pseud. (Little Prudy's Series.). N.D. Hurst & Co.
--Little Prudy's Captain Horace. May, Sophie, pseud. (Home Series for Girls). N.D. Hurst & Co.
--Little Prudy's Captain Horace. May, Sophie, pseud, 1 of 6 vols. (Illus.). 183p. (Little Prudy Stories). 1882. Set. Lee & Shepard.
--Little Prudy's Captain Horace and Little Prudy's Cousin Grace. May, Sophie, pseud. (Illus.). (Little Prudy Ser.: Vol. 2). N.D. Set of 3. Caldwell.
--Little Prudy's Cousin Grace. May, Sophie, pseud. (Illus.). (Editha Ser.). N.D. Caldwell.
--Little Prudy's Cousin Grace. May, Sophie, pseud. (Little Prudy Stories). N.D. Colby and Rich.
--Little Prudy's Cousin Grace. May, Sophie, pseud. (The Little Prudy Stories). N.D. Cupples & Leon Co.
--Little Prudy's Cousin Grace. May, Sophie, pseud. (Illus.). (Editha Series.). N.D. Dodge Publishing Co.
--Little Prudy's Cousin Grace. May, Sophie, pseud. (Little Prudy Ser.). N.D. Hurst & Co.
--Little Prudy's Cousin Grace. May, Sophie, pseud. (Home Series for Girls). N.D. Hurst & Co.
--Little Prudy's Cousin Grace. May, Sophie, pseud, 1 of 6 vols. (Illus.). (Little Prudy Stories). 1882. Set. Lee & Shepard.
--Little Prudy's Cousin Grace. May, Sophie, pseud. LC 42-26112. 4 p. l, 5-183 p. front. plates. 17 cm. (Little Prudy series). 1899. Lee and Shepard.
--Little Prudy's Dottie Dimple. May, Sophie, pseud. (The Little Prudy Stories). N.D. Cupples & Leon Co.
--Little Prudy's Dotty Dimple. May, Sophie, pseud. (Illus.). (Editha Ser.). N.D. Caldwell.
--Little Prudy's Dotty Dimple. May, Sophie, pseud. (Little Prudy Stories). N.D. Colby and Rich.
--Little Prudy's Dotty Dimple. May, Sophie, pseud. (Editha Series.). N.D. Dodge Publishing Co.
--Little Prudy's Dotty Dimple. May, Sophie, pseud. (Little Prudy Series.). N.D. Hurst & Co.
--Little Prudy's Dotty Dimple. May, Sophie, pseud. (Home Series for Girls). N.D. Hurst & Co.
--Little Prudy's Dotty Dimple. May, Sophie, pseud, 1 of 6 Vols. (Illus.). (Little Prudy Stories). 1882. Lee & Shepard.
--Little Prudy's Dotty Dimple. May, Sophie, pseud. (Illus.). 171p. N.D. Lee & Shepard.
--Little Prudy's Fairy Book. May, Sophie, pseud. (The Little Prudy Stories). N.D. Cupples & Leon Co.
--Little Prudy's Flyaway Series. May, Sophie, pseud, 6 vols. (Illus.). 1882. Set. Lee & Shepard.
--Little Prudy's Sister Susie. May, Sophie, pseud. (Little Prudy Stories). N.D. Colby and Rich.
--Little Prudy's Sister Susy. May, Sophie, pseud. (Illus.). (Editha Ser.). N.D. Caldwell.
--Little Prudy's Sister Susy. May, Sophie, pseud. (The Little Prudy Stories). N.D. Cupples & Leon Co.
--Little Prudy's Sister Susy. May, Sophie, pseud. (Illus.). (Editha Series.). N.D. Dodge Publishing Co.
--Little Prudy's Sister Susy. May, Sophie, pseud. (Little Prudy Series.). N.D. Hurst & Co.
--Little Prudy's Sister Susy. May, Sophie, pseud. (Home Series for Girls). N.D. Hurst & Co.
--Little Prudy's Sister Susy. May, Sophie, pseud, 1 of 6 vols. (Illus.). 189p. (Little Prudy Stories). 1882. Set. Lee & Shepard.
--Little Prudy's Story. May, Sophie, pseud. (The Little Prudy Stories). N.D. Lothrop, Lee & Shepard.
--Little Prudy's Story Book. May, Sophie, pseud. (Illus.). (Editha Ser.). N.D. Caldwell.
--Little Prudy's Story Book. May, Sophie, pseud. (Little Prudy Stories). N.D. Colby and Rich.
--Little Prudy's Story Book. May, Sophie, pseud. (Illus.). (Editha Series.). N.D. Dodge Publishing Co.
--Little Prudy's Story Book. May, Sophie, pseud. (Little Prudy Series.). N.D. Hurst & Co.
--Little Prudy's Story Book. May, Sophie, pseud, 1 of 6 vols. (Illus.). (Little Prudy Stories). 1882. Set. Lee & Shepard.
--Little Prudy's Story Book and Little Prudy's Dorothy Dimple. May, Sophie, pseud. (Illus.). (Little Prudy Ser.: Vol. 3). N.D. Set of 3. Caldwell.
--Lucy in Fairyland. May, Sophie, pseud. (Little Prudy's Children). N.D. Lothrop, Lee & Shepard.
--Lucy in Fairyland. May, Sophie, pseud. Gebfert, C. H. L., illus. 16cm. 165p. 1901. Lee & Shepard.
--Miss Thistledown. May, Sophie, pseud. LC 49-329621. 205 p. plates. 16 cm. (Her Little Prudy's Flyaway Ser., 6). 1874. Lee and Shepard.
--Miss Thistledown. May, Sophie, pseud, 1 of 6 vols. (Illus.). (Little Prudy's Flyaway Ser.). 1882. Lee & Shepard.
--Miss Thistledown. May, Sophie, pseud. LC 2-11144. 5, 9-205 p. front. plates. 16 1/2 cm. (Little Prudy's Flyaway Ser., Vol. 5). 1901. Lee and Shepard.

--The Odd One. May, Sophie, pseud. (Author of "Prudy" and "Dotty." A companion volume to "The Doctor's Daughter," "Quinnebasset Girls," "Our Helen" "The Asbury Twins "). (Illus.). 1882. Lee & Shepard.
--Our Helen. May, Sophie, pseud. LC 2-22396. 19cm. 372p. (Her Quinnebasset series). 1902. Lee & Shepard.
--Our Helen. May, Sophie, pseud. (Illus.). (Maidenhood Ser.). N.D. Lee & Shepard.
--Prudy Keeping House. May, Sophie, pseud. (Little Prudy's Flyaway Ser.). N.D. Colby and Rich.
--Prudy Keeping House. May, Sophie, pseud, 1 of 6 vols. (Illus.). (Little Prudy's Flyaway Ser.). 1882. Lee & Shepard.
--Prudy Keeping House. May, Sophie, pseud. LC 98-331. 192 p. front., plates. 16 1/2 cm. (Little Prudy's Flyaway Ser.). 1898. Lee and Shepard.
--Quinnebasset Girls. May, Sophie, pseud, 1 of 6 vols. LC 5-33644. (Illus.). (Quinnebasset Ser.). 1905. Set. Lee & Shepard.
--The Quinnebasset Series. May, Sophie, pseud, 4 vols. (Illus.). 1882. Set in box. Lee & Shepard.
--Santa Claus on Snow Shoes. May, Sophie, pseud. (Illus.). 8cm. 127p. 1898. DeWolfe, Fiske & Co.
--Sister Susy. May, Sophie, pseud. LC 20-16387. 4 p. l, 5-189 p. front. plates. 16 cm. (Little Prudy series, v.2). 1893. Lee and Shepard.
--The Twin Cousins. May, Sophie, pseud, 1 of 6 vols. (Illus.). (Flaxie Frizzle Stories). N.D. Set. Lee & Shepard.
--Wee Lucy. May, Sophie, pseud, 3 vols. (Illus.). (Little Prudy's Children: Vol. 3). N.D. Lee & Shepard.
--Wee Lucy's Secret. May, Sophie, pseud. LC 99-2506. vii, 192 p. front., 3 pl. 16 1/2 cm. (Little Prudy's children). 1899. Lee and Shepard.
--Wee Lucy's Secret. May, Sophie, pseud. (Illus.). (Little Prudy's Children). N.D. Lothrop & Shepard.

Clarke, Rebecca Sophia (1833-1906) & Round, William M. F.
--Wide Awake Pleasure Book "D". Containing "Quinnebasset Girls", "Child Marian", etc. May, Sophie, pseud. (Illus.). N.D. D. Lothrop & Co.

Clarke, Richard A
--The Crack in the Dish And Other Fables. Fitts, Clara E. Atwood, illus. LC 22-2254. 4 p. l, 146 p. 1 l, incl. illus., plates. front. 19 1/2 cm. 1922. Little, Brown and Company.
--The Forgetful Letter B: Fun-filled tales for very little people. Weage, Josephine, illus. LC 55-45818. (Illus.). 23cm. 71p. 1922. Reily & Lee.
--Picture Worlds. Fitts, Clara E. Atwood, illus. LC 24-9574. 5 p. l, 3-144 p. front. illus., plates. 19 1/2 cm. 1923. Little, Brown and Company.
--Pon-a-Time Tales. Fitts, Clara E. Atwood, illus. LC 22-9892. 5 p. l, 146 p. 1 l. incl. front., illus., plates 19 1/2 cm. 1922. Little, Brown and Company.

Clarke, Rosan
--Wings for Ruth. LC 46-3131. 183 p. front., plates. 19 1/2 cm. 1945. W. A. Wilde Company.

Clarke, Ruth
--Bonny the Pony. Lloyd, Stanley, illus. LC 48-18784. 19cm. 220p. 1948. Frederick Warne & Co.

Clarke, Sara K.
--Pet for Chandran. Turkle, Brinton Cassaday (1915-), illus. LC 61-8006. (ps). 1961. (ISBN 0-377-68911-4). Friend Pr.

Clarke, Sarah Jones see Shirley, Penn, pseud.

Clarke, Sarah Jones (1840-)
--The Happy Six. Shirley, Penn, pseud. LC 22-5169. 171 p. front., plates. 16 1/2 cm. (The Silver gate series, v.3). 1897. Lee and Shepard.
--Little Miss Weezy. Shirley, Penn, pseud. LC 22-5166. 141 p. front., plates. 17 cm. 1886. Lee and Shepard.
--Little Miss Weezy's Brother. Shirley, Penn, pseud. LC 22-51672. 164 p. front., plates. 16 1/2 cm. 1888. Lee & Shepard.
--The Merry Five. Shirley, Penn, pseud. LC 22-5152. 155 p. front., 7 pl. 17 cm. (Her Silver gate series). c.1896. Lee and Shepard.

Clarke, Simon
--Silly Simon. Eccles, Charles (1922-), illus. 1967. (ISBN 0-695-88002-0). (ISBN 0-695-48002-2). Follett Publishing.

Clarke, Tom Eugene (1915-)
--Alaska Challenge. LC 59-13159. 222 p. 22cm. 1959. Lothrop, Lee & Shepard Co.
--Back to Anchorage. LC 61-15444. 224 p. 22cm. 1961. Lothrop, Lee & Shepard.
--The Mounties Patrol the Sea. 1969. (ISBN 0-664-32445-2). Westminster Press.
--No Furs for the Czar. LC 62-16569. 191p. 22cm. 1962. Lothrop, Lee and Shepard Co.
--The Puddle Jumper: The Adventures of a Young Flyer in Alaska. LC 60-12036. 191 p. 22cm. 1960. Lothrop, Lee & Shepard Co.

Clarke, Ward, tr. see Zeggelen, Marie Christine Van.

Clarke, William Kemp Lowth (1879-)
--S. S. Peter and Paul. (Folk Lore And Fairy Tales). N.D. MacMillan Bks.

Clarkson, Edith Margaret (1915-)
--Susie's Babies: A True Story. Schwarz, Macy, illus. LC 60-10091. 73p. illus. 23cm. (gr. 3-6). 1960. (ISBN 0-8028-4005-1). Eerdmans.

Clarkson, Ewan (1929-)
--Halic: The Story of af a Gray Seal. Cuffari, Richard (1925-1978), illus. LC 74-95465. (Illus.). 158 p. 22cm. 1970. Dutton.
--The Running of the Deer. Stone, David Karl (1922-), illus. 1972. Dutton.
--Syla the Mink. 1968. Dutton.

Clarkson, Jan Nagel (1943-)
--Tricks Animals Play. LC 75-6066. (Illus.). 32p. (Book for Young Explorers Fourth Ser). (ps-3). 1975. Set Of 4. (ISBN 0-87044-167-1). Natl Geog.

Clarkson, L.
--Fly Away Fairies and Baby Blossoms. (Illus.). N.D. E P Dutton.

Claro, Joseph
--Condorman. (Illus.). 131p. (Orig.). (gr. 7-12). 1981. (ISBN 0-590-32022-X). Scholastic Inc.
--Herbie Goes Bananas. (Illus.). 96p. (gr. 3-7). 1980. (ISBN 0-590-31609-5). Scholastic Inc.
--I Can Predict the Future. Cuffari, Richard (1925-1978), illus. LC 72-1086. (Illus.). 96 p. 22cm. 1972. Lothrop, Lee & Shepard.
--My Bodyguard. 96p. (Orig.). 1981. (ISBN 0-590-31932-9, Schol Pap). Scholastic Inc.
--Snowball Express. (gr. 3-5). 1980. (ISBN 0-590-30359-7). Scholastic Inc.

Clason, Clyde B.
--Ark of Venus. (Illus.). (gr. 7-11). 1955. (ISBN 0-394-90917-8). Knopf: Distributed by Borzoi.

Claster, Nancy
--Romper Room Do Bees: A Book of Manners. Dart, Eleanor, illus. LC 56-14399. unpaged. illus. 21cm. (Little golden book, 273). 1956. Simon and Schuster.

Claston, W. J.
--The Mastery of the Air. (The Aviation Library). N.D. Dodge Pub. Co.

Clathrop, M. E., tr. see Spyri, Johanna Heusser.

Claude-Lafontaine, Pascale
--Monsieur Bussy, the Celebrated Hamster. Delhumeau, Annick, illus. LC 68-31154. (Illus.). 29cm. 34p. (gr. k-3). 1968. (ISBN 0-07-035780-3). (ISBN 0-07-035781-1). McGraw-Hill.

Claudine, pseud., see Hurwitz, Claudine.

Claudine (1929-)
--The Flight of the Animals. LC 70-153788. (Illus.). 28 p. 27cm. 1971. (ISBN 0-8193-0492-1). Parents' Magazine Press.

Claudy, Carl Harry (1879-)
--The Blue Grotto Terror. Valentine, A. C., illus. LC 34-322072. vii, 234 p. front. 19 1/cm. (His Adventures in the unknown). c.1934. Grosset & Dunlap.
--Dangerous Waters. Lassell, Charles, illus. LC 29-17046. 6 p. l., 11-296, 1 p. front., plates. 19 1/2 cm. c.1929. The Bobbs-Merill Company.
--The Girl Reporter. Parsons, Priscilla B., illus. 1930. Litle, Brown & Co.
--The Gold He Found. LC 28-19628. 4 p. l., 233, 1 p. front. 19 1/2 cm. 1928. D. Appleton & Company.
--The Land of No Shadow. Valentine, A. C., illus. LC 33-328470. vii, 214 p. front. 19 1/2 cm. (His Adventures in the unknown). c.1933. Grosset & Dunlap.
--The Mystery Men of Mars. Valentine, A. C., illus. LC 33-184604. vii, 216 p. front. 19 1/2 cm. (His Adventures in the unknown). c.1933. Grosset & Dunlap.
--Partners of the Forest Trail. Emerson, C. Chase, illus. LC 15-24005. 7 p. l., 225 p. front., plates. 19 1/2 cm. 1915. R. M. McBride & Co.
--Pirates by Force. Kraemer, Joseph L., illus. LC 17-13450. 303, 1 p. front., plates. 19 1/2 cm. c.1917. The Bobbs-Merrill Company.
--Tell-Me-Why Stories About Animals. Wrenn, Thomas N., illus. LC 14-176610. 7 p. l., 209 p. col. front., col. plates. 21 1/2 cm. 1914. McBride, Nast & Company.
--Tell-Me-Why Stories About Color and Sound. Wrenn, Thomas N., illus. LC 15-22070. 7 p. l., 235 p. col. front., col. plates. 21 1/2 cm. 1915. R. M. McBride & Company.
--Tell-Me-Why Stories About Great Discoveries. Wrenn, Thomas N., illus. LC 16-245705. x p., 1 l., 258 p. col. front., col. plates. 21 1/2 cm. 1916. R. M. McBride & Company.
--A Thousand Years a Minute. Valentine, A. C., illus. LC 33-3283. vii, 216 p. front. 19 1/2 cm. (His Adventures in the unknown). c.1933. Grosset & Dunlap.
--Treasures of Darkness: A Mystery. Chapman, Frederick Trench (1887-), illus. LC 33-28724. 5 p. l., 3-288 p. col. front. 20 1/2 cm. 1933. Doubleday, Doran & Company, Inc.

Claus, A.
--The Brave Little Tailor. N.D. (ISBN 0-07-011279-7). McGraw-Hill Book Company.
--Tom Thumb. N.D. (ISBN 0-07-011280-0). McGraw-Hill Book Company.

Clausen, John Henry
--Beak Hollins. Palmstrom, P. O., illus. LC 27-16097. 20cm. 100p. 1927. R. G. Badger.

Claveloux, Nicole
--Go, Go, Go, Grabote. Claveloux, Nicole, illus. LC 73-80924. (Illus.). 32p. (Harlin Quist Bks). (gr. 2-5). 1973. (ISBN 0-8252-0092-X). Dial.

Claverie, Jean (1946-)
--Shopping. LC 85-2423. p. cm. 1986, c.1985. (ISBN 0-394-87565-6). (ISBN 0-394-97565-0). Random House.

Claxton, Oliver
--Remus. Callahan, Vince, illus. LC 39-230407. 34 p. col. illus. 20 1/2 x 20 1/2 cm. 1939. Harper & Brothers.

Claxton, Philander Priestley (1862-), adapted by see Meissner, Marie.

Claxton, Philander Priestley, tr. see Grimm, Jakob Ludwig Karl (1785-1863) & Grimm, Wilhelm Karl.

Claxton, Philander Priestley, tr. see Meissner, Marie.

Clay, Beatrice
--Stories from King Arthur and His Round Table. Curtis, Dora, illus. 127 p. col. front., col. plates. 18 cm. (Half-title: Tales for children from many lands). 1913. J. M. Dent & Sons Limited.
--Stories of King Arthur and the Round Table. N.D. E P Dutton.

Clay, Catherine Lee
--Season of Love. LC 68-18442. 207 p. 25cm. 1968. Atheneum.

Clay, Charles
--Fur Trade Apprentice. Hogner, Nils (1893-1970), illus. LC 41-2318. viii, 380 p. front., illus., plates. 20 cm. 1940. Oxford University Press.
--Young Voyageur. LC 41-5102. viii p., 1 l., 409 p. 19 1/2 cm. 1938. Oxford University Press.

Clay, John Cecil (1875-)
--The Lover's Mother Goose. (Illus.). 1905. Bobbs-Merrill Company.

Clay, N. L.
--Eight Plays for Boys. N.D. (ISBN 0-435-21002-5). Heinemann Ed.

Clay, Oliver
--The Treasure Finders: Or, How the Adventurers of Four Countries Discovered a New Land. N.D. Duffield.

Clay, Well
--Adventures of a Raindrop. LC 40-11701. 2 p. l., 66 p. illus. 28 cm. c.1940. The Maplewood Press.

Clayman, Barbara
--The Dukes of Hazzard. (Illus.). 32p. (Movie & TV Tie-Ins Ser.). (gr. 5-8). 1983. (ISBN 0-87191-878-1). (ISBN 0-89812-287-2). Creative Ed.

Claypool, Jane, , see Miner, Jane Claypool.

Claypool, Jane, (1933-)
--Career Prep: Working In A Hospital. Miner, Jane Claypool. (Illus.). 64p. (Jem High Interest-Low Reading Level Ser.). (gr. 7 up). 1983. (ISBN 0-671-44889-7). Messner.
--Jasmine Finds Love. Miner, Jane Claypool. 1st ed. LC 82-13633. p. cm. (Floweromance). c.1982. (ISBN 0-664-32699-4). Westminster Press.
--A Love for Violet. Miner, Jane Claypool. LC 82-10980. p. cm. (Floweromance). c.1982. (ISBN 0-664-32697-8). Westminster Press.

Clayton, Addison
--Three Boys and Their Ambition. Ives, Sarah Noble, illus. LC 7-14588. 64 p. col. front., illus. 19 1/2 cm. c.1907. McLoughlin Brothers.

Clayton, Barbara, pseud., see Pluff, Barbara Littlefield.

Clayton, Barbara, pseud. (1926-)
--Decision for Sally. Pluff, Barbara Littlefield. LC 60-12747. 184 p. 22cm. 1960. Funk & Wagnalls.
--Ditto. Pluff, Barbara Littlefield. Willcox, Sandra, illus. LC 68-11903. (Illus.). 123 p. 21cm. 1968. Funk & Wagnalls.
--Halfway Hannah. Pluff, Barbara Littlefield. LC 64-11117. 184 p. 22cm. 1964. Funk & Wagnalls.
--One Special Summer. Pluff, Barbara Littlefield. Zemsky, Jessica, illus. LC 66-793486. 123p. illus. 23cm. (gr. 3-7). 1966. (ISBN 0-308-80026-5). Funk & Wagnalls.
--Pepper Pot. Pluff, Barbara Littlefield. LC 65-19339. 191 p. 22cm. 1965. Funk & Wagnalls.
--Second Best. Pluff, Barbara Littlefield. LC 63-8867. 184 p. 22 cm. 1963. Funk & Wagnalls.
--Skates for Marty. Pluff, Barbara Littlefield. LC 59-108946. 216p. 22cm. 1959. Funk & Wagnalls.
--Tomboy. Pluff, Barbara Littlefield. LC 61-12962. 183 p. 22cm. 1961. Funk & Wagnalls Co.

Clayton, Dean
--T-Shirt Factory: A Typewriting Simulation. (gr. 9-12). 1982. (ISBN 0-538-11700-1). SW Pub.

Clayton, Francis Treadway, tr. see Spyri, Johanna Heusser.

Clayton, Jacqueline
--Bunny Brothers. (Fireside Library). N.D. Thomas Nelson & Sons.

Clayton, Margaret
--Camping in the Forest: The Adventures of Five Children. (Illus.). 1910. Frederick Warne & Co.

Cleary, Beverly Bunn (1916-)
--Beezus and Ramona. Darling, Louis, Jr. (1916-1970), illus. LC 55-7623. (Illus.). 159 p. 21cm. (Morrow junior books). 1955. Morrow.
--Beezus & Ramona Stories. Darling, Louis, Jr. (1916-1970), illus. Incl. Henry & Beezus. LC 52-5930. 192p; Henry & Ribsy. LC 54-6402. 192p; Henry & the Clubhouse. LC 62-7161. 192p; Henry & the Paper Route. LC 57-8562. 192p; Henry Huggins. LC 50-8615; Beezus & Ramona. LC 55-7623. (Illus.). 160p. (gr. 4-6). 1973. Morrow.
--Dear Mr. Henshaw. Zelinsky, Paul O., illus. LC 83-5372. p. cm. 1983. (ISBN 0-688-02405-X). Morrow. **Awards: (JNM); (ALA).**
--Ellen Tebbits. Darling, Louis, Jr. (1916-1970), illus. LC 51-11430. (Illus.). 160 p. 21cm. (Morrow junior books). 1951. Morrow.
--Emily's Runaway Imagination. Krush, Joe (1918-) & Krush, Beth (1918-), illus. LC 61-10939. (Illus.). 221 p. 21cm. 1961. Morrow.
--Fifteen. Krush, Joe (1918-) & Krush, Beth (1918-), illus. LC 56-7509. (Illus.). 254 p. 22cm. (Morrow junior books). 1956. Morrow.
--Henry & Beezus. Darling, Louis, Jr. (1916-1970), illus. (Illus.). (gr. 3-7). 1952. (ISBN 0-688-21383-9). (ISBN 0-688-31383-3). Morrow.
--Henry and Ribsy. Darling, Louis, Jr. (1916-1970), illus. (gr. 3-7). 1954. William Morrow & Co.
--Henry and the Clubhouse. Darling, Louis, Jr. (1916-1970), illus. 1962. (ISBN 0-688-21721-4). William Morrow and Company.
--Henry and the Paper Route. Darling, Louis, Jr. (1916-1970), illus. LC 57-8562. (Illus.). 192 p. 22cm. (Morrow junior books). 1957. Morrow.
--Henry Huggins. Darling, Louis, Jr. (1916-1970), illus. 155p. (gr. 3-5). 1950. Morrow.
--The Hullabaloo ABC. Thollander, Earl Gustave (1922-), illus. LC 60-9710. unpaged. illus. 27cm. c.1960. Parnassus Press.
--Jean & Johnny. Krush, Beth (1918-) & Krush, Joe (1918-), illus. LC 59-7806. (Illus.). 284p. (Morrow junior books). (gr. 6-9). 1959. (ISBN 0-688-21740-0). (ISBN 0-688-31740-5). Morrow.
--Jean and Johnny. Stevens, Mary, illus. 1960. William Morrow & Co.
--The Luckiest Girl. LC 58-6667. 288 p. 21cm. (Morrow junior books). 1958. Morrow.
--Lucky Chuck. Higginbottom, Jeffrey Winslow (1945-), illus. LC 83-13386. (ps-3). 1984. (ISBN 0-688-02736-9). (ISBN 0-688-02738-5). Morrow.
--Mitch and Amy. Porter, George, illus. LC 67-1293. (Illus.). 222 p. 21cm. 1967. Morrow.
--The Mouse and the Motorcycle. Darling, Louis, Jr. (1916-1970), illus. LC 65-20956. (Illus.). 158 p. 21cm. 1965. W. Morrow. **Award: (ALA).**
--Otis Spofford. Darling, Louis, Jr. (1916-1970), illus. LC 53-6660. (Illus.). 191 p. 21cm. (Morrow junior books). 1953. Morrow.
--Ralph S. Mouse. Zelinsky, Paul O., illus. LC 82-3516. (Illus.). 160 p. 21cm. 1982. (ISBN 0-688-01452-6). W. Morrow.
--Ramona and Her Father. Tiegreen, Alan, illus. LC 77-1614. (Illus.). 186 p. 21cm. 1977. (ISBN 0-688-22114-9). (ISBN 0-688-32114-3). Morrow. **Awards: (IBBY); (BGH); (JNM).**
--Ramona and Her Mother. Tiegreen, Alan, illus. LC 79-10323. (Illus.). 207 p. 21cm. 1979. (ISBN 0-688-22195-5). (ISBN 0-688-32195-X). Morrow. **Award: (ALA).**
--Ramona Forever. Tiegreen, Alan, illus. LC 84-704. (Illus.). 21 cm. 182p. 1984. (ISBN 0-688-03785-2). (ISBN 0-688-03785-2). Morrow. **Award: (ALA).**
--Ramona Quimby, Age Eight. Tiegreen, Alan, illus. LC 80-28425. (Illus.). 190 p. 21cm. 1981. (ISBN 0-688-00477-6). (ISBN 0-688-00478-4). Morrow. **Awards: (ALA); (JNM).**
--The Ramona Quimby Diary. (Illus.). 160p. (gr. 3-7). 1984. (ISBN 0-688-03883-2, Morrow Junior Books). Morrow.
--Ramona the Brave. Tiegreen, Alan, illus. LC 74-16494. (Illus.). 189 p. 21cm. 1975. (ISBN 0-688-22015-0). Morrow.
--Ramona the Pest. Darling, Louis, Jr. (1916-1970), illus. LC 68-12981. (Illus.). 192 p. 21cm. 1968. (ISBN 0-688-21721-4). W. Morrow.
--The Real Hole. Stevens, Mary E. (1920-1966), illus. LC 60-5797. (Illus.). unpaged. (Morrow junior books). 1960. Morrow.
--Ribsy. Darling, Louis, Jr. (1916-1970), illus. LC 64-13263. (Illus.). 192 p. 21cm. 1964. Morrow.
--Runaway Ralph. Darling, Louis, Jr. (1916-1970), illus. LC 77-95786. 1970. (ISBN 0-688-21701-X). William Morrow and Company.

AUTHOR INDEX CLEVELAND, DAVID

--The Sausage at the End of the Nose. 1974. Children's Book Council.
--Sister of the Bride. Krush, Joe (1918-) & Krush, Beth (1918-), illus. LC 63-8802. (Illus.). 288 p. 21cm. 1963. Morrow.
--Socks. Darwin, Beatrice, illus. LC 72-10298. (Illus.). 156 p. 22cm. 1973. (ISBN 0-688-20067-2). Morrow.
--Two Dog Biscuits. Stevens, Mary E. (1920-1966), illus. LC 61-5022. (Illus.). unpaged. (Morrow junior books). 1961. Morrow.

Cleary, Jon (1917-)
--The Sundowners. 1965. Charles Scribner's Sons.

Cleary, Jon (1917-) & Clemens, Samuel Langhorne (1835-1910)
--The Sundowners. Twain, Mark, pseud. Powers, Richard M. Gorman (1921-), illus. LC 54-14473. 383p. 22cm. (Pt. col.). (Junior Deluxe Edition). 1965, c.1952. Scribners.

Cleary, Ruth, jt. auth. see Armando, Jeanne.

Cleary, Timothy, tr. see Limmer, Hans.

Cleaver
--How the Chipmunk Got Its Stripes. (ps-3). N.D. (ISBN 0-590-11960-5, Schol Pap). Scholastic Inc.

Cleaver, Bill, jt. auth. see Cleaver, Vera.

Cleaver, Bill (1920-1981) & Cleaver, Vera
--Delpha Green and Company. LC 79-172141. 141 illus. 22. 1972. (ISBN 0-397-31236-9). (ISBN 0-397-31344-6). Lippincott.
--Grover. Marvin, Frederic, illus. LC 69-12001. 22cm. 125p. 1970. Lippincott.

Cleaver, Denis (1911-)
--Pongo the Terrible. Backhouse, G. W., illus. LC 49-8397. 96 p. illus. 20 cm. 1949. Westminister Press.

Cleaver, Elizabeth Mrazik (1939-)
--The Enchanted Caribou. Cleaver, Elizabeth Mrazik (1939-), illus. 32p. 1985. (ISBN 0-689-31170-2). Atheneum. **Award: (ALA).**
--The Miraculous Hind. Cleaver, Elizabeth Mrazik (1939-), illus. 1973. HRW. **Award: (CLA).**

Cleaver, Elizabeth Mrazik (1939-), retold by.
--Petrouchka. Cleaver, Elizabeth Mrazik (1939-), illus. LC 79-14436. p. cm. 1979. (ISBN 0-689-30704-7). Atheneum. **Award: (CCCL).**

Cleaver, Hylton Reginald (1891-1961)
--The Term of Thrills. N.D. Frederick Warne & Co.

Cleaver, Nancy, jt. auth. see Tresselt, Alvin R.

Cleaver, Vera
--Sugar Blue. Nones, Eric Jon, illus. LC 83-19910. (Illus.). 160p. (gr. 5 up). 1984. (ISBN 0-688-02720-2). Lothrop.
--Sweetly Sings the Donkey. LC 85-40098. 150 p. 22cm. c.1985. (ISBN 0-397-32156-2). (ISBN 0-397-32157-0). Lippincott.

Cleaver, Vera, jt. auth. see Cleaver, Bill.

Cleaver, Vera & Cleaver, Bill (1920-1981)
--Dust of the Earth. (gr. 6-9). 1975. Harper & Row.
--Dust of the Earth. LC 75-18939. 159 p. 21cm. 1975. (ISBN 0-397-31650-X). Lippincott.
--Ellen Grae. 1st ed. Raskin, Ellen (1928-1984), illus. LC 67-19267. (Illus.). 89 p. 22cm. 1967. Lippincott.
--Hazel Rye. (gr. 6-8). 1983. Harper & Row.
--Hazel Rye. 1st ed. LC 81-48603. p. cm. c.1983. (ISBN 0-397-31951-7). (ISBN 0-397-31952-5). Lippincott. **Award: (ALA).**
--I Would Rather Be a Turnip. LC 78-141452. 159 p. 22cm. 1971. Lippincott.
--The Kissimmee Kid. LC 80-29262. 159 p. 22cm. c.1981. (ISBN 0-688-41992-5). (ISBN 0-688-51992-X). Lothrop, Lee & Shepard Books.
--Lady Ellen Grae. 1st ed. Raskin, Ellen (1928-1984), illus. LC 68-10981. (Illus.). 124 p. 22cm. 1968. Lippincott.
--A Little Destiny. LC 79-10322. 152 p. 22cm. c.1979. (ISBN 0-688-51904-0). Lothrop, Lee & Shepard Books.
--A Little Destiny. 1979. Morrow.
--Me Too. LC 73-7631. 158 p. 21cm. 1973. (ISBN 0-397-31485-X). Lippincott. **Award: (ALA).**
--The Mimosa Tree. LC 71-117236. 125 p. 21cm. 1970. Lippincott.
--The Mock Revolt. 1971. Harper.
--The Mock Revolt. LC 75-151467. 160 p. 21cm. 1971. Lippincott.
--Queen of Hearts. 1978. Harper.
--Queen of Hearts. LC 77-18252. 158 p. 21cm. c.1978. (ISBN 0-397-31771-9). Lippincott. **Award: (ALA).**
--Trial Valley. LC 76-54303. 158 p. 21cm. c.1977. (ISBN 0-397-31722-0). Lippincott.
--Where the Lilies Bloom. 1st ed. Spanfeller, James John (1930-), illus. LC 75-82402. (Illus.). 174 p. 22cm. 1970, c.1969. J. B. Lippincott Co.
--Where the Lilies Bloom. Spanfeller, James John (1930-), illus. 1969. Lippincott. **Awards: (BGH); (ALA).**
--The Whys and Wherefores of Littabelle Lee. LC 72-86929. (Illus.). 156 p. 22cm. 1973. Atheneum.

Cleek, Charles
--The Story of Ebird. LC 38-32017. 92, 2 p. illus. 20 cm. c.1938. W. Morrow & Co.

Cleghorn, Sarah Norcliffe (1876-) & Fisher, Dorothea Frances Canfield, Mrs. (1879-1958)
--Understood Betsy: A Play. LC 34-29151. xiii p., 2 l., 3-112 p. 19 cm. c.1934. Harcourt, Brace and Company.

Cleland, Davenport E.
--The White Kangaroo. N.D. Pott & Co.

Cleland, Robert Glass
--California Pageant: The Story of Four Centuries. Lufkin, Raymond H. (1897-), illus. 1946. Alfred A Knopf : distributed by Borzoi Books.

Clemence, Ruth
--Witchery Island. (Good Reading for Girls Ser.). N.D. Golden Press.

Clemens, Nancy
--Under Glass. Jones, Wilfred J. (1888-), illus. LC 37-16939. viii p., 1 l., 274 p. illus. 20 1/2 cm. 1937. Longmans. Green and Co.

Clemens, Samuel Langhorne see Twain, Mark, pseud.

Clemens, Samuel Langhorne, jt. auth. see Cleary, Jon.

Clemens, Samuel Langhorne (1835-1910)
--The Adventures of Huckleberry Finn. Twain, Mark, pseud. (Illus.). (Great Illustrated Classics). N.D. (ISBN 0-396-03482-9). Dodd, Mead & Company.
--The Adventures of Huckleberry Finn. Twain, Mark, pseud. Brehm, Worth, illus. 1951. Harper.
--The Adventures of Huckleberry Finn. McKay, Donald A. (1895-), illus. N.D. (ISBN 0-448-05451-5). (ISBN 0-448-06000-0). (ISBN 0-448-05900-2). 2.50(Popular). (ISBN 0-448-05800-6). Grosset & Dunlap Pub.
--The Adventures of Huckleberry Finn. Twain, Mark, pseud. Polseno, Jo, illus. LC 63-6887. vi, 344 p. illus. 20 cm. (Companion library). 1963. Grosset & Dunlap.
--The Adventures of Huckleberry Finn. Twain, Mark, pseud. Rockwell, Norman Percevel (1894-1978), illus. N.D. The Heritage Press.
--The Adventures of Tom Sawyer. Twain, mark, pseud. LC 76-359714. (Illus.). 22cm. 274p. 1902, c.1875. American Pub. Co.
--The Adventures of Tom Sawyer. Twain, Mark, pseud. (Great Illustrated Classics). N.D. (ISBN 0-396-04161-2). Dodd, Mead & Company.
--The Adventures of Tom Sawyer. Twain, Mark, pseud. LC 71-136455. (Illus.). xiii, 249 p. 25cm. (World book limited edition). c.1975. (ISBN 0-7166-3100-8). Field Enterprises Educational Corp.
--Adventures of Tom Sawyer. N.D. Rand McNally & Co.
--The Adventures of Tom Sawyer. Twain, Mark, pseud. Bolian, Polly (1925-), illus. LC 65-11928. 253 p. col. illus. 22 cm. (Whitman classics library). 1965. Whitman Pub. Co.
--The Adventures of Tom Sawyer. Twain, Mark, pseud. Bown, Derick, illus. LC 78-2796. p. cm. (Raintree's illustrated classics). 1978. (ISBN 0-8393-6205-6). Raintree Childrens Books.
--The Adventures of Tom Sawyer. Twain, Mark, pseud. Brehm, Worth, illus. 1938. Harper.
--The Adventures of Tom Sawyer. Twain, Mark, pseud. Davidson, Al, illus. LC 70-111663. (Illus.). 256 p. 29cm. 1970, c.1969. Childrens Press.
--The Adventures of Tom Sawyer. Twain, Mark, pseud. Falter, John Philip (1910-), illus. (Illus.). 297 p. 24cm. (Macmillan Classics, 39). 1962. Macmillan.
--The Adventures of Tom Sawyer. Twain, Mark, pseud. Polseno, Jo, illus. LC 63-6891. vi, 282 p. illus. 20 cm. (Companion library). 1963. Grosset & Dunlap.
--The Adventures of Tom Sawyer. Twain, Mark, pseud. Powers, Richard M. Gorman (1921-), illus. LC 54-14473. 271p. illus. 22cm. 1954. Junior Deluxe Editions.
--The Adventures of Tom Sawyer. Twain, Mark, pseud. Rockwell, Norman Percevel (1894-1978), illus. N.D. Heritage Press.
--Adventures of Tom Sawyer. Twain, Mark, pseud. Sutton, Felix (1910-), adapted by. Nielsen, Jon (1912-), illus. LC 55-42188. 64p. illus. 21cm. (Wonder Playbooks, 2524). 1955. Wonder Books.
--The Adventures of Tom Sawyer. Twain, Mark, pseud. 1st ed. Torbert, Floyd James (1922-), illus. LC 52-6373. 120 p. illus. 22 cm. (Winston Pixie Bks.). 1952. Winston.
--The Adventures of Tom Sawyer. Twain, Mark, pseud. Vallely, Henry E., illus. LC 45-5363. 2 p. l., 9-235 p. illus. 21 cm. c.1944. Whitman Publishing Co.
--The Adventures of Tom Sawyer. Twain, Mark, pseud. White, Anne Terry (1896-), ed. Helweg, Hans H. (1917-), illus. LC 56-14139. 96p. illus. 27cm. (Golden picture classics, CL-102-69). 1956. Simon and Schuster.
--A Connecticut Yankee in King Arthur's Court. Twain, Mark, pseud. Guilbeau, Honore Cooke (1907-), illus. 285p. N.D. Heritage Press.
--Huckleberry Finn. Twain, Mark, pseud. (Magnum Easy Eye Classic Ser). (gr. 7-12). N.D. Lancer.
--Huckleberry Finn. Twain, Mark, pseud. Brown, Verne B, adapted by. Fleishman, Seymour (1918-), illus. LC 51-10983. x, 314 p. illus. 22 cm. 1951. Scott, Foresman.
--Huckleberry Finn. Twain, Mark, pseud. Farr, Naunerle, ed. Redondo, Francisco, illus. LC 73-75468. (Illus.). footnotes. 64p. (Orig.). (Now Age Illustrated Ser.). (gr. 5-10). 1973. (ISBN 0-88301-207-3). (ISBN 0-88301-098-4). Pendulum Pr.
--Huckleberry Finn. Williams, Stanley T., intro. by. (Great Illustrated Classics). N.D. Dodd Mead & Co.
--Jim Baker's Bluejay Yarn. Twain, Mark, pseud. Brenner, Fred (1920-), illus. LC 63-15062. (Illus.). 21cm. 46p. 1963. Orion Press.
--Mark Twain's Adventures of Huckleberry Finn. Depew, Ollie (1888-), adapted by. LC 51-4404. vii, 221 p. illus. 21 cm. (Globe adapted classics). 1951. Globe Book Co.
--The Prince and the Pauper. Twain, Mark, pseud. Chorpenning, Charlotte Lee Barrows (1872-1955), ed. 1938. Dramatists Play Service.
--The Prince and the Pauper. Dempster, Dunbracco, illus. LC 73-79986. (Illus.). 224 p. 29cm. 1969. Childrens Press.
--The Prince and the Pauper. Twain, Mark, pseud. Hatherell, William, illus. 1909. Harper.
--The Prince and the Pauper: A Tale for Young People of All Ages. Twain, Mark, pseud. Hodgson, Robert, illus. LC 68-110444. xv, 248 p. 14 plates, illus, (incl. 4 col.) facism. 22 cm. (Children's Illustrated Classics: No. 80). 1968. Dent.
--The Prince and the Pauper: A Tale for Young People of All Ages. Twain, Mark, pseud. Hodgson, Robert, illus. (Illus.). xv, 248 p. 22cm. (Children's illustrated Classics, No. 80). 1968. E. P. Dutton.
--The Prince & The Pauper & Other Stories. (Illus.). (Great Il. Classics Ser). (gr. 7 up). N.D. (ISBN 0 396 05236 3). Dodd.
--Richard Brown and the Dragon: Retold from an Anecdote by Samuel Langhorne Clemens in A Tramp Abroad. 1st ed. Bright, Robert (1902-), ed. LC 52-9275. 81 p. illus. 21 cm. 1952. Doubleday.
--Tom Sawyer's Treasure Hunt. Twain, Mark, pseud. Chorpenning, Charlotte Lee Barrows, adapted by. 1937. French.

Clemens, Samuel Langhorne (1835-1910) & Grey, Zane
--Code of the West. N.D. Grosser & Dunlap.

Clement, Bertha (1852-)
--Happy Days at Grandfather's: A Story for Girls. Ireland, Mary Eliza Haines, Mrs. (1834-1927), tr. LC 18-13316. 177 p. incl. front., plates. 17 cm. 1902. U. B. Publishing House.
--Lottie's Second Year with the Werndorfs: A Continuation of "Happy Days at Grandfather's". Ireland, Mary Eliza Haines, Mrs. (1834-1927), tr. LC 18-17300. 2 p. l., 3-216 p. 17 cm. 1903. U. B. Publishing House.
--More Happy Days at Grandfather's. Ireland, Mary Eliza Haines, Mrs. (1834-1927), tr. LC 8-4367. iv, 7-178 p. 17 cm. 1906. United Brethren Publishing House.

Clement, Bonnie (1942-)
--Little Princess of the Flowers. LC 80-18635. p. cm. c.1980. (ISBN 0-87123-343-6). Bethany Fellowship.

Clement, Carol, ed. see Budapest, Zsuszanna.

Clement, H.
--Letty. (The Young Folks Ser.: No. 4). N.D. Fleming H. Revell Co.

Clement, Hal, pseud., see Stubbs, Harry Clement.

Clement, Hal, pseud. (1922-)
--Left of Africa. Stubbs, Harry Clement. 1st ed. Frolich, Dany, illus. LC 78-107359. (Illus.). 160 p., 1 leaf of plates. 29cm. c.1976. Aurian Society Press : Distributed by PDA Enterprises.
--Needle. Stubbs, Harry Clement. (Young Moderns Edition). 1950. Doubleday & Co.

Clement, Jane Tyson (1917-)
--The Sparrow. Hutteria Society of Brothers, ed. Mow, Kathy, illus. Moody, Ruby, intro. by. LC 68-21133. 1978. (ISBN 0-87486-009-1). Plough.
--The Sparrow, and Other Stories with Poems. Mow, Kathy, illus. LC 68-21133. (Illus.). viii, 198 p. 23cm. 1968. Plough Pub. House.
--The Sparrow: Five Stories & Seven Poems. Mow, Kathy, illus. LC 68-21133. (Illus.). (gr. 7 up). 1968. (ISBN 0-87486-004-0). Plough.

Clement, M. E.
--Bible Stories Simply Told. (Illus.). N.D. Thos Nelson & Sons.

Clement, Marguerite
--All the World Is Colour. L'Hardy, Pierre & L'Hardy, Germaine, Mrs., illus. LC 31-26526. 95 p. col. illus. 82 cm. N.D. Farrar and Rinehart.
--Flowers of Chivalry: Stories of Heroes and Heroines of Old France. Germaine, pseud. & L'Hardy, Pierre, illus. Denonian, Germaine. LC 34-24094. 3 p. l., 72 p. col. illus. 29 cm. 1934. Doubleday, Doran & Company, Inc.
--Once in France. Denonian, Germaine, illus. LC 27-5015. 5 p. l., 246 p. incl. illus., plates. col. front. 20 1/2 cm. 1927. Doubleday, Page & Company.
--Where Was Bobby?. Petersham, Maud Sylvia Fuller, Mrs. (1890-1971) & Petersham, Miska (1889-1960), illus. LC 28-29245. 3 p. l., 151 p. incl. illus. (part col.) plates (part col.) col. front., enl. plates. 20 cm. 1928. Doubleday, Doran & Company, Inc.

Clementia, pseud., see Feehan, Mary Edward.

Clements, Andrew (1949-), tr. see Bohdal, Susi.

Clements, Andrew (1949-), tr. see Sacre, Marie-Jose.

Clements, Bruce (1931-)
--Anywhere Else but Here. LC 80-11345. 151 p. 22cm. c.1980. (ISBN 0-374-30371-1). Farrar, Straus, Giroux.
--Coming About. 192p. 1984. (ISBN 0-374-31457-8). FS&G.
--The Face of Abraham Candle. LC 74-85365. 179 p. 22cm. (Bell book). 1969. Farrar, Straus & Giroux.
--From Ice Set Free. 224p. 1972. (ISBN 0-374-32468-9). Farrar, Straus and Giroux.
--I Tell a Lie Every So Often. LC 73-22356. (Illus.). 149 p. 21cm. 1974. (ISBN 0-374-33619-9). (ISBN 0-374-43539-1). Farrar, Straus and Giroux.
--Prison Window, Jerusalem Blue. LC 77-10081. p. cm. c.1977. Farrar, Straus & Giroux.
--Two Against the Tide. LC 67-19883. 199 p. 21cm. (Bell book). 1967. Farrar, Straus & Giroux.

Clements, Christine
--Slewfoot, the Despicable Monster. Marshall, David, illus. (Illus.). 100p. (ps-4). N.D. C Clements.

Clements, M. E
--Sheltering Arms;". Or, The Entrance of God's World Gives Light. LC 6-41706. 166 p. incl. front. 19 cm. 1891. T. Nelson and Sons.
--Sheltering Arms: Or, The Entrance of God's Word Gives Light, 1 of 3 vols. (Illus.). (The "Cords of Love" Ser.). N.D. Set. Thos Nelson & Sons.

Clemmer, Mary
--Ballads For Little Folks. (Illus.). N.D. Houghton, Mifflin And Co.

Clemons, Elizabeth, pseud., see Nowell, Elizabeth Cameron.

Clemons, Elizabeth
--Rodeo Days. Swanson, J. N., illus. LC 60-8353. 64p. (Sunset Junior Bks.). 1960. J. B. Lippincott.
--Rodeo Days. Nowell, Elizabeth Cameron. Swanson, J. N., illus. LC 60-8353. 64p. illus. 24cm. (Sunset junior book). 1960. Lane Book Co.
--Shells Are Where You Find Them. Gault, Joe, illus. 1960. Alfred A Knopf : distributed by Borzoi Books.
--Tide Pools and Beaches. Gault, Joe, illus. 1964. Alfred A Knopf : distributed by Borzoi Books.

Cleophas, M., Sr.
--Little Apple Tree's Wish. (Illus.). N.D. Dghtrs St Paul.

Clerici, Aurora Virginia
--A. V. C. Fairy Tales. 1st ed. LC 54-12282. 64p. 21cm. c.1955. Exposition Press.

Clery, Reginald Valentine see Hogarth, Peter & Clery, Val.

Clery, Val, jt. auth. see Hogarth, Peter.

Cleve, Valerie & Kruss, James (1926-)
--The Tailor and the Giant. Witt, Edith, illus. LC 70-166204. (Illus.). 27 p. 1972. Platt & Munk.

Cleveland
--In the Forecastle, 1 of 64 vols. (Young Library Library: No. 26). 1900. Set. Hurst & Co.

Cleveland, Anne Thornburn (1916-)
--The Life-Savers. Cleveland, Anne Thornburn (1916-), illus. LC 62-16389. c.1962. W. W. Norton.

Cleveland, David
--The Frog on Robert's Head. Ernst, Lisa Campbell, illus. LC 81-104. p. cm. 1981. (ISBN 0-698-20512-X). Coward, McCann, Geoghegan.

Cleveland, David & Karlin, Nurit
--The April Rabbits. LC 78-2044. (Illus.). 32 p. c.1978. (ISBN 0-698-20463-8). Coward, McCann & Geoghegan.

Cleveland, Edmund Janes (1878-)
--Philus, the Stable Boy of Bethlehem: And Other Children's Story- Sermons for Christmas and Other Days and Seasons of the Christian Year. Martin, Paul, illus. LC 27-19779. xv, 132 p. front., plates. 19 1/2 cm. 1927. Harper & Brothers.
Cleveland, Frank Mortimer (1871-)
--Aesop's Fables in Rhyme. MacDowell, Rowland Q., illus. LC 36-33980. 4 p. l., 132 p. front. (port.) illus. 23 cm. c.1936. P. R. Bucci.
Cleveland, H. W. S.
--Merchant Navigator. N.D. Harper & Brothers.
Cleveland, Helen M (0000-1909)
--Stories of Brave Old Times: Some Pen Pictures of Scenes Which Took Place Previous to or Connected with the American Revolution. LC 4-21999. 308 p. front., illus., plates, port. 20 1/2 cm. 1904. Lee and Shepard.
Cleveland, Helen M. (0000-1909) & Gay, Margaret
--Santa Claus' Home, with Other Stories and Rhymes for Mamma to Read Aloud. LC 65-72780. (Illus.). 47. 22cm. 1896. Arena Pub. Co.
Cleveland, Patience
--The Lion is Busy. Stuart, Liza, illus. LC 64-656. (Illus.). 31cm. 39p. c.1963. Atlantis Books.
Cleveland, Rawlings Junior High School
--One Winter's NIght and Other Plays for Assembly Programs. LC 28-30834. 60 p. incl. mounted front., 1 mounted illus. 23 cm. 1928. Rawlings Junior High School.
Cleveland, Reginald M
--Cop: Chief-of-Police Dogs. Bransom, Paul (1885-), illus. LC 28-28050. x p. 1 l., 131 p. col. front., plates part col. 24 cm. 1928. Milton Bradley Company.
--Cop: Chief of Police Dogs. Bransom, Paul (1885-), illus. N.D. Milton Bradley Co.
--Guard, Son of Cop. Megargee, Edwin, illus. LC 31-30261. 4 p. l., 247 p. front., illus., plates. 24 cm. 1931. Milton Bradley Company.
Cleveland Museum of Art see Kozloff, Arielle P.
Cleven, Cathrine Seward (1906-)
--Black Hawk, Young Sauk Warrior. Morrow, Gray, illus. LC 66-23538. (Illus.). 200 p. 20cm. (Childhood of famous Americans). 1966. Bobbs-Merrill.
--Fight Angel. LC 61-7935. 192p. illus. 22cm. 1961. Reilly Lee.
--John Hancock: New England Boy. Morrow, Gray, illus. LC 63-17665. 20cm. 200p. 1963. Bobbs-Merrill Co, Inc.
--Pirate Dog. Goldstein, Leslie, illus. LC 62-10032. 223p. illus. 22cm. 1962. Bobbs-Merrill.
--The Secret of the King's Field: A Story of France in the Eighteenth Century. 1st ed. Busch, Paul, illus. LC 52-10669. 203 p. illus. 22 cm. 1952. Bobbs-Merrill.
Cleven, Kathryn Seward see Cleven, Cathrine Seward.
Clevin, Joergen (1920-)
--Pete and Johnny to the Rescue. LC 74-4926. (Illus.). 57 p. 27cm. 1974. (ISBN 0-394-82995-6). Random House.
--Pete's First Day at School. LC 73-3683. (Illus.). 57 p. 27cm. 1973. (ISBN 0-394-82652-3). Random House.
Clewes, Dorothy Mary (1907-)
--Adopted Daughter. LC 68-9734. 191 p. 21cm. 1968. Coward-McCann.
--All the Fun of the Fair. Sofia, pseud. (1926-), illus. Zeiger, Sophia. LC 62-10428. 127p. illus. 20cm. (gr. 2-5). 1962. (ISBN 0-698-20003-9). Coward-McCann.
--The Birthday. Sofia, pseud. (1926-), illus. Zeiger, Sophia. LC 63-10178. 72 p. illus. 21 cm. 1963. Coward-McCann.
--A Boy Like Walt. LC 67-3473. 190 p. 21cm. 1967. Coward-McCann.
--The Branch Line. Sofia, pseud. (1926-), illus. Zeiger, Sofia. LC 63-14877. 128 p. illus. 20 cm. 1963. Coward-McCann.
--The End of Summer. LC 76-159756. 191 p. 22cm. 1971. Coward, McCann & Geoghegan.
--A Girl Like Cathy. (gr. 4-6). 1975. (ISBN 0-590-09152-2, Schol Trade Pap). Schol Bk Serv.
--The Golden Eagle,. A Mystery. LC 62-120331. 189p. 21cm. 1st U.S. edition. 1962. Coward-McCann.
--Guide Dog. Burchard, Peter Duncan (1921-), illus. LC 65-13284. (Illus.). 159 p. 21cm. 1965. Coward-McCann.
--The Happiest Day. N.D. E . M. Hale and Co.
--The Happiest Day. Sofia, pseud. (1926-), illus. Zeiger, Sophia. LC 58-970203. 64p. illus. 21cm. 1959. Coward-McCann.
--Henry Hare's Boxing Match. Turner, Patricia W., illus. LC 50-10216. 63 p. illus. (part col.) 14 cm. (Brown Burrows book, no. 1). 1950. Coward-McCann.
--Henry Hare's Earthquake. Turner, Patricia W., illus. LC 51-680. 63 p. illus. (part col.) 15 cm. (Brown Burrows book, no. 2). 1951. Coward-McCann.
--The Hidden Key. Sofia, pseud. (1926-), illus. Zeiger, Sophia. LC 61-134022. 119p. illus. 20cm. 1961. Coward-McCann.
--Hide and Seek. Sofia, pseud. (1926-), illus. Zeiger, Sophia. LC 60-121730. 64p. illus. 21cm. 1960. Coward-McCann.
--The Holiday. Sofia, pseud. (1926-), illus. Zeiger, Sofia. LC 64-17996. 64 p. illus. 21 cm. 1964. Coward-McCann.
--The Library. Lonette, Reisie Dominee (1924-), illus. LC 75-132595. (Illus.). 92 p. 20cm. 1971, c.1970. Coward-McCann.
--Missing from Home. LC 78-52826. p. cm. 1978, c.1975. (ISBN 0-15-254882-3). Harcourt Brace Jovanovich.
--The Mystery of the Blue Admiral. Moll, J. Marianne, illus. LC 54-8713. 20cm. 214p. (gr. 5-7). 1954. Coward-McCann, Inc.
--The Mystery of the Jade-Green Cadillac. Moll, J. Marianne, illus. LC 58-7002. (Illus.). 252 p. 20cm. 1958. Coward-McCann.
--The Mystery of the Lost Tower Treasure. Moll, J. Marianne, illus. LC 60-6867. 220p. illus. 20cm. 1960. Coward-McCann.
--The Mystery of the Midnight Smugglers. Moll, J. Marianne, illus. LC 64-10435. (Illus.). 256 p. 20cm. 1964. Coward-McCann.
--The Mystery of the Scarlet Daffodil. Moll, J. Marianne, illus. LC 52-13486. 246p. illus. 20cm. 1952, c.1953. Coward- McCann.
--Mystery of the Singing Strings. Moll, J. Marianne, illus. LC 61-825068. 256p. illus. 20cm. 1961. Coward-McCann.
--Mystery on Rainbow Island. Moll, J. Marianne, illus. LC 56-9947. 256p. illus. 20cm. 1st U.S. edition. 1957, c.1956. Coward-McCann.
--The Old Pony. Sofia, pseud. (1926-), illus. Zeiger, Sophia. LC 60-5676. 95p. illus. 20cm. c.1960. Coward-McCann.
--Roller Skates, Scooter, and Bike. Marshall, Constance Kay (1918-), illus. LC 66-13135. (Illus.). 115 p. 20cm. 1966. Coward-McCann.
--The Runaway. Sofia, pseud. (1926-), illus. Zeiger, Sofia. LC 57-10711. 63p. illus. 21cm. 1957. Coward-McCann.
--The Secret. N.D. E. M. Hale & Co.
--The Secret. Sofia, pseud. (1926-), illus. Zeiger, Sofia. LC 56-12084. 121p. illus. 20cm. 1956. Coward-McCann.
--Storm Over Innish. LC 73-4317. 132 p. 21cm. 1973. T. Nelson.
--The Wild Wood. Hawkins, Irene Beatrice (1906-), illus. LC 48-5767. 128 p. illus. (part col.) 23 cm. 1st U.S. edition. 1948. Coward-McCann.
Clief, Sylvia Worth Van see Heide, Florence Parry (1919-) & Van Clief, Sylvia Worth.
Clifford, David, jt. auth. see Rosenberg, Ethel Clifford.
Clifford, Ella, pseud., see Paull, Minnie E. Kenney.
Clifford, Ella
--Beside Still Waters. 258p. 1905. American Tract Society.
Clifford, Eth, pseud., see Rosenberg, Ethel Clifford.
Clifford, Eth, jt. auth. see Peterson, Willis.
Clifford, Eth, pseud. (1915-)
--Bear Before Breakfast. Rosenberg, Ethel Clifford. Oechsli, Kelly (1918-), illus. (Illus.). (gr. k-3). 1962. Putnam.
--Burning Star. Rosenberg, Ethel Clifford. Dillon, Leo (1933-) & Dillon, Diane (1933-), illus. LC 73-22064. xvi, 190 p. 22cm. 1974. (ISBN 0-395-18450-9). Houghton Mifflin.
--The Curse of the Moonraker. Rosenberg, Ethel Clifford. LC 77-24431. p. cm. 1977. (ISBN 0-395-25837-5). Houghton Mifflin.
--The Dastardly Murder of Dirty Peter. Rosenberg, Ethel Clifford. Hughes, George, illus. LC 81-6316. p. cm. (gr. 2-5). 1981. (ISBN 0-395-31671-5). Houghton Mifflin.
--Ground Afire: The Story of Death Valley. Rosenberg, Ethel Clifford. (gr. 5 up). 1965. (ISBN 0-695-43540-X). Follett.
--Harvey's Horrible Snake Disaster. Rosenberg, Ethel Clifford. 160p. (gr. 3-6). 1984. HM.
--Help! I'm a Prisoner in the Library. Rosenberg, Ethel Clifford. Hughes, George, illus. LC 79-14447. (Illus.). 105 p. 22cm. 1979. (ISBN 0-395-28478-3). Houghton Mifflin.
--Just Tell Me When We're Dead!. Rosenberg, Ethel Clifford. Hughes, George, illus. LC 83-10865. p. cm. 1983. (ISBN 0-395-33071-8). Houghton Mifflin.
--The Killer Swan. Rosenberg, Ethel Clifford. LC 80-17773. p. cm. 1980. (ISBN 0-395-29742-7). Houghton Mifflin Co.
--The Remembering Box. Rosenberg, Ethel Clifford. Diamond, Donna (1950-), illus. LC 85-10851. (Illus.). 70 p. 24cm. 1985. (ISBN 0-395-38476-1). Houghton Mifflin.
--The Rocking Chair Rebellion. Rosenberg, Ethel Clifford. LC 78-14834. p. cm. 1978. (ISBN 0-395-27163-0). Houghton Mifflin.
--The Strange Reincarnations of Hendrik Verloom. Rosenberg, Ethel Clifford. LC 82-11795. 115 p. 22cm. 1982. (ISBN 0-395-32433-5). Houghton Mifflin.
--Why Is an Elephant Called an Elephant. Rosenberg, Ethel Clifford. LC 69-12436. (Illus.). (gr. 1-3). 1966. (ISBN 0-672-50583-5). Bobbs.
--The Wild One. Rosenberg, Ethel Clifford. Stewart, Arvis L., illus. LC 74-8899. (Illus.). xiii, 206 p. 22cm. 1974. (ISBN 0-395-19491-1). Houghton Mifflin.
Clifford, Flora H., ed.
--Ring Songs and Games: The/Wheelock Girls' Song Book". Clifford, Flora H., compiled by. N.D. Milton Bradley Co.
Clifford, Gail
--But Rabbits Are Charming!. Walling, Robert S., illus. LC 46-209954. (Designed by Musso-Clifford). 28 p. col. illus. 28 x 22 cm. 1946. Clifford, Inc.
Clifford, Josephine, Mrs.
--Overland Stories. N.D. Claxton, Remsen, & Haffelfinger.
Clifford, Kathleen
--The Enchanted Glen: A Fairy Tale. Weed, Kim, illus. LC 46-129191. 48 p. illus. (part col.) 29 x 22 1/2 cm. 1945. Beverly Publishing Co.
Clifford, Laurie B. (1948-)
--Accept the Royal Challenge. (What If...Bks.). (gr. 5-9). 1984. (ISBN 0-8307-0940-1). Regal.
--The Million Dollar Night, No. 3. (gr. 5-7). 1983. (ISBN 0-8423-4284-2). Tyndale.
--The Peppermint Gang & Frog Heaven. 160p. (Peppermint Gang Ser.). (gr. 8-12). N.D. (ISBN 0-8423-0935-7). Tyndale.
--What if You Follow the Lone Cry?. LC 83-15960. (What If Bks.: No. 2). (gr. 5-9). 1983. (ISBN 0-8307-0913-4). Regal.
--What if You- Rescue the Royal Treasure?. LC 85-18313. p. cm. (What if- ? series ; 5). ((Series: Clifford, Laurie B., 1948-). (What if books ; 5.). c.1985. (ISBN 0-8307-1047-7). Regal Books.
--What if You Ride the Blue Bazoo. LC 83-15959. (What If Bks.: No. 1). (gr. 4-9). 1983. (ISBN 0-8307-0901-0). (ISBN 0-8307-0901-0). Regal.
--What if You Sneak Behind Enemy Lines. LC 84-1995. (What If Bks.: No. 3). (gr. 5-9). 1984. (ISBN 0-8307-0939-8). Regal.
--What If You...Blaze the Jet Trail?. LC 85-18287. p. cm. ("What if ..." series ; 6). ((Series: Clifford, Laurie B., 1948-). (What if books ; 6.). c.1985. (ISBN 0-8307-1048-5). Regal Books.
Clifford, Lucy Lane W. K., Mrs.
--Anyhow Stories, Moral and Otherwise Amd Wooden Tony, and Anyhow Story: Reprinted from The Last Touches. LC 75-32186. (Illus.). x, 146 23 p., 11 leaves of plates. 19cm. (Classics of Children's Literature, 1621-1932). 1977. (ISBN 0-8240-2298-X). Garland Pub.
--The Getting Well of Dorothy. Browne, Gordon Frederick (1858-1932), illus. 19cm. 251p. 1917. E. P. Dutton & Co.
Clifford, Margaret Cort see Clifford, Peggy, pseud.
Clifford, Mary Louise Beneway (1926-)
--Bisha of Burundi. Stubley, Trevor Hugh (1932-), illus. LC 72-83780. (Illus.). xii, 140 p. 21cm. 1973. (ISBN 0-690-14596-9). Crowell.
--Salah of Sierra Leone. Moon, Elzia, illus. LC 75-9665. (Illus.). 184 p. 21cm. 1975. (ISBN 0-690-00908-9). Crowell.
--Salah of Sierra Leone. Moon, Elzia, illus. 1975. Harper.
Clifford, Mollie Lee
--Polly, the Autobiography of a Parrot. Bridgman, Lewis Jesse (1857-1931), illus. LC 6-39759. (Illus.). 20cm. 268p. (Animal Autobiographical Ser.). 1906. Caldwell.
--Yoppy, the Autobiography of a Monkey. Bridgman, Lewis Jesse (1857-1931), illus. LC 5-21571. (Illus.). 20cm. 215p. (Animal Autobiographical Ser.). 1905. Caldwell.
Clifford, Peggy, pseud., see Clifford, Margaret Cort.
Clifford, Peggy, pseud. (1929-)
--Elliott. Clifford, Margaret Cort. Chwast, Jacqueline (1932-), illus. LC 67-25311. (Illus.). 118 p. 24cm. 1967. Houghton Mifflin.
--The Gnu and the Guru Go Behind the Beyond: A Cautionary Tale. Clifford, Margaret Cort. Von Schmidt, Eric (1931-), illus. LC 79-115450. (Illus.). 95 p. 27cm. 1970. Houghton Mifflin. **Award: (NYT).**
Clifford, Sandy
--The Roquefort Gang. Clifford, Sandy, illus. 1981. Houghton.
--The Roquefort Gang. Clifford, Sandy, illus. LC 80-20269. (Illus.). 79 p. 21cm. 1981. (ISBN 0-395-29521-1). Parnassus Press.
--The Smartest Person in the World. Clifford, Sandy, illus. LC 79-14138. (Illus.). 17cm. 47p. (gr. k-3). 1979. (ISBN 0-395-28411-2). Parnassus.
Clifford, W. K.
--Anyhow Stories, Moral & Otherwise. (Illus.). N.D. MacMillan.
Clifton, Fred
--Darl. (Illus.). 104p. (gr. 2-6). 1973. (ISBN 0-89388-098-1). Okpaku Communications.
Clifton, Lucille (1936-)
--All Us Come Cross the Water. 1st ed. Steptoe, John Lewis (1950-), illus. LC 72-76575. (Illus.). 32 p. 25cm. 1973. (ISBN 0-03-089262-7). Holt, Rinehart and Winston.
--Amifika. 1st ed. DiGrazia, Thomas (0000-1983), illus. LC 77-5887. (Illus.). 32 p. 26cm. c.1977. (ISBN 0-525-25548-6). Dutton.
--The Black B C's. Miller, Don (1923-), illus. (Illus.). 1970. E.P.Dutton & Co.
--The Boy Who Didn't Believe in Spring. 1st ed. Turkle, Brinton Cassaday (1915-), illus. LC 72-89844. (Illus.). 32 p. 1973. (ISBN 0-525-27145-7). Dutton.
--Don't You Remember?. 1st ed. Ness, Evaline Michelow, Mrs. (1911-), illus. LC 73-77448. (Illus.). 32 p. 23cm. 1973. (ISBN 0-525-28840-6). Dutton.
--Everett Anderson's Christmas Coming. 1st ed. Ness, Evaline Michelow, Mrs. (1911-), illus. LC 75-150025. (Illus.). 32 p. 1971. (ISBN 0-03-080219-9). (ISBN 0-03-080219-9). Holt, Rinehart and Winston.
--Everett Anderson's Friend. Grifalconi, Ann (1929-), illus. LC 75-32251. p. cm. c.1976. (ISBN 0-03-015161-9). Holt, Rinehart and Winston.
--Everett Anderson's Goodbye. 1st ed. Grifalconi, Ann (1929-), illus. LC 82-23426. (Illus.). 28 p. 22cm. c.1983. (ISBN 0-03-063518-7). Holt, Rinehart, and Winston. **Award: (CSKA).**
--Everett Anderson's Nine Month Long. Grifalconi, Ann (1929-), illus. LC 78-4202. p. cm. 1978, c.1979. (ISBN 0-03-043536-6). Holt, Rinehart, and Winston.
--Everett Anderson's Year. 1st ed. Grifalconi, Ann (1929-), illus. LC 73-22424. (Illus.). 31 p. 21cm. 1974. (ISBN 0-03-012736-X). Holt, Rinehart and Winston.
--Everett Anderson's 1 2 3. Grifalconi, Ann (1929-), illus. LC 76-25866. p. cm. c.1977. (ISBN 0-03-017441-4). Holt, Rinehart and Winston.
--Good, Says Jerome. 1st ed. Douglas, Stephanie, illus. LC 73-77462. (Illus.). 32 p. 26cm. 1973. (ISBN 0-525-30865-2). Dutton.
--The Lucky Stone. Payson, Dale (1943-), illus. LC 78-72862. p. cm. c.1979. (ISBN 0-440-05121-5). (ISBN 0-440-05122-3). Delacorte Press.
--My Brother Fine with Me. 1st ed. Barnett, Moneta (1922-1976), illus. LC 75-9621. p. cm. 1975. (ISBN 0-03-014171-0). Holt, Rinehart and Winston.
--My Friend Jacob. 1st ed. Di Grazia, Thomas (0000-1983), illus. LC 79-19168. (Illus.). 32 p. 26cm. c.1980. (ISBN 0-525-35487-5). Dutton.
--Some of the Days of Everett Anderson. 1st ed. Ness, Evaline Michelow, Mrs. (1911-), illus. LC 78-98922. (Illus.). 32 p. 1970. Holt, Rinehart and Winston.
--Sonora Beautiful. 1st ed. Garland, Michael, illus. LC 81-2094. p. cm. (Skinny book). c.1981. (ISBN 0-525-39680-2). (ISBN 0-525-39679-9). Dutton.
--Three Wishes. Douglas, Stephanie, illus. LC 75-5579. p. cm. 1976. (ISBN 0-670-71063-6). Viking Press.
--The Times They Used to Be. 1st ed. Jeschke, Susan (1942-), illus. LC 73-21859. (Illus.). 48 p. 22cm. 1974. (ISBN 0-03-012171-X). Holt, Rinehart and Winston.
Clifton, Oliver Lee, pseud., see Rathborne, St. George.
Clifton, Oliver Lee, pseud. (1854-1928)
--The Camp Fire Boys at Silver Fox Farm. Rathborne, St. George. (The Camp Fire Boys Ser.). N.D. Barse & Hopkins.
Clifton, Richard
--The Miller and the Toad. N.D. Sherman, French and Co.
Clifton, Sidney, tr. see Lohmeyer, Julius (1835-1903) & Schanz, Frieda.
Climo, Lindee
--Chester's Barn. Climo, Lindee, illus. (Illus.). (gr. 1 up). 1982. (ISBN 0-88776-132-1). Tundra Bks. **Award: (AFH).**
Climo, Shirley (1928-)
--The Cobweb Christmas. 1st ed. Lasker, Joseph Leon (1919-), illus. LC 81-43879. (Illus.). 32 p. 19cm. c.1982. (ISBN 0-690-04215-9). (ISBN 0-690-04216-7). Crowell.
--The Cobweb Christmas. Lasker, Joseph Leon (1919-), illus. 1982. Harper.
--Gopher, Tanker & the Admiral. McKeating, Eileen, illus. LC 83-45240. (Illus.). 128p. (gr. 2-6). 1984. (ISBN 0-690-04382-1, TYC-J). (ISBN 0-690-04383-X). Har-Row.
--Someone Saw a Spider: Spider Facts and Folktales. Zimmer, Dirk, illus. LC 84-45340. p. cm. c.1985. (ISBN 0-690-04435-6). (ISBN 0-690-04436-4). Crowell.
Climo, Shirley (1928-), retold by.
--Piskies, Spriggans, and Other Magical Beings: Tales from the Droll-Teller. 1st ed. Dos Santos, Joyce Audy, illus. LC 79-7839. p. cm. 1981. (ISBN 0-690-04063-6). (ISBN 0-690-04064-4). Crowell.

AUTHOR INDEX

COATES, HENRY

Clinard, Dorothy Long (1909-) & Newby, Dorothy D.
--The Hidey Hole. (Illus.). 1959. Duell, Sloan and Pearce Pub.
--The Hidey Hole: The Mystery of the Old Winslow Homestead. Orbaan, Albert F. (1913-), illus. LC 60-5443. (Illus.). 152 p. 21cm. 1960. Duell, Sloan and Pearce.
Cline, Charles Terry, Jr. (1935-)
--Damon. LC 74-16585. 320p. 1975. (ISBN 0-399-11429-7). Putnam.
Cline, Linda (1941-)
--Weakfoot. LC 74-26865. 175 p. 22cm. 1975. (ISBN 0-688-41697-7). (ISBN 0-688-51697-1). Lothrop, Lee & Shepard Co.
Cline, Nancy, jt. auth. see Weizenbach, John F.
Cline, Nancy, jt. auth. see Welzenbach, John F.
Clinton, Althea L., pseud., see Taylor, Alta Lucretia.
Clise, Michele
--My Circle of Bears. Burns, Marsha, photos by. (Orig.). 1st U.S. edition. 1981. (ISBN 0-914676-65-2, Star & Eleph Bks). Green Tiger Pr.
Clithero, Myrtle Ely see Clithero, Sally, pseud.
Clithero, Sally, pseud., see Clithero, Myrtle Ely.
Clithero, Sally, pseud. (1906-), compiled by
--Beginning-To-Read Poetry. Clithero, Myrtle Ely. Blegvad, Erik (1923-), illus. LC 67-21167 (Illus.). 30p. (Beginning-to-Read Ser.). (gr. 2-4). 1967. (ISBN 0-695-87150-1). (ISBN 0-695-47150-3). Follett.
Clive, Mary (1907-)
--Christmas with the Savages. Gough, Philip (1908-), illus. 177p. illus. 23cm. 1955. Macmillan.
--Christmas with the Savages. Gough, Philip (1908-), illus. LC 56-16394. (Illus.). 23cm. 177p. N.D. St Martin's Press.
Clodd, Edward (1840-1930)
--Tom Tit Tot: An Essay of Savage Philosophy in Folk-Tale. LC 67-23907. 249p. Repr. of 1898 ed. (Folk-lore Ser.). 1968 (Gale Reprints). Duckworth: Distributed by Singing Tree Press.
Cloke, Rene
--Barnaby's Cuckoo Clock. 25p. N.D. Pitman Publishing Corporation.
--The Flying Frog. 25p. 1958. Pitman Publishing Corporation.
--Little Folk's First book. (Illus.). N.D. Ferederick Warne & Co.
--Merry's New Hat. 25p. 1958. Pitman Publishing Corporation.
--My First Picture Book of Baby Animals. Cloke, Rene, illus. LC 80-20271. p. cm. c.1980. (ISBN 0-517-31090-2). Derrydale Books.
--My First Picture Book of Fairy Tales. Cloke, Rene, illus. LC 79-52797. (Illus.). 18 p. 34cm. 1979. (ISBN 0-517-29263-7). Derrydale Books.
--My First Picture Book of Nursery Rhymes. Cloke, Rene, illus. LC 79-52799. p. cm. 1979. (ISBN 0-517-29266-1). Derrydale Books.
--My First Picture Book of Poetry. Cloke, Rene, illus. LC 80-17144. p. cm. c.1980. (ISBN 0-517-31095-3). Derrydale Books.
--My First Picture Book of Telling the Time. Cloke, Rene, illus. LC 79-52800. (Illus.). 18 p. 34cm. 1979, c.1976. (ISBN 0-517-29267-X). Derrydale Books.
--My First Picture Book of Zoo Animals. Cloke, Rene, illus. LC 80-20280. p. cm. 1980. (ISBN 0-517-31097-X). Derrydale Books.
--My Treasury of Rhymes. Cloke, Rene, illus. LC 79-52802. (Illus.). 18 p. 34cm. (Derrydale fun time library). 1979, c.1974. (ISBN 0-517-29268-8). Derrydale Books.
--Tufty Paints His Door. 25p. 1958. Pitman Publishing Corporation.
Cloke, Rene, illus.
--Little Folk's Book of Nursery Rhymes. LC 62-18911. (Illus.). (gr. k-3). 1962. (ISBN 0-7232-0341-5). Warne.
--Little Folk's Book of Nursery Tales. LC 63-19182. 64 p. illus. (part col.) 25 cm. 1963. F. Warne.
Close, Elizabeth Taliaferro
--The Magic Ring: Children's Tales From Richard Wagner. LC 64-5648. 158 p. 21 cm. (A bookland juvenile). 1964. Carlton Press.
Closser, Lynne, ed. see Da Free, John.
Clot, S. & Quinel, Charles
--Legends of Britain. Moorehead, Caroline (1944-), adapted by. Dimpre, Henri & Sainte-Croix, Gaston De, illus. LC 68-54127. (Illus.). 189 p. 19cm. (Myths and legends). 1969, c.1968. World Pub. Co.
Cloud, Claude Carey (1899-) & Lentz, Harold B., illus.
--Little Red Riding Hood. LC 35-2. (Illus.). 18p. 23cm. 1934. Blue Ribbon Press.
--Little Red Riding-Hood. Little Red Riddinghood. LC 35-2. 18 p. incl. front., illus. (part col.) 24 cm. c.1934. Blue Ribbon Press.
Clouston, William Alexander (1843-1896)
--The Book of Noodles. N.D. Gale Reprint.
Cloutier, Helen H (1909-)
--Isle Royale Calling. LC 57-11346. (Illus.). 215 p. 21cm. 1957. Dodd, Mead.
--The Many Names of Lee Lu. Elmi, Don, illus. LC 60-136351. unpaged. illus. 24cm. c.1960. A. Whitman.
--Sim Barton: Girl Radio Operator. 1st ed. LC 53-20944. 171p. 21cm. 1952. Pageant Press.
Cloven, George & Steiner, Barbara A
--But Not Stanleigh. Cloven, Ruth LC 81-9265. (Illus.). 33 p. 29cm. c.1980. Stanleigh Co.
Clover, Alice Mary Ross (1892-) & Clover, Jack
--Joan Foster in Europe. LC 51-11588. viii, 243 p. 21cm. 1951. Dodd, Mead.
Clover, Jack, jt. auth. see Clover, Alice Mary Ross.
Clover, Samuel Travers (1859-)
--On Special Assignment. Laskey, H. G., illus. LC 3-14364. 20cm. 307p. 1903. Lothrop Pub. Co.
--Paul Travers' Adventures. Being a Faithful Narrative of a Boy's Journey Around the World... LC 20-16493. 5 p. l., 5-368, 1 p. front., plates. 19 1/2 cm. 1897. Way & Williams.
--Paul Travers' Adventures: Being a Faithful Narrative of a Boy's Journey Around the World...and How He Won His Reporter's Star. New ed. Emerson, C. Chase, illus. LC 1-6310. 4 p. l., 5-368 p. front., plates. 19 cm. 1901. Lothrop Publishing Company.
Clow, W. M
--The Old, Old Story. Pratt, William, illus. N.D. Dodge.
Cluff, Tom
--Minutemen of the Sea. N.D. Wilcox & Follett Co.
--Minutemen of the Sea. O'Sullivan, Tom, illus. (Illus.). (gr. 5 up). 1955. (ISBN 0-695-45810-8). Follett.
Clugston, Katharine Thatcher, adapted by see Stevenson, Richard.
Clure, Beth & Rumsey, Helen
--Can You Guess?. Smith, Bron, illus. LC 75-46434. (Illus.). 24cm. 33p. (I Can Do It Series). c.1976. (ISBN 0-8372-2170-6). Bowmar.
--Come with Me. Smith, Bron, illus. LC 75-46436. (Illus.). 15 p. (I can do it series). c.1976. (ISBN 0-8372-2169-2). Bowmar.
--Cowboy Can. Curry, Nancy, ed. Mandlin, Harvey, photos by. LC 68-19658. 12 color photos. 24p. (Bowmar Early Childhood Series). (ps-2). 1969. Bowmar.
--Me. Rupp, Jacques, illus. LC 67-28261. (Illus.). 21 p. (Bowmar early childhood series). 1968. Bowmar Pub. Corp.
--Me. rev. ed. Taylor, Paul L., illus. LC 72-178666. (Illus.). 16 p. (Manipulative series). 1971, c.1968. (ISBN 0-8372-0363-5). Bowmar.
--Surprise Boxes. Acosta, Karen, illus. LC 75-46430. (Illus.). 14 p. (I can do it series). c.1976. (ISBN 0-8372-2174-9). Bowmar.
--Telling Tails. Shubin, Steve, illus. LC 67-28262. (Illus.). 19 p. (Bowmar early childhood series). 1970, c.1968. Bowmar.
--Things I Like to Do. Rupp, Jacques, illus. LC 68-19660. (Illus.). 24cm. 21p. (Bowmar Early Childhood Series). (ps-2). 1969. Bowmar.
--Through the Day. Wysocki, Harry, illus. (Illus.). 24cm. 20p. (Bowmar Early Childhood Series). (ps-2). 1969. Bowmar.
--Where Is Home?. Rupp, Jacques, illus. LC 67-28263. (Illus.). 19 p. (Bowmar early childhood series). 1968. Bowmar Pub. Corp.
Clute, Tom, jt. auth. see Fritz, Jean Guttery.
Clutha, Janet Paterson Frame see Frame, Janet, pseud.
Clutton, C. & Posthumus, C.
--The Racing Car. 1962. Norton Company.
Clyde, Ahmad
--Cheng Ho's Voyage. Durkee, Noura, illus. LC 81-66951. (Illus.). 32p. (Orig.). (Children's Book Ser.). (gr. 3-7). 1981. (ISBN 0-89259-021-1). Am Trust Pubns.
Clyde, Anna M.
--Jack-a-Boy in Beast Land. LC 1-24852. 19cm. 139p. 1901. George W. Jacobs & Co.
--Jack-a-boy on Beast Land. (Lad and Lassie Series.). 1915. George W. Jacobs.
Clymer, Eleanor Lowenton see Bell, Janet, pseud.
Clymer, Eleanor Lowenton see Kinsey, Elizabeth, pseud.
Clymer, Eleanor Lowenton (1906-)
--The Adventure of Walter. Fetz, Ingrid (1915-), illus. LC 65-21711. 58p. col. illus. 14cm. (ps-4). 1965. (ISBN 0-689-20055-2). Atheneum.
--Belinda's New Spring Hat. Fiammenghi, Gioia (1929-), illus. LC 69-11524. (Illus.). 32 p. 23cm. 1969. F. Watts.
--Benjamin in the Woods. (Illus.). (gr. k-3). N.D. G&D.
--The Big Pile of Dirt. 1st ed. Shore, Robert (1924-), illus. (Illus.). 32 p. 1968. Holt, Rinehart and Winston.
--Chester. Keats, Ezra Jack (1916-1983), illus. LC 54-874962. 141p. illus. 21cm. 1954. Dodd, Mead.
--Chipmunk in the Forest. Fetz, Ingrid (1915-), illus. 1965. Atheneum.
--Chipmunk in the Forest. Fetz, Ingrid (1915-), illus. (Illus.). (gr. 2-5). 1972. (ISBN 0-689-70311-2, Aladdin). Atheneum.
--The Country Kittens. Bendick, Jeanne (1919-), illus. LC 47-12104. 1947. McBride.
--Engine Number Seven. 1st ed. Quackenbush, Robert Mead (1929-), illus. LC 74-20911. (Illus.). 46 p. 24cm. 1975. (ISBN 0-03-013701-2). Holt, Rinehart and Winston.
--The Get-Away Car. LC 78-7445. 149 p. 22cm. c.1978. Dutton.
--The Grocery Mouse. Bendick, Jeanne (1919-), illus. LC 45-5126. 94, 2 p. incl. col. front., illus. (part col.) 23 1/2 cm. 1945. R. M. McBride & Company.
--Hamburgers-and Ice Cream for Dessert. Doty, Roy (1922-), illus. LC 75-6753. (Illus.). 48 p. 23cm. 1975. (ISBN 0-525-31305-2). Dutton.
Harry, the Wild West Horse. Shortall, Leonard W., illus. LC 63-10375. (Illus.). 56 p. 22cm. 1963. Atheneum.
--Here Comes Pete. Boyle, Mildred, illus. LC 44-3968. 96 p. incl. col. front., col. illus. 23 1/2 cm. 1944. R. M. McBride & Company.
--Horatio. 1st ed. Quackenbush, Robert Mead (1929-), illus. LC 67-18999. (Illus.). 63 p. 17cm. 1968. Atheneum.
--Horatio. Quackenbush, Robert Mead (1929-), illus. (gr. k-3). 1974. Atheneum.
--Horatio Goes to the Country. 1st ed. Quackenbush, Robert Mead (1929-), illus. LC 78-5137. (Illus.). 63 p. 17cm. 1978. Atheneum.
--Horatio Solves a Mystery. 1st ed. Quackenbush, Robert Mead (1929-), illus. LC 79-22590. (Illus.). 59 p. 18cm. 1980. (ISBN 0-689-10999-7). Atheneum.
--Horatio's Birthday. 1st ed. Quackenbush, Robert Mead (1929-), illus. LC 76-09. (Illus.). 59 p. 17cm. 1976. (ISBN 0-689-30520-6). Atheneum.
--The Horse in the Attic. Lewin, Ted (1935-), illus. LC 83-6377. (Illus.). 96p. (gr. 3-6). 1983. (ISBN 0-02-719040-4). Bradbury Pr.
--The House on the Mountain. 1st ed. Carty, Leo (1931-), illus. LC 75-133123. (Illus.). 39 p. 23cm. 1971. (ISBN 0-525-32365-1). Dutton.
--How I Went Shopping and What I Got. 1st ed. Hyman, Trina Schart (1939-), illus. LC 70-182787. (Illus.). 33 p. 24cm. 1972. (ISBN 0-03-088589-2). (ISBN 0-03-088590-6). Holt, Rinehart and Winston.
--The Latch Key Club. Dillon, Corinne Boyd, illus. LC 49-10999. 282 p. illus. 22 cm. 1949. D. McKay Co.
--Leave Horatio Alone. 1st ed. Quackenbush, Robert Mead (1929-), illus. LC 74-75557. (Illus.). 63 p. 18cm. 1974. (ISBN 0-689-30405-6). Atheneum.
--Little Bear Island. Koering, Ursula (1921-), illus. LC 45-37860. 143 p. incl. front., illus. 22 cm. 1945. R. M. McBride & Company.
--Luke Was There. 1st ed. De Groat, Diane (1947-), illus. LC 73-7170. (Illus.). 74 p. 22cm. 1973. (ISBN 0-03-011161-7). Holt, Rinehart and Winston.
--Make Way for Water. Wonsetler, John Charles (1900-), illus. LC 53-10499. 63p. illus. 22cm. (Everyday Adventure Story). 1953. J. Messner.
--Me and the Eggman. 1st ed. Stone, David Karl (1922-), illus. LC 75-179054. (Illus.). 56 p. 22cm. 1972. (ISBN 0-525-34775-5). Dutton.
--Mister Piper's Bus. (Illus.). (gr. 3-5). 1961. (ISBN 0-8382-0537-2). Hale.
--Mr. Piper's Bus. Wiese, Kurt (1887-1974), illus. LC 61-6935. 92p. illus. 21cm. 1961. Dodd, Mead.
--My Brother Stevie. LC 67-3010. 76 p. 22cm. 1967. Holt, Rinehart and Winston.
--My Mother Is the Smartest Woman in the World. Kincade, Nancy, illus. LC 82-1685. (Illus.). 85 p. 22cm. 1982. (ISBN 0-689-30916-3). Atheneum.
--Not Too Small After All. O'Sullivan, Tom, illus. LC 55-9606. 55p. illus. 23cm. (gr. 2-4). 1955. F. Watts.
--Now That You Are Seven. Fetz, Ingrid (1915-), illus. LC 63-7239. 1963. Association Press.
--Patch. Kinsey, Elizabeth, pseud. Davis, James H., illus. LC 47-424. 32 p. col. illus. 27 1/2 x 23 1/2 cm. 1946. R. M. McBride & Company.
--Santiago's Silver Mine. 1st ed. Fetz, Ingrid (1915-), illus. LC 72-86930. (Illus.). 74 p. 21cm. 1973. (ISBN 0-689-30081-6). Atheneum.
--A Search for Two Bad Mice. Gill, Margery Jean (1925-), illus. LC 80-12789. p. cm. 1980. (ISBN 0-689-30771-3). Atheneum.
--Sociable Toby. N.D. E. M. Hale and Co.
--Sociable Toby. Fetz, Ingrid (1915-), illus. LC 55-118483. 81p. illus. 23cm. 1956. F. Watts.
--The Spider, the Cave, and the Pottery Bowl. 1st ed. Fetz, Ingrid (1915-), illus. LC 70-134806. (Illus.). 66 p. 21cm. 1971. Atheneum.
--Take Tarts As Tarts Is Passing. Doty, Roy (1922-), illus. LC 73-77463. (Illus.). 32 p. 23cm. 1974. (ISBN 0-525-40640-9). Dutton.
--Thirty-Three Bunn Street. Miller, Jane Judith (1925-), illus. LC 52-8687. 152 p. illus. 21 cm. 1952. Dodd, Mead.
--This Cat Came to Stay!. Kinsey, Elizabeth, pseud. Sibley, Don (1922-), illus. LC 55-5408. (Illus.). 157 p. 20cm. 1955. F. Watts.
--The Tiny Little House. 1st ed. Fetz, Ingrid (1915-), illus. LC 64-19559. 55 p. col. illus. 14 cm. 1964. Atheneum.
--Tommy's Wonderful Airplane. Wiese, Kurt (1887-1974), illus. LC 51-11020. 212 p. illus. 21 cm. 1951. Dodd, Mead.
--Treasure at First Base. Porter, Jean Macdonald (1906-), illus. LC 50-7782. (Illus.). 248 p. 21cm. 1950. Dodd, Mead.
--The Trolley Car Family. Koering, Ursula (1921-), illus. LC 47-306119. 256 p. illus. 21 cm. 1947. D. McKay Co.
--We Lived in the Almont. 1st ed. Stone, David Karl (1922-), illus. LC 74-116880. (Illus.). 102 p. 22cm. 1970. (ISBN 0-525-30050-Y). Dutton.
--Wheels. 1st ed. Goslin, Charles, illus. LC 65-215474. 1 v. (unpaged) illus. (part col.) 22 cm. (A Book to begin on). 1965. Holt, Rinehart and Winston.
--A Yard for John. Rev. ed. Boyle, Mildred, illus. LC 43-6176. 94 p., 1 l. incl. col. front., illus. (part col.) ccl. plates. 23 1/2 x 18 cm. 1943. R. M. McBride & Company.
Clymer, Susan
--The One & Only Bunbun. Forberg, Ati, pseud. (1925-), illus. Forberg, Beate Gropius. (Illus.). 64p. (Orig.). (gr. 3-5). 1983. (ISBN 0-590-32463-2). Scholastic Inc.
Clymer, Theodore
--Four Corners of the Sky: Poems, Chants, and Oratory. 1st ed. Brown, Marc Tolon (1946-), illus. LC 75-8893. (Illus.). 46, 2 p. 24cm. 1975. (ISBN 0-316-14761-3, Pub. by Atlantic Monthly Press). Little, Brown.
--The Travels of Atunga. 1st ed. Schoenherr, John Carl (1935-), illus. LC 73-3158. (Illus.). 31 p. 24cm. 1973. (ISBN 0-316-14760-5). Little, Brown.
Clymer, Theodore & Miles, Miska, pseud. (1899-)
--Horse and the Bad Morning. 1st ed. Martin, Patricia Miles. Morrill, Leslie H., illus. LC 81-12660. (Illus.). 32 p. 22cm. c.1982. (ISBN 0-525-45103-X). Dutton.
Clyne, Geraldine
--The Jolly Jump-Ups See the Circus: Jingling Bros., the Greatest Show. LC 44-9796. 13 p. col. illus. 27 cm. c.1944. McLoughlin Bros., Inc.
--Ten Toys. LC 39-2438. (Illus.). 32cm. 49p. 1938. McLoughlin Bros.
Clyne, Geraldine, ed. see Mother Goose.
Clyne, Patricia Edwards
--The Corduroy Road. Cary, Louis Favreau (1915-), illus. Cary, pseud. LC 73-3902. (Illus.). 93 p. 24cm. 1973. (ISBN 0-396-06815-4). Dodd, Mead.
--The Curse of Camp Gray Owl. LC 80-2783. (Illus.). 174 p. 22cm. c.1981. (ISBN 0-396-07922-9). Dodd, Mead.
--The Curse of the Grey Camp Owl. LC 80-2783. 176p. (gr. 5 up). 1981. Dodd.
--Ghostly Animals of America. Lewin, Ted (1935-), illus. LC 77-6487. p. cm. 1977. (ISBN 0-396-07465-0). Dodd, Mead.
--Strange & Supernatural Animals. Lewin, Ted (1935-), illus. (Illus.). (gr. 5 up). 1979. Dodd.
--Tunnels of Terror. Aloise, Frank E., illus. LC 74-25515. (Illus.). 157 p. 21cm. 1975. (ISBN 0-396-07073-6). Dodd, Mead.
Coalson, Glo, jt. auth. see Wasson, Valentina Pavlovna.
Coalson, Glo (1946-)
--Three Stone Woman. LC 75-157314. (Illus.). 32 p. 27cm. 1971. Atheneum.
Coalwell, Reg
--The Gibbles. LC 79-89080. (Illus.). 1979. (ISBN 0-89081-200-4). Harvest Hse.
Coates, Belle (1896-)
--Barn Cat. Henneberger, Robert G. (1921-), illus. LC 55-10140. (Illus.). 56 p. 21cm. 1955. Scribner.
--Little Maverick Cow. N.D. E. M. Hale & Co.
--Little Maverick Cow. Fulton, George, illus. LC 57-5167. (Illus.). 56 p. 21cm. 1957. Scribner.
--Mak. LC 81-6533. p. cm. c.1981. (ISBN 0-395-31603-0). Houghton Mifflin.
--The Sign of the Open Hand. Micale, Albert (1913-), illus. LC 62-9643. (Illus.). 63 p. 21cm. 1962. Scribner.
--That Colt Fireplug. Dennis, Wesley (1903-1966), illus. LC 58-6739. 65p. illus. 22cm. 1958. Scribner.
Coates, Ella Mary
--Four Little Indians. N.D. John C. Winston Co.
--Four Little Indians: Or, How Carroll "Got Even". LC 2-25757. 4 p. l., 11-262 p. front., plates. 19 1/2 cm. 1902. H. T. Coates & Company.
Coates, H. M., Mrs.
--The Beautiful Island. (Illus.). N.D. Pott, Young & Co.
Coates, Henry Troth (1843-1910), compiled by.
--Children's Book of Poetry. New ed. N.D. John C. Winston.

--The Children's Book of Poetry. Dore, Louis Christophe Paul Gustave (1832-1883), illus. (Illus.). N.D. Porter & Coates.
--The Children's Book of Poetry: Carefully Selected from the Works of the Best and Most Popular Writers for Children. LC 6-35055. viii, 525 p. incl. front., illus. 23 1/2 cm. 1879. Porter & Coates.
--The Children's Book of Poetry: Carefully Selected from the Works of the Best and Most Popular Writers for Children. Dore, Louis Christophe Paul Gustave (1832-1883), illus. LC 70-149101. (Illus.). viii, 525 p. 24cm. (Granger index reprint series). 1971. (ISBN 0-8369-6226-5). Books for Libraries Press.
--Fireside Stories, Old and New. (Illus.). N.D. Henry T. Coates & Co.

Coates, Joseph K

--The Gentle Dragon. LC 79-84574. 329 p. 22cm. c.1979. (ISBN 0-89882-001-4). Lane.

Coates, William B., ed.

--Stop, Look & Laugh. 1960. Nelson.

Coats, Alice Margaret (1905-)

--Story of Horace. (Illus.). 1937. Tri-Ocean Books.
--The Story of Horace. Coats, Alice Margaret (1905-), illus. LC 39-9214. 52 p. col. illus. 26 cm. c.1939. Coward McCann, Inc.

Coats, Claude, adapted by see Disney, Walt, Productions.

Coatsworth, David see Snake, Sam.

Coatsworth, Elizabeth, jt. auth. see Polland, Madeleine Angela Cahill.

Coatsworth, Elizabeth Jane (1893-), ed. see Beston, Henry B.

Coatsworth, Elizabeth Jane (1893-), ed. see Hudson, William Henry.

Coatsworth, Elizabeth Jane (1893-)

--Alice-all-by-Herself. 1966. Macmillan Company.
--Alice-All-by-Herself. De Angeli, Marguerite Lofft, Mrs. (1889-), illus. LC 37-24270. 6 p. l., 181 p. incl. illus., plates. col. front. 23 1/2 cm. 1937. The Macmillan Company.
--All-of-a-Sudden Susan. Cuffari, Richard (1925-1978), illus. LC 74-6200. (Illus.). 74 p. 22cm. 1974. (ISBN 0-02-722610-7). Macmillan.
--American Adventures, 1620-1945. Frankenberg, Robert Clinton (1911-), illus. LC 68-12079. (Illus.). viii, 229 p. 22cm. 1968. Macmillan.
--Aunt Flora. Lee, Manning De Villeneuve (1894-1980), illus. LC 53-9822. 64p. illus. 22cm. (Once-upon-a-time-in-America series). 1953. Macmillan.
--Away Goes Sally. 1969. MacMillan Publishing Company.
--Away Goes Sally. Sewell, Helen Moore (1896-1957), illus. LC 34-312986. 5 p. l., 122 p. incl. illus., plates. front. 28 1/2 cm. 1934. The Macmillan Company.
--Bess and the Sphinx. Loewenstein, Bernice, illus. LC 67-15543. (Illus.). 88 p. 22cm. 1967. Macmillan.
--The Big Green Umbrella. Sewell, Helen Moore (1896-1957), illus. LC 44-47950. 28 p. incl. col. front., illus. (part col.) 22 x 21 cm. (Story parade picture book). 1944. Grosset & Dunlap.
--Bob Bodden and the Good Ship Rover. Schroeder, Ted (1931-1973), illus. LC 68-11719. (Illus.). 48 p. 23cm. 1968. (ISBN 0-8116-4008-6). Garrard Pub. Co.
--Bob Bodden and the Seagoing Farm. Aloise, Frank E., illus. LC 71-103066. (Illus.). 47 p. 23cm. (Reading shelf book). 1970. (ISBN 0-8116-4020-5). Garrard Pub. Co.
--Boston Belles. Lee, Manning De Villeneuve (1894-1980), illus. LC 52-13288. (Illus.). 64 p. 21cm. (Once-upon-a-time-in-America series, 3). 1952. Macmillan.
--The Boy with the Parrot. 1968. MacMillan Publishing Company.
--The Boy with the Parrot. Bronson, Wilfrid Swancourt (1894-), illus. LC 30-10708. 7 p. l., 101, 1 p., 1 l. incl. front., illus., plates. double col. pl. 22 1/2 cm. 1930. The Macmillan Company.
--The Boy with the Parrott. 1964. MacMillan.
--Captain's Daughter. Ray, Ralph (1920-1952), illus. (gr. 7-9). N.D. (ISBN 0-02-042590-2). Macmillan.
--The Cat and the Captain. Kay, Gertrude Alice (1884-1939), illus. LC 27-18028. 6 p. l., 3-95 p. incl. illus., plates. col. front., col. plates. 16 1/2 cm. (The Little library). 1927. The Macmillan Company.
--The Cat and the Captain. Loewenstein, Bernice, illus. LC 73-6041. (Illus.). 56 p. 18cm. 1974. (ISBN 0-02-719070-6). Macmillan.
--The Cat Who Went to Heaven. Ward, Lynd Kendall (1905-1985), illus. LC 58-10917. (Illus.). 62 p. 24cm. 1958. Macmillan.
--The Cat Who Went to Heaven. Ward, Lynd Kendall (1905-1985), illus. 1967. Macmillan.
--The Cat Who Went to Heaven. Ward, Lynd Kendall (1905-1985), illus. LC 30-21929. 4 p. l., 57 p. illus., double pl. 23 1/2 cm. 1930. The Macmillan Company. **Award: (JNM).**
--The Cave. Houser, Allan C. (1914-), illus. LC 58-14982. (Illus.). 63 p. 24cm. 1958. Viking Press.
--Cherry Ann and the Dragon Horse. Lee, Manning de Villeneuve (1894-1980), illus. LC 55-13613. 64p. illus. 21cm. (Once-upon-a-time-in-America series). 1955. Macmillan.
--The Children Come Running. Duvoisin, Roger Antoine, et al. (1904-1980), illus. LC 60-513655. (Illus.). 93 p. 23cm. 1960. Golden Press.
--Cricket and the Emperor's Son. Palmer, Juliette (1930-), illus. LC 65-13333. (Illus.). v, 126 p. 21cm. 1965, c.1962. W. W. Norton.
--Cricket and the Emperor's Son. Yap, Weda (1894-), illus. LC 32-253926. 7 p. l., 112 p., 2 l. incl. illus., plates. front. 22 cm. 1932. The Macmillan Company.
--Daisy. Brown, Judith Gwyn (1933-), illus. LC 72-86796. (Illus.). 69 p. 22cm. 1973. Macmillan.
--Dancing Tom. 1967. MacMillan Publishing Company.
--Dancing Tom. Paull, Grace A. (1898-), illus. LC 38-330099. 49 p. illus. 18 1/2 x 18 1/2 cm. 1938. The Macmillan Company.
--Daniel Webster's Horses. Cary, Louis Favreau (1915-), illus. Cary, pseud. LC 78-130966. (Illus.). 47 p. 23cm. (A Reading shelf book). (American Folk Tales). 1971. (ISBN 0-8116-4025-6). Garrard Pub. Co.
--Desert Dan. Johnson, Eugene Harper, illus. LC 60-506852. 61p. illus. 24cm. 1960. Viking Press.
--Dog from Nowhere. Sibley, Don (1922-), illus. (Illus.). (gr. 1-5). 1958. (ISBN 0-06-021325-6). Har-Row.
--The Dog from Nowhere. Sibley, Don (1922-), illus. LC 59-2937. 80p. illus. 23cm. 1958. Row, Peterson.
--Dollar for Luck. Hauman, George (1890-1961) & Hauman, Doris, Mrs. (1897-), illus. LC 51-10202. (Illus.). 154 p. 21cm. 1951. Macmillan.
--Door to the North: A Saga of Fourteenth Century America. 1st ed. Chapman, Frederick Trench (1887-), illus. LC 50-10540. (Illus.). ix, 246 p. 22cm. (Land of the Free series). (gr. 5-7). 1950. Winston.
--Down Half the World. Bernstein, Zena, illus. (Illus.). (gr. 7 up). 1968. (ISBN 0-02-721470-2). Macmillan.
--Down Tumbledown Mountain. Watson, Aldren Auld (1917-), illus. LC 59-294. 80p. illus. 23cm. c.1958. Row, Peterson.
--Enchanted: An Incredible Tale. Frank, Mary (1933-), illus. LC 68-12649. (Illus.). 12 b&w line drawings. 160p. (gr. 7 up). 1968. (ISBN 0-394-91112-1). Pantheon.
--The Fair American. 1968. MacMillan Publishing Company.
--The Fair American. Sewell, Helen Moore (1896-1957), illus. LC 40-30714. 6 p. l., 132 p. front., illus. 23 1/2 cm. 1940. The Macmillan Company.
--First Adventure. Ray, Ralph (1920-1952), illus. LC 50-10427. (Illus.). 60 p. 21cm. 1950. Macmillan.
--Five Bushel Farm. Sewell, Helen Moore (1896-1957), illus. 1969. MacMillan Publishing Company.
--Five Bushel Farm. Sewell, Helen Moore (1896-1957), illus. LC 39-5776. 7 p. l., 152 p. incl. front., plates. 23 1/2 cm. 1939. The Macmillan Company.
--Forgotten Island. Paull, Grace A. (1898-), illus. LC 42-24436. 3 p. l., 65, 1 p. incl. front., illus. 21 x 16 cm. (Story parade adventure book). 1942. Grosset & Dunlap.
--The Fox Friend. Hamberger, John F. (1934-), illus. LC 66-111013. 1v. (unpaged) col. illus. 17x24cm. (gr. k-2). c.1966. (ISBN 0-02-720510-X). Macmillan.
--George and Red. Giovanopoulos, Paul Arthur (1939-), illus. LC 69-11293. (Illus.). 55 p. 21cm. 1969. Macmillan.
--The Golden Horse Shoe. 1968. MacMillan Publishing Company.
--The Golden Horseshoe. Lawson, Robert (1892-1957), illus. LC 35-18415. 7 p. l., 3-151, 2 p. incl. illus., plates. front. 21 cm. 1935. The Macmillan Company.
--Good Night. Aruego, Jose (1932-), illus. LC 79-175596. (Illus.). 32 p. 19cm. 1972. Macmillan.
--Grandmother Cat and the Hermit. Boker, Irving, illus. LC 70-99786. (Illus.). 87 p. 22cm. 1970. Macmillan.
--The Hand of Apollo. Jacques, Robin (1920-), illus. LC 65-18156. 77 p. illus. 22 cm. 1965. Viking Press.
--Here I Stay. Earle, Edwin (1887-1974), illus. (gr. 6-8). 1938. (ISBN 0-698-20058-6). Coward.
--Hide and Seek. Vaughan-Jackson, Genevieve (1913-), illus. LC 56-6017. unpaged. illus. 19cm. 1956. Pantheon.
--The House of the Swan. Voute, Kathleen (1892-), illus. LC 48-2030. 165 p. illus. 21 cm. 1948. Macmillan Co.
--Houseboat Summer. Davis, Marguerite (1889-), illus. LC 42-36173. 191, 1 p. incl. col. front., col. illus. 21 x 16 1/2 cm. 1942. The Macmillan Company.
--Indian Encouters: An Anthology of Stories and Poems. Chapman, Frederick Trench (1887-), illus. LC 60-8544. 264p. illus. 22cm. (gr. 6-8). 1960. Macmillan.
--Indian Mound Farm. Rocker, Fermin (1907-), illus. LC 69-18234. (Illus.). 62 p. 22cm. 1969. Macmillan.
--Jock's Island. Obligado, Lilian Isabel (1931-), illus. LC 63-18371. (Illus.). 75 p. 24cm. 1963. Viking.
--Jon the Unlucky. 1st ed. Nesbitt, Esta (1918-), illus. LC 64-12339. (Illus.). 94 p. 23cm. 1964. Holt, Rinehart and Winston.
--The Kitten Stand. Keeler, Katherine Southwick (1887-), illus. LC 46-2193. 28 p. incl. col. front., illus. (part col.) 23 x 20 1/2 cm. (Story parade picture book). 1945. Grosset & Dunlap.
--Knock at the Door. Bedford, Francis Donkin (1864-1950), illus. 4 p. l., 73, 1 p. col. front., illus. 19 x 21 1/2 cm. 1931. The Macmillan Company.
--The Last Fort. Shenton, Edward (1895-), illus. (Land of the Free Ser.). 1953. Holt, Rinehart and Winston.
--Last Fort. Shenton, Edward (1895-), illus. LC 52-5499. (Illus.). 250p. (Land of the Free Ser). (gr. 5-7). 1952. (ISBN 0-03-035580-X). HR&W.
--Lighthouse Island. Shimin, Symeon (1902-), illus. LC 67-18681. (Illus.). 62 p. 24cm. 1968. W. W. Norton.
--The Little Haymakers. Paull, Grace A. (1898-), illus. LC 49-50063. 79 p. illus. 21 cm. 1949. Macmillan.
--The Littlest House. 1967. MacMillan Company.
--The Littlest House. Davis, Marguerite (1889-), illus. LC 40-27309. 150, 2 p. incl. front., illus. 21 cm. 1940. The Macmillan Company.
--Lonely Maria. Ness, Evaline Michelow, Mrs. (1911-), illus. LC 60-4715. unpaged. illus. 22cm. 1960. Pantheon Books.
--Lucky Ones: Five Journeys Toward a Home. Doyle, Janet, illus. LC 68-20612. (Illus.). 12 b & w ils. 96p. (gr. 4-6). 1968. (ISBN 0-02-722630-1). Macmillan.
--Marra's World. Turska, Krystyna Zofia (1933-), illus. LC 75-9520. (Illus.). 83 p. 22cm. 1975. (ISBN 0-688-80007-6). (ISBN 0-688-84007-8). Greenwillow Books.
--Mountain Bride: An Incredible Tale. Thompson, George William (1925-), illus. 1954. Pantheon Books Inc.
--Mouse Chorus. Vaughan-Jackson, Genevieve (1913-), illus. LC 55-14821. (Illus.). unpaged. 20cm. 1955. Pantheon.
--Night and the Cat. Foujita, Taugouharu (1886-), illus. LC 50-10240. 55 p. illus. 25 cm. 1950. Macmillan.
--The Noble Doll. Politi, Leo (1908-), illus. LC 61-11676. (Illus.). 45 p. 25cm. 1961. Viking Press.
--Old Whirlwind: A Story of Davy Crockett. Lee, Manning de Villeneuve (1894-1980), illus. LC 53-12226. 64p. illus. 21cm. (Her Once-upon-a-time-in-America series, 5). 1953. Macmillan.
--The Peaceable Kingdom, and Other Poems. Eichenberg, Fritz (1901-), illus. LC 57-10238. unpaged. iluus. 16x24cm. c.1958. (ISBN 0-394-81484-3). Pantheon Books.
--The Peddler's Cart. Gay, Zhenya (1906-1978), illus. LC 56-7295. (Illus.). 151 p. 21cm. 1956. Macmillan.
--Pika and the Roses. Wiese, Kurt (1887-1974), illus. LC 59-671527. (Illus.). 32 p. 19cm. c.1959. Pantheon.
--The Place. Auerbach, Marjorie Hoffberg (1932-), illus. LC 65-10318. 72p. col. illus. 23cm. (gr. 4-6). 1966, c.1965. (ISBN 0-03-048480-4). Holt.
--Plum Daffy Adventure. Davis, Marguerite (1889-), illus. LC 47-301460. 161, 1 p., l., incl. front., illus. 21 x 16 cm. 1947. The Macmillan Company.
--Poems. 1968. MacMillan Publishing Company.
--Poems. Guthrie, Vee, illus. (Illus.). (gr. 4-6). 1957. (ISBN 0-02-721490-7). Macmillan.
--The Princess and the Lion. Ness, Evaline Michelow, Mrs. (1911-), illus. LC 62-21608. 77 p. illus. 22 cm. 1963. Pantheon. **Award: (ALA).**
--Pure Magic. Fetz, Ingrid (1915-), illus. LC 72-92435. (Illus.). 68 p. 22cm. 1973. (ISBN 0-02-721500-8). Macmillan.
--Ronnie and the Chief's Son. 1967. MacMillan Publishing company.
--Ronnie & the Chief's Son. Martin, Stefan (1936-), illus. LC 62-10637. (Illus.). (gr. 4-6). 1962. (ISBN 0-02-721600-4). Macmillan.
--The Secret. Bolognese, Donald Alan (1934-), illus. LC 64-17376. (Illus.). 31 p. 27cm. 1965. Macmillan.
--Silky: An Incredible Tale. Carroll, John, illus. 1953. Pantheon Books Inc.
--The Snow Parlor, and Other Bedtime Stories. Robinson, Charles (1931-), illus. LC 74-153923. (Illus.). 64 p. 24cm. 1971. (ISBN 0-448-21416-4). (ISBN 0-448-26186-3). Grosset & Dunlap.
--Sod House. 1967. MacMillan Publishing Company.
--The Sod House. Lee, Manning de Villeneuve (1894-1980), illus. LC 54-12898. (Illus.). 64 p. 21cm. 1954. Macmillan.
--Sparrow Bush. (gr. 4-6). N.D. G&D.
--The Sparrow Bush: Rhymes. Martin, Stefan (1936-), illus. LC 66-10787. 63p. illus. 24cm. c.1966. Norton.
--Summer Green. Unwin, Nora Spicer (1907-), illus. 1948. Macmillan.
--The Sun's Diary. (Poetry, Music & Art). (MacMillan Bks. for Boys & Girls). (gr. 4-6). N.D. MacMillan Bks.
--Sword of the Wilderness. Stein, Harve (1904-), illus. LC 36-221907. xii p., 1 l., 160 p. incl. front., illus. 21 cm. 1936. The Macmillan Company.
--Sword of Wilderness. 1967. MacMillan Publishing company.
--They Walk in the Night. 1st ed. Martin, Stefan (1936-), illus. LC 68-22727. (Illus.). 60 p. 1969. Norton.
--Thief Island. Wonsetler, John Charles (1900-), illus. LC 43-16555. 4 p. l., 118 p. illus. 21 cm. 1943. The Macmillan Company.
--A Toast to the King. Orr, Forrest W., illus. 1940. Coward-McCann, Inc.
--Tonio and the Stranger: A Mexican Adventure. Bronson, Wilfrid Swancourt (1894-), illus. LC 41-4720. 4 p. l., 3-69 p. incl. front., illus. 21 x 16 cm. (story parade adventure book). c.1941. Grosset & Dunlap.
--Toutou in Bondage. Handforth, Thomas Schofield (1897-1948), illus. LC 29-18666. 5 p. l., 56, 1 p. incl. illus., double plates. front. 22 1/2 cm. 1929. The Macmillan Company.
--Troll Weather. Arndt, Ursula, illus. LC 66-9612. (Illus.). 41 p. 22cm. 1967. Macmillan Co.
--Trudy and the Tree House. Davis, Marguerite (1889-), illus. LC 44-4327. 5 p. l., 113, 1 p. incl. front., illus. 21 cm. 1944. The Macmillan Company.
--Twelve Months Make a Year. Davis, Marguerite (1889-), illus. LC 43-6820. 198, 2 p. col. illus. 21 x 16 1/2 cm. 1943. The Macmillan Company.
--Under the Green Willow. Domanska, Janina, illus. LC 84-1471. (Illus.). 7 7/16 x 6 1/8. 24p. (14 pt.). (Anniversary). (gr. k-3). 1984, c.1971. (ISBN 0-688-03845-X). (ISBN 0-688-03846-8). Greenwillow.
--Under the Green Willow. Domanska, Janina, illus. LC 73-123131. (Illus.). color ils. 24p. (gr. k-2). 1971. (ISBN 0-02-722600-X). Macmillan.
--Up Hill and Down: Stories. 1st ed. Davis, James H., illus. LC 47-31436. 188 p. illus. 21 cm. 1947. A. A. Knopf.
--The Wanderers. Hyman, Trina Schart (1939-), illus. LC 70-182114. (Illus.). 112 p. 24cm. 1972. Four Winds Press.
--The Were-fox. Orig. Title: Pure Magic. 1973. MacMillan Publishing Company.
--The Were-Fox. Fetz, Ingrid (1915-), illus. LC 74-20675. p. cm. 1975. (ISBN 0-02-042760-3). Collier Books.
--The White Horse. Sewell, Helen Moore (1896-1957), illus. LC 42-21438. 6 p. l., 164 p. front., illus. 23 1/2 cm. 1942. The Macmillan Company.
--The Wishing Pear. 1966. MacMillan Publishing Company.
--The Wishing Pear. Ray, Ralph (1920-1952), illus. LC 51-13514. 64 p. illus. 21 cm. 1951. Macmillan.
--The Wonderful Day. Sewell, Helen Moore (1896-1957), illus. LC 46-3639. xiii, 126 p. incl. front., illus. 23 1/2 cm. 1946. The Macmillan Company.
--You Say You Saw a Camel!. Turkle, Brinton Cassaday (1915-), illus. LC 59-295. 23cm. 72p. 1958. Row Peterson.
--You Shall Have a Carriage. Pitz, Henry Clarence (1895-1976), illus. LC 41-178782. 4 p. l., 138 p., 1 l. front., illus. 21 cm. 1941. The Macmillan Company.

Coatsworth, Elizabeth Jane (1893-), ed.

--The Giant Golden Book of Cat Stories. Rojankovsky, Feodor Stepanovich (1891-1970), illus. LC 53-132729. 66p. illus. 33cm. (Giant golden book, 572). 1953. Simon and Schuster.
--The Giant Golden Book of Dog Stories. Rojankovsky, Feodor Stepanovich (1891-1970), illus. LC 53-434953. 66p. illus. 33cm. (Giant golden book, 578). 1953. Simon and Schuster.

Coatsworth, Elizabeth Jane (1893-) & Barnes, Kate, eds.

--The Giant Golden Book of Dogs, Cats, and Houses: 61 Stories and Poems. Rojankovsky, Feodor Stepanovich (1891-1970), illus. LC 57-1326. 124p. illus. 33cm. (Gaint golden book, 699). 1957. Simon and Schuster.

--Horse Stories. Rojankovsky, Feodor Stepanovich (1891-1970), illus. (Big Golden Book). 1954. Golden Press.

Coatsworth, Emerson S. see Snake, Sam.

Cobalt, Martin

--Pool of Swallows. LC 73-17033. 139 p. 21cm. 1974. (ISBN 0-8407-6387-5). T. Nelson.

Cobb, Alice, jt. auth. see Fahs, Sophia Blanche Lyon, Mrs.

Cobb, Alice (1909-)

--Come to Shanta Bhawan. Hutchinson, William Miller (1916-), illus. LC 63-8689. 142 p. illus. 21 cm. 1963. Friendship Press.

--Raising Cane on Huckleberry. Hutchinson, William Miller (1916-), illus. LC 59-6040. 137p. illus. 21cm. 1959. Friendship Press.

--The Swimming New York. LC 57-6166. 127p. illus. 20cm. 1957. Friendship Press.

--The Swimming Pool. LC 57-6166. 127p. illus. 20cm. 1957. Friendship Press.

Cobb, Alma French

--When I Was a Gay, Wee Child. Cobb, Alma French, illus. LC 43-3199. viii p., 1 l., 11-55 p. illus. 20 cm. c.1942. The Kaleidograph Press.

Cobb, Andy, pseud., see Russell, Marie.

Cobb, Ann

--Kinfolks: Kentucky Mountain Rhymes. N.D. Houghton Mifflin.

Cobb, Benjamin Franklin (1844-)

--Yankee Mother Goose. (Illus.). 1910. Hurst & Co.

--Yankee Mother Goose. Brison, Ella S., illus. LC 2-22416. 88p. col. illus. 26 1/2 x 22 1/2cm. 1902. Jamieson-Higgins.

Cobb, Bertha Browning Barnes, Mrs. (1867-1951) & Cobb, Ernest (1877-)

--Adam Lee. Doane, Lucy, illus. 325p. (gr. 6). N.D. G P Putnam's Sons.

--Adam Lee. Doane, Lucy, illus. LC 38-6690. 324, 1 p. incl. front., 1 illus., plates, map. pl. 17 1/2 cm. c.1938. The Arlo Publishing Company.

--Allspice. Bridgman, Lewis Jesse (1857-1931), illus. 220p. N.D. G. P. Putnam's Sons.

--Allspice: The Adventures of Daddy Fox, Ginger Bear, the Miller and the Miller's Wife. Bridgman, Lewis Jesse (1857-1931), illus. LC 25-4067. 5 p. l., 220 p. incl. front., plates. 17 1/2 cm. c.1925. The Arlo Publishing Company.

--Andre. 274p. N.D. G. P. Putnam's Sons.

--Andre. Bridgman, Lewis Jesse (1857-1931), illus. LC 30-9461. 4 p. l., 274 p. front., plates. 17 1/2 cm. c.1930. The Arlo Publishing Company.

--Anita. 285p. (gr. 6). N.D. G P Putnam's Sons.

--Anita: A Story of the Rocky Mountains. 4 p. l., 285 p. col. front., illus., plates (part col.) 19 1/2 cm. c.1920. Lothrop, Lee & Shepard Co.

--Anita: A Story of the Rocky Mountains. Pettibone, Anita & Bridgman, Lewis Jesse, illus. McClure, L. C., photos by. LC 20-18437. 1 p. l., 285 p. front., illus., plates. 17 1/2 cm. c.1920. The Arlo Publishing Company.

--Arlo. N.D. G. P. Putnam Sons.

--Clematis. LC 56-172276. 246p. illus. 18cm. 1955. Arlo Pub. Co.

--Clematis. N.D. G. P. Putnam's.

--Clematis. Cram, A. G. & Levis, Willis, illus. LC 17-30281. 4 p. l., 246 p. col. front., col. plates. 18 cm. c.1917. The Riverdale Press, Brookline.

--Dan's Boy. N.D. G. P. Putnam Sons.

--Dan's Boy. Bridgman, Jesse, illus. LC 26-2815. 4 p. l., 272 p. front., plates. 17 1/2 cm. c.1926. The Arlo Publishing Company.

--Pennie. N.D. G. P. Putnam Sons.

--Pennie. Bridgman, Lewis Jesse (1857-1931), illus. Parker, Mary Louise LC 28-26354. 4 p. l., 194 p. col. front., col. plates. 17 1/2 cm. c.1927. The Arlo Publishing Company.

--Robin. Doane, Lucy & Berry, K. W., illus. LC 34-4189. 4 p. l., 155 p. front., illus., plates. 19 cm. c.1934. G. P. Putnam's Sons.

Cobb, David

--The Adventures of Billy & Lilly, 4 bks. Incl. Dino the Dinosaur. (ISBN 0-582-53107-1); Football in Space. (ISBN 0-582-53106-3); Lilly's Flying Horse. (ISBN 0-582-53104-7); Tennis Star!. (ISBN 0-582-53105-5). (English As a Second Language Bk.). (gr. 1-5). 1981. Longman.

Cobb, Diane

--The Way Back. Cobb, Diane, illus. LC 72-87878. (Illus.). 78 p. 1972. Sufism Reoriented.

Cobb, Ernest, jt. auth. see Cobb, Bertha Browning Barnes, Mrs.

Cobb, Irvin Shrewsbury (1876-)

--Azam: The Story of an Arabian Colt and His Friends. N.D. Rand McNally & Co.

--Four Useful Pups. Blumenthal, M. U., illus. LC 40-10377. 34 p. illus. 21 x 19 cm. c.1940. Rand McNally & Company.

--From Place to Place. N.D. Grosset & Dunlap.

Cobb, James F.

--Martin the Skipper. (A Tale for Boys and Sea-faring Folks). N.D. Thomas Y. Crowell & Co.

--Martin the Skipper. N.D. Wells, Gardner, Darton & Co.'s.

--Off to California. N.D. Wells, Gardner, Darton & Co.'s.

--Silent Jim (Pub. by Society for Promoting Christian Knowledge). N.D. E. & J. b. young & Co.

--The Watchers on the Longships. (Illus.). 300p. N.D. T. Y. Crowell.

--Watchers On the Longships. N.D. Wells, Gardner, Darton & Co.'s.

Cobb, Lucy M & Hicks, Mary A.

--Animal Tales from the Old North State. Hogan, Inez (1895-), illus. LC 38-236265. 200 p. illus. 21 cm. 1938. E. P. Dutton & Co., Inc.

Cobb, Mabel

--Old Phoebe. Lewis, Claude Allen, illus. N.D. Beechhurst Press.

--Old Phoebe: The Story of an Elephant. Lewis, Claude Allen, illus. LC 46-18490. 128 p. incl. mounted col. front., illus plates. 23 1/2 cm. 1946. B. Ackerman, Inc.

Cobb, Mabel, jt. auth. see Lewis, Claude Allen.

Cobb, Mabel & Lewis, Claude Allen

--The Story of Pocahontas. LC 46-592. 1 p. l., 15, 1 p. col. illus. 28 1/2 cm. (Picfade series). c.1945. The American Crayon Company.

Cobb, Mary Coe

--The Secret Room. LC 53-672. 124p. 21cm. 1953. Meador Pub. Co.

Cobb, Meta R., jt. auth. see Stern, Edith Mendel, Mrs.

Cobb, Meta R. & Stern, Edith Mendel

--Joan Chooses Occupational Therapy. N.D. Dodd, Mead & Co.

Cobb, Sophia Dickinson

--Lucy's Lovers: Or, Hillsboro'farms,. LC 2953. 1 p. l., 5-423 p. 19 cm. (On cover: American girls' series). 1900. Lee and Shepard.

Cobb, Sylvanus, Jr.

--The Captive Bride. (The Eureka Detective Stories). N.D. J. S. Ogilvie Co.

--A Dark Plot. (The Eureka Detective Stories). N.D. J. S. Ogilvie Co.

--The Double Duel. (The Eureka Detective Stories). N.D. J. S. Ogilvie Co.

--The Gunmaker of Moscow. (Illus.). N.D. Caldwell.

--The King's Talisman. (The Eureka Detective Stories). N.D. J. S. Ogilvie Co.

Cobb, Winifred B.

--Brook Haven. (Illus.). (gr. 3-6). 1964. (ISBN 0-8111-0018-9). Naylor.

Cobban, Maclaren

--The Avenger of Blood. (Cassell's Popular Library of Fiction). N.D. Cassell's Popular Library of Ficton.

Cobbin, Ingram

--The Child's Story of The New Testament. (Illus.). (The Golden Day's Ser.). N.D. John C. Winston & Co.

Cobbin, Rev. Ingram

--Child's Story of the Gospel. (The Progressive Ser.). N.D. John C. Winston.

Cobble, Alice D

--Wembi, the Singer of Stories. Hallas, Doris, illus. LC 59-9700. 128p. illus. 22cm. (gr. 3-5). 1959. Bethany Press.

Cobbs, Price Mashaw, jt. auth. see Grier, William H.

Cobby, Maisie

--Jingles for Me to Play: I am Five. 24p. 1964. Pitman Publishing Corporation.

--Jingles for Me to Play: I am Seven. 24p. 1964. Pitman Publishing Corporation.

--Jingles for Me to Play: I am Six. 24p. 1964. Pitman Publishing Corporation.

--Rhymes for Me to Speak: I am six. 24p. 1964. Pitman Publishing Corporation.

--Sally on Holiday: Sally on the Farm. 63p. 1963. Pitman Publishing Corporation.

Cobden, Paul

--Going on a Mission, 1 of 6 vols. (Illus.). (Beckoning Ser.). 1882. Set. Lee & Shepard.

--Going on a Mission, 1 of 25 vols. (Illus.). (Pilgrim Ser. for Girls: No. 10). 1900. Lee & Shepard.

--Good Luck, 1 of 6 vols. (Illus.). (Beckoning Ser.). 1882. Lee & Shepard.

--Good Luck, 1 of 25 vols. (Illus.). (Pilgrim Ser. for Boys: No. 10). 1900. Lee & Shepard.

--Good Luck. LC 2-11145. 19cm. 218p. (Pilgrim Series for Boys, No. 10). (The Beckoning Ser.). 1901. Lee & Shepard.

--Little Lights Along the Shore. N.D. Bradley & Woodruff.

--Take a Peep, 1 0f 6 vols. (Illus.). (Beckoning Ser.). 1882. Lee & Shepard.

--Take a Peep, 1 of 25 vols. (Illus.). (Mayflower Ser. for Girls: No. 22). 1900. Lee & Shepard.

--Take a Peep. LC 2-22408. 19cm. 199p. (Mayflower Series for Girls, No. 22). (The Beckoning Ser.). 1902. Lee & Shepard.

--The Turning Wheel, 1 of 25 vols. (Illus.). (Pilgrim Ser. for Boys: No. 21). 1900. Lee & Shepard.

--The Turning Wheel, 1 of 6 vols. (Illus.). (Beckoning Ser.). N.D. Set. Lee & Shepard.

--Who Will Win?, 1 0f 6 vols. (Illus.). (Beckoning Ser.). 1882. Lee & Shepard.

Cober, Mary E.

--Remarkable History of Tony Beaver. Hayes, William Dimitt (1913-), illus. (Illus.). (gr. 5-7). 1968. (ISBN 0-679-25118-9). McKay.

Coble, Harold H.

--Man: Responsible & Caring. LC 77-75765. 1977. (ISBN 0-8054-5625-2). Broadman.

Coblentz, Catherine Cate, Mrs. (1897-1951)

--Animal Pioneers. Wiese, Kurt (1887-1974), illus. LC 36-22843. xii p., 2 l., 3-241 p. incl. front., illus., plates. 21 cm. 1936. Little, Brown, and Company.

--The Beggar's Penny. N.D. Longmans Green & Co.

--The Beggars' Penny. 1943. McKay.

--The Beggars' Penny. Van Stockum, Hilda Gerarda (1908-), illus. LC 43-151812. ix p., 1 l., 269 p. incl. front., illus. map. 23 1/2 cm. 1943. Longmans, Green and Co.

--The Bells of Leyden Sing. Van Stockum, Hilda Gerarda (1908-), illus. LC 44-7483. xi, 259 p. incl. fronts., illus. 21 1/2 cm. 1944. Longmans, Green and Co.

--The Blue and Silver Necklace. Earle, Edwin (1887-1974), illus. LC 37-341751. xiii p., 2 l., 3-242 p. incl. front., illus., plates. 21 cm. 1937. Little, Brown and Company.

--The Blue Cat of Castle Town. Holland, Janice (1913-1962), illus. LC 74-14930. (Illus.). 123 p. 23cm. 1974, c.1949. (ISBN 0-914378-05-8). Countryman Press.

--The Blue Cat of Castle Town. Holland, Janice (1913-1962), illus. 1983. Countryman.

--The Blue Cat of Castle Town. 1st ed. Holland, Janice (1913-1962), illus. LC 49-9614. 123 p. illus. 24 cm. 1949. Longmans, Green. **Award: (JNM).**

--The Falcon of Eric the Red. Pitz, Henry Clarence (1895-1976), illus. LC 42-36271. xi, 211 p. incl. front., illus., plates (part double) 22 1/2 cm. 1942. Longmans, Green and Co.

--Martin and Abraham Lincoln, Based on a True Incident. Engelbrecht, Trientja (1925-), illus. LC 47-4516. 24 p. col. illus. 24 cm. 1947. Childrens Press.

--Martin and Abraham Lincoln: Based on a True Incident. Engelbrecht, Trientja (1925-), illus. LC 47-4516. 24p. col. illus. 24cm. (gr. 2-6). 1967, c.1947. (ISBN 0-516-03545-2). Childrens.

--Scatter, the Chipmunk. Schwartz, Berta (1922-), illus. LC 46-3913. 25 p. col. illus. 23 1/2 x 18 1/2 cm. 1946. Childrens Press, Inc.

Coblentz, Stanton Arthur (1896-)

--Aesop's Fables. Syverson, Henry, illus. LC 67-29313. (Illus.). 87 p. 21cm. 1968. C. R. Gibson Co.

--The Wonder Stick. Glanckoff, Samuel (1894-), illus. LC 29-22397. vi p., 2 l., 309 p. front., plates. 19 1/2 cm. 1929. Cosmopolitan Book Corporations.

Coburn, Alvin Langdon, jt. auth. see Bantock, Granville, Sir.

Coburn, Claire Martha (1876-)

--Our Little Swedish Cousin. Bridgman, Lewis Jesse (1857-1931) & Woodberry, R. C., illus. LC 6-29041. vii p., 2 l., 109 p. front., 5 pl. 20 cm. 1906. L. C. Page & Company.

Coburn, Jewell Reinhart

--Encircled Kingdom: Legends and Folktales of Laos. Ullberg, Nena Grigorian, illus. LC 79-53838. (Illus.). 80 p., 2 p. of plates. 29cm. c.1979. (ISBN 0-918060-03-6). Burn, Hart.

Coburn, Jewell Reinhart, ed. see Duong, Van Quyen.

Coburn, Jewell Reinhart & Ullberg, Nena Grigorian

--Khmers, Tigers, and Talismans: From the History and Legends of Mysterious Cambodia. Ullberg, Nena Grigorian, illus. LC 77-14887. (Illus.). 93 p. 24cm. c.1978. (ISBN 0-918060-02-8). Burn, Hart.

Coburn, John Bowen (1914-)

--Anne and the Sand Dobbies: A Story About Death for Children and Their Parents. LC 64-24917. 121 p. 22 cm. 1964. Seabury Press.

Coburn, Oliver, tr. see Kruss, James.

Coburn, Walt (1889-)

--Stirrup High. Santee, Ross (1889-1965), illus. Gipson, Frederick Benjamin (1908-1973), intro. by. LC 57-11499. 190p. illus. 22cm. 1957. J. Messner.

Cocagnac, Augustine Maurice-Jean (1924-)

--Three Trees of the Samurai. LeFoll, Alain, illus. (Illus.). (gr. k up). 1970. (ISBN 0-531-04018-6). (ISBN 0-531-05018-1). Quist.

Cochran, Charlie Price

--Ridin' Down-N-Texas-Mebbe Round the World. (Illus.). (gr. 4-7). N.D. (ISBN 0-8181-0097-4). Pageant-Poseidon.

Cochran, Hamilton (1898-1977)

--Buccaneer Islands. Gay, Zhenya (1906-1978), illus. LC 41-16894. 3 p. l., 249 p. incl. front. (map) illus. 21 1/2 cm. 1941. T. Nelson & Sons.

--Pirates of the Spanish Main. Nesmith, Robert I, ed. (Illus.). (American Heritage Junior Library). 1961. Harper & Row Publishers.

Cochran, Louis

--The Story of the Lowly Gnome: When the Sea King's Daughter Came Out of the Sea; How the Red Rose Came to Be Red. LC 29-144031. 72 p. 21 cm. c.1929. Dorrance and Company.

Cochran, Martha Conney (1870-)

--Fur, Feathers and Fun: A Book for Children. Fernald, Anne, illus. LC 46-947. 62p. illus. 23 1/2cm. 1946, c.1945. Carleton Printing Co.

Cochran, Ruth Gilbert see Gilbert, Celia, pseud.

Cochran, Ruth Gilbert (1893-)

--Day Dale in "A Lady of High Degree". Gilbert, Celia, pseud. Rodgers, Richard H. (1876-1953), illus. LC 31-14193. (Lettered on Cover Day Dale in the Movies). 214 p. incl. front. 19 1/2 cm. c.1931. Barse & Co.

--Day Dale in "South Sea Siren". Gilbert, Celia, pseud. Rodgers, Richard H. (1876-1953), illus. LC 31-14192. 213 p. incl. front. 19 1/2 cm. c.1931. Barse & Co.

Cochrane, Louise Morley (1918-)

--Tabletop Theatres. Simunek, Kate, illus. LC 73-8348. (Illus.). 48 p. 25cm. 1st U.S. edition. 1974, c.1973. (ISBN 0-8238-0155-1). Plays, Inc.

Cock Robin

--The Courtship and Wedding of Cock Robin and Jenny Wren. Weir, Harrison William (1824-1906), illus. LC 51-54222. (With an account of the Doleful death of Cock Robin). 16p. col. illus. 19cm. 1951. Sheldon Blakeman.

--The Courtship, Merry Marriage, and Feast of Cock Robin and Jenny Wren, to Which is Added the Doleful Death of Cock Robin. Cooney, Barbara (1917-), illus. LC 65-17531. 1v.(unpaged) col. illus. 16x22cm. c.1965. Scribners. **Award: (ALA).**

--The Marriage of Cock & Jenny Wren. LC 57-34673. 20p. illus. 16cm. 1957, c.1956. University of Kentucky: Dist. by High Noon Press.

--The Old Story of Poor Cock Robin. Duffield, Kenneth Graham, ed. LC 20-20553. 62p., l. incl. col. front. illus. 14 1/2cm. c.1920. Altemus Co.

--The Story of Cock Robin. LC 80-492808. (Illus.). 4 p., 6 leaves of plates. 19cm. (Familiar Series). N.D. McLoughlin Bros.

Cocke, M. Ritchie Harrison

--Tales My Grandmother Told Me. 1953. The Dietz Press.

Cocke, Sarah Johnson, Mrs.

--Bypaths in Dixie: Folk Tales of the South. LC 11-257417. 316, 1 p. front., illus., plates. 21 cm. c.1911. E. P. Dutton & Company.

--Bypaths in Dixie: Folk Tales of the South. Edwards, Harry Stillwell, intro. by. LC 72-6501. (Illus.). 316 p. 22cm. (The Black Heritage Library Collection). 1972. (ISBN 0-8369-9164-8). Books for Libraries Press.

--Old Mammy Tales from Dixie Land. Edwards, Harry Stillwell, intro. by. 338 p. front., illus. (music) plates. 21 cm. N.D. E. P. Dutton & Company.

Cocke, Zitella

--The Grasshopper's Hop. (Illus.). (Editha Ser.). N.D. Caldwell.

--The Grasshopper's Hop and other Verses. Mora, Joseph Jacinto (1876-), illus. LC 1-11741. 12cm. 113p. 1901. Dana Estes & Co.

Cockefair, Ada Milam, jt. auth. see Cockefair, Edgar Augustus.

Cockefair, Edgar Augustus & Cockefair, Ada Milam

--The Story of You. LC 55-30999. unpaged. illus. 25cm. c.1955. Milam Publications.

Cockett, Mary

--Ash Dry, Ash Green. Stanley, Diana (1909-), illus. LC 68-15234. (Illus.). 64 p. 22cm. 1st U.S. edition. 1968, c.1966. Criterion Books.

--Look at the Little One. Palmer, Margaret, illus. LC 75-42224. (Illus.). 24 p. 21cm. 1976, c.1974. (ISBN 0-516-03585-1). Childrens Press.

--Magic and Gold: Tales from Northern Europe. 1st ed. Kesteven, Peter, illus. LC 78-79868. (Illus.). 69 p. 21cm. (The Pergamon English Library). 1970. Pergamon Press.

--Pelican Park. Francis, Frank, illus. LC 69-10775. (Illus.). 33 p. 30cm. 1969. F. Warne.

--Rosanna the Goat. Brown, Judith Gwyn (1933-), illus. LC 75-119006. (Illus.). 62 p. 21cm. 1970. Bobbs-Merrill.

--Snake in the Camp. Beales, Joan, illus. LC 75-41376. (Illus.). 23 p. 21cm. (Stepping stones). 1976, c.1975. (ISBN 0-516-03592-4). Childrens Press.

--Tower Raven. Launder, Sally, illus. (gr. 2-5). 1976. (ISBN 0-8277-4812-4). British Bk Ctr.

Cockrell, Emma Baldwin, Mrs.

--Kodak Sketches of Two Little Girls: A Story Book for Children. LC 19-16. 167 p. 8cm. 1900. The Idea Co.

Cockrell, Marian Brown (1909-)

--Revolt of Sarah Perkins. 1969. (ISBN 0-679-50272-6). McKay.

--Shadow Castle. Bailey, Olive, illus. LC 45-740846. 3 p. l., 122 p. col. front., illus. 23 cm. 1945. Whittlesey House, McGraw-Hill Book Company, Inc.

Codd, Carol

--Chooki and the Ptarmigan. Codd, Michael, illus. LC 76-27178. (Illus.). 32 p. 24cm. 1976. (ISBN 0-8027-6278-6). Walker.

Codrington, F. J.

--Bring-Brother: One of the Children-in-Blue from the Town of Lone Bamboo. N.D. Macmillan.

Codrington, Florence Isabel (1867-)

--Chopsticks. Jacobs, Helen M., et al., illus. (True Or Might-Be-True Stories). 1929. MacMillan Bks.

Cody, Grace Ethelwyn

--Elinor's Junior Hop. LC 11-23897. 5 p. l., 292 p., 1 l. col. front., col. plates. 20 cm. $1.50. 1911. D. Appleton and Company.

--Jacquette, a Sorority Girl. Post, Charles Johnson, illus. LC 8-3429. 6 p. l., 300 p. front., 5 pl. 17 1/2 cm. 1908. Duffield & Company.

Cody, Hiram Alfred

--The Fighting-Slogan. LC 26-15404. viii, 2, 11-285 p. 19 1/2 cm. c.1926. George H. Doran Company.

--Rod of the Lone Patrol. LC 16-21705. 348 p. 20 cm. c.1916. George H. Doran Company.

Cody, Sherwin (1868-1959)

--Four American Poets: William Cullen Bryant, Henry Wadsworth Longfellow, John Greenleaf Whittier, Oliver Wendell Holmes : a Book for Young Americans. LC 78-4033. (Illus.). 254 p. 23cm. (The Four Great Americans Ser.: No. 4). 1978, c.1899. (ISBN 0-8482-3506-1). Norwood Editions.

Cody, W. F.

--Adventures of Buffalo Bill. N.D. Harper & Bros.

Coe, Douglas, pseud., see Epstein, Beryl Williams.

Coe, Douglas, pseud. (1910-)

--The Burma Road. Epstein, Beryl Williams. Hoskins, Winfied, illus. LC 46-5738. 192 p. incl. front. (map) illus. 21 cm. 1946. J. Messner Inc.

Coe, Fanny E

--The First Book of Stories for the Story-Teller. LC 10-7955. xiii, 222 p., 1 l. 18 cm. c.1910. Houghton Mifflin Company.

--The Second Book of Stories for the Story-Teller. LC 13-9795. xiv, 209, 1 p. 18 cm. c.1913. Houghton Mifflin Company.

--The Second Book of Stories for the Story-Teller. 22cm. 209p. 1919. Houghton Mifflin Co.

Coe, Fanny E., ed. see Alcott, Louisa May.

Coe, Frederick Levi (1883-)

--Graven with Flint. Hallock, Robert, illus. LC 50-13164. (Illus.). 150 p. 21cm. 1950. Crowell.

--Knight of the Cross: A Story of the Crusades. King, Robin, pseud. (1919-), illus. Raleigh-King, Robin Victor Lethbridge. LC 51-11488. (Illus.). 245 p. 22cm. 1951. Sloane.

--Knight of the Cross: A Story of the Crusades. King, Robin, pseud. (1919-), illus. Raleigh-King, Robin Victor Lethbridge. N.D. William Morrow & Co.

Coe, Joyce

--The Donkey Who Served the King. (Illus.). (Arch Bk. Ser.: No. 15). (gr. k-3). 1978. (ISBN 0-570-06120-2). Concordia.

Coe, Lloyd (1899-1976)

--Boku and the Sound. Coe, Lloyd (1899-1976), illus. 32p. 1950. Thomas Y. Crowell.

--Boku and the Sound. Coe, Lloyd (1899-1976), illus. LC 53-8409. (Illus.). 32p. 1954. Thomas Y. Crowell Company.

--Charcoal. Coe, Lloyd (1899-1976), illus. LC 46-3214. 32 p. illus. (part col.) 17 x 26 cm. 1946. Thomas Y. Crowell Company.

Coe, R., Miss

--Leila Among The Mountains. N.D. Bradley & Woodruff.

Coe, Richard

--Crocodile. Howard, Alan (1922-), illus. (Illus.). (gr. 4-6). N.D. (ISBN 0-571-05985-6). Transatlantic.

Coen, Fabio

--The Redcomb and the Fox. Peltzer, Remi, illus. LC 79-635. p. cm. c.1979. (ISBN 0-394-84239-1). (ISBN 0-394-94239-6). Knopf.

Coen, Fabio, tr. see Despois, Pauline.

Coen, Fabio, tr. see Grimm, Jakob Ludwig Karl (1785-1863) & Grimm, Wilhelm Karl.

Coen, Fabio, tr. see Perrault, Charles.

Coerr, Eleanor, pseud., see Hicks, Eleanor B..

Coerr, Eleanor Beatrice (1922-)

--The Bell Ringer & the Pirates. Sandin, Joan (1942-), illus. LC 82-47700. (Illus.). 5 7/8 x 8 1/2. (18 pt.). (I Can Read Bks.). (gr. k-3). 1983. (ISBN 0-06-021354-X). (ISBN 0-06-021355-8). Har-Row.

--The Big Balloon Race. Croll, Carolyn, illus. LC 80-8368. p. cm. (I can read history book). c.1981. (ISBN 0-06-021352-3). (ISBN 0-06-021353-1). Harper & Row.

--The Mixed-up Mystery Smell. De Paola, Tomie, pseud. (1934-), illus. De Paola, Thomas Anthony. LC 75-20353. (Illus.). 45 p. 22cm. (see and read book). 1976. (ISBN 0-399-60957-1). Putnam.

--The Mystery of the Golden Cat. LC 68-13871. (Illus.). 68 p. 27cm. 1968. C. E. Tuttle Co.

--Twenty-Five Dragons. Daley, Joann, illus. LC 75-121412. (Illus.). 95 p. 23cm. 1971. (ISBN 0-695-80179-1). Follett.

--Waza Wins at Windy Gulch. McCaffery, Janet, illus. LC 76-21224. (Illus.). 44 p. 23cm. (See and read storybook). c.1977. Putnam.

Coffey, Brian

--Abecedarian. Hill, Sandra, illus. LC 77-359350. (Illus.). 30 p. 22cm. 1974. (ISBN 0-9500639-1-6). Advent Books.

Coffey, Helen Dairine (1933-), compiled by.

--The Dark Tower. (Illus.). 1967. (ISBN 0-689-20064-1). Atheneum Publishers.

--The Dark Tower: Nintenth Century Narrative Poems. LC 78-74508. (Illus.). Repr. of 1967 ed. (Children's Literature Reprint Ser.). (gr. 5 up). 1979. (ISBN 0-8486-0008-8). Core Collection.

Coffin, Charles Carleton (1823-1896)

--The Boys of '61. (Illus.). (Our Boy's Library). N.D. Dana Estes & Co.

--The Boys of '61: Or, Four Years of Fighting. New ed. (Illus.). (Charles Carleton Coffin's Famous War Stories). N.D. Dana Estes & Co.

--The Boys of '76. New ed. 419p. N.D. Harper & Bros.

--The Boys of '76. abr. new ed. Johnson, Charles F., ed. Roberts, Liam, illus. (Illus.). 320p. (gr. 5 up). N.D. (ISBN 0-87955-816-4). (ISBN 0-87955-216-6). O'Hara.

--Dan of Millbrook. (Illus.). N.D. Estes & Lauriat's.

--Dan of Millbrook: Author of "Boys of '61", "Winning His Way". Merrill, Frank Thayer (1848-), illus. N.D. Dana Estes and Company.

--Following the Flag. (Author of "The Boys of '76," "The Story of Liberty," "Our New Way 'Round the World" and "Boys of '61."). (The Carleton Series of Juveniles). N.D. Estes & Lauriat's.

--Following the Flag. N.D. James R. Osgood.

--Following the Flag. N.D. L. C. Page & Co.

--Four Years of Fighting. N.D. James R. Osgood.

--My Days & Nights on the Battlefield, 1 of 3 vols. (Illus.). (Carleton's Famous War Stories). N.D. Dana Estes & Co.

--My Days and Nights on the Battlefield. (Author of "The Boys of '76," "The Story of Liberty," "Our New Way 'Round the World" and "Boys of '61."). (The Carleton Series of Juveniles). N.D. Estes & Lauriat's.

--My Days and Nights on the Battlefield. N.D. James R. Osgood.

--My Days and Nights on the Battlefield. N.D. Page Co.

--Our New Way Round the World. N.D. James R. Osgood.

--Winning His Way. (Illus.). (The Rugby Ser.). N.D. A. L. Burt.

--Winning His Way. (Author of "The Boy of '76," "The Story of Liberty," "Our New Way 'Round the World" and "Boys of '61."). (The Carleton Series of Juveniles). N.D. Estes & Lauriat's.

--Winning His Way. N.D. James R. Osgood.

--Winning His Way. N.D. Page Co.

Coffin, Lewis & Long, Manning (1906-)

--The Fog Boat. Miret, Gil, illus. LC 57-11651. 128p. illus. 24cm. 1957. Lothrop, Lee Shepard.

Coffin, Patricia (1912-1974)

--The Gruesome Green Witch. Parnall, Peter (1936-), illus. LC 69-13168. (Illus.). 85 p. 25cm. 1969. Walker.

Coffin, Rebecca Jane, jt. ed. see Tchaika, Florence Esther Matthews, Mrs.

Coffin, Rebecca Jane & Hughes, Avah Willyn, eds.

--Picture Scripts. LC 37-279. v. illus. 16-22 cm. c.1935. E. Stern & Co., Inc.

Coffin, Roland F.

--An Old Sailor's Yarn: Tales of Many Seas. N.D. Funk & Wagnalls Co.

Coffman, Ramon, jt. ed. see Pape, Frank Cheyne.

Cogancherry, Helen, jt. auth. see Wright, Betty Ren.

Coggee, Jessie McGuire

--Rabbit Foot for Luck. Stevens, Mary E. (1920-1966), illus. LC 55-14813. 190p. illus. 22cm. 1955. Abingdon Press.

Coggins, Carolyn, jt. auth. see Holt, Jack.

Coggins, Herbert Leonard

--Busby & Co. Duvoisin, Roger Antoine (1904-1980), illus. LC 52-6010. 96 p. illus. 22 cm. 1952. Whittlesey House.

--I Am a Mouse. Brook, Judy (1926-), illus. LC 59-6671. (Illus.). 117 p. 21cm. 1959. Abelard-Schuman.

Coggins, Herbert Leonard, jt. auth. see Holt, Jack.

Coggins, Jack Banham (1914-)

--The Illustrated Book of Knights. Coggins, Jack Banham (1914-), illus. LC 57-14031. (Illus.). 105 p. 28cm. c.1957. Grosset & Dunlap.

--Young Viking. Coggins, Jack Banham (1914-), illus. (gr. 4-6). 1973 (Starline). Schol Bk Serv.

Coggins, Jack & Pratt, Fletcher (1897-1956)

--By Space Ship to the Moon. LC 58-10631. 56p. illus. 29cm. c.1958. Random House.

Coggins, Paschal Heston see Marlow, Sidney, pseud.

Coghill, Anne Louise Walker see Walker, Annie L., Miss.

Coghlan, W. E.

--St. George's Key, 1 of 16 Vols. (Illus.). (Warne's Incident and Adventure Library: No. 7). N.D. Scribner & Welford.

Cogswell, Coralie Norris see Howard, Coralie, pseud.

Cogswell, Frederick, jt. ed. see Lower, Thelma.

Cohen, Aaron, jt. auth. see Lindsay, Ann.

Cohen, Anthea (1913-)

--The Green Girl. (gr. 7 up). 1978. (ISBN 0-590-05371-X, Schol Pap). Scholastic Inc.

Cohen, Barbara (1932-)

--Benny. LC 77-242. 154 p. c.1977. (ISBN 0-688-41804-X). (ISBN 0-688-51804-4). Lothrop, Lee & Shepard.

--The Binding of Isaac. Mikolaycak, Charles (1937-), illus. LC 77-90367. (Illus.). 32 p. 22cm. c.1978. (ISBN 0-688-41830-9). (ISBN 0-688-51830-3). Lothrop Lee & Shepard.

--Bitter Herbs and Honey. LC 76-18132. p. cm. c.1976. (ISBN 0-688-41772-8). (ISBN 0-688-51772-2). Lothrop, Lee & Shepard.

--The Carp in the Bathtub. Halpern, Joan, illus. LC 72-1079. (Illus.). 26 cm. 48p. 1972. Lothrop, Lee, and Shepard Co.

--The Demon Who Would Not Die. Ivanov, Anatoly, illus. LC 82-1739. p. cm. 1982. (ISBN 0-689-30917-1). Atheneum.

--Fat Jack. LC 80-12510. p. cm. 1980. (ISBN 0-689-30772-1). Atheneum.

--Gooseberries to Oranges. 1st ed. Brodsky, Beverly, illus. LC 81-5774. (Illus.). 31 p. 26cm. c.1982. (ISBN 0-688-00690-6). (ISBN 0-688-00691-4). Lothrop, Lee & Shepard. **Award: (ALA).**

--Here Come the Purim Players!. Brodsky, Beverly, illus. LC 83-14878. 1984. (ISBN 0-688-02106-9). Lothrop.

--I Am Joseph. Mikolaycak, Charles (1937-), illus. LC 79-20001. (Illus.). (gr. 2 up). 1980. (ISBN 0-688-41933-X). (ISBN 0-688-51933-4). Lothrop. **Award: (ALA).**

--The Innkeeper's Daughter. LC 79-2421. 159 p. 22cm. c.1979. (ISBN 0-688-41906-2). (ISBN 0-688-51906-7). Lothrop, Lee & Shepard Books.

--King of the Seventh Grade. LC 82-15247. 190 p. 22cm. c.1982. (ISBN 0-688-01302-3). Lothrop, Lee & Shepard Books.

--Lovers' Games. 1st ed. LC 83-2641. 239 p. 22cm. 1983. (ISBN 0-689-30981-3). Atheneum.

--Metzgar's New York. LC 85-230. p. cm. 1985. (ISBN 0-688-05849-3). Lothrop, Lee & Shepard Books.

--Molly's Pilgrim. 1st ed. Deraney, Michael J., illus. LC 83-797. (Illus.). 32 p. 26cm. c.1983. (ISBN 0-688-02103-4). Lothrop, Lee & Shepard Books.

--Queen for a Day. LC 80-28115. 158 p. 22cm. c.1981. (ISBN 0-688-00437-7). (ISBN 0-688-00438-5). Lothrop, Lee & Shepard Books.

--R, My Name Is Rosie. LC 77-28867. 188 p. 22cm. c.1978. (ISBN 0-688-41839-2). (ISBN 0-688-51839-7). Lothrop, Lee & Shepard.

--Roses. Steptoe, John Lewis (1950-), illus. (Illus.). 224p. (gr. 6 up). 1984. (ISBN 0-688-02166-2). Lothrop.

--The Secret Grove. Deraney, Michael J., illus. LC 85-51146. (Illus.). 32 p. 24cm. c.1985. (ISBN 0-8074-0301-6). Union of American Hebrew Congregations.

--Thank You, Jackie Robinson. Cuffari, Richard (1925-1978), illus. LC 73-17703. (Illus.). 125 p. 22cm. 1974. (ISBN 0-688-41580-6). Lothrop, Lee & Shepard Co.

--Unicorns in the Rain. LC 79-22082. 164 p. 22cm. (Argo book). 1980. (ISBN 0-689-30735-7). Atheneum.

--Where's Florrie?. Halpern, Joan, illus. LC 75-40341. (Illus.). 44 p. 26cm. c.1976. (ISBN 0-688-41738-8). (ISBN 0-688-51738-2). Lothrop, Lee & Shepard.

Cohen, Barbara (1932-), retold by.

--Lovely Vassilisa. Ivanov, Anatoly, illus. LC 80-12494. p. cm. 1980. Atheneum.

--Yussel's Prayer. Deraney, Michael J., illus. LC 80-25377. (Illus.). 32 p. 25cm. 1981. (ISBN 0-688-00460-1). (ISBN 0-688-00461-X). Lothrop, Lee & Shepard Books. **Award: (ALA).**

Cohen, Barbara (1932-) & Lovejoy, Bahija Fattuhi (1914-), eds.

--Seven Daughters & Seven Sons. LC 81-8092. 220 p. 22cm. 1982. (ISBN 0-689-30875-2). Atheneum.

Cohen, Burton & Schroder, William

--Nelson Makes a Face. 1st ed. Schroder, William E., illus. LC 78-2000. (Illus.). 40 p. c.1978. (ISBN 0-688-41850-3). (ISBN 0-688-51849-4). Lothrop, Lee & Shepard Co.

Cohen, Caron Lee

--Sally Ann Thunder Ann Whirlwind Crockett. Dewey, Ariane (1937-), illus. LC 84-7978. (Illus.). 40 p. 24cm. (gr. 1-3). c.1985. (ISBN 0-688-04006-3). (ISBN 0-688-04007-1). Greenwillow Books.

--Wake up, Groundhog!. Cohen, Caron Lee, illus. LC 74-80322. (Illus.). 32 p. 20cm. 1975. (ISBN 0-517-51693-4). Crown Publishers.

Cohen, Daniel (1936-)

--America's Very Own Ghosts. Berenzy, Alix, illus. LC 84-18749. (Illus.). 48 p. 24cm. c.1985. (ISBN 0-396-08505-9). Dodd, Mead & Co.

--America's Very Own Monsters. Huffman, Tom, illus. LC 82-4961. (Illus.). 48 p. 24cm. c.1982. (ISBN 0-396-08069-3). Dodd, Mead.

--The Body Snatchers. LC 74-32115. (The Weird & Horrible Library). (gr. 6 up). 1975. (ISBN 0-397-31560-0, JBL-J). (ISBN 0-397-31610-0). Har-Row.

--The Body Snatchers. 160p. 1975. J B Lippincott Company.

--The Case of the Battling Ball Clubs. Overlie, George, illus. LC 79-84356. (Illus.). 32 p. 16cm. (Carolrhoda mini-mysteries). c.1979. (ISBN 0-87614-101-7). Carolrhoda Books.

--The Case of the Long-Lost Twin. Overlie, George, illus. LC 79-84357. (Illus.). 32 p. 16cm. (Carolrhoda mini-mysteries). c.1979. (ISBN 0-87614-094-0). Carolrhoda Books.

--The Case of the Missing Poodle. Overlie, George, illus. LC 79-84358. (Illus.). 30 p. 16cm. (Carolrhoda mini-mysteries). c.1979. (ISBN 0-87614-095-9). Carolrhoda Books.

--The Case of the Runaway Rabbit. Overlie, George, illus. LC 79-84359. (Illus.). 32 p. 16cm. (Carolrhoda mini-mysteries). c.1979. (ISBN 0-87614-096-7). Carolrhoda Books.

--The Case of the Spanish Stamps. Overlie, George, illus. LC 79-56197. (Illus.). 32 p. 16cm. (Carolrhoda mini-mystery). c.1980. (ISBN 0-87614-117-3). Carolrhoda Books.

--The Case of the Supermarket Swindle. Overlie, George, illus. LC 79-56199. (Illus.). 32 p. 16cm. (Carolrhoda mini-mystery). c.1980. (ISBN 0-87614-119-X). Carolrhoda Books.

--Everything You Need to Know About Monsters and Still Be Able to Get to Sleep. 1st ed. Stokes, Jack, illus. LC 79-6589. (Illus.). 118 p. 22cm. c.1981. (ISBN 0-385-15803-3). (ISBN 0-385-15804-1). Doubleday.

--Ghostly Animals. LC 76-23751. (Illus.). ix, 81 p. 25cm. 1977. (ISBN 0-385-11567-9). Doubleday.

--Ghostly Terrors. LC 81-43232. p. cm. 1981. (ISBN 0-396-07996-2). Dodd, Mead.

--The Greatest Monsters in the World. (Illus.). 81p. 18cm. (Archway Paperback). 1977, c.1975. (ISBN 0-671-29812-7). Pocket Books.

--The Headless Roommate and Other Tales of Terror. LC 80-18821. p. cm. c.1980. (ISBN 0-87131-327-8). M. Evans.

--The Magic of the Little People. Payson, Dale (1943-), illus. LC 73-19236. (Illus.). index. 96p. (gr. 3 up). 1974. (ISBN 0-671-32638-4). Messner.

--Monster Dinosaur. LC 82-48460. (Illus.). 192p. (gr. 3-6). 1983. (ISBN 0-397-31953-3, JBL-J). (ISBN 0-397-31954-1). Har-Row.

--Monster Hunting Today. LC 83-7496. (gr. 6-8). N.D. (ISBN 0-396-08184-3). Dodd.

--Monsters, Giants & Little Men from Mars. LC 74-4534. 256p. (gr. 4-7). 1975. (BFYR). Doubleday.

--Monsters You Never Heard of. LC 79-23641. (Illus.). (High Interest, Low Vocabulary Ser.). (gr. 4-9). 1980. Dodd.

--The Mystery of the Faded Footprint. Overlie, George, illus. LC 79-84360. (Illus.). 30 p. 16cm. (Carolrhoda mini-mysteries). c.1979. (ISBN 0-87614-097-5). Carolrhoda Books.

--The Mystery of the Hidden Camera. Overlie, George, illus. LC 79-84362. (Illus.). 32 p. 15cm. (Carolrhoda mini-mysteries). c.1979. (ISBN 0-87614-098-3). Carolrhoda Books.

--The Mystery of the Locked Door. Overlie, George, illus. LC 79-50786. (Illus.). 32 p. 16cm. (Carolrhoda mini-mysteries). c.1979. (ISBN 0-87614-099-1). Carolrhoda Books.

--The Mystery of the Marked Money. Overlie, George, illus. LC 79-50788. (Illus.). 32 p. 16cm. (Carolrhoda mini-mysteries). c.1979. (ISBN 0-87614-100-9). Carolrhoda Books.

--The Mystery of the Mellafeller Elephant. Overlie, George, illus. LC 79-56198. (Illus.). 32 p. 16cm. (Carolrhoda mini-mystery). c.1980. (ISBN 0-87614-118-1). Carolrhoda Books.

--The Mystery of the Missing Ring. Overlie, George, illus. LC 79-56200. (Illus.). 32 p. 16cm. (Carolrhoda mini-mystery). c.1980. (ISBN 0-87614-120-3). Carolrhoda Books.

--Natural History of Unnatural Things. LC 70-135444. (Illus.). photos. prints. (gr. 5 up). 1971. (ISBN 0-525-35655-X). Dutton.
--The Restless Dead: Ghostly Tales From Around the World. LC 83-27447. (Illus.). 112p. (High Interest, Low Vocabulary Ser.). (gr. 4). 1984. (ISBN 0-396-08325-0). Dodd.
--Science Fiction's Greatest Monsters. LC 80-1087. (Illus.). (High Interest-Low Vocabulary Ser.). (gr. 4-9). 1980. Dodd.
--Southern Fried Rat, and Other Gruesome Tales. Brier, Peggy, illus. 1983. Dutton.
--Southern Fried Rat and Other Gruesome Tales. Brier, Peggy, illus. LC 82-25120. (Illus.). 128 p. 22cm. c.1983. (ISBN 0-87131-400-2). M. Evans.
--The Tomb Robbers. LC 79-22760. (Illus.). 96p. (gr. 3-6). 1980. (ISBN 0-07-011566-4). McGraw.
--Vaccination and You. Petie, Haris, pseud. (1915-), illus. Petty, Roberta. LC 76-81388. (Illus.). 95 p. 22cm. 1969. J. Messner.
--Watchers in the Wild. Hamberger, John F. (1934-), illus. 1971. Little Brown & Co.
--The World's Most Famous Ghosts. LC 77-16857. (Illus.). 112 p. 22cm. c.1978. (ISBN 0-396-07543-6). Dodd, Mead.
--Young Ghosts. LC 78-4619. p. cm. c.1978. Dutton.

Cohen, David Solis see Shortent, Daisy, pseud.

Cohen, David Solis (1852-)
--The Stockings in the Barn. Shortent, Daisy, pseud. LC 15-6301. (Illus.). 18cm. 20p. 1891. Davis Brothers.

Cohen, Florence Chanock (1927-)
--Freedom Next Time. LC 70-147861. 192p. (gr. 7 up). 1971. (ISBN 0-671-32413-6). Messner.
--Portrait of Deborah. LC 61-6368. 191 p. 22cm. 1961. Messner.

Cohen, Floreva G
--Sneakers to Shul. Cooper, Zephyr, illus. LC 78-4920. (Illus.). 35 p. 25cm. c.1978. Board of Jewish Education of Greater New York.

Cohen, Jane, jt. auth. see Miller, Elizabeth Kubota.

Cohen, Joel H.
--Six Million Dollar Man & the Bionic Woman. (gr. 4-6). 1977. (ISBN 0-590-10340-7, Schol Pap). Scholastic Inc.

Cohen, John Michael (1903-), tr. see Cervantes Saavedra, Miguel de.

Cohen, Lenore
--Bible Tales for Very Young Children, 2 bks. Kishore, Penina, illus. (Illus.). N.D. Bk. 1. Bk. 2. UAHC.
--Came Liberty Beyond Our Hope: A Story of Hanukkah. Gaal, George, illus. (Illus.). (gr. 7-9). 1963. (ISBN 0-378-69661-0). Ritchie.
--Passover to Freedom. Greene, Lucille B., illus. (Illus.). (gr. 7-9). 1967. (ISBN 0-378-69653-X). Ritchie.

Cohen, Louise Maxwell see Corwen, Maxwell, pseud.

Cohen, Louise Maxwell (1884-)
--Ole Man Swordfish. Corwen, Maxwell, pseud. Horvath, Ferdinand Huszti (1891-), illus. LC 31-34143. 4 p. l., 125 p. col. front., illus. 26 cm. 1931. Falcon Publishing Co.

Cohen, Miriam see Hutchins, Pat, et al.

Cohen, Miriam (1926-)
--Bee My Valentine!". Hoban, Lillian (1925-), illus. LC 77-21950. (Illus.). 32 p. c.1978. (ISBN 0-688-80129-3). (ISBN 0-688-84129-5). Greenwillow Books.
--Best Friends. Hoban, Lillian (1925-), illus. LC 70-146620. (Illus.). 1 v (unpaged. (Collier juvenile paperbacks). 1973, c.1971. Collier Books.
--Best Friends. Hoban, Lillian (1925-), illus. LC 70-146620. 23cm. 32p. 1971. Macmillan.
--Born to Dance Samba. Fiammenghi, Gioia (1929-), illus. LC 83-47690. c.1984. (ISBN 0-06-021358-2). Harper & Row.
--First Grade Takes a Test. 1st ed. Hoban, Lillian (1925-), illus. LC 80-10316. (Illus.). 32 p. c.1980. (ISBN 0-688-80265-6). (ISBN 0-688-84265-8). Greenwillow Books.
--Jim Meets the Thing. 1st ed. Hoban, Lillian (1925-), illus. LC 81-1026. (Illus.). 32 p. c.1981. (ISBN 0-688-00616-7). (ISBN 0-688-00617-5). Greenwillow Books.
--Jim's Dog Muffins. Hoban, Lillian (1925-), illus. LC 83-14090. (Illus.). 8 x 7. 32p. (16 pt.). (gr. k-3). 1984. (ISBN 0-688-02564-1). (ISBN 0-688-02565-X). Greenwillow.
--Liar, Liar, Pants on Fire!. Hoban, Lillian (1925-), illus. LC 84-25869. (Illus.). 8 x 7. 32p. (14 pt.). (gr. k-3). 1985. (ISBN 0-688-04244-9). (ISBN 0-688-04245-7). Greenwillow.
--Lost in the Museum. 1st ed. Hoban, Lillian (1925-), illus. LC 78-16765. (Illus.). 32 p. c.1979. (ISBN 0-688-80187-0). (ISBN 0-688-84187-2). Greenwillow Books.
--The New Teacher. Hoban, Lillian (1925-), illus. LC 78-163239. (Illus.). 32 p. 1974, c.1972. Collier Books.
--No Good in Art. 1st ed. Hoban, Lillian (1925-), illus. LC 79-16566. (Illus.). 32 p. c.1980. (ISBN 0-688-80234-6). (ISBN 0-688-84234-8). Greenwillow Books.
--See You Tomorrow, Charles. Hoban, Lillian (1925-), illus. LC 82-11834. (Illus.). 8 x 7. 32p. (14 pt.). (gr. k-3). 1983. (ISBN 0-688-01804-1). (ISBN 0-688-01805-X). Greenwillow.
--So What?. 1st ed. Hoban, Lillian (1925-), illus. LC 81-20101. (Illus.). 32 p. c.1982. (ISBN 0-688-01202-7). (ISBN 0-688-01203-5). Greenwillow Books.
--Starring First Grade. Hoban, Lillian (1925-), illus. LC 84-5929. (Illus.). 9 7/8 x 8. 32p. (14 pt.). (gr. k-3). c.1985. (ISBN 0-688-04029-2). (ISBN 0-688-04030-6). Greenwillow.
--Tough Jim. Hoban, Lillian (1925-), illus. LC 73-19065. (Illus.). 32 p. 1974. (ISBN 0-02-722760-X). Macmillan.
--When Will I Read?. Hoban, Lillian (1925-), illus. LC 76-28320. (Illus.). 32 p. c.1977. (ISBN 0-688-80073-4). (ISBN 0-688-84073-6). Greenwillow Books.
--Will I Have a Friend?. Hoban, Lillian (1925-), illus. LC 67-5219. (Illus.). 1 v. (unpaged. 1967. Macmillan.

Cohen, Morton N. see Moreton, John, pseud.

Cohen, Octavus Roy (1891)
--The Valley of Olympus. LC 29-1677. 3 p. l., 297, 1 p. 19 1/2 cm. 1929. D. Appleton & Company.

Cohen, Paul, jt. auth. see Bernstein, Joanne Eckstein.

Cohen, Peter Zachary (1931-)
--The Authorized Autumn Charts of the Upper Red Canoe River Country. 1st ed. De Paola, Tomie, pseud. (1934-), illus. De Paola, Thomas Anthony. LC 73-134807. (Illus.). 48 p. 1972. Atheneum.
--Bee. Cuffari, Richard (1925-1978), illus. LC 74-19197. (Illus.). 187 p. 22cm. 1975. Atheneum.
--The Bull in the Forest. 1st ed. Bornschlegel, Ruth, illus. LC 69-18955. (Illus.). 86 p. 22cm. 1969. Atheneum.
--Calm Horse, Wild Night. 1st ed. LC 82-1746. (Illus.). vi, 168 p. 22cm. 1982. (ISBN 0-689-30918-X). Atheneum.
--Deadly Game at Stony Creek. Dease, Michael J., illus. LC 78-51772. (Illus.). (gr. 4-7). 1978. Dial Bks Young.
--Foal Creek. 1st ed. Moyler, Alan, illus. LC 72-75266. (Illus.). 214 p. 23cm. 1972. Atheneum.
--The Great Red River Raft. Fay, Anne, ed. (Illus.). 40p. (gr. 4up). 1984. (ISBN 0-8075-3039-5). A Whitman.
--Morena. Petie, Haris, pseud. (1915-), illus. Petty, Roberta. LC 71-115081. (Illus.). 140 p. 21cm. (Aladdin Book, A24). 1973, c.1970. Atheneum.
--The Muskie Hook. 1st ed. O'Sullivan, Tom, illus. LC 69-13525. (Illus.). 151 p. 22cm. 1969. Atheneum.
--The Muskie Hook. O'Sullivan, Tom, illus. 1972. Atheneum.

Cohen, S. Alan (1933-) & Hyman, Joan S.
--The Cookie Caper and Other Selections. LC 76-9102. p. cm. (Reading house series from Random House : Study-skills (orange). c.1976. (ISBN 0-394-04295-6). Random House.
--The Dragon Rag and Other Selections. LC 76-9124. p. cm. (Reading house series from Random House : Sound-symbol B (lime)). c.1976. (ISBN 0-394-04246-8). Random House.
--The Goose-Aroo and Other Selections. LC 76-9109. (Illus.). 91 p. 24cm. (Reading house series from Random House : Comprehension and vocabulary (orange)). c.1977. (ISBN 0-394-04284-0). Random House.
--How the Thunderbird Came to Be and Other Selections. LC 76-17002. (Illus.). 91 p. 24cm. (Reading house series from Random House : Study skills (yellow)). c.1977. (ISBN 0-394-04335-9). Random House.
--It's All in How You Look at It, and Other Selections. LC 76-48934. (Illus.). 92 p. 24cm. (reading house series from Random House : Comprehension and vocabulary (green)). c.1977. (ISBN 0-394-04424-X). Random House.
--The Magic Show and Other Selections. LC 76-40348. (Illus.). 91 p. 24cm. (Reading house series from Random House : Study skills (blue)). c.1977. (ISBN 0-394-04401-0). Random House.
--A Monkey Sings Rings Around Me and Other Selections. LC 76-9092. p. cm. (Reading house series from Random House : Comprehension and vocabulary (lime)). c.1976. (ISBN 0-394-04258-1). Random House.
--The Pied Piper of Hamelin, and Other Selections. LC 76-48059. (Illus.). 92 p. 24cm. (Reading house series from Random House : Study skills (green)). c.1977. (ISBN 0-394-04434-7). Random House.
--The Powder Keg Derby and Other Selections. LC 76-40346. (Illus.). 92 p. 24cm. (Reading house series from Random House : Structural analysis (blue)). c.1977. (ISBN 0-394-04381-2). Random House.
--Sheriff Sheridan Rides Again, and Other Selections. LC 76-48066. (Illus.). 92 p. 24cm. (Reading house series from Random House : Structural analysis (green)). c.1977. (ISBN 0-394-04414-2). Random House.
--Tumble, Grumble and Crumble and Other Selections. LC 76-9097. (Illus.). 91 p. 24cm. (Reading house series from Random House : Sound-symbol (orange)). c.1977. (ISBN 0-394-04273-5). Random House.
--We Like Drexel And Other Selections. LC 76-9124. (Illus.). 91 p. 24cm. (Reading house series from Random House : Sound-symbol B (lime)). c.1977. (ISBN 0-394-04246-8). Random House.
--What's for Dinner, Dad? and Other Selections. LC 76-17080. (Illus.). 91 p. 24cm. (Reading house series from Random House : Structural analysis (red)). c.1977. (ISBN 0-394-04348-0). Random House.
--You Don't Know Big Until You Weigh a Whale and Other Selections. LC 76-17003. (Illus.). 91 p. 24cm. (Reading house series from Random House : Sound symbol (yellow)). c.1977. (ISBN 0-394-04311-1). Random House.

Cohn, Emma, tr. see Severin, Jean.

Cohn, Norma
--Brother and Sister. LC 42-11047. 19cm. 31p. 1942. Oxford University Press.
--Little People in a Big Country. N.D. Oxford University Press.

Cohn, Robert see Garvey, Robert, pseud.

Coit, Dorothy (1889-)
--The Ivory Throne of Persia. N.D. J. B. Lippincott.
--Kai Khosru and Other Plays for Children As Produced by the King-Coit Children's Theatre. LC 34-42585. xx, 187 p. front., plates. 19 1/2 cm. c.1934. Theatre Arts, Inc.

Coit, Dorothy (1889-) & Firdausi, Shahnama
--The Ivory Throne of Persia. LC 29-18200. xiii, 241 p. col. front., plates. (part col.) 21 cm. 1929. Frederick A. Stokes Company.

Coit, Favida
--How the Rain Sprites were Freed. N.D. D. Lothrop Co.

Coit, John
--Cocobear Meets Butterbear. McCracken, Stephen, illus. LC 83-82638. (Illus.). 33p. (gr. 3-7). 1983. (ISBN 0-938694-14-6). JCP Corp VA.

Coke, Dorothy V.
--Mary Catherine & the Little Pig's Tail. (Illus.). 1981. (ISBN 0-533-04761-7). Vantage.

Coker, A. M.
--Crockside Lads. (Illus.). (Sunday-Hour Lib.). N.D. American Tract Society.
--Crookside Lads and Found on the Hills. (Illus.). 256p. 1905. American Tract Society.

Coker, Gylbert (1944-)
--Naptime. LC 78-50415. p. cm. 1978. (ISBN 0-440-06303-5). (ISBN 0-440-06304-3). Delacorte Press.

Colacino, Antonio
--More Adventures of Susan and Spotty. Colacino, Antonio, illus. LC 69-18319. (Illus.). 24 p. 22cm. 1969. Platt & Munk.

Colahan, Charles Edward (1906-)
--Blondie. LC 38-17569. 3 p. l., 9-253 p. 19 1/2 cm. N.D. Godwin,.

Colbeck, Alfred
--The Fall of the Staincliffes. (Illus.). (The Staincliffe Ser.: Vol. 1). N.D. Fleming H. Revell Co.

Colbert, Edwin Harris (1905-)
--Digging for Dinosaurs. Borja, Robert (1923-), illus. (Illus.). photos. (Adventures in Nature & Science Series). (gr. 3-7). 1960. (ISBN 0-516-01412-9). Childrens.

Colbert, Mildred
--Kutkos, Chinook Tyee. Williams, Keith Shaw, illus. LC 43-1544. xi, 228 p. illus., col. plates (1 double) 20 1/2 x 15 1/2 cm. c.1942. D.C. Heath and Company.

Colbin, Annemarie & Dalmais, Anne Marie
--The Adventures of Brownie and Puff. Giannini, Jean, illus. LC 74-142152. (Illus.). 60 p. 31cm. (Big golden book). 1971. Golden Press.

Colburn, T. S.
--Little Red Bowl. (gr. k-3). N.D. Carlton.

Colby, Carroll Burleigh (1904-1977)
--Gabbit: The Magic Rabbit. Colby, Carroll Burleigh (1904-1977), illus. LC 51-1099. 24cm. 30p. 1951. Coward-McCann, Inc.
--Night People. LC 61-8251. 48p. illus. 24cm. N.D. Coward McCann.
--Night People: Workers From Dawn to Dusk. new and rev. ed. LC 70-166591. (Illus.). 48 p. 28cm. (Colby books). 1971. Coward, McCann & Geoghegan.
--Strangely Enough. 192p. (gr. 7 up). 1972. (ISBN 0-8069-3918-4). (ISBN 0-8069-3919-2). Sterling.
--The Weirdest People in the World. LC 72-95221. (Illus.). 192 p. 21cm. 1973. (ISBN 0-8069-3922-2). Sterling Pub. Co.

Colby, Curtis
--Bill's Great Idea. Bergeron, Joseph R., illus. LC 73-14590. (Illus.). 27 p. 23cm. (His Adventures in the Glen series). 1973. (ISBN 0-88436-022-9). EMC Corp.
--The Fight for the Glen. Bergeron, Joseph R., illus. LC 73-14586. (Illus.). 30 p. 23cm. (His Adventures in the Glen series). 1973. EMC Corp.
--Goose Rescue. Bergeron, Joseph R., illus. LC 73-14585. (Illus.). 30 p. 23cm. (His Adventures in the Glen series). 1973. (ISBN 0-88436-018-0). EMC Corp.
--Night Watch in the Glen. Bergeron, Joseph R., illus. LC 73-14596. (Illus.). 31 p. 23cm. (His Adventures in the Glen series). 1973. (ISBN 0-88436-016-4). EMC Corp.
--Otter in Danger. Bergeron, Joseph R., illus. LC 73-14591. (Illus.). 30 p. 23cm. (His Adventures in the Glen series). 1973. (ISBN 0-88436-020-2). EMC Corp.
--Wilderness Adventure. Bergeron, Joseph R., illus. LC 73-14603. (Illus.). 30 p. 23cm. (His Adventures in the Glen series). 1973. (ISBN 0-88436-025-3). EMC Corp.

Colby, Fred Myron
--Brave Lads & Bonnie Lassies. (Illus.). N.D. Methodist Bk Concern.
--The Daughter of Pharaoh: A Tale of the Exodus. N.D. Methodist Bk Concern.

Colby, Harriet
--Where Is Johnny!. Davis, Rosemary, illus. LC 44-9407. 26 p. col. illus. 14 x 17 cm. 1944. Howell, Soukin.

Colby, J. Rose, jt. ed. see Jones, R.

Colby, James W. see J. W. C. , pseud.

Colby, Jean Poindexter (1909-)
--Dixie of Dover: A Boy and Dog Story. Stevens, Mary, illus. LC 58-8478. 21cm. 92p. 1958. Little, Brown and Company.
--The Elegant Eleanor. Nichols, Marie C. (1905-), illus. LC 58-8279. (Illus.). 27cm. 56p. 1958. Hastings House.
--Jenny. Nichols, Marie C. (1905-), illus. LC 57-10732. 20cm. 44p. 1957. Hastings House, Publishers, Inc.
--Jim the cat. Nichols, Marie C. (1905-), illus. LC 57-5514. 46p. illus. 24cm. 1957. Little Brown.
--Tear Down to Build Up. 1960. E M Hale.

Cole, Ann, et al. (1937-)
--Purple Cow to the Rescue. LC 82-47913. (Illus.). 160p. (gr. 1-5). 1982. (ISBN 0-316-15104-1). (ISBN 0-316-15106-8). Little.

Cole, Babette
--Don't Go Out Tonight. LC 81-43647. p. cm. (A Creepy Concertina Pop-up). 1982. (ISBN 0-385-18090-X). Doubleday.
--The Hairy Book. Cole, Babette, illus. LC 84-11496. (Illus.). 40p. (gr. 1-7). 1985. (ISBN 0-394-97026-8, BYR). (ISBN 0-394-87026-3). Random.
--Nungu and the Elephant. Cole, Babette, illus. LC 79-27777. (Illus.). 28 p. 24cm. 1980. (ISBN 0-07-011696-2). McGraw-Hill.
--Nungu and the Hippopotamus. Cole, Babette, illus. LC 78-12382. (Illus.). 28 p. 24cm. 1979. (ISBN 0-07-011695-4). McGraw-Hill.
--The Trouble with Mom. LC 83-7750. (Illus.). 30 p. 21cm. 1984. (ISBN 0-698-20597-9). Coward-McCann.
--The Trouble with Mom. Cole, Babette, illus. (Illus.). 32p. (gr. k-3). 1984. (ISBN 0-698-20597-9, Coward). Putnam Pub Group.

Cole, Bessie Mae Garton, ed.
--Treasure Chest: A Collection of Children's Choice Poems and Verses. 1st Ed. 1st ed. LC 51-3280. 167 p. 22 cm. 1951. De Vorss.

Cole, Brock
--The King at the Door. Cole, Brock, illus. LC 78-20064. (Illus.). 32 p. 22cm. (gr. k-3). c.1979. (ISBN 0-385-14718-X). (ISBN 0-385-14719-8). Doubleday.
--No More Baths. 1st ed. Cole, Brock, illus. LC 78-22790. (Illus.). 401 p. 22cm. c.1980. (ISBN 0-385-14714-7). (ISBN 0-385-14715-5). Doubleday.
--Nothing but a Pig. 1st ed. Cole, Brock, illus. LC 80-8643. (Illus.). 32 p. 22cm. c.1981. (ISBN 0-385-17064-5). (ISBN 0-385-17063-7). Doubleday.
--The Winter Wren. LC 84-1583. (Illus.). 32p. (gr. 2 up). 1984. (ISBN 0-374-38454-1). (ISBN 0-374-38454-1). FS&G.

Cole, Brock, jt. auth. see Banks, Lynne Reid.

Cole, Carol Cassidy
--Downy Wing & Sharp Ears. N.D. George Sully & Co.
--Velvet Paws & Shiny Eyes. N.D. George Sully & Co.

Cole, Duane
--Vagabond Cub. LC 67-5474. (Illus.). 183 p. 23cm. 1967. K. Cook Co.

Cole, Earl & Cole, Natalie Joyce Galatzer (1931-)
--Hooper: The What-What Owl. LC 63-16839. 1 v. (unpaged) col. illus. 25 cm. 1963. Duell, Sloan and Pearce.

Cole, Edna Earle
--The Good Samaritan, and Other Bible Stories Dramatized. Wagner, Harold, illus. LC 15-22987. 7 p. 3 l., 13-133 p. front., plates 19 1/2 cm. 1915. R. G. Badger; Etc., Etc.

Cole, Harold
--A Few Thoughts on Trout. Christensen, Betty, illus. LC 85-30742. p. cm. c.1985. (ISBN 0-671-60542-9). (ISBN 0-671-60531-3). Julian Messner.

Cole, Helen C.
--Po'-Nya - Her Story. (Illus.). 60p. (gr. k-2). 1976. (ISBN 0-682-48566-7). Exposition.

Cole, Henry I (1922-)
--Rory, the Spunky Monkey. LC 57-7260. unpaged. illus. 15x21cm. (Bookland juvenile). 1957. Comet Press Books.

Cole, Henry, Sir (1808-1882)
--The Most Delectable History of Reynard the Fox. Jacobs, Joseph (1854-1916), ed. Calderon, William Frank (1865-1943), illus. LC 17-27607. xxxvii, 260 p. incl. front., illus., 9 pl. 19 cm. (Cranford series). 1895. Macmillan and Co.

Cole, Joanna
--Aren't You Forgetting Something, Fiona?. Delaney, Ned, pseud. (1951-), illus. Delaney, Thomas Nicholas III. LC 83-13457. (Illus.). 39 p. 23cm. (ps-3). 1984, c.1983. (ISBN 0-8193-1121-9). Parents Magazine Press.
--Bony-Legs. Zimmer, Dirk, illus. LC 82-7424. p. cm. c.1983. (ISBN 0-517-54634-5). Crown.
--Bony-Legs. Zimmer, Dirk, illus. LC 85-5070. (Illus.). 47 p. 23cm. 1985, c.1983. (ISBN 0-02-722970-X). Four Winds Press.
--Bony-Legs. Zimmer, Dirk, illus. LC 82-7424. (Illus.). 48p. (ps-3). 1983. (ISBN 0-590-07882-8, Four Winds). (ISBN 0-517-54634-5). Scholastic Inc. **Award: (ALA).**
--A Chick Hatches. (Illus.). 48p. (gr. k-3). 1976. (ISBN 0-688-32087-2). Morrow. **Award: (ALA).**
--The Clown Arounds. Smith, Jerry, illus. LC 81-4662. p. cm. 1981. (ISBN 0-8193-1059-X). (ISBN 0-8193-1060-3). Parents Magazine Press.
--The Clown-Arounds Go on Vacation. Smath, Jerry, illus. LC 83-13480. (Illus.). 41 p. 23cm. (ps-3). 1984, c.1983. (ISBN 0-8193-1120-0). Parents Magazine Press.
--The Clown-Arounds Have a Party. Smath, Jerry, illus. LC 82-2128. (Illus.). 42 p. 23cm. c.1982. (ISBN 0-8193-1085-9). (ISBN 0-8193-1086-7). Parents Magazine Press.
--Fleas. Wrigley, Elsie, illus. (Illus.). index. 64p. (gr. 3-7). 1973. (ISBN 0-688-31844-4). Morrow.
--Get Well, Clown-Arounds!. Smath, Jerry, illus. LC 82-8148. p. cm. 1983. (ISBN 0-8193-1095-6). (ISBN 0-8193-1096-4). Parents Magazine Press.
--Golly Gump Swallowed a Fly. Weissman, Bari, illus. LC 81-11072. p. cm. 1982. (ISBN 0-8193-1069-7). Parents Magazine Press.
--The Secret Box. Sandin, Joan (1942-), illus. LC 78-140680. (Illus.). 39 p. 26cm. 1971. Morrow.
--Sweet Dreams, Clown-Arounds!. Smath, Jerry, illus. LC 85-6348. p. cm. 1985. (ISBN 0-8193-1138-3). Parents Magazine Press.

Cole, Joanna, compiled by.
--Best-Loved Folktales of the World. Schwarz, Jill Karla, illus. 1982. Doubleday.
--A New Treasury of Children's Poetry: Old Favorites and New Discoveries. Brown, Judith Gwyn (1933-), illus. LC 83-20821. 1984. (ISBN 0-385-18539-1). Doubleday.

Cole, Joanna & Darrow, Whitney, Jr. (1909-)
--Fun on Wheels. LC 76-54236. (Illus.). 32 p. 1977, c.1976. (ISBN 0-688-22102-5). (ISBN 0-688-32102-X). Morrow.

Cole, Joanne, jt. auth. see Cole, Michael.
Cole, Lois Dwight see Avery, Lynn, pseud.
Cole, Lois Dwight see Dudley, Nancy, pseud.
Cole, Lois Dwight see Dwight, Allan, pseud.
Cole, Lois Dwight see Eliot, Anne, pseud.
Cole, Lois Dwight see Lattin, Anne, pseud.
Cole, Lois Dwight (1903-1979), adapted by see Ewing, Juliana Horatia Gatty, Mrs.

Cole, Michael
--Bod and the Cherry Tree. Cole, Michael & Cole, Joanne, illus. LC 67-3569. (Illus.). 32 p. 17cm. 1967, c.1966. Follett Pub. Co.

Cole, Michael & Cole, Joanne
--Bod's Apple. Cole, Michael & Cole, Joanne, illus. LC 67-3565. (Illus.). 32 p. 17cm. 1967, c.1965. Follett Pub. Co.
--Bod's Dream. Cole, MIchael & Cole, Joanne, illus. LC 67-3568. (Illus.). 32 p. 17cm. 1967, c.1966. Follett Pub. Co.
--Bod's Present. Cole, Michael & Cole, Joanne, illus. LC 67-3566. (Illus.). 31 p. 17cm. 1967, c.1965. Follett Pub. Co.
--Wet Albert. Cole, Joanne & Cole, Michael, illus. LC 67-21153. (Illus.). 32 p. 25cm. 1968, c.1967. Follett Pub. Co.

Cole, Natalie
--Little Dog. (Illus.) (Little Book Ser). (gr. k-6). 1975. (ISBN 0-89409-001-1). Childrens Art.

Cole, Natalie Joyce Galatzer, jt. auth. see Cole, Earl.

Cole, Pamela McArthur
--The Story of the Golden Apple. LC 3-5527. 128 p. illus. 19 cm. c.1902. Richardson, Smith & Company.

Cole, Samuel Valentine
--The Great Grey King. N.D. Sherman, French and Co.

Cole, Sara, jt. auth. see McGill-Franzen, Anne.

Cole, Sheila Rotenberg (1939-)
--Meaning Well. Raynor, Paul, illus. LC 73-12225. (Illus.). 63 p. 21cm. 1974. (ISBN 0-531-02665-5). Watts.
--When the Tide Is Low. 1st ed. Wright-Frierson, Virginia, illus. LC 84-10023. (Illus.). 32p. (ps-1). 1985. (ISBN 0-688-04067-5). (ISBN 0-688-04066-7). Lothrop.

Cole, Stephen, pseud., see Webbe, Gale Dudley.

Cole, Stephen, pseud. (1909-)
--The Growing Season. Webbe, Gale Dudley. LC 66-11706. 150p. 22cm. (Ariel bks.). N.D. Farrar.
--Pitcher and I. Webbe, Gale Dudley. LC 63-9075. 156 p. 22 cm. 1963. Ariel Books.
--Pitcher and I. Webbe, Gale Dudley. 1963. E M Hale.

Cole, William Rossa (1919-)
--Aunt Bella's Umbrella. 1st ed. Chwast, Jacqueline (1932-), illus. LC 71-97252. (Illus.). 45 p. 20cm. 1970. Doubleday.
--A Boy Named Mary Jane, and Other Silly Verse. Banek, Yvette, illus. LC 75-34091. p. cm. 1976. (ISBN 0-531-01144-5). Watts.
--Frances Face-Maker. Ungerer, Tomi, pseud. (1931-), illus. Ungerer, Jean Thomas. LC 63-18465. (Illus.). 32p. (A Going-to-Bed Bk). (ps-2). 1971. (ISBN 0-529-03791-2). Collins Pubs.
--Frances Face-Maker: A Going-to-Bed Book. 1st ed. Ungerer, Tomi, pseud. (1931-), illus. Ungerer, Jean Thomas. LC 63-18465. 1 v. (unpaged) col. illus. 23 cm. 1963. World Pub. Co.
--Give Up?. Thaler, Mike (1936-), illus. LC 78-6842. (Illus.). (gr. 4-6). 1978. (ISBN 0-531-02249-8). Watts.
--Good Dog Poems. Sanderson, Ruth, illus. LC 80-21547. p. cm. 1980. (ISBN 0-684-16709-3). Scribner.
--Knock Knocks, the Most Ever. Thaler, Mike (1936-), illus. LC 75-33205. (Illus.). 96 p. 22cm. 1976. (ISBN 0-531-02428-8). (ISBN 0-531-01142-9). F. Watts.
--Knock Knocks You've Never Heard Before. Thaler, Mike (1936-), illus. LC 76-30386. (Illus.). 96 p. 22cm. 1977. (ISBN 0-531-00385-X). F. Watts.
--Oh, Such Foolishness!. De Paola, Tomie, pseud. (1934-), illus. De Paola, Thomas Anthony. LC 78-1622. (Illus.). (gr. 3-6). 1978. (ISBN 0-397-31807-3, JBL-J). Har-Row.
--Oh, That's Ridiculous. 1st ed. Ungerer, Tomi, pseud. (1931-), illus. Ungerer, Jean Thomas. LC 70-183934. (Illus.). index. 80p. (gr. 4-7). 1972. (ISBN 0-670-52107-8). Viking Pr.
--The Square Bear & Other Riddle Rhymers. (gr. k-3). 1977. (ISBN 0-590-10320-2). Scholastic Inc.
--That Pest Jonathan. Ungerer, Tomi, pseud. (1931-), illus. Ungerer, Jean Thomas. LC 73-77949. (Illus.). 32 p. 20cm. 1970. Harper & Row.
--What's Good for a Five-Year-Old?. 1st ed. Sorel, Edward (1929-), illus. LC 68-24760. (Illus.). 32 p. (His Books for young readers). (ps-1). 1969. (ISBN 0-03-086623-5). Holt, Rinehart & Winston.
--What's Good for a Six-Year-Old?. 1st ed. Fetz, Ingrid (1915-), illus. LC 65-21541. (Illus.). 32 p. 1965. Holt, Rinehart and Winston.
--What's Good for a Three-Year-Old?. Hoban, Lillian (1925-), illus. LC 73-13962. (Illus.). 32 p. (ps). 1974. (ISBN 0-03-007441-X). Holt, Rinehart and Winston.
--What's Good for a 4-Year-Old?. 1st ed. Ungerer, Tomi, pseud. (1931-), illus. Ungerer, Jean Thomas. LC 67-19062. (Illus.). (ps-k). 1967. (ISBN 0-03-062370-7). (ISBN 0-03-062375-8). (ISBN 0-03-080108-7). HR&W.

Cole, William Rossa (1919-), selected by.
--An Arkful of Animals: Poems for the Very Young. Munsinger, Lynn (1951-), illus. LC 78-70041. p. cm. 1978. (ISBN 0-395-27205-X). Houghton Mifflin.
--Beastly Boys and Ghastly Girls. Ungerer, Tomi, pseud. (1931-), illus. Ungerer, Jean Thomas. LC 80-25894. p. cm. 1980, c.1964. Philomel Books.
--Beastly Boys and Ghastly Girls. Ungerer, Tomi, pseud. (1931-), illus. Ungerer, Jean Thomas. LC 64-20962. (Illus.). 124 p. 24cm. 1964. World Pub. Co. **Award: (ALA).**
--The Birds and the Beasts Were There. Siegl, Helen (1924-), illus. LC 63-18467. (Illus.). 320 p. 24cm. 1963. World Pub. Co. **Award: (ALA).**
--The Birds and the Beasts Were There: Animal Poems. Siegl, Helen (1924-), illus. LC 77-3586. p. cm. 1977, c.1963. (ISBN 0-529-03742-4). Collins.
--A Book of Animal Poems. Parker, Robert Andrew (1927-), illus. LC 73-5141. (Illus.). 288 p. 24cm. 1973. (ISBN 0-670-17907-8). Viking Press.
--The Book of Giggles. Ungerer, Tomi, pseud. (1931-), illus. Ungerer, Jean Thomas. LC 71-128526. (Illus.). 98 p. 22cm. 1970. World Pub. Co.
--Book of Love Poems. Bo, Lars, illus. (Illus.). (gr. 7 up). 1965. (ISBN 0-670-17990-6). Viking Pr.
--A Book of Nature Poems. Parker, Robert Andrew (1927-), illus. LC 69-18257. (Illus.). 256 p. 24cm. 1969. (ISBN 0-670-18006-8). (ISBN 0-670-18007-6). Viking Press.
--A Case of the Giggles. Ungerer, Tomi, pseud. (1931-), illus. Ungerer, Jean Thomas. LC 67-15220. 2 v. col. illus. 14cm. 1967. World.
--Dinosaurs & Beasts of Yore. Natti, Susanna (1948-), illus. (Illus.). (gr. 3 up). 1979. (ISBN 0-399-20763-5, Philomel). Putnam Pub Group.
--Dinosaurs and Beasts of Yore: Poems. Natti, Susanna (1948-), illus. LC 78-31619. (Illus.). 62 p. 22cm. 1979. (ISBN 0-529-05511-2). Collins.
--Humorous Poetry for Children. 1st ed. Metzl, Ervine (1899-), illus. LC 55-5283. (Illus.). 124 p. 25cm. 1955. World Pub. Co.
--I Went to the Animal Fair. Rosselli, Colette (1916-), illus. LC 75-23020. (Illus.). (gr. k-3). N.D. (ISBN 0-529-03530-8, Philomel). Putnam Pub Group.
--I Went to the Animal Fair. Rosselli, Colette (1916-), illus. (Illus.). (gr. k-3). 1958. (ISBN 0-529-03529-4). (ISBN 0-529-03530-8). World Pub. **Award: (ALA).**
--I Went to the Animal Fair: A Book of Animal Poems. 1st ed. LC 58-9415. (Illus.). 45 p. 1958. World Pub. Co. **Award: (ALA).**
--I Went to the Animal Fair: A Book of Animal Poems. 1st ed. Rosselli, Colette (1916-), illus. LC 75-23020. p. cm. 1975, c.1958. (ISBN 0-529-03530-8). Collins.
--I'm Mad at You. Macclain, George, illus. LC 77-25497. (Illus.). (gr. 1-4). 1978. (ISBN 0-529-05363-2, Philomel). Putnam Pub Group.
--I'm Mad at You: Verses. MacClain, George, illus. LC 77-25497. (Illus.). 62 p. 22cm. c.1978. (ISBN 0-529-05363-2). Collins.
--Oh, How Silly!. 1st ed. Ungerer, Tomi, pseud. (1931-), illus. Ungerer, Jean Thomas. LC 74-123020. (Illus.). 94 p. 24cm. 1970. (ISBN 0-670-52095-0). Viking Press.
--Oh, Such Foolishness!. Poems. De Paola, Tomie, pseud. (1934-), illus. De Paola, Thomas Anthony. LC 78-1622. p. cm. c.1978. (ISBN 0-397-31807-3). Lippincott.
--Oh, What Nonsense. Ungerer, Tomi, pseud. (1931-), illus. Ungerer, Jean Thomas. LC 66-10249. 80p. (gr. 4-6). 1969. (ISBN 0-670-05025-3, Puffin). Penguin.
--Oh, What Nonsense. Ungerer, Tomi, pseud. (1931-), illus. Ungerer, Jean Thomas. LC 66-6763. (Illus.). 80p. illus 21cm. (gr. k-6). 1966. (ISBN 0-670-52117-5). Viking Pr.
--Oh What Nonsense. Ungerer, Tomi, pseud. (1931-), illus. Ungerer, Jean Thomas. LC 66-6763. 60p. 1966. (ISBN 0-670-52117-5). (ISBN 0-670-52118-3). Viking Press.
--Pick Me Up: A Book of Short, Short Poems. LC 78-165103. 192p. (gr. 5 up). 1972. (ISBN 0-02-722810-X). Macmillan.
--Poem Stew. Weinhaus, Karen Ann, illus. 1981. Harper.
--Poem Stew. 1st ed. Weinhaus, Karen Ann, illus. LC 81-47106. p. cm. c.1981. (ISBN 0-397-31963-0). (ISBN 0-397-31964-9). J.B. Lippincott.
--Poems for Seasons and Celebrations. 1st ed. Troyer, Johannes (1902-), illus. LC 61-12012. (Illus.). 191 p. 24cm. 1961. (ISBN 0-529-03660-6). World Pub. Co.
--Poems from Ireland. LC 77-132294. (Illus.). (Poems of the World). (gr. 7-12). 1972. (ISBN 0-690-63898-1, TYC-J). Har-Row.
--Poems of Magic and Spells. 1st ed. Bacon, Peggy, pseud. (1895-), illus. Bacon, Margaret Frances. LC 77-2938. p. cm. 1977, c.1960. (ISBN 0-529-03587-1). Collins.
--Poems of Magic and Spells. 1st ed. Bacon, Peggy, pseud. (1895-), illus. Bacon, Margaret Frances. LC 60-5802. (Illus.). 224 p. 25cm. 1960. World Pub. Co.
--Poems of Thomas Hood. (Illus.). (Poets Ser.). 1968. (ISBN 0-690-63791-8). (ISBN 0-690-63792-6). Thomas Y Crowell.
--The Poetry of Horses. LC 79-9228. p. cm. 1979. (ISBN 0-684-16330-6). Scribner.
--The Poets Tales. (Illus.). (gr. k-12). 1971. (ISBN 0-686-24424-9). (ISBN 0-686-24425-7). Collins Pubs.
--Poet's Tales: A New Book of Story Poems. rev. ed. Keeping, Charles William James (1924-), illus. LC 72-101841. (Illus.). line drawings. 320p. (gr. 7 up). 1971. (ISBN 0-529-00458-5). (ISBN 0-529-00459-3). World Pub.
--Rough Men, Tough Men: Poems of Action and Adventure. Arno, Enrico (1913-1981), illus. LC 78-85871. (Illus.). 255 p. 25cm. (gr. 7 up). 1969. (ISBN 0-670-60863-7). Viking Press.
--The Sea, Ships, & Sailors. Jacques, Robin (1920-), illus. (Illus.). 1967. (ISBN 0-670-62642-2). Viking Pr.

Cole, William Rossa (1919-) & Colmore, Julia, eds.
--The Poetry-Drawing Book. LC 60-10984. unpaged. illus. (part col.) 22x29cm. N.D. Simon and Schuster.

Coleick, E. Fenwick
--Adventures Of Pioneer Children. (Illus.). N.D. Robert Clarke & Co.

Coleman, Anita S.
--Singing Bells. Nankivel, Claudine, illus. LC 61-5572. (Illus.). (gr. k-2). N.D. Broadman.

Coleman, Bernard (1890-) & Eich, Estelle
--Eagle Wing. LC 56-8068. (Illus.). 22cm. 45p. 1956. Greenwich Book Publishers.

Coleman, Charles G
--The Shining Sword. 1st ed. LC 56-31266. 181p. 20cm. 1956. (ISBN 0-87213-086-X). Loizeaux Bros.

Coleman, David, jt. auth. see Fox, Phyllis W.

Coleman, Earl S (1910-)
--Rockets at Dawn. Cram, L. D. (1898-), illus. LC 54-7678. 193p. illus. 22cm. 1954. Longmans, Green.
--Sierra Quest. 1st ed. Cram, L D. (1898-), illus. LC 52-138807. 200p. illus. 22cm. 1953. Longmans, Green.
--Winners Losers. Murch, Frank J., illus. LC 53-7237. (Illus.). 184 p. 21cm. 1953. Longmans, Green.

Coleman, Eleanor S
--The Cross and the Sword of Cortes. LC 68-18332. 191 p. 22cm. 1968. Simon & Schuster.

Coleman, Gilbert Payson
--A Captain at Fifteen. LC 11-23833. 5 p. l., 309, 1 p. col. plates. 20 cm. 1911. D. Appleton and Company.

Coleman, H. T. J.
--Rhyme for a Penny. N.D. MacMillan.

Coleman, Helen
--Little Travelers around the World, visits to people of Other Lands. Bonawitz, George, illus. LC 7-37551. 2 p. l., iii-v, 110p. col. front., illus., plates. 30 1/2cm. 1907. A. S. Barnes & Co.

Coleman, Joseph
--The First Witch. (Illus.). (Pal Paperbacks,-Pal Skills II Ser.). (gr. 5-12). 1980. (ISBN 0-8374-3566-8). Xerox Ed Pubns.
--Missing Papers. (Illus.). (Pal Paperbacks, - Pal Skills II Ser.). (gr. 5-12). 1980. (ISBN 0-8374-3556-0). Xerox Ed Pubns.
--Space Wars. (Illus.). (Pal Paperbacks, - Pal Skills II Ser.). (gr. 5-12). 1980. (ISBN 0-8374-3563-3). Xerox Ed Pubns.

Coleman, Leslie
--Wiberforce, Detective. (gr. 4-7). 1978. (ISBN 0-8277-5435-3). British Bk Ctr.
--Wilberforce & the Blue Cave. (gr. 2-6). 1978. (ISBN 0-8277-5434-5). British Bk Ctr.
--Wilberforce the Whale. (gr. 2-6). 1978. (ISBN 0-8277-5433-7). British Bk Ctr.

Coleman, Lester L., jt. auth. see Clark, Bettina.

Coleman, Lonnie (1920-1982)
--Orphan Jim. LC 75-7253. 216p. 1975. Doubleday.

Coleman, Marion Reeves Moore (1900-)
--A Brigand, Two Queens, and a Prankster: Stories of Janosik, Queen Bona, Queen Kinga and the Sowizdrzal. LC 72-80394. 77 p. 18cm. 1972. (ISBN 0-910366-13-6). Cherry Hill Books.
--The Man on the Moon: The Story of Pan Twardowski. LC 77-155638. 54 p. 18cm. 1971. Cherry Hill Books.

Coleman, Mrs., et al., trs. see Segur, Sophie Rostopchine, Mrs.

Coleman, Pauline Mabel Hodgkinson
--The Beau Collector. LC 57-5234. 213p. 21cm. 1957. Dodd, Mead.
--The Different One. LC 55-56444. 244p. 21cm. 1955. Dodd, Mead.
--Not an Iota. LC 59-6002. 21cm. 212p. 1959. Dodd, Mead & Co.
--The Preposterous Voyage. LC 58-9971. 244 p. 21cm. 1958. Dodd, Mead.

Coleman, Ralph Pallen & Ferris, J. L. G., illus.
--Patriotic American Stories. (The Children's Bookshelf). N.D. John C. Winston.

Coleman, Robert William Alfred see Insight, James, pseud.

Coleman, Satis Narrona Barton, Mrs. (1878-)
--Another Dancing Time. Earle, Vana (1917-), illus. 32p. 1954. John Day Books.
--The Book of Bells. 187p. (gr. 6-9). 1938. John Day Books.
--Dancing Time: Music for Rhythmic Activities of Children. Earle, Vana (1917-), illus. 32p. 1952. John Day Books.
--The Gingerbread Man and Other Songs of the Children's Storybook Friends. Hambridge, Ruth, illus. LC 31-33747. 71, 1 p. col. illus. 20 x 28 cm. c.1931. The John Day Company.

--Jack Heaton, Wireless Operator. Owen, Robert Emmett (1878-), illus. LC 19-14938. 6 p. l., 245 p. front., illus., plates. 20 cm. c.1919. Frederick A. Stokes Company.

Collins, Burnita

--The Whistlepunk: Nat's Adventures in a Redwood Camp. Collins, Burnita, illus. LC 32-23572. 300 p. front., plates. 21 cm. c.1932. Lothrop, Lee & Shepard Co.

Collins, Carvel

--Sam Ward in the Gold Rush. N.D. Stanford University Press.

Collins, Dale see Fennimore, Stephen, pseud.

Collins, Dale (1897-)

--Bush Holiday. Fennimore, Stephen, pseud. MacKnight, Ninon (1908-), illus. Ninon, pseud. LC 49-8777. 242 p. illus. 21 cm. 1st U.S. edition. 1949. Doubleday.

--Robinson Carew, Castaway. Price, Christine Hilda (1928-1980), illus. LC 49-73347. 208 p. 22 cm. 1949. Rinehart.

--Shipmates Down Under. Busoni, Rafaello (1900-1962), illus. LC 50-6971. 188 p. illus. 20 cm. 1950. Holiday House.

Collins, David Raymond (1940-)

--If I Could, I Would. Oechsli, Kelly (1918-), illus. LC 78-27430. (Illus.). 46 p. 23cm. (Imagination book). c.1979. (ISBN 0-8116-4417-0). Garrard Pub. Co.

--Joshua Poole and Sunrise. Johnston, Clifford, illus. LC 80-118597. (Illus.). 32 p. 24cm. c.1980. (ISBN 0-8054-4260-X). Broadman Press.

--Joshua Poole and the Special Flowers. Johnston, Clifford, illus. LC 81-213175. (Illus.). 32 p. 24cm. c.1981. (ISBN 0-8054-4271-5). Broadman Press.

--Joshua Poole Hated School. Johnston, Clifford, illus. LC 77-361881. (Illus.). 31 p. 24cm. 1977, c.1976. (ISBN 0-8054-4236-7). Broadman Press.

--Kim Soo and His Tortoise. Cohen, Alix, illus. LC 73-112365. (Illus.). 48 p. 22cm. 1970. (ISBN 0-87460-226-2). (ISBN 0-87460-227-0). Lion Press.

--The One Bad Thing About Birthdays. 1st ed. Wiesner, David, illus. LC 80-23104. (Illus.). 32 p. 22cm. (Let me read book). c.1981. (ISBN 0-15-258288-6). (ISBN 0-15-258289-4). Harcourt Brace Jovanovich.

--A Spirit of Giving. Hall, Susan T. (1940-), illus. LC 78-108429. (Illus.). 32 p. 24cm. c.1978. (ISBN 0-8054-4238-3). Broadman Press.

--Walt Disney's Surprise Christmas Present. Locke, Vance, illus. LC 72-157403. (Illus.). 32 p. 27cm. 1971. (ISBN 0-8054-4317-7). Broadman Press.

Collins, David Raymond (1940-) & Witter, Evelyn

--The Golden Circle. Lindstrom, Annette, illus. LC 82-51215. p. cm. c.1983. (ISBN 0-938232-47-9). Winston-Derek Publishers.

Collins, Dean, jt. auth. see Anderson, Eva Greenslit.

Collins, Frederick A.

--Mirth and Mystery. 312p. N.D. Coward-McCann.

Collins, Harold

--The Difficulty at Deep End. Collins, Harold, illus. LC 78-101499. (Illus.). 109 p., 2 leaves of plates. 29cm. c.1978. Hallett Hall.

Collins, Hubert E.

--Warpath and Cattle Trail. Brown, Paul (1893-1958), illus. 320p. 1928. William Morrow & Co.

--Warpath and Cattle Trail. Brown, Paul (1893-1958), illus. Beard, Dan, frwd. by. 320p. 1933. William Morrow & Co.

Collins, Judith Graham (1942-)

--Josh's Scary Dad. LC 83-2752. p. cm. c.1983. (ISBN 0-687-20546-8). Abingdon.

Collins, Letta Ellen, Mrs. (1850-)

--Something about Santa Claus. LC 5-9054. (Illus.). 19 cm. 28p. 1905. Neale Publishing Co.

Collins, Meghan (1926-)

--Maiden Crown. LC 79-16201. (Illus.). 230 p. 22cm. 1979. (ISBN 0-395-28639-5). Houghton Mifflin.

--The Willow Maiden. Gal, Laszlo (1933-), illus. LC 85-1533. (Illus.). 38 p. 29cm. 1985. (ISBN 0-8037-0217-5). (ISBN 0-8037-0218-3). Dial Books for Young Readers.

Collins, Norman Richard (1907-1982)

--Black Ivory. 1948. Duell Sloan & Pearce.

Collins, Pat Lowery (1932-)

--Tumble, Tumble, Tumbleweed. Robinson, Charles (1870-1937), illus. LC 81-23968. (Illus.). 32. 1982. (ISBN 0-8075-8122-4). Whitman.

Collins, Patricia

--My Friend Andrew. Berelson, Howard (1940-), illus. LC 79-13191. p. cm. c.1979. (ISBN 0-13-608844-9). Prentice-Hall.

Collins, Rebecca

--Parent's Gift. N.D. Claxton, Remsen, & Haffelfinger.

Collins, Rebecca, compiled by.

--Child's Treasury: Verses for Little Children. (Illus.). N.D. Claxton, Remsen, and Haffelfinger.

Collins, Robert J

--The Legend of the Devil's Lode. Sneyd, Douglas, illus. LC 62-20654. 156 p. illus. 20 cm. (Secret circle mysteries, no. 3). c.1962. Little, Brown.

Collins, Ruth M

--Alphonse & Archibald. LC 53-995222. unpaged. illus. 26cm. 1953. Dodd, Mead.

--Alphonse & Archibald. N.D. E. M. Hale & Co.

--Horace, the Hound That Howled. LC 51-10443. 64 p. illus. 25 cm. 1951. Dodd, Mead.

--Septimus, the St. Bernard. LC 49-10588. 64 p. illus. 25 cm. 1949. Dodd, Mead.

Collins, Ruth Philpott (1890-1975)

--Flying Cow. Keats, Ezra Jack (1916-1983), illus. LC 63-17189. (Illus.). 22cm. 123p. (gr. 4-6). 1963. (ISBN 0-8098-2363-2). Walck.

--Hubba-Hubba: A Tale of the Sahara. Berson, Harold (1926-), illus. LC 68-26800. (Illus.). 96 p. 24cm. 1968. Crown Publishers.

--Krishna and the White Elephant. Keats, Jack Ezra (1916-1983), illus. LC 61-15208. 22cm. 119p. (School Library Journal). 1961. Henry Z. Walck, Inc., Publishers.

--The Mystery of the Giant Giraffe. Robinson, Charles (1931-), illus. LC 69-17909. (Illus.). 143 p. 22cm. 1969. H. Z. Walck.

Collins, Susan

--Frogmorton. Shepard, Ernest Howard (1879-1976), illus. 1956. Alfred A Knopf : distributed by Borzoi Books.

Collins, Trish (1927-)

--Grinkles: A Keen Halloween Story. Collins, Trish (1927-), illus. LC 80-22050. (Illus.). 32p. (Easy-Read Story Bks.). (gr. k-3). 1981. (ISBN 0-531-02471-7). (ISBN 0-531-04190-5). Watts.

Collins, Wilkie (1824-1889)

--The Moonstone. (Illus.). (Great Illustrated Classics). (gr. 9 up). 1955. (ISBN 0-396-03760-7). Dodd.

--The Moonstone. (The Astor Library). N.D. Dodd Mead and Co.

--The Moonstone. 1908. Harper & Bros.

--Moonstone. (Nelson Classics). N.D. Thomas Nelson & Sons.

--The Moonstone. (Keith Jennison Large Type Bks). (gr. 6 up). N.D. (ISBN 0-531-00239-X). Watts.

--The Moonstone. Laklan, Carli (1907-), abridged by. Brooks, Meredith, illus. LC 67-25786. (Illus.). 91 p. 21cm. (Pacemaker classics). 1967. Fearon Publishers.

--The Woman in White. N.D. Harper & Bros.

Collmann, Sophie Marie

--Tales from the Old World and the New. LC 16-15664. 5 p. l., 230 p. front., plates. 20 cm. 1916. Stewart & Kidd Company.

Collodi, Carlo, pseud., see Lorenzini, Carlo.

Collodi, Carlo, pseud. (1826-1890)

--The Adventures of Pinocchio. Lorenzini, Carlo. (Illus.). 272p. (The Illustrated Junior Library). 1982. (ISBN 0-448-11001-6, G&D). Putnam Pub Group.

--Pinocchio. Lorenzini, Carlo. N.D. Ginn & Co.

--Pinocchio. Lorenzini, Carlo. (Illus.). (Crowell's Every Land Series For Children). 1915. T Y Crowell.

--Pinocchio and Pip. Lorenzini, Carlo. (Illus.). N.D. William Collins Sons & Company Ltd.

--Walt Disney Productions Presents Pinocchio and the Isle of Fun. Lorenzini, Carlo. book club ed., 1st american. LC 84-186026. (Illus.). 42 p. 23cm. 1st U.S. edition. (Disneys Wonderful World of Reading). c.1984. (ISBN 0-394-86535-9). Random House.

Collodi, Carlo, pseud. (1826-1890) & Teahan, James T

--The Pinocchio of Carlo Collodi. Lorenzini, Carlo. Jaffars, Alexa, illus. LC 84-22245. (Illus.). xxxii, 206 p. 24cm. 1985. (ISBN 0-8052-3912-X). Schocken Books.

Collodi, Richard Henry

--Two Years Before the Mast. (Children's Classics Ser.). N.D. Macmillan.

Collver, Carol, jt. auth. see Blakey, Madge Beattie.

Collyer, Barbara & Foley, John R.

--Christmas in the Country. Worcester, Retta, illus. LC 50-10018. unpaged. illus. 21 cm. (Little golden book, 95). N.D. Simon and Schuster.

Colman, Hila see Crayder, Teresa, pseud.

Colman, Hila

--Accident. LC 80-20509. 154 p. 21cm. 1980. (ISBN 0-688-22238-2). (ISBN 0-688-32238-7). W. Morrow.

--After the Wedding. LC 75-11587. 189 p. 21cm. 1975. (ISBN 0-688-22043-6). (ISBN 0-688-32043-0). Morrow.

--The Amazing Miss Laura. LC 76-17316. p. cm. c.1976. (ISBN 0-688-22079-7). (ISBN 0-688-32079-1). Morrow.

--Andy's Landmark House. Rocker, Fermin (1907-), illus. LC 68-21088. (Illus.). 121 p. 22cm. 1969. Parents' Magazine Press.

--Benny, the Misfit. Raphael, Elaine, pseud. (1933-), illus. Bolognese, Elaine Raphael Chionchio. LC 72-7544. (Illus.). 117 p. 21cm. 1973. (ISBN 0-690-13201-8). (ISBN 0-690-13201-8). Crowell.

--The Best Wedding Dress. LC 60-8999. 221 p. 21cm. (Morrow junior books). 1960. Morrow.

--The Big Step. LC 57-7674. 192 p. 21cm. 1957. Morrow.

--The Boy Who Couldn't Make up His Mind. Greenwald, Sheila, pseud. (1934-), illus. Green, Sheila Ellen. LC 65-151796. 24p. col. illus. 23cm. (gr. 1-4). c.1965. Macmillan.

--Bride at Eighteen. LC 66-6354. 185 p. 21cm. 1966. Morrow.

--Car-Crazy Girl. LC 67-19244. 159 p. 21cm. 1967. Morrow.

--The Case of the Stolen Bagels. Porter, Patricia Grant, illus. LC 77-10029. p. cm. c.1977. (ISBN 0-517-53064-3). Crown Publishers.

--Chicano Girl. LC 73-4922. 191 p. 21cm. 1973. (ISBN 0-688-20082-6). Morrow.

--Christmas Cruise. LC 65-153375. 190p. 22cm. c.1965. Morrow.

--Classmates by Request. LC 64-19430. 192p. (gr. 7 up). 1964. (ISBN 0-688-21626-9). Morrow.

--Claudia, Where Are You?. LC 72-78340. 191 p. 21cm. 1969. W. Morrow.

--Confession of a Storyteller. LC 81-17325. p. cm. c.1981. (ISBN 0-517-53851-2). Crown Publishers.

--A Crown for Gina. LC 58-6814. 221 p. 21cm. 1958. Morrow.

--Daughter of Discontent. LC 74-155995. 191 p. 21cm. 1971. W. Morrow.

--Diary of a Frantic Kid Sister. LC 72-92388. 119 p. 22cm. 1973. (ISBN 0-517-50262-3). Crown Publishers.

--Ellie's Inheritance. LC 79-19009. p. cm. 1979. (ISBN 0-688-22204-8). (ISBN 0-688-32204-2). Morrow.

--End of the Game. Charles, Milton, photos by. LC 77-172982. (Illus.). line drawings. 96p. (gr. 5-7). 1971. (ISBN 0-529-00923-4). Collins-World.

--Ethan's Favorite Teacher. 1st ed. Wallner, John C. (1945-), illus. LC 74-31081. (Illus.). 32 p. 24cm. 1975. (ISBN 0-517-52114-8). Crown Publishers.

--The Family and the Fugitive. LC 70-39466. 191 p. 21cm. 1972. Morrow.

--The Family Trap. LC 82-12495. p. cm. 1982. (ISBN 0-688-01472-0). William Morrow.

--Friends and Strangers on Location. LC 74-3027. 190 p. 21cm. 1974. (ISBN 0-688-21785-0). (ISBN 0-688-21785-0). Morrow.

--The Girl from Puerto Rico. LC 61-10782. 222 p. 21cm. (Morrow junior books). 1961. Morrow.

--Girl Meets Boy. 144p. (gr. 7 up). 1982. (ISBN 0-590-31988-4). Scholastic Inc.

--The Happenings at North End School. LC 77-117224. 175 p. 21cm. 1970. Morrow.

--Julie Builds Her Castle. LC 59-7407. 21cm. 220p. (gr. 7 up). 1959. Morrow.

--Mixed-Marriage Daughter. LC 68-25483. 21cm. 191p. 1968. W. Morrow.

--Mrs. Darling's Daughter. LC 62-14366. 191 p. 21cm. 1962. Morrow.

--Nobody Has to Be a Kid Forever. LC 75-35810. 117 p. 22cm. 1976. (ISBN 0-517-52521-6). Crown Publishers.

--Nobody Told Me What I Need to Know. LC 84-8673. 176p. (gr. 7 up). 1984. (ISBN 0-688-03869-7, Morrow Junior Books). Morrow.

--Not for Love. LC 83-6120. 192p. (gr. 5 up). 1984. (ISBN 0-688-02419-X). Morrow.

--Peter's Brownstone House. Weisgard, Leonard Joseph, illus. (Illus.). (gr. 1-3). 1963. (ISBN 0-8382-0647-6). Hale.

--Peter's Brownstone House. Weisgard, Leonard Joseph (1916-), illus. LC 63-7380. (Illus.). (gr. k-3). 1963. (ISBN 0-688-21707-9). Morrow.

--Phoebe's First Campaign. LC 63-14206. 190 p. 21 cm. 1963. Morrow.

--Rachel's Legacy. LC 78-12783. 190 p. 21cm. 1978. (ISBN 0-688-22154-8). (ISBN 0-688-32154-2). Morrow.

--The Secret Life of Harold, the Bird Watcher. Robinson, Charles (1931-), illus. LC 77-17075. (Illus.). 70 p. 21cm. c.1978. (ISBN 0-690-01306-X). (ISBN 0-690-03830-5). Crowell.

--Something Out of Nothing. Trinkle, Sally, illus. LC 68-10257. (Illus.). 45 p. 22cm. 1968. Weybright and Talley.

--Sometimes I Don't Love My Mother. LC 77-23445. 190 p. 21cm. 1977. (ISBN 0-688-22121-1). (ISBN 0-688-32121-6). Morrow.

--Tell Me No Lies. LC 78-1285. 74 p. 24cm. c.1978. (ISBN 0-517-53229-8). Crown Publishers.

--That's the Way It Is, Amigo. Coalson, Glo (1946-), illus. LC 74-30398. (Illus.). 90 p. 21cm. 1975. (ISBN 0-690-00750-7). Crowell.

--Watch That Watch. Weisgard, Leonard Joseph (1916-), illus. LC 62-7091. (Illus.). (gr. k-3). 1962. (ISBN 0-688-31623-9). Morrow.

--Weekend Sisters. LC 85-5665. 170 p. 22cm. c.1985. (ISBN 0-688-05785-3). W. Morrow.

--What's the Matter with the Dobsons?. LC 80-18980. 113 p. 24cm. c.1980. (ISBN 0-517-53409-6). Crown Publishers.

Colman, Margery, pseud., see McCarthy, Margery Sybil.

Colman, Margery, pseud., ed.

--Bramble. McCarthy, Margery Sybil. Colman, Margery, pseud., illus. McCarthy, Margery Sybil. LC 48-5965. 32 p. illus. (part col.) 26 cm. 1st U.S. edition. 1948, c.1946. Coward McCann.

Colman, Mrs.

--Lu-Lu's Books for Boys: Containing "Boat Builders", "Child's Gem", "Grandfather's Stories", etc, 6 vols. (Illus.). N.D. James Miller.

Colman, Pamela Atkins Chandler, Mrs.

--The Child's Gem. A Holiday Gift. LC 15-12444. x, 11-106 p. incl. col. front., illus., plates 11 1/2 cm. 1844. T. H. Carter and Company.

--The Little Keepsake: Original and Selected. LC 15-18029. 108 p. incl. front., illus., plates. 10 cm. N.D. G. Colman.

Colman, Pamela Atkins Chandler, Mrs., ed.

--The Child's Gem. LC 6-39410. v. illus., plates (part col.) 10-12 cm. N.D. T. H. Carter and Company; Etc., Etc.

--The Child's Gem: For 1845. LC 15-12445. 1 p. l., viii, 9-95, 1 p. col. front., illus., plates. 12 cm. N.D. T. H. Carter and Company.

--The Mother's Present. A Holiday Gift for the Young. LC 15-171551. viii, 9-222 p. front., plates. 16 1/2 cm. 1847. S. Colman.

Colmey, Mary Jane

--Jamie Finds a Friend. Kleitz, Mary, illus. LC 68-24827. (Illus.). 1 v. (unpaged. 29cm. 46p. 1968. T. S. Denison.

--You Are the Captain. Furan, Barbara J., illus. LC 77-78273. (Illus.). 31 p. 29cm. 1969. T. S. Denison.

Colmore, Julia, jt. ed. see Cole, William Rossa.

Colmot, Marie, pseud., see Collin Delavaud, Marie Moreal De Brevans.

Coloane, Francisco (1910-)

--The Stowaway. Floherty, John Joseph, Jr. (1892-1964), illus. Breaux, Adele, tr. LC 64-23326. (Illus.). 23cm. 113p. 1964. (ISBN 0-87141-008-7). Manyland Books Inc.

Coloma, Luis P. (1851-1915)

--Perez the Mouse. Moreton, Ada Margarette Smith, Lady, ed. Vyse, George Howard, illus. LC 50-5154. (Illus.). 63 p. 19cm. 1950. Dodd, Mead.

--Perez the Mouse: Adapted from the Spanish of Padre Luis Coloma. Moreton, Ada Margarette Smith Moreton, Lady, ed. Vyse, George Howard, illus. LC 14-207413. vi, 7-39, 1 p. illus., 17 col. pl. (incl. front.) 14 cm. 1915. John Lane.

Colomb, Josephine Blanche Bouchet (1833-1892)

--Hermine's Triumphs. Vogel, Herman, illus. LC 6-30675. 1 p. l., 326 p. illus. 22 cm. 1892. D. Appleton and Company.

Colonius, Lillian (1911-)

--At the Zoo. Schroeder, Glenn, illus. (gr. 1-3). 1967. (ISBN 0-516-08398-8). Melmont.

--Here Comes the Fireboat. 1967. (ISBN 0-516-07701-5). Childrens Press.

--Here Comes the Fireboat. N.D. Elk Grove Press.

Colos, Francois, retold by.

--The Student Who Became King in Spite of Himself. 1st ed. Colos, Francois, illus. LC 72-80243. (Illus.). 32 p. 1974. (ISBN 0-03-091978-9). Holt, Rinehart and Winston.

Colquhoun, Archibald (1912-1964), tr. see Latini, Angela.

Colson, Elizabeth

--Friends of Ours. Young, Florence Liley, illus. LC 18-160216. 4 p. l., 86 p. front., plates. 20 cm. 1918. Missionary Education Movement of the United States and Canada.

Colson, Elizabeth & Chittenden, Anna G.

--The Child Housekeeper. Upton, Alice Leonore, illus. Riis, Jacob A., intro. by. (Music and Songs by Alice R. Baldwin). (Illus.). N.D. A. S. Barnes Co.

Colson, F. H.

--Stories and legends: First Greek Reader. N.D. St Martin's Press.

Colson, Thora

--Rinkin of Dragon's Wood. LC 65-21275. 83p. illus. 22cm. c.1965. Dutton.

--Rinkin of Dragon's Wood. Marriott, Patricia (1920-), illus. (Children's Illustrated Classics). N.D. E. P. Dutton & Co.

Colt, Florence Underwood

--Uncle Sam's Speaker for His Little Boys and Girls. LC 74-169710. (Illus.). xi, 254 p. 25cm. c.1899. Juvenile Pub. Co.

Colt, Martin, pseud., see Epstein, Samuel.

Colt, Martin, pseud. (1909-)

--The Riddle of the Hidden Pesos. Epstein, Samuel. Wonsetler, John Charles (1900-), illus. LC 48-6144. 216 p. illus. 21 cm. (A Roger Baxter Mystery). 1948. J. Messner.

--Favourite Stories from Hong Kong. (Favourite Stories Ser.). 1978. (ISBN 0-686-60358-3). Heinemann Ed.
--Favourite Stories from Malaysia. (Favourite Stories Ser.). 1972. (ISBN 0-686-60425-3). Heinemann Ed.
--Favourite Stories from Malaysia. bilingual ed. (Orig.). (The Favourite Stories Ser.). 1981. (ISBN 0-686-73752-0). Heinemann Ed.
--Favourite Stories from the Philippines. (Favourite Stories Ser.). 1978. (ISBN 0-686-60426-1). Heinemann Ed.
--Favourite Stories from the Philippines. bilingual ed. (The Favourite Stories Ser.). 1981. (ISBN 0-686-73754-7). Heinemann Ed.
--Further Favourite Stories from Asia. bilingual ed. (The Favourite Stories Ser.). (gr. 5). 1981. (ISBN 0-686-73756-3). Heinemann Ed.
--More Favourite Chinese Stories. bilingual ed. (Orig.). (The Favourite Stories Ser.). 1981. (ISBN 0-686-73757-1). Heinemann Ed.
--More Favourite Stories from Asia. bilingual ed. (Orig.). (The Favourite Stories Ser.). 1981. (ISBN 0-686-73758-X). Heinemann Ed.
--More Favourite Stories from Asia. (Favourite Stories Ser.). N.D. (ISBN 0-686-65637-7). Heinemann Ed.

Comber, Lilian see Beckwith, Lillian, pseud.

Combes, Lenora Fees
--Let's Go Shopping. Combes, Lenora Fees, illus. LC 48-7812. (Illus.). 21cm. 42p. (Little Golden Library). 1948. Simon and Shuster.

Comden, Betty (1919-) & Green, Adolph (1915-)
--Good Morning, Good Night. Shimin, Symeon (1902-), illus. LC 67-9541. (Illus.). 1 v (unpaged). 29cm. (Kin/Der owl book, KS17). 1967. Holt, Rinehart and Winston.

Comegys, Benjamin Bartis (1819-1901)
--Talks with Boys and Girls: Or, Wisdom Better than Gold. 237p. N.D. American Sunday-School Union.

Comfort, Elizabeth Maxwell
--Grizzly's Little Pard. N.D. Thomas Whittaker.
--The Little Heroine of Poverty Flat. N.D. Thomas Whittaker.

Comfort, George F., Mrs.
--Folks and Fairies. (Illus.). N.D. Harper & Brothers.

Comfort, John
--Don's Doings. N.D. Macmillan.
--Matt Desmond's Bit. N.D. Macmillan.

Comfort, Mildred Houghton (1886-)
--Alpine Paths. Gringhuis, Richard H. (1918-1974), illus. Gringhuis, Dirk, pseud. LC 53-10402. 128p. illus. 21cm. 1953. Beckley-Cardy.
--Herbert Hoover: Boy Engineer. Fiorentino, Al, illus. LC 65-14978. 200p. illus. 20cm. (Childhood of famous Amers.). c.1965. Bobbs.
--Kish of India. Paul, Arthur, illus. LC 53-11439. 128p. illus. 21cm. 1953. Beckley-Cardy.
--Little Lost Kitten: A Story of Williamsburg in the Days of George Washington. Lee, Manning De Villeneuve (1894-1980), illus. LC 56-834310. (Published with the Approval and Collaboration of Colonial Williamsburg, Williamsburg va.). unpaged. illus. 21cm. (Rand McNally elf book, 544). c.1956. Rand McNally.
--Moving Day. LC 58-6562. unpaged. illus. 21cm. c.1958. Rand McNally.
--Princess Isabel of Brazil. LC 68-57047. (Illus.). 14 drawings. index. 192p. (American Background Bks). (gr. 5-9). 1969. (ISBN 0-02-832120-0). Kenedy.
--Princess Isabel of Brazil and the Glittering Pen. Unada, pseud. (1927-), illus. Gliewe, Unada Grace. LC 68-57047. (Illus.). 183 p. 22cm. (American Background Books: No. 35). 1969. P. J. Kenedy.
--Search Through Pirate's Alley. Fleur, Anne Elizabeth (1901-), illus. Sari, pseud. LC 45-980919. viii, 200 p. incl. front., illus. 20 1/2 cm. 1945. W. Morrow and Co.
--Sergeant Preston and Yukon King. Lackey, William, illus. LC 55-8479. unpaged. illus. 21cm. (Rand McNally Elf Book, 500). c.1955. Rand McNally.
--Temple Town to Tokyo. Paul, Arthur, illus. LC 52-12934. 143 p. illus. 21 cm. 1952. Beckley-Cardy.
--Treasure on the Johnny Smoker. MacDonald, James, illus. LC 68-255. 219 p. illus. 22 cm. 1967. Denison.
--Treasure on the Johnny Smoker. MacDonald, James, illus. LC 47-31078. 219 p. illus. 21 cm. 1947. W. Morrow.
--Winter on the Johnny Smoker. Pitz, Henry Clarence (1895-1976), illus. LC 43-13574. v, 218 p. illus. 21 cm. 1943. W. Morrow & Comapny.

Comfort, Will Levington (1878-1932)
--Apache. c.1931. E. P. Dutton & Co.

Comins, Elizabeth Barker see Caxton, Laura, pseud.

Comins, Elizabeth Barker
--Hartwell Farm. N.D. John C. Winston.
--Marion Berkley. N.D. John C. Winston.
--The Story of Mistress Polly: Who Did Not Like to Shell Peas. Comins, Elizabeth Barker, illus. 16 p. illus. 16 x 20 cm. c.1890. L. Prang & Co.
--Why?. Comins, Elizabeth Barker, illus. LC 15-16829. 12 p. illus. 20 cm. c.1890. L. Prang & Co.

Comiskey, Florence Elizabeth
--Jamie's Adventure With a Magic Carpet, and Other Stories. Nagel, Stina (1918-), illus. 1959. Exposition Press.

Commager, Evan
--Beaux. LC 58-9778. (Illus.). 243 p. 22cm. 1958. Harper.
--Cousins. 1st ed. Bodecker, Niels Mogens (1922-), illus. LC 56-9437. (Illus.). 270 p. 22cm. 1956. Harper.
--Tenth Birthday. 1st ed. Sibley, Don (1922-), illus. LC 54-10845. (Illus.). 186 p. 21cm. 1954. Bobbs-Merrill.
--Valentine. LC 60-9457. 1961. (ISBN 0-06-021370-1). Har-Row.

Commager, Henry Steele (1902-), ed.
--Chestnut Squirrel. Weil, Lisl (1910-), illus. LC 52-7193. (Illus.). 122 p. 24cm. 1952. Houghton Mifflin.
--The St. Nicholas Anthology. (Illus.). 1983. Crown.
--The St. Nicholas Anthology. LC 83-11664. 1983, c.1975. (ISBN 0-517-42082-1). Greenwhich House.
--Treasury of Best-Loved Stories, Poems, Games, and Riddles from St. Nicholas Magazine. LC 84-13536. (Illus.). xiv, 586 p. 24cm. 1984, c.1978. (ISBN 0-517-44810-6). Greenwich House : Distributed by Crown Publishers.

Commins, Dorothy Berliner, selected by.
--The Big Book of Favorite Songs for Children. Schlesinger, Alice, illus. N.D. Grosset & Dunlap.
--Favorite Christmas Songs & Stories. Cunningham, Dellwyn, illus. (Illus.). (gr. 2-5). 1962. (ISBN 0-448-00321-X, G&D). Putnam Pub Group.
--Favorite Songs for Children. Schlesinger, Alice, illus. (Illus.). (ps). 1965. (ISBN 0-448-04210-X, G&D). Putnam Pub Group.
--Nursery Songs. Schlesinger, Alice, illus. (Illus.). (gr. k-3). N.D. Wonder.
--The Wonder Book of Nursery Songs. N.D (Wonder Books). Grosset & Dunlap.

Comparetti, Alice Pattee (1907-)
--Gregory's Angels. LC 78-188250. 168 p. 23cm. 1972. (ISBN 0-8028-3418-3). Eerdmans.

Compton, Herbert Eastwick
--A Free Lance in a Far Land. (Cassell's Popular Library of Fiction). N.D. Cassell's & Co's Pubs.
--A King's Hussar. (Cassell's Popular Library of Fiction). N.D. Cassell & Co.'s Pubs.

Compton, Margaret, pseud., see Harrison, Amelia Williams.

Compton, Margaret, pseud. (1852-1903)
--Bockers. Harrison, Amelia Williams. (The Vacation Ser.). N.D. Penn.
--Bockers. Harrison, Amelia Williams. Betts, John Henderson, illus. (Sunbeam Ser. for Young People). N.D. Penn Publishing Co.
--Bockers and his Chum Peggy. Harrison, Amelia Williams. McCullough, William A., illus. LC 1-8048. 19cm. 234p. 1896. Alpha Publishing Co.
--Bockers and His Chum Peggy. Harrison, Amelia Williams. McCullough, William A., illus. N.D. DeWolfe, Fiske & Co.
--The Green Door. Harrison, Amelia Williams. (Illus.). (The Little People's Ser.). N.D. Penn Publishing co.
--The Green Door. Harrison, Amelia Williams. Betts, John Henderson, illus. (The Vacation Ser.). 1901. Penn.

Compton, Ray, ed. see Meader, Stephen Warren.

Comstock, Enos Benjamin (1879-1945)
--Fairy Frolics. Comstock, Frances Bassett, illus. 64p. 1913. Rand, Mcnally & Co.
--More Tuck-Me-In Stories. N.D. Dodd, Mead & Co.
--More Tuck-Me-in Stories. Comstock, Enos Benjamin (1879-1945), illus. LC 23-13858. 79 p. col. front., illus., col. plates. 24 cm. c.1922. Moffat, Yard and Company.
--Mrs. Waterby and the Nine Little Waterbys. N.D. Dodd, Mead & Co.
--Tuck-Me-In Stories. N.D. Dodd, Mead & Co.
--Tuck-me-in Stories. Comstock, Enos Benjamin (1879-1945), illus. 25cm. 76p. 1917. Moffat, Yard & Co.
--When Mother Lets Us Tell Stories. N.D. Dodd, Mead & Co.
--When Mother Lets Us Tell Stories. Comstock, Enos Benjamin (1879-1945), illus. LC 18-11250. 2 p. l., 90 p. illus. 21 cm. 1917. Moffat, Yard and Company.

Comstock, Esther J.
--Vallejo & the Four Flags. Comstock, Floyd B., illus. LC 79-21636. (Illus.). xvi, 142p. (gr. 4). 1979. (ISBN 0-686-47318-3). Comstock Bon.

Comstock, Harriet Theresa, Mrs. (1860-), retold by see Andersen, Hans Christian.

Comstock, Harriet Theresa Smith, Mrs. (1860-), ed. see Andersen, Hans Christian.

Comstock, Harriet Theresa Smith, Mrs. (1860-)
--A Boy of a Thousand Years Ago. Varian, George, illus. LC 2-19878. 1 p. l., 196 p. front., illus., pl. 19 1/2 cm. 1902. Lee & Shepard.
--A Boy of a Thousand Years Ago. Varian, George, illus. 1905. Lee and Shepard Company.
--Camp Brave Pine. N.D. Thomas Y. Crowell Company.
--Cedric the Saxon. (Illus.). (The Children's Hour Series.). N.D. George H Doran.
--Cedric the Saxon. LC 1-21970. 1 p. l., 73 p. front., 4 pl. 19 cm. 1901. T. Whittaker.
--Janet of the Dunes. 297p. N.D. Little, Brown.
--A Little Dusky Hero. LC 2-21585. 4 p. l., 93 p. front. 19 1/2 cm. (golden hour series). 1902. T. Y. Crowell & Co.
--Little Dusky Hero. (Illus.). (Crowell's Happy Day Series.). 1915. T Y Crowell.
--Meg and the Others. O'Malley, M. Power, illus. LC 6-25997. 2 p. l., 149 p. front., plates. 19 1/2 cm. 1906. T. Y. Crowell & Co.
--Molly the Drummer Boy. LC 6372. (Illus.). 22 x 16cm. 60p. (Dainty Ser.). 1900. Henry Altemus Co.
--The Place Beyond the Winds. Potter, Harry Spafford, illus. LC 14-16759. 20cm. 386p. 1914. Doubleday, Page & Co.
--Princess Rags and Tatters. Thayer, Emma Redington Lee (1874-1973), illus. LC 12-21951. 5 p. l., 3-112 p. 1 l., col. front., col. plates, 19 1/2 cm. 1912. Doubleday, Page & Company.
--The Queen's Hostage. 319p. N.D. Little, Brown.
--Then Marched the Brave. Nicks, Anna S., illus. LC 4-21662. ix pl. 1 l., 13-136 p. incl. col. front., 4 pl. 19 cm. 1904. H. Altemus Company.
--Tower or Throne. LC 2-23295. 19cm. 274p. N.D. Little, Brown.
--Uhen the British Came. Comstock, Harriet Theresa Smith, Mrs. (1860-) & Wager-Smith, Curtis, illus. LC 4-21730. ix pl 1 l., 13-152 p. incl. col. front., 3 pl. 19 cm. (Altemus' Holly-tree series.). 1904. H. Altemus Company.
--An Unintentional Patriot. Eckman, F. A., illus. LC 6-35625. ix, 13-146 p. incl. front. ill. pl. 18 1/2cm. c.1906. Altemus Co.

Comstock, Harriet Theresa Smith, Mrs. (1860-), ed.
--Andersen's Fairy Tales. Comstock, Harriet Theresa Smith, Mrs. (1860-), illus. (Burt's Series of one Syllable Books). N.D. A. B. Burt Co.

Comstock, Raymond
--Lads Who Dared. LC 18-20779. xxi, 343 p. front., plates. 20 cm. 1918. G. P. Putnam's Sons.

Comyn, L. N.
--Christian Elliott: Or, Mrs. Danvers' Prize, 1 of 6 vols. (Illus.). (Julia Maitland Library). N.D. E P Dutton.

Conan, Grace Wilbur
--The Children's Year. N.D. Milton Bradley Co.

Conan Doyle, Arthur see Conaway, Judith (1948-) & Doyle, Arthur Conan, Sir.

Conan Doyle, Arthur see Doyle, Arthur Conan, Sir.

Conant, Chara Broughton
--Naomi, 1 of 50 vols. 305p. (Library of Best Authors). 1905. American Tract Society.
--Winnie Lorimer's Visit 1890. LC 12-31645. (Illus.). 19cm. 277p. N.D. American Tract Society.

Conant, H. C., tr. see Nieritz, Karl Gustav.

Conant, Helen S.
--The Butterfly Hunters. N.D. James R. Osgood.

Conant, James Bryant (1893-1978)
--The Hounds of the Baskervilles. N.D. New American Library.

Conant, Roger William (1895-)
--Hiking Westward: Being the Story of Two Boys Whose Ambition Led Them to Face Privations and Hardships in Their Quest of a Home in the Great West. Merrill, Frank Thayer (1848-), illus. LC 22-6936. 3 p. l., 409 p. col. front. 19 1/2 cm. c.1920. W. A. Wilde Company.

Conaway, Judith (1948-), adapted by see Verne, Jules.

Conaway, Judith (1948-)
--I Dare You!. Maloney, Katie, photos by. LC 76-46432. (Illus.). (Moods & Emotions Ser.). (gr. k-3). 1977. (ISBN 0-8172-0062-2). Raintree Pubs.
--I'll Get Even. Gubin, Mark, illus. LC 77-23455. p. cm. c.1977. (ISBN 0-8172-0964-6). Raintree Editions.
--A Long Trip to Work: A Turkish Worker Travels to Germany. Maloney, Katie, photos by. LC 77-730083. (Books & cassettes sold as 7 book set only). (Illus.). (A World of Our Own). (ps). 1977. (ISBN 0-89290-015-6). Soc for Visual.
--The New City People: A Guatemalan Family Makes the Big Move. Maloney, Katie, photos by. LC 77-730083. (Books & cassettes sold as 7 book set only). (Illus.). (A World of Our Own). (ps). 1977. (ISBN 0-89290-014-8). Soc for Visual.
--Unsolved Mysteries...with Sherlock Holmes & Dr. Watson. (gr. 7-9). 1976. (ISBN 0-89290-113-6). Soc for Visual.
--Was My Face Red. Maloney, Katie, photos by. LC 76-46635. (Illus.). (Interaction 1 Ser.). (gr. k-3). N.D. (ISBN 0-8172-0061-4, Raintree Editions). Raintree Pubs.
--Will I Ever Be Good Enough?. LC 76-45854. (Illus.). (Moods & Emotions). (gr. k-3). 1977. (ISBN 0-8172-0059-2). Raintree Pubs.

Conaway, Judith (1948-) & Doyle, Arthur Conan, Sir (1859-1930)
--Mysteries of Sherlock Holmes: Based on the Stories of Sir Arthur Conan Doyle. Miller, Lyle (1950-), illus. LC 81-15751. (Illus.). 95 p. 20cm. (Step-up Adventures). c.1982. (ISBN 0-394-85086-6). (ISBN 0-394-95086-0). Random House.

Conaway, Judith (1948-) & Lovelace, Delos Wheeler (1894-1967)
--King Kong. Berenstain, Michael (1951-), illus. LC 82-15078. (Illus.). 95 p. 20cm. (Step-up Adventures). c.1983. (ISBN 0-394-85617-1). (ISBN 0-394-95617-6). Random House.

Conder, E. R.
--Sleepy Forest. N.D. George Routledge & Sons.

Condon, Evangelus M
--The Elysium Fields. Condon, Evangelus M., illus. LC 30-3315. 2 p. l. 9-64 p. front. illus. 19 1/2 c. c.1929. R. G. Badger.

Condon, Helen Browne
--Cowbells for Forget-Me-Not. Beals, Dorothy Lee, illus. LC 42-23227. 3 p. l., 72 p., 1 l. incl. front., illus. 22 1/2 cm. 1942. T. Nelson and Sons.
--State College. Smith, Ralph C., illus. LC 38-36515. 316 p. front., plates. 22 cm. c.1938. The Penn Publishing Company.
--Two Career Girls. Smith, Ralph C., illus. LC 40-34537. 303 p. front. 22 cm. c.1940. Penn Publishing Company.

Condon, Randall Judson & Leavitt, Helen S., eds.
--Assembly Songs and Choruses for High Schools. LC 29-23902. 27cm. 236p. 1929. Ginn & Co.

Condon, Richard Thomas (1915-)
--The Whisper of the Axe. 1976. Dial.

Condor, Charles, illus.
--Beauty and the Beast. The Story of Beauty and the Beast, the Complete Fairy Story. Dowson, Ernest Christopher (1867-1900), tr. from Fr. LC 47-365813. 5 p. l., 118, 1 p. col. front., col. plates. 29 1/2 x 23 cm. 1908. John Lane.

Condor, Gladyn, pseud., see Davison, Gladys Patton.

Condor, Gladyn, pseud. (1905-)
--Escape to Life. Davison, Gladys Patton. LC 65-14317. viii. 148 p. 21 cm. 1965. Concordia Pub. House.

Cone, Gray Helen
--One, Two, Three, Four. Humphrey, Maud (1868-), illus. (Babes of the Year Ser.). N.D. Frederick A. Stokes Co.
--Tiny Toddlers: New Verses. Humphrey, Maud (1868-), illus. LC 16-4667. 7 l. col. front. illus. N.D. Frederick Stokes Co.

Cone, Helen Gray, jt. auth. see Humphrey, Maud.

Cone, Molly Lamken see More, Caroline, pseud.

Cone, Molly Lamken (1918-)
--The Amazing Memory of Harvey Bean. MacLean, Robert (1926-), illus. LC 79-27263. (Illus.). 83 p. 22cm. 1980. (ISBN 0-395-29181-X). Houghton Mifflin.
--Annie, Annie. Friedman, Marvin (1930-), illus. LC 69-19937. (Illus.). 112 p. 22cm. 1969. Houghton Mifflin.
--Call Me Moose. Loewenstein, Bernice, illus. LC 78-1026. (Illus.). 166 p. 22cm. 1978. (ISBN 0-395-26457-X). Houghton Mifflin.
--Crazy Mary. Holmes, Bea, illus. LC 66-12095. 135p. illus. 22cm. (gr. 7-9). c.1966. (ISBN 0-395-06701-4). Houghton.
--Dance Around the Fire. Friedman, Marvin (1930-), illus. LC 74-9382. (Illus.). 155 p. 22cm. 1974. (ISBN 0-395-19490-3). Houghton Mifflin.
--The Green, Green Sea: A Story of Greece. Estrada, Ric, illus. LC 68-24584. (Illus.). 40 p. 23cm. (Stories from many lands). 1968. Crowell.
--The House in the Tree: A Story of Israel. Shimin, Symeon (1902-), illus. LC 67-23664. (Illus.). 40 p. 24cm. 1968. T. Y. Crowell Co.
--Hurry, Henrietta. LC 66-8947. 160 p. 22cm. 1966. Houghton Mifflin.
--Mishmash. Shortall, Leonard W., illus. LC 62-10316. (Illus.). 114 p. 22cm. 1962. Houghton Mifflin.
--Mishmash and the Big Fat Problem. Shortall, Leonard W., illus. LC 81-20216. (Illus.). 112 p. 22cm. 1982. (ISBN 0-395-32078-X). Houghton Mifflin.

--The U-Boat Hunters. N.D. Charles Scribner's Sons.
--Wide Courses. N.D. Charles Scribner's Sons.

Connolly, James Edward (1949-)
--Why the Possum's Tail Is Bare, and Other North American Indian Nature Tales. Adams, Andrea, illus. LC 84-26871. p. cm. c.1985. (ISBN 0-88045-069-X). Stemmer House Publishers.

Connolly, Louise (1862-1927)
--Mrs. Chatterbox and Her Family. Merwin, Decie (1894-1961), illus. LC 27-23866. 6 p. l., 214 p. incl. front., plates. 20 1/2 cm. 1927. The Macmillan Company.

Connolly, Phyllis
--Cheers for Chippie. Connolly, Jerome Patrick (1931-), illus. LC 69-19948. (Illus.). 40 ils. 64p. (gr. 2-5). 1969. (ISBN 0-8178-4482-1). (ISBN 0-8178-4481-3). Harvey.

Connolly, Vera Leona (1888-)
--Judy Grant: Editor. LC 40-7709. viii p., 1 l., 301 p. 21 cm. 1940. Dodd, Mead and Company.

Connor, Brooke, jt. auth. see Kittelson, Pat.

Connor, Chris
--The Rat King's Daughter. (Illus.). 1978. (ISBN 0-7011-5016-5, Pub. by Chatto Bodley Jonathan). Merrimack Bk Serv.

Connor, Ellen, retold by.
--Two Little Frogs Happy Hop and Freddy Frog: From an Old Fable. Rutherford, Lorene, illus. LC 63-22564. 1v. (unpaged) col. illus. 22cm. c.1965. Naylor.

Connor, Glenn A
--Thunderbolt. vi p., 1 l., 9-317 p. 19 1/2 cm. 1928. G.H. Watt.

Connor, Grace
--Don't Disturb Daddy. N.D. (ISBN 0-8283-1158-7). Branden.

Connor, James (1944-)
--I, Dwayne Kleber. LC 74-120944. 126 p. 21cm. 1970. Young Scott Books.
--Surfing Summer. LC 78-82269. (Illus.). 159 p. 22cm. 1969. W. R. Scott.

Connor, John Hal
--Sandy: The Tin Soldier of the A.E.F. Wiese, Kurt (1887-1974), illus. LC 31-34005. 3 p. l., ix-xii, 114 p. incl. col. illus., col. plates., col. pl. 23 cm. 1931. Laidlaw Brothers.

Connor, Joyce Mary see Marlow, Joyce, pseud.

Connor, Ralph, pseud., see Gordon, Charles William.

Connor, Ralph, pseud. (1860-1937)
--Black Rock. Gordon, Charles William. (The Good Value Books). N.D. Grosset & Dunlap.
--Glengarry School Days. Gordon, Charles William. N.D. Grosset & Dunlap.
--Glengarry School Days: A Story of Early Days in Glengarry. Gordon, Charles William. 1902. Revell.

Connor, Seymour Vaughan (1923-)
--Adventure in Glory. 1965. Steck-Vaughn Company.

Connors, Thomas P & Glaser, Paul
--John Benton, Rookie Policeman. Kennedy, Stephen P., intro. by. LC 57-7165. 269 p. 21cm. (Dodd, Mead career books). 1957. Dodd, Mead.

Conover, Charlotte, ed.
--A Holiday Story Sampler for Young Readers. Chisholm, Christine, illus. LC 41-22512. 7 p. l., 17-166, 1 p. incl. col. front., illus., plates (part col.) 23 1/2 x 18 1/2 cm. 1941. A. Whitman & Company.

Conover, Chris, jt. auth. see Harris, Dorothy Joan.

Conover, Chris (1950-)
--The Gingerbread Boy. Conover, Chris (1950-), illus. (Illus.). (ps-1). N.D. (ISBN 0-8228-6403-7). Platt.
--Six Little Ducks. Conover, Chris (1950-), illus. LC 75-22155. (Illus.). 32 p. 24cm. c.1976. (ISBN 0-690-01036-2). (ISBN 0-690-01037-0). Crowell. **Award: (BGH).**

Conover, Chris (1950-), retold by.
--The Wizard's Daughter: A Viking Legend. Conover, Chris (1950-), illus. LC 84-12613. (Illus.). 31 p. 31cm. c.1984. (ISBN 0-316-15314-1). Little, Brown.

Conrad, Barnaby, Jr. (1922-)
--Zorro, a Fox in the City: A Novel. 1st ed. Conrad, Barnaby, Jr. (1922-), illus. LC 79-140379. (Illus.). 126 p. 22cm. 1971. Doubleday.

Conrad, Earl (1912-)
--The Premier. (gr. 11 up). N.D. Pyramid Pubns.

Conrad, Eleanor Bishop
--The Teddy-Bear Circus. Conrad, Eleanor Bishop, illus. LC 77-94100. (Illus.). 40 p. 29cm. 1969. T. S. Denison.

Conrad, H. D., tr. see Hoffmann, Franz.

Conrad, H. D., Mrs., tr. see Hoffmann, Franz.

Conrad, Joseph, pseud., see Korzeniowski, Josef Teodor Konrad Walecz.

Conrad, Joseph, pseud. (1857-1924)
--Heart of Darkness & the End of the Tether. Korzeniowski, Josef Teodor Konrad Walecz. (Magnum Easy Eye Classic Ser). (gr. 9 up). N.D. Lancer.
--Lord Jim. Korzeniowski, Josef Teodor Konrad Walecz. (Illus.). (Great Illustrated Classics). (gr. 9 up). 1961. (ISBN 0-396-04556-1). Dodd.
--Lord Jim. Korzeniowski, Josef Teodor Konrad Walecz. LC 44-22843. 1927. Doubleday.
--Lord Jim. Korzeniowski, Josef Teodor Konrad Walecz. (Magnum Easy Eye Classic Ser). (gr. 9-12). N.D. Lancer.
--Lord Jim. Korzeniowski, Josef Teodor Konrad Walecz (Pub. by Doubleday). (gr. 7-12). 1972 (Starline). Schol Bk Serv.
--Lord Jim. Korzeniowski, Josef Teodor Konrad Walecz. (Keith Jennison Large Type Bks). (gr. 9 up). 1966. (ISBN 0-531-00229-2). Watts.
--Sea Tales. Korzeniowski, Josef Teodor Konrad Walecz. (Windmill Bks.). 1937. Doubleday Doran & Co.
--Tales of the East and West. Zabel, Morton Dauwen, ed. N.D. Doubleday & Co.

Conrad, L. K., tr. see Bucher-Waldis, Angelika.

Conrad, Pam
--I Don't Live Here!. DeGroat, Diane (1947-), illus. LC 84-7125. (Illus.). 80p. (gr. 2-6). 1984. (ISBN 0-525-44080-1). (ISBN 0-525-44080-1). Dutton.
--Prairie Songs. Ludeck, Darryl S., illus. 1985. Harper & Roe.

Conrad, Sybil (1921-)
--Believe in Spring. LC 67-29446. 183 p. 21cm. 1967. Vanguard Press.
--Enchanted Sixteen. 1st ed. Ilsley, Velma Elizabeth (1918-), illus. LC 57-5751. (Illus.). 219 p. 21cm. 1957. Holt.
--The Golden Summer. 1st ed. Stevens, Mary E. (1920-1966), illus. LC 55-10565. 220p. illus. 22cm. 1955. Holt.
--Sorority Rebel. 1st ed. LC 58-13063. 158 p. 21cm. 1958. Holt.

Conrade, Mary S, et al.
--Songs in Season: For Primary and Intermediate Grades. LC 41-22476. 4 p. l., xiii, 9-144 p. 24 1/2 cm. c.1899. A. Flanagan.

Conrader, Constance Stone
--Blue Wampum. LC 58-6760. (Illus.). 184 p. 21cm. 1958. Duell, Sloan and Pearce.

Conrow, Herman (1874-)
--The Man in the Moon Is Talking. LC 47-27093. 133 p. 23 cm. 1946. Warwick Book Press.

Conroy, Jack, jt. auth. see Bontemps, Arna Wendell.

Conroy, Joseph P.
--Out to Win. LC 19-16099. 19cm. 181p. 1919. Benziger Brothers.

Considine, Kate & Schuler, Ruby
--One, Two, Three, Four. Lee, Robert J. (1921-), illus. LC 63-16413. (Illus.). 26 p. (Little owl book). c.1963. Holt, Rinehart and Winston.

Consky, Susan B.
--Beanie. 124p. 1951. Moody Press.
--Mischief on the Farm. (Illus.). 128p. (Childrens Bks). Orig. Title: Beanie and His Friends. (gr. 1-5). 1970. (ISBN 0-8024-1540-7). Moody.

Constable, Ethel Dana
--Blocks with Which We Build. Dulin, Dorothy, illus. LC 14-3903. 104 p. incl. front., illus. 19 cm. $0.3. 1914. A. Flanagan Company.

Constandne, Learie Nicholas (1902-)
--Cricket in the Sun. (Illus.). 23cm. 131p. 1946. S. Paul.

Constant, Alberta Wilson (1908-1981)
--Does Anyone Care About Lou Emma Miller?. 1st ed. LC 78-4774. (gr. 3-7). 1979. (ISBN 0-690-01335-3, TYC-J). (ISBN 0-690-03890-9). Har-Row.
--Miss Charity Comes to Stay. Darling, Louis, Jr. (1916-1970), illus. LC 59-5250. (Illus.). 249 p. 21cm. 1959. Crowell.
--The Motoring Millers. Krush, Beth (1918-) & Krush, Joe (1918-), illus. LC 69-11081. (Illus.). 358 p. 21cm. 1969. Crowell.
--Those Miller Girls. Krush, Joe (1918-) & Krush, Beth (1918-), illus. LC 65-18694. 303p. illus. 21cm. (gr. 5-9). c.1965. (ISBN 0-690-82109-3). Crowell. **Award: (ALA).**
--Willie & the Wildcat Well. Watson, Aldren Auld (1917-), illus. LC 62-7741. (Illus.). (gr. 5-9). 1962. (ISBN 0-690-89351-5, TYC-J). T Y Crowell. **Award: (ALA).**

Constantino, Joan & Constantino, Josephine
--Pepito at Capistrano. Patton, Lucia, illus. LC 43-12118. 32 p. illus. (part col.) 24 x 18 1/2 cm. 1943. A. Whitman & Company.

Constantino, Josephine, jt. auth. see Constantino, Joan.

Constiner, Merle
--Meeting at the Merry Fifer. LC 66-11772. 139p. 21cm. c.1966. Norton.
--The Rebel Courier and the Redcoats. LC 68-28722. 122 p. 21cm. 1968. Meredith Press.
--Sumatra Alley. LC 79-140080. 128 p. 21cm. 1971. (ISBN 0-8407-6126-0). T. Nelson.

Contemporary Perspectives, Inc.
--High Action Treasure Chest Books. (Incl. 44 bks., skill cards & tchr's guide). (gr. 4-6). 1981. (ISBN 0-87895-295-0). Modern Curr.

Contempre, Yvette
--The Tower of Babel. LC 79-65866. (Children's Art Ser.). N.D. (ISBN 0-382-06327-9). Silver.

Contreras, Primo
--Song of Time. N.D. Carlton Press Inc.

Converse, Berthae Harris, Mrs.
--Little Kin Chan. Schneder, Clara, illus. LC 29-18175. 5 p. l., 3-101, 1 p. col. front., illus. 18 1/2 cm. c.1929. Friendship Press.

Converse, Berthae Harris, Mrs. & Wagner, Mabel Garrett, Mrs.
--Kin Chan and the Crab: A Course on Japan for Primary Children. LC 27-16740. iv p., 1 l., 137 p. fold. pl. 19 1/2 cm. c.1927. Friendship Press.

Converse, Caroline
--Sea Babies. LC 33-36071. 2 p. l., 29 p. col. illus. 24 cm. c.1933. A. W. Hogue.
--The Sea Babies. (Illus.). 36p. (Sea Baby Ser.). N.D. Frederick A. Stokes.

Converse, F., ed. see Portor, Laura Spencer.

Converse, Frank H
--Adventures at Sea. LC 8-32331. x p., 2 l., 3-197, 1 p. front. 5 pl. 18 1/2 cm. (On verse of i.-p.: Harper's adventure series. p. $0.60.). 1908. Harper & Brothers.
--The Adventures of Tad. LC 13-23600. 285 p. front., plates. 18 1/2 cm. 1886. D. Lothrop and Company.
--Boys' Adventures: Containing: In Southern Seas, The Mystery of a Diamond, A Voyage to the Old Coast, 3 vols. (Illus.). N.D. International Book Co.
--Gold of Flat Top Mountain. (The Boys Own Library). N.D. David McKay.
--Gold of Flat Top Mountain, 39 vols. (Illus.). (Famous Books for Boys Ser.: No. 14). 1905. Set. H M Caldwell Co.
--The Gold of Flat-Top Mountain. 264p. (Medal Library: No. 57). 1900. Street & Smith.
--Happy-Go-Lucky-Jack. LC 6-27200. 300 p. front., plates. 19 cm. (On cover: Leather-clad tales, no. 36). c.1891. United States Book Company.
--Heir to a Million. LC 6-27199. 303 p. incl. front., plates. 19 cm. (On cover: Leather-clad tales. no. 31). c.1891. United States Book Company.
--In Search of an Unknown Race. (The Boys Own Library). N.D. David mcKay.
--In Search of an Unknown Race. LC 1-26273. 19cm. 249p. 1901. Street & Smith.
--In Southern Areas: Or, Jack Esbon's Eventful Voyage. LC 13-23598. 245 p. incl. front., plates. 16 1/2 cm. (Munsey's popular series, no. 17). 1888. F. A. Munsey & Company.
--In Southern Seas. (The Boys Own Library). N.D. David McKay.
--In Southern Seas. (Illus.). (St. Nicholas Series for Boys). N.D. International Book Co.
--In Southern Seas. (Illus.). 18cm. 245p. (Medal Library: No. 43). 1900. Street & Smith.
--The Island Treasure. LC 6-27198. (Illus.). (The Boys' Home Ser.). N.D. A. L. Burt.
--The Island Treasure: Or, Harry Darrel's Fortunes. 244 p. incl. front., plates. 19 1/2 cm. (On cover: Boys' home library, v. 1, no. 15). c.1888. A. L. Burt.
--The Island Treasure: Or, Harry Darrel's Fortune. (The Rugby Series for Boys and Girls). N.D. A. L. Burt Company.
--The Island Treasure: Or, Harry Darrel's Fortune. (Illus.). (The Alger Series for Boys). N.D. A. L. Burt's Pubs.
--The Island Treasure: Or, Harry Darrel's Fortune. (Wide Awake Boys Ser.). N.D. A. L. Burt.
--The Lost Gold Mine. (Illus.). (The Little People's Ser.). N.D. Penn Publishing Co.
--The Lost Gold Mine. LC 10-4188. 354 p. incl. front. plates. 18 1/2 cm. (Adventure Stories Ser.). 1896. The Penn Publishing Company.
--The Mystery of a Diamond. (The Boys Own Library). N.D. David McKay.
--The Mystery of a Diamond. LC 6-27197. N.D. F. H. Lovell & Company.
--The Mystery of a Diamond, 39 vols. (Illus.). (Famous Books for Boys Ser.: No. 18). 1905. Set. H M Caldwell Co.
--The Mystery of a Diamond. (Illus.). (St. Nicholas Series for Boys). N.D. International Book Co.
--The Mystery of a Diamond. 203p. (Medal Library: No. 49). 1900. Street & Smith.
--That Treasure. 18cm. 218p. (Medal Library: No. 65). 1900. Street & Smith.
--That Treasure: Or, Adventures of Frontier Life. LC 13-23599. 218 p. incl. front., pl. 16 1/2 cm. (Munsey's popular series, no. 13). 1888. F. A. Munsey.
--That Treasure: Or, Adventures of Frontier Life. LC 6-27196. 218 p. incl. front 16 1/2 cm. (On cover: Leather-clad tales. no. 11). c.1890. F. F. Lovell & Company.
--Van: Or, In Search of an Unknown Race. 249 p. front., plates. 19 cm. (On cover: Leather-clad tales, no. 37). c.1891. United States Book Company.
--A Voyage to the Gold Coast. (The Boys Own Library). N.D. David McKay.
--A Voyage to the Gold Coast. (Illus.). (St. Nicholas Series for Boys). N.D. International Book Co.

Conway, Doris M.
--When I Am Alone. (Illus.). (gr. 1-3). 1971. Vantage.

Conway, Helene
--The End Is the Beginning. LC 77-161554. 190 p. 23cm. 1972. (ISBN 0-695-80241-0). (ISBN 0-695-40241-2). Follett.
--A Year to Grow. Best, Allena Champlin, Mrs. (1892-1974), illus. Berry, Erick, pseud. LC 43-6174. vii p., 1 l., 224 p. illus. 21 cm. 1943. Longmans, Green and Co.

Conway, Laura
--Moment of Truth. LC 75-10081. 160p. 1975. (ISBN 0-8415-0382-6). Dutton.

Conway, Paul Gerard, ed.
--Stories Out of School. LC 35-12191. x p., 1 l., 331 p. front., plates. 21 cm. 1935. J. B. Pomfret.

Conway, Tim & Sparks, Ted
--They Went That-a-Way & That-a-Way. (gr. 4-6). 1979. (ISBN 0-590-08049-0). Scholastic Inc.

Conwell, Russell H.
--Little Bo. N.D. American Baptist Publication Society.

Conyers, Cassandra
--The Saggy Baggy Elephant. Campana, Manny, illus. LC 81-83343. (Illus.). 12 p. 25cm. (Golden sturdy shape book). c.1982. (ISBN 0-307-12266-2). Golden Press.

Conyers, DeWitt
--Poochie & Lickrish. Gantz, David, illus. (Illus.). 16p. (Golden Fuzzy Shape Bks.). (ps). 1983. (ISBN 0-307-25791-6, Golden Pr). Western Pub.

Conyers, DeWitt, selected by.
--Animal Poems for Children. Schweninger, Ann (1951-), illus. LC 81-84381. (Illus.). 20 p. 24cm. (Golden storytime book). c.1982. (ISBN 0-307-11954-8). (ISBN 0-307-61954-0). Golden Press.

Conyers, Dorothy
--Three Girls and a Hermit. N.D. Dutton.

Conyn, Cornelius
--A Zoo of My Own. DeWilde, Dick, illus. 192p. 1958. John Day & Co.

Cook, Alice Maria, Mrs.
--Poems for the Young. LC 22-22942. 24cm. 164p. 1888. Rand Avery Co.

Cook, Ann, jt. auth. see Blance, Ellen.

Cook, Anna B.
--The Village School Choir. (Illus.). N.D. James A. Moore.
--The Washerwoman's Daughter. (Illus.). N.D. James A. Moore.

Cook, Bernadine (1924-)
--Curious Little Kitten. (Illus.). (gr. k-2). 1956. (ISBN 0-8382-0193-8). Hale.
--The Curious Little Kitten. Charlip, Remy (1929-), illus. LC 56-10692. unpaged. illus. 20x26cm. c.1956. Young Scott Books.
--The Little Fish That Got Away. N.D. E. M. Hale & Co.
--The Little Fish that Got Away. 64p. 1965. Pitman Publishing Corporation.
--The Little Fish That Got Away. Johnson, Crockett, pseud. (1906-1975), illus. Leisk, David Johnson. LC 56-5419. (Illus.). unpaged. 20cm. (Young Scott books). c.1956. W. R. Scott.
--Looking for Susie. 1959. E M Hale.
--Looking for Susie. Shahn, Judith, illus. LC 59-1739. (Illus.). unpaged. c.1959. Young Scott Books.

Cook, Bertha Louise Drew see Yap, Weda, pseud.

Cook, Bertha Louise Drew (1904-)
--Abigail's Private Reason. Yap, Weda, pseud. Cook, Bertha Louise Drew (1904-), illus. Yap, Weda, pseud. LC 32-5750. (Illus.). 70 p. 16cm. 1932. The Macmillan Co.

Cook, Canfield
--The Flying Jet. Smith, Crosby, illus. LC 45-5182. v p., 1 l., 210 p. incl. front. 19 1/2 cm. 1945. Grosset & Dunlap.
--From the Ground up. LC 48-4521. 266 p. 21 cm. 1948. T. Y. Crowell Co.
--Lost Squadron. Dobias, Frank (1902-), illus. LC 43-10329. v, 216 p. incl. front. 19 1/2 cm. 1943. Grosset & Dunlap.
--Secret Mission. N.D. Grosset & Dunlap.
--Sky Attack. N.D. Grosset & Dunlap.
--Spitfire Pilot. N.D. Grosset & Dunlap.
--Springboard to Tokyo. Dobias, Frank (1902-), illus. LC 43-169581. v p., 1 l., 210 p. incl. front. 19 1/2 cm. 1943. Grosset & Dunlap.
--Wings Over Japan. Knight, Clayton (1891-1969), illus. LC 44-939795. v p., 1 l., 215 p. incl. front. 19 1/2 cm. 1944. Grosset & Dunlap.

Cook, David F.
--Uncle Dave's Bedtime Yarns. Moritz, Dolores, illus. LC 73-76238. (Illus.). xvi, 368 p. 24cm. 1973. Monitor Publications.

AUTHOR INDEX | **COOLIDGE, FLORENCE**

Cook, Eliza (1818-1889)
--The Old Arm-Chair. Humphrey, Lizzie B., illus. LC 25-4894. 20 x 17cm. 26p. 1886. D. Lothrop & Co.
Cook, Ella Booker
--The Ghost of Windy Hill. N.D. Vantage Press.
Cook, Emilie C.
--Winnie the Witch & the Frightened Ghost. Gilleo, Alma, ed. McKissack, Vernon, illus. LC 74-734865. (Books & cassettes sold as 10 book set only). (Illus.). (Holiday Tales). (ps). 1977. (ISBN 0-89290-012-1). Soc for Visual.
Cook, Frances Kerr, Mrs., ed.
--Red and Gold Stories. Cook, Frances Kerr, Mrs., illus. LC 27-16914. 128 p. incl. col. front., col. illus. 22 1/2 cm. c.1927. Albert Whitman Company.
--Today's Books of Yesterday: Well Told Tales from Modern Authors. LC 26-2786. 127 p. incl. col. front., illus., (part col.) 18 1/2 cm. ("A just-rite book"). c.1925. Albert Whitman Company.
Cook, Fred James (1911-)
--City Cop. LC 78-60284. (Signal Bks.). (gr. 9 up). 1979. Doubleday.
Cook, George S. (1920-)
--Fish Heads and Fire Ants. Vestal, Herman B., illus. LC 72-10111. (Illus.). 116 p. 23cm. 1973. (ISBN 0-201-09230-1). Young Scott Books.
Cook, Gladys Moon (1907-)
--Vashti & the Strange God. LC 74-29465. (Illus.). 1975. (ISBN 0-912692-57-X). Cook.
Cook, Howard Norton (1901-)
--Sammi's Army. LC 43-10173. 32 p. col. illus. 31 x 24 1/2 cm. 1943. Doubleday, Doran & Company, Inc.
Cook, Lyn, pseud., see Waddell, Evelyn Margaret.
Cook, Lyn, pseud. (1918-)
--The Bells on Finland Street. Waddell, Evelyn Margaret. Wyatt, Stanley, illus. LC 51-9740. (Illus.). 197 p. 22cm. 1950. Macmillan.
--Jady and the General. Waddell, Evelyn Margaret. Smith, Murray, illus. 1955. St Martin's Press.
--The Magic fiddler. Waddell, Evelyn Margaret. (Illus.). 1951. St Martin's Press.
--Pegeen and the Pilgrim. Waddell, Evelyn Margaret. Wheeler, Pat & Wheeler, Bill, illus. (Illus.). 1957. St Martin's Press.
--Rebel on the Trail. Waddell, Evelyn Margaret. Collins, Ruth M., illus. 1953. St Martin's Press.
--The Road to Kip's Cove. Waddell, Evelyn Margaret. Wheeler, William, illus. LC 62-678. (Illus.). 222 p. 22cm. 1962, c.1961. St. Martin's Press.
--Samantha's Secret Room. Waddell, Evelyn Margaret. McKibbin, Bill, illus. LC 64-12047. (Illus.). ix, 210 p. 22cm. 1964. St. Martin's Press.
Cook, Marcy
--Codecracker Two. (gr. 4-8). 1982. (ISBN 0-88488-236-5). Creative Pubns.
Cook, Marion Belden
--Five Cents to See the Monkey. Wohlberg, Meg (1905-), illus. LC 56-5080. 68p. illus. 22cm. 1956. Knopf.
--Terry's Ferry. 1st ed. Weihs, Erika (1917-), illus. LC 57-8960. (Illus.). 24cm. 45p. 1957. E. P. Dutton & Co.
--Waggles and the Dog Catcher. Darling, Louis, Jr. (1916-1970), illus. LC 51-5639. 64 p. illus. 21 cm. 1951. Morrow.
Cook, Marjorie (1920-)
--To Walk on Two Feet. LC 77-17369. 93 p. 21cm. c.1978. (ISBN 0-664-32628-5). Westminster Press.
Cook, Mary E
--Blackie and His Family. Bevans, Michael H., illus. LC 49-7904. vii, 69 p. illus. 21 cm. 1949. Brace.
Cook, Melva Janice (1919-)
--Cassie's Busy Day. Cassell, Robert H., illus. LC 82-72989. (ps). 1984. (ISBN 0-8054-4162-X). Broadman.
--Christmas at Kyle's House. D'Adamo, Anthony, illus. LC 64-10810. (Illus.). 32p. (ps). 1964. (ISBN 0-8054-4137-9). (ISBN 0-8054-4136-0). Broadman.
--I Know God Loves Me. Fleming, Stanley B., illus. 1960. Broadman Press.
Cook, Mercer, tr. see Thiam, Djibi.
Cook, Neil E
--Welcome--Stranger. LC 29-6456. 4 p. l., 232, 1 p. front. 19 1/2 cm. 1929. D. Appleton and Company.
Cook, Olive Rambo (1892-)
--Coon Holler. 1st ed. Voute, Kathleen (1892-), illus. LC 58-5974. (Illus.). 178 p. 22cm. 1958. Longmans, Green.
--Locket. Torrey, Helen (1901-), illus. LC 63-13179. (Illus.). 21cm. 148p. (gr. 4-6). N.D. McKay.
--Serilda's Star. 1st ed. Torrey, Helen (1901-), illus. LC 59-12747. (Illus.). 176 p. 21cm. 1959. Longmans, Green.
--The Sign at Six Corners. Lambo, Donald W. (1903-1966), illus. LC 65-141321. 210p. illus. 21cm. c.1965. (ISBN 0-679-20180-7). McKay.
Cook, Ray M.
--The Complete Sing-for-Fun Book. Cook, Samuel, ed. index. (gr. 2-12). 1974. (ISBN 0-8074-0004-1). UAHC.
Cook, Richard Yerkes (1845-)
--A Studious Boy Who Became a Great Man And Other Stories. LC 8-976624. 2 v. 21 cm. 1907. Printed for Private Distribution Press of E. Stern & Co., Inc.
Cook, Roderick, jt. auth. see Jayme, William North.
Cook, Samuel, ed. see Cook, Ray M.
Cook, Will
--The Speed Merchant. LC 64-24484. 148 p. 21cm. 1964. Duell, Sloan & Pearce.
--Speed Merchants. (gr. 7-9). 1964. (ISBN 0-696-80530-8). Hawthorn.
Cook, William Wallace
--His Friend the Enemy. Lowenheim, Frederick, illus. LC 3-3864. 19cm. 304p. 1903. G. W. Dillingham Co.
--Wilby's Dan. Falls, Charles Buckles (1874-1960), illus. LC 4-25684. 20 cm. 325p. 1904. Dodd, Mead & Co.
Cooke, Ann
--The Grandfather Clock. 1984. (ISBN 0-533-05997-6). Vantage.
Cooke, Anna B., tr.
--Grandmother's Curiosity Cabinet. N.D. E. P. Dutton.
Cooke, Arthur Owens (1867-1930)
--At the Zoo. 192p. N.D. Platt & Munk.
--At the Zoo. Austin, Winifred, illus. 27cm. 152p. 1931. Thomas Nelson & Sons.
--Blackbeard's Boy. Forrest, A. S., illus. LC 30-9745. (Illus.). 20cm. 304p. 1929. Thomas Nelson & Sons.
--Stories of France in Days of Old. 21cm. 146p. (In Days of Old Ser.). 1914. Frederick A. Stokes Co.
--Stories of Rome. (In Days of Old Ser.). N.D. Frederick A. Stokes.
Cooke, Barbara, pseud., see Alexander, Anne Barbara Cooke.
Cooke, Barbara, pseud. (1913-)
--My Daddy and I. Alexander, Anne Barbara Cooke. Satorsky, Cyril, illus. LC 61-7133. unpaged. illus. 21cm. 1961. Abelard-Schuman.
--Pete and the Mouse. Alexander, Anne Barbara Cooke. Rose, Gerald Hembdon Seymour (1935-), illus. 1964. Abelard-Schuman.
Cooke, Carrie A.
--From June to June, 1 of 20 vols. New ed. (Illus.). 350p. (Sunday-School Lib: No. 13). 1895. Set. Lothrop Pub. Co.
Cooke, Carrie A., selected by.
Young Folks' Speaker: A Collection of Prose & Poetry for Declamations, Recitations, & Elocutionary Exercises. (Illus.). N.D. Lothrop Publishing Co.
Cooke, David Coxe (1917-)
--Better Baseball for Boys. (Illus.). (gr. 3-6). 1959. (ISBN 0-8382-0070-2). Hale.
--How Atomic Submarines are Made. LC 67-7779. 64p. illus. 10 x 24cm. 1967. Dodd Mead.
--While the Crowd Cheers: All-American Sports Stories for All-American Boys. 1st ed. LC 53-82528. 186p. 20cm. 1953. Dutton.
Cooke, Donald Ewin (1916-)
--Johnny On-the-Spot. LC 55-6315. 188p. illus. 22cm. 1955. Nelson.
--Little Wolf Slayer. Pitz, Henry Clarence (1895-1976), illus. (Winston Adventure Bk.). 1958. Holt, Rinehart and Winston.
--Little Wolf Slayer: A Story of Philadelphia's First Quakers. 1st ed. Pitz, Henry Clarence (1895-1976), illus. LC 52-5489. 184 p. illus. 22 cm. (Winston adventure books). 1952. Winston.
--Men of Sherwood: New Tales of Robin Hood's Merry Band. Burchard, Peter Duncan (1921-), illus. LC 61-7624. (Illus.). 214p. (gr. 7-9). 1961. (ISBN 0-03-033045-9). HR&W.
--The Narrow Ledge of Fear. Geary, Clifford N. (1916-), illus. LC 54-5907. 191 p. 21cm. 1954. Nelson.
--Powder Keg (Pub. by Holt, Rinehart & Winston). (gr. 4-6). 1972 (Starline). Schol Bk Serv.
--Powder Keg: A Story of the Bermuda Gunpowder Mystery. 1st ed. Stein, Harve (1904-), illus. LC 53-7109. 179p. illus. 23cm. (Winston adventure books). 1953. Winston.
--A Race with the Wolves. Loh, George, illus. LC 65-14153. (Illus.). 41 p. 24cm. (Wise owl book, WC34). c.1965. Holt, Rinehart, and Winston.
--The Silver Horn of Robin Hood. 1st ed. Cooke, Donald Ewin (1916-), illus. LC 56-9656. (Illus.). 238 p. 24cm. 1956. Winston.
--Valley of Rebellion: A Story of America's First Armed Revolt Against British Authority. 1st ed. Pitz, Henry Clarence (1895-1976), illus. LC 55-6523. 210p. illus. 22cm. 1955. Winston.
Cooke, Donald Ewin (1916-), illus.
--The House that Jack Built. LC 63-8238. (Illustrations Adapted from Old Drawings by Frederick Richardson). (Illus.). 24 p. 24cm. (A Little Owl Bk.). 1963. Holt, Rinehart & Winston.
--The Old Woman and Her Pig. LC 63-8237. (Illustrations Adapted from Old Drawings by Frederick Richardson.). (Illus.). 24 p. 24cm. (A Little Owl Bk.). 1963. Holt, Rinehart and Winston.
Cooke, Donald Ewin (1916-) & Dukas, Paul (1865-1935)
--The Sorcerer's Apprentice: A Story of Magic Based Upon the Legend That Inspired the Ballad by Goethe, and Following Closely the Program of Paul Dukas' Famous Musical Fantasy "L'apprenti Sorcier". 1st ed. Cooke, Donald Ewin (1916-), illus. LC 47-11378. 56 p. illus. 24 cm. 1947. J. C. Winston Co.
Cooke, Donald Ewin (1916-) & Hoffmann, Ernst Theodor Amadeus (1776-1822)
--The Nutcracker of Nuremberg: A Christmas Fantasy Based Upon the Old Hoffmann Legend. Cooke, Donald Ewin (1916-), illus. LC 38-33219. x p., 4 l., 7-148 p. incl. plates (part col.) 23 cm. c.1938. The John C. Winston Company.
Cooke, Donald Ewin (1916-) & Scott, J. Denton
--Pug Invades the Fifth Column. LC 43-7516. 214 p. col. front., illus. 21 cm. 1943. David McKay Company.
Cooke, Donald Ewin (1916-) & Zhar-Ptitsa (1916-)
--The Firebird. Cooke, Donald Ewin (1916-), illus. LC 39-255682. 3 p. l., ix-xv, 144 p. incl. illus., plates. col. plates. 29 cm. c.1939. The John C. Winston Company.
Cooke, Edith Holden, Mrs.
--The Bratchets. Holden, Lansing Colton (1896-1938), illus. LC 40-7710. 50 p. incl. front., illus. 19 x 18 cm. c.1939. B. Bratchet, Ltd.
--The Bratchets. Holden, Lansing Colton (1896-1938), illus. LC 70-182779. (Illus.). 47 p. (Holt Owlet). 1972, c.1936. (ISBN 0-03-005701-9). Holt.
--The Bratchets. Holden, Lansing Colton (1896-1938), illus. LC 36-19095. 50 p. illus. 18 1/2 x 18 1/2 cm. c.1936. Oxford University Press.
Cooke, Edmund Vance (1866-1932)
--Cheerful Children. Scannell, Mae Herrick, illus. LC 26-11707. 91 p. illus. 20 cm. c.1923. Beckley-Cardy Company.
--Chronicles of the Little Tot: Poems About Children. DeLand, Clyde O., illus. 1905. Dodge.
--I Rule the House. (Poems About Children). c.1910. Dodge.
--Just Then Something Happened. LC 14-6796. xi p., 1 l., 322 p. col. front., col. plates 20 cm. c.1914. Dodge Publishing Company.
--The Story Club. Curtis, Eliza, illus. LC 12-29471. vi, 210 p. col. front., col. plates 22 cm. c.1912. Dodge Publishing Company.
--Told to the Little Tot. Pease, Bessie Collins, illus. LC 6-32672. 132 p. col. front., illus., col. plates. 22 cm. c.1906. Dodge Publishing Company.
Cooke, Edna W., illus.
--Mother Goose Nursery Rhymes. N.D. Cupples & Leon.
Cooke, Emogene
--Window Garden. N.D. Grosset & Dunlap.
Cooke, F. E.
--Guiding Lights. 232p. N.D. American Tract Scoiety.
Cooke, Flora Juliette (1864-)
--Nature Myths and Stories. Rev ed. Dulin, Dorothy, illus. LC 19-31. 159 p. col. front., illus. 19 cm. c.1919. A. Flanagan Company.
--Nature Myths and Stories: For Little Children. LC 14-4514. v, 2, 9-102 p. illus. 19 cm. (1864-). c.1913. A. Flanagan Company.
--Nature Myths and Stories for Little Children. rev. ed. LC 43-357757. v, 2, 9-102, 2 p. illus. 19 cm. c.1895. A. Flanagan.
--Nature Myths and Stories for Young Children. LC 44-29962. 92 p. 1 illus. 20 cm. 1893. A. Flanagan.
Cooke, Grace MacGowan, Mrs. (1863-)
--The Doings of the Dollivers: The Strange Adventures of a Doll Family. (Juvenile Ladder Library for Children). N.D. Macmillan.
--The Doings of the Dollivers: The Strange Adventures of a Doll Family. Linnell, Harry, illus. LC 10-28800. 8 p. l., 3-174 p. front., plates. 19 cm. 1910. Sturgis & Walton Company.
--The Fortunes of John Hawk: A Boy of Old New York 1781. Eltonhead, Frank, illus. LC 28-21823. xi, 355 p. front., plates. 20 cm. c.1928. The Century Co.
--A Gound Fiddle. Mudge, E. Lynn & Miles, E. B., illus. xi p., 1 l., 15-118 p. incl. front. 8 pl. 18 cm. 1904. H. Altemus Company.
--A Gourd Fiddle, 1 of 21 vols. Mudge, E. Lynn & Miles, E. B., illus. (Boys & Girls Booklovers Ser.: No. 10). 1905. Set. Henry Altemus Co.
--Son Riley Rabbit & Little Girl. N.D. Frederick A Stokes.
--Sonny Bunny Rabbit and His Friends. Barnes, Culmer, illus. LC 15-18275. 5 p. l., 210 p. col. front., col. plates. 21 cm. c.1915. Frederick A. Stokes Company.
Cooke, Grace MacGowan, Mrs. (1863-) & McQueen, Anne
--The Girls of Silver Spur Ranch. Williams, Florence White, illus. LC 13-17997. 2 p. l 252 p. col. front., pl. 20cm. c.1913. M. A. Donohue & Co.
Cooke, John Estes, pseud., see Baum, Lyman Frank.
Cooke, John Estes, pseud. (1856-1919)
--Justin Harley. Baum, Lyman Frank. (Illus.). N.D. Claxton, Remsen, and Haffelfinger.
Cooke, Laura S. H. Dimple
--Dopp. (Illus.). N.D. Houghton, Mifflin And Co.
Cooke, Marjorie Benton (0000-1920)
--Bambi. 1921. A. L. Burt Co.
Cooke, Muriel & The, Meadley Harpers
--Mrs. Calipher's House. Cooke, Sherman, illus. LC 43-151745. 63 p. col. illus. 23 1/2 x 17 1/2 cm. 1943. A. A. Knopf.
Cooke, Muriel & Cooke, Sherman
--A Tale of Whoa. LC 40-632. 32 p. incl. col. front., illus. (part col.) 19 x 25 cm. c.1939. David McKay Company.
Cooke, Rose Terry, Mrs. (1827-1892)
--Little Foxes. Neill, John Rea (1878-1943), illus. LC 4-21994. 98 p. incl. col. front., 8 pl. 19 cm. (Altemus' Holly-tree series). 1904. H. Altemus Company.
Cooke, Sherman, jt. auth. see Cooke, Muriel.
Cooke, Tom
--Big Bird's Color Game: Featuring Big Bird, a Jim Henson Sesame Street Muppet. LC 79-67616. (Illus.). 14 p. 25cm. (Golden sturdy shape book). c.1980. (ISBN 0-307-12254-9). Golden Press.
--The Care Bears' Book of Favorite Bedtime Stories. Cooke, Tom, illus. LC 83-23656. (Illus.). 80p. (ps-3). 1984. (ISBN 0-910313-20-2). (ISBN 0-910313-20-2). Parker Bro.
--Grover's Super Surprise Book: Featuring Jim Henson's Muppets. Cooke, Tom, illus. Penick, Ib, designed by. LC 77-93776. (Illus.). 14 p. (on double leaves). 24cm. (CTW Sesame Street pop up ; 12). c.1978. (ISBN 0-394-83841-6). Random House.
Cooke, Tom & Henson, Jim
--Bert and Ernie on the Go: Featuring Jim Henson's Sesame Street Muppets. Penick, Ib, designed by. LC 80-54574. (Illus.). 14 p. 24cm. (CTW Sesame Street Pop-up ; 15: No.). (ps-2). c.1981. (ISBN 0-394-84869-1). Random House : In Conjunction with Children's Television Workshop.
Cookson, Catherine McMullen (1906-)
--Blue Baccy. Jordan, Tessa, illus. LC 73-1749. (Illus.). 148 p. 21cm. 1973, c.1972. (ISBN 0-672-51830-9). Bobbs-Merrill.
--Go Tell It to Mrs. Golightly. LC 80-10318. 192 p. 22cm. 1980, c.1977. (ISBN 0-688-41965-8). (ISBN 0-688-51965-2). Lothrop, Lee & Shepard.
--Lanky Jones. LC 80-22676. 158 p. 22cm. c.1981. (ISBN 0-688-00430-X). (ISBN 0-688-00431-8). Lothrop, Lee & Shepard.
--The Mallen Lot. LC 73-16393. 320p. 1974. (ISBN 0-525-15073-0). Dutton.
--Mrs. Flannagan's Trumpet. LC 79-26352. 192 p. 22cm. 1980, c.1976. Lothrop, Lee & Shepard Books.
--The Nipper. Jordan, Tessa, illus. LC 73-159017. (Illus.). 171 p. 21cm. 1970. Bobbs-Merrill.
--Our John Willie. LC 73-22687. (Illus.). 191 p. 1974. (ISBN 0-672-51897-X). Bobbs-Merrill.
Cool, Joyce (1938-)
--The Kidnapping of Courtney Van Allen and What's Her Name. LC 80-28455. 175 p. 22cm. c.1981. (ISBN 0-394-84822-5). (ISBN 0-394-94822-X). Knopf : Distributed by Random House.
Cooley, Berta
--We Fell into Paradise. (gr. 4-12). 1978. (ISBN 0-89185-036-8). Anthelion Pr.
Cooley, Marjorie L
--The Dandelion Fairy and Gyp's License. LC 22-16173. 30 p. 19 cm. c.1922. Dorrance.
Coolidge, Elizabeth
--After Supper Songs. Coolidge, Elizabeth, illus. LC 99-124. (Illus.). 62p. 1898. H. S. Stone & Co.
--After Supper Songs: Words and Music for Children. Coolidge, Elizabeth, illus. (Illus.). N.D. Duffield & Co.
Coolidge, Florence Claudine
--Little Ugly Face and Other Indian Tales. (The Little Library Ser.). N.D. Macmillan.
--Little Ugly Face And Other Indian Tales. Petersham, Maud Sylvia Fuller, Mrs. (1890-1971) & Petersham, Miska (1889-1960), illus. LC 25-23505. vi, 181 p. col. illus. 19 cm. 1925. The Macmillan Company.

Coolidge, Grace
--Paddy-Paws. Carr, Warner, illus. N.D. Rand McNally.
Coolidge, Olivia Ensor (1908-)
--Come by Here. Johnson, Milton (1932-), illus. LC 72-115451. (Illus.). xi, 239 p. 22cm. 1970. Houghton Mifflin. **Award: (BGH).**
--Cromwell's Head. Wilson, Edward Arthur (1886-), illus. LC 55-9952. (Illus.). 262 p. 22cm. 1955. Houghton Mifflin.
--Egyptian Adventures. Low, Joseph (1911-), illus. LC 53-109890. 209p. illus. 22cm. (gr. 7-12). 1954. (ISBN 0-395-06719-7). Houghton Mifflin. **Award: (ALA).**
--Greek Myths. Sandoz, Edouard Marcel (1918-), illus. LC 49-5593. xi, 243 p. illus.24 cm. 1949. Houghton Mifflin Co.
--The King of Men. Raskin, Ellen (1928-1984), illus. LC 66-120966. 230p. illus 22 cm. (gr. 7up). 1966. (ISBN 0-395-06725-1). Houghton. **Award: (ALA).**
--Legends of the North. Sandoz, Edouard Marcel (1918-), illus. (Illus.). (gr. 7 up). 1951. (ISBN 0-395-06726-X). HM.
--The Maid of Artemis. Holmes, Bea, illus. LC 69-14724. (Illus.). x, 132 p. 22cm. 1969. Houghton Mifflin.
--Marathon Looks on the Sea. Schachner, Erwin, illus. LC 67-23307. (Illus.). viii, 246 p. 22cm. 1967. Houghton Mifflin.
--Men of Athens. Johnson, Milton (1932-), illus. LC 62-12249. (Illus.). 244 p. 22cm. 1962. Houghton Mifflin.
--People in Palestine. LC 64-19985. 212p. 22cm. c.1965. Houghton.
--Roman People. Lipinski deOrlov, Lino Sigismondo (1908-), illus. Lipinski, Lino S., pseud. LC 59-7481. (Illus.). 243 p. 22cm. 1959. Houghton Mifflin.
--Tales of the Crusades. Dore, Louis Christophe Paul Gustave (1832-1883), illus. LC 72-98516. (Illus.). ix, 225 p. 22cm. 1970. Houghton Mifflin.
--Trojan War. Sandoz, Edouard Marcel (1918-), illus. (Illus.). (gr. 7-12). 1952. (ISBN 0-395-06731-6). HM.

Coolidge, Susan, pseud., see Woolsey, Sarah Chauncey.

Coomaraswamy, Ananda Kentish (1877-1947) & Nivedita, Sr.
--Myths of the Hindus & Buddhists. (Illus.). (gr. 4-8). N.D. Dover.
Coombe, F.
--Her Friend and Mine. (Scribner-Blackie Series of books for young people). N.D. Charles Scribner's Sons.
Coombs, Charles I., ed. see Disney, Walter Elias.
Coombs, Charles Ira (1914-)
--Ace of the Argonne. Albright, Donn, illus. LC 67-23353. (Illus.). 157 p. 21cm. 1967. World Pub. Co.
--Alaska Bush Pilot. Naylor, Raymon, illus. LC 63-5597. (Illus.). 256 p. 20cm. (American adventure series). 1963. Harper & Row.
--Baseball Stories. (Illus.). (Young Readers Bookshelf). (gr. 4-7). N.D. (ISBN 0-8313-0020-5). Lantern.
--The Case of the Purple Mark. LC 55-5759. 192p. 21cm. 1955. Westminister Press.
--Celestial Space, Inc. LC 54-6985. (Illus.). 190 p. 22cm. 1954. Westminster Press.
--Countdown to Danger. McCann, Gerald (1916-), illus. LC 60-8994. (Illus.). (gr. 4-7). 1960. (ISBN 0-8313-0027-2). Lantern.
--Detective Stories. (Illus.). (Young Readers Bookshelf). (gr. 4-7). N.D. (ISBN 0-8313-0025-6). Lantern.
--Everygirls Teen-Age Stories. (Illus.). N.D. Lantern Press Inc.
--Frank Luke, Balloon Buster. Betts, Emmett A., ed. Naylor, Raymon, illus. LC 67-6277. (Illus.). 256 p. 20cm. (American adventures series). 1967. Harper & Row.
--Indoor Sports Stories. (Illus.). (Young Readers Bookshelf). (gr. 4-7). N.D. (ISBN 0-8313-0024-8). Lantern.
--Mystery of Satellite Seven. LC 57-8928. 160 p. 21cm. 1958. Westminister Press.
--Mystery Stories. (Illus.). (Young Readers Bookshelf). (gr. 4-7). N.D. (ISBN 0-8313-0023-X). Lantern.
--Railroad Stories. (Illus.). (Young Readers Bookshelf). (gr. 4-7). N.D. (ISBN 0-8313-0017-5). Lantern.
--Rocket Pioneer. Betts, Emmett Albert (1903-), ed. Naylor, Raymon, illus. LC 65-4178. 256p. illus. 20cm. (Amer. adventure ser.). c.1965. Harper.
--Sabre Jet Ace. Betts, Emmet A., ed. Ruth, Rod (1912-), illus. LC 59-16436. (Illus.). 20cm. 260p. (The American Adventure Ser.). 1959. Wheeler Pub. Co.
--Sleuth at Shortstop. N.D. E . M. Hale and co.
--Sleuth at Shortstop. LC 55-6990. 190p. illus. 21cm. 1955. Lantern Press.
--Stories of the Diamond. (Illus.). (Young Readers Bookshelf). (gr. 4-7). N.D. (ISBN 0-8313-0017-5). Lantern.
--Teen-Age Adventure Stories. LC 62-32. 254 p. illus. 22 cm. (Teen-age library). 1964, c.1948. Grosset & Dunlap.
--Teen-Age Adventure Stories. LC 48-9560. 254 p. illus. 21 cm. (Teen-age library). 1948. Lantern Press.
--Teen-Age Champion Sports Stories. Ricketts, William B., illus. LC 50-13583. 254 p. illus. 21 cm. 1950. Lantern Press.
--Teen-age Treasure Chest of Sports Stories. (The Teen-age Library). N.D. Grosset & Dunlap.
--Teen-Age Treasure Chest of Sports Stories. LC 48-7628. 250 p. illus. 21 cm. (Teen-age library). 1948. Lantern Press.
--Treasure under Coyote Hill. LC 56-7225. 191p. illus. 22cm. 1956. Westminister Press.
--Young Atom Detective. Lewis, Geoffrey Dean, illus. LC 58-5867. (Illus.). 21cm. 189p. (gr. 4-7). N.D. (ISBN 0-8313-0021-3). Lantern.
--Young Circus Detective. Geer, Charles Hand (1922-), illus. LC 54-10747. 192p. illus. 21cm. (Young heroes library). 1954. Lantern Press.
--Young Infield Rookie. (Young Heroes Library). N.D. Grosset & Dunlap.
--Young Infield Rookie. Geer, Charles Hand (1922-), illus. LC 54-728174. 188p. illus. 21cm. (Young heroes library). (gr. 4-7). 1954. (ISBN 0-8313-0018-3). Lantern Press.
--Young Pony Express Rider. (Young Heroes Library). N.D. Grosset & Dunlap.
--Young Pony Express Rider. Geer, Charles Hand (1922-), illus. LC 53-10374. 191p. illus. 21cm. (Young heroes library). 1953. Lantern Press.
--Young Ranch Detective. Priscilla, Louis, illus. LC 56-100117. 189p. illus. 21cm. (Young heroes library). (gr. 4-7). 1956. Lantern Press.
--Young Readers Atom Mystery. Lewis, Geoffrey Dean, illus. LC 62-217. 189 p. illus. 20 cm. (Young readersbookshelf26). 1961, c.1958. Grosset & Dunlap.
--Young Readers Baseball Mystery. Geer, Charles Hand (1922-), illus. LC 59-484. (Illus.). 20cm. 190p. 1959. Grosset & Dunlap.
--Young Readers Baseball Stories. Osborne, Richard N., illus. LC 53-11975. 190p. illus. 22cm. (Young readers bookshelf 3). 1953, c.1950. Grosset & Dunlap.
--Young Readers Baseball Stories. Osborne, Richard N., illus. LC 50-11857. (Illus.). 190 p. 21cm. (Young readers bookshelf). 1950. Lantern Press.
--Young Readers Basketball Stories. Geer, Charles Hand (1922-), illus. LC 54-613. 191p. illus. 22cm. (.Young readers bookshelf 13). 1954, c.1951. Grosset & Dunlap.
--Young Readers Basketball Stories. Geer, Charles Hand (1922-), illus. LC 51-14779. 191 p. illus. 21 cm. (Young readers bookshelf). 1951. Lantern Press.
--Young Readers Circus Mystery. Geer, Charles Hand (1922-), illus. LC 60-1366. (Illus.). 20cm. 192p. N.D. Grosset & Dunlap.
--Young Readers Detective Stories. Geer, Charles Hand (1922-), illus. LC 62-34. 192 p. illus. 21 cm. (Young readers bookshelf16). 1961, c.1951. Grosset & Dunlap.
--Young Readers Detective Stories. Geer, Charles Hand (1922-), illus. LC 52-6055. 192 p. illus. 21 cm. (Young readers bookshelf). 1951. Lantern Press.
--Young Readers Football Stories. Ricketts, William B., illus. LC 53-11976. 187p. illus. 22cm. (Young readers bookshelf 6). 1953, c.1950. Grosset & Dunlap.
--Young Readers Football Stories. Ricketts, William B., illus. LC 51-186. (Illus.). 187 p. 21cm. (Young readers bookshelf). 1950. Lantern Press.
--Young Readers Indoor Sports Stories. Geer, Charles Hand (1922-), illus. LC 62-235. 188 p. illus. 20 cm. (Young readers bookshelf21). 1961, c.1952. Grosset & Dunlap.
--Young Readers Indoor Sports Stories. Geer, Charles Hand (1922-), illus. LC 52-9875. 188 p. illus. 21 cm. (Young readers bookshelf). 1952. Lantern Press.
--Young Readers Mystery Stories. Geer, Charles Hand (1922-), illus. LC 53-119775. 192p. illus. 22cm. (Young readers bookshelf 8). 1953, c.1951. Grosset & Dunlap.
--Young Readers Mystery Stories. Geer, Charles Hand (1922-), illus. LC 51-11123. 192 p. illus. 21 cm. (Young readers bookshelf). 1951. Lantern Press.
--Young Readers Railroad Stories. Geer, Charles Hand (1922-), illus. LC 62-35. 192 p. illus. 21 cm. (Young readers bookshelf18). 1961, c.1953. Grosset & Dunlap.
--Young Readers Railroad Stories. Geer, Charles Hand (1922-), illus. LC 53-554297. 192p. illus. 21cm. (Young readers bookshelf). 1953. Lantern Press.
--Young Readers Ranch Mystery. Priscilla, Louis, illus. LC 60-1322. (Illus.). 20cm. 180p. (Young Readers Bookshelp: No. 25). 1960. Grosset & Dunlap.
--Young Readers Sports Treasury. Geer, Charles Hand (1922-), illus. LC 52-12497. 191 p. illus. 21 cm. (Young readers bookshelf). 1952. Lantern Press.
--Young Readers Stories of the Diamond. Geer, Charles Hand (1922-), illus. LC 62-36. 194 p. illus. 21 cm. (Young readers bookshelf). 1961, c.1951. Grosset & Dunlap.
--Young Readers Stories of the Diamond. Geer, Charles Hand (1922-), illus. LC 51-14778. 194 p. illus. 21 cm. (Young readers bookshelf). 1951. Lantern Press.
--Young Readers Water Sports Stories. Geer, Charles Hand (1922-), illus. LC 57-135831. 180p. illus. 20cm. (Young readers bookshelf 19). c.1952. Grosset & Dunlap.
--Young Readers Water Sports Stories. Geer, Charles Hand (1922-), illus. LC 52-14177. 189 p. illus. 21 cm. (Young readers bookshelf). 1952. Lantern Press.
--Young Sleuth at Shortstop. (Illus.). (gr. 6-9). 1955. Lantern.
Coombs, Francis Lovell (1876-)
--Young Crusoes of the Sky. Bayha, Edwin F., illus. LC 11-24133. 6 p. l., 3-380 p. incl. plates. front. 20 cm. 1911. The Century Company.
--The Young Railroaders: Tales of Adventure and Ingenuity. Masters, F. B., illus. LC 10-22056. x, 380 p. incl. plates. front. 20 cm. 1910. The Century Co.
Coombs, Patricia (1926-)
--Dorrie and the Amazing Magic Elixir. Coombs, Patricia (1926-), illus. LC 74-4206. (Illus.). 48 p. 26cm. 1974. (ISBN 0-688-41640-3). (ISBN 0-688-41640-3). Lothrop, Lee & Shepard Co.
--Dorrie and the Birthday Eggs. Coombs, Patricia (1926-), illus. LC 72-155748. (Illus.). 48 p. 26cm. 1971. Lothrop, Lee & Shepard.
--Dorrie and the Blue Witch. Coombs, Patricia (1926-), illus. LC 64-21196. (Illus.). 37, 11 p. 26cm. 1964. Lothrop, Lee and Shepard Co.
--Dorrie and the Dreamyard Monsters. Coombs, Patricia (1926-), illus. LC 77-1373. (Illus.). 47 p. 26cm. c.1977. (ISBN 0-688-41807-4). (ISBN 0-688-51807-9). Lothrop, Lee & Shepard.
--Dorrie and the Fortune Teller. Coombs, Patricia (1926-), illus. LC 73-4934. (Illus.). 47 p. 26cm. 1973. (ISBN 0-688-41533-4). (ISBN 0-688-41533-4). Lothrop, Lee & Shepard Co.
--Dorrie and the Goblin. Coombs, Patricia (1926-), illus. LC 72-1080. (Illus.). 48 p. 26cm. 1972. Lothrop, Lee & Shepard Co.
--Dorrie and the Halloween Plot. Coombs, Patricia (1926-), illus. LC 76-3643. (Illus.). 48 p. 26cm. c.1976. (ISBN 0-688-41764-7). (ISBN 0-688-51764-1). Lothrop, Lee & Shepard.
--Dorrie & the Haunted House. Coombs, Patricia (1926-), illus. LC 74-120159. (Illus.). ils., some color. 48p. (gr. 1-5). 1970. (ISBN 0-688-51108-2). Lothrop.
--Dorrie and the Screebit Ghost. Coombs, Patricia (1926-), illus. LC 79-4443. (Illus.). 48 p. 26cm. c.1979. (ISBN 0-688-41883-X). (ISBN 0-688-51883-4). Lothrop, Lee & Shepard.
--Dorrie and the Weather-Box. Coombs, Patricia (1926-), illus. LC 66-9138. (Illus.). 1 v. (unpaged. 26cm. 1966. Lothrop, Lee & Shepard Co.
--Dorrie and the Weather Box. Coombs, Patricia (1926-), illus. 1966. (ISBN 0-688-50986-X). William Morrow and Company.
--Dorrie and the Witch Doctor. Coombs, Patricia (1926-), illus. LC 67-25293. (Illus.). 1 v. (unpaged. 26cm. 1967. Lothrop, Lee & Shepard.
--Dorrie and the Witches' Camp. Coombs, Patricia (1926-), illus. LC 82-9986. p. cm. c.1983. (ISBN 0-688-01507-7). Lothrop, Lee & Shepard Books.
--Dorrie and the Witch's Imp. Coombs, Patricia (1926-), illus. LC 75-5504. (Illus.). 47 p. 26cm. 1975. (ISBN 0-688-41704-3). (ISBN 0-688-51704-8). Lothrop, Lee & Shepard.
--Dorrie and the Witchville Fair. 1st ed. Coombs, Patricia (1926-), illus. LC 80-10189. (Illus.). 48 p. 26cm. c.1980. (ISBN 0-688-41957-7). (ISBN 0-688-51957-1). Lothrop, Lee & Shepard Books.
--Dorrie and the Wizard's Spell. Coombs, Patricia (1926-), illus. LC 68-27601. (Illus.). 1 v. 48p. 26cm. 1968. Lothrop, Lee & Shepard Co.
--Dorrie's Magic. Coombs, Patricia (1926-), illus. (Illus.). 42 p. 26cm. 1962. Lothrop, Lee & Shepard.
--Dorrie's Play. Coombs, Patricia (1926-), illus. LC 65-22024. (Illus.). 1 v. (unpaged. 26cm. 1965. Lothrop, Lee and Shepard Co.
--Lisa and the Grompet. Coombs, Patricia (1926-), illus. LC 71-101471. (Illus.). 31 p. 21cm. 1970. Lothrop, Lee & Shepard.
--The Lost Playground. Coombs, Patricia (1926-), illus. LC 63-11672. (Illus.). 44 p. 24cm. 1963. Lothrop, Lee and Shepard Co.
--The Magic Pot. Coombs, Patricia (1926-), illus. LC 76-54876. p. cm. c.1977. (ISBN 0-688-41792-2). (ISBN 0-688-51792-7). Lothrop, Lee & Shepard Co.
--The Magician & McTree. Coombs, Patricia (1926-), illus. LC 83-11984. (Illus.). (gr. 1-4). 1984. (ISBN 0-688-02109-3). (ISBN 0-688-02109-3). Lothrop.
--Molly Mullett. Coombs, Patricia (1926-), illus. LC 74-22009. (Illus.). 38 p. 26cm. 1975. (ISBN 0-688-41692-6). (ISBN 0-688-51692-0). Lothrop, Lee & Shepard Co.
--Mouse Cafe. Coombs, Patricia (1926-), illus. LC 72-148481. (Illus.). 46 p. 21cm. 1972. Lothrop, Lee & Shepard Co. **Award: (NYT).**
--Tilabel. Coombs, Patricia (1926-), illus. LC 77-21039. (Illus.). 31 p. 26cm. (gr. 1-3). c.1978. (ISBN 0-688-41831-7). (ISBN 0-688-51831-1). Lothrop, Lea & Shepard Co.
--Waddy & His Brother. LC 63-16783. (Illus.). 24cm. (ps-1). 1963. Lothrop.
Coomer, George H.
--The Boys in the Forecastle. (St. Nicholas Series for Boys). N.D. International Book Co.
--The Boys in the Forecastle: A Story of Real Ships and Real Sailors. LC 1-307. 225p. (Munsey's Popular Ser.: No. 3). 1887. F. A. Munsey.
--The Boys in the Forecastle: A Story of Real Ships and Real Sailors. 18cm. 225p. (Medal Library: No. 75). 1900. Street & Smith.
--Miscellaneous Poems. LC 22-22953. 20cm. 168p. 1851. George H. Coomer.
--The Mountain Cave. (Illus.). (St. Nicholas Series for Boys). N.D. International Book Company.
--The Mountain Cave: Or, The Mystery of the Sierra Nevada. LC 3839. 205 p. 17 cm. (On cover: Medal library. no. 60). 1900. Street & Smith.
--The Old Man of the Mountains. (Illus.). (St. Nicholas Series for Boys). N.D. International Book Co.
--The Old Man of the Mountains. LC 6-30189. 1 p. l., 5-245 p. front., plates. 19 cm. (On cover: Leather-clad tales. no. 40). c.1891. United States Book Company.
--Old Merry's Travels on the Continent. (Illus.). (St. Nicholas Series for Boys). N.D. International Book Co.
--The Young Whaler. (Wide Awake Boys Ser.). N.D. A. L. Burt.
--The Young Whaler, 1 of 4 Vols. Davis, J. Watson, illus. (Sailing Order Ser.). N.D. Set. D Lothrop & Co.
--The Young Whaler: A Story of the Sea. Davis, J. Watson, illus. LC 3-11670. 20cm. 317p. (The Rubgy Series for Boys and Girls). 1903. A. L. Burt Company.
Coon, Alma S.
--The Mouse & the Mill & the Bottle Babies. Shoemaker, Kathryn E., illus. (Illus.). 44p. (ps-1). 1982. (ISBN 0-87935-061-X). Williamsburg.
Coon, B., jt. auth. see Rhode, H.
Coon, Martha Sutherland (1884-)
--Georgie's Capital. Keyser, Corinne, illus. LC 67-16905. (Illus.). 205 p. 22cm. (gr. 3-6). 1967. Harvey House.
Coon, Merlin Joseph (1917-)
--The Sea Horse. LC 52-40856. 135 p. illus. 22 cm. 1952. Academy Publishers.
Cooney, Barbara, jt. auth. see Grimm, Jakob Ludwig Karl.
Cooney, Barbara (1917-), adapted by see Chaucer, Geoffrey.
Cooney, Barbara (1917-), retold by see Grimm, Jakob Ludwig Karl (1785-1863) & Grimm, Wilhelm Karl.
Cooney, Barbara (1917-)
--Captain Pottle's House. Cooney, Barbara (1917-), illus. LC 48-130437. 6 p. l., 3-172, 1 p. incl. front., illus. 19 cm. 1943. Farrar & Rinehart, Inc.
--Cock Robin. Cooney, Barbara (1917-), illus. (Illus.). (gr. k-3). 1965. (ISBN 0-684-82013-7). Scribner.
--A Garland of Games & Other Diversions: An Alphabet Book. LC 69-15675. (Illus.). 31 p. 1969. Colonial Williamsburg; Distributed by Holt, Rinehart and Winston, New York.
--The Kelleyhorns. Cooney, Barbara (1917-), illus. LC 42-16138. 6 p. l., 3-259 p. front., illus. 21 cm. 1942. Farrar & Rinehart, Inc.
--King of Wreck Island. Cooney, Barbara (1917-), illus. LC 41-11236. 3 p. l., 3-91 p. illus. 24 cm. c.1941. Farrar & Rinehart Incorporated.
--The Little Juggler. LC 61-10576. (Illus.). 46 p. 24cm. (gr. 3-6). 1961. (ISBN 0-8038-4239-2). Hastings House.
--Miss Rumphius. Cooney, Barbara (1917-), illus. LC 85-40447. (Illus.). 32 p. (Picture puffins). 1985, c.1982. (ISBN 0-14-050539-3). Puffin Books.
--Miss Rumphius. Cooney, Barbara (1917-), illus. LC 82-2837. (Illus.). 32p. 1st U.S. edition. (gr. k-3). 1982. (ISBN 0-670-47958-6). Viking Pr. **Award: (ABA).**
Cooney, Barbara (1917-), illus.
--Demeter and Persephone: Homeric Hymn Number Two. Proddow, Penelope, tr. LC 76-155852. (Illus.). 48 p. 29cm. 1972. Doubleday.
--Spirit Child: A Story of the Nativity. Bierhorst, John (1936-), tr. LC 84-720. (Illus.). 32p. 1984. (ISBN 0-688-02609-5, Morrow Junior Books). (ISBN 0-688-02610-9). Morrow. **Award: (ALA).**

--The Prairie. (The Fairmount classics). N.D. Macrae Smith Co.
--The Prairie. (The Leather-Stocking Tales). N.D. Page Co.
--The Prairie. Davenport, Basil, intro. by. (Great Illustrated Classics). N.D. Dodd Mead & Co.
--The Prairie. Smith, Henry Nash, ed. 453p. 1950. Rinehart & Co.
--Precaution. N.D. G. P. Putnam's Sons.
--Red Rover. (Burt's Home Library). N.D. A L Burt Co.
--The Red Rover. (Illus.). (The Rugby Series for Boys). N.D. A. L. Burt's Pubs.
--Red Rover. N.D. G. P. Putnam's Sons.
--The Red Rover. Walker, S. Warren, intro. by. 534p. (Bison Book). 1963. University of Nebraska Press.
--The Redskins. N.D. G. P. Putnam's Sons.
--Satanstoe. N.D. G. P. Putnam's Sons.
--Satanstoe. Hough, L. Robert, illus. 426p. (Bison Bk). 1962. University of Nebraska Press.
--The Sea-Lions. N.D. G. P. Putnam's Sons.
--The Spy. (Famous Bks. for Young Americans). N.D. A. L. Burt Co.
--The Spy. (Illus.). (Great Illus. Classics). 1947. Dodd.
--The Spy. (Illus.). (Great Il. Classics). (gr. 9 up). 1949. (ISBN 0-396-02728-8). Dodd.
--The Spy. N.D. G. P. Putnam's Sons.
--The Spy. (Classics for Children). N.D. Ginn.
--The Spy. N.D. Grosset & Dunlap.
--The Spy. (Illus.). (Famous Books for Boys). N.D. H. M. Caldwell Co.
--The Spy. N.D. Houghton Mifflin Co.
--The Spy. (Riverside Bookshelf). N.D. Houghton Mifflin Co.
--The Spy. (Riverside Literature Ser.: 207). N.D. Houghton Mifflin Co.
--The Spy. (Sears Juvenile Classics). N.D. J.H.Sears & Co.
--The Spy. (Illustrated Cabinet Editions). (The Works of James Fenimore Cooper: No. 2). N.D. L. C. Page & Co.
--The Spy. (The Fairmount Classics). N.D. Macrae Smith.
--The Spy. (The Lake English Classics). N.D. Scott Foresman & Co.
--The Spy. Baldridge, Cyrus Leroy (1889-), illus. (Minton, Balch Library of Illustrated Classics). N.D. Minton Balch & Co.
--The Spy. Dahl, Curtis, intro. by. (Great Illustrated Classics). N.D. Dodd Mead & Co.
--The Spy: A Tale of Neutral Ground. (Modern Student's Library). N.D. Charles Scribner's Sons.
--Stories of the Woods: Or, Adventures of Leather-Stocking, Selected from the "Leather-Stocking Tales". Darley, Felix Octavius Carr (1822-1866), illus. LC 24-11854. 345 p. front., plates. 18 cm. 1863. J. G. Gregory.
--The Last of the Mohicans. (The People's Library). N.D. Funk & Wagnalls Co.
--The Two Admirals. (Illus.). (The Rugby Series for Boys). N.D. A. L. Burt's Pubs.
--The Two Admirals. N.D. G. P. Putnam's Sons.
--The Water Witch. (Burt's Home Library). N.D. A L Burt Co.
--Water Witch. (Illus.). (The Rugby Series for Boys). N.D. A. L. Burt's Pubs.
--The Water-Witch. N.D. G. P. Putnam's Sons.
--The Ways of the Hour. N.D. G. P. Putnam's Sons.
--Wept of Wish-ton-Wish. N.D. G. P. Putnam's.
--Wing and Wing. (Illus.). (The Rugby Series for Boys). N.D. A. L. Burt's Pubs.
--Wing and Wing. N.D. G. P. Putnam's Sons.
--Wyandotte. N.D. G. P. Putnam's Sons.

Cooper, James Fenimore (1789-1851) & Melville, Herman
--Adventures Afloat and Ashore. N.D. G. P. Putnam's Sons.

Cooper, Joan
--Lek of Thailand. (Illus.). (gr. 1-4). 1971. (ISBN 0-912472-09-X). Miller Bks.
--Monkey. (Illus.). (gr. 1-4). 1971. (ISBN 0-912472-10-3). Miller Bks.

Cooper, John R, pseud., see Stratemeyer Syndicate.

Cooper, John R., pseud.
--The College League Mystery. Stratemeyer Syndicate. Repr. of 1953 ed (Pub. by Garden City). (The Mel Martin Baseball Stories: Vol. 5). N.D. Books Inc.
--The College League Mystery. Stratemeyer Syndicate. LC 53-1824. 191p. illus. 20cm. (The Mel Martin Baseball Stories: Vol. 5). 1953. Garden City Books.
--The Fighting Shortstop. Stratemeyer Syndicate. Repr. of 1953 ed (Pub. by Garden City). (The Mel Martin Baseball Stories: Vol. 6). N.D. Books Inc.
--The Fighting Shortstop. Stratemeyer Syndicate. 192p. illus. 20cm. (The Mel Martin Baseball Stories: Vol. 6). 1953. Garden City Books.
--First Base Jinx. Stratemeyer Syndicate. Repr. of 1952 ed (Pub. by Garden City). (The Mel Martin Baseball Stories: Vol. 4). N.D. Books Inc.
--First Base Jinx. Stratemeyer Syndicate. LC 52-4488. 191 p. illus. 20 cm. (The Mel Martin Baseball Stories: Vol. 4). 1952. Garden City Books.
--First Base Jinx. Stratemeyer Syndicate. LC 81-23105. 206 p. 19cm. (The Mel Martin Baseball Stories: Vol. 4). 1982, c.1952. (ISBN 0-671-44539-1). (ISBN 0-671-44548-0). Wanderer Books.
--The Mystery at the Ball Park. Stratemeyer Syndicate. Repr. of 1947 ed (Pub. by Cupples & Leon). (The Mel Martin Baseball Stories: Vol. 1). N.D. Books Inc.
--The Mystery at the Ball Park. Stratemeyer Syndicate. LC 52-1482. 208 p. illus. 20 cm. Repr. of 1947 ed (Pub. by Cupples & Leon Co.). (The Mel Martin Baseball Stories: Vol. 1). 1952. Garden City Books.
--The Mystery at the Ball Park. Stratemeyer Syndicate. LC 81-21950. 201 p. 19cm. (The Mel Martin Baseball Stories: Vol. 1). 1982, c.1952. (ISBN 0-671-44536-7). (ISBN 0-671-44545-6). Wanderer Books.
--The Mystery at the Ball Park. Stratemeyer Syndicate. Schaare, C. Richard, illus. LC 47-23570. iii, 208 p. front. 19 1/2 cm. (The Mel Martin Baseball Stories: Vol. 1). 1947. Cupples & Leon Co.
--The Phantom Homer. Stratemeyer Syndicate. Repr. of 1952 ed (Pub. by Garden City). (The Mel Martin Baseball Stories: Vol. 3). N.D. Books Inc.
--The Phantom Homer. Stratemeyer Syndicate. LC 52-1483. 189 p. illus. 20 cm. (The Mel Martin Baseball Stories: Vol. 3). 1952. Garden City Books.
--The Phantom Homer. Stratemeyer Syndicate. 1st ed. LC 81-23091. 202 p. 19cm. (The Mel Martin Baseball Stories: Vol. 3). 1982. (ISBN 0-671-44538-3). (ISBN 0-671-44547-2). Wanderer Books.
--The Southpaw's Secret. Stratemeyer Syndicate. Repr. of 1947 ed (Pub. by Cupples & Leon). (The Mel Martin Baseball Stories: Vol. 2). N.D. Books Inc.
--The Southpaw's Secret. Stratemeyer Syndicate. LC 52-1484. 212 p. illus. 20 cm. Repr. of 1947 ed (Pub. by Cupples & Leon Co.). (The Mel Martin Baseball Stories: Vol. 2). 1952. Garden City Books.
--The Southpaw's Secret. Stratemeyer Syndicate. LC 81-22031. 204 p. 19cm. (The Mel Martin Baseball Stories: Vol. 2). 1982, c.1952. (ISBN 0-671-44537-5). (ISBN 0-671-44546-4). Wanderer Books.
--The Southpaw's Secret. Stratemeyer Syndicate. Schaare, C. Richard, illus. LC 47-30453. iii, 212 p. front. 20 cm. (The Mel Martin Baseball Stories: Vol. 2). 1947. Cupples & Leon Co.

Cooper, Joyce, retold by.
--More Adventures of Spider. Pinkney, Jerry (1939-), illus. (Illus.). (gr. k-4). 1972. (ISBN 0-590-03452-9). Scholastic Inc.

Cooper, Kay (1941-)
--C'mon Ducks!. LC 77-25089. (Illus.). 64p. (gr. 3 up). 1978. (ISBN 0-671-32905-7). Messner.

Cooper, Lee Pelham (1926-)
--Five Fables from France. Keeping, Charles William James (1924-), illus. LC 72-103941. (Illus.). 86 p. 22cm. 1970. (ISBN 0-200-71668-9). Abelard-Schuman.
--Pirate of Puerto Rico. Stone, David Karl (1922-), illus. (Illus.). 6 ils. (gr. 4-6). 1972. (ISBN 0-399-20240-4). Putnam.

Cooper, Lettice Ulpha (1897-)
--The Bear Who Was Too Big. Ives, Ruth, illus. LC 66-8946. (Illus.). 30 p. 27cm. 1966, c.1963. Follett Pub. Co.
--Blackberry's Kitten. (Illus.). (gr. 4-6). 1961. (ISBN 0-8382-0096-6). Hale.
--Blackberry's Kitten. Shillabeer, Mary Eleanor (1904-), illus. LC 63-13798. (Illus.). (gr. 1-4). 1963. (ISBN 0-8149-0291-X). Vanguard.
--Gunpowder, Treason and Plot. Grant, Elisabeth, illus. LC 70-120861. (Illus.). 119 p. 22cm. 1970. (ISBN 0-200-71570-4). Abelard-Schuman.
--The Twig of Cypress. LC 66-22211. x, 159p. 21cm. 1st U.S. edition. (gr. 6-9). 1966, c.1965. Washburn.

Cooper, Margaret C.
--Code Name: Clone. Bigelow, Christopher, illus. (Illus.). 192p. (gr. 4-6). 1982. (ISBN 0-8027-6474-6). (ISBN 0-8027-6475-4). Walker & Co.

Cooper, Margaret C & Burke, Rod
--Solution: Escape. LC 80-50496. p. cm. 1980. (ISBN 0-8027-6404-5). (ISBN 0-8027-6405-3). Walker.

Cooper, Margaret Rice
--The Great Bone Hunt. Goodwin, Harold (1919-), illus. LC 67-50. (Illus.). 1 v. (unpaged). 23cm. 1967. Macmillan.
--The Ice Palace. Goodwin, Harold (1919-), illus. LC 66-160998. 49p. illus. 23cm. (gr. 1-4). c.1966. Macmillan.

Cooper, Marjorie see Margie, pseud.

Cooper, Marjorie (1910-)
--Jeepers the Little Frog. 1965. (ISBN 0-8382-0380-9, Hale Giant Books). E. M. Hale and Company.
--Jeepers: The Little Frog. Cooper, Marjorie (1910-), illus. LC 66-140178. 1v. (unpaged) col. illus. 33cm. 1966. Rand McNally.

Cooper, Marjorie (1910-), illus.
--Mother Goose. Margie, pseud. LC 51-27548. (Illus.). 20cm. 24p. (Bonnie Spin-wheel Book). 1951. S. Lowe Co.
--Rumpelstiltskin. LC 63-112642. (Illus.). 22 p. 33cm. (Rand McNally giant book). 1967, c.1959. Rand McNally.

Cooper, Marjorie (1910-) & Lee, Manning De Villeneuve (1894-1980), illus.
--The Rand McNally Favorite Storybook. 96p. (gr. 4-8). 1976. (ISBN 0-528-05500-3). Rand.

Cooper, Matlie Lula, jt. auth. see Halladay, Anne M, Mrs.

Cooper, Mattie Lula (1914-)
--House on the Corner. Herric, Pru, illus. LC 63-8681. (Illus.). 21cm. 127p. 1963. Friendship Press.

Cooper, Merian C see Lovelace, Delos Wheeler.

Cooper, Mr., tr. see Berquin, Arnaud.

Cooper, Padraic, jt. auth. see Cooper, Elizabeth Keyser.

Cooper, Page (1891-)
--Amigo: Circus Horse. Pitz, Henry Clarence (1895-1976), illus. (Illus.). (gr. 4-6). N.D. (ISBN 0-448-02300-8). G&D.
--Red Tartar. 1st ed. LC 57-740452. 218p. 21cm. 1957. World Pub. Co.
--Silver Spurs to Monterey. 1st ed. Giesen, Herman D., illus. LC 56-5312. 217p. illus. 21cm. 1956. World Pub. Co.
--Thunder. 1st ed. Shenton, Edward (1895-), illus. LC 54-5346. 218p. illus. 21cm. 1954. World Pub. Co.
--Thunder. 1st ed. Shenton, Edward (1895-), illus. LC 56-9265. 218p. illus. 21cm. (World junior library). c.1954. World Pub. Co.

Cooper, Page (1891-), ed.
--Great Horse Stories. Brown, Paul (1893-1958), illus. N.D. Hanover House.

Cooper, Paul Fenimore
--Dindle. Cooper, Marion Erskine, illus. (Illus.). (gr. 4 up). 1963. (ISBN 0-399-60127-9). Putnam.
--Tal: His Marvelous Adventures With Noom-Zor-Noom. 305p. N.D. Frederick Ungar Publishing Co.
--Tal: His Marvelous Adventures with Noom-Zor-Noom. Reeves, Ruth, illus. LC 29-190096. x p., 1 l., 305 p. incl. front., illus., plates. 22 cm. c.1929. W. Morrow & Co.

Cooper, Peter
--The Secret Papers of Julia Templeton. 160p. (gr. 6-9). 1985. (ISBN 0-89272-197-9). Down East.

Cooper, Raymond K
--Teeny-Big. Hobson, Dorothy Ashbrook, illus. LC 53-31410. 56p. illus. 21cm. 1953. Christopher Pub. House.

Cooper, Samuel Williams (1860-1939)
--Think and Thank: A Tale. LC 74-27975. iv, 120 p. 21cm. (The Modern Jewish Experience). 1975, c.1890. (ISBN 0-405-06704-6). Arno Press.

Cooper, Susan (1935-)
--The Dark is Rising. Cober, Alan Edwin (1935-), illus. LC 72-85916. (Illus.). 216 p. 25cm. 1973. Atheneum. **Awards: (BGH); (ALA); (JNM); (CMA).**
--Dawn of Fear. Gill, Margery Jean (1925-), illus. LC 71-115755. (Illus.). 157 p. 21cm. 1970. Harcourt, Brace, Jovanovich.
--Greenwitch. LC 73-85319. 147 p. 25cm. 1974. (ISBN 0-689-30426-9). Atheneum.
--The Grey King. 1st ed. Heslop, Michael, illus. LC 75-8526. (Illus.). 208 p. 25cm. 1975. (ISBN 0-689-50029-7). Atheneum. **Awards: (JNM); (ALA); (CMA).**
--Jethro and the Jumbie. Bryan, Ashley F. (1923-), illus. LC 79-14667. p. cm. 1979. (ISBN 0-689-50140-4). Atheneum.
--Over Sea, Under Stone. Gill, Margery Jean (1925-), illus. LC 66-11199. (Illus.). 252 p. 21cm. 1st U.S. edition. 1966, c.1965. Harcourt, Brace & World.
--Over Sea, Under Stone. 1st ed. Gill, Margery Jean (1925-), illus. LC 79-10489. p. cm. (Voyager/HBJ book). 1979, c.1965. (ISBN 0-15-670542-7). Harcourt Brace Jovanovich.
--Seaward. LC 83-7055. p. cm. 1983. (ISBN 0-689-50275-3). Atheneum.
--The Silver Cow: A Welsh Tale. Hutton, Warwick (1939-), illus. LC 82-13928. (Illus.). 32 p. 26cm. 1983. (ISBN 0-689-50236-2). Atheneum. **Award: (ALA).**
--Silver on the Tree. Heslop, Michael, illus. LC 77-5361. ix, 269 p. 25cm. 1977. (ISBN 0-689-50088-2). Atheneum.

Cooper, Wendy Lowe (1919-)
--Alibi Children. Beetles, Peggy, illus. (gr. 3-6). 1958. (ISBN 0-685-20918-0). Verry.
--Laughing Lady. Fletcher, Geoffrey, illus. (Illus.). (gr. 3-6). 1957. (ISBN 0-685-21293-9). Verry.

Cooper, William E.
--The Lonely Tree. Cooke, Pati Kos, illus. (Illus.). 28p. (Orig.). 1983. (ISBN 0-911175-01-6). Elm Pubs.

Coopersmith, Harry (1903-), ed.
--Hebrew Songster: For Kindergarten and Primary Grades. Zion, Harriet, illus. LC 48-20536. iv, 88 p. illus. 23 cm. 1948. Jewish Education Committee of N.Y.
--More of the Songs We Sing. Oechsli, Kelly (1918-), illus. (Illus.). 288p. (gr. 4-10). 1970. (ISBN 0-8381-0217-4). United Syn Bk.
--New Jewish Song Book. LC 65-14593. (gr. 3-9). N.D. (ISBN 0-87441-060-6). Behrman.

Coopersmith, Jerome (1925-)
--A Chanukah Fable for Christmas. Hoff, Sydney (1912-), illus. LC 70-75587. (Illus.). 47 p. 27cm. 1969. Putnam.

Cope, Dawn & Cope, Peter
--Humpty Dumpty's Favourite Nursery Rhymes. (Illus.). 64p. 1981. (ISBN 0-03-059907-5). Webb & Bower.
--Red Riding Hood's Favourite Fairy Tales. (Illus.). 64p. 1981. (ISBN 0-03-059906-7). Webb & Bower.

Cope, Dawn & Cope, Peter, eds.
--Christmas Carols for Young Children. Le Mair, Henriette Willebeek (1889-1966), illus. (Illus.). 32p. (gr. 5-12). 1981. (ISBN 0-914510-12-6). Evergreen.

Cope, Herman
--The Bible Boy Taken Captive by the Indians. LC 75-7082. (Illus.). 35 p., 1 leaf of plates. 24cm. (The Garland Library of Narratives of North American Indian Captivities ; 59: No.). 1977. (ISBN 0-8240-1683-1). Garland Pub.

Cope, Peter, jt. auth. see Cope, Dawn.

Cope, Peter, jt. ed. see Cope, Dawn.

Copeland, Colene
--Priscilla. Harrison, Edith, illus. LC 81-80663. (Illus.). 212p. (Orig.). (gr. 3 up). 1981. (ISBN 0-939810-01-8). (ISBN 0-939810-02-6). Jordan Valley.

Copeland, Donald McKillop
--The True Book of Little People. Gehr, Mary, illus. LC 53-11749. (Illus.). 42 p. 22cm. 1953. Childrens Press.

Copeland, Helen (1920-)
--Duncan's World. Berson, Harold (1926-), illus. LC 67-23665. (Illus.). 220 p. 21cm. 1967. Crowell.
--Festival in the Park. Berson, Harold (1926-), illus. LC 70-106570. (Illus.). 224 p. 22cm. 1970. Crown Publishers.
--Meet Miki Takino. Werth, Kurt (1896-), illus. 1963. (ISBN 0-688-51001-9). William Morrow and Company.
--This Snake Is Good. Walker, Charles W., illus. LC 68-17076. (Illus.). 181 p. 21cm. 1968. Crowell.

Copeland, Walter, pseud., see Jerrold, Walter Copeland.

Copeland, William
--Five Hours From Isfahan. 1975. (ISBN 0-399-11431-9). G.P. Putnam's Sons.

Copenhaver, Laura Scherer
--An Adventurous Quest. 1903. United Lutheran Pub. House.

Copland, Aaron (1900-) & Denby, Edwin (1903-)
--The Second Hurricane. (A Play-Opera for high school performance). 27cm. 112p. 1938. C. C. Birchard & Co.

Copland, George Leonard
--Rollo MacBean and Co. Copeland, George Leonard, illus. LC 42-505827. 47 p. col. illus. 24 x 21 cm. 1942. Creative Age Press, Inc.

Copley, Esther Hewlett, Mrs.
--The Popular Grove: Or, Little Harry and His Uncle Benjamin. 15cm. 178p. (Tales for People and their Children). 1843. G. S. Appleton.

Copp, Andrew James see Copp, Jim, pseud.

Copp, DeWitt S.
--The Far Side. 199p. 1975. (ISBN 0-393-08723-9). Norton.

Copp, James
--Martha Matilda O'Toole. Kellogg, Steven (1941-), illus. LC 69-11971. (Illus.). 32 p. 27cm. 1969. Bradbury Press.

Copp, Jim, pseud., see Copp, Andrew James.

Copp, Jim, 3rd, pseud. (1916-)
--Martha Matilda O'toole. Copp, Andrew James. Kellogg, Steven (1941-), illus. N.D. Prentice-Hall.

Copp, Lillian Grace
--Joyous Peggy. Tandy, Russell H., illus. LC 31-14416. viii, 312 p. front., plates. 20 cm. 1931. Cupples & Leon Company.
--Sue Stanwood. McNulty, William C., illus. LC 27-2537. 4 p. l., 317 p. front., plates. 19 cm. 1927. L. C. Page & Company.

Copp, Theodore Bayard Fletcher (1902-)
--The Bridge of Bombers. Gregori, Leon (1919-), illus. LC 41-14550. v p., 1 l., 212 p. incl. front. 20 cm. c.1941. Grosset & Dunlap.
--The Mystery of Devil's Hand. Gregori, Leon (1919-), illus. LC 41-140455. vi p., 1 l., 214 p. incl. front. 20 cm. c.1941. Grosset & Dunlap.

--August, Die She Must. LC 83-15657. 180p. (gr. 5-9). 1984. (ISBN 0-689-31012-9). Atheneum.
--Axe-Time, Sword-Time. LC 75-29468. 204 p. 22cm. 1976. (ISBN 0-689-30498-6). Atheneum.
--Cabin in the Sky. LC 76-17. 197 p. 22cm. 1976. (ISBN 0-689-30521-4). Atheneum.
--A Candle to the Devil. Hamilton, Gail, pseud. 1st ed. Scribner, Joanne L. (1949-), illus. LC 75-9519. (Illus.). 180 p. 22cm. 1975. (ISBN 0-689-30478-1). Atheneum.
--Child of the Morning. 11 x 12 1/2. 120p. Repr. of 1982 ed (Pub. by Atheneum). (15 pt.). (gr. 6-9). N.D. Am Printing Hse.
--Child of the Morning. LC 81-8057. 112 p. 22cm. 1982. (ISBN 0-689-30876-0). Atheneum.
--The Clown. LC 75-8759. 188 p. 22cm. 1975. (ISBN 0-689-30465-X). Atheneum.
--A Dance to Still Music. Robinson, Charles (1931-), illus. LC 74-75558. 1974. (ISBN 0-689-30406-4). Atheneum.
--Don't Slam the Door When You Go. LC 72-75267. 198 p. 25cm. 1972. Atheneum.
--Face the Music. LC 85-7453. 178 p. 22cm. 1985. (ISBN 0-689-31139-7). Atheneum.
--The Faraway Island. LC 76-25152. 158 p. 22cm. 1977. (ISBN 0-689-30550-8). Atheneum.
--Hey, That's My Soul You're Stomping on. LC 77-13499. 122 p. 22cm. 1978. (ISBN 0-689-30617-2). Atheneum.
--I Wish You Love. Orig. Title: The Clown. (gr. 7-12). 1977. (ISBN 0-590-11861-7, Schol Pap). Scholastic Inc.
--The Lifestyle of Robie Tuckerman. LC 76-169036. 199 p. 21cm. 1971. (ISBN 0-8407-6162-7). T. Nelson.
--Lion on the Mountain. Dixon, Paige, pseud. 1st ed. Breslow, J. H., illus. LC 72-75268. (Illus.). 118 p. 22cm. 1972. Atheneum.
--The Loner: A Story of the Wolverine. 1st ed. Miller, Grambs, illus. LC 78-6843. (Illus.). 102 p. 22cm. 1978. (ISBN 0-689-30651-2). Atheneum.
--The Long Journey. 1st ed. Robinson, Charles (1931-), illus. LC 79-115067. (Illus.). 187 p. 22cm. 1970. Atheneum.
--Make No Sound. LC 77-2001. 148 p. 22cm. 1977. (ISBN 0-689-30580-X). Atheneum.
--Making It. LC 80-24769. 156 p. 22cm. c.1980. (ISBN 0-316-15731-7). Little, Brown.
--Me and You and a Dog Named Blue". LC 78-13746. 179 p. 22cm. 1979. (ISBN 0-689-30675-X). Atheneum.
--Meet Me at Tamerlane's Tomb. 1st ed. Robinson, Charles (1931-), illus. LC 74-19351. (Illus.). 152 p. 22cm. 1975. (ISBN 0-689-30446-3). Atheneum.
--The Mustang & Other Stories. (gr. 4-6). 1978. (ISBN 0-590-05389-2, Schol Pap). Scholastic Inc.
--Mystery on Ice. LC 84-21559. 144 p. 22cm. 1985. (ISBN 0-689-31089-7). Atheneum.
--The Person in the Potting Shed. LC 80-12299. p. cm. 1980. (ISBN 0-689-30774-8). Atheneum.
--Pimm's Cup for Everbody. Dixon, Paige, pseud. 1st ed. LC 75-45480. 142 p. 22cm. 1976. (ISBN 0-689-30523-0). Atheneum.
--Promises to Keep. Dixon, Paige, pseud. 1st ed. LC 74-75560. 165 p. 22cm. 1974. Atheneum.
--Rising Damp. LC 79-22675. 145 p. 22cm. 1980. (ISBN 0-689-30736-5). Atheneum.
--A Row of Tigers. 1st ed. Eitzen, Allan (1928-), illus. LC 69-13523. (Illus.). 165 p. 21cm. 1969. Atheneum.
--Sam. McGee, Barbara J. (1943-), illus. LC 67-18994. (Illus.). 219 p. 22cm. 1967. Atheneum.
--Sasha, My Friend. Shell, Richard L., illus. (Illus.). 1969. Atheneum Publishers.
--Sasha, My Friend. Shell, Richard L., illus. LC 69-18968. (Illus.). 203 p. 21cm. (Aladdin Book, A29). 1973, c.1969. Atheneum.
--The Search for Charlie. Dixon, Paige, pseud. 1st ed. LC 75-23187. 90 p. 22cm. 1976. (ISBN 0-689-30500-1). Atheneum.
--Silver Wolf. Dixon, Paige, pseud. 1st ed. Brewster, Ann, illus. LC 73-86932. (Illus.). 108 p. 22cm. 1973. Atheneum.
--A Star to the North. Angier, Bradford, illus. LC 79-11962. 156p. 1970. Nelson Junior Books.
--Strike!. LC 82-13759. p. cm. 1983. (ISBN 0-689-30952-X). Atheneum.
--This Is a Recording. 1st ed. Cuffari, Richard (1925-1978), illus. LC 73-154751. (Illus.). 168 p. 22cm. 1971. Atheneum.
--Titania's Lodestone. Hamilton, Gail, pseud. 1st ed. LC 74-19491. (Illus.). 200 p. 22cm. 1975. (ISBN 0-689-30449-8). Atheneum.
--A Trick of Light. 1st ed. Dabcovich, Lydia, illus. LC 75-175552. (Illus.). 117 p. 22cm. 1972. Atheneum.
--Watching Eyes (Pub. by Atheneum). (gr. 9 up). 1976. (ISBN 0-590-10238-9, Schol Trade Pap). Schol Bk Serv.
--A Watery Grave. LC 82-1726. 153 p. 22cm. 1982. (ISBN 0-689-30919-8). Atheneum.
--Which Witch Is Which. LC 83-3900. p. cm. (Escapade). 1983. (ISBN 0-689-31373-X). Atheneum.
--The Winds of Time. 1st ed. Owens, Gail, illus. LC 73-84823. (Illus.). 164 p. 22cm. 1974. (ISBN 0-689-30133-2). Atheneum.
--The Woman in Your Life. LC 84-2942. 192p. (gr. 8 up). 1984. (ISBN 0-689-31044-7). Atheneum.
--The Young Grizzly. Dixon, Paige, pseud. Miller, Grambs, illus. LC 73-84827. (Illus.). 106 p. 22cm. 1974. (ISBN 0-689-30137-5). Atheneum.
--You're Allegro Dead. LC 81-1906. p. cm. 1981. (ISBN 0-689-30840-X). Atheneum.

Corcoran, Brewer (1877-)
--The Bantam. LC 12-9964. v, 1 p., 1 l., 253, 1 p. front. 19 cm. 1912. Harper & Brothers.
--The Barbarian: Or, Will Bradford's School Days at St. Jo's. Rogers, Walter S., illus. LC 17-13. 4 p. l., 305 p. front., plates. 20 cm. 1917. The Page Company.
--The Boy Scouts at Camp Lowell. Bull, Charles Livingston (1874-1932), illus. LC 22-192177. 4 p. l., 305 p. front., plates. 20 cm. 1922. The Page Company.
--The Boy Scouts of Kendallville. Meister, Charles E., illus. LC 18-122169. 5 p. l., 270 p. front., plates. 20 cm. 1918. The Page Company.
--The Boy Scouts of the Wolf Patrol. Goss, John, illus. LC 20-3061. 5 p. l., 329 p. front., plates. 20 cm. 1920. The Page Company.
--Will Bradford's School Days: Or, the Barbarian. Goss, John, illus. N.D. L. C. Page.
--Will Bradford's School Days: Or, The Barbarian. Rogers, Walter S., illus. N.D. Page Co.

Corcoran, Charles
--Blackrobe. N.D. Bruce Publishing Co.

Corcoran, Jean Kennedy (1926-)
--Elias Howe, Inventive Boy. Fleur, Anne Elizabeth (1901-), illus. Sari, pseud. LC 62-9255. 200p. illus. (pt. col.) (Childhood of famous Amers.). c.1962. Bobbs.

Corcoran, Jean Kennedy (1926-), adapted by.
--Folk Tales of England. LC 63-14584. 124p. (gr. 4-7). N.D. (ISBN 0-672-50271-2). Bobbs.

Corcoran, Jean Kennedy (1926-) & Chall, Jeanne, eds.
--Folk Tales of North America. LC 62-22150. (Illus.). 123p. (gr. 4-7). 1962. (ISBN 0-672-50278-X). Bobbs.

Corcoran, Mark
--The Mystery of the Rebellious Robot. Corcoran, Mark, illus. LC 78-19703. p. cm. (Star Wars). c.1979. (ISBN 0-394-84086-0). (ISBN 0-394-94086-5). Random House.

Corcoran, Mary Roberta
--The Mary, John and Tommy Book. Baker, Aimee, illus. LC 30-18303. 5 p. l., 32 p. illus., pl. 22 cm. 1930. G. Banta Publishing Co.

Corcos, Loris
--Jonathan Bangs Said "No-O-O-O-O-O-O-O!. LC 46-20644. 35 p. col. illus. 15 x 23 cm. 1946. Lothrop, Lee and Shepard Co.
--Patches. Corcos, Loris, illus. LC 41-107843. 48 p. illus. (part col.) 24 x 31 cm. 1941. E. P. Dutton & Company, Inc.
--The Stuck-up Prince. LC 39-199090. 77 p. incl., col. front., col. illus. 19 cm. 1939. E. P. Dutton & Company, Inc.

Corcos, Lucille (1908-1973)
--Joel Gets a Dog. Corcos, Lucille (1908-1973), illus. LC 58-5200. 1958. Abelard-Schuman.
--Joel Gets a Haircut. Corcos, Lucille (1908-1973), illus. LC 52-14721. unpaged. illus. 27cm. 1952. Abelard Press.
--Joel Spends His Money. Corcos, Lucille (1908-1973), illus. LC 53-8358. unpaged. illus. 27cm. 1954. Abelard-Schuman.
--Jolly ABC Books of Toys. LC 54-15098. unpaged. illus. 21cm. (Jolly books, 218). c.1953. Jolly Books.

Cord, Barry, pseud., see Germano, Peter.

Corddry, Thomas I
--Kibby and the Red Elephant. Kock, Carl, illus. LC 72-13771. (Illus.). 111 p. 22cm. 1973. (ISBN 0-87955-106-2). (ISBN 0-87955-106-2). J. P. O'Hara.
--Kibby's Big Feat. Blake, Quentin (1932-), illus. LC 76-118927. (Illus.). 112 p. 24cm. 1970. Follett.

Cordell, Alexander, pseud., see Graber, Alexander.

Cordell, Alexander, pseud. (1914-)
--The Healing Blade. Graber, Alexander. LC 79-136816. (Illus.). 156 p. 22cm. 1971. (ISBN 0-670-36445-2). Viking Press.
--The Traitor Within. Graber, Alexander. Ambrus, Victor G., pseud. (1935-), illus. Ambrus, Gyozo Laszlo. LC 72-13250. (Illus.). 126 p. 22cm. 1st U.S. edition. 1973. (ISBN 0-8407-6294-1). T. Nelson.
--The White Cockade. Graber, Alexander. LC 74-102923. (Illus.). 138 p. 22cm. 1970. Viking Press.
--Witches' Sabbath. Graber, Alexander. LC 75-123023. (Illus.). 157 p. 22cm. 1970. Viking Press.

Cordier, Ralph Waldo, jt. auth. see Hugley, Laura Mengert.

Cordner, Elizabeth P., tr. from Ger.
--Christmas Stories and March Violets. 92p. N.D. George H. Ellis Co.

Core, Susie Pearl
--Children of the Cruces Trail. McKeown, Anne Cordts, illus. LC 48-15386. 72 p. illu. 20 x 22 cm. c.1946. North River Press.
--Christmas on the Isthmus. McKeown, Anne Cordts, illus. LC 35-23326. 62, 2 p. illus. 20 x 22 cm. c.1936. Clermont Press.
--Kris Kringle at the Cross-Roads. Chan, Irene, illus. LC 48-152196. viii, 95 p. illus. 20 x 22 cm. 1946. North River Press.
--An Odyssey of the Spanish Main. McKeown, Anne Cordts, illus. LC 38-1045. 64 p. illus. 20 x 22 cm. c.1937. Clermont Press.
--Panama's Jungle Book. McKeown, Anne Cordts, illus. LC 36-15935. 40 p. illus. 20 x 22 cm. c.1936. Clermont Press.

Coren, Alan (1938-)
--Arthur and the Great Detective. Astrop, John, illus. LC 79-23511. (Illus.). 74 p. 24cm. 1st U.S. edition. 1979. (ISBN 0-316-15736-8). Little, Brown.
--Arthur & the Purple Panic. Astrop, John, illus. LC 83-61281. (Illus.). 64p. (gr. 4-6). 1984. (ISBN 0-88186-001-8). Parkwest Pubns.
--Arthur the Kid. Astrop, John, illus. LC 77-26989. (Illus.). 73 p. 22cm. 1st U.S. edition. c.1977. (ISBN 0-316-15734-1). Little, Brown.
--Arthur's Last Stand. Astrop, John, illus. LC 79-14052. (Illus.). 74 p. 22cm. 1st U.S. edition. c.1977. (ISBN 0-316-15742-2). Little, Brown.
--Buffalo Arthur. Astrop, John, illus. LC 78-6398. (Illus.). 70 p. 22cm. 1st U.S. edition. c.1978. (ISBN 0-316-15738-4). Little, Brown.
--Klondike Arthur. Astrop, John, illus. LC 78-23176. (Illus.). 74 p. 22cm. 1st U.S. edition. 1979, c.1977. (ISBN 0-316-15733-3). Little, Brown.
--The Lone Arthur. Astrop, John, illus. LC 78-6459. (Illus.). 72 p. 22cm. 1st U.S. edition. c.1978. Little, Brown.
--Railroad Arthur. Astrop, John, illus. LC 77-28419. (Illus.). 74 p. 22cm. 1st U.S. edition. c.1977. (ISBN 0-316-15736-8). Little, Brown.

Corey, Dallas
--The Christmas Legend of Monkey Joe. LC 78-65591. (Illus.). 37 p. c.1978. Monkey Joe Enterprises.

Corey, Dorothy
--Everybody Takes Turns. Ann, Fay, ed. Axeman, Lois, illus. LC 79-18652. (Illus.). (Self-Starter Ser.). (ps-1). 1980. (ISBN 0-8075-2166-3). A Whitman.
--New Shoes!. Leder, Dora, illus. LC 84-17381. p. cm. 1985. (ISBN 0-8075-5583-5). A. Whitman.
--No Company Was Coming to Samuel's House: No Llegaban Invitados a la Casa De Samuel. Baker, Donald (1921-), illus. Baker, Marguerite Arguedas, tr. LC 76-21301. (Illus.). 40 p. 24cm. c.1976. (ISBN 0-87917-055-7). B. Ethridge-Books.
--Pepe's Private Christmas. Wallner, John C (1945-), illus. LC 78-6208. p. cm. c.1978. (ISBN 0-8193-0966-4). (ISBN 0-8193-0967-2). Parent's Magazine Press.
--Tomorrow You Can. Axeman, Lois, illus. 1977. Whitman.
--You Go Away. Axeman, Lois, illus. 32p. 1976. (ISBN 0-8075-9441-5). Albert Whitman.

Corey, Paul Frederick (1903-)
--Corn Gold Farm. LC 48-7831. 223 p. 21 cm. (Morrow junior books). 1948. W. Morrow.
--Five Acre Hill. MacDonald, James, illus. LC 46-18718. 5 p. l., 273 p. illus. 21 cm. 1946. W. Morrow & Company.
--The Little Jeep. Zander, Jack, illus. LC 46-22073. 51, 1 p. illus. (part col.) 24 1/2 cm. 1946. The World Publishing Company.
--Milk Flood. Busoni, Rafaello (1900-1962), illus. LC 56-10433. (Illus.). 189 p. 22cm. 1956. Abelard-Schuman.
--The Red Tractor. LC 44-61256. vii, 248 p. 21 cm. 1944. W. Morrow & Company.
--Shad Haul. LC 47-30678. 218 p. col. front. 21 cm. 1947. W. Morrow.

Coriell, Rebekah, jt. auth. see Coriell, Ron.

Coriell, Ron & Coriell, Rebekah
--Caring & Sharing. (Character Builders Ser.). (ps-2). 1980. (ISBN 0-8007-7013-7, Christian School Curricium). Revell.
--Doing Unto Others. (Character Builders Ser.). (ps-2). 1980. (ISBN 0-8007-7012-9, Christian School Curriculum). Revell.
--Faithful Followers. (Character Builders Ser.). (gr. 3-6). 1980. (ISBN 0-8007-7014-5, Christian School Curriculum). Revell.
--Fashioning the Faith. (Character Builders Ser.). (gr. 7-10). 1980. (ISBN 0-8007-7010-2, Christian School Curriculum). Revell.
--Happy Hearts. (Character Builders Ser.). (ps-2). 1980. (ISBN 0-8007-7006-4, Christian School Curriculum). Revell.
--His Mind, His Heart. (Character Builders Ser.). (gr. 7-10). 1980. (ISBN 0-8007-7002-1, Christian School Curriculum). Revell.
--Learning Lessons. (Character Builders Ser.). (ps-2). 1980. (ISBN 0-8007-7004-8, Christian School Curriculum). Revell.
--Learning to Listen. (Character Builders Ser.). (gr. 3-6). 1980. (ISBN 0-8007-7008-0, Christian School Curriculum). Revell.
--Listen, Look & Live. (Character Builders Ser.). (ps-2). 1980. (ISBN 0-8007-7001-3, Christian School Curriculum). Revell.
--Living Like Him. (Character Builders Ser.). (ps-2). 1980. (ISBN 0-8007-7005-6, Christian School Curriculum). Revell.
--Rejoicing in Truth. (Character Builder Ser.). (gr. 7-10). 1980. (ISBN 0-8007-7011-0, Christian School Curriculum). Revell.
--Seeing & Being Like Him. (Character Builders Ser.). (ps-2). 1980. (ISBN 0-8007-7000-5, Christian School Curriculum). Revell.
--True & Happy. (Character Builders Ser.). (gr. 3-6). 1980. (ISBN 0-8007-7009-9, Christian School Curriculum). Revell.
--Walking His Way. (Character Builders Ser.). (gr. 3-6). 1980. (ISBN 0-8007-7003-X, Christian School Curriculum). Revell.
--Wise Eyes & Wise Ways. (Character Builders Ser.). (gr. 3-6). 1980. (ISBN 0-8007-7015-3, Christian School Curriculum). Revell.

Cork, Denise
--The Gingerbread Man. Hutchings, illus. (Illus.). 14p. (Giant Board Bks.). (ps). 1972. (ISBN 0-528-82284-5). Rand.
--The Three Bears. Manchipp, Stephanie, illus. (Illus.). 14p. (Giant Board Bks.). (ps). 1972. (ISBN 0-528-82283-7). Rand.
--Three Little Pigs. Lupatelli, Anthony, illus. Lupatelli, pseud. (Illus.). 14p. (Giant Board Bks.). (ps). 1972. (ISBN 0-528-82282-9). Rand.

Corkery, Daniel (1878-1964)
--The Wager & Other Stories. (Illus.). 1950. Devin.

Corkran, Alice Abigail (0000-1916)
--Adventures of Mrs. Wishing to Be. (Illus.). N.D. Charles Scribner's Sons.
--Dora. (Illus.). (Scribner-Blackie series of books for young people). N.D. Charles Scribner's
--Down the Snow Stairs. Browne, Gordon Frederick (1858-1932), illus. (Romance and Language Series.). N.D. Dodge Publishing Cp.
--Down the Snow Stairs: Or, From Good Night to Good Morning. (Illus.). (The Little Women Ser.). N.D. A. L. Burt's Pubs.
--Down the Snow Stairs: Or, From Good Night to Good Morning. (Illus.). (The Wellesley Series for Girls). N.D. A. L. Burt.
--Joan's Adventures: At the North Pole and Elsewhere. (The Rugby Series for Boys and Girls). N.D. A. L. Burt Company.
--Joan's Adventures, At the North Pole and Elsewhere. (Illus.). (The Little Women Ser.). N.D. A. L. Burt's Pubs.
--Joan's Adventures at the North Pole and Elsewhere. (Scribner-Blackie Series of books for young people). N.D. Charles Scribner's
--Joan's Adventures,at the North Pole and Elsewhere. (Illus.). (The Wellesley Series for Girls). N.D. A. L. Burt.
--Margery Merton's Girlhood. (The Rugby Series for Boys and Girls). N.D. A. L. Burt Company.
--Margery Merton's Girlhood. (Illus.). (Fireside Ser. for Girls). N.D. A. L. Burt's Publications.
--Margery Merton's Girlhood. (Illus.). (The Meade Series for Girls). N.D. A. L. Burt.
--Margery Merton's Girlhood. (Illus.). (Scribner-Blackie Series of books for young people). N.D. Charles Scribner's Sons.
--Meg's Friend. (Illus.). (The Wellesley Series for Girls). N.D. A. L. Burt's Pubs.
--Meg's Friend. (Illus.). (Scribner-Blackie Series of books for young people). N.D. Charles Scribner's Sons.
--Meg's Friend: A Story for Girls. (Illus.). 1915. A L Burt & Co.
--Meg's Friend: A Story for Girls. (The Rugby Series for Boys and Girls). N.D. A. L. Burt Company.

Corlett, William (1938-)
--The Dark Side of the Moon. LC 76-57890. 160p. 1st U.S. edition. (gr. 6-9). 1977. (ISBN 0-87888-118-2). Bradbury Pr.
--The Gate of Eden. 1975. Bradbury Press.
--The Land Beyond. 1976. Brafbury Press.
--Return to the Gate. LC 76-57889. 163 p. 22cm. 1st U.S. edition. 1977, c.1975. (ISBN 0-87888-112-3). Bradbury Press.

Corley, Donald
--The Fifth Son of the Shoemaker. N.D. Robert M. McBride & Co.
--The Haunted Jester. N.D. Robert M. McBride & Co.
--The House of Lost Identity. N.D. Robert M. McBride & Co.

Cormack, Margaret Grant (1913-)
--Animal Tales from Ireland. Earle, Vana (1917-), illus. LC 55-9931. 63p. illus. 25cm. 1st U.S. edition. 1955, c.1954. J. Day Co.

AUTHOR INDEX

CORY, DAVID

--How the Rabbit Took a Ride. 1st ed. Phillips, W. F., illus. LC 62-12174. (Illus.). 194 p. 21cm. 1962, c.1959. Duell, Sloan and Pearce.

Cormack, Maribelle

--Timber Jack. 1952. Franklin Watts, Inc.

Cormack, Maribelle, jt. auth. see Alexander, William Prindle.

Cormack, Maribelle B. (1902-)

--Road to Down Under. Shenton, Edward (1895-), illus. LC 44-4111. 7 p. l., 3-301, 1 p. illus. 20 cm. 1944. D. Appleton-Century Company, Incorporated.

--Runner of the Trail. N.D. D. Appleton-Century Co.

--Wind of the Vikings: A Tale of the Orkney Isles. Lawson, Robert (1892-1957), illus. LC 37-5558. xviii p., 1 l., 259 p. incl. front., illus., plates. 21 cm. 1937. D. Appleton-Century Company, Incorporated.

Cormack, Maribelle B. (1902-) & Alexander, William Prindle (1881-)

--Horns of Gur. Brissaud, Pierre, illus. LC 40-27548. 4 p. l., 11-134 p. incl. illus., plates. 23 cm. c.1935. American Book Company.

--Horns of Gur. L'Allemand, Gordon, illus. LC 36-171. 4 p. l., 11-134 p. incl. illus., plates. 24 cm. c.1935. Suttonhouse, Ltd.

--Jacques: The Goatherd. Brissaud, Pierre, illus. LC 38-12119. xix, 1 p., 1 l., 225 p. incl. front., illus. 21 cm. 1938. D. Appleton-Century Company, Incorporated.

--Land for My Sons: Or, A Frontier Tale of the American Revolution. Justis, Lyle, illus. N.D. D. Appleton-Century Co.

--The Luck of the Comstocks: A Story of Block Island. Frommholz, Hilda, illus. LC 41-19199. xiv p., 1 l., 298 p. incl. front., illus. 20 cm. 1941. D. Appleton-Century Company Incorporated.

Cormack, Maribelle B. (1902-) & Bytovetzski, Pavel L.

--Swamp Boy. Hoskins, Winfield Scott, illus. LC 48-8860. (Illus.). 22cm. 200p. (gr. 10 up). N.D. (ISBN 0-679-20202-1). McKay.

--Swamp Boy: A Story of the Okefinokee Swamp in Georgia. LC 48-8860. 290 p. illus. 22 cm. 1948. D. McKay Co.

--Underground Retreat. (Dollar Mystery and Adventure Ser.). N.D. David McKay Co.

Cormier, Robert Edmund (1925-)

--After the First Death. LC 78-11770. 233 p. 22cm. c.1979. (ISBN 0-394-84122-0). (ISBN 0-394-94122-5). Pantheon Books.

--Beyond the Chocolate War: A Novel. LC 84-22865. 278 p. 22cm. c.1985. (ISBN 0-394-87343-2). (ISBN 0-394-97343-7). Knopf : Distributed by Random House.

--The Bumble Bee Flies Anyway: A Novel. LC 83-2458. p. cm. 1983. (ISBN 0-394-86120-5). (ISBN 0-394-96120-X). Pantheon Books.

--The Chocolate War: A Novel. LC 73-15109. 253 p. 22cm. 1974. (ISBN 0-394-82805-4). (ISBN 0-394-82805-4). Pantheon Books.

--Eight Plus One: Stories. LC 80-13512. p. cm. c.1980. (ISBN 0-394-84595-1). (ISBN 0-394-94595-6). Pantheon Books.

--I Am the Cheese: A Novel. LC 76-55948. 233 p. 22cm. c.1977. (ISBN 0-394-83462-3). Pantheon Books.

Cornelius, Annabel Bullock (1898-)

--Grandma's Make-up Stories: Animal Tales for Youngsters. 1st ed. Pomerantz, Norman, illus. LC 59-13577. (Illus.). 41 p. 21cm. 1960, c.1959. Greenwich Book Publishers.

Cornelius, Carol (1942-)

--Bobbin's Land. Altschuler, Franz (1923-), illus. LC 78-2399. (Illus.). 31 p. 25cm. (Concept book). c.1978. Child's World.

--Isabella Wooly Bear Tiger Moth. Altschuler, Franz (1923-), illus. LC 77-28423. (Illus.). 32 p. 25cm. (Concept book). c.1978. (ISBN 0-913778-97-4). Child's World.

Cornelius, Lilian

--Youngheart and Other Plays: With Notes on Simple Production. LC 36-33752. 4 p. l., 11-140 p. 19 cm. 1936. Greenberg.

Cornelius, Mary (1901-)

--Marc's Choice: A Story of the Time of Diocletian. Benson, Andrew, illus. LC 57-10380. 154p. illus. 22cm. (Catholic treasury books). 1957. Bruce Pub. Co.

Cornell, James, jt. auth. see Cornell, James Clayton, Jr.

Cornell, James Clayton, Jr. (1938-) & Cornell, James

--Mythical Monsters. (Illus.). (gr. 6-9). 1974. (ISBN 0-590-03163-5, Schol Pap). Scholastic Inc.

Cornell, Sarah B.

--Carl's Home. N.D. Henry Hoyt.

Corner, Julia

--The Shepherd Lord: Magnet Stories for Boys and Girls. (Illus.). N.D. Warne & Co.

Corney, Estelle

--Pa's Top Hat. Abrahams, Hilary Ruth (1938-), illus. (Illus.). 30 p. 26cm. 1981. (ISBN 0-233-97255-2). Andre Deutsch.

Corning, Mary Spring

--Miss Elliot's Girls. (Illus.). (The Wellesley Series for Girls). N.D. A. L. Burt.

--Miss Elliot's Girls: A Story for Young Girls. (The Girl Chums Ser.). N.D. A. L. Burt Company.

Cornish, Mary Taylor & Mother Goose

--Mother Goose Plays ... 3 v. 19 cm. 1926. March Brothers.

Cornish, Mary Taylor, jt. auth. see Yates, Patty M.

Cornish, Samuel James (1935-)

--Grandmother's Pictures. Johns, Jeanne, illus. LC 74-166371. (Illus.). 36 p. 23cm. 1974. (ISBN 0-912846-04-6). Bookstore Press.

--Grandmother's Pictures. Johns, Jeanne, illus. LC 75-33566. (Illus.). unpaged. 23cm. 1976, c.1974. (ISBN 0-87888-092-5). Bradbury Press. **Award: (ALA).**

--Walking the Streets with Mississippi John Hurt. Colvin, James, illus. LC 77-20288. p. cm. c.1978. (ISBN 0-8096-1762-5). Bradbury Press.

--Your Hand in Mine. 1st ed. Owens, Carl, illus. LC 74-103833. (Illus.). 32 p. 22cm. (Curriculum-related books). 1970. Harcourt, Brace & World.

Cornish, Samuel James (1935-) & Dixon, Lucian W., eds.

--Chicory: Young Voices from the Black Ghetto. LC 76-98620. 96 p. 19cm. 1969. Association Press.

Cornwall, Claudia

--Print-Outs: The Adventures of a Rebel Computer. (Illus.). 78p. (Orig.). 1982. (ISBN 0-919325-00-9, Pub. by Nerve Pr Canada). Gay Sunshine.

Cornwall, Ian Wolfram (1909-)

--Hunter's Half-Moon. Howard, M. Maitland (1898-) & Cornwall, W. J., illus. LC 68-15943. (Illus.). 158 p. 22cm. 1st U.S. edition. 1969, c.1967. Coward-McCann.

Cornwallis-West, George Frederick Myddleton (1874-)

--Us Dogs. Barker, Kathleen Frances (1901-1973), illus. LC 39-6112. xi, 1, 119 p. front., illus., plates. 22 cm. 1938. Country Life, Ltd.

Cornwell, David John Moore see Le Carre, John, pseud.

Cornwell, Susan P.

--Finland Family: Fancies Taken for Facts. N.D. Dodd & Mead.

Cornyn, John Hubert

--Around the Wigwam Fire. Varian, George, illus. 1921. Little, Brown.

Corona, Philip B.

--Mirror on the Wall: How it works. Bolian, Polly (1925-), illus. LC 64-12853. 19 x 24cm. 33p. 1964. Prentice-Hall.

Coronet see Tazewell, Charles.

Correll, Hal

--A Gift from the East. A Story of Christ. Caswell, Edward C., illus. LC 29-10222. 2 p. l., 7-228 p. plates. 20 cm. c.1928. David C. Cook Publishing Co.

--In the Service of the King. Holberg, Richard A. (1889-1942), illus. LC 30-9471. 32 p. plates. 19 cm. c.1929. David C. Cook Publishing Company.

Correy, Lee, pseud., see Stine, George Harry.

Corrigan, Barbara (1922-), illus.

--Parents Keep Out: Elderly Poems for Youngerly Readers. LC 51-13805. 137 p. illus. 21 cm. 1951. Little, Brown.

Corrigan, Helen Adeline (1909-)

--Holiday Ring: Festival Stories and Poems. Bennett, Rainey (1907-), illus. LC 75-15975. (Illus.). 256 p. 24cm. 1975. (ISBN 0-8075-3356-4). A. Whitman.

Corrin, Sara, ed. see Grimm, Jakob Ludwig Karl (1785-1863) & Grimm, Wilhelm Karl.

Corrin, Sara, ed. see Hughes, Shirley.

Corrin, Sara & Corrin, Stephen, eds.

--The Faber Book of Christmas Stories. Bennett, Jill (1947-), illus. LC 84-13552. 1984. (ISBN 0-571-13348-7). Faber.

--The Faber Book of Modern Fairy Tales. Strugnell, Ann, illus. LC 82-670034. (Illus.). 312 p. 23cm. c.1981. (ISBN 0-571-11768-6). Faber and Faber.

--More Stories for Seven-Year-Olds and Other Young Readers. Hughes, Shirley (1929-), illus. LC 79-670248. (Illus.). 183 p. 22cm. (gr. 1-3). 1979. (ISBN 0-571-11196-3). Faber and Faber.

--Mrs. Fox's Wedding. Le Cain, Errol John (1941-), illus. LC 79-3056. (Illus.). 30 p. c.1980. (ISBN 0-385-15761-4). (ISBN 0-385-15762-2). Doubleday.

--Once upon a Rhyme: One Hundred One Poems for Young Children. Bennett, Jill (1947-), illus. LC 82-5104. (Illus.). 160p. (gr. 1-4). 1982. (ISBN 0-571-11913-1). Faber & Faber.

--Pet Stories for Children. Bennett, Jill (1947-), illus. LC 85-4413. (Illus.). viii, 190 p. 23cm. 1985. (ISBN 0-571-13642-7). Faber and Faber.

--Round the Christmas Tree. Bennett, Jill (1947-), illus. LC 83-14015. p. cm. 1983. (ISBN 0-571-13151-4). Faber and Faber.

--Stories for Eight-Year-Olds. 1973. (ISBN 0-13-850180-7). P-H.

--Stories for Five Year-Olds & Other Young Readers. Hughes, Shirley (1929-), illus. (Illus.). 168p. (ps-5). 1973. (ISBN 0-571-10162-3). Faber & Faber.

--Stories for Seven-Year Olds: And Other Young Readers. Hughes, Shirley (1929-), illus. LC 66-1643. 188 p. illus. 22 cm. 1966, c.1964. Faber & Faber.

--Stories for Seven-Year-Olds & Other Young Readers. Hughes, Shirley (1929-), illus. (Illus.). 188p. (gr. 1-3). 1982. (ISBN 0-571-05823-X). Faber & Faber.

--Stories for Seven Year Olds & Other Young Readers. Hughes, Shirley (1929-), illus. LC 69-12871. (Illus.). 192p. 1st U.S. edition. (gr. k-3). 1969. (ISBN 0-531-01802-4). Watts.

--Stories for Six-Year-Olds and Other Young Readers. Hughes, Shirley (1929-), illus. LC 69-12872. (Illus.). 198 p. 23cm. 1969, c.1967. F. Watts.

--Stories for Tens & Over. Ambrus, Victor G., pseud. (1935-), illus. Ambus, Gyozo Laszlo. (Illus.). 240p. 1976. (ISBN 0-571-10873-3). Faber & Faber.

--Stories for Under-Fives. Hughes, Shirley (1929-), illus. (Illus.). 158p. (ps-5). 1974. (ISBN 0-571-10371-5). Faber & Faber.

--A Time to Laugh: Funny Stories for Children. Rose, Gerald Hembdon Seymour (1935-), illus. LC 84-28784. (Illus.). 205 p. 20cm. c.1985. (ISBN 0-571-13416-5). Faber and Faber.

--A Time to Laugh: Thirty Stories for Young Children. Rose, Gerald Hembdon Seymour (1935-), illus. 1980. Faber.

--A Time to Laugh: Thirty Stories for Young Children. Rose, Gerald Hembdon Seymour (1935-), illus. (Illus.). (ps-5). 1972. (ISBN 0-571-09950-5, Pub. by Faber & Faber). Merrimack Pub Cir.

Corrin, Stephen, jt. ed. see Corrin, Sara.

Corrin, Stephen, ed. see Grimm, Jakob Ludwig Karl (1785-1863) & Grimm, Wilhelm Karl.

Corrin, Stephen, ed. see Hughes, Shirley.

Corrin, Stephen, tr. see Andersen, Hans Christian.

Corrin, Stephen, tr. see Gernet, Nina Vladimirovna (1904-) & Jagdfeld, G.

Corrington, John William (1932-)

--The Bombardier. 1970. (ISBN 0-399-10096-2). G.P. Putnam's Sons.

--The Upper Hand. 1967. (ISBN 0-399-10829-7). G.P. Putnam's Sons.

Corse, Mary

--The House of Endless Doors. LC 23-1125. 62., 2 p. col. front. 21 cm. 1922. W. Ransom.

Corsello, Marguerite M.

--Who Said That?. A Child's Poem of Animal Sounds. McCue, Lisa, illus. (Illus.). 24p. (First Little Golden Bks.). (ps). 1982. (ISBN 0-307-11132-6, Golden Pr). Western Pub.

Corser, Joan D.

--The Tales of Mannikin & Bubbikin. Corser, Joan D., illus. (Illus.). 1984. (ISBN 0-533-05970-4). Vantage.

Corson, Hazel W (1906-)

--Peter and the Big Balloon. Marsh, William, illus. LC 60-6584. (Illus.). 95 p. 21cm. 1959. Benefic Press.

--Peter and the Moon Trip. Tiedemann, Berthold, illus. LC 57-314855. 96p. illus. 21cm. (Her Space travel books). 1957. Benefic Press.

--Peter and the Rocket Ship. (Air Age Books). N.D. Benefic Press.

--Peter and the Rocket Ship. James, William, illus. LC 55-3234. (Illus.). 96 p. 21cm. (Her Space travel books). 1955. Beckley-Cardy Co.

--Peter and the Rocket Team. Faulkner, John Frink, illus. LC 64-24984. 64 p. col. illus. 21cm. 1964. Benefic Press.

--Peter and the Two-Hour Moon. (Air Age Books). N.D. Benefic Press.

--Peter and the Two-Hour Moon. James, William, illus. LC 56-4957. (Illus.). 96 p. 21cm. (Her Space travel books). 1956. Beckley-Cardy Co.

--Peter and the Unlucky Rocket. Marsh, William, illus. LC 59-12336. (Illus.). 95 p. 21cm. 1959. Benefic Press.

Cort, D.

--The Minstrel Boy. 1961. MacMillan Co.

Cort, Howard R

--The Donakin Circus. N.D. Frederick A. Stokes.

Cort, John, jt. auth. see Cort, Margaret.

Cort, Margaret & Cort, John

--Little Oleg. LC 77-103606. (Illus.). 32 p. 26cm. 1971, c.1965. (ISBN 0-87614-007-X). Carolrhoda Books.

Cortese, James & Van Vliet, Claire

--What the Owl Said. LC 79-318076. (Illus.). 26 p. 31cm. c.1979. Janus Press.

Corvin, Michael

--The Magic Kite. 160p. N.D. British Book Centre.

Corvo, Baron

--Stories Toto Told Me, 1 of 6 vols. (The Bodley booklets Ser.: No. 6). 1900. John Lane.

Corwen, Maxwell, pseud., see Cohen, Louise Maxwell.

Corwin, David

--The Chipmunks' Merry Christmas. Scarry, Richard McClure (1919-), illus. (Little Golden Book). 1959. Golden Press.

Corwin, Judith Hoffman (1946-)

--Sleepytime, Sleepytime. (Illus.). (Peggy Cloth Bks.). (ps). 1979. (ISBN 0-448-46836-0). Platt.

Corwin, Norman Lewis (1910-)

--Dog in the Sky: The Authentic and Unexpurgated Odyssey of Runyon Jones. Gergely, Tibor (1900-1978), illus. LC 52-14606. 156 p. illus. 23 cm. 1952. Simon and Schuster.

Cory, David Magie (1872-1966)

--Adventures of Puss in Boots, Jr. (Puss in Boots, Jr.). (Twilight Tales Ser.: Vol. 1). 1917. Grosset & Dunlap.

--The Adventures of Puss in Boots, Jr. LC 17-23335. 6 p. l., 9-148, 1 p. incl. plates. 19 cm. (His Twilight tales v. 1). 1917. Harper & Brothers.

--The Adventures of Rag and Tag. Van Vredenburgh, Clara L., illus. N.D. Nourse.

--The Adventures of Young Mother Goose. Babcock, Elizabeth Jones, illus. LC 28-13254. 126 p., 1 l. incl. front., illus. 21 x 25 cm. c.1928. Grosset & Dunlap.

--Billy Bunny and Daddy Fox. (The Billy Bunny Books). N.D. Cupples & Leon Co.

--Billy Bunny and His Friends. Van Vredenburgh, Clara L., illus. LC 17-29189. 160 p. incl. front., illus. 24 cm. c.1917. George H. Doran Company.

--Billy Bunny and Robbie Redbreast. (The Billy Bunny Books). N.D. Cupples & Leon Co.

--Billy Bunny and the Friendly Elephant. (The Billy Bunny Books). N.D. Cupples & Leon Co.

--Billy Bunny and Timmie Chipmunk. (The Billy Bunny Books). N.D. Cupples & Leon Co.

--Billy Bunny and Uncle Bull Frog. (The Billy Bunny Books). N.D. Cupples & Leon Co.

--Billy Bunny and Uncle Lucky Lefthind-foot. (The Billy Bunny Books). N.D. Cupples & Leon Co.

--Chippewa Trail. LC 39-19704. 143 p. incl. front., illus. 22 cm. (His The little Indian series). c.1939. Grosset & Dunlap.

--Cowbells and Clover. LC 35-17389. 128 p. incl. front., illus. 26 cm. c.1935. Grosset & Dunlap.

--The Cruise of the Noah's Ark. (Little Journeys to Happyland). N.D. Grosset & Dunlap.

--Further Adventures of Puss in Books, Jr. (Puss in Boots, Jr.). (Twilight Tales Ser.: Vol. 2). N.D. Grosset & Dunlap.

--Further Adventures of Puss in Boots, Jr. LC 17-23336. 5 p. l., 13-125, 1 p. illus. 19 cm. (His Twilight tales v. 2). 1917. Harper & Brothers.

--Hawk Eye. LC 38-30612. 125 p. incl. front., illus. 22 cm. (His The little Indian series). c.1938. Grosset & Dunlap.

--The Iceberg Express. (Little Journeys to Happyland). N.D. Grosset & Dunlap.

--Little Indian. (The Little Indian Stories). c.1934. Grosset & Dunlap.

--Little Indian. Haynes, Lee, illus. LC 22-18676. 120 p. front., plates. 18 cm. (His Little Indian series, v. 1). c.1922. The Saalfield Publishing Company.

--Little Jack Rabbit & Big Brown Bear. Barbour, H. S., illus. (Little Jack Rabbit Bks.). N.D. Grosset & Dunlap.

--Little Jack Rabbit & Chippy Chipmunk. Barbour, H. S., illus. (Little Jack Rabbit Bks.). N.D. Grosset & Dunlap.

--Little Jack Rabbit & Danny Fox. Barbour, H. S., illus. (Little Jack Rabbit Bks.). N.D. Grosset & Dunlap.

--Little JAck RAbbit and Hungry Hawk. Barbour, H. S., illus. (Little Jack Rabbit Bks.). N.D. Grosset & Dunlap.

--Little Jack Rabbit and Miss Mousie. Barbour, H. S., illus. LC 25-10383. 128 p. col. front., col. plates. 20 cm. (His Little Jack Rabbit books). c.1925. Grosset & Dunlap.

--Little Jack Rabbit & Mr. Wicked Wolf. Barbour, H. S., illus. (Little Jack Rabbit bks.). N.D. Grosset & Dunlap.

--Little Jack Rabbit & Old Man Weasel. Barbour, H. S., illus. (Little Jack Rabbit bks.). N.D. Grosset & Dunlap.

--Little Jack Rabbit & Professor Crow. Barbour, H. S., illus. (Little Jack Rabbit Bks.). N.D. Grosset & Dunlap.

--Little Jack Rabbit and the Circus Elephants. Barbour, H. S., illus. LC 28-18253. vi, 7-128 p. col. front., col. plates. 20 cm. (His Little Jack Rabbit books). c.1928. Grosset & Dunlap.

--Little Jack Rabbit and the Policeman Dog. Barbour, H. S., illus. LC 25-10334. 128 p. col. front., col. plates. 20 cm. (His Little Jack Rabbit books). c.1925. Grosset & Dunlap.

--Little Jack Rabbit & the Squirrel Brothers. Barbour, H. S., illus. (Little Jack Rabbit Bks.). N.D. Grosset & Dunlap.

--Little Jack Rabbit & Uncle John Hare. Barbour, H. S., illus. (Little Jack Rabbit Bks.). N.D. Grosset & Dunlap.

--Little Jack Rabbit's Adventures. Barbour, H. S., illus. (Little Jack Rabbit Bks). N.D. Grosset & Dunlap.
--Little Jack Rabbit's Big Blue Book. LC 24-12451. x, 277 p. front. (port.) illus., col. plates. 23 cm. c.1924. Grosset & Dunlap.
--Little Jack Rabbit's Big Blue Book. c.1924. Harper & Bros.
--Little Jack Rabbit's Big Red Book. N.D. Harper & Bros.
--Little People of the Garden. rev. ed. LC 28-14270. 30p. illus. col. plates. 19 1/2cm. c.1928. Grosset & Dunlap.
--The Little Wilful Princess. Jones, Elizabeth Ivins, illus. LC 19-932. 97 p. front., illus. 24 cm. 1918. Moffat, Yard and Company.
--Lone Star. LC 36-8139. 128 p. incl. front., illus. 23 cm. (His The little Indian series). c.1936. Grosset & Dunlap.
--THe Magic Soap Bubble. (Little Journeys to Happyland). N.D. Grosset & Dunlap.
--The Magic Umbrella. (Little Journeys to Happyland). N.D. Grosset & Dunlap.
--Puss in Boots, Jr., and Old Mother Goose. (Puss in Books, Jr.). (Twilight Tales Ser.). N.D. Grosset & Dunlap.
--Puss in Boots, Jr., and Old Mother Goose. LC 20-14705. 4 p. l., 125. 1 p. illus. 19 cm. (His Twilight tales v. 5). c.1919. Harper & Brothers.
--Puss in Boots, Jr. and Robinson Crusoe. (Puss in Boots, Jr.). (Twilight Tales Ser.). N.D. Grosset & Dunlap.
--Puss in Boots, Jr., and the Good Gray Horse. (Puss in Boots, Jr.). (Twilight Tales Ser.). N.D. Grosset & Dunlap.
--Puss in Boots, Jr. and the Good Gray Horse. LC 21-14294. 4 p. l., 128, 1 p. illus. 19 cm. (His Twillight tales. v. 7). c.1921. Harper & Brothers.
--Puss in Boots, Jr. and the Manin the Moon. (Puss in Boots, Jr.). (Twilight Tales Ser.). N.D. Grosset & Dunlap.
--Puss in Boots, Jr., and Tom Thumb. (Puss in Boots, Jr.). (Twilight Tales Ser.). N.D. Grosset & Dunlap.
--Puss in Boots, Jr. and Tom Thumb. LC 21-14293. 4 p. l., 133, 1 p. illus. 19 cm. (His Twilight tales. v. 8). c.1921. Harper & Brothers.
--Puss in Boots, Jr., in Fairyland. (Puss in Boots, Jr.). (Twilight Tales Ser.). N.D. Grosset & Dunlap.
--Puss in Boots, Jr. in Fairyland. LC 18-11079. 4 p. l., 146, 1 p. illus. 18 cm. (His Twilight tales v. 4). 1918. Harper & Brothers.
--Puss in Boots, Jr. in New Mother Goose Land. LC 20-15064. 3 p. l., 121. 1 p. illus. 19 cm. (His Twilight tales v. 6). 1920. Harper & Brothers.
--Puss Junior and Robinson Crusoe. LC 22-19045. vi p., 1 l., 141, 1 p. illus. 19 cm. (His Twilight tales. v. 9). c.1922. Harper & Brothers.
--Puss Junior and the Man in the Moon. LC 22-19162. vi p., 1 l., 132, 1 p. illus. 19 cm. (His Twilight tales. v. 10). c.1922. Harper & Brothers.
--Pussin Boots, Jr., in New Mother Goose Land. N.D. Harper & Brothers.
--Raven Wing. LC 37-9863. 128 p. incl. front., illus. 23 cm. (His The little Indian series). c.1937. Grosset & Dunlap.
--Red Feather. LC 34-4685. 126 p. incl. front., illus. 23 cm. (His The little Indian series). c.1934. Grosset & Dunlap.
--Red Feather and Star Maiden. LC 35-4338. 127 p. incl. front., illus. 22 cm. (His The little Indian series). c.1935. Grosset & Dunlap.
--Star Boy. Haynes, Lee, illus. LC 22-18677. 119 p. front., plates. 18 cm. (His Little Indian series, v. 3). c.1922. The Saalfield Publishing Company.
--Sunny Meadow Stories. Taylor, Ethel Bonney, illus. N.D. Rand McNally & Co.
--Travels of Puss in Boots, Jr. (Puss in Boots, Jr.). (Twilight Tales Ser.: Vol.3). 1918. Grosset & Dunlap.
--Travels of Puss in Boots, Jr. LC 18-11080. 4 p. l., 150, 1 p. illus. 18 cm. (His Twilight tales v. 3). 1918. Harper & Brothers.
--Uncle Lucky. (Little Jack Rabbit Bks). N.D. Grosset & Dunlap.
--The Which Book: The Doings of Willie Crosspatch and Mary Sunshine. 80p. N.D. Nourse.
--White Feather. Haynes, Lee, illus. LC 22-18675. 120 p. front., plates. 18 cm. (His Little Indian series, v. 2). c.1922. The Saalfield Publishing Company.
--White Otter. LC 34-4686. 128 p. incl. front., illus. 23 cm. (His The little Indian series). c.1934. Grosset & Dunlap.
--The Wind Wagon. (Little Journeys to Happyland). N.D. Grosset & Dunlap.
--The Yellow Dog Trap. (The Little Jack Rabbit Bks). N.D. Grosset & Dunlap.

Cory, Fanny Young

--The Babes in the Wood. Cory, Fanny Young, illus. N.D. Bobbs-Merrill Co.
--The Fanny Cory Mother Goose. Cory, Fanny Young, illus. N.D. Bobbs-Merrill Co.
--Little Boy Blue. Cory, Fanny Young, illus. N.D. Bobbs-Merrill Co.
--Little Me: In Picture and Verse. Cory, Fanny Young, illus. LC 36-15964. 56 p. illus. 20 cm. c.1936. E. P. Dutton & Co., Inc.
--Our Baby Book. Cory, Fanny Young, illus. N.D. Bobbs-Merrill Company.
--Sonny Sayings. Cory, Fanny Young, illus. N.D. E. P. Dutton & Co.

Cory, George

--Head-on with Hurricane Camille. Baldini, Tony, illus. LC 79-21323. (Illus.). (Quest, Adventure, Survival Ser.). (gr. 4-8). 1980. (ISBN 0-8172-1565-4). Raintree Pubs.
--Head-On with Hurricane Camille. Baldini, Tony, illus. LC 79-21323. (Illus.). 46p. (Quest, Adventure, Survival Ser.). (gr. 4-9). 1982. (ISBN 0-8172-2060-7). Raintree Pubs.

Coryell, Hubert Vansant (1889-)

--Indian Brother. Pitz, Henry Clarence (1895-1976), illus. LC 35-17486. xv, 348 p. incl. front., illus., plates (part double) 22 cm. c.1935. Harcourt, Brace and Company.
--Klondike Gold. Sperry, Armstrong W. (1897-1976), illus. LC 38-29785. vi p., 1 l., 319 p. illus. 23 cm. 1938. The Macmillan Company.
--The Scalp Hunters. Jones, Wilfred J. (1888-), illus. LC 36-27422. x, 277 p. incl. front., plates. 22 cm. c.1936. Harcourt, Brace and Company.
--Tan-Ta-Ka Kills-with-a-Knife. Townsend, Lee (1895-), illus. LC 34-29555. viii p., 2 l., 3-305 p. incl. front., illus., plates. 21 cm. 1934. Little, Brown, and Company.

Coryell, Hugh (1913-)

--Terry and the Mysterious Monkey. 1st ed. Ressler, William, illus. LC 52-5482. 116 p. illus. 22 cm. 1952. Winston.

Coryell, John Russell (1851-1924)

--Diccon the Bold. (Illus.). (Roundabout Lib.). N.D. Henry T. Coates & Co.
--Diccon the Bold. (Roundabout Library). N.D. John C. Winston Co.
--Diccon the Bold: A Story of the Days of Columbus. LC 44-29774. vi, 279 p. front., plates. 20 cm. 1893. G. P. Putnam's Sons.
--Diego Pinzon and the Fearful Voyage He Took into the Unknown Ocean A. D. 1492. LC 12-19588. iv, 259 p. front., 29 pl. 19 cm. 1892. Harper & Brothers.
--The Man Who Stole Millions: Nick Carter's Special Train, Wanted for Murder; Three Complete Stories of the Exploits of Nicholas Carter ... LC 2804. 197 p. 19 cm. (On cover: Magnet detective library. no. 129). 1900. Street & Smith.
--Tommy's Money. (Harper's Young People Ser.). N.D. Harper & Brothers.

Cosby, William Henry, Jr. (1937-)

--Fat Albert's Survival Kit. (gr. 4-6). 1975. (ISBN 0-525-61532-6, Pub by Windmill Bks). Dutton.
--The Wit and Wisdom of Fat Albert. 1st ed. Filmation, illus. LC 73-9320. (Illus.). 64 p. 18cm. 1973. (ISBN 0-525-61004-9). Windmill Books.

Cosgrave, John O'Hara, II (1908-)

--Clipper Ship. 1963. MacMillan.

Cosgrove, Rachel R, pseud., see Payes, Cosgrove.

Cosgrove, Rachel R, pseud. (1922-) & Baum, Lyman Frank (1856-1919)

--The Hidden Valley of Oz: Founded on and Continuing the Famous Oz Stories by L. Frank Baum. Payes, Cosgrove. Gringhuis, Richard H. (1918-1974), illus. Dirk, pseud. LC 51-8226. 313 p. illus. 23 cm. 1951. Reilly & Lee Co.

Cosgrove, Stephen Edward (1945-)

--Bangalee. James, Robin, illus. LC 78-11059. p. cm. 1979. (ISBN 0-87191-666-5). Creative Education.
--Bangalee. James, Robin, illus. LC 78-101496. (Illus.). 32 p. 23cm. c.1976. (ISBN 0-915396-13-0). Serendipity Press Mankato, MN : Available in Hardcover from Creative Education.
--Bugglar Brothers. (Orig.). (Bugg Bks.). 1984. (ISBN 0-8431-1232-8). Price Stern.
--Bugglar Brothers. Reasoner, Charles, illus. LC 84-11557. (Illus.). 31 p. (Bugg books). c.1984. (ISBN 0-86592-305-1). Rourke Enterprises.
--Bumble B. Bear: A Gift for the Giving. Reasoner, Charles, illus. (Illus.). (Bear Board Bks.). 1984. (ISBN 0-8431-1386-3). Price Stern.
--Bumble B. Bear Cleans Up. Reasoner, Charles, illus. (Illus.). (Bear Board Bks.). 1984. (ISBN 0-8431-1169-0). Price Stern.
--Bumble B. Bear Rides in the Car. Reasoner, Charles, illus. (Illus.). (Bear Board Bks.). 1984. (ISBN 0-8431-1167-4). Price Stern.
--Bumble B. Bear Takes a Walk. Reasoner, Charles, illus. (Illus.). (Bear Board Bks.). 1984. (ISBN 0-8431-1170-4). Price Stern.
--Bumble B. Bear: The Christmas Tree. Reasoner, Charles, illus. (Illus.). (Bear Board Bks.). 1984. (ISBN 0-8431-1387-1). Price Stern.
--Cap'n Smudge. James, Robin, illus. LC 78-11063. p. cm. 1979. (ISBN 0-87191-659-2). Creative Education.
--Cap'n Smudge. James, Robin, illus. LC 78-101415. (Illus.). 32 p. 23cm. c.1977. (ISBN 0-915396-17-3). (ISBN 0-8431-0551-8). Serendipity Press.
--Catundra. James, Robin, illus. LC 78-64879. (Illus.). 32 p. 23cm. c.1978. (ISBN 0-87191-692-4). Creative Education.
--Chatterbox. Reasoner, Charles, illus. LC 85-42714. p. cm. (Whimsie storybook). c.1985. (ISBN 0-394-87456-0). Random House.
--Cooty-Doo. Reasoner, Charles, illus. 32p. (Orig.). (Bugg Bks.). 1984. (ISBN 0-317-11680-0). Price Stern.
--Cooty-Doo. Reasoner, Charles, illus. LC 85-2443. p. cm. (Bugg books). c.1984. (ISBN 0-86592-817-7). Rourke Enterprises.
--Crabby Gabby. James, Robin, illus. LC 85-14351. p. cm. 1985. (ISBN 0-86592-342-6). Rourke Enterprises.
--Cranky. Reasoner, Charles, illus. LC 85-42712. p. cm. (Whimsie storybook). c.1985. (ISBN 0-394-87454-4). Random House.
--Creole. James, Robin, illus. LC 78-11182. p. cm. 1978. (ISBN 0-87191-655-X). Creative Education.
--Creole. James, Robin, illus. LC 78-101428. (Illus.). 32 p. 23cm. (gr. 1-6). c.1975. (ISBN 0-915396-10-6). (ISBN 0-8431-0552-6). Serendipity Press.
--Crick-Ette. Reasoner, Charles, illus. LC 84-11554. (Illus.). 31 p. (Bugg books). c.1984. (ISBN 0-86592-303-5). Rourke Enterprises.
--Crickeette. (Orig.). (Bugg Bks.). 1984. (ISBN 0-8431-1226-3). Price Stern.
--Doodle Bugg. Reasoner, Charles, illus. 32p. (Orig.). (Bugg Bks.). 1984. (ISBN 0-8431-1213-1). Price Stern.
--Doodle Bugg. Reasoner, Charles, illus. LC 85-2442. p. cm. (Bugg books). c.1984. (ISBN 0-86592-816-9). Rourke Enterprises.
--Dragolin. James, Robin, illus. (Orig.). (Serendipity Storybks.). 1984. (ISBN 0-8431-1165-8). Price Stern.
--Dragolin. James, Robin, illus. LC 85-14400. p. cm. 1985. (ISBN 0-86592-344-2). Rourke Enterprises.
--The Dream Tree. James, Robin, illus. LC 78-10866. p. cm. 1979. (ISBN 0-87191-665-7). (ISBN 0-8431-0553-4). Creative Education.
--The Dream Tree. James, Robin, illus. LC 78-101425. (Illus.). 32 p. 23cm. c.1974. (ISBN 0-915396-06-8). Serendipity Press.
--Dune Bugg. (Illus.). 32p. (Crick-Ette Ser.). 1983. (ISBN 0-8431-1200-X). Price-Stern.
--Dune Bugg. (Illus.). 32p. (Bugg Ser.). 1983. (ISBN 0-8431-1206-9). Price Stern.
--Eevil Weevil. (Illus.). 32p. (Bugg Ser.). 1983. (ISBN 0-8431-1201-8). Price Stern.
--Eevil Weevil. Reasoner, Charles, illus. LC 84-11635. p. cm. (Bugg books). 1984. (ISBN 0-86592-307-8). Rourke Enterprises.
--Feather Fin. James, Robin, illus. (Illus.). 32p. (Orig.). (Serendipity Ser.). 1983. (ISBN 0-8431-0593-3). Price Stern.
--Feather Fin. James, Robin, illus. LC 84-15057. (Illus.). 31 p. 26cm. c.1984. (ISBN 0-86592-332-9). Rourke Enterprises.
--Flutterby. James, Robin, illus. LC 78-10870. p. cm. 1979. (ISBN 0-87191-664-9). Creative Education.
--Flutterby. James, Robin, illus. LC 78-101417. (Illus.). 32 p. 23cm. c.1976. (ISBN 0-915396-12-2). Serendipity Press.
--Flutterby Fly. James, Robin, illus. (Illus., Orig.). (Serendipity Storybks.). 1984. (ISBN 0-8431-1162-3). Price Stern.
--Flutterby Fly. James, Robin, illus. LC 85-14353. p. cm. 1985. (ISBN 0-86592-346-9). Rourke Enterprises.
--Gabby. (Orig.). (Serendipity Bks.). 1984. (ISBN 0-8431-0607-7). Price Stern.
--Gabby. James, Robin, illus. LC 84-15079. (Illus.). 31 p. 26cm. c.1984. (ISBN 0-86592-329-9). Rourke Enterprises.
--Giggle. Reasoner, Charles, illus. LC 85-42716. p. cm. (Whimsie storybook). (Whimsie storybook.). c.1985. (ISBN 0-394-87458-7). Random House.
--Gimme. Reasoner, Charles, illus. LC 85-1958. p. cm. (Whimsie storybook). (Whimsie storybook.). c.1985. (ISBN 0-394-87451-X). Random House.
--Glance. (Orig.). (Bugg Bks.). 1984. (ISBN 0-8431-1236-0). Price Stern.
--Glance. Reasoner, Charles, illus. LC 84-11553. (Illus.). 31 p. (Bugg books). c.1984. (ISBN 0-86592-302-7). Rourke Enterprises.
--Glitterby Baby. James, Robin, illus. LC 85-14354. p. cm. 1985. (ISBN 0-86592-340-X). Rourke Enterprises.
--The Gnome from Nome. James, Robin, illus. LC 78-11454. p. cm. 1979. (ISBN 0-87191-656-8). Creative Education.
--The Gnome from Nome. James, Robin, illus. LC 78-101418. (Illus.). 32 p. 23cm. c.1974. (ISBN 0-915396-01-7). Serendipity Press.
--Gobble and Gulp. Reasoner, Charles, illus. LC 85-42715. p. cm. (Whimsie storybook). c.1985. (ISBN 0-394-87457-9). Random House.
--Grampa Lop. 32p. (Orig.). (Serendipity Bks.). 1984. (ISBN 0-8431-1161-5). Price Stern.
--Grampa-Lop. James, Robin, illus. LC 84-15078. (Illus.). 31 p. 26cm. 1984, c.1981. (ISBN 0-86592-338-8). Rourke Enterprises.
--Hucklebug. James, Robin, illus. LC 78-11453. (Illus.). 32 p. 23cm. (Serendipity book). 1978, c.1975. (ISBN 0-87191-657-6). Creative Education.
--Hucklebug. James, Robin, illus. LC 78-101419. (Illus.). 32 p. 23cm. c.1975. (ISBN 0-915396-07-6). Serendipity Press.
--Humbugg. (Orig.). (Bugg Bks.). 1984. (ISBN 0-8431-1230-1). Price Stern.
--Humbugg. Reasoner, Charles, illus. LC 84-11632. (Illus.). 31 p. 17cm. (Bugg books). 1984. (ISBN 0-86592-309-4). Rourke Enterprises.
--Humbugs. (Illus.). 32p. (Bugg Ser.). 1983. (ISBN 0-8431-1202-6). Price Stern.
--In Search of the Saveopotomas. James, Robin, illus. LC 78-11135. p. cm. 1979. (ISBN 0-87191-661-4). Creative Education.
--In Search of the Saveopotomas. James, Robin, illus. LC 78-101404. (Illus.). 32 p. 23cm. c.1974. (ISBN 0-915396-00-9). Serendipity Press.
--Jake O'Shawnasey. (Illus.). (Serendipity Bks.). (gr. k-4). 1978. (ISBN 0-87191-654-1). Creative Ed.
--Jake O'Shawnasey. James, Robin, illus. (gr. 1-6). 1975. (ISBN 0-8431-0558-5). Price Stern.
--Jake O'Shawnasey. James, Robin, illus. LC 78-101420. (Illus.). 32 p. 23cm. c.1975. (ISBN 0-915396-08-4). Serendipity Press.
--Jingle Bear. James, Robin, illus. LC 85-14403. p. cm. 1985. (ISBN 0-86592-339-6). Rourke Enterprises.
--Jitterbugg. Reasoner, Charles, illus. (Illus., Orig.). (Bugg Bks.). 1984. (ISBN 0-8431-1216-6). Price Stern.
--Jitterbugg. Reasoner, Charles, illus. LC 85-2445. p. cm. (Bugg books). c.1984. (ISBN 0-86592-812-6). Rourke Enterprises.
--June Bugg. Reasoner, Charles, illus. LC 84-11555. (Illus.). 31 p. (Bugg books). c.1984. (ISBN 0-86592-301-9). Rourke Enterprises.
--June Bugs. (Illus.). 32p. (Bugg Ser.). 1984. (ISBN 0-8431-1203-4). Price Stern.
--Kartusch. James, Robin, illus. LC 78-65066. (Illus.). 32 p. 23cm. c.1978. (ISBN 0-87191-689-4). Creative Education.
--Katy-Didd. Reasoner, Charles, illus. (Illus., Orig.). (Bugg Bks.). 1984. (ISBN 0-8431-1214-X). Price Stern.
--Katy-Didd. Reasoner, Charles, illus. LC 85-2444. p. cm. (Bugg books). 1984. (ISBN 0-86592-815-0). Rourke Enterprises.
--Kiyomi. James, Robin, illus. (Illus., Orig.). (Serendipity Storybks.). 1984. (ISBN 0-8431-1164-X). Price Stern.
--Kiyomi. James, Robin, illus. LC 85-14430. p. cm. 1985. (ISBN 0-86592-343-4). Rourke Enterprises.
--Leo the Lop. James, Robin, illus. LC 78-10834. p. cm. 1979. (ISBN 0-87191-658-4). Creative Education.
--Leo the Lop. James, Robin, illus. LC 78-101401. (Illus.). 32 p. 23cm. c.1977. (ISBN 0-915396-16-5). Serendipity Press.
--Leo the Lop - Tail Three. James, Robin, illus. (Illus.). 32p. (Serendipity Bks). 1980. (ISBN 0-8431-0577-1). Price Stern.
--Leo the Lop: Tail Three. 32p. (Orig.). (Serendipity Bks.). 1984. (ISBN 0-8431-1160-7). Price Stern.
--Leo the Lop, Tail Three, Bk. 1. James, Robin, illus. (Illus.). 32p. (Serendipity Bks.). (gr. k-4). 1981. (ISBN 0-87191-791-2). Creative Ed.
--Leo the Lop: Tail Two. 32p. (Orig.). (Serendipity Bks.). 1984. (ISBN 0-8431-1159-3). Price Stern.
--Leo the Lop (Tail Two). James, Robin, illus. (Illus., Orig.). (Serendipity Books). (gr. k-6). 1979. (ISBN 0-8431-0572-0). Price Stern.
--Little Mouse on the Prairie. James, Robin, illus. LC 78-64877. (Illus.). 32 p. 23cm. (Serendipity book). c.1978. (ISBN 0-87191-690-8). Creative Education.
--Lord & Lady Bugg. (Orig.). (Bugg Bks.). 1984. (ISBN 0-8431-1233-6). Price Stern.
--Lord & Lady Bugg. Reasoner, Charles, illus. LC 84-11556. (Illus.). 31 p. (Bugg books). c.1984. (ISBN 0-86592-304-3). Rourke Enterprises.
--Love Bugg. (Orig.). (Bugg Bks.). 1984. (ISBN 0-8431-1231-X). Price Stern.
--Love Bugg. Reasoner, Charles, illus. LC 84-11562. (Illus.). 31 p. (Bugg books). c.1984. (ISBN 0-86592-306-X). Rourke Enterprises.
--Maui-Maui. James, Robin, illus. (Illus.). (Serendipity Bks.). (gr. k-6). 1979. (ISBN 0-8431-0573-9). Price Stern.
--Ming Ling. James, Robin, illus. 32p. (Orig.). (Serendipity Bks.). 1983. (ISBN 0-8431-0592-5). Price Stern.

--Uncle Bouqui of Haiti. Crockett, Lucy Herndon (1914-), illus. LC 42-18468. 126 p., 1 l. col. illus. 22 cm. 1942. W. Morrow and Company.

Courlander, Harold (1908-), compiled by.

--The Crest and the Hide, and Other African Stories of Heroes, Chiefs, Bards, Hunters, Sorcerers, and Common People. Vachula, Monica, illus. LC 81-9739. (Illus.). 137 p. 24cm. c.1982. (ISBN 0-698-20536-7). Coward, McCann & Geoghegan. **Award: (ALA).**

Courlander, Harold (1908-) & Eshugbayi, Ezekiel A., eds.

--Olode the Hunter, and Other Tales from Nigeria. 1st ed. Arno, Enrico (1913-1981), illus. LC 68-13370. (Illus.). 153 p. 20cm. 1968. Harcourt, Brace & World.

Courlander, Harold (1908-) & Herzog, George (1901-), eds.

--The Cow-Tail Switch And Other And Other West African Stories. LC 47-30108. 4 p. l., 143 p., 1 l. 24 cm. 1947. H. Holt and Company. **Award: (JNM).**

Courlander, Harold (1908-) & Prempeh, Albert Kofi, eds.

--Hat-Shaking Dance & Other Ashanti Tales from Ghana. Arno, Enrico (1913-1981), illus. LC 56-5872. (Illus.). (gr. 3-7). 1957. (ISBN 0-15-233615-X, HJ). HarBraceJ.

--Hat Shaking Dance and Other Tales from the Gold Coast. N.D. E . M. Hale and Co.

--The Hat-Shaking Dance and Other Tales from the Gold Coast. 1st ed. Arno, Enrico (1913-1981), illus. LC 56-587230. 115p. illus. 21cm. (gr. 3-7). 1957. (ISBN 0-15-233615-X). Harcourt, Brace.

Cournos, Helen Sybil Norton Kestner, jt. auth. see Cournos, John.

Cournos, John (1881-1966), ed. see Gogol, Nikolai Vasilevich.

Cournos, John, jt. ed. see Haydn, Hiram.

Cournos, John (1881-1966)

--A Boy Named John. Ishmael, Woodi (1914-), illus. LC 41-18711. 4 p. l., 117 p. incl. front., illus. 21 cm. 1941. C. Scribner's Sons.

Cournos, John (1881-1966) & Cournos, Helen Sybil Norton Kestner, pseud. (1893-)

--Famous British Poets. Cournos, Helen Sybil Norton Kestner. (Illus.). (gr. 7-9). 1952. (ISBN 0-396-03400-4). Dodd.

--Pilgrimage to Freedom. 1st ed. Norton, Sybil, pseud. Anderson, Rus, illus. LC 52-13064. 170p. illus. 21cm. 1953. Holt.

Coursen, Frances B.

--What the Dragon Fly Told the Children. (Illus.). N.D. Lothrop Lee & Shepard Co.

Court, Wesli, pseud., see Turco, Lewis.

Court, Wesli (1940-)

--Murgatroyd & Mabel. Michaels, Robert (1926-), illus. (Illus.). (gr. k-2). 1978. (ISBN 0-930000-06-4). Mathom.

Courtain, Patrick

--Mister Bird. Couratin, Patrick, illus. (Illus.). 24p. (gr. k up). N.D. Quist.

Courtney, Dayle

--Escape from Eden. Ham, John, illus. LC 81-5710. p. cm. ((Series: Courtney, Dayle.). (Thorne Twins adventure books.). (Thorne Twins Adventure Books). 1981. (ISBN 0-87239-467-0). Standard Pub.

--Flight to Terror. Ham, John, illus. LC 81-5632. p. cm. (Thorne Twins Adventure Books: 1). 1981. (ISBN 0-87239-467-0). Standard Pub.

--The Foxworth Hunt. Ham, John, illus. LC 82-5512. 221 p. 20cm. (Thorne Twins Adventure Bks.). c.1982. (ISBN 0-87239-553-7). Standard Pub.

--The Great UFO Chase. Ham, John, illus. LC 84-2445. (Illus.). 192p. (Orig.). (Thorne Twins Adventure Bks.). (gr. 6-10). 1984. (ISBN 0-87239-755-6). Standard Pub.

--The Hidden Cave. Ham, John, illus. LC 82-5510. p. cm. (Thorne Twins Adventure Bks.). 1982. (ISBN 0-87239-555-3). Standard Pub.

--The House That Ate People. Ham, John, illus. LC 83-4697. p. cm. (Thorne Twins Adventure Bks.: 15). 1983. (ISBN 0-87239-683-5). Standard Pub.

--The Ivy Plot. Ham, John, illus. LC 81-5631. p. cm. (Thorne Twins Adventure Books: 4). 1981. (ISBN 0-87239-469-7). Standard Pub.

--Jaws of Terror. Ham, John, illus. LC 82-5511. (Illus.). 191 p. 20cm. (Thorne Twins Adventure Bks.). c.1982. (ISBN 0-87239-554-5). Standard Pub.

--The Knife with Eyes. Ham, John, illus. LC 81-5624. p. cm. (Thorne Twins Adventure Bks.: 3). 1981. (ISBN 0-87239-469-7). Standard Pub.

--Mysterious Strangers. Ham, John, illus. LC 82-3320. (Illus.). 221 p. 20cm. (Thorne Twins Adventure Books: 8). c.1982. (ISBN 0-87239-552-9). Standard Pub.

--The Olympic Plot. Ham, John, illus. LC 84-2473. (Illus.). 192p. (Orig.). (Thorne Twins Adventure Bks.). (gr. 6-10). 1984. (ISBN 0-87239-756-4). Standard Pub.

--Omen of the Flying Light. Ham, John, illus. LC 81-5353. p. cm. (Thorne Twins Adventure Books: 6). N.D. (ISBN 0-87239-443-3). Standard Pub.

--Operation Doomsday. Ham, John, illus. LC 81-5655. p. cm. (Thorne Twins Adventure Books: 5). 1981. (ISBN 0-87239-466-2). Standard Pub.

--Secret of Pirates' Cave. Ham, John, illus. (Illus.). 192p. (Orig.). (Thorne Twins Adventure Bks.). (gr. 6-10). 1984. (ISBN 0-87239-758-0). Standard Pub.

--Shadow of Fear. Ham, John, illus. LC 83-4696. p. cm. (Thorne Twins adventure book ; 14). (Thorne Twins adventure books ; 14.). 1983. (ISBN 0-87239-682-7). Standard Pub.

--The Sinister Circle. Ham, John, illus. LC 83-4699. p. cm. (Thorne Twins Adventure Bks.: 16). 1983. (ISBN 0-87239-684-3). Standard Pub.

--Three-Ring Inferno. Ham, John, illus. LC 82-5561. (Illus.). 191 p. 20cm. (Thorne Twins Adventure Bks.: 7). c.1982. (ISBN 0-87239-551-0). Standard Pub.

--Tower of Flames. Ham, John, illus. LC 82-3270. (Illus.). 192 p. 20cm. (Thorne Twins Adventure Bks.). c.1982. (ISBN 0-87239-556-1). Standard Pub.

--The Trail of Bigfoot. Ham, John, illus. LC 83-4700. p. cm. (Thorne Twins Adventure Bks.: 13). 1983. (ISBN 0-87239-681-9). Standard Pub.

--The Unicorn Clue. Ham, John, illus. LC 84-6537. p. cm. 1984. (ISBN 0-87239-757-2). Standard Pub.

Courtney, E. S., Mrs.

--Twice Tried: or, the Three Influences, 1 of 3, Vol. 2. (Idle Words Ser.). N.D. Claxton, Remsen, & Haffelfinger.

Courtney, Gwendoline

--Those Verney Girls. LC 56-12473. 218p. 22cm. 1957. F. Watts.

Courtney, Jennifer L

--Pepito the Naughty Donkey. Manchipp, Ben, illus. LC 77-184642. (Illus.). 18 p. (Whitman scratch-and-sniff book). 1972. Western Pub. Co.

Courtright, Jane, jt. auth. see Courtright, John.

Courtright, John (1912-)

--Jolly Blue Boat. Courtright, Jane & Courtright, John (1912-), illus. (gr. 1-4). 1962. (ISBN 0-516-03039-6). Childrens.

Courtright, John (1912-) & Courtright, Jane

--Jolly Blue Boat. Courtright, John (1912-) & Courtright, Jane, illus. LC 47-24084. (Illus.). 20 x 27cm. 28p. 1947. Childrens Press.

Cousin, Virginia, pseud., see Townsend, Virginia Frances.

Cousin Alice, pseud., see Haven, Alice Bradley.

Cousin Bell

--Little Addie's Library, 12 Vols. (Illus.). 768p. N.D. Ira Bradley & Co's.

Cousin Ella

--Little Twigs. (Illus.). 280p. (Sunday-Hour Lib.). 1905. American Tract Society.

Cousin Kate, pseud., see McIntosh, Maria Jane.

Cousin Mary

--Holidays at Chestnut Hill, 1 of 25 vols. (Illus.). (Pilgrim Ser. for Boys: No. 13). 1900. Lee & Shepard.

Cousins, Lynne, illus.

--Tom, Tom, the Piper's Son & Other Rhymes. Snowdon, Lynda, compiled by. (Illus.). 12p. (First Nursery Rhyme Bks.). (ps-1). 1981. Crown.

Cousins, Sue Margaret (1905-)

--The Boy in the Alamo. Eggenhofer, Nicholas, illus. LC 83-72585. (Illus.). 180p (Pub. by Grosset & Dunlap). Orig. Title: We Were There at the Battle of the Alamo. 1983. (ISBN 0-931722-26-8). Corona Pub.

--Uncle Edgar and the Reluctant Saint. Cirlin, Edgar, illus. LC 48-9033. 49 p. illus. 20 cm. 1948. Farrar, Straus.

--We Were There at the Battle of the Alamo. Eggenhofer, Nicholas, illus. LC 58-5702. (Illus.). 22cm. 180p. (We were there books, 18). (gr. 4-9). 1958. (ISBN 0-448-05018-8). G&D.

Cousin Virginia, pseud., see Townsend, Virginia Frances.

Cousin Virginia, pseud. (1836-1920)

--Christmas Stocking. Townsend, Virginia Frances. 400p. N.D. Thomas O'Kane.

Cousin Zilpha (1865-)

--Link and Other Stories. (Illus.). 136p. N.D. American Tract Society.

--Sunny Bell. (Illus.). N.D. D. Lothrop & Co.

Coussens, Penrhyn Wingfield (1873-), ed.

--A Child's Book of Famous Stories. Smith, Jessie Willcox (1863-1935), illus. LC 41-5099. xi p., 1 l., 462, 1 p. col. front., col. plates. 23 cm. 1940. Garden City Publishing Co., Inc.

--A Child's Book of Stories. Smith, Jessie Willcox (1863-1935), illus. LC 34-28412. 25cm. 462p. (The Treasure House Bks.). 1934. Dodd, Mead & Co.

--A Child's Book of Stories. Smith, Jessie Willcox (1863-1935), illus. LC 11-25418. xi p., 1 l., 463 p. col. front., col. plates. 24 cm. 1911. Duffield & Company.

--The Diamond Story Book. Green, Ethel, illus. LC 14-17092. 7 p. l., 415, 2 p. col. front., col. plates. 20 cm. 1914. Duffield & Company.

--The Jade Story Book: Stories from the Orient. x, 369 p. col. front. 20 cm. (On verso of half-title: The jewel series). 1922. Duffield and Company.

--Poems Children Love: A Collection of Poems Arranged for Children and Young People of Various Ages. LC 72-98078. (Illus.). 333 p. 21cm. (Granger index reprint series). 1969. Books for Libraries Press.

--Poems Children Love: A Collection of Poems Arranged for Children and Young People of Various Ages. LC 8-23514. 4 p. l., 333 p. 20 cm. c.1908. Dodge Publishing Company.

--The Ruby Story Book: Tales of Courage and Heroism. Parrish, Maxfield, contrib. by. LC 16-18024. 6 p. l., 3-341, 2 p. col. front. 20 cm. (On verso of half-title: The jewel series). 1916. Duffield & Company.

--The Sapphire Story Book: Stories of the Sea. (Jewell Ser.). 1917. Duffield.

Coutant, Helen H. (1909-)

--First Snow. Vo-Dinh, Mai (1933-), illus. LC 74-1187. (Illus.). 30 p. 22cm. 1974. (ISBN 0-394-82831-3). (ISBN 0-394-92831-8). Knopf; Distributed by Random House.

--The Gift. Vo-Dinh, Mai (1933-), illus. LC 82-7810. (Illus.). 46 p. 22cm. c.1983. (ISBN 0-394-85499-3). (ISBN 0-394-95499-8). Knopf.

--Isle Royal Callingg. LC 67-2033. 23cm. 215p. 1966, c.1957. Eerdmans.

Couzens, Reginald C.

--The Stories of the Months and Days. N.D. Frederick A. Stokes.

--The Stories of the Months and Days. LC 70-124662. (Illus.). 160 p. 23cm. 1970. Gale Research Co.

Cove, Mary A.

--Puffee with the Ticklish Tummy. 1979. (ISBN 0-533-04079-5). Vantage.

Covell, Natalie Anne, jt. auth. see Crossen, Stacy Jo.

Coventry, Martha, tr. see Gallaz, Christopher & Innocenti, Roberto.

Coventry, Mary

--Lucy Cockoo. N.D. Transatlantic Arts.

Cover, Arthur Byron, ed. see Semple, Lorenzo.

Coville, Bruce (1950-)

--The Monster's Ring. Coville, Katherine (1939-), illus. LC 82-3436. (Illus.). 96p. (gr. 8-11). 1982. (ISBN 0-394-85320-2). (ISBN 0-394-95320-7). Pantheon.

--Sarah & the Dragon. Peck, Beth, illus. LC 83-48447. (Illus.). 48p. (gr. k-3). 1984. (ISBN 0-397-32069-8, JBL-J). (ISBN 0-397-32070-1). Har-Row.

Coville, Bruce (1950-) & Coville, Katherine (1939-)

--The Foolish Giant. LC 77-18522. (Illus.). 46 p. 24cm. (Lippincott I-like-to-read book). c.1978. (ISBN 0-397-31800-6). (ISBN 0-397-31801-4). Lippincott.

--Sarah's Unicorn. LC 79-2408. p. cm. (Lippincot I-like-to-read book). c.1979. (ISBN 0-397-31872-3). (ISBN 0-397-31873-1). Lippincott.

Coville, Katherine, jt. auth. see Coville, Bruce.

Covington, John P

--Motorcycle Racer. LC 78-121950. 144 p. 22cm. (Doubleday signal books). 1973. (ISBN 0-385-02325-1). Doubleday.

Cowan

--The King's Children. (Illus.). (Crowell's Young People Ser.). N.D. Thomas Y. Crowell.

Cowan, Elizabeth (1940-) & Davis, Karen

--Fairy Tales of the Sea. Hubbard, Fain, illus. LC 81-185228. (Illus.). v, 146 p. 23cm. 1981. Texas A&M University, Sea Grant College Program : Copies from Marine Information Service, Sea Grant College Program, Texas A&M University.

Cowan, John Franklin (1854-)

--Boy Campaigners of '61: A Story of the Patriotism, The Valor and the Very Manhood of the Youth Who Fought on Both Sides in the First Campaign of the "War Between States". LC 34-2344. 320 p. front. 20 cm. c.1933. W. A. Wilde Company.

--Capturing a King's Calabash. LC 34-31078. 188 p. incl. front. (port.) 20 cm. c.1934. Paradise of the Pacific.

--Colorado River Boy Boatmen. LC 33-2625. 143 p. 20 cm. c.1932. Printed by Frye & Smith for Stockton Press.

--The Jo-Boat Boys. Pierce, Winthrop H., illus. LC 12-31658. 2 p. l., 3-856 p. front., plates. 19 cm. (Crowell's Young People Ser.). c.1891. T. Y. Crowell & Co.

--The Mother of the King's Children: A Story of Church Blessings Through Christian Endeavor. LC 20-19338. iv, 5-433 p. front., plates. 19 cm. 1892. T. Y. Crowell & Co.

--Pilgrim's Progress. 368p. N.D. Pilgrims Press.

--The Pony Expressman. 368p. N.D. Pilgrim Press.

--The Pony Expressman. 368p. N.D. Sunday-School Library.

Cowan, S. K.

--Play: Picture-Book of Boys, Girls and Babies. Scannell, Edith, photos by. 1884. Marcus Ward & Co.

Coward, Noel

--The Noel Coward Song Book. 1953. Simon and Schuster.

Cowden-Clarke, Mary

--Uncle Peep, and I: A Child's Novel. N.D. Robert Brothers.

Cowdrey, Clara Blanche Waters Vickers Cowdrey, Mrs. (1860-)

--Baby Sister and Other Poems. LC 41-6237. 4 p. l., 2-19p., 1 l. 16cm. c.1941. Democrat News Print.

Cowell, Cyril (1888-)

--Your Book of Animal Drawing. Cowell, Cyril (1888-), illus. LC 63-22888. 64p. illus. 22cm. 1963. Faber & Faber Dist. Hollywood-by-the-Sea, Fla., Transatlantic.

Cowell, Eileen H., ed.

--Tell Me a Story. Bledsoe, Judith, illus. (gr. 3-6). 1962 (Puffin). Penguin.

Cowell, Phyllis Fair

--A Hugga Bunch Hello. Lipking, Ronald C., illus. LC 85-3592. (Illus.). 44 p. 29cm. c.1985. (ISBN 0-910313-90-3). Parker Bros.

--Your Best Wishes Can Come True. Ewers, Joe, illus. LC 83-23726. (A Tale from the Care Bears). c.1984. (ISBN 0-910313-18-0). Parker Bros.

Cowell, Vi

--Normie's Moose Hunt. (Illus.). (gr. 1-3). 1968. (ISBN 0-8382-1030-9). Hale.

Cowen, Eve, pseud., see Werner, Herman.

Cowen, Eve, pseud. (1926-)

--Catch the Sun. Werner, Herman. LC 80-82983. (Illus.). 64p. (SporTellers Ser.). (gr. 4 up). 1981. (ISBN 0-516-02261-X). Childrens.

--High Escape. Werner, Herman. LC 80-82986. (Illus.). 64p. (SporTellers Ser.). (gr. 4 up). 1981. (ISBN 0-516-02264-4). Childrens.

--Jungle Jenny. Werner, Herman. LC 78-72331. (Illus.). (Pacesetters Ser.). (gr. 4 up). 1979. (ISBN 0-516-02185-0). Childrens.

--Jungle Jenny. Werner, Herman. LC 78-72331. (Illus.). 57 p. 18cm. (Pacemaker bestellers book). c.1979. (ISBN 0-8224-5365-7). Fearon Pitman Publishers.

--Race to Win. Werner, Herman. LC 80-82988. (Illus.). 64p. (SporTellers Ser.). (gr. 4 up). 1981. (ISBN 0-516-02266-0). Childrens.

Cowes, Harriet L

--Tiny tot tales. N.D. Carlton Press.

Cowham, Hilda

--Fiddlesticks (Pub. by Society for Promoting Christian Knowledge). N.D. E. & J. B. Young & Co.

Cowles, Ginny (1924-)

--Nicholas. Hurd, Clement (1908-), illus. LC 74-11432. (Illus.). 39 p. 23cm. 1975. (ISBN 0-8164-3133-7). Seabury Press.

Cowles, Julia Darrow, Mrs., jt. auth. see Banta, Nathaniel Moore.

Cowles, Julia Darrow, Mrs. (1862-1919)

--The Children of Mother Goose. (The Children's Hour Bks). N.D. Grosset & Dunlap.

--The Children's Story Hour. Abbott, Ethelyn, illus. LC 24-22119. 128 p. col. illus. 19 cm. 1924. A. Flanagan Company.

--Favorite Tales for Story-Telling. LC 24-5200. 156 p. 19 cm. 1924. A. Flanagan Company.

--Going to School in Animal Land. Dulin, Dorothy, illus. LC 22-16146. 126 p. incl. col. front., col. illus. 19 cm. 1922. A. Flanagan Company.

--Going to School in Animal Land. Dulin, Dorothy, illus. LC 17-257681. 111 p. incl. front., illus. 19 cm. N.D. A. Flanagan Company.

--Jim Crow's Language Lessons. LC 3-17917. (Illus.). 19cm. 118p. (The Golden Hour Series for Young People). 1903. Thomas Y. Crowell.

--Myths from Many Lands. Dulin, Dorothy, illus. LC 24-22141. 124 p. col. illus. 19 cm. 1924. A. Flanagan Company.

--Our Little Athenian Cousin of Long Ago: Being the Story of Hero, a Boy of Athens. Goss, John, illus. LC 13-213583. xii, 125 p. col. front., plates. 20 cm. (little cousins of long ago series). 1913. L. C. Page & Company.

--Our Little Macedonian Cousin of Long Ago: Being the Story of Nearchus, a Boy of Macedonia and Companion of Alexander. Goss, John, illus. LC 15-152403. v. p., 1 l., 2 106 p. col. front., col. plates. 20 cm. (little cousins of long ago series.). 1915. The Page Company.

--Our Little Roman Cousin of Long Ago: Being the Story of Marcus, a Boy of Rome. Goss, John, illus. LC 13-8249. xiv, 118 p. col. front., plates. 20 cm. (Little cousins of long ago series). 1913. L. C. Page & Company.

--Our Little Saxon Cousin of Long Ago: Being the Story of Turgar, a Boy of Anglo-Saxons, in the Time of Alfred the Great. Packard, H. W., illus. LC 16-17363. 6 p. l., 112 p. col. front., plates. 20 cm. (Little cousins of long ago series). 1916. The Page Company.
--Our Little Spartan Cousin of Long Ago: Being the Story of Chartas. by julia darrow cowles ... illustrated by john goss. Goss, John, illus. LC 14-11805. viii p., 1 l., 2, 145 p. col. front., plates. 20 cm. (little cousins of long ago series). 1914. The Page Company.
--Twilight Folk Tales. Goss, John, illus. LC 24-22147. 128 p. col. illus. 19 cm. 1924. A. Flanagan Company.

Cowles, Julia Darrow, Mrs. (1862-1919), ed.
--Favorite Fairy Tales Retold: The First of a Series of Children's Classics. LC 15-6138. viii p., 1 l., 163 p. 18 cm. 1915. A. C. McClurg & Co.
--Favorite Folk Tales Retold: The Second of a Series of a Series of Children's Classics. LC 16-8361. viii p., 1 l., 169 p. 18 cm. 1916. A. C. McClurg & Co.
--Stories to Tell: Including Stories for Reproduction and Dramatization in the School Room ... LC 7-16749. 124 p. 18 cm. c.1906. A. Flanagan Company.

Cowles, Julia Darrow, Mrs. (1862-1919) & Abbott, Ethelyn
--The Child's Own Fairy Book. Dulin, Dorothy, illus. LC 24-22142. 127 p. col. illus. 1. cm. 1924. A. Flanagan Company.

Cowles, Kathleen, pseud., see Krull, Kathleen.

Cowles, Kathleen, pseud. (1952-)
--The Bugs Bunny Book. Krull, Kathleen. Baker, Darrell, illus. (Illus.). 24p. (ps-4). 1977. (ISBN 0-307-68913-1, Golden Pr). Western Pub.
--What Will I Be?. Krull, Kathleen. Connor, Eulala, illus. (A Young Reader Ser.). (gr. k-3). 1979. (ISBN 0-307-60174-9, Golden Pr). Western Pub.

Cowley, Cassia Joy (1936-)
--The Duck in the Gun. Sorel, Edward (1929-), illus. LC 68-21885. (Illus.). 40 p. 20cm. 1969. Doubleday.
--The Silent One. Greissle, Hermann, illus. LC 80-21853. (Illus.). 136 p. 22cm. c.1981. (ISBN 0-394-94761-4). (ISBN 0-394-84761-X). Knopf : Distributed by Random House.

Cowley, Malcolm, ed. see Whitman, Walt.

Cowley, R.
--Gamble for Victory. 1963. MacMillan Co.

Cowling, Tom Pierce
--Little Songs: A Book of Poems with Music for the Nursery. Govey, Lilian A, illus. N.D. George H Doran.

Cowper, E. E.
--Corporal Ida's Floating Camp. N.D. Macmillan.
--Girls on the Gold Trail. N.D. Thomas Nelson & Sons.
--Hit The Trail. N.D. Thomas Nelson & Sons.
--Peterina on the Rescue Trail. N.D. Thomas Nelson & Sons.

Cowper, Edith
--The Misadventures of I. M. P (Pub. by Society for Promoting CLhristian Knowledge). N.D. E. & J. B. Young & Co.
--Thekla Jansen (Pub. by Society for Promoting Christian Knowledge). N.D. E. & J. B. Young & Co.

Cowper, William (1731-1800)
--Diverting History of John Gilpin. Caldecott, Randolph (1846-1886), illus. LC 70-110579. (Illus.). color ils. 32p. (gr. k-3). 1970. (ISBN 0-200-72014-7). Abelard.
--The Diverting History of John Gilpin: Showing How He Went Farther Than He Intended, and Came Safe Home Again. Caldecott, Randolph (1846-1886), illus. LC 25-269051. 79 p. incl. plates. 19 cm. 1925. Frederick A. Stokes Company.
--John Gilpin's Ride. (Peter Possum Paperbacks Ser). 1967. (ISBN 0-531-05125-0). Watts.

Cox, Clyde L.
--Grandpa's Outdoor Stories for Children. Nair, Christina, illus. (Illus.). (gr. k-11). 1977. (ISBN 0-533-02718-7). Vantage.

Cox, David
--Ayu & the Perfect Moon. (Illus.). 32p. (ps-k). 1984. (ISBN 0-370-30533-7, Pub. by the Bodley Head). Merrimack Pub Cir.

Cox, David Samuel (1871-)
--Blackie Bear. LC 35-7528. v. col. illus. 21 cm. c.1935. National Art Company.

Cox, Elinor D
--Fairy Snow. 1st ed. Lyons, Dave, illus. LC 53-127063. 37p. illus. 24cm. 1953. Pageant Press.

Cox, George Williams (1827-1902), ed.
--Oliver Twist. N.D. Little, Brown & Co.
--Tales of Ancient Greece. 4th ed. 1879. A. C. McClurg & Co.

Cox, George Williams (1827-1902) & Newbolt, Henry, Sir, eds.
--Tales of the Gods and Heroes. (The Nelson Classics). N.D. Thomas Nelson & Sons.

Cox, John Harrington (1863-), adapted by see Nibelungenlied.

Cox, John Harrington (1863-), tr. see Nibelungenlied.

Cox, John Harrington (1863-), ed.
--Folk Tales of East and West. LC 12-23126. viii p., 2 l., 3-190 p., 1 l. 19 cm. (Knighthood series). 1912. Little, Brown, and Company.
--Knighthood in Germ and Flower: The Anglo-Saxon Epic, Beowulf, and the Arthurian Tale Sir Gawain and the Green Knight. Beowulf & Gawain and the Green Knight LC 10-216582. viii p., 3 l., 3-187 p. front., 3 pl. 19 cm. 1910. Little, Brown, and Company.

Cox, Kenyon (1856-1919)
--Mixed Beasts. LC 4-27337. 5 p. l., 132 p. illus. 20 cm. 1904. Fox, Duffield & Company.

Cox, Kris, jt. auth. see Cox, Mike.

Cox, Lee Sheridan (1916-)
--Andy & Willie. LC 67-24048. viii, 179 p. 22cm. 1967. Dutton.

Cox, Lillian
--Treasure Ship Sails East. N.D. MacMillan.

Cox, Mike, et al.
--Fire Drill. Wasserman, Dan, ed. Reese, Bob, illus. (Illus.). (Ten Word Bks.). (gr. k-1). 1979. (ISBN 0-89868-071-9). (ISBN 0-89868-082-4). ARO Pub.

Cox, Mike & Cox, Kris
--Flowers. Wasserman, Dan, ed. Reese, Bob, illus. (Illus.). (Ten Word Bks.). (gr. k-1). 1979. (ISBN 0-89868-076-X). (ISBN 0-89868-087-5). ARO Pub.

Cox, Miriam Stewart
--The Three Treasures: Myths of Old Japan. Fujii, Kingo, illus. LC 64-1104. 256p. illus. 24cm. c.1964. Harper.

Cox, Miriam Stewart, ed.
--The Magic and the Sword: The Greek Myths Retold. Price, Harold L (1912-), illus. LC 56-14418. 214p. illus. 24cm. 1956. Row, Peterson.

Cox, Palmer (1840-1924)
--Another Brownie Book. 144p. (The Brownie Ser.: No. 2). 1905. Century Co.
--Another Brownie Book. LC 66-24130. (Illus.). 144 p. 24cm. 1966. Dover Publications.
--Another Brownie Book. LC 67-16924. xi, 144p. illus. 24cm. 1967. McGraw.
--Another Brownie Book. LC 12-31637. 3 p. l., ix-xi, 144 p. illus. 26 x 21 cm. c.1890. The Century Co.
--Baby's Annual. Cox, Palmer (1840-1924), illus. LC 44-24047. 26cm. N.D. Lothrop Publishing Co.
--Bomba, the Merry Old King. Cox, Palmer (1840-1924), illus. (Palmer Cox Ser.). N.D. Hurst and Company.
--The Brownie and Prince Florimel: Or, Brownieland, Fairyland, and Demonland. LC 18-17665. 5 p. l., 3-246 p. front. (port.) illus. 22 cm. 1918. The Century Co.
--Brownie Clown of Brownie Town. LC 8-24452. 103 p. illus. (part col.) 18 x 24 cm. c.1908. The Century Co.
--The Brownie Primer. Cox, Palmer (1840-1924), illus. (Illus.). 110p. N.D. Century Co.
--Brownies. N.D. (ISBN 0-531-05105-6). Franklin Watts.
--Brownies Abroad. (Illus.). 144p. (The Brownies Ser.: No. 6). 1905. Century Co.
--The Brownies Abroad. LC 99-4638. 3 p. l., ix-xi 144 p. illus. 26 cm. c.1899. The Century Co.
--Brownies and the Farmer. Cox, Palmer (1840-1924), illus. (Palmer Cox Ser.). N.D. Hurst and Company.
--The Brownies Around the World. (Illus.). 144p. (The Brownies Ser.: No. 4). 1905. Century Co.
--The Brownies Around the World. LC 4-19415. 3 p. l., ix-xi, 144 p. illus. 26 cm. 1894. The Century Co.
--The Brownies at Home. (Illus.). 150p. (The Brownies Ser.: No. 3). 1905. Century Co.
--The Brownies at Home. LC 68-28403. (Illus.). xi, 144 p. 24cm. 1968. Dover Publications.
--The Brownies at Home. LC 4-19414. 3 p. l., ix-xi, 144 p. illus. 26 cm. 1893. The Century Co.
--The Brownies' Christmas Pudding and Other Brownie Stories. (Illus.). (The Young Folks Library). N.D. Caldwell.
--The Brownies' Christmas Pudding and Other Brownie Stories. (Illus.). (The Alcazar Classics). N.D. Caldwell.
--The Brownies in the Philippines, 7 vols. Cox, Palmer (1840-1924), illus. (Illus.). 144p. (The Brownies Ser.). 1905. Century Co.
--The Brownies in the Philippines. Cox, Palmer (1840-1924), illus. LC 4-27353. 3 p. l., ix-xi, 144 p. illus. 27 cm. 1904. The Century Co.
--The Brownies' Latest Adventures. LC 10-24485. 3 p. l., ix-xi, 1, 144 p. illus. 27 x 22 cm. c.1910. The Century Co.
--The Brownies Many More Nights. LC 13-213604. 5 p. l., 144 p. illus. 26 x 22 cm. 1913. The Century Co.
--The Brownies: Their Book. (Illus.). 144p. (The Brownie Ser.: No. 1). 1905. Century Co.
--The Brownies: Their Book. LC 67-16923. xi, 144p. illus. 25cm. 1967. McGraw.
--The Brownies: Their Book. LC 4-16127. xi, 144 p. illus. 25 cm. c.1887. The Century Co.
--The Brownies: Their Book. Cox, Palmer (1840-1924), illus. LC 64-25091. 144p. illus 24cm. 1964. Dover.
--The Brownies Through the Union. (Illus.). 144p. (The Brownies Ser.: No. 5). 1905. Century Co.
--The Brownies Through the Union. LC 4-19413. 3 p. l., ix-xl, 144 p. illus. 26 cm. 1895. The Century Co.
--Bugaboo Bill. Holdsworth, William Curtis, illus. LC 74-133198. (Illus.). 30 p. 29cm. (Ariel book). 1971. (ISBN 0-374-31010-6). Farrar, Straus & Giroux.
--Christmas Pudding and Other Brownie Stories. N.D. Hurst & Co.
--Cock Robin. Cox, Palmer (1840-1924), illus. (Palmer Cox Ser.). N.D. Hurst and Company.
--Grandmother Mouse's Tale. Cox, Palmer (1840-1924), illus. (Palmer Cox Ser.). N.D. Hurst and Company.
--Meddlesome Peter. Cox, Palmer (1840-1924), illus. (Palmer Cox Ser.). N.D. Hurst and Company.
--Monkey Jack. Cox, Palmer (1840-1924), illus. (Palmer Cox Ser.). N.D. Hurst and Company.
--Palmer Cox's Book of Fairy Stories and Pictures. (Illus.). (The St. Nicholas Ser.). N.D. Hurst and Company.
--Palmer Cox's Brownie Book, 11 vols. New ed. (Illus.). (Six to Sixteen Ser.: No. 11). 1905. Set. H M Caldwell Co.
--Palmer Cox's Brownies Book, 1 of 64 vols. (Young America Library: No. 32). 1900. Set. Hurst & Co.
--Palmer Cox's Fairy Book. (Illus.). 1910. Hurst & Co.
--Queer People with Paws and Claws: And Their Kweer Kapers ... LC 12-31638. 109 p. illus. 25 x 21 cm. c.1888. Hubbard Brothers.
--Queer Stories about Queer Animals: Told in Rhymes and Jingles. Cox, Palmer (1840-1924), illus. LC 5-25652. 96 p. illus. 26cm. c.1905. National Publishing Co.

Cox, Palmer (1840-1924) & Dodge, Mary Elizabeth Mapes (1831-1905)
--Childhood's Happy Day: A. B. C. book in colors. LC 54-49955. unpaged. illus. 26cm. c.1893. Star Pub. Co.

Cox, Palmer (1840-1924) & Douglas, Malcolm
--The Brownies in Fairyland. 110p. c.1925. Century Co.

Cox, Peter, jt. auth. see Hays, Wilma Pitchford.

Cox, Stephen A D
--Harry's Newspaper: Or, The Young Publisher. Smythe, Willard G., illus. LC 31-116. 215 p. incl. front., illus. 20 cm. (Adventure books for boys and girls). c.1930. A. Whitman & Co.

Cox, Stephen Angus
--The Dare Boys After Benedict Arnold. (Illus.). (The Dare Boys of 1776). N.D. A. L. Chatterton Co.
--The Dare Boys in the Red City. (Illus.). (The Dare Boys of 1776). N.D. A. L. Chatterton Co.
--The Dare Boys in Trenton. (Illus.). (The Dare Boys of 1776). N.D. A. L. Chatterton Co.
--The Dare Boys in Vincennes. Mencl, Rudolf, illus. LC 12-21318. 2 p. l., 9-193 p. incl. plates. front. 20 cm. c.1912. A. L. Chatterton Co.
--The Dare Boys in Virginia. (Illus.). (The Dare Boys of 1776). N.D. A. L. Chatterton Co.
--The Dare Boys of 1776. (Illus.). (The Dare Boys of 1776 Ser.). N.D. A. L. Chatterton Co.
--The Dare Boys on the Brandywine. (Illus.). (The Dare Boys of 1776). N.D. A. L. Chatterton Co.
--The Dare Boys on the Hudson. (Illus.). (The Dare Boys of 1776). N.D. A. L. Chatterton Co.
--The Dare Boys with General Greene. (Illus.). (The Dare Boys of 1776). N.D. A. L. Chatterton Co.
--The Dare Boys with Lafayette. (Illus.). (The Dare Boys of 1776). N.D. A. L. Chatterton Co.

Cox, Victoria, pseud., see Garretson, Victoria Diane.

Cox, Victoria, jt. auth. see Applebaum, Stan.

Cox, Victoria, pseud. (1945-) & Applebaum, Stan (1929-)
--Laughing Garbage Disposal. Garretson, Victoria Diane. Barlowe, Dorothea, illus. (Nature's Sanitation Corps Ser). 1974. (ISBN 0-307-12754-0, Golden Pr). (ISBN 0-307-62754-3). Western Pub.
--The Laughing Garbage Disposal. Garretson, Victoria Diane. Barlowe, Dorothea, illus. (Golden Ecology Ser.). (gr. 3-6). 1974. (ISBN 0-307-62754-3, Golden Pr). Western Pub.

Cox, Wallace Maynard (1924-1973) & Greenbaum, Everett
--The Tenth Life of Osiris Oaks. Fitzgerald, F. A., illus. LC 72-183195. (Illus.). 125 p. 22cm. 1972. (ISBN 0-671-65190-0). Simon and Schuster.

Cox, William N see Curtiss, Percy, pseud.

Cox, William N, Mrs.
--Richard Peters: Or, Could He Forgive Him. Curtiss, Percy, pseud. LC 21-12974. 6, 9-356 p. incl. front. plates. 17 cm. 1872. Graves & Ellis.

Cox, William Robert see Reeve, Joel, pseud.

Cox, William Robert (1901-)
--The Backyard Five. LC 73-2135. 215 p. 21cm. 1973. (ISBN 0-396-06810-3). Dodd, Mead.
--Battery Mates. LC 77-16871. p. cm. 1978. (ISBN 0-396-07525-8). Dodd, Mead.
--Big League Rookie. LC 65-17511. 147 p. 21cm. 1965. Dodd, Mead.
--Big League Sandlotters. LC 79-141029. 183 p. 21cm. 1971. (ISBN 0-396-06305-5). Dodd, Mead.
--Five Were Chosen: A Basket Ball Story. LC 56-8594. 181 p. 21cm. (gr. 7-9). 1956. (ISBN 0-396-03834-9). Dodd, Mead.
--Game, Set, and Match. LC 76-13140. 182 p. 22cm. c.1977. (ISBN 0-396-07400-6). Dodd, Mead.
--Goal Ahead. Reeve, Joel, pseud. LC 67-22811. 173 p. 22cm. 1967. (ISBN 0-87599-137-8). S. G. Phillips.
--Gridiron Duel. LC 59-6514. 21cm. 208p. 1959. Dodd, Mead & Co.
--Gunner on the Court. LC 72-2344. 176 p. 21cm. 1972. (ISBN 0-396-06613-5). Dodd, Mead.
--Home Court Is Where You Find It. LC 79-6641. 207 p. 22cm. c.1980. (ISBN 0-396-07798-6). Dodd, Mead.
--Jump Shot Joe. LC 68-27822. 182 p. 21cm. 1968. Dodd, Mead.
--Playoff. LC 72-7358. 148 p. 18cm. (Bantam pathfinder series). 1972. Bantam Books.
--Rookie in the Backcourt. LC 75-105289. 182 p. 21cm. 1970. Dodd, Mead.
--Tall on the Court. LC 64-12470. 209 p. 21cm. 1964. Dodd, Mead.
--Third and Eight to Go. LC 64-23287. 21cm. 178p. 1964. Dodd, Mead.
--Third and Goal. LC 73-162613. 182 p. 22cm. 1971. (ISBN 0-396-06381-0). Dodd, Mead.
--Trouble at Second Base. LC 66-12811. 181 p. 21cm. 1966. Dodd, Mead.
--The Unbeatable Five. LC 74-2596. 176 p. 21cm. 1974. (ISBN 0-396-06957-6). Dodd, Mead.
--The Valley Eleven. LC 67-26153. 217 p. 21cm. 1967. Dodd, Mead.
--The Wild Pitch. 22cm. 208p. 1963. Dodd, Mead.

Coxeter, P., jt. auth. see Piecewicz, A.

Coxhead, Mary
--Eyes for Chico. Hutchinson, William Miller (1916-), illus. LC 60-5026. 1960. Broadman Press.

Coy, Nancy
--Freedom Trail. LC 57-5414. (Illus.). 252 p. 21cm. 1958. Dodd, Mead.

Coyle, Charles W
--Gold!. Adventure in the Neveda Desert. Lefevre, Frank J., illus. LC 31-20070. 381 p. incl. front. plates. 20 cm. c.1931. Milton Bradley Company.

Coyle, Kathleen
--Brittany Summer. Floethe, Richard (1901-), illus. LC 40-33791. 4 p. l., 239, 1 p. col. front., col. plates. 22 x 19 cm. c.1940. Harper & Brothers.

Coyle, Lee Brown, illus.
--The Seventh Orge. N.D. Bruce Humphries.

Coyne, Anne
--A Shepherd and a King. 1939. Bruce Publishing Co.

Coze, Minerva De La see De la Coze, Minerva.

Cozzens, Samuel Woodworth (1834-1878)
--Crossing the Quicksands, 1 of 60 vols. (American Boys' Ser.: No. 14). 1900. Lee & Shepard.
--Crossing the Quicksands: Or, The Veritable Adventures of Hal and Ned upon the Pacific Slope, 1 of 3 Vols. (Illus.). (Young Trail-Hunters Ser.). 1882. Lee and Shepard.
--The Young Silver Seekers, 1 of 50 vols. (Illus.). (The Norwood Ser.: No. 6). 1900. Lee & Shepard.
--Young Silver Seekers. (Illus.). (The Live Boys' Ser.). N.D. Lee & Shepard.
--Young Silver Seekers: Or, Hal and Ned in the Marvelous Country. (Illus.). (Famous Books for Boys Ser.: No. 35). 1905. Set. H M Caldwell Co.
--The Young Silver Seekers: Or, Hal and Ned in the Marvellous Country. Completing the Young Trail Hunters' Series. LC 12-31640. 2 p. l., iii-xii, 13-343 p. front., plates. 18 cm. (His The young trail hunters' series v. 3). 1883. Lee and Shepard.
--The Young Silver-Seekers: Or, Hal and Phil in the Marvellous Country, 1 of 3 vols. (Illus.). (The Young Trail-Hunter Ser.). 1882. Lee & Shepard.
--The Young Trail Hunters. (Illus.). (Famous Books for Boys). N.D H. M. Caldwell Co.
--The Young Trail-Hunters, 1 of 3 vols. (Illus.). (The Young Trail-Hunter Ser.). 1882. Lee & Shepard.

--Young Trail Hunters, 1 of 60 vols. (Illus.). (American Boys' Ser.: No. 50). 1900. Lee & Shepard.
--Young Trail Hunters. (Illus.). (The Live Boys' Ser.). N.D. Lee & Shepard.
--The Young Trail Hunters: Or, The Wild Riders of the Plains. The Veritable Adventures of Hal Hyde and Ned Brown on Their Journey Across the Great Plains of the South-West. LC 4-29192. 235 p. front., illus., plates. 19 cm. (On cover: American boy's series v. 50). 1904. Lee and Shepard.
Crabb, Frederic N., Sr.
--The Adventures of Lulu May. 1959. Exposition Press.
Crabb, Lawrence James, Jr. (1944-) & Crabb, Lawrence James, Sr. (1912-)
--The Adventures of Captain Al Scabbard, No. 2. LC 80-27358. 128p. (Orig.). (gr. 6-8). 1981. (ISBN 0-8024-0281-X). Moody.
--The Adventures of Captain Al Scabbard Number Two, No.1. LC 80-272223. 128 p. 19cm. (gr. 6-8). c.1981. (ISBN 0-8024-0280-1). Moody Press.
Crabtree, Judith
--The Sparrow's Story: At the King's Command. (Illus.). 32p. (ps-1). 1983. (ISBN 0-19-554359-9). Oxford U Pr.
Craddock, Charles Egbert, pseud., see Murfree, Mary Noacilles.
Craddock, Charles Egbert, pseud. (1850-)
--The Champion. Murfree, Mary Noacilles. N.D. Houghton Mifflin.
--Down the Ravine: A Story for Young People. Murfree, Mary Noacilles. (Illus.). N.D. Houghton Mifflin & Co.
--The Story Of Keedon Bluffs. Murfree, Mary Noacilles. N.D. Houghton, Mifflin And Co.
--The Young Mountaineers. Murfree, MAry Norcilles. Fraser, Malcolm, illus. N.D. Houghton Mifflin.
Cradock, H C, Mrs.
--Everyday Stories. LC 20-18661. 243 p. 20 cm. c.1920. G. W. Jacobs & Company.
--Josephine is Busy. N.D. Frederick A Stokes.
--Josephine Keeps School. Appleton, Honor C., illus. LC 52-39446. 64 p. illus. 25 cm. N.D. Dodge Pub. Co. N. D.
--Josephine's Happy Family. N.D. Frederick A Stokes.
--Pamela's Teddy Bear. N.D. Thomas Nelson & Sons.
--Peggy and Joan. N.D. Barse & Co.
--Peggy's Twins. N.D. Macmillan.
--Where the Dolls Live. (Juvenile Ladder Library for Children). N.D. Macmillan.
--Where the Dolls Live. (Folk Lore and Fairy Tales). N.D. MacMillan Bks.
Craft, Kinuko Y.
--Mother Goose ABC. Craft, Kinuko Y., illus. LC 76-43213. (Illus.). 20 p. 32cm. (Cricket book). c.1977. (ISBN 0-8228-6513-0). Platt & Munk.
Craft, Ruth
--Carrie Hepple's Garden. Haas, Irene (1929-), illus. LC 78-397. (Illus.). 32 p. 24cm. 1979. (ISBN 0-689-50099-8). Atheneum.
--The King's Collection. Trimby, Elisa (1948-), illus. LC 78-8808. (Illus.). 40 p. 18cm. c.1978. (ISBN 0-385-14664-7). (ISBN 0-385-14665-5). (ISBN 0-385-14665-5). Doubleday.
--The Winter Bear. Blegvad, Erik (1923-), illus. LC 74-18178. (Illus.). 25 p. 22cm. 1975, c.1974. (ISBN 0-689-50017-3). Atheneum.
Crafton, Allen
--The Stranger Star. LC 23-8759. iv p., 1 l., 129 p. 20 cm. c.1923. G. Sully and Company.
Crafts, Annetta Stratford (1865-)
--Jupiter Jingles: Or, A Trip to Mysterland. LC 15-16801. 41 p. incl. double col. front., illus. 22 cm. c.1897. Laird & Lee.
--The Tale of a Tail: And Other Classic Rhymes for Children. LC 4-24474. (Illus.). 22 cm. 38p. 1904. Laird & Lee's Publications.
Crafts, F. W. & Main, P. H.
--Little Pilgrim Songs. N.D. E. Steiger & Co.
Crafts, F. W. & Merrill, B. J.
--Songs for Little Folks in the Home and School. N.D. E. Steiger & Co.
Crafts, Wilbur Fisk
--Talks and Stories About Prayer. 120p. N.D. American Tract Society.
Cragi, D. Cunningham
--Stories from Aunt Judy. (Queen's Treasures Ser.). N.D. Harcourt Brace & Co.
Cragin, Belle S.
--Peter and Tom: Or, Two Unlikely Heroes. (Illus.). (St. Nicholas Ser.). 1905. Set. A L Burt Co.
Cragin, Ethel Raymond
--The Hidden Treasure. Eulalie, pseud. (1896-), illus. Banks, Eulalie M.. LC 33-19483. 3 p. l., 9-41 p. illus. (part col. c.1932. Suttonhouse.
Cragin, Laura Ella
--Kindergarten Bible Stories. N.D. Fleming H. Revell Co.
--Kindergarten Stories for Sunday School and Home. N.D. George H Doran.
--Kindergarten Stories for the Sunday School and Home. (Illus.). 1903. Winona Publishing Co.
--Old Testament Stories for Little Children. N.D. Fleming H. Revell Co.
Cragin, Mary A. see Allison, Joy, pseud.
Craig, Allan
--Counting things and Magic Rings. N.D. (ISBN 0-8283-1585-X). Branden Press.
Craig, Anne Abbot Throop, Mrs. (1869-)
--The Dramatic Festival: A Consideration of the Lyrical Method As a Factor in Preparatory Education. LC 12-20806. xvii p., 1 l., 363 p. 19 cm. 1912. G. P. Putnam's Sons.
Craig, Diana, adapted by.
--Elijah: Messenger of God. Baxter, Leon, illus. LC 84-51683. (Illus.). 24p. (Bible Stories Ser.). (gr. 3 up). 1984. (ISBN 0-382-06943-9). (ISBN 0-382-06943-9). Silver.
--Jacob & Esau. Baxter, Leon, illus. LC 84-51684. (Illus.). 24p. (Bible Stories Ser.). (ps up). 1984. (ISBN 0-382-06944-7). (ISBN 0-382-06795-9). Silver.
--Moses & the Flight from Egypt. Baxter, Leon, illus. LC 84-50448. (Illus.). 24p. (Bible Stories Ser.). (gr. 3 up). 1984. (ISBN 0-382-06945-5). (ISBN 0-382-06797-5). Silver.
--The Young Moses. Baxter, Leon, illus. LC 84-50449. (Illus.). 24p. (Bible Stories Ser.). (gr. 3 up). 1984. (ISBN 0-382-06797-5). (ISBN 0-382-06946-3). Silver.
Craig, E. S. E
--The Wonderful Birthday. Evans, Gil, illus. LC 75-90287. (Illus.). 82 p. 24cm. 1969. Random House.
Craig, George
--Mr. Mizzen's Rocket. (Illus.). (ps-5). 1968. (ISBN 0-571-08669-1). Faber & Faber.
Craig, Hazel Thompson (1904-)
--Becky Lou in Grandmother's Days: Story, Scenes and Costumes. Craig, Sam (1904-), photos by. LC 61-180921. 61p. 29cm. (gr. 3-4). c.1961. Denison.
--Molly in Story Book Forest. Craig, Hazel Thompson (1904-), photos by. LC 64-17744. (Illus.). 29cm. 40p. 1964. T. S. Dennison.
Craig, Helen
--The Knight, the Princess & the Dragon. Craig, Helen, illus. LC 84-19419. (Illus.). 32p. (ps-2). 1985. (ISBN 0-394-97212-0). (ISBN 0-394-87212-6). Knopf.
--Mouse House Days of the Week. Craig, Helen, illus. LC 82-60211. (Illus.). 30p. (ps-1). 1983. (ISBN 0-394-85286-9). Random.
--Susie and Alfred in the Night of the Paper Bag Monsters. Craig, Helen, illus. LC 84-25045. (Illus.). 28 p. 24cm. 1st U.S. edition. c.1985. (ISBN 0-394-87427-7). (ISBN 0-394-97427-1). Knopf.
Craig, James, pseud., see Snell, Roy Judson.
Craig, John Ernest (1921-)
--The Last Canoe: A Novel. LC 79-11224. p. cm. 1979. (ISBN 0-698-20490-5). Coward, McCann & Geoghegan.
--The Long Return. Doremus, Robert (1913-), illus. LC 59-14305. (Illus.). 22cm. 255p. 1959. Bobbs-Merrill Co.
--No Word for Good-Bye. Aalto, Harri, illus. LC 77-166593. 190 p. 21cm. 1971, c.1969. (ISBN 0-698-20102-7). Coward, McCann & Geoghegan.
--Wagons West. Wyatt, Stanley, illus. LC 56-7420. 128p. illus. 21cm. 1956, c.1955. Dodd, Mead.
--Who Wants to Be Alone?. Orig. Title: Zach. (gr. 7-12). 1975. (ISBN 0-590-10168-4, Schol Trade Pap). Schol Bk Serv.
--Wormburners. Daniel, Alan (1939-), illus. (gr. 4-6). 1976. (ISBN 0-590-10282-6, Schol Pap). Schol Bk Serv.
--Zach. LC 72-76701. 254 p. 22cm. 1972. (ISBN 0-698-20187-6). (ISBN 0-698-30458-6). Coward, McCann & Geoghegan.
Craig-Knox, Isa
--Esther West. New ed. 1877. Cassell, Petter, & Galpin.
--Esther West, 1 of 4 Vols. (Illus.). (The Sisters' Library: No. 4). N.D. Cassell, Petter, Galpin.
--Peggy Ogilvie's Inheritance, 1 of 4 vols. (The School Girl's Library). N.D. Cassell, Petter, Galpin.
Craig, Lillian K
--The Curious Car. LC 31-1279. 94 p. incl. col. front., illus. (part col.) 20 cm. c.1930. The Bruce Publishing Co.
Craig, M. Jean
--The Dragon in the Clock Box. Oechsli, Kelly (1918-), illus. LC 62-17347. (Illus.). 48 p. 24cm. 1962. W. W. Norton. **Award: (ALA).**
--Little Monsters. (gr. k-3). 1976. (ISBN 0-590-10298-2, Schol Pap). Scholastic Inc.
--The Long and Dangerous Journey. Ohlsson, Ib (1935-), illus. LC 65-13339. 1 v.(unpaged) illus. (part col.) 27 cm. 1965. Norton.
--The Man Whose Name Was Not Thomas. Stanley, Diane (1943-), illus. LC 80-28417. p. cm. c.1981. (ISBN 0-385-15064-4). Doubleday.
--The New Boy on the Sidewalk. Greenwald, Sheila, pseud. (1934-), illus. Green, Sheila Ellen. LC 67-24280. 1 v. (unpaged) illus. 24 cm. c.1967. Norton.
--Not Very Much of a House. Almquist, Don (1929-), illus. LC 67-15455. (Illus.). 1 v. (unpaged). 26cm. 1967. W. W. Norton.
--Pomando. Arno, Enrico (1913-1981), illus. LC 69-17135. (Illus.). 90 p. 24cm. 1969. Norton.
--Spring is Like the Morning. Almquist, Don (1929-), illus. LC 65-13303. (Illus.). 24cm. 61p. N.D. G. P. Putnam Sons.
--Summer Is a Very Busy Day. Almquist, Don (1929-), illus. LC 67-14803. 64p. col. illus. 24cm. 1967. Putnam.
--What Did You Dream?. Gill, Margery Jean (1925-), illus. LC 64-12117. (Illus.). 42 p. 27cm. 1964. Abelard-Schuman.
--Where Do I Belong?. Cruz, Raymond (1933-), illus. LC 75-142530. (Illus.). 32 p. 1971. Four Winds Press.
Craig, M. Jean, retold by.
--The Adventures of Tom Thumb. Shekerjian, Haig & Shekerjian, Regina Tor, illus. (Illus.). (gr. k-3). 1972. (ISBN 0-590-00283-X). Scholastic Inc.
--Puss in Boots. Jones, Robert A., illus. 48p. (gr. k-3). 1970. (ISBN 0-590-00395-X). (ISBN 0-590-04400-1). Scholastic Inc.
--The Sand, the Sea, and Me. Newell, Audrey Townsend Walker, illus. LC 70-186175. (Illus.). 32 p. 1972. (ISBN 0-8027-6105-4). (ISBN 0-8027-6106-2). Walker.
--The Three Wishes. (gr. k-3). 1971. (ISBN 0-590-01621-0). Scholastic Inc.
Craig, M. Jean, adapted by see Grimm, Jakob Ludwig Karl (1785-1863) & Cooney, Barbara.
Craig, M. Jean, tr. see Brunhoff, Laurent De.
Craig, Margaret Maze (1911-1964)
--It Could Happen to Anyone. LC 61-14534. 215 p. 21cm. 1961. (ISBN 0-690-45472-4). Crowell.
--Julie. LC 52-8653. 247 p. 21 cm. 1952. Crowell.
--Marsha. 248p. 1955. Thomas Y. Crowell.
--Now That I'm Sixteen. LC 59-11392. 185 p. 21cm. 1959. Crowell.
--Now that I'm Sixteen. 1959. E M Hale.
--Three Who Met. LC 58-8705. (gr. 7 up). 1958. (ISBN 0-690-82393-2). T Y Crowell.
--Trish. N.D. Berkley.
--Trish. LC 51-1164. 242 p. 21 cm. 1951. Crowell.
Craig, Mary Francis see Shura, Mary Francis, pseud.
Craig, Mary Francis see Shura, Mary Francis.
Craig, Millie
--Mr. Peanut & Mr. Jellybean. Deel, Angi, illus. 1983. (ISBN 0-533-05480-X). Vantage.
Craig, Patricia, jt. auth. see Cadogan, Mary Rose.
Craig, Paula M
--Mr. Wiggle's Book. Foster, Celeste K., illus. LC 73-155574. (Illus.). 32 p. 1972. (ISBN 0-513-01177-3). Denison.
Craig, Stephanie, tr. see Reboul, Antoine.
Craige, J. K., tr. see Andersen, Hans Christian.
Craige, W. A., tr. see Andersen, Hans Christian.
Craigie, David, pseud., see Craigie, Dorothy M..
Craigie, Dorothy M. see Craigie, David, pseud.
Craigie, Dorothy M. (1908-)
--Dark Atlantis. Craigie, David, pseud. Craigie, Dorothy M. (1908-), illus. LC 53-12227. (Illus.). 220 p. 19cm. 1953. Macmillan.
--The Saucy Cockle. Craigie, Dorothy M. (1908-), illus. 1957. Abelard-Schuman.
--The Voyage of the Luna I. Craigie, David, pseud. Craigie, Dorothy M. (1908-), illus. Craigie, David, pseud. LC 49-11389. 252 p. illus. 21 cm. 1949. Messner.
Craigie, Hamilton
--The Longhorn Trail. (Western Stories for Boys). 1931. Grosset & Dunlap.
Craigie, Jessie K., tr. see Andersen, Hans Christian.
Craigie, Mary E
--Once Upon a Time: Stories for Children, Taken from the Ancient Gods and Heroes. LC 18-17307. 127 p. front., plates. 18 cm. 1876. G. P. Putnam's Sons.
--Once Upon a Time: Stories of the Ancient Gods and Heroes. (Illus.). N.D. G P Putnam's Sons.
Craigie, William Alexander, tr. see Andersen, Hans Christian.
Craigin, Louisa T.
--The Cedars, 1 of 18 vols. (Library of Romance Ser). N.D. Lothrop Pub Co.
--The Cedars: Lore of Child Life. Walker, C. Howard, illus. N.D. Lockwood, Brooks, and Co.
--Ellis Gray Long Ago: More of Child Life. Hale, Susan, designed by. (Illus.). N.D. Lockwood, Brooks, and Co.
--Long Ago, 1 of 18 vols. (Library of Romance Ser). N.D. Lothrop Pub Co.
--Sunshine, 1 of 18 vols. (Library of Romance Ser). N.D. Lothrop Pub. Co.
Craik, Dinah Maria Mulock see Mulock, Dinah Maria, pseud.
Craik, Dinah Maria Mulock (1826-1887), tr. see Witt, Henriette Elizabeth Guizot.
Craik, Dinah Maria Mulock, Mrs., jt. auth. see Kingsley, Charles.
Craik, Dinah Maria Mulock, Mrs. (1826-1887), selected by see Paton, Noel, Sir.
Craik, Dinah Maria Mulock, Mrs. (1826-1887)
--Adventures of a Brownie. (Famous Bks for Young Americans). N.D. A. L. Burt Co.
--Adventures of a Brownie. (Illus.). (The Little Women Series). N.D. A. L. Burt's Pubs.
--Adventures of a Brownie. (Illus.). (The Wellesley Series for Girls). N.D. A. L. Burt's Pubs.
--Adventures of a Brownie. (Illus.). (Pleasant Hour Ser.). N.D. Barse and Hopkins.
--Adventures of a Brownie. (Illus.). (The Rainy Day Ser.). N.D. Barse & Hopkins.
--Adventures of a Brownie. N.D. Grosset & Dunlap.
--Adventures of a Brownie. LC 98-334. 4 p. l., 7-161 p. front. (port.) illus. 16 cm. 1898. H. Altemus.
--The Adventures of a Brownie, 25 vols. (Illus.). (The Editha Ser.: No. 13). 1905. Set. H M Caldwell Co.
--Adventures of a Brownie. (Illus.). (The Young Folks Lib.). N.D. H. M. Caldwell Co.
--Adventures of a Brownie, 1 of 156 vols. (Illus.). (The Empyreal Lib.). N.D. H. M. Caldwell Co.
--The Adventures of a Brownie. (Illus.). 1882. Harper.
--The Adventures of a Brownie. (Harper's Young People Ser.). N.D. Harper & Brothers.
--Adventures of a Brownie. (Illus.). (Young People's Lib.). 1898. Henry Altemus Co.
--The Adventures of a Brownie. 1905. Henry Altemus Co.
--Adventures of a Brownie. (Illus.). (Vademecum Ser). N.D. Henry Altemus Company's Pub.
--Adventures of a Brownie. (Illus.). (Boys' and Girls' Classics). N.D. Henry Altemus Co.
--Adventures of a Brownie. Handy Volume, Large Type ed. (Illus.). (Beauxarts Ser.). N.D. Henry Altemus.
--Adventures of a Brownie. (Illus.). (Young People's Library). N.D. Henry Altemus.
--The Adventures of a Brownie. 1900. Hurst & Co.
--The Adventures of a Brownie. (Illus.). (The Cambridge Classics). N.D. Hurst and Company.
--The Adventures of a Brownie. (Illus.). (The Laurelhurst Ser.). N.D. Hurst and Company.
--The Adventures of a Brownie. (Illus.). (Alligator Classics). N.D. Hurst & Co.
--Adventures of a Brownie. (The Children's Classics). N.D. J.B. Lippincott.
--Adventures of a Brownie. N.D. MacMillan.
--The Adventures of a Brownie. LC 23-10255. 2 p. l., 7-128 p. front. (port.) illus. (part col.) 24 cm. c.1923. New York, Rand McNally & Company.
--The Adventures of a Brownie. (Illus.). 1910. Putnam.
--Adventures of a Brownie, 1 of 24 vols. (Illus.). (Children's Favorite Classics). 1900. T. Y. Crowell & Co.
--The Adventures of a Brownie. (Children's Home Library). 1915. T Y Crowell.
--The Adventures of a Brownie. (Children's Favorite Classics). N.D. Thomas Y. Crowell & Co.
--The Adventures of a Brownie. (Handy Volume Classics). N.D. Thomas Y. Crowell & Co.
--The Adventures of a Brownie. Barry, Etheldred Breeze (1870-), illus. (Cosy Corner Ser.). N.D. L. C. Page & Co.
--The Adventures of a Brownie. Brundage, Frances, illus. 2 p. l., 11-93 p. col. front., illus. 20 cm. (John Newbery series). c.1927. The Saalfield Publishing Company.
--The Adventures of a Brownie. DuBois, Jacqueline, illus. 55 p. front., illus. 21 cm. (Easy-to-read books). c.1934. The Saalfield Publishing Company.
--The Adventures of a Brownie. Hofsten, Hugo Von, illus. LC 7-24192. 48 p. col. front., 5 col. pl. 21 cm. (rainy day series). c.1907. Brewer, Barse & Co.
--The Adventures of a Brownie. McCracken, James, et al., illus. (gr. 2-4). N.D. A. Whitman & Co.
--The Adventures of a Brownie. Prittie, Edwin John, illus. x, 102 p. col. front., illus., col. pl. 21 cm. (The child's garden of charming books). c.1929. The John C. Winston Company.
--The Adventures of a Brownie. Seaman, Mary Lott, illus. (Little Library). N.D. Macmillan.
--The Adventures of a Brownie and The Little Lame Prince. LC 75-32175. (Illus.). viii, 114, 169 p. 19cm. (Classics of Children's Literature, 1621-1932). 1977. (ISBN 0-8240-2287-4). Garland Pub.
--The Adventures of a Brownie as told to my Child. LC 4-17535. (Illus.). 18cm. 139p. 1903. Harper & Brothers.
--The Adventures of a Brownie: As Told to My Child. LC 8-24462. 128 p. incl. illus., plates col. front. 24 cm. c.1908. McLoughlin Brothers.
--The Adventures of a Brownie As Told to My Child. LC 44-48093. 167 p. col. front., illus., plates. 17 cm. c.1893. T. Y. Crowell & Co.

--At Uncle Fred's Ranch. LC 29-12533. 4 p. l., 120 p. col. front., col. plates. 20 cm. (Her Points West series). c.1929. A. L. Burt Company.
--Canny: The Courageous. LC 31-32639. 240 p. 20 cm. c.1931. The World Syndicate Publishing Co.
--The Children of the Rising Sun. Lederer, Charlotte Bacskay, Mrs. (1872-), illus. LC 31-34192. v. col. fronts., illus. 20 cm. c.1931. The World Syndicate Publishing Company.
--Conquistador. Pitz, Henry Clarence (1895-1976), illus. LC 31-29199. ix p., 3 l., 3-288 p. plates. 23 cm. c.1931. Duffield and Green.
--David: The Incorrigible. LC 28-253458. 5 p. l., 3-246 p. 20 cm. c.1928. Rae D. Henkle Co., Inc.
--Evermay Ranch. Ullberg, Marjorie Lee, illus. LC 40-31800. 269 p. illus. 21 cm. c.1940. David McKay Company.
--The Grist Mill Ghost. LC 31-326381. 1 p. l., 9-224 p. 20 cm. c.1931. The World Syndicate Publishing Co.
--Holidays on the Ranch. LC 29-12534. 4 p. l., 120 p. col. front., col. plates. 20 cm. (Her Points West series). c.1929. A. L. Burt Company.
--Ki-Ki, Circus Trouper. Wiese, Kurt (1887-1974), illus. LC 37-21031. 63. 1 p. incl. col. front., col. illus. 24 cm. 1937. A. Whitman & Co.
--Libby Lou. (Points West Ser.). 1929. A L Burt Co.
--Little Moon. LC 29-12537. 4 p. l., 120 p. col. front., enl. plates. 20 cm. (Her Points West series). c.1929. A. L. Burt Company.
--The Mystery of Black Eagle Island. Dunkelberger, Ralph, illus. LC 27-16916. 309 p. front., plates. 20 cm. 1927. The Penn Publishing Company.
--The Mystery of Seal Islands. Bardwell, Harrison, pseud. LC 31-172776. 1 p. l., 9-223 p. 20 cm. c.1931. The World Syndicate Publishing Company.
--The Mystery of Seven Gables. Dunkelberger, Ralph, illus. LC 28-173806. 312 p. front., plates. 20 cm. 1928. The Penn Publishing Company.
--The Mystery Ship. Bardwell, Harrison, pseud. LC 31-17021. 3 p. l., 9-214 p. 20 cm. c.1931. The World Syndicate Publishing Co.
--Peter. Daru, Juliska, pseud. Lederer, Charlotte Bacskay, Mrs. (1872-), illus. LC 31-20526. 236 p. incl. front., plates. 21 cm. c.1931. E. P. Dutton & Co., Inc.
--Stephen the Valiant. Daru, Juliska, pseud. Lederer, Charlotte Bacskay, Mrs. (1872-), illus. LC 30-13550. 5 p. l., 3-264 p. col. front., illus. 21 cm. c.1930. E. P. Dutton & Co., Inc.
--Tenderfoot Ranchers. LC 29-12536. 4 p. l., 120 p. col. front., col. plates. 20 cm. (Her Points West series). c.1929. A L Burt Company.
--The Victors. Wier, Don, illus. LC 33-318808. xi, 254 p. plates. 23 cm. c.1933. Duffield and Green.
--With the Revolutionists in Bolivia. LC 31-16451. 2 p. l., 7-201 p. 20 cm. c.1931. The World Syndicate Publishing Company.
--Woolly West. LC 29-12535. 4 p. l., 120 p. col. front. col. plates. 20 cm. (Her Points West series). c.1929. A. L. Burt Company.

Craine, Edith Janice (1881-) & Burton, Alberta N.
--Happy Days Out West. Gregory, Dorothy Lake, illus. 129p. (gr. 2-3). N.D. Rand McNally & Co.
--Happy Days Out West for Littlebits. Gregory, Dorothy Lake, illus. LC 27-18318. 129 p. illus. col plates. 20 cm. c.1927. Rand, McNally & Company.
--Littlebits. Gregory, Dorothy Lake, illus. LC 26-15428. 133 p. illus., col. plates. 21 cm. c.1926. Rand, McNally & Company.

Craine, Edith Janice (1881-) & Moseley, L H
--The Fairway Bell. Rodgers, Richard H. (1876-1953), illus. LC 30-29984. 6 p. l., 3-267, 1 p. col. front., illus., col. plates. 21 cm. 1930. Duffield and Company.

Crake, Augustine David (1836-1890)
--Edwy the Fair: The First Chronicle of Aescendune. Holberg, Richard A. (1889-1942), illus. LC 28-29237. xi, 303 p. col. front., col. plates. 20 cm. 1928. Longmans, Green and Co.
--The Heir of Treherne. N.D. Thomas Whittaker.
--Stories from Old English History. N.D. Thomas Whittaker.
--The Victor's Laurel. N.D. Thomas Whittaker.

Cram, Emma C
--The David Stories. LC 17-12959. 6 p. l., 3-54 p. col. plates. 20 cm. c.1915. The Pilgrim Press.
--Uncle David's Little Nephew. LC 17-13190. 20cm. 66p. 1916. Pilgrim Press.

Cram, William Everett
--Little Beasts of Field & Wood. 1912. Small,Maynard & Co.

Cramer, Jesse Grant (1890-), tr. see Grundtvig, Svend Hersleb.

Cramer, Marie (1887-)
--The Diamond Princess. Cramer, Marie (1887-), illus. Hart, John G., tr. LC 31-23357. 56 p. col. front., illus., col. plates. 20 1/2 x 26 cm. c.1931. F. Warne & Co., Inc.

Cramer, R.
--Favorite French Fairy Tales. Couglass, Barbara, ed. N.D. Dodd Mead & Co.

Crameri, Talbot
--Snow at Tataru. Tuckwell, Jennifer, illus. LC 68-16551. (Illus.). 102 p. 19cm. (Trend books). 1969. Cheschire.

Crammond, Joan
--Zoo. (Illus.). index. 74p. (gr. 3-8). 1973. David & Charles.

Cramp, Walter Samuel (1867-), tr. see Lorenzini, Carlo.

Cramp, Walter Samuel (1826-1890), ed.
--Beppo. N.D. Small Maynard & Co.
--Collodi's Pinocchio: The Adventures of a Marionette. (Illus.). 212p. N.D. Dana Estes and Company.

Crampton, Bernie & Crampton, Cynthia
--Rocky and Sandy: The Story of Two Tortoises on the California Desert. LC 67-22488. (Illus.). l v. 61p. 1967. Ritchie Press.

Crampton, Charles Ward (1877-), ed. see Wollaston, Mary A.

Crampton, Cynthia, jt. auth. see Crampton, Bernie.

Crampton, G. E. E.
--Silver Sands: Pennie's Romance, 1 of 4 vols. (Sister Eleanor Ser.). 1872. D. Lothrop & Co.

Crampton, G. E. E., jt. auth. see Farman, Ella.

Crampton, Gertrude (1909-)
--The Funny Fixes of the Floogle Family. Maas, Dorothy, illus. LC 52-10702. (Illus.). 160 p. 23cm. (gr. 1-5). 1952. Bobbs-Merrill.
--Further Pottleby Adventures. Peck, Anne Merriman (1884-), illus. LC 51-12423. 93 p. illus. 20 cm. 1951. Aladdin Books.
--The Golden Christmas Book. Malvern, Corinne (1905-1956), illus. 1947. Simon & Schuster.
--The Golden Funny Book. Miller, John Parr (1913-), illus. LC 50-14110. 76 p. col. illus. 29 cm. (Big golden book, 469). 1950. Simon and Schuster.
--A Grab Bag of Fun. Jupo, Frank J. (1904-), illus. LC 53-1825. (Illus.). 128 p. 22cm. 1953. Aladdin Books.
--The Large & Growly Bear. Miller, John Parr (1913-), illus. LC 61-11965. (Illus.). 24p. (ps-4). 1961. (ISBN 0-307-60510-8, Golden Pr). Western Pub.
--Little Golden Funny Book. Miller, John Parr (1913-), illus. LC 50-7513. 42p. (Little Golden Library). 1950. Simon and Shuster.
--More Pottleby Adventures. 1st ed. Peck, Anne Merriman (1884-), illus. LC 50-7140. 82 p. illus. 20 cm. 1950. Aladdin Books.
--Noises and Mr. Flibberty-Jib. Wilkin, Eloise Burns (1904-), illus. LC 48-2210. 42 p. illus. (part col.) 21 cm. (The Little Golden Library: No. 29). 1947. Simon and Schuster.
--The Pottlebys. Peck, Anne Merriman (1884-), illus. LC 49-866642. 92 p. illus. 20 cm. 1949. Aladdin Books.
--Scuffy the Tugboat. Gergely, Tibor (1900-1978), illus. (Little Golden Book: 30). 1947. Simon and Schuster.
--Scuffy the Tugboat. Gergely, Tibor (1900-1978), illus. (Illus.). 24p. (ps-2). 1973. (ISBN 0-307-10490-7, Golden Pr). (ISBN 0-307-60490-X). (ISBN 0-307-60633-3, Golden Pr). Western Pub.
--Scuffy the Tugboat and His Adventures Down the River. Gergely, Tibor (1900-1978), illus. LC 55-342284. unpaged. illus. 21cm. (Little golden book, 244). 1955. Simon and Schuster.
--Tootle. Gergely, Tibor (1900-1978), illus. LC 48-3538. 42 p. illus. (part col.) 21 cm. (The Little Golden Library: No. 21). 1945. Simon and Schuster.
--Tootle, The Story of a Locomotive. Reed, Mary, ed. Gergely, Tibor (1900-1978), illus. LC 48-3538. (Little Golden Library). 1945. Simon & Schuster.

Crampton, Gertrude (1909-) & Brown, Margaret Wise (1910-1952)
--Train Stories. Gergely, Tibor (1900-1978) & Seiden, Art, illus. (Giant Little Golden Book). 1958. Golden Press.

Crampton, Patricia, ed. see Masefield, John Edward.

Crampton, Patricia, ed. see Von Walther, Gertrud.

Crampton, Patricia, tr. see Bomans, Godfried Jan Arnold.

Crampton, Patricia, tr. see Broger, Achim.

Crampton, Patricia, tr. see Damjan, Mischa.

Crampton, Patricia, tr. see Hartman, Evert.

Crampton, Patricia, tr. see Havrevold, Finn.

Crampton, Patricia, tr. see Hellberg, Hans-Eric.

Crampton, Patricia, tr. see Klink, Johanna Louise.

Crampton, Patricia, tr. see Koerner, Wolfgang.

Crampton, Patricia, tr. see Linde, Gunnel.

Crampton, Patricia, tr. see Sommerfelt, Aimee.

Crampton, Patricia, tr. see Swahn, Sven Christer.

Crampton, Patricia, tr. see Tenfjord, Johanne Marie Giaever.

Crampton, Patricia, tr. see Walther, Gertrud Von.

Crampton, Patricia, tr. see Wurthle, Fritz.

Cranch, Christopher Pearse (1813-1892)
--Kobboltozo, 1 of 3 vols. (Sequel to Last of the Huggermuggers). (Illus.). (Little Jacket Stories). 1882. Lee & Shepard.
--Kobboltozo: A Sequel to The Last of the Huggermuggers ... LC 19-1690. 3 p. l., 95 p. incl. front., illus., plates. 21 cm. (With his The story of the Huggermuggers. Boston, 1860). 1860. Mayhew & Baker.
--Kobboltozo: A Sequel to the Last of the Huggermuggers. With Illustrations. LC 2-15743. 1 p. l., vii-viii, 95 p. incl. illus., plates. front. 22 cm. 1857. Phillips, Sampson and Company.
--Last of the Huggermuggers. (Little Jacket Stories). N.D. Colby and Rich.
--Last of the Huggermuggers, 1 of 3 Vols. (Illus.). (Little Jacket Ser.). 1882. Lee & Shepard.
--The Last of the Huggermuggers: A Giant Story. (Illus.). (St. Nicholas Ser.). 1905. Set. A L Burt Co.
--Last of the Huggermuggers: A Giant Story. (Illus.). (The Ruby Series for Boys). 1915. A L Burt & Co.
--The Last of the Huggermuggers: A Giant Story ... LC 19-169137. 3 p. l., 70 p. front., illus., plates. 21 cm. (Added t.-p.: Giant hunting; or, Little Jacket's adventures). 1860. Mayhew & Baker.
--The Last of the Huggermuggers: A Giant Story. (The Rugby Series for Boys and Girls). N.D. A. L. Burt Company.

Crandall, Ruth
--Buzzy Bee Story Book. Sparks, Judith, ed. (Illus.). 24p. (A Happy Day Bk.). (gr. 1-3). 1980. (ISBN 0-87239-409-3). Standard Pub.

Crandall, Weller Robin
--Old King Grasshopper, the Mighty Rules of Grasshopper Land. Pratt, Alice, illus. LC 61-11965. (Illus.). 28 p. 36 x 29cm. (A Master-Craft Drawing and Story Book). 1939. B. Crandall.

Crandell, Helen Hopkins
--Little White Cotton. N.D. Frederick A. Stokes.
--Little White Cotton. N.D. J. B. Lippincott.

Crandell, Myra Clarke
--Enoch and the Brave un. Waterhouse, Charles (1924-), illus. LC 65-21598. 214 p. illus. 21 cm. 1965. McKay.
--Molly and the Regicides. Frame, Paul (1913-), illus. LC 68-16143. (Illus.). 255 p. 22cm. 1968. Simon and Schuster.

Crane, Alan (1901-)
--Gloucester Joe. LC 43-16590. 26cm. 30p. 1943. Thomas Nelson & Sons.
--Nick and Nan in Yucatan. LC 45-7023. 32 p. illus. (part col.) 26 cm. 1945. T. Nelson & Sons.
--Pepita Bonita. LC 42-203360. 39 p. col. illus. 23 x 19 cm. 1942. T. Nelson and Sons.

Crane, Arthur T
--The "From A. to Z Company". LC 11-31640. 64 p. incl. plates. 18 cm. c.1911. David C. Cook Publishing Co.

Crane, Barbara Joyce (1934-)
--The Baby Jay. (Illus.). (Crane Reading System-Eng. Ser.). (gr. k-2). 1977. (ISBN 0-686-74262-1). Crane Pub Co.

Crane, Caroline (1930-)
--Don't Look at Me That Way. LC 71-109228. 181 p. 22cm. 1970. Random House.
--A Girl Like Tracy. LC 66-15081. 186 p. 21cm. 1966. D. McKay Co.
--Lights Down the River. LC 64-11702. 216 p. 22 cm. 1964. Doubleday.
--Pink Sky at Night. LC 63-12882. 168 p. 22 cm. 1963. Doubleday.
--Stranger on the Road. LC 76-155599. 180 p. 22cm. 1971. (ISBN 0-394-82148-3). (ISBN 0-394-92148-8). Random House.
--Wedding Song. Werth, Kurt (1896-), illus. LC 67-211831. 183 p. 21cm. 1967. McKay.

Crane, Donn
--The Adventures of Five Little Scamps: Told. Crane, Donn, illus. LC 40-34106. 48 p. illus. (part col.) 20 x 21 cm. N.D. A. Whitman & Co.
--Flippy and Skippy: The Two Flying Squirrels. LC 40-14812. 48 p. illus. (part col.) 22 x 22 cm. c.1940. The John C. Winston Company.

Crane, Florence
--Gypsy Secret. LC 57-6468. 245 p. 21cm. 1957. Random House.

Crane, Laura Dent
--The Automobile Girls Along the Hudson: Or, Fighting Fire in Sleepy Hollow. (The Automobile Girls Series). N.D. Henry Altemus Co.
--The Automobile Girls at Chicago: Or, Winning Out Against Heavy Odds. LC 12-24628. 254 p. incl. front., plates. 20 cm. (Her The automobile girls series). c.1912. Henry Altemus Company.
--The Automobile Girls at Newport: Or, Watching the Summer Parade. (The Automobile Girls Series). N.D. Henry Altemus Co.
--The Automobile Girls at Palm Beach: Proving their Mettle Under Southern Skies. (The Automobile Girls Ser.). N.D. Henry Altemus Co.
--The Automobile Girls in the Berkshires: Or, The Ghost of Lost Man's Trail. (The Automobile Girls Series). N.D. Henry Altemus Co.

Crane, Louise, ed. see Holladay, Virginia.

Crane, Louise, Mrs.
--The Magic Spear, and Other Stories of China's Famous Heroes. N.D. Gale Reprint.
--The Magic Spear, and Other Stories of China's Famous Heroes. Yutang, Lin & Yee, Ching C., frwd. by. LC 38-870119. vi p., 1 l., xi-xx, 21-244, ix-x p. incl. illus., plates. 24 cm. c.1938. Random House.

Crane, Lucy, tr.
--Grimm's Tales. (Children's Favorite Classics). 1900. Thomas Y. Crowell Company.

Crane, Lucy, tr. see Grimm, Jakob Ludwig Karl (1785-1863) & Grimm, Wilhelm Karl.

Crane, Lucy, et al. (1842-1882), trs. see Grimm, Jakob Ludwig Karl (1785-1863) & Grimm, Wilhelm Karl.

Crane, Nathalia Clara Ruth (1913-)
--The Janitor's Boy. N.D. Thomas Seltzer : Dist. by Loring & Mussey.
--Janitor's Boy & Other Poems. LC 76-9892. (Children's Literature Reprint Ser). (gr. 3-5). 1976. (ISBN 0-8486-0003-7). Core Collection.

Crane, Nathalia Clara Ruth (1913-) & Feeney, Leonard (1897-1978)
--The Ark and the Alphabet: An Animal Collection. LC 39-31692. xii p., 1 l., 44 p. 19 cm. 1939. The Macmillan Company.

Crane, Stephen Townley (1871-1900)
--The Black Riders. N.D. Sherman, French & Co.
--Bride Comes To Yellow Sky. Johnson, V. C., illus. (Illus.). 40p. (Creative's Classics Ser.). (gr. 6-12). 1982. (ISBN 0-87191-827-7). Creative Ed.
--Great Stories of Heroism and Adventure. Halberstam, David (1934-), ed. x, 502 p. 21cm. 1967. Platt & Munk.
--The Little Regiment, and Other Episodes of the American Civil War. N.D. D. Appelton & Co.'s Pub.
--Maggie: A Girl of the Street. Jordan, Philip, illus. (Illus.). 1970. (ISBN 0-8131-0128-X). University Press of Kentucky.
--Maggie and Other Stories. Austin, ed. N.D. (ISBN 0-671-46574-0). Simon & Schuster.
--The Open Boat. Johnson, V. C., illus. (Illus.). 64p. (Creative's Classic Ser.). (gr. 6-12). 1982. (ISBN 0-87191-826-9). Creative Ed.
--Open Boat & Three Other Stories. Quackenbush, Robert Mead (1929-), illus. LC 68-10280. (Illus.). woodcuts. 96p. (Illustrated Editions). (gr. 7 up). 1968. (ISBN 0-531-01074-0). Watts.
--The Red Badge of Courage. N.D. Brown Book Company.
--The Red Badge of Courage. 1900. D. Appleton and Company.
--The Red Badge of courage. N.D. (ISBN 0-531-00270-5). Franklin Watts.
--The Red Badge of Courage. LC 72-192916. xli, 266 p. 22cm. (Thrushwood book). 1971, c.1952. (ISBN 0-448-02553-1). Grosset & Dunlap.
--The Red Badge of Courage. N.D. The Modern Library.
--The Red Badge of Courage. Curry, John Steuart (1897-1946), illus. 170p. N.D. Heritage Press.
--The Red Badge of Courage. Herzberg, Max J., ed. 1926. Appleton-Century-Crofts.
--The Red Badge of Courage. Herzberg, Max J., intro. by. (Illus.). N.D. Dodds, Mead & Co.
--The Red Badge of Courage. Sculley, Bradley (1897-) & Beatty, R. C., eds. LC 62-9512. 344p. 1962. (ISBN 0-393-09543-6). (ISBN 0-393-05320-2). Norton & Co.
--The Red Badge of Courage: An Episode of the American Civil War. Descombes, Roland, illus. LC 77-367913. (Illus.). 245 p. 21cm. 1976. The Franklin Library.
--The Red Badge of Courage: An Episode of the American Civil War. Mozley, Charles (1915-), illus. LC 78-31250. (Illus.). 22cm. 131p. (Children's Illustrated Classics). 1971. (ISBN 0-460-05090-7). E. P. Dutton.
--Red Badge of Courage & Other Stories. (Great Illustrated Classics). (gr. 9 up). 1979. Dodd.
--Red Badge of Courage & Other Stories. 368p. (Franklin Watts Classics). (gr. 7 up). 1969. (ISBN 0-531-00422-8). Watts.
--Stephen Crane: Great Stories of Heroism & Adventure. (Great Writers Collection). (gr. 7 up). N.D. Platt.
--The Third Violet. N.D. D. Appleton & Co.'s Pub.

Crane, Thomas (1843-) & Houghton, Ellen K. Bolton, illus.
--Abroad. LC 42-48366. 56 p. incl. col. front., col. illus. 22 x 18 1/2 cm. 1882. M. Ward & Co.

--Rooster Who Refused to Crow. (Illus.). (gr. 3-4). 1972. (ISBN 0-89375-050-6). Troll Assocs.

Crawford, William, Jr.

--Gore and Glory. (Dollar Mystery and Adventure Ser.). N.D. David McKay Co.

Crawley-Boevey, C. M.

--Jack. (Illus.). (The Little Men Ser.). N.D. A. L. Burt's Pubs.

--Jack: A Topsy Turvy Story. (Illus.). (The Rugby Ser.). N.D. A. L. Burt.

Crayder, Dorothy

--The Pluperfect of Love. Sedgwick, Paulita, illus. LC 79-154758. (Illus.). 184 p. 23cm. 1971. Atheneum.

--The Riddles of Mermaid House. LC 77-2863. 184 p. 22cm. 1977. (ISBN 0-689-30579-6). Atheneum.

--She and the Dubious Three. Ilsley, Velma Elizabeth (1918-), illus. LC 74-75559. (Illus.). 186 p. 22cm. 1974. (ISBN 0-689-30407-2). Atheneum.

--She, the Adventuress. Ilsley, Velma Elizabeth (1918-), illus. LC 72-86931. (Illus.). 188 p. 22cm. 1973. Atheneum.

--She, the Adventuress. Ilsley, Velma Elizabeth (1918-), illus. 1979. Atheneum.

Crayder, Dorothy, jt. auth. see McCully, Helen.

Crayder, Dorothy & Primavera, Elise

--The Joker and the Swan. LC 80-8722. p. cm. 1981. (ISBN 0-06-021363-9). (ISBN 0-06-021364-7). Harper & Row.

Crayder, Dorothy & Vaeth, Susan

--Ishkabibble!. Vaeth, Susan, illus. LC 75-30862. (Illus.). 100 p. 22cm. 1976. (ISBN 0-689-30499-4). Atheneum.

Crayder, Teresa, pseud., see Colman, Hila.

Crayder, Teresa, pseud.

--Cathy and Lisette. Colman, Hila. 1st ed. Copelman, Evelyn, illus. LC 64-11698. 143 p. 22cm. (Signal book). 1964. Doubleday.

--Sudden Fame. Colman, Hila. LC 66-16100. 151p. 22cm. 1966. Macmillan.

Creagh, Patrick (1930-), tr. see Reggiani, Renee.

Credle, Ellis (1902-)

--Across the Cotton Patch. LC 35-14724. 59 p. illus. 23 x 29 cm. 1935. T. Nelson and Sons.

--The Adventures of Tittletom. LC 49-10076. 79 p. illus. 21 cm. (Oxford books for boys and girls). 1949. Oxford Univ. Press.

--Andy and the Circus. Credle, Ellis (1902-), illus. LC 74-164968. (Illus.). 55 p. 27cm. 1971. (ISBN 0-8407-6164-3). (ISBN 0-8407-6165-1). T. Nelson.

--Big Doin's on Razorback Ridge. Credle, Ellis (1902-), illus. LC 56-6468. 125p. illus. 23cm. 1956. Nelson.

--Big Doin's on Razorback Ridge. Credle, Ellis (1902-), illus. LC 77-27803. (Illus.). 125 p. 24cm. 1978, c.1956. (ISBN 0-8407-6607-6). T. Nelson.

--Big Fraid, Little Fraid. LC 64-18739. (Illus.). 46p. 1964. Nelson Junior Books.

--Big Fraid, Little Fraid. Credle, Ellis (1902-), illus. (Illus.). (gr. k-3). 1964. (ISBN 0-525-66007-0). Lodestar Bks.

--Down, Down the Mountain. (Illus.). 1934. Lodestar.

--Down, Down the Mountain. LC 34-31981. 47 p. illus. 30 cm. 1934. T. Nelson and Sons.

--The Flop-Eared Hound. Townsend, Charles, illus. LC 38-27584. 61 p. illus. 24 cm. c.1938. Oxford University Press.

--The Goat That Went to School. Credle, Ellis (1902-), illus. LC 40-27461. 28 p. incl. col. front., illus. (part col.) 25 x 21 cm. (story parade picture book). c.1940. Grosset & Dunlap.

--Here Comes the Showboat. Credle, Ellis (1902-), illus. LC 49-11650. 95 p. illus., music. 25 cm. 1949. Nelson.

--Janey's Shoes. LC 48-4907. 28 p. illus. (part col.) 22 cm. (Story parade picture book). c.1944. Grosset & Dunlap.

--Johnny and His Mule. Townsend, Charles, illus. LC 46-7072. 44 p. illus. 19 1/2 x 19 cm. 1946. Oxford University Press.

--Johnny and His Mule. Townsend, Charles, photos by. (Illus.). 48p. 1946. Walck.

--Little Jeemes Henry. LC 36-10048. 2 p. l., 3-44, 1 p. illus. 23 cm. 1936. T. Nelson and Sons.

--Little Pest Pico. Townsend, Richard F., illus. LC 70-82911. (Illus.). 42 p. 27cm. 1969. T. Nelson.

--Monkey See, Monkey Do: A Folktale. LC 68-22745. (Illus.). 1 v. 46p. 27cm. 1968. T. Nelson.

--My Pet Peepelo. Townsend, Charles, illus. LC 48-7289. 62 p. illus. 25 cm. (Oxford books for boys and girls). 1948. Oxford Univ. Press.

--Pepe and the Parrot. LC 37-15465. 47 p. col. illus. 30 cm. 1937. T. Nelson and Sons.

--Pig-O-Wee: The Story of a Skinny Mountain Pig. LC 36-8047. 44 p. col. illus. 26 cm. c.1936. Rand, McNally & Company.

--Tall Tales from the High Hills. 1957. E M Hale.

--Tall Tales from the High Hills. 1957. Nelson Junior Books.

--Townsend. 1946. Oxford University Press.

Creed, Lisa (1953-) & Little River Elementary School (Bahama N.C.)

--The House Within Me: An Anthology of Poems by Children from Little River School. LC 81-882. 57 p. 22cm. c.1981. (ISBN 0-932112-10-2). Carolina Wren Press.

Creekmore, Raymond (1905-)

--Ali's Elephant. Creekmore, Raymond (1905-), illus. LC 49-9170. 40 p. illus. 27 cm. 1949. Macmillan Co.

--Fujio. Creekmore, Raymond (1905-), illus. LC 51-12194. (Illus.). unpaged. 26cm. 1951. Macmillan.

--Little Fu. Creekmore, Raymond (1905-), illus. LC 47-12198. 40 p. illus. 27 cm. 1947. Macmillan Co.

--Little Skipper. Creekmore, Raymond (1905-), illus. LC 50-7442. (Illus.). 40 p. 27cm. 1950. Macmillan.

--Lokoshi. Creekmore, Raymond (1905-), illus. N.D. Macmillan.

--Lokoshi Learns to Hunt Seals. Creekmore, Raymond (1905-), illus. LC 46-8620. 48 p. incl. front., illus. 26 1/2 x 21 cm. 1946. The Macmillan Company.

Creer, Maria J.

--My Mother's Diamonds. (Illus.). (The Girl's Own Favorite Ser.). N.D. E. P. Dutton & Co.

Cregan, Mairin

--Old John. Sewell, Helen Moore (1896-1957), illus. LC 36-8197. 6 p. l., 183 p., 1 l., incl. front., illus., plates. 23 cm. 1936. The Macmillan Company.

Creglow, Mary Elizabeth Rodhouse

--The Fairy Phlox: And Other Verses. McCain, Velura, illus. LC 31-152938. 61 p. incl. front., plates. 20 cm. c.1931. R. G. Badger.

Creighton, Beatrice

--Little Plays for Little Folks. LC 31-32228. 91 p. front., plates. 20 cm. c.1931. The Penn Publishing Company.

Creighton, Bessy E

--The Adventures of the Wandies. Creighton, Bessy E., illus. LC 27-74826. 32 p. illus. 24 cm. c.1926. Greenberg.

Creighton, David

--Deeds of Gods and Heroes. LC 67-9329. (Illus.). 216 p. 22cm. 1967. St. Martin's Press.

Creighton, Don, pseud., see Drury, Maxine Cole.

Creighton, Don, pseud. (1914-)

--Little League Ball Hawk. Drury, Maxine Cole. LC 68-11223. 163 p. 22cm. 1968. Steck-Vaughn Co.

--Little League Giant. Drury, Maxine Cole. LC 65-12084. 170 p. 22cm. 1965. Steck-Vaughn Co.

--Little League Old-Timers. Drury, Maxine Cole. LC 67-1511. 152 p. 22cm. 1967. Steck-Vaughn Co.

--Secret Little Leaguer. Drury, Maxine Cole. 1966. E M Hale.

--The Secret Little Leaguer. Drury, Maxine Cole. 170 p. 18cm. (Intext sportbook, 109). 1973, c.1966. (ISBN 0-88444-001-X). Intext Press.

--The Secret Little Leaguer. Drury, Maxine Cole. LC 66-12928. 170 p. 22cm. 1966. Steck-Vaughn Co.

Creighton, Katherine

--The Elves of Mount Fern. LC 22-18657. 106 p. col. front. 19 cm. c.1922. Dorrance.

--Nature Songs and Stories. 2 p. l., 76 p. illus. (incl. music) 19 x 25 cm. 1914. The Comstock Publishing Company.

Creighton, Susan

--Huggins and Kisses. Lipking, Ronald C., illus. LC 85-5676. p. cm. c.1985. (ISBN 0-910313-92-X). Parker Brothers.

--Hugs from the Heart. Ewers, Joe, illus. LC 85-9477. (Illus.). 32 p. 21cm. c.1985. (ISBN 0-87372-005-9). Parker Brothers.

Cremins, Robert

--My Animal Mother Goose. Cremins, Robert, illus. (ps-1). 1983. (ISBN 0-517-55098-9). Crown.

Cresher, G. R

--Adventures in the Snow. american ed. Hanson, Edward, illus. LC 65-23786. (Illus.). 22cm. 44p. (Peacemaker Story Books). 1965, c.1961. Fearon Pub.

--Around Home: Three Short Stories. rev. american ed. Brooks, Meredith, illus. LC 70-88776. (Illus.). 22cm. 42p. (Peacemaker Story Books). c.1969. Fearon.

Crespi, Francesca, illus.

--A Treasure Box of Fairy Tales: Hansel & Gretel, Rapunzel, Jack & the Beanstalk, & Aladdin. Jones, Olive, retold by. (Illus.). 1984. (ISBN 0-8037-0079-2). Dial Bks Young.

Crespi, Pachita, jt. auth. see Gay, Zhenya.

Crespi, Pachita (1900-)

--Cabita's Rancho: A Story of Costa Rica. Gay, Zhenya (1906-1978), illus. LC 42-117108. 207, 1 p. incl. front., illus. 21 cm. 1942. J. Messner, Inc.

--Gift of the Earth. LC 46-6398. 32 p. col. illus. 19 1/2 cm. 1946. C. Scribner's Sons.

Crespi, Pachita (1900-) & Lee, Jessica

--Mystery of the Mayan Jewels. Crespi, Pachita (1900-), illus. LC 45-31142. 2 p. l., 164 p. illus. 21 cm. 1945. C. Scribner's Sons.

Cressey, James

--The Dragon and George. Cole, Tamasin, illus. LC 79-15751. p. cm. 1979, c.1977. (ISBN 0-13-219154-7). Prentice-Hall.

--Fourteen Rats & a Rat-Catcher. Cole, Tamasin, illus. LC 77-4759. p. cm. 1977, c.1976. (ISBN 0-13-329920-1). Prentice-Hall.

--Max the Mouse. Cole, Tamasin, illus. LC 78-1027. p. cm. 1978, c.1977. (ISBN 0-13-566299-0). Prentice-Hall.

--Pet Parrot. Cole, Tamasin, illus. LC 78-468. p. cm. 1978, c.1977. Prentice-Hall.

Cresswell, Beatrix F.

--The Royal Progress of King Pepito. Greenaway, Kate (1846-1901), illus. LC 45-32788. (Illus.). 21cm. 48p. 1889. J. B. Young & Co.

Cresswell, Helen

--Absolute Zero: Being the Second Part of the Bagthorpe Saga. LC 77-12675. 174 p. 22cm. (The Bagthorpe Saga). c.1978. (ISBN 0-02-725550-6). Macmillan. **Award: (ALA).**

--At the Stroke of Midnight. Dinan, Carolyn, illus. (Illus.). 192p. (ps-2). 1974. (ISBN 0-00-195041-X). Collins-World.

--The Bagthorpe Saga: Ordinary Jack. Bennett, Jill (1947-), illus. 1977. Macmillan.

--Bagthorpes Abroad: Being the Fifth Part of The Bagthorpe Saga. LC 84-7125. 204p. (gr. 5-9). 1984. (ISBN 0-02-725390-2). Macmillan.

--Bagthorpes Haunted. LC 85-42798. 182 p. 22cm. 1st U.S. edition. (Bagthorpe Saga ; 6th pt.). c.1985. (ISBN 0-02-725380-5). Macmillan Pub. Co.

--Bagthorpes Unlimited: Being the Third Part of the Bagthorpe Saga. LC 78-3561. 180 p. 22cm. (The Bagthorpe Saga). 1978. (ISBN 0-02-725430-5). Macmillan. **Award: (ALA).**

--Bagthorpes Unlimited: Being the Third Part of the Bagthorpe Saga. Bennett, Jill (1947-), illus. LC 79-314414. (Illus.). 175 p. 21cm. ((Her). (Bagthorpe saga). 1978. Faber.

--Bagthorpes vs. the World: Being the Fourth Part of the Bagthorpe Saga. LC 79-13260. 193 p. 22cm. (The Bagthorpe Saga). (gr. 5up). 1979. (ISBN 0-02-725420-8). Macmillan.

--The Beachcombers. LeCain, Errol John (1941-), illus. LC 72-75348. 133 p. 22cm. 1972. Macmillan.

--The Bongleweed. Strugnell, Ann, illus. LC 73-4057. 138 p. 22cm. 1973. (ISBN 0-02-725500-X). Macmillan.

--Butterfly Chase. (Illus.). 31 p. 20cm. (puffin easy reader). 1975. (ISBN 0-14-050139-8). Penguin Books.

--Day on Big O. Hughes, Shirley (1929-), illus. LC 68-18509. (Illus.). 32p. (Beginning to Read Ser). (gr. 2-4). 1968. (ISBN 0-695-41906-4). Follett.

--Dear Shrink. LC 82-7728. 186 p. 22cm. 1982. (ISBN 0-02-725560-3). Macmillan.

--A Game of Catch. Forberg, Ati, pseud. (1925-), illus. Forberg, Beate Gropius. LC 76-46991. (Illus.). 43 p. 23cm. 1977. (ISBN 0-02-725440-2). Macmillan.

--Jumbo Spencer. De Larrea, Victoria, illus. LC 66-7764. 128p. illus. 22cm. (gr. 4-6). 1966, c.1963. Lippincott.

--The Night Watchmen. Floyd, Gareth (1940-), illus. LC 77-120717. (Illus.). 122 p. 21cm. 1969. Macmillan. **Award: (CMA).**

--Ordinary Jack: Being the First Part of the Bagthorpe Saga. LC 77-5146. (gr. 5 up). 1977. (ISBN 0-02-725540-9). Macmillan.

--The Piemakers. Brown, Judith Gwyn (1933-), illus. LC 80-14433. (Illus.). 114 p. 22cm. c.1980. (ISBN 0-02-725410-0). Macmillan.

--The Piemakers. Mars, Witold Tadeusz J. (1912-), illus. LC 68-14618. (Illus.). 142 p. 22cm. 1968. Lippincott.

--Pietro & the Mule. Eckersley, Maureen, illus. LC 71-119005. (Illus.). line drawings. 64p. (gr. 1-4). 1970. (ISBN 0-672-51304-8). Bobbs.

--The Secret World of Polly Flint. Felts, Shirley (1934-), illus. LC 83-24861. (Illus.). 176 p. 22cm. 1st U.S. edition. 1984, c.1982. (ISBN 0-02-725400-3). Macmillan. **Award: (ALA).**

--Two Hoots. Blanc, Martine, illus. LC 77-15854. (Illus.). 28 p. 18cm. (An Early Reader). 1978, c.1974. (ISBN 0-517-53280-8). Crown Publishers.

--Two Hoots and the Big Bad Bird. Blanc, Martine, illus. LC 77-15857. (Illus.). 28 p. 18cm. (An Early Reader). 1978, c.1975. (ISBN 0-517-53281-6). Crown Publishers.

--Two Hoots and the King. Blanc, Martine, illus. LC 78-55548. (Illus.). 28 p. 18cm. (An Early Reader). 1978, c.1977. (ISBN 0-517-53494-0). Crown Publishers.

--Two Hoots Go to the Sea. Blanc, Martine, illus. LC 77-15855. (Illus.). 28 p. 18cm. (An Early Reader). 1978, c.1974. (ISBN 0-517-53283-2). Crown Publishers.

--Two Hoots in the Snow. Blanc, Martine, illus. LC 78-55546. (Illus.). 27 p. 18cm. (An Early Reader). 1978, c.1975. (ISBN 0-517-53495-9). Crown Publishers.

--Two Hoots Play Hide-and Seek. Blanc, Martine, illus. LC 77-15856. (Illus.). 28 p. 18cm. (An Early Reader). 1978, c.1977. (ISBN 0-517-53282-4). Crown Publishers.

--Up the Pier. Floyd, Gareth (1940-), illus. LC 72-178939. (Illus.). 144 p. 21cm. 1971. (ISBN 0-571-09771-5). Faber and Faber.

--Up the Pier. Floyd, Gareth (1940-), illus. LC 79-178598. (Illus.). 144 p. 21cm. 1972, c.1971. Macmillan. **Award: (ALA).**

--Where the Wind Blows. Forberg, Ati, pseud. (1925-), illus. Forberg, Beate Gropius. LC 68-21124. (Illus.). 61 p. 25cm. 1968. Funk & Wagnalls.

--The White Sea Horse. Jacques, Robin (1920-), illus. LC 65-21662. 64p. illus. 21cm. 1st U.S. edition. (gr. 4-6). 1965, c.1964. (ISBN 0-397-30858-2). Lippincott.

--The Winter of the Birds. LC 75-34278. ix, 244 p. 22cm. 1976, c.1975. (ISBN 0-02-725510-7). Macmillan. **Award: (ALA).**

Creswick, Paul (1866-1947)

--Hasting the Pirate. Robinson, Thomas Heath (1869-1950), illus. LC 3-15219. 19cm. 303p. 1902. E. P. Dutton.

--Robin Hood. (McKay's Illustrated Classics). N.D. David McKay Co.

--Robin Hood. Wyeth, Newell Convers (1882-1945), illus. 1917. (ISBN 0-684-20780-X). Charles Scribner's Sons.

--Robin Hood. Wyeth, Newell Convers (1882-1945), illus. LC 17-29729. 362 p. col. plates. 25 cm. 1917. D. McKay.

--Robin Hood. Wyeth, Newell Convers (1882-1945), illus. 1921. David McKay.

--Robin Hood. Wyeth, Newell Convers (1882-1945), illus. LC 17-29729. (Illus.). 362 p. 24cm. (The Scribner Illustrated Classics). Orig. Title: Robin Hood and His Adventures, 1906. 1957. Scribner.

--Robin Hood. Wyeth, Newell Convers (1882-1945), illus. LC 84-10662. 362 p., 9 leaves of plates. (gr. 6-8). 1984. (ISBN 0-684-18162-2). (ISBN 0-684-18180-0). Scribners.

--Robin Hood and His Adventures. Robinson, Thomas Heath (1869-1950), illus. LC 4-888. 312 p. illus., 8 pl. 4 col. pl. (incl. front.) 22 cm. 1903. E. P. Dutton & Co.

Creswick, Paul (1866-1947) & Malory, Thomas, Sir (1410-1471)

--King Arthur: The Story of the Round Table. Westmarcott, Bernard (1887-) & D'Emo, L., illus. LC 25-21159. 2 p. l., 7-423 p. col. front., illus. 20 cm. c.1925. American Book Company.

Cretan, Gladys Yessayan (1921-)

--All Except Sammy. Shimin, Symeon (1902-), illus. LC 65-137124. 42p. col. illus. 22cm. c.1966. Atantic-Little.

--Because I Promised. Jefferson, Robert Louis (1929-), illus. LC 79-95197. (Illus.). 56 p. 24cm. 1970. (ISBN 0-687-02526-5). Abingdon Press.

--A Gift from the Bride. Fava, Rita (1932-), illus. LC 64-10172. 59 p. illus. 25 cm. 1964. Little Brown.

--A Hole, a Box, and a Stick. Frascino, Edward, illus. LC 72-1081. (Illus.). 32 p. 26cm. 1972. Lothrop, Lee & Shepard Co.

--Lobo. Coombs, Patricia (1926-), illus. LC 77-81924. (Illus.). 32 p. 22cm. 1969. Lothrop, Lee & Shepard Co.

--Lobo. Coombs, Patricia (1926-), illus. 1970. (ISBN 0-688-40035-3). William Morrow and Company.

--Lobo and Brewster. Coombs, Patricia (1926-), illus. LC 73-135295. (Illus.). 32 p. 21cm. 1971. Lothrop, Lee & Shepard Co.

--Me, Myself, and I. Bolognese, Donald Alan (1934-), illus. LC 73-85129. (Illus.). 32 p. 24cm. 1969. (ISBN 0-688-21645-5). Morrow.

--Messy Sally. Porter, Patricia Grant, illus. LC 72-177315. (Illus.). 32p. (gr. k-3). 1972. (ISBN 0-688-31885-1). Lothrop.

--Run Away, Habeeb!. Jefferson, Robert Louis (1929-), illus. LC 68-10703. (Illus.). 40 p. 25cm. 1968. Abingdon Press.

--Sunday for Sona. Flynn, Barbara (1928-), illus. LC 73-4935. (Illus.). 32 p. 22cm. 1973. (ISBN 0-688-41537-7). (ISBN 0-688-41537-7). Lothrop, Lee & Shepard.

--Ten Brothers with Camels. Ventura, Piero Luigi (1937-), illus. LC 73-84543. (Illus.). 30 p. 28cm. 1975. (ISBN 0-307-15690-7). Golden Press.

Crew, Fleming H., jt. auth. see Gall, Alice Crew, Mrs.

Crew, Fleming H (1882-)

--The More the Merrier: Stories. Hogner, Nils (1893-1970), illus. LC 52-9428. 121 p. illus. 21 cm. 1952. Oxford University Press.

Crew, Helen Cecilla Coale, Mrs. (1866-1941)

--Alanna. Esley, Joan, illus. LC 29-18155. 5 p. l., 233, 1 p. col. front., illus. 22 cm. 1929. Harper & Brothers.

--Day Before Yesterday. Scott, Janet Laura, illus. LC 35-19875. 6 p. l., 17-286 p. col. front., illus., col. plates. 20 cm. 1935. Harper & Brothers.

--Laughing Lad: A Story of Modern France. Berger, William Merritt (1872-), illus. LC 31-236806. xi, 221 p. incl. front., illus. 20 cm. c.1931. The Century Co.

--The Lost King. LC 29-17044. 5 p. l., 3-206 p. front., illus. (map) plates. 20 cm. c.1929. The Century Co.
--Peter Swiss. Hogeboom, Amy (1891-), illus. LC 34-31299. 6 p. l., 233 p. col. front., illus. 23 cm. 1934. Harper & Brothers.
--The Runaway Cousins: A Tale of Czechoslovakia. Voute, Kathleen (1892-), illus. LC 36-20253. 6 p. l., 3-225, 1 p. incl. plates. front. 21 cm. 1936. Little, Brown, and Company.
--The Shawl with Silver Bells. Brann, Esther, illus. LC 32-24060. xiii p., 1 l., 242 p. incl. front., illus., plates, geneal. tab. 21 cm. 1932. The Macmillan Company.
--Singing Seamen. Rodgers, Richard H. (1876-1953), illus. LC 30-22900. 5 p. l., 3-237 p. front., plates. 20 cm. c.1930. The Century Co.
--The Trojan Boy. Rodgers, Richard H. (1876-1953), illus. LC 28-197478. viii p., 2 l., 3-207 p. front., illus. (map) plates. 20 cm. c.1928. The Century Co.
--Under Two Eagles. Pitz, Henry Clarence (1895-1976), illus. LC 29-19781. x, 298 p. incl. plates. col. front. 21 cm. 1929. Little, Brown, and Company.

Crew, Helen Cicilla Coale, Mrs. (1866-1941)
--Saturday's Children. Freeman, Margaret (1893-), illus. LC 27-5457. x p., 3 l., 3-306 p. incl. plates. col. front. 21 cm. 1927. Little, Brown, and Company.

Crewdson, Jane Fox, Mrs. (1808-1863)
--Aunt Jane's Verses for Children. LC 24-31530. (Illus.). 16cm. 144p. 1855. Association of Friends.

Crewe-Jones, Florence, tr. see Malot, Hector Henri.

Crews, Donald
--Bicycle Race. LC 84-27912. (Illus.). 9 7/8 x 8. 24p. (16 pt.). (ps-1). 1985. (ISBN 0-688-05171-5). (ISBN 0-688-05172-3). Greenwillow.
--Carousel. Crews, Donald, illus. 1982. Greenwillow.
--Freight Train. Crews, Donald, illus. LC 78-2303. (Illus.). 22 p. c.1978. (ISBN 0-688-80165-X). (ISBN 0-688-84165-1). Greenwillow Books. **Award: (RCM).**
--Freight Train. Crews, Donald, illus. LC 84-11519. (Illus.). 24 p. (Picture puffins). 1985, c.1978. (ISBN 0-14-050480-X). Puffin Books.
--Harbor. Crews, Donald, illus. (Illus.). (ps-1). 1982. (ISBN 0-688-00861-5). (ISBN 0-688-00862-3). Greenwillow.
--Parade. Crews, Donald, illus. LC 82-20927. (Illus.). 9 7/8 x 8. 32p. (20 pt.). (gr. k-3). 1983. (ISBN 0-688-01995-1). (ISBN 0-688-01996-X). Greenwillow.
--School Bus. Crews, Donald, illus. LC 83-18681. (Illus.). unpaged. c.1984. (ISBN 0-688-02807-1). (ISBN 0-688-02808-X). Greenwillow Books.
--School Bus. Crews, Donald, illus. LC 85-576. (Illus.). 32 p. 1985, c.1984. (ISBN 0-14-050549-0). Puffin Books.
--Ten Black Dots. LC 85-14871. (Illus.). 8 1/4 x 8. 32p. (24 pt.). (ps-3). 1986. (ISBN 0-688-06067-6). (ISBN 0-688-06068-4). Greenwillow.
--Ten Black Dots. Crews, Donald, illus. LC 68-12514. (Illus.). 26 p. 17cm. 1968. Scribner.
--Truck. Crews, Donald, illus. LC 79-19031. (Illus.). 32 p. c.1980. (ISBN 0-688-80244-3). (ISBN 0-688-84244-5). Greenwillow Books. **Award: (ALA).**
--Truck. Crews, Donald, illus. LC 84-18137. (Illus.). 32 p. (Picture puffins). 1985, c.1980. (ISBN 0-14-050506-7). Puffin Books.
--We Read: A to Z. Crews, Donald, illus. LC 66-11500. (Illus.). 26 (i.e. 52) p. 21cm. 1967. Harper & Row.

Crichlow, Ernest, jt. auth. see Beim, Jerrold.

Crichton, Antoinette K. see A K C , pseud.

Crichton, Antoinette K.
--A Very Little Story for Very Little Children. A K C , pseud. LC 44-33360. 38 p. 19 cm. 1883. The Chas. M. Green Printing Company.

Crichton, Frances Elizabeth Sinclair, Mrs. (1877-1918)
--Peep-in-the-World. 10th impression. ed. McIntosh, Frank (1901-), illus. LC 29-15980. 4 p. l., 258 p. front., plates. 20 cm. 1929. Longmans, Green and Co.
--Peep-in-the-World. Rountree, Harry (1878-1950), illus. v, 258 p. front., pl. 20 cm. 1910. Longmans, Green & Co.

Crichton, John Michael (1942-)
--The Great Train Robbery. 1975. (ISBN 0-394-49401-6). Knopf.

Crichton, Marion Carrie
--Gus the Bus. 1967. (ISBN 0-516-07612-4). Childrens Press.
--Gus the Bus. Smith, Robert David (1932-), illus. LC 67-21057. (Illus.). 38 p. 24cm. 1967. Elk Grove Press.

Crichton, Michael see Crichton, John Michael.

Cridge, Annie Denton
--Crumb Basket. N.D. Colby and Rich.

Cridland, Margery
--The Baker. Knight, Clayton (1891-1969), illus. (gr. k-3). N.D. David McKay Co.

Criker, Blanche, ed.
--Five Great Dog Stories: Containing: Jack London's "The Call of the Wild"; John Brown's "Rab and His Friends"; Alfred Ollivant's "Bob, Son of Battle"; Marshall Saunders'"Beautiful Joe"; Ouida's "A Dog of Flanders". 356p. 1960. Dover Pub.

Crinkle, C.
--Voyages of Captain Crinkle. Lincoln, Edith (1883-), illus. N.D. Hesperian House.

Crippen, David (1936-)
--Two Sides of the River. Brown, David Scott (1936-), illus. LC 75-25512. (Illus.). 32 p. c.1976. (ISBN 0-687-42783-5). Abingdon Press

Crippen, P. G.
--Christmas and Christmas Love. (Legend and History Library). N.D. Dodge.

Crisp, Frank Robson (1915-)
--The Devil Diver. Powers, Richard M. Gorman (1921-), illus. LC 54-7832. 1954. Coward-McCann.
--The Golden Quest. Powers, Richard M. Gorman (1921-), illus. LC 53-8393. (Illus.). 276 p. 21cm. 1953. Coward-McCann.
--The Haunted Reef. Powers, Richard M. Gorman (1921-), illus. LC 52-7123. 250 p. illus. 21 cm. 1952. Coward-McCann.
--The Java Wreckmen. Powers, Richard M. Gorman (1921-), illus. LC 56-7139. (Illus.). 248 p. 21cm. 1956. Coward-McCann.
--The Manila Menfish. Powers, Richard M. Gorman (1921-), illus. LC 57-7425. 244 p. illus. 21 cm. 1957. Coward-McCann.
--The Sanguman: A Dirk Rogers Adventure. Williams, Patrick, illus. LC 67-1997. (Illus.). 160 p. 22cm. 1966, c.1965. C. McCutcheon.
--The Sea Ape. Powers, Richard M. Gorman (1921-), illus. LC 59-5236. (Illus.). 21cm. 254p. 1959. Coward-McCann Inc.
--The Sea Robbers. Powers, Richard M. Gorman (1921-), illus. LC 52-134187. 245 p. illus. 21 cm. 1953. Coward- McCann.
--The Treasure of Barby Swin. Powers, Richard M. Gorman (1921-), illus. LC 55-689393. 215 p. illus. 21 cm. 1955. Coward- McCann.

Crisp, William George
--White Gold in the Cassiar. LC 55-9828. 213 p. 21 cm. 1955. Dodd, Mead.

Crispin, Edmund, pseud., see Montgomery, Robert Bruce.

Crispin, Edmund, pseud. (1921-1978)
--Stars and Under. Montgomery, Robert Bruce. N.D. Transatlantic Arts Inc.

Criss, Inez Sandelin
--Two If by Sea or the Magic of Three: Episode Number. 1st. ed. Criss, Monica V, illus. (Illus.). 64 p. 22cm. (gr. 1-6). 1974, c.1973. (ISBN 0-682-47835-0). Exposition Press.

Criss, Mildred (1890-)
--Betty Lee in Paris. Barnhart, Nancy (1899-) & Lee, Mannning De Villeneuve (1894-1980), illus. LC 31-12263. viii, p., 2 l., 313 p. incl. illus., plates. front. 21 cm. (windmill books). 1931. Doubleday, Doran & Company, Inc.
--Betty Lee in Paris. Barnhart, Nancy (1889-) & Lee, Manning De Villeneuve (1894-1980), illus. LC 17-31456. viii p., 2 l., 313 p. incl. illus., plates. front. 21 cm. (Young moderns bookshelf). 1937. The Sun Dial Press, Inc.
--Isabella, Young Queen of Spain. Simont, Marc (1915-), illus. LC 41-19319. 5 p. l., 219 p. illus. 22 x 17 cm. 1941. Dodd, Mead & Company.
--Little Cabbages. Barnhart, Nancy (1889-), illus. LC 28-23668. viii p., 2 l., 313 p. incl. illus., plates. col. front. 21 cm. 1928. Doubleday, Doran & Company, Inc.
--Madeleine's Court on an Island in Paris. Brissaud, Pierre, illus. LC 38-20648. 3 p. l., 186 p. illus. 21 cm. 1938. Dodd, Mead & Company.
--Malou, a Little Swiss Girl. Lederer, Charlotte Bacskay, Mrs. (1872-), illus. LC 29-19520. 5 p. l., 280 p. incl. illus., plates. col. front. 21 cm. (gr. 7). 1929. Doubleday, Doran & Company, Inc.
--Martine and Michel: A Story of the French Jura Mountains. LC 37-22396. 6 p. l., 289 p. incl. illus., plates. col. front. 21 cm. (Young moderns bookshelf). 1937. The Sun Dial Press, Inc.
--Martine and Michel: A Story of the French Jura Mountains. Verpilleux, Emile Antoine (1888-), illus. LC 36-10610. 6 p. l., 289 p. incl. illus., plates front. 21 cm. (Young moderns books). 1936. Doubleday, Doran & Company, Inc.
--Martine and Michel: A Story of the Jura Mountains. LC 31-24262. 6 p. l., 289 p. incl. illus., plates, col. front. 21 cm. 1931. Doubleday, Doran & Company, Inc.
--Pocahontas, Young American Princess. Simont, Marc (1915-), illus. LC 43-7356. viii p., 1 l., 286 p. illus. 22 cm. 1943. Dodd, Mead & Company.
--The Red Caravan: The Wandering Adventures of Francesca. LC 40-11706. xi p., 1 l., 274 p. 21 cm. (Young moderns bookshelf). 1940. The Sun Dial Press.
--The Red Caravan: The Wandering Adventures of Francesca. Brissaud, Pierre, illus. Dimnet, Ernest, frwd. by. LC 34-21152. xi, 1 l., 274 p. col. front. 21 cm. 1934. Doubleday Doran & Company, Inc.

Crissey, Forrest (1864-1943)
--The Young Newspaper Scout: An Interesting Narrative of a Boy's Adventures in the Northwest During the Riel Rebellion. LC 75-302977. (Illus.). 194 p., 10 leaves of plates. 20cm. 1895. W. B. Conkey Co.

Crist, Eda Szecskay (1909-) & Crist, Richard Harrison
--China. LC 61-12710. 90 p. illus. 22 cm. 1961. Westminster Press.
--The Cloud-Catcher. Crist, Richard Harrison, illus. LC 56-5904. 143 p. illus. 22 cm. 1956. Abelard-Schuman.
--Excitement in Appleby Strees. Crist, Eda Szecskay (1909-) & Crist, Richard Harrison, illus. LC 50-8970. 27 p. illus. 25cm. (A Silver Star Book). 1950. Children's Press.
--Excitement in Appleby Street. N.D. Grosset & Dunlap.
--The Good Ship Spider Queen. 1st ed. Crist, Eda Szecskay (1909-) & Crist, Richard Harrison, illus. LC 53-5243. 184 p. illus. 21 cm. 1953. Bobbs Merrill.
--Mystery of Broken-Horse Chimneys. Crist, Richard Harrison, illus. LC 60-5038. 192p. 1960. Abelard-Schuman.
--The Secret of Turkeyfoot Mountain. Crist, Richard Harrison, illus. LC 57-6022. 22cm. 204p. 1957. Abelard-Schuman.

Crist, Richard, jt. auth. see Crist, Eda Szecskay.

Crist, Richard Harrison, jt. auth. see Crist, Eda Szecskay.

Cristini, Ermanno & Puricelli, Luigi
--In My Garden. (Illus.). 28p. N.D. (ISBN 0-907234-05-4, Pub. by Picture Bk Studio USA). Neugebauer Pr.
--In the Pond. Cristini, Ermanno & Puricelli, Luigi, illus. LC 84-972. (Illus.). 28p. 1984. (ISBN 0-907234-43-7, Pub. by Picture Bk Studio USA). Neugebauer Pr.
--In the Woods. LC 83-8153. p. cm. (Picture Book Studio Series). c.1983. (ISBN 0-907234-31-3). Neugebauer Press USA : Distributed by Alphabet Press.

Crocker, Beulah Mary
--An Exciting New Year's Day in Jungletown. LC 11-805. (Illus.). 16 p. 16 x 24cm. 1910. Press of Hahn & Harmon Company.

Crocker, Gladys Hosmer
--Twelve Classroom Plays for Primary Pupils. LC 40-17464. 51 p. 19 cm. 1939. Eldridge Entertainment House, Incorporated.

Crocker, Joan
--The Singing Cart. Crocker, Joan, illus. LC 45-104713. 4 p. l., 86 p. col. front., illus., col. plates. 21 1/2 x 19 cm. 1945. W. Morrow and Company.

Crockett, Davy
--The Adventures of Davy Crockett. Rev. ed. Thomason, John W., Jr., illus. 1955. Charles Scribner's Sons.

Crockett, Lucy Herndon (1914-)
--Capitan: The Story of an Army Mule. Crockett, Lucy Herndon (1914-), illus. LC 40-33796. 4 p. l., 354 p. illus. (incl. maps) col. double plates. 24 cm. c.1940. H. Holt and Company.
--Lucio and His Nuong: A Tale of the Philippine Islands. LC 39-27432. 54 p. col. illus. 30 cm. c.1939. H. Holt and Company.
--Pong Choolie, You Rascal--!. 1st ed. Crockett, Lucy Herndon (1914-), illus. LC 51-13516. 246 p. illus. 21 cm. 1951. Holt.
--Pong Choolie, You Rascal. Crockett, Lucy Herndon (1914-), illus. LC 51-13516. (Illus.). 246p. (gr. 5-7). 1966. (ISBN 0-03-059540-1). HR&W.
--Teru: A Tale of Yokohama. Crockett, Lucy Herndon (1914-), illus. LC 50-9944. (Illus.). 213 p. 21cm. 1950. Holt.
--That Mario. Crockett, Lucy Herndon (1914-), illus. LC 40-7101. 4 p. l., 181, 2 p. illus. 21 cm. c.1940. H. Holt and Company.
--The Year Something Almost Happened in Pinoso. LC 60-11488. (Illus.). 21cm. 150p. 1960. Pantheon.

Crockett, Maline
--More Stories to See & Share. Grover, Nina, illus. (Illus.). 64p. 1981. Deseret Bk.

Crockett, Samuel Rutherford (1860-1914)
--Sir Toady Crusoe: The Adventures of Two Boys and a Girl. Browne, Gordon Frederick (1858-1932), illus. LC 5-33499. 21cm. 356p. Repr. 1910. Frederick A. Stokes.
--The Surprising Adventures of Sir Toady Lion with Those of General Napoleon Smith: An Improving History for Old Boys, Young Boys, Good Boys, Bad Boys, Little Boys, Cowboys and Tom-Boys. 1910. Frederick A. Stokes.
--The Surprising Adventures of Sir Toady Lion with Those of General Napoleon Smith: An Improving History for Old Boys, Young Boys, Good Boys, Bad Boys, Little Boys, Cowboys, and Tom-Boys. Browne, Gordon Frederick (1858-1932), illus. LC 6-31590. xiv, 314 p. incl. front. illus. 21 cm. c.1897. F. A. Stokes Company.
--Sweetheart Travellers: A Child's Book for Children, for Women, and for Men. Browne, Gordon Frederick (1858-1932) & Groome, W. H. C., illus. 3 p. l., ix-xv, 314 p. incl. front., illus., plates. 21 cm. 1896. F. A. Stokes Company.
--Sweethearts at Home. LC 12-20564. 4 p. l., 311 p. col. front., col. plates. 21 cm. 1912. Frederick A. Stokes Company.

Crockett, Samuel Rutherford (1860-1914) & Scott, Walter, Sir (1771-1832)
--Red Cap Adventures. LC 8-24454. (Being the Second Series of Red Cap Tales Stolen from the Treasure Chest of the Wizard of the North. Original Author: Sir Walter Scott (1771-1832)). x 411 p. col. front., 15 col. pl 21 cm. 1908. The Macmillan Company; Etc.
--Red Cap Tales. LC 4-25381. (Stolen from the Treasure Chest of the Wizard of the North Which Theft is Humbly Acknowledged by S. R. Crockett. Original Author: Sir Walter Scott)1771-1832)). xii p., 1 l., 413 p. 16 col. pl. (incl. front.) 21 cm. 1904. The Macmillan Company; Etc., Etc.

Crofford, Emily Ardell (1927-)
--Stories from the Blue Road. Nobens, C. A., illus. LC 81-21229. (Illus.). 167 p. 23cm. c.1982. (ISBN 0-87614-189-0). Carolrhoda Books.

Crofford, Emily Ardell (1927-) & LaMarche, Jim
--A Matter of Pride. LC 81-3875. p. cm. c.1981. (ISBN 0-87614-171-8). Carolrhoda Books.

Croft, Aloysius
--Twenty One Saints. 1937. Bruce Pub Co.

Croft, Edith Fries, jt. ed. see Croft, Kenneth.

Croft, Kenneth & Croft, Edith Fries, eds.
--Selected Stories By American Authors. 128p. 1973. (ISBN 0-87789-074-9). English Language Services.
--Stories By Washington Irving. 132p. 1973. English Language Service.

Crofton, Helen Rose Ann Milman see Milman, Helen, pseud.

Crofton, Helen Rose Anne Milman, Mrs. (1857-)
--Jim's Conquest. Lance, Eveline, illus. LC 40-37549. 128 p. incl. fron. illus. 18 cm. N.D. E. Nister.

Crofts, Freeman Wills (1879-)
--Young Robin Brand, Detective. LC 48-556791. v, 208 p. 21 cm. (Junior red badge mystery). 1948. Dodd, Mead.

Crofut, William E., III (1934-)
--The Moon on the One Hand: Poetry in Song. Crofut, Susan, illus. Cooper, Kenneth, frwd. by. LC 74-18179. (Illus.). 64p. (gr. 1-9). 1975. (ISBN 0-689-50018-1, McElderry Bk). Atheneum. **Award: (ALA).**

Croix, Robert de La see De la Croix, Robert.

Croker, T. Crofton, ed.
--Irish Folk Stories for Children. (Illus.). 90p. (gr. 6 up). 1983. (ISBN 0-85342-690-2, Pub. by Mercier Pr Ireland). Irish Bk Ctr.

Croll, Carolyn
--Too Many Babas. Croll, Carolyn, illus. LC 78-22474. (Illus.). 5 7/8 x 8 1/2. 64p. (18 pt.). (I Can Read Bks.). (gr. k-3). 1979. (ISBN 0-06-021384-1). Har-Row.

Croll, Carolyn, jt. auth. see Flory, Jane Trescott.

Croll, Philip C., tr. see Hoffmann, Franz.

Croman, Dorothy Young, see Rosenberg, Dorothy.

Croman, Dorothy Young (1906-)
--Danger in Sagebrush Country. 144p. (Outlands Adventure Ser.). (gr. 4-7). 1984. (ISBN 0-8423-0514-9). Tyndale.
--Gather Around. LC 78-27450. (Illus.). 241 p. 24cm. (Functional Basic Reading Series). 1971. (ISBN 0-87076-180-3). Stanwix House.
--The Mystery of Steamboat Rock. Geer, Charles Hand (1922-), illus. LC 56-6617. (Illus.). 192 p. 21cm. 1956. Putnam.
--Trouble on the Blue Fox Islands: An Outlands Adventure. LC 84-52333. 188 p. 18cm. (WindRider books). c.1985. (ISBN 0-8423-7345-4). Tyndale House.

Crombie, Ruth
--Christopher, the Canary. Crombie, Ruth, illus. LC 35-17387. (Illus.). 48 p. 22cm. 1935. Whitman Publishing Co.

Crome
--Wilderness Family Pt. 2. (gr. 3-5). N.D. (ISBN 0-590-12113-8, Schol Pap). Scholastic Inc.

Cromie, Alice Hamilton (1914-)
--Nobody Wanted to Scare Her. Brinckloe, Julie Lorraine (1950-), illus. LC 73-20723. (Illus.). 139 p. 22cm. 1974. (ISBN 0-385-02845-8). (ISBN 0-385-02845-8). Doubleday.

Cromie, Robert Allen (1909-), ed.
--Where Steel Winds Blow. 1968. (ISBN 0-679-50146-0). McKay.

Cromie, William Joseph (1930-)
--Steven and the Green Turtle. Eaton, Tom (1940-), illus. LC 77-85040. (Illus.). 64 p. 23cm. (Science I can read book). (gr. k-3). 1970. (ISBN 0-06-021374-4). Harper & Row.
Crommelin, Emeline Gifford (1859-), ed.
--Famous Legends Adapted for Children. LC 4-4984. xiv, 181 p. incl. 9 pl. front. 19 cm. 1904. The Century Co.
--Famous Legends: The Leading Folk-Lore of Nine Countries, Forty-Two Legends in All. (Illus.). 196p. 1905. Century Co.
Crommelin, May
--My Friends: A Novel Birthday-Book. (Illus.). N.D. George Routldege.
Crompton, Anne Eliot (1930-)
--Deer Country. Kaufman, Maggie, illus. LC 72-76292. (Illus.). 128p. (gr. 7 up). 1973. (ISBN 0-316-16141-1, Pub. by Atlantic Monthly Pr). Little.
--The Ice Trail. LC 80-17062. p. cm. c.1980. (ISBN 0-416-30691-8). Methuen.
--The Lifting Stone. Sewall, Marcia (1935-), illus. LC 77-10607. (Illus.). 40 p. c.1978. (ISBN 0-8234-0325-4). Holiday House.
--Queen of Swords. LC 79-26496. 139 p. 22cm. c.1980. (ISBN 0-416-30611-X). Methuen.
--The Rain-Cloud Pony. Frame, Paul (1913-), illus. LC 76-47545. (Illus.). 127 p. 21cm. c.1977. (ISBN 0-8234-0295-9). Holiday House.
--The Sorcerer. Morrill, Leslie H., illus. LC 70-150048. (Illus.). 175 p. 21cm. 1971. Little, Brown.
--The Winter Wife: An Abenaki Folktale. Parker, Robert Andrew (1927-), illus. LC 74-19061. (Illus.). 47 p. 25cm. 1975. (ISBN 0-316-16143-8). Little, Brown.
Crompton, Frances Eliza
--The Children of Hermitage. Pendle, Alexy, illus. LC 78-144210. (Illus.). 152 p. 21cm. 1971. St. Martins Press.
--Friday's Child. (Illus.). N.D. E. P. Dutton & Co.
--Gatty and I. (Illus.). (Goldenrod Library Ser.). 1905. L. C. Page & Co.
--The Gentle Heritage. (Illus.). 188p. N.D. E. P. Dutton & Co.
--Little Swan Maidens. (Illus.). (Dainty Ser.). N.D. Henry Altemus Co.
--Master Bartlemy: Or, The Thankful Art. (Illus.). N.D. E. P. Dutton & Co.
--Messire, and Other Stories. LC 12-31664. 3 p. l., 117 p. front., plates. 19 cm. 1895. E. P. Dutton and Company.
--The Rose Carnation. N.D. E. P. Dutton & Co.
--The Rose-Carnation. (Illus.). (Dainty Ser.). N.D. Henry Altemus Co.
--Voyage of the Mary Adair. N.D. E. P. Dutton & Co.
--The Voyage of the Mary Adair, 1 of 15 vols. LC 6377. (Illus.). 21cm. 48p. (Dainty Ser. of Choice Gift Bks: No. 6). 1905. Set. Henry Altemus Co.
Crompton, Frances Eliza, jt. auth. see Winter, John Strange.
Crompton, George
--Spunky the Inchworm. N.D. Vantage Press Inc.
Crompton, Margaret
--The House Where Jack Lives. Gill, Margery Jean (1925-), illus. (Illus.). 30p. (ps-1). 1980. (ISBN 0-370-30027-0, Pub. by Chatto, Bodley Head & Jonathan). Merrimack Pub Cir.
Crompton, Patricia, tr. see Lindgren, Astrid Ericsson.
Crompton, Richmal, pseud., see Lamburn, Richmal Crompton.
Cromwell, R. N., Mrs.
--The Three Gifts. 125p. N.D. American Tract Society.
Crone, Glenn P.
--There Really Is a Santa Claus. Stone, David Karl (1922-), illus. (Illus.). 16 4-color ils. 16p. (gr. k-6). 1969. (ISBN 0-8042-2970-8). John Knox.
Crone, Ruth, jt. auth. see Brown, Marion Marsh.
Cronin, Archibald Joseph (1896-1981)
--The Citadel. (A novel). 1937. (ISBN 0-316-16158-6). Little.
--The Green Years. (A novel). 1944. (ISBN 0-316-16159-4). Little.
Cronin, Bernard see North, Eric, pseud.
Cronin, Bernard
--The Ant Men: A Science Fantasy Novel. North, Eric, pseud. 1st ed. Blaisdell, Paul & Schomburg, Alex, illus. 216 p. 21 cm. (Science fiction). 1955. Winston.
Crook, Beverly
--April's Witches. LC 71-141575. 219 p. 22cm. 1971. (ISBN 0-8114-7724-X). Steck-Vaughn Co.
--Fair Annie of Old Mule Hollow. LC 78-9291. (Illus.). 175 p. 21cm. c.1978. (ISBN 0-07-014487-7). McGraw-Hill.
Crook, James F
--Jack in the Mountains. Bull, Charles Livingston (1874-1932), illus. LC 26-10692. 4 p. l., 315 p. col. front., plates. 20 cm. c.1926. L. C. Page & Company.

Crooke, William (1848-1923), retold by.
--Talking Thrush and Other Tales from India. Robinson, William Heath (1872-1944), illus. Crooke, William, compiled by. N.D. E. P. Dutton & Co.
--The Talking Thrush: Stories of Birds and Beasts. Rouse, William Henry Denham (1863-), illus. xi, 217, 1 p. incl. front., illus., plates. 20 cm. 1938. J. M. Dent & Sons, Ltd.
Cropp, Ben
--Cheeky the Dolphin. (Illus.). 51p. 1968. Tri-Ocean Books.
Crosby
--Our Little Books for Little Folks. N.D. American Book Co.
Crosby, Adelaide Upton
--The Enchanted Butterflies. Clark, Susan H. Mrs., Mrs. & Crosby, Adelaide Upton, illus. LC 44-29958. 57 p. incl. front., plates. 21 1/2 x 17 1/2 cm. c.1895. Frederick A. Stokes Company.
Crosby, Alexander L. (1906-1980)
--Go Find Hanka!. 1970. (ISBN 0-516-08816-5). Childrens Press.
--Go Find Hanka!. Rounds, Glen Harold (1906-), illus. LC 72-119067. (Illus.). 44 p. 25cm. 1970. (ISBN 0-87464-154-3). Golden Gate Junior Books.
--One Day for Peace. LC 72-146306. 109 p. 21cm. 1971. Little, Brown.
--The World of Rockets. LC 65-226492. 79p. illus. (pt. col.) ports. 24cm. (Gateway bks. G-13). 1965. Random.
Crosby, Carroll
--Ronnie and the Wise Old Owl. Mayer, Marguarette, illus. LC 48-330361. 28 p. illus. (part col.) 24 cm. 1945, c.1944. Random House.
Crosby, Fanny
--Fanny Crosby's Story of Ninety-four Years. Jackson, S. Trevena, illus. N.D. Fleming H. Revell Co.
Crosby, John Campbell (1912-)
--Party of the Year. (General Ser.). 1980. (ISBN 0-8161-3067-1, Large Print Bks). G K Hall.
Crosby, Nina & Marten, Elizabeth
--The Zoo. (gr. 3-6). 1980. (ISBN 0-916456-73-0). Good Apple.
Crosby, Percy Leo (1891-)
--Skippy. (The Children's Favorite Ser.). N.D. Grosset & Dunlap.
--The Story of Skippy. LC 34-41057. 1 p. l., 7-316, 1 p. illus. 24 cm. (big big book). c.1934. Whitman Publishing Company.
Crosby, Ralph M.
--We Have Met the Enemy. N.D. Bobbs-Merrill Co.
Crosby, Ruth Avis, Mrs.
--A Trip with Mother Goose. LC 15-8290. 55 p. illus. 21 cm. 1904. W. B. Conkey Company.
Crosher, G. R. see Kesteven, G. R., pseud.
Crosher, G. R.
--Around the Town. Hanson, Edward, illus. LC 63-19807. (Illus.). 40 p. 22cm. (Pacemaker Story Bk.). 1963, c.1962. Fearon Publishers.
--A Bomb in the Submarine. american ed. Hanson, Edward, illus. LC 65-23737. 60 p. illus. 22 cm. (Pacemaker story books). 1965, c.1956. Fearon Publishers.
--By the Sea. Rev. American ed. Cate, Patricia, illus. LC 78-88778. (Illus.). 42. 22cm. (Pacemaker Story Bks.). c.1969. Fearon Publishers.
--Mystery Cottage. Hanson, Edward, illus. LC 63-19806. (Illus.). 60 p. 22cm. (Pacemaker Story Bks.). 1953, c.1950. Fearon Publishers.
--Night Adventure. rev. american ed. Carlson, Kenneth L., illus. LC 74-88777. (Illus.). 44 p. 22cm. (Pacemaker story books). 1969. Fearon Publishers.
--Ride on a Rainy Afternoon. american ed. Redman, Francis E., illus. LC 65-23729. 60 p. illus. 22 cm. (Pacemaker story books). 1965, c.1959. Fearon Publishers.
Crosland, Thomas William Hodgson (1886-1924)
--Little People: An Alphabet. Mayer, Henry, illus. LC 2-25634. 3 p. l., 94, 1 p. incl. col. pl. 14 x 9 cm. (dumpy books for children, 5). 1902. F. A. Stokes Company.
Croson, Bob
--Nick & Co. in a Fix. LC 85-13817. p. cm. (Lion paperback). c.1985. (ISBN 0-85648-953-0). Lion Pub.
Cross
--Pilgrim Boy. 144p. N.D. American Tract Society.
Cross, Belle
--The Silk Ladder. N.D. Vantage Press Inc.
Cross, Beverly, jt. auth. see Pemsteen, Hans.
Cross, D.
--Music Stories for Girls and Boys. N.D. Ginn & Co.
Cross, Elsa, Mrs.
--The Quest of the Golden Star. Herwig, William & Herwig, Mary, illus. LC 26-320. 4 p. l., 11-221 p. col. front., illus. 23 cm. 1925. The Printshop Company, Ltd.
Cross, F. J.
--Good Morning! Good Night!. (Illus.). 216p. 1905. Cassell & Co.

Cross, Genevieve Marion (1910-)
--The Fawn and the White Mountain Express. Ayer, Margaret (0000-1981), illus. LC 49-118378. 29 p. col. illus. 21 x 26 cm. c.1949. Cross Publications.
--Fluff and the Fireman: A Story. Cross, Genevieve Marion (1910-), illus. LC 47-12265. 26 p. illus. (part col.) 18 x 25 cm. c.1947. Cross Publications.
--The Little Heroes of Hartford. Brigham, William C., illus. LC 47-12360. 84 p. illus. (part col.) 22 cm. 1947. Cross Publications.
--My Bunny Book. Clement, Charles (1921-), illus. LC 52-7614. unpaged. illus. 31 cm. 1952. Cross Publications.
--The Pop-Corn Lamb and the Peppermint Sticks. LC 49-11838. 32 p. illus. (part col.) music. 21 x 26 cm. c.1949. Cross Publications.
--The Round-up at Bar-C Ranch. 1st ed. Vegh, Steven, illus. LC 50-11222. (Illus.). 34 p. 29cm. (Cross Books for Children). 1950. Cross Publications.
--Tommy and the Indians. Vegh, Steven, illus. LC 50-11223. (Illus.). 35 p. 29cm. (Cross Books for Children). 1950. Cross Publications.
--A Trip to the Yard. Hartwell, Marjorie & Dixon, Rachel, illus. LC 52-7615. unpaged. illus. 31 cm. 1952. Cross Publications; Distributed by Garden City Books.
--West with the Mounties. McGeehan, Robert (1933-), illus. LC 51-6289. (Illus.). 30. 29cm. 1951. Cross Publications, Dist. by Garden City Books.
Cross, Gerald, jt. auth. see Greene, Laura.
Cross, Gilbert Broadhead
--A Hanging at Tyburn. LC 83-6331. p. cm. 1983. (ISBN 0-689-31007-2). Atheneum.
--The Mystery at Loon Lake. LC 83-15871. 128p. (Escapade Ser.). (gr. 4-6). 1985. (ISBN 0-689-31381-0). Atheneum.
Cross, Gillian Clare (1945-)
--Born of the Sun. Edwards, Mark, ed. LC 84-3740. 1984, c.1983. (ISBN 0-8234-0528-1). Holiday House.
--The Dark Behind the Curtain. Parkins, David, illus. (Illus.). 159p. 1984. (ISBN 0-19-271457-0). Oxford University Prees.
--The Demon Headmaster. Rees, Gary & Thomas, Mark, illus. (Illus.). 174p. (gr. 3-7). 1983. (ISBN 0-19-271460-0, Pub. by Oxford U Pr Childrens). Merrimack Pub Cir.
--On the Edge. LC 84-48741. 176p. 1985. (ISBN 0-8234-0559-1). Holiday. **Award: (ALA).**
--Revolt at Ratcliffe's Rags. LC 80-515836. 144 p. 23cm. 1980. (ISBN 0-19-271439-2). Oxford University Press.
--A Whisper of Lace. (Illus.). 144p. 1982. (ISBN 0-19-271447-3, Pub. by Oxford U Pr Childrens). Merrimack Pub Cir.
Cross, Helen Reeder, pseud., see Broadhead, Helen Cross.
Cross, Helen Reeder, pseud. (1913-)
--A Curiosity for the Curious. Broadhead, Helen Cross. Tomes, Margot Ladd (1917-), illus. LC 77-3400. p. cm. 1977. (ISBN 0-698-20423-9). Coward, McCann & Geoghegan.
--Isabella Mine. Broadhead, Helen Cross. Stock, Catherine, illus. LC 81-12346. p. cm. c.1982. (ISBN 0-688-00885-2). Lothrop, Lee & Shepard Books.
Cross, John Keir (1914-1967)
--The Angry Planet: An Authentic First-Hand Account of a Journey to Mars in the Spaceship Albatross. Jacques, Robin (1920-), illus. LC 46-7564. viii p., 3 l., 239 p. incl. front., illus. 21 cm. (gr. 5-7). 1946. (ISBN 0-698-20006-3). Coward-McCann Inc.
--Blackadder, a Tale of the Days of Nelson and Trafalgar. 1st American Ed. ed. McFarlane, Stephen (1920-), compiled by. Jacques, Robin (1920-), illus. LC 51-5442. (The Various Documents Collected and Edited by Stephen MacFarlane and the Whole Now Presented for the First time in Book Form.). 223 p. illus. 21 cm. 1951. Dutton.
--The Other Side of Green Hills. Jacques, Robin (1920-), illus. LC 47-30953. 5 l., 9-190 p. illus. 21 cm. 1947. Coward-McCann.
--The Red Journey Back: A First-Hand Account of the Second and Third Martian Expeditions, by the Space-Ships Albatross and Comet. Jacques, Robin (1920-), illus. LC 54-6320. 252 p. 21cm. 1954. Coward-McCann.
--The Stolen Sphere: An Adventure and a Mystery. LC 53-6067. 220 p. 21cm. 1953, c.1952. Dutton.
Cross, Marguerite S.
--Whitie. Salsbury, Donald, illus. (Illus.). (gr. 5 up). 1977. (ISBN 0-533-02704-7). Vantage.
Cross, Milton John (1897-1975)
--New Milton Cross' Complete Stories of the Great Operas. rev. ed. 1955. Doubleday.
Cross, Peter
--Trouble for Trumpets. Cross, Peter, illus. LC 83-43115. (Illus.). (gr. 3 up). 1985. (ISBN 0-394-86513-8, BYR). (ISBN 0-394-96513-2). Random.
Cross & Kingsley
--Half a Sixpence. Ohayon, adapted by. (Illus.). (gr. 7-12). 1972 (Starline). Schol Bk Serv.

Crossen, Kendall Foster see Chambers, M. E., pseud.

Crossen, Kendell Foster (1910-)
--Wanted: Dead Men: A New Milo March Adventure. Chambers, M E, pseud. LC 65-14448. 188p. 21cm. (Rinehart suspense novel). c.1965. Holt.
Crossen, Stacy Jo. & Covell, Natalie Anne
--Me Is How I Feel: Poems. DeLarrea, Victoria, illus. (gr. 1-4). 1970. Dutton.
--Me Is How I Feel: Poems. De Larrea, Victoria, illus. LC 76-119120. (Illus.). 26 p. 22cm. 1970. (ISBN 0-8415-2020-8). McCall Pub. Co.
Crossland, Newton, Mrs.
--Hildred. N.D. George Routledge & Sons.
--The Island of the Rainbow. N.D. George Routledge & Sons.
Crossland, T. W. H., ed.
--Golden Numbers: Simple Stories and Amusing Pictures. (Illus.). N.D. McClure, Phillips & Co.
Crossley, B. Alice, jt. ed. see Burack, Abraham Saul.
Crossley, B. Alice, jt. ed. see Durrell, Donald DeWitt.
Crossley-Holland, Kevin (1941-)
--The Callow Pit Coffer. Gordon, Margaret (1939-), illus. LC 69-13440. (Illus.). 48 p. 1969, c.1968. Seabury Press.
--The Fire-Brother. Troughton, Joanna Margaret (1947-), illus. LC 74-24764. (Illus.). 46 p. 22cm. (Clarion Book). 1975, c.1974. (ISBN 0-8164-3143-4). Seabury Press.
--The Green Children. Gordon, Margaret (1939-), illus. LC 68-14087. (Illus.). 1 v. (unpaged. 1968, c.1966. Seabury Press.
--Havelok the Dane. Wildsmith, Brian Lawrence (1930-), illus. LC 65-21276. (Illus.). 22cm. 178p. (Children's Illustrated Classics). (gr. 5 up). 1965. Dutton.
--King Horn. Keeping, Charles William James (1924-), illus. LC 66-5568. 214p. illus. 22cm. 1966, c.1965. Dutton.
--The Pedlar of Swaffham. Gordon, Margaret (1939-), illus. LC 70-129208. (Illus.). 47 p. 1971. Seabury Press.
--The Sea Stranger. Troughton, Joanna Margaret (1947-), illus. LC 73-7125. (Illus.). 46 p. 22cm. 1974, c.1973. (ISBN 0-8164-3107-8). Seabury Press.
--Winter's Tales for Children Three. Floyd, Gareth (1940-), illus. (Illus.). (gr. 4-7). 1968. St Martin.
Crossley-Holland, Kevin (1941-), ed.
--Beowulf. Keeping, Charles William James (1924-), illus. Crossley-Holland, Kevin, tr. (gr. 6-9). 1984. Merrimack.
--The Faber Book of Northern Folk-Tales. Howard, Alan (1922-), illus. LC 83-14039. p. cm. 1983. (ISBN 0-571-13166-2). Faber and Faber.
--The Faber Book of Northern Legends. Howard, Alan (1922-), illus. LC 83-14124. p. cm. 1983. (ISBN 0-571-13165-4). Faber & Faber.
--Storm & Other Old English Riddles. Thistlethwaite, Miles (1945-), illus. Crossley-Holland, Kevin, tr. LC 74-125147. (gr. 7 up). 1970. (ISBN 0-374-37270-5). FS&G.
Crossley-Holland, Kevin, jt. auth. see Paton Walsh, Jill.
Crossley-Holland, Kevin, jt. auth. see Thomas, Gwyn.
Crossley-Holland, Kevin, ed. see Yeats, William Butler.
Crossman, David A.
--The Secret King. (Children's Theatre Playscript Ser.). 1971. (ISBN 0-88020-069-3). Coach Hse.
Croswell, Volney
--How to Hide a Hippopotamus. Croswell, Volney, illus. LC 58-11422. 1958. Dodd, Mead & Co. **Award: (NYT).**
--How to Hide a Hippopotamus. Croswell, Volney, illus. (Illus.). (gr. k-2). 1958. (ISBN 0-8382-0352-3). Hale.
Crothers, Samuel McChord (1857-1927)
--The Children of Dickens. Smith, Jessie Willcox (1863-1935), illus. N.D. Charles Scribner's Sons'.
--Miss Muffet's Christmas Party. anniversary ed. Moore, Anne Carroll, frwd. by. LC 29-12617. x, 106, 1 p. incl. illus., plates. front. 20 cm. c.1929. Houghton Mifflin Company.
Crottet, Robert, jt. auth. see Mendez, Enrique.
Crouch, Archie R.
--In His Hands. 1952. Friendship Press.
--Not by Might. 1956. Friendship Press.
Crouch, Howard E.
--Brother Dutton of Molokai. LC 58-12228. 148p. 1958. Bruce Pub Co.
Crouch, Julia
--Three Successful Girls. LC 25-23753. vii, 382 p. 19 cm. 1871. Hurd and Houghton.

--The Whiz Kid & the Secret of Riverton. (gr. 6 up). 1975. (ISBN 0-685-59402-5). BJ Pub Group.
--The Whiz Kid & the Secret of Riverton. (Orig.). 1976. (ISBN 0-515-03920-9). BJ Pub Group.
Crume, Vic, adapted by.
--Napoleon & Samantha. (Orig.). 1976. (ISBN 0-515-04140-8). BJ Pub Group.
--Napoleon and Samantha. Walt Disney Productions & Rafill, Stewart LC 76-27632. 127 p. 19cm. c.1976. (ISBN 0-515-04140-8). Pyramid Books.
--The Parent Trap. 112p. (gr. 4-6). 1969. (ISBN 0-590-02961-4). Scholastic Inc.
--The Sky's the Limit. (Orig.). (gr. 7 up). 1975. (ISBN 0-515-03804-0). BJ Pub Group.
Crump, Bonnie Lela
--Bobby Squirrel's Secrets. Crump, Bonnie Lela, illus. LC 30-3222. 2 p. l., 3-92 p. col. front., illus. 21 cm. c.1929. R. G. Badger.
Crump, Fred H., Jr. (1931-)
--Marigold & the Dragon. Crump, Fred H., Jr. (1931-), illus. (Illus.). (gr. k-3). 1964. (ISBN 0-8114-7537-9). Steck-V.
--Missy and the Duke: Missy y el Duque. LC 77-2554. (Illus.). 67 p. 29cm. c.1977. (ISBN 0-87917-058-1). Blaine Ethridge-Books.
--Ringo the Raccoon. Crump, Fred H., Jr. (1931-), illus. (Illus.). 16p. (Orig.). (gr. k-6). 1982. (ISBN 0-8249-8991-0). Ideals.
--The Teeny Weeny Genie. Crump, Fred H., Jr. (1931-), illus. LC 66-7619. 48p. col. illus. 22 x 25cm. (gr. 1-2). 1966. (ISBN 0-8114-7564-6). Steck-Vaughn.
Crump, James Irving, jt. ed. see Boy's Life Magazine Editors.
Crump, James Irving, jt. ed. see Brown, Reynold.
Crump, James Irving (1887-1979)
--The Birdsong Boys. Baldridge, Cyrus LeRoy (1889-), illus. LC 55-6834. 136p. illus. 21cm. 1955. Friendship Press.
--The Boy Scout Fire Fighters. Wrenn, Charles L., illus. LC 17-22010. 249 p. incl. front. plates. 20 cm. (On verso of t.-p.: The boy scout life series). c.1917. Barse & Hopkins.
--The Boy's Book of Fisheries. 1933. Dodd, Mead & Co.
--Boys' Life Book of Scout Stories. 1953. Doubleday & Co.
--The Cloud Patrol. Heaslip, William, illus. LC 29-2814. 188 p. front., plates. 20 cm. c.1929. Grosset & Dunlap.
--Craig of the Cloud Patrol. Heaslip, William, illus. LC 31-1926. 4 p. l., 3-242 p. front., plates. 20 cm. c.1931. Grosset & Dunlap.
--Jack Straw in Mexico: How the Engineers Defended the Great Hydro-Electric Plant. Crump, Leslie (1894-), illus. LC 14-15370. 4 p. l., 231 p. front., plates. 20 cm. 1914. McBride, Nast & Company.
--Jack Straw, Lighthouse Builder. Crump, Leslie (1894-), illus. LC 15-21628. 7 p. l., 242 p. front., plates. 20 cm. 1915. R. M. McBride & Company.
--Mog, the Mound Builder. N.D. Grosset & Dunlap.
--Mog: The Mound Builder. Schuyler, Remington (1884-1955), illus. Shetrone, H. C. LC 31-29493. xi, 228 p. front., plates. 21 cm. 1931. Dodd, Mead and Company.
--Mog, the Mound Builder. Schuyler, Remington (1884-1955), illus. 1931. Dodd, Mead & Co.
--Og, Boy of Battle. N.D. Grosset & Dunlap.
--Og-Boy of Battle. Bull, Charles Livingston (1874-1932), illus. LC 25-19114. 5 p. l., 289 p. front., plates. 21 cm. 1925. Dodd, Mead & Company.
--Og of the Cave People. Murray, Jack, illus. LC 35-16480. ix, 232 p. incl. illus., plates. front. 20 cm. 1935. Dodd, Mead & Company.
--Og of the Cave People. Murray, Jack, illus. N.D. Grosset & Dunlap.
--Og-Son of Fire. Bull, Charles Livingston (1874-1932), illus. LC 22-18648. 5 p. l., 198 p. front., plates. 21 cm. 1922. Dodd, Mead and Company.
--Og, Son of Og. LC 65-168214. viii, 211p. 21cm. c.1965. Dodd.
--Out of the Woods. LC 41-5508. 5 p. l., 269 p. incl. illus., plates. 21 cm. c.1941. Dodd, Mead & Co.
--The Pilot of the Cloud Patrol. Heaslip, William, illus. LC 29-10215. 220 p. front., plates. 20 cm. (Buddy Books for Boys). c.1929. Grosset & Dunlap.
--Scouts to the Rescue: Fictionized from the New Universal Chapter Play Starring Jackie Cooper, Illustrated with Scenes from the Motion Picture. Crump, James Irving (1887-1979), illus. LC 39-9213. 128 p. illus. 17 cm. c.1939. Rand, McNally & Company.
--Teen-Age Boy Scout Stories. Gaschke, Ronald, illus. LC 48-9559. 256 p. illus. 21 cm. (Teen-age library). 1948. Lantern Press.
Crump, James Irving (1887-1979), ed.
--Teen-age Boy Scout Stories. (The Teen-age Library). N.D. Grosset & Dunlap.
Crump, Leslie (1894-)
--Pip: The Yellow Pup Sees the U. S. A. LC 27-20373. 55 p. col. illus. 21 cm. c.1927. Dodd, Mead & Company.
Crunk, Tony
--Two Towns & the People Who Lived in Them. Hamblin, Melissa, illus. LC 78-57037. (Illus.). 44 p. 19cm. 1978. Vantage Point Press.
Cruse, Amy, Mrs. (1870-), ed.
--The Young Folk's Book of Epic Heroes. LC 27-6232. xiii. 318 p. col. front., illus., plates (part col.) 23 cm. (Romance of knowledge series). 1927. Little, Brown, and Company.
--The Young Folk's Book of Myths. LC 26-8642. xiii, 265 p. col. front., illus., plates (part col.) 23 cm. 1926. Little, Brown, and Company.
--The Young Folk's Book of Myths. xiii, 265 p. col. front., illus., plates (part col.) 23 cm. (Romance of knowledge series). 1935. Little, Brown, and Company.
Crutcher, Chris
--Running Loose: A Novel. LC 82-20935. p. cm. (gr. 10up). 1983. (ISBN 0-688-02002-X). Greenwillow Books.
Cruz, Manuel (1931-) & Cruz, Ruth
--A Chicano Christmas Story: Un Cuento Navideno Chicano. Cruz, Manuel, illus. LC 80-6944. (Illus.). 48 p. 23cm. (ps-5). c.1980. (ISBN 0-86624-000-4). Bilingual Educational Services.
Cruz, Raymond (1933-)
--The Knight and the Squire. 1st ed. Palacios, Argentina, ed. LC 78-20091. (A Retelling of the Adventures of Don Quixote and Sancho Panza, Based on Cervantes' "Don Quixote De la Mancha".). (Illus.). 96 p. 27cm. c.1979. (ISBN 0-385-12433-3). (ISBN 0-385-12434-1). Doubleday.
Cruz, Ruth, jt. auth. see Cruz, Manuel.
Cruz, Victor Hernandez, jt. ed. see Kohl, Herbert R.
Crysler, Mildred G
--Adventures in Underground Fairylands: A Fantasy Tour of the Carlsbad Caverns. LC 54-119082. 199p. illus. 21cm. 1955. Exposition Press.
Ctvrtek, Vaclav (1911-1976)
--Little Chalk Man. 1st ed. Batherman, Muriel (1926-), illus. LC 74-113050. (Illus.). color ils. 96p. (gr. 2 up). 1970. (ISBN 0-394-90489-3). Knopf.
Cuchulain
--The Boys' Cuchulain: Heroic Legends of Ireland. Hull, Eleanor (1860-1935), ed. Reid, Stephen (1873-1934), illus. (Illus.). 22 cm. 279p. 1910. Thomas Y. Crowell Co.
Cuchulain see Page, Eileen.
Cuddy, Lucy Alsanson, Mrs. & McCauley, Mary Weaver, Mrs.
--Jack and Jill, Little Miss Muffet, Six Little Mice and Yellow Pussy. LC 25-11958. 137 p. incl. front., illus. (incl. music) 18 cm. c.1925. Rand, McNally & Company.
Cuffari, Richard, jt. auth. see Barth, Edna.
Cuffari, Richard (1925-1978)
--Families Are Like That!. Stories to Read to Yourself. Cuffari, Richard (1925-1978), illus. LC 73-21647. (Illus.). 142 p. 21cm. 1975. (ISBN 0-690-00004-9). (ISBN 0-690-00433-8). Crowell.

Culbertson, Mary Haeseler & Culbertson, Polly
--The Bear Facts. Fennell, Paul J., illus. LC 48-9653. 30 p. illus. (part col.) 21 cm. 1948. J. C. Winston Co.
--Peter PT. Byrne, Annette, illus. LC 44-7834. 18cm. 26p. 1944. David McKay Co.
Culbertson, Polly, jt. auth. see Culbertson, Mary Haeseler.
Cule, William Edward
--Mabel's Prince Wonderful: Or, A Trip to Story Land. Mein, Will G., illus. N.D. E. P. Dutton & Co.
Culin, Charlotte
--Cages of Glass, Flowers of Time. LC 79-14460. p. cm. 1979. (ISBN 0-87888-157-3). Bradbury Press.
Cullen, Alan
--The Golden Fleece: A Play for Young People. LC 72-184045. (Illus.). 74 p. 23cm. c.1971. Anchorage Press.
Cullen, Countee, jt. auth. see Cat, Christopher.
Cullen, Countee (1903-1946)
--The Lost Zoo: A Rhyme for the Young, but Not Too Young. Sebree, Charles, illus. LC 40-34870. 6 p. l., 72 p., 1 l. col. front., col. plates. 24 cm. c.1940. Harper & Brothers.
--My Lives and How I Lost Them. Bennett, Rainey (1907-), illus. (Illus.). 189 p. 18cm. 1973, c.1971. Curtis Books.
--My Lives and How I Lost Them. Bennett, Rainey (1907-), illus. LC 70-118963. (Done by Christopher Cat, in Collaboration with Countee Cullen). (Illus.). 224p. c.1971. Follett Pub. Co.
Cullen, James J & Homerus
--Ulysses and the Cyclops: A Tale from Homer's Odyssey. 1st ed. Vallejo, Kay, illus. LC 57-191725. unpaged. illus. 24cm. 1956. Microclassics Press.
Culler, Lucy Yeend, Mrs.
--Violet. LC 22-23244. 46 p. 2 port. 18 x 14 cm. 1889. C. Lutz, Printing and Binding.
Culliford, Pierre see Delporte, pseud.
Culliford, Pierre see Peyo, pseud.
Cullison, Irene Margaret, adapted by see Mother Goose.
Cullum, Albert
--The Geranium on the Window Sill Just Died, but Teacher You Went Right on. LC 75-141525. (Illus.). 60 p. (gr. kup). c.1971. (ISBN 0-8252-0063-6). (ISBN 0-8252-0063-6). Harlin Quist.
--Murphy, Molly, Max, and Me. Galeron, henri, illus. LC 76-21411. (Illus.). 24 p. 26cm. c.1976. (ISBN 0-8252-0141-1). (ISBN 0-8252-0140-3). H. Quist.
--You Think Just Because You're Big, You're Right. LC 76-21406. (Illus.). 60 p., 1 leaf of plates. c.1976. (ISBN 0-8252-0145-4). Harlin Quist.
Cullum, Albert, adapted by see Shakespeare, William.
Culp, Louanna McNary (1901-1965)
--Languri: Little Monkey of India. Borcio, Vesna, illus. LC 64-16315. 63 p. illus. 25 cm. 1964. Golden Gate Junior Books.
Culp, William Maurice
--And a Duck Waddles Too. Wilson, Eulalie Banks, illus. LC 39-17802. 96 p. incl. col. front. illus. (part col.) 21 cm. 1939. A Whitman & Co.
--Jeremiah. Moore, Charleton D., illus. LC 32-31038. 96 p. incl. col. front., col. illus. 20 cm. N.D. Harr Wagner Publishing Company.
--Jeremiah the Cat. Wilson, Eulalie Banks, illus. LC 39-17645. 96 p. incl. col. front., illus. (part col.) 20 cm. 1939. A. Whitman & Co.
Culpeper, Josephine, Mrs.
--Bolax, Imp or Angel--Which?. LC 7-20704. 4 p. l., 207 p. front., plates. 20 cm. 1907. J. Murphy Company.
Culpepper, Linda Decker
--The New Song. LC 68-22283. 191 p. 22cm. 1968. Review and Herald Pub. Association.
Culpepper, Ruth C.
--New Home, New Friend. LC 60-9537. 311 p. illus. 19cm. 1960. Convention Press.
Cultice, Virginia C
--Kivi Speaks. Marshall, Daniel, illus. LC 74-853. (Illus.). 32 p. 26cm. 1975. (ISBN 0-688-41586-5). (ISBN 0-688-41586-5). Lothrop, Lee & Shepard.
Cumberlege, Vera G (1908-)
--Shipwreck. Mikolaycak, Charles (1937-), illus. LC 73-93553. (Illus.). 30 p. 1974. (ISBN 0-695-80478-2). Follett Pub. Co.
Cuming, Edward William Dirom (1862-)
--Three Jovial Puppies. Shepherd, J. A., illus. (Illus.). N.D. Caldwell.
--Wonders in Monsterland. Shepherd, J. A., illus. LC 2-14068. (Illus.). xii, 257. 19cm. N.D. Longmans, Green and Co.
Cumings, Art
--There's a Monster Eating My House. Cumings, Art, illus. LC 80-25378. p. cm. 1981. (ISBN 0-8193-1053-0). (ISBN 0-8193-1054-9). Parent Magazine Press.
Cumings, Art, jt. auth. see Quin-Harkin, Janet.
Cumings, Arthur see Cumings, Art.
Cumings, Elizabeth
--A Happy Discipline. (The Girl Chums Ser.). N.D. A L. Burt Co.
--Josephine in War Time. LC 14-215840. 5 p. l., 252 p. front., plates. 21 cm. c.1914. The Pilgrim Press.
--Miss Matilda Archambeau Van Dorn. N.D. Lothrop Pub. Co.
Cummin, Jane, jt. auth. see Denison, Carol.
Cumming, Marian
--All About Marjory. 1st ed. Martin, David Stone (1913-), illus. LC 50-14656. 148 p. illus. 21 cm. 1950. Harcourt, Brace.
--Clan Texas. 1st ed. Burchard, Peter Duncan (1921-), illus. LC 55-7609. 117p. illus. 22cm. 1955. Harcourt, Brace.
--Just Like Nancy. Sweet, Edward, illus. LC 52-11963. (Illus.). 174 p. 21cm. 1953. Harcourt, Brace.
--A Valentine for Candy. Suba, Susanne (1913-), illus. LC 59-9269. 160p. N.D. Harcourt, Brace.
Cumming, Primrose Amy (1915-)
--Ben: The Story of a Cart-Horse. Burdekin, Harold, illus. LC 40-3040. 94, 1 p. illus. 28 cm. c.1940. E. P. Dutton & Company.
--The Chestnut Filly. Lloyd, Stanley, illus. LC 40-33629. 190 p. incl. front., plates. 24 cm. 1940. M. S. Mill Co., Inc.
--The Mystery Pony. Tulloch, Maurice, illus. LC 57-11520. 213p. illus. 22cm. (Criterion book for young people). 1957. Criterion Books.
--Mystery Pony. Tulloch, Maurice, illus. LC 57-11520. (Illus.). (gr. 7 up). 1957. (ISBN 0-87599-024-X). S G Phillips.
--Rachel of Romney. Langley, Nina Scott, illus. LC 41-13398. viii, 180 p. illus. 22 x 17 cm. 1940. C. Scribner's Sons.
--Silver Snaffles: A Story of a Shetland Pony. Lloyd, Stanley, illus. LC 38-152220. 160 p. incl. front., plates. 24 cm. 1937. M. S. Mill Co., Inc.
--The Wednesday Pony. Lloyd, Stanley, illus. LC 40-30721. 190 p. incl. front., plates. 24 cm. 1939. M. S. Mill Co., Inc.
Cumming, William D., jt. auth. see Love, Stewart A.
Cummings, Betty Sue (1918-)
--Hew Against the Grain. LC 76-25593. 174 p. 25cm. 1977. (ISBN 0-689-30551-6). Atheneum.
--Let a River Be. LC 77-22647. 195 p. 22cm. 1978. (ISBN 0-689-30635-0). Atheneum.
--Now, Ameriky. LC 79-11750. 175 p. 24cm. 1979. (ISBN 0-689-30705-5). Atheneum.
--Turtle. Dodge, Susan, illus. LC 80-24062. (Illus.). 42 p. 22cm. 1981. (ISBN 0-689-30805-1). Atheneum.
Cummings, Edward Estlin (1894-1962)
--Fairy Tales. Eaton, John (1942-), illus. LC 75-8515. (Illus.). 36 p. 23cm. (Voyager book ; AVB 96). 1975, c.1965. (ISBN 0-15-629895-3). Harcourt Brace Jovanovich.
--Fairy Tales. Eaton, John (1942-), illus. LC 65-18727. 36p. illus. (pt. col.) 26cm. N.D. Harcourt.
--Hist Whist & Other Poems for Children. Firmage, George James (1928-), ed. Calsada, David, illus. (Illus.). (Liveright Bk.). 1983. (ISBN 0-87140-640-3). Norton.
Cummings, M. J.
--Little Toss. (Illus.). N.D. D. Lothrop & Co.
--Uncle Anthony. (Illus.). N.D. D. Lothrop Co.
Cummings, M. J. & Bray, R. M.
--Fern Glen Ser. Containing "Fern Glen," "Little Toss," "Uncle Anthony," and "Petite", 4 vols. N.D. D. Lothrop & Co.
Cummings, Mabel H., jt. auth. see Foster, Mary H.
Cummings, Pat
--Jimmy Lee Did It. LC 84-21322. (Illus.). 26 p. 22cm. c.1985. (ISBN 0-688-04632-0). (ISBN 0-688-04633-9). Lothrop, Lee & Shepard Books.
Cummings, Ray (1887-1957)
--The Man Who Mastered Time. N.D. A. C. McClurg.
--Tarrano the Conqueror. N.D. A. C. McClurg & Co.
Cummings, Walter Thies (1933-)
--The Girl in the White Hat. Cummings, Walter Thies (1933-), illus. (gr. k-3). 1959. (ISBN 0-07-014913-5). (ISBN 0-07-014914-3). McGraw. **Award: (NYT).**
--The Kid. Cummings, Walter Thies (1933-), illus. LC 60-11954. 26cm. 32p. 1960. (ISBN 0-07-014908-9). McGraw-Hill Book Company.
--Miss Esta Maude's Secret. LC 60-16945. (Illus.). 32 p. 26cm. c.1961. Whittlesey House.
--Miss Esta Maude's Secret. Cummings, Walter Thies (1933-), illus. LC 60-16945. 32p. 1961. (ISBN 0-07-014906-2). McGraw-Hill Book Company.
--Wickford of Beacon Hill. LC 61-17673. 32 p. illus. 26cm. c.1962. McGraw-Hill.
Cummins, Hester V. (1862-)
--Short Stories for Children. LC 15-16820. (Mainly in Verse). 38p. 16 1/2cm. 1893. Parrott & Sons.
Cummins, Kundry see Karroff, K. K. de, pseud.
Cummins, Kundry
--Stiggles. Karroff, K. K. de, pseud. Colman, Margery, pseud., illus. McCarthy, Margery Sybil. LC 45-8002. (Illus.). 32 p. 25cm. 1945. Coward-McCann.
Cummins, Maria Susanna (1827-1866)
--The Lamplighter. (Illus.). (The Wellesley Series for Girls). 1915. A L Burt & Co.
--The Lamplighter, 1 of 110 vols. (The Manhattan Ser.). N.D. A. L. Burt's Pubs.
--The Lamplighter, No. 81. (The Cornell Ser). N.D. A. L. Burt's Pubs.
--The Lamplighter. N.D. Donohue, Henneberry & Co.
--The Lamplighter. (Illus.). N.D. George Routledge & Sons.
--The Lamplighter. (The Good Value Books). N.D. Grosset & Dunlap.
--The Lamplighter. (Illus.). (Famous Books for Girls Ser.: No. 12). 1905. Set. H M Caldwell Co.
--The Lamplighter. (Illus.). (Caldwell's Illustrated Library of Famous Books by Famous Authors). N.D. H. M. Caldwell Co.
--The Lamplighter. (Illus.). (Berkeley Lib.). N.D. H. M. Caldwell Co.
--The Lamplighter. N.D. Houghton Mifflin Co.
--The Lamplighter. (Illus.). (Home Ser.). N.D. Hurst and Company.
--The Lamplighter. (Illus.). (Almonte Library). N.D. Hurst and Company.
--The Lamplighter. (Illus.). (St. Nicholas Series for Girls). N.D. International Book Co.
--The Lamplighter. (Sears Juvenile Classics). N.D. J.H.Sears & Co.
--The Lamplighter. (Illus.). (The Waldorf Lib.). N.D. T. Y. Crowell & Co.

--Little Red Caboose. Burchard, Peter Duncan (1921-), illus. (gr. k-3). N.D. Wonder.
--Pea Patch Island. Himler, Ronald Norbert (1937-), illus. LC 74-13641. (Illus.). 30 p. 28cm. 1975. (ISBN 0-307-15693-1). Golden Press.
--Raggedy Ann & Andy: The Little Grey Kitten. Goldsborough, June (1923-), illus. (Illus.). 24p. (ps-3). 1975. (ISBN 0-307-60139-0, Golden Pr). Western Pub.
--The Tail of Gregory. Berwick, Jean Shepherd (1929-), illus. LC 64-10544. i v. (unpaged) col. illus. 28 cm. 1964. Golden Gate Junior Books.
Curren, Polly (1917-) & Chall, Jeanne, eds.
--Folk Tales of Scandinavia. (Illus.). (gr. 4-7). 1962. (ISBN 0-672-50280-1). Bobbs.
Currey, Edward Hamilton
--Ian Hardy Fighting the Moors. LC 17-20423. 2 p. l., 13-320 p. col. front., col. plates. 20 cm. N.D. J. B. Lippincott Company.
Currey, John E. B
--Australian Sea Stories. Angus, Don, illus. LC 73-173095. (Illus.). 117 p. 26cm. (Southern cross series). 1972. (ISBN 0-304-93916-1). Cassell Australia.
Curriculum Adaptation Network for Bilingual Bicultural Education
--A Boy Named Manuel. LC 76-5999. (Illus.). 69 p. 28cm. c.1976. (ISBN 0-8120-0676-3). Barron's Educational Series, Inc.
Currie, Frances Isabelle
--Gala Day Books. (Illus.). N.D. Publications of the Methodist Book Concern.
--The One White Turkey, etc, 1 of 4 vols. (Illus.). (Gala Day Bks). N.D. Set. Methodist Bk Concern.
--The Sedwick's New Year, etc, 1 of 4 vols. (Illus.). (Gala Day Bks). N.D. Set. Methodist Bk Concern.
--A Sham Battle & a Real Hero, etc, 1 of 4 vols. (Illus.). (Gala Day Bks). N.D. Set. Methodist Bk Concern.
--A Tiff with the Tiffins. (Illus.). N.D. Publications of the Methodist Book Concern.
--Tom Paxton's Celebration, etc, 1 of 4 vols. (Illus.). (Gala Day Bks). N.D. Set. Methodist Bk Concern.
Currie, Jessie, illus.
--Sunshine and Showers. (No. 214). N.D. Raphael Tuck & Sons.
Curro, Evelyn Malone (1907-)
--The Great Circus Parade: A Story Without Words. LC 63-8839. unpaged (chiefly illus.) 17 x 24 cm. (Little owl book). 1963. Holt, Rinehart and Winston.
Curry, Cathy Babcock, tr. see Havrevold, Finn.
Curry, Daniel (1809-1887), ed.
--Young People's Scrap-Book: Containing Choice Selections, Narratives, Descriptive Pieces, Natural History, Scenes and Places, Personal Sketches, and Illustrated Poems. With More Than Three Hundred ... Wood-Cuts. LC 15-12460. 302 p. front., illus. 29 cm. 1884. Walden and Stowe.
Curry, E. S.
--The House of Her Prison (Pub. by Society for Promoting Christian Knowledge). N.D. E. & J. B. Young & Co.
Curry, Jane Louise (1932-)
--The Bassumtyte Treasure. LC 77-14381. 129 p. 22cm. 1978. (ISBN 0-689-50100-5). Atheneum.
--Beneath the Hill. 1st ed. Gobbato, Imero (1923-), illus. LC 67-2450. (Illus.). 255 p. 21cm. 1967. Harcourt, Brace & World.
--The Birdstones. LC 77-3392. 204 p. 22cm. 1977. (ISBN 0-689-50089-0). Atheneum.
--The Change-Child. Floyd, Gareth (1940-), illus. LC 69-13772. (Illus.). 174 p. 22cm. 1969. Harcourt, Brace & World. **Award: (ALA).**
--The Daybreakers. Robinson, Charles (1931-), illus. LC 72-94332. (Illus.). 191 p. 21cm. 1970. Harcourt, Brace & World.
--Down from the Lonely Mountain: California Indian Tales. Arno, Enrico (1913-1981), illus. LC 65-14114. (Illus.). (gr. 4-6). 1965. (ISBN 0-15-224142-6). HarBraceJ.
--Ghost Lane. LC 78-73399. (Illus.). 158 p. 22cm. 1979. (ISBN 0-689-50129-3). Atheneum.
--The Great Flood Mystery. LC 85-1322. (Illus.). 171 p. 22cm. 1985. (ISBN 0-689-50306-7). Atheneum.
--The Ice Ghosts Mystery. LC 74-190552. 215 p. 23cm. 1972. (ISBN 0-689-20578-3). Atheneum.
--The Lost Farm. Robinson, Charles (1931-), illus. LC 73-85320. (Illus.). 137 p. 22cm. 1974. (ISBN 0-689-30427-7). Atheneum.
--The Magical Cupboard. Robinson, Charles (1931-), illus. LC 75-43892. (Illus.). 138 p. 21cm. 1976. Atheneum.
--Mindy's Mysterious Miniature. Robinson, Charles (1931-), illus. LC 72-124842. (Illus.). 157 p. 21cm. 1970. (ISBN 0-15-254290-6). Harcourt Brace Jovanovich.
--Over the Sea's Edge. Robinson, Charles (1931-), illus. LC 70-152693. (Illus.). vii, 182 p. 21cm. 1971. (ISBN 0-15-259010-2). Harcourt Brace Jovanovich.
--Parsley Sage, Rosemary, & Time. Robinson, Charles (1931-), illus. LC 74-18181. (Illus.). 108 p. 21cm. 1975. (ISBN 0-689-50019-X). Atheneum Publishers.
--Poor Tom's Ghost. LC 76-28468. 178 p. 22cm. 1977. (ISBN 0-689-50072-6). Atheneum.
--The Shadow Dancers. LC 83-3733. p. cm. 1983. (ISBN 0-689-50276-1). Atheneum.
--The Sleepers. Floyd, Gareth (1940-), illus. LC 68-13368. (Illus.). 255 p. 21cm. 1968. Harcourt, Brace & World.
--The Watchers. LC 75-8582. (Illus.). 235 p., 1 leaf of plates. 22cm. 1975. (ISBN 0-689-50030-0). Atheneum.
--The Wolves of Aam. LC 80-24370. (Illus.). viii, 192 p. 22cm. (Agro book). 1981. (ISBN 0-689-50173-0). Atheneum.
--Woofus, the Woolly Dog. Winship, Florence Sarah, illus. LC 44-8061. (Illus.). 30 p. 28cm. (A Fuzzy Wuzzy Bk.). 1944. Whitman Publishing Co.
Curry, Jennie George (1892-)
--Tumbleweed Tales. Montgomery, Mary Elizabeth, illus. LC 73-17249. (Illus.). vii, 133 p. 22cm. 1973. (ISBN 0-8111-0504-0). Naylor Co.
Curry, Nancy
--An Apple Is Red. Mandlin, Harvey, photos by. LC 67-31186. 1v. (chiefly col. illus.) 21x23 cm. (Bowmar early childhood ser.). c.1967. Bowmar Pub Corp.
--A Beautiful Day for a Picnic. Mandlin, Harvey, photos by. (Illus.). 32 p. (Bowmar early childhood series). 1968. Bowmar Pub. Corp.
--Do You Suppose Miss Riley Knows?. Mandlin, Harvey, photos by. LC 67-31327. 1v. (unpaged) col. illus. 21x 23cm. (Bowmar early childhood ser.). c.1967. Bowmar Pub. Corp.
--The Littlest House. Rupp, Jacques, illus. LC 68-17032. (Illus.). 1 v. (unpaged. (Bowmar early childhood series). 1968. Bowmar Pub. Corp.
--My Friend Is Mrs. Jones. Mandlin, Harvey, photos by. LC 67-26369. (Illus.). 1 v. (Bowmar early childhood series). 1967. Bowmar Pub. Corp.
Curry, Nancy, ed. see Clure, Beth & Rumsey, Helen.
Curry, Nancy, ed. see Crume, Marion W.
Curry, Nancy, ed. see Jaynes, Ruth M.
Curry, Nancy, ed. see Radlauer, Ruth Shaw (1926-) & Radlauer, Edward.
Curry, Peggy Simpson (1911-)
--A Shield of Clover. LC 78-125653. 120 p. 21cm. 1970. McKay.
Curry, Peter
--The Good Night Book. 12p. (Peter Curry Board Bks.). 1984. (ISBN 0-8431-1049-X). Price Stern.
--You & Me-Me. 12p. (Orig.). (Peter Curry Board Bks.). 1984. (ISBN 0-8431-1048-1). Price Stern.
Curry, W. Lawrence, ed.
--Songs & Hymns for Primary Children. (gr. 1-3). 1978. (ISBN 0-664-10117-8). Westminster.
Curtain, Mary
--Armond & the First Christmas. (Illus.). (Arch Bk.: No. 16). 1979. (ISBN 0-570-06129-6). Concordia.
Curtayne, Alice
--More Tales of Irish Saints. (Illus.). N.D. Sheed & Ward, Inc.
--Twenty Tales of Irish Saints. 1955. Sheed & Ward, Inc.
Curtin, Jeremiah, tr. see Sienkiewocz, Henryk.
Curtin, Jeremiah (1840-1906)
--Fairy Tales of Eastern Europe. N.D. Vanguard Press.
--Fairy Tales of Eastern Europe. Hood, George W., illus. LC 14-19873. 2 p. l., vii p., 3 l., 259 p. col. front., col. plates 22 cm. 1914. McBride, Nast & Company.
--Hero-Tales of Ireland. Day, Maurice (1892-), illus. 282p. 1921. Little,Brown & Co.
--Wonder Tales from Russia. Day, Maurice (1892-), illus. LC 21-188709. vi p., 1 l., 270 p. col. front., illus., col. plates. 20 cm. 1921. Little, Brown & Company.
Curtin, Thomas
--Boy in the Oil Belt. N.D. Pageant Press, Inc.
Curtis, Agnes
--Christmas Comedies. 168p. N.D. T. S. Denison.
--Good Plays for Patriotic Holidays: A Collection of One-Act Patriotic Plays for the Upper Grammar Grades and Junior and Senior High Schools. LC 32-692226. 149 p. 18 cm. c.1932. T. S. Denison & Company.
--Holiday Plays for Young People. 110 p. 19 cm. c.1929. The Willis N. Bugbee Sompany.
Curtis, Alice Bertha
--Children of the Prairie. Holberg, Richard A. (1889-1942), illus. LC 38-29553. 108 p. illus. 23 cm. c.1938. Thomas Y. Crowell Company.
--Winter on the Prairie. Paull, Grace A. (1898-), illus. LC 45-35073. 2 p. l., 164 p. illus. 23 cm. 1945. Thomas Y. Crowell Company.
Curtis, Alice Turner, Mrs. (1860-1958)
--Anne Nelson, a Little Maid of Province Town. Lyndall, Isabel, illus. LC 10-26173. 21cm. 263p. 1910. R. F. Fenno & Co.
--A Frontier Girl of Chesapeake Bay. Price, Harriet Longstreet (1891-), illus. LC 34-35888. 292 p. front., plates. 20 cm. c.1934. The Penn Publishing Company.
--A Frontier Girl of Massachusetts. Coleman, Ralph Pallen, illus. LC 30-211809. 4 p. l., 7-266 p. front., illus., plates. 20 cm. c.1930. The Penn Publishing Company.
--A Frontier Girl of New York. Snyder, Harold E., illus. LC 31-29187. 275 p. front., illus., plates. 20 cm. c.1931. The Penn Publishing Company.
--A Frontier Girl of Pennsylvania. Price, Harriet Longstreet (1891-), illus. LC 37-14418. 277 p. front., plates. 20 cm. c.1937. The Penn Publishing Company.
--A Frontier Girl of Virginia. Coleman, Ralph Pallen, illus. LC 29-21423. 268 p. front., illus., plates. 20 cm. c.1929. The Penn Publishing Company.
--Grandpa's Little Girls. Smith, Wuanita (1866-), illus. (Grandpa's Little Girls Books). N.D. Penn Publishing Co.
--Grandpa's Little Girls. Smith, Wuanita (1866-), illus. LC 7-23941. 201 p. front., 4 pl. 20 cm. (Sunbeam Ser. for Young People). 1907. The Penn Publishing Company.
--Grandpa's Little Girls and Miss Abitha. Smith, Wuanita (1866-), illus. LC 11-139821. 206 p. front., plates. 20 cm. 1911. The Penn Publishing Company.
--Grandpa's Little Girls and their Friends. Smith, Wuanita (1866-), illus. LC 9-17451. 190p. (The Grandpa's Little Girls Books). 1909. Penn Publishing Co.
--Grandpa's Little Girls at School. Smith, Wuanita (1866-), illus. (The Grandpa's Little Girls Books). N.D. Penn Publishing Co.
--Grandpa's Little Girls at School. Smith, Wuanita (1866-), illus. LC 8-15325. 195 p. front., 4 pl. 20 cm. (Sunbeam Ser. for Young People). 1908. The Penn Publishing Company.
--Grandpa's Little Girls Grown Up. Smith, Wuanita (1866-), illus. (The Grandpa's Little Girls Books). N.D. Penn Publishing Co.
--Grandpa's Little Girls Grown up. Smith, Wuanita (1866-), illus. LC 12-12486. 204 p. front., plates. 20 cm. c.1912. The Penn Publishing Company.
--Grandpa's Little Girls' Houseboat Party. Smith, Wuanita (1866-), illus. (The Grandpa's Little Girls Books). N.D. Penn Publishing Co.
--The Little Heroine at School. Kennedy, J. W. Ferguson, illus. LC 9-18370. vii, 9-323 p. front., 5 pl. 20 cm. (Little heroine series). 1909. Lothrop, Lee & Shepard Co.
--A Little Heroine of Illinois: A Young Girl's Patriotism and Daring. Huybers, John, illus. LC 8-20020. vii, 258 p. front., 7 pl. 19 cm. (Little heroine series). 1908. Lothrop, Lee & Shepard Co.
--A Little Maid of Boston. James, Sandra, illus. LC 54-10331. 224p. illus. 29cm. 1954. Knopf.
--A Little Maid of Boston. Price, Harriet Longstreet (1891-), illus. LC 33-354862. 224 p. front., plates. 20 cm. c.1933. The Penn Publishing Company.
--A Little Maid of Bunker Hill. James, Sandra, illus. LC 52-8165. 239 p. illus. 20 cm. 1952. Knopf.
--A Little Maid of Bunker Hill. Smith, Wuanita (1866-), illus. LC 16-189105. 239 p. front., plates. 20 cm. 1916. The Penn Publishing Company.
--A Little Maid of Fort Pitt. James, Sandra, illus. LC 53-51000. 243p. illus. 20cm. 1953. Knopf.
--A Little Maid of Fort Pitt. Price, Harriet Longstreet (1891-), illus. LC 31-30599. 4 p. l., 7-243 p. front., plates. 20 cm. c.1931. The Penn Publishing Company.
--A Little Maid of Lexington. James, Sandra, illus. LC 55-7085. 220p. illus. 20cm. 1955. Knopf.
--A Little Maid of Lexington. Price, Harriet Longstreet (1891-), illus. LC 32-32567. 220 p. front., plates. 20 cm. c.1935. The Penn Publishing Company.
--A Little Maid of Maryland. James, Sandra, illus. LC 51-13022. 217 p. illus. 20 cm. 1952. Knopf.
--A Little Maid of Maryland. Little, Nat, illus. LC 23-13944. 217 p. front., plates. 20 cm. 1923. The Penn Publishing Company.
--A Little Maid of Massachusetts Colony. James, Sandra, illus. LC 51-11077. 224 p. illus. 20 cm. 1951. Knopf.
--A Little Maid of Massachusetts Colony. Smith, Wuanita (1866-), illus. LC 14-111437. 226 p. front., plates. 20 cm. 1914. The Penn Publishing Company.
--A Little Maid of Mohawk Valley. James, Sandra, illus. LC 52-8166. 203 p. illus. 20 cm. 1952. Knopf.
--A Little Maid of Mohawk Valley. Norcross, Grace, illus. LC 24-23083. 203 p. front., 20 cm. 1924. The Penn Publishing Company.
--A Little Maid of Mohawk Valley. Norcross, Grace, illus. LC 25-212691. 219 p. front., plates. 20 cm. 1925. The Penn Publishing Company.
--A Little Maid of Monmouth. James, Sandra, illus. LC 53-93155. 219p. illus. 20cm. 1953. Knopf.
--A Little Maid of Monmouth. Norcross, Grace & Smith, Wuanita (1866-), illus. LC 25-21269. (The Little Maid's Historical Stories). N.D. Penn.
--A Little Maid of Nantucket. James, Sandra, illus. LC 50-5737. 208 p. col. illus. 20 cm. 1950. Knopf.
--A Little Maid of Nantucket. Norcross, Grace, illus. LC 26-146731. 208 p. front., plates. 19 cm. 1926. The Penn Publishing Company.
--A Little Maid of Narragansett Bay. James, Sandra, illus. LC 54-53047. 231p. illus. 20cm. 1954. Knopf.
--A Little Maid of Narragansett Bay. Smith, Wuanita (1866-), illus. LC 15-158671. 231 p. front., plates. 20 cm. 1915. The Penn Publishing Company.
--A Little Maid of New Hampshire. James, Sandra, illus. LC 54-103334. 224p. illus. 20cm. 1954. Knopf.
--A Little Maid of New Hampshire. Price, Harriet Longstreet (1891-), illus. 224 p. front., plates. 20 cm. 1928. The Penn Publishing Company.
--A Little Maid of New Orleans. James, Sandra, illus. LC 49-804292. 224 p. col. illus. 20 cm. 1949. A. A. Knopf.
--A Little Maid of New Orleans. Price, Harriet Longstreet (1891-), illus. LC 30-30774. 224 p. front., plates. 20 cm. c.1930. The Penn Publishing Company.
--A Little Maid of Newport. 1st Borzoi ed. James, Sandra, illus. LC 55-8957. 224p. illus. 20cm. 1955. Knopf.
--A Little Maid of Newport. Smith, Wuanita (1866-) & Price, Hattie Longstreet, illus. LC 35-24895. 224 p. front., plates. 20 cm. c.1935. The Penn Publishing Company.
--A Little Maid of Old Connecticut. LC 18-189552. 213 p. front., plates. 20 cm. 1918. The Penn Publishing Company.
--A Little Maid of Old Connecticut. James, Sandra, illus. LC 53-5101. 213p. illus. 20cm. 1953. Knopf.
--A Little Maid of Old Maine. James, Sandra, illus. LC 53-9316. 214p. illus. 20cm. 1953. Knopf.
--A Little Maid of Old Maine. Pilsbry, Elizabeth, illus. LC 20-171725. 214 p. front., plates. 20 cm. 1920. The Penn Publishing Company.
--A Little Maid of Old New York. James, Sandra, illus. LC 51-11076. 224 p. illus. 20 cm. 1951. Knopf.
--A Little Maid of Old New York. Pilsbry, Elizabeth, illus. LC 21-211414. 224 p. front., plates. 20 cm. 1921. The Penn Publishing Company.
--A Little Maid of Old Philadelphia. James, Sandra, illus. LC 55-7086. 210p. illus. 20cm. 1955. Knopf.
--A Little Maid of Old Philadelphia. Smith, Wuanita (1866-) & Cooke, Edna, illus. LC 19-13842. (The Little Maid's Historical Stories). N.D. Penn.
--A Little Maid of Province Town. James, Sandra, illus. LC 54-103328. 212p. illus. 20cm. 1954. Knopf.
--A Little Maid of Province Town. Smith, Wuanita (1866-), illus. (The Little Maids' Historical Ser.). N.D. Penn Publishing LCo.
--A Little Maid of Province Town. Smith, Wuanita (1866-), illus. LC 13-186031. 212 p. front., plates. 20 cm. 1913. The Penn Publishing Company.
--A Little Maid of Quebec. 1st Borzoi ed. James, Sandra, illus. LC 55-895857. 224p. illus. 20cm. 1955. Knopf.
--A Little Maid of Quebec. Price, Harriet Longstreet (1891-), illus. LC 36-221758. 224 p. front. 20 cm. c.1936. The Penn Publishing Company.
--A Little Maid of South Carolina. James, Sandra, illus. LC 51-13023. 223 p. illus. 20 cm. 1952. Knopf.
--A Little Maid of South Carolina. Price, Harriet Longstreet (1891-), illus. LC 29-21425. 223 p. front., plates. 20 cm. c.1929. The Penn Publishing Company.
--A Little Maid of Ticonderoga. James, Sandra, illus. LC 54-5305. 216p. illus. 20cm. 1954. Knopf.
--A Little Maid of Ticonderoga. Smith, Wuanita (1866-), illus. LC 17-20858. 216 p. front., plates. 20 cm. 1917. The Penn Publishing Company.
--A Little Maid of Valley Forge. 1st Borzoi ed. James, Sandra, illus. LC 51-2641. 224 p. col. illus. 20 cm. 1951. Knopf.
--A Little Maid of Valley Forge. Price, Harriet Longstreet (1891-), illus. LC 37-34170. 224 p. front., plates. 20 cm. c.1937. The Penn Publishing Company.
--A Little Maid of Vermont. James, Sandra, illus. LC 48-6258. 224 p. col. illus. 20 cm. 1948. A. A. Knopf.
--A Little Maid of Vermont. Norcross, Grace, illus. LC 27-148011. 224 p. front., plates. 20 cm. 1927. The Penn Publishing Company.

Cutler, May Ebbitt (1923-)
--I Once Knew an Indian Woman. Johnson, Bruce, illus. (Illus.). 80p. (gr. 7-12). 1973. (ISBN 0-395-16044-8). HM.

Cutler, Uriel Waldo (1854-), ed. see Malory, Thomas, Sir.

Cutler, Uriel Waldo (1854-), ed.
--Stories of King Arthur. (Illus.). (Children's Favorite Classics). 1915. Thomas Y. Crowell.

Cutt, Margaret Nancy & Cutt, William Towrie (1898-)
--Hogboon of Hell & Other Strange Orkney Tales. Kennedy, Richard (1910-), illus. (Illus.). (gr. 2-7). 1979. (ISBN 0-233-97020-7). Andre Deutsch.

Cutt, William Towrie, jt. auth. see Cutt, Margaret Nancy.

Cutt, William Towrie (1898-)
--Seven for the Sea. LC 73-93556. (Illus.). 96 p. 23cm. 1974, c.1972. (ISBN 0-695-80480-4). (ISBN 0-695-40480-6). Follett.

Cutting, Dorothy L.
--Concerning Christopher; Fun With a Parrot. 1st ed. LC 54-12468. 42 p. 21cm. 1955. Exposition Press.

Cutting, Mary Stewart
--The Blossoming Rod. (The Christmas Ser.). N.D. A. B. Burt Company.
--Heart of Lynn. Stowe, Helen, illus. N.D. J.B. Lippincott.

Cutts, David, adapted by see Poe, Edgar Allan.

Cutts, David E., adapted by.
--Edgar Allan Poe's The Cask of Amontillado. Poe, Edgar Allan (1809-1849) LC 81-15997. (Illus.). 31 p. 24cm. c.1982. (ISBN 0-89375-622-9). (ISBN 0-89375-623-7). Troll Associates.
--The Gingerbread Boy. Goodman, Joan E, illus. LC 78-18069. (Illus.). 32 p. 25cm. c.1979. (ISBN 0-89375-122-7). Troll Associates.
--The House That Jack Built. Silverstein, Donald (1932-), illus. LC 80-106227. (Illus.). 32 p. 24cm. c.1979. (ISBN 0-89375-127-8). Troll Associates.

Cutts, David E., adapted by see Poe, Edgar Allan.

Cutts, E. L.
--Nuthurst. N.D. E. & J. B. Young & Co.

Cuyler, Margery
--Sir William & the Pumpkin Monster. Winborn, Marsha, illus. LC 84-610. (Illus.). (gr. 5-8). 1984. (ISBN 0-03-064032-6). (ISBN 0-03-064032-6). HR&W.
--The Trouble with Soap. LC 81-12636. 104 p. 22cm. c.1982. Dutton.

Cuyler, T. L.
--Cedar Christian, 1 of 103 vols. (The Pearl Library: No. 14). 1900. Set. Hurst & Co.
--Gold Dust, 1 of 50 vols. (Heart Life Classics). N.D. American Tract Society.

Czaja, Helen Manley
--The Beautiful Cow. Czaja, Micheal (1911-), illus. LC 44-6037. (Illus.). 55 p. 22 x 26cm. 1944. H. Holt and Company.

Czarnomski, Francis Bauer, tr. see Ossendowski, Ferdynand Antoni.

Czebatul, Anthony A.
--The Legend of Protogonos. 1984. (ISBN 0-533-06148-2). Vantage.

Czege, Albert Wass De see Wass De Czege, Elizabeth M. & Wass De Czege, Albert.

Czege, Elizabeth M. Wass De see Wass De Czege, Elizabeth M. & Wass De Czege, Albert.

Dabcovich, Lydia
--Follow the River. McLeod, Emilie Warren (1926-1982), ed. LC 80-10173. (Illus.). 32 p. 23cm. (Unicorn book). c.1980. (ISBN 0-525-30015-5). Dutton.
--Mrs. Huggins and Her Hen Hannah. Dabcovich, Lydia, illus. LC 85-4406. (Illus.). 24 p. c.1985. (ISBN 0-525-44203-0). Dutton.
--Sleepy Bear. LC 81-9729. (Illus.). 32 p. c.1982. (ISBN 0-525-39465-6). Dutton.

Dabrowska, Beata, tr. see Probst, Pierre.

Dacey, Philip (1939-)
--The Boy Under the Bed. LC 80-8858. (Poetry & Fiction Ser.). 1981. (ISBN 0-8018-2601-2). (ISBN 0-8018-2602-0). Johns Hopkins.

D'Achille, Gino, illus.
--King Solomon's Mines. LC 82-3843. (Illus.). 96p. (Step-Up Adventures Ser.: No. 5). (gr. 2-5). 1982. (ISBN 0-394-95275-8). (ISBN 0-394-85275-3). Random.

Dacquino, V. T
--Kiss the Candy Days Good-Bye. LC 82-70324. 129 p. 22cm. c.1982. (ISBN 0-440-04546-0). Delacorte Press.

Dada, Olubandele (1941-)
--West African Folk Tales. LC 73-127358. (Illus.). 67 p. 22cm. 1970. Dorrance.

D'Addio, Janie & Bach, Othello
--Monicas Hannukah House. McElroy, Darlene, illus. (Illus.). 64p. (gr. 2-8). 1983. (ISBN 0-914759-01-9). Preferred Pr.

Daddona, Mark
--Hoe, Hoe, Hoe: Watch My Garden Grow. Dadonna, Mark, illus. (Illus.). 1st U.S. edition. 1980. (ISBN 0-201-03079-9). (ISBN 0-201-03004-7). A-W.

Daem, Mary, pseud., see Daem, Thelma Mary Bannerman.

Daem, Mary, pseud. (1914-)
--The Dragon with a Thousand Wrinkles. Daem, Thelma Mary Bannerman. Brown, Marc Tolon (1946-), illus. LC 76-125134. (Illus.). 15 p. (Magic circle book). 1971. Ginn.
--The House on the Top of the Hill. Daem, Thelma Mary Bannerman. Leake, Donald, illus. LC 71-153909. (Illus.). 22 p. 24cm. (Magic circle book). 1971, c.1972. (ISBN 0-663-22978-2). Ginn.
--Lucky Lure at Arrow Point. Daem, Thelma Mary Bannerman. Whittam, Geoffrey William (1916-), illus. 1959. Abelard-Schuman.
--The Whistling Mountain. Daem, Thelma Mary Bannerman. Whittam, Geoffrey William (1916-), illus. 1960. Abelard-Schuman.

Daem, Thelma Mary Bannerman see Daem, Mary, pseud.

Daenecke, Eric (1914-)
--Tales of Mullah Nasir-ud-Din: Persian Wit, Wisdom and Folly. 1st ed. LC 60-4088. 22cm. 1960. Exposition Press.

Da Free, John
--I Am Happiness: A Rendering for Children of the Spiritual Adventure. Bodha, Daji & Closser, Lynne, eds. (Illus., Orig.). (gr. 2 up). 1982. (ISBN 0-913922-68-4). Dawn Horse Pr.

Daggett, Dorothy
--Please Read Me a Story. (Illus.). 40p. (ps). 1975. Dorrance.

Daggett, Hon R., ed.
--The Legends and Myths of Hawaii: The Fables and Folklore of a Strange People. Daggett, Hon R., illus. 1972. (ISBN 0-8048-1032-X). Charles E. Tuttle Co.

Dagliesh, Alice (1893-1979) & Rhys, Ernest (1859-), eds.
--The Land of Nursery Rhyme. Folkard, Charles James (1878-1963), illus. LC 32-35027. xvi, 240 p. col. front., illus., col. plates. 23 cm. 1932. E. P. Dutton & Co.

Dahl, Borghild Margarethe (1890-)
--The Cloud Shoes. 1st Ed ed. Helweg, Hans H. (1917-), illus. LC 57-8979. 60p. illus. 23cm. (gr. 2-6). 1957. (ISBN 0-525-28018-9). Dutton.
--The Daughter. Helweg, Hans H. (1917-), illus. LC 56-8290. (Illus.). 190 p. 21cm. 1956. Dutton.
--Homecoming. (gr. 9 up). 1960. (ISBN 0-525-32133-0). Dutton.
--I Wanted to See. 1967. MacMillan Publishing Company.
--Karen. LC 58-3056. 313 p. 21cm. 1958, c.1947. Dutton.
--Karen. LC 47-5201. 4 l., 3-313 p. 21 cm. 1947. Random House.
--A Minnetonka Summer. Lambo, Donald W. (1906-1966), illus. LC 60-11863. (Illus.). 21cm. 125p. 1960. E. P. Dutton & Co.
--Rikk of the Rendal Clan. Ohlsson, Ib (1935-), illus. LC 68-16858. (Illus.). 63 p. 24cm. 1968. Dutton.
--Stowaway to America. LC 59-5817. 21cm. 192p. (gr. 8 up). 1959. Dutton.
--This Precious Year. LC 64-10685. 159 p. 21cm. 1964. Dutton.
--Under This Roof. LC 61-12451. 22cm. 190p. (gr. 7 up). 1961. Dutton.

Dahl, Mary Bartlett
--Free Souls. LC 72-86296. (Illus.). 133 p. 22cm. 1969. Houghton Mifflin.

Dahl, Roald, jt. auth. see Disney, Walt, Productions.

Dahl, Roald (1916-)
--The BFG. Blake, Quentin (1932-), illus. LC 82-15548. p. cm. 1982. (ISBN 0-374-30469-6). Farrar, Straus, Giroux.
--The BFG. Blake, Quentin (1932-), illus. LC 85-566. (Illus.). 207 p. 20cm. 1985, c.1982. (ISBN 0-14-031597-7). Viking Penguin.
--Boy: Tales of Childhood. LC 84-48462. (Illus.). 176p. N.D. (ISBN 0-374-37374-4). (ISBN 0-374-37375-2). FS&G.
--Charlie and the Chocolate Factory. Schindelman, Joseph (1923-), illus. LC 72-22407. (Junior Deluxe Editions). (Illus.). 22cm. 178p. 1972, c.1964. Knopf.
--Charlie & the Chocolate Factory: A Play. George, Richard Robert (1943-), adapted by. 96p. (gr. 3-7). 1983. (ISBN 0-14-031125-4, Puffin). Penguin.
--Charlie and the Great Glass Elevator: The Further Adventures of Charlie Bucket and Willy Wonka, Chocolate-Maker Extraordinary. Schindelman, Joseph (1923-), illus. LC 72-2434. (Illus.). 161 p. 25cm. 1972. (ISBN 0-394-82472-5). (ISBN 0-394-82472-5). Knopf.
--Danny, the Champion of the World. Bennett, Jill (1947-), illus. LC 75-8971. (Illus.). 196 p. 24cm. (gr. 3 up). 1975. (ISBN 0-394-83103-9). (ISBN 0-394-93103-3). Knopf : Distributed by Random House.
--Dirty Beasts. Blake, Quentin (1932-), illus. LC 85-594. p. cm. (Picture puffins). 1985, c.1983. (ISBN 0-14-050435-4). Puffin Books.
--Dirty Beasts. Fawcett, Rosemary, illus. (Illus.). 32p. (gr. 1 up). 1984. (ISBN 0-374-31790-9). FS&G.
--The Enormous Crocodile. Blake, Quentin (1932-), illus. LC 77-5081. p. cm. 1977. (ISBN 0-394-83594-8). (ISBN 0-394-93594-2). Knopf : Distributed by Random House.
--Fantastic Mr. Fox. Chaffin, Donald, illus. LC 74-118704. (Illus.). 62 p. 24cm. 1970. (ISBN 0-394-90497-4). Knopf.
--George's Marvelous Medicine. Blake, Quentin (1932-), illus. LC 81-11811. (Illus.). 88 p. 24cm. 1982, c.1981. (ISBN 0-394-84600-1). (ISBN 0-394-94600-6). Knopf : Distributed by Random House.
--James & the Giant Peach. Burkert, Nancy Ekholm (1933-), illus. (Illus.). (gr. 3 up). 1961. (ISBN 0-394-81282-4). (ISBN 0-394-91282-9). Knopf.
--Kiss Kiss. 1960. Alfred A Knopf : distributed by Borzoi Books.
--Magic Finger. Du Bois, William Sherman Pene (1916-), illus. LC 66-18657. (Illus.). 40p. (gr. 1-5). 1966. (ISBN 0-06-021381-7, HarpJ). (ISBN 0-06-021382-5). Har-Row.
--The Magic Finger. Du Bois, William Sherman Pene (1916-), illus. LC 66-18657. (Illus.). 48p. (A Trophy Picture Bk.). (gr. 3-6). 1983. (ISBN 0-06-443045-6, Trophy). Har-Row.
--Roald Dahl's James and the Giant Peach: A Play. George, Richard, adapted by. LC 83-206783. 1983. (ISBN 0-14-031464-4). Penguin Books.
--Roald Dahl's Revolting Rhymes. Blake, Quentin (1932-), illus. LC 82-15263. p. cm. 1982. (ISBN 0-394-85422-5). Knopf.
--Someone Like You. 1953. Alfred A Knopf : distributed by Borzoi Books.
--The Twits. Blake, Quentin (1932-), illus. LC 80-18410. (Illus.). 76 p. 24cm. 1981, c.1980. (ISBN 0-394-84599-4). Knopf ; Distributed by Random House.
--The Witches. Blake, Quentin (1932-), illus. LC 83-14195. (Illus.). 160p. (gr. 6 up). 1983. (ISBN 0-374-38457-6). (ISBN 0-374-38458-4). FS&G. **Award: (ALA).**
--The Witches. Blake, Quentin (1932-), illus. LC 85-519. (Illus.). 206 p. 20cm. 1985, c.1983. (ISBN 0-14-031730-9). Puffin Books.
--The Wonderful Story of Henry Sugar & Six More. LC 77-5354. (gr. 7 up). 1977. (ISBN 0-394-83604-9). (ISBN 0-394-93604-3). Knopf.

Dahl, Roaldhard Robert (1916-), ed. see George, Richard Robert.

Dahlby, Edith L.
--My Own Book of Secrets. Hambleton, Joanne, illus. 1977. (ISBN 0-682-48776-7). Exposition.

Dahlin, Doris (1952-)
--The Sit-in Game. LC 72-9956. 96 p. 22cm. 1974, c.1972. (ISBN 0-670-64730-6). Viking Press.

Dahlstedt, Marden (1921-)
--Shadow of the Lighthouse. Brown, Judith Gwyn (1933-), illus. LC 73-88537. (Illus.). 159 p. 21cm. 1974. (ISBN 0-698-20291-0). (ISBN 0-698-20291-0). Coward, McCann & Geoghegan.
--The Stopping Place. Davis, Allen, illus. LC 75-43616. (Illus.). 160 p. 21cm. c.1976. (ISBN 0-399-20496-2). Putnam.
--The Terrible Wave. Robinson, Charles (1931-), illus. LC 72-76687. (Illus.). 125 p. 22cm. 1972. (ISBN 0-698-20188-4). (ISBN 0-698-20188-4). Coward, McCann & Geoghegan.

Dahlstrom, Tore
--Bread for the Giant. Muller, Gerda Maria, illus. LC 66-4002. 24 p. col. illus. 19 x 22 cm. (A Pere Caster Book). 1966. Golden Press.

Dailes, Ida, tr. see Zur Muhlen, Herminia.

Dailey, Alphabelle
--Novel Readings for Children. 96p. N.D. T. S. Denison & Co Inc.

Dailey, Alphabelle, et al.
--The Juvenile Recitation Book. 111p. N.D. T. S. Denison.

Dailey, Virginia
--The Honor of Lawrence House. LC 59-5559. 22cm. 181p. 1959. Duell, Sloan and Pearce Pub.
--The Keys to Lawrence House. LC 60-5447. 21cm. 181p. 1960. Duell, Sloan and Pearce Pub.
--Lassie of the Red Shield. LC 63-3779. 119 p. 21 cm. 1963. Zondervan Pub. House.

Daily, Dorothy Tinsley
--The Christmas Party. 1955. Friendship Press.

Daily Planet Staff
--The Daily Planet: Special Superman II Movie Edition. (Illus.). 40p. (gr. 3-7). 1981. (ISBN 0-394-85009-2). Random.

Daines, Lyman Luther, jt. auth. see Jacobsen, Virginia Budd, Mrs.

Dakkar, Prince
--The Trotting Twins. (Illus.). (gr. 5-7). N.D. Vantage.

Dale, Darley see Steele, Francesca Maria, pseud.

Dale, Darley
--The Black Donkey: Or, The Guernsey Boys. Steele, Francesca Maria, pseud. (Illus.). N.D. E J B Young.
--Cissy's Troubles. Steele, Francesca Maria, pseud. N.D. Thomas Whittaker.
--Little Bricks. Steele, Francesca Maria, pseud. N.D. Thomas Whittaker.

Dale, Handelsman, jt. auth. see Dale, R. B.

Dale, Jean N., ed.
--The Monkey's Paw. (Illus.). (Reading & Exercise Ser.). (gr. k-6). 1974. (ISBN 0-19-433623-9). Oxford U Pr.
--Tale from Tangier. (Illus.). (Reading & Exercise Ser.). (gr. k-6). 1974. (ISBN 0-19-433624-7). Oxford U Pr.

Dale, Jean N. & Sheeler, Willard D., eds.
--The Angry Sea. (Illus.). (Reading & Exercise Ser.). (gr. k-6). 1973. (ISBN 0-19-433620-4). Oxford U Pr.
--The Quite Man. (Reading & Exercise Ser.). (gr. k-6). 1974. (ISBN 0-19-433622-0). Oxford U Pr.
--The Whistler. (Reading & Exercise Ser.). (gr. k-6). 1973. (ISBN 0-19-433619-0). Oxford U Pr.
--Winds of Virtue. (Reading & Exercise Ser.). (gr. k-6). 1974. (ISBN 0-19-433621-2). Oxford U Pr.

Dale, Mamie Mary Elizabeth
--Willie Selville's Mission. Dale, W. T., ed. LC 1-17001. 186p. 1901. Mamie Dale Book and Tract Publishing Fund.

Dale, Margaret Jessy Miller see Miller, Margaret J., pseud.

Dale, Nathan Haskell
--The White Duckling and Other Stories. N.D. Thomas Y. Crowell Company.

Dale, Norman, pseud., see Denny, Norman George.

Dale, Norman, pseud. (1901-), tr. see Guillot, Rene.

Dale, Norman, tr. see Lobe, Mira.

Dale, Norman, pseud. (1901-)
--Casket & the Sword. Denny, Norman George. Docktor, Irv (1918-), illus. (Illus.). (gr. 3-7). 1956. (ISBN 0-06-021385-X). Har-Row.
--The Secret Motorcar. Denny, Norman George. 1954. E M Hale.
--The Six Stone Faces. Denny, Norman George. Dale, Norman, pseud. John, Diana, illus. LC 60-13111. (Illus.). 1960. A. S. Barnes & Co.

Dale, R. B. & Dale, Handelsman
--Benjamin & Sylvester. N.D. McGraw-Hill.

Dale, Ralph Alan
--When I Met Robin. Battaglia, Aurelius (1910-), illus. (Illus.). 31 p. 29cm. (Carousel book). 1968. L. W. Singer Co.

Dale, Ruth Bluestone
--Benjamin-and Sylvester Also. Handelsman, J. B., illus. LC 60-12412. (Illus.). 19 x 26cm. 32p. 1960. Whittlesey House.
--Do You Know a Cat?. Chen, Tony (1929-), illus. LC 68-6719. (Illus.). 31 p. 29cm. (Carousel book). 1968. L. W. Singer Co.

Dale, W. T., ed. see Dale, Mamie Mary Elizabeth.

Dalen, Peter van
--The Marshal of Granger. Dalen, Peter van, illus. N.D. Hesperian House.

Dalesman, compiled by.
--Yorkshire Legends. 2nd ed. (Illus.). 71p. (Orig.). 1976. (ISBN 0-686-64123-X). Legacy Bks.

Daley, C. F.
--The Skating Party, and Other Poems and Stories. Shepley, B. Annie, illus. (Illus.). 1891. Worthington Co.
--Sun Dials: How Mammas Tell Time and Other Poems and Stories. Shepley, B. Annie, illus. 1891. Warthington Co.
--When They Are Company, and Other Poems and Stories. Shepley, B. Annie, illus. (Illus.). 1891. Worthington Co.

Dalgliesch, Alice (1893-), ed. see Johnson, Richard.

Dalgliesh, Alice see Hutchins, Pat, et al.

Dalgliesh, Alice (1893-), ed. see Means, Philip Ainsworth.

Dalgliesh, Alice (1893-1979), ed. see Mother Goose.

Dalgliesh, Alice (1893-1979)
--Adam and the Golden Cock. Weisgard, Leonard Joseph (1916-), illus. LC 59-7206. (Illus.). 64 p. 21cm. 1959. Scribner.
--Along Janet's Road. Milhous, Katherine (1894-1977), illus. LC 46-3956. 6 p. l., 206 p. illus. 21 cm. 1946. C. Scribner's Sons.
--The Bears on Hemlock Mountain. Sewell, Helen Moore (1896-1957), illus. (Illus.). 64 p. 21cm. 1952. Scribner. **Award: (JNM).**
--The Blue Teapot: Sandy Cove Stories. Woodward, Hildegard (1898-), illus. LC 31-25419. 5 p. l., 73 p. col. front., illus., col. plates. 22 cm. 1931. The Macmillan Company.
--A Book for Jennifer: A Story of London Children in the Eighteenth Century and of Mr. Newbery's Juvenile Library. Milhous, Katherine (1894-1977), illus. LC 40-276418. 6 p. l., 3-114 p. illus., col. plates. 21 cm. 1940. C. Scribner's Sons.

Daly, Jim, pseud., see Stratemeyer, Edward L..
Daly, Jim, pseud. (1862-1930)
--Gentleman Jack: Or, From Student to Pugilist. Stratemeyer, Edward L.. (New York Five Cent Library: No. 14). 1892. Street & Smith.
--Gentleman Jack's Big Hit: Or, Downing the Prize Ring Fakirs. Stratemeyer, Edward L.. (New York Five Cent Library: No. 65). 1893. Street & Smith.
--Gentleman Jack's Debut: Or, The Ring Champion on the Stage. Stratemeyer, Edward L.. (New York Five Cent Library: No. 32). 1893. Street & Smith.
--Gentleman Jack's Mix-Up: Or, Settled Outside of the Prize Ring. Stratemeyer, Edward L.. (New York Five Cent Library: No. 46). 1893. Street & Smith.
--Gentleman Jack's Soft Mark: Or, Knocked Out in Three Rounds. Stratemeyer, Edward L.. (New York Five Cent Library: No. 61). 1893. Street & Smith.
--Gentleman Jack's Tour: Or, The Ring Champion and His Enemies. Stratemeyer, Edward L.. (New York Five Cent Library: No. 36). 1893. Street & Smith.
Daly, Kathleen
--Four Little Kittens. Saviozzi, Adriana Mazza (1928-), illus. (ps-1). 1957. (ISBN 0-307-60322-9, Golden Pr). Western Pub.
Daly, Kathleen, ed. see Hazelton, Elizabeth Baldwin.
Daly, Kathleen N.
--Captain Kangaroo. Seiden, Art & Schmidt, Edwin, illus. (Giant Little Golden Book). 1959. Golden Press.
--Captain Kangaroo and the Panda. Schmidt, Edwin, illus. (Little Golden Book). 1957. Golden Press.
--CBS Television's Captain Kangaroo. Seiden, Art, illus. LC 56-4761. (Illus.). 21cm. (Little Golden Book: 261). 1956. Simon & Schuster.
--Cristobalito. LC 76-27624. (Illus.). 128 p. 19cm. 1976. (ISBN 0-515-04139-4, Pyramid Books). BJ Pub. Group.
--Howdy Doody's Animal Friends. Seiden, Art, illus. LC 56-1899. unpaged. illus. 21 cm. (Little golden book, 252). 1956. Simon and Schuster.
--Ladybug, Ladybug. Smith, Susan Carlton (1923-), illus. LC 70-83816. (Illus.). 27 p. 18cm. 1969. American Heritage Press.
--Listen, Little, Tiger. Miller, John Parr (1913-), illus. N.D. Golden Press.
--Little Tiger Books. Miller, John Parr (1913-), illus. N.D. Golden Press.
--Little Tiger Colors Everything. Miller, J. P., illus. LC 65-203585. 1v. (unpaged) col. illus. 14x17cm. (Her A golden tiger bk.). 1965. Golden.
--Little Tiger Learns His ABC. Miller, John Parr (1913-), illus. LC 65-203403. 1v. (unpaged) col. illus. 14x17cm. (Her A golden tiger bk.). (gr. k-1). 1965. Golden.
--Little Tiger Takes a Trip. Miller, John Parr (1913-), illus. (Illus.). (gr. k-1). 1965 (Golden Pr). Western Pub.
--The Magic of Horses. Offerman, Lynn, ed. Helmer, Jean, illus. 64p. (gr. 3 up). 1985. (ISBN 0-671-49771-5, Little Simon). S&S.
--Making Friends. Cocca-Leffler, Maryann (1958-), illus. LC 83-25118. (Illus.). 42 p. 29cm. (Cabbage Patch Kids). c.1984. (ISBN 0-910313-27-X). Parker Bros.
--Mustang. (Orig.). (gr. 5 up). 1975. (ISBN 0-515-03897-0). BJ Pub Group.
--Mustangs!. Guarino, Joseph, illus. LC 75-15394. (Illus.). 18cm. 125p. (The Wonderful World of Disney). 1975. (ISBN 0-515-03897-0). Pyramid Communications.
--My Doctor Bag Book. Brown, Marc Tolon (1946-), illus. (Illus.). 24p. (Carry-Me Book). (ps-3). 1977. (ISBN 0-307-68851-8, Golden Pr). Western Pub.
--My Elephant Book. Battaglia, Aurelius (1910-), illus. LC 67-3023. (Illus.). 1 v. 25p. 33cm. (Big golden book). 1967, c.1966. Golden Press.
--My Little Golden Book About Travel. Gergely, Tibor (1900-1978), illus. LC 56-4678. unpaged. illus. 21 cm. (Little golden book, 269). 1956. Simon and Schuster.
--The New Puppy. Obligado, Lilian Isabel (1931-), illus. (Little Golden Book). 1959. Golden Press.
--Strawberry Shortcake and Pets on Parade. Sustendal, Pat, illus. LC 83-8164. (Illus.). 42 p. 29cm. c.1983. (ISBN 0-910313-06-7). Parker Brothers.
--Tiny Tiger Learns a Lot. Miller, John Parr (1913-), illus. (Illus.). (ps-k). 1976. (ISBN 0-307-13770-8, Golden Pr). (ISBN 0-307-63770-0). Western Pub.
--Tonka. (Orig.). 1976. (ISBN 0-515-04018-5). BJ Pub Group.
Daly, Kathleen N., as told by.
--Aladdin and His Magic Lamp. Hess, Lowell, illus. (Little Golden Book). 1959. Golden Press.
--Bruno Bear's Bedtime Book: A Collection of Stories and Poems for the Very Young. Hefter, Richard (1942-), illus. LC 76-1500. (Illus.). 60 p. 31cm. c.1976. (ISBN 0-88470-050-X). (ISBN 0-88470-051-8). Strawberry Books : Distributed by Larousse.
--Puss in the Boots. N.D. Golden Press.
--Raggedy Ann & Andy: An Adaptation. LC 76-47894. (Illus.). 91 p. 24cm. c.1977. (ISBN 0-672-52301-9). Bobbs-Merrill.
--The Three Bears. Rojankovsky, Feodor Stepanovich (1891-1970), illus. LC 67-5980. (Illus.). 24 p. 26cm. (Golden square book). 1967. Golden Press.
Daly, Kathleen N., ed. see Andersen, Hans Christian.
Daly, Kathleen N, adapted by see Perrault, Charles.
Daly, Kathleen N., adapted by see Pezzi, Maria Pia.
Daly, Maggie
--Kate Brennan, Model. LC 55-10063. 249 p. 21cm. 1956. Dodd, Mead.
Daly, Mary Maxine
--Juvenile Adventure Stories. 1st ed. Lyons, Dave, illus. LC 55-12376. 82 p. illus. 21 cm. 1955. Pageant Press.
Daly, Maureen
--Seventeenth Summer. LC 84-24637. 255 p. 21cm. 1985, c.1942. (ISBN 0-396-02322-3). Dodd, Mead.
Daly, Maureen, ed.
--Sixteen & Other Stories (Pub. by Dodd). (gr. 7-9). 1972. (ISBN 0-590-08015-6, Schol Trade Pap). Schol Bk Serv.
Daly, Maureen see McGivern, Maureen Daly.
Daly, Niki
--Ben's Gingerbread Man. LC 85-3327. p. cm. 1985. (ISBN 0-670-80806-7). Viking Penguin.
--Joseph's Other Red Sock. Daly, Niki, illus. LC 81-66440. (Illus.). 32 p. 23cm. 1st U.S. edition. 1982. (ISBN 0-689-50216-8). Atheneum.
--Monsters Are Like That. LC 85-3328. p. cm. 1985. (ISBN 0-670-80807-5). Viking Penguin.
--Teddy's Ear. LC 85-3329. p. cm. 1985. (ISBN 0-670-80808-3). Viking.
--Vim the Rag Mouse. Daly, Niki, illus. LC 79-63334. (Illus.). 32p. (ps-4). 1979. (ISBN 0-689-50141-2, McElderry Bk). Atheneum.
Daly, Robert Welter (1916-1975)
--Guns of Roman Nose. LC 57-7164. 179 p. 21 cm. 1957. Dodd, Mead.
--Guns of Yorktown. LC 53-8951. 181 p. 21 cm. 1953. Dodd, Mead.
Daly, T. A.
--Ring-Around-A-Rosy. (McKay's Indestructable Nursery). N.D. David McKay.
Daly, Thomas Augustine (1871-)
--Little Polly's Pomes. LC 14-115. 90 p. col. front., 7 col. pl. 25 cm. 1914. The Devin-Adair Company.
Dalziel, Edward (1817-1905) & Dalziel, George (1815-1902), illus.
--The Arabian Nights' Entertainments. (Illus.). 800p. N.D. George Routledge & Sons.
Dam, Cornelia H, Mrs.
--Indian Children of the Eastern Woodlands. Parker, Arthur Caswell (1881-1955), ed. Hall, Frances J., illus. LC 39-1389. vi, 39 p., 1 l. illus. (part col.) 28 cm. 1938. Orthovis Publishing Company.
Damashek, Sandy & Henson, James Maury (1936-)
--Follow the Leader: Featuring Jim Henson's Sesame Street Muppets. Cooke, Tom, illus. LC 81-81631. (Illus.). 26 p. 27cm. c.1981. (ISBN 0-307-23142-9). Western Pub. Co. : Children's Television Workshop.
D'Amato, Alex, jt. auth. see D'Amato, Janet Potter.
D'Amato, Janet Potter (1925-) & D'Amato, Alex (1919-)
--Blow Wind Blow. N.D (Wonder Books). Grosset & Dunlap.
--My First Book of Riddles. (ps-1). 1974. (ISBN 0-448-00745-2). Wonder.
--Wonder Book of Riddles. N.D (Wonder Books). Grosset & Dunlap.
D'Amelio, Dan (1927-)
--Silvabamba. LC 77-74837. (Illus.). 64p. (Pacesetters Ser.). (gr. 4 up). 1978. (ISBN 0-516-02158-3). Childrens.
--Taller Than Bandai Mountain: The Story of Hideo Noguchi. Banbery, Fred, illus. 160p. 1968. (ISBN 0-670-69285-9). (ISBN 0-670-69286-7). Viking Press.
Damjan, Mischa
--Atuk. Casty, Gian, illus. LC 66-12455. (Illus.). 1 v. (unpaged. 30cm. 1966, c.1964. Pantheon Books.
--The Big Squirrel and the Little Rhinoceros. 1st Ed. ed. LC 65-758778. 1v. (unpaged) col. illus. 30cm. 1965, c.1964. Norton.
--Clown Said No. (gr. k-3). 1963. (ISBN 0-07-015238-1). (ISBN 0-07-015239-X). McGraw.
--The False Flamingoes. Steadman, Ralph Idris (1936-), illus. LC 70-105399. (Illus.). 31 p. 29cm. 1970, c.1968. Scroll Press.
--Francesco & His Donkeys. Ineichen, Mona, illus. Crampton, Patricia, tr. (Illus.). 80p. 1981. (ISBN 0-905478-10-X, Pub. by Andersen-Hutchinson England). State Mutual Bk.
--Goodbye Little Bird. Duntze, Dorothee, illus. LC 82-20954. p. cm. 1983. (ISBN 0-571-12520-4). Faber and Faber.
--The Little Green Man. Kenelski, Maurice, illus. LC 76-166286. (Illus.). 32 p. 1972, c.1971. (ISBN 0-8193-0535-9). (ISBN 0-8193-0536-7). Parents' Magazine Press.
--The Little Prince and the Tiger Cat. Steadman, Ralph Idris (1936-), illus. (Illus.). 32 p. 30cm. 1968, c.1967. McGraw-Hill.
--The Little Sea Horse. Bellettati, Riccardo, illus. LC 82-20953. (Illus.). 29 p. 30cm. 1983. (ISBN 0-571-12519-0). Faber and Faber.
--The Magic Paintbrush. Eckert, Horst (1931-), illus. Janosch, pseud. LC 67-23015. (Illus.). 30 p. 28cm. 1967. H. Z. Walck.
--Mau, King of Cats. McGovern, Ann, adapted by. Buchi, Werner, illus. LC 63-7736. (Illus.). (gr. k-2). 1961. Putnam.
--The Wolf and the Kid. Velthuijs, Max (1923-), illus. LC 68-16312. (Illus.). 32 p. 30cm. 1968, c.1967. McGraw-Hill.
Damjan, Mischa, adapted by.
--Ivan and the Witch: A Russian Tale. Bogdanovic, Toma (1937-), illus. LC 78-76089. (Illus.). 32 p. 33cm. 1969. McGraw-Hill.
Dammann, Louis
--Folk & Fairy Tales in Verse. (gr. k-6). N.D. Vantage.
Dammast, Jeanie Selina
--High and Low: Or, Help Each Other. N.D. Thomas Nelson & Sons.
Damon, Dave, ed. see Damon, Valerie H.
Damon, Samuel Foster (1893-1971)
--The Day After Christmas. Bock, Vera, illus. LC 30-29568. 205, 1 p. incl. front., illus. 19 cm. 1930. A. & C. Boni.
Damon, Valerie H.
--Willo Mancifoot (and the Mugga Killa Whomps). Damon, Dave, ed. LC 83-50739. (Illus.). (gr. 2-6). 1985. (ISBN 0-932356-07-9). (ISBN 0-932356-08-7). Star Pubns Mo.
Dana, Barbara (1940-)
--Crazy Eights. LC 77-25645. viii, 194 p. 22cm. c.1978. (ISBN 0-06-021388-4). (ISBN 0-06-021389-2). Harper & Row.
--Rutgers and the Water-Snouts. Brenner, Fred (1920-), illus. LC 68-24330. (Illus.). 149 p. 21cm. 1969. Harper & Row.
--Spencer and His Friends. Chwast, Jacqueline (1932-), illus. LC 66-5956. 120p. illus 24cm. c.1966. Atheneum.
--Zucchini. 1st ed. Christelow, Eileen (1943-), illus. LC 80-8448. p. cm. 1982. (ISBN 0-06-021394-9). (ISBN 0-06-021395-7). Harper & Row.
Dana, Charles Anderson (1819-1897), tr. from Ger.
--Christmas Eve and Other Stories. LC 17-26994. 48 p. incl. front., illus., plates. 15 cm. 1852. Crosby & Nichols.
--German Fairy Tales. (Illus.). (St. Nicholas Series for Girls). N.D. International Book Co.
Dana, Dorathea, pseud., see Dankovszky, Dorathea.
Dana, Dorathea
--Goodbye Bunny Bangs. Dana, Dorathea, illus. 1956. Abelard-Schuman.
Dana, Doris
--The Elephant and His Secret. 1st ed. Frasconi, Antonio (1919-), illus. LC 78-75432. (Based on a fable by Gabriels Mistral). 40p. col. illus 27cm. 1974. (ISBN 0-689-30430-7). Atheneum.
Dana, Doris, tr. see Godoy Alcayaga, Lucila.
Dana, Doris, tr. see Mistral, Gabriela.
Dana, Doris & Godoy Alcayaga, Lucila (1889-1957)
--The Elephant and His Secret. El Elefante y Su Secreto. 1st ed. Frasconi, Antonio (1919-), illus. LC 73-75432. (Illus.). 40 p. 27cm. 1974. Atheneum.
Dana, J. J.
--Humpy Dumpy, 1 of 4 Vols. (Siver Lake Ser.). N.D. National Temperance Society.
--Mrs. Marsh's Help. 336p. N.D. T. Y. Crowell.
--Mrs. Marsh's Help. (The Ollie Library). N.D. Warren & Wyman.
Dana, John Cotton, ed. see Prescott, Della R.
Dana, Mary Pepperell (1914-), compiled by.
--The Jingle Book ... Dana, Mary Pepperell (1914-), illus. LC 41-1268. 16 1. col. illus. 26 x 22 cm. c.1940. W. R. Scott, Inc.
Dana, Mrs.
--Dana's Young Sailor. N.D. Harper & Brothers' Trade-List.
--Forecastle Tom. 1882. Harper's Trade-List.
Dana, Richard Henry, Jr. (1815-1882)
--Sir Wilfred Grenfell. (Children's Classics). N.D. Macmillan.
--The Story of Two Years Before the Mast. Beals, Frank Lee (1881-1972), ed. King, E. E., illus. LC 52-4447. 140 p. illus. 21 cm. (Famous story series). 1952. B. H. Sanborn.
--Two Years Before the Mast. (Illus.). (The Rugby Series for Boys). 1905. A. L. Burt's Pubs.
--Two Years Before the Mast. (Famous Bks. for Young Americans). N.D. A. L. Burt Co.
--Two Years Before the Mast. (Illus.). (The Round Table Ser.). N.D. A. L. Burt's Pubs.
--Two Years Before the Mast, 1 of 110 vols. (The Manhattan Ser.). N.D. A. L. Burt's Pubs.
--Two Years Before the Mast. (Great Illustrated Classics). N.D. Dodd, Mead & Co.
--Two Years Before the Mast. (The Children's Favorite Ser.). N.D. Grosset & Dunlap.
--Two Years Before the Mast. (Illus.). (Famous Books for Boys). N.D. H. M. Caldwell Co.
--Two Years Before the Mast. (Illus.). (Boys' and Girls' Classics). N.D. Henry Altemus Co.
--Two Years Before the Mast. (Riverside Literature Ser.). N.D. Houghton Mifflin Co.
--Two Year's Before the Mast, 1 of 64 vols. (Young America Library: No. 51). 1900. Set. Hurst & Co.
--Two Years Before the Mast. N.D. James R. Osgood.
--Two Years Before the Mast. (Magnum Easy Eye Classic Ser). (gr. 8-12). N.D. Lancer.
--Two Years Before the Mast. N.D. Macmillan.
--Two Years Before the Mast. 543p. N.D. Scott, Foresman & Co.
--Two Years Before the Mast. (Illus.). (Rainbow Classics). 1946. World Pub.
--Two Years before the Mast. Beals, Frank Lee (1881-1972), adapted by. Beals, Frank Lee, retold by. (Illus.). (Famous Story Ser.). N.D. Naylor.
--Two Years Before the Mast. Blaine, Mahlon, illus. (The Father & Son Library). N.D. Sears Publishing Co.
--Two Years Before the Mast. new & abr. ed. Fago, John Norwood, ed. Cruz, Ernest R., illus. (Illus.). (Now Age Illustrated III Ser.). (gr. 4-12). 1977. (ISBN 0-88301-282-0). (ISBN 0-88301-270-7). Pendulum Pr.
--Two Years Before the Mast. Hawley, Hattie L. & Gordon, Elizabeth H., eds. N.D. Charles Scribner's Sons'.
--Two Years Before the Mast. Mueller, Hans Alexander (1888-), illus. N.D. Heritage Press.
--Two Years Before the Mast. Newbolt, Henry, Sir, ed. (The Nelson Classics). N.D. Thomas Nelson & Sons.
--Two Years Before the Mast. Nichols, Dale William (1904-), illus. 400p. N.D. Heritage Press.
Dana Estes & Co, ed. see Clarke, Mary Cowden, Mrs.
Danaher, J.
--Six Detective Stories. 1975. MacMillan Publishing Company.
--Six Ghost Stories. 1972. MacMillan Publishing Company.
Danaher, Kevin (1913-)
--Folktales of the Irish Countryside. Berson, Harold (1926-), illus. LC 70-129213. (Illus.). x, 102 p. 24cm. 1970. D. White.
Danbury, Iris
--Chateau of Pines. (Good Reading for Girls Series). N.D. Golden Press.
Dane, Beatrice J., jt. ed. see Dane, George Ezra.
Dane, George Ezra (1904-) & Dane, Beatrice J., eds.
--Once There Was and Was Not. N.D. Doubleday Doran & Co.
--Once There Was and Was Not: Tales and Rhymes from Majorca. Wells, Rhea (1891-), illus. LC 31-26711. xiii, 269 p. col. front., illus., plates. 21 cm. 1931. Junior Literary Guild.
Danforth, Amy
--Animal Fair: Poems. Sturgill, Susan, illus. LC 83-172906. (Illus.). 56. c.1983. (ISBN 0-912883-00-6). Cricket Publications.
--Patchwork of Poems. Fleming, Denise, illus. (Illus.). 20p. (Orig.). (gr. 1-6). 1981. Dragonfly Pr.
Danforth, Wendy
--Ickle McNoo. Glasbergen, Randy, illus. LC 74-15502. (Illus.). 30 p. 29cm. 1974. Allied Publications.
Danglish, Edith M.
--Issac Beach Signalman. (Illus.). N.D. Society for Promoting Christian Knowledge.
Daniel, Alan, jt. auth. see Naylor, Phyllis Reynolds.
Daniel, Barlette
--I'll Take Manhattan. 144p. (Mirrors Ser.). (gr. 7 up). 1984. (ISBN 0-448-47725-4). Putnam Pub Group.
Daniel, Becky & Daniel, Charlie
--The Great Paper Airplane Factory. (gr. 2-6). 1978. (ISBN 0-916456-21-8). Good Apple.
--Rainbow Factory. (ps-2). 1982. (ISBN 0-86653-063-0). Good Apple.
Daniel, Charlie, jt. auth. see Daniel, Becky.
Daniel, Clarence
--Haunted Derbyshire. (Illus.). 80p. (Orig.). (gr. 6 up). 1975. (ISBN 0-913714-40-2). Legacy Bks.

Daniel, David
--The Complete Book of Bible Stories for Jewish Children. Einhorn, Ben, illus. LC 75-155841. (Illus.). 2 v. in 1. 25cm. 1971. (ISBN 0-87068-381-0). (ISBN 0-87068-380-2). Ktav Pub. House.
Daniel, Doris T.
--Pauline & the Peacock. Schoenewolf, Barbara B., illus. LC 80-50301. (Illus.). 64p. (Orig.). (ps-8). 1980. E C Temple.
Daniel, Elizabeth
--Happy Days: Photographs of Happy Boys and Girls. LC 37-2572. 1 p. l., 5-62, 1 p. illus. 17 cm. c.1937. Rand, McNally & Company.
--Happy Hours: Photographs of Happy Children, with Verses. LC 34-18526. 2 p. l., 7-62, 1 p. illus. 17 cm. c.1934. Rand, McNally & Company.
--Our Button Book. LC 38-18388. 1 p. l., 5-64 p. illus. 17 cm. c.1938. Rand McNally & Company.
Daniel, Ernie
--Back Tracking Bronco. (gr. 2 up). 1968. (ISBN 0-8059-1320-3). Dorrance.
--Guteater. LC 70-154864. 85p. (gr. 7 up). 1971. (ISBN 0-8059-1565-6). Dorrance.
Daniel, Frank, ed. see Mother Goose.
Daniel, Hawthorne, jt. auth. see Dickey, Herbert Spencer, Dr.
Daniel, Hawthorne, jt. auth. see Sherman, Harold Morrow.
Daniel, Hawthorne (1890-)
--Bare Hands: Being the Story of the Extraordinary Steam Boat That Was Built on Devil's Island off the Coast of Alaska by Four Shipwrecked Men. Jansson, Arthur August (1890-), illus. LC 29-4209. 5 p. l., 244 p. incl. plates. col. front. 20 cm. 1929. Coward-McCann, Inc.
--Broken Dykes: A Story of the Siege of Leyden. Voter, Thomas W., illus. LC 34-32403. 7 p. l., 185 p. incl. illus., plates 23 cm. 1934. The Macmillan Company.
--The Clipper Ship. Rigney, Francis Joseph (1882-), illus. 1928. Dodd, Mead & Co.
--Dorothy Stanhope--Virginian. Holberg, Richard A. (1889-1942), illus. LC 31-29419. 5 p. l., 3-279 p. col. front., illus., plates, port. 21 cm. c.1931. Coward-McCann, Inc.
--Fogbound. Greene, Hamilton, illus. LC 43-11743. 5 p. l., 257 p. col. front., illus. 22 1/2 cm. 1943. The John C. Winston Company.
--The Gauntlet of Dunmore. Pitz, Henry Clarence (1895-1976), illus. LC 26-16265. 7 p. l., 252 p. incl. front., plates. 20 cm. 1926. The Macmillan Company.
--Head Wind. Pont, Charles Ernest (1898-), illus. LC 36-819894. 5 p. l., 177 p. 22 cm. 1936. The Macmillan Company.
--The Honor of Dunmore. Pitz, Henry Clarence (1895-1976), illus. LC 27-878321. 7 p. l., 256 p. incl. front., plates. 19 cm. 1927. The Macmillan Company.
--The Lost Professor. Holberg, Richard A. (1889-1942), illus. LC 33-287257. 6 p. l., 3-269 p. col. front., illus. 21 cm. c.1933. Coward-McCann, Inc.
--Peggy of Old Annapolis. N.D. Grosset & Dunlap.
--Peggy of Old Annapolis. Holberg, Richard A. (1889-1942), illus. LC 30-257437. 6 p. l., 3-256 p. col. front., illus., plates. 21 cm. 1930. Coward-McCann Inc.
--The Red Rose of Dunmore. Blood, William C., illus. LC 28-22143. 5 p. l., 212 p. col. front., illus. 20 cm. 1928. The Macmillan Company.
--The Seal of the White Buddha: Being the Tale of a New England Girl in the Year 1847 Sailing Aboard Her Uncle's Clipper Ship to Distant China, and of the Mystery, Adventure and Great Good Fortune Which Befell Her. Holberg, Richard A. (1889-1942) & Tracy, Glenn, illus. LC 28-21377. 6 p. l., 3-271 p. col. front., plates. 22 cm. 1928. Coward-McCann, Inc.
--The Shadow of the Sword. Verpilleux, Emile Antoine (1888-), illus. LC 30-31026. 6 p. l., 3-221 p. incl. illus., plates (1 double) col. front. 23 cm. 1930. The Macmillan Company.
--Shuttle and Sword: The Adventures of a Weaver's Son in Old Flanders. Voter, Thomas W., illus. LC 32-12518. x p., 1 l., 168, 1 p. incl. front., illus. 23 cm. 1932. The Macmillan Company.
--Whampoa. Wiese, Kurt (1887-1974), illus. LC 41-16001. 5 p. l., 273 p. incl. front., illus., plates. 22 cm. 1941. Thomas Y. Crowell Company.
Daniel, Rebecca
--Abraham. Kreitman, Kay M., illus. (Illus.). 32p. (Our Greatest Heritage Ser.). (gr. 7-12). 1983. (ISBN 0-86653-133-5). Good Apple.
--Adam & Eve. Kreitman, Kay M., illus. (Illus.). 32p. (Our Greatest Heritage Ser.). (gr. 7-12). 1983. (ISBN 0-86653-131-9). Good Apple.
--Daniel. Kreitman, Kay M., illus. (Illus.). 32p. (Our Greatest Heritage Ser.). (gr. 7-12). 1983. (ISBN 0-86653-140-8). Good Apple.
--Jonah. Kreitman, Kay M., illus. (Illus.). 32p. (Our Greatest Heritage Ser.). (gr. 7-12). 1983. (ISBN 0-86653-141-6). Good Apple.
--Joseph. Kreitman, Kay M., illus. 32p. (Our Greatest Heritage Ser.). (gr. 7-12). 1983. (ISBN 0-86653-134-3). Good Apple.
--Joshua. Kreitman, Kay M., illus. (Illus.). 32p. (Our Greatest Heritage Ser.). (gr. 7-12). 1983. (ISBN 0-86653-136-X). Good Apple.
--Moses. Kreitman, Kay M., illus. (Illus.). 32p. (Our Greatest Heritage Ser.). (gr. 7-12). 1983. (ISBN 0-86653-135-1). Good Apple.
--Noah. Kreitman, Kay M., illus. (Illus.). (Our Greatest Heritage Ser.). (gr. 7-12). 1983. (ISBN 0-86653-132-7). Good Apple.
--Samson. Kreitman, Kay M., illus. (Illus.). 32p. (Our Greatest Heritage Ser.). (gr. 7-12). 1983. (ISBN 0-86653-[illegible]). Good Apple.
--Solomon. Kreitman, Kay M., illus. (Illus.). 32p. (Our Greatest Heritage Ser.). (gr. 7-12). 1983. (ISBN 0-86653-139-4). Good Apple.
--Women of the Old Testament. Kreitman, Kay M., illus. (Illus.). 32p. (Our Greatest Heritage Ser.). (gr. 7-12). 1983. (ISBN 0-86653-142-4). Good Apple.
Daniel, Robert, ed. see Austen, Jane.
Daniel-Rops, Henry
--Golden Legend of Young Saints. Newland, Mary Reed, illus. Intrator, Mira, tr. c.1960. P J Kennedy & Sons.
Daniel, Theo S., 3rd
--River Bottom Humor. LC 68-24262. (Illus.). port. 158p. (gr. 8 up). 1968. (ISBN 0-8111-0112-6). Naylor.
Daniell, Albert Scott see Daniell, David Scott, pseud.
Daniell, David Scott see Bowood, Richard, pseud.
Daniell, David Scott, pseud., see Daniell, Albert Scott.
Daniell, David Scott, pseud. (1906-1965)
--The Boy They Made King. Daniell, Albert Scott. Stobbs, William (1914-), illus. (Illus.). 1960. Duell, Sloan and Pearce Pub.
--By Jiminy. Daniell, Albert Scott. Valentine, Donald Graham (1929-), illus. (Illus.). (gr. 3-6). 1962. (ISBN 0-685-20988-1). Verry.
--The Dragon and the Rose. Daniell, Albert Scott. Stratton, Sheila, illus. LC 57-5131. 208p. illus. 22cm. 1957. Abelard-Schuman.
--Hunt Royal. Daniell, Albert Scott. Stobbs, William (1914-), illus. (Illus.). (gr. 5-9). 1958. (ISBN 0-685-21197-5). Verry.
--Mission for Oliver. Daniell, Albert Scott. Stobbs, William (1914-), illus. (Illus.). (gr. 5-9). 1959. (ISBN 0-685-21347-1). Verry.
--Polly & Oliver Pursued. Daniell, Albert Scott. Stobbs, William (1914-), illus. (Illus.). (gr. 5-9). 1964. (ISBN 0-685-21435-4). Verry.
--The Rajah's Treasure. Daniell, Albert Scott. Stobbs, William (1914-), illus. LC 61-11962. 21cm. 121p. 1960. Duell.
--Sandro's Battle. Daniell, Albert Scott. Spencer, Colin, illus. LC 62-15471. (Illus.). 21cm. 153p. 1962. Duell, Sloan & Pearce.
--Sea Fights. Daniell, Albert Scott. 1966. Lawrence Verry Inc.
Daniels, A. J.
--Told Out of School: Or, Humorous Yarns of School Life and Boyhood. (Illus.). (Story Books for Boys). N.D. Cassell & Co.'s Pubs.
Daniels, Guy (1919-), tr. see Afanasev, Aleksandr Nikolaevich.
Daniels, Guy (1919-), tr. see Bunin, Ivan Alexeyvich.
Daniels, Guy (1919-), tr. see Krylov, Ivan Andreevich.
Daniels, Guy, tr. see Maiakovskii, Vladimir Vladimirovich.
Daniels, Guy, tr. see Mikhalkov, Sergei Vladimirovich.
Daniels, Guy (1919-), tr. see Tolstoy, Leo Nikolaevich.
Daniels, Guy (1919-), ed.
--The Falcon Under the Hat: Russian Merry Tales and Fairy Tales. Rojankovsky, Feodor Stepanovich (1891-1970), illus. LC 68-26418. (Illus.). 111 p. 26cm. (gr. 7 up). 1969. Funk & Wagnalls.
--A Lermontov Reader. Daniels, Guy (1919-), tr. N.D. (ISBN 0-448-00209-4). Grosset & Dunlap.
--Tsar's Riddles Or, The Wise Little Girl. Galdone, Paul (1914-), illus. LC 67-3798. (Illus.). 32p. (gr. k-3). 1967. (ISBN 0-07-015332-9). McGraw.
Daniels, Jonathan (1902-1981)
--Mosby, Gary Ghost of the Confederacy. 1959. J. B. Lippincott.
Daniels, Neil, jt. auth. see Hudson, Anne.
Daniels, Patricia, adapted by.
--Aladdin and the Magic Lamp. Art, Temple, illus. Wagner, Betty Jane, afterword by. LC 79-27304. (Illus.). 23 p. 24cm. (Raintree Fairy Tales). c.1980. (ISBN 0-8393-0257-6). Raintree Childrens Books.
--Ali Baba and the Forty Thieves. Troughton, Joanna Margaret (1947-), illus. LC 79-27042. (Illus.). 23 p. 24cm. (Raintree Fairy Tales). c.1980. (ISBN 0-8393-0255-X). Raintree Childrens Books.
--Beauty and the Beast. Large, Annabel, illus. LC 79-28433. (Illus.). 23 p. 24cm. (Raintree Fairy Tales). c.1980. (ISBN 0-8393-0258-4). Raintree Childrens Books.
--Cinderella. Read, Maggie, illus. LC 79-28526. (Illus.). 23 p. 24cm. (Raintree Fairy Tales). c.1980. (ISBN 0-8393-0253-3). Raintree Childrens Books.
--Moby Dick: Or, the White Whale. Kelley, Gary, illus. LC 81-15386. (Original Authors: The Grimm Brothers.). p. cm. 1982. (ISBN 0-8172-1679-0). Raintree Publishers.
--Rumpelstiltskin. Nightingale, Sandy Ann, illus. LC 79-27140. (Illus.). 23 p. 24cm. (Raintree Fairy Tales). 1980. (ISBN 0-8393-0252-5). Raintree Childrens Books.
--Sinbad the Sailor. Webb, Roger (1939-), illus. LC 79-28588. (Illus.). 23 p. 24cm. (Raintree Fairy Tales). c.1980. (ISBN 0-8393-0256-8). Raintree Childrens Books.
--Sleeping Beauty. Tarrant, Carol, illus. LC 79-26974. (Illus.). 23 p. 24cm. (Raintree Fairy Tales). c.1980. (ISBN 0-8393-0254-1). Raintree Childrens Books.
--Snow White and the Seven Dwarfs. Spalding, Tony, illus. LC 79-28431. (Original Authors: The Grimm Brothers.). (Illus.). 23 p. 24cm. (Raintree Fairy Tales). c.1980. Raintree Childrens Books.
Daniels, Patricia, adapted by see Melville, Herman.
Daniels, Velma Seawell (1931-)
--Kat: The Story of a Calico Cat. O'Leary, Eileen, illus. LC 77-13738. (Illus.). 32 p. 29cm. (gr. k-7). 1977. (ISBN 0-88289-180-4). Pelican Pub. Co.
Daniels, W. H.
--That Boy, Who Shall Have Him?. (Illus.). N.D. Methodist Book Concern.
Danielski, S E
--Andrew, the Apostle. LC 66-32726. 1 v. (unpaged) illus. 21 cm. N.D. Dujarie Press.
Danielson, Frances Weld
--The Animal School and Other Stories. Atwood, Clara E., illus. LC 15-15301. 61 p. col. front., col. plates. 21 cm. c.1914. The Pilgrim Press.
--The Children's Christmas Tree. N.D. Pilgrim Press.
--Little Animal Stories. Atwood, Clara E., illus. LC 11-22547. ix, 172 p. front., plates. 21 cm. c.1911. The Pilgrim Press.
--Story Telling Time. Atwood, Clara E., illus. LC 12-24464. ix, 169, 1 p. col. front., col. plates. 21 cm. 1912. The Pilgrim Press.
Danielsson, Bengt Emmerick (1921-)
--Terry in the South Seas. Heyman, Pierre, illus. Spink, Reginald, tr. 216p. 1960. Reilly & Lee Company.
Danielsson, Bengt Emmerik (1921-)
--Terry's Kon-Tiki Adventure. Risch, L. & Risch, P., illus. (Illus.). (gr. 3-6). 1965. (ISBN 0-685-21601-2). Verry.
Danish, Barbara (1948-)
--The Dragon & the Doctor. Danish, Barbara (1948-), illus. (Illus.). 32p. (ps-3). 1971. (ISBN 0-912670-00-2). Feminist Pr.
Dank, Gloria
--The Forest of App. LC 83-1627. p. cm. 1983. (ISBN 0-688-02315-0). Greenwillow Books.
Dank, Gloria, jt. auth. see Dank, Milton.
Dank, Milton (1920-)
--The Dangerous Game. LC 77-23453. 157 p. 21cm. c.1977. (ISBN 0-397-31753-0). Lippincott.
--Game's End. LC 78-12625. 158 p. 21cm. c.1979. (ISBN 0-397-31821-9). Lippincott.
--Khaki Wings: A Novel. LC 80-65832. 180 p. 22cm. c.1980. (ISBN 0-440-04486-3). Delacorte Press.
--Red Flight Two. LC 81-176. p. cm. c.1981. (ISBN 0-440-07336-7). Delacorte Press.
Dank, Milton (1920-) & Dank, Gloria
--The Computer Caper. (Galaxy Gang Mystery Ser.). (gr. 5-9). 1983. (ISBN 0-385-29296-1). Delacorte.
--The Computer Game Murder. LC 85-1650. 119 p. 22cm. (Galaxy Gang mystery). c.1985. (ISBN 0-385-29411-5). Delacorte Press.
--The Three-D Traitor: A Galaxy Gang Mystery. LC 84-4324. 128p. (gr. 4-6). 1984. (ISBN 0-385-29345-3). Delacorte.
--Treasure Code: A Galaxy Gang Mystery. LC 84-15569. 128p. (gr. 4-6). 1985. (ISBN 0-385-29370-4). Delacorte.
Dankovszky, Dorathea see Dana, Dorathea, pseud.
Dankovszky, Dorathea
--Good Bye, Bunny Bangs. Dankovszky, Dorathea, illus. LC 56-5902. unpaged. illus. 23cm. 1956. Abelard Schuman.
--Sugar Bush. Dana, Dorathea, pseud. Dankovszky, Dorathea, illus. Dana, Dorathea, pseud. LC 47-30259. 174 p. incl. front., illus. col. plates. 22 cm. 1947. T. Nelson & Sons.
--The Unruly Robin. Dorkovszky, Dorathea, illus. LC 53-8357. 64p. illus. 22cm. 1953. Abelard Press.
Dann, Jack (1945-) & Dozois, Gardner Raymond (1947-), eds.
--Future Power. 1976. (ISBN 0-394-49420-2). Random.
Dann, Max
--Adventures with My Worst Best Friend. (Illus.). 122p. (gr. 3-7). 1984. (ISBN 0-19-554361-0, Pub. by Oxford U Pr Childrens). Merrimack Pub Cir.
--Bernice Knows Best. James, Ann, illus. (Illus.). 32p. 1st U.S. edition. (gr. 1-5). 1984. (ISBN 0-19-554414-5, Pub. by Oxford U Pr Childrens). Merrimack Pub Cir.
Dannay, Frederic see Queen, Ellery, pseud.
Dannecker, Hazel I.
--Fisherman Simms. Bradfield, Margaret, illus. LC 47-304263. 24 p. illus. (part col.) 18 x 26 cm. 1947. Abingdon-Cokesbury Press.
--Happy, Hero, & Judge. Robertson, Lilian, illus. 1950. Abelard.
--Happy, Hero and Judge. Robertson, Lilian, illus. LC 50-8716. 1950. Abindon-Cokesbury Press.
Dannenbaum, Marta, contrib. by see Beach, Ransford.
Danner, Catherine
--Buster Bulldozer. Stoddard, Mary Alice, illus. LC 53-22434. (Illus.). 17cm. (Tell a Tale Books). 1953, c.1952. Whitman Pub. Co.
Danska, Herbert (1928-)
--The Street Kids. Danska, Herbert (1928-), illus. LC 70-84568. (Illus.). 160 p. 24cm. 1970. Knopf.
Danton, Jane
--The Life Story of Baby Sandy. N.D. Rand McNally & Co.
Dantzic, Cynthia Maris (1933-)
--Stop Dropping Breadcrumbs on My Yacht. LC 74-2254. (Illus.). 32 p. 25cm. 1974. (ISBN 0-13-846998-9). Prentice-Hall.
D'Anvers, N., pseud., see Bell, Nancy R. E..
D'Anvers, N., pseud.
--Story of a Dog. Bell, Nancy R. E.. N.D. J. B. Lippincott Co.
Danziger, Paula (1944-)
--Can You Sue Your Parents for Malpractice?. A Novel. LC 78-72856. vii, 152 p. 21cm. c.1979. (ISBN 0-440-01050-0). Delacorte Press.
--The Cat Ate My Gymsuit. LC 74-8898. p. cm. 1974. (ISBN 0-440-01612-6). (ISBN 0-440-01612-6). Delacorte Press.
--The Divorce Express. LC 82-70318. (Illus.). 148 p. 22cm. c.1982. (ISBN 0-440-02035-2). Delacorte Press.
--It's an Aardvark-Eat-Turtle World. LC 84-17645. 132 p. 22cm. c.1985. (ISBN 0-385-29371-2). Delacorte Press.
--The Pistachio Prescription: A Novel. LC 77-86330. 154 p. 21cm. (gr. 7 up). c.1978. (ISBN 0-440-06936-X). Delacorte Press.
--There's a Bat in Bunk Five. LC 80-15581. p. cm. c.1980. (ISBN 0-440-08605-1). (ISBN 0-440-08606-X). Delacorte Press.
Darbois, Dominique
--Achouna, Boy of the Arctic. Darbois, Dominique, illus. LC 62-10391. 26cm. 47p. (Children of the World Books). c.1962. Follett Pub. Co.
--Agossou, Boy of Africa. Darbois, Dominique, illus. LC 62-10390. 47p. illus. 27cm. (Children of the world bks.). c.1962. Follett.
--Aslak, Boy of Lapland. Darbois, Dominique & Darbois, Dominique, illus. Greufebsteub, Sandra, adapted by. LC 67-15021. (Illus.). 48 p. 26cm. (Children of the world books). 1968. (ISBN 0-695-40572-1). Follett Pub. Co.
--Hassen, Boy Of The Desert. Darbois, Dominique, illus. 1961. (ISBN 0-695-43680-5). Follett Publishing.
--Kai Ming, Boy Of Hong Kong. Darbois, Dominique, illus. 1960. (ISBN 0-695-44780-7). Follett Publishing.
--Lakhmi, Girl of India. Darbois, Dominique, illus. LC 64-10552. (Illus.). 47 p. 27cm. (Children of the world books). 1964. (ISBN 0-695-44970-2). Follett Pub. Co.
--Noriko, Girl Of Japan. Darbois, Dominique, illus. 1964. (ISBN 0-695-46395-0). Follett Publishing.
--Rikka and Rindji: Children of Bali. Darbois, Dominique, illus. LC 59-14049. (Illus.). 47 p. 26cm. (Children of the world books). (gr. 3-5). c.1959. (ISBN 0-695-47750-1). Follett Pub. Co.
--Tacho, Boy of Mexico. Darbois, Dominique, illus. (Illus.). (gr. 3-5). 1961. (ISBN 0-695-48440-0). Follett.
Darby, Ada Claire, jt. auth. see Violette, Hallie Hall.
Darby, Ada Claire (1883-)
--Brave Venture: A Story of the First Thanksgiving;. 1st Ed ed. Floyd, James Torbert, illus. LC 52-12894. 184p. illus. 22cm. (Winston adventure books). 1953. Winston.
--Columbine Susan. Simon, Howard (1903-1979), illus. LC 40-33278. 5 p. l., 3-273, 1 p. incl. illus., plates. front. 20 cm. 1940. Frederick A. Stokes Company.

--Columbine Susan. Simon, Howard (1903-1979), illus. N.D. J. B. Lippincott Co.
--Gay Soeurette. Gilkison, Grace, Mrs., illus. LC 33-27392. 4 p. l., 312 p. incl. front., illus. 20 cm. 1933. Frederick A. Stokes Company.
--Hickory-Goody. Gilkison, Grace, Mrs., illus. LC 30-205862. 5 p. l., 277 p. incl. plates. col. front. 20 cm. 1930. Frederick A. Stokes Company.
--Island Girl. 1St Ed ed. Castle, Jane, illus. LC 51-11162. 215 p. illus. 21 cm. 1951. Lippincott.
--Jump Lively, Jeff!". Paull, Grace A. (1898-), illus. LC 42-19439. 279, 1 p. incl. front., illus. 21 cm. 1942. Frederick A. Stokes Company.
--Jump Lively Jeff!. Paull, GraceA. (1898-), illus. N.D. J. B. Lippincott.
--Keturah Came Round the Horn. Gilkison, Grace, Mrs., illus. N.D. J. B. Lippincott.
--Keturah Came 'round the Horn: A Story of Old California. Gilkison, Grace, Mrs., illus. LC 35-8215. 7 p. l., 296 p. incl. front., illus. 20 cm. 1935. Frederick A. Stokes Company.
--Look Away, Dixie Land!". Wright, Cameron, illus. LC 41-18351. viii p., 1 l., 339 p. illus. 21 cm. c.1941. Frederick A. Stokes Company.
--Look Away, Dixie Land!. Wright, Cameron, illus. N.D. J. B. Lippincott Co.
--Peace-Pipes at Portage: A Story of Old St. Louis. Gilkison, Grace, Mrs., illus. LC 38-27388. vii, 253 p. illus. 20 cm. 1938. Frederick A. Stokes Company.
--Pinafores and Pantalettes: Or, The Big Brick House. Chapman, Billie, illus. LC 27-14604. 5 p. l., 270 p. front., plates. 20 cm. c.1927. L. C. Page & Company.
--Pull Away, Boatman. 1St Ed ed. McGee, Millard, illus. LC 53-10215. 247p. illus. 21cm. 1953. Lippincott.
--Scally Alden. Woodring, Gaye, illus. LC 29-30082. 22cm. 241p. 1929. Laidlaw Bros.
--Skip-Come-a-Lou. LC 28-21492. 4 p. l., 243 p. col. front. 20 cm. 1928. Frederick A. Stokes Company.
--Skip-Come-A-Lou. N.D. J. B. Lippincott.
--Sometimes Jenny Wren. Gilkison, Grace, Mrs., illus. LC 31-200723. 5 p. l., 294 p. incl. plates. col. front., col. plates. 20 cm. 1931. Frederick A. Stokes Company.
--Sometimes Jenny Wren. Gilkison, Grace, Mrs., illus. N.D. J. B. Lippincott.
--Yonder the Golden Gate: A Story of Old San Francisco. Haste, Laurence B., illus. LC 39-20237. ix, 1, 341 p. illus. 22 cm. 1939. Frederick A. Stokes Company.

Darby, Gene Kegley (1921-)
--Doc, the Dog. Miller, Edward (1905-1974), illus. LC 77-78841. (Illus.). 48 p. 21cm. (Animal adventure series). 1970. Benefic Press.
--Gomar, the Gosling. Miller, Edward (1905-1974), illus. LC 75-78838. (Illus.). 47 p. 21cm. (Animal adventure series). 1969. Benefic Press.
--Hamilton, the Hamster. Miller, Edward (1905-1974), illus. LC 73-78840. (Illus.). 48 p. 21cm. (Animal adventure series). 1970. Benefic Press.
--Horace, the Horse. Miller, Edward (1905-1974), illus. LC 70-78842. (Illus.). 48 p. 21cm. (Animal adventure series). 1970. Benefic Press.
--Jerry Finds Ants. Nerlinger, Joe, illus. (Illus.). (gr. 2-4). 1964. (ISBN 0-8114-7583-2). Steck-V.
--Jerry Finds Bees. Nerlinger, Joe, illus. LC 67-14785. 48p. col. illus. 24cm. 1967. Steck-Vaughan.
--Jerry Finds Spiders. Nerlinger, Joe, illus. LC 69-11096. (Illus.). 48 p. 23cm. 1969. (ISBN 0-8114-7664-2). Steck-Vaughn Co.
--Leonard Discovers America. Nerlinger, Joe, illus. (Leonard and His Time Machine Ser.). (RL 1.6). N.D. (ISBN 0-201-40603-9). Addison-Wesley.
--Leonard Visits Dinosaur Land. Nerlinger, Joe, illus. (Time Machine Ser). (RL 2.0). N.D. (ISBN 0-201-40604-7). Addison-Wesley.
--Leonard Visits Sitting Bull. (Time Machine Ser.). (RL 2.2). N.D. (ISBN 0-201-40605-5). Addison-Wesley.
--Pat, the Parakeet. Miller, Edward (1905-1974), illus. LC 74-78843. (Illus.). 48 p. 21cm. (Animal adventure series). 1970. Benefic Press.

Darby, James M.
--In the Land of Taboos. (Illus.). (gr. 4-6). 1957. St Anthony.

Darby, Oscar Nolan
--Favorite Stories: Adapted by. Rogers, Carol, ed. LC 56-10051. 224p. illus. 22cm. 1956. Steck Co.

Darby, Oscar Nolan, ed. see Irving, Washington.
Darby, Oscar Nolan, jt. ed. see Pulliam, Roy Avron.
Darby, Oscar Nolan, ed. see Stevenson, Robert Louis.
D'Arcy, Margaretta, jt. auth. see Arden, John.
Darden, Dorothy
--Tales from the Four Winds. 1st ed. LC 56-840121. 88p. illus. 21cm. 1956. Pageant Press.

Dare, Elaine St. Johns
--My Friend God. 1st ed. Teichman, Dorothy, illus. LC 56-8315. 28cm. 44p. 1956. E. P. Dutton & Co.

Dare, Viola
--Little Poems for Little Folks. LC 30-4509. 2 p. l., 33p. 19 1/2cm. c.1930. Stratford Co.

Dareff, Hal (1920-)
--Fun with ABC and 1-2-3: An Alphabet and Counting Book in Rhyme. Hafner, Marylin (1925-), illus. LC 65-18659. 1 v. (unpaged) col. illus. 26cm. 1965. Parents Magazine Press.

DaRif, Andrea
--The Blueberry Cake that Little Fox Baked. DaRif, Andrea, illus. LC 84-444. 1984. (ISBN 0-689-50307-5). Atheneum.

Daring, Hope, pseud., see Johnson, Anna.
Daringer, Helen Fern (1892-)
--Adopted Jane. Seredy, Kate (1899-1975), illus. LC 47-30260. 4 p. l., 3-225 p. incl. illus., plates. 20 1/2 cm. 1947. Harcourt, Brace and Company.
--Bigity Anne. Sibley, Don (1922-), illus. LC 54-5152. (Illus.). 177 p. 21cm. 1954. Harcourt, Brace.
--Country Cousin. Godwin, Stephani & Godwin, Edward Fell (1912-), illus. LC 51-9582. 277 p. illus. 21 cm. (gr. 7 up). 1951. (ISBN 0-15-220190-4). Harcourt, Brace.
--Debbie of the Green Gate. Godwin, Edward Fell (1912-), illus. LC 50-5815. (Illus.). 232 p. 21cm. 1950. Harcourt, Brace.
--A Flower of Araby. Marokvia, Artur F. (1909-), illus. LC 58-5706. (Illus.). 188 p. 21cm. 1958. Harcourt, Brace.
--The Golden Thorn. Werth, Kurt (1896-), illus. LC 56-5873. (Illus.). 181 p. 21cm. 1956. Harcourt, Brace.
--Just Plain Betsy. Geer, Charles Hand (1922-), illus. LC 67-19890. (Illus.). 160 p. 21cm. 1967. Harcourt, Brace & World.
--Keepsake Ring. 1st ed. Godwin, Stephani & Godwin, Edward Fell (1912-), illus. LC 53-5432. 174p. illus. 22cm. 1953. Harcourt, Brace.
--Like a Lady. 1st ed. Knight, Susan, illus. LC 55-5235. 218p. illus. 21cm. (gr. 4-7). c.1955. (ISBN 0-15-245429-2). Harcourt, Brace.
--Mary Montgomery, Rebel. Seredy, Kate (1899-1975), illus. LC 48-6025. (Illus.). 222p. (gr. 7 up). 1948. (ISBN 0-15-252231-X, HJ). HarBraceJ.
--Pilgrim Kate. Seredy, Kate (1899-1975), illus. LC 49-7754. 252 p. 21 cm. N.D. Harcourt,Brce.
--Stepsister Sally. Price, Garrett W. (1896-1979), illus. LC 52-7083. (Illus.). 182p. (gr. 3-7). 1966. (ISBN 0-15-280321-1). (ISBN 0-15-684951-8). HarBraceJ.
--The Turnabout Twins. Geer, Garrett, illus. LC 60-10758. (Illus.). 154 p. 22cm. 1960. Harcourt, Brace.
--Yesterday's Daughter. Hampshire, Michael Allen, illus. LC 64-20224. 156 p. 20 cm. 1964. Harcourt, Brace & World.

Dark, Irene
--Norway. Bird, Frank, illus. LC 66-3957. (Illus.). unpaged. 16 x 21cm. (World dolls series). 1966. Pergamon.

Darke, Marjorie (1929-)
--The First of Midnight. Morris, Anthony, illus. LC 77-13435. (Illus.). 190 p. 22cm. 1978, c.1977. (ISBN 0-8164-3209-0). Seabury Press.
--A Question of Courage. Archer, Janet, illus. LC 75-8756. 208 p. 24cm. 1975. (ISBN 0-690-00789-2). Crowell.

Darley, Dale
--Great Spectacles. (Illus.). N.D. E & J B Young.

Darley, Felix Octavius Carr (1822-1888), illus.
--Aladdin: Or, The Wonderful Lamp. Alta ed. 1888. Porter & Coates.
--The Cooper Stories: Including: "Stories of the Prarie", "Stories of the Woods" & "Stories of the Sea", 3 vols. N.D. Houghton, Osgood & Co.

Darling, Edward (1907-1974)
--When Sparks Fly Upward. 144p. (gr. 6-8). 1970. (ISBN 0-679-24100-0). Washburn.

Darling, Esther Birdsall, Mrs.
--Baldy of Nome. 1947. A. A. Knopf.
--Baldy of Nome. Longstreet, Harriet Price, illus. N.D. Penn.
--Boris, Grandson of Baldy. N.D. Alfred A. Knopf.
--Luck of the Trail. (Young Moderns Edition). 1947. Doubleday & Co.
--Luck of the Trail. Dennis, Morgan (1891-1960), illus. LC 33-285913. 5 p. l., 309 p. cvol. front. 21 cm. 1933. Doubleday, Doran & Company, Inc.
--Luck of the Trail. Dennis, Morgan (1891-1960), illus. LC 39-24300. 5 p. l., 309 p. col. front. 21 cm. (Young moderns bookshelf). 1939. The Sun Dial Press, Inc.
--Navarre of the North. Bull, Charles Livingston (1874-1932), illus. LC 30-21938. 5 p. l., 268 p. front. 21 cm. 1930. Doubleday, Doran & Company, Inc.
--Navarre of the North: A Thrilling Story of the Grandson of Baldy of Nome. LC 35-76768. 5 p. l., 268 p. 21 cm. (Young moderns books). 1935. Doubleday, Doran & Company, Inc.
--Navarre of the North: A Thrilling Story of the Grandson of Baldy of Nome. LC 46-8617. 5 p. l., 268 p. 20 cm. (Young moderns). 1946. Doubleday & Co., Inc.
--Navarre of the North: A Thrilling Story of the Grandson of Baldy of Nome. LC 37-22649. 5 p. l., 268 p. front. 21 cm. (Young modern bookshelf). 1937. The Sun Dial Press, Inc.

Darling, Frank
--Fuzzie & the Drummer Boy. (Illus.). (gr. k-2). 1967. (ISBN 0-8382-0278-0). Hale.

Darling, Kathy, pseud., see Darling, Mary Kathleen.
Darling, Kathy, pseud. (1943-)
--Bug Circus. Darling, Mary Kathleen. Brown, Buck (1936-), illus. LC 76-17021. (Illus.). 47 p. 23cm. (For real book). c.1976. (ISBN 0-8116-4301-8). Garrard Pub. Co.
--The Easter Bunny's Secret. Darling, Mary Kathleen. Oechsli, Kelly (1918-), illus. LC 78-58521. (Illus.). 48 p. 23cm. (Garrard mystery book). c.1978. (ISBN 0-8116-6405-8). Garrard Pub. Co.
--Jack Frost and the Magic Paint Brush. Darling, Mary Kathleen. Oechsli, Kelly (1918-), illus. LC 76-14465. (Illus.). 47 p. 23cm. c.1977. (ISBN 0-8116-4402-2). Garrard Pub. Co.
--The Jelly Bean Contest. Darling, Mary Kathleen. Brown, Buck (1936-), illus. LC 72-3450. (Illus.). 61 p. 23cm. 1972. (ISBN 0-8116-6970-X). Garrard Pub. Co.
--Little Bat's Secret. Darling, Mary Kathleen. Szekeres, Cyndy (1933-), illus. LC 74-8175. (Illus.). 64 p. 24cm. 1974. (ISBN 0-8116-6975-0). Garrard Pub. Co.
--The Mystery in Santa's Toyshop. Darling, Mary Kathleen. Pierson, Lori, illus. LC 77-19090. (Illus.). 48 p. 23cm. (Garrard mystery book). c.1978. (ISBN 0-8116-6402-3). Garrard Pub. Co.
--Pecos Bill Finds a Horse. Darling, Mary Kathleen. Szekeres, Cyndy (1933-), illus. LC 79-12079. (Illus.). 40 p. 23cm. c.1979. (ISBN 0-8116-4047-7). Garrard Pub. Co.

Darling, Kathy, pseud. (1943-) & Wunder, Ira
--Paul and His Little-Big Dog. Darling, Mary Kathleen. Ray, Brian (1939-), illus. LC 77-22267. (Illus.). 32 p. 23cm. (For real book). c.1977. (ISBN 0-8116-4307-7). Garrard Pub. Co.

Darling, Lois MacIntyre (1917-) & Darling, Louis, Jr. (1916-1970)
--The Sea Serpents Around Us. Darling, Louis, Jr. (1916-1970) & Darling, Lois MacIntyre (1917-), illus. LC 65-16843. ix, 69p. illus. 18x25cm. c.1965. Little.

Darling, Louis, Jr., jt. auth. see Darling, Lois MacIntyre.
Darling, Marjorie
--Journey to Ankara. Creekmore, Raymond (1905-), illus. LC 54-12608. unpaged. illus. 27cm. 1954. Macmillan.

Darling, Mary Greenleaf (1848-)
--Battles at Home. LC 74-180995. (Illus.). 329 p. 20cm. 1877. Lee and Shepard.
--Battles at Home, 1 of 30 vols. (American Girls' Ser.: No. 1). 1900. Set. Lee & Shepard.
--A Girl of this Century: A Continuation of "We Four Girls". True, Lilian Crawford, illus. 1902. Lothrop, Lee & Shepard.
--In the World. LC 12-31529. 330 p. incl. front. plates. 18 cm. 1871. H. B. Fuller.
--In the World, 1 of 30 vols. (Sequel to "Battles at Home"). (American Girls' Ser.: No. 8). 1900. Set. Lee & Shepard.
--We Four Girls: A Summer Story for Girls. 1899. Lothrop, Lee & Shepard.

Darling, Mary Kathleen see Darling, Kathy, pseud.
Darlington, Edgar B. P.
--The Circus Boys Across the Continent: Or, Winning New Laurels on the Tanbark. (The Circus Boys Series). N.D. Henry Altemus Company.
--The Circus Boys in Dixie Land: Or, Winning the Plaudits of the Sunny South. (The Circus Boys Ser.). N.D. Henry Altemus Company.
--The Circus Boys on the Flying Rings: Or, Making the Start in the Sawdust Life. (The Circus Boys Series). N.D. Henry Altemus Company.
--The Circus Boys on the Mississippi: Or, Afloat with the Big Show on the Big River. LC 12-21151. 252 p. incl. front., plates. 20 cm. (His The circus boys series). c.1912. Henry Altemus Company.
--The Circus Boys on the Plains: Or, The Young Advance Agents Ahead of the Show. (The Circus Boys Series). N.D. Henry Altemus Company.

Darlington, Madge Fyffe (1890-)
--Out to Grandpa's: A Novel for the Young in Heart. LC 64-19190. 52 p. 22 cm. N.D. Greenwich Book Publishers,.
--Stories for the Kindergarten. LC 49-49341. vii, 106 p. 21 cm. 1949. Naylor.

Darlington, Sandy, ed. see Dranow, Ralph.
Darmand, Frances Ullmann (1904-)
--A Very, Very Special Day. Vroman, Tom, illus. LC 63-8176. unpaged. illus. 29 cm. 1963. Parents' Magazine Press.

Darnell, Eula K.
--Sonny & the Mountain. Darnell, Eula K., illus. LC 79-63420. (Illus.). 1979. (ISBN 0-533-04262-3). Vantage.
--A Trip to the Hospital: Memories. 1982. (ISBN 0-533-05085-5). Vantage.

Darnton, Maida Castelhun, Mrs., tr. see Fabricius, Johan Wigmore.
Darnton, Maida Castelhun, Mrs., tr. see Hamsun, Marie Andersen, Mrs.
Darnton, Maida Castelhun, Mrs., tr. see Mezger, Max.

Darrah, Jane, ed.
--Legends of Long Ago. LC 61-17995. (Illus.). 25cm. 371p. (Collier's Junior Classics Ser.). 1962. Crowell-Collier Pub.

Darrel, David
--Boo Baboon. Darrel, David, illus. LC 40-6445. 36 p. illus. 22 x 25 cm. c.1940. C. Scribner's Sons.

Darrell, Margery
--Once Upon a Time: The Fairy Tale World of Arthur Rackham. Rackham, Arthur (1867-1939), illus. LC 72-81255. (Illus.). 296 p. 24cm. (Studio book). 1972. (ISBN 0-670-52574-X). Viking Press.

Darrow, Whitney, Jr., jt. auth. see Cole, Joanna.
Darrow, Whitney, Jr., jt. auth. see Kahn, Joan.
Darrow, Whitney, Jr. (1909-)
--Animal Etiquette. LC 69-16868. 48 p. 18cm. 1969. Windmill Books.
--I'm Glad I'm a Boy!. I'm Glad I'm a Girl!. LC 72-107277. (Illus.). 41 p. 18cm. 1970. Windmill Books Inc.

Dart, Archa O
--Jack's Adventure. LC 37-158873. 148 p. illus. 20 cm. c.1936. Southern Publishing Association.
--Martha Jean of Idylwild. LC 38-326190. 254 p. incl. front., illus. 20 cm. c.1938. Review and Herald Publishing Association.

Dartnell, G. E.
--Ella's Locket, and What It Brought Her. N.D. Thomas Nelson and Sons.

Darton, Frederick Joseph Harvey
--The Canterbury Pilgrims. N.D. Frederick A. Stokes.
--The Story of the Canterbury Pilgrims. Kirk, Maria Louise (1860-), illus. (Fine Art Juveniles). N.D. Frederick A. Stokes.
--The Story of the Canterbury Pilgrims. Kirk, Maria Louise (1860-), illus. 1947. J. B. Lippincott.
--The Wonder Book of Beasts. 1909. Frederick A. Stokes.

Darton, Frederick Joseph Harvey, adapted by.
--Old English Stories. (Illus.). (The Children's Bookshelf). N.D. Dodge Publishing Company.

Darton, Frederick Joseph Harvey, jt. auth. see Johnson, Richard.
Daru, Juliska, pseud., see Craine, Edith Janice.
Daru, Juliska, pseud. (1881-)
--D: Stephen the Valiant. Craine, Edith Janice. Lederer, Charlotte Bacskay, Mrs. (1872-), illus. N.D. E. P. Dutton & Co.
--Peter. Craine, Edith Janice. Lederer, Charlotte Bacskay, Mrs. (1872-), illus. 1931. E. P. Dutton & Co.

Darwin, Bernard Richard Meirion (1876-) & Darwin, Elinor Mary Monsell, Mrs.
--Mr. Tootleoo and Co. LC 37-4469. 45 p. col. illus. 19 x 25 cm. 1936. Harper & Brothers.
--The Tale of Mr. Tootleoo. LC 26-276859. 46 p. col., plates. 20 x 27 cm. 1926. Harper & Brothers.
--Tootleoo Two. LC 29-13064. 42 p. col. plates. 20 x 27 cm. 1928. Harper & Brothers.

Darwin, Elinor Mary Monsell, jt. auth. see Darwin, Bernard Richard Meirion.
Darwin, Elinor Mary Monsell, Mrs., jt. auth. see Darwin, Bernard Richard Meirion.
Darwin, Gary
--Darwin's Thumb Tip Miracles. Fenton, Robert & Fenton, Irene, eds. Darwin, Gary, et al., illus. Darwin, Siegfried, intro. by. (Illus.). 129p. (Orig.). (gr. 8 up). 1981. (ISBN 0-939024-00-4). (ISBN 0-686-98459-5). (ISBN 0-939024-01-2). Rare Pub.

Daryl, Sydney
--A Life Voyage: Or, With the Tide. (Illus.). N.D. Scribner, Welford & Armstrong.

Das, Manoj
--Stories of Light & Delight. Mario, illus. (Illus.). (Nehru Library for Children). (gr. 2-8). 1979. (ISBN 0-89744-181-8). Auromere.

Dasent, George Webbe, Sir (1817-1896), tr. see Asbjornsen, Peter Christen.
Dasent, George Webbe, Sir (1817-1896), tr. see Asbjornsen, Peter Christen (1812-1885) & Moe, Jorgen Engebretsen.

--Miracle on Thirty Fourth Street. LC 47-4221. (gr. 7 up). N.D. (ISBN 0-15-160239-5). HarBraceJ.
--Miracle on Thirty-Fourth Street. De Paola, Tomie, pseud. (1934-), illus. De Paola, Thomas Anthony. 1984. Harcourt.

Daviess, Maria Thompson (1872-1924)
--The Elected Mother. N.D. Bobbs-Merrill Co.
--The Melting of Molly. N.D. Grosset & Dunlap.
--Miss Selina Lue and The Soap-Box Babies. Meylan, Paul J., illus. N.D. Bobbs-Merrill Company.
--Phyllis. 286p. N.D. Century Co.
--Sue Jane. Furman, E. A., illus. LC 12-22558. 5 p. l., 3-223 p. incl. plates. front. 20 cm. 1912. The Century Co.
--The Treasure Babies. King, W. B., illus. LC 11-234080. 4 p. l., 203, 1 p. front., plates. 20 cm. c.1911. The Bobbs-Merrill Company.

Davis, Alice Vaught
--Peter Penguin. Wise, Guy Brown (1895-), illus. LC 39-25880. (Illus.). 23 x 30cm. 32p. 1939. G. P. Putnam, Inc.
--Timothy Turtle. (Illus.). (gr. k-3). 1940. (ISBN 0-8382-0874-6). Hale.
--Timothy Turtle. Wiser, Guy Brown (1895-), illus. LC 40-32634. (Illus.). (gr. k-3). 1940. (ISBN 0-15-288268-1, HJ). HarBraceJ.
--Timothy Turtle. Wiser, Guy Brown (1895-), illus. LC 40-32634. (Illus.). (gr. 1-4). 1972. (ISBN 0-15-690450-0, VoyB). HarBraceJ.

Davis, Anne Pence
--Mimi at Camp: The Adventures of a Tomboy. LC 39-105261. 3 p. l., 13-251 p. 20 cm. c.1935. The Goldsmith Publishing Company.
--The Top Hand of Lone Tree Ranch. Savitt, Sam (1917-), illus. LC 60-9165. (Illus.). 81 p. 21cm. 1960. Crowell.
--Wishes Are Horses. Hauger, Madge, illus. LC 38-17086. vii p., 2 l., 275 p. illus. 22 cm. c.1938. Mathis, Van Nort & Co.

Davis, Antia
--The Little Yellow School Bus. N.D. Carlton Press.

Davis, Barbara Steincrohn
--Forest Hotel. Benvenuti, G., illus. (Illus.). 24p. (gr. k-1). 1976. (ISBN 0-307-60350-4, Golden Pr). Western Pub.
Scrubadubba Dragon. Dolezal, Carroll, illus. LC 70-150344. (Illus.). 32 p. 24cm. (gr. k-2). 1971. (ISBN 0-8114-7729-0). Steck-Vaughn Co.

Davis, Berrie (1922-)
--The Fourth Day of Fear. 1973. (ISBN 0-399-11232-4). G.P. Putnam's Sons.

Davis, Bette J (1923-)
--Freedom Eagle. Davis, Bette J. (1923-), illus. LC 72-1087. (Illus.). 61, 3 p. 25cm. 1972. Lothrop, Lee & Shepard Co.

Davis, Bette (1914-)
--Spiders, Crabs, and Creepy Crawlers: Two African Folktales. Arnott, Kathleen, ed. LC 78-1057. (Illus.). 46 p. 23cm. c.1978. (ISBN 0-8116-4412-X). Garrard Pub. Co.

Davis, Betty Elise
--Scotchtown Tale. Ayer, Margaret (0000-1981), illus. LC 46-7093. (Illus.). 21cm. 144p. 1946. T. Nelson & Sons.
--Young Tom Jefferson's Adventure Chest. Paflin, Roberta, pseud. (1903-), illus. Petty, Roberta Harris Pfafflin. LC 42-51180. 249 p. incl. front., plates. 21 cm. 1942. M. S. Mill Co., Inc.

Davis, Burke (1913-)
--Roberta E. Lee. Opper, John, illus. LC 56-11473. (The Sad but Almost True Story of the Rabbit Who Longed to BE Prettier Than Scarlett O'Hara or Anybody Else). unpaged. illus. 26 cm. (gr. 3-7). 1956. (ISBN 0-910244-07-3). J. F. Blair.

Davis, Burton Elsworth (1888-)
--Pet Poems. Liggera, John, illus. LC 54-9130. 66p. illus. 23cm. 1954. Vantage Press.

Davis, Carl Brandt, jt. auth. see Davis, Dorothy Brandt.

Davis, Caroline E. Kelly, Mrs. (1831-)
--Alice Haven. N.D. Bradley & Woodruff.
--Alice Haven. N.D. Henry Hoyt.
--Andy Hall: Or, The Mission Scholar in the Army. N.D. Henry Hoyt.
--Aunt Lois. N.D. Bradley & Woodruf's.
--Aunt Lois: Or, Happiness to Others. (The C. E. K. D. Library For Girls). N.D. Henry Hoyt.
--Baby's Christmas. N.D. Henry Hoyt.
--Benny the Newsboy, 1 of 12 vols. (Illus.). (Flowers for Children). N.D. D Lothrop.
--Benny the Newsboy, 1 of 12 vols. (Illus.). (Playmate Ser.). N.D. Set. Lothrop Publishing Co.
--Bernice, the Farmer's Daughter. (Illus.). 283p. N.D. A. I. Bradley & Co.'s Pub.
--Bernice, the Farmer's Daughter. N.D. Henry Hoyt.
--Billie's Good Friend, 1 of 12 vols. (Illus.). (Flowers for Children). N.D. D Lothrop.
--Billy's Good Friend, 1 of 12 vols. (Playmate Ser.). N.D. Set. Lothrop Publishing Co.
--Brave Donald, 1 of 12 vols. (Illus.). (Flowers for Children). N.D. D Lothrop.
--Brave Donald, 1 of 12 vols. (Playmate Ser.). N.D. Set. Lothrop Publishing Co.
--Cain and Abel, 1 of 25 vols. (Illus.). (Infant Lib.: No. 9). N.D. Set. A. I. Bradley & Co.'s Pub.
--Cain and Abel to the Tabernacle. (The Child Library). N.D. Henry Hoyt.
--Carrie Allison. N.D. Bradley & Woodruff.
--Chew Alley: Or, How to Make Sunshine. (Illus.). 400p. N.D. A. I. Bradley & Co.'s Pub.
--Chew Alley: Or, How to make Sunshine. (C. E. K. D. Library For Girls). N.D. Henry Hoyt.
--Child Bible Stories. (Illus.). N.D. Bradley & Woodruff.
--Child Jesus, 1 of 25 vols. (Illus.). (Infant Lib.: No. 9). N.D. Set. A. I. Bradley & Co.'s Pubs.
--Christmas Story. N.D. Bradley & Woodruff.
--Daisey Deane. N.D. Henry Hoyt.
--Daisy Deane, 1 of 25 vols. (Illus.). (Intermediate, Primary and Infant Libs.). N.D. A. I. Bradley & Co.'s Pubs.
--Daisy Lost and Daisy Found, 1 of 12 vols. (Illus.). (Flowers for Children). N.D. D Lothrop.
--Daisy Lost and Daisy Found, 1 of 12 vols. (Illus.). (Playmate Ser.). N.D. D Lothrop.
--Disobedient Walter, 1 of 12 vols. (Illus.). (Flowers for Children). N.D. D Lothrop.
--Disobedient Walter, 1 of 12 vols. (Illus.). (Playmate Ser.). N.D. D Lothrop.
--Dotty, 1 of 12 vols. (Illus.). (Flowers for Children). N.D. D Lothrop.
--Dotty, 1 of 12 vols. (Illus.). (Playmate Ser.). N.D. D Lothrop.
--Faithful In Least. N.D. Bradley & Woodruff.
--Faithful In Least. N.D. Henry Hoyt.
--Fireside Talks: Stories On The Commandment. N.D. Bradley & Woodruff.
--Flowers for Children, 12 vols. (Illus.). N.D. Set. D Lothrop.
--Frankie's Little Friend. N.D. Henry Hoyt.
--Frankie's Little Friend. (Illus.). 128p. N.D. Ira Bradley & Co.'s.
--Frankie's Little Meeting. (Illus.). 120p. N.D. Ira Bradley & Co's.
--Frankie's Work, 1 of 36 vols. (Illus.). (Primary Lib.: No. 8). N.D. Set. A. I. Bradley & Co.'s Pubs.
--Frankie's Work. N.D. Henry Hoyt.
--Frisk, 1 of 12 vols. (Illus.). (Playmate Ser.). N.D. D Lothrop.
--Froggy's Little Brother: Or, The Honest Street Sweeper. (Illus.). 294p. N.D. Ira Bradley & Co's.
--Gerty Harding's Mission. (Illus.). 260p. N.D. A. I. Bradley & Co.'s Pub.
--Gerty Harding's Mission. N.D. Henry Hoyt.
--Gold Bracelets. N.D. Bradley & Woodruff.
--Grace Hale. N.D. Bradley & Woodruff.
--Grace Hale. N.D. Henry Hoyt.
--Grace Martin. N.D. Henry Hoyt.
--Grandpa's Girl, 1 of 12 vols. (Illus.). (Flowers for Children). N.D. D Lothrop.
--Grandpa's Girl, 1 of 12 vols. (Playmate Ser.). N.D. Set. Lothrop Publishing Co.
--Granny Bright's Blanket. (Illus.). 459p. N.D. A. I. Bradley & Co.'s Pub.
--Granny Bright's Blanket. LC 42-43709. 18cm. 432p. (C. E. K. D. Library For Girls). 1873. Henry Hoyt.
--Heart's Delight. (Illus.). 432p. N.D. A. I. Bradley & Co.
--Hearts' Delight. LC 42-43709. 432 p. front., plates. 18 cm. c.1873. H. Hoyt.
--Heart's Delight. New ed. 1875. Henry Hoyt.
--Heart's Delight. (The C. E. K. D. Library For Girls). N.D. Henry Hoyt.
--Holidays At Home, 1 of 3 vols. (Illus.). 400p. (Picture Story Book Ser.). N.D. D. Lothrop & Co.
--Into the Highways. N.D. Bradley & Woodruff.
--Johnny's Captain. N.D. Bradley & Woodruff.
--Johnny's Captain. N.D. Henry Hoyt.
--Little Apple Blossom. N.D. Bradley & Woodruff.
--The Little Conqueror: Or, The Children's Comfort-Bags. N.D. Henry Hoyt.
--Little Maidie. (Part 1). N.D. Henry Hoyt.
--Little Maidie. (Part 2). N.D. Henry Hoyt.
--Little Maidie. (Part 3). N.D. Henry Hoyt.
--Little Maidie, 3 vols, Vols. 1-3. (Illus.). 532p. N.D. Ira Bradley & Co's.
--Little Three-Year Old. 1873. D. Lothrop & Co.
--Mary's Patience Bank. (Illus.). 226p. N.D. A. I. Bradley & Co.'s Pubs.
--Mary's Patience Bank. N.D. Henry Hoyt.
--Matty Frost. N.D. Henry Hoyt.
--Matty Frost. (Illus.). 152p. N.D. Ira Bradley & Co's.
--Miss Benedict's Way. (Illus.). 237p. 1905. American Tract Society.
--Miss Wealthy's Hope, 1 of 50 vols. (Illus.). 350p. (Sunday-School Lib: No. 14). N.D. Set. Lothrop Pub. Co.
--Molly's Verse, 1 of 36 vols. (Primary Lib.: No. 7). N.D. Set. A. I. Bradley & Co.'s Pubs.
--Nettie's Christmas Party, 1 of 12 vols. (Illus.). (Playmate Ser.). N.D. D Lothrop.
--Netty's Christmas Party, 1 of 12 vols. (Illus.). (Flowers for Children). N.D. D Lothrop.
--Netty's Christmas Party, 1 of 6 vols. (Playmate Ser.). N.D. Set. Lothrop Publishing Co.
--No Cross, No Crown. N.D. Bradley & Woodruff.
--No Cross No Crown. N.D. Henry Hoyt.
--The Old Barracks: Or, Seeking the Light. (Illus.). 344p. N.D. A. I Bradley & Co.'s Pubs.
--Old Barracks: Or, Seeking the Light. N.D. Henry Hoyt.
--Papa's Little Soldiers. N.D. Bradley & Woodruff.
--Papa's Little Soldiers. N.D. Henry Hoyt.
--The Parables. N.D. Bradley & Woodruff.
--The Parables. (The Child Library). N.D. Henry Hoyt.
--Penny Rust's Christmas. (Illus.). 267p. N.D. A. I. Bradley & Co.'s Pubs.
--Penny Rust's Christmas. N.D. Henry Hoyt.
--Playmate Series, 12 vols. (Illus.). N.D. D Lothrop.
--Rose's Dream, 1 of 12 vols. (Playmate Ser.). N.D. Set. Lothrop Publishing Co.
--Ruth Chenery. N.D. Bradley & Woodruff.
--Ruth Chenery. N.D. Henry Hoyt.
--The Squire's Daughter. N.D. Bradley & Woodruff.
--The Squire's Daughter. N.D. Henry Hoyt.
--The Sunny Path. N.D. Bradley & Woodruff.
--The Sunny Path. N.D. Henry Hoyt.
--The Tabernacle. N.D. Bradley & Woodruff.
--Tabernacle to Jonah. (The Child Library). N.D. Henry Hoyt.
--Talking Portraits, 1 of 12 vols. (Illus.). (Flowers for Children). N.D. D Lothrop.
--That Boy. (Illus.). (Child Life Ser.). N.D. D. Lothrop Co.
--That Boy, 1 of 4 vols. Curtis, Jessie, illus. (Merry Christmas Library). 1882. D Lothrop.
--Tina's Child-Life. (Illus.). (Morning Glory Ser.). N.D. D. Lothrop Co.
--Tina's Child-Life. (Golden Lily Ser.). N.D. D. Lothrop Co.
--Toady. N.D. Bradley & Woodruff.
--Two Babies. (Illus.). (Flowers for Children). N.D. D Lothrop.
--Two Babies, 1 of 12 vols. (Illus.). (Playmate Ser.). N.D. D Lothrop.
--Two Books. N.D. Bradley & Woodruff.
--Two Books. N.D. Henry Hoyt.
--Upward Path. N.D. Bradley & Woodruff.
--The Upward Path. N.D. Henry Hoyt.
--The Yachtville Boys. N.D. Bradley & Woodruff.
--Yachtville Boys. N.D. Henry Hoyt.

Davis, Caroline E. Kelly, Mrs. (1831-) & Hopkins, L. P., Mrs.
--Bartie and Willie. N.D. Bradley & Woodruff.
--Clever Little People. N.D. Bradley & Woodruff.
--Dead Monkey. N.D. Bradley & Woodruff.
--Grandmother True. N.D. Bradley & Woodruff.
--Ivan. N.D. Bradley & Woodruff.
--Mamma's Talks. N.D. Bradley & Woodruff.
--Molly's Verse. N.D. Bradley & Woodruff.
--Our Father In Heaven. N.D. Bradley & Woodruff.

Davis, Caroline E. Kelly, Mrs. (1831-) & Macdonald, George (1824-1905)
--A Double Story, 1 of 4 Vols. Curtis, Jessie, illus. (Little Mother Ser.). N.D. Set. D Lothrop & Co.
--Little Mother and Other Stories, 1 of 4 Vols. Curtis, Jessie, et al., illus. (Little Mother Ser.). N.D. Set. D Lothrop & Co.
--Little Mother Series, 4 vols. Curtis, Jessie, et al., illus. N.D. Set. D Lothrop.
--Papa's Boy, 1 of 4 vols. Curtis, Jessie, et al., illus. (Little Mother Ser.). N.D. Set. D Lothrop & Co.
--Robbie Meredith, 1 of 4 Vols. Curtis, Jessie, et al., illus. (Little Mother Ser.). N.D. Set. D Lothrop & Co.

Davis, Caroline (1900-)
--Jungle Child. Martinez, Jean, illus. LC 50-10363. (Illus.). 256 p. 22cm. 1950. Viking Press.
--The Roaring in the Glens. Bisset, Douglas, illus. LC 67-1120. (Illus.). 154 p. 22cm. 1967, c.1966. Abelard-Schuman.

Davis, Charles Belmont
--Her Own Sort and Others. N.D. Charles Scribner's Sons.

Davis, Charles Evan (1901-)
--Joe and Bob on Northland Trails. Higgins, Cardwell S., illus. LC 49-10650. 162 p. illus. 22 cm. 1949. J. Messner.
--Senior Days at Davenport High. Fleur, Anne Elizabeth (1901-), illus. Sari, pseud. LC 51-10056. 177 p. illus. 21 cm. 1951. Messner.

Davis, Christopher (1928-)
--Sad Adam, Glad Adam. Tusan, Stan (1936-), illus. LC 66-6326. 31p. illus. 22cm. (gr. 1-3). 1966. Crowell-Collier.

Davis, Clyde Brion (1894-1962)
--Eyes of Boyhood. LC 53-10221. 323 p. 22cm. 1953. Lippincott.
--North Woods Whammy. 1st ed. LC 51-9795. 219 p. 21 cm. 1951. Lippincott.
--Northend Wildcats. Shenton, Edward (1895-), illus. LC 38-34544. 5 p. l., 3-305, 1 p. incl. front., illus., plates. 20 cm. c.1938. Farrar & Rinehart, Inc.

Davis, Daphne
--The Donald Duck Book. Davis, Daphne, illus. (ps-1). 1964. (ISBN 0-307-68911-5, Golden Pr). Western Pub.

Davis, Daphne, jt. auth. see Disney, Walt, Productions.

Davis, David, compiled by.
--A Single Star: An Anthology of Christmas Poetry. Gill, Margery Jean (1925-), illus. (Illus.). 94p. 1978. (ISBN 0-370-01269-0, Pub. by Chatto Bodley Jonathan). Merrimack Pub Cir.

Davis, Dorcas
--Book of Maha, the Elephant. McCann, Gerald (1916-), illus. LC [illegible] (Illus.). (gr. 4-7). 1960. Lantern.

Davis, Dorothy Brandt & Davis, Carl Brandt
--The Tall Man. Davis, Dorothy Brandt & Davis, Carl Brandt, illus. LC 63-3596. unpaged. illus. 32 x 14 cm. 1963. Brethren Press.

Davis, Dorothy Brandt & Davis, Sarah Elizabeth
--The Little Man. Davis, Dorothy Brandt & Davis, Sarah Elizabeth, illus. LC 66-6597. 49p. col. illus. 19x28cm. 1966. Brethren Pr.
--The Middle Man. LC 64-4887. (Illus.). 23 x 25cm. 34p. 1964. Brethren Press.

Davis, Dorrit, jt. auth. see Epstein, Beryl Williams.

Davis, Douglas Fredell (1935-)
--The Lion's Tail. Himler, Ronald Norbert (1937-), illus. LC 79-23293. (Illus.). 32 p. 26cm. 1980. (ISBN 0-689-50153-6). Atheneum.
--There's an Elephant in the Garage. Kellogg, Steven (1941-), illus. LC 79-11378. (Illus.). 32 p. c.1979. (ISBN 0-525-41050-3). Dutton.

Davis, E.
--Snip and Whip and Some Other Boys. (Illus.). 1882. Lee & Shepard.

Davis, E. K (1937-)
--Mrs. Brisby's Remembering Game. Chandler, Jean (1927-), illus. LC 81-86489. (Illus.). 12 p. 21cm. (Little golden sniff it book). c.1982. (ISBN 0-307-13209-9). Golden Press.
--The Poky Little Puppy at the Fair. Chandler, Jean (1927-), illus. LC 81-81327. (Illus.). 12 p. 21cm. (Little Golden sniff it book). c.1981. (ISBN 0-307-13203-X). Golden Press.

Davis, Earle, ed. see Dickens, Charles John Huffam.

Davis, Edith Vezolles , ed. see Disney, Walt, Productions.
--Celia's Choice, How One Girl Solved Her Problems. Gretter, J. Clemens, illus. LC 33-24353. 319 p. incl. front., plates. 21 cm. c.1933. Lothrop, Lee & Shepard Co.
--The Magic Fiddle and What It Brought to Marie. Inglis, Antoinette, illus. LC 28-22658. 287 p. front., plates. 20 cm. c.1928. Lothrop, Lee & Shepard Co.
--One Girl's Way. Goss, John, illus. LC 30-24238. 314 p. front., plates. 21 cm. c.1930. Lothrop, Lee & Shepard Co.

Davis, Edna Clark
--Miss Polly Wiggles. Greene, Julia, illus. LC 25-176948. 335 p. front., plates. 21 cm. c.1925. Lothrop, Lee & Shepard Co.
--Polly Wiggles and Some Others. Greene, Julia, illus. LC 27-19200. 317 p. front., plates. 20 cm. c.1927. Lothrop, Lee & Shepard Co.

Davis, Edward E.
--Bruno the Pretzel Man. Simont, Marc (1915-), illus. LC 84-47630. (Illus.). 64p. (gr. 2-5). 1984. (ISBN 0-06-021398-1). (ISBN 0-06-021399-X). (ISBN 0-06-021399-X). HarpJ.

Davis, Eileen
--Happiness Around Her, a Tapestry of Youth. LC 47-3532. 5 p. l., 3-208 p. 20 1/2 cm. 1947. Random House.

Davis, Emmett A. (1948-)
--Clues in the Desert. Downing, Julie, illus. LC 83-8626. (Adventure Diary). c.1983. (ISBN 0-940742-29-2). Raintree Publishers.
--Only in Dreams. Urbanovic, Jackie, illus. LC 83-8627. (Illus.). 32p. (Imagination Bks.). (gr. k-3). 1983. (ISBN 0-940742-15-2, Pub. by Carnival Press). (ISBN 0-940742-15-2). Raintree Pubs.
--See No Evil. Franz, Jenny, illus. LC 83-8609. (Illus.). 32p. (Adventure Diaries). (gr. 3-6). 1983. (ISBN 0-940742-14-4, Pub. by Carnival Press). (ISBN 0-940742-14-4). Raintree Pubs.

Davis, Evangeline D
--Rabel Raider. 160p. 1975. J B Lippincott Company.

Davis, F. H., ed.
--Myths and Legends of Japan. (Myths Ser.). N.D. Frederick A. Stokes.

Davis, G. A., illus.
--The Yellow Dwarf, and Other Stories. LC 52-49162. 48 p. illus. 25 cm. (Aunt Fanny's Fairy Tales). c.1907. McLoughlin Bros.

Davis, George M., jt. auth. see Martin, Frank E.

Davis, Gibbs (1953-)
--Fishman and Charly. LC 82-23350. 166 p. 22cm. 1983. (ISBN 0-395-33882-4). Houghton Mifflin.
--Katy's First Haircut. Shute, Linda, illus. LC 85-2435. (Illus.). 32 p. 21cm. 1985. (ISBN 0-395-38942-9). Houghton Mifflin.
--Maud Flies Solo. LC 80-27084. p. cm. 1981. (ISBN 0-87888-173-5). Bradbury Press.
--The Other Emily. Shute, Linda, illus. 1983. Houghton.
--Swann Song. LC 81-18066. 179 p. 22cm. c.1982. (ISBN 0-87888-198-0). Bradbury Press.

Davis, Grace Emeline Tinker, Mrs.
--Mary Eliza's Wonder-Life: A Story About the Make-Believe Things. LC 13-26182. 5 p. l., 115 p. 21 cm. 1913. Sherman, French & Company.

Davis, Grania (1943-), adapted by see Gellek, Nazli.

Davis, Harriet Ide Eager (1892-1974)
--Elmira: The Girl who Loved Edgar Allen Poe. LC 66-9234. (Illus.). 137 p. 24cm. 1966. Houghton Mifflin.
--Tommy Tiptoe. Cooke, Edna W., illus. LC 24-14149. 75, 1 p. col. illus. 21 cm. 1924. A. A. Knopf.

Davis, Harriet Ide Eager (1892-1974) & Eager, John Howard (1848-)
--The Little Mouse. Willis, Bess Goe, illus. LC 22-30108. 62 p., 1l. incl. col. front., col. illus. 15 cm. c.1928. Henry Altemus Company.

Davis, Hazel H
--Davy Crockett. Moyers, William (1916-), illus. LC 55-9512. 64p. c.1955. Random House.
--General Jim. Theibert, Philip Richard, illus. LC 58-9110. 22cm. 192p. (gr. 5-9). 1958. (ISBN 0-8272-1201-1). Bethany Pr.

Davis, Helen Sarchet
--Good Livin'. A Farm Boy's Diary. 1st ed. LC 52-6085. 128 p. 22 cm. 1952. Exposition Press.

Davis, Hubert, ed.
--A January Fog Will Freeze a Hog, and Other Weather Folklore. Wallner, John C. (1945-), illus. 1977. Crown.

Davis, J. W, Mrs., tr. see Hartner, Eva.

Davis, J Walter
--The Gawktown Revival Club: A Satire on Hypocrites. LC 99-125. v. 16 degree. 1899. The Gleaner Pub. Co.

Davis, J. Watson, illus.
--The History of Tom Thumb. LC 5-21563. 22cm. 123p. 1905. A. L. Burt.
--The Story of Bluebeard and Other Stories. LC 5-21568. 23cm. 123p. 1905. A. L. Burt Co.

Davis, James Robert (1945-)
--Garfield A to Z Zoo. Christensen, Anne, ed. Fentz, Mike & Kuhn, Dave, illus. LC 83-17697. (Illus.). 24p. (Garfield Mini-Storybooks). (ps-5). 1984. (ISBN 0-394-86483-2, BYR). (ISBN 0-394-86483-2). Random.
--Garfield Book of the Seasons. Christensen, Anne, ed. Fentz, Mike & Kuhn, Dave, illus. LC 83-17814. (Illus.). 24p. (Garfield Mini-Storybooks). (gr. k-5). 1984. (ISBN 0-394-86482-4). (ISBN 0-394-86482-4). Random.
--Garfield Goes to a Picnic. Fentz, Mike, illus. LC 82-60879. (Illus.). 24p. (Sniffy Bks.). (ps-1). 1983. (ISBN 0-394-85634-1). Random.
--Garfield in Space. LC 83-6061. (Illus.). 32p. (Garfield Mini-Storybks.). (gr. k-5). 1983. (ISBN 0-394-86122-1). Random.
--Garfield Mix & Match Storybook. Davis, James Robert (1945-), illus. (Illus.). (Garfield Ser.). 1982. (ISBN 0-394-85444-6). Random.
--Garfield, the Knight in Shining Armor. Fentz, Mike, illus. LC 82-50232. (Illus.). 31 p. c.1982. (ISBN 0-394-85446-2). Random House.

Davis, Janet
--Completely Cowed. LC 69-16534. 21cm. 162p. 1968, c.1969. Chilton Book Co.

Davis, Janice
--Cowboy Jeans & Chili Beans. (Scratch-Sniff Color Ser.). (gr. 4-9). 1980. (ISBN 0-931318-04-1). Walnut AZ.
--Daisy Discovers Spring. Morris, Jill, illus. (Illus.). (gr. 4-9). N.D. (ISBN 0-931318-03-3). Walnut AZ.
--The Merry Christmas Mice. (Illus.). (Scratch-Sniff-Color Ser.). (gr. 4-9). 1978. (ISBN 0-931318-02-5). Walnut AZ.
--A Tale of the Butterscotch Bears. (Illus.). (Scratch-Sniff-Color Ser.). (gr. 4-9). 1980. (ISBN 0-931318-05-X). Walnut AZ.

Davis, Jennie
--I Can Talk to God Anytime, Anyplace. (ps-k). 1982. (ISBN 0-89693-205-2, Sonflower Bks). SP Pubns.
--In God's Great Way. Endres, Helen Elise, illus. LC 82-7446. (Illus.). 32p. (gr. 1-2). 1982. (ISBN 0-89693-201-X). Dandelion Hse.
--Julie's New Home: A Story about Being a Friend. Karch, Pat, illus. (Illus.). 30p. (Making Choices Ser.). (gr. k-3). 1983. (ISBN 0-516-06384-7). Childrens.
--Praise Him! Praise Him!. Hutton, Kathryn, illus. LC 82-7238. (Illus.). 32p. (ps-k). 1982. (ISBN 0-89693-208-7). Dandelion Hse.

Davis, Jesse
--Classics of the Royal Ballet. LC 79-10866. (Illus.). (gr. 4 up). 1980. (ISBN 0-698-20502-2). Putnam Pub Group.

Davis, Jim see Davis, James Robert.

Davis, John A (1945-)
--Tom Bard and Other Nortonville Boys. LC 12-31917. 408 p. front., plates. 18 cm. c.1882. Presbyterian Board of Publication.

Davis, John G.
--Taller Than Trees. LC 75-13392. 288p. 1975. (ISBN 0-385-11069-3). Doubleday.

Davis, John W., ed.
--Pinocchio Under the Sea. Della-Chiesa, Carolyn M. (1887-), tr. N.D. Macmillan.

Davis, Julia Adams (1900-)
--Mountains are Free. 1st ed. Nadejen, Theodore, illus. LC 30-22749. (Illus.). x, 250 p. 21cm. 1930. E. P. Dutton.
--No Other White Men (Pub. by Dutton). (gr. 7-12). 1972 (Starline). Schol Bk Serv.
--Peter Hale. Wiesenberg, Louis, illus. LC 39-20963. 246, 1 p. incl. front., illus. 21 cm. 1939. E. P. Dutton & Co., Inc.
--Remember and Forget. Pugh, Mabel (1891-), illus. LC 32-21195. 192 p. incl. front., plates. 20 cm. c.1932. E. P. Dutton & Company, Inc.

Davis, Karen, jt. auth. see Cowan, Elizabeth.

Davis, Katherine Kennicott, et al. (1892-)
--Little Drummer Boy. Keats, Ezra Jack (1916-1983), illus. LC 68-25714. (Illus.). full color ils. 32p. (gr. k-3). 1968. (ISBN 0-02-749530-2). Macmillan. **Award: (ALA).**
--The Little Drummer Boy. Keats, Ezra Jack (1916-1983), illus. LC 68-25714. (gr. k-3). 1972. (ISBN 0-02-044090-1, Collier). (ISBN 0-02-044080-4). Macmillan.

Davis, Katherine Wallace
--Pappina, a Little Italian Girl. LC 30-10989. (Illus.). 18cm. 171p. (Little People of Other Lands Ser.). 1928. A. Flanagan Company.

Davis, Lavinia Riker see Farmer, Wendell, pseud.

Davis, Lavinia Riker, Mrs. (1909-1961)
--Adventures in Steel. Dobias, Frank (1902-), illus. LC 38-113061. 8 p. l., 166 p. incl. front., plates. 20 cm. c.1938. Modern Age Books, Inc.
--Americans Every One. Weisgard, Leonard Joseph (1916-), illus. LC 42-36228. 5 p. l., 128 p. incl. illus., plates. (part col.) col. front. 21 cm. 1942. Doubleday, Doran & Co., Inc.
--Bicycle Commandos. Harvey, Alice, illus. LC 44-9413. 3 p. l., 186 p. incl. front., 1 illus., plates. 20 1/2 cm. N.D. Doubleday, Doran and Company, Inc.
--Buttonwood Island. Brown, Paul (1893-1958), illus. LC 40-305618. x p., 1 l., 299 p. front., illus. 21 cm. 1940. Doubleday, Doran & Company, Inc.
--Clown Dog. 1st ed. LC 61-6308. (Illus.). 25cm. 61p. 1961. Doubleday.
--Danny's Luck. Woodward, Hildegard (1898-), illus. (Illus.). (gr. 1-4). 1953. (ISBN 0-385-07755-6). Doubleday.
--Donkey Detectives. 1st ed. Porter, Jean Macdonald (1906-), illus. LC 55-7658. 220p. illus. 22cm. 1955. Doubleday.
--Fish Hook Island Mystery. MacKnight, Ninon (1908-), illus. Ninon, pseud. LC 45-8810. 5 p. l., 239 p. incl. illus., plates. 20 1/2 cm. 1945. Doubleday, Doran and Company, Inc.
--Grab Bag: Stories for Each and Every One. Fischer, Marjorie, Mrs., ed. Weisgard, Leonard Joseph (1916-), illus. LC 41-11985. 4 p. l., 312 p. illus. 21 cm. 1941. Doubleday, Doran & Company, Inc.
--Hearts in Trim. 1st ed. LC 54-6782. 216p. 22cm. 1954. Doubleday.
--Hobby Horse Hill. Brown, Paul (1893-1958), illus. LC 39-27311. 6 p. l., 270 p. incl. front., illus. 21 cm. 1939. Doubleday, Doran & Co., Inc.
--Island City: Adventures in Old New York. Spier, Peter Edward (1927-), illus. LC 61-12509. 256p. c.1961. Doubleday.
--It Happened On a Holiday. Porter, Jean Macdonald (1906-), illus. LC 58-12038. (Illus.). 22cm. 180p. 1958. Doubleday.
--Janey's Fortune. 1st ed. LC 57-7280. 240p. 22cm. 1957. Doubleday.
--The Keys to the City: Adventures in New York. Benjamin, Nora Gottheil (1899-), illus. LC 36-19164. 4 p. l., 264 p. incl. plates. 21 cm. 1936. C. Scribner's Sons.
--Melody, Mutton Bone, and Sam. Brown, Paul (1893-1958), illus. LC 47-11177. 245 p. illus. 21 cm. 1947. Doubleday.
--Peppermint Pond. Farmer, Wendell, pseud. 1St Ed ed. McClelland, John, illus. LC 50-9692. viii, 207 p. illus. 20 cm. 1950. Doubleday.
--Plow Penny Mystery. Brown, Paul (1893-1958), illus. LC 42-22580. 6 p. l., 275 p. illus. 21 cm. 1942. Doubleday, Doran & Company, Inc.
--Pony Jungle. Ross, Gordon, illus. LC 41-12025. 7 p. l., 309 p. col. illus. 21 cm. 1941. Doubleday, Doran & Co., Inc.
--Roger and the Fox. Woodward, Hildegard (1898-), illus. LC 47-11631. 43 p. col. illus. 21 x 26 cm. (Junior books). c.1947. Doubleday. **Award: (RCM).**
--Round Robin. Riswold, Gilbert, illus. 1962. Charles Scribner's Sons.
--Round Robin. Woodward, Hildegard (1898-), illus. LC 43-3408. 4 p. l., 147 p. illus. 21 x 17 1/2 cm. 1943. C. Scribner's Sons.
--Sandy's Spurs. Paull, Grace A. (1898-), illus. LC 51-13708. (Illus.). 246 p. 21cm. 1951. Doubleday.
--A Sea Between. LC 45-3449. 3 p. l., 266 p. 20 cm. 1945. Doubleday, Doran & Co., Inc.
--The Secret of Donkey Island. 1st ed. Porter, Jean Macdonald (1906-), illus. LC 52-11001. 246 p. illus. 20 cm. 1952. Doubleday.
--Skyscraper Mystery. Machetanz, Frederick (1908-), illus. LC 37-19847. viii p., 2 l., 204 p. incl. plates. front. 21 cm. 1937. C. Scribner's Sons.
--Spinney and Spike and the B-29. Shenton, Edward (1895-), illus. LC 44-6752. 3 p. l., 112 p., 1 l. illus. 21 cm. 1944. C. Scribner's Sons.
--Stand Fast and Reply. LC 43-159532. vi p., 1 l., 278 p. 21 cm. 1943. Doubleday, Doran & Company, Inc.
--Summer is Fun. Woodward, Hildegard (1898-), illus. LC 51-13709. 1951. Doubleday & Co.
--The Surprise Mystery. Farmer, Wendell, pseud. Harvey, Alice, illus. LC 43-9927. v p., 1 l., 181 p. illus. 20 cm. 1943. Doubleday, Doran & Company, Inc.
--We All Go Away. Warren, Dorothea, illus. LC 40-7100. 3 p. l., 112 p. illus. 21 x 18 cm. 1940. C. Scribner's Sons.
--We All Go to School. Warren, Dorothea, illus. LC 41-17945. 5 p. l., 156 p., 1 l. illus. (part col.) 21 x 17 cm. 1941. C. Scribner's Sons.
--The Wild Birthday Cake. 1st ed. Woodward, Hildegard (1898-), illus. LC 49-9354. (Illus.). 50 p. 26cm. (Junior books). c.1949. Doubleday. **Award: (RCM).**

Davis, Lois Carlile
--The Winter Donkey. LC 79-8654. 126 p. 21cm. 1980. (ISBN 0-233-97198-X). A. Deutsch.

Davis, Louise Littleton (1921-)
--More Tales of Tennessee. LC 78-15957. 192p. (gr. 6-12). 1978. (ISBN 0-88289-183-9). Pelican.
--Snowball Fight in the White House. Boehm, Linda, illus. LC 73-15782. (Illus.). 63 p. 24cm. 1974. (ISBN 0-664-32539-4). Westminster Press.

Davis, Lovesta Dorwin
--Arimathea's Gift. N.D. The Wartburg Press.

Davis, Lydia Henderson (1919-)
--South Sea Holiday. 1st Ed ed. Davis, Tom, illus. LC 56-8460. 204p. illus. 21cm. (Atlantic Monthly Press book). 1956. Little, Brown.

Davis, M. E. M., pseud., see Davis, Mary Evelyn Moore.

Davis, Mac
--Great Sports Humor. (Illus.). 128p. Repr. (gr. 3-9). 1973. (ISBN 0-448-11529-8, Pretzel Press). G&D.
--Great Sports Humor. LC 73-823. (Illus.). 128p. (Elephant Books). (gr. 3-9). 1976. (ISBN 0-448-12576-5, G&D). Putnam Pub Group.
--Teen-Age Baseball Jokes and Legends. N.D. Grosset & Dunlap.

Davis, Maggie S. (1942-)
--The Best Way to Ripton. Gammell, Stephen, illus. LC 82-2940. (Illus.). 32p. (ps-3). 1982. (ISBN 0-8234-0459-5). Holiday.
--Grandma's Secret Letter. Wallner, John C (1945-), illus. LC 80-23331. (Illus.). 32 p. 25cm. c.1982. (ISBN 0-8234-0382-3). Holiday House.
--Rickety Witch. Chorao, Ann Mckay Sproat (1936-), illus. LC 84-498. (Illus.). 32p. (ps-3). 1984. (ISBN 0-8234-0521-4). (ISBN 0-8234-0521-4). Holiday.

Davis, Marilyn
--The Little Fly. Davis, Laura, illus. (Illus.). (ps-2). 1977. (ISBN 0-682-48739-2). Exposition.

Davis, Mary Evelyn Moore see Davis, M. E. M., pseud.

Davis, Mary Evelyn Moore, Mrs. (1852-1909)
--Jaconetta: Her Boxes. Davis, M. E. M., pseud. LC 1-18550. 12cm. 152p. 1901. Houghton Mifflin & Co.
--Jaconetta: Her Loves. Davis, M. E. M., pseud. N.D. Houghton Mifflin.
--The Moons of Balbanca. 5 p. l., 180 p., 1 l. front., 5 pl. 20 cm. 1908. Houghton Mifflin Company.

Davis, Mary Gould, jt. auth. see Boggs, Ralph Steele.

Davis, Mary Gould, jt. auth. see Kalibala, Ernest Balintuma.

Davis, Mary Gould (1882-)
--Baker's Dozen. Brock, Emma Lillian (1886-1974), illus. LC 30-20065. (Illus.). (gr. 3-7). 1930. (ISBN 0-15-205691-2). HarBraceJ.
--The Handsome Donkey. Brock, Emma Lillian (1886-1974), illus. LC 33-27256. 5 p. l., 3-67 p. incl. illus., plates. col. front., col. plates. 24 cm. c.1933. Harcourt, Brace and Company.
--Sandy's Kingdom. Brock, Emma Lillian (1886-1974), illus. LC 35-273068. 5 p. l., 3-79 p. incl. illus., plates. front. 24 cm. c.1935. Harcourt, Brace & Company.
--With Cap and Bells: Humorous Stories to Tell and to Read Aloud. Bennett, Richard Michael (1899-), illus. LC 37-27464. xviii, 246 p. incl. front., illus., plates. 21 cm. c.1937. Harcourt, Brace and Company.

Davis, Mary Gould (1882-), ed.
--The Girl's Bk. of Verse. Fisher, Dorothea Frances Canfield, Mrs. (1879-1958), intro. by. N.D. J. B. Lippincott.
--The Girl's Book of Verse: A Treasury of Old and New Poems. Fisher, Dorothea Frances Canfield, Mrs. (1879-1958), intro. by. 1922. Frederick A. Stokes.
--Girl's Book of Verse: An Anthology. rev. ed. Munson, Amelia, intro. by. (gr. 7-9). 1952. (ISBN 0-397-30211-8). Lippincott.
--The Truce of the Wolf and Other Tales of Old Italy. Van Everen, Jay, illus. LC 31-280141. 5 p. l., 3-125, 1 p. incl. illus. (music) plates. front 24 cm. c.1931. Harcourt, Brace and Company. **Award: (JNM).**

Davis, Mary Hayes & Chow-Leung, eds.
--Chinese Fables and Folk Stories. LC 8-22958. 214 p. illus. 19 cm. (On cover: Eclectic readings). c.1908. American Book Company.
--Chinese Fables and Folk Stories. LC 76-48746. (Illus.). 214 p. 23cm. (Eclectic Readings). 1976, c.1908. (ISBN 0-8414-3813-7). Folcroft Library Editions.
--Chinese Fables and Folk Stories. LC 77-16314. (Illus.). 214 p. 23cm. (Eclectic Readings.). 1977, c.1908. (ISBN 0-8482-0566-9). Norwood Editions.

Davis, Mary Lee (1935-)
--Polly and the President. Jackson, Jan, illus. LC 67-15697. (Illus.). 32 p. 24cm. 1967. Lerner Publications Co.

Davis, Mary Montague, Mrs.
--Betty Bradford, Engineer. King, Ruth, illus. LC 30-14390. vii p., 1 l., 244 p. incl. illus. plates. front. 21 cm. 1930. The Macmillan Company.
--Dr. Pete of the Sierras. LC 28-11316. 4 p. l., 211 p. col. front. 21 cm. 1928. The Macmillan Company.

Davis, Mary Octavia (1901-)
--Going to the Fair. Dutz, pseud. (1901-), illus. Davis, Mary Octavia. LC 68-11220. (Illus.). 31 p. 24cm. 1968. Steck-Vaughn Co.
--Mouse Trail. LC 65-12511. 32p. illus. (pt. col.) 24cm. c.1965. Steck.
--Pinkie. Davis, Mary Octavia (1901-) & Dutz, illus. LC 52-11189. (Illus.). (gr. k-2). 1952. (ISBN 0-8114-7546-8). Steck-V.
--Rickie. Davis, Mary Octavia (1901-) & Dutz, illus. LC 55-7878. (Illus.). (gr. k-2). 1955. (ISBN 0-8114-7554-9). Steck-V.

Davis, May H.
--Do you See What I See?. Boyd, Robert, illus. (Illus.). 1975. (ISBN 0-682-48287-0). Exposition Press.

Davis, Milburn J.
--Smarty Pants. N.D. Carlton Press Inc.

Davis, Miriam K
--Maggie Pollard's Sacrifice. LC 12-31918. 222 p. front. 18 cm. 1883. Lutheran Publication Society.

Davis, Norman (1907-)
--Picken's Exciting Summer. 1950. Oxford University Press.
--Picken's Exciting Summer. Winslade, illus. LC 51-9583. 45 p. col. illus. 25 cm. 1948. Oxford University Press.
--Picken's Great Adventure. Winslade, illus. LC 50-15595. 45 p. col. illus. 25 cm. 1948. Oxford University Press.
--Picken's Great Adventure. Zogbaum, Rufus F., illus. LC 50-2468. (Illus.). 43 p. 24cm. (Oxford books for boys and girls). 1950, c.1949. Oxford University Press.
--Picken's Treasure Hunt. LC 55-5970. (Illus.). 64 p. 24cm. 1955. Oxford University Press.
--Picken's Treasure Hunt. 1955. Oxford University Press.

Davis, Ossie
--Escape to Freedom: The Story of Young Frederick Douglass. (gr. 5-9). 1978. (ISBN 0-670-29775-5). Viking Pr. **Awards: (CSKA); (ALA).**
--Langston: A Play. LC 82-70314. 144p. (gr. 7 up). 1982. (ISBN 0-440-04634-3). Delacorte.

Davis, Paxton (1925-)
--A Flag at the Pole: Three Soliloquies. Little, Harold, illus. LC 76-81. p. cm. 1976. (ISBN 0-689-30522-2). Atheneum.
--Ned. Little, Harold, illus. LC 78-4187. (Illus.). (gr. 5-9). 1978. (ISBN 0-689-30650-4). Atheneum.
--Three Days. LC 79-22676. (Illus.). 102 p. 21cm. 1980. Atheneum.

AUTHOR INDEX DAY, ARTHUR

Davis, Rebecca Blaine Harding, Mrs. (1831-1910)
--Kent Hampden. LC 12-318429. vii p., 1 l., 152 p. front., plates. 20 cm. 1892. C. Scribner's Sons.
--Natasqua. 2 p. l., 7-154 p. 19 cm. (On cover: Cassell's "rainbow" series). c.1886. Cassell & Company, Limited.
Davis, Reda
--Martin's Dinosaur. (Illus.). (gr. 2-4). 1959. (ISBN 0-8382-0505-4). Hale.
--Martin's Dinosaur. Slobodkin, Louis (1903-1975), illus. LC 59-7762. (Illus.). 40 p. 26cm. 1959. (ISBN 0-690-52147-2). Crowell.
Davis, Richard
--Space One. 155p. (gr. 7-12). 1975. (ISBN 0-200-71967-X). Transatlantic.
--Space Three: A Collection of Science Fiction Stories. LC 77-360699. 152 p. 23cm. 1976. Abelard.
Davis, Richard Harding (1864-1916)
--The Boy Scout. LC 14-9412. 17cm. 48p. 1914. Charles Scribner's Sons.
--The Boy Scout and Other Stories for Boys. LC 17-24696. 20cm. 323p. 1917. Charles Scribner's Sons.
--Cinderella and Other Stories. 1896. Charles Scribner's Sons.
--The King's Jackal. Gibson, Charles Dana, et al. (1867-1944), illus. 1898. Charles Scribner's Sons.
--The Lion and the Unicorn. Christy, Howard Chandler (1873-1952), illus. 20cm. 295p. 1910. C. Scribner's Sons.
--The Lion and the Unicorn. Christy, Howard Chandler (1873-1952), illus. 19 cm. 204p. 1899. Charles Scribner's Sons.
--The Lost Road. Morgan, Wallace, illus. 1913. Charles Scribner's Sons.
--The Man Who Could Not Lose. 1911. Charles Scribner's Sons.
--Once Upon a Time. 1910. Charles Scribner's Sons.
--Ranson's Folly. Remington, Frederic (1861-1909) & Clark, Walter Appleton, illus. 1902. Charles Scribner's Sons.
--The Red Cross Girl. Morgan, Wallace, illus. 1912. Charles Scribner's Sons.
--The Scarlet Car: The Princess Aline. 1910. Charles Scribner's Sons.
--Stories for Boys. LC 73-150472. (Illus.). 269 p. 21cm. (Short story index reprint series). 1971. (ISBN 0-8369-3812-7). Books for Libraries Press.
--Stories for Boys. LC 16-631829. 5 p. l., 204 p. front., plates. 19 cm. 1915. C. Scribner's Sons.
--Stories for Boys. LC 4-16128. 20cm. 204p. (Scribner's Series for Young People). 1891. Charles Scribner's Sons.
--The White Mouse. Gibbs, George, illus. 1909. Charles Scribner's Sons.
Davis, Robert Hobart (1869-)
--Tree Toad: The Story of a Bad Boy. McCloskey, John Robert (1914-1969), illus. N.D. J. P. Lippincott Co.
Davis, Robert P see Slattery, Duard G.
Davis, Robert (1881-)
--Gid Granger. Wilson, Charles Banks (1918-), illus. LC 45-106447. 4 p. l., 179 p., 1 l. illus. 20 cm. 1945. Holiday House, Inc.
--Hudson Bay Express. Pitz, Henry Clarence (1895-1976), illus. LC 42-506139. 262 p. illus. 20 1/2 cm. 1942. Holiday House.
--Padre Porko: A Gentlemanly Pig. 3rd print. enl. ed. Eichenberg, Fritz (1901-), illus. LC 48-8251. 197 p. illus. 20 cm. (gr. 4-6). 1948. (ISBN 0-8234-0085-9). Holiday House.
--Padre Porko, the Gentlemanly Pig. Eichenberg, Fritz (1901-), illus. LC 40-200782. 165 p. illus. 20 cm. c.1939. Holiday House.
--Partners of Powder Hole. David, Marshall, illus. LC 47-30291. 167 p. illus. 21 cm. c.1947. Holiday House.
--Pepperfoot of Thursday Market. Baldridge, Cyrus Leroy (1889-), illus. LC 41-853742. 187 p. illus. 20 cm. c.1941. Holiday House.
--That Girl of Pierre's. Goff, Lloyd Lozes (1919-), illus. LC 48-887602. 250 p. illus. 21 cm. 1948. Holiday House.
Davis, Rocky (1927-)
--Sundari: The Leopard in My Lap. 272p. 1974 (Barre-Westover). Crown.
Davis, Ruby, ed. see Clark, Barbara R.
Davis, Russell F
--Some Town You Brought Me to: A Novel. LC 76-87164. 146 p. 22cm. (gr. 7 up). 1969. Crown Publishers.
Davis, Russell Gerard (1922-) & Ashabranner, Brent Kenneth (1921-)
--Chief Joseph, War Chief of the Nez Perce. LC 62-12779. 190p. illus. 21cm. c.1962. McGraw.
--The Choctaw Code. (Illus.). 21cm. 152p. (Young pioneer bk.: No. 78008). 1966, c.1961. McGraw.
--The Choctaw Code. LC 61-9466. (Illus.). 152 p. 21cm. 1961. Whittlesey House.
--The Lion's Whiskers. Teason, James G., illus. (Tales of Africa). 1959. Little, Brown.
--Point Four Assignment. Miret, Gil, illus. 1959. Little, Brown and Company.
--Strangers in Africa. LC 63-18542. 149 p. 21cm. 1963. McGraw-Hill.
--Ten Thousand Desert Swords: The Epic Story of a Great Bedouin Tribe. Fisher, Leonard Everett (1924-), illus. LC 60-9336. 22cm. 158p. 1960. Little, Brown.
Davis, Ruth, jt. auth. see Freeman, Ritza.
Davis, S. & Kaye, M.
--Golden Thread. (Illus.). (gr. 2-7). N.D. Prayer Bk.
Davis, Sadie Holcombe
--Jesus, Once a Child. (Little Treasure Ser.). 1954. Broadman Press.
--When Jesus Was Here. Scott, Dorothy H., illus. (Illus.). (Little Treasure Series). (ps). 1957. (ISBN 0-8054-4211-1). Broadman.
Davis, Samuel Hoffman see Hoffman, Sam, pseud.
Davis, Samuel Hoffman
--A Boy Named Jesus. Hoffman, Sam, pseud. LC 56-36577. 66p. illus. 24cm. 1955. College Pub. Co.
Davis, Sarah Elizabeth, jt. auth. see Davis, Dorothy Brandt.
Davis, Susan
--Password to Heaven. Teasley, Rose, illus. LC 80-20515. p. cm. c.1980. (ISBN 0-8127-0298-0). Southern Pub. Association.
Davis, Susan Burdick (1878-), ed.
--Wisconsin Lore for Boys and Girls. LC 32-561. xv, 283 p. illus. (incl. ports.) 21 cm. 1931. E. M. Hale and Company.
Davis, Sydney K.
--Adventures of Aloysius. Weisman, Jerome, illus. (Illus.). (Highlights Handbooks Ser). (gr. 2-6). 1965. (ISBN 0-87534-128-4). Highlights.
Davis, Thomas A, ed. see Parker, Lois Mary.
Davis, Trivers James
--I Can Stop Any Time I Want. Davis, Allen, illus. (Illus.). 1974. (ISBN 0-13-444927-4). Prentice Hall.
Davis, Verne Theodore (1889-1973)
--The Devil Cat Screamed. Goldstein, Leslie, illus. LC 66-10249. 127 p. illus. 22 cm. 1966. Morrow.
--The Gobbler Called. Keats, Ezra Jack (1916-1983), illus. LC 63-14204. (Illus.). 160 p. 22cm. 1963. Morrow.
--Orphan of the Tundra. Lawrence, Judith Ann, illus. LC 68-28275. (Illus.). 112 p. 21cm. 1968. Weybright and Talley.
--The Runaway Cattle. Geer, Charles Hand (1922-), illus. LC 65-11040. 128p. illus. 23cm. c.1965. Morrow.
--Time of the Wolves. Keats, Ezra Jack (1916-1983), illus. LC 62-7720. (Illus.). 22cm. 127p. (gr. 3-6). 1962. Morrow.
Davis, W. J., Mrs., tr. see Heimburg, W.
Davis, William Angelo
--Dalton's Dream. N.D. Vantage Press Inc.
Davison, Frank Dalby (1893-1970)
--Children of the Dark People. 176p. 1962. Tri-Ocean Books.
--Children of the Dark People. O'Harris, Pixie, illus. LC 37-28774. xiii, 209 p. incl. front., illus., plates. 21 cm. 1937. Coward-McCann, Inc.
--Dusty. 1946. Coward-McCann, Inc.
--Red Heifer. Wallace, Frank, illus. (gr. 7-9). 1934. Coward-McCann, Inc.
Davison, Gladys Patton see Condor, Gladyn, pseud.
Davison, Mary
--Beechwood. (Illus.). N.D. E & J B Young.
--Grizzy's Story. (Illus.). N.D. E & J B Young.
--The Oliver Children. N.D. E. & J. B. Young & Co.
Davisson, Elizabeth Derr
--Polkadot of the Flying M Ranch. Kalab, Theresa, illus. LC 43-9418. 192 p. illus. 21 cm. 1943. E. P. Dutton and Company, Inc.
Dawes, C. Burr (1902-), tr. see Pradier, Mireille.
Dawes, Sarah Elizabeth, Mrs. (1832-)
--Bible Stories. (Handy Volume Classics). N.D. Thomas Y. Crowell & Co.
--Bible Stories for Children. LC 3-15427. 18cm. 366p. 1903. T. Y. Crowell & Co.
--Bible Stories for Young People. Fulleylove, John, illus. 350p. N.D. Thomas Y. Crowell Co.
--Ethel's Year at Ashton, 1 of 20 vols. New ed. (Illus.). 350p. (Sunday-School Lib: No. 13). N.D. Set. Lothrop Pub. Co.
--Hours With Mamma, 1 of 50 vols. (Illus.). 309p. (Model Library Number Three). N.D. Set. American Tract Society.
--Light From the Star of Bethlehem. LC 24-11114. (Illus.). 18cm. 69p. 1871. J. S. Locke & Co.
--Nellie at Grandpapa's. N.D. Bradley & Woodruff.
--Nellie at Home. N.D. Bradley & Woodruff.
--Nellie at School. N.D. Bradley & Woodruff.
--Nellie Series, 3 vols. (Illus.). 240p. N.D. Ira Bradley & Co's.
--Nellie Trying To Be Useful. N.D. Bradley & Woodruff.
--Nellie's Little Brother. N.D. Bradley & Woodruff.
--Nellie's Little Guest. N.D. Bradley & Woodruff.
--Pictures and Stories for Little Ones. 128p. N.D. American Tract Society.
--Rose and Her Pets. 128p. N.D. American Tract Society.
Dawley, Eloise K., jt. auth. see Oller, Marie.
Dawley, Muriel & McLaughlin, Roberta, eds.
--North American Indian Songs. (gr. 4 up). N.D. Bowmar.
Dawlish, Peter, pseud., see Kerr, James Lennox.
Dawlish, Peter, pseud. (1899-1963)
--The Boy Jacko. Kerr, James Lennox. Stobbs, William (1914-), illus. LC 62-21754. 22cm. 184p. 1963, c.1962. F. Watts.
Dawson, Alec John (1872-1951)
--Finn the Wolfhound. LC 63-7894. 20cm. 248p. (Voyager bk.: AVB39). 1966, c.1962. Harcourt.
--Finn the Wolfhound. Kennedy, Richard (1910-), illus. LC 62-53323. 251 p. illus. 21 cm. 1962. Brockhampton Press.
--Jan, a Dog and a Romance. LC 15-19862. 19cm. 279p. 1915. Harper & Brothers.
--Jan, Son of Finn. Armour, G. D., illus. LC 28-2064. vii, 312 p. front., plates 20 cm. c.1928. E. P. Dutton & Company.
--Jan Son of Finn. Kennedy, Richard (1910-), illus. (Illus.). [illegible]
Dawson, Alexandra D., jt. auth. see Carmichael, William Porter.
Dawson, C. E.
--Lion-Hearted: The Story of Bishop Hannington's Life Told for Boys and Girls, 8 Vols. (Illus.). N.D. E. & J. B. Young & Co.
Dawson, Carley
--Dragon Run. Ward, Lynd Kendall (1905-1985), illus. LC 55-9951. 202p. illus. 23cm. 1955. Houghton Mifflin.
--Mr. Wicker's Window. Ward, Lynd Kendall (1905-1985), illus. LC 52-5906. (Illus.). 272 p. 24cm. 1952. Houghton Mifflin.
--The Sign of the Seven Seas. Ward, Lynd Kendall (1905-1985), illus. LC 53-10983. (Illus.). 287 p. 22cm. 1954. Houghton Mifflin.
Dawson, Diane
--Larry. Dawson, Diane, illus. LC 78-103061. (Illus.). 22cm. 29p. c.1978. National Assn. for Visually Handicapped.
--Mixed-up Mother Goose. Kessler, Leonard P. (1921-), illus. LC 79-23357. p. cm. (Young Mother Goose Books). 1980. (ISBN 0-8116-7404-5). Garrard Pub. Co.
Dawson, Diane, jt. auth. see Barrett, Judith.
Dawson, Diane, jt. auth. see Greeley, Andrew Moran.
Dawson, Elmer A., pseud., see Stratemeyer Syndicate.
Dawson, Elmer A, pseud.
--Buck's Home Run Drive: Or, The Chester Boys Winning Against Odds. Stratemeyer Syndicate. Rogers, Walter S., illus. LC 31-3100. iv, 246 p. front., plates. 20 cm. (The Buck and Larry Baseball Stories: Vol. 4). 1931. Grosset & Dunlap.
--Buck's Winning Hit: Or, The Chester Boys Making a Record. Stratemeyer Syndicate. Rogers, Walter S., illus. LC 30-13806. iv, 216 p. front., plates. 20 cm. (The Buck and Larry Baseball Stories: Vol. 2). 1930. Grosset & Dunlap.
--Garry Grayson at Lenox High: Or, the Champions of the Football League. Stratemeyer Syndicate. Rogers, Walter S., illus. (The Garry Grayson Football Stories: Vol. 2). 1926. Grosset & Dunlap.
--Garry Grayson at Stanley Prep: Or, The Football Rivals of Riverview. Stratemeyer Syndicate. Rogers, Walter S., illus. (The Garry Grayson Football Stories: Vol. 5). 1927. Grosset & Dunlap.
--Garry Grayson Hitting the Line: Or, Stanley Prep on a New Gridiron. Stratemeyer Syndicate. Rogers, Walter S., illus. LC 29-10963. 2 p. l., 214 p. front. 20 cm. (The Garry Grayson Football Stories: Vol. 7). 1929. Grosset & Dunlap.
--Garry Grayson Showing His Speed: Or, a Daring Run on the Gridiron. Stratemeyer Syndicate. Rogers, Walter S., illus. (The Garry Grayson Football Stories: Vol. 4). 1927. Grosset & Dunlap.
--Garry Grayson's Double Signals: Or, Vanquishing the Football Plotters. Stratemeyer Syndicate. Rogers, Walter S., illus. LC 31-124580. iv, 217 p. front. 20 cm. (The Garry Grayson Football Stories: Vol. 9). 1931. Grosset & Dunlap.
--Garry Grayson's Double Signals: Or, Vanquishing the Football Plotters. Stratemeyer Syndicate. Rogers, Walter S., illus. Repr. of 1931 ed (Pub. by Grosset & Dunlap). (The Garry Grayson Football Stories: Vol. 9). N.D. Whitman Publishing Co.
--Garry Grayson's Football Rivals: Or, the Secret of the Stolen Signals. Stratemeyer Syndicate. Rogers, Walter S., illus. (The Garry Grayson Football Stories: Vol. 3). 1926. Grosset & Dunlap.
--Garry Grayson's Forward Pass: Or, Winning in the Final Quarter. Stratemeyer Syndicate. Condon, Gratham, illus. LC 32-12754. iv, 216 p. front. 20 cm. (The Garry Grayson Football Stories: Vol. 10). 1932. Grosset & Dunlap.
--Garry Grayson's Hill Street Eleven: Or, The Football Boys of Lenox. Stratemeyer Syndicate. Rogers, Walter S., illus. (The Garry Grayson Football Stories: Vol. 1). 1926. Grosset & Dunlap.
--Garry Grayson's Winning Kick: Or, Battling for Honor. Stratemeyer Syndicate. Rogers, Walter S., illus. LC 28-128097. iv, 218 p. front. 20 cm. (The Garry Grayson Football Stories: Vol. 6). 1928. Grosset & Dunlap.
--Garry Grayson's Winning Touchdown: Or, Putting Passmore Tech on the Map. Stratemeyer Syndicate. Rogers, Walter S., illus. LC 30-130970. iv, 216 p. front. 20 cm. (The Garry Grayson Football Stories: Vol. 8). 1930. Grosset & Dunlap.
--Garry Grayson's Winning Touchdown: Or, Putting Passmore Tech on the Map. Stratemeyer Syndicate. Rogers, Walter S., illus. Repr. of 1930 ed (Pub. by Grosset & Dunlap). (The Garry Grayson Football Stories: Vol. 8). N.D. Whitman Publishing Co.
--Larry's Fadeaway: Or, The Chester Boys Saving the Nine. Stratemeyer Syndicate. Rogers, Walter S., illus. LC 30-138051. iv, 244 p. front., plates. 20 cm. (The Buck and Larry Baseball Stories: Vol. 3). 1930. Grosset & Dunlap.
--Larry's Speedball: Or, The Chester Boys and the Diamond Secret. Stratemeyer Syndicate. Grubb, W. B., illus. iv, 246 p. front., plates. 20 cm. (The Buck and Larry Baseball Stories: Vol. 5). 1932. Grosset & Dunlap.
--The Pick-up Nine: Or, The Chester Boys on the Diamond. Stratemeyer Syndicate. Rogers, Walter S., illus. LC 30-13240. iv, 262 p. front., plates. 20 cm. (The Buck and Larry Baseball Stories: Vol. 1). 1930. Grosset & Dunlap.
Dawson, Francis Warrington (1878-)
--Buz and Fury. N.D. Bernard Publishing Co.
--Buz and Fury. Rogers, Walter S., illus. LC 24-1113. 219 p. 19 cm. 1923. The Honest Truth Publishing Co.
Dawson, Grace Strickler (1891-)
--The Butterfly Shawl: A Story of Spanish California, 1826. Barton, Loren, illus. LC 40-9444. 4 p. l., vii-x p., 1 l., 294 p. incl. illus., plates, col. front. 20 1/2 cm. 1940. Doubleday, Doran & Company, Inc.
--The Nuggets of Singing Creek. Barton, Loren, illus. LC 38-27436. 6 p. l., 304 p. incl. front., illus., plates. 21 cm. 1938. Doubleday, Doran & Company, Inc.
Dawson, Linda, jt. auth. see Furchgott, Terry.
Dawson, Mabel Louise
--The Girl Who Bought a Dream. LC 57-9803. 220p. 20cm. 1957. Arcadia House.
Dawson, Mary (1919-)
--Tecwyn: The Last of the Welsh Dragons. Fetz, Ingrid (1915-), illus. LC 67-513. (Illus.). 72 p. 24cm. 1967. Parents' Magazine Press.
--Tinker Tales: A Humpty Dumpty Book. Chwast, Jacqueline (1932-), illus. LC 73-3496. (Illus.). 68 p. 24cm. 1973. (ISBN 0-8193-0698-3). (ISBN 0-8193-0698-3). Parents' Magazine Press.
Dawson, Mitchell
--The Magic Firecrackers. Wiese, Kurt (1887-1974), illus. LC 49-11501. 192 p. illus. 22 cm. 1949. Viking Press.
--The Queen of Trent. new ed. (gr. 5-9). 1975. (ISBN 0-8277-4476-5). British Bk Ctr.
--The Queen of Trent. Keeping, Charles William James (1924-), illus. LC 61-5408. 21cm. 171p. 1961. Abelard-Schuman.

Dawson, Rosemary
--A Walk in the City. Dawson, Richard, illus. LC 50-7042. 30p. (gr. k-2). 1950. Viking.
--Walk in the City. Dawson, Richard, illus. (Illus.). (ps-1). 1960. (ISBN 0-670-74909-5). Viking Pr.

Dawson, Sarah Morgan
--A Confederate Girl's Diary. N.D. Houghton Mifflin.
Dawson, T. R.
--Five Classics of Fairy Chess. Dickins, A. S., pref. by. (Illus.). N.D. (ISBN 0-8446-4727-6). Peter Smith.
Dawson, Warrington see Dawson, Francis Warrington.
Day, Alexandra
--Good Dog, Carl. Day, Alexandra, illus. LC 85-70419. (Illus.). 36p. (Orig.). (ps up). 1985. (ISBN 0-88138-062-8, Star & Elephant Bks.). (ISBN 0-88138-052-0). Green Tiger Pr.
Day, Arthur Grove (1904-)
--Tommy Dane of Sonora. Burne, Harry H. A., illus. LC 29-18333. ix, 236 p. front., plates. 19 1/2 cm. $1.7. c.1929. The Century Co.
Day, Arthur Grove (1904-), ed.
--Melville's South Seas: An Anthology. (Illus.). (gr. 9 up). 1970. Hawthorn.

Day, Beth
--The Story of Johnikin. Hallowell, Elizabeth M., illus. 72p. (The Little Reader Ser.). N.D. American Baptist Pub. Society.
Day, Beth Feagles, jt. auth. see Day, Donald.
Day, Beth Feagles (1924-)
--Gene Rhodes: Cowboy (Eugene Manlove Rhodes). Bjorklund, Lorence F. (1913-1978), illus. LC 54-10583. 192p. illus. 22cm. 1954. J. Messner.
--The Little Professor of Piney Woods. N.D. Julian Messner, Inc.
Day, Beth Feagles (1924-) & Liley, Helen Margaret Irwin (1928-)
--The Secret World of the Baby. Nilsson, Lennart & Szasz, Suzanne Shorr, illus. LC 68-23670. (Illus.). 113 p. 27cm. 1968. Random House.
Day, Betsy A., jt. auth. see Wright, Betty Ren.
Day, Clarence Shepherd, Jr. (1874-1935)
--Life with Father. (Keith Jennison Large Type Bks). (gr. 9 up). 1966. (ISBN 0-531-00226-8). Watts.
Day, Donald (1899-) & Day, Beth Feagles (1924-)
--Will Rogers, the Boy Roper. Moyers, William (1916-), illus. LC 50-10083. (Illus.). 201 p. 21cm. 1950. Houghton Mifflin.
Day, Emily Foster
--The Menehunes. Wright, Spencer, illus. (For the Little Tots). N.D. Paul Elder & Company Catalogue.
Day, Geo T.
--African Adventure and Adventures. N.D. D. Lothrop Co.
Day, H.
--The Eagle Badge. (Harper's Selected Juveniles). N.D. Harper & Brothers.
Day, Harold W.
--Zip & Rip Stories: Adventures of the Two Little Raccoons. N.D. (ISBN 0-685-46326-5). Vantage.
Day, Holman Francis (1865-)
--The Rainy Day Railroad War. 5 p. l., 257 p. front., 8 pl. 19 cm. 1906. A. S. Barnes & Company.
--The Rainy Day Railroad War. LC 13-21260. 5 p. l., 256, 1 p. front., plates. 20 cm. 1913. Harper & Brothers.
Day, Lal Behari (1826-1894), compiled by.
--Folk-Tales of Bengal. N.D. Gale Reprint.
--Folk Tales of Bengal. N.D. MacMillan.
Day, Lillian (1893-), ed. see Andersen, Hans Christian.
Day, Mahlon
--New-York Street Cries, in Rhyme. Marcus, Leonard S., intro. by. LC 77-75122. (Illus.). 1977. Dover.
Day, Marguerite
--Tell 'Em Again Stories. N.D. Dodd, Mead & Co.
--Tell 'em Again Tales. Glackens, Louis M., illus. LC 24-27627. 3 p. l., 48 p. col. front., illus., col. plates. 27 cm. 1924. Duffield & Company.
Day, Michael E, jt. auth. see Whitmore, Carol.
Day, Price (1907-1978)
--Well, About the Penguin. Day, Price (1907-1978), illus. LC 39-31272. (Illus.). 21cm. 33p. 1939. Simon & Schuster.
Day, Rhonda, ed. see Garcia, Joseph G.
Day, Rosemary
--The Witch and the Owl. Riley, Terry, illus. LC 82-161804. (Illus.). 24 p. 27cm. 1981. (ISBN 0-460-06886-5). Dent.
Day, Samuel Phillips, retold by see Bunyan, John.
--Reynard the Fox. (Illus.). (Burt's Series of One Syllable Books). N.D. A. L. Burt's Pubs.
Day, Samuel Phillips, retold by. see Reynard the Fox. English.
Day, Thomas (1748-1789)
--The History of Little Jack. Blake, William (1757-1827), illus. LC 75-32149. (Illus.). 310 p. in various pagings. 16cm. (Classics of Children's Literature, 1621-1932). 1977. (ISBN 0-8240-2263-7). Garland Pub.
--The History of Little Jack. Blake, William (1757-1827), illus. LC 74-184683. (Illus.). 76 p. 14cm. 1850. W. P. Hazard.
--History of Little Jack and Other Stories. LC 7-30161. 110 p. col. front., illus. 20 cm. c.1906. McLoughlin Brothers.
--The History of Sandford and Merton. LC 22-180759. (Abridged from the Original: For the Amusement and instruction of Juvenile Minds). 110 p. 5 pl. 14 cm. 1796. Printed by Samuel Etheridge, and Sold by the Booksellers.
--The History of Sandford and Merton. new ed. Anderson, Alexander, pseud. (1804-1872), illus. Tuttle, George. LC 21-26827. 222 p. 8 pl. 15 cm. 1845. S. Babcock.
--The History of Sandford and Merton. the only complete american ed. LC 18-17296. viii, 9-538 p. front., plates. 20 cm. 1875. The World Publishing House.
--The History of Sandford and Merton. the only complete american edition. LC 25-137844. viii, 9-538 p. front., plates. 20 cm. 1856. W. P. Hazard.
--The History of Sandford and Merton. Anderson, Alexander (1775-1870), illus. LC 43-363020. 380 p. incl. front., illus. 17 1/2 cm. N.D. C. S. Francis & Co.
--The History of Sandford and Merton. Kramnick, Isaac, ed. LC 75-32143. 3 v. 19cm. (Classics of Children's Literature, 1621-1932). 1977. (ISBN 0-8240-2260-2). Garland Pub.
--The History of Sandford and Merton: A Work Intended for the Use of Children : Iii Volumes in One. LC 37-82797. vi, 7-408 p. 17 cm. 1801. Printed by Warner & Hanna, No. , Market-Street,Corner of South Gay-Street.
--The History of Sandford and Merton: A Work Intended for the Use of Children. 2d baltimore ed. LC 76-371854. 403 p. 17cm. 1809. Printed and Sold by Warner & Hanna.
--Sandford and Merton. (Illus.). N.D. Houghton, Mifflin & Co.
--Sandford and Merton, 1 of 5 Vols. (Illus.). (Standard Juveniles Ser.). N.D. Set. Houghton, Osgood & Co.
--Sandford and Merton. (Illus.). (St Nicholas Series for Boys). N.D. International Book Co.
--Sandford and Merton. (Illus.). N.D. J B Lippincott.
--Sandford and Merton, 1 of 16 Vols. (Illus.). (Warne's Incident and Adventure Library: Vol. 2). N.D. Scribner & Welford.
--Sandford and Merton. Godolphin, Mary, retold by. (Illus.). (Burt's Series of One Syllable Books). N.D. A. L. Burt's Pubs.
--Sandford and Merton. Hartley, Cecil, ed. (Illus.). N.D. George Routledge & Sons.
--Sandford and Merton: In Words of One Syllable. New ed. Godolphin, Mary, ed. (Illus.). N.D. James Miller.
--Sanford and Merton. N.D. D. Lothrop & Co.
--Sanford and Merton. (Illus.). N.D. Messrs. Roberts Brothers.
--Sanford and Merton. (The Youth's Cabinet of A. L. O. E. Presentation Popular Standard Bks.). N.D. Pott, Young, & Co.
--Sanford and Merton. (Incident and Adventure Library). N.D. R. Worthington & Co.
--The Story of Two Boys. Johnson, Clifton, retold by. LC 7-34311. 192 p. illus. 19 cm. (On cover: Eclectic reading). c.1907. American Book Company.
Day, Thomas (1748-1789) & Aesopus
--The Juvenile Classic Ser. Containing "Unexpected Pleasures," "Aesop's Fables," "Sanford and Merton," and "Evenings at Home". N.D. Set. D. Lothrop & Co.
Day, Veronique
--Landslide. Tomes, Margot Ladd (1917-), illus. Morgan, Margaret, tr. from Fr. LC 63-15543. (Illus.). 158 p. 21cm. 1963. Coward-McCann. **Award: (ALA).**
Day, Will, jt. auth. see Holland, David.
Day Lewis, Cecil (1904-1972)
--Dick Willoughby. LC 38-17012. 255 p. 21 cm. 1938. Random House.
--The Otterbury Incident. Ardizzone, Edward Jeffrey Irving (1900-1979), illus. (Illus.). 148p. 1978. (ISBN 0-370-01002-7, Pub. by Chatto Bodley Jonathan). Merrimack Pub Cir.
--The Otterbury Incident. Ardizzone, Edward Jeffrey Irving (1900-1979), illus. LC 49-10537. 160 p. illus. 21 cm. 1949. Viking Press.
--The Otterbury Incident. Ardizzone, Edward Jeffrey Irving (1900-1979), illus. LC 69-13056. (Illus.). 176 p. 21cm. (gr. 4-6). 1969, c.1948. World Pub. Co.
--Poetry for You: A Book for Boys & Girls on the Enjoyment of Poetry. (gr. 7-9). N.D. Soccer.
Day Lewis, Cecil (1904-1972), ed.
--The Echoing Green, 3 Vols. in 1. LC 45-20699. Repr. of 1937 ed (Pub. by Blackwell). (Granger Poetry Library). (gr. 6-10). 1976. (ISBN 0-89609-015-9). Granger Bk.
--The Echoing Green: An Anthology of Verse. LC 67-31313. 3 v. 19 cm. 1960. B. Blackwell.
Daynes, Leona Taylor
--Wee Rhymes for Wee Kiddies. Taylor, Rhea, illus. LC 21-14292. cover-title, 17 p. illus. (part col.) 30 cm. 1921. Child Lore Publishing Company.
Dayrell, Elphinstone (1869-1917)
--Why the Sun & the Moon Live in the Sky. Lent, Blair (1930-), illus. LC 68-15293. (Illus.). (gr. k-3). 1977. (ISBN 0-395-06741-3, Sandpiper). (ISBN 0-395-25381-0). HM.
--Why the Sun and the Moon Live in the Sky: An African Folktale. Lent, Blair (1930-), illus. (Illus.). 26 p. 24cm. (gr. k-2). 1968. (ISBN 0-395-06741-3). Houghton Mifflin. **Awards: (ALA); (RCM).**
Dayton, Dorothy (1947-)
--The Epic of Alexandra. Ingram, Virginia, illus. LC 79-22391. (Illus.). 113 p. 27cm. c.1979. (ISBN 0-89587-015-0). J. F. Blair.
Dayton, Laura
--I'd Rather Be Me. Laufer, Susan, illus. LC 78-72137. (Illus.). (gr. k-3). N.D. Dandelion Pr.
--Mommies & Daddies Work. Rogers, Terrance, illus. LC 78-73532. (Illus.). (ps-2). N.D. Dandelion Pr.
Dayton, Laura & Huggins, Susan
--Le Roy's Birthday Circus. Huggins, Susan, illus. LC 81-2205. p. cm. c.1981 (Dandelion Pr.). (ISBN 0-525-66744-X). Elsevier/Dutton.
Dayton, Mona
--Earth and Sky. Duvoisin, Roger Antoine (1904-1980), illus. LC 69-10204. (Illus.). 25 p. 27cm. 1969. Harper & Row.
Dazey, Agnes Christine Johnston, jt. auth. see Dazey, Frank M.
Dazey, Frank M. & Dazey, Agnes Christine Johnston
--Pepe, the Bad One. Hall, H. Tom, illus. LC 66-11920. 130p. illus. 23cm. 1966. Westminster.
De, La Fontaine Jean see La Fontaine, Jean de.
De, La Fontaine Jean see La Fontaine, Jean De (1621-1695) & Aesopus.
De, La Fontaine Jean see Larned, William Trowbridge & La Fontaine, Jean De.
De, La Fontaine Jean see La Fontaine, Jean De (1621-1695) & Gay, John.
Deachamps, Robert
--Let's Take a Walk: A Story Told in Pictures. Heller, Aaron & Deechamps, Robert, illus. LC 63-12415. (Illus.). 26 p. 24cm. 1963. Holt, Rhinehart and Winston.
Deakin, Irving
--Peter and the Wolf. rev. ed. Jones, Richard C. (1910-), illus. LC 40-32643. 47p. 1940. Oxford University Press.
Deakin, Michael
--The Children on the Hill: One Family's Bold Experiment with a New Way of Learning and Growing. LC 73-1731. 125 p. 22cm. 1973, c.1972. (ISBN 0-672-51843-0). Bobbs-Merrill.
De Amicis, Edmomdo see Amicis, Edmondo De.
De Amicis, Edmondo see Amicis, Edmondo de.
De Amicis, Edmondo see Amicis, Edmondo de (1846-1908) & Ruskin, John.
Dean (Thomas) and Son, London
--Dean's Moveable Book of Children's Sports and Pastimes. LC 44-333657. cover-title, 8 l. col. illus. 25 cm. N.D. Dean & Son.
Dean, Agnes Louise
--Devonshire Cream. Lathrop, Dorothy Pulis (1891-1980), illus. LC 50-1838. 49 p. illus. 23 cm. 1950. Unity Press.
--Good Luck, Mary Ann !. Wireman, Katharine Richardson, illus. LC 51-12140. 160 p. illus. 22 cm. 1951. Abingdon-Cokesbury.
--Let Us Be Merry. Morse, Dorothy Bayley (1906-1979), illus. LC 41-10783. xiii, 169, 1 p., 1 l. incl. front., illus. 21 cm. 1941. A. A. Knopf.
--Songs for My Grandmother. Schellens, S. S., illus. LC 45-100582. 83, 1 p. incl. front. (port.) plates. 22 cm. 1945. Unity Press, Inc.
Dean, Alexander (1893-), ed.
--Seven to Seventeen: Plays for School and Camp. 1st ed. LC 31-25175. xiii, 466 p. 21 cm. 1931. S. French.
Dean, Amber (1902-)
--Be Home By Eleven. 1973. (ISBN 0-399-11142-5). G.P. Putnam's Sons.
Dean, Anabel (1915-)
--Destruction Derby. LC 71-170772. (Illus.). 79 p. 22cm. (Racing wheels series). 1972. Benefic Press.
--Drag Race. LC 78-170771. (Illus.). 79 p. 21cm. (Racing wheels series). 1972. Benefic Press.
--Hot Rod. LC 74-170770. (Illus.). 80 p. 21cm. (Racing wheels series). 1972. Benefic Press.
--Indy 500. LC 72-170775. (Illus.). 80 p. 22cm. (Racing wheels series). 1972. Benefic Press.
--Pink Paint. LC 70-164853. (Illus.). 35 p. 1972. (ISBN 0-513-01213-3). T. S. Denison.
--Road Race. LC 79-170774. (Illus.). 79 p. 22cm. (Racing wheels series). 1972. Benefic Press.
--Stock Car Race. LC 75-170773. (Illus.). 79 p. 22cm. (Racing wheels series). 1972. Benefic Press.
--Willie Can Fly. Fuller, Nancy Lee, illus. LC 73-110301. (Illus.). 36 p. (ps-2). c.1970. (ISBN 0-513-00493-9). Denison.
--Willie Can Not Squirm. Fuller, Nancy Lee, illus. LC 70-110299. (Illus.). 36 p. 1970. T. S. Denison.
--Willie Can Ride. Fuller, Nancy Lee, illus. LC 70-110300. (Illus.). 36 p. 1970. T. S. Denison.
Dean, Bessie
--Let's Choose the Right. Dean, Bessie, illus. LC 76-29302. (Illus.). 64 p. 22cm. c.1976. (ISBN 0-88290-072-2). Horizon Publishers.
--Let's Learn the First Principles. Dean, Bessie, illus. LC 78-70366. (Illus.). 64 p. 22cm. c.1978. (ISBN 0-88290-104-4). Horizon Publishers.
--Let's Love One Another. Dean, Bessie, illus. LC 77-74492. (Illus.). 64 p. 22cm. c.1977. (ISBN 0-88290-077-3). Horizon Publishers.
--Paul's Letters. (Illus.). 72p. (Orig.). (Story Books to Color). (gr. k-5). 1981. (ISBN 0-88290-170-2). Horizon Utah.
--Stories Jesus Told: A Child's Coloring Book of the Parables of Jesus. (Illus.). (Children's Inspirational Coloring Bk.). (ps-6). 1979. (ISBN 0-88290-132-X). Horizon Utah.
Dean, C., jt. auth. see Dean, G. D.
Dean, Eva
--In Peanut Land. Dean, Eva, illus. (Illus.). N.D. R. F. Fenno & Co.
--In Peanut Land: Verses. Dean, Eva, illus. LC 7-37511. 137 p. front., illus. 27 cm. c.1907. I. Somerville & Company.
Dean, Frank
--Cowboy Fun. Rogers, Will, Jr., intro. by. LC 79-91384. (Illus.). 160p. 1980. (ISBN 0-8069-4608-3). (ISBN 0-8069-4609-1). Sterling.
Dean, G. D. & Dean, C.
--Lambs of the Fold. N.D. Pilgrim Press.
Dean, Graham M (1904-)
--Bob Gordon, Cub Reporter. LC 35-19987. 4 p. l., 280 p. col. front. 21 cm. 1935. Doubleday, Doran & Company, Inc.
--Bob Gordon, Cub Reporter. LC 39-24301. 4 p. l., 280 p. 21 cm. (Young moderns bookshelf). 1939. The Sun Dial Press, Inc.
--Daring Wings. LC 31-15415. 243 p. 20 cm. c.1931. The Goldsmith Publishing Co.
--Deadline for Jim. LC 61-12802. (Illus.). 22cm. 190p. 1961. Criterion Books.
--Dusty of the Double Seven. Lee, Manning De Villeneuve (1894-1980), illus. LC 48-1919. 189 p. illus. 22 cm. 1948. Viking Press.
--The Front Page Mystery. Lee, Manning De Villeneuve, illus. LC 31-5065. 5 p. l., 236, 1 p. front., illus. 20 cm. 1931. D. Appleton and Company.
--Gleaming Rails. Cavanagh, Paul, illus. LC 30-932631. 5 p. l., 228, 1 p. front., illus. 20 cm. 1930. D. Appleton and Company.
--Herb Kent: West Point Cadet. LC 36-40820. 5 p. l., 17-250 p. 20 cm. c.1936. The Goldsmith Publishing Company.
--Jim of the Press: A Young Reporter's Adventures with the Associated Press. LC 33-25378. 4 p. l., 312 p. front. 21 cm. 1933. Doubleday, Doran & Company, Inc.
--Jim of the Press: A Young Reporter's Adventures with the Associated Press. LC 38-239269. 4 p. l., 312 p. front. 21 cm. (Young moderns bookshelf). 1938. The Sun Dial Press, Inc.
--Riders of the Gabilans. Dennis, Wesley (1903-1966), illus. LC 44-7665. 191 p. illus. 21 cm. 1944. The Viking Press.
--The Sky Trail. LC 32-11201. 2 p. l., 13-253 p. 20 cm. c.1932. The Goldsmith Publishing Company.
--Wings Over the Desert. Dennis, Wesley (1903-1966), illus. LC 45-35211. 224 p. illus. 21 cm. 1945. The Viking Press.
Dean, Leigh
--The Looking Down Game. Giovanopoulos, Paul Arthur (1939-), illus. LC 68-13075. (Illus.). 34 p. 22cm. 1968. Funk & Wagnalls.
--Lulu's Back in Town. Coconis, Ted, pseud., illus. CoConis, Constantinos. LC 68-21125. (Illus.). 30 p. 23cm. 1968. Funk & Wagnalls.
--Rufus Gideon Grant. Giovanopoulos, Paul Arthur (1939-), illus. LC 79-104834. (Illus.). 62 p. 24cm. 1970. Scribner.
Dean, Leigh, jt. auth. see Lisker, Sonia O.
Dean, Leigh, adapted by see Menotti, Gian-Carlo.
Dean, Leon W. (1889-)
--Border Bullets. Tolford, Joshua (1909-), illus. LC 53-5409. (Illus.). 185 p. 22cm. 1953. Ariel Books.
--Green Mountain Boy: The Story of Seth Warner. Child, Charles Jesse (1901-), illus. LC 44-872. xii, 242 p. incl. front., illus. 21 cm. 1944. Farrar & Rinehart, Inc.
--Guns Over Champlain. LC 46-2716. 5 p. l., 3-245 p. 19 cm. 1946. Rinehart and Company, Inc.
--I Become a Ranger. LC 45-1954. 6 p. l., 3-240 p. incl. front. (map) 19 cm. 1945. Farrar & Rinehart Inc.
--Old Wolf: The Story of Israel Putnam. Gillette, Henry Sampson (1915-), illus. LC 42-200967. x p., 2 l., 3-276 p. illus. 21 cm. 1942. Farrar & Rinehart, Inc.
--Pirate Lair. Werth, Kurt (1896-), illus. LC 47-1583. 6 p. l., 3-246 p. incl. front., illus. 19 cm. 1947. Rinehart & Company, Inc.
--Royalton Raid. LC 49-836019. ix, 241 p. front., map. 20 cm. 1949. Rinehart.
--Stark of the North Country. Gillette, Henry Sampson (1915-), illus. LC 41-19200. viii p., 2 l., 3-277 p. illus. (incl. map) 21 cm. c.1941. Farrar & Rinehart.
--The White Ox: Being a Story of One Ezra Button and the Adventures That Befell Him in the Neighborhood of Lake Champlain in New England. Leamon, Tom, illus. LC 53-7093. (Illus.). 177 p. 22cm. 1953. Ariel Books.

AUTHOR INDEX DECKER, DUANE

Dean, Mary Bathurst
--Three Little Maids. Small, Frank O., illus. (Illus.). N.D. Lothrop.
Dean, Nell Marr (1910-)
--The Vet is a Girl. LC 59-12756. 21cm. 192p. (Romance for Young Moderns). 1959. Messner.
Deane, Shirley Joan (1920-)
--Vendetta. Ambrus, Victor G., pseud. (1935-), illus. Ambrus, Gyozo Laszlo. LC 67-20959. (Illus.). 146 p. 22cm. 1967. Viking Press.
De Angeli, Arthur Craig & De Angeli, Marguerite Lofft, Mrs. (1889-)
--The Empty Barn. De Angeli, Marguerite Lofft, Mrs. (1889-), illus. LC 66-10035. 60 p. illus. (part col.) 24 cm. 1966. Westminster Press.
De Angeli, Marguerite Lofft, Mrs., jt. auth. see De Angeli, Arthur Craig.
De Angeli, Marguerite Lofft, Mrs. (1889-)
--Black Fox of Lorne. De Angeli, Marguerite Lofft, Mrs. (1889-), illus. LC 56-8233. (Illus.). 1911p. (gr. 3-7). 1956. (ISBN 0-385-07581-2). (ISBN 0-385-08300-9). Doubleday. **Award: (JNM).**
--Bright April ... De Angeli, Marguerite Lofft, Mrs. (1889-), illus. LC 46-5341. 86, 2 p. incl. front., illus. (part col.) 22 x 22 cm. 1946. Doubleday & Company, Inc.
--Copper-Toed Boots. De Angeli, Marguerite Lofft, Mrs. (1889-), illus. LC 38-27989. 92 p. illus. (part col.) 26 cm. 1938. Doubleday, Doran & Company, Inc.
--The Door in the Wall. 1st ed. LC 49-11491. (Illus.). 111. 24cm. (Junior Bks.). 1949. Doubleday.
--The Door in the Wall: A Play. De Angeli, Marguerite Lofft, Mrs. (1889-), illus. LC 68-14179. (Illus.). 153 p. 22cm. 1968. Doubleday.
--The Door in the Wall. LC 49-11491. (Illus.). 120 p. 20cm. (Zephyr Books). 1973, c.1949. Doubleday.
--The Door in the Wall. De Angeli, Marguerite Lofft, Mrs. (1889-), illus. LC 64-7025. 120p. illus. (pt. col.) 24cm. 1964. Doubleday.
--The Door in the Wall: A Story of Medieval London. De Angeli, Marguerite Lofft, Mrs. (1889-), illus. LC 64-7025. (gr. 3-6). 1949. Doubleday. **Award: (JNM).**
--Elin's Amerika. De Angeli, Marguerite Lofft, Mrs. (1889-), illus. LC 41-21552. 96 p. illus. (part col.) 22 x 22 cm. 1941. Doubleday, Doran & Company, Inc.
--Fiddlestrings. De Angeli, Marguerite Lofft, Mrs. (1889-), illus. LC 73-82243. (Illus.). 143 p. 24cm. 1974. (ISBN 0-385-08218-5). (ISBN 0-385-08218-5). Doubleday.
--Friendship & Other Poems. De Angeli, Marguerite Lofft, Mrs. (1889-), illus. LC 79-6857. (Illus.). 48p. 1981. Doubleday.
--Goose Girl. De Angeli, Marguerite Lofft, Mrs. (1889-), illus. (Illus.). (gr. 1-3). N.D. (ISBN 0-385-05148-4). Doubleday.
--Henner's Lydia. De Angeli, Marguerite Lofft, Mrs. (1889-), illus. LC 36-35987. 70 p. illus. (part col.) 22 x 22 cm. 1936. Doubleday, Doran & Company, Inc.
--Henner's Lydia. De Angeli, Marguerite Lofft, Mrs. (1889-), illus. (gr. 3-5). 1963. Doubleday.
--Jared's Island. De Angeli, Marguerite Lofft, Mrs. (1889-), illus. LC 47-11632. 95 p. illus., map (on lining-papers) 25 cm. 1947. Doubleday.
--Just Like David. De Angeli, Marguerite Lofft, Mrs. (1889-), illus. LC 51-14087. (Illus.). 121 p. 21cm. 1951. Doubleday.
--The Lion in the Box. De Angeli, Marguerite Lofft, Mrs. (1889-), illus. LC 74-33676. p. cm. 1975. (ISBN 0-385-03317-6). (ISBN 0-385-03327-3). Doubleday.
--Marguerite De Angeli's Book of Nursery & Mother Goose Rhymes. LC 54-9838. (Illus.). (gr. k-5). 1954. (Zephyr). Doubleday. **Award: (ALA).**
--Petite Suzanne. De Angeli, Marguerite Lofft, Mrs. (1889-), illus. LC 37-31487. 88 p. illus. (part col.) 21 x 21 1/2 cm. 1937. Doubleday, Doran & Company, Inc.
--Shippack School: Being the Story of Eli Shrawder and of One Christopher Dock, Schoolmaster About the Year 1750. LC 39-27899. 88 p. illus. (part col.) 22 x 22 cm. 1939. Doubleday, Doran and Company, Inc.
--Skippack School. De Angeli, Marguerite Lofft, Mrs. (1889-), illus. (O.s.i.). (Illus.). (gr. 4-6). N.D. (ISBN 0-385-07913-3). (ISBN 0-385-07914-1). Doubleday.
--Skippack School: Being the Story of Eli Shrawder and of One Christopher Dock, Schoolmaster About the Year 1750. (Illus.). 92 p. 21cm. (Junior books). 1961, c.1939. Doubleday.
--A Summer Day with Ted and Nina. De Angeli, Marguerite Lofft, Mrs. (1889-), illus. LC 40-9445. 32 p. illus. (part col.) 20 x 18 cm. 1940. Doubleday, Doran & Company, Inc.
--Ted and Nina Go to the Grocery Store. De Angeli, Marguerite Lofft, Mrs. (1889-), illus. LC 36-27032. 32 p. illus. (part col.) 14 1/2 x 18 1/2 cm. 1935. Doubleday, Doran, & Company.
--Ted and Nina Have a Happy Rainy Day. De Angeli, Marguerite Lofft, Mrs. (1889-), illus. LC 36-8053. 32 p. illus. (part col.) 15 x 19 cm. 1936. Doubleday, Doran and Company, Inc.
--The Ted and Nina Story Book. De Angeli, Marguerite Lofft, Mrs. (1889-), illus. LC 64-14812. (Illus.). 96 p. 1965. Doubleday.
--Thee, Hannah!. De Angeli, Marguerite Lofft, Mrs. (1889-), illus. LC 40-27724. 88 p. illus. (part col.) 21 1/2 x 21 1/2 cm. 1940. Doubleday, Doran & Company, Inc.
--Turkey for Christmas. 1961. E. M. Hale.
--Turkey for Christmas. De Angeli, Marguerite Lofft, Mrs. (1889-), illus. LC 44-47779. 49 p. col. illus. 17 cm. 1944. The Westminster Press.
--Turkey for Christmas. De Angeli, Marguerite Lofft, Mrs. (1889-), illus. LC 65-103672. 48p. illus. (pt. col.) 25cm. c.1965. Westminster.
--Up the Hill. De Angeli, Marguerite Lofft, Mrs. (1889-), illus. LC 42-24961. (Illus.). 88 p. 1942. Doubleday, Doran & Company, Inc.
--Whistle for the Crossing. LC 70-42323. (Illus.). 107 p. 22cm. c.1977. (ISBN 0-385-11552-0). Doubleday.
--Yonie Wondernose. De Angeli, Marguerite Lofft, Mrs. (1889-), illus. LC 44-7326. 39 p. illus. (part col.) 26x24 cm. 1944. Doubleday, Doran & Company. **Award: (RCM).**
De Angeli, Marguerite Lofft, Mrs. (1889-), compiled by.
--Book of Nursery and Mother Goose Rhymes. LC 54-9838. (Illus.). 192 p. 32cm. 1954. Doubleday. **Awards: (ALA); (RCM).**
--A Pocket Full of Posies: A Merry Mother Goose. LC 61-11142. (Illus.). 28p. 27cm. c.1961. (ISBN 0-385-08060-3). Doubleday.
De Angulo, Jaime
--Indian Tales. De Angulo, Jaime, illus. (Illus.). 245p. 1962. (ISBN 0-8090-0049-0, AmCen). (ISBN 0-8090-5836-7). Hill & Wang.
De Aragon, Maximo
--The Pearl. LC 80-83435. (Illus.). 50p. (Orig.). (gr. 7-12). 1984. (ISBN 0-932906-08-7). Pan-Am Publishing Co.
De Aragon, Ray John
--City of Candy and Streets of Ice Cream. De Aragon, Rosa Maria, illus. LC 79-52960. (Illus.). 34 p. 19cm. (Miss Miffet Storytime Series). c.1979. (ISBN 0-932906-05-2). (ISBN 0-932906-04-4). Pan American Pub.
Dearborn, Blanche J
--Aleck and His Friends: A Health Reader. Keene, Charles Herbert, ed. LC 32-7487. 2 p. l., 139 p. col. illus. 19 cm. c.1932. Houghton Mifflin Company.
--Cuthbert. Benthem, Richard Van, illus. LC 52-31435. 111 p. illus. 25 cm. 1952. Wilcox and Follett Co.
Dearborn, Mary Hager, Mrs., jt. auth. see Hager, Luther George.
DeArmand, Frances Ullmann (1904-)
--A Very, Very Special Day. Vroman, Tom, illus. LC 63-8176. (Illus.). (gr. k-2). 1963. (ISBN 0-8193-0042-X, Four Winds). Scholastic Inc.
DeArmand, Frances Ullmann (1904-), ed.
--When Mother Was a Girl: Stories She Read Then. LC 64-11118. xiv. 209 p. 24 cm. 1964. Funk & Wagnalls.
Dearmer, Mabel
--The Cockyolly Bird. Dearmer, Mabel, illus. N.D. George H Doran & Co.
Dearmer, Percy, Mrs.
--Roundabout Rhymes. (Illus.). (Scribner-Blackie Series of books for young people). N.D. Charles Scribner's Sons.
Dearmin, Jennie Tarascou, jt. auth. see Peck, Helen Estelle.
DeArmond, Dale
--Berry Woman's Children. LC 84-29760. (Illus.). 40 p. 26cm. c.1985. (ISBN 0-688-05814-0). (ISBN 0-688-05815-9). Greenwillow Books.
Deary, Terry (1946-)
--The Custard Kid. Firmin, Charlotte (1954-), illus. LC 81-21693. (Illus.). 93 p. 23cm. (Good time library). 1982, c.1980. (ISBN 0-87614-188-2). Carolrhoda Books.
--The Lambton Worm. Firmin, Charlotte (1954-), illus. LC 82-1327. (Illus.). 88p. (The Good Time Library). (gr. 3-7). 1982. (ISBN 0-87614-196-3). Carolrhoda Bks.
Deason, May Cavin (1892-)
--A Potpourri of Poems for Children. Scofield, Mary, illus. LC 54-3028. 63p. illus. 20cm. 1954. Story Book Press.
Deasy, Isabel Josephine
--The Princess Eileen. Barnett, Ambrose M., Jr., illus. LC 18-544. 1 p. l., 50 p., 1 l. illus. 20 cm. c.1917. Cal., J. J. Newbegin.
Deasy, Michael
--City ABC's. Perron, Robert, illus. LC 74-81784. (Illus.). 32. 27cm. 1974. (ISBN 0-8027-6157-7). (ISBN 0-8027-6158-5). Walker.
Deat, Roma Riggs
--Troubles Gets Lost: A Story. McMillan, Frank, illus. LC 49-3931. 60 p. illus. (part col.) 23 x 28 cm. 1949. Pacific Press Pub. Assn.
DeBear, Constance, jt. auth. see Burger, Isabel.
De Beaumont, Marie (1711-1780)
--Beauty and the Beast. (Illus.). N.D. E. P. Dutton & Co.
De Beck, Billy
--Barney Google. N.D. David McKay Co.
Debengam, Frank
--In the Antartic. N.D. Transatlantic Arts, Inc.
Debenham, Mary H.
--Duty and Affection: Or, The Faithful Drummer Boy. N.D. Thomas Whittaker.
--Fairmeadows Farm. N.D. Thomas Whittaker.
--For King and Home. N.D. Thomas Whittaker.
--Household Troops: Or, Small Service is True Service (Pub. by Society for Promoting Christian Knowledge). N.D. E. & J. B Young & Co.
--A Little Candle. N.D. Thomas Whittaker.
--The Mavis and the Merlin. N.D. Thomas Whittaker.
--Moor and Moss. N.D. Thomas Whittaker.
--My God-Daughter. N.D. Thomas Whittaker.
--My Neighbor's Garden. N.D. Frederick Warner & Co.
--The Rules of this House. (The Welcome Library). N.D. Frederick Warne & Co.
--St. Helen's Well. N.D. Thomas Whittaker.
--Two Maiden Aunts. N.D. Thomas Whittaker.
--The Whispering Winds, and the Tales that They Told, 36 vols. (Illus.). (St. Nicholas Ser.). 1905. Set. A L Burt Co.
--The Whispering Winds, and the Tales that They Told. (Illus.). (The Wellesley Series for Girls). N.D. A. L. Burt.
--The Whispering Winds and the Tales that They Told. (Illus.). (Scribner-Blackie Series of books for young people). N.D. Charles Scribner's Sons.
Deblander, Gabriel
--The Fall of Icarus. LC 79-65865. (Children's Art Ser.). N.D. (ISBN 0-382-06329-5). Silver.
De Blumenthal, Kalamatiano, jt. ed. see Xenophontovna, Verra.
Debnam, Betty
--The Mini Spy Mystery Fun Book. (Illus.). 24p. (The Mini Page Fun Books). (gr. k-3). 1982. (ISBN 0-02-042820-0). Macmillan.
De Borhegyi, Suzanne Sims (1926-)
--The Secret of the Sacred Lake. Stone, David Karl (1922-), illus. LC 67-4762. (Illus.). 208 p. 21cm. (gr. 4-7). 1967. (ISBN 0-03-062500-9). (ISBN 0-03-062505-X). Holt, Rinehart and Winston.
De Bosschere, Jean see Bosschere, Jean De.
De Bosschere, Jean see Cervantes Saavedra, Miguel de.
De Bosschere, Jean (1878-)
--Folk Tales of Flanders. De Bosschere, Jean (1878-), illus. Jesse, F. Tennyson, tr. LC 19-26343. xii, 178, 1 p. incl. col. front., illus. 11 col. pl. 27 1/2 cm. 1918. Dodd, Mead & Company.
DeBosschere, Jean (1878-) & Morris, M. C. O.
--Christmas Tales of Flanders. (Illus.). N.D. (ISBN 0-8446-4516-8). Peter Smith Publisher, Inc.
De Botton, Jean
--Fou Fou Discovers America. De Botton, Jean, illus. LC 45-4452. 32 p. col. illus. 31 x 23 1/2 cm. 1945. "Les Arts De France.
De Brisville, Jean-Claude
--Big Bear. Bour, Daniele, illus. Mondello, Anita, tr. LC 76-54161. (Illus.). (ps-2). 1977. (ISBN 0-13-076216-4). P-H.
De Brunhoff, Jean see Brunhoff, Jean de.
De Brunhoff, Jean see Brunhoff, Jean De (1899-1937) & Brunhoff, Laurent De.
De Brunhoff, Laurent see Brunhoff, Jean De (1899-1937) & Brunhoff, Laurent De.
De Brunhoff, Laurent see Brunhoff, Laurent de.
De Bruyn, Monica Jean Grembowicz (1952-)
--The Beaver Who Wouldn't Die. De Bruyn, Monica Jean Grembowicz (1952-), illus. LC 75-2968. (Illus.). 32 p. 23cm. c.1975. (ISBN 0-695-80586-X). Follett Pub. Co.
--Lauren's Secret Ring. LC 79-27261. (Illus.). 32 p. 24cm. c.1980. (ISBN 0-8075-4391-8). A. Whitman.
--Six Special Places. De Bruyn, Monica Jean Grembowicz (1952-), illus. LC 75-6575. (Illus.). 32 p. 24cm. (gr. k-2). 1975. (ISBN 0-8075-7386-8). A. Whitman.
De Camp, Catherine Crook, jt. ed. see De Camp, Lyon Sprague.
De Camp, Catherine Crook (1907-), ed.
--Creatures of the Cosmos. Krush, Beth (1918-) & Krush, Joe (1918-), illus. LC 77-22748. 152 illus. 21. c.1977. (ISBN 0-664-32621-8). Westminster Press.
De Camp, Lyon Sprague (1907-) & De Camp, Catherine Crook (1907-), eds.
--Tales Beyond Time: From Fantasy to Science Fiction. Forberg, Ati, pseud. (1925-), illus. Forberg, Beate Gropius. LC 73-17035. (Large Print Books). (Illus.). 247 p. 25cm. 1973. (ISBN 0-8161-6165-8). G. K. Hall.
--Tales Beyond Time: From Fantasy to Science Fiction. Forberg, Ati, pseud. (1925-), illus. Forberg, Beate Gropius. LC 72-11950. (Illus.). 159, 1 p. 24cm. 1973. Lothrop, Lee & Shepard.
--Three Thousand Years of Fantasy and Science Fiction. LC 72-1099. 256 p. 24cm. 1972. (ISBN 0-688-40006-X). (ISBN 0-688-50006-4). Lothrop, Lee & Shepard Co.
De Camp, Rosemary
--Here, Duke!. (Illus.). (gr. 4-6). N.D. McKay.
De Campi, Anita
--The Mother Goose Parade. N.D. The Reilly & Britton Co.
--My Kindergarten Days. (Illus.). N.D. Bobbs-Merrill Company.
De Capella, F.
--Tales and Legends of the Middle Ages. Wilson, Henry, ed. (Illus.). (Tales and Legends Ser.). N.D. Benziger Brothers Pub.
DeCaprio, Annie
--The Bus from Chicago. 24p. 1965. Pitman Publishing.
--Bus from Chicago. (Early Start Pre School Readers). (gr. k-1). N.D. Wonder.
--The Dinosaur and the Dodo. 32p. 1965. Pitman Publishing.
--Dinosaur & the Dodo. Shapiro, Allen, illus. (Illus.). color ils. 32p. (Ready-To-Read Books) (gr. 2-3). 1969. (ISBN 0-448-02385-7). G&D.
--Dog & the Wolf. Lazzaro, Victor, illus. (Ready-To-Read Books). (gr. 2-3). 1969. (ISBN 0-448-02387-3). G&D.
--Getting the Lion and the Deer. 24p. 1965. Pitman Publishing Corporation.
--Happy Day. (Early Start Pre School Readers). (gr. k-1). N.D. Wonder.
--One Two Poems. 24p. 1965. Pitman Publishing.
--The Rabbit and the Turtle. 24p. 1965. Pitman Publishing.
--Willie and the Whale. 24p. 1965. Pitman Publishing.
De Caroline, tr. see Le Paillot, Jean.
De Cervantes Saavedra, Miguel see Cervantes Saavedra, Miguel de.
De Cesco, Federica
--The Prince of Mexico. Lobb, Frances, tr. LC 76-117169. 224 p. 21cm. 1970, c.1968. John Day Co.
--The Wind of the Camargue. LC 72-5366. 191 p. 23cm. 1973, c.1972. John Day Co.
De Charlieu, Hector see Charlieu, Hector De.
De Chatelain, Clara De Pontigny see Chatelain, Clara De Pontigny De.
Deck, Mary Celeste
--The Book About Kitties. LC 78-2497. p. cm. c.1978. (ISBN 0-8431-0457-0). Price/Stern/Sloan.
Decker, Clarence R.
--Modern Stories From Many Lands. Angoff, Charles, illus. 434p. 1972. (ISBN 0-87141-040-0). Manyland Books inc.
Decker, Della West
--Through Young Eyes. LC 36-22181. 3 p. l., ix-xi p., 15-87 p. illus. 20 cm. c.1936. The Kaleidograph Press.
Decker, Dorothy W.
--Stripe Presents the ABC's. Decker, Dorothy W., illus. (Illus.). 64p. (Stripe Adventure Ser.). (gr. k-3). 1984. (ISBN 0-87518-266-6, Gemstone Bks). Dillon.
--Stripe Visits New York. Decker, Dorothy W., illus. LC 85-6768. p. cm. 48p. (gr. k-3). c.1985. (ISBN 0-87518-267-4). Dillon Press.
Decker, Duane Walter see Wayne, Richard, pseud.
Decker, Duane Walter (1910-1964)
--The Big Stretch. LC 52-5071. (Morrow junior books). 1952. Morrow.
--The Catcher from Double-A. LC 50-5969. 188 p. 21 cm. 1950. Morrow.
--Clutch Hitter. Wayne, Richard, pseud. LC 51-9846. 201 p. 22 cm. 1951. Macrae Smith.
--Fast Man on a Pivot. LC 51-1377. 221 p. 21cm. (Morrow junior books). 1951. Morrow.
--The Gobbler Called. Keats, Ezra Jack (1916-1983), illus. 1963. Morrow.
--Good Field, No Hit. LC 47-30656. 208 p. 21 cm. 1947. M. S. Mill Co.
--The Grand-Slam Kid. LC 64-10257. 189 p. 21 cm. 1964. Morrow.
--Hit and Run. LC 49-1915. 188 p. 21 cm. 1949. M. S. Mill Co. and W. Morrow.
--Long Ball to Left Field. LC 58-7488. (Illus.). 217 p. 21cm. 1958. Morrow.
--Mister Shortstop. LC 54-6401. 185 p. 21cm. (Morrow junior books). 1954. Morrow.
--Rebel in Right Field. LC 61-8021. 190 p. 21cm. 1961. Morrow.
--Showboat Southpaw. LC 60-6870. 188 p. 21cm. (Morrow junior books). 1960. Morrow.
--Starting Pitcher. LC 48-2166. 187 p. 21 cm. 1948. M. S. Mill Co. and W. Morrow.
--Switch Hitter. LC 52-13876. 218p. 21cm. 1953. Morrow.
--Third Base Rookie. LC 59-5804. 186 p. 21cm. (Morrow junior books). 1959. Morrow.
--Wrong-Way Rookie. Wayne, Richard, pseud. LC 52-6762. 189 p. 22cm. 1952. Macrae Smith Co.

Decker, Malcolm
--The Rebel and the Turncoat. LC 49-8501. 250 p. 21 cm. 1949. Whittlesey House.
Decker, Margaret S.
--Mr. Billiwicket's Burro. (Illus.). 51p. (gr. k-5). 1980. (ISBN 0-913976-08-3). Discovery Bks.
--Mr. Billiwicket's Burro: Ten Stories. Berger, Charles J., illus. (Illus.). (gr. 1-3). 1980. (ISBN 0-682-49565-4). Exposition.
Decker, Marjorie Ainsborough, ed.
--The Christian Mother Goose Baby Album in Rhyme. Sparr, Theanna, illus. (Illus.). 30p. 1982. (ISBN 0-933724-12-8). Decker Pr Inc.
--The Christian Mother Goose Book. Hammond, Glenna Fae & Decker, Marjorie Ainsborough, illus. LC 78-78337. (Illus.). 111 p. 28cm. 1978. (ISBN 0-933724-00-4). Christian Mother Goose Book Co.
--The Christian Mother Goose Treasury. (Illus.). 112p. 1980. (ISBN 0-8007-1196-3). Revell.
--The Christian Mother Goose Treasury. 1st ed. Decker, Marjorie Ainsborough & Hammond, Glenna Fae, illus. LC 80-69167. (Illus.). 112p. 1st U.S. edition. (Christian Mother Goose Trilogy: Vol. II). (gr. k-4). 1980. (ISBN 0-933724-01-2). Decker Pr Inc.
--The Christian Mother Goose Treasury. 1st ed. Hammond, Glenna Fae & Decker, Marjorie Ainsborough, illus. LC 80-69167. (Illus.). 110 p. 28cm. 1980. (ISBN 0-933724-01-2). C.M.G. Productions.
--The Christian Mother Goose Trilogy, 3 Vols. Sparr, Theanna & Scott, Colleen M., illus. (Illus.). 580. 336p. (ps-4). 1983. (ISBN 0-933724-14-4). Decker Pr Inc.
--Life in Christian Mother Goose Land. LC 83-70989. (Illus.). 112p. (Christian Mother Goose Trilogy: Vol. III). (gr. k-4). 1983. (ISBN 0-933724-13-6). Decker Pr Inc.
Deckert, Alice Mae
--Prairie Pals. Eitzen, Allan (1928-), illus. LC 64-18734. 143 p. illus. 22 cm. 1964. Herald Press.
DeClements, Barthe (1920-)
--How Do You Lose Those Ninth Grade Blues?. 144p. (gr. 7 up). 1984. (ISBN 0-590-33195-7, Point). Scholastic Inc.
--How Do You Lose Those Ninth Grade Blues?. A Novel. LC 83-5750. 137 p. 22cm. (gr. 5-9). 1983. (ISBN 0-670-38122-5). Viking Press.
--Nothing's Fair in Fifth Grade. LC 80-29257. 137 p. 22cm. 1981. (ISBN 0-670-51741-0). Viking Press.
--Seventeen & In-Between. LC 84-5282. 22cm. 164p. (gr. 7-9). 1984. (ISBN 0-670-63615-0, Viking Kestrel). Viking.
Decoin, Didier (1945-)
--Catherine Marshall's Story Bible. Marshall, Catherine (1907-), retold by. LC 82-1361. (Illus.). 196 p. 33cm. 1982. (ISBN 0-8245-0447-X). Chosen.
De Coo, George
--Blinky. De Coo, George, illus. 40p. N.D. House of Field.
De Coster, Charles T.
--Flemish Legends. Delstanche, Albert, illus. Taylor, Harold, tr. LC 78-74513. (Illus.). Repr. of 1920 ed. (Children's Literature Reprint Ser.). (gr. 7 up). 1979. (ISBN 0-8486-0217-X). Core Collection.
DeCoster, Charles Theodore Henri see Coster, Charles Theodore Henri De & Delstanche, Albert.
De Czege, Albert Wass see Wass De Czege, Elizabeth M. & Wass De Czege, Albert.
De Czege, Elizabeth M. Wass see Wass De Czege, Elizabeth M. & Wass De Czege, Albert.
Dede, Vivian
--Mr. Dumb Jokes. 1982. (ISBN 0-570-08407-5). Concordia.
Dedera, Don & Robles, Bob
--Goodbye, Garcia, Adios. LC 75-43344. (Illus.). xvi, 131 p. 26cm. c.1976. (ISBN 0-87358-147-4). Northland Press.
Dee, as told by see Jackson, Elizabeth Rhodes.
Dee, M. M.
--Adventures of Dusty. (Illus.). 48p. (gr. k-4). 1984. (ISBN 0-937460-39-7). Hendrick-Long.
Dee, Ruby, ed.
--Glowchild, and Other Poems. LC 72-77858. xv, 111 p. 20cm. 1972. (ISBN 0-89388-040-X). Third Press, Joseph Okpaku Pub. Co.
Dee, Sylvia
--Dear Guest and Ghost. N.D. Macmillan.
--There Was a Little Girl. Alexander, James, illus. N.D. Macmillan.
Deegan, Paul Joseph (1937-)
--Almost a Champion. Henriksen, Harold, illus. LC 74-14517. (Illus.). 39 p. 23cm. (His Dan Murphy sports stories, 3). 1975. (ISBN 0-87191-402-6). Amecus Street; Distributed by Childrens Press, Chicago.
--Close but Not Quite. Henriksen, Harold, illus. LC 74-16334. (Illus.). 39 p. 23cm. (His Dan Murphy sports stories, 5). 1975. (ISBN 0-87191-405-0). Amecus Street; Distributed by Childrens Press, Chicago.
--Dan Moves up. Henriksen, Harold, illus. LC 74-17069. (Illus.). 39 p. 23cm. (His Dan Murphy sports stories, 4). 1975. (ISBN 0-87191-406-9). Amecus Street; Distributed by Childrens Press, Chicago.
--Important Decision. Henriksen, Harold, illus. LC 74-14514. (Illus.). 39 p. 23cm. (His Dan Murphy sports stories, 1). 1975. (ISBN 0-87191-401-8). Amecus Street; Distributed by Childrens Press, Chicago.
--The Team Manager. Keely, John, illus. LC 74-14515. p. cm. 1974. Creative Education.
--The Tournaments. Keely, John, illus. LC 74-14936. p. cm. (His A Dan Murphy story). 1974. (ISBN 0-87191-404-2). Creative Education.
Deer, Ada & Simon, R. E., Jr.
--Speaking Out. LC 70-136433. (Illus.). 1 color photo. 64p. (Open Door Bks). (gr. 6-12). 1970. (ISBN 0-516-04829-5). Childrens.
Deering, Fremont B., pseud., see Goldfrap, John Henry.
Deering, Fremont B., pseud. (1879-1917)
--The Border Boys Across the Frontier. Goldfrap, John Henry. (The Border Boys' Ser.). N.D. Hurst & Co.
--The Border Boys Along the St. Lawrence. Goldfrap, John Henry. (The Border Boys' Ser.). N.D. Hurst & Co.
--The Border Boys in the Canadian Rockies. Goldfrap, John Henry. (The Border Boys' Ser.). N.D. Hurst & Co.
--The Border Boys with the Mexican Rangers. Goldfrap, John Henry. (The Border Boys' Ser.). N.D. Hurst & Co.
Deering, Janet
--Eddie's Moving Day. Kaufman, Joe (1911-), illus. 32p. (Golden Beginning Reader Ser). (gr. k-2). 1969. (ISBN 0-307-61160-4, Golden Pr). Western Pub.
Deering, Mary S.
--An Average Boy's Vacation, No.1. (Forest City Ser.). N.D. Dresser, McLellan & Co.
--Phil, Rob and Louis: Or, Haps and Mishaps of Three Average Boys, No.2. (Forest City Ser.). N.D. Dresser, McLellan & Co.
Deerksen, Eva
--Polly Parrot. LC 52-4233. 62 p. illus. 19 cm. 1952. Moody Press.
De Faber, Cecilia Bohl see Caballero, Fernan, pseud.
Defoe, Daniel, jt. auth. see Politzer, Anie.
Defoe, Daniel (1661-1731)
--The Adventures of Robinson Crusoe. (Altemus' New Illustrated Young People's Library). N.D. Henry Altemus Company.
--The Adventures of Robinson Crusoe. (Illus.). (One-Syallable Ser.). N.D. Henry Altemus Co.
--The Adventures of Robinson Crusoe. (Illus.). (Children's Gift Ser.). N.D. Henry Altemus Company Publications.
--The Adventures of Robinson Crusoe. (Illus.). (Boys and Girls' Classics). N.D. Henry Altemus.
--Adventures of Robinson Crusoe. (World Famous Ser.). N.D. Lothrop, Lee & Shepard.
--The Adventures of Robinson Crusoe. (Globe Editions). N.D. Macmillan & Co.
--The Adventures of Robinson Crusoe. (Golden Treasury Ser.). N.D. Macmillan & Co.
--Adventures of Robinson Crusoe. Adams, William Taylor (1822-1897), ed. Optic, Oliver, pseud. (World-Famous Ser.). N.D. Lothrop, Lee & Shepard.
--Adventures of Robinson Crusoe. West, M., adapted by. N.D. Longmans Green & Co.
--The Adventures of Robinson Crusoe on His Island. Tilney, Frederick Colin, ed. Symington, J. A., illus. 18cm. 128p. (Tales for Children from Many Lands). N.D. E. P. Dutton & Co.
--An American Robinson Crusoe for American Boys and Girls: The Adaptation, with Additional Incidents. Allison, Samuel Buell, ed. LC 19-4447. 171 p. illus. 19 cm. c.1918. Educational Publishing Company.
--Defoe's Robinson Cursoe. Lambert, ed. (Classics for Children). N.D. Ginn and Company.
--The Life and Adventures of Robinson Crusoe. (Illus.). (Lubbock's Books). N.D. George Routledge & Sons.
--The Life and Adventures of Robinson Crusoe. Duvoisin, Roger Antoine (1904-1980), illus. LC 46-5868. 287, 1 p. col. front., illus., col. plates. 22 cm. (Half-title: Rainbow classics). 1946. The World Publishing Company.
--The Life and Strange Surprising Adventures of Robinson Crusoe, of York, Mariner: As Related by Himself. Pocock, Guy Noel (1880-), illus. LC 32-20984. vii p., 1 l., 11-352 p. col. front., col. plates. 23 cm. 1931. Garden City Publishing Company, Inc.
--The Life and Strange Surprizing Adventures of Robinson Crusoe of York, Mariner. (Illus.). 26cm. 284p. 1945. The Peter Pauper Press.
--The Life and Surprising Adventures of Robinson Crusoe. (Children's Classics). N.D. Macmillan.
--The Life and Surprising Adventures of Robinson Crusoe, of York, Mariner. Kauffmann, illus. LC 52-26364. 289 p. illus. 20 cm. (Caldwell's juvenile classics). N.D. H. M. Caldwell Co.
--A Little Book of Robinson Crusoe and Other Good Old Tales. LC 34-10382. (Illus.). 252 p. 14cm. (little big books). c.1934. McLoughlin Bros., Inc.
--Molly Flanders. N.D. Knopf.
--Molly Flanders. (Magnum Easy Eye Classic Ser). (gr. 10 up). N.D. Lancer.
--Molly Flanders. N.D. Modern Library.
--Molly Flanders. Marsh, Reginald (1898-1954), illus. 372p. N.D. Heritage Press.
--The Picture Book of Robinson Crusoe. Moore, Elizabeth C, Mrs., adapted by. Verpilleux, Emile Antoine (1888-), illus. LC 31-7410. 51, 1 p. incl. col. front., col. illus. 29 cm. 1931. The Macmillan Company.
--Robinson Crusoe. (Illus.). (The Rugby Series for Boys). N.D. A. L. Burt's Pubs.
--Robinson Crusoe. (Illus.). 576p. (The Excelsior Edition). 1879. American News Co.
--Robinson Crusoe. Repr. (The Caxton Edition). N.D. Belford, Clarke.
--Robinson Crusoe. (Illus.). 400p. Repr. (Royal Octavo Edition). N.D. Cassell, Petter, Galpin.
--Robinson Crusoe. N.D. Claxton, Remsen & Haffelfinger.
--Robinson Crusoe, 1 of 6 Vols. (Crusoe Library). N.D. Colby & Rich.
--Robinson Crusoe. (Illus.). Repr. (The Twilight Ser.: 14). N.D. Cupples & Leon.
--Robinson Crusoe. (One-Syllable Bks.). N.D. D. Appleton & co.
--Robinson Crusoe. (Heath's Home & School Classics Ser.). N.D. D C Heath.
--Robinson Crusoe. 20cm. 419p. (The Golden Books for Children). 1918. D. McKay Co.
--Robinson Crusoe. (McKay's Illustrated Classics). N.D. David Mckay Co.
--Robinson Crusoe, 1 of 4 Vols. (The Crusoe Library). N.D. Dodd, Mead.
--Robinson Crusoe. (Illus.). Repr. N.D. E. & J. B. Young & Co.
--Robinson Crusoe. N.D. E P Dutton.
--Robinson Crusoe. Repr. (Popular Illustrated). N.D. Fairbanks & Palmer.
--Robinson Crusoe. N.D. Frederick Warne & Co.
--Robinson Crusoe. (The Crusoe Bks.). N.D. G. W. Carleton & Co.
--Robinson Crusoe. (Doubleday Classics). N.D. Garden City Books.
--Robinson Crusoe. (The Children's Favorites). 1915. George W. Jacobs & Co.
--Robinson Crusoe. (Washington Square Classics Ser.). N.D. George W Jacobs.
--Robinson Crusoe. (Robinson Crusoe Library of English Classic Juvenile Bks.). N.D. George Routledge & Sons.
--Robinson Crusoe. (Treasure-Box of Wonder and Entertainment). N.D. George Routledge & Sons.
--Robinson Crusoe. (The Moss Wreath Library of Simple Stories for Children). N.D. George Routledge & Sons.
--Robinson Crusoe. (Classics for Children). N.D. Ginn.
--Robinson Crusoe. (The Good Value Books). N.D. Grosset & Dunlap.
--Robinson Crusoe. (Illus.). (Classics Illus. Ser.). N.D. (ISBN 0-685-74081-1). Guild Bks.
--Robinson Crusoe. (Illus.). 566p. (Juvenile Classics Ser.). 1905. Set. H M Caldwell Co.
--Robinson Crusoe. (Illus.). (Famous Books for Boys). N.D. H. M. Caldwell Co.
--Robinson Crusoe. N.D. Henry Altemus Company.
--Robinson Crusoe. (English Readings Ser.). N.D. Henry Holt.
--Robinson Crusoe, 1 of 6 vols. Repr. (Rose Valley Lib.). N.D. Set. Henry T. Coates & Co.
--Robinson Crusoe. (Illus.). (Ever New Books for Young People). N.D. Henry Altemus Company Publications.
--Robinson Crusoe. (Riverside Bookshelf). N.D. Houghton Mifflin Co.
--Robinson Crusoe, 1 of 64 vols. (Young America Library: No. 37). 1900. Set. Hurst & Co.
--Robinson Crusoe. (Young American Library). N.D. Hurst & Co.
--Robinson Crusoe. Repr. (Victoria Edition). 1882. J B Lippincott.
--Robinson Crusoe. (The Cottage Library). N.D. J. B. Lippincott.
--Robinson Crusoe. Holiday ed. N.D. J. S. Locke.
--Robinson Crusoe. (The Famous Library). N.D. James Miller.
--Robinson Crusoe. (Sears Juvenile Classics). N.D. J.H. Sears & Co.
--Robinson Crusoe. (The Winston Clear-Type Popular Classics). N.D. John C. Winston.
--Robinson Crusoe. (The Young People's Library). N.D. John C. Winston.
--Robinson Crusoe, 4. (The Children's Favorites). N.D. Leavitt & Allen Bros.
--Robinson Crusoe. (The World-Renowned Ser.). N.D. Leavitt & Allen Bros.
--Robinson Crusoe, 1 of 6 vols. (Illus.). Repr. (Crusoe Library). 1882. Lee & Shepard.
--Robinson Crusoe. (Royal Illuminated Library). N.D. Lee & Shepard.
--Robinson Crusoe. (Wild Life Ser.). N.D. Lee & Shepard.
--Robinson Crusoe. Abridged. (Class Books of English Literature). N.D. Longmans Green & Co.
--Robinson Crusoe. (The Washington Square Classics). N.D. Macrae Smith.
--Robinson Crusoe. (Casket of Juveniles). N.D. Mason, Baker & Pratt.
--Robinson Crusoe. (Aunt Louisa's Big Picture Bks.). N.D. McLoughlin Bros.
--Robinson Crusoe. (Miss Merryheart's Bks.). N.D. McLoughlin Bros.
--Robinson Crusoe. N.D. (ISBN 0-686-08949-9). Merrimack.
--Robinson Crusoe. (The Nelson Classics). N.D. Nelson Bks.
--Robinson Crusoe. N.D. Nichols & Hall.
--Robinson Crusoe. 1937. Oxford University Press.
--Robinson Crusoe. (Arabian Nights Library). N.D. Porter & Coates.
--Robinson Crusoe. (Rose Valley Library). N.D. Porter & Coates.
--Robinson Crusoe, 3 Vols. (Illus.). Repr. (Arabian Nights Library). N.D. Porter & Coates.
--Robinson Crusoe, 1of 6 Vols. (Illus.). Repr. (Rose Valley Library). N.D. Set. Porter & Coates.
--Robinson Crusoe. (The Youth's Cabinet of A. L. O. E. Presentation Popular Standard Bks.). N.D. Pott, Young, & Co.
--Robinson Crusoe. (Illus.). (Young People's Classics). N.D. R. F. Fenno & Co.
--Robinson Crusoe. (Wide, Wide World Library). N.D. R. Worthington.
--Robinson Crusoe. (Hopeful Enterprise Library). N.D. R. Worthington & Co.
--Robinson Crusoe. (Incident and Adventure Library). N.D. R. Worthington & Co.
--Robinson Crusoe. (Illus.). (The Junior Library Ser.: Vol. 11). N.D. Rand, McNally & Co.
--Robinson Crusoe. N.D. Scott,Foresman & Co.
--Robinson Crusoe, 1 of 24 vols. (Illus.). (Children's Favorite Classics). 1900. T. Y. Crowell & Co.
--Robinson Crusoe. (Illus.). (Children's Home Library). 1915. T Y Crowell.
--Robinson Crusoe, 1 of 15 vols. (Illus.). Repr. (Star Ser.). N.D. T. Y. Crowell.
--Robinson Crusoe. (The Illuminated Ser.). N.D. The American News Co.
--Robinson Crusoe. (Children's Favorite Classics). N.D. Thomas Y. Crowell Company.
--Robinson Crusoe. (The Crusoe Library). N.D. Thomas Nelson & Sons.
--Robinson Crusoe. (Illus.). Repr. N.D. Thomas Nelson & Sons.
--Robinson Crusoe, 1of4 vols. (Illus.). Repr. (Every Boy's Library). N.D. Thomas Nelson & Sons.
--Robinson Crusoe. (Illus.). (Collins' Juvenile Ser.). N.D. William Collins Co.
--Robinson Crusoe, Pts 1 & 2. (Illus.). N.D. William Collins Sons & Company.
--Robinson Crusoe. (Classic Ser.). N.D. World Publishing Co.
--Robinson Crusoe. Ayton- Symington, J., illus. LC 54-286572. 245p. illus. 21cm. (Children's illustrated classics). 1954. Dent.
--Robinson Crusoe. Ayton-Symington, J., illus. (Children's Illustrated Classics). N.D. E. P. Dutton & Co.
--Robinson Crusoe. Baldwin, James (1841-1925), ed. Chapman, Frederick Trench (1887-), illus. LC 51-12414. 185 p. illus. 20 cm. 1951. Aladdin Books.
--Robinson Crusoe. Ball, Robert (1890-), illus. LC 48-3220. ix. 309 p. illus. 23 cm. (Lippincott classics). 1948. J. B. Lippincott Co.
--Robinson Crusoe. Barnum, Jay Hyde (1888-1962), illus. LC 52-7222. (Adapted). (Illus.). unpage. 29cm. c.1952. Random House.
--Robinson Crusoe, Vols. 1 & 2. Biggs, J. R., illus. N.D. Penguin Books.
--Robinson Crusoe. Bown, Derick, illus. LC 78-3384. p. cm. (Raintree's illustrated classics). 1978. (ISBN 0-8393-6212-9). Raintree Childrens Books.
--Robinson Crusoe. Browne, Gordon Frederick (1858-1932), illus. (Illus.). (Scribner-Blackie Series of books for young people). N.D. Charles Scribner's Sons.
--Robinson Crusoe. Browne, Verne B., ed. Turkle, Brinton Cassaday (1915-), illus. LC 51-8883. 306 p. illus. 22 cm. 1951. Scott, Foresman.
--Robinson Crusoe. Castellon, Federico (1914-) & Codorniu, Federico, illus. (Illus.). 348 p. 24cm. (Macmillan classics, 15). 1962. Macmillan.
--Robinson Crusoe. Chisholm, Louey, ed. N.D. Thomas Nelson & Sons.
--Robinson Crusoe. Chorpenning, Charlotte Lee Barrows (1872-1955), adapted by. 1952. Children's Theatre Press.

Deitch, Gene & Hlavaty, Vratislav (1934-)
--A Visit from a Turtle. LC 74-469. (Illus.). 34 p. 24cm. 1974, c.1973. (ISBN 0-531-02727-9). (ISBN 0-531-02726-0). Watts.
Deitrick, Marion Rolfe Johnson (1903-)
--Johnny Mouse of Corregidor. De Wolfe, Henry, illus. LC 42-22576. 7 p. l., 13-134 p. illus. 22 1/2 cm. 1942. The Bobbs-Merrill Company.
Deitz (1947-)
--The Good Morning Grump. Dienemann, Debbie, illus. LC 81-22876. (Illus.). 30 p. (gr. k-3). c.1982. (ISBN 0-687-15520-7). (ISBN 0-687-15520-7). Abingdon.
De Jaeger, Charles
--Paul Is a Maltese Boy. LC 68-13444. (Illus.). 48 p. 22cm. (Children everywhere series). 1968, c.1965. Hastings House.
De Jaeger, Charles & Mauthner, Maria
--Christiane Lives in the Alps. De Jaeger, Charles, illus. LC 67-8837. 48 p. (chiefly illus. 22cm. (Children everywhere series). (Children Everywhere Series). 1967, c.1962. Hastings House.
Dejeans, Elizabeth
--The Moreton Mystery. N.D. Bobbs-Merrill Co.
--Nobody's Child. Keller, Arthur I., illus. N.D. Bobbs-Merrill Co.
--The Tiger's Coat. Keller, Arthur I., illus. N.D. Bobbs-Merrill Co.
De Jong, David Cornel, Tr, jt. auth. see Roggeveen, Leonard.
De Jong, David Cornel (1905-1967)
--Alexander the Monkey-Sitter. Weiss, Harvey (1922-), illus. LC 65-168445. 58p. col. illus. 22cm. c.1965. Atlantic-Little.
--Around the Dom. Lorraine, Walter Henry (1929-), illus. LC 64-12618. (Illus.). 187 p. 21cm. 1964. Holt, Rinehart and Winston.
--The Happy Birthday Egg. Weiss, Harvey (1922-), illus. LC 62-12376. (Illus.). 52 p. 22cm. 1962. Little, Brown.
--The Happy Birthday Umbrella. Weiss, Harvey (1922-), illus. LC 59-7342. (Illus.). 50 p. 22cm. 1959. Little, Brown.
--Looking for Alexander. Weiss, Harvey (1922-), illus. LC 63-7681. (Illus.). 59 p. 22cm. (Atlantic Monthly Press book). 1963. Little, Brown.
--Seven Sayings of Mr. Jefferson. Porter, Mildred Sophie, illus. LC 57-12732. (Illus.). (gr. 2-6). 1957. (ISBN 0-87466-024-6). (ISBN 0-87466-061-0). Parnassus.
--The Squirrel and the Harp. Spier, Jo, illus. LC 66-10194. 46p. illus. 22cm. (gr. k-3). 1966. (ISBN 0-02-726530-7). Macmillan.
De Jong, Dola (1911-)
--Between Home and Horizon. Mueller, Madeline, tr. from Dutch. LC 62-9472. 215 p. 22cm. 1962. Knopf.
--By Marvelous Agreement. LC 60-11422. 211 p. 22cm. 1960. Knopf.
--The House on Charlton Street. Riswold, Gilbert, illus. LC 62-9644. (Illus.). 157 p. 21cm. 1962. Scribner.
--The Level Land. Hoowij, Jan H., illus. LC 43-182012. 2 p. l., 164 p. illus. 29 1/2 cm. 1943. C. Scribner's Sons.
--Nikkernik, Nakkernak and Nokkernok. Hoowij, Jan H., illus. LC 42-21770. 4 p. l., 117 p. illus. 21 x 16 cm. 1942. C. Scribner's Sons.
--One Summer's Secret. LC 63-19114. 184 p. 21 cm. (Youth today novel). 1963. D. McKay Co.
--Return to the Level Land. LC 47-11424. 152 p. illus. 21 cm. 1947. C. Scribner's Sons.
--Sand for the Sandmen. Norton, Natalie, illus. LC 46-4801. 4 p. l., 87, 1 p. illus. (part col.) 21 cm. 1946. C. Scribner's Sons.
DeJong, Meindert (1906-)
--The Almost All-White Rabbity Cat. Vestal, Herman B., illus. LC 72-178599. (Illus.). 133p. (gr. 3-6). 1972. (ISBN 0-02-726560-9). Macmillan.
--Along Came a Dog. Sendak, Maurice Bernard (1928-), illus. LC 57-9265. (Illus.). 192p. (gr. 4-7). 1980. (ISBN 0-06-440114-6, Trophy). Har-Row.
--Along Came a Dog. Sendak, Maurice Bernard (1928-), illus. LC 57-9265. (Illus.). 172 p. 21cm. 1958. (ISBN 0-06-021421-X). Harper. **Awards: (IBBY); (ALA); (JNM).**
--Bells of the Harbor. Wiese, Kurt (1887-1974), illus. LC 41-23273. 6 p. l., 289 p. illus. 21 cm. 1941. Harper & Brothers.
--Big Goose & the Little White Duck. Burkert, Nancy Ekholm (1933-), illus. LC 63-15322. (Illus.). (gr. 1-5). 1963. (ISBN 0-06-021431-7, HarpJ). Har-Row.
--The Big Goose and the Little White Duck. Potter, Edna, illus. LC 38-32623. 4 p. l., 160 p. col. front., illus., col. plates. 22 cm. 1938. Harper & Brothers.
--The Big Goose and the Little White Duck. Potter, Edna, illus. LC 63-15322. (Illus.). 169 p. 23cm. 1963, c.1938. Harper & Row.
--Billy and the Unhappy Bull. Simont, Marc (1915-), illus. LC 46-8064. 6 p. l., 206 p. illus. 21 cm. 1946. Harper & Brothers.
--Cat That Walked a Week. Robinson, Jessie Berkowitz, illus. LC 43-16877. (Illus.). 148p. (gr. 1-5). 1943. (ISBN 0-06-021450-3, HarpJ). Har-Row.
--Dirk's Dog, Bello. Wiese, Kurt (1887-1974), illus. LC 39-27724. 4 p. l., 296 p. incl. illus., plates. col. front. 22 cm. (gr. 7-9). 1939. (ISBN 0-06-021456-2). Harper & Brothers.
--The Easter Cat. Hoban, Lillian (1925-), illus. LC 78-141933. (Illus.). 110 p. 20cm. 1973, c.1971. Collier Books.
--Far Out the Long Canal. Grossman, Nancy S. (1940-), illus. LC 64-20947. (Illus.). 231p. (gr. 3-7). 1964. (ISBN 0-06-021466-X, HarpJ). Har-Row. **Award: (ALA).**
--Good Luck Duck. Simont, Marc (1915-), illus. LC 50-6809. (Illus.). 24cm. 57p. (gr. 3-7). 1950. (ISBN 0-06-021475-9, HarpJ). Har-Row.
--Horse Came Running. Sagsoorian, Paul (1923-), illus. LC 71-99119. (Illus.). 9 full-page drawings. 160p. 147p. (gr. 4 up). 1970. (ISBN 0-02-726540-4). Macmillan.
--Horse Came Running. Sagsoorian, Paul (1923-), illus. LC 71-99119. 192p. (gr. 5-7). 1972. (ISBN 0-02-042800-6, Collier). Macmillan.
--House of Sixty Fathers. Sendak, Maurice Bernard (1928-), illus. LC 56-8148. (Illus.). (gr. 5 up). 1956. (ISBN 0-06-021481-3, HarpJ). Har-Row. **Awards: (IBBY); (ALA); (JNM).**
--Hurry Home Candy. Sendak, Maurice Bernard (1928-), illus. LC 53-8536. 244p. illus. 21cm. (gr. 4-6). 1953. (ISBN 0-06-021486-4). (ISBN 0-06-440025-5). Harper. **Award: (JNM).**
--Journey from Peppermint Street. (Illus.). (gr. 5 up). 1974. (ISBN 0-06-440011-5, Trophy). (ISBN 0-06-021488-0). Har-Row.
--Journey from Peppermint Street. McCully, Emily Arnold (1939-), illus. LC 68-27870. (Illus.). 242 p. 21cm. 1968. Harper & Row. **Awards: (NBA); (ALA).**
--Last Little Cat. McMullan, James (1934-), illus. LC 61-5765. (Illus.). (gr. 2-6). 1961. (ISBN 0-06-021501-1, HarpJ). Har-Row. **Award: (ALA).**
--The Little Cow and the Turtle. Sendak, Maurice Bernard (1928-), illus. LC 55-8822. (Illus.). 177 p. 21cm. (gr. 3-6). 1955. (ISBN 0-06-021511-9). Harper.
--The Little Stray Dog. Shenton, Edward (1895-), illus. LC 43-86957. 5 p. l., 51 p. illus. 22 1/2 cm. 1943. Harper & Brothers.
--The Mighty Ones: Great Men and Women of Early Bible Days. Schmidt, Harvey (1929-), illus. LC 68-27820. (Illus.). 282 p. 25cm. 1959. (ISBN 0-06-021521-6). Harper.
--Nobody Plays with a Cabbage. Allen, Thomas Burt (1928-), illus. (Illus.). 52 p. 24cm. (gr. 2-6). 1962. (ISBN 0-06-021531-3). Harper. **Award: (ALA).**
--Puppy Summer. Lobel, Anita Kempler (1934-), illus. LC 65-22160. (Illus.). 98p. (gr. 1-5). 1965. (ISBN 0-06-021540-2, HarpJ). Har-Row.
--Shadrach. Sendak, Maurice Bernard (1928-), illus. LC 53-5250. (Illus.). 192p. (gr. 3-6). 1980. (ISBN 0-06-440115-4, Trophy). Har-Row.
--Shadrach. Sendak, Maurice Bernard (1928-), illus. LC 53-5250. (Illus.). 182 p. 21cm. (gr. 1-5). 1953. (ISBN 0-06-021546-1). Harper. **Awards: (ALA); (JNM).**
--The Singing Hill. Sendak, Maurice Bernard (1928-), illus. LC 62-16414. (Illus.). 180 p. 21cm. (gr. 1-4). 1962. (ISBN 0-06-021556-9). Harper & Row. **Awards: (NYT); (ALA).**
--Smoke Above the Lane. Goodenow, Girard, illus. LC 51-9759. (Illus.). 58 p. 24cm. (gr. 1-5). 1951. (ISBN 0-06-021566-6). Harper.
--The Tower by the Sea. 1st ed. Comfort, Barbara (1916-), illus. (Illus.). 113 p. 22cm. (gr. 5 up). 1950. (ISBN 0-06-021576-3). Harper.
--The Wheel on the School. Sendak, Maurice Bernard (1928-), illus. LC 54-8945. (Illus.). 298p. (gr. 3-6). 1954. (ISBN 0-06-021585-2, HarpJ). (ISBN 0-06-021586-0). (ISBN 0-06-440021-2). Har-Row. **Awards: (JNM); (ALA).**
--Wheels Over the Bridge. Watson, Aldren Auld (1917-), illus. LC 41-5300. 6 p. l., 219, 1 p. illus., plates. 22 cm. c.1941. Harper & Brothers.
De Jonge, Joanne
--Anaku: The True Story of a Wolf. (Voyager Ser.). (gr. 5 up). 1979. (ISBN 0-8010-2894-9). Baker Bk.
--Crooked Footprints. (Rainbow Ser). (gr. 4-6). 1978. (ISBN 0-8010-2879-5). Baker Bk.
--Dandelions & Jumping Beans. (Rainbow Ser). (gr. 4-6). 1978. (ISBN 0-8010-2880-9). Baker Bk.
--Hummingbirds & Roadrunners. (Rainbow Ser). (gr. 4-6). 1978. (ISBN 0-8010-2882-5). Baker Bk.
DE Kay, Ormonde, Jr. (1923-)
--THe Adventure of Lewis and Clark. (Illus.). 1968. Random House.
--Snorkls & the Waterwitch. Wildman, George, illus. LC 83-4458. (Illus.). 32p. (ps-3). 1983. (ISBN 0-394-86086-1). Random.
De Kerosett, Marie Aline
--Friends in My Garden. LC 33-7570. 96 p. illus. 21 cm. c.1933. The Christopher Publishing House.
Dekker, Jan, tr. see Kavcic, Vladimir.
Dekker, Thomas
--The Shoemaker's Holiday. Lawlis, Merritt, ed. 1968. Barron.
De Kort, Kees
--Jesus Heals the Blind Man. De Kort, Kees, illus. (Illus.). 28p. (Children's Picture Books Series: Bk. 3). (ps). 1968. (ISBN 0-8066-9382-7). Augsburg.
De Kort, Kees, illus.
--Good Samaritan. (Illus.). (ps-3). 1970. (ISBN 0-8066-9385-1). Augsburg.
--Jesus Stills the Storm. Martinsen, Paul, tr. (Illus.). 28p. (ps-1). 1968. (ISBN 0-8066-9381-9). Augsburg.
--What the Bible Tells Us: Third Series, 4 bks. Incl. A Baby Called John. 28p. (ISBN 0-8066-1770-5, 10-0538); Jesus & a Little Girl. 28p. (ISBN 0-8066-1771-3, 10-3479); The Son Who Left Home. 28p. (ISBN 0-8066-1773-X, 10-5852); Jesus Goes Away. 28p. (ISBN 0-8066-1774-8, 10-3510). (gr. 1-4). 1980. Augsburg.
De Koven, Reginald, jt. auth. see Field, Eugene.
De Koven, Reginald & Field, Eugene
--The Field-De Koven Song Book. N.D. Charles Scribner's Sons.
De Kovend, James (1831-1879)
--Dorchester Polytechine Academy: Dr. Neverasole, Principal. LC 6-33295. 226 p. 18 cm. 1879. L. H. Morehouse.
DeKroyft, Helen Aldrich
--The Story of Little Jakey. 132p. 1876. Hurd & Houghton.
Del, Favero Agustina Santos see Ganz, Barbara & Noda, Phyllis.
De la, Fontaine Jean see La Fontaine, Jean de.
De La Bedolliere, Emile Gigault see La Bedolliere, Emile Gigault De.
De Laboulaye, Edouard Rene Lefebvre see Laboulaye, Edouard Rene Lefebvre de.
De La Brette, Jean
--My Uncle & the Cure. N.D. (ISBN 0-8149-0274-X). Vanguard.
Delach, Mary K & Karlovich, Helen
--Happy Mama and Her Auto-Fly. LC 76-8721. (Illus.). 67 p. 24cm. c.1976. (ISBN 0-914598-29-5). Padre Productions.
De la Coze, Minerva
--A Little Fairy Tale for Little People. 23p. 1983. (ISBN 0-533-05618-7). Vantage.
De la Croix, Robert
--Mysteries of the Sea. 256p. 1957. John Day Books.
--Ships of Doom. 192p. 1962. John Day & Co.
De Ladebat, Monique P.
--The Village that Slept. 1980. (ISBN 0-8398-2610-9, Gregg). G K Hall.
Delafield, Celia
--Mrs. Mallard's Ducklings. (Illus.). (gr. k-3). 1946. (ISBN 0-8382-0525-9). Hale.
--Mrs. Mallard's Ducklings. Weisgard, Leonard Joseph (1916-), illus. (Illus.). (gr. k-3). 1946. (ISBN 0-688-51200-3). Lothrop.
Delafield, Emily Prime
--Alice in Wonderland. LC 16-13442. (A Play Compiled from Lewis Carroll's Stories, Alice in Wonderland, and Through the Looking Glass and What Alice Found There). ix p., 1 l., 89 p., 1 l. col. front., col. plates. 21 cm. 1898. Dodd, Mead & Company.
Delafield, Emily Prime, compiled by see Carroll, Lewis.
De La Fontaine, Jean
--The Lion & the Rat: A Fable. Wildsmith, Brian Lawrence (1930-), illus. (Illus.). 32p. (ps-1). 1963. (ISBN 0-19-279607-0, Pub. by Oxford U Pr Childrens). Merrimack Pub Cir. **Award: (KGM).**
De La Fontaine, Jean see La Fontaine, Jean de.
DeLage, Ida (1918-)
--ABC Christmas. Beerworth, Roger, illus. LC 77-14604. (Illus.). 32 p. 24cm. (Once Upon an Abc). c.1978. (ISBN 0-8116-4355-7). Garrard Pub. Co.
--ABC Easter Bunny. Sloan, Ellen, illus. LC 78-14829. (Illus.). 32 p. 23cm. (Once Upon an Abc). c.1979. (ISBN 0-8116-4356-5). Garrard Pub. Co.
--ABC Fire Dogs. Sloan, Ellen, illus. LC 77-591. p. cm. 1977. (ISBN 0-8116-6072-9). Garrard Pub. Co.
--ABC Halloween Witch. Cunette, Lou, illus. LC 77-5469. (Illus.). 32 p. 23cm. (Once Upon an Abc). c.1977. (ISBN 0-8116-4353-0). Garrard Pub. Co.
--ABC Pigs Go to Market. Oechsli, Kelly (1918-), illus. LC 77-23317. (Illus.). a. c.1977. (ISBN 0-8116-6073-7). Garrard Pub. Co.
--ABC Pirate Adventure. Brown, Buck (1936-), illus. LC 77-3171. p. cm. 1977. (ISBN 0-8116-6074-5). Garrard Pub. Co.
--ABC Santa Claus. Brown, Judith Gwyn (1933-), illus. LC 77-5629. (Illus.). 32 p. 23cm. (Once Upon an Abc). c.1978. (ISBN 0-8116-4354-9). Garrard Pub. Co.
--ABC Triplets at the Zoo. Pierson, Lori, illus. LC 79-13265. (Illus.). 32 p. 23cm. (Once Upon an Abc). c.1980. (ISBN 0-8116-4357-3). Garrard Pub. Co.
--Beware! Beware! A Witch Won't Share. Schroeder, Ted (1931-1973), illus. LC 72-76326. (Illus.). 46 p. 23cm. 1972. (ISBN 0-8116-4059-0). Garrad Pub. Co.
--Bunny Hunt. Pierson, Lori, illus. LC 81-6516. p. cm. 1982. (ISBN 0-8116-6085-0). Garrard.
--A Bunny Ride. McVay, Tracy, illus. LC 74-14818. (Illus.). 32 p. 23cm. 1975. (ISBN 0-8116-6065-6). Garrard Pub. Co.
--Bunny School. McVay, Tracy, illus. LC 76-17625. (Illus.). 32 p. 23cm. c.1976. (ISBN 0-8116-6071-0). Garrard Pub. Co.
--The Farmer and the Witch. Miret, Gil, illus. LC 66-12674. 46p. col. illus 23cm. (Tall tales). (Old Witch Books). (gr. k-4). 1966. Garrard Pub. Co.
--Frannie's Flower. Sloan, Ellen, illus. LC 79-11724. (Illus.). 32 p. 23cm. c.1979. (ISBN 0-8116-6076-1). Garrard Pub. Co.
--Good Morning, Lady. McVay, Tracy, illus. LC 73-22084. (Illus.). 32 p. 23cm. 1974. (ISBN 0-8116-6051-6). Garrard Pub. Co.
--Hello, Come In. Mardon, John, illus. LC 71-156079. (Illus.). 39 p. 24cm. 1971. (ISBN 0-8116-6708-1). Garrard Pub. Co.
--The Old Witch and Her Magic Basket. Sloan, Ellen, illus. LC 78-58520. (Illus.). 48 p. 23cm. c.1978. Garrard Pub. Co.
--The Old Witch and the Crows. Smith, Marianne, illus. LC 81-13227. (Illus.). 45 p. 23cm. c.1983. (ISBN 0-8116-4067-1). Garrard Pub. Co.
--The Old Witch and the Dragon. Unada, pseud. (1927-), illus. Gliewe, Unada Grace. LC 78-11283. (Illus.). 48 p. 23cm. c.1979. (ISBN 0-8116-4064-7). Garrard Pub. Co.
--The Old Witch and the Ghost Parade. Taylor, Jody, illus. LC 77-18185. p. cm. 1978. (ISBN 0-8116-4062-0). Garrard Pub. Co.
--The Old Witch and the Snores. Miret, Gil, illus. LC 75-95748. (Illus.). 46 p. 23cm. (Tall tales books). 1970. Garrard Pub. Co.
--The Old Witch and the Wizard. Korach, Mimi (1922-), illus. LC 73-16039. (Illus.). 47 p. 23cm. 1974. (ISBN 0-8116-4060-4). Garrard Pub. Co.
--The Old Witch Finds a New House. Paris, Pat, illus. LC 79-11732. (Illus.). 44 p. 23cm. c.1979. (ISBN 0-8116-4065-5). Garrard Pub. Co.
--The Old Witch Gets a Surprise. Sloan, Ellen, illus. LC 80-24223. (Illus.). 48 p. 23cm. c.1981. (ISBN 0-8116-4066-3). Garrard Pub. Co.
--The Old Witch Goes to the Ball. Nebel, Gustave E., illus. LC 69-15830. (Illus.). 46 p. 23cm. (Reading shelf book). 1969. (ISBN 0-8116-4055-8). Garrard Pub. Co.
--The Old Witch's Party. Korach, Mimi (1922-), illus. LC 75-45232. (Illus.). 48 p. 23cm. c.1976. (ISBN 0-8116-4061-2). Garrard Pub. Co.
--Pilgrim Children Come to Plymouth. Vestal, Herman B., illus. LC 80-29180. (Illus.). 48p. (gr. 1-5). 1981. (ISBN 0-8116-6084-2). Garrard.
--The Pilgrim Children on the Mayflower. Dodson, Bert, illus. LC 79-21812. (Illus.). 48p. (Ida DeLage Bks.). (gr. 1-5). 1980. (ISBN 0-8116-4315-8). Garrard.
--Pink Pink. Mahan, Benton, illus. LC 72-11015. (Illus.). 40 p. 23cm. 1973. (ISBN 0-8116-6725-1). Garrard Pub. Co.
--Santa's Christmas Helper, Tinsel. Paris, Pat, illus. LC 80-28058. p. cm. (Tinsel, Christmas Fairy). 1981. (ISBN 0-8116-7650-1). Garrard Pub. Co.
--The Squirrel's Tree Party. McVay, Tracy, illus. LC 78-58523. (Illus.). 32 p. 23cm. c.1978. (ISBN 0-8116-6073-7). Garrard Pub. Co.
--Weeny Witch. Oechsli, Kelly (1918-), illus. LC 68-10173. (Illus.). 48 p. 23cm. (Reading shelf books). 1968. (ISBN 0-8116-4052-3). Garrard Pub. Co.
--What Does a Witch Need?. Schroeder, Ted (1931-1973), illus. LC 76-143305. (Illus.). 47 p. 23cm. (A Reading shelf book). 1971. (ISBN 0-8116-4058-2). Garrard Pub. Co.
--The Witchy Broom. Peaver, Walt, illus. LC 69-10373. (Illus.). 45 p. 23cm. (A Reading shelf book). 1969. (ISBN 0-8116-4054-X). Garrard Pub. Co.
DeLage, Ida (1918-) & Sloan, Ellen
--Am I a Bunny?. LC 77-11639. (Illus.). 31 p. 23cm. c.1978. (ISBN 0-8116-6072-9). Garrard Pub. Co.
Delagran, Louise, ed. see Masters, M.
Delagran, Louise, et al., eds. see Masters, M.
De Laguna, Frederica Annis (1908-)
--The Thousand March: Adventures of an American Boy with Garibaldi. Law, Daniel F., illus. LC 30-25619. viii, 266 p., 1 l. col. fornt., illus. 21 cm. 1930. Little, Brown, and Company.

AUTHOR INDEX DE LA

Delahaye, Gilbert (1923-)
--The Little Garage Man. N.D (Wonder Books). Grosset & Dunlap.
--Pamela Learns to Ride. Marlier, Marcel, illus. LC 68-60203. (Illus.). 29 p. 29cm. 1968. Hart Pub. Co.
De La Iglesia, Maria Elena (1936-)
--The Cat and the Mouse, and Other Spanish Tales. Low, Joseph (1911-), illus. LC 67-1012. (Illus.). 1 v. (unpaged). 24cm. 1966. Pantheon Books.
--Oak That Would Not Pay. Snyder, Jerome (1916-1976), illus. LC 68-24564. (Illus.). halftones. 40p. (gr. k-4). 1968. (ISBN 0-394-80927-0). (ISBN 0-394-90927-5). Pantheon.
Delamar, Gloria T.
--Children's Counting Out Rhymes, Fingerplays Jump Rope & Bounce-Ball Chants & Other Rhythms: A Comprehensive English-Language Reference. LC 82-24904. 224p. 1983. (ISBN 0-89950-064-1). McFarland & Co.
De La Mare, Colin
--They Walk Again. N.D. E. P. Dutton & Co.
Delamare, Henriette Eugenie
--Chiquita and a Mother's Heart: Two Stories. LC 23-16388. 219 p. front. 20 cm. c.1923. H. L. Kilner & Co.
--Five Birds in a Nest. LC 14-18504. 189 p. front. 19 cm. 1914. Benziger Brothers.
--The Little Apostle on Crutches. 1912. Benziger Brothers.
--The Reformation of Jimmy and Some Others. Young, Florence Liley, illus. LC 14-14541. 3 p. l., 352 p. front., plates. 20 cm. c.1914. Lothrop, Lee & Shepard Co.
--That Boy Gaston: A Story of French Home Life Before the War. LC 27-23864. 185 p. front. 20 cm. c.1927. H. L. Kilner & Co.
De La Mare, Walter John (1873-1956), ed. see Child Study Association of America.
De LaMare, Walter John (1873-1956), ed. see Jack and the Beanstalk.
De La Mare, Walter John (1873-1956)
--Bells and Grass. 128p. N.D. Viking Press.
--Bells & Grass. reissue ed. Lathrop, Dorothy Pulis (1891-1980), illus. (Illus.). (gr. 4 up). 1964. (ISBN 0-670-15625-6). Viking Pr.
--Broomsticks and Other Tales. 1925. Alfred A. Knopf.
--A Child's Day. Cadby, Carine & Cadby, Will, illus. N.D. Dutton.
--A Child's Day: A Book of Rhymes. Authorized. Bromhall, Winifred, illus. 1923. Henry Holt.
--Come Hither: A Collection of Rhymes and Poems for the Young of All Ages. new and rev. ed. Buckels, Alec, illus. 1928. Alfred A. Knopf.
--Come Hither: A Collection of Rhymes and Poems for the Young of all Ages. Chappell, Warren (1904-), illus. (Illus.). (gr. 3 up). 1957. (ISBN 0-394-40336-3). Knopf.
--Crossings: A Fairy Play. Lathrop, Dorothy Pulis (1891-1980), illus. 1923. Alfred A. Knopf.
--Down-Adown-Derry: A Book of Fairy Poems. Lathrop, Dorothy Pulis (1891-1980), illus. LC 76-9889. (Illus.). (Children's Literature Reprint Ser). (gr. 3-5). 1976. (ISBN 0-8486-0004-5). Core Collection.
--Down-Adown-Derry: Fairy Poems. Lathrop, Dorothy Pulis (1891-1980), illus. 193p. N.D. Henry Holt & Co.
--The Dutch Cheese. Lathrop, Dorothy Pulis (1891-1980), illus. 4 p. l., 3-75, 1 p. incl. illus., col. plates. col. front. 24 cm. 1931. A. A. Knopf.
--Eight Tales. 1971. (ISBN 0-87054-055-6). Arkham House Publishers Inc.
--The Magic Jacket. Kennedy, Paul Edward (1929-), illus. (Illus.). (gr. 4 up). 1962. (ISBN 0-394-91388-4). Knopf. **Award: (ALA).**
--Miss Jemima. Buckels, Alec, illus. LC 36-5636. 21cm. 39p. 1935. Artist and Writers Guild.
--Molly Whuppie. LeCain, Errol John (1941-), illus. LC 82-83099. 1983. (ISBN 0-374-35000-0). Farrar.
--Mr. Bumps and His Monkey. Lathrop, Dorothy Pulis (1891-1980), illus. 1942. Holt.
--Mr. Bumps and His Monkey. Lathrop, Dorothy Pulis (1891-1980), illus. LC 42-22581. v, 2, 69 p. illus. (part col.) 23 x 18 1/2 cm. 1942. The John C. Winston Company.
--Nursery Rhymes for Certain Times. Darwin, Elinor May (0000-1954) & Leathem, Moyra (1928-), illus. (Illus.). (gr. k-3). N.D. Transatlantic.
--Peacock Pie. 122p. (Fanfares Ser.). (gr. 4 up). 1980. (ISBN 0-571-18014-0). Faber & Faber.
--Peacock Pie: A Book of Rhymes. new ed. Cooney, Barbara (1917-), illus. (Illus.). (gr. 4 up). 1961. (ISBN 0-394-91486-4). Knopf.
--Peacock Pie: A Book of Rhymes. Crowe, Jocelyn (1906-), illus. LC 37-27029. 1936. Henry Holt & Co.
--Peacock Pie: A Book of Rhymes. Fraser, Claude Lovat (1890-1921), illus. N.D. Henry Holt & Co.
--Peacock Pie: A Book of Rhymes. Robinson, William Heath (1872-1944), illus. 1920. Henry Holt.
--Penny a Day. Kennedy, Paul Edward (1929-), illus. LC 60-13022. (Illus.). 22cm. 200p. (gr. 4 up). 1960. (ISBN 0-394-91493-7). Knopf.
--Poems for Children. N.D. Henry Holt & Co.
--Rhymes and Verses. Blaisdell, Elinore (1904-), illus. 344p. 1947. Henry Holt & Co.
--Songs of Childhood. (gr. 3 up). N.D. Dover.
--Songs of Childhood. LC 75-32200. Repr. of 1902 ed. (Classics of Children's Literature, 1621-1932: Vol. 61). 1976. (ISBN 0-8240-2310-2). Garland Pub.
--Songs of Childhood. Repr. of 1902 ed. 1916. Longmans,Green & Co.
--Stories from the Bible. N.D. David McKay Co.
--Stories from the Bible. Ardizzone, Edward Jeffrey Irving (1900-1979), illus. (Illus.). (gr. 2 up). 1961. (ISBN 0-394-91676-X). Knopf.
--Stories From the Bible. Nadejen, Theodore, illus. 393p. 1929. Cosmopolitan Book Corp.
--Story and Rhyme. 1921. Dutton.
--The Story of Miss Jemima. Farnam, Nellie H., illus. LC 40-30536. 3 p. l., 11-55, 1 p. incl. col. front., illus. (part col.) 22 cm. c.1940. Grosset & Dunlap.
--Tales Told Again. Howard, Alan (1922-), illus. (A new edition of Told Again, Containing 19 of the best fairy tales.). 1927. Borzoi.
--Tales Told Again. Howard, Alan (1922-), illus. 1959. Knopf
--This Year: Next Year. Jones, Harold (1904-), illus. LC 37-28483. 64 p. col. illus. 26 cm. 1937. H. Holt & Company, Inc.
--The Three Mulla-Mulgars. Lathrop, Dorothy Pulis (1891-1980), illus. LC 19-196000. 3 p. l., 11-275 p. col. front., illus., plates (part col.) 25 cm. 1919. A. A. Knopf.
--The Three Royal Monkeys. Eldridge, Mildred E. (1909-), illus. LC 48-8739. 277 p. illus. 22 cm. 1948. A. A. Knopf.
--Told Again: Old Tales Told Again. Watson, A. H., illus. LC 27-25042. 6 p. l., 248 p., 1 l. illus., col. plates. 23 cm. 1927. A. A. Knopf.
--The Warmint: A Poem. Ness, Eveline Michelow, Mrs. (1911-), illus. LC 76-454. 32p. col. ill. 11 x 16cm. c.1976. (ISBN 0-684-14663-0). Scribner.
De La Mare, Walter John (1873-1956), ed.
--Animal Stories. LC 40-27317. lvi, 420 p. illus. 22 cm. (gr. 3-7). 1940. (ISBN 0-684-20797-4). C. Scribner's Sons.
--Tom Tiddler's Ground: A Book of Poetry for Children. Gill, Margery Jean (1925-), illus. Clark, Leonard (1905-1981), frwd. by. LC 62-9471. 253p. illus. 25cm. 1962, c.1961. (ISBN 0-394-91757-X). Knopf.
DeLancey, Floy Winks
--When the Sun Goes Down. Gerhard, Mae, illus. LC 68-6465. (Illus.). 32 p. 29cm. (Carousel book). 1968. L. W. Singer Co.
Deland, Ellen Douglas (1860-1922)
--Alan Ransford. (Illus.). N.D. Harper & Brothers.
--Alan Ransford: A Story. Edwards, Harry C., illus. LC 6-33294. 2 p. l., 281 p. front., 7 pl. 19 cm. 1898. Harper & Brothers.
--Clyde Corners. Caswell, Edward C., illus. LC 18-22895. v p., 1 l., 319, 1 p. col. front., col. plates. 20 cm. 1918. D. Appleton and Company.
--Country Cousins. LC 13-210223. 4 p. l., 311, 1 p. col. front., col. plates. 20 cm. 1913. D. Appleton and Company.
--Cyntra. Caswell, Edward C., illus. LC 15-21789. 19cm. 315p. 1915. D. Appleton and Company.
--The Fortunes of Phoebe. LC 12-21919. 4 p. l., 318, 1 p. col. front., col. plates. 20 cm. 1912. D. Appleton and Company.
--The Friendship of Anne. (Illus.). 332p. 1910. W. A. Wilde.
--The Friendship of Anne: A Story. Stecher, William Frederick (1864-), illus. LC 7-26962. 332 p. front., 4 pl. 20 cm. c.1907. W. A. Wilde Company.
--The Girls of Dudley School. LC 11-23895. vii p., 1 l., 318 p., 1 l. col. front., col. plates. 20 cm. 1911. D. Appleton and Company.
--The Girls of Dudley School. LC 20-123401. vii p., 1 l., 318, 1 p. col, front., col. plates. 1. cm. 1919. D. Appleton and Company.
--In the Old Herrick House and Other Stories. LC 6-332935. 4 p. l., 3-282 p. front., plates. 19 cm. 1897. Harper & Brothers.
--Josephine. Mears, W. E., illus. LC 4-22672. 4 p. l., 272, 1 p. front., 3 pl. 19 cm. 1904. Harper & Brothers.
--Katrina. 340p. 1910. W. A. Wilde.
--Katrina. Stephens, Alice Barber (1858-1932), illus. 20cm. 340p. 1898. W. A. Wilde & Company.
--A Little Son of Sunshine: A Story for Boys and Girls. Mears, W. E., illus. LC 6-35941. 4 p. l., 283, 1 p. front., 3 pl. 20 cm. 1906. Harper & Brothers.
--Malvern. 341p. 1910. W. A. Wilde.
--Malvern: A Neighborhood Story. Stephens, Alice Barber (1858-1932), illus. LC 4-23572. 341 p. front., 4 pl. 20 x 16 cm. 1896. W. A. Wilde & Company.
--The Middleton Bowl, 1 of 21 vols. (Illus.). (Boys & Girls Booklovers Ser.: No. 20). 1905. Set. Henry Altemus Co.
--The Middleton Bowl. (Illus.). (Illustrated Cherrycroft Ser.). N.D. Henry Altemus Co.
--The Middleton Bowl. Smith-Wager, Curtis, illus. LC 5-38103. ix p., 1 l., 13-174 p. incl. front., 3 pl. 18 cm. c.1905. H. Altemus Company.
--Miss Appolina's Choice. Adams, Henrietta S., illus. LC 6-33592. ix, p., 1 l., 13-111 p. incl. front., illus., plates. 19 cm. c.1906. H. Altemus Company.
--Miss Betty of New York. Robinson, Rachael, illus. LC 8-31164. 3 p. l., 3-284 p., 1 l. front., 3 pl. 20 cm. 1908. Harper & Brothers.
--Oakleigh. LC 4-16129. 3 p. l., 233 p. front., 18 pl. 19 cm. 1896. Harper & Brothers.
--The Old Herrick House. (Illus.). N.D. Harper & Brothers.
--The Secret Stairs. LC 21-15254. 3 p. l., 270, 1 p. col. front. 20 cm. 1921. D. Appleton and Company.
--A Successful Venture. Stephens, Alice Barber (1858-1932), illus. LC 4-235717. 340 p. front., 4 pl. 20 x 16 cm. 1897. W. A. Wilde & Company.
--Three Girls of Hazelmere: A Story. 360p. 1910. W. A. Wilde.
--Three Girls of Hazelmere: A Story. Stecher, William Frederick (1864-), illus. LC 3-22320. 360 p. front., 4 pl. 20 cm. 1903. W. A. Wilde Company.
--The Waring Girls. Caswell, Edward C., illus. LC 17-241676. 4 p. l., 319, 1 p. col. front., col. plates. 20 cm. 1917. D. Appleton and Company.
Delaney, Antoinette
--The Butterfly. Delaney, Antoinette, illus. LC 77-72651. p. cm. c.1977. (ISBN 0-440-00890-5). (ISBN 0-440-00891-3). Delacorte Press.
--Monster Tracks?. Delaney, Antoinette, illus. LC 79-2671. p. cm. c.1981. (ISBN 0-06-021588-7). (ISBN 0-06-021589-5). Harper & Row.
Delaney, Antoinette, illus.
--Nursery Rhymes. LC 75-39339. (Illus.). (A Diorama Bk.). (ps-1). 1976. (ISBN 0-394-83260-4). Random.
Delaney, M. C.
--Henry's Special Delivery. McCue, Lisa, illus. LC 83-27480. (Illus.). 144p. (gr. 3-6). 1984. (ISBN 0-525-44081-X). (ISBN 0-525-44081-X). Dutton.
--The Marigold Monster. 1st ed. Delaney, Thomas Nicholas, III (1951-), illus. LC 82-14739. p. cm. c.1983. (ISBN 0-525-44023-2). Dutton.
Delaney, Thomas Nicholas, III (1951-)
--Bert and Barney. Delaney, Thomas Nicholas, III (1951-), illus. LC 79-10633. (Illus.). 32 p. 23cm. 1979. (ISBN 0-395-28377-9). Houghton Mifflin.
--One Dragon to Another. Delaney, Thomas Nicholas, III (1951-), illus. LC 75-33250. (Illus.). 48 p. 26cm. 1976. (ISBN 0-395-24209-6). Houghton Mifflin.
--Rufus the Doofus. LC 78-60493. (Illus.). 32 p. 25cm. 1978. (ISBN 0-395-27153-3). Houghton Mifflin.
--Terrible Things Could Happen. Delaney, Thomas Nicholas, III (1951-), illus. LC 82-10051. p. cm. c.1983. (ISBN 0-688-01282-5). Lothrop, Lee & Shepard Books.
--Two Strikes, Four Eyes. Delaney, Thomas Nicholas, III (1951-), illus. LC 76-14348. (Illus.). 32 p. 1976. (ISBN 0-395-24744-6). Houghton Mifflin.
--A Worm for Dinner. Delaney, Thomas Nicholas, III (1951-), illus. LC 76-62504. (Illus.). 32 p. 28cm. 1977. (ISBN 0-395-25153-2). Houghton Mifflin.
Delano, Edith Barnard, Mrs.
--June. N.D. Houghton Mifflin.
--To-Morrow Morning. N.D. Houghton Mifflin.
--Two Alike. LC 18-21684. vii, 1 p. 1 l., 263, 1 front., plates. 19 cm. 1918. Houghton Mifflin Company.
Delano, Frances J.
--Susanne. Barry, Etheldred Breeze (1870-), illus. LC 2-15348. (Illus.). 19cm. 130p. (Cosy Corner Ser.). 1903. L. C. Page & Co.
Delano, Hugh (1933-)
--Eddie: A Goalie's Story. LC 75-38345. (gr. 9 up). 1976. (ISBN 0-689-10715-3). Atheneum.
Delano, Jack, jt. auth. see Blanco, Tomas.
De Lany, Retta Lawrence
--Children's Rhymes and Verses. LC 9-129. 20cm. 64p. 1908. The Imperial Press.
De Laoulaye, Edouard Rene LeFebvre see Laoulaye, Edouard Rene LeFebvre de.
De La Pasture, Elizabeth Bonham (1866-)
--The Little Squire: A Story of Three. (Illus.). (Cassell's Popular Library of Ficton). N.D. Cassell & Co.'s Pubs.
Delaplaine, Eleanor Frances
--Our Neighborhood: Verses Written Between the Ages of 9 and 12. LC 35-215722. 72 p. illus., 21 cm. c.1935. Dorrance & Company.
DeLapp, Ardyce Lucile (1903-), ed.
--Stories That Teach: A Collection. LC 72-83557. 288 p. 21cm. 1972. (ISBN 0-8309-0077-2). Herald Pub. House.
De La Ramee, Marie Louise see Ouida, pseud.
De La Ramee, Marie Louise (1839-1908)
--Ariadne. Ouida, pseud. (Illus.). N.D. J. B. Lippincott Co.
--Beatrice Boville. Ouida, pseud. (Illus.). N.D. J. B. Lippincott Co.
--BeBee: Or, Two Little Wooden Shoes. Ouida, pseud. (Illus.). N.D. J. B. Lippincott Co.
--Bebee: Or, Two Little Wooden Shoes. Ouida, pseud. New ed. Barry, Etheldred Breeze (1870-), illus. (Illus.). N.D. Joseph Knight co.
--Bimbi: Stories for Children. Ouida, pseud. (Illus.). 239p. N.D. Dana Estes and Company.
--Bimbi: Stories for Children. Ouida, pseud. LC 61964. 2 p. l., 239 p. front., plates. 18 cm. (On cover: Home and school library.). 1900. Ginn & Company.
--Bimbi: Stories for Children. Ouida, pseud. LC [illegible]. 303 p. 19 cm. 1882. J. B. Lippincott & Co.
--Bimbi. Stories for Children. Ouida, pseud. Garrett, Edmund Henry (1853-1929), illus. LC 4-16835. 303 p. incl. front. 8 pl. 22 cm. 1892. J. B. Lippincott Company.
--Bimbi: Stories for Children. Ouida, pseud. Kirk, Maria Louise (1860-), illus. LC 10-22530. 212 p. col. front., 7 col. pl. 21 cm. 1910. J. B. Lippincott Company.
--Cecil Castlemaine's Gage. Ouida, pseud. N.D. Claxton, Remsen, and Haffelfinger.
--Cecil Castlemaine's Gage. Ouida, pseud. N.D. Little, Brown & Co.
--Chandos. Ouida, pseud. (Burt's Home Lib.). N.D. A. L. Burt's Pubs.
--Chandos. Ouida, pseud. N.D. G. W. Dillingham Co.
--The Child of Urbino. Ouida, pseud. (Illus.). (Children's Classics Ser.). N.D. Dana Estes and Company.
--The Child of Urbino & Meleagris Gallopavo. Ouida, pseud, 1 of 7 vols. New ed. (Illus.). (Bimbi Stories for Children). 1900. Set. J B Lippincott.
--The Child of Urbino and Moufflou. Ouida, pseud. (Illus.). (Every Boy's Library). N.D. Caldwell.
--The Child of Urbino and Moufflou. Ouida, pseud. x ed. (Children Hour Series.). N.D. Dodge Publishing Co.
--The Child of Urbino and Moufflou. Ouida, pseud. Barry, Etheldred Breeze (1870-), illus. LC 4272. 4 p. l., 11-85 p. incl. front., plates. 19 cm. c.1900. D. Estes & Company.
--The Child of Urbino. Raphael. Ouida, pseud. Jenkins, Sara D., ed. LC 2-17057. 64 p. incl. pl., port. 20 cm. c.1900. Educational Publishing Company.
--A Dog of Flanders. Ouida, pseud, 36 vols. (Illus.). (St. Nicholas Ser.). 1905. Set. A L Burt Co.
--A Dog of Flanders. Ouida, pseud. (Illus.). (The Rugby Ser.). N.D. A. L. Burt.
--A Dog of Flanders. Ouida, pseud. N.D. Grosset & Dunlap.
--A Dog of Flanders. Ouida, pseud. (Illus.). (The Young Folks Lib.). N.D. H. M. Caldwell Co.
--A Dog of Flanders. Ouida, pseud, 1 of 3 vols. (The Lakeside Series of Handy Volume Classics: No. 6). N.D. Set. H. M. Caldwell.
--A Dog of Flanders. Ouida, pseud, 1 of 156 vols. (Illus.). (The Empyreal Lib of Handy Volume Classics). N.D. H. M. Caldwell & Co.
--Dog of Flanders. Ouida, pseud. (Illus.). (Boys' and Girls' Classics). N.D. Henry Altemus Co.
--A Dog of Flanders. Ouida, pseud. New ed. (Illus.). (Vademecum Ser.). N.D. Henry Altemus.
--A Dog of Flanders. Ouida, pseud. Handy Volume, Large Type ed. (Illus.). (Beauxarts Ser.). N.D. Henry Altemus.
--Dog of Flanders. Ouida, pseud. (Illus.). 1900. J B Lippincott.
--A Dog of Flanders. Ouida, pseud. (Little Classics). N.D. James R Osgood & Co.
--A Dog of Flanders. Ouida, pseud. (Cosy Corner Ser.). N.D. L. C. Page & Co.
--A Dog of Flanders. Ouida, pseud. LC 14-22442. 15cm. 64p. (Maynard's English Classic Ser.). 1898. Maynard, Merrill.
--A Dog of Flanders. Ouida, pseud. 1900. Maynard Merrill & Co.
--A Dog of Flanders. Ouida, pseud. LC 6-33371. (Illus.). 17cm. 94p. 1891. Nims & Knight.
--A Dog of Flanders. Ouida, pseud. (Illus.). N.D. Putman's Trade List.
--A Dog of Flanders. Ouida, pseud. (Illus.). (Young People's Classics). N.D. R. F. Fenno & Co.
--A Dog of Flanders. Ouida, pseud. Brundage, Frances, illus. LC 27-332. (Illus.). 20cm. 90p. (John Newberry Ser.). 1926. Saalfield Publishing Co.
--A Dog of Flanders. Ouida, pseud. Fuller, Harvey K., illus. LC 27-23403. 128 p. incl. col. front., col. illus. 24 cm. (just right book). c.1927. A. Whitman Company.
--A Dog of Flanders. Ouida, pseud. Kirk, Maria Louise (1860-), illus. LC 15-10953. 78p. col. front., col. plates. 20cm. 20cm. 78p. c.1915. J. B. Lippincott.

--A Dog of Flanders. Ouida, pseud. Regina, illus. LC 31-5063. 128 p. incl. col. front., col. illus. 20 cm. c.1930. Beckley-Cardy Company.

--A Dog of Flanders. Ouida, pseud. Swart, Rose C., ed. MacDonall, Angus & Pohl, Hugo D., illus. LC 10-28801. (Illus.). 18cm. 100p. (The Canterbury Classics). 1910. Rand McNally & Company.

--A Dog of Flanders. Ouida, pseud. Tenggren, Gustaf (1896-1970), illus. 1949. Macmillan.

--A Dog of Flanders. Ouida, pseud. Tenggren, Gustaf (1896-1970), illus. LC 25-14715. 4 p. l., 104 p. incl. plates. col. front., col. plates. 17 cm. 1925. The Macmillan Company.

--A Dog of Flanders. Ouida, pseud. Weekes, Blanche E., ed. Fitz, John, Jr., illus. LC 28-30698. (Illus.). 21cm. viii, 84p. 1928. John C. Winston Company.

--A Dog of Flanders: A Christmas Story. Ouida, pseud. (Illus.). N.D. Joseph Knight Co.

--A Dog of Flanders: A Christmas Story. Ouida, pseud. (Cosy Corner Ser.). N.D. L. C. Page & Co.

--A Dog of Flanders: A Christmas Story. Ouida, pseud. Jenkins, Sara D., ed. LC 99-1671. 1 p. l., 5-77 p. illus., 2 pl. 18 cm. 18cm. 77p. c.1898. Educational Publishing Company.

--Dog of Flanders and Nurnberg Stove. Ouida, pseud. (Wonderland Ser.). N.D. Harper & Bros.

--Dog of Flanders and Other Stories. Ouida, pseud. (Children's Favorite Classics). N.D. Thomas Y. Crowell.

--A Dog of Flanders and Other Stories. Ouida, pseud. Garrett, Edmund Henry (1853-1929), illus. LC 6-33370. 4 p. l., 7-245 p. front., plates. 21 x 16 cm. 1893. J. B. Lippincott Company.

--A Dog of Flanders and Other Stories. Ouida, pseud. Leone, Mariano, illus. LC 65-171982. 192p. illus. 20cm. (Companion lib.). 1965. Grosset.

--Dog of Flanders & Other Stories. Ouida, pseud. Leone, Mariano, illus. (Illus.). (Companion Library). (gr. 7 up). 1965. (ISBN 0-448-05480-9, G&D). Putnam Pub Group.

--A Dog of Flanders And the Nurnberg Stove. Ouida, pseud. LC 2-8119. iv, 116 p. 18 cm. (Riverside literature series, no. 150). 1902. Houghton, Mifflin and Co.

--A Dog of Flanders: Being a Story of Friendship Closer than Brotherhood. Ouida, pseud. LC 6-6265. 21cm. 90p. 1906. Roycrafters.

--A Dog of Flanders, the Nurnberg Stove and Other Stories. Ouida, pseud. LC 35-27157. 3 p. l., 8-241 p. 21 cm. 1935. Grosset & Dunlap.

--A Dog of Flanders, the Nurnberg Stove, and Other Stories. Ouida, pseud. Kirk, Maria Louise (1860-), illus. LC 9-28210. 230 p. col. front., 7 col. pl. 21 cm. 1909. J. B. Lippincott Company.

--Findelkind. Ouida, pseud. (Illus.). (Children's Classics Ser.). N.D. Dana Estes and Company.

--Findelkind. Ouida, pseud. LC 1-290808. 1 p. l., 53 p. front., pl. 18 cm. 1900. Ginn & Company.

--Findelkind. Ouida, pseud. (Illus.). (Goldenrod Library Ser.). 1905. L. C. Page & Co.

--Findelkind. Ouida, pseud. Barry, Etheldred Breeze (1870-), illus. LC 1-23004. 3 p. l., 63 p. incl. illus., plates. front. 19 cm. (Cosy corner series). 1901. L. C. Page & Company.

--Flashes. Ouida, pseud. N.D. G. W. Dillingham.

--Folle Farine. Ouida, pseud. N.D. J.B. Lippincott Co.

--Friendship. Ouida, pseud. 1905. American News Co.

--Friendship. Ouida, pseud. (New Red Letter Ser). N.D. International Book Company.

--Friendship. Ouida, pseud. N.D. J. B. Lippincott Co.

--A House Party. Ouida, pseud. (Sunset Ser.). N.D. J. S. Ogilvie.

--A House Party. Ouida, pseud. N.D. Little, Brown & Co.

--In the Apple Country, & Findelkind. Ouida, pseud, 1 of 7 vols. New ed. (Bimbi Stories for Children). 1900. Set. J B Lippincott.

--The Little Earl. Ouida, pseud. (Illus.). (Every Boy's Library). N.D. Caldwell.

--The Little Earl. Ouida, pseud, 1 of 7 vols. New ed. 1900. Set. J B Lippincott.

--The Little Earl. Ouida, pseud. (The "Bimbi" Series of Children's Booklets). N.D. Thomas Y. Crowell.

--The Little Earl. Ouida, pseud. Barry, Etheldred Breeze (1870-), illus. LC 4327. 4 p. l., 11-82 p. incl. front., 5 pl. 19 cm. c.1900. D. Estes & Company.

--Moufflon: The Dog of Florence. Ouida, pseud. Jenkins, Sara D., tr. LC 31-29634. 80 p. incl. illus. (part col.) col. pl. 19 cm. c.1931. A. Whitman & Co.

--Moufflou, & Other Stories. Ouida, pseud, 1 of 7 vols. New ed. (Bimbi Stories for Children). N.D. Set. J B Lippincott.

--Moufflou and Other Stories. Ouida, pseud. Kirk, Maria Louise (1860-) & Garrett, Edmund Henry (1853-1929), illus. LC 18-1872. 88 p. col. front., plates (part col.) 20 cm. (On verso of half-title: The children's classics). 1917. J. B. Lippincott Company.

--The Nurnberg Store. (The Rugby Series for Boys and Girls). N.D. A.L. Burt Company.

--The Nurnberg Stove. Ouida, pseud, 36 vols. (Illus.). (St. Nicholas Ser.). 1905. Set. A L Burt Co.

--The Nurnberg Stove. Ouida, pseud. (Illus.). (The Rugby Ser.). N.D. A. L. Burt.

--The Nurnberg Stove. Ouida, pseud. (Illus.). (Children's Classics Ser.). N.D. Dana Estes and Company.

--The Nurnberg Stove. Ouida, pseud. LC 1-29031. 1 p. l., 98 p. front., pl. 18 cm. 1900. Ginn & Company.

--The Nurnberg Stove. Ouida, pseud, 1 of 7 vols. New ed. (Bimbi Stories for Children). 1900. Set. J B Lippincott.

--The Nurnberg Stove. Ouida, pseud. (The Children's Classics). N.D. J. B. Lippincott.

--The Nurnberg Stove. Ouida, pseud. LC 6-332901. (Illus.). 21cm. 123p. 1893. Joseph Knight Co.

--The Nurnberg Stove. Ouida, pseud. (The Cosy Corner Ser.). N.D. L C Page & Co.

--The Nurnberg Stove. Ouida, pseud. LC 6-33289. 73 p. 18 cm. (Maynard's English classic series.--no. 151). c.1895. Maynard, Merrill & Co.

--The Nurnberg Stove. Ouida, pseud. (Illus.). 1910. Putman.

--The Nurnberg Stove. Ouida, pseud. LC 6-33291. 101 p. incl. front. plates. 17 cm. 1895. R. F. Fenno & Company.

--The Nurnberg Stove. Ouida, pseud. (Illus.). N.D. R. F. Fenno & Co.

--The Nurnberg Stove. Ouida, pseud. (Illus.). (Crowell's Child Life Series.). 1915. T Y Crowell.

--The Nurnberg Stove. Ouida, pseud. (The "Bimbi" Series of Children's Booklets). N.D. Thomas Y. Crowell.

--The Nurnberg Stove. Ouida, pseud. Boyd, Frank (1893-), illus. 122p. illus. 17cm. (Little library). 1952, c.1928. Macmillan.

--The Nurnberg Stove. Ouida, pseud. Boyd, Frank (1893-), illus. LC 28-21897. 4 p. l., 138 p. incl. illus., plates. col. front. 17 cm. (Lettered on cover: The little library). 1928. The Macmillan Company.

--The Nurnberg Stove. Ouida, pseud. Brundage, Frances, illus. LC 27-18385. 3 p. l., 9-90 p., 1 l., col. front., illus. 20 cm. (John Newbery series). c.1927. The Saalfield Publishing Company.

--The Nurnberg Stove. Ouida, pseud. Kirk, Maria Louise (1860-), illus. LC 16-978220. 96 p. col. front., col. plates. 20 cm. 1916. J. B. Lippincott Company.

--The Nurnberg Stove. Ouida, pseud. Merchant, Elizabeth Lodor, ed. Prittie, Edwin John, illus. LC 30-5242. xi, 97 p. incl. col. front., illus., col. pl. 21 cm. (The child's garden of charming books). c.1929. The John C. Winston Company.

--The Nurnberg Stove and Other Stories. Ouida, pseud. Laite, Blanche Fisher, illus. LC 24-21354. vii, 296 p incl. front., illus. 18 cm. 1924. Ginn and Company.

--Provence Rose. Ouida, pseud, 1 of 7 vols. New ed. (Bimbi Stories for Children). 1900. Set. J B Lippincott.

--A Provence Rose. Ouida, pseud. (Illus.). (Goldenrod Library Ser.). 1905. L. C. Page & Co.

--Puck. Ouida, pseud. N.D. J. B. Lippincott.

--Puck. Ouida, pseud. N.D. Little, Brown & Co.

--Syrlin. Ouida, pseud. N.D. J. B. Lippincott.

--Two Little Wooden Shoes. Ouida, pseud, No.61. (Seaside Library Ser.). N.D. George Munro: American News Co.

--Two Little Wooden Shoes. Ouida, pseud. Garrett, Edmund Henry (1853-1929), illus. N.D. J.B. Lippincott.

--Two New Dog Stories and Another. Ouida, pseud. Thompson, Ivan Peronet, illus. LC 6390. (Illus.). 200p. 1900. Drexel Biddle's Pub.

--Under Two Flags. Ouida, pseud. Empire ed. 1905. American News Co.

--Under Two Flags. Ouida, pseud. (The Roxburghe Classics). N.D. Estes & Lauriat's.

--Under Two Flags. Ouida, pseud. popular ed. N.D. G. W. Dillingham.

--Under Two Flags. Ouida, pseud, 1 of 2 vol. et, Vol. I. (New Popular Two-Volume Sets Ser.: No. 20). N.D. International Book Co.

--Under Two Flags. Ouida, pseud. N.D. J. B. Lippincott.

--Under Two Flags. Ouida, pseud. N.D. J. S. Ogilvie Co.

De La Roche, Mazo (1885-1961)

--The Song of Lambert. Soper, Eileen Alice (1905-), illus. LC 56-6762. 52p. illus. 22cm. 1st U.S. edition. (Atlantic Monthly Press book). 1956, c.1955. Little, Brown.

De Larrabeiti, Michael

--The Borribles. LC 77-12743. (Illus.). 239 p. 22cm. 1978, c.1976. (ISBN 0-02-726700-8). Macmillan.

--Jeeno, Heloise & Igamor, The Long, Long Horse. Ambrus, Victor G., pseud. (1935-), illus. Ambrus, Gyozo Laszlo. (Illus.). 24p. (gr. 1-3). 1984. (ISBN 0-7207-1257-2). Merrimack Pub Cir.

De Larrea, Victoria, jt. auth. see Herold, Ann Bixby.

Delarue, Paul

--The Borzoi Book of French Folk-Tales. 1956. Borzoi.

--French Fairy Tales. abr. ed. Chappell, Warren (1904-), illus. LC 68-11171. line drawings. 128p. (gr. 5 up). 1968. (ISBN 0-394-81140-2). (ISBN 0-394-91140-7). Knopf.

De La Torre, Lillian, pseud., see McCue, Lillian Bueno.

De La Torre, Lillian, pseud. (1902-)

--The White Rose of Stuart: The Story of Flora Macdonald, Heroine of the '45. McCue, Lillian Bueno. LC 54-9873. 214p. illus. 22cm. 1954. T. Nelson.

Delaune, Jewel Lynn de Grummond

--Giraffes Can Be a Trouble. King, Robin, pseud. (1919-), illus. Raleigh-King, Robin Victor Lethbridge. LC 55-5469. 1955. E. P. Dutton & Co.

Delaune, Lynn De Grummond, jt. auth. see De Grummond, Lena Young.

DeLaurentis, Louise Budde (1920-)

--Etta Chipmunk. Spiegel, Lawrence M., illus. LC 62-17848. unpaged. illus. 29 cm. (gr. k-6). 1962. (ISBN 0-513-00321-5). T. S. Denison.

De La Valette, Andree

--Pierre and Nonetta. Fleur, Anne Elizabeth (1901-), illus. Sari, pseud. LC 48-10130. 92 p. illus. (part col.) 22 cm. c.1948. Saalfield Pub. Co.

Delavaud, Marie Moreal De Brevans Collin see Collin Delavaud, Marie Moreal De Brevans.

De La Vergne, George Harrison (1868-)

--At the Foot of the Rockies: Stories of Mountain and Plain, or, Boy Life on the Old Ranche. LC 2-10827. 209 p. 21 cm. 1902. The Abbey Press.

Del Barco, Lucy Salamanca see Salamanca, Lucy.

Delderfield, Eric Raymond (1909-)

--Eric Delderfield's Book of True Animal Stories. N.D. (ISBN 0-8008-2510-1). (ISBN 0-8008-2512-8). Taplinger.

Delderfield, Ronald Frederick (1912-1972)

--The Adventures of Ben Gunn: A Story of The Pirates of Treasure Island. Stobbs, William (1914-), illus. LC 57-9346. 263p. illus. 23cm. 1957, c.1956. Bobbs-Merrill.

--Too Few for Drums. LC 78-162712. 256p. (gr. 7 up). 1971. (ISBN 0-671-65195-1, Juveniles). S&S.

De Leeuw, Adele Louise (1899-)

--The Barred Road. LC 54-9574. 247 p. 22cm. 1954. Macmillan.

--The Barred Road. 2d ed. LC 64-23075. 247 p. 21 cm. 1964. Macmillan.

--Behold This Dream. LC 68-28839. 255 p. 21cm. 1968. (ISBN 0-07-016256-5). McGraw-Hill.

--Blue Ribbons for Meg. Schweitzer, Mac, illus. LC 50-5455. (Illus.). 145 p. 25cm. 1950. Little, Brown.

--The Boy with Wings. Vosburgh, Leonard W. (1912-), illus. LC 74-158560. (Illus.). 46 p. 1971. (ISBN 0-87874-001-5). Nautilus Books.

--Career for Jennifer. De Leeuw, Cateau Wilhelmina (1903-1975), illus. LC 41-21719. 3 p. l., 280 p. illus. 21 cm. 1941. The Macmillan Company.

--Casey Jones Drives an Ice Cream Train. Aloise, Frank E., illus. LC 74-152792. (Illus.). 38 p. 23cm. (Reading shelf book). (Tall Tales Bks.). 1971. (ISBN 0-8116-4029-9). Garrard Pub. Co.

--Clay Fingers. LC 48-8425. 230 p. 21 cm. 1948. Macmillan Co.

--Curtain Call. LC 49-115758. 213 p. 21 cm. 1949. Macmillan.

--Doctor Ellen. LC 44-9912. 3 p. l., 210 p. 21 cm. 1944. The Macmillan Company.

--Doll Cottage. LC 39-276378. 5 p. l., 268 p. illus. 21 cm. 1939. The Macmillan Company.

--Donny: The Boy Who Made a Home for Animals. Wohlberg, Meg, illus. LC 57-5520. (Illus.). 118 p. 21cm. 1957. Little, Brown.

--Every girls Adventure Stories. Burhans, Richard W., illus. LC 55-6989. 222p. illus. 21cm. (Everygirls library). 1955. Lantern Press.

--Future for Sale. LC 46-82412. 3 p. l., 211 p. 21 cm. 1946. The Macmillan Company.

--Gay Design. LC 42-22582. 279 p. 20 1/2 cm. 1942. The Macmillan Company.

--The Goat Who Ate Flowers. Hart, Marjorie, illus. LC 58-10489. (Illus.). 48 p. 24cm. 1958. Steck Co.

--Hawthorne House. LC 50-10100. 220 p. 21 cm. 1950. Macmillan.

--Horseshoe Harry and the Whale. Blake, Quentin (1932-), illus. LC 76-3529. (Illus.). 42 p. 26cm. c.1976. (ISBN 0-8193-0885-4). (ISBN 0-8193-0886-2). Parents' Magazine Press.

--Horseshoe Harry & the Whale. Blake, Quentin (1932-), illus. LC 76-3529. (Illus.). 48p. (gr. k-4). 1976. (ISBN 0-8193-0885-4). (ISBN 0-8193-0886-2). Scholastic Inc.

--Island Adventure: A Novel for Girls. De Leeuw, Cateau Wilhelmina (1903-1975), illus. LC 34-31079. 4 p. l., 276 p. illus. 20 cm. 1934. The Macmillan Company.

--John Henry, Steel-Drivin' Man. Laite, Gordon (1925-), illus. LC 66-20136. (Illus.). 40p. (American Folktales Ser.). (gr. 2-5). 1966. (ISBN 0-8116-4004-3). Garrard.

--Legends & Folk Tales of Holland. Kennedy, Paul Edward (1929-), illus. LC 63-17330. (Illus.). 157 p. 21cm. 1963. T. Nelson.

--Linda Marsh. LC 43-14086. 263 p. 21 cm. 1943. The Macmillan Company.

--Mickey the Monkey. Henneberger, Robert G. (1921-), illus. LC 52-5009. (Illus.). 116 p. 22cm. 1952. Little, Brown.

--Miss Fix-It. LC 66-11103. 229p. 22cm. c.1966. Macmillan.

--Nobody's Doll. Vaughan, Anne (1913-), illus. LC 46-3568. 3 p. l., 3-85, 1 p., 1 l. col. front., illus., col. plates. 22 cm. 1946. Little, Brown and Company.

--Old Stormalong: Hero of the Seven Seas. Oechsli, Kelly (1918-), illus. LC 67-16852. (Illus.). 3-color ils. 40p. (Reading Shelf-American Folktales Ser.). (gr. 2-5). 1967. (ISBN 0-8116-4005-1). Garrard.

--Old Stormalong: Hero of the Seven Seas. Oechsli, Kelly (1918-), illus. (Illus.). 44 p. 23cm. (Tall tales). c.1967. Garrard Pub. Co.

--The Patchwork Quilt. De Leeuw, Cateau Wilhelmina (1903-1975), illus. LC 43-15173. 6 p. l., 3-174, 1 p. illus., col. plates. 20 1/2 cm. 1943. Little, Brown and Company.

--Paul Bunyan and His Blue Ox. Schroeder, Ted (1931-1973), illus. LC 68-101710. (Illus.). 29 p. 22cm. (Reading shelf books). 1968. Garrard Pub. Co.

--Paul Bunyan Finds a Wife. Schroeder, Ted (1931-1973), illus. LC 69-11771. (Illus.). color ils. 32p. (American Folktales Ser.). (gr. 2-5). 1969. (ISBN 0-8116-4013-2). Garrard.

--Place for Herself. De Leeuw, Cateau Wilhelmina (1903-1975), illus. LC 37-20196. 20cm. 283p. 1937. Macmillan.

--Rika, a Dutch Girl's Vacation in Java. De Leeuw, Cateau Wilhelmina (1903-1975), illus. LC 32-24062. viii p., 1 l., 299 p. incl. front., illus. 20 cm. 1932. The Macmillan Company.

--The Rugged Dozen. LC 55-14977. 231p. 22cm. 1955. Macmillan.

--The Rugged Dozen Abroad. LC 60-15045. (Illus.). 22cm. 197p. 1960. Macmillan.

--The Story of Amelia Earhart. Beckhoff, Harry, illus. LC 55-6740. 181p. illus. 22cm. (Signature books 33). c.1955. Grosset & Dunlap.

--Title to Happiness. LC 47-11555. 222 p. 21 cm. 1947. Macmillan Co.

--Uncle Davy Lane, Mighty Hunter. Vestal, Herman B., illus. LC 79-110166. (Illus.). 48 p. 23cm. (A Reading shelf book). 1970. (ISBN 0-8116-4023-X). Garrard Pub. Co.

--The Whaling Adventure of Bowleg Bill. Blake, Quentin (1932-), illus. LC 76-3529. p. cm. c.1976. (ISBN 0-8193-0885-4). (ISBN 0-8193-0886-2). Parents' Magazine Press.

--Who Can Kill the Lion. Schroeder, Ted (1931-1973), illus. LC 66-20137. (Illus.). 48p. (Fantasy Ser.). (gr. k-4). 1966. (ISBN 0-8116-4051-5). Garrard.

--Who Can Kill the Lion?. Schroeder, Ted (1931-1973), illus. LC 66-201374. 40p. col. illus. 23cm. (Fantasy bks.). 1966. Garrard.

--With a High Heart. LC 45-9171. 4 p. l., 207 p. 21 cm. 1945. The Macmillan Company.

--Year of Promises. De Leeuw, Cateau Wilhelmina (1903-1975), illus. LC 36-9941. vii p., 1 l., 275 p. illus. 20 cm. 1936. The Macmillan Company.

De Leeuw, Adele Louise (1899-) & De Leeuw, Cateau Wilhelmina (1903-1975)

--Anim Runs Away. LC 38-12296. 22cm. 39p. 1938. Macmillan.

--Apron Strings. LC 59-7743. 21cm. 220p. 1959. The World Publishing Co.

--Breakneck Betty. LC 57-9465. 219 p. 21cm. 1957. World Pub. Co.

--The Caboose Club. LC 57-8039. 22cm. 150p. 1957. Little, Brown.

--Dina and Betsy. LC 40-32774. 138 p. incl. col. front., illus. (part col.) 21 x 17 cm. 1940. The Macmillan Company.

--The Expandable Browns. 1st ed. Sibley, Don (1922-), illus. LC 55-5187. 145p. illus. 22cm. c.1955. Little, Brown.

--Hideaway House. Candy, Robert (1920-), illus. LC 53-7322. (Illus.). 151 p. 22cm. 1953. Little, Brown.

--Love is the Beginning. LC 60-7486. 21cm. 217p. 1960. The World Publishing Co.

AUTHOR INDEX DEMAS, VIDA

--The Salty Skinners. Spilka, Arnold (1917-), illus. LC 64-10173. (Illus.). 169 p. 22cm. 1964. Little, Brown.
--Showboat's Coming!. LC 56-5735. (Illus.). 218 p. 21cm. 1956. World Pub. Co.
--The Strange Garden. Wohlberg, Meg (1905-), illus. LC 58-8480. (Illus.). 21cm. 90p. 1958. Little, Brown.

De Leeuw, Adele Louise (1899-) & Paradis, Marjorie Bartholomew (1886-1970)
--Dear Stepmother. LC 56-11572. 220 p. 22cm. 1956. Macmillan.
--The Golden Shadow. LC 51-13611. 218 p. 21cm. 218p. N.D. Macmillan.

De Leeuw, Cateau Wilhelmina see Hamilton, Kay, pseud.

De Leeuw, Cateau Wilhelmina see Lyon, Jessica, pseud.

De Leeuw, Cateau Wilhelmina, jt. auth. see De Leeuw, Adele Louise.

De Leeuw, Cateau Wilhelmina (1903-1975)
--Bright Gold: A Junior Novel. Lyon, Jessica, pseud. LC 53-10083. 208p. 22cm. 1953. Macrae Smith.
--Determined to Be Free. Lambo, Donald W. (1903-1966), illus. LC 63-9633. 176 p. illus. 21 cm. 1963. Nelson.
--Fear in the Forest. Vosburgh, Leonard W. (1912-), illus. LC 60-7290. (Illus.). 23cm. 127p. 1960. Nelson.
--For a Whole Lifetime: A Junior Novel. Lyon, Jessica, pseud. LC 49-6497. 221 p. 22 cm. 1949. Macrae-Smith-Co.
--The Gentle Heart. Hamilton, Kay, pseud. LC 49-7729. 255 p. 20 cm. 1949. Macrae-Smith-Co.
--Give Me Your Hand. LC 59-7343. (gr. 6-10). 1960. (ISBN 0-316-18029-7). Little.
--The Given Heart. Lyon, Jessica, pseud. LC 57-12004. 198p. 22cm. 1957. Macrae Smith.
--Not for One Alone: A Junior Novel. Lyon, Jessica, pseud. LC 55-10735. 191 p. 21cm. 1955. Macrae Smith.
--One Week of Danger (Pub. by Nelson). (gr. 4-6). 1972 (Starline). Schol Bk Serv.
--One Week of Danger. Werth, Kurt (1896-), illus. LC 59-5339. (Illus.). 23cm. 96p. 1959. Nelson.
--The Proud Air: A Junior Novel. Lyon, Jessica, pseud. LC 56-104384. 221p. 22cm. 1956. Macrae Smith.
--The Proving Years. Vosburgh, Leonard W. (1912-), illus. LC 62-10562. 158p. c.1962. Nelson.
--This My Desire: A Junior Novel. Lyon, Jessica, pseud. LC 52-10363. 208 p. 22 cm. 1952. Macrae Smith.
--To Have and Not Hold: A Junior Novel. Lyon, Jessica, pseud. LC 54-10362. 205 p. 21cm. 1954. Macrae Smith.
--Truth to Tell. Martin, Carl, illus. LC 65-19364. 212 p. 20 cm. (Whitman teen novels). 1965. Whitman Pub. Co.
--The Turn in the Road. Rethi, Lili (1894-), illus. LC 61-13832. 21cm. 143p. 1961. Nelson.
--Where Valor Lies. Plummer, William Kirtman, illus. LC 59-11509. 22cm. 106p. (Clarion Books). 1959. Doubleday.

DeLeeuw, Hendrik (1891-1977)
--Java Jungle Tales. Wiese, Kurt (1887-1974), illus. LC 33-30455. xvi, 311 p. incl. illus. (incl. map) plates, col. front. 21 cm. 1933. Doubleday, Doran & Company, Inc.
--Peewee the Mousedeer. Gergely, Tibor (1900-1978), illus. LC 43-7557. 71, 1 p. col. illus. 19 x 26 cm. c.1943. David McKay Company.

De Leon, Jacqueline, tr. see Amiot, Pierre.

De Lespinasse, Cobie Muyskens see Lespinasse, Cobie Muyskens De.

Delessert, Etienne (1941-)
--How the Mouse Was Hit on the Head by a Stone and So Discovered the World. Piaget, Jean (1896-1980), frwd. by. LC 79-158138. (Illus.). 32 p. 29cm. 1971. Good Book, Inc.

Delessert, Etienne (1941-) & Schmid, Eleonore (1939-)
--The Endless Party. LC 67-16287. (Illus.). 32 p. 29cm. 1967. H. Quist; Distributed in the U.S. and Canada by Crown Publishers, New York.
--The Tree. LC 67-500. (Illus.). 1 v. (unpaged). 24cm. ("A Harlin Quist book."). c.1966. H. Quist; Distributed by Crown Publishers.

Deletaille, Albertine
--At the Top of the House. Deletaille, Albertine, illus. LC 46-6399. 24p. N.D. Harcourt,.
--A Home for My Kittens. Hirsch, Constance, tr. LC 66-3794. 24p. col. illus. 19x 22cm. (Pere Castor bk.). c.1966. Golden Pr.

Deletaille, Albertine & Faucher, Paul (1898-)
--My Very Own Puppy. LC 66-3580. 1 v. (unpaged) col. illus. 21 cm. (Golden read-it-yourself book). 1966. Golden Press.

Delgado, Alan George (1909-)
--Hide the Slipper. Lewis, Edward, illus. (Illus.). (gr. 3-6). 1963. (ISBN 0-685-21177-0). Verry.
--Hot-Water Bottle Mystery. Lewis, Edward, illus. 144p. Orig. Title: The Very Hot Water Bottle. (gr. 4-6). 1970 (StarLine). Schol Bk Serv.
--Return Ticket. Lewis, Edward, illus. (Illus.). (gr. 3-6). 1965. (ISBN 0-685-21474-5). Verry.
--The Very Hot Water-Bottle. LC 64-15640. (Illus.). 119 p. 23cm. 1964. Follett Pub. Co.

Delgado, Eduard
--Alex's Adventures Downtown. Rovira, Francesc, illus. LC 85-29346. p. cm. 1986, c.1984. Distributed by Crown.

Delgado, Eduard & Rovira, Francesc
--Alex's Adventures at the Harbor. LC 85-29320. p. cm. 1985. (ISBN 0-517-60673-9). Derrydale Books : Distributed by Crown Publishers.

Delhumeau, Annick
--Bon Voyage, Hippopotamus. LC 63-15060. 1 v. (unpaged) col. illus. 28 cm. 1963. Orion Press.

Delibes, Leo (1836-1891)
--Coppelia. Murakami, Tsutomu, illus. (Pictorial Fontaine Ser.) (gr. 3-6). 1960. Silver

De Liefde, Jacob
--The Golden Cap: Or, the Beautiful Legend of Fastedina, & Adgillus, & Other Stories. (Illus.). 350p. N.D. Merrill.
--The Great Dutch Admirals. N.D. George Routledge & Sons.

De Liefde, John
--The Postman's Bag. (Illus.). N.D. George Routledge & Sons.
Walter's Escape. (Illus.). (The Home and Enterprise Library Ser.). N.D. Frederick Warne & Co.

De Lind, Robert
--Samantha's Halloween Plans. LC 78-50585. 1978. (ISBN 0-533-03633-X). Vantage.

DeLipman, M., illus.
--With Fire and Sword. 825p. N.D. Henry Altemus Co.

Delitzsch, Franz
--A Day in Capernaum. N.D. Claxton, Remsen & Haffelfinger.

Delius, John
--Our Baby's Animal Alphabet. (Illus.). 100p. N.D. Monarch Book Company.

Dell, Donna, pseud., see Narzakian, Donna Dell.

Dell, Ethel May
--The Odds and Other Stories. N.D. A L Burt Co.

Dell, Joan
--The Missing Boy. Greenwald, Sheila, pseud. (1934-), illus. Green, Sheila Ellen. LC 58-13305. 22cm. 192p. 1958. Putnam.

Dell, Stanley
--The Three-Four Kittens. Lamont, Jean, illus. LC 41-6044. 96p. N.D. Henry Holt & Co.

Della Chiesa, Carol, tr. see Carroll-Abbing, John Patrick.

Della-Chiesa, Carolyn M. (1887-), tr. see Davis, John W.

Della Chiesa, Carolyn M., tr. see Lorenzini, Carlo.

Della Chiesa, Carolyn M (1887-)
--Puppet Parade. Carter, Helene (1887-1960), illus. LC 32-25734. xiii, 242 p. incl. front., illus., plates. 20 cm. 1932. Longmans, Green and Co.
--Three of Salu: Around the Year in Northern Italy. Carter, Helene (1887-1960), illus. LC 23-7489. 179 p. incl. front., illus. 19 cm. (Children of the world). 1923. World Book Company.

Dellinger, Annetta E
--Hugging. Williams, Jenny (1939-), illus. LC 84-21505. (Illus.). 30 p. 25cm. (What Is It?). c.1985. (ISBN 0-89565-301-X). Child's World.
--My First Easter Book. Hohag, Linda Sommers, illus. LC 84-21512. (Illus.). 31 p. 25cm. c.1985. (ISBN 0-516-02904-5). Childrens Press.

Dellosa, Janet, jt. auth. see Carson, Patti.

Delmare, Henriette Eugenie
--Children of the Log Cabin. N.D. Benziger Bros.

De Lopez, Graciela Carrillo, jt. auth. see Rohmer, Harriet.

Delporte, pseud., jt. auth. see Peyo, pseud.

Del Ray, Lester see Wright, Kenneth, pseud.

Del Rey, Lester see St. John, Philip, pseud.

Del Rey, Lester see Van Lhin, Erik, pseud.

Del Rey, Lester (1915-)
--Attack from Atlantis. Roban, Paul, illus. LC 53-9312. 207 p. 22cm. (Science fiction). 1953. Winston.
--The Cave of Spears. Nicholas, Frank, illus. LC 57-9196. (Illus.). 206 p. 20cm. 1957. Knopf.
--The Infinite Worlds of Maybe. LC 66-8669. 192 p. 22cm. (Winston Science Fiction Ser.). 1966. Holt, Rinehart and Winston.
--Marooned on Mars. (Winston Science Fiction Ser.). 1952. Holt, Rinehart and Winston.
--Mission to the Moon. Schomburg, Alex, illus. LC 56-5093. 207 p. 22cm. (Science fiction novel). 1956. Winston.
--Moon of Mutiny. LC 79-459. 217 p. 22cm. (Gregg Press science fiction series). 1979, c.1961. (ISBN 0-8398-2518-8). Gregg Press.
--Moon of Mutiny. LC 61-14968. 217 p. 22cm. 1961. Holt, Rinehart and Winston.
--The Mysterious Planet. LC 52-14254. 209 p. 22cm. (Science fiction novel). 1953. Winston.
--Outpost of Jupiter. LC 63-10205. 191 p. 22cm. 1963. (ISBN 0-03-035845-0). Holt, Rinehart and Winston.
--A Pirate Flag for Monterey: The Story of the Sack of Monterey. 1st ed. Cooke, Donald Ewin (1916-), illus. LC 52-5488. 178 p. illus. 22 cm. (Winston adventure books). 1952. Winston.
--Prisoners of Space. LC 68-10427. 142 p. 21cm. 1967, c.1968. Westminster Press.
--Rocket from Infinity. LC 66-12029. 191p. 22cm. c.1966. Holt.
--Rockets Through Space. rev. ed. 1960. Holt, Rinehart and Winston.
--The Runaway Robot. 1965. E M Hale.
--The Runaway Robot. LC 65-10951. 176p. 21cm. c.1965. Westminster.
--Step to the Stars. Kocher, W. A., illus. LC 60-6399. 56p. (Winston Science Fiction Ser). (gr. 7-9). 1954. (ISBN 0-03-035720-9). HR&W.
--Step to the Stars: A Science Fiction Novel. 1st ed. Schomburg, Alex, illus. LC 54-8792. 211p. 22cm. (Science fiction). 1954. Winston.
Tunnel Through Time. 1966. E M Hale.
--Tunnel Through Time. LC 66-11916. 153p. 21cm. c.1966. Westminster.

Del Rey, Lester & Matschat, Cecile Hulse, eds.
--The Year After Tomorrow. N.D. John C. Winston Co.

Delstanche, Albert, jt. auth. see Coster, Charles Theodore Henri De.

Delton, Jina (1961-)
--Two Blocks Down. LC 80-8458. 148 p. 21cm. c.1981. (ISBN 0-06-021590-9). (ISBN 0-06-021591-7). Harper & Row.

Delton, Judy (1931-)
--Angel in Charge. Morrill, Leslie H., illus. LC 84-27862. (Illus.). 152 p. 22cm. 1985. (ISBN 0-395-37488-X). Houghton Mifflin.
--Back Yard Angel. Morrill, Leslie H., illus. LC 82-23409. (Illus.). 107 p. 22cm. 1983. (ISBN 0-395-33883-2). Houghton Mifflin.
--Bear & Duck on the Run. Tucker, Kathleen, ed. Munsinger, Lynn (1951-), illus. (Illus.). 32p. (Just for Fun Bks.). (ps-3). 1984. (ISBN 0-8075-0594-3). A Whitman.
--A Birthday Bike for Brimhall. Leary, June, illus. LC 83-21025. (Illus.). 56p. (Carolrhoda On My Own Bks.). (gr. k-4). 1985. (ISBN 0-87614-256-0). Carolrhoda Bks.
--Brimhall Comes to Stay. 1st ed. Szekeres, Cyndy (1933-), illus. LC 78-7524. (Illus.). 63 p. 22cm. (Fun-to-read book). c.1978. (ISBN 0-688-41863-5). (ISBN 0-688-51863-X). Lothrop, Lee & Shepard.
--Brimhall Turns Detective. Wyman, Cherie R., illus. LC 82-9582. p. cm. (Carolrhoda on My Own Books). c.1983. (ISBN 0-87614-203-X). Carolrhoda Books.
--Brimhall Turns to Magic. 1st ed. Degen, Bruce, illus. LC 78-12141. (Illus.). 62 p. 22cm. (Fun-to-read book). c.1979. (ISBN 0-688-41878-3). (ISBN 0-688-51878-8). Lothrop, Lee & Shepard Co.
--Duck Goes Fishing. Munsinger, Lynn (1951-), illus. LC 83-17116. p. cm. 1983. (ISBN 0-8075-1722-4). A. Whitman.
--The Elephant in Duck's Garden. Munsinger, Lynn (1951-), illus. LC 85-15531. p. cm. 1985. (ISBN 0-8075-1959-6). A. Whitman.
--The Goose Who Wrote a Book. Cleary, Catherine, illus. LC 81-15475. (Illus.). 40 p. 23cm. (Carolrhoda on my own books). c.1982. (ISBN 0-87614-179-3). Carolrhoda Books.
--Groundhog's Day at the Doctor. Maestro, Giulio (1942-), illus. LC 80-36718. (Illus.). 32 p. 24cm. c.1981. (ISBN 0-8193-1041-7). (ISBN 0-8193-1042-5). Parents Magazine Press.
--I Never Win!. Gilchrist, Cathy, illus. LC 80-27618. (Illus.). 32 p. 22cm. (Carolrhoda on my own books). c.1981. (ISBN 0-87614-139-4). Carolrhoda Books.
--I'll Never Love Anything Ever Again. Daniel, Alan (1939-), illus. LC 84-17271. 1984. (ISBN 0-8075-3521-4). A. Whitman.
--I'm Telling You Now. 1st ed. Hoban, Lillian (1925-), illus. LC 82-17714. (Illus.). 32 p. 22cm. c.1983. (ISBN 0-525-44037-2). E.P. Dutton.
--Kitty in High School. LC 84-523. 1984. (ISBN 0-317-07658-2). (ISBN 0-395-35334-3). HM.
--Kitty in the Middle. Robinson, Charles (1931-), illus. LC 78-31434. (Illus.). 135 p. 22cm. 1979. (ISBN 0-395-28004-4). Houghton Mifflin.
--Kitty in the Summer. Robinson, Charles (1931-), illus. LC 80-17665. (Illus.). 148 p. 22cm. 1980. (ISBN 0-395-29456-8). Houghton Mifflin.
--Lee Henry's Best Friend. Faulkner, John Frink (1922-), illus. LC 79-16902. p. cm. (Concept book/level 1). 1979. (ISBN 0-8075-4417-5). A. Whitman.
--My Mom Hates Me in January. Faulkner, John Frink (1922-), illus. LC 77-5749. (Illus.). 32 p. 24cm. c.1977. A. Whitman.
--My Mother Lost Her Job Today. Trivas, Irene, illus. LC 80-19067. p. cm. (Concept Book Level 1). 1980. (ISBN 0-8075-5359-X). A. Whitman.
--Near Occasion of Sin. LC 84-4597. 152 p. 22cm. c.1984. (ISBN 0-15-256738-0). Harcourt, Brace, Jovanovich.
--The New Girl at School. Hoban, Lillian (1925-), illus. LC 79-11409. (Illus.). (gr. k-3). 1979. Dutton.
--On a Picnic. Funai, Mamoru R. (1932-), illus. LC 78-1240. (Illus.). 64 p. 24cm. (Reading-on-my-own book). c.1979. (ISBN 0-385-12944-0). (ISBN 0-385-12945-9). Doubleday.
--Only Jody. Porter, Patricia Grant, illus. LC 81-20178. (Illus.). 95 p. 22cm. 1982. (ISBN 0-395-32080-1). Houghton Mifflin.
--Penny-Wise, Fun Foolish. Maestro, Giulio (1942-), illus. LC 77-1582. p. cm. c.1977. (ISBN 0-517-52996-3). Crown Publishers.
--A Pet for Duck and Bear. Munsinger, Lynn (1951-), illus. LC 82-1932. (Illus.). 32 p. 24cm. c.1982. (ISBN 0-8075-6522-9). A. Whitman.
--Rabbit Finds a Way. Lasker, Joseph Leon (1919-), illus. LC 74-23102. (Illus.). 32 p. 24cm. 1975. (ISBN 0-517-52030-3). Crown Publishers.
--Rabbit's New Rug. Brown, Marc Tolon (1946-), illus. p. cm. 1979. (ISBN 0-8193-1010-7). Parents' Magazine Press.
--Three Friends Find Spring. Maestro, Giulio (1942-), illus. LC 76-46294. (Illus.). 32 p. 26cm. c.1977. (ISBN 0-517-52888-6). Crown.
--Two Good Friends. Maestro, Giulio (1942-), illus. LC 73-88181. (Illus.). 32 p. 24cm. 1974. (ISBN 0-517-51401-X). Crown Publishers.
--Two Is Company. Maestro, Giulio (1942-), illus. LC 75-45180. (Illus.). 47 p. 24cm. c.1976. (ISBN 0-517-52601-8). Crown Publishers.
--A Walk on a Snowy Night. Rossner, Ruth, illus. 1982. Harper.

Delton, Judy (1931-) & Goldsborough, June
--It Happened on Thursday. LC 77-19086. (Illus.). 32 p. 24cm. (Concept books). c.1978. (ISBN 0-8075-3669-5). A. Whitman.

Delton, Judy (1931-) & Knox-Wagner, Elaine
--The Best Mom in the World. Faulkner, John Frink (1922-), illus. LC 78-27238. (Illus.). 32 p. 24cm. (Concept book/level 1). c.1979. (ISBN 0-8075-0665-6). A. Whitman.

Delton, Julie (1959-)
--My Uncle Nikos. Simont, Marc (1915-), illus. LC 81-43317. (Illus.). 32 p. 23cm. c.1983. (ISBN 0-690-04164-0). (ISBN 0-690-04165-9). Crowell.

De Luca, Angelo Michael (1912-) & Giuliano, William
--Selections from Italian Poetry. LC 66-10394. (Illus.). 128p. (Mod. For. Lang. Ser). (gr. 10 up). 1966. (ISBN 0-8178-3792-2). Harvey.

Delulio, Donata (1941-)
--The Day the Animals Left the Zoo. Delulio, John, illus. LC 70-162620. (Illus.). 43 p. 1972. Doubleday.

Delvavaud, Marie Moreal De Brevans Collin see Collin Delavaud, Marie Moreal De Brevans.

De Lyrienne, Richard
--The Quest of the Gilt-Edged Girl, 1 of 6 vols. (The Bodley Booklets Ser.: No. 3). 1900. Set. John Lane.

De Mar, Helena Harriet (1887-)
--Gobbledy Gook Meet Percy Peacock. Escourido, Joseph, illus. LC 55-163569. unpaged. illus. 21cm. (Aunty Mar book). 1954. Traversity Press.

De Marce, Roxanne, ed. see Rides At The Door, pseud. & Blackfeet Heritage Program.

Demaree, Doris C.
--Bible Stories for Children. Uptton, Clive, illus. Incl. Exciting Bible Adventures. (ISBN 0-87162-235-1, D1445); Followers of God. (ISBN 0-87162-236-X, D1446); Helping Others. (ISBN 0-87162-237-8, D1447); Bible Boys & Girls. 1970. (ISBN 0-87162-002-2, D1443); Bible Heroes. (ISBN 0-87162-004-9, D1444); Living for Jesus. (ISBN 0-87162-055-3, D1448). (Illus.). (Doris Demaree Ser). (gr. k-4). 1974. Warner Pr.

Demaree, Margaret
--A Christmas Greeting. LC 74. 48p. 1899. Jennings & Pye.

Demarest, Christopher Lynn (1951-)
--Benedict Finds a Home. Demarest, Christopher Lynn (1951-), illus. LC 81-15586. (Illus.). 32p. (ps-1). 1982. (ISBN 0-688-00154-8). (ISBN 0-688-00586-1). Lothrop.
--Clemens' Kingdom. Demarest, Christopher Lynn (1951-), illus. LC 82-12731. p. cm. c.1983. (ISBN 0-688-01655-3). (ISBN 0-688-01657-X). Lothrop, Lee & Shepard Books.

Demarest, Virginia
--The Fruit of Desire: A Novel. LC 10-15638. 2 p. l., 331, 1 p. 20 cm. 1910. Harper & Brothers.

Demas, Vida (1927-)
--First Person, Singular. 1974. (ISBN 0-399-11241-3). G. P. Putnam's Sons.

De Mattos, Alexander Louis Teixeira see Maeterlinck, Maurice.
De Maupassant, Guy (1850-1893)
--The Diamond Necklace & Four Other Stories. Quackenbush, Robert Mead (1929-), illus. (Illus.). (gr. 7 up). 1967. (ISBN 0-531-01065-1). Watts.
--Odd Number. 1889. (ISBN 0-06-012855-0, HarpT). Har-Row.
--Selected Short Stories. ultratype ed. (Franklin Watts Classics). (gr. 7 up). N.D. (ISBN 0-531-00423-6). Watts.
De Mejo, Oscar (1911-)
--The Forty-Niner. De Mejo, Oscar (1911-), illus. LC 84-48340. (Illus.). 48 p. c.1985. (ISBN 0-06-021577-1). (ISBN 0-06-021578-X). Harper & Row.
--There's a Hand in the Sky. LC 83-2320. (Illus.). 64 p. c.1983. (ISBN 0-394-85667-8). Pantheon Books.
--The Tiny Visitor. De Mejo, Oscar (1911-), illus. LC 81-222387. (Illus.). 64 p. c.1982. (ISBN 0-394-85256-7). Pantheon Books. **Award: (NYT).**
De Melik, Beatrice, Mrs., jt. auth. see Pease, Eleanor Fairchild, Mrs.
De Ment, Doyle L.
--The Adventures of Dewy Frost. 1965. Pageant Press INC.
Demerest, Ada Rose
--Junior Pageants: Pageants and Dramatic Programs Designed Especially for Junior Groups. LC 28-30. 93 p. illus. 24 cm. c.1927. The Standard Publishing Company.
De Mers, Joseph (1910-)
--Alice in Letterland: ABC. DeMers, Joseph (1910-), illus. LC 46-18717. 22 p. col. illus. 28 cm. 1946. Mercel Rodd Co.
--Smokey and the Red Fire Engine. De Mers, Joseph (1910-), illus. LC 48-451837. 26 p. illus. (part col.) 23 cm. 1945. Rogue Press M. Rodd Co., Distributors.
--Sugarfoot and the Merry-Go-Round. N.D. Wilcox & Follett Co.
--Sugarfoot and the Merry-Go-Round. De Mers, Joseph (1910-), illus. LC 46-5576. 24 p. col. illus. 29 cm. 1946. M. Rodd Co.
Demers, Paul (1943-)
--Oliver and Ophelia: A Tale of Opossums. Delaney, Jacqueline Keenan (1930-), illus. LC 85-6020. (Illus.). 20 p. c.1985. (ISBN 0-916897-04-4). Andrew Mountain Press.
De Messieres, Nicole (1930-)
--Reina, the Galgo. LC 81-9768. 211 p. 22cm. c.1981. (ISBN 0-525-66749-0). Elsevier/Nelson Books.
--Reina the Galgo. 160p. (gr. 7 up). 1981. (ISBN 0-525-66749-0). Lodestar Bks.
Demi, pseud., see Hitz, Demi.
Demi, pseud. (1942-)
--Cinderella on Wheels: Spin the Wheel-See the Action. Hitz, Demi. LC 82-2996. p. cm. c.1982. (ISBN 0-03-059473-1). Holt, Rinehart, and Winston.
--Follow the Line. Hitz, Demi. LC 81-4072. (Illus.). 48 p. 16cm. c.1981. (ISBN 0-03-059112-0). Holt, Rinehart and Winston.
--Hide & Seek with Wilma Worm. Hitz, Demi. LC 82-63207. (Illus.). 26p. (Follow-Me Bks.). (ps). 1983. (ISBN 0-394-86020-9). Random.
--The Leaky Umbrella. Hitz, Demi. LC 80-18803. (Illus.). 33 p. 21cm. c.1980. (ISBN 0-13-526962-8). Prentice-Hall.
--Liang and the Magic Paintbrush. Hitz, Demi. Demi, pseud. (1942-), illus. Hitz, Demi. LC 80-11351. (Illus.). 32 p. 21cm. c.1980. (ISBN 0-03-056289-9). Holt, Rinehart, and Winston.
--Three Little Elephants. Hitz, Demi. LC 80-53679. (Illus.). 22 p. 13cm. (Follow me book). c.1981. (ISBN 0-394-84760-1). Random House.
--Under the Shade of the Mulberry Tree. Hitz, Demi. LC 78-15733. (Illus.). 32 p. 27cm. c.1979. (ISBN 0-13-936476-5). Prentice-Hall.
--Watch Harry Grow!. Hitz, Demi. Demi, pseud. (1942-), illus. Hitz, Demi. LC 84-60109. (Illus.). 26p. (Follow-Me Bks.). (ps-1). 1984. (ISBN 0-394-86857-9, Pub. by BYR). Random.
--Where Is Willie Worm?. Hitz, Demi. LC 80-53680. (Illus.). 24 p. 13cm. (A Follow Me Book). c.1981. (ISBN 0-394-84759-8). Random House.
De Mille, Agnes, pseud., see Prude, Agnes George.
De Mille, Agnes, pseud. (1905-)
--Dance to the Piper. Prude, Agnes George. (Illus.). (Autobiography). (gr. 9 up). 1952. (ISBN 0-316-18034-3, Pub. by Atlantic Monthly Pr). Little.

De Mille, Alban Bertram (1873-), ed. see Hughes, Thomas.

De Mille, James (1837-1880)
--Among the Brigands. (Illus.). (Famous Books for Boys). N.D. H. M. Caldwell Co.
--Among the Brigands, 1 of 3 Vols. (James DeMille author of "B. O. A. C. Stories."). (Illus.). (The Young Dodge Club Ser.). 1882. Lee & Shepard.
--Among the Brigands, 1 of 50 vols. (Illus.). (The Norwood Ser.: No. 8). 1900. Lee & Shepard.
--The "B. O. W. C.", 1 of 6. (B. O. W. C. Stories). N.D. Colby and Rich.
--The "B. O. W. C, 1 Of 6 vols. (Illus.). (B. O. W. C. Stories). 1882. Set. Lee & Shepard.
--The B. O. W. C, 1 of 60 vols. (American Boys' Ser.: No. 8). 1900. Set. Lee & Shepard.
--The Boys of Grand Pre School, 1 of 6. (B. O. W. C. Stories). N.D. Colby and Rich.
--The Boys of Grand Pre School, 1 of 6 vols. (Illus.). 348p. (B.O. W. C. Stories). 1882. Set. Lee & Shepard.
--Boys of Grand Pre School, 1 of 60 vols. (American Boys' Ser.: No. 7). 1900. Set. Lee & Shepard.
--Fire in the Woods, 1 of 6. (B. O. W. C. Stories). N.D. Colby and Rich.
--Fire in the Woods, 1 of 6 vols. (Illus.). 323p. (B. O. W. C. Stories). 1882. Lee & Shepard.
--Fire in the Woods, 1 of 60 vols. (American Boys' Ser.: No. 16). 1900. Set. Lee & Shepard.
--The Lily & the Cross, 1 of 50 vols. (Illus.). (The Norwood Ser.: No. 9). 1900. Lee & Shepard.
--The Lily and the Cross: A Tale of Arcadia. N.D. Lee & Shepard.
--Lost in the Fog, 1 of 6. (B. O. W. C. Stories). N.D. Colby and Rich.
--Lost in the Fog, 1 of 6 Vols. (Illus.). 316p. (B. O. W. C. Stories). 1882. Lee & Shepard.
--Lost in the Fog, 1 of 60 vols. (Illus.). (American Boys' Ser.: No. 29). 1900. Lee & Shepard.
--Picked Up Adrift, 1 of 6 vols. (B. O. W. C. Stories). N.D. Colby and Rich.
--Picked Up Adrift, 1 of 6 Vols. (Illus.). (B. O. W. C. Series). 1882. Lee & Shepard.
--The Seven Hills, 1 of 3 Vols. (James DeMille author of B. O. W. C. Stories."). (Illus.). (The Young Dodge Club). 1882. Lee & Shepard.
--Treasure of the Sea, 1 of 60 vols. (Illus.). (American Boys' Ser.: No. 39). 1900. Lee & Shepard.
--The Treasure of the Seas, 1 of 6 Vols. (Illus.). (B. O. W. C. Stories). 1882. Lee & Shepard.
--Treasures of the Sea, 6 of 6. (B. O. W. C. Stories). N.D. Colby and Rich.
--The Winged Lion: Or, Stories of Venice, 1 of 50 vols. (Illus.). (The Norwood Ser.: No. 10). 1900. Lee & Shepard.
--The Winged Lion: Or, Stories of venice, 1 of 3 Vols. (James DeMille author of "B. O. W. C. Stories."). (Illus.). 1882cm. (The Young Dodge Club). N.D. Lee & Shepard.
--Young Dodge Club, 3 vols. (Illus.). 1882. Set. Lee & Shepard.
DeMille, Jancie F.
--Kendra's Surprise: A Child's First Visit to Zion. 1981. (ISBN 0-686-46196-7). Zion.
De Mille, William Churchill (1878-) & Barnard, Charles (1838-)
--The Forest Ring: A Fairy Fantasy. Sichel, Harold M. (1881-), illus. LC 14-201211. 180 p. col. front., illus., col. plates. 24 cm. c.1914. George H. Doran Company.
Deming, Dorothy (1893-)
--Anne Snow, Mountain Nurse. LC 47-11813. 272 p. 21 cm. (Career books). 1947. Dodd, Mead.
--Baffling Affair in the County Hospital. LC 62-15502. (Illus.). 21cm. 212p. 1962. Dodd, Mead.
--Curious Calamity in Ward Eight. LC 54-7078. 184p. illus. 21cm. 1954. Dodd, Mead.
--Hilda Baker, School Nurse. LC 55-9135. 244 p. 21cm. (Dodd, Mead career books). 1955. Dodd, Mead.
--Linda Kent, Student Nurse. LC 52-7213. 274 p. 21cm. (Career books). 1952. Dodd, Mead.
--Mysterious Discovery in Ward K. LC 59-9580. (Illus.). 21cm. 210p. 1959. Dodd, Mead.
--Nurse's Dilemma in the Private Corridor. LC 57-11547. (Illus.). 213 p. 21cm. 1957. Dodd, Mead.
--Nursing Assignment in El Salvador. LC 54-10703. 244 p. 21cm. (Career books). 1954. Dodd, Mead.
--Pam Wilson, Registered Nurse. N.D. Dodd, Mead &.
--Penny and Pam, Nurse and Cadet. LC 44-8833. 5 p. l., 230 p. 19 1/2 cm. (Career books). 1944. Dodd, Mead & Company.
--Penny Marsh and Ginger Lee: Wartime Nurses. LC 43-142909. 7 p. l., 3-236 p. 21 cm. (Career books). 1943. Dodd, Mead & Company.
--Penny Marsh Finds Adventure in Public Health Nursing. Warren, Dorothea, illus. 1940. Dodd, Mead & Co.
--Penny Marsh: Public Health Nurse. Warren, Dorothea, illus. 1938. Dodd, Mead &Co.
--Penny Marsh, R. N., Director of Nurses. (gr. 7-9). 1960. (ISBN 0-396-04426-3). Dodd.
--Penny Marsh: Supervisor of Public Health Nurses. Warren, Dorothea, illus. 1938. Dodd, Mead & Co.
--Sharon's Nursing Diary. LC 49-10591. vii, 272 p. 21 cm. (Dodd, Mead career books). 1949. Dodd, Mead.
--Strange Disappearance from Ward 2. LC 56-5435. (Illus.). 243 p. 21cm. 1956. Dodd, Mead.
--Sue Morris: Sky Nurse. LC 53-5099. 247p. 21cm. (Career books). 1953. Dodd, Mead.
--Trudy Wells, R. N., Pediatric Nurse. LC 57-5235. 244 p. 21cm. (Dodd, Mead career books). 1957. Dodd, Mead.
Deming, Edwin Willard (1860-1942)
--American Animal Life. N.D. Frederick A. Stokes.
--Children of the Wild. N.D. Frederick A. Stokes.
--Four Footed Wilderness People. N.D. Frederick A. Stokes.
--Little Indian Folk. N.D. Frederick A. Stokes.
--Little Red People. (Illus.). N.D. Frederick A. Stokes.
Deming, Norma H., jt. auth. see Jackson, Bennett B.
Deming, Richard (1922-)
--Dragnet: Case Histories from the Popular Television Series. authorized. Goozee, Dan, illus. LC 72-19986. (Illus.). 210 p. 20cm. 1970. Western Pub. Co.
Deming, Therese Osterheld, Mrs. (1874-)
--Cosel with Geronimo on His Last Raid: The Story of an Indian Boy. Deming, Edwin Willard (1860-1942), illus. LC 38-8781. xvii, 125 p. illus., col. plates. 24 cm. 1938. F. A. Davis Company.
--Indian Child Life. Deming, Edwin Willard (1860-1942), illus. LC 99-4899. 37 l. illus., 18 pl. (incl. front.) 21 x 29 cm. 1899. F. A. Stokes Company.
--Indian Child Life. Deming, Edwin Willard (1860-1942), illus. LC 32-12852. 37 l. illus., 18 col. pl. (incl. front.) 21 x 28 cm. c.1927. F. A. Stokes Company.
--Little Brothers of the West. Deming, Edwin Willard (1860-1942), illus. LC 2-23760. 26 p. col. front., illus., 5 col. pl. 26 cm. 1902. Frederick A. Stokes Company.
--Many Snows Ago. Deming, Edwin Willard (1860-1942), illus. LC 29-20979. 96 p. col. front., illus. (part col.) 21 x 28 cm. 1929. Frederick A. Stokes Company.
--Red Folk and Wild Folk. Deming, Edwin Willard (1860-1942), illus. 1902. Frederick A. Stokes Co.
--Wigwam Children. Deming, Edwin Willard (1860-1942), illus. N.D. Frederick A. Stokes.
Deming, Therese Osterheld, Mrs. (1874-) & Shaw, Thelma
--Red People of the Wooded Country. Deming, Edwin Willard (1860-1942), illus. N.D. Albert Whitman & Co.
De Miomandre, Francis (1880-)
--The Story of Pierre Pons. Guignebault, Paul, illus. Rich, Edwin Gile (1879-), tr. LC 29-17314. 95, 1 p. incl. front., illus. (part col.) 28 cm. c.1929. E. P. Dutton & Co., Inc.
De Miskey, Julian (1908-1976)
--Piccolo. De Miskey, Julian (1908-1976), illus. LC 68-6466. (Illus.). 32 p. 29cm. (Carousel book). 1968. L. W. Singer Co.
Demmer, Elly
--The Circus Mouse. Denner, Helga, illus. LC 63-15143. (Illus.). 30 p. 1963. Rand McNally.
De Monvel, Louis Maurice Boutet see Boutet De Monvel, Louis Maurice.
De Morgan, John (1848-)
--Old Ironsides: The United States Frigate Constitution, Terror of the High Seas, Captain Isaac Hull Commanding. Comstock, Enos Benjamin (1879-1945), illus. LC 33-21926. 3 p. l., 5-190 p. illus. 20 cm. c.1933. McLoughlin Bros., Inc.
--Taming the Barbary Pirates: Or, With Decatur and Somers in the Mediterranean. LC 33-21927. 3 p. l., 3-171 p. illus. 20 cm. c.1933. McLoughlin Bros., Inc.
--Taming the Barbary Pirates: Or, With Decatur and Somers in the Mediterranean. Comstock, Enos Benjamin (1879-1945), illus. LC 9-10649. 3 p. l., 3-171 p. col. front., illus. 21 cm. 1908. McLoughlin Bros.
--A Yankee Ship and a Yankee Crew in the Good Ship United States: Commodore John Barry Commanding. Comstock, Enos Benjamin (1879-1945), illus. LC 33-21925. 1 p. l., 5-186 p. incl. illus., plates. 20 cm. c.1933. McLoughlin Bros., Inc.
De Morgan, Mary
--Complete Fairy Tales. DeMorgan, William Frend & Crane, Walter (1845-1915), illus. LC 63-7489. (Illus.). 21cm. 412p. N.D. Franklin Watts.
--The Necklace of Princess Fiorimonde, & Other Stories. (Illus.). N.D. MacMillan.
--On a Pincushion, 2 vols, Repr. Of 1877 Ed. Incl. The Necklace of Princess Fiorimonde, & Other Stories. Repr. of 1880 ed. LC 75-32181. (Illus.). (Classics of Children's Literature, 1621-1932). 1977. Set. (ISBN 0-8240-2293-9). Garland Pub.
--On a Pincushion, and Other Fairy Tales. De Morgan, William Frend, illus. N.D. E. P. Dutton.
--Other Fairy Tales. N.D. E. P. Dutton & Co.
--Princess Girlikin: Or,The Fairy Thimble. incl. front illus. 22 cm. 256p. 1892. E. P. Dutton & Co.
--The Wind Fairies And Other Stories. Cockerell, Olive, illus. N.D. Dutton.
DeMorgan, Mary & DeMorgan, William Frend (1839-1917)
--On a Pincushion, and Other Stories. N.D. Duffield.
DeMorgan, Mary & DeMorgan, William Frend (1839-1917), eds.
--On a Pincushion, and Other Fairy Tales ; The Necklace of Princess Fiorimonde, and Other Stories. LC 75-32181. (Illus.). 426 p. in various pagings, 7 leaves of plates. 19cm. (Classics of Children's Literature, 1621-1932). 1977. (ISBN 0-8240-2293-9). Garland Pub.
DeMorgan, S. E.
--Algy's Lesson. N.D. Cassell Petter & Galpin.
DeMorgan, William Frend, jt. auth. see DeMorgan, Mary.
DeMorgan, William Frend, jt. ed. see DeMorgan, Mary.
De Mosa, Catherine Cornwall
--Blue Bucket Nuggets. 140p. N.D. Binfords & Mort.
Dempsey, Al, jt. auth. see Moore, Robin.
Dempsey, Vincent
--Cabin Boy. LC 56-7140. 1956. Coward-McCann.
Dempster, Al, ed.
--Walt Disney's Mother Goose. Disney, Walt, Studio, illus. (ps-1). 1952. (ISBN 0-307-60079-3, Golden Pr). Western Pub.
--Walt Disney's Pinocchio. N.D. Golden Press.
Dempster, Al, adapted by see Disney, Walt, Productions.
Dempster, Al, adapted by see Disney, Walt, Productions & Carroll, Lewis.
Dempster, Al, ed. see Disney, Walt, Productions & Lorenzini, Carlo.
Dempster, Al, ed. see Disney, Walt, Studio.
Dempster, Al, jt. ed. see Hench, John.
Dempster, William
--Paul Bunyan. LC 73-2033. (Illus.). 247 p. 29cm. (Educator classic library, 12). 1968. Classic Press.
--Paul Bunyan. Dempster, William, illus. LC 68-31320. (Illus.). 247 p. 29cm. 1973, c.1968. Childrens Press.
De Musset, Paul Edme see Musset, Paul Edme De.
Demuth, Averil
--The House in the Mountains. MacKnight, Ninon (1908-), illus. Ninon, pseud. LC 41-19425. ix, p., 1 l., 240 p. col. front., illus. 21 cm. c.1941. Harper & Brothers.
--Trudi and Hansel: A Story of the Austrian Tyrol. Lavrin, Nora Fry, illus. LC 38-24561. 173, 1 p. incl. col. front., illus. (part col.) 22 cm. c.1938. The John C. Winston Company.
DeMuth, Vivienne
--Ten Little Fingers, Ten Little Toes: Nursery Games and Finger Plays for the Very Young. DeMuth, Vivienne, illus. LC 79-51984. (Illus.). 20 p. 32cm. c.1979. (ISBN 0-525-69010-7, Gingerbread Bk.). (ISBN 0-525-69011-5). E. P. Dutton.
DeMuth, Vivienne, illus.
--The Busy Animal Dress-Up Book. (Illus.). (ps-1). 1979. (Gingerbread Bks). Dutton.
Denan, Corinne, retold by.
--Dragon and Monster Tales. Williams, Jenny (1939-), illus. LC 79-66329. (Illus.). 46 p. 23cm. c.1980. (ISBN 0-89375-325-4). Troll Associates.
--Giant Tales. Dodson, Bert, illus. LC 79-66330. (Illus.). 47 p. 23cm. c.1980. (ISBN 0-89375-328-9). (ISBN 0-89375-327-0). Troll Associates.
--Goblin Tales. Rogers, Jackie, illus. LC 79-66326. (Illus.). 48 p. 23cm. c.1980. (ISBN 0-89375-320-3). (ISBN 0-89375-319-X). Troll Associates.
--Hair-Raising Tales. Leightbown, Meredith, illus. LC 79-66334. (Illus.). 46 p. 23cm. c.1980. (ISBN 0-89375-334-3). (ISBN 0-89375-333-5). Troll Associates.
--Haunted House Tales. Toulmin-Rothe, Ann, illus. LC 79-66335. (Illus.). 44 p. 23cm. c.1980. (ISBN 0-89375-336-X). (ISBN 0-89375-335-1). Troll Associates.
--Once Upon a Time Tales. Lidbeck, Karin, illus. LC 79-66337. (Illus.). 46 p. 23cm. c.1980. (ISBN 0-89375-340-8). (ISBN 0-89375-339-4). Troll Associates.
--Strange and Eerie Tales. Baldwin-Ford, Pamela, illus. LC 79-66336. (Illus.). 46 p. 23cm. c.1980. (ISBN 0-89375-337-8). Troll Associates.
--Tales of Magic and Spells. Watling, James, illus. LC 79-66325. (Illus.). 48 p. 23cm. c.1980. (ISBN 0-89375-318-1). (ISBN 0-89375-317-3). Troll Associates.
--Tales of the Ugly Ogres. Craft, Kinuko Y., illus. LC 79-66333. (Illus.). 46 p. 23cm. c.1980. (ISBN 0-89375-332-7). (ISBN 0-89375-331-9). Troll Associates.

AUTHOR INDEX **DENNY, J.**

--Troll Tales. Parker, Edward, illus. LC 79-66327. (Illus.). 46 p. 23cm. c.1980. (ISBN 0-89375-322-X). (ISBN 0-89375-321-1). Troll Associates.
--Witch Tales. Baldwin-Ford, Pamela, illus. LC 79-66328. (Illus.). 46 p. 23cm. c.1980. (ISBN 0-89375-324-6). Troll Associates.
--Wizard Tales. Sweat, Lynn, illus. LC 79-66331. (Illus.). 45 p. 23cm. c.1980. (ISBN 0-89375-330-0). (ISBN 0-89375-329-7). Troll Associates.

De Nancrede, Edith & Smith, Gertrude Madeira
--Mother Goose Dances. 56 p. illus. 32 cm. c.1940. (ISBN 0-912222-04-2). H. T. FitzSimons Company.

DeNarvaez, Cynthia
--My Dear Dolphin. Greenberg, Jerry, photos by. LC 70-83821. (Illus.). 30 photos. (gr. 3-6). 1969. (ISBN 0-07-045889-8). (ISBN 0-07-045890-1). McGraw.

Denbury, Lorraine Mabel
--Story of Johnny Doggit. (Illus.). N.D. Vantage Press, Inc.

Denby, Edwin, jt. auth. see Copland, Aaron.

Dendel, Esther Sietman Warner see Warner, Esther S., pseud.

Dender, Jay, pseud., see Deindorfer, Robert Greene.

Dender, Jay, pseud. (1922-1983)
--Tom Harmon and the Great Gridiron Plot: An Original Story Featuring Tom Harmon, Famous Football Star, As the Hero. Deindorfer, Robert Greene. authorized. Vallely, Henry E., illus. LC 46-794048. 2 p. l., 9-251 p. illus. 20 1/2 cm. 1946. Whitman Publishing Co.

Denef, Ruth, tr. see Chrystoph, Paul.

Denef, Ruth, tr. see Wiemer, Rudolf Otto.

De Nervaud, Marie
--Scarum. LC 33-5768. vi, 317 p. 20 cm. c.1933. Duffield and Green.
--Scarum. LC 39-12437. 4 p. l., 3-250 p. 20 cm. c.1939. Grosset & Dunlap.

Denes, Gee & Harris, E. M.
--Christmas at Timothy's. N.D. Nelson Bks.
--Jennifer Goes to School. Denes, Gee, illus. LC 46-16347. 38, 2 p. col. illus. 23 1/2 x 20 cm. 1945. T. Nelson and Sons Limited.
--John and Jennifer and Their Pets. Denes, Gee illus. N.D. Thomas Nelson & Sons.
--John and Jennifer at the Farm. N.D. Nelson Bks.
--John and Jennifer at the Zoo. N.D. Nelson Bks.
--John and Jennifer Go Camping. Denes, Gee, illus. N.D. Thomas Nelson & Sons.
--John and Jennifer Go Travelling. Denes, Gee. illus. N.D. Thomas Nelson & Sons.

Dengler, Marianna Herron (1935-)
--Catch the Passing Breeze. Najaka, Marlies Merk, illus. LC 77-3159. 126 p. 22cm. c.1977. (ISBN 0-03-019426-1). Holt, Rinehart and Winston.
--A Pebble in Newcomb's Pond. Garry-McCord, Kathleen, illus. LC 78-14825. (Illus.). 160 p. 22cm. c.1979. (ISBN 0-03-044641-4). Holt, Rinehart and Winston.
--Vicki. 135p (Pub. by Holt, Rinehart & Winston). (gr. 7 up). 1980. (ISBN 0-590-31324-X). Scholastic Inc.

Dengler, Sandy
--The Arizona Longhorn Adventure. LC 80-18060. p. cm. 128p. (Pioneer Family Adventures). (gr. 5-8). c.1980. (ISBN 0-8024-0299-2). Moody Press.
--The Horse Who Loved Picnics. LC 80-10691. p. cm. (Pioneer Family Adventures). c.1980. (ISBN 0-8024-3589-0). Moody Press.
--The Melon Hound. LC 79-28218. p. cm. (The Pioneer Family Adventures ; 2: No.). c.1980. Moody Press.
--Mystery at McGeehan Ranch. LC 81-18694. p. cm. c.1982. (ISBN 0-8024-2972-6). Moody Press.
--Rescue in the Desert. LC 80-25563. 128 p. 18cm. (Pioneer Family Adventures: No.5). c.1981. (ISBN 0-8024-0874-5). Moody Press.
--Socorro Island Treasure. LC 82-22864. 126 p. 18cm. c.1983. (ISBN 0-8024-7813-1). Moody Press.
--Summer of the Wild Pig. LC 79-15609. 124 p. 19cm. (Pioneer Family Adventures). (gr. 6-8). c.1979. (ISBN 0-8024-8429-8). Moody Bible Institute.
--Three in One Pioneer Family Adventure Series. 1985. (ISBN 0-8024-6365-7). Moody.

Denice the Menace, Television Program see Memling, Carl (1918-1969) & Ketcham, Hank.

Denis, Armand (1896-1971)
--On Safari. 1963. E M Hale.

Denis, F. & Charnier, V.
--The True Robinson Crusoes: Stories of Adventure, 1 of 4. Russell, Charles, tr. from Fr. (Illus.). 220p. (The Album Library Ser.). N.D. Lee & Shepard.

Denis, L. & Charnier, V.
--The True Robinson Crusoes, 1 of 4. Russell, Charles, tr. (The True Crusoe Ser.). N.D. Cassell, Petter, & Galpin.

Denis, Michaela
--Leopard in My Lap. N.D. Julian Messner, Inc.

Denison, C.W Mrs. see Denison, Mary Andrews, Mrs.

Denison, C. W. Mrs. see Denison, Mary Andrews, Mrs.

Denison, C W Mrs. see Vance, Clara.

Denison, Carol
--Animal Stories. Szasz, Frank, illus. LC 63-4456. 95 p. illus. 27 cm. (Golden storytime book). 1963, c.1957. Golden Press.
--A Part-Time Dog for Nick. Miller, Jane Judith (1925-), illus. LC 59-6183. 1959. Dodd, Mead & Co.
--What Every Young Rabbit Should Know. Wiese, Kurt (1887-1974), illus. LC 48-102475. 64 p. illus. (part col.) 23 x 26 cm. 1948. Dodd, Mead.

Denison, Carol & Cummin, Jane
--Where Any Young Cat Might Be. Wiese, Kurt (1887-1974), illus. LC 56-8609. unpaged. illus. 23 x 26cm. 1956. Dodd, Mead.

Denison, Mary Andrews see Edson, N. I., pseud.

Denison, Mary Andrews see Vance, Clara, pseud.

Denison, Mary Andrews, Mrs., et al. (1826-1911)
--Entertaining and Useful Library for Young Ladies: Containing "Talbury Girls", "Violet Douglas", "Beulah Romney," etc, 14 vols. N.D. Set. D.Lothrop & Co.
--Select Library: Containing "Strawberry Hill," "Bright Days," "Overcoming," etc, 7 vols. N.D. Set. D. Lothrop & Co.

Denison, Mary Andrews, Mrs. (1826-1911)
--Anne and Tilly. (Saturday Afternoon Ser.). N.D. Alfred Martien.
--Anne's Beach Party. (Saturday Afternoon Ser.). N.D. Alfred Martien.
--Anne's New Life. (Saturday Afternoon Ser.). N.D. Alfred Martien.
--Anne's Saturday Afternoons. (Saturday Afternoon Ser.). N.D. Alfred Martien.
--Antoinette, 1 of 6 vols. (Illus.). N.D. Set. Bradley & Woodruff.
--Barbara. Edson, N. I., pseud. (Illus.). N.D. Lothrop Pub. Co.
--Barbara's Triumph. (Illus.). (St. Nicholas Series for Girls). N.D. International Book Co.
--Barbara's Triumphs, 31 vols. (Illus.). (Famous Books for Girls Ser.: No. 7). 1905. Set. H M Caldwell Co.
--Barbara's Triumphs: Or The Fdortunes of a Young Artist. (The Girls' Own Library). N.D. David McKay.
--Bessie Brown. N.D. Bradley & Woodruff's.
--The Blind Princess. N.D. Bradley & Woodruff's.
--Captain Molly, 1 of 30 vols. (American Girls' Ser.: No. 2). 1900. Set. Lee & Shepard.
--Dolly's Narrative, 1 of 6 vols. (Illus.). N.D. Set. Bradley & Woodruff.
--Ethel's Triumph. (Illus.). 422p. N.D. A. I. Bradley & Co.'s Pub.
--An Every-Day Heroine. Waugh, Ida, illus. (Keystone Ser.). N.D. Penn Publishing Co.
--An Everyday Heroine: A Story for Girls. Waugh, Ida, illus. (The Vacation Ser.). 1896. Penn.
--The Frenchman's Ward. (The Girls' Own Library). N.D. David McKay.
--Frenchman's Ward, 31 vols. (Illus.). (Famous Books for Girls Ser.: No. 8). 1905. Set. H M Caldwell Co.
--Glennandale. LC 21-15382. 1 p. l., 320 p. front., plates. 18 cm. 1882. American Baptist Publication Society.
--The Guardian's Trust. (The Girls' Own Library). N.D. David McKay.
--Guardian's Trust, 31 vols. (Illus.). (Famous Books for Girls Ser.: No 9). 1905. Set. H M Caldwell Co.
--Hannah's Triumph. (Denison Ser.). N.D. Alfred Martien.
--Her Secret. (Illus.). (Vacation Ser.). N.D. Penn Publishing Co.
--Her Secret: A Story for Girls. Lyndall, Isabel, illus. LC 4-21667. 3 p. l., 5-316 p. front., 6 pl. 19 cm. (Keystone Ser.). 1904. The Penn Publishing Company.
--Hidden Treasure. LC 21-15394. (Illus.). 18cm. iv, 301p. 1877. D. Lothrop.
--How She Helped Him. (Illus.). 212p. N.D. A. I. Bradley & Co.'s Pub.
--John Dane, 1 of 6 vols. (Illus.). N.D. Set. Bradley & woodruff.
--John Dane. LC 21-153933. v, 7-451 p. front. 18 cm. 1874. H. Holt.
--Kept from Idols. (Illus.). 376p. N.D. A. I. Bradley & Co.'s Pubs.
--Led to the Light. LC 21-15384. (Illus.). 16cm. vi, 352p. 1867. J. S. Claxton.
--The Little Folks of Redbow. LC 21-15395. 362 p. front., plates. 18 cm. 1875. H. A. Young & Co.
--No Mother Like Mine. LC 21-153921. v, 7-273 p. front., plates. 19 cm. 1880. I. Bradley & Co.
--A Noble Sister, 1 of 3, Vol. 1. (Denison Ser.). N.D. Alfred Martien.
--A Noble Sister. LC 21-153916. iv, 5-373 p. front., plates. 17 cm. (Added t.-p.: The Denison series). 1886. J. S. Claxton.
--Off the Track, 3 of 3, Vol. 3. (Denison Ser.). N.D. Alfred Martien.
--The Old Folly and Its Inhabitants. LC 31-194974. 2 p. l., 3-308 p. front., plates. 18 cm. 1882. American Baptist Publication Society.
--The Old Folly and Its Inhabitants. (Illus.). 308p. N.D. Sunday-School Publications.
--Opposite the Jail. LC 21-15390. (Illus.). 334p. 1883. A. I. Bradley & Co.'s Pubs.
--Opposite the Jail, Sequel, 1 of 6 vols. (Illus.). N.D. Set. Bradley & Woodruff.
--Orphan Anne. LC 75-310901. 16cm. 150p. (Saturday Afternoon Ser.). 1871. Alfred Martien.
--The Romance of a Schoolboy. (Illus.). N.D. Caldwell.
--The Romance of a Schoolboy. (Illus.). N.D. Merriam Company.
--Romilly Street. LC 76-366565. 142 p. 21cm. 1976. (ISBN 0-234-77800-8). Dobson.
--Sequel to Opposite the Jail: Or, On Trial for His Life. LC 21-15390. vi, 7-279 p. front., plates. 18 cm. 1883. I. Bradley & Co.
--Silent Tom. LC 21-15389. 377 p. front., plates. 18 cm. (Added t.-p.: The thousand dollar prize series). c.1872. D. Lothrop & Co.
--Silent Tom, 1 of 50 vols. (Young People's Library: No. 35). N.D. Set. Lothrop Publishing Co.
--Stolen from Home. (Illus.). 399p. N.D. A. I. Bradley & Co.'s Pubs.
--Stolen from Home. LC 21-15388. iv, 5-399 p. front., plates. 18 cm. c.1873. H. Holt.
--Stolen From Home. (Cousin John's Library). N.D. Henry Holt.
--Strawberry Hill. Vance, Clara, pseud. LC 21-15387. iv, 5-432 p. front., plates. 18 cm. 1870. D. Lothrop & Co.
--Sunshine Cottage. N.D. Bradley & Woodruff.
--The Talbury Girls. Vance, Clara, pseud. LC 21-153851. 487 p. front., plates. 17 cm. 1871. D. Lothrop & Co.
--What One Boy Can Do. LC 21-15386. v, 267 p. front. 19 cm. 1886. I. Bradley & Co.

Denison, Merrill
--Klondike Mike. N.D. World Publishing.

Denison, Muriel Goggin, Mrs.
--Happy Tramp. The Story of a Little Girl and Her Old English Sheep Dog. Bryan, Marguerite, illus. LC 42-14631. 5 p. l., 260 p. illus. 21 x 16 cm. 1942. Dodd, Mead & Company.
--Susannah: A Little Girl with the Mounties. Bryan, Marguerite, illus. LC 36-29007. ix, 299 p. incl. front., illus., plates. 21 cm. 1936. Dodd, Mead & Company.
--Susannah at Boarding School. Bryan, Marguerite, illus. LC 38-34547. ix p., 1 l., 344 p. illus. 21 cm. 1938. Dodd, Mead & Company.
--Susannah of the Mounties. LC 59-12361. (With illustrations from the motion picture featuring Shirley Temple). (Illus.). 1959. Random House Inc.
--Susannah of the Yukon. Bryan, Marguerite, illus. LC 37-29928. vii, 343 p. incl. front., illus., plates. 21 cm. 1937. Dodd, Mead & Company.
--Susannah Rides Again. Bryan, Marguerite, illus. LC 40-341073. 6 p. l., 329 p. illus. 21 x 16 cm. 1940. Dodd, Mead & Company.

Denker, Henry (1912-)
--That First Easter. Keats, Ezra Jack (1916-1983), illus. LC 58-5122. 128p. 1959. Thomas Y. Crowell Co.

Denker, Nan Watson (1885-)
--Aweigh on a Windjammer: An Adventure Book. LC 42-23953. 221 p. col. front., illus. 21 cm. 1942. W. A. Wilde Company.
--The Bound Girl, 1 of 36 vols. (Illus.). (Primary Lib.: No. 8). N.D. Set. A. I. Bradley & Co.'s Pubs.
--The Bound Girl. LC 57-5541. 183p. 22cm. 1957. Ariel Books.

Denman, Michael L., tr. see Granowsky, Alvin (1936-) & Tweedt, Joy Ann.

Denneborg, Heinrich Maria (1909-)
--Grisella the Donkey. Lemke, Horst (1922-), illus. Capouya, Emile (1922-), tr. LC 57-581185. 138p. illus. 22cm. 1957. D. McKay Co.
--Jan & the Wild Horse. Lemke, Horst (1922-), illus. Capouya, Emil, tr. from Ger. (gr. 4-7). N.D. McKay.
--Johnny and the Jester. Lemke, Horst (1922-), illus. LC 69-11222. (Illus.). 30 p. 27cm. 1969. Watts.
--The Only Horse for Jan. Lemke, Horst (1922-), illus. Capouya, Emile, tr. LC 61-6105. (Illus.). (gr. 3-7). 1961. McKay.

Denney, Diana Ross see Ross, Diana.

Denney, Diana (1910-)
--The Little Red Engine Gets a Name. Ross, Diana, Lewitt & Him, illus. LC 45-6094. 32 p. illus. (part col.) 17 1/2 x 24 1/2 cm. c.1945. Transatlantic Arts, Inc.

Denning, Ruth Miller
--Micko in the Land of Far Away: An Adventure Story for Children. 1st ed. LC 55-12462. 94p. illus. 21cm. 1956. Exposition Press.

Dennis, Clara G
--The All-Holidays Book of Jane and John. Stevens, Beatrice (1876-), illus. LC 29-19793. 96 p. col. front., illus., plates. 27 cm. c.1929. Marshall Jones Company.
--Cuddly Kitty and Busy Bunny. Wright, Alan & Anderson, Anne, illus. LC 27-18459. 96 p. incl. col. front., col. illus. 16 cm. 1927. T. Nelson & Sons.
--Podgy Puppy and Naughty Neddy. Wright, Alan & Anderson, Anne, illus. LC 27-18134. 96 p. incl. col. front., col. illus. 16 cm. 1927. T. Nelson & Sons.

Dennis, Clarence James (1876-1938) & Whitmore, Lee
--C. J. Dennis' Slippery-Dip: Fun for Kids. Whitemore, Lee, illus. LC 77-356059. (Illus.). 29 p. 30cm. 1976. (ISBN 0-207-13293-3). Angus and Robertson.

Dennis, G. R., ed. see Swift, Jonathan.

Dennis, June
--A Mike for Marion. 1st ed. Finch, Jean Rutherford, illus. LC 52-12135. 200p. illus. 21cm. 1952. Longmans, Green.

Dennis, Mary Boardman Cable, Mrs., ed. see Field, Eugene.

Dennis, Morgan (1891-1960)
--Burlap. Dennis, Morgan (1891-1960), illus. LC 45-4229. (Illus.). (gr. k-3). 1945. (ISBN 0-670-19582-0). (ISBN 0-670-19583-9). Viking Pr.
--Himself and Burlap on TV. LC 54-12999. (Illus.). 19 x 23cm. 41p. 1954. Viking Press.
--Kitten on the Keys. (Illus.). (gr. 2-4). 1961. (ISBN 0-8382-0410-4). Hale.
--Kitten on the Keys. Dennis, Morgan (1891-1960), illus. LC 61-7696. (gr. 2-4). 1961. (ISBN 0-670-41418-2). Viking Pr.
--The Pup Himself. LC 43-14818. 42 p. illus. 19 x 23 cm. 1943. The Viking Press.
--The Sea Dog. LC 58-3598. (Illus.). 21 x 24cm. 1958. Viking Press.
--Skit and Skat. Dennis, Morgan (1891-1960), illus. LC 51-9955. (Illus.). 42 p. 1951. Viking Press.

Dennis, Peter (1950-)
--The Lost Starship. Dennis, Peter (1950-), illus. LC 81-52500. (Illus.). 28 p. 20cm. (Starters Stories, Green: No. 4). c.1981. (ISBN 0-382-06579-4). Silver Burdett Co.

Dennis, Suzanne Easton (1922-)
--Answer Me That. Wood, Owen, illus. LC 69-12433. 23cm. 32p. (gr. k-3). N.D. (ISBN 0-672-50209-7). Bobbs.

Dennis, Wesley (1903-1966)
--A Crow I Know. N.D. E. M. Hale & Co.
--A Crow I Know. LC 57-3922. (Illus.). unpaged. 25cm. 1957. Viking Press.
--Flip. Dennis, Wesley (1903-1966), illus. LC 77-2563. 68p. (ps-1). 1977, c.1941. (ISBN 0-14-050203-3, Puffin). Penguin.
--Flip. Dennis, Wesley (1903-1966), illus. LC 41-2939. 63 p. illus. 25 x 21 cm. (ps-1). 1941. (ISBN 0-670-31876-0). The Viking Press.
--Flip and the Cows. Dennis, Wesley (1903-1966), illus. LC 42-22827. 63 p. illus. 24 1/2 x 21 cm. 1942. The Viking Press.
--Flip and the Morning. Dennis, Wesley (1903-1966), illus. LC 77-2004. p. cm. (ps-1). 1977, c.1951. (ISBN 0-14-050204-1). Puffin Books.
--Flip and the Morning. Dennis, Wesley (1903-1966), illus. LC 51-13521. unpaged. illus. 25 cm. 1951. Viking Press.
--Holiday. Dennis, Wesley (1903-1966), illus. LC 46-7878. 61 p. illus. 21 1/2 x 26 cm. 1946. The Viking Press.
--The Ice Bird. (Illus.). 32p. (Pub. by Robert Luce). 1981. Devon Pub.
--Palamino and Other Horses. Dennis, Wesley (1903-1966), illus. LC 50-9205. (Illus.). 22cm. 249p. 1950. World Pub. Co.
--Palomino and Other Horses. Dennis, Wesley (1903-1966), illus. LC 56-9266. 226p. illus. 21cm. (World junior library). 1956, c.1950. World Pub. Co.
--Tumble: The Story of a Mustang. Dennis, Wesley (1903-1966), illus. LC 66-9830. (Illus.). 48 p. 25cm. 1966. Hastings House.

Dennison, George Harris (1925-)
--And Then a Harvest Feast. Dennison, George Harris (1925-), illus. (Illus.). (gr. 2-6). 1973. (ISBN 0-394-82631-0). (ISBN 0-394-92631-5). Random.

Dennison, M. A., Mrs.
--The Child Angel. N.D Henry Hoyt.

Denny, J. K. H.
--The Clever Miss Follett. (Illus.). (Scribner-Blackie Series of books for young people). N.D. Charles Scribner's Sons.

Denny, Melcena Burns, jt. auth. see Isasi, Mirim Erena.

Denny, Norman (1928-), tr. see Ayme, Marcel.

Denny, Norman George see Dale, Norman, pseud.

Denny, Norman George (1901-)
--The Casket and the Sword. Dale, Norman, pseud. Docktor, Irv (1918-), illus. LC 56-10367. (Illus.). 230 p. 22cm. 1956. Harper.
--The Secret Motorcar. Dale, Norman, pseud. Shenton, Edward (1895-), illus. LC 56-5156. (Illus.). 186 p. 22cm. 1957, c.1954. Harper.
Denny, Norman George (1901-) & Filmer-Sankey, Josephine
--The Bayeux Tapestry. 1966. (ISBN 0-689-20076-5). Atheneum Publishers.
Denny, Walter A., as told to.
--Stories from the Old Ones. Daychild, William, illus. (Illus., Orig.). (gr. 4 up). 1979. (ISBN 0-686-27639-6). Rising Wolf.
Dennys, Nicholas Belfield
--The Folk-Lore of China. N.D. Gale Reprint.
Denosova, Alice, tr. see Horak, Jiri (1884-) & Carruth, Jane.
Densel, Mary
--Goldy and Goldy's Friends. 139p. N.D. E. P. Dutton.
--LLoyd Dalan. N.D. E. P. Dutton.
--Tel Tyler at School. 186p. (The Goldy Books). N.D. E. P. Dutton.
--Three Little Tylers. 162p. (The Goldy Books). N.D. E. P. Dutton.
Denslow, Joan, jt. auth. see Allen, Gwen.
Denslow, William Wallace (1856-1915), ed. see Mother Goose.
Denslow, William Wallace (1856-1915)
--Animal Fair. Denslow, William Wallace (1856-1915), illus. (Denslow's Picture Books for Children). 1904. G. W. Dillingham Co.
--Barnyard Circus. New ed. Denslow, William Wallace (1856-1915), illus. (Denslow's Picture Books for Children). 1904. G. W. Dillingham Co.
--Denslow's One Ring Circus: Containing: "One Ring Circus" "Zoo" "A B C Book" "Five Little Pigs" "Tom Thumb" "Jack and the Beanstalk". Denslow, William Wallace (1856-1915), illus. 1903. G. W. Dillingham Co.
--Five Little Pigs. Denslow, William Wallace (1856-1915), illus. (Denslow's Picture Books for Children). 1903. G. W. Dillingham Co.
--House that Jack Built. Denslow, William Wallace (1856-1915), illus. (Denslow's Picture Books For Children). 1903. G. W. Dilllingham Co.
--Humpty Dumpty. (Denslow's Picture Books for Children). N.D. G. W. Dillingham Co.
--Jack and the Beanstalk. Denslow, William Wallace (1856-1915), illus. (Denslow's Picture Books for Children). N.D. G. W. Dillingham Co.
--Little Red Riding Hood. Denslow, William Wallace (1856-1915), illus. (Denslow's Picture Books for Children). 1903. G. W. Dillingham Co.
--Mary Had a Little Lamb. Denslow, William Wallace (1856-1915), illus. (Denslow's Picture Books for Children). 1903. G. W. Dillingham Co.
--Mother Goose A B C Book. Denslow, William Wallace (1856-1915), illus. (Denslow's Picture Books for Children). 1904. G. W. Dillingham Co.
--Old Mother Hubbard. Denslow, William Wallace (1856-1915), illus. (Denslow's Picture Books for Children). 1903. G. W. Dillingham Co.
--Scarecrow and the Tin-Man. New ed. Denslow, William Wallace (1856-1915), illus. (Denslow's Picture Books for Children). 1904. G. W. Dillingham Co.
--Simple Simon. New ed. Denslow, William Wallace (1856-1915), illus. (Denslow's Picture Books for Children). 1904. G. W. Dillingham Co.
--Three Bears. Denslow, William Wallace (1856-1915), illus. (Denslow's Picture Books for Children). 1903. G. W. Dillingham & Co.
--Three Little Kittens. Denslow, William Wallace (1856-1915), illus. (Denslow's Picture Books for Children). 1904. G. W. Dillingham Co.
--Tom Thumb. Denslow, William Wallace (1856-1915), illus. (Denslow's Picture Books for Children). 1903. G. W. Dillingham Co.
--When I Grow Up. Denslow, William Wallace (1856-1915), illus. LC 9-2679. (Illus.). 26 cm. 104p. 1909. Century Co.
--Zoo. Denslow, William Wallace (1856-1915), illus. (Denslow's Picture Books for Children). 1903. G. W. Dillingham Co.
Denslow, William Wallace (1856-1915) & Bragdon, Dudley A
--Billy Bounce. Denslow, William Wallace (1856-1915), illus. LC 6-34681. 3 p. l., 5-279 p. col. front., illus., 14 col. pl. 23 cm. 1906. G. W. Dillingham Co.
Denslow, William Wallace (1856-1915) & West, Paul Clarendon (1871-1918)
--The Pearl and the Pumpkin. West, Paul Clarendon, illus. LC 4-28950. 239, 1 p. col. illus., 16 col. pl. 23 cm. c.1904. G. W. Dillingham Co.
Densmore, Frances
--Dakota & Ojibwe People in Minnesota. Musicant, Ivan, intro. by. LC 77-72282. (Illus.). 55p. (gr. 7-9). 1977. (ISBN 0-87351-111-5). Minn Hist.
Dent, Roma Riggs
--Beetle, the Little Truck. LC 49-2580. 55 p. illus. (part col.) 22 x 29 cm. c.1948. Books from Pents Road.
--Caw-Caw, the Crow. Baerg, Harry John (1909-), illus. LC 53-27784. 45p. illus. 24cm. 1953. Southern Pub. Association.
--Troubles Gets Lost. McMillan, Frank, illus. LC 49-3931. (Illus.). 28 x 28cm. 60p. 1949. Pacific Press Pub. Assoc.
--Troubles Goes Traveling: Story. McMillan, Frank, illus. LC 49-4189. 55 p. illus. (part col.) 22 x 28 cm. 1949. Pacific Press Pub. Assn.
Dentinger, Don
--Helga & the Christmas Star. Moriarty, Ed, Jr., illus. (Illus.). 32p. (Reading Readiness Ser.). (ps-2). 1981. (ISBN 0-941802-03-5). Creat Learning.
--If Animals Could Talk. Lantz, Carrie, illus. (Illus.). 32p. (Orig.). (Reading Readiness Ser.). (ps-2). N.D. (ISBN 0-941802-02-7). Creat Learning.
Denton, Clara Janetta Fort, Mrs.
--The Brownies' Quest: A Day with the Brownies. LC 5-39588. 100 p. illus. 17 x 14 cm. c.1905. A. Flanagan Company.
--Daisy Dells: Rhymes and Verses. Cheney, Garnett, illus. LC 27-224487. 222 p. incl. front., illus. (part col.) 24 cm. (just right book). c.1927. A. Whitman & Co.
--Denton's Best Plays and Dialogues. Dixon, Marjorie Howe, illus. (gr. 7-9). N.D. A. Whitman & Co.
--Denton's Fanciful Tales: Homespun and Cozy Corner Stories. Higgins, Violet Moore & Cochran, J. T., illus. LC 28-65314. 4 p. l., 7-126, 2, 7-125 p. col. front., illus. (part col.) 21 cm. (just right book). c.1927. A. Whitman and Company.
--Homespun Stories: The Wonder Book of Fanciful Tales. Higgins, Violet Moore, illus. LC 24-25204. 126 p. incl. front., illus. 19 cm. (Lettered on cover: Just right book). c.1924. A. Whitman and Company.
--Little People's Dialogues: Designed for Young People of Ten Years. LC 70-98080. 122 p. 21cm. (Granger index reprint series). 1969. Books for Libraries Press.
--Open Air Stories: Real Stories of Birds and Animals. Stone, Vera E., illus. LC 23-16328. 109 p. incl. col. front., col. illus. 19 cm. (Just right book). c.1923. Albert Whitman Company.
--Real Out-of-Door Stories: Real Stories of Birds, Insects and Animals. Stone, Vera E., illus. LC 22-19820. 3 p. l., 106 p. col. front., illus. (part col.) 20 cm. ("Just right book"). c.1922. Albert Whitman Company.
--Robin Redbreast's Home. Seeley, Sue, illus. LC 28-6533. 5 p. l., 7-124 p., 1 l., 7-110 p. front., illus. (part col.) 21 cm. ("A just right book"). c.1927. Albert Whitman Co.
--Runaway Nanny, and Other Delightful Stories. Dash, Joseph Eugene, illus. LC 55-45820. (Illus.). 19cm. 128p. (A Just Right Bk.). 1925. A. Whitman Co.
--Topsy on the Top Floor. (Lad and Lassie Series.). 1915. George W. Jacobs.
--Under the Plantain Leaf: A Day with Three Insects. LC 4-22667. 1 p. l., 5-94 p. illus. 17 cm. 1904. A. Flanagan Company.
Denton, John
--The Color Factory. Edwards, Peter William (1934-), illus. (Illus.). (gr. 1-3). 1976. (ISBN 0-14-050155-X, Puffin). Penguin.
Denton, Margaret G.
--The Man Who Made The Rain Walk. 1984. (ISBN 0-8062-2304-9). Carlton.
Denton, Phyllis
--Tales of the Twins. Denton, Phyllis, illus. LC 58-11767. (Illus.). 21cm. 85p. 1958. F. Warne.
Denver, John, pseud., see Deutschendorf, Henry John Jr..
Denver, John, pseud. (1944-)
--The Children & the Flowers. Deutschendorf, Henry John Jr.. Gullerud, Randi, illus. (Illus.). 24p. 1979. (ISBN 0-914676-28-8, Star & Eleph Bks). Green Tiger Pr.
Denzel, Justin Francis (1917-)
--Black Kettle: King of the Wild Horses. Amundsen, Richard E., illus. LC 73-14786. (Illus.). 48 p. 23cm. (Famous animal stories). (Famous Animal Stories). 1974. (ISBN 0-8116-4854-0). Garrard Pub. Co.
--Hiboy: Young Devil Horse. Savitt, Sam (1917-), illus. LC 80-10578. 48p. (Famous Animal Stories Ser.). (gr. 3). 1980. (ISBN 0-8116-4866-4). Garrard.
--Jumbo, Giant Circus Elephant. Amundsen, Richard E., illus. LC 72-9349. (Illus.). 48 p. 22cm. (Famous animal stories). 1973. (ISBN 0-8116-4850-8). Garrard Pub. Co.
--Sampson, Yankee Stallion. Hutchinson, William Miller (1916-), illus. LC 79-22793. (Illus.). 48 p. 23cm. (Famous animal stories). c.1980. (ISBN 0-8116-4865-6). Garrard Pub. Co.
--Scat, The Movie Cat. Vestal, Herman B., illus. LC 77-23300. (Illus.). 48 p. 23cm. (Famous animal stories). c.1977. (ISBN 0-8116-4861-3). Garrard Pub. Co.
--Snowfoot: White Reindeer of the Arctic. Oughton, Taylor (1925-), illus. LC 75-43634. (Illus.). 48 p. 23cm. (Famous animal stories). c.1976. (ISBN 0-8116-4858-3). Garrard Pub. Co.
--Wild Wing: Great Hunting Eagle. Vestal, Herman B., illus. LC 75-6829. (Illus.). 48 p. 23cm. (Famous animal stories). 1975. (ISBN 0-8116-4856-7). Garrard Pub. Co.
Denzel, Mary
--Goldy and Goldy's Friend. (Illus.). N.D. Publications of E. P. Dutton & Co.
Denzer, Ann Wiseman, pseud., see Wiseman, Ann Sayre.
Denzer, Ann Wiseman, pseud. (1926-)
--Tony's Flower. Wiseman, Ann Sayre. Denzer, Ann Wiseman (1926-), illus. LC 61-1623. (Illus.). (gr. 3-8). 1961. (ISBN 0-8149-0293-6). Vanguard.
De Onis, Harriet, tr. see Marichalar, Antonio.
De Osma, Lupe, illus.
--The Witches' Ride and Other Tales from Costa Rica. De Osma, Lupe, tr. LC 57-9110. 190p. illus. 21cm. (Morrow junior books). 1957. W. Morrow.
De Palencia, Isabel see Palencia, Isabel De.
De Paola, Thomas Anthony see De Paola, Tomie, pseud.
De Paola, Tomie, pseud., see De Paola, Thomas Anthony.
De Paola, Tomie, jt. auth. see Hall, Malcolm.
De Paola, Tomie, jt. auth. see Johnston, Susan T.
De Paola, Tomie, pseud. (1934-), tr. see Gauch, Patricia Lee.
De Paola, Tomie de see Hardendorff, Jeanne B.
De Paola, Tomie, pseud. (1934-)
--Andy (That's My Name). De Paola, Thomas Anthony. De Paola, Tomie, pseud. (1934-), illus. De Paola, Thomas Anthony. LC 73-4583. (Illus.). 32 p. 1973. (ISBN 0-13-036749-4). Prentice-Hall.
--Big Anthony & the Magic Ring. De Paola, Thomas Anthony. LC 78-23631. (Illus.). (gr. k-3). 1979. (ISBN 0-15-611907-2, VoyB). HarBraceJ.
--Big Anthony and the Magic Ring. De Paola, Thomas Anthony. De Paola, Tomie, pseud. (1934-), illus. De Paola, Thomas Anthony. LC 78-23631. (Illus.). 32 p. 29cm. 32p. (ps-3). c.1979. (ISBN 0-15-207124-5). Harcourt Brace Jovanovich. **Award: (ALA).**
--Bill and Pete. De Paola, Thomas Anthony. De Paola, Tomie, pseud. (1934-), illus. De Paola, Thomas Anthony. LC 78-5330. (Illus.). 32 p. c.1978. (ISBN 0-399-20646-9). Putnam.
--Charlie Needs a Cloak. De Paola, Thomas Anthony. LC 73-16365. (Illus.). 32 p. 23cm. 1974, c.1973. (ISBN 0-13-128355-3). Prentice-Hall.
--Charlie Needs a Cloak. De Paola, Thomas Anthony. De Paola, Tomie, pseud. (1934-), illus. De Paola, Thomas Anthony. (Illus.). 32p. (ps-2). 1982. (ISBN 0-13-128280-8, Pub. by Treehouse). P-H.
--The Clown of God. De Paola, Thomas Anthony. De Paola, Tomie, pseud. (1934-), illus. De Paola, Thomas Anthony. LC 78-3845. (Illus.). (gr. k up). 1978. (ISBN 0-15-219175-5, HJ). (ISBN 0-15-618192-4). HarBraceJ. **Award: (ALA).**
--The Clown of God. De Paola, Thomas Anthony. De Paola, Tomie, pseud. (1934-), illus. De Paola, Thomas Anthony. (Illus.). (gr. 2-3). N.D. (ISBN 0-590-30068-7, Schol Pap). Scholastic Inc.
--The Comic Adventures of Old Mother Hubbard & Her Dog. DePaola, Thomas Anthony. LC 80-19270. (Illus.). 32p. (ps-3). 1981. (ISBN 0-15-219541-6, HJ). (ISBN 0-15-219542-4). HarBraceJ.
--Country Farm. De Paola, Thomas Anthony. DePaola, Tomie, pseud. (1934-), illus. De Paola, Thomas Anthony. (Illus.). 9p. (Magic Windows Ser.). 1984. (ISBN 0-399-21056-3, Philomel). Putnam Pub Group.
--Fight the Night. De Paola, Thomas Anthony. De Paola, Tomie, pseud. (1934-), illus. De Paola, Thomas Anthony. LC 68-24424. (Illus.). 33 p. 26cm. 1968. Lippincott.
--Fin M'Coul: The Giant of Knockmany Hill. De Paola, Thomas Anthony. De Paola, Tomie, pseud. (1934-), illus. De Paola, Thomas Anthony. LC 80-22854. (Illus.). 32 p. 29cm. c.1981. (ISBN 0-8234-0384-X). (ISBN 0-8234-0385-8). Holiday House. **Award: (ALA).**
--The First Christmas. De Paola, Thomas Anthony. De Paola, Tomie, pseud. (1934-), illus. De Paola, Thomas Anthony. (Illus.). 6p. (A Festive Pop-Up Bk.). 1984. (ISBN 0-399-21070-9, Putnam). Putnam Pub Group.
--Flicks. De Paola, Thomas Anthony. LC 79-87514. (Illus.). 32 p. c.1979. (ISBN 0-15-228487-7). Harcourt Brace Jovanovich.
--Four Stories for Four Seasons. De Paola, Thomas Anthony. De Paola, Tomie, pseud. (1934-), illus. De Paola, Thomas Anthony. LC 76-8837. (Illus.). 24cm. 48p. (ps-3). 1977. (ISBN 0-13-330175-3, Pub. by Treehouse). (ISBN 0-13-330100-1). P-H.
--The Friendly Beasts: An Old English Christmas Carol. De Paola, Thomas Anthony. De Paola, Tomie, pseud. (1934-), illus. De Paola, Thomas Anthony. LC 80-15391. (Illus.). 32p. 1981. (ISBN 0-399-20739-2). (ISBN 0-399-20777-5). Putnam Pub Group. **Award: (ALA).**
--Giorgio's Village. De Paola, Thomas Anthony. De Paola, Tomie, pseud. (1934-), illus. De Paola, Thomas Anthony. LC 81-10699. (Illus.). 1 v. c.1982. (ISBN 0-399-20854-2). Putnam. **Award: (ALA).**
--Helga's Dowry: A Love story. De Paola, Thomas Anthony. De Paola, Tomie, pseud. (1934-), illus. De Paola, Thomas Anthony. LC 76-54953. (Illus.). 32p. (ps-3). 1977. (ISBN 0-15-233702-4, VoyB). (ISBN 0-15-233701-6). (ISBN 0-15-640010-3). HarBraceJ.
--The Hunter and the Animals: A Wordless Picture Book. De Paola, Thomas Anthony. LC 81-2875. p. cm. c.1981. (ISBN 0-8234-0397-1). (ISBN 0-8234-0428-5). Holiday House.
--Joe and the Snow. De Paola, Thomas Anthony. De Paola, Tomie, pseud. De Paola, Thomas Anthony. LC 68-30738. (Illus.). 32 p. 23cm. 1968. Hawthorn Books.
--The Journey of the Kiss. De Paola, Thomas Anthony. LC 78-107640. (Illus.). 39 p. 1970. Hawthorn Books.
--The Kids' Cat Book. De Paola, Thomas Anthony. De Paola, Tomie, pseud. (1934-), illus. De Paola, Thomas Anthony. LC 79-2090. (Illus.). 32p. (gr. k-3). 1979. (ISBN 0-8234-0365-3). Holiday.
--The Knight and the Dragon. De Paola, Thomas Anthony. De Paola, Tomie, pseud. (1934-), illus. De Paola, Thomas Anthony. LC 79-18131. (Illus.). 29 p. (gr. 1-3). c.1980. (ISBN 0-399-20707-4). (ISBN 0-399-20708-2). Putnam.
--The Lady of Gaudalupe. De Paola, Thomas Anthony. De Paola, Tomie, pseud. (1934-), illus. De Paola, Thomas Anthony. 1980. Holiday.
--Marianna May and Nursey. De Paola, Thomas Anthony. De Paola, Tomie, pseud. (1934-), illus. De Paola, Thomas Anthony. LC 82-9364. (Illus.). 32p. 1983. (ISBN 0-8234-0473-0). (ISBN 0-8234-0473-0). Holiday House.
--Michael Bird-Boy. De Paola, Thomas Anthony. De Paola, Tomie, pseud. (1934-), illus. De Paola, Thomas Anthony. LC 74-23563. (Illus.). 32 p. 1975. (ISBN 0-13-580803-0). Prentice-Hall.
--The Monsters' Ball. De Paola, Thomas Anthony. De Paola, Tomie, pseud. (1934-), illus. De Paola, Thomas Anthony. LC 73-98184. (Illus.). 31 p. 23cm. 1970. Hawthorn Books.
--Mother Goose Story Streamers. De Paola, Thomas Anthony. De Paola, Tomie, pseud. (1934-), illus. De Paola, Thomas Anthony. (Illus.). 28p. (ps-3). 1984. (ISBN 0-399-21004-0, Putnam). Putnam Pub Group.
--The Mysterious Giant of Barletta. De Paola, Thomas Anthony. DePaola, Tomie, pseud. (1934-), illus. De Paola, Thomas Anthony. LC 83-18445. (Illus.). 32p. (ps-3). 1984. (ISBN 0-15-256347-4, HJ). HarBraceJ.
--Nana Upstairs and Nana Downstairs. De Paola, Thomas Anthony. LC 77-26698. p. cm. (gr. 1-3). 1978, c.1973. (ISBN 0-14-050290-4, Puffin Bks.). Penguin.
--Nana Upstairs and Nana Downstairs. De Paola, Thomas Anthony. De Paola, Tomie, pseud. (1934-), illus. De Paola, Thomas Anthony. 1973. Penguin.
--Nana Upstairs and Nana Downstairs. De Paola, Thomas Anthony. De Paola, Tomie, pseud. (1934-), illus. De Paola, Thomas Anthony. LC 72-77965. (Illus.). 32 p. 20cm. 1973. (ISBN 0-399-20300-1). (ISBN 0-399-20300-1). Putnam.
--Noah & the Ark. De Paola, Thomas Anthony. De Paola, Tomie, pseud. (1934-), illus. De Paola, Thomas Anthony. (Illus.). 32p. (Orig.). (ps-4). 1983. (ISBN 0-86683-699-3). (ISBN 0-86683-819-8). Winston Pr.
--Now One Foot, Now the Other. De Paola, Thomas Anthony. De Paola, Tomie, pseud. (1934-), illus. De Paola, Thomas Anthony. LC 80-22239. (Illus.). 32 p. 20cm. c.1981. (ISBN 0-399-20774-0). (ISBN 0-399-20775-9). Putnam.

--The Three Straw Men. LC 72-76504. 143 p. 21cm. 1970. (ISBN 0-87686-008-0). Candlelight Press.
--The Watcher on the Heights. LC 66-8329. v. 152p. 22cm. 1966. Duell.
--Wilbur the Trusting Whippoorwill. N.D. Arkham House Publishers.
Derlyne, Gibson (1936-)
--How Fast Can it Go?. Carlin, Dag, illus. LC 67-20696. (Illus.). 19 x 24cm. 1967. Reilly & Lee.
Derman, Martha
--And Philippa Makes Four. LC 83-1631. 150 p. 22cm. c.1983. (ISBN 0-590-07905-0). (ISBN 0-590-07905-0). Four Winds Press.
--And Philippa Makes Four. LC 85-1446. p. cm. 1985. (ISBN 0-02-728670-3). Four Winds Press.
--And Philippa Makes Four. 1983. Scholastic.
--The Friendstone. LC 80-24711. 151 p. 22cm. c.1981. (ISBN 0-8037-2472-1). (ISBN 0-8037-2480-2). Dial Press.
Derman, Sarah Audrey (1915-)
--Big Top. N.D. Benefic Press.
--Monkey Island. N.D. Benefic Press.
--Plush. Gschwind, William, illus. LC 52-3629. (Illus.). 30cm. (gr. 1-3). 1952. (ISBN 0-695-47140-6). Follett.
--Poker Dog. (Easy To Read Books). N.D. Benefic Press.
--Pony Ring. (Easy To Read Books). N.D. Benefic Press.
--Pretty Bird. N.D. Benefic Press.
--The Snowman Who Wanted to Stay. Couri, Dorcas (1915-), illus. LC 48-428810. 29 p. col. illus. 29 cm. (Fuzzy Wuzzy book). c.1948. Whitman Pub. Co.
--Surprise Egg. (Easy to Read Books). N.D. Benefic Press.
Der Meer, Wybe J. van see Van Der Meer, Wybe J.
Dermer, Irwin
--Witch's Hat. Meeuwissen, Tony, illus. (Illus.). 1980. (ISBN 0-233-97800-3). Andre Deutsch.
Dermody, Daniel Elmer see Uncle Dan, pseud.
Dermody, Daniel Elmer
--The Goose Girls of the San Josquin: A Dan D Book for Girls. Uncle Dan, pseud. LC 21-9004. 1 p. l., 45p. 21cm. c.1921. Hurst's Print Shop.
DeRoin, Nancy (1934-)
--Jataka Tales. Lanyon, Ellen, illus. LC 74-20981. (Illus.). x, 82 p. 23cm. 1975. (ISBN 0-395-20281-7). Houghton Mifflin.
De Roo, Anne Louise (1931-)
--Cinnamon and Nutmeg. LC 73-19939. 191 p. 21cm. 1974. (ISBN 0-8407-6372-7). T. Nelson.
--Scrub Fire. LC 80-12267. p. cm. 1980. (ISBN 0-689-30775-6). Atheneum.
Derosa, Peter Clement (1932-)
--The Bee & the Rose. Hollander, Nicole, illus. LC 75-7543. (Illus.). 80p. (gr. 4-7). 1975. (ISBN 0-913592-54-4). Argus Comm.
De Roussan, Jacques (1929-)
--If I Came from Mars: Si J'etais Martien. LC 76-58700. (Illus.). 28 p. (Astronomy for Children). (gr. k-4). c.1977. (ISBN 0-912766-53-0). Tundra Books of Northern New York.
Derrick, Chris
--A Stormy Passage in a Boy's Life. N.D. Thomas Whittaker.
Derrig, Leslie A. & Westdyk, Roxanne H.
--Mommy in the Sky. Murphy, Anne, illus. LC 83-73248. (Illus.). 32p. (Orig.). (Working Mommy Ser.: Vol. 2). (gr. k-5). 1983. (ISBN 0-915479-68-0). Cottage Pub Co.
Derrydale, Reginald
--Beasts. Reed, Edward Tennyson (1860-1933), illus. LC 77-371973. (Illus.). 46 p. c.1977. (ISBN 0-8055-1222-5). (ISBN 0-8055-0316-1). Hart Pub. Co.
Derwent, Lavinia
--Macpherson. 1st ed. Clark, Dorothy (1897-), illus. LC 63-116577. 124p. illus. 22cm. c.1961. Bobbs-Merrill.
--Song of Sula. Seward, Prudence, illus. LC 76-370826. (Illus.). 125 p. 21cm. 1976. (ISBN 0-575-02092-X). Gollancz.
Desages, P., tr. see Verne, Jules.
De Saint-Pierre, Jacques Henri Bernardin (1737-1814)
--Paul and Virginia. Anderson, Alexander, illus. Williams, Helen Maria (1762-1827), tr. from Fr. LC 36-29328. v, 7-120 p. 11 1/2 cm. 1850. J. A. & U. P. James.
--Paul & Virginia. Anderson, Alexander (1775-1870), illus. Williams, Helen Maria (1762-1827), tr. from Fr. LC 21-17605. 1 p. l., v, 7-154 p. illus., plates. 17 1/2 cm. 1805. Published by Evert Duyckinck, No. Pearl-Street. L. Nichols, Printer.
--Paul and Virginia. Westall, Richard (1765-1836), illus. Williams, Helen Maria (1762-1827), tr. from Fr. LC 29-5764. iv, 5-96 p. front., plates. 15 x 13 cm. 1841. E. Walker.
--Paul and Virginia. Westall, Richard (1765-1836), illus. Williams, Helen Maria (1762-1827), tr. from Fr. LC 21-305317. iv, 5-96 p. front., plates. 15 cm. 1834. Lilly, Wait & Co.
De Saint Euxpery, Antoine Jean Baptiste Marie Roger (1900-1944)
--The Little Prince. Woods, Katherine (1886-), tr. LC 43-51110. 91, 3 p. incl. col. front., illus. (part col.) 23 x 18 1/2 cm. 1943. Reynal & Hitchcock.
De Saint-Pierre, Jaques Henri Barnardin, jt. auth. see Goldsmith, Oliver.
De Santis, George, illus.
--Mother Goose. (Illus.). color ils. 12p. (Action Bks). (ps-k). 1971. Platt.
DeSantis, Josephine
--Grubby: The Absent Minded Gopher. (Illus.). 64p. (ps-6). 1981. (ISBN 0-89962-226-7). Todd & Honeywell.
De Santis, Zerlina
--Castle Days & Gallant Knights. (ps-3). N.D. Dghtrs St Paul.
--A Child's Story of Ancient Days. (Illus.). (ps-3). N.D. Dghtrs St Paul.
--A Child's Story of the Baby Who Changed the World. Sue, illus. (Illus.). 45 p. 22cm. 1968. St. Paul Editions.
De Santo, Charles
--Dear Tim. LC 81-23744. 200p. (Orig.). 1982. (ISBN 0-8361-1991-6). Herald Pr.
De Saussure, Eric (1925-)
--The Secret of Hell's Kitchen: A Parable for Young People. De Saurrure, Eric (1925-), illus. LC 80-15583. (Illus.). 109 p. 24cm. 1980. (ISBN 0-8164-0460-7). Seabury Press.
Desbarats, Peter (1933-)
--Gabrielle and Selena. Grossman, Nancy S. (1940-), illus. LC 68-11498. (Illus.). 1 v. (unpaged. 22cm. 32p. 1968. Harcourt, Brace & World.
--Gabrielle and Selena. Grossman, Nancy S. (1940-), illus. LC 73-14661. (Illus.). 32 p. 21cm. (Voyager book, AVB87). 1974, c.1968. (ISBN 0-15-634080-1). Harcourt Brace Jovanovich.
Desbeaux, Emile
--Mattie's Secret. (Illus.). N.D. George Routledge & Sons.
Desbery, Peter, jt. auth. see Miklowitz, Gloria D.
Desch, John Michael
--Midnight Revels. Kraemer, Xavier, illus. LC 39-341614. 4 p. l., 77 p. incl. illus. plates. 24 cm. 1939. Sunset Press.
Des Chesnez, Baroness see Des Chesnez, Elizabeth Lair Martineau.
Des Chesnez, Elizabeth Lair Martineau (1829-)
--Uncle Grandesir's Matches. N.D. E. Claxton.
Des Chesnez, Elizabeth Lair Martineau (1829-)
--Lady Green Satin. (Roundabout Lilbrary). N.D. John C. Winston Co.
--Lady Green Satin and Her Maid Rosette. Alta ed. N.D. Porter & Coates.
--Lady Green Satin and Her Maid Rosette: Or, The History of Jean Paul and His Little White Mice. (Illus.). (Roundabout Lib.). N.D. Henry T. Coates & Co.
--Uncle Grandesire's Matches. (Illus.). (New Alta Lib.). N.D. Henry T. Coates & Co.
De Segur, Sophie Rostopchine (1799-1874)
--The Story of a Donkey, 1 of 12 vols. New ed. (Illus.). (Good Time Ser.: No. 7). 1905. Set. Henry Altemus Co.
De Selincourt, Aubrey (1894-1962)
--Odysseus the Wanderer. (Illus.). (gr. 4-7). 1956. (ISBN 0-8382-0604-2). Hale.
--Odysseus the Wanderer. Meredith, Norman, illus. LC 56-6206. 244p. 1956. Criterion Bks. Inc.
Deseret Sunday School Union Board & Primary Assn. General Board, eds.
--Church of Jesus Christ of Latter-Day Saints. LC 46-1434. (Illus.). 22cm. 506p. 1945. Deseret Book Co.
Desmond, Alice Curtis, Mrs. (1897-)
--Barnum Presents:. General Tom Thumb. N.D. Macmillan.
--Cleopatra's Children. LC 79-160859. (Illus.). photos. maps. charts. (gr. 9 up). 1971. Dodd.
--Feathers: The Story of a Rhea. Bronson, Wilfrid Swancourt (1894-), illus. LC 40-32635. 71, 1 p. illus. 22 x 17 cm. 1940. The Macmillan Company.
--For Cross and King. Collins, Kreigh (1908-), illus. LC 41-5699. 5 p. l., 297 p. incl. illus., plates. 21 cm. 1941. Dodd, Mead & Company.
--Jorge's Journey. De Muth, Flora Nash (1888-), illus. LC 42-11248. 22cm. 158p. 1942. Macmillan.
--The Lucky Llama. Bronson, Wilfrid Swancourt (1894-), illus. LC 39-25706. 62, 2 p. incl. front., illus. 22 cm. 1939. The Macmillan Company.
--The Sea Cats. Bronson, Wilfrid Swancourt (1894-), illus. LC 44-910020. v, 7-216 p. illus. 21 cm. 1944. The Macmillan Company.
--Soldier of the Sun: A Story of Peru in the Days of the Incas. Watson, Ernest W., illus. LC 39-21148. 6 p. l., 243 p. illus. 21 cm. 1939. Dodd, Mead and Company.
--The Talking Tree. Ray, Ralph (1920-1952), illus. LC 49-10434. vii, 177 p. illus. 22 cm. 1949. Macmillan Co.
--Teddy Koala, Mascot of the Marines. Savitt, Sam (1917-), illus. LC 62-9084. (Illus.). 24cm. 92p. 1962. Dodd, Mead.
--Titus of Rome. LC 75-38353. (Illus.). (gr. 7). 1976. Dodd.
Desmond, Alice Curtis, Mrs. (1897-) & Malkus, Alida Wright Sims, Mrs. (1899-)
--Boys of the Andes. Dobias, Frank (1902-), illus. LC 41-7510. 56 p. incl. col. front., illus. (part col.) 22 cm. (On cover: New World neighbors). c.1941. D. C. Heath and Company.
Desmurger, Marguerite, adapted by.
--Stories from Greek History. Pecnard, Jacques, illus. Whelpton, Barbara, tr. from Fr. LC 63-24733. (Illus.). 185p. illus. (pt. col.) map. 19cm. (Myths and legends; Holly bk.). 1965, c.1963. World.
Desnos, Robert
--Chantefables. Annen, Charles, illus. Annen, Sharon, tr. from Fr. LC 84-61257. (Illus.). 60p. (gr. 1-6). 1986. (ISBN 0-9613938-0-7). Penstemon Pr.
Desnoyers, Louis Claude Joseph Florence, jt. auth. see Buckland, James.
De Solla, Hilda
--Happy Days. N.D. Vantage Press.
Despain, Goldie Brown
--A Tiny Ant Who Scared a Horned Toad. Petie, Haris, pseud. (1915-), illus. Petty, Roberta. LC 74-90757. (Illus.). 31 p. 24cm. 1970, c.1969. Iantern Press.
De Spain, Pleasant
--Pleasant Journeys: Twenty-two Tales from Around the World, 2 vols. Lyttle, Kirk, illus. LC 79-5359. (Illus., Orig.). (gr. 1-4). 1979. (ISBN 0-916076-36-9). Vol. 1. (ISBN 0-916076-36-9). Vol. 2. (ISBN 0-916076-37-7). Writing.
Despois, Pauline, adapted by.
--Little Table, Get Set. Bourre, Martine, illus. Coen, Fabio, tr. LC 79-19163. (Original Authors: Brothers Grimm). (Illus.). 24p. (Goodnight Bks). (gr. 1). 1980. (ISBN 0-394-84381-9). Knopf.
Despois, Pauline, adapted by see Grimm, Jakob Ludwig Karl.
Dessent, Michael Harold (1942-)
--Baseball Becky. LC 81-18856. 150 p. 23cm. c.1982. (ISBN 0-916392-80-5). Oak Tree Publications.
Dessureau, Dora M.
--The World's Children. N.D. Pageant Press, Inc.
Destang, Francoise, jt. auth. see Paschos, Jacqueline.
D'Esterre
--Gerald and Dolly. 241p. N.D. A. I. Bradley & Co.'s Pub.
De Stolz
--Blanche and Beryl. N.D. George Routledge & Sons.
--The House on Wheels: Or, THe Stolen Child. (Illus.). N.D. Lee Shepard Pub.
Des Voignes, Jules Verne
--The Novelty Circus Company. LC 7-29151. 374 p. front. 4 pl. 21 cm. 1907. G. W. Jacobs & Company.
Dethier, Vincent Gaston (1915-)
--Newberry: The Life and Times of a Maine Clam. Litterer, Marie, illus. LC 81-66267. (Illus.). 85 p. 23cm. c.1981. (ISBN 0-89272-085-9). Down East Books.
Dethise, Jeanne
--Tibs and Her Four Kittens. Marlier, Marcel, illus. LC 68-6075. (Illus.). 28 p. 29cm. 1968. Hart Pub. Co.
--Tibs and Her Four Kittens. Marlier, Marcel, illus. 32p. N.D. (ISBN 0-87460-179-7). (ISBN 0-87460-178-9). Lion Press.
Detmold, Edward J. (1883-), illus.
--The Arabian Nights. Dahl, Curtis, intro. by. N.D. Dodd, Mead & Co.
De Treville, Stan
--Strange Beasts of the African Jumbles. LC 75-127491. (Illus.). 16 l. 31cm. 1970. Nash Pub.
De Trevino, Elizabeth Borton (1904-)
--A Carpet of Flowers. Crane, Alan H. (1901-), illus. LC 55-583873. 88p. illus. 22cm. 1955. Crowell.
--About Bellamy. Robinson, Jessie Berkowitz, illus. LC 40-33933. 5 p. l., 214 p. incl. front., illus. 21 cm. c.1940. Harper & Brothers.
--Beyond the Gates of Hercules: A Story of the Lost Atlantis. LC 75-149227. (An Ariel Bk.). 1975. Farrar, Strauss.
--Beyond the Gates of Hercules: A Tale of the Lost Atlantis. LC 75-149227. viii, 246 p. 21cm. (Ariel book). 1971. (ISBN 0-374-30673-7). Farrar, Straus & Giroux.
--A Carpet of Flowers: Una Alfombra de Flores. Miles, Cyril (1918-), illus. LC 75-17878. 125p. (gr. 4-7). 1975. (ISBN 0-88468-003-7). (ISBN 0-88468-003-7). Ethridge.
--Casilda of the Rising Moon: A Tale of Magic and Faith, of Knights and a Saint in Medieval Spain. LC 67-2939. 186p. 22cm. (An Ariel Bk.). 1967. Farrar, Strauss & Giroux.
--I, Juan De Pareja. LC 65-19330. xii, 180 p. 22cm. 1965. (Bell Books) Farrar, Straus. **Awards: (JNM); (ALA).**
--Nacar: The White Deer. Arno, Enrico (1913-1981), illus. LC 63-20019. 149 p. illus. 22 cm. (Bell book). 1963. (ISBN 0-374-35478-2). Farrar, Straus.
--Our Little Ethiopian Cousin: Children of the Queen of Sheba. LC 35-30569. vii, 1 p., 2 l., 134 p. front. (port.) illus. (map) plates. 19 1/2 cm. (Little Cousin Ser.). c.1935. L. C. Page & Company.
--Our Little Aztec Cousin of Long Ago: Being the Story of Cogotl and How He Won Honor Under His King. Cue, Harold, illus. LC 34-35310. x p., 2 l., 83 p. incl. col. front. plates. 19 1/2 cm. (little cousins of long ago series). c.1934. L. C. Page & Company.
--Pollyanna and the Secret Mission. (The Pollyanna Books). N.D. Grosset & Dunlap.
--Pollyanna in Hollywood. (The Pollyanna Bks.). N.D. Grosset & Dunlap.
--Pollyanna in Hollywood: The Seventh Glad Book. Taylor, H. Weston, illus. (The Pollyanna Bks.). N.D. Page Co.
--Pollyanna'a Castle in Mexico. (The Pollyanna Bks.). N.D. Grosset & Dunlap.
--Pollyanna's Castle in Mexico: The Eighth Glad Book. Cue, Harold, illus. (The Pollyanna Bks.). N.D. Page Co.
--Pollyanna's Door to Happiness. (The Pollyanna Bks.). N.D. Grosset & Dunlap.
--Pollyanna's Door to Happiness: The Ninth Glad bk. Cue, Harold, illus. (The Pollyanna bks.). N.D. L. C. Page.
--Pollyanna's Golden Horseshoe. (The Pollyanna Bks.). N.D. Grosset & Dunlap.
--Pollyanna's Golden Horseshoe: The/Tenth Glad Book. Tyng, Griswold, illus. (The Pollyanna Bks.). N.D. Page Co.
--Turi's Poppa. Arno, Enrico (1913-1981), illus. LC 68-29470. (Illus.). 186 p. 22cm. (Bell book). 1968. Farrar, Straus, and Giroux. **Award: (BGH).**
De Troyes, Chrestien (1928-)
--The Joy of the Court. Hieatt, Constance Bartlett (1922-), retold by. Baynes, Pauline Diana (1922-), illus. LC 73-101931. (Illus.). 71 p. 25cm. 1971. (ISBN 0-690-46572-6). Crowell.
De Troyes, Chrestien (1928-) & Von Eschenbach, Wolfram
--The Castle of Ladies. Hieatt, Constance Barlett, retold by. Laliberte, Norman (1925-), illus. LC 75-187945. (Illus.). x, 72 p. 25cm. 1973. (ISBN 0-690-18064-0). Crowell.
Dettinger, Alma
--Crazy Quilt Circus. Prouty, Esther, illus. LC 33-309908. 3 p. l., 52 p. incl. plates. 26 cm. c.1933. R. H. Cunningham.
Detzer, Clarice Nessley
--The Island Mail. Caswell, Edward C., illus. LC 26-21116. 198 p. front., plates. 19 cm. c.1926. Harcourt, Brace and Company.
Detzer, Karl William (1891-)
--Pirate of the Pine Lands: Being the Adventures of Young Tom Lansing. Anderson, Harold & Anderson, Allen, illus. LC 29-17730. 20cm. 302p. c.1929. The Bobbs-Merrill Company.
Deucher, Sybil
--Curtain Calls for Haydn and Bach. Greenwalt, Mary, illus. N.D. E. P. Dutton & Co.
--Curtain Calls for Mozart. Greenwalt, Mary, illus. N.D. E. P. Dutton & Co.
--Curtain Calls for Schubert. Greenwalt, Mary, illus. N.D. E. P. Dutton & Co.
--Edvard Grieg, Boy of the Northland. Greenwalt, Mary, illus. LC 46-6784. 165 p. illus. (incl. music) 24 cm. 1946. E. P. Dutton & Company, Inc.
--The Young Brahms. Godwin, Edward Fell (1912-) & Godwin, Stephani, illus. LC 49-10486. 152 p. illus. 25 cm. 1949. E. P. Dutton.
Deucher, Sybil, jt. auth. see Wheeler, Opal.

DeWitt, Cornelius Hugh (1905-)
--The Little Golden ABC. LC 51-1777. 28 p. col. illus. 21 cm. (Little golden library, 101). 1951. Simon and Schuster.

De Witt, Evelyn F
--Old Caboose. Kirn, Ann Minette (1910-), illus. LC 45-99844. 31, p. col. illus. 30 x 23 cm. 1945. Glade House, Inc.

DeWitt, James, pseud., see Lewis, Mildred D..

DeWitt, James, pseud. (1912-)
--In Pursuit of the Spanish Galleon. Lewis, Mildred D.. LC 61-12803. (Illus.). 189 p. 22cm. 1961. Criterion Books.
--In Pursuit Of The Spanish Galleon. Lewis, Mildred D.. 1961. (ISBN 0-8382-0364-7, Cadmus Books). E. M. Hale and Company.

DeWitt, Jim
--Jammy Donuts a Season After. LC 83-90481. (Illus.). 64p. (Orig.). (Poetry for Schools Ser.). (gr. 4-12). 1984. (ISBN 0-915199-04-1). Pen-Dec.

De Witt, Johanna
--The Littlest Reindeer. Erickson, Phoebe (1907-), illus. LC 46-178884. 28 p. col. illus. 23 1/2 cm. 1946. Childrens Press, Inc.

De Witt, Josephine (1907-)
--Cowboy Ken. DeWitt, Josephinee (1907-), illus. LC 43-11854. 40 p. illus. 22 1/2 x 27 1/2 cm. 1943. Oxford University Press.
--Felicia: The Curious Cow. DeWitt, Josephine (1907-), illus. LC 40-32217. 56 p. illus. 24 x 31 cm. 1940. T. Nelson and Sons.
--The Fisherman and His Cat. DeWitt, Josephine (1907-), illus. LC 37-14278. (Illus.). 21 x 23cm. 43p. 1937. T. Nelson and Sons.
--Michael Sebastian McKinley Smith. De Witt, Josephine, illus. LC 42-2894. 23cm. 46p. 1942. Thomas Nelson & Co.
--The Milkman's Baby. DeWitt, Josephine (1907-), illus. LC 38-17084. (Illus.). 22 x 19cm. 47p. 1938. T. Nelson and Sons.
--The Whale and the Ferryboat. DeWitt, Josephine (1907-), illus. LC 39-31691. (Illus.). 31cm. 46p. 1939. T. Nelson and Sons.

De Witt, Samuel Aaron (1891-)
--The Shoemaker of the Stars, and Other Poems. Fulda, Elizabeth, illus. LC 41-3679. 47p. incl. front. illus. 27 x 27 1/2cm. 1941, c.1940. Parnassus Press.

De Wohl, Louis
--St. Helena & the True Cross. Krigstein, Bernard (1919-), illus. LC 58-12490. (Illus.). 22cm. 190p. (Vision books, 27). (gr. 4-10). 1958. (ISBN 0-374-80228-9, Vision). FS&G.

De Wolfe, Morgan, pseud., see Williamson, Thames Ross.

Dewrance, Margaret
--Charters. Smith, Audrey, illus. (Illus.). (gr. 5-9). 1965. (ISBN 0-685-21004-9). Verry.
--Muthu. Grice, David, illus. LC 68-16327. 160p. illus. 21cm. (gr. 5up). c.1967. Roy.

Dews, Robert P. see Swed, Trebor, pseud.

Dews, Robert P. (1915-)
--Whichaway?. Swed, Trebor, pseud. LC 78-100644. iv, 153 p. 23cm. 1977. Rebel Books.

Dexter, Catherine
--Gertie's Green Thumb. Eagle, Ellen, illus. LC 82-21664. p. cm. c.1983. (ISBN 0-02-730200-8). Macmillan.
--The Oracle Doll. LC 85-42803. p. cm. c.1985. (ISBN 0-02-709810-9). Four Winds Press.

Dexter, Charles O., jt. auth. see Dykes, Jimmie.

Dexter, Patricia Egan
--Arrow in the Wind. LC 78-1714. 160 p. 21cm. c.1978. (ISBN 0-8407-6588-6). T. Nelson.
--The Boy Who Snuck in. Counts, Kathy, illus. LC 77-29126. (Illus.). 32 p. (Apple books). c.1978. (ISBN 0-570-07902-0). Concordia Pub. House.
--The Emancipation of Joe Tepper. LC 76-26594. p. cm. c.1976. (ISBN 0-8407-6519-3). T. Nelson.

Dey, Denny, jt. auth. see Grim, Gary.

Deyneka, Anita (1943-)
--Alexi and the Mountain Treasure. Taylor, Larry, illus. LC 78-72835. (Illus.). 111 p. 18cm. (Chariot books). c.1979. (ISBN 0-89191-062-X). D. C. Cook Pub. Co.
--Alexi's Secret Mission. Fleishman, Seymour (1918-), illus. LC 74-29466. (Illus.). 126 p. 18cm. (Orig.). (gr. 3-7). c.1975. (ISBN 0-912692-58-8). D. C. Cook Pub. Co.
--Fire!. LC 74-17731. (Illus.). 128p. (gr. 4-6). N.D. (ISBN 0-912692-49-9). Cook.
--Tanya and the Border Guard. LC 73-86825. (Illus.). 94 p. 18cm. 1973. (ISBN 0-912692-23-5). D. C. Cook Pub. Co.

D'Ham, Claude, illus.
--On the Farm. (Illus., Orig.). (Moments Ser.). 1975. (ISBN 0-85953-036-1, Pub. by Child's Play England). Playspaces.

Dhotre, Damoo & Taplinger, Richard
--Wild Animal Man. 1961. Little, Brown and Company.

Diamard, Lucy
--Story of Daniel. (Ladybird Series). 1958. Christian Literature Crusade.

Diamond, Donna (1950-), retold by see Grimm, Jakob Ludwig Karl (1785-1863) & Grimm, Wilhelm Karl.

Diamond, Donna (1950-), retold by.
--The Pied Piper of Hamelin. Diamond, Donna (1950-), illus. LC 80-12027. (Illus.). 31 p. 26cm. c.1981. (ISBN 0-8234-0415-3). Holiday House.
--Rumpelstiltskin. Diamond, Donna (1950-), illus. LC 83-90. (Original Authors:Jakob Ludwig Karl Grimm (1785-1863) & Wilhelm Karl Grimm (1786-1859)). (Illus.). 32p. (gr. k-3). 1983. (ISBN 0-8234-0488-9). Holiday.
--The Seven Ravens. Diamond, Donna (1950-), illus. LC 77-14252. (Illus.). (gr. k-3). 1979. (ISBN 0-670-63557-X). Viking Pr.
--Swan Lake. Diamond, Donna (1950-), illus. LC 79-11179. p. cm. c.1979. (ISBN 0-8234-0357-2). Holiday House.

Diamond, Lucy
--Moses Prince & Shepherd. (Illus.). (Ladybird Series). N.D. Christian Lit.
--Naaman and the Little Maid. (Ladybird Series). N.D. Christian Literature Crusade.
--Shepherd Boy of Bethlehem. (Illus.). (Ladybird Series). N.D. Christian Lit.
--Story of Joseph. (Ladybird Series). 1954. Christian Literature Crusade.
--Two stories Jesus Told. (Ladybird Series). 1959. Christian Literature Crudade.
--When He Was Just a Little Child. Grant, Constance, illus. LC 31-8615. 62 p. col. front., illus. 20 cm. 1930. Oxford University Press.

Diamond, Samson R., jt. auth. see Welcher, Rosalind.

Dian, Twila
--A Color & Story Album for Horse Lovers. Dian, Twila, illus. (Illus.). 32p. (Orig.). (gr. 3-8). 1982. (ISBN 0-89844-083-1). Troubador Pr.

Dias, Earl Joseph (1916-)
--Melodramas and Farces for Young Actors. LC 56-11516. 263p. 21cm. 1956. Plays, Inc.
--New Comedies for Teen-Agers: A Collection of One-Act, Royalty-Free Comedies, Farces, and Melodramas. LC 70-20912. 322 p. 21cm. 1970. (ISBN 0-8238-0012-1). Plays Inc.

Diaz, Abby Morton, Mrs. (1821-1904)
--Brave Little Goose Girl, 1 of 6 vols. (Illus.). (Story Tree Ser.). N.D. Set. Lothrop Publishing Co.
--The Cat's Arabian Nights. N.D. Lothrop,Lee & Shepard.
--Chronicles of the Stimpcett Family and Others. Sweeney, Morgan J., illus. Boz, pseud. LC 20-23142. 2 p. l., 9-256 p. incl. front., plates. 22 cm. 1882. D. Lothrop and Company.
--Crooked Pond School. (Hopeful Enterprise Library). N.D. Scribner, Welford & Armstrong.
--The Ellson Children, 1 of 6 vols. (Illus.). (Story Tree Ser.). N.D. Set. Lothrop Publishing Co.
--Flatiron and Red Cloak. (Illus.). (Crowell's Child Life Series.). 1915. T Y Crowell.
--The Flatiron and the Red Cloak. (Illus.). (Old Times At X-roads). 1901. Thomas Y. Crowell & Co.
--Jamie & Joe, 1 of 6 vols. x ed. (Story Tree Ser.). N.D. Set. Lothrop Publishing Co.
--The Jimmyjohns. (Illus.). N.D. D. Lothrop Co.
--The Jimmyjohns and Other Stories. LC 19-11347. 262 p. incl. front., illus., plates. 19 cm. 1878. J. R. Osgood and Company.
--The Jimmyjohns & Other Stories. (Illus.). N.D. Lothrop Publishing Co.
--The King's Lily and Rosebud. (Illus.). N.D. James R Osgood and Company.
--Lucy Maria. (Illus.). N.D. D. Lothrop & Co.
--Lucy Maria. 1873. James R. Osgood.
--Mercy Jane, 1 of 6 vols. (Illus.). (Story Tree Ser.). N.D. Set. Lothrop Publishing Co.
--Polly Cologne. 192 p. incl. front., illus., plates 18 cm. 1881. D. Lothrop & Company.
--Polly Cologne Series: Containing: "Polly Cologne" "The Jimmyjohns" "A Story Book for Children", 3 vols. N.D. D. Lothrop Co.
--Simple Traveller: Little Stories for Little Folks. LC 42-482853. (Illus.). 93 p. front., illus. 18 1/2 cm. c.1880. D. Lothrop and Company.
--A Story Book For Children. (Illus.). N.D. D. Lothrop & Co.
--A Story-Book for the Children. LC 19-11346. (Illus.). viii p., 1 l., 11-263 p. incl. front., illus. 19 cm. 1875. J. R. Osgood and Company.
--A Story-Book for the Young Folks. N.D. James R. Osgood.
--The Story of Polly Cologne. LC 4-16822. (Illus.). 18cm. 192p. 1881. Lothrop.
--Story Three Series: Containing: "Mercy Jane" "Jamie and Joe" "Tab and Her Kittens" "Brave Little Goose Girl" "The Ellson Children" "The Procession", 6 vols. (Illus.). N.D. D. Lothrop Co.
--Those People from Skyton and Nine Other Stories. LC 7-20864. (Illus.). 5 p. l., 9-107 p. incl. illus., 10 pl. front. 18 cm. c.1906. S. E. Cassino & Son.
--Vacation Days, 4 vols. (Illus.). N.D. D Lothrop.
--William Henry and His Friends. LC 21-12973. 1 p. l., 265 p. front., illus. 18 cm. 1872. J. R. Osgood and Company.
--William Henry and His Friends. LC 99-326010. 1 p. l., 265 p. front., illus. 19 cm. c.1899. Lothrop Publishing Company.
--The William Henry Letters. LC 20-23169. 1 p. l., 257 p. front., illus. 18 cm. 1870. Fields, Osgood, & Co.
--The William Henry Letters. 1 p. l., 257 p. front., illus. 19 cm. c.1899. Lothrop Publishing Company.
--The William Henry Letters. Moore, Annie Carroll (1871-1961), ed. LC 30-23904. 366 p. incl. front., illus. 21 cm. c.1930. Lothrop, Lee & Shepard Co.

Diaz, Abby Morton, Mrs. (1821-1904) & Mahony, Bertha E.
--Polly Cologne. Sweeney, Morgan J., illus. Boz, pseud. LC 30-24335. 215 p. incl. illus., plates. 21 cm. 1930. Lothrop, Lee & Shepard Co.

Di Certo, Joseph John (1933-)
--Looking into T. V. (Illus.). 96p. (gr. 4-6). 1983. (ISBN 0-671-45948-1). Messner.
--The Wall People: In Search of a Home. Marvin, Frederic, illus. LC 84-21535. (Illus.). 152 p. 22cm. 1985. (ISBN 0-689-31090-0). Atheneum.

Dichev, Stefan (1920-)
--Rali. Dicheva, Liljana, illus. LC 68-15493. (Illus.). 224 p. 22cm. (Window books). 1968, c.1961. Stackpole Books.

Dick, Dancing Ed.
--My Mind Is an Ocean: Poems, Koans, and Prophecies from Kids Seven to Twelve Years. LC 85-11333. p. cm. 1985. (ISBN 0-89370-881-X). Borgo Press.

Dick, Lois H.
--Devil on the Deck. 192p. (Orig.). 1984. (ISBN 0-8007-1201-3). Revell.

Dick, Mary
--The Little Swiss Guard. Jandolo, Rina de Felici, illus. LC 55-4651. 1955. Bruce Publishing Co.

Dick, Opal Wheeler
--Pep, the True Story of a Collie Dog. Baerg, Harry John (1909-), illus. LC 55-421972. 77p. illus. 24cm. 1955. Southern Pub. Association.

Dick, Philip Kindred, jt. auth. see Martin, Les.

Dick, Trella Lamson (1889-1974)
--Bridger's Boy. LC 65-18964. 160 p. 23 cm. 1965. Follett Pub. Co.
--Burro on the Beach. Lewin, Ted (1935-), illus. LC 67-3774. 192 p. 23cm. 1967. Follett Pub. Co.
--The Flag in Hiding. Bolognese, Donald Alan (1934-), illus. 1959. Abelard-Schuman.
--The Island on the Border: A Civil War Story. LC 63-8106. 160 p. 23 cm. 1963. Abelard Schuman.
--Tornado Jones. Stevens, Mary E. (1920-1966), illus. LC 53-12984. (Illus.). 286 p. 23cm. 1953. Wilcox & Follett Co.
--Tornado Jones on Sentinel Mountain. Stevens, Mary E. (1920-1966), illus. LC 55-7494. 224p. illus. 23cm. 1955. Follett Pub. Co.
--Tornado's Big Year. Stevens, Mary E. (1920-1966), illus. LC 56-9870. (Illus.). 224p. illus. 23cm. (gr. 5 up). 1956. (ISBN 0-695-48960-7). Follett Pub. Co.
--Valiant Vanguard. Bolognese, Donald Alan (1934-), illus. LC 60-7503. 191. 21cm. 1960. Abelard-Schuman.

Dickens, Charles John Huffam see Boz, pseud.

Dickens, Charles John Huffam, jt. auth. see Stockton, Frank Richard.

Dickens, Charles John Huffam, jt. auth. see Thackeray, William Makepeace.

Dickens, Charles John Huffam, jt. auth. see Yonge, Charlotte Mary.

Dickens, Charles John Huffam (1812-1870)
--The Adventures of Oliver Twist. 524p. N.D. Oxford University Press.
--The Bagman's Story. 48p. (Classic Short Stories). 1983. (ISBN 0-87191-922-2). Childrens Bk Co.
--Barnaby Rudge. 257p. N.D. D. Appleton & Co.
--Barnaby Rudge. (International Classics). N.D. Dodd Mead & Co.
--Barnaby Rudge. (Everyman's Library). N.D. E. P. Dutton.
--Barnaby Rudge. New ed. N.D. G. W. Carleton & Co.
--Barnaby Rudge. N.D. Oxford University Press.
--Barnaby Rudge. (Nelson Classics). N.D. Thomas Nelson & Sons.
--Barnaby Rudge. Daugherty, James Henry (1889-1974), illus. N.D. Heritage Press.
--Barnaby Rudge. Jackson, Alice F., retold by. (Illus.). (Classics REtold to Children). N.D. George W. Jacobs & Co.
--Bleak House. (Burt's Home Library). N.D. A L Burt Co.
--Bleak House. Ball, Robert (1890-), illus. N.D. Heritage Press.
--Bleak House. Cournos, John, intro. by. 830p. (Great Illustrated Classics). N.D. Dodd, Mead & Co.
--Boots of the Holly Tree Inn. (Harper Junior Classics Ser.). N.D. Harper & Bros.
--Boys from Dickens. N.D. John C. Winston Co.
--Captain Boldheart and Other Stories in A Holiday Romance. Pearse, Susan Beatrice, illus. LC 27-112183. 6 p. l., 5-135 p. incl. plates. col. front., 3 col. pl. 20 cm. (The Macmillan children's classics). 1927. The Macmillan Company.
--Captain Boldheart and The Magic Fishbone: Two Comedies. 1st ed. Knight, Hilary (1926-), illus. McCarthy, Mary, pref. by. LC 64-23074. (Illus.). 30cm. 48p. 1964. Macmillan.
--Charles Dickens' Children Stories, 1 of 15 vols. (Illus.). (Dainty Ser. of Choice Gift Bks: No. 2). 1905. Set. Henry Altemus Co.
--Charles Dickens Ghost Stories. Speirs, John Hastie (1906-), illus. LC 84-5679. p. cm. 1984. (ISBN 0-671-52590-5). Little Simon.
--Charles Dickens' Oliver Twist. Ross, J. K, adapted by. Kaplan, Shirley, illus. LC 68-8912. (Illus.). 64 p. 23cm. 1968. Lancelot Press.
--Charming Stories About Children. (The Standard Series for Young Folks). N.D. John C. Winston.
--Child Characters from Dickens. N.D. E P Dutton.
--The Children's Dickens: Stories Selected from the Various Tales by Charles Dickens. Wright, Gilbert S., illus. (Illus.). N.D. George H. Doran.
--Children's Stories. (Illus.). (Dainty Ser.). N.D. Henry Altemus Co.
--Children's Stories from Dickens. (Illus.). N.D. A. L. Chatterton.
--Children's Stories from Dickens. (Illus.). (Young People's Classics). N.D. R. F. Fenno & Co.
--A Child's Dream of a Star. Barry, Etheldred Breeze (1870-), illus. (Cosy Corner Ser.). N.D. L. C. Page & Co.
--A Child's History of England. Rhys, Ernest, ed. (Illus.). 18cm. 396p. (Everyman's Library). 1907. E. P. Dutton & Co.
--Child's Oliver Twist and David Copperfield. N.D. American Book Company.
--The Chimes. N.D. Thomas Y Crowell Co.
--Christmas Stories. (People's Duodecimo Edition). N.D. T. B. Peterson & Bros.
--Christmas Stories. (Cheap Paper Cover Edition). N.D. T. B. Peterson & Bros.
--Christmas Bks. and Stories, Two. Eliot, George, pseud. (1819-1880) & Hugo, Victor, illus. Evans, Marian. (Illustrated Cabinet Edition). N.D. L. C. Page & Co.
--Christmas Books. 270p. N.D. Funk & Wagnalls.
--Christmas Books. New ed. N.D. G. W. Carleton & Co.
--Christmas Books. N.D. J.B. Lippincott.
--Christmas Books. N.D. Oxford University Press.
--Christmas Books. (Collins New Classics). N.D. Williams Collins Sons.
--Christmas Books. Dixon, Arthur A., illus. (Collins' Illustrated Pocket Classics). N.D. Collins.
--Christmas Books. Eytinge, Sol, illus. (The Illustrated Diamond Edition). N.D. Charles R. Osgood.
--Christmas Books and Stories, 2 Vols. N.D. Houghton Mifflin Co.
--A Christmas Carol. (Embassy Ser.). N.D. Barse & Hopkins.
--A Christmas Carol. (Traymore Ser.). N.D. Barse & Hopkins.
--A Christmas Carol. (Savoy Ser.). N.D. Barse & Hopkins.
--A Christmas Carol. (Blackstone Ser.). N.D. Barse & Hopkins.
--A Christmas Carol. (Commodore Ser.). N.D. Barse & Hopkins.
--A Christmas Carol. (Illus.). (The Young Folks Library). N.D. Caldwell.
--A Christmas Carol. N.D. David McKay Co.
--A Christmas Carol. (Alexandrian Ser.). N.D. Dodge.
--A Christmas Carol. (Remarque Edition of Literary Masterpieces). N.D. Dodge.
--A Christmas Carol. (Brown Book Ser.). N.D. Dodge.
--A Christmas Carol, 25 vols. (Illus.). (The Editha Ser.: No. 17). 1905. Set. H M Caldwell Co.
--A Christmas Carol. (Altemus' Wyncote Ser.). N.D. Henry Altemus Co.
--A Christmas Carol. (Illus.). (Boys' and Girls' Classics). N.D. Henry Altemus Co.
--A Christmas Carol. (Riverside Literature Ser.). N.D. Houghton Mifflin Co.
--A Christmas Carol. N.D. Little Brown & Co.
--A Christmas Carol. (Class Books of English Literature). N.D. Longmans, Green & Co.
--A Christmas Carol. N.D. Longmans Green & Co.
--A Christmas Carol. (Children's Classics). N.D. Macmillan.
--A Christmas Carol. 315p. (The Lake English Classics). N.D. Scott Foresman & Co.
--A Christmas Carol. N.D. The Peter Pauper Press.
--A Christmas Carol. Boog, Carle Michel, illus. (The Cosy Corner Ser.). N.D. L C Page & Co.
--A Christmas Carol. Brock, Charles Edmond (1870-1938), illus. N.D. E. P. Dutton & Co.
--A Christmas Carol. Brock, Henry Matthew (1875-1960), illus. N.D. Dodd, Mead & Co.

--A Christmas Carol. Everett, Ethel F., illus. N.D. Thomas Y. Crowell Co.
--A Christmas Carol. Foreman, Michael (1938-), illus. 1983. Dutton.
--A Christmas Carol. Higginson, Thomas Wentworth (1823-1911), ed. (The Young Folks' Ser). N.D. Lee & Shepard.
--A Christmas Carol. Hildebrandt, Greg (1939-), illus. 1983. Simon and Schuster.
--A Christmas Carol. Hyman, Trina Schart (1939-), illus. 1983. Holiday.
--A Christmas Carol. Keller, Arthur I., illus. N.D. David McKay Co.
--The Christmas Carol. Lee, Julian, pseud. (1902-), adapted by Latham, Jean Lee. 1931. Dramatic Publishing Company.
--A Christmas Carol. Leech, John (1817-1864), illus. N.D. Charles E. Lauriat.
--A Christmas Carol. Michael, Arthur C., illus. N.D. George H. Doran.
--A Christmas Carol. Nichols, Spencer Baird (1875-), illus. N.D. Frederick A. Stokes.
--A Christmas Carol. Rackham, Arthur (1867-1939), illus. 147p. 1952. J. B. Lippincott Co.
--A Christmas Carol. Reed, Philip G. (1908-), illus. 148p. 1940. Holiday House.
--A Christmas Carol. Searle, Ronald William Fordham (1920-), illus. 54p. 1961. The World Publishing Co.
--A Christmas Carol. Shinn, Everett (1876-1953), illus. N.D. Garden City Publishing Co.
--A Christmas Carol. Sweaney, A., ed. (Oxford Progressive English Readers Ser.). (gr. k-6). 1975. (ISBN 0-19-580724-3). Oxford U Pr.
--A Christmas Carol. Winter, Milo Kendall (1888-1956), illus. N.D. Rand McNally & Co.
--A Christmas Carol. Young, William Mark, illus. N.D. Grosset & Dunlap.
--A Christmas Carol & the Cricket on the Hearth. (Illus.). 220p. 1st U.S. edition. Repr. of 1963 ed. (Childrens Illustrated Classics Ser). 1973. (ISBN 0-460-05059-1, Pub. by J. M. Dent England). Biblio Dist.
--A Christmas Carol and The Cricket on the Hearth. Brock, Charles Edmond (1870-1938), illus. (Illus.). (Children's Illustrated Classics). 1963. E.P. Dutton & Co.
--A Christmas Carol in Prose: Being a Ghost Story of Christmas. Groth, John (1908-), illus. 1963. Macmillan.
--Christmas Chimes. (Christmas Classics). N.D. Barse & Hopkins.
--Christmas in Dickens. Shinn, Everett (1876-1953), illus. LC 41-2455. 68 p. incl. col. front., illus. (part col.) 24 cm. c.1941. Garden City Publishing Co., Inc.
--Christmas Stories. N.D. A. L. Burt Co.
--Christmas Stories. (Burt's Home Library). N.D. A L Burt Co.
--Christmas Stories. N.D. Charles Scribner's Sons.
--Christmas Stories. 162p. N.D. D. Appleton & Co.
--Christmas Stories. (Everyman's Library). N.D. E. P. Dutton & Co.
--Christmas Stories. (Classics for Children). N.D. Ginn & Co.
--Christmas Stories. (Sears Juvenile Classics). N.D. J.H. Sears & Co.
--Christmas Stories. N.D. Oxford University Press.
--Christmas Stories, 2 Vols. (Illustrated Duodecimo Edition). N.D. T. B. Peterson & Bros.
--Christmas Stories. (Illustrated Octavo Edition). N.D. T. B. Peterson & Bros.
--Christmas Stories. (gr. 1-6). N.D. (ISBN 0-529-02826-3). World Pub.
--Christmas Stories. Cruickshank, Phiz (1815-1882) & Stone, Marcus, illus. N.D. St Martin's Press.
--Christmas Stories. Nichols, Spencer Baird (1875-), illus. N.D. Frederick A. Stokes.
--Christmas Stories, American Notes, and Pictures from Italy. N.D. W. J. Widdleton.
--Christmas Stories from Dickens. (Illus.). (Young People's Classics). N.D. R. F. Fenno & Co.
--Christmas Story: The Goblin Who Stole the Sexton. Nast, Thomas (1840-1902), illus. N.D. McLoughlin Bros.
--Christmas Tales. (International Classics). N.D. Dodd Mead & Co.
--Christmas Tales. Becker, May Lamberton, intro. by. (Illus.). (Great Il. Classics). (gr. 7 up). N.D. (ISBN 0-396-00416-4). Dodd.
--Christmas with Mr. Pickwick. N.D. The Peter Pauper Press.
--The Cricket on the Hearth. (Harper Junior Classics Ser.). N.D. Harper & Bros.
--The Cricket on the Hearth. (Riverside Literature Ser.). N.D. Houghton Mifflin Co.
--The Cricket on the Hearth. Bedford, Francis Donkin (1864-1950), illus. N.D. Frederick Warne & Co.
--The Cricket on the Hearth. rev. ed. Bedford, Francis Dowlkin (1864-1950), illus. (Illus.). (gr. 7-9). 1956. (ISBN 0-7232-0319-9). Warne.
--The Cricket on The Hearth. Brock, Charles Edmond (1870-1938), illus. N.D. E. P. Dutton & Co.
--The Cricket on the Hearth: A Fairy Tale of Home. LC 42-46711. 24cm. 32p. 1846. Harper & Brothers.
--David Copperfield. Higginson, Thomas Wentworth (1823-1911), ed. (The Young Folk's Ser). N.D. Lee & Shepard.
--David Copperfield. (Burt's Home Library). N.D. A L Burt Co.
--David Copperfield. Empire ed. 1905. American News Co.
--David Copperfield. 351p. N.D. D. Appleton & Co.
--David Copperfield. (Illus.). (Great Illus. Classics). 1943. Dodd.
--David Copperfield. (The International Classics). N.D. Dodd Mead & Co.
--David Copperfield. (Everyman's Library). N.D. E. P. Dutton & Co.
--David Copperfield. New ed. N.D. G. W. Carleton & Co.
--David Copperfield. (The Good Value Books). N.D. Grosset & Dunlap.
--David Copperfield. N.D. Harper & Bros.
--David Copperfield. N.D. Houghton Mifflin Co.
--David Copperfield, 2 of 15 Vols. New ed. (Illus.). 854p. (Lovell's Popular Illustrated Edidtion). N.D. John W. Lovell.
--David Copperfield, 2 Vols. N.D. Little, Brown & Co.
--David Copperfield. (The Works of Charles Dickens). N.D. Macmillan.
--David Copperfield. N.D. Modern Library.
--David Copperfield. N.D. Oxford University Press.
--David Copperfield. 941p. (The Lake English Classics). N.D. Scott Foresman & Co.
--David Copperfield. (People's Duodecimo Edition). N.D. T. B. Peterson & Bros.
--David Copperfield. (Cheap Paper Cover Edition). N.D. T. B. Peterson & Bros.
--David Copperfield, 2 Vols. (Illustrated Duodecimo Edition). N.D. T. B. Peterson & Bros.
--David Copperfield. (Illustrated Octavo Edition). N.D. T. B. Peterson & Bros.
--David Copperfield, Two. N.D. Thomas Nelson & Sons.
--David Copperfield. (Nelson Classics). N.D. Thomas Nelson & Sons.
--David Copperfield. N.D. W. J. Widdleton.
--David Copperfield. N.D. William Collins Sons & Company Ltd.
--David Copperfield. Austen, John, illus. 832p. N.D. Heritage Press.
--David Copperfield. Baker, Franklin T., ed. (Modern Students Library). N.D. Charles Scribner's Sons.
--David Copperfield. Barnard, Frederick (1847-1896), illus. (The Rittenhouse Classics). N.D. Macrae Smith Co.
--David Copperfield. Becker, Mary Lamberton, intro. by. (Great Illustrated Classics). N.D. Dodd, Mead & Co.
--David Copperfield. Benscoter, Grace A & Gehlmann, John, eds. LC 45-6682. xii, 398 p. incl. front. (map) illus. 20 1/2 cm. 1945. Globe Book Company.
--David Copperfield. Cruickshank, Phiz (1812-1882) & Stone, Marcus, illus. N.D. St Martin's Press.
--David Copperfield. Eliot, George, et al., pseud. (1819-1880), illus. Evans, Marian. (Illustrated Cabinet Edition). N.D. L. C. Page & Co.
--David Copperfield. Eytinge, Sol, illus. (The Illustrated Diamond Edition). N.D. James R. Osgood.
--David Copperfield. Groome, W. H. C., illus. (Collins' Illustrated Pocket Classics). N.D. Collins.
--David Copperfield. Jackson, Alice, retold by. Blaikie, F. M. B., illus. LC 79-14169. (Illus.). 21 cm. 157p. (Classics Retold To Children). N.D. George W. Jacobs & Co.
--David Copperfield. Paine, Merrill P. & Graves, Robert, eds. (gr. 9-10). 1934. (ISBN 0-15-345540-3). HarBraceJ.
--David Copperfield. Phiz, pseud. (1815-1882), illus. Browne, Hablot Knight. N.D. J.B. Lippincott.
--David Copperfield. Phiz, pseud. (1815-1882), illus. Browne, Hablot Knight. (The Rittenhouse Classics). N.D. Macrae Smith.
--David Copperfield. West, M., adapted by. N.D. Longmans Green & Co.
--Dickens' Christmas Carol. Shinn, Everett (1876-1953), illus. Barrymore, Lionel, frwd. by. N.D. John C. Winston.
--Dicken's Christmas Stories. (Heirloom Library). N.D. Chanticleer Bks.
--Dickens' Christmas Stories. (Classic Ser.). N.D. World Publishing Co.
--Dicken's Christmas Stories for Children. Bellow, Molly K., ed. 179p. 1902. Jamieson-Higgins Co.
--Dickens' New Stories. (People's Duodecimo Edition). N.D. T. B. Peterson & Bros.
--Dickens' Stories About Children. Burd, Clara Miller, illus. N.D. John C. Winston Co.
--Dickens' Stories About Children. Burd, Clara Miller, illus. (The Children's Bookshelf). N.D. John C. Winston.
--Dickens Stories for Children. (Illus.). (Children's Colored Classics). N.D. Sully and Kleinteich.
--Dickens' Xmas Stories for Children, 11 vols. New ed. Campbell, H. S., illus. (Six to Sixteen Ser.: No. 1). 1905. Set. H M Caldwell Co.
--Dickens's Tale of Two Cities. McRae, ed. (Classics for Children). N.D. Ginn and Company.
--Dombery & Son. Cournos, John, intro. by. 839p. (Great Illustrated Classics). N.D. Dodd, Mead & Co.
--Dombey and Son. Cruickshank, Phiz (1815-1882) & Stone, Marcus, illus. N.D. St Martin's Press.
--Dombey and Son. Jackson, Alice F., retold by (Illus.). (Classics Retold to children). N.D. George W. Jacobs & Co.
--Girls from Dickens. N.D. John C. Winston Co.
--Great Expectation. Cruickshank, Phiz (1815-1882) & Stone, Marcus, illus. N.D. St Martin's Press.
--Great Expectations. (Burt's Home Library). N.D. A L Burt Co.
--Great Expectations. N.D. Charles Scribner's Sons.
--Great Expectations. N.D. D. Appleton & Co.
--Great Expectations. (Illus.). (Great Illus. Classics). 1942. Dodd.
--Great Expectations. (Everyman's Library). N.D. E. P. Dutton & Co.
--Great Expectations. N.D. Houghton Mifflin Co.
--Great Expectations. (The Works of Charles Dickens). N.D. Macmillan.
--Great Expectations. N.D. Oxford University Press.
--Great Expectations. (People's Duodecimo Edition). N.D. T. B. Peterson & Bros.
--Great Expectations. (Cheap Paper Cover Edition). N.D. T. B. Peterson & Bros.
--Great Expectations. (Illustrated Octavo Edition). N.D. T. B. Peterson & Bros.
--Great Expectations. N.D. Thomas Nelson & Sons.
--Great Expectations. N.D. William Collins Sons & Company Ltd.
--Great Expectations. Ardizzone, Edward Jeffrey Irving (1900-1979), illus. 408p. N.D. Heritage Press.
--Great Expectations. Davis, Earle, ed. 493p. 1949. Rinehart & Co.
--Great Expectations, One. Eliot, George, et al., pseud. (1819-1880), illus. Evans, Marian. (Illustrated Cabinet Edition). N.D. L. C. Page & Co.
--Great Expectations. Floyd, Gareth (1940-) & Fraser, F. A., illus. LC 74-106512. (Illus.). 217 p. 23cm. (Lifetime library). 1970. American Education Publications.
--Great Expectations. Green, Charles, illus. (The Rittenhouse Classics). N.D. Macrae Smith.
--Great Expectations. Jackson, Alice F., retold by. (Illus.). (Classics Retold to Children). N.D. George W. Jacobs & Co.
--Great Expectations. Newbolt, Henry, Sir, ed. (The Nelson Classics). N.D. Thomas Nelson & Sons.
--Great Expectations. Pailthorpe, Frederic W., illus. (Great Illustrated Classics). N.D. Dodd, Mead & Co.
--Great Expectations. Stone, Marcus, illus. N.D. J.B.Lippincott.
--Great Expectations and Hard Times. N.D. St. Martin's Press.
--Hard Times. New ed. N.D. G. W. Carleton & Co.
--Hard Times. (Cheap Paper Cover Edition). N.D. T. B. Peterson & Bros.
--The Holly Tree and Other Christmas Stories. Shepard, Ernest Howard (1879-1976), illus. N.D. Charles Scribner's Sons.
--Holly-Tree Inn, Other Stories. (People's Duodecimo Edition). N.D. T. B.Peterson & Bros.
--The Life of Our Lord. (Illus.). 127 p., 10 leaves of plates. 25cm. 1981. Westminster Press.
--Little Dorrit. (Burt's Home Library). N.D. A L Burt Co.
--Little Dorrit. 330p. N.D. D. Appleton & Co.
--Little Dorrit. New ed. N.D. G. W. Carleton & Co.
--Little Dorrit. N.D. Oxford University Press.
--Little Dorrit. (People's Duodecimo Edition). N.D. T. B. Peterson & Bros.
--Little Dorrit. (Cheap Paper Cover Edition). N.D. T. B. Peterson & Bros.
--Little Dorrit, 2 Vols. (Illustrated Duodecimo Edition). N.D. T. B. Peterson & Bros.
--Little Dorrit. (Illustrated Octavo Edition). N.D. T. B. Peterson & Bros.
--Little Dorrit. N.D. W. J. Widdleton.
--Little Dorrit. Cournos, John, intro. by. 788p. (Great Illustrated Classics). N.D. Dodd, Mead & Co.
--Little Nell. Jackson, Alice F., retold by. (Illus.). (Classics Retold to Children). N.D. George W. Jacobs & Co.
--Little Purr-Purr People, and How They Tried to Be Folks. Boz, pseud. LC 17-1705. 16 p. illus. 13 x 16 cm. c.1887. Hamilton-Brown Shoe Company.
--The Magic Fish-Bone. Jaques, Faith (1923-), illus. LC 69-17741. (Illus.). 32 p. 1969. Harvey House.
--The Magic Fishbone. Rainbird, Alice, ed. N.D. Frederick Warne & Co.
--The Magic Fishbone. Slobodkin, Louis (1903-1975), illus. 26p. 1953. Vanguard Press.
--Martin Chuzzlewit. 342p. N.D. D. Appleton & Co.
--Martin Chuzzlewit. New ed. N.D. G. W. Carleton & Co.
--Martin Chuzzlewit. N.D. Oxford University Press.
--Martin Chuzzlewit. Brock, Henry Matthew (1875-1960), illus. (International Classics). N.D. Dodd Mead & Co.
--Martin Chuzzlewit. Eytinge, Sol, illus. (The Illustrated Diamond Edition). N.D. James R. Osgood.
--Mickey's Christmas Carol. Disney Studio Staff, adapted by. LC 84-9491. (Original Author: Charles Dickens, 1812-1870). (Illus.). (gr. k up). 1984. (ISBN 0-517-55525-5). Crown.
--The New Oxford Illustrated Dickens, 21 vols. Incl. The Old Curiosity Shop. Cattermole, George & Phiz, pseud. (1815-1882), illus. Browne, Hablot Knight. (Illus.). 1951. (ISBN 0-19-254506-X); Our Mutual Friend. Stone, Marcus, illus. (Illus.). 1952. (ISBN 0-19-254510-8); The Personal History of David Copperfield. Browne, Hablot Knight. (Illus.). (ISBN 0-19-254502-7); The Posthumous Papers of the Pickwick Club (Illus.). 1947. (ISBN 0-19-254501-9); Sketches by Boz: Illustrative of Every-Day Life & Every-Day People. Cruikshank, George (1792-1878), illus. (Illus.). 1957. (ISBN 0-19-254518-3); A Tale of Two Cities. (Illus.). 1949. (ISBN 0-19-254504-3); The Uncommercial Traveller, & Reprinted Pieces, Etc. Pinwell, G. J., et al., illus. (Illus.). 1958. (ISBN 0-19-254521-3); The Adventures of Oliver Twist. Cruikshank, George (1792-1878), illus. House, Humphry, intro. by. 1949. (ISBN 0-19-254505-1); American Notes & Pictures from Italy. Stone, Marcus, et al., illus. Sitwell, Sacheverell (1897-), intro. by. 1957. (ISBN 0-19-254519-1); Barnaby Rudge: A Tale of the Riots of 'Eighty. Cattermole, George & Browne, Hablot Knight (1815-1882), illus. Tillotson, Katheleen, intro. by. 1954. (ISBN 0-19-254513-2); Bleak House. Phiz, pseud. (1815-1882), illus. Browne, Hablot Knight. Sitwell, Osbert, intro. by. 1948. (ISBN 0-19-254503-5); Christmas Books. Farjeon, Eleanor (1881-1965), intro. by. (Illus.). 1954. (ISBN 0-19-254514-0); Christmas Stories. Dalziel, E. G., et al., illus. Lane, Margaret (1907-), intro. by. 1956. (ISBN 0-19-254517-5); Dealings with the Firm of Dombey, & Son, Wholesale, Retail, & for Exploration. Phiz, pseud. (1815-1882), illus. Browne, Hablot Knight. Garrod, H. W., intro. by. 1950. (ISBN 0-19-254507-8); Great Expectations. Dickens, Charles Page, Frederick, intro. by. 1953. (ISBN 0-19-254511-6); Hard Times for These Times. Walker, F. & Greiffenhagen, Maurice, illus. Foot, Dingle, intro. by. 1955. (ISBN 0-19-254515-9); The Life & Adventures of Martin Chuzzlewit. Phiz, pseud. (1815-1882), illus. Browne, Hablot Knight. Russell, Geoffrey, intro. by. 1951. (ISBN 0-19-254509-4); The Life & Adventures of Nicholas Nickleby. Phiz, pseud. (1815-1882), illus. Browne, Hablot Knight. Thorndike, Sybil, intro. by. 1950. (ISBN 0-19-254508-6); Little Dorrit. Phiz, pseud. (1815-1882), illus. Browne, Hablot Knight. Trilling, Lionel (1905-1975), intro. by. 1953. (ISBN 0-19-254512-4); Master Humphrey's Clock & a Child's History of England. Hudson, Derek Rommel (1911-), intro. by. 1958. (ISBN 0-19-254520-5); The Mystery of Edwin Drood. Fildes, Luke & Collins, Charles, illus. Roberts, S. C., intro. by. 1956. (ISBN 0-19-254516-7). (Illus.). (gr. 7 up). N.D. Set. (ISBN 0-19-254522-1). Boxed Set Ecrase. (ISBN 0-19-195252-4). Oxford U Pr.
--Nicholas Nickelby. (Everyman's Library). N.D. E. P. Dutton & Co.
--Nicholas Nickelby. Cruickshank, Phiz (1815-1882) & Stone, Marcus, illus. N.D. St Martin's Press.
--Nicholas Nickleby. (Burt's Home Library). N.D. A L Burt Co.
--Nicholas Nickleby. 340p. N.D. D. Appleton & co.
--Nicholas Nickleby. N.D. D. C. Heath & Co.
--Nicholas Nickleby. 1944. Dodd.
--Nicholas Nickleby. (Illus.). (Great Il. Classics - Titans). (gr. 9 up). N.D. (ISBN 0-396-05262-2). Dodd.
--Nicholas Nickleby. (Everyman's Library). N.D. E. P. Dutton.

--Nicholas Nickleby. New ed. N.D. G. W. Carleton & Co.
--Nicholas Nickleby. N.D. Harper & Bros.
--Nicholas Nickleby, 2 Vol. N.D. Houghton Mifflin Co.
--Nicholas Nickleby, 2 Vols. (Illustrated Cabinet Editions). (The Works of Charles Dickens: Vols. 9-10). N.D. L. C. Page & Co.
--Nicholas Nickleby. (The Nelson Classics). N.D. Nelson Bks.
--Nicholas Nickleby. N.D. Oxford University Press.
--Nicholas Nickleby. (People's Duodecimo Edition). N.D. T. B. Peterson & Bros.
--Nicholas Nickleby. (Cheap Paper Cover Edition). N.D. T. B. Peterson & Bros.
--Nicholas Nickleby, 2 Vols. (Illustrated Duodecimo Edition). N.D. T. B. Peterson & Bros.
--Nicholas Nickleby. (Illustrated Octavo Edition). N.D. T. B. Peterson & Bros.
--Nicholas Nickleby, 2 vols, Two. N.D. Thomas Nelson & Sons.
--Nicholas Nickleby. N.D. W. J. Widdleton.
--Nicholas Nickleby. Eytinge, Sol, illus. (The Illustrated Diamond Edition). N.D. James R. Osgood.
--Nicholas Nickleby. Jackson, Alice F., retold by. (Illus.). (Classics Retold to Children). N.D. George W. Jacobs & Co.
--Nicholas Nickleby. Royster, Salibelle (1895-1975), ed. LC 54-13376. (Illus.). 229 p. 21cm. 1954. Globe Book Co.
--Nicholas Nickleby. Spurrier, Steven, illus. N.D. Heritage Press.
--Old Curiosity. (People's Duodecimo Edition). N.D. T. B. Peterson & Bros.
--The Old Curiosity Shop. (Burt's Home Library). N.D. A L Burt Co.
--Old Curiosity Shop. 221p. N.D. D. Appleton & Co.
--The Old Curiosity Shop. 1943. Dodd.
--The Old Curiosity Shop. (Illus.). (Great Il. Classics - Titans). (gr. 9 up). 1967. (ISBN 0-396-05617-2). Dodd.
--The Old Curiosity Shop. (International Classics). N.D. Dodd Mead & Co.
--The Old Curiosity Shop. N.D. Funk & Wagnalls.
--The Old Curiosity Shop. (The People's Library). N.D. Funk & Wagnalls Co.
--Old Curiosity Shop. New ed. N.D. G. W. Carleton & Co.
--Old Curiosity Shop. N.D. Harper & Bros.
--The Old Curiosity Shop. abr. ed. 1976. (ISBN 0-590-10229-X). Schol Bk Serv.
--Old Curiosity Shop. (Cheap Paper Cover Edition). N.D. T. B. Peterson & Bros.
--Old Curiosity Shop, 2 Vols. (Illustrated Duodecimo Edition). N.D. T. B. Peterson & Bros.
--Old Curiosity Shop. (Illustrated Octavo Edition). N.D. T. B. Peterson & Bros.
--Old Curiosity Shop. (Nelson Classics). N.D. Thomas Nelson & Sons.
--Old curiosity shop. N.D. William Collins Sons & Company Ltd.
--The Old Curiosity Shop. Cruickshank, Phiz (1815-1882) & Stone, Marcus, illus. N.D. St Martin's Press.
--Old Curiosity Shop, Two. Eliot, George, et al., pseud. (1819-1880), illus. Evans, Marian. (Illustrated Cabinet Edition). N.D. L. C. Page & Co.
--Old Curiosity Shop. Eytinge, Sol, illus. (The Illustrated Diamond Edition). N.D. James R. Osgood.
--Old Curiosity Shop, and Sketches, Part 1. N.D. W. J. Widdleton.
--Oliver Twist. N.D. A. L. Burt Co.
--Oliver Twist. N.D. Bruce Humphries.
--Oliver Twist. N.D. Charles Scribner's Sons.
--Oliver Twist. (Collins' Illustrated Pocket Classics). N.D. Collins.
--Oliver Twist. 172p. N.D. D. Appleton & Co.
--Oliver Twist. 1941. Dodd.
--Oliver Twist. (Illus.). (Great Il. Classics). (gr. 9 up). 1979. Dodd.
--Oliver Twist. (Everyman's Library). N.D. E. P. Dutton & Co.
--Oliver Twist. New ed. N.D. G. W. Carleton & Co.
--Oliver Twist. (The Good Value Books). N.D. Grosset & Dunlap.
--Oliver Twist. (The Children's Favorite Ser.). N.D. Grosset & Dunlap.
--Oliver Twist. N.D. Harper & Bros.
--Oliver Twist. N.D. Houghton Mifflin Co.
--Oliver Twist. N.D. J. B. Lippincott.
--Oliver Twist. (Magnum Easy Eye Classic Ser). (gr. 9-12). N.D. Lancer.
--Oliver Twist. (The Works of Charles Dickens). N.D. Macmillan.
--Oliver Twist. (The Rittenhouse Classics). N.D. Macrae Smith.
--Oliver Twist. N.D. Oxford University Press.
--Oliver Twist. (gr. 7-12). 1972 (Starline). Schol Bk Serv.
--Oliver Twist. (People's Duodecimo Edition). N.D. T. B. Peterson & Bros.
--Oliver Twist. (Cheap Paper Cover Edition). N.D. T. B. Peterson & Bros.
--Oliver Twist, 2 Vols. (Illustrated Duodecimo Edition). N.D. T. B. Peterson & Bros.
--Oliver Twist. (Illustrated Octavo Edition). N.D. T. B. Peterson & Bros.
--Oliver Twist. N.D. William Collins Sons & Company Ltd.
--Oliver Twist. Cruikshank, George (1792-1878), illus. (The Macdonald Illustrated Classics). N.D. Coward-McCann.
--Oliver Twist. Cruikshank, George (1792-1878), illus. N.D. J.B Lippincott.
--Oliver Twist. Cruikshank, George (1792-1878), illus. 463p. N.D. Thomas Y. Crowell Co.
--Oliver Twist, One. Eliot, George, et al., pseud. (1819-1880), illus. Evans, Marian. (Illustrated Cabinet Edition). N.D. L. C. Page & Co.
--Oliver Twist. Eytinge, Sol, illus. (The Illustrated Diamond Edition). N.D. James R. Osgood.
--Oliver Twist. Jackson, Alice F., retold by. (Illus.). (Classics Retold to Children). N.D. George W. Jacobs & Co.
--Oliver Twist. Newbolt, Henry, Sir, ed. (The Nelson Classics). N.D. Thomas Nelson & Sons.
--Oliver Twist. Teague, Donald (1897-), illus. (Minton, Balch Library of Illustrated Classics). N.D. Minton Balch & Co.
--Oliver Twist and Great Expectations. N.D. W. J. Widdleton.
--Oliver Twist: Collins New Classics. N.D. William Collins Sons & Co.
--Our Mutual Friend. New ed. N.D. G. W Carleton & Co.
--Our Mutual Friend. Klots, Allen, intro. by. (Great Illustrated Classics). N.D. Dodd, Mead & Co.
--Our Mututal Friends, Two. N.D. Thomas Nelson & Sons.
--The Personal History of David Copperfield. ix, p., 1 l., 881 p. 22 cm. (Universal library). 1931. Grosset & Dunlap.
--The Pickwick Papers. 326p. N.D. D. Appleton & Co.
--Pickwick Papers. (Illus.). (Great Il. Classics - Titans). (gr. 9 up). 1967. (ISBN 0-396-05604-0). Dodd.
--Pickwick Papers. (Everyman's Library). N.D. E. P. Dutton & Co.
--The Pickwick Papers. New ed. N.D. G. W. Carleton & Co.
--Pickwick Papers. (People's Duodecimo Edition). N.D. T. B. Peterson & Bros.
--Pickwick Papers. (Cheap Paper Cover Edition). N.D. T. B. Peterson & Bros.
--Pickwick Papers, 2 Vols. (Illustrated Duodecimo Edition). N.D. T. B. Peterson & Bros.
--Pickwick Papers. (Illustrated Octavo Edition). N.D. T. B. Peterson & Bros.
--Pickwick Papers. N.D. W. J. Widdleton.
--The Pickwick Papers. Brock, Charles Edmond (1870-1938) & Gardner, Mary Ponton, illus. (Ebony Library). N.D. Dodd Mead & Co.
--The Posthumous Papers of the Pickwick Club. 1944. Dodd.
--The Signalman. Richardson, I. M, adapted by. Ashmead, Hal, illus. LC 81-19819. (Illus.). 31 p. 24cm. (Famous Tales of Suspense). (gr. 5-9). c.1982. (ISBN 0-89375-630-X). (ISBN 0-89375-631-8). Troll Associates.
--Silas Marner, One. Eliot, George, et al., pseud. (1819-1880), illus. Evans, Marian. (Illustrated Cabinet Edition). N.D. L. C. Page & Co.
--Stories and Sketches. (Collins' Illustrated Pocket Classics). N.D. Collins.
--Stories from Dickens. McSpadden, Joseph Walker (1874-), ed. Suba, Susanne (1913-), illus. LC 57-388334. 288p. illus. 22cm. 1957. Junior Deluxe Editions.
--Stories from Dickens Retold for Boys and Girls. (The Challenge Ser.). N.D. John C. Winston.
--A Tale of Two Cities. N.D. A. L. Burt Co.
--A Tale of Two Cities. 638p. (Merrill's English Texts). N.D. Charles E Merrill.
--A Tale of Two Cities. N.D. Charles Scribner's Sons.
--A Tale of Two Cities. (The Macdonald Illustrated Classics). N.D. Coward-McCann.
--A Tale of Two Cities. 144p. N.D. D. Appleton & Co.
--A Tale of Two Cities. N.D. D C Heath.
--A Tale of Two Cities. 1942. Dodd.
--A Tale of Two Cities. (The International Classics). N.D. Dodd Mead & Co.
--A Tale of Two Cities. (Everyman's Library). N.D. E. P. Dutton.
--A Tale of Two Cities. N.D. Funk & Wagnalls.
--A Tale of Two Cities. New ed. N.D. G. W. Carleton & Co.
--A Tale of Two Cities. (Classics for Children). N.D. Ginn.
--A Tale of Two Cities. N.D. Harper & Bros.
--A Tale of Two Cities. (English Readings Ser.). N.D. Henry Holt.
--A Tale of Two Cities. (Riverside Library). N.D. Houghton Mifflin Co.
--A Tale of Two Cities. (Riverside Literature Ser.: 161). N.D. Houghton Mifflin Co.
--A Tale of Two Cities. (Sears Juvenile Classics). N.D. J.H.Sears & Co.
--A Tale of Two Cities. N.D. Little, Brown & Co.
--A Tale of Two Cities. (Longmans' English Classics). N.D. Longmans Green & Co.
--A Tale of Two Cities. (The Works of Charles Dickens). N.D. Macmillan.
--A Tale of Two Cities. (The Rittenhouse Classics). N.D. Macrae Smith.
--A Tale of Two Cities. N.D. Modern Library.
--A Tale of Two Cities. N.D. Oxford University Press.
--A Tale of Two Cities. 533p. (The Lake English Classics). N.D. Scott Foresman & Co.
--A Tale of Two Cities. (People's Duodecimo Edition). N.D. T. B. Peterson & Bros.
--A Tale of Two Cities. (Cheap Paper Cover Edition). N.D. T. B. Peterson & Bros.
--A Tale of Two Cities, 2 Vols. (Illustrated Duodecimo Edition). N.D. T. B. Peterson & Bros.
--A Tale of Two Cities. (Illustrated Octavo Edition). N.D. T. B. Peterson & Bros.
--A Tale of Two Cities, Two. N.D. Thomas Nelson & Sons.
--A Tale of two Cities. N.D. W. J. Widdleton.
--A Tale of Two Cities. N.D. William Collins Sons & Company Ltd.
--A Tale of Two Cities. (Classic Ser.). N.D. World Publishing Co.
--A Tale of Two Cities. Barnard, Frederick (1847-1896), illus. (The Rittenhouse Classics). N.D. Macrae Smith Co.
--A Tale of Two Cities. Ben Sussan, Rene, illus. N.D. Heritage Press.
--A Tale of Two Cities. Busoni, Rafaello (1900-1962), illus. N.D. Grosset & Dunlap.
--A Tale of Two Cities. Clare, Andrea M., adapted by. LC 73-80400. (Illus.). 92 p. 21cm. (Pacemaker classic). 1973. (ISBN 0-8224-9228-8). Fearon Publishers.
--A Tale of Two Cities. Cruickshank, Phiz (1815-1882) & Stone, Marcus, illus. N.D. St Martin's Press.
--A Tale of Two Cities. Dixon, Arthur A., illus. (Collins' Illustrated Pocket Classics). N.D. Collins.
--A Tale of Two Cities. Dunn, Harvey T., illus. N.D. Cosmopolitan Book Co.
--A Tale of Two Cities. Dunn, Harvey T., illus. (McKay's Illustrated Classics). N.D. David McKay Co.
--A Tale of Two Cities, One. Eliot, George, et al., pseud. (1819-1880), illus. Evans, Marian. (Illustrated Cabinet Edition). N.D. L. C. Page & Co.
--A Tale of Two Cities. Eytinge, Sol, illus. (The Illustrated Diamond Edition). N.D. James R. Osgood.
--A Tale of Two Cities. Jackson, Alice F., retold by. (Illus.). (Classics Retold to Children). N.D. George W. Jacobs & Co.
--A Tale of Two Cities. Jellinek, Joanna, ed. LC 76-13406. (Illus.). 111 p., 8 leaves of plates. 25cm. 1976. (ISBN 0-679-20374-5). D. McKay Co.
--A Tale of Two Cities. Krapesh, Patti, adapted by. Shaw, Charles (1941-), illus. LC 79-24746. (Illus.). 48 p. 24cm. c.1980. (ISBN 0-8172-1658-8). Raintree.
--A Tale of Two Cities. Newbolt, Henry, Sir, ed. (The Nelson Classics). N.D. Thomas Nelson & Sons.
--A Tale of Two Cities. Phiz, pseud. (1815-1882), illus. Browne, Hablot Knight. N.D. J.B.Lippincott.
--A Tale of Two Cities. Toomey, Elizabeth & Kottmeyer, William, eds. (The Everyreader Library). N.D. Webster Publishing Co.
--Three Musketeers, Two. Eliot, George, et al., pseud. (1819-1880), illus. Evans, Marian. (Illustrated Cabinet Edition). N.D. L. C. Page & Co.
--Tiny Tim and Dot, and the Fairy Cricket, 1 of 12 Vols. Darley, Felix Octavius Carr (1822-1888), illus. (Dickens' Little Folks). N.D. Set. Clark & Maynard.
--The Two Daughters, 1 of 12 Vols. Darley, Felix Octavius Carr (1822-1888), illus. (Dickens' Little Folks). N.D. Set. Clark & Maynard.
--Uncommercial Traveler. Eytinge, Sol, illus. (The Illustrated Diamond Edition). N.D. Charles R. Osgood.
--Young David Copperfield. Abridged for Children 8-14 from Charles Dickens' Immortal Classic. 1st ed. Sidlowski, Loretta, adapted by. LC 56-143867. 126p. 22cm. 1957, c.1956. Greenwich Book Publishers.

Dickens, Charles John Huffam (1812-1870) & Fraser, Francis Arthur
--Great Expectations. Floyd, Gareth (1940-), illus. LC 76-6693. (Illus.). 588 p. 22cm. c.1977. (ISBN 0-8055-1198-9). (ISBN 0-8055-0283-1). Hart Pub. Co.

Dickens, Charles John Huffam (1812-1870) & Green, Charles
--The Old Curiosity Shop. N.D. Macrae Smith.

Dickens, Charles John Huffam (1812-1870) & Kaphan, Mortimer
--Tell Us a Dickens Story. Gilkison, Grace, Mrs., illus. LC 30-28845. 8 p. l., 11-199 p. incl. front., plates. 24 cm. 1930. Coward-McCann, Inc.

Dickens, Charles John Huffam (1812-1870) & Thackeray, William Makepeace
--The Magic Fishbone & The Rose and the Ring. Hogarth, Paul (1917-) & Thackeray, William Makepeace (1811-1863), illus. ("The Magic Fishbone" by Charles Dickens, illustrated by Paul Hogarth, bound with "The rose and the Ring", written and illustrated by William Makepeace Thackeray.). (Children's Illustrated Classics). N.D. E. P. Dutton & Co.

Dickens, Frank, pseud., see Huline-Dickens, Frank William.

Dickens, Frank, pseud. (1931-)
--Albert Herbert Hawkins: The Naughtiest Boy in the World ,and the Space Rocket. Huline-Dickens, Frank William. LC 78-318623. (Illus.). 32 p. 1978. (ISBN 0-510-22507-1). E. Benn.
--Albert Herbert Hawkins: The Naughtiest Boy in the World. Huline-Dickens, Frank William. LC 72-149044. (Illus.). 30 p. 1971. Scroll Press.
--Albert Herbert Hawkins, the Naughtiest Boy in the World, and the Space Rocket. Huline-Dickens, Frank William. Dickens, Frank, pseud. (1931-), illus. Huline-Dickens, Frank William. LC 77-74708. (Illus.). 32 p. (Benn book collection). c.1978. (ISBN 0-385-13327-8). Doubleday.
--Boffo: The Great Motor-Cycle Race. Huline-Dickens, Frank William. LC 77-22087. (Illus.). 33 p. 1978, c.1976. (ISBN 0-8193-0956-7). (ISBN 0-8193-0957-5). Parents' Magazine Press.
--Fly Away Peter. Huline-Dickens, Frank. Steadman, Ralph Idris (1936-), illus. LC 70-99917. (Illus.). 32 p. 1970, c.1963. Scroll Press.

Dickens, Mary Angela, ed.
--Children's Stories from Dickens. Copping, Harold (1863-1932), illus. (Raphael House Library). N.D. David McKay.

Dickens, Monica Enid (1915-)
--The Great Fire. Negri, Rocco (1932-), illus. LC 72-92201. (Illus.). 64 p. 22cm. 1973, c.1970. (ISBN 0-385-05672-9). (ISBN 0-385-05672-9). Doubleday.
--The House at World's End. LC 79-155818. 186 p. 22cm. 1971, c.1970. Doubleday.
--My Fair Lady. Loewe, Frederick (1904-) & Lazare, Gerald John (1927-), illus. LC 67-23546. (Illus.). 143 p. 20cm. 1967. Four Winds Press.
--Summer at World's End. LC 79-180070. 187 p. 22cm. 1972. Doubleday.
--World's End in Winter. LC 72-97253. 163 p. 22cm. 1973, c.1972. (ISBN 0-385-01766-9). (ISBN 0-385-01766-9). Doubleday.

Dickenson, Christine
--Getting It All Together. (gr. 7-12). 1976. (ISBN 0-590-10128-5, Schol Pap). Schol Bk Serv.

Dickerson, Fannie M.
--Mary Had a Little Lamb. Owen, Herbert Alvin, illus. LC 2-25319. 19 x 15cm. 96p. 1902. F. A. Stokes.

Dickerson, Grace Leslie, jt. auth. see Carper, Jean Elinor.

Dickerson, Louise
--Good Wife, Good Wife. Himler, Ronald Norbert (1937-), illus. LC 77-23397. p. cm. 1977. (ISBN 0-07-044837-X). (ISBN 0-07-044838-8). McGraw-Hill.

Dickey, Bess
--Steps of Youth. LC 43-11143. 89 p. illus. 19 1/2 cm. 1943. Dorrance and Company.

Dickey, Herbert Spencer, Dr. & Daniel, Hawthorne (1890-)
--Misadventures of a Tropical Medico. N.D. Dodd, Mead & Co.

Dickey, James Lafayette (1923-)
--Tucky the Hunter. Angel, Marie (1923-), illus. LC 78-9343. p. cm. c.1978. (ISBN 0-517-53258-1). Crown Publishers.

Dickey, Katharine S.
--Lottie of the Mill. N.D. J. B. Lippincott.

Dickey, Robert L. (1861-)
--Black Beauty. N.D. Barse and Hopkins.

Dickie, Francis
--Umingmuk of the Barrens. N.D. George Sully & Co.

Dickinson, Alice, jt. ed. see Lang, Andrew.

Dickinson, Asa Don (1876-), ed.
--Children's Book of Christmas Stories. N.D. Doubleday Doran & Co.
--The Children's Book of Thanksgiving Stories. LC 15-24888. x, 339 1 p. col. front., pl. 20 cm. 1915. Doubleday, Page & Company.
--Good Cheer Stories Every Child Should Know: Children's Thanksgiving Stories. LC 42-10319. 20cm. 339p. (What Every Child Should Know Library). 1941. Doubleday, Doran & Co.

--Pines for the King's Navy. 1st ed. Chavez, Edward, illus. LC 55-8094. 212p. illus. 21cm. 1955. Little, Brown.
--The Savage Summer. Winters, Denny, illus. LC 64-16550. 177 p. illus. 21 cm. 1964. Little, Brown.
--The Story of Andre. Shevis, Stell, illus. LC 78-73269. (Illus.). 82 p., 1 leaf of plates. c.1979. (ISBN 0-89272-052-2). Down East Books.
--Wilderness River. LC 61-10493. 183 p. 21cm. 1961. Little, Brown.
--The Year of the Big Cat. LC 76-97142. 180 p. 21cm. 1970. Little, Brown.

Dietzel, Paul Franklin (1924-) & Houghton, Everett
--Go, Shorty, Go!. LC 65-26500. 140 p. 22cm. 1965. Bobbs-Merrill.

Diffin, Charles Willard
--Gray Smoke: The Coyote of El Coronel. Alyn, illus. LC 40-32775. 32 p. illus. 26 x 25 cm. c.1940. Garden City Publishing Co., Inc.
--The Secret of the Sun-God's Cave. Alyn, illus. LC 42-24492. 224 p. front. (map) col. plates. 22 cm. 1942. R. M. McBride and Company.

DiFiori, Lawrence
--The Strawberry Mother Goose. DiFiori, Lawrence, illus. LC 75-3808. (Illus.). 32 p. 24cm. c.1975. (ISBN 0-88470-016-X). (ISBN 0-88470-017-8). Strawberry Books : Distributed by Larousse.
--Where's Goldie?. DiFiori, Lawrence, illus. LC 82-83381. (Illus.). 24p. (First Little Golden Bk.). (ps). 1983. (ISBN 0-307-10149-5, Golden Pr). (ISBN 0-307-10149-5). Western Pub.

Di Fiori, Lawrence, jt. auth. see Yolen, Jane Hyatt.

DiFranco, JoAnn
--Walt Disney: When Dreams Come True. LC 84-12173. (Illus.). 64p. (Taking Part Bks.). (gr. 3 up). 1985. (ISBN 0-87518-281-X). Dillon.

Digance, Richard
--Animal Alphabet. Gold, Diana, illus. (Illus.). 78p. 1981. (ISBN 0-7181-1960-6, Pub. by Michael Joseph). Merrimack Pub Cir.

Digby, Anne (1935-)
--A Horse Called September. LC 76-382638. 128 p. 21cm. 1976. (ISBN 0-234-77875-X). Dobson.
--A Horse Called September. LC 82-5560. 128 p. 22cm. c.1982. (ISBN 0-312-39143-9). St. Martin's Press.
--The Quicksilver Horse. LC 82-16830. p. cm. 1982. (ISBN 0-312-66083-9). St. Martin's Press.

DiGeorge
--The Twelve Days of Christmas. (Illus.). 1967. James H. Heineman Inc Publishers.

Di Girolamo, Vittorio (1928-)
--Bo & the Sad King. Di Girolamo, Vittorio, illus. Eagleson, John & Gray, Rockwell, trs. from Span LC 72-77542. (Illus.). 32p. 1st U.S. edition. (gr. 1-5). 1972. (ISBN 0-88344-039-3). Orbis Bks.

D'Ignazio, Frederick (1949-)
--Chip Mitchell: The Case of the Robot Warriors. 1st ed. Pearson, Larry, illus. LC 83-13529. p. cm. 128p. (gr. 5-9). c.1983. (ISBN 0-525-67140-4). Lodestar Books.
--Chip Mitchell: The Case of the Stolen Computer Brains. Pearson, Larry, illus. LC 82-9608. 128p. (gr. 5-9). cm. 1983, c.1982 (Lodestar). (ISBN 0-525-66790-3). Dutton.
--Chip Mitchell, the Case of the Stolen Computer Brains. Pearson, Larry, illus. LC 84-12868. p. cm. 1984, c.1982. (ISBN 0-8104-6826-3). Hayden Book Co.
--Katie and the Computer. Gilliam, Stan, illus. 1980. Creative Computing.

Dike, Helen
--Stories from the Great Metropolitan Operas. N.D. Random House.

Dikeman, Margaret
--Henry's Wagon. N.D. Garden City Publishing Co.
--Henry's Wagon. Cooper, Marjorie (1910-), illus. Margie, pseud. LC 46-22500. (Illus.). 27 x 21cm. 32p. 1946. John Martin's House.

Dikeman, Peg see Dikeman, Margaret.

Dikkens, Charlie
--Percy. Miller, Fred, illus. (Illus.). (Learning Human Values Ser.). (gr. 2 up). 1976. (ISBN 0-685-68998-0). (ISBN 0-685-68999-9). Bookworld Comm.

Dikty, T. E, ed.
--Every Boy's Book of Outer Space Stories. LC 60-13260. 283p. c.1960. F. Fell.

Di Lampedusa, Giuseppe
--Two Stories and a Memory. N.D. (ISBN 0-448-00227-2). Grosset & Dunlap.

Dilcer, Marjorie R.
--Grandfather's Strange Shepherd's Crook: A Christmas Story. (Illus.). 32p. (gr. 2-4). 1975. (ISBN 0-682-48173-4). Exposition.

Dillard, Polly Hargis (1916-)
--Bible for Me: Little treasure series. 1961. Broadman Press.
--My Book About Jesus. Kasey, Anne R., illus. (Illus.). 32 p. 21cm. 1968. Broadman Press.
--Peter & the Rain. Derwinski, Beatrice, illus. LC 58-5406. (Illus.). (ps-k). 1958. (ISBN 0-8054-4108-5). Broadman.
--Sunday with Stevie. Smalley, Janet (1893-), illus. LC 56-3006. 1956. Broadman Press.

Dillenbeck, Marsden V. see Grahame, Kenneth.

Dilliard, Maud Esther (1916-)
--Ahoy, Peggy Stewart. Bjorklund, Lorence F. (1913-1978), illus. LC 56-8309. (Illus.). 120p. 1956. Dutton.
--A Farm for Juliana. 1st ed. Orbaan, Albert F. (1913-), illus. LC 51-12225. 189 p. illus. 22 cm. 1951. Dutton.
--The Twins of Old Flatbush. 1st. ed. Orbaan, Albert F. (1913-), illus. LC 52-7797. 182 p. illus. 22 cm. 1952. Dutton.
--Wishing Boy of New Netherland. 1st ed. Orbaan, Albert F. (1913-), illus. LC 50-9299. 187 p. illus. 21 cm. 1950. Dutton.

Dilling, Hulda A & Welsh, Joanna
--Markets of the World. LC 42-5134. iii, 1, 92 p. illus. (part col.) 21 cm. c.1942. Lyons and Carnahan.

Dillingham, Elizabeth Thompson (1880-)
--The Rabbit Windmill: Joyful Stories for Holidays and Other Days. Richardson, Frederick (1862-1937) & Stephenson, Eunice, illus. LC 30-15101. x, 163 p. col. front., illus., col. plates. 23 cm. c.1930. The John C. Winston Co.
--Tell It Again" Stories. LC 11-31134. ix, 173 p. illus. 19 cm. c.1911. Ginn and Company.

Dillingham, Frances Bent
--Christmas-tree Scholar. (Illus.). (Sunshine Library for Young People). 1900. T. Y. Crowell & Co.
--Proud Little Baxter. (Illus.). 100p. N.D. Pilgrim Press.

Dillingham, Pegge
--Sound Comics. Fregosi, Claudia, illus. LC 77-28544. (Illus.). 32 p. 24cm. c.1978. (ISBN 0-13-823013-7). Prentice-Hall.

Dillion, Eilis
--The Lost Island. 248p. N.D. Funk & Wagnalls.

Dillon, Barbara (1927-)
--The Beast in the Bed. Conover, Chris (1950-), illus. LC 80-15069. p. cm. 1981. (ISBN 0-688-22254-4). (ISBN 0-688-32254-9). Morrow.
--The Good-Guy Cake. Tiegreen, Alan, illus. LC 80-14514. (Illus.). 64 p. 21cm. 1980. (ISBN 0-688-22240-4). (ISBN 0-688-32240-9). Morrow.
--Mr. Chill. Higginbottom, Jeffrey Winslow (1945-), illus. LC 85-5107. p. cm. 1985. (ISBN 0-688-04980-X). (ISBN 0-688-04981-8). W. Morrow.
--The Teddy Bear Tree. Rose, David S. (1947-), illus. LC 82-2301. (Illus.). 79 p. 21cm. 1982. (ISBN 0-688-01447-X). (ISBN 0-688-01450-X). Morrow.
--What's Happened to Harry?. Conover, Chris (1950-), illus. LC 81-11153. (Illus.). 125 p. 21cm. 1982. (ISBN 0-688-00763-5). Morrow.
--Who Needs a Bear?. DeGroat, Diane (1947-), illus. LC 80-26530. (Illus.). 63 p. 22cm. 1981. (ISBN 0-688-00445-8). (ISBN 0-688-00446-6). W. Morrow.

Dillon, E. V
--In a Glass Darkly. LC 74-82216. 167 p. 22cm. 1974. (ISBN 0-8059-2054-4). Dorrance.

Dillon, Eilis, et al. (1920-), eds.
--The Lucky Bag. Klaw, Barbara Van Doren (1920-), illus. Gale, Martin, pseud. (Illus.). 220p. (gr. 3-11). 1985. (ISBN 0-86278-064-0, Pub. by O'Brien Pr Ireland). Irish Bks Media.

Dillon, Eilis (1920-)
--Cats' Opera. Vanecek, Kueta, illus. (Illus.). (gr. 3-7). 1963. (ISBN 0-672-50244-5). Bobbs.
--The Coriander. Donahue, Vic, illus. LC 64-11119. (Illus.). 211 p. 21cm. 211p. 1964, c.1963. Funk & Wagnalls. **Award: (ALA).**
--The Cruise of the Santa Maria. Kennedy, Richard (1910-), illus. (Illus.). 189 p. 22cm. 1967. Funk & Wagnalls.
--A Family of Foxes. Donahue, Vic, illus. LC 65-11722. 119p. illus. 21cm. 1965, c.1964. (ISBN 0-308-80005-2). Funk & Wagnalls.
--Fort of Gold. Johnson, Eugene Harper, illus. LC 62-8606. (Illus.). 22cm. 182p. (gr. 7 up). 1962. (ISBN 0-308-80103-2). Funk & W.
--A Herd of Deer. Kennedy, Richard (1910-), illus. LC 72-100651. (Illus.). 189 p. 22cm. 1970, c.1969. Funk & Wagnalls.
--The House on the Shore. LC 56-7778. 250p. illus. 22cm. 1956, c.1955. Funk & Wagnalls.
--The Island of Horses. Kennedy, Richard (1910-), illus. LC 57-10583. (Illus.). 218 p. 22cm. 1957, c.1956. Funk & Wagnalls.
--King Big-Ears. Hamil, Thomas Arthur (1928-), illus. LC 63-7501. unpaged. illus. 24 cm. 1963. Norton.
--The Lion Cub. Kennedy, Richard (1910-), illus. LC 67-159. (Illus.). 87 p. 21cm. 1967, c.1966. Duell, Sloan and Pearce.
--The Lost Island. Kennedy, Richard (1910-), illus. LC 54-7760. 201p. 1954. Funk & Wagnalls.
--The Road to Dunmore and The Key: Two Stories. Kennedy, Richard (1910-), illus. LC 68-28726. (Illus.). 109 p. 21cm. 1968. Meredith Press.
--The San Sebastian. Kennedy, Richard (1910-), illus. LC 54-11301. 241p. illus. 22cm. 1954. Funk & Wagnalls.
--The Sea Wall. Mars, Witold Tadeusz J. (1912-), illus. LC 65-170246. 139p. illus. 22cm. (Bell bks.). (gr. 5-9). c.1965. (ISBN 0-374-36501-6). Farrar.
--The Seals. Kennedy, Richard (1910-), illus. LC 69-12151. (Illus.). 127 p. 21cm. 1969, c.1968. Funk & Wagnalls.
--The Shadow of Vesuvius. LC 77-21941. p. cm. c.1977. (ISBN 0-8407-6569-X). T. Nelson.
--The Singing Cave. Campbell, Stan, illus. LC 60-6424. (Illus.). 186 p. 22cm. 1960, c.1959. Funk & Wagnalls Co. **Award: (ALA).**
--Under the Orange Grove. Kennedy, Richard (1910-), illus. LC 75-85420. (Illus.). 86 p. 22cm. 1969, c.1968. Meredith Press.
--THe Wild Little House. 1957. E M Hale.
--The Wild Little House. Drummond, Violet Hilda (1911-), illus. LC 57-9162. 26cm. 31p. 1957. Criterion Bks. Inc.
--Wild Little House. Drummond, Violet Hilda (1911-), illus. (Illus.). (gr. k-3). 1957. (ISBN 0-87599-025-8). S G Phillips.
--The Wise Man on the Mountain. Chapman, Gaynor (1935-), illus. LC 69-18960. (Illus.). 40 p. 28cm. 1st U.S. edition. 1970, c.1969. Atheneum.

Dillon, George (1906-1968)
--Boy In The Wind. N.D. Viking Press.

Dillon, Joan L.
--Homer's Secret. (Illus.). (gr. k-4). N.D. Vantage.

Dillon, Marian
--Wide Awake Billy. McGregor Turney, Elaine, illus. (Illus.). 48p. 1st U.S. edition. (gr. 2-5). 1984. (ISBN 0-241-10984-1, Pub. by Hamish Hamilton England). David & Charles.

Dillwyn, E. A.
--Jill. N.D. MacMillan.
--Jill & Jack. N.D. MacMillan.

Di Lorenzo, Eve
--So They Went to the Country: A Story for Children. 1st ed. Di Lorenzo, Eve, illus. LC 53-9790. 72p. illus. 21cm. 1953. Exposition Press.

Dilts, Jerome Jay (1890-)
--Twins of the Loblolly. LC 38-110701. 259 p. illus. 20 cm. c.1938. The Limberlost Publishing Company.

Dim, Joan
--Recollections of a Rotten Kid: A Novel. LC 74-6530. 173 p. 22cm. c.1974. (ISBN 0-672-52024-9). Bobbs-Merrill.

Dimitrova, Lyumila, et al., trs. see Karaliichev, Angel.

Dimmick, Ruth Crosby
--The Bogie Man. Neale, Marguerite B., illus. LC 7-36209. 25cm. 71p. 1906. John C. Winston.

Dimock, Anthony Weston (1842-1918)
--Dick Among the Lumber-Jacks. Dimock, Julian A., illus. LC 10-16007. 5 p. l., 300 p. front., plates. 20 cm. 1910. Frederick A. Stokes Company.
--Dick Among the Miners. Dimock, Julian A., illus. LC 13-18972. 20cm. 293p. 1913. Frederick A. Stokes.
--Dick Among the Seminoles. Dimock, Julian A., illus. LC 11-205487. 5 p. l. 324 p. front., plates. 20 cm. 1911. Frederick A. Stokes Company.
--Dick in the Everglades. Dimock, Julian A., illus. LC 9-24266. x, 2 307 p. front. illus., 31 pl. 20 cm. 1909. F. A. Stokes Company.

Dimock, Edward Cameron, Jr. (1929-), ed.
--The Thief of Love. Dimock, Edward Cameron, tr. 306p. 1963. The University Of Chicago Press.

Dimock, Edwin
--Monsieur and Madame. Glackens, Louis M., illus. 1924. Harper & Bros.

Dimond, Jasper
--Noah's Ark. (Illus.). 48p. (gr. k-3). 1983. (ISBN 0-13-622951-4). P-H.

Dinan, Carolyn
--The Lunch Box Monster. Dinan, Carolyn, illus. LC 83-1694. p. cm. (gr. k-2). 1983. (ISBN 0-571-13153-0). Faber & Faber.
--Skipper & Sam. Dinan, Carolyn, illus. LC 84-3988. (Illus.). 96p. (gr. k-2). 1984. (ISBN 0-571-13154-9). (ISBN 0-571-13154-9). Faber & Faber.

Di Nemo, Dina
--The Four Seasons of Vienna: For Musical Children, in Four Parts. LC 45-3624. 75 p. 21 1/2 cm. 1945. House of Field-Doubleday, Inc.

Dines, Harry Glen (1925-)
--Gilly and the Whicharoo. Dines, Harry Glen (1925-), illus. LC 68-27702. (Illus.). 36 p. 26cm. 1968. Lothrop, Lee & Shepard Co.
--The Mysterious Machine. Dines, Harry Glen (1925-), illus. LC 57-7499. (Illus.). 140 p. 21cm. 1957. Macmillan.
--Pitidoe, the Color Maker. Dines, Harry Glen (1925-), illus. LC 59-11297. unpaged. illus. 27cm. 1959. Macmillan.
--Sir Cecil and the Bad Blue Beast. LC 70-125868. (Illus.). 46 p. 27cm. 1970. S. G. Phillips.
--A Tiger in the Cherry Tree. Dines, Harry Glen (1925-), illus. LC 58-10468. (Illus.). 27cm. 1958. Macmillan.
--The Useful Dragon of Sam Ling Toy. Dines, Harry Glen (1925-), illus. LC 56-10785. (Illus.). unpaged. 28cm. 1956. Macmillan.

Dinesen, Isak
--Seven Gothic Tales. N.D. The Modern Library.

Dingman, Briggs P
--By Ways Appointed. LC 36-71. 127 p. incl. front., illus. 19 cm. c.1935. The Bible Institute Colportage Ass'n.

Dingwell, Joyce
--The Drummer and the Song. (Good Reading for Girls Sr.). N.D. Golden Press.

Dini, Gary
--The Heart That Followed Me Home. Dini, Heidi, illus. LC 83-60738. (Illus.). 32p. (gr. 2-5). 1983. (ISBN 0-8091-6548-1). (ISBN 0-8091-6548-1). Paulist Pr.

Dinkelspiel, S. B., pseud., see Dickson, Samuel.

Dinkelspiel, S. B., pseud.
--Lady Rum-Di-Doodle-Dum's Children. Dickson, Samuel. (Illus.). N.D. Frederick Warne & Co.

Dinman, Louise Ed.
--Stories from Greek History for Children. LC 10-17599. (Illus.). 20cm. 235p. (Graded Supplementary Reading Ser.). 1909. Charles E. Merrill Co.

Dinneen, Betty (1929-)
--The Family Howl. Bernath, Stefen, illus. LC 80-25385. (Illus.). 89p. (gr. 4-7). 1981. (ISBN 0-02-732150-9). Macmillan.
--Lion Yellow. Robinson, Charles (1931-), illus. LC 74-19712. p. cm. 1975. (ISBN 0-8098-2428-0). H. Z. Walck.
--Lions & Karen. Parsons, Rita, illus. (Illus.). (gr. 7 up). 1964. (ISBN 0-685-21304-8). Verry.
--A Lurk of Leopards. Robinson, Charles (1931-), illus. LC 72-3205. (Illus.). viii, 215 p. 21cm. 1972. (ISBN 0-8098-3107-4). H. Z. Walck.
--Make Way for the Ark. LC 77-75412. p. cm. c.1977. (ISBN 0-679-20419-9). McKay.
--Striped Horses: The Story of a Zebra Family. Bernath, Stefen, illus. LC 82-7786. (Illus.). 96p. (gr. 4-6). 1982. (ISBN 0-02-732200-9). Macmillan.
--A Tale of Three Leopards. Emry-Perrot, Jennifer, illus. LC 78-22627. (Illus.). 1980. Doubleday.

Di Noto, Andrea
--The Great Flower Pie. Ehlert, Lois Jane (1934-), illus. (Illus.). 1973. (ISBN 0-87888-038-0). McKay.
--The Great Flower Pie: Story. Ehlert, Lois Jane (1934-), illus. LC 72-181742. (Illus.). 32 p. 27cm. (gr. k-3). 1973. (ISBN 0-87888-038-0). Bradbury Press.
--The Star Thief. Lobel, Arnold Stark (1933-), illus. LC 67-10017. (Illus.). (gr. k-2). 1967. (ISBN 0-02-732570-9). Macmillan.

Dinsmoor, Alice (1849-)
--The Goodwins. Keller, Theodore, illus. LC 31-24662. 184 p. front., illus., pl. 21 cm. 1931. Meador Publishing Company.

Dinwoodie, Hepburn
--Storms on the Labrador. LC 38-810542. 3 p. l., 314 p. incl. front., illus. 23 cm. c.1938. Oxford University Press.

Diole, Philippe V. (1908-)
--The Undersea Adventure. N.D. Julian Messner, Inc.

Dionetti, Michelle (1947-)
--The Day Eli Went Looking for Bear. Dos Santos, Joyce Audy, illus. LC 79-23885. (Illus.). 32 p. c.1980. (ISBN 0-201-02663-5). Addison-Wesley.
--Thalia Brown and the Blue Bug. Calvin, James, illus. LC 79-4160. (Illus.). 32 p. 25cm. c.1979. (ISBN 0-201-01399-1). Addison-Wesley Pub. Co.

Diop, Birago
--Tales of Amadou Koumba. (Illus.). 158p. 1966. (ISBN 0-19-913173-2). Oxford University Press.

Diot, Alain
--The Piano Man. Richelson, Geraldine (1922-), adapted by. Leander, Ed, pseud. Galeron, Henri, illus. LC 75-30312. (Illus.). 32 p. 18cm. 1975. (ISBN 0-8252-0138-1). H. Quist : Distributed by Dial/Delacorte Sales.
--Quality Educators, Ltd. Naprstek, Joel Langhorne, illus. LC 77-73532. (gr. 1 up). 1977. (ISBN 0-8252-0478-X). Quist.

Diot, Alain, jt. auth. see Leander, Ed.

Diot, Alain & Naprstek, Joel
--Better, Best, Bestest. LC 77-73532. (Illus.). 23 p. 19cm. c.1977. (ISBN 0-8252-0478-X). H. Quist.

Di Pietro, Nicola, tr. see Bertelli, Luigi.

AUTHOR INDEX DISNEY, WALT

Diqs, Isaak
--Bedouin Boyhood. LC 68-8134. (Illus.). maps. glossary. 180p. (Young Readers Ser). (gr. 9 up). 1969. (ISBN 0-275-25080-6). Praeger.
Di Quattro, Mary
--The Rag Doll Treasure Chest. Tracy, Clare, illus. (Illus.). 1982. (ISBN 0-533-05403-6). Vantage.
Diradour, Virginia
--A Pocketful of Verses. LC 68-23224. 27 p. 21cm. (Contemporary poets of Dorrance, 696). 1968. Dorrance.
Dirk, pseud., see Gringhuis, Richard H..
Dirksen, Everett McKinley (1896-) & Jeffers, H. Paul (1934-)
--Gallant Men: Stories of American Adventure. Zander, Hans (1937-), illus. (gr. 3 up). 1967. (ISBN 0-07-017031-2). McGraw.
Dirksen, Joan
--I'll Find My Love. 1957. Berkley Books.
--I'll Find My Love. LC 57-11277. 190p. 22cm. 1957. Messner.
Dirlam, Mary (1925-), compiled by.
--Hit Parade of Short Stories. LC 54-20966. 17cm. 126p. (A TAB Club Bk.). 1953. Scholastic Corp; Dist. By the Teen Age Book Club.
Disch, Thomas M. (1940-), ed.
--The New Improved Sun: An Anthology of Utopian S-F. LC 74-15866. (Illus.). 216p. 1975. (ISBN 0-06-011052-X, HarpT). Har-Row.
--The Ruins of Earth: An Anthology of Stories of the Immediate Future. 1971. (ISBN 0-399-10127-6). G. P. Putnam's Sons.
Diska, Pat
--Andy Says ... Bonjour!. Jenkyns, Chris (1924-), illus. LC 54-11522. (Illus.). unpaged. 27cm. 1954. Vanguard Press. **Award: (NYT).**
--Andy Says Bonjour. N.D. E. M. Hale & Co.
Disney, Walt see Disney, Walter Elias.
Disney, Walt, Productions
--A B C Mickey Mouse Alphabet Book. 32 p. col. illus. 24 cm. c.1936. Whitman Publishing Co.
--The Adventures of Mickey Mouse. Disney, Walt, Studio, illus. LC 57-52240. v. col. illus. 20 cm. c.1931. David McKay, Company.
--America. Disney, Walt, Studio, illus. LC 65-26172. (Illus.). 256 p. 27cm. (Wonderful worlds of Walt Disney). 1965. Golden Press.
--American Folklore. Authorized. Wright, Betty Ren, retold by. Disney, Walt, Studio, illus. Armstrong, Samuel & Moore, Sparky, eds. LC 56-146511. 252p. illus. 30cm. 1956. Whitman Pub. Co.
--The Aristocats. LC 73-15626. (Illus.). 48p. 1974. (ISBN 0-394-82553-5, BYR). (ISBN 0-394-92553-X). Random.
--Bambi in the Woods: Things to Touch, See, & Sniff. Disney, Walt, Productions, illus. LC 84-60292. (Illus.). 14p. (ps). 1984. (ISBN 0-394-86771-8, Pub. by BYR). Random.
--The Big Bad Wolf and Little Red Riding Hood. Disney, Walt, Studio, illus. LC 34-216942. 60, 4 p. incl. vol. front., illus. (part col.) 27 cm. c.1934. Blue Ribbon Books, Incorporated.
--The Black Hole. LC 79-10622. p. cm. (Walt Disney's wonderful world of reading). 1979. (ISBN 0-394-84279-0). Random House.
--Black Hole. (gr. 4-8). 1979. (ISBN 0-307-65306-4, Golden Pr). Western Pub.
--The Black Hole. Davis, Edith, ed. (Illus.). 48p. (gr. 1-7). 1979. (ISBN 0-307-13505-5, Golden Pr). Western Pub.
--Black Hole. Disney, Walter Elias (1901-1966), illus. 24p. (Young Reader). (ps-3). 1980. (ISBN 0-307-60105-6, Golden Pr). Western Pub.
--The Black Hole Storybook. Steneman, Shep, adapted by. LC 79-10623. (Illus.). (gr. 3 up). 1979. (ISBN 0-394-84278-2, BYR). (ISBN 0-394-94278-7). Random.
--Bongo. LC 48-10134. 32 p. illus. (part col.) 17 cm. (Story hour series). 1948. Whitman Pub. Co.
--Bongo. Starr, Edgar, illus. LC 47-12524. 26 p. col. illus. 34 cm. (Big golden book). 1947. Simon and Schuster.
--The Book of Tall Tales: Featuring "The Shaggy Dog". LC 77-74466. (Illus.). (Disney's World of Adventure). (gr. 2-6). 1978. (ISBN 0-394-83596-4, BYR). (ISBN 0-394-93596-9). Random.
--Cars! Cars! Cars!. Featuring "The Love Bug" & Other Fun on Wheels. LC 77-74465. (Illus.). (Disney's World of Adventure Ser.). (gr. 2-6). 1977. (ISBN 0-394-83598-0, BYR). (ISBN 0-394-93598-5). Random.
--The Circus Book Featuring "Toby Tyler". LC 77-74462. (Illus.). (Disney's World of Adventure). (gr. 2-6). 1978. (ISBN 0-394-83597-2, BYR). (ISBN 0-394-93597-7). Random.
--The Cold-Blooded Penguin. Edmunds, Robert, adapted by. Disney, Walt, Studio, illus. LC 44-510401. (From the Walt Disney Picture " The Three Caballeros"). 24 p. illus. (part col.) 20 x 17 1/2 cm. (On cover: Walt Disney's little library). 1944. Simon and Schuster.
--The Country Cousin. 20 p. col. illus. 27 x 24 cm. 1937. David McKay Company.
--The Detective Book Featuring "Emil & the Detectives". LC 77-74463. (Illus.). (Disney's World of Adventure Ser.). (gr. 2-6). 1978. (ISBN 0-394-83600-0, BYR). (ISBN 0-394-83600-6). Random.
--Disney Mini-Pops, 6 bks. (Illus.). (ps-1). 1977 (Pub by Windmill Bks). Dutton.
--Disney Read-Aloud Film Classics: Snow White. 1981. (Harmony). (Harmony). Crown.
--Disney's World of Adventure Presents The Book of Tall Tales. LC 77-74466. (Illus.). 59 p. 27cm. c.1978. (ISBN 0-394-83596-4). (ISBN 0-394-93596-9). Random House.
--Disney's World of Adventure Presents The Circus Book. LC 77-74462. (Illus.). 59 p. 26cm. (Disney's World of Adventure). c.1978. (ISBN 0-394-83597-2). (ISBN 0-394-93597-7). Random House.
--Disney's World of Adventure Presents The Detective Book. LC 77-74463. (Illus.). 61 p. 26cm. 1978. (ISBN 0-394-83600-6). (ISBN 0-394-93600-0). Random House.
--Disney's World of Adventure Presents The Outdoor Adventure Book. LC 77-74468. p. cm. 1977. (ISBN 0-394-83601-4). (ISBN 0-394-93601-9). Random House.
--Disney's World of Adventure Presents The Underwater Adventure Book. LC 77-90198. (Illus.). 59 p. 27cm. (Disney's World of Adventure). c.1978. (ISBN 0-394-83602-2). (ISBN 0-394-93602-7). Random House.
--Donald at Sea. Disney, Walt, Productions, illus. (Illus.). 10p. (Bathtime Bks.). (ps). 1984. (ISBN 0-394-86751-3, Pub. by BYR). Random.
--Donald Duck. Disney, Walt, Studio, illus. LC 37-3370. (Illus.). 27 x 21cm. 33p. 1936. Grosset & Dunlop.
--Donald Duck. Disney, Walt, Studio, illus. LC 35-43. (Illus.). 33cm. 14p. 1935. Whitman Publishing Co.
--Donald Duck and His Friends. Disney, Walt, Studio, illus. LC 37-16543. 45, 1 p. illus. 30 cm. c.1937. Whitman Publishing Company.
--Donald Duck and His Nephews. Disney, Walt, Studio, illus. LC 84-9346. 1984. (ISBN 0-89659-511-0). Abbeville Press.
--Donald Duck and the Green Serpent. LC 48-16135. 1 v. (unpaged) illus. 12 cm. (The Better Little Books 1432: No.). 1947. Whitman Pub. Co.
--Donald Duck and the Magic Stick. LC 74-16493. p. cm. (Disney's wonderful world of reading, v. 25). 1975. (ISBN 0-394-82564-0). (ISBN 0-394-92564-5). Random House.
--Donald Duck & the Super-Sticky Secret. Disney, Walter Elias (1901-1966), illus. 32p. (Tell-a-Tale Reader). (ps-3). 1980. (ISBN 0-307-68425-3, Golden Pr). Western Pub.
--Donald Duck and the Witch. Bedford, Annie North, pseud. (1915-), as told by Watson, Jane Werner. Bedford, Annie North, pseud. Disney, Walt, Studio, illus. Kelsey, Richard I., adapted by. LC 53-3497. (Based on the Motion Picture "Trick or Treats"). unpaged. illus. 21cm. (Little golden book, D34). 1953. Simon and Schuster.
--Donald Duck Goes Camping. Disney, Walt, Productions, illus. (Illus.). (Tell-a-Tale Readers). (gr. k-3). 1979. (ISBN 0-307-68609-4, Whitman). Western Pub.
--Donald Duck Has His Ups and Downs. Disney, Walt, Studio, illus. LC 37-16369. 24 p. col. illus. 24 x 22 cm. c.1937. Whitman Publishing Company.
--Donald Duck in Bringing up the Boys. LC 48-10133. 32 p. illus. (part col.) 17 cm. (Story hour series). 1948. Whitman Pub. Co.
--Donald's Penguin. A Walt Disney Book. LC 40-148133. 24 p. illus. (part col.) 24 cm. c.1940. Garden City Publishing Company, Inc.
--Dumbo. Disney, Walt, Studio, illus. (Illus.). (ps-3). 1976. (ISBN 0-307-66050-8, Golden Pr). Western Pub.
--Dumbo. Sanchez, Rene, tr. Disney, Walt Studio, illus. (Illus.). 24p. (ps-3). 1977. (ISBN 0-307-68841-0, Golden Pr). Western Pub.
--Elmer Elephant. Disney, Walt, Studio, illus. LC 37-848. 46, 1 p. col. illus. 22 cm. c.1936. David McKay Company.
--Fantasy on Parade. rev. ed. Disney, Walt, Productions, illus. LC 76-23970. (Illus.). 256 p. 27cm. (The Walt Disney Parade of Fun, Fact, Fantasy, and Fiction). c.1977. (ISBN 0-307-15600-1). Golden Press.
--Fantasy on Parade. Disney, Walt, Studio, illus. LC 77-116696. (Illus.). 23cm. 255p. 1970. Golden Press.
--Fantasyland. Disney, Walt, Studio, illus. LC 65-26170. (Illus.). 253 p. 27cm. (Wonderful Worlds of Disney). 1965. Golden Press.
--The Fox and the Hound. LC 80-85424. (Illus.). 33 p. 29cm. c.1981. (ISBN 0-307-16802-6). Golden Press.
--The Fox and the Hound: Lost & Found. LC 81-81326. (Illus.). 13 p. 22cm. (Little Golden Sniff It Book). c.1981. (ISBN 0-307-13202-1). Golden Press.
--The Fox Finds a Friend. LC 81-80061. (Illus.). 12 p. 24cm. (A Golden Sturdy Shape Book). c.1981. (ISBN 0-307-12261-1). Golden Press.
--Friends to Find. Disney, Walter Elias (1901-1966), illus. 24p. (Winnie-the-Pooh Hunny Pot Bks.). (ps-3). 1980. (ISBN 0-307-68874-7, Golden Pr). Western Pub.
--Fun Favorites. rev. ed. Disney, Walt, Productions, illus. LC 76-23975. (Illus.). 256 p. 27cm. (The Walt Disney Parade of Fun, Fact, Fantasy, and Fiction). c.1977. (ISBN 0-307-15598-6). Golden Press.
--Fun Favorites. Disney, Walt, Studio, illus. LC 73-116695. (Illus.). 256. 27cm. (Walt Disney Parade of Fun, Fact, Fantasy and Fiction). c.1970. Golden Press.
--The Giant Walt Disney Word Book. LC 72-78621. (Illus.). 141 p. 29cm. (Golden book). 1972. Golden Press.
--Golden Everything Workbook Box for Beginning Readers & Counters. (Illus.). (ps-6). 1979. (ISBN 0-307-13639-6, Golden Pr). Western Pub.
--The Golden Touch. LC 38-4577. 2 p. l., 9-212 p. col. front., illus., col. plates. 23 cm. c.1937. Whitman Publishing Company.
--Goofy Keeps Fit. (ps-1). 1979. (ISBN 0-307-61079-9, Golden Pr). (ISBN 0-307-11079-6). Western Pub.
--Goofy Minds the House. LC 75-5851. 42p. col. ill. 24cm. (Disney's wonderful world of reading ; 31). 1975, c.1977. (ISBN 0-394-82573-X). (ISBN 0-394-92573-4). Random House.
--Great Moments in Fiction. rev. ed. Disney, Walt, Studio, illus. LC 76-23592. (Illus.). 256 p. 27cm. (The Walt Disney Parade of Fun, Fact, Fantasy, and Fiction). c.1977. (ISBN 0-307-15601-X). Golden Press.
--Hiawatha. LC 37-23688. 20 p. col. illus. 27 x 24 cm. c.1937. David McKay Company.
--Hide & Seek. LC 80-85425. (Illus.). 24 p. 20cm. (Little Golden Books). c.1981. (ISBN 0-307-01056-2). Golden Press.
--The Hound Finds a Friend. LC 81-80060. (Illus.). 12 p. 25cm. (Golden Sturdy Shape Book). c.1981. (ISBN 0-307-12264-6). Golden Press.
--How Do You Do? I'm Winnie the Pooh. Disney, Walt, Studio, illus. (Illus.). 10p. (Bathtime Bks.). (ps). 1985. (ISBN 0-394-87029-8, BYR). Random.
--If I Met Winnie the Pooh. Disney Artists, illus. LC 77-95424. (Illus.). (Stretch Books). (gr. k-2). 1978. (ISBN 0-448-16150-8, G&D). Putnam Pub Group.
--Jokes & Riddles. Disney, Walter Elias (1901-1966), illus. 24p. (Winnie-the-Pooh Hunny Pot Bk.). (ps-3). 1980. (ISBN 0-307-68869-0, Golden Pr). Western Pub.
--Little Red Riding Hood and the Big Bad Wolf. Disney, Walt Studio, illus. LC 34-17655. 32 p. illus. 22 cm. c.1934. David McKay Company.
--The Love Bug. LC 78-13896. (Illus.). (Walt Disney's Wonderful World of Reading Ser.). (gr. k-3). 1979. (ISBN 0-394-84139-5, BYR). (ISBN 0-394-94139-X). Random.
--Mad Hatter's Tea Party. Watson, Jane Werner (1915-), retold by. Bedford, Anne North, pseud. Disney, Walt, Studio, illus. Kelsey, Richard I. & Griffith, Don, eds. LC 51-13856. (From the Motion Picture Based on the Story by Lewis Carroll). unpaged. illus. 21 cm. (Little golden library, D23). 1951. Simon and Schuster.
--Magic Tricks. Disney, Walter Elias (1901-1966), illus. 24p. (Winnie-the-Pooh Hunny Pot Bk.). (ps-3). 1980. (ISBN 0-307-68870-4, Golden Pr). Western Pub.
--Mickey and the Beanstalk. LC 48-10135. 32 p. illus. (part col.) 17 cm. (Story hour series). N.D. Whitman Pub. Co..
--Mickey and the Beanstalk. Campbell, Grant, illus. LC 47-111902. 32 p. illus. (part col.) 22 cm. 1947. Grosset and Dunlap.
--Mickey Mouse. LC 34-20210. 1 p. l., 7-316p. 1 p. front., illus. 11cm. (On cover: The Big Little Books). c.1933. Whitman Publishing Company.
--A Mickey Mouse A B C Story. LC 38-35049. 31 p. col. illus. 29 cm. c.1937. Whitman Publishing Co.
--Mickey Mouse and His Friends Wait for the County Fair. LC 37-16870. 24 p. col. illus. 24 x 22 cm. c.1937. Whitman Publishing Company.
--Mickey Mouse and His Horse Tanglefoot. LC 37-847. 2 p. l., 60 p. col. illus. 22 cm. c.1936. David McKay Company.
--Mickey Mouse and Pluto ... LC 38-127368. 66 p. illus. (part col.) 26 cm. c.1936. Whitman Publishing Company.
--Mickey Mouse and the Lazy Daisy Mystery. LC 48-16136. 286 p. illus. 12 cm. (The Better Little Books1433: No.). 1947. Whitman Pub. Co.
--Mickey Mouse and the Marvelous Smell Machine. LC 79-63295. (Illus.). 29 p. 25cm. (Golden scratch & sniff book). c.1979. (ISBN 0-307-13544-6). Golden Press.
--The Mickey Mouse Birthday Book. LC 78-55911. (Illus.). (Disney's Wonderful World of Reading Ser.). (ps-3). 1978. (ISBN 0-394-83963-3, BYR). (ISBN 0-394-93963-8). Random.
--Mickey Mouse Crusoe. LC 36-394. 70, 1 p. col. front., illus. 25 cm. c.1936. Whitman Publishing Company.
--The Mickey Mouse Fire Brigade ... LC 38-12737. 66 p. incl. front., illus. (part col.) 26 cm. c.1936. Whitman Publishing Co.
--Mickey Mouse Has a Busy Day. LC 37-163752. 24 p. col. illus. 24 x 22 cm. c.1937. Whitman Publishing Company.
--Mickey Mouse Has a Party: A School Reader. LC 38-85050. 48 p. col. illus. 25 cm. c.1938. Whitman Publishing Company.
--Mickey Mouse in Giantland. Disney, Walt, Studio, illus. LC 35-182632. 1 p. l., 45 p. col. illus. (part col.) 25 cm. c.1934. David McKay Company.
--Mickey Mouse in King Arthur's Court. LC 34-3732. 48 p. incl. front., illus. (part col.) 25 cm. c.1933. Blue Ribbon Books, Inc.
--Mickey Mouse in Pigmyland. LC 36-393. 70. 1 p. col. front., illus. 25 cm. c.1936. Whitman Publishing Company.
--Mickey Mouse Movie Stories. Disney, Walt, Studio, illus. LC 32-579. 4 p. l., 190 p. illus. 23 cm. c.1931. David McKay Company.
--Mickey Mouse Story Book. Disney, Walt, Productions, illus. LC 77-364831. (Illus.). 62 p. 22cm. c.1931. David McKay Company.
--Mickey Mouse the Boat-Builder. LC 38-15221. 28 p. col. illus. 18 x 21 cm. c.1938. Grosset & Dunlap.
--Mickey Mouse, the Mail Pilot. LC 34-20211. 1 p. l., 7-296, 1 p. front., illus. 11 cm. (On cover: The Big Little Books). c.1933. Whitman Publishing Company.
--Mickey Mouse Waddle Book. Disney, Walt, Studio, illus. LC 34-35884. 33 p. illus. (part col.) 26 cm. c.1934. Blue Ribbon Books, Incorporated.
--Mickey Mouse's Summer Vacation. LC 48-10136. 32 p. illus. (part col.) 17 cm. (Story hour series). 1948. Whitman Pub. Co.
--Mickey's Christmas Carol. Disney, Walt, Studio, illus. LC 82-84522. (Illus.). 32p. (Golden Melody Bks.). (ps). N.D. (ISBN 0-307-12236-0, Golden Bks). (ISBN 0-307-04592-7). Western Pub.
--Mickey's Magic Hat and the Cookie Carnival. LC 37-16371. 24 p. col. illus. 24 x 22 cm. c.1937. Whitman Publishing Company.
--The New Walt Disney Treasury. LC 72-155677. (Illus.). 93 p. 32cm. (Giant golden book). 1971. Golden Press.
--New Walt Disney Treasury. 1971. (ISBN 0-307-15546-3, Golden Pr). (ISBN 0-307-65546-6). Western Pub.
--Nursery Rhymes. (ps-1). 1979. (ISBN 0-307-61077-2, Golden Pr). Western Pub.
--Nursery Stories from Walt Disney's Silly Symphony. LC 38-4578. 2 p. l., 9-212 p. col. front., illus., col. pl. 23 cm. c.1937. Whitman Publishing Company.
--One Hundred and One Dalmations. Buettner, Carl, adapted by. Disney, Walt, Studio & McGary, Norman, illus. LC 61-2724. (Based on the Book by Dodie Smith). (Illus.). 29cm. (A Big Golden Bk.). 1961. Golden Press.
--One Hundred and One Dalmations. Buettner, Carl, adapted by. Disney, Walt, Studio & Mattinson, Sylvia, illus. LC 61-8485. (Illus.). 23cm. 59p. (A Golden Reading Adventures). 1961. Golden Press.
--The Outdoor Adventure Book. LC 77-74468. (Illus.). (Disney's World of Adventure). (gr. 2-6). 1977. (ISBN 0-394-83601-4, BYR). (ISBN 0-394-93601-9). Random.
--Peculiar Penguins. Disney, Walt, Studio, illus. LC 35-19029. 1 p. l., 45 p. col. illus. 22 cm. c.1934. David McKay Company.
--The Plot to Capture Robin Hood: From the Walt Disney Motion Picture "Robin Hood". authorized. LC 73-83837. (Illus.). 45 p. 31cm. 1973. Golden Press.
--Pluto and the Puppy. LC 37-16542. 36 p. incl. col. front., illus. (part col.) 27 x 25 cm. c.1937. Grosset and Dunlap.
--The "Pop-up" Silly Symphonies: Containing Babes in the Woods and King Neptune. Disney, Walt, Studio, illus. LC 34-3729. 48 p. incl. front., illus. (part col.) 25 cm. c.1933. Blue Ribbon Books, in.
--The Princess Who Never Laughed. LC 74-14699. 42 col. ill. 24. (Disney's wonderful world of reading, no. 24). 1975, c.1974. (ISBN 0-394-82565-9). (ISBN 0-394-92565-3). Random House.
--The Rescuers. authorized. LC 77-78389. (Illus.). 47 p. 26cm. (Kid's paperback). c.1977. (ISBN 0-307-12366-9). Golden Press.
--The Rescuers. authorized. LC 76-54412. (Illus.). 42 p. 24cm. (Disney's wonderful world of reading). c.1977. (ISBN 0-394-83456-9). (ISBN 0-394-93456-3). Random House.

--The Rescuers. Disney, Walt, Studio, illus. (Illus.). (ps-3). 1977. (ISBN 0-307-62366-1, Golden Pr). (ISBN 0-307-12366-9). Western Pub.
--Return to Oz. LC 84-43005. (Illus.). 48p. (Disney's Wonderful World of Reading Ser.: No. 54). (ps-3). N.D. (ISBN 0-394-97183-3, BYR). (ISBN 0-394-87183-9). Random.
--The Robber Kitten. Disney, Walt, Studio, illus. LC 35-33164. (Illus.). 23 x 26cm. 46p. 1935. David McKay Company.
--Robin Hood. Disney, Walt, Productions, illus. LC 73-83836. (Illus.). 92 p. 31cm. 1973. Golden Press.
--Robin Hood & the Great Coach Robbery. LC 73-18738. (Illus.). 48p. 1974. (ISBN 0-394-82554-3, BYR). (ISBN 0-394-92554-8). Random.
--Robin Hood to the Rescue: From the Walt Disney Motion Picture Robin Hood. LC 73-77489. (Illus.). 34 p. 28cm. 34p. 1973. Golden Press.
--The Runaway Lamb at the County Fair. Disney, Walt, Studio & Svendsen, Julius, illus. LC 50-5784. 31 p. illus. (part col.) 27 cm. (Walt Disney picture story book). 1949. Grosset and Dunlap.
--The Small One. LC 78-20718. p. cm. c.1979. (ISBN 0-394-84232-4). (ISBN 0-394-94232-9). Random House.
--Snow White and the Seven Dwarfs. Authorized. LC 42-32089. (Illus.). 23 x 25cm. 15p. 1938. Walt Disney Enterprises.
--Snow White and the Seven Dwarfs. Disney, Walt, Studio, illus. LC 38-57486. 41 p. illus. (part col.) 27 cm. c.1937. David McKay Company.
--Snow White and the Seven Dwarfs. Disney, Walt, Studio, illus. LC 38-152205. 38 p. illus. (part col.) 19 x 24 cm. c.1938. Grosset & Dunlap.
--The Sorcerer's Apprentice. LC 73-9891. (Illus.). 48p. 1974. (ISBN 0-394-82551-9, BYR). (ISBN 0-394-92551-3). Random.
--Stories from Other Lands. Disney, Walt, Studio, illus. LC 65-261732. (Illus.). 256 p. 27cm. (Wonderful worlds of Walt Disney). 1965. Golden Press.
--The Story of Casey, Jr. A Walt Disney Book. LC 41-20888. 28 p. illus. (part col.) 24 cm. c.1941. Garden City Publishing Company.
--The Story of Timothy's House: A Walt Disney Book. LC 41-20885. 28 p. illus. (part col.) 24 cm. c.1941. Garden City Publishing Company.
--That's What Friends Are for: Walt Disney Productions' The Fox and the Hound. LC 80-84782. (Illus.). 24 p. 21cm. (Golden Look-Look Book). c.1981. (ISBN 0-307-11859-2). Golden Press.
--Three Favorite Tales. book club ed. LC 75-8845. (Illus.). 45 p. 24cm. (Disney's wonderful world of reading). c.1975. (ISBN 0-394-82574-8). (ISBN 0-394-92574-2). Random House.
--The Three Orphan Kittens. Disney, Walt, Studio, illus. LC 35-33165. 46. 1 p. incl. col. front., illus. (part col.) 23 x 26 cm. c.1935. David McKay Company.
--Timid Elmer. LC 39-30880. 64 p. illus. 13 x 14 cm. c.1939. Whitman Publishing Company.
--The Tortoise and the Hare. Disney, Walt, Studio, illus. LC 35-331633. 48 p. incl. col. front., illus. (part col.) 23 x 26 cm. c.1935. David McKay Company.
--Treasure Chest. Disney, Walt, Studio, illus. LC 48-9886. 66 p. illus. (part col.) 29 cm. (Big golden book). 1948. Simon and Schuster.
--The Ugly Duckling. LC 40-4859. 64 p. illus. 13 x 14 cm. c.1939. Whitman Publishing Company.
--The Underwater Adventure Book Featuring "20,000 Leagues Under the Sea". LC 77-90198. (Disney's World of Adventure Ser.). (gr. 3-7). 1978. (ISBN 0-394-83602-2, BYR). (ISBN 0-394-93602-7). Random.
--The Walt Disney Annual. LC 37-172474. v. illus., col. plates. 35 x 28 cm. N.D. Whitman Publishing Co.
--Walt Disney Legends of Davy Crockett: Based on Walt Disney's Television Films and the Motion Picture Davy Crockett, King of the Wild Frontier, with Fess Parker. Authorized. Arens, Michael, illus. Burton, Ardis Edwards, ed. LC 55-12836. 283p. illus. 21cm. 1955. Whitman Pub. Co.
--The Walt Disney Parade. Disney, Walt, Studio, illus. LC 40-32218. 3 p. l., 3-176 p. illus. (part col.) plates 29 x 22 cm. c.1940. The Garden City Publishing Co., Inc.
--Walt Disney Pictures Presents Return to Oz. LC 84-43005. (Illus.). 44 p. 25cm. (Disney's Wonderful World of Reading: No. 54). c.1985. (ISBN 0-394-87183-9). (ISBN 0-394-97183-3). Random House.
--Walt Disney Presents The Jungle Book. Bedford, Anne North, pseud. Watson, Jane Werner (1915-), retold by. Disney, Walt, Productions, illus. LC 67-20158. (Original Author: Joseph Rudyard KIpley (1865-1936)). (Illus.). 76 p. 34cm. (Giant golden book). 1967. Golden Press.
--Walt Disney Production Presents 101 Dalmations. LC 74-10829. (Illus.). 42 p. 24cm. (Disney's wonderful world of reading, no. 23). 1975, c.1974. (ISBN 0-394-82571-3). (ISBN 0-394-82571-3). Random House.
--Walt Disney Productions' Exploring the Hundred Acre Wood. LC 80-51162. (Illus.). 48 p. 21cm. (Disney's Adventures of Winnie-the-Pooh). c.1980. (ISBN 0-307-23206-9). Golden Press.
--Walt Disney Productions Presents A Christmas Surprise for Uncle Scrooge. LC 81-23559. p. cm. (Disney's Wonderful World of Reading ; 51). c.1981. (ISBN 0-394-85111-0). (ISBN 0-394-95111-5). Random House.
--Walt Disney Productions Presents A Narrow Escape. book club ed., 1st american. LC 84-241373. (Illus.). 44 p. 23cm. (Disney's World of Wonderful Reading). c.1984. (ISBN 0-394-86537-5). Random House.
--Walt Disney Productions Presents "Brer Rabbit & His Friends". (Illus.). (Disney's Wonderful World of Reading Ser.: No. 13). (ps-3). 1974. (ISBN 0-394-82774-0, BYR). (ISBN 0-394-92774-5). Random.
--Walt Disney Productions Presents "Brer Rabbit Gets Tricked". Book Club , 1st american ed. LC 81-149123. (Illus.). 41 p. 24cm. (Disney's Wonderful World of Reading). c.1981. (ISBN 0-394-84806-3). (ISBN 0-394-94904-8). Random House.
--Walt Disney Productions Presents Brer Rabbit Saves His Skin. book club ed., 1st american. LC 79-106653. (Illus.). 41 p. 25cm. (Disney's wonderful world of reading). c.1979. (ISBN 0-394-94159-4). (ISBN 0-394-84159-X). Random House.
--Walt Disney Productions Presents Button Soup. LC 74-28376. p. cm. (Disney's wonderful world of reading ; 28). 1975. (ISBN 0-394-82562-4). Random House.
--Walt Disney Productions Presents Donald Duck's Birthday. Book club ed. LC 82-18554. 1st U.S. edition. (Disney's Wonderful World of Reading). c.1983. (ISBN 0-394-85735-6). Random House.
--Walt Disney Productions Presents Donald Duck, Mountain Climber. LC 78-112190. (Illus.). 42 p. 25cm. (Disney's wonderful world of reading). c.1978. (ISBN 0-394-84078-X). (ISBN 0-394-94078-4). Random House.
--Walt Disney Productions Presents Donald Duck's Tallest Tale. LC 80-146357. (Illus.). 42 p. 24cm. (Disney's wonderful world of reading). c.1980. (ISBN 0-394-84740-7). (ISBN 0-394-94740-1). Random House.
--Walt Disney Productions Presents "Goofy and the Miller". Book club ed. Disney, Walt, Productions, illus. LC 79-101112. (Illus.). 42 p. 24cm. 1st U.S. edition. (Disney's Wonderful World of Reading). c.1978. (ISBN 0-394-84119-0). (ISBN 0-394-94119-5). Random House.
--Walt Disney Productions Presents "Goofy and the Magic Fish". book club ed., 1st american. LC 79-117840. (Illus.). 42 p. 24cm. (Disneys wonderful world of reading). c.1979. (ISBN 0-394-84158-1). (ISBN 0-394-94158-6). Random House.
--Walt Disney Productions Presents Goofy and the Pirate Treasure. LC 80-121110. (Illus.). 44 p. 24cm. (Disney's wonderful world of reading). c.1980. (ISBN 0-394-84538-2). (ISBN 0-394-94538-7). Random House.
--Walt Disney Productions Presents Goofy's Gags. LC 74-2043. (Illus.). 46 p. 24cm. (Disney's wonderful world of reading, 19). (No.19). (ps-3). 1974. (ISBN 0-394-82558-6). (ISBN 0-394-92558-0). Random House.
--Walt Disney Productions Presents Hiawatha and the Big Flood. book club ed., 1st american. LC 84-178977. (Illus.). 38 p. 22cm. (Disney's Wonderful World of Reading). c.1984. (ISBN 0-394-86560-X). Random House.
--Walt Disney Productions Presents Lady and the Tramp. Book Club , 1st american ed. LC 81-168246. (Illus.). 42 p. 25cm. (Disney's Wonderful World of Reading). c.1981. (ISBN 0-394-84955-8). Random House.
--Walt Disney Productions Presents Li'l Wolf and the Three Little Pigs. LC 84-185762. (Illus.). 42 p. 23cm. (Disney's Wonderful World of Reading). c.1984. (ISBN 0-394-86596-0). Random House.
--Walt Disney Productions Presents Lucky Puppy. LC 79-106706. (Illus.). 42 p. 25cm. (Disney's wonderful world of reading). c.1978. (ISBN 0-394-84117-4). (ISBN 0-394-94117-9). Random House.
--Walt Disney Productions Presents Merry Christmas, Uncle Scrooge McDuck!. Book Club , 1st american ed. LC 81-127825. (Illus.). 44 p. 25cm. (Disney's Wonderful World of Reading). c.1980. (ISBN 0-394-84781-4). (ISBN 0-394-94781-9). Random House.
--Walt Disney Productions Presents Mickey and the Haunted House: A Book of Hidden Surprises. LC 84-60291. (Illus.). 10 p. 24cm. c.1984. (ISBN 0-394-86772-6). Random House.
--Walt Disney Productions Presents Mickey and the Magic Cloak. LC 75-23314. p. cm. (Disney's wonderful world of reading ; 36). 1975. (ISBN 0-394-82566-7). (ISBN 0-394-92566-1). Random House.
--Walt Disney Productions Presents Mickey's Counting Book. LC 82-18554. (Disney's Wonderful World of Reading). c.1983. (ISBN 0-394-85735-6). Random House.
--Walt Disney Productions Presents Mickey's Christmas Carol. LC 84-4860. (Based on A Christmas Carol by Charles Dickens, 1812-1870). (Disney's Wonderful World of Reading). 1984, c.1982. (ISBN 0-394-85615-5). Random House.
--Walt Disney Productions Presents Mowgli and Kaa the Python. LC 81-203048. (Illus.). 42 p. 24cm. (Disney's Wonderful World of Reading). c.1981. (ISBN 0-394-85109-9). Random House.
--Walt Disney Productions Presents Robin Hood and the Great Coach Robbery. LC 73-18738. (Illus.). 42 p. 25cm. (Disney's wonderful world of reading). 1974. (ISBN 0-394-82554-3). (ISBN 0-394-82554-3). Random House.
--Walt Disney Productions Presents Robin Hood Spins Gold. LC 79-101630. (Illus.). 44 p. 25cm. (Disney's wonderful world of reading). c.1979. Random House.
--Walt Disney Productions Presents Scamp Saves the House. LC 81-140476. (Illus.). 44 p. 25cm. (Disney's Wonderful World of Reading). c.1980. (ISBN 0-394-84817-9). Random House.
--Walt Disney Productions Presents Scamp to the Rescue. book club ed. LC 80-146346. (Illus.). 42 p. 24cm. 1st U.S. edition. (Disney's wonderful world of reading). c.1980. (ISBN 0-394-84741-5). (ISBN 0-394-94741-X). Random House.
--Walt Disney Productions Presents Sindbad the Sailor. LC 79-103963. (Illus.). 41 p. 25cm. (Disney's wonderful world of reading). c.1978. (ISBN 0-394-84118-2). (ISBN 0-394-94118-7). Random House.
--Walt Disney Productions Presents "The Aristocats". authorized. LC 73-18764. (Illus.). 24 p. 32cm. (Big golden book). 1970. Golden Press Book.
--Walt Disney Productions Presents "The Aristocats". LC 73-15626. (Illus.). 42 p. 24cm. (Disney's wonderful world of reading, no. 14). 1974, c.1973. (ISBN 0-394-82553-5). (ISBN 0-394-82553-5). Random House.
--Walt Disney Productions Presents "The Black Hole". LC 79-10622. (Illus.). (Walt Disney's Wonderful World of Reading: No. 47). (ps-3). 1979. (ISBN 0-394-84279-0, BYR). (ISBN 0-394-94279-5). Random.
--Walt Disney Productions Presents The Love Bug. LC 78-13896. (Illus.). 42 p. 25cm. (Disney's wonderful world of reading ; 45). c.1979. (ISBN 0-394-84139-5). (ISBN 0-394-94139-X). (ISBN 0-394-94139-X). Random House.
--Walt Disney Productions Presents The Mystery Box. LC 80-107389. (Illus.). 42 p. 25cm. (Disney's wonderful world of reading). c.1979. (ISBN 0-394-84358-4). (ISBN 0-394-94358-9). Random House.
--Walt Disney Productions Presents "the Rescuers". LC 76-54412. (Illus.). (Disney's Wonderful World of Reading: No. 37). (ps-2). 1977. (ISBN 0-394-83456-9, BYR). (ISBN 0-394-93456-3). Random.
--Walt Disney Productions Presents "The Small One". LC 78-20718. (Illus.). (Walt Disney's Wonderful World of Reading: No. 46). (ps-3). 1979. (ISBN 0-394-84232-4, BYR). (ISBN 0-394-94232-9). Random.
--Walt Disney Productions Presents The Haunted House. LC 75-16430. 24cm. 44p. (Disney's wonderful world of reading ; 34). (Disney's Wonderful World of Reading Ser.: No.33). (ps-3). 1975. (ISBN 0-394-82570-5). (ISBN 0-394-92570-X). Random House.
--Walt Disney Productions Presents The Mice and the Circus. book club ed., 1st american. LC 79-129723. (Illus.). 42 p. 25cm. (Disney's wonderful world of reading). c.1979. (ISBN 0-394-84357-6). (ISBN 0-394-94357-0). Random House.
--Walt Disney Productions Presents The Magic Grinder. LC 75-11995. p. cm. (Disney's wonderful world of reading ; 33). 1975. (ISBN 0-394-82575-6). (ISBN 0-394-92575-0). Random House.
--Walt Disney Productions Presents "The Mystery of the Missing Peanuts". LC 75-1088. (Illus.). 48p. (Disney's Wonderful World of Reading Ser.: No. 30). (gr. 1-2). 1975. (ISBN 0-394-82572-1, BYR). (ISBN 0-394-92572-6). Random.
--Walt Disney Productions Presents Three Aristocrats in Trouble. Book Club , 1st american ed. LC 81-166663. (Illus.). 40 p. 25cm. (Disney's Wonderful World of Reading). c.1981. (ISBN 0-394-84846-2). Random House.
--Walt Disney Productions Presents Three Favorite Tales. LC 75-8845. p. cm. (Disney's wonderful world of reading ; 32). 1975. (ISBN 0-394-82574-8). (ISBN 0-394-92574-2). Random House.
--Walt Disney Productions Presents Tod & Copper from The Fox & the Hound. LC 81-2619. (Illus.). 48p. (Walt Disney's Wonderful World of Reading Ser.: No. 50). (ps-3). 1981. (ISBN 0-394-84819-5). (ISBN 0-394-94819-X). Random.
--Walt Disney Productions Presents Tod & Vixey from The Fox & the Hound. LC 81-5209. (Illus.). 48p. (Walt Disney's Wonderful World of Reading Ser.: No. 51). (ps-3). 1981. (ISBN 0-394-84904-3). (ISBN 0-394-94904-8). Random.
--Walt Disney Productions' Sir Brian and the Dragon. LC 80-51163. (Illus.). 21cm. 48p. (Disney's Adventures of Winnie-the-Pooh). c.1980. Golden Press.
--Walt Disney Productions' The Black Hole Poster Book. LC 79-18556. p. cm. c.1979. (ISBN 0-517-53892-X). Harmony Books.
--Walt Disney's Adventures of Mickey Mouse. 50th birthday ed. LC 77-26356. (Illus.). 128 p. 22cm. 1978. (ISBN 0-679-50854-6). D. McKay Co.
--Walt Disney's Adventures of Robin Hood. LC 53-13533. (Illus.). 29cm. 46p. (Walt Disney Library). 1955. Simon and Schuster.
--Walt Disney's Alice Favorites. LC 73-3257. (Illus.). 189 p. 25cm. 1973. Danbury Press.
--Walt Disney's Alice in Wonderland Finds the Garden of Live Flowers. Watson, Jane Werner (1915-), retold by. Disney, Walt, Studio, illus. Grant, Campbell, adapted by. LC 51-40026. unpaged. illus. 21 cm. (Little golden library, D20). 1951. Simon and Schuster.
--Walt Disney's Alice in Wonderland Meets the White Rabbit. Watson, Jane Werner (1915-), retold by. Disney, Walt, Studio, illus. Dempster, Al, adapted by. LC 51-13084. (From the Motion Picture Based on the Story by Lewis Carroll.). unpaged. illus. 21 cm. (Little golden library, D19). 1951. Simon and Schuster.
--Walt Disney's Andy Burnett. Verral, Charles Spain (1904-), adapted by. Dreany, E. Joseph, illus. LC 58-14641. (Based on the stories by Stewart Edward White). (Illus.). 29cm. 42p. (Big Golden book: 305). 1958. Simon & Schuster.
--Walt Disney's "Bambi". LC 41-22153. 52 p. incl. col. front., illus. (part col.) 4 col. pl. 29 x 23 cm. c.1941. Simon and Schuster.
--Walt Disney's Bambi. Grant, Bob, adapted by. Disney, Walt, Studio, illus. LC 48-6666. (Based on the Original by Felix Salten). (Illus.). 21cm. 42p. (The Little Golden Library). 1948. Simon and Schuster.
--Walt Disney's Bear Country. Godwin, Stephani & Godwin, Edward Fell (1912-), illus. LC 55-23675. (Story Adapted from the Walt Disney True-Life Adventure Motion Picture 'Bear Country). unpaged. illus. 17cm. (Tell-a-tale books, 2554). c.1954. Whitman Pub. Co.
--Walt Disney's Beaver Valley. Werner, Jane (1915-), adapted by. 1956. Golden Press.
--Walt Disney's Beaver Valley. Wright, Betty Ren, adapted by. Hartwell, Marjorie, illus. LC 55-236762. (Story Adapted from the Walt Disney True-Life Adventure Motion Picture 'Beaver Valley'). unpaged. illus. 17cm. (Tell-a-tale books, 2553). c.1954. Whitman Pub. Co.
--Walt Disney's Ben and Me. Authorized. Klein, Earl, adapted by. Disney, Walt, Studio, illus. LC 54-371853. unpaged. illus. 22cm. (Cozy-corner book). c.1954. Whitman Pub. Co.
--Walt Disney's Bongo. Grant, Campbell, adapted by. Disney, Walt, Studio, illus. LC 49-131. (Illus.). 20cm. 42p. (The Little Golden Library). 1948. Simon and Schuster.
--Walt Disney's Chip 'n' Dale at the Zoo. Bedford, Annie North, pseud. (1915-) & Bosche, Bill, eds. Watson, Jane Werner. Disney, Walt, Studio, illus. LC 54-3718. unpaged. illus. 21cm. (Little golden book, D38). 1954. Simon and Schuster.
--Walt Disney's Christmas Treasury. LC 78-14209. p. cm. 1978. (ISBN 0-89659-004-6). Abbeville Press.
--Walt Disney's Cinderella. LC 74-22325. (Illus.). 48p. (Disney's Wonderful World of Reading Ser.: No. 16). (ps-3). 1974. (ISBN 0-394-82552-7, BYR). (ISBN 0-394-92552-1). Random.
--Walt Disney's Cinderella. LC 82-243726. (Illus.). 1 v. 25cm. (Pop-Up Movie-Go-Round Book). c.1981. (ISBN 0-671-44898-6). Windmill Books.
--Walt Disney's Cinderella. Authorized. Disney, Walt, Productions, illus. Wheeler, George, adapted by. LC 55-18080. unpaged. illus. 17cm. (Tell-a-tale books, 964). c.1954. Whitman Pub. Co.

AUTHOR INDEX

DISNEY, WALT

--Walt Disney's Circus. LC 44-47737. 28 p. col. illus. 28 1/2 cm. 1944. Simon and Schuster.
--Walt Disney's Come Play with Donald Duck. Disney Walt Productions, illus. Terrazas, Ernest, adapted by. LC 49-13824. 32 p. illus. (part col.) 22 cm. (Walt Disney picture-story books). 1948. Grosset and Dunlap.
--Walt Disney's Come Play with Mickey Mouse. Disney, Walt, Productions, illus. Gonzales, Manuel, adapted by. LC 49-130. 32 p. illus. (part col.) 22 cm. (Walt Disney picture-story books). 1948. Grosset and Dunlap.
--Walt Disney's Come Play with Pluto Pup. Disney, Walt, Productions, illus. Svendsen, Julius, adapted by. LC 49-137. 32 p. illus. (part col.) 22 cm. (Walt Disney picture-story books). 1948. Grosset & Dunlap.
--Walt Disney's Come Play with the Seven Dwarfs. Disney, Walt, Productions, illus. Svendsen, Julius, adapted by. LC 49-139. 32 p. illus. (part col.) 22 cm. (Walt Disney picture-story books). 1948. Grosset & Dunlap.
--Walt Disney's Davy Crockett and Mike Fink: The Adventures of the King of the Wild Frontier and the King of the River, on the Ohio and the Mighty Mississippi. Disney, Walt, Studio, illus. LC 56-13563. (Illus.). 45 p. 29cm. (Walt Disney library, 433). c.1955. Simon and Schuster.
--Walt Disney's Davy Crockett, King of the Wild Frontier. Shapiro, Irwin (1911-), retold by. Disney, Walt, Studio, illus. Crawford, Mel (1925-), ed. LC 55-14724. unpaged. illus. 21cm. (Little golden library, D45). 1955. Simon and Schuster.
--Walt Disney's Davy Crockett's Keelboat Race. Shapiro, Irwin (1911-), retold by. Disney, Walt, Studio, illus. Crawford, Mel (1925-), adapted by. unpaged. illus. 21cm. (Mickey Mouse Club book, D47). 1955. Simon and Schuster.
--Walt Disney's Disneyland on the Air. Disney, Walt, Studio, illus. Bedford, Annie North, pseud. (1915-) & Armstrong, Samuel, eds. Watson, Jane Werner. LC 55-4120. unpaged. illus. 21cm. (Little golden book, D43). 1955. Simon and Schuster.
--Walt Disney's Donald and Mickey, Cub Scouts. LC 50-2913. (Illus.). 21cm. 24p. (A Cozy-Corner Bk.). 1950. Whitman.
--Walt Disney's Donald Duck and Chip 'n' Dale. Authorized. Disney, Walt, Studio, illus. Walsh, Stan & Wolfe, Gene, eds. LC 55 17930. unpaged. illus. 17cm. (Tell-a-tale books, 945). c.1954. Whitman Pub. Co.
--Walt Disney's Donald Duck and the Hidden Gold. Disney, Walt, Studio, illus. Watson, Jane Werner (1915-) Taliaferro, Al, adapted by. LC 51-13375. 78 p. illus. 19 cm. (Young readers' library). 1951. Simon and Schuster.
--Walt Disney's Donald Duck and the Magic Mailbox. LC 78-50650. (Illus.). 24 p. 21cm. (Golden look-look book). 1980, c.1979. (ISBN 0-307-11851-7). Golden Press.
--Walt Disney's Donald Duck and the Mouseketeers: Told by Annie North Bedford; Pseud. Bedford, Annie North, pseud. (1915-) & Armstrong, Samuel, eds. Watson, Jane Werner. Disney, Walt, Studio, illus. LC 56-590415. unpaged. illus. 21cm. (Mickey Mouse Club book, D53). 1956. Simon and Schuster.
--Walt Disney's Donald Duck and the New Birdhouse. Authorized. Disney, Walt, Studio, illus. Moores, Richard (1909-) & McGary, Norm, eds. LC 56-59079. unpaged. illus. 17cm. (Tell-a-tale books, 2577). c.1956. Whitman Pub. Co.
--Walt Disney's Donald Duck and the Wishing Star. Authorized. Disney, Walt, Studio, illus. Gonzales, Manuel & MacLaughlin, Don, eds. LC 52-4221. unpaged. illus. 21 cm. (Cozy-corner book). N.D. Whitman Pub. Co.
--Walt Disney's Donald Duck Goes to Disneyland. Authorized. Disney, Walt, Studio, illus. Banta, Milt & Boyle, Neil, eds. LC 55-4275. unpaged. illus. 17cm. (Tell-a-tale books, 2559). c.1955. Whitman Pub. Co.
--Walt Disney's Donald Duck Goes to Disneyland. Authorized. Disney, Walt, Studio & Banta, Milt, illus. LC 55-4275. (Illus.). 17cm. (Tell-a-Tale Bks.). 1955. Whitman Pub. Co.
--Walt Disney's Donald Duck in A Bit of a Hit. Authorized. Disney, Walt, Studio, illus. Strobl, Tony & Boyle, Neil, eds. LC 56-425855. unpaged. illus. 22cm. (Mickey Mouse Club). 1956. Whitman Pub. Co.
--Walt Disney's Donald Duck in Disneyland. Bedford, Annie North, pseud. (1915-), retold by Watson, Jane Werner. Disney, Walt, Studio, illus. Grant, Campbell, adapted by. LC 55-20573. unpaged. illus. 21cm. (Little golden library, D44). 1955. Simon and Schuster.
--Walt Disney's Donald Duck in Help Wanted. Authorized. Disney, Walt, Studio, illus. Wheeler, George, adapted by. LC 55-3189. unpaged. illus. 21cm. (Cozy-corner book). c.1955. Whitman Pub. Co.
--Walt Disney's Donald Duck in the High Andes. LC 43-17659. (From the Walt Disney Feature Production "Saludos Amigos"). 32 p. illus. (part col.) 21 1/2 x 17 1/2 cm. N.D. Artists & Writers Guild, Inc., Grosset & Dunlap Distributors.
--Walt Disney's Donald Duck, Prize Diver. Bedford, Annie North, pseud. (1915-), as told by Watson, Jane Werner. Disney, Walt, Studio & Boyle, Neil, illus. LC 56-1965. (Illus.). 21cm. 24p. (Walt Disney's Mickey Mouse Club Bks.). 1956. Simon and Schuster.
--Walt Disney's Donald Duck's Christmas Tree. Bedford, Annie North, pseud. (1915-), as told by Watson, Jane Werner. Disney, Walt, Studio, illus. Moore, Bob, adapted by. LC 55-4113. unpaged. illus. 21cm. (Little golden book, D39). 1954. Simon and Schuster.
--Walt Disney's Donald Duck's Happy Day Book: Featuring Huey, Dewey, and Louie. LC 83-82598. (Illus.). 10 p. 18cm. c.1984. (ISBN 0-307-06040-3). Golden Book.
--Walt Disney's Donald Duck's Lucky Day. LC 51-38463. unpaged. illus. 17 cm. (Tell-a-tale books). N.D. Whitman Pub. Co.
--Walt Disney's Donald Duck's Safety Book. Bedford, Annie North, pseud. (1915-), retold by Watson, Jane Werner. Disney, Walt, Studio, illus. Gonzales, Manuel & Wheeler, George, eds. LC 55-100041. unpaged. illus. 21cm. (Little golden book, D41). 1955, c.1954. Simon and Schuster.
--Walt Disney's Donald Duck's Toy Sailboat. Bedford, Annie North, pseud. (1915-), retold by Watson, Jane Werner. Disney, Walt, Studio, illus. Armstrong, Samuel, adapted by. LC 54-14963. (From the Motion Picture "Chips Ahoy"). unpaged. illus. 21cm. (Little golden book. D40). 1954. Simon and Schuster.
--Walt Disney's "Donald's Lucky Day". Story and Pictures from the Donald Duck Production. LC 39-90602. 20 p. col. illus. 24 x 29 cm. c.1939. Whitman Publishing Company.
--Walt Disney's Dumbo. Bedford, Annie North, pseud. (1915-), ed. Watson, Jane Werner. Disney, Walt, Studio, illus. LC 47-1968. 42 p. illus. (part col.) 20 1/2 x 17 cm. 1947. Simon and Schuster.
--Walt Disney's Dumbo. Bedford, Annie North, pseud. (1915-), as told by Watson, Jane Werner. Disney, Walt, Studio, illus. Kelsey, Dick, adapted by. LC 55-14836. unpaged. illus. 33cm. (Walt Disney's library, 428). 1955. Simon and Schuster.
--Walt Disney's Dumbo Favorites. LC 73-3259. (Illus.). 189 p. 24cm. 1973. Danbury Press.
--Walt Disney's "Dumbo of the Circus". LC 41-20884. 52 p. illus. (part col.) 20 x 26 cm. c.1941. Garden City Publishing Co.
--Walt Disney's "Dumbo". The Story of the Little Elephant with the Big Ears. LC 41-242593. 12 p. illus. (part col.) 28 x 26 cm. c.1941. Walt Disney Productions.
--Walt Disney's Famous Seven Dwarfs: An Authorized Book of the Walt Disney Characters. LC 42-32090. (From the Original Snow White and the Seven Dwarfs). cover-title, 20 p. illus. (part col.) 29 x 26 cm. c.1938. Walt Disney Enterprises.
--Walt Disney's Famous Seven Dwarfs: An Authorized Book of the Walt Disney Movies. LC 38-35052. 11 p. col. illus. 32 x 33 cm. c.1938. Whitman Publishing Co.
--Walt Disney's "Forest Friends from Snow White". Disney, Walter Elias (1901-1966), illus. LC 38-35057. 28 p. illus. (part col.) 24 cm. c.1938. Grosset & Dunlap.
--Walt Disney's Goofy and the Tiger Hunt. Authorized. Disney, Walt, Studio, illus. Moores, Dick & Armstrong, Samuel, eds. LC 55-223135. unpaged. illus. 17cm. (Tell-a-tale books, 2555). c.1954. Whitman Pub. Co.
--Walt Disney's "Gulliver Mickey. LC 74-23399. (Illus.). 48p. (Disney's Wonderful World of Reading Ser.: No. 27). (gr. 1-2). 1975. (ISBN 0-394-82561-6, BYR). (ISBN 0-394-92561-0). Random.
--Walt Disney's Hiawatha: Based on the Walt Disney Motion Picture 'Hiawatha.'. LC 53-8195. unpaged. illus. 21cm. (Little golden library, D31). 1953. Simon and Schuster.
--Walt Disney's Jiminy Cricket, Fire Fighter. Bedford, Annie North, pseud. (1915-), as told by Watson, Jane Werner. Disney, Walt, Studio & Armstrong, Samuel, illus. LC 56-1898. (Illus.). 21cm. (Walt Disney's Mickey Mouse Club Bks.). 1956. Simon and Schuster.
--Walt Disney's Johnny Appleseed. Parmalee, Ted, adapted by. Disney, Walt, Studio, illus. LC 49-9960. 42 p. illus. (part col.) 21 cm. 21cm. 42p. (Little golden library. Walt Disney's little library.D11). 1949. Simon and Schuster.
--Walt Disney's Lady. Authorized. Armstrong, Samuel, adapted by. Disney, Walt, Studio, illus. LC 55-22848. unpaged. illus. 21cm. (Cozy-corner book, 2405). c.1954. Whitman Pub. Co.
--Walt Disney's Lady. Authorized. Hubbard, Allen & Wolfe, Gene, eds. Disney, Walt, Studio, illus. LC 55-27083. unpaged. illus. 17cm. (Tell-a-tale books). 1955, c.1954. Whitman Pub. Co.
--Walt Disney's Lady and the Tramp. Disney, Walt, Studio, illus. Coats, Claude, adapted by. LC 55-14192. unpaged. illus. 83cm. (Big golden book, 582). 1955. Simon and Schuster.
--Walt Disney's Lady: From the Motion Picture 'Lady and the Tramp.'. Disney, Walt, Studio, illus. Greene, Ward Armstrong, Samuel, adapted by. LC 55-1615. unpaged. illus. 21cm. (Little golden book, D 42). 1955, c.1954. Simon and Schuster.
--Walt Disney's Lambert the Sheepish Lion. LC 79-129830. (Illus.). 24cm. 42p. (Disney's Wonderful World of Reading). c.1977. Random House.
--Walt Disney's Li'l Bad Wolf Stories. LC 78-50652. (Illus.). 48 p. 26cm. (Kid's paperback). c.1978. (ISBN 0-307-12078-3). Golden Press.
--Walt Disney's Little Man of Disneyland. Bedford, Annie North, pseud. (1915-), as told by Watson, Jane Werner. Disney, Walt, Studio, illus. Kelsey, Dick, adapted by. LC 55-13898. unpaged. illus. 21cm. (Mickey Mouse Club book, D46). 1955. Simon and Schuster.
--Walt Disney's Mary Poppins. Bedford, Anne North, pseud. (1915-), ed. Watson, Jane Werner. Clarke, Grace Dalles, illus. (Mary Poppins Original Stories by P. L. Travers). (Illus.). photos. (gr. k-2). 1964. (ISBN 0-307-10850-3, Golden Pr). Western Pub.
--Walt Disney's Mickey and His Friends. LC 76-62521. (Illus.). 48 p. 26cm. (Kid's paperback). c.1977. (ISBN 0-307-12364-2). Golden Press.
--Walt Disney's Mickey and the Beanstalk. LC 73-7584. p. (Disney's wonderful world of reading, #11). 1974. (ISBN 0-394-82550-0). (ISBN 0-394-92550-5). Random House.
--Walt Disney's Mickey Mouse & Donald Duck at the Circus. (Illus.). (Colorforms Bks.). (ps-2). 1973. (ISBN 0-394-82656-6, BYR). Random.
--Walt Disney's Mickey Mouse and Pluto Pup. Beecher, Elizabeth, retold by. Disney, Walt, Studio, illus. Grant, Campbell, adapted by. LC 53-2894. unpaged. illus. 21cm. (Little golden library, D32). 1953. Simon and Schuster.
--Walt Disney's Mickey Mouse and the Missing Mouseketeers. Bedford, Annie North, pseud. (1915-), as told by Watson, Jane Werner. Disney, Walt, Studio, illus. Svendson, Julius & Totten, Bob, eds. LC 56-59185. unpaged. illus. 21cm. (Mickey Mouse Club book, D57). 1956. Simon and Schuster.
--Walt Disney's Mickey Mouse Flies the Christmas Mail. Bedford, Annie North, pseud. (1915-), as told by Watson, Jane Werner. Disney, Walt, Studio, illus. Svendson, Julius & Boyle, Neil, eds. LC 56-58195. unpaged. illus. 21cm. (Walt Disney's Mickey Mouse club books, D 53). 1956. Simon and Schuster.
--Walt Disney's Mickey Mouse Goes Christmas Shopping. Bedford, Annie North, pseud. (1915-), retold by Watson, Jane Werner. Disney, Walt, Studio, illus. Moore, Bob & Atencio, Xavier, eds. LC 53-352510. unpaged. illus. 21cm. (Little golden book, D33). 1953. Simon and Schuster.
--Walt Disney's Mickey Mouse in the Wild West. LC 73-76289. (Illus.). 45 p. 31cm. 1973. Golden Press.
--Walt Disney's Mickey Mouse, the Kitten Sitters. LC 79-10803. (Illus.). 24 p. 32cm. 1979, c.1976. Golden Press.
--Walt Disney's Mother Goose. Disney, Walt, Studio, illus. LC 49-10465. 28 p. col. illus. 34 cm. 1949. Simon and Schuster.
--Walt Disney's Mother Goose. Disney, Walt, Studio, illus. (Illus.). (gr. k-2). 1970. (ISBN 0-307-10878-3, Golden Pr). (ISBN 0-307-60878-6). Western Pub.
--Walt Disney's Mystery in Disneyville. Moores, Richard (1909-), illus. Moores, Richard & Gonzales, Manuel, adapted by. LC 49-48823. 126 p. col. illus. 18 cm. (Golden story book, 7). 1949. Simon and Schuster.
--Walt Disney's Noah's Ark. Bedford, Annie North, pseud. (1915-), retold by Watson, Jane Werner. Disney, Walt, Studio, illus. Grant, Campbell, adapted by. LC 52-10799. unpaged. illus. 21 cm. (Little golden library, D28). 1952. Simon and Schuster.
--Walt Disney's One Hundred One Dalmations. LC 74-10829. (Illus.). 48p. (Disney's Wonderful World of Reading: No. 23). (ps-3). 1975. (ISBN 0-394-82571-3, BYR). (ISBN 0-394-92571-8). Random.
--Walt Disney's Pedro: The Story of a Little Airplane. LC 43-17618. 32 p. illus. (part col.) 21 1/2 x 17 1/2 cm. c.1943. Artists & Writers Guild, Inc., Grosset & Dunlap, Distributors.
--Walt Disney's Perri and Her Friends. Bedford, Annie North, pseud. (1915-), adapted by Watson, Jane Werner. LC 57-13501. (Based on the Story By Felix Salten, 1869-1945). (Illus.). (A Mickey Mouse Club Bk.). 1956. Simon and Schuster.
--Walt Disney's Perri: From the Walt Disney Motion Picture of Felix Salten's Original Story,. Kelaey, Dick, illus. Brown, Emily, adapted by. LC 57-1301. unpaged. illus. 33cm. (Big golden book, 415). 1957. Simon and Schuster.
--Walt Disney's Peter & the Wolf. LC 74-6423. (Illus.). 48p. (Disney's Wonderful World of Reading Ser.: No. 20). (ps-3). 1974. (ISBN 0-394-82563-2, BYR). (ISBN 0-394-92563-7). Random.
--Walt Disney's Peter Pan. Disney, Walt, Studio, illus. Armstrong, Samuel, adapted by. LC 52-4581. unpaged. illus. 21 cm. (Cozy corner book). N.D. Whitman Pub. Co.
--Walt Disney's Peter Pan and the Indians. Bedford, Annie North, pseud. (1915-), retold by Watson, Jane Werner. Disney, Walt, Studio, illus. Mack, Brice & Kinney, Dick, eds. LC 52-4578. unpaged. illus. 21 cm. (Little golden library, D26). 1952. Simon and Schuster.
--Walt Disney's Peter Pan and the Pirates: From the Motion Picture "Peter Pan" Based on the Story by Sir James M. Barrie. Disney, Walt, Studio, illus. LC 52-4579. unpaged. illus. 21 cm. (Little golden library, D25). 1952. Simon and Schuster.
--Walt Disney's Peter Pan and Wendy. Watson, Jane Werner (1915-), retold by. Bedford, Annie North, pseud. Disney, Walt, Studio, illus. LC 52-4580. unpaged. illus. 21 cm. (Little golden library, D24). 1952. Simon and Schuster.
--Walt Disney's Peter Pan Favorites. LC 73-3261. (Illus.). 189 p. 24cm. 1973. Danbury Press.
--Walt Disney's Peter Pan: From the Motion Picture "Peter Pan". Disney, Walt, Studio & Hench, John, illus. Dempster, Al LC 52-12789. unpaged. illus. 34 cm. (Big golden book, 570). N.D. Simon and Schuster.
--Walt Disney's Pinocchio. (Illus.). (Disney's Wonderful World of Reading Ser.: No. 10). (ps-3). 1973. (ISBN 0-394-82626-4, BYR). (ISBN 0-394-92626-9). Random.
--Walt Disney's Pinocchio. Disney's Pinocchio, illus. Collodi, Carlo, pseud. LC 48-6665. (Based on the Story by Carlo Lorengini(1826-1890)). 42 p. illus. (part col.) 21 cm. (Little golden library. Walt Disney's little library,D8). 1948. Simon and Schuster.
--Walt Disney's Pinocchio Favorites. LC 73-3260. (Illus.). 189 p. 24cm. 1973. Danbury Press.
--Walt Disney's Pluto Pup Goes to Sea. Bedford, Annie North, pseud. (1915-), as told by Watson, Jane Werner. Disney, Walt, Studio & Gracey, Yale, illus. LC 52-12317. (Illus.). 21cm. (The Little Golden Library). 1952. Simon and Schuster.
--Walt Disney's Pluto Pup Goes to Sea. Watson, Jane Werner (1915-), retold by. Bedford, Annie North, pseud. Disney, Walt, Studio, illus. Gracey, Yale, adapted by. LC 52-12317. unpaged. illus. 21 cm. (Little golden library, D30). 1952. Simon and Schuster.
--Walt Disney's Pooh Sleepytime Stories. LC 79-63296. (Illus.). 45 p. 27cm. 1980, c.1979. (ISBN 0-307-13735-X). Golden Press.
--Walt Disney's Robin Hood. Bedford, Annie North, pseud. (1915-), ed. Watson, Jane Werner. LC 55-13899. (Illus.). 21cm. (A Mickey Mouse Club Bk.). 1955. Simon and Schuster.
--Walt Disney's Robin Hood. Watson, Jane Werner (1915-), retold by. Disney, Walt, Studio, illus. LC 55-13899. unpaged. illus. 21cm. (Mickey Mouse Club book, D48). 1955. Simon and Schuster.
--Walt Disney's Savage Sam. Memling, Carl (1918-1969), retold by. Gipson, Frederick Benjamin (1908-1973) Crawford, Mel (1925-), illus. LC 63-5083. 1 v. (unpaged) col. illus. 33 cm. (Big golden book). 1963. Golden Press.
--Walt Disney's Seven Dwarfs Find a House: Told by Annie North Bedford; Pseud. Bedford, Annie North, pseud. (1915-), retold by Watson, Annie Werner. Disney, Walt, Studio, illus. Svendson, Julius, adapted by. LC 52-2381. unpaged. illus. 21 cm. (See-saw books, S-2). 1952. Simon and Schuster.
--Walt Disney's Sleeping Beauty. book club ed. LC 73-21794. (Illus.). 44 p. 25cm. (Disney's wonderful world of reading). c.1974. (ISBN 0-394-82798-8). (ISBN 0-394-92798-2). Random House.
--Walt Disney's Snow White and the Seven Dwarfs: An Authorized Book of the Walt Disney Movie. LC 38-35051. 15 p. illus. (part col.) 34 cm. c.1938. Whitman Publishing Co.
--Walt Disney's Snow White and the Seven Dwarfs. limited. LC 78-19232. p. cm. c.1978. (ISBN 0-932240-00-3). Circle Fine Art Press.

--Walt Disney's Snow White and the Seven Dwarfs. LC 84-252773. (Illus.). 24 p. 19cm. (A Golden Melody Book). c.1984. (ISBN 0-307-12249-2). Golden Book.

--Walt Disney's Snow White and the Seven Dwarfs. LC 80-22776. p. cm. c.1980. (ISBN 0-517-54328-1). (ISBN 0-517-54327-3). Harmony Books.

--Walt Disney's Snow White and the Seven Dwarfs. LC 37-39107. (Adapted from Grimm's Fairy Tales). 79 1 p. illus. (part col.) 33 cm. 1937. Harper & Brothers.

--Walt Disney's Snow White & the Seven Dwarfs. (Illus.). (Disney's Wonderful World of Reading Ser.: No. 8). (ps-3). 1973. (ISBN 0-394-82625-6, BYR). (ISBN 0-394-92625-0). Random.

--Walt Disney's Snow White and the Seven Dwarfs. LC 49-7173. (Adapted from Grimm's Fairy Tales). 42 p. illus. (part col.) 20 cm. (Little golden books. Walt Disney's little library, D4). 1948. Simon and Schuster.

--Walt Disney's Snow White and the Seven Dwarfs. Watson, Jane Werner (1915-), adapted by. Disney, Walt, Studio & Disney, Walt, Studio, illus. LC 52-9930. (Taken from the Original Snow White and the Seven Dwarfs.). unpaged. illus. 34 cm. (A Big Golden Book, 451). 1952. Simon and Schuster.

--Walt Disney's Snow White Favorites. LC 73-3256. (Illus.). 189 p. 24cm. 1973. Danbury Press.

--Walt Disney's Snow White Visits the Seven Dwarfs. book club ed., 1st american ed.. LC 80-109120. (Illus.). 42 p. 24cm. (Disney's wonderful world of reading). c.1979. (ISBN 0-394-84356-8). (ISBN 0-394-94356-2). Random House.

--Walt Disney's So Dear to My Heart. Palmer, Helen Marion (1898-1967), adapted by. Disney, Walt, Studio & Peet, Bill, illus. LC 50-3122. (Based on the Novel by Sterling North, 1906-). (Illus.). 18cm. 125p. (A Golden Story Bk.). 1950. Simon & Schuster.

--Walt Disney's Stormy. Souza, Paul, illus. LC 54-312431. unpaged. illus. 21cm. (Cozy-corner book, 2404). c.1954. Whitman Pub. Co.

--Walt Disney's Story Book of Peter Pan. Bedford, Annie North, pseud. (1915-), adapted by Watson, Jane Werner. LC 53-2326. (From the Walt Disney Motion Picture.Based on the Story by Sir James Barrie). 112p. illus. 28cm. (Big golden book, 571). 1953. Simon and Schuster.

--Walt Disney's Storybook Friends. LC 75-34634. (Illus.). 44 p. 29cm. c.1976. (ISBN 0-307-13767-8). Golden Press.

--Walt Disney's Surprise Package. Palmer, Helen Marion, pseud. (1898-1967), adapted by Geisel, Helen. Disney, Walt, Studio, illus. LC 49-133. 76 p. illus. (part col.) 33 c. (Giant golden book). 1948. Simon and Schuster.

--Walt Disney's "The Adventures of Mr. Toad". LC 81-2783. (Adapted from "The Wind in the Willows"). (Illus.). 48p. (Walt Disney's Wonderful World of Reading Ser.: No. 49). (ps-3). 1981. (ISBN 0-394-84818-7). (ISBN 0-394-94818-1). Random.

--Walt Disney's The Adventures of Mr. Toad. Hench, John, adapted by. Disney, Walt, Studio, illus. LC 49-11343. (Story Adapted from Kenneth Grahame's "The Wind in the Willows"). (Illus.). 34cm. 25p. (A Big Golden Bk.). 1949. Simon and Schuster.

--Walt Disney's The Aristocats. LC 73-15626. p. cm. (Disney's wonderful world of reading, no. 14). 1974. (ISBN 0-394-82553-5). (ISBN 0-394-92553-X). Random House.

--Walt Disney's "The Brave Little Tailor". LC 74-1253. (Illus.). 48p. (Disney's Wonderful World of Reading Ser.: No. 18). (ps-3). 1974. (ISBN 0-394-82559-4, BYR). (ISBN 0-394-92559-9). Random.

--Walt Disney's The Life of Donald Duck. LC 41-19721. 72 p. illus. (part col.) 29 cm. c.1941. Random House.

--Walt Disney's The Practical Pig. LC 40-14814. 24 p. illus. (part col.) 24 cm. c.1940. Garden City Publishing Company, Inc.

--Walt Disney's The Three Little Pigs. LC 48-10774. 42 p. illus. (part col.) 21 cm. (Little Golden Library. Walt Disney's Little Library, D 10). 1948. Simon and Schuster.

--Walt Disney's The Ugly Duckling. Bedford, Annie North, pseud. (1915-), as told by Watson, Jane Werner. Disney, Walt, Studio, illus. MacLaughlin, Don, adapted by. LC 52-2383. unpaged. illus. 21 cm. (Little golden library, D22). 1952. Simon and Schuster.

--Walt Disney's The Wise Little Hen. LC 38-12738. cover-title, 10 p. col. illus. 83 cm. c.1937. Western Printing & Lithographing Co.

--Walt Disney's Thumper. LC 42-15005. (Story Based on the Character Created by Walt Disney for the Motion Picture Bambi). (Illus.). 21 x 17cm. 32p. 1942. Grosset & Dunlap.

--Walt Disney's "Travels With Pooh.". LC 82-238669. (Illus.). 33 p. 29cm. (A Dutton Read a Long Book). c.1982. (ISBN 0-525-69700-4). E.P. Dutton.

--Walt Disney's Treasury. Fletcher, Steffi, compiled by. Disney, Walt, Studio, illus. Werner, Jane, compiled by. LC 54-16. (Illus.). 140 p. 33cm. (Giant golden book, 706). 1953. Simon and Schuster.

--Walt Disney's Twenty Thousand Leagues Under the Sea. Huemer, Dick, ed. Schroeder, Rod & Steel, John, illus. LC 55-3370. 21 cm. 282p. (Whitman Famous Classics). 1955. Whitman Pub. Co.

--Walt Disney's Uncle Remus Stories. Palmer, Helen Marion, pseud. (1898-1967), retold by Geisel, Helen. Dempster, al (1848-1908) & Justice, Bill, illus. LC 47-11931. (Based on the Original Stories by Joel Chandler(1848-1908)). 42 p. illus. (part col.) 21 cm. (Little Golden library). (A Little Golden Book). 1947. Simon and Schuster.

--Walt Disney's Water Birds: Story Adapted from the Walt Disney True-Life Adventure Motion Picture 'Water Birds'. Wright, Betty Ren & Hanson, Alice, eds. Hartwell, Marjorie, illus. LC 56-1049. unpaged. illus. 17cm. (True-life adventures). c.1955. Whitman Pub. Co.

--Walt Disney's "Winnie the Pooh & Tigger Too". LC 75-20349. (Illus.). 48p. (Disney's Wonderful World of Reading Ser: No. 35). (ps-3). 1976. (ISBN 0-394-82569-1, BYR). (ISBN 0-394-92569-6). Random.

--Walt Disney's 20,000 Leagues Under the Sea: Based on the Famous Jules Verne Novel, from the Motion Picture "Twenty Thousand Leagues Under the Sea". Huemer, Richard Martin (1898-), adapted by. Schroeder, Rod & Steel, John, illus. LC 55-3370. 282p. illus. 21cm. (Whitman famous classics, 1541). 1955. Whitman Pub. Co.

--Walt Disney's 20,000 Leagues Under the Sea: From the Original Story by Jules Verne. Beecher, Elizabeth, retold by. Disney, Walt, Studio, illus. Grant, Campbell, adapted by. LC 55-14007. 63p. illus. 29cm. (Big golden book, 483). c.1954. Simon and Schuster.

--Walt Dsney Productions Presents All Is Well That Ends Well. LC 79-124192. (Illus.). 42 p. 25cm. (Disney's wonderful world of reading). c.1979. (ISBN 0-394-84236-7). (ISBN 0-394-94236-1). Random House.

--The Wise Little Hen. Disney, Walt, Studio, illus. LC 35-18. 48 p. incl. col. front., illus. (part col.) 23 x 26 cm. c.1934. David McKay Company.

Disney, Walt, Productions & Aberson, Helen

--Walt Disney's Dumbo, the Flying Elephant. LC 78-112087. (Illus.). 42 p. 25cm. (Disney's wonderful world of reading). c.1978. (ISBN 0-394-84093-3). (ISBN 0-394-94093-8). Random House.

Disney, Walt, Productions & Andersen, Hans Christian (1805-1875)

--Walt Disney's Through the Picture Frame. Edmunds, Robert, adapted by. LC 44-51049. 24 p. illus. (part col.) 20 x 17 1/2 cm. (On cover: Walt Disney's little library). Orig. Title: Ole Lukoie. 1944. Simon and Schuster.

Disney, Walt, Productions & Ayer, Jean Y.

--Mickey Mouse and His Friends. LC 37-7713. 3 p. l., 102 p. illus. (part col.) 21 cm. 1937. T. Nelson and Sons.

Disney, Walt, Productions & Barrie, James Matthew, Sir (1860-1937)

--Walt Disney Presents Peter Pan. authorized. LC 77-6171. (Story and Pictures Adapted from the Walt Disney Animated Motion Picture "Peter Pan"). (Illus.). 210 p. 20cm. 1969. Whitman Book Division, Western Pub. Co.

Disney, Walt, Productions & Baruch, Dorothy Walter (1899-1962)

--Walt Disney's Dumbo of the Circus. Disney, Walt, Studio, illus. LC 48-10785. 90 p. col. illus. 22 cm. (Walt Disney Story Books). 1948. D. C. Heath.

Disney, Walt, Productions & Bedford, Annie North, pseud. (1915-)

--Walt Disney's Jiminy Cricket: Fire Fighter. Told by Annie North Bedford; Pseud. Watson, Jane Werner. Disney, Walt, Studio, illus. Armstrong, Mel, adapted by. LC 56-189804. unpaged. illus. 21cm. (Walt Disney's Mickey Mouse Club books, D50). 1956. Simon and Schuster.

Disney, Walt, Productions & Brown, Margaret Wise (1910-1952)

--Little Pig's Picnic and Other Stories. Disney, Walt, Studio, illus. LC 39-21181. 3 p. l., 102 p. col. illus. 22 cm. (Walt Disney Story Books). c.1939. D. C. Heath and Company.

Disney, Walt, Productions & Carey, Mary

--Walt Disney's Donald Duck and the Lost Mesa Ranch. Anderson, Al & Strobl, Anthony, illus. LC 67-1601. (Illus.). 156 p. 22cm. (Whitman Tween-Age Book). 1966. Whitman Pub. Co.

Disney, Walt, Productions & Carroll, Lewis, pseud. (1832-1898)

--Walt Disney's Alice in Wonderland. From the Motion Picture Based on the Story by Lewis Carroll. Dodgson, Charles Lutwidge. Disney, Walt, Studio, illus. Dempster, Al, adapted by. LC 51-10158. unpaged (chiefly illus.) 34cm. (Big golden book). c.1951. Simon and Schuster.

Disney, Walt, Productions & Dahl, Roald (1916-)

--The Gremlins. LC 43-8278. 52 p. incl. col. front., illus. (part col.) 28 1/2 x 23 cm. 1943. Random House.

Disney, Walt, Productions & Davis, Daphne

--Walt Disney's The Donald Duck Book. Pratt, Hawley & White, Al, illus. LC 64-57442. (Illus.). 1 v. (unpaged. 22cm. (Golden book for kindergarten). 1964. Golden Press.

Disney, Walt, Productions & Disney, Walter Elias (1901-1966)

--Mickey Mouse in "Ye Olden Days" with "Pop-up" Picture. LC 34-169. (Illus.). 1 p. l., 5-60 (i.e. 62) p. 13cm. (midget pop-up books). c.1934. Blue Ribbon Press.

Disney, Walt, Productions & Grahame, Kenneth (1859-1932)

--Walt Disney's Magnificent Mr. Toad. based on "The Wind in the Willows" by Kenneth Grahame. Disney, Walt, Studio, illus. Hench, John, adapted by. LC 49-48503. 32 p. illus. (part col) 27 cm. (Walt Disney picture-story book). 1949. Grosset & Dunlap.

--Walt Disney's Story of the Reluctant Dragon. LC 41-5100. 72 p. illus. (part col.) 28 x 29 cm. c.1941. Garden City Publishing Company.

--Walt Disney's The Adventures of Mr. Toad. Disney, Walt, Studio, illus. LC 49-11343. 25 p. col. illus. 34 cm. (Big golden book). 1949. Simon and Schuster.

Disney, Walt, Productions & Harris, Joel (1848-1908)

--Walt Disney's Brer Rabbit Rides the Fox. Geisel, Helen (1898-1967), as told by. Palmer, Marion, pseud. LC 47-2110. (Based on the Motion Picture Walt Disney Presents Uncle Remus in "Song of the South" and other Walt Disney adaptations of the original Uncle Remus Stories). 32 p. illus. (part col.) 21 1/2 x 17 1/2 cm. 1946. Grosset and Dunlap.

--Walt Disney's The Wonderful Tar Baby. Geisel, Helen (1898-1967), ed. LC 47-210. 32 p. illus. (part col.) 21 1/2 x 17 1/2 cm. 1946. Grosset & Dunlap.

--Walt Disney's Uncle Remus Stories. Geisel, Helen (1898-1967), ed. Dempster, Al & Justice, Bill, illus. LC 47-4662. 1 l., 7-92 p. illus. (part col.) 33 cm. (Giant Golden Books). 1947. Simon and Schuster.

Disney, Walt, Productions & Lorenzini, Carlo (1826-1890)

--Pinocchio and His Puppet Show Adventure. Collodi, Carlo, pseud. LC 73-395. (Illus.). 42 p. 25cm. (Disney's wonderful world of reading, 10). 1973. (ISBN 0-394-82626-4). (ISBN 0-394-82626-4). Random House.

--Walt Dinsey's Pinocchio. Collodi, Carlo, pseud. LC 42-31386. cover-title, 12 p. col. illus. 33 cm. 1940. Whitman Publishing Co.

--Walt Disney's "Figaro and Cleo". Collodi, Carlo, pseud. LC 40-7807. 27 p. col. illus. 23 cm. c.1940. Random House.

--Walt Disney's "Honest John and Giddy". Collodi, Carlo, pseud. LC 40-7808. 27 p. col. illus. 23 cm. c.1940. Random House.

--Walt Disney's "Jiminy Cricket". Collodi, Carlo, pseud. LC 40-780940. 27 p. illus. (part col.) 23 cm. c.1940. Random House.

--Walt Disney's Pinocchio. Collidi, Carlo, pseud. Disney, Walt, Studio, illus. Dempster, Al & Fletcher, Steffi, eds. LC 54-1236. unpaged. illus. 36cm. (Big golden book, 580). 1954, c.1953. Simon and Schuster.

--Walt Disney's Pinocchio Picture Book. Collodi, Carlo, pseud. LC 42-31387. cover-title, 12 p. col. illus. 33 cm. 1940. Grosset & Dunlap.

--Walt Disney's Version of "Pinocchio". Collodi, Carlo, pseud. LC 40-10098. (Based on Collodi's Pinocchio). 48 p. illus. (part col.) 18 x 24 cm. c.1939. Grosset & Dunlap.

--Walt Disney's Version of Pinocchio. Collodi, Carlo, pseud. LC 39-31271. 76 p. incl. illus. (part col.) col. pl. 29 cm. 1939. Random House.

--Walt Disney's Version of Pinocchio. Collodi, Carlo, pseud. LC 42-31388. (Based on a Famous Story). 24 p. illus. (part col.) 19 x 18 cm. c.1940. Whitman Publishing Company.

Disney, Walt, Productions & Memling, Carl (1918-1969)

--Walt Disney's The Sword in the Stone. LC 63-5904. (Suggested by the original story The sword in the stone by Th. H. White Pictures by the Walt Disney Studio). unpaged. illus. 33 cm. (big golden book). 1963. Golden Press.

Disney, Walt, Productions & Montgomery, Rutherford George (1894-)

--Walt Disney's El Blanco: The Legend of the White Stallion. Authorized. Stevens, Gloria, illus. LC 61-1300. (Illus.). 23cm. 124p. 1961. Golden Press.

Disney, Walt, Productions & North, Sterling (1906-1974)

--Walt Disney's So Dear to My Heart. Disney, Walt, Studio, illus. Palmer, Helen Marion, pseud. (1898-1967), adapted by Geisel, Helen. LC 50-3122. 125 p. col. illus. 18 cm. (Golden story book, 12). 1950. Simon and Schuster.

Disney, Walt, Productions & Prokofiev, Sergei Sergeevich (1891-1953)

--Walt Disney's Peter and the Wolf. LC 47-11901. 42 p. illus. (part col.) 21 cm. (The Little Golden Library: D5). 1947. Simon and Schuster.

Disney, Walt, Productions & Saldinger, Frances

--Walt Disney's Story Land: 72 Favorite Stories Adapted from Walt Disney Films. Disney, Walt, Productions, illus. LC 62-20158. (Illus.). 382 p. 1962. Golden Press.

Disney, Walt, Productions & Salten, Felix (1869-1945)

--Bambi's Fragrant Forest: Based on the Original Story by Felix Salten. LC 74-33127. (Based on the original story by Felix Salten). (Illus.). 26 p. (Golden fragrance book). 1975. (ISBN 0-307-13530-6). Golden Press.

--Walt Disney's Bambi. Disney, Walt, Studio, illus. LC 48-6666. 42 p. illus. (part col.) 21 cm. (Little golden library. Walt Disney's little library. D7). 1948. Simon and Schuster.

--Walt Disney's Bambi. Salzmann, Siegmund. Purnell, Idella (1901-), as told by. Chambers, Whittaker, tr. LC 44-2357. 3 p. l., 101, 1 p. illus. (part col.) 22 cm. 1944. D. C. Heath and Company.

--Walt Disney's Bambi. Salzmann, Siegmund. LC 42-8751. (Based on Original Story by Felix Salten). 32 p. illus. (part col.) 22 x 18 cm. c.1942. Grosset & Dunlap.

--Walt Disney's Bambi. LC 50-7819. 28 p. col. illus. 29 cm. (Fuzzy golden book). 1949. Simon and Schuster.

Disney, Walt, Productions & Schuchmann, Mary

--Walt Disney's Wild Animal Babies. authorized. Ruth, Rod (1912-) & Disney, Walt, Studio, illus. LC 66-4022. 1 v. (chiefly col. illus.) 32 cm. (Whiteman juveniles). 1965. Whitman Pub. Co.

Disney, Walt, Productions & Travers, Pamela Lyndon (1906-)

--Walt Disney's Mary Poppins. Fraser, Betty M., pseud. (1928-) & Pineo, Craig M., illus. Fraser, Elizabeth Marr. LC 64-7482. (Based on the Walt Disney Motion Picture.). (Illus.). 48 p. 33cm. (Big golden book). 1964. Golden Press.

Disney, Walt, Productions & Watson, Jane Werner (1915-)

--Walt Disney's Goofy, Movie Star. Bedford, Annie North, pseud. unpaged. illus. 21cm. (Mickey Mouse Club book, D52). 1956. Simon and Schuster.

--Walt Disney's Mary Poppins: Based on the Walt Disney Motion Picture. Clarke, Grace Dalles, illus. LC 64-57446. 1 v. (unpaged) col. illus. 33 cm. 1964. Golden Press.

--Walt Disney's Mickey Mouse Picnic. Disney, Walt, Studio, illus. LC 50-12283. (Illus.). 20cm. 28p. (The Little Golden Library). 1950. Simon and Schuster.

--Walt Disney's Perri and Her Friends: Based on the Book 'Perri,'. Disney, Walt, Studio, illus. LC 57-13501. unpaged. illus. 21cm. (Mickey Mouse club book, D54). 1957. Simon and Schuster.

Disney, Walt, Productions & Williams, Chester Sidney (1907-)

--The Victory March: Or, The Mystery of the Treasure Chest. LC 42-18952. 12 p. col. illus. 25 x 20 1/2 cm. 1942. Random House.

Disney, Walt, Studio

--Bambi, Friends of the Forest. (Illus.). (gr. k-3). 1976. (ISBN 0-307-60132-3, Golden Pr). Western Pub.

--Bambi Saves the Day. (ps-3). 1976. (Windmill). Dutton.

--Bambi's Big Day. (ps-1). 1977. (Windmill). Dutton.

--Brer Rabbit & the Tar Baby. Disney, Walt, Studio, illus. (Illus.). (ps-3). 1976. (ISBN 0-307-66058-3, Golden Pr). Western Pub.

--Cinderella's Castle. Disney, Walt, Studio, illus. (Illus.). (ps-1). 1975. (ISBN 0-307-68940-9, Golden Pr). Western Pub.

--Disney Mini-Pops, 6 bks. Incl. Bambi's Big Day; Donald's Company Trip; Mickey's Circus Adventure; Pinocchio & the Puppet Theater; Scrooge McDuck & the Vacant Lot; Snow White's Party. (Illus.). (ps-1). 1977. (Pub by Windmill Bks). Dutton.

--Donald Duck & the Magic Mailbox. (Golden Look-Look Bks.). (ps-3). 1978. (ISBN 0-307-61851-X, Golden Pr). (ISBN 0-307-11851-7). Western Pub.

--Donald Duck & the Witch Next Door. Disney, Walt, Studio, illus. (Illus.). (ps-3). 1976. (ISBN 0-307-60217-6, Golden Pr). Western Pub.

--Donald Duck, It's Play Time!. 24p. (A Big Picture Bks.). (gr. k-3). N.D. (ISBN 0-307-60828-X, Golden Pr). (ISBN 0-307-10828-7). Western Pub.
--Donald Duck: The Play Along Book. (Illus.). (Play & Learn Ser.). (ps-k). 1977. (ISBN 0-307-10741-8, Golden Pr). Western Pub.
--Donald Duck's Toy Train. (Illus.). 24p. (gr. k-3). 1976. (ISBN 0-307-60018-1, Golden Pr). Western Pub.
--Donald's Camping Adventure. (ps-1). 1977. (Windmill). Dutton.
--Gingerbread Man. Disney, Walt, Studio, illus. (Illus.). (ps-3). 1976. (ISBN 0-307-66081-8, Golden Pr). Western Pub.
--The Haunted Mansion. (Illus.). (ps-3). 1976. (ISBN 0-307-66061-3, Golden Pr). Western Pub.
--Heidi. Disney, Walt, Studio, illus. (Original Author: Johanna Heusser Spyri, 1827-1901). (Illus.). (ps-3). 1976. (ISBN 0-307-66085-0, Golden Pr). Western Pub.
--Hello, Winnie-the-Pooh!. (Contains 2 Little Golden Books, 2 Tell-A-Tale Books, 1 Shape Book & an activity book.). (Boxed Golden Bks. Ser.). (ps-2). 1977. (ISBN 0-307-13692-2, Golden Pr). Western Pub.
--If I Met Mickey Mouse. Duenewald, Doris, ed. Disney, Walt, Studio, illus. LC 77-95420. (Illus.). 1978. (ISBN 0-448-16151-6, G&D). Putnam Pub Group.
--The Jungle Book. Disney, Walt, Studio, illus. (gr. k-3). 1979. (ISBN 0-307-67585-8, Golden Pr). Western Pub.
--Mickey Mouse & the Great Lot Plot. Disney, Walt, Studio, illus. (Illus.). 24p. (gr. k-3). 1976. (ISBN 0-307-60129-3, Golden Pr). Western Pub.
--Mickey Mouse & the Marvelous Smell Machine. (Illus.). (A Golden Fragrance Bk.). (gr. k-3). 1979. (ISBN 0-307-64544-4, Golden Pr). (ISBN 0-307-13544-6). Western Pub.
--Mickey Mouse & the Sunken Treasure. (ps-3). 1976. (Windmill). Dutton.
--Mickey Mouse, Hideaway Island. 24p. (A Big Picture Bks.). (gr. k-3). 1979. (ISBN 0-307-60829-8, Golden Pr). (ISBN 0-307-10829-5). Western Pub.
--Mickey Mouse Says I Can, Can You?. Klimo, Kate, ed. Disney, Walt, Studio, illus. (Illus.). 6p. 1982. (ISBN 0-671-45821-3, Little Simon). S&S.
--Mickey Mouse Takes a Vacation. (ps-3). 1976. (Windmill). Dutton.
--Mickey's Christmas Carol. Disney, Walt, Studio, illus. (Illus.). 32p. (Golden Melody Bks.). (ps). N.D. (ISBN 0-307-12236-0, Golden Bks). Western Pub.
--Mickey's Circus Adventure. (ps-1). 1977. (Windmill). Dutton.
--New Walt Disney Treasury, Ten Favorite Stories. Disney, Walt Studio, illus. (Illus.). 96p. (gr. 6-12). 1971. (ISBN 0-307-15546-3, Golden Pr). Western Pub.
--Old MacDonald Duck Had a Farm. (ps-3). 1976. (Windmill). Dutton.
--Pinocchio & the Puppet Theater. (ps-1). 1977. (Windmill). Dutton.
--Pooh Sleepytime Stories. (Illus.). (A Golden Story Bk.). (gr. k-3). 1979. (ISBN 0-307-63735-2, Golden Pr). (ISBN 0-307-13735-X). Western Pub.
--Scrooge McDuck & the Vacant Lot. (ps-3). 1977. (Windmill). Dutton.
--Snow White and the Seven Dwarfs. LC 38-35052. 11p. col. illus. 32 x 33cm. c.1938. Whitman.
--Snow White & the Seven Dwarfs. Disney, Walt, Studio, illus. (Illus.). 24p. (Young Reader Ser.). (gr. k-3). 1976. (ISBN 0-307-60066-1, Golden Pr). (ISBN 0-307-10451-6). Western Pub.
--Snow White and the Seven Dwarfs. Disney, Walt, Studio, illus. LC 38-12740. 94p. illus. 28 1/2cm. c.1938. Whitman.
--Snow White's Party. (ps-1). 1977. (Windmill). Dutton.
--Tigger & Winnie-the-Pooh. Disney, Walt, Studio, illus. (Illus.). (ps-1). 1968. (ISBN 0-307-68948-4, Golden Pr). Western Pub.
--The Walt Disney Golden Song Book. (Illus.). 96p. (gr. 1-6). 1971. (ISBN 0-307-16825-5, Golden Pr). (ISBN 0-307-65811-2). Western Pub.
--Walt Disney's Alice in Wonderland. Dempster, Al, ed. (Illus.). 1951. (ISBN 0-307-10426-5, Golden Pr). (ISBN 0-307-60426-8). Western Pub.
--Walt Disney's Bambi. (Illus.). (gr. k-3). 1941. (ISBN 0-307-10450-8, Golden Pr). (ISBN 0-307-60450-0). Western Pub.
--Walt Disney's Chicken Little. Disney, Walt, Studio, illus. (Illus.). 24p. (ps-1). 1983. (ISBN 0-307-10436-2, Golden Pr). Western Pub.
--Walt Disney's Christmas Parade. 1977. (ISBN 0-307-11191-1, Golden Pr). Western Pub.
--Walt Disney's Cinderella. Disney, Walt, Studio, illus. (Illus.). (ps-2). 1950. (ISBN 0-307-60114-5, Golden Pr). Western Pub.
--Walt Disney's Grandpa Bunny: From the Motion Picture "Funny Little Bunnies". Watson, Jane Werner (1915-), ed. Disney, Walt, Studio, illus. Kelsey, Richard I. & Justice, Bill, eds. LC 51-39070. unpaged. illus. 21 cm. (Little golden library, D21). 1951. Simon and Schuster.
--Walt Disney's Lady. Disney, Walt, Studio, illus. (Illus.). 24p. (gr. k-3). 1976. (ISBN 0-307-60103-X, Golden Pr). Western Pub.
--Walt Disney's Li'l Bad Wolf Stories. (Kids Paperbacks). (ps-3). 1978. (ISBN 0-307-62078-6, Golden Pr). (ISBN 0-307-12078-3). Western Pub.
--Walt Disney's Mary Poppins. Bedford, Anne North, pseud. (1915-), ed. Watson, Jane Werner. Disney, Walt Studio, illus. (Illus.). (ps-3). 1976. (ISBN 0-686-86879-X, Golden Pr). Western Pub.
--Walt Disney's Mickey Mouse in the Wild West. Disney, Walt, Studio, illus. 48p. (gr. 2-6). 1973. (ISBN 0-307-15778-4, Golden Pr). Western Pub.
--Walt Disney's Mickey Mouse: The Kitten Sitters. (ps-3). 1979. (ISBN 0-307-10823-6, Golden Pr). Western Pub.
--Walt Disney's Peter & the Wolf. Disney, Walt, Studio, illus. (Illus.). (gr. k-3). 1976. (ISBN 0-307-60056-4, Golden Pr). Western Pub.
--Walt Disney's Pinocchio. Disney, Walt, Studio, illus. (Based on the Story by Carlo Lorengini(1826-1890)). (Illus.). (gr. k-3). 1953. (ISBN 0-307-10580-6, Golden Pr). (ISBN 0-307-60580-9). Western Pub.
--Walt Disney's Pooh's Schoolhouse. (ps-3). 1978. (ISBN 0-307-13738-4, Golden Pr). (ISBN 0-307-63738-7). Western Pub.
--Walt Disney's Robin Hood. Disney, Walt, Studio, illus. (gr. 3-7). 1973. (ISBN 0-307-16816-6, Golden Pr). (ISBN 0-307-10492-3). (ISBN 0-307-60492-6). Western Pub.
--Walt Disney's Robin Hood to the Rescue. Disney, Walt, Studio, illus. foldout. (ps-2). 1973. (ISBN 0-307-15004-6, Golden Pr). Western Pub.
--Walt Disney's Snow White & the Seven Dwarfs. Disney, Walt, Studio, illus. (Illus.). 24p. (ps-1). 1983. (ISBN 0-307-11451-1, Golden Pr). Western Pub.
--Walt Disney's Story Land. (Illus.). (gr. 1-5). 1962. (ISBN 0-307-16547-7, Golden Pr). (ISBN 0-307-66547-X). Western Pub.
--Walt Disney's Storybook Friends. (Illus.). (ps-k). 1979. (ISBN 0-307-15526-9, Golden Pr). Western Pub.
--Walt Disney's "The Adventures of Mr. Toad". Disney, Walt Studio & Hench, John, illus. (Adapted form the Disney Movie, "Ichabod and Mr. Toad"). (Big Golden Book: 424). 1949. Simon and Schuster.
--Walt Disney's the Love Bug, Herbie's Special Friend. Disney, Walt, Studio, illus. (Illus.). 24p. (gr. k-3). 1976. (ISBN 0-307-60130-7, Golden Pr). Western Pub.
--Walt Disney's the Plot to Capture Robin Hood. Disney, Walt, Studio, illus. (gr. k-3). 1973. (ISBN 0-307-13754-6, Golden Pr). Western Pub.
--Walt Disney's Winnie-the-Pooh Meets Tigger. (Illus.). 1973. (ISBN 0-307-10869-4, Golden Pr). (ISBN 0-307-60869-7). Western Pub.
--Winnie the Pooh: Hungry for Honey. Disney, Walt, Studio, illus. (Illus.). (ps-k). 1979. (ISBN 0-307-12152-6, Golden Pr). Western Pub.

Disney, Walt, Studio, illus.
--Bambi's Forest Friends. (Illus.). 8p. (Golden Cloth Bks.). (ps). 1982. (ISBN 0-307-11501-1, Golden Pr). Western Pub.
--Donald Duck's House. (Illus.). 8p. (Golden Cloth Bks.). (ps). 1982. (ISBN 0-307-11502-X, Golden Pr). Western Pub.
--Uncle Remus Brer Rabbit Stories. (Kids Paperbacks). (ps-4). 1977. (ISBN 0-307-62359-9, Golden Pr). (ISBN 0-307-12359-6). Western Pub.
--Walt Disney Character Tubby Book. (Illus.). 10p. (Tubby Bks.). (ps). 1980. (ISBN 0-671-41334-1, Pub. by Windmill). S&S.
--Walt Disney's Mickey & His Friends. (Illus.). (Kids Paperbacks). (ps-4). 1977. (ISBN 0-307-62364-5, Golden Pr). (ISBN 0-307-12364-2). Western Pub.
--Walt Disney's Nursery Tales. 1971. (ISBN 0-307-12068-6, Golden Pr). (ISBN 0-307-62068-9). Western Pub.
--Winnie-the-Pooh's Book of Toys. (Illus.). 8p. (Golden Cloth Bks.). (ps). 1982. (ISBN 0-307-11504-6, Golden Pr). Western Pub.

Disney, Walter Elias see Disney, Walter Elias.

Disney, Walter Elias, jt. auth. see Disney, Walt, Productions.

Disney, Walter Elias (1901-1966), as told by see Greene, Ward.

Disney, Walter Elias (1901-1966)
--Alice in Wonderland. Disney, Walt, Studio, illus. (Illus.). (Walt Disney Square Bks.). (gr. k-3). 1978. (ISBN 0-307-66086-9, Golden Pr). Western Pub.
--Alice in Wonderland Meets White Rabbit. Disney, Walt, Studio, illus. (Illus.). (ps-3). 1977. (ISBN 0-307-60019-X, Golden Pr). Western Pub.
--Aristocats. Disney, Walt, Studio, illus. (Illus.). 24p. (ps-2). 1976. (ISBN 0-307-66076-1, Golden Pr). Western Pub.
--Bambi. (Illus.). (ps). 1979. (Gingerbread). Dutton.
--The Bambi Book. (ps-1). 1966. (ISBN 0-307-68930-1, Golden Pr). Western Pub.
--Bambi Gets Lost. 1982. (ISBN 0-531-05159-5). Watts.
--The Big Bad Wolf. N.D. Blue Ribbon Books INc.
--Bremen Town Musicians. Disney, Walt, Studio, illus. (Illus.). (ps-3). 1976. (ISBN 0-307-66080-X, Golden Pr). Western Pub.
--Cinderella. Disney, Walt, Productions, illus. (Illus.). 10p. (Disney Movie-Go-Round Bks.). (ps-3). 1982. (ISBN 0-671-44898-6). Windmill Bks.
--Donald & the Chipmunks. 1982. (ISBN 0-531-05160-9). Watts.
--Donald Duck. (Illus.). (ps). 1979. (Gingerbread). Dutton.
--Donald Duck & the Golden Helmet. (Illus.). 36p. 1981. (ISBN 0-89659-178-6). Abbeville Pr.
--Donald Duck & the One Bear. Disney, Walt, Studio, illus. (Illus.). (ps-3). 1977. (ISBN 0-307-60039-4, Golden Pr). Western Pub.
--Donald Duck: Instant Millionaire. Disney, Walter Elias (1901-1966), illus. (Illus.). (Young Reader Ser.). (gr. k-3). 1979. (ISBN 0-307-60140-4, Golden Pr). Western Pub.
--Donald's Treasure Hunt. 1982. (ISBN 0-531-05158-7). Watts.
--The Emperor's New Clothes. Disney, Walt, Studio, illus. (Illus.). (Walt Disney Square Bks.). (gr. k-3). 1978. (ISBN 0-307-66088-5, Golden Pr). Western Pub.
--Favorite Nursery Tales. Disney, Walt, Studio, illus. (Illus.). (ps-3). 1977. (ISBN 0-307-12068-6, Golden Pr). Western Pub.
--Goldilocks & the Three Bears. Disney, Walt, Studio, illus. (Illus.). (Walt Disney Square Bks.). (gr. k-3). 1978. (ISBN 0-307-66089-3, Golden Pr). Western Pub.
--Goofy & the Chimps. 1982. (ISBN 0-531-05161-7). Watts.
--Goofy on Cave Man Island. (Illus.). 36p. 1981. (ISBN 0-89659-179-4). Abbeville Pr.
--The Grasshopper & the Ants. Disney, Walt, Studio, illus. (Illus.). (Walt Disney Square Bks.). (gr. k-3). 1978. (ISBN 0-307-66090-7, Golden Pr). Western Pub.
--Hansel & Gretel. Disney, Walter Elias (1901-1966), illus. (Illus.). (ps-3). 1976. (ISBN 0-307-66078-8, Golden Pr). Western Pub.
--How the Camel Got His Hump. Disney, Walter Elias (1901-1966), illus. (Illus.). (ps-3). 1976. (ISBN 0-307-66074-5, Golden Pr). Western Pub.
--Johnny Appleseed. Disney, Walter Elias (1901-1966), illus. (Illus.). (ps-3). 1976. (ISBN 0-307-66054-0, Golden Pr). Western Pub.
--The Jungle Book. (Illus.). (ps). 1979. (Gingerbread). Dutton.
--Lady & the Tramp. (Illus.). (ps). 1979. (Gingerbread). Dutton.
--Lady & the Tramp. Disney, Walt, Studio, illus. (Illus.). (Walt Disney Square Bks.). (gr. k-3). 1978. (ISBN 0-307-66091-5, Golden Pr). Western Pub.
--Lambert the Sheepish Lion. Disney, Walt, Studio, illus. (Illus.). (Walt Disney Square Bks.). (gr. k-3). 1978. (ISBN 0-307-66092-3, Golden Pr). Western Pub.
--Little Red Hen. Disney, Walt, Studio, illus. (Illus.). (Walt Disney Square Bks.). (gr. k-3). 1978. (ISBN 0-307-66093-1, Golden Pr). Western Pub.
--Mary Poppins. Disney, Walt, Studio, illus. (Illus.). (Walt Disney Square Bks.). (gr. k-3). 1978. (ISBN 0-307-66094-X, Golden Pr). Western Pub.
--Mickey & the Beanstalk. Disney, Walter Elias (1901-1966), illus. (Illus.). (ps-3). N.D. (ISBN 0-307-66057-5, Golden Pr). Western Pub.
--Mickey Mouse. (Illus.). (ps). 1979. (Gingerbread). Dutton.
--Mickey Mouse & Goofy: The Big Bear Scare. Disney, Walt, Studio, illus. (Young Reader Ser.). (gr. k-3). 1979. (ISBN 0-307-60318-0, Golden Pr). Western Pub.
--Mickey Mouse & the Mouseketeers: Ghost Town Adventures. Disney, Walt, Studio, illus. (Illus.). (gr. k-3). 1977. (ISBN 0-307-60135-8, Golden Pr). Western Pub.
--Mickey Mouse & the Second Wish. Disney, Walt, Studio, illus. (Illus.). (Tell-a-Tale Readers). (gr. k-3). 1973. (ISBN 0-307-68418-0, Whitman). Western Pub.
--Mickey Mouse & the World's Friendliest Monster. Disney, Walt, Studio, illus. (Illus.). (Tell-a-Tale Readers). (gr. k-3). 1976. (ISBN 0-307-68605-1, Whitman). Western Pub.
--Mickey Mouse: Best Neighbor Contest. Disney, Walt, Studio, illus. (Illus.). (gr. k-3). 1977. (ISBN 0-307-60134-X, Golden Pr). Western Pub.
--Mickey Mouse, Brave Little Tailor. Disney, Walter Elias (1901-1966), illus. (Illus.). (ps-2). 1976. (ISBN 0-307-66059-1, Golden Pr). Western Pub.
--Mickey Mouse Club. Disney, Walter Elias (1901-1966), illus. (Illus.). 24p. Repr. of 1975 ed. (ps-2). 1977. (ISBN 0-307-68997-2, Golden Pr). Western Pub.
--Mickey Mouse Joins the Foreign Legion. (Illus.). 36p. 1981. (ISBN 0-89659-175-1). Abbeville Pr.
--The Mickey Mouse Magic Book, Bk.25. (Illus.). (Disney's Wonderful World of Reading). 1975. (ISBN 0-394-82567-5). (ISBN 0-394-92567-X). Random House.
--The Mickey Mouse Make-it Book, Bk.21. (Illus.). (Disney's Wonderful World of Reading). 1974. (ISBN 0-394-82555-1). (ISBN 0-394-92555-6). Random House.
--Mickey Mouse Meets Robin Hood. (Illus.). 36p. 1981. (ISBN 0-89659-176-X). Abbeville Pr.
--Mickey Mouse: Missing Mouseketeers. Disney, Walt, Studio, illus. (Illus.). (gr. k-3). 1977. (ISBN 0-307-60057-2, Golden Pr). Western Pub.
--Mickey Mouse Movie Stories. Disney, Walter Elias (1901-1966), illus. (Bk. 2). N.D. David McKay Co.
--Mickey Mouse the Boat-Builder. N.D. Grosset & Dunlap.
--Mickey Mouse: The Kitten Sitters. Disney, Walt, Studio, illus. (Illus.). (Young Reader Ser.). (gr. k-3). 1976. (ISBN 0-307-60133-1, Golden Pr). (ISBN 0-307-10823-6). Western Pub.
--Mickey's Lucky Day. 1982. (ISBN 0-531-05162-5). Watts.
--More Mother Goose. Disney, Walt, Studio, illus. (Illus.). (Walt Disney Square Bks.). (gr. k-2). 1978. (ISBN 0-307-66095-8, Golden Pr). Western Pub.
--The Mouseketeer's Train Ride. Disney, Walt, Studio, illus. (Illus.). (gr. k-2). 1977. (ISBN 0-307-68894-1, Golden Pr). Western Pub.
--Old MacDonald Had a Farm. 1979. (ISBN 0-531-05145-5). Watts.
--One Hundred & One Dalmations. Disney, Walter Elias (1901-1966), illus. (Illus.). (ps-3). 1976. (ISBN 0-307-66082-6, Golden Pr). Western Pub.
--Pecos Bill. Disney, Walter Elias (1901-1966), illus. (Illus.). (ps-3). 1976. (ISBN 0-307-66079-6, Golden Pr). Western Pub.
--Pinocchio. (Illus.). (ps). 1979. (Gingerbread). Dutton.
--Pinocchio. Disney, Walt, Productions, illus. (Illus.). 10p. (Disney-Movie-Go-Round Bks.). (ps-3). 1982. (ISBN 0-671-44899-4). Windmill Bks.
--Robin Hood. (Illus.). (Big Picture Book Ser.). (ps-3). 1973. (ISBN 0-307-60492-6). Western Pub.
--Robin Hood. Disney, Walt, Studio, illus. (Illus.). (Walt Disney Square Bks.). (gr. k-3). 1978. (ISBN 0-307-66096-6, Golden Pr). Western Pub.
--The Seven Dwarfs & Their Diamond Mine. Disney, Walter Elias (1901-1966), illus. (Illus.). (ps-3). 1976. (ISBN 0-307-66051-6, Golden Pr). Western Pub.
--Sleeping Beauty. Disney, Walter Elias (1901-1966), illus. (Illus.). (ps-3). 1976. (ISBN 0-307-66083-4, Golden Pr). Western Pub.
--Snow White and the Seven Dwarfs. (gr. 2 up). 1979. (ISBN 0-448-15923-6, G&D). Putnam Pub Group.
--Snow White and the Seven Dwarfs. (Illus.). 1979. (ISBN 0-670-65381-0, Studio). Viking Pr.
--Snow White & the Seven Dwarfs. Disney, Walt, Productions, illus. (Illus.). 10p. (Disney Movie-Go-Round Bks.). (ps-3). 1982. (ISBN 0-671-44897-8). Windmill Bks.
--The Story of Mickey Mouse and the Smugglers. LC 77-364832. (Illus.). 316 p. 24cm. c.1935. Whitman Publishing Co.
--Swiss Family Robinson. (Illus.). 376p. N.D. Cassell Publishing Co.
--Swiss Family Robinson. Disney, Walter Elias (1901-1966), illus. (Illus.). (ps-3). 1976. (ISBN 0-307-66075-3, Golden Pr). Western Pub.
--Three Little Pigs. N.D. Blue Ribbon Books Inc.
--Three Little Pigs. (Illus.). (ps-3). 1976. (ISBN 0-307-66077-X, Golden Pr). Western Pub.
--Thumper. N.D. Grosset & Dunlap.
--Thumper's Race. Disney, Walter Elias (1901-1966), illus. (Illus.). (ps-3). 1976. (ISBN 0-307-66052-4, Golden Pr). Western Pub.
--The Walt Disney Pinocchio. N.D. Random House.
--Walt Disney's A Day With Donald Duck. Bedford, Annie North, pseud. (1915-), adapted by Watson, Jane Werner. Armstong, Samuel, illus. (Illustrations by Walt Disney Studio, adapted by Samuel Armstrong.). (Disney's Liitle Golden Book). 1956. Golden Press.

--Walt Disney's African Lion. 1956. Golden Press.

--Walt Disney's Alice in Wonderland Finds the Garden of Live Flowers. Werner, Jane, pseud. (1915-), adapted by Watson, Jane Werner. Grant, Campbell (1909-), illus. (Illustrations adapted). (Disney's Little Golden Book). 1951. Golden Press.

--Walt Disney's "Bambi". Disney, Walt, Studio, illus. (Big Golden Book). 1949. Golden Press.

--Walt Disney's Bambi. Grant, Bob, illus. (Illustrations adapted). Reissue of 1947 ed. (Disney's Little Golden book). 1960. Golden Press.

--Walt Disney's "Bambi". A Disney Read-Aloud Film Classic. (Illus.). (gr. 3-5). 1982. (ISBN 0-517-54463-6, Harmony). (ISBN 0-517-54462-8). Crown.

--Walt Disney's "Bambi & His Friends". (Walt Disney Board Bk.). 1974. (ISBN 0-307-11526-7, Golden Pr). Western Pub.

--Walt Disney's "Bedknobs & Broomsticks: A Disney Movie Special. (Illus.). 32p. (ps). 1971. (ISBN 0-307-10489-3, Golden Pr). Western Pub.

--Walt Disney's Ben and Me. Grant, Campbell (1909-), illus. LC 54-14961. (Illustrations adapted). 21cm. (Disney Little Golden Book). 1954. Golden Press.

--Walt Disney's Bongo. Starr, Edgar, illus. (Illustrations adapted). (Big Golden Book). 1947. Golden Press.

--Walt Disney's "Brer Rabbit and His Friends". From the Motion Picture "Song of the South.". LC 73-15623. (Illus.). 42 p. 24cm. (Disney's Wonderful World of Reading, no. 13). 1974, c.1973. (ISBN 0-394-82774-0). (ISBN 0-394-82774-0). Random House.

--Walt Disney's Chip "n" Dale at the Zoo. Bedford, Annie North, pseud. (1915-), adapted by Watson, Jane Werner. Bosche, Bill, illus. (Illustrations adapted). (Disney's Little Golden Book). 1954. Golden Press.

--Walt Disney's Cinderella. LC 73-22325. p. cm. (Disney's wonderful world of reading, 16). 1974. (ISBN 0-394-82552-7). (ISBN 0-394-82552-7). Random House.

--Walt Disney's "Cinderella". (Illus.). (gr. k-3). 1950. (ISBN 0-307-10425-7, Golden Pr). (ISBN 0-307-60425-X). Western Pub.

--Walt Disney's Cinderella. Grant, Campbell (1909-), illus. (Illustrations adapted). (Disney's Little Golden Book). 1957. Golden Press.

--Walt Disney's Cinderella. Werner, Jane, adapted by. Worcester, Retta, illus. (Illustrations adapted). (Big Golden Book). 1950. Golden Press.

--Walt Disney's Cinderella's Friends. Werner, Jane, adapted by. Dempster, Al, illus. (Illustrations adapted). (Disney's Little Golden Book). 1957. Golden Press.

--Walt Disney's Circus Board Book. (Illus.). 12p. (ps-2). 1975. (ISBN 0-307-11302-7, Golden Pr). Western Pub.

--Walt Disney's Darby O'Gill. Gantz, David, illus. Bedford, Annie North (1915-), as told by. (Illustrations adapted). (Disney Little Golden Book). 1959. Golden Press.

--Walt Disney's Davy Crockett. Beecher, Elizabeth, adapted by. Schmidt, Al, illus. LC 55-3291. (Original Illustrations by Walt Disney Studio). (Big Golden Book). 1955. Golden Press.

--Walt Disney's Davy Crockett and Mike Fink. Braddock, Jonathan, adapted by. Crawford, Mel (1925-), illus. 1956. Golden Press.

--Walt Disney's Davy Crockett and Mike Fink. Shapiro, Irwin, adapted by. Disney, Walt, Studio, illus. (Big Golden Book). 1956. Golden Press.

--Walt Disney's Donald and the Witch. Bedford, Annie North, pseud. (1915-), adapted by Watson, Jane Werner. Kelsey, Richmond I., illus. (Illustrations adapted). (Disney's Little Golden Book). 1953. Golden Press.

--Walt Disney's Donald Duck and Santa Claus. Bedford, Annie North, pseud. (1915-), adapted by Watson, Jane Werner. Dempster, Al, illus. (Illustrations adapted). (Disney's Little Golden Book). 1952. Golden Press.

--Walt Disney's Donald Duck Board Book. (Illus.). 12p. (ps-2). 1975. (ISBN 0-307-11304-3, Golden Pr). Western Pub.

--Walt Disney's "Donald Duck, It's Play Time!". LC 80-13827. (Illus.). 24 p. 32cm. c.1980. (ISBN 0-307-10828-7). Golden Press.

--Walt Disney's Donald Duck, Prize Diver. Bedford, Annie North, pseud. (1915-), adapted by Watson, Jane Werner. Boyle, Neil, illus. (Illustrations adapted). (Disney's Little Golden Book). 1956. Golden Press.

--Walt Disney's Donald Duck Treasury. Bedford, Annie North, pseud. (1915-), adapted by Watson, Jane Werner. Disney, Walt, Studio, illus. (Giant Little Golden Book). 1957. Golden Press.

--Walt Disney's Donald Duck Treasury. Bedford, Annie North, pseud. (1915-) & Kelsey, Dick, eds. Watson, Jane Werner. LC 60-4293. (Big Golden Book). 1960. Golden Press.

--Walt Disney's Donald Duck's Adventure. Bedford, Annie North, pseud. (1915-), adapted by Watson, Jane Werner. Grant, Campbell (1909-), illus. LC 50-12176. (Illustrations adapted). (Disney's Little Golden Book). 1950. Golden Press.

--Walt Disney's Donald Duck's Christmas Carol. Bedford, Annie North, pseud. (1915-), adapted by Watson, Jane Werner. McGray, Norm, illus. (Original Illustrations by Walt Disney Studio, adapted by Norm McGray). (Disney's Little Golden Book). 1960. Golden Press.

--Walt Disney's Donald Duck's Toy Train. Werner, Jane, adapted by. Kelsey, Richmond I. & Justice, Bill, illus. LC 40-14813. (Illustrations adapted). (Disney's Little Golden Book). 1951. Golden Press.

--Walt Disney's "Donald Duck's World Tour". (Walt Disney Board Bk). 1974. (ISBN 0-307-11528-3, Golden Pr). Western Pub.

--Walt Disney's Dumbo. Bedford, Annie North, pseud. (1915-), adapted by Watson, Jane Werner. Kelsey, Richmond I., illus. (Adapted from the Walt Disney film. Illustrations also adapted). (Big Golden Bk). 1955. Golden Press.

--Walt Disney's Dumbo. Disney, Walt, Studio, illus. (Disney's Little Golden Book). 1946. Golden Press.

--Walt Disney's Elmer Elephant Plus Peculiar Penguins. LC 78-19231. p. cm. 1978. (ISBN 0-679-20602-7). McKay.

--Walt Disney's "Fairy Tale Friends". (Illus.). 12p. (ps-2). 1975. (ISBN 0-307-11306-X, Golden Pr). Western Pub.

--Walt Disney's Goofy, Movie Star. Bedford, Annie North, pseud. (1915-), adapted by Watson, Jane Werner. Armstrong, Samuel, illus. (Illustrations adapted). (Disney's Little Golden Book). 1956. Golden Press.

--Walt Disney's "Goofy's Forest Fun". (Walt Disney Board Bk). 1974. (ISBN 0-307-11529-1, Golden Pr). Western Pub.

--Walt Disney's "It's a Small World". (Illus.). 32p. (Golden Melody Bks.). (ps-2). 1983. (ISBN 0-307-12248-4, Golden Pr). Western Pub.

--Walt Disney's "Lady & the Tramp". A Walt Disney Board Book. 12p. (ps). 1975. (ISBN 0-307-11531-3, Golden Pr). Western Pub.

--Walt Disney's Little Man of Disneyland. Bedford, Annie North, pseud. (1915-), adapted by Watson, Jane Werner. Kelsey, Richmond I., illus. (Illustrations adapted). (Disney's Little Golden book). 1955. Golden Press.

--Walt Disney's Lucky Puppy. Watson, Jane Werner (1915-), adapted by. Hubbard, Allen & Bestor, Don, illus. (Original Illustrations by Walt Disney Studio.). (Disney's Little Golden Book). 1960. Golden Press.

--Walt Disney's Mad Hatter's Tea Party. Werner, Jane, adapted by. Kelsey, Richmond I. & Griffith, Don, illus. (Illustrations adapted). (Disney's Little Golden Books). 1951. Golden Press.

--Walt Disney's "Mickey Mouse & His Friends. (Illus.). 12p. (ps-2). 1975. (ISBN 0-307-11307-8, Golden Pr). Western Pub.

--Walt Disney's Mickey Mouse and His Space Ship. Werner, Jane, adapted by. Banta, Milton & Ushler, John, illus. (Illustrations adapted). (Disney's Little Golden Book). 1952. Golden Press.

--Walt Disney's Mickey Mouse and Pluto Pup. Bedford, Annie North, pseud. (1915-), adapted by Watson, Jane Werner. Gracey, Yale, illus. (Illustrations adapted). Reissue of 1953 ed. (Disney's Little Golden Book). 1959. Golden Press.

--Walt Disney's Mother Goose. Dempster, Al, illus. (Illustrations adapted). Reissue of 1956 ed. (Disney's Little Golden Book). 1959. Golden Press.

--Walt Disney's Nomads of the North. DuBois, Gaylord, adapted by. Greene, Hamilton, illus. (A Golden Reading Adventure). 1960. Golden Press.

--Walt Disney's Odyssey of an Otter. Greene, Hamilton & Dresser, Lawrence T., illus. (An Animal Adventure Book). 1960. Golden Press.

--Walt Disney's Old Yeller. Lindquist, Willis, as told by. Doremus, Robert (1913-), illus. LC 58-14642. (Original illustrations by the Walt Disney Studio.). 33cm. 28p. (Big Golden Book). 1958. Golden Press.

--Walt Disney's Old Yeller. Shapiro, Irwin, as told by. Schmidt, Edwin & Dreany, E. Joseph, illus. (Disney's Little Golden Book). 1957. Golden Press.

--Walt Disney's Once upon a Wintertime. Oreb, Tom, illus. Oreb, Tom, ed. Disney Walt, Studio, illus. (Illustrations adapted). (Disney's Little Golden Book). 1950. Golden Press.

--Walt Disney's Perri. 1958. Golden Press.

--Walt Disney's Peter and the Wolf. Kelsey, Richmond I., illus. (Illustrations adapted). (Disney's Little Golden Book). 1956. Golden Press.

--Walt Disney's Pinocchio. Fletcher, Steffi, adapted by. Dempster, Al, illus. (Illustrations adapted). (Big Golden Book). 1954. Golden Press.

--Walt Disney's Pinocchio. Grant, Campbell (1909-), illus. (Illustrations adapted). (Disney's Little Golden book). 1948. Golden Press.

--Walt Disney's Robin Hood. Bedford, Annie North, pseud. (1915-), retold by Watson, Jane Werner. (Disney's Little Golden Book). 1955. Golden Press.

--Walt Disney's Santa's Toy Shop. Dempster, Al, illus. LC 50-14111. (Illustrations adapted). (Disney's Little Golden book). 1950. Golden Press.

--Walt Disney's Seven Dwarfs Find a House. Bedford, Annie North, pseud. (1915-), adapted by Watson, Jane Werner. Svendsen, Julius (1919-), illus. Reissue of 1953 ed. (Disney's Little Golden Book). 1958. Golden Press.

--Walt Disney's Shaggy Dog. Verral, Charles Spain, adapted by. Cellini, Joseph (1924-), illus. LC 59-4409. (Disney's Little Golden Book). 1959. Golden Press.

--Walt Disney's Sleeping Beauty. Watson, Jane Werner, ed. Disney, Walt, Studio, illus. (Giant Golden Book). 1957. Golden Press.

--Walt Disney's Sleeping Beauty. Watson, Jane Werner & Svendson, Julius, eds. Eyvind, Earl & Svendson, Julius, illus. (Illustrations adpated. Originals by Walt Disney Studio). (Big Golden Book). 1959. Golden Press.

--Walt Disney's Snow White and the Seven Dwarfs. O'Brien, Ken & Dempster, Al, illus. (Illustrations adapted). Reissue of 1948 ed. (Disney's Little Golden Book). 1957. Golden Press.

--Walt Disney's So Dear to My Heart. Palmer, Helen, adapted by. Peet, Bill, pseud. (1915-), illus. Peet, William Bartlett. (Illustrations adapted). (Golden Story Bk.). 1949. Golden Press.

--Walt Disney's Storytime Book. Grant, Campbell (1909-), adapted by. Grant, Campbell (1909-) & Grant, Bob, illus. (Original illustrations by Walt Disney Studio.). (Giant Little Golden Bk.). 1958. Golden Press.

--Walt Disney's Surprise Package. Disney, Walter Elias (1901-1966), illus. 1944. Simon & Schuster.

--Walt Disney's Surprise Package. Palmer, Helen Marion, adapted by. Disney, Walt, Studio, illus. (Giant Golden Bk.). 1944. Golden Press.

--Walt Disney's The Adventures of Mr. Toad. Hench, John, illus. (Illustrations Adapted). (Big Golden Book). 1949. Golden Press.

--Walt Disney's The Adventures Of Robin Hood. (Big Golden Book). 1956. Golden Press.

--Walt Disney's The Adventures of Zorro. Werstein, Irving, adapted by. Steel, John, illus. (Big Golden Book). 1958. Golden Press.

--Walt Disney's The Cold-Blooded Penguin. Edmunds, Robert, adapted by. Disney, Walt, Studio, illus. (Disney's Little Golden Book). 1944. Golden Press.

--Walt Disney's The Great Locomotive Chase. Verral, Charles Spain, adapted by. Kaye, Graham, illus. (Big Golden Book). 1956. Golden Press.

--Walt Disney's Tiny Movie Stories. Disney, Walt, Studio, illus. (Tiny Golden Book). 1950. Golden Press.

--Walt Disney's Toby Tyler. Memling, Carl (1918-1969), adapted by. Crawford, Mel (1925-), illus. (A Golden Reading Adventure Bk.). 1960. Golden Press.

--Walt Disney's Toby Tyler. Memling, Carl (1918-1969), adapted by. McKim, Sam, illus. LC 61-4929. (Disney's Little Golden Book). 1960. Golden Press.

--Walt Disney's Tonka. Beecher, Elizabeth, adapted by. Greene, Hamilton, illus. LC 59-4448. 23cm. 00p. (Big Golden Bk.). 1959. Golden Press.

--Walt Disney's Treasure Chest. Disney, Walt, Studio, illus. (Big Golden Bk.). 1948. Golden Press.

--Walt Disney's Twenty Thousand Leagues Under the Sea. Grant, Campbell (1909-) & Beecher, Elizabeth, illus. LC 55-14007. (Adapted from Walt Disney film. Pictures adapted from the Walt Disney Studio.). 29cm. 63p. (Big Golden Bk.). 1954. Golden Press.

--Walt Disney's Uncle Remus Stories. Palmer, Marion, adapted by. Dempster, Al & Justice, Bill, illus. (Illustrations adapted). Reissue of 1947 ed. (Giant Golden Bk.). 1959. Golden Press.

--Walt Disney's Westward Ho, The Wagons. Coombs, Charles I. & Schmidt, Al, eds. LC 56-14332. (Big Golden Book). 1956. Golden Press.

--Walt Disney's Winnie-the-Pooh's Blanket Book. (Illus.). (ps). 1980. (Gingerbread). Dutton.

--Walt Disney's Zorro. Verral, Charles Spain, adapted by. Steel, John, illus. (Disney's Little Golden Book). 1958. Golden Press.

--Winnie Puh. Disney, Walter Elias (1901-1966), illus. Sanchez, Rene, tr. from Eng. (Illus.). 24p. Orig. Title: Winnie-the-Pooh Book. (ps-3). 1977. (ISBN 0-307-68827-5, Golden Pr). Western Pub.

--Winnie the Pooh. (Illus.). (ps). 1979. (Gingerbread). Dutton.

--Winnie-the-Pooh & His Friends. Disney, Walter Elias (1901-1966), illus. (Illus.). (ps-3). 1976. (ISBN 0-307-68957-3, Golden Pr). Western Pub.

--Winnie-the-Pooh & the Blustery Day. Disney, Walter Elias (1901-1966), illus. (Illus.). (ps-3). 1976. (ISBN 0-307-66053-2, Golden Pr). Western Pub.

--Winnie-the-Pooh & the Honey Tree. Disney, Walter Elias (1901-1966), illus. (Illus.). (ps-3). 1976. (ISBN 0-307-66055-9, Golden Pr). Western Pub.

--The Wizard of Oz. Disney, Walter Elias (1901-1966), illus. (Illus.). (ps-3). 1976. (ISBN 0-307-66084-2, Golden Pr). Western Pub.

Disney, Walter Elias (1901-1966), adapted by.

--Treasure Island. Disney, Walter Elias (1901-1966), illus. (Original Author: Robert Louis Stevenson, 1850-1894). (Illus.). (ps-3). 1976. (ISBN 0-307-66060-5, Golden Pr). Western Pub.

Disney, Walter Elias (1901-1966), illus.

--The Cold Blooded Penguin. LC 41-51040. 18cm. 24p. 1944. Simon & Schuster.

Disney, Walter Elias (1901-1966) & Bedford, Annie North, pseud. (1915-)

--Walt Disney's Mickey and the Missing Mouseketeers. Watson, Jane Werner. Disney, Walt, Studio, illus. (Disney's Little Golden Book). 1956. Golden Press.

--Walt Disney's Perri. Watson, Jane Werner. (Disney's Little Golden Book). 1956. Golden Press.

--Walt Disney's Scamp. Watson, Jane Werner. McGray, Norm & Rinaldi, Joe, eds. Disney, Walt, Studio, illus. (Disney's Little Golden Book). 1957. Golden Press.

--Walt Disney's Scamp's Adventure. Watson, Jane Werner. Rinaldi, Joe & Boyle, Neil, eds. Disney, Walt, Studio, illus. Reissue of 1958 ed. (Disney's Little Golden Book). 1960. Golden Press.

--Walt Disney's Sleeping Beauty. Watson, Jane Werner. Disney, Walt, Studio, illus. Svendson, Julius & Armitage, Frank, eds. (Adapted by Julius Svendson, Frank Armitage, Walt Peregoy.). (Disney's Liitle Golden Book). 1957. Golden Press.

Disney, Walter Elias (1901-1966) & Beutter, Carl

--Walt Disney's Donald Duck, Lost and Found. Grant, Bob & Totten, Bob, illus. (Disney's Little Golden Book). 1960. Golden Press.

Disney, Walter Elias (1901-1966) & Greene, Ward

--Walt Disney's Lady and the Tramp. Armstrong, Samuel, illus. (Based on the story by Ward Greene.Illustrations adapted). (Big Golden Bk.). 1955. Golden Press.

Disney, Walter Elias (1901-1966) & Lindquist, Willis

--The Walt Disney's Littlest Outlaw. Disney, Walt, Studio & Greene, Hamilton, illus. (Illustrations Adapted.). 1956. Golden Press.

--Walt Disney's Robin Hood. Greene, Hamilton, illus. 1956. Golden Press.

Disney, Walter Elias (1901-1966) & Montgomery, Rutherford

--Walt Disney's "Weecha the Raccoon". Dresser, Lawrence T., illus. LC 60-4856. (An Animal Adventure Book). 1960. Golden Press.

Disney, Walter Elias (1901-1966) & Peet, Bill (1915-)

--Walt Disney's Goliath II. Peet, Bill, pseud. (1915-), illus. Peet, William Bartlett. (Disney's Little Golden Book). 1959. Golden Press.

Disney, Walter Elias (1901-1966) & Porter, Eleanor Hodgman

--Walt Disney's "Pollyanna". Beecher, Elizabeth, adapted by. Hedstrom, Karen, illus. (Based on the story by Eleanor H. Porter.). (Disney's Little Golden Book). 1960. Golden Press.

Disney, Walter Elias (1901-1966) & Shapiro, Irwin

--Walt Disney's Davy Crockett. Crawford, Mel (1925-), illus. (Illustrations adapted). (Disney's Little Golden Book). 1955. Golden Press.

--Walt Disney's "Davy Crockett". Stewart, Norton, illus. 1955. Golden Press.

--Walt Disney's Davy Crockett's Keelboat Race. Crawford, Mel (1925-), illus. (Illustrations adapted). (Disney's Little Golden Book). 1955. Golden Press.

Disney, Walter Elias (1901-1966) & Sinclair, Lewis

--Walt Disney's Bongo. Grant, Campbell (1909-), illus. (Based on a story by Sinclair Lewis. Illustrations adapted. Originals by Walt Disney Studio). (Disney's Little Golden Book). 1957. Golden Press.

--The Infinity Clue. Stratemeyer Syndicate. Morrill, Leslie H., illus. LC 81-10329. p. cm. (The Hardy Boys Ser.: Vol. 70). c.1981. (ISBN 0-671-42342-8). (ISBN 0-671-42343-6). Wanderer Books.

--The Jungle Pyramid. Stratemeyer Syndicate. LC 76-14297. (Illus.). 180 p. 20cm. (The Hardy Boys Ser.: Vol. 56). c.1977. (ISBN 0-448-08956-4). (ISBN 0-448-18956-9). Grosset & Dunlap.

--The Lone Eagle of the Border: Or, Ted Scott and the Diamond Smugglers. Stratemeyer Syndicate. Rogers, Walter S., illus. LC 29-2815. vi, 214 p. front. 20 cm. (The Ted Scott Flying Ser.: Vol. 8). c.1929. Grosset & Dunlap.

--Lost at the South Pole: Or, Ted Scott in Blizzard Land. Stratemeyer Syndicate. Rogers, Walter S., illus. LC 30-2682. vi, 214 p. front. 20 cm. (The Ted Scott Flying Ser.: Vol. 11). c.1930. Grosset & Dunlap.

--The Mark on the Door. Stratemeyer Syndicate. rev. ed. LC 67-20847. (Illus.). 175 p. 20cm. (The Hardy Boys Ser.: Vol. 13). 1967. Grosset & Dunlap.

--The Mark on the Door. Stratemeyer Syndicate. Gretter, J. Clemens, illus. LC 34-14005. (Written for the Stratemeyer Syndicate by Harriet Stratemeyer Adams, 1894-1982, under the pseudonym, Franklin W. Dixon). iv, 219 p. front. 20 cm. (The Hardy Boys Ser.: Vol. 13). c.1934. Grosset & Dunlap.

--The Masked Monkey. Stratemeyer Syndicate. LC 71-180994. (Illus.). 178 p. 20cm. (The Hardy Boys Ser.: Vol. 51). 1972. (ISBN 0-448-08951-3). Grosset & Dunlap.

--The Melted Coins. Stratemeyer Syndicate. Laune, Paul Sidney (1899-), illus. LC 44-2023. vi p., 1 l., 215 p. incl. front. 19 1/2 cm. (The Hardy Boys Ser.: Vol. 23). 1944. Grosset & Dunlap.

--The Melted Coins. Stratemeyer Syndicate. rev. ed. Svenson, Andrew E. (1910-1975), rev. by. LC 78-86722. (Illus.). 180 p. 20cm. (The Hardy Boys Ser.: Vol. 23). 1970. Grosset & Dunlap.

--The Missing Chums. Stratemeyer Syndicate. rev. ed. (Illus.). (The Hardy Boys Ser.: Vol. 4). 1962. Grosset & Dunlap.

--The Missing Chums. Stratemeyer Syndicate. Rogers, Walter S., illus. iv, 214 p. front. 20 cm. (The Hardy Boys Ser.: Vol. 4). c.1928. Grosset & Dunlap.

--The Mummy Case. Stratemeyer Syndicate. Morrill, Leslie H, illus. LC 80-15921. (Illus.). 180 p. 19cm. (The Hardy Boys Ser.: Vol. 63). c.1980. (ISBN 0-671-41117-9). (ISBN 0-671-41112-8). Wanderer Books.

--The Mysterious Caravan. Stratemeyer Syndicate. LC 74-10463. (Illus.). 182 p. 20cm. (The Hardy Boys Ser.: Vol. 54). 1975. (ISBN 0-448-08954-8). Grosset & Dunlap.

--The Mystery at Devil's Paw. Stratemeyer Syndicate. LC 59-16010. (Illus.). 183 p. 20cm. (The Hardy Boys Ser.: Vol. 38). 1959. Grosset & Dunlap.

--The Mystery at Devil's Paw. Stratemeyer Syndicate. rev. ed. Adams, Harriet Stratemeyer (1894-1982), rev. by. LC 73-2184. (Illus.). 180 p. 20cm. (The Hardy Boys Ser.: Vol. 38). 1973. (ISBN 0-448-08938-6). Grosset & Dunlap.

--The Mystery of Cabin Island. Stratemeyer Syndicate. rev. ed. LC 66-11316. (Illus.). 178p. illus. 20cm. (The Hardy Boys Ser.: Vol. 8). 1966. Grosset.

--The Mystery of Cabin Island. Stratemeyer Syndicate. Rogers, Walter S., illus. LC 29-16920. iv, 214 p. front. 20 cm. (The Hardy Boys Ser: Vol. 8). c.1929. Grosset & Dunlap.

--The Mystery of Smuggler's Cove. Stratemeyer Syndicate. Morrill, Leslie H., illus. LC 80-15921. (Illus.). 181 p. 19cm. (The Hardy Boys Ser.: Vol. 64). c.1980. (ISBN 0-671-41117-9). (ISBN 0-671-41112-8). Wanderer Books.

--The Mystery of the Aztec Warrior. Stratemeyer Syndicate. LC 64-2160. (Written for the Stratemeyer Syndicate by Harriet Stratemeyer Adams, 1894-1982, under the pseudonym, Franklin W. Dixon). (Illus.). 178 p. 20cm. (The Hardy Boys Ser.: Vol. 43). 1964. Grosset & Dunlap.

--The Mystery of the Chinese Junk. Stratemeyer Syndicate. (Illus.). (The Hardy Boys Ser.: Vol. 39). (gr. 5-9). 1960. Grosset & Dunlap.

--The Mystery of the Desert Giant. Stratemeyer Syndicate. LC 61-1196. (Illus.). 182 p. 20cm. (The Hardy Boys Ser.: Vol. 40). 1961. Grosset & Dunlap.

--The Mystery of the Flying Express. Stratemeyer Syndicate. Laune, Paul Sidney (1899-), illus. vi, 217 p. incl. front. 20 cm. (The Hardy Boys Ser.: Vol. 20). c.1941. Grosset & Dunlap.

--The Mystery of the Samurai Sword. Stratemeyer Syndicate. Morrill, Leslie H., illus. LC 79-17393. p. cm. Repr. of 1979 ed. (The Hardy Boys Ser.: Vol. 60). 1979. (ISBN 0-671-34011-5). (ISBN 0-671-95497-0). Messner.

--The Mystery of the Spiral Bridge. Stratemeyer Syndicate. LC 66-10713. (Written for the Stratemeyer Syndicate by Andrew E. Svenson, 1910-1975, under the pseudonym, Franklin W. Dixon). 177p. illus. 20cm. (The Hardy Boys Ser.: Vol. 45). 1966. Grosset.

--Mystery of the Stone Idol. Stratemeyer Syndicate. Morrill, Leslie H., illus. LC 80-21896. p. cm. (The Hardy Boys Ser.: Vol. 65). c.1981. (ISBN 0-671-42289-8). (ISBN 0-671-42290-1). Wanderer Books.

--The Mystery of the Whale Tattoo. Stratemeyer Syndicate. LC 68-12750. (Illus.). 174 p. 20cm. (The Hardy Boys Ser.: Vol. 47). 1968. Grosset & Dunlap.

--Night of the Werewolf. Stratemeyer Syndicate. Morrill, Leslie H., illus. LC 79-17046. p. cm. (The Hardy Boys Ser.: Vol. 59). c.1979. (ISBN 0-671-95520-9). Wanderer Books.

--The Outlaw's Silver. Stratemeyer Syndicate. Morrill, Leslie H., illus. LC 81-11467. p. cm. (The Hardy Boy Ser.: Vol. 67). c.1981. (ISBN 0-671-42336-3). (ISBN 0-671-42337-1). Wanderer Books.

--Over the Jungle Trails: Or, Ted Scott and the Missing Explorers. Stratemeyer Syndicate. Rogers, Walter S., illus. LC 29-18703. vi, 214 p. incl. front. 20 cm. (The Ted Scott Flying Ser.: Vol. 10). c.1929. Grosset & Dunlap.

--Over the Ocean to Paris: Or, Ted Scott's Daring Long Distance Flight. Stratemeyer Syndicate. Rogers, Walter S., illus. LC 27-184750. vi, 214 p. front. 20 cm. (The Ted Scott Flying Ser.: Vol. 1). c.1927. Grosset & Dunlap.

--Over the Rockies with the Air Mail: Or, Ted Scott Lost in the Wilderness. Stratemeyer Syndicate. Rogers, Walter S., illus. LC 27-221526. vi, 214 p. front. 20 cm. (The Ted Scott Flying Ser.: Vol. 3). c.1927. Grosset & Dunlap.

--The Pentagon Spy. Stratemeyer Syndicate. Morrill, Leslie H., illus. LC 79-24463. (Illus.). 182 p. 19cm. (The Hardy Boys Ser.: Vol. 61). c.1980. (ISBN 0-671-95570-5). Wanderer Books : Distributed by Simon & Schuster.

--The Phantom Freighter. Stratemeyer Syndicate. rev. ed. LC 75-115957. (Illus.). 181 p. 20cm. (The Hardy Boys Ser.: Vol. 26). 1970. (ISBN 0-448-08926-2). Grosset & Dunlap.

--The Phantom Freighter. Stratemeyer Syndicate. Tandy, Russell H., illus. LC 47-16694. vi p., 1 l., 216 p. incl. front. 19 1/2 cm. (The Hardy Boys Ser.: Vol. 26). 1947. Grosset & Dunlap.

--The Pursuit Patrol: Or, Chasing the Platinum Pirates. Stratemeyer Syndicate. Hazelton, Isaac Brewster, illus. LC 43-1149. vii p., 1 l., 214 p. incl. front. 19 1/2 cm. (The Ted Scott Flying Ser.: Vol. 20). 1943. Grosset & Dunlap.

--Rescued in the Clouds: Or, Ted Scott, Hero of the Air. Stratemeyer Syndicate. Rogers, Walter S., illus. LC 27-19177. vi, 214 p. front. 20 cm. (The Ted Scott Flying Ser.: Vol. 2). c.1927. Grosset & Dunlap.

--The Roaring River Mystery. Stratemeyer Syndicate. Frame, Paul (1913-), illus. LC 83-16927. p. cm. (The Hardy Boys Ser.: Vol. 80). c.1984. (ISBN 0-671-49722-7). (ISBN 0-671-49721-9). Wanderer Books, Simon & Schuster.

--The Search for the Lost Flyers: Or, Ted Scott Over the West Indies. Stratemeyer Syndicate. Rogers, Walter S., illus. LC 28-126602. vi, 216 p. front. 20 cm. (The Ted Scott Flying Ser.: Vol. 5). c.1928. Grosset & Dunlap.

--The Secret Agent on Flight 101. Stratemeyer Syndicate. (Illus.). 176 p. 20cm. (The Hardy Boys Ser.: Vol. 46). 1967. Grosset & Dunlap.

--The Secret of Pirates' Hill. Stratemeyer Syndicate. LC 57-13572. (Illus.). 213 p. 20cm. (The Hardy Boys Ser.: Vol. 36). 1957, c.1956. Grosset & Dunlap.

--The Secret of Pirates' Hill. Stratemeyer Syndicate. rev. ed. (Illus.). (The Hardy Boys Ser.: Vol. 36). 1972. Grosset & Dunlap.

--The Secret of Skull Mountain. Stratemeyer Syndicate. rev. ed. LC 66-31247. (Illus.). 177 p. 20cm. (The Hardy Boys Ser.: Vol. 27). 1966. Grosset & Dunlap.

--The Secret of Skull Mountain. Stratemeyer Syndicate. Tandy, Russell H., illus. LC 48-5428. (Written for the Stratemeyer Syndicate by Harriet Stratemeyer Adams, 1894-1982, under the pseudonym, Franklin W. Dixon). vi, 212 p. front. 20 cm. (The Hardy Boys Ser.: Vol. 27). 1948. Grosset & Dunlap.

--The Secret of the Caves. Stratemeyer Syndicate. rev. ed. LC 66-8426. (Illus.). 175p. illus. 20cm. (The Hardy Boys Ser.: Vol. 7). 1965, c.1964. Grosset.

--The Secret of the Caves. Stratemeyer Syndicate. Rogers, Walter S., illus. LC 29-10214. iv, 210 p. front. 20 cm. (The Hardy Boys Ser.: Vol. 7). c.1929. Grosset & Dunlap.

--The Secret of the Lost Tunnel. Stratemeyer Syndicate. rev. ed. LC 68-24655. (Illus.). 174 p. 20cm. (The Hardy Boys Ser.: Vol. 29). 1968. Grosset & Dunlap.

--The Secret of the Lost Tunnel. Stratemeyer Syndicate. Tandy, Russell H., illus. LC 50-5627. 210 p. front. 20 cm. (The Hardy Boys Ser.: Vol. 29). 1950. Grosset & Dunlap.

--The Secret of the Old Mill. Stratemeyer Syndicate. rev. ed. (Illus.). (The Hardy Boys Ser.: Vol. 3). 1962, c.1961. Grosset & Dunlap.

--The Secret of the Old Mill. Stratemeyer Syndicate. Rogers, Walter S., illus. LC 27-18474. iv, 212 p. front. 20 cm. (The Hardy Boys Ser.: Vol. 3). c.1927. Grosset & Dunlap.

--The Secret of Wildcat Swamp. Stratemeyer Syndicate. rev. ed. LC 69-14267. (Illus.). 178 p. 20cm. (The Hardy Boys Ser.: Vol. 31). 1969. Grosset & Dunlap.

--The Secret of Wildcat Swamp. Stratemeyer Syndicate. Pell, Roy, illus. LC 52-7162. 212 p. illus. 20 cm. (The Hardy Boys Ser.: Vol. 31). 1952. Grosset & Dunlap.

--The Secret Panel. Stratemeyer Syndicate. rev. ed. LC 74-86693. (Illus.). 178 p. 20cm. (The Hardy Boys Ser.: Vol. 25). 1969. Grosset & Dunlap.

--The Secret Panel. Stratemeyer Syndicate. Tandy, Russell H., illus. LC 46-2072. (Written for the Stratemeyer Syndicate by Harriet Stratemeyer Adams, 1894-1982, under the pseudonym, Franklin W. Dixon). vi p., 1 l., 212 p. incl. front. 19 cm. (The Hardy Boys Ser.: Vol. 25). 1946. Grosset & Dunlap.

--The Secret Warning. Stratemeyer Syndicate. rev. ed. LC 66-12695. 176p. illus. 20cm. (The Hardy Boys Ser.: Vol. 17). 1966. Grosset.

--The Secret Warning. Stratemeyer Syndicate. Laune, Paul Sidney (1899-), illus. LC 38-9831. iv, 220 p. front. 20 cm. (The Hardy Boys Ser.: Vol. 17). c.1938. Grosset & Dunlap.

--The Shattered Helmet. Stratemeyer Syndicate. LC 72-90825. (Illus.). 180 p. 19cm. (The Hardy Boys Ser.: Vol. 52). 1973. (ISBN 0-448-08952-1). Grosset & Dunlap.

--The Shore Road Mystery. Stratemeyer Syndicate. rev. ed. LC 64-55755. (Illus.). 178 p. 20cm. (The Hardy Boys Ser.: Vol. 6). 1964. Grosset & Dunlap.

--The Shore Road Mystery. Stratemeyer Syndicate. Rogers, Walter S., illus. LC 28-220648. iv, 212 p. front. 20 cm. (The Hardy Boys Ser.: Vol. 6). c.1928. Grosset & Dunlap.

--The Short-Wave Mystery. Stratemeyer Syndicate. rev. ed. (Illus.). (The Hardy Boys Ser.: Vol. 24). 1966. Grosset & Dunlap.

--The Short-Wave Mystery. Stratemeyer Syndicate. Tandy, Russell H., illus. LC 45-1618. (Illus.). vi, 217 p. 20cm. (The Hardy Boys Ser.: Vol. 24). 1945. Grosset & Dunlap.

--The Sign of the Crooked Arrow. Stratemeyer Syndicate. rev. ed. LC 71-100119. (Illus.). 178 p. 20cm. (The Hardy Boys Ser.: Vol. 28). 1970. Grosset & Dunlap.

--The Sign of the Crooked Arrow. Stratemeyer Syndicate. Tandy, Russell H., illus. LC 49-1194. vii, 214 p. illus. 20 cm. (The Hardy Boys Ser.: Vol. 28). 1949. Grosset & Dunlap.

--The Sinister Signpost. Stratemeyer Syndicate. rev. ed. (Illus.). (The Hardy Boys Ser.: Vol. 15). 1968. Grosset & Dunlap.

--The Sinister Signpost. Stratemeyer Syndicate. Gretter, J. Clemens, illus. LC 36-189676. (Written for the Stratemeyer Syndicate by Harriet Stratemeyer Adams, 1894-1982, under the pseudonym, Franklin W. Dixon). iii, 215 p. front. 20 cm. (The Hardy Boys Ser.: Vol. 15). c.1936. Grosset & Dunlap.

--Sky Sabotage. Stratemeyer Syndicate. Frame, Paul (1913-), illus. LC 83-1240. p. cm. (The Hardy Boys Ser.: Vol. 79). 1983, c.1982. (ISBN 0-671-47556-8). (ISBN 0-671-47557-6). Wanderer Books.

--The Skyfire Puzzle. Stratemeyer Syndicate. LC 85-11440. p. cm. (The Hardy Boys Ser.). c.1985. (ISBN 0-671-49732-4). (ISBN 0-671-49731-6). Wanderer Books.

--South of the Rio Grande: Or, Ted Scott on a Secret Mission. Stratemeyer Syndicate. Rogers, Walter S., illus. LC 28-181198. vi, 215 p. front. 20 cm. (The Ted Scott Flying Ser.: Vol. 6). c.1928. Grosset & Dunlap.

--The Sting of the Scorpion. Stratemeyer Syndicate. LC 78-57930. (Illus.). 180 p., 1 leaf of plates. 20cm. (The Hardy Boys Ser.: Vol. 58). c.1979. (ISBN 0-448-08958-0). Grosset & Dunlap.

--The Stone Idol. Stratemeyer Syndicate. Morrill, Leslie H., illus. (Illus.). 192p. (The Hardy Boys Ser.: Vol. 65). (gr. 3-7). 1981. (ISBN 0-671-42289-8). (ISBN 0-671-42290-1). Wanderer Bks.

--The Submarine Caper. Stratemeyer Syndicate. LC 81-3361. p. cm. (The Hardy Boys Ser.: Vol. 68). c.1981. (ISBN 0-671-42338-X). (ISBN 0-671-42339-8). Wanderer Books.

--The Swamp Monster. Stratemeyer Syndicate. Arico, Diane, ed. 192p. (The Hardy Boys Ser.). (gr. 8-12). 1985. (ISBN 0-671-55054-3). (ISBN 0-671-55048-9). Wanderer Bks.

--The Mystery of the Flying Express. Stratemeyer Syndicate. rev. ed. Svenson, Andrew E. (1910-1975), rev. by. LC 73-106327. (Illus.). 177 p. 20cm. Reissue of 1941 ed. (The Hardy Boys Ser.: Vol. 20). 1970. (ISBN 0-448-08920-3). Grosset & Dunlap.

--Through the Air to Alaska: Or, Ted Scott's Search in Nugget Valley. Stratemeyer Syndicate. Rogers, Walter S., illus. LC 30-150992. vi, 216 p. front. 20 cm. (The Ted Scott Flying Ser.: Vol. 12). c.1930. Grosset & Dunlap.

--Tic-Tac-Terror. Stratemeyer Syndicate. Morrill, Leslie H., illus. LC 81-19749. (Illus.). 201 p. 20cm. (The Hardy Boys Ser.: Vol. 74). c.1982. (ISBN 0-671-42356-8). (ISBN 0-671-42357-6). Wanderer Books.

--The Tower Treasure. Stratemeyer Syndicate. rev. ed. Adams, Harriet Stratemeyer (1894-1982), rev. by. LC 59-2529. (Illus.). 180 p. 20cm. (The Hardy Boys Ser.: Vol. 1). 1959. Grosset & Dunlap.

--The Tower Treasure. Stratemeyer Syndicate. Rogers, Walter S., illus. (The Hardy Boys Ser.: Vol. 1). 1927. Grosset & Dunlap.

--Track of the Zombie. Stratemeyer Syndicate. Morrill, Leslie H., illus. LC 81-16132. (Illus.). 185 p. 20cm. (The Hardy Boys Ser.: Vol. 71). c.1982. (ISBN 0-671-42348-7). (ISBN 0-671-42349-5). Wanderer Books.

--Trapped at Sea. Stratemeyer Syndicate. Orloff, Denis, illus. LC 82-4793. (Illus.). 181 p. 20cm. (The Hardy Boys Ser.: Vol. 75). c.1982. (ISBN 0-671-42362-2). (ISBN 0-671-42363-0). Wanderer Books.

--The Twisted Claw. Stratemeyer Syndicate. rev. ed. LC 77-86667. (Illus.). 177 p. 20cm. (The Hardy Boys Ser.: Vol. 18). 1969. Grosset & Dunlap.

--The Twisted Claw. Stratemeyer Syndicate. Laune, Paul Sidney (1899-), illus. LC 39-2924. (Written for the Stratemeyer Syndicate by Harriet Stratemeyer Adams, 1894-1982, under the pseudonym, Franklin W. Dixon). iii, 217 p. front. 19 cm. (The Hardy Boys Ser.: Vol. 18). c.1939. Grosset & Dunlap.

--The Vanishing Thieves. Stratemeyer Syndicate. Morrill, Leslie H., illus. LC 80-26013. (Illus.). 179 p. 19cm. (The Hardy Boys Ser.: Vol. 66). c.1981. (ISBN 0-671-42291-X). (ISBN 0-671-42292-8). Wanderer Books.

--The Viking Symbol Mystery. Stratemeyer Syndicate. LC 63-1130. (Illus.). 175 p. 20cm. (The Hardy Boys Ser.: Vol. 42). 1963. Grosset & Dunlap.

--The Voodoo Plot. Stratemeyer Syndicate. Morrill, Leslie H., illus. (Illus.). 192p. (The Hardy Boys Ser.: Vol. 72). (gr. 3-7). 1982. (ISBN 0-671-42350-9). (ISBN 0-671-42351-7). Wanderer Bks.

--The Wailing Siren Mystery. Stratemeyer Syndicate. rev. ed. (Illus.). 177 p. 20cm. (The Hardy Boys Ser.: Vol. 30). 1968. Grosset & Dunlap.

--The Wailing Siren Mystery. Stratemeyer Syndicate. Tandy, Russell H., illus. LC 51-1496. (Written for the Stratemeyer Syndicate by Harriet Stratemeyer Adams, 1894-1982, under the pseudonym, Franklin W. Dixon). 214 p. front. 20 cm. (The Hardy Boys Ser.: Vol. 30). 1951. Grosset & Dunlap.

--What Happened at Midnight. Stratemeyer Syndicate. rev. ed. LC 67-66297. (Illus.). 173 p. illus. 20 cm. (The Hardy Boys Ser.: Vol. 10). 1967. Grosset & Dunlap.

--What Happened at Midnight. Stratemeyer Syndicate. Rogers, Walter S., illus. LC 31-124574. iv, 213 p. front. 20 cm. (The Hardy Boys Ser.: Vol. 10). c.1931. Grosset & Dunlap.

--While the Clock Ticked. Stratemeyer Syndicate. rev. ed. (Illus.). (The Hardy Boys Ser.: Vol. 11). 1962. Grosset & Dunlap.

--While the Clock Ticked. Stratemeyer Syndicate. Gretter, J. Clemens, illus. LC 32-201957. iv, 213 p. front. 20 cm. (The Hardy Boys Ser.: Vol. 11). c.1932. Grosset & Dunlap.

--The Witchmaster's Key. Stratemeyer Syndicate. LC 75-17392. (Illus.). 179 p. 20cm. (The Hardy Boys Ser.: Vol. 55). 1977, c.1976. (ISBN 0-448-08955-6). Grosset & Dunlap.

--The Yellow Feather Mystery. Stratemeyer Syndicate. LC 54-8546. (Illus.). 216p. 20cm. (The Hardy Boys Ser.: Vol. 33). 1953. Grosset & Dunlap.

--The Yellow Feather Mystery. Stratemeyer Syndicate. rev. ed. LC 78-158746. (Illus.). 181 p. 20cm. (The Hardy Boys Ser.: Vol. 33). 1971. (ISBN 0-448-08933-5). Grosset & Dunlap.

Dixon, Franklin W., jt. auth. see Keene, Carolyn.

--The Snow Fox: A Tale of Canada. Dobrin, Arnold (1928-), illus. (Illus.). 32 p. 1968. Coward-McCann.
--Taro and the Sea Turtles: A Tale of Japan. Dobrin, Arnold (1928-), illus. LC 66-8326. 1 v. (unpaged) illus. (pt. col.) 21x26cm. (gr. k-3). 1966. (ISBN 0-698-30352-0). Coward.
--To Katmandu: A Story of Nepal. Dobrin, Arnold (1928-), illus. LC 74-132296. (Illus.). 48 p. 23cm. (Stories from many lands). 1972. (ISBN 0-690-82730-X). (ISBN 0-690-82731-8). Crowell.

Dobrin, Norma Zane
--El Loro de Juan. Dobrin, Arnold (1928-), illus. LC 63-7220. (Illus.). 32 p. 24cm. 1963. Golden Gate Junior Books.

Dobsinsky, P.
--Enchanted Castle & Other Tales. (Illus.). (Illustrated Juvenile Classics). (gr. 1-4). N.D. Tudor.

Dobson, Austin
--Jack & His Brothers. N.D. Thomas Nelson & Sons.

Dobson, Austin, Mrs.
--Cherryburn and Other Stories. (Illus.). 128p. (The Steadfast Ser.). N.D. Fleming H. Revell co.

Dobson, Danae & Dobson, James Clayton, Jr. (1936-)
--Woof!. A Bedtime Story About a Dog. Bellile, Dennis, illus. LC 79-64635. (Illus.). 31 p. c.1979. (ISBN 0-8499-0142-1). Word Books.

Dobson, James Clayton, Jr., jt. auth. see Dobson, Danae.

Dobson, Kenneth
--Hector, The Stowaway Dog. Spier, Peter Edward (1927-), illus. 1958. Little, Brown.

Dobson, Millicent
--Hero: The Biggest Cat in the World. Gorman, Terry, illus. LC 55-6890. 126p. illus. 23cm. 1955. Coward-McCann.

Dock, Phyllis
--Little Hawk: A Story of a Morgan Stallion. Berzinsky, Mary, illus. (Illus.). 96 p. 21cm. 1967. Highlands Press.

Docker, Rolf (1916-)
--Marius. Aas, Tonje S., illus. Stallybrass, Oliver George Weatherhead (1925-), tr. from Norwegian. LC 72-91069. (gr. 4-6). 1970. (ISBN 0-15-252096-1). HarBraceJ.

Dockery, Wallene T. (1941-)
--Gabby's Christmas Wish. Zook, Maurine (1929-), illus. LC 78-11802. p. cm. 1978. (ISBN 0-88319-042-7). Shoal Creek Publishers.

Dr. Seuss, pseud., see Geisel, Theodor Seuss.

Dodd, Edward Howard see Hill, W. M., pseud.

Dodd, Edward Howard (1905-)
--Tales of Maui. Hill, W. M., pseud. Boullaire, Jacques, illus. LC 64-11516. 74 p. illus. 24 cm. 1964. (ISBN 0-396-05056-5). Dodd, Mead.

Dodd, Edward (1904-)
--Chipper the Beaver. (Illus.). 63 p. 22cm. (See and read beginning to read book). 1968. Putnam.
--Flapfoot. Dodd, Edward (1904-), illus. LC 68-55403. (Illus.). 29cm. 31p. (A Carousel Bk.). 1968. L. W. Singer Co.

Dodd, Lee Wilson
--The Sly Giraffe. N.D. E P Dutton.

Dodd, Loring Holmes, jt. auth. see Dodd, Ruth Esleeck.

Dodd, Loring Holmes (1879-)
--Wag Tales. Dodd, Loring Holmes (1879-), illus. LC 66-20134. 64p. col. illus. 18cm. 1966. Dresser.

Dodd, Loring Holmes (1879-) & Dodd, Ruth (1881-)
--The Puppy Book: The Story of Wendy, the Puppy Named for Barrie's Famous Heroine. Dodd, Loring Holmes (1879-), illus. N.D. Lothrop Lee & Shepard Co.

Dodd, Lynley Stuart (1941-)
--The Apple Tree. north american ed. LC 85-9774. p. cm. 1985, c.1983. (ISBN 0-918831-28-8). (ISBN 0-918831-08-3). G. Stevens.
--Hairy Maclary's Bone. north american ed. LC 85-9772. (Illus.). 36 p. 1985, c.1984. (ISBN 0-918831-26-1). (ISBN 0-918831-06-7). G. Stevens.
--The Nickle Nackle Tree. LC 77-12493. (Illus.). 38 p. 22cm. 1978, c.1976. (ISBN 0-02-732610-1). Macmillan.
--The Smallest Turtle. north american ed. LC 85-9771. p. cm. 1985, c.1983. (ISBN 0-918831-27-X). (ISBN 0-918831-07-5). G. Stevens.

Dodd, Madeline
--All Kinds Of Cow. Tsugami, Kyuzo, illus. 1965. (ISBN 0-695-80270-4). (ISBN 0-695-40270-6). Follett Publishing.

Dodd, Ruth, jt. auth. see Dodd, Loring Holmes.

Dodd, Ruth Esleeck, Mrs. (1881-)
--The Cocky Cocker Book: A cur-tail-ed history of Li'l' Miss Muffet. Dodd, Loring Holmes (1879-), illus. LC 36-7373. N.D. Bruce Humphries, Inc.

Dodd, Ruth Esleeck (1881-) & Dodd, Loring Holmes (1879-)
--The Cocky Cocker Book. Dodd, Loring Holmes (1879-), illus. N.D. Dresser, Chapman & Grimes Inc.

Dodd, Wayne Donald see Wayne, Donald, pseud.

Dodd, Wayne Donald (1930-)
--A Time of Hunting. LC 75-4779. 128 p. 22cm. 1975. (ISBN 0-8164-3151-5). Seabury Press.

Dodds, Myrta Hazlett, Mrs.
--Children of Sunny Syria. Ayer, Margaret (0000-1981), illus. LC 36-20140. 22cm. 147p. 1936. Thomas Y. Crowell Co.
--White Camels of the Singing Sands. Ayer, Margaret (0000-1981), illus. LC 39-10763. 4 p. l., 149 p. incl. front., illus. (part col.) 23 cm. 1939. Thomas Y. Crowell Company.

Dodge, Alice A.
--Jerry and His Friends. 300p. (Honor-bright Library). N.D. Lockwood, Brooks, & Co. for American Tract Society.
--Kate Woodman: Or, the Heart Revealed. (Illus.). 229p. N.D. American Tract Society.
--Pleasant Grove. 208p. (Pleasant-grove Ser.). N.D. Lockwood, Brooks, & Co. for American Tract Society.
--Progress. N.D. Hurd & Houghton for American Tract Society.
--Progress: the Sequel to Jerry. 346p. (Honor-bright Library). N.D. Lockwood, Brooks, & Co. for American Tract Society.
--Rebe's Common Sense. (Illus.). 320p. N.D. American Tract Society.
--Way to Be Happy. 64p. (Moss-rose Stories). N.D. Lockwood, Brooks, & Co. for American Tract Society.

Dodge, Bertha Sanford (1902-)
--The Story of Nursing. Corrigan, Barbara (1922-), illus. 1954. Little, Brown.

Dodge, Daniel Kilham (1867-), tr. see Westergaard, A. C.

Dodge, David Francis (1910-)
--Shear the Black Sheep. LC 42-17799. 4 p. l., 285 p. 21 cm. 1942. The Macmillan Company.

Dodge, Louis (1870-)
--Everychild: A Story Which the Old May Interpret to the Young and Which the Young May Interpret to the Old. Laite, Blanche Fisher, illus. LC 21-158229. ix p., 2 l., 3-284 p. col. front., col. plates. 22 cm. 1921. C. Scribner's Sons.
--The Sandman's Forest: A Story for Large Persons to Read to Small Persons. Bransom, Paul (1885-), illus. LC 18-18745. viii p. 1 l., 293 p. col. front.,col. plates. 21 cm. 1918. C. Scribner's Sons.
--The Sandman's Mountain: A Story for Large Persons to Read to Small Persons. Bransom, Paul (1885-), illus. LC 20-170105. ix, 2 278 p. col. front., col. plates. 21 cm. 1920. C. Scribner's Sons.

Dodge, Mary Abigail see Hamilton, Gail, pseud.

Dodge, Mary Abigail (1833-1896)
--Little Folk Life. Hamilton, Gail, pseud. LC 54-49956. 18cm. 219p. 1872. Harper.
--Little Folk Life. Hamilton, Gail, pseud. (Part 1). N.D. Wm. F. Gill & Co.
--Little Folk Life. Hamilton, Gail, pseud. (Part 2). N.D. Wm. F. Gill & Co.

Dodge, Mary Elizabeth Mapes, jt. auth. see Cox, Palmer.

Dodge, Mary Elizabeth Mapes, Mrs. (1831-1905)
--Baby Days. N.D. Appleton Century Co.
--Donald and Dorothy. LC 22-5171. xii, 355 p. incl. front., illus., plates. 20 cm. 1883. Roberts Brothers.
--Donald and Dorothy. LC 21-20595. xii, 355 p. incl. front., illus., plates. 19 cm. 1890. Roberts Brothers.
--Donald and Dorothy. LC 2-11735. 2 p. l., vii-xii p., 1 l., 355 p. incl. front., illus., plates 20 cm. 1901. The Century Co.
--A Few Friends and How They Amused Themselves. A Tale in Nine Chapters ... LC 26-23548. 182 p. 18 cm. 1869. J. B. Lippincott & Co.
--The Golden Gate. LC 8-31461. (Illus.). 17cm. 228p. 1903. M. A. Donohue & Co.
--Hans Bricker: Or, The Silver Skates. (The Scribner's School of Reading). N.D. Charles Scribner's Sons.
--Hans Brinker. (Boy's Library of Pluck and Action). N.D. Charles Scribner's Sons.
--Hans Brinker. Good Value ed. N.D. Grosset & Dunlap.
--Hans Brinker. (Sears Juvenile Classics). N.D. J.H.Sears & Co.
--Hans Brinker. (The Winston Clear-Type Popular Classics). N.D. John C. Winston.
--Hans Brinker. (The Nelson Classics). N.D. Nelson Bks.
--Hans Brinker. (Classic Ser.). N.D. World Publishing Co.
--Hans Brinker. Baldridge, Cyrus LeRoy (1889-), illus. N.D. (ISBN 0-448-05462-0, Companion Library). Grosset & Dunlap.
--Hans Brinker. Noe, Eva, illus. LC 26-143441. 2 p. l., iii-iv. 242 p. col. front., illus. 25 cm. (Sears illustrated juveniles). c.1926. J. H. Sears & Company, Inc.
--Hans Brinker. Rhead, Louis John (1857-1926) & Schoonover, Frank Earle (1877-1972), illus. (Rhead's Illustrated Juveniles). N.D. Harper & Bros.
--Hans Brinker. Rudolph, Norman Guthrie (1896-1983), illus. (Winston Pixie Bks.). 1953. Holt, Rinehart and Winston.
--Hans Brinker. Sewell, Helen Moore (1896-1957) & Boyle, Mildred, illus. LC 36-3138. 20cm. 300p. (The Thorndike Library). 1936. Appleton-Century-Crofts, Inc.
--Hans Brinker. Shoemaker, Edna Cooke, illus. (The Washington Square Classics). N.D. Macrae Smith.
--Hans Brinker and the Silver Skates. Chorpenning, Charlotte Lee Barrows (1872-1955), adapted by. 1938. Children's Theatre Press.
--Hans Brinker: Or, The Silver Skates. LC 15-198641. x p., 2 l., 3-380 p. col. front., col. plates. 22 cm. 1915. C. Scribner's Sons.
--Hans Brinker: Or, the Silver Skates. (Illus.). (Six to Sixteen Ser.). N.D. Caldwell.
--Hans Brinker Or The Silver Skates. 1969. (ISBN 0-516-04248-3). Childrens Press.
--Hans Brinker: Or, The Silver Skates. N.D. Hurst & Co.
--Hans Brinker: Or, the Silver Skates. (Magnum Easy Eye Classic Ser). (gr. 5-8). N.D. Lancer.
--Hans Brinker: Or, The Silver Skates. Fleur, Anne Elizabeth 1901-, illus. Sari, pseud. LC 40-6695. 247 p. illus. 19 cm. c.1940. McLoughlin Brothers, Inc.
--Hans Brinker: Or, The Silver Skates. LC 85-42970. p. cm. (Puffin classics). 1985. (ISBN 0-14-035042-X). Puffin Books.
--Hans Brinker, or the Silver Skates. abr. ed. 224p. (gr. 4-6). 1968. (ISBN 0-590-08540-9, Schol Trade Pap). Schol Bk Serv.
--Hans Brinker: Or, The Silver Skates. (Illus.). N.D. Sully and Kleinteich.
--Hans Brinker: Or, The Silver Skates. Baldridge, Cyrus Leroy (1889-), illus. (Illus.). (gr. 4-6). 1945. (ISBN 0-448-05811-1, G&D). (ISBN 0-448-05462-0). (ISBN 0-448-06011-6). Putnam Pub Group.
--Hans Brinker: Or, The Silver Skates. Baumhauer, Hans (1913-), illus. LC 56-662. 295p. illus. 21cm. (Children's illustrated classics). 1955. Dent.
--Hans Brinker: Or the Silver Skates. Baumhauer, Hans (1913-), illus. (Illus.). (Children's Illustrated Classics). 1956. E.P. Dutton & Co.
--Hans Brinker: Or, The Silver Skates. Burd, Clara Miller, illus. LC 25-10421. (The Children's Bookshelf). 1925. John C. Winston.
--Hans Brinker: Or, The Silver Skates. Carsey, Alice, illus. LC 17-251249. 239 p. col. front., illus., col. plates. 23 cm. c.1917. Whitman Publishing Co.
--Hans Brinker: Or, the Silver Skates. Dierks, Dennis A., illus. LC 76-79992. (Illus.). afterword. 256p. 29cm. (Fun-to-Read Classics Ser). (gr. 4 up). 1969. (ISBN 0-516-04248-3). Childrens.
--Hans Brinker: Or, The Silver Skates. new amsterdam ed. Doggett, Allen B., illus. LC 4-16130. xiv, 396p. illus. 21cm. 1896. Scribner.
--Hans Brinker: Or, The Silver Skates. Edwards, George Wharton (1859-1950), illus. LC 15-19864. (Illus.). 22cm. 380p. 1915. Scribner.
--Hans Brinker: Or, The Silver Skates. Edwards, George Wharton (1859-1950), illus. LC 74-170401. (Illus.). 329 p. 23cm. (Scribner illustrated classics). 1974, c.1915. (ISBN 0-684-20800-8). (ISBN 0-684-20800-8). Scribner.
--Hans Brinker: Or, The Silver Skates. Enright, Maginel Wright, illus. LC 18-26968. 345 p. col. plates. 25 cm. 1918. D. McKay.
--Hans Brinker Or The Silver Skates. Galdone, Paul (1914-), illus. N.D. Doubleday.
--Hans Brinker: Or, The Silver Skates. Galdone, Paul (1914-), illus. LC 54-14472. (Illus.). 319 p. 22cm. 1954. Junior Deluxe Editions.
--Hans Brinker: Or, The Silver Skates. Higgins, Violet Moore, illus. LC 29-24738. 320 p. incl. front., illus. 23 cm. c.1929. A. Whitman & Company.
--Hans Brinker: Or, The Silver Skates. Hilpert, Ruth Ewing, Mrs., ed. LC 25-104216. xiv, 325 p. col. front., illus., col. plates. 21 cm. c.1925. The John C. Winston Company.
--Hans Brinker: Or, The Silver Skates. Lawson, George, illus. LC 33-20979. 4 p. l., 7-407 p. col. front., plates. 21 cm. c.1933. The Saalfield Publishing Company.
--Hans Brinker: Or, The Silver Skates. McNaughton, B. F., illus. LC 34-31445. 1 p. l., 7-92 p. illus. 30 cm. c.1934. Whitman Publishing Company.
--Hans Brinker: Or, The Silver Skates. Mencl, Rudolf, illus. LC 13-12867. 261 p. col. front., illus., col. plates. 24 cm. c.1913. Graham & Matlack.
--Hans Brinker: Or, The Silver Skates. Osborne, Helen, illus. LC 43-9535. 1 p. l., 9-252 p. front., illus. 21 cm. 1943. The Saalfield Publishing Company.
--Hans Brinker: Or, The Silver Skates. Rhead, Louis John (1857-1926), illus. LC 24-19419. ix, 341 p. incl. illus., plates. col. front. 24 cm. c.1924. Harper and Brothers.
--Hans Brinker: Or, The Silver Skates. Rhys, Ernest, ed. 17cm. 246p. (Everyman's Library for Young People). 1914. E. P. Dutton & Co.
--Hans Brinker: Or The Silver Skates. Spier, Peter Edward (1927-), illus. LC 58-10858. (Illus.). 345 p. 21cm. 1958. Scribner.
--Hans Brinker: Or, The Silver Skates. Thorndike, Edward Lee (1874-), ed. vii, 309 p. incl. front., illus. 20 cm. (Thorndike library). c.1936. D. Appleton-Century Company, Incorporated.
--Hans Brinker: Or, The Silver Skates. complete and unabridged. Van Stockum, Hilda Gerarda (1908-), illus. Becker, May Lamberton, intro. by. LC 74-27247. (Illus.). 335 p. 21cm. 335p. (Rainbow classics). 1975. (ISBN 0-529-05025-0). (ISBN 0-529-05026-9). Collins.
--Hans Brinker: Or, The Silver Skates. Van Stockum, Hilda Gerarda (1908-), illus. Becker, May Lamberton, intro. by. LC 46-25118. (Illus.). 22cm. 335p. (Rainbow Classics). 1946. World Pub. Co.
--Hans Brinker: Or, the Silver Skates. Van Stockum, Hilda Gerarda (1908-), illus. (Illus.). (Rainbow Classics). (gr. 7 up). 1948. (ISBN 0-529-02848-4). World Pub.
--Hans Brinker: Or, the Silver Skates. rev. ed. Van Stockum, Hilda Gerarda (1908-), illus. LC 72-9971. (Illus.). (Rainbow Classics Ser.). (gr. k-6). 1973. (ISBN 0-529-05026-9). World Pub.
--Hans Brinker: Or, The Silver Skates. Winter, Milo Kendall (1888-1956), illus. LC 36-17126. 352 p. col. front., illus., col. plates. 29 cm. (Windermere series). c.1936. Rand, McNally & Company.
--Hans Brinker: Or, The Silver Skates. Wyeth, Newell Convers (1882-1945) & Hurd, Peter (1904-1984), illus. LC 32-21421. 7 p. l., 305 p. incl. col. front., col. plates 23 cm. c.1932. Garden City Publishing Co., Inc.
--Hans Brinker: Or, The Silver Skates, a Story of Life in Holland. new ed. with sixty original illustrations. LC 43-40891. 3 p. l., 11-20 p., 1 l., 21-377 p. incl. illus., plates. front. 19 cm. 1887. C. Scribner's Sons.
--Hans Brinker: Or, The Silver Skates: a Story of Life in Holland. LC 4-16130. xiv, p., 1 l., 393 p. incl. front., illus., plates. 21 cm. 1896. C. Scribner's Sons.
--Hans Brinker: Or, The Silver Skates; a Story of Life in Holland. LC 16-620213. 2 p. l., 3-375 p. col. front., col. plates. 20 cm. (Ranally series). c.1916. Rand, McNally & Company.
--Hans Brinker: Or, The Silver Skates, a Story of Life in Holland. LC 3-27263. (Illus.). 20cm. 347p. 1879. Scribner.
--Hans Brinker: Or, The Silver Skates, A Story of Life in Holland. LC 43-80891. (Illus.). 19cm. 377p. 1887. Scribner.
--Hans Brinker: Or, The Silver Skates; a Story of Life in Holland. Baldridge, Cyrus LeRoy (1889-), illus. LC 46-1508. xv p., 1 l., 289 p. col. front., illus., col. plates. 20 1/2 cm. (Illustrated Junior Library). 1945. (ISBN 0-448-05911-8). (ISBN 0-448-05811-1). Grosset & Dunlap.
--Hans Brinker: Or, The Silver Skates; a Story of Life in Holland. new amsterdam ed. Doggett, Allen B., illus. LC 7-739. xiv p., 1 l., 393 p. incl. front., illus. plates. 20 cm. 1902. C. Scribner's Sons.
--Hans Brinker: Or, The Silver Skates; a Story of Life in Holland. Kredel, Fritz (1900-1973), illus. LC 63-6890. xiv, 298 p. illus. 20 cm. 20cm. 208p. (Companion library). 1963. Grossett & Dunlap.
--Hans Brinker: Or, The Silver Skates, a Story of Life in Holland. Lowe, Orton, ed. Gallagher, Sears (1869-1955), illus. LC 18-519. (Illus.). 18cm. 355p. c.1917. Ginn.
--Hans Brinker: Or, The Silver Skates, a Story of Life in Holland. Winter, Milo Kendall (1888-1956), illus. LC 16-6202. (Illus.). 20cm. 375p. (Rand McNally Ser.). 1916. Rand, McNally.
--Hans Brinker: Or, The Story of the Silver Skates. 1st ed. Rudolph, Norman Guthrie (1896-1983), illus. LC 52-13678. 120p. illus. 22cm. (Pixie books). 1953. Winston.
--Hans Brinker: The Silver Skates. (Famous Bks. for Young Americans). N.D. A. L. Burt Co.
--The Hole in the Dike. Carle, Eric (1929-), illus. LC 74-23562. (Illus.). 32 p. 28cm. 1975, c.1974. (ISBN 0-690-00676-4). Crowell.
--Irvington Stories. New, rev. & enlarged. Darley, Felix Octavius Carr (1822-1888), illus. LC 8-294164. (Illus.). 251 p. 19cm. c.1898. M. A. Donohue.
--Irvington Stories. New, rev. & enlarged. Darley, Felix Octavius Carr (1822-1888), illus. LC 98-1116. (Illus.). 251 p. 18cm. 251p. 1898. W. L. Allison Co.

--Alice's Adventures Under Ground: Being a Facsimile of the Original Ms. Book Afterwards Developed into "Alice's Adventures in Wonderland". Carroll, Lewis, pseud. LC 20-13900. viii p., 2 l., facsim. (2 p. l., 89, 1 p., illus.), 91-95, 1 p. 19 cm. 1886. Macmillan and Co.
--Alice's Adventures Under Ground: Being a Facsimile of the Original Ms. Book Afterwards Developed into "Alice's Adventures in Wonderland". Carroll, Lewis, pseud. LC 80-8599. p. cm. 1980. (ISBN 0-8317-0240-0). Mayflower Books.
--Alice's Adventures Under Ground: Being a Facsimile of the Original Ms. Book Afterwards Developed into "Alice's Adventures in Wonderland". Carroll, Lewis, pseud. Dodgson, Charles Lutwidge (1832-1898), illus. Carroll, Lewis, pseud. LC 33-1141. 5 p. l., 91 p. illus. 20 cm. 1932. The Macmillan Company.
--The Animated Picture Book of Alice in Wonderland. Carroll, Lewis, pseud. Wehr, Julian, illus. LC 45-7535. 24 p. illus. (part col.) 20 x 26 cm. 1945. Grosset and Dunlap.
--The Annotated Alice: Alice's Adventures in Wonderland & Through the Looking Glass. Carroll, Lewis, pseud. Gardner, Martin (1914-), ed. Tenniel, John, Sir (1820-1914), illus. LC 60-7341. (Illus.). 351 p. 28cm. 1960. C. N. Potter.
--Jabberwocky, and More Nonsense. Carroll, Lewis, pseud. Taback, Simms, illus. LC 63-9161. 63 p. col. illus. 21 cm. 1964. Dell Pub. Co.
--Jabberwocky and Other Frabjous Nonsense. Carroll, Lewis, pseud. Taback, Simms, illus. (Illus.). 48 p. 29cm. 1967, c.1964. H. Quist, Distributed by Crown Publishers.
--Journeys in Wonderland. Carroll, Lewis, pseud. derrydale 1979 ed. Tenniel, John, Sir (1820-1914), illus. LC 79-18860. (Illus.). ix, 192, 224 p., 2 leaves of plates. 21cm. 1979. (ISBN 0-517-30132-6). Derrydale Books.
--The Lewis Carroll Book. Carroll, Lewis, pseud. Herrick, Richard, ed. Tenniel, John, Sir (1820-1914) & Holiday, Henry (1839-1927), illus. LC 31-319378. xix, 439 p. illus. 21 cm. 1931. L. MacVeagh, The Dial Press.
--Lewis Carroll's Alice in Wonderland. Carroll, Lewis, pseud. Steadman, Ralph Idris (1936-), illus. LC 73-82899. (Illus.). 108 p. 32cm. 1973. (ISBN 0-517-50135-X). C. N. Potter; Distributed by Crown.
--Lewis Carroll's Jabberwocky. Carroll, Lewis, pseud. Zalben, Jane Breskin (1950-), illus. Humpty Dumpty, annotations by. LC 77-75040. (Illus.). 32 p. 1977. (ISBN 0-7232-6145-8). F. Warne.
--Lewis Carroll's Through the Looking Glass, and What Alice Found There. Carroll, Lewis, pseud. Steadman, Ralph Idris (1936-), illus. LC 72-87337. (Illus.). 143 p. 32cm. 1973. C. N. Potter; Distributed by Crown.
--The Mad Gardener's Song. Carroll, Lewis, pseud. 1st ed. Morrison, Sean, illus. LC 67-20458. (Illus.). 1 v. (unpaged. 24cm. 1967. Bobbs-Merrill.
--The Nursery Alice. Carroll, Lewis, pseud. Tenniel, John, Sir (1820-1914), illus. Carroll, Lewis, pseud. LC 79-12419. p. cm. (Mayflower facsimile classics). 1979. (ISBN 0-8317-6478-3). Mayflower Books.
--The Nursery "Alice ". Carroll, Lewis, pseud. Tenniel, John, Sir (1820-1914) & Thomson, E. Gertrude, illus. Gardner, Martin (1914-), intro. by. LC 66-24136. (Illus.). xi, 56, 7 p. 25cm. 1966. McGraw-Hill.
--The Pig-Tale. Carroll, Lewis, pseud. Lubin, Leonard B., illus. LC 74-13424. (Illus.). 30 p. 27cm. 1975. (ISBN 0-316-13006-0). Little, Brown. **Award: (NYT).**
--The Story of Sylvie and Bruno. Carroll, Lewis, pseud. facsim. ed. LC 79-22513. p. cm. (Facsimile Classics Series). 1980. Mayflower Books.
--Sylvie and Bruno. Carroll, Lewis, pseud. Furniss, Harry (1854-1925), illus. LC 75-32196. (Illus.). xi, 400 p. 21cm. (Classics of Children's Literature, 1621-1932). 1976. (ISBN 0-8240-2307-2). Garland Pub.
--Sylvie and Bruno. Carroll, Lewis, pseud. Furniss, Harry (1854-1925), illus. LC 7-747. xxiii, 400 p. incl. front., illus. 19 cm. 1898. Macmillan and Co., Limited.
--Sylvie and Bruno. Carroll, Lewis, pseud. Furniss, Harry (1854-1925), illus. LC 67-28170. (Illus.). xxiv, 400 p. 19cm. (Legacy library facsimile). 1967. University Microfilms.
--Through the Looking-Glass. Carroll, Lewis, pseud. LC 42-114. vi, 198 p. front., illus. 19 cm. (Editha series. 21). 1913. H. M. Caldwell Co.
--Through the Looking Glass. Carroll, Lewis, pseud. Tenniel, John, Sir (1820-1914), illus. N.D. Publications of Bruce Humphries.
--Through the Looking Glass. Carroll, Lewis, pseud. Tenniel, John, Sir (1820-1914), illus. LC 77-77325. p. cm. 1977. (ISBN 0-312-80374-5). St. Martin's Press.
--Through the Looking-Glass. Carroll, Lewis, pseud. Tenniel, John, Sir (1820-1914), illus. LC 46-25179. 98 p. col. illus. 27 x 20 1/2 cm. 1946. Whittlesey House, McGraw-Hill Book Company, Inc.
--Through the Looking-Glass and What Alice Found There. Carroll, Lewis, pseud. LC 4842. 167 p. incl. front., illus. 16 cm. c.1900. W. B. Conkey Company.
--Through the Looking-Glass and What Alice Found There. Carroll, Lewis, pseud. Hughes, Franklin, illus. LC 31-24653. 4 p. l., 129 p., 1 l. col. plates. 29 cm. 1931. Cheshire House.
--Through the Looking-Glass and What Alice Found There. Carroll, Lewis, pseud. Kay, Gertrude Alice (1884-1939) & Tenniel, John, Sir (1820-1914), illus. LC 29-24874. 235, 5 p. col. front., illus., col. plates. 21 cm. (stories all children love series). c.1929. J. B. Lippincott Company.
--Through the Looking-Glass and What Alice Found There. Carroll, Lewis, pseud. Milner, Florence Cushman, Mrs. & Cory, Fanny Young, illus. LC 17-294931. 218 p. front., (port.) illus., pl. 18 cm. (Half-title: The Canterbury classics ...). c.1917. Rand McNally & Company.
--Through the Looking-Glass and What Alice Found There. Carroll, Lewis, pseud. Newell, Peter (1862-1924), illus. LC 2-24101. xiv, xiii-xvi p., 1 l., 211 p. front. (port.) pl. 23 cm. 1902. Harper & Brothers.
--Through the Looking-Glass and What Alice Found There. Carroll, Lewis, pseud. Pease, Bessie Collins, illus. LC 9-16128. viii p., 1 l., 185 p. col. front., illus., col. plates. 22 cm. c.1909. Dodge Publishing Company.
--Through the Looking-Glass And What Alice Found There. Carroll, Lewis, pseud. Tenniel, John, Sir (1820-1914), illus. LC 27-8514. 230 p. illus. 18 cm. (On cover: Seaside library. Pocket edition. no. 789). 1886. G. Munro.
--Through the Looking-Glass And What Alice Found There. Carroll, Lewis, pseud. Tenniel, John, Sir (1820-1914), illus. LC 27-8513. 5 p. l., 224 p. front., illus. 18 cm. (On cover: Lovell's library. no. 481). 1885. J. W. Lovell Company.
--Through the Looking-Glass: And What Alice Found There. Carroll, Lewis, pseud. Tenniel, John, Sir (1820-1914), illus. LC 4-19547. 5 p. l., 224 p. front., illus. 19 cm. 1891. Macmillan and Co.
--Through the Looking-Glass And What Alice Found There. Carroll, Lewis, pseud. Tenniel, John, Sir (1820-1914), illus. viii, 2 p., 3 l., 224 p. incl. front., illus. 19 cm. 1902. The Macmillan Company.
--Through the Looking-Glass And What Alice Found There. Carroll, Lewis, pseud. Tenniel, John, Sir (1820-1914), illus. LC 42-1194. xiv p., 4 l., 5-198, 2 p. incl. front., illus. 24 cm. c.1941. The Heritage Press.
--Through the Looking-Glass, And What Alice Found There. Carroll, Lewis, pseud. Tenniel, John, Sir (1820-1914), illus. LC 67-349. (Illus.). 224 p. 20cm. (Legacy library facsimile). 1966. University Microfilms.
--The Walrus and the Carpenter. Carroll, Lewis, pseud. Cattaneo, Tony, illus. LC 74-81671. (Illus.). 24 p. 18cm. (Stuff and nonsense books). 1974. (ISBN 0-7232-1813-7). F. Warne.
--The Walrus and the Carpenter and Other Poems. Carroll, Lewis, pseud. Rose, Gerald Hembdon Seymour (1935-), illus. LC 69-10834. (Illus.). 32 p. 1969, c.1968. Dutton.

Dodgson, Charles Lutwidge (1832-1898) & Peake, Mervyn Laurence (1911-1968)
--Alice's Adventures in Wonderland & Through the Looking Glass. Carroll, Lewis, pseud. Tenniel, John, Sir (1820-1914), illus. LC 79-64115. p. cm. 1979, c.1978. (ISBN 0-8052-3716-X). Schocken Books.

Dodgson, Charles Lutwidge (1832-1898) & Tenniel, John, Sir (1820-1914), illus.
--Alice Through the Looking-Glass. Carroll, Lewis, pseud. giant illustrated. LC 76-62759. (Illus.). 96 p. 28cm. 1977. (ISBN 0-85670-216-1). Academy Editions.
--Alice's Adventures in Wonderland. Carroll, Lewis, pseud. Zimmermann, Antonie, tr. LC 74-78778. (Illus.). 178 p. 21cm. 1974. (ISBN 0-486-20668-8). Dover Publications.
--Alice's Adventures in Wonderland, & Through the Looking Glass: Both with the Illustrations of John Tenniel & The Hunting of the Snark. Carroll, Lewis, pseud. LC 77-17651. (Illus.). 291 p. 21cm. 1978. (ISBN 0-8052-0594-2). Schocken Books.

Dodgson, J. H
--Little Murphy: A Tale for All Sorts of Children. LC 71-158345. (Illus.). 143 p. 21cm. 1971. (ISBN 0-396-06386-1). Dodd, Mead.

Dodley, Bernard F J
--Tuffy Taylor. LC 53-2926. 248p. 22cm. 1953, c.1931. Bruce Pub. Co.

Dodsley, Robert (1703-1764) & Aesopus
--Select Fables of Aesop and Other Fabulists ... new ed. LC 20-19620. iv, 5-228 p. front. 17 cm. 1786. Printed and Sold by Joseph Cruishank, in Market-Street, Between Second and Third-Streets.
--Select Fables of Aesop and Other Fabulists ... iv, 5-215 p. 14 cm. N.D. Printed and Sold by Peter Stewart, in Second-Street, Ninth Door Above Chestnut-Street.
--Select Fables of Esop and Other Fabulists. In Three Books. new ed. 209, 6 p. illus. 17 cm. N.D. Printed and Sold by Benjamin Johnson, High-Street.

Dodson, Bert
--Lazy Jack: An English Folk Tale. Dodson, Bert, illus. LC 78-18070. (Illus.). 34 p. 24cm. (gr. k-4). c.1979. (ISBN 0-89375-123-5). (ISBN 0-89375-123-5). Troll Associates.

Dodson, Fitzhugh James (1923-)
--I Wish I Had a Computer That Makes Waffles-. Teaching Your Child with Modern Nursery Rhymes. 1st ed. Lowenheim, Alfred (1947-), illus. LC 78-13178. p. cm. c.1978. (ISBN 0-916392-27-9). Oak Tree Publications.

Dodson, Fitzhugh James (1923-) & Reuben, Paula (1932-)
--The Carnival Kidnap Caper. LC 79-20260. p. cm. c.1979. (ISBN 0-916392-40-6). Oak Tree Publications.

Dodson, Kenneth MacKenzie (1907-)
--Away All Boats. (A novel). (gr. 9 up). 1954. (ISBN 0-316-18830-1). Little.

Dodson, Owen Vincent (1914-1983)
--Boy at the Window. LC 51-9471. 224p. Repr. of 1951 ed. (gr. 7 up). 1977. (ISBN 0-374-30929-9). FS&G.

Dodson, Susan (1941-)
--The Creep. LC 79-1102. 218 p. 22cm. c.1979. (ISBN 0-590-07599-3). Four Winds Press.
--Have You Seen This Girl?. LC 81-69516. 182 p. 22cm. c.1982. (ISBN 0-590-07633-7). Four Winds Press.
--Shadows Across the Sand. LC 83-5469. (Illus.). 224p. (gr. 6 up). 1983. (ISBN 0-688-02426-2). Lothrop.

Dodworth, Dorothy L.
--A Dangerous Day for Mrs. Doodlepunk. Dodworth, Dorothy L., illus. LC 54-9912. (Illus.). unpaged. (Young Scott books 528). 1954. Scott.
--Look Out, Mrs. Doodlepunk. Orig. Title: A Dangerous Day for Mrs. Doodlepunk. (gr. 2-3). 1971. (ISBN 0-590-00105-1, Schol Pap). Schol Bk Serv.
--Mrs. Doodlepunk Trades Work. Dodworth, Dorothy L., illus. LC 57-9711. (Illus.). unpaged. (Young Scott books). c.1957. W. R. Scott.

Doederlein, Gertrude
--Kamla's Good Day. 46p. 1954. Augsburg Pub.
--The Music Box Maker. Mickelson, Melva, illus. LC 57-9722. (Illus.). 23cm. 1957. Augsburg Pub.

Doepke, Frederick W.
--Sod Pod. (gr. k-5). N.D. Carlton.

Doerksen, Eva
--Polly Parrot. LC 52-4233. (Illus.). 19cm. 62p. 1952. Moody Press.

Doheny, Margaret A
--Play Awhile: A Dramatic Reader for the Second School Year. LC 16-15054. 3 p. l., v-xi, 178 p. col. front., illus., col. plates. 19 cm. 1916. Little, Brown and Company.

Doherty, Geoffrey Donald, ed.
--Aspects of Science Fiction. (gr. 9 up). 1959. (ISBN 0-7195-2215-3). Transatlantic.
--Second Orbit: A New Science Fiction Anthology for Schools. LC 66-1600. 218p. 19cm. (Albemarle lib. for schs.). 1966, c.1965. J. Murray.

Doherty, Ivy R. Duffy see Hardwick, Sylvia, pseud.

Doherty, Ivy R. Duffy (1922-)
--Here I Am, Em B!. LC 80-20185. (Illus.). 95 p. 21cm. (Penguin series). c.1981. Review and Herald Pub. Association.
--My Magic Carpet Never Wears Out. Bohlmann, Siegfried E., illus. LC 63-177603. 125 p. illus. 23 cm. 1963. Review and Herald Pub. Association.
--No Need for a Magic Carpet. Baerg, Harry John (1909-), illus. LC 62-14165. 128p. illus. 23cm. 1962. Review and Herald Pub.
--Prisoner in the Beech Tree. Converse, John, illus. LC 72-77019. 22 cm. 127p. (Penguin Ser.). 1972. Review and Herald Pub.

Doherty, John Stephen
--Mystery of Hidden Harbor. LC 63-8735. (gr. 6-9). 1963. Doubleday.

Doherty, Peg, ed.
--Time Bomb & Other Stories of Mystery & Suspense. (gr. 7-12). 1972. (ISBN 0-590-09273-1, Schol Trade Pap). Schol Bk Serv.

Doi, Hiroyuki (1914-) & Reynolds, Barbara Leonard
--The Story of Leopons. (Illus.). 46 p. 21cm. 1967. Putnam.

Doisneau, Robert, ed. see Gregor, Arthur S.

Doisneau, Robert & Gregor, Arthur
--One, Two, Three, Four, Five: Verses. 1956. J. B. Lippincott.

Doisy, Louisa
--Helen May: Or, Unto Her Life's End. N.D. T. Whittaker.

Dolan, Edward Francis, Jr. (1924-)
--Great Mysteries of the Air. (Illus.). (gr. 4 up). 1983. (ISBN 0-396-08185-1). Dodd.

Dolan, Ellen M.
--Jack the Ship Boy. 1967. (ISBN 0-07-017363-X). McGraw.
--Sandro, Student Painter. Dolan, Ellen M., adapted by. Wabbes, Marie, illus. LC 72-2388. (Illus.). 26 p. (Children of other times). c.1968. Webster Division, McGraw-Hill.

Dolan, Ellen M., adapted by.
--Bill of the Pony Express. Wabbes, Marie, illus. LC 67-5517. (Original Text by Marion Clark). (Illus.). 19 x 21cm. (Children of Other Times). 1967. Webster Division, McGraw-Hill.
--Oliver, the Page. Wabbes, Marie, illus. LC 67-5516. (Original Text by Marcel Vermeulen). (Illus.). 19 x 21cm. (Children of Other Times). 1967. Webster Division, McGraw-Hill.

Dolan, Ellen M., adapted by see Dolan, Ellen M.

Dolan, Ellen M., adapted by see Onclincx, Georges.

Dolan, Ellen M, adapted by see Vermeulen, Marcel.

Dolan, Lenore K
--The Children's Own Play Book. 145 p. 18 cm. c.1931. Paine Publishing Company.
--Short Plays and Pageants for All Occasions and Grades. 142 p. 19 cm. c.1930. Eldridge Entertainment House, Inc.

Dolan, Mike
--Ziggy & His Friends. (Illus.). 1980. (ISBN 0-516-09203-0). Childrens.

Dolan, Sheila
--The Wishing Bottle. Morrill, Leslie H., illus. LC 79-13061. (Illus.). 81 p. 22cm. 1979. (ISBN 0-395-28479-1). Houghton Mifflin.

Dolbier, Maurice Wyman (1912-)
--The Half-Pint Jinni and Other Stories. Thomas, Allan (1901-), illus. LC 48-7634. 242 p. illus. 21 cm. 1948. Random House.
--Jenny, the Bus That Nobody Loved. Gergely, Tibor (1900-1978), illus. LC 44-748430. 1 p. l., 7-43, 1 p. illus. (part col.) 28 1/2 cm. c.1944. Random House.
--Lion in the Woods. N.D. E . M. Hale and Co.
--A Lion in the Woods. 1st ed. Henneberger, Robert G. (1921-), illus. LC 54-8322. 114p. illus. 22cm. c.1955. Little, Brown.
--The Magic Shop. Eichenberg, Fritz (1901-), illus. LC 46-5290. 3 p. l., 3-74, 1 p. col. illus. 22 cm. 1946. Random House.
--Paul Bunyan. Fisher, Leonard Everett (1924-), illus. LC 59-6145. (Illus.). (Legacy: Ser.). (gr. 4-7). 1959. (ISBN 0-394-80159-8). (ISBN 0-394-90159-2). Random.
--Torten's Christmas Secret. Henneberger, Robert G. (1921-), illus. LC 51-12428. (Illus.). (gr. 1-4). 1951. (ISBN 0-316-18914-6). Little.

Dolch, Edward William (1889-)
--In the Woods. (Dolch First Reading Books). 1958. Garrard Press.
--Some Are Small. (Dolch First Reading Books). 1959. Garrard Press.

Dolch, Edward William (1889-) & Dolch, Marguerite Pierce (1891-)
--Aesop's Stories. (Illus.). (Pleasure Reading Ser). (gr. 3-12). 1951. (ISBN 0-8116-2602-4). Garrard.
--Andersen Stories. (Illus.). (Pleasure Reading Ser.). (gr. 3-12). 1956. (ISBN 0-8116-2601-6). Garrard.
--Animal Stories. Dolch, Marguerite Pierce (1891-), illus. LC 53-842. (Illus.). (Basic Vocabulary Ser.). (gr. 1-6). 1952. (ISBN 0-8116-2501-X). Garrard.
--Animal Stories in Basic Vocabulary. (Illus.). 163 p. 21cm. (Basic vocabulary series). 1952. Garrard Press.
--Bear Stories. Forsythe, Charles, illus. LC 58-14549. (Basic Vocabulary Ser.). (gr. 1-6). 1957. (ISBN 0-8116-2510-9). Garrard.
--Bear Stories in Basic Vocabulary. Forsythe, Charles, illus. (Illus.). 165 p. 21cm. (Basic vocabulary series). 1957. Garrard Press.
--Bible Stories. (Pleasure Reading Ser.). (gr. 3-12). 1950. (ISBN 0-8116-2609-1). Garrard.
--Big, Bigger, Biggest. (First Reading Bks.). (gr. 1-4). 1959. (ISBN 0-8116-2807-8). Garrard.
--Circus Stories in Basic Vocabulary. Wallace, Dee, illus. LC 57-18990. 166p. illus. 21cm. (Basic vocabulary series). 1956. (ISBN 0-8116-2512-5). Garrard Press.
--Dog Pals. Matera, Fran, illus. LC 63-22908. 64 p. col. illus. 21 cm. (His A first reading book). N.D. Garrard Pub. Co.,.

AUTHOR INDEX DONAHEY, MARY

--Dog Stories in Basic Vocabulary. Johnson, Bernette & Kerr, Robert S., illus. LC 55-18081. (Illus.). 169 p. 22cm. (Basic vocabulary series). 1954. (ISBN 0-8116-2508-7). Garrard Press.
--Elephant Stories in Basic Vocabulary. Wallace, Dee, illus. LC 56-47392. (Illus.). 165 p. 21cm. (Basic vocabulary series). 1956. Garrard Press.
--Fairy Stories. (Pleasure Reading Ser.). (gr. 3-12). 1950. (ISBN 0-8116-2600-8). Garrard.
--Famous Stories. (Pleasure Reading Ser). (gr. 3-12). 1955. (ISBN 0-8116-2603-2). Garrard.
--Far East Stories. (Pleasure Reading Ser). (gr. 3-12). 1953. (ISBN 0-8116-2606-7). Garrard.
--Folk Stories in Basic Vocabulary. Dolch, Marguerite Pierce (1891-), illus. LC 53-843 159p. illus. 21cm. (Basic vocabulary series). 1952. (ISBN 0-8116-2500-1). Garrard Press.
--Friendly Birds. Rogers, Carol, illus. 64 p. illus. 21 cm. (First reading book). c.1959. Garard Press.
--Greek Stories. Dolch, Marguerite Pierce (1891-), illus. (Pleasure Reading Ser.). (gr. 3-12). 1955. (ISBN 0-8116-2607-5). Garrard.
--Gulliver's Stories. (Pleasure Reading Ser). (gr. 3-12). 1960. (ISBN 0-8116-2611-3). Garrard.
--Gulliver's Stories. Vayssieres, Jean J., illus. (Illus.). (gr. k-3). 1976. (ISBN 0-590-09850-0, Schol Pap). Scholastic Inc.
--Horse Stories in Basic Vocabulary. Forsythe, Charles, illus. LC 61-4901. (Illus.). 161 p. 21cm. (Basic vocabulary series). 1958. (ISBN 0-8116-2514-1). Garrard Press.
--I Like Cats. (First Reading Books Ser). (gr. 1-4). 1959. (ISBN 0-8116-2809-4). Garrard.
--In the Woods. Borja, Robert (1923-), illus. LC 63-6689. (Illus.). 64 p. 21cm. c.1958. Garrard Press.
--Irish Stories in Basic Vocabulary. Mowry, Carmen, illus. LC 63-6698. 165 p. illus. 21 cm. (Basic vocabulary series). c.1958. Garrard Press.
--Ivanhoe. Foster, George, illus. LC 61-4981. (Pleasure Reading Ser). (gr. 3-12). 1961. (ISBN 0-8116-2612-1). Garrard.
--Lion and Tiger Stories in Basic Vocabulary. Forsythe, Charles, illus. LC 57-14055. (Illus.). 165 p. 22cm. (Basic vocabulary series). 1957. (ISBN 0-8116-2511-7) Garrard Press.
--Lodge Stories in Basic Vocabulary. Jackson, Billy M. (1891-), illus. LC 57-14056. (Illus.). 163 p. 21cm. (Basic vocabulary series). (gr. 1-6). 1957. Garrard Press.
--Monkey Friends. Forsythe, Charles, illus. LC 63-6690. 63 p. illus. 21 cm (First reading book). 1958. Garrard Press.
--More Dog Stories in Basic Vocabulary. Johnson, Eugene Harper, illus. (Illus.). 164 p. 22cm. (Basic vocabulary series). 1962. (ISBN 0-8116-2515-X). Garrard Press.
--Navaho Stories. Jackson, Billy M., illus. LC 58-14550. (Illus.). (Dolch Basic Vocabulary Ser.). (gr. 1-6). 1957. (ISBN 0-8116-2507-9). Garrard.
--Old World Stories. (Dolch Pleasure Reading Ser.). (gr. 3-12). 1952. (ISBN 0-8116-2605-9). Garrard.
--On the Farm. (Illus.). (Dolch First Reading Books Ser.). (gr. 1-4). 1958. (ISBN 0-8116-2804-3). Garrard.
--Once There Was a Bear. McCann, Gerald (1916-), illus. LC 62-51596. (Illus.). 63 p. 21cm. (First reading book). c.1962. Garrard Pub. Co.
--Once There Was a Cat. Hauge, Carl & Hauge, Mary, illus. LC 61-4975. (Illus.). 63 p. 22cm. (First reading books). c.1961. Garrard Press.
--Once There Was a Dog. O'Sullivan, Tom, illus. LC 62-51595. (Illus.). 64 p. 21cm. (First reading book). c.1962. Garrard Pub. Co.
--Once There Was a Monkey. Shannon, Kenyon, illus. LC 62-2249. (Illus.). 62 p. 21cm. (First reading book). c.1962. Garrard Press.
--Once There Was a Rabbit. Patterson, Robert (1899-), illus. LC 61-4976. (Illus.). 63 p. 21cm. (First reading books). c.1961. Garrard Press.
--Once There Was an Elephant. Moyers, William (1916-), illus. LC 61-4980. (Illus.). 64 p. 21cm. (First reading books). c.1961. Garrard Press.
--Pleasure Reading Series. LC 51-936. (Illus.). v. 21cm. N.D. Garrard Press.
--Pueblo Stories: In Basic Vocabulary. Kerr, Robert S., illus. LC 55-11203. 160p. illus. 22cm. (Basic vocabulary series). 1956. (ISBN 0-8116-2503-6). Garrard Press.
--Robin Hood Stories. (Dolch Pleasure Reading Ser.). (gr. 3-12). 1957. (ISBN 0-8116-2604-0). Garrard.
--Robinson Crusoe. (Dolch Pleasure Reading Ser.). (gr. 3-12). 1958. (ISBN 0-8116-2610-5). Garrard.
--Some Are Small. Kettelkamp, Larry Dale (1933-), illus. LC 63-22868. 62 p. col. illus. 21 cm. (Dolch first reading book1). c.1959. Garrard Pub. Co.
--Stories from Alaska. Heldt, Carl, illus. (Illus.). 168 p. 22cm. (Folklore of the world). 1961. Garrard Press.
--Stories from Canada. Miret, Gil, illus. LC 64-11100. (Illus.). 21cm. vii, 168p. (Folklore of the World). 1964. Garrard Pub. Co.
--Stories from France. Laite, Gordon (1925-), illus. LC 63-71202. 167 p. illus. 21 cm. (Folklore of the world). 1963. Garrard Pub. Co.
--Stories from Hawaii. Schroeder, Ted (1931-1973), illus. (Illus.). 167 p. 22cm. (Folklore of the world). 1960. Garrard Press.
--Stories from India. Laite, Gordon (1925-), illus. LC 61-5487. (Illus.). 21cm. 168p. (Folklore of the World). 1961. Garrard Press.
--Stories from Italy. Browning, Colleen (1929-), illus. (Illus.). 168 p. 21cm. (Folklore of the world). 1962. Garrard Pub. Co.
--Stories from Japan. Hawkinson, John Samuel (1912-) & Hawkinson, Lucy Ozone (1924-1971), illus. LC 60-9706. (Illus.). 168 p. 21cm. (Folklore of the world). 1960. Garrard Press.
--Stories from Mexico. De Soto, Ernest, illus. LC 60-97096. (Illus.). 168 p. 21cm. (Folklore of the world). 1960. Garrard Press.
--Stories from Old China. Moy, Seong (1921-), illus. LC 63-15960. vii, 166 p. col. illus. 21 cm. (Folklore of the world). 1964. Garrard Pub. Co.
--Stories from Old Egypt. Laite, Gordon (1925-), illus. LC 64-10127. vii, 168 p.col. illus. 21 cm. (Folklore of the world). 1964. Garrard Pub. Co.
--Stories from Old Russia. Lewicki, James, illus. LC 63-13627. vii, 168 p. col. illus. 21 cm. (Folklore of the world). 1964. Garrard Pub. Co.
--Stories from Spain. Bolognese, Donald Alan (1934-), illus. LC 62-7207. (Illus.). 168 p. 21cm. (Folklore of the world). 1962. Garrard Press.
--Tepee Stories, in Basic Vocabulary. Kerr, Robert S., illus. (Illus.). 165 p. 22cm. (Basic vocabulary series). 1956. Garrard Press.
--Tommy's Pets. (Dolch First Reading Books Ser.). (gr. 1-4). 1958. (ISBN 0-8116-2802-7). Garrard.
--Why Stories. Dolch, Marguerite Pierce (1891-), illus. (Dolch Basic Vocabulary Ser.). (gr. 1-6). 1958. (ISBN 0-8116-2502-8). Garrard.
--Why" Stories in Basic Vocabulary. Dolch, Marguerite Pierce (1891-), illus. LC 53-844. 160p. illus. 21cm. (Basic vocabulary series). 1952. Garrard Press.
--Wigwam Stories in Basic Vocabulary. Kerr, Robert S., illus. LC 55-11205. 165p. illus. 22cm. (Basic vocabulary series). 1956. Garrard Press.
--Zoo Is Home. (First Reading Books Ser). (gr. 1-4). 1958. (ISBN 0-8116-2801-9). Garrard.

Dolch, Edward William (1889-) & Scott, Walter, Sir (1771-1832)
--Ivanhoe for Pleasure Reading. Foster, George, illus. LC 61-4981. (Illus.). 166 p. 21cm. (Their Pleasure reading series 1B). 1961. Garrard Press.

Dolch, Marguerite Pierce, jt. auth. see Dolch, Edward William.

Dolch, Marguerite Pierce, Mrs., jt. auth. see Dolch, Edward William.

Dolch, Marguerite Pierce (1891-)
--Animal Stories from Africa. Morton, Lee Jack, Jr. (1928-), illus. LC 75-8862. p. cm. (Dolch Folklore of the world). 1975. (ISBN 0-8116-2563-X). Garrard Pub. Co.
--Once There Was a Coyote. Hauge, Carl & Hauge, Mary, illus. LC 75-2124. (Illus.). 64 p. 21cm. (First reading book). 1975. (ISBN 0-8116-2816-7). Garrard Pub. Co.
--Stories from Africa. Smith, Vincent D., illus. LC 75-5888. (Illus.). vii, 168 p. 22cm. (Folklore of the world). 1975. (ISBN 0-8116-2562-1). Garrard Pub. Co.
--True Cat Stories in Basic Vocabulary. Dolch, Marguerite Pierce (1891-), illus. LC 75-2146. (Illus.). vii, 157 p. 22cm. (Basic vocabulary series). 1975. (ISBN 0-8116-2516-8). Garrard Pub. Co.

Dole, Charles Fletcher
--Crib and Fly: A Tale of Two Terriers. N.D. D C Heath & Co.

Dole, Charles Fletcher (1845-1927), ed. see Ingelow, Jean.

Dole, Charles Fletcher, ed. see Segur, Sophie Rostopchine, Mrs.

Dole, Helen B., tr. see Baumbach, Rudolf.

Dole, Helen B., tr. see Spyri, Johanna Heusser.

Dole, Helen James Bennett, Mrs. (1857-1944), tr. see Spyri, Johanna Heusser.

Dole, Nathan Haskell, tr. see Tolstoy, Leo Nikolaevich.

Dole, Nathan Haskell, Mrs., tr. see Brentano, Clemens Maria.

Dole, Nathan Haskell (1852-1935), tr.
--The White Duckling And Other Stories. LC 13-980966. 5 p. l., 126 p. col. front., col. plates. 22 cm. c.1913. Thomas Y. Crowell Co.

Dolens, Joel
--Betty's Sad Teddy Bear. LC 66-15965. (Illus.). 16 p. 30cm. (Read-aloud picture book). 1967, c.1966. Follett Pub. Co.
--A Day at the Zoo. LC 66-15966. (Illus.). 16 p. 30cm. (Read-aloud picture book). 1967, c.1966. Follett Pub. Co.
--Jimmy Paints His House. Dolens, Joel, illus. LC 66-15967. (Illus.). 16 p. (Read-aloud picture book). 1967, c.1966. Follett Pub. Co.

Doleski, Teddi
--The Hurt. McNichols, William Hart, illus. LC 83-60737. (Illus.). 32p. (gr. 2-5). 1983. (ISBN 0-8091-6551-1). (ISBN 0-8091-6551-1). Paulist Pr.

Dolgin, Gail, jt. auth. see Karl, Terry.

Dolim, Mary Nuzum (1925-)
--Miss Mac. LC 63-20490. vii, 152 p. 22 cm. 1963. Van Nostrand.

Dolim, Mary Nuzum (1925-) & Kakacek, Gen.
--Four Hands for Mercy. LC 65-25532. vii, 135p. 21cm. c.1965. Van Nostrand.

Dolinger, Jane
--Veronica. 1958. Fleet Pub Corp.

Dolsen, Harriet
--Cloud Islands. Santa Claus Island, Feather Island, Candy Island. LC 44-303024. 58 p. incl. front., pl. 14 1/2 x 12 cm. 1880. W. B. Smith and Co.

Dolson, Bobbie Jane Van see Aitken, Dorothy Lockwood.

Dolson, Bobbie Jane Van see Armistead, Charles.

Dolson, Bobbie Jane Van see Degering, Etta Fowler.

Dolson, Bobbie Jane Van see Dewees, Eleanor.

Dolson, Bobbie Jane Van see Meseraull, Elaine & Van Dolson, Bobbie Jane.

Doman, Bruce K.
--Goodbye Mommy. Melton, David (1934-), illus. LC 77-79632. (Illus.). 86p. (The Gentle Revolution Ser.). 1982. (ISBN 0-936676-00-0). Better Baby.

Domanska, Janina
--Busy Monday Morning. Domanska, Janina, illus. LC 83-25362. (Illus.). 9 7/8 x 8. 32p. (30 pt.). (ps-1). c.1985. (ISBN 0-688-03833-6). (ISBN 0-688-03834-4). (ISBN 0-688-03834-4). Greenwillow.
--Din Dan Don, It's Christmas. Domanska, Jamina, illus. LC 75-8509. (Illus.). 34 p. 1975. (ISBN 0-688-80003-3). (ISBN 0-688-84003-5). Greenwillow Books. **Award: (ALA).**
--I Saw a Ship a-Sailing. LC 75-185147. (Illus.). 33 p. 1972. Macmillan.
--King Krakus and the Dragon. Domanska, Janina, illus. LC 78-12934. (Illus.). 36 p. 27cm. c.1979. (ISBN 0-688-80189-7). (ISBN 0-688-84189-9). Greenwillow Books. **Award: (NYT).**
--Little Red Hen. Domanska, Janina, illus. LC 72-92436. (Illus.). 32 p. 1973. (ISBN 0-02-732820-1). Macmillan.
--Look, There Is a Turtle Flying. LC 68-12082. (Illus.). 1 v. (unpaged. 27cm. 1968. Macmillan.
--Marek, the Little Fool. LC 81-6966. (Illus.). 32 p. c.1982. (ISBN 0-688-00912-3). (ISBN 0-688-00913-1). Greenwillow Books.
--Marilka. Domanska, Janina, illus. LC 79-101729. 32 p. (chiefly col. illus. 22cm. 1970. Macmillan.
--Master of the Royal Cats. Domanska, Jamina, illus. LC 65-27335. 1 v. (unpaged) col. illus. 27 cm. N.D. Seabury Press,.
--Palmiero & the Ogre. Domanska, Janina, illus. LC 67-10028. (Illus.). 1v. (unpaged) Col. illus. 21x26 cm. (gr. k-3). 1967. Macmillan.
--A Scythe, a Rooster, and a Cat. Domanska, Janina, illus. LC 80-17445. (Illus.). 32 p. 25cm. c.1981. (ISBN 0-688-80308-3). (ISBN 0-688-84308-5). Greenwillow Books.
--Spring Is. Domanska, Janina, illus. LC 75-25953. (Illus.). 32 p. 26cm. c.1976. (ISBN 0-688-80026-2). (ISBN 0-688-84026-4). Greenwillow Books.
--The Tortoise and the Tree. Domanska, Janina, adapted by. LC 77-14572. (Illus.). 36 p. 26cm. c.1978. (ISBN 0-688-80132-3). (ISBN 0-688-84132-5). Greenwillow Books.
--The Tortoise and the Tree. Domanska, Janina, illus. (ps-2). 1978. Morrow.
--The Turnip. Domanska, Janina, illus. LC 69-18235. (Illus.). 32 p. 1969. Macmillan.
--What Do You See?. LC 73-6052. (Illus.). 32 p. 26cm. 1974. (ISBN 0-02-732830-9). Macmillan.
--What Happens Next?. Domanska, Janina, illus. LC 82-24219. p. cm. 1983. (ISBN 0-688-01748-7). (ISBN 0-688-01749-5). Greenwillow Books.

Domanska, Janina, ed.
--The Best of the Bargain. LC 76-13010. (Adapted from a Polish Folktale). (Illus.). 36 p. 26cm. c.1977. (ISBN 0-688-80062-9). (ISBN 0-688-84062-0). Greenwillow Books.
--If All the Seas Were One Sea. Domanska, Janina, illus. LC 73-146621. 31 p. (chiefly col. illus.). 26cm. 1971. Macmillan. **Awards: (ALA); (BGH); (RCM).**
--Why So Much Noise?. Domanska, Janina, illus. LC 65-20258. 1 v. (unpaged) col. illus. 23 cm. (gr. k-3). 1965. (ISBN 0-06-021691-3). Harper & Row.

Dombrovskii, Anatolii [illegible]
--In the White Stone's Shadow. LC 81-193590. (Illus.). 70 p. 23cm. 1979. Progress Publishers.

Dombrowski Zu Papros und Krusvic, Kathe Schonberger Von see K. O. S, pseud.

Dombrowski Zu Papros und Krusvic, Kathe Schonberger Von (1881-)
--Abdalla and the Donkey: A Tale of Woe and Joy for Children from Eight to Eighty Years. Dombrowski, Kos, illus. LC 28-22882. (Fiction). (MacMillan Bks. for Boys & Girls). (gr. 4-6). N.D. MacMillan Bks.
--Boga. K. O. S, pseud. Dombrowski zu Papros und Krusvic, Kathe SchonbergerVon (1881-), illus. K. O. S, pseud. LC 28-22383. vii. 96 p. col. front., illus., col. plates. 26 cm. (Macmillan Books for Boys and Girls). 1928. The Macmillan Company.

Dombrowski Zu Papros und Krusvic, Kathe Schonberger Von (1881-), ed.
--The Fat Camel of Bagdad: A New Tale of Abdallah's Adventures, for Children from Eight to Eight Years. Dombrowski Zu Papros und Krusvic, Kathe Schonberger Von (1881-), illus. LC 29-212124. xi p., 1 l., 156 p. incl. plates. col. front. 20 cm. 1929. The Macmillan Company.

Dominic, Mary (1917-)
--Little Nellie of Holy God. N.D. Bruce Publishing Company.

Dominick, Bayard
--Joe, a Porpoise. (gr. 4-6). N.D. G&D.
--Joe, a Porpoise. Coe, Richard (1923-), illus. (Illus.). (gr. 3-5). 1968. (ISBN 0-8392-3067-2). Astor-Honor.
--Sam, a Goat. Coe, Richard (1923-), illus. LC 68-21359. (Illus.). 20 p. 26cm. 1968. Astor-Honor.

Dominque, Otis G
--Poems for Boys and Girls. LC 66-20506. 39 p. illus. 20 cm. (Contemporary poets of Dorrance, 620). 1966. Dorrance.

Domjan, Joseph Spiri (1907-)
--Hungarian Heroes & Legends. Domjan, Joseph Spiri (1907-), illus. (Illus.). (gr. 7 up). 1963. (ISBN 0-442-02166-6). Van Nos Reinhold.
--I Went to the Market: An Old Czechoslovakian Folksong. LC 74-109198. (Illus.). 16 p. 17cm. (Bill Martin instant reader). c.1970. (ISBN 0-03-084592-0). Holt, Rinehart and Winston.
--Little Cock. Hardendorff, Jeanne B., ed. Domjan, Joseph Spiri (1907-), illus. LC 70-82409. (Illus.). 14 color woodcuts. 40p. 26cm. 32p. (gr. 1-4). 1969. (ISBN 0-397-31084-6). Lippincott.
--The Proud Peacock. Domjan, Joseph Spiri (1907-), illus. LC 65-14144. 1 v. (unpaged) col. illus. 29 cm. (Wise owl book, WL07). 1965. Hold, Rinehart, and Winston.

Domke, Todd
--Grounded. LC 81-14267. 186 p. 22cm. c.1982. (ISBN 0-394-85163-3). (ISBN 0-394-95163-8). Knopf : Distributed by Random House.

Don-Carlos, Louisa Cooke, Mrs.
--The Mouse Miller, and Other Stories. LC 17-12861. 1 p. l., 118 p. 19 cm. c.1917. Davis & Bond.

Donahey, Mary Augusta Dickerson, Mrs. (1876-)
--The Adventures of a Happy Dolly. (Six Fairy Tales). N.D. Barse & Hopkins.
--Apple Pie Inn. Jones, Henrietta, illus. LC 42-194443. 5 p. l., 222 p. incl. front., illus. 21 1/2 cm. 1942. Thomas Y. Crowell Company.
--Best Tales for Children. Trippe, Uldene, illus. 173 p. incl. col. fronts., col. illus. 24 cm. (World-wide "Just right" book). c.1924. A. Whitman Anc Company.
--The Castle of Grumpy Grouch. (Six Fairy Tales). N.D. Barse & Hopkins.
--The Castle of Grumpy Grouch. (Illus.). 151p. N.D. Edward Stern & Co.
--The Castle of Grumpy Grouch. Doane, Pelagie (1906-1966), illus. LC 48-6759. 162 p. illus. 21 cm. 1948. Random House.
--Down Spider Web Lane: A Fairy Tale. (Six Fairy Tales). N.D. Barse & Hopkins.
--Down Spider Web Lane: A Fairy Tale. Kay, Gertrude Alice (1884-1939), illus. LC 9-22269. 130 p. col. front., illus., 5 col. pl. 26 cm. 1909. E. Stern & Co., Inc.

--Lady Teddy Comes to Town. Donahey, William (1883-1970), illus. LC 19-15675. 4 p. l., 231 p. col. front. 20 cm. c.1919. Small, Maynard & Company.
--The Magical House of Zur. (Six Fairy Tales). N.D. Barse & Hopkins.
--Marty Lu. LC 25-18704. 5 p. l., 221 p. col. front. 21 cm. 1925. Doubleday, Page & Company.
--Marty Lu. LC 39-15657. 5 p. l., 221 p. col. front. 21 cm. (Young moderns bookshelf). 1937. The Sun Dial Press, Inc.
--Marty Lu's Treasure. Bischoff, Ilse Marthe (1903-), illus. LC 27-20263. vi p., 2 l., 250 p. incl. illus., plates. col. front. 21 cm. 1927. Doubleday, Page & Company.
--Mysterious Mansions. McNab, Allan, illus. LC 32-24672. vi p., 2 l., 230 p. front. 20 cm. 1932. Doubleday, Doran & Company, Inc.
--Peter and Prue. LC 24-22685. 258 p. col. front., illus., col. plates. 20 cm. c.1924. Rand, McNally & Company.
--The Prince Without a Country. LC 16-15842. 125 p. col. front., col. plates. 26 cm. c.1916. Barse & Hopkins.
--The Spanish McQuades: The Lost Treasure of Zavala. Donahey, William (1883-1970) & Beebe, Robb, illus. LC 31-15690. viii p., 3 l., 252 p. incl. illus., plates, col. front. 21 cm. 1931. Doubleday, Doran & Company, Inc.
--Tales to Be Told to Children. LC 15-25941. 160 p. 19 cm. 1915. The Howell Company.
--The Talking Bird and Wonderful Wishes of Jacky and Jean. Falls, Charles Buckles (1874-1960), illus. LC 23-1448. 3 p. l., 11-146 p. col. front., col. plates. 24 cm. 1920. A. Whitman & Company.
--The Tavern of Folly. Galdone, Paul (1914-), illus. LC 30-21953. 5 p. l., 269 p. col. front. 21 cm. 1930. Doubleday, Doran & Company, Inc.
--Through the Little Green Door. (Six Fairy Tales). N.D. Barse & Hopkins.
--Through the Little Green Door. Kay, Gertrude Alice (1884-1939), illus. N.D. Edward Stern & Co.
--The Wonderful Wishes of Jacky and Jean. Falls, Charles Buckles (1874-1960), illus. LC 5-41639. 146 p. incl. col. front. 5 col. pl. 26 cm. 1905. A. Wessels Company.

Donahey, William (1883-1970)
--Adventures of the Teenie Weenies. Donahey, William (1883-1970), illus. N.D. Rand McNally & Co.
--Adventures of the Teenie Weenies. Donahey, William (1883-1970), illus. LC 20-17323. 128 p. col. front., illus., col. plates. 29 cm. c.1920. The Reilly & Lee Co.
--Alice and the Teenie Weenies. Donahey, William (1883-1970), illus. LC 28-61175. 2 p. l., 7-105 p. incl. front., illus. 25 cm. c.1927. The Reilly & Lee Co.
--Down the River with the Teenie Weenies. Donahey, William (1883-1970), illus. N.D. Rand McNally & Co.
--Tennie Weenie Days. Dohaney, William (1883-1970), illus. LC 44-20106. 65 p. incl. col. front., illus. (part col.) 24 1/2 cm. 1944. Whittlesey House, McGraw-Hill Book Company, Inc.
--Teenie Weenie Neighbors. Donahey, William (1883-1970), illus. LC 45-10595. 68 p. incl. col. front., illus. (part col.) 22 1/2 cm. 1945. Whittlesey House, McGraw-Hill Book Company, Inc.
--Teenie Weenie Town. Donahey, William (1883-1970), illus. LC 42-24964. 71, 1 p. incl. col. front., illus., col. plates. 25 cm. 1942. Whittlesey House, McGraw-Hill Book Company, Inc.
--The Teenie Weenies Book. Kishbaugh, Allan, intro. by. LC 84-80569. (Illus.). 90p. (Orig.). N.D. (ISBN 0-88138-035-0, Star & Elephant Bks.). Green Tiger Pr.
--The Teenie Weenies Down the River. Donahey, William (1883-1970), illus. 1921. Reilly & Lee.
--The Teenie Weenies in the Wildwood. Donahey, William (1883-1970), illus. N.D. Rand McNally & Co.
--The Teenie Weenies in the Wildwood. Donahey, William (1883-1970), illus. LC 23-112927. 120 p. col. front., illus., col. plates. 27 cm. c.1923. The Reilly & Lee Co.
--The Teenie Weenies Under the Rosebush. Donahey, William (1883-1970), illus. N.D. Rand McNally & Co.

Donahue, Bob & Donahue, Marilyn
--Things That Go Bump in the Night, & Other Fears. 1983. (ISBN 0-8423-7083-8). Tyndale.

Donahue, Cheney
--My Children's Stories. Lyons, Dave, illus. LC 55-12048. 1955. Pageant Press, Inc.

Donahue, Elvira, ed.
--The News Time Fun Time Book. Blake, Bud, pseud. (1918-), illus. Blake, Julian Watson. (Illus.). 21cm. 64p. c.1964. Scholastic.

Donahue, John
--The Cookie Jar and Other Plays. LC 73-91050. (Illus.). xx, 178 p., 2 leaves of plates. 23cm. 1975. (ISBN 0-8166-0708-7). University of Minnesota Press.

Donahue, John & Jenkins, Linda Walsh
--Five Plays from the Children's Theatre Company of Minneapolis. LC 73-91051. (Illus.). xvii, 240 p., 2 leaves of plates. 23cm. 1975. University of Minnesota Press.

Donahue, Marilyn, jt. auth. see Donahue, Bob.

Donahue, Marilyn Cram
--The Crooked Gate. pennypincher ed. LC 83-27227. 128 p. 18cm. 1984, c.1979. (ISBN 0-89191-831-0). Chariot Books.
--The Crooked Gate. LC 79-51743. 1979. (ISBN 0-89191-185-5). Cook.
--The Music Plays Past Midnight. LC 83-70900. 125 p. 18cm. c.1983. (ISBN 0-89191-756-X). Chariot Books.
--To Catch a Golden Ring. LC 80-68312. 128 p. 18cm. 1984. (ISBN 0-89191-330-0). Chariot Books.
--To Catch a Golden Ring. (gr. 4-9). 1980. (ISBN 0-89191-330-0). Cook.
--Violets Grow in Secret Places. LC 84-15559. 128p. (Pennypincher Ser.). (gr. 5-9). 1984. (ISBN 0-89191-885-X, Chariot Books). Cook.

Donahue, Millicent
--Jam 'n Crackers. LC 75-155360. (Illus.). 124 p. 21cm. 1971. (ISBN 0-8158-0260-9). Christopher Pub. House.

Donaldson, Bryan (1921-)
--Petey the Penguin & His Pink Pajamas. (Illus.). (gr. k-3). 1963. (ISBN 0-87167-119-0). Allied Fla.

Donaldson, Elaine, adapted by.
--Scrooge. LC 71-127561. (Adapted from a screenplay by Leslie Bricusse based on the novel, "A Christmas Carol" by Charles John Huffam Dickens, 1812-1870). (Illus.). 128 p. 29cm. 1970. Cinema Center Films.

Donaldson, Ellen Miller, Mrs.
--In Blue Bird Time. Lupprian, Hildegard (1897-), illus. LC 26-85513. 8 p. l., 160 p. col. front., col. illus., col. plates. 22 cm. 1926. Milton Bradley Company.
--Little Papoose Listens. Lupprian, Hildegard (1897-), illus. N.D. Milton Bradley Co.
--Moons of Long Ago. Cassell, Charles, illus. N.D. Milton Bradley Co.

Donaldson, Lois, jt. auth. see Sperry, Portia Howe.

Donaldson, Lois (1898-), ed. see Sixtus, Albert.

Donaldson, Lois (1898-)
--In the Mouse's House. N.D. Albert Whitman & Co.
--Karl's Wooden Horse. Bergmann, Ann (1911-), illus. LC 75-115894. (Illus.). 32 p. 1970. (ISBN 0-8075-4107-9). A. Whitman.
--Karl's Wooden Horse. Bergmann, Ann (1911-), illus. LC 31-29426. (Illus.). 18 1/2 x 21cm. 32p. 1931. Laidlaw Brothers.
--Kylle Kluk: The Story of the Youngest Chick Hero of All Denmark. Moe, Louis Maria Niels Peder Halling (1858-), illus. LC 31-28467. 24 p. illus. (part col.) 23 x 31 cm. 1931. Laidlaw Brothers.
--One Hundred Fairy Tales. Anderson, Anne & Wellman, Mauriete, illus. LC 37-218244. 1 p. l., 7-123 p. illus., col. plates. 35 cm. c.1937. Whitman Publishing Company.
--Scouting for Washington. Wickham, Wilmer, illus. LC 51-13187. 64 p. illus. 21 cm. 1951. Whitman.
--Smoky, the Lively Locomotive. LC 46-393145. 33 p. col. illus. 19 1/2 x 21 1/2 cm. 1945. A. Whitman & Company.

Donaldson, Margaret C (1926-)
--Journey into War. Stubbs, Joanna, illus. LC 79-64796. (Illus.). 152 p. 22cm. 1979. (ISBN 0-233-97109-2). A. Deutsch.
--The Moon's on Fire. Stubbs, Joanna, illus. LC 80-65664. (Illus.). 138 p. 22cm. 1980. (ISBN 0-233-97249-8). A. Deutsch.

Donaldy, Ernestine, jt. ed. see Norton, Alice Mary.

Donauer, Friedrich
--Swords Against Carthage. Cooper, F. T., tr. LC 61-12878. (Illus.). (gr. 7-11). 1932. (ISBN 0-8196-0112-8). Biblo.

Donavan, Hobart
--Desert Stallion. Riley, William, illus. LC 53-7631. (Illus.). 181 p. 21cm. 1953. Knopf.

Don Bluth Productions, jt. auth. see Shankman, Sarah.

Dondney, Sarah
--Stories of Girlhood: Or, The Brook and the River. 192p. N.D. Cassell, Petter, & Galpin.

Donelly, Eleanor C.
--Klondike Picnic. N.D. Benziger Brothers.

Doney, Meryl
--The Kind Stranger. Round, Graham, illus. (Illus.). 16p (Pub. by Lion Publishing). 1982. (ISBN 0-86683-666-7). Winston Pr.
--The Lost Sheep. Round, Graham, illus. (Illus.). 16p (Pub. by Lion Publishing). 1982. (ISBN 0-86683-663-2). Winston Pr.
--The Loving Father. Round, Graham, illus. (Illus.). 16p (Pub. by Lion Publishing). 1982. (ISBN 0-86683-665-9). Winston Pr.
--The Two Houses. Round, Graham, illus. (Illus.). 16p (Pub. by Lion Publishing). 1982. (ISBN 0-86683-664-0). Winston Pr.

Doney, Meryl, ed.
--Now We Have a New Baby. Fort, Jane, illus. (Illus.). 16p (Pub. by Lion). Orig. Title: Now We have a New Baby. 1983. (ISBN 0-686-43064-6). Winston Pr.

Dong, Jim, jt. auth. see Robles, Al.

Donleavy, James Patrick (1926-)
--The Ginger Man. N.D. Berkly Bks.

Donlon, Yolande
--Third Time Lucky. 1976. (J Wade). Dial.

Donna, Natalie (1934-1979)
--Boy of The Masai. Larsen, Peter, photos by. 60p. 1964. Dodd, Mead & Co.

Donnell, Annie Hamilton
--Camp Fidelity Girls. Ahrens, Ellen Wetherald, illus. LC 3-23482. 3 p. 1, 273 p. front., 5 pl. 20 cm. 1903. Little, Brown, and Company.
--Glory and the Other Girl. LC 7-26346. 63 p. illus 18 cm. c.1907. D. C. Cook Publishing Company.
--Judith Lynn: A Story of the Sea. LC 6-41271. 64 p. illus. 18 cm. c.1906. D. C. Cook Publishing Company.
--Rebecca Mary. Green, Elizabeth Shippen, illus. (Girls' Library). 1905. Harper & Bros.

Donnelly, Eleanor Cecilia (1838-1917), ed.
--Amy's Music Box And Other Little Stories and Verses for Children. LC 12-320972. 206 p. 17 cm. c.1896. H. L. Kilner & Co.
--Little Compliments of the Season, and Other Tiny Rhymes for Tiny Readers. Simple Verses, Original, Selected and Translated, for Namedays, Birthdays, Christmas, New Year, and Other Festive and Social Occasions. LC 16-9618. 128 p. incl. front. illus. 18 cm. 1887. Benziger Brothers.
--Petronilla, and Other Stories. 1896. Benziger Brothers.

Donnelly, Elfie
--Offbeat Friends. Bell, Anthea, tr. LC 82-7995. 119 p. 24cm. 1st U.S. edition. 1982. (ISBN 0-517-54617-5). Crown. **Award: (ALA).**
--So Long, Grandpa. Bell, Anthea, tr. from Ger. LC 81-3241. 92 p. 24cm. 1981, c.1980. (ISBN 0-517-54423-7). Crown Publishers. **Award: (ALA).**
--Tina into Two Won't Go. Bell, Anthea, tr. from Ger. LC 83-5563. p. cm. 1983. (ISBN 0-590-07912-3). Four Winds Press.

Donnelly, Katherine Fair, ed. see Bato, Joseph.

Donnelly, M. A., ed.
--Best Book of Sports Stories. Freire, J., illus. LC 66-9501. (Illus.). 278 p. 25cm. (Best book series). 1966. Doubleday.

Donnison, Polly
--William the Dragon. Donnison, Polly, illus. LC 72-94138. (Illus.). 16 x 24cm. 60p. (ps-3). 1973. (ISBN 0-698-30510-8, Coward). (ISBN 0-698-20258-9). Putnam Pub Group.

Donohue, Dina
--Mr. Harty Comes for Christmas. Unada, pseud. (1927-), illus. Gliewe, Unada Grace. LC 78-104871. (Illus.). 32 p. 24cm. c.1978. (ISBN 0-8170-0771-7). Judson Press.

Donovan, D. J
--The Adventures of Starbeem and Re-Koil. Skrocki, Edward A., illus. LC 67-5499. 1 v. (unpaged) col. illus. 28 cm. 1967. House of Ideas.
--Now Mildred. Skrocki, Edward A., illus. LC 68-6778. (Illus.). 28cm. 40p. 1968. House of Ideas.

Donovan, Edward Joseph (1904-)
--Adventure on Ghost River. LC 60-5454. 21cm. 150p. 1960. Duell, Sloan and Pearce Pub.
--Adventure on Sunset Trail. LC 61-11958. 21cm. 150p. 1961. Duell Sloan & Pearce.

Donovan, J. B.
--Bill Speed on Hot Ice. 1971. (ISBN 0-87508-644-6). Chr Lit.
--Bill Speed-Special Squad. 1971. (ISBN 0-87508-645-4). Chr Lit.
--Laughing Horses. 1971. (ISBN 0-87508-713-2). Chr Lit.

Donovan, John (1928-)
--Family: A Novel. LC 75-37409. 116 p. 22cm. c.1976. (ISBN 0-06-021721-9). (ISBN 0-06-021722-7). Harper & Row. **Award: (ALA).**
--Good Old James. Stevenson, James Walker (1929-), illus. LC 74-20387. (Illus.). 24 p. 20cm. 1975. (ISBN 0-06-021703-0). (ISBN 0-06-021704-9). Harper & Row.
--I'll Get There It Better Be Worth The Trip. LC 69-15539. 208p. (gr. 7 up). 1969. (ISBN 0-06-021717-0, HarpJ). (ISBN 0-06-021718-9). Har-Row.
--The Little Orange Book. Caputo, Mauro, illus. LC 61-5003. (Illus.). unpaged. 18cm. (Morrow junior books). 1961. Morrow.
--Remove Protective Coating a Little at a Time. LC 73-4977. 101 p. 22cm. 1973. (ISBN 0-06-021719-7). (ISBN 0-06-021719-7). Harper & Row.
--Wild in the World. LC 74-159044. 128p. (gr. 5 up). 1971. (ISBN 0-06-021702-2, HarpJ). Har-Row.

Donovan, Mary Ellen (1860-)
--An Unwilling Traveler. LC 17-15976. 2 p. l., 240 p. 19 cm. 1917. B. Herder Book Co.

Donovan, Mary Rose, illus.
--Wee Folks and Mother. N.D. George W. Jacobs & Co.

Donze, Sara Lee
--The Robin and the Thorn: An Easter Story for Children. LC 65-12134. 1v. (unpaged) illus. 22cm. c.1965. (ISBN 0-8066-0525-1). Augsburg.

Doob, Leonard William (1909-), ed.
--Ants Will Not Eat Your Fingers: African Poems. (gr. 7 up). 1966. (ISBN 0-8027-6008-2). Walker & Co.
--A Crocodile Has Me by the Leg: African Poems. Wangboje, Solomon Irein, illus. LC 67-23097. (Illus.). 1 v. (unpaged). 24cm. 1967. Walker.

Dooley, Bernard F J
--The Lair of the Wolves. LC 35-1088. 3 p. l., 276 p. front. 20 cm. c.1934. The Bruce Publishing Company.
--Paul Hart Comes Through. LC 27-5949. iv p., 1 l., 257 p. 19 cm. c.1926. P. J. Kenedy & Sons.
--Scouting for Secret Service. LC 23-469. iv, 259 p. 20 cm. c.1922. P. J. Kenedy & Sons.
--Servant of the King. N.D. Bruce Publishing Co.
--Tuffy Taylor. 1953. Bruce Publishing Co.
--Tuffy Taylor. LC 32-202535. vi p., 1 l., 296 p. front. 19 cm. c.1931. The Bruce Publishing Company.

Dooley, Eddie
--Under the Goal Posts. (Thrilling! Exciting! Football Stories). N.D. Grosset & Dunlap.

Dooley, Fern Pascoe
--Joey's Ghost Pumpkin. Woodson, Jack, pseud. (1913-), illus. Woodson, John Waddie Jr.. LC 81-69695. (Illus.). 64 p. 22cm. c.1982. (ISBN 0-8054-4515-3). Broadman Press.

Doone, Radko (1896-)
--Nuvat, the Brave: An Eskimo Robinson Crusoe. Walleen, Hans Alex, illus. LC 34-16903. 7 p., 1 l., 13-194 p. incl. illus., plates. 23 cm. c.1934. Macrae Smith Company.
--Red Beards of the Yellow River. Deitch, Harry, illus. LC 39-31690. viii p., 1 l., 11-223 p. illus. 23 cm. c.1939. Macrae Smith Company.

Doop, Katherine Elizabeth (1863-)
--Bobby and Betty in the Country. Brand, Mary Spoor, illus. 20cm. 224p. 1927. Rand McNally & Co.
--Bobby and Betty with the Workers. Brand, Mary Spoor, illus. 20cm. 199p. 1923. Rand McNally & Co.

Doorly, Eleanor
--Insect Man. Gibbings, Robert (1889-), illus. N.D. Penguin Bks.

Dootson, Lily Lee
--A Riddle Book. Biers, Clarence, illus. 152p. (gr. 1-2). N.D. Rand McNally & Co.

Dor, Ana, pseud., see Ceder, Georgiana Dorcas.

Dorcheff, George (1893-)
--Stories and Legends of Two Worlds. 1st ed. Nagel, Stina (1918-), illus. LC 60-50594. (Illus.). 22cm. 125p. 1960. Exposition Press.

Dorcy, Mary Jean, Sr. (1914-)
--Rosary Stories for Little Folk. 1940. Bruce Publishing Co.

Dore, Louis Christophe Paul Gustave (1832-1883), illus.
--Adventures Of Munchausen. N.D. Cassell.
--Dore's Popular Fairy Tales. N.D. James Miller.
--Droll Stories. English ed. (Illus.). 1888. R Worthington.
--Fairy Tales Told Again. N.D. Cassell, Petter & Galpin.
--French Fairy Tales. Coleman, Mrs., tr. N.D. Porter & Coates.
--Standard Fairy Tales, 1 of 3 Vols. (Illus.). (Famous Fairy Library). N.D. Set. Porter & Coates.

Doremus, Robert (1913-), illus.
--Spooks and Spirits and Shadowy Shapes. LC 49-11186. 167 p. illus. 20 cm. 1949. Aladdin Books.

Dorey, Jacques
--Three and the Moon. 1929. Alfred A. Knopf.

Dorian, Edith Mc Ewen (1900-)
--Ask Dr. Christmas. Unwin, Nora Spicer (1907-), illus. LC 51-13205. (Illus.). 144 p. 21cm. 1951. Whittlesey House.
--High-Water Cargo. Orr, Forrest W., illus. LC 65-63574. 224p. illus., map, 22cm. bibl. 1965. Rutgers.
--High-Water Cargo. Orr, Forrest W., illus. LC 50-6928. (Illus.). 216 p. 21cm. 1950. Whittlesey House.
--No Moon on Graveyard Head. (Illus.). (gr. 6-9). 1953. (ISBN 0-8382-0593-3). Hale.
--No Moon on Graveyard Head. LC 53-10626. (gr. 7 up). 1953. (ISBN 0-07-017624-8). McGraw.
--Trails West and Men Who Made Them. N.D. Whittlesey House.

--The Twisted Shadow. LC 67-2721. (Illus.). 167 p. 20cm. (Young pioneer edition). 1967, c.1956. McGraw-Hill.
--The Twisted Shadow. LC 56-10310. 167p. illus. 21cm. 1956. Whittlesey House.

Dorian, Edith Mc Ewen (1900-) & Wilson, W. N.
--Animals That Made U. S. History. LC 64-22952. 112p. illus. 26cm. bibl. c.1964. Whittlesey-McGraw.

Dorian, Marguerite
--Alligator's Toothache. LC 61-11915. (Illus.). (ps-3). 1962. Lothrop.
--When the Snow Is Blue. Dorian, Marquerite, illus. LC 59-15453. (Illus.). unpaged. 27cm. 1960. Lothrop, Lee and Shepard Co.

Dorio, Evelyn
--Pigalee Pink. 96p. 1979. (ISBN 0-9603118-4-X). MD Dhu
--Pigalee Pink & Other Stories. Davenport, May, illus. Davenport, May, intro. by. LC 79-56540. (Illus.). 95p. (gr. 3-6). 1979. Davenport.

Dorison, K. J.
--Dear Mr. ASPCA: Letters from School Children to the American Society for the Prevention of Cruelty to Animals. Lazarus, Mell (1927-), illus. American Society for the Prevention of Cruelty to Animals Mapel, Eolliam LC 65-16708. 1 v. (unpaged) illus. 16 x 16 cm. c.1965. Taplinger.

Dorliae, Peter Gondro (1935-)
--Animals Mourn for Da Leopard & Other West African Tales. Wangboje, Solomon Irein, illus. LC 74-84167. (Illus.). 12 linoleum cuts. 80p. (gr. 5 up). 1970. (ISBN 0-672-50918-0). Bobbs.

Dorman, N. B (1927-)
Laughter in the Background. LC 80-23941. 158 p. 21cm. c.1980. (ISBN 0-525-66714-8). Elsevier/Nelson Books.

Dorman, Sonya (1924-)
--Planet Patrol. LC 78-1566. (gr. 6-10). 1978. (ISBN 0-698-20435-2, Coward). Putnam Pub Group.

Dornblaster, Irene La Wall see La Wall, Irene, pseud.

Dornblatt, Leah
--Tova's Happy Purim: In Yerusholayim. Backman, Aidel, illus. (Illus.). (ps-4). N.D. (ISBN 0-87306-989-7). Feldheim.

Dorr, Henry C.
--Mohawk Peter and Other Stories. N.D. Cornhill Publishing Company.

Dorr, Julia C. R.
--In Kings' House: A Romance of the Days of Queen Anne. Merrill, Frank Thayer (1848-), illus. N.D. L. C. Page.

Dorrance, Ward & Morby, Thomas
--The White Hound Stories. Gordon, Caroline, illus. 205p. 1959. University of Missouri Press.

Dorre, Pamela
--Wind Over Stonehenge. LC 77-75947. (Illus.). 64p. (Pacesetters Ser.). (gr. 4 up). 1978. (ISBN 0-516-02175-3). Childrens.

Dorreth, Velma
--Pie Face. Thorne, Diana (1894-), illus. LC 47-24777. (Illus.). 22cm. 14p. (A Cozy-Corner Bk.). 1947. Whitman Pub. Co,.

Dorritt, Susan
--Jason's Lucky Day. Goodall, John Strickland (1908-), illus. LC 58-5788. 1958. Abelard-Schuman.
--Jellybean: The Puppy Who Was Born in the Time of the Snow. Marriott, Patricia (1920-), illus. LC 56-11023. unpaged. illus. 27cm. 1957. Abelard-Schuman.
--The Learning Book. Donald, Elizabeth, illus. LC 60-13917. 26cm. 1960. Abelard-Schuman.
--Wait Till Sunday. Duvoisin, Roger Antoine (1904-1980), illus. LC 57-6516. unpaged. illus. 27cm. c.1957. Abelard-Schuman.
--Wait Till Sunday. Duvoisin, Roger Antoine (1904-1980), illus. (Illus.). (gr. 1-3). 1957. (ISBN 0-8382-0924-6). Hale.

Dorros, Arthur
--Alligator Shoes. Dorros, Arthur, illus. LC 82-2409. (Illus.). 24p. (ps-k). 1982. (ISBN 0-525-44001-1). Dutton.
--Pretzels. Dorros, Arthur, illus. LC 81-1021. (Illus.). 55 p. 22cm. (Greenwillow Read-Alone Books). c.1981. (ISBN 0-688-00668-X). (ISBN 0-688-00669-8). Greenwillow Books.

Dorsey, Anna Hanson McKenney, Mrs. (1815-1896)
--The Old House at Glenaran. LC 12-31936. 408 p. 19 cm. 1887. J. Murphy & Co.
--Tom Boy. LC 12-31938. (Bound With her "Two Ways". Baltimore, 1891). 262 p. plan. 19 cm. 1891. J. Murphy & Co.
--Tom Boy. 3d ed. LC 42-26412. (Bound With her "Two Ways". Baltimore, c1891). 262 p. illus. (plan) 18 1/2 cm. c.1891. John Murphy Company.
--Two Ways. LC 12-319372. 220 p. 19 cm. 1891. J. Murphy & Co.
--Two Ways. LC 42-26411. 220 p. 18 1/2 cm. c.1891. J. Murphy Company.

Dorsey, Charles James
--Golden Playdays. Kaji, Elsa & Anderson, J. P., illus. LC 54-46565. unpaged. illus. 31cm. (The Tickle Toe Ser.). 1954, c.1922. Children's Pub. Co.
--Playday Rhymes. Kaji, Elsa & Anderson, J. P., illus. LC 53-52545. 16p. illus. 31cm. (The Tickle Toe Ser.). 1953, c.1922. Children's Pub. Co.
--Rhymes of Golden Childhood. Kaji, Elsa & Anderson, J. P., illus. LC 54-46566. unpaged. illus. 31cm. (The Tickle Toe Ser.). 1954, c.1922. Children's Pub Co.
--Rockabye Rhymes. Kaji, Elsa & Anderson, J. P., illus. LC 53-52905. (The Tickle Toe Ser.). 1953, c.1922. Children's Pub Co.

Dorsey, Ella Loraine (1853-1935)
--Jet, the War-Mule, And Other Stories for Boys and Girls. LC 12-31930. 307 p. 17 1/2 cm. 1894. The Ave Maria.
--Midshipman Bob. 265p. N.D. Ave Maria Publications.
--Pickle and Pepper. (Illus.). N.D. Benziger Brothers' Pub.
--The Taming of Polly. LC 12-31985. 3 p. l., 5-244 p. front. 19 1/2 cm. 1897. Benziger Brothers.

Dorsky, Blanche
--Harry: A True Story. Batherman, Muriel (1926-), illus. LC 77-3308. (Illus.). 32 p. 24cm. c.1977. (ISBN 0-13-384198-7). Prentice-Hall.

Dorsman, Charlotte K
--White Wolf. LC 47-12176. 128 p. front. 20 cm. 1947. Dorrance.

Dorson, Richard Mercer (1916-1981)
--American Folklore. 313p. 1959. The University Of Chicago Press.
--American Negro Folktales. N.D. (ISBN 0-8446-1990-6). Peter Smith Publisher, Inc.
--Folk Legends of Japan. Noguchi, Yoshie, illus. 1971. (ISBN 0-8048-0191-6). Charles E. Tuttle Co.

Doskocilova, Hana (1936-)
--Animal Tales. Armstrong, William Howard (1914-), ed. Hanak, Mirko, illus. Merriam, Eve (1916-), tr. 32p. (gr. 1-3). 1971. (ISBN 0-385-00298-X). (ISBN 0-385-01182-2). Doubleday.

Doss, Helen Grigsby (1918-)
--All the Children of the World. Knapp, Audrie L., illus. LC 58-3311. 20cm. 1958. (ISBN 0-687-01064-0). Abingdon Press.
--A Brother the Size of Me. (Illus.). (gr. 2-6). 1957. (ISBN 0-316-19063-2). Little.
--A Brother the Size of Me. 1 st. ed. Patterson, Robert (1899-), illus. LC 57-8040. 88p. illus. 22cm. 1957. (ISBN 0-316-19063-2). Little, Brown.
--The Family Nobody Wanted. (gr. 7-10). N.D. (ISBN 0-590-08530-1, Schol Pap). Scholastic Inc.
--Friends Around the World. Knapp, Audrie L., illus. LC 59-7499. (Illus.). 24 p. 20cm. 1959. Abingdon Press.
--Jonah. Kohn, Norman, illus. LC 64-14791. 111 p. illus., map (on lining papers) 25 cm. 1964. Abingdon Press.
--King David. Kohn, Norman, illus. LC 67-7319. (Illus.). 143 p. 25cm. 1967. Abingdon Press.
--Young Readers' Book of Bible Stories. Armstrong, Tom, illus. LC 76-95199. (Illus.). 384 p. 29cm. 1970. Abingdon Press.

Dos Santos, Joyce Audy
--The Diviner. LC 79-9616. p. cm. c.1980. (ISBN 0-397-31909-6). (ISBN 0-397-31910-X). Lippincott.
--Henri and the Loup-Garou. LC 81-9445. (Illus.). 40 p. 19cm. c.1982. (ISBN 0-394-84950-7). Pantheon Books.
--Sand Dollar, Sand Dollar. LC 79-3019. (Illus.). 32 p. c.1980. (ISBN 0-397-31891-X). (ISBN 0-397-31894-4). Lippincott.
--Sand Dollar, Sand Dollar. Dos Santos, Joyce Audy, illus. (gr. 1-3). 1980. Harper.

Dostoevsky, Fyodor Mikhailovich (1821-1881)
--Crime & Punishment. (Illus.). (Great Il. Classics - Titans). (gr. 9 up). 1963. (ISBN 0-396-04873-0). Dodd.
--Crime & Punishment. 764p. (Ultratype Eds). (gr. 7 up). N.D. (ISBN 0-531-00418-X). Watts.
--Talking Crocodile. Campbell, M. Rudolph, adapted by. Piussi-Campbell, Judy, illus. LC 68-30681. (Illus.). 48p. (ps-3). 1968. (ISBN 0-689-20089-7). (ISBN 0-689-20090-0). Atheneum.

Dotey, Clara
--Blind Jakey, 1 of 5 vols. (Sunny Dell Ser.). N.D. D. Lothrop & Co.
--Blind Jakey. 144p. N.D. Hurd & Houghton for American Tract Society.
--Blind Jakey. 144p. N.D. Lockwood, Brooks & Co. for American Tract Society.

Dotts, Maryann J. (1933-)
--I Am Happy. Hughey, Harriette, illus. LC 70-127373. 22cm. 32p. 1971. (ISBN 0-687-18203-4). Abingdon Press.

Dotty, Andes
--My Little Library. Hampton, Blake, illus. LC 64-1568. 3 v. col. illus. 13 cm. 1963. Rutledge Books.

Doty, Douglas Zabriskie
--Andy's Adventures on Noah's Ark. Glackens, Louis M., illus. LC 2-28289. 21cm. 218p. 1902. J. F. Taylor & Co.

Doty, Jean Slaughter see Slaughter, Jean.

Doty, Jean Slaughter (1929-)
--Can I Get There by Candlelight?. Lewin, Ted (1935-), illus. LC 79-24466. (Illus.). 111 p. 22cm. c.1980. (ISBN 0-02-732670-5). Macmillan.
--The Crumb. LC 75-33648. 122 p. +mcm. 122p. c.1976. (ISBN 0-688-80035-1). (ISBN 0-688-84035-3). Greenwillow Books.
--Dark Horse. Chhuy, Dorothy Haskell, illus. LC 82-21651. (Illus.). 122 p. 22cm. 1983. (ISBN 0-688-01703-7). Morrow.
--Gabriel. Lewin, Ted (1935-), illus. LC 73-6045. (Illus.). 138 p. 21cm. 1974. (ISBN 0-02-732740-X). Macmillan.
--If Wishes Were Horses. LC 84-882. 132p. (gr. 5-9). 1984. (ISBN 0-02-733020-6). (ISBN 0-02-733020-6). Macmillan.
--The Monday Horses. LC 77-13310. 149 p. 22cm. c.1978. (ISBN 0-688-80134-X). (ISBN 0-688-84134-1). Greenwillow Books.
--Summer Pony. Savitt, Sam (1917-), illus. LC 74-20801. p. cm. 1975. (ISBN 0-02-042950-9). Collier Books.
--Summer Pony. Savitt, Sam (1917-), illus. LC 72-90991. (Illus.). 121 p. 21cm. 1973. (ISBN 0-02-732750-7). Macmillan.
--The Valley of the Ponies. Chhuy, Dorothy Haskell, illus. LC 81-19381. p. cm. c.1982. (ISBN 0-02-732790-6). Macmillan.
--Winter Pony. Lewin, Ted (1935-), illus. LC 74-19044. (Illus.). 106 p. 22cm. 1975. (ISBN 0-02-732760-4). Macmillan.
--Yesterday's Horses. LC 84-42981. 114 p. 22cm. c.1985. (ISBN 0-02-733040-0). Macmillan.

Doty, Julia Van Duyn (1882-)
--True Stories About the Bears of Yellowstone National Park. Stewart, Martha Ross, illus. LC 47-20011. 63 p. illus. 20 x 19 1/2 cm. 1947. Printed by Stevens & Wallis, Inc.

Doty, Roy, created by see Preston, David R.

Doty, Roy (1922-)
--Gunga, Your Din-Din Is Ready: Son of Puns, Gags, Quips, and Riddles. LC 75-24624. (Illus.). 64 p. 24cm. c.1976. (ISBN 0-385-11521-0). Doubleday.
--King Midas Has a Gilt Complex. LC 77-19226. (Illus.). 64 p. 25cm. c.1979. (ISBN 0-385-13488-6). (ISBN 0-385-13489-4). Doubleday.
--Old One-Eye Meets His Match. LC 77-90369. (Illus.). 60 p. 22cm. (Fun-to-read book). c.1978. (ISBN 0-688-41825-2). (ISBN 0-688-51825-7). Lothrop, Lee & Shepard.
--Pinocchio Was Nosey: Grandson of Puns, Gags, Quips and Riddles. LC 76-51805. (Illus.). 63 p. 24cm. c.1977. (ISBN 0-385-12919-X). (ISBN 0-385-12920-3). Doubleday.
--Puns, Gags, Quips, and Riddles: A Collection of Dreadful Jokes. LC 73-13116. (Illus.). 64 p. 25cm. 1974. (ISBN 0-385-06051-3). (ISBN 0-385-06051-3). Doubleday.
--Q's Are Weird O's: More Puns, Gags, Quips, and Riddles. LC 74-17379. (Illus.). 64 p. 25cm. 1975. (ISBN 0-385-02403-7). (ISBN 0-385-02403-7). Doubleday.
--Tinkerbell Is a Ding-a-Ling. LC 79-6973. (Illus.). 64 p. 24cm. c.1980. (ISBN 0-385-13490-8). (ISBN 0-385-13491-6). Doubleday.

Doty, William Lodewick (1919-1979)
--Crusaders of the Great River, Marquette and Joliet. Lynch, Donald, illus. LC 58-13116. 180p. illus. 22cm. (Banner Books). 1958. Benziger Bros.

Doubleday, Russell (1872-)
--Cattle Ranch to College. (Every Boy's Library). N.D. Grosset & Dunlap.
--Cattle Ranch to College. MacDonald, Janet, illus. N.D. Doubleday Doran.
--Cattle-Ranch to College: The True Tale of a Boy's Adventures in the Far West. LC 99-4905. xii p., 2 l., 347 p. front., 23 pl. 21 cm. 1899. Doubleday & McClure Co.
--Cattle Ranch to College: The True Tale of a Boy's Adventures in the Far West. LC 36-10611. x p., 1 l., 347 p. front., illus., plates. 20 1/2 cm. (Young moderns books). 1936. Doubleday, Doran & Company, Inc.
--Cattle Ranch to College: The True Tale of a Boy's Adventures in the Far West. LC 37-22394. x p., 1 l., 347 p. front., illus., plates. 20 1/2 cm. (Young moderns bookshelf). 1937. The Sun Dial Press, Inc.
--A Gunner Aboard the Yankee. (Every Boy's Library). N.D. Grosset & Dunlap.
--A Gunner Aboard the "Yankee". From the Diary of Number Five of the Afterport Gun; the Yarn of the Cruise and Fights of the Naval Reserves in the Spanish-American War. Lewis, H. H., ed. LC 98-1498. xv, 312 p. incl. front. 26 pl. (part col.) 21 cm. 1898. Doubleday & McClure Co.
--A Year in a Yawl: A True Tale of the Adventures of Four Boys in a Thirty-Foot Yawl. LC 1-25443. viii p., 1 l., 365 p. front., 15 pl. 21 cm. 1901. Doubleday, Page & Co.
--A Year in a Yawl: A True Tale of the Adventures of Four Boys in a Thirty-foot Yawl. (Illus.). N.D. Grosset & Dunlap.

Doubtfire, Dianne Abrams (1918-)
--Escape on Monday. (gr. 7-12). 1974. (ISBN 0-590-03018-3). Scholastic Inc.
--A Girl Called Rosemary. (gr. 7-12). 1977. (ISBN 0-590-09243-X, Schol Pap). Schol Bk Serv.
--Girl in Cotton Wool. (gr. 7-12). 1976. (ISBN 0-590-01512-5, Schol Trade Pap). Schol Bk Serv.

Doudney, Sarah (1842-)
Faith Harrowby: Or, The Smuggler's Cave. N.D. Thomas Nelson & Sons.
--Under False Colors. (Illus.). (Fireside Series for Girls). N.D. A. L. Burt's Pubs.
--Under False Colors. (Illus.). (The Wellesley Series for Girls). N.D. A. L. Burt.
--Under False Colors. (Illus.). (Scribner-Blackie Series of books for young people). N.D. Charles Scribner's Sons.
--Under False Colors: A Story of Two Girls' Lives (The Rugby Series for Boys and Girls) N.D. A. L. Burt Company.

Dougherty, Joanna Foster see Foster, Joanna.

Dougherty, Katherine
--A Street of Churches. Brown, Judith Gwyn (1933-), illus. N.D. (ISBN 0-687-39953-X). Abingdon Press.

Doughtie, Charles
--Gabriel Wrinkles. Saxon, Charles D., illus. LC 59-6072. (The Bloodhound who could'nt smell). 1959. Dodd, Mead & Co.
--High Henry: The Cowboy Who Was Too Tall To Ride A Horse. Gregg, Don, illus. LC 60-13903. 26cm. 1960. Dodd, Mead & Co.

Doughty, Bix L.
--Noah & the Great Ark. 1978. (ISBN 0-87602-163-1). Anchorage.

Doughty, Gertrude
--Pam Robin and Stumps. N.D. J. B. Lippincott Co.

Doughty, S. P., Mrs.
--Little Stories for Little Folks. N.D. New Church Books.
--Mountains & Molehills: And Other Christmas Tales. N.D. Massachusetts New-Church Union.
--Trifles: Or, Little Stories about Little Things. N.D. Massachusetts New-Church Union.
--Willie Benton: Or, The Soldier's Boy and Other Stories. N.D. Massachusetts New-Church Union.

Doughty, Wayne Dyre
--Crimson Moccasins. LC 66-11497. 214 p. 22cm. 1966. Harper & Row.

Douglas, Alan
--Tenderfoot Squad. LC 30-1353. 2 p. l., 11-185 p. front. 19 cm. (His The Hickory Ridge boy scouts). 1919. The New York Book Company.

Douglas, Amanda Minnie (1837-1916)
--Almost As Good As a Boy. Davidson, Bertha G., illus. LC 4038. 2 p. l., iii-iv p., 1 l., 375 p. front., 7 pl. 19 cm. 1900. Lee and Shepard.
--Almost As Good as a Boy. Davidson, Bertha G., illus. 1905. Lee and Shepard Company.
--The Children in the Little Old Red House. Wyman, Louise, illus. LC 12-8140. 4 p. l., 344 p. front., plates. 19 1/2 cm. (Her Little red house series). 1912. Lothrop, Lee & Sherpard Co.
--Clover's Princess. (Illus.). (Illustrated Holly-Tree Ser.). N.D. Henry Altemus Co.
--Clover's Princess. Neill, John Rea (1878-1943), illus. LC 4-21719. ix p., 1 l., 13-95 p. incl. col. front., 6 pl. 19 cm. 1904. H. Altemus Company.
--Drifted Asunder: or, The Tide of Fate. N.D. William F. Gill.
--An Easter Lily. Gonzalez, A. D., illus. LC 6-348076. ix p., 1 l., 13-115 p. incl. front., illus., plates. 18 1/2 cm. c.1906. H. Altemus Company.
--The Girls at Mount Morris. LC 14-10728. 3 p. l., 317 p. front., plates. 19 1/2 cm. c.1914. M. A. Donohue & Co.
--Hannah Ann: A Sequel to A Little Girl in Old New York. LC 6-33460. 4 p. l., 375 p. 19 1/2 cm. (The "little girl" series). 1897. Dodd, Mead & Company.
--Helen Grant at Aldred House. Brooks, Amy (0000-1931), illus. LC 5-29990. 4 p. l., 339 p. front., 5 pl. 19 cm. (Her The Helen Grant books). 1905. Lee and Shepard.
--Helen Grant, Graduate. Brooks, Amy (0000-1931), illus. LC 8-23553. 4 p. l., 399 p. front., 5 pl. 19 cm. (Her Helen Grant books). 1908. Lothrop, Lee & Shepard Co.
--Helen Grant in College. Brooks, Amy (0000-1931), illus. LC 6-32682. vii, 352 p. front., 5 pl. 19 cm. (Her The Helen Grant books). 1906. Lothrop, Lee & Shepard Co.

--Helen Grant, Senior. Brooks, Amy (0000-1931), illus. LC 7-26596. 4 p. l., 405 p. front., 5 pl. 19 cm. (Her The Helen Grant books). c.1907. Lothrop, Lee & Shepard Co.
--Helen Grant, Teacher. Brooks, Amy (0000-1931), illus. LC 9-22620. 4 p. l., 439 p. front., plates. 19 cm. (Her Helen Grant books). 1909. Lothrop, Lee and Shepard Co.
--Helen Grant's Decision. Brooks, Amy (0000-1931), illus. (The Helen Grant Stories). 1910. Lothrop,Lee & Shepard.
--Helen Grant's Friends. Brooks, Amy (0000-1931), illus. LC 4-22660. 4 p. l., 402 p. front., 5 pl. 19 cm. 1904. Lee and Shepard.
--Helen Grant's Harvest Year. Hoxie, Bertha Davidson, illus. LC 11-11894. 4 p. l., 412 p. front., plates. 19 cm. (Her The Helen Grant books). 1911. Lothrop, Lee & Shepard Co.
--Helen Grant's Schooldays. Brooks, Amy (0000-1931), illus. LC 3-238889. vii, 391 p. front., 5 pl. 19 cm. 1903. Lee and Shepard.
--How Bessie Kept House, 1 of 21 Vols. (Illus.). (Boys & Girls Booklovers Ser.: No. 15). N.D. Set. Henry Altemus Co.
--How Bessie Kept House. (Illus.). (Illustrated Cherrycroft Ser.). N.D. Henry Altemus Co.
--How Bessie Kept House. Leopold, L. R., illus. LC 3-25215. ix p., 1 l., 13-121 p. incl. front., 2 pl. 18 cm. 1903. H. Altemus Company.
--In the Ranks. (Kathie's Stories for Young People). N.D. Colby and Rich.
--In the Ranks. LC 6-33459. 4 p. l., 7-278 p. front., plates. 16 1/2 cm. 17cm. 4p. (Added t.-p.: Kathie's stories. 5). 1872. Lee and Shepard.
--In the Ranks. (Illus.). (Kathie's Stories For Young People). 1872. Lee & Shepard.
--In the Ranks, 1 of 6 Vols. (Illus.). (Kathie's Stories for Young People). 1882. Lee & Shepard.
--In the Ranks. LC 99-40. 12cm. 278p. (Kathie Stories). 1899. Lee and Shepard.
--In the Ranks, 1 of 6 Vols. (Illus.). (The Kathie Ser.). 1905. Lee and Shepard Company.
--In the Ranks. (The Kathie Stories: Vol.). 1800. Lothrop,Lee & Shepard.
--The Kathie Series, 6 Vols. (Illus.). 1905. Lee and Shepard Company.
--Kathie's Aunt Ruth. (Kathie's Stories for Young People). N.D. Colby and Rich.
--Kathie's Aunt Ruth. LC 6-33458. 4 p. l., vii-viii, 9-257 p. front., plates. 16 1/2 cm. (Added t.-p.: Kathie's stories. 2). 1871. Lee and Shepard.
--Kathie's Aunt Ruth, 1 of 6 vols. (Author of "In Trust."). (Illus.). (Kathie's Stories For Young People). 1882. Lee & Shepard.
--Kathie's Aunt Ruth. LC 99-20. 257p. 1898. Lee & Shepard.
--Kathie's Aunt Ruth, 1 of 6 Vols. (Illus.). (The Kathie Ser.). 1905. Lee and Shepard Company.
--Kathie's Harvest Days. (Kathie's Stories for Young People). N.D. Colby and Rich.
--Kathie's Harvest Days. LC 6-33457. 4 p. l., 7-272 p. front., plates. 16 1/2 cm. (Added t.-p.: Kathie's stories 6). 1872. Lee and Shepard.
--Kathie's Harvest Days, 1 of 6 vols. (Illus.). (Kathie's Stories for Young People). 1882. Lee & Shepard.
--Kathie's Harvest Days. LC 99-3763. 272 p. pl. 12 cm. (Kathie's stories, v. 6). 1899. Lee & Shepard.
--Kathie's Harvest Days, 1 of 6 Vols. (Illus.). (The Kathie Ser.). 1905. Lee and Shepard Company.
--Kathie's Soldiers. (Kathie's Stories for Young People). N.D. Colby and Rich.
--Kathie's Soldiers. LC 6-33456. 4 p. l., 7-262 p. front., plates. 16 1/2 cm. (Added t.-p.: Kathie's stories 4). 1872. Lee and Shepard.
--Kathie's Soldiers, 1 of 6 vols. (Illus.). (Kathie's Stories for Young People). 1882. Lee & Shepard.
--Kathie's Soldiers, 1 of 6 Vols. (Illus.). (The Kathie Ser.). 1905. Lee and Shepard Company.
--Kathie's Soldiers. (The Kathie Stories: Vol. 4). 1899. Lothrop,Lee & Shepard.
--Kathie's Stories for Young People, 6 vols. (Illus.). 1882. Set. Lee & Shepard.
--Kathie's Summer at Cedarwood. (Kathie's Stories for Young People). N.D. Colby and Rich.
--Kathie's Summer at Cedarwood. LC 6-33455. 4 p. l., vii-viii, 9-278 p. front., plates. 16 1/2 cm. (Added t.-p.: Kathie's stories. 3). 1871. Lee and Shepard.
--Kathie's Summer at Cedarwood, 1 of 6 vols. (Illus.). (Kathie's Stories For Young People). 1882. Lee & Shepard.
--Kathie's Summer at Cedarwood. 278p. 1898. Lee & Shepard.
--Kathie's Summer at Cedarwood, 1 of 6 Vols. (Illus.). (The Kathie Ser.). 1905. Lee and Shepard Company.
--Kathie's Three Wishes. (Kathie's Stories for Young People). N.D. Colby and Rich.
--Kathie's Three Wishes. LC 6-33454. 4 p. l., vii-viii, 9-260 p. front., plates. 16 1/2 cm. (Added t.-p.: Kathie's stories. 1). 1871. Lee and Shepard.
--Kathie's Three Wishes, 1 of 6 vols. (Illus.). (Kathie's Stories for Young People). 1882. Lee & Shepard.
--Kathie's Three Wishes. 260p. 1898. Lee & Shepard.
--Kathie's Three Wishes, 1 of 6 Vols. (Illus.). (The Kathie Ser.). 1905. Lee and Shepard Company.
--Larry. LC 6-33408. ix, 242 p. front. (port.) 19 cm. 1893. Lee and Shepard.
--Larry: A Prize Story. 1900. Lee & Shepard.
--A Little Girl in Old Baltimore. (The Little Girl Ser.). N.D. A. L. Burt Company.
--A Little Girl in Old Baltimore. LC 7-29566. 4 p. l., 344 p. 19 1/2 cm. (On verso of half-title: The "little girl" series). 1907. Dodd, Mead and Company.
--A Little Girl in Old Boston. (The Little Girl Ser.). N.D. A. L. Burt Company.
--A Little Girl in Old Boston. LC 98-579. 3 p. l., 372 p. 19 1/2 cm. (The "Little Girl" Series). c.1898. Dodd, Mead and Company.
--A Little Girl in Old Chicago. (The Little Girl Ser.). N.D. A. L. Burt Company.
--A Little Girl in Old Chicago. LC 4-24513. 3 p. l., 324 p. 19 1/2 cm. (Her The "little girl" series). 1904. Dodd, Mead and Company.
--A Little Girl in Old Chicago. (Phenix Ser.). N.D. Dodd, Mead & Company.
--A Little Girl in Old Detroit. (The Little Girl Ser.). N.D. A. L. Burt Co.
--A Little Girl in Old Detroit. LC 2-21991. 4 p. l., 362 p. 19 1/2 cm. (The "Little girl" series). 1902. Dodd, Mead & Company.
--A Little Girl in Old New Orleans. (The Little Girl Ser.). N.D. A. L. Burt Company.
--A Little Girl in Old New Orleans. LC 1-25423. 3 p. l., 325 p. 19 1/2 cm. ("Little Girl" Series). 1901. Dodd, Mead & Company.
--A Little Girl In Old New York. (The Little Girl Ser.). N.D. A. L. Burt Company.
--A Little Girl in Old New York. LC 6-33407. 3 p. l., 5-367 p. 19 1/2 cm. (The "little girl" series). 1896. Dodd, Mead & Company.
--A Little Girl in Old New York. (The Phenix ser.). 1896. Dodd, Mead & Co.
--A Little Girl in Old Philadelphia. (The Little Girl Ser.). N.D. A. L. Burt Company.
--A Little Girl in Old Philadelphia. LC 99-5392. vii, 371 p. 19 1/2 cm. 1899. Dodd, Mead and Company.
--A Little Girl in Old Pittsburgh. (The Little Girl Ser.). N.D. A. L. Burt Company.
--A Little Girl in Old Pittsburgh. LC 9-25634. 3 p. l., 335 p. 20 cm. (Her Little girl series). 1909. Dodd, Mead and Company.
--A Little Girl in Old Quebec. (The Little Girl Ser.). N.D. A. L. Burt Company.
--A Little Girl in Old Quebec. LC 6-34045. 311 p. 20 cm. (Her The "Little Girl" Series). 1906. Dodd, Mead.
--A Little Girl in Old Salem. (The Little Girl Ser.). N.D. A. L. Burt Company.
--A Little Girl in Old Salem. LC 8-28061. 3 p. l., 306 p. 19 1/2 cm. (Her The "Little Girl" Series). 1908. Dodd, Mead and Company.
--A Little Girl in Old San Francisco. (The Little Girl Ser.). N.D. A. L. Burt Company.
--A Little Girl in Old San Francisco. 4 p. l., 330 p. 19 1/2 cm. (Her The "little girl" series). 1905. Dodd, Mead and Company.
--A Little Girl in Old St. Louis. (The Little Girl Ser.). N.D. A. L. Burt Company.
--A Little Girl in Old St. Louis. 4 p. l., 323 p. 19 1/2 cm. (The "Little Girl" Series). 1903. Dodd, Mead & Company.
--A Little Girl in Old Washington. LC 5025. 3 p. l., 319 p. 19 1/2 cm. (The "little girl" series). 1900. Dodd, Mead and Company.
--A Little Girl of Long Ago. (The Little Girl Series). N.D. A. L. Burt Company.
--A Little Girl Ser. (The Little Girl Ser.). N.D. A. L. Burt Company.
--The Little Missionary, 1 of 12 vols. (Illus.). (Illustrated Holly-Tree Ser.: No. 4). 1905. Henry Altemus Co.
--A Little Missionary. Garber, Daniel, illus. LC 4-21663. 19 cm. 95p. 1904. H. Altemus Co.
--Lottie Eames. (The Girlhood Ser.). 1873. Lee & Shepard.
--A Modern Cinderella. LC 14-9411. 3 p. l., 297 p. front., plates. 19 1/2 cm. c.1913. M. A. Donohue & Co.
--Nelly Kinnard's Kingdom. (The Douglas Novels). 1904. Lothrop, Lee & Shepard.
--The Old Woman who Lived in a Shoe. (The Douglas Novels). N.D. Lothrop, Lee & Shepard.
--The Old Woman Who Lived in a Shoe. 1873. Shepard & Gill.
--The Old Woman Who Lived in a Shoe. 380 p. front., plates. 17 1/2 cm. 1875. W. F. Gill and Company.
--The Old Woman Who Lived In a Shoe. 400p. 1875. Wm. F. Gill & Co.
--The Red House Children at Grafton. Wyman, Louise, illus. LC 13-6894. 4 p. l., 352 p. front., plates. 19 1/2 cm. (Her Little red house series). 1913. Lothrop, Lee & Shepard Co.
--The Red House Children Growing up. Wyman, Louise, illus. LC 16-13746. vii, 346 p. incl. front. plates. 19 1/2 cm. (Her Little red house series). 1916. Lothrop, Lee & Shepard Co.
--The Red House Children's Vacation. Wyman, Louise, illus. LC 14-6287. 4 p. l., 351 p. front., plates. 19 1/2 cm. (Her Little red house series). 1914. Lothrop, Lee & Shepard Co.
--The Red House Children's Year. Wyman, Louise, illus. LC 15-800328. 4 p. l., 326 p. front., plates. 19 1/2 cm. (Her Little red house series). 1915. Lothrop, Lee & Shepard Co.
--Santa Claus Land. (Illus.). 1900. Lee & Shepard.
--Santa Claus Land. 1873. Shepard & Gill.
--Santa Claus Land. N.D. Wm. F. Gill & Co.
--Seven Daughters. (The Girlhood Ser.). 1873. Lee & Shepard.
--Seven Daughters. LC 7-1246. 369 p. incl. front. plates. 18 cm. (Maidenhood Series). 1874. Lee and Shepard.
--Seven Daughters, 1 of 30 vols. (American Girls' Ser.: No. 20). 1900. Set. Lee & Shepard.
--There's No Place Like Home. N.D. William F. Gill.
--What Charlie Found To Do. (Illus.). (Dainty Ser.). N.D. Henry Altemus Co.

Douglas, Amanda Minnie (1837-1916) & Brine, Mary D.
--Tim's Partner, and Other Stories. N.D. D. Lothrop & Co.

Douglas, Ann
--The Bald Mountain. N.D. Vantage Press.

Douglas, Barbara, retold by see Perrault, Charles (1628-1703) & Aulnoy, Marie Catherine Jumelle de Berneville.

Douglas, Barbara (1930-)
--Good as New. Brewster, Patience, illus. (ps-1). 1982. (ISBN 0-688-41983-6). (ISBN 0-688-51983-0). Lothrop.

Douglas, Betty Tomlinson
--Mr. Hoot and the Firefly. Tomlinson, Ted A., illus. LC 65-20940. vii, 37 p. illus. 22 cm. 1965. Naylor Co.

Douglas, Edith Owen
--The Witch Cake. LC 48-17792. 63 p. 23 cm. c.1947. Exposition Press.

Douglas, Emily Taft (1899-)
--Appleseed Farm. Vaughan, Anne (1913-), illus. LC 48-5822. 127 p. illus. 21 cm. 1948. Abingdon-Cokesbury Press.

Douglas, George Brisbane Scott, Sir (1856-), ed.
--Scottish Fairy and Folk Tales. (Illus.). (Fairly and Folk Tales Ser.). N.D. Charles Scribner's Sons.
--Scottish Fairy Tales. Torrance, J., illus. (The Fairy Library). N.D. A. L. Burt Co.

Douglas, Gilbert
--The Bulldog Attitude. LC 57-10552. 181 p. 21cm. 1957. Crowell.
--Hard to Tackle. LC 56-9799. 208 p. 21cm. 1956. Crowell.
--Hardnose. LC 57-5865. 213 p. 21cm. 1957. Crowell.

Douglas, Hester
--The Land Where Jesus Christ Lived: A Tale for the Young. N.D. Thomas Nelson & Sons.

Douglas, James McM., pseud., see Butterworth, William Edmund III.

Douglas, James McM., pseud. (1929-)
--Hunger for Racing. Butterworth, William Edmund III. Mott, Herb, illus. (Illus.). (Putnam Sports Shelf). (gr. 7-10). 1967. (ISBN 0-399-60271-2). Putnam Pub Group.
--A Long Ride on a Cycle. Butterworth, William Edmund III. LC 79-179379. (Illus.). 191 p. 21cm. 1972. Putnam.
--Racing to Glory. Butterworth, William Edmund III. (Illus.). 192p. (Sports Shelf Ser). (gr. 5-9). 1969. (ISBN 0-399-20193-9). Putnam.
--The Twelve Cylinder Screamer. Butterworth, William Edmund III. 1970. G P Putman's Sons.

Douglas, John Scott
--Fate of the Clipper Westwind. LC 53-8399. 250 p. 21cm. 1953. Dodd, Mead.
--Northward the Whalers Go. LC 52-10603. 230 p. 21cm. 1952. Dodd, Mead.
--The Secret of the Undersea Bell. LC 51-13649. 242 p. 21cm. 1951. Dodd, Mead.

Douglas, Julia
--Deerhurst. (Illus.). 385p. N.D. A. I. Bradley & Co.'s Pub.
--Steady and True. (Illus.). 250p. N.D. A. I. Bradley & Co.'s Pubs.

Douglas, Laura W.
--The Mystery of Crooknose. N.D. (ISBN 0-685-32935-6). Assoc Bk.

Douglas, Malcolm
--My Odd Little Folk. Rhymes and Verses About Them. With Some Others. Birch, Reginald Barthurst (1856-1943) & Hopkins, L., illus. LC 14-6561. viii, 143 p. 24 cm. c.1893. H. Altemus.

Douglas, Malcolm, jt. auth. see Cox, Palmer.

Douglas, Marian, pseud., see Robinson, Annie Douglas Green.

Douglas, Marion
--In the Poverty Year. (Illus.). (The From Nine to Twelve Ser.). N.D. Thomas Y. Crowell & Co.
--In the Poverty Year. (The "Bimbi" Series of Children's Booklets). N.D. Thomas Y. Crowell.

Douglas, Marjory Stoneman (1890-)
--Alligator Crossing: A Novel. LC 59-11428. 192p. illus. 21cm. (The Your Fair Land Ser.). 1959. J. Day Co.
--Freedom River. Shenton, Edward (1895-), illus. (Illus.). (gr. 5 up). 1953. (ISBN 0-684-20802-4). Scribner.
--Freedom River: Florida, 1845;. Shenton, Edward (1895-), illus. LC 53-12263. 264p. illus. 21cm. (Strength of the Union). 1953. Scribner.

Douglas, Mrs.
--Two Rose Trees: A Story for Girls. (Illus.). N.D. E. P. Dutton & Co.

Douglas, Penelope
--Lucie Attwell Read Me A story Pop Up Book. Attwell, Mabel Lucie (1879-1964), illus. (Illus.). (ps-3). N.D. Merry Thoughts.

Douglas, Robert Dick
--A Boy Scout in the Grizzly Country. N.D. G. P. Putnam Sons.

Douglass, Barbara (1930-)
--The Chocolate Chip Cookie Contest. Nones, Eric Jon, illus. LC 84-5682. (Illus.). 32 p. 26cm. c.1985. (ISBN 0-688-04043-8). (ISBN 0-688-04044-6). Lothrop, Lee & Shepard.
--Good As New. 1st ed. Brewster, Patience, illus. LC 80-21406. (Illus.). 32 p. 26cm. c.1982. (ISBN 0-688-41983-6). Lothrop, Lee & Shepard Books.
--The Great Town & Country Bicycle Balloon Chase. Newsom, Carol, illus. LC 83-14877. (Illus.). 32p. (gr. k-3). 1984. (ISBN 0-688-02231-6). (ISBN 0-688-02232-4). Lothrop.
--Sizzle Wheels. McLaughlin, James (1948-), illus. LC 80-39750. (Illus.). 173 p. 21cm. c.1981. (ISBN 0-664-32680-3). Westminster Press.
--Skateboard Scramble. 1st ed. Stein, Alex, illus. LC 78-12480. (Illus.). 91 p. 21cm. c.1979. (ISBN 0-664-32641-2). Westminster Press.

Douglass, Charles York (1884-) & Douglass, Harriet Walden, Mrs.
--All for the Love of Laddie: Written for Children and Those Who Love Them ... LC 15-10282. ix, 323 p. col. front., illus., plates (part col.) 21 cm. $3.00. 1915. The Knickerbocker Press.

Douglass, Harriet Walden, Mrs., jt. auth. see Douglass, Charles York.

Douty, Esther Morris (1909-1978)
--Ball in the Sky: John Wise, America's Pioneer Balloonist. 1st ed. Gorsline, Douglas Warner (1913-1985), illus. LC 56-6226. 90p. illus. 22cm. 1956. Holt.

Dow, Ethel Constance (1890-)
--The Diary of a Birthday Doll. N.D. Barse & Hopkins.
--The Diary of a Birthday Doll. Smith, Louise Clark & Nosworthy, Florence England, illus. 88p. N.D. Edward Stern & Co.
--Mother's Hero. Lyndall, Isabel, illus. (Illus.). N.D. Edward Stern & Co.
--Mother's Hero. Weber, Sarah Stilwell & Lyndall, Isabel, illus. N.D. Barse & Hopkins.
--Mother's Hero. Weber, Sarah Stilwell & Foster, John M., illus. N.D. Barse & Co.
--The Proud Roxana. Wierman, Eugenie, illus. 136p. N.D. Edward Stern & Co.

Dow, Katharine
--My Time of Year. Erhard, Walter (1920-), illus. LC 61-8582. (Illus.). (gr. k-3). 1961. (ISBN 0-8098-1073-5). Walck. **Award: (NYT).**

Dowd, Emma C
--Doodles: The Sunshine Boy. Kirk, Maria Louise (1860-), illus. LC 15-8937. vii, 1 p., 1 l., 347, 1 p., 1 l. col. front., col. plates. 18 cm. $1.00. 1915. Houghton Mifflin Company.
--The Owl and the Bobolink: Verses for Young Readers. Troth, Emma, illus. LC 14-8817. xvii p., 1 l., 175, 1 p., 1 l. front., plates. 19 1/2 cm. $1.10. 1914. Houghton Mifflin Company.
--Polly and the Princess. (Growing Literature Ser.). N.D. Grosset & Dunlap.
--Polly and the Princess. LC 17-29865. vii, 1 p., 1 l., 388, 2 p. col. front., col. plates. 20 cm. $1.35. 1917. Houghton Mifflin Company.
--Polly of Lady Gay Cottage. (Growing Literature Ser.). N.D. Grosset & Dunlap.
--Polly of Lady Gay Cottage. Deremeaux, Irma, illus. N.D. Houghton Mifflin.
--Polly of the Hospital Staff. (Growing Literature Ser.). N.D. Grosset & Dunlap.
--Polly of the Hospital Staff. Deremeaux, Irma, illus. N.D. Houghton Mifflin.
--When Polly was Eighteen. N.D. Houghton Mifflin.

--A Study in Scarlet. Bd. with The Sign of Four. (gr. 10 up). N.D. (ISBN 0-425-02838-0, S2747, Medallion). Berkley Pub.
--Study in Scarlet, and the Sign of the Four. N.D. Harper & Bros.
--Tales of Sherlock Holmes. N.D. Triangle Books.
--Tales of Sherlock Holmes. Dinnerstein, Harvey (1928-), illus. (gr. 9 up). 1963. (ISBN 0-02-732920-8). Macmillan.
--The White Company. (The Children's Favorite Ser.). N.D. Grosset & Dunlap.
--The White Company. Daugherty, James Henry (1889-1974), illus. (Harper Junior Classics Ser.). N.D. Harper & Bros.
--The White Company. Johansen, Anders D., illus. (The Father & Son Library). N.D. Sears Publishing Co.
--White Company. Wyeth, Newell Convers (1882-1945), illus. (Illustrated Classics). (gr. 7 up). N.D. McKay.

Doyle, Arthur Conan, Sir (1859-1930) & Chesterton, Gilbert Keith
--Tales of Mystery & Suspense. (gr. 9 up). 1980. Boxed Set. (ISBN 0-307-13622-1, Golden Pr). Western Pub.

Doyle, Brian (1930-)
--Up to Low. 1982. Groundwood Douglas & McIntyre. **Award: (CLA).**

Doyle, Elizabeth
--Strawberry Shortcake & the Birthday Surprise. Sustendal, Pat, illus. LC 83-8168. (Illus.). 40p. (Strawberry Shortcake Ser.). (ps-3). 1983. (ISBN 0-910313-11-3). Parker Bro.

Doyle, Emma Lyons
--Hawaiian Mother Goose: The Nonsense Rhymes of Tutu Nene. Myhre, Ethelyn, illus. Mother Goose LC 44-7833. 48 p. illus. 31 cm. 1944. Tongg Publishing Company.

Doyle, Fredric Clyde
--Smoky Ridge. Kalab, Theresa, illus. LC 44-4501. vii, 128 p. plates. 21 cm. 1944. Longmans, Green and Co.

Doyle, Martha Claire MacGowan see James, Martha, pseud.

Doyle, Martha Claire MacGowan Mrs. (1869-)
--The Boys of Pigeon Camp: Their Luck and Fun. James, Martha, pseud. Kennedy, J. W. Ferguson, illus. LC 7-27158. 3 p. l., 224 p. front., 5 pl. 20 cm. (Her Pigeon camp series). 1907. Lothrop, Lee & Shepard Co.
--The Hero of Pigeon Camp: Or, How Lucci Made Good. James, Martha, pseud. Kennedy, J. W. Ferguson, illus. 233 p. front., 5 pl. 20 cm. (Her Pigeon Camp series). 1908. Lothrop, Lee & Shepard Co.
--Jack Tenfield's Star: A Story for Boys and Some Girls. James, Martha, pseud. Copeland, Charles, illus. 325p. 1905. Lee and Shepard Company.
--Jack Tenfield's Star: A Story of Yankee Pluck. James, Martha, pseud. Copeland, Charles, illus. LC 4-21724. 20 1/2cm. 304p. 1904. Lothrop,Lee & Shepard.
--Jimmie Suter And the Boys of Pigeon Camp. James, Martha, pseud. Picknell, George W., illus. LC 6-29531. v p., 1 l., 245 p. front., 5 pl. 19 1/2 cm. (Her Pigeon camp series). 1906. Lothrop, Lee & Shepard Co.
--Little Miss Dorothy: The Wonderful Adventures of Two Little People. James, Martha, pseud. (Illus.). (The Wellesley Series for Girls). 1915. A L Burt & Co.
--My Friend Jim: A/Story of Real Boys and for them. James, Martha, pseud. Merrill, Frank Thayer (1848-), illus. LC 1-24912. 19 1/2cm. 212p. 1901. Lothrop,Lee & Shepard.
--Tom Wintstone: Wide Awake. James, Martha, pseud. Dunton, W. Herbert, illus. 234p. 1902. Lee & Shepard.
--Little Miss Dorothy: The Story of the Wonderful Adventures of Two Little People. James, Martha, pseud. Davis, J. Watson, illus. LC 1-10010. 2 p. l., iii-iv p., 1 l., 277 p. front., plates. 18 cm. 1901. A. L. Burt.

Doyle, Richard (1824-1883)
--Beauty and the Beast. Ryskamp, Charles, frwd. by. 48p. 1973. (ISBN 0-87598-042-2). The Pierpont Morgan Library.

Doyle, Richard (1824-1883), illus.
--The Doyle Fairy Book. Montalba, Anthony R., tr. Green, F. G., intro. by. N.D. Frederick A. Stokes Co.

Doyle, Robert J.
--Tuffy. Scherschel, Frank J., illus. LC 42-19357. 64 p. illus. 26 x 21 cm. 1942. Simon and Schuster.

Doyle, Tim
--Born Loser. Mooney, Thomas J., ed. Rich, Harry & Smolinski, Dick, illus. (Illus., Orig.). (Beginning Pal Paperbacks Ser.). (gr. 7-12). 1977. (ISBN 0-8374-3465-3). Xerox Ed Pubns.

Dozier, Grady
--False Echoes. 244p. (Orig.). 1984. (ISBN 0-931290-84-8). Alchemy Bks.

Dozois, Gardner Raymond, jt. ed. see Dann, Jack.

Dozois, Gardner Raymond (1947-), ed.
--Another World: Adventures in Otherness. (gr. 7 up). 1977. (ISBN 0-695-80695-5). (ISBN 0-695-40695-7). Follett.

Drady, Alan (1903-)
--Red Morton Waterboy. Hall, T. Victor, illus. LC 32-22564. 1932. Appleton Century Co.
--Rodney Newton. LC 29-21422. 5 p. l., 283 p. 19 1/2 cm. c.1929. P. J. Kenedy & Sons.
--That Cathedral Team. LC 35-22398. 5 p. l., 238 p. 19 cm. c.1935. P. J. Kenedy & Sons.

Drago, Harry Sinclair (1888-1979)
--Many Beavers: The Story of a Cree Indian Boy. Bjorklund, Lorence F. (1913-1978), illus. LC 67-2769. 126p. illus. 24cm. 1967. (ISBN 0-396-05488-9). Dodd.

Dragonet, Edward, pseud., see Williamson, Thames Ross.

Dragonwagon, Crescent see Parsons, Ellen, pseud.

Dragonwagon, Crescent (1952-)
--Always, Always. Zeldich, Arieh (1949-), illus. LC 83-22199. (Illus.). 32 p. 24cm. c.1984. (ISBN 0-02-733080-X). Macmillan.
--Coconut. Tafuri, Nancy, illus. LC 83-47691. c.1984. (ISBN 0-06-021759-6). Harper & Row.
--I Hate My Brother Harry. 1st ed. Gackenbach, Dick, illus. LC 82-47706. p. cm. c.1983. (ISBN 0-06-021757-X). (ISBN 0-06-021758-8). Harper & Row.
--If You Call My Name. Palladini, David Mario (1946-), illus. LC 78-22480. p. cm. c.1981. (ISBN 0-06-021743-X). (ISBN 0-06-021744-8). Harper & Row.
--Jemima Remembers. Howell, Troy, illus. LC 84-855. (Illus.). 32 p. 24cm. c.1984. (ISBN 0-02-733070-2). Macmillan.
--Jemina Remembers. Howell, Troy, illus. 1980. Macmillan.
--Katie in the Morning. 1st ed. Day, Betsy A., illus. LC 82-47709. p. cm. c.1983. (ISBN 0-06-021729-4). (ISBN 0-06-021730-8). Harper & Row.
--Strawberry Dress Escape. Hoban, Lillian (1925-), illus. LC 74-14074. (Illus.). 32 p. 27cm. 1975. (ISBN 0-684-13912-X). Scribner.
--When Light Turns into Night. Parker, Robert Andrew (1927-), illus. LC 74-2634. (Illus.). 32 p. 1975. (ISBN 0-06-021739-1). (ISBN 0-06-021740-5). Harper & Row.
--Will It Be Okay?. Shecter, Ben (1935-), illus. LC 76-48859. (Illus.). 32 p. 23cm. c.1977. (ISBN 0-06-021737-5). Harper & Row.
--Wind Rose. Himler, Ronald Norbert (1937-), illus. LC 75-25414. (Illus.). 32p. (ps-3). 1976. (ISBN 0-06-021741-3, HarpJ). (ISBN 0-06-021742-1). Har-Row.
--The Year It Rained: A Novel. LC 84-42980. p. cm. c.1985. (ISBN 0-02-733110-5). Macmillan.
--Your Owl Friend. Bornstein-Lercher, Ruth (1927-), illus. LC 76-58725. p. cm. c.1977. (ISBN 0-06-021731-6). (ISBN 0-06-021734-0). Harper & Row.

Dragonwagon, Crescent (1952-) & Zindel, Paul (1936-)
--To Take a Dare. LC 80-8441. 249 p. 22cm. c.1982. (ISBN 0-06-026858-1). (ISBN 0-06-026859-X). Harper & Row.

Dragoumis, Julia D.
--Tales of a Greek Island. 1912. Houghton Mifflin.
--Under Greek Skies. LC 13-22450. xxi, 305 p. col. front., plates. 20 cm. (On verso of half-title: Little schoolmates series, ed. by F. Converse). c.1913. E. P. Dutton & Company.

Dragt, Tonke
--The Towers of February: A Diary by an Anonymous (for the Time Being) Author with Added Punctuation and Footnotes. LC 75-22154. (Illus.). 251 p. 21cm. 1975. (ISBN 0-688-22044-4). (ISBN 0-688-32044-9). Morrow.

Drake
--Cavendish, And Dampier. N.D. Harper & Brothers'.

Drake, Burgess
--The Book of Lyonne. Peake, Mervyn Lawrence (1911-1968), illus. N.D. British Book Centre.

Drake, Elizabeth (1948-)
--The Last Score. LC 81-65908. 183 p. 22cm. c.1981. (ISBN 0-590-07796-1). Four Winds Press.

Drake, Emily Hopkins
--Natalie and the Brewsters. Buttera, F. J., illus. LC 31-240708. 307 p. front., 1 illus. (music) plates. 19 1/2 cm. c.1931. Lothrop, Lee & Shepard Co.

Drake, Ensign Robert L., pseud., see Hayes, Clair Wallace.

Drake, J. B., Mrs., jt. auth. see Bourhill, E. J, Mrs.

Drake, John, ed. see Stevenson, Robert Louis.

Drake, M. E., Mrs.
--Fanny's Autobiography. 278p. N.D. Pilgrim Press.

Drake, Margaret Parsons
--Bright Horizon. LC 54-7182. 256p. 21cm. 1953, c.1954. Avalon Books.

Drake, Robert L., pseud., see Hayes, Clair Wallace.

Drake, Samuel Adams (1833-1905)
--Book of New England Legends & Folk Lore. LC 76-157254. (Illus.). (gr. 9 up). 1971. (ISBN 0-8048-0990-9). C E Tuttle.
--A Book of New England Legends and Folk-lore: In Prose and Poetry. 477p. Repr. of 1901 ed. 1969 (Gale Reprints). Singing Tree Press.
--Myths and Fables of Today. 1901. Lothrop, Lee & Shepard.
--The Young Vigilantes: A Story of California Life in the Fifties. Bridgman, Lewis Jesse (1857-1931), illus. LC 4-22666. 284 p. front., 5 pl. 19 cm. 1904. Lee and Shepard.

Drake, Stan, jt. auth. see Starr, Leonard.

Drake-Brochman, H., ed. see Parker, K. Langloh.

Dralle, Elizabeth Mary (1910-)
--Angel in the Tower. Dralle, Elizabeth Mary (1910-), illus. LC 62-14956. (Illus.). 101p. (gr. 2-6). 1962. (ISBN 0-374-30330-4). FS&G.

Drama League of America
--Plays for Children. Oglebay, Kate, ed. LC 15-5526. 16 p. 19 1/2 cm. $0.2. 1915. Rogers & Hall, Printers.

Drama League of America & Alden, Alice Wight (1865-)
--Dickon Goes to the Fair And Other Plays. BEst, A. Starr, Mrs., intro. by. xi p., 2 l., 17-204 p./19 1/2 cm. (The Drama league junior play series Contains music.). c.1927. George H. Doran Company.

Dranow, Ralph
--The Woman Who Knocked out Sugar Ray. Darlington, Sandy & Reynolds, Julie, eds. Reynolds, Julie, illus. LC 81-70081. (Illus.). 192p. (Orig.). 1982. (ISBN 0-9604152-5-4). Arrowhead Pr.

Draper, jt. auth. see Hunt.

Draper, Cena Christopher (1907-)
--Dandy and the Mystery of the Locked Room. Minnis, Pat Burrows, illus. LC 73-90492. (Illus.). 224 p. 22cm. 1974. (ISBN 0-8309-0114-0). Independence Press.
--Papa Says: The Story of My Sister Bianca. LC 56-5244. 222p. 22cm. c.1956. Liveright Pub. Corp.
--Ridge Willoughby. Rice, Elizabeth (1913-), illus. LC 52-9975. 119 p. illus. 24 cm. 1952. Steck Co.
--Rim of the Ridge. Weiss, Emil (1896-1965), illus. LC 65-15263. 157 p. illus. 21 cm. 1965. Criterion Books.
--The Worst Hound Around. LC 78-25687. 115 p. 21cm. c.1979. (ISBN 0-664-32643-9). Westminster Press.

Draper, Delores
--The Doll Book. Ike, Jane Hori, illus. (Illus.). (gr. k-2). 1977. (ISBN 0-307-68917-4, Golden Pr). Western Pub.

Draper, Edythe
--Wonder. 448p. (gr. 1-4). 1984. (ISBN 0-8423-8385-9). Tyndale.

Draper, Kate, jt. auth. see Charnin, Martin Jay.

Dravich, Jay
--Dreams of Cloud Dancing. 1st ed. Gullikson, Karen, illus. LC 82-90408. (Illus.). 156 p. 23cm. c.1982. (ISBN 0-9604258-2-9). (ISBN 0-9604258-3-7). Tari Book Publishers.
--Tales for a Child's Heart. Bernard, Lisa, illus. LC 80-50009. (Illus.). 121 p. 24cm. c.1980. Tari Book Publishers.

Drawbaugh, Susan M.
--What Pet Will I Get?. LC 77-83881. 1977. (ISBN 0-89430-017-2). Palos Verdes.

Drawson, Blair (1943-)
--Do Something Special on Your Birthday. (ps-3). N.D. (ISBN 0-590-05799-5, Schol Pap). Scholastic Inc.
--I Like Hats. (ps-3). N.D. (ISBN 0-590-05800-2, Schol Pap). Scholastic Inc.

Drayson, Alfred Wilks (1827-1901)
--The Gentleman Cadet. (Illus.). N.D. E. P. Dutton & Co.

Drayton, Grace Gebbie (1877-)
--Baby Bears. N.D. The Century Co.
--Bettina's Bonnet. (Illus.). (The Kiddie Ser.). 1915. Harper & Brothers.
--Bunny's Birthday. (Illus.). (The Kiddie Ser.). N.D. Harper & Brothers.
--G. G. Drayton's Jumble Book. (Illus.). (The Kiddie Ser.). N.D. Harper & Brothers.

Drazin, Judith
--Stage Fever. 94p. (gr. 7-10). 1984. (ISBN 0-241-11073-4, Pub. by Hamish Hamilton England). David & Charles.

Draznin, Boris
--Marshmellowterra: The Land of Marshmallow People & Whimsical Animals. Green, Bruce, illus. (Illus.). 96p. (gr. 7-12). 1982. (ISBN 0-682-49914-5). Exposition.

Drdek, Richard E
--The Game. LC 68-14182. 142 p. 22cm. 1968. Doubleday.
--Horace the Friendly Octopus. Veno, Joseph, illus. LC 65-9787. 128 p. col. illus. 24 cm. 1965. Allyn and Bacon.
--Lefty's Boy. LC 76-78699. 204 p. 22cm. 1969. Doubleday.
--Street Dog. Crichlow, Ernest T. (1914-), illus. LC 68-1882. (Illus.). 24cm. 48p. (Carousel Book). 1967. L. W. Singer Co.

Drdek, Richard E & Hansen, Mary Lewis (1933-)
--Fields and Fences. Sheldon, William D., ed. (Illus.). 223 p. 24cm. (Sheldon basic reading series. Centennial ed.). 1968. Allyn and Bacon.
--Town and Country. Sheldon, William D., ed. (Illus.). 254 p. 24cm. (Sheldon basic reading series. Centennial ed.). 1968. Allyn and Bacon.

Dreany, E. Joseph
--Bible Stories from the Old Testamemt. 1960. Maxton Pub Corp.
--Indians in Pop-up Action Pictures. LC 51-7236. unpaged. illus. 27 cm. N.D. Maxton Publishers.

Dreger, Georgia E
--A Different Dream. Woodson, Jack, pseud. (1913-), illus. Woodson, John Waddie Jr. LC 81-67750. (Illus.). 96 p. 20cm. c.1982. (ISBN 0-8054-4806-3). Broadman Press.

Dreifus, Miriam W
--Brave Betsy. Greenwald, Sheila, pseud. (1934-), illus. Green, Sheila Ellen. LC 61-8000. (Illus.). 46 p. 23cm. 1961. Putnam.
--Timmy Gets His Horse. Teichman, Dorothy, illus. LC 61-5689. (Illus.). 44 p. 23cm. 1961. Putnam.

Dreiser, Theodore Herman Albert (1871-1945)
--The "Genius". LC 23-12168. x p., 2 l., 9-736 p. 20 cm. c.1923. Boni and Liveright.
--Sister Carrie. Simpson, Claude Mitchell (1910-1976), ed. LC 59-1819. (gr. 9 up). 1959. (ISBN 0-395-05134-7, RivEd). HM.

Drennan, G. D., retold by.
--Peter Pan: Retold In Story Form From J. M. Barrie's Play. N.D. Barse & Hopkins.

Dresbach, Elsa (1907-)
--Beasties. Day, Maurice (1892-), illus. LC 52-17540. 64 p. illus. 19 cm. 1951. Pacific Books.

Drescher, Henrik
--Looking for Santa Claus. LC 84-4419. (Illus.). 32p. (ps-1). 1984. (ISBN 0-688-02997-3). (ISBN 0-688-02999-X). Lothrop.
--Rudy and Buster and the Look-Alikes. LC 85-225. p. cm. 1985. (ISBN 0-688-05816-7). (ISBN 0-688-05817-5). Lothrop, Lee & Shepard Books.
--Simon's Book. Drescher, Henrik, illus. LC 82-24931. (Illus.). 36 p. 26cm. c.1983. (ISBN 0-688-02085-2). Lothrop, Lee & Shepard Books. **Award: (NYT).**
--The Strange Appearance of Howard Cranebill, Jr. Drescher, Henrik, illus. LC 82-71. (Illus.). 33 p. 25cm. c.1982. (ISBN 0-688-00961-1). (ISBN 0-688-00962-X). Lothrop, Lee & Shepard. **Award: (NYT).**

Drescher, Joan Elizabeth, jt. auth. see Bartoli, Jennifer.

Drescher, Joan Elizabeth (1939-)
--I'm in Charge. LC 81-8225. (Illus.). 32 p. c.1981. (ISBN 0-316-19330-5). Little, Brown.
--The Marvelous Mess. Drescher, Joan Elizabeth (1939-), illus. LC 79-25949. (Illus.). 32 p. 1980. (ISBN 0-395-29160-7). Houghton Mifflin.
--Max and Rufus. Drescher, Joan Elizabeth (1939-), illus. LC 82-3061. (Illus.). 32 p. 1982. (ISBN 0-395-32435-1). Houghton Mifflin.

Dreslov, Aksel
--A Rivera, A Town, A Poet: A Walk Together With Hans Christian Andersen. 149p. 1962. Dufour Editions.
--The Singing Chameleon. 1963. Dufour Editions.
--Where The Leopard Passes: "Here is A Magnificent Children's Book, & An African One.". Hawkins, Sheila (1905-), illus. 134p. 1963. Dufour Editions.

Dresser, Elizabeth, jt. auth. see Gulick, Peggy.

Dressler, Marie
--The Life Story of an Ugly Duckling. N.D. Robert M McBride.

Dressman, John (1947-)
--On the Cliffs of Acoma: A Pueblo Story with a Short History Acoma. LC 83-20177. 1984. (ISBN 0-86534-021-8). Sunstone Press.

Drew, Elizabeth A. (1887-1965) & Joseph, Michael (1897-), eds.
--Puss in Books: A Collection of Stories About Cats. Wheelan, Albertine Randall (1863-), illus. LC 32-35923. xv, 1, 275 p. front., plates. 21 cm. 1932. Dodd, Mead & Company.

Drew, Louise, illus.
--In the Morning: Twenty Bible Verses. N.D. Abingdon Press.

Drew, Mina P., jt. auth. see Barr, Henrietta C.

Drew, Patricia Mary (1938-)
--Spotter Puff. Drew, Patricia Mary (1938-), illus. (Illus.). 30p. 1st U.S. edition. (gr. k-3). 1979. (ISBN 0-7011-5053-X, Pub. by Chatto Bodley Jonathan). Merrimack Pub Cir.

Drewe, Beatrice
--Toby & the Aqualung. (Illus.). 1975. (ISBN 0-685-86601-7). State Mutual Bk.
--Toby & the Treasure. (Illus.). 1976. (ISBN 0-685-86602-5). State Mutual Bk.

AUTHOR INDEX

DUBANEVICH, ARLENE

Drewery, Mary (1918-)
--Devil in Print. Stobbs, William (1914-), illus. LC 66-116886. 216p. illus., map. 21cm. 1st U.S. edition. 1966, c.1963. McKay.
--Hamid and the Palm Sunday Donkey. Gray, Reginald S., illus. LC 67-26848. (Illus.). 22cm. 124p. 1st U.S. edition. 1968, c.1967. Hastings.
Drezy, Baroness Emmuska see Orczy, Emma Magdelena Rosalia Maria Josefa Barbara.
Driggs, Howard Roscoe (1873-)
--Ben, the Wagon Boy. LC 44-534483. vii, 108 p. incl. col. front., illus. 23 1/2 cm. 1944. Stevens & Wallis.
--George, the Handcart Boy. 1st ed. Hales, J. Rulon, illus. LC 52-12499. 20cm. 1952. Alladin Books.
--Jacko and the Dingo Boy. Palmer, Herman, illus. LC 24-221202. 5 p. l., 109 p. col. illus. 20 cm. 1924. The University Publishing Company.
--Nick Wilson: Pioneer Boy Among the Indians. 1st ed. Bjorklund, Lorence F. (1913-1978), illus. LC 51-12429. 88 p. illus. 20 cm. 1951. Aladdin Books.
--Nick Wilson: Pioneer Boy Among the Indians. Bjorklund, Lorence F. (1913-1978), illus. N.D. E. P. Dutton & Co.
--Pitch Pine Tales. 1st ed. Bjorklund, Lorence F. (1913-1978), illus. LC 51-3815. ix, 101 p. illus. 20 cm. 1951. Aladdin Books.
--Pitch Pine Tales. Bjorklund, Lorence F. (1913-1978), illus. N.D. E. P. Dutton & Co.
--The Pony Express Goes Through. Jackson, William H., illus. N.D. J. B. LIppincott Co.
--When Grandfather Was a Boy: Stories. Hales, J. Rulon, illus. LC 57-408515. 88p. illus. 24cm. 1957. Deseret Book Co.
Driggs, Howard Roscoe (1873-) & King, Sara S.
--Rise of the Lone Star. Deming, Edwin Willard (1860-1942), illus. N.D. J. B. Lippincott Co.
Driggs, Laurence La Tourette (1876-)
--The Adventures of Arnold Adair, American Ace. Watson, Henry S., illus. LC 18-9775. 1918. Little Brown & Co.
--Arnold Adair with the English Aces: Being the Further Flying Adventures of an American Aviator. Watson, Henry S., illus. LC 22-19054. 5 p. l., 321 p. front., plates. 19 1/2 cm. $1.7. 1922. Little, Brown, and Company.
--Heroes of Aviation. N.D. Little Brown & Co.
--On Secret Air Service. N.D. Little Brown & Co.
Drillien, Berengere, tr. see Margueritte, Paul (1860-1918) & Margueritte, Victor.
Drillien, Berengere, tr. see Mille, Pierre.
Drinan, Neil
--Seven Tales of the Forstranan. Beresford, Alexandra, illus. LC 80-112763. (Illus.). 64 p. 27cm. c.1979. (ISBN 0-89742-019-5). Dawne-Leigh Publications.
Drinkwater, Jennie Maria see Conklin, Jennie Maria Drinkwater.
Drinkwater, John (1882-1937), ed.
--All About Me: Poems for a Child. Brock, Henry Matthew (1875-1960), illus. LC 28-22486. 104 p. illus. 21 cm. 1928. Houghton Mifflin Company.
--More About Me: Poems for a Child. Brock, Henry Matthew (1875-1960), illus. LC 33-333072. 109, 1 p. illus. 21 cm. 1930. Houghton Mifflin Company.
--The Way of Poetry. LC 73-116399. 272 p. 21cm. (Granger index reprint Series). 1970, c.1922. Books for Libraries Press.
--The Way of Poetry: An Anthology for Younger Readers. LC 22-19944. xxx p., 1 l., 240 p. 19 1/2 cm. 1922. Houghton Mifflin Company.
Driscoll, Charles Benedict (1885-)
--Doubloons: The Story of Buried Treasure. Cimino, Harry, illus. N.D. Farrar & Rinehart.
--Driscoll's Book of Pirates. Amory, Montfort, illus. LC 34-38323. (Illus.). 23cm. 124p. 1934. David M. Mc.Kay Co.
--Treasure Aboard. Amory, Montfort, illus. LC 31-29817. 5 p. l., 3-272 p. col. front., illus. 21 cm. c.1931. Farrar & Rinehart, Incorporated.
Driscoll, James R.
--The Brighton Boys at Chateau-Thierry. (The Brighton Boys Ser.). N.D. John C. Winston.
--The Brighton Boys at St. Mihiel. (The Brighton Boys Ser.). N.D. John C. Winston.
--The Brighton Boys in the Argonne Forest. (The Brighton Boys Ser.). N.D. John C. Winston.
--The Brighton Boys in the Flying Corps. (The Brighton Boys Ser.). N.D. John C. Winston.
--The Brighton Boys in the Radio Service. (The Brighton Boys Ser.). N.D. John C. Winston.
--The Brighton Boys in the Submarine Fleet. LC 18-105370. 256 p. incl. front. plates. 19 cm. (His The Brighton boys series). 1918. The John C. Winston Company.
--The Brighton Boys in the Submarine Treasure Ship. (The Brighton Boys Ser.). N.D. John C. Winston.
--The Brighton Boys in the Trenches. (The Brighton Boys Ser.). N.D. John C. Winston.
--The Brighton Boys in Transatlantic Flight. (The Brighton Boys Ser.). N.D. John C. Winston.
--The Brighton Boys with the Battle Fleet. (The Brighton Boys Ser.). N.D. John C. Winston.
--The Brighton Boys with the Engineers at Cantigny. (The Brighton Boys Ser.). N.D. John C. Winston.
Driver, Olive Elizabeth Wagner (1905-)
--The Christmas Story: Told in Verse. Driver, Olive Elizabeth Wagner (1905-), illus. LC 51-12331. unpaged. illus. 29 cm. 1951. Exposition Press.
Driz, Ovsei Ovseevich (1908-1971) & Neugroschel, Joachim
--The Boy and the Tree. LC 78-4119. p. cm. 1978. (ISBN 0-13-080929-2). Prentice-Hall.
Drizari, Nelo (1900-)
--Four Seas to Dreamland: The Autobiography of an Albanian Boy on Horseback. LC 76-365077. v. 139 p. 23cm. (Illyrian saga book). c.1969. Publication Research Features.
Dromgoole, William Allen, Miss (1860-1934)
--The Best of Friends. (Illus.). (Cosy Corner Ser.). N.D. L. C. Page & Co.
--A Boy's Battle. (Illus.). (Every Boy's Library). N.D. Caldwell.
--A Boy's Battle, 1 of 25 vols. (Illus.). (The Young of Heart Ser.: No. 8). N.D. Set. Dana Estes & Co.
--A Boy's Battle. (Children's Hour Series.). N.D. Dodge Publishing Co.
--A Boy's Battle. LC 98-142. 91 p. incl. 4 pl. front. 19 cm. (On verse of half-title: The young of heart series, 8). 1898. Estes & Lauriat.
--The Faffier's Dog and His Fellows. Sacker, Amy M., illus. (Cosy corner ser.). N.D. L. C. Page & Co.
--The Farrier's Dog and His Fellow. Sacker, Amy M., illus. LC 12-31943. 5 p. l., 75 p. front., illus. 18 1/2 cm. 1897. L.C. Page and Company (Incorporated).
--The Fortunes of the Fellow. (Cosy Corner Ser.). N.D. L. C. Page & Co.
--The Fortunes of the Fellow: A Companion Book to The Farrier's Dog and His Fellow. LC 98-860. 122 p. incl. front., illus., plates. 18 1/2 cm. 1898. L. C. Page and Company (Incorporated).
--Harum Scarem Joe. (Illus.). (Every Boy's Library). N.D. Dodge Publishing cp.
--Harum Scarum Joe. (Illus.). (Every Boy's Library). N.D. Caldwell.
--Harum-Scarum Joe. Meynelle, Louis, illus. LC 99-3345. 77 p. incl. front., plates. 19 cm. (On verse of half-title: The young of heart series. v. 17). 1899. D. Estes & Company.
--Hero-Chums. (Illus.). (Every Boy's Library). N.D. Caldwell.
--Hero-Chums, 1 of 25 vols. (Illus.). (The Young of Heart Ser.: No. 1). N.D. Set. Dana Estes & Co.
--Hero-Chums. LC 12-31942. 147 p. incl. front., 4 pl. 19 cm. 1898. Estes and Lauriat.
--A Moonshiner's Son. (The Vacation Ser.). N.D. Penn.
--A Moonshiner's Son. (Adventure Stories for Boys). N.D. Penn.
--A Moonshiner's Son. (The Outdoor Bks.). N.D. Penn Publishing Co.
--A Moonshiner's Son. Carter, F. A., illus. (Illus.). (The Little People's Ser.). N.D. Penn Publishing Co.
--Rare Old Chums. (Illus.). (Editha Ser.). N.D. Caldwell.
--Rare Old Chums. (Illus.). (Editha Series.). N.D. Dodge Publishing Co.
--Rare Old Chums. Barry, Etheldred Breeze (1870-), illus. LC 98-1499. 99 p. incl. 5 pl. front. 19 cm. (On verse of half-title: The young of heart series, v. 5). 1898. D. Estes & Company.
--Rare Old Chums. Barry, Etheldred Breeze (1870-), illus. (The Cosy Corner Ser.). N.D. L C Page & Co.
--Three Little Crackers from Down in Dixie. Barry, Etheldred Breeze (1870-), illus. LC 98-1204. 249 p. incl. front., illus., plates. 20 cm. 1898. L. C. Page and Company.
Drown, Lessie Mae
--School Days. Nye, Vernon Paul, illus. LC 46-406. 159 p. illus. 21 cm. 1945. Review and Herald Publishing Association.
Drowne, Tatiana Balkoff, tr. see Ershov, Petr Pavlovich.
Drowne, Tatiana Balkoff (1913-)
--But Charlie Wasn't Listening. Meredith, Helen (1913-), illus. LC 60-4735. 30p. illus. (part col.) 21x26cm. c.1960. Pantheon Books.
--I Am from Siam. Meredith, Helen (1913-), illus. LC 61-3401. (Illus.). (gr. k-3). 1961. (ISBN 0-394-91271-3). Pantheon.
--Little Magic Horse. Bock, Vera, illus. N.D. Macmillan.
--Take Wing!. Meredith, Helen (1913-), illus. (Illus.). 40 p. 1963. Viking Press.
Druce, Robert
--Eye of Innocence: Children & Their Poetry. (gr. 3 up). 1965. Verry.
Drucker, Boris
--Henrietta. Drucker, Boris, illus. LC 65-22827. 1v. (unpaged) (chiefly col. illus.) 19x21cm. (ps-3). c.1965. Abelard.
Drukker, Hazel see Silberman, Hazel Lenore Drukker, Mrs.
Drummond, Henry (1851-1897)
--Baxter's Second Innings: A Book for Boys. LC 12-31885. 19cm. 32p. 1892. James Pott.
--The Greatest thing in the World. N.D. Branden Press.
--The Lowell Lectures on the Ascent of Man. Wain, Louis, illus. LC 4-168360. xi, 346 p. 20 cm. 1894. J. Pott & Co.
--The Monkey that Would Not Kill. Lenski, Lois (1893-1974), illus. LC 29-26904. (Illus.). 19cm. vii, 91p. 1929. Dodd, Mead & Company.
--The Monkey That Would Not Kill. Wain, Louis, illus. LC 4-16836. 6 p. l., 115 p. incl. 15 pl. front. 18 1/2 cm. 1898. Dood, Mead and Company.
Drummond, Mrs.
--Emily Vernon. (Carters' Fireside Library). N.D. Robert Carter & Brothers.
Drummond, Susan (1933-)
--The Grinnies' Secret: Story and Pictures. LC 81-11192. p. cm. c.1981. (ISBN 0-933114-09-5). (ISBN 0-933114-08-7). Red Hen Press.
Drummond, Violet Hilda (1911-)
--The Charming taxicab. Drummond, Violet Hilda (1911-), illus. N.D. Transatlantic Arts, Inc.
--The Flying Postman. Drummond, Violet Hilda (1911-), illus. LC 64-14149. 1 v. (unpaged) illus. (part col.) 27 cm. 1964. Constable Young Books, New York, H. Z. Walck.
--The Flying Postman. Drummond, Violet Hilda (1911-), illus. 1948. Houghton Mifflin Co.
--The Flying Postman. Drummond, Violet Hilda (1911-), illus. LC 49-7589. 48 p. col. illus. 23 cm. (Porpoise books). 1948. Penguin Books.
--Miss Anna Truly. Drummond, Violet Hilda (1911-), illus. LC 49-5471. 38 p. col. illus. 23 cm. 1949. Houghton Mifflin Co.
--Mr. Finche's Pet Shop. Drummond, Violet Hilda (1911-), illus. LC 54-7769. 1954. Oxford University Press.
--Mrs. Easter and the Storks. Drummond, Violet Hilda (1911-), illus. LC 59-12790. (Illus.). 26cm. 31p. 1960. A. S. Barnes & Co. **Award: (KGM).**
--Mrs. Easter's Parasol. Drummond, Violet Hilda (1911-), illus. (Illus.). (ps-5). N.D. (ISBN 0-571-11134-3). Faber & Faber.
--Phewtus the Squirrel. Drummond, Violet Hilda (1911-), illus. LC 67-90193. 48p. col. front., col. illus. 25cm. 1966. Constable Young Bks.
--Phewtus the Squirrel. Drummond, Violet Hilda (1911-), illus. LC 39-32123. 32p. 1939. Oxford University Press.
--Phewtus the Squirrel. rev. ed. Drummond, Violet Hilda (1911-), illus. (Illus.). (ps-1). 1966. Verry.
Druon, Maurice Samuel Roger Charles (1918-)
--Tistou of the Green Thumb. New, Revised. Duheme, Jacqueline, illus. Hare, Humphrey, tr. (Illus.). LC 58-11642. 178 p. 21cm. (gr. 4 up). 1958. (ISBN 0-684-20803-2). Scribner. **Award: (ALA).**
Drury, John, jt. auth. see Drury, Maxine Cole.
Drury, John (1918-) & Drury, Maxine Cole (1914-)
--Danger Afloat. LC 51-13994. 158 p. illus. 21 cm. 1951. Nelson.
--The Rosemont Riddle. Galdone, Paul (1914-), illus. LC 53-7242. 191p. 22cm. 1953. T. Nelson.
Drury, Lola Ross & Bush, Paine L.
--For Love of Liberty. Blair, Lois, illus. LC 40-348731. 2 p. l., 346 p. illus. 20 cm. c.1940. Mathis, Van Nort & Company.
Drury, Maxine Cole see Creighton, Don, pseud.
Drury, Maxine Cole, jt. auth. see Drury, John.
Drury, Maxine Cole (1914-)
--George and the Long Rifle. Stein, Harve (1904-), illus. LC 57-10525. (Illus.). 117 p. 21cm. 1957. Longmans, Green.
--Glory for Gil. LC 64-11512. 184 p. 22cm. 1964. D. McKay Co.
--Half A Team. McCann, Gerald (1916-), illus. 1960. David McKay Company Inc.
--Half a Team. 1st ed. McCann, Gerald (1916-), illus. LC 60-11977. (Illus.). 21cm. 184p. 1960. Longmans, Green.
--Liberty Boy. Bock, Vera, illus. LC 67-28222. (Illus.). vi, 218 p. 21cm. 1967. D. McKay Co.
--Marty and the Major. 1st ed. Manget, Jeanne C., illus. LC 55-51852. 150p. illus. 21cm. c.1955. Little,Brown.
--Two Princes, One Witch, & Miss Katie O'Flynn. (ps-3). 1969. (ISBN 0-13-935106-X). P-H.
Drury, Maxine Cole (1914-) & Drury, John (1918-)
--A Career for Carol. Caddell, Foster (1921-), illus. LC 58-8937. (Illus.). 216 p. 22cm. 1958. Longmans, Green.
Drury, Roger Wolcott (1914-)
--The Champion of Merrimack County. Wegner, Fritz (1924-), illus. 1976. Little.
--The Finches' Fabulous Furnace. Blegvad, Erik (1923-), illus. LC 71-129909. (Illus.). 149 p. 22cm. 1971. Little, Brown.
Druzhkov, Y.
--The Adventures of Pencil & Screwbolt. 135p. 1973. (ISBN 0-8285-1097-0, Pub. by Progress Pubs USSR). Imported Pubns.
Dr. Who (Television Program), jt. auth. see Whitaker, David.
Dryden, Cecil Pearl (1887-)
--By Sea on the Tonquin. 1956. LC 56-[illegible] 634p. diagrs. 21cm. 1956. Caxton Republication of the Report.
--Mr. Hunt and the Fabulous Plan. Driessen, Beatrice, illus. LC 58-5325. (Illus.). 343 p. 22cm. 1958. Caxton Printers.
Dryer, Marion M
--Snoopy Gets a Name. Gehr, Mary, illus. LC 46-7449. 32 p. incl. front., illus. (part col.) 26 cm. 1946. The Children's Company.
Drysdale, Walter Gow
--Tommy Knockers: Folklore of the Gold Mines. 1st ed. Rice, George E, Jr., illus. LC 76-14328. (Illus.). iii, 66, 3 p. 22cm. c.1976. A. H. Drysdale.
Drysdale, William (1852-1901)
--The Beach Patrol. New ed. 318p. (Brain and Brawn Ser.). 1930. W. A. Wilde Co.
--The Beach Patrol. Copeland, Charles, illus. 318p. (Brain and Brawn Ser.). c.1897. W. A. Wilde.
--Cadet Standish of the St. Louis. 354p. (Brain and Brawn Ser.). 1910. W. A. Wilde Co.
--Cadet Standish of the St. Louis: A Story of Our Naval Campaign in Cuban Waters. Burgess, H., illus. LC 99-19559. 354 p. front., plates. 20 cm. c.1899. W. A. Wilde & Company.
--The Fast Mail: The Story of a Train Boy. Copeland, Charles, illus. LC 7-18996. 328 p. front., plates. 19 1/2 cm. (Half-title: Brain and brawn series). c.1896. W. A. Wilde & Company.
--The Mystery of Abel Forefinger. LC 7-18995. 3 p. l., 208 p. front., plates. 19 cm. 1894. Harper & Brothers.
--Pine Ridge Plantation. (Illus.). (Crowell's Young People Ser.). N.D. Thomas Y. Crowell.
--The Treasury Club. (Illus.). 330p. 1910. W. A. Wilde & Co.
--The Treasury Club: A Story of the Treasury Department, Illustrating How Important a Factor Is Money in Our National Life. Copeland, Charles, illus. LC 5027. 1 p. l., 5-330 p. front., plates 19 1/2 cm. (United States government series). c.1900. W. A. Wilde Company.
--The Young Consul. (Illus.). 356p. 1910. W. A. Wilde Co.
--The Young Consul: A Story of the Department of State. Copeland, Charles, illus. LC 1-31431. 356 p. front., plates. 20 cm. (On verso of half-title: The United States government series). c.1901. W. A. Wilde Company.
--The Young Reporter. 300p. (Brain and Brawn Ser.). 1910. W. A. Wilde Co.
--The Young Reporter: A Story of Printing House Square. Copeland, Charles, illus. LC 7-18994. 298 p. front., plates. 19 1/2 cm. (Half-title: Brain and brawn series). 1895. W. A. Wilde & Company.
--The Young Supercargo: A Story of the Merchant Marine. 352p. (Brain and Brawn Ser.). 1910. W. A. Wilde Co.
--The Young Supercargo: A Story of the Merchant Marine. Copeland, Charles, illus. LC 98-14. 352 p. front., plates. 20 cm. (Half-title: Brain and brawn series). c.1898. W. A. Wilde & Company.
D.S.C & S.C.D
--The Young Pupil's Keepsake. LC 14-22484. 4 p. l., 9-72 p. 16 cm. 1861. J. Munroe and Company.
Duane, Diane
--Deep Wizardry. LC 84-15566. (Illus.). 272 p., 1 p. of plates. 22cm. c.1985. (ISBN 0-385-29373-9). Delacorte.
--So You Want to be a Wizard. (gr. 5-9). 1983. (ISBN 0-385-29305-4). Delacorte.
Duane, Mary Morris
--Barn Yard Ditties. Page, Gilbert, illus. LC 38-96. 3 p. l., 38p. illus. 23 1/2cm. c.1937. Chapman & Grimes.
Duarte, Margarida E.
--Legend of the Palm Tree. (gr. 4-6). N.D. (ISBN 0-448-02970-7). G&D.
Dubanevich, Arlene
--Pig William. Dubanevich, Arlene, illus. LC 85-5776. p. cm. 1985. (ISBN 0-02-733200-4). Bradbury Press.

--Pigs in Hiding. Dubanevich, Arlene, illus. LC 83-1409. (Illus.). 32p. (ps-1). 1983. (ISBN 0-590-07872-0, Four Winds). (ISBN 0-590-07872-0). Scholastic Inc.

DuBay, W.

--The Trap. Spiegle, Dan, illus. (Illus.). 24p. (Masters of the Universe Storybooks). (gr. k-3). 1983. (ISBN 0-307-11795-2, Golden Pr). Western Pub.

Dubelaar, Thea

--Maria. Post, Mance, illus. LC 82-2134. (Illus.). 154 p. 21cm. 1982. Morrow.

Dubkin, Lois Knudson (1911-)

--Quiet Street. Palmer, Juliette (1930-), illus. LC 63-7998. (Illus.). unpaged. 27cm. c.1963. Abelard-Schuman.

DuBois, Elizabeth

--Wally's Summer. (gr. k-2). N.D. Carlton.

Dubois, Frances, jt. auth. see Dubois, Gertrude.

Du Bois, Gaylord

--Barry Blake of the Flying Fortress. White, J. R., illus. LC 43-22854. 2 p. l., 9-248 p. illus. 20 1/2 cm. (Fighters for freedom series). 1943. Whitman Publishing Company.

--The Lone Ranger. Laune, Paul Sidney (1899-), illus. LC 37-5757. v, 218p. front. 19cm. c.1937. Grosset & Dunlap.

--The Long Rider and the Treasure of Vanished Men. Vallely, Henry E., illus. LC 46-78807. 2 p. l., 9-248 p. illus. 20 1/2 cm. 1946. Whitman Publishing Company.

--The Pony Express. Fletcher, Sydney E., illus. LC 44-8196. 32p. illus. (part. col) 23cm. c.1944 (Artists & Writers Guild). Grosset & Dunlap.

DuBois, Gaylord, jt. auth. see Lebeck, Oskar.

DuBois, Gaylord, adapted by see Disney, Walter Elias.

DuBois, Gaylord, adapted by see Stevenson, Robert Louis.

Dubois, Gertrude & Dubois, Frances

--Peter and Penny Plant a Garden. LC 36-198271. x, p., 1 l., 210 p. incl. front., illus. 20 cm. 1936. Frederick A. Stokes Company.

--Peter and Penny Plant a Garden. Lawson, Marie Abrams (1894-1956), illus. 1936. J. B. Lippincott Co.

Du Bois, Mary Constance (1879-)

--Captain Madeleine. Berger, William Merritt (1872-), illus. LC 28-21184. 6 p. l., 3-276 p. front., plates. 19 1/2 cm. $1.7. 1928. The Century Co.

--Comrade Rosalie. Rahn, A. D., illus. LC 19-14911. 6 p. l., 3-473 p. front., plates 19 1/2 cm. 1919. The Century Co.

--Elinor Arden, Royalist. Renda, W., illus. LC 4-27355. 6 p. l., 283 p. incl. front., plates, ports. 20 cm. 1904. The Century Co.

--The Girls of Old Glory. Rahn, A. D., illus. LC 18-17612. 6 p. l., 3-422 p. front., plates. 19 1/2 cm. 1918. The Century Co.

--The Lass of the Silver Sword. Relyea, Charles M., illus. LC 9-26142. ix, 418 p. incl. 21 pl. front. 20 cm. 1909. The Century Co.

--The League of the Signet Ring. Relyea, Charles M., illus. LC 10-216381. 6 p. l., 3-391 p. incl. plates. front. 20 cm. $1.5. 1910. The Century Co.

--Mother's Story Box. LC 33-29996. 171 p. front., illus. 21 cm. c.1933. The Abingdon Press.

--Patsy of the Pet Shop. Caddy, Alice, pseud. (1896-1977), illus. Burman, Alice Caddy. LC 37-20063. xi p., 1 l., 242 p. incl. front., illus., plates. 20 cm. 1937. D. Appleton-Century Company Incorporated.

--Shadow Cove Mystery. Parks, Elise, illus. LC 40-4718. xi p., 1 l., 310 p. incl. front., illus. 20 cm. 1940. D. Appleton-Century Company, Incorporated.

--White Fire. Relyea, Charles M., illus. LC 23-124350. 6 p. l., 3-475 p. front., plates. 19 1/2 cm. 1923. The Century Co.

Dubois, Rochelle Lynn Holt (1879-)

--A Legend in His Time. Sheppard, Susan, illus. (Illus., Orig.). (gr. 8-10). 1979. (ISBN 0-934536-01-5). Merging Media.

DuBois, Shirley Graham see Graham, Shirley, pseud.

Du Bois, Shirley Graham (1907-1977)

--The Story of Pocahontas. Meadowcroft, Enid La Monte (1898-1966), ed. Cooper, Mario (1905-), illus. LC 52-13749. (Illus.). 22cm. 180p. (Signature Books: No. 21). 1953. Grosset & Dunlap.

DuBois, Theodora McCormick (1890-)

--Banjo the Crow. Torrey, Helen (1901-), illus. LC 43-464728. 4 p. l., 141, 1 p. front., illus. 24 1/2 cm. 1943. Houghton Mifflin Company.

--Diana Can Do It. LC 37-19882. 212p. illus. 22cm. 1937. Houghton Mifflin.

--Diana's Feathers. LC 35-14889. 5 p. l., 244 p. incl. front., illus. 21 1/2 cm. 1935. Houghton Mifflin Company.

--Heroes in Plenty ... LC 45-8222. 2 p. l., 220 p. 20 1/2 cm. 1945. Doubleday, Doran and Company, Inc.

--The High King's Daughter. Hardy, John, illus. LC 65-19334. 184p. illus. 22cm. (Ariel bk.). c.1965. Farrar.

--The High King's Daughter. Hardy, John, illus. (Illus.). (gr. 7-9). 1965. FS&G.

--Rich Boy, Poor Boy. LC 61-11323. 192p. (Ariel Bks.). 1961. Farrar, Straus & Giroux.

--Tiger Burning Bright. LC 63-16477. xi, 239 p. illus. 22 cm. 1964. Ariel Books.

--Tiger Burning Bright. (Illus.). (gr. 7-11). 1964. (ISBN 0-374-37557-7). FS&G.

--The Traveling Toys. Peat, Fern Bisel, Mrs. (1893-), illus. LC 34-35886. 201 p. incl. col. front., illus. col. plates. 22 1/2 cm. c.1934. The Penn Publishing Company.

--We Merrily Put to Sea. 1st ed. Porter, Jean MacDonald (1906-), illus. LC 50-9337. 247 p. illus. 21 cm. 1950. Doubleday.

Du Bois, William Sherman Pene (1916-)

--The Alligator Case. Du Bois, William Sherman Pene (1916-), illus. LC 65-11446. (Illus.). 63 p. 24cm. 1965. (ISBN 0-06-021746-4). Harper & Row.

--Bear Circus. Du Bois, William Sherman Pene (1916-), illus. (Illus.). 48p. (gr. k-3). 1973. (ISBN 0-670-05085-7, Puffin). Penguin.

--Bear Circus. Du Bois, William Sherman Pene (1916-), illus. LC 76-153665. (Illus.). color ils. 48p. (Viking Seafarer Ser.). (gr. k-3). 1971. (ISBN 0-670-15073-8). Viking Pr. **Award: (NYT).**

--Bear Circus. Du Bois, William Sherman Pene (1916-), illus. LC 76-153665. (Illus.). 48 p. 29cm. 1976, c.1971. (ISBN 0-670-15073-8). Viking Press.

--Bear Party. Du Bois, William Sherman Pene (1916-), illus. 48p. (ps-2). 1969. (ISBN 0-670-05015-6, Puffin). Penguin.

--Bear Party. Du Bois, William Sherman Pene (1916-), illus. LC 51-14823. unpaged. illus. 21 cm. 1951. Viking Press. **Award: (RCM).**

--Bear Party. Du Bois, William Sherman Pene (1916-), illus. (Illus.). (ps-2). 1963. (ISBN 0-670-15124-6). (ISBN 0-670-90000-1). (ISBN 0-670-90502-X). Viking Pr.

--Call Me Bandicoot. Du Bois, William Sherman Pene (1916-), illus. LC 77-120733. (Illus.). (gr. 5-7). 1970. (ISBN 0-06-024697-9, HarpJ). (ISBN 0-06-024698-7). Har-Row.

--Elizabeth, the Cow Ghost. Du Bois, William Sherman Pene (1916-), illus. LC 36-10049. 17cm. 47p. 1936. Nelson.

--Elizabeth, the Cow Ghost. Du Bois, William Sherman Pene (1916-), illus. LC 64-9770. (Illus.). 26cm. 41p. (gr. k-4). 1964. (ISBN 0-670-29202-8). Viking Pr.

--The Flying Locomotive. Du Bois, William Sherman Pene (1916-), illus. 1941. Viking Press.

--The Forbidden Forest. Du Bois, William Sherman Pene (1916-), illus. LC 77-25651. (Illus.). 56 p. 29cm. c.1978. (ISBN 0-06-024699-5). (ISBN 0-06-024700-2). Harper & Row. **Award: (NYT).**

--Gentleman Bear. Du Bois, William Sherman Pene (1916-), illus. LC 84-48320. (Illus.). 80p. (gr. k up). N.D. (ISBN 0-374-32533-2). FS&G.

--The Giant. Du Bois, William Sherman Pene (1916-), illus. LC 54-12910. (Illus.). 124 p. 25cm. 1954. Viking Press. **Award: (ALA).**

--Giant Otto. Du Bois, William Sherman Pene (1916-), illus. LC 33-23264. 1936. Viking Press.

--The Great Geppy. 1946. Viking.

--The Great Geppy. Du Bois, William Sherman Pene (1916-), illus. LC 40-6302. 92 p. illus. (part col.) 25 1/2 cm. 1940. (ISBN 0-670-34903-8). The Viking Press.

--The Horse in the Camel Suit. Du Bois, William Sherman Pene (1916-), illus. LC 67-16478. (Illus.). 79 p. 24cm. 1967. (ISBN 0-06-021747-2). Harper & Row.

--Lazy Tommy Pumpkinhead. Du Bois, William Sherman Pene (1916-), illus. LC 66-8207. (Illus.). 28 p. 21cm. 1966. (ISBN 0-06-021750-2). Harper & Row.

--Lion. (Illus., Pub. by Viking Pr). (Viking Seafarer Ser). (gr. 1-3). 1974. (ISBN 0-670-05093-8, Puffin). Penguin.

--Lion. (Illus.). 32p. (ps-3). 1983. (ISBN 0-14-050417-6, Puffin). Penguin.

--Lion. 1981. (ISBN 0-670-42950-3). Viking Pr.

--Lion. Du Bois, William Sherman Pene (1916-), illus. LC 56-13707. (Illus.). 36 p. 26cm. 1956. (ISBN 0-670-42950-3). Viking Press. **Awards: (ALA). ; (RCM).**

--Lion. Du Bois, William Sherman Pene (1916-), illus. (Illus.). 1 v. (unpaged. 22cm. (Viking Seafarer book). 1974. (ISBN 0-670-05093-8). Viking.

--Mother Goose for Christmas. Du Bois, William Sherman Pene (1916-), illus. LC 72-91406. (Illus.). 48p. (gr. k-3). 1973. (ISBN 0-670-49007-5). Viking Pr.

--Otto & the Magic Potatoes. Du Bois, William Sherman Pene (1916-), illus. LC 79-102919. (Illus.). 48p. 26cm. (gr. 3-5). 1970. (ISBN 0-670-52986-9). Viking Pr.

--Otto at Sea. LC 36-23363. 16 x 16 cm. 40p. 1936. Viking Press.

--Otto at Sea: The Adventures of Otto. Du Bois, William Sherman Pene (1916-), illus. LC 58-3548. (Illus.). 37 p. 26cm. 1958. (ISBN 0-670-52999-0). Viking Press.

--Otto in Africa. Du Bois, William Sherman Pene (1916-), illus. LC 61-7700. (Illus.). 35 p. 26cm. 1961. Viking Press.

--Otto in Texas. Du Bois, William Sherman Pene (1916-), illus. LC 59-16422. (Illus.). 45 p. 26cm. 1959. Viking Press.

--Peter Graves. Du Bois, William Sherman Pene (1916-), illus. LC 50-10429. (Illus.). (gr. 5-9). 1950. (ISBN 0-670-54942-8). Viking Pr.

--Porko Von Popbutton. Du Bois, William Sherman Pene (1916-), illus. LC 69-14445. (Illus.). 80 p. 22cm. 1969. (ISBN 0-06-021754-5). Harper & Row.

--Pretty Pretty Peggy Moffitt. Du Bois, William Sherman Pene (1916-), illus. LC 68-10786. (Illus.). 32 p. 21cm. 1968. Harper & Row.

--Squirrel Hotel. Du Bois, William Sherman Pene (1916-), illus. LC 79-17958. (Illus.). 47 p. 25cm. (Gregg Press Children's Literature Series). 1979, c.1951. (ISBN 0-8398-2606-0). Gregg Press.

--Squirrel Hotel. Du Bois, William Sherman Pene (1916-), illus. 1952. Viking Press.

--Three Little Pigs. Du Bois, William Sherman Pene (1916-), illus. (Illus.). (gr. k-3). 1978. (ISBN 0-14-050196-7, Puffin). Penguin.

--Three Little Pigs. Du Bois, William Sherman Pene (1916-), illus. (Illus.). (ps-1). 1962. (ISBN 0-670-70812-7). Viking Pr.

--The Three Policemen: Or, Young Bottsford of Farbe Island. Du Bois, William Sherman Pene (1916-), illus. LC 38-22017. 92 p. illus. (part col.) 25 1/2 cm. 1938. The Viking Press.

--The Three Policemen: Or, Young Bottsford of Farbe Island. Du Bois, William Sherman Pene (1916-), illus. (Illus.). (gr. 2-5). 1960. (ISBN 0-670-70912-3). Viking Pr.

--Topsy-Turvy Emperor of China. Du Bois, William Sherman Pene (1916-), illus. Singer, Isaac Bashevis (1904-) & Shub, Elizabeth, trs. from Yiddish LC 71-121805. (Illus.). 15 color ils. 48p. (gr. 1-5). 1971. (ISBN 0-06-025677-X). (ISBN 0-06-025678-8). Har-Row.

--The Twenty-One Balloons. 1948. Viking.

--The Twenty-One Balloons. Du Bois, William Sherman Pene (1916-), illus. LC 47-2533. 5 p. l., 3-179, 1 p. incl. front., illus. 24 cm. 1947. (ISBN 0-670-73441-1). The Viking Press. **Award: (JNM).**

Du Bois, William Sherman Pene (1916-) & Lee, Po

--The Hare & the Tortoise & The Tortoise & the Hare: La Liebre y la Tortuga & La Tortuga y la Liebre. Du Bois, William Sherman Pene (1916-), illus. LC 77-146125. (Illus.). 48 p. 1972. Doubleday.

Du Bose, Horace M.

--The Gang of Six: A Story of the Boy Life of To-day. LC 7-12694. 147p. 19cm. 1906. M. E. Church, South, Smith & Lamar Agents.

Du Bose, La Rocque Russ (1926-)

--Aye, Aye, Sir. McGee, Millard, illus. LC 58-7740. 173p. illus. 22cm. 1958. Lothrop, Lee & Shepard.

--Wild Horse, Wild Rider. LC 67-20463. 186 p. 22 cm. 1967. Steck-Vaughn Co.

Dubov, N.

--A Boy by the Sea. 199p. 1974. (ISBN 0-8285-1114-4, Pub. by Progress Pubs USSR). Imported Pubns.

--The Fugitive. 139p. 1977. (ISBN 0-8285-1151-9, Pub. by Progress Pubs USSR). Imported Pubns.

Dubrovin, Vivian (1931-)

--Baseball Just for Fun. Leo, Judith, illus. LC 74-10867. p. cm. 22cm. 30p. (Her Summer fun/winter fun). 1974. (ISBN 0-88436-136-5). (ISBN 0-88436-136-5). EMC Corp.

--A Better Bit and Bridle. Inderieden, Nancy, illus. LC 75-20346. p. cm. (Her Saddle up!). 1975. (ISBN 0-88436-201-9). (ISBN 0-88436-202-7). EMC Corp.

--A Chance to Win. Inderieden, Nancy, illus. LC 75-20081. (Illus.). 39 p. 24cm. (Her saddle up!). 1975. (ISBN 0-88436-203-5). (ISBN 0-88436-204-3). EMC Corp.

--The Magic Bowling Ball. LC 74-10869. p. cm. (Her Summer fun/winter fun). 1974. (ISBN 0-88436-130-6). (ISBN 0-88436-131-4). EMC Corp.

--Open the Gate. Inderieden, Nancy, illus. LC 75-20026. p. cm. (Her Saddle up!). 1975. (ISBN 0-88436-207-8). (ISBN 0-88436-208-6). EMC Corp.

--Rescue on Skis. Leo, Judith, illus. LC 74-11004. p. cm. (Her Summer fun/winter fun). 1974. (ISBN 0-88436-134-9). (ISBN 0-88436-134-9). EMC Corp.

--The Track Trophy. Leo, Judith, illus. LC 74-10931. p. cm. (Her Summer fun/winter fun). 1974. (ISBN 0-88436-132-2). (ISBN 0-88436-132-2). EMC Corp.

--Trailering Troubles. Inderieden, Nancy, illus. LC 75-20362. p. cm. (Her Saddle up!). 1975. (ISBN 0-88436-205-1). (ISBN 0-88436-206-X). EMC Corp.

Dubsky, Dora

--Sing and Dance. Gordon, Ayala, illus. 48p. N.D. Frederick Ungar Publishing Co Inc.

Duc, pseud., see Ducourant, Bernard.

Duchacek, Ivo Duka see Duka, Ivo, pseud.

Duchacek, Ivo Duka (1913-) & Kolda, Helena (1928-)

--Martin and His Friend from Outer Space. Duka, Ivo, pseud. LC 55-552422. 95p. illus. 23cm. 1955. Harper.

--The Secret of the Two Feathers. Duka, Ivo, pseud. LC 54-6337. 88p. illus. 23cm. 1954. Harper.

Du Chaillu, Paul Belloni (1831-1903)

--Adventures In The Great Forest Of Equatorial Africa And The Country Of The Dwarfs. (Illus.). N.D. Harper & Brothers' Trade-List.

--The Country of the Dwarfs. (Illus.). 1882. Harper's Trade-List.

--The Country of the Dwarfs, 1 of 5 vols. (Illus.). (Bks for Boys). N.D. Set. Harper & Brothers.

--Gorilla Country. N.D. Harper & Bros.

--In African Forest and Jungle. Perard, Victor Semon (1870-1957), illus. LC 3-24208. xii p., 1 l., 193 p. front., 23 pl. 20 1/2 cm. 1903. C. Scribner's Sons.

--Ivar the Viking: A Romantic History Based Upon Authentic Facts of the Third and Fourth Centuries. LC 4-16456. xxiv, 307 p. facsim. 19 cm. 1893. C. Scribner's Sons.

--King Mombo. Perard, Victor Semon (1870-1957), illus. LC 2-22175. xvi, 225 p. front., pl. 20 1/2 cm. 1902. C. Scribner's Sons.

--The Land of the Long Night. Burns, W. J., illus. N.D. Charles Scribner's Sons.

--Lost in the Jungle. (Illus.). (Happy Home Library). N.D. E. P. Dutton & Co.

--Lost in the Jungle. (Illus.). 1882. Harper's Trade-List.

--Lost in the Jungle, 1 of 5 vols. (Illus.). (Bks for Boys). N.D. Set. Harper & Brothers.

--Lost in the Jungle. Best, Allena Champlin, Mrs. (1892-1974), illus. Berry, Erick, pseud. LC 62-518726. 269p. 20cm. 1962. Harper.

--Lost in the Jungle: Narrated for Young People. LC 79-159939. (Illus.). viii, 260 p. 22cm. 1971. Gryphon Books.

--My Apingi Kingdom. (Illus.). 1882. Harper's Trade-List.

--My Apingi Kingdom, 1 of 5 vols. (Illus.). (Bks for Boys). N.D. Set. Harper & Brothers.

--Stories of the Gorilla Country, 1 of 5 vols. (Illus.). (Bks for Boys). N.D. Set. Harper & Brothers.

--Wild Life Under the Equator. (Illus.). 1882. Harper's Trade-List.

Duchesne, Janet (1930-)

--Richard Goes Sailing. LC 67-19769. (Illus.). 48 p. 24cm. 1968, c.1966. Delacorte Press.

Duchess, pseud., see Hungerford, Margaret Wolfe Hamilton.

Duckett, Eleanor Shipley, jt. auth. see Milner-White, Eric.

Duckles, Vincent Harris (1913-)

--The Ducks Come to the Farm. Havel, Victor, illus. LC 50-23546. 18 p. col. illus. 22 cm. (Bonnie book). N.D. John Martin's House.

Duckworth, Elisabeth, adapted by see Hille-Brandts, Lene.

Duckworth, Elisabeth, adapted by see Lybeck, Sebastian.

Duckworth, Elizabeth, tr. see Lybeck, Sebastian.

Ducornet, Erica (1650-1705), adapted by see Aulnoy, Marie Catherine Jumelle de Berneville.

Ducornet, Erica (1943-) & Ducornet, Guy

--Shazira Shazam and the Devil. LC 76-117552. (Illus.). 32 p. 1970. (ISBN 0-13-807875-0). Prentice-Hall.

Ducornet, Guy, jt. auth. see Ducornet, Erica.

Ducorron, Charles Alexander Francis

--The Boy King of the Cannibal Islands. Eskridge, Robert Lee, illus. LC 32-25464. 1932. Bobbs Merrill Co.

Ducourant, Bernard see Duc, pseud.

Ducourant, Bernard (1932-)

--Stevie Searches for Buried Treasure. Duc, pseud. LC 68-29534. 31 cm. 32p. 1968. Hart Pub. Co.

Duddington, Nataliia Aleksandrovna Ertel, tr. see Afanasev, Aleksandr Nikolaevich.

Dudek, J. B.

--Lullaby. N.D. Bruce Humphries.

Dudevant, Amandine Lucile Aurore Dupin see Sand, George, pseud.

Dudevant, Mme. see Sand, George, pseud.

Dudley, Albertus True (1866-)

--At the Home Plate. Copeland, Charles, illus. LC 10-162383. ix, 316 p. front., plates. 20 cm. (His Stories of the Triangular league). c.1910. Lothrop, Lee & Shepard Co.

--Following the Ball. Copeland, Charles, illus. LC 3-13826. xi, 316 p. front., 3 pl. 20 cm. 1903. Lee and Shepard.

--A Full-Back Afloat: Being an Account of Dick Melvin's Vacation Voyage. Copeland, Charles, illus. LC 8-17995. ix, 310 p. front., 5 pl. 20 cm. (Phillips Exeter series). 1908. Lothrop, Lee & Shepard Co.

--The Great Year. Copeland, Charles, illus. LC 7-237180. ix, 302 p. front., 5 pl. 20 cm. (Phillips Exeter series). 1907. Lothrop, Lee & Shepard Co.

--The Half-Miler. Goss, John, illus. LC 13-172497. 332 p. front., plates. 20 cm. (Phillips Exeter series). 1913. Lothrop, Lee & Shepard Co.

--In the Line. Copeland, Charles, illus. LC 5-17278. xiii, 309 p. front., 3 pl. 20 cm. (Phillips Exeter series). 1905. Lee and Shepard.

--The King's Powder. Goss, John, illus. LC 23-124468. 414 p. front., plates. 20 cm. c.1923. Lothrop, Lee & Shepard Co.

--Making the Nine. Copeland, Charles, illus. LC 4-18895. xiii, 332 p. front., 7 pl. 20 cm. (Phillips Exeter series). 1904. Lee and Shepard.

--The Pecks in Camp. Copeland, Charles, illus. LC 11-21863. vii p, 1 l., 335 p. front., plates. 20 cm. (Phillips Exeter series). 1911. Lothrop, Lee & Shepard Co.

--The School Four. (Stories of the Triangular League). N.D. Lothrop, Lee & Shepard.

--A Spy of Seventy-Six. Cue, Harold, illus. LC 33-251909. 323 p. front., plates. 21 cm. c.1933. Lothrop, Lee & Shepard Co.

--The Unofficial Prefect. Wood, Franklin T. & Skimore, T. D., illus. LC 16-170690. ix, 11-254 p. front., plates. 20 cm. (His Stories of the Triangular league). 1916. Lothrop, Lee & Shepard Co.

--With Mask and Mitt. Copeland, Charles, illus. LC 6-18584. xiii, 300 p. front., 7 pl. 20 cm. (Phillips Exeter series). 1906. Lothrop, Lee & Shepard Co.

--The Yale Cup. Copeland, Charles, illus. LC 8-10279. xi, 301 p. front., 5 pl. 20 cm. (Phillips Exeter series). 1908. Lothrop, Lee & Shepard Co.

Dudley, Bide

--Bolivar Brown. Wood, Harry, illus. LC 21-16376. (Harper's Selected Juveniles). 1921. Harper & Brothers.

Dudley, Dessalee Ryan, Mrs., jt. auth. see Troxell, Eleanor.

Dudley, Ernest (1908-)

--An Elephant Called Slowly. (gr. 6-10). N.D. Pyramid Pubns.

Dudley, Margaret, jt. auth. see De Leuw, Adele Louise.

Dudley, Martha (1912-)

--Bad Mousie. Engelbrecht, Trientja (1925-), illus. LC 66-13971. 1 v. (unpaged) illus. (part col.) 22 cm. 1966. (ISBN 0-516-03414-6). Childrens Press.

--Bad Mousie: Donica's Story. Engelbrecht, Trientja (1925-), illus. LC 47-202288. 36 p. illus. (part col.) 19 1/2 x 17 cm. (Star-bright book. S-303). 1947. Childrens Press, Inc.

Dudley, Maywill

--A Picture Story Book for Children. Containing the Stories of Peter Rabbit, Red Riding Hood, The Three Little Pigs, Cinderella, and Three Bears. Dudley, Maywill, illus. LC 34-40517. 3-30 p. illus. (part col.) 31 cm. c.1934. Whitman Publishing Company.

Dudley, Nancy, pseud., see Cole, Lois Dwight.

Dudley, Nancy, pseud. (1903-1979)

--Linda Goes on a Cruise. Cole, Lois Dwight. Sofia, pseud. (1926-), illus. Zeiger, Sophia. LC 57-13158. (Illus.). 23cm. 1958. Coward-McCann.

--Linda Goes to a TV Studio. Cole, Lois Dwight. Sofia, pseud. (1926-), illus. Zeiger, Sophia. LC 57-7428. unpaged. illus. 23cm. 1957. Coward-McCann.

--Linda Goes to the Hospital. Cole, Lois Dwight. Sofia, pseud. (1926-), illus. Zeiger, Sophia. LC 53-9359. (Illus.). 47 p. 23cm. 1953. Coward-McCann.

--Linda Travels Alone. Cole, Lois Dwight. Sofia, pseud. (1926-), illus. Zeiger, Sophia. LC 55-6888. (Illus.). unpaged. 23cm. 1955. Coward-McCann.

--Linda's First Flight. Cole, Lois Dwight. Sofia, pseud. (1926-), illus. Zeiger, Sophia. LC 56-71418. unpaged. illus. 23cm. 1956. Coward-McCann.

Dudley, Ruth Hubbell (1905-)

--Hank and the Kitten. Darling, Louis, Jr. (1916-1970), illus. LC 49-9997. 62 p. illus. 21 cm. (Morrow junior books). 1949. W. Morrow.

--The Tiptop Wish. Galdone, Paul (1914-), illus. LC 58-6585. 115p. 1958. Thomas Y. Crowell Co.

Dudley-Smith, Trevor see Trevor, Elleston, pseud.

Dudney, Sarah

--Miss Willowburn's Offer. (Illus.). (Scribner-Blackie Series of books for young people). N.D. Charles Scribner's Sons.

Dudochkin, Petr Petrovich

--Which Is the Best Place?. Ginsburg, Mirra (1919-), adapted by. Duvoisin, Roger Antoine (1904-1980), illus. LC 75-31946. (Illus.). 28 p. 26cm. c.1976. (ISBN 0-02-735980-8). Macmillan.

Duecy, Charles M.

--The Odd Adventures of the Electrical Pussy Cat. Duecy, Charles M., illus. 1964. Vantage Press.

Dueland, Joy Vivian

--Barn Kitten, House Kitten. Dueland, Joy Vivian, illus. (Illus.). 1978. (ISBN 0-931942-00-4). Phunn Pubs.

--Beaver Boy. Dueland, Joy Vivian, illus. LC 70-125135. (Illus.). 30 p. 23cm. (Magic circle book). 1971. Ginn.

--Dear Tabby. Dueland, Joy Vivian, illus. (Illus.). 1978. (ISBN 0-931942-02-0). Phunn Pubs.

--Julia Kitten's Kitchen. Dueland, Joy Vivian, illus. (Illus.). 1978. (ISBN 0-931942-01-2). Phunn Pubs.

--Kitten in the Manger. Dueland, Joy Vivian, illus. (Illus.). 1981. Phunn Pubs.

--The Pine Tree That Went to Sea. Cary, Louis Favreau (1915-), illus. Cary, pseud. LC 77-125137. (Illus.). 24 p. 24cm. (Magic circle book). 1971. Ginn.

Duenewald, Doris, ed.

--Bad News Bears Go to Japan Activity Book. (Illus.). (Elephant Books Ser.). (gr. k-7). 1978. (ISBN 0-448-16175-3, G&D). Putnam Pub Group.

--The Play Money Book. (Illus.). (Elephant Bks.). 1978. (ISBN 0-448-16163-X, G&D). Putnam Pub Group.

Duenewald, Doris, ed. see Altman, Margery.

Duenewald, Doris, ed. see Bel Geddes, Barbara.

Duenewald, Doris, ed. see Benson, Murray & Ladd, Fred.

Duenewald, Doris, ed. see Disney, Walt, Studio.

Duenewald, Doris, ed. see Fujikawa, Gyo.

Duenewald, Doris, ed. see Hoch, Edward D.

Duenewald, Doris, ed. see Mother Goose.

Duenewald, Doris, ed. see Tallarico, Tony.

Duest, Marianne

--Barbie in Television. Patterson, Robert (1899-), illus. LC 64-17312. 181 p. illus. 21 cm. c.1964. Random House.

Duff, Annis, jt. auth. see Adshead, Gladys Lucy.

Duff, Jim

--Whiz, the Elf Who Made Christmas Special. Tjames, Jerry, illus. (Illus.). (Story Book Ser.). (ps-5). 1980. (ISBN 0-89305-030-X). (ISBN 0-89305-031-8). Anna Pub.

Duff, Maggie, pseud., see Duff, Margaret K..

Duff, Maggie, pseud.

--Dancing Turtle. Duff, Margaret K.. Horvath, Maria (1948-), illus. LC 80-24683. (Illus.). 32 p. 27cm. c.1981. (ISBN 0-02-733010-9). Macmillan Pub. Co.

--Johnny and His Drum. Duff, Margaret K.. Robinson, Charles (1931-), illus. LC 73-182533. (Illus.). 30 p. 24cm. 1972. (ISBN 0-8098-1192-8). H. Z. Walck.

--The Princess and the Pumpkin. Duff, Margaret K.. Stock, Catherine, illus. LC 79-24060. (Illus.). 32 p. 26cm. c.1980. (ISBN 0-02-733000-1). Macmillan.

Duff, Maggie, pseud., retold by

--Rum Pum Pum: A Folk Tale from India. Duff, Margaret K.. Aruego, Jose (1932-) & Dewey, Ariane (1937-), illus. LC 77-12389. (Illus.). 32 p. c.1978. (ISBN 0-02-732950-X). Macmillan.

Duff, Margaret K. see Duff, Maggie, pseud.

Duffe, Marcelle Laval

--New Amsterdam Colonial Days. Holland, Janice (1913-1962), illus. LC 42-14632. 35p. col. illus. 22cm. c.1942. Row, Peterson & Co.

--New England Colonial Days. Holland, Janice (1913-1962), illus. LC 41-8538. (Illus.). 22cm. 36p. (Basic Social Education Ser.). 1941. Peterson and Company.

--Southern Colonial Days. Holland, Janice (1913-1962), illus. LC 42-10024. 36p. col. illus. 22cm. c.1942. Row, Peterson & Co.

Duffey, Arthur

--For Old Donchester: Or, Archie Hartley and His Schoolmates. Goss, John, illus. LC 12-20640. 3 p. l., 350 p. front., plates. 20 cm. 1912. Lothrop, Lee & Shepard Co.

--On the Cinder Path: Or, Archie Hartley's First Term at Donchester. N.D. Lothrop,Lee & Shepard.

Duffield, tr. see Cervantes Saavedra, Miguel de.

Duffield, Elizabeth M

--Lucile: Bringer of Joy. Taylor, M. P., illus. LC 17-127147. vi p., 1 l., 303 p. front. plates. 20 cm. c.1917. Sully and Kleinteich.

--Lucile on the Heights. Gooch, Thelma, illus. LC 18-12206. 2 p. l., iii-iv p., 2 l., 301 p. front., plates. 20 cm. c.1918. G. Sully & Company.

--Lucile the Torch Bearer. Taylor, M. P., illus. LC 15-230008. 4 p. l., 296 p. front., plates, 20 cm. c.1915. Sully and Kleinteich.

--Lucile Triumphant. Taylor, M. P., illus. LC 16-231441. vi p. 1 l., 306 p. front., plates. 20 cm. c.1916. Sully and Kleinteich.

Duffield, J. W.

--Bert Wilson at Panama. LC 54-1110. 49cm. 205p. (The Famous Bert Wilson Books). 1914. George Sully & Co.

--Bert Wilson at Panama. (Illus.). (The Bert Wilson Books, Second Ser.). N.D. Sully and Kleinteich.

--Bert Wilson at the Wheel. LC 13-9475. 4 p. l., 222 p. front., plates. 20 cm. (His The Bert Wilson series. 1). 1913. Sully and Kleinteich.

--Bert Wilson in the Rockies. (The Famous Bert Wilson Bks). N.D. George Sully & Co.

--Bert Wilson in the Rockies. (Illus.). (The Bert Wilson Books, Second Ser.). N.D. Sully and Kleinteich.

--Bert Wilson, Marathon Winner. (The Famous Bert Wilson Bks). N.D. George Sully & Co.

--Bert Wilson, Marathon Winner. (Illus.). (The Bert Wilson Books, First Ser.). N.D. Sully and Kleinteich.

--Bert Wilson on the Gridiron. (The Famous Bert Wilson Bks). N.D. George Sully & Co.

--Bert Wilson on the Gridiron. (Illus.). (The Bert Wilson Books, Second Ser.). N.D. Sully and Kleinteich.

--Bert Wilson, Wireless Operator. (The Famous Bert Wilson Bks). N.D. George Sully & Co.

--Bert Wilson, Wireless Operator. (Illus.). (The Bert Wilson Books, First Ser.). N.D. Sully and Kleinteich.

--Bert Wilson's Fade-Away Ball. 1st ed. LC 13-10990. (Illus.). 205p. (The Bert Wilson Books). 1913. Sully and Kleinteich.

--Bert Wilson's Twin-Cylinder Racer. LC 14-6565. 19cm. 212p. (The Famous Bert Wilson Bks). 1914. George Sully & Co.

--Bert Wilson's Twin Cylinder Racer. (Illus.). (The Bert Wilson Books, Second Ser.). N.D. Sully and Kleinteich.

--Radio Boys in the Secret Service: Or, Cast Away on an Iceberg. LC 26-23557. 255p. front. 19 1/2cm. (Radio Boys Ser.). c.1922. M. A. Donohue & Co.

Duffield, Kenneth Graham

--Little Black Rabbit. Burroughs, John F., illus. LC 18-851334. 233 p. incl. col. front., plates. 19 cm. c.1918. Henry Altemus Company.

--The Three Bears And Other Stories. Gallagher, J. L. & Hoopes, Margaret Campbell, illus. LC 57-140875. 64p. illus. 26cm. 1957. Platt &Munk Co.

Duffield, Kenneth Graham, ed. see Cock Robin.

Duffield, Lois, jt. auth. see Ousley, Odille.

Duffill, James

--Picture Talks on the Gospels: Sixty Original Stories and Talks Illustrating the Gospels for the Church's Year. LC 36-10589. 2 p. l., 97 p. 19 cm. 1935. The Faith Press, Ltd.

Duffus, Helen Millcete

--The Strawberry Girls. LC 29-17788. 4 p. l., 3-242 p. 20 cm. 1929. Duffield and Company.

Duffus, Robert Luther (1888-1972)

--That Was Alderbury: A Novel. LC 41-12727. 5 p. l., 3-327 p. 21 cm. 1941. The Macmillan Company.

Duffy, James

--The Revolt of the Teddy Bears: A May Gray Mystery. McClintock, Barbara LC 84-15522. (Illus.). 72 p. 22cm. c.1985. (ISBN 0-517-55533-6). Crown Publishers.

Duffy, Marguerite R., ed. see Andersen, Hans Christian.

Duffy, Olive

--Chatter Charmers. N.D. Carlton Press Inc.

Dugan, LeRoy, illus.

--Heroes of the Old Testament, No. 3. 96p. (Orig.). (gr. k-4). 1981. (ISBN 0-87123-703-2). Bethany Hse.

Dugan, Michael Gray (1947-)

--Nonsense Places: An Absurd Australian Alphabet. Stackpool, Walter (1917-), illus. LC 77-364521. (Illus.). 34 p. 1976. (ISBN 0-00-185021-0). Collins.

Dugan, Michael Gray (1947-), ed.

--Stuff & Nonsense. Niland, Deborah (1951-), illus. LC 76-53610. (Illus.). 79 p. 22cm. 1st U.S. edition. 1977, c.1974. (ISBN 0-529-05337-3). Collins World.

Dugan, William J.

--The Ball Book. Dugan, William J., illus. LC 64-57439. (Illus.). unpaged. 22cm. (Golden bk. for kindergarten). 1964. Golden.

--Bill Dugan's Busy Town. Dugan, William J., illus. LC 70-81957. (Illus.). 62 p. 30cm. 1969. Golden Press.

--The Bug Book. LC 66-9495. (Illus.). 24 p. 22cm. (Golden book for kindergarten). c.1965. Golden Press.

--The Christmas Angel Book. (Illus.). 24 p. 22cm. (Golden book for kindergarten). c.1965. Golden Press.

--The Red Little Golden Book of Fairy Tales. Dugan, William J., illus. (Little Golden Book). 1958. Golden Press.

--Sam Squirrel Goes to the City. Dugan, William J., illus. LC 73-83814. (Illus.). 27 p. 27cm. 1969. American Heritage Press.

Duganne, Phyllis

--Ruthie. Williamson, Ada Clendenin, illus. LC 21-14706. 4 p. l., 272 p. front., plates. 20 cm. 1921. Harcourt, Brace and Company.

Du Genestoux, Magdeleine (1885-)

--Peepo and His Dog: An Algerian Adventure. Pecoud, A., illus. Haas, Merle S. (1896-1985), tr. LC 37-17025. 256 p. incl. front., illus. 21 cm. c.1937. Random House.

Duggan, Janie Prichard

--The Little Acrobat: A Story of Italy. Bickford, Nana French, illus. LC 19-14939. vii p., 1 l., 185 p. front., plates. 20 cm. 1919. Little, Brown, and Company.

--Little Cuba Libre: A Story of Cuban Patriots for Children Young and Old. Bickford, Nana French, illus. LC 18-16020. 6 p. l., 3-282 p. front., plates. 20 cm. 1918. Little, Brown, and Company.

Duggan, Mary M (1921-)

--Old Hawk's Gold. LC 66-7041. 124p. 22cm. 1966. (ISBN 0-8114-7639-1). Steck.

Duggan, Maurice Noel (1922-1975)

--Fabulous McFanes. (Illus.). 118p. (gr. 3-7). 1974. (ISBN 0-8002-0461-1). Intl Pubns Serv.

--Falter Tom and the Water Boy. Rowell, Kenneth, illus. LC 59-12200. 64p. 1959. Criterion Bks, Inc.

--Falter Tom & the Water Boy. Rowell, Kenneth, illus. LC 59-12200. (Illus.). (gr. 3-6). 1959. (ISBN 0-87599-027-4). S G Phillips.

Dugmore, Arthur Radclyffe (1870-)

--Adventures in Beaver Stream Camp. (Every Boy's Library). N.D. Grosset & Dunlap.

--Adventures in Beaver Stream Camp: Lost in the Northern Wilds. Dugmore, Arthur Radclyffe (1870-), illus. LC 18-189541. xi, 341, 1 p. incl. front., illus. plates. 20 cm. 1918. Doubleday, Page & Company.

--Two Boys in Beaver-Land: A Book of the Woods. Dugmore, Arthur Radclyffe (1870-), illus. LC 20-219651. 2 p. l., 3-245, 1 p. front., illus. 20 cm. 1920. Doubleday, Page & Company.

Dugo, Andre, pseud., see Szenes, Andre.

Dugo, Andre, pseud. (1895-)

--The Calf that Flew Away. Szenes, Andre. 1st ed. LC 50-12596. 32 p. illus. 26cm. (gr. k-2). 1950. Henry Holt & co.

--The Dogcatcher's Dog. Szenes, Andre. 1st ed. Dugo, Andre, pseud. (1895-), illus. Szenes, Andre. LC 52-9035. (Illus.). unpaged. 26 cm. 1952. Holt. **Award: (NYT).**

--Joe The Bluebird & Carl The Cardinal. Szenes, Andre. N.D. E. M. Hale & Co.

Du Jardin, Judy, jt. auth. see Du Jardin, Rosamond Neal.

Du Jardin, Rosamond Neal (1902-1963)

--Boy Trouble. (gr. 4-9). 1953. (ISBN 0-397-30229-0, JBL-J). Har-Row.

--Boy Trouble: A Tobey Heydon Story. 1st ed. LC 53-542319. 183p. 21cm. 1953. Lippincott.

--Class Ring. LC 51-9796. (gr. 4-9). 1951. (ISBN 0-397-30184-7, JBL-J). Har-Row.

--Class Ring: A Tobey Heydon Story. 1st ed. LC 51-9796. 207 p. 21 cm. 1951. Lippincott.

--Double Date. LC 52-5102. 191 p. 21cm. 1952. Lippincott.

--Double Feature. LC 53-8910. (gr. 4-9). 1953. (ISBN 0-397-31599-6). Lippincott.

--Double Wedding. LC 59-12354. (gr. 4-9). 1959. (ISBN 0-397-30446-3, JBL-J). Har-Row.

--Double Wedding. 192p. 1958. J. B. Lippincott.

--A Man for Marcy. LC 54-11687. 21cm. 182p. N.D. Berkley.

--A Man for Marcy. LC 54-8109. (gr. 4-9). 1954. (ISBN 0-397-30272-X). Lippincott.

--Marcy Catches up. 1st ed. LC 52-8791. 190 p. 21 cm. 1952. (ISBN 0-397-30215-0). Lippincott.

--One of the Crowd. LC 61-15257. (gr. 4-9). 1961. (ISBN 0-397-30582-6, JBL-J). Har-Row.

--Practically Seventeen. LC 49-10520. 213 p. 21 cm. 1949. J. B. Lippincott Co.

--Practically Seventeen. (gr. 7-12). 1973. (ISBN 0-590-02397-7, Schol Trade Pap). Schol Bk Serv.

--Practically Seventeen. 208p. (gr. 7 up). 1982. (ISBN 0-590-02397-7). Scholastic Inc.

--Real Thing. (gr. 4-9). 1956. (ISBN 0-397-30344-0, JBL-J). Har-Row.

--The Real Thing: A Tobey Heydon Story. 1st ed. LC 56-107267. 192p. 21cm. 1956. Lippincott.

--Senior Prom. (gr. 4-9). 1957. (ISBN 0-397-30388-2, JBL-J). Har-Row.

--Senior Prom. 1st ed. LC 57-108668. 192p. 21cm. 1957. Lippincott.

--Showboat Summer. 1st ed. LC 55-10652. 192p. 21cm. 1955. (ISBN 0-397-30311-4). Lippincott.

--Someone to Count On. LC 62-18008. (gr. 4-9). 1962. (ISBN 0-397-30636-9, JBL-J). Har-Row.

--Someone to Count on. LC 62-18008. 185 p. 21cm. 1962. Lippincott.

--Wait for Marcy. 1st ed. LC 50-14655. 221 p. 21 cm. 1950. Lippincott.

--Wedding in the Family. LC 58-10145. 192 p. 21cm. 1958. (ISBN 0-397-30441-2). Lippincott.

AUTHOR INDEX DUNHAM, KATHARINE

--Little Old Lady of Cliffside: Norway in Story, Song, and Pictures. Frankel, Simon, illus. unpaged. illus. and phonodisc (2s. 7in. 78rpm.) in pocket. 19x20cm. (Merry-go-round books). c.1954. Winston.

Dumas, Gerald J. (1930-)
--Rabbits Rafferty. Tripp, Wallace Whitney (1940-), illus. (Illus.). 196 p. 22cm. 1968. Houghton Mifflin.

Dumas, Philippe (1940-)
--Caesar, Cock of the Village. Dumas, Philippe (1940-), illus. Engel, Deirdre, tr. from Fr. (Illus.). 1st U.S. edition. (gr. k-4). 1980. (ISBN 0-13-110189-7). P-H.
--Laura Loses Her Head. (Illus.). 64p. (ps-3). 1981. (Pub. by Gollancz England). David & Charles.
--Lucie, the Tale of a Donkey. LC 78-26630. p. cm. 1979, c.1977. (ISBN 0-13-541169-6). Prentice-Hall.
--The Story of Edward. Dumas, Philippe (1940-), illus. LC 76-28720. (Illus.). 48 p. c.1977. (ISBN 0-8193-0869-2). Parents' Magazine Press. **Award: (BGH).**

Du Maurier, Daphne (1907-)
--Flight of the Falcon. LC 65-10613. (gr. 9 up). N.D. (ISBN 0-385-05355-X). Doubleday.
--Rebecca. 1948. Doubleday.

Du Mond, Frank L.
--Tall Tales of the Catskills. Parnall, Peter (1936-), illus. LC 68-18456. (Illus.). 192p. (gr. 3-7). 1968. (ISBN 0-689-20091-9). (ISBN 0-689-20092-7). Atheneum.

Dumont, Melaine
--Coco, the Monkey: a Story for Children. Harnard, Lois, tr. N.D. Claxton, Remsen, & Haffelfinger.
--Velvet Coat, the Cat. Harnard, Lois, tr. (Illus.). N.D. Claxton, Remsen, and Haffelfinger.

Dumpledon, Bernard & Miller, Muriel
--Brunel's Three Ships. N.D. British Book Centre.

Dun, Marie de Nervaud
--Scarum. LC 33-5768. (Illus.). 20cm. 317p. 1933. Duffield & Green.
--Scarum. LC 39-12437. (Illus.). 20cm. 250p. 1939. Grosset & Dunlap.

Dunaway
--Bragon the Dragon Calendar Capers. (gr. 1-4). 1978. (ISBN 0-916456-36-6). Good Apple.

Dunaway, et al.
--Bragon the Dragon Tells Time. (gr. 1-4). 1978. (ISBN 0-916456-37-4). Good Apple.

Dunaway, Anna Brownell
--Joystone Manor. LC 39-80075. 276 p. front. 20 cm. c.1939. W. A. Wilde Company.

Dunbar, Aldis
--Once There Was a Prince, 8. N.D. Little, Brown & Co.
--Sons O'Connor. Colum, Padraic (1881-1972), intro. by. N.D. E. P. Dutton & Co.
--Sons O'Cormac. new ed. Horvath, Ferdinand Huszti (1891-), illus. Colum, Padraic (1881-1972), intro. by. N.D. E. P. Dutton & Co.

Dunbar, Jane Thorpe
--Little People's Out-of-Door Melodies. Lamb, F. Mortimer, illus. LC 23-16570. 3 p. l., 5-65 p. illus. 20 cm. c.1923. The Four Seas Company.

Dunbar, Paul Laurence (1872-1906)
--Complete Poems of Paul Laurence Dunbar. (gr. 7 up). 1913. Dodd.
--Little Brown Baby. Rodgers, Bertha, ed. Best, Allena Champlin, Mrs. (1892-1974), illus. Berry, Erick, pseud. LC 40-4721. xiv, 106 p. incl. plates. 21cm. 1940. (ISBN 0-396-01993-5). Dodd, Mead & Company.

Dunbar, Robert Everett (1926-)
--Into Jupiter's World. Hamilton, Jack D (1941-), photos by. LC 80-25526. (Illus.). 89 p. 22cm. (Triumph book). 1981. (ISBN 0-531-04266-9). F. Watts.

Dunboyne
--Aunt Lily's Motto: A Tale. (Illus.). N.D. E & J B Joung.
--Fritz and his Friends: A Tale. N.D. E & J B Young & Co.
--Letty's Mission. (Illus.). N.D. Publications of E. P. Dutton & Co.
--Some Great Thing. N.D. Thomas Whittaker.

Duncan, Ardinelle Beam (1913-)
--Twirly Hurly, the Helicopter Rabbit. Bath, Lorna, illus. LC 62-18883. (Illus.). (gr. k-2). 1962. (ISBN 0-87482-015-4). Wake-Brook.

Duncan, Betty L.
--Ollie the Octopus. Duncan, Betty L., illus. LC 75-324021. (Illus.). 38 p. c.1974. (ISBN 0-533-01339-9). Vantage Press.

Duncan, Carl Dudley (1895-), ed. see Shackelford, Frederick H.

Duncan, Cleo
--Fiddlesticks Joins the Family. Corvus, John, illus. LC 64-19468. 1 v. (unpaged) col. illus. 21 cm. 1964. United Church Press.

Duncan, Cora Tousley
--Nora Nobody And Other Poems For Childern. 1st ed. Inman, Peggy Duncan, illus. LC 56-5810. 92p. illus. 21cm. 1956. Vantage Press.

Duncan, Eula Griffin, Mrs. & Cannon, Alice
--Big Road Walker. Eichenberg, Fritz (1901-), illus. LC 40-34007. x, 121 p. illus. 24 cm. 1940. Frederick A. Stokes Company.
--Big Road Walker. Eichenberg, Fritz (1901-), illus. 1940. J. B. Lippincott Co.

Duncan, Frances
--Mary's Garden and How It Grew. N.D. D. Appleton-Century Co.

Duncan, Fred B.
--Deepwater Family. LC 69-15707. (Illus.). 20 photos. old prints. 192p. (gr. 5 up). 1969. (ISBN 0-394-91041-9). Pantheon.

Duncan, Glenn & Barrett, John
--The Puggle Tales. Mendez, Phil, illus. 32p. 1984. (ISBN 0-8431-1726-5). Price Stern.

Duncan, Gregory, pseud., see McClintock, Marshall.

Duncan, Gregory, pseud. (1906-1967)
--Dick Donnelly of the Paratroops: Story. McClintock, Marshall. Kirn, Francis, illus. LC 45-954164. 3 p. l., 11-248 p. illus. 20 1/2 cm. (Fighters for freedom series). 1944. Whitman Publishing Company.
--March Anson and Scoot Bailey of the U.S. Navy. McClintock, Marshall. Vallely, Henry E., illus. LC 45-953. 3 p. l., 11-248 p. illus. 20 1/2 cm. (Fighters for freedom series). 1944. Whitman Publishing Company.

Duncan, Jane, pseud., see Cameron, Elizabeth Jane.

Duncan, Jane, pseud. (1910-1976)
--Brave Janet Reachfar. Cameron, Elizabeth Jane. Hedderwick, Mairi (1939-), illus. LC 74-8693. (Illus.). 32 p. 26cm. 1975. (ISBN 0-8164-3130-2). Seabury Press.
--Camerons Ahoy!. Cameron, Elizabeth Jane. Ambrus, Victor G., pseud. (1935-), illus. Ambrus, Gyozo Laszlo. LC 68-17646. 8, 184 p. illus. 23 cm. (B 68-06011). 1968. St. Martin's P.
--Camerons at the Castle. Cameron, Elizabeth Jane. Ambrus, Victor G., pseud. (1935-), illus. Ambrus, Gyozo Laszlo. LC 64-18789. vii, 151p. illus. 23cm. 1965, c.1964. Macmillan.
--Camerons at the Castle. Cameron, Elizabeth Jane. Ambrus, Victor G., pseud. (1935-), illus. Ambrus, Gyozo Laszlo. (Illus.). (gr. 4-6). N.D. St Martin.
--Camerons Calling. Cameron, Elizabeth Jane. Ambrus, Victor G., pseud. (1935-), illus. Ambrus, Gyozo Laszlo. LC 66-16608. vi. 186p. illus. 23cm. c.1966. St. Martin's Press.
--Camerons on the Hills. Cameron, Elizabeth Jane. Ambrus, Victor G., pseud. (1935-), illus. Ambrus, Gyozo Laszlo. (Illus.). (gr. 4-6). 1963. St Martin.
--Camerons on the Train. Cameron, Elizabeth Jane. Ambrus, Victor G., pseud. (1935-), illus. Ambrus, Gyozo Laszlo. (Illus.). (gr. 4-6). 1963. St Martin.
--Janet Reachfar and Chickabird. Cameron, Elizabeth Jane. Hedderwick, Mairi (1939-), illus. LC 77-12709. p. cm. 1978. (ISBN 0-8164-3203-1). Seabury Press.
--Janet Reachfar and the Kelpie. Cameron, Elizabeth Jane. Hedderwick, Mairi (1939-), illus. LC 75-44166. (Illus.). 32 p. 26cm. 1976. (ISBN 0-8164-3169-8). Seabury Press.

Duncan, John M
--Down the Mast Road. LC 56-7557. 191p. 21cm. 1956. Whittlesey House.
--Twelve Days 'til Trenton. 21cm. 155p. (Young pioneer bk.: No. 78009). 1967, c.1958. McGraw.
--Twelve Days 'Til Trenton. N.D. McGraw-Hill.
--Twelve Days 'til Trenton. LC 57-14688. 155 p. 21cm. 1958. Whittlesey House.

Duncan-Jones, C M , ed.
--English Folklore Stories. N.D. Macmillan.
--A London Sparrow & Mignonette. N.D. Macmillan.
--Stories from Ballads. N.D. Macmillan.
--Stories from France. N.D. Macmillan.
--Stories from Wales. N.D. Macmillan.

Duncan, Julia K., pseud., see Stratemeyer Syndicate.

Duncan, Julia K., pseud.
--Doris Force at Barry Manor: Or, Mysterious Adventures between Classes. Stratemeyer Syndicate. Repr. of 1932 ed (Pub. by Henry Altemus Co.). (The Doris Force Ser.: Vol. 4). N.D. Goldsmith Publishing Co.
--Doris Force at Barry Manor: Or, Mysterious Adventures Between Classes. Stratemeyer Syndicate. Gooch, Thelma, illus. LC 32-21438. iv, 5-218 p. front., plates. 20 cm. (The Doris Force Ser.: Vol. 4). 1932. Henry Altemus Co.
--Doris Force at Barry Manor: Or, Mysterious Adventures between Classes. Stratemeyer Syndicate. Gooch, Thelma, illus. Repr. of 1932 ed (Pub. by Henry Altemus Co.). (The Doris Force Ser.: Vol. 4). N.D. M. A. Donohue & Co.
--Doris Force at Cloudy Cove: Or, The Old Miser's Signature. Stratemeyer Syndicate. Gooch, Thelma, illus. Repr. of 1931 ed (Pub. by Henry Altemus Co.). (The Doris Force Ser.: Vol. 2). N.D. Goldsmith Publishing Co.
--Doris Force at Cloudy Cove: Or, The Old Miser's Signature. Stratemeyer Syndicate. Gooch, Thelma, illus. LC 21-18088. iv, 5-218 p. front., plates. 20 cm. (The Doris Force Ser.: Vol. 2). 1932. Henry Altemus Co.
--Doris Force at Locked Gates: Or, Saving a Mysterious Fortune. Stratemeyer Syndicate. Gooch, Thelma, illus. LC 31-12370. iv, 5-212 p. front., plates. 20 cm. (The Doris Force Ser.: Vol. 1). 1931. Henry Altemus Co.
--Doris Force at Locked Gates: Or, Saving a Mysterious Fortune. Stratemeyer Syndicate. Gooch, Thelma, illus. Repr. of 1931 ed (Pub. by Henry Altemus Co.). (The Doris Force Ser.: Vol. 1). N.D. M. A. Donohue & Co.
--Doris Force at Raven Rock: Or, Uncovering the Secret Oil Well. Stratemeyer Syndicate. Gooch, Thelma, illus. Repr. of 1932 ed. (The Doris Force Ser.: Vol. 3). N.D. Goldsmith Publishing Co.
--Doris Force at Raven Rock: Or, Uncovering the Secret Oil Well. Stratemeyer Syndicate. Gooch, Thelma, illus. LC 32-19826. iv, 5-216 p. front., plates. 20 cm. (The Doris Force Ser.: Vol. 3). 1932. Henry Altemus Co.

Duncan, Kathleen M
--Crispin's Castle. LC 78-21525. 100 p. 21cm. (Pathfinder Ser.). c.1979. (ISBN 0-310-37821-1). Zondervan Pub. House.
--Sally and the Shepherdess. LC 78-24324. 102 p. 21cm. (Pathfinder Ser.). 1979. (ISBN 0-310-37801-X). Zondervan.

Duncan, Lois Steinmetz see Kerry, Lois, pseud.

Duncan, Lois Steinmetz (1934-)
--Daughters of Eve. LC 79-14918. 239 p. 24cm. c.1979. (ISBN 0-316-19550-2). Little, Brown.
--Debutante Hill. LC 58-9902. 212 p. 21cm. 1958. Dodd, Mead.
--Down a Dark Hall. LC 74-5294. 181 p. 21cm. 1974. (ISBN 0-316-19547-2). Little, Brown.
--From Spring to Spring: Poems & Photographs. LC 82-11100. (Illus.). 96p. (gr. 3-7). 1982. (ISBN 0-664-32695-1). Westminster.
--Game of Danger. LC 62-13000. (gr. 7-10). 1962. (ISBN 0-396-04698-3). Dodd.
--A Gift of Magic. Stewart, Arvis L., illus. LC 70-150053. (Illus.). 183 p. 22cm. 1971. Little, Brown.
--Giving Away Suzanne. Weisgard, Leonard Joseph (1916-), illus. LC 63-18060. (Illus.). (gr. k-3). 1963. (ISBN 0-396-06401-9). Dodd.
--Horses of Dreamland. Diamond, Donna (1950-), illus. LC 84-21759. p. cm. c.1985. (ISBN 0-316-19554-5). Little, Brown.
--Hotel for Dogs. Shortall, Leonard W., illus. LC 77-142824. 165 p. 22cm. 1971. (ISBN 0-395-12364-X). Houghton Mifflin.
--I Know What You Did Last Summer. LC 73-8829. 199 p. 21cm. 1973. (ISBN 0-316-19546-4). Little Brown.
--Killing Mr. Griffin. LC 77-27658. 243 p. 22cm. c.1978. (ISBN 0-316-19549-9). Little, Brown.
--The Littlest One in the Family. Larsen, Suzanne Kesteloo (1930-), illus. LC 60-6024. (Illus.). 27cm. 1960. Dodd, Mead & Co.
--Locked in Time. LC 85-23. 210 p. 22cm. c.1985. (ISBN 0-316-19555-3). Little, Brown.
--The Middle Sister. LC 60-9593. 180 p. 21cm. 1960. Dodd, Mead.
--Peggy. LC 70-113440. 249 p. 21cm. 1970. Little, Brown.
--Ransom. LC 66-13196. 187 p. 22cm. 1966. Doubleday.
--Season of the Two-Heart. LC 64-20632. 213 p. 21cm. 1964. Dodd, Mead.
--Silly Mother. Larsen, Suzanne Kesteloo (1930-), illus. LC 62-9214. (Illus.). (gr. k-3). 1962. Dial.
--Stranger with My Face. LC 81-8299. 250 p. 21cm. c.1981. (ISBN 0-316-19551-0). Little, Brown.
--Summer of Fear. LC 76-8264. p. cm. c.1976. (ISBN 0-316-19548-0). Little, Brown.
--The Terrible Tales of Happy Days School. 1st ed. Henstra, Friso (1928-), illus. LC 82-14945. p. cm. c.1983. (ISBN 0-316-19541-3). Little, Brown.
--They Never Came Home. LC 69-11006. 192 p. 22cm. 1969. Doubleday.
--The Third Eye. LC 83-26777. (gr. 7up). 1984. (ISBN 0-316-19553-7). Little.

Duncan, Mary Lundie (1814-1840)
--Rhymes for My Children. LC 38-35064. 82 p. plates. 15 x 12 cm. 1850. R. Carter & Brothers.

Duncan, Norman (1871-1916)
--The Adventures of Billy Topsail: A Story for Boys. LC 6-16512. 3 p. l., 5-331 p. front., illus. (map) plates. 21 cm. 1906. F. H. Revell Company.
--Billy Topsail & Company: A Story for Boys. LC 10-22535. 318 p. front., plates. 21 cm. c.1910. Fleming H. Revell Company.
--Billy Topsail, M. D. A Tale of Adventure with Doctor Luke of the Labrador. LC 16-21055. 317 p. front., plates. 21 cm. c.1916. Fleming H. Revell and Company.
--Billy Topsail with Doctor Luke of the Labrador. (Every Boy's Library). N.D. Grosset & Dunlap.
--Christmas Eve at Topmast Tickle. (Idyll Envelope Ser.). N.D. Fleming H Revell.
--Doctor Luke of The Labrador. N.D. Fleming H. Revell Co.
--The Suitable Child. Green, Elizabeth Shippen, illus. (Illus.). N.D. Fleming H Revell.

Duncan, Philip
--Waggery Town. Duncan, Philip, illus. LC 35-17386. N.D. Harper & Bros.

Duncan, Riana
--A Nutcracker in a Tree: A Book of Riddles. Duncan, Riana, illus. LC 80-67492. (Illus.). 32p. (gr. k-3). 1981. Delacorte.

Duncan, Robert Lipscomb (1927-)
--The Dragons at the Gate. LC 75-11572. 288p. 1975. (ISBN 0-688-02937-X). Morrow.

Duncan, Ronald Frederick Henry, jt. ed. see Harewood, Maria Donata Stein Lascelles.

Duncan, Thomas, ed. see Ward-Jackson, Annis.

Duncombe, Frances Riker (1900-)
--Cassie's Village. Mars, Witold Tadeusz J. (1912-), illus. 1965. (ISBN 0-688-41181-9). William Morrow and Company.
--Cissie's Village. Mars, Witold J. (1912-), illus. LC 65-10091. (Illus.). 22cm. 221p. N.D. Lothrop, Lee and Shepard Co.
--Clarinda. Straeter, Angela, illus. LC 44-4616. 133 p. illus. 24 cm. 1944. Holt.
--Eemi: The Story of a Clown. Hill, Marjorie, illus. LC 47-2537. 2 p. l., 38, 2 p., 1 l. col. illus. 20 1/2 cm. 1946. H. Holt and Company
--Ghost at Garnet Lodge. LC 49-11176. 280p. 1949. William Sloan Associates.
--Ghost at Garnet Lodge. Stevens, Mary E. (1920-1966), illus. N.D. William Morrow & Co.
--High Hurdles. Mason, Eleanor Iselin, illus. LC 41-29827. 5 p. l., 3-249 p. illus., plates. 22 cm. c.1941. H. Holt and Company.
--Hoo! Hoo! De Witt!. Lamont, Jean, illus. LC 39-31801. 31, 1 p. illus. (part col.) 22 cm. c.1939. H. Holt and Company.
--The Quetzal Feather. Mars, Witold Tadeusz J. (1912-), illus. LC 67-22597. (Illus.). 255 p. 22cm. 1967. Lothrop, Lee & Shepard Co.
--Summer of the Burning. Cuffari, Richard (1925-1978), illus. LC 75-42956. (Illus.). 176 p. 22cm. c.1976. (ISBN 0-399-20513-6). Putnam.

Dundas, Mrs.
--The Little Cap. (The Little Gipsey Ser.). N.D. The American News Co.
--Wrecked, not Lost. (Illus.). (Child Life Ser.). N.D. D. Lothrop Co.
--Wrecked, Not Lost: Or, The Pilot and His Companions, 1 of 6 vols. (Illus.). (Holiday Tales Library). N.D. E P Dutton.

Dungan, Alice Blackburn
--This Is Petra. LC 37-36390. 223 p. 21 cm. c.1937. J. B. Lippincott Company.

Dunham, Curtis
--The Amazing Adventures of Bobbie in Bugabooland (Next Door to Fairyland). A Cheerful Chronicle for Children Not Younger Than Seven. Kerr, George F., illus. LC 7-31415. 6 p. l., 214 p., 1 l. col. front., illus., plates (partly col.) 25 cm. 1907. The Bobbs-Merrill Company.
--The Golden Goblin: Or, The Flying Dutchman, Junior; a Pleasant Fantasy for Children Based on the Most Fascinating of All Undying Legends; Told in Prose and Verse. Kerr, George F., illus. 6 p. l., 189, 1 p. col. front., illus, 7 col. pl. 25 cm. 1906. Bobbs-Merrill Company.
--Two In a Zoo. Herford, Oliver (1863-1935), illus. LC 4-24497. 25 cm. 148p. 1904. Bobbs-Merrill Co.

Dunham, Curtis, compiled by.
--Wurra-Wurra: A Legend of Saint Patrick at Tara. Innes, John, illus. LC 11-4621. (Illus.). 16cm. 98p. 1911. Fitzgerald.

Dunham, Edith
--Diary of a Mouse. Pease, Bessie Collins, illus. N.D. Dodge.
--Jogging Round the World: Riders and Drivers With Curious Steeds or Vehicls in Strange Lands and At Home. LC 3-37163. 78 p. incl. front., illus. pl. 26 x 21 cm. 1905. Frederick A. Stokes Company.

Dunham, Geoff
--Mudlark. Dunham, Geoff, illus. LC 63-17186. (Illus.). (gr. k-3). 1963. (ISBN 0-8098-1088-3). Walck.

Dunham, John L. (1939-) & Klinger, Gene
--Someday I'm Going to Be Somebody. LC 70-101740. (Illus.). 63 p. 19cm. (Open door book). 1970. Childrens Press.

Dunham, Katharine (1910-)
--Kasamance: A Fantasy. LC 73-92612. (gr. 7 up). 1974. (ISBN 0-89388-128-7). Okpaku Communications.

Dunham, Lillian Shackleton & Walton, Gertrude H
--Two Short Plays for Little Folks: "Red Riding Hood's Reward"The Good Ghost. 13 p. 19 cm. (On cover: Eldridge juvenile plays). c.1932. Eldridge Entertainment House, Inc.
Dunham, Mabel
--Kristli's Trees. Dewdney, Selwyn, illus. 1948. Hale. **Award: (CLA).**
Dunham, Montrew Goetz (1919-)
--Abner Doubleday: Young Baseball Pioneer. Morrow, Gray, illus. LC 65-23665. 200 p. col. illus. 20 cm. (Childhood of famous Americans). 1965. Bobbs-Merrill.
--George Westinghouse: Young Inventor. Morrow, GRay, illus. LC 63-11195. 200 p. illus. 20 cm. (Childhood of famous Americans). 1963. Bobbs-Merrill.
--Oliver Wendell Holmes, Jr. Boy of Justice. Robinson, Jerry, illus. LC 61-12319. 200p. col. illus. (Childhood of famous Americans). c.1961. Bobbs.
Dunhill, James
--Bernadino and the Huks. LC 66-641. 58p. illus. 21cm. (World adventure stories, v.2). 1966, c.1965. F. Muller.
--Bernardino & the Huks. (gr. 9 up). N.D. Soccer.
--The Deserted Highway. LC 66-642. 62p. illus. 21cm. (World adventure stories, v.4). 1966, c.1965. F. Muller.
--Holiday in Hong Kong. LC 66-6402. 58p. illus. 21cm. (World adventure stories, v.3). 1966, c.1965. F. Muller.
--Mel in Malaya. LC 66-639. 61p. illus. 21cm. (World adventure stories, v.1). 1966, c.1965. F. Muller.

Dunlap, Julia, jt. auth. see Hosmer, Margaret Kerr, Mrs.

Dunlap, Marion Wallace
--Magic Fruit Garden. N.D. E. P. Dutton & Co.
Dunlap, Mary J.
--Children Hour. 1983. (ISBN 0-8062-2188-7). Carlton.
Dunlap, Maurice Pratt (1882-) & Sturluson, Snorri
--Stories of the Vikings. Tenggren, Gustaf (1896-1970), illus. LC 23-16489. 5 p. l., 342 p. col. front., plates. 20 cm. c.1923. The Bobbs-Merrill Company.
Dunleavy, Janet Egleson see Frank, Janet, pseud.
Dunlop, Agnes Mary Robertson see Kyle, Elisabeth, pseud.
Dunlop, Agnes Mary Robertson see Ralston, Jan, pseud.
Dunlop, Agnes Mary Robertson (0000-1982), ed. see Jones, Robinson Godfrey.
Dunlop, Eileen Rhona (1938-)
--Elizabeth, Elizabeth. Farmer, Peter, illus. LC 76-46578. (Illus.). 185 p. 24cm. 1977, c.1975. (ISBN 0-03-019311-7). Holt, Rinehart and Winston.
--Fox Farm. LC 78-14091. (Illus.). 149 p., 1 leaf of plates. 22cm. 1979, c.1978. (ISBN 0-03-049051-0). Holt, Rinehart and Winston.
--Fox Farm. LC 78-40466. 149 p. 23cm. 1978. (ISBN 0-19-271428-7). Oxford University Press.
--The House on Mayferry Street. Gili, Phillida, illus. LC 77-5744. (Illus.). 204 p. 22cm. 1977, c.1976. (ISBN 0-03-020686-3). Holt, Rinehart and Winston.
--The Maze Stone. LC 82-22232. 1983. (ISBN 0-698-20587-1). Putnam.
Dunlop, Emma E
--Have You Snuzzled a Wuzzle Today?. LC 85-2141. p. cm. c.1985. (ISBN 0-394-87495-1). Random House.
Dunmore, Patricia
--Morrie Mouse's Birthday Treat. (Illus.). 50p. (gr. k-3). 1976. (ISBN 0-685-67459-2). Intl Pubns Serv.
Dunn, Antonia
--Candy Cane for Katie. 1st ed. Robinson, Jessie Berkowitz, illus. LC 41-24261. (Illus.). 17cm. 29p. 1941. Harper & Brothers.
Dunn, Byron Archibald (1842-)
--Battling for Atlanta. LC 4696. 380 p. front., illus. (ports.) plates, map. 19 cm. (The young Kentuckians series no. 3). 1900. A. C. McClurg & Co.
--The Boy Scouts of the Shenandoah. St. John, J. Allen, illus. LC 16-20109. vi p., 2 l., 355 p. front., plates. 19 cm. (His The young Virginians series). 1916. A. C. McClurg & Co.
--The Courier of the Ozarks. Delay, H. S., illus. LC 12-21764. ix p., 1 l., 363 p. front., plates. 20 cm. (His The young Missourians series). 1912. A. C. McClurg & Co.
--From Atlanta to the Sea. LC 21-12975. 408 p. incl. front. plates. 19 cm. (His Young Kentuckian's series). 1901. A. C. McClurg & Co.
--General Nelson's Scout. LC 98-14118. 320 p. front., plates. 19 cm. 1898. A. C. McClurg and Company.
--The Last Raid. Delay, H. S., illus. LC 14-162182. 3 p. l., iii-iv, 2 p., 1 l., 344 p. front., plates. 19 cm. (His The young Missourians series). 1914. A. C. McClurg & Co.
--On General Thomas's Staff. LC 99-3921. 379 p. front., 13 pl. 19 cm. (young Kentuckians series). 1899. A. C. McClurg and Compaby.
--Raiding with Morgan. LC 3-25540. 2 p. l., 7-334 p., 1 l. front., 9 pl. 20 cm. (young Kentuckians series). 1903. A. C. McClurg & Co.
--The Scout of Pea Ridge. Delay, H. S., illus. LC 11-262537. ix p., 1 l., 344 p. front., plates. 19 cm. (His The young Missourians series). 1911. A. C. McClurg & Co.
--Scouting for Sheridan. St. John, J. Allen, illus. LC 18-22966. 6 p. l., 389 p. front., plates. 19 cm. (His The young Virginians series). 1918. A. C. McClurg & Co.
--Storming Vicksburg. Delay, H. S., illus. LC 13-20572. 6 p. l., 361 p. front., plates. 19 cm. (His The young Missourians series). 1913. A. C. McClurg & Co.
--With the Army of the Potomac. St. John, J. Allen, illus. LC 17-252861. vi p., 2 l., 322 p. front., plates. 19 cm. (His The young Virginians series). 1917. A. C. McClurg & Co.
Dunn, Elizabeth
--Sugar and Spice and Other Candy Stories. LC 61-1579. c.1960. Grosset & Dunlap.
Dunn, Joseph Allan Elphinstone (1872-1941)
--Boru: The Story of an Irish Wolfhound. 195 p. 21 cm. (Famous dog stories). 1961, c.1926. Grosset & Dunlap.
--Boru: The Story of an Irish Wolfhound. Megargee, Edwin, illus. xiii p., 1 l., 195 p. front., illus., plates. 21 cm. 1936. Dodd, Mead & Company.
--Buffalo Boy. (Buddy Bks for Boys). N.D. Grosset & Dunlap.
--Buffalo Boy. Rozen, Jerome, illus. LC 29-2811. 224 p. front., plates. 20 cm. c.1929. Grosset & Dunlap.
--Jim Morse, Gold Hunter. N.D. Small,Maynard & Co.
--Jim Morse, South Sea Trader. LC 19-14707. 6 p. l., 239 p. front., plates. 20 cm. c.1919. Small, Maynard & Company.
--The Odyssey of Boru. Megargee, Edwin, illus. LC 27-1385. xi p., 2 l., 195 p. front., illus., plates. 21 cm. 1926. Dodd, Mead and Company.
--Young Eagle of the Trail. Machtey, illus. LC 31-12454. 3 p. l., 216 p. front., plates. 20 cm. c.1931. Grosset & Dunlap.
Dunn, Judy, pseud., see Spangenberg, Judith Dunn.
Dunn, Judy, pseud. (1942-)
--The Animals of Buttercup Farm. Spangenberg, Judith Dunn. Dunn, Phoebe, illus. LC 81-4892. p. cm. 1981. (ISBN 0-394-84798-9). (ISBN 0-394-94798-3). Random House.
--Friends. Spangenberg, Judith Dunn. Dunn, Phoebe & Dunn, Tris, illus. LC 77-125914. (Illus.). 40 p. 1971. (ISBN 0-87191-046-2). Creative Educational Society.
--The Little Duck. Spangenberg, Judith Dunn. Dunn, Phoebe, illus. LC 75-36467. (Illus.). 32p. (Picturebacks Ser). (ps-1). 1976. (ISBN 0-394-83247-7, BYR). Random.
--The Little Goat. Spangenberg, Judith Dunn. Dunn, Phoebe, illus. LC 77-91658. (Illus.). 32 p. 21cm. (Random House picture book). c.1978. (ISBN 0-394-83872-6). (ISBN 0-394-93871-2). Random House.
--The Little Kitten. Spangenberg, Judith Dunn. Dunn, Phoebe, illus. LC 82-16711. p. cm. c.1982. (ISBN 0-394-95818-7). (ISBN 0-394-85818-2). Random House.
--The Little Lamb. Spangenberg, Judith Dunn. Dunn, Phoebe, illus. LC 76-24167. (Pictureback Library Editions). (ps-2). 1978. (ISBN 0-394-93455-5, BYR). Random.
--The Little Puppy. Spangenberg, Judith Dunn. Dunn, Phoebe, illus. LC 84-2031. 1984. (ISBN 0-394-96595-7). Random.
--The Little Rabbit. Spangenberg, Judith Dunn. Dunn, Phoebe, illus. LC 79-5241. (Illus.). 32 p. 21cm. c.1980. (ISBN 0-394-84377-0). (ISBN 0-394-94377-5). Random House.
Dunn, Judy, pseud. (1942-) & Dunn, Tris
--Having Fun. Spangenberg, Judith Dunn. Dunn, Phoebe, illus. LC 70-128851. (Illus.). 48 p. 1971. (ISBN 0-87191-067-5). Creative Educational Society.
--Things. Spangenberg, Judith Dunn. Dunn, Phoebe, illus. LC 68-17818. (Illus.). 48 p. 1968. Doubleday.
Dunn, Julia Mills
--The Helpful Club. LC 15-21866. 67 p. 15 cm. (On cover: Library series. v. 2, no. 2). 1891. Woman's Temperance Publishing Association.
Dunn, L. R.
--Lizzie Hagar, 1 of 25 vols. (Illus.). (Selected Bks for Sunday School: No. 21). N.D. Set. Methodist Bk Concern.
Dunn, Marion Herndon (1920-)
--Tenase Brave. Moore, June (1942-), illus. LC 74-128453. (Illus.). v, 104 p. 23cm. 1971. (ISBN 0-87695-106-X). Aurora Publishers.
Dunn, Martha Baker
--Anne of Memory Street. N.D. L. C. Page & Co.
--The Sleeping Beauty. (Illus.). (Editha Ser.). N.D. Caldwell.
--The Sleeping Beauty. (Illus.). (Goldenrod Library Ser.). 1905. L. C. Page & Co.
--Sleeping Beauty. Modern Ver ed. Sacker, Amy M., illus. (Cosy Corner Ser.). N.D. L. C. Page & Co.
--The Sleeping Beauty: A Modern Version. Barry, Etheldred Breeze (1870-), illus. LC 12-31946. 5 p. l., 13-97 p. incl. front., illus., plates. 19 cm. 1898. L. C. Page and Company.
Dunn, Mary Lois (1930-)
--The Man in the Box: A Story from Vietnam. LC 68-19488. (Illus.). 155 p. 21cm. 1968. McGraw-Hill.
Dunn, Mary Lois (1930-) & Mayhar, Ardath (1930-)
--The Absolutely Perfect Horse. LC 82-47726. p. cm. c.1983. (ISBN 0-06-021773-1). (ISBN 0-06-021774-X). Harper & Row.
Dunn, Mildred, ed.
--Courage to Win: Stories for Boys. LC 67-16361. 144 p. 21cm. 1967. Broadman Press.
Dunn, Theo, jt. auth. see Battle, Gerald Nichols.
Dunn, Tris, jt. auth. see Dunn, Judy.
Dunnahoo, Terry (1927-)
--This Is Espie Sanchez. LC 76-14807. p. cm. 1976. (ISBN 0-525-41130-5). Dutton.
--Who Cares About Espie Sanchez?. LC 75-12577. 152 p. 22cm. 1975. (ISBN 0-525-42690-6). Dutton.
--Who Needs Espie Sanchez?. LC 77-7147. p. cm. 1977. (ISBN 0-525-42704-X). Dutton.
Dunne, Agnes M., jt. tr. see Miller, Sophie Antoinette.
Dunne, John William (1875-)
--The Jumping Lions of Borneo. Robinson, Irene Bowen, Mrs. (1891-), illus. LC 38-10960. 2 p. l., 60 p. illus. 31 cm. c.1938. H. Holt and Company.
--St. George and the Witches. Coe, Lloyd (1899-1976), illus. LC 39-25042. viii p., 1 l., 206 p. plates. 21 cm. c.1939. H. Holt and Company.
Dunne, Mary Collins (1914-)
--Alaskan Summer. Grant, Elisabeth, illus. LC 68-13229. (Illus.). 160 p. 22cm. 1968. (ISBN 0-200-71536-4). Abelard-Schuman.
--Gregory Gray and the Brave Beast. Axeman, Lois, illus. LC 72-1462. (Illus.). 46 p. 24cm. 1972. (ISBN 0-516-03467-7). Childrens Press.
--Hoby & Stub. LC 80-18449. 156 p. 22cm. 1981. (ISBN 0-689-30806-X). Atheneum.
--Reach Out, Ricardo. LC 72-141866. 157 p. 22cm. 1971. (ISBN 0-200-71759-6). Abelard-Schuman.
--The Secret Of Captives Cave. LC 76-25228. p. cm. c.1976. (ISBN 0-399-20547-0). Putnam.
Dunne, Peter Finley
--Mr. Dooley Says. N.D. Charles Scribner's Sons.
Dunnegan, H. C.
--Caroline Had a Dream and Other Tales. N.D. Carlton Press.
Dunnett, Dorothy (1923-)
--Pawn in Frankincense. 1969. (ISBN 0-399-10623-5). G. P. Putnam's Sons.
--The Ringed Castle. 1972. (ISBN 0-399-10912-9). G. P. Putnam's Sons.
Dunnett, Margaret Rosalind (1909-)
--Ladies and Gentlemen. Gardiner, Jill, illus. LC 77-352832. (Illus.). 158 p. 21cm. 1976. (ISBN 0-233-96785-0). Deutsch.
--No Pets Allowed & Other Animal Stories. Rush, Peter (1937-), illus. LC 80-2692. (Illus.). 144p. (gr. 2-7). 1981. (ISBN 0-233-97103-3). Andre Deutsch.
Dunning, A. K., Mrs., jt. auth. see Hazelton, Mabel.
Dunning, Annie Ketchum, Mrs. (1831-)
--Grace Avery's Influence. N.D. D. Lothrop & Co.
--Grace Westervelt: Or, The Children of the Covenant. A Sequel to "Theodore". LC 12-32626. 311 p. front., plates. 18 cm. c.1876. Presbyterian Board of Publication.
--The Minister's Wife. N.D. American Sunday-School Union.
--Ralph Waring's Money. N.D. American Sunday-School Union.
--A Story of Four Lives, 1 of 5 vols. (Illus.). (Favorite Books for Girls). N.D. D. Lothrop & Co.
--Trifles. N.D. D. Lothrop & Co.
Dunning, Arthur Stephen, Jr. (1924-), ed.
--Mad Sad & Glad. (gr. 7-9). 1972. (ISBN 0-590-09188-3, Schol Trade Pap). Schol Bk Serv.
--Mad Sad & Glad. Repr. (Starbright Editions). (gr. 7-12). 1973. Schol Bk Serv.
Dunning, Arthur Stephen, Jr. (1924-) & Lueders, Edward, eds.
--Reflections on a Gift of Watermelon Pickle & Other Modern Verse. LC 66-8763. (Illus.). (gr. 7 up). 1966. (ISBN 0-688-41231-9). (ISBN 0-688-51231-3). Lothrop.
--Reflections on a Gift of Watermelon Pickle and Other Modern Verse. 1966. (ISBN 0-688-41231-9). William Morrow and Company.
--Some Haystacks Don't Even Have Any Needle and Other Complete Modern Poems. (Illus.). color ils. 192p. (gr. 7 up). 1969. (ISBN 0-688-41445-1). Lothrop. **Award: (ALA).**
Dunnington, Tom, illus.
--Animals. LC 83-25213. (Illus.). 32p. (The Shape of Poetry Ser.). (gr. k-3). 1984. (ISBN 0-89565-264-1). Childs World.
Dunnington, Tom, jt. auth. see Greene, Carol.
Dunnington, Tom, ed. see Blyton, Enid Mary.
Dunrea, Olivier
--Eddy B, Pigboy. Dunrea, Olivier, illus. LC 83-2832. (Illus.). 22 p. 19cm. 1983. (ISBN 0-689-50277-X). Atheneum.
--Fergus and Bridey. Dunrea, Olivier, illus. LC 84-19828. (Illus.). 32 p. c.1985. (ISBN 0-8234-0554-0). Holiday House.
--Mogwogs on the March!. Dunrea, Olivier, illus. LC 85-5493. p. cm. c.1985. (ISBN 0-8234-0578-8). Holiday House.
--Ravena. Dunrea, Olivier, illus. LC 82-23244. (Illus.). 32p. (ps-3). 1984. (ISBN 0-8234-0487-0). (ISBN 0-8234-0487-0). Holiday.
Dunsany, Edward John Moreton Drax Plunkett (1878-1957)
--Fifty-One Tales. 138p. N.D. Little , Brown & Co.
--Tales of Three Hemispheres. N.D. Bruce Humphries, Inc.
Dunsing, Dorothy May
--The Seminole Trail. 1st ed. Toschik, Larry (1922-), illus. LC 56-9215. 211p. illus. 21cm. 1956. Longmans, Green.
--Swamp Shadows. Ray, Ralph (1920-1952), illus. LC 48-7182. 226 p. illus. 22 cm. 1948. Longmans, Green.
--War Chant. 1st ed. Johnson, Eugene Harper, illus. LC 54-767925. 176p. 21cm. 1954. Longmans, Green.
Dunstan, Maryjane, jt. auth. see Garlan, Patricia Wallace.
Dunster, H. P.
--Tales of Lancastrian Times. N.D. Potts, Young & Co.
Dunton, Edith Kellogg see Warde, Margaret, pseud.
Dunton, Edith Kellogg (1875-)
--Betty Wales & Co. Warde, Margaret, pseud. LC 38-12747. 358 p. front. 19 cm. 1926. The Penn Publishing Company.
--Betty Wales & Co. Warde, Margaret, pseud. Nagel, Eva M., illus. (The Betty Wales Bks.). N.D. Grosset & Dunlap.
--Betty Wales and Co. Warde, Margaret, pseud. Nagel, Eva M., illus. (The Betty Wales Books). N.D. Penn Publishing Co.
--Betty Wales & Co. A Story for Girls. Warde, Margaret, pseud. Nagel, Eva M., illus. LC 9-24325. 358 p. front., 6 pl. 20 cm. 1909. The Penn Publishing Company.
--Betty Wales, B. A. Warde, Margaret, pseud. LC 36-986619. 5, 9-345 p. 19 cm. 1936. The Penn Publishing Company.
--Betty Wales, B. A. Warde, Margaret, pseud. Nagel, Eva M., illus. (The Betty Wales Bks.). N.D. Grosset & Dunlap.
--Betty Wales, B. A. A Story for Girls. Warde, Margaret, pseud. Nagel, Eva M., illus. LC 8-24449. 345 p. front., 6 pl. 20 cm. 1908. The Penn Publishing Company.
--Betty Wales Decides. Warde, Margaret, pseud. Nagel, Eva M., illus. (The Betty Wales Bks.). N.D. Grosset & Dunlap.
--Betty Wales Decides. Warde, Margaret, pseud. Nagel, Eva M., illus. (The Betty Wales Books). N.D. Penn Publishing Co.
--Betty Wales Decides: A Story for Girls. Warde, Margaret, pseud. Nagel, Eva M., illus. LC 11-24819. 357 p. front., plates. 20 cm. 1911. The Penn Publishing Company.
--Betty Wales, Freshman. Warde, Margaret, pseud. LC 32-17527. 3, 7-369 p. front. 19 cm. 1929. The Penn Publishing Company.
--Betty Wales, Freshman. Warde, Margaret, pseud. Nagel, Eva M., illus. (The Betty Wales Bks.). N.D. Grosset & Dunlap.
--Betty Wales, Freshman. Warde, Margaret, pseud. Nagel, Eva M., illus. (The Betty Wales Books). N.D. The Penn Publishing Co.
--Betty Wales, Freshman: A Story for Girls. Warde, Margaret, pseud. Nagel, Eva M., illus. LC 4-21668. 369 p. front., 6 pl. 19 cm. (Keystone Ser.). 1904. The Penn Publishing Company.
--Betty Wales, Freshman: A Story for Girls. Warde, Margaret, pseud. Nagel, Eva M., illus. LC 13-23589. 2 p. l., 3-369 p. front., plates. 20 cm. 1912. The Penn Publishing Company.
--Betty Wales, Junior. Warde, Margaret, pseud. LC 34-6034. 344 p. front. 19 cm. c.1934. The Penn Publishing Company.
--Betty Wales, Junior. Warde, Margaret, pseud. Nagel, Eva M., illus. (The Betty Wales Bks.). N.D. Grosset & Dunlap.

--Dragonfall Five & the Space Cowboys. Stern, Simon (1943-), illus. LC 74-19036. (Illus.). 22cm. 96p. (gr. 3-6). 1975. (ISBN 0-688-41680-2). (ISBN 0-688-51680-7). Lothrop.
--Dragonfall Five and the Space Cowboys. Stern, Simon (1943-), illus. 1975. (ISBN 0-688-41680-2). William Morrow and Company.

Earnshaw, Judith, ed.
--Sprouts on Helicon. (gr. 9 up). N.D. (ISBN 0-233-95784-7). Transatlantic.

Earring, Monica F.
--Prairie Legends. Robinson, Pat, illus. (Indian Culture Ser.). (gr. 6-9). 1978. (ISBN 0-89992-069-1). Mt Coun Indian.

East, Anna M.
--Daniel's Odyssey. 1981. (ISBN 0-8062-1834-7). Carlton.
--Teensie & Beensie: The Adventures of Mother Rabbit's Children & Their Woodland Friends. 2nd ed. Smith, Kathleen E., illus. (Illus.). (ps-3). 1971. (ISBN 0-682-47226-3). Exposition.

East, Ben (1898-)
--The Last Eagle. (Illus.). 320p. 1974. Crown.

East, Ben (1898-), ed.
--Mistaken Journey. Dahl, Jack, illus. LC 79-53775. p. cm. (Survival). 1979. (ISBN 0-89686-046-9). (ISBN 0-89686-054-X). Crestwood House.

East, Ben (1898-) & Schroeder, Howard
--Grizzly!. Dahl, Jack, illus. LC 79-53748. (Illus.). 47 p. 23cm. (Survival). c.1979. (ISBN 0-89686-045-0). (ISBN 0-89686-053-1). Crestwood House.

Easterly, Lane, ed.
--Great Bible Stories for Children. N.D. (ISBN 0-8407-4988-0). Nelson.
--Great Bible Stories for Children. N.D. (ISBN 0-8407-5351-9). Nelson.

Easthill, Ruth
--Little Red Hen. The Story of the Little Red Hen. Easthill, Ruth, illus. LC 37-21958. 34 p. illus. (part col.) 17 cm. c.1937. Whitman Publishing Co.
--Three Little Ducks. Easthill, Ruth, illus. LC 37-21957. 34 p. illus. (part col.) 17 cm. c.1937. Whitman Publishing Co.

Eastlake, William Derry (1917-)
--Dancers in the Scalp House. LC 75-16135. 245p. (Richard Seaver Bk). 1975. (ISBN 0-670-25467-3). Viking Pr.

Eastman, Charles Alexander (1858-)
--Indian Boyhood. 247p. 1914. (ISBN 0-486-22037-0). Dover Books.
--Indian Boyhood. N.D. Gale Reprint.
--Indian Child Life. Varian, George, illus. LC 13-17131. vii p., 2 l., 160 p., 1 l. front., plates. 19 cm. 1913. Little, Brown, and Company.
--Indian Scout Craft and Lore. 190p. Orig. Title: Indian Scout Talks. 1914. (ISBN 0-486-22995-5). Dover Books.
--Red Hunters and the Animal People. LC 74-7964. p. cm. 1976. (ISBN 0-404-11852-6). AMS Press.
--The Red Hunters and the Animal People. LC 4-31055. (Illus.). 20cm. 248p. (Harper's Selected Juveniles.). 1901. Harper & Brothers.

Eastman, Charles Alexander (1858-) & Eastman, Elaine Goodale, Mrs. (1863-)
--Wigwam Evenings: Sioux Folk Tales. Deming, Edwin Willard (1860-1942), illus. LC 9-26010. xvi. 253 p. incl. illus., plates, front. 19 cm. 1909. Little, Brown and Company.

Eastman, David, adapted by.
--Sherlock Holmes: The Adventure of the Empty House. Eitzen, Allan (1928-), illus. LC 81-11673. (Illus.). 32p. (gr. 5-9). 1982. (ISBN 0-89375-616-4). (ISBN 0-89375-617-2). Troll Assocs.
--Sherlock Holmes: The Adventure of the Speckled Band. Eitzen , Allan, illus. LC 81-11694. (Illus.). 32p. (gr. 5-9). 1982. (ISBN 0-89375-618-0). (ISBN 0-89375-619-9). Troll Assocs.
--Sherlock Holmes: The Final Problem. Eitzen, Allan (1928-), illus. LC 81-11609. (Illus.). 32p. (gr. 5-9). 1982. (ISBN 0-89375-612-1). (ISBN 0-89375-613-X). Troll Assocs.
--Sherlock Holmes: The Red-Headed League. Eitzen, Allan (1928-), illus. LC 81-11619. (Illus.). 32p. (gr. 5-9). 1982. (ISBN 0-89375-614-8). (ISBN 0-89375-615-6). Troll Assocs.

Eastman, David, (1859-1930), adapted by see Doyle, Arthur Conan, Sir.

Eastman, Elaine Goodale see Goodale, Elaine (1863-) & Goodale, Dora Read.

Eastman, Elaine Goodale, Mrs., jt. auth. see Eastman, Charles Alexander.

Eastman, Elaine Goodale, Mrs. (1863-)
--Indian Legends Retold. Varian, George, illus. 161p. 1919. Little, Brown.
--The Luck of Oldacres. Bailey, William J., illus. LC 28-19753. 6 p. l., 3-239 p. front., plates. 19 1/2 cm. 1928. The Century Co.
--Yellow Star: A Story of East and West. De Cora, Angel & Star, William Lone, illus. LC 11-23870. 6 p. l., 3-272 p. front., plates. 19 1/2 cm. 1911. Little, Brown, and Company.

Eastman, Frances Whitteir (1915-)
--We Belong Together. 128p. 1960. Friendship Press.

Eastman, Fred (1886-)
--Pursuit of the Flying Baby: A Faithful Account of the Strange Happenings to William Thompson After His Mother Told Him to Mind the Baby. Regina & Ludwig, illus. LC 28-30279. 5 p. l., 237 p. col. front., col. illus. 20 1/2 cm. c.1928. Willett, Clark & Colby.

Eastman, Julia Arabella, jt. auth. see Edson, N. I.

Eastman, Julia Arabella (1837-1911)
--Kitty Kent, 1 of 6 vols. (Illus.). N.D. Lothrop.
--Kitty Kent. (Illus.). (The Kitty Kent Library). N.D. Set. Ward & Drummond.
--Kitty Kent's Troubles. LC 20-19316. 488 p. front., plates. 18 cm. (On cover: The young folks' library, no. 3). 1884. D. Lothrop & Co.
--Kitty Kent's Troubles, 1 of 50 vols. (Illus.). 350p. (Sunday-School Lib: No. 14). N.D. Set. Lothrop Pub. Co.
--Kitty Kent's Troubles. N.D. Pilgrims Press.
--The Ridgemont Ser. Containing "The Romney's of Ridgemont," "School-days of Beulah Romney," and "Kitty Kent's Troubles", 3 vols. N.D. Set. D. Lothrop & Co.
--The Rommeys of Ridgemont, 1 of 50 vols. (Illus.). 350p. (Sunday-School Lib: No. 14). N.D. Set. Lothrop Pub. Co.
--The Romneys of Ridgemont, 1 of 6 vols. (Illus.). N.D. D Lothrop.
--School Days of Beulah Romney, 1 of 6 vols. (Illus.). N.D. D. Lothrop Co.
--School Days of Beulah Romney, 1 of 50 vols. (Illus.). 350p. (Sunday-School Lib: No. 14). N.D. Set. Lothrop.
--Short Comings and Long Goings, 1 of 6 vols. (Illus.). N.D. D Lothrop.
--Short-Comings and Long-Goings: Or, The Boys and Girls of Glencairn. LC 20-16475. 3 p. l., 5-269 p. front., plates. 17 1/2 cm. (Added t.-p.: New $500 prize series). 1871. D. Lothrop & Co.
--Striking for the Right, 1 of 6 vols. (Illus.). N.D. Lothrop Pub. Co.
--Young Rick, 1 of 50 vols. (Illus.). 350p. (Sunday-School Lib: No. 14). N.D. Set. Lothrop Pub. Co.
--Young Rick, 1 of 6 vols. Eytinge, Sol, illus. (Illus.). (Eastman's (Julia A.) Books). N.D. D Lothrop & Co.
--Young Rick. Eytinge, Sol, illus. (Illus.). N.D. Lothrop Pub. Co.
--Young Rick Library: Containing "Young Rick", "Two Fortune Seekers" and "My Little Gentlemen", 3 vols. N.D. Set. D. Lothrop & Co.

Eastman, Julia Arabella (1837-1911) & Fell, Archie
--Our Daughter's Library: Containing "New Commandment", "Mrs. Thorne's Guests", "Neighbor's House" and "Strawberry Hill", 4 vols. N.D. Set. D. Lothrop & Co.

Eastman, Max Forrester (1883-1969)
--Venture. LC 27-24010. 4 p. l., 398 p. 19 1/2 cm. 1927. A. & C. Boni.

Eastman, Patricia
--Sometimes Things Change. Fleishman, Seymour (1918-), illus. LC 83-10090. p. cm. (Rookie Reader). 1983. (ISBN 0-516-02044-7). (ISBN 0-516-42044-5). Childrens Press.

Eastman, Philip Dey, jt. auth. see McKie, Roy.

Eastman, Philip Dey (1909-)
--The Alphabet Book. LC 73-16859. 32 p. (chiefly col. illus. 21cm. 1974. (ISBN 0-394-82818-6). Random House.
--Are You My Mother?. Eastman, Philip Dey (1909-), illus. LC 60-13495. (Illus.). 63 p. 24cm. (Beginner books, B-18). 1960. Beginner Books; Distributed by Random House.
--The Best Nest. Eastman, Philip Dey (1909-), illus. LC 68-28459. (Illus.). 63 p. 24cm. 1968. Beginner Books.
--Big Dog ... Little Dog: A Bedtime Story. LC 73-2677. (Illus.). 32 p. 21cm. 1973. (ISBN 0-394-82669-8). (ISBN 0-394-82669-8). Random House.
--Big Dog- Little Dog: A Bedtime Story. LC 81-12070. p. cm. c.1981. (ISBN 0-394-85142-0). Random House.
--Everything Happens to Aaron. Incl. In the Summer; In the Autumn; In the Winter; In the Spring. (Take-Along Bks). (ps-1). 1976. Set. (ISBN 0-394-83330-9, BYR). Random.
--Everything Happens to Aaron, 4 Bks. Eastman, Philip Dey (1909-), illus. (Illus.). (Take Along Books Ser). (ps-1). 1967. Set. (ISBN 0-394-81051-1). (ISBN 0-394-91051-6). Random.
--Everything Happens to Aaron in the Autumn. LC 67-20862. (Illus.). 16cm. 23p. (Take-along bks.). 1967. Random.
--Everything Happens to Aaron in the Spring. (Illus.). 16cm. 23p. (Take-along bks.). 1967. Random.
--Everything Happens to Aaron in the Summer. LC 67-20863. (Illus.). 16cm. 23p. (Take-along bks.). 1967. Random.
--Everything Happens to Aaron in the Winter. LC 67-20865. (Illus.). 16cm. 23p. (Take-along bks.). 1967. Random.
--Flap Your Wings. Eastman, Philip Dey (1909-), illus. LC 77-87822. (Illus.). 36 p. 24cm. (Random House early bird book). 1969. Random House.
--Flap Your Wings. Eastman, Philip Dey (1909-), illus. LC 76-24164. (Illus.). 32 p. 21cm. (Random House pictureback). (Best book club ever). c.1977. (ISBN 0-394-83565-4). Random House.
--Go, Dog, Go!. LC 61-7069. (Illus.). 64 p. 24cm. (Beginner books, B-20). 1961. Beginner Books.
--Sam & the Firefly. Eastman, Philip Dey (1909-), illus. LC 58-11966. (Illus.). 62 p. 24cm. 1958. Beginner Books; Distributed by Random House.
--What Time Is It?. LC 79-63902. (Illus.). 21 p. 16cm. c.1979. (ISBN 0-394-84267-7). Random House.

Eastman, Sophie E.
--Finding His Footprints. N.D. Lockwood, Brooks, & Co. for American Tract Society.

Easton, Theodore Sydney
--The Secret of the Wallowa Cave. LC 34-12884. 5 p. l., 3-127, 1 p. col. front., illus. 20 1/2 cm. 1934. Metropolitan Press.

Easton, Violet
--Elephants Never Jump: Story. Sole, Vendrell Carme (1944-), illus. LC 85-47937. p. cm. c.1985. (ISBN 0-87113-049-1). Atlantic Monthly Press.

Eastwick, Ivy Ethel Olive
--A Camel for Saida. Fortnum, Peggy, pseud. (1919-), illus. Nuttall-Smith, Margaret Emily Noel. LC 64-23329. 127 p. illus. (part col.) 28 cm. 1964. Roy Publishers.
--Cherry stones garden swings. Jones, A. Robert, illus. LC 62-11144. (Illus.). 19cm. 63p. N.D. Abingdon Press.
--Deck the Stable. Unwin, Nora Spicer (1907-), illus. LC 60-9816. (Illus.). unpaged. illus 20cm. (gr. 2-5). 1960. McKay.
--Fairies and Suchlike. Merwin, Decie (1894-1961), illus. LC 46-5907. 63 1 p. col. illus. 20 x 17 1/2 cm. 1946. E. P. Dutton & Company Inc.
--I Rode the Black Horse Far Away. Jones, Robert A., illus. (Illus.). (ps-5). N.D. (ISBN 0-687-18553-X). Abingdon.
--I Rode the Black Horse Far Away: Poems. LC 60-6814. (Illus.). 63 p. 19cm. 1960. Abingdon Press.
--Rainbow Over All: Poems. Siberell, Anne, illus. LC 67-2931. (Illus.). 64 p. 24cm. 1967. D. McKay Co.
--Seven Little Popovers. Lisowski, Gabriel (1946-), illus. LC 79-19010. (Illus.). 32 p. 27cm. c.1979. (ISBN 0-695-41291-4). Follett Pub. Co.
--Traveler's Joy Poems. Merwin, Decie (1894-1961), illus. LC 60-5303. 47p. illus. 21cm. 1960. Mckay.

Eastwick, Ivy Ethel Olive & Swinger, Marlys
--In and Out the Windows: Happy Poems for Children. Barth, Gillian, illus. LC 73-90841. (Illus.). 71 p. 24cm. 1969. Plough Pub. House.

Eastwood, Edna (1894-)
--Saints Courageous: Stories for Boys and Girls. Gaard, Emma, illus. LC 48-970128. 189 p. illus. 21 cm. 1948. Morehouse-Gorham Co.
--When the Time Comes: A Story of Holy Week and Easter. LC 53-13447. 97p. 23cm. c.1953. Vantage Press.

Eastwood, Frances
--Geoffrey the Lollard, 1 of 10 vols. (Popular Stories). N.D. Dodd, Mead & Co.
--Marcella of Rome, 1 of 10 vols. (Popular Stories). N.D. Dodd, Mead & Company.

Eaton, Anne Thaxter (1881-1971), ed. see Alcott, Louisa May.

Eaton, Anne Thaxter (1881-1971), ed.
--The Animals' Christmas. Angelo, Valenti (1897-), illus. (Illus.). (gr. 4 up). 1944. (ISBN 0-670-12800-7). Viking Pr.
--A Round Dozen. 1963. (ISBN 0-670-60877-7). Viking Pr.
--Welcome Christmas: A Garland of Poems. Angelo, Valenti (1897-), illus. (Illus.). (gr. 4 up). 1955. (ISBN 0-670-75708-X). Viking Pr.

Eaton, Evelyn Sybil Mary (1902-)
--Canadian Circus. Ward, Ella Hanson, illus. LC 39-14800. ix, 11-240 p. front., plates. 21 cm. 1939. T. Nelson and Sons, Ltd.
--John--Film Star: A Novel for Boys. Matthew, Jack (1911-) & Vox, Maximilien, illus. LC 37-10699. vii, 246 p. col. front., illus. 20 1/2 cm. 1937. T. Nelson and Sons, Ltd.

Eaton, Frances
--Dollikins and the Miser. Taylor, W. L., illus. LC 44-29778. 3 p. l., 11-235 p. incl. illus., plates. front. 21 1/2 x 17 1/2 cm. 1890. D. Lothrop Company.
--A Queer Little Princess and Her Friends. Bridgman, Lewis Jesse (1857-1931), illus. LC 12-32019. 3 p. l., 11-359 p. incl. illus., plates, front. 21 1/2 x 17 cm. c.1888. D. Lothrop Company.

Eaton, Harriette Grace
--Bunya-Bunya Magic. LC 55-11717. 61p. 22cm. 1955. Creative Press.

Eaton, Jeanette
--The Story of Light. Schwartz, Max, illus. LC 28-16135. 76p. col. front., illus. 19cm. (City and Country Ser.). 1928. Harper & Brothers.

Eaton, Jeanette, jt. auth. see Collier, Virginia M.

Eaton, Jeanette, jt. auth. see Finta, Alexander.

Eaton, Jeanette (1886-1968)
--Betsy's Napoleon. Brissaud, Pierre, illus. LC 36-27454. 6 p. l., 3-274 p. col. front., plates. 21 cm. 1936. W. Morrow and Company.
--Daughter of the Seine. 1929. Harper. **Award: (JNM).**

Eaton, M. A., ed. see Longfellow, Henry Wadsworth.

Eaton, Seymour (1859-1916)
--Adventures of the Traveling Bears. (The Traveling Bear Ser.). N.D. Barse & Hopkins.
--More About Teddy B. and Teddy G. The Roosevelt Bears: Being Volume Two Depicting Their Further Travels and Adventures. Culver, R. K., illus. LC 7-26344. 129 p. col. front., illus. (part col.) 28 1/2 x 21 1/2 cm. 1907. E. Stern & Company, Inc.
--Prince Domino and Muffles. Twelvetrees, C, illus. 146p. N.D. Edward Stern & Co.
--The Roosevelt Bears Abroad. Culver, R. K., illus. LC 8-23562. 178 p. col. front., illus. (partly col.) 28 1/2 cm. 1908. E. Stern & Co., Inc.
--The Roosevelt Bears Go to Washington. Campbell, V. Floyd (0000-1906), illus. (Illus.). (gr. 6 up). 1981. Dover.
--The Roosevelt Bears: Their Travels and Adventures. Campbell, V. Floyd (0000-1906), illus. LC 79-52525. (Illus.). 180 p. 24cm. 1979. (ISBN 0-486-23819-9). Dover Publications.
--The Roosevelt Bears: Their Travels and Adventures. Campbell, V. Floyd (0000-1906), illus. LC 6-20453. 180 p. 1 l., col. front., illus. (part col.) 28 1/2 x 22 cm. 1906. E. Stern & Company, Inc.
--Teddy-B & Teddy-G: The Bear Detectives. Wrightman, Francis P. & Sweeny, William K., illus. LC 9-22618. 178 p. col. front., illus. (partly col.) 28 1/2 cm. 1909. E. Stern & Co., Inc.
--Traveling Bear Detectives. (The Traveling Bear Ser.). 1921. Barse & Hopkins.
--Traveling Bears Across the Sea. (The Traveling Bear Ser.). N.D. Barse & Hopkins.
--Traveling Bears at Play. (The Traveling Bears Ser.). N.D. Barse & Hopkins.
--Traveling Bears' Birthday. (The Traveling Bear Ser.). 1921. Barse & Hopkins.
--Traveling Bears in England. (The Traveling Bears Ser.). N.D. Barse & Hopkins.
--Traveling Bears in New York. (The Traveling Bear Ser.). N.D. Barse & Hopkins.
--Traveling Bears In Outdoor Sports. (The Traveling Bear Ser.). N.D. Barse & Hopkins.
--Traveling Bears in the East and West. (The Traveling Bear Ser.). N.D. Barse & Hopkins.

Eaton, Tom (1940-)
--Flap. Eaton, Tom (1940-), illus. LC 72-1383. (Illus.). 117 p. 26cm. 1972. Delacorte Press.
--The Organized Week. Eaton, Tom (1940-), illus. (gr. 7-12). 1977. (ISBN 0-590-09858-6). Scholastic Inc.
--Otis G. Firefly's Phantasmagoric Almanac & Calendar. Eaton, Tom (1940-), illus. (Illus.). (gr. 7-12). 1975. (ISBN 0-590-09936-1, Schol Trade Pap). Schol Bk Serv.

Eaton, Walter Prichard (1878-)
--Adventures of the Duck Family. Rose, Carl (1903-1971), illus. LC 33-136. 111 p. incl. front., illus. 20 cm. c.1932. W. A. Wilde Company.
--Boy Scouts at Crater Lake: A Story of Crater Lake National Park and High Cascades. Kiser, Fred H., illus. LC 23-121226. 292 p. front., plates 19 1/2 cm. c.1922. W. A. Wilde Company.
--Boy Scouts at the Grand Canyon: A Story of the Rainbow Country. LC 33-486. 304 p. front., plates. 19 1/2 cm. 1932. W. A. Wilde Company.
--Boy Scouts in Death Valley. LC 30-337503. 2 p. l., 307 p. front., plates. 19 1/2 cm. c.1939. W. A. Wilde Company.
--Boy Scouts in Glacier Park: The Adventures of Two Young Easterners in the Heart of the High Rockies. Kiser, Fred H., illus. LC 18-26969. 336 p. front., plates. 19 1/2 cm. c.1918. W. A. Wilde Company.
--Boy Scouts in the Dismal Swamp. Copeland, Charles, illus. LC 13-26563. 10, 13-304 p. incl. front., 1 illus. 19 1/2 cm. c.1913. W. A. Wilde Company.
--Boy Scouts in the Green Mountain Trail: A Story of the Long Trail. LC 29-19026. 317 p. front., plates. 19 1/2 cm. 1929. W. A. Wilde Company.

--Boy Scouts in the White Mountains: The Story of a Long Hike. Merrill, Frank Thayer (1848-), illus. LC 15-1291. 2 p. l., 9, 13-301 p. col. front., plates. 19 1/2 cm. c.1914. W. A. Wilde Company.
--The Boy Scouts of Berkshire. Copeland, Charles, illus. LC 12-21317. 313 p. incl. col. front., 1 illus. 20 cm. c.1912. W. A. Wilde Company.
--Boy Scouts of the Wildest Patrol: The Adventures of Peanut As a Young Scout Master. Merrill, Frank Thayer (1848-), illus. LC 15-21436. 10, 13-302 p. incl. col. front., illus. (map) pl. 19 1/2 cm. c.1915. W. A. Wilde Company.
--Boy Scouts on Katahdin: A Story of the Maine Woods. LC 24-25740. 315 p. front., plates. 19 1/2 cm. c.1924. W. A. Wilde Company.
The Cow That Lived in a House. Ross, Carl (1903-1971), illus. LC 35-1324. 41 p. incl. front., illus. 20 cm. c.1934. W. A. Wilde Company.
--Hawkeye's Roommate: A Story of Hampshire School. Martin, P. L. & Cue, Harold, illus. LC 28-28085. viii, 9-316 p. front. 19 1/2 cm. c.1927. W. A. Wilde Company.
--The Idyl of Twin Fires. N.D. W. A. Wilde Co.
--The Man Who Found Christmas. Stone, Walter King, illus. N.D. W. A. Wilde Co.
--On the Edge of the Wilderness. Bull, Charles Livingston (1874-1932), illus. 320p. N.D. W. A. Wilde.
--Peanut-Cub Reporter. Merrill, Frank Thayer (1848-), illus. N.D. W. A. Wilde.

Eavey, Louise Bone (1900-)
--A Child's Shining Pathway of Christian Nursery Rhymes. Murphy, Emmy Lou Osborne (1910-), illus. LC 61-627. 57p. illus. 20cm. 1960. Zondervan.

Eber, Christine Engla
--Just Momma and Me. LC 75-30308. (Illus.). 36 p. 26cm. c.1975. (ISBN 0-914996-09-6). Lollipop Power.

Eber, Christine Engla, jt. auth. see Atkinson, Mary Ella.

Eber, Dorothy Margaret Harley, jt. auth. see Pitseolak, Peter.

Eberhard, Wolfram (1909-), ed.
--Chinese Fairy Tales and Folk Tales. Eberhard, Wolfram (1909-), tr. N.D. E. P. Dutton & Co.
--Folktales of China. Eberhard, Wolfram (1909-), tr. N.D. (ISBN 0-671-48127-4). Simon & Schuster (Washington Square Press).
--Folktales of China. Eberhard, Wolfram (1909-), tr. 312p. 1965. The University Of Chicago Press.

Eberle, Irmengarde see Allen, Allyn, pseud.

Eberle, Irmengarde (1898-1979)
--A Circus of Our Own. Wiese, Kurt (1887-1974), illus. LC 48-839594. 162 p. illus. 22 cm. 1948. Dodd, Mead.
--Come Be My Friend. N.D. E. M. Hale & Co.
--Come Be My Friend. Riger, Bob, illus. LC 56-5170. 149p. illus. 21cm. 1956. Dodd. Mead.
--The Dog Who Came to Visit. Payne, Roger, illus. LC 67-23074. (Illus.). 95 p. 22cm. 1967. Abelard-Schuman.
--Evie & Cookie. Slobodkin, Louis (1903-1975), illus. LC 57-52560. (Illus.). 122p. (gr. 2-4). 1957. (ISBN 0-394-81134-8). (ISBN 0-394-91134-2). Knopf.
--Evie & the Wonderful Kangaroo. Slobodkin, Louis (1903-1975), illus. LC 55-8945. (Illus.). 22cm. 128p. (gr. 2-4). 1955. (ISBN 0-394-81135-6). Knopf.
--A Family to Raise. Bostelmann, Else, illus. LC 39-27436. (Illus.). 92. 21cm. 1939. Holiday House.
--The Favorite Place. Perl, Susan (1922-1983), illus. LC 56-7437. 135p. illus. 20cm. c.1957. F. Watts.
--Fawn in the Woods. Hess, Lilo, photos by. LC 62-7151. (Illus.). 42. 24cm. 1962. Crowell.
--A Good House for a Mouse. Wilkin, Eloise Burns (1904-), illus. LC 40-690174. 31 p. illus. 23 1/2 cm. c.1940. J. Messner Inc.
--Hop, Skip, and Fly: Stories of Small Creatures. Bostelmann, Else, illus. LC 37-27416. (Illus.). 70. 21cm. 1937. Holiday House.
--Johnny's Island Ark. Savitt, Sam, illus. LC 60-5584. (Illus.). 89p. 21cm. 1960. F. Watts.
--Lone Star Fight. Townsend, Lee (1895-), illus. LC 54-112373. 292p. illus. 21cm. 1954. Dodd, Mead.
--Lorie. Stevens, Mary E. (1920-1966), illus. LC 50-9950. 174 p. illus. 22 cm. 1950. Whittlesey House.
--Mountain Holiday. Brudi, Theresa, illus. LC 76-140090. (Illus.). 123 p. 22cm. 1971. (ISBN 0-200-71754-5). Abelard-Schuman.
--Mustang on the Prairie. Cellini, Joseph (1924-), illus. LC 68-22476. (Illus.). 89 p. 22cm. 1968. Doubleday.
--Pete & the Mouse. Rose, Gerald Hembdon Seymour (1935-), illus. LC 64-17818. (Illus.). 26cm. 41p. (ps-3). 1964. Abelard.
--Phoebe-Belle. Eichenberg, Fritz (1901-), illus. LC 41-197220. 63, 1 p. illus. 22 1 / 2cm. c.1941. The Greystone Press.
--Picture Stories for Children. (Illus.). 28cm. 89p. 1921. Frederick A. Stokes Co.
--Picture Stories for Children: A Rebus. Eberle, Irmengarde (1898-1979). illus. LC 84-4352. (Illus.). 60p. (ps-3). 1984, c.1921. (ISBN 0-385-29340-2). Delacorte.
--The Right Dog for Joe. Porter, Jean Macdonald (1906-), illus. LC 49-487740. vii, 197 p. illus. 21 cm. 1949. Dodd, Mead.
--Robins and the Window Sill. Scott, Myron E., photos by. LC 58-6604. 42p. illus. 24cm. 1958. Crowell.
--Rosemary's Secret. Koering, Ursula (1921-), illus. LC 58-6199. (Illus.). 140 p. 21cm. 1958. Random House.
--The Steam Shovel Family. Moran, Constance Oehler (1898-), illus. LC 48-6715. 187 p. illus. 21 cm. 1948. D. McKay Co.
--Too Many Shoes and Stockings. Brashears, C. Walton, illus. LC 47-80. (Illus.). 26cm. 34p. N.D. Reynal & Hitchcock.
--Too Many Shoes and Stockings. Brashears, Walton, illus. (gr. k-9). N.D. David McKay Co.
--Town Without Grown-Ups. LC 41-14768. 255 1 p., incl. front., illus. (incl. plan) 22 cm. c.1941. J. Messner, Inc.
--The Very Good Neighbors. De Muth, Flora Nash (1888-), illus. LC 45-5355. 95, 1 p. illus. (part col.) 21 cm. 1945. J. B. Lippincott Company.
--The Visiting Jimpsons. Kreps, Ruth, illus. (gr. 3-7). N.D. David McKay Co.
--The Visiting Jimpsons. Kreps, Ruth, illus. LC 46-7720. 4 p. l., 11-188 p. incl. illus., plates. 21 cm. 1946. Reynal & Hitchcock.
--We'll Take the Skyway. LC 43-453. 3 p. l., 233 p. 21 cm. 1942. Thomas Y. Crowell Company.

Eberle, Paul (1928-) & Eberle, Shirley (1929-)
--The Adventures of Mrs. Pussycat. De Rosa, Anthony, illus. LC 72-5093. (Illus.). 94 p. 25cm. 1972. (ISBN 0-13-014142-9). (ISBN 0-13-014126-7). Prentice-Hall.

Eberle, Shirley, jt. auth. see Eberle, Paul.

Eberling, Georgia Moore
--One Winter. Wind, Betty, illus. LC 58-3344. (Illus.). 119p. 21cm. 1958, c.1957. Concordia Pub. House.
--When Jesus was a Little Boy. Evans, Katherine Floyd (1901-1964), illus. LC 54-11854. unpaged. illus. 25cm. 1954. Children's Press.
--When Jesus Was a Little Boy. Evans, Katherine Floyd (1901-1964), illus. N.D. Grosset & Dunlap.

Eberman, Gilbert Willis (1917-)
--Clatsop Drumbeats: Poetry. (Indian Culture Ser.). (gr. 5). 1973. (ISBN 0-89992-040-3). MT Coun Indian.

Eberstadt, Frederick, jt. auth. see Eberstadt, Isabel Nash.

Eberstadt, Isabel Nash & Eberstadt, Frederick
--What Is for My Birthday?. Weisgard, Leonard Joseph (1916-), illus. LC 61-5322. (Illus.). 24cm. 31p. (ps up). 1961. (ISBN 0-316-20537-0). Little.
--Where Did Tuffy Hide?. Weisgard, Leonard Joseph (1916-), illus. LC 57-8041. unpaged illus. 24cm. c.1957. Little, Brown.
--Who Is at the Door?. Weisgard, Leonard Joseph (1916-), illus. LC 59-7344. (Illus.). unpaged. 24cm. 1960, c.1959. Little, Brown.

Eberts, Marjorie & Gisler, Margaret
--Pancakes, Crackers, and Pizza: A Book About Shapes. Hayes, Stephen, illus. LC 84-7699. (Illus.). 31 p. 19cm. (A Rookie Reader). c.1984. (ISBN 0-516-02063-3). Childrens Press.

Ebetz, Eva K
--Victory Drums. Driscoll, June, illus. LC 55-137555. 235p. illus. 21cm. 1955. St. Anthony Guild Press.

Eby, Lois Christine see Lawson, Patrick, pseud.

Eby, Lois Christine (1908-)
--Marked for Adventure. 148p. 1960. Chilton Books.
--Patty Lynn at the Grand Canyon. Lawson, Patrick, pseud. LC 60-6308. (Illus.). 182p. 21cm. 1960. Dodd, Mead.
--Patty Lynn: Daughter of the Rangers. Lawson, Patrick, pseud. LC 59-6602. (Illus.). 175 p. 21cm. 1959. Dodd, Mead.
--Star-Crossed Stallion. Lawson, Patrick, pseud. LC 54-9508. 183 p. 22cm. 1954. Dodd, Mead.
--Star-Crossed Stallion's Big Chance. Lawson, Patrick, pseud. Stenbery, Algot, illus. LC 57-9750. (Illus.). 239 p. 21cm. 1957. Dodd, Mead.

Eby, Richard E.
--The Amazing Lamb of God: Bedtime Stories to be Read to Children. (Illus.). 128p. 1983. (ISBN 0-8007-1336-2). Revell.

Echols, Ula Waterhouse
--Knights of Charlemagne. Pitz, Henry Clarence (1895-1976), illus. LC 28-27683. xviii, 362 p. incl. plates. col. front 24 cm. 1928. Longmans, Green and Co.
--Robin Hood. McCracken, James, illus. LC 32-300276. vii, 9-128 p. col. front., illus., plates. (part col.) 23 1/2 cm. c.1932. A. Whitman & Co.

Eckblad, Edith Berven (1923-)
--Danny's Orange Christmas Camel. Wallerstedt, Don, illus. LC 72-121962. (Illus.). 32 p. 22cm. 1970. Augsburg Pub. House.
--Danny's Straw Hat. Mulder, Jeanne, illus. LC 62-9099. (Illus.). 22cm. 1962. Augsburg Pub. House.
--Kindness Is a Lot of Things. Rutherford, Bonnie & Rutherford, Bill, illus. LC 65-20124. 1v. (unpaged) illus. (pt. col.) 19cm. 1966, c.1965. C. R. Gibson.
--A Smile Is to Give. Lee, Robert J. (1921-), illus. LC 70-88714. (Illus.). 25 p. 19cm. 1969. Rand McNally.
--Soft As the Wind. Roberts, Jim, illus. LC 74-79365. (Illus.). 31 p. 22cm. 1974. (ISBN 0-8066-1428-5). Augsburg Pub. House.

Ecke, Wolfgang (1927-)
--The Bank Holdup. Rettich, Rolf & Langenfass, Hansjorg, illus. LC 81-21024. (Illus.). 138 p. 22cm. 1982. (ISBN 0-13-056168-1). Prentice-Hall.
--The Castle of the Red Gorillas. Rettich, Rolf, illus. LC 82-23122. p. cm. c.1983. Prentice-Hall.
--The Face at the Window. Rettich, Rolf, illus. Humphries, Stella, tr. from Ger. LC 79-15628. (Illus.). 1st U.S. edition. (gr. 5-9). 1979. (ISBN 0-13-299115-2). P-H.
--The Face at the Window. Rettich, Rolf, illus. (Illus.). 128p. (gr. 5-9). 1983. (ISBN 0-13-299081-4, Pub. by Treehouse Bks). P-H.
--Flight Toward Home. LC 78-89582. (Illus.). 116 p. 22cm. 1970. Macmillan.
--The Invisible Witness. Rettich, Rolf, illus. (Illus.). (gr. 5-9). 1981. (ISBN 0-13-505529-6). P-H.
--The Midnight Chess Game. Rettich, Rolf & Langenfass, Hansjorg, illus. LC 84-26564. p. cm. 1st U.S. edition. 1985, c.1983. (ISBN 0-13-582826-0). Prentice-Hall.
--The Stolen Paintings. LC 81-8644. p. cm. 1981, c.1979. (ISBN 0-13-846865-6). Prentice-Hall.

Eckenrode, Hamilton James (1881-)
--Told in Story, American History... LC 22-23734. v. 19 cm. c.1922. Johnson Publishing Company.

Ecker, Alica C.
--Peter and The Icicle Elf. N.D. Carlton Press.

Ecker, B. A
--Independence Day. LC 82-22810. 205 p. 18cm. (Avon Flare Book). c.1983. (ISBN 0-380-82990-8). Avon Books.

Eckerson, Margaret H.
--Flossy and Bossy Stories. (Illus.). (Play and Study Ser.). N.D. D. Lothrop Co.
--Little Pharisee Series, 6 vols. N.D. Pilgrims Press.

Eckert, Allan W. (1931-)
Blue Jacket: War Chief of the Shawnees. 1969. Little, Brown and Company.
--The Dark Green Tunnel. Wiesner, David, illus. LC 83-12078. (Illus.). 256p. (gr. 7up). 1984. (ISBN 0-316-20881-7). Little.
--Incident at Hawk's Hill. Schoenherr, John Carl (1935-), illus. LC 73-20418. 279p. 24cm. 1974, c.1971. (ISBN 0-8161-6176-3). G. K. Hall.
--Incident at Hawk's Hill. Schoenherr, John Carl (1935-), illus. LC 77-143718. (Illus.). xvii, 173 p. 21cm. 1971. Little, Brown. **Awards: (ALA); (JNM).**
--Johnny Logan: A Novel. LC 83-12078. vi, 217 p. 22cm. c.1983. (ISBN 0-316-20880-9). Little Brown.
--The Wand: The Return to Mesmeria. Wiesner, David, illus. LC 85-162. (Illus.). 214 p. 24cm. (Bk. 2 in the Mesmerian annals). c.1985. (ISBN 0-316-20882-5). Little, Brown.

Eckert, Horst see Janosch, pseud.

Eckert, Horst (1931-)
--The Crocodile Who Wouldn't Be King. Janosch, pseud. Eckert, Horst (1931-), illus. Janosch, pseud. LC 70-151811. (Illus.). 31 p. 27 x 28cm. 1971. Putnam.
--Dear Snowman. Janosch, pseud. Eckert, Horst (1931-), illus. Janosch, pseud. LC 70-107784. (Illus.). 32 p. (ps-3). 1970, c.1969. (ISBN 0-529-00926-9). World Pub. Co.
--Joshua and the Magic Fiddle. Janosch, pseud. Eckert, Horst (1931-), illus. Janosch, pseud. (Illus.). 32 p. 1968. World Pub. Co.
--Just One Apple. Janosch, pseud. Eckert, Horst (1931-), illus. Janosch, pseud. LC 66-11924. 1v. (unpaged) col. illus. 28cm. 1966, c.1965. Walck.
--The Magic Auto. Janosch, pseud. Eckert, Horst (1931-), illus. Janosch, pseud. LC 73-167758. (Illus.). 24 p. 26cm. 1971. Crown Publishers.
--The Thieves and the Raven. Janosch, pseud. Eckert, Horst (1931-), illus. Janosch, pseud. LC 73-91029. (Illus.). 32 p. 1970. Macmillan.
--Tonight at Nine. Janosch, pseud. Eckert, Horst (1931-), illus. Janosch, pseud. LC 67-19925. 1v. (unpaged) col. illus. 20x26cm. (gr. k-3). 1967. (ISBN 0-8098-1128-6). Walck.
--The Yellow Auto Named Ferdinand. Janosch, pseud. Eckert, Horst (1931-), illus. Janosch, pseud. LC 72-11083. (Illus.). 32 p. 1st U.S. edition. 1973. (ISBN 0-87614-043-6). Carolrhoda Books.

Eckford, Eugenia
--Wonder Windows: Pictures and Stories of Art in Many Lands. N.D. E. P. Dutton & Co.

Eckrich, James Frederick see James, Frederick, pseud.

Eckrich, James Frederick (1924-)
--Cloud Hoppers. James, Frederick, pseud. Evans, Katherine Floyd (1901-1964), illus. LC 49-5951. 38 p. illus. (part col.) 23 cm. 1949. Childrens Press.

Economakis, Olga
--Oasis of the Stars. Lent, Blair (1930-), illus. LC 65-20389. (Illus.). 1 v. (unpaged. 24cm. 1965. Coward-McCann.

Ecuyer, Lee
--Zippy Goes to School: A Real Live Animal Book. Westelin, Albert G. & Ecuyer, Lee, photos by. LC [illegible]. unpaged. illus. 21cm. (Rand McNallybook-elf book, 489). c.1954. Rand McNally.
--Zippy, the Chimp. Mitchell, Benn, photos by. LC 54-7245. unpaged. illus. 21cm. (Rand McNally book-elf book, 487). c.1953. Rand McNally.
--Zippy's Birthday Party: A Real Live Animal Book. LC 55-8191. unpaged. illus. 21cm. (Rand McNally elf book, 506). c.1955. Rand McNally.

Ed, Carl
--Harold Teen. 48p. (C & L Famous Comics in Book Form: No. 1). N.D. Cupples & Leon Co.

Edda, Samundar see Pyk, Ann Phillips.

Edda Snorra Sturlusonar
--Norse Stories. Mabie, Hamilton Wright (1846-1916), retold by. Wright, George, illus. LC 1-26271. (Illus.). vii, 250. 20cm. 1901. Dodd, Mead and Company.
--Norse Stories. Mabie, Hamilton Wright (1846-1916) & Bates, Katharine Lee (1850-1929), eds. Wright, George, illus. LC 2-14856. viii, 304 p. front., pl. 17 1/2 cm. 1902. Rand, McNally & Company.
--Norse Stories. Mabie, Hamilton Wright (1846-1916), retold by. LC 1-11828. 169p. 18cm. 1882. Roberts Brothers.
--Norse Tales. Mabie, Hamilton Wright, retold by. LC 1-129078. vii, 250. 17cm. 1900. Dodd, Mead and Company.

Edda Snorra Sturlusonar, jt. auth. see Brown, Abbie Farwell.

Eddy, Daniel Clarke (1823-1896)
--The Alps and the Rhine. (The Percy Family). N.D. Andrew F. Graves.
--Baltic to Vesuvius. (The Percy Family). N.D. Andrew F. Graves.
--England and Scotland. (The Percy Family). N.D. Andrew F. Graves.
--Paris to Amsterdam. (The Percy Family). N.D. Andrew F. Graves.
--Visit to Ireland. (The Percy Family). N.D. Andrew F. Graves.
--Walter in Athens. (Crowell's Library For Young People). N.D. Thomas Y. Crowell & Co.'s Catalogue.
--Walter in Athens, 1 of 6. Whitney, E. J., illus. (Walter's Tour in the East). N.D. Sheldon & Co.
--Walter in Constantinople. (Crowell's Library For Young People). N.D. Thomas Y. Crowell & Co.'s Catalogue.
--Walter in Constantinople, 1 of 6. Whitney, E. J., illus. (Walter's Tour in the East). N.D. Sheldon & Co.
--Walter in Damascus. (Crowell's Library For Young People). N.D. Thomas Y. Crowell & Co.'s Catalogue.
--Walter in Damascus. Whitney, E. J., illus. (Walter's Tour in the East). N.D. Sheldon & Co.
--Walter In Egypt. (Crowell's Libraray For Young People). N.D. Thomas Y. Crowell & Co.'s Catalogue.
--Walter in Egypt, 1 of 6. Whitney, E. J., illus. (Walter's Tour in the East). N.D. Sheldon & Co.
--Walter in Jerusalem. (Crowell's Library For Young People). N.D. Thomas Y. Crowell & Co.'s Catalogue.
--Walter in Jerusalem, 1 of 6. Whitney, E. J., illus. (Walter's Tour in the East). N.D. Sheldon & Co.
--Walter in Samaria. (Crowell's Library For Young People). N.D. Thomas Y. Crowell & Co.'s Catalogue.
--Walter in Samaria, 1 of 6. Whitney, E. J., illus. (Walter's Tour in the East). N.D. Sheldon & Co.
--The Young Man's Friend. N.D. Andrew F. Graves.
--The Young Woman's Friend. N.D. Andrew F. Graves.
--The Young Woman's Friend. (The Young Ladies' Library). N.D. Estes & Lauriat's.

Eddy, Sarah J., compiled by.
--Friends and Helpers. (Illus.). 231p. N.D. Dana Estes and Company.

Edel, May
--The Story of Our Ancestors. Danska, Herbert (1928-), illus. 1955. Little, Brown.

--The Story of People. Danska, Herbert (1928-), illus. 1953. Little, Brown.
Edelberg, Linda R., adapted by see Bischoff, Helmut & Winter, Klaus.
Edelberg, Linda R., tr. see Winter, Klaus (1928-) & Bischoff, Helmut.
Edell, Celeste
--Here Come the Clowns. Fisher, Leonard Everett (1924-), illus. LC 57-12208. (Illus.). 155p. 21cm. 1958. Putnam.
--Lynn Palmer, Caterer. LC 60-7051. 192. 21cm. (A Career Romance for Young Moderns). 1960. Messner.
--A Present from Rosita. N.D. E . M. Hale and Co.
--A Present from Rosita. Fax, Elton Clay (1909-), illus. LC 52-12718. (Illus.). 179 p. 21cm. 1952. J. Messner.
Edelman, Elaine
--I Love My Baby Sister (Most of the Time). Watson, Wendy McLeod (1942-), illus. LC 83-25623. (Illus.). 24 p. 21cm. c.1984. (ISBN 0-688-02245-6). (ISBN 0-688-02247-2). Lothrop, Lee & Shepard.
--I Love My Baby Sister (Most of the Time). Watson, Wendy McLeod (1942-), illus. LC 85-574. (Illus.). 28 p. 18cm. (Picture puffins). 1985, c.1984. (ISBN 0-14-050547-4). Puffin Books.

Edelman, Elaine & Gundersheimer, Karen
--Boom-De-Boom. LC 79-18130. (Illus.). 30 p. c.1980. (ISBN 0-394-84341-X). (ISBN 0-394-94341-4). Pantheon Books.

Edelman, Lily Judith (1915-1981)
--The Sukkah & the Big Wind. Kessler, Leonard P. (1921-), illus. (Illus.). (Holiday Series of Picture Story Books). (gr. k-2). 1956. (ISBN 0-8381-0716-8). United Syn Bk.

Edelmann, Heinz, illus.
--Prince Ring: Icelandic Fairy Tale. 32p. (Collection of Fairy Tales Ser.). 1983. (ISBN 0-87191-951-6). Childrens Bk Co.

Edelstadt, Vera (1903-)
--A Steam Shovel for Me!. Romano, Emanuele (1897-1984), illus. LC 33-23678. 56 p. illus. (part col.) 26 cm. 1933. Frederick A. Stokes Company.
--A Steam Shovel for Me. Romano, Emanuele (1897-1984), illus. 1932. J. B. Lippincott Co.
--Young Fighters of the Soviets. Florian, illus. LC 44-7948. 5 p. l., 3-104 p. illus., col. plates. 20 1/2 cm. 1944. A. A. Knopf.

Edens, Cooper
--Emily & the Shadow Shop. Dowers, Patrick, illus. (Illus.). 40p. 1982. (ISBN 0-914676-63-6, Star & Eleph Bks). Green Tiger Pr.
--If You're Afraid of the Dark, Remember the Night Rainbow. LC 80-105693. (Illus.). 40 p. 22cm. c.1979. (ISBN 0-914676-26-1). (ISBN 0-914676-27-X). Green Tiger Press.
--Inevitable Papers. (Illus.). 40p. 1982. (ISBN 0-914676-94-6, Star & Eleph Bks). Green Tiger Pr.
--Phenomenal Alphabet. Eide, Joyce, illus. LC 84-144745. (A Star & Elephant Book). c.1983. (ISBN 0-914676-91-1). Green Tiger Press.
--The Starcleaner Reunion. LC 79-122663. (Illus.). 34 p. c.1979. (ISBN 0-914676-31-8). Green Tiger Press.
--With Secret Friends. (Illus.). 44p. 1981. (ISBN 0-914676-57-1, Star & Eleph Bks). Green Tiger Pr.
Edens, Cooper & Poltarnees, Welleran, eds.
--Weird & Wonderful. (Illus., Orig.). N.D. (ISBN 0-914676-66-0, Star & Eleph Bks). Green Tiger Pr.
Edersheim
--Robbie and His Mother. 132p. N.D. Congregational Sunday-School and Publishing Society.
Edey, Birdsall Otis, Mrs.
--Six Giants and a Griffin. (Illus.). (Harper's Selected Juveniles). N.D. Harper & Brothers Trade-List.
Edey, Marion
--Open the Door: Rhymes for Children. Grider, Dorothy (1915-), illus. LC 49-5616. 79 p. illus. 21 cm. 1949. C. Scribner's Sons.
Edgar, John G.
--The Boy Crusaders. (The Popular Library). N.D. The American News Co.
--Boy Princes. N.D. American News Co.
--Cavaliers and Roundheads. 1875. Scribner, Welford, & Armstrong.
--Great Men and Gallant Deeds. (Jutland Ser.). N.D. Colby and Rich.
--War of the Roses. (Illus.). N.D. Scribner, Welford & Armstrong.
Edgar, Kenneth
--Starfire. (Illus., Orig.). (gr. 3 up). 1961. (ISBN 0-910286-13-2). Boxwood.
Edgar, Madalen G., selected by.
--Stories from Morris. (Illus.). (Children's Favorite Classics). N.D. Thomas Y. Crowell.
--A Treasury of Verse, for Little Children. (Illus.). 127, 1 p. front. 19 cm. c.1914. Thomas Y. Crowell Company.
--A Treasury of Verse for Little Children. 1882- ed. Pogany, Willy (1882-1955), illus. LC 28-26845. 255, 1 p. col. front., illus., col. plates. 23 cm. c.1923. The Macmillan Company.
--A Treasury of Verse for School and Home. Chilman, Eric, illus. LC 26-14189. xix, 523 p. col. front., illus., col. plates. 23 1/2 cm. c.1926. Thomas Y. Crowell Company.
Edgar, Madalen G., selected by see Scott, Walter, Sir.
Edgar, Pamela & Matz, Dale
--Adventures of Jason: Mythical Magical Journey into Self-Discovery. Domez, Lee, illus. LC 85-9695. (Illus.). 58 p. 21cm. c.1985. (ISBN 0-941992-05-5). Los Arboles Publications.
Edgeworth, Maria, et al. (1767-1849)
--Waste Not, Want Not, and Other Stories: And Other Stories. O'Shea, Michael Vincent (1866-), ed. Barbauld, Anna Letitia Aiken, Mrs. (1743-1825), illus. LC 3-11331. vii, 84 p. incl. front., illus. 19 cm. (On cover: Heath's home and school classics, no. 20). 1901. D. C. Heath & Co.
Edgeworth, Maria, jt. auth. see Barker, Sale, Mrs.
Edgeworth, Maria (1767-1849)
--The Absentee. N.D. Harper & Brothers.
--All For the Best and Other Stories, 1 of 3 Vols. (Illus.). (Edgeworth's Popular Library). N.D. Set. James Miller.
--Belinda. N.D. George Routledge & Sons.
--The Birthday Present and Other Stories. (Illus.). (Editha Ser.). N.D. Caldwell.
--The Birthday Present and Other Stories. (Illus.). (Editha Series). N.D. Dodge Publishing Co.
--The Bracelets. (My Favorite Library). N.D. George Routledge & Sons.
--Early Lessons. Foster, Birket, illus. N.D. George Routledge & Sons.
--Edgeworth's Moral and Popular Tales, 1 of 8 Vols. (Illus.). (Warne's Home Sunshine Library). N.D. Scribner & Welford.
--Edgeworth's Popular LIbrary: Containing "All for the Best, and Other Stories", "Moral Tales" and "Popular Tales", 3 vols. (Illus.). N.D. Set. James Miller.
--The False Key. (Illus.). (Children Hour Series.). N.D. Dodge Publishing Co.
--The False Key. (My Favorite Library). N.D. George Routledge & Sons.
--The False Key and Other Stories. (Illus.). (Every Boy's Library). N.D. Caldwell.
--The Fireside Story Book ... LC 44-27435. 62, 3-63, 3-63 p. front., plates. 14 1/2 x 12 1/2 cm. 1854. C. G. Henderson & Co.
--Forgive and Forget. (Children's Hour Series.). N.D. Dodge Publishing Co.
--Forgive and Forget. (My Favorite Library). N.D. George Routledge & Sons.
--Forgive and Forget and Other Stories. (Illus.). (Every Boy's Library). N.D. Caldwell.
--Frank. N.D. E P Dutton.
--Frank. N.D. George Routledge & Sons.
--Frank, 2 vols. 1882. Harper's.
--Frank, 2 Vols. (The Edgeworth Library). N.D. Kelly, Piet & Co.
--Frank. (Illus.). N.D. R. Worthington.
--Frank, Rosamond, Harry and Lucy. (Warne's Home Circle Library). N.D. Frederick Warne & Co.
--Harry and Lucy. (Illus.). N.D. George Routledge & Sons.
--Harry and Lucy, 2 vols. 1882. Harper's.
--Harry and Lucy, 2 Vols. (The Edgeworth Library). N.D. Kelly, Piet & Co.
--Harry and Lucy: To Which Are Added The Little Dog Trusty, The Cherry Orchard, and The Orange Man. new ed. LC 6-26305. 192 p. col. front 16 1/2 cm. 1856. G. Routledge and Sons.
--Helen. N.D. George Routledge & Sons.
--Helen. (Warne's Star Ser.). N.D. Scribner & Welford.
--Lazy Lawerence and Other Stories. (Illus.). (Every Boy's Library). N.D. Dodge Publishing Co.
--Lazy Lawrence. (My Favorite Library). N.D. George Routledge & Sons.
--Lazy Lawrence and Other Stories. (Illus.). (Every Boy's Library). N.D. Caldwell.
--The Little Merchants. (My Favorite Library). N.D. George Routledge & Sons.
--Little Plays: Being an Additional Volume of The Parent's Assistant, Published from the Manuscript, and Ornamented with Engravings from Original Designs. LC 77-360183. (Illus.). 59, 57, 69 p., 1 leaf of plates. 15cm. 1827. T. T. Ash.
--Little Plays for Children: Being a Continuation of The Parent's Assistant. LC 77-360181. (Illus.). 178 p., 1 leaf of plates. 15cm. 1827. W. Burgess, Jr.
--The Mimic. (My Favorite Library). N.D. George Routledge & Sons.
--Moral and Popular Tales. (Illus.). N.D. J B Lippincott & Co.
--Moral and Popular Tales, 1 of 8 Vols. (Illus.). (Warne's Victoria Gift Books Ser.: Vol. 6). N.D. R. Worthington.
--Moral Tales. LC 42-44503. 516 p. plates. 16 cm. 1856. C. G. Henderson & Co.
--Moral Tales, 2 vols. 1882. Harper's.
--Moral Tales. (Illus.). (St. Nicholas Series for Boys). N.D. International Book Co.
--Moral Tales, 1 of 3 Vols. (Illus.). (Edgeworth's Popular Library). N.D. Set. James Miller.
--Moral Tales for Young People. new ed. LC 65-444392. vi, 414 p. illus. 17 cm. N.D. New York, G. Routledge.
--Moral Tales for Young People. The/Feminist Controversy in England, 1788-1810. LC 73-22194. 3 v. 21cm. 1974. (ISBN 0-8240-0856-1). Garland Pub.
--The Orphans. (My Favorite Library). N.D. George Routledge & Sons.
--The Parent's Assistant. LC 75-32150. v. 19cm. (Classics of Children's Literature, 1621-1932). 1976. (ISBN 0-8240-2264-5). Garland Pub.
--Parent's Assistant. 1882. Harper's.
--The Parents Assistant, 1 of 5 Vols. (Illus.). (Standard Juvenile Ser.: Vol. 4). N.D. Set. Houghton, Osgood & Co.
--Parent's Assistant. (Illus.). (St. Nicholas Series for Children). N.D. International Bo. Co.
--Parents' Assistant. (Illus.). N.D. R. Worthington.
--The Parent's Assistant: Or, Stories for Children. (Illus.). N.D. James Miller.
--The Parent's Assistant: Or, Stories for Children. LC 75-300560. (Illus.). 576 p. 16cm. N.D. Monroe & Francis.
--The Parent's Assistant: Or, Stories for Children. new illustrated complete. LC 6-26299. xi, 12-535 p. front., pl. 17 1/2 cm. 1853. W. P. Hazard.
--The Parent's Assistant: Or, Stories for Children. Fraser, F. A., illus. (Illus.). N.D. George Routledge.
--The Parent's Assistant: Or, Stories for Children. Hammond, Chris, illus. LC 4-17537. (Illus.). xix, 463. 20cm. 1897. The Macmillan Company.
--The Parents' Assistant: Or, Stories for Children. Phiz, pseud. (1815-1882), illus. Browne, Hablot Knight. (Illus.). N.D. George Routledge & Sons.
--The Parent's Assistant: Or, Stories for Children. Ritchie, Anne Isabella Thackeray, Lady (1837-1919), ed. LC 4-17537. xix, 463, 2 p. incl. front., illus. 20 cm. 1897. Macmillan and Co., Limited.
--Popular Tales. N.D. George Routledge & Sons.
--Popular Tales, 2 vols. 1882. Harper's Trade-List.
--Popular Tales. (Illus.). (St. Nicholas Series for Boys). N.D. International Book Co.
--Popular Tales. N.D. James Miler.
--Popular Tales, 1 of 3 Vols. (Illus.). (Edgeworth's Popular Library). N.D. Set. James Miller.
--Popular Tales. N.D. R. Worthington.
--The Purple Jar. (My Favorite Library). N.D. George Routledge & Sons.
--Rosamond. N.D. E P Dutton.
--Rosamond. (Illus.). N.D. George Routledge & Sons.
--Rosamond. 1882. Harper's.
--Rosamond. (The Edgeworth Library). N.D. Kelly, Piet & Co.
--Rosamond. LC 21-2683. 2 v. 13 1/2 cm (v. 2: 13 cm. 1808. Published by Jacob Johnson, No. Market-Street; Adams, Printer.
--Rosamond. (Illus.). N.D. R. Worthington.
--Rosamond: A Sequel to Early Lessons. LC 42-26187. 2 v. col. plates. 14 1/2 cm. 1821. J. Maxwell.
--Rosamond and Other Tales: In Words of One Syllable. N.D. E P Dutton.
--Simple Susan. (Illus.). (Editha Series.). N.D. Dodge Publishing Co.
--Simple Susan and Other Tales. Burd, Clara Miller, illus. LC 29-24090. 5 p. l., 216 p. incl. illus., plates. col. front., col. plates. 19 1/2 cm. (The Macmillan children's classics). 1929. The Macmillan Company.
--Simple Susan: Told to the Children. Chisholm, Louey, as told by. Allen, Olive, illus. LC 14-14234. xi, 111 p. 8 col pl. (incl. front.) 15 cm. (Half-title: Told to the children series, ed. by Louey Chisholm no. 31). 1907. E. P. Dutton & Co.
--Stories for Children. N.D. Macmillian & Co.
--Stories for Children. N.D. R. Worthington.
--Tales from Maria Edgeworth. Thomson, Hugh (1860-1920), illus. LC 8-30023. 21cm. 411p. (Fine Art Juveniles). 1908. Frederick A. Stokes.
--Tales from Maria Edgeworth. Thomson, Hugh (1860-1920), illus. Dobson, Austin, intro. by. LC 8-30023. xxiv, 411, 1 p. incl. front., illus., plates., 21 cm. 1908. W. Gardner, Darton & Co.
--Tales That Never Die. Welsh, Charles (1850-), ed. LC 8-21924. xiii p., 1 l., v-vii, 458 p. front. (port.) 24 pl. 19 1/2 cm. c.1908. H. M. Caldwell Co.
--To-Morrow. Or, The Dangers of Delay. LC 21-2684. 108 p. 14 cm. 1813. Published by Evert Duyckinck, No. Pearl-Street; C. W. Bunce, Printer.
--Waste Not, Want Not; and the Barring Out: Two Tales, with a Biographical Introduction and Notes. 1 p. l., v-x, 11-98 p. 18 cm. (Riverside literature series, no. 44). c.1889. Houghton, Mifflin and Company.
--Waste Not, Want Not Stories. Johnson, Clifton (1865-), retold by. LC 5-38491. (Illus.). 260p. 19cm. (Eclectic Readings). 1905. American Book Company.
Edgeworth, Maria (1767-1849) & Abbott, Jacob
--Forgotten Stories of Long Ago. Lucas, E. V., selected by. N.D. Frederick A. Stokes Co.
Edgeworth, Maria (1767-1849) & Edgeworth, Richard Lovell (1744-1817)
--Edgeworth's Harry and Lucy. With an Address to Mothers, the Stories of Little Dog Trusty, The Orange Man, and The Cherry Orchard ... LC 41-32450. 264 p. illus. 16 1/2 cm. N.D. Munroe & Francis.
Edgeworth, Maria (1767-1849) & Lamb, Charles (1775-1834)
--The Blue Jar Story Book. LC 7-30432. 112 p. col. fron., illus. 19 1/2 cm. 1906. McLoughlin Brothers.
Edgeworth, Maria (1767-1849) & Taylor, Jane (1783-1824)
--Waste Not, Want Not, and Other Stories. ed. O'Shea, Michael Vincent (1866-) & Bodwell, W. P., illus. LC 4-18949. vii, 84 p. incl. front., illus. 20 cm. (Heath's home and school classics). 1904. Heath & Co.
Edgeworth, Richard Lovell, jt. auth. see Edgeworth, Maria.
Edgington, Evelyn
--Their Angels. (Illus.). (ps-3). N.D. Vantage.
Edgley, Leslie
--A Dirty Business. 1969. (ISBN 0-399-10212-4). G. P. Putnam's Sons.
Edgun, pseud., see Hatch, Mary Cottam.
Edholm, Lizette M
--The Merriweather Girls and the Mystery of the Queen's Fan. LC 32-11203. 3 p. l., 13-245 p. 19 1/2 cm. c.1932. The Goldsmith Publishing Company.
--The Merriweather Girls at Good Old Rockhill. LC 32-11200. 3 p. l., 13-244 p. 19 1/2 cm. c.1932. The Goldsmith Publishing Company.
--The Merriweather Girls in Quest of Treasure. LC 32-11199. 3 p. l., 13-245 p. 19 1/2 cm. c.1932. The Goldsmith Publishing Company.
--The Merriweather Girls on Campers' Trail. LC 32-112061. 3 p. l., 13-249 p. 19 1/2 cm. c.1932. The Goldsmith Publishing Company.
--Ship Ahoy!. LC 34-33676. vi, 13-78 p. incl. front., illus. 19 1/2 cm. (Our changing world). 1934. T. Nelson and Sons.
Edick, Grace Willard, jt. auth. see Wiley, Belle.
Edinger, Norman
--Why Santa Claus wore false whiskers. 1964. Exposition Press Inc.
Editions les Belles Images Staff, tr. from Fr.
--Little Red Riding Hood. 16p. (Orig.). (Butterfly bks). (ps-2). 1976. (ISBN 0-8467-0222-3, Pub. by Two Continents). Hippocrene Bks.
--Mother Goose Rhymes. (Illus., Orig.). 1st U.S. edition. (Butterfly Bks). (gr. 1-2). 1977. (ISBN 0-8467-0331-9, Pub. by Two Continents). Hippocrene Bks.
--The Three Bears. 16p. (Orig.). (Butterfly Bks). (ps-2). 1976. (ISBN 0-8467-0221-5, Co-Pub by Editions les Belles Images). Two Continents.
Editors of Reader's Digest, selected by.
--Best Loved Books for Young Readers. 1st ed. LC 66-12161. (Illus.). v. 20cm. 1966. Reader's Digest Association.
Edland, Elisabeth
--The Children's King and Other Plays for Children: With Chapters on Dramatizing with Children. LC 28-6204. 78 p. 19 cm. c.1928. The Abingdon Press.
--Plum Blossoms: For Intermediate or Older Junior Groups. LC 25-8461. 59 p. incl. illus., pl. 17 1/2 cm. c.1925. The Abingdon Press.
Edler, Timothy J.
--The Adventures of Crawfish-Man. Edler, Timothy J., illus. (Illus.). 40p. 1st U.S. edition. (Tim Edler's Tales from the Atchafalaya Ser.). (gr. k-8). 1979. (ISBN 0-931108-04-7). Little Cajun.
--Coocan: Boy of the Swamp. (Illus.). (Tim Edler's Tales from the Atchafclaya Ser.). (gr. k-8). 1983. (ISBN 0-931108-09-8). Little Cajun.
--Crawfish-Man Rescues Ron Guidry. (Illus.). (Tim Edler's Tales from the Atchafalaya). (gr. k-8). 1980. (ISBN 0-931108-05-5). Little Cajun.
--Crawfish-Man's Night Befo' Christmas. (Illus.). 40p. (gr. k-8). 1984. (ISBN 0-931108-12-8). Little Cajun.
--Dark Gator. (Illus.). (Tim Edler's New Swamp Wars Ser.). (gr. k-8). 1980. (ISBN 0-931108-06-3). Little Cajun.

--Maurice the Snake & Gaston the Near-Sighted Turtle: Tim Edler's Tales from the Atchafalaya. (Illus.). (gr. k-8). 1977. (ISBN 0-931108-00-4). Little Cajun.

--Rhombus: The Cajun Unicorn. (Illus.). 40p. (Tim Edler's Tales from the Atchafalaya Ser.). (gr. k up). 1984. (ISBN 0-931108-10-1). Little Cajun.

--Santa's Cajun Christmas Adventure. Edler, Timothy J., illus. (Illus.). 48p. (Tim Edler's Tales from the Atchafalaya Ser.). (gr. k-8). 1981. (ISBN 0-931108-07-1). Little Cajun.

--T-Boy & the Trial for Life. (Illus.). (Tim Edler's Tales from the Atchafalaya Ser.). (gr. k-8). 1978. (ISBN 0-931108-02-0). Little Cajun.

--T-Boy in Mossland. Edler, Timothy J., illus. LC 78-111707. (Illus.). 42 p. 28cm. (Tim Edler's Tales from the Atchafalaya ; no. 3). 1978. (ISBN 0-931108-03-9). Little Cajun Books.

Edman, Irwin

--Adam, the Baby, and the Man from Mars. N.D. Houghton Mifflin Co.

Edman, Polly, jt. auth. see Jensen, Virginia Allen.

Edmison, John P. (1831-1912), ed.

--Stories from the Norseland. Smith, Wuanita (1866-) & Bowker, A. R., illus. LC 9-28187. 20cm. 337p. (Classic Stories). 1909. Penn Publishing Co.

Edmond, A. M., Mrs.

--Over the Sea: Scenes and Incidents in Other Lands. (Illus.). 180p. N.D. Sunday-School Publications.

Edmonds, Edith

--Mark's Tropical Fish. Mitchell, Charlie, illus. 48p. 1st U.S. edition. (Lead-off Bks.). (gr. 1-4). 1976. (ISBN 0-87955-112-7). (ISBN 0-87955-712-5). O'Hara.

Edmonds, Elmer Valentine (1888-)

--Atomic 'Enery Goes Prospecting. 1st ed. LC 53-128021. 210p. 21cm. 1953. Pageant Press.

--Atomic 'Enery Goes Prospecting, Vol. II. N.D. Pageant Press, Inc.

--Atomic 'Enery Tries Deep Sea Exploring. 1st ed. LC 54-66978. 220p. 21cm. 1954. Pageant Press.

--Atomic 'Enery Tries Deep Sea Exploring, Vol. III. N.D. Pageant Press, Inc.

--Resourceful Atomic 'Enery, Vol. I. N.D. Pageant Press, Inc.

Edmonds, Ivy Gordon, jt. auth. see Ikkyu, Osho.

Edmonds, Ivy Gordon (1917-)

--The Bounty's Boy: A Novel. Walker, Gil, illus. LC 62-19322. (Illus.). 189 p. 22cm. 1962. Bobbs-Merrill.

--The Case of the Marble Monster & Other Stories. 112p. Orig. Title: Ooka the Wise. (gr. 4-6). 1969. (ISBN 0-590-08024-5). Scholastic Inc.

--Joel of the Hanging Gardens. Parker, Bob, illus. LC 66-10896. 148p. illus. 21cm. c.1966. Lippincott.

--The Magic Dog. (Illus.). 128p. (gr. 5-9). 1982. (ISBN 0-525-66757-1). Lodestar Bks.

--Ooka the Wise, Tales of Old Japan. Yamazaki, Sanae, illus. 1961. Bobbs.

--Trickster Tales. Morrison, Sean, illus. LC 66-84065. (Illus.). 147 p. 21cm. 1966. Lippincott.

Edmonds, Mary D

--Out of the Net. Bayler, Dorothy, illus. LC 40-27596. 253, 1 p. incl. front., illus., plates. 21 cm. c.1940. Oxford University Press.

Edmonds, Paul, pseud., see Kuttner, Henry.

Edmonds, Paul, pseud. (1915-1958)

--Rhymes for Children. Kuttner, Henry. Edmonds, Paul, pseud. (1915-1958), illus. Kuttner, Henry. LC 41-5697. 40p. illus. (part. col.) 27 1/2 x 21 1/2cm. c.1940. Expression Co.

Edmonds, Richard W

--Young Captain Barney. LC 56-6182. 248p. 21cm. 1956. Macrae Smith.

Edmonds, Walter Dumaux (1903-)

--Beaver Valley. Morrill, Leslie H., illus. LC 79-129899. (Illus.). 70 p. 21cm. 1971. Little, Brown.

--Bert Breen's Barn. LC 75-2157. (Illus.). 270 p. 22cm. 1975. (ISBN 0-316-21166-4). Little, Brown. **Award: (NBA).**

--The Big Barn. 1930. Little, Brown & Co.

--Cadmus Henry. 1949. (ISBN 0-8382-1056-2, Cadmus Books). E. M. Hale and Company.

--Cadmus Henry. Lee, Manning De Villeneuve (1894-1980), illus. LC 49-10592. (Illus.). 22cm. 137p. (gr. 7-9). 1949. Dodd.

--Corporal Bess: The Story of a Boy and a Dog. Lee, Manning de Villeneuve (1894-1980), illus. LC 52-10920. (Illus.). 182 p. 22cm. 1952. Dodd, Mead.

--Drums Along the Mohawk. (The story of the pioneers of the Mohawk Valley during the Revolution). (gr. 7 up). 1936. (ISBN 0-316-21142-7, Pub. by Atlantic Monthly Pr). Little.

--Hound Dog Moses and the Promised Land. Gropper, William (1897-1977), illus. LC 54-9234. unpaged. illus. 24cm. 1954. Dodd, Mead.

--In the Hands of the Senecas. (A novel). (gr. 7-9). 1947. (ISBN 0-316-21143-5, Pub. by Atlantic Monthly Pr). Little.

--The Matchlock Gun. Lantz, Paul (1908-), illus. LC 41-17547. x p., 2 l., 50 p. illus., double col. plates. 25 x 20 cm. 1941. Dodd, Mead & Company. **Award: (JNM).**

--Mr. Benedict's Lion. Lee, Doris Emrick (1905-1983), illus. LC 50-10167. (Illus.). vi, 154 p. 22cm. 1950. Dodd, Mead.

--The Night Raider and Other Stories. LC 80-17491. p. cm. c.1980. (ISBN 0-316-21141-9). Little, Brown.

--Seven American Stories. Bock, William Sauts Netamux'we (1939-), illus. LC 69-10657. (Illus.). 400 p. 25cm. 1970. Little, Brown.

--The South African Quirt. 1985. Little Brown.

--The Story of Richard Storm. Bock, William Sauts Netamux'we (1939-), illus. LC 73-9603. (Illus.). 30 p. 1974. Little, Brown.

--They Had a Horse. Gorsline, Douglas Warner (1913-1985), illus. LC 62-9083. (Illus.). 60 p. 24cm. 1962. Dodd, Mead.

--Time to Go House. Victor, Joan Berg (1942-), illus. LC 69-17752. (Illus.). 137 p. 21cm. 1969. Little, Brown.

--Tom Whipple. Lantz, Paul (1908-), illus. LC 42-23438. ix p., 1 l., 70 p. illus. (part col.) 25 x 20 cm. 1942. Dodd, Mead & Company.

--Two Logs Crossing: John Haskell's Story. Gergely, Tibor (1900-1978), illus. LC 43-17980. 5 p. l., 82, 1 p. illus. 22 1/2 cm. 1943. Dodd, Mead & Company.

--Uncle Ben's Whale. Gropper, William (1897-1977), illus. LC 55-86352. unpaged. illus. 24cm. 1955. Dodd, Mead. **Award:(NYT).**

--Wilderness Clearing. De Martelly, John Stockton (1903-), illus. LC 44-9706. xi, 156 p. plates. 21 cm. 1944. Dodd, Mead & Company.

--Wilderness Clearing. Simont, Marc (1915-), illus. 1958. Dodd.

--Wolf Hunt. 1st ed. Bock, William Sauts Netamux'we (1939-), illus. LC 73-108171. (Illus.). 112 p. 21cm. 1970. Little, Brown.

Edmondson, Madeleine

--Anna Witch. DuBois, William Sherman Pene (1916-), illus. LC 81-43653. p. cm. c.1982. (ISBN 0-385-17393-8). Doubleday.

--The Witch's Egg. Chorao, Ann Mckay Sproat (1936-), illus. 1974. Houghton.

--The Witch's Egg. Chorao, Ann Mckay Sproat (1936-), illus. LC 72-97769. (Illus.). 47 p. 24cm. 1974. (ISBN 0-8164-3100-0). Seabury Press.

Edmunds, Robert, adapted by see Disney, Walter Elias.

Edmunds, Robert, adapted by see Disney, Walt, Productions.

Edmunds, Robert, adapted by see Disney, Walt, Productions & Andersen, Hans Christian.

Edmundson, Bess

--Melinda's Doll House. Pennington, Pat, illus. LC 63-21924. 150 p. illus. 21 cm. c.1963. Dorrance.

Edmundson, Norah Mary

--The Lavender Garden and Other Stories. Howard, C. M., illus. Potter, Helen Beatrix (1866-1943), frwd. by. N.D. Frederick Warne & Co.

Edsall, Marian Stickney (1920-)

--Our Auto Trip. Grider, Dorothy (1915-), illus. LC 52-33575. 21cm. 29p. (Rand McNally book-elf book, 457). 1952. Rand McNally.

Edson, Billy D.

--Lone's Christmas Boots & Other Tales from the Mother Lode. 95p. 1982. (ISBN 0-682-49916-1). Exposition.

Edson, N. I., pseud., see Denison, Mary Andrews.

Edson, N. I.

--Silent Tom. N.D. D. Lothrop & Co.

Edson, N. I., jt. auth. see Farman, Ella.

Edson, N. I. & Eastman, Julia A.

--The One Thousand Dollar Prize Series, Part First: Containing "Striking for the Right," "Silent Tom," "Evening Rest,"etc, 8 vols. N.D. D. Lothrop & Co.

Edstrom, O. E

--Epp's Trip to the Moon. LC 45-5903. 117 p. 20 1/2 cm. 1945. House of Field Inc.

Educational Publishing Corporation Darien, Conn, ed.

--Tell Us a Story!. A Collection of Short Stories for Children of All Ages ... LC 44-40334. iii, 75 p. illus. 21 1/2 cm. 1944. Educational Publishing Corporation.

Educational Research Council of America

--Power Plant Worker. Ferris, Theodore H., et al., eds. Briggs, Henry J., illus. McKlroy, Louis A., intro. by. (Illus.). 36p. (Real People at Work Ser. K). (gr. 3). 1975. (ISBN 0-89247-089-5). Changing Times.

Edward, Ernest, ed.

--Kate Greenaway Treasury. LC 67-23363. (Illus.). 1977. (ISBN 0-529-00313-9, Philomel). Putnam Pub Group.

Edward, Leo

--Poppy Ott and the Stuttering Parrot. (The Poppy Ott Bks). N.D. Grosset & Dunlap.

Edwards, Amelia Ann Blandford (1831-1892)

--In the Days of My Youth. N.D. International.

--The Phantom Coach. Richardson, I. M, adapted by. Ashmead, Hal, illus. LC 81-19862. (Illus.). 32 p. 24cm. (Famous Tales of Suspense). c.1982. (ISBN 0-89375-634-2). (ISBN 0-89375-635-0). Troll Associates.

Edwards, Anne (1927-)

--The Bible for Young Readers: the Old Testament. Front, Charles & Christian, David, illus. LC 68-20534. (Illus.). 369 p. 19cm. 1968, c.1967. Golden Press.

Edwards, Annette

--Baby's Day. Pointer, Priscilla, illus. LC 53-29589. unpaged. illus. 21cm. (Treasure books, 859). 1953. Treasure Books.

--Baby's First Book. Schad, Helen, illus. LC 54-150975. unpaged. illus. 21cm. (Wonder books, 606). 1953. Wonder Books.

--My First Book of Farm Animals. Wilde, Irma, illus. LC 53-2369. unpaged. illus. 21cm. (Treasure books, 858). c.1953. Treasure Books.

Edwards, Arthur Bennet

--The Story of the Stork. LC 20-8887. 12p. 31cm. c.1920. Wall Street Text Co. (Syra).

Edwards, Bertram, pseud., see Edwards, Herbert Charles.

Edwards, Bertram, pseud. (1912-)

--The Mystery of Barrowmead Hill. Edwards, Herbert Charles. Spilka, Arnold (1917-), illus. LC 59-5115. 21cm. 181p. 1959. David McKay Co.

--Strange Traffic. Edwards, Herbert Charles. Kennedy, Richard (1910-), illus. LC 60-6285. 21cm. 151p. 1960. David McKay.

Edwards, Beverly

--My House. Edwards, Beverly, illus. LC 66-15993. (Illus.). 23cm. c.1966. McGraw-Hill.

--My Pets. Edwards, Beverly, illus. LC 66-159952. 1v. (unpaged) col. illus. 23cm. 1966. McGraw.

--My Toys. Edwards, Beverly, illus. LC 66-15994. (Illus.). 23cm. c.1966. McGraw-Hill.

--My Zoo. Edwards, Beverly, illus. LC 66-15992. (Illus.). 23cm. c.1966. McGraw-Hill.

Edwards, Brian, jt. auth. see Edwards, Lynne.

Edwards, Bruce

--Rachel Noble's Experience, 1 of 4 Vols. (The Red Bridge Ser.). N.D. National Temperance Society.

Edwards, C. M., Mrs.

--My Sister Margaret: A Temperance Story. 1873. Nelson & Phillips.

--Rainbow Side.(Illus.).N.D.Methodist Book Concern.

--The Rainbow Side: A Sequel to "The Itinerant.". LC 12-32016. 296 p. incl. front., 3 pl. 17 1/2 cm. c.1858. Carlton & Porter.

--Sister Margaret. (Illus.). N.D. Methodist Book Concern.

Edwards, Cassie

--Heart Strings, No. 3. 192p. (First Romance Ser.). (gr. 6-12). 1982. (ISBN 0-8439-1153-0, Leisure Bks). Nordon Pubns.

Edwards, Cecile Pepin (1916-)

--Champlain, Father of New France. Chapman, Frederick Trench (1887-), illus. LC 55-14814. 127p. illus. 21cm. (Makers of America). 1955. Abingdon Press.

--John Alden: Steadfast Pilgrim. Orr, Forrest W., illus. LC 65-10519. 191p. col. illus., col. maps. 22cm. (Piper bks.). c.1965. Houghton.

--John Alden: Steadfast Pilgrim. Orr, Forrest W., illus. LC 65-10519. 191 p. col. illus. maps. 22 cm. (piper books. 1965. Houghton Mifflin.

--King Phillip. 1962. Houghton Mifflin Company.

--Luck for the Jolly Gale. Stein, Harve (1904-), illus. N.D. Abelard.

--Luck for the Jolly Gale. Stein, Harve (1904-), illus. LC 47-30424. 22cm. 189p. 1947. Abingdon-Cokesbury Press.

--Party for Suzanne. Castle, Jane, illus. LC 52-11648. 191 p. illus. 22 cm. 1952. Abingdon-Cokesbury Press.

--Roger Williams: Defender of Freedom. Stein, Harve (1904-), illus. LC 57-13928. 128p. illus. 21cm. (Makers of America). 1957. Abingdon Press.

Edwards, Charles Austin McNally (1917-)

--Son of the Mohawks. Cooper, Mario (1905-), illus. LC 55-14356. 188p. illus. 21cm. 1955. Bouregy & Curl.

Edwards, Clara McKinney

--The Wonderful Gift. Morgan, Dorothy Rittenhouse, illus. LC 27-21326. 21cm. 160p. 1927. The Four Seas Co.

Edwards, Clayton, ed. see Cervantes Saavedra, Miguel de.

Edwards, Clayton, ed. see Longfellow, Henry Wadsworth.

Edwards, Clifford Q

--Summer at Sea. LC 73-84576. (Illus.). 107 p. 23cm. 1973. Word Books.

Edwards, Dorothy Lee

--Oscar, the Business Rabbit. Snell, Carroll, photos by. LC 40-12855. 70 p., 1 l. front., illus. 21 x 21 cm. c.1940. E. P. Dutton & Co., Inc.

Edwards, Dorothy (1914-1982)

--My Naughty Little Sister & Bad Harry's Rabbit. Hughes, Shirley (1929-), illus. LC 80-18501. p. cm. 1st U.S. edition. 1980, c.1977. (ISBN 0-13-608935-6). Prentice-Hall.

--My Naughty Little Sister and Bad Harry's Rabbit. Hughes, Shirley (1929-), illus. 1981. Prentice.

--A Wet Monday. Williams, Jenny (1939-), illus. LC 76-12405. p. cm. 1976. (ISBN 0-688-32081-3). (ISBN 0-688-27081-6). Morrow.

--The Witches & the Grinnygog. 176p. (gr. 5-8). 1983. (ISBN 0-571-11720-1). Faber & Faber.

Edwards, Eleanor Middleton, compiled by.

--Great Mystery Stories. Stone, David Karl (1922-), illus. LC 62-52907. 191 p. illus. 23 cm. (Sunrise library). 1960. Hart Pub. Co.

--Great Stories About Animals. Lawn, John, illus. LC 67-17991. (Illus.). 191 p. 23cm. (Sunrise library). 1967. Hart Pub. Co.

--Great Stories About Dogs. Baldwin, Richard, illus. LC 64-24884. 191p. illus. 23cm. (Sunrise lib.). c.1965. Hart.

--Great Stories About Horses. Greene, Hamilton, illus. LC 63-18759. (Illus.). 191 p. 23cm. (Sunrise library). 1963. Hart Pub. Co.

Edwards, Elizabeth, pseud., see Inderlied, Mary Elizabeth.

Edwards, Elizabeth, pseud. (1945-)

--The Proving Ground. Inderlied, Mary Elizabeth. N.D. Zondervan Publishing House.

--Trappings. Inderlied, Mary Elizabeth. N.D. Zondervan Publishing House.

Edwards, Eva D

--Haruko: Child of Japan. LC 35-2102. viii, 200 p. incl. front., illus. 19 1/2 cm. c.1934. Harr Wagner Publishing Company.

Edwards, Eva D & Sung, Sze Ai

--Ling Ling, Child of China. LC 39-341601. vi, 217 p. illus. (incl. ports.) 21 cm. 1939. Harr Wagner Publishing Company.

Edwards, Florence Dunn

--Menino. Hellmuth, Mary, illus. LC 40-131662. 2 p. l., 20 p. col. front., illus. (part col.) 24 cm. c.1940. Grosset & Dunlap.

Edwards, G. N., jt. ed. see Hughes, Rosalind.

Edwards, Gunvor

--Cat Samson. (ps-3). N.D. (ISBN 0-8277-5407-8). (ISBN 0-8277-5406-X). British Bk Ctr.

Edwards, Gunvor, tr. see Unnerstad, Edith Totterman.

Edwards, Harvey (1929-)

--Leise: Danish Girl from Drager. Abrahamsen, Leise (1918-), illus. Spring, Ira, photos by. LC 78-96317. 48 illus. 22. N.D. (ISBN 0-15-243822-X). Hardcourt Brace Jovanovich.

Edwards, Harvey (1929-) & Spring, Ira (1918-)

--Lars Olav: A Boy of Norway. Spring, Ira (1918-), illus. LC 69-17115. (Illus.). photos. (gr. 4-7). 1969. (ISBN 0-15-243605-7). (ISBN 0-15-243606-5). HarBraceJ.

Edwards, Hazel

--Honey, the Hospital Dog: Story. north american ed. Chisholm, Jane, illus. LC 85-14863. p. cm. (Easy-to-Read Animal Adventures). 1985. (ISBN 0-918831-46-6). (ISBN 0-918831-24-5). G. Stevens.

Edwards, Herbert Charles see Edwards, Bertram, pseud.

Edwards, Jane Campbell (1932-)

--What Happened to Amy. LC 61-11924. 22cm. 191p. 1961. Lothrop Lee & Shepard.

--What Happened to Amy? (Pub. by Lothrop). (gr. 7-12). 1972. (ISBN 0-590-09071-2, Schol Trade Pap). Schol Bk Serv.

Edwards, Jean, ed.

--Four Winds: A Poetry Anthology. LC 78-74815. 3 v. in 1. 20cm. (Granger poetry library). 1979. (ISBN 0-89609-133-3). Granger Book Co.

Edwards, John Emlyn

--Twigwidge. Sharp, Caroline, illus. LC 76-383970. (Illus.). 128 p. 22cm. 1976. (ISBN 0-237-44852-1). Evans Bros.

Edwards, Josephine Cunnington (1904-)

--Kamwendo. Padgett, Jim, illus. LC 66-3983. 91p. illus. 21cm. 1966. Southern Pub. Assn.

--Reuben's Portion. Malmeda, Joseph W., illus. LC 57-48120. (Illus.). 208p. 20cm. 1957. Southern Pub. Association.

--Secret in the Hayloft. LC 73-97798. 21cm. 192p. (gr. 4-9). 1969. Southern Pub.

--Sibande & Other Stories. Nye, Vernon Paul, illus. LC 66-28815. 22cm. 96p. (gr. 4-6). N.D. Pacific Pr Pub Assn.

--Swift Arrow. LC 67-17867. (Illus.). v, 116 p. 22cm. 1967. Pacific Press Pub. Association.

--Tales from Africa. Malmeda, Joseph W., illus. LC 56-14568. 255p. illus. 24cm. 1956. Southern Pub. Association.

--Unto, A Knowledge of the Truth. Collins, Fred, illus. LC 61-11982. (Illus.). 190p. 22cm. 1961. Review and Herald Pub. Association.

Edwards, Julie see Andrews, Julie.

Edwards, Julie (1935-)

--Mandy. Brown, Judith Gwyn (1933-), illus. LC 76-157901. (Illus.). 7 ils. 128p. (gr. 3-7). 1971. (ISBN 0-06-021802-9, HarpJ). (ISBN 0-06-021803-7). Har-Row.

Edwards, June, adapted by.
--Huckleberry Finn. Craft, Kinuko Y., illus. Twain, Mark, pseud. LC 79-24312. (Original Author: Samuel Langhorne Clemens (Mark Twain), 1835-1910). (Illus.). 48 p. 24cm. c.1980. (ISBN 0-8172-1651-0). Raintree Publishers.
--Tom Sawyer. Naprstek, Joel Langhorne, illus. LC 80-22095. (Original Author: Samuel Langhorne Clemens (Mark Twain), 1835-1910). (Illus.). 48 p. 24cm. (Raintree Short Classics Series). c.1981. (ISBN 0-8172-1665-0). Raintree Publishers.
--Treasure Island. LC 79-24100. (Original Author: Robert Louis Stevenson, 1850-1894). (Illus.). 47 p. 24cm. c.1980. (ISBN 0-8172-1655-3). Raintree Publishers.
Edwards, June, adapted by see Twain, Mark.
Edwards, Kate Flournoy (1877-1980)
--Rhymes for Good Times & Some Other Verses. Edwards, Kate Flournoy (1877-1980), illus. (Illus.). 6 halftones. 64p. (gr. 1-5). 1971. (ISBN 0-910220-08-5). (ISBN 0-910220-09-3). Larlin Corp.
--Rhymes For Good Times and Some Other Verses. Edwards, Kate Flournoy (1877-1980), illus. N.D. Norman S. Berg Publisher.

Edwards, Leo, pseud., see Leo, Edward Edson.

Edwards, Lilly Rust
--Grandmother's Stories. Rust, Alice & Knox, Mary, illus. LC 34-448181. 37 p. illus. 23 cm. c.1933. Printed by the Michie Company.
Edwards, Linda Strauss
--The Downtown Day. Edwards, Linda Strauss, illus. LC 82-4645. p. cm. 1983. (ISBN 0-394-95407-6). Knopf.
--The Downtown Day. Edwards, Linda Strauss, illus. 1983. Pantheon.
Edwards, Lynne (1943-) & Edwards, Brian (1937-)
--Dead As the Dodo. LC 72-6957. (Illus.). 36 p. 27cm. 1973. (ISBN 0-8193-0640-1). (ISBN 0-8193-0640-1). Parents' Magazine Press.
Edwards, Malcolm
--Constellations: Stories of the Future. 192p. (gr. 5-9). 1984. (ISBN 0-575-02838-6, Pub. by Gollancz England). David & Charles.
Edwards, Mark
--Small Songs for Young Readers. LC 59-10120. 41 p. 20cm. (Contemporary poets of Dorrance series, no. 509). 1959. Dorrance.
Edwards, Mark, ed. see Cross, Gillian Clare.
Edwards, Mary Ellen, illus.
--Little Red Riding Hood. (Illus.). N.D. White, Stokes & Allen.
Edwards, Mary Roxie Lane (0000-1922)
--In Daddy Jesse's Kingdom. LC 23-2030. 106 p. incl. front. 20 1/2 cm. 1922. The J. W. Burke Company.
Edwards, May
--The Hobo Hound. Suba, Susanne (1913-), illus. LC 48-6064. 31 p. illus. (part col.) 26 cm. (Slottle library). 1947. Rand, McNally.
Edwards, Michelle
--Misha, the Minstrel. Edwards, Michelle, illus. LC 84-62336. (Illus.). 25 p. 29cm. 1985. (ISBN 0-930100-19-0). Holy Cow! Press.
Edwards, Monica Le Doux Newton (1912-)
--Dolphin Summer. Whittam, Geoffrey William (1916-), illus. LC 79-137462. (Illus.). 192 p. 21cm. 1971, c.1963. Hawthorn Books.
--The Midnight Horse. LC 50-12968. 278 p. 22cm. 1950. Vanguard Press.
--Storm Ahead. N.D. Penguin Bks.
--White Riders. N.D. Penguin Bks.
Edwards, Page L., Jr. (1941-)
--Scarface Joe. LC 83-20667. 128p. 1984. (ISBN 0-590-07899-2). (ISBN 0-590-07899-2). Four Winds Press.
--Scarface Joe. (gr. 6-8). 1984. Scholastic.
Edwards, Roselyn see Alexander, Marge, pseud.
Edwards, Roselyn (1929-)
--Busy Boys & Girls. (Illus.). (ps-k). N.D. Southern Pub.
--Mamma's Bean Sweater, and Other Stories. LC 73-81312. (Illus.). 128p. 22cm. 1967. Review and Herald Pub. Association.
--The Secret of the Siren And Other Stories. LC 75-102114. (Illus.). 126 p. 22cm. (Penguin series). 1970. Review and Herald Pub. Association.
--The Treasure of Lower Butternut. Greer, Arlo, illus. LC 73-172828. (Illus.). 90p. 21cm. c.1972. Review and Herald Pub. Association.
Edwards, Roy (1922-), tr. see Rutgers van der Loeff-Basenau, Anna Maria Margaretha.
Edwards, Roy, tr. see Rutgers van der Loeff-Basenau, Anna Maria Margarethe.
Edwards, Sally Cary (1929-)
--George Midgett's War. 1985. Scribner's.
--Isaac and Snow. Hampshire, Michael Allen, illus. LC 72-89759. (Illus.). 123 p. 22cm. 1973. (ISBN 0-698-20244-9). (ISBN 0-698-20244-9). Coward, McCann & Geoghegan.
--When the World's on Fire. Lebenson, Richard, illus. LC 70-179381. (Illus.). 125 p. 21cm. 1972. Coward, McCann & Geoghegan.

Edwards, Tryon (1809-1894), ed.
--Select Poetry for Children and Youth. LC 16-9619. 1 p. l., x, 11-285 p. 18 cm. 1852. M. W. Dodd.
Edwards, Winifred
--The Money tree and other stories. N.D. Vantage Press, Inc.
Edwardson, Cordelia
--Miriam Lives in a Kibbutz. Rivkin-Brick, Anna (1908-), illus. LC 75-155754. (Illus.). photos. 48p. (gr. 4-6). 1971. (ISBN 0-688-51365-4). Lothrop.
Edwardson, E., ed. see Spenser, Edmund (1552-1599) & Malory, Thomas Sir.
Edwin, Maribel
--The Hidden House. LC 64-1825. 21cm. 218p. 1965. Nelson.
Edwin, Samuel
--Captain Noah and his ark. Fielding, Lola, illus. (Illus.). 48p. 1965. Abelard-Schuman.
Edwina
--Sinbad Again!. 92p. N.D. Coward-McCann.
--Sinbad: Or, A Dog's Life. 96p. N.D. Coward-McCann.
Eells, Elsie Spicer, Mrs. (1880-), retold by.
--The Brazilian Fairy bk. N.D. J. B. Lippincott.
--The Brazilian Fairy Book. Hood, George W., illus. LC 26-13568. x p., 2 l., 3-193 p. col. front., col. plates. 21 cm. 1926. Frederick A. Stokes Company.
--Fairy Tales from Brazil: How and Why Tales from Brazilian Folk-Lore. Barton, Helen M., illus. LC 17-25892. xiii, 210 p. front., plates. 20 1/2 cm. 1917. Dodd, Mead & Company.
--The Islands of Magic: Legends, Folk and Fairy Tales from the Azores. Brock, Emma Lillian (1886-1974), illus. LC 22-20316. xii, 289 p. incl. front., illus., plates. 19 1/2 cm. c.1922. Harcourt, Brace and Company.
--The Magic Tooth and Other Tales from the Amazon. N.D. Little Brown & Co.
--Tale of Enchantment from Spain. Petersham, Maud Sylvia Fuller, Mrs. (1890-1971) & Petersham, Miska (1889-1960), illus. 1956. (ISBN 0-396-03119-6). Dodd, Mead & Company.
--Tales from the Amazon. Choate, Florence & Curtis, Elizabeth, illus. LC 20-18503. (Illus.). (gr. 4-6). 1938. Dodd.
--Tales of Enchantment from Spain. Petersham, Maud Sylvia Fuller, Mrs. (1890-1971) & Petersham, Miska (1889-1960), illus. LC 50-5917. vi, 173 p. illus. (part col.) 21 cm. 1950. Dodd, Mead.
--Tales of Enchantment from Spain. Petersham, Maud Sylvia Fuller, Mrs. (1890-1971) & Petersham, Miska (1889-1960), illus. LC 20-17754. p., 3 l., 3-173 p. col. front., illus., col. plates. 21 cm. c.1920. Harcourt, Brace and Howe.
--Tales of Giants from Brazil. Barton, Helen M., illus. LC 18-18503. 6 p. l., 3-179 p. front., plates. /20 1/2 cm. 1918. Dodd, Mead and Company.

Eells, May Worthington
--Honorable Lunch: Nancy's Home Economics Experiences in Japan. LC 57-12483. 273p. 21cm. (Career books). 1957. Dodd, Mead.
--Sally and Her Homemaking. Byran, Marguerite, illus. LC 41-16481. 250 p. illus. 21 cm. (Career books). 1941. Dodd, Mead.
--Sally and Her Kitchens: The Story of Sally Lewis' Career in Home Economics. Bryan, Marguerite, illus. LC 39-22927. 256 p. illus. 21 cm. (Career books). 1939. Dodd, Mead.
--Sally, Army Dietitian. LC 44-4722. 210 p. illus. 21 cm. (Dodd, Mead career books). 1944. Dodd, Mead.
--A Touch of Parsley: A Young Home Economist in Business. LC 48-7428. ix, 245 p. 21 cm. (Career books). 1948. Dodd, Mead.
Efron, Marshall & Olsen, Alfa-Betty (1947-)
--Bible Stories You Can't Forget, No Matter How Hard You Try. Barrett, Ron (1937-), illus. LC 76-9853. (Illus.). xi, 79 p. 24cm. c.1976. (ISBN 0-525-26500-7). Dutton.
Egan, Evelyn & Hurlbert, Delpha
--Adventures Fishing. Orloff, Gregory, illus. LC 59-12335. (Illus.). 100p. 23cm. (Outdoor Adventure Ser.). 1959. Benefic Press.
Egan, Frank
--The Fairy Isle of Coosanure. Dunne, Jeanette, illus. (Illus.). 96p. (gr. 3-7). 1981. (ISBN 0-905473-70-1, Pub. by Wolfhound Pr Ireland). Irish Bks Media.
Egan, Joseph Burke (1879-)
--New Found Tales from Many Lands. Richardson, Frederick (1862-1937), illus. LC 30-5146. xv, 352 p. col. front., illus., col. plates. 22 1/2 cm. (The Children's Bookshelf). c.1929. The John C. Winston Company.
--Wings of Flame: Everyday Fables. Prittie, Edwin John, illus. LC 30-9535. xv, 1 365 p. col. front., illus., col. plates. 23 1/2 cm. (The Children's Bookshelf). c.1929. The John C. Winston Company.
Egan, Margaret
--Hospital Summer. LC 68-21060. 187 p. 22cm. 1968. Doubleday.

Egan, Maurice Francis (1852-1924)
--The Adventurers. LC 22-21205. 224 p. front. 18 1/2 cm. 1922. H. L. Kilner & Co.
--Belinda: A Story of New York. LC 2-1783. 3 p. l., 5-276 p. 19 cm. 1901. H. L. Kilner & Co.
--Belinda's Cousins: A Tale of Town and Country. LC 4-67. 315p. 19cm. 1903. H. L. Kilner.
--The Boys in the Block. LC 6-37560. 85 p. 15 1/2 cm. 1924. Benziger Brothers.
--The Chatelaine of the Roses: A Romance of St. Bartholomew's Night, and Other Tales. LC 6-37559. 218 p. 19 cm. c.1897. H. L. Kilner & Co.
--The Flower of the Flock and The Badgers of Belmont. LC 7-1247. 279 p. front. 19 1/2 cm. 1895. Benziger Brothers.
--A Garden of Roses: Stories and Sketches. LC 6-37558. 278 p. 17 1/2 cm. 1887. T. B. Newman & Co.
--How They Worked Their Way, and Other Tales. Stories of Duty. LC 6-37557. 256 p. front. 18 cm. 1892. Benziger Brothers.
--In a Brazilian Forest and Three Brave Boys. LC 98-2166. 2 p. l., 7-219 p. 19 cm. c.1898. H. L. Kilner & Co.
--Jack Chumleigh at Boarding-School. LC 99-5216. 280 p. 18 1/2 cm. c.1899. H. L. Kilner & Co.
--Jack Chumleigh: Or, and Friends and Foes. LC 6-37556. 2 p. l., 3-251 p. 19 cm. 1896. J. Murphy & Co.
--Jasper Thorn: A Story of New York Life. LC 6-37555. 308 p. 19 cm. c.1897. H. L. Kilner & Co.
--The Leopard of Lancianus and Other Stories. LC 98-2167. 2 p. l., 7-229 p. 19 cm. c.1898. H. L. Kilner & Co.
--Some Pleasant Tales for Boys and Girls. 64 p. 15 1/2 cm. (On cover: Catholic library, v. 25). 1898. C. Wildermann.
--St. Martin's Summer. LC 5-24846. 307 p. 19 cm. c.1905. H. L. Kilner & Co.
--The Watson Girls: A Washington Story. 2d ed. LC 1-30977. 196 p. 18 cm. c.1900. H. L. Kilner & Co.
--The Watsons of the Country. LC 5-24200. 303 p. 19 cm. c.1905. H. L. Kilner & Co.
Egan, Maurice Francis (1852-1924), ed.
--The Best Stories by the Foremost Catholic Authors. LC 10-23945. 10 v. 16 cm. c.1901. Benziger Brothers.
Egan, Robert, tr. see Protter, Eric & Protter, Nancy.
Egar, Edward
--Red Head. N.D. E. M. Hale & Co.
Ege, Nezahet Nurettin
--Turgut Lives in Turkey. Kalab, Theresa, illus. LC 39-276408. vi p., 2 l., 230 p. incl. front., illus. 21 cm. 1939. Longmans, Green and Co.
Eger, Jeffrey
--The Statue in the Harbor: A Story of Two Apprentices. LC 85-61511. p. cm. 1985, c.1986. (ISBN 0-382-09146-9). (ISBN 0-382-09145-0). Silver Burdett Co.
Egermeier, Elsie Emilie (1890-)
--Bible Picture A B C Bk. 63p. N.D. Reilly & Lee Co.
--Bible Story Book. N.D. Reilly & Lee.
--Bible Story Book. new ed. Hall, Arlene Stevens, ed. Uptton, Clive, illus. LC 68-23397. (A Complete Narration from Genesis to Revelation for Young & Old). (Illus.). 576 p. 25cm. 1969. Warner Press.
--Bible Story Book. deluxe ed. Hall, Arlene Stevens, ed. Uptton, Clive, illus. LC 71-9004. (A Complete Narration from Genesis to Revelation for Young & Old). (Illus.). 576, 64, 16 p. 24cm. 1969. Warner Press.
--Egermeier's Bible Picture ABC Book. N.D. Warner Press.
--Egermeier's Bible Story Bk. Rev. ed. 645p. N.D. Reilly & Lee Co.
--Egermeier's Bible Story Book. Uptton, Clive, illus. LC 77-26856. p. cm. 1978, c.1969. (ISBN 0-13-246850-6). Prentice-Hall.
--Egermeier's Favorite Bible Stories. (gr. k-6). 1965. (ISBN 0-87162-014-6). Warner Pr.
--Picture-Story Life of Christ: Adapted from Bible Story Book. LC 40-14699. vii, 8-292 p. incl. illus., col. plates. plates. 23 cm. c.1940. The Warner Press.
--Picture-Story Life of Jesus. Hall, Arlene Stevens, ed. LC 65-14972. 1966, c.1965. Warner.
Egerton, George, tr. see Hansson, Ola.
Eggleston, Edward (1837-1902)
--The Book of Queer Stories and Stories Told on a Cellar Door. LC 6-37554. 132 p. 19 cm. 1871. Adams, Blackmer, & Lyon Publishing Co.
--The Cellar Door Club, and other Stories. (Juvenile Classics). 1874. Henry L. Shepard & Co.
--A Christmas Story. N.D. Adams, Blackmer, & Lyon Co.
--The Circuit Rider. N.D. Charles Scribner's Sons.
--The Circuit Rider: A Tale of the Heroic Age. N.D. (ISBN 0-8446-1167-0). Peter Smith Publisher, Inc.

--The Hoosier School-Boy. LC 6-37553. ix p., 1 l., 9-181 p. incl. front., 4 pl. 19 cm. 1883. C. Scribner's Sons.
--The Hoosier School-Boy. edition specially arranged by the author for use as a reader in schools, and with the addition of definitions and occasional notes and questions. vii p., 1 l., 139 p. front, 4 pl. 19 cm. 1890. C. Scribner's Sons.
--The Hoosier School-Boy. LC 36-138811. xi p., 1 l., 194 p. incl. plates. 19 1/2 cm. c.1936. C. Scribner's Sons.
--The Hoosier School Boy. (Scribner's Series for Young People). N.D. Charles Scribner's Sons.
--The Hoosier School-Boy. LC 66-8851. (Illus.). vi, 261 p. 21cm. 1966, c.1883. P. Smith.
--Mr. Blake's Walking-Stick: A Christmas Story for Boys and Girls. LC 6-37552. 3 p. l., 9-60 p. 18 1/2 x 12 cm. 1870. Adams, Blackmer, & Lyon Publishing Co.
--Queer Stories for Boys and Girls. LC 6-375514. vi, 186 p. 18 cm. 1884. C. Scribner's Sons.
--Queer Stories for Boys and Girls. LC 77-89717. vi, 186 p. 20cm. (Children's Literature Reprint Series). 1977. (ISBN 0-8486-0214-5). Core Collection Books.
--Roxy. N.D. Charles Scribner's Sons.
--The Schoolmaster's Stories: For Boys and Girls. LC 6-37550. 279 p. incl. front., illus., plates. 19 cm. 1874. H. L. Shepard & Co.
--The Schoolmaster's Stories: For Boys and Girls. LC 72-84567. p. cm. 1974, c.1874. (ISBN 0-403-03057-9). Scholarly Press.
--Stories of American Life and Adventure: Third Reader Grade. LC 4-18015. 214 p. incl. front., illus. 19 cm. (Eclectic school readings). c.1895. American Book Company.
--Stories of Great Americans for Little Americans. (Eclectic School Readings). N.D. American Book Company.
Eggleston, Edward (1837-1902), illus.
--Saint Nicholas Book of Plays and Operettas. Hapgood, T. B., designed by. 225p. (New Books for Boys and Girls). 1900. The Century Co.
Eggleston, George Cary (1839-1911)
--The Bale Marked Circle X: A Blockade Running Adventure. Emerson, C. Chase, illus. LC 2-13613. 376 p. front., 3 pl. 20 cm. 1902. Lothrop Publishing Company.
--The Big Brother: A Story of Indian War. LC 4-16132. 182 p. front., 4 pl. 20 cm. (The big brother series, v. 1). 1875. G. P. Putnam's Sons.
--Camp Venture: A Story of the Virginia Mountains. McCullough, William A., illus. LC 1-31859. 4 p. l., 11-401 p. front., plates. 18 cm. c.1901. Lothrop Publishing Company.
--Captain Sam. (Illus.). 212p. (Putnam's Knickerbocker Ser.). N.D. G. P. Putnam's Sons.
--Captain Sam: Or, The Boy Scouts of 1814. LC 4-16133. 2 p. l., 7-212 p. plates. 20 cm. (Big Brother Series, v. 2). 1876. G. Putnam's Sons.
--Jack Shelby. (The Eggleston Juveniles). N.D. Lothrop,Lee & Shepard.
--Joe Lambert's Ferry. LC 7-1502. 150 p. front., plates. 18 cm. (On cover: Peace Island series). c.1883. D. Lothrop and Company.
--The Last of the Flatboats: A Story of the Mississippi and Its Interesting Family of Rivers. LC 3185. 382 p. front., plates, map. 19 1/2 cm. c.1900. Lothrop Publishing Company.
--Long Knives: The Story of How They Won the West. Merrill, Frank Thayer (1848-), illus. LC 7-27159. 2 p. l., iii, 2 p., 1 l., 393 p. front. 5 pl. 19 1/2 cm. 1907. Lothrop, Lee & Shepard Co.
--Running the River: A Story of Adventure and Success. LC 4-6738. vi, p., 1 l., 295 p. front., illus., 5 pl. 19 cm. 1904. A. S. Barnes & Company.
--The Signal Boys. (Illus.). (Putnam's Knickerbocker Ser.). N.D. G. P. Putman's Sons.
--The Signal Boys: Or, Captain Sam's Company. LC 4-16134. 2 p. l., 218 p. front. (map) 4 pl. 20 cm. (Big brother series. v. 3). 1878. G. P. Putnam's Sons.
--Strange Stories from History for Young People. LC 6-37549. x p., 1 l., 13-243 p. incl. front., plates. 16 1/2 cm. (Harper's young people series). 1886. Harper & Brothers.
--What Happened at Quasi. (The Eggleston Juveniles). N.D. Lothrop,Lee & Shepard.
--Wreck of the "Red Bird", 1 of 5 Vols. (Illus.). (Big Brother Ser.). N.D. G. P. Putnam's Sons.
--The Wreck of the Red Bird: A Story of the Carolina Coast. LC 4-31664. vii, 216 p. 6 pl. (incl. front.) 20 cm. 1882. G. P. Putnam's Sons.
--The Wreck of the Red Bird: A Story of the Carolina Coast. LC 4-18929. v, p., 1 l., 216 p. 6 pl. (incl. front.) 20 cm. (On cover: The Knickerbocker series). 1903. G. P. Putnam's Sons.
Eggleston, George Cary (1839-1911) & Freeman, Mary Eleanor Wilkins, Mrs. (1862-)
--Little Lads. LC 4-24502. (Illus.). 24cm. 188p. 1904. Saalfield Publishing Co.

AUTHOR INDEX EISNER, LEONARD

Eggleston, Joyce Smith
--Things That Grow. LC 57-9989. (Illus.). unpaged. 21cm. (Look, read, learn). 1958. Melmont Publishers.
Eggleston, Margaret White, Mrs. (1878-)
--Around the Camp Fire with the Older Boys. LC 21-22329. ix p., 2 l., 13-132 p. 19 1/2 cm. $1.25. c.1921. George H. Doran Company.
--Fireside Stories for Girls in Their Teens. LC 21-926. xii p., 1 l., 15-144 p. 19 1/2 cm. c.1921. George H. Doran Company.
--Kathie's Diary: Leaves from an Old, Old Diary. LC 26-4063. viii p., 3 l., 13-339 p. 1 illus., plates (1 double, col.) ports. 20 cm. c.1926. George H. Doran Company.
--More Fireside Stories for Girls in Their Teens. LC 28-6525. x, 153 p. 19 1/2 cm. 1928. Doubleday, Doran & Company, Inc.
--The Red Stocking and Other Christmas Stories. LC 37-36930. viii p., 2 l. 153 p. 19 1/2 cm. 1937. Harper & Brothers.
Eggleston, N. H., Mrs.
--Daughters of the Prairie. 301p. N.D. Hurd & Houghton for American Tract Society.
--Daughters of the Prairie, 1 of 4 vols. 301p. (The Prairie Library). N.D. Lockwood, Brooks, & Co. for American Tract Society.
Eglash, Albert
--How a Little Girl Became a Great Hunter: The Story of Mtuto Tembo. (Illus.). 40p. (Orig.). 1983. (ISBN 0-935320-01-6). San Luis Quest.
--My Mom's Not Dead. (Illus.). 60p. (Orig.). 1983. (ISBN 0-935320-03-2). San Luis Quest.
Egloff, Lee G.
--The Adventures of Brald. 1980. (ISBN 0-533-04192-9). Vantage.
Eglsaer, Marie-Therese
--Figaro. (Illus.). 80p. 1984. (ISBN 0-89962-371-9). Todd & Honeywell.
E. H., tr. see Topelius, Zakarias.
Ehmcke, Susanne (1906-) & Steiner, Heiri
--Necklace for Laurie. Crawford, Elizabeth D., tr. from Ger. LC 70-22251. (Illus.). 27 p. 29cm. 1971, c.1970. (ISBN 0-15-256750-X). Harcourt Brace Jovanovich.
Ehre, Edward, jt. ed. see Marsh, Irving T.
Ehrensperger, Harold A.
--Change of Heart. 176p. 1954. Friendship Press.
Ehret, Walter & Evans, George
--International Book of Christmas Carols. (Illus.). (gr. 4 up). 1963. (ISBN 0-13-471607-8). P-H.
Ehrhardt, Von Reinhold (1900-)
--The Clock in the Tower. Watts, Anna Bernadette (1942-), illus. (gr. 3-7). N.D. Scroll Pr.
--Kikeri: Or, The Proud Red Rooster. Watts, Anna Bernadette (1942-), illus. LC 75-97446. (Illus.). 32 p. 1969. World Pub. Co.
--Kikeri: Or, The Proud Red Rooster. Watts, Anna Bernadette (1942-), illus. LC 75-97446. 28cm. 32p. (gr. 7 up). 1970. (ISBN 0-529-00914-5). (ISBN 0-529-00915-3). World Pub.
Ehrlich, Amy (1942-), retold by see Andersen, Hans Christian.
Ehrlich, Amy (1942-)
--Annie and the Kidnappers. Shortall, Leonard W. & Starr, Leonard, illus. LC 82-3697. (Illus.). 64 p. 20cm. c.1982. Random House.
--Annie Finds a Home. Shortall, Leonard W. & Starr, Leonard, illus. LC 81-15910. (Illus.). 32 p. 21cm. (Random House pictureback). c.1982. (ISBN 0-394-85161-7). Random House.
--Bunnies All Day Long. Henry, Marie H., illus. LC 84-20031. (Illus.). 25 p. 24cm. 1985. (ISBN 0-8037-0185-3). Dial Books for Young Readers.
--Bunnies and Their Grandma. Henry, Marie H., illus. LC 84-20030. (Illus.). 23 p. 24cm. 1985. (ISBN 0-8037-0186-1). Dial Books for Young Readers.
--The Everyday Train. Alexander, Martha G (1920-), illus. LC 76-12922. 20cm. 32p. c.1977. (ISBN 0-8037-2191-9). (ISBN 0-8037-2192-7). Dial Press.
--Leo, Zack and Emmie. Kellogg, Steven (1941-), illus. LC 81-2604. p. cm. c.1981. (ISBN 0-8037-4761-6). (ISBN 0-8037-4760-8). Dial Press.
--The Wild Swans. Jeffers, Susan, illus. LC 81-65843. (Original Author: Hans Christian Andersen, 1805-1875). p. cm. c.1981. (ISBN 0-8037-9381-2). (ISBN 0-8037-9391-X). Dial Press.
--Zeek Silver Moon. (Illus.). unpaged. 26cm. (Pied piper book). 1976, c.1972. (ISBN 0-8037-9891-1). Dial Press.
--Zeek Silver Moon. Parker, Robert Andrew (1927-), illus. LC 70-181787. (Illus.). 32 p. 27cm. 1972. Dial Press.
Ehrlich, Amy (1942-), adapted by.
--Annie: The Storybook Based on the Movie. LC 81-15416. p. cm. (Movie Storybooks). 1982. (ISBN 0-394-85087-4). (ISBN 0-394-95087-9). Random House.
--Cinderella. Jeffers, Susan, illus. LC 85-1685. (Original Author :Charles Perrault (1628-1705)). p. cm. 1985. (ISBN 0-8037-0205-1). (ISBN 0-8037-0206-X). Dial Books for Young Readers.
--The Ewoks & the Lost Children. LC 84-18379. (Illus.). 48p. (ps-2). 1985. (ISBN 0-394-97186-8, BYR). (ISBN 0-394-87186-3). Random.
--The Ewoks and the Lost Children. LC 84-18379. (Adapted from a Screenplay by Bob Carrou, Story by George Lucas). (Illus.). 42 p. 29cm. c.1985. (ISBN 0-394-87186-3). (ISBN 0-394-97186-8). Random House.
--The Ramdom House Book of Fairy Tales. Goode, Diane (1949-), illus. 224p. 1985. (ISBN 0-394-85693-7). (ISBN 0-394-95693-1). Random House.
Ehrlich, Bettina Bauer see Bettina, pseud.
Ehrlich, Bettina Bauer (1903-)
--Castle in the Sand. Bettina, pseud. Ehrlich, Bettina Bauer (1903-), illus. Bettina, pseud. LC 51-10033. (Illus.). 47p. 26cm. 1951. Harper.
--Cocolo. Bettina, pseud. LC 48-9303. 32p. 1948, c.1945. Harper.
--Cocolo Comes to America. Bettina, pseud. LC 49-11840. (Illus.). 32p. 1949. Harper.
--Cocolo's Home. Bettina, pseud. Ehrlich, Bettina Bauer (1903-), illus. Bettina, pseud. LC 50-10831. (Illus.). 32 p. 35cm. c.1950. Harper.
--The Goat Boy. Bettina, pseud. Ehrlich, Bettina Bauer (1903-), illus. Bettina, pseud. LC 66-4739. 24p. col. illus. 25cm. 1st U.S. edition 1966, c.1965. Norton.
--A Horse for the Island. Bettina, pseud. Ehrlich, Bettina Bauer (1903-), illus. Bettina, pseud. LC 52-7883. (Illus.). 213 p. 22cm. 1952. Harper.
--Of Uncles and Aunts. Bettina, pseud. 1st American ed. LC 64-9759. (Illus.). 23cm. 1964, c.1963. W. W. Norton.
--Pantaloni. Bettina, pseud. Ehrlich, Bettina Bauer (1903-), illus. Bettina, pseud. LC 57-9103 (Illus.). unpaged. 34cm. c.1957. Harper. **Award: (ALA).**
--Piccolo. Bettina, pseud. Ehrlich, Bettina Bauer (1903-), illus. Bettina, pseud. LC 54-8948. (Illus.). 64 p. 13cm. 1954. Harper.
--Trovoto. Bettina, pseud. LC 59-9319. (Illus.). 47p. 29cm. 1959. Ariel Books.
Ehrmann, Mary B., jt. auth. see Bailey, Carolyn Sherwin.
Ehrmann, Naftoli Hertz
--Stories by Judaeus. Backman, Aidel, illus. LC 82-100257. (Illus.). 206 p. 22cm. c.1980. (ISBN 0-86517-002-9). Lightbooks : Distributor, Z. Berman Books.
Ehrsam, Theodore, ed. see Browing, Peter.
Eich, Estelle, jt. auth. see Coleman, Bernard.
Eichelberger, Rosa Kohler (1896-)
--Big Fire in Baltimore. Schnedier, Rex, illus. LC 78-31311. (Illus.). 204 p. 23cm. 1979. (ISBN 0-916144-36-4). (ISBN 0-916144-37-2). Stemmer House.
--Bronko. Rainnie, Hedley, illus. LC 55-5914. 192 p. illus. 24 cm. (Morrow junior books). 1955. Morrow.
Eichenberg, Eduard
--What the Birds Did at Hazel's Orchard. LC 16-21975. 3 p., l., 76 p. front. 20 cm. $1.0. 1916. Printed for J. J. Newbegin, by J. H. Nash.
Eichenberg, Fritz (1901-)
--Ape in a Cape: An Alphabet of Odd Animals. 1st ed. Eichenberg, Fritz (1901-), illus. LC 52-6908. unpaged. illus. 29 cm. 1952. Harcourt, Brace. **Award: (RCM).**
--Ape in a Cape: An Alphabet of Odd Animals. Eichenberg, Fritz (1901-), illus. (Illus.). 1 v. (unpaged. 23cm. (Voyager Book). 1973, c.1952. (ISBN 0-15-607830-9). Harcourt.
--Ape in a Cape: An Alphabet of Odd Animals. Eichenberg, Fritz (1901-), illus. LC 65-29408. 1 v. (chiefly col. illus.) 29 cm. N.D. Harcourt, Brace & World.
--Dancing in the Moon: Counting Rhymes. Eichenberg, Fritz (1901-), illus. LC 55-8674. (Illus.). 21p. illus. 27cm. (gr. k-3). 1956. (ISBN 0-15-221443-7, HJ). HarBraceJ. **Award: (ALA).**
Eichenberg, Fritz (1901-) & Musaus, Johann Karl
--Poor Troll: The Story of Ruebezahl and the Princess. Eichenberg, Fritz (1901-), illus. LC 82-795. p. cm. c.1981. (ISBN 0-916144-94-1). Stemmer House Publishers.
Eichler, Margrit (1942-)
--Martin's Father. 2d ed. Magennis, Bev, illus. LC 77-81779. (Illus.). 30 p. c.1977. (ISBN 0-914996-17-7). (ISBN 0-914996-16-9). Lollipop Power.
Eicke, Edna
--The Children Who Got Married. LC 69-16869. (Illus.). 32 p. 24cm. 1969. Windmill Books.
--What's Your Name. Eicke, Edna, illus. (Illus.). (gr. 1-6). 1968. (ISBN 0-06-021804-5, Dist. by Har-Row). Windmill Bks.
Eicke, Edna & Kraus, Robert (1925-)
--Lillian, Morgan and Teddy. LC 70-148459. (Illus.). 32 p. 24cm. 1971. (ISBN 0-87807-022-2). Windmill Books.
Eifert, Virginia S.
--Buffalo Trace. Lee, Manning de Villeneuve (1894-1980), illus. (Illus.). (gr. 8 up). 1955. (ISBN 0-396-03703-8). Dodd. **Award: (ALA).**
Eige, Lillian E.
--The Kidnapping of Mr. Huey. LC 82-48610. 160p. (gr. 6 up). 1983. (ISBN 0-06-021798-7, HarpJ). (ISBN 0-06-021799-5). Har-Row.
Eilert, Bernd, jt. auth. see Waechter, Friedrich Karl.
Eiloart, Mrs.
--Archie Blake. N.D. George Routledge & Sons.
--The Boy with an Idea. 1873. G. P. Putnam's Sons.
--The Boy with and Idea, 1 of 15 Vols. (Illus.). (Warne's Hopeful Enterprise Library). N.D. Scribner & Welford.
--The Boys of Beechwood. (Illus.). (Routledge's Wecome Series of Boys' Books). N.D. George Routledge & Sons.
--Chris Fairlie's Boyhood. (Warne's Adventure Library). N.D. Frederick Warne & Co.
--Cris Fairlie's Boyhood: A Tale of an Old Town, 1 of 15 Vols. (Illus.). (Warne's Hopeful Enterprise Library). N.D. Scribner & Welford.
--Cris Fairlie's Boyhood: Tales of an Old Town, 1 of 8 Vols. (Illus.). (Warne's Victoria Gift Books Ser.). N.D. R. Worthington.
--Ernie Elton at Home and at School. N.D. George Routledge & Sons.
--Ernie Elton at School, and What Came of his Going There. N.D. George Routledge & Sons.
--Ernie Elton, the Lazy Boy. N.D. George Routledge & Sons.
--Johnny Jordan and His Dog. N.D. George Routledge & Sons.
--Tom Dunstone's Troubles. N.D. George Routledge & Sons.
--The Young Squire, 1 of 8 Vols. (Illus.). (Warne's Victoria Gift Books Ser.: No. 4). N.D. R. Worthington.
--The Young Squire, 1 of 15 Vols. (Illus.). (Warne's Hopeful Enterprise Library). N.D. Scribner & Welford.
Eimerl, Sarel Henry (1925-), adapted by see Swift, Jonathan.
Einberg, Elizabeth
--Ann & Peter in Southern Germany. Toothill, Harry, illus. LC 60-861. 20cm. 144p. (The Kennedys abroad). (gr. 7 up). 1960, c.1959. F. Muller: London. Distributed by Sportshelf: New York.
Einhorn, David
--The Seventh Candle and Other Folk Tales of Eastern. Schloss, Ezekiel, illus. Pashin, Gertrude, tr. from Yiddish. (Illus.). 1968. (ISBN 0-87068-369-1). Ktav Publishing House Inc.
Einsel, Naiad, jt. auth. see Minshull, Evelyn White.
Einsel, Walter (1926-)
--Did You Ever See?. 64p. (ps-1). 1962. (ISBN 0-201-09169-0, Young Scott Bks). A-W.
--Did You Ever See?. LC 62-2378. (Illus.). 64p. (gr. k-3). 1969. (ISBN 0-590-08034-2, Schol Pap). Scholastic Inc.
Eiseley, Loren Corey (1907-1977)
--The Immense Journey. 1957. (ISBN 0-394-43014-X). Random.
Eiseman, Alberta (1925-)
--Candido. Obligado, Lilian Isabel (1931-), illus. (Illus.). (gr. k-2). 1967. (ISBN 0-02-733300-0). Macmillan.
--Candido: A Story. Obligado, Lilian Isabel (1931-), illus. LC 65-20191. 1 v. (unpaged) illus. (part col.) 22 x 29 cm. 1965. Macmillan.
--The Guest Dog. Porter, George, illus. LC 68-55404. (Illus.). 48p. 24cm. (A Carousel Bk.). 1968. L. W. Singer.
--The Sunday Whirligig. Lonette, Reisie Dominee (1924-), illus. LC 77-2000. 24cm. 40p. 1977. Atheneum.
Eiseman, Alberta (1925-) & Eiseman, Nicole
--Gift from a Sheep: The Story of How Wool Is Made. Sugarman, Tracy (1921-), illus. LC 79-10629. (Illus.). 52 p. 22cm. (gr. 4-5). 1979. (ISBN 0-689-30707-1). Atheneum.
Eiseman, Alberta (1925-) & Sladkus, Ingrid
--Monica: The Story of a Young Magazine Apprentice. 184p. 21cm. (Dodd, Mead career books). 1957. Dodd, Mead.
--Skate to a Mountain Song. LC 66-11577. 134p. 21cm. c.1966. Macmillan.
Eiseman, Nicole, jt. auth. see Eiseman, Alberta.
Eisen, Anthony T. Fon see Fon Eisen, Anthony.
Eisen, Anthony T. Fon see Fon Eisen, Anthony

Eisenberg, Azriel Louis (1903-) & Globe, Leah Ain (1900-), eds.
--Sabra Children: Stories of Fun and Adventure in Israel. Josephson, Gabe, illus. LC 73-94343. (Illus.). xi, 239 p. 24cm. 1970. J. David Publishers.
Eisenberg, Eleanor
--The Pretty House That Found Happiness. Warren, Betsy, pseud. (1916-), illus. Warren, Elizabeth Avery. LC 64-17592. (Illus.). 31p. 22 x 25cm. 1964. Steck Co.
--The Pretty House That Found Happiness. rev. ed. Warren, Betsy, pseud. (1916-), illus. Warren, Elizabeth Avery. LC 74-10936. (Illus.). 31 p. 25cm. 1974. (ISBN 0-8114-7767-3). Steck-Vaughn Co.
Eisenberg, Harvey, illus.
--M-G-M's Tom and Jerry and Their Friends: M-G-M Cartoons. (Golden Story Book). 1949. Golden Press.
Eisenberg, Harvey, ed. see Archer, Peter & Loew's Incorporated.
Eisenberg, Harvey & MacLaughlin, Don, illus.
--M-G-M's Tom and Jerry: M-G-M Cartoons. (Golden Story Book). 1951. Golden Press.
--M-G-M's Tom and Jerry Meet Little Quack: M-G-M Cartoons. Reissue of 1953 ed. (Little Golden Book). 1958. Golden Press.
Eisenberg, Lisa, jt. auth. see Hall, Katy.
Eisenberg, Lisa, jt. auth. see McMullan, Kate.
Eisenberg, Lisa (1949-)
--Falling Star. LC 79-52653. (Illus.). 64p. (Laura Brewster Mysteries Ser.). (gr. 4 up). 1980. (ISBN 0-516-02205-0). Childrens.
--Falling Star. LC 79-52653. (Laura Brewster Bks.). 1980. (ISBN 0-8224-1081-8). Pitman Learning.
--Fast-Food King. LC 79-52564. (Illus.). 64p. (Laura Brewster Mysteries Ser.). (gr. 4 up). 1980. (ISBN 0-516-02206-7). Childrens.
--Fast-Food King. LC 79-52654. (Laura Brewster Bks.). 1980. (ISBN 0-8224-1082-6). Pitman Learning.
--Fast-Food King. Lichtenstein, Karl, illus. LC 79-52564. (Illus.). 58 p. 18cm. (Pacemaker book). (A Laura Brewster Book). c.1980. (ISBN 0-8224-1082-6). Fearon Pitman Publishers.
--Golden Idol. LC 79-52655. (Illus.). 64p. (Laura Brewster Mysteries Ser.). (gr. 4 up). 1980. (ISBN 0 516 02207 5). Childrens.
--Golden Idol. LC 79-52655. (Laura Brewster Bks.). 1980. (ISBN 0 8224 1083 4). Pitman Learning.
--House of Laughs. LC 79-52656. (Illus.). 64p. (Laura Brewster Mysteries Ser.). (gr. 4 up). 1980. (ISBN 0-516-02208-3). Childrens.
--House of Laughs. LC 79-52656. (Laura Brewster Bks.). 1980. (ISBN 0-8224-1084-2). Pitman Learning.
--Killer Music. LC 79-52657. (Illus.). 64p. (Laura Brewster Mysteries Ser.). (gr. 4 up). 1980. (ISBN 0-516-02209-1). Childrens.
--Killer Music. LC 79-52657. (Laura Brewster Bks.). 1980. (ISBN 0-8224-1085-0). Pitman Learning.
--Laura Brewster Books, 6 bks. (gr. 6 up). 1980. (ISBN 0-8224-1080-X). Pitman Learning.
--Man in the Cage. LC 80-65912. 75 p. 18cm. (Pacemaker book). (Talespinners: I). c.1981. (ISBN 0-8224-6728-3). Fearon Education.
--Tiger Rose. LC 79-52658. (Illus.). 64p. (Laura Brewster Mysteries Ser.). (gr. 4 up). 1980. (ISBN 0-516-02210-5). Childrens.
Tiger Rose. LC 79-52658. (Laura Brewster Bks.). 1980. (ISBN 0-8224-1086-9). Pitman Learning.
Eisenberg, Miriam, jt. auth. see Eisenberg, Philip.
Eisenberg, Monroe, jt. auth. see Francis, Dorothy Brenner.
Eisenberg, Philip (1917-)
--We Were There With Charles Darwin on H. M. S. Beagle. Kluckhohn, Clyde K., contrib. by. Vestal, Herman B., illus. LC 60-16154. (Illus.). 178p. 22cm. (We Were There Bks.). 1960. Grosset & Dunlop.
--Won Kim's Ox. Eisenberg, Hilda, illus. (Illus.). (gr. 3-5). 1956. (ISBN 0-695-49660-3). Follett.
Eisenberg, Philip (1917-) & Eisenberg, Miriam
--The Brave Gives Blood. Ames, Lee Judah (1921-), illus. LC 54-6763. 62p. illus. 22cm. (Everyday science stories). 1954. J. Messner.
Eisenberg, Phyllis Rose
--A Mitzvah Is Something Special. Jeschke, Susan (1942-), illus. LC 77-25664. (Illus.). 30 p. 23cm. c.1978. (ISBN 0-06-021807-X). (ISBN 0-06-021808-8). Harper & Row.
Eisenberg, Ronald Lee (1945-)
--The Iguana Corps of the Haganah. LC 77-83948. (Illus.). 120 p. 23cm. c.1977. (ISBN 0-8197-0456-3). Bloch Pub. Co.
Eisenhower, Julie Nixon
--Julie Eisenhower's Favorite Stories. LC 74-84357. (Illus.). 124 p. 29cm. c.1974. Saturday Evening Post Library.
Eisenstat, Jane Sperry see Sperry, J. E., pseud.
Eisenstein, Judith K. & Prensky, Frieda, eds.
--Songs of Childhood. Gordon, Ayala, illus. (Illus.). index. 322p. (ps-3). N.D. (ISBN 0-8381-0722-2). United Syn Bk.
Eisenstein, Phyllis (1946-)
--Born to Exile. Fabian, Stephen E. (1930-), illus. LC 77-78598. (Illus.). 202 p. 20cm. (Arkham House science fiction novel). 1978. (ISBN 0-87054-082-3). Arkham House.
Eisner, Helen Geller
--The Little Boy Who did not Know Why. Cannon, Marian, illus. LC 46-7369. 19 x 17 cm. 35p. 1946. Lothrop Lee & Shepard.
Eisner, Leonard
--Mystery of Broken Wheel Ranch. (Botel Interesting Reading Ser.). (gr. 3-5). N.D. Penns Valley.

Eisner, William Erwin (1917-)
--Ghostly Jokes & Ghastly Riddles. Eisner, William Erwin (1917-), illus. (Illus.). (gr. 2-6). 1979. (ISBN 0-89437-079-0). Baronet.
--Spaced-Out Jokes. Eisner, William Erwin (1917-), illus. (Illus.). (gr. 2-6). 1979. (ISBN 0-89437-080-4). Baronet.
Eitzen, Ruth Carper (1924-)
--Ti Jacques: A Story of Haiti. Eitzen, Allan (1928-), illus. LC 76-158688. (Illus.). 41 p. 23cm. (Stories from many lands). 1972. (ISBN 0-690-82429-7). (ISBN 0-690-82430-0). Crowell.
--Ti Jacques: A Story of Haiti. Eitzen, Allan (1928-), illus. LC 76-158688. (Illus.). (Stories from Many Lands Ser). (gr. k-4). 1972. (ISBN 0-690-82429-7, TYC-J). Har-Row.
Eivind, R.
--Finnish Legends for English Children. (Illus.). 214p. (The Children's Library). N.D. MacMillian & Co.
Ekeroth, Marianne G.
--My Own Little Cat. Nordin, G., illus. (Illus.). (gr. 2-5). 1963. (ISBN 0-698-30248-6). Coward.
Ekker, Ernst Alfred, jt. auth. see Baum, Willi.
Ekrem, Selma
--Turkish Fairy Tales. Bayrak, Loba, illus. (Illus.). (gr. 4-6). 1964. (ISBN 0-442-02261-1). Van Nos Reinhold.
El Cid Campeador
--The Tale of the Warrior Lord: El Cantar De Mio Cid. Sherwood, Merriam (1892-), tr. LC 30-269025. xvii, 1 p., 1 l., 156 p. incl. col. front., illus. (incl. map) plates. 23 1/2cm. c.1930. Longmans, Green & Co.
El-Shamy, Hasan, ed.
--Folktales of Egypt. El-Shamy, Hasan, tr. (Folktales of the World Ser.). 1980. Univ. of Chicago Press.
Ela, Chipman P.
--The Banjo Timepiece. 2nd ed. 210p. 1978. (ISBN 0-9607464-0-4). C P Ela.
Elam, Elizabeth (1914-)
--Chuffer. Langford, Dan, illus. LC 49-105934. 48 p. illus. 22 cm. 1949. J. C. Winston Co.
Elam, Richard Mace, Jr. (1920-)
--Cave of Living Treasure. LC 58-18557. (Illus.). 21cm. 222p. (gr. 4-7). 1958. Lantern.
--Science Fiction Stories. (Illus.). (Young Readers Bookshelf). (gr. 4-7). N.D. (ISBN 0-8313-0033-7). Lantern.
--Teen-Age Science Fiction Stories. Geer, Charles Hand (1922-), illus. 254 p. illus. 22 cm. (Teen-age library, 26). 1961, c.1952. Grosset & Dunlap.
--Teen-Age Science Fiction Stories. Geer, Charles Hand (1922-), illus. Leyson, Burr W. LC 52-11200. 254 p. illus. 21 cm. 1952. Lantern Press.
--Teen-Age Super Science Stories. Vaughn, Frank E., illus. 253 p. illus. 21 cm. (Teen-age library). 1961, c.1957. Grosset & Dunlap.
--Teen-Age Super Science Stories. Vaughn, Frank E., illus. LC 57-8908. 253p. illus. 21cm. 1957. Lantern Press.
--Teen-Age Treasure Hunt: The Cave of Living Treasure. Prezio, Victor, illus. 222 p. illus. 21 cm. (Teen-age library). 1961, c.1948. Grosset & Dunlap.
--Young Readers Science Fiction Stories. Prezio, Victor, illus. 191 p. illus. 20 cm. 1961, c.1957. Grosset & Dunlap.
--Young Readers Science Fiction Stories. Prezio, Victor, illus. LC 57-8909. 191p. illus. 22cm. 1957. Lantern Press.
--Young Stowaways in Space. McCann, Gerald (1916-), illus. LC 60-13785. (Illus.). 21cm. 191p. (gr. 4-7). 1960. Lantern.
--Young Visitor to Mars. (Young Heroes Library). N.D. Grosset & Dunlap.
--Young Visitor to Mars. Geer, Charles Hand (1922-), illus. LC 53-10375. 256p. illus. 21cm. (Young heroes library). 1953. (ISBN 0-8313-0031-0). Lantern Press.
--Young Visitor to the Moon. LC 65-12603. 191 p. 21 cm. 1965. Lantern Press.
Elam, Richard Mace, Jr. (1920-), ed.
--Teen-Age Suspense Stories. (gr. 6-10). 1963. (ISBN 0-8313-0047-7). Lantern.
Elarson, Georgina
--Little Workers in the Kitchen. 1979. (ISBN 0-8163-0240-5). Pacific Pr Pub Assn.
Elbert, Mary K.
--Number Men. Owens, Lillian, illus. Bd. with Jane & the Lost Shoe. (gr. 3-6). N.D. Vantage.
Elborn, Andrew
--Bird Adalbert. Bohdal, Susi (1951-), illus. LC 83-8165. (Illus.). 28p. Orig. Title: Der Schone Vogel Adalbert. (gr. 4 up). 1983. (ISBN 0-907234-45-3, Pub. by Picture Bk Studio USA). Neugebauer Pr.
Elbow, Meg
--The Rootomom Tree. Munsinger, Lynn (1951-), illus. LC 77-26696. (Illus.). 44 p. 24cm. 1978. (ISBN 0-395-26452-9). Houghton Mifflin.
El Comancho, pseud., see Phillips, Walter Shelley.
El Comancho, pseud.
--The Sandman: His Indian Stories. Phillips, Walter Shelley. El Comancho, pseud., illus. Phillips, Walter Shelley. (The Sandman Ser.). N.D. Page Co.
Elder, Art
--The Blue Streak and Doctor Medusa. Kirn, Francis, illus. LC 46-6207. 3 p. l., 11-248 p. illus. 20 1/2 cm. 1946. Whitman Publishing Company.
Elder, Jacob D. (1913-)
--Song Games from Trinidad and Tobago. LC 64-25264. 119p. 26cm. (American Folklore Society. Bibliographical and Special Ser.: Vol. 6). 1965, c.1962. Univ. of Texas. Box Univ. Stn.
Elder, Joseph, ed.
--The Farthest Reaches. (gr. 7 up). N.D. S&S.
Elder, Michael Aiken (1931-)
--Tony Behind the Scenes: A Story of the Theatre. Crockford, J. J., illus. (Illus.). (gr. 8 up). N.D. Transatlantic.
Elderdice, James Raymond (1889-)
--The Last Ditch: A Story of Panama and the Canal Zone. LC 15-13357. vi p., 1 l., 295 p. front., plates. 19 1/2 cm. c.1915. Rand McNally & Company.
--T. Haviland Hicks, Freshman. Avison, George F. (1885-), illus. LC 15-18723. 5 p. l., 305 1 p. col. front., col. plates. 19 cm. 1915. D. Appleton and Company.
--T. Haviland Hicks, Junior. Avison, George F. (1885-), illus. LC 16-7497. 5 p. l., 333 1 p. col. front., col. plates. 19 1/2 cm. 1916. D. Appleton and Company.
--T. Haviland Hicks, Sophomore. Rigney, Francis Joseph (1882-), illus. LC 15-25465. 5 p. l., 333, 1 p. front., illus. 19 cm. 1915. D. Appleton and Company.
Eldon, Magdalen
--Bumble. Eldon, Magdalen, illus. N.D. Charles Scribner's Sons.
--Snow Bumble. LC 52-120285. unpaged. illus. 26cm. 1952. Scribner.
Eldred, Warren L
--The Boys of Brookfield Academy. Scott, Arthur O., illus. LC 10-8938. 6 p. l., 381 p. front., plates. 20 1/2 cm. 1910. Lothrop, Lee & Shepard Co.
--Camp St. Dunstan. Scott, Arthur O., illus. 5 p. l., 325 p. incl. plan. front., plates. 20 1/2 cm. (St. Dunstan series). 1911. Lothrop, Lee & Shepard Co.
--Classroom & Campus. Scott, Arthur O., illus. 1912. Lothrop, Lee.
--The Crimson Numbers. Scott, Arthur O., illus. LC 10-152370. 6 p. l., 324 p. front., plates. 21 cm. (St. Dunstan series). c.1910. Lothrop, Lee & Shepard Co.
--The Lookout Island Campers. Scott, Arthur O., illus. LC 9-16110. 5 p. l.,341 p. front., 5 pl. 20 1/2 cm. 1909. Lothrop, Lee & Shepard Co.
--The Oak Street Boys' Club. LC 11-223335. ix, 2 p., 1 l., 344 p. front., plates. 20 1/2 cm. 1911. Lothrop, Lee & Shepard Co.
--St. Dunstan Boy Scouts. Scott, Arthur O., illus. LC 13-8247. 4 p. l., 335 p. front., plates. 20 1/2 cm. (St. Dunstan series). 1913. Lothrop, Lee & Shepard Co.
--The Townsend Twins, Camp Directors. Relyea, Charles M., illus. LC 13-21023. 6 p. l., 3-376 p. incl. front., plates. 20 cm. 1913. The Century Co.
Eldridge, Ethel J., Mrs., adapted by.
--Ling, Grandson of Yen-Foh. Wiese, Kurt (1887-1974), illus. LC 36-151628. 29, 3 p. incl. col. front., col. illus. 24 cm. 1936. A. Whitman & Co.
--Yen-Foh, a Chinese Boy. Wiese, Kurt (1887-1974), illus. LC 35-272901. 29, 3 p. incl. col. front., col. illus. 24 cm. 1935. A. Whitman & Co.
Eldridge, Roger
--The Shadow of the Gloom-World. LC 77-26200. 191 p. 22cm. 1978, c.1977. (ISBN 0-525-39235-1). Dutton.
Eldridge, Ruby
--The Legend of the Gray Castle. (Illus.). (gr. 5-7). N.D. Vantage.
Eleanor, Mary, Mother (1903-)
--Afiong: A Story of West Africa. Rev ed. Paschal, Mary, illus. LC 59-10975. 96p. illus. 22cm. 1959. Bruce Pub. Co.
The, Electric Company
--Tickle Yourself Again with Riddles. Smollin, Michael J., illus. LC 78-19699. (Illus.). (gr. k-3). 1979. (ISBN 0-394-84152-2, BYR). Random.
--Tickle Yourself with Riddles. Smollin, Michael J., illus. LC 77-90197. (ps-4). 1978. (ISBN 0-394-83783-5, BYR). Random.
Eleven Sophomores
--Stories for Children. (Illus.). 1875. Messrs. Roberts Brothers.
--Stories for Children. (Illus.). 1882. Roberts Brothers.
Elfers, Robert A.
--Four from Moonbeam. 144p. 1962. Friendship Press.
Elgin, Jill, illus.
--Hans Christian Andersen. (Read-Aloud Bks.). (gr. k-3). N.D. (ISBN 0-685-22278-0). Wonder.
Elgin, Kathleen (1923-), retold by.
--The First Book of Mythology: Greek and Roman. Elgin, Kathleen (1923-), illus. LC 55-9600. 61p. illus. 23cm. (First books, 67). (gr. 4-6). c.1955. (ISBN 0-531-00589-5). F. Watts.
--The First Book of Norse Legends. Elgin, Kathleen (1923-), illus. LC 56-10066. 69p. illus. 23cm. (First books, 72). c.1956. Watts.
Elias, Edith L., Mrs.
--The Children's Robinson Crusoe. N.D. Dodd Mead & Co.
--Periwinkle's Island. Benatar, Molly, illus. LC 21-11138. 239 p. col. front., illus., col. plates. 19 cm. 1920. W. & R. Chambers, Ltd.
Elias, Horace Jay (1910-), adapted by see Stevenson, Robert Louis.
Elias, Horace Jay (1910-)
--The Computer That Went Bananas. (Illus.). 96p. (gr. 3-8). 1974. (ISBN 0-06-087073-7, HW). Har-Row.
--Flash Gordon & the Sand World of Mongo. (Illus.). (gr. 5 up). 1976. (ISBN 0-06-465051-0, PBN). B&N Imports.
--The Flintstone Storybook. Hanna Barbera Productions,Inc, illus. LC 77-94035. (Illus.). (ps-2). 1978. (ISBN 0-448-14744-0, G&D). Putnam Pub Group.
--The Flintstones. (Illus.). 96p (Pub. by Hanna-Barbera Productions, Inc.). (gr. k-3). 1975. (ISBN 0-06-087076-1, HW). Har-Row.
--The Flintstones: Fred & Barney Lay an Egg. (Illus.). 96p. (gr. 3-8). 1974. (ISBN 0-06-087070-2, HW). Har-Row.
--Flintstones: Fred, Mayor for a Day. 1974. (ISBN 0-06-087076-1, HW). Har-Row.
--The Flintstones Storybook. hanna-barbera authorized. LC 77-94035. (Illus.). 79 p. 24cm. c.1978. (ISBN 0-448-14744-0). Grosset & Dunlap.
--The Flintstones: The Bedrock Connection. (Illus.). 96p (Pub. by Hanna-Barbera Productions, Inc.). (gr. k-3). 1975. (ISBN 0-06-087078-8, HW). Har-Row.
--The Flintstones: Volunteer Fireman. (Illus.). 96p (Pub. by Hanna-Barbera Productions, Inc.). (gr. k-3). 1975. (ISBN 0-06-087077-X, HW). Har-Row.
--Gentlemen Farmers. (Illus.). 96p. (gr. 3-8). 1974. (ISBN 0-06-087072-9, HW). Har-Row.
--Tom & Jerry & the Real Gone Goose. (Illus.). (gr. 3-8). 1976. (ISBN 0-06-465052-9, PBN). B&N Imports.
--Yogi Bear: How Does Your Garden Grow. 1974. (ISBN 0-06-087075-3, HW). Har-Row.
Elias, Horace Jay (1910-), adapted by.
--The Wizard of Oz: With Pictures from the MGM Classic Starring Judy Garland. LC 76-319. (Original Author: Lyman Frank Baum, 1856-1919). (Illus.). 127 p. 28cm. c.1976. (ISBN 0-448-12432-7). Grosset & Dunlap.
Elias, Horace Jay (1910-) & Bigelow, Lori
--The Costume Party: A New Lori Bigelow Story. LC 79-112448. (Illus.). 29cm. 28p. c.1979. Watertower Books.
Eliason, Peter
--The Comeuppance of Dipsey Dolan. 162p. (Orig.). (Michael the Archangel Ser.). (gr. 2-10). 1984. (ISBN 0-916777-34-0). W P Allen.
Elieff, De Anne
--Andy the Real "Live" Toy Airplane. Kelly, Carolyn, illus. (Illus.). 24p. (ps-5). 1983. (ISBN 0-86666-099-2). GWP.
Elinson, H.
--Down Our Street. 20p. 1975. (ISBN 0-8285-1132-2, Pub. by Progress Pubs USSR). Imported Pubns.
Eliot, Anne, pseud., see Cole, Lois Dwight.
Eliot, Anne, pseud. (1903-1979)
--Dorie of Dogtown Common. Cole, Lois Dwight. Werth, Kurt (1896-), illus. LC 62-11143. (Illus.). 21cm. 184p. (gr. 3-7). 1962. (ISBN 0-687-11207-9). Abingdon.
--Shadows Waiting. Cole, Lois Dwight. (gr. 7-9). 1969. Hawthorn.
Eliot, Ethel Cook, Mrs. (1890-)
--Buttercup Days. N.D. Doubleday Page & Co.
--The Dryad and the Hired Boy. McCarthy, C. J., illus. LC 18-25355. 6 p. l., 276 p. col. front., paltes. 21 cm. 1928. Doubleday, Doran & Company, Inc.
--Fireweed. LC 25-18698. viii p., 1 l., 311 p. front. 19 1/2 cm. c.1925. Doubleday, Page & Co.
--The Gay Mystery. King, Ruth, illus. LC 31-18175. viii p., 1 l., 268 p., 1 l. front. illus., plates. 21 cm. 1931. Doubleday, Doran & Company, Inc.
--The House on the Edge of Things. Fremont-Smith, Frances Eliot, illus. LC 23-14206. 5 p. l., 100 p. col. front., illus. col. plates. 23 1/2 cm. c.1923. Beacon Press.
--The Little Black Coal. LC 23-12865. 6 p. l., 3-109 p. incl. col. illus., col. plates. col. front. 19 1/2 cm. 1923. Frederick A. Stokes Company.
--The Little House in the Fairy Wood. Hatt, Mabel K., illus. LC 18-17241. 3 p. l., 121 p. col. front., col. plates. 21 1/2 cm. c.1918. Frederick A. Stokes Company.
--Storey Manor: A Mystery. LC 37-22395. 5 p. l., 246 p. col. front. 30 1/2 cm. (Young moderns bookshelf). 1937. The Sun Dial Press, Inc.
--Storey Manor: A Mystery. LC 42-511223. 5 p. l., 246 p. 20 1/2 cm. (Young moderns bookshelf). 1942. The Sun Dial Press.
--Storey Manor: A Mystery. Custis, Eleanor Parke, illus. LC 27-19214. 5 p. l., 246 p. col. front. 19 1/2 cm. 1927. Doubleday, Page & Company.
--The Vanishing Comrade. LC 24-23600. 3 p. l., v-vi p., 1 l., 282 p. front. 19 1/2 cm. 1924. Doubleday, Page & Company.
--The Vanishing Comrade. Riley, Nicholas F., illus. LC 31-256444. 3 p. l., v-vi p., 1 l., 282 p. front. 20 1/2 cm. (the windmill books. 1931. Doubleday Doran & Company, Inc.
--Waul & Dyke, Inc. Ryan, Douglas, illus. LC 26-20760. 5 p. l., 244 p. front., plates. 19 1/2 cm. c.1926. Doubleday, Page & Co.
--The Wind Boy. Bromhall, Winifred, illus. LC 23-15471. 6 p. l., 288 p. incl. illus., plates. col. front. 21 cm. 1923. Doubleday, Page & Company.
--The Wind Boy. Hallock, Robert, illus. LC 45-8601. 244 p. illus. 21 cm. 1945. The Viking Press.
Eliot, Frances (1901-)
--Pablo's Pipe. Eliot, Frances (1901-), illus. LC 36-27297. 22cm. 48p. 1936. E. P. Dutton & Co.
--The Traveling Coat. Eliot, Frances (1901-), illus. LC 37-27459. 20x27 1/2cm. 1937. E. P. Dutton & Co.
Eliot, George, pseud., see Evans, Marian.
Eliot, George Fielding (1894-1971)
--The Eagles of Death. De Beaulieu, G., illus. LC 31-74132. 282 p., 1 l. col. front., plates. 20 cm. c.1930. Warne & Co., Inc.
Eliot, George, pseud. (1819-1880)
--Adam Bede. Evans, Marian. (Great Illustrated Classics -Titans). (gr. 9 up). N.D. (ISBN 0-396-06601-1). Dodd.
--Adam Bede. Evans, Marian. 1952. Grove Press.
--Adam Bede. Evans, Marian, 2 Vols. (Riverside Edition). N.D. Houghton Mifflin Co.
--Adam Bede. Evans, Marian. (New International Library). N.D. John C. Winston Co.
--Adam Bede. Evans, Marian. (The Luxembourg Illustrated Library). N.D. Thomas Y. Crowell Company.
--Adam Bede. Evans, Marian. Haight, Gordon S., ed. 551p. 1949. Rinehart & Co.
--Adam Bede. Evans, Marian. Newbolt, Henry, Sir, ed. (The Nelson Classics). N.D. Thomas Nelson & Sons.
--Adam Bede. Evans, Marian. Wylie, Laura Johnson, intro. by. (Modern Student's Library). N.D. Charles Scribner's Sons'.
--Arabian Nights. Evans, Marian. N.D. Hurst & Co.
--How Lisa Loved The King. Evans, Marian. (Illus.). N.D. D. Lothrop & Co.
--Little Tom and Maggie. Evans, Marian. Merrill, Frank Thayer (1848-), illus. N.D. Dana Estes and Company.
--Middlemarch. Evans, Marian. 1950. Grove Press.
--The Mill on the Floss. Evans, Marian. N.D. A. L. Burt Co.
--The Mill on the Floss. Evans, Marian. N.D. Charles R. Osgood.
--The Mill on the Floss. Evans, Marian. N.D. D. C. Heath & Co.
--The Mill on the Floss. Evans, Marian, Nos.174-175. (Lakeside Library Ser.). N.D. Donnelley, Loyd & Co.
--The Mill on the Floss. Evans, Marian. (Everyman's Library). N.D. E. P. Dutton & Co.
--The Mill on the Floss. Evans, Marian, No.11. (Seaside Library Ser.). 1878. George Munro: Dist. by American News Co.
--The Mill on the Floss. Evans, Marian. 1951. Grove Press.
--The Mill on the Floss. Evans, Marian, 2 Vols. (Riverside Edition). N.D. Houghton Mifflin Co.
--Mill on the Floss. Evans, Marian, Two. (Illustrated Cabinet Edition). N.D. L. C. Page & Co.
--The Mill on the Floss. Evans, Marian. 548p. N.D. Little, Brown & Co.
--The Mill on the Floss. Evans, Marian. 510p. (The Lake English Classics). N.D. Scott Foresman & Co.
--The Mill on the Floss. Evans, Marian. N.D (Standard and Holiday Books). The American News Co.
--The Mill on the Floss. Evans, Marian. (Standard Library). N.D. Thomas Y. Crowell & Co.

Elliot, Geraldine, pseud., see Bingham, Evangeline Marquerite Ladys Elliot.
Elliot, Geraldine, pseud., see Bringham, Evangeline Marquerite Ladys Elliot.
Elliot, Geraldine, pseud. (1899-)
--The Hunter's Cave: A Book of Stories Based on African Folk-Tales. Bringham, Evangeline Marquerite Ladys Elliot. Hawkins, Sheila (1905-), illus. LC 62-17713. 174 p. illus. 23 cm. 1962. Dufour Editions.
--The Long Grass Whispers. Bingham, Evangeline Marquerite Ladys Elliot. Hawkins, Sheila (1905-), illus. LC 62-17712. 132 p. illus. 23 cm. (Classic Bks.). 1962. Dufour Editions.
--The Long Grass Whispers. Bingham, Evangeline Marquerite Ladys Elliot. Hawkins, Sheila (1905-), illus. LC 39-23641. vii p., 2 l., 132 p. incl. illus., plates. 26 1/2 cm. c.1939. G.P. Putnam's Sons.
--The Long Grass Whispers. Bingham, Evangeline Marquerite Ladys Elliot. Hawkins, Sheila (1905-), illus. LC 68-21826. (Illus.). vii, 132 p. 21cm. 1968, c.1939. Schocken Books.
--The Long Grass Whispers: A Book of African Folk Tales. Bingham, Evangeline Marquerite Ladys Elliot. Hawkins, Sheila (1905-), illus. LC 68-21826. (Illus.). (gr. 3-7). 1970. (ISBN 0-8052-0260-9). Schocken.
--The Singing Chameleon: A/Book of African Stories Based on Local Customs, Proverbs and Folk-Lore. Hawkins, Sheila (1905-), illus. LC 63-10442. (Illus.). 168p. 22cm. 1963. Dufour Edisons.
--Where the Leopard Passes: A Book of African Folk Tales. Bingham, Evangeline Marquerite Ladys Elliot. Hawkins, Sheila (1905-), illus. LC 68-21827. (Illus.). vii, 133 p. 21cm. 1968, c.1949. Schocken Books.
Elliot, Irene Constance
--A Real Quaker. LC 57-59615. 37p. (A Bookland Juvenile). 1957. Comet Press Books.
Elliot, James William (1833-1915), ed.
--Mother Goose Set to Music. 111p. N.D. McLoughlin Bros.
Elliot, Kathleen Morrow, Mrs.
--Jo-Yo's Idea. Duvoisin, Roger Antoine (1904-1980), illus. LC 39-278581. 3 p. l., 3-114, 2 p. incl. col. front., illus. (part col.) 23 1/2 cm. 1939. A.A. Knopf.
--Riema, Little Brown Girl of Java. Duvoisin, Roger Antoine (1904-1980), illus. LC 37-21373. 3 p. l., 53, 1 p. illus. (part col.) 23 cm. 1937. A.A. Knopf.
--Soomoon, Boy of Bali. Duvoisin, Roger Antoine (1904-1980), illus. LC 38-28943. 2 p. l., vii-viii, 3-88, 1 p. illus. (part col.) 23 cm. 1938. A.A. Knopf.
Elliot, Madge, pseud., see Eytinge, Margaret Winship.
Elliot, Madge, pseud.
--The Ball of the Fruits. Eytinge, Margaret Winship. Pierson, P. R. B., illus. LC 15-242. 15, 1 p. col illus., pl. 20 cm. 1872. Baldwin.
Elliot, Madge, pseud. & Langford, Laura Carter Halloway, Mrs. (1848-)
--Original Christmas Stories ... Eytinge, Margaret Winship. LC 16-3394. 31 p. col. illus. 20 cm. 1873. Baldwin, the Clothier.
Elliot, Margaret
--When the Night Crow Flies. Dunbar, Colin, illus. (gr. 2-7). 1977. (ISBN 0-8277-5386-1). (ISBN 0-8277-5385-3). British Bk Ctr.
Elliot, S. H.
--Emily Maria. 72p. N.D. American Tract Scoiety.
Elliott, Alan Curtis (1952-)
--On Sunday the Wind Came. Bonners, Susan, illus. LC 79-19083. (Illus.). 32 p. c.1980. (ISBN 0-688-22218-8). (ISBN 0-688-32218-2). Morrow.
Elliott, Bob & Goulding, Ray
--Bob and Ray's Linda Lovely and the Fleebus. Smollin, Michael J., illus. 1960. Dodd, Mead & Co.
Elliott, Brian
--Strawberry Shortcake & Baby Needs a Name. Gatie, John, illus. (Illus.). 40p. (Strawberry Shortcake Ser.). (ps-3). 1984. (ISBN 0-910313-21-0). Parker Bro.
Elliott, Emilia, pseud., see Jacobs, Caroline Emilia.
Elliott, Gertrude, illus.
--The First Little Golden Book of Fairy Tales. (Little Golden Book: 9). 1942. Simon and Schuster.
--The Golden Book of Fairy Tales. LC 47-1301. 42 p. illus. (part col.) 20 x 17 cm. (On cover: The Little golden library. 9). 1946. Simon and Schuster.
--The Little Golden Book of Fairy Tales. (Little Golden Book). 1942. Golden Press.
--Nursery Rhymes. LC 49-4192. 28 p. col. illus. 21 cm. (Little golden library, 59). 1949, c.1948. Simon and Schuster.
Elliott, Glynn S. see Mrs E. , pseud.
Elliott, Harley (1940-)
--The Tiger's Spots. Elliott, Harley (1940-), illus. LC 76-45383. 42 col. illus. 23. (Crossing Press series of children's stories). c.1976. (ISBN 0-912278-79-X). (ISBN 0-912278-80-3). Crossing Press.
Elliott, James William (1833-1915)
--Mother Goose Melodies Set to Music. Dalziel, George (1815-1902) & Dalziel, Edward (1817-1905), illus. LC 46-33462. 5 p. l., 110, 1 p. front., illus. 19 1/2 cm. 1873. G. W. Carleton & Co.
--Mother Goose: Or, National Nursery Rhymes and Nursery Songs. Dalziel, George (1815-1902) & Dalziel, Edward (1817-1905), illus. p. front., illus. 27 cm. 1872. Novello, Ewer, and Co.
--Mother Goose: Or National Nursery Rhymes & Nursery Songs. Dalziel, George (1815-1902) & Dalziel, Edward (1817-1905), illus. (Illus.). 111p. Repr. of 1873 ed. (Pub. by George Routledge & Sons). 1981. Doll Works.
--Mother Goose's Nursery Rhymes and Nursery Songs. Dalziel, George (1815-1902) & Dalziel, Edward (1817-1905), illus. LC 19-7344. 2 p. l., 110, 1 p. illus. 23 1/2 cm. N.D. McLoughlin Bros.
--National Nursery Rhymes and Nursery Songs. Dalziel, George (1815-1902) & Dalziel, Edward (1817-1905), illus. LC 46-33464. 4 p. l., 110, 1 p. front., illus. 27 cm. N.D. Lee & Walker, W. H. Boner & Co.
Elliott, James William (1833-1915) & Bentley, J. M.
--Little Folks' Album of Music. (Illus.). N.D. Cassell, Petter, Galpin.
Elliott, Lydia S.
--Found In the Forest. Valentine, Donald Graham (1929-), illus. LC 58-9087. (Illus.). 222p. 21cm. 1958. F. Warne.
Elliott, Mary Belson, compiled by see Barbauld, Anna Letitia Aikin, Mrs.
Elliott, Mary Belson, Mrs.
--No Time Like the Present. LC 24-6646. 36 p. fold. front., plates. 15 cm. 1839. H. Benton.
Elliott, Miss
--Round the Mulberry Bush. Elliott, Miss, illus. (gr. k-3). N.D. Harper & Bros.
Elliott, Roberta
--Kirsti & the Bear. Gronqvist, Eija, illus. LC 65-12611. (Illus.). 24cm. 127p. 1st U.S. edition. (gr. 3-5). 1965. (ISBN 0-15-243008-3). HarBraceJ.
Elliott, Ruth, Mrs.
--Margery's Christmas Box. N.D. Bradley & Woodruff.
Ellis, Anne Leo
--Dabble Duck. Truesdell, Susan G., illus. LC 83-47692. (Illus.). 32p. (ps-2). 1984. (ISBN 0-06-021817-7). (ISBN 0-06-021818-5). HarpJ.
Ellis, Charles & Weir, Frank
--I'd rather be a president. 1956. Simon & Schuster.
Ellis, Constance Turner
--God is with Us: Verses. Sabine, Mary, illus. LC 49-1571. 48p. col. illus. 27cm. 1949. C. Wildermann Co.
Ellis, David, tr. see Melancon, Claude.
Ellis, Edward Sylvester see Carleton, Captain Latham C., pseud.
Ellis, Edward Sylvester see Gordon, Colonel H. R., pseud.
Ellis, Edward Sylvester see Jayne, Lieutenant R. H., pseud.
Ellis, Edward Sylvester see Lisle, Seward D., pseud.
Ellis, Edward Sylvester, jt. auth. see Alger, Horatio, Jr.
Ellis, Edward Sylvester (1840-1916)
--Across Texas, 1 of 3 Vols. (Roundabout Library). (Wild-Wood Library Ser.: Vol. 3). N.D. Set. John C. Winston Co.
--Across Texas. LC 6-37818. iv, 349 p. front., plates. 19 1/2 cm. (Wild-woods series, v. 3). (Roundabout Lib.). c.1893. Porter & Coates.
--Adrift in the Wilds. (Illus.). (The Alger Series for Boys). N.D. A. L. Burt's Pubs.
--Adrift in the Wilds, 1 of 3 vols. (The Adventure Ser.). N.D. Set. A. L. Burt's Pubs.
--Adrift In The Wilds: Or, The Adventures of Two Shipwrecked Boys. LC 7-2726. (Illus.). 19cm. 279p. (Boy's Home Library, v.1, no.3.). 1887. A. L. Burt.
--Adrift on the Pacific: A Boys's Story of the Sea and it's Perils. Davis, J. Watson, illus. (The Rugby Series for Boys and Girls). N.D. A. L. Burt Company.
--The Adventure Series, 3 vols. N.D. Set. A. L. Burt's Pubs.
--Alden Among the Indians: Or, The Search for the Missing Pony Express Rider. Prittie, Edwin John, illus. LC 9-18060. 323 p. col. front., 3 pl. 19 1/2 cm. (Half-title: The Overland series. v. 2). c.1909. The J.C. Winston Company.
--Alden, the Pony Express Rider: Or, Racing for Life. Prittie, Edwin John, illus. LC 9-18061. 19 1/2cm. 330p. (The Overland series: v.1). 1909. John C. Winston.
--An American King. LC 4-3955. 19cm. 482p. (Colonial Ser.: No. 1). 1903. H. T. Coates & Co.
--An American King, 1 of 3 Vols. (Colonial Ser.: Vol. 1). N.D. Set. John C. Winston Co.
--Among the Esquimaux. (Vacation Ser.). N.D. Penn Publishing Co.
--Among the Esquimaux: Or, Adventures Under the Arctic Circle. (Adventure Stories). N.D. Penn Publishing Co.
--Among the Esquimaux: Or, Adventures Under the Arctic Circle. LC 6-37817. 317 p. incl. front. plates. 19 cm. 1894. The Penn Publishing Company.
--Arthur Helmuth. 308 p. incl. front., plates. 19 cm. (On cover: Leather-clad tales, no. 33). c.1891. United States Book Company.
--Astray in the Forest. (Illus.). (Story Books for boys). N.D. Cassell & Co.'s Pubs.
--Black Partridge: Or, The Fall of Fort Dearborn. Gordon, Colonel H. R., pseud. LC 6-17000. 2 p. l., 302 p. front., 7 pl. 21 cm. 1906. E.P. Dutton & Company.
--Blazing Arrow, 1 of 3 Vols. (War Chief Ser.). N.D. Set. John C. Winston Co.
--Blazing Arrow: A Tale of the Frontier. LC 4328. iv, 289 p. front., plates. 19 cm. (War chief series, no. 2). 1900. H. T. Coates & Co.
--The Boy Hunters of Kentucky. (Illus.). (Story Books for Boys). N.D. Cassell & Co's Pubs.
--The Boy Patriot. Davis, J. Watson, illus. (Illus.). (The Continental Ser.). N.D. A. L. Burt' Pubs.
--The Boy Patriot. A Story of Jack, the Young Friend of Washington. Davis, J. Watson, illus. LC 4697. 3 p. l., 302 p. front., plates. 19 1/2 cm. c.1900. A. L. Burt.
--Boy Patrol Around the Council Fire. Prittie, Edwin John, illus. 314p. (The Boy Patrol Ser.). 1913. John C. Winston.
--Boy Patrol on Guard. (The Boy Patrol Ser.). N.D. John C. Winston.
--Brave Billy. Strehlan, Carl A., illus. LC 7-20871. 360 p. front., 3 pl. 19 1/2 cm. (Half-title: Bound to win series no. 1). c.1907. The J. C. Winston Company.
--Brave Tom. (Brave and Honest Ser.: Vol. 1). N.D. Merriam Company.
--Brave Tom: Or, The Battle that Won, 1 of 3 vols. (Illus.). (Roundabout Lib.). (Brave and Honest Ser.: Vol. 1). N.D. Set. Henry T. Coates & Co.
--Brave Tom: Or, The Battle that Won, 1 of 3 Vols. (Roundabout Library). (Brave and Honest Ser.: Vol. 1). N.D. Set. John C. Winston Co.
--Brave Tom: Or, The Battle That Won. LC 6-37816. 231 p. front., plates. 19 1/2 cm. (Brave and Honest Series, no. 1). c.1894. The Merriam Company.
--Cabin in the Clearing, 1 of 3 Vols. (Roundabout Library). (Wyoming Ser.: Vol. 3). N.D. Set. John C. Winston Co.
--Cabin in the Clearing, 1 of 3 vols. (Roundabout Lib.). (Wyoming Ser.: No. 3). 1891. Set. Porter & Coates.
--The Cabin in the Clearing: A Tale of the Frontier. 438 p. front., plates. 17 1/2 cm. (His Wyoming series, no. 3). c.1890. Porter & Coates.
--Camp Fire and Wigwam, 1 of 3 vols. (Illus.). (Log Cabin Ser.: Vol. 2). N.D. Set. Henry T. Coates & Co.
--Camp Fire and Wigwam. 388p. (Log Cabin Ser.: No.2). 1885. John C. Winston.
--Camp Fire and Wigwam. LC 7-39305. (Illus.). 19cm. 383p. (Log Cabin Ser.: No. 2). 1907. John C. Winston.
--Camp-Fire and Wigwam. LC 6-37815. iv, 5-388 p. front., plates. 16 1/2 cm. ("Log cabin series", no. 2). c.1885. Porter & Contes.
--Camp in the Mountains. (Deerfoot Ser.: No.2). N.D. John C. Winston.
--The Camp in the Mountains. LC 6-37814. iv, 5-366 p. front., plates. 17 1/2 cm. (Deerfoot series, no. 2). c.1887. Porter & Coates.
--The Campers Out. (Vacation Ser.). N.D. Penn Publishing Co.
--The Campers Out: Or, the Right Path and the Wrong. 363p. (The Vacation Ser.). 1893. Penn.
--The Campers Out: Or, The Right Path and the Wrong. LC 6-37813. 363 p. incl. front. plates. 19 cm. (Adventure Stories Ser.). 1893. The Penn Publishing Company.
--Captain of the Camp: Or, Ben the Young Boss. Prittie, Edwin John, illus. 280p. (The Catamount Camp Ser.). 1910. John C. Winston.
--Captured by Indians. (Illus.). (Story Books for Boys). N.D. Cassell & Co's Pubs.
--Catamount Camp. Prittie, Edwin John, illus. 316p. (The Catamount Camp Ser.). 1910. John C. Winston.
--The Cave in the Mountain. Jayne, Lieutenant. R. H., pseud. (Wide Awake Boys Ser.). N.D. A. L. Burt.
--The Cave in the Mountain: A Sequel to "In the Pecos Country.". Jayne, Lieutenant R. H., pseud. LC 6-37812. 295 p. incl. front., plates. 19 1/2 cm. (War whoop series, no. 4). c.1894. The Merriam Company.
--The Cave in the Mountains. Jayne, Lieutenant R. H., pseud. (Illus.). N.D. Thompson & Thomas.
--Check 2134, 1 of 39 Vols. (Illus.). (Famous Books for Boys Ser.: No. 4). 1905. Set. H M Caldwell Co.
--Check 2134. 275p. (Medal Library: No. 41). 1900. Street & Smith.
--Check 2134. 275 p. incl. front. plates. 19 cm. (On cover: Leather-clad tales, no. 42). c.1891. United States Book Company.
--Comrades True. (Vacation Ser.). N.D. Penn Publishing Co.
--Comrades True: Or, Perseverance Versus Genius. LC 6-37810. iv, 7-319 p. front., plates. 18 1/2 cm. 1895. The Penn Publishing Company.
--Comrades True: Or, Perseverance Versus Genius. LC 24-28516. iv, 7-319 p. front. 19 cm. (Adventure Stories Ser.). 1908. The Penn Publishing Company.
--Cowmen and Rustlers. LC 98-340. 322p. (Roundabout Library). (Northwest Ser.: No. 2). 1898. H. T. Coates & Co.
--Cowmen and Rustlers, 1 of 3 Vols. (The Northwest Ser.: Vol. 2). N.D. Set. John C. Winston Co.
--The Cromwell of Virginia, 1 of 3 Vols. (Colonial Ser.: Vol. 2). N.D. Set. John C. Winston Co.
--The Cromwell of Virginia: A Story of Bacon's Rebellion. LC 4-33124. 380p. 19cm. (Colonial Ser.). 1904. H. T. Coates.
--The Daughter of the Chieftain. (Illus.). (Story Books for Boys). N.D. Cassell & Co.'s Pubs.
--Deerfoot in the Forest. Davis, J. Steeple, illus. LC 5-28020. 366 p. col. front., 7 pl. 19 cm. (Half-title: New Deerfoot series no. 1). 1905. The J. C. Winston Co.
--Deerfoot in the Mountains. Davis, J. Steeple, illus. LC 5-28021. 19cm. 363p. (New Deerfoot Ser.: No.3). 1905. John C. Winston.
--Deerfoot on the Prairies. Davis, J. Steeple, illus. LC 5-28019. 7, 1, 1 1., 9-366 incl. col. front. 7 pl. 19. 366p. (New Deerfoot Ser.: No.2). 1905. John C. Winston.
--Dorsey, the Young Inventor. LC 99-4908. v, 297 p. front, 1 illus., 5 pl. 17 1/2 cm. (True grit series). 1899. Fords, Howard & Hulbert.
--Dorsey, the Young Inventor, 1 of 3 Vols. (True Grit Ser.). N.D. Set. John C. Winston Co.
--Down the Mississippi. LC 12-32067. iv, 5-323 p. front., plates. 17 1/2 cm. (His "Great river series" no. 1). c.1886. Cassell & Company, Limited.
--The "F" Cipher. 20cm. 292p. (Idle Moments Ser.: No. 19). 1892. The Price-McGill Co.
--Fighting to Win: The Story of a New York Boy. Davis, J. Watson, illus. LC 7-9548. 1 p. l., 304 p. front., plates. 19 1/2 cm. c.1907. A. L. Burt Company.
--Fire, Snow & Water: Or, Life in the Lone Land. Dougherty, Louis R., illus. LC 9-14937. 324 p. incl. front. 3 pl. 19 1/2 cm. c.1908. The J. C. Winston Company.
--The Flying Boys in the Sky. Prittie, Edwin John, illus. 304p. (The Flying Boys Ser.: Vol.1). 1911. John C. Winston.
--The Flying Boys to the Rescue. Prittie, Edwin John, illus. 304p. (The Flying Boys Ser.: Vol.2). 1911. John C. Winston.
--Footprints in the Forest. 387p. (Log Cabin Ser.: No.3). 1886. John C. Winston.
--Footprints in the Forest. LC 12-32297. iv, 5-387 p. front., plates. 17 1/2 cm. ("Log cabin series." no. 3). c.1886. Porter & Coates.
--The Forest Messengers. Prittie, Edwin John, illus. 4 p. l., 340 p. col. front., 3 pl. 19 1/2 cm. (Half-title: Paddle your own canoe series no. 1). c.1907. The J.C. Winston Company.
--Four Boys: Or, the Story of a Forest Fire, 1 of 3 vols. (Illus.). (Roundabout Lib.). (Through on Time Ser.: Vol. 3). N.D. Set. Henry T. Coates & Co.
--Four Boys: Or, The Story of a Forest Fire, 1 of 3 Vols. (Roundabout Library). (Through on Time Ser.: Vol. 3). N.D. Set. John C. Winston Co.
--Four Boys: Or, The Story of a Forest Fire. LC 6-37809. 263 p. front., plates. 20 1/2 cm. (On cover: Through on time series no. 3). c.1896. The Merriam Company.
--From Low to High Gear. Kennedy, J. W. Ferguson, illus. LC 6-23705. 4 p. l., 11-329 p. front., 7 pl. 19 1/2 cm. c.1906. D. Estes & Company.
--From Tent to White House. (The Boys' Own Library). N.D. David McKay.
--From Tent to White House, 39 vols. (Illus.). (Famous Books for Boys Ser.: No. 13). 1905. Set. H M Caldwell Co.
--From the Throttle to the President's Chair: A Story of American Railway Life. LC 12-32291. v, 375 p. front., plates. 19 1/2 cm. c.1892. Cassell Publishing Company.

--Trailing Geronimo: Or, Campaigning with Crook. Prittie, Edwin John, illus. LC 8-23529. 353 p. col. front., 3 pl. 19 cm. (Half-title: The Arizona series (v. 2))). c.1908. The J. C. Winston Company.
--True Blue: A Story of Luck and Pluck. Kennedy, J. W. Ferguson, illus. LC 3-13059. 19.5 cm. 360p. 1903. Dana Estes and Company.
--True to his Trust. (Vacation Ser.). N.D. Penn Publishing Co.
--True to His Trust. Davis, J. Steeple, illus. (Adventure Stories). N.D. Penn Publishing Co.
--True to His Trust. Davis, J. Steeple, illus. LC 6-377913. 329 p. incl. front. plates. 18 1/2 cm. 1897. The Penn Publishing Company.
--Two Boys in Wyoming, 1 of 3 Vols. (The Northwest Ser.: Vol. 3). N.D. Set. John C. Winston Co.
--Two Boys in Wyoming: A/Tale of Adventure. LC 98-1017. 19 1/2cm. 309p. (Roundabout Library). (Northwest Ser.: No. 3). 1898. H. T. Coates & Co.
--Uncrowning a King: A Tale of King Philip's War. LC 6-38415. 312 p. front., 7 pl. 19 1/2 cm. 1896. New Amsterdam Book Company.
--Uncrowning a King: A Tale of King Philip's War. Davis, J. Steeple, illus. (Historical Stories for Boys). N.D. Penn.
--Unlucky Tib. Bridgman, Lewis Jesse (1857-1931), illus. LC 9-17239. 20cm. 332p. 1909. D. Estes & Co.
--Unlucky Tib. Kennedy, J. W. Ferguson, illus. (Illus.). (Low to High Gear Ser.). N.D. Dana Estes & Co.
--Up the Forked River: Adventures in South America. Lisle, Seward D., pseud. N.D. John C. Winston Co.
--Up the Forked River: Or, Adventures in South America. Lisle, Seward D., pseud. LC 4-26244. 20cm. 304p. (Strange Adventure Ser.: No. 2). 1904. H. T. Coates & Co.
--Up the Tapajos: Or, Adventures in Brazil. LC 12-32078. iv, 5-326 p. front., plates. 17 1/2 cm. (His "Great river series", no. 2). c.1886. Cassell & Company, Limited.
--Upside Down: An Automobile Story for Boys. LC 9-14820. 2 p. l., 9-242 p. front., 3 pl. 19 1/2 cm. c.1909. The J. C. Winston Company.
--A Waif of the Mountains. 12cm. 312p. 1900. The Mershon Co.
--The White Mustang. Jayne, Lieutenant R. H., pseud, 39 vols. (Illus.). (Famous Books for Boys Ser.: No. 32). 1905. Set. H M Caldwell Co.
--The White Mustang. Jayne, Lieutenant R. H., pseud. LC 1-24918. 12cm. 342p. 1901. Street & Smith.
--White Mustang,. A Tale of the Lone Star State. Jayne, Lieutenant R. H., pseud. (The Wild Advanture Ser.). N.D. David McKay.
--The White Mustang. A Tale of the Lone Star State. Jayne, Lieutenant R. H., pseud. LC 6-37790. 342 p. front., plates. 19 cm. (Wild adventure series, no. 2). c.1889. F. F. Lovell & Company.
--The Wild Man of the Woods. A Mystery of the Wilderness. Carleton, Captain Latham C., pseud. LC 17-576. 1 p. l., 5-127 p. incl. plates. 19 cm. (On cover: The boy's Dashaway Series. no. 7). c.1892. G. Munro.
--The Wilderness Fugitives, 1 of 3 vols. (Illus.). (Roundabout Lib.). (River and Wilderness Ser.: Vol. 2). N.D. Set. Henry T. Coates & Co.
--The Wilderness Fugitives, 1 of 3 Vols. (Roundabout Library). (River and Wilderness Ser.: Vol. 2). N.D. Set. John C. Winston Co.
--The Wilderness Fugitives: A Sequel to the River Fugitives. LC 6-37789. 253 p. incl. front., plates. 19 cm. (River and wilderness series, no. 2). c.1893. The Price-McGill Company.
--Wolf Ear the Indian. (Illus.). (Story Books for Boys). N.D. Cassell & Co's Pubs.
--The Wonderful Story of Old. LC 4-32687. (Illus.). 20cm. 348p. 1904. M. W. Hazen Co.
--Work and Win. Davis, J. Watson, illus. (Illus.). N.D. A. L. Burt.
--The Worst Boy. LC 12-240563. 286 p. front., plates. 19 cm. c.1912. American Tract Society.
--Wyoming, 1 of 3 vols. (Roundabout Library). (Wyoming Valley Ser.: Vol. 1). N.D. Set. John C. Winston Co.
--Wyoming. 321 p. incl. front. plates. 17 1/2 cm. (Wyoming Valley series, no. 1). c.1888. Porter & Coates.
--Wyoming, 1 of 3 vols. (Roundabout Lib.). (Wyoming Valley Ser.: Vol. 1). 1891. Set. Porter & Coates.
--The Young Conductor: Or, Winning His Way, 1 of 3 vols. (Illus.). (Roundabout Lib.). (Through on Time Ser.). N.D. Set. Henry T. Coates & Co.
--The Young Conductor: Or, Winning His Way, 1 of 3 Vols. (Roundabout Library). (Through on Time Ser.). N.D. Set. John C. Winston Co.
--The Young Gold Seekers of the Klondike. Carter, F. A., illus. LC 99-3524. 311 p. front., plates. 19 cm. (Adventure Stories Ser.). 1899. The Penn Publishing Company.
--A Young Hero: Or, Fighting to Win. LC 7-2714. 235 p. incl. front. 19 1/2 cm. (On cover: Boys' home library, v. 1, no. 13). c.1888. A. L. Bury.
--A Young Hero: Or, Fighting to Win. (Illus.). (The Boys' Library Ser.). N.D. A. L. Burt.
--A Young Hero: Or, Fighting to Win. (Illus.). (The Alger Series for Boys). N.D. A. L. Burt's Pubs.
--The Young Pioneers: Or, Better to be Born Plucky than Rich. Davis, J. Watson, illus. LC 9-25812. 20cm. 286p. 1908. A. L. Burt Co.
--The Young Ranchers: Or, Fighting the Sioux. LC 6-37787. iv, 284 p. front., plates. 19 1/2 cm. (On cover: "Forest and prairie series," no. 3). c.1895. H. T. Coates & Co.
--The Young Ranchers: Or, Fighting the Sioux, 1 of 3 vols. (Illus.). (Roundabout Lib.). (Forest and Prairie Ser.: Vol. 3). N.D. Set. Henry T. Coates & Co.
--The Young Ranchers: Or, Fighting the Sioux, 1 of 3 Vols. (Roundabout Library). (Forest and Prairie Ser.: Vol. 3). N.D. Set. John C. Winston Co.
--The Young Scout. (Illus.). (The Alger Series for Boys). N.D. A. L. Burt's Pubs.
--The Young Scout, 1 of 3 vols. (The Adventure Ser.). N.D. Set. A. L. Burt's Pubs.
--The Young Scout. The Story of a West Point Lieutenant. LC 6-37788. 1 p. l., 275 p. front., plates. 19 cm. c.1895. A. L. Burt.

Ellis, Edward Sylvester (1840-1916) & Chipman, William Pendleton
--The Cruise of the Firefly. Prittie, Edwin John, illus. LC 6-21383. 305 p. front., 3 pl. 19 1/2 cm. (Half-title: Up and doing series). c.1906. The J. C. Winston Company.

Ellis, Edwin J.
--Doda's Birthday. N.D. Pott, Young & Co.

Ellis, Ella Thorp (1928-)
--Celebrate the Morning. 1st. ed. LC 72-75269. 177 p. 22cm. 1972. Atheneum.
--Hallelujah. McWilliams, Ginnie, illus. LC 76-4810. (Illus.). 208 p. 24cm. 1976. (ISBN 0-689-30536-2). Atheneum.
--Hugo and the Princess Nena. LC 82-16315. p. cm. 1983. (ISBN 0-689-30953-8). Atheneum.
--Riptide. Snyder, Joel, illus. LC 69-18966. (Illus.). 201 p. 22cm. 1969. Atheneum.
--Riptide. Snyder, Joel, illus. LC 69-18966. (Illus.). 201 p. 21cm. (Aladdin Book, A25). 1973, c.1969. Atheneum.
--Roam the Wild Country. 1st. ed. Schlesinger, Bret, illus. LC 67-18990. (Illus.). 212 p. 22cm. 1967. Atheneum.
--Sleepwalker's Moon. LC 79-22665. 234 p. 22cm. 1980. Atheneum.
--Where the Road Ends. 1st. ed. LC 73-84824. 197 p. 22cm. 1974. (ISBN 0-689-30134-0). Atheneum.

Ellis, Griffith Ogden (1869-), ed. see The, American Boy.

Ellis, Griffith Ogden (1869-), intro. by.
--The American Boy Adventure Stories. LC 46-7628. (Illus.). 20cm. 408p. (Young Moderns). 1946. Doubleday & Co.

Ellis, Hamilton
--Trains & Tractors. (Illus.). (ps-7). 1957. (ISBN 0-685-21621-7). Verry.

Ellis, Herbert, pseud., see Wilson, Lionel.

Ellis, James
--Run For Your Life, Open Door. 1970. (ISBN 0-516-04846-5). (ISBN 0-516-14846-X). Childrens Press.

Ellis, Jessie Croft
--Mary Ann of Old Kentucky. LC 47-15857. 5 p. l., 50 p. illus. (ports.) 20 cm. 1946. The Dietz Printing Company.

Ellis, Jim
--Jumping Frog from Jasper County: Advertising-As I Lived It. (Illus.). 256p. 1970. (ISBN 0-200-71693-X). Abelard.

Ellis, John Breckenridge (1870-)
--The Little Fiddler of the Ozarks: A Novel. N.D. Laidlaw Bros.
--The Red Box Clew. N.D. Fleming H. Revell Co.

Ellis, John Samuel (1873-)
--The Boy From Reifel's Ranch. (Bks. for Boy Scouts). 1915. Abingdon Press.
--The Boy from Reifels Ranch. LC 15-7278. 3 p. l., 5-302 p. front., plates. 19 1/2 cm. c.1915. The Abingdon Press.

Ellis, Joyce K.
--The Big Split. moody press rev. ed. LC 82-23948. p. cm. 1983, c.1979. (ISBN 0-8024-0190-2). Moody Press.
--The Big Split. LC 78-21262. (Illus.). 168 p. 20cm. c.1979. (ISBN 0-8407-5671-2). T. Nelson.
--Snowmobile Trap. LC 81-38363. (Illus.). 166 p. 20cm. c.1981. T. Nelson.

Ellis, Joyce K., compiled by.
--Saved by a Broken Pole & Other Stories. 75p. (Orig.). (gr. 2-6). 1980. (ISBN 0-89323-007-3). BMA Pr.

Ellis, Joyce K. & Lynn, Claire, eds.
--Tell Me A Story Lord Jesus. Broky, Kenneth, illus. (Illus.). 44p. (Orig.). (gr. 1-3). 1981. (ISBN 0-89323-023-5). BMA Pr.

Ellis, Judy, pseud., see Blumenthal, Judith Louise Teitler.

Ellis, Katharine Ruth
--The Wide Awake Girls. (The Wide Awake Girls Ser.). N.D. Little Brown & Co.

Ellis, Leo Roy (1909-)
--The Bronc Tattoo. LC 66-12580. 192 p. 22 cm. 1966. Funk & Wagnall.
--King Rooster. LC 65-11723. 214p. illus. 22cm. c.1965. Funk & Wagnalls.
--Nights of Danger. Donahue, Vic, illus. LC 64-11120. 123p. illus. 21cm. c.1964. Funk &Wagnalls.

Ellis, Louise (1948-)
--The Alphavegetabet. LC 77-363404. (Illus.). 56 p. 26cm. c.1976. (ISBN 0-02-976730-X). Collier Macmillan Canada.

Ellis, Mary Jackson (1916-)
--Gobble, Gobble, Gobble. Sears, Jewel, illus. LC 56-12429. 29cm. 1956. T. S. Denison.
--Spaghetti Eddie. Myers, Sylvia, illus. LC 57-126992. unpaged. illus. 29cm. 1957. T. S. Denison.
--Swimmer Is a Hopper. Moline, Earl Warren, Jr., illus. LC 57-14566. unpaged. illus. 29cm. 1957. T. S. Denison.

Ellis, Melvin Richard (1912-)
--Caribou Crossing: A Novel. LC 70-141013. (Illus.). 183 p. 22cm. 1971. (ISBN 0-03-086227-2). (ISBN 0-03-086228-0). (ISBN 0-03-089729-7). Holt, Rinehart and Winston.
--An Eagle to the Wind. LC 77-10930. 143 p. 22cm. c.1978. (ISBN 0-03-022766-6). Holt, Rinehart and Winston.
--Flight of the White Wolf. LC 75-98916. (Illus.). 195 p. 22cm. 1970. Holt, Rinehart and Winston.
--Ghost Dog of Killicut. Amundsen, Richard E., illus. LC 70-81696. (Illus.). 125 p. 22cm. 1969. Four Winds Press.
--Hurry Up Harry Hanson. LC 76-182121. 176 p. 22cm. 1972. Four Winds Press.
--Ironhead. LC 68-24761. 151 p. 22cm. 1968. Holt, Rinehart and Winston.
--No Man for Murder. LC 72-91651. 212 p. 22cm. 1973. Holt, Rinehart and Winston.
--Sad Song of the Coyote. LC 67-2306. 127 p. 22cm. 1967. Holt, Rinehart and Winston.
--Sidewalk Indian. LC 73-13980. 198p. (gr. 7 up). 1974. (ISBN 0-03-012076-4). HR&W.
--When Lighting Strikes. 160p. 1970. Four Winds Press.
--When Lightning Strikes. LC 72-124187. 144 p. 22cm. 1970. Four Winds Press.
--Wild Goose, Brother Goose. (gr. 5-8). 1972 (Tempo). G&D.
--The Wild-Horse Killers. LC 75-22156. 191 24. 1976. (ISBN 0-03-014866-9). Holt, Rinehart and Winston.
--The Wild Runners. LC 74-117293. 183 p. 22cm. 1970. Holt, Rinehart and Winston.

Ellis, Mrs.
--The Brewer's Family. N.D. Dodd & Mead.

Ellis, Patsy, jt. auth. see Torriani, Aimee.

Ellis, Patsy & Torriani, Aimee (1900-)
--Amber Eyes. LC 47-4397. 98 p. illus. 21 cm. 1947. St. Meinrad's Abbey.

Ellis, Sarah Stickney, Mrs. (1812-1872)
--The Brother and Sister, and Other Tales. new ed. LC 42-29020. 216 p. front. (port.) 15 1/2 cm. 1848. E. Walker.
--Irish Girl and other Poems. LC 24-22544. 19cm. 263p. 1844. T. Cowerpath & Co.

Ellison, Eugenia Adams
--Exiled Heart: The Ballad of Sam Huston. Ellison, Marky, illus. LC 65-223667. 70p. illus., maps, port. 22cm. c.1965. Naylor.
--Teacher, Teacher, Don't Whip Me. Ellison, Marky, illus. (gr. 1-3). N.D. (ISBN 0-8158-0089-4). Chris Mass.

Ellison, Fred P., tr. see Queiroz, Rachel de.

Ellison, Lucile Watkins (1907-1979)
--Butter on Both Sides. Brown, Judith Gwyn (1933-), illus. LC 79-15808. p. cm. 1979. (ISBN 0-684-16281-4). Scribner.
--The Tie That Binds. Brown, Judith Gwyn (1933-), illus. LC 80-27113. (Illus.). x, 130 p. 22cm. c.1981. (ISBN 0-684-16875-8). Scribner.
--A Window to Look Through. Brown, Judith Gwyn (1933-), illus. LC 81-23186. (Illus.). x, 118 p. 22cm. c.1982. (ISBN 0-684-17438-3). Scribner.

Ellison, Lynne
--The Green Bronze Mirror. N.D. (ISBN 0-8149-0298-7). The Vanguard Press.

Ellison, Virginia Howel see Mapes, Mary A., pseud.

Ellison, Virginia Howell see Mapes, Mary A., pseud.

Ellison, Virginia Howell see Howell, Virginia.

Ellison, Virginia Howell see Mussey, Virginia Howell.

Ellison, Virginia Howell (1910-)
--Surprise!. Mapes, Mary A., pseud. Fredenthal, David, photos by. LC 44-9414. 15 x 18 cm. 18p. 1944. Howell, Soskin.
--Training Pants. Sturtevant, Harriet, illus. LC 46-2025. 23 x 18 cm. 24p. 1946. Howell, Soskin.

Ellman, Maureen C.
--Talk to Me. Ellman, Ronald B., illus. Bugart, Herbert J., pref. by. LC 78-56138. (Illus.). 64p. (gr. 1-8). 1979. (ISBN 0-686-30184-6). Ellman Studio.

Ellsberg, Edward (1891-)
--I Have Just Begun to Fight: The Story of John Paul Jones. Foster, Gerald, illus. LC 42-8144. x p. 1 l., 269 p. incl. illus., plates, diagrs. col. front., col. plates. 22 cm. 1942. Dodd, Mead, & Company.
--Ocean Gold. LC 35-13555. 3 p. l., 263 p. 19 1/2 cm. 1935. Dodd, Mead & Company.
--Spanish Ingots. Rogers, Hubert, illus. LC 36-18206. vii, 299 p. incl. front., illus. plates. 21 cm. 1937. Dodd, Mead & Company.
--Submarine Treasure. Rogers, Hubert, illus. LC 53-4005. (Illus.). vii, 299 p. 21cm. 1953, c.1936. Dodd, Mead.
--Thirty Fathoms Deep. Crump, Leslie (1894-), illus. LC 30-18863. 5 p. l., 268 p. front., plates. 19 1/2 cm. c.1930. Dodd, Mead & Company.
--Treasure Below. LC 40-8961. 3 p. l., 305 p. 21 cm. 1940. Dodd, Mead & Company.

Ellsworth, Daisy & Henson, Jim, pseud. (1928-)
--What Did You Bring?. Featuring Jim Henson's Sesame Street Muppets. Henson, James Maury. Stevenson, Nancy W., illus. LC 79-57466. (Illus.). 28 p. 27cm. c.1980. (ISBN 0-307-23107-0). Western Pub. Co.

Ellsworth, Helen (1882-)
--The Blue Jays in the Sierras. Ellsworth, Helen (1882-), illus. LC 18-108387. 19 1/2cm. 205p. 1918. The Century Co.

Ellsworth, Mary, illus.
--Bedtime Stories. LC 42-1192. 34 p. illus. (part col.) 30 1/2 x 25 1/2 cm. c.1941. The Saalfield Publishing Company.
--The Colorful Story Book. LC 41-14766. 1 p. l., 7-86 p. illus. (part col.) 31 x 26 cm. c.1941. The Saalfield Publishing Company.
--Three Famous Stories. LC 41-17546. 34 p. illus. (part col.) 30 1/2 x 26 cm. c.1941. The Saalfield Publishing Company.

Ellwitz, Yvonne
--Little Angel Lost. (gr. 2-4). 1970. Vantage.

Elmendorf, Lawrence, ed. see Mother Goose.

Elmer, Irene Elizabeth (1937-)
--Anthony's Father. MacClain, George, illus. LC 72-149332. (Illus.). 44 p. 23cm. 1972. (ISBN 0-399-20272-2). (ISBN 0-399-60741-2). Putnam.
--Boy Who Ran Away. Mathews, Sally, illus. LC 63-23143. (Illus.). (Arch Bks: Set 1). (gr. 3-5). 1964. (ISBN 0-570-06001-X). Concordia.
--A Lodestone and a Toadstone. Sidjakov, Nicolas (1924-), illus. LC 69-11538. (Illus.). 40 p. 27cm. 1969. Knopf.
--Mandragora's Dragon. Van Sciver, Ruth (1915-), illus. (Illus.). (gr. k-3). 1964. (ISBN 0-687-23124-8). Abingdon.

Elmo, ed.
--Dimples. (Illus.). N.D. Belford, Clarke & Co's.
--Little Bright Eyes. (Illus.). N.D. Belford, Clarke & Co.
--Sparkles for Bright Eyes. (Illus.). N.D. Belford, Clarke & Co's.

Elmore, Patricia
--Susannah and the Blue House Mystery. Wallner, John C (1945-), illus. LC 79-20491. (Illus.). 164 p. 22cm. c.1980. (ISBN 0-525-40525-9). Dutton.
--Susannah and the Poison Green Halloween. Schick, Joel (1945-), illus. LC 82-2493. (Illus.). 106 p. 22cm. c.1982. (ISBN 0-525-44019-4). Dutton.

Elmslie, Theodora C.
--His Lordship's Puppy. Waugh, Ida, illus. (Sunbeam Ser. for Young People). 1900. Penn.
--His Lordship's Puppy. Waugh, Ida, illus. (Illus.). (The Little People's Ser.). N.D. Penn Publishing Co.
--Little Lady of Lavender. Scannell, Edith & H L E, illus. LC 12-31972. 320 incl. front., illus. plates. 19. 1894. American Sunday-School Union.
--The Little Lame Lord: Or, The Child of Cloverlea. (Illus.). 265p. 1898. The Union Press.
--The Pilgrim Child. LC 12-31973. 178 p. incl. front., illus., plates. 20cm. c.1896. The American Sunday-School Union.
--Those Midsummer Fairies. LC 12-31974. 352 p. front., illus., illus., plates. 19 1/2cm. 1895. The American Sunday-School Union.

E. L. P
--Nobody but Nan. N.D. Methodist Book Concern.
--Nobody But Nan. N.D. Nelson & Phillips.

Els, Betty Vander
--The Bombers' Moon. 129p. 1985. (ISBN 0-374-30864-0). Farrar Strauss.

Elsasser, Ruth, illus.
--Cinderella. Collis, J., tr. from Ger. (Illus.). 23p. (gr. 2-3). 1978. (ISBN 0-85440-332-9, Pub. by Steinerbooks). Anthroposophic.
Elsbree, Elizabeth Sellers (1901-)
--Across the Isthmus. Winslow, Earle B. (1884-), illus. LC 35-14580. vi. 7-68 p. incl. front., illus., map. 19 1/2cm. (our changing world. 1935. T. Nelson and Sons.
Elsdale, May
--Stella's Cup: Or, The Boy Artist. (Illus.). (Warne's Home Circle Library). N.D. Frederick Warne & Co.
E L S E, pseud., see Estey, Henry G..
Elsea, Matilda Mahaffey, ed.
--Choice Poems for Elementary Grades. LC 44-26979. 3 p. l., 9-230, 17 p. 23 cm. 1943. The Edwards Press
Elsie-Jean, pseud., see Stern, Elizabeth Gertrude Levin.
Elsie-Jean, pseud., see Stern, Elsie Jean.
Elsie-Jean, pseud. (1898-1954)
--Adventure of Fairy Tinkle Toes. Stern, Elizabeth Gertrude Levin. Franz, Erik, illus. N.D. A. B. Burt Co.
--Old Fables For You and Pictures Too. Stern, Elizabeth Gertrude Levin. Duval, Estelle, illus. LC 28-7330. (Lettered by Erik Franz) 47p col. illus. 281/2cm. 1927. Thomas Nelson & Sons.
--Wild Flowers and Elves. Stern, Elizabeth Gertrude Levin. Ries, Gerta, illus. LC 28-1286. 32 p. col. illus. 28 1/2cm. 1927. T. Nelson & Sons.
Elsingham, H.
--A Story of Ancient Wales. N.D. Thomas Whittaker.
Elson, Marilyn
--Duffy on the Farm. McCue, Lisa, illus. LC 83-82600. (Illus.). 20 p. 32cm. c.1984. (ISBN 0-307-10407-9). (ISBN 0-307-60404-7). Golden.
Elson, William Harris (1856-1935) & Gray, William Scott (1885-1960)
--Dick and Jane: Basic Pre-Primer. LC 76-28489. p. cm. (Series: Curriculum Foundation Series : Life-Reading Service.). 1976, c.1936. (ISBN 0-688-03126-9). Morrow.
--More Dick and Jane Stories. 48p. N.D. Scott, Foresman & Co.
Elting, Mary, jt. auth. see Folsom, Franklin Brewster.
Elting, Mary, ed. see Folsom, Michael.
Elting, Mary (1906-)
--The Big Red Pajama Wagon. Anderson, Betty, illus. LC 50-892. 32 p. col. illus. 17cm. (Tell-a-tale Books). c.1950. Whitman.
--Helicopter Mystery. Floherty, John Joseph, Jr. (1892-1964), illus. LC 58-13928. (Illus.). 22cm. 178p. (gr. 3-6). 1968. (ISBN 0-8178-3172-X). Harvey.
--Lady, the Little Blue Mare. Winship, Florence Sarah, illus. LC 50-39808. 21cm. 32p. 1950. Whitman.
--Miss Polly's Animal School. (Easy Readers Ser.). (gr. k-3). N.D. Wonder.
--The Mysterious Milk Robber: And Other Stories. Koering, Ursula (1921-), illus. LC 77-89780. (Illus.). 302 p. 22cm.(gr. 3-6). 1970. (ISBN 0-8178-4562-3). Harvey.
--Smoky. Reed, Veronica, pseud. (1916-), illus. Sherman, Theresa. LC 47-5590. 32 p. col. illus. 17 cm. (Tell-a-tale books). c.1947. Whitman Pub. Co.
--Speckles & the Triplets. Stevens, Mary, illus. LC 49-5065. 17cm. 32p. (Tell-a-tale books). c.1949. Whitman Pub. Co.
--What's going on Here. Stanforth, Deirdre, illus. LC 68-21300. 63 p. col. illus. 22cm. (Easy Reader). 1968. Grosset & Dunlap.
--Wheels and Noises. Dauber, Elizabeth, illus. LC 50-6644. (Illus.). 42 p. 21cm. (Wonder book for children, 524). 1950. Wonder Books.
--Who Lives on the Farm. Jackson, Pauline (1918-), illus. LC 50-31159. 41 p. col. illus. 21cm. 1949. Wonder Books.
--Wishes & Secrets. Stevens, Mary, illus. LC 56-13042. 151p. illus. 22cm. 1956. Bobbs-Merrill Co.
Elting, Mary (1906-) & Goodman, Ann Davidow (1932-)
--Dinosaur Mysteries. Swan, Susan Elizabeth (1944-), illus. LC 79-55035. (Illus.). 64p. (Bronto Bks). (gr. 3-8). 1980. (ISBN 0-448-13617-1). (ISBN 0-686-64320-8). Platt.
--Dinosaur Mysteries. Swan, Susan Elizabeth (1944-), illus. (Illus.). 64p. (gr. 1-7). 1980. (ISBN 0-448-47487-5, G&D). Putnam Pub Group.
Elting, Mary (1906-) & Gossett, Margaret
--Patch. Koering, Ursula (1921-), illus. LC 48-7934. 156 p. illus. 20 cm. 1948. Doubleday.
Elton, Emily D.
--A Mince Pie Dream, a Book of Children's Verse: A Book of Children's Verse. Mansfield, Blanche McManus (1869-), illus. LC 14-22737. 75 p. col. front., col. plates. 23cm. c.1897. E. R. Herrick & Company.
Elton, Packer
--Roy Rogers an the Trail of Zeros: An Original Story Featuring Roy Rogers. Gleicher, Al, illus. LC 54-33172. 282 p. illus. 20cm. 1954. Whitman.
Elwart, Joan Potter (1927-)
--Animal Babies. Seiden, Art & Ker, Edith, illus. LC 67-1942. (Illus.). 1 v. (unpaged. 30cm. (Whitman Small World Library Book). 1966. Whitman Pub. Co.
--Daisy Tells. Warren, Betsy, pseud. (1916-), illus. Warren, Elizabeth Avery. LC 66-12031. 32p col. illus. 19x24cm. c.1966. (ISBN 0-8114-7511-5). Steck.
--Hey! Let's Go. Reiss, John J., illus. Haas, Arthur P., photos by. LC 67-6488. (Illus.). 28 p. 22cm. (Whitman big tell-a-tale). 1966. Whitman Pub. Co.
--Right Foot, Wrong Foot. Warren, Betsy, pseud. (1916-), illus. Warren, Elizabeth Avery. LC 68-19557. (Illus.). 32 p. 27cm. 1968. Steck-Vaughn Co.
--What Hides Inside?. Michal, Marie, illus. LC 72-2803. (Illus.). 20 p. 16cm. (Downy book). 1972. (ISBN 0-528-82449-X). Rand McNally.
Elwell, Edward Henry (1825-1890)
--The Boys of Thirty-Five. (Illus.). (Our Boys' Prize Library). N.D. Lee & Shepard.
--The Boys of Thirty-Five: A Story of a Seaport Town. LC 12-32121. 2 p. l., 9-255 p. 17 1/2cm. 1884. Lee and Shepard.
Elwell, Peter
--The King of the Pipers. LC 83-22176. (Illus.). 32 p. 24cm. c.1984. (ISBN 0-02-733460-0). Macmillan.
Elwes, A. T
--The Lion and Tiger Toy-Book. (Illus.). N.D. George Routledge.
Elwes, Alfred (0000-1888)
--Frank and Andrea. (Cabinet of Adventure). N.D. Pott, Young & Co.
--Frank and Andrea: Forest Life in the Island of Sardinia. Dudley, Robert, illus. N.D. Pott, Young & Co.
--Guy Rivers: A Boy's Struggles in the Great World. N.D. Pott, Young & Co.
--Luke Ashley: School Life in Holland. N.D. Pott, Young & Co.
--Paul Blake. (Illus.). (St. Nicholas Series for Boys). N.D. International Book Co.
--Swift and Sure: or, The Career of Two Brothers. N.D. Thomas Nelson & Sons.
Elwes, Alfred (0000-1888) & Horne, Richard Henry (1802-1884)
--Pictures of Comical People: With Stories About Them. For Children of All Ages. Grandville, Jean Ignace Isidore Gerard (1803-1847), illus. LC 44-49400. 4 p. l., 7-304 p. front., illus., plates. 17 cm. 1856. C. S. Francis and Company.
Elwood, Roger, ed. see Binder, Eando, pseud. (1911-1974) & O'Donnell, K. M.
Elwood, Roger, ed. see Blackwood, Algernon, et al.
Elwood, Roger (1943-), ed. see Giles, Gordon, et al.
Elwood, Roger (1943-), ed. see Holly, J. Hunter, pseud. (1932-) & Malzberg, Barry N.
Elwood, Roger (1943-), compiled by see Jones, Raymond F., et al.
Elwood, Roger (1943-), ed. see Lytle, B. J. & Orgill, Michael Thomas.
Elwood, Roger (1943-), ed. see Orgill, Michael Thomas (1946-) & Louden, Leo.
Elwood, Roger, ed. see Zebrowski, George (1945-) & Goldsmith, Howard.
Elwood, Roger, ed. see Zebrowski, George (1945-) & Malzberg, Barry N.
Elwood, Roger (1943-)
--Tomorrow: New Worlds of Science Fiction. LC 75-17783. 218 p. 22 cm. 1975. (ISBN 0-87131-185-2). M. Evans.
Elwood, Roger (1943-), ed.
--Children of Infinity: Original Science Fiction Stories for Young Readers. Morgan, Jacqui, illus. LC 72-8930. (Illus.). 24cm. 192p. (gr. 6 up). 1973. (ISBN 0-531-02599-3). Watts.
--Crisis: Ten Original Stories of Science Fiction. LC 73-19901. 224p. (gr. 6 up). 1974. (ISBN 0-525-66374-6). Elsevier-Nelson.
--Crisis: Ten Original Stories of Science Fiction. 1st. ed. LC 73-19901. 176 p. 21cm. 1974. (ISBN 0-8407-6374-3). T. Nelson.
--Dystopian Visions. LC 75-25544. 204p. 1975. (ISBN 0-13-222216-7). P-H.
--The Gifts of Asti, and Other Stories of Science Fiction. LC 74-18132. 216 p. 23cm. 1975. (ISBN 0-695-80534-7). (ISBN 0-695-40534-9). Follett Pub. Co.
--Horror Tales: Spirits, Spells & the Unknown. Baumgartner, Robert, illus. Zebrowski, George (1945-), intro. by. LC 74-14061. (Illus.). 123 p. 27cm. 1974. (ISBN 0-528-82469-4). (ISBN 0-528-82470-8). Rand McNally.
--Horror Tales: Spirits, Spells, & the Unknown. Baumgartner, Robert, illus. (Illus.). 128p. (gr. 5-12). 1974. (ISBN 0-528-80181-3). Rand.
--The Learning Maze and Other Science Fiction. LC 73-20094. 191 p. 22cm. 1974. (ISBN 0-671-32661-9). J. Messner.
--Monster Tales; Vampires, Werewolves, and Things. Altschuler, Franz (1923-), illus. Block, Robert, intro. by. LC 73-12069. (Illus.). 117 p. 27cm. 1973. (ISBN 0-528-82506-2). (ISBN 0-528-82506-2). Rand McNally.
--Monster Tales: Vampires, Werewolves, & Things. Altschuler, Franz (1923-), illus. Block, Robert, intro. by. 128p. (gr. 5-7). 1973. (ISBN 0-528-82506-2). (ISBN 0-528-80199-6). Rand.
--More Science Fiction Tales: Crystal Creatures, Bird-Things, & Other Weirdies. Ruth, Rod (1912-), illus. LC 74-12283. (Illus.). 123 p. 27cm. 1974. (ISBN 0-528-82471-6). (ISBN 0-528-82472-4). Rand McNally.
--Night of the Sphinx & Other Stories. Groenjes, Kathleen, illus. LC 73-21482. (Illus.). 23cm. 48p. (Science Fiction Bks). Orig. Title: When the Cold Came & Other Stories. (gr. 4-8) 1974. (ISBN 0-8225-0954-7). Lerner Pubns.
--The Other Side of Tomorrow: Original Science Fiction Stories About Young People of the Future. Danska, Herbert (1928-), illus. LC 73-3046. (Illus.). vii, 207 p. 24cm. 1973. (ISBN 0-394-82468-7). (ISBN 0-394-92468-1). Random House.
--The Science Fiction Annual, No. 1. 192p. 1975. (ISBN 0-87131-185-2). M. Evans & Company.
--Science Fiction Tales: Invaders, Creatures and Alien Worlds. Ruth, Rod (1912-), illus. LC 73-9799. (Illus.). 124 p. 27cm. 1973. (ISBN 0-528-82504-6). (ISBN 0-528-82504-6). Rand McNally.
--Survival from Infinity: Original Science Fiction Stories for Young Readers. Morgan, Jacqui, illus. LC 73-14696. (Illus.). viii, 174 p. 24cm. 1974. (ISBN 0-531-02666-3). Watts.
--Tomorrow, New Worlds of Science Fiction. LC 75-17783. 228p. (gr. 7 up). 1975. (ISBN 0-87131-185-2). M Evans.
Ely, Jean, jt. auth. see Feldman, Anne.
Ely, Luise, jt. auth. see Gould, Carmen.
Ely, Richard T.
--English's Boy's Book Battle Lyrics. (Illus.). N.D. Harper &Brothers.
--Stories from English History. (Illus.). N.D. Harper & Brothers.
Ely, Wilmer Mateo
--The Boy Chums Cruising in Florida Waters: Or, The Perils and Dangers of the Fishing Fleet. (The Boy Chum Ser.). N.D. A. L. Burt.
--The Boy Chums in the Florida Jungle: Or, Charlie West and Walter Hazard with the Seminole Indians. (The Boy Chum Ser.). N.D. A. L. Burt.
--The Boy Chums in the Forest: Or, Hunting for Plume Birds in the Florida Everglades. (The Boy Chums Ser.). N.D. A. L. Burt.
--The Boy Chums in the Gulf of Mexico: Or, A Dangerous Cruise with the Greek Spongers. (The Boy Chum Ser.). N.D. A. L. Burt.
--The Boy Chums on Haunted Island: Or, Hunting for Pearls in the Bahama Islands. (The Boy Chum Ser.). N.D. A. L. Burt.
--The Boy Chums on Indian River: Or, the Boy Partners of the Schooner "Orphan". (The Boy Chum Ser.). N.D. A. L. Burt.
--The Boy Chums' Perilous Chums: Or, Searching for Wreckage on the Florida Coast. (The Boy Chum Ser.). N.D. A. L. Burt.
--The Boy Truckers: A Story of Florida. Davis, J. Watson, illus. LC 5-24181. 1 p., l., 308 p. front., pl. 19 1/2cm. c.1905. A. L. Burt Co.
--The Young Plume Hunters. Davis, J. Watson, illus. (Illus.). N.D. A. L. Burt.
--The Young Treasure Seekers: The Adventures of Charley West and Walter Hazard on a Perilous Cruise Hunting for Treasure. Davis, J. Watson, illus. LC 11-12058. 2 p. l., 3-298 p. front., plates. 19 1/2cm. (boy chums series). c.1911. A. L. Burt Company.
Elzbieta
--Dikou and the Snivelly Snoak. LC 84-20458. (Illus.). 32 p. 22cm. 1985, c.1984. (ISBN 0-8120-5622-1). Barron's.
--Dikou, the Little Troon Who-Walks-at-Night. LC 84-20484. (Illus.). 29 p. 22cm. 1985, c.1984. (ISBN 0-8120-5621-3). Barron's.
--Little Mops and the Butterfly. LC 73-10373. 32 p. of illus. 19cm. Orig. Title: Here and There. 1974, c.1972. (ISBN 0-385-06793-3). (ISBN 0-385-06793-3). Doubleday.
--Little Mops and the Moon. LC 73-10374. 32 p. of illus. 19cm. Orig. Title: Summer Riddles; Little Mops Tries to Capture the Moon. 1974, c.1972. (ISBN 0-385-06797-6). (ISBN 0-385-06797-6). Doubleday.
--Little Mops at the Seashore. LC 73-10375. 32 p. of illus. 19cm. Orig. Title: What Could be Nicer?. 1974, c.1972. (ISBN 0-385-06792-5). (ISBN 0-385-06792-5). Doubleday.
Emanuel, Elizabeth, jt. auth. see Thayer, Marjorie.
Emberley, Barbara Anne (1932-)
--Simon's Song. Emberley, Edward Randolph (1931-), illus. LC 70-79117. (Illus.). 32 p. 19cm. 1969. Prentice-Hall.
Emberley, Barbara Anne (1932-), adapted by.
--Drummer Hoff. Emberley, Edward Randolph (1931-), illus. LC 67-28189. (Adapted from a Folk Verse). (Illus.). 32 p. 1967. Prentice-Hall. **Award: (RCM).**
--Night's Nice. Emberley, Edward Randolph (1931-), illus. LC 62-15898. (Illus.). 26 p. 19cm. 1963. Doubleday.
--One Wide River to Cross. Emberley, Edward Randolph (1931-), illus. LC 66-207031. 1v. (unpaged) illus. 20x27cm. 1966. Prentice. **Awards: (ALA); (RCM).**
--One Wide River to Cross. Emberley, Edward Randolph (1931-), illus. (Illus.). woodcut illus. 32p. (gr. k-3). 1970 (Schol Trade Pap). Schol Bk Serv.
--The Story of Paul Bunyan. Emberley, Edward Randolph (1931-), illus. (Illus.). 32 p. 28cm 1963. Prentice-Hall.
Emberley, Edward Randolph, jt. auth. see Emberley, Barbara Anne.
Emberley, Edward Randolph (1931-)
--A Birthday Wish. 1st. ed. Emberley, Edward Randolph (1931-), illus. LC 77-5147. (Illus.). 32 p. 26cm. c.1977. (ISBN 0-316-23409-5). Little, Brown.
--Cock a Doodle Doo. Emberley, Edward Randolph (1931-), illus. LC 64-13270. 1 v. (chiefly illus.) 17. 1964. Little, Brown and Company.
--Ed Emberley Little Drawing Book of Weirdoes. Emberley, Edward Randolph (1931-), illus. (gr. 1 up). 1973. (ISBN 0-316-23605-5). Little.
--Ed Emberley Little Drawing Books. Emberley, Edward Randolph (1931-), illus. (gr. 1 up). 1978. (ISBN 0-316-23614-4). Little.
--Ed Emberley's ABC. Emberley, Edward Randolph (1931-), illus. LC 77-28099. (Illus.). 58 p. c.1978. (ISBN 0-316-23408-7). Little, Brown.
--Green Says Go. LC 68-21165. (Illus.). 32 p. 27cm. 1968. Little, Brown.
--Klippity Klop. 1st. ed. Emberley, Edward Randolph (1931-), illus. LC 74-6308. (Illus.). 32 p. 20cm. 1974. (ISBN 0-316-23607-1). Little, Brown.
--London Bridge Is Falling Down. Emberley, Edward Randolph (1931-), illus. (Illus.). (The verses, the tune, the rules & the historical background of the favorite children's game). (gr. k-3). 1967. (ISBN 0-316-23588-1). (ISBN 0-316-23416-8). Little.
--The Parade Book. 1st ed. Emberley, Edward Randolph (1931-), illus. LC 62-123784. (Illus.). 28 p. 1962. Little, Brown.
--Rosebud. Emberley, Edward Randolph (1931-), illus. LC 66-11006. (Illus.). 26cm. 32p. (A picture book version of the "wish-I-were-different" theme for turtles). (ps up). 1966. (ISBN 0-316-23412-5). Little.
--The Wing on a Flea: A Book About Shapes. Emberley, Edward Randolph (1931-), illus. (Illus.). (ps up). 1961. (ISBN 0-316-23600-4). Little. **Award: (NYT).**
--The Wizard of Op. 1st. ed. Emberley, Edward Randolph (1931-), illus. LC 75-20345. (Illus.). 32 p. 25cm. 1975. (ISBN 0-316-23610-1). Little, Brown.
Emblen, Betty J., jt. auth. see Emblen, Donald Lewis.
Emblen, Donald Lewis (1918-) & Emblen, Betty J.
--The Palomino Boy. Ward, Lynd Kendall (1905-1985), illus. LC 48-10353. 189 p. 21 cm. 1948. Viking Press.
Embleton, Elisabeth
--Little Red Riding Hood. Carruth, Jane & Embleton, Gerry, illus. LC 74-14342. p. cm. (Collins-World fairy tales in color). 1975, c.1973. (ISBN 0-529-05225-3). (ISBN 0-529-05226-1). Collins-World.
Embry, Margaret Jacob (1919-1975)
--Blue-Nosed Witch. Rose, Carl (1903-1971), illus. (Illus.). 48p. (gr. 3-6). 1956. (ISBN 0-8234-0011-5). Holiday.
--Kid Sister. Freeman, Don (1908-1978), illus. LC 58-3775. (Illus.). 165 p. 20cm. 1958. Holiday House.
--Mister Blue. Turkle, Brinton Cassaday (1915-), illus. 72p. (gr. k-3). 1969 (Schol Trade Pap). Schol Bk Serv.
--Mr. Blue. Turkle, Brinton Cassaday (1915-), illus. LC 63-25004. (Illus.). 71 p. 21cm. 1963. Holiday House.
--My Name Is Lion. Glattauer, Ned, illus. LC 70-119803. (Illus.). 46 p. 24cm. 1970. Holiday House.

--Peg-Leg Willy. Grifalconi, Ann (1929-), illus. LC 66-8626. (Illus.). 1 v. (unpaged. 21cm. 1966. Holiday House.
--Shadi. LC 70-141407. 92 p. 22cm. 1971. (ISBN 0-8234-0186-3). Holiday House.

Embury
--Blind Girl, and Other Tales. 1882. Harper's Trade-List.

Embury, Lucy (1883-)
--The Listening Man. Hamilton, Russell, illus. LC 40-32776. xii, 283 p. illus. 24cm. c.1940. J. Messner, Inc.
--Painted Saints. Alexander, Guy, illus. LC 38-33010. 192 p. illus. 23 1/2cm. 1938. The Viking Press.

Emecheta, Florence Onye Buchi (1944-)
--The Moonlight Bride. LC 82-17816. 77 p. 22cm. 1983, c.1980. (ISBN 0-8076-1062-3). (ISBN 0-8076-1063-1). G. Braziller.
--Nowhere to Play: Based on a story by the author's twelve-year-old daughter Christy. Archer, Peter Kingsley (1926-), illus. LC 80-40596. (Illus.). 72 p. 21cm. c.1980. (ISBN 0-85031-366-X). Allison & Busby : Distributed in the U.S.A. by Schocken Books.
--The Wrestling Match. LC 82-17750. 74 p. 22cm. 1983, c.1980. (ISBN 0-8076-1060-7). (ISBN 0-8076-1061-5). G. Braziller.

Emerson, Alice B., pseud., see Stratemeyer Syndicate.

Emerson, Alice B., pseud.
--Betty Gordon and Her School Chums: Or, Bringing the Rebels to Terms. Stratemeyer Syndicate. Rogers, Walter S., illus. LC 24-14875. 2 p. l., 210 p. front. 19 1/2cm. (The Betty Gordon Ser.: Vol. 7). 1924. Cupples & Leon Co.
--Betty Gordon and the Hale Twins: Or, An Exciting Vacation. Stratemeyer Syndicate. Tandy, Russell H., illus. LC 29-112892. 1 p. l., 204 p. front. 19 1/2 cm. (The Betty Gordon Ser.: Vol. 12). 1929. Cupples & Leon Co.
--Betty Gordon and the Lost Pearls: Or, A Mystery of the Seaside. Stratemeyer Syndicate. Willis, Bess Goe, illus. (The Betty Gordon Ser.: Vol. 10). 1927. Cupples & Leon Co.
--Betty Gordon and the Mystery Girl: Or, The Secret at Sundown Hall. Stratemeyer Syndicate. LC 32-13784. 2 p. l., 208 p. front. 19 1/2 cm. (The Betty Gordon Ser.: Vol. 15). 1932. Cupples & Leon Co.
--Betty Gordon at Boarding School: Or, The Treasure of Indian Chasm. Stratemeyer Syndicate. Gooch, Thelma, illus. (The Betty Gordon Ser.: Vol. 4). 1921. Cupples & Leon Co.
--Betty Gordon at Bramble Farm: Or, The Mystery of a Nobody. Stratemeyer Syndicate. Gooch, Thelma, illus. (The Betty Gordon Ser.: Vol. 1). 1920. Cupples & Leon Co.
--Betty Gordon at Mountain Camp: Or, The Mystery of Ida Bellethorne. Stratemeyer Syndicate. Gooch, Thelma, illus. (The Betty Gordon Ser.: Vol. 5). 1922. Cupples & Leon Co.
--Betty Gordon at Mystery Farm: Or, Strange Doings at Rocky Ridge. Stratemeyer Syndicate. Tandy, Russell H., illus. LC 30-168918. 2 p. l., 204 p. front. 19 1/2 cm. (The Betty Gordon Ser.: Vol. 13). 1930. Cupples & Leon Co.
--Betty Gordon at Ocean Park: Or, School Chums on the Boardwalk. Stratemeyer Syndicate. Gooch, Thelma, illus. 2 p. l., 206 p. front. 19 1/2cm. (The Betty Gordon Ser.: Vol. 6). 1923. Cupples & Leon Co.
--Betty Gordon at Rainbow Ranch: Or, Cowboy Joe's Secret. Stratemeyer Syndicate. Townsend, Ernest N., illus. (The Betty Gordon Ser.: Vol. 8). 1925. Cupples & Leon Co.
--Betty Gordon in Mexican Wilds: Or, The Secret of the Mountains. Stratemeyer Syndicate. (Illus.). (The Betty Gordon Ser.: Vol. 9). 1926. Cupples & Leon Co.
--Betty Gordon in the Land of Oil: Or, The Farm That Was Worth a Fortune. Stratemeyer Syndicate. Gooch, Thelma, illus. (The Betty Gordon Ser.: Vol. 3). 1920. Cupples & Leon Co.
--Betty Gordon in Washington: Or, Strange Adventures in a Great City. Stratemeyer Syndicate. Gooch, Thelma, illus. (The Betty Gordon Ser.: Vol. 2). 1920. Cupples & Leon Co.
--Betty Gordon on No-Trail Island: Or, Uncovering a Queer Secret. Stratemeyer Syndicate. Suk, A., illus. LC 31-14179. 2 p. l., 207 p. front. 19 1/2cm. (The Betty Gordon Ser.: Vol. 14). 1931. Cupple & Leon Co.
--Betty Gordon on the Campus: Or, The Secret of the Trunk Room. Stratemeyer Syndicate. Townsend, Ernest N., illus. LC 28-157939. 2 p. l., 208 p. front. 19 1/2cm. (The Betty Gordon Ser.: Vol. 11). 1928. Cupples & Leon Co.
--Ruth Fielding and Baby June. Stratemeyer Syndicate. LeBeuthillier, M. J., illus. LC 31-14339. 2 p. l., 210 p. front. 19 1/2cm. (The Ruth Fielding Ser.: Vol. 27). 1931. Cupples & Leon Co.
--Ruth Fielding and Her Crowning Victory: Or, Winning Honors Abroad. Stratemeyer Syndicate. Tandy, Russell H., illus. LC 34-5903. 2 p. l., 210 p. front. 19 1/2cm. (The Ruth Fielding Ser.: Vol. 30). 1934. Cupples & Leon Co.
--Ruth Fielding and Her Double. Stratemeyer Syndicate. Tandy, Russell H., illus. LC 32-13785. 2 p. l., 204 p. front. 19 1/2cm. (The Ruth Fielding Ser.: Vol. 28). 1932. Cupples & Leon Co.
--Ruth Fielding and Her Great Scenario: Or, Striving for the Motion Picture Prize. Stratemeyer Syndicate. Willis, Bess Goe, illus. (Vol. 23). 1927. Cupples & Leon Co.
--Ruth Fielding and Her Greatest Triumph: Or, Saving Her Company from Disaster. Stratemeyer Syndicate. Tandy, Russell H., illus. LC 33-9285. 2 p. l., 202 p. front. 19 1/2cm. (The Ruth Fielding Ser.: Vol. 29). 1933. Cupples & Leon Co.
--Ruth Fielding and the Gypsies: Or, The Missing Pearl Necklace. Stratemeyer Syndicate. Rogers, Walter S., illus. LC 16-23592. 2 p. l., 204 p. front. 19cm. (The Ruth Fielding Ser.: Vol. 8). 1915. Cupples & Leon Co.
--Ruth Fielding at Briarwood Hall: Or, Solving the Campus Mystery. Stratemeyer Syndicate. (Illus.). (The Ruth Fielding Ser.: Vol. 2). 1913. Cupples & Leon Co.
--Ruth Fielding at Cameron Hall: Or, A Mysterious Disapperance. Stratemeyer Syndicate. Townsend, Ernest N., illus. LC 28-157918. 2 p. l., 210 p. front. 19 1/2cm. (The Ruth Fielding Ser.: Vol. 24). 1928. Cupples & Leon Co.
--Ruth Fielding at College: Or, The Missing Examination Papers. Stratemeyer Syndicate. Owen, Robert Emmett (1878-), illus. (The Ruth Fielding Ser.: Vol. 11). 1917. Cupples & Leon Co.
--Ruth Fielding at Golden Pass: Or, The Perils of an Artificial Avalanche. Stratemeyer Syndicate. (Illus.). (The Ruth Fielding Ser.: Vol. 21). 1925. Cupples & Leon Co.
--Ruth Fielding at Lighthouse Point: Or, Nita the Girl Castaway. Stratemeyer Syndicate. (The Ruth Fielding Ser.: Vol. 4). 1913. Cupples & Leon Co.
--Ruth Fielding at Silver Ranch: Or, Schoolgirls Among the Cowboys. Stratemeyer Syndicate. (Illus.). (The Ruth Fielding Ser.: Vol. 5). 1913. Cupples & Leon Co.
--Ruth Fielding at Snow Camp: Or, Lost in the Backwoods. Stratemeyer Syndicate. (Illus.). (The Ruth Fielding Ser.: Vol. 3). 1913. Cupples & Leon Co.
--Ruth Fielding at Sunrise Farm: Or, What Became of the Ruby Orphans. Stratemeyer Syndicate. (Illus.). (The Ruth Fielding Ser.: Vol. 7). 1915. Cupples & Leon Co.
--Ruth Fielding at the War Front: Or, The Hunt for The Lost Soldier. Stratemeyer Syndicate. Owen, Robert Emmett (1878-), illus. (The Ruth Fielding Ser.: Vol. 14). 1918. Cupples & Leon Co.
--Ruth Fielding Clearing Her Name: Or, The Rivals of Hollywood. Stratemeyer Syndicate. LC 29-112909. (Illus.). 2 p. l., 210 p. front. 19 1/2cm. (The Ruth Fielding Ser.: Vol. 25). 1929. Cupples & Leon Co.
--Ruth Fielding Down East: Or, The Hermit of Beach Plum Point. Stratemeyer Syndicate. Owen, Robert Emmett (1878-), illus. (The Ruth Fielding Ser.: Vol. 16). 1920. Cupples & Leon Co.
--Ruth Fielding Down in Dixie: Or, Great Days in the Land of Cotton. Stratemeyer Syndicate. Rogers, Walter S., illus. (The Ruth Fielding Ser.: Vol. 10). 1916. Cupples & Leon Co.
--Ruth Fielding Homeward Bound: Or, A Red Cross Worker's Ocean Perils. Stratemeyer Syndicate. (Illus.). (The Ruth Fielding Ser.: Vol. 15). 1919. Cupples & Leon Co.
--Ruth Fielding in Alaska: Or, The Miners of Snow Mountain. Stratemeyer Syndicate. (Illus.). (The Ruth Fielding Ser.: Vol. 22). 1926. Cupples & Leon Co.
--Ruth Fielding in Moving Pictures: Or, Helping the Dormitory Fund. Stratemeyer Syndicate. Rogers, Walter S., illus. (The Ruth Fielding Ser.: Vol. 9). 1916. Cupples & Leon Co.
--Ruth Fielding in Talking Pictures: Or, The Prisoners of the Tower. Stratemeyer Syndicate. LC 30-13352. (Illus.). 2 p. l., 208 p. front. 19 1/2cm. (The Ruth Fielding Ser.: Vol. 26). 1930. Cupples & Leon Co.
--Ruth Fielding in the Far North: Or, The Lost Motion Picture Company. Stratemeyer Syndicate. LC 24-14874. (Illus.). 2 p. l. 206 p. front. 19 1/2cm. (The Ruth Fielding Ser.: Vol. 20). 1924. Cupples & Leon Co.
--Ruth Fielding in The Great Northwest: Or, The Indian Girl Star of the Movies. Stratemeyer Syndicate. Gooch, Thelma, illus. (The Ruth Fielding Ser.: Vol. 17). 1921. Cupples & Leon Co.
--Ruth Fielding in the Red Cross: Or, Doing Her Bit for Uncle Sam. Stratemeyer Syndicate. (Illus.). (The Ruth Fielding Ser.: Vol. 13). 1918. Cupples & Leon Co.
--Ruth Fielding in the Saddle: Or, College Girls in the Land of Gold. Stratemeyer Syndicate. Owen, Robert Emmett (1878-), illus. LC 38-94274. 2 p. l., 208 p. front. 19 1/2cm. (The Ruth Fielding Ser.: Vol. 12). 1938, c.1917. Cupples & Leon Co.
--Ruth Fielding of the Red Mill: Or, Jasper Parloe's Secret. Stratemeyer Syndicate. (Illus.). (The Ruth Fielding Ser.: Vol. 1). 1913. Cupples & Leon Co.
--Ruth Fielding on Cliff Island: Or, The Old Hunter's Treasure Box. Stratemeyer Syndicate. Rogers, Walter S., illus. (The Ruth Fielding Ser.: Vol. 6). 1915. Cupples & Leon Co.
--Ruth Fielding on the St. Lawrence: Or, The Queer Old Man of the Thousand Islands. Stratemeyer Syndicate. Gooch, Thelma, illus. LC 22-9874. 2 p. l., 208 p. front. 19 1/2cm. (The Ruth Fielding Ser.: Vol. 18). 1922. Cupples & Leon Co.
--Ruth Fielding Treasure Hunting: Or, A Moving Picture That Became Real. Stratemeyer Syndicate. Gooch, Thelma, illus. (The Ruth Fielding Ser.: Vol. 19). 1923. Cupples & Leon Co.

Emerson, Caroline Dwight (1891-1973)
--Father's Big Improvements. Ayer, Margaret (0000-1981), illus. LC 36-194387. 5 p. l., 148 p. illus. 19 1/2cm. 1936. Frederick A. Stokes Company.
--Father's Big Improvements. Ayer, Margaret (0000-1981), illus. N.D. J. B. Lippincott Co.
--A Hat-Tub Tale: Or, On the Shores of the Bay of Fundy. Lenski, Lois (1893-1974), illus. LC 28-19759. ix, 185 p. incl. front., illus. 22 1/2cm. 1928. E.P. Dutton & Company.
--Indian Hunting Grounds. Schuyler, Remington (1884-1955), illus. LC 38-295482. 5 p. l., 3-191 p. incl. front., (map) illus. 21cm. 1938. Frederick A. Stokes Company.
--Indian Hunting Grounds. Schuyler, Remington (1884-1955), illus. N.D. J. B. Lippincott Co.
--The Little Green Car. Galdone, Paul (1914-), illus. LC 46-7349. 28 p. illus. (part. col.) 23 x 21 cm. (Story parade picture book). 1946. Grosset & Dunlap.
--The Magic Tunnel. Lufkin, Raymond H. (1897-), illus. N.D. J. B. Lippincott Co.
--The Magic Tunnel. Robinson, Jerry, illus. LC 68-27271. (Illus.). 122 p. 22cm. 1968, c.1964. Four Winds Press.
--The Magic Tunnel: A Story of Old New York. Lufkin, Raymond H. (1897-), illus. LC 40-30715. 4 p. l., 120 p. col. illus. 21 1/2cm. 1940. Frederick A. Stokes Company.
--A Merry-Go-Round of Modern Tales. Lenski, Lois (1893-1974), illus. LC 27-152151. vii p., 1 l., 173 p. illus. 22 1/2cm. 1927. E.P. Dutton & Company.
--Mickey Sees the U.S.A. Disney, Walt, Studio, illus. LC 44-5957. 3 p. l., 138 p. illus. (part col.) 22 cm. (On cover: Walt Disney story books). 1944. D. C. Heath and Company.
--Mr. Nip & Mr. Tuck: Being a Sequel to "A Hat-Tub Tale". rev. ed. Lenski, Lois (1893-1974), illus. LC 30-20202. v, 173 p. front., illus. 22 1/2 cm. 1930. E. P. Dutton & Company.
--Mr. Nip & Mr. Tuck in the Air. Nims, W. C., illus. LC 46-17780. 160 p. illus. 21 cm. 1946. E. P. Dutton and Company, Inc.
--School Days in Disneyville. Rev. ed. Disney, Walt, Studio, illus. LC 39-21182. 3 p. l., 102 p. col. illus. 21 1/2 cm. (On cover: Walt Disney story books). 1939. D. C. Heath and Company.

Emerson, Donald Conger (1913-)
--Court Decision. LC 67-15044. 218 p. 21cm. 1967. D. McKay Co.
--Span Across a River. LC 66-12127. 248p. 21cm. c.1966. McKay.

Emerson, Edith, illus.
--The Song of Roland. Sherwood, Merriam (1892-), tr. 1938. Mckay.

Emerson, Elizabeth U.
--Songs of Sunshine for Kindergarten School and Home. 8cm. 89p. 1900. O. Ditson Co.

Emerson, Elizabeth U. & Brown, L. Kate
--Stories in Songs for Kindergarten: Home and School. N.D. E. Steiger & Co.

Emerson, H. H. & Brothers, Dalziel, illus.
--The May Blossom: Or, the Princess and Her People. (Illustrated from Original Paintings by H. H. Emerson(the principal illustrator of "Afternoon Tea.")). 1882. A. C. Armstrong.

Emerson, Irving
--The Song-Land. N.D. Brown & Gross.

Emerson, Joyce, tr. see Baumann, Hans.
Emerson, Joyce, tr. see Benary-Isbert, Margot.
Emerson, Joyce, tr. see Braumann, Franz.
Emerson, Joyce, tr. see Guillot, Rene.
Emerson, Joyce, tr. see Hutterer, Franz.
Emerson, Joyce, tr. see Loisy, Jeanne.

Emerson, Ralph Waldo (1803-1882)
--Poems of Ralph Waldo Emerson. Adams, James Donald (1891-1968), ed. Burnett, Virgil, illus. LC 65-23774. (Illus.). (Poets Ser.). (gr. 4 up). 1965. (ISBN 0-690-63436-6). T Y Crowell.
--We Thank Thee. Blaisdell, Elinore (1904-), illus. LC 56-17225. unpaged. illus. 22cm. (A Coxy Corner book). 1955. Whitman Pub. Co.

Emerson, Sybil Davis (1895-)
--Jacques at the Window. Emerson, Sybil Davis (1895-), illus. LC 36-21192. 149, 3 p. incl. front., illus. 21 1/2 cm. c.1936. Thomas Y. Crowell Company.
--Pigeon House Inn. LC 39-21788. 4 p. l., 151, 1 p. illus. (part col.) 23 1/2 cm. 1939. Thomas Y. Crowell Company.

Emerson, Victoria & Thompson, James J.
--Into the World. Draper, J. Everett, illus. LC 50-10801. 125 p. illus. 20 cm. 1950. Woman's Press.

Emery, Anne Eleanor McGuigan (1907-)
--Bright Horizons. Vartanian, Raymond J., illus. LC 47-2059. v, 218 p. incl. front., illus. 19 1/2 cm. 1947. G. P. Putnam's Sons.
--Campus Melody. LC 55-5315. 189p. 22cm. 1955. Westminster Press.
--Carey's Fortune. LC 72-82412. 171 p. 21cm. 1969. Westminster Press.
--County Fair: A 4-H Romance. LC 53-7887. 222 p. 22cm. 1953. Macrae Smith.
--Danger in a Smiling Mask. LC 68-28107. 176 p. 21cm. 1968. Westminster Press.
--Dinny Gordon, Freshman. LC 59-8240. 190 p. 22cm. 1959. Macrae Smith.
--Dinny Gordon, Junior. LC 64-14874. 169 p. 22 cm. 1964. Macrae Smith.
--Dinny Gordon, Senior. LC 65-24902. 169 p. 22cm. 1965. Macrae Smith.
--Dinny Gordon, Sophomore. LC 61-15105. (gr. 7-10). 1961. (ISBN 0-8255-3115-2). Macrae.
--A Dream to Touch. LC 58-8726. 190 p. 21cm. 1958. Macrae Smith.
--First Love, Farewell. LC 58-9096. 21cm. 171p. (gr. 5-9). 1958. (ISBN 0-664-32202-6). Westminster.
--First Love, True Love. LC 56-5376. 191p. 22cm. c.1956. Westminster Press.
--First Orchid for Pat. LC 57-912676. 187p. 21cm. 1957. Westminster Press.
--Free Not to Love. LC 74-20764. 139 p. 21cm. 1975. (ISBN 0-664-32563-7). Westminster Press.
--Going Steady. LC 50-7106. 189 p. 22cm. 1950. Westminster Press.
--Hickory Hill. LC 55-107345. 206p. 21cm. (Her A4- H romance). 1955. Macrae Smith.
--High Note, Low Note. LC 54-5273. 214p. 21cm. 1954. Westminster Press.
--Jennie Lee, Patriot. LC 66-18337. 176p. 21cm. 1966. Westminster.
--Losing Game. 1965. E M Hale.
--Married on Wednesday: A Junior Novel. LC 57-6646. 223p. 22cm. 1957. Macrae Smith.
--Mountain Laurel. LC 48-3951. xii, 239 p. illus. 20 cm. 1948. G. P. Putnam's Sons.
--Mystery of the Opal Ring. LC 67-19695. 175 p. 21cm. 1967. Westminster Press.
--The Popular Crowd. LC 61-6766. 21cm. 171p. (gr. 7-10). 1961. (ISBN 0-664-32254-9). Westminster.
--Scarlet Royal. Lee, Manning De Villeneuve (1894-1980), illus. LC 52-10367. 223 p. illus. 22 cm. 1952. Macrae Smith.
--Scarlet Royal. Lee, Manning De Villeneuve (1894-1980), illus. LC 76-23407. 223 21. 1976, c.1952. (ISBN 0-664-32604-8). Westminster Press.
--Senior Year. Krush, Beth (1918-), illus. LC 49-8568. 208 p. illus. 21 cm. 1949. Westminster Press.
--The Sky Is Falling. LC 79-113472. 159 p. 21cm. 1970. Westminster Press.
--Sorority Girl. Horwitz, Richard, illus. LC 52-7049. 191 p. 22cm. 1952. Westminster Press.
--A Spy in Old Detroit. (Illus.). (gr. 6-9). 1963. (ISBN 0-8382-0786-3). Hale.
--A Spy in Old Detroit. Vestal, Herman B., illus. LC 63-12792. (Illus.). 22cm. 206p. (gr. 3-7). 1963. Rand.
--A Spy in Old New Orleans. Weiss, Emil (1896-1965), illus. LC 60-8262. (Illus.). 21cm. 237p. (gr. 3-6). 1960. (ISBN 0-528-80098-1). Rand.
--A Spy in Old Philadelphia. Vestal, Herman B., illus. LC 58-8953. (Illus.). 21cm. 208p. (gr. 3-6). 1958. (ISBN 0-528-80100-7). Rand.
--A Spy in Old West Point. Bjorklund, Lorence F. (1913-1978), illus. (Illus.). (gr. 6-12). 1965. (ISBN 0-528-87648-1). Rand.
--A Spy in Old West Point. Bjorklund, Lorence F. (1913-1978), illus. LC 65-19441. 191p. illus. 22cm. c.1965. Rand McNally.
--A Spy in Old West Point. Bjorklund, Lorence F. (1913-1978), illus. LC 65-19441. (Illus.). 22cm. 191p. (gr. 4-6). 1965. (ISBN 0-528-80093-0). Rand.

AUTHOR INDEX ENGSTROM, THEODORE

--Stepfamily. LC 79-26908. 141 p. 21cm. c.1980. (ISBN 0-664-32660-9). Westminster Press.
--Sweet Sixteen. LC 56-104377. 188p. 21cm. 1956. Macrae Smith Co.
--That Archer Girl. LC 59-11557. 21cm. 175p. 1959. (ISBN 0-664-32223-9). Westminster Press.
--Tradition. King, Ruth, illus. LC 47-30021. 250 p. 21 cm. 1946. The Vanguard Press, Inc.
--Vagabond Summer. LC 52-11539. 183 p. 22cm. 1953. Westminster Press.

Emery, Anne Eleanor McGuigan (1907-)
--The Losing Game. LC 65-10078. 141 p. 21 cm. c.1965. Westminster Press.

Emery, Carlyle
--Twinkle Town Tales... Story in Rhyme. Henderson, Arthur, illus. LC 29-3494. v. col. illus. 21 1/2 cm. c.1920. Hamilton-Brown Shoe Company.

Emery, Mabel Sarah (1859-)
--Real Children in Many Lands: A Series of Visits Through the Stereoscope. LC 5-20731. 222 p. 19 1/2 cm. c.1905. Underwood & Underwood.
--Real Children in Many Lands: A Series of Visits Through the Stereoscope, new ed., rev. and enl. LC 14-2950. 254 p. 19 1/2 cm. c.1914. Underwood & Underwood.
--When We Were Little. Clark, Edith N., illus. LC 13-319684. 96 p. incl. front., 6 pl. 21 cm. 1894. Universalist Publishing House.

Emery, Russell Guy (1908-)
--Action at Third. LC 57-6642. (Illus.). 190 p. 22cm. 1957. Macrae Smith.
--Adventure North. Lee, Manning De Villeneuve (1894-1980), illus. LC 47-2850. 246 p. illus. 21 1/2 cm. 1947. Macrae-Smith-Company.
--Gray Line and Gold. LC 51-14001. 207 p. 22 cm. 1951. Macrae Smith.
--High, Inside!. (Famous Sports Stories). N.D. Grosset & Dunlap.
--High, Inside!. LC 48-8595. 208 p. 22 cm. 1948. Macrae Smith Co.
--Hyland of the Hawks. LC 55-6449. 208 p. 21cm. 1955. Macrae Smith.
--Rebound. LC 55-10737. 190p. 21cm. 1955. Macrae Smith.
--Relief Pitcher. N.D. Macrae Smith Co.
--T-Quarterback. N.D. Grosset & Dunlap.
--T-Quarterback. LC 49-6498. 201 p. 22 cm. 1949. Macrae Smith Co.
--Warren of West Point. LC 50-10023. 202 p. 21cm. 1950. Macrae Smith.
--Wings Over West Point. Deitch, Harry, illus. LC 40-329829. 4 p. l., 11-297 p. illus. 21 cm. c.1940. Macrae-Smith Company.

Emery, Samuel
--Chickens and Vegetables, Incorporated. LC 26-15470. 3 p. l., 103, 1 p. 19 1/2 cm. 1926. D. Appleton and Company.

Emett, Frederick Rowland (1906-)
--New World for Nellie. LC 52-6903. (Illus.). 29cm. 38p. 1952. Harcourt, Brace.

Emley, Mabel R.
--Her Romance and the Value of a Trained Mind. LC 19-13889. 31 p. 19 1/2cm. c.1919. Saulsbury Pub.

Emlin, James
--Stories in Verse for Children. Emlin, James, illus. LC 2-29410. 20cm. 79p. 1902. J. C. Winston Co.

Emmett, Bruce (1949-)
--Rooftop Wizard: A Storybook with Magic Tricks. Emmett, Bruce (1949-), illus. LC 74-1140. (Illus.). 47 p. 26cm. 1974. (ISBN 0-13-782425-4). Prentice-Hall.

Emmett, Elizabeth
--The Land He Loved, a Story of Old Narragansett. Parmelee, Lydia H., illus. LC 40-30537. 3 p. l., 291 p. illus. 21 cm. 1940. The Macmillan Company.
--Secret in a Snuffbox. Parmelee, Lydia H., illus. LC 41-15010. 3 p. l., 268 p. illus. 21 cm. 1941. The Macmillan Company.

Emmons, Ramona Ware, jt. auth. see Pope, Billy N.

Emmrich, Dorothy, tr. see Capuana, Luigi.

Emmrich, Dorothy, tr. see Ubertis-Gray, Corinna Teresa.

E. M. P
--The Story of a Pin: Or, The Changes and Chances of an Eventful Life. (Illus.). N.D. Thomas Nelson & Sons.

Emrich, Duncan Black MacDonald see MacDonald, Blackie, pseud.

Emrich, Duncan Black MacDonald, jt. ed. see Jaquith, Priscilla.

Emrich, Duncan Black MacDonald (1908-), ed.
--The Hodgepodge Book: An Almanac of American Folklore; Containing All Manner of Curious, Interesting, and Out-of-the-Way Information Drawn from American Folklore, and Not to Be Found Anywhere Else in the World; As Well As Jokes, Conundrums, Riddles, Puzzles, and Other Matter Designed to Amuse and Entertain-All of It Most Instructive and Delightful. MacDonald, Blackie, pseud. Ohlsson, Ib (1935-), illus. LC 72-77811. (Illus.). 367 p. 24cm. 1972. Four Winds Press.
--Nonsense Book. Macdonald, Blackie, pseud. Ohlsson, Ib (1935-), illus. LC 77-105339. (Illus.). 240p. 272p. (gr. 7 up). 1970. (ISBN 0-590-07157-2, Four Winds). Scholastic Inc.
--Riddles & Jokes & Foolish Facts. MacDonald, Blackie, pseud. Ohlsson, Ib (1935-), illus. (gr. 4-6). 1976. (ISBN 0-590-04281-5). Scholastic Inc.
--The Whim-Wham Book. MacDonald, Blackie, pseud. Ohlsson, Ib (1935-), illus. LC 75-9872. (Illus.). 335 p. 24cm. 1975. (ISBN 0-590-07315-X). Four Winds Press.

Emrich, Marion Vallat (1910-)
--The Child's Book of Folklore. Korson, George Gershon (1899-), ed. LC 47-11876. xv, 240 p. illus. 21 cm. 1947. Dial Press.
--The Child's Book of Folklore. Korson, George Gershon (1899-), ed. Cosgrave, John O'Hara, II (1908-1968), illus. LC 68-57607. xv, 240 p. illus. 21 cm. 1964. Dial Press.

Enault, Louis (1824-1900)
--The Captain's Dog. (Illus.). (Sunshine Library for Young People). 1900. T. Y. Crowell & Co.
--The Captain's Dog. (Illus.). N.D. Thomas Y. Crowell Co.'s Catalogue.
--The Captain's Dog. Grabianski, Janusz (1928-1976), illus. LC 76-146804. (Illus.). 32 p. 29cm. 1971. (ISBN 0-531-01984-5). Watts.

Encking, Louise Franziska (1879-)
--The Little Gardeners. N.D. Albert Whitman & Co.
--The Toymaker. Kukenthal, Fritz, illus. N.D. Albert Whitman & Co.

Encking, Louise F., tr. see Hoffmann, Ernst Theodor Amadeus.

Encking, Louise Franziska (1879-), retold by see Thelen, Gerda.

Enderle, Judith A., jt. auth. see Tessler, Stephanie Gordon.

Enderle, Judith Ann, jt. auth. see Tessler, Stephanie Gordon.

Enderle, Judith Ann (1941-)
--Good Junk. Gibbons, Gail (1944-), illus. LC 80-26315. (Illus.). 32 p. c.1981. (ISBN 0-525-66720-2). Elsevier/Nelson Books.

Endersby, Frank
--The Boy & the Horse. Endersby, Frank, illus. (Illus.). 16p. 1980. (ISBN 0-85953-098-1, Pub. by Child's Play England). Playspaces.

Endicott, Ruth Belmore, pseud., see Stratemeyer Syndicate.

Endicott, Ruth Belmore, pseud.
--Carolyn of the Corners. Stratemeyer Syndicate. Repr. of 1918 ed (Pub. by Dodd, Mead & Co.). (The Carolyn Ser.: Vol. 1). 1919. Grosset & Dunlap.
--Carolyn of the Corners. Stratemeyer Syndicate. Caswell, Edward C., illus. (The Carolyn Ser.: Vol. 1). 1918. Dodd, Mead & Co.
--Carolyn of the Sunny Heart. Stratemeyer Syndicate. Repr. of 1919 ed (Pub. by Dodd, Mead & Co.). (The Carolyn Ser.: Vol. 2). 1920. Grosset & Dunlap.
--Carolyn of the Sunny Heart. Stratemeyer Syndicate. Caswell, Edward C., illus. (The Carolyn Ser.: Vol. 2). 1919. Dodd, Mead & Co.

Endicott, W. E., tr.
--Sons of the Saddle. (Juvenile Classics). 1874. Henry L. Shepard & Co.

Endore, Gamuel Gay (1900-1970), tr. see Loti, Pierre.

Enerson, Laura
--Our Library Lives in a Bus. 1st ed. Robin, pseud. (1915-), illus. Roberts, Eric. LC 77-71462. (Illus.). 45 p. 1977. Cover Pub. Co.

Enete, William Walters (1893-)
--Sammy Writes a Book. LC 39-34138. 112 p. illus. (incl. ports.) 20 cm. c.1939. Broadman Press.

Engdahl, Sylvia Louise (1933-)
--Beyond the Tomorrow Mountains. 1st ed. Cuffari, Richard (1925-1978), illus. LC 72-86934. (Illus.). 257 p. 25cm. 1973. Atheneum.
--The Doors of the Universe. LC 80-18804. p. cm. 1981. (ISBN 0-689-30807-8). Atheneum.
--Enchantress from the Stars. 1st ed. Shackell, Rodney, illus. LC 74-98609. (Illus.). 275 p. 27cm. 1970. Atheneum. **Award: (JNM).**
--The Far Side of Evil. Cuffari, Richard (1925-1978), illus. LC 77-134808. (Illus.). 292 p. 21cm. (Aladdin Book, A28). 1973, c.1971. Atheneum.
--Journey Between Worlds. 1st ed. McCrea, James Craig, Jr. (1920-) & McCrea, Ruth Pirman (1921-), illus. LC 72-115076. (Illus.). 235 p. 23cm. 1970. Atheneum.
--My World Is Earth. Cuffari, Richard (1925-1978), illus. LC 78-11317. p. cm. 1979. (ISBN 0-689-30678-4). Atheneum.
--This Star Shall Abide. 1st ed. Cuffari, Richard (1925-1978), illus. LC 79-175553. (Illus.). 247 p. 25cm. 1972. Atheneum.

Engdahl, Sylvia Louise (1933-), ed.
--Anywhere, Anywhen: Stories of Tomorrow. LC 76-5485. x, 301 24. 324p. (gr. 6-12). 1976. (ISBN 0-689-30537-0). Atheneum.

Engdahl, Sylvia Louise (1933-) & Roberson, Rick James (1956-), eds.
--Universe Ahead: Stories of the Future. Cuffari, Richard (1925-1978), illus. LC 75-8849. p. cm. 1975. (ISBN 0-689-30471-9). Atheneum.

Engebrecht, Patricia Ann (1935-)
--The Promise of Moonstone: A Novel. 1st. ed. LC 82-20659. p. cm. c.1983. (ISBN 0-8253-0123-8). Beaufort Books.
--Under the Haystack. 1st. ed. LC 72-14225. 124 p. 22cm. 1973. (ISBN 0-8407-6296-8). T. Nelson.

Engebretson, Betty
--What Happened to George?. Friend, Esther, illus. LC 47-6458. 40 col. illus. 31. N.D. Rand McNally & Co.
--What Happened to George!. Opitz, Marge, illus. LC 58-6561. (Illus.). 21cm. (Tip-Top Elf Book: 1006). 1958. Rand McNally.

Engel, Beth Bland (1921-)
--Big Words. LC 82-5036. p. cm. c.1982. (ISBN 0-525-66779-2). Lodestar Books.
--Ride the Pine Sapling. LC 77-25672. 199 p. 21cm. c.1978. (ISBN 0-06-021815-0). (ISBN 0-06-021816-9). Harper & Row.

Engel, Deirdre, tr. see Dumas, Philippe.

Engel, Dolores
--Voyage of the Kon-Tiki. Bale, Gary, illus. LC 78-26766. (Illus.). (Raintree Great Adventures). (gr. 3-6). 1979. (ISBN 0-8393-0151-0). Raintree Pubs.

Engel, Erna Michaelis
--Nature Rhymes for Little Folks. LC 25-23615. 160p. illus. 21 1/2cm. c.1925. Erie Printin Co.

Engelbach, Alfred H.
--Bertie and His Sister: A Domestic Story. (Illus.). N.D. E & J B Young.
--Gretchen's Troubles. N.D. Pott, Young & Co.
--Gretchen's Troubles: Or, A Story of German Peasant Life for Girls. (Illus.). N.D. E. & J. B. Young & Co.
--Kitty Bligh's Birthday. (Illus.). N.D. E & J B Young.
--Monsieur Jack: A Tale of the Old War Time. (Illus.). N.D. E & J B Young.
--Ned Lyttleton's Little One: A Tale of a Traveller. (Illus.). N.D. E & J B Young.
--Poor Little Gaspard's Drum. (Illus.). N.D. E & J B Young.
--Poor Little Gaspard's Drum. N.D. Pott, Young & Co.
--Two Campaigns, 1 of 4 Vols. (Illus.). (Rosamond's Book Shelf). N.D. Set. Pott, Young & Co.
--The Wreck of the Osprey. (Illus.). (Ellerslie House Library). N.D. Methodist Bk Concern.
--Wreck of the Osprey. (Ellerslie House Library). N.D. Nelson & Phillips.
--The Wreck of the Osprey: A Story for Boy. (Illus., Pub. by Society for Promoting Christian Knowledge). N.D. E & J B Young.

Engelbert, Irene Butler
--Can Green Tomatoes Hatch? And Other Stories. McDonald, Ralph J., illus. LC 75-1932. (Illus.). 127 p. 21cm. (Crown book). 1975. (ISBN 0-8127-0095-3). Southern Pub. Association.
--Listen, my Children. Baerg, Harry John (1909-), illus. LC 58-17825. 126 p. illus. 23cm. 1957. Herald Pub. Association.
--Old Stubborn & Other Stories. Granstaff, William (1925-), illus. (gr. 4-6). N.D. Southern Pub.

Engelhard, Georgia
--Peterli and the Mountain. Gekiere, Madeleine (1919-), illus. LC 54-5586. (Illus.). 39 p. 24cm. 1954. Lippincott.

Engelhardt, James F.
--Let Freedom Ring. (Children's Theatre Playscript Ser.). 1975. (ISBN 0-88020-035-9). Coach Hse.

Engeman, Jack
--My first days at school. (Illus.). N.D. Bobbs-Merrill Co, Inc.

Engen, Sadie O.
--John Tay: Messenger to Pitcairn. (Trailblazer Ser.). 1981. (ISBN 0-8163-0405-X). Pacific Pr Pub Assn.

England, George Allan (1877-)
--Adventure Isle. Lee, Manning De Villeneuve (1894-1980), illus. LC 26-16359. vii, 269 p. front, plates. 19 1/2 cm. c.1926. The Century Co.

Engle, Alice E.
--The Story of Four Acorns. (Illus.). N.D. D. Lothrop & Co.

Engle, Eloise Hopper (1923-)
--Countdown for Cindy. LC 62-11630. 191 p. 22cm. 1962. C. S. Hammond.
--Dawn Mission: A Flight Nurse in Korea. Zeller, Dorothy N., frwd. by. LC 62-7786. 190p. c.1962. John Day.
--Princess of Paradise. Hawaii's Last Queen. LC 62-14902. 183p. 21cm. (Daughters of valor ser.). c.1962. John Day.
--Sea Challenge: The Epic Voyage of Magellan. Mott, Herb, illus. LC 62-10582. 221p. 22cm. c.1962. Hammond.

Engle, Joanna
--Cap'n Kid Goes to the South Pole. Paris, Pat, illus. LC 82-61013. (Illus.). 32p. (Sea World Mini Storybooks). (gr. 1-6). 1983. (ISBN 0-394-85643-0). Random.

Engle, Paul Hamilton (1908-)
--Golden Child. Fisher, Leonard Everett (1924-), illus. (Illus.). (gr. 4-6). N.D. (ISBN 0-525-30772-9). Dutton.
--Who's Afraid?. Prohaska, Ray (1901-), illus. LC 63-8303. 63 p. illus. 30 cm. (Modern masters book for children). 1963. Crowell-Collier Press.

Engle, William
--The G-Men Smash the "Professor's" Gang. Beebe, Robb (1891-), illus. LC 37-809. viii p., 1 l., 205 p. front. 19 cm. (The G. Men Stories). c.1936. Grosset & Dunlap.

Englebert, Victor (1933-)
--Camera on Africa: The World of an Ethiopian Boy. Englebert, Victor (1933-), photos by. 96p. N.D. Harcourt Brace Jovanovich.
--Camera on Ghana: The World of a Young Fisherman. Englebert, Victor (1933-), photos by. 96p. N.D. Harcourt Brace Jovanovich.
--Camera on the Sahara: The World of Three Young Nomads. Englebert, Victor (1933-), photos by. 64p. N.D. Harcourt Brace Jovanovich.
--The Goats of Agadez. Englebert, Victor (1933-), photos by. LC 72-76363. (Illus.). 48p. (gr. k-4). 1973. (ISBN 0-15-231118-1, HJ). HarBraceJ.

Englefield, Cicely (1893-)
--A House for a Mouse. Englefield, Cicely (1893-), illus. LC 38-8841. 41, 2 p. illus. 15 1/2 cm. 1937. Oxford University Press.
--Katie the Caterpillar. Englefield, Cicely (1893-), illus. LC 33-8842. 41, 2 p. illus. 15 1/2 cm. 1937. Oxford University Press.
--The Tail of a Guinea Pig. Englefield, Cicely (1893-), illus. LC 38-8907. (Illus.). 16cm. 43p. 1937. Oxford Univ. Press.

English, Douglas (1870-)
--Beasties Courageous. (Illus.). N.D. Cassell & Co.
--Beasties Courageous. N.D. Funk & Wagnalls.
--A Book of Nimble Beasts. (Illus.). N.D. Dana Estes & Co.
--Wee Tim'rous Beasties. (Illus.). N.D. Cassell & Co.
--Wee Tim'rous Beasties. N.D. Funk & Wagnalls.

English Folk Dance & Song Society
--English Folk Dancing. 1975. (ISBN 0-8277-4094-8). British Bk Ctr.

English, James Wilson (1915-)
--Border Adventure. LC 52-13709. 224 p. 21 cm. 1952. Abelard Press.
--The Rin Tin Story. N.D. Dodd, Mead & Co.
--Tailbone Patrol. Wells, Peter (1912-), illus. LC 55-13588. 186 p. illus. 21 cm. 1955. Holiday House.
--Tops in Troop 10. Shortall, Leonard W., illus. LC 66-11104. 168p. illus. 21cm. 1966. (ISBN 0-02-733580-1). Macmillan.

English, Mary Secrest
--Aunt Mary's Wonderland: Short Stories for Children. LC 84-204943. x, 93 p. 22cm. c.1984. E. Uhlan Associates.
--Aunt Mary's Wonderland: Short Stories for Children. (ps-2). 1984. (ISBN 0-682-40228-1). Exposition Pr FL.

English, Thomas Dunn (1819-1902)
--Fairy Stories and Wonder Tales. Noll, Florence English, ed. Tucker, Elizabeth S., illus. LC 12-32105. 6 p. l., 303 p. front., plates. 19 cm. c.1897. Frederick A. Stokes Company.
--The Little Giant. The Big Dwarf and Two Other Wonder-Tales for Boys and Girls from Eight to Eighty Years Old. Noll, Arthur Howard, ed. Perkins, Lucy Fitch, Mrs. (1865-1937), illus. LC 4-28199. 3 p. l., v-vi p., 3 l., 13-150 p. front., illus., plates. 25 1/2 cm. 1904. A. C. McClurg & Co.

English, Thomas Hopkins (1895-), ed. see Harris, Joel Chandler.

Engstrom, Theodore Wilhelm (1916-), ed.
--Bedtime Stories for Boys and Girls. LC 51-14472. 162 p. illus. 24 cm. 1951. Zondervan Pub. House.
--Bible Stories for Boys & Girls. Doares, Robert G., illus. (Illus.). (gr. k-4). 1971. (ISBN 0-310-24211-8). Zondervan.

Engvick, William, ed. see Wilder, Alec.

Ennis, Frank (1917-)
--Benny and the Birds. Bisch, Charlene, illus. LC 52-67535. unpaged. illus. 29 cm. c.1952. Tell Well Press.
Enoch, Lora L., jt. auth. see Rogers, Ethel.
Enos, Larry J.
--Backcourt Mischief. LC 77-73463. iii, 151 p. 19cm. 1977. Adams Press.
Enrick
--Wishes. (gr. 1-4). 1970. (ISBN 0-07-019425-4). (ISBN 0-07-019426-2). McGraw.
Enright, Dennis Joseph (1920-)
--Beyond Land's End. LC 80-476920. 139 p. 21cm. 1979. (ISBN 0-7011-2352-4). Chatto & Windus.
--The Joke Shop. LC 76-27570. 124 21. 1976. (ISBN 0-679-20385-0). D. McKay Co.
--Wild Ghost Chase. (Illus.). 138p. (gr. 4-7). 1980. (ISBN 0-7011-2285-4, Pub. by Chatto Bodley Jonathan). Merrimack Pub Cir.
Enright, Elizabeth (1909-1968)
--Borrowed Summer and Other Stories. Enright, Elizabeth (1909-1968), illus. 1946. Rinehart.
--A Christmas Tree for Lydia. Enright, Elizabeth (1909-1968), illus. LC 51-8255. 14cm. 38p. 1951. Rinehart.
--Doublefields: Memoirs and Stories. Enright, Elizabeth (1909-1968), illus. 1967. Harcourt Brace.
--The Four-Story Mistake. Enright, Elizabeth (1909-1968), illus. LC 42-22828. 6 p. l., 3-177 p. col. front., col. illus. 21 1/2 cm. 1942. Farrar & Rinehart, Inc.
--Gone-Away Lake. 1st ed. Krush, Joe (1918-) & Krush, Beth (1918-), illus. LC 57-7172. (Illus.). 192 p. 21cm. 1957. Harcourt, Brace. **Awards: (ALA); (JNM).**
--Kintu: A Congo Adventure. Enright, Elizabeth (1909-1968), illus. LC 35-19682. 5 p. l., 3-54 p. incl. illus. (part col.) col. plates. 20 cm. 1935. Farrar and Rinehart, Inc.
--The Melendy Family: Containing "The Saturdays" "The Four-Story Mistake" & "Then There Were Five". Enright, Elizabeth (1909-1968), illus. LC 47-30925. (Illus.). 241p. (gr. 4-6). 1947. (ISBN 0-03-032840-3). HR&W.
--The Moment Before the Rain. Enright, Elizabeth (1909-1968), illus. 1955. Harcourt Brace.
--Return to Gone-Away. Krush, Joe (1918-) & Krush, Beth (1918-), illus. LC 61-6113. (Illus.). 191 p. 19cm. (Voyager Book, 74). 1973, c.1961. (ISBN 0-15-676900-X). Harcourt.
--The Riddle of the Fly and Other Stories. Enright, Elizabeth (1909-1968), illus. 1959. Harcourt Brace.
--The Saturdays. Enright, Elizabeth (1909-1968), illus. LC 41-17880. 6 1, 3-175 incl. col. front., col. illus. 21. 1941. (ISBN 0-03-089690-8). Farrar & Rinehart.
--The Sea is All Around. Enright, Elizabeth (1909-1968), illus. LC 40-27691. (Illus.). 124p. (gr. 4-6). 1940. (ISBN 0-03-062690-0). HR&W.
--Spiderweb for Two: A Melendy Maze. Enright, Elizabeth (1909-1968), illus. LC 51-13712. (Illus.). 209 p. 22cm. 1951. Rinehart.
--Tatsinda. 1st ed. Haas, Irene (1929-), illus. LC 63-7888. (Illus.). 80 p. 23cm. 1963. (ISBN 0-15-284276-4). Harcourt, Brace & World. **Award: (ALA).**
--Then There Were Five. Enright, Elizabeth (1909-1968), illus. LC 44-7330. 6 p. l., 3-241 p. incl. front., illus. 21 cm. 1944. Farrar & Rinehart, Inc.
--Thimble Summer. Enright, Elizabeth (1909-1968), illus. LC 38-27586. (Illus.). 5 p.l., 3-124 p. col. front 22cm. 1938. Farrar & Rinehart, Incorporated. **Award: (JNM).**
--Thimble Summer. Enright, Elizabeth (1909-1968), illus. LC 66-43350. 124 p. illus. (part col.) 22 cm. c.1938. Holt, Rinehart and Winston.
--Thimble Summer. Enright, Elizabeth (1909-1968), illus. 1976. Holt.
--Zeee. 1st ed. Haas, Irene (1929-), illus. LC 65-10064. (Illus.). 46 p. 20cm. 1965. (ISBN 0-15-299955-8). Harcourt, Brace & World.
Enright, Walter J. Pat (1879-)
--Al Alligator, and How He Learned to Play the Banjo. Enright, Walter J. Pat (1879-), illus. LC 47-31039. 98 p. illus. (part col.) 26 cm. 1947. Dodd, Mead.
--Sailor Jim's Cave: A Mystery of Buried Treasure in Florida. Enright, Walter J. Pat (1879-), illus. LC 51-13651. 270 p. illus. 21 cm. 1951. Dodd, Mead.
Enriquez, C. M.
--Khyberie: The Story of a Pony on the Indian Frontier. N.D. MacMillan.
Ensdaile, S. K.
--Discipline for Penelope. N.D. MacMillan.
Enslow, Ella, jt. auth. see Harlow, Alvin Fay.
Ensor, Dorothy
--The Adventures of Hatim Tai. Baynes, Pauline Diana (1922-), illus. LC 62-6508. (An adaptation of Duncan Forbe's Translation of the original legends). (Illus.). 21cm. 89p. 1962, c.1960. H. Z. Walck.
Enters, Angna
--Silly Girl. N.D. Houghton Mifflin Co.
Entwhistle, Mary, jt. auth. see Chalmers, Muriel.
Entwistle, Mary
--Little Children of Mission Lands. LC 25-7501. 199 p. front., illus., plates. 20 cm. $1.75. c.1925. George H. Doran Company.
Entwistle, Mary & Harris, Elizabeth (1883-)
--The Call Drum: African Stories and Studies for Primary Children. teachers ed. LC 28-24840. 4p. l., 3-138p. 20cm. c.1928. Friendship Press.
Ephron, Delia (1944-)
--Santa and Alex. 1st ed. Primavera, Elise, illus. LC 83-14848. (Illus.). 46 p. c.1983. (ISBN 0-316-24300-0). Little, Brown.
Epictetus
--Epictetus. (Classics for Children). N.D. Ginn and Company.
Epp, Margaret Agnes see Goossen, Agnes, pseud.
Epp, Margaret Agnes (1913-)
--Anita and the Driftwood House. 127p. 1957. Moody Press.
--Call of the Wahoa & Other Adventures. 128p. (Pre-Teen Bks.). (gr. 4-7). 1971. (ISBN 0-8024-3110-0). Moody.
--Great Frederick & Other Stories. line drawings. 128p. (gr. 7 up). 1971. (ISBN 0-8024-1325-0). Moody.
--Prairie Princess. Doares, Robert G., illus. LC 67-14389. 127p. illus. 20cm. 1967. Moody.
--The Princess and the Pelican. Doares, Robert G., illus. LC 68-18888. (Illus.). 127 p. 20cm. 1968. Moody Press.
--Princess Rides a Panther. Doares, Robert G., illus. LC 76-123156. (Illus.). 128p. (Juvenile Fiction Ser.). (gr. 1-5). 1970. Moody.
--Runaway at the Running K. (gr. 6-8). 1972. (ISBN 0-8024-0079-5, MG). Moody.
--Sarah & the Darnley Boys. 120p. (gr. 6-12). 1981. (ISBN 0-88207-490-3). Victor Bks.
--Sarah and the Lost Friendship. LC 78-65203. (Illus.). 131 p. 20cm. (Winner book). (Prairie Adventure Ser.). c.1979. (ISBN 0-88207-483-0). Victor Books.
--Sarah & the Magic Twenty-Fifth. Doares, Robert G., illus. LC 76-50172. (Illus.). 131 p. 20cm. (Winner book). (Prairie Adventure Ser.). c.1977. (ISBN 0-88207-477-6). Victor Books.
--Sarah & the Mystery of the Hidden Boy. LC 79-65043. 144p. (gr. 2-6). 1979. (ISBN 0-88207-485-7). Victor Bks.
--Sarah & the Pelican. Doares, Robert G., illus. LC 76-50171. (Illus.). 132 p. 20cm. (Winner book). (Prairie Adventure Ser.). c.1977. (ISBN 0-88207-476-8). Victor Books.
Eppenstein, Louise (1892-)
--Sally goes shopping alone. Friend, Esther, illus. LC 40-82434. 11-44p. col. front., col. ill. 29 1/2 x 191/2cm. c.1940. Platt & Munk.
--Sally goes to the Circus Alone. Staples, Jean, illus. LC 52-14344. 44 p. illus. 24cm. 1952, c.1953. Platt & Munk.
--Sally Goes Traveling Alone. Staples, Jean, illus. LC 48-5159. 44 p. illus. 24 cm. 1947. Platt & Munk Co.
Epperson, Eleanor & Epperson, John
--Timberjack and the Chief. LC 84-62904. (Illus.). v. 1. 23cm. c.1984. (ISBN 0-9614114-0-6). Pillar Point Press.
Epperson, John, jt. auth. see Epperson, Eleanor.
Eppes, Allen
--Dairy Maid. LC 40-35813. 253 p. 19 1/2 cm. c.1940. Gramercy Publishing Co.
Epstein, Anne Merrick (1931-)
--Good Stones. Meddaugh, Susan (1944-), illus. LC 77-23188. (Illus.). 204 p. 22cm. 1977. (ISBN 0-395-25154-0). Houghton Mifflin.
--Stone Man, Stone House. 1st ed. Schongut, Emanuel, illus. LC 71-136297. (Illus.). 48 p. 22cm. 1972. Doubleday.
Epstein, Beryl Williams see Coe, Douglas, pseud.
Epstein, Beryl Williams, jt. auth. see Allen, Adam.
Epstein, Beryl Williams, jt. auth. see Epstein, Samuel.
Epstein, Beryl Williams (1910-)
--Lucky, Lucky White Horse. Carpenter, Mia, illus. LC 64-19607. 59 p. illus. 23 cm. 1965. Harper & Row.
Epstein, Beryl Williams (1910-) & Davis, Dorrit
--Two Sisters and Some Hornets. Wells, Rosemary, illus. LC 70-179102. (Illus.). 32 p. 24cm. 1972. Holiday House.
Epstein, Beryl Williams (1910-) & Epstein, Samuel (1909-)
--Change for a Penny. Powers, Richard M. Gorman (1921-), illus. LC 59-11429. 21cm. 254p. 1959. Coward-McCann Inc.
Epstein, Len, jt. auth. see Haynes, Henry Louis.
Epstein, Leslie (1936-)
--Stanley the Starfish. LC 79-17987. p. cm. 1980. (ISBN 0-03-052081-9). Holt, Rinehart and Winston.
Epstein, Morris, jt. ed. see Schloss, Ezekiel.
Epstein, Morris (1921-1973)
--My Holiday Story Book. rev. ed. (gr. 4-5). 1958. (ISBN 0-87068-368-3). Ktav.
Epstein, Perle Sherry (1938-)
--Monsters: Their Histories, Homes & Habits. LC 72-97496. 128p. (gr. 6-9). 1973. Doubleday.
Epstein, Samuel see Allen, Adam, pseud.
Epstein, Samuel see Campbell, Bruce, pseud.
Epstein, Samuel see Colt, Martin, pseud.
Epstein, Samuel, jt. auth. see Epstein, Beryl Williams.
Epstein, Samuel (1909-)
--The Black Thumb Mystery. Campbell, Bruce, pseud. LC 50-6596. vii, 216 p. front. 20 cm. (His The Ken Holt mystery stories, 3). 1950. Grosset & Dunlap.
--The Clue of the Coiled Cobra. Campbell, Bruce, pseud. LC 51-4333. 214 p. front. 20 cm. (His The Ken Holt mystery stories, 5). 1951. Grosset & Dunlap.
--The Clue of the Marked Claw. Campbell, Bruce, pseud. LC 50-9256. vii, 211 p. front. 20 cm. (His The Ken Holt mystery stories, 4). 1950. Grosset & Dunlap.
--The Mystery of the Galloping Horse. Campbell, Bruce, pseud. LC 54-8547. 212 p. illus. 20 cm. (His Ken Holt mystery stories, 9). 1954. Grosset & Dunlap.
--The Mystery of the Gallows Cliff. Campbell, Bruce, pseud. LC 60-1209. 184p. 20cm. (Ken Holt Mystery). 1960. Grosset & Dunlop.
--The Mystery of the Green Flame. Campbell, Bruce, pseud. LC 55-1065. (Illus.). 212p. 20cm. (Ken Holt Mystery). 1955. (ISBN 0-396-05215-0). Grosset & Dunlop.
--The Mystery of the Grinning Tiger. Campbell, Bruce, pseud. LC 56-323635. 209 p. illus. 20 cm. (His A Ken Holt mystery 11). 1956. Grosset & Dunlap.
--The Mystery of the Plumed Serpent. Campbell, Bruce, pseud. LC 62-3498. 176 p. illus. 20cm. (His The Ken Holt Mystery Stories). 1962. Grosset & Dunlap.
--The Mystery of the Vanishing Magician. Campbell, Bruce, pseud. LC 57-13573. 215 p. illus. 20 cm. (His Ken Holt mystery stories 12). 1957, c.1956. Grosset & Dunlap.
--Peter Platypus. Montana, Bob (1920-1975), illus. LC 46-6209. 3 p. l., 23, 1 p. col. illus. 28 x 22 cm. 1946. R. Speller.
--The Riddle of the Stone Elephant. Campbell, Bruce, pseud. LC 49-6829. vii, 213 p. front. 20 cm. (Ken Holt mystery stories, 2). 1949. Grosset & Dunlap.
--The Secret of Hangman's Inn. Campbell, Bruce, pseud. LC 51-7744. 213 p. illus. 20 cm. (His Ken Holt mystery stories, 6). 1951. Grosset & Dunlap.
--The Secret of Skeleton Island. Campbell, Bruce, pseud. LC 49-6774. vii, 214 p. front. 20 cm. (Ken Holt mystery stories, 1). 1949. Grosset & Dunlap.
Epstein, Samuel (1909-) & Epstein, Beryl Williams (1910-)
--The Andrews Raid: Or, The Great Locomotive Chase, April 12, 1862. Powers, Richard M. Gorman (1921-), illus. LC 56-9953. 253 p. illus. 22 cm. 1956. Coward-McCann.
--Grandpa's Wonderful Glass. Elgin, Jill, illus. Moore, Lilian (Illus.). (gr. k-3). N.D. G&D.
--Hurricane Guest. Miller, Marilyn Jean (1925-), illus. LC 64-11174. (Illus.). 57 p. 24cm. (Random House easy to read library, R-33). 1964. Random House.
--Jackknife for a Penny. Avillez, Martim, illus. LC 57-14897. (Illus.). 247 p. 21cm. 1958. Coward-McCann.
--Mister Peale's Mammoth. Avillez, Martim, illus. LC 76-49644. (Illus.). 63 p. 21cm. c.1977. (ISBN 0-698-20402-6). Coward, McCann & Geoghegan.
--Pick It up. De Paola, Tomie, pseud. (1934-), illus. De Paola, Thomas Anthony. LC 70-151759. (Illus.). 32 p. 22cm. 1971. (ISBN 0-8234-0194-4). Holiday House.
--Spring Holidays. Schroeder, Ted (1931-1973), illus. LC 64-12340. (Illus.). 64 p. 25cm. (Holiday book). 1964. Garrard Pub. Co.
--Take This Hammer. 1st ed. De Paola, Tomie, pseud. (1934-), illus. De Paola, Thomas Anthony. LC 69-10910. (Illus.). 32 p. 22cm. 1969. Hawthorn Books.
--Who Needs Holes?. De Paola, Tomie, pseud. (1934-), illus. De Paola, Thomas Anthony. LC 72-92634. (Illus.). 30 p. 22cm. 1970. Hawthorn Books.
Epstein, Sherrie S
--Penny, the Medicine Maker: The Story of Penicillin. Springer, Mark, illus. LC 60-14006. (Illus.). unpaged. 27cm. 1960. Medical Books for Children.
Erckmann, Emile (1822-1899) & Chatrian, Alexandre (1826-1890)
--The Story of a Peasant: Including; "The States General", "The Country in Danger", "Year One of the Republic", & "Citizen Bonaparte, 4 Vols. (Illus.). (Juvenile Series). N.D. Dodd, Mead & Co.
Erdman, Loula Grace (0000-1976)
--A Bluebird Will Do. LC 72-6881. 213 p. 21cm. 1973. (ISBN 0-396-06717-4). Dodd, Mead.
--Fair is the Morning. 1945. David McKay Company Inc.
--Fair Is the Morning. LC 45-8645. 3 p. l., 186 p. illus. 21 cm. 1945. Longmans, Green and Co., Inc.
--The Good Land. LC 59-9617. 182 p. 21cm. 1959. Dodd, Mead.
--My Sky Is Blue. (gr. 9 up). 1953. (ISBN 0-679-20123-8). McKay.
--My Sky Is Blue. (Willow Bks.). (gr. 8 up). N.D. Pyramid Pubns.
--Room to Grow. Handville, Robert, illus. LC 62-17013. (Illus.). 242 p. 21cm. 1962. Dodd, Mead.
--Save Weeping for the Night. LC 74-25522. ix, 205 p. 21cm. 1975. (ISBN 0-396-07087-6). Dodd, Mead.
--Separate Star. 1944. David McKay Company Inc.
--Separate Star. Holland, Janice (1913-1962), illus. LC 44-32445. 3 p. l., 200 p. 21 cm. 1944. Longmans, Green and Co.
--The Wide Horizon: A Story of the Texas Panhandle. LC 56-6865. 245 p. 21cm. 1956. Dodd, Mead.
--The Wind Blows Free. LC 52-7603. 242 p. 21 cm. 1952. Dodd, Mead.
--A Wonderful Thing: And Other Stories. LC 64-13886. viii, 244 p. 21cm. 1964. (ISBN 0-396-04979-6). Dodd, Mead.
Erdoes, Richard, ed. see Lame Deer, et al.
Erdoes, Richard (1912-)
--The Green Tree House. Erdoes, Richard (1912-), illus. LC 65-23267. 1v. (unpaged) illus. (pt. col.) 29cm. c.1965. Dodd.
Erdoes, Richard (1912-), ed.
--American Indian Legends. Goble, Paul (1933-), illus. LC 76-8660. p. cm. 1976. (ISBN 0-394-83181-0). (ISBN 0-394-93181-5). Pantheon Books.
--The Sound of Flutes & Other Indian Legends. Goble, Paul (1933-), illus. LC 76-8660. (Illus.). 1976. (ISBN 0-394-93181-5). Pantheon. **Award: (ALA).**
Erens, Pamela
--A Flight For Freedom. (Illus.). (gr. 6-12). 1977. (ISBN 0-915288-32-X). Shameless Hussy.
Erfft, Shirley
--Little Things Mean a Lot. 1982. (ISBN 0-8062-1897-5). Carlton.
Erger, Connie, jt. auth. see Erger, Gene.
Erger, Gene & Erger, Connie
--Ko of Menehuneland: The Adventures of a Hawaiian Elf-Boy. Takamoto, Jane M., illus. LC 62-18938. (Illus.). 48p. (gr. 3-8). N.D. C E Tuttle.
Erickson
--Carl Bartlett: A Story for Boys. 1900. Hurst & Co.
Erickson, Carol A. & Ross, Gail J.
--Susie the Snaice. 1974. (ISBN 0-87506-051-X). Campus.
Erickson, D. S.
--The Wadsworth Boys. N.D. D. Lothrop & Co.
Erickson, John R.
--Alkali County Tales. Holmes, Gerald L., illus. (Illus.). 100p. (Orig.). (gr. 3up). 1984. (ISBN 0-916941-06-X). (ISBN 0-9608612-8-9). Maverick Bks.
--Cowboys are Partly Human. Holmes, Gerald L., illus. 110p. (Orig.). (gr. 3 up). 1983. (ISBN 0-9608612-6-2). (ISBN 0-9608612-4-6). Maverick Bks.
--The Further Adventures of Hank the Cowdog. Holmes, Gerald L., illus. 93p. (Orig.). (Hank the Cowdog Ser.: 2nd.). (gr. 3). 1983. (ISBN 0-9608612-7-0). (ISBN 0-9608612-5-4). Maverick Bks.
--Hank the Cowdog: It's a Dog's Life. (Illus.). 100p. (Orig.). (Hank the Cowdog Ser.). (gr. 3). N.D. (ISBN 0-916941-04-3). (ISBN 0-9608612-9-7). Maverick Bks.
Erickson, Lorene, jt. ed. see Leo, Kathleen R.
Erickson, Phoebe, jt. auth. see Potter, Helen Beatrix.
Erickson, Phoebe (1907-)
--Black Penny. 1st ed. Erickson, Phoebe (1907-), illus. LC 51-11084. (Illus.). 183 p. 22cm. 1951. Knopf.
--Cattail House. Erickson, Phoebe (1907-), illus. LC 49-8989. 36 p. illus. (part col.) 23 cm. 1949. Childrens Press.
--Cattail House. new ed. Erickson, Phoebe (1907-), illus. unpaged, illus. 25 cm. 1962, c.1949. Childrens Press.
--Daniel Coon: The Story of a Pet Raccoon. Erickson, Phoebe (1907-), illus. LC 54-7478. (Illus.). 179 p. 22cm. 1954. (ISBN 0-394-91068-0). Knopf.
--Double or Nothing. Erickson, Phoebe (1907-), illus. LC 58-7762. (Illus.). 24cm. 127p. (gr. 2-6). 1958. (ISBN 0-06-021840-1). Har-Row.
--Double or Nothing. Erickson, Phoebe (1907-), illus (Pub. by Har-Row). (gr. 4-6). 1972 (Starline). Schol Bk Serv.
--Just Follow Me. Erickson, Phoebe (1907-), illus. (Illus.). (gr. 1-3). N.D. (ISBN 0-695-84560-8). (ISBN 0-695-44560-X). Follett.

Escoula, Yvonne (1916-)
--Six Blue Horses: A Novel. Vaughn, Ciba, tr. LC 70-103044. 160p. (gr. 5-9). 1970. (ISBN 0-87599-162-9). S G Phillips.

Esenwein, Joseph Berg (1867-), ed.
--Adventures to Come. LC 37-21643. 4 p. l., 13-187 p. col. front., illus. 22 cm. (World of adventure series, ed. by J. B. Esenwein). c.1937. McLoughlin Bros. Inc.

--Calling All Boys. LC 37-21641. 3 p. l., 11-190 p. col. front., illus. 22 cm. (World of adventure series, ed. by J. B. Esenwein). c.1937. McLoughlin Bros. Inc.

--Field and Campus. LC 37-21646. 2 p. l., 11-188 p. col. front., illus 23 cm. (World of adventure series, ed. by J. B. Esenwein). c.1937. McLoughlin Bros. Inc.
--Real Stories for Real Girls. LC 37-21645. 188 p., 1 l. incl. col. front., illus. 22 cm. (World of adventure series, ed. by J. B. Esenwein). c.1937. McLoughlin Bros. Inc.
--Spirited Horses and Daring Dogs. LC 37-21644. 185 p. incl. col. front., illus. 22 cm. (World of adventure series). c.1937. McLoughlin Bros. Inc.
--Sport and Adventure. LC 37-21647. (World of adventure series). N.D. McLoughlin Bros. Inc.

Eshugbayi, Ezekiel A., jt. ed. see Courlander, Harold.

Eskil, Ragna B.
--Good Plays for School Days. 119p. N.D. T. S. Denison & Co Inc.

Eskridge, Robert Lee (1891-)
--South Sea Playmates. N.D. Bobbs Merrill Co.
--Umi: The Hawaiian Boy Who Became a King. Eskridge, Robert Lee, illus. LC 36-31570. 103, 2 p. incl. col. front., illus. (part col.) 23 1/2 cm. c.1936. The John C. Winston Company.

Esley, Joan
--The Visit. Wilkin, Eloise Burns (1904-), illus. LC 80-12934. (Illus.). 32 p. 31cm. c.1980. (ISBN 0-528-82286-1). Rand McNally.

Espeland, Pamela Lee (1951-)
--The Story of Arachne. Kennedy, Susan, illus. LC 80-15621. (Illus.). 32 p. 24cm. (Myths for Modern Children Ser.). c.1980. (ISBN 0-87614-130-0). Carolrhoda Books.
--The Story of Baucis and Philemon. Overlie, George, illus. LC 80-27674. (Illus.). 32 p. 24cm. (Myths for modern children ser.). c.1981. (ISBN 0-87614-140-8). Carolrhoda Books.
--The Story of Cadmus. Sandland, Reg, illus. LC 80-15640. p. cm. (myths for modern childern ser.). c.1980. (ISBN 0-87614-128-9). Carolrhoda Books.
--The Story of King Midas. Overlie, George, illus. LC 80-15691. p. cm. (myths for modern childern ser.). c.1980. (ISBN 0-87614-129-7). Carolrhoda Books.
--The Story of Pygmalion. Cleary, Catherine, illus. LC 80-15792. (Illus.). 30 p. 24cm. (Myths for Modern Childern Ser.). c.1981. (ISBN 0-87614-127-0). Carolrhoda Books.
--Theseus and the Road to Athens. Sandland, Reg, illus. LC 80-27713. (Illus.). 32 p. 24cm. (Myths for modern children ser.). c.1981. (ISBN 0-87614-141-6). Carolrhoda Books.

Espeland, Pamela Lee (1951-) & Waniek, Marilyn Nelson (1946-)
--The Cat Walked Through the Casserole: And Other Poems for Children. Hyman, Trina Schart (1939-) & Knight, Hilary, illus. LC 84-11381. (Illus.). 40p. (gr. k-4). c.1984. (ISBN 0-87614-268-4). Carolrhoda Bks.

Espenscheid, Gertrude
--The Oh Ball. Espenscheid, Gertrude Elliott, illus. (Illus.). (ps-1). 1966. (ISBN 0-06-021851-7, HarpJ). Har-Row.

Espenscheid, Gertrude Elliott, jt. ed. see Smith, Dorothy Hall.

Espy, Rosalie & Martin, Clyde Inez
--Fun with Dusty. Mastri, Fiore, illus. LC 58-25227. (Illus.). 22cm. 128p. 1958. W. S. Benson.

Essex, Rosamund Sibyl (1900-)
--Into the Forest. LC 65-203731. 156p. 21cm. 1st U.S. edition. 1965, c.1963. Coward.

Estabrook, Irene, jt. auth. see Gilstrap, Robert Lawrence.

Estcourt, Doris
--California Holiday. Brock, Charles Edmond (1870-1938), illus. LC 38-9431. 255 p. incl. illus., plates, map. col. front. 20 1/2 cm. c.1937. Dodd, Mead & Company.
--Little Elephant Comes to Town. Mountain, M. K., illus. LC 39-8130. 118 1 p. illus. (part col.) 20 1/2 cm. 1939. Oxford University Press.

Estep, Irene Compton
--Pioneer Buckaroo. Tiedemann, Berthold, illus. LC 58-2874. (Illus.). 160p. 23cm. (Pioneer Ser.). 1958. Benefic Press.
--Pioneer Pilgrim. Tiedemann, Berthold, illus. LC 59-8831. (Illus.). 160p. 23cm. 1959. Benefic Press.

Ester, Dana, compiled by.
--The Home Book of Poetry. new ed. (Illus.). N.D. Estes & Lauriat.

Estes, Eleanor (1906-1979)
--The Alley. 1st ed. Ardizzone, Edward Jeffrey Irving (1900-1979), illus. LC 64-23042. (Illus.). 283 p. 20cm. 1964. Harcourt, Brace & World.
--The Coat-Hanger Christmas Tree. 1st ed. Suba, Susanne (1913-), illus. LC 73-75433. (Illus.). 77 p. 22cm. 1973. (ISBN 0-689-30416-1). Atheneum.
--Ginger Pye. Estes, Eleanor (1906-1979), illus. LC 51-10446. (Illus.). 250 p. 22cm. 1951. (ISBN 0-15-230930-6). Harcourt, Brace. **Award: (JNM).**
--Ginger Pye. Estes, Eleanor (1906-1979), illus. 1972. Harcourt.
--The Hundred Dresses. Slobodkin, Louis (1903-1975), illus. LC 44-8063. 3 p. l., 80 p., 1 l. illus. (part col.) 22 x 17 cm. 1944. Harcourt, Brace and Company. **Award: (JNM).**
--The Hundred Dresses. Slobodkin, Louis (1903-1975), illus. LC 73-12940. (Illus.). 80 p. 24cm. (Voyager book, AVB 88). 1974, c.1944. (ISBN 0-15-642350-2). Harcourt Brace Jovanovich.
--A Little Oven. N.D. E. M. Hale & Co.
--A Little Oven. Estes, Eleanor (1906-1979), illus. LC 55-7064. (Illus.). unpaged. c.1955. Harcourt, Brace.
--Lollipop Princess: A Play for Paper Dolls in One Act. Estes, Eleanor (1906-1979), illus. LC 67-25602. (Illus.). (gr. 3-7). 1967. (ISBN 0-15-248160-5). (ISBN 0-15-248161-3). HarBraceJ.
--The Lost Umbrella of Kim Chu. 1st ed. Ayer, Jacqueline (1930-), illus. LC 78-59156. (Illus.). 85 p. 21cm. 1978. (ISBN 0-689-50111-0). Atheneum.
--The Middle Moffat. 1st ed. Slobodkin, Louis (1903-1975), illus. LC 42-36272. (Illus.). 5 p.l., 3-317 p. incl. plates. 21cm. 1942. Harcourt, Brace and Company. **Award: (JNM).**
--The Middle Moffat. 1st ed. Slobodkin, Louis (1903-1975), illus. LC 79-11970. p. cm. (Voyager/HBJ book). 1979, c.1942. Harcourt Brace Jovanovich.
--Miranda the Great. Ardizzone, Edward Jeffrey Irving (1900-1979), illus. LC 67-1409. (Illus.). 79 p. 22cm. 1967. Harcourt, Brace & World.
--The Moffat Museum. 1st ed. Estes, Eleanor (1906-1979), illus. LC 83-8427. (Illus.). 262 p. 21cm. c.1983. (ISBN 0-15-255086-0). Harcourt Brace Jovanovich.
--The Moffats. Slobodkin, Louis (1903-1975), illus. LC 41-51893. 5 p. l., 3-290 p., 1 l. incl. front., illus., plates. 21 cm. c.1941. Harcourt, Brace and Company.
--Pinky Pye. 1st ed. Ardizzone, Edward Jeffrey Irving (1900-1979), illus. LC 58-5708. (Illus.). 192 p. 21cm. 1958. Harcourt, Brace. **Award: (ALA).**
--Pinky Pye. Ardizzone, Edward Jeffrey Irving (1900-1979), illus. LC 75-31581. p. cm. (Voyager book ; AVB 100). 1976, c.1958. (ISBN 0-15-671840-5). Harcourt Brace Jovanovich.
--Rufus M. Slobodkin, Louis (1903-1975), illus. LC 43-51239. 4 p. l., 3-320 p. incl. illus., plates. front. 20 1/2 cm. 1943. Harcourt, Brace and Company. **Award: (JNM).**
--Sleeping Giant & Other Stories. Estes, Eleanor (1906-1979), illus. LC 48-9223. (Illus.). 23cm. 101p. (gr. 1-5). 1948. (ISBN 0-15-275851-8, HJ). HarBraceJ.
--The Sun and the Wind and Mr. Todd. Slobodkin, Louis (1903-1975), illus. LC 43-3609. 96 p. col. illus. 28 cm. 1943. Harcourt, Brace and Company.
--The Tunnel of Hugsy Goode. 1st ed. Ardizzone, Edward Jeffrey Irving (1900-1979), illus. LC 79-167833. (Illus.). x, 244 p. 22cm. 1971, c.1972. (ISBN 0-15-291100-6). Harcourt Brace Jovanovich.
--The Witch Family. 1st ed. Ardizzone, Edward Jeffrey Irving (1900-1979), illus. LC 60-11250. (Illus.). 186 p. 22cm. 1960. Harcourt, Brace.

Estes, Rose
--The Case of the Dancing Dinosaur. Vincente, illus. LC 83-63444. (Illus.). 128p. (Find Your Fate Mystery Ser.: No. 2). (gr. 4-7). 1985. (ISBN 0-394-96431-4, BYR). (ISBN 0-394-86431-X, BYR). Random.

--Children of the Dragon. Lundgren, Carl, illus. LC 84-22318. (Illus.). 224p. (gr. 4-9). 1985. (ISBN 0-394-96433-0, BYR). (ISBN 0-394-86433-6). Random.

--Circus of Fear. LC 83-50050. 160p. (Dungeons & Dragons Endless Quest Book Ser.). (gr. 5up). 1983. (ISBN 0-394-72102-0). Random.

--Revenge of the Rainbow Dragons. LC 82-51206. (Illus.). (The Endless Quest Book: No.6). c.1983. (ISBN 0-88038-021-7). TSR.

Estes, Shirley Potter
--Robbie's Friend George. Inderieden, Nancy, illus. LC 75-128815. (Illus.). 32 p. 1972. (ISBN 0-87614-018-5). Carolrhoda Books.

Estey, Henry G. see E L S E, pseud.

Estey, Henry G., Mrs.
--Three Girls and Their Motto. E L S E, pseud. LC 12-320189. 2 p. l., 3-200 p. front., plates. 18 1/2 cm. c.1893. American Baptist Publication Society.
--Walter Harley's Conquest. E L S E, pseud. LC 12-32015. 2 p. l., 3-240 p. front., plates. 18 1/2 cm. c.1889. American Baptist Publication Society.

Esther, Haakon, jt. auth. see Fife, Dale Odile.

Estoril, Jean, pseud., see Allan, Mabel Esther.

Estoril, Jean, pseud. (1915-)
--Ballet for Drina. Allan, Mabel Esther. LC 58-9223. (gr. 5-10). N.D. (ISBN 0-8149-0299-5). Vanguard.
--Drina Dances in Italy. Allan, Mabel Esther. LC 61-15484. (Illus.). 192 p. 22cm. 1962, c.1961. Vanguard Press.

Estrada, Doris Perkins (1923-)
--Periwinkle Jones. Stover, Jo Ann (1931-), illus. LC 65-15091. (Illus.). 94p. illus. 22cm. (gr. 3-5). 1965. (ISBN 0-385-05566-8). Doubleday.

Etchemendy, Teje
--Tales of Old Russia. Etchemendy, Teje, illus. LC 64-17444. (Illus.). 93 p. 29cm. 1964. Rand McNally.

Etchison, Birdie Lee (1937-)
--Me and Greenley. Converse, James, illus. LC 81-6487. (Illus.). 124 p. 20cm. 1981. (ISBN 0-8361-1966-5). Herald Press.
--Strawberry Mountain. Converse, James, illus. LC 81-7093. p. cm. 1982. (ISBN 0-8361-1981-9). Herald Press.

Etheridge, Mary Lee
--Dick and Joe: Or, Two of a Kind. LC 12-32103. 138 p. incl. front., plates. 23 cm. c.1893. De Wolfe, Fiske & Co.
--Mistress Muff and Her Friends. Andrews, illus. (Illus.). N.D. DeWolfe, Fiske & Co.

Etherton, Roy
--The Day It Rained in Colors. 1981. (ISBN 0-89191-099-9). Caroline Hse.

Ethridge, Willie Snow, Mrs.
--Going to Jerusalem. N.D. The Vanguard Press.
--It's Greek To Me. N.D. The Vanguard Press.
--Let's Talk Turkey. N.D. The Vanguard Press.
--There's Yeast in the Middle East. N.D. The Vanguard Press.
--This Little Pig Stayed Home. N.D. Vanguard Press.

Etkin, Anne Dunwody Little (1923-)
--All at Sea. Etkin, Anne Dunwody Little (1923-), illus. LC 61-1252. 68p. illus. 20cm. 1961. S. Etkin.

Ets, Marie Hall, jt. auth. see Tarry, Ellen.

Ets, Marie Hall, Mrs. (1893-)
--Another Day. Ets, Marie Hall, Mrs. (1893-), illus. LC 53-2892. (Illus.). 40 p. 1953. Viking Press.
--Automobiles for Mice. Ets, Marie Hall, Mrs. (1893-), illus. (Illus.). 31 p. 1964. Viking Press.
--Bad Boy, Good Boy. Ets, Marie Hall, Mrs. (1893-), illus. LC 67-8523. (Illus.). 49 p. 27cm. 1967. Crowell.
--Beasts and Nonsense. LC 52-13290. 64 p. illus. 24 cm. 1952. Viking Press. **Award: (NYT).**
--Cow's Party. Ets, Marie Hall, Mrs. (1893-), illus. LC 58-14712. (Illus.). 32 p. 27cm. 1958. Viking Press.
--Elephant in a Well. 1st ed. Ets, Marie Hall, Mrs. (1893-), illus. LC 74-183935. (Illus.). 30 p. 1972. (ISBN 0-670-29169-2). Viking Press.
--Gilberto and the Wind. LC 77-16274. p. cm. 1978, c.1963. (ISBN 0-14-050276-9). Puffin Books.
--Gilberto and the Wind. Ets, Marie Hall, Mrs. (1893-), illus. LC 63-8527. (Illus.). 32 p. 26cm. 1963. Viking Press. **Award: (ALA).**
--In the Forest. Ets, Marie Hall, Mrs. (1893-), illus. (Illus., Pub. by Viking Pr). (Picture Puffins Ser). (ps-2). 1976. (ISBN 0-14-050180-0, Puffin). Penguin.
--In the Forest. Ets, Marie Hall, Mrs. (1893-), illus. LC 78-15459. p. cm. 1978, c.1944. (ISBN 0-14-050180-0). Puffin Books.
--In the Forest. Ets, Marie Hall, Mrs. (1893-), illus. LC 44-7727. (Illus.). 45 p. 1944. The Viking Press. **Award: (RCM).**
--Jay Bird. 1st ed. Ets, Marie Hall, Mrs. (1893-), illus. LC 73-19590. (Illus.). 40 p. 19cm. 1974. (ISBN 0-670-40608-2). Viking Press.
--Just Me. Ets, Marie Hall, Mrs. (1893-), illus. LC 78-11458. p. cm. 1978, c.1965. (ISBN 0-14-050325-0). Puffin Books.
--Just Me. Ets, Marie HAll, Mrs. (1893-), illus. LC 65-13349. (Illus.). 32 p. 1965. Viking Press. **Awards: (ALA); (RCM).**
--Little Old Automobile. Ets, Marie Hall, Mrs. (1893-), illus. LC 48-4046. (Illus.). 27cm. 32p. (ps-1). 1948. (ISBN 0-670-43264-4). Viking Pr.
--Mister Penny. Ets, Marie Hall, Mrs. (1893-), illus. LC 35-12185. (Illus.). 21 x 28cm. 47p. (ps-3). 1935. (ISBN 0-670-48074-6). Viking Pr.
--Mister Penny's Circus. Ets, Marie Hall, Mrs. (1893-), illus. (Illus.). 64 p. 28cm. 1961. Viking Press.
--Mister Penny's Race Horse. Ets, Marie Hall, Mrs. (1893-), illus. LC 56-14110. (Illus.). 63 p. 27cm. 1956. Viking Press. **Awards: (ALA); (RCM).**
--Mr. T. W. Anthony Woo: The Story of a Cat and a Dog and a Mouse. Ets, Marie Hall, Mrs. (1893-), illus. (Illus.). 54 p. 1951. Viking Press. **Award: (RCM).**
--Oley: The Sea Monster. Ets, Marie Hall, Mrs. (1893-), illus. LC 47-30113. (Illus.). 30 x 23cm. 32p. (ps-3). 1947. (ISBN 0-670-52394-1). (ISBN 0-670-52395-X). Viking Pr.
--Play with Me. Ets, Marie Hall, Mrs. (1893-), illus. LC 55-14845. (Illus.). 31 p. 26cm. 1955. Viking Press. **Awards: (IBBY); (ALA); (RCM).**
--The Story of a Baby. Ets, Marie Hall, Mrs. (1893-), illus. 64p. N.D. Viking Press.
--Talking Without Words: I Can. Can You?. Ets, Marie Hall, Mrs. (1893-), illus. LC 68-27568. (Illus.). unpaged. 19 x 25 cm. 1968. Viking Press. **Award: (NYT).**

Ets, Marie Hall, Mrs. (1893-) & Labastida, Aurora
--Nine Days to Christmas. Ets, Marie Hall, Mrs. (1893-), illus. (Illus.). 48 p. 29cm. 1959. Viking Press. **Award: (RCM).**

Etter, Lester Frederick (1904-)
--Big Down Gamble. Chauncy, Francis, illus. LC 68-23789. (Illus.). 124 p. 22cm. 1968. Hastings House.
--Bull Pen Hero. LC 66-186047. 212p. 22cm. c.1966. Bobbs.
--Cool Man on the Court. Kramer, Frank, illus. LC 76-85230. (Illus.). 125 p. 22cm. 1969. Hastings House.
--Fast Break Forward. Chauncy, Francis, illus. LC 72-79494. (Illus.). 128 p. 22cm. 1969. Hastings House.
--Get Those Rebounds. Calvin, James, illus. LC 77-17217. 119 illus. 22. 1977. (ISBN 0-8038-2685-0). Hastings House.
--Golden Gloves Challenger. Chauncy, Francis, illus. LC 67-25610. (Illus.). 125 p. 22cm. 1967. Hastings House.
--Morning Glory Quarterback. LC 65-26516. 215p. 22cm. c.1965. Bobbs.
--Soccer Goalie. Chauncy, Francis, illus. LC 69-14456. (Illus.). 127 p. 22cm. 1969. Hastings House.

Ettinger, Betty
--Joan and Jack. Ettinger, Betty, illus. LC 35-9706. 24 x 28cm. 20p. 1935. Grosset & Dunlap.

Etzkorn, Leo Rudolph, jt. auth. see Wade, Mary Hazelton Blanchard, Mrs.

Etzkorn, Leo Rudolph, jt. auth. see Pike, Henry Lee Mitchell.

Eu, March K.
--Sons of Chong. McFadden, S. Michele, ed. (Illus.). (gr. 3 up). 1978. (ISBN 0-89262-022-6). Career Pub.

Eubanks, L. E
--Swamps of Mystery. LC 45-13599. 93 p. 18 cm. 1944. The Wartburg Press.

Eubanks, L. E., jt. auth. see Garrett, Wouter Van.

Eudaly, Marie Saddler
--Dickie in Mexico. Crawford, Selma & Eudaly, N. Hoyt, photos by LC 53-352481. unpaged. illus. 19x24cm. 1951. Broadman Press.

Eugenie

--Jenny's Surprise Summer. Eugenie, illus. (Illus.). LC 80-85033. 24p. (Little Golden Bks.). (ps). 1981. (ISBN 0-307-02047-9, Golden Pr). (ISBN 0-307-60247-8). Western Pub.

--Wickedishrag. Eugenie, illus. LC 68-21795. (Illus.). 26 p. 19cm. (Stardust books). 1968. C. R. Gibson Co.

Eulalie, pseud., see Banks, Eulalie M..

Eulalie, pseud. (1896-), illus.
--Mother Goose Rhymes. Banks, Eulalie M.. LC 80-83934. (Illus.). 48p. Repr. of 1953 ed. (ps-1). 1981. (ISBN 0-448-40114-2). (ISBN 0-448-13946-4). Platt.
--Mother Goose Rhymes. Banks, Eulalie M.. (Illus.). 48p. (ps-3). 1978. (ISBN 0-448-40114-2, G&D). Putnam Pub Group.
--Nursery Time. Banks, Eulalie M.. (Illus.). (Gingerbread Bks). (ps-1). 1979. Dutton.
--Nursery Time. Banks, Eulalie M.. LC 79-64688. (Illus.). 10 p. 21cm. (Gingerboard book). c.1979. (ISBN 0-525-69403-X). Gingerbread House.
--The True Mother Goose. Banks, Eulalie M.. LC 79-1948. (Illus.). (ps-2). 1979. (Gingerbread Bks). (Gingerbread Bks.). Dutton.
--The True Mother Goose. Banks, Eulalie M.. LC 79-1948. (Illus.). 20 p. 32cm. c.1979. (ISBN 0-525-69004-2). Gingerbread House.

AUTHOR INDEX EVANS, PAULINE

Eulenspiegel, Till
--The Wicked Tricks of Tyl Uilenspiegel. Williams, Jay (1914-1978), retold by. Henstra, Friso (1928-), illus. LC 77-7884. (Illus.). 51 p. 24cm. c.1978. (ISBN 0-590-07478-4). Four Winds Press.
Eunson, John Dale (1904-)
--The Day They Gave Babies Away. Gorsline, Douglas Warner (1913-1985), illus. LC 72-84484. (Illus.). 57 p. 22cm. (Ariel book). 1970. Farrar, Straus and Giroux.
--Up on the Rim. LC 70-102063. (gr. 7 up). 1970. (ISBN 0-374-38053-8). FS&G.
Eure, James Bruce
--The Swamp Angel. 1st. ed. 187 p. 21cm. 1974. (ISBN 0-682-47878-4). Exposition Press.
Eustis, Helen
--Mr. Death & the Red-Headed Woman. Reinhard, Michl, illus. (Illus.). 40p. (Orig.). (gr. 7 up). 1983. (ISBN 0-88138-013-X, Star & Eleph Bks). Green Tiger Pr.
Eutemey, Loring
--Let's Hear It for the Queen. Childress, Alice (1920-), illus. LC 76-16075. p. cm. 1976. (ISBN 0-698-20388-7). Coward, McCann & Geoghegan.
Evans, A. W., tr. see France, Anatole.
Evans, Augusta J.
--Beulah. (The Good Value Books). N.D. Grosset & Dunlap.
--Inez. (The Good Value Books). N.D. Grosset & Dunlap.
Evans, Charles Seddon (1883-), retold by see Morris, William.
Evans, Charles Seddon (1883-), as told by see Reynard the Fox. English.
Evans, Charles Seddon (1883-1944)
--Cinderella. Rackham, Arthur (1867-1939), illus. 26cm. 110p. 1919. J. B. Lippincott.
--Cinderella. Rackham, Arthur (1867-1939), illus. LC 78-18392. (Illus.). 110 p. 24cm. 1978. (ISBN 0-14-004907-X). Penguin Books.
--Cinderella. Rackham, Arthur (1867-1939), illus. LC 72-81681. (Illus.). 110 p. 25cm. (Studio book). 1972. (ISBN 0-670-22255-0). Viking Press.
--The Sleeping Beauty. Rackham, Arthur (1867-1939), illus. LC 76-165392. (Illus.). 110 p. 24cm. 1971. (ISBN 0-486-22756-1). Dover.
--The Sleeping Beauty. Rackham, Arthur (1867-1939), illus. LC 21-573436. 110 p., 1 l. incl. col. front., illus., col. plates. 26 cm. 1920. J. B. Lippincott Co.
--The Sleeping Beauty. Rackham, Arthur (1867-1939), illus. LC 72-81682. (Illus.). 110 p. 24cm. (Studio book). 1972. (ISBN 0-670-65096-X). Viking Press.
Evans, Charlotte S.
--Jon-Colin's Tree. (Illus.). 32p. (gr. k-2). 1975. (ISBN 0-682-48198-X). Exposition.
Evans, Clifford L.
--The Special Tree in Paw Paw's Orchard. Teague, Barbara, illus. LC 77-360601. (Illus.). 27 p. 29cm. c.1976. Study-Learning Associates.
Evans, David A
--Race on the Mountain. LC 63-7737. 147 p. illus. 21 cm. 1963. Putnam.
Evans, Doris Portwood
--Breakfast with the Birds. Chen, Tony (1929-), illus. LC 78-165485. (Illus.). 48 p. 24cm. 1972. (ISBN 0-399-20250-1). (ISBN 0-399-60766-8). Putnam.
--Mr. Charley's Chopsticks. Cuffari, Richard (1925-1978), illus. LC 79-183553. (Illus.). 62 p. 23cm. (Break-of-day book). 1972. Coward, McCann & Geoghegan.
Evans, E. K. & Best, Allena Champlin, Mrs. (1892-1974)
--Mr. Jones and Mr. Finnegan. Berry, Erick, pseud. 32p. 1941. Oxford University Press.
Evans, Earlene G.
--I Love You, Ugly Old Hag!. Vango, Eugene, illus. 1981. (ISBN 0-533-04488-X). Vantage.
Evans, Edna Hoffman (1913-)
--Bill and the Bird Bander. Evans, W. J., photos by. N.D. John C. Winston.
--Bob Vincent: Veterinarian. 1st ed. Oehler, Bernice Olivia (1881-), illus. LC 49-1263. 192 p. illus. 21 cm. 1949. E. P. Dutton.
--Sunstar and Pepper: Scouting with Jeb Stuart. Park, Anna Elizabeth, illus. LC 47-4639. viii, 294 p. illus. 21 cm. 1947. Univ. of North Carolina Press.
--Written with Fire: The story of Cattle Brands. 1962. Holt, Rinehart and Winston, Inc.
Evans, Edward Everett (1893-)
--The Planet Mappers. LC 55-5211. 242p. 21cm. 1955. Dodd, Mead.
Evans, Edward Radcliffe Garth Russell (1881-)
--Noel Howard: Midshipman. LC 35-10479. x, 246 p. col. front., plates. 21 cm. 1935. F. Warne & Co., Ltd.
Evans, Ernestine
--The Story of the Harbor. Lozowick, Louis (1892-1973), illus. LC 28-16136. 3 p. l., 60 p. col. front., illus. 19 1/2 cm. (City and Country Ser.). 1928. Harper & Brothers.
Evans, Eubule A.
--The Pride of the Village. N.D. E. & J. B. Young & Co.
--The Professor's Daughter. (Illus.). N.D. E & J B Young.
--Young Pirates. N.D. E.& J. B. Young & Co.
Evans, Eva Knox, Mrs. (1905-)
--Araminta. Best, Allena Champlin, Mrs. (1892-1974), illus. Berry, Erick, pseud. LC 35-5698. 84 p. incl. front., illus., plates. 22 cm. c.1935. Minton, Balch and Company.
--Araminta's Goat. Best, Allena Champlin, Mrs. (1892-1974), illus. Berry, Erick, pseud. LC 38-27722. 92 p. incl. front., illus., plates. 22 cm. c.1938. G. P. Putnam's Sons.
--Emma Belle and Her Kinfolks. Gag, Flavia (1907-1979), illus. LC [illegible] p. incl. front., illus., plates. 21 cm. c.1940. G. P. Putnam's Sons.
--Jerome Anthony. Best, Allena Champlin, Mrs. (1892-1974), illus. Berry, Erick, pseud. LC 36-171287. 88 p. incl. front., illus., plates. 22 cm. c.1936. G. P. Putnam's Sons.
--Key Corner. Best, Allena Champlin, Mrs. (1892-1974), illus. Berry, Erick, pseud. LC 38-973237. 206 p. incl. front., illus., plates. 21 cm. c.1938. G. P. Putnam's Sons.
--The Lost Handkerchiefs. Gag, Flavia (1907-1979), illus. LC 41-14048. 64 p. col. illus. 21 cm. c.1941. G. P. Putnam's Sons.
--Skookum. Rev. ed. Busoni, Rafaello (1900-1962), illus. LC 46-8277. 78 p. illus. 22 cm. 1946. Putnam.
--Skookum. Frankenberg, Robert Clinton (1911-), illus. LC 66-14589. (Illus.). 80 p. 22cm. (Merit books). 1966. Houghton Mifflin.
--Sleepy Time. Champion, Reed, illus. LC 62-7538. (Illus.). 40 p. 22cm. 1962. Houghton Mifflin.
--The Snow Book. Watson, Aldren Auld (1917-), illus. LC 65-10589. 72p. illus. 21cm. c.1965. Little.
--The Story of Su-Su. Earle, Vana (1917-), illus. LC 53-11362. (Illus.). 31 p. 24cm. c.1953. D. McKay Co.
--A Surprise for Araminta. Eshner, Ann, illus. LC 42-6763. (Illus.). 22cm. 28p. (Story Parade Picture Book). 1942. Grosset & Dunlap.
--That Lucky Mrs. Plucky. Stover, Jo Ann (1931-), illus. (Illus.). 63 p. 22cm. 1961. D. McKay Co.
--Tim's Place. 192p. (gr. 6-8). N.D. G. P. Putnam's Sons.
--Where Do You Live?. Darwin, Beatrice, illus. (Illus.). 31 p. 22cm. (Golden beginning reader). 1960. Golden Press.
--Why We Live Where We Live. Koering, Ursula (1921-), illus. (Illus.). (gr. 2-6). 1953. (ISBN 0-316-25828-8). Little.
Evans, F. C.
--Puffin, Puma & Co. (Poetry, Music And Art). N.D. MacMillan Bks.
Evans, Florence Adele (1879-)
--Alice's Adventures in Pictureland. Wheelan, Albertine Randall (1863-), illus. LC 1-29182. 192 p. incl. front., illus. plates. 24 x 18 1/2 cm. 1900. The Dodge Publishing Company.
--Jewel Story Book. Fry, W. H., illus. LC 3-19179. 102 p. front., 3 pl. 19 x 16 cm. 1903. The Saalfield Pub. Company.
--A Tale of Pierrot and His Cat. 76 p. col. front., col. pl. 23 1/2 x 31 cm. 1901. Dodge Pub. Co.
--The Woodland Elf. Williams, Carll B., illus. 212 p. incl. front., 3 pl. 19 x 17 cm. c.1906. The Saalfield Publishing Company.
Evans, George, jt. auth. see Ehret, Walter.
Evans, Gwendolen Mary
--The House in the Little Green Wood. Evans, Gwendolen Mary, illus. N.D. Frederick Warne & Co.
--Turn Again Lane. N.D. Frederick Warne & Co.
Evans, Hope H., ed.
--The Outback & Beyond: Stories from the Last Frontier. LC 72-75426. 264p. (gr. 7-9). 1973. (ISBN 0-385-05528-5). (ISBN 0-385-05019-4). Doubleday.
Evans, Hubert Reginald (1892-)
--Derry: Airedale of the Frontier. N.D. Grosset & Dunlap.
--Derry, Airedale of the Frontier. Yohn, F. C., illus. LC 28-21167. 4 p. l., 253 p. front., plates. 21 cm. 1928. Dodd, Mead & Company.
--Derry, of Totem Creek. Sellen, H. E. M., illus. LC 30-24082. vii, 252 p. front., plates, 21 cm. 1930. Dodd, Mead & Company.
--Derry's Partner. N.D. Grosset & Dunlap.
--Derry's Partner. Schoonover, Frank Earle (1877-1972), illus. LC 29-172607. 5 p. l., 268 p. front., plates. 21 cm. 1929. Dodd, Mead & Company.
--Forest Friends: Stories of Animals, Fish and Birds West of the Rockies. 1926. Judson Press.
--Mountain Dog. LC 56-5106. 21cm. 168p. 1956. Westminster Press.
--The Silent Call. Sellen, H. E. M., illus. LC 30-10044. 4 p. l., 248 p. front., plates. 21 cm. 1930. Dodd, Mead and Company.
Evans, Ian Andrews
--Choisissez Vos Roles: Graded Sketches for Young Actors by I. A. Evans. LC 67-102749. vii, 102p. 21cm. 1967. Macmillan.
Evans, Idrisyn Oliver (1894-)
--Gadget City: A Story of Ancient Alexandria. LC 46-58652. 256 p. incl. front., illus. (incl. map) diagrs. 18 1/2 cm. 1945. F. Warne and Co., Ltd.
Evans, J. A.
--I Know the Truck Driver. (Illus.). 1970. G P Putman's Sons.
Evans, Julia Rendell see Hobson, Polly, pseud.
Evans, Katherine Floyd, jt. auth. see Hetherington, Mildred Lyon.
Evans, Katherine Floyd (1901-1964)
--A Donkey for Abou. Evans, Katherine Floyd (1901-1964), illus. LC 64-13160. (Illus.). 42 p. 27cm. 1964. Abelard-Schuman.
--Flowers for Mother. Evans, Katherine Floyd (1901-1964), illus. LC 48-1891. 32 p. col.illus. 24 cm. 1948. D. McKay Co.
--The Ladybug Who Wouldn't Fly Home. Evans, Katherine Floyd (1901-1964), illus. LC 48-20694. 36 p. col. illus. 26 cm. 1945. Wilcox & Follett Co.
--Little Bear Bumble. Evans, Katherine Floyd (1901-1964), illus. LC 56-8574. (Illus.). 32 p. 24cm. 1956. Whitman.
--The Little Juggler. Evans, Katherine Floyd (1901-1964), illus. 1960. Bruce Pub Co.
--The Little Tree. Evans, Katherine Floyd (1901-1964), illus. LC 57-66. unpaged. illus. 21cm. (Christian child's stories, 9). 1956. Bruce Pub. Co.
--Maid and Her Pail Of Milk. Evans, Katherine Floyd (1901-1964), illus. 1959. E M Hale.
--The Mice That Ate Iron. Evans, Katherine Floyd (1901-1964), illus. LC 63-13328. (Illus.). unpaged. 25cm. 1963. A. Whitman.
--Mice That Ate Iron. Evans, Katherine Floyd (1901-1964), illus. 1963. E M Hale.
--Michael Angelo Mouse. Evans, Katherine Floyd (1901-1964), illus. LC 48-35872. 28 p. col. illus. 24 cm. 1945. Wilcox & Follett Co.
--One Good Deed Deserves Another. Evans, Katherine Floyd (1901-1964), illus. LC 64-16366. (Illus.). 33 p. 24cm. 1964. A. Whitman.
--Raphael's Cat. Evans, Katherine Floyd (1901-1964), illus. LC 61-15554. 29cm. (gr. k-3). 1961. (ISBN 0-672-50460-X). Bobbs.
Evans, Katherine Floyd (1901-1964), retold by.
--The Boy Who Cried Wolf. Evans, Katherine Floyd (1901-1964), illus. (Illus.). 32 p. 24cm. c.1960. A. Whitman.
--A Bundle of Sticks. Evans, Katherine Floyd (1901-1964), illus. LC 62-11070. (Illus.). unpaged. 24cm. 1962. A. Whitman.
--Bundle Of Sticks. Evans, Katherine Floyd (1901-1964), illus. 1962. (ISBN 0-8382-0128-8, Cadmus Books). E. M. Hale and Comapny.
--Camel in the Tent. Evans, Katherine Floyd (1901-1964), illus. 32p. N.D. Albert Whitman & Company.
--Camel In The Tent. Evans, Katherine Floyd (1901-1964), illus. LC 61-13328. unpaged. illus. 25cm. 1961. (ISBN 0-8382-0143-1, Cadmus Books). E. M. Hale and Company.
--The Maid and Her Pail of Milk. Evans, Katherine Floyd (1901-1964), illus. (Illus.). 32 p. 24cm. c.1959. A. Whitman.
--The Man, the Boy, and the Donkey. Evans, Katherine Floyd (1901-1964), illus. (Illus.). 31 p. 24cm. c.1958. A. Whitman.
Evans, Larry
--Fantastic Journey. (Illus.). (Posterbook Ser.). 1978. (ISBN 0-912300-89-2). Troubador Pr.
--Invisibles Two. (Illus.). 40p. (Orig.). 1981. (ISBN 0-89844-028-9). Troubador Pr.
--Space Warp (Warrior Robot Patrol). Evans, Larry, illus. (Illus.). 32p. (Orig.). 1978. (ISBN 0-912300-98-1). Troubador Pr.
Evans, Lawton Bryan (1862-1934)
--Heroes of Troy. Lotave, Carl, illus. LC 24-13954. 3 p. l., 446 p. front., plates 21 1/2 cm. c.1924. Milton Bradley Company.
--Old Time Tales. Ottendorff, E. Pollak, illus. LC 22-128958. vi, 336 p. col. front., col. plates. 21 1/2 cm. c.1922. Milton Bradley Company.
--The Pathfinder. (MacMillan Bks. for Boys & Girls). (gr. 7-9). N.D. MacMillan Bks.
--With Pack and Saddle: Famous American Frontier Stories. Ewing, R. A., illus. 1930. Milton Bradley Co.
Evans, Lawton Bryan (1862-1934), ed.
--Worth While Stories for Every Day. LC 17-128641. iv. vii-xiii, 424 p. 21 cm. 1917. Milton Bradley Company.
Evans, Lena
--The Little Pioneer. LC 33-207291. 2 p. l., 3-68, 2 p. 19 1/2 cm. (The Junior Classic Ser.). 1932. D. C. Doran.
Evans, Lewis
--Stories from Fancyland. N.D. Macmillan.
Evans, Marguerite Florence Helene Jervis, Mrs. see Barcynska, Countess, pseud.
Evans, Marguerite Florence Helene Jervis, Mrs. (1894-)
--Rose O' the Sea: A Romance. Barcynska, Countess, pseud. LC 20-17652. 3 p. l., 3-334 p., 1 l. col. front. 19 1/2 cm. 1920. Houghton Mifflin Company.
Evans, Marguerite Florence Helene Jervis, Mrs. (1894-), ed.
--The Little Mother Who Sits at Home. Barcynska, Countess, pseud. LC 15-5601. viii p., 1 l., 196 p. col. front. 18 1/2 cm. c.1915. E. P. Dutton & Coompany.
Evans, Mari (1923-)
--I Look at Me. 1974. (ISBN 0-88378-081-X). (ISBN 0-685-41469-8). Third World.
--J. D. 1st ed. Pinkney, Jerry (1939-), illus. LC 72-89129. (Illus.). 58 p. 24cm. 1973. (ISBN 0-385-08247-9). (ISBN 0-385-08247-9). Doubleday.
--Jim Flying High. 1st ed. Bryan, Ashley F. (1923-), illus. LC 78-22628. (Illus.). 32 p. 27cm. c.1979. (ISBN 0-385-14129-7). (ISBN 0-385-14130-0). Doubleday.
Evans, Marian see Eliot, George, pseud.
Evans, Mark
--Pepito, the Little Dancing Dog: The Story of Xavier Cugat's Chihuahua. Cugat, Xavier (1900-), illus. LC 78-65354. (Illus.). 32 p. 29cm. c.1979. (ISBN 0-87592-063-2). Scroll Press.
Evans, Max (1925-)
--My Pardner. Bjorklund, Lorence F. (1913-1978), illus. LC 75-187421. (Illus.). 106 p. 24cm. 1972. (ISBN 0-395-13725-X). Houghton Mifflin.
--My Pardner. Bjorklund, Lorence F. (1913-1978), illus. LC 84-2238. (Illus.). 1984, c.1972. (ISBN 0-8263-0699-3). University of New Mexico Press.
--Southwest Wind. (Illus.). (gr. 9 up). 1958. (ISBN 0-8111-0181-9). Naylor.
Evans, Melvin (1911-)
--The Tiniest Sound. 1st ed. Young, Ed (1931-), illus. LC 69-12696. (Illus.). 48 p. 22cm. 1969. Doubleday.
Evans, Nancy, jt. auth. see Banks, Ann.
Evans, Patricia Healy, pseud., see Carpenter, Patricia Healy Evans.
Evans, Patricia Healy, pseud. (1920-)
--Jump Rope Rhymes. Carpenter, Patricia Healy Evans. Evans, Patricia Healy, pseud. (1920-), illus. Carpenter, Patricia Healy Evans. N.D. Porpoise Bookshop.
--Rimbles; a Book of Children's Classic Games, Rhymes, Songs, and Sayings. Carpenter, Patricia Healy Evans. Fiammenghi, Gioia (1929-), illus. LC 61-9504. 157p. 27cm. 1961, c.1955. Doubleday.
Evans, Pauline Rush, ed.
--Best Book of Adventure Stories. McCurry, Charles & Noonan, Dan, illus. LC 64-16228. (Illus.). 283 p. 25cm. (Her Best Bks. Ser.). 1964. Doubleday.
--Best Book of Animal Stories. McCurry, Charles & Ball, Robert, illus. LC 64-16229. (Illus.). 283 p. 24cm. 1964. Doubleday.
--Best Book of Bedtime Stories. Sibley, Don (1922-), illus. LC 66-12182. 288 p. illus. (part col.) 24 cm. (Her Best book series). 1966. Doubleday.
--Best Book of Dog Stories. McCurry, Charles & Cellini, Joseph (1924-), illus. LC 64-16230. (Illus.). 278 p. 24cm. 1964. Doubleday.
--Best Book of Fairy Tales. Le Moult, Adolph & Wilde, Irma, illus. 286p. illus. (part col.) 24cm. (Her Best Bks. Ser.). N.D. Doubleday.
--Best Book of Fun and Nonsense. McCurry, Charles & Wilde, George A., illus. LC 64-16231. 287p. illus. (pt. col.) 24cm. (Her Best bk. ser.). 1964, c.1957. Doubleday.
--Best Book of Horse Stories. Houlihan, Ray & Noonan, Dan, illus. LC 64-16233. (Illus.). 278 p. 24cm. (Her Best Bks. Ser.). 1964. Doubleday.
--Best Book of Mystery Stories. McCurry, Charles, illus. LC 65-19864. 284p. illus. (pt. col.) 24cm. (Best Bk. Ser.). 1965, c.1958. Doubleday.
--Best Book of Read Aloud Stories. Le Moult, Adolph & Wilde, George A., illus. LC 66-12184. 283 p. illus. (part col.) 24 cm. (Her Best Bks. Ser.). 1966. Doubleday.
--Best Book of Stories of Boys and Girls. McCurry, Charles & Sibley, Donald (1922-), illus. LC 65-19866. (Illus.). 284 p. 24cm. (Best Bks. Ser.). 1965. Doubleday.
--Best Book of Stories of Boys and Girls. Color Illus. McCurry, Charles & Sibley, Donald (1922-), illus. LC 65-19866. 284p. illus. (pt. col.) 24cm. (Best Bk. Ser.). 1965, c.1958. Doubleday.
--The Family Treasury of Children's Stories. 1st ed. Sibley, Don (1922-), illus. LC 56-9600. (Illus.). 3 v. 22cm. 1956. Doubleday.
--The Family Treasury of Children's Stories, 2 vols. Sibley, Don (1922-), illus. LC 63-12311. 2v. (486;498p.) illus. 22cm. 1963, c.1956. Doubleday.

--Good Housekeeping's Best Book of Adventure Stories. 1st ed. Noonan, Daniel, illus. LC 57-12951. 382p. illus. 21cm. 1957. Good Housekeeping Magazine Distributed by Prentice-Hall, Englewood Cliffs, N.J.
--Good Housekeeping's Best Book of Bedtime Stories. 1st ed. Sibley, Don (1922-), illus. LC 57-12953. 384p. illus. 21cm. 1957. Good Housekeeping Magazine; Distributed by Prentice-Hall.
--Good Housekeeping's Best Book of Dog Stories. Collim, Joseph, illus. LC 58-10523. (Illus.). 21cm. 384p. 1958. Prentice-Hall.
--Good Housekeeping's Best Book of Fairy Tales. 1st ed. Wilde, Irma, illus. LC 57-12954. 383p. illus. 21cm. 1957. Good Housekeeping Magazine Distributed by Prentice-Hall, Englewood Cliffs, N.J.
--Good Housekeeping's Best Book of Fun and Nonsense. 1st ed. Wilde, George A., illus. LC 57-12955. 384p. illus. 21cm. 1957. Good Housekeeping Magazine Distributed by Prentice-Hall, Englewood Cliffs, N.J.
--Good Housekeeping's Best Book of Horse Stories. Noonan, Daniel, illus. LC 58-10445. (Illus.). 21cm. 384p. 1958. Prentice-Hall.
--Good Housekeeping's Best Book of Nature Stories. 1st ed. Hunter, Mel (1927-), illus. LC 57-12956. 383p. illus. 21cm. 1957. Good Housekeeping Magazine Distributed by Prentice-Hall, Englewood Cliffs, N.J.

Evans, Ruth
--The Jungle of Tonza Mara. Smith, Lawrence Beall (1909-), illus. LC 63-9593. 69 p. illus. 27 cm. 1963. Macmillan.

Evans, Shirlee (1931-)
--Tree Tall and the Whiteskins. Ponter, James J., illus. LC 85-13952. (Illus.). 104 p. 20cm. 1985. (ISBN 0-8361-3402-8). Harald Press.

Evans, Wainwright
--The Thunder Bird. Dobias, Frank (1902-), illus. LC 34-33283. viii p., 1 l., 11-70 p. incl. front., illus. 20 cm. (Our changing world). 1934. T. Nelson and Sons.

Evansen, Virginia Besaw (1921-)
--The Flea Market Mystery. Abel, Raymond (1911-), illus. LC 77-16863. (Illus.). 188 p. 22cm. c.1978. (ISBN 0-396-07521-5). Dodd, Mead.
--Nancy Kelsey. Lantz, Paul (1908-), illus. (Illus.). (gr. 7 up). 1965. McKay.
--Sierra Summit. Thomas, Allan (1901-), illus. LC 67-15045. (Illus.). ix, 245 p. 21cm. 1967. D. McKay Co.

Evarts, Hal George (1887-)
--The Bald Face and Other Animal Stoires. Bull, Charles Livingston (1874-1932), illus. 317p. 1921. Alfred A. Knopf.
--Fur Sign. Hunt, Lynn Bogue, illus. LC 22-17940. v. 225 p. front. 20 cm. 1922. Little, Brown, and Company.
--Jerbo: The Jumper. Nelson, Don, illus. LC 30-23231. 41 p. illus. 24 cm. c.1930. Whitman Publishing Company.
--Kobi of the Sea. Nelson, Don, illus. LC 30-232322. 42 p. illus. 24 cm. c.1930. Whitman Publishing Company.
--Phantom, the White Mink. Nelson, Don, illus. LC 30-23233. 41 p. illus. 24 cm. c.1930. Whitman Publishing Company.
--The Shaggy Legion. 307p. 1930. Little, Brown & Co.
--Swift, the Kit Fox. Nelson, Don, illus. LC 30-23234. 40 p. illus., pl. 24 cm. c.1930. Whitman Publishing Company.

Evarts, Hal George, Jr. (1915-)
--Bigfoot. LC 73-1329. 190 p. 22cm. 1973. (ISBN 0-684-13388-1). Scribner.
--Jay-Jay and the Peking Monster. LC 77-27426. 185 p. 22cm. c.1978. (ISBN 0-684-15547-8). Scribner.
--Jedediah Smith, Trail Blazer of the West. Krigstein, Bernard (1919-), illus. LC 58-13310. (Illus.). 192 p. 21cm. 1959, c.1958. Putnam.
--Mission to Tibet. LC 72-120362. 190 p. 22cm. 1970. Scribner.
--The Pegleg Mystery. LC 75-174650. 189 p. 22cm. 1972. (ISBN 0-684-12686-9). Scribner.
--The Purple Eagle Mystery. LC 75-27704. 218 p. 22cm. c.1976. (ISBN 0-684-14531-6). Scribner.
--The Secret of the Himalayas. LC 62-14034. 185 p. 21cm. 1962. Scribner.
--Smugglers' Road. LC 68-12515. 192p. 22cm. 1968. Scribners.
--The Talking Mountain. LC 66-18540. 192 p. 22 cm. 1966. Scribner.
--Treasure River. LC 64-16182. (Illus.). 186 p. 22cm. 1964. Scribner.

Evatt, Harriet, Mrs. (1895-)
--An Army in Pigtails. Evatt, Harriet, Mrs. (1895-), illus. LC 62-18094. 42p. illus. (pt. col.) 29cm. (gr. 1-5). c.1962. (ISBN 0-672-50210-0). Bobbs.
--Big Indian and Little Bear. Evatt, Harriet, Mrs. (1895-), illus. LC 54-10851. unpaged. illus. 23cm. c.1954. Bobbs-Merrill.
--Davy Crockett, Big Indian, and Little Bear. Evatt, Harriet, Mrs. (1895-), illus. LC 55-10898. unpaged. illus. 22cm. c.1955. Bobbs-Merrill.
--Mystery of Lonesome Manor. Stone, David Karl (1922-), illus. LC 62-11980. (Illus.). 22cm. 187p. (gr. 3-7). 1962. (ISBN 0-672-50402-2). Bobbs.
--The Mystery of the Alpine Castle. 1st ed. Evatt, Harriet, Mrs. (1895-), illus. LC 51-13204. 242 p. illus. 23 cm. 1951. Bobbs-Merrill.
--The Mystery of the Creaking Windmill. Evatt, Harriet, Mrs. (1895-), illus. LC 45-7649. 243 p. incl. front., illus. 22 cm. 1945. The Bobbs-Merrill Company.
--The Mystery of the Old Merchant's House. 1st ed. Evatt, Harriet, Mrs. (1895-), illus. LC 47-30682. 226 p. illus. 23 cm. 1947. Bobbs-Merrill Co.
--The Papoose Who Wouldn't Keep Her Stockings on. Evatt, Harriet, Mrs. (1895-), illus. LC 54-6507. unpaged. illus. 27cm. c.1954. Bobbs-Merril.
--The Red Canoe. Evatt, Harriet, Mrs. (1895-), illus. LC 40-30187. 137 p. illus. 26 cm. c.1940. The Bobbs-Merrill Company.
--The Secret of Solitary Cove. Kennedy, Paul Edward (1929-), illus. LC 64-15676. 144 p. illus. 22 cm. 1964. Bobbs-Merrill.
--The Secret of the Old Coach Inn. Stone, David Karl (1922-), illus. LC 59-14304. (Illus.). 22cm. 191p. 1959. Bobbs-Merrill Co, Inc.
--The Secret of the Ruby Locket. Evatt, Harriet, Mrs. (1895-), illus. LC 43-13839. 245 p. incl. front., illus. 22 1/2 cm. 1943. The Bobbs-Merrill Company.
--The Secret of the Singing Tower. 1st ed. Evatt, Harriet, Mrs. (1895-), illus. LC 53-9868. 243p. illus. 23cm. 1953. Bobbs-Merrill.
--The Secret of the Whispering Willow. 1st ed. Evatt, Harriet, Mrs. (1895-), illus. LC 50-5905. (Illus.). 282 p. 22cm. 1950. Bobbs-Merrill.
--The Snow Owl's Secret. Evatt, Harriet, Mrs. (1895-), illus. LC 46-734529. 243 p. incl. front., illus. 22 cm. 1946. The Bobbs-Merrill Company.
--Suzette's Family. LC 41-16066. 132 p. 1 l. illus. 26 cm. c.1941. The Bobbs-Merrill Company.
--You Can't Keep a Squirrel on the Ground. LC 61-7922. 29cm. 47p. (gr. k-3). 1961. (ISBN 0-672-50596-7). Bobbs.

E. V. B. , illus.
--Beauty and the Beast: An Old Tale Retold. N.D. Scribner & Welford.
--Child's Play. N.D. Scribner & Welford.
--A New Child's Play. N.D. Scribner & Welford.

Eve, Esme, illus.
--Mother Goose. N.D. Grosset & Dunlap.

Eve, Esme, et al., illus.
--Three-Hundred-Sixty Five Animal Stories. new ed. (Illus.). color ils. 240p. 1st U.S. edition. (ps). 1971. (ISBN 0-307-16554-X, Golden Pr). Western Pub.

Eve, Esme & Mamlock, Gwyneth, illus.
--Three Hundred Sixty-Six Goodnight Stories. (Illus.). 1969. (ISBN 0-307-15568-4, Golden Pr). Western Pub.

Eveleth, Alice Towne
--Top O' the Day. LC 32-33417. 138 p. 19 cm. c.1932. Dorrance & Co., Inc.

Evelyn, Constance
--Miss Nettie's Girls. (Illus.). 256p. N.D. Ira Bradley & Co's.

Evelyn-Marie (1927-)
--Daniel Scott and the Monster. Lang, Irene, illus. LC 85-13369. p. cm. 1985. (ISBN 0-9614746-1-0). Barry Books.

Evenhuis, Gertie (1932-)
--Locked Harbor. Richter, Eva, tr. (gr. 4 up). 1967. Macmillan.
--What About Me?. Stenberg, Ron, illus. Salway, Lance, tr. LC 76-373952. (Illus.). 93 p. 18cm. (Puffin books). 1976, c.1974. (ISBN 0-14-030795-8). Puffin Books.
--What About Me?. 1st. ed. Stenberg, Ron, illus. Salway, Lance, tr. LC 76-27312. 96 21. 1976, c.1974. (ISBN 0-8407-6524-X). T. Nelson.

Everard, Walker
--Sir Walter's Ward. (Illus.). (Scribner-Blackie Series of books for young people). N.D. Charles Scribner's Sons.

Everden, Margery (1916-)
--The Runaway Apprentice. Wong, Jeanyee, illus. 21cm. 138p. N.D. Random House.

Everds, Martha
--Love Is. 1st ed. Bacon, Paul (1913-), illus. LC 78-92866. (Illus.). 36 l. 20cm. 1969. Doubleday.

Everds, Marty
--Lionel, the Lazy Lion. Everds, Marty, illus. LC 60-6253. (Illus.). 21cm. 41p. (gr. k-2). 1960. (ISBN 0-690-49520-X). T Y Crowell.
--The Mob from Wobbly Woods. Evards, John, illus. (Illus.). (ps-2). 1980. (Gingerbread). Dutton.

Everett, Ethel
--Nursery Rhymes. N.D. Thomas Nelson & Sons.
--Old Fairy Tales. N.D. Thomas Nelson & Sons.

Everett-Green, Evelyn (1856-1932)
--Afterthought House (Pub. by Society for Promoting Christian Knowledge). N.D. E. & J. B. Young & Co.
--Barbara's Brothers. Taylor, Ethel Bonney & Taylor, R., illus. (Illus.). 447p. 1887. American Sunday-School Union.
--Barbara's Brothers. Taylor, Ethel Bonney & Taylor, R., illus. (Illus.). 447p. N.D. Ira Bradley & Co's.
--Birdie's Resolve: And How it was accomplished. N.D. Thomas Nelson & Sons.
--Bruno and Bimba. (Illus.). 256p. N.D. E. P. Dutton & Co.
--Carol Carew. (The Girls Own Library). N.D. David McKay.
--The City of the Golden Gate. 1909. Dodge.
--A Clerk of Oxford and His Adventures in the Baron's War. 1897. Nelson.
--Clive's Conquest. (Illus.). 64p. 1905. American Tract Society.
--Dare Lorimer's Heritage. 1892. Bradley and Woodruff.
--Dick Whistler's Tramp. 1891. Revell.
--The Doctor's Dozen. 1892. American Sunday School Union.
--Don Carlos (Pub. by Society for Promoting Christian Knowledge). N.D. E. & J. B. Young & Co.
--Dulcie & Tottie: Or, The Story of an Old Fashioned Pair. 1889. Thos Nelson & Sons.
--Dulcie's Little Brother: Or, Doings at Little Monksholm. 1887. Thos Nelson & Sons.
--Dulcie's Love Story. 1891. Thos Nelson & Sons.
--Dunalton: Or, The Story of Jack & His Guardians. N.D. Thos Nelson & Sons.
--Esther's Charge. (Illus.). (Fireside Series for Girls). 1899. A. L. Burt's Pubs.
--Esther's Charge. (Illus.). (The Wellesley Series for Girls). N.D. A. L. Burt's Pubs.
--Evil May Day: A Story of Fifteen Hundred and Seventeen. 1893. Nelson.
--Fallen Fortunes: Being the Adventures of a Gentleman of Quality in the Days of Queen Anne. 1902. Nels.
--Fighting the good Fight: Or, The Successful Influence of Well-Doing. N.D. Thos Nelson & Sons.
--Fir-Tree Farm. 1891. Revell.
--Gladys or Gwenyth?. The Story of a Mistake. N.D. Thomas Nelson & Sons.
--Golden Gwendolyn. 1893. Bradley.
--A Gordon Highlander. 1901. Nelson.
--The Great Show: Or, Bunny's Birthday. 1893. Revell.
--The Heir of Hascombe Hall: A Tale of the Days of the Early Tudors. 1900. Nelson.
--The Heiress of Wylmington. N.D. Thomas Nelson & Sons.
--Her Husbands's Home. (Illus.). 384p. N.D. A. I. Bradley & Co.'s Pub.
--In the Days of Chivalry: A Tale of the Times of the Black Prince. 1893. Nelson.
--In the Wars of the Roses. N.D. Thomas Nelson & Sons.
--Judith, the Money-Lender's Daughter. 1896. Bradley.
--The King's Butterfly. Dixon, Arthur A., illus. 1900. Dutton.
--Little Lady Val: A Tale of the Days of Good Queen Bess. Dixon, Arthur A., illus. (Illus.). (Dainty Ser.). N.D. Henry Altemus Co.
--Little Lois. (Illus.). N.D. Thomas Nelson & Sons.
--Little Miss Vixen. 1893. Revell.
--Little Ruth's Lady. 1890. Carter.
--The Lord of Dynevor: A Tale in the Time of Edward the First. 1892. Nelson.
--Loyal Hearts. N.D. Thos Nelson & Sons.
--Marcus Stratford's Change: Or, Roy's Temptation. 1890. Bradley and Woodruff.
--Miss Marjorie of Silvermead. 1901. G. W. Jacobs.
--Miss Uraca. 1894. Bradley.
--Molly Melville. (Illus.). 1897. Thomas Nelson & Sons.
--Mrs. Romaine's Household. 1891. Bradley and Woodruff.
--Namesakes: The Story of a Secret. 1893. Revell.
--Odeyne's Marriage. (Illus.). 384p. 1900. E. P. Dutton & Company.
--Old Miss Audrey: A Chronicle of a Quiet Village. 1893. Revell.
--Olive Roscoe: Or, The New Sister. 1896. Nelson.
--Oliver Langton's Ward. 1890. Bradley Woodruff.
--A Pair of Pickles. (Illus.). 191p. 1899. A. I. Bradley & Co.'s Pub.
--Pat the Lighthouse Boy. 1894. Ward and Drummond.
--The Percevals: Or, A Houseful of Girls. 1890. Revell.
--Princess Fairstar: A Story of the Days of Charles I. Micheal, F. H., illus. 1902. Dutton.
--Roger Trehern. Orig. Title: The Conscience of Roger Trehern. 1903. American Tract Society.
--Secret Chamber at Chad. (Illus.). N.D. Thomas Nelson & Sons.
--The Secret of Maxshelling. 1901. Dutton.
--Sir Aylmer's Heir. (Illus.). 1890. Thomas Nelson & Sons.
--Sister: A Chronicle of Fair Haven. Finnemore, J., illus. N.D. Thomas Nelson & Sons.
--The Stronger Will. 1890. Bradley Woodruff.
--Summer Holiday. (Illus.). 80p. (The Rosebud Ser.). N.D. Fleming H. Revell Co.
--Sydney's Secret: Or, Honesty Is the Best Policy. (Illus.). N.D. E & J B Young.
--Tom Tufton's Toll. 1898. Nelson.
--Tom Tufton's Travels. 1898. Nelson.
--True to the Last: Or, My Boyhood's Hero. N.D. Thos Nelson & Sons.
--Vera's Trust. N.D. Thos Nelson & Sons.
--The Willful Willoughbys. (Illus.). 317p. N.D. A. I. Bradley & Co.'s Pub.
--The Willful Willoughbys: A Cathedral City Story. 1893. Revell.
--Winning the Victory: Or, Di Pennington's Reward. N.D. Thos Nelson & Sons.

Everett-Green, Evelyn (1856-1932) & Bedford, H. Louise
--Priscilla: A Story for Girls. Bacon, John H., illus. 1900. Thomas Nelson & Sons.

Everett-Green, Evelyn (1856-1932) & Fletcher, Evelyn
--Holidays at the Farm. 1913. Dutton.

Everett, William (1839-1910)
--Changing Base: Or, What Edward Rice Learnt. (Royal Club Ser.). N.D. Colby and Rich.
--Changing Base: or, What Edward Rice Learnt at school, 1 of 2 vols. LC 12-32128. (Illus.). 18cm. 282p. (The Royal Club Ser.). 1868. Lee & Shepard.
--Double Play: Or, How Joe Hardy Chose His Friends. (Royal Club Ser.). N.D. Colby and Rich.
--Double Play: or, How Joe Hardy Chose His Friends, 1 of 2 vols. (Illus.). (The Royal Club Series). 1882. Lee & Shepard.
--Thine, Not Mine: A Sequel to "Changing Base.". LC 12-32127. vii p., 1 l., 7-297 p. front., plates. 18 cm. 1891. Roberts Brothers.

Everett-Green, Evelyn, jt. auth. see Brown, Janet.

Evernden, Margery (1916-)
--Davy Crockett & His Coonskin Cap. (Children's Theatre Playscript Ser.). 1956. (ISBN 0-88020-025-1). Coach Hse.
--The Frog Princess & the Witch. (Children's Theatre Playscript Ser.). 1963. (ISBN 0-88020-028-6). Coach Hse.
--The Golden Trail. Ward, Lynd Kendall (1905-1985), illus. LC 52-5856. (Illus.). 179 p. 21cm. 1952. Random House.
--The Happiest Family in the World. LC 85-88. p. cm. 1985. (ISBN 0-688-04638-X). Lothrop, Lee & Shepard Books.
--King Arthur's Sword. (Children's Theatre Playscript Ser.). 1959. (ISBN 0-88020-034-0). Coach Hse.
--The King of the Golden River. (Children's Theatre Playscript Ser.). 1955. (ISBN 0-88020-033-2). Coach Hse.
--The Kite Song. LC 84-4367. 192p. (gr. 6-9). 1984. (ISBN 0-688-01200-0). Lothrop.
--Knight of Florence. Busoni, Rafaello (1900-1962), illus. LC 50-8606. (Illus.). vi, 133 p. 21cm. 1950. Random House.
--Lyncoya. LC 73-7528. 212 p. 21cm. 1973. (ISBN 0-8098-3115-5). H. Z. Walck.
--Rumpelstiltskin. (Children's Theatre Playscript Ser.). 1955. (ISBN 0-88020-051-0). Coach Hse.
--The Secret of Han Ho. (Children's Theatre Playscript Ser.). 1956. (ISBN 0-88020-052-9). Coach Hse.
--The Secret of the Porcelain Fish. Handforth, Thomas Schofield (1897-1948), illus. LC 47-30267. 5 p. l., 3-147, 3 p. incl. front., illus. 22 cm. 1947. Random House.
--Simon's Way. Newfeld, Frank (1928-), illus. LC 63-10908. (Illus.). 224 p. 21cm. 1963. H. Z. Walck.
--The Sword with the Golden Hilt. Soles, William, illus. LC 50-10430. 132 p. illus. 24 cm. 1950. (ISBN 0-87004-037-5). Caxton Printers.
--Wilderness Boy. LC 55-10106. 218 p. 21cm. 1955. Putnam.

Evers, Alf, jt. auth. see Evers, Helen Dean Bryant.

Evers, Alf (1905-)
--Abner's Cabin. Weisgard, Leonard Joseph (1916-), illus. LC 57-7541. unpaged. illus. 28cm. c.1957. F. Watts.
--The Baby Bunny. Seiden, Bea Rabin, illus. LC 51-9324. unpaged. illus. 21 cm. (Wonder books, 548). 1951. Wonder Books.
--The Baldhead Mountain Expedition. Geer, Charles Hand (1922-), illus. LC 59-7865. 205p. illus. 21cm. 1959. Macmillan.
--Bobby's Happy Day. Cooper, Marjorie (1910-), illus. LC 52-10981. unpaged. illus. 26cm. 1953. Rand McNally.
--Brave Little Steam Shovel. Stone, David Karl (1922-), illus. LC 51-25841. (Illus.). 21cm. 41p. (gr. k-3). N.D. Wonder.

--Buddy, the Little Taxi. Corwin, Eleanor, illus. LC 52-18199. unpaged. illus. 21 cm. (Rand McNally book-elf book, 456). N.D. Rand McNally.
--The Colonel's Squad. Sewell, Helen Moore (1896-1957), illus. LC 52-14345. (Illus.). 200 p. 22cm. 1952. Macmillan.
--A Day on the Farm: A/Rand McNally Book-Elf Book. Grider, Dorothy (1915-), illus. LC 48-798572. (Illus.). 21cm. 40p. 1948. Rand McNally and Co.
--The Deer-Jackers. Parker, Lewis, illus. LC 64-11759. 152p. illus. 22cm. c.1965. Macmillan.
--The Goose Who Played the Piano. Cunningham, Dellwyn, illus. LC 51-14550. unpaged. illus. 21 cm. (Wonder books, 567). 1951. Wonder Books.
--Little Bobo and His Blue Jacket. Brice, Tony, illus. LC 44-3055. (Illus.). 23 x 20cm. 40p. 1944. Rand McNally.
--Little Bobo and His Blue Jacket. Brice, Tony, illus. LC 53-29587. unpaged. illus. 21cm. (Rand McNally book-elf book, 472). c.1953. Rand McNally.
--Little Bobo and His Blue Jacket. Brice, Tony, illus. LC 55-90298. unpaged. illus. 33cm (Rand McNally giant book). 1955, c.1953. Rand McNally.
--The Little Engine that Laughed. Seiden, Art, illus. LC 50-12279. 29 col. illus. 29. (Treasure books). 1950. Grosset & Dunlap.
--Open the Door. Polseno, Jo, illus. LC 60-5581. unpaged. illus. 27cm. 1960. F. Watts.
--Slick in Me and the Fallon Case. 1st ed. Klinger, Charles, illus. LC 52-13065. 175p illus. 21cm. 1953. Holt.
--There's No Such Animal. Grom, Bogdan, illus. LC 58-10141. (Illus.). 24cm. (gr. k-3). 1958. Lippincott.
--The Three Kings of Saba. Sewell, Helen Moore (1896-1957), illus. LC 55-9509. unpaged. illus. 26cm. c.1955. Lippincott. **Awards: (NYT); (ALA).**
--The Treasure of Watchdog Mountain. Burchard, Peter Duncan (1921-), illus. LC 55-13716. 74p. illus. 24cm. 1955. Macmillan.

Evers, Helen see Ivarson, Siane, pseud.

Evers, Helen Dean Bryant
--Little Hippo and His Red Bicycle. Brice, Tony, illus. LC 48-3306. (Illus.). 23cm. 40p. 1945. Rand McNally.
--The Three Little Kittens. Brice, Tony, illus. Bryant. LC 38-16757. 82 p. col. illus. 17 cm. c.1933. Rand, McNally & Company.

Evers, Helen Dean Bryant & Evers, Alf (1905-)
--All About Copy-Kitten: The Complete Adventures of Copy-Kitten, As First Told in Copy-Kitten, and More About Copy-Kitten. LC 40-14675. 121 p. illus. 20 x 18 cm. c.1940. Rand McNally & Company.
--Benny and his birds. LC 41-15926. 48p. col. illus. 20 x 30cm. c.1941. Rand McNally & Co.
--Chatterduck. LC 43-3613. 41 p. col. illus. 19 1/2 x 16 1/2 cm. c.1943. Rand McNally & Company.
--Cheeky Chipmunk. LC 46-3681. 44 p. col. illus. 19 1/2 x 17 cm. c.1945. Rand McNally & Company.
--Copy-Kitten. LC 37-540320. 57 p. illus. 20 x 17 cm. c.1937. Rand, McNally & Company.
--Copy Kitten. LC 57-8253. (Illus.). 22cm. (A Rand McNally Elf Book). 1957. Rand McNally.
--Crosspatch. LC 49-883082. 41 p. illus. 20 cm. c.1949. Rand McNally.
--Crybaby Calf. LC 41-2940. 57 p. col. illus. 20 x 17 cm. c.1941. Rand McNally & Company.
--Crybaby Calf. LC 57-7311. unpaged. illus. 22 cm. (Rand McNally elf book, 547). 1957. Rand McNally.
--Frankie. LC 39-271285. 57 p. illus. 20 cm. c.1939. Rand, McNally & Company.
--Fussbunny. LC 44-2951. 40 p. col. illus. 19 1/2 x 17 cm. c.1944. Rand McNally & Company.
--Fussbunny. LC 55-11972. (Illus.). 21cm. 1955. Rand McNally.
--The Happy Hen. LC 33-243483. 32 p. illus. 20 x 24 cm. c.1933. Farrar & Rinehart, Incorporated.
--The House the Pecks Built. LC 40-311183. 48 p. col. illus. 26 x 20 cm. c.1940. Rand McNally & Company.
--Little Goosie-Gosling. LC 34-29547. 63 p. illus. 17 cm. c.1934. Farrar & Rinehart, Incorporated.
--A Little Lamb. LC 35-14571. 61 p. illus. 17 cm. c.1935. Farrar & Rhinehart, Incorporated.
--The Merry Mouse. LC 36-195633. 63 p. illus. 17 cm. c.1936. Farrar & Rinehart, Incorporated.
--Moonymouse. LC 48-6030. 41 p. col. illus. 20 cm. 1948. Rand McNally.
--Moonymouse. LC 58-8220. (Illus.). 22cm. (Tip-top Elf Bks.). 1958. Rand McNally.
--More About Copy-Kitten. LC 40-71058. 57 p. illus. 20 cm. c.1940. Rand McNally & Company.
--Mr. Scrunch. LC 39-23864. 48 p. illus. 26 cm. c.1939. Rand McNally & Company.
--Playboy Penguin. LC 43-15776. 26 p. col. illus. 19 1/2 x 17 cm. c.1943. Rand McNally & Company.
--The Plump Pig. LC 38-10449. 55 p. illus. 20 x 17 cm. c.1938. Rand, McNally & Company.
--Plump Pig. LC 56-71070. unpaged. illus. 21cm. (Rand McNally elf book, 542). c.1956. Rand McNally.
--Pokey Bear. LC 42-6280. 41 p. col. illus. 20 x 17 cm. c.1942. Rand McNally & Company.
--Sloppy Joe. LC 47-1533. 41 p. col. illus. 19 1/2 x 17 cm. c.1947. Rand McNally & Company.
--This Little Pig. LC 32-28833. 32 p. col. illus. 20 x 24 cm. c.1932. Farrar & Rinehart, Incorporated.

Everson, Dale Millar (1928-)
--The Different Dog. Galdone, Paul (1914-), illus. LC 60-5796. (Illus.). (Morrow junior books). (gr. k-3). 1960. Morrow.
--Mrs. Popover Goes to the Zoo. McCaffery, Janet, illus. LC 63-11777. unpaged illus. 21 x 24 cm. 1963. Morrow.

Everson, Florence McClurg & Everson, Howard
--The Coming of the Dragon Ships. 1st. ed. D'Aulaire, Edgar Parin (1898-), illus. LC 31-23194. 128, 1 p. incl. illus., plates, col. front., col. plates. 22 cm. 1931. E. P. Dutton & Co., Inc.
--The Secret Cave. Wakefield, Lucina Smith, illus. LC 30-201632. 101 p. incl. col. front., col. illus. 20 cm. c.1930. E. P. Dutton & Co.

Everson, Florence McClurg & Power, Effie Louise (1873-)
--Early Days in Ohio: A Story of a Pioneer Family of the Western Reserve. Richards, George Mather (1880-), illus. LC 28-25554. xi, 265 p. incl. plates. front. 20 cm. 1928. E. P. Dutton & Co., Inc.

Everson, Howard, jt. auth. see Everson, Florence McClurg.

Everton, Macduff (1947-)
--El Circo Magico Modelo: Finding the Magic Circus. Everton, Macduff (1947-), illus. LC 79-88199. (Illus.). 32 p. c.1979. (ISBN 0-87614-106-8). Carolrhoda Books.

Every, Dale Van
--The Captive Witch. N.D. Jullian Messner, Inc.

Every, Philip Cochrane, pseud., see Burnford, Sheila.

Evey, Ethel L. (1915-)
--Stowaway to Texas. LC 83-11363. p. cm. 1983, c.1982. (ISBN 0-89896-102-5). (ISBN 0-89896-101-7). Larksdale Press.

Evison, Millicent
--The Good-for-Nothing Graysons. Wilson, F. Vaux, illus. LC 28-22311. 310 p. front., plates. 20 cm. c.1928. Lothrop, Lee & Shepard Co.
--Peggy Pretend. Hubon, Edna F. Hart, illus. LC 22-6601. 5 p. l., 319 p. front., plates. 21 cm. 1922. Lothrop, Lee & Shepard Co.
--Rainbow Gold. Duphiney, Wilfred I., illus. LC 21-6501. 362 p. front., plates. 21 cm. c.1920. Lothrop, Lee & Shepard Co.

Evslin, Bernard, et al. (1922-)
--Heroes & Monsters of Greek Myths. bibl. notes. 112p. (gr. 7-9). 1970. (ISBN 0-590-01555-9). Scholastic Inc.

Evslin, Bernard (1922-)
--Adventures of Ulysses. Hunter, William (1942-), illus. (Illus.). 160p. (gr. 7-9). 1970. (ISBN 0-590-02973-8, Schol Trade Pap). Schol Bk Serv.
--Dolphin Rider & Other Greek Myths. (gr. 4-6). 1976. (ISBN 0-590-00128-0, Schol Pap). Schol Bk Serv.
--Gods, Demigods, & Demons. (gr. 7-12). 1976. (ISBN 0-590-10131-5, Schol Trade Pap). Schol Bk Serv.
--The Greek Gods. (gr. 7-12). 1972. (ISBN 0-590-06350-2, Schol Pap). Scholastic Inc.
--Greeks Bearing Gifts: The Epics of Achilles & Ulysses. LC 76-16039. (Illus.). 336p. 1976. (ISBN 0-590-17431-2, Four Winds). Scholastic Inc.
--The Green Hero: Early Adventures of Finn McCool. Bascove, Barbara, illus. LC 74-23851. (Illus.). 181 p. 24cm. 1975. (ISBN 0-590-07121-1). Four Winds Press.
--Heraclea: A Legend of Warrior Women. Bitzer, Lucy Martin, illus. LC 77-17967. (Illus.). 257 p. 24cm. c.1978. (ISBN 0-590-07405-9). Four Winds Press.
--Hercules. Smith, Joseph A. (1936-), illus. (gr. 4-8). 1984. (ISBN 0-688-02748-2). Morrow.
--Heroes, Gods & Monsters of the Greek Myths. Hofmann, William, illus. LC 67-23541. (Illus.). (gr. 7 up). 1967. (ISBN 0-590-07059-2, Four Winds). Schol Bk Serv.
--Signs and Wonders. Mikolaycak, Charles (1937-), illus. LC 81-2188. p. cm. c.1981. (ISBN 0-590-07686-8). Four Winds Press.
--Signs & Wonders: Tales from the Old Testament. Mikolaycak, Charles (1937-), illus. (Illus.). 352p. (gr. 7 up). 1982. (ISBN 0-590-07686-8, Four Winds). Scholastic Inc.

Ewald, Carl (1856-1908)
--The Battle of the Bees and Other Stories. Sperry, Margaret (1905-), adapted by. Phillips, Lily R, illus. LC 76-44621. (Illus.). 114 p. 24cm. c.1977. (ISBN 0-8448-1039-8). Crane, Russak.
--The Four Seasons. Teixeira de Mattos, Alexander Louis (1865-1921), tr. LC 13-21310. 21cm. 187p. 1913. Dodd, Mead & Co.
--The Old Willow-Tree and Other Stories. Lee, G. E. & Jacobs, Helen M., illus. Teixeira De Mattos, Alexander Louis (1865-1921), tr. LC 23-26847. 3 p. l., 9-157 p. incl. illus., plates. col. front., col. plates. 22 cm. 1923. Frederick A. Stokes Company.
--The Queen Bee. Smith, George Charles Moore (1858-), tr. from Danish. LC 9-11051. (Illus.). 22 x 17cm. 125p. 1908. T. Nelson & Sons.
--The Spider, and Other Stories. 1st ed. Woodman, Bill, illus. Le Gallienne, Eva (1899-), tr. LC 79-8043. (Illus.). 86 p. 23cm. c.1980. (ISBN 0-690-04042-3). (ISBN 0-690-04043-1). Crowell.
--The Spider and Other Stories. Woodman, Bill, illus. Le Gallienne, Eva (1899-), tr. from Danish. LC 79-8043. (Illus.). 96p. 1980. (ISBN 0-690-04042-3, 1980). (ISBN 0-690-04043-1). Har-Row.
--Two-legs. Bride, John & Jacobs, Helen, illus. Teixeria de Mattos, Alexander Louis (1865-1921), tr. from Danish. 22cm. 160p. 1922. Frederick A. Stokes Co.

Ewart, Gavin Buchanan (1916-)
--The Batsford Book of Light Verse for Children. LC 79-307917. (Illus.). 160 p. 23cm. 1979. (ISBN 0-7134-0916-9). Batsford.

E. W. B.
--Archibald Hamilton. (Fern Glen Ser.). N.D. D. Lothrop Co.

Ewell, Gale, pseud., see Brown, Ethel Poole.

Ewen, David (1907-)
--Haydn, a Good Life. Kohs, Marion R., illus. LC 46-11803. 5 p. l., 3-245 p. 1 l. illus. 24 1/2 cm. 1946. H. Holt and Company.

Ewers, John Keith (1904-)
--Written in Sand. 1st ed. Johnson, Avery Fischer (1906-), illus. LC 47-4736. 160 p. illus. 21 cm. 1947. E. P. Dutton.

Ewing, Frank Calvin (1888-)
--I-a-Goo and His Forest Friends. Clare, Ernie, illus. LC 48-6821. v, 110 p. illus. 26 cm. 1948, c.1947. Foster & Stewart Pub. Corp.

Ewing, Juliana Horatia Gatty, jt. auth. see Molesworth, Mary Louisa Stewart, Mrs.

Ewing, Juliana Horatia Gatty, Mrs. (1841-1885)
--Benjy in Beastland. (Illus.). (The Children's Friend Ser.). N.D. Little, Brown and Company.
--The Blue Bells on the Lea and Ten Other Tales in Verse, 1 of 6 Vols. Andre, Richard, illus. (Illus.). (Blue Bell Ser.). 1884. E. & J. B. Young & Co.
--Blue or Red: Or, The Discontented Lobster. Andre, Richard, illus. 1883. Young.
--Brothers of Pity and other Stories. (Illus.). N.D. E & J B Young.
--Brothers of Pity and Other Tales of Beasts and Men. 1882. E. & J. B. Young & Co.
--The Brownies, 25 vols. (Illus.). (The Editha Ser.: No. 15). 1905. Set. H M Caldwell Co.
--The Brownies, 1 of 183 vols. Pocket ed. (The Universal Library). 1900. Hurst & Co.
--The Brownies. (Illus.). (Alligator Classics). N.D. Hurst & Co.
--The Brownies. (Every Boy's and Every Girl's Ser.). N.D. The Macmillan Co.
--The Brownies. Milhous, Katherine (1894-1977), illus. LC 46-11850. 20cm. 50p. (gr. 1-4). 1946. Charles Scribner's Sons.
--The Brownies and Other Stories, 36 vols. (Illus.). (St. Nicholas Ser.). 1905. Set. A L Burt Co.
--The Brownies and Other Stories. (Illus.). (The Wellesley Series for Girls). N.D. A. L. Burt.
--The Brownies and Other Stories. (Queens Treasure Ser.). N.D. Harcourt Brace.
--The Brownies, and Other Stories. Shepard, Ernest Howard (1879-1976), illus. LC 54-11696. 239p. illus. 21cm. (Children's illustrated classics). 1954. Dent.
--Brownies & Other Stories. Shepard, Ernest Howard (1879-1976), illus. (Illus.). (Children's Illustrated Classics). (gr. 3-6). 1954. (ISBN 0-525-27252-6). Dutton.
--The Brownies and Other Tales, 1 of 18 Vols. N.D. E & J B Young & Co.
--The Brownies and Other Tales. Cruikshank, George (1792-1878), illus. (The Ewing Books: Vol. VI). N.D. Frederick Stokes.
--The Brownies and Other Tales. Cruikshank, George (1792-1878), illus. 1901. Hurst.
--Daddy Darwin's Dovecot. (Illus.). (Every Boy's Library). N.D. Caldwell.
--Daddy Darwin's Dovecot. (Illus.). (Every Boy's Library). N.D. Dodge Publishing Co.
--Daddy Darwin's Dovecot. (Illus.). (The Children's Friend Ser.). N.D. Little, Brown and Company.
--Daddy Darwin's Dovecot. (Illus.). (Sunshine Library). 1915. Thomas Y Crowell.
--Daddy Darwin's Dovecot. Barry, Etheldred Breeze (1870-), illus. LC 98-726. 3 p. l., 11-78 p. incl. plates. front. 19 cm. (On verso of half-title: The young of heart series. 4). 1898. D. Estes & Company.
--Daddy Darwin's Dovecot, 1 of 25 vols. Barry, Etheldred Breeze (1870-), illus. LC 98-726. (Illus.). (The Young of Heart Ser.: No. 4). 1898. Set. Dana Estes & Co.
--Daddy Darwin's Dovecot. Caldecott, Randolph (1846-1886), illus. LC 13-7130. 22cm. 52p. N.D. E. & J. B. Young & Co.
--Daddy Darwin's Dovecot. Caldecott, Randolph (1846-1886), illus. N.D. Robert Brothers.
--Daddy Darwin's Dovecot: A Country Tale. LC 6-39110. 64 p. col. front., illus. 20 cm. c.1906. McLoughlin Borthers.
--Daddy Darwin's Dovecot: A Country Tale. Caldecott, Randolph (1846-1886), illus. 1884. E. J. B. Young & Co.
--Daddy Darwin's Dovecot: Melchior's Dream and Other Stories. (Illus.). 1910. Little, Brown & Co.
--Dandelion Clocks and Other Tales. Browne, Gordon Frederick, et al. (1858-1932), illus. 1887. Young.
--Doll's Housekeeping, 1 of 6 Vols. Andre, Richard, illus. (Illus.). (Blue Bell Ser.). N.D. E. & J. B. Young & Co.
--The Dolls Wash. Andre, Richard, illus (Pub. by Society for Promoting Christian Knowlwdge). N.D. E & J B Young.
--Flat Iron for a Farthing. (The Rugby Series for Boys and Girls). N.D. A. L. Burt Company.
--A Flat Iron for a Farthing, 1 of 5 vols. (Juliana H. Ewing's Wks.). N.D. Set. A. L. Burt's Pubs.
--Flat Iron for a Farthing. (Illus.). (The Little Men Ser.). N.D. A. L. Burt's Pubs.
--A Flat Iron for a Farthing. N.D. E & J B Young.
--A Flat Iron for a Farthing. (Queen's Treasure Ser.). N.D. Harcourt Brace & Co.
--Flat-Iron for a Farthing, 1 of 103 vols. (The Pearl Library: No. 24). 1900. Set. Hurst & Co.
--Flat Iron for a Farthing. (Home Series for Girls). N.D. Hurst & Co.
--A Flat-Iron for a Farthing. (Illus.). (St. Nicholas Series for Girls). N.D. International Book Co.
--A Flat Iron for a Farthing, 1 of 9 Vols. (Illus.). (Complete Works of Julia Ewing). N.D. International Book Co.
--A Flat-Iron for a Farthing. (Illus.). 1910. Little Brown & Co.
--A Flat-Iron for a Farthing. (Illus.). N.D. Robert Brothers.
--A Flat Iron for a Farthing: Or, Some Passages in the Life of an Only Son. 1884. Roberts.
--A Flat Iron for a Farthing: Or, Some Passages in the Life of an Only Son. Allingham, Helen Paterson (1848-1926), illus. (The Ewing Books: Vol. I). N.D. Frederick A Stokes Co.
--Grandmother's Spring. Andre, Richard, illus (Pub. by Society for Promoting Christian Knowledge). 1885. E & J B Young.
--A Great Emergency. (Illus.). (Every Boy's Library). N.D. Caldwell.
--A Great Emergency. N.D. E & J B Young.
--A Great Emergency, 1 of 32 vols, Vol. 5. (Illus.). (Famous Books for Girls). N.D. H. M. Caldwell Co.
--A Great Emergency. Barry, Etheldred Breeze (1870-), illus. LC 12-32122. vi p., 1 l., 166 p. incl. illus., plates. front. 19 cm. (On cover: Cosy corner series). 1897. L. C. Page and Company.
--A Great Emergency: And A Very Ill-Tempered Family. Avery, Gillian, intro. by. LC 69-14799. (Illus.). 174 p. 21cm. Reissue of 1874 ed. (Victorian revivals). 1969. (ISBN 0-8052-3087-4). (ISBN 0-8052-0225-0). Schocken Books.
--A Great Emergency and other Stories. (Queen's Treasure Ser.). N.D. Harcourt Brace & Co.
--A Great Emergency, and Other Tales. (Illus.). (The Ewing Books: Vol. VII). N.D. Frederick Stokes.
--A Great Emergency, and other Tales. (Illus.). (St. Nicholas Series for Girls). N.D. International Book Co.
--A Great Emergency and Other Tales, 1 of 9 vol. set. (Illus.). (Complete Works of Juliana Ewing). N.D. International Book Co.
--A Great Emergency and Other Tales. (Illus.). N.D. Little Brown & Co.
--A Great Emergency, and Other Tales. (Illus.). 1877. Robert Brothers.
--A Great Emergency, and Other Tales. LC 9-3012. 284 p. front., pl. 17 cm. 1886. Roberts Brothers.
--Jackanapes, 98 vols. (The Rugby Ser.). 1905. Set. A L Burt Co.
--Jackanapes. (Illus.). (The Little Men Ser.). N.D. A. L. Burt's Pubs.
--Jackanapes. (The Cornell Ser.: No. 71). N.D. A. L. Burt's Pubs.
--Jackanapes, 25 vols. (Illus.). (The Editha Ser.: No. 18). 1905. Set. H M Caldwell Co.

--Jackanapes. (Illus.). (The Young Folks Lib.). N.D. H. M. Caldwell Co.
--Jackanapes, 1 of 32 vols, Vol. 9. (Illus.). (Famous Books for Girls). N.D. H. M. Caldwel Col.
--Jackanapes. N.D. Harcourt Brace & Co.
--Jackanapes, 1 of 12 vols. New ed. (Illus.). (Good Time Ser.: No. 3). 1905. Set. Henry Altemus Co.
--Jackanapes, 1 of 103 vols. (The Pearl Library: No. 37). 1900. Set. Hurst & Co.
--Jackanapes. (Illus.). (Home Ser.). N.D. Hurst and Company.
--Jackanapes. N.D. John C. Winston Co.
--Jackanapes. (Illus.). N.D. Little Brown & Co.
--Jackanapes. (Illus.). (The Children's Friend Ser.). N.D. Little, Brown and Company.
--Jackanapes. (Handy Volume Classics). N.D. Thomas Y. Crowell & Co.
--Jackanapes. Bruce, Josephine, illus. 58p. 1903. D C Heath.
--Jackanapes. Rev. ed. Bruce, Josephine, illus. LC 2-15209. 4 p. l., 71 p. front., plates 19 cm. 1902. D. Estes & Company.
--Jackanapes. Caldecott, Randolph (1846-1886), illus. LC 13-20465. (Illus.). 21cm. 47p. 1884. E. and J. B. Young and Co.
--Jackanapes. Caldecott, Randolph (1846-1886), illus. LC 50-18481. (Illus.). 22cm. 47p. N.D. E. S. Gorham.
--Jackanapes. Caldecott, Randolph (1846-1886), illus. Willard, J. H., intro. by. LC 3-5181. vii, 1 9-128 p. front., illus. 20 cm. 1903. Henry Altemus Company.
--Jackanapes. Caldecott, Randolph (1846-1886), illus. LC 63-56365. (Illus.). 21cm. 47p. 1883. J. B. Young.
--Jackanapes. Caldecott, Randolph (1846-1886), illus. LC 74-230186. (Illus.). 18cm. 60p. 1884. Roberts Bros.
--Jackanapes. Gordon, Frederick C., illus. LC 12-32125. 80 p. incl. front., illus., plates. 22 x 17 cm. 1893. E. P. Dutton & Company.
--Jackanapes. Noble-Ives, Sarah, illus. LC 6-35731. 72p. col. front., illus. pl. 19 1/2cm. c.1906. McLoughlin Bros.
--Jackanapes. Norris, E., ed. LC 6-12561. 1 p. l., iii, 1 5-94 p. illus. 16 cm. (Young people's library of choice literature). c.1906. Educational Publishing Company.
--Jackanapes. Sacker, Amy M., illus. LC 12-32129. 4 p. l., 60 p. front., illus. 19 cm. (On cover: Cosy corner series). 1895. Joseph Knight Company.
--Jackanapes. Sacker, Amy M., illus. (The Cosy Corner Ser.). N.D. L C Page & Co.
--Jackanapes. rev ed. Trent, W. P., ed. Bruce, Josephine, illus. LC 6391. 58p. incl. front., ill. pl. 19cm. (The Story Book Ser.: No. 1). 1900. Heath & Co.
--Jackanapes. Trent, W. P, ed. (Heath's Home and School Classics.). 1910. Heath & Co.
--Jackanapes. Tudor, Tasha (1915-), illus. LC 48-8949. 61 p. illus. (part col.) 20 cm. 1948. Oxford Univ. Press.
--Jackanapes. Tudor, Tasha (1915-), illus. 64p. 1948. Walck.
--Jackanapes and Daddy Darwin. (Illus.). (The Boys' and Girls' Books). N.D. Little, Brown and Company.
--Jackanapes and Daddy Darwin. (Children's Favorite Classics). 1900. Thomas Y. Crowell & Co.
--Jackanapes and Other Stories. N.D. Grosset & Dunlap.
--Jackanapes and other Stories. (Queen's Treasure Ser.). N.D. Harcourt Brace & Co.
--Jackanapes: And Other Stories. Bryant, Sara Cone (1873-), ed. Gallagher, Sears (1869-1955), illus. LC 18-82. v, 271 p. illus. 18 cm. c.1917. Ginn and Company.
--Jackanapes, and Other Tales. (Illus.). (St. Nicholas Series for Girls). N.D. International Book Co.
--Jackanapes and Other Tales, 1 of 9 Vols. Set. (Illus.). (Complete Works of Juliana Ewing). N.D. International Book Co.
--Jackanapes and Other Tales. Tarrant, Percy, illus. LC 27-27786. 5 p. l., 9-267 p. col. front., col. plates. 20 cm. (Newbery classics). 1927. David McKay Company.
--Jackanapes, and Other Tales: Mrs. Ewing Stories, 1 of 9 Vols. N.D. Robert Brothers.
--Jackanapes, and The Brownies. LC 2-13793. 18cm. v, 90p. (Riverside Literature Ser.(no.151)). 1902. Houghton Mifflin Co.
--Jackanapes and The peace egg. Weekes, Blanche Ethel, intro. by. Fitz, John, Jr., illus. LC 28-14243. x. 95p. col. front., 21cm. c.1928. John C. Winston.
--Jackanapes, Daddy Darwin's Dovecot, and Other Stories. LC 12-32124. 220 p. col. front., illus., plates. 17 cm. c.1893. T. Y. Crowell & Co.
--Jackanapes: Daddy Darwin's Dovecot, and The Story of a Short Life. xvi, 231 p. incl. illus., plates. 18 cm. (Half-title: Everyman's library, ed. by Ernest Rhys. For young people). 1916. J. M. Dent & Sons, Ltd.
--Jackanapes, Together with Daddy Darwin's Dovecot and Lob Lie-by-the-Fire. Caldecott, Randolph (1846-1886), illus. LC 67-7461. (Illus.). 184 p. 24cm. (Legacy library facsimile). 1966. University Microfilms.
--Jacknapes and Other Stories. (The Nelson Classics). N.D. Nelson bks.
--Jan of the Windmill. (The Rugby Series for Boys and Girls). N.D. A. L. Burt Company.
--Jan of the Windmill. (Illus.). (Fireside Ser. for Girls). N.D. A. L. Burt's Publications.
--Jan of the Windmill. (Illus.). (The Wellesley Series for Girls). N.D. A. L. Burt's Pubs.
--Jan of the Windmill. (The Cornell Ser.: No. 72). N.D. A. L. Burt's Pubs.
--Jan of the Windmill. N.D. E & J B Young.
--Jan of the Windmill, 1 of 32 vols, Vol. 10. (Illus.). (Famous Books for Girls). N.D. H. M. Caldwell Co.
--Jan of the Windmill. (Queen's Treasure Ser.). N.D. Harcourt Brace & Co.
--Jan of the Windmill, 1 of 103 vols. (The Pearl Library: No. 40). 1900. Set. Hurst & Co.
--Jan of the Windmill. (Illus.). (St. Nicholas Series for Girls). N.D. International Book Co.
--Jan of the Windmill, 1 of 9 vol. set. (Illus.). (Complete Works of Juliana Ewing). N.D. International Book Co.
--Jan of the Windmill. (Illus.). 1910. Little Brown & Co.
--Jan of the Windmill. (Illus.). N.D. Robert Brothers.
--Jan of the Windmill. (Every Boy's and Every Girl's Ser.). N.D. The Macmillan Co.
--Jan of the Windmill. Allingham, Helen Paterson (1848-1926), illus. (The Ewing Bks.: Vol. V). N.D. Frederick Stokes.
--Jan of the Windmill. Allingham, Helen Paterson (1848-1926), illus. LC 60-51384. (Illus.). 23cm. 242p. (gr. 4-6). 1960. (ISBN 0-8098-2341-1). Walck.
--Jan of the Windmill. Wheelhouse, M. V., illus. (Queen's Treasures Ser.). N.D. Macmillan Co.
--Jan of the Windmill. A Story of the Plains. LC 4-17538. x, 310 p. front., plates. 18 cm. 1904. Little. Brown, and Company.
--Jan of the Windmill. A Story of the Plains. LC 31-35239. x, 310 p. front. 17 cm. (Half-title: Town and country series). 1877. Roberts Brothers.
--Jan of the Windmill: A Story of the Plains. Allingham, Helen Paterson (1848-1926), illus. LC 60-51384. (Illus.). 242 p. 23cm. 1960. H. Z. Walck.
--Juliana H. Ewing's Works, 5 vols. N.D. Set. A. L. Burt's Pubs.
--Juliana Horatia Ewing's Works, 11 vols. (Illus.). 19cm. 1909. Little, Brown & Co.
--The Land of Lost Toys. 82p. 1900. Little, Brown & Co.
--Land of the Lost Toys. (Illus.). (The Children's Friend Ser.). N.D. Little, Brown and Company.
--Last Words. 277p. N.D. Little, Brown.
--Last Words. A Final Collection of Stories. Murphy, H. D., illus. LC 12-32126. 2 p. l., iii-iv, 2, 9-285 p. front. (port.) plates. 19 x 16 cm. 1891. Roberts Brothers.
--Little Boy and Wooden Horses, 1 of 6 Vols. Andre, Richard, illus. (Illus.). (Blue Bell Ser.). N.D. E. & J. B. Young & Co.
--Little Lame Prince. (Illus.). (The Empyreal Library of Handy Volume Classics). N.D. H. M. Caldwell Co.
--Little Lame Prince. (Illus.). (The Young Folks Lib.). N.D. H. M. Caldwell Co.
--Lob-Lie-by-the-Fire. N.D. Harcourt Brace & Co.
--Lob Lie-by-the-Fire. (Illus.). 1910. Little Brown & Co.
--Lob-Lie-By-The-Fire. 349p. (Stories for Young People). N.D. Little, Brown.
--Lob Lie By the Fire. (Children's Favorite Classics). 1900. Thomas Y. Crowell & Co.
--Lob Lie-by-the-Fire. Ivins, Florence Wyman, illus. LC 37-20322. 144 p. incl. illus., plates. 21 cm. c.1937. Oxford University Press.
--Lob Lie-by-the-Fire. Lurie, Alison, pref. by. Bd. with Jackanapes. Repr. of 1884 ed; Daddy Darwin's Dovecot. Repr. of 1884 ed. LC 75-32178. (Illus.). 180 p. in various pagings. 19cm. Repr. of 1874 ed. (Classics of Children's Literature, 1621-1932). 1977. (ISBN 0-8240-2290-4). Garland Pub.
--Lob-Lie-by-the-Fire, and Other Stories. (Illus.). (The Wellesley Series for Girls). N.D. A. L. Burt.
--Lob-Lie-by-the Fire, and other Stories. (Queen's Treasures Ser.). N.D. Harcourt Brace & Co.
--Lob-Lie-By-the-Fire, and Other Tales, 36 vols. (Illus.). (St. Nicholas Ser.). 1905. Set. A L Burt Co.
--Lob Lie-by-the Fire & the Story of a Short Life. (Illus.). 184p. 1st U.S. edition. (Childrens Illustrated Classics Ser.). 1964. (ISBN 0-460-05063-X, Pub. by J. M. Dent England). Biblio Dist.
--Lob Lie-by-the-Fire: Or, The Luck of Lingborough, and Other Stories. LC 4-16837. 245 p. col. front., illus., plates. 17 cm. 1893. T. Y. Crowell & Co.
--Lob Lie-by-the-Fire: Or, The Luck of Lingborough and Other Tales. Cruikshank, George (1792-1878), illus. 1875. Young.
--Lob Lie-by-the-Fire: Or, the Luck of Lingborough and the Story of a Short Life. Caldecott, Randolph (1846-1886) & Brock, Henry Matthew (1875-1960), illus. (Illus.). (Children's Illustrated Classics). 1964. E.P. Dutton & Co.
--Lob Lie-by-the Fire: Or, The Luck of Lingborough. Caldecott, Randolph (1846-1886), illus. Evans, Edmund (1826-1905), contrib. by. LC 38-7696. 72 p. incl. front., illus. 22 cm. 1885. Society for Promoting Christian Knowledge.
--Lob-Lie-by-the-Fire, The Brownies and Other Tales. (Illus.). (St. Nicholas Series for Girls). N.D. International Book Co.
--Lob-Lie-By-The-fire, The Brownies, and Other Tales, 1 of 9 vol. set. (Illus.). (Complete Works of Juliana Ewing). N.D. International Book Co.
--Lob lie-by-the-fire, The Brownies, and Other Tales. (Illus.). N.D. Robert Brothers.
--Madam Liberality, 25 vols. (Illus.). (The Editha Ser.: No. 24). 1905. Set. H M Caldwell Co.
--Madam Liberality. Barry, Etheldred Breeze (1870-), illus. LC 1-17665. 74p. 1901. L. C. Page & Co.
--Mary's Meadow. LC 5953. 1 p. l., 93 p. front., plates. 20 cm. 1900. Little, Brown and Company.
--Mary's Meadow. (Illus.). (The Children's Friend Ser.). N.D. Little, Brown and Company.
--Mary's Meadow and Letter from a Little Garden. Browne, Gordon Frederick (1858-1932), illus. Evans, Edmund, contrib. by. LC 33-7799. 96 p. incl. front., illus. 22 cm. 1886. Society for Promoting Christian Knowledge.
--Mary's Meadow and Letters from a Little Garden. Browne, Gordon Frederick (1858-1932), illus (Pub. by Society for Promoting Christian Knowledge). 1886. E. & J. B. Young & Co.
--Mary's Meadow, and Other Stories. (Queen's Treasure Ser.). N.D. Harcourt Brace & Co.
--Mary's Meadow: And Other Tales of Fields and Flowers, 1 of 18 Vols. N.D. E & J B Young & Co.
--Melchior's Dream (Pub. by Society for Promoting Christian Knowledge). N.D. E. & J. B. Young & Co.
--Melchior's Dream, and Other Stories. (Queen's Treasure Ser.). N.D. Harcourt Brace & Co.
--Melchior's Dream, and Other Tales. (Illus.). (St. Nicholas Series for Girls). N.D. International Book Co.
--Melchior's Dream and Other Tales, 1 of 9 vol. set. (Illus.). (Complete Works of Juliana Ewing). N.D. Internationa Book Co.
--Melchior's Dream, and Other Tales. Browne, Gordon Frederick (1858-1932), illus. (The Ewing Book: Vol. VIII). N.D. Frederick Stokes.
--Melchior's Dream and other Tales: Mrs. Ewing Work, 1 of 18 Vols. N.D. E.& J B Young Co.
--Melchior's Dream, Brothers of Pity and Other Tales. (Illus.). 17 cm. 356p. 1886. Robert Brothers.
--Melchoir's Dream. N.D. E & J B Young.
--Melchoir's Dream and other Stories. (Queen's Treasure Ser.). N.D. Harcourt Brace & Co.
--The Mill Stream. Andre, Richard, illus (Pub. by Society for Promoting Christian Knowledge). N.D. E & J B Young.
--Mother's Birthday Reviews and Seven Other Tales in Verse. Andre, Richard, illus. 1888. Young.
--Mrs. Overtheway's Remembrances. (Illus.). N.D. E & J B Young.
--Mrs. Overtheway's Remembrances. LC 75-32171. xi, 168 21. Reissue of 1869 ed. (Classics of Children's Literature, 1621-1932). 1977. (ISBN 0-8240-2283-1). Garland Pub.
--Mrs. Overtheway's Remembrances, 1 of 32 vols, Vol. 18. (Illus.). (Famous Books for Girls). N.D. H. M. Caldwell Co.
--Mrs. Overtheway's Remembrances. (Queen's Treasure Ser.). N.D. Harcourt Brace & co.
--Mrs. Overtheway's Remembrances. (Illus.). 1910. Little Brown & Co.
--Mrs. Overtheway's Remembrances. Pasquier, J. A. & Wolf, J., illus. 1881. Roberts.
--Mrs. Overtheway's Remembrances. Pasquier, J. A. & Wolf, J., illus. LC 23-1954. 17cm. 274p. 1887. Roberts Brothers.
--Mrs. Overtheway's Remembrances. Pasquier, J. A. & Wolf, J., illus. LC 46-36235. 5 p. l., 3-274 p. incl. front. plates. 17 cm. 1889. Roberts Brothers.
--Mrs. Overtheway's Remembrances. Wolf, J., illus. (The Ewing Books: Vol. IV). N.D. Frederick Stokes.
--Mrs. Overtheway's Remembrances, and Other Tales. (Illus.). (St. Nicholas Series for Girls). N.D. International Book Co.
--Mrs. Overtheway's Remembrances and Other Tales, 1 of 9 vol. set. (Illus.). (Complete Works of Juliana Horatia). N.D. International Book Co.
--Mrs. Overtheway's Remembrances & Other Tales. Rhys, Ernest, ed. 18cm. 300p. (Everyman's Library for Young People). 1916. E. P. Dutton & Co.
--Old-Fashioned Fairy Tales, 1 of 18 Vols. New Ed. ed. N.D. E & J B Young & Co.
--Old-Fashioned Fairy Tales: Brothers of Pity and Other Tales of Beast and Men. (Illus.). 1910. Little Brown & Co.
--Papa's Poodle and Other Pets, 1 of 6 Vols. Andre, Richard, illus. (Illus.). (Blue Bell Ser.). N.D. E. & J. B. Young & Co.
--The Peace Egg and a Christmas Mumming Play, 1 of 18 Vols. Browne, Gordon Frederick (1858-1932), illus. Society for Promoting Christian Knowledge LC 42-357121. 58 p. incl. front., illus. 21 cm. 1887. Society for Promoting Christian Knowledge.
--Red and Blue: Or, the Disconted Lobster. (Illus.). N.D. E & J B Young.
--Six to Sixteen. (Illus.). (Fireside Ser. for Girls). N.D. A. L. Burt's Publications.
--Six to Sixteen, 1 of 5 vols. (Juliana H. Ewing's Wks.). N.D. Set. A. L. Burt's Pubs.
--Six to Sixteen. (Illus.). (The Wellesley Series for Girls). N.D. A. L. Burt's Pubs.
--Six to Sixteen. (Illus.). (The Meade Series for Girls). N.D. A. L. Burt.
--Six to Sixteen, No. 142. (The Cornell Ser.). N.D. A. L Burt's Pubs.
--Six to Sixteen. (Illus.). N.D. E & J B Young.
--Six to Sixteen. LC 75-32179. (Illus.). 19cm. vii, 296p. Repr. of 1875 ed. (Classics of Children's Literature, 1621-1932: Vol. 42). 1977. (ISBN 0-8240-2291-2). Garland Pub.
--Six to Sixteen, 1 of 31 vols. (Illus.). (Famous Books for Girls Ser.: No. 21). 1905. Set. H M Caldwell Co.
--Six to Sixteen, 1 of 32 Vols, Vol. 22. (Illus.). (Famous Books for Girls). N.D. H. M. Caldwell Co.
--Six to Sixteen. N.D. HArcourt Brace & Co.
--Six to Sixteen. (Queen's Treasure Ser.). N.D. Harcourt Brace & Co.
--Six to Sixteen. (Illus.). (St. Nicholas Series for Girls). N.D. International Book Co.
--Six to Sixteen, 1 of 9 vol. set. (Illus.). (Complete Works of Juliana Horatia). N.D. International Book Co.
--Six to Sixteen. (Every Boy's and Every Girl's Ser.). N.D. The Macmillan Co.
--Six to Sixteen: A Story for Girls. (Illus.). N.D. Little Brown & Co.
--Six to Sixteen: A Story For Girls. (Illus.). 1875. Messrs. Roberts Brothers.
--Six to Sixteen: A Story for Girls. Allingham, Helen Paterson (1848-1926), illus. (The Ewing Books: Vol. II). N.D. Frederick Stokes.
--Six to Sixteen: A Story for Girls. Allingham, Helen Paterson (1848-1926), illus. LC 75-32179. (Illus.). x, vii, 296 p., 9 leaves of plates. 19cm. (Classics of Children's Literature, 1621-1932). 1976. (ISBN 0-8240-2291-2). Garland Pub.
--Six to Sixteen. A Story for Girls. Allingham, Helen Paterson (1848-1926), illus. LC 4-17539. iv, 296 p. front., plates. 17 cm. 1904. Little, Brown, and Company.
--Snap Dragons. (Illus.). (The Sunshine Library for Young People). N.D. Thomas Y. Crowell.
--Snap-Dragons: A Tale of Christmas Eve, and Old Father Christmas, an Old-Fashioned Tale of the Young Days of a Grumpy Old Godfather. Browne, Gordon Frederick (1858-1932), illus. Evans, Edmund, contrib. by. LC 20-23161. 68 p. incl. front., illus. 21 cm. 1888. Society for Promoting Christian Knowledge.
--Snap-Dragons and Other Stories, 25 vols. (Illus.). (The Editha Ser.: No. 23). 1905. Set. H M Caldwell Co.
--Snapdragons: A Tale of Christmas Eve, and Old Father Christmas: An Old-Fashioned Tale of the Young Days of a Grumpy Old Godfather. Browne, Gordon Frederick (1858-1932), illus. LC 20-23161. 1888. Young.
--A Soldiers Children. Andre, Richard, illus (Pub. by Society for Promoting Christian Knowledge). N.D. E & J B Young.
--A Soldier's Children and Five Other Tales in Verse. Andre, Richard, illus. 1883. Young.
--Stories. Cooke, Edna W., illus. LC 20-26995. 5 p., l., 3-426 p. col. front., col. plates. 25 cm. 1920. Duffield and Company.
--The Story of a Short Life. (Illus.). (Fireside Ser. for Girls). N.D. A. L. Burt's Publications.
--The Story of a Short Life, 1 of 5 vols. (Juliana H. Ewing's Wks.). N.D. Set. A. L. Burt's Pubs.
--The Story of a Short Life. (Illus.). (The Wellesley Series for Girls). N.D. A. L. Burt's Pubs.
--The Story of a Short Life, 1 of 12 vols. New ed. (Illus.). (Good Time Ser.: No. 10). 1905. Set. Henry Altemus Co.

--From Long Ago and Many Lands: Stories for Children Told Anew. Baldridge, Cyrus Leroy (1889-), illus. LC 48-10958. xviii, 205 p. illus. 24 cm. (Beacon educational ser.). 1948. Beacon Press.
--Red, Yellow and Black: Tales of Indians, Chinese and Africans. LC 18-19806. 2 p. l., 7-215 p. plates, port. 19 cm. c.1918. The Methodist Book Concern.

Fahs, Sophia Blanche Lyon, Mrs. (1876-1978) & Cobb, Alice (1909-)
--Old Tales for a New Day: Early Answers to Life's Eternal Questions. Stair, Gobin (1912-), illus. LC 80-84076. (Illus.). xvi, 201 p. 24cm. 1981, c.1980. (ISBN 0-87975-138-X). Prometheus Books.

Fahs, Sophia Blanche Lyon, Mrs. (1876-1978) & Spoerl, Dorothy T.
--Beginnings: Earth, Sky, Life, Death. rev. ed. (gr. 4-7). 1958. (ISBN 0-8070-1974-7). Beacon Pr.

Fahy, Julian
--Ants to Zebra: Animal Verses for Children. 1st ed. Reindollar, Eleanor, illus. LC 53-9786. 92p. illus. 15 x 21cm. 1953. Exposition Press.

Fair, Martha Harris, et al.
--Shakespeare's Plays for Young People. Pigford, Barbara, illus. (Illus.). 37p. (Orig.). 1st U.S. edition. 1982. (ISBN 0-911181-01-6). Harris Learning.

Fair, Martha Harris & Ragsdale, Karl S., eds.
--Mother Goose Bustin' Loose. Pigford, Barbara, illus. (Illus.). 18p. (Orig.). 1st U.S. edition. (gr. k-8). 1982. (ISBN 0-911181-02-4). Harris Learning.

Fair, Sylvia (1933-)
--The Bedspread. Fair, Sylvia (1933-), illus. LC 81-11152. (Illus.). 32 p. 26cm. 1982. (ISBN 0-688-00877-1). W. Morrow.

Fairbairn, Ann, pseud., see Tait, Dorothy.

Fairbairn, Ann, pseud. (1902-1972)
--That Man Cartwright. Tait, Dorothy. (gr. 6 up). 1970. Crown.

Fairbairn, Barbara
--The Little Pig Who Ate a Four-Leaf Clover. Fairbairn, Barbara, illus. LC 28-18559. 102 p. col. illus., col. pl 24 cm. c.1928. Rand. McNally & Company.

Fairbairn, D. N.
--The Flying Sunbeam. Anderson, Betty, illus. LC 50-34274. (Illus.). 32. (Tell-A-Tale Bks.). 1950. Whitman.

Fairbairn, Mrs.
--Gerald and Dot, 1 of 12 Vols. (Dickory Dot Series.). N.D. Thomas Whittaker.

Fairbanks, Arthur
--The Mythology of Greece and Rome. N.D. D. Appleton-Century Co.

Fairfax, Jane, ed. see Vestly, Anne Catharina.

Fairfax-Lucy, Brian (1898-1974) & Pearce, Ann Philippa (1920-)
--The Children of the House. Sergeant, John, illus. LC 68-24418. (Illus.). 190 p. 22cm. 1968. Lippincott.

Fairfax, Virginia
--The Camp's Strange Visitors. LC 36-9239. 256p. 20cm. (The Girl Scouts Mystery Ser.). 1936. A. L. Burt Company.
--The Curious Quest. LC 34-147621. 3 p. l., 5-250 p. front. 21 cm. (Girl Scouts Mystery Ser.). c.1934. A. L. Burt Company.
--The Mysterious Camper. 253p. (The Girl Scouts Mystery Ser.). 1933. A. L. Burt Co.
--The Mysterious Camper. LC 33-11401. 253 p. front. 21 cm. (Girl Scouts Mystery Ser.). N.D. Chicago.
--The Secret of Camp Pioneer. LC 23-11402. 252 p. front. 21 cm. (Girl Scouts Mystery Ser.). c.1933. A. L. Burt Company.
--The Secret of Halliday House. LC 33-114002. 238 p. front. 21 cm. (Her The girl scouts mystery series). N.D. A. L. Burt.
--Su Won and Her Wonderful Tree. 1st ed. Morse, Dorothy Bayley (1906-1979), illus. LC 49-10287. 151 p. illus. 21 cm. 1949. E.P. Dutton.
--The Trail of the Gypsy Eight. (The Girl Scouts Mystery Series). 1933. A. L. Burt Co.

Fairfax, Virginia & Buie, Hallie
--Ke Sooni. Smalley, Janet (1893-), illus. LC 48-5411. 127 p. illus. 21 cm. 1947. Friendship Press.

Fairfield, Frances, jt. auth. see Heath, Virginia.

Fairgrieve, James, jt. auth. see Young, Ernest.

Fairholme, Elizabeth (1910-) & Powell, Pamela
--Esmeralda Ahoy!. 1st ed. Spier, Peter Edward (1927-), illus. LC 59-11591. (Illus.). 212 p. 22cm. 1959. Doubleday.

Fairless, Caroline
--Hambone. Edelson, Wendy, illus. (Illus.). 48p. 1980. (ISBN 0-912766-97-2). Tundra Bks.

Fairman, Joan Alexandra (1935-)
--A Penny Saved. Petie, Haris, pseud. (1915-), illus. Petty, Roberta. LC 78-143702. (Illus.). 32 p. 24cm. 1971. Lantern Press.

Fairman, Paul W.
--Five Knucklebones. 1st ed. Berger, Vivian, illus. LC 70-182784. (Illus.). 164 p. 21cm. 1972. (ISBN 0-03-088592-2). Holt, Rinehart and Winston.
--The Forgetful Robot. 1st. ed. LC 68-24762. 163 p. 22cm. 1968. Holt, Rinehart and Winston.
--The Ghost of Graveyard Hill. (The Partridge Family Ser.: No.4). (gr. 4-12). 1971. Curtis.
--Terror by Night. (The Partridge Family Ser.: No.5). (gr. 4-12). 1971. Curtis.

Fairmont, Ethel
--Rhymes for Kindly Children. Gruelle, John Barton (1880-1938), illus. N.D. A. L. Burt Co.
--Rhymes for Kindly Children: Modern Mother Goose Jingles. Gruelle, John Barton (1880-1938), illus. LC 37-4767. 127 p. incl. col. illus., col. plates. 27 cm. c.1937. The Wise-Parslow Company.

Fairstar, Mrs., ed.
--Memoirs of a London Doll, Written by Herself. 1957. Macmillan.

Fairweather, Jessie Home
--The Happiest Christmas. Wilde, Irma, illus. LC 55-419920. unpaged. illus. 17 cm. (Tell-a-tale books, 2516). 1955. Whitman Pub. Co.
--Matilda, MacElroy and Mary. Robinson, Ira Edwin (1927-), illus. LC 50-38004. 32p. col. illus. 17cm. (Tell-a-tale books). c.1950. Whitman Pub. Co.

Faison, Mabel Hubbard
--Scalawag the Scottie. Foy, Ottilie, illus. LC 40-7525. 168 p. illus. 21 cm. c.1940. American Book Company.

Faizi, Abul-Oasim & Blyth, Hugh Featherstone
--The Wonderlamp. Stevenson, Don, adapted by. LC 81-23648. p. cm. 1983, c.1981. (ISBN 0-933770-19-7). Kalimat Press.

Falconer, Rebecca see Becky, pseud.

Falconer, Rebecca (1919-)
--Tall Enough Tommy. Becky, pseud. LC 48-21618. 25 p. col. illus. 24 cm. 1948. Childrens Press.

Falconnet, Paulette, jt. auth. see D'Assaily, Gisele.

Falk, Ann Mari (1922-)
--Matthew Blows Bubbles. Ware, Kay (1916-) & Sutherland, Lucille, eds. Wikland, Ilon (1930-), illus. LC 64-6415. (Illus.). 23cm. (The Read for Fun Ser.). 1964. Webster Division, McGraw-Hill.
--A Place of Her Own. MacMillan, Annabelle, pseud. (1922-), tr. from Ingen vanlig Stin. Quick, Annabelle. LC 64-23043. 127 p. 21cm. 1st U.S. edition. 1964. Harcourt, Brace & World.
--Who Is Erika?. Macmillan, Annabelle, pseud. (1922-), tr. Quick, Annabelle. LC 63-17706. 124 p. 21cm. 1st U.S. edition. 1963. Harcourt, Brace & World.

Falk, Elsa (1888-)
--Akio & the Moon Goddess. Kraynak, George, illus. (Illus.). (gr. 4-6). 1961. (ISBN 0-695-40240-4). Follett.
--The Borrowed Canoe: A Story of the Hupa Indians of Northern California. Falk, Elsa (1888-), illus. LC 70-88722. (Illus.). 47 p. 27cm. 1969. (ISBN 0-378-62083-5). Ward Ritchie Press.
--Fence Across the Trail. Stein, Harve (1904-), illus. LC 57-8282. (Illus.). 96 p. 23cm. 1957. Follett Pub. Co.
--Fire Canoe. Frankenberg, Robert Clinton (1911-), illus. LC 56-112170. 188p. illus. 23cm. 1956. (ISBN 0-695-42730-X). Follett Pub. Co.
--Fog Island. Bennett, Rainey (1907-), illus. LC 53-129857. 189p. illus. 23cm. 1953. (ISBN 0-695-42940-X). Wilcox and Follett Co.
--Shoes for Matt. O'Sullivan, Tom, illus. (Illus.). (gr. 4-6). 1960. (ISBN 0-695-47850-8). Follett.
--Tohi: A chumash indian boy. 1965. Melmont Publishers, Inx.
--Tohi, A Chumash Indian Boy. Falk, Elsa (1888-), illus. LC 59-5031. (Illus.). 37p. 22cm. (Look, Read, Learn). 1959. Melmont Publishers.
--Winter Journey. (gr. 7 up). 1955. (ISBN 0-695-49520-8). Follett.
--Winter Journey. O'Sullivan, Tom, illus. LC 55-7504. 222p. illus. 23cm. 1955. Follett Pub. Co.

Falk, Lee Harrison see Robertson, Dale.

Falkberget, Johan Petter (1879-)
--Broomstick and Snowflake: From the Norwegian of Johan Falkberget. Sewell, Helen Moore (1896-1957), illus. Welhaven, Thekia (1891-), tr. LC 33-29353. 4 p. l., 3-88 p. front., illus. 23 cm. 1933. The Macmillan Company.

Falken, Linda C.
--Ella in the Castle. Conte, Patrizia & Vanetti, Giorgio, illus. (Illus.). 16p. (Golden Magical Places Ser.). (ps-k). 1984. (ISBN 0-307-17100-0, Golden Bks). Western Pub.

Falkner, John Meade (1808-1932)
--Moonfleet. Kredel, Fritz (1900-1973), illus. (Illus.). (gr. 7 up). 1951. (ISBN 0-316-27382-1). Little.

Fall, Thomas, pseud., see Snow, Donald Clifford.

Fall, Thomas, pseud. (1917-)
--Goat Boy of Brooklyn. Snow, Donald Clifford. Rocker, Fermin (1907-), illus. LC 68-28740. (Illus.). 192 p. 21cm. 1968. Dial Press.

Fallada, Hans, pseud., see Ditzen, Rudolf.

Falls, Charles Buckles (1874-1960)
--The Modern A B C Book. LC 30-29346. 32 p. col. illus. 31 cm. 1930. The John Day Company.

Falls, Gregory A.
--The Pushcart War. (Orig.). 1984. (ISBN 0-87602-248-4). Anchorage.

Fanchiotti, Marguerite
--A Bow in the Cloud. Leatham, Moyra (1928-), illus. LC 34-2192. 226p. 22cm. 1954. Oxford University Press. **Award: (ALA).**
--A Bow in the Clouds. 227p. (gr. 6-8). 1954. Walck.
--Stories From The Bible. Kiddell-Monroe, Joan (1908-), illus. 248p. 1957. Walck.

Fanciulli, Giuseppe (1881-)
--The Little Blue Man. Sweet, May MacDaniel, Mrs. (1865-), tr. LC 26-18628. xii. 1. 197, 1 p. front., illus., plates. 22 cm. 1926. Houghton Mifflin Company.

Fanelli, Jenny, ed. see Brandel, Marc.

Fanelli, Jenny, ed. see Karman, Janice & Bagdasarian, Ross.

Fanelli, Jenny, ed. see Sewell, Anna.

Fang, Yi-K'Iun, jt. auth. see Faucher, Paul.

Fannin, Cole
--Gene Autry and the Golden Stallion. Authorized. Hampton, John, illus. LC 55-20863. (Illus.). 282p. 21cm. 1954. Whitman Pub. Co.
--Rin Tin Tin and the Ghost Wagon Train. Arens, Michael, illus. 1959. Golden Press.
--Roy Rogers and the Brasada Bandits: An Original Story Featuring Roy Rogers, King of the Cowboys, the Famous Motion Picture, Radio, and Television Star, As the Hero. Authorized. Arens, Michael, illus. LC 55-3580. 282p. illus. 21cm. 1955. Whitman Pub. Co.

Fanning, Robbie (1947-)
--One Hundred Butterflies. LC 79-14776. 189 p. 21cm. c.1979. (ISBN 0-664-32654-4). Westminster Pres.

Fanshawe, Elizabeth
--Rachel. Charlton, Michael Alan (1923-), illus. LC 76-9944. (Illus.). 29 p. 1st U.S. edition. 1977, c.1975. (ISBN 0-87888-098-4). Bradbury Press.

Fant, Louie Judson, Jr. (1931-)
--Noah. new ed. Castillo, Romulo & Paul, Frank A., illus. (Illus.). 14p. 1973. (ISBN 0-917002-70-9). Joyce Media.

Fante, John Thomas (1911-) & Borchert, Rudolf (1928-)
--Bravo, Burro!. Hirsh, Marilyn (1944-), illus. LC 70-98186. (Illus.). 127 p. 23cm. 1st U.S. edition. 1970. Hawthorn Books.

Faralla, Dana (1909-)
--The Magnificent Barb. Laune, Paul Sidney (1899-), illus. (Illus.). (gr. 4-6). 1951. (ISBN 0-448-02282-6). G&D.
--The Singing Cupboard. Ardizzone, Edward Jeffrey Irving (1900-1979), illus. LC 63-14269. (Illus.). 93 p. 22cm. 1963, c.1962. Lippincott.
--Swanhilda-of-the-Swans. Berson, Harold (1926-), illus. LC 64-19052. (Illus.). 95 p. 23cm. 1964. Lippincott.
--The Willow In the Attic. Fava, Rita (1932-), illus. LC 60-7615. 96p. 1960. J. B. Lippincott.
--The Wonderful Flying-Go-Round. 1st ed. Berson, Harold (1926-), illus. LC 65-19721. 94 p. illus. 25 cm. 1965. World Pub. Co.
--The Wooden Swallow. Worth, Wendy, illus. LC 67-278. 94 p. illus. 25 cm. 1966. World Pub. Co.

Faralone, pseud., see Smith, Elizabeth A..

Farber, jt. auth. see Knoepfel.

Farber, Norma (1909-1984)
--All Those Mothers at the Manger. Lloyd, Megan, illus. LC 85-42610. p. cm. 1985, c.1979. (ISBN 0-06-021869-X). (ISBN 0-06-021870-3). Harper & Row.
--As I Was Crossing Boston Common. Lobel, Arnold Stark (1933-), illus. LC 75-6520. (Illus.). 32 p. 1975, c.1973. (ISBN 0-525-25960-0). E. P. Dutton. **Award: (ALA).**
--Blanquette. Gusman, Annie, illus. LC 78-5141. p. cm. 1980, c.1979. (ISBN 0-201-01924-8). Addison-Wesley.
--Did You Know It Was the Narwhale?. 1st ed. Vizbara, Carole, illus. LC 67-18997. (Illus.). 1 v. (unpaged. 22cm. 1967. Atheneum.
--How Does it Feel to Be Old?. Hyman, Trina Schart (1939-), illus. 1979. Dutton.
--How the Hibernators Came to Bethlehem. Cooney, Barbara (1917-), illus. LC 78-64630. p. cm. 1979, c.1966. (ISBN 0-8027-6352-9). (ISBN 0-8027-6353-7). Walker.
--How the Left-Behind Beasts Built Ararat. Frasconi, Antonio (1919-), illus. LC 77-14650. (Illus.). 30 p. 27cm. 1978. (ISBN 0-8027-6313-8). (ISBN 0-8027-6314-6). Walker.
--How to Ride a Tiger. Schumacher, Claire, illus. LC 83-4289. p. cm. 1983. (ISBN 0-395-34553-7). Houghton Mifflin.
--Mercy Short: A Winter Journal, North Boston, 1692-93. LC 82-5013. p. cm. c.1982. (ISBN 0-525-44014-3). Dutton.
--Never Say Ugh! to a Bug. Aruego, Jose (1932-), illus. LC 78-13948. (Illus.). 32p. (gr. k-3). 1979. (ISBN 0-688-80140-4). (ISBN 0-688-84140-6). Greenwillow.
--A Ship in a Storm on the Way to Tarshish. Chess, Victoria (1939-), illus. LC 77-23288. (Illus.). 32 p. 26cm. c.1977. (ISBN 0-688-80096-3). (ISBN 0-688-84096-5). Greenwillow Books.
--Six Impossible Things Before Breakfast: Stories & Poems. De Paola, Tomie, pseud. (1934-), illus. De Paola, Thomas Anthony. LC 76-40264. (Illus.). 48 p. 24cm. c.1977. (ISBN 0-201-01969-8). Addison-Wesley.
--Small Wonders: Poems. Mizumura, Kazue, illus. LC 78-31282. (Illus.). 23cm. 31p. (gr. 2-5). 1979. (ISBN 0-698-20484-0, Coward). Putnam Pub Group.
--There Goes Feathertop!. 1st ed. Brown, Marc Tolon (1946-), illus. LC 78-12096. (Illus.). 32 p. 22cm. (Unicorn book). c.1979. (ISBN 0-525-29667-0). Dutton.
--There Once Was a Woman Who Married a Man. Dabcovich, Lydia, illus. LC 78-1036. (Illus.). 32 p. 24cm. c.1978. (ISBN 0-201-01947-7). Addison-Wesley. **Award: (NYT).**
--This Is the Ambulance Leaving the Zoo. 1st ed. De Paola, Tomie, pseud. (1934-), illus. De Paola, Thomas Anthony. LC 74-23761. (Illus.). 32 p. 1975. (ISBN 0-525-41125-9). Dutton.
--Three Wanderers from Wapping. Mikolaycak, Charles (1937-), illus. LC 77-24730. (Illus.). 62 p. 24cm. c.1978. (ISBN 0-201-01968-X). Addison-Wesley.
--Up the Down Elevator. Gusman, Annie, illus. LC 79-13199. p. cm. 1979. (ISBN 0-201-01924-8). Addison-Wesley.
--Where's Gomer?. 1st ed. Du Bois, William Sherman Pene (1916-), illus. LC 74-4039. (Illus.). 32 p. 1974. (ISBN 0-525-42590-X). Dutton.

Farde, H. A.
--The Old Ship: Or, Better than Strength. (Illus.). N.D. E. P. Dutton & Co.

Farge, Phyllis La see La Farge, Phyllis.

Farge, Sheila La see Bodker, Cecil.

Farge, Sheila La see Gripe, Maria Kristina.

Farge, Sheila La see La Farge, Sheila.

Fargo, Lucille Foster (1880-)
--Come, Colors, Come. LC 40-14195. xvi p., 1 l., 283 p. incl. front., illus., plates. 21 cm. c.1940. Dodd, Mead & Company.
--Marian-Martha. Warren, Dorothea, illus. LC 36-27388. xiii, 257 p. incl. front., illus., plates. pl. 21 cm. 1936. Dodd, Mead & Company.
--Prairie Chautauqua. Ogg, Oscar John (1908-1971), illus. LC 43-14769. xii, 2, 254 p. illus. 21 cm. 1943. Dodd, Mead & Company.
--Prairie Girl. Gannett, Ruth Chrisman Arens (1896-1979), illus. LC 37-19750. xi, 276 p. incl. front., illus., plates. 21 cm. 1937. Dodd, Mead & Company.

Faris, John Thompson (1871-1949)
--Nolichucky Jack. Cammerota, D., illus. LC 27-18324. 10 p. 3 l., 15-288 p. col. front., plates. 20 cm. c.1927. J. B. Lippincott Company.

Faris, Lillie A.
--Bible Stories for Young People. 256p. N.D. Platt & Munk Co.
--New Testament Stories. 128p. N.D. Platt & Munk Co.
--Old Testament Stories. (Popular Story Ser.). N.D. Platt & Munk Co.

Farjam, Faridah
--The Crystal Flower & the Sun. new & rev. ed. Jabbari, Ahmad, ed. Nodjoumi, Nikzad, illus. Jabbari, Ahmad, tr. from Persian. (Illus.). 24p. (Orig.). 1st U.S. edition (Pub. by Lerner Publications). (gr. k up). 1983. (ISBN 0-939214-16-4). Mazda Pubs.
--The Crystal Flower and the Sun: An Original Persian Folk Story: Gul-i bulur va Khvuarshid. Nodjoumi, Nikzad, illus. LC 71-128814. (Illus.). 24 p. 25cm. 1972. (ISBN 0-87614-017-7). Carolrhoda Books.

Farjam, Faridah & Azaad, Meyer
--Uncle New Year: An Original Persian Folk Story. Mesghali, Farsheed, illus. LC 77-128810. (Illus.). 24 p. 25cm. 1972. (ISBN 0-87614-014-2). Carolrhoda Books.
--Uncle Noruz (Uncle New Year). Jabbari, Ahmad, ed. Mesghali, Farsheed, illus. Jabbari, Ahmad, tr. from Persian. (Illus.). 24p. (Orig.). 1st U.S. edition (Pub. by Lerner Publications). (gr. k up). 1983. (ISBN 0-939214-14-8). Mazda Pubs.

Farjeon, Annabel
--The Siege of Trapp's Mill. LC 73-84826. 132p. 22cm. 1974, c.1972. (ISBN 0-689-30136-7). Atheneum.

Farjeon, Benjamin Leopold (1833-1903)
--The Golden Land: Or, Links from Shore to Shore. Browne, Gordon Frederick (1858-1932), illus. Evans, Edmund, contrib. by. LC 41-332581. viii, 9-344 p. front., illus., plates. 19 cm. 1886. Ward, Lock, & Co.

--Lucy and Their Majesties, a Comedy in Wax. Cory, Fanny Young & Varian, George, illus. LC 4-27354. (Illus.). viii, 322. 20cm. 1904. The Century Co.

Farjeon, Benjamin Leopold (1833-1903) & Allen, Grant

--Three Times Tried, and Other Stories. N.D. Thomas Y. Crowell & Co.'s Catalogue.

Farjeon, Eleanor (1881-1965)

--Ameliaranne and the Magic Ring. Pearse, Susan Beatrice, illus. LC 34-5412. 63 p. illus. (part col.) 21 cm. 1933. David McKay Company.

--Ameliaranne at the Seaside. Pearse, Susan Beatrice, illus. N.D. David McKay Co.

--Ameliaranne's Washing-Day. Pearse, Susan Beatrice, illus. LC 34-38723. 60 p. illus. (part col.) 21 cm. 1934. David McKay Company.

--Around the Seasons: Poems by Eleanor Farjeon. Paton, Jane Elizabeth (1934-), illus. LC 69-10731. (Illus.). color ils. 32p. 1st U.S. edition. (gr. k-3). 1969. (ISBN 0-8098-1143-X). Walck.

--A Book for Eleanor Farjeon: A Tribute to Her Life and Work, 1881-1965. Ardizzone, Edward Jeffrey Irving (1900-1979), illus. Lewis, Naomi, intro. by. LC 66-14765. 184 p. illus. 23 cm. 1st U.S. edition. 1966. H. Z. Walck.

--Cherrystones. 1st american ed. Morton-Sale, Isobel (1904-) & Morton-Sale, John (1901-), illus. LC 44-7070. 58, 3 p., 1 l. incl. front., illus. 21 cm. (Stokes book). 1944. J. B. Lippincott Company.

--The Children's Bells: A Selection of Poems. Fortnum, Peggy, pseud. (1919-), illus. Nuttall-Smith, Margaret Emily Noel. LC 60-6484. (Illus.). 212 p. 24cm. 1st U.S. edition. 1960. (ISBN 0-8098-2342-X). H. Z. Walck.

--Come Christmas. Field, Rachel Lyman (1894-1942), illus. LC 28-6996. viii p., 2 l., 3-62 p. illus. (part col.) 20 cm. 1928. Frederick A. Stokes Company.

--Come Christmas. Field, Rachel Lyman (1894-1942), illus. N.D. J. B. Lippincott.

--Eleanor Farjeon's Book. Ardizzone, Edward Jeffrey Irving (1900-1979), illus. LC 64-314136. 208 p. illus. 18 cm. (Puffin Books, PS 141). c.1960. Penguin Books.

--Eleanor Farjeon's Book: Stories, Verses, Plays. Graham, Eleanor (1896-), ed. Ardizzone, Edward Jeffrey Irving (1900-1979), illus. (Illus.). 207 p. 18cm. (Puffin Book, PS141). 1973, c.1960. Penguin.

--Eleanor Farjeon's Poems for Children. Wakefield, Lucina Smith, illus. LC 51-11164. (Illus.). 236p. 21cm. (gr. 4-6). 1951. (ISBN 0-397-30193-6). Lippincott.

--A First Chap-Book of Rounds. Garside, John, illus. (Music by Herbert Farjeon). 1919. E P Dutton.

--The Glass Slipper. 159p. Repr. 1981. (ISBN 0-89966-360-5). Buccaneer Bks.

--The Glass Slipper. 108p. Repr. 1981. (ISBN 0-89967-034-2). Harmony & Co.

--The Glass Slipper. Shepard, Ernest Howard (1879-1976), illus. LC 55-3820. (From the play of the same name by Eleanor & Herbert Farjeon). 175p. illus. 23cm. 1955. Oxford University Press.

--The Glass Slipper. Shepard, Ernest Howard (1879-1976), illus. LC 56-773. 187p. illus. 22cm. 1956, c.1955. (ISBN 0-670-34196-7). Viking Press.

--Grannie Gray: Children's Plays and Games. Fortnum, Peggy, pseud. (1919-), illus. Nuttall-Smith, Margaret Emily Noel. 135p. illus., music 22cm. 1956. Oxford University Press.

--Italian Peep Show. Ardizzone, Edward Jeffrey Irving (1900-1979), illus. (Illus.). 96 p. 22cm. 1960. H. Z. Walck.

--Italian Peep Show. Thornycroft, Rosalind (1891-), illus. N.D. J. B. Lippincott.

--Italian Peep Show and Other Tales. Thornycroft, Rosalind (1891-), illus. LC 27-4058. 6 p. l., 146 p. col. front., illus. (part col.) 22 cm. 1926. Frederick A. Stokes Company.

--Jim at the Corner. N.D. Henry Z. Walck Inc.

--Jim at the Corner. Ardizzone, Edward Jeffrey Irving (1900-1979), illus. LC 58-3746. (Illus.). 101 p. 22cm. 1958. H. Z. Walck.

--Joan's Door. Townsend, Will, illus. LC 27-2895. 127, 1 p. incl. front., illus. 19 cm. 1927. Frederick A. Stokes Company.

--Kaleidoscope. Ardizzone, Edward Jeffrey Irving (1900-1979), illus. LC 63-17499. (Illus.). (gr. 4-7). 1963. (ISBN 0-8098-2365-9). Walck.

--Kaleidoscope. Lathrop, Dorothy Pulis (1891-1980), illus. 1929. Frederick A. Stokes Co.

--Katy Kruse at the Seaside: Or, The Deserted Islanders. LC 33-929158. 32 p. col. front., col. plates. 26 cm. 1932. David McKay Company.

--Ladybrook. LC 31-6269. 4 p. l., 3-310 p., 1 l. incl. geneal. tab. 20 cm. 1931. Frederick A. Stokes Company.

--The Little Bookroom. Ardizzone, Edward Jeffrey Irving (1900-1979), illus. (Illus.). Repr. (New Oxford Library Ser.). (gr. 4 up). 1979. (ISBN 0-19-277099-3). Oxford U Pr.

--The Little Bookroom. Ardizzone, Edward Jeffrey Irving (1900-1979), illus. LC 83-49007. p. cm. (Godine Storytellers). 1984. (ISBN 0-87923-522-5). Oxford University Press.

--The Little Bookroom: Eleanor Farjeon's Short Stories for Children. Ardizzone, Edward Jeffrey Irving (1900-1979), illus. LC 56-865665. 302p. illus. 23 cm. 1956. Oxford University Press. **Awards: (ALA); (CMA).**

--The Little Bookroom: Eleanor Farjeon's Short Stories for Children. Ardizzone, Edward Jeffrey Irving (1900-1979), illus. LC 60-15908. (Illus.). (gr. 4-7). 1956. (ISBN 0-8098-2323-3). Walck.

--Martin Pippin in the Apple Orchard. Brock, Charles Edmond (1870-1938), illus. 1922. Frederick A. Stokes.

--Martin Pippin in the Apple Orchard. Kennedy, Richard (1910-), illus. (Illus.). (gr. 1-7). 1961. (ISBN 0-397-30571-0). Lippincott.

--Martin Pippin in the Daisy-Field. Morton-Sale, Isobel (1904-) & Morton-Sale, John (1901-), illus. LC 38-27125. 6 p. l., 320 p. col. front., illus. 21 cm. 1938. Frederick A. Stokes Company.

--Martin Pippin in the Daisy-Field. Morton-Sale, Isobel (1904-) & Morton-Sale, John (1901-), illus. LC 63-9857. 294 p. illus. 22 cm. 1963, c.1937. Lippincott.

--Mighty Men ... LC 25-200476. v. illus. 20 cm. N.D. D. Appleton and Company.

--Mighty Men. Chesterman, Hugh, illus. Barnes, C. C., intro. by. LC 26-21020. xii p., 1 l., 213, 1 p. illus. 19 cm. c.1926. D. Appleton and Company.

--Mr. Garden. Paton, Jane Elizabeth (1934-), illus. LC 66-13951. 39p. illus. (pt. col.) 26cm. 1st U.S. edition. 1966, c.1965. (ISBN 0-8098-2045-5). Walck.

--Mrs. Malone. Ardizzone, Edward Jeffrey Irving (1900-1979), illus. LC 62-14055. (Illus.). 24 p. 15cm. 1962. H. Z. Walck.

--The New Book of Days. 1961. (ISBN 0-8098-2348-9). David McKay Company.

--Nursery Rhymes of London Town. (Illus.). 1952. Dufour.

--The Old Nurse's Stocking-Basket. Ardizzone, Edward Jeffrey Irving (1900-1979), illus. LC 65-24112. 102p. illus. 21cm. 1966, c.1965. Walck.

--The Old Nurse's Stocking-Basket. Whydale, E. Herbert, illus. LC 31-21899. 4 p. l., 3-154 p., 1 l. incl. illus., plates. col. front. 22 cm. 1931. Frederick A. Stokes Company.

--The Old Sailor's Yarn Box. 6 p. l., 143 p. incl. illus., plates. 22 cm. 1934. Frederick A. Stokes Company.

--The Old Sailor's Yarn Box. N.D. J. B. Lippincott.

--One Foot in Fairyland: Sixteen Tales. Lawson, Robert (1892-1957), illus. LC 38-29547. v p., 2 l., 3-261 p. illus. 22 cm. 1938. Frederick A. Stokes Company.

--One Foot in Fairyland Sixteen Tales. Lawson, Robert (1892-1957), illus. N.D. J. B. Lippincott.

--Over the Garden Wall. Raverat, Gwendolen Mary (1885-1957), illus. LC 33-27358. ix, 156 p. illus. 20 cm. 1933. Frederick A. Stokes Company.

--Over the Garden Wall. Raverat, Gwendolen Mary (1885-1957), illus. N.D. J. B. Lippincott.

--Paladins in Spain. Tozer, Katharine, illus. LC 38-242229. 168, 4 p. incl. col. front. plates. 21 cm. (Horizon books). 1937. T. Nelson and Sons Ltd.

--The Perfect Zoo. Burrell, Kathleen, illus. 1929. David McKay Co.

--The Perfect Zoo. Kruse, Katy, photos by. N.D. David McKay Co.

--Poems for Children. LC 51-11164. 236 p. 21 cm. 1951. Lippincott.

--A Prayer for Little Things. Jones, Elizabeth Orton (1910-), illus. LC 45-4536. 15 p. col. illus. 20 1/2 cm. 1945. Houghton Mifflin Company.

--A Second Chap-Book of Rounds. Garside, John, illus. (Music by Herbert Farjeon). 1919. E P Dutton.

--The Silver Curlew. Shepard, Ernest Howard (1879-1976), illus. LC 53-39525. 182p. illus. 23cm. 1953. Oxford University Press. **Award: (ALA).**

--The Silver Curlew. Shepard, Ernest Howard (1879-1976), illus. (Illus.). 162 p. 22cm. 1954, c.1953. Viking Press.

--Sing for Your Supper. Morton-Sale, Isobel (1904-) & Morton-Sale, John (1901-), illus. LC 38-18120. 137, 1 p. incl. front., illus. 20 cm. 1938. Frederick A. Stokes Company.

--Sing for Your Supper: A Book of Verse for Boys and Girls. Morton-Sale, John (1901-) & Morton-Sale, Isobel (1904-), illus. N.D. J. B. LIppincott Co.

--Singing Games for Children. Littlejohns, J., illus. 1919. Dutton.

--The Tale of Tom Tiddler: With Rhymes of London Town. Tealby, Norman, illus. LC 30-12299. x p., 1 l., 241 p. incl. front., illus. 22 cm. 1930. Frederick A. Stokes Company.

--Ten Saints. 1936. (ISBN 0-8098-2305-5). David McKay Company.

--Then There Were Three: Being Cherrystones, The Mulberry Bush, The Starry Floor. Morton-Sale, Isobel (1904-) & Morton-Sale, John (1901-), illus. LC 65-21664. (Illus.). 174 p. 23cm. 1965. (ISBN 0-397-30839-6). Lippincott.

--Westwoods. Smith, May, illus. LC 36-5637. 40p. 1935. Artists and Writer's Guild.

--The Wonders of Herodotus. Nelson, Edmund, illus. LC 38-3166. ix, 11-176 p. incl. col. front., illus. 21 cm. (Horizon books. no. 11). 1937. T. Nelson and Sons Ltd.

Farjeon, Eleanor (1881-1965) & Farjeon, Herbert

--Heroes and Heroines. N.D. E. P. Dutton & Co.

Farjeon, Eleanor (1881-1965) & Mayne, William James Carter (1928-), eds.

--A Cavalcade of Kings. Ambrus, Victor G., pseud. (1935-), illus. Ambrus, Gyozo Laszlo. LC 65-14643. (Illus.). 237 p. 26cm. 1965, c.1964. H. Z. Walck.

--Cavalcade of Queens. Ambrus, Victor G., pseud. (1935-), illus. Ambrus, Gyozo Laszlo. LC 65-23251. (Illus.). (gr. 4-7). 1965. (ISBN 0-8098-2381-0). Walck.

Farjeon, Eve Annabel (1919-)

Maria Lupin. Hunt, James, illus. LC 67-19580. (Illus.). 160 p. 21cm. 1967. Abelard-Schuman.

--The Siege of Trapp's Mill. LC 73-84826. 132 p. 22cm. 1974, c.1972. Atheneum.

Farjeon, Herbert, jt. auth. see Farjeon, Eleanor.

Farjeon, L. B.

--Dr. Glennie Revenge. N.D. Rand McNally.

FArley, Agnes, tr. see France, Anatole.

Farley, Carol J. (1936-)

--Bunch on McKellahan Street. LC 75-152736 (Illus.). map. 256p. (gr. 4-6). 1971. (ISBN 0-531-01992-6). Watts.

--The Garden Is Doing Fine. 1st ed. Sweat, Lynn, illus. LC 75-9516. (Illus.). 185 p. 22cm. 1975. (ISBN 0-689-30475-7). Atheneum.

--Loosen Your Ears. Nicklaus, Carol, illus. LC 76-25206. p. cm. 1977. (ISBN 0-689-30553-2). Atheneum.

--The Most Important Thing in the World. LC 73-9675. (Illus.). vi, 133 p. 22cm. 1974. (ISBN 0-531-02663-9). F. Watts.

--Ms. Isabel Cornell, Herself. LC 79-22667. 145 p. 25cm. 1980. (ISBN 0-689-30740-3). Atheneum.

--Mystery in the Ravine. Escourido, Joseph, illus. LC 67-637. (Illus.). 114 p. 21cm. 1967. F. Watts.

--The Mystery of the Fiery Message. Newsom, Carol, illus. LC 82-13867. (Illus.). 106 p. 19cm. (Avon/Camelot book). c.1983. (ISBN 0-380-81927-9). Avon Books.

--Mystery of the Fog Man. Escourido, Joseph, illus. LC 66-12121. 116p. illus. 21cm. c.1966. Watts.

--Sergeant Finney's Family. Shortall, Leonard W., illus. LC 78-79667. (Illus.). 240 p. 22cm. 1969. F. Watts.

--Settle Your Fidgets. 1st. ed. Lazarevich, Mila (1942-), illus. LC 77-1650. (Illus.). 147 p. 22cm. 1977. (ISBN 0-689-30604-0). Atheneum.

--Twilight Waves. LC 81-1417. p. cm. 1981. (ISBN 0-689-30842-6). Atheneum.

Farley, Harriet (1817-1907)

--Christmas Stories: Told in a Happy Home (Hazelnook) in New England. LC 44-29960. 2 p. l., 7-256 p. 18 1/2 cm. (On cover: Lovell's library. Vol. 9, no. 473). 1884. John W. Lovell Company.

Farley, Helen Hall Moyer see Gilmore, Ernest, pseud.

Farley, Helen Hall Moyer, Mrs.

--The Blakes and the Blooms: Or, What Can Be Done by Earnest Hearts and Willing Hands. Gilmore, Ernest, pseud. LC 12-32574. 287 p. front., plates. 18 cm. 1884. Presbyterian Board of Publication.

--The Children's Hour. Gilmore, Ernest, pseud. (Illus.). N.D. Cassell, Petter, Galpin.

--Christine's Text. Gilmore, Ernest, pseud, 1 of 4 Vols. Penney, L., ed. 72p. (The Never-Begin Ser.). N.D. Per set in box 3.00. National Temperance Society.

--Griffin Alley Folk: Or, Pearls from the Slums. Gilmore, Ernest, pseud. LC 12-32571. 256 p. front., plates. 18 cm. 1886. Presbyterian Board of Publication.

--A Pot of Daisies. Gilmore, Ernest, pseud. LC 12-32572. 127p. 19cm. 1895. The National Temperance Society and Publication House.

--Sweetheart. Gilmore, Ernest, pseud. LC 12-32573. 84p. 22cm. 1896. American Tract Society.

--Sweetheart. Gilmore, Ernest, pseud. (Illus.). 84p. 1905. American Tract Society.

Farley, Karin

--Canal Boy. LC 77-91564. (Illus.). (Wholesome Adventure for Boys Gift Set Ser.). (gr. 5-8). 1978. (ISBN 0-89191-106-5). Cook.

Farley, Leonard V, jt. auth. see Hubbard, Freeman Henry.

Farley, Walter Lorimer (1915-)

--Big Black Horse. N.D. E. M. Hale & Co.

--Big Black Horse. Schucker, James, illus. LC 53-6288. (Adapted from "The Black Stallion"). (Illus.). 64 p. 29cm. 1953. Random House.

--The Black Stallion. Ward, Keith, illus. LC 41-218827. ix, 273 p. incl. illus., plates. 21 cm. 1941. Random House.

--The Black Stallion and Flame. Eldridge, Harold, illus. LC 60-10029. (Illus.). 240 p. 21cm. 1960. Random House.

--The Black Stallion and Satan. Menasco, Milton, illus. LC 49-6117. 208 p. illus. 21 cm. 1949. Random House.

--The Black Stallion and the Girl. Draper, Angie, illus. LC 75-147884. (Illus.). 214 p. 22cm. 1971. (ISBN 0-394-92145-3). Random House.

--Black Stallion Challenged!. Draper, Angie, illus. LC 64-15094. (Illus.). 246p. illus. 22cm. (gr. 5-9). 1964. (ISBN 0-394-80617-4, BYR). (ISBN 0-394-90617-9). (ISBN 0-394-84371-1). Random.

--The Black Stallion: Comic Book Album. Genin, Robert, adapted by. Faure, Michel, illus. LC 83-60188. (Illus.). 48p. (Black Stallion Comic Bks.). (gr. 3-7). 1983. (ISBN 0-394-86025-X). Random.

--The Black Stallion Legend. LC 83-1870. p. cm. 1983. (ISBN 0-394-86026-8). (ISBN 0-394-96026-2). Random House.

--The Black Stallion Mystery. Singer, Mel, illus. LC 57-7527. (Illus.). 202 p. 21cm. 1957. Random House.

--The Black Stallion Picture Book. LC 78-20653. p. cm. c.1979. (ISBN 0-394-84174-3). (ISBN 0-394-94174-8). Random House.

--The Black Stallion Returns. Eldridge, Harold, illus. LC 45-8763. 6 p. l., 3-229 p. incl. col. front., illus., plates. 19 1/2 cm. 1945. Random House.

--The Black Stallion Returns: Movie Storybooks. Spinner, Stephanie (1943-), ed. Farley, Tim, photos by. LC 82-3861. (Illus.). 64p. (gr. 2-7). 1982. (ISBN 0-394-85412-8). (ISBN 0-394-95412-2). Random.

--The Black Stallion Revolts. Eldridge, Harold, illus. LC 53-6284. (Illus.). 305 p. 21cm. 1953. Random House.

--The Black Stallion's Courage. LC 56-5471. (Illus.). 242 p. 21cm. 1956. Random House.

--The Black Stallion's Filly. Menasco, Milton, illus. LC 52-7216. (Illus.). 309 p. 21cm. 1952. Random House.

--The Black Stallion's Ghost. Draper, Angie, illus. LC 77-81313. (Illus.). 187 p. 22cm. 1969. Random House.

--The Black Stallion's Sulky Colt. Eldridge, Harold, illus. LC 54-7011. (Illus.). 248 p. 22cm. 1954. Random House.

--The Blood Bay Colt. Menasco, Milton, illus. LC 50-9584. (Illus.). 307 p. 21cm. 1950. Random House.

--The Great Dane, Thor. Cellini, Joseph. (1924-), illus. LC 67-271. (Illus.). 207 p. 24cm. 1966. Random House.

--The Horse-Tamer. Schucker, James, illus. LC 58-9030. (Illus.). 175 p. 21cm. 1958. Random House.

--The Horse That Swam Away. Summers, Leo, illus. LC 65-10486. (Illus.). 75 p. 23cm. 1965. Random House.

--The Island Stallion. Ward, Keith, illus. LC 48-8397. vii, 247 p. illus. 21 cm. 1948. Random House.

--The Island Stallion Races. Eldridge, Harold, illus. LC 55-6065. (Illus.). 256 p. 21cm. 1955. Random House.

--The Island Stallion's Fury. Eldridge, Harold, illus. LC 51-11818. (Illus.). 243 p. 21cm. 1951. Random House.

--Larry and the Undersea Raider. Jackson, P. K., illus. LC 42-11249. 225p. 1942. Random House.

--Little Black, a Pony. Schucker, James, illus. LC 61-7789. (Illus.). 24cm. 60p. (Beninner Bks., B-21). (gr. 1-2). 1961. (ISBN 0-394-80021-4). (ISBN 0-394-90021-9). Beginner.

--Little Black Goes to the Circus. Schucker, James, illus. LC 63-13866. (Illus.). 59 p. 24cm. 1963. Beginner Books.

--The Little Black Pony Races. Schucker, James, illus. LC 68-14491. (Illus.). 61 p. 24cm. 1968. Random House.

--Man O' War. Draper, Angie, illus. (Illus.). 326 p. 24cm. 1962. Random House.

--Son of the Black Stallion. Menasco, Milton, illus. LC 47-3369. viii, 3-330 p. incl. front., illus. 20 1/2 cm. 1947. Random House.

--Walter Farley's Black Stallion Books, 4 bks. Incl. The Black Stallion. LC 41-21882; The Black Stallion Returns. LC 45-8763; The Black Stallion & Satan. LC 49-6117; The Black Stallion Mystery. LC 57-7527. (gr. 4-9). 1979. Boxed Set. (ISBN 0-394-84176-X, BYR). Random.

Farman, Ella

--Allie Bird Ser. Containing "A Little Woman," "Grandma Crosby's Household," and "A Girl's Money", 3 vols. N.D. Set. D. Lothrop & Co.

--Anna Maylie Ser. Containing "Annie Maylie", "Willie Lee", "Zina", etc, 4 vols. N.D. Set. D. Lothrop & Co.

--The Doll Doctor, and Other Stories. (Illus.). N.D. D. Lothrop & Co.

--Good-for-nothing Polly: A Story for Boys. (Illus.). N.D. D. Lothrop & Co.

--Sugar Plums: A Book of Sweets for the Children. Northam, C. A., illus. (Illus.). N.D. D. Lothrop & Co.

Farman, Ella, jt. auth. see Hallowell, S. C., Mrs.

Farman, Ella & Crampton, G. E. E.

--Entertaining and Instructive Library for Girls: Containing "Rose and Millie", "Edith Prescott", "Little Toss", "Petite," etc, 12 vols. N.D. Set. D. Lothrop & Co.

Farman, Ella & Edson, N. I.

--Hidden Treasure Ser. Containing "Hiden Treasure," "Barbara", "Mrs. Hurd's Niece", and "Fabrics", 4 vols. N.D. Set. D. Lothrop & Co.

Farman, Sara E.

--Goldie's Adventures. N.D. D. Lothrop Co.

Farmayan, Jo

--The Wonderful Lamp from Isfahan. Sherman, Harriet, illus. LC 77-37093. 1973. (ISBN 0-07-019960-4). (ISBN 0-07-019960-4). McGraw-Hill.

Farmer, Clifford

--Joe of Rollingacres. LC 25-39457. viii, 317 p. front., plates. 20 cm. c.1924. The Cornhill Publishing Company.

Farmer, F. V.

--Boy and Girl Heroes. (Everychild's Series). N.D. Macmillan.

Farmer, Penelope, tr. see Oz, Amos.

Farmer, Penelope Jane (1939-)

--A Castle of Bone. LC 78-190553. 151 p. 22cm. 1972. Atheneum.

--Charlotte Sometimes. Connor, Chris, illus. LC 69-13773. (Illus.). 192 p. 21cm. 1st U.S. edition. 1969. Harcourt, Brace & World.

--Daedalus and Icarus. Connor, Chris, illus. LC 71-96318. (Illus.). 47 p. 25cm. 1st U.S. edition. 1971. (ISBN 0-15-221212-4). Harcourt Brace Jovanovich.

--Emma in Winter. Spanfeller, James John (1930-), illus. LC 66-7481. (Illus.). 160 p. 21cm. 1st U.S. edition. 1966. Harcourt, Brace & World.

--The Magic Stone. Kaufmann, John (1931-), illus. LC 64-20225. 223 p. illus. 20 cm. 1st U.S. edition. 1964. Harcourt, Brace & World.

--Sea Gull. Ribbons, Ian (1924-), illus. LC 66-11200. 47p. illus. 21cm. 1st U.S. edition. c.1966. (ISBN 0-15-271086-8). (ISBN 0-15-271087-6). Harcourt.

--The Serpent's Teeth: The Story of Cadmus. Connor, Chris, illus. LC 76-137760. (Illus.). 48 p. 25cm. 1st U.S. edition. 1972, c.1971. (ISBN 0-15-272904-6). (ISBN 0-15-272905-4). Harcourt, Brace, Jovanovich.

--The Story of Persephone. McCallum, Graham (1943-), illus. LC 73-4923. (Illus.). 48 p. 25cm. 1973. (ISBN 0-688-20084-2). (ISBN 0-688-20084-2). Morrow.

--The Summer Birds. Spanfeller, James John (1930-), illus. LC 62-12822. (Illus.). (gr. 4-6). 1962. (ISBN 0-15-282485-5, HJ). HarBraceJ. **Awards: (ALA); (CMA).**

--William and Mary: A Story. LC 74-76272. 160 p. 22cm. 1974. (ISBN 0-689-50005-X). Atheneum.

--The Year King. LC 77-3165. p. cm. 1977. (ISBN 0-689-50090-4). Atheneum.

Farmer, Philip Jose (1918-)

--The Fabulous Riverboat. 1971. (ISBN 0-399-10273-6). G. P. Putnam's Sons.

Farmer, Philip Jose (1918-), compiled by.

--Mother Was a Lovely Beast: A Feral Man Anthology, Fiction and Fact About Humans Raised by Animals. LC 74-11117. xiii, 246 p. 22cm. 1974. (ISBN 0-8019-5964-0). Chilton Book Co.

Farmer, Wendell, pseud., see Davis, Lavinia Riker.

Farmer, Wendell

--Bicycle Detectives. Harvey, Alice, illus. (Young Moderns Edition). 1953. Doubleday & Co.

Farnagle, A. E. & Smith, W. Hovey

--Farnagle's Fables for Children & Adults. Crawford, Kimberly Ann, illus. (Illus.). 64p. (Orig.). (gr. 1-5). 1984. (ISBN 0-916565-04-1). Whitehall Pr.

Farnam, Suzanne Silveruys (1898-) & McCarroll, Marion Clyde (1893-1977)

--Suzanne of Belgium. N.D. E. P. Dutton & Co.

Farnham, Arthur L. & Farnham, Lorraine J.

--Teddy's Trip to Africa. 1982. (ISBN 0-533-05288-2). Vantage.

Farnham, Lorraine J., jt. auth. see Farnham, Arthur L.

Farnol, Jeffery see Farnol, John Jeffery.

Farnol, John Jeffery (1878-1952)

--The Amateur Gentleman. N.D. Little, Brown & Co.

--Black Bartlemy's treasure. N.D. Little, Brown & Co.

--The Geste of Duke Jocelyn. N.D. Little, Brown & Co.

--The Honourable Mr. Tawnish. Brock, Charles Edmond (1870-1938), illus. LC 13-22290. 4 p. l., 165 p. col. front., col. plates. 20 cm. 1913. Little, Brown, and Company.

--The Loring Mystery. N.D. Little, Brown & Co.

--Our Admirable Betty. N.D. Little, Brown & Co.

--Peregrine's Progress. N.D. Little, Brown & Co.

--The Shadow and Other Stories. N.D. Little, Brown & Co.

Farnsworth, Alice G.

--Murder by Default. LC 75-30160. 104p. (Orig.). 1976. (ISBN 0-89185-017-1). (ISBN 0-89185-016-3). Anthelion Pr.

Farnsworth, C. H.

--Grammar School Songs. N.D. Charles Scribner's Sons.

Farnsworth, Frances Joyce, Mrs.

--Baby Hippo's Jungle Journey. LC 28-28940. 102 p. front., plates. 24 cm. c.1928. The Abingdon Press.

--Cubby in Wonderland. LC 32-33418. 140 p. incl. front., illus. 21 cm. c.1932. The Abingdon Press.

--Cubby in Wonderland. LC 52-13020. 140p. illus. 21cm. (National parks and monuments ser.). 1953, c.1932. University of New Mexico Press.

--Cubby in Wonderland. Rev. ed. LC 58-12810. (Illus.). 120p. 21cm. 1958. University of New Mexico Press.

--Cubby Returns. N.D. University of New Mexico Press.

--Cubby Returns. LC 35-7602. 170 p. incl. front., illus. 21 cm. c.1935. The Abingdon Press.

--Cubby Returns to Yellowstone. (Illus.). 1958. University of New Mexico Press.

--Cubby Returns to Yellowstone. 1st Rev. ed. LC 61-13116. (Illus.). 147p. 21cm. Orig. Title: Cubby Returns, 1935. 1961. University of New Mexico Press.

--Mr. Possum Visits the Zoo: And Other Nature Stories. LC 26-17651. 69 p. front. 23 cm. c.1926. The Abingdon Press.

--Mrs. Humming Bird's Double: And Other Nature Stories. King, George A., illus. LC 30-23659. 106 p. front., plates. 24 cm. c.1930. The Abingdon Press.

--Tike and Tiny in the Tetons. LC 54-7821. 162p. illus. 20cm. 1954. University of New Mexico Press.

--Winged Moccasins: The Story of Sacajawea. Bjorklund, Lorence F. (1913-1978), illus. LC 54-6765. 189p. illus. 22cm. 1954. J. Messner.

Farnsworth, Marcia

--Precious. (gr. 4-7). N.D. Carlton.

Farnsworth, Vesta J., Mrs.

--Stories Mother Told. LC 25-9139. 176 p. incl. front. (port.) illus. 20 cm. c.1925. Review and Herald Publishing Association.

Farnum, Mabel Adelaide (1887-)

--Our Little Vatican City Cousin. Beaton, Monica, illus. LC 34-35681. 6 p. l., 96 p. col. front., plates. 20 cm. (The little cousin series). c.1934. L. C. Page & Company.

Farny, H. F., illus.

--Patience: Or, The Poet and the Milkmaid. LC 16-18658. (Founded on Gilbert and Sullivan's Opera, Patience; Adapted for Children). (Illus.). 14p. 1882. P. G. Thomson.

Farquarharson, Martha

--Elsie's Girlhood. N.D. Dodd & Mead.

--Holidays at Roselands. N.D. Dodd & Mead.

Farquhar, Margaret Cutting (1905-), ed.

--Favorite Stories to Read Aloud. N.D. Grosset & Dunlap.

Farquhar, Margaret Cutting (1905-) & Weigle, Oscar, eds.

--A Bedtime Treasury of Children's Stories. Wolf, Ann, illus. LC 60-16093. 512p. col. illus. 24cm. N.D. Grosset & Dunlap.

Farquhar, Silas Edgar, ed. see Dalgliesh, Alice.

Farquhar, Silas Edgar (1887-1965) & Hill, Patty Smith (1868-), eds.

--Childcraft ... teachers' ed. LC 40-5654. 14 v. col. fronts. (v. 1-11) illus. (part col.) col. plates, double map, diagrs. 25 1/2 cm (v. 13-14: 25 1/2 x 35 1/2 cm. c.1939. The Quarrie Corporation.

Farquharson, Martha, pseud., see Finley, Martha.

Farr, Diana Pullein-Thompson see Pullein-Thompson, Josephine Mary Wedderburn & Pullein-Thompson, Diana.

Farr, Diana Pullein-Thompson see Pullein-Thompson, Diana.

Farr, Finis King (1904-1982)

--The Elephant Valley. 1967. Arlington House.

Farr, Naunerle, ed. see Clemens, Samuel Langhorne.

Farr, Naunerle, ed. see Hawthorne, Nathaniel (1804-1864) & Trinidad, Angel.

Farr, Naunerle, ed. see Poe, Edgar Allan.

Farr, Naunerle, ed. see Stoker, Bram.

Farr, Naunerle C., adapted by.

--Ivanhoe. Taloac, Gerry, illus. LC 78-51546. (Original Author: Sir Walter Scott, 1771-1832). (Illus.). 62 p. 21cm. (Now age illustrated series). 1979, c.1978. (ISBN 0-88301-327-4). (ISBN 0-88301-315-0). Pendulum Press.

--The Last of the Mohicans. Carrillo, Fred, illus. LC 77-79441. (Original Author: James Fenimore Cooper, 1789-1851). (Illus.). 62 p. 21cm. (Now age books illustrated). c.1977. (ISBN 0-88301-267-7). Pendulum Press.

Farrant, Leda (1927-)

--The Daughter of the Sun & Other Stories. Kahiga, Samuel (1940-), illus. (Illus.). 1969. (ISBN 0-19-519511-6). Oxford U Pr.

Farrant, Trevor, jt. auth. see Rotsler, William.

Farrar, Charles Alden John (0000-1893)

--Down the West Branch: Or Camps and Tramps Around Katahdin ... LC 12-32169. 5 p. l., vii-viii, 13-311 p. front., plates. 18 cm. (Added t.-p.: Lake and forest series. By Charles A. J. Farrar). 1886. Lee and Shepard.

--Down the West Branch: Or, Camps & Tramps Around Katahdin, 1 of 50 vols. (Illus.). (The Norwood Ser.: No. 11). 1900. Lee & Shepard.

--Eastward Ho!. Or, Adventures at Rangeley Lakes. (Illus.). (The Norwood Ser.). 1900. Lee & Shepard.

--Eastward, Ho!. Or, Adventures at Rangeley Lakes. (Illus.). (Lake and Forest Ser.). N.D. Lee & Shepard.

--Up the North Branch: A Summer's Outing, 1 of 50 vols. (Illus.). (The Norwood Ser.: No. 13). 1900. Lee & Shepard.

--Up the North Branch: A Summer's Outing. (Illus.). (Lake And Forest Ser.). N.D. Lee & Shepard.

--Wild Woods Life: Or A Trip to Parmachenee. (Illus.). (The Norwood Ser.). 1900. Lee & Shepard.

--Wild Woods Life: Or, A Trip to Parmachenee. (Illus.). (Lake And Forest Ser.). N.D. Lee & Shepard.

Farrar, Francis Albert

--Old Greek Nature Stories. 256 p. front., plates 19 cm. (Half-title: Told through the ages). 1926. L. Macveagh, The Dial Press.

Farrar, Frederic William (1831-1903)

--Eric: Little by Little. N.D. Albert Mason.

--Eric: Or, Little by Little, 1 of 3 Vols. (The College Library). N.D. Set. E P Dutton & Co.

--Eric, or Little by Little. LC 75-32199. (Illus.). Repr. of 1892 ed. (Classics of Children's Literature, 1621-1932: Vol. 60). 1976. (ISBN 0-8240-2309-9). Garland Pub.

--Eric: Or, Little by Little. (gr. 7-9). N.D. MacMillan Bks.

--Eric: Or, Little by Little. Avery, Gillan Elise (1926-), pref. by. LC 75-32199. (Illus.). viii, 368 p. 1 leaf of plates. 19cm. Reissue of 1892 ed. (Classics of Children's Literature, 1621-1932). 1977. (ISBN 0-8240-2309-9). Garland Pub.

--Eric: Or, Little by Little, A Tale of Roslyn School. LC 24-27987. 2 p. l., ix-x, 11-366 p. front. 19 cm. (On cover: College library). 1890. E. P. Dutton & Company.

--Eric: Or, Little by Little, A Tale of Roslyn School. 304 p. front. 20 cm. (On cover: The college library). N.D. W. L. Allison Co.

--Eric: Or, Little by Little, A Tale of Roslyn School. 24th ed. Browne, Gordon Frederick (1858-1932), illus. LC 49-40041. xiv, 368 p. illus. 19 cm. 1891. A.C. McClurg.

--Eric: Or, Little by Little, A Tale of Roslyn School. Traver, George A., illus. LC 2-12949. 1 p. l., 7-366 p. front., pl. 21 cm. 1902. E. P. Dutton & Company.

--Julian Home. N.D. E P Dutton.

--Julian Home. (gr. 7-9). N.D. MacMillan Bks.

--St. Winifred. (gr. 7-9). N.D. MacMillan Bks.

--St. Winifred: Or, The World of School, 1 of 3 Vols. (The College Library). N.D. Set. E P Dutton & Co.

--St. Winifred's: Or, The World of School. LC 49-41828. 411 p. 20 cm. (The College Library). 1878. E.P. Dutton.

--St. Winifred's: Or, The World of School. Browne, Gordon Frederick (1858-1932), illus. LC 6-38977. 6, vii-viii, 9-424 p. front. illus. 19 cm. (On cover: The college library). 1897. W. L. Allison Co.

--The Three Homes. New ed. N.D. E. P. Dutton

Farrar, John Chipman (1896-1974)

--Indoor and Outdoor Plays for Children: Including The Magic Sea Shell. Bromhall, Winifred & Ludlum, Mary M., illus. LC 33-929. 201 p. incl. col. front., illus., col. plates. 21 cm. c.1933. Noble and Noble.

--The Magic Sea Shell, and Other Plays for Children. Ludlum, Mary M., illus. LC 23-16995. viii p., 3 l., 15-155 p. incl. illus., plates. 20 cm. c.1923. George H. Doran Company.

--Songs for Johnny-Jump-Up. Leach, Rita, illus. LC 30-28188. xii, 55 p. incl. front., illus. 20 cm. 1930. R. R. Smith, Inc.

Farrar, Richard Bartlett, Jr. (1939-)

--Hungry Snowbird. (Illus.). (A Break-of-Day Bk.). 1975. (ISBN 0-698-30557-4). Coward, McCann & Geoghegan.

Farrar, S. E., jt. auth. see Cushing, Henriette.

Farrar, Susan Clement (1917-)

--Samantha on Stage. Sanderson, Ruth, illus. LC 78-64958. (Illus.). 164 p. 22cm. c.1979. (ISBN 0-8037-7574-1). (ISBN 0-8037-7577-6). Dial Press.

Farre, Rowena

--Seal Morning. (gr. 7-9). 1972. (ISBN 0-590-02215-6, Schol Pap). Scholastic Inc.

Farrell, Anne A. (1916-)

--Eight Days at Guara. Lacis, Astra, illus. LC 76-365578. (Illus.). 183 p. 22cm. 1976. (ISBN 0-340-20573-3). Hodder & Stoughton.

--Night-Time is a Quiet Time. Farrell, Anne A. (1916-), illus. LC 68-14966. (Illus.). 1 v. (unpaged. 19cm. 1968. C. R. Gibson Co.

--Poems for a Little Boy. Farrell, Anne A. (1916-), illus. LC 71-83843. (Illus.). 27 p. 19cm. (Stardust books). 1969. C. R. Gibson Co.

--Poems for a Little Girl. Farrell, Anne A. (1916-), illus. LC 78-83842. (Illus.). 27 p. 19cm. (Stardust books). 1969. C. R. Gibson Co.

Farrell, Gene

--Junior Days at Mountain View. LC 47-425. 88 p. 20 cm. 1946. Wm. B. Eerdmans Publishing Company.

--A New Garment. LC 48-199191. 121 p. 21 cm. 1948. W.B. Eerdmans Pub. Co.

Farrell, James Thomas (1904-1979)

--The Silence of History. N.D. Doubleday & Co.

Farrell, Kate, jt. ed. see Koch, Kenneth.

Farrell, Maria Owens

--Peter the Great. Strezki, Frances, illus. LC 32-35930. 4 p. l., 157, 1 p. front., plates. 14 cm. c.1932. Marya Press.

Farrell, Muriel, jt. auth. see Kravetz, Nathan.

Farrell, Sherrie

--Gabriel's Very First Birthday. (Illus.). 1976. (ISBN 0-686-16512-8). Pacific Pipeline.

Farrington, Frank

--Sunny Sam. Kirkbride, E. R., illus. 1921. Reilly & Lee.

Farrington, Harry Webb (1880-), selected by.

--Cher Ami. LC 27-969. 64 p. illus. 21 cm. c.1926. Rough and Brown Press.

Farrington, Selwyn Kip, Jr. (1904-)

--Bill, The Broadbill Swordfish. Hunt, Lynn Bogue, illus. LC 42-19165. 48p. N.D. Coward-McCann.

--Tony the Tuna. 1976. (ISBN 0-911660-25-9). Yankee Peddler.

Farris, Stella

--The Magic Blanket. Farris, Stella, illus. LC 80-111628. (Illus.). 28 p. 16cm. (Bedtime book). c.1979. (ISBN 0-06-021879-7). Harper & Row.

--The Magic Bubble-Pipe. Farris, Stella, illus. LC 78-108162. (Illus.). 28 p. 16cm. (Bedtime book). 1978. (ISBN 0-06-021878-9). Harper & Row.

--The Magic Castle. Farris, Stella, illus. LC 78-108161. (Illus.). 27 p. 17cm. (Bedtime book). 1978. (ISBN 0-06-021877-0). Harper & Row.

--The Magic Castle Fairytale Book. Payson, DAle (1943-), illus. (Illus.). (Special Pop-Up Bks.). (ps-3). 1978. (ISBN 0-394-83548-4, BYR). Random.

--The Magic Teddy Bear. Farris, Stella, illus. LC 79-2394. (Illus.). (ps-2). 1979. (ISBN 0-06-021880-0, HarpJ). Har-Row.

Farrow, Dorothy Parmlee Potter, Mrs. (1886-)

--Little Brown Hen. Dobias, Frank (1902-), illus. LC 41-17040. 48 p. col. illus. 17 x 18 cm. 1941. The Macmillan Company.

Farrow, George Edward (1866-1920)

--Adventures in Wallypug Land. (Illus.). (The Wellesley Series for Girls.). 1915. A L Burt & Co.

--Adventures in Wallypug Land. (The Rugby Ser.). N.D. A. L. Burt Company.

--Adventures in Wallypug Land. (Illus.). (The Little Women Ser.). N.D. A. L. Burt's Pubs.

--Dick, Marjorie and Fidge. (The Rugby Ser.). N.D. A. L. Burt Company.

--Dick, Marjorie and Fidge: The Adventures of Three Little People. (Illus.). (The Wellesley Series for Girls). N.D. A. L. Burt.

--The Missing Prince. Furniss, Harry (1854-1925) & Furniss, Dorothy, illus. LC 21-16839. xiii p., 1 l., 198 p. incl. front., illus., plates. 22 cm. 1897. Dodd, Mead and Company.

--The Wallypug of Why. Furniss, Harry (1854-1925) & Furniss, Dorothy, illus. (Illus.). N.D. Dodd, Mead & Co.

Farrow, Peter & Lampert, Diane

--Twyllyp. Farrow, Peter, illus. LC 63-12378. 60 p. illus. 23 cm. (an astor book. 1963. (ISBN 0-8392-3040-0). I. Obolensky.

Farrow, Rachi

--Charlie's Dream. Farrow, Rachi, illus. LC 77-4320. (Illus.). 32 p. c.1978. (ISBN 0-394-83595-6). (ISBN 0-394-93595-0). Pantheon Books.

Farrow, Tiera

--Lawyer in Petticoats. N.D. Vantage Press Books.

Favata, Raymond
--The Romper Room Song Book of Musical Adventures: Alphabetcha!. Favata, Raymond, illus. LC 83-23185. (Illus.). 64p. (ps-2). 1984. (ISBN 0-89845-055-1). Caedmon.
--The Romper Room Song Book of Musical Adventures: Quick Draw!. Favata, Raymond, illus. LC 83-23186. (Illus.). (ps-2). 1984. (ISBN 0-89845-054-3). Caedmon.
Fawsett, Marise
--Hooly: Stories of a Country Mouse. Fawsett, Marise, illus. LC 39-9938. 4 p. l., 3-126. 1 p. col. front., col. plates. 16 cm. 1939. Old County Road Press.
Fay, Ann, ed. see Bernstein, Joanne Eckstein, et al.
Fay, Ann, ed. see Christian, Mary Blount.
Fay, Ann, ed. see Vande Velde, Vivian.
Fay, Anne, ed. see Cohen, Peter Zachary.
Fay, Anne, ed. see Latta, Richard.
Fay, Erica
--Kings and Heroes. Quiller-Couch, Arthur Thomas, Sir (1863-1944), frwd. by. 84p. N.D. G P Putnam's Sons.
Fay, Leo Charles, et al. (1920-), eds. see Rosenberg, Ethel Clifford, et al.
Fay, Leo Charles (1920-) & Ross, Ramon Royal
--Lost and Found. LC 72-186168. (Illus.). 72 p. 20cm. (Young America basic reading program. Level 4). 1972. (ISBN 0-8361-1480-9). Lyons & Carnahan.
Faye-Lund, Hans, jt. auth. see Holmvik, Oyvind.
Fayerweather, Margaret Doane Gardiner, Mrs. (1883-)
--Anne Alive! A Year in the Life of a Girl of New York State. Roosevelt, Anna Eleanor, Mrs. (1884-1962) LC 33-25690. xiii p., l., 17-303 p. incl. front., illus., plates. 20 cm. 1933. R. M. McBride & Company.
--Anne at Large: The Further Adventures of "Anne Alive". King, Ruth, illus. LC 34-40672. ix, 350 p. incl. illus., plates. 19 1/2 cm. c.1934. Robert M. McBride & Company.
--Anne at Work: Further Adventures of "Anne Alive". King, Ruth, illus. LC 35-25830. x p., 2 l., 3-289 p. incl. illus., plates. front. 19 1/2 cm. c.1935. R. M. McBride & Company.
Fazio, Rebecca S.
--The Do-Anything Wagon. 32p. (gr. 3-5). 1978. Dorrance.
Fea, Henry R.
--Adventure in the Sierras. Kidder, Harvey, illus. LC 67-15294. (Illus.). iii, 179 p. 22cm. (Ginn reading program.). (Ginn Book Length Stories). 1970, c.1959. Ginn.
--Maggie's Caravan. 1965. David Mckay Company.
--Maggie's Caravan. Lewis, Richard William (1933-1966), illus. LC 65-21600. 126 p. illus. 21 cm. 1965. I. Washburn.
--Operation Cannonball. Lambo, Donald W. (1903-1966), illus. LC 74-82643. (Illus.). 144 p. 21cm. 1969. Ives Washburn.
--The Wild One. 1964. David McKay Company Inc.
--The Wild One. LC 64-12613. 120 p. illus. 1964. Washburn.
Feagles, Anita MacRae (1927-)
--Casey, the Utterly Impossible Horse. Wilson, Dagmar (1916-), illus. LC 60-50242. 95 p. illus. 22 cm. 1960. Young Scott Books.
--Genie & Joe Maloney. Sibley, Don (1922-), illus. 64p. (gr. 2-5). 1962. (ISBN 0-201-09197-6, Young Scott Bks). A-W.
--The Genie and Joe Maloney. Sibley, Don (1922-), illus. (Illus.). 62 p. 21cm. 1962. W. R. Scott.
--He Who Saw Everything: The Epic of Gilgamesh. 64p. 1966. (ISBN 0-201-09215-8). Addision-Wesley.
--Me, Cassie. LC 68-15258. 158 p. 22cm. 1968. Dial Press.
--Queen Sara & the Messy Fairies. Grossman, Nancy S. (1940-), illus. LC 68-15339. (Illus.). 66 p. 27cm. 1968. Young Scott Books.
--The Sea Rock. 1st ed. Arnaud, Read, illus. LC 68-11887. (Illus.). 56 p. 26cm. 1968. Bobbs-Merrill.
--Sophia Scarlotti and Ceecee. LC 78-12630. 164 p. 22cm. 1979. (ISBN 0-689-30680-6). Atheneum.
--A Stranger in the Spanish Village. Rev. ed. De Diego, Julio, illus. LC 64-13578. 71 p. illus. 22 cm. 1964. Young Scott Books.
--Thor & the Giants. Russell, Gertrude B., illus. LC 68-27024. (Illus.). color ils. 48p. (gr. 1-5). 1968. (ISBN 0-201-09365-0, A-W Childrens). A-W.
--Thor and the Giants: An Old Norse Legend. Barrer-Russell, Gertrude (1921-), illus. LC 68-27024. (Illus.). 1 v. (unpaged. 29cm. 1968. Young Scott Books.
--The Tooth Fairy. LC 62-2377. unpaged. illus. 19 cm. 1962. Young Scott Books.
--Twenty-Seven Cats Next Door. Shipman, Robert A., illus. 72p. 1965. (ISBN 0-201-09379-0). Addision-Wesley.
--Twenty-Seven Cats Next Door. Shipman, Robert A., illus. LC 65-12581. 71 p. illus. 22 cm. 1965. Young Scott Books.
--The Year the Dreams Came Back. LC 76-4469. 146 p. 22cm. 1976. Atheneum.
Feagles, Anita MacRae (1927-), retold by.
--Autun & the Bear. Barrer-Russell, Gertrude (1921-), illus. 48p. (gr. k-4). 1967 (Young Scott Bks). A-W.
--Autun and the Bear: An Old Icelandic Legend. rev. ed. Barrer-Russell, Gertrude (1921-), illus. LC 67-4610. (Illus.). 48 p. 28cm. 1967. Young Scott Books.
--He Who Saw Everything:. The Epic of Gilgamesh. Gonzalez, Xavier, illus. LC 66-11409. (Illus.). 63p. 28cm. 1966. Young Scott Books.
Feague, Mildred H. (1915-)
--The Little Indian and the Angel. DeGrazia, Ted, pseud. (1909-1982), illus. DeGrazia, Ettore. LC 76-101597. (Illus.). 45 p. 22cm. 1970. Childrens Press.
--Little Sky Eagle and the Pumpkin Drum. DeGrazia, Ted, pseud. (1909-1982), illus. DeGrazia, Ettore. LC 73-123805. (Illus.). 42 p. 22cm. 1972. (ISBN 0-516-03572-X). Childrens Press.
Fearing, Kenneth (1902-1961)
--The Big Clock. Nelson, James, intro. by. LC 68-20832. 175p. 1968. (ISBN 0-393-08565-1). Norton & Co.
Fearon, Ethelind E.
--Little Dog. Simon, Howard (1903-1979), illus. LC 53-674556. 194p. illus. 22cm. 1955. Lothrop, Lee & Shepard Co.
Fecher, Constance (1911-)
--Heir to Pendarrow. LC 77-85363. 192p. (gr. 7 up). 1969. (ISBN 0-374-32937-0). FS&G.
--The Leopard Dagger. LC 72-97002. 179 p. 21cm. 1973. (ISBN 0-374-34377-2). Farrar, Strauss and Giroux.
--The Link Boys. 1st ed. Cuffari, Richard (1925-1978), illus. LC 75-149219. (Illus.). 177 p. 21cm. (Ariel book). 1971. (ISBN 0-374-34497-3). Farrar, Straus & Giroux.
--Tom Hawke (Pub. by FS&G). Orig. Title: The Link Boys. (gr. 5-7). 1972 (Starline). Schol Bk Serv.
--Tom Hawke. (gr. 4-6). 1972. (ISBN 0-590-09381-9, Schol Trade Pap). Schol Bk Serv.
--Venture for a Crown. 150 p. 22cm. (Ariel book). 1968. Farrar, Straus & Giroux.
Fechner, Amrei
--I Am a Little Dog. Kimber, Robert, tr. LC 82-25294. p. cm. 1983, c.1982. (ISBN 0-8120-5514-4). Barron's Educational Series, Inc.
--I am a Little Elephant. Kimber, Robert, tr. (Little Animal Stories Ser.). (ps). 1984. (ISBN 0-8120-5586-1). Barron.
--I am a Little Lion. Kimber, Robert, tr. (Little Animal Stories Ser.). (ps). 1984. (ISBN 0-8120-5585-3). Barron.
--I Am a Little Pony. Kimber, Rita, illus. Kimber, Robert, tr. LC 85-3899. p. cm. 1985. (ISBN 0-8120-5667-1). Barron's Educational Series.
Fechner, Amrei, jt. auth. see Spanner, Helmut.
Fechter, Alyce Shinn (1909-)
--M'Toto: The Adventures of a Baby Elephant. Garbutt, Bernard (1900-), illus. LC 64-8134. 96 p. illus. 24 cm. 1965. McGraw-Hill.
Feczko, Kathy
--The Great Bunny Race. Jones, John Ralph (1935-), illus. LC 84-8634. (Illus.). 32p. (Giant First-Start Readers Ser.). (gr. k-12). 1985. (ISBN 0-8167-0357-4). (ISBN 0-8167-0437-6). Troll Assocs.
--Umbrella Parade. Borgo, Deborah Colvin, illus. LC 84-8650. (Illus.). 30 p. 24cm. c.1985. (ISBN 0-8167-0356-6). (ISBN 0-8167-0436-8). Troll Associates.
Feder, Jane (1940-)
--Beany. Gundersheimer, Karen, illus. LC 78-10416. (Illus.). 32 p. 12 x 23 cm. c.1979. (ISBN 0-394-83734-7). (ISBN 0-394-93734-1). Pantheon Books. **Award: (ALA).**
--The Night-Light. McCrady, Lady (1951-), illus. LC 79-20687. (Illus.). 31 p. 21cm. c.1980. (ISBN 0-8037-6604-1). (ISBN 0-8037-6605-X). Dial Press.
Feder, Joseph Marvin (1891-) & Tribble, Evelyn H.
--Judy Page, Medical Technologist: A Novel. LC 46-335945. 4 p. l., 11-219 p. 22 cm. 1946. The William-Frederick Press.
Feder, Paula Kurzband (1935-)
--Where Does the Teacher Live?. 1st ed. Hoban, Lillian (1925-), illus. LC 78-13157. (Illus.). 48 p. 24cm. (A Fat Cat Book). c.1979. (ISBN 0-525-42586-1). Dutton.
Feder, Robert Arthur see Arthur, Robert, pseud.
Feder-Tal, Karah
--The Ring. Langer, Tsofia, illus. Dixon, Adrienne, tr. LC 65-15444. 192p. illus. 21cm. (gr. 5-10). c.1965. Abelard.
--The Stone of Peace. Evers, Alie, illus. Kousbroek, H. R., tr. LC 61-5792. (Illus.). 187p. 20cm. Orig. Title: Dutch. 1961. Abelard-Schuman.
Federal Theatre Project (U.S.) see Swortzell, Lowell Stanley.
Federation of Women's Zionists of Great Britian and Ireland
--Silver Wing and Golden Harp. (Illus.). N.D. A. S. Barnes & Co.
Federico, Helen
--ABC. LC 63-2139. unpaged. illus. 31 cm. (Golden happy books). c.1963. Golden Press.
Federlein, Anne Cairns
--Play in Preschool Mainstreamed and Handicapped Settings. LC 80-65612. (Illus.). ix, 102 p. 28cm. c.1981. (ISBN 0-86548-035-4). Century Twenty One Pub.
Fedor, Peter & Leo, Veronica
--The Bird of Happiness. (gr. 1-3). 1976. (ISBN 0-8277-4659-8). British Bk Ctr.
Fedorov, Vadim Dmitrievich
--An Ordinary Magic Watch. Loskutova, Tatyana & Mokhova, Nina, illus. Beveridge, Nancy, tr. (Illus.). 144 p. 24cm. c.1977. Ardis.
Fedoseev, Grigorii Anisimovich
--Pashka of Bear Ravine. Victor, Joan Berg (1942-), illus. White, Anne Terry (1896-), tr. LC 67-20222. (Illus.). 224p. (gr. 5 up). 1967. (ISBN 0-394-91883-5). Pantheon.
Feehan, Mary Edward see Clementia, pseud.
Feehan, Mary Edward, Sr.
--The Quest of Mary Selwyn. Clementia, pseud. LC 17-25128. 245p. 19cm. 1917. Benziger Brothers.
Feehan, Mary Edward, Sr. (1878-)
--Bab Comes into Her Own. Clementia, pseud. LC 26-8492. 4 p. l., 298 p. front. 19 cm. c.1925. Matre & Co.
--Bird-a-Lea. Clementia, pseud. Waddell, James A., illus. LC 21-136089. 357 p. front., plates. 20 cm. c.1920. Extension Press.
--Mostly Mary. Clementia, pseud. LC 21-17980. 154 p. incl. front. 19 cm. c.1921. Matre & Company.
--New Neighbors at Bird-a-Lea. Clementia, pseud. LC 32-9937. 288 p. front. 19 1/2 cm. c.1932. The Bookery.
--The Selwyns in Dixie. Clementia, pseud. LC 23-18214. 4 p. l., 261 p. front. 19 1/2 cm. c.1923. Matre & Co.
--Uncle Frank's Mary. Clementia, pseud. LC 17-25125. 4 p. l., 5-265 p. front. 19 cm. 1917. Benziger Brothers.
--Uncle Frank's Mary: The First of a Series. Clementia, pseud. LC 16-25096. 434 p. front. 19 1/2 cm. c.1916. M. A. Donohue & Company.
--Wilhelmina. Clementia, pseud. LC 40-1008. 3 p. l., 265 p. front. 19 1/2 cm. 1940. Frederick Pustet Co., Inc.
Feehan, Mary Edward, Sr. (1878-), as told by.
--The Story of Berta and Beth. Clementia, pseud. Wilhelmina, illus. LC 40-10079. 158 p. col. front. illus. 19 cm. c.1924. Matre & Company.
Feehan, May Agnes
--Ann of Greystones. LC 37-339052. 4 p. l., 227 p. 20 1/2 cm. c.1937. P. J. Kenedy & Sons.
--Princess Mamselle. LC 28-30852. 3 p. l., 133 p. front. 20 cm. c.1928. The Bookery.
Feelings, Muriel Grey (1938-)
--Moja Means One: Swahili Counting Book. Feelings, Thomas (1933-), illus. LC 76-134856. (Illus.). 24 x 27 cm. 32p. 1971. Dial Press. **Award: (ALA).**
--Zamani Goes to Market. Feelings, Thomas (1933-), illus. LC 70-97032. (Illus.). 44 p. 24cm. 1970. Seabury Press.
Feeney, Leonard, jt. auth. see Crane, Nathalia Clara Ruth.
Feeney, Stephanie
--A Is for Aloha. Hammid, Hella, illus. LC 80-5462. (Illus.). 64p. (ps-k). 1980. (ISBN 0-8248-0722-7). UH Pr.
Fegan, Camilla (1939-)
--Late for Hallowe'en. Armitage, Eileen, illus. (Illus.). 107 p. 22cm. 1st U.S. edition. 1967, c.1966. Criterion Books.
Fehr, Howard Franklin (1901-1982)
--Five Is 5. Strimban, Robert & Strimban, Jack, illus. LC 63-16418. (Illus.). 1 v. (unpaged. (Little owl book). c.1963. Holt, Rinehart and Winston.
--Number Patterns Make Sense. LC 65-14137. 1 v. (unpaged) col. illus. 29 cm. (Wise owl book, WA11). 1965. Holt, Rinehart and Winston.
Fehse, Willi Richard (1906-) & Petis De la Croix, Francois (1653-1713)
--The Thousand and One Days. Holle, Erich, illus. Bell, Anthea, tr. from Fr. LC 76-149325. (Illus.). 213 p., 6 plates. 22cm. 1971. (ISBN 0-200-71724-3). Abelard-Schuman.
Feil, Hila (1942-)
--The Ghost Garden. 1st ed. Quirk, Thomas, illus. LC 75-29277. (Illus.). 236 p. 22cm. 1975, c.1976. (ISBN 0-689-30501-X). Atheneum.
--The Windmill Summer. Brenner, Fred (1920-), illus. LC 77-183172. (Illus.). 128 p. 21cm. 1972. (ISBN 0-06-021887-8). (ISBN 0-06-021888-6). Harper & Row.
Fein, Bill
--They All Depend on You. Bramer, Pat, illus. LC 82-81044. (Illus.). 50p. 1983. (ISBN 0-86666-097-6). GWP.
Fein, Harry H.
--The Flying Chinaman. Rea, Gardner (1892-1966), illus. 1938. Alfred A. Knopf.
Feinberg, Harold S., jt. auth. see Ryder, Joanne.
Feiner, Ruth
--Cat Across the Path. N.D. J. B. Lippincott.
Feinerman, Tehilla, tr. see Peretz, Isaac Loeb.
Feininger, Lyonel (1871-1956)
--The Kin-der-Kids: All Thirty-One Strips in Full Color. Feininger, Lyonel (1871-1956), illus. (Illus.). 32p. (Orig.). 1980. Dover.
Feinman, Jeffrey (1943-)
--Freebies for Kids. (gr. 4 up). 1979. (ISBN 0-671-33009-8). Wanderer Bks.
Feinman, Jeffrey (1943-) & Schwartz, Betty (1927-)
--Freebies for Kids. Rev. Updated. 208p. 1983. (ISBN 0-671-42657-5). Wanderer Bks.
Feinstein, Alan Shawn (1931-)
--Folk Tales from Persia. Paxson, Diana L., illus. LC 77-124199. (Illus.). 100 p. 22cm. 1971. (ISBN 0-498-06846-3). A. S. Barnes.
--Folk Tales from Portugal. Paxson, Diana L., illus. LC 74-146754. (Illus.). 102 p. 22cm. 1972. (ISBN 0-498-01031-7). A. S. Barnes.
--Folk Tales from Siam. Pibulsongram, Pat, illus. LC 68-27219. (Illus.). 90 p. 22cm. 1969. A. S. Barnes.
Feinstein, Joe
--A Silly Little Kid. Richards, John Paul, illus. LC 74-76605. (Illus.). 32 p. 27cm. 1969. Steck-Vaughn Co.
Feist, Bertha E
--Grunty Grunts and Smiley Smile Indoors. Brater, M. P., illus. LC 20-20552. 62 p. 1 l. incl. col. front., col. illus. 14 1/2 cm. c.1920. Henry Altemus Company.
Feistel, Sally, jt. auth. see Meshover, Leonard.
Fejes, Claire (1920-)
--Enuk, My Son. LC 73-77417. (Illus.). 32 p. 29cm. 1969. Pantheon Books.
Feld, Friedrich, pseud., see Rosenfeld, Friedrich.
Feld, Friedrich, pseud.
--The Day the Town Went Silent. (gr. 4-6). 1972 (Starline). Schol Bk Serv.
--Marvellous Matches. LC 66-10787. (Illus.). (gr. 4-7). 1961. (ISBN 0-8075-4978-9). A Whitman.
--Mystery of the Musical Umbrella. (Illus.). (Gateway Ser, No. 24). (gr. 3-5). 1962. (ISBN 0-394-80124-5). Random.
Felder, Eleanor
--X Marks the Spot. Hafner, Marylin (1925-), illus. LC 70-132599. (Illus.). 32 p. 19cm. 1972. Coward, McCann & Geoghegan.
Feldman, Alan (1945-)
--Lucy Mastermind. Trivas, Irene, illus. LC 85-10094. (Illus.). 115 p. 22cm. c.1985. (ISBN 0-525-44155-7). E.P. Dutton.
Feldman, Charles
--Songs of the Wilshire Boulevard Temple Camps. Schoolman, Leonard A., ed. LC 78-128769. 68p. (Orig.). (gr. 8 up). 1970. UAHC.
Feldmar, Andrew, tr. see Gardonyi, Geza.
Felgate, Cynthia & Whitley, Jay, eds.
--Play School Stories. 64p. (Play School Books Ser.). (gr. k). N.D. (ISBN 0-563-07151-6). BBC.
Felix, Monique
--Further Adventures of a Little Mouse Trapped in a Book. Felix, Monique, illus. (Illus.). 32p. 1983. (ISBN 0-88138-009-1, Star & Eleph Bks). Green Tiger Pr.
--The Further Adventures of the Little Mouse Trapped in a Book. Felix, Monique, illus. (ps-k). 1984. Green Tiger.
--If I Were a Sheep. Felix, Monique, illus. (Illus.). 12p. (Orig.). 1982. (ISBN 0-914676-67-9, Pub. by Envelope Bks). Green Tiger Pr.
--Miam, Miam. Felix, Monique, illus. (Illus.). N.D. (ISBN 2-8265-0046-5, Pub. by Envelope Bks). Green Tiger Pr.
--The Story of a Little Mouse Trapped in a Book. Felix, Monique, illus. (Illus.). 28p. 1980. (ISBN 0-914676-52-0, Star & Eleph Bks). Green Tiger Pr.
Fell, Archie, pseud., see Capron, Mary J..
Fell, Archie, pseud.
--Apron-Strings and Which Way They Pulled. Capron, Mary J.. 270p. (Apron-Strings Library). N.D. Thomas Y. Crowell.
--Apron Strings, and Which Way They Pulled. Capron, Mary J.. (Apron Strings Library). N.D. Warren & Wyman.
--Baby Clover. Capron, Mary J.. (Illus.). (Baby Clover Ser.). N.D. D. Lothrop Co.
--Bonnie Bell Series. Capron, Mary J., 48 vols. (Illus.). 1882. Set in a box. D Lothrop.
--Charley and his Chums. Capron, Mary J., 1 of 6 vols. (Illus.). (Baby Clover Ser.). N.D. D. Lothrop Co.
--Dumpy. Capron, Mary J., 1 of 6 vols. (Illus.). (Baby Clover Ser.). N.D. D. Lothrop Co.
--Mrs. Thorne's Guests: Or, Salt with Savor and without. Capron, Mary J.. (Illus.). N.D. D. Lothrop & Co.

--Tover Tangle. Capron, Mary J.. (Crowell's Library For Young People). N.D. Thomas Y. Crowell & Co.'s Catalogue.
--The Tover Tangle: and How it was Straightened Out. Capron, Mary J.. (The Apron Strings Library). N.D. Warren & Wyman.
--The Tover Tangle, and the Way it Was Straightened Out. Capron, Mary J.. 330p. (Apron-Strings Library). N.D. T. Y. Crowell.
--A Trip to Lotus Land. 1917. John Lane.
--Twisty Clover Series: Includes "Twisty's Trials," "Charley and His Chums," "Baby Clover," "Twisty's Tumbles," "Twisty's Album," and "Dumpy.". Capron, Mary J., 6 vols. (Illus.). N.D. Set. D. Lothrop.
--Twisty's Album. Capron, Mary J.. (Illus.). (Baby Clover Ser.). N.D. D. Lothrop Co.
--Twisty's Trials. Capron, Mary J.. (Illus.). (Baby Clover Ser.). N.D. D. Lothrop Co.
--Twisty's Tumbles. Capron, Mary J.. (Illus.). (Baby Clover Ser.). N.D. D. Lothrop Co.

Fell, Archie, jt. auth. see Eastman, Julia Arabella.

Fell, Archie, pseud. & Shaw, Jennie R.
--Our Daughter's Library; Containing "The New Commandment," "Mrs. Thorne's Guest," "Neighbor's House,"and "Katharine's Experience". Capron, Mary J., 4 vols. N.D. Set. D. Lothrop & Co.

Fellowes, Edward Colton
--Stories of the Stone Age: A Boy's Life in 16,000 B.C. LC 25-23613. 5 p. l., 3-170 p. col. front., col. plates. 24 cm. c.1925. Small, Maynard & Company.

Fellows, Edward B., ed.
--The Excelsior Annual: Or, Pupil's Gift, for 1849 ... LC 15-12459. 1 p. l., xi, 12-264 p. front., plates. 17 cm. 1848. Nafis & Cornish.

Fellows, Muriel H.
--The Land of Little Rain: A Story of Hopi Indian Children. Fellows, Muriel H., illus. LC 36-16937. 121 p. incl. col. front., illus. (part col.) 23 cm. 1936. The John C. Winston Company.
--Little Magic Painter: A Story of the Stone Age. Fellows, Muriel H., illus. LC 38-27460. 111, 1 p. incl. col. front., illus. (part. col.) 23 cm. c.1938. The John C. Winston Company.

Fells, Dorothy
--Tale to Tell: Legends from Many Lands. Roberts, Doreen (1922-), illus. (Illus.). (gr. 3 up). 1965. Verry.

Felsen, Henry Gregor (1916-)
--Anyone for Cub Scouts?. Galdone, Paul (1914-), illus. LC 54-5923. 150p. illus. 20cm. 1954. Scribner.
--Bertie Comes Through. 1st ed. Toan, Jane, illus. LC 47-5731. 212 p. illus. 21 cm. 1947. E. P. Dutton.
--Bertie Makes a Break. 1st ed. Toan, Jane, illus. LC 49-6245. (Illus.). 22cm. 192p. N.D. E.P.Dutton.
--Bertie Takes Care. 1st ed. Toan, Jane, illus. LC 48-8140. 184 p. illus. 21 cm. 1948. E. P. Dutton.
--Boy Gets Car. LC 60-13886. 314 p. 22cm. 1960. Random House.
--The Boy Who Discovered the Earth. Shortall, Leonard W., illus. LC 55-10141. 140p. illus. 20cm. 1955. Scribner.
--Crash Club. LC 58-9880. 282 p. 21cm. 1958. Random House.
--Cub Scout at Last!. Henneberger, Robert G. (1921-), illus. LC 52-13939. (Illus.). (gr. 2-5). 1952. (ISBN 0-684-12785-7, ScribT). Scribner.
--Cub Scout at Last. Henneberger, Robert G. (1921-), illus. 1952. Trade Publications.
--Davey Logan, Interne. LC 50-5739. 191 p. 21cm. 1950. Dutton.
--Flying Correspondent: A Seth Rantoul Story. Ishmael, Woodi (1914-), illus. LC 47-1830. 3 p. l., 9-218 p. illus. 21 cm. 1947. E. P. Dutton and Company, Inc.
--Hot Rod. LC 50-8827. 188 p. 20cm. 1950. Dutton.
--Jungle Highway: Three Young Americans Meet Adventure in the Building of the Pan American Highway. LC 42-6004. 5 p. l., 13-218, 1 p. 1 illus. 21 cm. 1942. E. P. Dutton and Company, Inc.
--Navy Diver. LC 42-19934. 223 p. incl. forms. 21 cm. 1942. E. P. Dutton and Company, Inc.
--Some Follow the Sea. LC 44-1667. 192 p. plates. 21 cm. 1944. Books, Inc., Distributed by E. P. Dutton & Co., Inc.
--Street Rod. LC 53-5030. 277 p. 21cm. 1953. Random House.
--Struggle Is Our Brother. Ishmael, Woodi (1914-), illus. LC 43-1890. 5 p. l., 15-220 p. incl. front., illus., plates (1 double) 21 cm. 1943. E. P. Dutton & Company, Inc.
--Submarine Sailor. LC 43-111383. 208 p. plates. 21 cm. 1943. E. P. Dutton & Co., Inc.
--Two and the Town. Shigaki, Tack, illus. N.D. Charles Scribner's Sons.

Felt, Sue (1924-)
--Contrary Woodrow. Felt, Sue (1924-), illus. LC 58-7155. (Illus.). unpaged. c.1958. Doubleday.
--Hello-Goodbye. Felt, Sue (1924-), illus. N.D. Doubleday & Co.
--Rosa-Too-Little. Felt, Sue (1924-), illus. LC 50-9505. (Illus.). 30 p. (Junior books). 1950. Doubleday.

Felton, Harold William (1902-)
--Big Mose: Hero Fireman. Laite, Gordon (1925-), illus. LC 69-11774. (Illus.). color ils. 40p. (American Folktales Ser.). (gr. 2-5). 1969. (ISBN 0-8116-4017-5). Garrard.
--Bowleg Bill: Seagoing Cow-Puncher. Moyers, William (1916-), illus. LC 57-11282. (Illus.). 21cm. 174p. (gr. 5-9). 1957. (ISBN 0-13-080424-X). P-H.
--Cowboy Jamboree: Western Songs & Lore. Watson, Aldren Auld (1917-), illus. Carmer, Carl Lamson (1893-1976), frwd. by. (Illus.). (gr. 5-9). 1951. (ISBN 0-394-91056-7). Knopf.
--Fire-Fightin' Mose. Watson, Aldren Auld (1917-), illus. LC 55-6100. (Illus.). 173p. (gr. 7-11). 1955. Knopf.
--Gib Morgan, Oil Driller. Sagsoorian, Paul (1923-), illus. LC 72-1535. (Illus.). 94 p. 24cm. 1972. (ISBN 0-396-06583-X). Dodd, Mead.
--A Horse Named Justin Morgan. Fisher, Leonard Everett (1924-), illus. LC 62-9171. (Illus.). 160 p. 23cm. 1962. Dodd, Mead.
--John Henry & His Hammer. Watson, Aldren Auld (1917-), illus. (Illus.). (gr. 5-9). 1950. (ISBN 0-394-91291-8). Knopf.
--Mike Fink, Best of the Keelboatmen. Watson, Aldren Auld (1917-), illus. (Illus.). (gr. 4-6). 1960. (ISBN 0-396-04344-5). Dodd.
--New Tales from Pecos Hill. N.D. E. M. Hale and Co.
New Tall Tales of Pecos Bill. 1958. E M Hale.
--New Tall Tales of Pecos Bill. Moyers, William (1916-), illus. LC 58-12185. (Illus.). 164 p. 21cm. 1958. Prentice-Hall.
--Pecos Bill & the Mustang. Shortall, Leonard W., illus. LC 65-17809. (Illus.). (gr. k-2). 1965. (ISBN 0-13-655589-6). (ISBN 0-13-655597-7). P-H.
--Pecos Bill: Texas Cowpuncher. 1949. A. A. Knopf.
--Sergeant O'Keefe & his Mule: Balaam. Fisher, Leonard Everett (1924-), illus. LC 62-15500. 24cm. 96p. 1962. Dodd, Mead & Co.
--True Tall Tales of Stormalong: Sailor of the Seven Seas. Sandin, Joan (1942-), illus. LC 68-22880. (Illus.). 64 p. 24cm. 1968. Prentice-Hall.
--William Phips & The Treasure Ship. Smith, Alvin (1933-), illus. 160p. 1965. Dodd, Mead & Co.
--The World's Most Truthful Man: Tall Tales Told by Ed Grant in Maine. Grant, Ed, as told by. 150p. 1961. Dodd, Mead & Co.

Felton, Harold William (1902-), ed.
--Legends of Paul Bunyan. Bennett, Richard Michael (1899-), illus. 1947. A. A. Knopf.

Felton, Ronald Oliver see Welch, Ronald, pseud.

Fender, Kay
--Odette: A Bird in Paris. Dumas, Philippe (1940-), illus. LC 77-6352. p. cm. 1st U.S. edition. 1977. (ISBN 0-13-630525-3). Prentice-Hall.

Fenisong, Ruth
--Boy Wanted. Cassel, Lili, pseud. (1924-), illus. Wronker, Lili Cassel. LC 64-11833. (Illus.). 148 p. 22cm. 1964. Harper & Row.

Fenley, Florence (1898-1971)
--Heart Full of Horses. (Illus.). N.D. (ISBN 0-8111-0575-X). The Naylor Company.

Fenn, Eleanor Frere, Lady (1743-1813)
--Fables in Monosyllables. LC 70-127865. (Illus.). xxiv, 112, xii, 64 p. 16cm. (Early Children's Books). 1970. Johnson Reprint Corp.
--Fables in Monosyllables. LC 21-2685. 2 p. l., ix-xiv, 15-60 p.; ix, 11-38 p. incl. fronts., illus. 16 1/2 cm. 1798. Printed for Thomas Dobson, at the Stone House No. , South Second Street.

Fenn, George Manville, jt. auth. see Gibbon, Charles.

Fenn, George Manville, jt. auth. see Meade, L. T.

Fenn, George Manville (1831-1909)
--Adventures of Working Men, 1 of 6 vols. (The Notable Library). N.D. Cassell, Petter, Galpin.
--Beneath the Sea. Bridgman, Lewis Jesse (1857-1931), illus. N.D. T. Y. Crowell & Co.
--The Black Tor, 1 of 11 vols. (Popular Bks for Boys). 1900. Set. J B Lippincott.
--Brownsmith's Boy. (Illus.). (Scribner-Blackie Series of Books for Young People). N.D. Charles Scribner's Sons.
--Bunyip Land. (Illus.). (Scribner-Blackie Series of Books for Young People). N.D. Charles Scribner's Sons.
--Cinnamon Garden. N.D. E. & J. B. Young & Co.
--Commodore Junk. (Boys Own Library). N.D. David McKay.
--Commodore Junk. 18cm. 347p. (Medal Library: No. 37). 1900. Street & Smith.
--The Crystal Hunters: A Boys's Adventures in Higher Alps. N.D. Wessels & Bissell Co.
--Cutlass and Cudgel. Schonberg, John, illus. N.D. Brentano's Publications.
--Devon Boys. (Illus.). (Scribner-Blackie series of books for young people). N.D. Charles Scribner's Sons.
--Diamond Dyke. (Illus.). N.D. E. P. Dutton & Co.
--Dick o'the Fens. (Illus.). (Scribner-Blackie series of books for young people). N.D. Charles Scribner's Sons.
--The Dingo Boys. (The Boys Own Library). N.D. David McKay.
--The Dingo Boys. (Illus.). (Special Juvenile Titles Ser). N.D. International Book Co.
--The Dingo Boys. 18cm. 265p. (Medal Library: No. 74). 1900. Street & Smith.
--Draw Swords. (Illus.). N.D. E. P. Dutton & Co.
--Featherland,. Or How the Birds Lived at Greenlawn. (Illus.). N.D. Publications of E. P. Dutton & Co.
--First in the Field. (Illus.). (Ajax Ser.). N.D. Dodd, Mead & Co.
--Fixed Bayonets. (Illus.). N.D. E. P. Dutton.
--Frank and Saxon (Pub. by Society for Promoting Christian Knowledge). N.D. E. & J. B. Young & Co.
--Friends I Have Made, 1 of 6 vols. (Illus.). (The Notable Library). N.D. Cassell, Petter, Galpin.
--Gil the Gunner: Or, The Youngest Officer in the East. (1831-1909). N.D. E. J. B. Young & Co.
--The Golden Magnet. (Illus.). (Scribner-Blackie Series of books for young people). N.D. Charles Scribner's Sons.
--The Golden Magnet. (The Boys Own Library). N.D. David McKay.
--The Golden Magnet. (Illus.). (St. Nicholas Series for Boys). N.D. International Book Co.
--The Grand Chaco. (The Boys Own Library). N.D. David McKay.
--The Grand Chaco. (Illus.). (Special Juvenile Titles Ser). N.D. International Book Co.
--Hollowdell Grange: Or, Holiday Hours in a Country Home. N.D. George Routledge & Sons.
--In the King's Name. (Scribner-Blackie Series of books for young people). N.D. Charles Scribner's Sons.
--Jack at Sea (Pub. by Society for Promoting Christian Knowledge). N.D. E. & J. B. young & Co.
--King Robert's Page. (Illus.). N.D. E. P. Dutton & Co.
--Life's Eclipse (Pub. by Society for Promoting Christian Knowledge). N.D. E. & J. B. Young & Co.
--The Little Skipper. N.D. E. P. Dutton & Co.
--The Little Skipper, 1 of 15 vols. (Illus.). (Dainty Ser. of Choice Gift Bks: No. 11). 1905. Set. Henry Altemus Co.
--Menhardoc. (Illus.). (Scribner-Blackie Series of books for young people). N.D. Charles Scribner's Sons.
--Mother Carey's Chicken. (Illus.). (The Round Table Ser.). N.D. A. L. Burt's Pubs.
--Mother Carey's Chicken. (Illus.). (The Rugby Series for Boys). N.D. A. L. Burt's Pubs.
--Mother Carey's Chicken. (Illus.). (Scribner-Blackie Series of books for young people). N.D. Charles Scribner's Sons.
--Mother Carey's Chicken: Her Voyage to the Unknown Isle. (The Rugby Ser.). 1905. Set. A L Burt Co.
--Nat the Naturalist. (Illus.). (The Round Table Ser.). N.D. A. L. Burt's Pubs.
--Nat the Naturalist. (Illus.). (The Rugby Series for Boys). N.D. A. L. Burt's Pubs.
--Nat the Naturalist. (Illus.). (Scribner-Blackie Series of books for young people). N.D. Charles Scribner's Sons.
--Nat the Naturalist: A Boy's Adventures in the Eastern Seas. 1905. Set. A L Burt Co.
--Ned Leger (Pub. by Society for Promoting Christian Knowledge). N.D. E. & J. B. Young & Co.
--Nic Revel: Or, A White Slave's Adventure in Alligator. (Illus.). N.D. E. P. Dutton & Co.
--Off to the Wilds. (Author of "Ship Ahoy," "The Parson of Dumford" and "The Treasure Hunters," a story of adventure in Zululand.). (Illus.). 340p. N.D. T. Y. Crowell.
--Our Soldier Boy. N.D. E. P. Dutton & Co.
--Our Soldier Boy, 1 of 15 vols. (Illus.). (Dainty Ser. of Choice Gift Bks: No. 10). 1905. Set. Henry Altemus Co.
--Patience Eins. (Illus.). (Scribner-Blackie Series of books for young people). N.D. Charles Scribner's Sons.
--Planter Jack (Pub. by Society for Promoting Christian Knowledge). N.D. E. & J. B. Young & Co.
--The Powder Monkey. LC 77-377750. (Illus.). 52 p. 20cm. (Altemus' rose carnation series). c.1906. H. Altemus Co.
--The Powder Monkey. (Illus.). (Dainty Ser.). N.D. Henry Altemus Co.
--Quicksilver. (Illus.). (Scribner-Blackie Series of books for young people). N.D. Charles Scribner's Sons.
--The Rajah of Dah. N.D. Thomas Whittaker.
--Real Gold: A Story of Adventure. N.D. Thomas Whittaker.
--Sail Ho!. Or, A Boy at Sea. N.D. E. J. B. Young & Co.
--Syd Belton: The Boy who Would Not Go to Sea. (Illus.). N.D. Wessels & Bissell Co.
--To the West. N.D. E & J B Young.
--Treasure Hunters, No.6. (Lakeside Library Ser.). N.D. Donnelley, Loyd & Co.
--Uncle Bart (Pub. by Society for Promoting Christian Knowledge). 1900. E. & J. B. Young & Co.
--Vince the Revel. (Illus.). N.D. E. P. Dutton & Co.
--The Weathercock. (The Boys Own Library). N.D. David McKay.
--The Weathercock. (Illus.). (Special Juvenile Titles Ser). N.D. International Book Co.
--The Weathercock. LC 1-94281. (Illus.). 19cm. 349p. 1901. Street & Smith.
--The Young Castellan, 1 of 11 vols. (Popular Bks for Boys). 1900. Set. J B Lippincott.
--The Young Castellan: A Tale of the English Civil War. LC 12-321702. 1 p. l., 5-344 p. front., plates. 20 cm. 1895. J. B. Lippincott Company.
--A Young Hero. (Illus.). (Dainty Ser.). N.D. Henry Altemus Co.
--Young Robin Hood. (Dainty Ser.). N.D. E. P. Dutton & Co.
--Young Robin Hood. LC 6398. (Illus.). 20cm. 72p. 1900. H. Altemus Co.
--Young Robin Hood, 1 of 15 vols. (Illus.). (Dainty Ser. of Choice Gift Bks: No. 4). 1905. Set. Henry Altemus Co.
--Yussuf the Guide. (Illus.). (The Round Table Ser.). N.D. A. L. Burt's Pubs.
--Yussuf the Guide. (Illus.). (The Rugby Series for Boys). N.D. A. L. Burt's Pubs.
--Yussuf the Guide. (Illus.). (Scribner-Blackie Series of books for young people). N.D. Charles Scribner's Sons.
--Yussuf the Guide: A Story of Adventure in Asia Miner. (The Rugby Ser.). 1905. Set. A L Burt Co.
--Yussuf the Guide: A Story of Adventure in Asia Minor. (The Rugby Ser.). N.D. A. L. Burt Company.

Fenn, George Manville (1831-1909) & Garrett, Edward
--Story Upon Story: Twelve Tales, Crisp Original and Interesting. (No. 408). N.D. Raphael Tuck & Sons.

Fenn, George Manville (1831-1909) & Glasgow, Geraldine R.
--Little People's Book of Wild Animals. (Illus.). N.D. E. P. Dutton & Co.

Fennema, Ilona
--Dirk's Wooden Clogs. Apol, Georgette, illus. LC 78-473291. (Illus.). 29cm. 30p. 1969. Oxford Univ. Press.
--Dirk's Wooden Shoes. Apol, Georgette, illus. LC 75-11785. (Illus.). 30 p. 29cm. 1970. Harcourt, Brace & World.

Fenner, Carol Elizabeth (1929-)
--Christmas Tree on the Mountain. Fenner, Carol Elizabeth (1929-), illus. LC 64-6753. (Illus.). (gr. k-3). 1966. (ISBN 0-15-217880-5, HJ). HarBraceJ.
--Christmas Tree on the Mountain. 1st. ed. Fenner, Carol Elizabeth (1929-), illus. LC 66-6993. 1. v. (unpaged) col. illus. 29x14cm. 1966. Harcourt.
--Ice Skates. Forberg, Ati, pseud. (1925-), illus. Forberg, Beate Gropius. (Illus.). 48p. Repr (Pub. by Random House). 1980. (ISBN 0-590-30376-7). Scholastic Inc.
--Lagalag, the Wanderer. Fenner, Carol Elizabeth (1929-), illus. LC 68-11499. (Illus.). 1 v. (unpaged. 23cm. 40p. 1968. Harcourt, Brace & World.
--The Skates of Uncle Richard. Forberg, Ati, pseud. (1925-), illus. Forberg, Beate Gropius. LC 78-55910. p. cm. 1978. (ISBN 0-394-83553-0). (ISBN 0-394-93553-5). Random House.
--Tigers in the Cellar. Fenner, Carol Elizabeth (1929-), illus. (Illus.). 32 p. 26cm. 1963. Harcourt, Brace & World.

Fenner, Marian Warner Wildman see Wildman, Marian Warner.

Fenner, Phyllis Reid (1899-1982), compiled by.
--Adventure: Rare & Magical. Pitz, Henry Clarence (1895-1976), illus. LC 45-811683. (Illus.). 22cm. 178p. (gr. 3-7). 1945. (ISBN 0-394-80894-0). (ISBN 0-394-90894-5). Knopf.
--Behind the Wheel: Stories of Cars on Road and Track. Geer, Charles Hand (1922-), illus. LC 64-17610. (Illus.). 221 p. 22cm. 1964. Morrow.
--Brother Against Brother: Stories of the War Between the States. (gr. 7-11). 1975. (ISBN 0-688-21126-7). Morrow.
--Brother Against Brother: Stories of the War Between the States. Lohse, William R., illus. LC 57-8588. 192p. illus. 22cm. 1957. Morrow.
--Circus Parade: Stories of the Big Top. 1st ed. Ames, Lee Judah (1921-), illus. LC 54-9183. (Illus.). 174p. illus. 25cm. (gr. 3-7). 1954. (ISBN 0-394-81030-9). (ISBN 0-394-91030-3). Knopf.

--Consider the Evidence, Stories of Mystery & Suspense. Geer, Charles Hand (1922-), illus. LC 73-792. (Illus.). 192p. (gr. 7 up). 1973. (ISBN 0-688-20080-X). Morrow.
--Contraband: Stories of Smuggling the World Over. Geer, Charles Hand (1922-), illus. (Illus.). (gr. 7 up). 1967. (ISBN 0-688-31183-0). Morrow.
--Cowboys, Cowboys, Cowboys: Stories of Roundups & Rodeos, Branding & Bronco-Busting;. Lee, Manning De Villeneuve (1894-1980), illus. LC 50-6387. 287 p. illus. 25 cm. 1950. F. Watts.
--Crack of the Bat: Stories of Baseball. 1st ed. LC 51-13014. 160 p. 25cm. (Borzoi books for young people). 1952. Knopf.
--Danger Is the Password: Stories of Wartime Spies. Geer, Charles Hand (1922-), illus. LC 65-18510. 220p. illus. 22cm. (gr. 7 up). c.1965. Morrow.
--The Dark and Bloody Ground: Stories of the American Frontier. Geer, Charles Hand (1922-), illus. LC 63-12631. (Illus.). 223 p. 22cm. 1963. William Morrow.
--Demons and Dervishes: Tales with More-Than-Oriental Splendor. Pitz, Henry Clarence (1895-1976), illus. LC 46-7371. 5 p. l., 183 p., 2 l. incl. front., illus. 21 1/2 cm. 1946. (ISBN 0-394-91099-0). A. A. Knopf.
--Desperate Moments: Stories of Escapes & Hurried Journeys. Geer, Charles Hand (1922-), illus. LC 77-155496. (Illus.). halftones. (gr. 7 up). 1971. (ISBN 0-688-31233-0). Morrow.
--Dogs, Dogs, Dogs. N.D. Grosset & Dunlap.
--Dogs, Dogs, Dogs: An Anthology of Short Stories. 1951. Franklin Watts, Inc.
--A Dog's Life: Stories of Champions, Hunters, and Faithful Friends. 1st ed. Bloom, Lloyd, illus. LC 78-6580. (Illus.). 192 p. 22cm. 1978. (ISBN 0-688-22156-4). (ISBN 0-688-32156-9). Morrow.
--Elephants, Elephants, Elephants: An Anthology of Short Stories. 1952. Franklin Watts, Inc.
--The Endless Dark: Stories of Underground Adventure. Marchesi, Stephen, illus. LC 77-5494. (Illus.). 192 p. 22cm. 1977. (ISBN 0-688-22122-X). (ISBN 0-688-32122-4). Morrow.
--Feasts and Frolics: Special Stories for Special Days. 1st ed. Durney, Helen R., illus. LC 49-11219. xii, 159 p. illus. 25 cm. 1949. A. A. Knopf.
--Feasts and Frolics: Special Stories for Special Days. Durney, Helen R., illus. LC 67-90305. 159 p. illus. 1967. A. A. Knopf.
--Finders Keepers: Stories of Treasure Seekers. Geer, Charles Hand (1922-), illus. LC 75-77317. (Illus.). 11 ils. note. 224p. (gr. 7 up). 1969. (ISBN 0-688-21293-X). Morrow.
--Fools and Funny Fellows: More "Time to Laugh" Tales. 1st ed. Pitz, Henry Clarence (1895-1976), illus. LC 47-6433. 6 l., 3-185 p. illus. 22 cm. 1947. A. A. Knopf.
--Full Forty Fathoms: Stories of Underwater Adventure. Eagle, Michael (1942-), illus. LC 75-6942. (Illus.). 192 p. 22cm. 1975. (ISBN 0-688-22037-1). (ISBN 0-688-32037-6). Morrow.
--Fun, Fun, Fun: An Anthology of Short Stories. 1953. Franklin Watts, Inc.
--Gentle Like a Cyclone: Stories of Horses and Their Riders. Bjorklund, Lorence F. (1913-1978), illus. LC 74-2499. (Illus.). 190 p. 22cm. 1974. (ISBN 0-688-21821-0). (ISBN 0-688-21821-0). Morrow.
--Ghosts, Ghosts, Ghosts. (Illus.). (gr. 5-9). 1952. (ISBN 0-8382-0283-7). Hale.
--Ghosts, Ghosts, Ghosts. Lee, Manning De Villeneuve (1894-1980), illus. (Illus.). (Terrific Triple Titles Ser.). (gr. 4-6). 1952. (ISBN 0-531-01676-5). Watts.
--Ghosts, Ghosts, Ghosts: An Anthology of Short Stories. Lee, Manning De Villeneuve (1894-1980), illus. 281p. 1955. Franklin Watts, Inc.
--Ghosts, Ghosts, Ghosts: Stories of Spooks and Spirits, Haunts and Hobgoblins, Werewolves and Will-O'-the-Wisps. Rev. ed. Lee, Manning De Villeneuve (1894-1980), illus. LC 52-13331. 281p. illus. 25cm. 1952. F. Watts.
--Giants & Witches, and a Dragon or Two. Pitz, Henry Clarence (1895-1976), illus. LC 43-16225. 6 p. l., 3-206 p., 2 l. illus. 22 cm. 1943. A. A. Knopf.
--Giants and Witches and a Dragon or Two. Pitz, Henry Clarence (1895-1976), illus. 1959. Knopf.
--Giggle Box; Funny Stories for Boys and Girls. 1st ed. Steig, William (1907-), illus. LC 50-10106. (Illus.). 144 p. 25cm. (Borzoi books for young people). 1950. Knopf.
--Giggle Box: Funny Stories for Boys and Girls. 1st ed. Steig, William (1907-), illus. LC 67-90587. 144 p. illus. 25 cm. (Borzoi books for young people). 1966. Knopf.
--Horses, Horses, Horses: Palominos and Pintos, Polo Ponies and Plow Horses, Morgans and Mustangs. Crowell, Pers (1910-), illus. LC 49-760221. 285 p. illus. 24 cm. (gr. 4-6). 1949. (ISBN 0-531-01690-0). F. Watts.
--Hunter & the Hunted: Stories of Field & Forest. Geer, Charles Hand (1922-), illus. LC 68-21003. (Illus.). 10 ils. 192p. (gr. 7 up). 1968. (ISBN 0-688-21412-6). Morrow.
--Indians, Indians, Indians: Stories of Tepees and Tomahawks, Wampum Belts & War Bonnets, Peace Pipes & Papooses. Lee, Manning De Villeneuve (1894-1980), illus. LC 50-4869. 287 p. illus. 25 cm. 1950. Watts.
--Keeping Christmas: Stories of the Joyous Season. Werner, Honi, illus. LC 79-15590. (Illus.). 221 p. 22cm. 1979. (ISBN 0-688-22206-4). (ISBN 0-688-32206-9). Morrow.
--Kick-off: Stories of Football. 174 p. 25cm. (Borzoi books for young people). (gr. 3-7). 1960. (ISBN 0-394-91301-9). Knopf.
--Lift Line: Stories of Downhill and Cross-Country Skiing. Lorenz, Albert (1941-), illus. LC 76-4803. 206p. ill. 22 cm. 208p. (gr. 7 up). c.1976. (ISBN 0-688-22076-2). (ISBN 0-688-32076-7). Morrow.
--Magic Hoofs: Horse Stories from Many Lands. Pitz, Henry Clarence (1895-1976), illus. LC 51-10060. (Illus.). 278 p. 22cm. (gr. 3-7). 1951, c.1941. Knopf.
--Midnight Prowlers: Stories of Cats and Their Enslaved Owners. Gershinowitz, George, illus. LC 81-3953. p. cm. 1981. (ISBN 0-688-00704-X). Morrow.
--No Time for Glory: Stories of World War II. Lohse, William R., illus. LC 62-11900. 223 p. 22cm. (gr. 7 up). 1962. (ISBN 0-688-21776-1). Morrow.
--Open Throttle: Stories of Railroads & Railroad Men. Geer, Charles Hand (1922-), illus. LC 66-6179. (Illus.). (gr. 7 up). 1966. (ISBN 0-688-21735-4). Morrow.
--Over There!. Stories of World War I. Lohse, William R., illus. LC 61-11218. 191 p. 22cm. (gr. 7 up). 1961. Morrow.
--Perilous Ascent: Stories of Mountain Climbing. Geer, Charles Hand (1922-), illus. LC 71-124350. (Illus.). 190 p. 22cm. (gr. 7 up). 1970. (ISBN 0-688-21734-6). W. Morrow.
--Pirates, Pirates, Pirates: Stories of Cutlasses and Corsairs, Buried Treasure and Buccaneers, Ships and Swashbucklers. Lee, Manning De Villeneuve (1894-1980), illus. LC 51-9851. 287 p. illus. 25 cm. (gr. 5-8). 1951. Watts.
--The Price of Liberty: Stories of the American Revolution. Lohse, William R., illus. LC 60-5187. (Illus.). 191 p. 22cm. 1960. W. Morrow.
--Princesses & Peasant Boys: Tales of Enchantment. Pitz, Henry Clarence (1895-1976), illus. LC 44-9752. 7 p. l., 3-188 p. incl. front., illus. 22 cm. 1944. A. A. Knopf.
--Quick Pivot; Stories of Basketball. LC 65-21562. 177p. 25cm. 22cm. 191p. (gr. 5 up). c.1965. Knopf.
--Speed, Speed, Speed. (Illus.). (gr. 6 up). 1950. (ISBN 0-8382-0782-0). Hale.
--Speed, Speed, Speed: An Anthology of Short Stories. Lohse, William R., illus. 256p. (gr. 4-7). 1954. Franklin Watts, Inc.
--Speed, Speed, Speed: Stories of Races and Chases in Hot Rods and Jets, Trains and Planes, Submarines and Speedboats. Lohse, William R., illus. LC 54-9826. 246p. illus. 25cm. 1954. F. Watts.
--Stories of the Sea. Werth, Kurt (1896-), illus. (Illus.). (gr. 5-9). 1953. (ISBN 0-394-91678-6). Knopf.
--There Was a Horse: Folktales from Many Lands. Pitz, Henry Clarence (1895-1976), illus. LC 41-10472. 5 p. l., 281, 2 p. incl. front., illus. 21 1/2 cm. (Tales of many lands). 1941. A. A. Knopf.
--Time to Laugh: Funny Tales from Here and There. Pitz, Henry Clarence (1895-1976), illus. LC 42-19684. 6 p. l., 3-240 p., 2 l. incl. col. front., illus. 20 1/2 cm. 1942. A. A. Knopf.
--Where Speed Is King: Stories of Racing Adventure. Geer, Charles Hand (1922-), illus. LC 78-39618. (Illus.). 192 p. 22cm. 1972. Morrow.
--Wide-Angle Lens: Stories of Time and Space. Ingraham, Erick, illus. LC 80-16992. 223 p. 22cm. 1980. (ISBN 0-688-32241-7). (ISBN 0-688-32241-7). Morrow.
--With Might and Main: Stories of Skill and Wit. 1st ed. Pitz, Henry Clarence (1895-1976), illus. LC 48-8738. ix, 190 p. illus. 23 cm. 1948. A. A. Knopf.
--Yankee Doodle: Stories of the Brave and the Free. 1st ed. Maxwell, John Alan, illus. LC 51-11070. 214 p. illus. 22 cm. (gr. 3-7). 1951. (ISBN 0-394-91841-X). Knopf.

Fenner, Phyllis Reid (1899-1982) & Hughes, Avah Willyn, eds.
--Entrances and Exits: A Book of Plays for Young Actors. Kramer, Frank, illus. LC 60-11919. 276p. illus. 21cm. (gr. 4-6). c.1960. (ISBN 0-396-04431-X). Dodd, Mead.

Fenner, Phyllis Reid (1899-1982) & McCrea, Mary, eds.
--More Stories for Fun and Adventure: Some Short, Some Long, Some Quiet, Some Exciting; Everyday and Magical Adventure. LC 64-14215. 190p. 21cm. (gr. 4-9). c.1964. (ISBN 0-381-99834-7). John Day.
--Stories for Fun & Adventure. (Illus.). (gr. 4-6). 1961. (ISBN 0-8382-0800-2). Hale.
--Stories for Fun and Adventure: A Collection for All Boys and Girls Who Love Good Stories. LC 61-11831. 190p. c.1961. John Day.
--Strange but True: Stories of Many Things. LC 79-101465. (Illus.). xi, 211 p. 21cm. 1970. John Day Co.

Fennimore, Stephen, pseud., see Collins, Dale.

Fenollosa, Mary McNeill, Mrs.
--Blossoms from a Japanese Garden: A Book of Child-Verses. LC 13-23199. vii, 60 p. mounted col. front., mounted col. plates. 22 x 17 cm. 1913. Frederick A. Stokes Company.

Fenten, D. X (1932-)
--Harvesting the Sea. LC 76-101905. (Illus.). 63 p. 25cm. 1970. Lippincott.

Fenton, Alfred H.
--Dana of the "Sun,". D'Emo, Leon, illus. N.D. Farrar & Rinehart.
--Oliver Hazard Perry. Hake, Gordon, illus. N.D. Farrar & Rinehart.

Fenton, Carroll Lane (1900-1969)
--Goldie is a Fish. Fenton, Carroll Lane (1900-1969), illus. 1961. John Day.
--The Moon for Young Explorers. (Illus.). 1963. (ISBN 0-381-99828-2). John Day.
--Weejack and His Neighbors. Fenton, Carroll Lane (1900-1969), illus. LC 44-3161. 128 p. illus. 21 cm. 1944. The John Day Company.
--Wild Folk at the Pond. Fenton, Carroll Lane (1900-1969), illus. 127p. (gr. 4-6). 1948. John Day Bks.
--Wild Folk at the Seashore. Fenton, Carroll Lane (1900-1969), illus. 96p. (The Wild Folks Bks.). 1959. John Day Co.
--Wild Folk in the Mountains. Fenton, Carroll Lane (1900-1969), illus. LC 58-7468. 96p. (The Wild Folk Bks.). 1958. John Day & Co.
--Wild Folk In the Woods. Fenton, Carroll Lane (1900-1969), illus. 128p. (The Wild Folk Bks.). 1952. John Day & Co.

Fenton, Carroll Lane (1900-1969) & Adams, Mildred
--Worlds in the Sky. Fenton, Carroll Lane (1900-1969), illus. 96p. 1963. John Day Co.

Fenton, Carroll Lane (1900-1969) & Alice, Epstein
--Cliff Dwellers of Walnut Canyan. Orbaan, Albert F. (1913-), illus. 63p. 1960. John Day & Co.

Fenton, Carroll Lane (1900-1969) & Carswell, Evelyn Medicus (1919-)
--Wild Folk in the Desert. Fenton, Carroll Lane (1900-1969), illus. LC 58-10610. (Illus.). 128 p. 23cm. 128p. 1958. J. Day Co.

Fenton, Carroll Lane (1900-1969) & Fenton, Mildred Adams
--Riches From The Earth. Fenton, Carroll Lane (1900-1969), illus. 160p. 1953. John Day & Co.

Fenton, Edward, tr. see Zei, Alki.

Fenton, Edward (1917-)
--Aleko's Island. 1st ed. Davis, Dimitris (1905-), illus. LC 48-8879. 246 p. illus. 21 cm. 1948. Doubleday.
--The Big Yellow Balloon. 1st ed. Ohlsson, Ib (1935-), illus. LC 67-15962. (Illus.). 1 v. (unpaged. 48p. 1967. Doubleday.
--Duffy's Rocks. 1st ed. LC 73-14594. 198 p. 22cm. 1974. (ISBN 0-525-28940-2). Dutton.
--Fierce John. Du Bois, William Sherman Pene (1916-), illus. N.D. Doubleday.
--Fierce John. Du Bois, William Sherman Pene (1916-), illus. LC 69-11809. (Illus.). 2 color line drawings. halftones. 64p. (ps-2). 1969. (ISBN 0-03-072925-4). HR&W.
--Fierce John: A Story. Du Bois, William Sherman Pene (1916-), illus. LC 69-11809. (Illus.). 59 p. 22cm. 1969, c.1959. Holt, Rinehart and Winston.
--The Golden Doors. 1st ed. Fiammenghi, Gioia (1929-), illus. LC 57-7281. (Illus.). 262 p. 22cm. 1957. Doubleday.
--Hidden Trapezes. 1st ed. Lonette, Reisie Dominee (1924-), illus. LC 50-9411. viii, 239 p. illus. 21 cm. 1950. Doubleday.
--An Island for a Pelican. Davis, Dimitris (1905-), illus. (Illus.). 60 p. 25cm. 1963. Doubleday.
--An Island for a Pelican. Davis, Dimitris (1905-), illus. 1963. (ISBN 0-8382-0372-8, Cadmus Books). E. M. Hale and Company.
--A Matter of Miracles. 1st ed. LC 67-14212. (Illus.). 22 cm. 239p. 1967. Holt, Rinehart, and Winston.
--The Nine Questions. Hodges, Cyril Walter (1909-), illus. LC 59-11592. 235p. 1959. Doubleday.
--Once Upon a Saturday. 1st ed. Fava, Rita (1932-), illus. LC 58-9201. (Illus.). 232 p. 22cm. 1958. Doubleday.
--Penny Candy. 1st ed. Gorey, Edward St. John (1925-), illus. LC 69-11959. (Illus.). 46 p. 22cm. 1970. Holt, Rinehart and Winston.
--Phantom of Walkaway Hill. 1961. E M Hale.
--The Phantom of Walkaway Hill. Stover, Jo Ann (1931-), illus. LC 61-7605. (Illus.). 260 p. 22cm. 1961. Doubleday.
--The Refugee Summer. LC 81-12593. p. cm. 1982. (ISBN 0-440-07404-5). Delacorte Press.
--The Riddle of the Red Whale. 1st ed. LC 66-8825. 207p. 22cm. 1966. (ISBN 0-385-07056-X). Doubleday.
--Us and the Duchess. 1st ed. Lonette, Reisie Dominee (1924-), illus. LC 47-31028. 208 p. illus. 21 cm. 1947. Doubleday.

Fenton, Edward (1917-) & La Bedolliere, Emile Gigault De (1812-1883)
--Nine Lives: Or, The Celebrated Cat of Beacon Hill. Galdone, Paul (1914-), illus. (Illus.). 62 p. 27cm. 1951. Pantheon.
--Nine Lives or the Celebrated Cat of Bacon Hill. N.D. E. M. Hale and Co.

Fenton, Erma B.
--Bruce & the Steam Engine. (Illus.). (ps-1). N.D. Vantage.

Fenton, Irene, ed. see Darwin, Gary.

Fenton, Mildred Adams, jt. auth. see Fenton, Carroll Lane.

Fenton, Robert, ed. see Darwin, Gary.

Fenton, William
--Fury & the Lone Pine Mystery. Ushler, John, illus. 1959. Golden Press.

Fenty, A. A, adapted by see Braithwaite, P. A.

Fenwick, Elizabeth (1920-)
--Cockleberry Castle. 1st ed. Lonette, Reisie Dominee (1924-), illus. LC 62-8925. 73 p. illus. 22 cm. 1963. Pantheon.

Fenwick, Iva Doren
--The Seventh Dream. Koski, Barbara, illus. LC 56-8424. 126p. illus. 21cm. 1956. Comet Press

Ferber, Edna (1887-1968)
--Cimarron. (gr. 9 up). N.D. (ISBN 0-448-01014-3). G&D.

Ferdenzi, Til, jt. auth. see Berra, Lawrence Peter.

Ferdinand, Raimund
--The Spendthrift: A musical fairy tale in three acts. Tramer, Erwin, tr. 204p. N.D. Frederick Ungar Publishing Co.

Fergus, Meryl
--Discovering at the Zoo. Self, Margaret M., ed. (Illus.). 32p. (Orig.). (ps-5). 1974. (ISBN 0-8307-0306-3). Regal.

Ferguson, Constance (1920-)
--Green Gates Mystery. LC 76-6111. 142 p. 21cm. c.1976. (ISBN 0-8309-0161-2). Independence Press.

Ferguson, Dale, jt. auth. see Giblin, James Cross.

Ferguson, Donald
--The Scranton High Boys at Ice Hockey. (The Scranton High Boys Ser.). N.D. World Pub.
--The Scranton High Boys On the Cinder Path. (The Scranton High Boys Ser.). N.D. World Publishing Co.
--The Scranton High Boys Out for the Pennant. (The Scranton High Boys Ser.). N.D. World Publishing Co.
--Scranton High Chums. (Scranton High Boys Ser.). N.D. World Publishing Co.

Ferguson, Ruby Constance Annie
--A Horse of Her Own. Caney, illus. LC 50-6535. 192 p. illus. 21 cm. 1950. Dodd, Mead.
--Jill Enjoys Her Ponies. Caney, illus. LC 55-706021. 160p. illus. 22cm. 1955, c.1954. Dodd, Mead.
--Jill Has Two Ponies. Caney, illus. LC 53-5155. 152p. illus. 21cm. 1953, c.1952. Dodd, Mead.
--A Stable for Jill. Caney, illus. LC 51-10432. 152 p. illus. 21 cm. 1951. Dodd, Mead.

Fergusson, Adam (1932-)
--Roman Go Home. 1969. (ISBN 0-399-10705-3). G. P. Putnam's Sons.

Fergusson, Heather
--Adventures of a Monkey King: Book I. Hing Sum Lau, illus. (Illus.). 64p. (Adventures of a Monkey King Ser.). (gr. 4-7). 1982. (ISBN 0-942056-01-9). Character Bks.

Ferm, Betty (1926-)
--False Idols. 1974. (ISBN 0-399-11405-X). G. P. Putnam's Sons.
--Flair for Fashion. LC 67-21623. 192 p. 21cm. (Career-romance for young moderns). 1967. J. Messner.

Ferman, Edward Lewis (1937-), ed.
--Best from Fantasy & Science Fiction: A Special Twenty-Fifth Anniversary Anthology. LC 73-9024. 336p. 1974. Doubleday.

Ferman, Edward Lewis (1937-) & Malzberg, Barry N. (1939-), eds.
--Final Stage: The Ultimate Science Fiction Anthology. LC 73-91122. 352p. 1974. (ISBN 0-88327-035-8, Charterhouse). McKay.

Fern, Eugene A. (1919-)
--Birthday Presents. Fern, Eugene A. (1919-), illus. LC 67-2665. 1 v. (unpaged) col. illus. 19 cm. (Ariel book). 1967. Farrar, Straus & Giroux.
--The King Who Was Too Busy. LC 66-11705. 47p. col. illus. 27cm. (Ariel bks.). c.1966. Farrar.

AUTHOR INDEX FIDELER, NANCY

--Lorenzo and Angelina. (Illus.). 31 p. 1968. Farrar, Straus & Giroux.
--The Most Frightened Hero. Fern, Eugene A. (1919-), illus. LC 61-5888. (Illus.). unpaged. 28cm. 1961. Coward-McCann.
--Pepito's Story. 1960. E M Hale.
--Pepito's Story. Fern, Eugene A. (1919-), illus. LC 60-5251. (Illus.). unpaged. 26cm. c.1960. Ariel Books.
--What's He Been Up to Now?. Fern, Eugene A. (1919-), illus. (Illus.). (gr. k-3). 1961. Dial.

Fernald, Helen Clark (1888-)
--Jonathan's Doorstep. Walker, Nedda, illus. LC 43-512636. vii, 1, 280 p. illus. 21 cm. 1943. Longmans, Green and Co.
--Plow the Dew Under. 1st ed. LC 52-9666. 301 p. 21 cm. 1952. Longmans, Green.
--Smoke Blows West. MacDonald, James, illus. LC 37-27444. x p., 1 l., 288 p. incl. front., illus. 20 1/2 cm. 1937. Longmans, Green and Co.
--The Shadow of the Crooked Tree. (Illus.). (gr. 10 up). 1965. (ISBN 0-679-20177-7). McKay.

Fernald, Helen Clark (1888-) & Slocombe, Edwin M.
--River Empire. Eadie, Eleanor Osborn & Peck, Gladys, illus. LC [illegible] vi, 218 p. illus. 22 cm. 1940. Longmans, Green and Co.
--The Scarlet Fringe. Sanchez, Carlos M. (1908-), illus. LC 31-25970. xvii, 236 p. incl. front., illus., plates. 20 1/2 cm. 1931. Longmans, Green and Co.

Fernandes, Albert
--The Cabin Beyond. N.D. Meador Publishing Co.

Fernandez, Peter
--Bedtime Bible Stories For Childern. Elliot, John, illus. 128p. 1969. (ISBN 0-668-02049-0). ARco Books.

Fernando, adapted by see Dobowski, Cathy East.

Fernhain, Elsie Von, tr. see Ireland, Mary Eliza Haines, Mrs.

Ferntheil, Carol
--Bible Adventures. Mills, Donald, illus. (Illus.). (Basic Bible Readers Ser.). (gr. 3). 1963. (ISBN 0-87239-260-0). Standard Pub.
--I Read About God's Gifts. Gohman, Vera Kennedy (1922-), illus. (Illus.). (Basic Bible Readers Ser.). (gr. 2). 1962. (ISBN 0-87239-259-7). Standard Pub.
--I Read About God's Love. March, Jane, illus. (Illus.). (Basic Bible Readers Ser.). (gr. 1). 1962. (ISBN 0-87239-258-9). Standard Pub.
--If You Had Been in Bethlehem: Diorama Book. (gr. k-3). 1977. (ISBN 0-87239-166-3). Standard Pub.
--Noah's Ark: Diorama Book. (gr. k-3). 1977. (ISBN 0-87239-167-1). Standard Pub.

Ferraro, Renato, jt. auth. see Peg, Gianni.

Ferrars, E. X., pseud., see Brown, Morna Davis.

Ferrars, E. X., pseud. (1907-)
--Hunt the Tortoise. Brown, Morna Davis (Pub. by Doubleday). (gr. 8 up). 1972. Curtis.
--The Shape of a Stain. Brown, Morna Davis (Pub. by Doubleday). (gr. 8 up). 1972. Curtis.

Ferres, A.
--His First Kangaroo. (Scribner-Blakie Series of books for young people). N.D. Charles Scribner's Sons.

Ferris, Anita Brockway (1881-)
--Giovanni: Stories of an Italian Boy. LC 17-24279. vi, 90 p. incl. front., illus. 19 c. 1917. Missionary Education Movement of the United States and Canada.
--The Honorable Crimson Tree: And Other Tales of China; a Book for Boys and Girls. ix, 11-136 p. incl. front., illus., music. 19 1/2 cm. 1919. Everyland Press.
--The Magic Box. LC 22-14189. 3 p.l, 103 p. front., plates. 19 1/2 cm. c.1922. Council of Women for Home Missions and Missionary Education Movement of the United States and Canada.

Ferris, Bernice Dodge
--Tales of Cats, Catastrophes, and Kittens: Stories in Verse. 1st ed. Otteson, Madalene, illus. LC 55-12125. 20p. illus. 21cm. 1955. ExpositionPress.

Ferris, Elmer Ellsworth (1861-)
--Jerry at the Academy. Shinn, Everett (1876-1953), illus. LC 40-33279. viii p., 3 l., 321 p. incl. front., illus., plates. 20 1/2 cm. 1940. Doubleday, Doran & Company, Inc.
--Jerry of Seven Mile Creek. Fogarty, Thomas, Jr., illus. LC 38-27438. 6 p. l., 281 p. incl. front., illus., paltes. 20 1/2 cm. 1938. Doubleday, Doran & Company, Inc.

Ferris, Helen Josephine (1890-1969)
--Dody and Captain Jinks. Paull, Grace A. (1898-), illus. LC 39-289764. 64 p. incl. col. front., illus. (part col.) 22 cm. 1939. Doubleday, Doran & Company, Inc.
--Tommy and His Dog, Hurry. Wood, Ruth, illus. LC 44-4921. 5 p. l., 130 p. front., illus. 20 cm. 1944. Doubleday, Doran & Co., Inc.
--Watch Me said the Jeep. 1st ed. Gergely, Tibor (1900-1978), illus. LC 44-41896. (Illus.). 28p. 21 x 26cm. 1944. Garden City Publishing.

Ferris, Helen Josephine (1890-1969), ed.
--Adventure Waits: A Book of Adventure Stories for Girls. Morris, Beth Krebs, illus. LC 28-22457. 6 p. l., 3-309 p. incl. front., plates. 21 1/2 cm. c.1928. Harcourt, Brace and Company.
--The Brave & the Fair. Ness, Evaline Michelow, Mrs. (1911-), illus. LC 60-5841. (Illus.). 22cm. 242p. 1960. (ISBN 0-03-033625-2). HR&W.
--Favorite Poems, Old and New: Selected for Boys and Girls. Smith, Kay Lovelace & Weisgard, Leonard Joseph (1916-), illus. LC 65-25155. (Illus.). 27cm. 375p. (Compton's beginner's bookshelf). 1965. Compton.
--Favorite Poems, Old & New: Selected for Boys and Girls. 1st ed. Weisgard, Leonard Joseph (1916-), illus. LC [illegible] (gr. [illegible]) 1957. Doubleday.
--Girl Scout Stories: Second Book. N.D. Doubleday Doran & Co.
--Girls, Girls, Girls: Stories of Love, Courage, and the Quest for Happiness. LC 56-7435. 241p. 24cm. (Terrific triple title series). 1957, c.1956. F. Watts.
--Love Comes Riding: Stories of Romance and Adventure for Girls. Morris, Beth Krebs, illus. LC 29-24079. vi p., 3 l., 3-315 p. incl. front., plates. pl. 21 cm. c.1929. Harcourt, Brace and Company.
--Love's Enchantment. Bock, Vera, illus. (gr. 7-12). N.D. Doubleday Bks.
--Time of Understanding: Stories of Girls Learning to Get Along with Their Parents. (gr. 7 up). 1963. (ISBN 0-531-01815-6). Watts.

Ferris, Helen Josephine (1890-1969) & Kimball, Alice Mary, eds.
--Girl Scout Short Stories. LC 26-4062. v. col. front., illus. plates (part col.) 26 cm. N.D. Pub. for Girl Scouts, Inc., by Doubleday, Page & Company.

Ferris, James Cody, pseud., see Stratemeyer Syndicate.

Ferris, James Cody, pseud.
--The X Bar X Boys and the Sagebrush Mystery. Stratemeyer Syndicate. Laune, Paul Sidney (1899-), illus. LC 39-19904. vii, 216 p. incl. front. 19 1/2 cm. (The X Bar X Boys Ser.: Vol. 18). 1939. Grosset & Dunlap.
--The X Bar X Boys at Copperhead Gulch. Stratemeyer Syndicate. Rev. ed. Gretter, J. Clemens, illus. LC 33-15492. iii, 219 p. front. 19 1/2 cm. (The X Bar X Boys Ser.: Vol. 12). 1933. Grosset & Dunlap.
--The X Bar X Boys at Grizzly Pass. Stratemeyer Syndicate. Rev. ed. Rogers, Walter S., illus. LC 29-16919. iv, 218 p. front. 19 1/2 cm. (The X Bar X Boys Ser.: Vol. 8). 1929. Grosset & Dunlap.
--The X Bar X Boys at Nugget Camp. Stratemeyer Syndicate. Rogers, Walter S., illus. LC 28-54069. iv, 216 p. front. 19 1/2 cm. (The X Bar X Boys Ser.: Vol. 6). 1928. Grosset & Dunlap.
--The X Bar X Boys at Rustlers' Gap. Stratemeyer Syndicate. Rogers, Walter S., illus. LC 29-2813. iv, 218 p. front. 19 1/2 cm. (The X Bar X Boys Ser.: Vol. 7). 1929. Grosset & Dunlap.
--The X Bar X Boys at the Round-Up. Stratemeyer Syndicate. Rogers, Walter S., illus. (The X Bar X Boys Ser.: Vol. 5). 1927. Grosset & Dunlap.
--The X Bar X Boys at the Strange Rodeo. Stratemeyer Syndicate. Rev. ed. Gretter, J. Clemens, illus. LC 35-8864. iv, 212 p. front. 19 1/2 cm. (The X Bar X Boys Ser.: Vol. 14). 1935. Grosset & Dunlap.
--The X Bar X Boys at Triangle Mine. Stratemeyer Syndicate. Laune, Paul Sidney (1899-), illus. LC 38-18386. iii, 218 p. front. 19 1/2 cm. (The X Bar X Boys Ser.: Vol. 17). 1938. Grosset & Dunlap.
--The X Bar X Boys Branding the Wild Herd. Stratemeyer Syndicate. Rev. ed. Gretter, J. Clemens, illus. LC 34-14004. iv, 215 p. front. 19 cm. (The X Bar X Boys Ser.: Vol. 13). 1934. Grosset & Dunlap.
--The X Bar X Boys Following the Stampede. Stratemeyer Syndicate. Laune, Paul Sidney (1899-), illus. LC 42-17482. 4 p. l., 211 p. incl. front. 19 cm. (The X Bar X Boys Ser.: Vol. 21). 1942. Grosset & Dunlap.
--The X Bar X Boys Hunting the Prize Mustangs. Stratemeyer Syndicate. Laune, Paul Sidney (1899-), illus. LC 37-815288. iii, 220 p. front. 19 1/2 cm. (The X Bar X Boys Ser.: Vol. 16). 1937. Grosset & Dunlap.
--The X Bar X Boys in Smoky Valley. Stratemeyer Syndicate. 1st ed. Gretter, J. Clemens, illus. LC 32-12765. iv, 219 p. front. 19 1/2 cm. (The X Bar X Boys Ser.: Vol. 11). 1932. Grosset & Dunlap.
--The X Bar X Boys in the Haunted Gully. Stratemeyer Syndicate. Laune, Paul Sidney (1899-), illus. LC 40-792988. vii, 216 p. incl. front. 19 1/2 cm. (The X Bar X Boys Ser.: Vol. 19). 1940. Grosset & Dunlap.
--The X Bar X Boys in Thunder Canyon. Stratemeyer Syndicate. Rogers, Walter S., illus. (The X Bar X Boys Ser.: Vol. 2). 1926. Grosset & Dunlap.
--The X Bar X Boys Lost in the Rockies. Stratemeyer Syndicate. Rogers, Walter S., illus. LC 30-2691. iv, 211 p. front. 19 1/2 cm. (The X Bar X Boys Ser.: Vol. 9). 1930. Grosset & Dunlap.
--The X Bar X Boys on Big Bison Trail. Stratemeyer Syndicate. Rogers, Walter S., illus. (The X Bar X Boys Ser.: Vol. 4). 1927. Grosset & Dunlap.
--The X Bar X Boys on the Ranch. Stratemeyer Syndicate. Rogers, Walter S., illus. (The X Bar X Boys Ser.: Vol. 1). 1926. Grosset & Dunlap.
--The X Bar X Boys on Whirlpool River. Stratemeyer Syndicate. Rogers, Walter S., illus. (The X Bar X Boys Ser.: Vol. 3). 1926. Grosset & Dunlap.
--The X Bar X Boys Riding for Life. Stratemeyer Syndicate. Rogers, Walter S., illus. LC 31-13348. iv, 216 p. front. 19 1/2 cm. (The X Bar X Boys Ser.: Vol. 10). 1931. Grosset & Dunlap.
--The X Bar X Boys Seeking the Lost Troopers. Stratemeyer Syndicate. Laune, Paul Sidney (1899-), illus. LC 41-[illegible] v, 213 p. incl. front., 19 1/2 cm. (The X Bar X Boys Ser.: Vol. 20). 1941. Grosset & Dunlap.
--The X Bar X Boys with the Secret Rangers. Stratemeyer Syndicate. 1st ed. Gretter, J. Clemens, illus. LC 36-18966. iii, 215 p. front. 19 1/2 cm. (The X Bar X Boys Ser.: Vol. 15). 1936. Grosset & Dunlap.

Ferris, Jean
--Amen, Moses Gardenia. 1st ed. LC 83-14153. 200p. 1983. (ISBN 0-374-30252-9). Farrar Straus Giroux.

Ferris, Theodore H., et al., eds. see Educational Research Council of America.

Ferro, Beatriz
--Caught in the Rain. 1st ed. Sambin, Michele, illus. LC 79-2513. (Illus.). 25 p. 22cm. c.1980. (ISBN 0-385-15625-1). Doubleday.

Ferry, Charles (1927-)
--O Zebron Falls!. LC 77-9986. 213 p. 22cm. 1977. (ISBN 0-395-25839-1). Houghton Mifflin.
--One More Time. LC 84-20507. 171 p. 22cm. 1985. (ISBN 0-395-36692-5). Houghton Mifflin.
--Raspberry One. LC 82-25476. 232 p. 22cm. 1983. (ISBN 0-395-34069-1). Houghton Mifflin.
--Up in Sister Bay. Lewin, Ted (1935-), illus. LC 75-15799. (Illus.). 228 p. 22cm. 1975. (ISBN 0-395-21409-2). Houghton Mifflin.

Ferry, G.
--An Adventure with the Apaches. N.D. Benziger Bros.

Ferry, Gabriel, pseud., see Bellemare, Louis De.

Fessenden, Katharine (1896-1974)
--Old Testament Story: Adam to Jonah. (Illus.). (gr. 4-6). 1960. (ISBN 0-8098-2344-6). Walck.

Fessenden, Laura Canfield Spencer Dayton, Mrs. (0000-1924)
--Moon Children. Campbell, R. J., illus. LC 2-22304. 2 p. l., 7-91, 2 p. col. illus. 28 1/2 cm. 1902. Jamieson-Higgins Co.
--Two Thousand and Two: Childlife One Hundred Years from Now. Campbell, R. J., illus. LC 3-13818. 22cm. 184p. 1902. Jamieson-Higgins Co.

Festetits, Kate Neely Hill, Mrs. (1837-)
--Doris Selwyn: Or, A Girl's Influence. LC 6-39237. 3 p. l., 5-335 p. front., plates. 18 1/2 cm. c.1887. American Baptist Publication Society.
--Doris Selwyn: Or, A Girl's Influence. (Illus.). 353p. N.D. Sunday-School Publications.
--Eunice and Laura: Or, The Right Use of Prayer. (Illus.). 320p. N.D. Sunday-School Publications.
--Eunice and Laura: Or,Three Dreadful Days. LC 6-39238. 2 p. l., 3-320 p. front., plates. 18 1/2 cm. c.1886. American Baptist Publication Society.
--Florry Forrester: Or, Three Dreadful Days. LC 6-39239. 2 p. l., 3-320 p. front., plates. 18 1/2 cm. c.1886. American Baptist Publication Society.
--The Flower-Mission, and What Grew Out of It. LC 6-39240. viii, 9-224 p. incl. front. plates. 17 1/2 cm. c.1879. American Sunday-School Union.
--From Post to Pillar. LC 6-39241. 3 p. l., 5-304 p. front., plates. 18 1/2 cm. c.1889. American Baptist Publication Society.
--From Post to Pillar. (Illus.). 304p. N.D. Sunday-School Publications.
--In Mother's Place: Or, The Jay Family. LC 6-39242. 385 p. front., pl. 19 1/2 cm. c.1892. The American Sunday-School Union.
--Irma: The Little Musician. 2 p. l., 3-249 p. front., plates. 17 1/2 cm. c.1885. American Baptist Publication Society.
--Irma, the Little Musician. (Illus.). 248p. N.D. Sunday-School Publications.
--Leslie Rossiter: What She Was Born for, 1 of 60 vols. LC 6-39244. 3 p. l., 5-318 p. front., plates. 18 1/2 cm. (Crescent Lib.). c.1891. Set. American Baptist Publication Society.
--The Old Academy: How the Church Was Rebuilt. LC 6-39245. 3 p. l., 5-288 p. front., plates. 18 1/2 cm. c.1890. American Baptist Publication Society.
--Picnics and Parties: Or, Aunt Sally's Experiences. LC 6-39246. 224 p. front., plates. 17 1/2 cm. c.1880. American Baptist Publication Society.
--Poor Children's Picnic. 106p. N.D. Sunday-School Publications.
--Stephen Hardee. LC 6-39247. 279 p. front., pl. 18 1/2 cm. c.1897. The American Sunday-School Union.
--That Horrid Sarah. [illegible] front., plates. 17 1/2 cm. c.1879. American Baptist Publication Society.
--That Horrid Sarah: The Story of a Young Girl. 206p. N.D. Sunday-School Publications.
--A Year at Dangerfield. LC 6-39249. 2 p. l., 3-288 p. front., plates. 18 1/2 cm. c.1895. American Baptist Publication Society.

Fetter, Margherita Gardner, Mrs.
--Flying Bunnies around the World. LC 38-10334. [illegible] illus. 28 1/2cm. c.1938. Booklover.

Fettig, Art
--The Three Robots. Carpenter, Joe, illus. LC 80-84356. (Illus.). 96p. 1981. (ISBN 0-9601334-0-2). Growth Unltd.
--The Three Robots Find a Grandpa. Carpenter, Joe, illus. LC 84-80378. (Illus.). 96p. (Orig.). 1984. (ISBN 0-9601334-8-8). Growth Unltd.

Fota, Ingrid, jt. auth. see Hurwitz, Johanna.

Feuerlicht, Roberta Strauss (1931-)
--The Legends of Paul Bunyan. Werth, Kurt (1896-), illus. LC 65-27805. 128p. illus. 22cm. (Amer. in the making). c.1966. Collier.
--The Legends of Paul Bunyan. Werth, Kurt (1896-), illus. (gr. 7 up). 1966 (CCPr). Macmillan.

Feuillet, Octave (1821-1890)
--Punch: His Life and Adventures. Bertell, Charles Albert D'Arnould (1820-1882), illus. McPharlin, Paul (1903-1948), tr. LC 46-5941. 128 p. incl. col. front., illus. (part col.) 19 cm. 1946. Didier.
--The Story of Mr. Punch. Gable, J. Harris (1902-), tr. LC 29-17659. 7 l., 13-139, 1 p. col. front., illus. 21 1/2 cm. c.1929. E. P. Dutton & Co., Inc.

Feustel, Gunther
--Jose: A Tale from South America. Baltzer, Hans (1900-), illus. Humphries, Stella, tr. LC 67-24091. (Illus.). 2-color ils. 96p. (gr. 4-8). 1968. (ISBN 0-440-04256-9, Sey Lawr). Delacorte.

Few, Frank
--The Boomerang maker. (Illus.). 48p. 1963. Tri-Ocean Books.

Fey, James Taylor
--Long, Short, High, Low, Thin, Wide. Russell, Janie, illus. LC 75-158705. (Illus.). 32 p. (Young math book). 1971. (ISBN 0-690-50549-3). (ISBN 0-690-50550-7). Crowell.

Feydy, Anne Lindbergh (1940-)
--Osprey Island. Smith, Maggie Kaufman, illus. LC 74-9379. (Illus.). 164 p. 22cm. 1974. (ISBN 0-395-19498-9). Houghton Mifflin.

Fezandie, Hector
--Felicia and the Sandman. LC 36-7828. 153 p. illus. 22 cm. c.1936. T. F. Kyle.
--Felicia and the Sandman. Perard, Victor Semon (1870-1957), illus. LC 35-16052. 2 p. l., 7-158 p. illus. 22 cm. c.1935. The Somerset Press.
--The Land of Lost Dolls: Or, Really-Truly and Otherwise. Perard, Victor Semon (1870-1957), illus. LC 37-36929. x, 11-229, 1 p. col. front., illus., col. plates. 24 cm. 1937. T. F. Kyle.

F. F. G
--Little Nan: Or, A Living Remembrance. N.D. E. P. Dutton & Co.

Ffolliott, Rosemary (1934-) & Ledbetter, Gordon
--De Bever Hall: The Story of a Stately Dolls House. LC 76-383912. (Illus.). 75 p. 29cm. 1976. (ISBN 0-7156-1018-X). G. Duckworth.

Ficowski, Jerzy
--Sister of the Birds, and Other Gypsy Tales. Mikolaycak, Charles (1937-), illus. Borski, Lucia Merecka, tr. LC 76-11619. (Illus.). 72 p. 20cm. c.1976. (ISBN 0-687-38596-2). Abingdon.

Fiddler, Daniel
--Freddy Firefly. (Illus.). (gr. k-3). 1978. (ISBN 0-89185-185-2). Anthelion Pr.

Fideler, Nancy B. see Lawrence, Anne, pseud.

Fideler, Nancy B. see Raymond, Nancy, pseud.

Fideler, Nancy B. (1918-)
--The Clown's Clock Book. Lawrence, Anne, pseud. Gringhuis, Richard H. (1918-1974), illus. Dirk, pseud. LC 47-3012. 28 p. col. illus. 26 1/2 x 22 1/2 cm. (On cover: Story hour library). 1946. The Fideler Company.

--Susanna B. And William C. Field, Rachel Lyman (1894-1942), illus. LC 34-30550. 62, 2 p. col. illus. 14 1/2 cm. 1934. W. Morrow & Company.
--Taxis & Toadstools. Field, Rachel Lyman (1894-1942), illus. (Illus.). (gr. 3-6). 1926. (ISBN 0-385-07520-0). (ISBN 0-385-07115-9). Doubleday.
--The Yellow Shop. Field, Rachel Lyman (1894-1942), illus. LC 31-28324. 3 p. l. 62 p. col. illus. 14 1/2 cm. 1931. Doubleday, Doran & Company, Inc.
Field, Rachel Lyman (1894-1942), ed.
--American Folk & Fairy Tales. Freeman, Margaret (1893-), illus. LC 27-25017. (Illus.). 23cm. 302p. (gr. 3-7). 1929. (ISBN [illegible]) [illegible].
Fielde, A. M.
--Chinese Fairy Tales. N.D. G. P. Putnam's Sons.
Fieldhouse, Felice., Mrs.
--Yukon Holiday. Lufkin, Raymond H. (1897-), illus. LC 40-13168. 3 p. l., 230 p. illus. 20 cm. 1940. Longmans, Green and Co.
Fielding, Alfred
--Shanghaied;. A Novel for Boys who Love Ships and the Sea. 1st ed. LC 57-12578. 139p. 21cm. 1937. Greenwich Book Publishers
Fielding, Archibald (1900-)
--The Net Around Joan Ingilby. LC 28-22463. 3 p. l., 3-302 p. 1 l. 19 1/2 cm. 1928. A. A. Knopf.
Fielding, Henry
--Tom Jones. N.D. The Modern Library.
Fielding, Jane, ed. see Bridges, Thomas Charles.
Fielding, Loraine Hornaday
--French Heels to Spurs. James, Will, intro. by. N.D. D. Appleton-Century Co.
Fielding, Sally (1933-)
--Kate and the Mystery Ponies. LC 85-13816. p. cm. (Lion Paperback). c.1985. (ISBN 0-85648-959-X). Lion Pub.
Fielding, Sarah (1710-1768)
--The Governess: Or, Little Female Academy. LC 77-396017. (Illus.). 20cm. vii, 375p. (The Juvenile library). 1968. Oxford Univ. Press.
Fields, E. M.
--Mixed Pickles. (The Rugby Series for Boys and Girls). N.D. A. L. Burt Company.
Fife, Alta, jt. auth. see Fife, Austin.
Fife, Austin & Fife, Alta
--Saints Of Sage & Saddle. (Illus.). N.D. (ISBN 0-8446-1179-4). Peter Smith Publisher, Inc.
Fife, Dale Odile (1910-)
--Adam's ABC. Robertson, Don (1933-), illus. LC 77-132590. (Illus.). 63 p. 1971. Coward, McCann & Geoghegan.
--Bluefoot. Bordigoni, Idelette, illus. LC 68-27700. (Illus.). 40 p. 26cm. 1968. Lothrop, Lee & Shepard Co.
--The Boy Who Lived in the Railroad Depot. Fetz, Ingrid (1915-), illus. LC 68-18822. (Illus.). 72 p. 24cm. 1968. Coward-McCann.
--Destination Unknown. LC 81-4209. p. cm. c.1981. (ISBN 0-525-28624-1). Dutton.
--Dog Called Dunkel. Alain, pseud. (1904-), illus. Brustlein, Daniel. LC 66-13136. (Illus.). (gr. k-3). 1966. (ISBN 0-698-30063-7). Coward.
--The Fish in the Castle. Miller, Marilyn Jean (1925-), illus. LC 65-20378. 45p. illus. 23cm. c.1965. Coward.
--Follow That Ghost!. 1st ed. Drescher, Joan Elizabeth (1939-), illus. LC 79-11370. (Illus.). 58 p. 23cm. (Unicorn book). c.1979. (ISBN 0-525-30010-4). Dutton.
--Imagine That!. Black, Ben, illus. LC 73-81588. (Illus.). 24 p. 23cm. (Magic circle book). 1974. (ISBN 0-663-25469-8). Ginn.
--Joe and the Talking Christmas Tree. Tomes, Margot Ladd (1917-), illus. LC 68-31067. (Illus.). 48 p. 23cm. 1968. Coward-McCann.
--The Little Park. LaSalle, Janet (1926-), illus. LC 73-7322. (Illus.). 32 p. 19cm. 1973. (ISBN 0-8075-4634-8). A. Whitman.
--North of Danger. Esther, Haakon, illus. LC 77-26199. (Illus.). 72 p. 22cm. (Unicorn book). c.1978. (ISBN 0-525-36035-2). Dutton.
--Ride the Crooked Wind. Cuffari, Richard (1925-1978), illus. LC 72-89766. (Illus.). 95 p. 21cm. 1973. (ISBN 0-698-20249-X). (ISBN 0-698-20249-X). Coward, McCann & Geoghegan.
--Rosa's Special Garden. De John, Marie, illus. LC 84-17223. p. cm. 1984. (ISBN 0-8075-7115-6). A. Whitman.
--The Sesame Seed Snatchers. Kossin, Sandy (1926-), illus. (Illus.). 112p. (gr. 2-5). 1983. (ISBN 0-395-34826-9). HM.
--Stork for the bell tower. 48p. 1964. Coward McCann, Inc.
--Walk a Narrow Bridge. 186 p. 21cm. 1966. Coward-McCann.
--What's New, Lincoln?. Galdone, Paul (1914-), illus. LC 73-105949. (Illus.). 59 p. 24cm. 1970. Coward-McCann.
--What's the Prize, Lincoln?. Galdone, Paul (1914-), illus. LC 76-152231. (Illus.). 63 p. 24cm. 1971. Coward, McCann & Geoghegan.
--Who Goes There, Lincoln?. Galdone, Paul (1914-), illus. LC 74-83016. (Illus.). 62 p. 24cm. 1975. (ISBN 0-698-30565-5). Coward, McCann & Geoghegan.
--Who'll Vote for Lincoln?. Galdone, Paul (1914-), illus. LC 76-57127. (Illus.). 63 p. 24cm. c.1977. (ISBN 0-698-30665-1). Coward, McCann & Geoghegan.
--Who's in Charge of Lincoln?. Galdone, Paul (1914-), illus. LC 65-13286. (Illus.). 61 p. 24cm. 1965. Coward-McCann.
Fifield, Flora & Langner, Nola (1930-)
--Pictures for the Palace. LC 57-12263. (Illus.). (gr. k-3). N.D. (ISBN 0-8149-0301-0). Vanguard.
Figes, Eva (1932-), tr. see Borchers, Elisabeth.
Figes, Eva (1932-)
--Banger. Stubbs, Joanna, illus. LC 68-9413. (Illus.). (gr. k-2). 1968. (ISBN 0-87460-035-9). (ISBN 0-87460-045-6). Lion.
--The Musicians of Bremen. Lemke, Horst (1922-), illus. (gr. k-3). 1975. (ISBN 0-8277-4484-6). British Bk Ctr.
--Scribble Sam. Stubbs, Joanna, illus. LC 79-157106. full color ils. 32p. (gr. k-2). 1971. (ISBN 0-679-20167-X). McKay.
Figueroa, John Louis (19[illegible]-)
--Antonio's World. 1st ed. Morales, Samuel E., illus. LC 75-126790. (Illus.). 60 p. 20cm. (Challenger book. La raza series). 1970. Hill and Wang Distributed by Random House.
Figueroa, Pablo (1938-)
--Enrique: A Challenge Book. Negron, Bill, illus. LC 79-126791. 57p. (La Raza Ser.). (gr. 5-10). 1970 (Challenger, Challenger). Hill & Wang.
Figyelmessy, Elisa Haldeman, Mrs.
--Two Boys in the Tropics. LC 10-220551. x p., 1 l., 345, 1 p. front., plates. 20 cm. 1910. The Macmillan Company.
Filbert, Mary A.
--And Then They Were There. (gr. 4-7). N.D. Carlton.
Filleal, Marion
--Marion: or, The Smuggler's Wife. (Illus.). N.D. E & J B Young.
Fillebrown, Rebekah Huddell Miller, Mrs. (1863-)
--Betty Corbin. LC 13-317. 2 p. l., 70 p. 19 1/2 cm. 1912. Broadway Publishing Company.
--Rhymes of Happy Childhood. Prittie, Edwin John, illus. LC 9-555. 25cm. 119p. 1908. J. C. Winston.
Filleul, Marianne
--The Squatter's Home (Pub. by Society for Promoting Christian Knowledge). N.D. E. & J. B Young & Co.
Filley, Chauncey I., Mrs.
--What Nobody Ever Told Me. N.D. Methodist Book Concern.
Filligham, Patricia
--Anna's Elephant. (Illus.). 33p. 1983. (ISBN 0-318-00210-8). Warthog Pr.
Fillmore, A. D.
--Nightingale: Sunday School Singer. N.D. Applegate, Pounsford & Co.
Fillmore, Myrtle
--Wee Wisdom's Way. Heitland, Wilmot E., illus. LC 22-6614. 95 p. col. front., plates. 23 1/2 cm. N.D. Unity Press.
Fillmore, Parker Hoysted (1878-1944), retold by.
--Czechoslovak Fairy Tales. Matulka, Jan (1890-), illus. LC 19-17830. x p., 2 l., 3-245, 1 p. incl. col. front., illus. plates. 21 cm. 1919. Harcourt, Brace and Howe.
--Fillmore Folk Tales: Selected for Young Folks from "Mighty Mikko" and "The Laughing Prince". Harper, Wilhelmina (1884-1973), selected by. Van Everen, Jay, illus. LC 26-27492. 4 p. l., 3-222 p. illus. 21 cm. 1926. Harcourt, Brace and Company.
--Laughing Prince. Van Everen, Jay, illus. LC 21-18687. (Illus.). (gr. 4-6). 1921. (ISBN 0-15-243639-1). HarBraceJ.
--A Little Question in Ladies' Rights. O'Neill, Rose Cecil (1874-), illus. LC 16-18918. 79 p. incl. front., illus., pl. 18 1/2 cm. 1916. John Lane Company.
--Mighty Mikko: A Book of Finnish Fairy Tales and Folk Tales. Van Everen, Jay, illus. LC 22-20322. xvi, 314, 1 p. incl. illus., plates. col. front. 21 cm. c.1922. Harcourt, Brace and Company.
--The Shoemaker's Apron: A Second Book of Czechoslovak Fairy Tales and Folk Tales. Matulka, Jan (1890-), illus. LC 20-176790. xiii, 280 p., 1 l. incl. illus., plates. col. front. 21 cm. 1920. Harcourt, Brace and Howe.
--The Stuffed Parrot. Britcher, Phyllis, illus. LC 31-22801. 6 p. l., 3-174 p. incl. illus., plates. col. front., col. plates. 19 1/2 cm. c.1931. Harcourt, Brace and Company.
--The Wizard of the North: A Tale from the Land of Heroes. Everen, Jay Van, illus. LC 23-14976. xv p., 2 l., 3-213 p. incl. front., plates. 20 1/2 cm. c.1923. Harcourt, Brace and Company.
Fillmore, Parker Hoysted (1878-1944) & Love, Katheine, eds.
--The Shepherd's Nosegay. N.D. E . M. Hale and Co.
--The Shepherd's Nosegay: Stories from Finland and Czechoslovakia. Arno, Enrico (1913-1981), illus. LC 58-11558. 192p. 1958. Harcourt, Brace and Co Inc.
Filmer, John, illus.
--Illustrated Book of Songs for Children. (Illus.). N.D. James Miller.
--Illustrated Book of Songs For Children. (Illus.). N.D. Thomas R. Knox & Co.
Filmer-Sankey, Josephine, jt. auth. see Denny, Norman George.
Filosa, Dorothea
--Parsley the Horse. Filosa, Dorothea, illus. LC 40-30538. 2 p. illus. [illegible] c.1940. Garden City Publishing Co., Inc.
--Susi. Filosa, Dorothea, illus. LC 39-30378. 32 p. col. illus. 28 cm. c.1939. Garden City Publishing Co., Inc.
Filson, Brent
--The Puma. LC 77-12853. 112 p. 22cm. (Doubleday signal book). c.1979. (ISBN 0-385-12983-1). Doubleday.
--Smoke Jumpers. LC 76-56289. 135 p. 22cm. (Doubleday signal book). c.1976. (ISBN 0-385-12790-1). Doubleday.
Finch, Donald George (1937-)
--She Waits for Me. (gr. 8-12). 1977. (ISBN 0-912472-16-2). Miller Bks.
Finch, Nora Jane (1845-)
--Colliery Jim: The Autobiography of a Mine Mule. LC 4-22854. 171 p. front., illus. 18 1/2 cm. c.1904. A. Flanagan Company.
Finch, Phillip
--Haulin'. LC 74-22838. 240p. 1975. (ISBN 0-385-01313-2). Doubleday.
Findlay, Phillip
--Alice and the Ox Goad. (Daisy Dell Stories). N.D. Henry A. Young.
--Playing Soldier. (Daisy Dell Ser.). N.D. Henry A. Young.
--Rosa Dale's Friends. (Daisy Dell Ser.). N.D. Henry A. Young.
--Sadie's Adventures. (Daisy Dell Ser.). N.D. Henry A. Young.
--Shepherdess of Daisy Dell. (Daisy Dell Ser.). N.D. Henry A. Young.
--Work for Play. (Daisy Dell Stories). N.D. Henry A. Young.
Fine, Aaron
--Peter Plants a Pocketful. LC 55-5969. 31p. (Oxford Books for Boys & Girls). 1955. Oxford University Press.
--The School Bus Picnic. Fine, Aaron, illus. LC 54-57378. unpaged. illus. 22 cm. 1954. Holt.
Fine, Anne (1947-)
--The Granny Project. LC 83-5592. 167p. 1983. (ISBN 0-374-32763-7). FS&G.
--The Summer-House Loon. LC 78-19515. 126 p. 21cm. 1979, c.1978. (ISBN 0-690-03933-6). (ISBN 0-690-03934-4). Crowell.
Fine, Janice & Watt, Lois
--Benito and the Bootstraps. Brigham, Barbara, illus. LC 79-134696. (Illus.). 47 p. 22cm. 1970. (ISBN 0-8111-0381-1). Naylor Co.
Fine, Warren (1943-)
--The Mousechildren and the Famous Collector. 1st ed. Mayer, Mercer (1943-), illus. LC 79-96013. (Illus.). 57 p. 27cm. 1970. Harper & Row.
Finely, Martha (1828-1909)
--Elsie's Young Folks. (The Elsie Books). N.D. Dodd, Mead & Co.
Finfer, Celentha & Wasserberg, Esther
--Grandfather Dear. Greenberg, Irwin, illus. (Illus.). 30 p. 21cm. (A Follett beginning-to-read book). 1968. Follett.
--Grandmother Dear. Matthews, Ray, illus. 1966. (ISBN 0-695-83455-X). (ISBN 0-695-43455-1). Follett Publishing.
Finger, Charles Joseph (1871-1941)
--Bobbie and Jock and the Mailman. Finger, Helen, illus. LC 38-27780. 2 p. l., 155, 1 p. illus. 21 cm. c.1938. H. Holt and Company.
--Bushrangers. Honore, Paul (1885-), illus. N.D. Robert M. McBride &.
--Cape Horn Snorter: A Story of the War of 1812, and of Gallant Days with Captain Porter of the U.S. Frigate, Essex. Rev. ed. Pitz, Henry Clarence (1895-1976), illus. LC 39-23188. 5 p. l., 263 p. incl. front., illus. 22 cm. 1939. Houghton Mifflin Company.
--Courageous Companions. Daugherty, James Henry (1889-1974), illus. LC 29-20115. 7 p. l., 304, 1 p. incl. front., illus., plates. 23 cm. c.1929. Longmans, Green and Co.
--The Distant Prize: Or, A Bk. About Rovers, Rangers, and Rascals. N.D. D. Appleton-Century Co.
--A Dog at His Heel. Pitz, Henry Clarence (1895-1976), illus. N.D. John C. Winston.
--Five Little Midway. Pitz, Henry Clarence (1895-1976), illus. N.D. Grosset & Dunlap.
--Five Little Peppers Grown-up. Pitz, Henry Clarence (1895-1976), illus. N.D. Grosset & Dunlap.
--Give a Man a Horse. Pitz, Henry Clarence (1895-1976), illus. LC 36-27461. x, 340 p. col. front., illus. 22 cm. c.1938. The John C. Winston Company.
--Golden Tales from Faraway. Finger, Helen, illus. LC 40-7296. xi, 233 p. incl. col. front., illus. 23 cm. c.1940. The John C. Winston Company.
--High Water in Arkansas. Pitz, Henry Clarence (1895-1976), illus. N.D. Grosset & Dunlap.
--Highwaymen. Honore, Paul (1885-), illus. (Boys' Own Edition). N.D. Robert M. McBride &.
--The Magic Tower. Finger, Helen, illus. LC 34-34200. 118 p. illus. 21 cm. 1933. The Kings Arms Press, Duffield & Green.
--The Spreading Stain: A Tale for Boys and Men with Boys' Hearts. LC 27-22474. 5 p. l., 245 p. col. front. 20 1/2 cm. 1927. Doubleday Page & Co.
--Tales from Silver Lands. LC 24-26940. 6 p. l., 225 p. col. front., illus., col. plates. 23 1/2 cm. 1924. Doubleday, Page & Company. **Award: (JNM).**
--Tales from Silver Lands. (Illus.). 20cm. 206p. (Zephyr bks.). 1972, c.1924. Doubleday.
--Tales Worth Telling. Honore, Paul (1885-), illus. LC 27-21055. 4 p. l., 3-250 p. col. front., illus., col. plates. 21 cm. c.1927. The Century Co.
--When Guns Thundered at Tripoli. Pitz, Henry Clarence (1895-1976), illus. LC 37-22969. 5 p. l., 3-290 p. col. front., illus. 21 cm. c.1937. H. Holt and Company.
--The Yankee Captain in Patagonia. Pitz, Henry Clarence (1895-1976), illus. LC 41-4721. 4 p. l., 74, 1 p. incl. front., illus. 21 x 10 cm. (story parade adventure book). c.1941. Grosset & Dunlap.
Fingland, Randy & Schneider, Andrea
--Dinosaur Cooler. (Illus.). 1980. Crosscut Saw.
Fink, Augusta (1916-)
--To Touch the Sky. LC 71-141157. (Illus.). 101 p. 25cm. 1971. (ISBN 0-87464-170-5). Golden Gate Junior Books.
Fink, Clarence Mervyn (1913-)
--Young Chad Seal of Los Angeles. Nichols, Charles A., illus. LC 51-93588. (Illus.). 48. 20cm. 1951. Story Book Press.
Fink, Dale B
--Mr. Silver and Mrs. Gold. LC 79-15924. p. cm. (gr. 4-8). 1980. (ISBN 0-87705-447-9). Human Sciences Press.
Fink, Joanne, adapted by see Melville, Herman.
Fink, Joanne (1954-), retold by.
--William Tell. Fromm, Hieronimus (1802-1870), illus. LC 84-50434. (Original Author: Friedrich Schiller, 1759-1805). (Illus.). 26 p., 1 leaf of plates. 26cm. (Classics for Kids). 1984. (ISBN 0-382-06806-8). Silver Burdett Co.
Finkel, George Irvine (1909-1975)
--Cloudmaker. LC 65-14027. 163p. 23cm. c.1965. Roy.
--James Cook, Royal Navy. LC 74-181042. (Illus.). 213 p. 18cm. (Puffin books). 1973. (ISBN 0-14-030596-3). Penguin Books.
--The Long Pilgrimage. LC 69-13079. (Illus.). 319 p. 22cm. 1969, c.1967. Viking Press.
--The Loyal Virginian. LC 68-27570. 288p. (gr. 7 up). 1968. (ISBN 0-670-44368-9). (ISBN 0-670-44369-7). Viking Pr.
--The Loyal Virginian. 1968. Viking Press.
--Watch Fires to the North. LC 67-24857. 311 p. maps. 22 cm. 1967. Viking Press.
Finkleman, Ken, jt. auth. see Rotsler, William.
Finlay, Ian Hamilton (1925-)
--Poems to Hear & See. LC 71-133557. (Illus.). color ils. 48p. (gr. 5 up). 1971. (ISBN 0-02-735210-2). Macmillan.
Finlay, Roger Thompson (1860-)
--The Wonder Island Boys. Adventures on Strange Islands. LC 17-29184. 242 p. front., illus., plates. 19 1/2cm. c.1915. The New York Book Company.
--The Wonder Island Boys. Capture and Pursuit. LC 14-11051. 2 p. l., 238 p. front., illus., plates. 19 1/2cm. c.1914. The New York Book Company.
--The Wonder Island Boys. Exploring the Island. LC 14-11048. 2 p. l., 238 p. front., illus., plates. 19 1/2cm. c.1914. The New York Book Company.
--The Wonder Island Boys. The Castaways. LC 14-11050. 2 p. l., 238 p. front., illus., plates, diagrs. 19 1/2cm. c.1914. The New York Book Company.
--The Wonder Island Boys. The Conquest of the Savages. LC 14-11049. c.1914. The New York Book Company.
--The Wonder Island Boys. The Mysteries of the Caverns. LC 14-11047. 2 p. l., xii, 11-234 p. front., illus., plates. 19 1/2cm. c.1914. The New York Book Company.
--The Wonder Island Boys. The Tribesmen. LC 14-11046. 2 p. l., 238 p. front., illus., plates. 19 1/2cm. c.1914. The New York Book Company.
--The Wonder Island Boys. Treasures of the Islands. LC 17-29183. 234 p. front., illus. (incl. maps) plates. 19 1/2cm. c.1915. The New York Book Company.

Finlay, Winifred Lindsay Crawford McKissack (1910-)
--Beadbonny Ash. LC 75-19082. 192 p. 21cm. 1975, c.1973. (ISBN 0-8407-6436-7). T. Nelson.
--Danger at Black Dyke. LC 68-31174. (Illus.). 186 p. 22cm. 1968. S. G. Phillips.
Finlay, Winifred Lindsay Crawford McKissack (1910-), retold by.
--Cap O' Rushes And Other Folk Tales: And Other Folk Tales. Ambrus, Victor G, pseud. (1935-), illus. Ambrus, Gyozo Laszlo. (Illus.). 122 p. 22cm. 1974. (ISBN 0-8382-1096-1). E. M. Hale.
--Folk Tales from Moor and Mountain. Ambrus, Victor G., pseud. (1935-), illus. Ambrus, Gyozo Laszlo. LC 72-98027. (Illus.). 128 p. 22cm. 1970, c.1969. Roy Publishers.
--Folk Tales from the North. Ambrus, Victor G., pseud. (1935-), illus. Ambrus, Gyozo Laszlo. LC 69-10886. (Illus.). 127 p. 23cm. 1969, c.1968. F. Watts.
--Tattercoats, and Other Folk Tales. Hughes, Shirley (1929-), illus. LC 77-364936. (Illus.). 118 p. 23cm. 1977, c.1976. (ISBN 0-8178-5532-7). Harvey House.
Finlayson, Ann (1925-), adapted by see Thane, Elswyth.
Finlayson, Ann (1925-)
--Greenhorn on the Frontier. Mars, Witold Tadeusz J. (1912-), illus. LC 73-93587. (Illus.). 209 p. 23cm. 1974. F. Warne.
--House Cat. Berson, Harold (1926-), illus. LC 73-93588. (Illus.). 48 p. 24cm. 1974. F. Warne.
--Rebecca's War. Streeter, Sherry, illus. LC 78-183735. (Illus.). 280 p. 23cm. 1972. F. Warne.
--Redcoat in Boston. Landa, Peter, illus. LC 75-150364. (Illus.). 279 p. 23cm. 1971. F. Warne.
--Runaway Teen. 1st ed. Copelman, Evelyn, illus. LC 63-8739. (Illus.). 143 p. 22cm. (Signal book). 1963. Doubleday.
--The Silver Bullet. LC 78-6575. 223 p. 21cm. c.1978. T. Nelson.
--A Summer to Remember. 1st ed. Johnson, Ray (1900-), illus. LC 64-11707. (Illus.). 144 p. 22cm. (Signal book). 1964. Doubleday.
Finley, Jean
--The Blue Domers. LC 28-119248. 4 p. l., 118 p. col. front., col. plates. 19 1/2cm. (Her Blue Domers series). c.1928. A.L. Burt Company.
--The Blue Domers' Alphabet Zoo. LC 28-10515. 4 p. l., 119 p. col. front., col. plates. 19 1/2cm. (Her Blue Domers series). c.1928. A.L. Burt Company.
--The Blue Domers and the Hidden Shanty. LC 30-10607. 4 p. l., 120 p. col. front., col. plates. 19 1/2cm. (Her Blue Domers series). c.1930. A.L. Burt Company.
--The Blue Domers and the Magic Flute. LC 28-141216. 4 p. l., 120 p. col. front., col. plates. 19 1/2cm. (Her Blue Domers series). c.1928. A.L. Burt Company.
--The Blue Domers and the Wishing Tree. LC 28-14405. 4 p. l., 120 p. col. front., col. plates. 19 1/2cm. (Her Blue Domers series). c.1928. A.L. Burt Company.
--The Blue Domers in the Deep Woods. LC 28-105144. 4 p. l., 120 p. col. front., col. plates. 19 1/2cm. (Her Blue Domers series). c.1928. A.L. Burt Company.
--The Blue Domers' Nest. LC 30-10606. 4 p. l., 117 p. col. front., col. plates. 19 1/2cm. (Her Blue Domers series). c.1930. A.L. Burt Company.
--The Blue Domers Under Winter Skies. LC 28-131701. 4 p. l., 119 p. col. front., col. plates. 19 1/2cm. (Her Blue Domers series). c.1928. A.L. Burt Company.
Finley, Maeve O'Reilly
--Haiku for You: One Hundred and One Fun Readings For Boys and Girls. 1st ed. LC 65-292795. 46 p. 21 cm. 1966. Vantage Press.
Finley, Martha see Farquharson, Martha, pseud.
Finley, Martha (1828-1909)
--Casella: Or, The Children of the Valleys. Farquharson, Martha, pseud. LC 12-32332. x, 11-389 p. 17 1/2cm. 1869. J.B. Lippincott & Co.
--Cassella, 1 of 7 vols. (The Finley Lib.). N.D. Set. Dodd, Mead & Co.
--Christmas with Grandma Elsie. LC 3-22357. 1 p. l., 317 p. front. 18 1/2cm. c.1888. Dodd, Mead & Company.
--Elsie and Her Loved Ones. LC 3-29273. 299p. (The Elsie Books). 1903. Dodd, Mead & Co.
--Elsie and Her Namesakes. LC 5-35593. 2 p. l., 306 p. front. 18 1/2cm. (The Elsie Bks.). 1905. Dodd, Mead and Company.
--Elsie and the Raymonds. (The Famous Elsie Bks). N.D. A L Burt Co.
--Elsie and the Raymonds. LC 12-324879. 324 p. 18cm. c.1889. Dodd, Mead and Company.
--Elsie and the Raymonds, 1 of 5 vols. (The Elsie Bks.). N.D. Set. Dodd, Mead & Company.
--Elsie at Home, 1 of 25 vols. LC 12-323349. 1 p. l., 295 p. 18cm. (The Finley Bks.). c.1897. Dodd, Mead and Company.
--Elsie at Ion, 1 of 25 vols. LC 12-323306. 1 p. l., 291 p. 18 1/2cm. (The Finley Bks.). c.1893. Dodd, Mead & Company.
--Elsie at Ion. (The Elsie Books). N.D. Dodd, Mead & Co.
--Elsie at Nantucket. 301p. Repr. 1981. (ISBN 0-89966-333-8). Buccaneer Bks.
--Elsie at Nantucket. LC 12-323291. (A Sequel to Elsie's New Relations). 2 p. l., 3-334 p. pl. 17 1/2cm. c.1884. Dodd, Mead & Company.
--Elsie At Nantucket, 1 of 25 vols. (The Finley Bks.). N.D. Set. Dodd, Mead & Company.
--Elsie at Nantucket. 302p. Repr. 1980. (ISBN 0-89967-011-3). Harmony & Co.
--Elsie at the World's Fair, 1 of 25 vols. (The Elsie Bks). N.D. Set. Dodd, Mead & Co.
--Elsie At Viamede. (The Famous Elsie Bks). N.D. A L Burt Co.
--Elsie at Viamede, 1 of 25 vols. LC 3-22358. 1 p. l., 293 p. 18 1/2cm. (The Finley Bks.). c.1892. Dodd, Mead & Company.
--Elsie Dinsmore. (The Famous Elsie Bks). N.D. A. B. Burt Co.
--Elsie Dinsmore. LC 35-334261. 2 p. l., 316 p. 19 1/2cm. 1930. A.L. Burt Company.
--Elsie Dinsmore. LC 74-15737. (Illus.). 342 p. 24cm. (Popular Culture in America). 1974, c.1896. (ISBN 0-405-06372-5). Arno Press.
--Elsie Dinsmore. (The Elsie Bks.). N.D. Dodd & Mead.
--Elsie Dinsmore, 1 of 25 vols. (The Finley Bks.). N.D. Set. Dodd, Mead & Company.
--Elsie Dinsmore. (The Phoenix Ser.). N.D. Dodd, Mead & Co.
--Elsie Dinsmore. LC 75-32168. xii, 288 p. 19cm. (Classics of Children's Literature, 1621-1932). 1977, c.1867. (ISBN 0-8240-2281-5). Garland Pub.
--Elsie Dinsmore. N.D. Grosset & Dunlap.
--Elsie Dinsmore. (Home Series for Girls). N.D. Hurst & Co.
--Elsie Dinsmore. Christy, Howard Chandler (1873-1952), illus. LC 12-32492. vi, 7-299 p. incl. illus., plates. front. 22cm. (Phenix Ser.). c.1897. Dodd, Mead & Company.
--Elsie Dinsmore. Muheim, Henry, illus. LC 43-15176. 1 p. l., 9-252 p. front., illus. 20 1/2 cm. 1943. The Saalfield Publishing Company.
--Elsie in the South, 1 of 25 vols. LC 99-5398. 1 p. l., 324 p. pl. 12cm. (The Finley Bks.). 1899. Dodd, Mead & Co.
--Elsie on the Hudson and Elsewhere, 1 of 25 vols. LC 98-1215. 2 p. l., 329 p. 18 cm. (The Finely Bks.). 1898. Dodd, Mead and Company.
--Elsie Yachting with the Raymonds. (The Famous Elsie Bks). N.D. A L Burt Co.
--Elsie Yachting with the Raymonds, 1 of 25 vols. LC 20-19347. 3 p. l., 3-280 p. front. 28cm. (The Finley Bks.). c.1890. Dodd, Mead and Company.
--Elsie's Children. 243p. Repr. (The Famous Elsie Bks.). 1981. (ISBN 0-89966-336-2). Buccaneer Bks.
--Elsie's Children. 1877. Dodd, Mead & Company.
--Elsie's Children, 1 of 25 vols. (The Elsie Bks). N.D. Set. Dodd, Mead & Co.
--Elsie's Friends at Woodburn. LC 12-323316. 334 p. front. 18 1/2cm. c.1887. Dodd, Mead & Company.
--Elsie's Friends at Woodburn. (The Elsie Bks). N.D. Dodd, Mead & Co.
--Elsie's Girlhood. complete authorized. LC 35-334291. (A Sequel to "Elsie Dinsmore" and "Elsie's Holidays at Roseland"). 2 p. l., 371 p. 19 1/2cm. (The Elsie Bks.). 1930. A.L. Burt Company.
--Elsie's Girlhood. LC 11-15097. (A Sequel to "Elsie Dinsmore" and "Elsie's Holidays at Roselands"). 3 p. l., 3-422 p. front., plates. 18cm. (The Elsie Bks.). 1872. Dodd & Mead.
--Elsie's Girlhood, 1 of 25 vols. (The Elsie Bks). N.D. Set. Dodd, Mead & Co.
--Elsie's Holidays at Roseland. (The Elsie Bks). N.D. A. L. Burt Co.
--Elsie's Holidays at Roseland. (The Elsie Bks). N.D. Dodd, Mead & Co.
--Elsie's Journey on Inland Waters. LC 12-32346. 1 p. l., 283 p. front. 18cm. (The Elsie Bks.). 1895. Dodd, Mead and Company.
--Elsie's Kith and Kin. (The Elsie Books). N.D. Dodd, Mead & Co.
--Elsie's Motherhood. 243p. Repr. 1981. (ISBN 0-89966-335-4). Buccaneer Bks.
--Elsie's Motherhood. complete authorized. LC 35-33428. (A Sequel to "Elsie's Womanhood"). iv, 348 p. 19 1/2cm. (The Elsie Bks.). 1930. Chicago, A.L. Burt Company.
--Elsie's Motherhood, 1 of 25 vols. (A Sequel to Elsie's Womanhood). (The Elsie Bks). 1876. Set. Dodd, Mead & Co.
--Elsie's Motherhood. LC 4-25677. (A Sequel to "Elsie's Womanhood"). iv, 348 p. front. 18 1/2cm. (The Elsie Bks.). 1904. Dodd, Mead and Company.
--Elsie's New Relations, 1 of 25 vols. (The Elsie Bks). N.D. Set. Dodd, Mead & Co.
--Elsie's New Relations: What They Did and How They Fared at Ion. LC 13-324902. 324 p. front., plates. 17 1/2cm. c.1883. Dodd, Mead & Company.
--Elsie's Vacation. N.D. Dodd, Mead & Company.
--Elsie's Vacation and After Events, 1 of 25 vols. LC 12-32489. 1 p. l., 292 p. front. (port.) 18 1/2cm. (The Finley Bks.). c.1891. Dodd, Mead, and Company.
--Elsie's Widowhood. LC 3-223619. (A Sequel to "Elsie's Children"). vi, 7-331 p. front. 18 1/2cm. (The Elsie Bks.). c.1880. Dodd, Mead & Company.
--Elsie's Winter Trip. (The Elsie Bks). N.D. Dodd, Mead & Co.
--Elsie's Womanhood. LC 35-33427. (A Sequel to "Elsie's Girlhood"). iv, 343 p. 19 1/2cm. (The Elsie Bks.). 1930. A.L. Burt Company.
--Elsie's Womanhood. LC 3-22360. (A Sequel to "Elsie's Girlhood"). iv, 343 p. front. 18 1/2cm. (The Elsie Bks.). 1901. Dodd, Mead & Company.
--Elsie's Young Folks in Peace and War ... LC 1-29038. 1 p. l., 285 p. front. 12cm. 1900. Dodd, Mead & Co.
--Grandmother Elsie. LC 3-223622. (A Sequel to "Elsie's Widowhood"). 298 p. front. 18 1/2cm. c.1882. Dodd, Mead & Company.
--Grandmother Elsie, 1 of 25 vols. (The Elsie Bks). N.D. Set. Dodd, Mead & Co.
--Mildred and Elsie. (The Mildred Ser.). N.D. A. L. Burt Co.
--Mildred and Elsie. (The Mildred Ser.). N.D. Set. Dodd, Mead & Company.
--Mildred at Home. (The Mildred Ser.). N.D. A. L. Burt Co.
--Mildred At Home, 1 of 7 vols. (The Mildred Ser.). N.D. Set. Set. Dodd, Mead & Company.
--Mildred at Home: With Something About Her Relatives and Friends. LC 12-324851. 327 p. front., 2 pl. 17 1/2cm. c.1884. Dodd, Mead & Company.
--Mildred at Roselands. (The Mildred Ser.). N.D. A. L. Burt.
--Mildred at Roselands, 1 of 7 vols. (Mildred Series). N.D. Set. Dodd, Mead & Co.
--Mildred Keith. (The Mildred Ser.). N.D. A. L. Burt Co.
--Mildred Keith, 1 of 6 vols. (The Mildred Ser.). N.D. Set. Set. Dodd, Mead & Company.
--Mildred's Boys and Girls. (The Mildred Ser.). N.D. A. L. Burt Co.
--Mildred's Boys and Girls. LC 12-32328. (A Sequel to "Mildred's Married Life"). 346 p. front., plates. 17 1/2cm. (The Mildred Ser.). c.1886. Dodd, Mead, and Company.
--Mildred's Married Life, 1 of 7 vols. (The Mildred Ser.). N.D. Set. Dodd, Mead & Co.
--Mildred's Married Life: Or, a Winter with Elsie Dinsmore. (The Mildred Ser.). N.D. A. L. Burt Co.
--Mildred's New Daughter, 1 of 7 vols. (The Mildred Ser.). N.D. Set. Dodd, Mead & Co.
--Mildred's New Daughters. (The Mildred Ser.). N.D. A. L. Burt Co.
--Mysie's Work, and How She Did It. LC 12-32333. 360 p. front., plates. 15 1/2cm. c.1864. Presbyterian Board of Publication.
--A New Elsie Book. (The Finley Bks.). N.D. Set. Dodd, Mead & Co.
--An Old-Fashioned Boy, 1 of 7 vols. (The Finley Lib.). N.D. Set. Dodd, Mead & Co.
--An Old-Fashioned Boy. (Phoenix Ser.). N.D. Dodd, Mead & Company.
--Our Fred: Or, Seminary Life at Thurston, 1 of 7 vols. (The Finley Lib.). N.D. Set. Dodd, Mead & Co.
--Signing the Contract, and What it Cost, 1 of 7 vols. (The Finley Lib.). N.D. Dodd, Mead & Co.
--The Thorn in the Nest, 1 of 7 vols. (The Finley Lib.). N.D. Set. Dodd, Mead & Co.
--The Tragedy of Wild River Valley, 1 of 7 vols. (The Finley Lib.). N.D. Dodd, Mead & Co.
--Twiddledetwit. LC 98-583. 12cm. 127p. 1898. Dodd, Mead & Co.
--The Two Elsies. LC 3-223590. 302 p. front. 18cm. (The Elsie Bks.). c.1885. Dodd, Mead & Company.
--Wanted, a Pedigree, 1 of 7 vols. (The Finley Lib.). N.D. Set. Dodd, Mead & Co.

Finley, Ruth E.
--The Fireside Book of Ghost Stories. Wagenknecht, Edward, ed. N.D. Grosset & Dunlap.

Finley, Tom
--Diabolus Seeks Revenge. Finley, Tom, illus. LC 82-15069. (Illus.). 96p. (gr. 7 up). 1982. (ISBN 0-8307-0839-1). Regal.
Finley, Virginia & Mason, Beverly
--A Cat Called Room Eight. Martin, Valerie (1948-), illus. LC 66-14332. 59 p. illus. 27 cm. 1966. (ISBN 0-399-60085-X). Putnam.
Finley, William Lovell (1876-)
--Little Bird Blue. Horsfall, Robert Bruce (1869-1948), illus. LC 15-26652. 7 p. l., 3-60 p. 1 l. incl. front., illus., plates. 19 1/2cm. 1915. Houghton Mifflin Company.
Finn, Francis James (1859-1928)
--Ada Merton. LC 6-41133. 173 p. 17 1/2cm. 1896. B. Herder.
--Ada Merton. 4th ed. LC 8-30420. 173 p. 17 1/2cm. 1898. B. Herder.
--The Best Foot Forward, 1 of 8 vols. (Illus.). (Father Finn's Stories). N.D. Set. Benizger Brothers' Pub.
--The Best Foot Forward, and Other Stories. LC 287. v, 5-244 p. front. 19 1/2cm. 1900. Benziger Brother.
--Bobbie in Movieland. LC 21-17981. 206 p. incl. front. 19cm. 1921. Benziger Brothers.
--But Thy Love and Thy Grace. Svendsen, Charles C., illus. LC 1-255460. 138 p. incl. front. (port.) plates. 19cm. 1901. Benziger Brothers.
--Candles' Beams. LC 26-17771. 256 p. front. 19cm. 1926. Benziger Brothers.
--Claude Lightfoot: Or, How the Problem Was Solved, 1 of 8 vols. LC 6-41136. 245 p. front. 19 1/2cm. 1893. Benziger Brothers.
--Cupid of Campion. LC 16-21053. 232 p. front. 19cm. $0.8. 1916. Benziger Brothers.
--Ethelred Preston: Or, The Adventures of a Newcomer, 1 of 8 vols. LC 6-41135. 200 p. incl. front. 19 1/2cm. 1896. Benziger Brothers.
--Facing Danger. LC 19-161490. 197 p. 19cm. 1919. Benziger Brothers.
--The Fairy of the Snows. N.D. Benziger Bros.
--Harry Dee: Or, Making It Out, 1 of 8 vols. LC 6-411342. 284 p. front. 19 1/2cm. 1893. Benziger Brothers.
--His First and Last Appearance. Svendsen, Charles C., illus. 213 p. incl. front. (port.) illus. 20 1/2cm. 1900. Benziger Brothers.
--His Luckiest Year: A Sequel to "Lucky Bob,". LC 18-19297. 256 p. incl. front. 19cm. 1918. Benziger Brothers.
--Lord Bountiful. LC 23-17343. viii, 9-237 p. front. 19cm. 1923. Benziger Brothers.
--Lucky Bob. LC 17-28190. 248 p. front. 19cm. 1917. Benziger Brothers.
--Mostly Boys. 152 p. front. 17 1/2cm. 1895. Benziger Brothers.
--Mostly Boys: Short Stories, 1 of 8 vols. enl. ed. LC 6-411380. 224 p. front. 19 1/2cm. 1897. Benziger Brothers.
--My Strange Friend. LC 7-305. 70 p. 15 1/2cm. 1897. Benziger Brothers.
--My Strange Friend. (Our Boys' and Girls' Lib.). N.D. Benziger Brothers' Pub.
--New Faces and Old: Short Stories. LC 6-41139. 137 p. 17 1/2cm. 1896. B. Herder.
--New Faces and Old: Short Stories. 4th ed. LC 8-30421. 137 p. 17 1/2cm. 1897. B. Herder.
--On the Run. LC 22-23916. 222 p. front. 19cm. 1922. Benziger Brother.
--Percy Wynn: Or, Making a Boy of Him, 1 of 8 vols. (Illus.). (Father Finn's Stories). N.D. Set. Benziger Brothers' Pub.
--Percy Wynn: Or, Making a Boy of Him. LC 6-411411. viii, 9-216 p. incl. front. 19cm. c.1889. Catholic Companion Print.
--Sunshine and Freckles. LC 25-19911. vi, 7-192 p. front. 19cm. 1925. Benziger Brothers.
--That Football Game: And What Came of It. LC 4-16135. 256 p. front. 19 1/2cm. 1897. Benziger Brothers.
--That Football Game: and What Came of It, 1 of 8 vols. (Illus.). (Father Finn's Stories). N.D. Set. Benziger Brothers' Pub.
--That Office Boy. N.D. Benziger Bros.
--Tom Playfair: Or, Making a Start. 255 p. front. 19 1/2cm. 1892. Benziger Brothers.
--Tom Playfair: Or, Making a Start, 1 of 8 vols. (Illus.). (Father Finn's Stories). N.D. Set. Benziger Brothers' Pub.
Finn-Thiele
--The Wager of Gerald O'Rourke. N.D. Benziger Brothers.
Finn, William Joseph (1881-) & Scholastica, Mary (1893-), eds.
--Song Wings. Oehler, Bernice Olivia (1881-), illus. LC 42-4472. 75, 5 p. illus. 21 1/2 cm. (Youth music series.). c.1940. C. C. Birchard & Company.
Finnegan, Edward G.
--Children's Bible Stories. Stahl, Ben F. & Fleishman, Seymour (1918-), illus. LC 75-18758. (Illus.). (Treasure House Bks). (ps-12). 1978. Delair.
--A Treasure House Book of Children's Bible Stories. Stahl, Ben F. & Fleishman, Seymour (1918-), illus. LC 75-18758. (Illus.). 253 p. 29cm. c.1977. (ISBN 0-8326-1803-9). Consolidated Book Publishers.

--A Lantern in the Window. Johnson, Eugene Harper, illus. LC 57-7564. (Illus.). 126 p. 23cm. 1957. T. Nelson.
--Like Nothing at All. Weisgard, Leonard Joseph (1916-), illus. LC 60-9159. (Illus.). (ps-3). 1979. (ISBN 0-690-49379-7, TYC-J). Har-Row.
--Like Nothing at all. Weisgard, Leonard Joseph (1916-), illus. LC 62-12213. (Illus.). 40p. 1962. J. Thomas Y Crowell Company.
--Listen, Rabbit. Shimin, Symeon (1902-), illus. LC 64-10860. (Illus.). (gr. k-3). 1964. (ISBN 0-690-49592-7, TYC-J). Har-Row. **Award: (ALA).**
--My Cat Has Eyes of Sapphire Blue. Angel, Marie (1923-), illus. LC 72-13925. (Illus.). 24 p. 1973. (ISBN 0-690-56637-9). Crowell.
--My Cousin Abe. Vosburgh, Leonard W. (1912-), illus. LC 62-159860. 285p. 22cm. c.1962. Nelson. **Award: (ALA).**
--My First Hanukkah Book. Kiedrowski, Priscilla, illus. Child's World (Firm) LC 84-21510. (Illus.). 31 p. 25cm. c.1985. (ISBN 0-516-02905-3). Childrens Press.
--My Mother and I. Mizumura, Kazue, illus. LC 67-3271. (Illus.). 32 p. 26cm. 1967. Crowell.
--Nine Cheers for Christmas: A Christmas Pageant. 1945. Row Peterson.
--No Accounting for Tastes. Gaulke, Gloria & Taylor, Paul, illus. LC 72-89030. (Illus.). 42 p. 27cm. (Bowmar nature series). 1973. (ISBN 0-8372-0868-8). Bowmar.
--Now That Days Are Colder. Laite, Gordon (1925-), illus. LC 72-89024. (Illus.). 42 p. 27cm. (Bowmar nature series). 1973. (ISBN 0-8372-0862-9). Bowmar.
--Off to the Gold Fields. Powers, Richard M. Gorman (1921-), illus. LC 55-10006. 158p. illus. 21cm. 1955. T. Nelson.
--Once We Went on a Picnic. Chen, Tony (1929-), illus. LC 75-9836. (Illus.). 25 p. 1975. (ISBN 0-690-00955-0). (ISBN 0-690-00956-9). Crowell.
--Out in the Dark and Daylight. Owens, Gail, illus. LC 78-22492. (Illus.). 151 p. 21cm. c.1980. (ISBN 0-06-021902-5). (ISBN 0-06-021903-3). Harper & Row.
--Over the Hills to Nugget. James, Sandra, illus. LC 49-11177. 121p. 1949. Aladdin Books.
--Plays About Our Nation's Songs: Royalty-Free Plays, Pageants, and Programs Dramatizing in Songs and Scenes the Story of America Growing. 188p. 21cm. c.1962. Plays, Inc.
--Rabbits, Rabbits. 1st ed. Niemann, Gail, illus. LC 82-48849. p. cm. c.1983. (ISBN 0-06-021896-7). (ISBN 0-06-021899-1). Harper & Row.
--Runny Days, Sunny Days. Fisher, Aileen Lucia (1906-), illus. (Illus.). 126p. illus. 24cm. (gr. 1-4). 1958. (ISBN 0-200-00012-8). Abelard.
--Secret in the Barrel. Orig. Title: Off to the Gold Fields. (gr. 4-6). N.D (StarLine). Schol Bk Serv.
--Set the Stage for Christmas. 1948. Row Peterson.
--Sing, Little Mouse. Shimin, Symeon (1902-), illus. LC 68-11061. (Illus.). 36 p. 27cm. 1969. Crowell.
--Skip (Pub. by Nelson). (gr. 4-6). 1972 (Starline). Schol Bk Serv.
--Skip. Vaughan-Jackson, Genevieve (1913-), illus. LC 58-10587. 157p. 1958. Nelson.
--Skip Around the Year. Fiammenghi, Gioia (1929-), illus. LC 67-8315. (Illus.). 1 v. (unpaged). 22cm. 56p. (Crowell holiday book). 1967. Crowell.
--Sleepy Heads. Thomas, Phero, illus. LC 72-89028. (Lettering by Paul Taylor). (Illus.). 42 p. (Bowmar nature series). 1973. (ISBN 0-8372-0866-1). Bowmar.
--Summer of Little Rain. Stevens, Gloria, illus. LC 61-6806. (Illus.). 159 p. 24cm. 1961. Nelson.
--Tail Twisters. Pucci, Albert John (1920-), illus. LC 72-89025. (Lettering by Paul Taylor). (Illus.). 43 p. 25cm. (Bowmar nature series). 1973. (ISBN 0-8372-0863-7). Bowmar.
--That's Why. LC 46-16159. 96 p. illus. 21 cm. 1946. T. Nelson & Sons.
--Trapped by the Mountain Storm. Collins, J. Fred, illus. 1950. Aladdin Books.
--A Tree to Trim: A Christmas Play. 1945. Row Peterson.
--Up the Windy Hill: A Book of Merry Verse with Silhouettes. Fisher, Aileen Lucia (1906-), illus. LC 53-6805. 128p. illus. 24cm. 1953. Abelard Press.
--Up, up the Mountain. Riswold, Gilbert, illus. (Illus.). 32 p. 26cm. 1968. T. Y. Crowell Co.
--Valley of the Smallest: The/Life Story of a Shrew. Zallinger, Jean Day (1918-), illus. (Illus.). 1966. Crowell. **Award: (IBBY).**
--We Went Looking. Angel, Marie (1923-), illus. LC 68-13578. (Illus.). 25 p. 22cm. 1968. (ISBN 0-690-87150-3). (ISBN 0-690-87151-1). Crowell.
--What Happened to Toyland. 1945. Row Peterson.
--Where does Everyone Go?. Adams, Adrienne (1906-), illus. LC 61-6135. 1961. T. Crowell.
--Witches Beware. 1948. Play Club.
--You Don't Look Like Your Mother," Said the Robin to the Fawn. Forberg, Ati, pseud. (1925-), illus. Forberg, Beate Gropius. LC 72-89029. (Lettering by Paul Taylor). (Illus.). 42 p. 32cm. (Bowmar nature series). 1973. (ISBN 0-8372-0867-X). Bowmar.

Fisher, Aileen Lucia (1906-) & Rabe, Olive Hanson (0000-1968)
--Patriotic Plays and Programs. LC 56-7109. 418p. 21cm. 1956. Plays, Inc.
--United Nations Plays and Programs. rev. ed. (gr. 3-12). 1961. (ISBN 0-8238-0021-0). Plays Inc Pub.
--We Alcotts: The Story of Louisa M. Alcott's Family As Seen Through the Eyes of "Marmee," Mother of Little Women. Raskin, Ellen (1928-1984), illus. (Illus.). 278 p. 22cm. 1968. Atheneum.
--We Dickinsons: The Life of Emily Dickinson As Seen Through the Eyes of Her Brother Austin. Raskin, Ellen (1928-1984), illus. LC 65-21723. 246 p. illus. 22 cm. 1965. Atheneum.

Fisher, Alfred Hugh (1867-)
--Frolics with Uncle Yule. LC 29-1665. 63 p. illus. 28 cm. 1928. Hale, Cushman & Flint.

Fisher & Brother, Philadelphia
--Fun for Little People. LC 32-21967. cover-title, p. 33-40. col. illus. 14 cm. (Fisher and brother's funny toys). N.D. Fisher & Brother.
--Little Red Riding -Hood: The History of Little Red Riding-Hood. LC 32-30571. 8 p. illus. 15 cm. (Fisher's toy books). N.D. Fisher & Brother.
--Merry Making Riddles. LC 32-30566. cover-title, p. 55-62. col. illus. 14 cm. (Fisher and brother's funny toys). N.D. Fisher & Brother.
--Merry Stories by a Merry Little Man. LC 32-30567. cover-title, p. 9-16 col. illus. 14 cm. (Fisher and brother's funny toys). 1860. Fisher & Brother.
--Rhymes for Very Little People. LC 28-202892. cover-title, p. 68-75. col. illus. 14 cm. (Fisher and brother's funny toys). N.D. Fisher & Brother.

Fisher, Ann (1893-)
--The Lost Dove: The Story of Two Doves, Talsy and Jeeper. Luke, Keye, illus. LC 53-7408. 118p. illus. 28cm. 1953. House-Warven.

Fisher, Anne Benson (1898-)
--Bears, Pirates and Silver Lace: Stories of Old California. Nesbitt, Philip, illus. LC 44-9408. 5 p. l., 134 p. col. front., illus., plates (part col.) 20 1/2 cm. 1944. (ISBN 0-8323-0155-8). (ISBN 0-8323-0255-4). Binfords & Mort.
--Stories California Indians Told. N.D. E . M. Hale and Co.
--Stories California Indians Told. Robbins, Ruth (1917-), illus. LC 57-8065. (Illus.). (gr. 3-7). 1957. (ISBN 0-395-27723-X). Parnassus.

Fisher, Barbara, ed. see Wilkins, Sarah & Mennella, Roxanna.

Fisher, Barbara (1940-)
--Big Harold & Tiny Enid. (Illus.). 26p. (Orig.). (gr. 1-3). 1975. (ISBN 0-934830-01-0). Ten Penny.
--Car Boy. Fisher, Barbara (1940-), illus. (Illus.). 29p. (Orig.). (gr. k-2). 1977. (ISBN 0-934830-02-9). Ten Penny.
--Dan. Fisher, Barbara (1940-), illus. (Illus.). 20p. (Orig.). (gr. k-5). 1981. (ISBN 0-934830-19-3). Ten Penny.
--Max St. Peter McBride & Theodora. Fisher, Barbara (1940-), illus. (Illus.). 58p. (Orig.). (gr. k-3). 1981. (ISBN 0-934830-20-7). Ten Penny.
--Philpin's Tree. (Illus.). 12p. (Orig.). (gr. 1-3). 1976. (ISBN 0-934830-00-2). Ten Penny.

Fisher, Barbara (1940-) & Spiegel, Richard (1947-), eds.
--Poetry Hunter, No. 1. (Illus.). 92p. (Orig.). (gr. k-6). 1981. (ISBN 0-934830-21-5). Ten Penny.

Fisher, Barbara (1940-) & Spiegel, Richard Alan (1947-), eds.
--In Search of a Song, Vol. 3. (Illus.). 64p. (Orig.). (gr. 1-6). 1982. (ISBN 0-934830-27-4). Ten Penny.
--In Search of a Song: PS-114, Vol. 1. (Illus.). 90p. (Orig.). (gr. k-6). 1981. (ISBN 0-934830-25-8). Ten Penny.
--In Search of a Song: PS-276, Vol. 2. (Illus.). 90p. (Orig.). (gr. k-6). 1981. (ISBN 0-934830-26-6). Ten Penny.
--More Poetry Hunter. (Illus.). 92p. (Orig.). 1981. (ISBN 0-934830-23-1). Ten Penny.
--Still More Poetry Hunter. (Illus.). 36p. (Orig.). (gr. k-6). 1981. (ISBN 0-934830-24-X). Ten Penny.
--Subway Slams. (Illus.). 48p. (Orig.). (gr. k-8). 1981. (ISBN 0-934830-22-3). Ten Penny.

Fisher, Clavin Cargill (1912-)
--A Spy at Ticonderoga. Johns, Jeanne, illus. LC 75-14203. (Illus.). 143 p. 22cm. 1975. (ISBN 0-912944-30-7). Berkshire Traveller Press.

Fisher, Cyrus T., pseud., see Teilhet, Darwin Le Ora.

Fisher, Cyrus T., pseud.
--Ab Carmody's Treasure. Block, Lou, illus. 280p. (gr. 7-10). N.D. Henry Holt & Co.

Fisher, David
--The Criminal Career of Vinegar Tom. Fisher, David, illus. LC 63-7059. (Illus.). 1 v. (unpaged. 26cm. 1963. Abelard-Schuman.
--Tilly Ballooning. Fisher, David, illus. LC 61-5409. (Illus.). 48p. 1961. Abelard-Schumann.

Fisher, Dorothea Frances Canfield, Mrs., jt. auth. see Cleghorn, Sarah Norcliffe.

Fisher, Dorothea Frances Canfield, Mrs., jt. auth. see Lichtenberger, Andre.

Fisher, Dorothea Frances Canfield, Mrs. (1879-1958), ed. see Richards, Laura Elizabeth Howe, Mrs.

Fisher, Dorothea Frances Canfield, Mrs. (1879-1958)
--The Bent Twig. 334p. Repr. 1981. (ISBN 0-89966-343-5). Buccaneer Bks.
--The Bent Twig. 340p. Repr. 1981. (ISBN 0-89967-018-0). Harmony & Co.
--Made-to-Order Stories. Lathrop, Dorothy Pulis (1891-1980), illus. N.D. Harcourt Brace & Co.
--Nothing Ever Happens and How It Does: Sixteen True Stories. Bristol, Esther Boston (1876-), illus. LC 40-31720. ix, 180 p. illus. 21 cm. 1940. The Beacon Press.
--Our Independence and the Constitution. Doremus, Robert (1913-), illus. LC 50-10543. 188 p. col. illus. 22 cm. (Landmark books 5). 1950. Random House.
--Paul Revere and the Minute Men. Price, Norman Mills (1877-1951), illus. LC 50-11711. 181 p. col. illus. 22 cm. (Landmark books 4). 1950. Random House.
--Something Old, Something New: Stories of People Who Are America. Shipman, Mary Dana, illus. LC 49-10969. 191 p. illus. 21 cm. 1949. W. R. Scott.
--Tell Me a Story: A Book of Stories to Tell to Children. Gergely, Tibor (1900-1978), illus. LC 40-8050. 64p. (The Crabtree Basic Ser.). N.D. University Publishing Co.
--Understood Betsy. 2 p. l., 271 p. col. front. 21 cm. 1937. Grosset & Dunlap.
--Understood Betsy. 2nd ed. LC 70-158839. (Illus.). (gr. 4 up). 1972. (ISBN 0-03-086639-1). HR&W.
--Understood Betsy. 1st Rev. ed. Alexander, Martha G. (1920-), illus. LC 70-158839. (Illus.). 211 p. 22cm. 1971, c.1972. (ISBN 0-03-086639-1). (ISBN 0-03-086640-5). Holt, Rinehart, and Winston.
--Understood Betsy. Barnes, Catherine J. (1918-), illus. LC 46-22774. 4 p. l., 213 p. illus. 21 cm. 1946. H. Holt and Company.
--Understood Betsy. Williamson, Ada Clendenin, illus. LC 17-23050. 3 p. l., 271 p. front., plates. 19 1/2 cm. 1917. H. Holt and Company.

Fisher, Edward
--The Animal Song Book. 1963. St Martin's Press.

Fisher, Ellen
--Tell Me, Cat. Tiffany, Virginia, illus. (ps-1). 1970. (ISBN 0-307-10813-9, Golden Pr). Western Pub.

Fisher, Garyl G
--The Legend of Teton Tony (King of the Mountain Rams). Lyon, Norma Madge, illus. LC 74-24352. (Illus.). 29 p. and phonodisc (2s. 7 in. 33 1/3 rpm.) in pocket. 22cm. 1971. Distributed by Pix-Audio Productions.
--The Yellowstone Adventures of Pretty Paw and Little Claw. Lyon, Norma Madge, illus. LC 74-16537. (Illus.). 38 p. 22cm. 1970. Parliament Publishers.

Fisher, Harriet Irene
--Aunt Hattie's Bible Stories. 1941. Moody.
--The Story of Jesus. 126p. 1949. Moody.

Fisher, L
--Susie's Hair. (Illus.). 1965. Holt, Rinehart and Winston, Inc.

Fisher, Laura Harrison (1934-)
--Amy and the Sorrel Summer. 1st ed. Greenwald, Sheila, pseud. (1934-), illus. Green, Sheila Ellen. LC 64-14575. 190 p. illus. 22 cm. 1964. Holt, Rinehart and Winston.
--Charlie Dick. 1st ed. Negri, Rocco (1932-), illus. LC 74-80326. (Illus.). 170 p. 22cm. 1972. (ISBN 0-03-081499-5). (ISBN 0-03-081603-3). Holt, Rinehart and Winston.
--Never Try Nathaniel. LC 68-10077. 216 p. 22cm. 1968. Holt, Rinehart and Winston.
--You Were Princess Last Time. Grossman, Nancy S. (1940-), illus. LC 65-22943. (Illus.). 158p. (gr. 5-7). 1965. (ISBN 0-03-053455-0). (ISBN 0-03-053460-7). HR&W.

Fisher, Lena Leonard
--Lantern Stories. N.D. Abingdon Press.
--Lantern Stories. LC 13-80571. 96 p. 19 cm. $0.5. c.1913. Eaton & Mains.

Fisher, Leonard Everett, jt. auth. see Fisher, Margery M.

Fisher, Leonard Everett (1924-)
--Across the Sea from Galway. Fisher, Leonard Everett (1924-), illus. LC 75-9513. (Illus.). 103 p. 23cm. 1975. (ISBN 0-590-07345-1). Four Winds Press.
--Boxes! Boxes!. LC 83-14761. (Illus.). 26 p. 32p. (ps-1). 1984. (ISBN 0-670-18334-2, Viking Kestrel). Viking.
--The Death of Evening Star: The Diary of a Young New England Whaler. 1st ed. Fisher, Leonard Everett (1924-), illus. LC 75-164719. (Illus.). 125 p. 25cm. 1972. Doubleday. **Award: (ALA).**
--A Head Full of Hats. Fisher, Leonard Everett (1924-), illus. LC 62-10133. (Illus.). 32 p. 26cm. 1962. Dial Press.
--Letters from Italy. Fisher, Leonard Everett (1924-), illus. LC 76-42462. (Illus.). 100 p. 24cm. c.1977. (ISBN 0-590-07408-3). Four Winds Press.
--Noonan: A Novel About Baseball, ESP, and Time Warps. LC 77-80887. (Illus.). 125 p. 24cm. c.1978. (ISBN 0-385-11692-6). (ISBN 0-385-11693-4). Doubleday.
--Pumpers, Boilers, Hooks and Ladders: A Book of Fire Engines. Fisher, Leonard Everett (1924-), illus. (Illus.). 34 p. 1961. Dial Press.
--Pushers, Spads, Jennies and Jets: A Book of Airplanes. LC 61-12906. (Illus.). unpaged. 1961. Dial Press.
--A Russian Farewell. Fisher, Leonard Everett (1924-), illus. LC 80-342. p. cm. c.1980. (ISBN 0-590-07525-X). Four Winds Press.
--Storm at the Jetty. LC 80-24402. (Illus.). 32 p. 1981. (ISBN 0-670-67214-9). Viking Press.
--Sweeney's Ghost. 1st ed. Fisher, Leonard Everett (1924-), illus. LC 73-9027. (Illus.). 133 p. 24cm. 1975. (ISBN 0-385-08800-0). (ISBN 0-385-08800-0). (ISBN 0-385-08800-0). Doubleday.
--The Warlock of Westfall. 1st ed. Fisher, Leonard Everett (1924-), illus. LC 73-82625. (Illus.). 119 p. 25cm. 1974. (ISBN 0-385-07125-6). (ISBN 0-385-07125-6). Doubleday.

Fisher, Leonard Everett (1924-), adapted by.
--The Seven Days of Creation. Fisher, Leonard Everett (1924-), illus. LC 81-2952. (Illus.). 32p. (ps-3). 1981. (ISBN 0-8234-0398-X). Holiday. **Award: (ALA).**

Fisher, Lois I (1948-)
--Puffy P. Pushycat, Problem Solver. Payson, Dale (1943-), illus. LC 82-19833. p. cm. 1983. (ISBN 0-396-08119-3). Dodd, Mead.
--Rachel Vellars, How Could You?. LC 83-27481. c.1984. (ISBN 0-396-08327-7). Dodd, Mead.
--Radio Robert. LC 84-24706. 128p. (gr. 4 up). 1985. (ISBN 0-396-08503-2). Dodd, Mead.
--Sarah Dunes, Weird Person. LC 80-2780. 152 p. 21cm. c.1981. (ISBN 0-396-07929-6). Dodd, Mead.
--Wretched Robert. LC 81-17526. 110 p. 21cm. c.1982. (ISBN 0-396-08039-1). Dodd, Mead.

Fisher, Lois Jeannette (1909-)
--Bible Picture Stories. (Illus.). N.D. Childrens Press Inc.
--Bill and His Neighbors. N.D. Houghton Mifflin Co.
--Lois and Looie: Inside a TV Show. Fisher, Lois Jeannette (1909-) & Murr, Karl, illus. LC 51-12197. unpaged. illus. 24 cm. 1951. Children's Press.

Fisher, Lucretia
--The Butterfly and the Stone. Jardine, Thomas, illus. LC 80-29260. p. cm. 1981. (ISBN 0-916144-69-0). Stemmer House Publishers.
--Two Monsters: A Fable. Jardine, Thomas, illus. LC 76-21684. (Illus.). 48 p. 1976. (ISBN 0-916144-07-0). (ISBN 0-916144-08-9). Stemmer House.

Fisher, Margery M & Fisher, Leonard Everett (1924-)
--But Not Our Daddy. LC 62-15393. (Illus.). 25 p. 22cm. 1962. Dial Press.

Fisher, Margery Tuner (1913-), ed. see Horne, Richard Henry.

Fisher, Margery Turner (1913-), ed.
--Open the Doors. LC 67-13821. 397 p. illus. 23 cm. 1967, c.1965. World Pub. Co.

Fisher, Miriam Louise Scharfe (1939-)
--Pamela Goes to School. Rev. ed. Bigham, John C., illus. LC 62-18927. unpaged. illus. 23 cm. reading-go-round books. c.1962. E. C. Seale.

Fisher, Paul R. (1960-)
--The Ash Staff. LC 79-11731. 179 p. 22cm. 1979. (ISBN 0-689-30708-X). Atheneum.
--The Hawks of Fellheath. LC 79-22080. (Illus.). 211 p. 22cm. 1980. (ISBN 0-689-30741-1). Atheneum.
--Mont Cant Gold. LC 80-23851. (Illus.). 251 p. 22cm. 1981. (ISBN 0-689-30808-6). Atheneum.
--The Princess and the Thorn. LC 80-12309. (Illus.). 237 p. 22cm. 1980. (ISBN 0-689-30776-4). Atheneum.

Fisher, Richard
--The Very First Time. N.D. Doubleday.

Fisher, Robert, ed.
--Amazing Monsters: Verses to Thrill and Chill. Allen, Rowena, illus. LC 82-1493. p. cm. 1982. (ISBN 0-571-11850-X). Faber and Faber.

--Roy Blakeley's Tangled Trail. (The Roy Blakeley Bks.). N.D. Grosset & Dunlap.
--Roy Blakeley's Wild Goose Chase. Durant, Charles, illus. LC 30-39538. vi, 218 p. front. 19 1/2 cm. c.1930. Grosset & Dunlap.
--Skinny McCord. (The Buddy Bks For Boys). N.D. Grosset & Dunlap.
--Skinny McCord. Hastings, Howard Livingston (1887-), illus. LC 28-6171. vi p., 1 l., 235 1 p. front., plates. 19 1/2 cm. c.1928. Grosset & Dunlap.
--Spiffy Henshaw. (The Buddy Bks for Boys). N.D. Grosset & Dunlap.
--Spiffy Henshaw. Hastings, Howard Livingston (1887-), illus. LC 29-10958. 3 p. l., 214 p. front., plates. 19 1/2 cm. c.1929. Grosset & Dunlap.
--The Story of Terrible Terry. (Buddy Bks. for Boys). N.D. Grosset & Dunlap.
--The Story of Terrible Terry. Hastings, Howard Livingston (1887-), illus. LC 30-12297. vi, 217 p. front., plates. 19 1/2 cm. c.1930. Grosset & Dunlap.
--Tom Slade at Bear Mountain. Hastings, Howard Livingston (1887-), illus. LC 25-100635. vi p., 1 l., 221 p. front., plates. 19 1/2 cm. c.1925. Grosset & Dunlap.
--Tom Slade at Black Lake. (The Tom Slade Bks.). N.D. Grosset & Dunlap.
--Tom Slade at Shadow Isle. Hastings, Howard Livingston (1887-), illus. LC 28-211859. vi, 211 p. front., plates. 19 1/2 cm. c.1928. Grosset & Dunlap.
--Tom Slade at Temple Camp. Rogers, Walter S., illus. LC 17-9347. 3 p. l., 209 p. front., plates. 20 cm. c.1917. Grosset & Dunlap.
--Tom Slade, Boy Scout. (The Tom Slade Bks.). N.D. Grosset & Dunlap.
--Tom Slade, Forest Ranger. (The Tom Slade Bks.). N.D. Grosset & Dunlap.
--Tom Slade in the Haunted Cavern. Hastings, Howard Livingston (1887-), illus. LC 29-110908. vi p., 1 l., 211 p. front., 1 illus., plates. 19 1/2 cm. (His Tom Slade books). c.1929. Grosset & Dunlap.
--Tom Slade in The North Woods. (The Tom Slade Bks). N.D. Grosset & Dunlap.
--Tom Slade, Motorcycle Dispatch Bearer. (The Tom Slade Bks.). N.D. Grosset & Dunlap.
--Tom Slade on a Transport. LC 19-2189. vi, 198 p. front., plates. 19 1/2 cm. c.1918. Grosset & Dunlap.
--Tom Slade on Mystery Trail. (The Tom Slade Bks.). N.D. Grosset & Dunlap.
--Tom Slade on Overlook Mountain. Hastings, Howard Livingston (1887-), illus. LC 23-101001. 4 p. l., 229 p. front., plates. 19 1/2 cm. c.1923. Grosset & Dunlap.
--Tom Slade on the River. (The Tom Slade Bks.). N.D. Grosset & Dunlap.
--Tom Slade Picks a Winner. (The Tom Slade Bks.). N.D. Grosset & Dunlap.
--Tom Slade,. The Boy Scout of the Moving Pictures. N.D. Grosset & Dunlap.
--Tom Slade With the Boys Over There. (The Tom Slade Bks.). N.D. Grosset & Dunlap.
--Tom Slade with the Colors. (The Tom Slade Bks.). N.D. Grosset & Dunlap.
--Tom Slade with the Flying Corps. (The Tom Slade Bks.). N.D. Grosset & Dunlap.
--Tom Slade's Double Dare. Owen, Robert Emmett (1878-), illus. LC 22-3896. 3 p. l., 216 p. front., plates. 19 1/2 cm. c.1922. Grosset & Dunlap.
--Uncle Sam's Outdoor Magic: Bobby Cullen with the Reclamation Workers. LC 16-22050. 4 p. l., 3-312, 1 p. front., plates. 19 1/2 cm. 1916. Harper & Brothers.
--Westy Martin. (The Westy Martin Bks.). N.D. Grosset & Dunlap.
--Westy Martin in the Land of the Purple Sage. Hastings, Howard Livingston (1887-), illus. LC 29-10221. 3 p. l., 199 p. front., plates. 19 1/2 cm. (His Westy Martin books). c.1929. Grosset & Dunlap.
--Westy Martin in the Rockies. (The Westy Martin Bks.). N.D. Grosset & Dunlap.
--Westy Martin in the Sierras. Machtey, illus. LC 31-13100. 3 p. l., 205 p. front., plates. 19 1/2 cm. (His Westy Martin books). c.1931. Grosset & Dunlap.
--Westy Martin in the Yellowstone. LC 24-194207. viii, 229 p. front., plates. 19 1/2 cm. c.1924. Grosset & Dunlap.
--Westy Martin on the Mississippi. Hastings, Howard Livingston (1887-), illus. LC 30-122967. 3 p. l., 210 p. front. 19 1/2 cm. (His Westy Martin books). c.1930. Grosset & Dunlap.
--Westy Martin on the Old Indian Trail. Hastings, Howard Livingston (1887-), illus. LC 28-18112. vi, 210 p. front., plates. 19 1/2 cm. (His Westy Martin books). c.1928. Grosset & Dunlap.
--Westy Martin on the Sante Fe Trail. (The Westy Martin Bks.). N.D. Grosset & Dunlap.
--Wigwag Weigand. Hastings, Howard Livingston (1887-), illus. LC 29-10213. vi, 214 p. front., plates. 19 1/2 cm. (The Buddy Books for Boys). c.1929. Grosset & Dunlap.

Fitzpatrick, Edward Augustus (1884-)
--Religious Poems for Little Folks. LC 36-23540. 128 p. incl. front., illus. 19 cm. (Half-title: Poetry helps for the Highway to heaven series). c.1936. The Bruce Publishing Company.

Fitzpatrick, Eva & Stubbs, Joanna
--Kirsty at the Lodge. (Illus.). (ps-5). N.D. (ISBN 0-571-09769-3). Faber & Faber.

Fitzpatrick, Kathleen
--The Weans of Rowallan. Bacon, Peggy, pseud. (1895-), illus. Bacon, Margaret Frances. LC 37-25068. xviii, 236 p. incl. front., illus. 19 1/2 cm. 1937. Coward-McCann, Inc.

Fitzroy, Olivia
--The Island of Birds. Sheppard, Raymond, illus. (Illus.). 252p. 1960. (ISBN 0-685-21256-4). Lawrence Verry Inc.

Fitzsimmons, Cortland
--Crimson Ice. N.D. Grosset & Dunlap.
--Death on the Diamond. N.D. Grosset & Dunlap.
--Seventy-Thousand Witnesses. (Detective Stories for Boys). N.D. Grosset & Dunlap.

Fitzsimons, Ruth Marie Mangan
--Christopher Listens. Beaton, Ruth, illus. LC 67-16463. (Illus.). (Second Grade Bk. Ser.). (gr. 2-3). 1967. (ISBN 0-513-00315-0). Denison.
--Make Believe with Mike. Smith, Riley K., photos by. (Illus.). 64 p. 28cm. 1968. T. S. Denison.

Fix, Betty S. (1900-)
--The Adventures of Idabell and Wakefield. LC 46-211011. v. col. illus. 29 x 28 1/2 cm. N.D. The Crosby House.

Fix, Philippe, jt. auth. see Fix, Rejane.

Fix, Philippe & Fix, Rejane
--Pink Elephant with Golden Spots. Fix, Philippe & Fix, Rejane, illus. (Illus.). 32p. (ps). 1971. (ISBN 0-307-60889-1, Golden Pr). Western Pub.

Fix, Rejane, jt. auth. see Fix, Philippe.

Fix, Rejane & Fix, Philippe
--The Kangaroo with a Hole in Her Pocket. Fix, Philippe, illus. LC 76-159827. (Illus.). 27 p. 33cm. 1971. Golden Press.

Fjell, Ingemar
--Jack Fox, Licensed Detective. Torrell, Staffan, illus. LC 68-18399. (Illus.). 147 p. 22cm. 1968. Coward-McCann.

Flack, Dora Dutson (1919-)
--Christmas Magic: A Treasury of Christmas Memories. LC 77-81884. x, 70 p. 23cm. 1977. (ISBN 0-88494-322-4). Bookcraft.

Flack, Marjorie see Hutchins, Pat, et al.

Flack, Marjorie (1897-1958)
--All Around the Town: The Story of a Boy in New York. Flack, Marjorie (1897-1958), illus. LC 29-21927. viii p., 1 l., 283 p. incl. illus., plates. col. front. 20 1/2 cm. 1929. Doubleday, Doran & Company, Inc.
--Angus and the Cat. Flack, Marjorie (1897-1958), illus. LC 31-32343. 32 p. illus. (part col.) 18 x 26 c. 1931. Doubleday, Doran & Company, Inc.
--Angus and the Ducks. Flack, Marjorie (1897-1958), illus. LC 30-26829. 32 p. illus. (part col.) 17 1/2 x 25 1/2 cm. 1930. Doubleday, Doran & Company, Inc.
--Angus and the Ducks. Flack, Marjorie (1897-1958), illus. 1939. Doubleday.
--Angus Lost. 1st ed. Flack, Marjorie (1897-1958), illus. LC 32-21558. (Illus.). 32p. 17 x 25cm. (Junior Bks.). 1932. Doubleday, Doran & Company.
--Angus Lost. Flack, Marjorie (1897-1958), illus. 1941. Doubleday.
--Ask Mister Bear. Flack, Marjorie (1897-1958), illus. (gr. k-3). 1968. (ISBN 0-02-735390-7). Macmillan.
--Ask Mr. Bear. LC 32-22192. 32 p. col. illus. 21 cm. 1932. The Macmillian Company.
--Ask Mr. Bear. Flack, Marjorie (1897-1958), illus. (Illus.). 38 p. 21cm. (ps-1). 1958, c.1932. Macmillan.
--Away Goes Jonathan Wheeler. 1st ed. Larsson, Hilma (1920-), illus. LC 44-7576. 25 p. col. illus. 20 x 22 cm. c.1944. Garden City Publishing Co., Inc.
--The Boats on the River: Story. Barnum, Jay Hyde (1888-1962), illus. LC 46-11852. 31 p. col. illus. 26 x 31 1/2 cm. 1946. (ISBN 0-670-17725-3). The Viking Press. **Award: (RCM).**
--Christopher. Flack, Marjorie (1897-1958), illus. LC 35-192787. 40 p. illus. (part col.) 17 cm. N.D. C. Scribner's Sons.
--The Happy Birthday Letter. N.D. Houghton Mifflin co.
--Humphrey;. One Hundred Years Along The Wayside Withe a box Turtle. Flack, Marjorie (1897-1958), illus. LC 34-41052. 90 p. incl. col. front., illus. (part col.) plates (part. col.; part double) 27 1/2 cm. 1934. Doubleday, Doran & Company, Inc.
--I See a Kitty: A Story. Flack, Marjorie (1897-1958), illus. LC 43-17839. cover-title, 16 p. col. illus. 19 1/2 x 19 1/2 cm. 1943. The Garden City Publishing Co.
--Lucky Little Lena. Flack, Marjorie (1897-1958), illus. LC 37-36656. 38 p. col. illus. 22 cm. 1937. The Macmillan Company.
--The New Pet. Flack, Marjorie (1897-1958), illus. LC 43-512317. 32 p. illus. (part col.) 26 cm. 1943. Doubleday, Doran & Co., Inc.
--Restless Robin. 1937. E M Hale.
--The Restless Robin. Flack, Marjorie (1897-1958), illus. LC 37-37588. 46 p. col. illus. 19 x 23 cm. 1937. Houghton Mifflin Company.
--The Story About Ping. Wiese, Kurt (1887-1974), illus. LC 77-23403. p. cm. 1977, c.1933. (ISBN 0-14-050241-6). Puffin Books.
--The Story About Ping. Wiese, Kurt (1887-1974), illus. LC 33-29356. (Illus.). 32 p. 23cm. c.1933. The Viking Press.
--Tim Tadpole and the Great Bullfrog. LC 34-107538. 32 p. illus. (part col.) 20 cm. 1934. Doubleday, Doran & Company, Inc.
--Tim Tadpole and the Great Bullfrog. (Illus.). 1 v. (unpaged). 24cm. (Zephyr Book). 1973, c.1934. Doubleday.
--Topsy. Flack, Marjorie (1897-1958), illus. LC 35-677110. 32 p. illus. (part col.) 18 x 26 cm. 1935. Doubleday, Doran & Company, Incorporated.
--Topsy and Angus and the Cat. (Illus.). 18 x 26cm. 64p. 1935. Junior Literary Guild.
--Wag-Tail Bess. Flack, Marjorie (1897-1958), illus. LC 33-24660. 32 p. illus. (part col.) 18 x 26 cm. 1933. Doubleday, Doran & Company, Inc.
--Wait for William. 1935. E M Hale.
--Wait for William. Holberg, Richard A. (1889-1942) & Flack, Marjorie (1897-1958), illus. LC 35-185659. 33 p. illus. (part col.) 21 x 24 cm. c.1935. Houghton Mifflin Company.
--Walter, the Lazy Mouse. 1937. E M Hale.
--Walter, the Lazy Mouse. Flack, Marjorie (1897-1958), illus. LC 37-17507. 80 p. col. illus. 20 cm. 1937. Doubleday, Doran & Co., Inc.
--Walter, the Lazy Mouse. Flack, Marjorie (1897-1958), illus. LC 38-10339. 80 p. illus. 20 cm. 1937. The Junior Literary Guild Corporation.
--Walter, the Lazy Mouse. Szekeres, Cyndy (1933-), illus. (Illus.). 95 p. 24cm. 1963. Doubleday.
--What to do About Molly. Flack, Marjorie (1897-1958) & Larsson, Karl, illus. N.D. Houghton Mifflin Co.
--William and His Kitten. Flack, Marjorie (1897-1958), illus. LC 36-36264. 32 p. illus. (part col.) 20 x 24 cm. 1938. Houghton Mifflin Company.
--Willy Nilly. Flack, Marjorie (1897-1958), illus. LC 36-127516. 32 p. col. illus. 25 cm. N.D. The Macmillan Company.

Flack, Marjorie (1897-1958) & Benet, William Rose (1886-1950)
--Adolphus: Or, The Adopted Dolphin & Pirate's Daughter. LC 41-25515. 32 p. illus. 26 x 22 cm. 1941. Houghton Mifflin Company.

Flack, Marjorie (1897-1958) & Larsson, Karl
--Pedro. Larsson, Karl, illus. LC 40-7108. 96 p. incl. col. front., illus. (part col.) 23 x 19 cm. 1940. The Macmillan Company.

Flack, Marjorie (1897-1958) & Lomen, Helen
--Taktuk, an Arctic Boy. Flack, Marjorie (1897-1958), illus. LC 28-23541. 5 p. l., 139 p. incl. illus., plates. col. front. 21 cm. 1928. Doubleday, Doran & Company, Inc.

Flack, Naomi John White see Sellers, Naomi, pseud.

Flack, Naomi John White
--Charley's Clan. Sellers, Naomi, pseud. Unada, pseud. (1927-), illus. Gliewe, Unada Grace. LC 73-7470. (Illus.). 40 p. 23cm. 1973. (ISBN 0-8075-1124-2). A. Whitman.
--The Little Elephant Who Liked to Play. Sellers, Naomi, pseud. Mitsuhashi, Yoko, illus. LC 73-77986. (Illus.). 32 p. 23cm. (Magic circle book). 1974. (ISBN 0-663-25473-6). Ginn.

Flagg, Elisha (1885-)
--Rookie. Flagg, James Montgomery (1877-), illus. LC 4-7601. 62 p., 1 l. incl. front., plates. 24 1/2 cm. 1940. A. Whitman & Co.

Flagg, Elizabeth E
--The Flower by the Prison. LC 7-149101. 3 p. l., 5-323 p. front., plates. 18 cm. (Added t.-p.: New $500 prize series). 1871. N. H., G. T. Day & Co.

Flagg, Elizabeth E. & Atkinson, Mary E.
--New Five Hundred Dollar Prize Series, Part First: Containing "Short Comings and Long Goings," "One Year of My Life," "Hester's Happy Summer," etc, 6 vols. N.D. Set. D. Lothrop & Co.

Flagg, Mildred Buchanan, Mrs. (1886-)
--A Boy of Salem. Hamaker, William B., illus. Hart, Albert Bushnell, intro. by. LC 39-29724. ix, 13-171 p. incl. front., illus. 22 1/2 cm. 1939. T. Nelson and Sons.
--Plymouth Maid. LC 37-5365. 86 p. incl. front., illus. 19 1/2 cm. (Our changing world). 1937. T. Nelson and Sons.

Flaherty, Robert
--Louisiana Story. LC 77-159156. (Illus.). photos. 32p. (gr. 2 up). 1971. (ISBN 0-87807-032-X). (ISBN 0-87807-033-8). Windmill Bks.
--Nanook of the North. (Illus.). photos. 32p. 1971. (ISBN 0-87807-024-9). (ISBN 0-87807-025-7). Windmill Bks.

Flakkeberg, Ardo
--Sea Broke Through. Spier, Peter Edward (1927-), illus. (Illus.). (gr. 5-7). 1960. (ISBN 0-394-91591-7). Knopf.

Flanagan, Harley
--Stories & Illustrations. Flanagan, Harley, illus. Ginsberg, Allen (1926-), intro. by. LC 79-305058. (Illus.). 28 p. 21cm. c.1976. (ISBN 8-7875-9406-4). Charlatan Press.

Flanagan, Richard
--The Hunting Variety. 1973. (ISBN 0-399-11218-9). G.P. Putnam's Sons.

Flanders, E. H.
--Fifteen Songs From Looking Out of Jimmie. N.D. E. P. Dutton & Co.
--Looking Out of Jimmy. Pogany, Willy (1882-1955), illus. N.D. E. P. Dutton & Co.

Flanders, Isadore Elizabeth
--The Keeper of the Stars. LC 40-361073. viii, 9-32 p. 20 cm. c.1940. The Christopher Publishing Hose.

Flanders, Michael Henry (1922-1975)
--Captain Noah and His Floating Zoo. King, Harold (1945-), illus. LC 73-7053. (Illus.). 33 p. 24cm. 1973, c.1972. (ISBN 0-672-51841-4). Bobbs-Merrill.
--Creatures Great & Small. Minale, Marcello (1938-), illus. LC 65-22940. (Illus.). 40p. (gr. k-4). 1965. (ISBN 0-03-053485-2). (ISBN 0-03-053490-9). HR&W.
--The Sloth and the Gnu. Swan, Peter Charles (1921-), illus. LC 74-81668. (Illus.). 24 p. 18cm. (Stuff and nonsense books). 1974. (ISBN 0-7232-1811-0). F. Warne.

Flanders, Mildred Glawson (1897-)
--Land of the Free: A/Pioneer Story for Children. LC 55-43390. (Illus.). 20cm. 1949. Northam Pub. House.

Flashner, Amy, tr. see Timmermans, Felix.

Flather, J. H., ed. see Lamb, Charles (1775-1834) & Lamb, Mary Ann.

Flatz, Prunella C. Pott
--Hedgehog's Jacket: A Traditional Story. Flatz, Prunella C. Potts, illus. LC 67-25208. (Illus.). 1 v. 14cm. 48p. 1967. Hart Pub. Co.

Flaubert, Gustave (1821-1880)
--Golden Tales from Flaubert. (Golden Tales from Great Writers). N.D. Dodd, Mead & Co.
--Three Tales. N.D. Knopf.

Flaurier, Noel
--Young Folks Christmas Book. 96p. N.D. T. S. Denison & Co Inc.

Flavius, Josephus
--Josephus Flavius' Works, 3 vols. (Illus.). N.D. Lovell, Coryell & Co.

Flax, Zena, ed.
--The Old Fashioned Children's Storybook. LC 82-80875. (Illus.). 64p. 1982. (ISBN 0-448-12537-4, G&D). Putnam Pub Group.
--The Old-Fashioned Children's Storybook. Greenaway, Kate (1846-1901) & Rackham, Arthur (1867-1939), illus. Lewis, Naomi, frwd. by. (Illus.). 64p. 1980. (ISBN 0-671-41540-9). Wanderer Bks.

Flaxman, Traudi see Traudi, pseud.

Flaxman, Traudi (1942-)
--Kostas the Rooster. Traudi, pseud. Pinkney, Jerry (1939-), illus. LC 68-14071. (Illus.). 1&4 color ils. 32p. 26cm. (ps-1). 1968. (ISBN 0-688-51171-6). Lothrop.

Flayderman, Phillip Charles (1930-1969), ed.
--Great Narrative Poems. (gr. 9 up). 1968. Pyramid Pubns.
--One Hundred Great Poems. (gr. 9 up). N.D. Pyramid Pubns.

Fleharty, Ed
--Western Tales for Children. LC 57-31474. 55p. illus. 21cm. c.1956. College Pub. Co.

Fleischer, Leonore
--Blind Sunday. 171p. (gr. 7 up). 1982. (ISBN 0-590-32155-2, Wishing Star Bks). Scholastic Inc.

Fleischer, Leonore, adapted by.
--The Picture Storybook of the Neverending Story. LC 83-25463. c.1984. (ISBN 0-385-19380-7). Doubleday.

Fleischman, Albert Sidney (1920-)
--The Bloodhound Gang in the Case of Princess Tomorrow. Morrison, Bill (1935-), illus. LC 80-19518. (Illus.). 62 p. 19cm. 64p. (The Bloodhound Gang Ser.). c.1981. (ISBN 0-394-94674-X). (ISBN 0-394-84674-5). Random House/Children's Television Workshop.
--The Bloodhound Gang in the Case of the Cackling Ghost. Rao, Anthony, illus. LC 80-20059. (Illus.). 63 p. 19cm. c.1981. (ISBN 0-394-94673-1). (ISBN 0-394-84673-7). Random House/Children's Television Workshop.
--The Bloodhound Gang in the Case of the Flying Clock. Harmuth, William, illus. LC 80-28056. p. cm. 64p. (Bloodhound Gang Bks). 1981. (ISBN 0-394-84765-2). (ISBN 0-394-94765-7). Random House/Children's Television Workshop.
--The Bloodhound Gang in The Case of the Secret Message. Harmuth, William, illus. LC 80-28469. (Illus.). 64p. (Bloodhound Gang Bks.). (gr. 2-4). 1981. (ISBN 0-394-94764-9). (ISBN 0-394-84764-4). Random.
--The Bloodhound Gang in the Case of the Two Hundred & Sixty-Four Pound Burglar. Morrison, Bill (1935-), illus. Children's Television Workshop LC 81-12066. (Illus.). 62 p. 20cm. (Bloodhound Gang Books). 1982. (ISBN 0-394-95108-5). (ISBN 0-394-85108-0). Random House, Children's Television Workshop.
--The Bloodhound Gang's Secret Code Book. Morrison, Bill (1935-), illus. LC 82-3682. (Illus.). 64p. (A Three-Two-One Contact Bk.). (gr. 3-7). 1983. (ISBN 0-394-85231-1). Random.
--By the Great Horn Spoon!. Von Schmidt, Eric (1931-), illus. LC 63-13459. 198 p. illus. 21 cm. 1963. Little, Brown.
--Chauncy & the Grand Rascal. Von Schmidt, Eric (1931-), illus. LC 66-14903. (Illus.). (Chauncy strikes out on his own & goes from one hilarious adventure to another). (gr. 4-6). 1966. (ISBN 0-316-28575-7, Pub. by Atlantic Monthly Pr). Little.
--The Ghost in the Noonday Sun. Chappell, Warren (1904-), illus. LC 65-10794. (A hair-raising ghost & pirate Story). (Illus.). 173p. (gr. 4-6). 1965. (ISBN 0-316-28576-5, Pub. by Atlantic Monthly Pr). Little.
--The Ghost on Saturday Night. 1st ed. Von Schmidt, Eric (1931-), illus. LC 73-14751. (Illus.). 57 p. 22cm. 1974. (ISBN 0-316-28583-8). Little, Brown.
--The Hey Hey Man. 1st ed. Westcott, Nadine Bernard, illus. LC 78-31702. (Illus.). 31 p. 24cm. c.1979. (ISBN 0-316-26001-0, Atlantic Monthly Pr). Little, Brown.
--Humbug Mountain. 1st ed. Von Schmidt, Eric (1931-), illus. LC 78-9419. (Illus.). 149 p. 21cm. c.1978. (ISBN 0-316-28569-2). Little, Brown. **Award: (BGH).**
--Jim Bridger's Alarm Clock, and Other Tall Tales. Von Schmidt, Eric (1931-), illus. LC 78-5854. p. cm. c.1978. (ISBN 0-525-32795-9). E. P. Dutton.
--Jingo Django. 1st ed. Von Schmidt, Eric (1931-), illus. LC 75-140481. (Illus.). 172 p. 21cm. 1971. Little, Brown. **Award: (ALA).**
--Kate's Secret Riddle Book. Bottner, Barbara (1943-), illus. LC 76-56160. (Illus.). 32 p. 22cm. (Easy-read story book). 1977. (ISBN 0-531-00377-9). Watts.
--Longbeard the Wizard. Bragg, Charles, illus. LC 79-97140. (Illus.). (gr. k-3). 1970. (ISBN 0-316-28574-9). Little.
--McBroom and the Beanstalk. 1st ed. Lorraine, Walter Henry (1929-), illus. LC 77-22177. (Illus.). 40 p. 26cm. c.1977. (ISBN 0-316-28570-6). Little, Brown.
--McBroom and the Big Wind. Lorraine, Walter Henry (1929-), illus. LC 81-15659. (Illus.). 40 p. 25cm. 1982. (ISBN 0-316-28543-9). (ISBN 0-316-28544-7). Little, Brown.
--McBroom and the Big Wind. 1st ed. Werth, Kurt (1896-), illus. LC 67-15450. (Illus.). 46 p. 24cm. 1967. Norton.
--McBroom and the Great Race. 1st ed. Lorraine, Walter Henry (1929-), illus. LC 79-22609. (Illus.). 57 p. 24cm. c.1980. (ISBN 0-316-28568-4). Little, Brown.
--McBroom Tells a Lie. 1st ed. Lorraine, Walter Henry (1929-), illus. LC 76-8396. (Illus.). 46 p. 22cm. c.1976. (ISBN 0-316-28572-2). Little, Brown.
--McBroom Tells the Truth. Lorraine, Walter Henry (1929-), illus. LC 81-1035. p. cm. 1981. (ISBN 0-316-28550-1). (ISBN 0-316-28552-8). Little, Brown.
--McBroom Tells the Truth. Werth, Kurt (1896-), illus. 1966. Norton.
--McBroom the Rainmaker. Lorraine, Walter Henry (1929-), illus. LC 81-17143. (Illus.). 40 p. 25cm. 1982. (ISBN 0-316-28541-2). (ISBN 0-316-28542-0). Little, Brown.
--McBroom the Rainmaker. Werth, Kurt (1896-), illus. LC 73-4458. (Illus.). 1 v. (unpaged. 24cm. (Thistle Book). 1973. (ISBN 0-448-21479-2). Grosset & Dunlap.
--McBroom's Almanac. Lorraine, Walter Henry (1929-), illus. LC 83-9043. (Illus.). vii, 88 p. 25cm. c.1984. (ISBN 0-316-26009-6). Little, Brown.
--McBroom's Ear. Lorraine, Walter Henry (1929-), illus. LC 81-15636. (Illus.). 40 p. 25cm. (gr. 3up). 1982. (ISBN 0-316-28539-0). (ISBN 0-316-28540-4). Little, Brown.
--McBroom's Ear. 1st ed. Werth, Kurt (1896-), illus. LC 71-77856. (Illus.). 48 p. 24cm. 1969. W. W. Norton.
--McBroom's Ghost. Frankenberg, Robert Clinton (1911-), illus. LC 72-153928. (Illus.). 48 p. [illegible] 1971. [illegible] Grosset & Dunlap.
--McBroom's Ghost. Lorraine, Walter Henry (1929-), illus. LC 81-1118. (Illus.). 43 p. 25cm. 1981, c.1971. (ISBN 0-316-28547-1). (ISBN 0-316-28549-8). Little, Brown.
--McBroom's Popcornmobile. Lorraine, Walter Henry (1929-), illus. 1976. Little Brown and Company.
--McBroom's Zoo. Lorraine, Walter Henry (1929-), illus. LC 81-15052. (Illus.). 40 p. 25cm. 1982. (ISBN 0-316-28536-6). (ISBN 0-316-28538-2). Little, Brown.
--McBroom's Zoo. Werth, Kurt (1896-), illus. LC 72-75784. (Illus.). 46 p. 24cm. (Thistle book). 1972. (ISBN 0-448-21444-X). (ISBN 0-448-21444-X). Grosset & Dunlap.
--Me and the Man on the Moon-Eyed Horse. 1st ed. Von Schmidt, Eric (1931-), illus. LC 76-26595. (Illus.). 37 p. 22cm. c.1977. (ISBN 0-316-28571-4). Little, Brown.
--Mr. Mysterious & Company. 1st ed. Von Schmidt, Eric (1931-), illus. LC 62-7105. (Illus.). 151 p. 21cm. 1962. Little, Brown.
--Mr. Mysterious's Secrets of Magic. Von Schmidt, Eric (1931-), illus. (Illus.). 96p. (gr. 4-6). 1975. (ISBN 0-316-28584-6, Pub. by Atlantic Monthly Pr). Little.
--The Wooden Cat Man. 1st ed. Yang, Jay (1941-), illus. LC 70-170169. (Illus.). 48 p. 1972. (ISBN 0-316-28581-1). Little, Brown.

Fleischman, H. Samuel
--Gang Girl. 1st ed. Walker, Shirley, illus. LC 67-17269. (Illus.). 143 p. 22cm. (Doubleday signal books). 1967. Doubleday.

Fleischman, Paul
--The Animal Hedge. Dabcovich, Lydia, illus. LC 82-2404. (Illus.). 32p. (gr. 2-5). 1983. (ISBN 0-525-44002-X). Dutton.
--The Birthday Tree. Sewall, Marcia (1935-), illus. LC 78-22155. (Illus.). 32 p. c.1979. (ISBN 0-06-021915-7). (ISBN 0-06-021916-5). Harper & Row.
--Coming-&-Going Men: Four Tales. Gaul, Randy, illus. LC 84-48336. (Illus.). 160p. (Charlotte Zolotow Bk.). (gr. 6up). 1985. (ISBN 0-06-021883-5). (ISBN 0-06-021884-3). HarpJ.
--Finzel the Farsighted. 1st ed. Sewall, Marcia (1935-), illus. LC 83-1416. (Illus.). 46 p. 23cm. c.1983. (ISBN 0-525-44057-7). E.P. Dutton.
--Graven Images: Three Stories. 1st ed. Glass, Andrew, illus. LC 81-48649. (Illus.). 96p. (A Charlotte Zolotow Bk.). (gr. 6 up). 1982. (ISBN 0-06-021906-8, HarpJ). (ISBN 0-06-021907-6). Har-Row. **Awards: (ALA); (JNM).**
--The Half-a-Moon Inn. 1st ed. Jacobi, Kathy, illus. LC 79-2010. (Illus.). 88 p. 21cm. c.1980. (ISBN 0-06-021917-3). (ISBN 0-06-021918-1). Harper & Row.
--I Am Phoenix: Poems for Two Voices. Nutt, Ken (1951-), illus. LC 85-42615. (Illus.). 51 p. 24cm. c.1985. (ISBN 0-06-021881-9). (ISBN 0-06-021882-7). Harper & Row.
--Path of the Pale Horse. 1st ed. LC 82-48611. ix, 147 p. 22cm. c.1983. (ISBN 0-06-021904-1). (ISBN 0-06-021905-X). Harper & Row.
--Phoebe Danger, Detective, in The Case of the Two-Minute Cough. Apple, Margot, illus. LC 82-15616. p. cm. 1983. (ISBN 0-395-33226-5). Houghton Mifflin.

Fleischman, Sid see Fleischman, Albert Sidney.

Fleischmann, Harriet (1904-)
--Great Enchantment. (gr. 8-10). 1967. (ISBN 0-8019-5202-6). Chilton.

Fleischmann, Peter
--Alexander & the Car with a Missing Headlight. Schindel, Morton, adapted by. (Illus.). (ps up). 1967. (ISBN 0-670-11202-X). Viking Pr.

Fleisher, Michael Lawrence (1942-)
--The Great Superman Book. 1979. (Harmony). Crown.

Fleisher, Robbin & Forberg, Ati, pseud. (1925-)
--Quilts in the Attic. Forberg, Beate Gropius. LC 78-3597. (Illus.). 31 p. 24cm. c.1978. (ISBN 0-02-735420-2). Macmillan.

Fleishman, Seymour (1918-)
--Four Cheers for Camping. Fleishman, Seymour (1918-), illus. LC 63-13329. (Illus.). unpaged. 24cm. 1963. A. Whitman.
--Gumbel, the Fire-Breathing Dragon. Fleishman, Seymour (1918-), illus. LC 74-94563. (Illus.). 32 p. 26cm. 1970. Harvey House.
--Too Hot in Potzburg. Fleishman, Seymour (1918-), illus. LC 81-11498. p. cm. 1981. (ISBN 0-8075-8024-4). A. Whitman.
--Where's Kit?. Fleishman, Seymour (1918-), illus. LC 62-11071. (Illus.). unpaged. 24cm. 1962. A. Whitman.

Fleming, Alice Mulcahey (1928-)
--Doctors in Petticoats. 160p. 1964. J B Lippincott Co.
--The Little Maelstrom. 317p. N.D. Meador Publishing Co.

Fleming, Alice Mulcahey (1928-), ed.
--America Is Not All Traffic Lights: Poems of the Midwest. photos. 84p. (gr. 7 up). 1976. (ISBN 0-316-28590-0). Little.
--Hosannah the Home Run: Poems About Sports. (Illus.). (gr. 7 up). 1972. (ISBN 0-316-28588-9). Little.

Fleming, Christopher Le see Potter, Helen Beatrix (1866-1943) & Le Fleming, Christopher.

Fleming, Denise, illus.
--The Charmkins Sniffy Adventure. (Illus.). 24p. (Sniffy Bks.). (gr. 3-5). 1983. (ISBN 0-394-86115-9). Random.
--It Feels Like Christmas!. A Book of Surprises to Touch, See, and Sniff. LC 84-60622. (Illus.). 10 p. 24cm. c.1984. (ISBN 0-394-86862-5). Random House.

Fleming, Elizabeth P
--Gift from the Mikado. Smalley, Janet (1893-), illus. LC 58-5129. (Illus.). 176 p. 21cm. 1958. Westminster Press.
--The Merry Adventures of Robin Hood Harlan. Hall, H. Tom, illus. LC 62-10577. (Illus.). 176p. 23cm. 1962. Westminster Press.
--Redcloud & Co. Smalley, Janet (1893-), illus. LC 59-6021. (Illus.). 191p. 21cm. 1959. Westminster Press.
--The Spell on the Stones. Helms, Georgeanne, illus. LC 61-7704. (Illus.). 160p. 21cm. 1961. Westminster Press.
--The Takula Tree. 1964. E M Hale.
--The Takula Tree. Jefferson, Robert Louis (1929-), illus. LC 64-10518. 175 p. illus. 22 cm. 1964. Westminster Press.

Fleming, Emma L.
--The Green Forest. (Illus.). 64p. (gr. 1-2). 1972. (ISBN 0-682-47530-0). Exposition.

Fleming, Guy, illus.
--Baba Yaga's Geese & Other Russian Stories. LC 73-77852. (Illus.). 128p. (Midland Bks.: No. 222). (gr. 1-6). 1973. (ISBN 0-253-10500-5). (ISBN 0-253-20222-1). Ind U Pr.

Fleming, Harry
--Terry & Sid. (Illus.). (Jet Ser). (gr. 7-11). 1963. Verry.

Fleming, Ian Lancaster (1908-1964)
--Chitty Chitty Bang Bang. (gr. 3-5). 1980. (ISBN 0-590-03428-6). Scholastic Inc.
--Chitty Chitty Bang Bang. Burningham, John MacKintosh (1936-), illus. 159p. Repr. of 1964 ed. 1964. (ISBN 0-88411-983-1). Amereon Ltd.
--Chitty-Chitty-Bang-Bang. Burningham, John Mackintosh (1936-), illus. (gr. 2-4). 1964. (ISBN 0-394-81021-X). Random.
--Chitty Chitty Bang Bang. Perkins, Albert Rogers (1904-1975), adapted by. Tobey, Barney, illus. LC 68-28461. (Illus.). 72p. (gr. k-3). 1968. (ISBN 0-394-80053-2). (ISBN 0-394-90053-7). Beginner.

Fleming, Lisa, pseud., see Reno, Esther Watson.

Fleming, Lisa
--Up and Down the Street. 1953. Oxford University Press.

Fleming, Lora
--A Birthday Cake for Mother. (Mini-Bk). (gr. 1-4). 1971. (ISBN 0-912472-12-X). Miller Bks.

Fleming, Lucy Ward Randolph (1847-)
--Alice Withrow: Or, The Summer at Home. LC 12-32192. 241 p. front., plates. 19 cm. c.1886. T. Y. Crowell & Co.

Fleming, Patricia Crew
--Rico, the Young Rancher. Yap, Weda (1894-), illus. LC 42-10031. 64 p. incl. col. front., illus. (part col.) 21 1/2 cm. (Half-title: New world neighbors). c.1942. D. C. Heath and Company.

Fleming, Rachel M.
--Round the World in Folk Tales. N.D. Harcourt Brace & Co.

Fleming, Susan (1932-)
--Countdown at Thirty-Seven Pinecrest Drive. Krush, Beth (1918-) & Krush, Joe (1918-), illus. LC 82-8337. (Illus.). 132 p. 22cm. c.1982. (ISBN 0-664-32694-3). Westminster Press.
--The Pig at Thirty-Seven Pinecrest Drive. 1st ed. Krush, Beth (1918-) & Krush, Joe (1918-), illus. LC 80-22391. (Illus.). 127 p. 21cm. (gr. 3-5). c.1981. (ISBN 0-664-32676-5). Westminster Press.
--Trapped on the Golden Flyer. 1st ed. Stein, Alex, illus. LC 77-15941. (Illus.). 125 p. 21cm. c.1978. (ISBN 0-664-32627-7). Westminster Press.

Fleming, W. H.
--The Hunted Piccanninies. Edmunds, Kay, illus. LC 28-30779. 1948. E. P. Dutton & Co.

Fleming, Waldo, pseud., see Williamson, Thames Ross.

Fletcher, A.
--Florence Egerton, 1 of 103 vols. (The Pearl Library: No. 25). 1900. Set. Hurst & Co.

Fletcher, Adele Whitely (1898-)
--The Mystery of Blue Star Lodge. 1st ed. Kocsis, James C. (1936-), illus. Paul, James, pseud. LC 65-14020. (Illus.). 143 p. 22cm. (Signal book). 1965. Doubleday.

Fletcher, Charlie May see Simon, Charlie May Hogue, pseud.

Fletcher, Charlie May Hogue see Simon, Charlie May, pseud.

Fletcher, Cynthia H.
--My Jesus Pocketbook of Nursery Rhymes. Sherman, Erin, illus. LC 80-52041. (Illus.). 32p. (Orig.). (ps). 1980. (ISBN 0-937420-00-X). Stirrup Assoc.

Fletcher, David, pseud., see Barber, Dulan F..

Fletcher, David, pseud. (1940-)
--Confetti for Cortorelli. Barber, Dulan F.. Thompson, George William (1925-), illus. LC 57-6597. (Illus.). 146 p. 22cm. 1957. Pantheon.
--The King's Goblet. Barber, Dulan F.. LC 62-14271. 311 p. 22cm. 1962. Pantheon Books.
--Mother O'pearl: Three Tales. Barber, Dulan F.. Obrant, Susan (1946-), illus. LC 78-117460. (Illus.). 101 p. 24cm. 1970. Pantheon Books.
--Village of Hidden Wishes. Barber, Dulan F.. Stefula, D., illus. LC 60-7025. (Illus.). (gr. 4-7). 1960. Pantheon.

Fletcher, Dorothy
--Week of Dream Horses. Borelli, Theresa, illus. (Illus.). (Envelope Bk.). 1984. (ISBN 0-88138-017-2). Green Tiger Pr.

Fletcher, Elizabeth S.
--The Christmas Story. N.D. Carlton.

Fletcher, Evelyn, jt. auth. see Everett-Green, Evelyn.

Fletcher, Evelyn, jt. auth. see Weedon, Lucy L.

Fletcher, Evelyn, jt. auth. see Hover, M. A.

Fletcher, Helen Jill (1910-)
--Show and Tell. Renfro, Ed., illus. LC 68-18772. (Illus.). 1 v. (unpaged. 22cm. 1968. Platt & Munk.

Fletcher, Helen Jill (1910-), ed.
--The Trumpet Books of Laughs. Vartanian, Raymond J., illus. LC 55-3582. unpaged. illus. 26cm. (Trumpet book, BT50). 1955. S. Gabriel Sons.

Fletcher, Inglis Clark, Mrs. (1888-)
--Men of Albemarle. LC 42-229963. 566 p. 21 1/2 cm. 1942. The Bobbs-Merrill Company.
--Raleigh's Eden. A Novel. LC 40-301009. 662 p. 21 1/2 cm. c.1940. The Bobbs-Merrill Company.
--The White Leopard: A Tale of the African Bush. Rev ed. Wiese, Kurt (1887-1974), illus. LC 31-234704. 304 p. incl. front., illus., plates. 22 1/2 cm. c.1931. The Bobbs-Merrill Company.

Fletcher, Jesse C.
--The Wimpy Harper Story. 1967. Broadman Press.

Fletcher, Lawrence
--Into the Inknown. (Cassell's Popular Library of Fiction). N.D. Cassell & Co.'s Pubs.

Fletcher, Mabel
--Old Settler Stories. (Everychild's Ser.). N.D. Macmillan.

Fletcher, Mary, jt. ed. see Fletcher, Terry.

Fletcher, Robert Howe (1850-)
--Marjorie and Her Papa. Birch, Reginald Bathurst (1856-1943), illus. 97p. N.D. Century Co.
--Marjorie and Her Papa. Birch, Reginald Bathurst (1856-1943), illus. Fletcher, Robert Howe, designed by. N.D. DeWolfe, Fiske & co.
--Marjorie and Her Papa, How They Wrote a Story and Made Pictures for It. Birch, Reginald Bathurst (1856-1943), illus. LC 12-32201. 2 p. l, 3-66 p., 1 l illus. 26 cm. 1891. The Century Co.

Fletcher, Sarah
--My Bible Story Book: Bible Stories for Small Children. Kueker, Don, illus. LC 73-91810. (Illus.). 71 p. 28cm. 1974. (ISBN 0-570-03423-X). Concordia Pub. House.
--My Stories About God's People. Kueker, Don, illus. (Illus.). 32p. (ps-3). 1974. (ISBN 0-570-03426-4). Concordia.
--My Stories About Jesus. Kueker, Don, illus. (Illus.). 32p. (ps-3). 1974. (ISBN 0-570-03428-0). (ISBN 0-570-03427-2). Concordia.

Fletcher, Steffi
--Betsy McCall's Paper Doll Story Book. Miloche, Hilda & Kane, Wilma, illus. (Big Golden Book). 1954. Golden Press.
--Gene Autry. Crawford, Mel (1925-), illus. LC 55-3222. unpaged. illus. 21cm. (Little golden library, 230). 1955. Simon and Schuster.
--The Lone Ranger. Dreany, E. Joseph, illus. LC 56-468135. unpaged. illus. 21cm. (Little golden book, 263). 1956. Simon and Schuster.

--M-G-M's Tom and Jerry's Party. LC 55-3188. unpaged. illus. 21cm. (Little golden book, 235). 1955. Simon and Schuster.

Fletcher, Steffi, adapted by see Disney, Walter Elias.

Fletcher, Steffi, compiled by see Disney, Walt, Productions.

Fletcher, Steffi, ed. see Disney, Walt, Productions & Lorenzini, Carlo.

Fletcher, Terry & Fletcher, Mary, eds.
--Children's Writers & Illustrators Workshop Presents ... Superbook: A Super Collection of Fun, Fact, Fiction, and Fantasy. Children's Writers & Illustrators Workshop LC 77-92773. (Illus.). 128 p. 27cm. 1st U.S. edition. 1977. (ISBN 0-8120-0991-6). Barron's Educational Series.

Fletcher, Winifred Bell
--Squiddle, the Squid with a Smile on His Middle. Alexander, Betty, illus. LC 52-18684. unpaged. illus. 22 cm. (Aloha books for children). N.D. Pacific Pub. Co.

Flettrich, Terry
--House in the Bend of Bourbon Street. Lo-An, illus. (Illus.). 1974. (ISBN 0-88289-015-8). Pelican.

Fleur, Anne Elizabeth see Sari, pseud.

Fleur, Anne Elizabeth, jt. auth. see Vaughn, Dorothea B., Mrs.

Fleur, Anne Elizabeth (1901-)
--The Bad Donkey, and Other Animal Stories. Sari, pseud. Fleur, Anne Elizabeth (1901-), illus. Sari, pseud. LC 42-1195. (Illus.). 17cm. 60p. (The Little Color Classics). 1942. McLoughlin Bros., Inc.
--A Coat for Kleintje. Sari, pseud. LC 39-13753. (Illus.). 24p. N.D. Grosset & Dunlap.
--The Ducks of Dingle Dell, and Other Stories. Sari, pseud. Fleur, Anne Elizabeth (1901-), illus. Sari, pseud. LC 41-3988. (Illus.). 17 x 13cm. 62p. 1941. McLoughlin Bros. Inc.
--The Gingerbread Boy. Sari, pseud. N.D. Grosset & Dunlap.
--Jeanne-Marie Goes to Market. Sari, pseud. Fleur, Anne Elizabeth (1901-), illus. Sari, pseud. LC 38-23924. 24p. 1938. Grosset & Dunlap.
--Little Red Riding Hood. Sari, pseud. Fleur, Anne Elizabeth (1901-), illus. Sari, pseud. LC 41-22145. 58 p. incl. col. front., illus. (part col.) 17 x 14 cm. (The little color classics). c.1941. McLoughlin Bros., Inc.
--The Magic Ring. Sari, pseud. Fleur, Anne Elizabeth (1901-), illus. Sari, pseud. LC 43-4183. 60 p. incl. col. front., illus. (part col.) 17 1/2 x 13 1/2 cm. (Little color classics). 1943. McLoughlin Brothers, Inc.
--Make-Believe Stories. Sari, pseud. Fleur, Anne Elizabeth (1901-), illus. Sari, pseud. LC 42-19760. 59 p. incl. col. front., illus. (part col.) 17 1/2 x 13 1/2 cm. (On cover: The Little color classics ... 807). 1942. McLoughlin Bros., Inc.
--Rumpelstiltskin. Sari, pseud. Fleur, Anne Elizabeth (1901-), illus. Sari, pseud. LC 41-22778. (Illus.). 59 p. (Little color classics). c.1941. McLoughlin Bros., Inc.
--Sari's Mother Goose. Sari, pseud. Fleur, Anne Elizabeth (1901-), illus. Sari, pseud. LC 50-11226. 38 p. col. illus. 29 cm. 1949. Bell Pub. Co.
--Sleeping Beauty. Sari, pseud. Fleur, Anne Elizabeth (1901-), illus. Sari, pseud. N.D. Grosset & Dunlap.
--Sleeptime Stories. Sari, pseud. Fleur, Anne Elizabeth (1901-), illus. Sari, pseud. LC 41-19204. (Illus.). 32p. 1941. McLoughlin Bros., Inc.
--Sunny Tales. Sari, pseud. Fleur, Anne Elizabeth (1901-), illus. Sari, pseud. LC 42-1757. 60 p. incl. col. front., illus. (part col.) 17 cm. (The Little color classics). c.1942. McLoughlin Bros., Inc.
--Ten Little Servants. Sari, pseud. LC 39-12109. 24p. N.D. Grosset & Dunlap.
--The Toy Shop. Sari, pseud. Lancaster, A. F., illus. LC 43-48576. 60 p. incl. col. front., illus. (part col.) 17 1/2 x 13 1/2 cm. (Little color classics). 1943. McLoughlin Brothers, Inc.
--The White Goat, A Story of Switzerland. Sari, pseud. LC 38-29406. (Illus.). 24p. 21 x 22cm. 1938. Grosset & Dunlop.
--The Winkle Twinkle Pup, and Other Stories. Sari, pseud. Fleur, Anne Elizabeth (1901-), illus. Sari, pseud. LC 41-2095. 62 p. incl. col. front., illus. (part col.) 17 1/2 x 13 1/2 cm. (On cover: The little color classics). c.1941. McLoughlin Bros., Inc.

Fleuron, Svend (1874-)
--Flax, Police Dog. Aldin, Cecil Charles Windsor (1870-1935), illus. Nash, Elizabeth Gee, Mrs., tr. LC 31-28365. 5 p. l, 230, 3 p. incl. plates. front. 22 1/2 cm. 1931. H. Holt and Company.
--The Grey Hare: A Romance of the Danish Fields. LC 39-32380. 4 p. l, 3-177 p. illus. 19 1/2 cm. c.1939. Farrar & Rinehart, Inc.

Fleury, Barbara Frances (1907-)
--Luckypiece. Rev. ed. Hauman, George (1890-1961), illus. LC 36-22338. 6 p. l, 146 p. illus. 19 1/2 cm. 1936. The Macmillan Company.
--The Runaway Deer. Somppi, Lilly, illus. LC 38-9833. (Illus.). 32p. 22cm. 1938. The Macmillan Co.

Flexer, George
--Snorkel. Victorine, James, illus. (Illus.). (ps-2). 1975. (ISBN 0-13-815316-7). P-H.

Flexner, Hortense (1885-)
--Chipper. King, Wyncie (1884-), illus. LC 41-17881. 46, 2 p. illus. 22 cm. c.1941. Frederick A. Stokes Company.
--Chipper. King, Wyncie (1884-), illus. N.D. J. B. Lippincott.
--Puzzle Pond. King, Wyncie (1884-), illus. LC 48-7858. 63p. 1948. J. B. Lippincott Co.
--The Wishing Window. King, Wyncie (1884-), illus. LC 42-2519. 63 p. illus. 21 1/2 cm. 1942. Frederick A. Stokes Company.
--The Wishing Window. King, Wyncie (1884-), illus. Fisher, Dorothea Frances Canfield, Mrs. (1879-1958), frwd. by. 1942. J. B. Lippincott Co.

Flight, John W.
--Moses: Egyptian Prince, Law-Giver. 1942. (ISBN 0-8070-1984-4). (ISBN 0-8070-1985-2). Beacon Pr.

Flint, Annie Austin (1866-)
--Sunbeam Stories and Others. Keith, Dora Wheeler & Nugent, Meredith, illus. LC 44-30629. 97, 1 p. front., illus., plates 21 cm. 1897. Bonnell, Silver & Company.

Flint, Timothy (1780-1840)
--Little Henry, the Stolen Child. LC 73-104452. 143 p. 23cm. 1970. (ISBN 0-8398-0558-6). Literature House.
--The Lost Child. LC 73-104452. Repr. of 1830 ed. 1970. (ISBN 0-8398-0558-6). Gregg.

Flintan, Douglas L
--There Really Is a Father Christmas. Hoene, Mary Jane, illus. LC 38-128441. 4 p. l, 73 p. illus. 26 cm. c.1938. Willet, Clark & Company.

Floethe, Louise Lee (1913-)
--Birthday Presents. (Illus.). (gr. k-3). 1964 (Vision). FS&G.
--Bittersweet Summer. Floethe, Richard (1901-), illus. LC 64-21429. 249 p. 22cm. 1964. Ariel Books.
--Blueberry Pie. Floethe, Richard (1901-), illus. LC 62-9645. (Illus.). 32 p. 26cm. c.1962. (ISBN 0-684-13457-8). Scribner.
--Cowboy on the Ranch. Floethe, Richard (1901-), illus. LC 59-16485. (Illus.). (gr. 1-5). 1959. (ISBN 0-684-13158-7). Scribner.
--Farmer & His Cows. N.D. E. M. Hale & Co.
--The Farmer and His Cows. Floethe, Richard (1901-), illus. LC 57-14036. unpaged. illus. 21x26cm. c.1957. Scribner.
--Floating Market. Floethe, Richard (1901-), illus. LC 69-14971. (Illus.). 36 p. 28cm. 1969. Farrar, Straus & Giroux.
--Fountain of the Friendly Lion. Floethe, Richard (1901-), illus. LC 66-13708. (Illus.). (gr. k-4). 1966. (ISBN 0-684-82044-7). Scribner.
--If I Were Captain. Floethe, Richard (1901-), illus. LC 56-893910. (Illus.). (gr. k-2). 1956. (ISBN 0-684-20812-1). Scribner.
--The New Roof. Floethe, Richard (1901-), illus. LC 65-10482. 1v. (unpaged) col. illus. 26cm. c.1965. (ISBN 0-684-20813-X). Scribners.
--Sara. Floethe, Richard (1901-), illus. LC 61-6969. (Illus.). 121p. 22cm. 1961. Ariel.
--Terry Sets Sail. Floethe, Richard (1901-), illus. LC 58-7760. (Illus.). 58p. 1958. Harper & Brothers.
--A Thousand and One Buddhas. Floethe, Richard (1901-), illus. (Illus.). 56p. 1967. (ISBN 0-374-37524-0). Farrar, Straus and Giroux.
--Triangle X. Floethe, Richard (1901-), illus. LC 60-5777. (Illus.). (gr. 2-6). 1960. (ISBN 0-06-021925-4, HarpJ). Har-Row.
--The Winning Colt. Floethe, Richard (1901-), illus. LC 56-11145. 90p. illus. 22cm. 1956. Sterling Pub. Co.
--A Year to Remember. Floethe, Richard (1901-), illus. LC 57-11654. 252 p. 22cm. 1957. Lothrop, Lee & Shepard.

Floherty, John Joseph, Jr. (1892-1964)
--Behind the Silver Shield. Rev. ed. 208p. 1960. J. B. Lippincott.
--Flowing Gold. Floherty, John Joseph, Jr. (1892-1964), illus. 224p. 1957. J. B. Lippincott.
--Forest Ranger. 143p. 1956. J. B. Lippincott.
--Men Against Crime: The Inside Story of T Men. 1946. J. B. Lippincott.
--Our F.B.I. An Inside Story. 1951. J. B. Lippincott.
--Television Story. Rev. ed. 160p. 1957. J. B. Lippincott.
--Troopers All: Stories of State Police. 148p. 1954. J. B. Lippincott.
--White Terror: Adventures With the Ice Patrol. 1947. J. B. Lippincott.

Floherty, John Joseph, Jr. (1892-1964) & McGrady, Mike
--Skin Diving Adventures. 160p. 1962. J B Lippincott Company.
--Whirling Wings. 160p. 1961. J B Lippincott Company.
--Youth and the F.B.I. 159p. 1960. J B Lippincott Company.

Flood, L. L., jt. auth. see Loughlin, Burren.

Flood, Richard T
--The Fighting Shortstop. Ames, Lee Judah (1921-), illus. LC 54-6488. (Illus.). 210 p. 22cm. 1954. Houghton Mifflin.
--The Fighting Southpaw. Candy, Robert (1920-), illus. LC 54-122411. 180p. illus. 22cm. (Famous Sports Stories). 1954, c.1949. Grosset & Dunlap.
--The Fighting Southpaw. Candy, Robert (1920-), illus. LC 49-10532. 180 p. illus. 22 cm. 1949. Houghton Mifflin Co.
--Pass That Puck!. (Famous Sports Stories). N.D. Grosset & Dunlap.
--Pass That Puck. Hartman, C. L., illus. 136 p. illus. 22 cm. 1949. Houghton Mifflin Co.
--Penalty Shot. Candy, Robert (1920-), illus. LC 55-9953. (Illus.). 180 p. 22cm. 1955. Houghton Mifflin.
--The Point After. Candy, Robert (1920-), illus. LC 51-11764. 216 p. illus. 22 cm 1951. Houghton Mifflin.

Flora, James Royer (1914-)
--Charlie Yup and His Snip-Snap Boys. Flora, James Royer (1914-), illus. LC 59-6562. 34p. 1959. Harcourt, Brace and Co Inc.
--The Day the Cow Sneezed. Flora, James Royer (1914-), illus. LC 57-9740. (Illus.). unpaged. 29cm. c.1957. Harcourt, Brace.
--The Day the Cow Sneezed. Flora, James Royer (1914-), illus. LC 75-8746. p. cm. (Voyager book ; AVB 98). 1975, c.1957. (ISBN 0-15-624213-3). Harcourt Brace Jovanovich.
--The Fabulous Firework Family. Flora, James Royer (1914-), illus. LC 55-7610. (Illus.). unpaged. 29cm. 1955. Harcourt, Brace. **Award: (ALA).**
--Fishing with Dad. Flora, James Royer (1914-), illus. LC 67-18865. (Illus.). 1 v. (unpaged) 26cm. 1967. Harcourt, Brace & World.
--Grandpa's Farm: Four Tall Tales. Flora, James Royer (1914-), illus. LC 65-17989. (Illus.). 1 v. (unpaged). 29cm. (gr. 1-4). 1965. (ISBN 0-15-232340-6). Harcourt, Brace & World.
--Grandpa's Ghost Stories. 1980. (ISBN 0-689-70469-0, Aladdin). Atheneum.
--Grandpa's Ghost Stories. Flora, James Royer (1914-), illus. LC 78-108947. (Illus.). 28 p. 26cm. (ps-4). 1978. (ISBN 0-689-50112-9, McElderry Bk.). Atheneum.
--Grandpa's Witched-up Christmas. Flora, James Royer (1914-), illus. LC 81-12843. (Illus.). 32 p. 26cm. 1982. (ISBN 0-689-50232-X). Atheneum.
--The Great Green Turkey Creek Monster. Flora, James Royer (1914-), illus. LC 75-43894. (Illus.). 32 p. 30cm. 1976. (ISBN 0-689-50060-2). Atheneum.
--The Joking Man. Flora, James Royer (1914-), illus. LC 68-25185. (Illus.). 1 v. 32p. 24cm. 1968. Harcourt, Brace & World.
--Kangaroo for Christmas. (Illus.). (gr. 1-3). 1962. (ISBN 0-8382-0397-3). Hale.
--Kangaroo for Christmas. Flora, James Royer (1914-), illus. LC 62-14243. (Illus.). (gr. k-3). 1962. (ISBN 0-15-242026-6, HJ). (ISBN 0-15-242027-4). HarBraceJ.
--Leopold, the See-Through Crumbpicker. Flora, James Royer (1914-), illus. LC 61-6114. (Illus.). unpaged. 26cm. 1961. Harcourt, Brace & World.
--Little Hatchy Hen. Flora, James Royer (1914-), illus. LC 69-18624. (Illus.). 32 p. 29cm. 1969. Harcourt, Brace & World. **Award: (ALA).**
--My Friend Charlie. Flora, James Royer (1914-), illus. LC 64-16265. (Illus.). (gr. k-3). 1964. (ISBN 0-15-256336-9). HarBraceJ.
--Pishtosh, Bullwash & Wimple. Flora, James Royer (1914-), illus. LC 71-190554. (Illus.). 32 p. 24cm. 1972. Atheneum.
--Sherwood Walks Home. Flora, James Royer (1914-), illus. LC 66-16004. (Illus.). (gr. 1-3). 1966. (ISBN 0-15-273735-9, HJ). HarBraceJ.
--Stewed Goose. Flora, James Royer (1914-), illus. LC 73-75434. (Illus.). 30 p. 24cm. (gr. k-3). 1973. (ISBN 0-689-30417-X). Atheneum.
--Wanda and the Bumbly Wizard. LC 79-54683. (Illus.). 32 p. 27cm. 1980. (ISBN 0-689-50154-4). Atheneum.

Flora, Margaret
--Animal-land Children: Or, The Contest for the Magic Glasses. Hodge, Helen Geraldine, illus. 20cm. 128p. 1919. Beckley-Cardy Co.

Floren, Lee see Lang, Grace, pseud.

Floren, Lee (1910-)
--Forever this Love. LC 57-13558. 221p. 21cm. 1957. Avalon Books.

Florence, James, jt. auth. see Cusack, Ellen Dymphna.

Florence, Lee see Nelson, Marguerite, pseud.

Florentz, Christopher
--So Wild a Dream. Spohn, Cliff, illus. LC 78-14773. p. cm. (Pacesetters). 1979. (ISBN 0-516-02172-9). Childrens Press.

Florian
--Select Fables: With notes, exercises, & vocabulary. (Illus.). (Primary Ser.). N.D. MacMillan.

Florian, Douglas (1950-)
--Airplane Ride. LC 83-45048. (Illus.). 32p. (ps-2). 1984. (ISBN 0-690-04364-3, TYC-J). (ISBN 0-690-04365-1). Har-Row.
--A Bird Can Fly. Florian, Douglas (1950-), illus. 1980. Greenwillow.
--The City. LC 81-43312. (Illus.). 32 p. 24cm. c.1982. (ISBN 0-690-04166-7). (ISBN 0-690-04167-5). Crowell Junior Books.

Florich
--Little May and Her Lost A. (Illus.). N.D. Estes & Lauriat's.

Flory, Arthur, jt. auth. see Flory, Jane Trescott.

Flory, Jane Trescott (1917-)
--The Bear on the Doorstep. Croll, Carolyn, illus. LC 80-10952. (Illus.). 32 p. 1980. (ISBN 0-395-29239-5). Houghton Mifflin.
--Clancy's Glorious Fourth. Flory, Jane Trescott (1917-), illus. LC 64-15915. 168 p. illus. 22 cm. 1964. Houghton Mifflin.
--Faraway Dream. Flory, Jane Trescott (1917-), illus. (Illus.). 219 p. 22cm. 1968. Houghton Mifflin.
--Farmer John. LC 50-34275. (Illus.). 32p. 17cm. (Tell-a-Tale Bks.). 1950. Whitman.
--The Golden Venture. LC 75-43899. (Illus.). 232 p. 22cm. 1976. (ISBN 0-395-24377-7). Houghton Mifflin.
--The Great Bamboozlement. LC 81-17862. (Illus.). 145 p. 22cm. (gr. 5-9). 1982. (ISBN 0-395-31859-9). Houghton Mifflin.
--The Hide-Away Ducklings. Flory, Jane Trescott (1917-), illus. LC 46-7370. 32 p. illus. (part col.) 24 x 21 cm. 1946. Grosset and Dunlap.
--How Many?. LC 44-7128. (Illus.). 22p. 16 x 15cm. 1944. H. Holt and Company.
--It Was a Pretty Good Year. LC 77-21782. p. cm. 1977. (ISBN 0-395-25835-9). Houghton Mifflin.
--The Liberation of Clementine Tipton. LC 74-8180. (Illus.). 213 p. 22cm. 1974. (ISBN 0-395-19493-8). Houghton Mifflin.
--The Lost and Found Princess. Flory, Jane Trescott (1917-), illus. LC 78-24323. (Illus.). 48 p. 23cm. 1979. Houghton Mifflin.
--Miss Plunkett to the Rescue. Sims, Blanche, illus. LC 82-15797. p. cm. 1983. (ISBN 0-395-33072-6). Houghton Mifflin.
--Mist on the Mountain. 1966. E M Hale.
--Mist on the Mountain. Flory, Jane Trescott (1917-), illus. LC 66-12097. 249 p. illus. 22 cm. 1966. Houghton Mifflin.
--Mr. Snitzel's Cookies. Flory, Jane Trescott (1917-), illus. LC 50-14878. 33p. 1950. Rand McNally & Co.
--Once Upon a Windy Day. LC 47-26191. 32 p. col. illus. 17 cm. (Tell-a-tale books). c.1947. Whitman Pub. Co.
--One Hundred and Eight Bells. LC 63-15281. 219 p. illus. 22 cm. 1963. Houghton Mifflin.
--Peddler's Summer. Flory, Jane Trescott (1917-), illus. LC 60-5210. (Illus.). 158 p. 22cm. 1960. Houghton Mifflin.
--Ramshackle Roost. Croll, Carolyn, illus. LC 75-184245. (Illus.). 181 p. 22cm. 1972. (ISBN 0-395-13728-4). Houghton Mifflin.
--The Runaway Train. Flory, Jane Trescott (1917-), illus. LC 51-34961. unpaged. illus. 23 cm. (Avon toy book). N.D. Avon Kiddie Books.
--Snooty, the Pig Who Was Proud. LC 45-829. 32 p. col. illus. 17 x 14 1/2 cm. (On cover: Tell-a-tale books). c.1944. Whitman Publishing Co.
--Timothy, The Little Brown Bear. Flory, Jane Trescott (1917-), illus. LC 49-5067. 33 p. col. illus. 17 c. (Rand McNally book). c.1949. Rand McNally.
--Too Little Fire Engine. Flory, Jane Trescott (1917-), illus. N.D. Grosset & Dunlap.
--The Too Little Fire Engine. Flory, Jane Trescott (1917-), illus. LC 50-3446. (Illus.). 41p. 21cm. 1950. Wonder Books.
--Tune for the Towpath. (Illus.). (gr. 4-6). 1962. (ISBN 0-8382-0903-3). Hale.
--Tune for the Towpath. Flory, Jane Trescott (1917-), illus. (Illus.). (gr. 4-6). 1962. (ISBN 0-395-06764-2). HM.
--We'll Have a Friend for Lunch. Croll, Carolyn, illus. LC 73-18452. (Illus.). 32 p. 28cm. 1974. (ISBN 0-395-18448-7). Houghton Mifflin.
--The Wide-Awake Angel. N.D. Grosset & Dunlap.
--The Wide Awake Angel. Flory, Jane Trescott (1917-), illus. LC 45-8203. 32 p. col. illus. 24 x 20 1/2 cm. 1945. Grosset and Dunlap.

Flory, Jane Trescott (1917-) & Croll, Carolyn
--The Unexpected Grandchildren. LC 77-5085. (Illus.). 30 p. 22cm. 1977. (ISBN 0-395-25797-2). Houghton Mifflin.

Flory, Jane Trescott (1917-) & Flory, Arthur
--Cow in the Kitchen. (gr. k-3). N.D. Lothrop Bks.
Flournoy, Valerie (1952-)
--The Best Time of Day. Ford, George Cephas, Jr., illus. LC 77-91641. p. cm. 1979. (ISBN 0-394-83799-1). (ISBN 0-394-83786-X). Random House.
--The Patchwork Quilt. Pinkney, Jerry (1939-), illus. LC 84-1711. (Illus.). 32 p. 28cm. c.1985. (ISBN 0-8037-0097-0). (ISBN 0-8037-0098-9). Dial Books for Young Readers. **Awards: (CSKA); (ALA).**
Flournoy, Valerie (1952-) & De Groat, Diane (1947-)
--The Twins Strike Back. LC 79-21960. (Illus.). 32 p. 25cm. c.1980. (ISBN 0-8037-8691-3). (ISBN 0-8037-8692-1). Dial Press.
Flower, Elliott (1863-)
--Nurse Norah's up-to-date Fairy Tales. Cory, Fanny Young, illus. LC 3-24534. 18cm. 163p. 1903. J. Pott & Co.
Flower, Jane
--The Puzzle Box Mystery. Earle, Vana (1917-), illus. LC 61-15863. (Illus.). 126p. 21cm. 1961. Sterling Pub. co.
Flower, Jessie Graham
--Grace Harlowe. (The Grace Harlowe Overseas Series). N.D. Henry Altemus Co.
--Grace Harlowe with the American Army on the Rhine. (The Grace Harlowe Overseas Ser.). N.D. Henry Altemus Co.
--Grace Harlowe with the Red Cross in France. (The Grace Harlowe Overseas Ser.). N.D. Henry Altemus Co.
--Grace Harlowe with the U.S. Troops in the Argonne. (The Grace Harlowe Overseas Ser.). N.D. Henry Altemus Co.
--Grace Harlowe with the Yankee Shock Boys at St. Quentin. (The Grace Harlowe Overseas Ser.). N.D. Henry Altemus Co.
--Grace Harlowe's First Year at Overton College. (The College Girls Ser.). N.D. Henry Altemus Company.
--Grace Harlowe's Fourth Year of Overton College. 248 p. incl. front., plates. 19 1/2 cm. (Her The college girls series). c.1914. Henry Altemus Company.
--Grace Harlowe's Golden Summer. (The College Girls Ser.). N.D. Henry Altemus Company.
--Grace Harlowe's Junior Year at High School: Or, Fast Friends in the Sororities. LC 13-19427. 256 p. incl. front., plates. 19 1/2 cm. (Her The high school girls series). c.1911. Henry Altemus Company.
--Grace Harlowe's Overland Riders Among the Border Guerillas. LC 24-254187. 255 p. incl. front., illus. 19 1/2 cm. (Her Grace Harlowe's overland series). c.1924. Henry Altemus Company.
--Grace Harlowe's Overland Riders at Circle O Ranch. LC 23-772241. 239 p. incl. front., illus. 19 1/2 cm. (Her Grace Harlowe's overland riders series). c.1923. Henry Altemus Company.
--Grace Harlowe's Overland Riders in the Black Hills. LC 23-772118. 256 p. incl. front., plates. 19 1/2 cm. (Her Grace Harlowe's overland riders series). c.1923. Henry Altemus Company.
--Grace Harlowe's Overland Riders in the Great North Woods. LC 21-197693. 255 p. incl. front., plates. 19 1/2 cm. (Her Grace Harlowe's overland riders series). c.1921. Henry Altemus Company.
--Grace Harlowe's Overland Riders in the High Sierras. 251 p. incl. front., illus. 19 1/2 cm. (Her Grace Harlowe's overland riders series). c.1923. Henry Altemus Company.
--Grace Harlowe's Overland Riders in the Yellowstone National Park. LC 23-7723. 236 p. incl. front., plates. 19 1/2 cm. (Her Grace Harlowe's overland riders series). c.1923. Henry Altemus Company.
--Grace Harlowe's Overland Riders on the Great American Desert. LC 21-649977. 255 p. incl. front., illus. 19 1/2 cm. (Her Grace Harlowe's overland riders series). c.1921. Henry Altemus Company.
--Grace Harlowe's Overland Riders on the Lost River Trail. 255 p. incl. front., illus. 19 1/2 xm. (Her Grace Harlowe's overland riders series). c.1924. Henry Altemus Company.
--Grace Harlowe's Overland Riders on the Old Apache Trail. 255 p. incl. front., illus. 19 1/2 cm. (Her Grace Harlowe's overland riders series). c.1921. Henry Altemus Company.
--Grace Harlowe's Plebe Year at High School: Or, The Merry Doings of the Oakdale Freshmen Girls. LC 12-24685. 255 p. incl. front., plates. 19 1/2 cm. (Her The high school girls series). c.1910. Henry Altemus Company.
--Grace Harlowe's Problem. LC 16-18487. 256 p. incl. front., plates. 19 1/2 cm. (Her The college girls series). c.1916. Henry Altemus Company.
--Grace Harlowe's Return to Overton Campus. LC 15-17760. 256 p. incl. front., plates. 19 1/2 cm. (Her The college girls series). c.1915. Henry Altemus Company.
--Grace Harlowe's Second Year at Overton College. (The College Girls Series). N.D. Henry Altemus Company.
--Grace Harlowe's Senior Year at High School: Or, The Parting of the Ways. LC 13-19428. 256 p. incl. front., plates. 19 1/2 cm. (Her The high school girls series). c.1911. Henry Altemus Company.
--Grace Harlowe's Sophomore Year at High School: Or, The Record of the Girl Chums in Work and Athletics. LC 13-194253. 252 p. incl. front., plates. 19 1/2 cm. (Her The high school girls series). c.1911. Henry Altemus Company.
--Grace Harlowe's Third Year at Overton College. (The College Girls Ser.). N.D. Henry Altemus Company.
Flower, Phyllis
--The Barn Owl. Pape, Cherryl, illus. LC 76-58686. (Illus.). 5 7/8 x 8 1/2. 64p. (18 pt.). (Nature I Can Read Bks.). (gr. k-3). 1978. (ISBN 0-06-021919-X) Har-Row.
Flowerdew, Phyllis
--The Pedro Bks Ser. Smith, Virginia, illus. Incl. A Hat for Pedro; Hats for Donkeys; Mr. Carlos & the Baby; Mrs. Carlos Wants a Car; Pedro; Pedro & the Cars; Pedro & the Kitten; The Wrong Donkey. (Ea. bk 24p.). (Illus.). (gr. k-2). 1978. (ISBN 0-8372-2590-6). Bowmar-Noble.
Flowers, Lee S.
--The Mystery of Lookout Mountain. N.D. Christopher Publishing House.
Floy, Henry, jt. auth. see Snow, Sophia P.
Floy, James C.
--Harry Budd: Or, History of an Orphan Boy 16th ed. (Illus.). N.D. Methodist Bk Concern.
Floyd, James C.
--Some Gentle Moving Thing. 2nd ed. McBride, Michael, illus. LC 82-60198. (Illus.). 70p. (gr. 7-9). 1982. (ISBN 0-938232-11-8). Winston-Derek.
Floyd, Keith (1939-)
--Sandman's Land. LC 77-364597. 39 p. 22cm. c.1976. (ISBN 0-88967-018-8). Tree Frog.
Floyd, Lucy & Lasky, Kathryn (1944-)
--Agatha's Alphabet, with Her Very Own Dictionary. Leder, Dora, illus. LC 75-15660. (Illus.). 57 p. 31cm. 1975. (ISBN 0-528-82145-8). (ISBN 0-528-80149-X). Rand McNally.
Floyd, Silas Xavier (1869-)
--Floyd's Flowers: Or, Duty and Beauty for Colored Children, Being One Hundred Short Stories Gleaned from the Storehouse of Human Knowledge and Experience ... Adams, John Henry, illus. LC 78-168050. (Illus.). 326 p. 19cm. 1975. (ISBN 0-404-00048-7). AMS Press.
--Floyd's Flowers: Or, Duty and Beauty for Colored Children; Being One Hundred Short Stories Gleaned from the Storehouse of Human Knowledge and Experience... Rev ed. Adams, John Henry, illus. LC 5-28018. 326 p. front. (2 port.) illus. 21 cm. c.1905. Hertel, Jenkins & Co.
--The New Floyd's Flowers: Short Stories for Colored People, Old and Young; Greatly Rev. and Enl. with ABC's Supplement. Howard, Alice C, Mrs., ed. LC 22-3017. 317, 3 p. incl. front. (port.) illus., plates. 20 cm. c.1922. Austin Jenkins Co.
Floyer, Edith L.
--Molly's Heroine. N.D. Thomas Nelson & Sons.
Fluckiger, Alfred (1898-)
--Tuck, the Story of a Snow-Hare. Huxtable, Grace, illus. Fyleman, Rose, tr. LC 51-147524. 154p. illus. 20cm. N.D. Coward-McCann.
Flugge, Klauss, tr. see Janosch.
Flynn, Charlotte
--Dangerous Beat. (Orig.). (Moonstone Ser.: No. 3). (gr. 5 up). 1985. (ISBN 0-671-50783-4). Archway.
Flynn, Edwin A
--The Story of Oswald Page: A Boy from Arizona. LC 18-14534. 212 p. 19 1/2 cm. c.1918. P.J. Kenedy & Sons.
Flynn, Harry Eugene (1877-) & MacLean, Ray Butts (1873-), eds.
--Voices of Verse ... LC 33-35364. 4 v. illus. 19 1/2 cm. 1933. Lyons & Carnahan.
--Voices of Verse ... LC 44-1796. 4 v. illus. 20 1/2 cm. N.D. Lyons & Carnahan.
Flynn, Rose
--Peggy Plants a Tree. Howe, Gertrude Herrick (1902-), illus. LC 41-5507. 4 p. l., 60, 8 p. col. front., illus. 21 cm. 1941. C. Scribner's Sons.
Foa, Eugenie Rodrigues-Gradis (0000-1853)
--Little Robinson Crusoe of Paris. Oldham, Marion Mildred, illus. Olcott, Julia, tr. from Fr. LC 25-214196. 160 p. col. front., col. plates. 21 cm. (The stories all children love series). c.1925. J.B. Lippincott Company.
--The Strange Search. Cooke, Sherman, illus. Pendleton, Amena, tr. from Fr. LC 29-13367. 202 p. col. front., col. plates. 21 cm. (The stories all children love series). 1928. J.B. Lippincott Company.
Foa, Eugenie Rodrigues-Gradis (0000-1853), tr.
--Mystery of Castle Pierrefitte. Pendleton, Amena, Tr LC 27-21019. xi p., 1 l., 226 p. incl. illus., plates. col. front. 20 cm. 1927. Longmans, Green and Co.
Fodor, et al.
--The Good Health For Better Living Program: Good Health For You. Incl. No. 1. 174p. (24 pt.). (gr. 1, 4-0901); No. 2. 204p. (20-22 pt.). (gr. 2, 4-0902); No. 3. 246p. (18-20 pt.). (gr. 3, 4-0903); No. 4, 3 vols. 552p. (16-18 pt.). (gr. 4, 4-0904); No. 5, 3 vols. 628p. (16-18 pt.). (gr. 5, 4-0905); No. 6, 3 vols. 628p. (16-18 pt.). (gr. 6, 4-0906); No. 7, 3 vols. 750p. (16-18 pt.). (gr. 7, 4-0907); No. 8, 3 vols. 750p. (16-18 pt.). (gr. 8, 4-0908). 11 x 12 1/2. Repr. of 1983 ed (Pub. by Laidlaw). (16-24 pt.). N.D. Am Printing Hse.
Fogel, Barbara R
--What's the Biggest?. Wolff, Barbara, illus. LC 66-15411. 115p. illus. 24cm. c.1966. Random.
Fogle, Willa
--Our Father. Fogle, Peter, illus. LC 57-16378. 60p. illus. 23cm. 1956. Scrivener.
Fogler, Doris & Nicol, Nina, Mrs.
--Rusty Pete of the Lazy AB. Fogler, Doris, illus. LC 29-9920. 5 p. l., 3-106 p. incl. illus., plates. col. front., col. pl. 21 x 19 1/2 cm. 1929. The Macmillan Company.
Foldes, Jolan (1903-)
--Rudi Finds a Way. Jemne, Elsa Laubach (1888-), illus. LC 41-16895. 151 p. illus. 21 cm. c.1941. J. B. Lippincott Company.
Folds, Thomas M.
--Where is the Fire?. LC 47 30695. (Illus.). 35p. 29cm. 1947. Houghton Mifflin Co.
Foley, Anna Bernice Williams (1902-)
--The Gazelle & the Hunter. Magnuson, Diana, illus. LC 79-18880. (Illus.). 64p. (Folk Tales Ser.). (gr. 2-6). 1980. (ISBN 0-516-06480-0). Childrens.
--The Gazelle and the Hunter: A Persian Folk Tale. Magnuson, Diana, illus. LC 79-18880. p. cm. 1980. (ISBN 0-89565-104-1). Child's World.
--Spaceships of the Ancients. Hoffmann, Lee Kolozsi, illus. LC 78-59116. (Illus.). 61 p. 24cm. c.1978. Veritie Press.
--Star Stories. Gurvin, Abe, illus. (gr. 1-4). 1970. (ISBN 0-525-39899-6). Dutton.
--Star Stories. Gurvin, Abe, illus. LC 74-104124. 48p. 1970. (ISBN 0-8415-2004-6). McCall Publishing Company.
--A Walk Among Clouds. McLean, Mina Gow, illus. LC 79-18295. p. cm. c.1980. (ISBN 0-89565-105-X). Child's World.
--Why the Cock Crows Three Times. Anderson, Rondi Marie, illus. LC 79-19088. p. cm. c.1980. (ISBN 0-89565-106-8). Child's World.
Foley, Arthur
--Breezy adventure. N.D. Bruce Humphries, Inc.
Foley, George F., Jr.
--Sinbad of the Coast Guard. Gray, George R., illus. N.D. Dodd, Mead & Co.
Foley, James Williams (1874-)
--Boys and Girls. N.D. E P Dutton.
--Friendly Rhymes. N.D. E P Dutton.
--Sing a Song of Sleepy Head: Being Readable Rhymes for Curious Children. LC 22-20935. 6 p. l., 3-123, 1 p. incl. front., illus. plates. 21 cm. c.1922. E. P. Dutton & Company.
--Tales of the Trail. N.D. E P Dutton.
--Voices of Song. N.D. E P Dutton.
Foley, John R., jt. auth. see Collyer, Barbara.
Foley, Julia R, tr.
--The Wonderful Voyage of Little Pierre, and Other Stories from the French. LC 25-11367. 56 p. 19 1/2 cm. c.1925. The Christopher Publishing House.
Foley, June (1944-)
--It's No Crush, I'm in Love!. LC 81-15214. 215 p. 22cm. c.1982. (ISBN 0-440-04119-8). Delacorte Press.
--Love by Any Other Name. LC 82-72752. 216 p. 22cm. c.1983. (ISBN 0-440-04865-6). Delacorte Press.
Foley, Mary Louise Munro (1933-)
--The Caper Club. Stone, David Karl (1922-), illus. LC 76-79227. (Illus.). 80 p. 24cm. (Carousel book). 1969. L. W. Singer.
--The Sinister Studios of KESP-TV. Febland, David, illus. (Illus.). 96p. (Orig.). (Twistaplot Bks.: No. 5). (gr. 7 up). 1983. (ISBN 0-590-32827-1). Scholastic Inc.
--Somebody Stole Second. Heinly, John (1932-), illus. LC 74-176033. (Illus.). 45 p. 23cm. 1972. Delacorte Press.
--Tackle Twenty-Two. Heinly, John (1932-), illus. LC 78-50425. (Illus.). (gr. 1-3). 1978. Delacorte.
--The Train of Terror. Febland, David, illus. (Illus.). 96p. (Orig.). (Twistaplot Bks.: No. 2). (gr. 7 up). N.D. (ISBN 0-590-32499-3). Scholastic Inc.
Foley, Tom, illus.
--Sakshi Gopal: A Witness for the Wedding. Greene, Joshua, retold by. (Illus.). 16p. 1st U.S. edition. (gr. 1-4). 1981. (ISBN 0-89647-010-5). Bala Bks.
Folinsbee, J. P. (1902-)
--Everygirls Nurse Stories. Furman, Abraham Loew, ed. McCann, Gerald (1916-), illus. LC 59-13375. 21cm. 223p. (Everygirls Library). 1959. Lantern Press.
Folkard, Charles James (1878-1963)
--Teddy Tail's Alphabet. N.D. Macmillan.
Follansbee, Pauline
--Puppet Show. N.D. Dorrance & Co.
Follen, Eliza Lee Cabot, Mrs. (1787-1860), tr. see Montgolfier, Adelaide De.
Follen, Eliza Lee Cabot, Mrs. (1787-1860)
--The Birthday, 1 of 5 vols. (Illus.). (Well-Spent Hour Library). N.D. Thomas Y. Crowell.
--Conscience, 1 of 12 vols. (Illus.). (Twilight Stories). 1882. Set. Lee & Shepard.
--Hymns, Songs, and Fables, for Young People. rev. and enl. from the last ed. [illegible] p. 16 cm. 1847. W. Crosby and H. P. Nichols.
--Little Songs, 1 of 3 vols. (Illus.). (Baby Ballad Ser.). 1882. Lee & Shepard.
--Little Songs. LC 12-82288. 96 p. incl. front., illus. 17 cm. 1856. Whittemore, Niles and Hall.
--Little Songs. Humphrey, Lizzie B., illus. LC 15-1593. 76 p. incl. front., illus. 18 cm. 1875. Lee and Shepard.
--Little Songs, for Little Boys and Girls... LC 15-2593. 66 p. incl. front., illus. 12 cm. 1833. L. C. Bowles.
--Made-up Stories, 1 of 12 vols. (Illus.). (Twilight Stories). 1882. Lee & Shepard.
--Made-up Stories. (Illus.). (The Old Garret Stories). 1900. Set. Lee & Shepard.
--Mrs. Follen's Little Songs & New Songs for Little People. (Illus.). 1900. Lee & Shepard.
--Peddler of Dust Sticks, 1 of 12 vols. (Illus.). (Twilight Stories). 1882. Lee & Shepard.
--Piccolissima, 1 of 12 vols. (Illus.). (Twilight Stories). 1882. Set. Lee & Shepard.
--Sequel to "The Well-Spent Hour: Or, The Birth-Day. LC 30-14033. vi, 154 p. front., pl. 16 cm. 1832. Carter and Hendee.
--The Talkative Wig, 1 of 12 vols. (Illus.). (Twilight Stories). 1882. Set. Lee & Shepard.
--Three Little Kittens. Cooper, Marjorie (1910-), illus. LC 68-13402. (Illus.). 22 p. (incl. lining papers). 33cm. (Rand McNally giant book). 1968, c.1966. Rand McNally.
--Traveller's Stories, 1 of 12 vols. (Illus.). (Twilight Stories). 1882. Lee & Shepard.
--Travellers' Stories, 1 of 6 vols. (Illus.). (The Old Garret Stories). 1900. Set. Lee & Shepard.
--True Stories about Dogs, 1 of 12 vols. (Illus.). (Twilight Stories). 1882. Lee & Shepard.
--True Stories About Dogs & Cats. Billings, illus. LC 30-140841. 96 p. incl. front., illus. 15 1/2 cm. (Half-title: Mrs Follen's twilight stories no. 1). 1856. Whittemore, Niles & Hall.
--Twilight Stories, 12 vols. (Illus.). 1882. Set. Lee & Shepard.
--Two Festivals, 1 of 12 vols. (Illus.). (Twilight Stories). 1882. Set. Lee & Shepard.
--The Well-Spent Hour, 1 of 5 vols. (Illus.). (Well-Spent Hour Library). N.D. Thomas Y. Crowell.
--What Animals Do and Say, 1 of 12 vols. (Illus.). (Twilight Stories). 1882. Lee & Shepard.
--What Animals Do and Say, 1 of 6 vols. (Illus.). (The Old Garret Stories). N.D. Set. Lee & Shepard.
--When I was a Girl, 1 of 12 vols. (Illus.). (Twilight Stories). 1882. Lee & Shepard.
--When I was a Girl, 1 of 6 vols. (Illus.). (The Old Garret Stores). N.D. Set. Lee & Shepard.
--Who Speaks Next?, 1 of 12 vols. (Illus.). (Twilight Stories). 1882. Set. Lee & Shepard.
--Who Spoke Next. (Illus.). (The Old Garret Stories). 1900. Set. Lee & Shepard.
Follet, Helen Thomas, Mrs. (1884-1970)
--Men of Sulu Sea. N.D. Charles Scribner's.
--Ocean Outposts. N.D. Charles Scribner's Sons.
Follett, Barbara Newhall (1914-)
--The House Without Windows & Eepersip's Life There. LC 27-2812. 5 p. l., 166 p., 1 l. 19 1/2 cm. 1927. A. A. Knopf.
--The Voyage of the Norman D. 1928. Alfred A. Knopf.
Follett, Dwight W.
--Gunner and The Dombo. Nelson, Don, photos by. LC 45-7781. (Illus.). 32p. N.D. Wilcox & Follett Co.
Follett, Garth
--The Circus. N.D. Wilcox & Follett Co.
Follett, Helen Thomas, Mrs. (1884-1970)
--House Afire!. Sperry, Armstrong W. (1897-1976), illus. LC 41-52014. 4 p. l., 102 p. illus. 22 cm. 1941. C. Scribner's Sons.
Folley, Helen
--Island on Guard. N.D. Charles Scribner's Sons.
Folmsbee, Beulah
--Guki the Moon Boy, and Other Plays. LC 28-20718. 5 p. l., 3-155 p., 1 l. incl. front., illus., plates, diagrs. 21 cm. c.1928. Harcourt, Brace & Company.
Folsom, A. P. & Folsom, M. T., eds.
--Young Folks' Poetry. N.D. Lothrop Pub. Co.
Folsom, Franklin Brewster see Brewster, Benjamin, pseud.

Folsom, Franklin Brewster see Nesbit, Troy, pseud.
Folsom, Franklin Brewster (1907-)
--The Baby Elephant. Brewster, Benjamin, pseud. Burchard, Peter Duncan (1921-), illus. LC 50-10325. (Illus.). 32p. 21cm. 1950. Wonder Books.
--Beyond the Frontier. rev. ed. Floherty, John Joseph, Jr. (1892-1964), illus. (Illus.). 249 p. 22cm. 1968. Harvey House.
--The Big Book of the Real Circus. Brewster, Benjamin, pseud. Phillips, Gail, illus. 1951. Grosset & Dunlap.
--Diamond Cave Mystery. library ed. Floherty, John Joseph, Jr. (1892-1964), illus. LC 62-10795. (Illus.). 282 p. 22cm. (His A wilderness mystery). 1962. Harvey House.
--Forest Fire Mystery. Floherty, John Joseph, Jr. (1892-1964), illus. (Illus.). 282cm. (Wilderness Mystery Ser). (gr. 4-7). 1963. (ISBN 0-8178-4062-1). Harvey.
--The Hidden Ruin. LC 57-6509. 217p. 22cm. 1957. Funk & Wagnalls.
--The Hidden Ruin. Floherty, John Joseph, Jr. (1892-1964), illus. LC 66-31472. (Illus.). 243 p. 22cm. (His A Wilderness mystery). 1966. Harvey House.
--Indian Mummy Mystery. Floherty, John Joseph, Jr. (1892-1964), illus. LC 62-10796. (Illus.). 282 p. 22cm. (His A wilderness mystery). (gr. 5-7). 1962. (ISBN 0-8178-4032-X). Harvey House.
--The Jinx of Payrock Canyon. Nesbit, Troy, pseud. Koering, Ursula (1921-), illus. LC 55-828. (Illus.). 282p. 21cm. 1954. Whitman.
--Mystery at Payrock Canyon. Floherty, John Joseph, Jr. (1892-1964), illus. LC 62-17253. (Illus.). (Wilderness Mystery Ser). (gr. 4-7). 1962. (ISBN 0-8178-4051-6). (ISBN 0-8178-4052-4). Harvey.
--Mystery at Rustlers Fort. Floherty, John Joseph, Jr. (1892-1964), illus. LC 60-14421. (Illus.). 22 cm. 282p. (Wilderness Mystery Series). 1960. (ISBN 0-8178-4021-4). Harvey House, Inc Publishers.
--Oscar the Baby Elephant. Brewster, Benjamin, pseud. Burchard, Peter Duncan (1921-), illus. N.D. Wonder Books.
--Sand Dune Pony Mystery. Floherty, John Joseph, Jr. (1892-1964), illus. (Illus.). 282p. (Wilderness Mystery Ser). (gr. 3-6). 1960. (ISBN 0-8178-4011-7). (ISBN 0-8178-4012-5). Harvey.
--Search in the Desert. Highsmith, Mary & Highsmith, Stanley, illus. LC 55-11098. 200p. illus. 22cm. 1955. Funk & Wagnalls.
Folsom, Franklin Brewster (1907-) & Elting, Mary (1906-)
--It's a Secret. Brewster, Benjamin, pseud. Myers, Bernice, illus. LC 50-10300. unpaged. col. illus. 21 cm. (Wonder books, 540). 1950. Wonder Books.
--The Real Book of American Tall Tales. 1st ed. Danska, Herbert (1928-), illus. LC 52-12391. 192p. illus. 21cm. (Real books R30). 1952. Garden City Books, by Arrangement with F. Watts New York.
Folsom, M. T., jt. ed. see Folsom, A. P.
Folsom, Marcia McClintock & Folsom, Michael
--Easy As Pie: A Guessing Game of Sayings. Kent, Jack, pseud. (1920-), illus. Kent, John Wellington. LC 84-14978. (Illus.). 64 p. 24cm. c.1985. (ISBN 0-89919-303-X). Clarion Books.
Folsom, Michael
--Keep Your Eyes Open. Dauber, Elizabeth, illus. LC 65-21506. 60 p. col. illus. 22 cm. 1965. Grosset & Dunlap.
--The Secret Story of Pueblo Bonito. Elting, Mary, ed. Elgin, Kathleen (1923-), illus. (Science and Parade Series). 1963. Harvey House, Inc, Publishers.
Folsom, Michael, jt. auth. see Folsom, Marcia McClintock.
Foltz, Marie B.
--My Old Country Grandfather. N.D. Vantage Press.
Foltz, Mary Jane
--Awani. Silverman, Melvin Frank (1931-1966), illus. LC 64-12039. 128p. illus. 22cm. c.1964. Morrow.
--Nicolau's Prize. Turkle, Brinton Cassaday (1915-), illus. LC 67-2709. (Illus.). 91 p. 21cm. 1967. McGraw-Hill.
--Tuchin's Mayan Treasure. Silverman, Melvin Frank (1931-1966), illus. LC 63-9961. (Illus.). 63 p. 22cm. 1963. Morrow.
Fon Eisen, Anthony T. (1917-)
--Bond of the Fire. LC 65-13080. (Illus.). 188 p. 21cm. 1965. World Pub. Co.
--The Magnificent Mongrel. Geer, Charles Hand (1922-), illus. LC 78-101848. (Illus.). 125 p. 21cm. 1970. World Pub. Co.
--Storm, Dog of Newfoundland. (gr. 5-11). N.D. Charles Scribner's Sons.
--The Prince of Omeya. LC 64-20000. 318 p. map. 21 cm. 1964. World Pub. Co.
Fonhus, Mikkjel
--Jaampa, The Silver Fox. 244p. N.D. G. P. Putnam's Sons.
Fontaine, Don
--All Those in Favor. LC 54-5673. 250p. 21cm. 1954. Prentice-Hall.
Fontaine, Jan
--The Spaghetti Tree. Runyon, Anne Marshall, illus. LC 79-118526. (Illus.). 44 p. 22cm. (gr. k-4). c.1979. (ISBN 0-934926-00-X). Talespinner Publications.
Fontaine, Jean de La see De La Fontaine, Jean.
Fontaine, Robert Louis
--Humorous Monologues for Teenagers. Rev. ed. 1971. (ISBN 0-8238-0125-X). Plays, Inc.
--Humorous Skits for Young People: A Collection of Royalty-Free Short Plays and Easy-to-Perform Comedy Sketches. LC 77-359195. vi, 184 p. 21cm. (gr. 6-12). c.1976. (ISBN 0-8238-0210-8). Plays, Inc.
Fontana, Ugo, illus.
--The Magic Butterfly, and Other Fairy Tales of Central Europe. Obligado, George (1908-), tr. LC 63-24445. (Illus.). 37cm. 62p. (A Golden Giant Book). 1963. Golden Press.
--The Magic Butterfly & Other Slavic Fairy Tales. N.D. Golden Press.
Fontane, Theodor (1819-1898)
--Sir Ribbeck of Havelland. Hogrogian, Nonny (1932-), illus. Shub, Elizabeth, tr. from Ger. LC 69-12746. (Illus.). 32 p. 1969. Macmillan. **Award: (ALA).**
Fontannza, Luciennec & Ker Wilson, Barbara (1929-)
--The Willow Pattern Story. Fontannaz, Lucienne, illus. (Illus.). 1984. (ISBN 0-207-13848-6, Pub. by Salem Hse Ltd). Merrimack Pub Cir.
Fontanosa, Napoleon E., II
--Shoes Story. 32p. 1984. (ISBN 0-89962-373-5). Todd & Honeywell.
Fontenot, Mary Alice (1910-)
--Clovis Crawfish and Etienne Escargot. Vincent, Eric, illus. Gilmore, Jeanne & Gilmore, Robert, contrib. by. LC 79-119985. (Illus.). 27 p. 29cm. c.1979. Acadiana Press.
--Clovis Crawfish & Etienne Escargot. Vincent, Eric, illus. 32p. (gr. k-6). 1982. (ISBN 0-88289-368-8). Pelican.
--Clovis Crawfish and Etienne Escargot. Vincent, Eric, illus. LC 84-18895. p. cm. 1985, c.1979. (ISBN 0-88289-368-8). Pelican Pub. Co.
--Clovis Crawfish & Petit Papillon. Graves, Keith, illus. LC 83-27325. (Illus.). 52p. Repr. (gr. k-5). 1985. (ISBN 0-88289-448-X). (ISBN 0-88289-448-X). Pelican.
--Clovis Crawfish and the Orphan Zo-Zo. Vincent, Eric, illus. LC 81-17740. p. cm. c.1982. (ISBN 0-88289-312-2). Pelican Pub. Co.
--Clovis Crawfish and the Singing Cigales. Vincent, Eric, illus. LC 81-5608. p. cm. (1910-). 1981. (ISBN 0-88289-270-3). Pelican Pub. Co.
Foot, Katherine B.
--The Rovings of a Restless Boy. 12cm. 294p. 1901. The Mershon Co.
--The Sea Captain's Children. Merrill, Frank Thayer (1848-), illus. LC 9-19835. 18cm. 128p. 1905. S. E. Cassino & Son.
Foote, Agnes Cope
--Huckleberry Island. Hall, Kleber, illus. LC 38-29542. 6 p. l., 3-259, 1 p. incl. front., illus., plates. 21 cm. 1938. Little, Brown and Company.
--The Sea Bird Islands. Wyeth, Andrew Newell (1917-), illus. LC 39-23637. 6 p. l., 3-254 p. incl. front., plates. 21 cm. 1939. Little, Brown and Company.
Foote, Darby Mozelle (1942-)
--Baby Love & Casey Blue. LC 74-16597. 320p. 1975. (ISBN 0-399-11436-X). Putnam.
Foote, Doreen
--Dude Girl. LC 51-11026. 194 p. 21 cm. 1951. Dodd, Mead.
Foote, Edward Bliss (1829-1906)
--Science in Story: Sammy Tubbs, the Boy Doctor and "Sponsie," the Troublesome Monkey. LC 12-32188. (Illus.). 15 x 11cm. (Murray Hill Ser.). 1874. Murray Hill Publishing.
Foote, Evelyn Carter
--A Very Special Spring. LC 81-67749. 95 p. 20cm. 1982, c.1981. (ISBN 0-8054-7317-3). Broadman Press.
Foote, John McFarland (1883-), ed. see Hale, Edward Everett.
Foote, John McFarland (1883-), ed. see Hale, Edward Everett (1822-1909) & Hubbard, Elbert.
Foote, John McFarland (1883-), ed.
--Patriotic American Stories. (The Winston Clear-Type Popular Classics). N.D. John C. Winston.
Foote, John Taintor (1881-)
--Dumb-Bell and Others. (Famous Dog Stories). N.D. Grosset & Dunlap.
--Dumbell of Brookfield. N.D. Grosset & Dunlap.
--Hoofbeats. (Illus.). (gr. 7-9). N.D. (ISBN 0-448-02278-8). G&D.
--Hoofbeats. (Famous Horse Stories). N.D. Grosset & Dunlap.
--Trub's Diary. LC 28-10884. vi p., 1 l., 269, 1 p. 19 1/2 cm. 1928. D. Appleton & Company.
Foote, Kate, jt. auth. see Kaler, James Otis.
Foote, Mary Hallock, Mrs. (1847-)
--The Little Fig-tree Stories. Foote, Mary Hallock, Mrs. (1847-), illus. 183p. 1899. Houghton Mifflin & Co.
Foote, Timothy Gilson (1926-) & Chartier, Normand (1945-)
--The Great Ringtail Garbage Caper. Chartier, Normand (1945-), illus. LC 79-21238. (Illus.). 66 p. 22cm. 1980. (ISBN 0-395-28759-6). Houghton Mifflin.
Foote-Smith, Elizabeth (1913-)
--Gentle Albatross. LC 75-44098. 1976. (ISBN 0-399-11730-X). Putnam.
Footman, David John (1895-)
--A Pretty Pass: Or, Just a Little Careless. LC 33-7560. 5 p. l., 3-309 p. 20 cm. 1933. W. Morrow and Company.
Forberg, Ati, pseud., see Forberg, Beate Gropius.
Forberg, Ati, jt. auth. see Fleisher, Robbin.
Forberg, Ati, pseud. (1925-), ed.
--On a Grass-Green Horn: Old Scotch and English Ballards. Forberg, Beate Gropius. Forberg, Ati, pseud. (1925-), illus. Forberg, Beate Gropius. LC 65-21715. 52p. illus. 26cm. (gr. 4 up). c.1965. (ISBN 0-689-20105-2). Atheneum.
Forberg, Beate Gropius see Forberg, Ati, pseud.
Forbes, Bryan (1926-)
--International Velvet. 1978. (ISBN 0-8317-4950-4, Mayflower Bks). Smith Pubs.
Forbes, Colin, pseud., see Sawkins, Raymond Harold.
Forbes, Colin, pseud. (1923-)
--Year of the Golden Ape. Sawkins, Raymond Harold. 256p. 1974. (ISBN 0-525-23895-6). Dutton.
Forbes, Cora Belle
--Elizabeth's Charm-String. LC 3-25552. xiii, 238 p., 1 l. front., illus., 9 pl. 19 1/2 cm. 1903. Little, Brown, and Company.
Forbes, Edith Emerson, ed.
--Favourites of a Nursery of Seventy Years Ago: And Some Others of Later Date. LC 16-23416. ix p., 2 l., 620 p., 1 l. incl. front., illus. 18 1/2 cm. 1916. Houghton Mifflin Company.
Forbes, Esther (1891-1967)
--Johnny Tremain. Ward, Lynd Kendall (1905-1985), illus. Stauffer, Ruth Matilda (1865-), notes by. LC 45-4020. ix, 2, 256, xx p. col. front., illus. (incl map) plates. 21 cm. 1945. Houghton Mifflin Company.
--Johnny Tremain: A Novel for Old & Young. Ward, Lynd Kendall (1905-1985), illus. LC 43-16483. 4 p. l., 256 p. col. front. 21 cm. 1943. Houghton Mifflin Company. **Award: (JNM).**
--A Mirror for Witches. N.D. Houghton Mifflin Co.
--Miss Marvel. N.D. Houghton Mifflin Co.
--O Genteel Lady. N.D. Houghton Mifflin Co.
--Rainbow on the Road. 1954. Houghton Mifflin Co.
--Running of the Tide. N.D. Houghton Mifflin Co.
Forbes, Gerritt Van Husen (1795-1863)
--New-York Evening Tales: Or, Uncle John's True Stories About Natural History ... LC 21-2688. 4 v. fronts., illus. 18 cm. 1833. M.Day.
Forbes, Graham B., pseud., see Stratemeyer Syndicate.
Forbes, Graham B., pseud.
--The Boys of Columbia High in Camp: Or, The Rivalry of the Old School League. Stratemeyer Syndicate. Rogers, Walter S., illus. (The Boys of Columbia High Ser.: Vol. 8). 1920. Grosset & Dunlap.
--The Boys of Columbia High in Track Athletics: Or, A Long Run that Won. Stratemeyer Syndicate. Rogers, Walter S, illus. (The Boys of Columbia High Ser.: Vol. 6). 1913. Grosset & Dunlap.
--The Boys of Columbia High in Winter Sports: Or, Stirring Doings on Skates and Iceboats. Stratemeyer Syndicate. Rogers, Walter S., illus. (The Boys of Columbia High Ser.: Vol. 7). 1915. Grosset & Dunlap.
--The Boys of Columbia High on the Diamond: Or, Winning Out by Pluck. Stratemeyer Syndicate. Rogers, Walter S., illus. (The Boys of Columbia High Ser.: Vol. 2). 1912, c.1911. Grosset & Dunlap.
--The Boys of Columbia High on the Gridiron: Or, The Struggle for the Silver Cup. Stratemeyer Syndicate. Rogers, Walter S., illus. (The Boys of Columbia High Ser.: Vol. 4). 1912, c.1911. Grosset & Dunlap.
--The Boys of Columbia High on the Ice: Or, Out for the Hockey Championship. Stratemeyer Syndicate. Rogers, Walter S., illus. (The Boys of Columbia High Ser.: Vol. 5). 1912, c.1911. Grosset & Dunlap.
--The Boys of Columbia High on the River: Or, The Boat Race Plot that Failed. Stratemeyer Syndicate. Rogers, Walter S., illus. (The Boys of Columbia High Ser.: Vol. 3). 1912, c.1911. Grosset & Dunlap.
--The Boys of Columbia High: Or, The All Around Rivals of the School. Stratemeyer Syndicate. Rogers, Walter S., illus. (The Boys of Columbia High Ser.: Vol. 1). 1912, c.1911. Grosset & Dunlap.
--Frank Allen after Big Game: Or, With Guns and Snowshoes in the Rockies. Stratemeyer Syndicate. (The Frank Allen Ser.: Vol. 15). 1927. Garden City Publishing Co., Inc.
--Frank Allen and His Motor Boat: Or, Racing to Save a Life. Stratemeyer Syndicate. LC 26-18102. 1 p. l., 216 p. 19 cm. (The Frank Allen Ser.: Vol. 10). 1926. Garden City Publishing Co., Inc.
--Frank Allen and His Rivals: Or, The Boys of Columbia High in Track Athletics. Stratemeyer Syndicate. LC 26-22299. 1 p. l., 230 p. plates. 19 cm. (The Frank Allen Ser.: Vol. 4). Orig. Title: The Boys of Columbia High in Track Athletics; or, A Long Run that Won. 1926. Garden City Publishing Co., Inc.
--Frank Allen at Gold Fork: Or, Locating the Lost Claim. Stratemeyer Syndicate. LC 26-18103. 1 p. l., 214 p. 19 cm. (The Frank Allen Ser.: Vol. 9). 1926. Garden City Publishing Co., Inc.
--Frank Allen at Old Moose Lake: Or, the Trail in the Snow. Stratemeyer Syndicate. (The Frank Allen Ser.: Vol. 12). 1926. Garden City Publishing Co., Inc.
--Frank Allen at Rockspur Ranch: Or, The Old Cowboy's Secret. Stratemeyer Syndicate. LC 26-14124. 1 p. l., 214 p. 19 cm. (The Frank Allen Ser.: Vol. 8). 1926. Garden City Publishing Co., Inc.
--Frank Allen at Zero Camp: Or, The Queer Old Man of the Hills. Stratemeyer Syndicate. LC 27-1244. 1 p. l., 216 p. 18 1/2 cm. (The Frank Allen Ser.: Vol. 13). 1926. Garden City Publishing Co., Inc.
--Frank Allen, Captain of the Team: Or, The Boys of Columbia High on the Gridiron. Stratemeyer Syndicate. LC 26-223242. 2 p. l., 232 p. 19 cm. (The Frank Allen Ser.: Vol. 11). Orig. Title: The Boys of Columbia High on the Gridiron; or, The Struggle for the Silver Cup. 1926. Garden City Publishing Co., Inc.
--Frank Allen, Head of the Crew: Or, The Boys of Columbia High on the River. Stratemeyer Syndicate. LC 26-223012. 2 p. l., 229 p. 19 cm. (The Frank Allen Ser.: Vol. 6). Orig. Title: The Boys of Columbia High on the River; or, The Boat Race Plot that Failed. 1926. Garden City Publishing Co., Inc.
--Frank Allen in Camp: Or, Columbia High and the School League Rivals. Stratemeyer Syndicate. 1 p. l., 214 p. plates. 19 cm. (The Frank Allen Ser.: Vol. 7). Orig. Title: The Boys of Columbia High in Camp; or, The Rivalry of the old School League. 1926. Garden City Publishing Co., Inc.
--Frank Allen in Winter Sports: Or, Columbia High on Skates and Iceboats. Stratemeyer Syndicate. 1 p. l., 236 p. plates. 18 1/2 cm. (The Frank Allen Ser.: Vol. 3). Orig. Title: The Boys of Columbia High in Winter Sports; or, Stirring Doings on Skates and Iceboats. 1926. Garden City Publishing Co., Inc.
--Frank Allen, Pitcher: Or, The Boys of Columbia High on the Diamond. Stratemeyer Syndicate. LC 26-223002. 2 p. l., 227 p. plates. 19 cm. (The Frank Allen Ser.: Vol. 5). Orig. Title: The Boys of Columbia High on the Diamond ; or, Winning Out by Pluck. 1926. Garden City Publishing Co., Inc.
--Frank Allen Playing to Win: Or, The Boys of Columbia High on the Ice. Stratemeyer Syndicate. LC 26-603122. 2 p. l., 229 p. plates. 18 1/2 cm. (The Frank Allen Ser.: Vol. 2). Orig. Title: The Boys of Columbia High on the Ice; or, Out for the Hockey Championship. 1926. Garden City Publishing Co., Inc.
--Frank Allen Snowbound: Or, Fighting for Life in the Big Blizzard. Stratemeyer Syndicate. (The Frank Allen Ser.: Vol. 14). 1927. Garden City Publishing Co., Inc.
--Frank Allen's Schooldays: Or, The All-Around Rivals of Columbia High. Stratemeyer Syndicate. LC 26-603423. 2 p. l., 227 p. plates. 19 cm. (The Frank Allen Ser.: Vol. 1). Orig. Title: The Boys of Columbia High; or, The All Around Rivals of the School. 1926. Garden City Publishing Co., Inc.
Forbes, Helen Cady
--Apple Pie Hill. Barte, Eleanore, illus. LC 30-10707. 5 p. l., 154 p. incl. plates. 19 1/2 cm. 1930. The Macmillan Company.
--Araminta. Martin, Paul, illus. LC 27-24269. vii p., 1 l., 229 p. col. front., plates. 19 1/2 cm. 1927. The Macmillan Company.
--Mario's Castle. De Angeli, Marguerite Lofft, Mrs. (1889-), illus. LC 28-21061. vii, 198 p. col. front., plates. 19 1/2 cm. 1928. The Macmillan Company.
--Mary and Marcia, Partners. Wood, Harrie (1902-), illus. LC 26-16368. 5 p. l., 3-159 p. inc. front., plates. 19 1/2 cm. 1926. The Macmillan Company.
Forbes, J. H. see Locker, Arthur, pseud.

--Hornblower Takes Command. Griggs, G. P., selected by. Whittam, Geoffrey William (1916-), illus. LC 65-173245. 223p. illus. 20cm. 1st U.S. edition. (Cadet ed. of Hornblower, v.2). (gr. 7 up). 1965, c.1937. (ISBN 0-316-28898-5). Little.
--Hornblower's Triumph. Griggs, G. P., ed. Whittam, Geoffrey William (1916-), illus. LC 65-173257. 223p. illus. 20cm. 1st U.S. edition. (Cadet ed. of Hornblower, v.4). (gr. 7 up). 1965, c.1945. (ISBN 0-316-28900-0). Little.
--Lieutenant Hornblower. (gr. 7 up). 1952. (ISBN 0-316-28907-8). Little.
--Lord Hornblower. (gr. 7 up). 1946. (ISBN 0-316-28908-6). Little.
--Lord Hornblower. (Keith Jennison Large Type Bks). (gr. 6 up). N.D. (ISBN 0-531-00228-4). Watts.
--Mr. Midshipman Hornblower. (gr. 7 up). 1950. (ISBN 0-316-28909-4). Little.
--Poo-Poo & the Dragons. Lawson, Robert (1892-1957), illus. LC 42-17225. viii, 142, 1p. incl. front., illus. 22cm. 1942. Little, Brown.

Forester, Dexter J., pseud., see Goldfrap, John Henry.

Forester, Dexter J., pseud. (1879-1917)
--Bungalow Boys. Goldfrap, John Henry. (The Bungalow Boys Ser.). N.D. Hurst & Co.

Forgatsch, Olive H.
--A World of Wonder: Poetry for Children. LC 82-90106. (Illus.). 60p. (gr. 2-5). 1982. (ISBN 0-9608784-0-8). Rainbow Child Bks.

Forgey, William W. (1942-)
--Campfire Stories: Things That Go Bump in the Night. LC 85-2429. 160p. (Orig.). 1985. (ISBN 0-934802-23-8). (ISBN 0-934802-23-8). ICS Bks.

Forgirts, M. A. D.
--Sunshine Cottage. N.D. Henry Hoyt.

Forman, Frieda, jt. auth. see Masey, Mary Louise.

Forman, Henry James (1879-1966)
--The Man Who Lived in a Shoe. 334p. N.D. Little,Brown & Co.
--The Pony Express. N.D. Grosset & Dunlap.

Forman, Henry James (1879-1966) & Woods, Walter
--The Pony Express: A Romance. LC 25-22450. viii, 308 p. front., plates, 19 1/2 cm. c.1925. Grosset & Dunlap.

Forman, James Douglas (1932-)
--A Ballad for Hogskin Hill. LC 79-16563. 229 p. 22cm. c.1979. (ISBN 0-374-30497-1). Farrar, Straus, Giroux.
--Call Back Yesterday. LC 81-14416. p. cm. 1981. (ISBN 0-684-17168-6). Scribner.
--Ceremony of Innocence. LC 73-106177. 249 p. 21cm. 1970. Hawthorn Books.
--The Cow Neck Rebels. LC 77-88783. (Illus.). 272 p. 22cm. (Bell book). 1969. Farrar, Straus & Giroux.
--Doomsday Plus Twelve. LC 84-18221000001. p. cm. 1984. (ISBN 0-684-18221-1). Scribner.
--A Fine, Soft Day. LC 78-11127. 245 p. 22cm. c.1978. (ISBN 0-374-32301-1). Farrar, Straus, Giroux.
--Follow the River. LC 75-1448. 185 p. 21cm. 1975. (ISBN 0-374-32424-7). Farrar, Straus and Giroux.
--Freedom's Blood. LC 78-23265. 114, 1 p. 25cm. 1979. (ISBN 0-531-02866-6). F. Watts.
--Horses of Anger. LC 67-15004. 249 p. 22cm. (Bell book). 1967. Farrar, Straus & Giroux.
--The Life and Death of Yellow Bird. LC 73-82697. 215 p. 21cm. 1973. (ISBN 0-374-34408-6). Farrar, Straus and Giroux.
--My Enemy, My Brother. LC 80-28140. p. c. c.1981. (ISBN 0-525-66735-0). Elsevier/Nelson Books.
--My Enemy, My Brother. LC 75-80282. 250 p. 21cm. 1969. Meredith Press.
--People of the Dream. LC 76-188271. (Illus.). 227 p. 21cm. 1972. (ISBN 0-374-35804-4). Farrar, Straus & Giroux.
--The Pumpkin Shell. LC 81-7774. p. cm. c.1981. (ISBN 0-374-36159-2). Farrar/Straus/Giroux.
--Ring the Judas Bell. LC 65-11619. 218 p. 22cm. 1965 (Bell Books). Farrar. **Award: (ALA).**
--The Shield of Achilles. LC 66-14036. 211 p. 22cm. 1966 (Bell). Farrar.
--The Skies of Crete. LC 63-20018. 181 p. 22cm. (Bell book). 1963. Farrar, Straus.
--So Ends This Day. LC 78-125148. 247 p. 21cm. (Bell book). 1970. Farrar, Straus & Giroux.
--Song of Jubilee. LC 74-149224. 185 p. 21cm. (Bell book). 1971. (ISBN 0-374-37142-3). Farrar, Straus and Giroux.
--The Survivor. LC 76-2478. 272 p. 21cm. c.1976. (ISBN 0-374-37312-4). Farrar, Straus & Giroux.
--Three for Freedom. LC 73-18742. p. cm. 1974. (ISBN 0-394-82386-9). (ISBN 0-394-82386-9). Random House.
--The Traitors. LC 68-23747. xii, 238 p. 22cm. (Bell book). 1968. Farrar, Straus & Giroux.
--The White Crow. LC 76-62530. p. cm. c.1976. (ISBN 0-374-38386-3). Farrar, Straus and Giroux.

Forman, Joan
--The Princess in the Tower. Sanders, Beryl, illus. (Illus.). 96p. (gr. 1-4). 1978. (ISBN 0-571-09911-4). Faber & Faber.

Forman, Leona Shluger (1940-)
--Bico: A Brazilian Raft Fisherman's Son. LC 69-14328. (Illus.). 92, 4 p. 25cm. 1969. Lothrop, Lee & Shepard Co.

Forman, Werner, jt. auth. see Burland, Cottie Arthur.

Fornatora, Nancy
--Planetanimals: Mission Zapton. Lewis, Jean, ed. Costanza, John, illus. LC 84-61163. (Illus.). 48p. (ps-3). 1984. (ISBN 0-448-18965-8). Putnam Pub Group.

Forney, Inor
--Nhan: A Boy of Viet-Nam. Forney, Inor, illus. LC 75-77116. (Illus.). 25 p. 21cm. 1969. C. E. Tuttle Co.

Forrest, Gene
--Bon Repos. 1975. (ISBN 0-682-48340-0). Exposition Press.

Forrest, Hal
--Tailspin Tommy: The Mystery of the Midnight Patrol. Stevens, Mark, adapted by. Beebe, Robb (1891-), illus. LC 37-3372. v, 218 p. front. 19 cm. c.1936. Grosset & Dunlap.

Forrest, Hal & Chaffin, Glen
--Tailspin Tommy. N.D. Cupples & Leon Co.

Forrest, John L, retold by see Reinke de Vos & Reynard the Fox. English.

Forrest, Linn Argyle, jt. auth. see Blackerby, Alva W.

Forrest, Neil
--Fiddling Freddy, 6 Vols. (The Golden Thread Ser.). N.D. Anson D. F. Randolph & Co.
--Fiddling Freddy, 1 of 3 Vols. (The Jack and Rosy Library: No. 3). N.D. Anson D. F. Randolph & Co.
--Honest and Earnest, 1 of 6 Vols. (The Golden Thread Ser.: No. 2). N.D. Anson D. F. Randolph & Co.
--Honest and Earnest, 1 of 3 Vols. (The Jack and Rosy Library: No. 2). N.D. Anson D. F. Randolph & Co.
--Jack and Rosy, 1 of 6 Vols. (The Golden Thread Ser.: No. 3). N.D. Anson D. F. Randlph & Co.
--Jack and Rosy, 1 of 3 Vols. (Jack and Rosy Library). N.D. Anson D. F. Randolph & Co.
--The Jack and Rosy Library: Including: "Jack and Rosy", "Honest and Earnest", & "Fiddling Freddy". N.D. A. D. F. Randolph & Co.

Forrester, Alfred Henry (1804-1872)
--Fairy Tales, Comprising Patty and Her Pitcher, Tiny and Her Vanity, The Giant and the Dwarf, The Selfish Man, Peter and His Goose, The Giant Hands. Crowquill, Alfred, pseud. (1804-1872), illus. Forrester, Alfred Henry. LC 15-27763. 181 p. incl. front., illus. 17 1/2 cm. 1857. G. Routledge & Co.

Forrester, Dexter J., pseud., see Goldfrap, John Henry.

Forrester, Francis, pseud., see Wise, Daniel.

Forrester, Francis, pseud. (1813-1898)
--Ben Blinker: or, Maggie's Golden Motto, and What It Did for her Brother. Wise, Daniel. N.D. Lee & Shepard.
--Dick Duncan. Wise, Daniel, 1 of 5 Vols. (Glen Morris's Stories). N.D. Set. Nelson & Phillips.
--Dick Duncan: A Boy Who Loved Mischief. Wise, Daniel, 1 of 5 vols. (Illus.). (Glen Morris Stories Ser.). N.D. Set. Methodist Bk Concern.
--Elbert's Return: Or, Foxy at Home Again. Wise, Daniel, 1 of 6 vols. (Illus.). (Hollywood Ser.: Vol. 6). N.D. Set. Methodist Bk Concern.
--Elbert's Return: or, "Foxy" at Home Again. Wise, Daniel. (Hollywood Ser.). 1875. Perkinpine & Higgins.
--Florence Baldwin's Pic-Nic. Wise, Daniel. (Hollywood Ser.). 1875. Perkinpine & Higgins.
--Florence Baldwin's Picnic: And What a Game of It, 1 of 6 Vols. Wise, Daniel, illus. (Illus.). (Hollywood Ser.). N.D. Set. Methodist Book Concern.
--Florence Rewarded: Or, Priscilla the Beautiful. Wise, Daniel, 1 of 6 vols. (Illus.). (Hollywood Ser.: Vol. 4). N.D. Set. Methodist Bk Concern.
--Glen Morris Stories Ser. Wise, Daniel, 5 Vols. (Illus.). N.D. Methodist Book Concern.
--Guy Carlton. Wise, Daniel, 1 of 5 Vols. (Glen Morris's Stories). N.D. Set. Nelson & Phillips.
--Guy Carlton: A Boy Who Belonged to the "Try Company". Wise, Daniel, 1 of 5 vols. (Illus.). (Glen Morris Stories Ser.). N.D. Set. Methodist Bk Concern.
--Jessie Carlton: A Girl Who Fought with Little Impulse. Wise, Daniel, 1 of 5 vols. (Illus.). (Glen Morris Stories Ser.). N.D. Set. Methodist Bk Concern.
--Katie Carlton.Wise, Daniel, 1 of 5 Vols. (Glen Morris's Stories). N.D. Set. Nelson & Phillips.
--Katie Carlton: A Proud, Vain Girl. Wise, Daniel, 1 of 5 vols. (Illus.). (Glen Morris Stories Ser.). N.D. Set. Methodist Bk Concern.
--Lionel's Courage: Or, Clementine's Great Peril. Wise, Daniel, 1 of 6 vols. (Illus.). (Hollywood Ser.: Vol. 3). N.D. Set. Methodist Bk Concern.
--Lionel's Pluck: or, Clementine's Great Peril. Wise, Daniel. (Hollywood Ser.). 1875. Perkinpine & Higgins.
--Little Peachblossom: Or, Rambles in Central Park. Wise, Daniel. (Illus.). N.D. Methodist Book Concern.
--Little Peachblossom: Or, Rambles in Central Park. Wise, Daniel. N.D. Nelson & Phillips.
--Mattie Sherwood. Wise, Daniel, 1 of 5 Vols. (Glen Morris's Stories). N.D. Set. Nelson & Phillips.
--Nat and his Chum: or, the Friendly Rivals. Wise, Daniel. (Hollywood Ser.). 1875. Perkinpine & Higgins.
--Nat and His Chum: The Friendly Rivals. Wise, Daniel, 1 of 6 Vols. (Illus.). N.D. Set. Methodist Book Concern.
--Priscilla the Beautiful: or, Florence Rewarded. Wise, Daniel. (Hollywood Ser.). 1875. Perkinpine & Higgins.
--Stephen and His Temper: Or, The Children of Hollywood. Wise, Daniel, 1 of 6 Vols. N.D. Set. Methodist Book Concern.
--Stephen and his Tempter. Wise, Daniel. (Hollywood Ser.). 1875. Perkinpine & Higgins.
--Walter Sherwood: An Easy, Good-natured Boy. Wise, Daniel, 1 of 5 vols. (Illus.). (Glen Morris Stories Ser.). N.D. Set. Methodist Bk Concern.
--Winwood Cliff: Or, The Sailor's Son. Wise, Daniel, Vol. 1. (The Winwood Cliff Ser.). N.D. Lee & Shepard.

Forrester, Izola Louise (1878-)
--The Door in the Mountain. LC 28-24698. 320 p. front., plates 19 cm. c.1928. Macrae Smith Company.
--The Girls of Bonnie Castle ... Parry, Anna W., illus. LC 1-29041. 277 p. front., pl. 12 cm. 1900. G. W. Jacobs & Co.
--Greenacre Girls. (The Greenacre Ser.). N.D. Macrae Smith.
--Greenacre Girls. Garrett, Anna, illus. LC 15-23062. 331 p. front., plates. 20 cm. $1.2. 1915. G. W. Jacobs & Company.
--Jack O' Lantern. Price, Harriet Longstreet (1891-), illus. LC 27-20588. 3 p. l., 9-318 p. front., plates. 19 cm. c.1927. Macrae Smith Company.
--Jean of Greenacres. (The Greenacre Ser.). N.D. George W Jacobs.
--Jean of Greenacres. (The Greenacre Ser.). N.D. Macrae Smith.
--Jean of Greenacres. Garrett, Anna, illus. LC 17-13218. 344 p. incl. col. front. col. plates. 1917. G. W. Jacobs & Company.
--Kit of Greenacre Farm. (The Greenacre Ser.). N.D. Macrae Smith.
--Kit of Greenacre Farm. Garrett, Anna, illus. LC 19-8318. 312 p. col. front., col. plates. 20 cm. 1919. G. W. Jacobs & Company.
--The Polly Page Camping Club. LC 15-12252. 4 p. l., 7-301 p. front., plates. 20 cm. $1.0. 1915. G. W. Jacobs & Co.
--The Polly Page Camping Club. (The Polly Page Bks.). N.D. Macrae Smith.
--The Polly Page Motor Club. LC 14-619. 4 p. l., 7-345 p. front., plates. 20 cm. c.1913. G. W. Jacobs & Co.
--The Polly Page Motor Club. (The Polly Page Bks.). N.D. Macrae Smith.
--The Polly Page Ranch Club. LC 11-35888. 328 p. front., 4 pl. 20 cm. c.1911. G. W. Jacobs & Co.
--The Polly Page Ranch Club. (The Polly Page Bks.). N.D. Macrae Smith.
--The Polly Page Yacht Club. LC 10-28495. 4 p. l., 7-351 p. front., plates, 20 cm. $1.2. c.1910. G. W. Jacobs & Co.
--The Polly Page Yacht Club. (The Polly Page Bks.). N.D. Macrae Smith.
--Rook's Nest. LC 1-24906. 328p. 12cm. 1901. G. W. Jacobs & Co.
--The Secret of the Blue Macaw. Landau, Jacob (1917-), illus. LC 36-32330. 303 p. incl. front., illus. (part double) 19 1/2 cm. c.1936. Macrae Smith Company.
--Us Fellers. (Illus.). N.D. George W. Jacobs & Co.

Forrester, John (1943-)
--Bestiary Mountain. LC 85-5685. p. cm. 1985. (ISBN 0-02-735530-6). Bradbury Press.

Forrester, Victoria (1940-)
--Bears & Theirs. LC 81-15071. (Illus.). 94 p. 15cm. 1982. (ISBN 0-689-30913-9). Atheneum.
--The Candlemaker & Other Tales. Boulet, Susan Beddon, illus. LC 83-15658. (Illus.). 64p. (ps up). 1984. (ISBN 0-689-31013-7). Atheneum.
--A Latch Against the Wind. LC 84-21526. (Illus.). 48 p. 23cm. 1985. (ISBN 0-689-31091-9). Atheneum.
--The Magnificent Moo. Forrester, Victoria (1940-), illus. LC 82-13781. (Illus.). 40p. (ps-1). 1983. (ISBN 0-689-30954-6). Atheneum.
--Oddward. 1st ed. Forrester, Victoria (1940-), illus. LC 81-12908. (Illus.). 44 p. 15cm. 1982. (ISBN 0-689-30912-0). Atheneum.
--The Touch Said Hello. LC 82-3894. (Illus.). 32p. (ps-2). 1982. (ISBN 0-689-30947-3). Atheneum.
--Words to Keep Against the Night. Forrester, Victoria (1940-), illus. LC 83-2624. 1983. (ISBN 0-689-30984-8). Atheneum.

Forsee, Frances Aylesa
--Miracle for Mingo. 1st ed. Reed, Veronica, pseud. (1916-), illus. Sherman, Theresa. LC 56-9272. 159p. illus. 21cm. 1956. Lippincott.
--Too Much Dog. 1st ed. Johnson, Eugene Harper, illus. LC 57-103272. 192p. illus. 21cm. 1957. Lippincott.
--The Whirly Bird. 1st ed. Two Arrows, Tom, illus. LC 55-7982. 224p. illus. 21cm. 1955. Lippincott.

Forsee, Frances Aylesa, retold by.
--They Trusted God: Bible Stories. Ziol, Hank, illus. LC 79-90565. (Illus.). viii, 188 p. 24cm. c.1980. (ISBN 0-87510-122-4). Christian Science Pub. Society.

Forsey, Maude S
--Mollie Hazeldne's Schooldays. LC 24-21081. ix, 11-297, 1 p. front., plates. 19 1/2 cm. 1924. T. Nelson and Sons, Ltd.

Forshay-Lundford, Cin
--Walk Through Cold Fire. LC 84-17643. 224p. (gr. 7 up). 1985. (ISBN 0-385-29395-X). Delacorte.

Forsman, Bettie
--From Lupita's Hill. 1st ed. Hampshire, Michael Allen, illus. LC 72-86936. (Illus.). 265 p. 22cm. 1973. Atheneum.

Forsslund, Karl Erik (1872-1941)
--The Tomten and the Fox. Lindgren, Astrid Ericsson (1907-), adapted by. Wiberg, Harald Albin (1908-), illus. LC 65-25501. (Illus.). v. (unpaged. 1965, c.1966. Coward-McCann. **Award: (ALA).**

Forst, S
--Pipkin. Jacques, Robin (1920-), illus. LC 73-113188. (Illus.). viii, 130 p. 24cm. 1970. Delacorte Press.

Forster, Edward, tr.
--Arabian Nights' Entertainments. 1048p. N.D. D. Appleton & Co.
--Arabian Nights' Entertainments. N.D. James Miller.

Forster, Frederick J
--On the Road to Make-Believe. Trippe, Uldene, illus. LC 24-27702. 128 p. incl. col. front., col. illus. 32 cm. c.1924. Rand, McNally & Company.
--Tippytoes Comes to Town. Trippe, Uldene, illus. LC 26-18492. 96 p. illus. (part col.) 27 cm. c.1926. Rand, McNally & Company.

Forster, Logan
--Desert Storm. Hubbard, Frank, illus. LC 55-5078. 218p. illus. 21cm. 1955. Dodd, Mead.
--Mountain Stallion. Forster, Jessie, illus. LC 56-5489. (Illus.). 241 p. 21cm. 1958. Dood, Mead.
--Revenge. McCann, Gerald (1916-), illus. LC 60-11921. (Illus.). 268p. 21cm. 1960. Dodd, Mead.
--Run Fast! Run Far!. McCann, Gerald (1916-), illus. LC 62-17011. (Illus.). 243 p. 22cm. 1962. Dodd, Mead.
--Tamarlane, Strange Son of Desert Storm. McCann, Gerald (1916-), illus. LC 59-9622. (Illus.). 254p. 21cm. 1959. Dodd, Mead.

Forsyth, Clarence
--Old Songs for Young America. Ostertag, Blanche, illus. (Illus.). 1900. Doubleday, Page & Co.

Forsyth, Elizabeth H., jt. auth. see Hyde, Margaret Oldroyd.

Forsyth, Gloria
--Pelican Prill. 1st ed. Henneberger, Robert G. (1921-), illus. LC 56-8292. 128p. illus. 21cm. 1956. Dutton.

Fort, John (1942-)
--June the Tiger. 1st ed. Loewenstein, Bernice, illus. LC 75-12603. p. cm. 1975. (ISBN 0-316-28925-6). Little, Brown.

Forte, Imogene
--The Puppet Factory. LC 83-82048. (Illus.). 96p. (gr. 2-6). 1984. (ISBN 0-86530-036-4). Incentive Pubns.

Forte, Imogene & MacKenzie, Joy
--For the Love of Ladybug. Harvey, Gayle S., illus. LC 77-83783. (Illus.). (Days of Wonder Hardback). (ps). 1978. (ISBN 0-913916-42-0). Incentive Pubns.
--From Here to the Edge of the World. LC 77-83785. (Illus.). (Days of Wonder Paper Set). (ps). 1979. (ISBN 0-913916-90-0). Incentive Pubns.
--Monsters Come in Several Sizes. LC 77-83786. (Illus.). 64p. (Days of Wonder Paper Set). 1979. (ISBN 0-913916-91-9). Incentive Pubns.

--Rodney, the Overseer. Castlemon, Harry, pseud. White, George G., illus. LC 12-313481. iii, 456 p. front., plates. 20 cm. (His Castlemon's war series v. 5). c.1892. Porter & Coates.
--Rodney, the Partisan. Castlemon, Harry, pseud, 1 of 6 Vols. (War Ser.). N.D. Set. John C. Winston Co.
--Rodney the Partisan. Castlemon, Harry, pseud. White, George G., illus. LC 12-312747. 424 p. front., plates. 20 cm. (His Castlemon's war series). c.1890. Porter & Coates.
--Roughing It Series: Containing: George in Camp, George at the Wheel, George at the Fort. Castlemon, Harry, pseud, 3 Vols. (Illus.). 1882. Set. Porter & Coates.
--A Sailor in Spite of Himself. Castlemon, Harry, pseud. LC 12-31248. iv, 415 p. front., plates. 20 cm. 1898. H. T. Coates & Co.
--A Sailor in Spite of Himself. Castlemon, Harry, pseud, 1 of 3 Vols. (Afloat and Ashore Ser.). N.D. Set. John C. Winston Co.
--Sailor Jack, the Trader. Castlemon, Harry, pseud, 1 of 6 Vols. (War Ser.). N.D. Set. John C. Winston Co.
--Sailor Jack, the Trader. Castlemon, Harry, pseud. White, George G., illus. LC 12-312533. iii, 467 p. front., plates. 20 cm. (His Castlemon's war series v. 6). c.1893. Porter & Coates.
--Snagged and Sunk. Castlemon, Harry, pseud, 1 of 3 Vols. (Roundabout Library). (Forest and Stream Ser.). N.D. Set. John C. Winston Co.
--Snagged and Sunk: Or, The Adventures of a Canvas Canoe. Castlemon, Harry, pseud. LC 12-312522. 419 p. front., plates. 17 cm. (His Forest and Stream Ser. v. 2). c.1888. Porter & Coates.
--Snowed Up. Castlemon, Harry, pseud. (Frank Nelson Ser.). N.D. John C. Winston.
--Snowed up: Or, The Sportsman's Club in the Mountains. Castlemon, Harry, pseud. LC 4-770786. vi, 7-301 p. incl. front. 20 cm. (His Frank Nelson series). 1904. H. T. Coates & Co.
--Snowed Up: Or, The Sportsman's Club in the Mountains. Castlemon, Harry, pseud, 1 of 3 vols. (Illus.). (His Frank Nelson Ser.). 1876. Porter and Coates.
--The Sportman's Club in the Saddle. Castlemon, Harry, pseud, 1 of 3 Vols. Faber, Hermann, illus. (Sportsmen Club Ser.). N.D. Porter & Coates.
--The Sportsman Club Among the Trapper. Castlemon, Harry, pseud. (The Sportsman Club Ser.). N.D. John C. Winston.
--The Sportsman's Club Afloat. Castlemon, Harry, pseud, 1 of 3 vols. LC 12-32354. iv, 5-277 p. front., plates. 18 cm. (Sportsman's Club Ser.). c.1874. Porter & Coates.
--The Sportsman's Club Afloat. Castlemon, Harry, pseud. LC 7-100497. iv, 5-277 p. front., plates. 19 cm. (Sportsman Club Ser.). c.1902. The J. C. Winston Co.
--The Sportsman's Club Among the Trappers. Castlemon, Harry, pseud, 1 of 3 Vols. (Sportsman's Club Ser.). N.D. John C. Winston.
--The Sportsman's Club Among the Trappers. Castlemon, Harry, pseud, 1 of 3 vols. Bensell, Edmund B., illus. (Illus.). (Sportsman's Club Ser.). N.D. Set. Henry T. Coates & Co.
--The Sportsman's Club in the Saddle. Castlemon, Harry, pseud, 1 of 3 Vols. (Sportsman's Club Ser.). N.D. John C. Winston.
--Steel Horse. Castlemon, Harry, pseud, 1 of 3 Vols. (Roundabout Library). (Forest and Stream Ser.). N.D. Set. John C. Winston Co.
--The Steel Horse: Or, The Rambles of a Bicycle. Castlemon, Harry, pseud. LC 12-32295. 2 p. l., 418 p. front., plates. 18 cm. c.1888. Porter & Coates.
--The Steel Horse: Or, the Rambles of a Bicyle. Castlemon, Harry, pseud, 1 of 3 vols. (Illus.). (Roundabout Lib.). (Forest and Stream Ser.). N.D. Set. Henry T. Coates & Co.
--A Struggle for a Fortune. Castlemon, Harry, pseud. (Illus.). (The Boy's Own Authors Ser.). N.D. Dana Estes & Co.
--A Struggle for a Fortune. Castlemon, Harry, pseud. Fry, W. H., illus. LC 2-19998. 298 p. front., plates. 20 cm. 1902. The Saalfield Publishing Co.
--The Ten-Ton Cutter. Castlemon, Harry, pseud, 1 of 3 vols. (Illus.). (Afoat and Ashore Ser.). N.D. Set. Henry T. Coates & Co.
--The Ten-Ton Cutter. Castlemon, Harry, pseud, 1 of 3 Vols. (Afloat and Ashore Ser.). N.D. Set. John C. Winston Co.
--The Young Wild Fowler. Castlemon, Harry, pseud. (Rod and Gun Club Ser.). N.D. John C. Winston.
--Tom Newcomb. Castlemon, Harry, pseud, 1 of 3 Vols. (Go-Ahead Ser.). N.D. Set. John C. Winston Co.
--Tom Newcomb. Castlemon, Harry, pseud, 3 Vols. (Illus.). (Go-Ahead Ser.). N.D. Porter & Coates.
--True to His Color. Castlemon, Harry, pseud, 1 of 6 vols. (Illus.). (War Ser.). N.D. Henry T. Coates & Co.
--True to His Colors. Castlemon, Harry, pseud, 1 of 6 Vols. (War Ser.). N.D. Set. John C. Winston Co.
--Two Ways of Becoming a Hunter. Castlemon, Harry, pseud, 1 of 3 vols. (Illus.). (Roundabout Lib.). (Hunter Ser.). N.D. Henry T. Coates & Pub.
--Two Ways of Becoming a Hunter. Castlemon, Harry, pseud, 1 of 3 Vols. (Roundabout Library). (Hunter Ser.). N.D. Set. John C. Winston Co.
--Two Ways of Becoming a Hunter. Castlemon, Harry, pseud. LC 12-31250. iv, 391 p. front., plates. 20 cm. c.1892. Porter & Coates.
--The White Beaver. Castlemon, Harry, pseud, 1 of 3 vols. (Illus.). (Roundabout Lib.). (Pony Express Ser.). N.D. Set. Henry T. Coates & Co.
--The White Beaver. Castlemon, Harry, pseud, 1 of 3 Vols. (Pony Espress Ser.). N.D. Set. John C. Winston Co.
--Winged Arrow's Medicine. Castlemon, Harry, pseud. (Illus.). N.D. Caldwell.
--Winged Arrow's Medicine: Or, The Massacre at Fort Phil Kearney. Castlemon, Harry, pseud. LC 1-11744. 298 p. incl. front. plates. 20 cm. 1901. The Saalfield Publishing Company.
--The Young Game-Warden. Castlemon, Harry, pseud. LC 12-32350. iv, 5-411 p. front., plates. 20 cm. c.1896. H. T. Coates & Co.
--The Young Game Warden. Castlemon, Harry, pseud, 1 of 3 vols. (Illus.). (Houseboat Ser.). N.D. Set. Henry T. Coates & Co.
--The Young Game Warden. Castlemon, Harry, pseud, 1 of 3 Vols. (The Houseboat Ser.). N.D. Set. John C. Winston Co.
--The Young Wild-Fowlers. Castlemon, Harry, pseud. LC 12-31249. iv, 5-376 p. front., plates. 17 cm. (His Rod and gun series v. 3). c.1885. Porter & Coates.
--The Young Wild Fowlers. Castlemon, Harry, pseud, 1 of 3 vols. (Rod & Gun Ser.). 1891. Set. Porter & Coates.

Fosdick, Harry Emerson (1878-1969)
--Jesus of Nazareth. 1959. Random House.

Foslien, Dagmar
--The Fantastic Fashion Show. Paris, Pat & Shackelford, Jeanie, illus. LC 83-24933. (Illus.). 42 p. 29cm. (Rose-Petal Place). c.1984. (ISBN 0-910313-50-4). Parker Bros.

Foss, Claude William (1855-1935), tr. see Topelius, Zakarias.

Foss, Claude William (1855-1935), selected by.
--At Yuletide, 2 vols. (Illus.). 1905. Set. Augustana Book Concern.

Foss, Michael
--Traditional Nursery Rhymes and Children's Verse. LC 77-364503. (Illus.). 5, 184 p. 25cm. 1976. (ISBN 0-7181-1556-2). Joseph.

Fossner, A. K., jt. auth. see Tripp, Edward.

Foster, Alan Dean, jt. auth. see Lynn, Haney.

Foster, Bennett
--The Owl Hoot Trail. N.D. World Publishing.

Foster, Birket, illus.
--Chimes for Childhood: A Collection of Songs for Little Folks. N.D. Estes and Lauriat's Publications.

Foster, Birket & Leech, Dore, illus.
--Christmas in Song and Story. N.D. R. Worthington.

Foster, Birket & Millais, illus.
--Chimes for Childhood. (Illus.). 208p. N.D. Lee & Shepard.

Foster, Carl
--Two Little Every-Day Folks. Hallowell, Elizabeth M., illus. LC 98-1509. 112 p. illus., pl. 12 degrees. 1898. American Baptist Pub. Soc.

Foster, Cecil (1876-)
--White Indian Girl. LC 52-130781. 235p. 20cm. c.1953. Dorrance.

Foster, Celeste K.
--Casper, the Caterpillar. Foster, Celeste K., illus. (Illus.). (Nature & Science Bk.). (gr. k-6). N.D. Denison.
--Jonathan & the Octopus. Foster, Celeste K., illus. LC 58-13731. (Illus.). (Third Grade Bk.). (gr. 3-4). 1958. Denison.

Foster, Charles (1822-1887)
--Fables and Allegories for Young and Old. LC 44-30634. 512 p. illus. 23 1/2 cm. 1885. C. Foster.
--First Steps. N.D. (ISBN 0-686-13586-5). Believers Bkshelf.
--First Steps: Bible Stories for Children. (Illus.). (gr. 5-8). 1960. (ISBN 0-8024-0023-X). Moody.
--First Steps For Little Feet In Gospel Paths. 328p. N.D. Charles Foster Publishing Company.
--The Story of the Bible: From Genesis to Revelation. 704p. N.D. Charles Foster Publishing Company.
--The Story of The Gospel: Our Saviour's Life on Earth. 366p. N.D. Charles Foster Publishing Company.

Foster, Constance J.
--This Rich World. N.D. Robert M. McBride & Co.

Foster, Doris Van Liew (1899-)
--Feather in the Wind: The Story of a Hurricane. Forberg, Ati, pseud. (1925-), illus. Forberg, Beate Gropius. LC 75-171616. (Illus.). 32 p. 26cm. 1972. Lothropp, Lee & Shepard Co.
--Honker Visits the Island. Werth, Kurt (1896-), illus. LC 62-15613. (Illus.). (ps-4). 1962. Lothrop.
--Tell Me, Little Boy. Duvoisin, Roger Antoine (1904-1980), illus. LC 53-7795. unpaged. illus. 26cm. c.1953. Lothrop, Lee & Shepard.
--Tell Me, Mr. Owl. Stone, Helen (1904-), illus. LC 56-915579. unpaged. illus. 26cm. (ps-3). c.1957. (ISBN 0-688-51071-X). Lothrop, Lee & Shepard.

Foster, Ed
--Tejanos. Negron, Bill, illus. Santos, Richard G., intro. by. LC 72-129037. (Illus.). xi, 48 p. 20cm. (Challenger book. La raza series). 1970. (ISBN 0-394-02020-0). Hill and Wang; Distributed by Random House.

Foster, Edith Francis
--Jimmy Crow. (Illus.). (Rebus Books for Little Folks). N.D. Dana Estes and Company.
--Marigold. Foster, Edith Francis, illus. LC 6-23704. 4 p. l., 11-252 p. front., 7 pl. 19 cm. c.1906. D. Estes & Company.
--Marigold's Winter. Foster, Edith Francis, illus. LC 6-19723. 275 p. front., 7 pl. 20 cm. c.1908. D. Estes & Company.
--Mary N' Mary. Foster, Edith Francis, illus. LC 5-19417. (Illus.). 19cm. 290p. (The Girls' Own Authors Ser.). 1905. Dana Estes & Co.
--Puss in the Corner. (Illus.). (Rebus Books for Little Folks). N.D. Dana Estes and Company.

Foster, Edith Francis & Johnson, Margaret
--Picture Stories for Little Folks. Foster, Edith Francis & Johnson, Margaret, illus. N.D. L. C. Page & Co.

Foster, Edna Abigail, Mrs.
--Hortense. Ayer, Mary, illus. 1905. Lee and Shepard Company.

Foster, Elizabeth C (1881-) & Williams, Slim, pseud. (1881-1974)
--The Friend of the Singing One. Williams, Clyde C.. Rocker, Fermin (1907-), illus. LC 67-19002. (Illus.). 122 p. 22cm. 1967. Atheneum.
--The Long Hungry Night. Coalson, Glo (1946-), illus. LC 72-86937. (Illus.). 149 p. 22cm. 1973. Atheneum.

Foster, Elizabeth Vincent (1905-1963)
--Gigi in America: The Further Adventures of a Merry-Go-Round Horse. Cote, Phyllis N. (1921-), illus. LC 46-3686. 2 p. l., 123, 1 p. illus. 24 1/2 cm. 1946. Houghton Mifflin Company.
--Gigi in America: The Further Adventures of a Merry-Go Round Horse. Cote, Phyllis N. (1921-), illus. LC 83-17485. c.1984. (ISBN 0-913028-69-X). North Atlantic Books.
--Gigi: The Story of a Merry-Go-Round Horse. Bischoff, Ilse Marthe (1903-), illus. LC 83-19329. (Illus.). 124p (Pub. by Houghton Mifflin). (gr. 4-8). 1984. (ISBN 0-913028-55-X). North Atlantic.
--Gigi: The Story of a Merry-Go-Round Hourse. Bischoff, Ilse Marthe (1903-), illus. LC 43-16551. 6 p. l., 118 p. col. front., illus. 24 1/2 cm. 1943. Houghton Mifflin Company.
--The House at Noddy Cove. Cote, Phyllis N. (1921-), illus. LC 49-7992. (Illus.). 107p. 22cm. 1949. Houghton Mifflin Co.
--The Islanders. N.D. Houghton Mifflin Co.
--Lyrico: The Only Horse of His Kind. LC 79-114000. (Illus.). 230p. (gr. 3-7). 1970. (ISBN 0-87645-027-3). Gambit.

Foster, Emilie
--Heaven Children: Or, Frolics at the Funny Old House on Funny Street. (Illus.). N.D. E. P. Dutton & Co.
--Teddy and His Friends. (Illus.). N.D. Dodd, Mead & Co.

Foster, Genevieve Stump (1893-1979)
--Andrew Jackson. LC 51-13713. 112 p. illus. 20 cm. (Her An initial biography). 1951. Scribner.
--Augustus Caesar's World. Foster, Genevieve Stump (1893-1979), illus. (Illus.). (gr. 5-11). 1949. (ISBN 0-684-13148-X). Scribner.

Foster, Hal, pseud., see Foster, Harold Rudolf.

Foster, Harold Rudolf see Foster, Hal, pseud.

Foster, Harold Rudolf see Harold, Hal, pseud.

Foster, Harold Rudolf (1892-1982)
--The Medieval Castle. Foster, Hal, pseud. Foster, Harold Rudolf (1892-1982), illus. Foster, Hal, pseud. LC 57-7693. 126p. illus. 22cm. 1957. Hastings House.
--The Minks' Cry. Foster, Hal, pseud. 1st ed. LC 81-70740. (Illus.). 92 p. 19cm. 1982. (ISBN 0-941920-00-3). Bay Press.
--Prince Valiant & the Golden Princess. Foster, Hal, pseud. Foster, Harold Rudolf (1892-1982), illus. Foster, Hal, pseud. (Illus.). 250 drawings. 128p. (Prince Valiant Ser: Vol 5). (gr. 4-6). 1968. (ISBN 0-8038-5729-2). Hastings.
--Prince Valiant and the Golden Princess. Foster, Hal, pseud. Trell, Max (1900-), adapted by. LC 55-11638. 127p. illus. 26cm. (His Prince Valiant, book 5). 1955. Hastings House.
--Prince Valiant & the Three Challenges. Foster, Hal, pseud. Foster, Harold Rudolf (1892-1982), illus. Foster, Hal, pseud. LC 60-15997. (Illus.). 27cm. 96p. (Prince Valiant Ser.: Vol 7). (gr. 4-6). 1960. (ISBN 0-8038-5731-4). Hastings.
--Prince Valiant Fights Attila the Hun. Harold, Hal, pseud. Foster, Harold Rudolf (1892-1982), illus. LC 52-11807. 127p. illus. 26cm. 1952. Hastings House.
--Prince Valiant in the Days of King Arthur. Foster, Hal, pseud. Foster, Harold Rudolf (1892-1982), illus. Foster, Hal, pseud. LC 54-630. unpaged. illus. 20cm. (Treasure books, 874). 1954. Treasure Books.
--Prince Valiant in the Days of King Arthur. Foster, Hal, pseud. Trell, Max, adapted by. LC 51-14151. 128p. illus. 26cm. (His Prince Valiant, book 1). 1951. Hastings House.
--Prince Valiant in the New World. Foster, Hal, pseud. Foster, Harold Rudolf (1892-1982), illus. Foster, Hal, pseud. LC 56-12353. 95p. illus. 26cm. (His Prince Valiant, book 6). 1956. Hastings House.
--Prince Valiant on the Inland Sea. Foster, Hal, pseud. Foster, Harold Rudolf (1892-1982), illus. Foster, Hal, pseud. (Illus.). 250 drawings. 128p. (Prince Valiant Ser.: Vol 3). (gr. 4-6). 1968. (ISBN 0-8038-5727-6). Hastings.
--Prince Valiant on the Inland Sea. Foster, Hal, pseud. Trell, Max (1900-), adapted by. Foster, Harold Rudolf (1892-1982), illus. Foster, Hal, pseud. LC 53-12931. 128p. illus. 26cm. (His Prince Valiant, book 3). 1953. Hastings House.
--Prince Valiant's Perilous Voyage. Foster, Hal, pseud. Trell, Max (1900-), adapted by. Foster, Harold Rudolf (1892-1982), illus. Foster, Hal, pseud. LC 54-132391. (Illus.). 26cm. 128p. (Prince Valiant Ser.: Vol 4). (gr. 4-6). 1954. (ISBN 0-8038-5728-4). Hastings.

Foster, Isabel
--Ray's Reward. LC 11-24112. 2 p. l., 163 p. front. 19 cm. 1911. Reid Publishing Company.
--The True Possession. LC 7-40277. (Illus.). 15p. 18cm. 1907. W. J. C. Dulany.

Foster, James
--Captured by the Arabs. LC 33-112659. 4 p. l., 244 p., 1 l. front. 21 cm. (His Exploration series). c.1933. A. L. Burt Company.
--The Forest of Mystery. LC 35-8286. 254 p. front. 21 cm. 21cm. 254p. (His Exploration series). (Exploration Series). c.1935. A. L. Burt Company.
--Lost in the Wilds of Brazil. LC 33-11386. 4 p. l., 243 p., 1 l. front. 21 cm. (His Exploration series). c.1933. A. L. Burt Company.
--Secrets of the Andes. LC 33-253673. 4 p. l., 245 p., 1 l. front. 21 cm. (His Exploration series). c.1933. A. L. Burt Company.

Foster, James Ralph (1890-), ed.
--The World's Great Folktales. 1st ed. LC 53-775226. 330p. 22cm. 1953. Harper.

Foster, Joanna (1928-)
--Pete's Puddle. LC 50-14113. 21cm. 21p. 1950. Houghton Mifflin Co.
--Pete's Puddle. 1st ed. Darwin, Beatrice, illus. LC 69-11596. (Illus.). 32 p. 19cm. 1969. Harcourt, Brace & World.

Foster, John Lawrence (1930-), compiled by.
--A First Poetry Book. Orr, Chris (1943-) & White, Martin, illus. (Illus.). 128p. 1982. (ISBN 0-19-918112-8, Pub. by Oxford U Pr Childrens). (ISBN 0-19-918113-6). Merrimack Pub Cir.
--A First Poetry Book. Orr, Chris (1943-) & White, Martin, illus. LC 80-482689. (Illus.). 128 p. 23cm. 1979. (ISBN 0-19-918113-6). (ISBN 0-19-918112-8). Oxford University Press.
--A Fourth Poetry Book. (Illus.). 144p. (Poetry Anthologies). (gr. 4-7). 1983. (ISBN 0-19-918152-7, Pub by Oxford U Pr Childrens). (ISBN 0-19-918151-9). Merrimack Pub Cir.
--A Second Poetry Book. Orr, Charles & White, Martin, illus. (Illus.). 128p. 1982. (ISBN 0-19-918136-5, Pub. by Oxford U Pr Childrens). (ISBN 0-19-918137-3). Merrimack Pub Cir.
--A Third Poetry Book. (Illus.). 144p. (Poetry Anthologies). (gr. 3-6). 1983. (ISBN 0-19-918140-3, Pub by Oxford U Pr Childrens). (ISBN 0-19-918139-X). Merrimack Pub Cir.

Foster, John Thomas (1925-)
--The Gallant Gray Trotter. Savitt, Sam (1917-), illus. LC 73-11988. (Illus.). 248 p. 22cm. 1974. (ISBN 0-396-06869-3). Dodd, Mead.
--Marco and That Curious Cat. Bjorklund, Lorence F. (1913-1978), illus. LC 70-123499. (Illus.). 186 p. 24cm. 1970. Dodd, Mead.
--Marco and the Sleuth Hound. Bjorklund, Lorence F. (1913-1978), illus. LC 69-16200. (Illus.). 153 p. 24cm. 1969. Dodd, Mead.
--Marco and the Tiger. Bjorklund, Lorence F. (1913-1978), illus. LC 67-2453. (Illus.). 127 p. 24cm. 1967. Dodd, Mead.

Foster, Joseph O'Kane see Foster, O'Kane, pseud.

--Red Raspberry Crunch. Fox, Charles Philip (1913-), illus. LC 77-10841. (Illus.). 29 p. 22cm. c.1978. (ISBN 0-679-20435-0). McKay.
--Snowball, the Trick Pony. Fox, Charles Philip (1913-), illus. LC 64-16405. (Illus.). 29cm. 32p. (ps-3). 1964. Reilly & Lee.
--When Autumn Comes. LC 67-8036. 1 v. (unpaged) illus. 29 cm. (Easy-to-read photo-story book for children). c.1966. Reilly & Lee.
--When Spring Comes. LC 64-22919. 1 v. (chiefly illus.) 29 cm. (Easy-to-read photo-story book for children). 1964. Reilly & Lee Co.
--When Summer Comes. Fox, Charles Philip (1913-), illus. LC 66-15163. 1 v. (unpaged) illus. 29 cm. (Easy-to-read photo-story for children). 1966. Reilly & Lee Co.
--When Winter Comes. (Illus.). 34p. 1962. Reilly & Lee Company.

Fox, Dorothea Warren (1914-)
--Follow Me, the Leader. Fox, Dorothea Warren (1914-), illus. LC 68-26078. (Illus.). 32 p. 24cm. 1968. Parents' Magazine Press.
--Miss Twiggley's Tree. LC 66-935315. 1v. (unpaged) col. illus. 26cm. 1966. Parents' Mag.

Fox, E.
--Roller Bears and the Safeway Tribe. (Fiction). (MacMillan Bks. for Boys & Girls). (gr. 4-6). N.D. MacMillan Bks.

Fox, Edward Seccomb (1911-)
--Hunger Valley. LC 65-10625. 189 p. 22 cm. 1965. Doubleday.
--Massacre Inlet. LC 65-19907. 184p. map (on lining paper) 22cm. c.1965. Doubleday.

Fox, Ethel C.
--Nelly's Confirmation: Or, I'm Not Good Enough. N.D. E. & J. B. Young & Co.
--The Polished Jewel. N.D. E. & J. B Young & Co.

Fox, Florence Cornelia (1861-1933)
--The Fox Mother Goose. N.D. G.P. Putnam's Sons.
--The Story of a Friendly Cow, Lily of Willowreed. LC 37-11250. iii, 86 p. illus. 20 cm. c.1937. American Book Company.

Fox, Frances Margaret (1870-)
--The Adventures of Blackberry Bear. Comstock, Enos Benjamin (1879-1945), illus. LC 18-18407. vii, 131 p. col. front., col. plates. 22 cm. 1918. Moffat, Yard & Company.
--Adventures of Sonny Bear. Carr, Warner, illus. LC 17-9574. 80 p. incl. col. front., illus. (part col.) 20 cm. c.1916. Rand, McNally & Company.
--Angeline Goes Traveling. Gregory, Dorothy Lake, illus. LC 27-183198. vii, 1, 256 p. col. front., illus., col. plates. 20 cm. c.1927. Rand, McNally & Company.
--Betty of Old Mackinaw. Barry, Etheldred Breeze (1870-), illus. 5 p. l., 109 p. incl. illus., pl. front. 19 cm. (Cosy corner series). 1901. L. C. Page & Company.
--Brother Billy. Barry, Etheldred Breeze (1870-), illus. LC 4-28963. (Illus.). 19 cm. 128p. (Cosy Corner Ser.). 1905. L. C. Page & Co.
--Carlota: A Story of the San Gabriel Mission. Ridgeway, Ethelind, illus. LC 8-25745. ix p., 2 l., 179 p. col. front., 5 col. pl. 20 cm. (On verso of half-title: Roses of St. Elizabeth series). 1908. L. C. Page & Company.
--The Country Christmas. Barry, Etheldred Breeze (1870-), illus. LC 7-24154. 4 p. l., 111 p. incl. illus. plates. front. 19 cm. (Cosy corner series). 1907. L. C. Page & Company.
--Doings of Little Bear. Carr, Warner, illus. 20 cm. 80p. 1915. Rand McNally.
--Ellen Jane. Gregory, Dorothy Lake, illus. N.D. Rand McNally.
--Farmer Brown and the Birds. Barry, Etheldred Breeze (1870-), illus. LC 3859. 72 p. incl. front., illus., plates. 19 cm. (On cover: Cosy corner series). 1900. L. C. Page & Company.
--Gay Legends of the Saints. 169p. N.D. Sheed & Ward.
--How Christmas Came to the Mulvaneys. Appleton, J. H., illus. LC 5-20775. 5 p. l., 113 p. incl. illus. 4 pl. front. 19 cm. (Cosy corner series). 1905. L. C. Page & Company.
--Janey. LC 25-22382. 151 p. incl. front., illus. col. plates. 18 cm. c.1925. Rand, McNally & Company.
--The Kinderkins. Brey, Laura, illus. N.D. Rand McNally.
--Legend of the Christ Child. 91p. N.D. Charles Scribner's Sons.
--Little Bear & His Friends. Beem, Frances M., illus. N.D. Rand McNally.
--Little Bear at Work and Play. Carr, Warner, illus. N.D. Rand McNally.
--Little Bear Stories. Harris, Walt, illus. LC 24-30601. 177, 1 p. incl. front., illus. 19 cm. c.1924. Rand, McNally & Company.
--Little Bear's Adventures. Beem, Frances M., illus. N.D. Rand McNally.
--Little Bear's Book. N.D. Rand McNally & Co.
--Little Bear's Ins and Outs. LC 28-18731. 64 p. incl. col. front., illus. (part col.) 20 cm. c.1928. Rand, McNally & Company.
--Little Bear's Laughing Times. Beem, Frances M., illus. N.D. Rand McNally.
--Little Bear's Playtime. Beem, Frances M., illus. N.D. Rand McNally.
--Little Bear's Ups & Downs. Beem, Frances M., illus. N.D. Rand McNally.
--The Little Cat That Could Not Sleep. Suba, Susanne (1913-), illus. LC 41-11114. 31 p. illus. (part col.) 23 x 20 cm. 1941. E. P. Dutton & Co., Inc.
--The Little Giant's Neighbours. (Illus.). (Cosy Corner Ser.). N.D. L. C. Page & Co.
--Little Lady Marjorie. (Illus.). (Princess series). N.D. L. C. Page & Co.
--Little Lady Marjorie. Barry, Etheldred Breeze (1870-), illus. LC 3-23894. 21cm. 286p. 1904. L. C. Page & Co.
--Little Mossback Amelia. Downer, Marion (1892-1971), illus. LC 39-21666. 3 p. l., 13-86 p. illus. (incl. map) 23 cm. 1939. E. P. Dutton and Company, Inc.
--Little Toad. LC 38-27781. 79 p. incl. illus., plates. 22 cm. 1938. The Vicking Press.
--The Magic Canoe: A Frontier Story of the American Revolution. Breuer, Matilda, illus. LC 30-31490. 4 p. l., 11-271 p. illus., col. plates. 20 cm. c.1930. Laidlaw Brothers.
--Mary Anne's Little Indian And Other True Stories for Children. Anoil, Dorothy O'Reilly, illus. 87 p. incl. front., illus. 18 cm. c.1913. A. Flanagan Company.
--Mother Nature's Little Ones. (Illus.). (Cosy Corner Ser.). N.D. L. C. Page & Co.
--Nancy Davenport. Eger, Ruth Caroline, illus. LC 28-18294. vii, 1, 261 p. col. front., illus., col. plates. 20 cm. c.1928. Rand, McNally & Company.
--Nannette. Gruelle, Justin C., illus. LC 29-18176. 80 p. incl. col. front., illus. (part col.) 21 cm. (Lettered on cover: The Volland Inglenook series). c.1929. The P. F. Volland Company.
--Nan's Christmas Boarder. Withingtion, Elizabeth R. & Martin, Gertrude E., illus. LC 24-24461. 6 p. l., 99 p. incl. front., illus., plates. 20 cm. 1924. L. C. Page & Company (Incorporated).
--The Rainbow Bridge: A Story. Merrili, Frank Thayer (1848-), illus. 254 p. incl. col. front. 20 cm. c.1905. W. A. Wilde Company.
--Seven Christmas Candles. Barry, Etheldred Breeze (1870-), illus. LC 9-28075. 5 p. l., 191, 1 p. col. front., 5 col. pl. 20 cm. (On cover: Roses of Saint Elizabeth series). 1909. L. C. Page & Company.
--Seven Little Wise Men. Barry, Etheldred Breeze (1870-), illus. LC 10-28802. 12 cm. 73p. (The Roses Ser.). 1910. L. C. Page & Co.
--Sister Sally. LC 25-11042. 105 p. illus., col. plates. 21 cm. c.1925. Rand, McNally & Company.
--True Monkey Stories. Gergely, Tibor (1900-1978), illus. LC 41-13405. 55, 1 p. illus. (part col.) 26 x 21 cm. c.1941. Lothrop, Lee & Shepard Company.
--Uncle Sam's Animals. LC 27-19000. xvii, 206 p. front., plates. 20 cm. c.1927. The Century Co.
--What Gladys Saw. (Illus.). 318p. N.D. W. A. Wilde Co.
--The Wilding Princess. Perkins, John Edward, illus. LC 29-13435. 79 p. illus., col. plates. 21 cm. (Volland Inglebook series). c.1929. The P. F. Volland Company.

Fox, Genevieve May
--Army Surgeon. 1944. Little, Brown & Co.
--Bonnie, Island Girl. 1st ed. Weissfeld, Mary Morton, illus. LC 54-5138. 242p. illus. 20cm. 1954. Little, Brown.
--Border Girl. Hauman, George (1890-1961) & Hauman, Doris, Mrs. (1897-), illus. LC 39-23640. viii p., 2 l., 3-272 p. incl. illus., plates. col. front. 21 cm. 1939. Little, Brown and Company.
--Cynthia of Bee Tree Hollow. Orr, Forrest W., illus. LC 48-4520. 212 p. illus. 20 cm. 1948. Little, Brown.
--Green Treasure. Orr, Forrest W., illus. LC 41-20167. vi, 258, 1 p. incl. illus., plates. col. front. 20 cm. 1941. Little, Brown and Company.
--Lona of Hollybush Creek. Orr, Forrest W., illus. LC 35-27308. 7 p. l., 3-275, 1 p., 1 l. incl. col. front., illus., plates. 21 cm. 1935. Little, Brown, and Company.
--Mountain Girl. Orr, Forrest W., illus. LC 32-3902. vi p., 2 l., 3-262 p. incl. illus., plates. col. front. 21 cm. 1932. Little, Brown, and Company.
--Mountain Girl Comes Home. Orr, Forrest W., illus. LC 34-2641. 5 p. l., 3-249, 1 p. incl. illus., plates. col. front. 21 cm. 1934. Little, Brown, and Company.
--Susan of the Green Mountains. Orr, Forrest W., illus. LC 37-21638. x p., 2 l. 3-275 p. incl. plates. col. front 21 cm. 1937. Little, Brown and Company.

Fox, Grace
--The Hairy Brown Angel and Other Animal Tails. Dunham, Darwin, illus. LC 76-45040. (Illus.). 132 p. 20cm. (Winner book). c.1977. (ISBN 0-88207-475-X). Victor Books.
--The Peanut Butter Hamster, and Other Animal Tails. Johnson, Richard (1953-), illus. LC 78-65204. (Illus.). 132 p. 20cm. (Winner book). c.1979. (ISBN 0-88207-484-9). Victor Books.

Fox, Jane L., illus.
--Another Mix or Match Storybook. LC 75-7163. (Illus.). 9p. (ps-1). 1975. (ISBN 0-394-83112-8, BYR). Random.

Fox, John William, Jr. (1862-1919)
--Erskine Dale-Pioneer. N.D. Charles Scribner's Sons.
--The Heart of the Hills. N.D. Charles Scribner's Sons.
--Little Shepherd of Kingdom Come. (Illus.). 250p. (Thrushwood Books). (gr. 5-11). 1970. G&D.
--Little Shepherd of Kingdom Come. Wyeth, Newell Convers (1882-1945), illus. (Illus.). (Illustrated Classics Ser). (gr. 7-11). 1931. (ISBN 0-684-20824-5). Scribner.
--The Trail of the Lonesome Pine. N.D. Charles Scribner's Sons.
--The Trail of the Lonesome Pine. N.D. Grosset & Dunlap.

Fox, Kaye
--Pussy Afloat: Tibby's Own Story of Adventure. LC 37-5085. 4 p. l., 7-227, 1 p. illus. 20 cm. c.1936. Fleming H. Revell Company.

Fox, L., jt. auth. see Hollander, Zander.
Fox, Martin A., jt. auth. see Bisconti, Patrick R.
Fox, Mary Virginia (1919-)
--Ambush at Fort Dearborn. Bjorklund, Lorence F. (1913-1978), illus. LC 62-8318. (Illus.). 173 p. 21cm. (gr. 4-6). 1962. St. Martin's Press.
--Apprentice to Liberty. Silverman, Melvin Frank (1931-1966), illus. LC 60-6809. (Illus.). 160p. 22cm. 1960. Abingdon Press.
--Treasure of the Revolution. Cary, pseud. (1915-), illus. Cary, Louis Favreau. LC 61-7047. (Illus.). 191p. 22cm. 1961. Abingdon Press.

Fox, Michael Wilson (1937-)
--Dr. Fox's Fables: Lessons from Nature. LC 80-18345. p. cm. c.1980. (ISBN 0-87491-291-1). (ISBN 0-87491-516-3). Acropolis Books.
--Lost Dogs Three. (gr. 4-6). 1979. (ISBN 0-590-05753-7). Scholastic Inc.
--Ramu and Chennai, Brothers of the Wild. Hampshire, Michael Allen, illus. LC 75-10453. (Illus.). 127 p. 23cm. (gr. 5-8). c.1975. (ISBN 0-698-20338-0). Coward, McCann & Geoghegan.
--Sundance Coyote. Gates, Dee, illus. LC 73-88534. (Illus.). 93 p. 23cm. 1974. (ISBN 0-698-20284-8). (ISBN 0-698-20284-8). Coward, McCann & Geoghegan.
--The Touchlings. Herman, Pat, illus. LC 80-27959. (Illus.). 65 p. 24cm. c.1981. (ISBN 0-87491-293-8). (ISBN 0-87491-517-1). Acropolis Books.
--Vixie, the Story of a Little Fox. Perrott, Jennifer, illus. LC 73-77426. (Illus.). 91 p. 23cm. 1973. (ISBN 0-698-20275-9). (ISBN 0-698-20275-9). Coward, McCann & Geoghegan.
--Whitepaws: a Coyote-Dog. Gammell, Stephen, illus. LC 78-11312. (Illus.). 73p. (gr. 6-8). 1979. (ISBN 0-698-20478-6, Coward). Putnam Pub Group.
--Wild Dogs Three. LC 76-46305. (Illus.). 64 p. c.1977. (ISBN 0-698-20400-X). Coward, McCann & Geoghegan.
--The Wolf. Frace, Charles, illus. LC 72-76700. (Illus.). 95 p. 23cm. 1973. Coward, McCann & Geoghegan.

Fox, Natalie, jt. auth. see Hoke, Helen L., Mrs.
Fox, Paula (1923-)
--Blowfish Live in the Sea. LC 75-122740. 116 p. 22cm. 1970. (ISBN 0-13-077602-5). Bradbury Press.
--Dear Prosper. McLachlin, Steve, illus. LC 68-17111. (Illus.). 67 p. 22cm. 1968. D. White.
--Good Ethan. Lobel, Arnold Stark (1933-), illus. LC 72-93810. (Illus.). 32 p. 24cm. 1973. (ISBN 0-87888-057-7). Bradbury Press.
--How Many Miles to Babylon?. 128p. (gr. 3-6). 1982. (ISBN 0-590-32391-1, Apple Paperbacks). Scholastic Inc.
--How Many Miles to Babylon?. Giovanopoulos, Paul Arthur (1939-), illus. LC 79-25802. (Illus.). 128p. (gr. 5-7). 1980. (ISBN 0-02-735590-X). Bradbury Pr.
--How Many Miles to Babylon. Giovanopoulos, Paul Arthur (1939-), illus. LC 67-19301. (Illus.). 8 line drawings, 117p. (gr. 4-8). 1967. D White.
--Hungry Fred. Wells, Rosemary, illus. LC 69-11970. (Illus.). 39 p. 24cm. 1969. Bradbury Press.
--The King's Falcon. Keith, Eros, illus. LC 69-13322. (Illus.). 56 p. 23cm. 1969. Bradbury Press.
--A Likely Place. Ardizzone, Edward Jeffrey Irving (1900-1979), illus. LC 66-16101. (Illus.). 57 p. 21cm. 1967. Macmillan.
--The Little Swineherd, and Other Tales. Lubin, Leonard B., illus. LC 78-5435. p. cm. c.1978. Dutton.
--Maurice's Room. Fetz, Ingrid (1915-), illus. LC 66-10167. (Illus.). 63 p. 22cm. 1966. Macmillan.
--Maurice's Room. Fetz, Ingrid (1915-), illus. LC 85-7200. (Illus.). 63 p. 23cm. 1985, c.1966. (ISBN 0-02-735490-3). Macmillan.
--One-Eyed Cat. Trivas, Irene, illus. LC 84-10964. 192p. (gr. 6-8). c.1984. (ISBN 0-02-735540-3). Bradbury Pr. **Award: (JNM).**
--A Place Apart. LC 80-36717. 183 p. 21cm. c.1980. (ISBN 0-374-35985-7). Farrar Straus Giroux.
--Portrait of Ivan. Lambert, Saul (1928-), illus. LC 74-93085. (Illus.). 131 p. 22cm. 1969. Bradbury Press. **Award: (ALA).**
--Portrait of Ivan. Lambert, Saul (1928-), illus. LC 84-20476. (Illus.). 131 p. 22cm. 1985. (ISBN 0-02-735550-0). Bradbury Press.
--The Slave Dancer. Keith, Eros, illus. LC 73-80642. (Illus.). 192p. (gr. 5-8). 1973. (ISBN 0-02-735560-8). Bradbury Pr. **Awards: (JNM); (ALA).**
--The Stone-Faced Boy. MacKay, Donald A. (1895-), illus. LC 68-9053. (Illus.). 106 p. 22cm. 1968. Bradbury Press. **Award: (ALA).**

Fox, Philip Charles
--When Spring Comes. (Illus.). 32p. 1964. Reilly & Lee.

Fox, Phyllis W. & Coleman, David
--Cinderella. (Musical Children's Theatre Playscript Ser.). 1978. (ISBN 0-88020-002-2). (ISBN 0-88020-003-0). Coach Hse.

Fox, Robert Barlow (1930-)
--Little Injun, Big Injun, Mormon Injun. LC 72-88909. 135 p. 24cm. c.1972. (ISBN 0-88290-013-7). Horizon Publishers.

Fox, Robin, adapted by.
--Le Poulet: A Rooster Who Laid Eggs. (Illus.). N.D. (ISBN 0-685-11509-7). French & Eur.

Fox, Robin, jt. auth. see Palazzo, Tony.
Fox, Robin, ed. see Berri, Claude.
Fox, Siv Cedering (1939-)
--The Blue Horse & Other Night Poems. Carrick, Donald (1929-), illus. LC 78-12793. (Illus.). 32p. (ps-3). 1979. (ISBN 0-395-28952-1, Clarion). HM.

Fox, Siv Cedering (1939-) & Carrick, Donald (1929-)
--The Blue Horse, and Other Night Poems. LC 78-12793. (Illus.). 30 p. 26cm. c.1979. (ISBN 0-8164-3226-0). Seabury Press.

Fox, Sonia
--Cindy Lou. Harrington, Betty, illus. (Illus.). (See & Read Storybook Ser). (gr. k-3). 1960. (ISBN 0-399-60098-1). Putnam.

Fox, Sonny (1925-)
--Funnier Than the First One: A New Joke Book. Gray, Bob (1928-), illus. LC 70-189883. (Illus.). 92 p. 23cm. 1972. (ISBN 0-399-20252-8). (ISBN 0-399-20252-8). Putnam.
--Funnier Than the First One: A New Joke Book. Gray, Bob (1928-), illus. (Illus.). 95 p. 18cm. (Berkley medallion book). 1974, c.1972. (ISBN 0-425-02536-5). Putnam.
--Funnier Than the First One: Another Joke Book. (Illus.). (gr. 4-9). 1972. (ISBN 0-399-60770-6). Putnam Pub Group.
--Jokes and How to Tell Them. LC 65-25461. (Illus.). 93 p. 23cm. 1965. Putnam.

Fox, Sonny (1925-) & Gray, Bob (1928-)
--Jokes and Tips for the Joke Teller. LC 76-353743. (Illus.). 92 p. 23cm. c.1976. (ISBN 0-399-20457-1). (ISBN 0-399-60947-4). Putnam.

Fox, William Wellington (1909-)
--From Bones To Bodies. 1959. (ISBN 0-8382-0270-5, Cadmus Books). E. M. Hale and Company.
--Rocks and Rain and the Rays of the Sun. LC 58-7379. 90 p. illus. 22 cm. 1958. H. Z. Walck.

Foxton, Thomas see Bunyan, John.
Foyle, Kathleen
--The Little Black Calf. Johnston, Arnrid, illus. LC 52-9513. 45p. illus. cm. 1952. F. Warne.
--The Little Good People: Folk Tales of Ireland. Fraser, Peter, illus. LC 50-4681. xi, 163 p. illus. (part col.) 21 cm. c.1949. Warne.

Fradin, Dennis Brindell (1945-)
--Bad Luck Tony. Scribner, Joanne L. (1949-), illus. LC 77-5888. p. cm. c.1977. (ISBN 0-13-055541-X). Prentice-Hall.
--Beyond the Mountain, Beyond the Forest. Maggard, John, illus. LC 78-6611. (Illus.). 46 p. 24cm. (Early Man). c.1978. (ISBN 0-516-03853-2). Childrens Press.
--Cara. Daley, Joann, illus. LC 77-6270. p. cm. 1977. (ISBN 0-516-03438-3). Childrens Press.
--Cave Painter. Maggard, John, illus. LC 77-16623. p. cm. (Early Man). 1978. (ISBN 0-516-03852-4). Childrens Press.
--The New Spear. Dunnington, Tom, illus. LC 78-11060. (Illus.). 45 p. 25cm. (Early Man). (gr. 2-5). c.1979. (ISBN 0-516-03854-0). Childrens Press.
--North Star. Neebe, William, illus. LC 77-26558. p. cm. (Early Man). 1978. (ISBN 0-516-03851-6). Children's Press.

--One Winter. (gr. 6-10). 1985. (ISBN 0-8038-5401-3). Hastings.

Fradin, Morris

--Hey-Ey-Ey, Lock!. Watson, Carol Stuart, illus. LC 73-91394. (Illus.). vi, 112 p. 27cm. 1st U.S. edition. 1974. See-and-Know Press.

Fraelich, Richard Oddly (1924-)

--Gretchen: Hit The Ball. Spiegel, Lawrence M., illus. LC 61-18089. 29cm. 40p. (Children's Picture Bks.). 1962. T. S. Denison & Co.

--Our Week in School. (First Grade Read-to Bks.). (gr. 1-3). N.D. Denison.

Fragasso, Philip M. (1950-)

--Good News Bad News. LC 80-15582. 138 p. 22cm. c.1980. (ISBN 0-201-03197-3). Addison-Wesley.

--Good News Bad News. LC 84-46020. p. cm. 1985, c.1980. (ISBN 0-201-03197-3). Crowell.

Frame, Janet, pseud., see Clutha, Janet Paterson Frame.

Frame, Janet, pseud. (1924-)

--Mona Minim and the Smell of the Sun. Clutha, Janet Paterson Frame. Jacques, Robin (1920-), illus. LC 69-18077. (Illus.). 94 p. 24cm. 1969. G. Braziller.

Frame, Paul (1913-), illus.

--Ali Baba & the Forty Thieves. White, Anne T., adapted by. Bd. with Abu Kir & Abu Sir. LC 68-11513. (Illus.). 96p. (Reading Shelf-Myths, Tales & Legends Ser.). (gr. 4-7). 1968. (ISBN 0-8116-4200-3). Garrard.

Frame, Paul (1913-) & Grimm, Jakob Ludwig Karl (1785-1863)

Sleeping Beauty. Mellon, Joseph, adapted by. LC 78-72129. (Illus.). 31 p. 23cm. 1979. (ISBN 0-89799-050-1). Dandelion Press.

Frampton, David, jt. auth. see Fieg, Victor P.

France, Anatole, pseud., see Thibault, Jacques Anatole Francois.

Frances, Margaret

--Rose Carleton's Reward. 283p. N.D. Chase & Hall.

Frances, Marian

--Mr. Mac-A-Doodle. (Illus.). (gr. 1). 1972. (ISBN 0-89375-045-X). Troll Assocs.

--Witch on a Motorcycle. new ed. (Illus.). (gr. 3-4). 1972. (ISBN 0-89375-047-6). Troll Assocs.

France, Anatole, pseud. (1844-1924)

--Bee: The Princess of the Dwarfs. Thibault, Jacques Anatole Francois. Robinson, Charles (1870-1937), illus. N.D. E. P. Dutton & Co.

--The Elm Tree on the Mall. Thibault, Jacques Anatole Francois. Willcocks, M. P., tr. N.D. Dodd, Mead & Co.

--Girls and Boys. Thibault, Jacques Anatole Francois. De Monvel, Boutet R., illus. N.D. Duffield.

--Golden Tales of Anatole France. Thibault, Jacques Anatole Francois. N.D. Dodd, Mead & Co.

--In All France: Children in Town and Country. Thibault, Jacques Anatole Francois. Enders, Lucille, illus. Wippern, Adolphus George (1868-), tr. LC 30-27928. 110 p., 1 l. incl. col. front., col. illus. 23 cm. (Young-heart books telling about other nations' young life). c.1930. A. Whitman & Co.

--Jocasta and the Famished Cat. Thibault, Jacques Anatole Francois. FArley, Agnes, tr. N.D. Dodd, Mead & Co.

--Little Sea Dogs And Other Tales of Childhood. Thibault, Jacques Anatole Francois. Foster, Marcia Lane (1897-), illus. May, James Lewis (1873-), tr. LC 26-26041. 6 p. l., 149 p. col. front., illus., col. plates. 23 cm. 1925. John Lane.

--The Man Who Married a Dumb Wife. Thibault, Jacques Anatole Francois. Page, Curtis Hidden, tr. N.D. Dodd, Mead & Co.

--Our Children. Thibault, Jacques Anatole Francois. De MOnvel, Boutet R., illus. N.D. Duffield.

--Penguin Island. Thibault, Jacques Anatole Francois. Evans, A. W., tr. N.D. Dodd, Mead & Co.

--The Wicker-Work Woman. Thibault, Jacques Anatole Francois. Willcocks, M. P., tr. N.D. Dodd, Mead & Co.

France, Tab

--Rhymes for Young Ghouls. N.D. Vantage Press Inc.

Frances, Emily, pseud., see Stover, W. N..

Frances, Esteban, jt. auth. see Heathers, Anne.

Franchere, Ruth

--Cesar Chavez. 1970. (ISBN 0-690-18383-6). (ISBN 0-690-18384-4). Thomas Y. Crowell.

--Hannah Herself. 1968. (ISBN 0-8382-0313-2, Cadmus Books). E. M. Hale and Company.

--Hannah Herself. LC 64-13908. 176 p. 21cm. 1964. T. Y. Crowell Co.

--Stampede North. LC 69-11296. (Illus.). 218 p. 21cm. 1969. Macmillan.

--The Travels of Colin O'Dae. Bjorklund, Lorence F. (1913-1978), illus. LC 66-775953. 261p. illus. 21cm. (gr. 7 up). 1966. (ISBN 0-690-83458-6). Crowell.

--Willa. Weisgard, Leonard Joseph (1916-), illus. LC 58-7324. (Illus.). 169 p. 21cm. 1958. Crowell.

Franchi, Anna (1867-)

--The Little Lead Soldier. N.D. Alfred A. Knopf.

--The Little Lead Soldier. Woodruff, Sarah Frances (1848-), tr. LC 19-18836. 186 p. col. front., illus., col. plates. 22 cm. 1919. The Penn Publishing Company.

Franchot, Annie Wood

--The Big Four and One More. LC 23-17653. 49 p. col. front., pl. 20 cm. 1923. F. H. Oakleaf Co.

--Bobs, King of the Fortunate Isle. Haywood, Carolyn (1898-) & Smith, Jessie Willcox (1863-1935), illus. LC 28-25547. vii p., 3 l., 3-210 p. incl. illus., paltes. col. front. 21 cm. c.1928. E. P. Dutton & Co., Inc.

--Bugs and Wings and Other Things. Cady, Walter Harrison (1877-1970) & Smith, Jessie Willcox (1863-1935), illus. LC 18-22752. ix, 99 p. col. front., illus., col. plates. 22 cm. c.1918. E. P. Dutton & Company.

--Max: A Midnight Adventure. LC 22-96569. 6 p. l., 3-46 p. col. front. 20 cm. c.1921. E. P. Dutton & Company.

--War Babies. Davis, Mary Louise, illus. LC 14-22140. viii p., 1 l., 61 p. col. front., illus., plates (part col.) 24 cm. 1914. The University Press.

--The White Giant and the Black Giant. Gamble, James, illus. LC 25-1294. 4 p. l., 3-72 p. front., illus. 24 cm. c.1924. E. P. Dutton & Company.

Francillon, Robert Edward (1841-1919)

--Gods and Heroes: Or, The Kingdom of Jupiter. authorized american. LC 42-47700. x, 285 p. 18 cm. (On cover: Classics for children). 1896. Ginn & Company.

--Gods and Heroes: Or, The Kingdom of Jupiter. Gallagher, Sears (1869-1955), illus. LC 15-19999. (Illus.). 361p. 18cm. 1915. Ginn & Company.

Francis, Anna B

--Pleasant Dreams. 1st ed. LC 83-6171. (Illus.). 32 p. c.1983. (ISBN 0-03-060574-1). Holt, Rinehart and Winston.

Francis, Dorothy Brenner (1926-)

--Adventure at Riverton Zoo. Scholz, Catherine, illus. LC 66-17001. 176p. illus. 22cm. 1966. Abingdon.

--Adventure at Riverton Zoo. Scholz, Catherine, illus. (Illus.). (gr. 5-8). N.D. (ISBN 0-687-00889-1). Abingdon.

--Another Kind of Beauty. LC 76-124878. 223 p. 22cm. 1970. Criterion Book.

--The Flint Hills Foal. Oughton, Taylor (1925-), illus. LC 76-4812. p. cm. 1976. (ISBN 0-687-13189-8). Abingdon Press.

--The Ghost of Graydon Place. 192p. (Orig.). (gr. 7 up). 1982. (ISBN 0-590-32545-0, Windswept). Scholastic Inc.

--Golden Girl. (gr. 7-12). 1975. (ISBN 0-590-09914-0, Schol Pap). Schol Bk Serv.

--Laugh at the Evil Eye. LC 70-123181. 189 p. 22cm. 1970. J. Messner.

--Murder in Hawaii. (gr. 7-12). 1974. (ISBN 0-590-06105-4, Schol Trade Pap). Schol Bk Serv.

--Mystery of the Forgotten Map. Lazare, Gerald John (1927-), illus. LC 68-13784. (Illus.). 188 p. 23cm. (Merit mystery). 1968. Follett Pub. Co.

--Piggy-Bank Minds and Forty Nine Other Object Lessons for Children. LC 76-49639. 127 p. 19cm. c.1977. (ISBN 0-687-31420-8). Abingdon.

--Two Against the Arctic. (Orig.). 1976. (ISBN 0-515-04026-6). BJ Pub Group.

--The Warning. 192p. (Orig.). (gr. 7-12). 1984. (ISBN 0-590-33250-3, Windswept Bks). Scholastic Inc.

Francis, Dorothy Brenner (1926-) & Eisenberg, Monroe

--Run of the Sea Witch. LC 77-13501. (Illus.). 158 p. 23cm. c.1978. Abingdon.

Francis, Frank

--The Magic Wallpaper. LC 79-118811. (Illus.). 27 p. 1970. Abelard-Schuman.

--Natasha's New Doll. Francis, Frank, illus. LC 73-935. (Illus.). 29 p. 26cm. 1974, c.1971. (ISBN 0-87955-700-1). Ohara Publications.

--Timimoto's Great Adventure. Francis, Frank, illus. LC 70-8063. (Illus.). 28 p. 27cm. 1969. Holiday House.

Francis, Frank, jt. auth. see Wood, Joyce.

Francis, H. D., jt. auth. see Streeter, Floyd Benjamin.

Francis, Helen Dannefer (1915-)

--Basketball Bones. Neale, Sidnee, illus. LC 62-16189. (Illus.). 118p. 22cm. 1962. Hastings House.

--Big Swat. LC 63-17803. 192 p. 22 cm. 1963. Follett Pub. Co.

--Double Reverse. LC 58-9202. 22cm. 214p. 1958. Doubleday.

--Football Flash. Kramer, Frank, illus. LC 61-11990. (Illus.). 22cm. 128p. 1961. Hastings House.

--Martha Norton: Operation Fitness U.S.A. Torbert, Floyd James (1922-), illus. LC 63-16168. 120 p. illus. 22 cm. 1963. Hastings House.

--Operation Fitness U.S.A. LC 63-16168. 120 p. illus. 22 cm. 1963. Hastings House.

Francis, Jane Shaw, jt. auth. see Mother Goose.

Francis, Joseph Greene (1849-1930)

--A Book of Cheerful Cats and Other Animated Animals. LC 16-5303. 1892. The Century Co.

--A Book of Cheerful Cats and Other Animated Animals. LC 67-28172. (Illus.). ix, 45 l. (Legacy library facsimile). 1967. University Microfilms.

--A Book of Cheerful Cats and Other Animated Animals. Francis, Joseph Greene (1849-1930), illus. LC 3-14833. x p., 1 l., 45 numb. l. illus. 17 x 23 1/2cm. 1903. Century Co.

--The Joyous Aztecs. Francis, Joseph Greene (1849-1930), illus. N.D. Appleton Century Co.

Francis, Joseph Greene (1849-1930) & Shepherd, J. C., illus.

--Funny Stories About Funny People in Rhymes, Pictures and Jingles. LC 6-751. 96 p. illus. 26 x 21 cm. c.1905. National Publishing Company.

Francis, Laurence H., ed.

--The Boys of Mirthfield Academy. (Illus.). N.D. Dana Estes and Company.

--Chatterbox Circus. Weir, Harrison William (1824-1906), illus. (Our "Chatterbox" Picture Books). N.D. Dana Estes and Company.

--Chatterbox Menagerie. Weir, Harrison William (1824-1906), illus. (Our "Chatterbox" Picture Books). N.D. Dana Estes and Company.

--Chatterbox Picture Book. Weir, Harrison William (1824-1906), illus. (Our "Chatterbox" Picture Books). N.D. Dana Estes and Company.

--Chatterbox Wild West. Weir, Harrison William (1824-1906), illus. (Our "Chatterbox" Picture Books). N.D. Dana Estes and Company.

--Chatterbox Zoo. Weir, Harrison William (1824-1906), illus. (Our "Chatterbox" Picture Book). N.D. Dana Estes and Company.

--Schoolboys of Rookesbury: Or, The Boys of the Fourth Form. (Illus.). N.D. Dana Estes and Company.

--Through Thick and Thin: Or, School Days at St. Egbert's. (Illus.). N.D. Dana Estes and Company.

Francis, May E (1880-)

--Jim Bowie's Lost Mine. 2nd rev., enl. ed. LC 66-234279. 98p. illus. 20cm. N.D. Naylor.

Francis, Philip W.

--The Remarkable Adventures of Little Boy Pip ... Johnson, Merle, illus. LC 7-36090. 3 p. l., 60 p., 1 l. col. front., illus., col. plates. 23 cm. c.1907. P. Elder & Company.

Francis, Sally R.

--The Goat That Went to School. Tamburine, Jean (1930-), illus. LC 53-18613. unpaged. illus. 21cm. (Rand McNally book-elf book, 469). 1953, c.1952. Rand McNally.

--The Puppy that Found a Home. Grider, Dorothy (1915-), illus. N.D. Rand McNally & Co.

--Scat, Scat. Collison, Elizabeth E., illus. LC 40-32636. (Illus.). 30p. 20 x 15 1/2cm. 1940. The Platt & Munk Co.

--Scat! Scat!. Powell, Linda K., illus. LC 76-56956. (Illus.). 18 p. 32cm. (Cricket book). c.1977. (ISBN 0-448-13056-4). Platt & Munk : Special Library Edition Distributed by Grosset & Dunlap.

Franciscan Sisters, illus.

--Come Listen to a Story. N.D. Vantage Press.

Franck, Frederick (1909-)

--My Friend in Africa. 1960. Bobbs-Merrill Co.

Franck, Harry Alverson (1881-1962)

--Marco Polo, Junior. 293p. N.D. Century Co.

Franco, Eloise

--Little Stories. LC 77-132050. (Illus.). 66 p. 21cm. 1970. (ISBN 0-8158-0251-X). Christopher Pub. House.

Franco, Joan E

--Joan's Vacation Days. Meline, Eva E., illus. LC 78-140518. (Illus.). 24 p. 21cm. (William-Frederick juvenile). 1971. William-Frederick Press.

Franco, Marjorie

--Love in a Different Key. LC 83-10653. 154 p. 22cm. 1983. (ISBN 0-395-34827-7). Houghton Mifflin.

--So Who Hasn't Got Problems?. LC 78-31410. 153 p. 22cm. 1979. (ISBN 0-395-27814-7). Houghton Mifflin.

Francois, Andre (1915-)

--Crocodile Tears. Francois, Andre (1915-), illus. LC 56-11622. unpaged. illus. 9x27cm. 1956. R. Delpire.

--Crocodile Tears. Francois, Andre (1915-), illus. 1956. Universe Books Inc. **Award: (NYT).**

--Crocodile Tears: Larmes De Crocodile. rev. ed. Francois, Andre (1915-), illus. (Fr). color illus. (gr. 3-7). 1964. (ISBN 0-87663-049-2). Universe.

--Jack and the Beanstalk: English Fairy Tale. american ed. LC 83-71178. c.1983. (ISBN 0-87191-947-8). Creative Education.

--You Are Ri-Di-Cu-Lous. Francois, Andre (1915-), illus. LC 72-77422. (Illus.). 32 p. 1970. Pantheon Books. **Award: (NYT).**

Francois, Paul

--The Hare and the Tortoise. Simon, Romain (1915-), illus. (From the Pere Castor Library). 1966. Golden Press.

Francois, Victor E.

--The Two Deaf Men. N.D. (ISBN 0-8283-1243-5). Branden Press.

Francoise, pseud., see Seignobosc, Francoise.

Frandon, Ramona & Hunt, Dave

--The Story of Superman: Four Little Library Books. Frandon, Ramona & Hunt, Dave, illus. LC 75-17774. (Illus.). (ps). 1980. Pap. (ISBN 0-394-84416-5, BYR). Random.

Frandsen, Karen G.

--I Started School Today. Frandsen, Karen G., illus. LC 83-23169. (Illus.). 32p. (Childhood Fantasies & Fears Ser.). (ps-2). 1984. (ISBN 0-516-03495-2). Childrens.

Frank, Florence Kiper, Mrs. (1865-1976)

--Three Plays for a Children's Theatre. LC 27-7098. 5 p. l., 3-128 p. front. 20 cm. 1926. H. Vinal.

Frank, Jane

--Monica Mink. Frank, Jane, illus. LC 48-9558. 24 p. illus. 23 x 25 cm. 1948. Vanguard Press.

Frank, Janet, pseud., see Dunleavy, Janet Egleson.

Frank, Janet, pseud. (1928-)

--Daddies. Dunleavy, Janet Egleson. Gergely, Tibor (1900-1978), illus. LC 54-1147. (Little Golden Book). 1954. Golden Press.

--Davy Crockett & the Indians. Dunleavy, Janet Egleson. Young, Cliff, illus. LC 56-720. unpaged. illus. 21cm. (Magic talking books, T-19). 1955. J. C. Winston Co.

--Happy Days: What Children Do the Whole Day Through. Dunleavy, Janet Egleson. Dart, Eleanor, illus. LC 55-12633. unpaged. illus. 21cm. (Little golden library, 247). 1955. Simon and Schuster.

Frank, Josette (1893-), ed. see Barrie, James Matthew, Sir.

Frank, Josette, jt. ed. see Lang, Andrew.

Frank, Josette (1893-), ed.

--More Poems to Read to the Very Young. Wilson, Dagmar (1916-), illus. LC 67-21917. (Illus.). 1 v. (unpaged). 33cm. 1968. Random House.

--Peter Pan. Goode, Diane (1949-), illus. LC 82-13288. (Edited from James Matthew Barrie's "Peter Pan and Wendy"). p. cm. (Looking glass library). 1983, c.1957. (ISBN 0-394-85717-8). (ISBN 0-394-95717-2). Random House.

--Poems to Read to the Very Young. Wilkin, Eloise Burns (1904-), illus. LC 82-518. (Illus.). 45 p. 28cm. c.1982. (ISBN 0-394-95188-3). Random House.

--Poems to Read to the Very Young. Wilson, Dagmar (1916-), illus. LC 61-78722. unpaged. col. illus. 33cm. c.1961. Random.

Frank, Mabel Livingston, jt. auth. see Zucca, Mana.

Frank, Mary, jt. auth. see Mason, Arthur.

Frank, Pat Harry Hart (1907-1964)

--Alas, Babylon. LC 59-5405. (gr. 10 up). N.D. (ISBN 0-397-00097-9). Har-Row.

Frank, Phil

--Travels with Farley. LC 80-24730. (Illus.). 96p. 1980. (ISBN 0-89844-023-8). Troubador Pr.

Frank, Phil & Frank, Susan

--Subee Lives on a Houseboat. Forrester, Bruce, photos by. LC 79-26354. (Illus.). 64p. (gr. 4 up). 1980. (ISBN 0-671-33055-1). Messner.

Frank, R., pseud., see Ross, Frank Xavier.

Frank, R. Donavan

--The Brave Traitor. (American history series). N.D. A. S. Barnes & Co,Inc.

--The Brave Traitor. (Illus.). (American History Series). N.D. A. S. Barnes & Company, Inc.

--The Cutter. (Illus.). (American History Series). N.D. A. S. Barnes & Company, Inc.

--The Ironclads. (Illus.). (American History Series). N.D. A. S. Barnes & Company, Inc.

Frank, R., Jr., pseud. (1914-)

--Flashing Harpoons: The/Story Of Whales And Whaling. Ross, Frank Xavier. Cosgrave, John O'Hara, II (1908-1968), illus. 1958. (ISBN 0-690-30704-7). Thomas Y. Crowell.

Frank, Susan, jt. auth. see Frank, Phil.

Frank, Yvonne Elizabeth (1921-)

--Children's Hour: Station Y. E. F. LC 32-25847. 114 p. incl. front., illus. pl. 22 cm. c.1932. The Macaulay Company.

Frankau, Pamela (1908-1967)

--The Devil We Know. LC 39-8914. 6 p. l., 3-495 p. 21 cm. 1939. E. P. Dutton & Company, Inc.

Frankau, Ronald

--Oh! Dear, Dear!. Onslow, Lola, illus. N.D. Frederick Warne & Co.

Frankay, Mary Evelyn Atkinson see Atkinson, M. E., pseud.

Franke, Simon (1880-)
--The Last of the Zuider Zee. Dom, Pol, illus. Mussey, June Barrows (1910-), tr. from Dutch. LC 37-38048. 192, 1 p. incl. front., illus., plates, double map. 24 cm. c.1937. Stackpole Sons.

Frankel, Alona
--The Family of Tiny White Elephants. Frankel, Alona, illus. LC 79-53771. (Illus.). 41 p. 17cm. 1980, c.1978. (ISBN 0-8120-5372-9). Barron's.
--Once Upon a Potty. LC 79-53769. (Illus.). 1st U.S. edition. (ps-3). 1980. (ISBN 0-8120-5371-0). Barron.

Frankel, Bernice
--Half-As-Big and the Tiger. Weisgard, Leonard Joseph, illus. LC 61-5084. (Illus.). unpaged. 24cm. 1961. F. Watts.
--The Seven Monkeys. Fellin, Peter, illus. LC 62-15076. (Illus.). 22cm. (A Wonderful World Bk.). 1962. A. S. Barnes.
--Tag-Along. Kenne, Alex, illus. LC 62-16582. (Illus.). 27cm. 1962. Parents' Magazine Press.
--Timothy and Alexander the Great. Jacks, Flo, illus. LC 62-10185. (Illus.). 22cm. (A Wonderful World Bk.). 1962. Barnes.

Frankel, Charles (1917-1979)
--The Bear & the Beaver. Crawford, Bill, pseud. (1913-1982), illus. Crawford, William Hulfish. LC 51-13201. unpaged. illus. 22 cm. 1951. Sloane.
--The Bear and the Beaver. Crawford, Bill, pseud. (1913-1982), illus. Crawford, William Hulfish. N.D. William Morrow & Co.

Frankel, Haskel (1926-)
--Adventure in Alaska. Accurso, Anthony, illus. LC 63-11207. (Illus.). 142 p. 22cm. (Signal book). 1963. Doubleday.
--Big Band. McDaniel, J. W., illus. LC 65-19867. (Illus.). 143 p. 22cm. (Doubleday signal books). 1965. Doubleday.
--Pro Football Rookie. Liese, Charles, illus. LC 64-19297. (Illus.). 144 p. 22cm. (Signal book). 1964. Doubleday.
--Rodeo Roundup. Bjorklund, Lorence F. (1913-1978), illus. LC 62-8929. (Illus.). 144 p. 22cm. (Signal book). 1962. Doubleday.

Frankel, Julie & Scheier, Michael
--The Wildfire Romance Fill-In Book. (Illus.). 80p. (Orig.). (Wildfire Extra Ser.). (gr. 7 up). 1984. (ISBN 0-590-33214-7, Wildfire). Scholastic Inc.

Frankel, Tamara Wien (1922-)
--Boys & Girls & Puppy Dogs. Frankel, Simon, illus. LC 49-1764. 28 p. col. illus. 22 cm. (Bonnie book). 1948. John Martin's House.
--The Weeping Pussy Willow. Frankel, Simon, illus. LC 48-16377. 32 p. col. illus. 23 cm. (Merry-go-round book). 1947. J. Martin's House.

Frankel, Walter
--The Lion Who Lay Down, Rolled Over, & Said Grr. 1979. (ISBN 0-533-03951-7). Vantage.

Franken, Klaus (1913-)
--Puzzlers for Young Detectives. LC 69-19484. (Illus.). 112 p. 21cm. 1969. Sterling Pub. Co.

Franken, Rose, Mrs. & Lewin, Jane
--Mr. Dooley Jr. A Comedy for Children. LC 34-4278. 2 p. l., 72, 2 p. diagrs. 19 cm. 1932. S. French; Etc., Etc.

Frankenberg, Lloyd, ed. see Burns, Robert.

Frankenberger, Samuel (1879-)
--Youngster Rimes. LC 38-31053. 96 p. 21 cm. c.1938. The Christopher Publishing House.

Frankenstein, Gustavus
--The Little Boy and the Elephant. Verbeek, Gustave, illus. LC 4-21078. (Illus.). 110p. 18cm. 1904. C. Altemus Company.

Frankenstein, Louise Michelbacher, Mrs. (1904-), ed.
--Junior Play-Readings. LC 35-27406. ix, 141 p. 20 cm. 1935. S. French.

Frankl, Liselotte
--Peter & His New Brother. Frank, Josette (1893-), intro. by. LC 49-7835. 22 p. col. illus. 27 cm. (Chanticleer junior book). c.1948. Chanticleer Press.

Franklin, Benjamin (1706-1790)
--A Bird in the Hand: Sayings from Poor Richard's Almanack. Petersham, Maud Sylvia Fuller, Mrs. (1890-1971) & Petersham, Miska (1889-1960), illus. LC 51-8266. unpaged. illus. 27 cm. 1951. Macmillan.
--The Whistle. Overlie, George, illus. LC 72-12487. (Illus.). 32p. (Seedling Bks). (gr. 2-6). 1974. (ISBN 0-8225-0282-8). Lerner Pubns.

Franklin, Freida Kenyon see Brown, F. K., pseud.

Franklin, Freida Kenyon (1921-)
--Last Hurdle. Brown, F. K., pseud. Spier, Peter Edward (1927-), illus. 208p (Pub. by T Y Crowell). (gr. 5-9). 1970. (ISBN 0-8152-0504-X). Apollo Eds.

Franklin, Frieda Kenyon (1921-)
--Last Hurdle. Spier, Peter Edward (1927-), illus. LC 53-8427. (Illus.). 202 p. 21cm. 1953. Crowell.

Franklin, George Cory (1872-)
--Back of Beyond. 1st ed. Moyers, William (1916-), illus. LC 52-11817. 192 p. illus. 21 cm. (American heritage series). 1952. Aladdin Books.
--Bravo, The Bummer. Cram, L. D. (1898-), illus. LC 53-10985. (Illus.). 121 p. 22cm. 1954. Houghton Mifflin.
--Indian Uprising. Hofmann, William, illus. LC 62-12250. (Illus.). 117p. 22cm. 1962. Houghton Mifflin.
--Mining the Iron Mask. 1st ed. Moyers, William (1916-), illus. LC 51-13269. 204 p. illus. 22 cm. 1952. Ariel Books.
--Monte. (Illus.). N.D. Houghton Mifflin.
--Pancho. Moyers, William (1916-), illus. LC 52-11454. (Illus.). 152 p. 22cm. 1953. Houghton Mifflin.
--Pedro, the Road Runner. Moyers, William (1916-), illus. LC 57-7453. (Illus.). 94 p. 22cm. (Hastings House easy reading series book). 1957. Hastings House.
--Pioneer Horse. Moyers, William, illus. LC 59-9721. (Illus.). 22 cm. 115p. 1960. Houghton Mifflin.
--Rocky, the Famous Bull Elk. Burger, Carl Victor (1888-1967), illus. LC 57-12089. (Illus.). 22 cm. 138p. 1958. Houghton Mifflin.
--Sheba, a Grizzly Bear. Cram, L. D. (1898-), illus. LC 53-7094. (Illus.). 176 p. 22cm. 1953. Ariel Books.
--Shorty's Mule. Moyers, William (1916-), illus. LC 52-5914. (Illus.). 25 cm. 45p. 1952. Houghton Mifflin.
--Son of Monte. Cram, L. D. (1898-), illus. LC 56-5542. (Illus.). 22 cm. 137p. 1956. Houghton Mifflin.
--Trails West. Bjorklund, Lorence F. (1913-1978), illus. LC 60-9089. (Illus.). 21 cm. 184p. 1960. Houghton Mifflin.
--Tricky: The Adventures of a Red Fox. Cram, L. D. (1898-), illus. LC 49-7632. v. 136 p. illus. 24 cm. 1949. Houghton Mifflin Co.
--Tuffy. Cram, L. D. (1898-), illus. LC 54-9046. (Illus.). 148 p. 22cm. 1954. Houghton Mifflin.
--Wild Animals of the Southwest. (Illus.). N.D. Houghton Mifflin.
--Wild Horses of the Rio Grande. (Illus.). (gr. 5-8). N.D. (ISBN 0-395-06774-X). HM.
--Zorra. N.D. E . M. Hale and Co.
--Zorra: A Fox of the Mountains. Cram, L. D. (1898-), illus. LC 57-7205. (Illus.). 118 p. 22cm. 1957. Houghton Mifflin.

Franklin, Harold (1920-)
--Run a Twisted Street. LC 75-117229. 175 p. 21cm. 1970. Lippincott.

Franklin, Joseph, pseud., see Warren, Joseph Franklin.

Franklin, Josephine
--Cousin Regulus. (Martin and Nelly Stories). N.D. Thompson, Brown & Co.
--Little Bessie. (Martin and Nelly Stories). N.D. Thompson, Brown & Co.
--Martin. (Martin and Nelly Stories). N.D. Thompson, Brown & Co.
--Martin and Nelly. (Martin and Nelly Stories). N.D. Thompson, Brown & Co.
--Martin and the Miller. (Martin and Nelly Stories). N.D. Thompson, Brown & Co.
--Martin on the Mountain. (Martin and Nelly Stories). N.D. Thompson, Brown & Co.
--Nelly and Her Boat. (Martin and Nelly Stories). N.D. Thompson, Brown & Co.
--Nelly and Her Fiends. (Martin and Nelly Stories). N.D. Thompson, Brown & Co.
--Nelly's First School Days. (Martin and Nelly Stories). N.D. Thompson, Brown & Co.
--Nelly's Visit. (Martin and Nelly Stories). N.D. Thompson, Brown & Co.
--Trouting, or Gipsying in the Woods. (Martin and Nelly Stories). N.D. Thompson, Brown & Co.
--Zelma. (Martin and Nelly Stories). N.D. Thompson, Brown and.

Franklin, Nora
--Little Crib-Curtain Stories. N.D. D. Lothrop Co.

Franklyn, Julian (1899-1970), ed.
--More Stories from the Arabian Nights. Sinclair, McDonald, illus. Burton, Richard, Sir (1821-1890), tr. from Arabic. (Illus.). 1957. Associated Booksellers.

Franko, Ivan (1856-1916)
--Fox Mykyta. Kurelek, William (1927-1977), illus. Melnyk, Bohdan (1914-), tr. LC 78-66434. (Illus.). 148 p. 26cm. c.1978. (ISBN 0-88776-112-7). Tundra Books.

Franshaw, C. F.
--Bennie, the Little Singer. (Illus.). 80p. (The Heartsease Ser.). N.D. Fleming H. Revell Co.

Frantz, Evelyn M. (1927-)
--A Bonnet for Virginia. LC 78-6472. 140 p. 21cm. c.1978. (ISBN 0-87178-101-8). Brethren Press.

Franz, Agnes, jt. auth. see Nieritz, Karl Gustav.

Franzen, Greta
--Great Ship Vasa. LC 72-150019. (Illus.). bibl. index. 96p. (gr. 7 up). 1971. (ISBN 0-8038-2647-8). Hastings.

Franzen, Nils-Olof (1916-)
--Agaton Sax & Lispington's Grandfather Clock. Blake, Quentin (1932-), illus. (gr. 2-7). 1979. (ISBN 0-233-96964-0). Andre Deutsch.
--Agaton Sax & the Big Rig. Blake, Quentin (1932-), illus. LC 80-2693. (Illus.). 128p. (gr. 2-7). 1981. (ISBN 0-233-96754-0). Andre Deutsch.
--Agaton Sax and the Diamond Thieves. Blake, Quentin (1932-), illus. Ramsden, Evelyn, tr. from Swedish. LC 79-64183. (Illus.). 110 p. 21cm. 1980. (ISBN 0-233-95724-3). A. Deutsch.
--Agaton Sax and the Diamond Thieves. Blake, Quentin (1932-), illus. Ramsden, Evelyn, tr. from Swedish. LC 67-5968. (Illus.). 110 p. 21cm. 1st U.S. edition. (Seymour Lawrence book.). 1967. Delacorte Press.
--Agaton Sax and the Incredible Max Brothers. Blake, Quentin (1932-), illus. LC 70-106902. (Illus.). 126 p. 22cm. 1970. Delacorte Press.
--Agaton Sax and the Scotland Yard Mystery. Blake, Quentin (1932-), illus. LC 69-19428. (Illus.). 128 p. 21cm. 1969. Delacorte Press.

Frary, Marie Harriette (1883-) & Stebbins, Charles Maurice (1871-), eds.
--The Crystal Palace and Other Legends. Martini, Herbert E., illus. LC 10-1364. 124 p. front., plates. 19 cm. 1910. Stebbins and Company.
--The Sunken City and Other Stories. Martini, Herbert E., illus. LC 14-914. 124 p. front., plates. 19 cm. c.1913. Milton Bradley Company.

Frascino, Edward
--Eddie Spaghetti. LC 77-11850. (Illus.). 114 p. 21cm. c.1978. (ISBN 0-06-021908-4). (ISBN 0-06-021909-2). Harper & Row.
--Eddie Spaghetti on the Homefront. 1st ed. LC 82-48847. p. cm. c.1983. (ISBN 0-06-021894-0). (ISBN 0-06-021895-9). Harper & Row.
--My Cousin the King. LC 85-3647. p. cm. c.1985. (ISBN 0-13-608423-0). Prentice-Hall.

Frascino, Edward, jt. auth. see Barry, Robert Everett.

Frascino, Edward, jt. auth. see Gray, Nigel.

Frasconi, Antonio (1919-)
--See and Say, Guarda E Parla, Mira y Habla, Regarde et Parle: A Picture Book in Four Languages. 1st ed. Frasconi, Antonio (1919-), illus. LC 55-86758. unpaged. illus. 27cm. 1955. Harcourt, Brace. **Award: (NYT).**
--The Snow and the Sun: A South American Folk Rhyme in Two Languages. Frasconi, Antonio (1919-), illus. LC 61-12342. 32p. (gr. k-3). 1961. (ISBN 0-15-276565-4, HJ). HarBraceJ. **Awards: (NYT); (ALA).**

Frasee, Laura, ed. see Andersen, Hans Christian.

Fraser, A. A.
--Raromi: Or, The Moari Chief's Heir, 1 of 12_Vols. (Illus.). (The Progress Ser). N.D. Fleming H Revell.

Fraser, Amy Stuart (1892-), ed.
--Dae Ye Min' Langsyne?. A Pot-Pourri of Games, Rhymes, and Ploys of Scottish Childhood. Dear, Constance & Dear, Brian, illus. LC 75-521164. (Illus.). xiv, 210 p. 23cm. 1975. (ISBN 0-7100-8233-9). Routledge & Paul.

Fraser, Anthea
--Whistler's Lane. 246p. 1975. Dodd.

Fraser, Antonia Pakenham, Lady (1932-)
--King Arthur and The Knights of the Round Table. Fraser, Rebecca, illus. 1971. Borzoi Books.
--King Arthur and the Knights of the Round Table. Fraser, Rebecca, illus. LC 73-141597. (Illus.). 192 p. 24cm. 1st U.S. edition. 1970. (ISBN 0-394-92156-9). Knopf Distributed by Random House.
--Robin Hood. 1st American ed. Fraser, Rebecca, illus. LC 77-141598. (Illus.). 207p. 24cm. c.1971. (ISBN 0-394-92157-7). Knopf.

Fraser, Beatrice & Fraser, Ferrin L.
--Arturo and Mr. Bang. Storrs, William W., illus. LC 63-11649. unpaged. illus. 29 cm. (gr. k-2). 1963. (ISBN 0-672-50212-7). Bobbs-Merrill.
--Bennie, the Bear Who Grew Too Fast. Duvoisin, Roger Antoine (1904-1980), illus. LC 56-9151. unpaged. illus. 26cm. c.1956. Lothrop, Lee & Shepard.

Fraser, Bessie Boyd
--Animal Sillies. 1st ed. Koski, Barbara, illus. LC 55-121991. (Illus.). unpaged. c.1955. Comet Press Books.

Fraser, Betty M., pseud., see Fraser, Elizabeth Marr.

Fraser, Betty M., pseud. (1928-), illus.
--My Little Library: A Christmas Garland of Carols, Holiday Rhymes, Prayers, and Graces. Fraser, Elizabeth Marr. LC 64-54932. 3v. col. illus. 13cm. c.1964. Dist. New York, Macmillan.

Fraser, C. F, Mrs.
--Master Frisky. (Illus.). (Sunshine Library). 1915. Thomas Y Crowell.
--Master Sunshine. LC 12-32406. 2 p. l., 54 p. front. 20 cm. (Sunshine Library for Young People). c.1898. T. Y. Crowell & Company.
--Strawberry Hill. (Illus.). (Sunshine Library for Young People). 1900. T. Y. Crowell & Co.

Fraser, Chelsea Curtis (1876-)
--Around the World in Ten Days. N.D. World Publishing Co.
--Around the World in Ten Days. Hastings, Howard Livingston (1887-), illus. LC 22-15973. ix, 310 p. col. front., plates (part col.) 20 cm. c.1922. Thomas Y. Crowell Company.
--The Boy Hikers Homeward Bound. LC 19-14796. 3 p. l., 301 p. front., plates. 21 cm. c.1919. Thomas Y. Crowell Company.
--The Boy Hikers: Or, Doing Their Bit for Uncle Sam. LC 19-4515. 5 p. l., 304 p. front., plates. 21 cm. 1918. Thomas Y. Crowell Company.
--Heroes of the Wilds. LC 23-11084. x, 2, 372 p. front., plates, ports. 21 cm. c.1923. Thomas Y. Crowell Company.
--Work-a-Day Heroes. LC 21-172173. v, 314 p. front., plates. 20 cm. c.1921. Thomas Y. Crowell Company.

Fraser, Claude Lovat (1890-1921)
--Nursery Rhymes. Fraser, Claude Lovat (1890-1921), illus. 26 cm. 47p. 1946. A. A. Knopf.

Fraser, Edith Emily Rose Oram (1903-)
--A Boy Hears Stories From the Old Testament. Padgett, Jim, illus. (Illus.). (gr. 1-3). 1967. (ISBN 0-687-03889-8). Abingdon.

Fraser, Elise Parker (1903-)
--The House on Parnassus. LC 53-13451. 94p. 20cm. 1953. Van Kampen Press.
--The Secret Fortress: Three Adventure Stories Based on Historical Facts. LC 55-20746. 96p. 21cm. 1955. Scripture Press.
--Trail of Gold: Fascinating Stories of Adventure in Early California, Based on Historical Truth. LC 54-37826. 103p. illus. 20cm. 1954. Scripture Press, Book Division.

Fraser, Elizabeth Marr see Fraser, Betty M., pseud.

Fraser, Ferrin L
--If I Could Fly--. LC 29-135852. 56 p. illus. 20 cm. c.1929. J. H. Sears & Company, Inc.

Fraser, Ferrin L., jt. auth. see Buck, Frank.

Fraser, Ferrin L., jt. auth. see Fraser, Beatrice.

Fraser, Ferrin L. & Buck, Frank (1882-)
--Tim Thomson in the Jungle. N.D. D. Appleton-Century Co.

Fraser, Frances
--Bear Who Stole the Chinook & Other Stories. (Illus.). (gr. 3-5). 1959. (ISBN 0-8382-0061-3). Hale.

Fraser, Francis Arthur, jt. auth. see Dickens, Charles John Huffam.

Fraser, Georgia
--The White Captain. LC 30-256203. vi, 319 p. col. front. 22 cm. 1930. Little, Brown, and Company.

Fraser, James Howard (1934-)
--Las Posadas: A Christmas Story. DeGrazia, Nick, illus. LC 63-21618. 1 v. (unpaged) illus. 19 cm. 1963. Northland Press.

Fraser, John (1931-)
--The Babysitter. 1969. (ISBN 0-399-10066-0). G. P. Putnam's Sons.

Fraser, Kathleen (1937-)
--Stilts, Somersaults, and Headstands: Game Poems Based on a Painting. Brueghel, Pieter (1515-1569), illus. LC 68-12236. (Illus.). 37 p. 24cm. 1968. (ISBN 0-689-20109-5). Atheneum.

Fraser, Kathleen (1937-) & Levy, Miriam F.
--Adam's World: San Francisco. Hipshman, Helen D., illus. LC 71-150801. (Illus.). color ils. halftones. 32p. (gr. k-2). 1971. (ISBN 0-8075-0174-3). A Whitman.

Fraser, L
--Nursery Rhymes. N.D. Knopf.

Fraser, Peter Shaw (1932-)
--Punch and Judy. 1970. Van Nostrand Reinhold Company.

Fraser, Phyllis Maurine (1915-), ed. see Mother Goose.

Fraser, Phyllis Maurine (1915-), ed.
--Mother Goose. Elliott, Miss, illus. (Little Golden Book). 1955. Golden Press.
--This Little Piggy and Other Counting Rhymes. Paflin, Roberta, pseud. (1903-), illus. Petty, Roberta Harris Pfafflin. LC 42-50766. 41, 1 p. illus. (part col.) 20 1/2 x 17 1/2 cm. (On cover: The Little golden library, 12). 1942. Simon and Schuster, Inc.

Fraser-Tytler, C. C.
--Jonathan. N.D. Henry Holt.

Fraser, William Alexander (1859-)
--The Outcasts. Heming, Arthur Henry Howard (1870-), illus. v. 1 p., 1 l., 137, 1 p. front., plates. 21 cm. 1901. Charles Scribner's Sons.
--The Sa'-Zada Tales. Heming, Arthur Henry Howard (1870-), illus. LC 5-32686. xii, 231 p. front., illus., 23 pl. 21 cm. 1905. C. Scribner's Sons.

Frauca, Harry
--Striped Wolf. Melrose, Genevieve, illus. (Illus.). 16 ils. 109p. (gr. 3-7). 1971. (ISBN 0-535-00031-6). Tri-Ocean.

AUTHOR INDEX

FREEMAN, GAIL

Fraydas, Stan (1918-)
--Hoppy, the Curious Kangaroo. Fraydas, Stan (1918-), illus. LC 52-37326. unpaged. illus. 21 cm. (Wonder books, 579). (ps-1). 1952. Wonder Books.
Fraydas, Stan (1918-), illus.
--The Strawberry Storybook to Color. (Illus.). 80p. (A Strawberry Shortcake Bk.). (ps-3). 1980. (ISBN 0-394-84574-9). Random.
Frazar, Douglas
--Perseverance Island. N.D. Lothrop, Lee & Shepard.
Frazee, Steve (1909-)
--Lassie: Lost in the Snow. (gr. 3 up). 1979. (ISBN 0-307-21504-0, Golden Pr). Western Pub.
--Lassie: The Mystery of Bristlecone Pine. (gr. 3 up). 1979. (ISBN 0-307-21505-9, Golden Pr). Western Pub.
--Lassie: The Secret of the Smelter's Cave. (gr. 3 up). 1979. (ISBN 0-307-21514-8, Golden Pr). Western Pub.
--Lassie: Trouble at Panter's Lake. (gr. 3 up). 1979. (ISBN 0-307-21515-6, Golden Pr). Western Pub.
--Year of the Big Snow: John Charles Fremont's Fourth Expedition. LC 62-[illegible]. 000p. illus. (gr. 7-9). c.1962. (ISBN 0-03-035175-8). Holt.
Frazer, James E.
--Tales of Pudding Hill: True Animal Stories from New Hampshire. 1st ed. Frazer, James E. & White, Jean, illus. LC 75-318144. (Illus.). 143 p. 22cm. 1975. (ISBN 0-682-48096-7). Exposition Press.
Frazer, James George, Sir (1854-1941) & Frazer, Lilly Grove, Lady
--Pasha the Pom: The Story of a Little Dog. Brock, Henry Matthew (1875-1960), illus. LC 39-1754. 5 p. l., 117 p. front., plates. 20 cm. 1937. David McKay Company.
Frazer, Lilly Grove, Lady
--The Singing Wood. Brock, Henry Matthew (1875-1960), illus. LC 31-34196. ix, 144 p. col. front., illus. 21 cm. 1931. The Macmillan Company.
Frazer, Lilly Grove, Lady, jt. auth. see Frazer, James George, Sir.
Frazer, Shamus
--The Crocodile Dies Twice. (Oxford Progressive English Readers Ser.). (gr. k-6). 1971. (ISBN 0-19-638231-9). Oxford U Pr.
--A Time of Darkness. Ibrahim, Abdullah, illus. (Illus.). (Oxford Progressive English Readers Ser.). (gr. k-6). 1975. (ISBN 0-19-580719-7). Oxford U Pr.
Frazier, Neta Lohnes (1890-)
--By-Line Dennie. LC 47-5876. 249 p. illus. 21 cm. 1947. T. Y. Crowell Co.
--The General's Boots. Voorhies, Stephen J., illus. LC 65-141282. (Illus.). x, 195 p. 22cm. 1965. D. McKay Co.
--Little Rhody. 1st ed. Moon, Henrietta Jones, illus. LC 52-14122. 152p. illus. 22cm. 1953. Longmans, Green.
--The Magic Ring. Voute, Kathleen (1892-), illus. LC 59-12749. (Illus.). 149 p. 22cm. 1959. Longmans, Green.
--My Love Is a Gypsy. 1st ed. LC 52-5638. 183 p. 21 cm. 1952. Longmans, Green.
--One Long Picnic. Lambo, Donald W. (1903-1966), illus. LC 62-11931. (Illus.). 22 cm. 170p. (gr. 4-6). 1962. (ISBN 0-679-25104-9). McKay.
--Rawhide Johnny. 1st ed. Toschik, Larry (1922-), illus. LC 57-105271. 180p. illus. 21cm. 1957. Longmans, Green.
--Rawhide Johnny. Toschik, Larry (1922-), illus. (gr. 6-9). 1957. (ISBN 0-679-20157-2). McKay.
--Secret Friend. 1st ed. Moon, Henrietta Jones, illus. LC 56-9216. 148p. illus. 23cm. 1956. Longmans, Green.
--Somebody Special. 1st ed. Moon, Henrietta Jones, illus. LC 54-9204. 148p. illus. 22cm. 1954. Longmans, Green.
--Something of My Own. 1st ed. LC 60-11344. 212p. 21cm. 1960. Longmans, Green.
--Stout-Hearted Seven. LC 73-5240. 174 p. 22cm. 1973. (ISBN 0-15-281450-7). Harcourt Brace Jovanovich.
--Young Bill Fargo. 1st ed. Crowell, Pers (1910-), illus. LC 55-8308. 202p. illus. 22cm. 1956. Longmans, Green.
Frechette, Annie Howells, Mrs.
--The Farm's Little People: Sequel to "On Grandfather's Farm ". LC 12-32405. 107 p. col. front., illus. 19 cm. c.1897. American Baptist Publication Society.
--On Grandfather's Farm. LC 12-32404. 85 p. col. front., illus. 19 cm. c.1897. American Baptist Publication Society.
Frederic, Harold
--The Lawton Girl. N.D. Charles Scribner's Sons.
Frederick, Lee, pseud., see Nussbaum, Albert F..
Frederick, Lee, pseud. (1934-)
--Crash Dive. Nussbaum, Albert F.. LC 78-15596. (Illus.). (Pacesetters Ser.). (gr. 4 up). 1978. (ISBN 0-516-02167-2). Childrens.
Frederick, Phil R.
--The Golden City. (Illus.). (gr. 1-3). N.D. Vantage.
Frederick, Vera M & Laudermilk, Pat
--Life with the Bushy Browntails. LC 80-136554. (Illus.). 32 p. c.1980. Frederick.
Fredericks, Alfred, illus.
--Knightly Legends of Wales: Or, The Boy's Mabinogion. Lanier, Sidney (1842-1881), intro. by. N.D. Charles Scribner's Sons.
Fredericks, Alfred, jt. auth. see Moore, Clement Clarke.
Fredericks, Arnold, pseud., see Kummer, Frederic Arnold.
Fredericks, Arnold, pseud. (1873-1943)
--The Ivory Snuff Box. Kummer, Frederic Arnold. (Detective Stories for Boys). N.D. Grosset & Dunlap.
Fredericks, Fred (1929-)
--Rebel. Fredericks, Fred (1929-), illus. (Illus.). (gr. 7-9). 1972 (Starline). Schol Bk Serv.
Fredericksen, Hazel (1897-)
--He Who runs Far. 256p. 1970. Addision-Wesley.
--He-Who-Runs-Far. Houser, John (1935-), illus. LC 75-120947. (Illus.). 248 p. 23cm. 1970. Young Scott Books.
Fredlee
--The Magic of Sea Shells. Romashko, Sandra, illus. LC 76-12931. (Illus.). 36 p. (Creative development series). c.1976. Windward Pub.
Fredricks, Jane S.
--Back from Bahia de los Muertos. Katherine, M., illus. 1972. (ISBN 0-682-47460-6). Exposition Press
--Three Wheels to Baja. Myrto, Katherine, illus. (Illus.). 160p. (gr. 5 up). 1973. (ISBN 0-682-47639-0). Exposition.
Fredricks, P. C.
--Battle at the Blue Line. Shields, Kenneth M., illus. LC 77-90327. (Illus.). 132 p. 20cm. (Winner book). c.1978. (ISBN 0-88207-482-2). Victor Books.
Free, Ann Cottrell
--Forever the Wild Mare. Savitt, Sam (1917-), illus. LC 63-18061. xxi, 178 p. illus. 21 cm. 1963. Dodd. Mead.
Free, John Da see Da Free, John.
Freed, Eleazar
--The Mystery of the Silver Fish, and Other Stories of Adventure. 1st ed. Kaplan, Seymour R., illus. LC 56-7785. 191p. illus. 22cm. 1956. Jewish Publication Society of America.
Freed, Gladys Hazel
--In the Time of the Lily. LC 76-376127. 140 p. 22cm. c.1975. (ISBN 0-533-01726-2). Vantage Press.
Freed, Margaret M., jt. auth. see Bird, Harriet.
Freedman, B Margaret, jt. auth. see Williams, Jay.
Freedman, Barnett (1901-), illus.
--Oliver Twist. 460p. N.D. Heritage Press.
Freedman, Benedict (1919-) & Freedman, Nancy (1920-)
--Mrs. Mike. (Illus.). 256p. 1947. (ISBN 0-698-10260-6, Coward). Putnam Pub Group.
Freedman, Chuck, jt. auth. see Platt, Kin.
Freedman, Jonathan (1950-)
--The Man Who'd Bounce the World. LC 79-10772. p. cm. 1979. (ISBN 0-932284-14-0). (ISBN 0-932284-16-7). Turtle Island Press.
Freedman, Nancy, jt. auth. see Freedman, Benedict.
Freedman, Paul I.
--Oh Brother, Oh Friend. (Illus.). 128p. 1982. (ISBN 0-89962-220-8). Todd & Honeywell.
Freedman, Russell Bruce (1929-)
--Animal Architects. Kalmenoff, Matthew, illus. LC 79-141404. (Illus.). 126 p. 21cm. 1971. (ISBN 0-8234-0182-0). Holiday House.
--Children of the Wild West. LC 83-5133. (Illus.). 128p. (gr. 3-6). 1983. (ISBN 0-89919-143-6, Clarion). HM. **Award: (ALA).**
--Two Thousand Years of Space Travel. (Illus.). 256p. (gr. 7 up). 1963. (ISBN 0-8234-0123-5). Holiday.
Freedman, Sally
--Monster Birthday Party. Tucker, Kathleen, ed. Dawson, Diane, illus. LC 83-17088. (Illus.). 32p. (Just for Fun Bks.). (gr. k-3). 1983. (ISBN 0-8075-5259-3). A Whitman.
Freehof, Lillian B. Simon (1906-)
--Candle Light Stories. Bearman, Jane Ruth (1917-), illus. (gr. 1-3). 1951. (ISBN 0-8197-0251-X). Bloch.
--The Captive Rabbi: The Story of R. Meir of Rothenburg. Gold, Albert, illus. LC 65-17046. viii, 198 p. illus. 22 cm. (Covenant Bks.: No.18). 1965. Jewish Publication Society of America.
--The Ghost of Garina Street. LC 59-14255. 21 cm. 157p. 1959. Abelard-Schuman.
--The Savage. LC 60-13926. 21 cm. 191p. 1960. Abelard-Schuman.
--Second Bible Legend Book. Port, Lillian, illus. (Bible Legend Books). N.D. Union of American Hebrew Congregation.
--Star Light Stories: Holiday & Sabbath Tales. Robinson, Jessie Berkowitz, illus. LC 52-14301. 96 p. illus. 28 cm. 1952. Bloch Pub. Co.
--Starlight Stories, 1 of 12 vols. (Sunday-School Lib: No. 12). N.D. Set. Lothrop Pub. Co.
--Stories of King David. (Illus.). (gr. 4-7). 1952. (ISBN 0-8276-0162-X). Jewish Pubn.
--Stories of King Solomon. (Illus.). (gr. 4-7). 1955. (ISBN 0-685-13310-9). Jewish Pubn.
--Third Bible Legend Book. Busoni, Rafaello (1900-1962), illus. (gr. 4 up). N.D. UAHC.
Freehoff, William Adolph (1889-)
--The Young Farmer at College. Boyer, Ralph L., illus. LC 17-29625. 330 p. front., plates. 20 cm. 1917. The Penn Publishing Company.
--The Young Farmer at Work. Humphreys, Donald S., illus. LC 24-520321. 316 p. front., plates. 19 cm. 1924. The Penn Publishing Company.
Freeling, Anne
--Ranjit of the Circus Ring. Marriott, Patricia (1920-), illus. LC 59-9897. (Illus.). 207p. 21cm. 1959. Roy Publishers.
Freeman, Austin R.
--The Red Thumb Mark. 1967. (ISBN 0-393-08506-6). Norton & Co.
Freeman, Barbara Constance (1906-)
--A Book by Georgina. Freeman, Barbara Constance (1906-), illus. LC 67-18672. (Illus.). 180 p. 21cm. 1968, c.1962. Norton.
--Broom-Adelaide. Freeman, Barbara Constance (1906-), illus. LC 65-154490. 124p. illus. 22cm. 1st U.S. edition. 1965. (ISBN 0-316-29291-5, Pub. by Atlantic Monthly Pr.). Little.
--A Haunting Air. LC 76-371499. (Illus.). 158 p. 21cm. 1976. (ISBN 0-333-19484-5). Macmillan.
--A Haunting Air. Freeman, Barbara Constance (1906-), illus. LC 77-2810. (Illus.). 158 p. 22cm. 1977, c.1976. (ISBN 0-525-31528-4). Dutton.
--Lucinda. Freeman, Barbara Constance (1906-), illus. LC 67-15452. (Illus.). 206 p. 21cm. 1967, c.1965. W. W. Norton.
--The Name on the Glass. Freeman, Barbara Constance (1906-), illus. LC 66-11769. (Illus.). 236 p. 21cm. 1966, c.1964. Norton.
--The Other Face. LC 76-19057. 151 p. 22cm. 1976, c.1975. (ISBN 0-525-36453-6). Dutton.
--A Pocket of Silence. LC 78-6392. 22 cm. 171p. 1978, c.1977. Dutton.
--Timi. LC 62-4183. (Illus.). (Faber Fanfares Ser.). (gr. 1-4). 1979. (ISBN 0-571-11350-8). Faber & Faber.
--Timi. Freeman, Barbara Constance (1906-), illus. LC 62-4183. 22 cm. 37p. 1961. Transatlantic Arts.
--Timi, the Tale of a Griffin. Bileck, Marvin (1920-), illus. LC 72-85796. (Illus.). 48 p. 24cm. (gr. 2-5). 1970. (ISBN 0-448-26151-0). Grosset & Dunlap.
Freeman, Don, jt. auth. see Freeman, Lydia.
Freeman, Don (1908-1978)
--Add-a-Line Alphabet. LC 68-12895. (Illus.). 32 p. 30cm. 1968. Golden Gate Junior Books.
--Beady Bear. Freeman, Don (1908-1978), illus. LC 76-50658. p. cm. 1977. (ISBN 0-14-050197-5). Puffin Books.
--Beady Bear. Freeman, Don (1908-1978), illus. LC 54-12295. (Illus.). 48 p. 19 x 25 cm. 1954. Viking Press.
--Bearymore. Freeman, Don (1908-1978), illus. LC 78-18281. (Illus.). 32 p. 19 x 23 cm. 1979, c.1976. (ISBN 0-14-050279-3). Puffin Books.
--Bearymore. Freeman, Don (1908-1978), illus. LC 76-94. (Illus.). 22 x 26 cm. 40p. (gr. k-3). 1976. (ISBN 0-670-15174-2). Viking Press.
--Botts, the Naughty Otter. Freeman, Don (1908-1978), illus. LC 63-14753. unpaged. illus. 24 x 26 cm. 1963. Golden Gate Junior Books.
--The Chalk Box Story. Freeman, Don (1908-1978), illus. (ps-2). 1976. Harper.
--The Chalk Box Story. Freeman, Don (1908-1978), illus. LC 76-10169. (Illus.). 40 p. 15 x 19 cm. c.1976. (ISBN 0-397-31699-2). Lippincott.
--Come Again, Pelican. Freeman, Don (1908-1978), illus. LC 61-11671. (Illus.). 44 p. 23 x 28 cm. 1961. Viking Press.
--Corduroy. Freeman, Don (1908-1978), illus. (Illus.). 32 p. 21cm. (ps-1). 1968. Viking Press.
--Cyrano the Crow. Freeman, Don (1908-1978), illus. LC 60-4440. (Illus.). 28 cm. 47p. (ps-3). 1960. (ISBN 0-670-25267-0). Viking Pr.
--Dandelion. Freeman, Don (1908-1978), illus. (gr. k-3). 1982. (ISBN 0-941078-11-6). (ISBN 0-941078-09-4). (ISBN 0-941078-10-8). Live Oak Media.
--Dandelion. Freeman, Don (1908-1978), illus. LC 77-2562. 1977, c.1964. (ISBN 0-14-050218-1). Puffin Books.
--Dandelion. Freeman, Don (1908-1978), illus. LC 64-21472. (Illus.). 22 x 26 cm. 48p. (ps-2). 1964. (ISBN 0-670-25532-7). Viking Pr.
--Flash the Dash. Freeman, Don (1908-1978), illus. LC 72-94227. (Illus.). 47 p. 20 x 24 cm. 1973. (ISBN 0-516-08722-3). Childrens Press.
--Fly High, Fly Low. Freeman, Don (1908-1978), illus. LC 57-13961. (Illus.). 56 p. 29cm. 1957. Viking Press. **Awards: (ALA); (RCM).**
--Forever Laughter. Freeman, Don (1908-1978), illus. LC 73-97826. (Illus.). 64 p. 20 x 24 cm. 1970. Golden Gate Junior Books.
--The Guard Mouse. Freeman, Don (1908-1978), illus. LC 67-2452. (Illus.). 47 p. 29cm. 1967. Viking Press.
--The Guard Mouse. Freeman, Don (1908-1978), illus. (gr. k-2). 1982. Viking.
--Hattie the Backstage Bat. Freeman, Don (1908-1978), illus. LC 72-123017. (Illus.). 32 p. 23 x 29 cm. 1970. Viking Press.
--Inspector Peckit. Freeman, Don (1908-1978), illus. LC 72-190715. (Illus.). 32 p. 27cm. 1972. (ISBN 0-670-39925-6). Viking Press.
--Mop Top. Freeman, Don (1908-1978), illus. N.D. E. M. Hale & Co.
--Mop Top. Freeman, Don (1908-1978), illus. LC 78-11246. p. cm. 1978, c.1955. (ISBN 0-14-050326-9). Puffin Books.
--Mop Top. Freeman, Don (1908-1978), illus. LC 55-14876. (Illus.). 48 p. 26cm. 1955. Viking Press.
--The Night the Lights Went Out. Freeman, Don (1908-1978), illus. LC 58-3489. (Illus.). 48 p. 24cm. 1958. Viking Press.
--Norman the Doorman. Freeman, Don (1908-1978), illus. LC 77-27071. p. cm. 1978, c.1959. (ISBN 0-14-050288-2). Puffin Books.
--Norman The Doorman. Freeman, Don (1908-1978), illus. LC 59-16171. 21 x 26 cm. 64p. 1959. Viking Press.
--The Paper Party. Freeman, Don (1908-1978), illus. LC 76-53848. (Illus.). 40 p. 20 x 23 cm. (Picture Puffin). (Picture Puffin Ser.). 1977, c.1974. (ISBN 0-14-050212-2). Puffin Books.
--The Paper Party. Freeman, Don (1908-1978), illus. LC 74-1365. (Illus.). 40 p. 22 x 28 cm. 1974. (ISBN 0-670-53804-3). Viking Press.
--Penguins of All People!. Freeman, Don (1908-1978), illus. LC 75-136815. (Illus.). 32 p. 23 x 29 cm. 1971. (ISBN 0-670-54617-8). Viking Press.
--A Pocket for Corduroy. Freeman, Don (1908-1978), illus. (Illus.). 1980. (ISBN 0-14-050352-8, Puffin). Penguin.
--A Pocket for Corduroy. Freeman, Don (1908-1978), illus. LC 77-16123. (Illus.). 32 p. 21cm. 1978. (ISBN 0-670-56172-X). Viking Press.
--Quiet! There's a Canary in the Library. Freeman, Don (1908-1978), illus. LC 69-15398. (Illus.). 48 p. 21 x 27 cm. 1969. (ISBN 0-87464-066-0). (ISBN 0-87464-067-9). Golden Gate Junior Books.
--Quiet! There's a Canary inthe Library. 1969. (ISBN 0-516-08737-1). Childrens Press.
--A Rainbow of My Own. Freeman, Don (1908-1978), illus. LC 78-11136. p. cm. 1978, c.1966. (ISBN 0-14-050328-5). Puffin Books.
--A Rainbow of My Own. Freeman, Don (1908-1978), illus. LC 66-13983. 1 v. (unpaged) col. illus. 22 x 24 cm. 32p. 1966. Viking Press.
--The Seal and the Slick. Freeman, Don (1908-1978), illus. LC 73-16118. (Illus.). 32 p. 1974. Viking Press.
--Ski Pup. Freeman, Don (1908-1978), illus. LC 63-8532. (Illus.). 56 p. 29cm. 1963. Viking Press.
--Space Witch. Freeman, Don (1908-1978), illus. LC 59-16352. (Illus.). 47 p. 26cm. 1959. Viking Press.
--Space Witch. Freeman, Don (1908-1978), illus. 1979. Viking.
--Tilly Witch. LC 78-11304. p.cm. 1978, c.1969. (ISBN 0-14-050262-9). Puffin Books.
--Tilly Witch. Freeman, Don (1908-1978), illus. LC 72-85867. (Illus.). 32 p. 27cm. 1969. Viking Press.
--Tilly Witch. Freeman, Don (1908-1978), illus. (Illus.). 32p. 23cm. (Viking seafarer books). 1975, c.1969. (ISBN 0-670-05100-4). Viking Press.
--The Turtle and the Dove. Freeman, Don (1908-1978), illus. LC 64-12499. (Illus.). 43 p. 24cm. 1964. Viking Press.
--Will's Quill. Freeman, Don (1908-1978), illus. LC 77-23024. (Illus.). 32 p. 23cm. (Picture Puffin). 1977, c.1975. (ISBN 0-14-050215-7). Puffin Books.
--Will's Quill. Freeman, Don (1908-1978), illus. LC 74-32382. (Illus.). p. cm. 28 cm. 32p. 1975. Viking Press.
Freeman, Dorothy Rhodes
--Arturo, Bernardo, Carlotta. Miake, L. K., illus. LC 77-89539. (Illus.). 71p. 28cm. 1969. Elk Grove Press.
--The Friday Surprise. Murphy, Mary (1923-), illus. LC 68-55789. (Illus.). 42 p. 24cm. 1968. Elk Grove Press.
--A Home for Memo. Garbutt, Bernard (1900-), illus. LC 68-54692. (Illus.). 54 p. 24cm. 1968. Elk Grove Press.
Freeman, Gail
--Alien Thunder: A Novel. LC 82-9578. p. cm. 1982. (ISBN 0-87888-206-5). Bradbury Press.

--Out from Under: A Novel. LC 81-18154. !66 p. 22cm. c.1982. (ISBN 0-87888-188-3). Bradbury Press.

Freeman, Godfrey

--The Owl and the Mirror. Kiddell-Monroe, Joan (1908-), illus. LC 61-11961. (Illus.). 116p. 21cm. 1961, c.1960. Duell, Sloan and Pearce.

Freeman, Grace M.

--Little Voices. N.D. Augustana Book Concern.

Freeman, Harrop Arthur, jt. auth. see Freeman, Ruth Nimmo St. John.

Freeman, Ira Maximilian, jt. auth. see Freeman, Mae Blacker.

Freeman, Ira Maximillian, jt. auth. see Freeman, Mae Blacker.

Freeman, James Dillet (1912-)

--Once Upon a Christmas: Stories. Lattimer, Evan, illus. LC 78-53345. (Illus.). 173 p. 26cm. c.1978. (ISBN 0-916438-14-7). Unity Books.

Freeman, James Midwinter see Ranger, Robin, pseud.

Freeman, Jean Todd (1929-)

--Cynthia and the Unicorn. Weisgard, Leonard Joseph (1916-), illus. LC 65-18039. 1 v32 p col. illus. 26 cm. 1967. Norton.

Freeman, Leila Crocheron

--Nip and Tuck. Freeman, Leila Crocheron, illus. LC 26-13669. 156 p., 1 l., incl. illus., plates. col, front., col plates. 30 cm. c.1926. J. H. Sears & Company, Inc.

--Nip and Tuck in Toyland. Freeman, Leila Crocheron, illus. LC 27-21070. 160 p. incl. illus., plates. col. front., col. plates. 30 cm. c.1927. J. H. Sears & Company, Inc.

Freeman, Lucy (1950-)

--The Eleven Steps. Brinckloe, Julie Lorraine (1950-), illus. LC 74-825. (Illus.). 43 p. 1975. (ISBN 0-385-04766-5). (ISBN 0-385-04766-5). (ISBN 0-385-04766-5). Doubleday.

Freeman, Lydia (1907-) & Freeman, Don (1908-1978)

--Chuggy and the Blue Caboose. LC 51-10258. (Illus.). 48 p. 23 x 28 cm. 1951. Viking Press.

--Pet of the Met. Freeman, Lydia & Freeman, Don, illus. LC 53-8719. (Illus.). 63 p. 1953. Viking Press. **Award: (ALA).**

Freeman, M. R.

--Steady and Strong. N.D. Pott & Co.

Freeman, Madeline A.

--A Horse for Running Buffalo. Daniel, Alan (1939-), illus. LC 72-173245. (Illus.). vii, 88 p. 23cm. 1972. Van Nostrand Reinhold.

Freeman, Mae Blacker (1907-)

--Do You Know About Stars?. Solonovich, George, illus. LC 70-123070. (Illus.). 26 p. 24cm. (Very first science book). 1970. Random House.

--Fun with Ballet. (Illus.). (gr. 4-6). 1952. (ISBN 0-394-80276-4, BYR). (ISBN 0-394-90276-9). Random.

--Space Base. Mora, Raul Mina, illus. LC 71-182290. (Illus.). 63 p. 26cm. 1972. (ISBN 0-531-02029-0). Watts.

Freeman, Mae Blacker (1907-) & Freeman, Ira Maximillian (1905-)

--The Sun, the Moon, & the Stars. rev. ed. Martin, Rene (0000-1977), illus. LC 78-64604. (Illus.). (gr. 2-4). 1979. (ISBN 0-394-80110-5, BYR). (ISBN 0-394-90110-X). Random.

--You Will Go to the Moon. rev. ed. Ames, Lee Judah (1921-), illus. LC 75-158389. (Illus.). 60 p. 24cm. 1971. (ISBN 0-394-82340-0). (ISBN 0-394-92340-5). Beginner Books.

Freeman, Margaret (1893-)

--Hidden Treasure: Parables for Kids. LC 81-16669. (Illus.). 96p. (Orig.). (gr. 4-9). 1982. (ISBN 0-87239-499-9). Standard Pub.

Freeman, Mary Eleanor Wilkins, jt. auth. see Greene, Ellin.

Freeman, Mary Eleanor Wilkins see Wilkins, Mary Eleanor.

Freeman, Mary Eleanor Wilkins see Wilkins, Mary Eleanor, Mrs.

Freeman, Mary Eleanor Wilkins, Mrs., jt. auth. see Eggleston, George Cary.

Freeman, Mary Eleanor Wilkins, Mrs. (1852-1930)

--The Adventures of Ann: Stories of Colonial Times. LC 22-10844. 92 p. incl. front., plates. 20 cm. c.1886. D. Lothrop and Company.

--Comtort Pease and Her Gold Ring. LC 12-32358. 45p. 18cm. (The Renaissance Booklets). 1895. Fleming H. Revell Co.

--Comfort Pease and Her Gold Ring. LC 42-19685. 45p. 18cm. (The Looking Upward Booklets). 1895. Fleming H. Revell.

--Doc Gordon. Merrill, Frank Thayer (1848-), illus. LC 42-40196. 20cm. 322p. 1906. The Authors and Newspaper Association.

--The Pot of Gold and other Stories. LC 42-39921. (Illus.). 18cm. 336p. 1892. Lothrop, Lee & Shepard Co.

--Princess Rosetta and the Popcorn Man, from The Pot of Gold. Greene, Ellin, Mrs. (1918-), ed. Hyman, Trina Schart (1939-), illus. LC 77-135296. (Illus.). 48 p. 24cm. 1971. Lothrop, Lee & Shepard Co.

--Silence & other Stories. LC 42-40197. 20cm. 336p. 1898. Harper & Brothers.

--Little Lassies. LC 4-24501. (Illus.). 24cm. 188p. 1904. Saalfield Publishing Co.

Freeman, Ritza (1875-) & Davis, Ruth (1877-)

--Norse Tales: Retold for Little Children and Others Who Care to Read Them. LC 12-8400. 112, 1 p. illus. 21 cm. 1912. A. C. McClurg & Co.

Freeman, Ruth Nimmo St. John (1901-) & Freeman, Harrop Arthur (1907-)

--Captain and Mate. Blair, Robert N., illus. LC 40-9446. (Illus.). 32p. 17 x 20cm. 1940. A. Whitman.

--Chips and Little Chips. Smith, Eldred M., illus. LC 39-27536. (Illus.). 32p. 17 x 20cm. (Junior Press Books). 1939. A. Whitman.

--Sparks and Little Sparks. Blair, Robert N., illus. LC 40-13972. (Illus.). 32p. 17 x 20cm. (Junior Press Bks.). 1940. A. Whitman.

Freeman, Tony

--Blimps. LC 78-38826. (Illus.). 48p. (On the Move Ser.). (gr. 3-6). 1979. (ISBN 0-516-03882-6). (ISBN 0-516-43882-4). Childrens.

Freer, Marjorie Mueller

--Gay Enterprises. LC 52-13549. 176 p. 21 cm. (Romance for young moderns). 1952. J. Messner.

--House of Holly. LC 54-10584. 188p. 21cm. (Romance for young moderns). 1954. J. Messner.

--Orchids for April. LC 57-6587. 189p. 21cm. (Romance for young moderns). 1957. J. Messner.

--Roberta: Interior Decorator. LC 47-11054. 5 l., 3-209 p. 20 cm. 1947. J. Messner.

--A School for Suzanne. LC 59-12759. 190p. 21cm. (A Romance for Young Moderns). 1959. Messner.

--Showcase for Diane. N.D. Julian Messner, Inc.

--Tours by Terry. LC 58-6013. 160p. 22cm. (A Romance for Young Moderns). 1958. Messner.

Frees, Harry Whittier

--Animal Land on the Air. Frees, Harry Whittier, photos by. LC 29-19191. 254, 1 p. incl. front., illus., plates. 21 cm. c.1929. Lothrop, Lee & Shepard Co.

--Four Little Bunnies. Frees, Harry Whittier, photos by. LC 35-2892. 61 p. illus. 14 x 17 cm. c.1935. Rand, McNally & Company.

--Four Little Kittens. Frees, Harry Whittier, photos by. LC 34-22038. 61 p. illus. 14 x 17 cm. c.1934. Rand, MacNally & Company.

--The Four Little Kittens' Christmas. Frees, Harry Whittier, photos by. LC 39-21565. 61 p. illus. 14 x 17 cm. c.1939. Rand MacNally & Company.

--Four Little Puppies. Frees, Harry Whittier, photos by. LC 35-28918. 61 p. illus. 14 x 17 cm. c.1935. Rand, McNally & Company.

--The Little Folks of Animal Land. Frees, Harry Whittier, photos by. LC 16-2211. 252, 1 p. incl. front., illus. plates. 21 x 18 cm. 1915. Lothrop, Lee & Shepard Co.

--The Little Kittens' Nursery Rhymes. N.D. Rand McNally & Co.

--More About the Four Little Kittens. Frees, Harry Whittier, photos by. (Illus.). 14 x 17 cm. 61p. 1938. Rand McNally & Co.

--The Sandman: His Animal Stories. Frees, Harry Whittier, photos by. LC 17-794678. 273 p. incl. front., illus. 20 cm. 1916. The Page Company.

--The Sandman: His Bunny Stories. Frees, Harry Whittier, photos by. viii, 13-274 p. front., illus. 20 cm. (On verso of half-title: Sandman stories). 1918. The Page Company.

--The Sandman: His Kittycat Stories. Frees, Harry Whittier, photos by. LC 18-7910. 5 p. l., 13-277 p. incl. front., plates. 20 cm. 1917. The Page Company.

--The Sandman: His Puppy Stories. Frees, Harry Whittier, photos by. LC 21-2092. 4 p. l., 13-292 p. front., illus. 20 cm. (On verso of half-title: Sandman stories). 1920. The Page Company.

--The Story of Bill Bunny. Frees, Harry Whittier, photos by. LC 37-1662. 32 p. illus. 31 cm. c.1937. Rand, McNally & Company.

--Toodles and Her Friends. LC 36-8054. 61 p. illus. 14 x 17 cm. c.1936. Rand, McNally & Company.

Freethy, Vernon F.

--Assignment in Danger. Hodges, Cyril Walter (1909-), illus. LC 57-6602. 180p. 21cm. 1957. D. McKay Co.

--Dangerous Homecoming. LC 62-7766. (Illus.). 21 cm. 151p. 1962. McKay.

Fregosi, Claudia Anne Marie (1946-)

--Almira's Violets. LC 75-26996. (Illus.). 32 p. 23cm. c.1976. (ISBN 0-688-80028-9). Greenwillow Books.

--Are There Spooks in the Dark?. Fregosi, Claudia Anne Marie (1946-), illus. LC 76-9789. p. cm. c.1976. (ISBN 0-590-07451-2). Four Winds Press.

--A Gift. LC 76-9015. (Illus.). 32 p. 24cm. c.1976. (ISBN 0-13-356220-4). Prentice-Hall.

--The Happy Horse. LC 76-54894. (Illus.). 36 p. 26cm. c.1977. (ISBN 0-688-80087-4). (ISBN 0-688-84087-6). Greenwillow Books.

--The Mammoth, the Owl, and the Crab. LC 74-13836. (Illus.). 31 p. 21cm. 1975. (ISBN 0-02-735690-6). Macmillan.

--The Pumpkin Sparrow: Adapted from a Korean Folktale. LC 76-13027. (Illus.). 32 p. 26cm. c.1977. (ISBN 0-688-80060-2). (ISBN 0-688-84060-4). Greenwillow Books.

--Snow Maiden. LC 78-27495. p. cm. c.1979. (ISBN 0-13-815340-X). Prentice-Hall.

--Sun Grumble. LC 73-6046. (Illus.). 32 p. 1974. (ISBN 0-02-735740-6). Macmillan.

Freiligrath-Kroeker, Kate, Mrs. (1845-1904)

--Alice in Wonderland: and Other Fairy Plays for Children. (Illus.). 143p. N.D. Dick & Fitzgerald.

--Fairy Tales from Bretano. (Illus.). (St. Nicholas Series for Girls). N.D. International Book Company.

Freiligrath-Kroeker, Kate, Mrs. (1845-1904), tr. see Brentano, Clemens Maria.

Freivogel, Esther

--All Around the City. Lattimore, Eleanor Frances (1904-), illus. LC 38-20484. (Illus.). 95p. 23cm. 1938. Friendship Press.

Fremantle, Anne Jackson (1910-)

--The Greatest Bible Stories. N.D. Stephen Daye Press.

--The Island of Cats. Sapieha, Christine, illus. LC 63-12381. 1 v. (unpaged) illus. 24 cm. (Astor book). 1964. I. Obolensky.

Fremantle, Anne Jackson (1910-), ed.

--Christmas Is Here: A Catholic Selection of Stories & Poems. (Illus.). (gr. 3-7). 1955. (ISBN 0-8044-2214-1, Stephen Daye Pr). Ungar.

Fremlin, Robert

--Three Friends. Tripp, Wallace Whitney (1940-), illus. LC 74-13802. (Illus.). 63 p. 21cm. 1975. Little, Brown.

Fremont, Lance

--The Mystery of the Cougar's Yellow Eye. (Orig.). (Voyager Ser.). 1982. (ISBN 0-8010-3506-6). Baker Bk.

Frenaye, Francis, tr. see MacOrlan, Pierre.

French, Allen (1870-), intro. by see Njala.

French, Allen (1870-1946)

--The Golden Eagle. Relyea, Charles M., illus. LC 17-243993. 7 p. l., 3-219 p. incl. front., plates. 20 cm. 1917. The Century Co.

--The Junior Cup. Rosenmeyer, Bernard J., illus. LC 4-17525. vii, 246 p. incl. plates. front. 20 cm. 1902. The Century Co.

--The Lost Baron: A Story of England in the Year 1200. Wyeth, Andrew Newell (1917-), illus. LC 40-7289. 4 p. l., 252 p. col. front., illus. 22 cm. 1940. Houghton Mifflin Company.

--Pelham and His Friend Tim. Grunwald, Ch., illus. LC 6-32675. viii p., 1 l., 391 p. front. 4 pl. 19 cm. 1906. Little, Brown, and Company.

--The Red Keep: A Story of Burgundy in the Year 1165. Wyeth, Newell Convers (1882-1945) & Wyeth, Andrew Newell (1917-), illus. LC 38-22018. 4 p. l., 309, 1 p. col. front. illus. 22 cm. 1938. Houghton Mifflin Company.

--Rolf and the Viking Bow. LC 64-239971. 186p. 24cm. (Companion bk. ser.). 1964. Walker.

--The Runaway. Relyea, Charles M., illus. LC 14-16941. 7 p. l., 3-368 p. incl. front., plates. 20 cm. 1914. The Century Co.

--Sir Marrok: A Tale of the Days of King Arthur. LC 2-22659. xiii, 281 p. incl. plates. front. 19 cm. (St. Nicholas books). 1902. The Century Co.

--The Story of Grettir the Strong. 10 ed. 1957. E. P. Dutton & Co.

--Story of Grettir, the Strong. Bennett, F. I., illus. (Illus.). (gr. 5-9). N.D. (ISBN 0-525-40178-4). Dutton.

--The Story of Rolf and the Viking's Bow. Pitz, Henry Clarence (1895-1976), illus. LC 24-21612. xii p., 1 l., 289 p. col. front., col. plates. 23 cm. (Beacon Hill book-shelf). 1924. Little, Brown, and Company.

--The Story of Rolf and the Viking's Bow. Rosenmeyer, Bernard J., illus. LC 4-24565. (Illus.). 408p. 1904. Little, Brown and Company.

French, Anne Warner see Warner, Anne.

French, Anne Warner, Mrs. (1869-1913)

--Sunshine Jane. LC 14-3106. vi, 279 p. front. 19 cm. 1914. Little, Brown, and Company.

French, Barbara

--Arlo and Alice: A Story of Two Lion Cubs. N.D. Vantage Press Inc.

French, Charles Wallace (1858-), ed. see Sewell, Anna.

French, Dorothy Kayser (1926-)

--I Don't Belong Here. LC 79-26905. 103 p. 21cm. c.1980. (ISBN 0-664-32664-1). Westminster Press.

--The Mystery of the Old Oil Well. Polseno, Jo, illus. LC 63-16926. 150 p. illus. 21 cm. 1963. F. Watts.

--Pioneer Saddle Mystery. LC 75-12418. 21 cm. 176p. c.1975. (ISBN 0-8313-0113-9). Lantern Press.

--Swim to Victory. LC 79-82403. 189 p. 22cm. 1969. Lippincott.

--A Try at Tumbling. LC 75-117237. 203 p. 21cm. 1970. Lippincott.

French, Fiona (1944-)

--Aio, the Rainmaker. French, Fiona (1944-), illus. (Illus.). (ps-6). 1978. (ISBN 0-19-279704-2). Oxford U Pr.

--The Blue Bird. French, Fiona (1944-), illus. LC 79-188900. (Illus.). 38 p. 29cm. 1972. (ISBN 0-8098-1194-4). H. Z. Walck.

--City of Gold. French, Fiona (1944-), illus. LC 74-644. (Illus.). 32 p. 29cm. 1974. (ISBN 0-8098-1220-7). H. Z. Walck.

--Future Story. LC 83-22317. (Illus.). 32 p. 29cm. 1st U.S. edition. 1984. (ISBN 0-911745-35-1). Peter Bedrick Books : Distributed in the USA by Harper & Row.

--Hunt the Thimble. French, Fiona (1944-), illus. (Illus.). (ps-6). 1978. (ISBN 0-19-279719-0). Oxford U Pr.

--Jack of Hearts. French, Fiona (1944-), illus. LC 78-19284. (Illus.). 24 p. 29cm. 1st U.S. edition. 1970. Harcourt, Brace & World.

--King Tree. LC 73-164375. (Illus.). 38 p. 29cm. 1973. (ISBN 0-19-279687-9). Oxford University Press.

--King Tree. French, Fiona (1944-), illus. LC 73-618. (Illus.). 31 p. 29cm. 1973. (ISBN 0-8098-1205-3). H. Z. Walck.

--Matteo. French, Fiona (1944-), illus. (Illus.). (ps-3). 1978. (ISBN 0-19-279713-1). Oxford U Pr.

French, Gillette, illus.

--One to Ten: A Number Book. LC 42-1760. 60 p. incl. col. front., illus. (part col.) 17 cm. (Little color classics). 1942. McLoughlin Bros, Inc.

French, Henry Willard (1854-)

--The Lance of Kahana: A Story of Arabia. 1920. Lothrop.

--The Lance of Kanana: A Story of Arabia. Garrett, Edmund Henry (1853-1929), illus. LC 7-140889. 172 p. incl. plates. front. 19 cm. c.1892. D. Lothrop Company.

--The Lance of Kanana: A Story of Arabia. Garrett, Edmund Henry (1853-1929), illus. LC 16-10345. 165 p. col. front., col. plates. 19 cm. c.1916. Lothrop, Lee & Shepard Co.

--The Lance of Kanana: A Story of Arabia. Jones, Wilfred J. (1888-), illus. LC 32-14435. 165 p. col. front. illus., col. plates. 23 cm. c.1932. Lothrop, Lee & Shepard Co.

--Oscar Peterson: Ranchman and Ranger. LC 7-12793. 4 p. l., 380 p. incl. illus., plates. front 21 cm. 1893. D. Lothrop Company.

--Through Arctics and Tropics. (Illus.). N.D. Lothrop Pub. Co.

French, Henry William, jt. auth. see Downing, Marlton.

French, Howard Dean

--The Lost Cricket. N.D. Abingdon Press.

French, Joseph Lewis

--The Jolly Roger. N.D. Milton Bradley Co.

French, Joseph Lewis, ed.

--Great Sea Stories. Pratt, William V., frwd. by. N.D. Tudor.

French, Kersti, tr. see Gripe, Maria Kristina.

French, Laura (1949-)

--Dragon's Ransom. LC 83-91424. 160p. (Endless Quest Bks.). (gr. 5up). 1984. (ISBN 0-394-72465-8). Random.

--Fat Albert & the Cosby Kids: Getting It Together. Hazleton & Willoughby, illus. (Illus.). (Tell-a-Tale Readers). (gr. k-3). 1975. (ISBN 0-307-68598-5, Whitman). Western Pub.

--The Santa Claus Book. Ruth, Rod (1912-), illus. LC 75-43398. (Illus.). 14 p. 33cm. (Golden play and learn book). c.1976. (ISBN 0-307-10733-7). Golden Press.

French, Lillie Hamilton (1854-1939)

--Hezekiah's Wives. LC 2-9818. xi, 116 p., 1 l. front. 19 cm. 1902. Houghton, Mifflin and Co.

French, Marion Flood (1920-)

--Mister Bear Goes to Boston. Weil, Lisl (1910-), illus. (Illus.). (ps-3). 1955. (ISBN 0-695-86020-8). (ISBN 0-695-46020-X). Follett.

--Mr. Bear Goes to Town. N.D. Wilcox & Follett Co.

French, Marion N., pseud., see Horowitz, Caroline.

French, Michael (1944-)

--Lifeguards Only Beyond This Point. LC 84-7660. 191 p. 23cm. c.1984. (ISBN 0-399-21098-9). Pacer Books.

--Lifeguards Only Beyond This Point. LC 84-7660. 208p. (Pacer Bks.). (gr. 7 up). 1984. (ISBN 0-399-21098-9). Putnam Pub Group.

--Pursuit. LC 82-70319. 192p. (gr. 7 up). 1982. (ISBN 0-440-06887-8). Delacorte.

--Soldier Boy. LC 85-19167. p. cm. 1986, c.1985. (ISBN 0-448-47768-8). Pacer Books.

--The Throwing Season. LC 79-53598. 216 p. 22cm. c.1980. (ISBN 0-440-08600-0). Delacorte Press.

Friedman, Irene
--Away We Go!. Friedman, Irene, illus. LC 76-46216. (Illus.). 17 p. 31cm. (Cricket book). c.1977. (ISBN 0-8228-6517-3). Platt & Munk.
Friedman, Judi, jt. auth. see Aylesworth, Jim.
Friedman, Judith & Sonnenblick, Carol
--Attack Pack. 128p. (gr. 4-12). 1982. (ISBN 0-9609616-0-7). New Dir Pr.
Friedman, Pauline
--Grandma's Rhymes and Stories. 48p. N.D. P Shalom Publication Inc.
Friedman, Rita, jt. auth. see Reiss, Elayne.
Friedman, Rose
--Dan Dooley's Lucky Star. Earle, Vana (1917-), illus. LC 58-3604. (Illus.). 21 cm. 45p. (Easy-to-Read Bks.). (gr. k-3). 1958. (ISBN 0-687-10204-9). Abingdon.
--Paddy McGuire and the Patriotic Squirrel. Kamen, Gloria (1923-), illus. LC 63-7970. 62 p. illus. 21 cm. 1963. Abingdon.
--Tim Tomkins, Circus Boy. Jackson, Polly, illus. LC 52-11649. unpaged. illus. 22 cm. 1952. Abingdon-Cokesbury Press.
--A Whistle for Tootles. Bradfield, Margaret, illus. LC 55-14815. unpaged. illus. 22cm. 1955. Abingdon Press.
Friedman, Sara Ann, jt. auth. see Schick, Alice.
Friedman, Warner George, jt. auth. see Gelman, Rita Golden.
Friedrich, Emmy Friederike Charlotte Kuhne see Rhoden, Emma von, pseud.
Friedrich, Emmy Friederike Charlotte Kuhne (1832-1885)
--An Obstinate Maid. Rhoden, Emma von, pseud. Waugh, Ida, illus. Ireland, Mary Eliza Haines, Mrs. (1834-1927), tr. from Ger. LC 98-1387. (Illus.). 323p. 1898. G. W. Jacobs & Co.
--Taming a Tomboy. Tr. from the Twenty-Fifth Edition of Emily Rhoden's "Der Trotzkopf," and Adapted for American Readers. Oswald, Felix Leopold (1845-1906), tr. LC 98-98. 236 p. front., 2 pl. 20 cm. 1898. W. L. Allison Co.
--The Young Violinist. Williams, Carll B., illus. Ireland, Mary Eliza Haines, Mrs. (1834-1927), tr. LC 6-34814. 140 p. incl. 3 pl. front. 20 cm. c.1906. The Saalfield Publishing Company.
Friedrich, Irma
--The Separated Island: One Summer at Martha's Vineyard. LC 40-7020. 234 p. incl. front., illus. 21 cm. c.1940. J. Messner, Inc.
Friedrich, Otto Alva, jt. auth. see Friedrich, Priscilla.
Friedrich, Otto Alva (1929-), ed. see Friedrich, Priscilla.
Friedrich, Otto Alva (1929-) & Friedrich, Priscilla
--The Marshmallow Ghosts. Adams, Adrienne (1906-), illus. N.D. Lothrop.
Friedrich, Priscilla
--Noah's Shark's Ark. Friedrich, Otto Alva (1929-), ed. Fellin, Peter, illus. LC 61-13923. (Illus.). 22 cm. (Wonderful World Bks.). N.D. A . S. Barnes & Co, Inc.
Friedrich, Priscilla, jt. auth. see Friedrich, Otto Alva.
Friedrich, Priscilla & Friedrich, Otto Alva (1929-)
--The April Umbrella. Duvoisin, Roger Antoine (1904-1980), illus. LC 63-11670. unpaged. illus. 26 cm. c.1963. Lothrop, Lee & Shepard.
--The Christmas Star. Groedel, Burton, illus. LC 62-15072. (Illus.). (A Wonderful World Bk.). 1962. Barnes.
--Clean Clarence. Slobodkin, Louis (1903-1975), illus. LC 58-10713. (Illus.). unpaged. 24cm. 1959. Lothrop, Lee & Shepard.
--The Easter Bunny That Over Slept. Adams, Adrienne (1906-), illus. 1956. (ISBN 0-688-41066-9). William Morrow and Company.
--The Easter Bunny That Overslept. Adams, Adrienne (1906-), illus. LC 57-5998. (Illus.). unpaged. 26cm. c.1957. Lothrop, Lee and Shepard Co.
--The Easter Bunny That Overslept. Adams, Adrienne (1906-), illus. LC 82-13013. 1983, c.1957. (ISBN 0-688-01540-9). (ISBN 0-688-01541-7). Lothrop, Lee & Shepard.
--The League of Unusual Animals. Rogers, Carol, illus. LC 65-12085. 44p. col. illus. 27cm. c.1965. Steck.
--The Wishing Well in the Woods. Duvoisin, Roger Antoine (1904-1980), illus. 1960. William Morrow and Company.
Friedrich, Ralph
--The Naughty Badger: A Favorite Story from Japan. Suzuki, Toshio, illus. LC 60-6925. (Original Author: Kachikachiyama). unpaged. illus. 27cm. 1960. C. E. Tuttle.
--The Rabbit who Lost His Fur: A Favorite Story from Japan. Suzuki, Toshio, illus. LC 60-6924. (Original Author: Inaba no shirousagi). unpaged. illus. 27cm. 1960. C. E. Tuttle.
Friel, Bessie
--Pipes O'Ben Mor. N.D. Vantage Press, Inc.
Friel, Ted, jt. auth. see Carkhuff, Robert R.
Friend, Esther, illus.
--Little Red Riding Hood. LC 51-21210. (Illus.). 33p. 17cm. (A Rand McNally Book-Elf Junior). 1950. Rand McNally.
--The Three Wishes. N.D. Rand McNally & Co.
Friend, James Trambert
--Science Fiction Quizzle Book for Boys & Girls. Favata, Raymond & Irrera, Paul, illus. LC 51-7128. 62 p. illus. 30 cm. (gr. 3-8). 1951. S. Gabriel Sons.
Friend Magazine
--Children's Stories from Around the World. LC 76-49807. (Illus.). 1976. Deseret Bk.
Friend, Morton
--Lop Ear and Little Gray. Obligado, Lilian Isabel (1931-), illus. LC 68-6251. (Illus.). 23 p. 29cm. (Carousel book). 1968. L. W. Singer Co.
Friendlich, Dick, pseud., see Friendlich, Richard J..
Friendlich, Dick, pseud. (1909-)
--All-Pro Quarterback. Friendlich, Richard J.. LC 63-8806. 222 p. 21 cm. 1963. Westminster Press.
--Backstop Ace. LC 61-5221. 21 cm. 187p. (gr. 7-10). 1961. (ISBN 0-664-32246-8). Westminster.
--Baron of the Bull Pen. Friendlich, Richard J.. LC 54-7928. 184p. 21cm. c.1954. Westminster Press.
--Baron of the Bull Pin. Friendlich, Richard J.. ed. 1955. (ISBN 0-664-32115-1). Westminster Press.
--Clean up Hitter. Friendlich, Richard J.. LC 56-8414. 176 p. 21cm. 1956. Westminster Press.
--Full Court Press. Friendlich, Richard J.. LC 62-7521. 187 p. 21cm. 1962. Westminster Press.
--Fullback from Nowhere. Friendlich, Richard J.. LC 67-1296. 192 p. 21cm. 1967. Westminster Press.
--Goal Line Stand. Friendlich, Richard J.. LC 51-12711. 188 p. 21cm. 1951. Westminster Press.
--Gridiron Crusader. Friendlich, Richard J.. LC 58-10280. 176p. 21cm. 1958. Westminster Press.
--Lead-off Man. Friendlich, Richard J.. LC 59-10280. 191p. 21cm. 1959. Westminster Press.
--Left End Scott. Friendlich, Richard J.. LC 55-8087. 192 p. 21cm. 1955. Westminster Press.
--Line Smasher. Friendlich, Richard J.. LC 52-7119. 194 p. 21cm. 1952. Westminster Press.
--Pinch Hitter. Friendlich, Richard J.. 1965. E M Hale.
--Pinch Hitter. Friendlich, Richard J.. LC 65-10967. 187 p. 21cm. 1965. Westminster Press.
--Pivot Man. Friendlich, Richard J.. LC 49-10823. 191 p. 22 cm. 1949. Westminister Press.
--Play Maker. Friendlich, Richard J.. LC 53-6134. 188 p. 22cm. 1953. Westminster Press.
--Relief Pitcher. Friendlich, Richard J.. 1964. E M Hale.
--Relief Pitcher. Friendlich, Richard J.. LC 64-10519. 176 p. 21 cm. 1964. Westminster Press.
--The Sweet Swing. Friendlich, Richard J.. LC 67-19123. 225 p. 22cm. 1968. Doubleday.
--Touchdown Maker. Friendlich, Richard J.. LC 65-19939. 234p. 22cm. c.1966. Doubleday.
--Warrior Forward. Friendlich, Richard J.. LC 50-9211. 190 p. 22cm. 1950. Westminster Press.
Friendlich, Richard J. see Friendlich, Dick, pseud.
Friermood, Elisabeth Hamilton (1903-)
--Ballad of Calamity Creek. LC 62-15946. 214 p. 22cm. 1962. Doubleday.
--Candle in the Sun. Schwartz, Daniel (1929-), illus. LC 55-9981. (Illus.). 255 p. 22cm. 1955. Doubleday.
--Circus Sequins. LC 68-22749. 240 p. 22cm. 1968. Doubleday.
--Doc Dudley's Daughter. LC 65-19876. 238 p. 22cm. 1965. Doubleday.
--Focus the Bright Land. LC 67-19065. 240 p. 22cm. 1967. Doubleday.
--Geneva Summer: A Romance of College Camp. 1st Ed. 1st ed. LC 52-10128. 224 p. 21 cm. 1952. Doubleday.
--Head High, Ellen Brody. LC 58-9185. 210 p. 22cm. 1958. Doubleday.
--Hoosier Heritage. 1st ed. Hallock, Robert, illus. LC 54-5210. 221p. illus. 22cm. 1954. Doubleday.
--Jo Allen's Predicament. LC 59-11594. 238 p. 22cm. 1959. Doubleday.
--The Luck of Daphne Tolliver. 1st ed. LC 61-12522. 239p. 22cm. 1961. Doubleday.
--Molly's Double Rainbow. 1st ed. Bolian, Polly (1925-), illus. LC 66-7755. 223p. illus. 22cm. (gr. 7-9). 1966. (ISBN 0-385-06991-X). Doubleday.
--One of Fred's Girls. LC 72-116136. 229 p. 22cm. 1970. Doubleday.
--Peppers' Paradise. LC 70-79969. 259 p. 22cm. 1969. Doubleday.
--Promises in the Attic. 1st ed. LC 56-9391. 226p. 22cm. 1960. Doubleday.
--Promises in the Attic. LC 60-12790 (Pub. by Doubleday). (gr. 5-9). 1975. (ISBN 0-913428-14-0). Landfall Pr.
--That Jones Girl. Reynolds, Doris, illus. LC 56-9391. (Illus.). 252 p. 22cm. 1956. Doubleday.
--The Wabash Knows The Secret. N.D. E . M. Hale and Co.
--The Wabash Knows the Secret. 1st ed. Paull, Grace a. (1898-), illus. LC 51-10775. ix, 239 p. illus. 21 cm. 1951. Doubleday.
--Whispering Willows. LC 64-19325. 239 p. 22cm. 1964. Doubleday.
--The Wild Donahues. LC 63-18233. 208 p. 22cm. 1963. Doubleday.
Fries, Chloe
--No Place to Hide. LC 78-12884. p. cm. 1978. (ISBN 0-87191-678-9). Creative Education.
Fries, Chloe & Tomlinson, Richard H.
--The Full of the Moon. E. J. Abrams Associates, illus. LC 78-70805. (Illus.). 56 p. 24cm. 1980, c.1978. (ISBN 0-87191-686-X). Creative Education.
Fries, Jurgen Nikolaus (1823-1894)
--The Emigrants. Ireland, Mary Eliza Haines, Mrs. (1834-1927), tr. LC 20-23155. 94 p. front., pl. 19 cm. 1918. Lutheran Book Concern.
--Twilight and Dawn: A Story for Children. LC 26-18322. 124 p. front., pl. 17 cm. c.1926. Augustana Book Concern.
Friesel, Uwe (1939-)
--Tim, the Peacemaker. Wilkon, Jozef (1930-), illus. LC 72-145822. (Illus.). 22 p. 29cm. 1971, c.1970. Scroll Press.
Friesen, Elizabeth Langeman (1916-)
--The Martin Family. LC 77-368228. (Illus.). 198 p. 22cm. c.1976. (ISBN 0-919213-04-9). S.N.
Fright, Henry
--The Search for the Talisman. (Illus.). (Scribner-Blackie series of books for young people). N.D. Charles Scribner's Sons.
Friis-Baastad, Babbis Ellinor (1921-1970)
--Don't Take Teddy. McKinnon, Lise Somme, tr. from Norwegian. LC 67-15480. 218p. 22cm. (gr. 5 up). 1967. (ISBN 0-684-13213-3). Scribners. **Award: (MLB).**
--Kristy's Courage. Geer, Charles Hand (1922-), illus. McKinnon, Lise Somme, tr. LC 65-18728. (Illus.). 21cm. 159p. (gr. 4-6). 1965. (ISBN 0-15-243370-8, HJ). HarBraceJ.
Friis-Baastad, Babbis see Baastad, Babbis Friis.
Frimmer, Steven (1928-)
--Neverland: Fabled Places & Fabulous Voyages of History & Legend. (Illus.). (gr. 7 up). 1976. (ISBN 0-670-50625-7). Viking Pr.
Frisbee, Lucy Post
--John Burroughs, Boy of Field and Stream. Morrow, Gray, illus. LC 64-13111. (Illus.). 200p. (Childhood of Famous Americans). 1964. Bobbs-Merrill.
--John F. Kennedy: Young Statesman. Fiorentino, Al, illus. LC 64-24807. 200 p. col. illus. 20 cm. (Childhood of famous Americans). 1964. Bobbs-Merrill.
Frisbie, William Albert (1867-)
--A B C Mother Goose. Bartholomew, Charles Lewis (1869-), illus. Bart, pseud. LC 5-5902. 56 p. col. illus. 32 cm. 1905. Rand, McNally & Company.
--The Bandit Mouse and Other Tales. Bartholomew, Charles Lewis (1869-), illus. Bart, pseud. LC 5226. 96 p. col. illus. 32 cm. 1900. Rand, McNally & Company.
--The Funny Adventures of Captain Pip. Bartholomew, Charles Lewis (1869-), illus. Bart, pseud. (Illus.). N.D. Rand McNally & Co.
--Natural History Stories for Children. (Illus.). 1910. Rand McNally & Co.
--The Pirate Frog. Bartholomew, Charles Lewis (1869-), illus. Bart, pseud. 96p. col. illus. N.D. Rand, McNally & Co.
--Puggery Wee: The Story of Three Elephants. Bart, illus. 80p. N.D. Rand, McNally & Co.
--The Shanghai Twins. (Illus.). N.D. Rand McNally & Co.
--Snap Shots. (Illus.). 1910. Rand McNally & Co.
Frisch, Wilhelmine
--The Storks of Lillegaard. Jauss, Anne Marie (1907-), illus. LC 50-9951. (Illus.). 231 p. 23cm. 1950. Bobbs-Merrill.
Frischkorn, Rebecca, jt. auth. see Sedgwick, Kate.
Friscia, Sal
--Ignorant Monkeys & Other Tales from India. Friscia, Sal, illus. LC 75-153977. (gr. 1-5). 1971. (ISBN 0-394-92319-7). (ISBN 0-394-82319-2). Pantheon.
Frisinger, Nellie
--Jeff & Jenny and the Kidnapping. LC 78-55337. (Illus.). 127 p. 20cm. (Jeff & Jenny adventure series). c.1978. (ISBN 0-89636-005-9). Accent Books.
--Jeff & Jenny at Camp Pinecrest. 128p. (Orig.). (Jeff & Jenny Adventure Ser.). (gr. 4-6). 1984. (ISBN 0-89636-121-7). Accent Bks.
--Jeff & Jenny on the Chinchilla Ranch. LC 77-75132. (Illus.). 127 p. 29cm. (Jeff & Jenny adventure series). c.1977. (ISBN 0-916406-73-3). Accent Books.
--Jeff & Jenny Winter in Alaska. LC 77-81775. (Illus.). 127 p. 19cm. (Jeff & Jenny adventure series). c.1977. (ISBN 0-916406-82-2). Accent Books.
Friskey, Margaret Richards (1901-)
--Adventure Begins at Home: Pictures by Children. LC 46-11854. 47 p. illus. (part col.) 28 1/2 x 21 cm. 1946. Childrens Press, Inc.
--Adventure for Beginners. Evans, Katherine Floyd (1901-1964), illus. LC 45-584. 28 p. col. illus. 26 x 20 1/2 cm. 1944. Wilcox & Follett Co.
--Annie and the Wooden Skates: A Story of Arlington in the 1840's. Patton, Lucia, illus. LC 42-7638. 62 p. col. front., illus., plates (part col.) 21 x 16 cm. 1942. Oxford University Press.
--Annie Lee and the Wooden Skates. rev. ed. Wiskur, Darrell D., illus. LC 69-14691. (Illus.). 94 p. 24cm. 1969. Childrens Press.
--Captain Joe. Evans, Katherine Floyd (1901-1964), illus. LC 47-29369. 37 p. illus. (part col.) 19 1/2 x 17 cm. (Story-book science series). 1947. Childrens Press, Inc.
--Chicken Little: Count-to-Ten. Evans, Katherine Floyd (1901-1964), illus. LC 46-1775. 28 p. col. illus. 19 1/2 x 26 cm. 1946. Childrens Press, Inc.
--Chipmunk Moves. Patton, Lucia, illus. LC 46-8551. 32 p. col. illus. 27 x 22 1/2 cm. 1946. David McKay Company.
--Corporal Crow. Patton, Lucia, illus. 32 p. col. illus. 26 1/2 x 22 1/2 cm. 1944. David McKay Company.
--A Goat Afloat. Patton, Lucia, illus. LC 42-15597. 32 p. illus. (part col.) 24 x 19 cm. (A Read-It-Yourself Story). 1942. A. Whitman & Company.
--Grandfather Frog: Patton/Lucia The Busy Loafer. LC 41-89591. 40 p. col. illus. 27 x 22 cm. c.1941. David McKay Company.
--The House That Ran Away. Patton, Lucia, illus. LC 43-17322. 32 p. illus. (part col.) 24 x 18 1/2 cm. (A Read-It-Yourself Story). 1943. A. Whitman & Company.
--Indian Two Feet and His Eagle Feather. Hawkinson, John Samuel (1912-) & Hawkinson, Lucy Ozone (1924-1971), illus. LC 67-20101. (Illus.). 1 v. (unpaged. 24cm. 1967. Children's Press.
--Indian Two Feet & His Horse. Evans, Katherine Floyd (1901-1964), illus. (Illus.). 64p. (gr. k-3). 1959. (ISBN 0-516-03501-0). Childrens.
--Indian Two Feet & His Horse. Keats, Ezra Jack (1916-1983), illus. LC 59-3589. (Illus.). 24 cm. (gr. 2-3). N.D. (ISBN 0-590-08056-3). (ISBN 0-590-04394-3). Scholastic Inc.
--Indian Two Feet and His Horse. El Indio Dos Pies y Su Caballo. LC 61-4978. (Illus.). unpaged. 24cm. 1961. Childrens Press.
--Indian Two Feet and the ABC Moose Hunt. LC 77-4467. p. cm. 1977. (ISBN 0-516-03500-2). Childrens Press.
--Indian Two Feet and the Grizzly Bear. Hawkinson, John Samuel (1912-), illus. LC 74-7481. (Illus.). 31 p. 25cm. 1974. (ISBN 0-516-03508-8). Childrens Press.
--Indian Two Feet and the Wolf Cubs. Hawkinson, John Samuel (1912-), illus. LC 75-159788. (Illus.). 64 p. 24cm. 1971. (ISBN 0-516-03506-1). Childrens Press.
--Indian Two Feet Rides Alone. Hawkinson, John Samuel (1912-), illus. LC 80-12688. p. cm. 1980. (ISBN 0-516-03523-1). Children Press.
--John Alden and the Pilgrim Cow. Wiskur, Darrell D., illus. LC 72-1455. (Illus.). 93 p. 23cm. 1972. (ISBN 0-516-03153-8). Childrens Pr.
--Johnny and the Monarch. Podendorf, Illa E. (1903-1983), ed. Evans, Katherine Floyd (1901-1964), illus. LC 46-3968. 24 p. col. illus. 23 1/2 x 18 1/2 cm. 1946. Childrens Press, Inc.
--Johnny Cottontail. Patton, Lucia, illus. LC 46-38072. 32 p. col. illus. 26 1/2 x 22 1/2 cm. 1946. David McKay Company.
--The Mystery of Rackety's Way. Eckart, Frances, illus. LC 69-14687. (Illus.). 32 p. 25cm. 1969. Childrens Press.
--Mystery of the Broken Bridge. LC 52-2853. (Illus.). unpaged. 24cm. (Silver star book). 1952. Childrens Press.
--Mystery of the Farmer's Three Fives. Hawkinson, John Samuel (1912-) & Hawkinson, Lucy Ozone (1924-1971), illus. LC 63-9707. (Illus.). 1 v. (unpaged. 23cm. (Reading laboratory book). 1963. Childrens Press.
--Mystery of the Gate Sign. Evans, Katherine Floyd (1901-1964), illus. LC 58-14614. (Illus.). unpaged. 25cm. 1958. Childrens Press.
--Mystery of the Magic Meadow. Eckart, Frances, illus. LC 68-12826. (Illus.). 1 v. 29 p. 25cm. 1968. Childrens Press.

Frost, Arthur Burdett (1851-1928)
--The Bull Calf & Other Stories. N.D. Charles Scribner's Sons.
--The Bull Calf, And Other Tales. LC 69-17099. (Illus.). 154 p. 1969. Dover Publications.
Frost, Bernice
--Children's Songs for Every Day. Schubert, Marie (1890-), illus. LC 31-10498. 80 p. col. illus, 25 cm. c.1931. American Book Company.
Frost, Betty
--Voyage of the Vagabond. LC 81-22858. (Illus.). 44 p. 18cm. (Perspectives book). c.1982. (ISBN 0-87879-296-1). Academic Therapy Publications.
Frost, Daniel, as told by see Kauffman, Reginald Wright.
Frost, Erica, pseud., see Supraner, robyn.
Frost, Erica, pseud. (1930-)
--Harold and the Dinosaur Mystery. Supraner, Robyn. Sims, Deborah, illus. LC 78-60123. (Illus.). 48 p. 23cm. (Troll easy-to-read mystery). c.1979. (ISBN 0-89375-088-3). Troll Associates.
--I Can Read About Ballet. Supraner, robyn. LC 74-24927. (Illus.). (gr. 2-4). 1975. (ISBN 0-89375-063-8). Troll Assocs.
--I Can Read About Ghosts. Supraner, robyn. LC 74-24964. (Illus.). (gr. 2-4). 1975. (ISBN 0-89375-065-4). Troll Assocs.
--Mystery of the Midnight Visitors. Supraner, Robyn. Gamache, Ann, illus. LC 78-18038. (Illus.). 48 p. 23cm. (Troll easy-to-read mystery). c.1979. (ISBN 0-89375-094-8). Troll Associates.
--Mystery of the Runaway Sled. Supraner, Robyn. Grant, Alice Leigh (1947-), illus. LC 78-60124. (Illus.). 48 p. 23cm. (Troll easy-to-read mystery). (gr. 2-4). c.1979. (ISBN 0-89375-077-8). Troll Associates.
Frost, Erica, pseud. (1930-) & Harvey, Paul (1926-)
--Case of the Missing Chick. Supraner, Robyn. Frost, Erica, pseud. (1930-), illus. LC 78-18036. (Illus.). 48 p. 23cm. (Troll easy-to-read mystery). (gr. 2-4). c.1979. (ISBN 0-89375-080-8). Troll Associates.
Frost, F., jt. auth. see Coles, R. R.
Frost, Frances Mary (1905-1959), adapted by see Menotti, Gian Carlo.
Frost, Frances Mary, ed. see Zinger, Oleg & Windmuller, Isle.
Frost, Frances Mary (1905-1959)
--American Caravan. Townsend, Lee (1895-), illus. LC 44-9099. 64 p. col. illus. 26 x 19 1/2 cm. 1944. Whittlesey House, McGraw-Hill Book Company.
--The Cat That Went to College. LC 51-12677. (Illus.). 64 p. 24cm. 1951. Whittlesey House.
--Christmas in the Woods. Watson, Aldren Auld (1917-), illus. LC 76-3835. (Illus.). 24p. (ps-3). 1976. (ISBN 0-06-021922-X, HarpJ). (ISBN 0-06-021923-8). Har-Row.
--Christmas in the Woods. Watson, Aldren Auld (1917-), illus. 1942. Harper & Brothers.
--Fireworks For Windy Foot. Townsend, Lee (1895-), illus. LC 56-9625. (Illus.). 112p. 1952. McGraw-Hill Book Company.
--Fireworks for Windy Foot. Townsend, Lee (1895-), illus. LC 56-9625. 176p. illus. 21cm. (gr. 4-7). 1956. (ISBN 0-07-022577-X). Whittlesey House.
--Little Fox. Dennis, Morgan (1891-1960), illus. LC 52-9452. (Illus.). 112 p. 22cm. 1952. Whittlesey House.
--Little Naturalist. Werth, Kurt (1896-), illus. LC 59-11930. (Illus.). 24 cm. 47p. (gr. 2-5). 1959. (ISBN 0-07-022569-9). McGraw.
--Little Whistler. (ps-3). 1966. (ISBN 0-07-022571-0). McGraw.
--The Little Whistler: Poems. Duvoisin, Roger Antoine (1904-1980), illus. LC 49-107652. 48 p. illus. (part col.) 24 cm. 1949. Whittlesey House.
--Maple Sugar for Windy Foot. Townsend, Lee (1895-), illus. (gr. 4-7). 1950. (ISBN 0-07-022575-3). McGraw.
--Maple Sugar for Windy Foot. Townsend, Lee (1895-), illus. LC 50-5418. 184 p. illus. 21 cm. 1950. Whittlesey House.
--Rocket Away!. Galdone, Paul (1914-), illus. Coles, Robert R., frwd. by. LC 53-5187. (Illus.). 48 p. 26cm. 1953. Whittlesey House.
--Sleigh Bells for Windy Foot. Townsend, Lee (1895-), illus. LC 48-4522. 184 p. illus. 21 cm. 1948. (ISBN 0-07-022578-8). Whittlesey House.
--Then Came Timothy. Bennett, Richard Michael (1899-), illus. LC 50-9412. (Illus.). 155 p. 21cm. 1950. Whittlesey House.
--Windy Foot at the County Fair. Townsend, Lee (1895-), illus. LC 47-2847. 153 p. incl. front., illus. 21 cm. 1947. (ISBN 0-07-022580-X). Whittlesey House, McGraw-Hill Book Company, Inc.
Frost, Frances Mary (1905-1959), ed.
--Legends of the United Nations. LC 43-14971. xi, 323 p. illus. 21 cm. 1943. Whittlesey House, McGraw-Hill Book Company, Inc.
Frost, John (1800-1859)
--The Youth's Book of the Seasons: Or, Nature Familiarly Developed. LC 15-2594. 2 p. l., vii-viii, 9-304 p. front., illus. 15 cm. 1835. Carey, Lea & Blanchard.
Frost, Kelman
--Exiles in the Sahara. Linton, Anne, illus. LC 64-14905. 159 p. illus., map. 23 cm. 1964. Abelard-Schuman.
--Men of the Mirage. LC 69-14323. 160 p. 22cm. 1969. Lothrop, Lee & Shepard.
--The Riddle of the Caid's Jewels. LC 69-10322. (Illus.). 23cm. 160p. 1969. Abelard-Schuman.
--Sahara Trail. LC 74-660. 121p. (gr. 6-9). 1974. (ISBN 0-8407-6382-4). Elsevier-Nelson.
--Son of the Sahara. Ambrus, Victor G., pseud. (1935-), illus. Ambrus, Gyozo Laszlo. LC 64-252689. 207p. illus. 21cm. 1965, c.1962. Roy.
--Stallion of the Desert. Pickard, Charles, illus. LC 66-10156. 167 p. illus. 22 1/2 15/. (B66-6198). 1966. Etc. Abelard-Schuman.
Frost, L. H.
--Lynda Newton. (Illus.). N.D. D. Lothrop Co.
Frost, Lesley (1899-1983)
--Digging Down to China. Hudnut, R., illus. (Illus.). 64p. (gr. 1-4). 1968. Devin.
--Not Really!. Eleven Jolly Stories. Reid, James (1907-), illus. Untermeyer, Louis (1885-1977), intro. by. LC 39-31797. 126 p. illus. 21 cm. c.1939. Coward-McCann, Inc.
--Really Not Really. Remington, Barbara, illus. LC 62-18041. (Illus.). 61 p. 27cm. 1962. Channel Press.
Frost, Marie
--Adventures with Peter Panda. Hutton, Kathryn, illus. (gr. k-3). 1978. (ISBN 0-87239-184-1). Standard Pub.
Frost, Robert Lee (1874-1963)
--Come in & Other Poems. large type ed. (Keith Jennison Bks). (gr. 7 up). N.D. (ISBN 0-531-00176-8). Watts.
--In the Clearing. Turkle, Brinton Cassaday (1915-), illus. LC 62-11578. 48p. (gr. 9 up). 1962. (ISBN 0-03-031010-5). HR&W.
--Stopping by Woods on a Snowy Evening. Jeffers, Susan, illus. LC 78-8134. p. cm. 1978. (ISBN 0-525-40115-6). Dutton. **Award: (ALA).**
--Stories for Lesley. Sell, Roger S., ed. Chappell, Warren (1904-), illus. LC 83-19756. 1984. (ISBN 0-8139-0979-1). University Press of Virginia.
--A Swinger of Birches: Poems of Robert Frost for Young People. Koeppen, Peter, illus. Fadiman, Clifton Paul (1904-), intro. by. LC 82-5517. (Illus.). (gr. 4 up). 1982. (ISBN 0-916144-92-5). (ISBN 0-916144-93-3). Stemmer Hse.
--You Come Too: Favorite Poems for Young Readers. Nason, Thomas Willoughby (1889-), illus. LC 59-12940. (Illus.). 94 p. 22cm. 1959. Holt.
Frost, William Henry (1863-1902)
--The Court of King Arthur: Stories from the Land of the Round Table. Burleigh, Sydney Richmond (1853-1931), illus. LC 44-34787. xii, 302 p. front., illus., plates 19 cm. 1896. C. Scribner's Sons.
--Fairies and Folk of Ireland. Burleigh, Sydney Richmond (1853-1931), illus. LC 5707. xvi, 290 p. front., illus., pl. 19 cm. 1900. C. Scribner's Sons.
--The Knights of the Round Table. Burleigh, Sydney Richmond (1853-1931), illus. 19cm. 281p. 1910. C. Scribner's Sons.
--The Knights of the Round Table: Stories of King Arthur and the Holy Grail. Burleigh, Sydney Richmond (1853-1931), illus. LC 44-35023. xiv, 281 p. front., illus., plates. 19 cm. 1897. C. Scribner's Sons.
--The Wagner Story Book: Firelight Tales of the Great Music Dramas. Burleigh, Sydney Richmond (1853-1931), illus. LC 4-11743. 5 p. l., 245 p. 11 pl. (incl. front.) 19 cm. 1894. C. Scribner's Sons.
Froud, Brian
--Goblins. Froud, Brian, illus. LC 83-16236. (Illus.). 5 double leaves. 30cm. 1983. (ISBN 0-02-735520-9). MacMillan Pub. Co.
Frumin, Natasha, retold by see Silverman, Maida.
Fry, Christopher, pseud. (1907-), tr. see Colette, Sidonie Gabrielle (1873-1954) & Ravel, Maurice.
Fry, Christopher (1907-)
--The Boat That Mooed. Weisgard, Leonard Joseph (1916-), illus. LC 65-15183. (Illus.). 26cm. 30p. (ps-2). 1965. (ISBN 0-02-735720-1). Macmillan.
Fry, Clara W. T
--Little Splendid's Vacation. Fry, Clara W. T., illus. (Illus.). 165p. N.D. American Unitarian Association.
Fry, Dorothy Whipple
--Rainbows & Echoes from Fairyland. N.D. Bruce Humphries.
--The Rescue of Silver Bell. N.D. Bruce Humphries.
Fry, Edward Bernard (1925-)
--Barco de Vela en el Viento: Sailboat in the Wind. Weber, Jim, illus. Gunning, Monica Owen (1930-), tr. (Illus.). 15p. (Storybooks for Beginners Ser.: Bk. 4). (gr. 1). 1980. (ISBN 0-89061-215-3). Jamestown Pubs.
--Barco de Vela: Sailboat. Weber, Jim, illus. Gunning, Monica (1930-), tr. (Illus.). 15p. (Storybooks for Beginners Ser.: Bk. 3). (gr. 1). 1980. (ISBN 0-89061-214-5). Jamestown Pubs.
Fry, Elizabeth Stafford
--Bully Bulfrog & His Home in Rainbow Valley. (True to Nature Ser.). N.D. Rand McNally.
--Bully Bullfrog's Queer Relations. Beem, Frances M., illus. (True to Nature Ser.). N.D. Rand McNally.
Fry, Margaret
--My Name Is John: A Book for Boys Named John. LC 31-2829. 63 p. incl. front., illus. 21 cm. 1930. Thomas S. Rockwell Company.
--My Name Is Mary. Chisolm, Christine, illus. LC 30-22022. 64 p. incl. front., illus. 21 cm. 1930. Thomas S. Rockwell Company.
Fry, Rosalie Kingsmill (1911-)
--Bandy Boy's Treasure Island. Fry, Rosalie Kingsmill (1911-), illus. LC 41-10786. 29 p. col. illus. 15 x 12 cm. 1941. E. P. Dutton & Co., Inc.
--A Bell for Ringelblume. 1st ed. Fry, Rosalie Kingsmill (1911-), illus. LC 57-5337. 89p. illus. 21cm. 1957. Dutton.
--Bumblebuzz. Fry, Rosalie Kingsmill (1911-), illus. LC 38-19923. 25 p. incl. col. front., col. illus. 25 cm. 1938. E. P. Dutton & Company, Inc.
--The Castle Family. Gill, Margery Jean (1925-), illus. LC 66-10393. (Illus.). 127 p. 21cm. 1966, c.1965. Dutton.
--Cinderella's Mouse, and Other Fairy Tales. 1st ed. Fry, Rosalie Kingsmill (1911-), illus. LC 53-60705. 85p. illus. 23cm. 1953. Dutton.
--Deep in the Forest. Fry, Rosalie Kingsmill (1911-), illus. N.D. Dodd, Mead & Co.
--The Echo Song. Fry, Rosalie Kingsmill (1911-), illus. LC 62-10382. 21cm. 100p. 1962. E. P. Dutton & Co.
--Fly Home, Colombina. Fry, Rosalie Kingsmill (1911-), illus. LC 60-6006. 21cm. 123p. 1960. E. P. Dutton & Co.
--A Ghost, a Witch, & Goblin. Fry, Rosalie Kingsman (1911-), illus. (Illus.). (gr. 2-3). 1971 (StarLine). Schol Bk Serv.
--Gypsy Princess. Gough, Philip (1908-), illus. LC 74-81717. (Illus.). 90 p. 22cm. 1969. Dutton.
--Ladybug! Ladybug!. Fry, Rosalie Kingsmill (1911-), illus. 35 p. col. illus. 22 cm. 1940. E. P. Dutton & Co., Inc.
--Matelot, Little Salior of Brittany. Fry, Rosalie Kingsmill (1911-), illus. LC 58-12565. 21cm. 128p. 1958. E. P. Dutton & Co.
--Mountain Door. Fry, Rosalie Kingsmill (1911-), illus. LC 61-5868. (Illus.). 21cm. 128p. (gr. 2-5). 1961. Dutton.
--Mungo. Ilsley, Velma Elizabeth (1918-), illus. LC 76-184126. (Illus.). 123 p. 21cm. 1972. (ISBN 0-374-35097-3). Farrar, Straus & Giroux.
--Pipkin Sees the World. Fry, Rosalie Kingsmill (1911-), illus. LC 51-12027. (Illus.). 96 p. 23cm. 1951. Dutton.
--Promise of the Rainbow. Jacques, Robin (1920-), illus. LC 65-11787. 127p. illus. 22cm. (gr. 3-6). 1965. (ISBN 0-374-36139-8). BellBks. Dist. Farrar, C.
--Riddle of the Figurehead. Fry, Rosalie Kingsmill (1911-), illus. LC 63-8596. (Illus.). 21cm. 157p. (gr. 3-7). 1963. (ISBN 0-525-38253-4). Dutton.
--Secret of the Ron Mor Skerry. Fry, Rosalie Kingsmill (1911-), illus. LC 59-5842. 21cm. 126p. Orig. Title: Child of the Western Isles. 1959. E. P. Dutton & Co.
--September Island. Gill, Margery Jean (1925-), illus. LC 64-106902. 112p. illus. 21cm. (gr. 3-7). c.1965. (ISBN 0-525-39129-0). Dutton.
--Snowed up. Jacques, Robin (1920-), illus. LC 76-125142. (Illus.). 124 p. 21cm. (Ariel book). 1970. Farrar, Straus & Giroux.
--Whistler in the Mist. Jacques, Robin (1920-), illus. LC 68-29467. (Illus.). 139 p. 22cm. 1968. Farrar, Straus, and Giroux.
--The Wind Call. Fry, Rosalie Kingsmill (1911-), illus. LC 56-1787. 115p. illus. 19cm. 1955. Dent.
--The Wind Call. Fry, Rosalie Kingsmill (1911-), illus. N.D. E. P. Dutton & Co.
Fry, Sarah Maria, Mrs.
--The Lost Key. (Illus.). (Books for Everbody). N.D. American Tract Society.
--The Lost Key. LC 12-32513. 252 p. front., plates. 16 cm. (On cover: Series for youth). 1860. Presbyterian Board of Publication.
--Young Hop Pickers. 98p. N.D. Presbyterian Committe of Publication.
Frye, Burton C. (1920-), ed.
--Saint Nicholas Anthology. (gr. 5 up). 1969. (ISBN 0-696-77906-4). Hawthorn.
--A St. Nicholas Anthology: The Early Years. Darling, Richard L., frwd. by. LC 73-91010. (Illus.). 439 p. 25cm. 1969. (ISBN 0-696-77906-4). Meredith Press.
Frye, Dean
--The Lamb & the Child. Duvoisin, Roger Antoine (1904-1980), illus. LC 63-15109. (Illus.). 32 p. 26cm. 1963. McGraw-Hill Book Co.
Frye, Dean, ed. see Heywood, John.
Frye, Pearl (1917-)
--Alberta for Short. 1st ed. Frye, Pearl (1917-), illus. LC 53-7304. 118p. illus. 21cm. 1953. Little, Brown.
Fryer, J. G., jt. auth. see Fryer, Jane Eayre, Mrs.
Fryer, Jane Eayre, Mrs. (1876-)
--Easy Steps in Housekeeping: Or, Mary Frances' Adventures Among the Doll People. Greene, Julia, illus. LC 15-163221. xiv, 2 p., 1 l., 19-253 p. col. front., illus., col. plates. 24 cm. c.1914. Printed by the John C. Winston Company.
--The Mary Frances Housekeeper: Or, Adventures Among the Doll People. Greene, Julia, illus. LC 14-19361. xiv, 2 p., 1l., 19-253 p. col. front., illus., col. plates. 24 cm. c.1914. The John C. Winston Co.
--The Mary Frances Story Book: Or, Adventures Among the Story People. Prittie, Edwin John, illus. LC 22-2052. 329 p. col. front., col. illus., col. plates. 24 cm. c.1921. The John C. Winston Company.
--Stories of Every Day Heroes. LC 21-1522. 20cm. 259p. (The Young American Story Books). 1920. John C. Winston.
--Stories of Everyday Friends. Cooke, Edna W., illus. LC 21-152322. 2 p. l., ix-xiii, 228 p. illus. (part co.) 19 cm. (Her Young American story book. v. 1). c.1920. The John C. Winston Company.
--Stories of Everyday Wonders. Cooke, Edna W., illus. LC 21-1522. 2 p. l., vii-xii, 259 p. illus. 20 cm. (Her Young American story book. v. 2). c.1920. John C. Winston Co.
Fryer, Jane Eayre, Mrs. (1876-) & Fryer, J. G.
--The Bible Story Book for Boys and Girls. N.D. John C. Winston.
Fryer, Kathleen, jt. auth. see Tempest, Margaret Mary.
Fryer, Mary Beacock (1929-)
--Escape: Adventures of a Loyalist Family. Clarke, Stephen, illus. LC 77-358606. (Illus.). 152 p. 22cm. c.1976. (ISBN 0-460-91410-3). J. M. Dent.
Fuchs
--African Decameron. (gr. 10 up). N.D. G&D.
Fuchs, Erich (1916-)
--Journey to the Moon. Fuchs, Erich (1916-), illus. LC 74-103151. (Illus.). color ils. 32p. (ps-3). 1970. (Sey Lawr). (Sey Lawr). Delacorte.
Fuchs, Gertraut
--Pajaro-Cu-Cu: Animal Rhymes for Everywhere. 1967. Atheneum Publishers.
Fuchs, Gertraut, jt. ed. see Wolf, Ingrid.
Fuchshuber, Annegert
--A Christmas Star. Fuchshuber, Annegert, illus. (Illus.). (gr. k-6). N.D. (ISBN 0-685-24604-3). Merry Thoughts.
--Most Beautiful Star in the World. (gr. k-3). N.D. (ISBN 0-685-28653-3). Merry Thoughts.
--The Wishing Hat. Fuchshuber, Annegert, illus. Crawford, Elizabeth D., tr. from Ger. LC 76-54237. (Illus.). 30 p. 24cm. 1977. (ISBN 0-688-22100-9). (ISBN 0-688-32100-3). Morrow.
Fuentes, Vilma M.
--The Monkey & the Crocodile. Inis, Ninabeth R., illus. (Illus.). 31p. (Orig.). (Mandaya & Mansaka Tales Ser.: No. 1). (gr. k-2). 1984. (ISBN 971-10-0127-6, Pub. by New Day Philippines). Cellar.
Fuess, Claude Moore (1885-)
--All for Andover: The School Life of Steve Fisher and His Friends. Goss, John, illus. LC 25-8154. 368 p. front., plates. 20 cm. c.1925. Lothrop, Lee & Shepard Co.
--The Andover Way. Goss, John, illus. LC 26-11251. 335 p. front., plates. 20 cm. c.1926. Lothrop, Lee & Shepard Co.
--Peter Had Courage: A Story for Boys. Dotterer, Lloyd J., illus. LC 27-19189. 327 p. front., plates. 20 cm. c.1927. Lothrop, Lee & Shepard Co.
Fufuka, Karama, pseud., see Morgan, Sharon Antonia.
Fufuka, Karama, pseud. (1951-)
--My Daddy Is a Cool Dude, and Other Poems. Morgan, Sharon Antonia. Fufuka, Mahiri, illus. LC 74-2883. (Illus.). 48 p. 24cm. 1975. (ISBN 0-8037-6187-2). (ISBN 0-8037-6188-0). Dial Press.

Funk, Charles E

--The Lucky Knife: A Western Adventure Story for Young People. 1st. ed. LC 53-850556. 134p. 21cm. 1953. Exposition Press.

Funk, Frances Ellen

--Playtime Round the World. Hubbard, Eleanore Mineah, illus. N.D. A. Whitman & Co.

Funk, Ruth S.

--Adventure of Debbie, Kenney & Jackie. Meyd, Orella S., illus. (Illus.). (ps-1). 1969. (ISBN 0-682-46963-7). Exposition.

Funk, Thompson see Battles, Edith

Funk, Tom (1911-)

--I Read Signs. Funk, Thompson (1911-), illus. LC 62-2070. (Illus.). 20cm. 40p. (gr. k-3). 1962. (ISBN 0-8234-0058-1). Holiday.

Funk, Tom see Funk, Thompson.

Furan, Paul, jt. auth. see Hull, Jesse Redding.

Furbush, Lydia

--Circus Parade. LC 42-11043. 26cm. 1942. MacMillan.

--Humpty Dumpty and Some other Funny People. N.D. MacMillan.

--Jack and the Beanstalk. N.D. MacMillan.

--Pied Piper. N.D. MacMillan.

Furchgott, Terry (1948-)

--Nanda in India. Furchgott, Terry (1948-), illus. (Illus.). 32p. (ps-3). 1983. (ISBN 0-233-96860-1). Andre Deutsch.

Furchgott, Terry (1948-) & Dawson, Linda

--Phoebe and the Hot Water Bottles. Furchgott, Terry (1948-), illus. LC 77-370380. (Illus.). 32 p. 26cm. 1979. (ISBN 0-233-96860-1). Deutsch.

Furlong, May

--Jordan Fairy Tales. Caldwell, Margaret, illus. LC 25-22409. 59 p. col. illus. 24 cm. c.1925. Jordan Publishing Company.

--The Lost Log Cabin. Young, Elsa Goldy, photos by. LC 33-33688. 23p. 1933. A. Whitman & Co.

--A Modern Knight: His Adventures. Young, Elsa Goldy, illus. LC 25-21160. 59 p. col. illus. 24 cm. (Jordan juvenile series). c.1925. Jordan Publishing Company.

Furman, Abraham Loew (1902-), ed. see Allen, Merritt Parmelee, et al.

Furman, Abraham Loew (1902-), ed. see Annixter, Paul.

Furman, Abraham Loew, ed. see Folinsbee, J. P.

Furman, Abraham Loew (1902-), ed. see Priestley, Lee Shore.

Furman, Abraham Loew (1902-), ed. see Rathjen, Carl Henry.

Furman, Abraham Loew (1902-), ed. see Richards, Steve, et al.

Furman, Abraham Loew (1902-), ed. see Stephens, William M.

Furman, Abraham Loew (1902-), ed. see Stoutenburg, Adrien Pearl, et al.

Furman, Abraham Loew (1902-), ed. see Strong, Paschal Neilson, et al.

Furman, Abraham Loew (1902-), ed. see Woolgar, George Jack.

Furman, Abraham Loew (1902-), ed.

--Everygirls Adventure Stories. (Illus.). (gr. 6-10). N.D. (ISBN 0-8313-0053-1). Lantern.

--Everygirls Career Stories. LC 57-13576. 221p. illus. 21cm. (Everygirls library). 1957, c.1954. Grosset & Dunlap.

--Everygirls Career Stories. LC 54-10748. 221p. illus. 21cm. (Everygirls library). 1954. Lantern Press.

--Everygirls Companion. LC 68-11184. 192 p. 21cm. 1968. Lantern Press.

--Everygirls Dog Stories. LC 63-10914. 192 p. 21cm. 1963. Lantern Press.

--Everygirls Horse Stories. N.D. Grosset & Dunlap.

--Everygirls Mystery Stories. Lake, Albert L., illus. LC 54-7283. (Illus.). 21cm. 222p. (gr. 6-10). 1954. (ISBN 0-8313-0061-2). Lantern.

--Everygirls Romance Stories. LC 57-13574. 223p. illus. 22cm. (Everygirls library). c.1955. Grosset & Dunlap.

--Everygirls Romance Stories. LC 55-6988. 223p. illus. 21cm. (Everygirls library). 1955. Lantern Press.

--Haunted Stories. revised edition. 163 p. 18cm. 1975, c.1965. Pocket Books.

--Horse Stories. (Illus.). (Young Readers Bookshelf). (gr. 4-7). N.D. Lantern.

--More Teen-Age Ghost Stories. LC 65-10915. 191 p. 21cm. 1963. Lantern Press.

--More Teen-Age Haunted Stories. LC 67-12010. 189 p. 22cm. (Teen-age library). 1967. Lantern Press.

--Nature Stories. (Young Reader's Bookshelf). (gr. 4-7). N.D. Lantern.

--Teen-Age Dog Stories. Osborne, Richard N., illus. LC 49-49573. 256 p. illus. 21 cm. 1949. Lantern Press.

--Teen-Age Double Agent Stories. (gr. 6-10). N.D. Lantern.

--Teen-Age Fishing Stories. McCann, Gerald (1916-), illus. LC 60-13784. (Illus.). 253 p. 21cm. 1960. Lantern Press.

--Teen-Age Frontier Stories. Prezio, Victor, illus. LC 58-13556. (Illus.). 256 p. 21cm. 1958. Lantern Press.

--Teen-Age Ghost Stories. Cobbledick, Carol, illus. LC 61-12780. (Illus.). 189 p. 21cm. 1961. Lantern Press.

--Teen-Age Ghost Stories. Cobbledick, Carol, illus. (Illus.). 189 p. 21cm. 1967. Lantern Press.

--Teen-Age Great Rescue Stories. LC 64-15172. 190 p. 21cm. 1964. Lantern Press.

--Teen-Age Haunted Stories. 190 p. 21cm. 1965. Lantern Press.

--Teen-Age Horse Stories. Osborne, Richard N., illus. LC 50-7134. 252 p. illus. 21 cm. 1950. Lantern Press.

--Teen-age Nurse Stories. McCann, Gerald (1916-), illus. LC 61-1866. (Illus.). 223p. 22cm. (The Teen-age Library). 1959. Grosset & Dunlop.

--Teen-Age Sea Stories. Cirlin, Edgar, illus. LC 48-9926. 252 p. 21 cm. (Teen-age library). 1948. Lantern Press.

--Teen-Age Spy Stories. LC 67-19632. 191 p. 21cm. (Teen-age library). 1967. Lantern Press.

--Teen-Age Stories. Prezio, Victor, illus. LC 61-1797. (Illus.). 188p. 22cm. (The Teen-Age Library). 1959. Grosset & Dunlop.

--Teen-Age Stories of the Diamond. Ricketts, William B., illus. LC 50-11856. 253 p. illus. 21 cm. 1950. Lantern Press.

--Teen-Age Suspense Stories. LC 63-17988. 187p. 22cm. c.1963. Lantern.

--Teenage Space Adventures. LC 75-189828. 192 p. 21cm. 1972. Lantern Press.

--Young Readers Adventure Stories. Osborne, Richard N., illus. LC 53-11981. 192p. illus. 22cm. (Young readers bookshelf1). 1953, c.1950. Grosset & Dunlap.

--Young Readers Adventure Stories. Osborne, Richard N., illus. LC 50-8782. 192 p. illus. 21 cm. (Young readers bookshelf). 1950. Lantern Press.

--Young Readers Animal Stories. Osborne, Richard N., illus. LC 53-11982. 189p. illus: 22cm. (Young readers bookshelf2). 1953, c.1950. Grosset & Dunlap.

--Young Readers Animal Stories. Osborne, Richard N., illus. LC 50-7046. 189 p. illus. 21 cm. (Young readers bookshelf). 1950. Lantern Press.

--Young Readers Dog Stories. Osborne, Richard N., illus. LC 53-11983. 191p. illus. 22cm. (Young readers bookshelf No. 5). 1953, c.1951. Grosset & Dunlap.

--Young Readers Dog Stories. Osborne, Richard N., illus. LC 50-11005. 191 p. illus. 21 cm. (Young readers bookshelf). N.D. Lantern Press.

--Young Readers Horse Stories. (Young Readers Bookshelf). N.D. Grosset & Dunlap.

--Young Readers Horse Stories. Geer, Charles Hand (1922-), illus. (Illus.). 191 p. 21cm. (Young readers bookshelf). 1951. Lantern Press.

--Young Readers Indian Stories. (Young Readers Bookshelf). N.D. Grosset & Dunlap.

--Young Readers Indian Stories. Geer, Charles Hand (1922-), illus. LC 51-10260. (Illus.). 189p. 21cm. (Young Readers Bookshelf). 1951. Lantern Press.

--Young Readers Nature Stories. Prezio, Victor, illus. (Illus.). 188 p. 21cm. 1959. Lantern Press.

--Young Readers Outdoor Sports Stories. Geer, Charles Hand (1922-), illus. LC 51-8304. 190 p. illus. 21 cm. (Young readers bookshelf). 1951. Lantern Press.

--Young Readers Pioneer Stories. Geer, Charles Hand (1922-), illus. LC 52-9004. 189 p. illus. 21 cm. (Young readers bookshelf). 1951. Lantern Press.

--Young Readers Sports Adventures. LC 68-11182. 192 p. 21cm. 1968. Lantern Press.

--Young Readers Sports Stories. Osborne, Richard N., illus. LC 53-11986. 189p. illus. 22cm. (Young Readers bookshelf No. 11). 1953, c.1950. Grosset & Dunlap.

--Young Readers Sports Stories. Osborne, Richard N., illus. LC 50-14012. 189 p. illus. 21 cm. (Young readers bookshelf). 1950. Lantern Press.

--Young Readers Wild Life Stories. Geer, Charles Hand (1922-), illus. LC 52-7986. 191 p. illus. 21 cm. (Young readers bookshelf). N.D. Lantern Press.

Furman, Joshua Robert (1932-), ed.

--More Teen-Age Football Stories. LC 74-21888. 154 p. 22cm. 1975. (ISBN 0-8313-0110-4). Lantern Press.

--Teen-Age Basketball Stories. (The Teen-Age Library). N.D. Grosset & Dunlap.

--Teen-Age Basketball Stories. Ricketts, William B., illus. LC 50-5060. 254 p. illus. 22 cm. (Teen-age library). 1949. Lantern Press.

--Teen-Age Gridiron Stories. (The Teen-Age Library). N.D. Grosset & Dunlap.

--Teen-Age Gridiron Stories. Osborne, Richard N., illus. LC 50-12893. 250 p. illus. 21 cm. 1950. Lantern Press.

Furman, Victoria

--Five in a Tent. LC 66-13334. 200p. 22cm. c.1966. Parents Mag. Lib. Ed.

Furneaux, Rupert (1908-)

--The Great Treasure Hunts. 1969. (ISBN 0-8008-3625-1). Taplinger.

Furnell, George

--Left Hand Wood. Lambourne, Nigel (1919-), illus. LC 71-91973. (Illus.). 219 p. 23cm. (Follett merit mystery). 1970, c.1967. (ISBN 0-695-40074-6). Follett Pub. Co.

Furniss, Ruth Pine, Mrs.

--Snow: A Love-Story. LC 29-18542. 248 p. 20 cm. N.D. Harcourt.

Furnivall, F J, jt. auth. see Bland, Edith Nesbit, Mrs.

Furrer, Juerg (1939-)

--Tortoise Island. Stanton, Henry B., ed. Furrer, Juerg (1939-), illus. Huerlimann, Bettina, tr. LC 74-19055. 29cm. 32p. 1975. (ISBN 0-201-02359-8). Addison-Wesley.

Furstenberg, William, retold by.

--Weekly Reader Books Presents The Wizard of Oz. Denslow, William Wallace (1856-1915), illus. LC 84-217302. (Original Author: Lyman Frank Baum, 1856-1919). (Illus.). 45 p. 23cm. c.1984. Weekly Reader Books.

Furth, Dori

--Back in Time for Supper. Weil, Lisl (1910-), illus. LC 47-11446. 27cm. 33p. (gr. 1-3). 1947. David McKay Co.

Furukawa, Mel, jt. auth. see Yolen, Jane Hyatt.

Furukawa, Toshi see Kanzawa, Toshiko, pseud.

Futamata, Eigoro (1932-)

--How Not to Catch a Mouse. Futamata, Eigoro (1932-), illus. LC 70-179981. (Illus.). 43 p. 1972. (ISBN 0-8348-2006-4). (ISBN 0-8348-2006-4). Weatherhill.

Futcher, Jane

--Crush. LC 81-13721. 255 p. 22cm. c.1981. (ISBN 0-316-29749-6). Little, Brown.

Futcher, P. H.

--Giants and Dwarfs. N.D. Harvard University Press.

Futrelle, Jacques

--Thinking Machine: Adventures of a Mastermind. Beck, Charles, illus. (Illus.). (gr. 5-10). 1965 (Four Winds). Schol Bk Serv.

--Thinking Machine: Adventures of a Mastermind. Beck, Charles, illus. (Illus.). (gr. 4-6). 1972 (StarLine). Schol Bk Serv.

Las, F. W.

--The Girl and Her Home. N.D. Houghton Mifflin Co.

Fyleman, Rose, tr. see Fluckiger, Alfred.

Fyleman, Rose Amy (1877-1957)

--The Adventure Club. Watson, A. H., illus. LC 26-16149. 138 p. incl. plates. col. front. 21 cm. c.1926. George H. Doran Company.

--The Doll's House. (Illus.). N.D. Thomas Nelson & Sons.

--The Doll's House. Best, Allena Champlin, Mrs. (1892-1974), illus. Berry, Erick, pseud. LC 31-21430. viii p., 1 l., 99, 1 p. incl. illus., plates. col. front. 21 cm. 1931. Doubleday, Doran & Company, Inc.

--Eight Little Plays for Children. N.D. Doubleday & Co.

--Eight Little Plays for Children. LC 25-7220. 94 p. 21 cm. c.1925. George H. Doran Company.

--Fairies & Chimneys. LC 79-9893. (Children's Literature Reprint Ser.). (gr. 2-5). 1976. (ISBN 0-8486-0005-3). Core Collection.

--Fairies and Chimneys. N.D. Doubleday & Co.

--Fairies and Chimneys. 1920. George H Doran.

--Fairies and Friends. 1926. Double Doran & Co.

--The Fairy Flute. 1923. George H Doran.

--The Fairy Green. 1923. George H Doran.

--Fifty-One New Nursery Rhymes. Burroughes, Dorothy Mary Burroughes, illus. LC 32-289811. viii p., 1 l., 98, 2 p. incl. 1 col. illus., col. plates. 23 x 30 cm. 1932. Doubleday, Doran and Company, Inc.

--Forty Good-Morning Tales. Best, Allena Champlin, Mrs. (1892-1974), illus. Berry, Erick, pseud. LC 29-108863. vi p., 2 l., 121 p. col. front., illus., col. plates. 21 cm. 1929. Doubleday, Doran & Company, Inc.

--Forty Good-Night Tales. Grosvenor, Thelma Cudlipp, illus. LC 24-22818. vi p., 2 l., 11-131 p. col. front., illus., col. plates. 21 cm. c.1924. George H. Doran Company.

--Gay Go up. Merwin, Decie (1894-1961), illus. LC 30-24243. 6 p. l., 3-106 p. incl. front., illus., plates. 21 cm. 1930. Doubleday, Doran & Company, Inc.

--Katy Kruse at the Seashore: The Further Adventures of These Cunning Dolls at the Beach. N.D. David McKay Co.

--The Katy Kruse Dolly Book. LC 27-22201. 22cm. 32p. 1927. Doubleday Doran & Co.

--The Katy Kruse Play Book. Druse, Katy, illus. LC 30-24338. 31p. 1930. David McKay Co.

--Letty: A Study of a Child. LC 27-19638. xii p., 1 l., 15-142 p. incl. front., illus., plates. 21 cm. c.1927. George H. Doran Company.

--A Little Christmas Book. N.D. Doubleday Doran & Co.

--Nine New Plays for Children. Halsey, Eleanor L., illus. LC 35-582. 128 p. incl. front., illus. 19 cm. (Half-title: The "Little theatre" series). 1934. T. Nelson and Sons, Ltd.

--Picture Rhymes from Foreign Lands. Karrick, Valery (1869-1948), illus. N.D. J. B. Lippincott.

--Picture Rhymes from Foreign Lands. Karrik, Valerian Vil'iamovich (1869-1942), illus. LC 35-273109. vii p., 1 l., 70 p. incl. front., illus. 22 cm. 1935. Frederick A. Stokes Company.

--Pipe and Drum. Mountfort, Irene, illus. N.D. J. B. Lippincott.

--A Princess Comes to Our Town. Lindsay, Gertrude, illus. LC 28-28388. 5 p. l., 158 p. incl. illus., plates. col. front. 21 cm. 1928. Doubleday, Doran & Company, Inc.

--The Rainbow Cat. Grosvenor, Thelma Cudlipp, illus. LC 23-17905. 117 p. col. front., illus., col. plates 21 cm. 1923. George H. Doran Company.

--The Rose Fyleman Fairy Book. 1923. George H Doran.

--The Strange Adventures of Captain Marwhopple. LC 32-6660. viii p., 1 l. 166 p. incl. illus., plates. col. front. 21 cm. 1932. Doubleday, Doran & Company, Inc.

--Tea Time Tales. Best, Allena Champlin, Mrs. (1892-1974), illus. Berry, Erick, pseud. LC 30-7798. viii p., 1 l., 246 p. incl. illus., plates. col. front. 21 cm. 1930. Doubleday, Doran & Company, Inc.

Fyleman, Rose Amy (1877-1957), ed.

--A'Piping Again. Mountfort, Irene, illus. N.D. Frederick A. Stokes.

--Bells Ringing: An Anthology of Verse for Young Children. Mountfort, Irene, illus. LC 40-336. viii, 88 p. illus. 19 cm. c.1939. Frederick A. Stokes Company.

--Here We Come A' Piping. LC 37-28505. 5 p. l., 83 p. illus. 19 cm. 1937. Frederick A. Stokes Company.

--Nursery Rhymes from Many Lands. Karrik, Valerian Vil'iamovich (1869-1942), illus. LC 73-118168. (Illus.). 70 p. 21cm. 1971. (ISBN 0-486-22450-3). Dover.

--Pipe & Drum: An Anthology of Verse for Young Children. LC 78-74510. (Illus.). 88 p. 23cm. 1979. (ISBN 0-8486-0010-X). Core Collection Books.

--Pipe & Drum. An Anthology of Verse for Young Children. Mountfort, Irene, illus. LC 72-435. (Illus.). 88 p. 23cm. (Granger index reprint series). 1972. (ISBN 0-8369-6360-1). Books for Libraries Press.

--Pipe and Drum: An Anthology of Verse for Young Children. Mountfort, Irene, illus. 1940. Frederick A. Stokes.

--Round the Mulberry Bush: Being a Book of Stories and Verse for Children from Six to Twelve. LC 28-21059. 192 p. col. front., illus. col. plates. 26 cm. c.1928. Dodd, Mead & Company.

--Sugar and Spice: A Collection of Nursery Rhymes, New and Old. Scott, Janet Laura, illus. LC 36-4918. 3 p. l., 11-61 p. illus. 29 cm. c.1935. Whitman Publishing Company.

Fyleman, Rose Amy (1877-1957), ed.

--Here We Come A'Piping. LC 77-94813. (Illus.). 83 p. 20cm. (Granger poetry library). 1978. (ISBN 0-89609-085-X). Granger Book Co.

Fyleman, Rose Amy (1877-1957) & Wilson, E. M. D.

--Billy Monkey: A True Tale of a Capuchin. Leslie, Cecil, illus. LC 38-2757. xii p., 1 l., 152, 1 p. col. front., illus. 19 cm. 1937. T. Nelson & Sons.

Fyson, Jennifer Grace (1904-)

--Friend Fire and the Dark Wings. Large, Annabel, illus. LC 83-670208. (Illus.). 136 p. 23cm. 1983. (ISBN 0-19-271467-8). Oxford University Press.

--The Journey of the Eldest Son. Ambrus, Victor G., pseud. (1935-), illus. Ambrus, Gyozo Laszlo. LC 67-1021. (Illus.). 214 p. 21cm. 1st U.S. edition. 1967, c.1965. Coward-McCann.

--The Three Brothers of Ur. Ambrus, Victor G., pseud. (1935-), illus. Ambrus, Gyozo Laszlo. LC 67-1014. (Illus.). 254 p. 21cm. 1st U.S. edition. 1967, c.1964. Coward McCann.

Gabel, Rya, tr. see Panova, Vera Fedorovna.

Gaber, Susan

--Favorite Poems for Children Coloring Book. (Illus.). 48p. (Orig.). (ps-3). 1980. Dover.

Gable, J. Harris (1902-), tr. see Feuillet, Octave.

Gabler, Grace

--A Child's Alphabet. Gabler, Grace, illus. LC 47-22539. (Illus.). 22cm. 32p. (Puffin Picture Book: Bk. 46). 1946. Penguin Books.

Gabriel, Gilbert Wolf (1890-)

--The Adventures of Peterkin. Ohrenschall, Helen E., illus. LC 16-16075. 153 p. col. front., illus., col. plates. 24 cm. c.1916. S. Gabriel Sons & Company.

Gabriel, Vera, jt. auth. see Schroeder, Mary N.

Gachet, Jacqueline

--The Ladybug. Gachet, Jacqueline, illus. LC 76-113738. (Illus.). 25 p. 27cm. 1970. (ISBN 0-8415-2011-9). Good Book, Inc.; Distributed by McCall Pub. Co.

Gaidar
--A Tale About a War Secret. 24p. 1975. (ISBN 0-8285-1642-1, Pub. by Progress Pubs USSR). Imported Pubns.
Gaige, Grace (1881-), ed.
--Recitations for Younger Children. LC 27-24176. xviii, 215 p. 19 1/2 cm. 1927. D. Appleton and Company.
--Recitations for Younger Children. LC 78-74816. xviii, 215 p. 21cm. (Granger Poetry Library). 1979. (ISBN 0-89609-134-1). Granger Book Co.
--Recitations: Old and New, for Boys and Girls. LC 24-28790. xxiii, 466 p. 21 cm. 1924. D. Appleton and Company.
--Recitations: Old and New, for Boys and Girls. LC 78-73486. xxiii, 466 p. 20cm. (Granger Poetry Library). 1979. (ISBN 0-89609-112-0). Granger Book Co.
Gail, Otto Willi (1896-)
--By Rocket to the Moon: The Story of Hans Hardt's Miraculous Flight. Gail, Otto Willi (1896-), illus. xi, 303 p. illus. 21 cm. 1950. Dodd, Mead.
--By Rocket to the Moon: The Story of Hans Hardt's Miraculous Flight. Gail, Otto Willi (1896-), illus. LC 31-13233. xi, 303 p. col. front., col. plates. 22 cm. c.1931. Sears Publishing Company, Inc.
Gaines, Charles K.
--Gorgo: A Romance of Old Athens. LC 76-3311. Repr. of 1903 ed (Pub. by Grosset & Dunlap). (gr. 6 up). 1976. (ISBN 0-8265-1203-8). Vanderbilt U Pr.
Gaines, Edith
--Mr. Impossible. 19p. (Stories From the Black History Ser.). N.D. New Day Press.
Gaines, Edith see McCluskey, John.
Gaines, Edith & Smith, Martha
--Jubilee Day: WildFire. 25p. N.D. (ISBN 0-913678-09-0). New Day Press.
Gaines, Ernest J. (1933-)
--A Long Day in November. Bolognese, Donald Alan (1934-), illus. LC 70-147131. (Illus.). 137 p. 22cm. 1971. Dial Press.
Gaines, M. C, ed.
--Picture Stories from the Bible: The New Testament in Full-Color Comic-Strip Form. Cameron, Don, illus. LC 80-51593. (Illus.). 143 p. 27cm. c.1980. (ISBN 0-8108-1422-6). Scarf Press.
--Picture Stories from the Bible: The Old Testament in Full-Color Comic-Strip Form. Cameron, Don, illus. LC 79-66064. (Illus.). 222 p. 26cm. c.1979. (ISBN 0-934386-01-3). Scarf Press.
Gaines, Ruth Louise (1877-)
--Helping France. N.D. E P Dutton.
--Ladies of Grecourt. N.D. E P Dutton.
--Little Light (Lucita). A Child's Story of Old Mexico. Enright, Maginel Wright, illus. LC 13-193371. xii, 99, 1 p. col. front., illus., col. plates. 20 cm. c.1913. Rand. McNally & Company.
--Treasure Flower: A Child of Japan. Gaines, Louise (1877-), illus. 6 p. l., xi-xxviii, 205 p. col. front., illus., plates (part col.) 20 cm. (On verso of half-title: "Little schoolmates" series). c.1916. E. P. Dutton & Company.
--A Village of Picardy. N.D. E P Dutton.
Gaines, Ruth Louise (1877-) & Read, G. W.
--The Village Shield. (Little Schoolmates). N.D. E. P. Dutton & Co.
Gainham, Sara, pseud., see Ames, Rachel.
Gainham, Sara, pseud. (1922-)
--Maculan's Daughter. Ames, Rachel. 1974. (ISBN 0-399-11255-3). G. P. Putnam's Sons.
Gainier-Raymond, Philippe
--The Tangled Web. Ortzen, Len, tr. N.D. Pantheon Books.
Gaither, Bill & Gaither, Gloria
--God Can. Jones, Aletha & Lerner, Sheralyn, illus. (Illus.). (Especially for Children Ser.: Vol. 10). (ps-8). 1977. (ISBN 0-914850-12-1). Impact Tenn.
--God Loves to Talk to Boys While They're Fishin. Jones, Aletha, illus. LC 75-18967. (Illus.). 32p. (Especially for Children Ser.: Vol. 5). (ps-8). 1975. (ISBN 0-914850-52-0). Impact Tenn.
--I'm a Promise. Jones, Aletha, illus. (Illus.). (Especially for Children Ser.: Vol. 8). 1977. (ISBN 0-914850-10-5). Impact Tenn.
--Jesus, I Heard You Had a Big House, Vol. 7. Jones, Aletha, illus. (Illus.). (Especially for Children Ser.). (ps-8). 1977. (ISBN 0-914850-09-1). Impact Tenn.
--Let All the Little Children Praise the Lord. Jones, Aletha & Lerner, Sheralyn, illus. (Illus.). (Especially for Children Ser.: Vol. 12). (ps-8). 1977. (ISBN 0-914850-18-0). Impact Tenn.
--This Is the Day That the Lord Hath Made. Jones, Aletha, illus. (Especially for Children Ser.: Vol. 9). (ps-8). 1977. (ISBN 0-914850-11-3). Impact Tenn.
--This Little Light of Mine. Jones, Aletha, illus. LC 75-18968. (Illus.). 32p. (Especially for Children Ser.: Vol. 6). (ps-8). 1975. (ISBN 0-914850-29-6). Impact Tenn.
Gaither, Frances Ormond Jones, Mrs. (1889-)
--Little Miss Cappo. Woodward, Hildegard (1898-), illus. LC 37-296536. ix p., 1 l., 254 p. incl. illus., plates. 22 cm. 1937. The Macmillan Company.
--The Painted Arrow. Paz, Henry, illus. LC 31-3402. ix p., 1 l., 244 p. incl. illus, plates. col. front. 21 cm. 1931. The Macmillan Company.
--The Scarlet Coat. Stein, Harve (1904-), illus. LC 34-338683. 5 p. l., 205 p. illus. 23 cm. 1934. The Macmillan Company.
Gaither, Gloria, jt. auth. see Gaither, Bill.
Gal, Laszlo (1933-), illus.
--The Moon Painters and Other Estonian Folk Tales. Maas, Selve, tr. 1971. (ISBN 0-670-48832-1). Viking Press.
--Siegfried: The Mighty Warrior. LC 68-1941. (Illus.). 136 p. 29cm. (Young pioneer book). 1967. McGraw-Hill.
Galang, Ricardo C., jt. auth. see Acacio, Arsenio B.
Galbraith, Clare Kearnes (1919-)
--Victor. 1st ed. Commerford, William, illus. LC 73-150054. (Illus.). 48 p. 25cm. 1971. Little, Brown.
Galbraith, Esther E., ed.
--Plays Without Footlights. 358p. 1945. Harcourt, Brace and Co Inc.
Galbraith, Kathryn Osebold
--Come Spring. LC 79-12311. 198 p. 22cm. 1979. (ISBN 0-689-50142-0). Atheneum.
--Katie Did. Ramsey, Ted, illus. LC 82-3981. (Illus.). 32p. (ps-2). 1982. (ISBN 0-689-50237-0, McElderry Bk). Atheneum.
--Something Suspicious. LC 85-4003. p. cm. 1985. (ISBN 0-689-50322-9). Atheneum.
--Spots Are Special!. Dawson, Diane, illus. LC 75-28179. (Illus.). 32 p. 1976. (ISBN 0-689-50038-6). Atheneum.
Galdar, Arkadii Petrovich
--Timur and His Gang. Gay, Zhenya (1906-1978), illus. Voynow, Zina, tr. LC 43-16875. vii, 2 125 p. illus. 21 cm. 1943. C. Scribner's Sons.
Galde, Dorothy A
--Danger Comes to Squirrel Valley. LC 78-24080. (Illus.). 125 p. 17cm. c.1979. (ISBN 0-8024-1175-4). Moody Press.
Galdone, Joanna
--Amber Day: A Very Tall Tale. Galdone, Paul (1914-), illus. LC 77-18179. (Illus.). 40 p. c.1978. (ISBN 0-07-022686-5). McGraw-Hill.
--Gertrude the Goose Who Forgot. Galdone, Paul (1914-), illus. LC 73-19583. (Illus.). lv. (unpaged. 1975. (ISBN 0-531-02735-X). Franklin Watts.
--Honeybee's Party. Galdone, Paul (1914-), illus. (Illus.). 32p. (gr. k-3). 1972. (ISBN 0-531-02550-0). Watts.
--The Little Girl and the Big Bear. Galdone, Paul (1914-), illus. LC 80-13853. (Illus.). 40 p. c.1980. (ISBN 0-395-29029-5). Houghton Mifflin/Clarion Books.
Galdone, Joanna, retold by.
--The Tailypo: A Ghost Story. Galdone, Paul (1914-), illus. LC 77-23289. 26cm. 32p. c.1977. (ISBN 0-8164-3191-4). Seabury Press.
Galdone, Paul, jt. auth. see Fife, Dale Odile.
Galdone, Paul, jt. auth. see Goodman, George Jerome Waldo.
Galdone, Paul, jt. auth. see Leverich, Kathleen.
Galdone, Paul (1914-), retold by see Aesopus.
Galdone, Paul (1914-), ed. see Grimm, Jakob Ludwig Karl.
Galdone, Paul (1914-), ed. see Grimm, Jakob Ludwig Karl (1785-1863) & Grimm, Wilhelm Karl.
Galdone, Paul, jt. ed. see Jacobs, Joseph.
Galdone, Paul (1914-), retold by see The, Three Bears.
Galdone, Paul (1914-), retold by see Three Little Pigs.
Galdone, Paul (1914-)
--Cat Goes Fiddle-I-Fee. Galdone, Paul (1914-), illus. LC 85-2686. (Illus.). 40 p. 20cm. c.1985. (ISBN 0-89919-336-6). Clarion Books.
--The First Seven Days: The Story of the Creation from Genesis. Galdone, Paul (1914-), illus. 1962. Crowell.
--The Gingerbread Boy. Galdone, Paul (1914-), illus. (ps-1). 1983. Houghton.
--The Gingerbread Boy. Galdone, Paul (1914-), illus. LC 74-11461. (Illus.). 40 p. 1975. (ISBN 0-8164-3132-9). Seabury Press.
--The Greedy Old Fat Man: An American Folk Tale. Galdone, Paul (1914-), illus. LC 83-2057. (Illus.). 32p. (ps-3). 1983. (ISBN 0-89919-188-6, Clarion). HM.
--Little Tuppen: An Old Tale. Galdone, Paul (1914-), illus. LC 67-1646. (Illus.). 20cm. 32p. (ps-3). 1967. (ISBN 0-395-28804-5, Clarion). Seabury Press.
--The Magic Porridge Pot. Galdone, Paul (1914-), illus. 1976. Houghton Mifflin.
--The Magic Porridge Pot. Galdone, Paul (1914-), illus. LC 76-3531. (Illus.). 32 p. 20cm. c.1976. (ISBN 0-8164-3173-6). Seabury Press.
--The Moving Adventures of Old Dame Trot and Her Comical Cat. Galdone, Paul (1914-), illus. LC 72-3611. (Illus.). 32 p. 1973. (ISBN 0-07-022692-X). McGraw-Hill.
--Old Woman & Her Pig. Galdone, Paul (1914-), illus. (gr. k-3). 1961. (ISBN 0-07-022721-7, GB). McGraw.
--The Old Woman and Her Pig. Galdone, Paul (1914-), illus. LC 59-14958. (Illus.). 32p. 19 x 23cm. 1960. Whittlesey House.
--Paddy the Penguin. Galdone, Paul (1914-), illus. 32p. 1959. Thomas Y. Crowell.
--The Strange Servant. LC 77-4563. p. cm. c.1977. (ISBN 0-394-83453-4). (ISBN 0-394-93453-9). Knopf.
--The Teeny-Tiny Woman. Galdone, Paul (1914-), illus. LC 84-4311. (Illus.). 32p. (ps-3). 1984. (ISBN 0-89919-270-X, Clarion). HM.
--The Turtle and the Monkey. LC 82-9596. p. cm. 1983, c.1982. (ISBN 0-89919-145-2). Clarion Books.
Galdone, Paul (1914-), retold by.
--The Amazing Pig: An Old Hungarian Tale. Galdone, Paul (1914-), illus. LC 80-16990. (Illus.). 32 p. c.1981. (ISBN 0-395-29101-1). Houghton Mifflin/Clarion Books.
--Androcles & the Lion. Galdone, Paul (1914-), illus. LC 75-81606. (Illus.). 39 p. 1970. McGraw-Hill.
--Cinderella. Galdone, Paul (1914-), illus. LC 78-7614. (Original Author: Charles Perrault, 1628-1703). (Illus.). 40 p. 29cm. c.1978. (ISBN 0-07-022684-9). McGraw-Hill.
--The Elves and the Shoemaker. Galdone, Paul (1914-), illus. LC 83-14979. c.1984. (ISBN 0-89919-226-2). Clarion Books.
--The Hare and The Tortoise: The House That Jack Built. Galdone, Paul (1914-), illus. 1962. (ISBN 0-07-022713-6). McGraw Hill Book Company.
--Henny Penny. Galdone, Paul (1914-), illus. (gr. k-2). 1973. Houghton Mifflin.
--Henny Penny. Galdone, Paul (1914-), illus. (Illus.). 32 p. 1968. Seabury Press.
--The History of Mother Twaddle & the Marvelous Achievements of Her Son Jack. Galdone, Paul (1914-), illus. LC 73-9726. (Illus.). 1 v. (unpaged). 29cm. 1974. (ISBN 0-8164-3112-4). Seabury Press.
--History of Simple Simon. Galdone, Paul (1914-), illus. (gr. k-6). 1966. (ISBN 0-07-022706-3). (ISBN 0-07-022707-1). McGraw.
--House That Jack Built. Galdone, Paul (1914-), illus. LC 61-7577. (Illus.). 26cm. 32p. (gr. k-3). 1961. (ISBN 0-07-022719-5, GB). McGraw.
--The House That Jack Built. Galdone, Paul (1914-), illus. N.D. (ISBN 0-07-022718-7). McGraw-Hill Book Company.
--The Life of Jack Sprat, His Wife & His Cat. Galdone, Paul (1914-), illus. LC 69-16254. (Illus.). 40 p. 1969. McGraw Hill.
--The Little Red Hen. Galdone, Paul (1914-), illus. (gr. k-2). 1973. Houghton Mifflin.
--The Little Red Hen. Galdone, Paul (1914-), illus. LC 72-97770. (Illus.). 40 p. 20cm. 1973. Seabury Press. **Award: (ALA).**
--Little Tom Tucker. Galdone, Paul (1914-), illus. LC 78-116664. (Illus.). 39 p. N.D. McGraw-Hill.
--The Monkey and the Crocodile: A Jataka Tale from India. Galdone, Paul (1914-), illus. (gr. k-3). 1969. Houghton Mifflin.
--The Monkey and the Crocodile: A Jataka Tale from India. Galdone, Paul (1914-), illus. LC 78-79939. (Illus.). 32 p. 30cm. 1969. Seabury Press.
--The Monster & the Tailor: A Ghost Story. Galdone, Paul (1914-), illus. LC 82-1246. (Illus.). 32 p. 26cm. c.1982. (ISBN 0-89919-116-9). Clarion Books.
--Obedient Jack. Galdone, Paul (1914-), illus. LC 72-131155. (Illus.). 27cm. 40p. (gr. k-3). 1971. (ISBN 0-531-01970-5). Watts.
--Old Mother Hubbard & Her Dog. Galdone, Paul (1914-), illus. (Illus.). (gr. k-3). 1960. (ISBN 0-07-022723-3, GB). McGraw. **Award: (ALA).**
--Puss in Boots. Galdone, Paul (1914-), illus. LC 75-25505. (Illus.). 32 p. 29cm. c.1976. (ISBN 0-8164-3159-0). Seabury Press.
--Rumpelstiltskin. Galdone, Paul (1914-), illus. LC 84-12741. (Illus.). 32p. 1st U.S. edition. (ps-3). 1985. (ISBN 0-89919-266-1, Clarion). HM.
--Shadrach, Meshach & Abednego. Galdone, Paul (1914-), illus. (Illus.). (gr. 1-4). 1965. (ISBN 0-07-022708-X). McGraw. **Award: (ALA).**
--The Three Billy Goats Gruff. Galdone, Paul (1914-), illus. LC 72-85338. (Illus.). 32p. (ps-3). 1973. (ISBN 0-395-28812-6, Clarion). HM.
--The Three Wishes. Galdone, Paul (1914-), illus. LC 61-15909. (Illus.). 32p. (gr. k-3). 1961. (ISBN 0-07-022714-4, GB). McGraw. **Award: (ALA).**
--What's in Fox's Sack?. An Old English Tale. Galdone, Paul (1914-), illus. LC 81-10251. (Illus.). 32 p. c.1982. (ISBN 0-89919-062-6). Clarion Books.
--The Wise Fool. Galdone, Paul (1914-), illus. LC 67-20226. (Based on a Tale from the Third Book of Pantagruel by Francois Rabelais). (Illus.). 29cm. 32p. 1968. Random House.
Gale, Agnes Spofford Cook, Mrs., adapted by.
--The Story of Ulysses, for Boys and Girls. LC 25-5344. (Illus.). 153p. 19cm. 1897. Public-School Publishing Co.

Gale, Agnes Spofford Cook, Mrs., retold by see Homerus.

Gale, Agnes Spofford Cook, Mrs., jt. ed. see McMurry, Lida Brown, Mrs.

Gale, Agnes Spofford Cook, Mrs. & Homerus
--The Story of Ulysses: For Boys and Girls. LC 25-5344. 2 p. l., 7-153, viii p. illus. 19 cm. 1897. Public-School Publishing Co.
Gale, Elizabeth see Gale, Mary Elizabeth.
Gale, Elizabeth Wright
--I'm Glad. Baldwin, Marilyn, illus. LC 69-18148. (Illus.). 24 p. 21cm. 1969. (ISBN 0-8170-0422-X). Judson Press.
--My Two Families. Woodend, James, illus. LC 69-18149. (Illus.). 24 p. 21cm. 1969. Judson Press.
Gale, Helen Mary (1912-)
--Jimmy Wins a Prize. Ilona, pseud., illus. Segner, Ellen. LC 47-16341. (Illus.). 32p. 22 x 19cm. 1946. John Martin's House, Inc.
--Minnie the Moo. Stearns, Sharon (1912-), illus. LC 66-15968. (Illus.). 16 p. (Read-aloud picture book). 1967, c.1966. Follett Pub. Co.
Gale, Leah
--Alfie: The Playful Elephant: Darien, Elsie, illus. LC 66-15964. (Illus.). 16 p. (Read-aloud picture book). 1967, c.1966. Follett Pub. Co.
--The Alphabet from A to Z. Blake, Vivienne, illus. LC 42-24232. 42p. illus. 20 1/2 x 17 1/2cm. (On cover: The/Little Golden Library. 3). 1942. Simon & Schuster.
--The Animals of Farmer Jones. Freund, Rudolf (1915-1969), illus. LC 42-24235. (Illus.). 42p. 21 x 18cm. (A Little Golden Bk.). 1942. Simon and Schuster.
--The Animals of Farmer Jones. New ed. Scarry, Richard McClure (1919-), illus. LC 53-4414. unpaged. illus. 21cm. (Little golden book, 211). 1953. Simon and Schuster.
--Animals of Farmer Jones. Scarry, Richard McClure (1919-), illus. (ps-1). 1970. (ISBN 0-307-60282-6, Golden Pr). Western Pub.
--Hurdy-Gurdy Holiday. 1st ed. Latham, Barbara (1896-), illus. LC 42-25660. (Illus.). 48p. 31 x 25cm. 1942. Harper & Brothers.
Gale, Leah, ed.
--Favorite Bedtime Stories. Elliott, Miss, illus. LC 43-15364. 52 p. illus. (part col.) 28 1/2 x 22 1/2 cm. c.1943. Artist and Writers Guild, Inc., Random House, Distributors.
--Favorite Tales of Long Ago. Elliott, Miss, illus. LC 43-153662. 93 p. incl. col. front., illus. (part col.) 28 1/2 x 23 cm. 1943. Artists and Writers Guild, Inc., Random House, Distributors.
--Nursery Songs. Malvern, Corinne (1905-1956), illus. (Little Golden Book: 7). 1942. Simon and Schuster.
Gale, Martha
--The Lost Lamb. N.D. American Tract Society.
Gale, Martin, pseud., see Klaw, Barbara Van Doren.
Gale, Mary Elizabeth
--Circus Babies. McKee, John Dukes, illus. 9 cm. 112p. (gr. 2-4). N.D. Rand McNally & Co.
--Ellen Drew. Westmacott, Bernard (1887-), illus. LC 38-24739. 6 p. l., 3-242 p. incl. front., plates., 21 cm. c.1938. G. P. Putnam's Sons.
--How the Animals Came to the Circus. Carr, Warner, illus. N.D. Rand McNally.
--Julia Valeria. (Illus.). (gr. 7-10). 1951. (ISBN 0-399-20109-2). Putnam.
--Katrina Von Ost and the Silver Rose. De Angeli, Marguerite Lofft, Mrs. (1889-), illus. LC 34-4342. 4 p. l., 3-294 p. front., illus. 21 cm. c.1934. G. P. Putnam's Sons.
--Little Sonny Sunfish. Riley, Garada Clark, illus. LC 24-172474. 64 p. incl. col. front., illus. (part col.) 20 cm. c.1923. Rand, McNally & Company.
--Seven Beads of Wampum. Lawson, Robert (1892-1957), illus. LC 36-10942. vii, 298 p. incl. front., illus. 21 cm. c.1936. G. P. Putnam's Sons.
--The Winged Boat. Stein, Harve (1904-), illus. LC 42-18495. 4 p. l., 3-190 p. col. front., illus. (part col.) 21 cm. 1942. G. P.Putnam's Sons.
Gale, Mary H (1902-)
--The Bantling. 1st ed. LC 52-2644. 170 p. 21 cm. 1952. Pageant Press.
Gale, Zona (1874-1938)
--The Christmas Party. Latham, Jean Lee (1902-), adapted by. 1930. Dramatic Publishing Company.
--Miss Lulu Bett. Kelsey, Lella B., ed. (Appleton Modern Literature Ser.). N.D. Appleton-Century-Crofts.

Galea'i Fa'apouli, Sano M
--My Days Are Made of Butterflies. Martin, William Ivan, Jr. (1916-), adapted by. Herman, Victor J. (1919-), illus. LC 77-109208. (Illus.). 32 p. 17cm. (Bill Martin instant reader). c.1970. (ISBN 0-03-084599-8). Holt, Rinehart and Winston.
Galeron, Henri
--When. Larmoth, Jeanine, adapted by. LC 77-73525. (Illus.). (gr. 3 up). 1977. (ISBN 0-8252-9267-0). Quist.
Galeron, Henri, jt. auth. see Goldthwaite, John.
Galgano, Ruth H
--The Wishing Star. 1st. ed. LC 52-14551. 88p. 21cm. 1952. Pageant Press.
Galinsky, Ellen (1942-)
--The Baby Cardinal. Galinsky, Ellen (1942-) photos by. LC 77-5083. (Illus.). 32 p. c.1977. (ISBN 0-399-20596-9). Putnam.
--Catbird. Galinsky, Ellen (1942-), photos by. LC 71-166589. (Illus.). 48 p. 1971. Coward, McCann & Geoghegan.
Gall, Alice Crew, Mrs. (1878-1949)
--Mary and Her Kitchen Garden. Stanley, Lee Wright, illus. LC 18-17668. ix 1 1., 11-52 , 1 1, col. fron., illus., col. plates. 24. 1917. George H Doran.
--Mother McGrew and Bartholomew Bull Frog. Stanley, Lee Wright (1882-), illus. (The Mother Mcgrew Bks.). N.D. Cupples & Leon Co.
--Mother McGrew and Caroline Crow. Stanley, Lee Wright (1882-), illus. (The Mother McGrew Bks.). N.D. Cupples & Leon Co.
--Mother McGrew and Daniel Donkey. Stanley, Lee Wright (1882-), illus. (The Mother McGrew Bks.). N.D. Cupples & Leon Co.
--Mother McGrew and Gerald Giraffe. Stanley, Lee Wright (1882-), illus. (The Mother McGrew Bks.). N.D. Cupples & Leon Co.
--Mother McGrew and Kate Kangaroo. Stanley, Lee Wright (1882-), illus. (The Mother McGrew Bks.). N.D. Cupples & Leon Co.
--Mother McGrew and Oliver Owl. Stanley, Lee Wright (1882-), illus. (The Mother McGrew Bks.). N.D. Cupples & Leon Co.
--Mother McGrew and Susanna Snail. Stanley, Lee Wright (1882-), illus. (The Mother McGrew Bks.). N.D. Cupples & Leon Co.
--Mother McGrew and Tommy Turkey. Stanley, Lee Wright (1882-), illus. (The Mother McGrew Bks.). N.D. Cupples & Leon Co.
--Mother McGrew and William Woodpecker. Stanley, Lee Wright (1882-), illus. (The Mother McGrew Bks.). N.D. Cupples & Leon Co.
Gall, Alice Crew, Mrs. (1878-1949) & Crew, Fleming H (1882-)
--The Adventures of Toby Spaniel. Carlson, George L., illus. LC 28-236785. 6 p. l., 3-172, 2 p. col. front., illus., col. plates. 23 cm. 1928. Duffield & Company.
--All the Year Round. N.D. Oxford University Press.
--All the Year Round. Bostelmann, Else, illus. LC 63-22755. (Illus.). (gr. k-3). 1944. (ISBN 0-8098-1012-3). Walck.
--Bushy Tail. Bostelmann, Else, illus. LC 41-52061. 164 p. incl. col. front. illus. (part col.) 24 cm. c.1941. Oxford University Press.
--Each in His Way: Stories of Famous Animals. Wiese, Kurt (1887-1974), illus. LC 37-28691. 180 p. incl. front., illus., plates. 23 cm. c.1937. Oxford University Press.
--Flat Tail. Kihn, W. Langdon, illus. LC 35-22959. 126, 1 p. incl. col. front., illus., col. plates. 24 cm. c.1935. Oxford University Press.
--Flat Tail. Kihn, W. Langdon, illus. 1935p. 1928. Walck.
--Here & There & Everywhere. Hogner, Nils (1893-1970), illus. LC 50-6620. 56 p. col. illus. 17 cm. 1950. Oxford University Press.
--Little Black Ant. N.D. Henry Z. Walck Inc.
--Little Black Ant. Torrey, Helen (1901-), illus. 128 p. incl. front., illus. 24 cm. c.1936. Oxford University Press.
--Ringtail. LC 58-12900. (Illus.). 21 cm. 119p. 1958. Henry Z. Walck Inc.
--Ringtail. Reid, James (1907-), illus. LC 33-24919. 119, 1 p. incl. front., illus. 24 cm. c.1933. Oxford University Press.
--The Royal Mimkin. Masline, Camille, illus. LC 34-29561. 128 p. incl. front. illus. 24 cm. 1934. Oxford University Press.
--Splasher. LC 45-977313. 136 p. illus. (part col.) 21 cm. 1945. Oxford University Press.
--The Top of the World. Hogner, Nils (1893-1970), illus. LC 39-25150. 110 p. incl. front., illus., plates. 24 cm. c.1939. Oxford University Press.
--Wagtail. Wiese, Kurt (1887-1974), illus. LC 32-200502. 4 p. l., 131, 1 p., 1 l., front., illus. 24 cm. c.1932. Oxford University Press.
--Wagtail. Wiese, Kurt (1887-1974), illus. N.D. Walck.
--Winter Flight. Hogner, Nils (1893-1970), illus. LC 49-8198. 108 p. illus. 24 cm. 1949. Oxford Univ. Press.
Gallagher, Elizabeth Lucy (1870-) & Peroni, Carlo, eds.
--Irish Songs and Airs Arranged for Children to Play and Sing. LC 36-364695. 55 p. 31 cm. 1936. E. L. Gallagher & Company.
Gallagher, Louise Barnes
--Frills and Thrills: The Career of a Young Fashion Designer. Cralick, Jeva, illus. (Dodd, Mead Career Bks.). N.D. Dodd, Mead & Co.
--Mary Bray, Fashion Designer. LC 45-5122. 5 p. l., 210 p. 19 1/2 cm. (Career books). 1945. Dodd, Mead & Company.
Gallagher, Louise Barnes & Hyndman, Jane Andrews Lee (1912-1978)
--Buttons and Beaux. Wyndham, Lee, pseud. LC 53-10611. 276p. 21cm. (Career books). 1953. Dodd, Mead.
Galland, Antonio (1646-1715), tr. see Dixon, E.
Gallant, Kathryn
--The Flute Player of Beppu. Wiese, Kurt (1887-1974), illus. LC 60-5677. (Illus.). 43 p. 21cm. c.1960. Coward-McCann.
--Jonathan Plays With The Wind. 1958. (ISBN 0-8382-0391-4, Cadmus Books). E. M. Hale And Company.
--Jonathan Plays with the Wind. Ramirez, Carl, illus. LC 58-10190. (Illus.). unpaged. 21cm. c.1958. Coward McCann.
Gallaway, Ruth Kinser (1918-)
--Kay Karls. LC 54-15099. 138p. 20cm. 1953. White Wing Pub. House & Press.
Gallaz, Christopher & Innocenti, Roberto
--Rose Blanche. Innocenti, Roberto, illus. Coventry, Martha & Graglia, Richard, trs. 1985. Creative Education. **Awards: (MLB); (ALA).**
Gallegos, Albert M
--Wise Owl of the Ballet. LC 77-17860. p. cm. 1977. (ISBN 0-87695-206-6). Aurora Publishers.
Galler, Helga
--Little Nerino. Galler, Melga, illus. LC 82-183080. (Illus.). 24 p. c.1982. (ISBN 0-907234-13-5). Neugebauer Press.
Gallery, Daniel V. (1901-1977)
--Cap'n Fatso. 192p. 1969. Norton & Co.
--Stand by-y-y to Start Engines. 218 p. 22cm. 1966. W. W. Norton.
Gallery, Douglas C.
--Country Cousin. N.D. Vantage Press.
Gallico, Paul William (1897-1976)
--The Abandoned. 1950. Borzoi Books.
--The Boy Who Invented the Bubble Gun. 272p. 1974. (ISBN 0-440-01789-0). Delacorte Press.
--The Day Jean-Pierre Joined the Circus. Fiammenghi, Gioia (1929-), illus. LC 69-17353. (Illus.). 74 p. 24cm. 1969. Watts.
--The Day Jean-Pierre Was Pignapped. Dulieu, Jean, pseud. (1921-), illus. Van Oort, Jan. LC 65-18120. 44p. illus. (pt. col.) 27cm. 1st U.S. edition. 1965, c.1964. Doubleday.
--Day Jean-Pierre Went Round the World. Fiammenghi, Gioia (1929-), illus. (Illus.). (gr. 1-3). 1965. (ISBN 0-385-07766-1). Doubleday.
--The Day Jean-Pierre Went Round the World. Fiammenghi, Gioia (1929-), illus. LC 66-154148. (Illus.). N.D. (ISBN 0-385-06437-3). Doubleday.
--The Day the Guinea Pig Talked. Dulieu, Jean, pseud. (1921-), illus. Van Oort, Jan. LC 64-11181. 27cm. 44p. N.D. Doubleday & Co.
--The House That Wouldn't Go Away. LC 79-53599. xi, 234 p. 22cm. c.1979. (ISBN 0-440-03496-5). (ISBN 0-440-03497-3). Delacorte Press.
--Ludmila. Lonette, Reisie Dominee (1924-), illus. LC 59-8002. (Illus.). 63p. 18cm. Orig. Title: Ludmila, a Legend of Lichtenstein, 1955. 1959. Doubleday.
--Mrs. Arris Goes to Moscow. 224p. 1975. Delacorte Press.
--The Small Miracle. Lonette, Reisie Dominee (1924-), illus. LC 52-10401. 58 p. illus. 20 cm. 1st U.S. edition. 1952. Doubleday.
--The Snow Goose. 1941. Borzoi Books.
--Snow Goose. (gr. 9 up). 1941. (ISBN 0-394-44593-7). Knopf.
--The Zoo Gang. 1971. (ISBN 0-698-10417-X). Coward.
Gallienne, Eva Le see Andersen, Hans Christian.
Gallienne, Eva Le see Ewald, Carl.
Gallo, Donald R, ed.
--Sixteen: Short Stories by Outstanding Writers for Young Adults. LC 84-3250. xii, 179 p. 22cm. c.1984. (ISBN 0-385-29346-1). Delacorte Press.
Gallo, Giovanni
--The Lazy Beaver. Samsa, Ermanno, illus. LC 82-18937. p. cm. 1983. (ISBN 0-399-20965-4). Philomel Books.
Gallo, Valerie
--Guess Who. Gallo, Valerie, illus. (Illus.). 10 halftones.24p. (Orig.). (Childrens Ser). (gr. 3 up). 1969. (ISBN 0-911718-14-1). Malter-Westerfield.
Gallup, Lucy
--Independent Bluebird. Darling, Louis, Jr. (1916-1970), illus. (Illus.). 22cm. 61p. (gr. 3-6). 1959. Morrow.
--Spinning Wings. Alexandroff, Dimitri, illus. LC 56-9715. 95p. illus. 21cm. 1956. Morrow.
Galon, Anne see Golon, Sergeanne.
Galsworthy, John (1867-1933)
--Awakening. Sauter, R. H., illus. LC 20-20951. 63, 1 p. col. front., illus. (part col) 26 cm. c.1920. C. Scribner's Sons.
Galt, Denham
--The Bear That Had No Bump of Locality. Kirkham, Bettie, illus. (Illus.). 1983. (ISBN 0-533-05290-4). Vantage.
Galt, Thomas Franklin, Jr. (1908-)
--Peter Zenger, Fighter for Freedom. Ray, Ralph (1920-1952), illus. LC 51-13010. 242 p. illus. 21 cm. 1951. Crowell.
--The Rise of the Thunderer. Mackey, John, illus. LC 54-5537. 196p. illus. 21cm. 1954. Crowell.
--Seven Days from Sunday. Freeman, Don (1908-1978), illus. (Illus.). (gr. 5 up). 1956. (ISBN 0-690-72879-4). T Y Crowell.
--Volcano. Ray, Ralph (1920-1952), illus. LC 46-3355. 4 p. l., 102 p. incl. front., illus. 24 1/2 cm. 1946. C. Scribner's Sons.
Galuski, Dawn
--A Fairy Tale for Kelly. Kuo, Anna, illus. (Illus.). 1977. (ISBN 0-533-02816-7). Vantage.
Galvean, Thelma
Poppy, Patchy & the Magic Star. Brown, Pat, illus. LC 75-41885. (Illus.). (ps-3). 1976. (ISBN 0-916542-00-9). (ISBN 0-916542-01-7). NELP.
Gambill, Henrietta (1912-), ed. see Hayes, Wanda.
Gambill, Henrietta, ed. see Shelton, Ingrid.
Gambill, Henrietta (1912-)
--Happy Times with the Lollipop Dragon. Sparks, Judith, ed. Peters, Luther J., illus. LC 81-86701. (Illus.). 24p. (Orig.). (Happy Day Bks.). (ps-3). 1982. (ISBN 0-87239-538-3). Standard Pub.
Gamec, Hazel S.
--The Magic Pencil Counting Book. Gamec, Hazel S., illus. (Illus.). 12p. 1980. (ISBN 0-938042-00-9). Printek.
Gamerman, Martha (1941-) & Wallner, Alexandra (1946-)
--Trudy's Straw Hat. LC 76-25864. (Illus.). 32 p. c.1977. (ISBN 0-517-52846-0). Crown Publishers.
Gamm, David Bernard (1948-)
--Child's Play: 15 Scripture Passages Arranged for Dramatic Presentation by Children in Grades Three Through Eight. LC 78-51069. (Illus.). 95 p. 28cm. c.1978. (ISBN 0-87793-150-X). Ave Maria Press.
Gammell, Stephen
--And Then the Mouse ... Three Stories. Hall, Malcolm (1945-), illus. LC 79-19411. (Illus.). 61 p. 21cm. c.1980. (ISBN 0-590-07618-3). Four Winds Press.
--Git Along, Old Scudder. Gammell, Stephen, illus. LC 82-13996. p. cm. c.1983. (ISBN 0-688-01674-X). Lothrop, Lee & Shepard Books.
--Once Upon MacDonald's Farm. Gammell, Stephen, illus. LC 80-23956. (Illus.). 32 p. 21cm. c.1981. (ISBN 0-590-07792-9). Four Winds Press.
--Once Upon MacDonald's Farm. Gammell, Stephen, illus. LC 84-29356. (Illus.). 32 p. 21cm. 1985, c.1981. (ISBN 0-02-737210-3). Four Winds Press.
--The Story of Mr. and Mrs. Vinegar. Gammell, Stephen, illus. LC 81-12347. (Illus.). 32 p. 17cm. c.1982. (ISBN 0-688-00889-5). Lothrop, Lee & Shepard.
--Wake-up, Bear-It's Christmas!. Gammell, Stephen, illus. LC 81-5019. (Illus.). 32 p. 26cm. c.1981. (ISBN 0-688-00692-2). (ISBN 0-688-00693-0). Lothrop, Lee & Shepard Books.
--Wake Up, Bear- It's Christmas!. Gammell, Stephen, illus. LC 84-4923. 1984, c.1981. (ISBN 0-14-050475-3). Puffin Books.
Gammell, Stephen, jt. auth. see McIlwraith, Maureen Mollie Hunter McVeigh.
Gammon, David J.
--The Mystery of Monster Lake. Davies, Frank, illus. LC 62-20652. 156 p. illus. 20 cm. (Secret circle mysteries, no. 1). c.1962. Little, Brown.
--The Secret of Spaniards Rock. Wheeler, William, illus. LC 64-10555. 158 p. illus. 20 cm. (Secret circle mysteries, no. 10). 1964, c.1963. Little, Brown.
Gammond, Peter (1925-)
--The Magic Flute. LC 79-67162. (Master Works of Opera Ser.). N.D. (ISBN 0-382-06312-0). Silver.
Gamoran, Mamie Goldsmith, Mrs. (1900-)
--Hillel's Happy Holidays. Gezari, Temina Nimtzowitz, illus. LC 39-25040. xv, 205 p. illus. 23 cm. (Union graded series, edited by E. Gamoran). 1939. The Union of American Hebrew Congregations.
Gampert, John, illus.
--Return of the Jedi. LC 83-60019. (Illus.). 16p. (Pop-Up Bks.). (gr. 1-5). 1983. (ISBN 0-394-86016-0). (ISBN 0-394-86016-0). Random.
Gandolfo, C., illus.
--Jesus in the Gospel. Daughters of St. Paul LC 80-69. (Illus.). 289 p. 25cm. c.1980. St. Paul Editions.
Ganguli, Kisari Mohan, tr. see Seeger, Elizabeth.
Gann, Ernest Kellogg (1910-)
--Brain 2000. LC 79-7048. 372 p. 22cm. 1980. (ISBN 0-385-14393-1). Doubleday.
Gannett, Ruth Chrisman Arens, jt. auth. see Bailey, Carolyn Sherwin.
Gannett, Ruth Stiles (1923-)
--The Dragons of Blueland. Gannett, Ruth Chrisman Arens (1896-1979), illus. 1951. Random House, Inc.
--Elmer and the Dragon. Gannett, Ruth Chrisman Arens (1896-1979), illus. (Illus.). 1951. Random House Inc.
--Katie and the Sad Noise. Simmons, Ellie, illus. LC 61-7767. (Illus.). unpaged. 24cm. 1961. Random House.
--My Father's Dragon. Gannett, Ruth Chrisman Arens (1896-1979), illus. LC 48-6527. 86 p. illus., col. map (on lining-papers) 21 cm. 1948. Random House. **Award: (JNM).**
--The Wonderful House-Boat-Train. Eichenberg, Fritz (1901-), illus. LC 49-11981. 63 p. illus. 22 cm. 1949. Random House.
Gannon, Robert Haines (1931-)
--Great Survival Adventures. Cohen, Gil, illus. LC 73-3691. (Illus.). 149 p. 22cm. 1973. (ISBN 0-394-82600-0). (ISBN 0-394-82600-0). Random House.
Gannon, W., ed. see Mother Goose.
Gano
--Grandpa's Carlie: Or, the Young Soldier. Gand, illus. (Illus.). 152p. N.D. American Tract Society.
Gans, Manfred & Torah Umesorach; National Society for Hebrew Day Schools
--Yeshiva Children Write Poetry: From the Heart ... We Sing : a Collection of Poems Published Under the Auspices of Torah Umesorah, the National Society for Hebrew Day Schools, the National Conference of Yeshiva Principals, and the American Jewish Museum of Art and Culture. LC 76-376138. (Illus.). xiii, 145 p. 26cm. c.1976. (ISBN 0-88482-742-9). Hebrew Pub. Co.
Gans, Margaret (1916-)
--Pam and Pam. Gans, Margaret (1916-), illus. LC 76-79582. (Illus.). 32 p. 25cm. 1969. (ISBN 0-516-03564-9). Childrens Press.
--Three Presents for Jamie. Gans, Margaret (1916-), illus. LC 72-79581. (Illus.). 32 p. 25cm. 1969. Childrens Press.
Gans, Roma (1894-)
--Birds at Night. Aliki, pseud. (1929-), illus. Brandenberg, Aliki Liacouras. LC 68-11062. 33p. illus. 21 x 23cm. 1968. T. Y. Crowell.
--The Wonder of Stones. Berg, Joan, pseud. (1942-), illus. Victor, Joan Berg. LC 63-15087. 1 v. (unpaged) illus. (part col.) 21 x 23 cm. (Let's-read-and-find-out books). 1963. Crowell.
Gant, Elizabeth, ed. see Irving, Washington.
Gant, Elizabeth & Gant, Katherine, eds.
--Little Red Riding Hood. Aloise, Frank E., illus. LC 69-10613. (Illus.). 45 p. 29cm. 1969. Abingdon Press.
Gant, Katherine, jt. ed. see Gant, Elizabeth.
Gant, Katherine, ed. see Irving, Washington.
Gant, Phyllis, pseud., see Hill, Phyllis.
Gant, Phyllis, pseud. (1922-)
--Islands. Hill, Phyllis. LC 74-190645. 288 p. 23cm. 1973. (ISBN 0-340-16536-7). Hodder and Stoughton.
Gant, Roland
--French Fairy Tales. Morris, Patricia, illus. Morris, Patricia, tr. 1956. Dufour.
--French Folk & Fairy Tales. Takakjian, Portia, illus. LC 63-15570. 192 p. illus. 22 cm. (Folk and fairy tales from many lands). 1963, c.1956. Putnam.
Ganton, Doris L. (1931-)
--Lucky, the Horse That Nobody Wanted. LC 77-357200. (Illus.). 143 p. 19cm. c.1976. (ISBN 0-919654-56-8). Hancock House Publishers.
Gantos, Jack, pseud., see Gantos, John Bryan Jr..
Gantos, Jack, pseud. (1951-)
--Rotten Ralph. Gantos, John Bryan Jr.. Rubel, Leslie, illus. LC 75-34101. p. cm. 1976. (ISBN 0-395-24276-2). Houghton Mifflin.
--Rotten Ralph's Rotten Christmas. Gantos, John Bryan Jr.. Rubel, Nicole (1953-), illus. LC 84-644. (Illus.). 32p. (ps-3). 1984. (ISBN 0-395-35380-7). HM.
--Sleepy Ronald. Gantos, John Bryan Jr.. Rubel, Nicole (1953-), illus. LC 76-13599. (Illus.). 30 p. 1976. (ISBN 0-395-24743-8). Houghton Mifflin.
--Willy's Raiders. Gantos, John Bryan Jr.. Rubel, Nicole (1953-), illus. LC 79-5264. (Illus.). 33 p. 24cm. c.1980. (ISBN 0-8193-1015-8) (ISBN 0-8193-1016-6). Parents Magazine Press.

AUTHOR INDEX GARIS, HOWARD

--Maxie Searching for Her Parents: Or, The Mystery in Australian Waters. LC 32-140202. 2 p. l., 204 p. front. 19 1/2 cm. (Her Maxie series). c.1932. Cupples & Leon Company.

Gardner, Elva Babcock

--Mohanraj: A High-Caste Boy of India. Munson, Harold W. (1920-), illus. LC 54-9981. 147p. illus. 23cm. 1954. Pacific Press Pub. Association.

--Thumby: A Story of India. LC 40-34274. 124 p. incl. front., illus., plates. 20 cm. c.1940. Review and Herald Publishing Association.

Gardner, Ernest, jt. ed. see Kingsley, Charles.

Gardner, Fred (1941-)

--The Lioness Who Made Deals. 1st ed. Krahn, Fernando (1935-), illus. LC 72-77859. (Illus.). 22 p. 26cm. 1969. Norton.

Gardner, Gerald (1929-) & Caruso, Dee

--The World's Greatest Athlete. (gr. 7-12). 1975. (ISBN 0-590-03755-2, Schol Pap). Scholastic Inc.

Gardner, Grace H.

--Kid Stuff. 1971. (ISBN 0-685-70662-1). M Jones.

--The Lazy Robin: A hurricane story for small folks. Smith, Flo, illus. LC 57-13383. unpaged. illus. 22cm. (The William-Frederick juvenile Ser.). 1958. William-Frederick Press.

--The Peanut Elephant. Reed, Barbara, illus. LC 57-10169. 15p. (The William-Frederick juvenile Ser.). 1957. William-Frederick Press.

--Pixie Pie, for Pixies!. LC 62-10881. 163 p. illus. 23 cm. (William-Frederick juvenile). 1963. William Frederick Press.

--Teacher Tells a Story: Stories and Verses for Tiny Tots. LC 54-10262. 43p. 22cm. 1954. William-Frederick Press.

--Teacher Tells More Tales: In Prose and Rhyme and Pictures. LC 56-5385. (Illus.). 87p. 23cm. 1956. William-Frederick Press.

--Twin Tales. LC 62-10880. (Illus.). 42p. 22cm. 1962. William-Frederick Press.

Gardner, H. C., Mrs.

--A King's Daughter: With other Stories from Real Life. 379p. N.D. Nelson & Phillips.

--Mehetabel. N.D. Nelson & Phillips.

--Rosamond Dayton. 234p. N.D. Nelson & Phillips.

Gardner, Horace John

--Let's Celebrate Christmas: Parties, Plays, Legends, Carols, Poetry, Stories. Potter, Edna, illus. (Illus.). (gr. 6-12). 1940. (ISBN 0-8260-3320-2). Ronald Pr.

Gardner, Horace John, jt. auth. see Young, William P.

Gardner, Hugh

--Tales from the Marble Mountain. Kiddell-Monroe, Joan (1908-), illus. LC 69-12145. (Illus.). 249 p. 23cm. 1969, c.1949. Meredith Press.

Gardner, John Champlin, Jr. (1933-1982)

--A Child's Bestiary. Gardner, John Champlin, Jr. (1933-1982) & Gardner, Joel, illus. LC 77-3945. (Illus.). (gr. 4 up). 1977. (ISBN 0-394-83483-6). (ISBN 0-394-93483-0). Knopf.

--Dragon, Dragon, & Other Timeless Tales. Shields, Charles (1944-), illus. LC 75-2542. 1975. (ISBN 0-394-83122-5). (ISBN 0-394-93122-X). Knopf.

--Gudgekin, the Thistle Girl, & Other Tales. Sporn, Michael, illus. LC 76-4819. (Illus.). 59 p. 24cm. c.1976. (ISBN 0-394-83276-0). Knopf.

--The King of the Hummingbirds and Other Tales. Sporn, Michael, illus. LC 76-42457. (Illus.). (gr. 4 up). 1977. (ISBN 0-394-83319-8). (ISBN 0-394-93319-2). Knopf.

Gardner, John Edmund (1926-)

--The Return of Moriarty. 356p. 1974. (ISBN 0-399-11382-7). Putnam.

--The Revenge of Moriarty. 1976. (ISBN 0-399-11664-8). Putnam.

Gardner, Karen

--Sense Books, 5 bks. Incl. My Life As an Eye. (ISBN 0-87879-115-9); My Life As an Ear. (ISBN 0-87879-116-7); My Life As a Tongue. (ISBN 0-87879-117-5); My Life As a Hand. (ISBN 0-87879-118-3); My Life As a Nose. (ISBN 0-87879-119-1). (gr. 3-6). 1975. Set. (ISBN 0-685-55192-X). Acad Therapy.

Gardner, Keith

--Diamonds, Bks 1. 20p. (The Adventures of Captain Roy). 1962. Pitman Publishing Corporation.

--The Five Men, Bk. 4. 16p. (The Adventures of Captain Roy). 1962. Pitman Publishing Corporation.

--Hansel and Gretel. 28p. (The Adventures of Captain Roy). 1964. Pitman Publishing Corporation.

--The Rescue, Bk. 3. 16p. (The Adventures of Captain Roy). 1962. Pitman Publishing Corporation.

Gardner, Lewis, jt. auth. see Burger, John Robert.

Gardner, Lillian Soskin (1907-)

--Dill Martin, Cub Scout, from Bobcat to Wolf. Stevens, Mary E. (1920-1966), illus. (Illus.). 190p. 22cm. 22cm. 1960, c.1952. F. Watts.

--Exactly Like Ben's. N.D. E. M. Hale & Co.

--Exactly Like Ben's. Mitchell, Michael, illus. LC 55-11847. 83p. illus. 22cm. c.1956. F. Watts.

--From Bobcat to Wolf: The Story of Den Seven, Pack Four. Stevens, Mary E. (1920-1966), illus. LC 52-11059. (Illus.). 190 p. 22cm. 1952. F. Watts.

--Oldest the Youngest and the one in the Middle. (Illus.). 61p. 27 cm. N.D. E. M. Hale and Co.

--The Oldest, the Youngest, & the One in the Middle. Stolberg, Doris, illus. LC 54-5949. (Illus.). 64 p. 27cm. 1954. F. Watts.

--Sal Fisher at Girl Scout Camp. Stevens, Mary E. (1920-1966), illus. LC 59-9797. (Illus.). 217 p. 21cm. 1959. F. Watts.

--Sal Fisher, Brownie Scout. Stevens, Mary E. (1920-1966), illus. LC 53-8612. (Illus.). 192 p. 20cm. 1953. F. Watts.

--Sal Fisher's Fly-up Year: A Brownie Scout Story. Stevens, Mary E. (1920-1966), illus. LC 57-7544. 214p. illus. 20cm. 1957. F. Watts.

--Somebody Called Booie. Sibley, Don (1922-), illus. LC 55-5409. (Illus.). 55 p. 23cm. 1955. Watts.

Gardner, Lucile Blake

--Birds and animals go to school. LC 51-3770. 1951. Dallas, Story Book Press.

Gardner, Martin, ed. see Baum, Lyman Frank.

Gardner, Martin (1914-), ed. see Dodgson, Charles Lutwidge.

Gardner, Martin (1914-)

--Never Make Fun of a Turtle, My Son. Alcorn, John (1935-), illus. LC 68-28912. (Illus.). color ils. 48p. (gr. 1-5). 1969. (ISBN 0-671-65032-7, Juveniles) (ISBN 0-671-65033-5). S&S.

Gardner, Mary

Nature Stories. Blossom, Ethel & Babbitt, Helen, illus. LC 12-12462. vi, 2, 255 p. illus. 18 cm. (Half-title: Everychild's series). 1912. The Macmillan Company.

Gardner, Mercedes (1905-) & Smith, Jean Shannon (1918-)

--Scooter and the Magic Star. Johnson, Bob (1950-), illus. LC 79-20922. (Illus.). 95 p. (Adventures of Scooter). c.1979. (ISBN 0-89742-033-0). (ISBN 0-89742-032-2). Dawne-Leigh Publications.

Gardner, Richard A. (1931-)

--The Bridge. LC 63-15918. 155 p. 21cm. 1963. J. Day Co.

--Danny & the Great Ape Komba. Orbaan, Albert F. (1913-), illus. (Illus.). 1962. John Day.

--Doctor Gadner's Fairy Tales for Today's Children. Lowenheim, Alfred (1947-), illus. (Illus.). 1974. (ISBN 0-13-216960-6). P-H.

--Dorothy and the Lizard of Oz. LC 80-12787. 1980. (ISBN 0-933812-03-5). Creative Therapeutics.

--Dr. Gardner's Fables for Our Times. Myers, Robert Eugene (1924-), illus. LC 80-26098. c.1981. (ISBN 0-933812-06-X). Creative Therapeutics.

--Dr. Gardner's Fairy Tales for Today's Children. Lowenheim, Alfred (1947-), illus. LC 80-16187. 1980. (ISBN 0-933812-02-7). Creative Therapeutics.

--Dr. Gardner's Modern Fairy Tales. Lowenheim, Alfred (1947-), illus. LC 83-10149. 1983, c.1977. (ISBN 0-933812-09-4). Creative Therapeutics.

--Dr. Gardner's Stories About the Real World. Lowenheim, Alfred (1947-), illus. LC 80-16542. p. cm. 1980. (ISBN 0-933812-04-3). Creative Therapeutics.

Gardner, Sandra

--Six Who Dared. (Teens reading on a 2-3rd grade level). (Illus.). 64p. (A Jem Bk.). 1981. (ISBN 0-671-43513-2). Messner.

Gardonyi, Geza (1863-1922)

--Slave of the Huns. Ambrus, Victor G., pseud. (1935-), illus. Ambrus, Gyozo Laszlo. Feldmar, Andrew, tr. Ambrus, Victor G., frwd. by. LC 70-84166. (Illus.). 357 p. 21cm. 1970, c.1969. (ISBN 0-672-50500-2). Bobbs-Merrill.

Garehime, Ed. D

--Mr. Jelly Bean. Garehime, Marianne E, illus. LC 77-82261. (Illus.). 61 p. 27 cm. c.1977. (ISBN 0-918822-01-7). Deem Corp.

Garelick, May (1910-)

--Double Trouble. Getz, Arthur, illus. LC 58-11855. (Illus.). 29 cm. 117p. 1958. Thomas Y. Crowell Co.

--Down to the Beach. Cooney, Barbara (1917-), illus. LC 72-87069. (Illus.). 45 p. 1973. Four Winds Press.

--Here Comes the Bride. Lasker, Joseph Leon (1919-), illus. LC 64-13586. l v. (unpaged) col. illus. 22 cm. 1964. Young Scott Books.

--Look at the Moon. Weisgard, Leonard Joseph (1916-), illus. LC 68-27023. (Illus.). 32 p. 28cm. 1969. Young Scott Books.

--Runaway Plane. Sumichrast, Jozef (1948-), illus. LC 73-522. (Illus.). 32 p. 23cm. (Lead-off book). 1973. (ISBN 0-87955-108-9). (ISBN 0-87955-108-9). J. P. O'Hara.

--Sounds of a Summer Night. Montresor, Beni (1926-), illus. LC 63-2380. (Illus.). unpage. 1963. Young Scott Books.

--What Makes a Bird a Bird?. Weisgard, Leonard Joseph (1916-), illus. LC 69-15973. (Illus.). 32 p. 1969. Follett Pub. Co.

--Where Does the Butterfly Go When It Rains. LC 61-2006. 32p. (ps-1). 1961. (ISBN 0-201-09401-0, A-W Childrens). A-W.

--Where Does the Butterfly Go When It Rains. Weisgard, Leonard Joseph (1916-), illus. (Illus.). (gr. k-2). 1961. (ISBN 0-8382-0938-6). Hale.

--Where Does the Butterfly Go When It Rains?. Weisgard, Leonard Joseph (1916-), illus. (Illus.). 32p. (gr. k-3). 1970. (ISBN 0-590-02538-4). Scholastic Inc.

--Who Likes It Hot?. Turkle, Brinton Cassaday (1915-), illus. LC 72-77804. (Illus.). 31 p. 1972. Four Winds Press.

--Wild Ducks and Daffodils. Ross, Clare Romano (1922-), illus. LC 65-12580. l v. (unpaged) col. illus. 20 x 25 cm. 1965. Young Scott Books.

--Winter's Birds. Hurd, Clement (1908-), illus. LC 64-13585. l v. (unpaged) col. illus. 25 cm. 1965. Young Scott Books.

Garfield, Brian Wynne (1939-), ed.

--War Whoop & Battle Cry. (gr. 7-9). 1972 (Starline). Schol Bk Serv.

Garfield, James B.

--Follow My Leader. (Illus.). (gr. 4-6). 1975. (ISBN 0-590-09107-7, Schol Trade Pap). Schol Bk Serv.

--Follow My Leader. Greiner, Robert, illus. LC 59-2701. (Illus.). (gr. 4-7). 1957. (ISBN 0-670-32332-2). Viking Pr.

--They Like You Better. Greiner, Robert, illus. LC 59-2701. (Illus.). 190 p. 21cm. 1959. Viking Press.

Garfield, Leon (1921-)

--The Apprentices. 1 st. american ed. LC 77-21770. viii, 315 p. 24cm. 1978. (ISBN 0-670-12978-X). Viking Press.

--Black Jack. Maitland, Anthony Jasper (1935-), illus. (Illus.). 1968. Longmans. **Award: (CMA).**

--Black Jack. Maitland, Antony Jasper (1935-), illus. LC 69-13455. (Illus.). 243 p. 22cm. 1969, c.1968. Pantheon Books.

--The Boy and the Monkey. Ridley, Trevor, illus. LC 73-76148. (Illus.). 47 p. 23cm. (Long-ago children series). 1970, c.1969. Watts.

--The Confidence Man. LC 78-14770. 1979. (ISBN 0-670-23723-X). Viking Press.

--Devil in the Fog. Maitland, Antony Jasper (1935-), illus. LC 67-270. 205 p. illus. 22 cm. 1st U.S. edition. 1966. Pantheon Books.

--The Drummer Boy. Maitland, Antony Jasper (1935-), illus. LC 75-101184. (Illus.). 10 line drawings. 192p. (gr. 7 up). 1970. (ISBN 0-394-90855-4). Pantheon. **Award: (CMA).**

--Fair's Fair. Schindler, Steven D., illus. LC 81-43136. (Illus.). 32p. (gr. k-3). 1983. (ISBN 0-385-17962-6). (ISBN 0-385-17963-4). Doubleday.

--Footsteps. LC 80-65834. 196 p. 22cm. c.1980. (ISBN 0-440-02634-2). Delacorte Press. **Award: (BGH).**

--The Ghost Downstairs. Maitland, Antony Jasper (1935-), illus. LC 75-175954. (Illus.). 107 p. 24cm. 1972. (ISBN 0-394-82410-5). (ISBN 0-394-92410-X). Pantheon Books. **Award: (ALA).**

--Jack Holborn. Maitland, Antony Jasper (1935-), illus. LC 65-1904. 199 p. illus. 23 cm. 1964. Constable Young Books.

--Jack Holborn. Maitland, Antony Jasper (1935-), illus. LC 65-20655. (Illus.). 250 p. 22cm. 1965. Pantheon Books.

--The King in the Garden. Bragg, Michael, illus. LC 84-10064. (Illus.). 32 p. 28cm. c.1984. (ISBN 0-688-04106-X). Lothrop, Lee & Shepard.

--King Nimrod's Tower. Bragg, Michael, illus. LC 81-86470. (Illus.). 32 p. 28cm. 1st U.S. edition. c.1982. (ISBN 0-688-01288-4). Lothrop, Lee & Shepard Books.

--Mister Corbett's Ghost. Cober, Alan Edwin (1935-), illus. LC 68-12653. (Illus.). 87 p. 24cm. 1968. Pantheon Books. **Award : (NYT).**

--The Night of the Comet: A Comedy of Courtship Featuring Bostock and Harris. LC 79-50670. (gr. 5-9). 1979. Delacorte.

--The Pleasure Garden. 288p. 1976. (ISBN 0-670-56012-X). Viking Pr.

--The Prisoners of September. 1975. Viking Press.

--The Restless Ghost: Three Stories. Lambert, Saul (1928-), illus. LC 70-77424. (Illus.). 132 p. 22cm. 1969. Pantheon Books.

--Smith. Maitland, Antony Jasper (1935-), illus. LC 67-20223. (Illus.). 218 p. 22cm. 1st U.S. edition. 1967. Pantheon Books. **Awards: (BGH); (CMA).**

--The Sound of Coaches. Lawrence, John (1933-), illus. LC 73-20931. 256 p. 22cm. 1974. (ISBN 0-670-65834-0). Viking Press.

--The Strange Affair of Adelaide Harris. Wegner, Fritz (1924-), illus. LC 72-160360. (Illus.). 223 p. 22cm. 1971. Pantheon Books.

Garfield, Leon (1921-), compiled by.

--Strange Fish and Other Stories. LC 74-14419. 92p. 24cm. 1974. (ISBN 0-688-40059-0). (ISBN 0-688-50059-5). Lothrop Lee & Shepard.

Garfield, Leon (1921-) & Blishen, Edward (1920-)

--The God Beneath the Sea. Blum, Zevi, illus. LC 79-138549. (Illus.). 212 p. 24cm. 1971. (ISBN 0-394-82130-0). Pantheon Books. **Award: (CMA).**

--The Golden Shadow. Keeping, Charles William James (1924-), illus. LC 73-168682. (Illus.). 159 p. 24cm. 1973. (ISBN 0-582-15162-7). Longman Young Books.

--The Golden Shadow. Keeping, Charles William James (1924-), illus. LC 73-1402. (Illus.). 159 p. 24cm. 1973. (ISBN 0-394-82704-X). (ISBN 0-394-82704-X). Pantheon Books.

Garfield, Leon (1921-) & Bragg, Michael

--The Writing on the Wall. LC 82-24938. (Illus.). 32p. (gr. 1-3). 1983. (ISBN 0-688-02112-3). Lothrop.

Garfield, Lillian E.

--See My Toys. Brice, Tony, illus. LC 48-3911. 33 p. col. illus. 17 cm. (Rand McNally book, 611). 1948, c.1947. Rand, McNally.

Garfield, Nancy

--The Dancing Monkey. Negri, Rocco (1932-), illus. LC 72-110309. (Illus.). 48 p. 22cm. 1970. Putnam.

--The Tuesday Elephant. Feelings, Thomas (1933-), illus. LC 68-11063. (Illus.). 44 p. 26cm. 1968. T. Y. Crowell Co.

Garfield, Robert, pseud., see Jackson, Kathryn.

Garfield, Robert, jt. auth. see Bechdolt, John Ernest.

Garfield, Robert, pseud. & Jackson, Byron

--The Penny Puppy, and Other Dog Stories. Jackson, Kathryn. LC 49-48612. (Robert Garfield is the joint pseudonym of Kathryn Jackson and Byron Jackson). 125 p. col. illus. 18 cm. (Golden story books, 9). 1949. Simon and Schuster.

--Train Stories. Jackson, Kathryn. LC 49-49193. (Robert Garfield is the joint pseudonym of Kathryn Jackson and Byron Jackson). 126 p. col. illus. 18 cm. (Golden story books, 6). 1949. Simon and Schuster.

Garfinkel, Bernard see Martin, Janet, pseud.

Garfinkel, Bernard Max see Allen, Robert, pseud.

Garfinkel, Bernard Max (1929-)

--Jamie and the Leopard. Sugita, Yutaka (1930-), illus. LC 69-20247. (Illus.). 26 p. 25cm. c.1967. Platt & Munk.

--My Growing Up Book. Ahlberg, Janet, illus. LC 77-185970. (Illus.). 68 p. 29cm. 1972. Platt & Munk.

--This Is Yellow and This Is Red. Allen, Robert, pseud. Witt, Edith, illus. LC 72-78044. (Illus.). 26 p. N.D. Platt & Munk.

--The Zoo Book: A Child's World of Animals. Sahula, Peter (1935-), photos by. LC 68-19577. (Illus.). 1 v. (unpaged). 21cm. 1968. Platt & Munk.

Garibaldi, Gerald (1951-)

--He Gave Himself to the Sea. Bachaus, Ken, illus. LC 79-21326. (Illus.). (Quest, Adventure, Survival Ser.). (gr. 4-8). 1980. (ISBN 0-8172-1561-1). Raintree Pubs.

--Nightmare in a Sea of Mud. Shaw, Charles (1941-), illus. LC 79-22418. (Illus.). 46 p. 24cm. c.1980. (ISBN 0-8172-1558-1). Raintree Publishers.

Garis, Cleo Fausta, pseud., see Clancy, Cleo Faust Garis.

Garis, Cleo Fausta, pseud.

--Missing at Marshlands. Clancy, Cleo Faust Garis. LC 34-9913. 249 p. front. 20 1/2 cm. (Her Arden Blake mystery series). c.1934. A. L. Burt Company.

--Mystery of Jockey Hollow. Clancy, Cleo Faust Garis. LC 34-8051. 255 p. front. 20 1/2 cm. (Her Arden Blake mystery series). c.1934. A. L. Burt Company.

--The Orchard Secret. Clancy, Cleo Faust Garis. 250 p. front. 20 1/2 cm. (Her Arden Blake mystery series). c.1934. A. L. Burt Company.

Garis, Howard Roger see Davidson, Marion, pseud.

Garis, Howard Roger see Sperry, Raymond, pseud.

Garis, Howard Roger (1873-1962)

--Adventures of the Galloping Gas Stove. (The Happy Home Ser.). N.D. Grosset & Dunlap.

--Adventures of the Prancing Piano. (The Happy Home Ser.). N.D. Grosset & Dunlap.

--Adventures of the Runaway Rocking Chair. (The Happy Home Ser.). N.D. Grosset & Dunlap.

--Adventures of the Sailing Sofa. (The Happy Home Ser.). N.D. Grosset & Dunlap.

--Adventures of the Sliding Foot Stool. (The Happy Home Ser.). N.D. Grosset & Dunlap.

--Adventures of the Traveling Table. (The Happy Home Ser.). N.D. Grosset & Dunlap.

--The Adventures of Uncle Wiggily: The Bunny Rabbit Gentleman with the Twinkling Pink Nose. Campbell, Lang (1886-), illus. LC 24-3954. (Illus.). 32p. 28cm. 1924. C. F. Graham & Co.

The Bear Hunt. LC 30-9480. 2 p. l., 260 p. front., plates. 20 cm. (His Dick and Janet Cherry series). c.1930. McLoughlin Bros., Inc.

--Buddy and Brighteyes Pig. (The Famous Uncle Wiggily Bed Time Ser.). N.D. A. L. Burt Company.
--Buddy and His Chum: Or, A Boy's Queer Search. LC 30-13350. 2 p. l., 210 p. front. 19 1/2 cm. (His Buddy books). c.1930. Cupples & Leon Company.
--Buddy and His Cowboy Pal: Or, A Boy on a Ranch. LC 35-6274. 2 p. l., 207 p. front. 19 1/2 cm. (His Buddy books). c.1935. Cupples & Leon Company.
--Buddy and His Flying Balloon: Or, A Boy's Mysterious Airship. LC 31-14189. 2 p. l., 206 p. front. 19 1/2 cm. (His Buddy books). c.1931. Cupples & Leon Company.
--Buddy and His Fresh-Air Camp: Or, A Boy and the Unlucky Ones. LC 47-11899. 210 p. front. 20 cm. (His The Buddy books). 1947. Cupples & Leon.
--Buddy and His Winter Fun: Or, A Boy in a Snow Camp. LC 29-11407. 3 p. l., 208 p. front. 19 1/2 cm. (His Buddy books). c.1929. Cupples & Leon Company.
--Buddy and the Arrow Club: Or, A Boy and the Long Bow. LC 37-947231. 2 p. l., 208 p. front. 19 1/2 cm. (His Buddy books). c.1937. Cupples & Leon Company.
--Buddy and the G-Man Mystery: Or, A Boy and a Strange Cipher. LC 45-155287. 2 p. l., 212 p. front. 19 1/2 cm. (His The Buddy books). c.1944. Cupples & Leon Company.
--Buddy and the Indian Chief: Or, A Boy Among the Navajos. LC 36-897414. 2 p. l., 207 p. front. 19 1/2 cm. (His Buddy books). c.1936. Cupples & Leon Company.
--Buddy and the Secret Cave: Or, A Boy and the Crystal Hermit. LC 34-62089. 2 p. l., 209 p. front. 19 1/2 cm. (His Buddy books). c.1934. Cupples & Leon Company.
--Buddy at Lost River: Or, A Boy and a Gold Mine. LC 38-17568. iii, 203 p. front. 19 1/2 cm. (His Buddy books). c.1938. Cupples & Leon Company.
--Buddy at Pine Beach: Or, A Boy on the Ocean. LC 31-14190. 2 p. l., 208 p. front. 19 1/2 cm. (His Buddy books). c.1931. Cupples & Leon Company.
--Buddy at Rainbow Lake: Or, A Boy and His Boat. LC 30-13351. 2 p. l., 210 p. front. 19 1/2 cm. (His Buddy books). c.1930. Cupples & Leon Company.
--Buddy at Red Gate: Or, A Boy on a Chicken Farm. LC 41-7695. iii, 209 p. front. 19 1/2 cm. (His Buddy books. no. 17). c.1941. Cupples & Leon Company.
--Buddy in Deep Valley: Or, A Boy on a Bee Farm. LC 40-6306. iii, 212 p. front. 19 1/2 cm. (His Buddy books). c.1940. Cupples & Leon Company.
--Buddy in Dragon Swamp: Or, A Boy on a Strange Hunt. iv, 208 p. front. 19 1/2 cm. (His Buddy books). 1942. Cupples & Leon Company.
--Buddy in School: Or, A Boy and His Dog. LC 29-114098. 2 p. l., 210 p. front. 19 1/2 cm. (His Buddy books). c.1929. Cupples & Leon Company.
--Buddy on Floating Island: Or, A Boy's Wonderful Secret. 2 p. l., 210 p. front. 19 1/2 cm. (His Buddy books). c.1933. Cupples & Leon Company.
--Buddy on Mystery Mountain: Or, A Boy's Strange Discovery. LC 32-136862. 2 p. l., 210 p. front. 19 1/2 cm. (His Buddy books). c.1932. Cupples & Leon Company.
--Buddy on the Farm: Or, A Boy and His Prize Pumpkin. LC 29-11408. 2 p. l., 212 p. front. 19 1/2 cm. (His Buddy books). c.1929. Cupples & Leon Company.
--Buddy on the Trail: Or, A Boy Among the Gypsies. LC 39-11051. iii, 204 p. front. 19 1/2 cm. (His Buddy books). c.1939. Cupples & Leon Company.
--Buddy's Victory Club: Or, A Boy and a Salvage Campaign. LC 43-9391. 3 p. l., 209 p. front. 19 1/2 cm. (His The Buddy books). 1943. Cupples & Leon Company.
--Bully and Bawly No-Tail: The Jumping Frogs. Wisa, Louis, illus. LC 15-5449. 207 p. incl. col. front. col. plates. 20 cm. (His Bedtime stories). c.1915. R. F. Fenno & Company.
--Bully and Bawly No-Trail. (The Famous Uncle Wiggily Bed Time Ser.). N.D. A. L. Burt Company.
--Camp Fire Girls on the Ice: Or, The Mystery of a Winter Cabin. Davidson, Marion, pseud. LC 13-25715. 5, 9-273 p. front., plates. 19 1/2 cm. (His The Camp fire girls series $1.00). c.1913. R. F. Fenno & Company.
--The Camp Fire Girls: Or, The Secret of an Old Mill. Davidson, Marion, pseud. LC 13-25714. 6, 9-296 p. front., plates. 19 1/2 cm. (His The Camp fire girls series) $1.00). c.1913. R. F. Fenno & Company.
--Chad of Knob Hill: The Tale of a Lone Scout. Martin, Paul, illus. LC 29-20984. 6 p. l., 3-298 p. incl. illus., plates. col. front. 20 1/2 cm. 1929. Little, Brown, and Company.
--Charlie and Arabella Chick. (The Famous Uncle Wiggily Bed Time Ser.). N.D. A. L. Burt Company.
--Curly and Floppy Twisty Tail. (The Famous Uncle Wiggily Bed Time Ser.). N.D. A. L. Burt Company.
--The Curlytops and Their Pets: Or, Uncle Toby's Strange Collection. (The Curlytops Ser.). N.D. Cupples & Leon Co.
--The Curlytops and Their Playmates: or, Jolly Times Through the Holidays. (The Curlytops Ser.). N.D. Cupples & Leon Co.
--The Curlytops at Cherry Farm: Or, Vacation Days in the Country. (The Curlytops Ser.). N.D. Cupples & Leon Co.
--The Curlytops at Happy House: Or, The Mystery of the Chinese Vase. LC 31-141912. vi, 212 p. incl. front. 19 1/2 cm. (His Curlytops series). c.1931. Cupples & Leon Company.
--The Curlytops at Silver Lake: Or, On the Water With Uncle Ben. (The Curlytops Ser.). N.D. Cupples & Leon Co.
--The Curlytops at Sunset Beach: Or, What Was Found in the Sand. Greene, Julia, illus. LC 24-14877. 2 p. l., 246 p. front., plates. 19 1/2 cm. (His Curlytops series). c.1924. Cupples & Leon Company.
--The Curlytops at the Circus: Or, The Runaway Elephant. LC 32-13687. 2 p. l., 208 p. front. 19 1/2 cm. (His Curlytops series). c.1932. Cupples & Leon Company.
--The Curlytops at Uncle Frank's: Or, Little Folks on Ponyback. (The Curlytops Ser.). N.D. Cupples & Leon Co.
--The Curlytops Growing up: Or, Winter Sports and Summer Pleasures. Greene, Julia, illus. LC 28-15794. vi, 248 p. incl. front. plates. 19 1/2 cm. (His Curlytops series). c.1928. Cupples & Leon Company.
--The Curlytops in a Summer Camp: Animal Joe's Menagerie. (The Curlytops Ser.). N.D. Cupples & Leon Co.
--The Curlytops in the Woods: Or, Fun at the Lumber Camp. Greene, Julia, illus. LC 30-1312. 2 p. l., 246 p. front., plates. 19 1/2 cm. (His Curlytops series). c.1923. Cupples & Leon Company.
--The Curlytops on Star Island: Or, Camping Out With Grandpa. (The Curlytops Ser.). N.D. Cupples & Leon Co.
--The Curlytops Snowed in: Or, Grand Fun with Skates and Sleds. Greene, Julia, illus. LC 33-324512. 2 p. l., 246 p. front. 19 1/2 cm. (His The Curlytops series). N.D. Cupples & Leon Company.
--The Curlytops Touring Around: or, Delightful Days in Pleasant Places. (The Curlytops Ser.). N.D. Cupples & Leon Co.
--Daddy takes Us Camping. (The "Daddy" Ser.). N.D. A. L. Burt Co.
--Daddy Takes Us Coasting. (The "Daddy" Ser.). N.D. A. L. Burt Co.
--Daddy Takes Us Fishing. (The "Daddy" Ser.). N.D. A. L. Burt Co.
--Daddy Takes Us Hunting Birds. Dean, Eva, illus. LC 16-21982. 1 p. l., 9-160 p. col. front., plates. 20 1/2 cm. (His The daddy series for little folks). c.1916. R. F. Fenno & Company.
--Daddy Takes Us Hunting Flowers. (The "Daddy" Ser.). N.D. A. L. Burt Co.
--Daddy Takes Us Skating. (The "Daddy" Ser.). N.D. A. L. Burt Co.
--Daddy Takes Us to the Circus. (The "Daddy" Ser.). N.D. A. L. Burt Co.
--Daddy Takes Us to the Farm. (The "Daddy" Ser.). N.D. A. L. Burt Co.
--Daddy Takes Us to the Garden. (The "Daddy" Ser.). N.D. A. L. Burt Co.
--Daddy Takes Us to the Woods. (The "Daddy" Ser.). N.D. A. L. Burt Co.
--Dick Hamilton's Airship: or, A Young Millionaire in the Clouds. (The Dick Hamilton Ser.). N.D. Grosset & Dunlap.
--Dick Hamilton's Cadet Days: Or, The Handicap of a Millionaire's Son. LC 10-11474. vi, 271 p. front., plates. 19 1/2 cm. (On cover: Dick Hamilton series) $0.60.). c.1910. Grosset & Dunlap.
--Dick Hamilton's Football Team: Or, A Young Millionaire on the Gridiron. (The Dick Hamilton Ser.). N.D. Grosset & Dunlap.
--Dick Hamilton's Fortune: or, The Stirring Doings of a Millionaire's Son. LC 9-20283. 19.5 cm. 275p. (The Dick Hamilton Ser.). 1909. Grosset & Dunlap.
--Dick Hamilton's Steam Yacht: or, A Young Millionaire and the Kidnappers. (The Dick Hamilton Ser.). N.D. Grosset & Dunlap.
--Dick Hamilton's Touring Car: or, Young Millionaire's Race for a Fortune. (The Dick Hamilton Ser.). N.D. Grosset & Dunlap.
--Dickie and Nellie Fliptail. (Bed Time Animal Stories). (The Famous Uncle Wiggily Ser.). N.D. A. L. Burt Company.
--Dottie and Willie Flufftail. (Bedtime Animal Stories). (The Famous Uncle Wiggily Bed Time Ser.). N.D. A. L. Burt Company.
--The Face in the Dismal Cavern. LC 30-9480. 1 p. l., 254 p. front., plates. 20 cm. (His Rick and Ruddy series). c.1930. McCloughlin Bros., Inc.
--From Office Boy to Reporter: Or, The First Step in Journalism. LC 7-23465. vi, 311 p. front., plates. 19 cm. (On verso of t.-p.: The great newspaper series). c.1907. Chatterton-Peck Company.
--From Office Boy to Reporter: Or, the First Step in Journalism. (The Newspaper Ser.). N.D. Grosset & Dunlap.
--The Gypsy Camp. LC 30-11383. 2 p. l., 264 p. front., plates. 20 cm. (His Dick and Janet Cherry series). c.1930. McLoughlin Bros., Inc.
--The Island Boys: Or, Fun and Adventures on Lake Modok. LC 12-22865. 2 p. l., 9-275 p. front., plates. 20 cm. (His The Island boys series). c.1912. R. F. Fenno & Company.
--Isle of Black Fire. LC 4-31049. 20cm. 301p. 1904. J. B. Lippincott Co.
--Jacke and Jumpo Kinky tail. (Bedtime Animal Stories). (The Famous Uncle Wiggily Bed Time Ser.). N.D. A. L. Burt Co.
--Jackie and Peetie Bow-Wow. (Bedtime Animal Stories). (The Famous Uncle Wiggily Bed Time Ser.). N.D. A. L. Burt Company.
--Jackie and Peetie Bow Wow. Wisa, Louis, illus. LC 12-22866. 1 p. l., 9-197, 1 p. col. front., col. plates. 20 cm. (His Bedtime stories). c.1912. R. F. Fenno & Company.
--Johnnie and Billie Bushytail. Wisa, Louis, illus. LC 11-23707. 20.5 cm. 229p. (Bedtime Stories). 1910. R. F. Fenno & Co.
--Johnny and Billy Bushytail. (Bedtime Animal Stories). (The Famous Uncle Wiggily Bed Time Ser.). N.D. A. L. Burt Company.
--Joie, Tommie and Kittie Kat. (Bedtime Animal Stories). (The Famous Uncle Wiggily Bed Time Ser.). N.D. A. L. Burt Company.
--Jollie and Jillie Longtail. (Bedtime Animal Stories). (The Famous Uncle Wiggily Bed Time Ser.). N.D. A. L. Burt Company.
--Larry Dexter and the Bank Mystery: Or, A Young Reporter in Wall Street. LC 12-18017. vi, 208 p. front. 19 1/2 cm. (His The young reporter series). c.1912. Grosset & Dunlap.
--Larry Dexter and the Stolen Boy: Or, A Young Reporter on the Lakes. LC 12-180188. vi, 205 p. front. 19 1/2 cm. (His The young reporter series). c.1912. Grosset & Dunlap.
--Larry Dexter in Belgium: or, A Young War Correspondent's Double Mission. (Illus.). (The Young Reporter Ser.). N.D. Grosset & Dunlap.
--Larry Dexter, Reporter: Or, Strange Adventures in a Great City. LC 7-23942. vi, 313 p. front., plates. 19 cm. (On verso of t.-p.: The great newspaper series). 1907. Chatterton-Peck Company.
--Larry Dexter's Great Search: Or, the Hunt for the Missing Millionaire. LC 9-17208. 19.5 cm. 247p. (The Great Newspaper Ser.). 1909. Grosset & Dunlap.
--The Little Golden Book of Uncle Wiggily. Crawford, Mel (1925-), illus. LC 53-8197. unpaged. illus. 21cm. (Little golden library, 148). 1953. Simon and Schuster.
--Lulu, Alice and Jimmie Wibblewobble. (Bedtime Animal Stories). (The Famous Uncle Wiggily Bed Time Ser.). N.D. A. L. Burt Company.
--Lulu, Alice and Jimmie Wibblewobble. Wisa, Louis, illus. LC 12-12490. 2 p. l., 9-195 p. col. front., col. plates. 20 1/2 cm. (Bedtime stories). c.1912. R. F. Fenno & Company.
--Mystery Boys at Round Lake. Nicholas, H. G., illus. LC 31-18070. 343 p. incl. front. plates. 19 1/2 cm. c.1931. Milton Bradley Co.
--Mystery Boys in Ghost Canyon. Nicholas, H. G., illus. LC 31-113830. 3 p. l., 353 p. front., plates. 19 cm. c.1930. Milton Bradley Co.
--The Mystery of the Brass Bound Box. LC 30-9479. 2 p. l., 262 p. front., plates. 20 cm. (His Rick and Ruddy series). c.1930. McLoughlin Bros., Inc.
--Nannie and Billie Wagtail. (Bedtime Animal Stories). (The Famous Uncle Wiggily Bed Time Ser.). N.D. A. L. Burt Company.
--Neddie and Beckie Stubtail. (Bedtime Animal Stories). (The Famous Uncle Wiggily Bed Time Ser.). N.D. A. L. Burt Company.
--On the Showman's Trail. LC 30-9477. 2 p. l., 256 p. front., plates. 20 cm. (His Rick and Ruddy series). c.1930. McLoughlin Bros., Inc.
--Rick and Ruddy Afloat: The Cruise of a Boy and His Dog. King, W. B., illus. LC 22-10394. 2 p. l., 262 p. front., plates. 19 cm. 1922. Milton Bradley Company.
--Rick and Ruddy in Camp: The Adventures of a Boy and His Dog. Winter, Milo Kendall (1888-1956), illus. LC 22-2001. 2 p. l., 254 p. front., plates. 20 cm. 1921. Milton Bradley Company.
--Rick and Ruddy on the Trail. King, W. B., illus. LC 24-116552. 2 p. l., 256 p. front., plates. 19 cm. (His Rick and Ruddy series). 1924. Milton Bradley Company.
--Rick and Ruddy Out West. King, W. B., illus. LC 23-12519. 3 p. l., 254 p. front., 1 illus., plates. 19 cm. (His Rick and Ruddy series). 1923. Milton Bradley Company.
--Rick and Ruddy: The Story of a Boy and His Dog. Goss, John, illus. LC 20-23176. 2 p. l., 282 p. col. front., plates. 20 cm. 1920. Milton Bradley Company.
--Rocket Riders Across the Ice: Or, Racing Against Time. LC 33-11384. 3 p. l., 231 p. front. 20 1/2 cm. (His Rocket riders series). c.1933. A. L. Burt Company.
--Rocket Riders in Stormy Seas: Or, Trailing the Treasure Divers. LC 33-11382. 4 p. l., 246 p. front. 20 1/2 cm. (His Rocket riders series). c.1933. A. L. Burt Company.
--Rocket Riders in the Air: Or, A Chase in the Clouds. LC 34-8046. 4 p. l., 7-251 p. front. 20 1/2 cm. (His Rocket riders series). c.1934. A. L. Burt Company.
--Rocket Riders Over the Desert: Or, Seeking the Lost City. LC 33-11383. 3 p. l., 250 p. front. 20 1/2 cm. (His Rocket riders series). c.1933. A. L. Burt Company.
--Sammie and Susie Littletail. (Bedtime Animal Stories). (The Famous Uncle Wiggily Bed Time Ser.). N.D. A. L. Burt Company.
--Sammie and Susie Littletail. (Illus.). N.D. R. F. Fenno & Co.
--Saving the Old Mill. LC 30-948482. 2 p. l., 264 p. front., plates. 20 cm. (His Dick and Janet Cherry series). c.1930. McLoughlin Bros., Inc.
--The Second Adventures of Uncle Wiggily: The Bunny Rabbit Gentleman and His Muskrat Lady Housekeeper. Campbell, Lang (1886-), illus. LC 74-192121. (Illus.). 32 p. 29cm. c.1925. C. E. Graham.
--The Secret of Lost River. LC 30-9483. 2 p. l., 254 p. front., 1 illus., plates. 20 cm. (His Rick and Ruddy series). c.1930. McLoughlin Bros., Inc.
--Shipwrecked on Christmas Island. LC 30-9485. 2 p. l., 249 p. front., plates. 20 cm. (His Dick and Janet Cherry series). c.1930. McLoughlin Bros., Inc.
--Snarlie the Tiger. LC 16-219814. 178 p. incl. col. front. col. plates. 21 x 17 cm. (His Circus animal stories). c.1916. R. F. Fenno & Company.
--Swept from the Storm. LC 30-113843. 1 p. l., 282 p. front., plates. 20 cm. (His Rick and Ruddy series). c.1930. McLoughlin Bros., Inc.
--Tam of the Fire Cave. LC 27-17532. 4 p. l., 257, 1 p. front. 19 1/2 cm. 1927. D. Appleton and Company.
--Teddy and the Mystery Cat. LC 37-9719. 2 p. l., 204 p. front. 19 1/2 cm. (His Teddy series). c.1937. Cupples & Leon Company.
--Teddy and the Mystery Deer. LC 40-630411. iii p., 1 l., 207 p. front. 19 1/2 cm. (His Teddy series). c.1940. Cupples & Leon Company.
--Teddy and the Mystery Dog. 2 p. l., 209 p. front. 19 1/2 cm. (His Teddy series). c.1936. Cupples & Leon Company.
--Teddy and the Mystery Goat. LC 41-127281. iii p., 1 l., 206 p. front. 19 1/2 cm. (His Teddy series). c.1941. Cupples & Leon Company.
--Teddy and the Mystery Monkey. LC 36-176967. 2 p. l., 207 p. front. 19 1/2 cm. (His Teddy series). c.1936. Cupples & Leon Company.
--Teddy and the Mystery Parrot. LC 38-175672. iii, 1, 210 p. front. 19 1/2 cm. (His Teddy series). c.1938. Cupples & Leon Company.
--Teddy and the Mystery Pony. LC 39-110521. iii, 1, 208 p. front. 19 1/2 cm. (His The Teddy series). c.1939. Cupples & Leon Company.
--Those Smith Boys on the Diamond: Or, Nip and Tuck for Victory. LC 12-228688. 273 p. incl. front. plates. 20 cm. (His Those Smith boys series). c.1912. R. F. Fenno & Company.
--Those Smith Boys: Or, The Mystery of the Thumbless Man. LC 10-216404. viii, 9-270 p. incl. col. front. col. plates. 20 1/2 cm. $1.2. c.1910. R. F. Fenno & Company.
--Three Little Trippertrots: How They Ran Away and How They Got Back Again. LC 12-17659. 6, 151 p. incl. plates. col. front., col. plates. 25 cm. c.1912. Graham & Matlack.
--Three Little Trippertrots on Their Travels: The Wonderful Things They Saw and the Wonderful Things They Did. LC 12-17658. 160 p. incl. plates. col. front., col. plates. 25 cm. $0.6. c.1912. Graham & Matlack.
--Tom Cardiff in the Big Top. LC 30-9482. 3 p. l., 256 p. front., plates. 20 cm. (His Tom Cardiff series). c.1930. McLoughlin Bros., Inc.
--Tom Cardiff in the Big Top. King, W. B., illus. LC 27-3823. 3 p. l., 256 p. front., plates. 19 cm. (His Tom Cardiff series). c.1927. Milton Bradley Company.
--Tom Cardiff's Circus. LC 30-94817. 3 p. l., 269 p. front., plates. 20 cm. (His Tom Cardiff series). c.1930. McLoughlin Bros., Inc.
--Tom Cardiff's Circus. King, W. B., illus. LC 26-7449. 3 p. l., 269 p. front., plates. 19 cm. (His Tom Cardiff series). 1926. Milton Bradley Company.

Garland, Hannibal Hamlin (1860-1940)

--Boy Life on the Prairie. N.D. Frederick Ungar Publishing Co.

--Boy Life on the Prairie. N.D. Harper & Brothers.

--Boy Life on the Prairie. McElderry, Bruce R., Jr. (1900-1970), intro. by. 1961. (ISBN 0-8032-5070-3). Nebraska Press.

--A Little Norsk: Or, Ol' Pap's Flaxen. LC 6-40721. 17cm. 157p. 1892. D. Appleton & Co.

--The Long Trail. Spayd, Barbara Grace, ed. LC 35-28731. lxvii, 332 p. front., plates. 19 cm. 1935. Harper & Brothers.

--The Long Trail: A Story of the Northwest Wilderness. LC 7-15590. 4 p. l., 262, 1 p. front., 7 pl. 19 1/2 cm. 1907. Harper & Brothers.

--Prairie Song and Western Story. Center, Stella Stewart (1878-), compiled by. Garland, Constance, illus. LC 29-5443. 17cm. 365p. 1928. Allyn & Bacon.

Garland, Helen C.

--Almost Too Late. N.D. Bradley & Woodruff.

Garland, Jennie

--Giddie Garland. N.D. Fleming H. Revell Co.

Garland, John

--Ross Grant, Gold Hunter. Boyer, Ralph L., illus. LC 16-13744. 384 p. front., illus. (maps) plates. 20 cm. 1916. The Penn Publishing Company.

--Ross Grant in Miners' Camp. Boyer, Ralph L., illus. LC 18-13904. 384 p. front., plates. 20 c. 1918. The Penn Publishing Company.

--Ross Grant on the Trail. Boyer, Ralph L., illus. LC 17-208594. 380 p. front., illus. (map) plates. 20 cm. 1917. The Penn Publishing Company.

--Ross Grant, Tenderfoot. Boyer, Ralph L., illus. (The Ross Grant Ser.). N.D. Penn.

Garland, Rosemary, ed.

--My Bedtime Book of Two-Minute Stories. Escott, Tony & Wellman, Sally, illus. LC 70-96773. (Illus.). 123 p. 29cm. 1970, c.1969. Grosset & Dunlap.

Garland, Sarah

--Going Shopping. Kroupa, Melanie, ed. Garland, Sarah, illus. LC 84-71902. (Illus.). 32p. 1st U.S. edition. (ps-k). 1985. (ISBN 0-87113-001-7). Atlantic Monthly.

--Having a Picnic. Kroupa, Melanie, ed. Garland, Sarah, illus. LC 84-71901. (Illus.). 32p. 1st U.S. edition. (ps-k). 1985. (ISBN 0-87113-002-5). Atlantic Monthly.

--Henry and Fowler. Garland, Sarah, illus. LC 76-371736. (Illus.). 32 p. 20cm. 1976. (ISBN 0-370-01800-1). Bodley Head.

--Henry and Fowler. Garland, Sarah, illus. LC 76-42160. (Illus.). 32 p. 20cm. 1977, c.1976. (ISBN 0-684-14866-8). Scribner.

--The Joss Bird. Garland, Sarah, illus. LC 74-25. (Illus.). 32 p. 20cm. 1975, c.1974. (ISBN 0-684-13846-8). Scribner.

--Potter Brownware: A Picture Book. Garland, Sarah, illus. LC 77-70271. (Illus.). 26 p. 20cm. c.1977. (ISBN 0-684-15044-1). Scribner.

--Rose & Her Bath. Garland, Sarah, illus. (Illus.). (ps-5). 1970. (ISBN 0-571-08728-0). (ISBN 0-571-11017-7). Faber & Faber.

--Rose, the Bath & the Merboy. Garland, Sarah, illus. (Illus.). 32p. (ps-5). N.D. (ISBN 0-571-09581-X). Faber & Faber.

Garlits, Don & Yates, Brock

--King of the Dragsters: The Story of Big Daddy (Don) Garlits. rev. & enl. ed. Hurst, George H, Jr., frwd. by. LC 75-115685. (Illus.). 246p. 1970. (ISBN 0-8019-5592-0). Chilton.

Garman, R. H.

--Jolly Times. Garman, R. H., illus. (Illus.). 1910. Hurst & Co.

--Jungle Larks. Garman, R. H., illus. (Illus.). N.D. Laird & Lee's Publications.

--Monkey Shines. Garman, R. H., illus. (Illus.). 24p. 1910. Hurst & Co.

Garn, Bernard J., Dr.

--A Visit to the Dentist. Krusz, Arthur, illus. N.D. Grosset & Dunlap.

--Visit to the Dentist. Krusz, Arthur, illus. (Illus.). (gr. k-3). 1959. (ISBN 0-448-02866-2). Wonder.

Garn, Doris, adapted by see Bragg, Mabel Caroline.

Garn, Doris, ed. see Ford, Ford Madox.

Garner, Alan (1935-)

--The Aimer Gate. Foreman, Michael (1938-), illus. LC 78-20964. (Illus.). 79 p. 21cm. 1979, c.1978. (ISBN 0-529-05506-6). Collins.

--Alan Garner's Book of British Fairy Tales. Collard, Derek, illus. LC 85-4586. p. cm. 1985. (ISBN 0-385-29425-5). Delacorte Press.

--Alan Garner's Fairy Tales of Gold. Foreman, Michael (1938-), illus. LC 80-15240. p. cm. c.1980. (ISBN 0-399-20759-7). Philomel Books.

--A Cavalcade of Goblins. Turska, Krystyna Zofia (1933-), illus. LC 69-17905. (Illus.). viii, 227 p. 26cm. 1969. H. Z. Walck. **Award: (ALA).**

--Elidor. Keeping, Charles William James (1924-), illus. LC 78-8379. p. cm. 1978. (ISBN 0-00-184202-1). Collins.

--Elidor. Keeping, Charles William James (1924-), illus. LC 67-3174. 185 p. 21cm. 1967, c.1965. H. Z. Walck.

--Granny Reardun. Foreman, Michael (1938-), illus. LC 78-8141. p. cm. 1979, c.1977. (ISBN 0-529-05505-8). Collins.

--The Guizer. LC 75-42040. (Illus.). 224p. (gr. 7 up). 1976. (ISBN 0-688-86001-X). Greenwillow.

--The Guizer: A Book of Fools. LC 75-42040. p. cm. 1976, c.1975. (ISBN 0-688-80043-2). Greenwillow Books.

--The Lad of the Gad. 128p. (gr. 5 up). 1981. (ISBN 0-399-20784-8, Philomel). Putnam Pub Group.

--The Moon of Gomrath. LC 77-16425. 160 p. 22cm. 1979, c.1963. (ISBN 0-00-184503-9). Collins & World.

--The Moon of Gomrath. LC 67-19922. 184 p. 21cm. 1967, c.1963. H. Z. Walck.

--The Old Man of Mow. Hill, Roger, illus. LC 72-98165. (Illus.). 47 p. 29cm. 1970, c.1967. Doubleday.

--The Owl Service. LC 79-10140. p. cm. 1979, c.1967. (ISBN 0-529-05520-1). Collins.

--The Owl Service. LC 68-23885. 202 p. 21cm. 1968, c.1967. H. Z. Walck. **Award: (ALA).**

--Red Shift. LC 73-584. 197 p. 22cm. 1973. (ISBN 0-02-735870-4). Macmillan.

--The Stone Book. Foreman, Michael (1938-), illus. LC 77-351982. (Illus.). 61 p. 21cm. 1976. (ISBN 0-00-184777-5). Collins.

--The Stone Book. Foreman, Michael (1938-), illus. LC 78-7965. (Illus.). 63 p. 21cm. 1978, c.1976. (ISBN 0-529-05503-1). Collins.

--The Stone Book. Foreman, Michael (1938-), illus. 1978. Putnam.

--Tom Fobble's Day. Foreman, Michael (1938-), illus. LC 78-26927. (Illus.). 72 p. 21cm. 1979, c.1977. (ISBN 0-529-05507-4). Collins.

--Tom Fobble's Day. Foreman, Michael (1938-), illus. 1979. Putnam.

--The Weirdstone: A Tale of Alderley. LC 61-10076. 224 p. 21cm. 1961, c.1960. F. Watts.

--The Weirdstone of Brisingamen. (Illus.). (gr. 5 up). 1979. (ISBN 0-399-20806-2, Philomel). Putnam Pub Group.

--The Weirdstone of Brisingamen: A Tale of Alderley. LC 78-24635. (Illus.). 224 p. 22cm. 1979, c.1960. (ISBN 0-529-05519-8). Collins.

--The Weirdstone of Brisingamen: A Tale of Alderley. rev. ed. LC 69-17914. 253 p. 21cm. 1969, c.1963. H. Z. Walck.

Garner, Claud Walton, jt. auth. see Knight, Ruth Adams.

Garner, Claud Wilton (1891-)

--Sam Houston: Texas Giant. LC 68-14623. xxiv, 344 p. 23cm. 1969. Naylor Co.

Garner, Elvira C., Mrs. (1895-)

--Ezekiel. Garner, Elvira C., Mrs. (1895-), illus. (gr. 1-3). 1937. Henry Holt & Co.

--Ezekiel Travels. Garner, Elvira C., Mrs. (1895-), illus. 1937. Henry Holt & Co.

--Little Cat Lost. Thorne, Diana (1894-), illus. LC 43-14767. 28 p. col. illus. 26 x 26 cm. 1943. J. Messner, Inc.

--Little Cat Lost. Thorne, Diana (1894-), illus. N.D. Veritas Press.

--Sarah Faith Anderson: Her Book. Garner, Elvira C., Mrs. (1895-), illus. LC 39-34159. 106 p. col. illus. 21 cm. c.1939. J. Messner, Inc.

--Way Down in Tennessee. Garner, Elvira C., Mrs. (1895-), illus. LC 41-8632. 96 p. illus. (part col.) 23 1/2 x 18 cm. c.1941. J. Messner, Inc.

Garner, Sam, ed. see Scribbs, Buck.

Garnett, Charles, Mrs.

--Three Little Heroes. N.D. Thomas Whittaker.

--Young Six Foot, and What Became of Him. (Illus.). N.D. E & J B Young.

Garnett, David (1892-1981)

--Lady Into Fox. Garnett, R. A., illus. Starrett, Vincent, intro. by. LC 66-3435. 90p. 1966. (ISBN 0-393-08533-3). Norton & Co.

Garnett, Emmeline, ed.

--Seasons: A Cycle of Verse. (gr. 7-11). 1966. FS&G.

Garnett, Eve C. R.

--Family from One End Street. Garnett, Eve C. R., illus. (Illus.). 1976. (ISBN 0-14-030007-4, Puffin). Penguin.

--Family From One End Street. Garnett, Eve C. R., illus. 1937. Vanguard. **Award: (CMA).**

--Family from One End Street. Garnett, Eve C. R., illus. (Illus.). (gr. 4-7). 1960. (ISBN 0-8149-0302-9). Vanguard.

--The Family from One End Street and Some of Their Adventures. Garnett, Eve C. R ., illus. LC 61-17. (Illus.). 208 p. 23cm. 1960. Vanguard Press.

--Further Adventures of the Family from One End Street. Garnett, Eve C. R., illus. LC 56-12040. (Illus.). 254 p. 22cm. 1956. (ISBN 0-8149-0303-7). Vanguard Press.

--Holiday at the Dew Drop Inn: A One End Street Story. Garnett, Eve C. R., illus. LC 62-11218. 292 p. illus. 22 cm. c.1962. Vanguard Press.

Garnett, Eve C. R., retold by.

--A Book of the Season: An Anthology. Garnett, Eve C. R., illus. LC 61-3857. 80p. illus. (part col.) 26cm. N.D. Bentley.

Garnett, Henry

--The Blood Red Crescent. Ciriello, illus. (A Clarion Book). 1960. Doubleday.

--Gamble for a Throne. Jackson, Peter, illus. (Illus.). 1959, c.1958. A. S. Barnes.

--The Red Bonnet. Houlihan, Ray, illus. LC 64-13852. 190p. illus. 22cm. c.1964. Doubleday.

Garnett, L. M. J.

--Greek Wonder Tales. (Folk Lore and Fairy Tales). (MacMillan Bks. For Boys & Girls). (gr. 4-6). N.D. MacMillan Bks.

--Ottoman Wonder Tales. (Folk Lore and Fairy Tales). (MacMillan Bks. For Boys & Girls). (gr. 4-6). N.D. MacMillan Bks.

Garnett, Louise Ayres, Mrs.

--The Merrymakers. LC 18-17512. 80 p. illus. (incl. music) col. plates. 27 cm. c.1918. Rand, McNally & Company.

--The Muffin Shop. Dunlap, Hope, illus. LC 9-7088. 29.5 x 24.5 cm. 79p. 1908. Rand McNally.

--The Rhyming Ring. Dunlap, Hope, illus. LC 11-14159. 30cm. 64p. 1910. Rand McNally & Co.

Garnett, Porter, designed by.

--The Lark Almanack. N.D. Doxey's Pubs.

Garnett, Richard Duncan Carey (1923-)

--Jack of Dover. Oakley, Graham (1929-), illus. LC 66-28886. (Illus.). (gr. 3-7). 1966. (ISBN 0-8149-0305-3). Vanguard.

--A Trumpet Sounds. 1st ed. Werth, Kurt (1896-), illus. 191. 22p. 1962. Doubleday.

--Undersea Treasure. Dickens, Jane, illus. (Illus.). (gr. 7 up). 1960. (ISBN 0-8149-0307-X). Vanguard.

--White Dragon. Oakley, Graham (1929-), illus. (Illus.). (gr. 7 up). 1964, c.1963. (ISBN 0-8149-0306-1). Vanguard.

Garnholz, Terry & Shank, Marcia

--Fun with Fables. Iwasaki, Nan, illus. (Basic Set includes: read-along book, activity book, cassete, parent's manual & box. Ensemble includes: Basic set plus 8 boxed crayons, scissors, paste & carrying case.). (Illus.). 36p. (FunThinkers Ser.). (gr. 1-5). 1983. (ISBN 0-88679-028-X). (ISBN 0-88679-025-5). Educ Insights.

--Ten Best-Loved Aesop's Fables for Today's Reader. Iwasaki, Nan, illus. (Basic Set includes: reading (read-along) book, cassette, activity book, parent's manual & box. Ensemble includes: Basic Set plus 8 boxed regular crayons, scissors, paste stick & carrying case.). (Illus.). 24p. (FunThinkers Ser.). (gr. 1-5). 1983. (ISBN 0-88679-028-X). (ISBN 0-88679-025-5). Educ Insights.

Garnier, Charles Marie Georges (1869-)

--Legends of Ireland. Giannini, Jean, illus. Vyse, Leslie, tr. from Fr. LC 68-54128. (Illus.). 190 p. 19cm. (Myths and legends.). 1969, c.1968. World Pub. Co.

Garr, Anton, ed. see Massaro, Cora D.

Garrard, Phillis

--Banana Tree House. Hader, Berta Hoerner (1890-1976) & Hader, Elmer Stanley (1889-1973), illus. LC 38-29526. 108 p. incl. col. front., illus. (part col.) 28 1/2 cm. c.1938. Coward-McCann, Inc.

--The Book of Ralf: A Story of the Middle Ages. Moment, John, illus. LC 52-10703. (Illus.). 279 p. 21cm. 1952. Bobbs-Merrill.

--Jenny's Secret Island: A Story of Bermuda. Sweeney, Dan, illus. LC 43-59303. ix, 277 p. col. front., illus. 22 cm. 1943. The John C. Winston Company.

--Running Away with Nebby. Pogany, Willy (1882-1955), illus. LC 44-418831. 144 p. incl. col. front., illus. (part col.) 24 x 18 1/2 cm. 1944. David McKay Company.

--Those Cartwright Twins. Best, Allena Champlin, Mrs. (1892-1974), illus. Berry, Erick, pseud. LC 32-22976. 5 pl. l., 288, 1 p. front., illus. 19 1/2 cm. 1932. D. Appleton and Company.

Garretson, Victoria Diane see Cox, Victoria, pseud.

Garrett, Edward, pseud., see Mayo, Isabella Fyvie.

Garrett, Edward, jt. auth. see Fenn, George Manville.

Garrett, Edward, ed. see Aesopus.

Garrett, Edward, pseud. (1843-1914)

--An Israelite Indeed. Mayo, Isabella Fyvie. (Stories for All Seasons). N.D. Dodd & Mead.

--A Chance Child. Mayo, Isabella Fyvie, 2 Sets in 1. (Mayo Ser.). N.D. Dodd, Mead & Co.

--The Dead Sin. Mayo, Isabella Fyvie, 2 Sets In 1. (Mayo Ser.). N.D. Dodd, Mead & Co.

--Magic Flower Pot. Mayo, Isabella Fyvie. 272p. N.D. Cassell, Petter, Galpin.

--The Old Mirror. Mayo, Isabella Fyvie, 2 Sets in 1. (Mayo Ser.). N.D. Dodd, Mead & Co.

--The Salt of the Earth. Mayo, Isabella Fyvie, 2 Sets In 1. (Mayo Ser.). N.D. Dodd, Mead & Co.

--Stories for all Seasons. Mayo, Isabella Fyvie, 8 Vols. N.D. N. Tibbals & Sons.

--Well W'thout Water. Mayo, Isabella Fyvie. (Stories for All Seasons). N.D. Dodd & Mead.

--White as Snow. Garrett, Ruth, illus. N.D. A. D. F. Randolph.

--White as Snow. Mayo, Isabella Fyvie. (Illus.). N.D. Set. Cheap Sunday-School Library.

Garrett, Edward, pseud. (1843-1914), adapted by

--Aesop's Fables. Mayo, Isabella Fyvie. N.D. George Routledge & Sons.

Garrett, Helen (1895-)

--Angelo the Naughty One. Politi, Leo (1908-), illus. (Illus.). 40p. (gr. k-3). 1970. (ISBN 0-670-05047-4, Puffin). Penguin.

--Angelo: The Naughty One. Politi, Leo (1908-), illus. LC 44-827718. 40 p. incl. col. front., col. illus. 26 1/2 x 20 1/2 cm. 1944. (ISBN 0-670-12568-7). The Viking Press.

--The Brothers from North Bay. Mays, Lewis Victor, Jr. (1927-), illus. LC 66-10226. 222 p. illus. 23 cm. c.1966. Westminster Press.

--Jobie. Moran, Constance Oehler (1898-), illus. LC 42-18954. 3 p. l., 9-205, 1 p. incl. illus., plates. 22 x 18 cm. 1942. J. Messner, Inc.

--Mr. Flip Flop. MacKenzie, Garry (1921-), illus. LC 48-10104. 41 p. illus. (part col.) 26 cm. 1948. Viking Press.

--Polly Roughhouse. Hall, Myron S., illus. LC 51-14093. 95 p. illus. 25 cm. 1951. Viking Press.

--Rufous Redtail. Jaques, Francis Lee (1887-1969), illus. (Illus.). 160p. 1947. Viking Press.

--Tophill Road. Bell, Corydon Whitten (1894-), illus. LC 50-6975. 251 p. illus. 22 cm. 1950. Viking Press.

Garrett, Ruth, jt. auth. see Garrett, Edward. pseud.

Garrett, William A. (1890-1967)

--The Grand Buffalo: An Adventure at the Back of Beyond for Big and Little Folk. Edwards, Mary Stella, illus. LC 26-18640. xi 1, 146, 1 p. col. front., illus., plates (part col.) 20 cm. 1926. D. Appleton and Company.

Garrett, Wouter Van & Eubanks, L. E.

--Change of Heart and Other Stories for Boys. LC 48-2016. 59 p. 18 cm. c.1946. Wartburg Press.

Garretto

--Gloglo: The Story of a Little Circus Seal. Garretto, illus. Lombroso, Irena K., tr. from Ital. LC 53-13364. 57p. illus. 23cm. 1953. Roy Publishers.

Garrigue, Sheila (1931-)

--All the Children Were Sent Away. LC 75-33600. 192p. (gr. 3-6). 1976. (ISBN 0-02-736630-8). Bradbury Pr.

--All the Children Were Sent Away: A Novel. LC 75-33600. 171 p. 22cm. c.1976. (ISBN 0-87888-093-3). Bradbury Press.

--Between Friends. LC 77-90952. 160 p. 22cm. c.1978. (ISBN 0-87888-133-6). Bradbury Press.

--The Eternal Spring of Mr. Ito. LC 85-5687. p. cm. 1985. (ISBN 0-02-737300-2). Bradbury Press.

Garrigues, Ellen E., ed. see Eliot, George.

Garrison, Adra Coffman

--The Door Santa Unlocked. 40p. 1962. Golden Bell Press.

--Fuzzy Wuzzy Bear and Other Short Stories. LC 53-12137. 56p. 23cm. 1954. Vantage Press.

Garrison, Christian Bascom (1942-)

--The Dream Eater. Goode, Diane (1949-), illus. LC 78-55213. p. cm. 1978. (ISBN 0-87888-134-4). Bradbury Press.

--Flim and Flam & the Big Cheese. Goode, Diane (1949-), illus. LC 75-33567. (Illus.). 32 p. 24cm. c.1976. (ISBN 0-87888-096-8). Bradbury Press.

--Little Pieces of the West Wind. Goode, Diane (1949-), illus. LC 75-887. (Illus.). 32 p. c.1975. (ISBN 0-87888-105-0). Bradbury Press.

Garrison, Lieut Frederick, pseud., see Sinclair, Upton Beall.

Garrison, Lieut Frederick, pseud. (1878-1968)

--A Cadet's Honor. Sinclair, Upton Beall. (The Boys' Own Library). N.D. David McKay.

--Off for West Point: Or, Mark Mallory's Struggle. Sinclair, Upton Beall. (The Boys' Own Library). N.D. David McKay.

--On Guard. Sinclair, Upton Beall. (The Boys' Own Library). N.D. David McKay.

--On Guard. Sinclair, Upton Beall. LC 3-17001. 283p. (Boys Own Library). c.1903. Street & Smith.

--The Treasure West Point: Or, Mark Mallory's Celebration. Sinclair, Upton Beall. (The Boys' Own Library). N.D. David McKay.

--The West Point Rivals. Sinclair, Upton Beall. (The Boys Own Library). N.D. David McKay.

Garrison, Wendell Phillips (1840-1907), ed.

--Bedside Poetry. N.D. D. Lothrop Co.

--Good-Night Poetry: Bedside Poetry: A Parent's Assistant in Moral Discipline. LC 16-9615. 2 p. l., vii-xiv, 143 p. 17 1/2 cm. 1891. Ginn and Company.

Garrold, Richard Phillip (1874-1920)
--The Black Brotherhood and Some of Its Sisters: A Story of Home and School. LC 12-21602. 384 p. front. 20 1/2 cm. 1912. Benziger Brothers.
--Freddy Carr and his Friends. N.D. Benziger Bros.
--Freddy Carr's Adventures. N.D. Benziger Bros.
--The Man's Hand and Other Stories. LC 49-41550. 196 p. plates, port. 18 cm. (The St. Nicholas Ser.). 1908. Benziger Bros.

Garrott, Hal
--First-Aide to Santa-Claus. Gardner, Mary Ponton, illus. LC 29-21005. x p. 1 l., 164 p. 24 cm. 1929. R. M. McBride & Company.
--Snythergen. Walker, Dugald Stewart (1888-1937), illus. LC 23-18643. 4 p. l., 157 p. inl. illus., plates. col. front., col. plates. 23 1/2 cm. 1923. R. M. McBride & Company.
--Squiffer. Walker, Dugald Stewart (1888-1937), illus. LC 24-29552. viii p., 1 l., 226 p., 1 l. incl. illus., plates. col. front. 23 cm. 1924. R. M. McBride & Company.

Garry-McCord, Kathleen, illus.
--Dick Whittington. LC 80-28171. p. cm. c.1981. (ISBN 0-89375-482-X). (ISBN 0-89375-483-8). Troll Associates.

Garshin, Vsevolod Mikhailovich (1855-1888)
--The Traveling Frog. Pinkney, Jerry (1939-), illus. Rudolph, Marguerita (1908-), tr. from Russian. LC 66-9386. 32p. illus. (pt. col.) 26cm. 1966. McGraw.

Garson, Eugenia & Haufrecht, Herbert, eds.
--Laura Ingalls Wilder Songbook. Williams, Garth Montgomery (1912-), illus. LC 68-24327. (Illus.). 160p. (gr. 4 up). 1968. (ISBN 0-06-021933-5, HarpJ). (ISBN 0-06-021934-3). Har-Row.

Garst, Doris Shannon (1899-)
--The Burro Who Sat Down. Loeffler, Gisella (1900-), illus. (Illus.). 1961. A. S. Barnes & Company, Inc.
--Cowboy Boots. Hargens, Charles, Jr. (1893-), illus. LC 46-25286. 191 p. illus. 21 1/2 cm. 1946. Abingdon-Cokesbury Press.
--Crazy About Horses. Dennis, Wesley (1903-1966), illus. LC 57-10737. 247p. illus. 22cm. 1957. Hastings House.
--Crazy Horse. 1950. (ISBN 0-8382-0185-7, Cadmus Books). E. M. Hale and Company.
--Crazy Horse. (Illus.). 1950. Houghton Mifflin.
--Dick Wootton, Trail Blazer of Raton Pass. LC 56-6787. 192p. 22cm. 1956. Messner.
--The Golden Bird. Ghikas, Panos (1923-), illus. LC 56-5546. 152p. illus. 22cm. 1956. Houghton Mifflin.
--A Horse & a Hero. Stevens, Mary E. (1920-1966), illus. (Illus.). (gr. 6-9). 1962. (ISBN 0-8038-2994-9). Hastings.
--A Horse and a Hero: A Wyoming Romance. Stevens, Mary E. (1920-1966), illus. LC 62-19877. (Illus.). 159 p. 22cm. (gr. 6-9). 1962. (ISBN 0-8038-2994-9). Hastings House.
--James Bowie and His Famous Knife. 192 p. 22cm. 1955. J. Messner.
--Jim Bridger. (Illus.). 1952. Houghton Mifflin.
--John Jewitt's Adventure. McKay, Donald A. (1895-), illus. LC 55-5215. (Illus.). 211 p. 22cm. 1955. Houghton Mifflin.
--Marching with Coronado. LC 41-12314. 5 p. l., 157 p. 23 1/2 cm. c.1941. Suttonhouse.
--Red Eagle. Buel, Hubert, illus. (Illus.). (gr. 4-6). 1959. (ISBN 0-8038-6295-4). Hastings.
--Rusty at Ram's Horn Ranch. Creekmore, Raymond (1905-), illus. LC 51-12150. (Illus.). 191 p. 22cm. 1951. Abingdon-Cokesbury Press.
--Scotty Allan: King of the Dog-Team Drivers. N.D. Julian Messner, Inc.
--Silver Spurs for Cowboy Boots. Hargens, Charles, Jr. (1893-), illus. LC 49-6994. 192 p. illus. 22 cm. 1949. Abingdon-Cokesbury Press.
--The Story of Buffalo Bill. N.D. Binfords & Mort.
--Tall in the Saddle. Ricketts, Ralph E., illus. 22 cm. 100p. 1960. Hastings House.
--Ten Gallon Hat. 1st ed. Moyers, William (1916-), illus. LC 53-7091. (Illus.). 215 p. 22cm. 1953. Ariel Books.
--Wish on an Apple. Nielsen, Jon (1912-), illus. LC 48-82997. 191 p. illu. 22 cm. 1948. Abingdon-Cokesbury Press.

Garst, Warren Edward (1922-)
--Texas Trail Drive. Tolford, Joshua (1909-), illus. LC 52-9362. (Illus.). 214 p. 24cm. 1952. Ariel Books.

Garstin, Norman
--Suitors of Aprille: A Fairy Story. (Illus.). 1900. John Lane.

Garten, Jan
--The Alphabet Tale. Batherman, Muriel (1926-), illus. LC 64-12425. (Illus.). 55 p. 1964. Random House.

Garten, Jan, jt. auth. see Batherman, Muriel.

Garth, Williams
--The Tiny Golden Library. 1964. Golden Press.

Garthwaite, Jimmy, pseud., see Garthwaite, Wymond Bradbury.

Garthwaite, Jimmy, pseud. (1895-)
--Bread An' Jam. Garthwaite, Wymond Bradbury. Garthwaite, Jimmy, pseud. (1895-), illus. Garthwaite, Wymond Bradbury. LC 28-23145. xii p., 1 l., 88 p., 1 l. illus. 21 1/2 cm. 1928. Harper & Brothers.
--Chicken Little. Garthwaite, Wymond Bradbury. (Playroom Rag Bks.). N.D. Harper & Bros.
--Puddin' An' Pie. Garthwaite, Wymond Bradbury. Garthwaite, Jimmy, pseud. (1895-), illus. Garthwaite, Wymond Bradbury. LC 29-233561. vii p., 1 l., 96 p. illus. 21 1/2 cm. 1929. Harper & Brothers.
--Skipper Jack. Garthwaite, Wymond Bradbury. Garthwaite, Jimmy, pseud. (1895-) & Camille, Jean, illus. Garthwaite, Wymond Bradbury. LC 37-30180. 30, 1 p. col. illus. 20 1/2 cm. c.1937. H. Holt and Company.
--The Zoo Book. Garthwaite, Wymond Bradbury. (Nursery Ser.). N.D. Harper & Bros.

Garthwaite, Marion Hook (1893-)
--Bright Particular Star. LC 58-6016. 190 p. 22cm. 1958. Messner.
--Coarse Gold Gulch. Krush, Beth (1918-) & Krush, Joe (1918-), illus. LC 56-9055. (Illus.). 217 p. 22cm. 1956. Doubleday.
--Holdup on Bootjack Hill. 1st ed. Summers, Leo, illus. 168. 22p. 1962. Doubleday.
--Holdup on Bootjack Hill. Summers, Leo, illus. (Illus.). (gr. 5-8). 1962. (ISBN 0-8382-0335-3). Hale.
--The Locked Crowns. Vestal, Herman B., illus. LC 63-12880. 223p. illus. 22cm. c.1963. Doubleday.
--Mario, A Mexican Boy's Adventure. 1st ed. Solbert, Ronni, pseud. (1925-), illus. Solbert, Romaine G.. 107. 22p. 1960. Doubleday.
--The Mystery of Skull Cap Island. 1st ed. Goldstein, Leslie, illus. LC 59-7906. (Illus.). 185 p. 22cm. 1959. Doubleday.
--Shaken Days. Koering, Ursula (1921-), illus. LC 52-13634. (Illus.). 204 p. 21cm. 1952. J. Messner.
--Tomas and the Red Headed Angel. Bjorklund, Lorence F. (1913-1978), illus. LC 50-10108. (Illus.). 190 p. 23cm. 1950. Messner.
--The Twelfth Night Santons. 1st ed. Lubell, Winifred A. Milius (1914-), illus. LC 64-18227. 62 p. col. illus. 20 cm. 1965. Doubleday.
--You Just Never Know. LC 55-9854. 192 p. 22cm. 1955. Messner.

Garthwaite, Wymond Bradbury see Garthwaite, Jimmy, pseud.

Gartman, Louise (1920-)
--Kensil Takes Over. LC 64-13756. 176 p. 22 cm. 1964. Westminster Press.

Gartner, Chloe Maria (1916-)
--Mistress of the Highlands. 352p. 1st U.S. edition. 1976. (ISBN 0-688-02998-1). Morrow.

Gartner, John F
--Ace Pitcher: A Rock Taylor Baseball Story. LC 53-9605. 215p. 21cm. 1953. Dodd, Mead.
--Cager's Challenge: A Rock Taylor Sports Story. LC 54-9437. 212 p. 21cm. 1955. Dodd, Mead.
--Rock Taylor, Football Coach. 1952. Dodd Mead & Co.
--Sons of Mercury: A Rock Taylor Sports Story. LC 56-5187. 179p. 21cm. 1956. Dodd, Mead.

Gartner, P. & Winkler, R.
--Mugel the Giant. N.D. Longmans, Green & Co.

Garve, Andrew, pseud., see Winterton, Paul.

Garve, Andrew, pseud. (1908-)
--Ashes of Loda. Winterton, Paul. large-type ed. (gr. 10 up). N.D. (ISBN 0-06-011446-0, HarpT). Har-Row.

Garvey, Robert, pseud., see Cohn, Robert.

Garvey, Robert, pseud. (1908-)
--Happy Holiday!. Cohn, Robert. Schloss, Ezekiel, illus. LC 53-7473. 88p. illus. 26cm. 1953. Ktav Pub. House.
--What Feast? And Other Tales. Cohn, Robert. Matulay, Laszlo (1912-), illus. LC 73-17013. (Illus.). 94 p. 24cm. 1974. (ISBN 0-87068-403-5). Ktav Pub. House.

Garvin, John W., ed.
--Canadian Verse for Boys and Girls. N.D. Thomas Nelson & Sons.

Gary, Charles L
--Flower Fables. Watson, Carol Stuart, illus. LC 78-13576. p. cm. 1978. (ISBN 0-914440-24-1). EPM Publications.

Garyson, C.
--Alberti and the Tempio Malatestiano. 20p. 1957. Pierpont Morgan Library.

Gascoigne, Bamber (1935-)
--Why the Rope Went Tight. Gascoigne, Christina (1938-), illus. LC 80-85378. (Illus.). 26 p. 24cm. 1st U.S. edition. c.1981. (ISBN 0-688-00590-X). Lothrop, Lee & Shepard Books.

Gascoigne, Christina (1938-), illus.
--Old King Cole and Other Nursery Rhymes. LC 85-1867. p. cm. 1985. (ISBN 0-394-87487-0). (ISBN 0-394-97487-5). Random House.

Gask, Lilian (1865-)
--Babes of the Wild. N.D. Thomas Y. Crowell Company.
--Brave Dogs. Hardy, M. D., illus. LC 28-7883. 157, 1 p. col. front., plates (part col.) 19 1/2 cm. 1927. Thomas Y. Corwell Co.
--Folks Tales from Many Lands. Pogany, Willy (1882-1955), illus. 300p. N.D. Thomas Y. Crowell Co.
--The Hundred Best Animals. N.D. Thomas Y. Crowell Company.
--Pig Tales, 1 of 4 vols. (Little People's Natural History Box). N.D. Dodge.
--Pig Tales, 1 of 4 Vols. (Little People's Natural History Box). N.D. Dutton.
--Squirrel Tales, 1 of 4 vols. (Little People's Natural History Box). N.D. Dutton.
--Squirrel Tales. (Little People's Natural History Box). N.D. Dodge.
--Stories About Bears. N.D. Thomas Y. Crowell Company.
--A Treasury of Animal Stories. (The Treasury Series for Children). N.D. Thomas Y. Crowell Co.
--A Treasury of Folk Tales. LC 18-260860. 123 p. incl. front., illus. 19 cm. 1917. Thomas Y. Crowell Company.

Gaskin, Arthur, Mrs.
--The Travellers and other Stories. Gaskin, Arthur, Mrs. & Evans, Edmund, illus. (Illus.). N.D. George Routledge & Sons.

Gaskin, Carol
--The Forbidden Towers. Price, T. Alexander, illus. LC 84-16219. (Illus.). 128p. (The Forgotten Forest Ser.). (gr. 3-7). 1985. (ISBN 0-8167-0324-8). (ISBN 0-8167-0325-6). Troll Assocs.
--The Magician's Ring. Price, T. Alexander, illus. LC 84-8499. (Illus.). 128p. (The Forgotten Forest Ser.). (gr. 3-7). 1985. (ISBN 0-8167-0320-5). (ISBN 0-8167-0321-3). Troll Assocs.
--Master of Mazes. Price, T. Alexander, illus. LC 84-24015. (Illus.). 128p. (The Forgotten Forest Ser.). (gr. 3-7). 1985. (ISBN 0-8167-0322-1). (ISBN 0-8167-0323-X). Troll Assocs.
--The War of the Wizards. Price, T. Alexander, illus. LC 84-2663. (Illus.). 128p. (The Forgotten Forest Ser.). (gr. 3-7). 1985. (ISBN 0-8167-0319-1). (ISBN 0-8167-0318-3). Troll Assocs.

Gaskin, Catherine (1929-)
--The Lynmara Legacy. LC 75-14987. 408p. 1976. (ISBN 0-385-11205-X). Doubleday.

Gaskoin, H., Mrs.
--Children's Treasury of Bible Stories, 1 of 3 pts, Pt. I. MacLear, G. F., ed. (Old Testament). N.D. Set. MacMillan.
--Children's Treasury of Bible Stories, 1 of 3 pts, Pt. II. MacLear, G. F., ed. (New Testament). N.D. MacMillan.
--Children's Treasury of Bible Stories, 1 of 3 pts, Pt. III. MacLear, G. F., ed. (Three Apostles: St. James, St.Paul, St. John). N.D. MacMillan.

Gaspard, Helen
--Doctor Dan, the Bandage Man. Malvern, Corinne (1905-1956), illus. Reissue of 1957 ed. (Little Golden Book). 1957. Golden Press.
--Doctor Dan, the Bandage Man. Malvern, Corinne (1905-1956), illus. (Little Golden Book: 111). 1950. Simon and Schuster.

Gaspari, illus.
--The Warrior & The Princess & Other South American Fairy Tales. N.D. Golden Press.

Gass, Emma Butler
--Paco of the Peorias. Gass, Alan, illus. LC 37-5364. (Illus.). 84p. incl. front., 19 1/2cm. 1937. T. Nelson & Sons.

Gasser, Doris L.
--Socrates, the Snowman. (Illus.). 1980. (ISBN 0-682-49446-1). Exposition.

Gaston, Susan
--New Boots for Salvador. Schwartz, Lydia, illus. LC 72-84097. (Illus.). 48 p. 29cm. 1972. (ISBN 0-378-62659-0). W. Ritchie Press.
--Ticket for Salvador. Schwartz, Lydia, illus. (Illus.). 48p. (gr. 3 up). 1971. (ISBN 0-8402-1238-0). Nash Pub.

Gasztold, Carmen Bernos De see De Gasztold, Carmen Bernos.

Gatch, Jean
--School Makes Sense-Sometimes!. Turnbull, Susan, illus. LC 80-10281. p. cm. 1980. (ISBN 0-87705-494-0). Human Sciences Press.

Gate, Ethel May
--All the King's Trumpets. Mountfort, Irene, illus. LC 30-261908. 176 p. col. front., illus. 21 1/2 cm. 1929. Yale University Press.
--The Broom Fairies, and Other Stories. LC 18-20087. 110 p. 18 1/2 cm. 1917. Yale University Press.
--The Broom Fairies, and Other Stories. Petersham, Maud Sylvia Fuller, Mrs. (1890-1980) & Petersham, Miska (1889-1960), illus. LC 22-20459. 110 p., 1 l. front., plates. 18 1/2 cm. 1922. Yale University Press.
--The Fortunate Days. Knowlton, Vianna, illus. LC 22-218318. 4 p. l., 127, 1 p., 1 l. plates. 20 cm. 1922. Yale University Press; Etc., Etc.
--Punch & Robinetta. Field, Rachel Lyman (1894-1942), illus. LC 23-15852. 2 p. l., 118, 2 p. front., illus., plates. 20 1/2 cm. 1923. Yale University Press; Etc., Etc.
--Tales from the Enchanted Isles. Lathrop, Dorothy Pulis (1891-1980), illus. LC 26-180911. 3 p. l., 118 p., 1 l. col. front., illus. 25 cm. 1926. Yale University Press.
--Tales from the Secret Kingdom. LC 19-16217. 93, 1 p. mounted illus. 20 cm. 1919. Yale University Press.

Gately, George
--Heathcliff: Wanted. (Illus.). (Heathcliff Cartoons Ser.). 1979. (ISBN 0-685-65051-0). G&D.

Gatenby, Rosemary (1918-)
--The Season of Danger. LC 74-10008. 188p. 1974. (ISBN 0-396-06998-3). Dodd.

Gates, Doris (1901-)
--Becky & The Bandit. (Ginn Book-Lenght Stories). 1955. Ginn & Co.
--Blue Willow. Lantz, Paul (1908-), illus. LC 40-32435. 172p. (gr. 4-6). 1976. (ISBN 0-14-030924-1, Puffin). Penguin -.
--Blue Willow. Lantz, Paul (1908-), illus. (Illus.). (gr. 4-7). 1940. (ISBN 0-670-17557-9). Viking Pr. **Award: (JNM).**
--The Cat and Mrs. Cary. Bacon, Peggy, pseud. (1895-), illus. Bacon, Margaret Frances. (Illus.). 216 p. 22cm. 1962. Viking Press. **Award: (ALA).**
--The Elderberry Bush. Obligado, Lilian Isabel (1931-), illus. LC 67-20958. (Illus.). 160 p. 21cm. 1967. Viking Press.
--A Fair Wind for Troy. Mikolaycak, Charles (1937-), illus. LC 76-27738. 24cm. 84p. 1976. (ISBN 0-670-30505-7). Viking Press.
--A Fair Wind for Troy. Mikolaycak, Charles (1937-), illus. LC 83-43167. 1984. (ISBN 0-14-031718-X). Viking Press.
--A Filly for Melinda. LC 83-14617. 180p. (gr. 3-7). 1984. (ISBN 0-670-31328-9, Viking Kestrel). Viking.
--A Filly for Melinda: A Novel. LC 84-18118. p. cm. 1985. (ISBN 0-14-031834-8). Puffin Books.
--The Golden God, Apollo. CoConis, Ted, pseud., illus. CoConis, Constantinos. LC 83-4002. (Illus.). 110 p. 20cm. 1983. (ISBN 0-14-031647-7). Penguin Books.
--The Golden God, Apollo. 1st ed. CoConis, Ted, pseud., illus. CoConis, Constantinos. LC 72-91397. (Illus.). 110 p. 25cm. 1973. (ISBN 0-670-34412-5). Viking Press.
--Little Vic. Seredy, Kate (1899-1975), illus. LC 51-13558. 160 p. illus. 22 cm. 1951. Viking Press.
--Lord of the Sky, Zeus. Handville, Robert, illus. LC 72-80514. (Illus.). 126 p. 25cm. 1972. (ISBN 0-670-44051-5). Viking Press.
--Mightiest of Mortals, Heracles. Cuffari, Richard (1925-1978), illus. LC 83-43166. (Illus.). 96p. (Greek Myths Ser.). (gr. 4-6). 1975. (ISBN 0-670-47556-4). (ISBN 0-14-031531-4). Viking Pr.
--A Morgan for Melinda. 189p. (gr. 3-7). 1982. (ISBN 0-14-031524-1, Puffin). Penguin.
--A Morgan for Melinda: A Novel. LC 79-19786. 189 p. 22cm. 1980. (ISBN 0-670-48932-8). Viking Press.
--My Brother Mike. LC 48-10103. 191 p. illus. 21 cm. 1948. Viking Press.
--North Fork. LC 45-351712. 211 p. 21 cm. 1945. The Viking Press.
--River Ranch. Landau, Jacob (1917-), illus. (Illus.). (gr. 4-7). 1949. (ISBN 0-670-60030-X). Viking Pr.
--Sarah's Idea. Chanslor, Marjorie Torrey Hood (1899-), illus. Torrey, Marjorie, pseud. (Illus.). (gr. 3-5). 1938. (ISBN 0-670-61881-0). Viking Pr.
--Sensible Kate. Chanslor, Marjorie Torrey Hood (1899-), illus. Torrey, Marjorie, pseud. LC 43-51256. (Illus.). (gr. 4-6). 1943. (ISBN 0-670-63374-7). Viking Pr.
--Sensible Kate. Chanslor, Marjorie Torrey Hood (1899-), illus. Torrey, Marjorie, pseud. (Illus.). 192p. (gr. 4-6). 1970. (ISBN 0-670-05039-3, Seafarer). Viking Pr.
--Trouble for Jerry. Chanslor, Marjorie Torrey Hood (1899-), illus. Torrey, Marjorie, pseud. LC 44-9336. 179 p. illus., pl. 20 1/2 cm. 1944. The Viking Press.
--Two Queens of Heaven, Aphrodite and Demeter. Hyman, Trina Schart (1939-), illus. LC 83-8136. p. cm. (The Greek Myths Ser.). 1983. (ISBN 0-14-031646-9). Puffin Books.
--Two Queens of Heaven, Aphrodite, Demeter. Hyman, Trina Schart (1939-), illus. LC 73-17423. (Illus.). 94 p. 25cm. 1974. (ISBN 0-670-73680-5). Viking Press.
--The Warrior Goddess, Athena. Bolognese, Donald Alan (1934-), illus. LC 72-80515. (Illus.). 121 p. 25cm. 1972. (ISBN 0-670-74996-6). Viking Press.

Gates, Eleanor (1875-1951)
--Pa Hardy. LC 86-5252. 3 p. l., 9-313 p. 19 cm. 1936. Green Circle Books.
--Phoebe. LC 19-3419. 4 p. l., 11-375 p. 19 1/2 cm. 1919. G. Sully and Company.
--Piggie. Conway, Gordon, pseud. (1875-1961), illus. Hamilton, Charles Harold St. John. LC 19-18402. x, 331 p. incl. front., illus. 19 1/2 cm. 1919. D. Appleton and Company.

--The Poor Little Rich Girl. LC 12-24819. 4 p. l., 447 p. front., plates. 19 1/2 cm. 1912. Duffield & Company.
--The Poor Little Rich Girl. LC 75-32203. xii, 447 p. 19cm. (Classics of Children's Literature, 1621-1932). 1976, c.1912. (ISBN 0-8240-2313-7). Garland Pub.
--The Poor Little Rich Girl. N.D. Grosset & Dunlap.
--The Prairie Girl. N.D. Grosset & Dunlap.
--The Rich Little Poor Boy. LC 22-2347. viii p., 1 l., 419 p. 19 1/2 cm. 1922. D. Appleton and Company.

Gates, Floy Perkinson (1880-)
--Hey, Mr. Grasshopper!. Angelo, Valenti (1897-), illus. LC 49-54147. 60p. illus. 21cm. 1949. Priv. Print.

Gates, Frieda (1933-)
--Monsters & Ghouls: Costumes & Lore. Gates, Frieda (1933-), illus. LC 79-5385. (Illus.). 48p. 1st U.S. edition. (gr. 4-9). 1980. (ISBN 0-8027-6378-2). (ISBN 0-8027-6379-0). Walker & Co.

Gates, Josephine Scribner, Mrs. (1859-1930)
--The April Fool Doll. Keep, Virginia, illus. LC 9-30444. 25cm. 152p. 1908. Bobbs-Merrill Co.
--The Book of Live Dolls: An Omnibus for Children. 103, 1 104 p., 1 l., 140, 1 p., 1 l., front., illus. , plates. 21 cm. 1931. Bobbs-Merrill.
--The Book of Live Dolls: An Omnibus for Children. Rogers, Mabel & DeFrehn, Sarah E., illus. LC 46-889. 193 p. col. front., illus., col. plates. 22 cm. 1945. The Bobbs-Merrill Company.
--Captain Billie Leads the Way to the Land of "I Don't Want To.". LC 15-5297. 4 p. l., 7-93 p. col. front., illus., col. plates. 16 cm. 1914. Dodd, Mead and Company.
--The Doll that was Lost and Found. Niles, Helen J., illus. LC 3-81960. 23cm. 137p. 1903. The Franklin Printing and Engraving Co.
--The Land of Delight: Child Life on a Pony Farm. Gates, Josephine Scribner, Mrs. (1859-1930), illus. LC 15-7118. 6 p. l., 3-114, 2 p. front., plates. 22 cm. $1.0. 1915. Houghton, Mifflin Company.
--Little Girl Blue. Keep, Virginia, illus. N.D. Houghton Miffliln Co.
--Little Girl Blue Lives in the Woods till She Learns to Say Please. Keep, Virginia, illus. LC 10-25832. 16cm. 53p. 1910. Houghton Mifflin Co.
--Little Girl Blue Plays. N.D. Houghton Mifflin.
--Little Girl Blue Plays I Spy. (Illus.). 16cm. 61p. 1913. Houghton Mifflin Co.
--Little Red, White and Blue. Keep, Virginia, illus. LC 6-30466. 5 p. l., 118 p. front., illus., 9 pl. 24 1/2 cm. 1906. The Bobbs-Merrill Company.
--The Live Dolls' Busy Days. Keep, Virginia, illus. LC 84-8041. p. cm. 1985, c.1907. (ISBN 0-940070-15-4). Doll Works.
--The Live Dolls' Busy Days. Keep, Virginia, illus. LC 7-30164. 4 p. l., 104 p. 1 l., front., illus., 9 pl. 24 1/2 cm. 1907. The Bobbs-Merrill Company.
--The Live Doll's House Party. Keep, Virginia, illus. LC 84-6117. (Reprint of 1906 Bobbs Merrill Ed.). 1984, c.1906. Doll Works.
--The Live Dolls' House Party. Keep, Virginia, illus. LC 6-28222. 5 p. l., 102, 2 p. front., illus., pl. 24 1/2 cm. 1906. The Bobbs-Merrill Company.
--The Live Dolls in Fairyland. Keep, Virginia, illus. LC 13-1308. 4 p. l., 135, 1 p. col. front., illus., col. plates. 24 cm. 1911. The Bobbs-Merrill Company.
--The Live Dolls in Wonderland: An Omnibus for Children. LC 46-7881. 205 p. col. front., illus., col. plates. 22 1/2 cm. 1946. The Bobbs-Merrill Company.
--The Live Doll's Party Days. Keep, Virginia, illus. LC 10-26376. 24cm. 159p. 1910. Bobbs-Merrill Co.
--The Live Doll's Party Days. Keep, Virginia, illus. LC 10-26376. (Illus.). 159p. Repr. of 1910 ed. (Pub. by Bobbs-Merill Co.). 1981. Doll Works.
--The Live Dolls: Play Days. Keep, Virginia, illus. LC 8-25990. 3 p. l., 106 p. 1 l., front., illus., plates. 24 1/2 cm. 1908. The Bobbs-Merrill Company.
--More About Live Dolls. Keep, Virginia, illus. LC 3-26962. xi, 104, 1 p. incl. col. front., illus., plates. 25 cm. 1903. The Franklin Printing & Engraving Company.
--More About the Live Dolls. Keep, Virginia, illus. (Illus.). N.D. Bobbs-Merrill.
--Nannette and the Baby Monkey. N.D. Houghton Mifflin Co.
--Nannette Goes to Visit Her Grandmother. LC 16-7660. 3 p. l., 5-52, 2 p. col. front., col. plates. 16 1/2 cm. 1915. Houghton Mifflin Company.
--The Secret of the Live Dolls. Archibald, A. L., illus. LC 24-21427. 3 p. l., 149, 1 p., 1 l., illus. 20 cm. 1924. The Bobbs-Merrill Company.
--The Story of Live Dolls. Keep, Virginia, illus. LC 1-24915. (Illus.). 103p. Repr. of 1901 ed. (Pub. by Bobbs-Merrill). 1981. Doll Works.
--The Story of Live Dolls. Keep, Virginia, illus. 4 p. l., 103 p. incl. front., illus., plates. 25 cm. 1901. The Bobbs-Merrill Company.
--The Story of the Lost Doll. Keep, Virginia, illus. LC 5-35529. 5 p. l., 108, 1 p. front., illus., 9 pl. 24 1/2 cm. 1905. The Bobbs-Merrill Company.
--The Story of the Mince Pie. Rae, John (1882-1963), illus. LC 16-19953. 7 p. l., 148 p. front., illus., 8 pl. 24 1/2 cm. 1916. Dodd, Mead and Company.
--The Story of the Three Dolls. Keep, Virginia, illus. LC 5-38492. 7 p. l., 148 p. front, illus., 8 pl. 24 1/2 cm. c.1905. The Bobbs-Merrill Company.
--Sunshine Annie. Cory, Fanny Young, illus. LC 10-19381. 4 p. l., 147, 1 p. col. front., col. plates. 20 1/2 cm. $1.2. 1910. The Bobbs-Merrill Company.
--Tommy Sweet-tooth and Little Girl Blue. Churbuck, Esther V., illus. LC 11-28436. 16 x 14cm. 64p. 1911. Houghton Mifflin Co.
--The Turkey Doll. LC 12-29035. 61, 1 p. col. front., illus., col. plates, 19 1/2 cm. 1912. Houghton Mifflin Company.

Gates, Josephine Scribner, Mrs. (1859-1930) & Salter, Mary Turner
--One Day in Betty's Life. Stuart, Bertha, illus. N.D. Bobbs-Merrill Co.

Gates, Natalie
--Decoy in Diamonds. 1971. (ISBN 0-399-10202-7). G. P. Putnam's Sons.

Gates, Wende Devlin (1918-) & Devlin, Harry (1918-)
--Cranberry Christmas. Devlin, Harry (1918-), illus. LC 76-2524. (Illus.). 38 p. 26cm. c.1976. (ISBN 0-8193-0844-7). Parents' Magazine Press.

Gathje, Curtis
--The Disco Kid. Bertol, Carole, photos by. LC 79-11495. (Illus.). 88 p. 22cm. (Triumph book). 1979. (ISBN 0-531-02895-X). (ISBN 0-531-02513-6). F. Watts.

Gathorne-Hardy, Jonathan G. (1933-)
--Airship Ladyship Adventure. 1977. Harper.
--The Airship Ladyship Adventure. Coalson, Glo (1946-), illus. LC 76-54218. (Illus.). 219 p. 21cm. 1st U.S. edition. c.1977. (ISBN 0-397-31727-1). Lippincott.
--Jane's Adventures in and Out of the Book. LC 80-29185. p. cm. 1981. (ISBN 0-87951-122-2). Overlook Press.
--Operation Peeg. Coalson, Glo (1946-), illus. 1974. Harper.
--Operation Peeg. Coalson, Glo (1946-), illus. LC 74-8908. p. cm. 1st U.S. edition. 1974, c.1972. (ISBN 0-397-31594-5). Lippincott.

Gatland & Jeffries
--Robots. (World of the Future Ser.). (gr. 5-9). 1979. (ISBN 0-86020-240-2, Usborne-Hayes). (ISBN 0-88110-003-X). (ISBN 0-86020-241-0). EDC.

Gatti, Attilio (1896-)
--Adventure in Black and White. Wiese, Kurt (1887-1974), illus. LC 43-8277. 5 p. l., 172 p. illus. 21 cm. 1943. C. Scribner's Sons.
--Kamanda: An African Boy. Gatti, Attilio, Mrs. (1896-) & Gatti, Attilio (1896-), photos by LC 53-12532. 200 p. illus. 23 cm. 1953. McBride Co.
--Kamanda: An African Boy. 1st ed. Gatti, Attilio, Mrs. (1896-) & Gatti, Attilio (1896-), photos by LC 41-17548. 148, 1 p. incl. front. (port.) illus. 22 cm. 1941. R. M. McBride and Company.
--Saranga, the Pygmy. Wiese, Kurt (1887-1974), illus. LC 39-276512. vi, 236 p. illus., col. pl. 21 cm. 1939. C. Scribner's Sons.
--The Wrath of Moto. Bransom, Paul (1885-), illus. LC 41-17946. 5 p. l., 160 p. illus. 24 x 18 1/2 cm. 1941. C. Scribner's Sons.

Gatty, Juliana Horatia see Ewing, Juliana Horatia Gatty, Mrs.

Gatty, Margaret Scott, Mrs. (1809-1873)
--Alice and Adolphus. (Carters' Fireside Library). N.D. Robert Carter & Brothers.
--Aunt Judy's Tales. (Carters' Fireside Library). N.D. Robert Carter & Brothers.
--Circle of Blessing, 1 of 2 vols. (Parables from Nature: No. 2). N.D. Robert Carter.
--Motes in the Sunbeam, 1 of 2 vols. (Parables from Nature). N.D. Robert Carter.
--Parables from Nature. (Queen's Treasure Ser.). N.D. Harcourt Brace & Co.
--Parables from Nature. xiv., 302 p., 1 l., 17 1/2 cm. (Half-title: Everyman's library, ed. by Ernest Thys. For young people). 1908. J.M. Dent & Co.,.
--Parables from Nature. (Carters' Fireside Library). N.D. Robert Carter & Brothers.
--Parables from Nature. Cope, Charles West (1811-1890) & Calderon, H., illus. LC 42-20898. viii, 196 p. front., plates. 20 1/2 cm. 1861. D. Appleton and Co.
--Parables from Nature. De Longpre, Paul (1855-1911), illus. LC 19-29051. 2 v. fronts., illus. 21 1/2 cm. 1893. G.P. Putnam's Sons.
--Parables from Nature. Hunt, William Holman (1827-1910), illus. Johnson, Diane, pref. by. LC 75-32180. (Illus.). x, 492 p., 33 leaves of plates. 19cm. (Classics of Children's Literature ; 1621-1932). 1976. (ISBN 0-8240-2292-0). Garland Pub.
--Worlds not Realized. (Alice and Adolphus). N.D. Robert Carter.

Gauch, Patricia Lee (1934-)
--Aaron and the Green Mountain Boys. Tomes, Margot Ladd (1917-), illus. LC 70-169246. (Illus.). 62 p. 23cm. (Break-of-day book). 1972. Coward, McCann & Geoghegan.
--Christina Katerina & the Box. Burn, Doris (1923-), illus. LC 71-133926. (Illus.). 48 p. 26cm. 1971. Coward, McCann & Geoghegan.
--Christina Katerina & the First Annual Grand Ballet. Burn, Doris (1923-), illus. LC 72-94136. (Illus.). 48 p. 26cm. 1973. (ISBN 0-698-20256-2). (ISBN 0-698-20256-2). Coward, McCann & Geoghegan.
--Fridays. LC 79-17047. 160 p. 22cm. c.1979. (ISBN 0-399-20703-1). Putnam.
--Grandpa and Me. Shimin, Symeon (1902-), illus. LC 72-88877. (Illus.). 32 p. 27cm. 1972. Coward, McCann and Geoghegan.
--The Green of Me. LC 78-6606. 156 p. 22cm. c.1978. (ISBN 0-399-20647-7). Putnam.
--Kate Alone. LC 80-15592. 107 p. 22cm. c.1980. (ISBN 0-399-20738-4). Putnam.
--The Little Friar Who Flew. De Paola, Tomie, pseud. (1934-), illus. De Paola, Thomas Anthony. (Illus., Orig.). (ps-4). 1980. (ISBN 0-399-20714-7). (ISBN 0-399-20741-4). Putnam Pub Group.
--Morelli's Game. LC 81-13880. p. cm. c.1981. (ISBN 0-399-20825-9). Putnam.
--My Old Tree. Burn, Doris (1923-), illus. LC 77-98449. (Illus.). 47 p. 26cm. 1970. Coward-McCann.
--Night Talks. LC 82-25001. p. cm. c.1983. (ISBN 0-399-20911-5). Putnam.
--On to Widecombe Fair. Hyman, Trina Schart (1939-), illus. LC 76-48151. (Illus.). 31 p. c.1978. (ISBN 0-399-20563-2). Putnam. **Award: (BGH).**
--Once Upon a Dinkelsbuhl. De Paola, Tomie, pseud. (1934-), tr. Paola, Thomas Anthony. LC 76-29356. (Illus.). 32 p. c.1977. (ISBN 0-399-20560-8). Putnam.
--A Secret House. Tomes, Margot Ladd (1917-), illus. LC 70-114755. (Illus.). 32 p. 26cm. 1970. Coward McCann.
--This Time. Tomes, Margot Ladd (1917-), illus. LC 74-79706. (Illus.). 43 p. 24cm. 1974. (ISBN 0-698-30552-3). (ISBN 0-698-20300-3). (ISBN 0-698-30552-3). Coward, McCann & Geoghegan.
--This Time, Tempe Wick?. Tomes, Margot Ladd (1917-), illus. LC 74-79706. (Illus.). 48p. (gr. 2-6). 1974. (ISBN 0-698-20300-3, Coward). Putnam Pub Group.
--The Year the Summer Died. LC 85-19244. p. cm. c.1985. (ISBN 0-399-21114-4). Putnam.

Gauch, Patricia Lee (1934-) & Alleman, Tillie Pierce
--Thunder at Gettysburg. Gammell, Stephen, illus. LC 75-7561. (Illus.). 46 p. 25cm. c.1975. (ISBN 0-698-20329-1). Coward, McCann & Geoghegan.

Gaul, Cecelia Catherine, jt. ed. see Jones, Llewellyn.

Gault, Clare (1925-) & Gault, Frank (1926-1982)
--The Day the Stars Played the Monsters. (Illus.). (gr. 5-8). 1974. (ISBN 0-590-06857-1, Schol Pap). Schol Bk Serv.
--Norman Joins the Football Team. Myers, Bernice, illus. (Illus.). (gr. k-3). 1975. (ISBN 0-590-09931-0). Scholastic Inc.
--Norman Plays Basketball. Myers, Bernice, illus. (gr. k-3). 1978. (ISBN 0-590-05394-9). Scholastic Inc.
--Norman Plays Ice Hockey. Myers, Bernice, illus. (Illus.). (gr. k-3). 1976. (ISBN 0-590-10144-7). Scholastic Inc.
--Norman Plays Second Base. Myers, Bernice, illus. (Illus.). (gr. k-3). 1974. (ISBN 0-590-03197-X). Scholastic Inc.
--Norman Plays Soccer. Myers, Bernice, illus. (Illus.). 32p. 1981. (ISBN 0-590-31795-4). Scholastic Inc.

Gault, Frank, jt. auth. see Gault, Clare.

Gault, William Campbell (1910-)
--Backfield Challenge. 1st ed. 160 p. 21cm. 1967. Dutton.
--The Big Stick. 1st ed. LC 75-5821. 121 p. 22cm. 1975. (ISBN 0-525-26520-1). Dutton.
--Bruce Benedict, Halfback. 1st ed. LC 57-8964. 192 p. 21cm. 1957. Dutton.
--The Checkered Flag. 1st ed. LC 64-13917. 192 p. 21 cm. 1964. Dutton.
--Cut-Rate Quarterback. LC 77-4174. 133 p. 22cm. c.1977. (ISBN 0-525-28450-8). Dutton.
--Dead Hero. N.D. E. P. Dutton & Co.
--Dim Thunder. 1st ed. Butterfield, Edwin A., Jr., illus. LC 58-9569. (Illus.). 184 p. 22cm. 1958. Dutton.
--Dirt Track Summer. 1st ed. LC 61-5871. 191 p. 21cm. 1961. Dutton.
--Drag Strip. LC 59-14058. 185 p. 21cm. 1959. Dutton.
--Gallant Colt. 1st ed. LC 54-8852. (Illus.). 188 p. 21cm. 1954. Dutton.
--Gasoline Cowboy. 1st ed. LC 73-15784. 146 p. 22cm. 1974. (ISBN 0-525-30352-9). Dutton.
--The Karters. 1st ed. LC 65-21278. 186 p. 21cm. 1965. Dutton.
--The Last Lap. LC 72-78085. 132 p. 18cm. (Dutton anytime books). 1974, c.1972. (ISBN 0-525-45022-X). Dutton.
--Little Big Foot. 1st ed. LC 63-15750. 160 p. 21cm. 1963. Dutton.
--The Lonely Mound. 1st ed. 158 p. 21cm. 1967. Dutton.
--The Long Green. 1st ed. LC 65-12179. 160 p. 21cm. 1965. Dutton.
--Mr. Fullback. 1st ed. LC 53-8246. (Illus.). 187 p. 21cm. 1953. Dutton.
--Mr. Quarterback. 1st ed. LC 55-8326. (Illus.). 190 p. 22cm. 1955. Dutton.
--The Oval Playground. LC 68-24721. 157 p. 21cm. 1968. Dutton.
--Quarterback Gamble. 1st ed. LC 72-102743. 137 p. 21cm. 1970. Dutton.
--Quarterback Gamble. 137 p. 20cm. (Dutton anytime books, AB07). 1973, c.1970. (ISBN 0-525-45015-7). Dutton.
--Road-Race Rookie. 1st ed. (gr. 7 up). N.D. (ISBN 0-525-38480-4). Dutton.
--Rough Road to Glory. 1st ed. (gr. 7 up). 1958. (ISBN 0-525-38676-9). Dutton.
--Showboat in the Backcourt. 1st ed. LC 75-35517. 122 p. 22cm. c.1976. (ISBN 0-525-39280-7). Dutton.
--Speedway Challenge. 1st ed. LC 56-8288. 189 p. 21cm. 1956. Dutton.
--Stubborn Sam. 1st ed. LC 69-13361. 158 p. 21cm. 1969. Dutton.
--The Sunday Cycles. LC 79-52049. p. cm. 1979. (ISBN 0-396-07715-3). Dodd, Mead.
--Sunday's Dust. 1st 312-66-011381 ed. (gr. 5 up). 1966. (ISBN 0-525-40517-8). Dutton.
--Super Bowl Bound. LC 80-1015. p. cm. 1980. (ISBN 0-396-07889-3). Dodd, Mead.
--Thin Ice. 1st ed. LC 78-7863. 151 p. 22cm. c.1978. (ISBN 0-525-41070-8). E. P. Dutton.
--Through the Line. 1st ed. LC 61-12450. 191 p. 21cm. 1961. Dutton.
--Thunder Road. 1st ed. LC 52-8251. (Illus.). 188 p. 21cm. 1952. Dutton.
--Trouble at Second. 1st ed. LC 72-95469. 148 p. 22cm. 1973. (ISBN 0-525-41570-X). Dutton.
--Two-Wheeled Thunder. 1st ed. LC 62-7832. 184 p. 21cm. 1962. Dutton.
--The Underground Skipper. LC 74-23769. 134 p. 22cm. 1975. (ISBN 0-525-41843-1). E. P. Dutton.
--Wheels of Fortune: Four Racing Stories. LC 63-8587. 157 p. 21cm. 1963. (ISBN 0-525-42495-4). Dutton.
--Wild Willie, Wide Receiver. LC 74-5006. 147 p. 22cm. 1974. (ISBN 0-525-42788-0). Dutton.

Gaunt, Michael, pseud., see Robertshaw, James Denis.

Gaunt, Michael, pseud. (1911-)
--Brim Sails Out. Robert Shaw, James Denis. Tresilian, Cecil Stuart (1891-), illus. LC 67-2766. (Illus.). 158 p. 21cm. 1967, c.1965. Coward-McCann.
--Brim's Boat. Robertshaw, James Denis. Tresilian, Cecil Stuart (1891-), illus. LC 66-13128. 127p. illus. 24cm. 1st U.S. edition. 1966, c.1964. Coward.

Gause, Lynne
--Matu and Matsue. Thomas, Ora Ann, illus. LC 73-86775. (Illus.). 32 p. 23cm. 1973. (ISBN 0-87716-048-1). Moore Pub. Co.

Gauss, Charlotte Wilhelmina, jt. auth. see Gauss, Marianne.

Gauss, Marianne (1885-)
--Adventure in the West. N.D. Beechhurst Press.
--Adventure in the West. Gauss, Charlotte Wilhelmina (1891-), illus. LC 44-4514. 188 p. incl. front., illus. 21 cm. 1944. B. Ackerman, Incorporated.
--Firecracker: The Wild Bronco. LC 37-9726. 32 p. incl. col. front illus. N.D. Albert Whitman & Co.
--Kickapoo: The Fighting Bronco. LC 38-16007. 32 p. incl. col. front illus. 24 cm. N.D. Albert Whitman & Co.

Gauss, Marianne (1885-) & Gauss, Charlotte Wilhelmina (1891-)
--Bang of the Diamond Tail. LC 35-18564. (Illus.). 30p. 24cm. (Junior Press Bks.). 1935. A. Whitman & Co.

Gaussen, L.
--The World's Birthday. N.D. Thomas Nelson & Sons.

Gauthier, Josie O.
--Wild Flower Story and Painting Book. N.D. Cupples & Leon Co.

Gauthier, Villare Henry, jt. auth. see Colette, Sidonie Gabrielle.

AUTHOR INDEX GEE, MAURINE

Gautier, Judith (1846-1917)
--The Memoirs of a White Elephant. Smith, L. H. & Kite, S. B., illus. Harvey, Sarah A. B., Mrs. (1846-), tr. LC 10-32442. 7 p. l., 3-233 p. front., plates 23 1/2 cm. $1.5. 1916. Duffield & Company.
Gautier, Theophile, jt. auth. see De Girardin, Emile.
Gautier, Theophile (1811-1872)
--Giselle: Or, the Willis. Brown, Marcia (1918-), illus. Verdy, Violette, tr. (Illus.). 64p. (gr. 7 up). 1970. (ISBN 0-07-023057-9). (ISBN 0-07-023058-7). McGraw.
--Tales from Gautier. (The Lotus Library of Continental Masterpieces). N.D. Brentano's.
Gaver, Becky, jt. auth. see Ciardi, John Anthony.
Gavighusrt, Walter
--Buffalo Bill's Great Wild West Show. 1957. Random House.
Gavorse, Joseph
--The Story of Phaethon, Son of Appollo. Fiene, Ernest (1894-), illus. LC 33-6058. 3 p. l., 11-32p., illus. 03cm. c.1932. Society of American Bibliophlies.
Gavy, illus.
--Mary Had a Little Lamb. N.D. Rand McNally & Co.
Gawain and the Green Knight see Cox, John Harrington.
Gawthorpe, Grace B
--Canary Village. Potter, Edna, illus. LC 30-208196. 5 p. l., 118 p. incl. col. front., col. illus. 20 cm. 1930. Frederick A. Stokes Company.
--Chicken Town. Potter, Edna, illus. 5 p. l., 118 p. incl. front., illus. 19 1/2 cm. 1931. Frederick A. Stokes Company.
--Chicken Town. Potter, Edna, illus. N.D. J. B. Lippincott.
--Dog City. Dennis, Morgan (1891-1960), illus. LC 32-241349. 4 p. l., 136 p. incl. col. front., col. illus. 20 cm. 1932. Frederick A. Stokes Company.
--Dog City. Dennis, Morgan (1891-1960), illus. N.D. J. B. Lippincott Co.
Gay, Amelia, pseud., see Hogarth, Grace Weston Allen.
Gay, Amelia, pseud. (1905-)
--Lucy's League. Hogarth, Grace Weston Allen. 1st ed. Unwin, Nora Spicer (1907-), illus. LC 51-9589. 208 p. illus. 21 cm. 1951. Harcourt, Brace.
Gay, Charles
--Ball And Hoop. N.D. American Sunday-School Union.
Gay, Douglas & Gay, Kathlyn (1930-)
--Road Racing. LC 81-80007. (Illus.). 56p. (Free Time Fun). (gr. 5). 1982. (ISBN 0-8178-0021-2). Harvey.
Gay, Eleanor
--Hi, Ho for the Country. N.D. Grosset & Dunlap.
Gay, Jan
--The Mutt Book. 1st ed. Gay, Zhenya (1906-1978), illus. LC 32-25852. 161 p. illus., double col. plates. 23 cm. 1932. Harper & Brothers.
Gay, Jan, jt. auth. see Gay, Zhenya.
Gay, Joana
--Red Shoes. LC 48-15200. 111 p. illus. 21 cm. 1947. De Vorss.
Gay, John
--Fables. 1905. Appleton and Co.
--Red Dust on the Green Leaves. Owen, Harrison, illus. Bruner, Jerome, intro. by. LC 73-77698. (gr. 7-12). 1973. (ISBN 0-88253-219-7). (ISBN 0-88253-220-0). Intercult Pr.
Gay, John, jt. auth. see La Fontaine, Jean De.
Gay, Kathlyn, jt. auth. see Gay, Douglas.
Gay, Kathlyn (1930-)
--Beth Donnis: Speech Therapist. LC 68-149390. 21cm. 190p. (Career Romance Ser.). (gr. 7 up). 1968. (ISBN 0-671-62360-5). Messner.
--Girl Pilot. LC 66-7940. 187p. 22cm. (Career romance for young mods.). 1966. Messner.
Gay-Kelly, Doreen
--Bea's Best Friend. Gay-Kelly, Doreen, illus. LC 74-22302. (Illus.). 32 p. 24cm. 1975. (ISBN 0-13-072538-2). Prentice-Hall.
Gay, Margaret, jt. auth. see Cleveland, Helen M.
Gay, Michel
--The Christmas Wolf. Gay, Michel, illus. LC 83-1441. (Illus.). 32p. Orig. Title: Le Loup Noel. (gr. k-3). 1983. (ISBN 0-688-02291-X). (ISBN 0-688-02290-1). Greenwillow.
--Little Boat. Gay, Michel, illus. LC 84-42985. (Illus.). 28 p. 16cm. c.1985. (ISBN 0-02-737550-1). (ISBN 0-02-737540-4). Macmillan.
--Little Plane. Gay, Michel, illus. LC 84-42986. (Illus.). 28 p. 16cm. c.1985. (ISBN 0-02-737510-2). (ISBN 0-02-737500-5). Macmillan.
--Little Truck. Gay, Michel, illus. LC 84-42983. (Illus.). 28 p. 16cm. c.1985. (ISBN 0-02-737530-7). (ISBN 0-02-737520-X). Macmillan.
--Rabbit Express. Gay, Michel, illus. LC 84-29608. (Illus.). 36 p. 1985, c.1982. (ISBN 0-688-04647-9). (ISBN 0-688-04648-7). Morrow.
--Take Me for a Ride. Gay, Michel, illus. LC 84-19088. (Illus.). 32p. (ps). c.1983. (ISBN 0-688-04135-3, Morrow Junior Books). (ISBN 0-688-04136-1, Morrow Junior Books). Morrow.
Gay, Peter
--XYZ. Gay, Peter, illus. LC 30-4749. 60 p. col. illus. 27 1/2 cm. c.1930. The Golden Drake Press.
Gay, Romney, pseud., see Britcher, Phyllis.
Gay, Romney, ed. see Mother Goose.
Gay, Romney, pseud. (1900-)
--Bonny's Wish. Britcher, Phyllis. N.D. Grosset & Dunlap.
--Cinder. Britcher, Phyllis. N.D. Grosset & Dunlap.
--Conny and Uncle Dick. Britcher, Phyllis. N.D. Grosset & Dunlap.
--Five Little Finger Playmates. Britcher, Phyllis. Steiner, Charlotte, illus. LC 50-1836. 41p. col. illus. 21cm. (Wonder books, 522). 1959, c.1949. Grosset & Dunlap.
--Five Little Playmates: A Book of Finger-Play. Britcher, Phyllis. rev ed. LC 41-3680. 61p. illus. (part col.). c.1941. Grosset & Dunlap.
--Nursery Tales. Britcher, Phyllis. N.D. Grosset & Dunlap.
--The Tale of Jeremy Gray. Britcher, Phyllis. rev ed. Gay, Romney, pseud. (1900-), illus. Britcher, Phyllis. LC 35-29216. 1 p. l., 41 p. illus. (part col.) 24 cm. c.1935. Greenberg.
--The Tale of Jeremy Gray. Britcher, Phyllis. Gay, Romney, pseud. (1900-), illus. Britcher, Phyllis. LC 48-2106. 29 p. col. illus. 19 cm. 1948. Grosset & Dunlap.
--The Tale of the Corally Crothers. Britcher, Phyllis. N.D. Grosset & Dunlap.
--Toby and Sue. Britcher, Phyllis. N.D. Grosset & Dunlap.
--Tommy Grows Wise. Britcher, Phyllis. N.D. Grosset & Dunlap.
Gay, Romney, pseud. (1900-), ed.
--Romney Gay's Big Picture Book: Rhymes and Pictures of Children at Play. Britcher, Phyllis. Gay, Romney, pseud. (1900-), illus. Britcher, Phyllis. LC 47-111916. 52 p. col. illus. 29 cm. 1947. Grosset and Dunlap.
--Romney Gay's Book of Nursery Tales. Britcher, Phyllis. Gay, Romney, pseud. (1900-), illus. Britcher, Phyllis. LC 42-8279. 2 p. l., 9-43, 1 p. incl. col. front., illus. (part col.) 23 1/2 x 22 cm. 1942. Grosset & Dunlap.
--Romney Gay's Picture Book of Poems. Britcher, Phyllis. Gay, Romney, pseud. (1900-), illus. Britcher, Phyllis. LC 40-11023. 2 p. l., 36 p. incl. col. front., illus. (part col.) 23 x 22 cm. c.1940. Grosset & Dunlap.
Gay, Zhenya (1906-1978)
--Bits and Pieces. Gay, Zhenya (1906-1978), illus. LC 58-1638. (Illus.). 25cm. 63p. 1958. Viking Press.
--Dear Friends. Gay, Zhenya (1906-1978), illus. LC 59-8968. (Illus.). 47p. (gr. k-3). 1959. (ISBN 0-06-021930-0, HarpJ). Har-Row.
--I'm Tired of Lions. Gay, Zhenya (1906-1978), illus. LC 61-1809. (Illus.). 40p. (ps-1). 1961. (ISBN 0-670-39360-6). Viking Pr.
--Jingle Jangle. Gay, Zhenya (1906-1978), illus. LC 53-2662. 79p. illus. 24cm. 1953. Viking Press.
--Look!. Gay, Zhenya (1906-1978), illus. LC 52-12233. unpaged. illus. 26 cm. 1952. Viking Press.
--Sakimura. Gay, Zhenya (1906-1978), illus. LC 37-31483. 37p. N.D. Viking Press.
--Small One. Gay, Zhenya (1906-1978), illus. LC 58-3524. (Illus.). 31 p. 26cm. 1958. Viking Press.
--What's Your Name?. N.D. E. M. Hale & Co.
--What's Your Name?. Gay, Zhenya (1906-1978), illus. LC 55-14310. (Illus.). 47 p. 24cm. 1955. Viking Press.
--Who is it?. Gay, Zhenya (1906-1978), illus. N.D. E. M. Hale & Co.
--Who Is It. Gay, Zhenya (1906-1978), illus. (Illus.). (ps-1). 1957. (ISBN 0-670-76476-0). Viking Pr.
--Who's Afraid?. Gay, Zhenya (1906-1978), illus. LC 65-18147. 32p. col. illus. 27cm. c.1965. Viking.
--Wonderful Things!. Gay, Zhenya (1906-1978), illus. LC 54-12396. (Illus.). 62 p. 28cm. 1954. Viking Press.
Gay, Zhenya (1906-1978) & Crespi, Pachita (1900-)
--A Fish Story. LC 39-32606. (Illus.). 27p. 23 x 23cm. 1939. Garden City Publishing Co.
--Happy Birthday. Gay, Zhenya (1906-1978) & Crespi, Pachita (1900-), illus. 36p. N.D. Viking Press.
--Manuelito of Costa Rica. Gay, Zhenya (1906-1978) & Crespi, Pachita (1900-), illus. LC 40-30188. 26cm. 40p. 1940. Julian Messner Inc.
--One Hundred Seventy Cats. Gay, Zhenya (1906-1978) & Crespi, Pachita (1900-), illus. LC 39-27652. 26cm. 27p. 1939. Random House.
Gay, Zhenya (1906-1978) & Gay, Jan
--The Goat Who Wouldn't Be Good: A Story of Norway. Gay, Zhenya (1906-1978), illus. LC 31-22248. 39p. 1931. William Morrow & Co.
--Pancho and His Burro. Gay, Zhenya (1906-1978), illus. LC 30-22894. 26cm. 32p. 1930. William Morrow & Co.
--The Shire Colt. Gay, Zhenya (1906-1978), illus. 1931. Doubleday Doran.
Gaye, Selina, adapted by see Josika, Nicholas.
Gayler, Marjorie
--It's the New Sound. Ede, Janina (1937-), illus. vii, 139p. illus. 21cm. 1966, c.1965. Whitman.
Gaylets, Grace
--The Alphabet of Ships For Childern. N.D. Vantage Press INc.
Gaylord, Glance, pseud., see Bradley, Warren Ives.
Gaylord, Glance, pseud. (1847-1868)
--After Years. Bradley, Warren Ives. 1867. Henry Hoyt.
--The Boys at Dr. Murray's. Bradley, Warren Ives. (Illus.). 340p. N.D. A. I. Bradley & Co.'s Pub.
--The Boys at Dr. Murray's. Bradley, Warren Ives. (Illus.). N.D. Andrew F Graves.
--Boy's at Dr. Murray's. Bradley, Warren Ives, 1 of 5 Vols. (Illus.). (Rainford Ser.: No. 5). N.D. Ward & Drummond.
--The Boys At Dr.Murray's. Bradley, Warren Ives. N.D. Bradley & Woodruff's.
--Bright Nook: Or, Aunt Maggie's Corner. Bradley, Warren Ives. (Illus.). N.D. Publications of the Methodist Book Concern.
--Culm Rock. Bradley, Warren Ives. N.D. Henry Hoyt.
--Culm Rock: The Story of a Year: What It Brought and What It Taught. Bradley, Warren Ives. Gaylord, Glance, pseud. LC 41-26703. 482 p. front., plates. 18 cm. 1867. H. Hoyt.
--Donald Deane. Bradley, Warren Ives. (Glance Gaylord Ser.). N.D. Henry A. Young.
--Gay Cottage. Bradley, Warren Ives. 144p. (Gay Cottage Stories). N.D. Lockwood, Brooks, & Co. for American Tract Society.
--Gilbert Star and His Lessons. Bradley, Warren Ives, 1 of 5 Vols. (Illus.). (Rainford Ser.). N.D. Ward & Drummond.
--Gilbert Starr and His Lessons. Bradley, Warren Ives. (The Rainford Ser.). N.D. Andrew F. Graves.
--Gilbert Starr and His Lessons. Bradley, Warren Ives, 1 of 6 vols. (Rainford Ser.). N.D. Set. Bradley & Woodruff.
--Gilbert's Last Summer at Rainford. Bradley, Warren Ives. (The Rainford Ser.). N.D. Andrew F. Graves.
--Gilbert's Last Summer at Rainford. Bradley, Warren Ives, 1 of 6 vols. (Rainford Ser.). N.D. Set. Bradley & Woodruff.
--Gilbert's Last Summer At Rainford. Bradley, Warren Ives, 1 of 5 Vols. (Illus.). (Rainford Ser.: No. 2). N.D. Ward & Drummond.
--Jack Arcombe. Bradley, Warren Ives. (The Rainford Ser.). N.D. Andrew F. Graves.
--Jack Arcombe. Bradley, Warren Ives, 1 of 4 vols. (Rainford Ser.). N.D. Set. Bradley & Woodruff.
--Jack Arcombe. Bradley, Warren Ives, 1 of 5 vols. (Illus.). (Rainford Ser.: No. 13). N.D. Ward & Drummond.
--Miss Patience Hathaway. Bradley, Warren Ives. (Glance Gaylord Ser.). N.D. Henry A. Young.
--Mr. Pendleton's Cup. Bradley, Warren Ives. (Glance Gaylord Ser.). N.D. Henry A. Young.
--Rainford Series: Containing: Gilbert Starr and his Lessons, Gilbert Starr's Last Summer,Will Rood's Friendship, Jack Arcombe. Bradley, Warren Ives, 4 vols. (Illus.). N.D. Ira Bradley & Co's.
--Uncle Downes' Home. Bradley, Warren Ives. 156p. (Chip-Basket Stories). N.D. Lockwood, Brooks, & Co. for American Tract Society.
--Will Rood's Friendship. Bradley, Warren Ives, 1 of 4 vols. (Rainford Ser.). N.D. Set. Bradley & Woodruff.
--Will Rood's Friendship. Bradley, Warren Ives. LC 81-186724. (Illus.). 254 p., 3 leaves of plates. 18cm. (Rainford series). (Rainford series.). 1867. Graves & Young.
--Will Rood's Friendship. Bradley, Warren Ives, 1 of 5 Vols. (Illus.). (Rainford Ser.: No. 4). N.D. Ward & Drummond.
Gaylord, Ilsien Nathalie
--Little Sea-Folk. N.D. Little Brown & Co.
--Sandman Time. LC 15-14522. c.1915. R. G. Badger.
Gaynor, Jessie Love Smith, Mrs. (1863-1921) & Holmes, Lora L.
--Songs and Scissors. Barr, Ethel Elaine, illus. LC 2-23507. 62 p. illus. 30 x 23 1/2 cm. c.1902. Clayton F. Summy Co.
Gaynor, Jessie Love Smith, Mrs. (1863-1921) & Riley, Alice Cushing Donaldson (1867-)
--The House That Jack Built: Operetta for Children. LC 2-13864. 2 p. l., 103 p. 29 cm. 1902. C. F. Summy Co.; Etc., Etc.
--Songs of the Child-World. No. 1-3. LC 41-22477. 3 v. 26 1/2 cm. N.D. The John Church Company.
Gayton, Daniel F.
--Butterball. Furan, Barbara J., illus. LC 71-79570. (Illus.). 32 p. 29cm. 1969. T. S. Denison.
Gaze, Harold
--Coppertop: The Queer Adventures of a Quaint Child. Gaze, Harold, illus. LC 24-8810. 4 p l., vii-x p., 1 l. 338 p. col. front., illus., col. plates. 24 cm. c.1924. Harper & Brothers.
--The Goblin's Glen: A Story of Childhood's Wonderland. Gaze, Harold, illus. LC 24-21032. ix, 241 p. col. front., col. plates. 21 cm. 1924. Little, Brown, and Company.
--The Merry Piper: Or, The Magical Trip of the Sugar Bowl Ship. Gaze, Harold, illus. LC 26-12767. 4 p. l., 247 p. col. front., illus. col. plates. 22 cm. 1925. Little, Brown & Company.
Geach, Patricia Sullivan (1916-)
--Joe's Palomino Pal. LC 70-117197. (Illus.). 96 p. 21cm. (Crown book). 1970. Southern Pub. Association.
Gearhart
--Tale of the Widow's Sons. N.D. Muhlenberg Press.
Gearhart, Robert Harris (1885-) & United Lutheran Church in America. Board of Publication
--The Keeper of the King's Inn: A Christmas Interlude. LC 41-22951. 75 p. illus., plates (1 col.) 20 cm. c.1941. The Board of Publication of the United Lutheran Church in America.
Geary, Clifford N. (1916-)
--Ticonderoga: A Picture Story. Geary, Clifford N. (1916-), illus. 1953. David McKay.
Gebaroff, Ara Jennings
--Stefanie Was the Good One. Fickle, Frank, illus. LC 49-50104. 99 p. illus. 24 cm. 1949. Caxton Printers.
Gebhardt, Hertha Von
--The Girl from Nowhere. Brun, Helen, illus. Kirkup, James (1927-), tr. 192p. 1957. Criterion Bks. Inc.
Gebhardt, Marie-Louise
--The Foolish Old Man Who Moved Mountains: Stories, Songs, and Sayings from China. Aberle, Edith & Tureck, Karen, illus. LC 68-57232. (Illus.). 128 p. 1969. Friendship Press.
Geddes, Betty G.
--When Children Play. Emery, Don Woodruff, illus. LC 51-9069. 92 p. illus. 22 cm. 1950. Exposition Press.
Gedo, Leopold
--Who Is Johnny?. Gedo, Leopold, illus. Seredy, Kate (1899-1975), tr. from Hungarian. LC 39-30548. 242, 1 p. illus. 22 cm. 1939. The Viking Press.
Gee, Annie L.
--The Victory That Overcometh (Pub. by Society for Promoting Christian Knowledge). N.D. E. & .J B. Young & Co.
Gee, Hugh & Gee, Sally
--Belinda and Father Christmas. LC 49-7836. (Illus.). 28p. 32cm. (A Chanticleer Junior Bk.). 1948. Chanticleer Press.
--Belinda and the Magic Journey. LC 49-2337. 29 p, col. illus. 32 cm. N.D. Garden City Publishing Co.
Gee, John
--Timbertoes. (Illus.). (Highlights Handbooks Ser). (gr. k-2). 1967. (ISBN 0-87534-133-0). Highlights.
Gee, Maurice Gough (1931-)
--The Half-Men of O. (Illus.). 204p. 1983. (ISBN 0-19-558081-8, Pub. by Oxford U Pr Childrens). Merrimack Pub Cir.
--Under the Mountain. LC 81-482751. 155 p. 22cm. N.D. (ISBN 0-19-558040-0). Oxford University Press.
--The World Around the Corner. Hebley, Gary, illus. LC 81-120975. (Illus.). 72 p. 22cm. 1980. (ISBN 0-19-558061-3). Oxford University Press.
Gee, Maurine H.
--Chicano, Amigo. Lewin, Ted (1935-), illus. LC 70-174578. (Illus.). 96 p. 21cm. 1972. Morrow.
--Firestorm. Geer, Charles Hand (1922-), illus. LC 68-10363. (Illus.). 94 p. 21cm. 1968. W. Morrow.
--Flood Hazard. Geer, Charles Hand (1922-), illus. LC 66-103792. (Illus.). (gr. 3-7). 1966. (ISBN 0-688-21302-2). Morrow.
--Jeff & the River. (Illus.). (gr. 4-6). 1961. (ISBN 0-8382-0381-7). Hale.
--Jeff and the River. Geer, Charles Hand (1922-), illus. 1961. William Morrow & Co.
--Timothy & the Snakes. Geer, Charles Hand (1922-), illus. (Illus.). (gr. 3-6). 1960. Morrow.
Gee, Myrtle Garrison, adapted by see O'Ryan, Francis & O'Ryan, Anna Wynne.
Gee, Sally, jt. auth. see Gee, Hugh.

Geelhaar, Anne
--Happy Harry and the Scarecrow. Koenig, Marion, adapted by. Meyer-Rey, Ingeborg, illus. LC 79-86130. (Illus.). 26 p. 27cm. 1969, c.1967. Childrens Press.
Geer, Charles Hand (1922-)
--Dexter & the Deer Lake Mystery. Geer, Charles Hand (1922-), illus. (gr. k-3). N.D. (ISBN 0-448-21176-9). G&D.
--Dexter and the Deer Lake Mystery. Geer, Charles Hand (1922-), illus. LC 65-133374. 138p. illus. 22cm. c.1965. Norton.
--Soot Devil. Geer, Charles Hand (1922-), illus. LC 76-130849. (Illus.). 130 p. 21cm. 1971. (ISBN 0-448-21405-9). Grosset & Dunlap.
Geering, Gerald Leroy (1932-)
--Once Upon a Star. Gerring, Gerald Leroy (1922-), illus. (Illus.). 63 p. 21cm. 1973. (ISBN 0-533-00474-8). Vantage.
Geffen, Pauline Felix
--The Prince of Wails. Millard, C. E., illus. LC 26-19867. 63, 1 p. incl. col. front., illus. (part col.) 25 cm. c.1926. Simon and Schuster.
Geffner, Anne
--A Child Celebrates the Jewish Holidays. Myerson, Alissa Meg, illus. LC 79-51011. (Illus.). 60 p., 1 leaf of plates. 23cm. 1980, c.1979. (ISBN 0-916634-07-8). Double M Press.
Gegner, R.
--Parade of the Animal Kingdom. 1967. MacMillam Publishing Company.
Gehlmann, John, ed. see Dickens, Charles John Huffam.
Gehm, Katherine
--Happiness Is Smiling. Brophy, Ruth, illus. LC 65-231886. 1v. (unpaged) col. illus. 29cm. c.1966. Denison.
Gehr, Mary
--Littlest Circus Seal. LC 59-2856. (Illus.). 24 cm. 1952. Childrens Press Inc.
Gehres, Ethel Maltby
--Wag: A Friendly Dog. N.D. John C. Winston.
Gehrman, Bernadine Louise (1908-)
--Toto. Snyder, Corynne, illus. LC 48-151995. 72 p. illus. 24 cm. 1945, c.1946. Wartburg Press.
Gehrt, Vicky Edwards
--Lily-Fair Learns a Lesson. Paris, Pat & Borgo, Deborah Colvin, illus. LC 83-25001. (Illus.). 44 p. 29cm. (Rose-Petal Place). c.1984. (ISBN 0-910313-51-2). Parker Bros.
--A Matter of Music. Paris, Pat & Thornley, Jean, illus. (Rose-Petal Place Ser.). 1984. (ISBN 0-910313-64-4). Parker Bro.
Geibel, James
--The Blond Brother. LC 78-16330. 201 p. 22cm. c.1979. (ISBN 0-399-20653-1). Putnam.
Geibel, Marguerite Turney
--Norma's Friends: A Story of Talents. Hoopes, Florence J. & Dukes, John, illus. LC 27-19199. 326 p. front., plates. 20 cm. c.1927. Lothrop, Lee & Shepard Co.
Geijerstam, Brita Af (1902-)
--Mia-Pia. Wikland, Ilon (1930-), illus. Oldenburg, Richard, tr. LC 61-7917. (Illus.). 89p. 24cm. 1961. Bobbs-Merrill.
Geijerstam, Gustaf Af (1858-1909)
--Big and Little Brothers. McKee, John Dukes, illus. Lifschultz, Burton Benjamin, tr. LC 30-28847. (Illus.). 158 p. incl. front., plates. 21 cm. 1930. Thomas S. Rockwell Company.
--My Boys: A Holiday Book for Big and Little. Larsson, Karl, illus. Huebsch, Alfhild Lamm, Mrs. (1887-), tr. from Swedish. LC 33-22298. 4 p. l., 3-186 p. incl. plates. 21 cm. 1933. The Viking Press.
Geikie, Evelyn Cunningham, ed.
--The Old Farm Gate: Stories and Poems for Little People. (Illus.). N.D. George Routledge.
--Two Little Friends. (Illus.). N.D. Geroge Routledge.
--The Young Coasters. (Illus.). N.D. George Routledge.
Geikie, John C.
--Adventures in Canada: Or, Life in the Woods. (Roundabout Lib.). N.D. Henry T. Coates & Co.
--Adventures in Canada: Or, Life in the Woods, 4 vols. (Roundabout Library). (Bear Hunters' Library). N.D. John C. Winston Co.
Geis, Bernard see Carroll, Elsie Frances Caruana.
Geis, Darlene, adapted by see Spyri, Johanna Heusser.
Geis, Darlene, adapted by see Verne, Jules.
Geis, Darlene see Carroll, Elsie Frances Caruana.
Geis, Darlene Stern see Kelly, Ralph, pseud.
Geis, Darlene Stern see London, Jane, pseud.
Geis, Darlene Stern
--Big-Little Dinosaur. (gr. k-3). N.D. Wonder.
--Design for Ann. LC 49-8502. 212 p. 21 cm. 1949. T. Y. Crowell Co.
--Dinny the Dinosaur. N.D (Wonder Books). Grosset & Dunlap.
--The Little Circus Train That Led the Parade. Kelly, Ralph, pseud. Klett, Walter, illus. LC 55-2681. unpaged. illus. 21cm. (Magic talking books, T-8). 1955. Winston.
--The Little Train That Won a Medal. Loeb, Anton, illus. LC 47-11558. 40 p. illus. (part col.) 25 cm. (wonder book for children). 1947. Wonder Books; Distributed by Random House.
--The Musical Toy Parade. London, Jane, pseud. Setterberg, Carl, illus. LC 55-2229. (Illus.). 21cm. (Magic Talking Books). 1955. J. C. Winston.
--The Mystery of the Thirteenth Floor. 1st ed. Bloch, Georgia, illus. LC 53-613955. 208p. illus. 22cm. 1953. Winston.
--The Rattle Rattle Train. N.D. Grosset & Dunlap.
--Rattle Rattle Train. (Illus.). (gr. k-3). 1957. Wonder.
--The Speedy Little Taxi. Frater, Hal, illus. LC 55-10587. unpaged. illus. 21cm. (Magic talking books, T3). 1955. J. C. Winston Co.
--Walt Disney's Treasury of Silly Symphonies. Disney, Walt, Productions, illus. LC 80-28072. p. cm. 1981. (ISBN 0-8109-0813-1). H. N. Abrams.
Geis, Darlene Stern, ed.
--Walt Disney's Treasury of Children's Classics. LC 78-3529. p. cm. 1978. (ISBN 0-8109-0812-3). H. N. Abrams.
Geis, Darlene Stern & Brahms, Johannes (1833-1897)
--The Singing Baby Book. Bobertz, Carl, illus. LC 56-169607. unpaged. illus. 21cm. (Magic talking books, T-14). 1955. J. C. Winston Co.
Geisel, Helen see Palmer, Helen Marion, pseud.
Geisel, Helen (1898-1967), as told by see Disney, Walt, Productions & Harris, Joel.
Geisel, Helen (1898-1967), ed. see Disney, Walt, Productions & Harris, Joel Chandler.
Geisel, Theodor Seuss see Dr. Seuss, pseud.
Geisel, Theodor Seuss see LeSieg, Theo., pseud.
Geisel, Theodor Seuss see Seuss, Dr., pseud.
Geisel, Theodor Seuss, jt. auth. see Poddany, Eugene.
Geisel, Theodor Seuss (1904-)
--And to Think That I Saw It on Mulberry Street. Dr. Seuss, pseud. Geisel, Theodor Seuss (1904-), illus. Dr. Seuss, pseud. (Illus.). (gr. 1-3). 1937. (ISBN 0-8382-0039-7). Hale.
--And to Think That I Saw It on Mulberry Street. Dr. Seuss, pseud. Geisel, Theodor Seuss (1904-), illus. Dr. Seuss, pseud. LC 37-38873. 32 p. illus. (part col.) 28 cm. 1937. (ISBN 0-8149-0387-8). Th Vanguard Press.
--Bartholomew & the Oobleck. Dr. Seuss, pseud. Geisel, Theodor Seuss (1904-), illus. Dr. Seuss, pseud. LC 49-11423. (Illus.). (gr. k-3). 1949. (ISBN 0-394-80075-3, BYR). (ISBN 0-394-90075-8). (ISBN 0-394-84539-0). Random. **Award: (RCM).**
--The Butter Battle Book. Dr. Seuss, pseud. Geisel, Theodor Seuss (1904-), illus. Dr. Seuss, pseud. LC 83-21286. (Illus.). 48p. (gr. 5up). 1984. (ISBN 0-394-86580-4, BYR). (ISBN 0-394-96580-9). (ISBN 0-394-86716-5). Random.
--Cat in the Hat. Dr. Seuss, pseud. Geisel, Theodor Seuss (1904-), illus. Dr. Seuss, pseud. LC 56-5470. (Illus.). (gr. 1-2). 1957. (ISBN 0-394-80001-X). (ISBN 0-394-90001-4). Beginner.
--The Cat in the Hat. Dr. Seuss, pseud. Geisel, Theodor Seuss (1904-), illus. Dr. Seuss, pseud. LC 56-5470. (Illus.). 61 p. 24cm. 1957. Houghton Mifflin.
--The Cat in the Hat. Dr. Seuss, pseud. Geisel, Theodor Seuss (1904-), illus. Dr. Seuss, pseud. LC 57-6466. (Illus.). 61 p. 24cm. 1957. Random House.
--Cat in the Hat Comes Back. Dr. Seuss, pseud. Geisel, Theodor Seuss (1904-), illus. Dr. Seuss, pseud. LC 58-9017. (Illus.). (gr. k-3). 1958. (ISBN 0-394-80002-8). (ISBN 0-394-90002-2). Beginner.
--The Cat in the Hat Comes Back. Dr. Seuss, pseud. Geisel, Theodor Seuss (1904-), illus. Dr. Seuss, pseud. LC 58-9017. 24cm. 61p. 1958. Random House.
--Cat in the Hat in English and French. Dr. Seuss, pseud. Geisel, Theodor Seuss (1904-) & Vallier, Jean, illus. Dr. Seuss, pseud. (Illus.). (French Beginner Books). (ps-3). 1967. (ISBN 0-394-80171-7). Beginner.
--The Cat in the Hat in English & Spanish. Dr. Seuss, pseud. Geisel, Theodor Seuss (1904-), illus. Dr. Seuss, pseud. Rivera, Carlos, tr. (Spanish Beginner Bks: No. 1). (gr. 1-2). 1967. (ISBN 0-394-81626-9). (ISBN 0-394-91626-3). Beginner.
--Cat in the Hat Songbook. Dr. Seuss, pseud. Geisel, Theodor Seuss (1904-), illus. Dr. Seuss, pseud. LC 67-21921. (Illus.). (gr. k-3). 1967. (ISBN 0-394-81695-1). (ISBN 0-394-91695-6). Beginner.
--Did I Ever Tell You How Lucky You Are?. Dr. Seuss, pseud. Geisel, Theodor Seuss (1904-), illus. Dr. Seuss, pseud. LC 73-5742. (Illus.). 47 p. 29cm. 1973. (ISBN 0-394-82719-8). (ISBN 0-394-82719-8). Random House.
--Dr. Seuss Storytime. Dr. Seuss, pseud. Geisel, Theodor Seuss (1904-), illus. Dr. Seuss, pseud. LC 74-736. (Illus.). 4 v. 29cm. 1974. (ISBN 0-394-15327-8). Random House.
--Dr. Seuss's ABC. Dr. Seuss, pseud. Geisel, Theodor Seuss (1904-), illus. Dr. Seuss, pseud. LC 63-9810. (Illus.). (gr. k-3). 1963. (ISBN 0-394-80030-3). (ISBN 0-394-90030-8). Beginner.
--Dr. Seuss's ABC. Dr. Seuss, pseud. Geisel, Theodor Seuss (1904-), illus. Dr. Seuss, pseud. LC 63-17261. (Illus.). 63p. 24cm. 1963. Beginner Books.
--Dr. Seuss's Sleep Book. Dr. Seuss, pseud. Geisel, Theodor Seuss (1904-), illus. Dr. Seuss, pseud. LC 62-17157. (Illus.). (gr. 3-7). 1962. (ISBN 0-394-80091-5, BYR). (ISBN 0-394-90091-X). Random.
--The Eye Book. LeSieg, Theo, pseud. McKie, Roy, illus. LC 68-28463. (Illus.). 29p. 24cm. (A Bright and Early Bk.). 1968. Random House.
--Five Hundred Hats of Bartholomew Cubbins. Dr. Seuss, pseud. Geisel, Theodor Seuss (1904-), illus. Dr. Seuss, pseud. (Illus.). (gr. 1-3). 1938. (ISBN 0-8382-0006-0). Hale.
--Five Hundred Hats of Bartholomew Cubbins. Seuss, Dr., pseud. Geisel, Theodor Seuss (1904-), illus. Dr. Seuss, pseud. LC 38-30610. (Illus.). (gr. k-3). 1938. (ISBN 0-8149-0388-6). Vanguard.
--The Foot Book. Dr. Seuss, pseud. Geisel, Theodor Seuss (1904-), illus. Dr. Seuss, pseud. LC 68-28462. (Illus.). 32 p. 24cm. (Bright & early book). 1968. Random House.
--Fox in Socks. Dr. Seuss, pseud. Geisel, Theodor Seuss (1904-), illus. Dr. Seuss, pseud. LC 65-10484. (Illus.). 61p. (gr. k-3). 1965. (ISBN 0-394-80038-9). (ISBN 0-394-90038-3). Beginner.
--Great Day for up!. Dr. Seuss, pseud. Blake, Quentin (1932-), illus. Dr. Seuss, pseud. LC 74-5517. (Illus.). 28 p. 24cm. (Bright & early book, 19). 1974. (ISBN 0-394-82913-1). (ISBN 0-394-82913-1). Beginner Books.
--Green Eggs & Ham. Dr. Seuss, pseud. Geisel, Theodor Seuss (1904-), illus. Dr. Seuss, pseud. LC 60-13493. (Illus.). 24cm. 62p. (gr. 1-2). 1960. (ISBN 0-394-80016-8). (ISBN 0-394-90016-2). Beginner.
--Happy Birthday to You. Dr. Seuss, pseud. Geisel, Theodor Seuss (1904-), illus. Dr. Seuss, pseud. LC 59-8475. (Illus.). (gr. 1-5). 1959. (ISBN 0-394-80076-1, BYR). (ISBN 0-394-90076-6). Random.
--Hooper Humperdink ... ? Not Him!. Dr. Seuss, pseud. Martin, Charles E (1910-), illus. LC 76-747. (Illus.). 40 p. 24cm. (Bright & Early Book 22). c.1976. (ISBN 0-394-83286-8). Beginner Books.
--Hop on Pop. Dr. Seuss, pseud. Geisel, Theodor Seuss (1904-), illus. Dr. Seuss, pseud. LC 63-9810. 24cm. 64p. (gr. 1-2). 1963. (ISBN 0-394-80029-X). (ISBN 0-394-90029-4). Beginner.
--Horton Hatches the Egg. Dr. Seuss, pseud. Geisel, Theodor Seuss (1904-), illus. Dr. Seuss, pseud. LC 40-277753. (Illus.). (gr. k-3). 1940. (ISBN 0-394-80077-X, BYR). (ISBN 0-394-90077-4). Random.
--Horton Hears a Who. Dr. Seuss, pseud. Geisel, Theodor Seuss (1904-), illus. Dr. Seuss, pseud. LC 54-7012. (Illus.). (gr. k-3). 1954. (ISBN 0-394-80078-8, BYR). (ISBN 0-394-90078-2). Random.
--How the Grinch Stole Christmas. Dr. Seuss, pseud. Geisel, Theodor Seuss (1904-), illus. Dr. Seuss, pseud. (Illus.). (gr. k-3). 1957. (ISBN 0-394-80079-6, BYR). (ISBN 0-394-90079-0). Random.
--Hunches in Bunches. Geisel, Theodor Seuss. Dr. Seuss, pseud. Geisel, Theodor Seuss (1904-), illus. Dr. Seuss, pseud. (Illus.). 48p. (gr. 1-5). 1982. (ISBN 0-394-95502-1). (ISBN 0-394-85502-7). Random.
--I Can Lick Thirty Tigers Today & Other Stories. Dr. Seuss, pseud. Geisel, Theodor Seuss (1904-), illus. Dr. Seuss, pseud. LC 71-86940. (Illus.). (gr. k-3). 1969. (ISBN 0-394-80094-X, BYR). (ISBN 0-394-90094-4). Random.
--I Can Read with My Eyes Shut!. Dr. Seuss, pseud. LC 78-7193. (Illus.). (A Beginner Bk.). (gr. 1-3). 1978. (ISBN 0-394-83912-9). (ISBN 0-394-93912-3). Beginner.
--I Can Read with My Eyes Shut. Dr. Seuss, pseud. Geisel, Theodor Seuss (1904-), illus. Dr. Seuss, pseud. LC 78-7193. 24cm. 40p. 1978. (ISBN 0-394-83912-9). (ISBN 0-394-93912-3). Beginner Books.
--I Had Trouble in Getting to Solla Sollew. Geisel, Theodor Seuss (1904-), illus. Dr. Seuss, pseud. LC 65-23994. (Illus.). (ps-3). 1965. (ISBN 0-394-80092-3, BYR). (ISBN 0-394-90092-8). Random.
--I Wish That I Had Duck Feet. Lesieg, Theo, pseud. Tobey, Barney, illus. LC 65-21211. 64 p. col. illus. 24 cm. "b-40. 1959. Beginner Books.
--I Wish That I Had Duck Feet. Lesieg, Theo, pseud. Tobey, Barney, illus. LC 65-21211. (Illus.). 64 p. 24cm. 1965. Beginner Books.
--I Wish That I Had Duck Feet. Lesieg, Theo, pseud. Tobey, Barney, illus. LC 67-957696. 64p. col. illus. 24cm. (I can read it all by myself ser., beginner bks.). 1967. Glasgow. Collins.
--I Wish That I Had Duck Feet. Lesieg, Theo, pseud. Tobey, Barney, illus. LC 65-212111. 64p. col. illus. 24cm. (Beginner bk., 40). c.1965. Random.
--If I Ran the Circus. Dr. Seuss, pseud. Geisel, Theodor Seuss (1904-), illus. Dr. Seuss, pseud. LC 56-9469. (Illus.). (gr. k-3). 1956. (ISBN 0-394-80080-X, BYR). (ISBN 0-394-90080-4). Random.
--If I Ran the Zoo. Dr. Seuss, pseud. Geisel, Theodor Seuss (1904-), illus. Dr. Seuss, pseud. LC 50-10185. (Illus.). 64p. (gr. k-3). 1950. (ISBN 0-394-80081-8, BYR). (ISBN 0-394-84545-5). Random. **Award: (RCM).**
--In a People House. Dr. Seuss, pseud. McKie, Roy, illus. LC 75-37406. (Illus.). 28 p. 24cm. (Bright & early book, BE12). 1972. (ISBN 0-394-82395-8). (ISBN 0-394-82395-8). Random House.
--King's Stilts. Dr. Seuss, pseud. Geisel, Theodor Seuss (1904-), illus. Dr. Seuss, pseud. LC 39-25149. (Illus.). (gr. k-3). 1939. (ISBN 0-394-80082-6, BYR). (ISBN 0-394-90082-0). Random.
--Lorax. Dr. Seuss, pseud. Geisel, Theodor Seuss (1904-), illus. Dr. Seuss, pseud. LC 74-158378. (Illus.). 29cm. 70p. 1971. (ISBN 0-394-82337-0, BYR). (ISBN 0-394-92337-5). Random.
--The Many Mice of Mr. Brice. Sieg, Theo Le, pseud. McKie, Roy, illus. LC 73-273. (Illus.). 20 p. 24cm. (Bright and Early Books for Beginning Beginners. BE 15). N.D. (ISBN 0-394-82670-1). Random House.
--Marvin K. Mooney, Will You Please Go Now?. Dr. Seuss, pseud. LC 72-1441. (Illus.). 28p. 24cm. (A Bright and Early Bk.). 1972. Random House.
--McElligot's Pool. Dr. Seuss, pseud. Geisel, Theodor Seuss (1904-), illus. Dr. Seuss, pseud. N.D. E. M. Hale & Co.
--McElligot's Pool. Dr. Seuss, pseud. Geisel, Theodor Seuss (1904-), illus. Dr. Seuss, pseud. LC 47-4895. (Illus.). 56 p. 29cm. (gr. k-3). 1947. (ISBN 0-394-80083-4, BYR). (ISBN 0-394-90083-9). Random House. **Award: (RCM).**
--Mister Brown Can Moo, Can You. Dr. Seuss, pseud. Geisel, Theodor Seuss (1904-), illus. Dr. Seuss, pseud. LC 73-117. (Illus.). 36p. (Bright & Early Book Ser). (ps-1). 1970. (ISBN 0-394-80622-0, BYR). (ISBN 0-394-90622-5). Random.
--My Book About Me, by Me Myself. I Wrote It! I Drew It!. Dr. Seuss, pseud. McKie, Roy, illus. LC 75-85289. (Illus.). 60 p. 29cm. 1969. Beginner Books.
--Oh, Say Can You Say?. Dr. Seuss, pseud. Geisel, Theodor Seuss (1904-), illus. Dr. Seuss, pseud. LC 78-20716. (Illus.). (gr. 1-4). 1979. (ISBN 0-394-84255-3, BYR). (ISBN 0-394-94255-8). Beginner.
--On Beyond Zebra. Dr. Seuss, pseud. Geisel, Theodor Seuss (1904-), illus. Dr. Seuss, pseud. (Illus.). (gr. 1-3). 1955. (ISBN 0-8382-0613-1). Hale.
--On Beyond Zebra. Dr. Seuss, pseud. Geisel, Theodor Seuss (1904-), illus. Dr. Seuss, pseud. (ps-3). 1955. (ISBN 0-394-80084-2, BYR). (ISBN 0-394-90084-7). Random.
--On Beyond Zebra. Dr. Seuss, pseud. Geisel, Theodor Seuss (1904-), illus. Dr. Seuss, pseud. LC 55-9321. (Illus.). (gr. k-3). 1955. (ISBN 0-394-80094-X). (ISBN 0-394-90094-4). Random.
--One Fish Two Fish Red Fish Blue Fish. Dr. Seuss, pseud. Geisel, Theodor Seuss (1904-), illus. Dr. Seuss, pseud. LC 60-7180. (Illus.). (gr. 1-2). 1960. (ISBN 0-394-80013-3). (ISBN 0-394-90013-8). Beginner.
--Please Try to Remember the First of October!. Geisel, Theodor Seuss. Sieg, Theo le, pseud. Cumings, Art, illus. LC 77-4504. (Illus.). 41 p. 24cm. c.1977. (ISBN 0-394-83563-8). Beginner Books.
--A Prayer For a Child. Dr. Seuss, pseud. Geisel, Theodor Seuss (1904-), illus. Dr. Seuss, pseud. 1958. Random House Inc.
--Scrambled Eggs Super. Dr. Seuss, pseud. Geisel, Theodor Seuss (1904-), illus. Dr. Seuss, pseud. (Illus.). (gr. k-3). 1953. (ISBN 0-394-90085-5). Random.
--The Shape of Me and Other Stuff. Dr. Seuss, pseud. Geisel, Theodor Seuss (1904-), illus. Dr. Seuss, pseud. LC 73-2297. (Illus.). 29 p. 25cm. (Bright & early book, BE 16). 1973. (ISBN 0-394-82687-6). (ISBN 0-394-82687-6). Beginner Books.

--Sneetches & Other Stories. Dr. Seuss, pseud. Geisel, Theodor Seuss (1904-), illus. Dr. Seuss, pseud. (Illus.). (gr. k-4). 1961. (ISBN 0-394-80089-3, BYR). (ISBN 0-394-90089-8). Random.
--Ten Apples up on Top!. Lesieg, Theo, pseud. Geisel, Theodor Seuss (1904-), illus. Lesieg, Theo, pseud. LC 61-7068. (Illus.). 59 p. 24cm. 1961. Beginner Books.
--There's a Wocket in My Pocket!. Dr. Seuss, pseud. Geisel, Theodor Seuss (1904-), illus. LC 74-5516. (Illus.). 28 p. 24cm. (Bright & early book, 18). 1974. (ISBN 0-394-82920-4). (ISBN 0-394-82920-4). Beginner Books.
--Thidwick: The Big-Hearted Moose. Dr. Seuss, pseud. Geisel, Theodor Seuss (1904-), illus. Dr. Seuss, pseud. (Illus.). (gr. k-3). 1948. [illegible] 0-394-90086-3). Random.
--Tribune. Dr. Seuss, pseud. Geisel, Theodor Seuss (1904-), illus. Dr. Seuss, pseud. N.D. The Vanguard Press.
--Yertle the Turtle & Other Stories. Dr. Seuss, pseud. Geisel, Theodor Seuss (1904-), illus. Dr. Seuss, pseud. LC 58-9011. (Illus.). (gr. k-3). 1958. (ISBN 0-394-80087-7, BYR). (ISBN 0-394-90087-1). Random.

Geiser, Florence, tr. see Siebe, Josephine.

Geisert, Arthur
--The Orange Scarf. Di Grazia, Thomas (0000-1983), illus. LC 73-93547. (Illus.). 32 p. 1970. Simon and Schuster.
--Pa's Balloon & Other Pig Tales. Geisert, Arthur, illus. LC 83-18552. (Illus.). 96p. (gr. k-3). 1984. (ISBN 0-395-35381-5). HM.

Geismer, Barbara Peck
--Very Young Verses. 1945. E M Hale.

Geismer, Barbara Peck & Suter, Antoinette Brown, eds.
--Very Young Verses. Bronson, Mildred, illus. LC 45-2306. xii p., 1 l., 210 p. illus. 20 cm. 1945. Houghton Mifflin Company.

Geiss, Tony
--The Four Seasons: Featuring Jim Henson's Muppets ... Cooke, Tom, illus. Children's Television Workshop & Sesame Street LC 79-10142. p. cm. c.1979. (ISBN 0-307-10820-1). (ISBN 0-307-60820-4). Western Pub. Co.

Geiss, Tony, et al.
--The Sesame Street Bedtime Storybook. Cooke, Tom, et al., illus. LC 77-93774. (Illus.). (ps-2). 1978. (ISBN 0-394-83843-2, BYR). (ISBN 0-394-93843-7). Random in conjunction with Children's Television Workshop.

Geiss, Tony, jt. auth. see Freudberg, Judy.

Geissler, Rudolph, illus.
--Our Country Home. N.D. Pott, Young, & Co.

Geist, Karen
--Adventures of Sara Kitten. 1980. (ISBN 0-8062-1316-7). Carlton.

Geist, Stanley, ed.
--French Stories and Tales. N.D. Simon & Schuster (Washington Square Press).

Geister, Edna
--Eleventh Child. LC 33-32921. 5 p. l., 204 p. front., plates. 20 cm. 1933. Harper & Brothers.

Gekiere, Madeleine (1919-)
--The Frilly Lily and The Princess. Gekiere, Madeleine (1919-), illus. 32p. 1960. J. B. Lippincott.
--Who Gave Us ... Peacocks! Planes! & Ferris Wheels!. unpaged. illus. 26cm. c.1953. Pantheon Books. **Award: (NYT).**

Geld, Ellen Bromfield (1932-)
--The Jungley One. Horn, Herbert, illus. LC 57-651794. 83p. illus. 25cm. 1957. Dodd, Mead.

Geldart, Thomas, Mrs.
--Emilie, the Peacemaker. N.D. George Routledge & Sons.
--The Geldart Series, 6 Vols. Gilbert, John Clitherae, illus. N.D. Sheldon & Co.
--Glimpses of Our Island Home. N.D. George Routledge & Sons.
--Mary Leigh: Or, Purpose in Life. (Illus.). N.D. Scribner, Welford & Armstrong.
--May Dundas: Or, the Force of Example. N.D. George Routledge & Sons.
--Truth is Everything. N.D. George Routledge & Sons.

Geldert, Grace, pseud., see Boylan, Grace Duffie.

Geldmacher, Horst, jt. auth. see Blesh, Rudi.

Gelhen, H. F.
--Nell's School Days. (Illus.). (Scribner-Blackie Series of Books for Young People). N.D. Charles Scribner's Sons.

Gelin, Irene
--Momo: A Story in Verse. (Illus.). 32p. (gr. 3-5). 1976. (ISBN 0-682-48475-X). Exposition.

Geline, Robert
--Trapped in the Deep. Wacker, Jack, illus. LC 79-21988. (Illus.). 46p. (Quest, Adventure, Survival). (gr. 4-9). 1982. (ISBN 0-8172-2073-9). Raintree Pubs.

Gelineau, R. Phyllis
--Songs in Action. LC 73-6679. (Illus.). xiii, 315 p. 24cm. 1974. (ISBN 0-07-023071-4). McGraw-Hill Book Co.

Gellek, Nazli
--Golden Foot. Stone, Karen, adapted by. White, Rosalyn, illus. LC 81-473415. (Illus.). 2 p. 29cm. (Jataka Tales Ser.). c.1976. (ISBN 0-913546-28-3). Dharma Pub.
--The Hunter and the Quail. McKeon, Ken (1945-), adapted by. Garbett, Rachel, illus. LC 81-474051. (Illus.). 24 p. 28cm. (Tales of the Buddha). c.1976. (ISBN 0-913546-30-5). Dharma Pub.
--The King and the Mangoes. Davis, Grania (1943-), adapted by. Johnson, Sheila, illus. LC 81-473347. (Illus.). 24 p. 29cm. (Tales of the Buddha). (Jataka tales). c.1975. (ISBN 0-913546-27-5). Dharma Pub.
--The Proud Peacock and the Mallard. Davis, Grania (1943-), adapted by. Christman, Anne, illus. LC 81-473413. (Illus.). 24 p. 29cm. (Tales of the Buddha). (Jataka tales). c.1976. Dharma Pub.
--Three Wise Birds. Stamler, Suzanne, adapted by. Nolan, Gary William, illus. LC 81-473416. (Illus.). 25 p. 29cm. (Jataka tales series). 1976. (ISBN 0-913546-29-1). Dharma Pub.

Gellek, Nazli, jt. auth. see Beven, Annette.

Geller, Barry (1932-)
You Turned the Fables on Me: As Aesop Complained to the Brothers Grimmly. Geller, Barry (1932-), illus. LC 79-108400. (Illus.). 80 p. 26cm. c.1978. (ISBN 0-8431-0477-5). Price/Stern/Sloan.

Geller, Norman
--The First Seven Days. (Illus.). 32p. (gr. 1-4). 1983. (ISBN 0-915753-00-6). N Geller Pub.

Gellert, Judith (1925-)
Wild Jeff. Gellert, Judith (1925-), photos by. LC 70-142080. (Illus.). 32 p. 29cm. 1971. Platt & Munk.

Gellhorn, Martha Ellis (1908-)
--What Mad Pursuit: A Novel. LC 34-36550. 5 p. l., 278 p. 20 cm. 1934. Frederick A. Stokes Company.

Gellibrand, Emma
--J. Cole. (Illus.). (Every Boy's Library). N.D. Caldwell.
--J. Cole. N.D. Dodge.
--J. Cole (Pub. by Society for Promoting Christian Knowledge). N.D. E. & J. B. Young & Co.
--J. Cole. (Illus.). (The Kingship Ser.). N.D. Fleming H Revell.
--J. Cole. (Illus.). (The Editha Ser.). 1905. Set. H M Caldwell Co.
--J. Cole. (Illus.). (Boys' and Girls' Classics). N.D. Henry Altemus Co.
--J. Cole. (Laddie Ser.). N.D. Henry Altemus Co.
--J. Cole. LC 12-32415. 2 p. l., 86 p. front., plates. 22 cm. c.1896. T. Y. Crowell & Company.
--J. Cole. (Illus.). (Sunshine Library for Young People). 1900. T. Y. Crowell & Co.
--J. Cole. (Illus.). (Crowell's Child Life Series.). 1915. T Y Crowell.
--J. Cole. Kirk, Maria Louise (1860-), illus. (The Children's Classics). N.D. J. B. Lippincott.
--Kitty and Harry, 1 of 12 Vols. (Dickkory Dock Series.). N.D. Thomas Whittaker.
--Why the Robin's Breast is Red. (Illus.). 1910. Fleming H Revell.

Gellie, Mary E.
--Dolly Dear. N.D. E. P. Dutton & Co.
--Fearless Frank: Or, The Captain's Children. (Illus.). N.D. Publications of E. P. Dutton & Co.
--The New Girl. (Illus.). (The Girl's Own Favorite Ser.). N.D. E. P. Dutton & Co.
--Stephen the Schoolmaster. N.D. E P Dutton.
--Venturesome Twins. (Illus.). N.D. E P Dutton.

Gelman, Rita Golden (1937-)
--Benji at Work. (Illus.). 32p. (gr. 3-7). 1980. (ISBN 0-590-31504-8). Scholastic Inc.
--Benji Takes a Dive at Marineland. (gr. 3-7). N.D. (ISBN 0-590-31547-1). Scholastic Inc.
--Cats & Mice. (gr. k-3). 1978. (ISBN 0-590-11832-3). Scholastic Inc.
--Dumb Joey. 1st ed. Pelavin, Cheryl (1946-), illus. LC 72-76580. (Illus.). 55 p. 24cm. 1973. Holt, Rinehart and Winston.
--Favorite Riddles, Knock-Knocks & Nonsense. Gerberg, Mort, illus. (Illus.). 48p. 1980. (ISBN 0-590-31287-1). Scholastic Inc.
--Hello, Cat, You Need a Hat. (ps-3). 1980. (ISBN 0-590-05793-6, Schol Pap). Scholastic Inc.
--Hey, Kid!. Nicklaus, Carol, illus. LC 76-55364. (Illus.). 32 p. 22cm. (Easy-read story book). 1977. (ISBN 0-531-00376-0). F. Watts.

Gelman, Rita Golden (1937-) & Friedman, Warner George (1934-)
--Uncle Hugh: A Fishing Story. LC 78-4918. p. cm. c.1978. (ISBN 0-15-292789-1). Harcourt Brace Jovanovich.

Gelman, Rita Golden (1937-) & Richter, Joan (1930-)
--Professor Coconut and the Thief. McCully, Emily Arnold (1939-), illus. LC 76-27846. (Illus.). 63 p. 24cm. c.1977. (ISBN 0-03-016931-3). Holt, Rinehart and Winston.

Gelman, Steve (1934-)
--Baseball Bonus Kid. 1st ed. Floherty, John Joseph, Jr. (1892-1964), illus. LC 61-12525. (Illus.). 141 p. 22cm. (Signal book). 1961. Doubleday.
--Evans of the Army. 1st ed. Bolle, Frank, illus. LC 64-11699. (Illus.). 142 p. 22cm. (Signal book). 1964. Doubleday.
--Football Fury. 1st ed. Sugarman, Tracy (1921-), illus. LC 62-8954. (Illus.). 140 p. 22cm. (Signal book). 1962. Doubleday.
--Young Olympic Champions. (gr. 4-6). N.D. (ISBN 0-448-25957-5). G&D.

Gemme, Leila Boyle (1942-)
--Ten-Speed Taylor. Hockerman, Dennis, illus. LC 78-1263. (Illus.). 63 p. 21cm. (Springboard books). c.1978. (ISBN 0-8075-7771-5). A. Whitman.

Gemmell, John, jt. auth. see Fotheringham, E. M.

Gemmill, Jane Pancoast Brown (1898-)
--Joan Wanted a Kitty. De Angeli, Marguerite Lofft, Mrs. (1889-), illus. LC 37-27417. 150, 2 p. incl. col. front., illus. (part col.) 21 cm. c.1937. The John C. Winston Company.
--The Little Bear and the Princess. Barker, Carol Minturn (1938-), illus. LC 61-7140. 22cm. 60p. 1961. Abelard Schumann.

Gemming, Elisabeth (1932-), tr. see Bolliger, Max.

Gemming, Elizabeth (1932-), tr. see Ranucci, Renato.

Gendel, Evelyn W. (1916-1977)
--Tortoise and Turtle. Knight, Hilary, illus. LC 60-10990. 1960. Simon and Schuster.
--Tortoise and Turtle Abroad. Knight, Hilary (1926-), illus. LC 63-7317. 55 p. illus. 27 cm. 1963. Simon and Schuster.

Gendron, Val
--Behind the Zuni Masks. 1958. David McKay Company Inc.
--Behind the Zuni Masks. Thomas, Allan (1901-), illus. LC 58-8331. (Illus.). 214 p. 21cm. 1958. Longmans, Green.
--The Fork in the Trail. 1st ed. Quinn, Sidney, illus. LC 52-7182. 208 p. illus. 21 cm. 1952. Longmans, Green.
--Outlaw Voyage. 1st ed. Vosburgh, Leonard W. (1912-), illus. LC 55-8247. (Illus.). 21cm. 221p. 1955. World Pub. Co.
--Powder and Hides. 1954. David McKay Company Inc.
--Powder and Hides. LC 54-7681. (Illus.). 230 p. 21cm. 1954. Longmans, Green.

Gendron, Val & McGill, David A.
--Whales. Barss, William (1916-), illus. LC 65-14461. 30p. col. illus. 21cm. (Follett beginning sci. bks.). c.1965. Follett.

Gene, Betsy
--Sir Abernathy. Lacy, Jacqueline, illus. LC 63-90596. (Illus.). 25cm. 31p. 1963. E. C. Seale.

General Protestant Episcopal Sunday School Union and Church Book Society, jt. auth. see Haven, Alice Bradley, Mrs.

General Protestant Episcopal Sunday School Union and Church Book Society, jt. auth. see Sanford, D. P., Mrs.

Generowicz, Witold
--The Train. LC 82-73216. (Illus.). 30 p. c.1982. (ISBN 0-8037-8834-7). Dial Press.

The, Genesis Project, ed.
--Songs for Sunshine & Rain: Genesis Project Songbook. Brown, Gill, illus. (Illus.). 48p. (Orig.). 1st U.S. edition. 1981. (ISBN 0-86702-010-5). Genesis Project.

Genestoux, Magdeleine Du see Du Genestoux, Magdeleine.

Genevoix, Maurice Charles-Louis (1890-1980)
--Rrou. Thorne, Diana (1894-), illus. Rosman, Alice Grant, tr. LC 32-24665. viii, 224 p. incl. front., illus. 23 cm. 1932. Minton, Balch & Company.

Geng, Veronica, ed.
--In a Fit of Laughter: An Anthology of Modern Humor. Smith, Richard, illus. LC 78-75893. 27 ils. 320p. (gr. 7 up). 1969. Platt.

Genin, Robert, adapted by see Farley, Walter Lorimer.

Genone, Hudor, pseud., see Roe, William James.

Gensler, Kinereth D & Nyhart, Nina
--The Poetry Connection: An Anthology of Contemporary Poems with Ideas to Stimulate Children's Writing. LC 78-14926. p. cm. c.1978. (ISBN 0-915924-08-0). Teachers & Writers Collaborative.

Gentile, Gennaro L & McKissack, Vernon
--The Mouse in the Manger. LC 78-72944. (Illus.). 77 p. c.1978. (ISBN 0-87793-165-8). Ave Maria Press.

Gentle, Mary (1956-)
--A Hawk in Silver. LC 84-20145. 237 p. 22cm. 1985, c.1977. (ISBN 0-688-04213-9). (ISBN 0-688-04213-9). Lothrop, Lee & Shepard.

George, Alice
--Dolly's Doings. Price, Harriet Longstreet (1891-), illus. LC 14-18503. 215 p. incl. front., illus. 20 cm. 1914. The Penn Publishing Company.

George, Charles
--A Christmas Story. N.D. T. S. Denison.
--The Night Before Christmas. N.D. T. S. Denison.
--Sleepy Head. N.D. T. S. Denison.
--Streamlined Cinderella. N.D. T. S. Denison.

George, David L.
--Freddie Freighliner to the Rescue. Reese, Bob, illus. (Illus.). 32p. (Adventures of Freddie Freightliner Ser.). (gr. k-3). 1983. (ISBN 0-516-02496-5). Childrens.
--Freddie Freightliner Goes to Hawaii. Murphy, Carol, ed. (Illus.). (gr. k-6). 1983. (ISBN 0-89868-136-7). (ISBN 0-89868-137-5). ARO PUB.
--Freddie Freightliner Goes to Hollywood. Murphy, Carol, ed. (Illus.). (gr. k-6). 1982. [illegible] ARO Pub.
--Freddie Freightliner Goes to Kennedy Space Center. Murphy, Carol, ed. (Illus.). (gr. k-6). 1982. (ISBN 0-89868-134-0). (ISBN 0-89868-133-2). ARO PUB.
--Freddie Freightliner Helps the Fire Department. Murphy, Carol, ed. (Illus.). (gr. k-6). 1983. (ISBN 0-89868-134-0). (ISBN 0-89868-135-9). ARO PUB.
--Freddie Freightliner Learns to Talk. Murphy, Carol, ed. (Illus.). (gr. k-6). 1981. (ISBN 0-89868-126-X). (ISBN 0-89868-127-8). ARO PUB.
--Freddie Freightliner Series. Murphy, Carol, ed. (Illus.). (gr. k-6). N.D. (ISBN 0-89868-124-3). (ISBN 0-89868-125-1). ARO PUB.
--Freddie Freightliner to the Rescue. Murphy, Carol, ed. (Illus.). (gr. k-6). 1982. (ISBN 0-89868-130-8). (ISBN 0-89868-131-6). ARO PUB.

George, Ema
--Around the World with Santa Claus. Asselin, Roberta, illus. LC 37-10696. (Illus.). 35p. 27cm. 1936. Suttonhouse Ltd.

George, Harry S.
--Demo of Seventieth Street. Quackenbush, Robert Mead (1929-), illus. LC 79-109124. (Illus.). 160p. (gr. 4-7). 1971. (ISBN 0-8098-2412-4). Walck.

George, Jean Craighead, jt. auth. see George, John Lothar.

George, Jean Craighead (1919-)
--All Upon a Sidewalk. 1st ed. Bolognese, Donald Alan (1934-), illus. LC 74-5229. (Illus.). 48 p. 22cm. 1974. (ISBN 0-525-25462-5). Dutton.
--All Upon a Stone. Bolognese, Donald Alan (1934-), illus. LC 75-101929. (Illus.). 48 p. 19cm. 1971. (ISBN 0-690-05533-1). Crowell. **Award: (ALA).**
--Coyote in Manhattan. Kaufmann, John (1931-), illus. LC 68-13579. (Illus.). 203 p. 21cm. 1968. T. Y. Crowell Co.
--The Cry of the Crow. LC 79-2016. 160p. (gr. 5 up). 1980. (ISBN 0-06-021956-4, HarpJ). (ISBN 0-06-021957-2). Har-Row.
--The Cry of the Crow. LC 79-2016. 160p. (A Trophy Bk.). (gr. 5 up). 1982. (ISBN 0-06-440131-6, Trophy). Har-Row.
--The Cry of the Crow: A Novel. LC 79-2016. 149 p. 21cm. c.1980. (ISBN 0-06-021956-4). (ISBN 0-06-021958-0). Harper & Row.
--Going to the Sun. George, Jean Craighead (1919-), illus. LC 75-25403. 132 p. 22cm. c.1976. (ISBN 0-06-021941-6). (ISBN 0-06-021942-4). Harper & Row.
--Going to the Sun. George, Jean Craighead (1919-), illus. 132p. 20cm. (Harper Trophy Book). 1977, c.1976. (ISBN 0-06-440088-3). Harper & Row.
--The Grizzly Bear with the Golden Ears. Catania, Tom, illus. 1982. Harper.
--The Grizzly Bear with the Golden Ears. Schoenherr, John Carl (1935-), illus. LC 80-7908. p. cm. 1981. (ISBN 0-06-021965-3). (ISBN 0-06-021966-1). Harper & Row.
--Gull Number Seven-Three-Seven. George, Jean Craighead (1919-), illus. LC 64-16531. (Illus.). 198p. (gr. 5-10). 1964. (ISBN 0-690-36171-8, TYC-J). Har-Row. **Award: (ALA).**
--Hold Zero!. LC 66-6356. 161p. 21cm. c.1966. Crowell.
--The Hole in the Tree. George, Jean Craighead (1919-), illus. LC 57-5348. (Illus.). 23cm. 54p. 1957. Dutton.
--Hook a Fish, Catch a Mountain. George, Jean Craighead (1919-), illus. LC 74-23884. 129 p. 22cm. 1975. (ISBN 0-525-32155-1). Dutton.
--Julie of the Wolves. Schoenherr, John Carl (1935-), illus. LC 73-4584. (Illus.). 212 p. 25cm. 1973, c.1972. (ISBN 0-8161-6102-X). G. K. Hall.
--Julie of the Wolves. Schoenherr, John Carl (1935-), illus. LC 72-76509. (Illus.). 170 p. 22cm. 1972. (ISBN 0-06-021943-2). (ISBN 0-06-021944-0). Harper & Row. **Awards: (JNM); (ALA).**
--The Moon of the Bears. Shepard, Mac, illus. (The Thirteen Moons). (gr. 3-6). 1967. (ISBN 0-690-55537-7). (ISBN 0-690-55538-5). Thomas Y. Crowell.

--The Moon of the Chickarees. Schoenherr, John Carl (1935-), illus. (The Thirteen Moons). 1968. (ISBN 0-690-55540-7). (ISBN 0-690-55541-5). Thomas Y. Crowell.
--The Moon of the Deer. Zallinger, Jean Day (1918-), illus. LC 69-13637. (Illus.). 40 p. 23cm. (Her The thirteen moons). 1969. Crowell.
--The Moon of the Moles. Levering, Robert, illus. (The Thirteen Moons). 1969. (ISBN 0-690-55552-0). (ISBN 0-690-55553-9). Thomas Y. Crowell.
--The Moon of the Monarch Butterflies. Tinkelman, Murray (1933-), illus. LC 68-13581. (Illus.). 40 p. 23cm. (Her The thirteen moons). 1968. Crowell.
--The Moon of the Mountain Lions. Lubell, Winifred A. Milius (1914-), illus. LC 68-21951. (Illus.). 39 p. 23cm. (Her Thirteen moons). 1968. T. Y. Crowell.
--Moon of the Winter Bird. Mizumura, Kazue, illus. (Illus.). (Thirteen Moons Ser). (gr. 4-6). 1970. (ISBN 0-690-55570-9). (ISBN 0-690-55571-7). T Y Crowell.
--My Side of the Mountain. George, Jean Craighead (1919-), illus. LC 59-7799. (Illus.). 178 p. 21cm. 1959. Dutton. **Award: (JNM).**
--One Day in the Desert. Brenner, Fred (1920-), illus. LC 82-45924. (Illus.). 48p. (gr. 5-7). 1983. (ISBN 0-690-04340-6, TYC-J). (ISBN 0-690-04341-4). Har-Row.
--Red Robin Fly Up!. George, Jean Craighead (1919-), illus. 1963. Reader's Digest.
--River Rats, Inc. LC 78-12318. 136 p. 22cm. c.1979. (ISBN 0-525-38455-3). Dutton.
--Snow Tracks. George, Jean Craighead (1919-), illus. LC 58-5232. (Illus.). 61 p. 23cm. 1958. Dutton.
--The Summer of the Falcon. George, Jean Craighead (1919-), illus. LC 62-16543. (Illus.). 153 p. 21cm. 1962. Crowell.
--The Talking Earth. LC 82-48850. p. cm. c.1983. (ISBN 0-06-021975-0). (ISBN 0-06-021976-9). Harper & Row.
--The Wentletrap Trap. Shimin, Symeon (1902-), illus. LC 77-4834. 25cm. 32p. 1977. (ISBN 0-525-42310-9). Dutton.
--Who Really Killed Cock Robin: An Ecological Mystery. LC 76-157944. 22cm. 149p. (gr. 4-7). 1971. Dutton.
--The Wounded Wolf. Schoenherr, John Carl (1935-), illus. LC 76-58711. (Illus.). 32 p. c.1978. (ISBN 0-06-021949-1). (ISBN 0-06-021950-5). Harper & Row.

George, John Lothar (1916-) & George, Jean Craighead (1919-)
--Bubo, the Great Horned Owl. George, Jean Craighead (1919-), illus. (Illus.). (gr. 6-9). 1954. (ISBN 0-525-27308-5). Dutton.
--Dipper of Copper Creek. George, Jean Craighead (1919-), illus. LC 56-8306. (Illus.). 183p. (American Wood & Tales Ser.). (gr. 5-9). 1956. (ISBN 0-525-28724-8). Dutton.
--Masked Prowler: The Story of a Raccoon. George, Jean Craighead (1919-), illus. 1950. Dutton.
--Meph, the Pet Skunk. George, Jean Craighead (1919-), illus. LC 52-7799. (Illus.). 180 p. 22cm. (American woodland tables). 1952. Dutton.
--Vison, the Mink. George, Jean Craighead (1919-), illus. (Illus.). (gr. 6-9). 1949. (ISBN 0-525-42037-1). Dutton.
--Vulpes, the Red Fox. George, Jean Craighead (1919-), illus. 184p. 1948. Dutton.

George, Katharine, et al.
--The Dog Watch & Other Stories. Uczen, Rebecca, illus. LC 81-67685. (Illus.). 48p. (Orig.). (gr. 4-6). 1981. (ISBN 0-9607638-0-5). Cobblestone Pub.

George, Richard Robert (1943-), adapted by see Dahl, Roald.

George, Richard Robert (1943-)
--Roald Dahl's Charlie and the Chocolate Factory: A Play. Dahl, Roaldhard Robert (1916-), ed. LC 76-16202. p. cm. 1976. (ISBN 0-394-83370-8). Knopf.

George, Sidney Charles (1898-)
--Amat's Elephant. 1959. Macmillan.
--The Blue Ray. (Three Star Bks.). N.D. Frederick Warne & Co.
--Burma Story. 1948. Warne.
--Daughters of Arabia. 1958. Warne.
--Eagle of the Desert. 1944. Warne.
--Hidden Treasure. (Illus.). 73p. 1972. David & Charles.
--Lost Empire. 1937. Warne.
--Midshipman's Luck. 1955. Warne.
--Pirates of the Lagoon. 1946. Warne.
--Red Goddess. 1939. Warne.
--Two Spies. 1948. Warne.

Georgel
--Cat Tales. (Illus.). 32p. (gr. 1-7). 1972. (ISBN 0-912954-03-5). Edmond Pub Co.

Georgiady, Nicholas P. & Romano, Louis G. (1921-)
--Gertie the Duck. Wilson, Dagmar (1916-), illus. (Illus.). (Beginning-to-Read Ser.). (gr. 1-3). 1959. (ISBN 0-695-43363-6). (ISBN 0-685-10942-9). Follett.
--Our National Anthem. McCann, Gerald (1916-), illus. (Illus.). (gr. 2-4). 1963. (ISBN 0-695-46680-1). Follett.

Georgiana
--Animal Jingles. Peller, Jackie, illus. LC 50-38006. (Illus.). 32p. 17cm. (Tell-a-Tale Bks.). 1950. Whitman.
--Dr. Goat. Clement, Charles (1921-), illus. LC 50-4107. (Illus.). 32p. 17cm. (Tell-a-Tale Bks.). 1950. Whitman.
--Let's Play. Gavy, illus. LC 53-22436. unpaged. illus. 17cm. (Tell-a-tale books). 1953, c.1952. Whitman Pub. Co.
--Puffy. Porter, Genevieve, illus. unpaged. illus. 17cm. (Tell-a-tale books). c.1952. Whitman Pub. Co.
--Teddy's Surprise. Suzanne, illus. LC 52-36194. unpaged. illus. 17 cm. (Tell-a-tale books). N.D. Whitman Pub. Co.
--That Donkey. Grider, Dorothy (1915-), illus. unpaged. illus. 17cm. (Tell-a-tale books). c.1954. Whitman Pub. Co.

Georgin, Steven Demetre see Stevens, Cat, pseud.

Georgiou, Constantine (1927-)
--The Clock. Lipscomb, Bernard, illus. (Illus.). 37 p. 25cm. 1967. Harvey House.
--The Nest. Tudor, Bethany, illus. LC 72-76396. (Illus.). 37 p. 25cm. 1972. (ISBN 0-8178-4891-6). (ISBN 0-8178-4891-6). Harvey House.
--Proserpina: The Duck That Came to School. Lipscomb, Bernard, illus. (Illus.). 60 p. 27cm. 1968. Harvey House.
--Rani, Queen of the Jungle. Sandin, Joan (1942-), illus. LC 70-88154. (Illus.). 32 p. 26cm. 1970. (ISBN 0-13-753053-6). Prentice-Hall.
--Rani, Queen of the Jungle. Sandin, Joan (1942-), illus. (Illus.). 1 v. (unpaged. 23cm. 1974, c.1970. (ISBN 0-13-753061-7). Prentice Hall.

Gerard, F.
--The Scarlet Beast. N.D. Longmans Green & Co.

Gerard, Jane (1930-)
--Jet Stewardess. LC 62-10200. 188 p. 21cm. (Career romance for young moderns). 1962. Messner.
--Overseas Teacher. LC 63-8647. 190 p. 21cm. (Career romance for young moderns). 1963. Messner.

Gerard, Mary Gold see Wheeler, Jane, pseud.

Gerard, Mary Gold (1908-)
--In They Go!. Cummings, Alison, illus. LC 56-25012. unpaged. illus. 22cm. (Cozy-corner book). c.1955. Whitman Pub. Co.

Gerard, Mary Gold (1908-), ed.
--Bedtime Stories for Wide-Awake Children. Wheeler, Jane, pseud. LC 39-22041. (Illus.). 72. 31cm. 1939. McLoughlin Brothers Inc.

Gerard, Morice
--Jock o' th' Beach. N.D. Thomas Nelson & Sons.

Geras, Adele Daphne (1944-)
--Apricots at Midnight and Other Stories from a Patchwork Quilt. Caldwell, Doreen, illus. LC 82-1728. (Illus.). 24cm. 141p. 1982, c.1977. (ISBN 0-689-30921-X). Atheneum.
--The Girls in the Velvet Frame. LC 79-12352. 149 p. 21cm. 1979, c.1978. (ISBN 0-689-30729-2). Atheneum. **Award: (ALA).**
--Other Echoes. LC 81-8080. p. cm. 1982. (ISBN 0-689-30877-9). (ISBN 0-689-30877-9). Atheneum.
--Snapshots of Paradise: Love Stories. LC 84-2934. 180p. (gr. 8 up). 1984. (ISBN 0-689-31045-5). Atheneum.
--Voyage. LC 82-13760. 193 p. 22cm. 1983. (ISBN 0-689-30955-4). Atheneum.

Gerber, Merrill Joan (1938-)
--Name a Star for Me: A Novel. LC 82-4788. p. cm. 1983. (ISBN 0-670-50389-4). (ISBN 0-670-50389-4). Viking.
--Please Don't Kiss Me Now. LC 80-25575. 218 p. 22cm. c.1981. (ISBN 0-8037-6792-7). Dial Press.

Gerber, William (1908-)
--Gooseberry Jones. Morris, Dudley Henry (1912-), illus. LC 47-30791. 96 p. illus. 22 cm. 1947. G. P. Putnam's Sons.
--Judishus. Mack, Gwynne Dresser, illus. LC 46-1714. (Illus.). 21cm. viii, 25p. 1946. W. Hebbard.

Gerber, William (1908-) & Goish, Genevive
--The Rings on Woot-Kew's Tail: Indian Legends of the Origin of the Sun, Moon & Stars. (Indian Culture Ser.). (gr. 3-9). 1973. (ISBN 0-89992-059-4). MT Coun Indian.

Gerberding, Elizabeth Sears, Mrs.
--The Golden Chimney. LC 1-25730. 213p. 1902. A. M. Robertson.

Gerdeman, Leah, jt. auth. see Griffin, Thomas H.

Gerdes, Florence Marie, retold by see Vergilius Maro, Publius.

Gerds, Gretchen
--Steve and the Burro's Secret. Weiss, Emil (1896-1965), illus. LC 59-15448. (Illus.). 21cm. 110p. 1960. Lee & Shepard.

Gere, Frances Kent
--Boy of Babylon. LC 41-17549. ix, 118 p. illus. 24 x 19 cm. c.1941. Longmans, Green and Co.
--Once Upon a Time in Egypt. LC 37-28711. 71 p. incl. col. front., illus. (part col.) 22 x 27 cm. 1937. Longmans, Green and Co.

Geren, Carl
--Shell Hunter. Maggard, John, illus. LC 77-1161. (Illus.). 47 p. 24cm. c.1977. (ISBN 0-516-03611-4). Childrens Press.

Gerez, Toni De see De Gerez, Toni.

Gergely, Marta
--Invitation to the Zoo. Rona, Emy (1904-), illus. LC 67-27289. (Illus.). 36 p. 34cm. 1968, c.1967. Lion Press.

Gergely, Tibor (1900-1978)
--Baby Wild Animals from A to Z. Gergely, Tibor (1900-1978), illus. LC 72-86428. (Illus.). 32cm. 24p. (A Golden Sturdy Happy Bk.). 1973. Golden Press.
--Busy Day, Busy People. LC 73-2448. (Illus.). 32 p. 21cm. 1973. (ISBN 0-394-82686-8). Random House.
--Emily's Moo. Gergely, Tibor (1900-1978), illus. (Illus.). (Golden Beginning Reader Ser). (ps-k). 1969. (ISBN 0-307-61154-X, Golden Pr). Western Pub.
--The Noah's Ark Book. LC 68-7748. (Illus.). 24 p. 22cm. (Golden book for kindergarten). c.1966. Golden Press.
--Scuffy the Tugboat. Gergely, Tibor (1900-1978), illus. (Illus.). (ps-1). 1972. (ISBN 0-307-68928-X, Golden Pr). Western Pub.
--Tibor Gergely's Great Big Book of Bedtime Stories. (Big Giant Bk). 1967. (ISBN 0-307-16529-9, Golden Pr). Western Pub.

Gergely, Tibor (1900-1978), ed.
--Bedtime Stories. Gergely, Tibor (1900-1978), illus. LC 72-191156. (Illus.). 48 p. 31cm. 1972. Golden Press.
--The Golden Storytime Book of Nursery Tales. Gergely, Tibor (1900-1978), illus. 1957. Golden Press.
--Great Big Book of Bedtime Stories. Gergely, Tibor (1900-1978), illus. LC 67-20159. (Illus.). 384 p. 27cm. 1967. Golden Press.
--The Great Big Fire Engine Book. Gergely, Tibor (1900-1978), illus. LC 50-12946. 1950. Simon & Schuster.
--Noah's Ark. Gergely, Tibor (1900-1978), illus. (Illus.). 24p. (ps). 1983. (ISBN 0-307-11482-1, Golden Pr). Western Pub.

Gerhard, Mae, illus.
--The Golden Bird: Folk Tales from Slovenia. Dekker, Jan & Lencek, Helen, trs. 160p. 1969. World Publishing Company.
--Sounds are High, Sounds are Low. (A Golden Science Reader Bk.). N.D. Golden Press.

Gerin, Winifred (1901-1981)
--Young Fanny Burney. 1961. Nelson.

Geringer, Laura (1948-)
--A Three Hat Day. Lobel, Arnold Stark (1933-), illus. LC 85-42640. (Illus.). 32 p. 24cm. c.1985. (ISBN 0-06-021988-2). (ISBN 0-06-021989-0). Harper & Row. **Award: (ALA).**

Gerler, William Robert (1917-)
--A Pack of Riddles. 1st ed. Maestro, Giulio (1942-), illus. LC 75-6781. (Illus.). 80 p. 20cm. 1975. (ISBN 0-525-36530-3). E. P. Dutton.

Gerlinger, Lorena
--Alvin, the Snowmobile. Gerlinger, Lorena, illus. (Illus.). 11p. (ps). 1976. (ISBN 0-9606712-4-2). L Gerlinger.
--The Easter Story. (Illus.). 14p. 1972. (ISBN 0-9606712-1-8). L Gerlinger.
--Sam Takes a Boat Ride. (Illus.). 12p. 1972. (ISBN 0-9606712-0-X). L Gerlinger.

German, Don (1931-)
--Mattie's Money Tree. Guida, Lisa Chauncy, illus. LC 84-11849. (Illus.). 94p. (gr. 2-4). 1984. (ISBN 0-664-32716-8). (ISBN 0-664-32716-8). Westminster.

German, Edward, Sir (1862-1936) & Kipling, Joseph Rudyard (1865-1936)
--The Just So Song Book. 3 p. l., 62 p. 24 cm. 1903. Page & Company.

Germano, Peter see Cord, Barry, pseud.

Germano, Peter
--Dry Range. Cord, Barry, pseud. LC 55-10201. 224 p. 20cm. 1955. Arcadia House.

Gernand, Adeline (1927-)
--The Mouse That Saved Christmas. 1st ed. White, Lynda, illus. LC 74-166365. (Illus.). 47 p. 1972. (ISBN 0-533-00475-6). Vantage Press.

Gernet, Nina Vladimirovna (1904-)
--Clever Masha. 15p. 1974. (ISBN 0-8285-1123-3, Pub. by Progress Pubs USSR). Imported Pubns.

Gernet, Nina Vladimirovna (1904-) & Jagdfeld, G.
--Katya and the Crocodile. Nightingale, Paula, illus. Corrin, Stephen, tr. from Russian. LC 74-373968. (Illus.). 21cm. 104p. 1968. (ISBN 0-900675-09-8). Gerrards Cross, Smythe.
--Katya & the Crocodile. Nightingale, Paula, illus. Corrin, Stephen, tr. (Illus.). 103p. (gr. 1-4). 1969. (ISBN 0-900675-09-8). Transatlantic.

Geronimi, Clyde
--Chips Quips. Geronimi, Clyde, illus. (Illus.). 55p. (gr. 4 up). 1983. (ISBN 0-939126-09-5). Back Bay.

Gerould, Gordon Hall (1877-)
--Filibuster. LC 24-9267. 4 p. l., 274, 1 p. front. 20 cm. 1924. D. Appleton and Company.

Gerrard, Jean
--Matilda Jane. Gerrard, Roy (1935-), illus. LC 83-48082. (ps up). N.D. (ISBN 0-374-34865-0). (ISBN 0-374-34865-0). FS&G.

Gerrard, Jean, jt. auth. see Gerrard, Roy.

Gerrard, Roy (1935-)
--The Favershams. LC 82-82390. 1983, c.1982. (ISBN 0-374-32292-9). Farrar, Straus & Giroux.
--Sir Cedric. Gerrard, Roy (1935-), illus. LC 84-6111. (Illus.). 32p. 1984. (ISBN 0-374-36959-3). (ISBN 0-374-36959-3). Farrar, Straus & Giroux. **Award: (NYT).**

Gerrard, Roy & Gerrard, Jean
--Matilda Jane. (Illus.). 32p. 1st U.S. edition. (ps-6). 1981. (Pub. by Gollancz England). David & Charles.

Gerrick, David J.
--Terror Tales for Teenagers. (gr. 5 up). 1979. Dayton Labs.

Gerrold, David (1944-) & Niven, Laurence Van Cott (1938-)
--The Flying Sorcerers. LC 76-40477. p. cm. 1976, c.1971. Aeonian Press.

Gerry, Margarita Spalding, Mrs.
--Philippa at the Chateau. LC 22-23119. 4 p. l., 306, 1 p. front., plates. 20 cm. c.1922. Harper & Brothers.
--Philippa's Experiments. LC 23-17271. 3 p. l., 313 p. front., plates. 20 cm. 1923. Harper & Brothers.
--Philippa's Fortune. LC 21-20439. 20cm. 305p. (Harper's Selected Juveniles). 1921. Harper & Brothers.

Gersbach, Jo R.
--The Case of the Buried Money Bags. (gr. 5-8). 1978. (ISBN 0-87881-065-X). Mojave Bks.
--The Unchewed Clue. (gr. 5-7). 1977. (ISBN 0-8181-0397-3). Pageant-Poseidon.

Gershator, Phillis (1942-)
--Honi and His Magic Circle. 1st ed. Rieger, Shay (1929-), illus. LC 79-84731. (Illus.). 48 p. 24cm. 1980, c.1979. (ISBN 0-8276-0167-0). Jewish Publication Society of America.

Gerson, Corinne (1927-)
--The Closed Circle. Korach, Mimi (1922-), illus. (Illus.). 122 p. 20cm. 1968. Funk & Wagnalls.
--Good Dog, Bad Dog. McCully, Emily Arnold (1939-), illus. LC 83-2635. p. cm. 1983. (ISBN 0-689-30986-4). Atheneum.
--How I Put My Mother Through College. LC 80-21681. 136 p. 22cm. 1981. (ISBN 0-689-30810-8). Atheneum.
--Like a Sister. Korach, Mimi (1922-), illus. (Illus.). (gr. 7-11). 1954. Funk & W.
--Oh, Brother. LC 81-8052. p. cm. 1982. (ISBN 0-689-30878-7). Atheneum.
--Tread Softly. LC 78-72199. 133 p. 22cm. c.1979. (ISBN 0-8037-9058-9). (ISBN 0-8037-9059-7). Dial Press.

Gerson, Corinne (1927-) & Ilsley, Velma Elizabeth (1918-)
--Son for a Day. 1st ed. LC 79-22613. (Illus.). 140 p. 22cm. 1980. (ISBN 0-689-30742-X). Atheneum.

Gerson, Emily Goldsmith, Mrs.
--A Modern Esther: And Other Stories for Jewish Children. Furman, C. T., illus. LC 10-6183. 212 p. illus. 20 cm. 1906. J. H. Greenstone.
--The Picture Screen. (Illus.). (Little Maid Ser.). N.D. Hurst and Company.

Gerson, Mary-Joan
--Omoteji's Baby Brother. Moon, Elzia, illus. LC 73-19251. (Illus.). 48 p. 1974. (ISBN 0-8098-1217-7). H. Z. Walck.
--Why the Sky Is Far Away: A Folktale from Nigeria. Meryman, Hope, illus. LC 73-17343. (Illus.). 32 p. 1974. (ISBN 0-15-296310-3). Harcourt Brace Jovanovich.

Gerson, Oscar
--Poetry for the Grades. (gr. 5-8). 1921. Franklin Publishing and Supply Co., Inc.

Gerson, Thomas Isaac, jt. auth. see Hood, Flora Mae.

Gerson, Trina
--Holiday Songs. Gerson, Ivan, illus. 84p. (ps-7). 1984. (ISBN 0-9605878-2-9). Anirt Pr.

Gerson, Virginia
--The Happy Heart Family. LC 39-27797. 64 p. col. front., illus., col. plates. 26 cm. 1939. Dodd, Mead & Company.
--The Happy Heart Family. LC 4-24475. 35p. incl. col. pl. 25 1/2cm. 1904. Duffield & Co.
--The Happy Heart Family. LC 7-25079. 5 p. l., 9-64 p. col. front., illus. (part col.) col. plates. 26 x 21 cm. 1907. Duffield & Company.
--Little Blossoms. LC 17-1347. 20 p. col. illus. 24 cm. 1885. White, Stokes & Allen.
--Little Dignity: Picture and Rhymes of Olden Times. Gerson, virginia, illus. N.D. George Routledge & Sons.
--Merry Little People. LC 17-1345. 20 p. col. illus. 24 cm. 1885. White, Stokes & Allen.

--Sun, Moon, And Stars. (Agnes Giberne's Scientific Series). N.D. American Tract Society.
--Will Foster and My Brother Paul: Or, Real Heroes. (Illus.). 484p. N.D. A. I. Bradley & Co.'s Pubs.
--Will Foster of the Ferry. LC 42-26899. v, 7-484 p. front., plates. 18 cm. 1885. I. Bradley & Co.
--Worls's Foundation. (Agnes Giberne's Scientific Series). N.D. American Tract Society.
Gibke, Carl H. & Bower, Mary Ruth
--Peter Pigeon. James, Sandra, illus. LC 41-13406. (Illus.). 32p. 21 x 19cm. 1941. Grosset & Dunlop.
Giblin, James Cross (1933-)
--Chimney Sweeps: Yesterday and Today. Tomes, Margot Ladd (1917-), illus. LC 81-43878. (Illus.). 64p. (gr. 4-8). 1982. (ISBN 0-690-04192-6, TYC-J). (ISBN 0-690-04193-4). Har-Row. **Award: (ALA).**
--The Truth About Santa Claus. LC 85-47541. p. cm. c.1985. (ISBN 0-690-04483-6). (ISBN 0-690-04484-4). T.Y. Crowell. **Award: (ALA).**
Giblin, James Cross (1933-) & Ferguson, Dale
--The Scarecrow Book. (Illus.). (gr. 2-4). 1980. Crown. **Award: (ALA).**
Gibson, Arthur S.
--Adventures of the Pig Family. (Illus.). N.D. E. P. Dutton & Co.
--March Hares and Their Friends. (Illus.). N.D. Publications of E. P. Dutton & Co.
Gibson, C. D. & Wiles, Irving R.
--The Bachelor's Christmas, and Other Stories. N.D. Charles Scribner's Sons.
Gibson Company Editors
--Poems of Childhood. Victor, Joan Berg (1942-), illus. LC 69-16103. (Illus.). line drawings. 128p. (gr. 6). 1969. (ISBN 0-8378-1781-1). Gibson.
Gibson, Edward W., jt. auth. see Gibson, Mary Richards.
Gibson, Ella
--Martha's Secret Wish. Lonette, Reisie Dominee (1924-), illus. LC 61-11922. (Illus.). 22cm. 174p. (gr. 4-6). 1961. (ISBN 0-688-41144-4). Lothrop.
Gibson, Enid
--The Golden Cockerel: Three Stories of Magic and Witchcraft from Russian Opera. Theobalds, Prue, illus. LC 63-18709. 53 p. illus. 22 cm. (Young reader's guides to music). 1963. H. Z. Walck.
Gibson, Gertrude Hevener (1906-)
--Cat-Cat. Wiskur, Darrell D., illus. LC 70-123804. (Illus.). 32 p. 25cm. 1970. (ISBN 0-516-03429-4). Childrens Press.
Gibson, Harry Clark (1912-)
--The Blue-and-Gold Man. LC 61-15816. 144 p. 21cm. 1961. Duell Sloan and Pearce.
Gibson, Helen & Herbert, Galina
--An Australian Christmas. LC 80-156499. p. cm. 1980, c.1961. Cobbers.
Gibson, J.
--Memory Bay. N.D. Longmans, Green & Co.
Gibson, James C. & Wilson, Raymond (1925-), eds.
--Rhyme and Rhythm. Morgan, Violet (1898-), illus. LC 67-54286. 4 v. illus. 22 cm. 1965. Macmillan.
Gibson, Josephine, pseud., see Hine, Alfred Blakelee.
Gibson, Josephine, pseud. (1915-)
--Is There a Mouse in the House. Hine, Alfred Blakelee. Hine, Sesyle Joslin. Bodecker, Niels Mogens (1922-), illus. LC 64-175981. (Illus.). (gr. k-3). 1965. Macmillan.
Gibson, Katharine (1893-)
--Arrow Fly Home. Ray, Ralph (1920-1952), illus. LC 45-3044. ix, 146 p., 2 l. incl. illus., plates. 21 cm. 1945. Longmans, Green & Co.
--Bow Bells. Bock, Vera, illus. LC 43-15324. xiii, 124, 1 p. incl. front., plates. 22 cm. 1943. Longmans, Green and Co.
--Cinders. 1939. (ISBN 0-679-25032-8). David McKay Company.
--Cinders. 1939. (ISBN 0-8382-0171-7, Cadmus Books). E. M. Hale and Company.
--Cinders. Bock, Vera, illus. LC 39-27654. 6 p. l., 3-132, 1 p. incl. illus., plates. 20 cm. 1939. Longmans, Green and Co.
--The Golden Bird and Other Stories. Sommer, Edwin G., illus. Walker, Caroline Burnite, intro. by. LC 27-22680. xiii p., 2 l., 163 p. incl. illus., plates. col. front., col. plates. 23 cm. 1927. The Macmillan Company.
--The Golden Bird and Other Stories. Sommer, Edwin G., illus. Walker, Caroline Burnite, intro. by. LC 41-38143. xiii p., 2 l., 151 p. incl. col. front., illus. 22 cm. 1935. The Macmillan Company.
--Jock's Castle. Bock, Vera, illus. LC 40-13169. 139, 1 p. incl. illus., plates (1 double) 24 cm. c.1940. Longmans, Green & Co.
--Nathaniel's Witch. Bock, Vera, illus. LC 41-20738. viii, 136 p. incl. illus., plates. 24 cm. 1941. Longmans, Green and Co.
--The Oak Tree House. 1936. David McKay Company Inc.
--The Oak Tree House. LC 36-274283. 127, 1 p. incl. front., illus., plates. 20 cm. 1936. Longmans, Green and Co.
--The Tall Book of Bible Stories. Chaiko, Ted, illus. LC 57-10952. (Illus.). 128p. (Tall Bks.). (gr. k-3). 1980. (ISBN 0-06-021935-1, HarpJ). (ISBN 0-06-021936-X). Har-Row.
--To See the Queen. 1954. E M Hale.
--To See the Queen. 1st ed. Funk, Clotilde Embree, illus. LC 54-9205. (Illus.). 21cm. 144p. 1954. Longmans, Green.
Gibson, Katharine (1893-), ed.
--Fairy Tales. Read, Isobel, illus. LC 51-227. 380 p. illus. (part col.) 27 cm. 1950. Whitman Pub. Co.
--The Tenggren Tell-It-Again Book. Tenggren, Gustaf (1896-1970), illus. LC 42-21077. vii, 199, 1 p. illus. (part col.) 28 1/2 cm. 1942. Little, Brown and Company.
Gibson, Lydia
--The Teacup Whale. LC 34-31289. (Illus.). 19 x 21cm. 23p. 1934. Farrar & Rinehart.
Gibson, Mary Richards & Gibson, Edward W.
--My First Snowflake. Gibson, Mary Richards, illus. LC 63-21260. (Illus.). (gr. k-3). 1963. (ISBN 0-87167-121-2). Allied Fla.
Gibson, Michael
--LeMans. Schulke, Flip Dora, photos by. 192p. (Twice around the Clock). 1964. G P Putnam's Sons.
--Monte Carlo Rally. (Illus.). 128p. 1959. Franklin Watts, Inc.
Gibson, Myra Tomback
--What Is Your Favorite Smell, My Dear?. LC 64-24433. 1 v. (unpaged) col. illus. 24 cm. 1964. Grosset & Dunlap.
--What Is Your Favorite Thing to Hear?. LC 66-9819. (Illus.). 1 v. (unpaged. 24cm. 1966. Grosset & Dunlap.
--What Is Your Favorite Thing to See?. LC 68-29965. (Illus.). 39 p. 24cm. 1968. Grosset & Dunlap.
--What Is Your Favorite Thing to Touch?. LC 65-20021. 1 v. (unpaged) col. illus. 23 cm. 1965. Grosset & Dunlap.
Gibson, Myron Bartlett (1858-)
--Herm and I. Fassitt, H. Norah, illus. LC 6-37918. ix p., 1 l., 13-116 p. incl. front., illus., plates. 19 cm. c.1906. H. Altemus Company.
Gibson, Sarah
--Donald and His Friends. (Illus.). 122p. N.D. American Tract Society.
Gibson, W. H.
--Camp Life. N.D. Harper & Bros.
Gibson, Walter, ed.
--Rod Sterling's Twilight Zone. (gr. 7-9). N.D. G&D.
--Rogues Gallery: A Variety of Mystery Stories. Spina, Paul, illus. LC 68-22469. (Illus.). 20 linecuts. 416p. (gr. 7 up). 1969. (ISBN 0-385-09371-3). Doubleday.
Gibson, Walter Brown see Adams, Andy, pseud.
Gibson, Walter Brown (1897-), adapted by see Serling, Rod.
Gibson, William (1914-)
--Monday after the Miracle. LC 83-45070. 160p. 1983. (ISBN 0-689-11396-X). Atheneum.
Gick, Georg Johannes
--The Shepherd's Pipe: Songs from the Holy Night. Swinger, Marlys, ed. Maendel, Maria Arnold & Barth, Gillian, illus. LC 71-85805. (Illus.). ix, score. 31cm. 99p. 1969. (ISBN 0-87486-010-5). Plough Pub. House.
Gick, Georg Johannes & Swinger, Marlys
--Shepherd's Pipe Songs from the Holy Night: A Christmas Cantata for Children's Voices or Youth Choir. Choral ed. Maendel, Maria Arnold, illus. Clement, Jane Tyson (1947-), intro. by. LC 71-85805. (Illus.). . 20p color ils. 100p. 64p. 1969. (ISBN 0-87486-010-5). (ISBN 0-87486-011-3). (ISBN 0-686-66331-4). Plough.
Gidal, Sonia Epstein (1922-)
--My Village in England. Gidal, Nachum, illus. (Illus.). 83 p. 27cm. 1963. Pantheon Books.
Gidal, Sonia Epstein (1922-) & Gidal, Tim
--Sons of the Desert. (Illus.). (gr. 5-6). 1960. (ISBN 0-394-91653-0). Pantheon.
Gidal, Tim, jt. auth. see Gidal, Sonia Epstein.
Giddings, Thaddeus Philander (1869-) & Earhart, Will (1871-), eds.
--The Magic of Song. LC 34-18823. 176 p. col. front., illus. 24 cm. (Music education series). c.1934. Ginn and Company.
--Songs of Childhood. LC 30-16915. 144 p. col. illus. 21 x 17 cm. (Music education series). c.1923. Ginn and Company.
Giegling, John A (1935-)
--Black Lightning: Three Years in the Life of a Fisher. Schoenherr, John Carl (1935-), illus. LC 75-328938. (Illus.). 127 p. 23cm. c.1975. (ISBN 0-698-20333-X). Coward, McCann & Geoghegan.
--Warrior of the Skies. Perrott, Jennifer, illus. LC 75-97663. (Illus.). vi, 135 p. 22cm. 1970. Doubleday.
Giehrl, Emmy Aschenbrenner (1837-)
--Master Fridolin. A Christmas Story. LC 12-32520. 96 p. 16 cm. 1897. Benziger Brothers.
--The Three Little Kings. LC 12-32524. 88 p. 16 cm. 1897. Benziger Brothers.
Gielow, Martha Sawyer (1854-1933), ed.
--Mammy's Reminiscences: A Collection of Plantation Dialect Stories, Character Sketches and Cradle Songs. (Illus.). 1905. A S Barnes & Co.
--The Whispering Fairy: Constructive Stories for Children. LC 23-18210. 50 p. 17 cm. 1923. J. F. Rowny Press.
Gies, Darlene
--Dinny: The Big-Little Dinosaur. N.D. Grosset & Dunlap.
Giesbrecht, Johnny
--The Angry Atheist. LC 75-38709. 156 p. 18cm. c.1976. (ISBN 0-8024-0223-2). Moody Press.
--The Winning of Gary Hastings. LC 76-12636. 128 p. 18cm. c.1976. (ISBN 0-8024-9563-X). Moody Press.
Giff, Patricia Reilly (1935-)
--The Almost Awful Play. Natti, Susanna (1948-), illus. LC 84-17922. p. cm. 1985. (ISBN 0-14-050530-X). Puffin Books.
--The Almost Awful Play. Natti, Susanna (1948-), illus. LC 83-17101. (Illus.). 28 p. 32p. (gr. 1-3). 1984. (ISBN 0-670-11458-8, Viking Kestrel). Viking.
--December Secrets. Sims, Blanche, illus. LC 85-32536. p. cm. (Kids of the Polk Street School). (No. 4). 1986, c.1984. (ISBN 0-385-29495-6). Delacorte Press.
--Fourth-Grade Celebrity. Morrill, Leslie H., illus. LC 79-50678. (Illus.). 117 p. 22cm. c.1979. (ISBN 0-440-02725-X). (ISBN 0-440-02726-8). Delacorte Press.
--The Gift of the Pirate Queen. Rutherford, Jenny, illus. LC 82-70310. 164 p. 22cm. c.1982. (ISBN 0-440-02970-8). (ISBN 0-440-02972-4). Delacorte Press.
--The Girl Who Knew It All. Morrill, Leslie H., illus. LC 79-50677. (Illus.). 118 p. 22cm. c.1979. (ISBN 0-440-03137-0). Delacorte Press.
--Have You Seen Hyacinth Macaw?. 1984. Delacorte.
--Have You Seen Hyacinth Macaw: A Mystery. Kramer, Anthony, illus. LC 80-68729. (Illus.). 128p. (gr. 4-7). 1981. Delacorte.
--Left-Handed Shortstop. Morrill, Leslie H., illus. (Illus.). (gr. 4-6). 1984. (ISBN 0-385-28533-7). (ISBN 0-385-28534-5). Delacorte.
--Left-Handed Shortstop: A Novel. Morrill, Leslie H., illus. LC 80-65835. (Illus.). 128p. (gr. 5-8). 1980. Delacorte.
--Loretta P. Sweeny, Where Are You?. Kramer, Anthony, illus. (Illus.). (gr. 4-8). 1983. (ISBN 0-385-29298-8). (ISBN 0-385-29299-6). Delacorte.
--Next Year I'll Be Special. Hafner, Marylin (1925-), illus. LC 79-19174. (Illus.). 32 p. 26cm. c.1980. (ISBN 0-525-35810-2). Dutton.
--Purple Climbing Days. Sims, Blanche, illus. LC 85-32542. p. cm. (Kids of the Polk Street School). (No. 9). 1986, c.1985. (ISBN 0-385-29500-6). Delacorte Press.
--Rat Teeth. Morrill, Leslie H., illus. LC 83-16601. (Illus.). 144p. (gr. 4-6). 1984. (ISBN 0-385-29339-9). (ISBN 0-385-29309-7). Delacorte.
--Say "Cheese". Sims, Blanche, illus. LC 85-32549. p. cm. (Kids of the Polk Street School). (No. 10). 1986, c.1985. (ISBN 0-385-29501-4). Delacorte Press.
--Suspect. Marchesi, Stephen, illus. LC 81-12657. (Illus.). 72 p. 22cm. (Skinny book). c.1982. (ISBN 0-525-45108-0). Dutton.
--Today Was a Terrible Day. Natti, Susanna (1948-), illus. LC 83-24482. 1984, c.1980. (ISBN 0-14-050453-2). Penguin Books.
--Today Was a Terrible Day. Natti, Susanna (1948-), illus. LC 79-12420. (Illus.). 25 p. 23cm. 1980. (ISBN 0-670-71830-0). Viking Press.
--The Valentine Star. Sims, Blanche, illus. LC 85-30757. p. cm. (The Kis of the Polk Street School: No. 6). 1986, c.1985. (ISBN 0-385-29497-2). Delacorte Press.
--Watch Out, Ronald Morgan!. Natti, Susanna (1948-), illus. LC 84-19623. (Illus.). 24, 1 p. 24cm. 1985. (ISBN 0-670-80433-9). Viking Kestrel.
--The Winter Worm Business: A Novel. Morrill, Leslie H., illus. LC 81-65490. 128p. (gr. 4-8). 1981. Delacorte.
Gifford, Douglas, ed.
--Warriors, Gods and Spirits from Central and South American Mythology. Sibbick, John, illus. (gr. 5-8). 1983. Schocken.
Gifford, Griselda (1931-)
--Jenny & the Sheep Thieves. (Illus.). 1975. (Pub. by Gollancz England). David & Charles.
Gift, Theo
--Pretty Miss Bellew. N.D. Henry Holt.
Giggins, Aileen Cleveland (1882-)
--A Little Princess of the Patio. Williamson, Ada Clendenin, illus. (The Little Princess Stories). N.D. Penn Publishing Co.
--A Little Princess of the Ranch. Williamson, Ada Clendenin, illus. (The Little Princess Stories). N.D. Penn Publishing Co.
Gikow, Louise
--Boober Fraggle's Celery Souffle. Oechsli, Kelly (1918-), illus. LC 84-6858. (Illus.). (ps-2). 1984. (ISBN 0-03-000722-4). HR&W.
--Boober Fraggle's Ghosts. Di Fiori, Lawrence, illus. LC 85-881. (Illus.). 40 p. 27cm. c.1985. Muppet Press : Holt, Rinehart and Winston.
--Boober Fraggle's Recipe. Oechsli, Kelly (1918-), illus. LC 84-6858. c.1984. Holt, Rhinehart, and Winston.
--Follow That Fraggle!. Lanza, Barbara, illus. LC 85-5479. (Illus.). 32 p. 22cm. c.1985. (ISBN 0-03-004558-4). Holt, Rinehart, and Winston.
--Goldilocks: Baby Piggy's Ghosts. Smollin, Michael J., illus. LC 84-22348. (Illus.). 32p. (Picturebacks Ser.). (ps-3). 1985. (ISBN 0-394-87223-1, BYR). Random.
--The Legend of the Doozer Who Didn't. McClintock, Barbara, illus. LC 84-6623. (Illus.). (Fraggle Rock Bks.). (ps-2). 1984. (ISBN 0-03-000717-8). (ISBN 0-03-004563-0). HR&W.
--Sprocket's Christmas Tale. McCue, Lisa, illus. LC 84-6526. (Illus.). (Fraggle Rock Bks.). (gr. 1-4). 1984. (ISBN 0-03-000708-9). HR&W.
--What's A Fraggle?. McClintock, Barbara, illus. LC 83-22779. (Illus.). 1984. (ISBN 0-03-071086-3). (ISBN 0-03-071889-9). HR&W.
Gikow, Louise & Henson, Jim, pseud.
--Jim Henson Presents Goldilocks, Baby Piggy's Dream Starring the Muppet Babies. Henson, James Maury. Smollin, Michael J., illus. LC 84-22348. (Illus.). 32 p. 21cm. (Random House pictureback). 1985. (ISBN 0-394-87223-1). Random House.
Gil, Ann G.
--Wilson Worm. Goodrich, Marye, illus. 1983. (ISBN 0-533-05737-X). Vantage.
Gilbert, Agnes Joan Sewell (1931-)
--Summerhill Summer. LC 67-15863. 208 p. 21cm. 1967. Bethany Press.
Gilbert, Alice
--Poems from Sharon's Lunch Box. Gilbert, Ellen, illus. LC 77-107037. (Illus.). 63 p. 22cm. 1972. Delacorte Press.
Gilbert, Ann Taylor, Mrs., jt. auth. see Taylor, Jane.
Gilbert, Ann Taylor, Mrs. (1782-1866) & Taylor, Jane (1783-1824)
--Greedy Dick. (Illus.). (The Little Ones' Library Ser.). N.D. Frederick A. Stokes Co.
Gilbert, Anthony, pseud., see Malleson, Lucy Beatrice.
Gilbert, Ariadne, jt. auth. see Gilbert, Edith Laura.
Gilbert, Bil
--The Weasels. Fraser, Betty M., pseud. (1928-), illus. Fraser, Elizabeth Marr. 1970. Pantheon Books.
Gilbert, Brenda G.
--Mortimer. Leinwand, Benna, illus. (Illus.). 1977. (ISBN 0-533-02290-8). Vantage.
Gilbert, Celia, pseud., see Cochran, Ruth Gilbert.
Gilbert, Charles Benajah, jt. auth. see Price, Lillian Louise.
Gilbert, Charles Benajah, jt. ed. see Harris, Ada Van Stone.
Gilbert, Constance, jt. auth. see Potter, Grace Elizabeth.
Gilbert, Daniel Branden, jt. auth. see Wyatt, Isabel.
Gilbert, Dorothy
--Can I Make Another One. (Illus.). N.D. Taplinger.
Gilbert, Douglas
--Floyd Gibbons: Knight of the Air. N.D. Robert M. McBride & Co.
Gilbert, Edith Laura (1872-)
--The Making of Meenie. Goddard, Margaret, illus. LC 4-21664. (Illus.). 20cm. 186p. 1904. Lee and Shepard.
Gilbert, Edith Laura (1872-) & Gilbert, Ariadne
--The Frolicsome Four. Bruce, Josephine, illus. LC 3-13619. viii p., 1 l., 199 p. front., 7 pl. 20 cm. 1903. Lee and Shepard.
Gilbert, Elliot (1924-)
--A Cat Story. Gilbert, Elliot (1924-), illus. LC 63-9088. (Illus.). 17 x 24cm. (A Little Owl Bk.). 1963. Holt, Rinehart and Winston.
Gilbert, Harriett (1948-)
--Running Away. LC 79-1937. 266 p. 21cm. c.1979. (ISBN 0-06-021972-6). (ISBN 0-06-021973-4). Harper & Row.
Gilbert, Harry (1946-)
--Sarah's Nest. 144p. (gr. 7 up). 1981. (ISBN 0-571-11596-9). Faber & Faber.
Gilbert, Helen Earle
--Doctor Trotter & His Big Gold Watch. Bradfield, Margaret, illus. LC 48-8295. (Illus.). 32p. (ps-2). 1948. (ISBN 0-687-11257-5). Abingdon.
--Dr. Trotter & His Big Gold Watch. N.D. E. M. Hale & Co.
--Dr. Trotter and His Big Gold Watch. Bradfield, Margaret, illus. LC 48-8295. 32 p. illus. (part col.) 22 x 27 cm. 1948. Abingdon-Cokesbury Press.

--Growing-up Summer. Hauge, Carl, illus. LC 76-11480. (Illus.). 173 p. 18cm. c.1976. D. C. Cook Pub. Co.
--Never Miss a Sunset. LC 74-29050. 237 p. 18cm. 1975. (ISBN 0-912692-56-1). D. C. Cook Pub. Co.

Gili, Phillida
--Demon Daisy's Dreadful Week. LC 80-80539. (ps-k). 1980. (ISBN 0-531-04179-4). Watts.
--Fanny and Charles, A Regency Escapade: Or, the Trick That Went Wrong. LC 83-5850. (Illus.). 28p. (gr. 5up). 1984, c.1983. (ISBN 0-670-30697-5, Viking Kestrel). Viking.
--The Lost Ears. Gili, Phillida, illus. (Illus.). 32p. (ps-k). 1981. (ISBN 0-531-04065-8). Watts.

Gilkison, Grace, Mrs.
--The King's Christmas Pudding. LC 29-21632. 63 p. incl. illus., col. plates. 21 cm. 1929. Coward McCann Inc.
--Little Arthur. Gilkison, Grace, Mrs., illus. LC 31-24447. x p., 1 l., 126 p. incl. illus., plates. col. front. 21 cm. 1931. Doubleday, Doran & Company, Inc.
--The Sparrow of Ulm And Four Other Famous Birds: A Starling, a Stork, a Jackdaw, and Some Geese. LC 31-240757. vii p., 2 l., 71 p. incl. illus., plates. col. front. 17 cm. (little library). 1931. The Macmillan Company.
--Two Mice and a King. Gilkison, Grace, Mrs., illus. LC 29-20243. 3 p. l., 54, 3 p. incl. illus., col. plates. 17 cm. (The little library). 1929. The Macmillan Company.

Gilkison, Grace, Mrs., illus.
--Told Under the Green Umbrella: Favorite Folk Tales, Fairy Tales, and Legends. Association for Childhood Education; Literature Committee LC 78-101086. (Illus.). viii, 188 p. 22cm. (Umbrella books). 1977, c.1930. Macmillan.

Gill, Bob (1931-)
--A to Z. 1st ed. Gill, Bob (1931-), illus. LC 62-8289. unpaged. illus. 31 x 14cm. 1962. Little Brown.
--I Keep Changing. LC 71-148052. (Illus.). 32 p. 22cm. 1971. Scroll Press.
--Ups & Downs. LC 73-20417. (Illus.). 32 p. 22cm. 1974. Addison-Wesley.

Gill, Bob (1931-) & Reid, Alastair (1926-)
--Balloon for a Blunderbuss. LC 60-15682. (Illus.). (gr. k-3). 1961. (ISBN 0-06-024855-6). Har-Row.

Gill, Derek Lewis Theodore (1919-)
--Tom Sullivan's Adventures in Darkness. LC 76-13405. (Illus.). (gr. 7 up). 1976. (ISBN 0-679-20377-X). McKay.

Gill, Elizabeth B., ed.
--Tales from the Arabian Nights. (Illus.). (gr. 1-4). 1964. (ISBN 0-394-80772-3). Random.

Gill, Ellen Hawley & Vranna, Claudia
--What Is a Brother?. Gill, Ellen Hawley, illus. LC 68-31764. (Illus.). 44 p. (Read-by-yourself books). 1968. Houghton Mifflin.

Gill, Frances
--The Little Days. Winter, Milo Kendall (1888-1956), illus. LC 19-2554. 23cm. 50p. N.D. Houghton Mifflin.
--Windy Leaf. LC 24-24919. 58 p. col. front. 20 cm. 1924. The Macmillan Company.

Gill, George
--Movement Plays and Action Songs. 67p. N.D. E. Steiger.

Gill, Jill
--Tiger & Leopard. Gill, Jill, illus. LC 73-134673. (Illus.). 31 p. 29cm. c.1971. Vanguard Press.

Gill, Joan
--Hush, Jon!. Sugarman, Tracy (1921-), illus. LC 67-18666. (Illus.). 47 p. 24cm. 1968. Doubleday.
--Sara's Granny and the Groodle. Chwast, Seymour (1931-), illus. LC 69-12695. (Illus.). 32 p. 29cm. 1969. Doubleday. **Award: (NYT).**

Gill, Kathleen R.
--Snow on the Sea. 128p. (gr. 4-8). 1982. (ISBN 0-89962-254-2). Todd & Honeywell.

Gill, Mabel Spicer
--Huttee Boy of the Jungle. Carmack, Paul R., illus. LC 29-21175. xviii p., 1 l., 184 p. incl. front., illus. 19 cm. c.1929. G. Sully and Company, Inc.

Gill, Margaret B.
--Tell Me About Susan. (Illus.). 18 ils. (gr. k-3). 1971. (ISBN 0-682-47332-4). Exposition.

Gill, Richard C., jt. auth. see Hoke, Helen L., Mrs.

Gill, Richard Cochran
--Flying Death: A Manga Story. Doyle, Merrill D., illus. LC 43-4724. 20cm. 238p. 1942. Henry Holt & Co.
--Kalu the Llama. Hogner, Nils (1893-1970), illus. LC 30-20723. 35 p. illus. 21 cm. N.D. Henry Holt & Co.
--Manga: An Amazon Jungle Indian. N.D. Grosset & Dunlap.
--Manga, an Amazon Jungle Indian. Stoops, Herbert Morton, illus. LC 37-22823. viii p., 2 l., 268 p. incl. illus., plates, maps. 21 cm. 1937. Frederick A. Stokes Company.
--Manga: An Amazon Jungle Indian. Stoops, Herbert Morton, illus. N.D. J. B. Lippincott.
--The Volcano of Gold: A Manga Story. Stoops, Herbert Morton, illus. LC 38-27785. ix p., 1 l., 256 p. incl. illus., plates, maps. 22 cm. 1938. Frederick A. Stokes Company.
--The Volcano of Gold: A Manga Story. Stoops, Herbert Morton, illus. N.D. J. B. Lippincott.

Gill, Richard Cochran & Hoke, Helen
--Paco Goes to the Fair. Gannett, Ruth Chrisman Arens (1896-1979), illus. LC 40-14540. 28cm. 80p. (gr. 3-5). 1940. Henry Holt & Co.

Gill, William Fearing (1844-1917), ed.
--The Horn of Plenty of Home Poems and Home Pictures. LC 15-23991. 190 p., 1 l. incl. illus., plates. front. 22 cm. 1876. W. F. Gill and Company.

Gillen, Michael see Foster, Mitchell, pseud.

Gillen, Michael (1911-)
--Tony's Good Luck. Foster, Mitchell, pseud. Gillen, Michael (1911-), illus. Foster, Mitchel, pseud. LC 55-7276. 22cm. 46p. 1955. Whittlesey House.

Gilleo, Alma
--The Easter Basket Mystery. Bargielski, Pat, illus. (Books & cassettes sold as 10 book set only). (Illus.). (Holiday Tales). (primer). N.D. (ISBN 0-89290-011-3). Soc for Visual.
--The Mystery of the Missing Valentines. McQueen, Lucinda, illus. (Books & cassettes sold as 10 book set only). (Illus.). (Holiday Tales). (ps). 1977. (ISBN 0-89290-010-5). Soc for Visual.

Gilleo, Alma, ed.
--Donkey-Lettuce, 10 bks. Axeman, Lois, illus. LC 74-734826. (Illus.). (Fairy Tales of the Brothers Grimm Cassette Bks). 1976. (ISBN 0-89290-007-5). Soc for Visual.
--The Elves & the Shoemaker. Laite, Gordon (1925-), illus. LC 65-2642. (Illus.). (Holiday Tales). (ps). 1977. (ISBN 0-89290-013-X). Soc for Visual.
--The Four Servants. Robison, Don, illus. LC 74-734828. (Illus.). 16p. (Fairy Tales of the Brothers Grimm Cassette Bks Ser.). 1976. (ISBN 0-89290-009-1). Soc for Visual.
--The Golden Buttons. Sharp, Gene (1923-), illus. LC 74-734827. (Illus.). 16p. (Fairy Tales of the Brothers Grimm Cassette Bks). (ps). 1976. (ISBN 0-89290-008-3). (ISBN 0-685-70098-4). Soc for Visual.
--The Goose-Girl, 10 bks. & one cassette. Biegel, Cecilia, illus. LC 74-734823. (Illus.). 16p. (Fairy Tales of the Brothers Grimm Cassette-Bks). (ps). 1976. Set. (ISBN 0-89290-005-9). Soc for Visual.
--Hans Clodhopper, 10bks. & one cassette. Hamblin, George, illus. LC 76-730154. (Illus.). (Hans Christian Andersen Cassette Bks). 1976. Set. (ISBN 0-89290-002-4). Soc for Visual.
--It's Perfectly True. Hamblin, George, illus. LC 76-730153. (Illus.). 16p. (Hans Christian Andersen Cassette Bks). 1976. (ISBN 0-89290-001-6). Soc for Visual.
--King Grisly-Beard, 10 bks. & one cassette. Stasiak, Krystyna, illus. LC 74-734822. (Illus.). 16p. (Fairy Tales of the Brothers Grimm Cassette Bks). (ps). 1976. (ISBN 0-89290-004-0). Soc for Visual.
--The Little Mermaid, 10 bks. Shelton, Harley, illus. LC 76-730155. (Illus.). (Hans Christian Andersen Cassette Bks). 1976. (ISBN 0-89290-003-2). (ISBN 0-685-70093-3). Soc for Visual.
--The Water of Life, 10 bks. & one cassette. Robertson, Robert, illus. LC 74-734825. (Illus.). (Fairy Tales of the Brothers Grimm Cassette Bks). 1976. Set. (ISBN 0-89290-006-7). Soc for Visual.
--The Wild Swans, 10 bks. & one cassette. Stasiak, Krystyna, illus. LC 76-730152. (Illus.). (Hans Christian Andersen Cassette Bks). 1976. Set. (ISBN 0-89290-000-8). (ISBN 0-685-70090-9). Soc for Visual.

Gilleo, Alma, ed. see Cook, Emilie C.

Gillespie, D. Craig
--Weeple People. Hamilton, Garry Clark, illus. LC 72-175348. (Illus.). 35 p. 1971, c.1972. (ISBN 0-07-023221-0). (ISBN 0-07-023220-2). McGraw-Hill.

Gillespie, Moya, tr. see Bobrowski, Johannes.

Gillespie, Robert B.
--Heads You Lose. 224p. 1985. (ISBN 0-396-08549-0). Dodd.

Gillespie, Thomas Haining
--Zoo-Man Stories. Fullerton, Len, illus. LC 60-15474. 121 p. illus. 19 cm. (His Zoo-man series, 2). 1960. Taplinger Pub. Co.

Gillett-Driggs
--The Texas Ranger. N.D. World Book Co.

Gillett, Mary
--Bugles at the Border. Tucker, Bruce, illus. LC 68-25853. (Illus.). x, 220 p. 22cm. 1968. J. F. Blair.

Gillham, Bill, pseud., see Gillham, William Edward Charles.

Gillham, Bill, pseud.
--The Early Words Picture Book. Gillham, William Edward Charles. Grainger, Sam, illus. LC 83-1802. p. cm. 1983. (ISBN 0-698-20583-9). Coward-McCann.
--Home Before Long. Gillham, William Edward Charles. Mosley, Francis, illus. 1984. Andre Deutsch.
--My Brother Barry. Gillham, William Edward Charles. (Illus.). 96p. (gr. 2-7). 1982. (ISBN 0-233-97358-3). Andre Deutsch.
--A Place to Hide. Gillham, William Edward Charles. Majewska, Maria, illus. (Illus.). 112p. (gr. 2-6). 1983. (ISBN 0-233-97496-2). Andre Deutsch.
--Septimus Fry or How Mrs. Fry Had the Cleverest Baby in the World. Gillham, William Edward Charles. Augarde, Steve (1950-), illus. LC 80-65661. (Illus.). 32p. (ps-3). 1981. (ISBN 0-233-97253-6). Andre Deutsch.

Gillham, Charles Edward (1898-)
--Beyond the Clapping Mountains. Chanimun, illus. (gr. 4-6). 1964. (ISBN 0-02-735950-6). Macmillan.
--Beyond the Clapping Mountains: Eskimo Stories from Alaska. Chanimun, illus. 1943. Macmillan.
--Medicine Men of Hooper Bay. Chanimun, illus. (Illus.). (gr. 4-6). 1966. (ISBN 0-02-735990-5). Macmillan.

Gillham, George Halsey
--The Adventures of William Tucker in a Shantyboat on the Mississippi. Thomson, Rodney, illus. LC 27-18264. vii, 2, 260, 1 p. front., plates. 20 cm. 1927. Houghton Mifflin Company.

Gillham, William Edward Charles see Gillham, Bill, pseud.

Gillian, Strickland W. (1869-)
--Danny and Fanny and Spot, the Fox Terrier Hero. 2 ed. Eger, Ruth Caroline, illus. LC 42-81291. 32 p. illus. 21cm. 1942, c.1939. Rand McNally & Co.
--Danny and Fanny: The Laurel Cliff Twins. Eger, Ruth Caroline, illus. LC 28-23670. 96 p. illus. (part col.) 24 cm. c.1928. Rand, McNally & Company.

Gilliat, E.
--Dorothy Dymoke: A Story of the Pilgrimage of Grace. (Illus.). N.D. E & J B Young.
--The King's Reeve. N.D. E. P. Dutton & Co.

Gillies, Mary E.
--Little Lizzie. Juv ed. (Illus.). N.D. Cassell & Co.
--Roger Fildyke's Secret. N.D. E. J B Young & Co.
--Voyage of the Constance in the Polar Seas. (The Boy's Library of Adventure). N.D. Pott, Young, & Co.

Gillies, R. C.
--Story of Stories: A Life of Jesus Christ. N.D. MacMillan.

Gilligan, Edmund (1899-1973)
--Sea Dog. 1st ed. Schule, Clifford H., illus. LC 54-8010. (Illus.). 177 p. 21cm. (Borzoi books for young people). 1954. Knopf.
--Shoe the Wild Mare. Bennett, Richard Michael (1899-), illus. LC 56-8894. 112p. illus. 22cm. (Borzoi books for young people). 1956. Knopf.

Gilliland, Cleburne Hap see Shows, Harry B. & Gilliland, Hap.

Gilliland, Cleburne Hap (1918-), ed. see Dygert, Janice.

Gilliland, Cleburne Hap (1918-)
--Coyote's Pow-Wow. (Indian Culture Ser.). (gr. 1-6). 1972. (ISBN 0-89992-022-5). MT Coun Indian.
--How the Dogs Saved the Cheyennes. (Indian Culture Ser.). (gr. 1-4). 1972. (ISBN 0-89992-017-9). MT Coun Indian.

Gilliland, Hap, jt. auth. see Shows, Harry B.

Gillis, Adolph & Benet, William Rose, eds.
--Poems for Modern Youth. N.D. Houghton Mifflin & Co.

Gillis, Everett A.
--Goldie. Gillis, Paul, illus. (Illus.). 64p. (Orig.). (gr. 3-7). 1982. (ISBN 0-938328-02-6). Pisces Pr TX.

Gillisater, Pia, jt. auth. see Gillisater, Sven.

Gillisater, Sven & Gillisater, Pia
--Pia's Journey to the Holy Land. N.D. Hartcourt Brace & World Inc.

Gillmore, Inez Haynes
--The Ollivant Orphans. N.D. Henry Holt.
--Phoebe & Ernest. N.D. Henry Holt.
--Phoebe, Ernest & Cupid. N.D. Henry Holt.

Gillooly, William P.
--Mickey the Angel. Ahern, Margaret McCrohan (1921-), illus. LC 53-5587. 116p. illus. 25cm. 1953. Newman Press.

Gilman, Arthur (1837-1909)
--Tales of the Pathfinders. LC 12-325678. 225, 1 p. incl. 1 illus., plates, plan. front. 19 cm. c.1884. D. Lothrop and Company.

Gilman, Arthur (1837-1909), ed.
--Magna Charta Stories. LC 12-32568. 192 p. incl. front., illus. plates. 18 cm. c.1882. D. Lothrop and Company.

Gilman, Bradley (1857-1932)
--The Kingdom of Coins and the Queer People Who Lived There. Merrill, Frank Thayer (1848-), illus. LC 42-32094. 5 p. l., 9-82 p. front., illus. 19 cm. 1894. Roberts Brothers.
--Musical Journey of Dorothy and Delia. (Illus.). (The Sunshine Library). N.D. Thomas Y. Crowell & Co.
--A Son of the Desert. Oakley, Thornton (1881-), illus. LC 9-26147. xi, 363 p. incl. 15 pl. front. 20 cm. 1909. The Century Co.

Gilman, Caroline Howard, Mrs. (1794-1888)
--A Gift Book of Stories and Poems for Children. LC 15-17153. 5 p. l., 9-176 p., 1 l., 9-179, 1 p. illus. 17 cm. 1850. C. S. Francis & Co.

Gilman, Caroline Howard, Mrs. (1794-1888) & Jervey, Caroline Howard
--Stories and Poems by Mother and Daughter. LC 51-48703. 296 p. illus. 18 cm. 1872. Lee & Shepard.

Gilman, Charles Lewis (1882-)
--The Fox Patrol in the North Woods. Mero, Lee, illus. LC 12-7624. 67 p. incl. col. front., illus. (partly col.) 23 cm. 1912. The Buzza Company.
--The Fox Patrol in the Open. Mero, Lee, illus. LC 12-7186. 70 p. incl. col. front., illus. (partly col.) 23 cm. 1912. The Buzza Company.
--The Fox Patrol on the River. Mero, Lee, illus. LC 12-7185. 71 p. incl. col. front., illus. (partly col.) 23 cm. 1912. The Buzza Company.

Gilman, Dorothy see Butters, Dorothy Gilman.

Gilman, Dorothy Foster (1891-)
--Suprising Antonia. Gooch, Thelma, illus. LC 23-375518. 5 p. l., 269 p. front., plates. 20 cm. 1923. L. C. Page and Company (Incorporated).

Gilman, Dorothy (1923-)
--The Calico Year. LC 52-14001. 223 p. 22cm. 1953. Macrae Smith.
--Carnival Gypsy. LC 50-7159. 217 p. 22cm. 1950. Macrae-Smith.
--Four-Party Line: A Junior Novel. LC 54-10361. 198 p. 22cm. 1954. Macrae Smith.
--Girl in Buckskin. LC 56-9969. 190 p. 21cm. 1956. Macrae Smith.
--Masquerade. LC 61-8303. 190 p. 22cm. 1961. Macrae Smith.
--The Maze in the Heart of the Castle. LC 82-45198. p. cm. 1983. (ISBN 0-385-17817-4). Doubleday.
--Ragamuffin Alley. LC 51-13078. 206 p. 22cm. 1951. Macrae Smith.
--Ten Leagues to Boston Town. LC 62-19162. 187 p. 22cm. 1962. Macrae Smith.
--Witch's Silver. LC 59-8239. 190 p. 22cm. 1959. Macrae Smith.

Gilman, Elizabeth L., et al., eds.
--Picnic Adventures. Sheahan, Henry Beston. Cosgrave, John O'Hara, II (1908-1968), illus. LC 40-7600. 192 p. col. illus. 21 cm. c.1940. Farrar & Rinehart, Inc.

Gilman, Robert Cham, pseud., see Coppel, Alfred.

Gilman, Robert Cham, pseud. (1921-)
--The Navigator of Rhada. Coppel, Alfred. LC 69-13774. (gr. 7 up). 1969. (ISBN 0-15-256725-9). HarBraceJ.
--The Starkahan of Rhada. Coppel, Alfred. LC 70-102441. (gr. 7-9). 1970. (ISBN 0-15-279126-4). HarBraceJ.
--The Rebel of Rhada. Coppel, Alfred. 192p. N.D. (ISBN 0-15-265793-2). Harcourt Brace Jovanovich.

Gilmartin, Thelma
--What Happens to Me When I Fish the Sea and a Fish Catches Me?. Barton, Kent, illus. LC 76-12929. (Illus.). 36 p. (Creative development series). c.1976. (ISBN 0-89317-009-7). Windward Pub.

Gilmer, Robert D.
--The Trial of the Sparrow for Killing Cock Robin. LC 15-20735. (Illus.). 16p. 27cm. 1889. Russell Brothers.

Gilmore, Beatrice Vivienne
--Beyond the Crystal Cave. LC 46-1161. 163, 1 p. illus. 22 cm. 1946. The Colt Press.

Gilmore, Edith Spacil (1920-)
--Betty Carroll's Adventure: A Novel for Girls. LC 56-9158. 188p. 22cm. 1957. Lothrop, Lee & Shepard.

Gilmore, Emily
--The Boys of Riverton. LC 12-32575. 270 p. front., plates. 18 cm. 1887. Presbyterian Board of Publication and Sabbath-School Work.

Gilmore, Ernest, pseud., see Farley, Helen Hall Moyer.

Gilmore, Iris, jt. auth. see Talmadge, Marian.

Gilmore, Jeanne see Fontenot, Mary Alice.

Gilmore, M. Jacqueline
--The Secret of Scared Acres. Armington, Jean, illus. LC 27-19184. 330 p. front., plates. 20 cm. c.1927. Lothrop, Lee & Shepard Co.

Gilmore, Mary A
--Katie, a Daughter of the King. LC 98-1735. 4 p. l., 5 84 p. front. 19 cm. 1891. G. W. Jacobs & Co.

Gilmore, Mary Cameron (1865-1962) & Pender, Lydia Podger (1907-)
--Poems for Playtime. Gulloch, June, illus. LC 60-28115. (Illus.). 26p. 33cm. 1969. Hamlyn.
Gilmore, Parker
--Travel, War and Shipwreck. N.D. E. P. Dutton & Co.
Gilmore, Robert see Fontenot, Mary Alice.
Gilmour, Bruce
--Lovers. LC 74-18307. (Illus.). 1975. (ISBN 0-688-00333-8). Morrow.
Gilmour, Harriet B. (1939-)
--Why Wembley Fraggle Couldn't Sleep. McClintock, Barbara, illus. LC 84-19286. (Illus.). 32 p. 22cm. c.1985. (ISBN 0-03-004557-6). Holt, Rinehart, and Winston.
Gilmour, Margaret
--[illegible] at the Circus. Pearse, Susan Beatrice, illus. LC 31-19278. 63 p. illus. (part col.) 21 cm. c.1931. David McKay Company.
--The Seven Little Spillikins. Govey, Lilian A., illus. N.D. David McKay Co.
--Trying Toby and the Punch and Judy Show. Orr, Jack, illus. N.D. David McKay Co.
Gilow, Betty & Tickle, Phyllis Alexander (1934-)
--It's No Fun to Be Sick: By Paula & Her Friends. (Illus.). 1976. (ISBN 0-918518-02-4). [illegible] TN.
Gilroy, Frank Daniel, jt. auth. see Gilroy, Ruth G.
Gilroy, Ruth G & Gilroy, Frank Daniel (1925-)
--Little Ego. Obligado, Lilian Isabel (1931-), illus. LC 78-124289. (Illus.). 57 p. (Gulliver House book). 1970. Simon and Schuster.
Gilroy, Thomas Laurence (1951-)
--In Bikole: Modern Stories of Life in a West African Village. Vachula, Monica, illus. LC 78-3271. (Illus.). (gr. 7 up). 1978. (ISBN 0-394-83722-3). Knopf: Distributed by Random House.
Gilson, Barbara
--Beyond the Dragon Door. N.D. Frederick Warne & Co.
Gilson, Charles James Louis (1878-)
--Held by Chinese Brigands. LC 21-18800. 5 p. l., 302 p. col. front. 20 cm. 1921. Dodd, Mead and Company.
--The Scarlet Hand. LC 21-188082. 4 p. l., 308 p. col. front. 20 cm. 1921. Dodd, Mead and Company.
--Taboo. N.D. Frederick Warne & Co.
--The Yellow Mask. LC 45-8307. 256 p. incl. map. front. 20 cm. 1943. F. Warne and Co. Ltd.
--The Zulu Trail. LC 26-19113. 4 p. l., 253 p. front. 20 cm. 1926. Doubleday, Page & Company.
Gilson, Jamie (1933-)
--Can't Catch Me, I'm the Gingerbread Man. LC 80-39748. 188 p. 22cm. c.1981. (ISBN 0-688-00435-0). (ISBN 0-688-00436-9). Lothrop, Lee & Shepard Books.
--Dial Leroi Rupert, DJ. 1st ed. Wallner, John C. (1945-), illus. LC 79-4662. (Illus.). 126 p. 22cm. c.1979. (ISBN 0-688-41888-0). (ISBN 0-688-51888-5). Lothrop, Lee & Shepard.
--Do Bananas Chew Gum?. LC 80-11414. 158 p. 22cm. c.1980. (ISBN 0-688-41960-7). (ISBN 0-688-51960-1). Lothrop, Lee & Shepard Books.
--Harvey, the Beer Can King. Wallner, John C. (1945-), illus. LC 78-1807. p. cm. c.1978. (ISBN 0-688-41845-7). (ISBN 0-688-51845-1). Lothrop, Lee & Shepard.
--Hello, My Name Is Scrambled Eggs. Wallner, John C. (1945-), illus. LC 84-10075. (Illus.). 160p. (gr. 4-6). 1985. (ISBN 0-688-04095-0). Lothrop.
--Thirteen Ways to Sink a Sub. 1st ed. Edwards, Linda Strauss, illus. LC 82-141. (Illus.). 140 p. 22cm. c.1982. (ISBN 0-688-01304-X). Lothrop, Lee & Shepard.
--Thirteen Ways to Sink a Sub. Edwards, Linda Strauss, illus. (Illus.). (gr. 3-7). 1982. (ISBN 0-688-01304-X). Morrow.
Gilson, Jennie S see Sunshine, Susan, pseud.
Gilson, Jennie S
--Bedtime Stories. Sunshine, Susan, pseud. LC 30-10341. 1 p. l., 5-114 p., 1 l. illus. 22 cm. c.1930. Printed by the Highland Press.
Gilstrap, Robert Lawrence (1933-)
--Ten Texas Tales. Warren, Betsy, pseud. (1916-), illus. Warren, Elizabeth Avery. LC 63-19972. ix, 142 p. illus. 21 cm. c.1963. Steck Co.
Gilstrap, Robert Lawrence (1933-) & Estabrook, Irene, eds.
--The Sultan's Fool & Other North African Tales. Greco, Robert, illus. LC 58-13065. (Illus.). 95p. (gr. 4-6). 1958. (ISBN 0-03-045480-8). HR&W.
Gimbel, Mary, jt. auth. see Cott, Jonathan.
Gincano, John Anthony & Hunter, Kay
--The Whitewashed Elephant. LC 36-17400. 24 p. illus. (part col.) 25 x 29 cm. c.1936. Grosset and Dunlap.
Gindhart, Issac D. (1878-)
--Muskrat Meadows at Hemlock Hall. Carrasco, Rudolph & Aspen, Marjorie, illus. LC 62-19703. 157p. illus. 21cm. c.1962. Fleet Pub. Corp.
Gindhart, James D. (1878-)
--The Story of the Muskrat War. Aspen, Marjorie, illus. LC 42-5138. (Illus.). 30p. 24cm. 1941. The Eldon Press.
Gingerbread Boy
--The Gingerbread Boy. Holdsworth, William Curtis, illus. LC 68-23751. 25p. illus. 21x23cm. 1968. Farrar.
--The Gingerbread Boy. Wehr, Julian, illus. LC 45-1341. 18 p. col. illus. 22 x 17 1/2 cm. c.1943. Duenewald Printing Corporation.
--The Gingerbread Boy. Wehr, Julian, illus. LC 43-136783. 24 p. col. illus. 22 x 17 cm. 1943. E. P. Dutton & Co., Inc.
--The Gingerbread Man. Scarry, Richard McClure (1919-), illus. LC 53-2893. unpaged. illus. 21cm. (Little golden library, 165). 1953. [illegible]
--The Gingerbread Man. Ireson, Barbara Francis (1927-), ed. Rose, Gerald Hembdon Seymour (1935-), illus. LC 64-20789. 1 v. (unpaged) col. illus. 26 cm. N.D. Norton, , C.
--The Gingerbread Man. Tate, Sally, illus. LC 48-153181. 40 p. col. illus. 22 cm. (Cozy corner book). c.1947. Whitman Pub. Co.
--The Gingerbread Man. Wadsworth, Wallace Carter (1894-1933), ed. Burrows, Peggy, illus. LC 51-[illegible]. unpaged. illus. 17cm. (Rand McNally book-elf junior, 635). c.1954. Rand McNally.
--The Gingerbread Man. Wadsworth, Wallace Carter (1894-1933), ed. Leaf, Anne Sellers, illus. LC 67-4732. 1 v. (unpaged) col. illus. 33 cm. (Rand McNally giant book). c.1965. Rand McNally.
Gingras, Grace, ed. see Dumas, Alexandre.
Gingras, Louis & Rainboldt, Jo
--Coyote & Kootenai. (gr. 2-6). 1977. (ISBN 0-89992-067-5). MT Coun Indian.
Gingrich, Arnold, ed.
--The Bedside Esquire. N.D. Grosset & Dunlap.
Ginn, ed. see Ruskin, John.
Ginnings, Harriett Wilcoxen see Harriett, pseud.
Ginnings, Harriett Wilcoxen (1905-)
--Animal ABC. Ginnings, Harriett Wilcoxen (1905-), illus. LC 49-515939. 31 p. col. illus. 17 cm. (Tell-a-tale books). c.1949. Whitman Pub. Co.
Ginsberg, Benjamin
--The Sibling Rivalry Monster. Muhlback, Alice, illus. LC 85-17474. p. cm. 1985. (ISBN 0-89594-184-8). The Crossing Press.
Ginsburg, Mirra (1919-), ed. see Chukovsky, Kornei Ivanovich.
Ginsburg, Mirra (1919-), adapted by see Dudochkin, Petr Petrovich.
Ginsburg, Mirra (1919-), retold by see Kharms, Daniil.
Ginsburg, Mirra, adapted by see Suteyev, Vladimir Grigorevich.
Ginsburg, Mirra, tr. see Aitmatov, Chingiz.
Ginsburg, Mirra, tr. see Bulychev, Kirill Vsevolodovich.
Ginsburg, Mirra, tr. see Obukhova, Lidiia Alekseevna.
Ginsburg, Mirra, tr. see Suteyev, Vladimir Grigorevich.
Ginsburg, Mirra (1919-)
--Kitten from One to Ten. Maestro, Giulio (1942-), illus. LC 79-24510. (Illus.). 32 p. 21cm. c.1980. (ISBN 0-517-53972-1). Crown.
--Little Rystu. Chen, Tony (1929-), illus. LC 76-30485. (Illus.). 32 p. 26cm. c.1978. (ISBN 0-688-80097-1). (ISBN 0-688-84097-3). Greenwillow Books.
--The Magic Stove. Heller, Linda (1944-), illus. LC 82-12523. (Illus.). 32 p. 26cm. c.1983. (ISBN 0-698-20566-9). Coward, McCann & Geoghegan.
--The Moonsweeper. 1976. MacMillan Publishing Company.
--Striding Slippers. Murdocca, Salvatore, illus. LC 77-12035. (Illus.). 32 p. 26cm. c.1978. (ISBN 0-02-736370-8). Macmillan.
--The Strongest One of All: Based on a Caucasian Folktale. Aruego, Jose (1932-) & Dewey, Ariane (1937-), illus. LC 76-44326. (Illus.). 32 p. 26cm. c.1977. (ISBN 0-688-80081-5). (ISBN 0-688-84081-7). Greenwillow Books.
--Where Does the Sun Go at Night?. Aruego, Jose (1932-) & Dewey, Ariane (1937-), illus. 1980. Greenwillow.
--Where Does 'the Sun Go at Night?. Aruego, Jose (1932-) & Dewey, Ariane (1937-), illus. LC 79-16151. (Illus.). 32 p. 26cm. c.1981. (ISBN 0-688-80245-1). (ISBN 0-688-84245-3). Greenwillow Books.
Ginsburg, Mirra (1919-), ed.
--The Air of Mars, and Other Stories of Time and Space. LC 75-34279. ix, 141 p. 22cm. c.1976. (ISBN 0-02-736160-8). Macmillan.
--The Fisherman's Son. Chen, Tony (1929-), illus. LC 78-31852. (Adapted from a Georgian Folktale). (Illus.). 33 p. 26cm. c.1979. (ISBN 0-688-80216-8). (ISBN 0-688-84216-X). Greenwillow Books.
--The Fox and the Hare. Nolden, Victor, illus. LC 75-90993. (Illus.). 33 p. 1969. Crown Publishers.
--How the Sun Was Brought Back to the Sky. Aruego, Jose (1932-) & Dewey, Ariane (1937-), illus. LC 74-19060. (Illus.). 32 p. 1975. (ISBN 0-02-735750-3). Macmillan.
--How Wilka Went to Sea, and Other Tales from West of the Urals. Mikolaycak, Charles (1937-), illus. LC 73-78877. (Illus.). 128 p. 24cm. 1975. (ISBN 0-517-50536-3). Crown Publishers. **Award: (ALA).**
--The Kaha Bird: Tales from the Steppes of Central Asia. Cuffari, Richard (1925-1978), illus. LC 70-166532. (Illus.). 159 p. 22cm. 1971. Crown Publishers.
--Last Door to Aiya: A Selection of the Best New Science Fiction from the Soviet Union. 192 p. 22cm. 1968. S. G. Phillips.
--The Lazies: Tales of the Peoples of Russia. Parry, Marian (1924-), illus. LC 72-92437. (Illus.). 70 p. 24cm. 1973. (ISBN 0-02-735840-2). Macmillan.
--The Master of the Winds and Other Tales from Siberia. Arno, Enrico (1913-1981), illus. LC 79-127520. (Illus.). 158 p. 22cm. 1970. Crown Publishers.
--The Night It Rained Pancakes. Florian, Douglas (1950-), illus. LC 79-16137. (Adapted from a Russian Folktale). (Illus.). 55 p. 22cm. (Greenwillow read-along books). c.1980. (ISBN 0-688-80241-9). (ISBN 0-688-84241-0). Greenwillow Books.
--One Trick Too Many: Fox Stories from Russia. Siegl, Helen (1924-), illus. LC 72-711. (Illus.). 39 p. 24cm. 1973. Dial Press.
--Pampalche of the Silver Teeth. Negri, Rocco (1932-), illus. Ginsburg, Mirra, tr. LC 75-6794. (Illus.). 32 p. c.1976. (ISBN 0-517-52241-1). Crown.
--The Proud Maiden, Tungak, and the Sun: A Russian Eskimo Tale. Galanin, Igor, illus. LC 73-19060. (Illus.). 31 p. 23cm. 1974. (ISBN 0-02-736260-4). Macmillan.
--The Sun's Asleep Behind the Hill. 1st ed. Zelinsky, Paul O., illus. LC 81-6615. (Illus.). 32 p. c.1982. (ISBN 0-688-00824-0). (ISBN 0-688-00824-0). Greenwillow Books.
--Three Rolls and One Doughnut. Lobel, Anita Kempler (1934-), illus. LC 70-120293. (Illus.). 52 p. 26cm. 1970. Dial Press.
The Twelve Clever Brothers and Other Fools. Mikolaycak, Charles (1937-), illus. 1979. Harper.
--The Twelve Clever Brothers and Other Fools: Russian Folk Tales. Mikolaycak, Charles (1937-), illus. LC 79-2409. p. cm. c.1979. (ISBN 0-397-31822-7). (ISBN 0-397-31862-6). Lippincott.
--Two Greedy Bears: Adapted from a Hungarian Folk Tale. Aruego, Jose (1932-) & Dewey, Ariane (1937-), illus. LC 76-8819. (Illus.). 32p. (ps-2). 1976. (ISBN 0-02-736450-X). Macmillan.
--What Kind of Bird is That?. Maestro, Giulio (1942-), illus. LC 72-91703. (Adapted from the Russian Story by V. Suteyev). (Illus.). 30p. 28cm. 1973. (ISBN 0-517-50255-0). Crown Publishers.
Ginther, Mary Pemberton
--Beth Anne Goes to School. Ginther, Mary Pemberton, illus. LC 20-1216. 332 p. front., plates. 19 cm. 1919. The Penn Publishing Company.
--Beth Anne Herself. Ginther, Mary Pemberton, illus. LC 15-205940. 352 p. front., plates. 19 cm. 1915. The Penn Publishing Company.
--Beth Anne: Really-for-Truly. Ginther, Mary Pemberton, illus. 357 p. front., plates. 19 cm. 1916. The Penn Publishing Company.
--Beth Anne's New Cousin. Ginther, Mary Pemberton, illus. LC 17-167296. 320 p. front., plates. 19 cm. 1917. The Penn Publishing Company.
--Betsy Hale. Ginther, Mary Pemberton, illus. LC 23-131056. 2 p. l., 7-269 p. front., plates. 19 cm. c.1923. The John C. Winston Company.
--Betsy Hale Succeeds. Ginther, Mary Pemberton, illus. LC 23-13104. 2 p. l., 7-256 p. front., plates. 19 cm. c.1923. The John C. Winston Company.
--Betsy Hale Tries. Ginther, Mary Pemberton, illus. LC 23-131061. 2 p. l., 7-254 p. front., plates. 19 cm. c.1923. The John C. Winston Company.
--Hilda of Grey Cot. Ginther, Mary Pemberton, illus. LC 24-340223. 5 p. l., 9-330 p. front., plates. 20 cm. 1923. The Penn Publishing Co.
--Hilda of Laudis and Company. Ginther, Mary Pemberton, illus. LC 24-174561. 302 p. front., plates. 20 cm. 1924. The Penn Publishing Company.
--Hilda of the Green Smock. Ginther, Mary Pemberton, illus. LC 25-199084. 312 p. front., plates. 20 cm. 1925. The Penn Publishing Company.
--Hilda of the Three Star Ranch. Ginther, Mary Pemberton, illus. LC 26-197330. 306 p. front., plates. 20 cm. 1926. The Penn Publishing Company.
--The Jade Necklace. (Mystery Bks. for Girls). N.D. Cupples & Leon Co.
--The Jade Necklace. LC 29-10437. 309 p. front., plates. 20 cm. c.1929. Macrae Smith Company.
--Miss Pat and Company, Limited. (The "Miss Pat" Ser.). N.D. John C. Winston.
--Miss Pat and Her Sisters. (The "Miss Pat" Ser.). N.D. John C. Winston.
--Miss Pat at Artemis Lodge. (The "Miss Pat" Ser.). N.D. John C. Winston.
--Miss Pat at School. LC 16-2370. 323 p. front. 19 cm. c.1915. The John C. Winston Company.
--Miss Pat in Buenos Ayres. (The "Miss Pat" Ser.). N.D. John C. Winston.
--Miss Pat in the Old World. LC 15-13358. 295 p. front. 19 cm. c.1915. The John C. Winston Company.
--Miss Pat's Career. (The "Miss Pat"). N.D. John C. Winston.
--Miss Pat's Great Idea. (The "Miss Pat" Ser.). N.D. John C. Winston.
--Miss Pat's Holidays at Greycroft. (Miss Pat Ser.). N.D. John C. Winston.
--Miss Pat's Problem. (The Miss Pat Ser.). N.D. John C. Winston.
--The Secret Stair. (Mystery Bks. for Girls). N.D. Cupples & Leon Co.
--The Secret Stair. Ginther, Mary Pemberton, illus. LC 20-117074. 293 p. front., plates. 19 cm. c.1928. Macrae Smith Company.
--The Thirteenth Spoon: A Mystery Story for Girls. LC 30-10469. 5 p. l., 9-308 p. 20 cm. c.1930. Macrae Smith Company.
Gioffre, Marisa
--Starstruck. LC 85-2153. p. cm. 1985. (ISBN 0-590-32834-4). Scholastic.
Giordano, Dick & Andru, Ross, illus.
--Wonder Woman. Penick, Ib, designed by. LC 79-56150. (Illus.). 14 p. 24cm. (Pop-up book). c.1980. (ISBN 0-394-84411-4). Random House.
Giordano, Joe, jt. auth. see Carey, Mary Virginia.
Giovannetti, Pericle
--Max. Giovannetti, Pericle, illus. LC 76-50008. (Illus.). 96p. (ps-12). 1977. (ISBN 0-689-50082-3, McElderry Bk). Atheneum.
Giovanni, Nikki (1943-)
--Ego-Tripping and Other Poems for Young People. Ford, George Cephas, Jr., illus. LC 73-81745. (Illus.). 37 p. 24cm. 1974, c.1973. (ISBN 0-88208-020-2). L. Hill; Distributed by Independent Publishers Group.
--Ego Tripping & Other Poems for Young Readers. Ford, George Cephas, Jr., illus. LC 73-81745. (Illus.). 48p. 1st U.S. edition. (gr. 2-7). 1974. (ISBN 0-88208-020-2). (ISBN 0-88208-019-9). Lawrence Hill.
--Spin a Soft Black Song: Poems for Children. Bible, Charles (1937-), illus. LC 76-163572. (Illus.). 64 p. 27cm. 1971. (ISBN 0-8090-8795-2). Hill and Wang.
--Spin a Soft Black Song: Poems for Children. rev. ed. Martins, George, illus. LC 84-19287. (Illus.). 57 p. 24cm. 1985. Hill and Wang.
--Vacation Time: Poems for Children. 1st ed. Russo, Marisabina, illus. LC 79-91643. (Illus.). 59 p. 22cm. 1980. (ISBN 0-688-03657-0). Morrow.
Giovetti, illus.
--My Book of Goldilocks and the Three Bears. LC 62-18013. (Illus.). 33cm. (Giant Maxton Book). 1962. Maxton Pub. Corp.
Gipson, Frederick Benjamin (1908-1973) see Disney, Walt, Productions.
Gipson, Frederick Benjamin (1908-1973)
--Curly and the Wild Boar. 1st ed. Himler, Ronald Norbert (1937-), illus. LC 77-25644. (Illus.). 88 p. 22cm. c.1979. (ISBN 0-06-022014-7). (ISBN 0-06-022015-5). Harper & Row.
--Hound-Dog Man. LC 49-7116. 1949. (ISBN 0-06-011540-8, HarpT). (ISBN 0-06-011541-6). Har-Row.
--Little Arliss. Himler, Ronald Norbert (1937-), illus. (Illus.). 83 p. 19cm. (Harper Trophy Book). 1980, c.1978. (ISBN 0-06-440108-1). Harper & Row.
--Old Yeller. Burger, Carl Victor (1888-1967), illus. LC 56-8780. (Illus.). 1956. (ISBN 0-06-011545-9, HarpT). (ISBN 0-06-011546-7). (ISBN 0-06-011548-3). Har-Row. **Award: (JNM).**
--Recollection Creek. Burger, Carl Victor (1888-1967), illus. LC 58-7764. (Illus.). 23cm. 248p. (gr. 5 up). 1959. (ISBN 0-06-022021-X, HarpJ). Har-Row.
--Savage Sam. Burger, Carl Victor (1888-1967), illus. LC 62-7948. (Illus.). 214 p. 22cm. 1962. Harper.
--The Trail-Driving Rooster. Simont, Marc (1915-), illus. LC 55-6345. (Illus.). 79 p. 22cm. 1955. Harper.
Gipson, Morrell (1920-), ed. see Calling All Girls.
Gipson, Morrell (1920-)
--City Country ABC. Weisgard, Leonard Joseph (1916-), illus. LC 48-1037. 48 p. col. ill. 28cm. c.1946. Garden City Pub. Co.

--Favorite Nursery Tales. 1st ed. Schindler, Steven D., illus. LC 82-45304. (Illus.). 30 p. 29cm. c.1983. (ISBN 0-385-17960-X). Doubleday.
--Hello Peter. Hurd, Clement (1908-), illus. LC 48-766303. 31 p. col. illus. 20 x 22 cm. (Junior books). 1948. Doubleday.
--Mr. Bear Squash-You-All-Flat. LC 50-1924. 44p. 1950. Grosset & Dunlap.
--The Surprise Doll. Lerch, Steffie E. (1908-), illus. LC 51-2727. 43 p. col. illus. 21 cm. (Wonder books, 519). 1949. Grosset & Dunlap.
Gipson, Morrell (1920-), retold by.
--Rip Van Winkle. San Souci, Daniel, illus. LC 83-20624. (Original Author: Washington Irving, 1783-1859). (Illus.). 32p. (ps-3). 1984. (ISBN 0-385-18757-2). (ISBN 0-385-18758-0). (ISBN 0-385-18758-0). Doubleday.
Girard, Hazel B
--A Giant Walked Among Them: Half-Tall Tales of Paul Bunyan and His Loggers. Girard, Marv, illus. LC 77-81432. 168 p. c.1977. M. Jones Co.
Girard, Linda Walvoord
--You Were Born on Your Very First Birthday. Kieffer, Christa, illus. LC 82-13700. p. cm. (Concept book/Level 1). 1982. (ISBN 0-8075-9455-5). A. Whitman.
Girardin, Emile De see De Girardin, Emile & Gautier, Theophile.
Girardin, Marie Alfred Jules (1832-1888)
--The Adventures of Johnny Ironsides. Bayard, Emile, illus. Frith, Henry, tr. LC 42-35710. 4 p. l., 300 p. front., illus., plates. 20 cm. 1884. G. Routledge and Sons.
Gire, Ken, Jr.
--The Christmas Duck. Neely, Keith R. (1943-), illus. (Illus.). 133p. (Sower Ser.). 1983. (ISBN 0-88062-112-5). Mott Media.
Girion, Barbara (1937-)
--The Boy with the Special Face. Palmer, Heidi (1948-), illus. LC 78-51986. (Illus.). 32 p. c.1978. (ISBN 0-687-03909-6). Abingdon.
--A Brief Season. LC 84-1217. 150 p. 1984. (ISBN 0-684-18088-X). Scribner.
--The Chicken Bone Wish. Cuffari, Richard (1925-1978), illus. (Illus.). 160p. (gr. 3-6). 1982. (ISBN 0-590-31783-0, Apple Paperbacks). Scholastic Inc.
--A Handful of Stars. LC 81-14476. p. cm. 1981. (ISBN 0-684-17167-8). Scribner.
--In the Middle of a Rainbow. LC 83-3300. 197 p. 22cm. c.1983. (ISBN 0-684-17885-0). Scribner.
--Joshua, the Czar, and the Chicken Bone Wish. Cuffari, Richard (1925-1978), illus. LC 78-15012. p. cm. 1978. (ISBN 0-684-15929-5). Scribner.
--Like Everybody Else. LC 80-21850. p. cm. 1980. (ISBN 0-684-16715-8). Scribner.
--Misty and Me. LC 79-15925. p. cm. 1979. (ISBN 0-684-16227-X). Scribner.
--A Tangle of Roots. LC 78-27243. 154 p. 22cm. c.1979. (ISBN 0-684-16074-9). Scribner.
Girl Scouts of the U. S. A.
--Brownies' Own Songbook. Roos, Ann, et al., eds. 48p. (gr. 1-3). 1968. (ISBN 0-88441-351-9). GS.
--The Ditty Bag. Tobitt, Janet E., compiled by. (gr. 4-12). N.D. GS.
--Girl Scout Pocket Songbook: For Juniors, Cadettes, Seniors, & Leaders. 56p. (gr. 5-12). 1972. (ISBN 0-88441-306-3). GS.
--Promenade All. Tobitt, Janet E., compiled by. (gr. 7 up). N.D. (ISBN 0-88441-356-X). GS.
--Sing High! Sing Low!. Sanders, Mary A., compiled by. (gr. 1 up). N.D. (ISBN 0-88441-355-1). GS.
--Skip to My Lou: For Brownies, Juniors, Cadettes, Seniors & Leaders. 32p. (gr. 1-8). 1958. (ISBN 0-88441-307-1). GS.
Girling, Zoe, ed.
--Polish Fairy Tales. Cook, Hazel, illus. LC 68-13806. (Illus.). 190 p. 23cm. (World fairy tale collections). 1968, c.1959. Follett Pub. Co.
Girls of Lady Eden's School, London
--Just How Stories. Steele, Derek, illus. (Illus.). 23p. (ps-3). 1981. (ISBN 0-224-01713-6, Pub. by Chatto-Bodley-Jonathan). Merrimack Pub Cir.
Girolamo, Vittorio Di see Di Girolamo, Vittorio.
Giruad, Jean & Charlier, Jean-Michel
--The Man with the Silver Star. (Illus.). 48p. (Lt. Blueberry Ser.). N.D. (ISBN 2-205-06578-5). Dargaud Pub.
Girvan, Helen Masterman, Mrs. (1891-)
--Blue Treasure: The Mystery of Tamarind Court. O'Brien, Harriet, illus. LC 37-21027. 5 p. l., 273 p. incl. front., illus. 20 cm. c.1937. Farrar & Rinehart, Inc.
--The Clue in the Antique Clock. LC 57-9677. 192 p. 22cm. 1957. Westminister Press.
--Disappearance at Lake House. (gr. 5-9). 1959. (ISBN 0-664-32216-6). Westminster.
--Down Bayberry Lane. LC 55-8361. 204p. 21cm. 1955. Westminster Press.
--End of a Golden String. 1st ed. Low, Vaike, illus. LC 52-7800. (Illus.). 192 p. 21cm. 1952. Dutton.
--Felicity Way. Howe, Gertrude Herrick (1902-), illus. LC 42-5828. 6 p. l., 3-274 p. incl. illus., plates. 20 cm. 1942. Farrar & Rinehart, Inc.
--The Frightened Whisper. LC 63-10969. 175 p. 21 cm. 1963. Westminster Press.
--Hidden Pond. 1st ed. Orbaan, Albert F. (1913-), illus. LC 51-10519. (Illus.). 192 p. 21cm. 1951. Dutton.
--The Hidden Treasure. LC 68-10526. 190 p. 21cm. 1968. Westminster Press.
--The House at 231. Haemer, Alan, illus. LC 40-14196. 6 p. l., 3-305 p. front., illus. 20 cm. c.1940. Farrar & Rinehart Inc.
--The Light in the Mill. Hopkins, Joseph, Jr., illus. LC 46-642884. 5 p. l., 3-246 p. illus. 19 1/2 cm. 1946. Rinehart & Company, Inc.
--The Missing Masterpiece. LC 65-16308. 192 p. 21 cm. 1965. Westminster Press.
--Mystery of the Unwelcome Visitor. LC 61-7957. 21cm. 188p. (gr. 7-10). 1961. (ISBN 0-664-32258-1). Westminster.
--Patty and the Spoonbill. Low, Vaike, illus. LC 53-10797. 218p. illus. 22cm. 1953. Funk & Wagnalls.
--Phantom on Skis. Haemer, Alan, illus. N.D. Rinehart & Co.
--The Seventh Step: Mystery at Cedarhead. Howe, Gertrude Herrick (1902-), illus. LC 49-836431. 238 p. illus. 21 cm. 1949. Rinehart.
--Shadow in the Greenhouse. LC 70-119566. 188 p. 21cm. 1970. Westminster Press.
--The White Tulip. Howe, Gertrude Herrick (1902-), illus. LC 44-700. viii, 280 p. illus. 20 cm. 1944. Farrar & Rinehart, Inc.
Girzone, Joseph F.
--Kara, the Lonely Falcon. 1979. (ISBN 0-533-03971-1). Vantage.
--Kara, The Lonely Falcon. Molloy, Eideen, illus. (Illus.). 52p. Repr. of 1979 ed (Pub. by Vantage Press). (gr. 7up). 1983. (ISBN 0-911519-05-X). Richelieu Court.

Gischler, Pearl Clements, jt. auth. see Hayden, Gwendolen Lampshire.

Gischler, Pearl Clements (1903-) & Hayden, Gwendolyn Lampshire (1904-)
--Christmas Tree Farm. Anderson, Victor (1904-), illus. LC 51-11433. 104 p. col. illus. 21 cm. 1951. Pacific Press Pub. Association.
--Mystery at Christmas Tree Farm. Anderson, Victor (1904-), illus. LC 75-142731. (Illus.). 128 p. 22cm. (Penguin series). (gr. 7 up). 1971. Review and Herald Pub. Association.
Gisler, Margaret, jt. auth. see Eberts, Marjorie.
Gissing, Vera, tr. see Hejna, Olga.
Gittings, Ella Beecher
--Margery's Vacation. LC 12-32570. 308 p. front., 2 pl. 19 cm. c.1891. Congregational Sunday-School and Publishing Society.
Gittings, James A.
--Down Strange Streets. Krieger, David, illus. LC 68-26733. (Illus.). 160 p. 21cm. 1968. Friendship Press.
Gittings, Joan Grenville Manton see Manton, Jo, pseud.
Gittings, Robert William Victor, jt. auth. see Manton, Jo.
Gittins, Anne, ed.
--Tales from the South Pacific Islands. Kealiinohomoku, Tom, illus. LC 76-5411. 26cm. 89p. 1976. (ISBN 0-916144-02-X). Stemmer House Publishers.
Giuliano, William
--Pat, Lad & the Sleepy Pig. (Illus.). 4 colors. 131p. (Easy Road to Reading Improvement Ser). (gr. 1-4). 1966. (ISBN 0-8178-6012-6). Harvey.
--Rednose, the Elf. (Illus.). 4 colors. 161p. (Easy Road to Reading Improvement Ser). (gr. 1-6). 1966. (ISBN 0-8178-6052-5). Harvey.
--Rednose the Elf. Ribas, Marta, illus. (Illus.). 161p. (The Easy Road to Reading Improvement Ser.). (gr. 1-3). 1966. (ISBN 0-9606420-1-3). Marand Pub Co.
Giuliano, William, jt. auth. see De Luca, Angelo Michael.
Gladd, Arthur Anthony (1913-)
--Galleys East!. Vosburgh, Leonard W. (1912-), illus. LC 61-5514. 270p. c.1961. Dodd, Mead.
--The Saracen Steed. Vosburgh, Leonard W. (1912-), illus. LC 60-6312. 21cm. 240p. 1960. Dodd, Mead & Co.
Gladden, Washington (1836-1918)
--Santa Claus on a Lark and Other Christmas Stories. LC 4-16136. 2 p. l., 178 p. illus. 24 cm. 1890. The Century Co.
Gladstone, Gary (1935-)
--Hey, Hey, Can't Catch Me!. LC 70-124315. (Illus.). 32 p. 27cm. N.D. Van Nostrand Reinhold Co.
Gladstone, George, Mrs.
--Sailing Orders. (Golden Lily Ser.). N.D. D. Lothrop Co.
--Sailing Orders, 1 0f 30 vols. (Illus.). (Morning Glory Ser). N.D. Lothrop Pub. Co.
--Tom Gillies. 349p. N.D. Congregational Sunday-School and Publishing Society.
--Tom Gillies,. The Knots He Tied and Untied. (Illus.). 220p. N.D. E P Dutton & Co.
--Tom Gillies: The Nots he Tied and untied. 1873. Henry A. Young.
--Uncle Max. (Golden Lily Ser.). N.D. D. Lothrop Co.
--Uncle Max, 1 of 30 vols. (Illus.). (Morning Glory Ser). N.D. Lothrop Pub. Co.
--Watchman Halfdan and His Little Grand-daughter. (Illus.). 80p. (The Rosebud Ser). N.D. Fleming H. Revell Co.
Gladstone, Josephine see Marquand, Josephine, pseud.
Gladstone, Lise
--The Inside Kid. Asch, Frank (1946-), illus. LC 76-55735. (Illus.). 47 p. 22cm. c.1977. (ISBN 0-07-023361-6). (ISBN 0-07-023362-4). McGraw-Hill.
Gladwyn, Gilbert
--On Papa's Lap. 92p. N.D. American Tract Society.
Glagoleva, Fainna, tr. see Aleksin, Anatolii Georgievich.
Glagoleva, Fainna, tr. see Perovskaya, Olga.
Glagoleva, Fainna, tr. see Raskin, A.
Glanville, Ada H.
--Queen Dido's Treasure. Cosimini, Roland F., illus. LC 30-25449. 4 p. l., 3-242 p. 1 l. col. front., illus. 21 cm. 1930. Little, Brown, and Company.
Glanville, Brian Lester (1931-)
--Goalkeepers Are Different. LC 72-79792. 154 p. 22cm. 1972. (ISBN 0-517-50070-1). Crown Publishers.
Glanzer, Herta
--Pep and Pepper. Baerg, Harry John (1909-), illus. LC 57-44037. 77p. illus. 24cm. 1957. Southern Pub. Association.
Glaser, Byron, jt. auth. see Neumeier, Marty.
Glaser, Dianne Elizabeth (1937-)
--Amber Wellington, Daredevil. Glaser, Marvin, illus. LC 74-78854. (Illus.). 116 p. 22cm. 1975. (ISBN 0-8027-6197-6). Walker.
--Amber Wellington, Witch Watcher. Glaser, Marvin, illus. LC 75-43991. (Illus.). 120 p. 22cm. 1976. (ISBN 0-8027-6245-X). (ISBN 0-8027-6246-8). Walker.
--The Diary of Trilby Frost. LC 75-37080. 189 p. 22cm. c.1976. (ISBN 0-8234-0277-0). Holiday House. **Award: (ALA).**
--Summer Secrets. LC 77-3820. 126 p. 22cm. c.1977. (ISBN 0-8234-0305-X). Holiday House.
Glaser, Dianne Elizabeth (1937-) & Stone, David Karl (1922-)
--The Case of the Missing Six. LC 77-16443. (Illus.). 156 p. 21cm. c.1978. (ISBN 0-8234-0318-1). Holiday House.
Glaser, Michael
--Does Anyone Know Where a Hermit Crab Goes?. Glaser, Michael, illus. LC 82-84341. (Illus.). 32p. (Orig.). (ps-3). 1983. (ISBN 0-911635-00-9). Knickerbocker.
Glaser, Milton (1929-) & Glaser, Shirley
--If Apples Had Teeth. Glaser, Milton (1929-), illus. LC 60-13399. 1960. Alfred A Knopf : distributed by Borzoi Books.
Glaser, Paul
--Squad Room Detective: A John Benton Story. LC 60-959251. 272p. 21cm. (Dodd, Mead career books). c.1960. Dodd, Mead.
Glaser, Paul, jt. auth. see Connors, Thomas P.
Glaser, Shirley, jt. auth. see Glaser, Milton.
Glasgow, Aline
--Honschi. Chen, Tony (1929-), illus. LC 72-669. (Illus.). 33 p. 28cm. 1972. (ISBN 0-8193-0596-0). (ISBN 0-8193-0597-9). Parents' Magazine Press.
--The Journey of Akbar. Kocsis, James C. (1936-), illus. Paul, James, pseud. LC 67-22251. (Illus.). 116 p. 21cm. 1967. Dial Press.
--Old Wind & Liu Li-San. LC 62-17254. (Illus.). (gr. 2-5). 1962. (ISBN 0-8178-3301-3). (ISBN 0-8178-3302-1). Harvey.
--The Pair of Shoes. Shimin, Symeon (1902-), illus. LC 69-18223. (Illus.). 48 p. 1971. Dial Press.
Glasgow, Ellen Anderson Gholson (1874-1945)
--The Battle-Ground. Baer, W. F. & Smith, W. Granville, illus. viii p., 1 l., 512 p. col. front., plates. 20 cm. 1902. Doubleday, Page & Co.
--Vein of Iron. LC 35-27270. (Modern Classic Ser.). (gr. 10 up). N.D. (ISBN 0-15-193497-5). HarBraceJ.
Glasgow, Geraldine
--Little Jack Hamilton. (Illus.). 1900. Thomas Nelson & Sons.
Glasgow, Geraldine R., jt. auth. see Fenn, George Manville.
Glasier, Jessie C.
--Gaining the Heights. N.D. Standard Publishing Co.
Glaspell, Susan
--Cherished and Shared of Old. Harvey, Alice, illus. N.D. Julian Messner Inc.
Glass, Andrew
--Jackson Makes His Move: Story and Pictures. Glass, Andrew, illus. LC 81-15957. (Illus.). 44 p. (gr. k-3). c.1982. (ISBN 0-7232-6207-1). F. Warne.
--My Brother Tries to Make Me Laugh. Glass, Andrew, illus. LC 83-14989. (Illus.). 32p. (ps-1). 1984. (ISBN 0-688-02257-X). (ISBN 0-688-02259-6). LOthrop.
Glass, Dudley
--The Spanish Goldfish. Bestall, A. E., illus. N.D. Frederick Warne & Co.
Glass, Esther Eby
--Aunt Nan & the Miller Five. LC 61-15954. (Illus.). 22cm. 128p. (gr. 4-9). 1961. (ISBN 0-8361-1309-8). Herald Pr.
--Larry and Kathy. Moon, Ivan, illus. LC 64-10186. 136 p. illus. 22 cm. 1964. Herald Press.
--Miller Five. Eitzen, Allan (1928-), illus. LC 58-13396. (Illus.). 22cm. 117p. (gr. 4-9). 1958. (ISBN 0-8361-1400-0). Herald Pr.
Glass, Isabel
--Fifth Avenue Store Only. 1974. (ISBN 0-399-11330-4). G. P. Putnam's Sons.
Glass, Malcolm Sanford, jt. ed. see Paton, M. Joe.
Glass, Paul, ed.
--Songs and Stories of Afro-Americans. Cuffari, Richard (1925-1978), illus. LC 72-145735. (Illus.). 61 p. 29cm. 1971. (ISBN 0-448-02467-5). Grosset & Dunlap.
--Songs & Stories of the North American Indians. (Illus.). 2 colors. 64p. (gr. 3-5). 1968. G&D.
Glass, Paul & Singer, Louis C.
--Songs of Hill & Mountain Folk. (Orig.). (gr. 5 up). N.D. (ISBN 0-448-01485-8). G&D.
--Songs of the Sea. (Orig.). (gr. 9 up). N.D. (ISBN 0-448-01489-0). G&D.
--Songs of Town & City Folk. (Orig.). (gr. 5 up). N.D. G&D.
Glasscock, Joyce
--Cowboy Eddie. Grider, Dorothy (1915-), illus. LC 50-4794. 21cm. 33p. N.D. Rand McNally & Co.
Glasser, Barbara
--Leroy Oops. 1st ed. Morton, Lee Jack, Jr. (1928-), illus. LC 77-144120. (Illus.). 16 p. 24cm. 1971. (ISBN 0-402-14028-1). Cowles Book Co.
Glasser, Barbara & Blustein, Ellen
--Bongo Bradley. Johnson, Bonnie Helene, illus. LC 73-337. (Illus.). 153 p. 22cm. 1973. Hawthorn Books.
Glasser, Judy, jt. auth. see Long, Claudia.
Glassford, Eva Belle (1915-)
--The Giant Step. LC 53-12270. 235p. 20cm. 1953. Dorrance.
Glassmacher, W. J. & Keller, Robert S., eds.
--Songs for Children: Over 200 Songs, Stories and Games. cover-title, 192 p. illus. 31 cm. (Everybody's favorite series, no. 5). c.1934. Amsco Music Sales Co.
Glassman, Leo M. (1897-)
--Janie's Wonderful Journey. Marcel, Delia, illus. LC 48-9470. 163 p. illus. 24 cm. 1948. Beechhurst Press.
Glasstone, Richard
--Better Ballet. (Illus.). (Better Bks). (gr. 7 up). N.D. (ISBN 0-7182-1453-6, SpS). Sportshelf.
Glauber, Uta Heil (1936-)
--How the Willow Wren Became King. Glauber, Uta Heil (1936-), illus. LC 72-115092. (Illus.). 31 p. 29cm. 1970. Abelard-Schuman.
Glaus, Marlene (1933-)
--Two Very Special Times. N.D. Carlton Press Inc.
Glazer, Joan I.
--Literature for Early Childhood. (Illus.). 240p. 1981. (ISBN 0-675-08039-8). Merrill.
Glazer, Lee
--Cookie Becker Casts a Spell. Apple, Margot, illus. LC 79-13268. (Illus.). 47 p. 22cm. c.1980. (ISBN 0-316-31582-6). Little, Brown.
Glazer, Tom (1914-), ed.
--Do Your Ears Hang Low?. Lazarevich, Mila (1942-), illus. LC 78-20072. (Illus.). (gr. 1-3). 1980. Doubleday.
--Eye Winker, Tom Tinker, Chin Chopper. Himler, Ronald Norbert (1937-), illus. (Illus.). 1978. Doubleday.
--Eye Winker, Tom Tinker, Chin Chopper: A Collection of Musical Finger Plays. LC 72-97497. (Illus.). 64p. (gr. 1-7). 1973. Doubleday.
--Music for Ones & Twos: Songs & Games for the Very Young Child. Weinhaus, Karen T., illus. LC 82-45199. (Illus.). 96p. (ps). 1983. (ISBN 0-385-14252-8). Doubleday.
--On Top of Spaghetti. 1st ed. Garcia, Tom, illus. LC 81-43042. (Illus.). 32 p. 29cm. c.1982. (ISBN 0-385-14250-1). Doubleday.
--On Top of Spaghetti. Seiden, Art, illus. LC 67-82. 21p. col. illus. 29cm. (Nursery treasure bks.). 1966. Grosset.
--Songs of Peace, Freedom, & Protest. 1970. (ISBN 0-679-50222-X). McKay.
--Tom Glazer's Treasury of Folk Songs for the Family. Seiden, Art, illus. (gr. 4 up). N.D. (ISBN 0-448-02956-1). G&D.
--Tom Glazer's Treasury of Songs for Children. (Illus.). N.D. (ISBN 0-686-74302-4). J R Pubns.

Goble, Paul (1933-), retold by.
--Star Boy. Goble, Paul (1933-), illus. LC 82-20599. p. cm. 1983. (ISBN 0-87888-210-3). Bradbury Press.
Goble, Paul (1933-) & Goble, Dorothy
--Brave Eagle's Account of the Fetterman Fight. Goble, Paul (1933-), illus. (Illus.). (gr. 5 up). 1972. (ISBN 0-394-92314-6). Pantheon.
--The Friendly Wolf. Goble, Paul (1933-), illus. LC 76-353731. (Illus.). 32 p. 26cm. 1974. (ISBN 0-87888-104-2). Bradbury Press.
--The Friendly Wolf. Goble, Paul (1933-), illus. 1975. E.P. Dutton & Co.
--Lone Bull's Horse Raid. Goble, Paul (1933-), illus. LC 73-76546. (Illus.). 63 p. 27cm. 1973. (ISBN 0-87888-059-3). Bradbury Press.
--Red Hawk's Account of Custer's Last Battle. Goble, Paul (1933-) & Goble, Dorothy, illus. 1970. Pantheon.
Gobright, L. A.
--Jack and Jill for Old and Young. N.D. Claxton,Remsen & Haffelfinger.
Gochnour, Mozelle
--Pee Wee: A Story for Little Girls. LC 37-357. 84 p. 19 cm. c.1937. Dorrance and Company.
Goda, Mary
--Adventures of Ricky Chick. Walstad, Chi Chi, illus. LC 70-156810. (Illus.). 32 p. 29cm. 1972. (ISBN 0-513-01154-4). Denison.
Godal, Eric
--Spotty, The Flying Dog. Godal, Eric, illus. LC 46-1553. 32 p. illus. 26 cm. 1915. Veritas Press.
Goddard, Anthea
--The Aztec Skull. LC 76-56606. 152 p. 21cm. 1977. (ISBN 0-8027-6285-9). Walker.
Goddard, Bob, pseud., see Goddard, Robert.
Goddard, Julia Bachope (0000-1896)
--The Boy and the Constellations. 1875. Scribner, Welford, & Armstrong.
--Fairy Tales in Other Land. LC 1-30584. 2 p., l., iii-iv, 9-189 p. front., illus. 19 cm. c.1901. The Mershon Company.
--Fairy Tales in Other Lands. LC 20-6035. 3 p. l., iii-iv, 9-189 p. front., illus. 20 cm. c.1892. Cassell Publishing Company.
--The Four Cats of the Tipperton's and Other Stories about Animals, 1 of 6 vols. (Illus.). 230p. (The Evening Hour Library). N.D. Cassell, Petter,Galpin.
--Ursula's Stumbling Block: Or, Pride Comes Before A Fall. Juv ed. N.D. Cassell & Co.
--Worth More than Gold, 1 of 6 vols. (Illus.). (The Fan Library). N.D. Cassell, Petter,Galpin.
Goddard, Kate Cox
--Chatterbox Child. LC 36-4192. 2 p. l., 46 p. 19 cm. c.1936. John P. Smith Company, Inc.
--Chatterbox Child. LC 38-3234. 3 p. l., 46 p. illus. 20 cm. c.1937. The Platt & Munk Co., Inc.
--Eight Fairy Tales. Piper, Watty, pseud. (1870-1845), ed. Bragg, Mabel Caroline. LC 38-19251. 96 p. illus. (part col.) 21 cm. c.1938. The Platt & Munk Co., Inc.
--Eight Nursery Tales. Piper, Watty (1870-1945), ed. LC 38-19406. (Illus.). 96p. 21cm. 1938. The Platt & Munk Co. Inc.
--My Little World. LC 36-41932. 2 p. l., 37 p. 19 cm. c.1936. John P. Smith Company, Inc.
--My Little World. LC 38-3237. 1 p. l., 37 p. illus. 20 cm. c.1937. The Platt & Munk Co., Inc.
--Poems for Little Ears. LC 36-4194. 2 p. l., 43 p. 19 cm. c.1936. John P. Smith Company, Inc.
--Poems for Little Ears. LC 38-3233. 2 p. l., 43 p. illus. 20 cm. c.1937. The Platt & Munk Co., Inc.
--Poems for Little Ears. LC 44-8470. 3 p. l., 130 p. illus. 20 cm. 1944. The Platt & Munk Co., Inc.
Goddard, Kate Cox, jt. auth. see McCrady, Elizabeth F.
Goddard, Richard
--The Children's Entertainment Book. 100p. N.D. T. S. Denison & Co Inc.
Goddard, Robert see Goddard, Bob, pseud.
Goddard, Robert
--The Little Jester Who Couldn't Laugh. Goddard, Bob, pseud. Smith, Ben, illus. LC 67-2704. (Illus.). 32 p. 24cm. 1967. (ISBN 0-8114-7534-4). Steck-Vaughn Co.
Godden, Rumer (1907-), ed. see Dickinson, Emily.
Godden, Rumer (1907-), tr. see De Gasztold, Carmen Bernos.
Godden, Rumer (1907-)
--Candy Floss. Adams, Adrienne (1906-), illus. LC 60-1642. (Illus.). 63 p. 25cm. 1960. Viking Press.
--The Diddakoi. Glegg, Creina, illus. 1972. Viking Press.
--The Doll's House. Saintsbury, Dana, illus. 128p. N.D. Viking Press.
--The Dolls' House. Tudor, Tasha (1915-), illus. LC 48-83248. 125 p. col. illus. 21 cm. 1948. Viking Press.
--The Dolls' House. Tudor, Tasha (1915-), illus. (Illus.). 136 p. 21cm. 1962. Viking Press.
--The Dragon of Og. Baynes, Pauline Diana (1922-), illus. LC 81-2620. p. cm. 1981. (ISBN 0-670-28168-9). Viking Press.
--Episode of Sparrows. (gr. 9 up). 1955. (ISBN 0-670-29757-7). Viking Pr.
--The Fairy Doll. Adams, Adrienne (1906-), illus. 1956. Macmillan. **Award: (CMA).**
--The Fairy Doll. Adams, Adrienne (1906-), illus. (Illus.). (gr. 2-6). 1956. (ISBN 0-670-30547-2). (ISBN 0-670-30548-0). Viking Pr. **Award: (ALA).**
--Four Dolls. Baynes, Pauline Diana (1922-), illus. LC 83-14157. (Illus.). 144p. (gr. 4-6). 1984. (ISBN 0-688-02801-2). (ISBN 0-688-02801-2). Greenwillow.
--Home Is the Sailor. Primrose, Jean Logan (1917-), illus. (Illus.). 128 p. 22cm. 1964. Viking Press. **Award: (ALA).**
--Impunity Jane: The Story of a Pocket Doll. Adams, Adrienne (1906-), illus. LC 54-3211. (Illus.). 47 p. 21cm. 1954. Viking Press. **Award: (ALA).**
--In Noah's Arc. 1949. Viking Press.
--A Kindle of Kittens. Byrnes, Lynne, illus. LC 78-15931. p. cm. 1979. (ISBN 0-670-41301-1). Viking Press.
--The Kitchen Madonna. Barker, Carol Minturn (1938-), illus. (Illus.). 89 p. 24cm. 1967. Viking Press.
--The Kitchen Madonna. Bryan, James, illus. LC 67-24858. (Illus.). 89 p. 24cm. 1967. Viking Press.
--Little Plum. Primrose, Jean Logan (1917-), illus. LC 63-8526. (Illus.). 97 p. 24cm. 1963. Viking Press. **Award: (ALA).**
--Miss Happiness and Miss Flower. Primrose, Jean Logan (1917-), illus. (Illus.). 81 p. 24cm. 1961. Viking Press. **Awards: (ALA); (CMA).**
--Mouse House. 1960. Viking.
--Mouse House. Adams, Adrienne (1906-), illus. (Illus.). 63 p. 24cm. 1957. Viking Press. **Award: (ALA).**
--The Mousewife. Rev. ed. Holder, Heidi, illus. 1982. Viking.
--The Mousewife. Saintsbury, Dana, illus. LC 51-10262. (Illus.). 48 p. 23cm. 1951. Viking Press.
--Mr. McFadden's Hallowe'en. Strugnell, Ann, illus. LC 75-20483. 127 p. 22cm. 1975. (ISBN 0-670-49271-X). Viking Press.
--The Old Woman Who Lived in a Vinegar Bottle. 1st ed. Hedderwick, Mairi (1939-), illus. LC 77-168563. (Illus.). 48 p. 28cm. 1972, c.1970. (ISBN 0-670-52318-6). Viking Press. **Award: (ALA).**
--Operation Sippacik. Bryan, James, illus. LC 69-13078. (Illus.). 109 p. 22cm. 1969. Viking Press.
--The Peacock Spring: A Western Progress. LC 75-31701. 286p. 1st U.S. edition. 1976. (ISBN 0-670-54558-9). Viking Pr.
--The Rocking Horse Secret. Smith, Juliet Stanwell, illus. LC 77-25489. (Illus.). 87 p. 21cm. 1978, c.1977. (ISBN 0-670-60243-4). Viking Press.
--St. Jerome & the Lion. Primrose, Jean Logan (1917-), illus. (Illus.). (gr. 4 up). 1961. (ISBN 0-670-61548-X). Viking Pr.
--The Story of Holly and Ivy. 1961. Viking.
--Story of Holly & Ivy. Adams, Adrienne (1906-), illus. LC 58-14964. (Illus.). 24cm. 64p. (gr. 2-6). 1958. (ISBN 0-670-67459-1). Viking Pr.
--The Story of Holly & Ivy. Cooney, Barbara (1917-), illus. LC 84-25799. (Illus.). 31 p. 28cm. c.1985. (ISBN 0-670-80622-6). Viking Kestrel.
--The Valiant Chatti Maker. Roy, Jeroo, illus. LC 83-7000. p. cm. 1983. (ISBN 0-670-74236-8). Viking Press.
Gode, Alexander, tr. see Van Iterson, Siny Rose.
Gode, Alison, tr. see Van Iterson, Siny Rose.
Godfrey, Elsa, illus.
--Count to Ten in No Man's Valley. LC 81-50716. (Illus.). 24p. (Shape Bks.). (ps-1). 1981. (ISBN 0-394-84980-9). Random.
Godfrey, George H., ed. see Bulfinch, Thomas.
Godfrey, Hollis (1874-)
--Dave Morrell's Battery. Wood, Franklin T., illus. LC 12-22564. 5 p. l., 289 p. front., plates. 19 cm. (Young captains of industry). 1912. Little, Brown, and Company.
--For the Norton Name. Fogarty, Thomas (1873-), illus. LC 9-24949. x p., 1 l., 238 p., 1 l. incl. front. 6 pl. 19 cm. (Young captains of industry). 1909. Little, Brown, and Company.
--Jack Collerton's Engine. Burgess, H., illus. LC 10-21637. ix p., 1 l., 285 p. front., illus., 7 pl. 19 cm. (Young captains of industry). 1910. Little, Brown, and Company.
Godfrey, Maude Corey
--The Biggle De Boo and the Big Boo Hoo. Whitney, H., illus. LC 31-34004. 1 p. l., 36 p. illus. 24 cm. 1931. Printed by A. R. F. Brandes.
Godfrey, Vincent Hubbard
--John Holmes at Annapolis. LC 27-18255. 3 p. l., 201 p. front., plates. 20 cm. 1927. Houghton Mifflin Company.
Godley, Elizabeth, Mrs.
--Green Outside. LC 32-8459. xvi, 55, 1 p. incl. col. front., illus. 22 cm. 1932. The Viking Press.
Godolphin, Mary, retold by.
--Aesop's Fables. (Burt's Series of One Syllable Books). N.D. A. B. Burt Co.
--Aesop's Fables, 1 of 6 vols. (Illus.). (One-Syllable Books, Cassell's Ser.: No. 3). N.D. Cassell, Petter, Galpin.
--Robinson Crusoe. N.D. George Routledge & Sons.
--Sandford and Merton, in Words of One Syllable. N.D. James Miller.
--Swiss Family Robinson. N.D. Educational Publishing Company.
Godolphin, Mary, adapted by see Aesopus.
Godolphin, Mary, retold by see Aikin, John (1747-1822) & Barbauld, Anna Letitia Aikin, Mrs.
Godolphin, Mary, retold by see Bunyan, John.
Godolphin, Mary, ed. see Day, Thomas.
Godolphin, Mary, adapted by see Defoe, Daniel.
Godolphin, Mary, adapted by see Wyss, Johann David Von.
Godophin, Mary, retold by see Aesopus.
Godoy Alcayaga, Lucila, jt. auth. see Dana, Doris.
Godoy Alcayaga, Lucila (1889-1957)
--Crickets and Frogs: A Fable. Frasconi, Antonio (1919-), illus. Dana, Doris, tr. from Span. LC 72-77131. (Illus.). 32 p. 24cm. 1972. Atheneum.
Godwin, Charlotte
--The Broken Doll. Long, Joy, illus. (Illus.). (ps-3). 1979. (ISBN 0-686-24535-0). CLCB Pr.
--The Unbroken Promise. Long, Joy, illus. (Illus.). (ps-5). 1979. (ISBN 0-686-24536-9). CLCB Pr.
Godwin, Edward F., jt. auth. see Godwin, Stephani Allfree.
Godwin, Frank (1889-), illus.
--King Arthur and His Knights. N.D. John C. Winston.
Godwin, Sarah
--The Little Brown Monkey. Winebrenner, Mildred, illus. LC 38-6963. 22 p., 1 l., illus. 31 cm. 1937. The Berkshire Press.
--Tizzie, the Brown Monkey. Winebrenner, Mildred, illus. LC 39-6115. 18, 1 p. col. illus. 29 cm. 1938. The Berkshire Press.
Godwin, Stephani Allfree & Godwin, Edward F.
--Out of the Strong. LC 55-8691. 183 p. 22cm. (Oxford books for boys and girls). 1955. Oxford University Press.
--Roman Eagle. LC 51-12460. 211 p. illus. 22 cm. 1951. Oxford University Press.
Godwin, William (1756-1836), ed.
--The Book of Fables. Selections from Esop and Other Authors. LC 30-140357. 1 p. l., 5-240 p. illus. 19 cm. 1856. R. B. Collins.
--Fables, Ancient and Modern. Greene, David L., pref. by. LC 75-32153. (Illus.). 2 v. in 1. 16cm. (Classics of Children's Literature, 1621-1932). 1976. (ISBN 0-8240-2267-X). Garland Pub. Co.
Goe, Dagmar
--Mr. and Mrs. Pumpkinseed. 1st. ed. Goe, Dagmar, illus. LC 56-11590. 19p. illus. 21cm. 1956. Exposition Press.
Goehren, Caroline Von see Von Goehren, Caroline.
Goepp, Elisabeth Wennins see Meg, Elisabeth, pseud.
Goes, Bertha
--Freshmen at Arden. LC 31-28579. 5 p. l., 3-256 p. 20 cm. c.1931. H. Holt and Company.
Goethe, Johann Wolfgang Von see Reynard the Fox. English & Von Goethe, Johann Wolfgang.
Goethe, Johann Wolfgang Von (1749-1832)
--The Fairy Tale of the Green Snake & the Beautiful Lily. new ed. Carlyle, Thomas (1795-1881), illus. Allen, Paul M., intro. by. bibl. footnotes. 96p. 1976. (ISBN 0-685-61970-2, Steinerbooks). Garber Comm.
Goetz, Delia, tr. see Alegria, Fernando.
Goetz, Delia (1898-)
--The Burro of Barnegat Road. Van Stockum, Hilda Gerarda (1908-), illus. LC 45-8119. 4 p. l., 3-205, 1 p. incl. illus., plates. 21 cm. 1945. Harcourt, Brace and Company.
--The Hidden Burro. Morse, Dorothy Bayley (1906-1979), illus. LC 49-9780. 128 p. illus. 21 cm. (Morrow junior books). 1949. W. Morrow.
--Islands of the Ocean. Darling, Louis, Jr. (1916-1970), illus. LC 64-10732. 64 p. illus. 22 cm. 1964. Morrow.
--Letters from Guatemala. Knight, Katharine, illus. LC 41-7511. 56 p. incl. col. front., illus. (part col.) 22 cm. (On cover: New world neighbors). c.1941. D. C. Heath and Company.
--Panchita: A Little Girl of Guatemala. Chase, Charlotte Anna, illus. LC 41-51862. 6 p. l., 3-180 p. incl. col. front., col. illus., col. plates. 23 cm. c.1941. Harcourt, Brace and Company.
Goetz, Lee Garrett (1932-)
--Camel in the Sea. Galdone, Paul (1914-), illus. LC 65-27776(Illus.). 58p. (gr. 2-5). 1966. (ISBN 0-07-023648-8). McGraw.
Goetzman, Anne, illus.
--True Story of the Tooth Fairy. (gr. k-3). N.D. (ISBN 0-448-01886-1). G&D.
Goff, Beth
--Where Is Daddy?. The Story of a Divorce. Perl, Susan (1922-1983), illus. LC 69-14608. (Illus.). 25 p. 22cm. 1969. Beacon Press.
--Where Is Daddy?. The Story of a Divorce. Perl, Susan (1922-1983), illus. LC 85-1317. p. cm. 1985. (ISBN 0-8070-2305-1). Beacon Press.
Goff, Charles J
--Moonlight Man. LC 40-29654. 2 p. l., 7-146 p. illus. 21 cm. 1940. Meador Publishing Company.
Goff, Lloyd Lozes (1919-)
--Run, Sandpiper, Run. Goff, Lloyd Lozes (1919-), illus. LC 57-6000. unpaged. illus. 26cm. 1957. Lothrop, Lee and Shepard.
Goffe, Toni
--Toby's Animal Rescue Service. (Illus.). 48p. 1st U.S. edition. (ps-3). 1982. (Pub. by Hamish Hamilton England). David & Charles.
Goffstein, Marilyn Brooke (1940-)
--Across the Sea. Goffstein, Marilyn Brooke (1940-), illus. LC 68-29500. (Illus.). 1 v. 38p. 18cm. 1968. Farrar, Straus, and Giroux.
--Brookie and Her Lamb. Goffstein, Marilyn Brooke (1940-), illus. LC 67-26372. (Illus.). 13cm. 31p. 1967. Farrar, Straus and Giroux.
--Daisy Summerfield's Style. LC 75-7499. p. cm. 1975. (ISBN 0-440-05402-8). Delacorte Press.
--Family Scrapbook. Goffstein, Marilyn Brooke (1940-), illus. LC 78-51435. (Illus.). 48 p. 23cm. 1978. (ISBN 0-374-32269-4). Farrar, Straus, Giroux. **Award: (ALA).**
--Fish for Supper. Goffstein, Marilyn Brooke (1940-), illus. LC 75-27598. (Illus.). 31 p. c.1976. (ISBN 0-8037-2571-X). (ISBN 0-8037-2572-8). Dial Press. **Award: (ALA).**
--The Gats!. Goffstein, Marilyn Brooke (1940-), illus. LC 66-124629. (Illus.). (gr. k-3). 1966. (ISBN 0-394-81180-1). Pantheon.
--Goldie, the Dollmaker. LC 79-85369. 18cm. 55p. 1969. Farrar, Straus and Giroux.
--Laughing Latkes. LC 80-68118. (Illus.). 31 p. 17cm. 1980. (ISBN 0-374-34364-0). Farrar, Straus, Giroiux.
--Little Schubert. Goffstein, Marilyn Brooke (1940-), illus. 1972. Harper & Row Pub.
--Me and My Captain. Goffstein, Marilyn Brooke (1940-), illus. LC 74-6699. (Illus.). 31 p. 18cm. 1974. (ISBN 0-374-34901-0). Farrar/Straus/Giroux.
--My Crazy Sister. Goffstein, Marilyn Brooke (1940-), illus. LC 76-2286. (Illus.). 20cm. 40p. (gr. k-3). 1976. Dial Bks Young.
--My Noah's Ark. Goffstein, Marilyn Brooke (1940-), illus. LC 77-25666. 19cm. 31p. c.1978. (ISBN 0-06-022022-8). (ISBN 0-06-022023-6). Harper & Row. **Award: (ALA).**
--Natural History. Goffstein, Marilyn Brooke (1940-), illus. LC 79-7318. (Illus.). 30 p. 19cm. 1979. (ISBN 0-374-35498-7). Farrar, Straus & Giroux. **Award: (NYT).**
--Neighbors. Goffstein, Marilyn Brooke (1940-), illus. LC 78-19491. (Illus.). 30 p. 22cm. c.1979. Harper & Row.
--Sleepy People. Goffstein, Marilyn Brooke (1940-), illus. LC 66-7286. 1966. Farrar, Straus & Giroux.
--Two Piano Tuners. Goffstein, Marilyn Brooke (1940-), illus. LC 71-106399. (Illus.). 65 p. 21cm. 1970. Farrar, Straus and Giroux.
--The Underside of the Leaf. LC 75-188252. 150p. 23cm. 1972. (ISBN 0-374-38031-7). Farrar, Strauss and Giroux.
Goggins, Elizabeth
--Billy Boy. LC 33-196524. 2 p. l., 3-30 p. illus. 20 cm. c.1932. Suttonhouse.
Gogol, Nikolai Vasilevich (1809-1852)
--The Fair at Sorochintsi: A Nikolai Gogol Story. Ray, Deborah (1940-), adapted by. Ray, Deborah (1940-), illus. LC 69-18633. (Illus.). 31 p. 26cm. 1969. (ISBN 0-8255-7645-8). Macrae Smith.
--Taras Bulba: A Tale of the Cossacks. Gay, Zhenya (1906-1978), illus. Hapgood, Isabel Florence (1850-1928), tr. from Russian. LC 31-23463. 284 p. col. front., plates. 21 cm. 1931. A. A. Knopf.
--Taras Bulba and Other Tales. Cournos, John (1881-1966), ed. xvii, 311 p. 17 cm. (Half-title: Everyman's library, ed. by Ernest Rhys. Fiction. no. 740). 1917. J. M. Dent & Sons, Ltd.
--Tarras Bulba. 1915. Alfred A. Knopf.
Gohman, Fred Joseph (1918-)
--Mystery at Indian Island. Gohman, Fred Joseph (1918-), illus. LC 63-10916. (Illus.). 21cm. 100p. (gr. 6-10). 1963. (ISBN 0-8313-0062-0). Lantern.
--Spider Webb Mysteries. LC 68-23985. (Illus.). 185 p. 22cm. 1969. Lantern Press.
Gohman, Vera
--It's Fun to Live at Happy House. N.D. Warner Press.

Going, Charles Buxton, jt. auth. see Corbin, Marie Overton.
Going, T William, ed. see March, William.
Goins, Ellen Haynes (1927-)
--Big Diamond's Boy. LC 76-54877. 160 p. 21cm. c.1977. (ISBN 0-8407-6528-2). T. Nelson.
--David's Pockets. Goins, Ellen Haynes (1927-), illus. LC 75-39837. (Illus.). 32 p. 1972. (ISBN 0-8114-7744-4). Steck-Vaughn Co.
--Horror at Hinklemeyer House. Papas, William (1927-), illus. LC 73-118961. (Illus.). 4-color ils. 27cm. 32p. (ps-3). 1971. (ISBN 0-695-80169-4). (ISBN 0-695-40169-6). Follett.
--Omar, the Undercover Cat. Goins, Ellen Haynes (1927-), illus. LC 68-19560. (Illus.). 32 p. 24cm. 1968. Steck-Vaughn Co.
--She Was Scared Silly. Goins, Ellen Haynes (1927-), illus. LC 77-150343. (Illus.). 32 p. 1971. (ISBN 0-8114-7728-2). Steck-Vaughn Co.
Goish, Genevive, jt. auth. see Gerber, William.
Goitein, E David
--Wonderful Tales of a Wonderful People. LC 24-19333. viii, 229 p. front., plates. 20 cm. 1924. E. P. Dutton & Company.
Gold, Doris B. (1919-), adapted by.
--Stories for Jewish Juniors: A Storybook for Boys and Girls. LC 66-178003. 222p. illus. (pt. col.) 24cm. 1967. Johathan David.
Gold, Herbert (1924-)
--The Young Prince and the Magic Cone. 1st ed. Brinckloe, Julie Lorraine (1950-), illus. LC 72-87753. (Illus.). 68 p. 25cm. 1973. (ISBN 0-385-01519-4). (ISBN 0-385-01519-4). Doubleday.
Gold, Michael (1894-)
--Charlie Chaplin's Parade. Soglow, Otto (1900-1975), illus. LC 30-23892. (Illus.). 62p. 22 x 23cm. 1930. Harcourt, Brace & Company.
Gold, Ned
--Eight Who Wrestled Death. Antonishak, Tom, illus. LC 79-23215. (Illus.). 46p. (Quest, Adventure, Survival). (gr. 4-9). 1982. (ISBN 0-8172-2056-9). Raintree Pubs.
Gold, Phyllis, pseud., see Goldberg, Phyllis.
Gold, Phyllis, pseud. (1941-)
--Please Don't Say Hello. Goldberg, Phyllis. Baker, Carl, photos by. LC 74-13185. (Illus.). 45 p. 24cm. (New juvenile series on the exceptional child). 1975. (ISBN 0-87705-211-5). Human Sciences Press.
Gold, Robert Stanley (1924-), ed.
--Point of Departure: Nineteen Stories of Youth & Discovery. 196p. (gr. 7 up). 1971 (Sey Lawr). Delacorte.
Gold, Sharlya
--Amelia Quackenbush. LC 73-7129. (Illus.). 153 p. 22cm. 1973. (ISBN 0-8164-3104-3). Seabury Press.
--The Potter's Four Sons. Maidoff, Jules, illus. LC 71-78723. (Illus.). 48 color linecuts. 48p. (gr. 10 up). 1969. (ISBN 0-385-05738-5). (ISBN 0-385-06662-7). Doubleday.
--The Potter's Four Sons: A Fable. Maidoff, Jules, illus. LC 71-787239. (Illus.). 44 p. 27cm. 1970. Doubleday.
--Time to Take Sides. LC 76-8265. p. cm. c.1976. (ISBN 0-8164-3177-9). Seabury Press.
Goldberg, David S., jt. auth. see Stitt, Edward Walmsley.
Goldberg, Irving (1904-), ed.
--The Magician and Other Stories. Kruckman, Herbert Lincoln (1904-), illus. LC 59-25323. 99p. illus. 28cm. 1957. Kinderbuch Publishers.
--Narrow Escape and Other Stories. Kruckman, Herbert Lincoln (1904-), illus. LC 59-25323. 84p. illus. 28cm. 1957. Kinderbuch.
--Yiddish Stories for Young People. Kruckman, Herbert Lincoln (1904-), illus. LC 68-6845. (Illus.). 254 p. 23cm. 1966. Kinderbuch Publishers.
Goldberg, Isaac (1887-1938), ed.
--Brazilian Tales. N.D. Four Seas.
--Brazilian Tales. Goldberg, Isaac (1887-1938), tr. LC 64-22035. 96p. 1965. Publications of Bruce Humphries.
Goldberg, Israel see Learsi, Rufus, pseud.
Goldberg, Israel (1887-)
--Prince of Judah and Other Stories of a Great Journey. Learsi, Rufus, pseud. Berger, Vivian, illus. LC 62-21985. 143 p. illus. 24 cm. 1962. Shengold Publishers.
--Shimmele. Learsi, Rufus, pseud. Maxwell, Stanley, illus. LC 40-10081. 6 p. l., 3-116, 1 p. incl. illus., plates. 20 cm. 1940. Behrman's Jewish Book House.
--Shimmele and His Friends. Learsi, Rufus, pseud. Maxwell, Stanley, illus. LC 40-10060. (Illus.). 113p. 20cm. 1940. Behrman's Jewish Book House.
Goldberg, Leah (1911-1970)
--Eli Lives in Israel. Riwkin-Brick, Anna (1908-), photos by. LC 65-1561. 1v. (unpaged) illus. 22cm. (gr. k-3). 1965, c.1964. Macmillan.
--Little Queen of Sheba. Rivkin-Brick, Anna (1908-), illus. N.D. Union of American Hebrew Congregations.
--Room for Rent. Katz, Avner, illus. LC 70-179558. (Illus.). 24 p. 23cm. 1972. Ward Ritchie Press.
Goldberg, Martha (1907-)
--Big Horse, Little Horse. Hamil, Thomas Arthur (1928-), illus. LC 60-14296. (Illus.). 41 p. 23cm. 1960. Macmillan.
--Boy Who Loved Horses. (gr. k-3). 1976. (ISBN 0-590-09892-6). Scholastic Inc.
--Lunch Box Story. Tobias, Beatrice, illus. LC 51-11000. 32p. 1951. Holiday House.
--Twirly Skirt. Stone, Helen (1904-), illus. LC 54-10557. 47p. 1954. Holiday House.
--Wait for the Rain. Price, Christine Hilda (1928-1980), illus. LC 52-13413. unpaged. illus. 20 cm. 1952. Holiday House.
Goldberg, Minerva J., jt. auth. see Jones, William Edward.
Goldberg, Moses Hyam (1940-)
--The Men's Cottage. (Orig.). 1980. (ISBN 0-87602-229-8). Anchorage.
Goldberg, Phyllis see Gold, Phyllis, pseud.
Goldberg, Stan J. (1939-) & Chess, Victoria (1939-)
--The Adventures of Stanley Kane. Chess, Victoria (1939-), illus. LC 73-75320. (Illus.). 32 p. 28cm. 1973. (ISBN 0-15-201599-X). Harcourt Brace Jovanovich.
Goldberg, Yatta G.
--A Gift of Challahs. Zakutinsky, R., ed. Backman, Aidel, illus. (Illus.). 32p. (Orig.). (gr. k-6). 1981. (ISBN 0-911643-00-1). Aura Pub.
Goldberger, Judith M
--The Looking Glass Factor. LC 79-11405. p. cm. c.1979. (ISBN 0-525-34148-X). Dutton.
Goldberger, Miriam, ed.
--New Girl & Other Stories of Teen Life. (gr. 7-12). 1974. (ISBN 0-590-03196-1, Schol Trade Pap). Schol Bk Serv.
--Teenager in Love. (gr. 7-9). 1972. (ISBN 0-590-09208-1, Schol Pap). Scholastic Inc.
The, Golden Goose
--The Golden Goose. Brooke, Leonard Leslie (1862-1940), illus. 24 p. illus. (part col.) 26 cm. (On cover: Leslie Brooke's children's books). N.D. F. Warne & Co., Ltd.
--The Golden Goose: A Picture Book. Stobbs, William (1914-), illus. LC 67-168605. 31p. col. illus. 19x26cm. 1967. McGraw.
Golden, Grace Blaisdell (1899-)
--Seven Dancing Dolls. Stone, David Karl (1922-), illus. LC 61-13147. 96p. c.1961. Bobbs.
Golden, MacDonald, pseud., see Brown, Margaret Wise.
Golden, MacDonald, pseud. (1910-1952)
--Little Lost Lamb. Brown, Margaret Wise. 1st ed. Weisgard, Leonard Joseph (1916-), illus. LC 45-10477. (Illus.). 40 p. c.1945. (ISBN 0-385-07750-5). Doubleday, Doran & Co., Inc. **Award: (RCM).**
The, Golden Magazine for Boys and Girls
--Walt Disney's Annual for Boys and Girls. no. 1-ed. LC 66-8405. v. col. illus. 29 cm. 1966. Golden Press.
Golden, Nancy, retold by.
--Raggedy Ann & Andy Giant Treasury: Four Adventures Plus Twelve Short Stories. LC 84-17654. (Original Author: Johnny Gruelle 1880-1938). (Illus.). 88 p. 29cm. 1984. (ISBN 0-517-45594-3). Derrydale Books : Distributed by Crown.
Golden Press, ed.
--Golden Book of Story Time Tales. Kane, Sharon Koester, illus. (Illus.). 1961 (Golden Pr). Western Pub.
Golden Press Editors
--The Golden Book of Story Time Tales. Kane, Sharon Koester, illus. LC 62-15234. 164p. col. illus. 28cm. c.1962. Golden Press.
Golden Rod
--The Bad Boy in the Country. (Humorous Books Ser.). N.D. J. S. Ogilvie.
Goldfeder, Cheryl, pseud., see Pahz, Anne Cheryl.
Goldfeder, Cheryl, pseud. (1949-) & Goldfeder, James, pseud. (1943-)
--The Girl Who Wouldn't Talk. Pahz, Anne Cheryl. Pahz, James Alon. 1974. National Association of the Deaf.
Goldfeder, James, jt. auth. see Goldfeder, Cheryl.
Goldfrank, Helen Colodny see Kay, Helen, pseud.
Goldfrap, John Henry see Deering, Fremont B., pseud.
Goldfrap, John Henry see Forrester, Dexter J., pseud.
Goldfrap, John Henry see Lawton, Capt. Wilbur, pseud.
Goldfrap, John Henry see Payson, Lieut. Howard, pseud.
Goldfrap, John Henry see Payson, Lieut. Howard, pseud.
Goldfrap, John Henry see West, Marvin, pseud.
Goldfrap, John Henry (1879-1917)
--Border Boys Across the Frontier. Deering, Fremont B., pseud. (Border Boys Ser.). N.D. A. L. Burt Co.
--Border Boys Along the St. Lawrence River. Deering, Fremont B., pseud. (Border Boys Ser.). N.D. A. L. Burt Co.
--Border Boys in the Canadian Rockies. Deering, Fremont B., pseud. (Border Boys SEr.). N.D. A. L. Burt Co.
--The Border Boys on the Trail. Deering, Fremont B., pseud. (Border Boys Ser.). N.D. A. L. Burt Co.
--The Border Boys on the Trail. Deering, Fremont B., pseud. Wrenn, Charles L., illus. LC 11-11561. 307 p. front., plates. 20 cm. c.1911. Hurst & Company.
--Border Boys with the Mexican Rangers. Deering, Fremont B., pseud. (Border Boys Ser.). N.D. A. L. Burt Co.
--Border Boys with the Texas Rangers. Deering, Fremont B., pseud. (Border Boys SEr.). N.D. A. L. Burt Co.
--The Border Boys with the Texas Rangers. Deering, Fremont B., pseud. LC 12-18551. 296 p. front., plates. 20 cm. (The Border Boys Ser.). c.1912. Hurst & Company.
--The Boy Aviators' Flight for a Fortune. Lawton, Capt. Wilbur, pseud. Wrenn, Charles L., illus. LC 12-16364. 299 p. front., plates. 20 cm. (The Boy Aviators Ser.). c.1912. Hurst & Company.
--The Boy Aviators in Africa. Lawton, Capt. Wilbur, pseud. (The Boy Aviators' Ser.). N.D. Hurst & Co.
--The Boy Aviators in Nicaragua: Or, In League with the Insurgents. Lawton, Capt. Wilbur, pseud. LC 12-24632. 336 p. 20 cm. (The Boy Aviators Ser.). c.1910. Hurst & Company.
--The Boy Aviators in Record Flight. Lawton, Capt. Wilbur, pseud. (The Boy Aviator Ser.). N.D. Hurst & Co.
--The Boy Aviators on Secret Service: Or, Working with Wireless. Lawton, Capt. Wilbur, pseud. LC 26-22312. 326 p. front., illus. 20 cm. (His Boy aviators' series). 1910. Hurst & Company.
--The Boy Aviators' Polar Dash. Lawton, Capt. Wilbur, pseud. (The Boy Aviators' Ser.). N.D. Hurst & Co.
--The Boy Aviators' Treasure Quest: Or, The Golden Galleon. Lawton, Capt. Wilbur, pseud. LC 12-246336. 291 p. incl. plates. front. 20 cm. (His Boy aviators' series). c.1910. Hurst and Company.
--The Boy Aviators with the Air Raiders. Lawton, Capt. Wilbur, pseud. (The Boy Aviators' Ser.). N.D. Hurst & Co.
--The Boy Scouts at the Panama-Pacific Exposition. Payson, Lieut. Howard, pseud. Wrenn, Charles L., illus. LC 15-13838. 303 p. front., plates. 20 cm. c.1915. Hurst & Company.
--The Boy Scouts for Uncle Sam. Payson, Lieut. Howard, pseud. Wrenn, Charles L., illus. LC 12-20638. 292 p. front., plates. 20 cm. (The Boy Scout Ser.). c.1912. Hurst & Company.
--The Boy Scouts of the Eagle Patrol. Payson, Lieut. Howard, pseud. LC 11-8476. 302 p. incl. front., plates. 20 cm. (The Boy Scout Ser.). c.1911. Hurst & Company.
--The Boy Scouts on Belgian Battlefields. Wrenn, Charles L., illus. LC 18-4346. 312 p. front., plates. 20 cm. c.1915. Hurst & Company.
--The Boy Scouts on the Range. Payson, Lieut. Howard, pseud. LC 11-11449. 306 p. front., plates. 20 cm. (The Boy Scout Ser.). c.1911. Hurst & Company.
--The Bungalow Boys Along the Yukon. Forrester, Dexter J., pseud. (The Bunglaow Boys Ser.). N.D. Hurst & Co.
--The Bungalow Boys in the Great Northwest. Forrester, Dexter J., pseud. (The Bunglaow Boys Ser.). N.D. Hurst & Co.
--The Bungalow Boys Marooned in the Tropics. Forrester, Dexter J., pseud. (The Bunglaow Boys Ser.). N.D. Hurst & Co.
--The Bungalow Boys North of Fifty-Three. Forrester, Dexter J., pseud. (The Bunglaow Boys Ser.). N.D. Hurst & Co.
--The Bungalow Boys on the Great Lakes. Forrester, Dexter J., pseud. Burnham, J. Paul, illus. LC 12-15563. 295 p. front., plates. 20 cm. (The Bungalow Boys Ser.). 1912. Hurst & Company.
--The Dreadnought Boys Aboard a Destroyer. Lawton, Capt. Wilbur, pseud. (The Dreadnought Boys Ser.). N.D. Hurst & Co.
--The Dreadnought Boys in Home Waters. Lawton, Capt. Wilbur, pseud. (The Dreadnought Boys Ser.). N.D. Hurst & Co.
--The Dreadnought Boys on a Submarine. Lawton, Capt. Wilbur, pseud. (The Dreadnought Boys Ser.). N.D. Hurst & Co.
--The Dreadnought Boys on Aero Service. Lawton, Capt. Wilbur, pseud. (The Dreadnought Boys Ser.). N.D. Hurst & Co.
--The Dreadnought Boys on Battle Practice. Lawton, Capt. Wilbur, pseud. LC 12-187921. 305 p. front., plates. 20 cm. (The Dreadnought Boy Ser.). c.1911. Hurst & Company.
--The Dreadnought Boys' World Cruise. Lawton, Capt. Wilbur, pseud. (The Dreadnought Boys Ser.). N.D. Hurst & Co.
--The Motor Rangers' Cloud Cruiser. West, Marvin, pseud. LC 12-12134. 286 p. front., plates. 20 cm. (The Motor Rangers Ser.). c.1912. Hurst & Company.
--The Motor Rangers' Lost Mine. West, Marvin, pseud. (The Motor Rangers' Ser.). N.D. Hurst & Co.
--The Motor Rangers on Blue Water. West, Marvin, pseud. (The Motor Rangers' Ser.). N.D. Hurst & Co.
--The Motor Rangers Through the Sierras. West, Marvin, pseud. (The Motor Rangers' Ser.). N.D. Hurst & Co.
--The Motor Rangers Touring for the Trophy. West, Marvin, pseud. (The Motor Rangers' Ser.). N.D. Hurst & Co.
--The Motor Rangers' Wireless Station. West, Marvin, pseud. (The Motor Rangers' Ser.). N.D. Hurst & Co.
Goldhammer, Carole K.
--The Underground Light Bulb. (Illus.). (gr. 7-12). 1972 (Starline). Schol Bk Serv.
Goldie, Fay
--Zulu Boy. LC 68-17327. 104p. illus. 22cm. 1968. St. Martins.
Goldilocks
--Goldilocks: Or, The Three Bears. N.D. E. P. Dutton & Co.
Goldin, Augusta R. (1906-)
--Ducks Don't Get Wet. LC 65-11647. (Illus.). (Crocodile Paperback Ser.). (gr. k-3). 1965. (ISBN 0-690-01258-6, TYC-J). Har-Row.
--My Toys. Friend, Esther, illus. LC 55-8197. unpaged. illus. 17cm. (Rand McNally junior elf book, 633). c.1955. Rand McNally.
--Spider Silk. Low, Joseph (1911-), illus. LC 64-18164. 1 v. (unpaged) illus. (part col.) 21 x 23 cm. (Let's-read-and-find-out books). 1964. Crowell.
--Straight Hair, Curly Hair. Emberley, Edward Randolph (1931-), illus. LC 66-12669. 1 v. (unpaged) illus. (pt. col.) 22cm. (Let's-read-and-findout bks.). 1966. Crowell.
Goldin, Diana & Heckel, Inge
--A Tale of Two Williams. Mydans, Carl, photos by. LC 77-12708. p. cm. 1977. (ISBN 0-87099-172-8). Metropolitan Museum of Art.
Goldin, Hyman Elias (1881-), ed.
--The Magic Ring and Other Medieval Jewish Tales. LC 46-772284. 249 p. incl. front., illus. 22 cm. 1946. Hebrew Publishing Company.
--Treasury of Bible Stories. (gr. 9 up). N.D. Twayne.
Goldin, Marilyn
--The Story of the Very Small Tree. Clapp, Martha, illus. LC 66-15729. (Illus.). (ps-3). 1966. Abelard.
Golding, Harry
--The Book of the Clock. Tarrant, Margaret Winifred (1888-), illus. N.D. George Sully & Co.
Golding, Vautier
--The Story of David Livingstone. LC 6-35312. viii, 118 p. col. front. (port.) 7(col. pl., map. 15 x 12 cm. (Half-title: The children's heroes series, ed. by J. Lang). 1906. T. C. & E. C. Jack.
Golding, William Gerald (1911-)
--Lord of the Flies. Forster, Edward Morgan (1879-1970), contrib. by. (gr. 9 up). 1978. (ISBN 0-698-10219-3, Coward). Putnam Pub Group.
Goldman, Katie
--In the Wings. LC 82-70200. 166 p. 22cm. c.1982. (ISBN 0-8037-3968-0). Dial Press.
Goldman, Phyllis W. (1927-) & Jaffe, Grace
--Whatever Happened to Yes?. Seiden, Art, illus. LC 72-126122. (Illus.). 24 p. 1970. (ISBN 0-8027-6084-8). (ISBN 0-8027-6085-6). Walker.
Goldman, Susan (1939-)
--Cousins Are Special. Goldman, Susan (1939-), illus. LC 78-11924. p. cm. (Self-starter books). 1978. (ISBN 0-8075-1317-2). A. Whitman.
--Grandma Is Somebody Special. Goldman, Susan (1939-), illus. LC 76-18980. (Illus.). 32 p. 19cm. (Self-starter). c.1976. (ISBN 0-8075-3034-4). A. Whitman.
--Grandpa and Me Together. LC 79-18244. (Illus.). 32 p. 19cm. (Self-starter books). c.1980. (ISBN 0-8075-3036-0). A. Whitman.
--Grandpa & Me Together. Tucker, Kathleen, ed. LC 79-18244. (Illus.). (Self-Starter Ser.). (ps-2). 1980. (ISBN 0-8075-3036-0). A Whitman.
Goldman, William W. (1931-)
--Wigger. 1st ed. Le Cain, Errol John (1941-), illus. LC 74-4497. (Illus.). 63 p. 22cm. 1974. Harcourt Brace Jovanovich.
Goldreich, Gloria
--Lori. LC 78-14387. 181 p. 22cm. c.1979. Holt, Rinehart and Winston.
--Season of Discovery. LC 76-40482. p. cm. 21cm. 156p. c.1976. (ISBN 0-8407-6523-1). T. Nelson.
Goldreich, Gloria, ed.
--A Treasury of Jewish Literature: From Biblical Times to Today. LC 81-6967. 256p. (gr. 5 up). 1982. (ISBN 0-03-053831-9). HR&W.

Goldsborough, Edmund Kennedy, Jr. (1882-)
--The Dream Adventures of Little Bill. Hudson, illus. LC 10-14674. 162 p. front., plate. 20 cm. c.1910. Broadway Publishing Co.

Goldsborough, June, jt. auth. see Delton, Judy.

Goldsborough, June (1923-)
--The Gingerbread Boy. Goldsborough, June (1923-), illus. (Illus.). (Action Bk). (ps-2). N.D. Platt.
--I Can Do It by Myself. Goldsborough, June (1923-), illus. (Illus.). 14p. (Golden Sturdy Bk.). 1981. (ISBN 0-307-12123-2, Golden Pr). Western Pub.
--Little Puppy. McClain, Mary, illus. (Illus.). 12p. (Shaggies Ser.). (ps-2). 1982. (ISBN 0-671-43159-5, Little Simon). S&S.
--Mother Goose on the Farm. Goldsborough, June (1923-), illus. (Illus.). (Tell-a-Tale Readers). (ps-1). 1975. (ISBN 0-307-68587-X, Whitman). Western Pub.
--The Real Book of First Stories. Goldsborough, June (1923-), illus. LC 73-7200. (Illus.). 59 p. 29cm. 1973. (ISBN 0-528-82190-3). (ISBN 0-528-82190-3). Rand McNally.
--Stories to Grow On. Goldsborough, June (1923-), illus. (Illus.). 64p. (ps-3). N.D. (ISBN 0-528-82420-1). Rand.
--The Story of Peter Rabbit. Goldsborough, June (1923-), illus. (ps). 1969. Platt.
--What's in the Woods?. Goldsborough, June (1923-), illus. LC 76-10271. (Illus.). 31 p. 24cm. c.1976. (ISBN 0-13-955054-2). Prentice-Hall.

Goldsen, Bernette, retold by.
--Jack and the Beanstalk. Calvi, Gian, illus. LC 77-86147. (Illus.). 34 p. 21cm. (Random House Pictureback). (Best book club ever). c.1978. (ISBN 0-394-83870-X). (ISBN 0-394-83478-X). Random House.

Goldsmid, Paula
--Did You Ever. (Illus.). 30p. (Orig.). (ps-k). 1971. (ISBN 0-914996-01-0). Lollipop Power.

Goldsmith-Carter, George
--Lord of the Chained. (gr. 5-12). 1972. (ISBN 0-688-40036-1). (ISBN 0-688-50036-6). Lothrop.

Goldsmith, Christine
--The Red Rooster Stories. Berlind, Gary Wayne, illus. LC 47-94097. 54 p., 1 l. incl. front., illus. 25 cm. c.1944. House of Field, Inc.

Goldsmith, Elsie Helen Borg, Mrs. (1885-)
--Gewallopus: The Story of a Playful Horse. Mager, Gus, illus. LC 26-23677. 84 p. incl. col. front., illus., col. plates. 24 cm. 1926. A. & C. Boni.

Goldsmith, Howard, jt. auth. see Zebrowski, George.

Goldsmith, Howard, ed. see Blackwood, Algernon, et al.

Goldsmith, Howard (1943-)
--Invasion Twenty-Two Hundred A. D. LC 78-22320. (Signal Bk.). 1979. Doubleday.
--The Shadow & Other Strange Tales. (Illus.). (gr. 4-7). 1977. (ISBN 0-685-03662-6). Xerox Ed Pubns.
--Terror by Night & Other Strange Tale. (Illus.). (gr. 7-10). N.D. (ISBN 0-685-03664-2). Xerox Ed Pubns.
--Toto, the Timid Turtle. Chan, Shirley, illus. LC 80-15096. p. cm. 1980. (ISBN 0-87705-525-4). Human Sciences Press.
--What Makes a Grumble Smile?. Eaton, Tom (1940-), illus. LC 76-25210. (Illus.). 48 p. 23cm. (Imagination book). c.1977. (ISBN 0-8116-4403-0). Garrard Pub. Co.
--The Whispering Sea. LC 76-11632. 22cm. 131p. 1976. (ISBN 0-672-52199-7). Bobbs-Merrill.

Goldsmith, Howard (1943-) & Mason, Alice Leedy, eds.
--Maggie the Mink. Flint, Russ, illus. LC 84-23090. p. cm. (Teaching Tales). c.1984. (ISBN 0-516-09123-9). Childrens Press.

Goldsmith, Margaret, tr. see Tetzner, Lisa.

Goldsmith, Milton (1861-)
--The Adventure of Walter and the Rabbit. (Illus.). (The Happy Hour Series.: No. 3). 1915. Cupples & Leon.
--Bennie and Jennie. (Illus.). (The Sunbonnet Series: No. 2). 1915. Cupples & Leon.
--Dorothy's Doll: A Nursery Tale. (Illus.). (The Happy Hours Series.: No. 2). 1915. Cupples & Leon.
--Jingles of the Zoo. (Illus.). (The Happy Hours Series.). 1915. Cupples & Leon.
--Little Karl. (Illus.). (The Sunbonnet Series.). 1915. Cupples & Leon.
--Little Susie Sunbonnet. (Illus.). (The Sunbonnet Series: No. 4). 1915. Cupples & Leon.
--The Magic Doll: A Fairy Tale. (Illus.). (The Happy Hour Ser.: No. 1). 1915. Cupples & Leon.
--The Strange Adventures of Prince Charming: A Story for the Young & Old. Superior, Rose S., illus. LC 19-19665. 1 p. l., 126 p. col. front., illus. col. plates. 25 cm. c.1919. McLoughlin Brothers, Inc.
--The Sunbonnet Twins. (Illus.). (The Sunbonnet Ser.: No. 1). 1915. Cupples & Leon.
--A Victim of Conscience: A Novel. LC 3-12814. iv, 318 p. front. 3 pl. 20 cm. 1903. H. T. Coates & Company.

Goldsmith, Oliver, jt. auth. see Caldecott, Randolph.

Goldsmith, Oliver, jt. auth. see Merington, Marguerite.

Goldsmith, Oliver (1728-1744)
--Vicar of Wakefield. Handy Volume, Large Type ed. (Illus.). (Beauxarts Ser.). N.D. Henry Altemus.

Goldsmith, Oliver (1728-1774)
--The Deserted Village. (Clarendon Press Ser.). N.D. Macmillian.
--The Deserted Village. Billings, Hammatt (1818-1874), illus. (Illus.). (Violet Ser.). N.D. Henry T. Coates & Co.
--Goldsmith's Vicar of Wakefield. (Classics for Children). N.D. Ginn and Company.
--The History of Little Goody Two Shoes. Merchant, Elizabeth Lodor, ed. Newbery, John (1713-1767), illus. Giles Gingerbread Price, Harriet Longstreet (1891-), illus. LC 30-21163. xiv p., 1 l., 96 p. col. front., illus., col. pl. 21 cm. c.1930. The John C. Winston Company.
--The History of Little Goody Two Shoes: Otherwise Called Mrs. Margery Two Shoes, with the Means by Which She Aquired Her Learning and Wisdom, and in Consequence Therof Her Estate; Set Forth at Large ... Woodward, Alice Bolingbroke (1862-), illus. LC 24-239224. xiv p., 1 l., 91 p. incl. illus., plates. col. front. 17 cm. (On cover: The Little library). (gr. 2-4). 1924. (ISBN 0-02-736280-9). The Macmillan Company.
--She Stoops to Conquer. N.D. The Macmillan Co.
--The Traveller and the Deserted Village. Barrett, A, notes by. N.D. MacMillian.
--The Vicar of Wakefield. N.D. A. C. McClurg & Co.
--The Vicar of Wakefield. (Burt's Home Library). N.D. A L Burt Co.
--Vicar of Wakefield. (Eclectic English Classics). N.D. American Book Co.
--Vicar of Wakefield. (The Cornell Ser.: No. 175). N.D. B. L. Burt's Pubs.
--Vicar of Wakefield. (Illus.). (The Young Folks Library). N.D. Caldwell.
--Vicar of Wakefield. (Choice Ser. of Choice Bks.). N.D. Cassell, Petter, & Galpin.
--Vicar of Wakefield. N.D. D. Lothrop Co.
--The Vicar of Wakefield. N.D. E. P. Dutton & Co.
--Vicar of Wakefield. (The Roxburghe Classics). N.D. Estes & Lauriat's.
--Vicar of Wakefield. (Illus.). (The Empyreal Library of Handy Volume Classics). N.D. H. M. Caldwell Co.
--The Vicar of Wakefield. (Illus.). (The Exquisite Ser.). N.D. H. M. Caldwell Co.
--Vicar of Wakefield. (Illus.). (The Chateau Ser). N.D. H. M. Caldwell Co.
--Vicar of Wakefield. N.D. Harper & Brothers.
--The Vicar of Wakefield. (New Alta Lib.). N.D. Henry T. Coates & Co.'s.
--Vicar of Wakefield. Handy Volume, Large Type ed. (Illus.). (Petit-Trianon Ser.). N.D. Henry Altemus.
--The Vicar Of Wakefield. (Illus.). N.D. Houghton, Mifflin & Co.
--The Vicar of Wakefield. (New Aldine Ser). N.D. International Book Co.
--Vicar of Wakefield. (New International Library). N.D. John C. Winston co.
--Vicar of Wakefield. (New Acorn Library). N.D. John C. Winston & Co.
--Vicar of Wakefield. (Illus.). (The Laurel Ser.). N.D. Joseph Knight Co.
--The Vicar of Wakefield. (Magnum Easy Eye Classic Ser.). (gr. 7 up). N.D. Lancer.
--The Vicar of Wakefield. N.D. Lee & Shepard.
--The Vicar of Wakefield. N.D. Longmans,Green & Co.
--Vicar of Wakefield, 1 of 4 Vols. (Library of Celebrated Books). N.D. R. Worthington.
--The Vicar of Wakefield. 287p. (The Lake English Classics). N.D. Scott Foresman & Co.
--The Vicar of Wakefield. N.D. Silver, Burdett.
--Vicar of Wakefield, 1 of 56 vols. (Illus.). (The Colonial Lib.). 1900. T. Y Crowell & Co.
--Vicar of Wakefield. (Illus.). (Handy Volume Classics). 1900. T. Y. Crowell & Co.
--Vicar of Wakefield, 1 of 56 vols. (The Faience Lib.). N.D. T. Y. Crowell & Co.
--Vicar of Wakefield. (The New Astor Library of Prose). N.D. T. Y. Crowell & Co.
--Vicar of Wakefield, 1 of 67 vols. (The Westminster Series of Poetry and Prose). N.D. T. Y. Crowell & Co.
--Vicar of Wakefield, 1 of 4 Vols. (Illus.). (The Standard Juvenile Library). N.D. Set. Thomas Nelson & Sons.
--The Vicar of Wakefield. (Standard Literature Ser.: No. 45). N.D. University Publishing Co.
--The Vicar of Wakefield. (Classic Ser.). N.D. World Publishing Co.
--The Vicar of Wakefield, 1 Vol. (Illus.). N.D. Worthington Company.
--The Vicar of Wakefield. Austen, John, illus. 256p. N.D. Heritage Press.
--The Vicar of Wakefield. Bewick, Thomas (1753-1828), illus. 1873. G. P. Putnam's Sons.
--Vicar of Wakefield. Dobson, Austin, notes by. (Illus.). N.D. D. Appleton & Co.
--The Vicar of Wakefield. James, Henry, intro. by. (Illus.). 325p. N.D. The Century Co.
--The Vicar of Wakefield. Macmillan, M., ed. N.D. St. Martin's Press.
--The Vicar of Wakefield. Mulready, William, illus. (Illus.). N.D. Thos Nelson & Sons.
--The Vicar of Wakefield. Rackham, Arthur (1867-1939), illus. N.D. David McKay Co.
--The Vicar of Wakefield. Willmott, R. A., memoir by. N.D. George Routledge & Sons.
--The Vicar of Wakefield & Other Writings. N.D. The Modern Library.
--The Vicar of Wakefield, She Stoops to Conquer and Other Poems. Vulliamy, C. E., intro. by. (Collins New Classics). N.D. William Collins Sons & Co.
--The Vicar of Wakefield: She Stoops to Conquer the Deserted Village and Others. N.D. William Collins Sons & Company Ltd.
--The Vicar Wakefield. Maclise, Mulready, illus. N.D. Charles Scribner Sons.

Goldsmith, Oliver (1728-1774) & De Saint-Pierre, Jaques Henri Barnardin (1737-1814)
--Vicar of Wakefield: Paul and Virginia, 1 of 4 Vols, Vols. 4 & 5. (Illus.). (Library of Classic Fiction, No. 2). N.D. Set. Porter & Coates.

Goldsmith, Oliver (1728-1774) & Jones, Giles
--Goody Two-Shoes: A Facsimile Reproduction of the Edition of 1766. Welsh, Charles (1850-1914), ed. Newbery, John (1713-1767), illus. LC 68-31083. (Illus.). xxiv, 156 p. 16cm. 1970. Singing Tree Press.
--The History of Goody Two-Shoes. To Which Is Added, The Rhyming Alphabet, or, Tom Thumb's Delight ... LC 24-2873. 30 p. incl. front. illus. 10 cm. N.D. Printed by Sheldon & Goodwin.
--The History of Little Goody Two-Shoes: An Account of the Means by Which She Acquired Her Learning and Wisdom, and, in Consequence Thereof, Her Estate. LC 41-27884. 2 p. l., vii-xxii, 1, 38, 1 p., 1 l. incl. front., illus. 19 cm. 1941. Printed at the Redcoat Press.
--The History of Little Goody Two-Shoes: Otherwise Called Mrs. Margery Twoshoes; with the Means by Which She Acquired Her Learning and Wisdom, and in Consequence Thereof Her Estate. LC 22-5874. 158 p. incl. front., illus. 13 cm. 1787. By Isaiah Thomas and Sold, Wholesale and Retail, at His Book Store.
--The History of Little Goody Twoshoes: Otherwise Called Mrs. Margery Twoshoes; with the Means by Which She Acquired Her Learning and Wisdom, and in Consequence Thereof Her Estate. Mumford, Lawrence Quincy (1903-), ed. Newbery, John (1713-1767), illus. LC 71-9264. (Illus.). 7, 158 p. 13cm. 1969. Printed by the Meriden Gravure Co.

Goldsmith, Ruth M. (1919-)
--Phoebe Takes Charge. LC 82-13955. 241 p. 22cm. 1983. (ISBN 0-689-50266-4). Atheneum.

Goldsmith, Sophie L., adapted by see Pyle, Howard.

Goldstein, Frances
--Children's Treasure Hunt Travel to Belgium & France. Goldstein, Frances, illus. LC 80-85012. (Illus.). 230p. (Orig.). (Children's Treasure Hunt Travel Guide Ser.). (gr. k-12). 1981. (ISBN 0-933334-02-8). Paper Tiger Pap.

Goldstein, Julius (1905-)
--Tiny Toot Train. Pollard, Nancy D. (1925-), illus. LC 51-27542. (Illus.). 24p. 20cm. (A Bonnie Spinwheel Bk.). 1951. S. Lowe Co.
--Wild West Shows. Carbe, Nino (1909-), illus. LC 51-28016. (Illus.). 23p. 20cm. (Bonnie Movie Bks.). 1951. S. Lowe Co.

Goldstein, Rhoda
--The Cat Who Loved the Sea. Ebert, Len, illus. LC 68-20544. (Illus.). 32 p. 25cm. 1968. Prentice-Hall.

Goldstein, Rose B.
--Songs to Share. Schloss, Ezekiel, illus. (Illus.). 64p. (ps-5). N.D. (ISBN 0-8381-0720-6). United Syn Bk.

Goldstein, Sam
--Animalimericks: Book I-Wild Cats. (Illus.). 16p. (Orig.). (Limericklets (Limerick Booklets) Ser.: No. 2). 1982. (ISBN 0-938338-10-2). Winds World Pr.
--Homonymericks. 16p. (Orig.). (Limericklets (Limerick Booklets) Ser.: No. 1). 1982. (ISBN 0-938338-09-9). Winds World Pr.

Goldston, Robert Conroy (1927-), ed. see Irving, Washington.

Goldston, Robert Conroy (1927-)
--The Legend of the Cid. Stephane, illus. LC 63-19010. (Illus.). (gr. 7 up). 1963. (ISBN 0-672-50353-0). Bobbs.

Goldston, Robert Conroy (1927-), adapted by.
--The Song of Roland. LC 64-17117. (gr. 7 up). 1964. (ISBN 0-672-50505-3). Bobbs.
--The Song of Roland. Stephane, illus. LC 64-17117. 117p. illus. 24cm. 1964. , C.

Goldsweig, Beryl
--Artemus Flint: Detective. (gr. 7-12). 1975. (ISBN 0-590-09886-1). Scholastic Inc.

Goldszmit, Henryk see Korczak, Jamusz, pseud.

Goldszmit, Henryk (1878-1943)
--Matthew, the Young King. Korczak, Jamusz, pseud. Sulkin, Edith & Sulkin, Sidney (1918-), eds. Lorentowicz, Irena (1910-), illus. LC 45-3237. 256 p. illus. 21 cm. 1945. Roy Publishers.

Goldthwait, Priscilla
--Night of the Wall. McMains, Denny, illus. LC 64-18042. 126 p. illus. 21 cm. 1964. Putnam.

Goldthwaite, John
--Eggs Amen!. Couratin, Patrick, illus. (Illus.). 32p. (Harlin Quist Bks). (gr. 3 up). 1973. (ISBN 0-8252-0134-9). Dial.
--Eggs Amen. Lapointe, Claude, illus. (gr. 4 up). 1976. (ISBN 0-8252-0133-0). Quist.

Goldthwaite, John & Galeron, Henri
--Roll Call: The Story of Noah's Ark & the World's First Losers. LC 78-70570. (Illus.). 24 p. 23cm. c.1978. (ISBN 0-8252-7482-6). (ISBN 0-8252-7481-8). Harlin Quist.

Golish, Vitold De
--Mamba-Kan: The Story of a Baby Elephant. LC 54-12838. (Illus.). unpaged. 27cm. 1954. J. Day Co.

Goll, Reinhold Weimar (1897-)
--The Moon Twins and the Treasure. Hoover, Russell, illus. LC 78-61141. (Illus.). 97 p. 23cm. c.1978. Elkins Park Press.
--Pedro Sails with Columbus. LC 81-90281. v, 87 p. 22cm. c.1981. R.W. Goll.
--Spaceship to Planet Veta. James, G. Oliver, illus. LC 62-10296. (Illus.). 21cm. 160p. 1962. Westminster Press.
--Three Weird Animals & a Flying Monster. (gr. 6-9). 1981. (ISBN 0-686-30642-2). R W Goll.
--Through Space to Planet T. large type ed. James, G. Oliver, illus. LC 63-15466. 156 p. illus. 21 cm. (gr. 3-6). 1963. (ISBN 0-664-20250-0). Westminster Press.
--Valley Forge Rebel. LC 73-94391. (Illus.). 159 p. 22cm. 1974. (ISBN 0-8059-1994-5). Dorrance.

Gollancz, I., ed. see Lamb, Charles (1775-1834) & Lamb, Mary Ann.

Gollancz, I., ed. see Shakespeare, William (1564-1616) & Lamb, Charles.

Goller, Claudine
--Algonkians of the Eastern Woodlands. 48p. (Native Peoples Ser.). (gr. 2-4). 1984. (ISBN 0-531-04683-4). Watts.

Gollob, Barbara Kowal, tr. see Jucker, Sita.

Gollob, Barbara Kowal, tr. see Wiemer, Rudolf Otto.

Gollomb, Joseph (1881-)
--That Year at Lincoln High. Caswell, Edward C., illus. LC 18-19510. 3 p. l., 290 p. front., plates. 20 cm. 1918. The Macmillan Company.
--Tiger at City High. LC 46-6544. 4 p. l., 3-212 p. 21 cm. 1946. Harcourt, Brace and Company.
--Tuning in at Lincoln High. LC 25-18872. 5 p. l., 255 p. front., plates. 20 cm. 1925. The Macmillan Company.
--Up at City High. LC 45-2837. 4 p. l., 3-217 p. 21 cm. 1945. Harcourt, Brace and Company.
--Window on the World. 208p. N.D. Harcourt, Brace & Co.
--Working Through at Lincoln High. LC 23-12338. 5 p. l., 228 p. front. 20 cm. 1923. The Macmillan Company.

Gollub, Morris, illus.
--That's Our Cleo. (Illus.). 1979. (ISBN 0-307-21566-0, Golden Pr). Western Pub.

Golmgren, Virginia C.
--Here's Susie. N.D. (ISBN 0-685-32928-3). Assoc Bk.

Golon, Anne see Golon, Sergeanne.

Golon, Sergeanne (1903-1972)
--Angelique and the Demon. 1973. (ISBN 0-399-11193-X). G. P. Putnam's Sons.
--The Temptations of Angelique. Barnett, Marguerite, tr. from Fr. 1970. (ISBN 0-399-10791-6). G. P. Putnam's Sons.

Gombrich, Lisboth, tr. see Hakansson, Gunvor.

Gomes, Bernadette
--Maile & the Marvelous One. Hall, Pat, illus. LC 84-4715. (Illus.). (Treasury of Children's Hawaiian Stories Ser.). (gr. 3-6). 1984. (ISBN 0-916630-40-4). Pr Pacifica.

Gomez, Ronald, jt. auth. see Hunter, Julius.

Gomez, Victoria
--Scream Cheese & Jelly. Schick, Joel (1945-), illus. 64p. (gr. 3-7). 1981. (ISBN 0-590-31266-9, Schol Pap). Scholastic Inc.
--Scream Cheese & Jelly!. Jokes, Riddles, & Puns. Schick, Joel (1945-), illus. LC 79-14575. (Illus.). (gr. 2-6). 1979. (ISBN 0-688-41916-X). (ISBN 0-688-51916-4). Lothrop.

--Let's Go to a Dairy. Abel, Raymond (1911-), illus. (Illus.). (Let's Go Ser). (gr. 1-3). 1956. (ISBN 0-399-60363-8). Putnam.
--The Ransom Note. Keane, Raymond, illus. LC 78-51340. (Illus.). 40 p. 22cm. (Weekly Reader Children's Book Club edition). c.1978. (ISBN 0-88375-216-6). Xerox Education Publications.
Goodspeed, Peter (1944-)
--Hugh and Fitzhugh. Nicklaus, Carol, illus. LC 73-19370. (Illus.). 28 p. 28cm. 1974. (ISBN 0-8228-7575-6). Platt & Munk.
--A Rhinoceros Wakes Me Up in the Morning: A Bedtime Tale. Panek, Dennis, illus. LC 81-21556. p. cm. 1982. (ISBN 0-87888-201-4). Bradbury Press.
--A Rhinoceros Wakes Me Up in the Morning: A Bedtime Tale. Panek, Dennis, illus. LC 83-19175. 1984, c.1982. (ISBN 0-14-050453-2). Penguin Books.
Goodwin, Alice Howland Goodwin, Mrs. (1835-), tr. see Spyri, Johanna Heusser.
Goodwin, Christina
--After Schooldays. N.D. Lothrop Pub. Co.
--Grammar School Fridays. 182p. N.D. Lothrop Pub. Co.
Goodwin, Elizabeth Sage see Sage, Betty, pseud.
Goodwin, Elizabeth Sage
--Rhymes of If and Why. Sage, Betty, pseud. Robinson, Boardman, illus. N.D. Dodd, Mead & Co.
--Rhymes of If and Why. Sage, Betty, pseud. Robinson, Boardman, illus. LC 27-23026. 28cm. 30p. 1927. Duffield.
--Rhymes of Read Children. Sage, Betty, pseud. Smith, Jessie Willcox (1863-1935), illus. LC 3-28929. 1903. Duffield.
Goodwin, Hal, pseud., see Goodwin, Harold Leland.
Goodwin, Harold Leland see Blaine, John, pseud.
Goodwin, Harold Leland see Goodwin, Hal, pseud.
Goodwin, Harold Leland see Savage, Blake, pseud.
Goodwin, Harold Leland (1914-)
--The Feathered Cape. LC 47-18420. 188 p. 21 1/2 cm. 1947. The Westminster Press.
--A Microphone for David. Goodwin, Harold Leland. Goodwin, Hal, pseud. 1939. Alfred A. Knopf.
--A Microphone for David. Goodwin, Hal, pseud. LC 42-16715. 20cm. 239p. 1942. Wm. Penn Publishing Corp.
Goodwin, Harold (1919-)
--Cargo. Goodwin, Harold (1919-), illus. LC 84-11027. (Illus.). 128p. (gr. 5-7). 1984. (ISBN 0-02-736870-X). Bradbury Pr.
--Magic Number. LC 78-75609. (Illus.). 97 p. 23cm. 1969. Bradbury Press.
--Top Secret: Alligators!. Goodwin, Harold (1919-), illus. LC 74-81695. (Illus.). 94 p. 22cm. 1975. (ISBN 0-87888-102-6). Bradbury Press.
--Top Secret: Alligators. Goodwin, Harold (1919-), illus. 1975. E.P. Dutton & Co.
Goodwin, John Lonnen (1912-)
--Freddy Fribs, Flea. Jones, Richard C. (1910-), illus. LC 38-14701. 2 p. l., 3-55, 1 p. illus. (part col.) 24 cm. 1938. McFarlane, Warde, McFarlane.
Goodwin, John Lonnen (1912-) & Chappel, Warren
--The Pleasant Pirate. LC 40-31301. 1940. Alfred A. Knopf.
Goodwin, Karl H, compiled by.
--Tennyson's Fairies and Other Stories. LC 14-1829. iv, 320 p. illus. 17 cm. 1889. D. Lothrop Company.
Goodwin, Mary J.
--The Ghost of Bennett's Villa. LC 79-88506. (Illus.). 1st U.S. edition. (gr. 5 up). 1981. (ISBN 0-932632-05-X). (ISBN 0-932632-03-3). MJG Co.
Goodwin, Maud Wilder, jt. ed. see Bellamy, Blanche Wilder.
Goodwin, Murray
--Alonzo and the Army of Ants. Komoda, Kiyoaki (1937-), illus. LC 66-15678. 104 p. illus. 23 cm. 1966. Harper & Row.
--The Underground Hideaway. Parnall, Peter (1936-), illus. LC 68-10207. (Illus.). 130 p. 22cm. 1968. Harper & Row.
Goody, Phyllis B.
--Danny and the Anaconda. 1st ed. Beardsley, Susan, illus. LC 76-364944. (Illus.). 40 p. c.1975. (ISBN 0-682-48427-X). Exposition Press.
--Julio, the Shoeshine Boy. Beardsley, Susan, illus. (gr. 2-5). 1977. (ISBN 0-682-48790-2). Exposition.
Goody Two Shoes
--The Story of Little Goody Two-Shoes: Who from a State of Rags and Care, and Having Shoes but Half a Pair, Their Fortune and Their Fame Would Fix, and Gallop in a Coach and Six. Gillespie, Jessie, illus. LC 44-40370. 33, 1 p. illus. (part col.) 21 x 19 cm. 1944. Grosset & Dunlap.
Goody Two Shoes & Newbery, John (1713-1767)
--The History of Little Goody Two-Shoes. LC 75-32141. 15cm. 311p. (Classics of children's literature, 1621-1932). 1977. (ISBN 0-8240-2257-2). Garland Pub.
Goodyear, R. A. H.
--The Captain & the Kings: A Public School Story. Lumley, Savile, illus. N.D. Macmillan.
--Fifth Form at Beck House. (MacMillan Bks. for Boys & Girls). (gr. 7-9). N.D. MacMillan Bks.
--The New Boy at Baxtergate. (MacMillan Bks. for Boys & Girls). (gr. 7-9). N.D. MacMillan Bks.
Goold-Adams, Deenagh
--The Toad in the Greenhouse. N.D. Transatlantic Arts.
Goolden, Barbara (1900-)
--Trouble for the Tabors. Greer, Charles, illus. LC 67-22007. (Illus.). 186 p. 21cm. 1967. I. Washburn.
Goor, Nancy, jt. auth. see Goor, Ron.
Goor, Ron & Goor, Nancy
--In the Driver's Seat. LC 81-43885. (Illus.). 96p. (gr. 1-4). 1982. (ISBN 0-690-04176-4, TYC-J). (ISBN 0-690-04177-2). Har-Row.
Goossen, Agnes, pseud., see Epp, Margaret Agnes.
Goossen, Agnes, pseud. (1913-)
--Mystery at Pony Ranch. Epp, Margaret Agnes. 128p. 1963. Moody.
Gopal, Oodith (1936-)
--Beyond the Bamboo Bridge. LC 74-981241. 95 p. 26cm. (Mauritius writers series). c.1969. S.N.
Gordon, A. C.
--More Solv-a-Crime. (gr. 7 up). 1978. (ISBN 0-590-11878-1). Scholastic Inc.
Gordon, Anna Adams (1853-)
--Toots, and Other Stories: Old Fashioned Stories and Jingles for New Fashioned Little Folk. 2nd ed. LC 10-13528. 196p. 19cm. 1906. Gordon.
Gordon, Bernard E.
--Once There Was a Passenger Pigeon. (gr. 1-4). 1976. (ISBN 0-8098-5003-6). Walck.
Gordon, Bernard Ludwig, jt. auth. see Gordon, Esther Saranga.
Gordon, Caroline
--Old red and Other Stories. 1963. Charles Scribner's Sons.
Gordon, Charles William see Connor, Ralph, pseud.
Gordon, Charles William (1860-1937)
--Glengarry School Days: A Story of Early Days in Glengarry. Connor, Ralph, pseud. 1902. Revell.
Gordon, Clarence (1835-1920)
--Boarding-School Days. Darley, Felix Octavius Carr (1822-1888) & Nast, Thomas (1840-1902), illus. LC 79-302967. (Illus.). iv, 291 p., 8 leaves of plates. 18cm. 1873. Hurd and Houghton.
Gordon, Colonel H. R., pseud., see Ellis, Edward Sylvester.
Gordon, Donald, pseud., see Payne, Donald Gordon.
Gordon, Donald, pseud. (1924-)
--Leap in the Dark. Payne, Donald Gordon. LC 76-142391. 222p. (gr. 7 up). 1971. Morrow.
Gordon, Dorothy Lerner (1893-1970), ed.
--Around the World in Song. Conover, Alida Van R., illus. Schelling, Ernest, Dr., frwd. by. LC 30-23571. xiv, 94, 2 p. illus. 28 cm. 1930. E. P. Dutton & Co., Inc.
--Around the World in Song. Conover, Alida Van R., illus. Schelling, Ernest, Dr., frwd. by. LC 33-2048. xiv, 95, 1 p. illus. 23 cm. (On cover: The Dorothy Gordon song-book series). c.1933. E. P. Dutton & Co., Inc.
--Dorothy Gordon's Treasure Bag of Game Songs. Reed, Veronica, pseud. (1916-), illus. Sherman, Theresa. Buchman, Adele LC 39-27246. 5 p. l., 13-93 p. incl. front., illus. 23 x 17 cm. c.1939. E. P. Dutton & Co., Inc.
--Sing It Yourself: Collection of Folk Songs from "The Young People's Concert Hour". Conover, Alida Van R., illus. Gartlan, George H., frwd. by. LC 28-30036. 8 p. l., 3-82 p. incl. front., illus. 31 cm. c.1928. E. P. Dutton & Co., Inc.
--Sing It Yourself: Folk Songs of All Nations. Conover, Alida Van R., illus. Gartlan, George H., frwd. by. LC 33-2049. 6 p. l., 3-84 p. incl. front., illus 23 cm. (On cover: The Dorothy Gordon song-book series). c.1933. E. P. Dutton & Co., Inc.
Gordon, E. V., jt. auth. see Tolkien, Ronald Reuel.
Gordon, Elizabeth H., ed. see Dana, Richard Henry, Jr.
Gordon, Elizabeth M.
--The Mighty Hunter. Wylie, Charles, illus. (Illus.). N.D. Dodd, Mead & Company.
--The Mighty Hunter in Toyland. Wylie, Charles, illus. 21 x 26cm. 36p. 1908. Dodd, Mead & Co.
--Two Teddy Bears in Toyland. Wylie, Charles, photos by. LC 8-241. 22cm. 34p. 1907. Dodd, Mead & Co.
Gordon, Elizabeth (1866-1922)
--Billy Bunny's Fortune. Enright, Maginel Wright, illus. LC 37-19343. 40 p. col. illus. 19 cm. 1937. Algonquin Publishing Company.
--Bird Children. Ross, M. T. Penny, illus. (Gift Juveniles). N.D. A. L. Burt Co.
--Bird Children: The Little Playmates of the Flower Children. 6th ed. Ross, M. T. Penny, illus. LC 12-24066. 4 p. l., 11-95, 1 p. col. illus. 24 cm. c.1912. P. V. Volland & Company.
--Buddy Jim. Rae, John (1882-1963), illus. (Gift Juveniles). N.D. A. L. Burt Co.
--Buddy Jim. Rae, John (1882-1963), illus. 93 p. col. illus. 24 cm. c.1922. P. F. Volland Company.
--Butterfly Babies' Book. Ross, M. T. Penny, illus. N.D. Rand McNally.
--Dolly & Molly & the Farmer Man. Beem, Frances M., illus. (The Dolly & Molly Ser.). N.D. Rand McNally.
--Dolly & Molly at the Circus. Beem, Frances M., illus. (The Dolly & Molly Ser.). N.D. Rand McNally.
--Dolly & Molly at the Seashore. Beem, Frances M., illus. (The Dolly & Molly Ser.). N.D. Rand McNally.
--Dolly & Molly on Christmas Day. Beem, Frances M., illus. (The Dolly & Molly Ser.). N.D. Rand McNally.
--Flower Children. Ross, M. T. Penny, illus. (Gift Juveniles). N.D. A. L. Burt Co.
--Flower Children: The Little Cousins of the Field and Garden. LC 40-633324. 92 p. col. illus. 25 cm. c.1939. The Wise-Parslow Company.
--Granddad Coco Nut's Party. Ross, M. T. Penny, illus. N.D. Rand McNally.
--I Wonder Why?. Ross, M. T. Penny, illus. 20cm. 72p. (gr. 1-2). N.D. Rand McNally & Co.
--Katherine: The Komical Kow. Tower, Lew, illus. 40p. (Sunny Bks.). N.D. P. F. Volland Co.
--Loraine and the Little People. Ross, M. T. Penny, illus. LC 15-20985. 73, 1 p. incl. front., illus. (part col.) 20 cm. c.1915. Rand, McNally & Company.
--Loraine and the Little People of Spring. Lee, Ella Dolbear, illus. LC 19-2277. 64 p. illus. (part col.) 21 cm. c.1918. Rand, McNally & Company.
--Loraine & the Little People of Summer. McCracken, James, illus. N.D. Rand McNally.
--More Really So Stories. Rosse, Herman, illus. (Gift Juveniles). N.D. A. L. Burt Co.
--Mother Earth's Children. Richardson, Frederick (1862-1937), illus. (Gift Juveniles). N.D. A. L. Burt.
--Mother Earth's Children: The Frolics of the Fruits and Vegetables. 2d ed. Ross, M. T. Penny, illus. LC 14-18740. 95, 1 p. col. illus. 24 cm. c.1914. P. F. Volland & Co.
--Really So Stories. Rae, John (1882-1963), illus. LC 24-7484. 96 p. col. illus. 24 cm. (On cover: Volland "Happy children books"). c.1924. P. F. Volland Company.
--Really So Stories. Rae, John (1882-1963), illus. LC 37-4882. 96 p. col. illus. 25 cm. c.1937. The Wise-Parslow Company.
--Realy-So-Stories. Rae, John (1882-1963), illus. (Gift Juveniles). N.D. A. L. Burt Co.
--The Tale of Johnny Mouse. Barney, Maginel Wright, Mrs. (1881-1966), illus. 40p. (Sunny Bks.). N.D. P. F. Volland Co.
--The Turned Into's. Scott, Janet Laura, illus. (Gift Juveniles). N.D. A. L. Burt Co.
--Watermellon Pete. Wilson, Clara Powers, illus. N.D. Rand McNally.
--Wild Flower Children: The Little Playmates of the Fairies. Scott, Janet Laura, illus. LC 19-2276. 84 p. col. illus. 24 cm. c.1918. P. F. Volland Company.
Gordon, Elizabeth (1866-1922) & Priest, Jane
--More Really-So Stories. Rae, John (1882-1963), illus. LC 30-1567. 95, 1 p. illus. (part col.) 24 cm. (On cover: Volland "Happy children books"). c.1929. P. F. Volland Company.
Gordon, Esther Saranga (1935-) & Gordon, Bernard Ludwig (1931-)
--If an Auk Could Talk. Ford, Pamela B., illus. (gr. k-3). 1980. (ISBN 0-8098-6200-X). Walck.
--Once There Was a Giant Sea Cow. Ford, Pamela B., illus. (Illus.). (gr. k-3). 1980. (ISBN 0-679-20851-8). McKay.
--There Really Was a Dodo. Di Fiori, Lawrence, illus. LC 73-19252. (Illus.). 32p. (gr. 1-4). 1974. (ISBN 0-8098-1218-5). Walck.
Gordon, Ethel Edison (1915-)
--The Freebody Heiress. LC 74-82981. 279p. 1975. (ISBN 0-679-50515-6). McKay.
--So Far From Home. LC 69-13638. 21cm. 168p. 1969. (ISBN 0-690-74867-1). Thomas Y. Crowell.
--Where Does the Summer Go?. 172 p. 21cm. 1967. T. Y. Crowell Co.
Gordon, Eva Lucretia & Hall, Jennie
--Nature Stories for Children: A Spring Book. v, 1, 90 p. col. illus. 20 cm. c.1927. Mentzer, Bush & Co.
--Nature Stories for Children: An Autumn Book. LC 26-18314. 3 p. l., 88 p. col. illus. 20 cm. c.1926. Mentzer, Bush & Co.
Gordon, Frederick, pseud., see Stratemeyer Syndicate.
Gordon, Frederick, pseud.
--Bob Bouncer's Schooldays: Or, The Doings of a Real, Live Everyday Boy. Stratemeyer Syndicate. (Illus.). (Up and Doing Ser.: Vol. 3). 1912. Graham & Matlack.
--The Fairview Boys Afloat and Ashore: Or, The Young Crusoes of Pine Island. Stratemeyer Syndicate. (Illus.). Repr. of 1914 ed (Pub. by Graham & Matlack). (Fairview Boys Ser: Vol. 1). Orig. Title: The Young Crusoes of Pine Island; or, The Wreck of the Puff. 1917. C. E. Graham Co.
--The Fairview Boys Afloat and Ashore: Or, The Young Crusoes of Pine Island. Stratemeyer Syndicate. (Illus.). Reissue of 1912 ed. (Fairview Boys Ser.: Vol. 1). Orig. Title: The Young Crusoes of Pine Island; or, The Wreck of the Puff. 1914. Graham & Matlack.
--The Fairview Boys and their Rivals: Or, Bob Bouncer's Schooldays. Stratemeyer Syndicate. (Illus.). Repr. of 1914 ed (Pub. by Graham & Matlack). (Fairview Boys Ser.: Vol. 3). Orig. Title: Bob Bouncer's Schooldays; or, The Doings of a Real, Live Everyday Boy. 1917. C. E. Graham Co.
--The Fairview Boys and Their Rivals: Or, Bob Bouncer's Schooldays. Stratemeyer Syndicate. (Illus.). Reissue of 1912 ed. (Fairview Boys Ser.: Vol. 3). Orig. Title: Bob Bouncer's Schooldays; or, The Doings of a Real, Live, Everyday Boy. 1914. Graham & Matlack.
--The Fairview Boys at Camp Mystery: Or, The Old Hermit and his Secret. Stratemeyer Syndicate. Repr. of 1914 ed (Pub. by Graham & Matlack). (Fairview Boys Ser.: Vol. 4). 1917. C. E. Graham Co.
--The Fairview Boys at Camp Mystery: Or, The Old Hermit and His Secret. Stratemeyer Syndicate. Mencl, Rudolf, illus. (Illus.). (Fairview Boys Ser.: Vol. 4). 1914. Graham & Matlack.
--The Fairview Boys at Lighthouse Cove: Or, Carried out to Sea. Stratemeyer Syndicate. Repr. of 1914 ed (Pub. by Graham & Matlack). (Fairview Boys Ser.: Vol. 5). 1917. C. E. Graham Co.
--The Fairview Boys at Lighthouse Cove: Or, Carried Out to Sea. Stratemeyer Syndicate. Mencl, Rudolf, illus. (Illus.). (Fairview Boys Ser.: Vol. 5). 1914. Graham & Matlack.
--The Fairview Boys on a Ranch: Or, Riding with the Cowboys. Stratemeyer Syndicate. Owen, Robert Emmett (1878-), illus. (Illus.). (Fairview Boys Ser.: Vol. 6). 1917. C. E. Graham Co.
--The Fairview Boys on Eagle Mountain: Or, Sammy Brown's Treasure hunt. Stratemeyer Syndicate. (Illus.). Repr. of 1914 ed (Pub. by Graham & Matlack). (Fairview Boys Ser.: Vol. 2). Orig. Title: Sammy Brown's Treasure Hunt; or, Lost in the Mountains. 1917. C. E. Graham Co.
--Sammy Brown's Treasure Hunt: Or, Lost in the Mountains. Stratemeyer Syndicate. LC 12-16327. (Illus.). 125 p. incl. front., plates. 23 cm. (Up and Doing Ser.: Vol. 2). 1912. Graham & Matlack.
--The Fairview Boys on Eagle Mountain: Or, Sammy Brown's Treasure Hunt. Stratemeyer Syndicate. (Illus.). Reissue of 1912 ed. (Fairview Boys Ser.: Vol. 2). Orig. Title: Sammy Brown's Treasure Hunt; or, Lost in the Mountains. 1914. Graham & Matlack.
--The Young Crusoes of Pine Island: Or, The Wreck of the Puff. Stratemeyer Syndicate. LC 12-248157. (Illus.). 126 p. incl. front., plates., 23 cm. (Up and Doing Ser.: Vol. 1). 1912. Graham & Matlack.
Gordon, Gordon, jt. auth. see Gordon, Mildred.
Gordon, Grace
--Patsy Carroll at Wilderness Lodge. Owen, Robert Emmett (1878-), illus. LC 17-22564. vi p., 1 l., 340 p. front., plates, 20 cm. c.1917. Cupples & Leon Company.
--Patsy Carroll in Old New England. Gooch, Thelma, illus. LC 21-130635. vi p., 2 l., 308 p. incl. front. plates. 20 cm. (Her Patsy Carroll series). c.1921. Cupples & Leon Company.
--Patsy Carroll in the Golden West. 320p. (The Patsy Carroll Ser.). N.D. Cupples & Leon Company.
--Patsy Carroll Stories for Girls. vi, 340 p., 2 l., 310 p., 1 l., 308 p., 1 l., 308 p. front. 21 cm. (Her Patsy Carroll series). c.1935. Cupples & Leon Co.
--Patsy Carroll Stories for Girls: Four Complete Books for Girls. LC 35-6462. 21cm. (Patsy Carroll Ser.). 1935. Cupples & Leon co.
--Patsy Carroll Under Southern Skies. (The Patsy Carroll Ser.). N.D. Cupples & Leon Company.
Gordon, Harry
--The River Motor Boat Boys on the Amazon: Or, The Secret of Cloud Island. (The River Motor Boat Boys Ser.). N.D. A. L. Burt Company.

--The River Motor Boat Boys on the Colorado: Or, The Clue in the Rockies. (The River Motor Boat Boys Series). N.D. A. L. Burt Company.
--The River Motor Boat Boys on the Columbia: Or, The Confession of A Photograph. (The River Motor Boat Boys Ser.). N.D. A. L. Burt Company.
--The River Motor Boat Boys on the Mississippi: Or, The Trail to the Gulf. (The River Motor Boat Boys Ser.). N.D. A. L. Burt Company.
--The River Motor Boat Boys on the Ohio: Or, The Three Blue Lights. (The River Motor Boat Boys Ser.). N.D. A. L. Burt Company.
--The River Motor Boat Boys on the Rio Grande: Or, In Defense of the Rambler. (The River Motor Boat Boys Ser.). N.D. A. L. Burt Company.
--The River Motor Boat Boys on the St. Lawrence: Or, The Lost Channel. (The River Motor Boat Boys Ser.). N.D. A. L. Burt Company.
--The River Motor Boat Boys on the Yukon: Or, The Lost Mine of Rainbow Bend. (The River Motor Boat Boys Ser.). N.D. A. L. Burt Company.

Gordon, Isabel (1916-)
--The ABC Hunt. Gordon, Isabel (1916-), illus. LC 61-11670. (Illus.). 19 x 24cm. 30p. 1961. Viking Press.

Gordon, Janet, pseud. see Hardy, Robina F.

Gordon, John Llewellyn (1932-)
--An Hour in the Morning. 1st ed. Gough, Philip (1908-), illus. LC 73-19671. (Illus.). 153 p. 23cm. 1974, c.1971. (ISBN 0-525-32295-7). Dutton.
--A Time in a City. 1st ed. Jacques, Robin (1920-), illus. LC 74-23813. (Illus.). 158 p. 22cm. 1975, c.1972. (ISBN 0-525-41340-5). E. P. Dutton.
--A Time in a City. Jacques, Robin (1920-), illus. LC 75-330419. (Illus.). 160 p. 23cm. 1972. (ISBN 0-19-271341-8). Oxford University Press.

Gordon, John William (1925-)
--The Edge of the World. LC 83-2783. 186 p. 22cm. 1st U.S. edition. 1983. (ISBN 0-689-50279-6). Atheneum.
--The Ghost on the Hill. LC 76-28316. p. cm. 1977, c.1976. Viking Press.
--The Giant Under the Snow: A Story of Suspense. Negri, Rocco (1932-), illus. LC 74-105479. 21cm. 200p. 1970. (ISBN 0-06-022031-7). Harper & Row.
--The Giant Under the Snow: A Story of Suspense. Negri, Rocco (1932-), illus. (Illus.). 200 p. 20cm. (Harper trophy book). 1975, c.1970. (ISBN 0-06-440064-6). Harper & Row.
--The House on the Brink. LC 73-135784. 120p. (Suspense Story Ser). (gr. 7 up). 1971. (ISBN 0-06-022029-5, HarpJ). (ISBN 0-06-022028-7). Har-Row.

Gordon, Katharine Parker Sleeper, Mrs.
--Fresh Flowers for Children. new ed., with additions. Billings, illus. LC 15-17171. viii, 9-176 p. front., plates. 18 cm. 1852. J. Munroe and Company.
--Fresh Flowers for My Children. LC 15-17170. vii, 9-140 p. incl. 4 pl. front., illus., plates. 15 cm. 1842. S. G. Simpkins.

Gordon, Louise, illus.
--Circus Land. (Illus.). (Shape Board Play Bks.). (ps-2). 1978. (ISBN 0-89828-009-5). Tuffy Bks.
--Mother Goose Rhymes. (Illus.). (Shape Play Bks.). (ps-2). 1976. (ISBN 0-89828-000-1). Tuffy Bks.
--The Shoelace Book of Rhymes. (Illus.). (Shape Board Play Bks.). (ps-2). 1978. (ISBN 0-89828-006-0). Tuffy Bks.

Gordon, Margaret (1939-)
--A Paper of Pins. LC 74-8767. (Illus.). 32 p. 26cm. 1975. (ISBN 0-8164-3131-0). Seabury Press.
--The Supermarket Mice. LC 84-235797. (Illus.). 32 p. 28cm. 1984. (ISBN 0-525-44145-X). Dutton.
--Wilberforce Goes on a Picnic. Gordon, Margaret (1939-), illus. LC 82-3476. (Illus.). 32p. (ps). 1982. (ISBN 0-688-01481-X). Morrow.
--Wilberforce Goes to a Party. LC 85-40383. p. cm. 1985. (ISBN 0-670-80148-8). Viking Kestrel.

Gordon, Margery & King, Marie B.
--A Magic World: An Anthology of Poetry. N.D. Appleton-Century-Crofts.
--Verse of Our Day. N.D. Appleton-Century-Crofts.

Gordon, Mary Daniel (1893-)
--The Crystal Ball. Gordon, Mary Daniel (1893-), illus. LC 20-17022. 3 p. l., 235 p. col. front., illus., col. plates. 21 cm. 1920. Little, Brown, and Company.

Gordon, Mildred (1912-1979) & Gordon, Gordon (1912-)
--Catnapped! The Further Adventures of Undercover Cat: The/Further Adventures of Undercover Cat. LC 74-5915. 192p. 1974. Doubleday.
--That Darn Cat. (gr. 4-6). 1973. (ISBN 0-590-08613-8). Scholastic Inc.
--Undercover Cat. (gr. 9 up). 1963. Doubleday.

Gordon, Patricia see Howard, Joan, pseud.

Gordon, Patricia (1904-)
--The Boy Jones. Adams, Adrienne (1906-), illus. LC 43-13044. 158 p. incl. plates. 22 cm. 1943. The Viking Press.
--The Heir to Christmas. MacKenzie, Garry (1921-), illus. LC 53-12456. 55p. illus. 22cm. 1953. Viking Press.
--The Light in the Tower. Howard, Joan, pseud. Adams, Adrienne (1906-), illus. LC 57-11650. unpaged. illus. 26cm. 1957. Lothrop, Lee & Shepard Co.
--Not-Mrs.-Murphy. Boyer, Ralph L., illus. LC 42-25518. 121, 1 p. illus. 20 cm. 1942. The Viking Press.
--The Oldest Secret. MacKenzie, Garry (1921-), illus. LC 53-2613. 128p. illus. 22cm. 1953. Viking Press.
--Rommany Luck. Busoni, Rafaello (1900-1962), illus. LC 46-118238. 206 p. illus. 21 cm. 1946. The Viking Press.
--Story of Louisa May Alcott. Howard, Joan, pseud. Meadowcroft, Enid La Monte, Mrs. (1898-1966), ed. Smith, Flora, illus. LC 55-10739. (Illus.). (gr. 4-6). 1955. (ISBN 0-448-05635-6, Sign). G&D.
--The Story of Mark Twain. Howard, Joan, pseud. Meadowcroft, Enid La Monte, Mrs. (1898-1966), ed. McKay, Donald A. (1895-), illus. LC 53-812678. 174p. illus. 22cm. (Signature books, 23). 1953. Grosset & Dunlap.
--The Summer Is Magic. Howard, Joan, pseud. Adams, Adrienne (1906-), illus. LC 52-14179. (Illus.). 182 p. 22cm. 1952. Lothrop, Lee & Shepard.
--The Taming of Giants. Howard, Joan, pseud. MacKenzie, Garry (1921-), illus. LC 50-8852. 57 p. 26cm. 1950. Viking Press.
--The Thirteenth Is Magic. Howard, Joan, pseud. Adams, Adrienne (1906-), illus. LC 50-11061. (Illus.). 169 p. 22cm. N.D. Lothrop, Lee & Shepard Co.
--Uncle Sylvester. Howard, Joan, pseud. MacKenzie, Garry (1921-), illus. LC 50-6943. 45p. 1950. Oxford University Press.
--The Witch of Scrapfaggot Green. Du Bois, William Sherman Pene (1916-), illus. LC 48-119215. 78 p. illus. 26 cm. 1948. Viking Press.

Gordon, Patricia (1904-) & Adams, Adrienne (1906-)
--The Boy Jones. LC 79-19011. p. cm. (Gregg Press Children's Literature Ser.). 1979. (ISBN 0-8398-2608-7). Gregg Press.

Gordon, Paul Herman (1902-)
--The Scout of the Golden Cross. LC 21-278. 5 p. l., 208, 4 p col. front., illus. 20 cm. 1920. H. Holt and Company.

Gordon, Selma, pseud., see Lanes, Selma Gordon.

Gordon, Selma, pseud. (1929-)
--Amy Loves Goodbyes. Lanes, Selma Gordon. Goldsborough, June (1923-), illus. LC 66-5101. (Illus.). (ps-3). 1966. Platt.

Gordon, Sharon
--Christmas Surprise. Magine, John (1921-), illus. (Illus.). 32p. (gr. k-2). 1980. (ISBN 0-89375-373-4). (ISBN 0-89375-273-8). Troll Assocs.
--Dinosaur in Trouble. Harvey, Paul (1926-), illus. (Illus.). 32p. (gr. k-2). 1980. (ISBN 0-89375-374-2). (ISBN 0-89375-274-6). Troll Assocs.
--Drip Drop. Page, Don (1946-), illus. LC 81-5112. p. cm. c.1981. (ISBN 0-89375-507-9). (ISBN 0-89375-508-7). Troll Associates.
--Easter Bunny's Lost Egg. Magine, Sharon, illus. (Illus.). 32p. (gr. k-3). 1980. (ISBN 0-89375-375-0). (ISBN 0-89375-275-4). Troll Assocs.
--First Day of Spring. Willis, Christine, illus. LC 81-2750. p. cm. c.1981. (ISBN 0-89375-531-1). (ISBN 0-89375-532-X). Troll Associates.
--Friendly Snowman. Magine, John (1921-), illus. (Illus.). 32p. (gr. k-2). 1980. (ISBN 0-89375-377-7). (ISBN 0-89375-277-0). Troll Assocs.
--Maxwell Mouse. Rosenberg, Amye, illus. LC 81-4653. p. cm. c.1981. (ISBN 0-89375-501-X). (ISBN 0-89375-502-8). Troll Associates.
--Pete the Parakeet. Harvey, Paul (1926-), illus. (Illus.). 32p. (gr. k-2). 1980. (ISBN 0-89375-384-X). (ISBN 0-89375-284-3). Troll Assocs.
--Play Ball, Kate!. Page, Don (1946-), illus. LC 81-4855. p. cm. c.1981. (ISBN 0-89375-525-7). (ISBN 0-89375-526-5). Troll Associates.
--Sam the Scarecrow. Silverstein, Donald (1932-), illus. (Illus.). 32p. (gr. k-2). 1980. (ISBN 0-89375-387-4). (ISBN 0-89375-287-8). Troll Assocs.
--The Spelling Bee. Garcia, Tom, illus. LC 81-4648. p. cm. c.1981. (ISBN 0-89375-535-4). (ISBN 0-89375-536-2). Troll Associates.
--Surprise Party. Hall, Susan T. (1940-), illus. LC 81-4869. p. cm. c.1981. (ISBN 0-89375-521-4). (ISBN 0-89375-522-2). Troll Associates.
--Three Little Witches. Sims, Deborah, illus. (Illus.). 32p. (gr. k-2). 1980. (ISBN 0-89375-390-4). (ISBN 0-89375-290-8). Troll Assocs.
--Tick Tock Clock. Page, Don (1946-), illus. LC 81-11393. (Illus.). 32 p. 24cm. (Now I know). c.1982. (ISBN 0-89375-676-8). (ISBN 0-89375-677-6). Troll Associates.
--What a Dog. Sims, Deborah, illus. (Illus.). 32p. (gr. k-2). 1980. (ISBN 0-89375-393-0). (ISBN 0-89375-293-2). Troll Assocs.

Gordon, Sheila
--A Monster in the Mailbox. 1st ed. De Luna, Tony, illus. LC 78-4600. p. cm. c.1978. Dutton.

Gordon, Shirley (1921-)
--The Boy Who Wanted a Family. Robinson, Charles (1931-), illus. LC 79-2003. (Illus.). 89 p. 23cm. c.1980. (ISBN 0-06-022051-1). (ISBN 0-06-022052-X). Harper & Row.
--Crystal Is My Friend. Frascino, Edward, illus. LC 77-11853. (Illus.). 32 p. 23cm. c.1978. (ISBN 0-06-022112-7). (ISBN 0-06-022113-5). Harper & Row.
--Crystal Is the New Girl. Frascino, Edward, illus. LC 75-25400. (Illus.). 31 p. 23cm. c.1976. (ISBN 0 06 022024 4). (ISBN 0 06 022025 2). Harper & Row.
--Grandma Zoo. Darrow, Whitney, Jr. (1909-), illus. LC 78-52402. p. cm. c.1978. (ISBN 0-06-022049-X). (ISBN 0-06-022050-3). Harper & Row.
--The Green Hornet Lunchbox. Graham, Margaret Bloy (1920-), illus. LC 79-86295. (Illus.). 31 p. 21cm. (Sandpiper books). 1973, c.1970. Houghton.
--Happy Birthday, Crystal. Frascino, Edward, illus. LC 80-8941. p. cm. c.1981. (ISBN 0-06-022006-6). (ISBN 0-06-022007-4). Harper & Row.
--Me and the Bad Guys. Frascino, Edward, illus. LC 79-9611. p. cm. c.1980. (ISBN 0-06-022116-X). (ISBN 0-06-022117-8). Harper & Row.

Gordon, Stables (1815-1906)
--England's Hero Prince. N.D. E. P. Dutton & Co.

Gordon, Violet
--Who's Who at the Zoo: Swinging Animal Tales,. LC 72-95113. (Illus.). 55 p. 22cm. 1973. (ISBN 0-8059-1819-1). Dorrance.

Gordon, William John
--The Treasure Finder. N.D. Frederick Warne & Co.

Gordon, William John, compiled by.
--Warne's Pleasure Book for Boys. LC 72-177246. 1v. (unpaged) ill. col. 23cm. 1924. F. Warne.

Gordon, William John, tr. see Rousselet, Louis.

Gore, John, ed.
--Three Howard Sisters. N.D. Transatlantic Arts.

Gore, Margaret
--Dust & Dreams. (gr. 5-9). 1975. (ISBN 0-8277-4478-1). British Bk Ctr.

Gorecka-Egan, Erica, illus.
--Polish Folk Tales. Borski, Lucia Mereka, Mrs., tr. LC 47-12588. 123 p. col. illus. 24 cm. 1947. Sheed & Ward.

Gorelick, Molly C. (1920-) & Graeber, Jean Boreman (1909-)
--Fire on Sun Mountain. (Illus.). photos. drawings. (Rescue Ser., Vol. 1: Vol.). (gr. 3-7). 1967. (ISBN 0-378-68023-4). Ritchie.
--Flood at Dry Creek. LC 67-15076. (Illus.). (Rescue Ser.; Vol.2). (gr. 3-7). 1967. (ISBN 0-378-68033-1). Ritchie.
--Fog Over Sun City. (Illus.). photos. drawings. (Rescue Ser.: Vol. 3). (gr. 6-9). 1968. (ISBN 0-378-68053-6). Ritchie.
--Snow Storm at Green Valley. LC 68-30701. (Illus.). 42 p. 24cm. (Rescue series, no. 5). 1968. (ISBN 0-378-68063-3). Ward Ritchie Press; Distributed by Golden Gate Junior Books, San Carlos, Calif.
--Storm at Sand Point. (Illus.). photos. drawings. (Rescue Ser.: Vol. 5). (gr. 5-9). 1967. (ISBN 0-378-68043-9). Ritchie.

Goren, Louis M.
--Fancies and Songs. 156p. N.D. Meador Publishing Co.

Gorey, Edward St. John (1925-)
--The Bug Book. 1st ed. LC 60-10151. unpaged. illus. 14cm. 1959. Looking Glass Library.
--Dracula: A Toy Theatre. Gorey, Edward St. John (1925-), illus. (Illus.). (Encore Edition). (gr. 1 up). 1979. (ISBN 0-684-17369-7, ScribJ). Scribner.
--The Dwindling Party. Gorey, Edward St. John (1925-), illus. LC 81-85698. (Illus.). 12p. (Pop-Up Bks.). 1982. (ISBN 0-394-85129-3). Random.
--Fletcher and Zenobia Save the Circus. Chess, Victoria (1939-), illus. LC 70-173831. (Illus.). 63 p. 21cm. 1971. (ISBN 0-396-06415-9). Dodd, Mead.
--Haunted Looking Glass. (Illus.). (Looking Glass Library). (gr. 3 up). 1959. (ISBN 0-394-80459-7). Random.
--The Tunnel Calamity. Gorey, Edward St. John (1925-), illus. (Illus.). 9p. (Orig.). (Magic Windows Ser.). 1984. (ISBN 0-399-21055-5, Putnam). Putnam Pub Group.
--The Wuggly Ump. LC 63-12404. (Illus.). 14 x 16cm. 1963. Lippincott.

Gorey, Edward St. John (1925-) & Neumeyer, Peter Florian (1929-)
--Donald & the... Gorey, Edward St. John (1925-), illus. (Illus.). 42p (Pub. by Addison Wesley), 1977. (ISBN 0-88496-203-2). Capra Pr.
--Donald Has a Difficulty. (Illus.). 48p. 1982. (ISBN 0-88496-175-3). Capra Pr.

Gorey, Edward St. John, jt. auth. see Chess, Victoria.

Gorfinkle, Lillian
--Bianca. Rosenberg, Silvia, illus. LC 59-6445. 61p. illus. 24cm. 1959. Rand McNally.

Gorham, Elsie
--Rainy Day in the Nursery. (Illus.). 1882. Lee & Shepard.
--Rainy Days, 1 of 4 vols. (Illus.). (Rainy Day Library). N.D. Set. Lee & Shepard.

Gorham, J. C., retold by.
--Alice in Wonderland. (Burt's Series of one Syllable Books). N.D. A. L. Burt Co.
--Black Beauty. (Burt's Series of One Syllable Books). N.D. A. L. Burt Co.
--Swiss Family Robinson. (Burt's Series of One Syllable Books). N.D. A. L. Burt Co.

Gorham, J. C, ed. see Sewell, Anna.

Gorham, J. C, Mrs., ed. see Dodgson, Charles Lutwidge.

Gorky, Maxim, pseud., see Peshkov, Alexiri Maximovich.

Gorky, Maxim, pseud. (1868-1936)
--Danko's Burning Heart. Peshkov, Alexiri Maximovich. Wettlin, Margaret, tr. 24p. 1983. (ISBN 0-8285-2756-3, Pub. by Raduga Pubs USSR). Imported Pubns.
--The Little Sparrow. Peshkov, Alexiri Maximovich. 11p. 1975. (ISBN 0-8285-1194-2, Pub. by Progress Pubs USSR). Imported Pubns.
--Tales from Gorky. Peshkov, Alexiri Maximovich. (The Lotus Library of Continental Masterpieces). N.D. Brentano's.
--Tales of Two Countries. Peshkov, Alexiri Maximovich. N.D. B.W.Huebsch.

Gorman, John B.
--Bonga Donga, the Snow Dog. (gr. 4-7). N.D. Carlton.
--Bonga Donga, the snow dog. Gorman, Bettye Sue, illus. LC 68-5933. 19p. illus. 21cm. N.D. J. P. Bell.

Gorman, Nana & Gorman, Papa
--Billy & Bonnie Meet Christopher Caterpillar. (Illus.). 32p. (ps-3). 1984. (ISBN 0-89962-415-4). Todd & Honeywell.

Gorman, Papa, jt. auth. see Gorman, Nana.

Gormley, Beatrice (1942-)
--Best Friend Insurance. McCully, Emily Arnold (1939-), illus. LC 83-5715. 1983. (ISBN 0-525-44066-6). Dutton.
--Fifth Grade Magic. McCully, Emily Arnold (1939-), illus. LC 82-9439. (Illus.). 131 p. 21cm. c.1982. (ISBN 0-525-44007-0). Dutton.
--The Ghastly Glasses. McCully, Emily Arnold (1939-), illus. LC 85-10112. (Illus.). 117 p. 21cm. c.1985. (ISBN 0-525-44215-4). Dutton.
--Mail-Order Wings. McCully, Emily Arnold (1939-), illus. LC 81-3283. p. cm. c.1981. (ISBN 0-525-34450-0). Dutton.

Gormly, Grace
--Juvenile Jewels. LC 40-2894. 64 p. 22 cm. c.1940. The Pyramid Press.

Gorney, Inor
--Nhan A Boy of Vietnam. 1969. (ISBN 0-8048-0412-5). Charles E. Tuttle.

Gorog, Judith
--Caught in the Turtle. Sanderson, Ruth, illus. LC 83-8154. p. cm. 1983. (ISBN 0-399-20981-6). Philomel Books.
--A Taste for Quiet and Other Disquieting Tales. Titherington, Jeanne, illus. LC 82-289. (Illus.). 128 p. 24cm. c.1982. (ISBN 0-399-20922-0). Philomel.

Gorse, Golden, pseud., see Wace, M. A..

Gorse, Golden, pseud.
--Moorland Mousie. Wace, M. A.. Edwards, Lionel Dalhousie Robertson (1878-), illus. LC 30-24235. vii, 106 p. front., plates. 26 cm. 1929. Country Life Ltd.
--Older Mousie. Wace, M. A.. Edwards, Lionel Dalhousie Robertson (1878-), illus. N.D. Charles Scribner's Sons.
--Older Mousie. Wace, M. A.. Edwards, Lionel Dalhousie Robertson (1878-), illus. LC 34-19490. vii, 1, 101, 1 p. front., plates. 26 cm. 1934. Country Life, Ltd.

Gorska, Halina
--Prince Godfrey, the Knight of the Star of the Nativity: Twelve Wondrous Tales Recorded by Master Johannes Sarabandus. His Majesty's Astrologer. Lorentowicz, Irena (1910-), illus. Braun, Roman, tr. from Polish. Fenner, Phyllis Reid (1899-1982), intro. by. LC 46-7452. xv, 1, 206, 1 p. incl. col. plates. col. plates. 22 cm. 1946. Roy Publishers.

Gorsline, Douglas Warner (1913-1985)
--Farm Boy. Gorsline, Douglas Warner (1913-1985), illus. LC 50-6586. (Illus.). 186 p. 22cm. 1950. Viking Press.

Gorsline, Sally Marie (1928-), ed.
--Nursery Rhymes. Gorsline, Douglas Warner (1913-1985), illus. LC 76-24168. (Illus.). 32 p. 21cm. (Random House pictureback). 1978, c.1977. (ISBN 0-394-93550-0). (ISBN 0-394-83550-6). Random House.

Goscinny, Rene
--Dalton City. Morris, illus. Nolan, Frederick W., tr. from Fr. (Illus.). 47p. (Lucky Luke). (gr. 4-9). 1972. (ISBN 0-340-17199-5). Larousse.
--Nicholas & the Gang Again. Sempe, illus. Bell, Anthea, tr. (gr. 4-7). 1977. (ISBN 0-8277-5403-5). British Bk Ctr.
--Nicholas & the Gang at School. Sempe, illus. Bell, Anthea, tr. (gr. 4-7). 1977. (ISBN 0-8277-5402-7). British Bk Ctr.

Gose, J. Gordon, jt. auth. see Jones, Maynard.

Gosh, Prince
--The Jungle Folk. N.D. Small,Maynard & Co.

Goshorn, Elizabeth
--Shoestrings. LC 75-14624. 30p. ill. 15 x 23cm. c.1975. (ISBN 0-87614-052-5). Carolrhoda Books.

Gosling, Arthur W, ed.
--How the Monkey Got His Short Tail,. LC 29-20005. 149 p. illus. 20 cm. c.1929. Democrat Printing Company.

Gosling, Thomas Warrington, ed. see Hughes, Thomas.

Goss, Charles Frederick
--Chickoryville S. S. N.D. Winona Publishing Co.
--Little Saint Sunshine. Keep, Virginia, illus. N.D. Bobbs-Merrill Co.

Goss, Clay (1946-)
--Bill Pickett: Black Bulldogger. 1st ed. Hall, Chico (1940-), illus. LC 76-126793. (Illus.). 56 p. 20cm. (Challenger book. Black series). 1970. Hill and Wang; Distributed by Random House.

Goss, Janet L. & Harste, Jerome C.
--It Didn't Frighten Me!. Romney, Steve, pseud. (1920-), illus. Bingley, David Ernest. LC 84-52558. (Illus.). 24 p. 22cm. (Predictable Reading Books). c.1985. (ISBN 0-87406-001-X). Willowisp Press.

Goss, Warren Lee (1835-)
--In the Navy: Or, Father Against Son; a Story of Naval Adventures in the Great Civil War, '61-'65. LC 12-32631. 1 p. l., v-xi, 399 p. front., plates. 19 cm. (Warren Lee Goss's War Bks.). c.1898. T. Y. Crowell & Co.
--Jack Alden. (Illus.). (Crowell's Young People Ser.). N.D. Thomas Y. Crowell.
--Jack Alden: A Story of Adventures in the Virginia Campaigns, '61-'65. LC 4-16137. xii, 402 p. incl. front. plates. 19 cm. (Warren Lee Goss's War Bks.). 1895. T. Y. Crowell & Co.
--Jack Gregory: A Boy's Adventures in the War of the Revolution. LC 23-11041. x p., 1 l., 270 p. col. front., col. plates. 21 cm. c.1923. Thomas Y. Crowell Company.
--Jed: A Boy's Adventures in the Army of '61-'65. LC 4-16138. 2 p. l., 404 p. front., plates. 19 cm. 1889. T. Y. Crowell & Co.
--Jed's Boy: A Story of Adventures in the Great World War. LC 19-14942. vi p., 1 l., 235 p. front., plates. 21 cm. c.1919. Thomas Y. Crowell Company.
--Tom Clifton: Or, Western Boys in Grant and Sherman's Army, '61-'65. LC 12-32704. 2 p. l., vii-xii, 427 p. front., plates. 19 cm. (Warren Lee Goss's War Bks.). c.1892. T. Y. Crowell & Co.

Gosselink, Marion G.
--Riggly Triggly Land. N.D. Pageant Press INC.

Gosselink, Sara Elizabeth (1893-)
--At Dawning. N.D. Wm. B. Eerdmans Publishing Co.
--Beside the Syrian Sea. N.D. E. P. Dutton & Co.
--The Blue Robe. N.D. Wm. B. Eerdmans Publishing Co.
--The Captive's Return. N.D. E. P. Dutton & Co.
--A Donkey for the King. 1st ed. LC 55-14408. 89p. 21cm. 1955. Eerdmans.
--The Honored Guest. N.D. Wm. B. Eerdmans Publishing Co.
--The King's Gardener. LC 47-29258. 20cm. 77p. N.D. W. B. Eerdman's Pub. Co.
--Lucius the Centurion. N.D. E. P. Dutton & Co.
--The Physician of Galilee. N.D. E. P. Dutton & Co.
--The Royal Inn. N.D. E. P. Dutton & Co.
--Shepherd Boy of Bethlehem. 1st ed. LC 55-144093. 89p. 21cm. 1955. Eerdmans.
--Stephen Collins' Christmas. N.D. Wm. B. Eerdmans Publishing Co.
--Through the Roof. LC 46-18712. 101 p., 1 l. 20 cm. 1946. Wm. B. Eerdmans Publishing Company.

Gossett, Adelaide L. J.
--Lullaby and Cradle Songs. (Illus.). N.D. E. P. Dutton & Co.

Gossett, Margaret
--The Kitten's Secret. Barton, Mary, illus. LC 50-10327. 1950. Wonder Books.

Gossett, Margaret, ed.
--The Real Book of Jokes. 1st ed. Winik, Leon, illus. LC 54-5472. 220p. illus. 22cm. (Real books R44). 1954. Garden City Books, by Arrangement with F. Watts.

Gossett, Margaret, jt. auth. see Elting, Mary.

Gothard, Bill
--The Eagle Story. LC 81-85536. (Illus.). 63p. (gr. 3-12). 1982. (ISBN 0-916888-07-X). Inst Basic Youth.

Gottesman, Meir Uri
--Shpeter. Jones, Yochanan & Koenig, Cara Sue, illus. LC 81-81311. (Illus.). v. 1-2. 29cm. (Judaica Youth Series). N.D. (ISBN 0-910818-35-5). (ISBN 0-910818-36-3). Judaica Press.

Gottfredson, Floyd, intro. by.
--Mickey Mouse. LC 78-15264. (Illus.). 204p. (Walt Disney Best Comics Ser.). 1978. (ISBN 0-89659-005-4). Abbeville Pr.

Gottfried, Polly
--Some Things Are for Keeping. Dugan, William J., illus. LC 67-7748. (ps-3). 1967. (ISBN 0-8054-4602-8). Broadman.

Gottlieb, Gerald (1923-)
--Adventures of Ulysses. Savage, Steele (1900-), illus. LC 59-5522. (Illus.). 22cm. 170p. (World Landmark Ser.: No. 40). (gr. 5-9). 1959. (ISBN 0-394-80540-2, BYR). (ISBN 0-394-90540-7). Random.

Gottlieb, Robin, tr. see Frere, Maud.

Gottlieb, Robin (1928-)
--Mystery Aboard the Ocean Princess. Korach, Mimi (1922-), illus. LC 67-39371. 125p. illus. 21cm. 1967. Funk & Wagnalls.
--Mystery of the Forgotten Diamond. 192p. c.1962. Funk & Wagnalls.
--Mystery of the Jittery Dog-Walker. Korach, Mimi (1922-), illus. LC 66-12581. (Illus.). 21cm. 126p. (gr. 3-7). 1966. (ISBN 0-308-80022-2). Funk & W.
--Mystery of the Marco Polo Ring. Korach, Mimi (1922-), illus. LC 68-11904. (Illus.). 128 p. 21cm. 1968. Funk & Wagnalls.
--Mystery of the Silent Friends. Brule, Al, illus. LC 64-11121. 116 p. illus. 21 cm. 1964. Funk & Wagnalls.
--Secret of the Unicorn. Korach, Mimi (1922-), illus. LC 65-11724. (Illus.). 21cm. 115p. (gr. 3-7). 1965. (ISBN 0-308-80017-6). Funk & W.
--So Much Can Happen. LC 63-8868. 183 p. illus. 23 cm. 1963. Funk & Wagnalls.
--That Summer in Paris. LC 61-6813. 22cm. 182p. (gr. 7-11). 1961. (ISBN 0-308-80183-0). Funk & W.

Gottlieb, William Paul (1917-)
--Farmyard Friends. Gottlieb, William Paul (1917-), illus. LC 56-59040. unpaged. illus. 21cm. (Little golden book, 272). 1956. Simon and Schuster.
--The Four Seasons. Gottlieb, William Paul (1917-), illus. LC 57-127347. unpaged. illus. 33cm. (Big golden book, 413). c.1957. Simon and Schuster.
--Laddie and the Little Rabbit. Gottlieb, William Paul (1917-), illus. LC 52-4204. unpaged. illus. 21cm. (Little golden library, 116). 1952. Simon and Schuster.
--Laddie, the Superdog. Gottlieb, William Paul (1917-), illus. LC 54-9026. unpaged. illus. 21cm. (Little golden book, 185). 1954. Simon and Schuster.
--The New Kittens. Gottlieb, William Paul (1917-), illus. (Little Golden Book). 1957. Golden Press.
--Pal and Peter. Gottlieb, William Paul (1917-), illus. (Little Golden Book). 1956. Golden Press.
--Pal and Peter. Gottlieb, William Paul (1917-), illus. LC 56-4679. unpaged. illus. 21cm. (Little golden book, 285). 1956. Simon and Schuster.
--A Pony for Tony. Gottlieb, William Paul (1917-), illus. LC 55-14337. unpaged. illus. 21cm. (Little golden book, 220). 1955. Simon and Schuster.
--Tiger's Adventure. Gottlieb, William Paul (1917-), illus. LC 54-14964. unpaged. illus. 21cm. (Little golden book, 208). 1954. Simon and Schuster.

Gottschalck, Oscar Hunt von (1865-)
--In Gnome Man's Land. LC 3-26163. (Illus.). 58p. 22cm. 1903. F. A. Stokes Company.
--Innocent Industries: Or, Kindergarten Tales for Industrious Infants. 50 p. illus. 29 cm. 1903. R. H. Russell.
--Lives of the Haunted. LC 3-2776. (Illus.). 64p. 23 x 30cm. 1902. R. H. Russell.

Gottschalk, Elin Toona (1937-)
--In Search of Coffee Mountains. LC 77-15071. p. cm. 21cm. 203p. c.1977. (ISBN 0-8407-6558-4). T. Nelson.

Gottschalk, Fruma Kasdan (1900-), retold by.
--The Runaway Soldier, and Other Tales of Old Russia. Lissim, Simon (1900-1981), illus. LC 46-25275. x p., 1 l., 161 p., 1 l. illus., col. plates. 21 x 16 cm. 1946. A. A. Knopf.
--Two Short Stories: The Stationmaster, and A Shot. LC 48-1937. 17cm. 72p. (Graded Russian Readers, Book 2). (The Heath-Chicago Russian Ser.). 1946. D. C. Heath.
--The Youngest General: A Story of Lafayette. Busoni, Rafaello (1900-1962), illus. LC 49-8467. vii, 169, iii p. illus. 22 cm. 1949. A. A. Knopf.

Gotwalt, Helen Louise Miller
--Gold Medal Plays for Holidays: Thirty Royalty-Free, One-Act Plays for Children. LC 58-5793. 432 p. 21cm. 1958. Plays, Inc.

Goudey, Alice E. (1898-)
--Butterfly Time. Nonnast, Marie (1924-), illus. LC 64-16185. 1 v. (unpaged) col. illus. 26 cm. 1964. Scribner.
--Danny Boy, the Picture Pony. LC 52-12454. 94 p. illus. 19 cm. 1952. Scribner.
--The Day We Saw the Sun Come up. Adams, Adrienne (1906-), illus. LC 61-5787. (Illus.). unpaged. 26cm. 1961. Scribner. **Awards: (ALA); (RCM).**
--The Good Rain. 1st ed. Unwin, Nora Spicer (1907-), illus. LC 50-9637. (Illus.). 31p. 27cm. 1950. Aladdin Books.
--Good Rain. Unwin, Nora Spicer (1907-), illus. N.D. E. P. Dutton & Co.
--Graywings. Nannast, Marie, illus. LC 63-10388. 63 p. illus. (part col.) 21 cm. 1964. Scribner.
--Here Come the Bears. MacKenzie, Garry (1921-), illus. LC 54-5924. (Illus.). 19 cm. 92p. (Encore Ser.). (gr. 1-5). 1954. (ISBN 0-684-13365-2, ScribJ). Scribner.
--Here Come the Beavers!. MacKenzie, Garry (1921-), illus. LC 57-11559. 94p. illus. 19cm. 1957. Scribner.
--Here Come the Cottontails!. MacKenzie, Garry (1921-), illus. LC 65-153531. 93p. illus. (pt. col.) 19cm. N.D. Scribners.
--Here Come the Deer. MacKenzie, Garry (1921-), illus. LC 55-6915. (Illus.). 19 cm. 92p. (gr. 1-5). 1955. (ISBN 0-684-82094-3). Scribner.
--Here Come the Elephants. (Illus.). (Encore Edition). (gr. 1-5). 1965. (ISBN 0-684-15835-3, ScribJ). Scribner.
--Here Come the Elephants!. MacKenzie, Garry (1921-), illus. LC 55-10139. 92p. illus. 19cm. 1955. Scribner.
--Here Come the Lions!. MacKenzie, Garry (1921-), illus. LC 56-6140. 94p. illus. 19cm. 1956. Scribner.
--Here Come the Seals!. MacKenzie, Garry (1921-), illus. LC 57-5169. 93p. illus. 19cm. 1957. Scribner.
--Here Come the Whales!. MacKenzie, Garry (1921-), illus. LC 56-10259. 94p. illus. 19cm. 1956. Scribner.
--Here Come the Wild Dogs. MacKenzie, Garry (1921-), illus. LC 58-6740. 19cm. 91p. 1958. Scribner.
--Houses from the Sea. Adams, Adrienne (1906-), illus. (Illus.). (gr. k-4). 1959. (ISBN 0-684-12458-0, ScribJ). (ISBN 0-684-12783-0). Scribner. **Award: (RCM).**
--Jupiter and the Cats. Brown, Paul (1893-1958), illus. LC 53-2661. 90p. illus. 19cm. 1953. Scribner.
--The Merry Fiddlers. Garbutt, Bernard (1900-), illus. LC 51-3816. (Illus.). 22cm. 47p. 1951. Aladdin Books.
--Smokey, the Well-Loved Kitten. Wohlberg, Meg (1905-), illus. LC 52-9005. 21cm. 1952. Lothrop, Lee and Shepard.
--Sunnyvale Fair. Galdone, Paul (1914-), illus. LC 62-9081. (Illus.). unpaged. 22cm. 1962. Scribner.

Goudge, Elizabeth (1900-1984)
--The Blue Hills. Watson, Aldren Auld (1917-), illus. LC 42-235544. 266 p. incl. col. illus., col. plates. 21 cm. 1942. Coward-McCann.
--Christmas Book. (gr. 7 up). 1967. Coward.
--I Saw Three Ships. Tomes, Margot Ladd (1917-), illus. LC 75-88867. (Illus.). 60 p. 24cm. 1st U.S. edition. 1969. Coward McCann.
--Linnets and Valerians. LC 80-28785. p. cm. (Gregg Press Children's Literature Ser.). 1981, c.1964. (ISBN 0-8398-2750-4). Gregg Press.
--Linnets and Valerians. Ribbons, Ian (1924-), illus. LC 64-17997. 290 p. 21cm. 1964. Coward-McCann. **Award: (ALA).**
--The Little White Horse. Hodges, Cyril Walter (1909-), illus. LC 47-185962. vi, 286 p. col. front., illus., col. plates. 18 cm. 1946. Gregg Press.
--The Little White Horse. Hodges, Cyril Walter (1909-), illus. Flanagan, Kate, intro. by. LC 79-17992. (Illus.). 280 p. 21cm. (Gregg Press Children's Literature Ser.). 1980, c.1946. (ISBN 0-8398-2607-9). Gregg Press. **Award: (CMA).**
--The Lost Angel. (Illus.). 1971. (ISBN 0-698-10220-7, Coward). Putnam Pub Group.
--The Reward of Faith. Unwin, Nora Spicer (1907-), illus. 1951. Coward-McCann, Inc.
--The Sister of the Angels. Hodges, Cyril Walter (1909-), illus. 1939. Coward-McCann, Inc.
--Smoky House. Floethe, Richard (1901-), illus. LC 40-277303. 286 p. incl. col. illus., col. plates. 21 cm. c.1940. Coward-McCann.
--The Valley of Song. Floethe, Richard (1901-), illus. LC 52-12096. 281 p. illus. 22 cm. 1952. Coward-McCann.
--The Well of the Star. LC 41-24257. 4 p. l., 3-42 p. 19 cm. c.1941. Coward-McCann, Inc.

Gouffe, Marie
--Treasures Beyond the Snows. Sellon, Michael B., illus. LC 77-95392. (Illus.). 103 p. 22cm. (Quest book for children). 1970. Theosophical Pub. House.

Gough, Clifford
--Sixty Selected Poems and Songs for Our Little Ones. N.D. Meador Publishing Co.

Gough, Irene
--The Golden Lamb. Murray, Joy, illus. LC 68-20643. (Illus.). 41 p. 22cm. 1968. Lerner Publications Co.

Gould, Carmen & Ely, Luise
--Showtime with Hoky Horse: A Creative Dramatics Book for Young Play-Makers. Aloise, Frank E., illus. LC 63-9577. 25p. col. illus. 29cm. (Young owl bk., YL7). 1964. Holt.

Gould, Chester (1900-1985)
--Dick Tracy, Ace Detective: An Original Story Based on the Famous Newspaper Strip "Dick Tracy". authorized. LC 43-22699. 3 p. l., 11-248 p. illus. 20 1/2 cm. 1913. Whitman Publishing Company.
--Dick Tracy and Dick Tracy Jr., and How They Captured Stooge Viller. (Dick Tracy and Dick Tracy Jr. Ser.). N.D. Cupples & Leon Co.
--Dick Tracy Meets the Night Crawler: An Original Story Based on the Famous Newspaper Strip "Dick Tracy". LC 45-10592. 3 p. l., 11-247 p. illus. 20 cm. 1945. Whitman Publishing Company.
--How Dick Tracy and Dick Tracy Jr. Caught the Racketeers. (Dick Tracy and Dick Tracy, Jr. Ser.). N.D. Cupples & Leon Co.

Gould, Dorothea Louise Knauff (1899-)
--Little Acres: The Story of Two Puppies. Aninger, Elizabeth Zickler, illus. LC 44-63762. 28 p. illus. 24 x 22 cm. 1944. The Rhinestone Press.

Gould, Edith Kingdon
--The Poems of Edith Kingdon Gould. LC 35-60. 56 p. front. (port.) 22 cm. c.1934. W. H. Sadlier, Inc.

Gould, Elizabeth Lincoln (0000-1914), adapted by see Alcott, Louisa May.

Gould, Elizabeth Lincoln (0000-1914)
--The Admiral's Granddaughter. Smith, Wuanita (1866-), illus. LC 7-23940. 202 p. front., 4 pl. 20 cm. (Sunbeam Ser. for Young People). 1907. The Penn Publishing Company.
--The Admiral's Little Companion. Smith, Wuanita (1866-), illus. LC 12-211420. 223 p. front., plates. 20 cm. 1912. The Penn Publishing Company.
--The Admiral's Little Housekeeper. Smith, Wuanita (1866-), illus. LC 10-160909. 202 p. front., plates. 20 cm. (Sunbeam Ser. for Young People). 1910. The Penn Publishing Company.
--The Admiral's Little Secretary. (The Admiral Ser.). N.D. Penn.
--Barbara and the Five Little Purrs. Bruce, Josephine, illus. N.D. Dodge.
--Barbara and the Five Little Purrs. Bruce, Josephine, illus. LC 9-20913. 5 p. l., 115 p. incl. illus., plates. col. front., col. plates. 20 cm. c.1908. H. M. Caldwell Co.
--Cap'n Gid. (The Outdoor Bks.). N.D. Penn.
--Felicia. Bruce, Josephine, illus. LC 8-19571. 192 p. front., 4 pl. 20 cm. (Sunbeam Ser. for Young People). 1908. The Penn Publishing Company.
--Felicia Visits. LC 10-16091. 202 p. front., plates. 20 cm. (Sunbeam Ser. for Young People). 1910. The Penn Publishing Company.
--Felicia Visits. Bruce, Josephine & Price, Mary L., illus. LC 10-16091. 20cm. 202p. (The Felicia Ser.). N.D. Penn Publishing Co.
--Felicia's Folks. (The Felicia Ser.). N.D. Penn.
--Felicia's Friends. Bruce, Josephine, illus. LC 9-16109. 186 p. front., 4 pl. 20 cm. 1909. The Penn Publishing Company.
--Grandma. (The Outdoor Bks.). N.D. Penn.
--Little Polly Prentiss. Waugh, Ida & Otis, Elizabeth, illus. (The Polly Prentiss Ser.). N.D. Penn Publishing Co.
--Little Polly Prentiss. Waugh, Ida, illus. LC 2-14858. iii, 192 p. front., plates. 20 cm. (Sunbeam Ser. for Young People). 1902. The Penn Publishing Company.
--Polly Prentiss Goes a-Visiting. Otis, Elizabeth, illus. LC 13-18602. 200 p. front., plates. 20 cm. 1913. The Penn Publishing Company.
--Polly Prentiss Goes a-Visiting. Waugh, Ida & Otis, Elizabeth, illus. (The Polly Prentis Ser.). N.D. Penn Publishing Co.
--Polly Prentiss Goes to School. LC 12-19160. 205 p. front., plates. 20 cm. 1912. The Penn Publishing Company.

Grabianski, Janusz (1928-1976), illus.
--Grimm's Fairy Tales. (Original Authors: The Brothers Grimm). (Illus.). (gr. 4-6). 1966. Hawthorn.
Grabo, Carl Henry (1881-)
--The Cat in Grandfather's House. Iserman, M. F., illus. LC 20-20590. 192 p. col. front., illus., col. plates. 22 cm. c.1929. Laidlaw Brothers.
--Peter and the Princess. Neill, John Rea (1878-1943), illus. 1921. Reilly & Lee.
Graboff, Abner (1919-)
--Do Catbirds Wear Whiskers?. LC 67-14805. 1 v. (unpaged) illus. 24cm. 1967. Putnam.
--Do You See What I See?. Graboff, Abner (1919-), illus. (gr. k-3). 1976. (ISBN 0-590-10124-2, Schol Pap). Schol Bk Serv.
--A Fresh Look at Cats. LC 63-13856. unpaged. illus. 23 cm. 1963. F. Watts.
--In a Cat's Eye. (Illus.). 1976. (ISBN 0-912846-25-9). Bookstore Pr.
Graboff, Abner (1919-), illus.
--Old Macdonald Had a Farm. (Illus.). 32p. (gr. k-3). 1970. (ISBN 0-590-01622-9). (ISBN 0-590-09098-4). Scholastic Inc.
--Old Macdonald Had a Farm. Repr. (Starbright Editions). (gr. k-3). 1973. Schol Bk Serv.
Grace, Betty
--The Cat with the Green Whiskers. 1st ed. LC 55-12481. 53p. illus. 21cm. c.1955. Pageant Press.
Grace, Fran
--Branigan's Dog. LC 81-6188. p. cm. 1981. (ISBN 0-87888-186-7). Bradbury Press.
--A Very Private Performance. LC 83-6378. p. cm. 1983. (ISBN 0-02-736650-2). Bradbury Press.
Grace, Nancy
--Earrings for Celia. Siegl, Helen (1924-), illus. LC 63-8506. (Illus.). 45 p. 19cm. 1963. Pantheon.
Grace, Skaar A
--Boy and His Horse. N.D. E . M. Hale and Co.
Gracey, Jean
--Good Morning. Schimmer, Florence & Schimmer, Wim, illus. (A Golden Answer Book). 1962. Golden Press.
Gracey, Yale, adapted by see Disney, Walt, Productions.
Gracia, Debbie
--My Birthday on Christmas Day. Aragon, Hilda, illus. (Illus.). 30p. (Orig.). 1st U.S. edition. (ps-7). 1980. (ISBN 0-915347-05-9). Pueblo Acoma Pr.
Gracza, Margaret Young (1928-), tr. see Hertz, Grete Janus.
Graeber, Charlotte Towner
--Grey Cloud. Bloom, Lloyd, illus. LC 79-14673. (Illus.). 124 p. 22cm. c.1979. (ISBN 0-590-07600-0). Four Winds Press.
--In, Out, and About Catfish Pond. Stockman, Jack (1951-), illus. LC 83-23957. (Illus.). 64 p. 20cm. (I Love to Read). c.1984. (ISBN 0-89191-798-5). Chariot Books.
--In, Out & about Catfish Pond. Stockman, Jack (1951-), illus. (Illus.). (Early Readers Ser.). (gr. 1-4). 1984. (ISBN 0-89191-841-8). (ISBN 0-89191-798-5). Cook.
--Mustard. Diamond, Donna (1950-), illus. LC 81-20764. (Illus.). 42 p. 19cm. c.1982. (ISBN 0-02-736690-1). Macmillan.
--The Thing in Katy's Attic. McCully, Emily Arnold (1939-), illus. LC 84-8117. (Illus.). 80p. (gr. 1-4). 1984. (ISBN 0-525-44146-8). (ISBN 0-525-44146-8). Dutton.
--Up, Down, and Around the Rain Tree. Stockman, Jack (1951-), illus. LC 83-23155. (Illus.). 64 p. 20cm. (I Love to Read). c.1984. (ISBN 0-89191-786-1). Chariot Books.
--Up, Down, & Around the Raintree. Stockman, Jack (1951-), illus. (Early Readers Ser.). (gr. 1-4). 1984. (ISBN 0-89191-840-X). (ISBN 0-89191-786-1). Cook.
Graeber, Jean Boreman, jt. auth. see Gorelick, Molly C.
Graeber, Jean Boreman (1909-)
--Bantie and Her Chicks. Hendrickson, June, illus. LC 59-5029. 22cm. 31p. (Look, Read, Learn Ser.). 1959. Melmont Publishers.
Graef, Robert A., illus.
--The Six Happy Goats. LC 43-4182. 62 p. incl. col. front., illus. (part col.) 17 1/2 x 18 1/2 cm. (Little color classics). 1943. McLoughlin Brothers, Inc.
--The Sleeping Beauty, and Other Fairy Tales. LC 42-1756. (Illus.). 59p. 17cm. (The Little Color Classics). 1942. McLoughlin Bros. Inc.
Grafe, Blanche
--Down in the Valley. 1982. (ISBN 0-533-05143-6). Vantage.
Graff, Carolyn
--The Frightening Flight of Toby Airplane. LC 78-78368. (Illus.). 26p. 1980. (ISBN 0-533-04212-7). Vantage.
Graff, Polly Anne Colver see Colver, Anne.
Graff, Polly Anne Colver, jt. auth. see Graff, S. Stewart.
Graff, Polly Anne Colver (1908-)
--Borrowed Treasure. Krigstein, Bernard (1919-), illus. LC 58-9941. 83 p. illus. 21 cm. (Borzoi books for young people). 1958. Knopf.
--Bread-and-Butter Indian. Williams, Garth Montgomery (1912-), illus. LC 64-11872. (Illus.). 96 p. 22cm. 1964. Holt, Rinehart and Winston.
--Bread-and-Butter Journey. 1st ed. Williams, Garth Montgomery (1912-), illus. LC 73-80315. (Illus.). 101 p. 22cm. 1970. Holt, Rinehart, and Winston.
--Lucky Four. Orbaan, Albert F. (1913-), illus. LC 60-12843. 150 p. illus. 21 cm. 1960. Duell, Sloan and Pearce.
--Nobodys Birthday. Bileck, Marvin (1920-), illus. LC 59-10020. unpaged. illus. 23 cm. 1961. Knopf.
--Old Bet. Palazzo, Tony (1905-1970), illus. LC 57-5255. (Illus.). 28cm. 1957. Knopf.
--Secret Castle. Low, Vaike, illus. LC 60-5512. 113 p. illus. 21 cm. (Borzoi books for young people). 1960. (ISBN 0-394-81599-8). Knopf.
--Shamrock Cargo: A Story of the Irish Potato Famine. Gretzer, John, illus. LC 52-5487. 182 p. illus. 22 cm. (Winston adventure books). 1952. Winston.
--Theodosia: Daughter of Aaron Burr. rev. ed. LC 62-10213. 182 p. 22 cm. 1962. Holt, Rinehart and Winston.
--Theodosia, Daughter of Aaron Burr. Blaisdell, Elinore (1904-), illus. LC 41-3684. 21cm. 291p. 1941. Farrar & Rinehart.
--Yankee Doodle Painter. 1st ed. Ames, Lee Judah (1921-), illus. LC 55-8949. 175 p. illus. 21 cm. 1955. Knopf.
Graff, Polly Anne Colver (1908-) & Graff, S. Stewart (1908-)
--The Wayfarer's Tree. LC 72-89842. 103 p. 22cm. 1973. (ISBN 0-525-42290-0). Dutton.
Graff, S. Stewart, jt. auth. see Graff, Polly Anne Colver.
Graff, S. Stewart (1908-) & Graff, Polly Anne Colver (1908-)
--Squanto: Indian Adventurer. Doremus, Robert (1913-), illus. LC 65-10158. 80p. col. illus. 23cm. (Amer. Indian). c.1965. Garrard.
Grafton, Ann, pseud., see Owens, Thelma Phlegar.
Grafton, Ann, pseud. (1905-)
--I, Roger Ellis, Know It All. Owens, Thelma Phlegar. Obligado, Lilian Isabel (1931-), illus. LC 69-12153. (Illus.). 128 p. 22cm. 1969. Funk & Wagnalls.
Grag, Wanda
--Nothing At All. N.D. E. M. Hale & Co.
Graglia, Richard, tr. see Gallaz, Christopher & Innocenti, Roberto.
Graha, Vera M.
--Treasure in the Covered Wagon. Simon, Howard (1903-1979), illus. 191p. 1952. J. B. Lippincott Co.
Graham, Ada (1931-) & Graham, Frank, Jr. (1925-)
--Coyote Song. Tyler, D. D., illus. LC 78-50436. (Audubon Readers Ser.: No. 4). (gr. 5 up). 1978. Delacorte.
--Jacob & Owl. Stoke, Frank & Stoke, Dorothea, photos by (Illus.). (gr. 3-7). 1981. (ISBN 0-698-20516-2, Coward). Putnam Pub Group.
--Jacob and Owl: A Story. (Illus.). 1982. Putnam.
--Jacob and Owl: A Story. Stoke, Frank & Stoke, Dorothea, photos by LC 81-3119. (Illus.). 63 p. 24cm. c.1981. (ISBN 0-698-20516-2). Coward, McCann & Geoghegan.
--The Mystery of the Everglades. (Illus.). 1975. (ISBN 0-394-82318-4). (ISBN 0-394-92318-9). Random House.
Graham, Al (1897-)
--Down with Dinosaurs: Verses. Palazzo, Tony (1905-1970), illus. LC 63-16820. 61 p. illus. 19 cm. 1963. Duell, Sloan and Pearce.
--The Mouse with the Small Guitar. Palazzo, Tony (1905-1970), illus. LC 47-11971. (Illus.). 35p. 24cm. 1947. R. Welch Co.
--The Rhymes of Squire O'Squirrel. Palazzo, Tony (1905-1970), illus. LC 63-10360. 60 p. illus. 28 cm. 1963. Duell, Sloan and Pearce.
--Songs for a Small Guitar. 1st ed. Palazzo, Tony, pseud. (1905-1970), illus. Palazzo, Anthony D.. LC 62-8531. (Illus.). 59p. 29cm. 1962. Duell, Sloan and Pearce.
--Timothy Turtle. Palazzo, Tony (1905-1970), illus. (Illus., Pub. by Viking Pr). (Viking Seafarer Ser). (gr. k-3). 1970. (ISBN 0-670-05035-0, Puffin). Penguin.
--Timothy Turtle. Palazzo, Tony (1905-1970), illus. (Illus.). (ps-2). 1946. (ISBN 0-670-71579-4). Viking Pr. **Award: (RCM).**
Graham, Al (1897-), retold by.
--The Pied Piper. Palazzo, Tony (1905-1970), illus. LC 63-20602. 1 v. (unpaged) col. illus. 29 cm. (Splendor book). c.1963. Duell, Sloan and Pearce.
Graham, Alberta Powell
--Strike Up the Band. N.D. Nelson Bks.
Graham, Alice H.
--The Desert Ballet. 1970. (ISBN 0-912472-01-4). Miller Books.
Graham, Andrew J
--The Lost Document: A Story of the Northwest. LC 36-298167. 80 p., 1 l. incl. front., pl. 14 x 11 cm. N.D. Printed by F. F. Henning.
Graham, Benzell
--That Big Broozer. (Illus.). (gr. 3-5). 1959. (ISBN 0-8382-0850-9). Hale.
--That Big Broozer. Galdone, Paul (1914-), illus. (Illus.). (gr. 3-6). 1959. Morrow.
Graham, Bob
--First There Was Frances. LC 85-17141. p. cm. 1986, c.1985. (ISBN 0-02-737030-5). Bradbury Press.
--Libby, Oscar & Me. LC 84-45430. (Illus.). 32 p. 26cm. 1985, c.1984. (ISBN 0-911745-89-0). Bedrick/Blackie : Distributed by Harper and Row.
--Libby, Oscar & Me. LC 84-18213. p. cm. 1st U.S. edition. 1985. (ISBN 0-399-21232-9). Putnam.
--Pearl's Place. Graham, Bob, illus. LC 85-47503. (Illus.). 32 p. 27cm. 1st U.S. edition. 1985, c.1983. (ISBN 0-87226-019-4). P. Bedrick Books : Distributed by Harper and Row.
--Pete & Roland. (Illus.). 28p. (gr. 1). 1983. (ISBN 0-00-184344-3, Pub. by W Collins Australia). Intl Schol Bk Serv.
Graham, Brenda Knight (1942-)
--The Pattersons & the Goat Men. LC 80-68468. (gr. 5-9). 1981. (ISBN 0-8054-4803-9). Broadman.
--The Pattersons and the Mysterious Airplane. Shaw, Charles (1941-), illus. LC 79-6022. (Illus.). 96 p. 21cm. c.1980. (ISBN 0-8054-4802-0). Broadman Press.
--The Pattersons at Turkey Hill House. Shaw, Charles (1941-), illus. LC 79-52002. (Illus.). 89 p. 22cm. c.1979. (ISBN 0-8054-4801-2). Broadman Press.
Graham-Cameron, Mike
--Cats. Herbert, Helen, illus. (Illus.). (Dinosaur Ser.). (gr. 2-5). 1978. (ISBN 0-85122-151-3, Pub. by Dino Pub). Merrimack Pub Cir.
Graham, Carolyn
--The Electric Elephant & Other Stories. (Illus., Orig.). 1982. (ISBN 0-19-503229-2). Oxford U Pr.
--Jazz Chants for Children. (Illus.). 1979. (ISBN 0-19-502496-6). (ISBN 0-19-502497-4). (ISBN 0-19-502575-X). tchrs' ed & cassette 15.00x. (ISBN 0-19-502576-8). Oxford U Pr.
Graham, Eleanor (1896-), ed. see Barrie, James Matthew, Sir.
Graham, Eleanor (1896-), ed. see Farjeon, Eleanor.
Graham, Eleanor (1896-1984), ed.
--Children Who Lived in a Barn. 224p. (Story Books). (gr. 2-5). 1975. (ISBN 0-14-030091-0, Puffin). Penguin.
--Eleanor Farjeon's Book. (gr. 4-6). 1973. (ISBN 0-14-030141-0, Puffin). Penguin.
--Famous Fairy Tales. (gr. k-3). N.D. (ISBN 0-448-00505-0, Wonder Books). Grosset & Dunlap.
--Favorite Nursery Tales ... Dixon, Rachel Taft, illus. LC 46-215719. 41 p. illus. (part col.) 25 x 19 cm. 1946. Wonder Books.
--Happy Holidays: Stories, Legends and Customs of Red Letter Days. Ellingford, Priscilla M., illus. 1933. E. P. Dutton & Co.
--Puffin Book of Verse. (gr. 3-5). 1953. (ISBN 0-14-030072-4, Puffin). Penguin.
--A Puffin Quartet of Poets:. Eleanor Farjeon, James Reeves, E.V. Rieu and Ian Serraillier. Bloomfield, Diana, illus. LC 58-2901. (Illus.). 189p. 18cm. (Puffin Bks.). 1958. Penguin Books.
--A Thread of Gold: An Anthology of Poetry. Gill, Margery Jean (1925-), illus. LC 75-99030. (Illus.). 96 p. 21cm. (Granger index reprint series). 1969, c.1964. Books for Libraries Press.
--Three Little Kittens and Other Nursery Tales. Dixon, Rachel Taft, illus. N.D. Grosset & Dunlap.
--Welcome Christmas!. Legends, Carols, Stories, Riddles. Ellingford, Priscilla M., illus. 1932. Dutton.
Graham, Ennis, pseud., see Molesworth, Mary Louisa Stewart.
Graham, Ennis, pseud. (1842-)
--Carrots. Molesworth, Mary Louisa Stewart. (Series of Works for the Young). N.D. Macmillan & Co.
--A Christmas Child. Molesworth, Mary Louisa Stewart. Crane, Walter (1845-1915), illus. (Illus.). N.D. Macmillian.
--Christmas Tree Land. Molesworth, Mary Louisa Stewart. (Illus.). N.D. Macmillian.
--Tell Me a Story. Molesworth, Mary Louisa Stewart. (Series of Books for the Young). N.D. Macmillan & Co.
Graham, Frank, Jr., jt. auth. see Graham, Ada.
Graham, Gail B.
--The Beggar in the Blanket & Other Vietnamese Tales. Bryan, Brigitte, illus. LC 77-85548. (Illus.). 95 p. 23cm. 1970. Dial Press.
--Cross-Fire: A Vietnam Novel. Martin, David Stone (1913-), illus. LC 71-175953. (Illus.). 135 p. 22cm. 1972. (ISBN 0-394-82380-X). (ISBN 0-394-92380-4). Pantheon Books.
Graham, Harriet
--Peanuts, Popped Corn, & Lemonade. 1982. (ISBN 0-533-05286-6). Vantage.
--The Ring of Zoraya. LC 81-8082. p. cm. 1982. (ISBN 0-689-30880-9). Atheneum.
--The Street That Disappeared. LC 76-380238. 176 p. 21cm. 1976. (ISBN 0-233-96781-8). Deutsch.
--Thomas and the Rag Man's Coat. LC 74-12291. p. cm. 1975, c.1974. (ISBN 0-87599-215-3). S. G. Phillips.
Graham, Helen Holland
--Little Don Pedro. 1959. (ISBN 0-8382-0445-7, Cadmus Books). E. M. Hale And Company.
--Little Don Pedro. Borten, Helen Jacobson (1930-), illus. LC 59-11280. (Illus.). 61 p. 21cm. c.1959. Abelard-Schuman.
Graham, Helen Holland & Huff, Barbara A.
--Taco, the Snoring Burro. Borten, Helen Jacobson (1930-), illus. LC 57-543817. unpaged. illus. 21cm. 1957. Abelard-Schuman.
Graham, Henry H
--Molly Fox And Other Stories. LC 37-109223. v, 7-119 p. illus. 19 cm. c.1937. The Warner Press.
Graham, Hugh, pseud., see Barrows, Ruth Marjorie.
Graham, Janet Pollock
--The Enchanted Wood. 1st ed. Kilgore, Al, illus. LC 54-12534. 102p. illus. 24cm. 1954. Pageant Press.
Graham, Janette Sargeant
--Challenge of the Coulee. LC 54-7682. (Illus.). 197 p. 21cm. 1954. Longmans, Green.
--Madcap Jeanie. Doane, Pelagie (1906-1966), illus. 21cm. 207p. N.D. Dodd, Mead & Co.
--The Secret of Plenty House. LC 52-10469. 216 p. 21cm. 1952. Dodd, Mead.
--Venture at Lake Tahogan. 1st ed. LC 56-6169. 174p. 22cm. 1956. Longmans, Green.
Graham, John (1926-)
--Crowd of Cows. Rojankovsky, Feodor Stepanovich (1891-1970), illus. LC 68-11500. (gr. k-3). 1968. (ISBN 0-15-220980-8). (ISBN 0-15-220981-6). HarBraceJ.
--I Love You, Mouse. De Paola, Tomie, pseud. (1934-), illus. De Paola, Thomas Anthony. LC 76-8022. 22cm. 32p. c.1976. (ISBN 0-15-238005-1). Harcourt Brace Jovanovich.
--I Love You, Mouse. De Paola, Tomie, pseud. (1934-), illus. De Paola, Thomas Anthony. LC 78-6214. p. cm. (Voyager/HBJ book). 1978, c.1976. (ISBN 0-15-644106-3). Harcourt Brace Jovanovich.
Graham, Judy
--Bird's Eye. (Illus.). 1981. (ISBN 0-914676-62-8, Star & Eleph Bks). Green Tiger Pr.
Graham, Kennon, pseud., see Harrison, David Lee.
Graham, Kennon, pseud. (1937-)
--Bugs Bunny, In Escape from Noddington Castle. Harrison, David Lee. Baker, Darrell, illus. 24p. (A Big Picture Bks.). (gr. k-3). 1979. (ISBN 0-307-10827-9, Golden Pr). (ISBN 0-307-60827-1). Western Pub.
--Bugs Bunny-Kingdom of Dimly. Harrison, David Lee. Baker, Darrell, illus. (Illus.). 24p. (ps-k). N.D. (ISBN 0-307-10827-9, Golden Pr). Western Pub.
--Lassie & the Secret Friend. Harrison, David Lee. Schaar, Robert, illus. (Illus.). 32p. (ps-1). 1972. (ISBN 0-307-60059-9, Golden Pr). Western Pub.
--Lassie's Big Clean-up Day. Harrison, David Lee. Schaar, Robert, illus. 24p. (Young Reader Ser.). (ps-3). 1980. (ISBN 0-307-60311-3, Golden Pr). Western Pub.
--My Little Book About Flying. Harrison, David Lee. Irvin, Fred M. (1914-), illus. (Illus.). (Tell-a-Tale Readers). (gr. k-3). 1979. (ISBN 0-307-68646-9, Whitman). Western Pub.
--Smokey Bear Saves the Forest. Harrison, David Lee. Gantz, David, illus. (Illus.). (Tell-a-Tale Readers). (gr. k-3). 1971. (ISBN 0-307-68463-6, Whitman). Western Pub.
Graham, Lillian S., jt. auth. see Wackerbarth, Marjorie.
Graham, Lorenz Bell (1902-)
--Carolina Cracker. 1972. Houghton Mifflin.
--David He No Fear. Grifalconi, Ann (1929-), illus. LC 71-109898. (Illus.). color ils. (gr. 2-5). 1971. (ISBN 0-690-23265-9, TYC-J). Har-Row.
--Detention Center. 1972. Houghton Mifflin.
--God Wash the World and Start Again. Ross, Clare Romano (1922-), illus. LC 75-109900. (Illus.). 40 p. 21cm. 1971, c.1946. (ISBN 0-690-33295-5). Crowell.
--Hongry Catch the Foolish Boy. Brown, James, Jr., illus. LC 77-184981. (Illus.). (gr. 2-5). 1973. (ISBN 0-690-40112-4). T Y Crowell.
--How God Fix Jonah. Calapai, Letterio (1903-), illus. 1946. Reynal.
--I, Momolu. Biggers, John Thomas (1924-), illus. LC 66-6820. (Illus.). 226 p. 21cm. 1966. Crowell.

--North Town. LC 65-12503. (gr. 7 up). 1965. (ISBN 0-690-58750-3). T Y Crowell.
--Return to South Town. LC 75-33712. 245 p. 21cm. c.1976. (ISBN 0-690-01081-8). Crowell.
--A Road Down in the Sea. LC 74-113854. (Illus.). (gr. 5-9). 1971. (ISBN 0-690-70501-8). T Y Crowell.
--Runaway. 1972. Houghton Mifflin.
--Song of the Boat. Dillon, Leo (1933-) & Dillon, Diane (1933-), illus. LC 74-5183. (Illus.). 40 p. 21cm. 1975. (ISBN 0-690-75231-8). (ISBN 0-690-75232-6). Crowell. **Awards: (ALA); (BGH).**
--South Town. (gr. 7 up). 1958. (ISBN 0-695-48220-3). Follett.
--Stolen Car. 1972. Houghton Mifflin.
--Tales of Momolu. Calapai, Letterio (1903-), illus. LC 16 V0V0. 4 p. l. 7 160 p. incl. illus., plates. 21 cm. 1946. Reynal & Hitchcock.
--Whose Town?. LC 69-13639. 246 p. 21cm. 1969. Crowell.

Graham, Lynda
--Pinky Marie: The Story of Her Adventure with the Seven Bluebirds. Kirn, Ann Minette (1910-), illus. LC 40-375512. 16 p. illus. (part col.) 27 x 24 cm. c.1939. The Saalfield Publishing Company.

Graham, Margaret Althea (1924-)
--Marilyn's Adventures. LC 63-15741. 119 p. 21 cm. 1963. Zondervan Pub. House.

Graham, Margaret Bloy, jt. auth. see Zion, Eugene.

Graham, Margaret Bloy (1920-)
--Be Nice to Spiders. Graham, Margaret Bloy (1920-), illus. LC 67-17101. (Illus.). 1 v. (unpaged. 25cm. (ps-2). 1967. Harper & Row.
--Benjy and the Barking Bird. Graham, Margaret Bloy (1920-), illus. LC 79-129856. (Illus.). 31 p. 29cm. (ps-1). 1971. (ISBN 0-06-022079-1). Harper & Row.
--Benjy's Boat Trip. Graham, Margaret Bloy (1920-), illus. LC 77-6893. (Illus.). 32 p. 29cm. c.1977. (ISBN 0-06-022092-9). (ISBN 0-06-022093-7). Harper & Row.
--Benjy's Dog House. LC 72-9854. (Illus.). 31 p. 29cm. 1973. Harper & Row.

Graham, Marguerite
--Fairy Fantasies. Scharff, Adrian, illus. LC 40-34281. 32 l. illus. 29 x 22 cm. c.1940. F. Lunning, Inc.

Graham, Mary
--Grandfather's Last Work. N.D. American Sunday-School Union.

Graham, Mary Nancy, ed.
--Book of Christmas Carols. Doane, Pelagie (1906-1966), illus. N.D. Grosset & Dunlap.
--Fifty Favorite Songs--Fun to Sing--Easy to Play. N.D. Grosset & Dunlap.
--Fifty Songs for Boys and Girls: The Original Tunes. Scott, Janet Laura, illus. LC 36-7179. 3 p. l., 9-60 p. illus. 21 x 21 cm. c.1935. Whitman Publishing Co.

Graham, Mary Stuart Campbell see Stuart, Mary, pseud.

Graham, Percy
--Essential Songs. LC 37-17543. 200 p. col. front., col. paltes 21 x 17 cm. c.1937. American Book Company.

Graham, Rosemary
--Flying O'Flynn. MacDonald, Catriona, illus. N.D. Dodd, Mead & Co.

Graham, Ruth Morris
--The Happy Sound. Zander, Hans (1937-), illus. LC 69-15981. (Illus.). 32 p. 27cm. 1970. Follett.

Graham, Shirley, pseud., see Du Bois, Shirley Graham.

Graham, Shirley, pseud. (1906-1977)
--Jean Baptiste Pointe De Sable, Founder of Chicago. DuBois, Shirley Graham. LC 53-9746. 180 p 22cm. 1953. J. Messner.
--The Story of Phillis Wheatley. Du Bois, Shirley Graham. LC 49-10767. 176 p. illus., port. 22 cm. N.D. J. Messner.
--The Story of Pocahontas. Du Bois, Shirley Graham. Meadowcroft, Enid La Monte, Mrs. (1898-1966), ed. Cooper, Mario (1905-), illus. LC 52-13749. 180p. illus. 22cm. (Signature books, 21). 1953. (ISBN 0-448-05621-6). Grosset & Dunlap.

Graham, Terry Lynne (1949-)
--Fingerplays and Rhymes: For Always and Sometimes. Graham, Terry Lynne (1949-), illus. LC 84-10937. (Illus.). 148, 8 p. 29cm. c.1984. (ISBN 0-89334-083-9). Humanics Ltd.
--Let Loose on Mother Goose. LC 81-80248. (Illus.). 96p. (gr. k-1). 1982. (ISBN 0-86530-030-5). Incentive Pubns.

Graham, Tom, pseud., see Lewis, Sinclair.

Graham, Vera M.
--Treasure in the Covered Wagon: A Story of the Oregon Trail. 1st ed. Simon, Howard (1903-1979), illus. LC 52-7459. 191 p. illus. 21 cm. 1952. Lippincott.

Grahame, Elspeth, ed. see Grahame, Kenneth.

Grahame, Gordon Hill (1889-)
--Maple Leaf Holiday. Vartanian, Raymond J., illus. LC 48-4361. 92 p. illus. (part col.) 22 cm. (Saalfield treasure book). c.1948. Saalfield Pub. Co.

Grahame, Hugh
--Runaway Airplane. Brice, Tony, illus. 17 x 13cm. 61p. 1943. Rand McNally & Co.

Grahame, Kenneth, jt. auth. see Disney, Walt, Productions.

Grahame, Kenneth (1859-1932), ed. see Field, Eugene.

Grahame, Kenneth (1859-1932)
--The Adventures of Mole, Rat & Toad. Palazzo-Craig, Janet, adapted by. Baer, Mary Alice, illus. LC 81-16422. (Illus.). 32p. (The Wind in the Willows Ser.). (gr. 2-5). 1982. (ISBN 0-89375-636-9). (ISBN 0-89375-637-7). Troll Assocs.
--The Battle at Toad Hall. Palazzo-Craig, Janet, adapted by. Baer, Mary Alice, illus. LC 81-16407. (Illus.). 32p. (The Wind in the Willows Ser.). (gr. 2-5). 1982. (ISBN 0-89375-642-3). (ISBN 0-89375-643-1). Troll Assocs.
--Bertie's Escapade. Shepard, Ernest Howard (1879-1976), illus. LC 49-10255. 41 p. illus. 20 cm. 1949. J. B. Lippincott Co.
--Dream Days. 1898. Lane.
--Dream Days. rev. ed. 1899. Lane.
--The First Whisper of "The Wind in the Willows". Grahame, Elspeth, ed. 1945. Lippincott.
--The Golden Age. LC 75-32198. (Illus.). Repr. of 1900 ed. (Classics of Children's Literature, 1621-1932: Vol. 59). 1976. (ISBN 0-8240-2308-0). Garland Pub.
--The Golden Age. 1895. Stone and Kimball.
--The Golden Age & Dream Days. (gr. 4-6). 1964. Dufour.
--The Headswoman, 1 of 6 vols. (The Bodley Booklets Ser.; No. 5). 1900. Set. John Lane.
--Kenneth Grahame's The Wind in the Willows. Cole, Babette, illus. LC 83-80060. c.1983. (ISBN 0-03-063862-3). Holt, Rhinehart, and Winston.
--Mole's Christmas: Or Home Sweet Home. Gooding, Beverley, illus. LC 82-12333. (Illus.). 32p. (gr. k-3). 1983. (ISBN 0-13-599738-0). P-H.
--More Adventures with Mr. Toad. Palazzo-Craig, Janet, adapted by. Baer, Mary Alice, illus. LC 81-16412. (Illus.). 32p. (The Wind in the Willows Ser.). (gr. 2-5). 1982. (ISBN 0-89375-640-7). (ISBN 0-89375-641-5). Troll Assocs.
--The Open Road: From The Wind in the Willows. Gooding, Beverley, illus. LC 79-22614. (Illus.). 32 p. 28cm. c.1979. (ISBN 0-684-16471-X). Scribner.
--The Reluctant Dragon. Fortnum, Peggy, pseud. (1919-), illus. Nuttall-Smith, Margaret Emily Noel. LC 64-7840. 75p. illus. 19cm. N.D. Dufour.
--The Reluctant Dragon. 1st ed. Hague, Michael R., illus. LC 83-209. p. cm. c.1983. Holt, Rinehart, and Winston.
--The Reluctant Dragon. Prestopino, Gregorio, illus. LC 68-21713. (Illus.). 43 p. 29cm. 1968. Grosset & Dunlap.
--The Reluctant Dragon. Shepard, Ernest Howard (1879-1976), illus. 58p. Repr. of 1938 ed. 1953. Holiday House.
--The River Bank: From, "The Wind in the Willows". Adams, Adrienne (1906-), illus. LC 77-3167. (Illus.). 30 p. 27cm. c.1977. (ISBN 0-684-15046-8). Scribner.
--Wayfarers All: From the Wind in the Willows. Gooding, Beverley, illus. (Illus.). 32p. (Encore Edition). (gr. 1 up). 1981. (ISBN 0-684-16876-6, ScribJ). Scribner.
--The Wind in the Willow. Milne, Alan Alexander (1882-1956) & Rackman, Arthur (1867-), eds. LC 62-5755. (Illus.). 25cm. 199p. (The Heritage Illustrated Bookshelf). 1966, c.1945. Heritage Press.
--The Wind in the Willows. LC 85-13538. p. cm. 1985. (ISBN 0-915361-32-9). Adama Books.
--Wind in the Willows. (Illus.). 224p. (Illustrated Junior Library). 1981. (ISBN 0-448-11028-8, G&D). Putnam Pub Group.
--The Wind in the Willows. (Deluxe Illustrated Classics Ser.). 1977. (ISBN 0-307-12218-2, Golden Pr). Western Pub.
--The Wind in the Willows. Barnhart, Nancy (1889-), illus. LC 8-29339. 3 p. l., 302 p. front. 20 cm. 1908. C. Scribner's Sons.
--The Wind in the Willows. Barnhart, Nancy (1889-), illus. 4 p. l., 350 p., 1 l. col. front., illus., col. pl. 21 cm. 1923. C. Scribner's Sons.
--The Wind in the Willows. Bransom, Paul (1885-), illus. N.D. Charles Scribner's Sons.
--The Wind in the Willows. Burningham, John Mackintosh (1936-), illus. LC 82-16022. p. cm. 1983. (ISBN 0-670-77120-1). Viking Press.
--The Wind in the Willows. Clark, Roberta Carter, illus. LC 67-1926. (Illus.). 254 p. 20cm. (Companion library). 1966. Grosset & Dunlap.
--The Wind in the Willows. Cuffari, Richard (1925-1978), illus. LC 67-410. 220 p. illus. (part col.) 24 cm. (Illustrated junior library). 1966. Grosset & Dunlap.
--The Wind in the Willows. Cuffari, Richard (1925-1978), illus. LC 67-24101. (Illus.). 128 p. 28cm. 1967. Grosset & Dunlap.

--The Wind in the Willows. Hague, Michael R., illus. LC 80-12509. (Illus.). 204 p., 2 leaves of plates. 27cm. c.1980. (ISBN 0-03-056294-5). Ariel Books : Holt, Rinehart and Winston.
--The Wind in the Willows. Rackham, Arthur (1867-1939), illus. N.D. Dial Press Inc.
--The Wind in the Willows. Rackham, Arthur (1867-1939), illus. Milne, Alan Alexander (1882-1956), intro. by. 190 p. illus. 25 cm. (the heritage illustrated bookshelf. 1959, c.1940. Heritage Press.
--The Wind in the Willows. Rackham, Arthur (1867-1939), illus. LC 40-83707. 244, 2 p. col. mounted front., col. mounted plates. 29 cm. 1940. The Limited Editions Club.
--The Wind in the Willows. Robertson, Graham, illus. (Illus.). 322p. 1908. Scribner.
--The Wind in the Willows. Shepard, Ernest Howard (1879-1976), illus. LC 33-27298. 3 p. l., 312 p. illus. 20 cm. 1933. C. Scribner's Sons.
--The Wind in the Willows. Shepard, Ernest Howard (1879-1976), illus. LC 35-4803. vi p., 1 l., 312 p. illus. 19 cm. (Modern standard authors). c.1935. C. Scribner's Sons.
--The Wind in the Willows. Shepard, Ernest Howard (1879-1976), illus. LC 53-2610. 259p. illus. 21cm. 1953. Scribner.
--The Wind in the Willows. Shepard, Ernest Howard (1879-1976), illus. LC 60-5241 (Illus.). 241 p. 24cm. 1960. Scribner.
--The Wind in the Willows. Shepard, Ernest Howard (1879-1976), illus. (Illus.). x, 307 p. 21cm. 1964. Scribner.
--The Wind in the Willows. Shepard, Ernest Howard (1879-1976), illus. Dillenbeck, Maraden V. & Brooke, Ellen W., intro. by. LC 64-21732. x, 307p. illus. 21cm. (Scribner sch. paperbacks, SSP4). 1967. Scribners.
--The Wind in the Willows. Shepard, Ernest Howard (1879-1976), illus. LC 83-11573. (Illus.). x, 244 p., 8 leaves of plates. 24cm. 1983, c.1981. (ISBN 0-684-17957-1). Scribner.
--The Wind in the Willows. unabridged. Stone, David Karl (1922-), illus. LC 68-19470. (Illus.). 254 p. 22cm. (Golden Press classics library). 1968. Golden Press.
--The Wind in the Willows. Tudor, Tasha (1915-), illus. LC 66-14847. (Tasha Tudor is the legal name change for Starling Burgess.). 255 p. illus. (part col.) 24 cm. 1966. World Pub. Co.
--The Wind in the Willows Pop-up-Book. Cole, Babette, illus. LC 83-80060. (Illus.). 12p. (gr. k-4). 1983. (ISBN 0-03-063862-3). HR&W.

Grahame, Kenneth (1859-1932), ed.
--The Cambridge Book of Poetry for Children. LC 16-10825. xv, 288 p. 21 cm. c.1916. G. P. Putnam's Sons; Etc., Etc.
--The Cambridge Book of Poetry for Children. LC 16-8599. 2 v. 20 cm. 1916. The University Press.
--The Cambridge Book of Poetry for Children. New. ed. Raverat, Gwendolen Mary (1885-1957), illus. LC 33-74082. xvii, 238 p. illus. 21 cm. c.1933. G. P. Putnam's Sons.
--The Cambridge Book of Poetry for Children. New. ed. Raverat, Gwendolen Mary (1885-1957), illus. LC 33-135112. xvi, 235, 1 p. illus. 21 cm. 1932. The University Press.

Grahame, Kenneth (1859-1932) & Green, Peter (1924-)
--The Wind in the Willows. LC 82-14080. xxvi, 150 p. 19cm. (The World's Classics). 1983. (ISBN 0-19-281640-3). Oxford University Press.

Grahame, Nellie
--Little Robbie. 139p. N.D. American Tract Society.
--Our Father, 1 of 50 vols. (Illus.). 64p. (Model Library: No.4). 1905. Set. American Tract Society.

Grahame-White, Claude (1879-) & Harper, Harry (1880-)
--The Air King's Treasure: A Story of Adventure with Airship & Aeroplane. Tennant, Dudley, illus. LC 35-28567. vi p., 1 l., 312 p. col. front., 3 col. pl. 21 cm. 1913. Cassell and Company, Ltd.

Grahamer, Kenneth
--Lullaby Land. Robinson, Charles (1870-1937), illus. N.D. Charles Scribner's Sons.

Gramatky, Hardie (1907-1979)
--Bolivar. Gramatky, Hardie (1907-1979), illus. (Illus.). (gr. k-3). 1961. (ISBN 0-399-60063-9). Putnam.
--Creeper's Jeep. Gramatky, Hardie (1907-1979), illus. LC 48-4403. 64 p. col. illus. 25 cm. 1948. G. P. Putnam's Sons.
--Happy's Christmas. Gramatky, Hardie (1907-1979), illus. LC 70-121940. (Illus.). 58 p. 24cm. 1970. Putnam.
--Hercules. Gramatky, Hardie (1907-1979), illus. (Illus.). color ils. 72p. (gr. k-3). 1960. (ISBN 0-399-60240-2). Putnam Pub Group.
--Hercules: The Story of an Old-Fashioned Fire Engine. Gramatky, Hardie (1907-1979), illus. LC 40-341089. 72 p. incl. col. front., illus. (part col.) 26 x 20 cm. c.1940. G. P. Putnam's Sons.

--Homer & the Circus Train. Gramatky, Hardie (1907-1979), illus. LC 57-145590. (Illus.). (gr. k-3). 1957. (ISBN 0-399-60263-1). Putnam.
--Little Toot. (Illus.). (gr. 1-3). 1939. (ISBN 0-8382-0473-2). Hale.
--Little Toot. (Illus.). (gr. k-3). 1959. (ISBN 0-399-20144-0). (ISBN 0-399-60422-7). Putnam Pub Group.
--Little Toot. Gramatky, Hardie (1907-1979), illus. LC 30-24222. 93 p. incl. col. front., illus. (part col.) 21 x 19 cm. c.1939. G. P. Putnam's Sons.
--Little Toot. Gramatky, Hardie (1907-1979), illus. LC 78-4801. (Illus.). 94 p. 20cm. 1978, c.1967. (ISBN 0-399-20144-0). (ISBN 0-399-60422-7). (ISBN 0-399-20649-3). Putnam.
--Little Toot on the Grand Canal. Gramatky, Hardie (1907-1979), illus. LC 68-15048. (Illus.). 86 p. 21cm. 1968. Putnam.
--Little Toot on the Mississippi. Gramatky, Hardie (1907-1979), illus. LC 73-76717. (Illus.). 89 p. 21cm. 1973. (ISBN 0-399-20364-8). (ISBN 0-399-20364-8). Putnam.
--Little Toot on the Thames. Gramatky, Hardie (1907-1979), illus. LC 64-19439. (Illus.). 87 p. 21cm. 1964. Putnam.
--Little Toot Through the Golden Gate. LC 75-10450. (Illus.). 86 p. 21cm. c.1975. (ISBN 0-399-20483-0). Putnam.
--Loopy. Gramatky, Hardie (1907-1979), illus. LC 41-17579. 72 p. incl. col. front., illus. (part col.) 26 x 20 cm. c.1941. G. P. Putnam's Sons.
--Nikos & the Sea God. Gramatky, Hardie (1907-1979), illus. LC 63-15536. 1 v. (unpaged) col. illus. 25 cm. 1963. Putnam.
--Sparky: The Story of a Little Trolley Car. Gramatky, Hardie (1907-1979), illus. LC 52-9833. (Illus.). 66 p. 24cm. 1952. Putnam.

Gram-Swing, Betty, tr. see Gruger, Heribert.

Granberg, Wilbur John (1906-)
--Johnny Gets Out the Vote. 1st ed. Fleur, Anne Elizabeth (1901-), illus. Sari, pseud. LC 52-12502. 174 p. illus. 20 cm. 1952. Aladdin Books.
--Johnny Wants to Be a Policeman. Cummings, Alison, illus. LC 51-12409. 79 p. illus. 20 cm. 1951. Aladdin Books.
--Sons of the Big Muddy: Dakota Territory in the 1880's. 1st ed. Medler, James V., illus. LC 54-6149. 192p. illus. 21cm. (American heritage). 1954. Aladdin Books.

Grand, Gordon
--Colonel Weatherford and His Friends. N.D. The Derrydale Press.

Grandma, pseud., see Styer, Harriet Wasson.

Grandma Moses, pseud., see Moses, Anna Mary Robertson.

Grandma Moses, pseud. (1860-1961), illus.
--The Night Before Christmas. Moses, Anna Mary Robertson, illus. (Illus.). (ps-4). 1962. (ISBN 0-394-80741-3). Random.

Grandmother Hope
--Lottie Wilde's Picnic. (Illus.). N.D. Thomas Y. Crowell & Co.

Grane, Hillis, pseud., see Svenson, Hilda.

Granger, Carol
--Jailer Who Changed His Mind: Paul & Silas. (Illus.). color ils. 32p. (Orig.). (Arch Bks: Set 8). (ps-4). 1971. (ISBN 0-570-06058-3). Concordia.

Granger, Margaret Jane see Granger, Peg, pseud.

Granger, Muriel
--Three Hundred Sixty-Five Bible Stories and Verses. LC 72-94289. (Illus.). 237 p. 29cm. (gr. k-6). 1973. (ISBN 0-307-16819-0). Golden Press.

Granger, Peg, pseud., see Granger, Margaret Jane.

Granger, Peg, pseud. (1925-1977)
--After the Picnic. Granger, Margaret Jane. LC 67-15710. 159 p 22cm. 1967. Lothrop, Lee & Shepard.
--Canyon of Decision. Granger, Margaret Jane. 192 p. 22cm. 1967. Criterion Books.

Granick, Harry (1898-)
--Run, Run. 1941. Golden Press.
--Run, Run!. Duncan, Gregor, illus. 21cm. 276p. 1941. Simon & Schuster.

Granite, Harvey R, jt. ed. see Stanchfield, Jo M.

Granite, Harvey R. (1927-) & Black, Millard H. (1912-), eds.
--Counterpoints. LC 76-147103. (Illus.). 168 p. 24cm. (Houghton Mifflin action series). 1971. (ISBN 0-395-12056-X). Houghton Mifflin.
--Ventures. LC 71-144317. (Illus.). 152 p. 24cm. (Houghton Mifflin action series). 1971. (ISBN 0-395-12050-0). Houghton Mifflin.
--Vibrations. LC 79-147101. (Illus.). 152 p. 24cm. (Houghton Mifflin action series). 1971. (ISBN 0-395-12052-7). Houghton Mifflin.

Granite School District see Stavros, Joyce.

Grannan, Mary
--Happy Playtime. N.D. John C. Winston Co.
--Just Mary Stories. 153p. N.D. G. P. Putnam's Sons.

--Maggie Muggins and Her Animal Friends. Zalusky, Bernard, illus. LC 59-9000. 26cm. 60p. 1959. Pennington Press.
--Maggie Muggins Bedtime Stories. Stern, Lonnie, illus. LC 59-12327. 26cm. 57p. 1959. Pennington Press.
--Maggie Muggins by the Sea. Stern, Lonnie, illus. LC 59-12328. 26cm. 59p. 1959. Pennington Press.
--Maggie Muggins Stories: A Recent Selection of the Famous Canadian Radio Stories. Schmidt, Edwin, illus. LC 50-10544. v, 202 p. illus. 21 cm. 1950. Winston.
--This is Maggie Muggins. Zalusky, Bernard, illus. LC 59-8998. 26cm. 60p. 1959. Pennington Press.
--The Wonderful World of Maggie Muggins. Stern, Lonnie, illus. LC 59-12329. 26cm. 59p. 1959. Pennington Press.
Granniss, Anna Jane (1856-)
--A Christmas Snowflake. (Illus.). N.D. Anna J. Granniss.
Granowsky, Alvin (1936-) & Tweedt, Joy Ann (1951-)
--Chicken Salad Soup. Denman, Michael L., tr. LC 84-9047. (Illus.). 31 p. 21cm. (Modern Curriculum Press Beginning to Read Series). c.1985. (ISBN 0-87895-882-7). (ISBN 0-87895-894-0). Modern Curriculum Press.
--Computer Park. Denman, Michael L., illus. LC 84-9051. (Illus.). 31 p. 21cm. (Modern Curriculum Press Beginning to Read Series). c.1985. (ISBN 0-87895-884-3). (ISBN 0-87895-896-7). Modern Curriculum Press.
--The Computer Rules. Denman, Michael L., illus. (Illus.). 31 p. 21cm. (Modern Curriculum Press Beginning to Read Series). c.1985. (ISBN 0-87895-883-5). (ISBN 0-87895-895-9). Modern Curriculum Press.
--The Fastest One of All. Denman, Michael L., illus. LC 84-9004. (Illus.). 31 p. 21cm. (Modern Curriculum Press Beginning to Read Series). c.1985. (ISBN 0-87895-885-1). (ISBN 0-87895-897-5). Modern Curriculum Press.
--Robert's Robot. Denman, Michael L., illus. LC 84-9083. (Illus.). 31 p. 21cm. (Modern Curriculum Press Beginning to Read Series). c.1985. (ISBN 0-87895-886-X). (ISBN 0-87895-898-3). Modern Curriculum Press.
--Who Said That?. Denman, Michael L., illus. LC 84-9001. (Illus.). 31 p. 21cm. (Modern Curriculum Press Beginning to Read Series). c.1985. (ISBN 0-87895-887-8). (ISBN 0-87895-887-8). Modern Curriculum Press.
Grant, Alice Leigh (1947-), illus.
--Friends Are Like That!. Stories to Read to Yourself. 1st ed. Child Study Children's Book Committee at Bank Street, selected by. LC 78-22513. (Illus.). 114 p. 24cm. c.1979. (ISBN 0-690-03979-4). (ISBN 0-690-03980-8). Crowell.
Grant, Alice Victoria
--Debbie's Pussy Cat. (Illus.). (gr. k-3). 1969. (ISBN 0-682-46823-1). Exposition.
--My Puppy Choo. 1967. (ISBN 0-682-45657-8). Exposition Press.
Grant, Bob, adapted by see Disney, Walt Productions.
Grant, Bruce (1893-1977)
--Cyclone. Frankenberg, Robert Clinton (1911-), illus. 190p. 1959. The World Publishing Company.
--Davy Crockett, American Hero. Timmins, William Frederick, illus. LC 55-10219. unpaged. illus. 21cm. (A Rand McNally Elf Book: No. 523). c.1955. Rand McNally.
--Eagle of the Sea. (Illus.). (gr. 7 up). 1949. (ISBN 0-528-87658-9). Rand.
--Leopard Horse Canyon: The Story of the Lost Appaloosas. LC 57-7406. 221 p. 21cm. 1957. World Pub. Co.
--Longhorn: A Story of the Chisholm Trail. Giesen, Herman D., illus. LC 56-9253. (Illus.). 215 p. 21cm. 1956. World Pub. Co.
--Pancho, a Dog of the Plains. 1st ed. Galdone, Paul (1914-), illus. LC 58-9417. 21cm. 1958. World Pub. Co.
--Ride, Gaucho. Savitt, Sam (1917-), illus. LC 69-13054. (Illus.). 159 p. 21cm. 1969. World Pub. Co.
--Six Gun: A Story of the Texas Rangers. 1st ed. Landau, Jacob (1917-), illus. LC 55-824917. 223p. illus. 21cm. 1955. World Pub. Co.
--The Star-Spangled Rooster. Mars, Witold Tadeusz J. (1912-), illus. LC 61-12013. 119p. 25cm. c.1961. World Pub. Co.
--Warpath,. A Tale of the Plains Indians. Landau, Jacob (1917-), illus. LC 54-8170. (Illus.). 220 p. 21cm. 1954. World Pub. Co.
--Zachary, the Governor's Pig. Frankenberg, Robert Clinton (1911-), illus. 144p. 1960. The World Publishing Company.
Grant, Bruce (1893-1977), ed.
--The Adventures of Robin Hood and His Merry Men: Starring Richard Greene. Authorized. Timmins, William Frederick, illus. LC 55-124571. unpaged. illus. 21cm. (Rand McNally elf book, 532). 1956, c.1955. Rand McNally.
Grant, Campbell (1909-), adapted by see Disney, Walter Elias.
Grant, Campbell, adapted by see Disney, Walt, Productions.
Grant, Captain George Hook (1896-)
--Boy Overboard!. Spier, Peter Edward (1927-), illus. 21cm. 100p. 1961. Little, Brown and Company.
Grant, Clara Louise
--Ukelele and Her New Doll. Grant, Campbell (1909-), illus. (Little Golden Book). 1951. Golden Press.
--Ukelele and Her New Doll. Grant, Campbell (1909-), illus. 21cm. 28p. (Little Golden Book: 102). 1951. Simon and Schuster.
Grant, Clara Odessa Winkler (1901-)
--The Heart of a Child. LC 38-10699. 82 p. 19 cm. c.1938. Golden Rule Publishing Company.
Grant, Cynthia D (1950-)
--Big Time. LC 81-8075. 158 p. 22cm. 1982. (ISBN 0-689-30879-5). Atheneum.
--Hard Love. LC 83-2603. p. cm. 1983. (ISBN 0-689-30985-6). Atheneum.
--Joshua Fortune. LC 80-11983. p. cm. 1980. (ISBN 0-689-30777-2). Atheneum.
--Summer Home. LC 81-1921. p. cm. 1981. (ISBN 0-689-30872-8). Atheneum.
Grant, Davidno, jt. auth. see Leonardo Da Vinci.
Grant, Dorothy Fremont (1900-)
--Adventurous Lady: Margaret Brent of Maryland. Grant, Douglas, illus. LC 57-10094. (American background books). N.D. P.J. Kenedy.
Grant, Eva H. (1913-1977)
--A Cow for Jaya. Hampshire, Michael Allen, illus. LC 72-85618. (Illus.). 62 p. 23cm. (Break-of-day book). 1973. (ISBN 0-698-20232-5). (ISBN 0-698-20232-5). Coward, McCann & Geoghegan.
--Will I Ever Be Older?. Lexa, Susan, illus. Hollingsworth, Charles, intro. by. LC 80-24782. p. cm. c.1981. (ISBN 0-8172-1340-6). Raintree Childrens Books.
Grant, Eva H. (1913-1977) & Mayo, Gretchen
--I Hate My Name. Hollingsworth, Charles, intro. by. LC 80-14428. (Illus.). 31 p. 24cm. c.1980. (ISBN 0-8172-1362-7). Raintree Childrens Books.
Grant, Forsyth A.
--Chums at Last: A Tale of School Life. (Illus.). N.D. Thomas Nelson & Sons.
Grant, Gordon H. (1875-1962)
--The Half Deck. N.D. Little Brown & Co.
--The Secret Voyage. LC 42-174761. 60, 3 p. illus. (part col.) 23 cm. 1942. W. Morrow and Co.
Grant, Gwendoline Ellen (1940-)
--The Lily Pickle Band Book. Chamberlain, Margaret, illus. (Illus.). 128p. 1st U.S. edition. (gr. 2-6). 1983. (ISBN 0-434-94137-9, Pub. by W. Heinemann). David & Charles.
Grant, Hilda Kay (1910-)
--Samuel Cunard, Pioneer of the Atlantic Steamship. LC 67-23076. (Illus.). 192 p. 22cm. 1967. Abelard-Schuman.
Grant, James
--Adventures of Rob Roy. (St. Nicholas Series for Boys). N.D. International Book Co.
--Dick Rodney: Adventures of an Eton Boy. N.D. Nichols & Hall.
--Dick Rodney: Or, the Adventures of an Eton Boy. N.D. George Routledge & Sons.
--Fairer than a Fairy. (Railway Library). N.D. George Routledge & Sons.
--Jack Manly: His Adventures by Sea and Land. N.D. George Routledge & Sons.
--Rob Roy's Adventures, 1 of 3 Vols. (Illus.). (The Rob Roy Library of Adventure). N.D. Set. George Routledge & Sons.
Grant, Jan
--Our New Baby. Lanier, Philip, illus. LC 79-22048. p. cm. 1980. (ISBN 0-516-03938-5). Childrens Press.
Grant, Jim
--The Fableous Land of Parenteenia. Brame, Herb, illus. LC 77-175487. (Illus.). 128 p. 22cm. 1972. (ISBN 0-8024-2508-9). Moody Press.
Grant, Joan
--The Blue Faience Hippopotamus. (Illus.). 60p. (Star & Elephant Ser.). 1984. (ISBN 0-88138-020-2). Green Tiger Pr.
Grant, Joan Marshall, pseud., see Kelsey, Joan Marshall.
Grant, Joan Marshall, pseud. (1907-)
--Redskin Morning, and Other Stories. Kelsey, Joan Marshall. Lavers, Ralph, illus. LC 78-20226. p. cm. (The Works of Joan Grant). 1979. (ISBN 0-405-11787-6). Arno Press.
--The Scarlet Fish and Other Stories. Kelsey, Joan Marshall. Lavers, Ralph, illus. LC 78-20229. (Illus.). 80 p., 7 leaves of plates. 21cm. (Works. 1979.). (The Complete Works of Joan Grant). 1980. (ISBN 0-405-11790-6). Arno Press.
Grant, Joseph Clarence (1908-) & Huemer, Richard Martin (1898-)
--Baby Weems. Benchley, Robert, intro. by. LC 41-11231. (Adapted from the Walt Disney's Production of The Reluctant Dragon). 64 p. illus. 25 cm. 1941. Doubleday, Doran and Company, Inc.
Grant, Leigh (1947-), tr. see Hazen, Barbara Shook.
Grant, Louise (1909-)
--The Fort & the Flag. Grant, Louise (1909-), illus. LC 76-40904. (Illus.). 73 p. 22cm. (Bicentennial historiettes series). 1977. (ISBN 0-915892-09-X). Regional Center for Educational Training.
Grant, Matthew G, pseud., see May, Julian.
Grant, Matthew G, pseud. (1931-)
--Squanto: The Indian Who Saved the Pilgrims. May, Julian. Nelson, John (1928-) & Henriksen, Harold, illus. LC 73-12813. (Illus.). 30 p. 25cm. (His Gallery of great American series. Indians of America). 1974. (ISBN 0-87191-270-8). Creative Education; Distributed by Childrens Press, Chicago.
--A Walk in the Mountains. May, Julian. LC 71-163272. (Illus.). 31 p. 29cm. 1971. Reilly & Lee Books.
Grant, Maude Margaret (1876-)
--Pastime Stories for Boys and Girls. Eulalie, pseud. (1896-), illus. Banks, Eulalie M.. LC 25-814. vi, 202 p. illus. (part col.) 20 cm. c.1924. The Southern Publishing Company.
--Windmills and Wooden Shoes. Cleveland, Bess Bruce, illus. LC 20-17229. (Illus.). 112p. 19cm. 1919. The Southern Publishing Co.
Grant, Myrna Lois (1934-)
--Ivan and the Daring Escape. De Velasco, Joe E., illus. LC 76-8683. (Illus.). 167 p. 18cm. 1976. (ISBN 0-8423-1847-X). Tyndale House Publishers.
--Ivan & the Moscow Circus. (gr. 4-8). 1980. (ISBN 0-8423-1843-7). Tyndale.
--Ivan & the Secret in the Suitcase. (Ivan Ser.). (gr. 3-8). 1975. (ISBN 0-8423-1849-6). Tyndale.
--Ivan and the Star of David. De Velasco, Joe E, illus. LC 77-72439. (Illus.). 142 p. 18cm. c.1977. (ISBN 0-8423-1845-3). Tyndale House Publishers.
Grant, Neil (1938-)
--Barbarossa, the Pirate King. (gr. 7-9). 1972. Hawthorn.
Grant, Robert (1852-)
--Jack Hall: Or, The School Days of an American Boy. Attwood, Francis G., illus. LC 4-17526. vi p., 1 l., 394 p. incl. illus., plates, front. 20 cm. 1903. C. Scribner's Sons.
--Jack Hall: Or, The School Days of an American Boy. Attwood, Francis G., illus. LC 8-3371. vi, 394 p. incl. front., plates. 20 cm. 1888. Jordan, Marsh and Company.
--Jack in the Bush: Or, A Summer on a Salmon River. Merrill, Frank Thayer (1848-), illus. LC 4-16826. 374 p. incl. front., 5 pl. 20 cm. 1893. C. Scribner's Sons.
Grant, Roy E., jt. auth. see Jordan, Myra J.
Grant, Sandy
--Hey, Look at Me!. A City ABC. Mulvehill, Larry, photos by. LC 73-81976. (Illus.). 31 p. 1973. (ISBN 0-87888-060-7). Bradbury Press.
Grant, Vernon
--A Monster is Loose in Tokyo. 1972. Charles E. Tuttle.
--Mr. Mixie Dough. Grant, Vernon, illus. LC 34-40514. 40 p. col. illus. 32 cm. c.1934. Whitman Publishing Company.
--Tinker Tim: The Toy Maker. LC 34-40515. 1 p. l., 5-29 p. col. illus. 31 cm. c.1934. Whitman Publishing Company.
Granville-Barker, Harley (1877-1946) & Harrison, G. B., eds.
--The Penny Fiddle. Ardizzone, Edward Jeffrey Irving (1900-1979), illus. N.D. Doubleday & Co.
--The Seige and fall of Troy. Hodges, Cyril Walter (1909-), illus. N.D. Doubleday & Co.
Granville, Paulina T., tr. see Leander, Richard.
Grapewin, Charley
--Meg Randall. N.D. Liveright Publications.
Gras, Felix
--The Reds of the Midi. Ward, Bertha Evans, ed. N.D. D. Appleton-Century Co., Inc.
Grasso, Mary Ellen Cipolla
--Jody. (Illus.). (gr. k-2). N.D. Vantage.
Grater, Dilys see Owen, Dilys, pseud.
Grattan, Peter, tr. see Crattan, Madeleine.
Grattan-Smith, T E
--True Blue: The Adventures of Mel, Ned, and Jum. 3 p. l., 257 p. col. front., plates. 20 cm. 1920. H. Holt and Company.
Grau, Shirley Ann (1929-)
--The Black Prince and Other Stories. 1955. Borzoi Press.
--The Condor Passes. 1971. Borzoi Books.
Grautoff, Christiane (1917-)
--The Stubborn Donkey. Jauss, Anne Marie (1907-), illus. LC 49-11179. 46 p. illus, (part col.) 23 cm. 1949. Aladdin Books.
--The Stubborn Donkey. Jauss, Anne Marie (1907-), illus. N.D. E. P. Dutton & Co.
--The Tale That Grew. Jauss, Anne Marie (1907-), illus. LC 55-10371. unpaged. illus. 22cm. 1955. Sterling Pub. Co.
Gravel, Fern, pseud., see Hall, James Norman.
Gravel, Fern, pseud. (1887-1951)
--Oh Millersville!. Hall, James Norman. Andrews, Clarence A., tr. LC 41-3646. (Illus.). 128p (Pub. by The Prairie Press). 1981. (ISBN 0-934582-01-7). (ISBN 0-934582-01-7). Midwest Heritage.
Gravelle, Kim
--Inuk: The Eskimo Who Hated the Snow. Gravelle, Kim, illus. LC 75-5656. (Illus.). 45 p. 24cm. 1975. (ISBN 0-516-03477-4). Childrens Press.
Gravengaard, Hans Peter
--Christmas Again. N.D. Chapman & Grimes.
Graver, Mary Byrd
--Jerry, the Pet Crow: Stories for Children. 1st ed. Shaw, Roderick, illus. LC 55-102951. 46p. illus: 21cm. 1955. Exposition Press.
Graves, Affleck
--Little Thumbamonk. N.D. Transatlantic Arts.
Graves, Alfred Percival (1846-), compiled by.
--The Irish Fairy. Denham, George, illus. (Illus.). 355p. 1909. Frederick A. Stokes.
Graves, Alida W
--A Little Maiden's Victory. LC 12-32624. 174 p. front., 2 pl. 19 cm. c.1896. American Tract Society.
--Sunshine Mary. LC 12-32625. 300 p. front., plates. 18 cm. c.1884. Presbyterian Board of Publication.
Graves, Andrew F.
--Broken Pitcher. N.D. Thomas Y. Crowell & Co.'s Catalogue.
--Luke Darrell. (Crowell's Library For Young People). N.D. Thomas Y. Crowell & Co.'s Catalogue.
--Mabel Ross. (Crowell's Library For Young People). N.D. Thomas Y. Crowell & Co.'s Catalogue.
Graves, Buddy
--Tin Flakes. N.D. Carlton Press.
Graves, Carolyn E.
--Skip-A-Star. (gr. 4-7). N.D. (ISBN 0-8181-0185-7). Pageant-Poseidon.
Graves, Charles Parlin see Parlin, John, pseud.
Graves, Charles Parlin (1911-1972)
--Annie Oakley, the Shooting Star. Cary, Louis Favreau (1915-), illus. Cary, pseud. LC 61-9734. (Illus.). 78 p. 23cm. (Discovery book). 1961. Garrard Press.
--Mickey-Angelo. Watson, Aldren Auld (1917-), illus. 122p. c.1962. Funk & Wagnalls.
Graves, Clay & Bradford, Ed
--Hurry up, Christmas!. LC 75-11504. p. cm. 1975. (ISBN 0-8116-6068-0). Garrard Pub. Co.
Graves, Elizabeth M.
--Hey, Horses. Palazzo, Tony (1905-1970), illus. LC 65-10400. (Reading Shelf-Animal Books Ser). (gr. 1-3). 1965. (ISBN 0-8116-6504-6). Garrard.
Graves, John Alexander, III (1920-)
--Blue & Some Other Dogs. (Illus.). 29p. 1981. (ISBN 0-88426-058-5). Encino Pr.
--Goodbye to a River. 1960. Borzoi.
Graves, Pat
--No Strings Attached. (Illus.). 1st U.S. edition. (gr. 7-12). 1976. (ISBN 0-89137-801-4). Quality Pubns.
--Seventh Street Angels. Curtis, Kathy, illus. (Illus.). 1st U.S. edition. (gr. 4-6). 1976. (ISBN 0-89137-800-6). Quality Pubns.
Graves, Richard, tr. see Guillot, Rene.
Graves, Robert, ed. see Dickens, Charles John Huffam.
Graves, Robert (1895-)
--An Ancient Castle. Graves, Elizabeth, illus. Thomas, William D., afterword by. LC 81-17204. (Illus.). 72p. 1st U.S. edition. 1981. (ISBN 0-935576-06-1). Kesend Pub Ltd.
--Ann at Highwood Hall: Poems for Children. Ardizzone, Edward Jeffrey Irving (1900-1979), illus. LC 66-104455. 48p. col. illus. 25cm. 1966, c.1964. Doubleday.
--The Big Green Book. Sendak, Maurice Bernard (1928-), illus. (Illus.). 63 p. 23cm. 1968. Crowell-Collier Press.
--The Big Green Book. Sendak, Maurice Bernard (1928-), illus. LC 84-42972. (Illus.). 62 p. 1985, c.1962. (ISBN 0-02-504450-8). Macmillan.
--Fairies & Fusiliers. 1918. Knopf.
--Greek Gods and Heroes. 1st ed. Davis, Dimitris (1905-), illus. LC 60-12438. (Illus.). 160 p. 25cm. 1960. Doubleday. **Award: (ALA).**
--Penny Fiddle: Poems for Children. Ardizzone, Edward Jeffrey Irving (1900-1979), illus. LC 61-11140. (Illus.). 24cm. 62p. (gr. 4-6). N.D. (ISBN 0-385-07983-4). Doubleday.
--The Poor Boy Who Followed His Star. Meyer-Wallace, Alice, illus. LC 68-8516. (Illus.). 43 p. 25cm. 1969, c.1968. Doubleday.
--Two Wise Children. Pinto, Ralph, illus. LC 72-2081. (Illus.). 32 p. 22cm. 1966. Quist; Distributed by Crown Publishers.
Graves, Sarah Bridge
--The Short-Tailed Whale. N.D. Bruce Humphries, Inc.
--The Story of Spots Baby. Spencer, Rebecca, illus. LC 37-3911. 19 p. illus. 22 x 28 cm. 1937. Falmouth Book House.

Graves, Sharol, jt. auth. see Ortiz, Simon J.
Graves, W. A.
--My Pearl, 1 of 103 vols. (The Pearl Library: No. 65). 1900. Set. Hurst & Co.
Graveson, Caroline C
--The Farthing Family: A Story of a London Family in the Seventeenth Century. LC 52-6146. 211 p. illus. 20 cm. 1951. Contemporary Books.
Gray, Abel
--A Story for Boys, 1 of 25 vols. (Illus.). (Pilgrim Ser. for Boys: No. 2). 1900. Lee & Shepard.
Gray, Annie Joslyn see Gray, Joslyn.
Gray, Bea
--Stay, Boy. LC 73-84494. (Illus.). 48 p. 22cm. 1973. (ISBN 0-8059-1902-3). Dorrance.
Gray, Belle
--Friend of Bitul Pony Hill. Wronn, Charile L., illus. LC 29-216883. 316 p. front., plates. 20 cm. c.1929. Barse & Co.
Gray, Bob, jt. auth. see Fox, Sonny.
Gray, Catherine & Gray, Jim (1947-)
--Tammy and the Gigantic Fish. 1st ed. Joyce, Bill, illus. LC 82-47732. p. cm. c.1983. (ISBN 0-06-022138-0). (ISBN 0-06-022139-9). Harper & Row.
Gray, Charles Wright, ed.
--'Dawgs!'. An Anthology of Stories About Them. LC 25-18715. ix, 342 p. 21 cm. 1925. H. Holt and Company.
--"Dawgs!". An Anthology of Stories About Them. LC 37-30672. ix, 342 p. 21 c. N.D. The Sun Dial Press.
--Hosses: An Anthology of Short Stories. vi p., 2 l., 3-382 p. 21 cm. c.1927. H. Holt and Company.
--'Hosses'. An Anthology of Short Stories. LC 38-3169. vi p., 2 l., 3-382 p. 21 cm. 1937. The Sun Dial Press, Inc.
--Real Dogs: An Anthology of Short Stories. 5 p. l., 3-352 p. 22 cm. 1933. Garden City Publishing Company, Inc.
--Real Dogs: An Anthology of Short Stories. LC 26-17475. 5 p. l., 3-325 p. 21 cm. c.1926. H. Holt and Company.
--Real Dogs: An Anthology of Short Stories. LC 37-7134. 5 p. l., 3-352 p. 21 cm. 1937. The Sun Dial Press.
Gray, Clarence, jt. auth. see Ritt, William.
Gray, Elizabeth Janet see Vining, Elizabeth Gray.
Gray, Elizabeth Janet (1902-)
--Adam of the Road. Lawson, Robert (1892-1957), illus. (Illus.). 317 p. 20cm. (Seafarer Book). 1973, c.1970. (ISBN 0-670-05080-6). Viking.
--Beppy Marlowe. Barton, Loren, illus. (Illus.). (gr. 5-10). 1936. (ISBN 0-670-15824-0). (ISBN 0-670-15825-9). Viking Pr.
--Cheerful Heart. (Illus.). (gr. 4-7). 1959. (ISBN 0-670-21375-6). Viking Pr.
--Fair Adventure. (gr. 7-11). 1940. (ISBN 0-670-30490-5). Viking Pr.
--Meggy Macintosh. (gr. 5-10). 1930. (ISBN 0-670-46641-7). Viking Pr.
--Meredith's Ann. (Windmill Bks.). N.D. Doubleday Doran & Co.
--Merediths' Ann: An Out-of-Doors Story for Girls. LC 27-191833. 5 p. l., 267 p. col. front. 21 cm. 1927. Doubleday, Page & Company.
--Penn. Whitney, George Gillett, illus. 320p. N.D. Viking Press.
--Sandy. LC 45-3446. 233 p. col. front. 21 cm. 1945. The Viking Press.
Gray, Elmer L.
--Furious & Free. (gr. 10up). 1984. (ISBN 0-317-01661-X). Broadman.
Gray, Emma J.
--A Golden Week. (Illus.). N.D. Methodist Bk Concern.
Gray, Ernest Alfred
--The Dog That Marched to Moscow. N.D. A. S. Barnes & Co.
--The Fifth Testament. LC 61-8564. 159p. (Wonderful world book). c.1961. Barnes.
--Roman Eagle, Celtic Hawk. Hall, Douglas (1931-), illus. (Illus.). 21cm. 255p. (A Wonderful World Bk.). 1959. A. S. Barnes & Co.
Gray, Frederick Turell (1804-1855), ed.
--My Teacher's New Year's Present: For the Year 1850. LC 15-2565. 1 p. l., v-vii, 9-64 p. front., illus. 13 cm. 1850. B. H. Greene.
--My Teacher's New Year's Present: Or, Select Biography of the Young. LC 15-2564. v, 6-96 p. front., illus. 13 cm. 1847. B. H. Greene.
Gray, Genevieve Stuck (1920-)
--Alaska Woman. Inderieden, Nancy, illus. LC 77-7040. (Illus.). 40 p. 24cm. (Time of Danger, Time for Courage). 1977. (ISBN 0-88436-386-4). EMC Corp.
--Break-in. Brooks, Nan, illus. LC 73-4505. (Illus.). 32 p. 23cm. (Her Girl stuff series). 1973. (ISBN 0-912022-64-7). EMC Corp.
--Casey's Camper. Mathieu, Joseph (1945-), illus. LC 72-10410. (Illus.). 39 p. 27cm. 1973. (ISBN 0-07-024202-X). (ISBN 0-07-024202-X). McGraw-Hill.

--The Dark Side of Nowhere. Inderieden, Nancy, illus. LC 77-7110. p. cm. (Time of Danger, Time for Courage). 1977. (ISBN 0-88436-390-2). (ISBN 0-88436-391-0). EMC Corp.
--Ghost Story. Matus, Greta (1938-), illus. LC 74-22049. (Illus.). 45 p. 22cm. 1975. (ISBN 0-688-41686-1). (ISBN 0-688-51686-6). Lothrop, Lee, and Shepard Co.
--Has Anyone Seen Buddy Bascom?. Inderieden, Nancy, illus. LC 77-7926. (Illus.). 40 p. 24cm. (Time of Danger, Time for Courage). 1977. (ISBN 0-88436-384-8). (ISBN 0-88436-385-6). EMC Corp.
--Hot Shot. Brooks, Nan, illus. LC 73-4585. (Illus.). 28 p. 23cm. (Her Girl stuff series). 1973. (ISBN 0-912022-62-0). (ISBN 0-912022-62-0). EMC Corp.
--How Far, Felipe?. Guffalcoul, Ann (1929-), illus. LC 77-11846. (Illus.). 63 p. 22cm. (I can read history book). c.1978. (ISBN 0-06-022107-0). (ISBN 0-06-022108-9). Harper & Row.
--I Know a Bus Driver. (Illus.). 48p. (Community Helper Bks.). (gr. 1-3). 1972. (ISBN 0-399-60703-X). Putnam Pub Group.
--Keep an Eye on Kevin: Safety Begins at Home. Madden, Donald B. (1927-), illus. LC 72-5136. (Illus.). 40 p. 24cm. 1973. (ISBN 0-688-40014-0). Lothrop, Lee & Shepard Co.
--A Kite for Bennie. Sowell, Floyd (1929-), illus. LC 77-39319. (Illus.). 40 p. 26cm. 1972. (ISBN 0-07-024197-X). (ISBN 0-07-024198-8). McGraw-Hill.
--The Magic Bears. Jones, Gary B, illus. LC 75-29316. (Illus.). 36 p. 24cm. (Her Blessingway, tales of a Navajo family). 1975. (ISBN 0-88436-223-X). (ISBN 0-88436-224-8). EMC Corp.
--The Secret of the Mask. Jones, Gary B., illus. LC 75-30708. p. cm. (Her Blessingway, tales of Navajo family). c.1975. (ISBN 0-88436-221-3). (ISBN 0-88436-222-1). EMC Corp.
--Send Wendell. Shimin, Symeon (1902-), illus. LC 73-17414. (Illus.). 33 p. 26cm. 1974. (ISBN 0-07-024195-3). (ISBN 0-07-024195-3). McGraw-Hill.
--The Seven Wishes of Joanna Peabody. Fax, Elton Clay (1909-), illus. LC 72-75017. (Illus.). 61 p. 22cm. 1972. Lothrop, Lee & Shepard.
--Sore Loser. Krush, Beth (1918-) & Krush, Joe (1918-), illus. LC 73-22056. (Illus.). 74 p. 21cm. 1974. (ISBN 0-395-18589-0). Houghton Mifflin.
--The Spiderweb Stone. Jones, Gary B., illus. LC 75-30529. p. cm. (Her Blessingway, tales of a Navajo family). c.1975. (ISBN 0-88436-219-1). (ISBN 0-88436-220-5). (ISBN 0-88436-220-5). EMC Corp.
--Stand-off. Brooks, Nan, illus. LC 73-4722. (Illus.). 39 p. 23cm. (Her Girl stuff series). 1973. (ISBN 0-912022-68-X). (ISBN 0-912022-69-8). EMC Corp.
--Stray. Brooks, Nan, illus. LC 73-4587. (Illus.). 36 p. 23cm. (Her Girl stuff series). 1973. (ISBN 0-912022-66-3). (ISBN 0-912022-66-3). EMC Corp.
--Tall Singer. Jones, Gary B., illus. LC 75-30531. p. cm. (Her Blessingway, tales of a Navajo family). c.1975. (ISBN 0-88436-217-5). (ISBN 0-88436-218-3). EMC Corp.
--Two Tickets to Memphis. Inderieden, Nancy, illus. LC 77-23394. (Illus.). 40 p. 24cm. (Time of Danger, Time for Courage). 1977. (ISBN 0-88436-388-0). (ISBN 0-88436-389-9). EMC Corp.
--Varnell Roberts, Super-Pigeon. Friedman, Marvin (1930-), illus. LC 75-12576. (Illus.). 113 p. 23cm. 1975. (ISBN 0-395-21408-4). Houghton Mifflin.
--The Yellow Bone Ring. Mars, Witold Tadeusz J. (1912-), illus. LC 70-156921. (Illus.). 159 p. 22cm. 1971. Lothrop, Lee and Shepard Co.
Gray, Harold Lincoln (1894-1968)
--Arf: The Life & Hard Times of Little Orphan Annie, 1935-1945. Capp, Al, pseud. (1909-1979), intro. by Caplin, Alfred Gerald. (Illus.). cartoons. (gr. 5 up). 1970. (ISBN 0-87000-098-5). Arlington Hse.
--Little Orphan Annie. 86p. (Famous Sixty Cents Quarto Comics). (The Famous Little Orphan Annie Ser.). N.D. Cupples & Leon Co.
--Little Orphan Annie, a Willing Helper. 86p. (The Famous Little Orphan Annie Ser.). N.D. Cupples & Leon Co.
--Little Orphan Annie & Little Orphan Annie in Cosmic City. (Illus.). 1974. Dover.
--Little Orphan Annie and the Gila Monster Gang: A Story Based on the Famous Newspaper Strip "Little Orphan Annie,". authorized. LC 45-12224. 3 p. l., 11-248 p. illus. 20 1/2 cm. 1944. Whitman Publishing Company.
--Little Orphan Annie and the Haunted House. 86p. (Famous Sixty Cents Quarto Comics). (The Famous Little Orphan Annie Ser.). N.D. Cupples & Leon Co.
--Little Orphan Annie and Uncle Sam. 86p. (The Famous Little Orphan Annie Ser.). N.D. Cupples & Leon Co.

--Little Orphan Annie Bucking the World. 86p. (Famous Sixty Cents Quarto Comics). (The Famous Little Orphan Annie Ser.). N.D. Cupples & Leon Co.
--Little Orphan Annie in Cosmic City. 86p. (The Famous Little Orphan Annie Ser.). N.D. Cupples & Leon.
--Little Orphan Annie in the Circus. 86p. (Famous Sixty Cents Quarto Comics). (The Famous Little Orphan Annie Ser.). N.D. Cupples & Leon Co.
--Little Orphan Annie in the Great Depression. Gray, Harold Lincoln (1894-1968), illus. (Illus.). 58p. (Orig.). 1979. Dover.
--Little Orphan Annie, Shipwrecked. 86p. (The Famous Little Orphan Annie Ser.). N.D. Cupples & Leon Co.
Capp, Helen Winifred Frost, Mrs.
--My Folks: As Told by Little Orphan Annie. Gray, Harold Lincoln (1894-1968), illus. LC 40-83631. 1 p. l., 5-30 p. illus. 23 cm. c.1940. Whitman Publishing Company.
Gray, Hester
--Kitty Barton: A Simple Story for Children. (Illus.). 1882. Lee & Shepard.
Gray, J. M. L.
--Hello Kitty's Button Book. Gray, J. M. L., illus. (Illus.). (Do It Cloth Bks.). (pb). 1982. (ISBN 0-394-85430-6). Random.
--Hello Kitty's Christmas Book. Gray, J. M. L., illus. LC 82-80921. (Illus.). 16 p. 19cm. (Hummingbird book). c.1982. (ISBN 0-394-85432-2). Random House.
Gray, Jenny, adapted by.
--Treasure Island. Grove, David, illus. LC 70-133537. (Original Author: Robert Louis Stevenson, 1850-1894). 21cm. 92p. (Pacemaker Classics). 1970. Fearon Publishers.
Gray, Jim, jt. auth. see Gray, Catherine.
Gray, Joan
--The Ball Boys on the Bay. LC 75-162024. (Illus.). 51 p. 22cm. 1971. (ISBN 0-8059-1580-X). Dorrance.
Gray, John E., retold by.
--India's Tales & Legends. Kiddell-Monroe, Joan (1908-), illus. (Illus.). (Myths & Legends Ser). (gr. 4-6). 1961. (ISBN 0-8098-2349-7). Walck.
Gray, John Rufus (1886-)
--Tall Tales of Deadeye Bob. Evans, Phyllis Riley, illus. LC 78-61623. (Illus.). 108 p. 21cm. c.1978. Gray.
Gray, Joslyn
--Black-Eyed Susan. Caswell, Edward C., illus. LC 24-10846. 4 p. l., 221 p. plates. 20 cm. 1924. C. Scribner's Sons.
--Bouncing Bet. LC 21-7123. 4 p. l., 230 p. front., plates. 20 cm. 1921. C. Scribner's Sons.
--Elsie Marley: Honey. LC 18-174959. 4 p. l., 267 p. front., plates. 19 cm. 1918. C. Scribner's Sons.
--The January Girl. LC 20-6864. 4 p. l., 211 p. front., plates. 20 cm. 1920. C. Scribner's Sons.
--Kathleen's Probation. LC 18-9076. 4 p. l., 228 p. front., plates. 19 cm. 1918. C. Scribner's Sons.
--The Newcomer in Penny Lane. Caswell, Edward C., illus. LC 22-17039. 4 p. l., 214 p. front., plates. 20 cm. (Penny lane books). c.1922. C. Scribner's Sons.
--The Old Mary Metcalf Place. Gooch, Thelma, illus. LC 23-72829. 4 p. l., 187 p. front., plates. 20 cm. 1923. C. Scribner's Sons.
--The Other Miller Girl. LC 22-8710. 4 p. l., 24 p. front., plates. 20 cm. 1922. C. Scribner's Sons.
--Rosemary Greenway. LC 19-15554. 4 p. l., 555 p. front., plates. 20 cm. 1919. C. Scribner's Sons.
--Rusty Miller. 4 p. l., 248 p. front., plates. 20 cm. 1919. C. Scribner's Sons.
Gray, Lawson
--Old Ire. A Reminiscence. LC 4440. 168 p. 20 cm. 1900. B. Herder.
Gray, Leslie & Stang, Judit (1921-1977), illus.
--The Magic Realm of Fairy Tales. (Illus.). 220 p. 27cm. (Whitman library of giant books). 1968. Whitman Pub. Division, Western Pub. Co.
Gray, Louisa M.
--Ada and Gerty. 336p. 1905. American Tract Society.
--Ada and Gerty: Hand in Hand Heavenward. (Illus.). N.D. Thomas Nelson & Sons.
--Children of Abbotsmuir Manse. (Illus.). N.D. Thomas Nelson & Sons.
--Little Miss Wardlaw. N.D. Thos Nelson & Sons.
--Mine Own People. N.D. Thos Nelson & Sons.
--Nelly's Teachers, & What They Learned. (Illus.). N.D. Thos Nelson & Sons.
Gray, Margaret
--The Donkey's Tale. (Illus.). 32p. 1984. (ISBN 0-8307-0963-0). Regal.
Gray, Marvin M (1921-)
--The Abominable Snowman. Gray, Cleve, illus. LC 61-19808. 21cm. 142p. 1961. Vantage Press.
Gray, Mary Ann
--The Truth About Fathers. LC 81-21571. 192p. (gr. 7 up). 1982. (ISBN 0-02-736700-2). Bradbury Pr.
Gray, Mary Richards, tr. see Spillmann, Joseph.

Gray, Merrilee, jt. auth. see Hoburg, Maryanne Regal.
Gray, Nicholas Stuart (1922-1981)
--The Apple Stone. Keeping, Charles William James (1924-), illus. LC 69-16293. (Illus.). 230 p. 22cm. 1st U.S. edition. 1969. Meredith Press.
--Boys. Adler, Robin, photos by. photos. Orig. Title: Boy: Cats with Everything. (gr. 7 up). 1969. (ISBN 0-696-54039-8). Hawthorn.
--The Edge of Evening. Stewart, Charles William (1915-), illus. (Illus.). (gr. 5 up). N.D. (ISBN 0-571-10795-8). Faber & Faber.
--The Further Adventures of Puss in Boots. Hatch, W. M., illus. (Illus.). (ps-5). 1971. (ISBN 0-571-09641-7). Faber & Faber.
--Grimbold's Other World. Keeping, Charles William James (1924-), illus. LC 68-13777. (Illus.). 184 p. 21cm. 1st U.S. edition. 1968, c.1963. (ISBN 0-8015-0342-6). Meredith Press.
--Mainly in Moonlight. Stewart, Charles William (1915-), illus. (Illus.). 160p. 1st U.S. edition. (Faber Fanfare Ser.). 1979. (ISBN 0-571-11332-X). Faber & Faber.
--Mainly in Moonlight: Ten Stories of Sorcery and the Supernatural. Keeping, Charles William James (1924-) illus. (Illus.). 181 p. 21cm. 1st U.S. edition. 1967, c.1965. Meredith Press.
--Over the Hills to Fabylon. Gray, Nicholas Stuart (1922-1981), illus. LC 70-102417. (Illus.). 197 p. 21cm. 1st U.S. edition. 1970. Hawthorn Books.
--Over the Hills to Fabylon. Gray, Nicholas Stuart (1922-1981), illus. 1954. Oxford Univ. Pr. Award: (CMA).
--A Wind from Nowhere. LC 78-321970. 155 p. 21cm. 1978. (ISBN 0-571-11182-3). Faber.
Gray, Nigel (1941-)
--The Deserter. 1st ed. Lewin, Ted (1935-), illus. LC 76-58693. p. cm. c.1977. (ISBN 0-06-022061-9). (ISBN 0-06-022062-7). Harper & Row.
Gray, Nigel (1941-) & Frascino, Edward
--It'll All Come Out in the Wash. LC 78-22482. (Illus.). 32 p. 21cm. c.1979. (ISBN 0-06-022067-8). (ISBN 0-06-022074-0). Harper & Row.
Gray, Patricia Clark see Clark, Virginia, pseud.
Gray, Patricia Clark see Gray, Patsey, pseud.
Gray, Patricia Clark
--Barefoot a Thousand Miles. LC 83-40391. 96p. 1984. (ISBN 0-8027-6528-9). Walker & Co.
--Blue Ribbon Summer. LC 68-16568. 201 p. 21cm. 1968. W. W. Norton.
--The Doggone Roan. Frame, Paul (1913-), illus. LC 57-10715. 192p. illus. 21cm. 1957. Coward-McCann.
--The Flag Is up. LC 73-119358. 159 p. 21cm. 1970. T. Nelson.
--Heads up. Shortall, Leonard W., illus. LC 56-995471. 191p. illus. 21cm. 1956. Coward-McCann.
--Jumping Jack. LC 65-133356. 159p. illus. 21cm. c.1965. Norton.
--Norah's Ark. (gr. 4-6). N.D. (ISBN 0-448-26012-3). G&D.
--Norah's Ark. 1st ed. LC 66-8360. 158p. 21cm. 1966. Norton.
--Show Ring Rogue. Savitt, Sam (1917-), illus. LC 63-10163. 157 p. illus. 21 cm. 1963. Coward-McCann.
--Star Bright. LC 64-17532. 128 p. 21 cm. 1964. Norton.
--Star Lost. LC 65-22678. 154p. 21cm. c.1965. Norton.
--Star, the Sea Horse. LC 68-19423. 153 p. 21cm. 1968. W. W. Norton.
--Thatch Cat. (gr. 4-8). 1978. (ISBN 0-8277-5431-0). British Bk Ctr.
Gray, Patrick Leopold (1864-)
--Prairie Chickens: A Tale of the Twining of Little Heart-Strings. LC 30-2762. 3 p. l., 9-160 p. 20 cm. c.1929. R. G. Badger.
Gray, Patsey, pseud., see Gray, Patricia Clark.
Gray, Patsey, pseud.
--Challenger. Gray, Patricia Clark. Savitt, Sam (1917-), illus. 1959. Coward-McCann Inc.
--Diving Horse. Gray, Patricia Clark. Savitt, Sam (1917-), illus. (Illus.). 1959. Coward McCann, Inc.
--Four-H Filly. Gray, Patricia Clark. Shortall, Leonard W., illus. 21cm. 236p. 1958. Coward-McCann Inc.
--Galloping Gold. Gray, Patricia Clark. Shortall, Leonard W., illus. 1958. Coward-McCann Inc.
--Horse in Her Heart. Gray, Patricia Clark. Savitt, Sam (1917-), illus. (Illus.). 1960. Coward McCann, Inc.
--Horsepower. Gray, Patricia Clark. LC 66-11770. 170p. 21cm. c.1966. Norton.
--Loco the Bronc. Gray, Patricia Clark. Savitt, Sam (1917-), illus. 1961. Coward McCann, Inc.
--Lucky Star. Gray, Patricia Clark. 1st ed. LC 67-15454. 168p. 21cm. 1967. Norton.
Gray, Patsy see Gray, Patsey.

Gray, Phoebe
--Little Sir Galahad. (Illus.). N.D. Small, Maynard & Co.
Gray, Robert
--Gray Wolf. (gr. 5-9). N.D. (ISBN 0-448-26154-5). G&D.
Gray, Rockwell, tr. see Di Girolamo, Vittorio.
Gray, Rosalie, pseud., see Mann, D. H..
Gray, Rosalie
--Willie and Birdie. 352p. (The Golden Rod Lib.). N.D. American Tract Society.
Gray, Ruth Sanford (1900-)
--God's Good Gifts. Gray, Ruth Sanford (1900-), illus. LC 53-5800. unpaged. illus. 25cm. c.1952. Broadman Press.
Gray, Simon
--Wise Child. (Illus.). 84p. 1968. (ISBN 0-87250-023-3). (ISBN 0-87250-024-1). David White Company.
Gray, Violet Gordon
--Margery Morris. Williamson, Ada Clendenin, illus. LC 17-29733. 342 p. front., plates. 19 cm. 1917. The Penn Publishing Company.
--Margery Morris--Mascot. Williamson, Ada Clendenin, illus. LC 20-4535. 352 p. front., plates. 19 cm. 1919. The Penn Publishing Company.
--Margery Morris and Plain Jane. Williamson, Ada Clendenin, illus. LC 20-142952. 1 p. l., 5-319 p. front., plates. 19 cm. 1920. The Penn Publishing Company.
--Margery Morris in the Pine Woods. Williamson, Ada Clendenin, illus. (The Margery Morris Books). N.D. Penn.
Gray, Walter T., pseud., see Victor, Metta Victoria Fuller.
Gray, Walter T., pseud. (1831-1855)
--The Bad Boy at Home and Abroad. Victor, Metta Victoria Fuller. (Sunset Ser.). N.D. J. S. Ogilvie.
--The Bad Boy at Home: And His Experiences in Trying to Become an Editor ... Victor, Metta Victoria Fuller. Gray, Walter T., pseud. (1831-1855), illus. Victor, Metta Victoria Fuller. LC 12-326472. 140 p. illus. 18 cm. c.1885. J. S. Ogilvie & Company.
--A Bad Boy's Diary: As Related by Himself. Victor, Metta Victoria Fuller. Johnson, Merle, illus. LC 30-12333. vi, 7-276 p. front., plates. 19 cm. 1911. J. S. Ogilvie Publishing Company.
Gray, William Bittle (1891-)
--Fish Tales and Ocean Odd Balls. LC 79-88265. 210p. 1971. (ISBN 0-498-07440-4). A. S. Barens & Company.
Gray, William Scott, jt. auth. see Elson, William Harris.
Gray, William Scott, jt. ed. see Arbuthnot, May Hill.
Graybill, Kathryn
--Cassie and the General. Werth, Kurt (1896-), illus. LC 62-15982. 95p. 21cm. c.1962. Nelson.
Graydon, Grace
--The Busy Bo-Peeps. Preston, Chloe, illus. N.D. David McKay.
Graydon, William Murray (1864-1946)
--The Butcher of Cawnpore. (The Boys Own Library). N.D. David McKay.
--Camp in the Snow: Boys Winter camp Life in Northern New England. (The Famous Adventure Ser.). N.D. David Mckay.
--The Camp in the Snow. (The Boys Own Library). N.D. David McKay.
--Campaigning with Braddock. (The Boys Own Library). N.D. David McKay.
--Canoe Boys and Camp Fires: Or, Adventures on Winding Water. (The Enterprise Bks.). N.D. Grosset & Dunlap.
--Canoe Boys and Campfires. New ed. (Alert Ser.). N.D. Grosset & Dunlap.
--Canoe Boys and Campfires: Or, Adventures on Winding Waters. LC 7-23535. 2 p. l., 9-286 p. front., plates. 19 cm. c.1907. Chatterton-Peck Company.
--Down the Susquehanna. (The Rugby Series for Boys and Girls). N.D. A. L. Burt Company.
--Exiled to Siberia. Carter, F. A., illus. LC 3677. 1 p. l., v-vi, 7-333 p. front., plates. 19 cm. (Adventure Stories Ser.). 1900. The Penn Publishing Company.
--From Lake to Wilderness. (The Boys Own Library). N.D. Davild McKay.
--In Barracks and Wigwam. (The Boys Own Library). N.D. David McKay.
--In Barracks and Wigwam. LC 3-864. 1 p. l., 5-240 p. 18 cm. (On cover: Medal library, no. 36). c.1900. Street & Smith.
--In Fort and Prison. (The Boys Own Library). N.D. David McKay.
--In the Days of Washington: A Story of the American Revolution. LC 6-44856. 319 p. front., plates. 19 cm. (Historical Stories Ser. for Boys and Girls). 1896. The Penn Publishing Company.
--Jungles and Traitors. (The Boys Own Library). N.D. David McKay.
--The Princess of the Purple Palace. LC 1-25438. v. 1 p., 1 l., 288 p. 20 cm. 1901. McClure, Phillips & Company.
--The River of Darkness. (Illus.). N.D. Thompson & Thomas.
--With Puritan and Pequot. De Land, Clyde O., illus. LC 4-10928. 4 p. 1 l., 5-398 p. front., 6 pl. 19 cm. (Historical Stories Ser. for Boys and Girls). 1904. The Penn Publishing Company.
Graydon, William R
--Full Sail for Tripoli. LC 68-25857. 159 p. 24cm. 1968. Golden Gate Junior Books.
--The Yellow Shoes. Payzant, Charles, illus. LC 63-12548. 58 p. illus. 26 cm. 1963. Golden Gate Junior Books.
Grayland, Valerie Merle Spanner
--Baby Sister. Cooper, Marjorie (1910-), illus. (Illus.). (gr. k-2). 1964. (ISBN 0-8382-0057-5). Hale.
--Baby Sister. Cooper, Marjorie (1910-), illus. LC 65-14636. 1v. (unpaged) col. illus. 32cm. 1965, c.1964. Rand McNally.
Grayson, David
--The Friendly Road. N.D. Grosset & Dunlap.
Grayson, Donald
--Bob Steele Afloat in the Clouds. (Motor Power Ser.). N.D. David McKay.
--Bob Steele From Auto to Airship. (Motor Power Ser.). N.D. David McKay.
--Bob Steele in Strange Waters. (Motor Power Ser.). N.D. David McKay.
--Bob Steele on High Gear. (Motor Power Ser.). N.D. David McKay.
--Bob Steele's Last Flight. (Motor Power Ser.). N.D. David McKay.
--Bob Steele's Motor Boat. (Motor Power Ser.). N.D. David McKay.
--Bob Steele's Motor Cycle. (Motor Power Ser.). N.D. David McKay.
--Bob Steele's New Aeroplane. (Motor Power Ser.). N.D. David McKay.
--Bob Steele's Winning Race. (Motor Power Ser.). N.D. David McKay.
Grayson, M. H. & Haine, Hector Emanuel, eds.
--On with the Play. LC 70-401282. v. 22cm. (Book One). N.D. Jacaranda.
Grayson, Marion F. (1906-1976)
--Let's Do Fingerplays. Weyl, Nancy, illus. LC 62-10217. (Illus.). (ps-3). 1962. (ISBN 0-88331-003-1). Luce.
Grayson, Marion F. (1906-1976), compiled by.
--Let's Count and Count Out. McClintock, Deborah Derr, illus. LC 75-11372. xiv, 104p. ill. 27cm. c.1975. Robert B. Luce.
Gray Wolf, Peter, pseud., see Sexton, Bernard.
Greaves, Griselda, ed.
--Burning Thorn. index. notes. 208p. 1st U.S. edition. (gr. 7 up). 1971. (ISBN 0-02-736740-1). Macmillan.
Greaves, Margaret (1914-)
--Cat's Magic. LC 80-8451. p. cm. 1981. (ISBN 0-06-022122-4). (ISBN 0-06-022123-2). Harper & Row.
--The Dagger & the Bird. Kubinyi, Laszlo (1937-), illus. LC 74-2624. (Illus.). 144p. (Story of Suspense Ser.). (gr. 4 up). 1975. (ISBN 0-06-022091-0, HarpJ). Har-Row.
--The Dagger and the Bird: A Story of Suspense. Kubinyi, Laszlo (1937-), illus. LC 74-2624. (Illus.). 133 p. 21cm. 1975. (ISBN 0-06-022090-2). (ISBN 0-06-022091-0). Harper & Row.
--Gallimaufry Books, 4 bks. McDonald, Jill, illus. Greaves, Margaret (1914-), intro. by. Incl. The Snowman of Biddle, & Other Stories. LC 74-10323. 64p. (ISBN 0-8372-1051-8); The Rainbow Sun, & Other Stories. LC 74-10325. 64p. (ISBN 0-8372-1052-6); King Solomon & the Hoopoes, & Other Stories. LC 74-10326. 80p. (ISBN 0-8372-1053-4); The Great Bell of Peking, & Other Stories. LC 74-10327. 80p. (Illus.). 1st U.S. edition. (gr. 3-6). 1975. (ISBN 0-8372-2016-5). Bowmar-Noble.
--Kate Crackernuts. Crespi, Francesca, illus. LC 85-4439. p. cm. 1985. (ISBN 0-8037-0225-6). Dial Books for Young Readers.
--A Net to Catch the Wind. Gammell, Stephen, illus. LC 78-20265. (Illus.). 47 p. 21cm. c.1979. (ISBN 0-06-022104-6). (ISBN 0-06-022105-4). Harper & Row.
--Stone of Terror. LC 74-2614. 176p. (Story of Suspense Ser). (gr. 7-12). 1974. (ISBN 0-06-022089-9, HarpJ). Har-Row.
--Stone of Terror: A Story of Suspense. LC 74-2614. 215 p. 21cm. 1974. (ISBN 0-06-022088-0). (ISBN 0-06-022089-9). Harper & Row.
Greaves, Margaret (1914-), retold by.
--Mother Cuspen. Crespi, Francesca, illus. LC 85-4438. p. cm. 1985. (ISBN 0-8037-0225-6). Dial Books for Young Readers.
--The Witch Cat. Crespi, Francesca, illus. LC 85-4440. p. cm. 1985. (ISBN 0-8037-0225-6). Dial Books for Young Readers.
--The Witch's Servant. Crespi, Francesca, illus. LC 85-4436. p. cm. 1985. (ISBN 0-8037-0225-6). Dial Books for Young Readers.
Gredsted, Torry (1885-)
--Jorn. Sawyer, Astrid Rosing, tr. 21cm. 251p. 1938. Reilly & Lee.
Gree, Alain (1936-)
--The All-Color Activity Book of Animals. Camps, Luis, illus. LC 75-7599. (Illus.). 26 p. 31cm. 1st U.S. edition. (All-color activity book). c.1974. Little, Brown.
--Sally and Billy at the Seaside. Gree, Alain (1936-), illus. LC 67-25209. (Illus.). 28 p. 29cm. 1967. Hart Pub. Co.
--Sally and Billy in the Woods. Gree, Alain (1936-), illus. LC 68-64470. (Illus.). 28 p. 28cm. 1968, c.1963. Hart Pub. Co.
--Sally & Billy Look at Ships. Gree, Alain, illus. (gr. k-3). N.D. (ISBN 0-87460-168-1). (ISBN 0-87460-169-X). Lion.
--Sally and Billy on the Farm. Gree, Alain (1936-), illus. LC 67-25210. (Illus.). 28 p. 29cm. 1967. Hart Pub. Co.
--Tell Me About Color. Gree, Gerard, illus. Chapman, Alexandra, tr. from Fr. LC 71-179404. (Illus.). 21 p. 27cm. 1972. (ISBN 0-448-02934-0). (ISBN 0-448-02934-0). Grosset & Dunlap.
--Tommy Discovers Colors. Gree, Gerard, illus. Bd. with Tommy Measures Everything. (Illus.). 24p. (gr. k-2). 1972. G&D.
Greeley, Andrew Moran (1928-) & Dawson, Diane
--Nora Maeve and Sebi. LC 76-18047. (Illus.). 64 p. 23cm. c.1976. (ISBN 0-8091-0214-5). (ISBN 0-8091-1974-9). Paulist Press.
Greeley, Valerie
--Farm Animals. (Illus.). (ps). 1970. Harper.
--Field Animals. (Illus.). 1984. Harper.
--Pets. (Illus.). 1984. Harper.
--Pets. LC 83-22509. (Illus.). 12p. 1st U.S. edition. 1984. (ISBN 0-911745-21-1). P Bedrick Bks.
--Zoo Animals. (Illus.). 1984. Harper.
Green
--Loon. 32p. N.D. Oddo Publishing Inc.
--Splash and Trickle. 32p. N.D. Oddo Publishing Inc.
Green, A.
--Our Haunted Kingdom. N.D. New VeiwPoints.
Green, Adam, pseud., see Weisgard, Leonard Joseph.
Green, Adam, pseud. (1916-)
--The Funny Bunny Factory. Weisgard, Leonard Joseph. Weisgard, Leonard Joseph (1916-), illus. 26p. col. illus. 30cm. 1967, c.1950. Grosset.
Green, Adolph, jt. auth. see Comden, Betty.
Green, Alexander
--Scarlet Sails. Nesbitt, Esta (1918-), illus. Whitney, Thomas Porter (1917-), tr. (Illus.). (gr. 5 up). 1967. (ISBN 0-684-82105-2). Scribner.
Green, Allen Ayrault
--The Land of Lost. (Illus.). N.D. Small, Maynard & Co.
Green, Anne M (1922-)
--Good-by, Gray Lady. LC 64-19569. (Illus.). 183 p. 22cm. 1964. Atheneum.
--To Race Again. Orbaan, Albert F. (1913-), illus. LC 61-7097. 195p. illus. 21cm. 1961. T. Nelson.
--The Valley Cup. Frame, Paul (1913-), illus. LC 62-10564. 208p. illus. 22cm. 1962. T. Nelson.
Green, Ava E.
--The Dark Night and Other Stories. N.D. Vantage Press.
Green, Barbara, jt. ed. see Yolen, Jane Hyatt.
Green, Ben K.
--Wild Cow Tales. 1969. Borzoi Books.
Green, C. S.
--Thrilling Stories of the Rebellion. (Illus.). (St. Nicholas Series for Boys). N.D. International Book Co.
Green, Carl, jt. auth. see Sanford, William.
Green, Carl R & Sanford, William R (1927-)
--Ghost of Frankenstein. Schroeder, Howard, ed. LC 84-29231. (Illus.). 48 p. 23cm. (Movie Monsters). c.1985. (ISBN 0-89686-261-5). Crestwood House.
--Tarantula. Schroeder, Howard, illus. LC 84-20067. (Adapted from a Screenplay by Martin Berkeley). (Illus.). 48 p. 23cm. c.1985. (ISBN 0-89686-264-X). Crestwood House.
--Werewolf of London. Schroeder, Howard, ed. LC 84-19910. (Illus.). 48 p. 23cm. c.1985. (ISBN 0-89686-265-8). Crestwood House.
Green, Cecile Stith
--The Tale of Theodore Bear. Lysaker, Gene, illus. LC 65-22300. 32p. col. illus. 26cm. 1965. Oddo.
--The Tale of Theodore Bear. Lysaker, Gene, illus. LC 68-56812. (Illus.). (gr. 1-2). 1968. (ISBN 0-87783-038-X). Oddo.
--The Tale of Theodore Bear. Lysaker, Gene, illus. (Illus.). (gr. 1-2). 1978. (ISBN 0-89508-060-5). Rainbow Bks.
Green, Charles, jt. auth. see Dickens, Charles John Huffam.
Green, Clarence David (1895-1983)
--Watch the Tides. Castle, Jane, illus. LC 61-2308. unpaged. illus. 21cm. 1961. Holiday House.
Green, Dana Saintsbury
--The Squirrel That Remembered. Green, Dana Saintsbury, illus. LC 51-12145. 60 p. illus. 22 cm. 1951. Viking Press.
Green, Diane Huss
--The Lonely War of William Pinto. LC 68-21173. 171 p. 22cm. 1968. Little, Brown.
--Ski Country. Brackett, Ward, illus. LC 65-5025. (Illus.). 158 p. 22cm. 1965. Allyn and Bacon.
Green, Dorothy
--Juno's Adventure: Antics of an Airedale; a Story. 1st. ed. Markham, R. L., illus. (Illus.). 1 v. (unpaged). 22cm. 1974. (ISBN 0-682-48005-3). Exposition.
Green, E. M.
--Child of the Caravan: Or, The Boy Musicaian. (Illus.). 256p. N.D. E. P. Dutton & Co.
--When We Were Children. Burton, W. G., illus. N.D. E. P. Dutton & Co.
Green, Edwin (1880-1932)
--Air Monster. LC 32-11205. 3 p.l., 13-245 p. 20cm. c.1932. The Goldsmith Publishing Company.
Green, Ellen Everett
--Squib and His Friends. (The Rugby Series for Boys and Girls). N.D. A. L. Burt Company.
Green, Emma Martha (1858-)
--The Laird of Glentyre: A Story of Scotland. LC 14-19134. xviii p., 3 l., 3-226 p. col. front., plates. 20 cm. (On verso of half-title: Little schoolmate series, ed. by F. Converse). c.1914. E. P. Dutton & Company.
Green, Fitzhugh (1888-)
--Anchor's Aweigh. LC 27-9856. 4 p. l., 270, 1 p. front. 20 cm. 1927. D. Appleton and Company.
--Bob Barlett, Master Mariner. (Girls' Books by Girls). N.D. G. P. Putnam Sons.
--Dick Byrd, Air Explorer. N.D. G. P. Putnam Sons.
--Fought for Annapolis. Wilson, Henry B., frwd. by. LC 25-4986. vii p., 1 l., 270, 1 p. front. 20 cm. 1925. D. Appleton and Company.
--Hold 'em, Navy. Byrd, Richard Evelyn (1888-1957), frwd. by. LC 26-200565. 4 p. l., 263, 1 p. front. 19 cm. 1926. D. Appleton and Company.
--Martin Johnson, Lion Hunter. (Girls' Books by Girls). N.D. G. P. Putnam Sons.
--Midshipmen All. Sims, William S., frwd. by. LC 25-194350. 4 p. l., 271, 1 p. front. 20 cm. 1925. D. Appleton and Company.
--The Mystery of the Erik. LC 23-344005. vi p., 1 l., 287, 1 p. col. front., 1 illus. (map) 20 cm. 1923. D. Appleton and Company.
--Roy Andrews, Dragon Hunter. (Girls' Books by Girls). N.D. G. P. Putnam Sons.
--Uncle Sam's Sailors. LC 26-991498. 4 p. l., 284, 1 p. front., illus. 20 cm. 1926. D. Appleton and Company.
--Won for the Fleet: A Story of Annapolis. LC 22-209572. 6 p. l., 281 p. front., plates. 20 cm. c.1922. E. P. Dutton & Company.
Green Grass Grows All Around
--The Green Grass Grows All Around: A Traditional Folk Song. Hoffmann, Hilde (1927-), illus. LC 68-10032. 1 v. (unpaged) col. illus. 26cm. c.1968. Macmillan.
Green, Hannah
--I Never Promised You a Rose Garden. LC 64-11018. 1964. (ISBN 0-03-043725-3). HR&W.
--In the City of Paris. Chen, Tony (1929-), illus. LC 81-43649. (Illus.). 32 p. 27cm. c.1985. (ISBN 0-385-15692-8). (ISBN 0-385-15693-6). Doubleday.
Green, Huss Diane
--Lenny's Surprise Piano. (Illus.). 1963. Golden, Gate Junior Books.
Green, Ivah E.
--Splash & Trickle. Connor, Bil, illus. (Illus.). (gr. 2-3). 1978. (ISBN 0-89508-062-1). Rainbow Bks.
--Splash and Trickle: A Conservation Story; the Adventures of Two Raindrops. Connor, Bil, illus. LC 68-56818. (Illus.). 32 p. 26cm. 1968. Oddo Pub.
--Where Is Duckling Three?. Le Blanc, Lee, illus. LC 68-16402. (Illus.). 32 p. 26cm. (Easy-to-read book.). (The Wonderful World of Children's Books). 1968. Oddo Pub.
Green, Ivah E. & Bromwell, Alice
--Woody, the Litte Wood Duck. Mason, George Frederick (1904-), illus. LC 55-8536. 63p. ill. 22cm. 1955. Abelard Schuman.
Green, Janet
--The Six. LC 78-1433. p. cm. 1978. (ISBN 0-8038-6753-0). Hastings House.
--Us,. Inside a Teenage Gang. Brown, Lance, photos by. LC 82-3089. (Illus.). 126 p. 22cm. 1982, c.1975. (ISBN 0-8038-6753-0). Hastings House Publishers.
Green, Kate (1846-1901)
--Marigold Garden. LC 72-3992. (Peter Possum Paperbacks Ser). 1967. (ISBN 0-531-05120-X). Watts.
Green, Kathleen
--Leprechaun Tales. 1st ed. De Larrea, Victoria, illus. (Illus.). 127 p. 21cm. 1968. Lippincott.

--Philip and the Pooka. De Larrea, Victoria, illus. LC 66-10897. 93p. illus. 22cm. c.1966. Lippincott.

Green, Laura

--Help: Getting to Know About Needing & Giving. Mayo, Gretchen, illus. LC 80-81082. 32p. (Juvenile Ser.). 1981. (ISBN 0-87705-402-9). Human Sci Pr.

Green, Levi Worthington (1858-)

--The Boy Fugitives in Mexico. LC 14-19136. 5 p. l., 277, 1 p. front., plates. 19 cm. 1914. Houghton Mifflin Company.

--Two American Boys in the War Zone. LC 15-21627. 5 p. l., 282 p., 1 l. front., plates. 20 cm. 1915. Houghton Mifflin Company.

Green, Lila, ed.

--Folktales and Fairytales of Africa. Pinkney, Jerry (1939-), illus. Grumm, Frank, designed by. LC 67-16761. 96p. col. illus. 25cm. (Folk lit. around the world). 1967. Silver Burdett.

--Folktales of Spain and Latin America. Silverstein, Donald (1932-), illus. LC 67-16760. (Illus.). 96 p. 25cm. (Fold literature around the world). 1967. Silver Burdett.

--Tales from Africa. Pinkney, Jerry (1939-), illus. LC 78-54623. (Illus.). 96 p. 25cm. (The World Folktale Library). c.1979. (ISBN 0-382-03330-7). Silver Burdett Co.

--Tales from Hispanic Lands. Silverstein, Donald (1932-), illus. LC 78-54624. (Illus.). 96 p. 25cm. (The World Folktale Library). c.1979. (ISBN 0-382-03349-3). Silver Burdett Co.

Green, Margaret Murphy (1926-), ed.

--The Big Book of Animal Fables. Green, Margaret Murphy (1926-), illus. LC 65-22100. (Illus.). 240 p. 25cm. 1965. F. Watts.

The Big Book of Animal Stories. Grabianski, Janusz (1928-1976), illus. LC 61-688913. 236p. illus. 25cm. 1961. F. Watts. **Award: (NYT).**

--The Big Book of Wild Animals. Grabianski, Janusz (1928-1976), illus. LC 63-7132. (Illus.). 236 p. 25cm. 1964. F. Watts.

Green, Marion

--The Magician Who Lived on the Mountain. american ed. Dyke, John (1935-), illus. LC 78-57506. p. cm. 1978, c.1977. (ISBN 0-516-03539-8). Childrens Press.

Green, Mary McBurney (1896-)

--Everybody Eats. Bloch, Lucienne (1909-), illus. LC 50-6493. 24cm. 20p. 1950. Young Scot Books.

--Everybody Eats. Glannon, Edward John (1911-), illus. LC 48-7868. 24cm. 20p. 1946. W. R. Scott.

--Everybody Eats. Klein, Louis, illus. LC 61-16070. 21 x 24cm. 1961. Young Scott Books.

--Everybody Grows Up. Granda, Sheila, illus. LC 69-11257. 27cm. 48p. 1969. F. Watts.

--Everybody Has a House. Bendick, Jeanne (1919-), illus. LC 44-4337. 24 x 21cm. 20p. 1944. W. R. Scott.

--Everybody Has a House. Klein, Louis, illus. LC 61-16071. 21 x 24cm. 1961. Young Scott Books.

--Is It Hard? Is It Easy?. Bloch, Lucienne (1909-), illus. 20 p. col. illus. 21 x 23 cm. c.1948. W. R. Scott.

--Is It Hard? Is It Easy. Gittleman, Len, illus. LC 60-501698. unpaged. illus. 27cm. (Young Scott books). c.1960. W. R. Scott.

--When Will I Whistle?. Berson, Harold (1926-), illus. LC 67-18242. (Illus.). 47 p. 27cm. 1967. F. Watts.

--Whose Little Red Jacket?. De Luna, Tony, illus. LC 65-11584. 1 v. (unpaged) col. illus. 26 cm. 1965. F. Watts.

Green, Melinda

--Bembelman's Bakery. Seuling, Barbara (1937-), illus. LC 77-22858. (Illus.). 32 p. 24cm. c.1978. (ISBN 0-8193-0913-3). (ISBN 0-8193-0914-1). Parents' Magazine Press.

--Rachel's Recital. Green, Melinda, illus. LC 79-1510. (Illus.). 47 p. 25cm. c.1979. (ISBN 0-316-32634-8). Little, Brown.

Green, Morton (1937-)

--Blue Skies Magic. Price, Hugh, illus. LC 72-80121. (Illus.). 24 p. 23cm. (Magic circle book). 1974. (ISBN 0-663-29159-3). Ginn.

Green, Nancy

--ABU Kassim's Slippers. Mars, Witold Tadensz J. (1912-), illus. LC 63-17801. 26cm. 32p. 1963. Follette Co.

--The Bigger Giant. N.D. Follette Co.

--The Bigger Giant. 32p. (gr. k-3). 1969. (ISBN 0-590-08014-8, Schol Pap). Schol Bk Serv.

Green, Nathan (1827-1919)

--The Tall Man of Winton and His Wife. LC 26-3675. 303 p. 16 cm. (Gem library, v. 2). 1872. Cumberland Presbyterian Board of Publication.

Green, Norma Berger (1925-), ed.

--Bears, Bees, and Birch Trees: Russian Riddles and Rhymes. Green, Norma Berger (1925-), illus. LC 72-79882. (Illus.). 32 p. 1973. (ISBN 0-385-02186-0). (ISBN 0-385-02186-0). Doubleday.

Green, Peter, jt. auth. see Grahame, Kenneth.

Green, Phyllis (1932-)

--Bagdad Ate It. Schick, Joel (1945-), illus. LC 79-1160. (Illus.). 32 p. 22cm. (Easy-read story book). 1980. (ISBN 0-531-03429-1). Franklin Watts.

--Eating Ice Cream with a Werewolf. Stren, Patti, illus. LC 82-47727. p. cm. 1983. (ISBN 0-06-022140-2). (ISBN 0-06-022141-0). Harper & Row.

--The Empty Seat. LC 79-21813. p. cm. 1979. (ISBN 0-525-66660-5). Elsevier/Nelson Books.

--The Faster Quitter in Town. 48p. 1972. (ISBN 0-201-09170-4). Addision-Wesley.

--The Fastest Quitter in Town. Lynch, Lorenzo (1932-), illus. LC 84-43142. p. cm. 1985, c.1972. (ISBN 0-201-09170-4). Harper & Row.

The Fastest Quitter in Town. Lynch, Lorenzo (1932-), illus. LC 72-761. (Illus.). 62 p. 23cm. 1972. (ISBN 0-201-09170-4). Young Scott Books.

--Gloomy Louie. Wallner, John C. (1945-), illus. LC 79-28533. (Illus.). 63 p. 21cm. 1980. (ISBN 0-8075-2962-1). A. Whitman.

--Grandmother Orphan. LC 77-22856. p. cm. c.1977. (ISBN 0-8407-6556-8). T. Nelson.

--Grandmother Orphan. Orellana, Ramon F., illus. 1975. (ISBN 0-87955-210-7). J. Philip O'Hara Inc.

--Ice River. Crowell, James (1936-), illus. LC 74-28382. (Illus.). 48 p. 22cm. 1975. (ISBN 0-201-02582-5). Addison-Wesley.

--Mildred Murphy, How Does Your Garden Grow?. Pinkney, Jerry (1939-), illus. LC 76-28459. (Illus.). 89 p. 22cm. c.1977. (ISBN 0-201-02594-9). Addison-Wesley.

--Nantucket Summer. LC 74-10276. 122 p. 21cm. 1974. (ISBN 0-8407-6403-0). Nelson.

--A New Mother for Martha. Luks, Peggy, illus. LC 78-16731. (Illus.). 32 p. 24cm. c.1978. Human Sciences Press.

--Nicky's Lopsided, Lumpy, but Delicious Orange. LC 78-4599. p. cm. c.1978. (ISBN 0-201-02590-6). Addison-Wesley.

--Uncle Roland, the Perfect Guest. Farrell, Mary Beth, illus. LC 82-5019. (Illus.). 32p. (ps-2). 1983. (ISBN 0-590-07885-2, Four Winds). (ISBN 0-517-54755-4). Scholastic Inc.

--Walkie-Talkie. LC 77-14154. 1978. (ISBN 0-201-02630-9, A-W Childrens). A-W.

--Wild Violets. LC 76-56124. 104 p. 21cm. c.1977. (ISBN 0-8407-6531-2). T. Nelson.

Green, Richard L., ed.

--Strange Adventures in Time. Adamson, George Worsley (1913-), illus. (Illus.). (Children's Illustrated Classics Ser.). (gr. 4-7). 1975. (ISBN 0-525-40412-0). Dutton.

Green, Robert James

--Hawk of the Nile. Miller, Shane (1907-), illus. LC 62-12450. 212p. illus. 21cm. 1962. St. Martin's Press.

--Kor and the Wolf Dogs. Lewis, Geoffrey Dean, illus. LC 56-9157. 220p. illus. 22cm. c.1956. Lothrop, Lee &Shepard.

--Patriot Silver. Bjorklund, Lorence F. (1913-1978), illus. LC 61-7888. 183p. illus. 21cm. (gr. 5-9). 1961. St. Martin's Press.

--Two Swords for a Princess. LC 57-11731. 217p. 21cm. 1957. Lothrop, Lee & Shepard.

--The Whistling Sword. Bjorklund, Lorence F. (1913-1978), illus. LC 62-14163. 159p. 21cm. c.1962. St. Martin's.

Green, Robert W.

--The Ebony Tree & the Spirit of Christmas. (Illus.). 48p. (gr. 2-4). 1975. (ISBN 0-682-48174-2). Exposition.

Green, Roger Gilbert Lancelyn (1918-), ed. see Carroll, Lewis.

Green, Roger Gilbert Lancelyn (1918-), ed. see Ballantyne, Robert Michael.

Green, Roger Gilbert Lancelyn (1918-), ed. see Dodgson, Charles Lutwidge.

Green, Roger Gilbert Lancelyn (1918-), selected by see Molesworth, Mary Louisa Stewart, Mrs.

Green, Roger Gilbert Lancelyn (1918-), ed. see Poe, Edgar Allan.

Green, Roger Gilbert Lancelyn (1918-)

--Adventures of Robin Hood. (Orig.). (gr. 2-5). 1956. (ISBN 0-14-030101-1, Puffin). Penguin.

--Beauty and the Bear and Other Tales. 79p. N.D. British Book Centre.

--A Book of Myths. (Illus.). Repr. of 1965 ed. (Childrens Illustrated Classics Ser). 1976. (ISBN 0-460-05066-4, Pub. by J. M. Dent England). Biblio Dist.

--Folk Tales of the World. Johnstone, Janet Grahame & Johnstone, Anne Grahame, illus. 1966. Ginn.

--Heroes of Greece & Troy. Copley, Heather (1920-) & Chamberlain, Christopher (1918-), illus. LC 61-14925. (Illus.). (gr. 8 up). 1961. (ISBN 0-8098-3036-1). Walck.

--King Arthur & His Knights of the Round Table. (Orig.). (gr. 5-7). 1974. (ISBN 0-14-030073-2, Puffin). Penguin.

--The Land Beyond the North. Hall, Douglas (1931-), illus. LC 59-1337. 157p. illus. 21cm. 1959, c.1958. H.Z. Walck.

--The Luck of Troy. 176p. (Puffin Story Bks.). (gr. 4up). 1976. (ISBN 0-14-030305-7, Puffin). Penguin.

--The Luck of Troy. Gill, Margery Jean (1925-), illus. LC 64-25457. 159 p. illus. 21 cm. (gr. 4-8). 1965. (ISBN 0-8023-1050-8). Dufour.

--Luck of Troy. Gill, Margery Jean (1925-), illus. 176p. (gr. 1-6). 1961. (ISBN 0-14-030305-7, Puffin). Penguin.

--The Luck of Troy. Gill, Margery Jean (1925-), illus. (Illus.). 18cm. 174p. (Puffin bks.: PS 305). 1967. Penguin.

--Mystery at Mycenae: An Adventure Story of Ancient Greece. Gill, Margery Jean (1925-), illus. LC 59-12798. 136p. illus. 21cm. (Wonderful world book). 1959. Barnes.

--Myths of the Norsemen. Wildsmith, Brian Lawrence (1930-), illus. 1970. (ISBN 0-14-030464-9, Puffin). Penguin.

--Once Upon a Time. Kubasts, Voljtech, illus. 1963. Golden Press.

--Once Upon a Time: Folk and Fairy Tales of the World. LC 63-15612. 30cm. 140p. 1962. Golden Press.

--Sleeping Beauty and Other Tales. Cloke, Rene, illus. 78p. 1947. British Book Centre Inc.

--Tale of Troy. (Illus., Orig.). (gr. 5-7). 1974. (ISBN 0-14-030120-8, Puffin). Penguin.

--Tales from Shakespeare. Beer, Richard, illus. (Illus.). (gr. 5 up). 1965. (ISBN 0-689-20120-6). (ISBN 0-689-20117-6). Atheneum.

--Tales of Greek Heroes. (Orig.). (gr. 5-7). 1974. (ISBN 0-14-030119-4, Puffin). Penguin.

--Tales the Muses Told. Bolognese, Donald Alan (1934-), illus. LC 65-22661. (Illus.). (gr. 8 up). 1965. (ISBN 0-8098-2383-7). Walck.

--The Wonderful Stranger: A Holiday Romance. Baynes, John, illus. N.D. British Book Centre.

Green, Roger Gilbert Lancelyn (1918-), ed.

--An All-Around Boy. N.D. Lentilhon & Co.

--Book of Myths. Kiddell-Monroe, Joan (1908-), illus. (Illus.). (Children's Illustrated Classics). (gr. 2-6). N.D. (ISBN 0-525-26968-1). Dutton.

--A Book of Myths. Kiddell-Monroe, Joan (1908-), illus. LC 65-3519. viii, 184 p. illus. (part col.) 22 cm. (C.I.C. series, no. 66). 1965. J. M. Dent.

--Book of Nonsense. Folkard, Charles James, et al. (1878-1963), illus. (gr. 2-7). 1956. (ISBN 0-525-26996-7). Dutton.

--The Book of Nonsense. Folkard, Charles James, et al. (1878-1963), illus. LC 56-12852. (Illus.). 22cm. 266p. (The Children's Illustrated Classics). c.1956. Dutton.

--A Cavalcade of Dragons. Turska, Krystyna Zofia (1933-), illus. LC 72-118776. (Illus.). xi, 256 p. 26cm. 1970. (ISBN 0-8098-2413-2). H. Z. Walck.

A Cavalcade of Magicians. Ambrus, Victor G., pseud. (1935-), illus. Ambrus, Gyozo Laszlo. LC 72-6877. (Illus.). xii, 274 p. 26cm. 1973. (ISBN 0-8098-2422-1). H. Z. Walck.

--The Hamish Hamilton Book of Other Worlds. Ambrus, Victor G., pseud. (1935-), illus. Ambrus, Gyozo Laszlo. LC 77-367379. (Illus.). xiii, 239 p. 26cm. 1976. (ISBN 0-241-89244-9). Hamilton.

--Modern Fairy Stories. Shepard, Ernest Howard (1879-1976), illus. LC 56-6632. 270p. illus. 22cm. (Children's illustrated classics). 1955. Dent.

--Modern Fairy Stories. Shepard, Ernest Howard (1879-1976), illus. (Illus.). (Children's Illustrated Classics). (gr. 3-6). 1956. (ISBN 0-525-35049-7). Dutton.

--Myths from Many Lands. Grahame Johnstone, Anne & Grahame Johnstone, Janet, illus. LC 66-255008. 77p. col. illus. 31cm. 1966, c.1965. Purnell.

--Myths of the Norsemen. Wildsmith, Brian Lawrence (1930-), illus. (Illus.). (gr. 4-8). 1964. (ISBN 0-370-01049-3) Dufour.

--Old Greek Fairy Tales. Shepard, Ernest Howard (1879-1976), illus. LC 79-89814. (Illus.). 186 p. 20cm. 1969, c.1958. Roy Publishers.

--Saga of Asgard. N.D. Penguin Bks.

--Strange Adventures in Time. (Illus.). 192p. 1st U.S. edition. (Childrens Illustrated Classics Ser). 1974. (ISBN 0-460-05097-4, Pub. by J. M. Dent England). Biblio Dist.

--Tale of Ancient Israel. Keeping, Charles William James (1924-), illus. (gr. 3-7). 1969. Dutton.

--The Tale of Thebes. Jordan, Jael Michal (1949-), illus. LC 76-22979. (Illus.). xiii, 102 p., 3 leaves of plates. 23cm. 1977. (ISBN 0-521-21410-6). (ISBN 0-521-21434-3). Cambridge University Press.

--Tales of Ancient Egypt. 1968. (ISBN 0-8098-3074-4). David McKay Company.

--Tales of Ancient Egypt. Copley, Heather (1920-), illus. (Illus.). 183 p. 18cm. (Puffin bks.). 1972, c.1967. (ISBN 0-14-030438-X). Penguin Bks. in Assn. with Bodley Head.

--Tales of Ancient Egypt. Raphael, Elaine, pseud. (1933-), illus. Bolognese, Elaine Raphael Chionchio. 1968. Penguin.

--Tales of Make-Believe. Toothill, Harry, illus. LC 60-52205. 235p. illus. 22cm. (Children's illustrated classics). (NO. 48). 1960. Dent.

--Tales of Make-Belive. Toothill, Harry, illus. LC 60-52205. (Illus.). 22cm. 235p. (Children's Illustrated Classics). 1960. Dutton.

--Tales of the Greeks and Trojans. Grahame Johnstone, Anne & Grahame Johnstone, Janet, illus. LC 66-25499. 77p. col. illus. 31cm. 1966, c.1963. Purnell.

--Ten Tales of Adventure. (Illus.). 204p. 1st U.S. edition. (Children Illustrated Classics Ser). 1972. (ISBN 0-460-05093-1, Pub. by J. M. Dent England). Biblio Dist.

--Ten Tales of Detection. (Illus.). 220p. 1st U.S. edition. Repr. of 1967 ed. (Childrens Illustrated Classics Ser). 1968. (ISBN 0-460-05072-9, Pub. by J. M. Dent England). Biblio Dist.

--Ten Tales of Detection. Ribbons, Ian (1924-), illus. (Illus.). (Children's Illustrated Classics Ser.). (gr. 7 up). 1967. (ISBN 0-525-40882-7). Dutton.

--Thirteen Uncanny Tales. (Illus.). 218p. 1st U.S. edition. (Childrens Illustrated Classics Ser). 1970. (ISBN 0-460-05085-0, Pub. by J. M. Dent England). Biblio Dist.

--Thirteen Uncanny Tales. Ogden, Ray, illus. LC 74-481905. 22cm. 201p. (Children's illustrated classics: No. 85). (gr. 6 up). 1970. Dutton.

Green, Roger J.

--The Fear of Samuel Walton. (Illus.). 234p. (gr. 6 up). 1984. (ISBN 0-19-271474-0, Pub. by Oxford U Pr Childrens). Merrimack Pub Cir.

Green, Sheila Ellen see Greenwald, Sheila, pseud.

Green Tiger Press, ed.

--Bubbles & Bubble Blowers. (Illus.). 12p. 1982. (ISBN 0-88138-000-8, Pub. by Envelope Bks). Green Tiger Pr

--The Dream Pedlar. (Illus.). 96p. 1st U.S. edition. 1982. (ISBN 0-914676-58-X, Star & Eleph Bks). Green Tiger Pr.

--Flying Horses. 12p. (Orig.). 1982. (ISBN 0-88138-005-9, Pub. by Envelope Bks). Green Tiger Pr.

--Kites. (Illus.). 12p. (Envelope Bks.). 1983. (ISBN 0-686-88575-9). Green Tiger Pr.

--Mermaids. (Illus.). 12p. (Orig.). 1982. (ISBN 0-88138-001-6, Pub. by Envelope Bks). Green Tiger Pr.

--Women with Long Hair. (Illus.). 12p. (Orig.). 1982. (ISBN 0-88138-006-7, Pub. by Envelope Bks). Green Tiger Pr.

Green, Walter D & Hauge, Patricia A.

--Grandfather's Treat: A Story. 1st. ed. Marham, Robert L., illus. 32 p. 22cm. (gr. 1-4). 1974. (ISBN 0-682-47946-2). Exposition Press.

Green, Warren Sherman (1924-)

--Elmo, the Christmas Glork. Green, Warren Sherman (1924-), illus. LC 51-14940. unpaged. illus. 14 x 22 cm. 1951. Pageant Press.

Greenawalt, Ethel M.

--Autumn in God's World. N.D. Standard Pub.

Greenaway, Kate (1846-1901)

--A Apple Pie. Evans, Edmund (1826-1905), illus. LC 17-13047. 22 l. col. illus. 22 x 26 1/2 cm. 1886. G. Routledge and Sons.

--Chatterbox Hall. Greenaway, Kate (1846-1901), illus. (Illus.). N.D. Worthington Company.

--Fairy Gifts: Or, A Wallet of Wonders. Greenaway, Kate (1846-1901), illus. N.D. E P Dutton.

--The Kate Greenaway Treasury. Ernest, Edward, ed. Greenaway, Kate (1846-1901), illus. LC 67-23363. 319p. illus. (pt. col.), ports. 27cm. 1967. World.

--The Kate Greenaway Treasury: An Anthology of the Illustrations and Writings of Kate Greenaway. Greenaway, Kate (1846-1901), illus. (Illus.). 319 p. 27cm. 1967. World Pub. Co.

--Kate Greenaway's Birthday Book for Children. N.D. Frederick Warne & Co.

--Kate Greenaway's Birthday Book for Children. Barker, Lucy Davis (1841-), contrib. by. Barker, Mrs Sale, pseud. Greenaway, Kate (1846-1901), illus. LC 12-32656. (Illus.). 126p. 10 x 10cm. 1880. G. Routledge.

--Kate Greenaway's Birthday Book for Children: Special De-Luxe Leather-Bound Edition. N.D. Frederick Warne & Co.

--Kate Greenaway's Family Treasury. LC 79-16363. p. cm. 1979. (ISBN 0-517-31005-8). Derrydale Books.

--Kate Greenaway's Mother Goose: Or, The Old Nursery Rhymes. Greenaway, Kate (1846-1901), illus. LC 78-61430. (Illus.). 55 p. 27cm. 1978. (ISBN 0-517-26289-4). Gramercy Pub. Co.

--The Language of Flowers. Greenaway, Kate (1846-1901), illus. (Greenaway's Picture Books Ser.). N.D. Frederick Warne & Co.

--Marigold Garden. (Illus.). (gr. k-3). 1885. (ISBN 0-7232-1800-5). Warne.

--Marigold Garden. Greenaway, Kate (1846-1901), illus. 56 p. incl. col. front., col. illus. 25 1/2 cm. 1910. F. Warne & Co.

--Marigold Garden. Greenaway, Kate (1846-1901) & Evans, Edmund (1826-1905), illus. LC 30-1004. 60 p. incl. col. front., col. illus. 27 1/2 x 23 cm. 1885. G. Routledge and Sons.

--Mother Goose. Greenaway, Kate (1846-1901), illus. (Illus.). 12p. Repr. of 1890 ed (Pub. by Warne). (ps-5). 1973. (ISBN 0-914510-04-5). Evergreen.
--Mother Goose & Nursery Rhymes. Greenaway, Kate (1846-1901), illus. (Illus.). 32p. (Kate Greenaway). (gr. k up). 1972. World Pub.
--Mother Goose: Or, The Old Nursery Rhymes. Greenaway, Kate (1846-1901), illus. LC 79-66806. (Illus.). 80 p. 29cm. c.1979. (ISBN 0-89009-305-9). Castle Books.
--Mother Goose: Or, The Old Nursery Rhymes. Greenaway, Kate (1846-1901), illus. LC 64-36652. (Illus.). 52 p. 17cm. 1964. F. Warne.
--Songs & Games. Greenaway, Kate (1846-1901), illus. (Illus.). 32p. (gr. k up). 1972. World Pub.
--Starlight Stories Told to Bright Eyes and Listening Ears. Greenaway, Kate (1846-1901), illus. N.D. Publications of E. P. Dutton & Co.
--Under the Window. (Illus.). (gr. 1-4). 1879. (ISBN 0-7232-1799-8). Warne.
--Under the Window. Greenaway, Kate (1846-1901), illus. 1910. Warne.
--Under the Window: A Beautiful Volume of Rhymes for Children. LC 13-2489. 24cm. 64p. N.D. George Routledge.
--Under the Window: Pictures and Rhymes for Children. Evans, Edmund (1826-1905), illus. LC 13-2489. (Illus.). 64p. 24cm. 1878. G. Routledge.

Greenaway, Kate (1846-1901), adapted by.
--Under the Window: Pictures and Rhymes for Children. Greenaway, Kate (1846-1901), illus. LC 15-240. (Illus.). 64p. 24 x 18cm. 1880. G. Routledge & Sons.

Greenaway, Kate (1846-1901) & Moore, Anne Carroll (1871-1961)
--Kate Greenaway Treasury. Ernest, Edward & Lowe, Patricia Tracy, eds. Greenaway, Kate (1846-1901), illus. (Illus.). (gr. 6 up). 1967. (ISBN 0-529-00313-9). World Pub.

Greenbaum, Everett, jt. auth. see Cox, Wallace Maynard.

Greenberg, Barbara (1940-)
--The Bravest Babysitter. Paterson, Diane R. Cole (1946-), illus. LC 77-71516. (Illus.). 32 p. 21cm. c.1977. (ISBN 0-8037-0363-5). (ISBN 0-8037-0364-3). Dial Press.

Greenberg, David
--Slugs. 1st ed. Chess, Victoria (1939-), illus. LC 82-10017. (Illus.). 31 p. c.1983. (ISBN 0-316-32659-3). Little, Brown.

Greenberg, Dorothy Rossen
--Siege Hero. Borja, Robert (1923-), illus. LC 64-661296. 142p. illus. (pt. col.) map. 21cm. bibl. c.1965. Reilly & Lee.

Greenberg, Eliezer, jt. ed. see Howe, Irving.

Greenberg, Evelyn Levow (1923-)
--The Little Tractor Who Traveled to Israel. Levy, Israel, illus. LC 49-3022. 48 p. illus. 21 cm. 1949. Behrman House.

Greenberg, Jan (1942-)
--Bye, Bye, Miss American Pie. LC 85-47590. 149 p. 22cm. 1985. (ISBN 0-374-31012-2). Farrar, Straus, Giroux.
--The Iceberg and Its Shadow. LC 80-20060. p. cm. c.1980. (ISBN 0-374-33624-5). Farrar, Straus and Giroux.
--No Dragons to Slay. 1st ed. LC 83-17200. p. cm. 1983. (ISBN 0-374-35528-2). Farrar, Straus, Giroux.
--The Pig-Out Blues. LC 82-2552. p. cm. 1982. (ISBN 0-374-35937-7). Farrar, Straus & Giroux.
--A Season in-Between. LC 79-17997. p. cm. c.1979. (ISBN 0-374-36564-4). Farrar Straus Giroux.

Greenberg, Joanne Goldenberg (1932-)
--Summering: A Book of Short Stories. 1966. Holt, Rinehart and Winston.

Greenberg, Martin Harry, jt. auth. see Asimov, Isaac.

Greenberg, Martin Harry, jt. ed. see Asimov, Isaac.

Greenberg, Martin Harry (1941-), ed. see Warrick, Patricia Scott.

Greenberg, Martin Harry, jt. ed. see Waugh, Charles G.

Greenberg, Martin Harry (1941-) & Olander, Joseph D, eds.
--Run to Starlight: Sports Through Science Fiction. LC 75-8005. vi, 383 22. 1975. (ISBN 0-440-07401-0). Delacorte Press.

Greenberg, Polly (1932-), ed. see Henton, Gladys.

Greenberg, Polly (1932-)
--The Devil Has Slippery Shoes. 1969. MacMillan Publishing Company.
--If You Really Believe It. 1976. Macmillan Company.

Greenberg, Robert A., ed.
--Gulliver's Travels. 1961. (ISBN 0-393-05321-0). (ISBN 0-393-09568-1). Norton & Co.

Greenberg, Sylvia S. & Raskin, Edith L.
--Home-Made Zoo. 1952. David McKay Co.

Greenbie, Sydney (1889-) & Institute of Pacific Relations. American Council
--An American Boy Visits the Orient. Seacord, Alice Nicholson, illus. LC 47-2707. vii, 311 p. incl. front. (map) illus. 21 1/2 cm. 1946. Webster Publishing Company.

Greenburg, Dan (1936-)
--Jumbo the Boy and Arnold the Elephant. 1st ed. Perl, Susan (1922-1983), illus. LC 69-12434. (Illus.). 47 p. 29cm. 1969. Bobbs-Merrill.

Greenburg, Joanne
--Jack and the Beanstalk. Walsh, Michael Sean, illus. LC 80-20571. (Illus.). 48 p. 25cm. c.1981. (ISBN 0-8299-1033-6). West Pub. Co.

Greene
--The Babei the Mill: And Zanina, the Flower Girl of Florence. (Illus.). N.D. Thomas Nelson & Sons.
--Bound by a Spell: Or, The Haunted Witch of the Forest. Juv ed. Browne, Gordon Frederick (1858-1932), illus. 376p. N.D. Cassell & Co.
--On Angels Wings: The Story of Little Violet of Edelsheim. (Illus.). N.D. Thomas Nelson & Sons.
--The Phantom Picture. (Illus.). N.D. Thomas Nelson & Sons.
--The Star in the Dustheap. (Warne's Golden Link Ser.). N.D. Frederick Warne & Co.

Greene, Anne Bosworth, Mrs. (1877-)
--Greylight. Relyea, Charles M., illus. LC 24-20509. 5 p. l., 3-222 p. front., plates. 19 1/2 cm. $1.7. c.1924. The Century Co.
--The White Pony in the Hills. Relyea, Charles M., illus. LC 27-9452. ix, 254 p. front., plates. 19 1/2 cm. c.1927. The Century Co.

Greene, Belle C.
--The Hobbledehoy: The Story of one Betwixt Boy and Man. (Illus.). N.D. Lothrop Pub. Co.

Greene, Bette (1934-)
--Morning Is a Long Time Coming. LC 76-42933. 261 p. 22cm. c.1978. (ISBN 0-8037-5496-5). Dial Press.
--Philip Hall Likes Me, I Reckon, Maybe. Lilly, Charles, illus. LC 74-2887. (Illus.). 135 p. 22cm. 1974. (ISBN 0-8037-6098-1). (ISBN 0-8037-6098-1). Dial Press. **Award: (JNM).**
--Summer of My German Soldier. LC 73-6025. 230 p. 22cm. 1973. Dial Press. **Award: (ALA).**
--Them That Glitter and Them That Don't. LC 82-13020. p. cm. 1983. (ISBN 0-394-84692-3). Knopf : Distributed by Random House.

Greene, Carla (1916-)
--Animal Doctors: What Do They Do?. Kessler, Leonard P. (1921-), illus. LC 67-14065. (Illus.). 5 7/8 x 8 1/2. 64p. (18 pt.). (I Can Read Bks.). (gr. k-3). 1967. (ISBN 0-06-022078-3). Har-Row.
--Before the Dinosaurs. Cuffari, Richard (1925-1978), illus. LC 70-119376. (Illus.). 80 p. 24cm. 1971, c.1970. Bobbs-Merrill.
--Cowboys: What Do They Do?. Kessler, Leonard P. (1921-), illus. LC 72-183160. (Illus.). 64p. (I Can Read Books). (gr. k-3). 1972. (ISBN 0-06-022081-3, HarpJ). (ISBN 0-06-022082-1, HarpJ). Har-Row.
--Doctors and Nurses, What Do They Do?. Kessler, Leonard P. (1921-), illus. LC 62-13313. 64 p. illus. 22 cm. (I can read book). 1963. Harper & Row.
--Holiday in a Trailer. Van Pelt, Harold L., photos by. LC 55-2998. 31p. illus. 20x21cm. (Look, read, learn). 1955. Melmont Publishers.
--A Hotel Holiday. Hoffman, William L., photos by. LC 55-24391. (Illus.). 31 p. 1954. Melmont Publishers.
--I Want to Be a Baker. Williamson, Audrey, illus. LC 56-4237. unpaged. illus. 25 cm. 1956. Childrens Press.
--I Want to Be a Ballet Dancer. Gehr, Mary, designed by. LC 59-16080. unpaged. illus. 25cm. 1959. Childrens Press.
--I Want to Be a Baseball Player. Eckart, Frances, illus. LC 61-10089. 25cm. 32p. 1961. Childrens Press.
--I Want to Be a Bus Driver. Evans, Katherine Floyd (1901-1964), illus. LC 57-9582. 25cm. 32p. ('I want to be' books). c.1957. Childrens Press.
--I Want to Be a Carpenter. Eckart, Frances, illus. LC 59-160816. 25cm. 32p. 1959. Childrens Press.
--I Want to Be a Coal Miner. Williamson, Audrey, illus. LC 57-3256. 25cm. 32p. 1957. Childrens Press.
--I Want to Be a Cowboy. LaSalle, Janet (1926-), illus. LC 60-6673. 25cm. 32p. 1960. Childrens Press.
--I Want to Be a Dairy Farmer. Eckart, Frances, illus. LC 57-95782. 25cm. 32p. ('I want to be' books). c.1957. Childrens Press.
--I Want to Be a Dentist. Wilde, Irma, illus. LC 60-11152. unpaged. illus. 25cm. 1960. Childrens Press.
--I Want to Be a Doctor. Eckart, Frances, illus. LC 58-3321. 25cm. 32p. 1958. Childrens Press.
--I Want to Be a Farmer. Wilde, George A. & Wilde, Irma, illus. LC 59-735. 25cm. 32p. 1959. Childrens Press.
--I Want to Be a Fireman. Wilde, George A. & Wilde, Irma, illus. LC 59-358825. 25cm. 32p. 1959. Childrens Press.
--I Want to Be a Fisherman. Hawkinson, Lucy Ozone (1924-1971) & Hawkinson, John Samuel (1912-), illus. LC 57-956. unpaged. illus. 25cm. ('I want to be' books). c.1957. Childrens Press.
--I Want to Be a Homemaker. Eckart, Frances, illus. 25cm. 32p. 1961. Childrens Press.
--I Want to Be a Librarian. Eckart, Frances, illus. LC 60-667488. 25cm. 32p. 1960. Childrens Press.
--I Want to Be a Mechanic. Gehr, Mary, designed by. LC 59-3587. unpaged. illus. 25cm. 1959. Childrens Press.
--I Want to Be a News Reporter. Eckart, Frances, illus. LC 58-3322. 25cm. 32p. 1958. Childrens Press.
--I Want to Be a Nurse. Krehbiel, Becky & Krehbiel, Evans, illus. LC 57-955. unpaged. illus. 25cm. ('I want to be' books). c.1957. Childrens Press.
--I Want to Be a Pilot. Gates, Richard, illus. LC 57-3434. 25cm. 32p. 1957. Childrens Press.
--I Want to Be a Policeman. Rogers, Carol, illus. (Illus.). 32 p. 25cm. 1958. Childrens Press.
--I Want to Be a Postman. Evans, Katherine Floyd (1901-1964), illus. LC 58-146155. 25cm. 32p. 1958. Childrens Press.
--I Want to Be a Restaurant Owner. Rogers, Carol, illus. LC 59-16079. 25cm. 32p. 1959. Childrens Press.
--I Want to Be a Road-Builder. Wilde, George A. & Wilde, Irma, illus. (Illus.). 32 p. 25cm. 1958. Childrens Press.
--I Want to Be a Scientist. LaSalle, Janet (1926-), illus. LC 61-10087. 25cm. 32p. 1961. Childrens Press.
--I Want to Be a Ship Captain. Palm, Felix, illus. LC 62-156368. 25cm. 32p. 1962. Childrens Press.
--I Want to Be a Space Pilot. LC 61-10090. (Illus.). unpaged. 25cm. 1961. Childrens Press.
--I Want to Be a Storekeeper. Eckart, Frances, illus. LC 58-14617. 25cm. 32p. 1958. Childrens Press.
--I Want to Be a Teacher. Johnson, Vie, illus. LC 57-3488. unpaged. illus. 25cm. 1957. Childrens Press.
--I Want to Be a Telephone Operator. Gehr, Mary, designed by. LC 58-146181. unpaged. illus. 25cm. 1958. Childrens Press.
--I Want to Be a Train Engineer. Havel, Victor, illus. LC 56-4236. unpaged. illus. 25cm. ('I want to be' books). 1956. Childrens Press.
--I Want to Be a Truck-Driver. Wilde, George A. & Wilde, Irma, illus. 25cm. 32p. 1958. Childrens Press.
--I Want to Be a Zoo-Keeper. Eckart, Frances, illus. 25cm. 32p. 1957. Childrens Press.
--I Want to Be an Airplane Hostess. Eckart, Frances, illus. LC 60-11153. 25cm. 32p. 1960. Childrens Press.
--I Want to Be an Animal Doctor. Eckart, Frances, illus. LC 56-4392. 25cm. 32p. 1956. Childrens Press.
--I Want to Be an Orange Grower. Williamson, Audrey, illus. LC 56-4393. 25cm. 32p. 1956. Childrens Press.
--Manuel, Young Mexican-American. Petie, Haris, pseud. (1915-), illus. Petty, Roberta. LC 78-88735. (Illus.). 47 p. 24cm. 1969. Lantern Press.
--Moses: The Great Lawgiver. Lewis, Anne, illus. (Illus.). 45 p. 27cm. 1968. Harvey House.
--A Motor Holiday. (Illus.). 31 p. (Look, read, learn). 1956. Melmont Publishers.
--Policemen and Firemen: What Do They Do?. Kessler, Leonard P. (1921-), illus. LC 62-8036. 64p. illus. 22cm. (I can read book). 1962. Harper.
--Soldiers & Sailors: What Do They Do?. Kessler, Leonard P. (1921-), illus. LC 63-15325. (Illus.). 5 7/8 x 8 1/2. 64p. (18 pt.). (I Can Read Bks.). (gr. k-3). 1963. (ISBN 0-06-022096-1). Har-Row.
--Soldiers and Sailors: What Do They Do?. Kessler, Leonard P. (1921-), illus. (Illus.). 64 p. 23cm. (I can read book). 1963. Harper & Row.
--A Trip on a Bus. (Illus.). 62 p. 23cm. 1964. Lantern Press.
--A Trip on a Jet. LC 60-13783. 59p. illus. 23cm. 1960. Lantern Press.
--A Trip on a Plane. LC 57-8272. unpaged. illus. 25cm. 1957. Lantern Press.
--A Trip on a Ship. Watson, William R., illus. LC 58-5876. 59p. illus. 23cm. 1958. Lantern Press.
--A Trip on a Train. LC 56-13026. unpaged. illus. 22cm. 1956. Lantern Press.
--Trip to the Aquarium. (Illus.). (gr. 1-5). 1967. (ISBN 0-8313-0066-3). Lantern.
--A Trip to the Zoo. (Illus.). N.D. (ISBN 0-8313-0109-0). Lantern Press Inc.
--Truck Drivers: What Do They Do?. Kessler, Leonard P. (1921-), illus. LC 67-4192. (Illus.). 5 7/8 x 8 1/2. 64p. (18 pt.). (I Can Read Bks.). (gr. k-3). 1967. (ISBN 0-06-022099-6). Har-Row.

Greene, Carol (1906-)
--Christmas on the Street: The Secret of the Second Basement. Halpern, Herb & Boyancheck, Dave, photos by LC 84-15523. (Illus.). 44 p. 29cm. c.1984. (ISBN 0-570-04107-4). Concordia Pub. House.
--A Computer Went a-Courting: A Love Song for Valentine's Day. Dunnington, Tom, illus. LC 83-7346. (Illus.). 27 p. 25cm. (Sing-along holiday stories). c.1983. (ISBN 0-516-08232-9). Childrens Press.
--The Dancing Bear, and Other Stories. Szeghy, Joe, illus. LC 73-78026. (Illus.). 63 p. 1973. (ISBN 0-570-06993-9). Concordia Pub. House.
--Hi, Clouds. LC 82-19854. p. cm. (Rookie Reader). 1983. (ISBN 0-516-02036-6). Childrens Press.
--Hinny Winny Bunco. 1st ed. Winter, Jeanette, illus. LC 81-47720. (Illus.). 63 p. 19cm. c.1982. (ISBN 0-06-022128-3). (ISBN 0-06-022129-1). Harper & Row. **Award: (ALA).**
--Ice Is- Whee!. LC 82-19855. p. cm. (Rookie Reader). 1983. (ISBN 0-516-02037-4). Childrens Press.
--The Insignificant Elephant. Gantner, Susan, illus. 1985. (ISBN 0-15-238730-7). Harcourt Brace & Jovanovich.
--Kiri & the First Easter. (Illus.). 32p. (Arch Bks: Set 9). (ps-4). 1972. (ISBN 0-570-06064-8). Concordia.
--Please, Wind?. Sharp, Gene (1923-), illus. LC 82-4548. (Illus.). 31 p. 19cm. (A Rookie Reader). c.1982. (ISBN 0-516-42033-X). Childrens Press.
--Rain! Rain!. Frederick, Larry, illus. LC 82-9509. (Illus.). 31 p. 19cm. (A Rookie Reader). c.1982. (ISBN 0-516-42034-8). (ISBN 0-516-02034-X). Childrens Press.
--Seven Baths for Naaman. (Illus.). 48p. (I Can Read a Bible Story Ser.: No. 2). (gr. 2-4). 1977. (ISBN 0-570-07321-9). (ISBN 0-570-07315-4). Concordia.
--Shine, Sun!. LC 82-19853. p. cm. (Rookie Reader). 1983. (ISBN 0-516-02038-2). (ISBN 0-516-42038-0). Childrens Press.
--Snow Joe. Sharp, Paul (1927-), illus. LC 82-9403. (Illus.). 31 p. 19cm. (A Rookie Reader). c.1982. (ISBN 0-516-02035-8). (ISBN 0-516-42035-6). Childrens Press.
--The Super Snoops and the Missing Sleepers. Sharp, Gene (1923-), illus. LC 75-34178. (Illus.). 31 p. 25cm. c.1976. (ISBN 0-516-03610-6). Childrens Press.
--The Truly Remarkable Day. Willman, Gordon, illus. LC 75-313208. (Illus.). 48 p. 26cm. c.1974. (ISBN 0-570-03424-8). Concordia Pub. House.
--Welcome the Stranger. Boyanchek, Dave, illus. LC 84-14941. c.1984. (ISBN 0-570-04105-8). Concordia Pub. House.
--The World's Biggest Birthday Cake. LC 85-16664. p. cm. (Sing-along holiday stories). 1985. (ISBN 0-516-08233-7). Childrens Press.

Greene, Carol (1906-) & Dunnington, Tom
--The Thirteen Days of Halloween. Dunnington, Tom, illus. LC 83-7347. (Illus.). 29 p. 25cm. (Sing-along holiday stories). c.1983. (ISBN 0-516-08231-0). Childrens Press.

Greene, Charles Walter (1881-)
--The Treasure of Liassi: A Tale of High Adventure. LC 53-10292. 222p. 23cm. 1954. Vantage Press.

Greene, Constance Clarke (1924-)
--Al(Exandra) the Great. LC 81-16058. 133 p. 22cm. 1982. (ISBN 0-670-11197-X). Viking.
--Ask Anybody: A Novel. LC 82-17624. p. cm. 1983. (ISBN 0-670-13813-4). Viking Press.
--Beat the Turtle Drum. Diamond, Donna (1950-), illus. LC 76-14772. p. cm. 1976. (ISBN 0-670-15241-2). Viking Press. **Award: (ALA).**
--Dotty's Suitcase. LC 80-10949. 147 p. 22cm. 1980. (ISBN 0-670-28050-X). Viking Press.
--Double-Dare O'Toole. LC 81-5102. 168p. (gr. 5-9). 1981. (ISBN 0-670-28053-4). Viking Pr.
--The Ears of Louis. Langner, Nola (1930-), illus. LC 74-8694. (Illus.). 90 p. 23cm. 1974. (ISBN 0-670-28718-0). Viking Press.
--Getting Nowhere. LC 77-5164. p. cm. 1977. (ISBN 0-670-33762-5). Viking Press.
--A Girl Called Al. Barton, Byron (1930-), illus. LC 69-18255. (Illus.). 127 p. 22cm. 1969. Viking Press. **Award: (ALA).**
--The Good-Luck Bogie Hat. LC 70-162674. 126 p. 22cm. 1971. (ISBN 0-670-34550-4). Viking Press.
--I and Sproggy. McCully, Emily Arnold (1939-), illus. LC 78-6096. (Illus.). 155 p. 22cm. 1978. (ISBN 0-670-38980-3). Viking Press.
--I Know You, Al. Barton, Byron (1930-), illus. LC 75-9741. (Byron Barton is the legal name change of Byron Vartanian.). p. cm. 1975. (ISBN 0-670-39048-8). Viking Press.
--Isabelle Shows Her Stuff. LC 84-40255. 144p. (gr. 8-12). 1984. (ISBN 0-670-41103-5, Viking Kestrel). Viking.

--Blissful Joy and the SATs: A Multiple-Choice Romance. Green, Sheila Ellen. LC 81-23692. 143 p. 22cm. c.1982. (ISBN 0-316-32673-9). Little, Brown.

--Give Us a Great Big Smile, Rosy Cole. Green, Sheila Ellen. LC 80-24319. p. cm. c.1981. (ISBN 0-316-32672-0). Little, Brown. **Award: (ALA).**

--The Hot Day. Green, Sheila Ellen. Greenwald, Sheila, pseud. (1934-), illus. Green, Sheila Ellen. LC 79-172342. (Illus.). 32 p. 24cm. 1972. Bobbs-Merrill.

--It All Began with Jane Eyre: Or, The Secret Life of Franny Dillman. Green, Sheila Ellen. LC 79-26901. (Illus.). 117 p. 22cm. c.1980. (ISBN 0-316-32671-2). Little, Brown.

--The Mariah Delany Lending Library Disaster. Green, Sheila Ellen. Greenwald, Sheila, pseud. (1934-), illus. Green, Sheila Ellen. LC 77-23020. p. cm. 1977. (ISBN 0-395-25836-7). Houghton Mifflin.

--Mat Pit and the Tunnel Tenants. Green, Sheila Ellen. LC 72-1391. (Illus.). 127 p. 21cm. 1972. (ISBN 0-397-31379-9). Lippincott.

--Miss Amanda Snap. Green, Sheila Ellen. Greenwald, Sheila, pseud. (1934-), illus. Green, Sheila Ellen. LC 72-75883. (Illus.). 31 p. 24cm. 1972. Bobbs-Merrill.

--Rosy Cole's Great American Guilt Club. Green, Sheila Ellen. LC 85-47876. p. cm. c.1985. (ISBN 0-87113-044-0). Atlantic Monthly Press.

--The Secret in Miranda's Closet. Green, Sheila Ellen. Greenwald, Sheila, pseud. (1934-), illus. Green, Sheila Ellen. LC 76-62499. (Illus.). 138 p. 22cm. 1977. (ISBN 0-395-25152-4). Houghton Mifflin.

--The Secret Museum. Green, Sheila Ellen. LC 73-16192. (Illus.). 127 p. 21cm. 1974. (ISBN 0-397-31497-3). Lippincott.

--Valentine Rosy. Green, Sheila Ellen. LC 84-9694. (Illus.). 89 p. 21cm. c.1984. (ISBN 0-316-32708-5). Little, Brown.

--Will the Real Gertrude Hollings Please Stand up?. Green, Sheila Ellen. 1st ed. LC 83-974. 162 p. 22cm. c.1983. (ISBN 0-316-32707-7). Little, Brown.

--Willie Bryant and the Flying Otis. Green, Sheila Ellen. Greenwald, Sheila, pseud. (1934-), illus. Green, Sheila Ellen. LC 76-105738. (Illus.). 153 p. 24cm. 1971. (ISBN 0-448-21390-7). Grosset & Dunlap.

Greenway, John (1919-), ed.

--Don't Talk to My Horse: Tall Tales from the U.S.A. Perl, Susan (1922-1983), illus. LC 67-16762. 96p. col. illus. 25cm. (Folk literature around the world). 1968. Silver Burdett.

--Gormless Tom And Other Tales From the British Isles. Palmer, Janice, illus. LC 68-10788. (Illus.). 96 p. 25cm. (Folk literature around the world). 1968. Silver Burdett Co.

--The Primitive Reader: An Anthology of Myths,Tales,Songs,Riddles,and Proverbs. LC 65-21986. 211p. (Folk-lore Ser.). 1965 (Gale Reprints). Folklore Associates.

--Tales from the British Isles. Palmer, Janice, illus. LC 78-56058. (Illus.). 96 p. 25cm. (The World Folktale Library). c.1979. (ISBN 0-382-03353-1). Silver Burdett Co.

--Tales from the United States. Perl, Susan (1922-1983), illus. LC 78-54626. (Illus.). 96 p., 1 leaf of plates. 25cm. (The World Folktale Library). c.1979. (ISBN 0-382-03351-5). Silver Burdett Co.

Greenwood, Ann

--A Pack of Dreams. Colonna, Bernard, illus. LC 78-467. p. cm. c.1978. (ISBN 0-13-647784-4). Prentice-Hall.

Greenwood, Edward Alister (1930-)

--Obstreperous. Greenwood, Edward Alister (1930-), illus. LC 79-8610. (Illus.). color ils. 48p. (gr. k-3). 1970. (ISBN 0-689-20509-0). Atheneum.

--V. I. P. Very Important Plant. (Picture Ser.). (gr. 3 up). 1976. (ISBN 0-14-050127-4, Puffin). Penguin.

Greenwood, F. A.

--Moon Maiden and Other Stories. 1891. Macmilliam.

Greenwood, Grace, pseud., see Lippincott, Sara Jane Clarke.

Greenwood, James

--Legends of Savage Life. Griset, Ernest, illus. N.D. G. P. Putnam's Sons.

--Peter's Adventures. Griset, Ernest, illus. N.D. George Routledge & Sons.

--The Purgatory of Peter the Cruel. Griset, Ernest, illus. LC 16-341491. 164 p. incl. front., illus., plates. 23 x 20 cm. 1868. G. Routledge & Sons.

Greenwood, Marion

--The Nursery A.B.C. Book. LC 3-594. (Illus.). 112p. 25cm. 1902. National Publishing Company.

Greenwood, Nat

--Belvedere: A Pooch Full of Tricks. (Anytime Bks Ser). (gr. 1 up). 1975. (ISBN 0-525-45028-9, Anytime Bks). Dutton.

Greenwood, Ted see Greenwood, Edward Alister.

Greer, Blanche

--The Black Swan & the Green See Saw. Sarnoff, Arthur, illus. LC 75-261399. (Illus.). 26cm. (gr. 5 up). 1977, c.1975. Dennis-Landman.

Greer, Gery & Ruddick, Bob

--Max and Me and the Time Machine. 1st ed. LC 82-48762. p. cm. c.1983. (ISBN 0-15-294819-8). Harcourt Brace Jovanovich.

Greer, Hazel McElhany

--As the Stars Forever. LC 65-25024. 88p. 22cm. (Destiny bk., D-105). 1966, c.1965. Pacific Pr. Pub.

Greey, Edward (1835-1888)

--The Golden Lotus. 1882. Lee & Shepard.

Greff, Marie

--Golden Cage. (gr. 3 up). N.D. (ISBN 0-8283-1157-9). Branden.

Greg, R. P, ed.

--A Selection of Old Nursery Rhymes. LC 78-1058. 58 p. 23cm. 1978. (ISBN 0-8414-4482-X). Folcroft Library Editions.

--A Selection of Old Nursery Rhymes. LC 74-17263. 58 p. 23cm. 1974. (ISBN 0-88305-232-6). Norwood Editions.

Gregg, Alan, pseud., see Mallette, Gertrude Ethel.

Gregg, Alan

--The Creeping Peril Mystery. Powers, Richard M. Gorman (1921-), illus. 1952. Doubleday & Co.

--The Mustery of Batty Ridge. LC 46-20367. 3 p. l., 213 p. 20 cm. 1946. Doubleday & Company, Inc.

--The Mystery of Flight 24. Hopkins, Joseph, Jr., illus. (gr. 7-11). 1947. Doubleday Bks.

--The Mystery of the King Turtle. Bernbach, Graham, Jr., illus. 1943. Doubleday Doran & Co.

--Skywinder Mystery. 1942. Doubleday Doran & Co.

Gregg, Ernest

--And the Sun God Said: That's Hip. Beazer, G. Falcon, illus. LC 72-76495. (Illus.). 24 p. 24cm. (gr. 5up). 1972. (ISBN 0-06-022114-3). (ISBN 0-06-022115-1). Harper & Row.

Gregg, Jess

--Baby Boy. 1973. (ISBN 0-399-11158-1). G. P. Putnam's Sons.

Gregg, John, pseud., see Crawford, John.

Gregg, Leslie

--Four Golden Everything Workbooks: Featuring Marvel Superheroes. Ordway, Jerry, illus. 48p. (ps). 1980. (ISBN 0-307-13624-8, Golden Pr). Western Pub.

Gregg, Mary Kirby, Mrs. (1817-1893) & Kirby, Elizabeth (1823-1873)

--Aunt Martha's Corner Cupboard. (Illus.). (The Favorite Lib.). N.D. DeWolfe, Fiske & Co.

--Aunt Martha's Corner Cupboard. N.D. Educational Publishing Company.

--Aunt Martha's Corner Cupboard. (Illus.). (Young People's Lib.). N.D. Henry Altemus Co.

--Aunt Martha's Corner Cupboard. (Illus.). N.D. Thomas Nelson & Sons.

--Aunt Martha's Corner Cupboard: Or, Stories About Tea, Coffee, Sugar, Rice, Etc. American ed. Rocheleau, William Francis, ed. LC 4-21561. 160 p. illus. 20 cm. c.1898. A. Flanagan Co.

--The Bundle of Sticks: Or, Love and Hate. (Illus.). N.D. George Routledge & Sons.

--Discontented Children and How They Were Cured. (Illus.). N.D. E. P. Dutton & Co.

--Julia Maitland: Or, Pride Goes Before a Fall, 1 of 6 Vols. (Illus.). (Julia Maitland Library). N.D. E P Dutton.

--Lucy Neville and Her Schoolfellows. N.D. R. Worthington.

--Thy Kingdom Come: A Tale for Boys and Girls. (Illus.). N.D. Thos Nelson & Sons.

Gregg, Nancy E. (1939-)

--Happy Holiday Happenings. Gramma Gregg's Enterprises, illus. LC 79-26359. (Illus.). 120 p. 19cm. (Her Gramma Gregg's stories.). (Gramma Gregg's stories.). c.1979. (ISBN 0-87961-105-7). (ISBN 0-87961-104-9). Naturegraph Publishers.

--The Harvest Hoedown. LC 79-18258. (Illus.). 96p. 19cm. c.1979. (ISBN 0-87961-098-0). (ISBN 0-87961-097-2). Naturegraph Publishers.

--Sir Bastian Skunk's First Thanksgiving and Year: Son of Father Time. Gramma Gregg's Enterprises, illus. LC 79-22608. (Illus.). 72 p. 19cm. c.1979. (ISBN 0-87961-103-0). (ISBN 0-87961-102-2). Naturegraph Publishers.

--Training the Racoon Boys. Gramma Greggs Enterprises, illus. LC 79-19325. (Illus.). 72 p. 19cm. (Her Gramma Gregg stories). (Gramma Gregg's stories.). c.1979. (ISBN 0-87961-101-4). (ISBN 0-87961-100-6). Naturegraph Publishers.

Gregor, Arthur, jt. auth. see Doisneau, Robert.

Gregor, Arthur S, jt. auth. see Koffler, Camilla.

Gregor, Arthur S. (1923-)

--Animal Babies. Koffler, Camilla (0000-1955), illus. Ylla, pseud. 1976. Harper.

--Does Poppy Live Here?. Duvoisin, Roger Antoine (1904-1980), illus. LC 57-6009. unpaged. illus. 26cm. c.1957. Lothrop, Lee & Shepard Co.

--One, Two, Three, Four, Five Verses. Doisneau, Robert, ed. (gr. 1-6). 1956. (ISBN 0-397-30322-X). Lippincott.

Gregor, Elmer Russell (1878-)

--Camping in the Winter Woods: Adventures of Two Boys in the Maine Woods. LC 12-24058. 5 p. l., 379, 1 p. front., plates. 20 cm. 1912. Harper & Brothers.

--Camping on Western Trails: Adventures of Two Boys in the Rocky Mountains. LC 13-210598. 332, 1 p. front., plates. 20 cm. 1913. Harper & Brothers.

--Captain Jim Mason. LC 24-24139. 3 p. l., 252, 1 p. front. 20 cm. 1924. D. Appleton and Company.

--Jim Mason, Backwoodsman. LC 23-9858. vi p., 1 l., 282, 1 p. 20 cm. 1923. D. Appleton and Company.

--Jim Mason, Scout. LC 23-13687. v, 1 p., 1 l., 273, 1 p. front. 20 cm. 1923. D. Appleton and Company.

--Mason and His Rangers. LC 26-161523. 3 p. l., 244, 1 p. front. 20 cm. 1926. D. Appleton and Company.

--The Medicine Buffalo. LC 25-156701. 3 p. l., 263, 1 p. col. front. 20 cm. 1925. D. Appleton and Company.

--The Mystery Trail. LC 27-19897. v, 224, 1 p. front. 20 cm. 1927. D. Appleton and Company.

--The Red Arrow: An Indian Tale. LC 15-18571. 5 p. l., 282, 1 p. front., plates. 19 cm. 1915. Harper & Brothers.

--Running Fox. LC 18-21578. vii, 317, 1 p. front. 19 cm. 1918. D. Appleton and Company.

--Spotted Deer. LC 22-6161. 3 p. l., 239, 1 p. front. 20 cm. 1922. D. Appleton and Company.

--The Spotted Pony. Rodgers, Richard H. (1876-1953), illus. LC 30-21334. v, 1 p., 1 l., 237, 1 p. front., illus. 20 cm. 1930. D. Appleton and Company.

--Three Sioux Scouts. LC 22-17974. 3 p. l., 252, 1 p. col. front. 20 cm. 1922. D. Appleton and Company.

--Three Wilderness Scouts. LC 28-23095. 3 p. l., 238, 1 p. front. 20 cm. (His Jim Mason series). 1928. D. Appleton and Company.

--The War Chief. LC 27-4080. 3 p. l., 236, 1 p. front. 19 cm. 1927. D. Appleton and Company.

--The War Eagle. LC 26-9912. 3 p. l., 223, 1 p. front. 20 cm. 1926. D. Appleton and Company.

--War-Path and Hunting Trail. (Harper's Young People Ser.). N.D. Harper & Brothers.

--War Path and Hunting Trail: Adventures of Indian Boys. LC 16-11582. 4 p. l., 202, 1 p. front. 20 cm. 1916. Harper & Brothers.

--The War Trail. LC 21-16804. 3 p. l., 257, 1 p. col. front. 20 cm. 1921. D. Appleton and Company.

--White Otter. LC 17-8586. 3 p. l., 312 p. front., illus. 20 cm. 1917. D. Appleton and Company.

--The White Wolf. LC 21-68026. 3 p. l., 267, 1 p.col. front. 20 cm. 1921. D. Appleton and Company.

Gregor, Emmy (1887-)

--The Elephant Who Came to Tea. Mayer, Fred, illus. LC 48-15197. 30p. illus. 26cm. 1947. Emmy Gregor.

Gregor, Kay

--Randy at the Rodeo. Moyers, William (1916-), illus. LC 50-12281. 29cm. 28p. (Treasure Bks.). 1950. Grosset & Dunlap.

Gregorian, Joyce Ballou (1946-)

--The Broken Citadel. LC 75-8869. (Illus.). 373 p. 25cm. 1975. (ISBN 0-689-30476-5). Atheneum.

--Castledown. LC 76-47627. 371 p. 25cm. 1977. (ISBN 0-689-30566-4). Atheneum.

Gregorich, Barbara

--Beep, Beep: Grades K-2. Hoffman, Joan, ed. Taber, Ed, illus. (Illus.). 16p. (Orig.). (Start to Read Ser.). (gr. k-2). 1984. (ISBN 0-88743-007-4). Sch Zone Pub Co.

--The Gum on the Drum: Grades K-2. Hoffman, Joan, ed. Sandford, John, illus. (Illus.). 16p. (Orig.). (Start to Read! Ser.). (gr. k-2). 1984. (ISBN 0-88743-004-X). Sch Zone Pub Co.

--I Want a Pet: Grades K-2. Hoffman, Joan, ed. Schneider, Rex, illus. (Illus.). 16p. (Orig.). (Start to Read! Ser.). (gr. k-2). 1984. (ISBN 0-88743-003-1). Sch Zone Pub Co.

--Nine Men Chase a Hen: Grades K-2. Hoffman, Joan, ed. Sandford, John, illus. (Illus.). 16p. (Orig.). (Start to Read! Ser.). (gr. k-2). 1984. (ISBN 0-88743-009-0). Sch Zone Pub Co.

--Rhyming Pictures: Preschool. Hoffman, Joan, ed. Pape, Richard, illus. (Illus.). 32p. (A Get Ready! Bk.). (ps). 1983. (ISBN 0-938256-53-X). Sch Zone Pub Co.

Gregorovius, Ferdinand (1862-)

--Little Snow White and Other Stories in Rhyme. Forst, Arthur, illus. LC 25-5007. 78 p. illus., col. plates. 22 cm. c.1924. The Christopher Publishing House.

Gregorowski, Christopher (1940-)

--Why a Donkey Was Chosen. Browne, Caroline, illus. LC 75-24951. (Illus.). 31 p. c.1975. (ISBN 0-385-11569-5). Doubleday.

Gregory, Diana Jean (1933-)

--The Fog Burns off by Eleven O'clock. LC 80-26790. 134p. 1st U.S. edition. (gr. 4-8). 1981. (ISBN 0-201-04139-1, A-W Childrens). A-W.

--The Fog Burns off by 11 O'clock. LC 84-40756. p. cm. 1985, c.1981. (ISBN 0-201-04139-1). Lippincott.

--I'm Boo ... That's Who!. Mohn, Susan Spellman, illus. LC 84-40762. p. cm. 1985, c.1979. (ISBN 0-201-02628-7). Lippincott.

--There's a Caterpillar in My Lemonade. LC 84-40794. 1985, c.1980. (ISBN 0-201-03603-7). Lippincott.

--There's a Caterpillar in My Lemonade. Thieme, Channing, illus. LC 80-17067. p. cm. c.1980. (ISBN 0-201-03603-7). Addison-Wesley Pub. Co.

Gregory, Frank M., illus.

--The Doll and Her Friends. N.D. Brentano's Publications.

--The School For Scandal. N.D. Dodd, Mead & Company.

Gregory, Horace Victor (1898-1982)

--Alphabet for Joanna: A Poem. 1st ed. Bryson, Bernarda (1905-1977), illus. LC 63-17965. 24 p. illus. (part col.) 14 cm. 1963. Holt, Rinehart and Winston.

Gregory, Horace Victor (1898-1982) & Zaturenska, Marya (1902-1982), eds.

--The Crystal Cabinet. 1967. MacMillan Publishing company.

--The Crystal Cabinet: An Invitation to Poetry. Bloomfield, Diana, illus. 1962. Holt.

--The Silver Swan: Poems of Romance and Mystery from William Blake to W. H. Auden. Schmidt, Rosalie Petrash, illus. LC 71-687. (Illus.). xxiv, 195 p. 18cm. 1968. Collier Books.

--Silver Swan: Poems of Romance & Mystery. Bloomfield, Diana, illus. LC 66-12031. (Illus.). 219p. (gr. 7-9). 1966. (ISBN 0-03-056260-0). HR&W.

Gregory, Isabella Augusta Persse, Lady (1852-1932)

--The Golden Apple. Gregory, Margaret, illus. LC 16-21257. 21.5 cm. 117p. 1916. G. P. Putnam's Sons.

--Irish Legends for Children. Boland, Frances, illus. (Illus.). 90p. (gr. 6 up). 1983. (ISBN 0-85342-691-0, Pub. by Mercier Pr Ireland). Irish Bk Ctr.

--The Kiltartan Poetry Book. N.D. G. P. Putnam's Sons.

Gregory, Jackson

--Judith of Blue Lake Ranch. N.D. Charles Scribner's Sons.

--The Short Cut. N.D. Grosset & Dunlap.

Gregory, John (1928-)

--The Tinker and the Cobbler: Twelve Poems, with Some Things to Do, and Other Poems. 1st ed. Forder, Roy, illus. LC 68-22493. (Illus.). xii, 59 p. (The Pergamon English Library). 1969. Pergamon Press.

Gregory, Justina, tr. see Levine, David.

Gregory, Louise F

--Mamma Nelly and I: The Story of Thinking Doll. 167p. N.D. Edward Stern & Co.

Gregory, Mary Huston

--Once Upon a Time Stories by. LC 6-35624. 268 p. 20 cm. 1906. General Publishing Co.

Gregory, Miriam

--My Furry Bear. Piequet Press Staff, ed. Gregory, Miriam, illus. (Illus.). 43p. (Orig.). (gr. 3-5). 1985. (ISBN 0-914275-02-X). Piequet Pr.

Gregory, O. B.

--Naamah & Elisha. (The Read About It Series: No.83). N.D. (ISBN 0-08-017261-X). British Bk Ctr.

Gregory, Patrick, tr. see Levine, David.

Greif, Martin (1938-)

--The St. Nicholas Book. Greif, Martin (1938-), illus. LC 76-5089. (Illus.). 59 p. 22cm. 1976. (ISBN 0-87663-234-7). Main Street/Universe Books.

--The St. Nicholas Book: A Celebration of Christmas Past. rev. ed. Greif, Martin (1938-), illus. LC 84-15460. (Illus.). 80p. (gr. 8). 1984. (ISBN 0-915590-51-4). Main Street.

Greifenstein, Sandra, tr. see Bruna, Dick.

Greifenstein, Sandra, tr. see Maillard, Claude.

Greiner, N. Gretchen, ed.

--A Batch of the Best. (gr. 3 up). 1979. (ISBN 0-307-21623-3, Golden Pr). (ISBN 0-307-61623-1, Golden Pr). Western Pub.

--A Batch of the Best;. Stories for Girls. Ericksen, Barbara M., illus. LC 76-121762. (Illus.). 211p. 20cm. (Whitman Classics). 1970. Western Pub. Co.

Grifalconi, Ann (1929-)
--City Rhythms. LC 65-26514. (Illus.). 1 v. (unpaged. 29cm. 1965. Bobbs-Merrill Co.
--The Matter with Lucy: An Album. LC 72-88758. (Illus.). 26 p. 24cm. 1973. (ISBN 0-672-51741-8). Bobbs-Merrill Co.
--The Toy Trumpet. Grifalconi, Ann (1929-), illus. LC 68-29300. (Illus.). 32 p. 29cm. 1968. (ISBN 0-672-50543-6). Bobbs-Merrill.
Griffen, Elizabeth L., adapted by.
--Shaggy Dog. photos. 96p. (gr. 4-9). 1970. (ISBN 0-590-02401-9). Scholastic Inc.
Griffin, Bernard, jt. auth. see Kibel, Mary.
Griffin, Elsie Hazeltine (1908-) & Warren, Letty (1924-)
--Pickwick Penguin and Willy Wallaby Discover America. Kendall, illus. LC 49-4528. 51 p. illus. 20 cm. 1949. Story Book Press.
Griffin, Gillett Good (1928-)
--A Mouse's Tale. LC 52-147092. unpaged. illus. 15x17cm. c.1952. Abelard Press.
Griffin, Ida Mary
--Over the Hills and Far Away. Thrigg, C. Louise, illus. LC 19-7169. 36 p., 1 l. illus. 29 cm. c.1919. Saulsbury Publishing Company, Incorporated.
Griffin, Judith Berry
--The Magic Mirrors. Crichlow, Ernest T. (1914-), illus. LC 79-132596. (Illus.). 58 p. 18cm. 1971. Coward, McCann & Geoghegan.
--Phoebe the Spy. (gr. 4-6). 1979. (ISBN 0-590-05758-8). Scholastic Inc.
Griffin, Thomas H & Gerdeman, Leah
--Arnie Trades His Coat. LC 77-359925. (Illus.). 29 p. 22cm. c.1976. (ISBN 0-89393-001-6). Carroll & Halleck.
--Wake up, Rodney!. LC 76-55299. (Illus.). 27 p. 23cm. c.1977. (ISBN 0-89393-002-4). Carroll & Halleck.
Griffin, Velma
--Circus Daze. LC 57-5398. 189p. illus. 22cm. 1957. Westminster Press.
--Fair Prize. LC 56-55690. 185p. 22cm. 1956. Westminster Press.
--Mystery Mansion. Kendrick, Alcy, illus. LC 58-5481. 172p. illus. 21cm. 1958. Westminster Press.
Griffis, Faye Campbell
--Lantern in the Valley. Bock, Vera, illus. LC 56-10393. 136p. illus. 21cm. 1956. Macmillan.
Griffis, William Elliot, jt. ed. see Ayrton, Matilda Chaplin, Mrs.
Griffis, William Elliot (1843-1928)
--The Arabian Nights Entertainment, 4 vols. (Illus.). N.D. Lothrop Pub. Co.
--Belgian Fairy Tales. LC 19-15590. 3 p. l., 252 p. col. front. 21 cm. c.1919. Thomas Y. Crowell Company.
--Brave Little Holland. (Illus.). (Riverside Juvenile Classics). N.D. Houghton Mifflin Co.
--Dutch Fairy Tales for Young Folks. LC 18-20689. iii, 220 p. col. front., col. plates. 21 cm. c.1918. Thomas Y. Crowell Company.
--The Fire-Fly's Lovers, and Other Fairy Tales of Old Japan. ix, 166 p. col. front., 7 col. pl. 20 cm. c.1908. T. Y. Crowell & Co.
--In the Mikado's Service. 361p. N.D. W. A. Wilde.
--Japanese Fairy Tales. 219p. N.D. Thomas Y. Crowell Co.
--Japanese Fairy World. Stories from the Wonder-Lore of Japan. LC 13-33862. vi p., 1 l., 304 p. 11 pl. 16 cm. 1880. J. H. Barhyte.
--Swiss Fairy Tales. LC 20-139799. v. 260 p. col. front., col. plates. 21 cm. c.1920. Thomas Y. Crowell Company.
--The Unmannerly Tiger, and Other Korean Tales. LC 11-18973. (Illus.). xi, 155 p. c.1911. Thomas Y. Crowell Company.
--Welsh Fairy Tales. LC 21-15510. 3 p. l., 204 p. col. front., col. plates. 21 cm. c.1921. Thomas Y. Crowell Company.
Griffith, Bonnie
--The Tree House Gang: Puppet Plays for Children. 48p. (Orig.). (gr. k-6). 1983. (ISBN 0-87239-648-7). Standard Pub.
Griffith, Don, ed. see Disney, Walt, Productions.
Griffith, Eleanor Glendower
--Cho-Cho and the Health Fairy: Six Stories. 5th ed. Gillespie, Jessie, illus. LC 24-21855. 40 p. illus. 17 x 15 cm. 1921. Child Health Organization of America.
--Cho-Cho and the Health Fairy: Six Stories. Gillespie, Jessie, illus. 39 p. incl. illus. (part col.) 18 cm. 1922. Macmillan Company.
Griffith, Fay
--Hidalgo and the Gringo Train. 1st ed. Oechsli, Kelly (1918-), illus. LC 58-5233. 89p. illus. 21cm. 1958. Dutton.
Griffith, Fitzclarence
--Sparky the Rascal. 1984. (ISBN 0-533-06143-1). Vantage.
Griffith, George P.
--Popper Gander: A Mother Goose Transition Book Designed for Parents and Teachers;. LC 68-48847. viii, 95 p. illus. 23 cm. c.1966. Gander Publishers.
Griffith, Helen Sherman, Mrs. (1873-)
--Hail, Virginia!. Willis, Bess Goe, illus. LC 30-9466. 288 p. incl. front. 19 cm. c.1930. The Penn Publishing Company.
--Her Father's Legacy: A Story for Girls. Waugh, Ida, illus. iv, 5-345 p. front., plates. 19 cm. (Keystone Ser.). 1901. The Penn Publishing Company.
--Her Wilful Way: A Story for Girls. Waugh, Ida, illus. iv, 360 p. front., pl. 19 cm. (Keystone Ser.). 1902. The Penn Publishing Company.
--Latty of the Circus. LC 9-19834. 20cm. 333p. (Vacation Ser.). (The Letty Bks.). 1909. Penn Publishing Co.
--Letty and Miss Grey. Balano, Paula Himmelsbach, illus. LC 17-133174. 320 p. front., plates. 19 cm. 1917. The Penn Publishing Company.
--Letty and the Twins. LC 10-12168. 307 p. front., plates. 19 cm. 1910. The Penn Publishing Company.
--Letty at the Conservatory. Balano, Paula Himmelsbach, illus. LC 15-63426. 319 p. front., plates. 19 cm. 1915. The Penn Publishing Company.
--Letty Grey--Heiress. Balano, Paula Himmelsbach, illus. LC 18-18885. 341 p. front., plates. 19 cm. 1918. The Penn Publishing Company.
--Letty of the Circus. (The Letty Books). N.D. Penn.
--Letty's Good Luck. Balano, Paula Himmelsbach, illus. LC 14-122081. 320 p. front., plates. 19 cm. (The Letty Bks.). 1914. The Penn Publishing Company.
--Letty's New Home. Jones, Frances D., illus. LC 11-31131. 20cm. 312p. (The Letty Bks.). 1911. Penn Publishing Co.
--Letty's Sister. Jones, Frances D., illus. LC 12-206374. 320 p. front., plates. 19 cm. 1912. The Penn Publishing Company.
--Letty's Springtime. Balano, Paula Himmelsbach, illus. 317 p. front., plates. 19 cm. 1916. The Penn Publishing Company.
--Letty's Treasure. Jones, Frances D., illus. 319 p. front., plates. 19 cm. 1913. The Penn Publishing Company.
--Louie Maude. Price, Harriet Longstreet (1891-), illus. LC 24-520288. 212 p. front. 19 cm. 1924. The Penn Publishing Company.
--Louie Maude and the Caravan. Price, Harriet Longstreet (1891-), illus. LC 25-19832. 2 p. l., 9-207 p. front. 20 cm. 1925. The Penn Publishing Company.
--Louie Maude and the Mary Ann. Sweeney, Nora, illus. LC 27-14802. 2 p. l., 9-206 p. front. 20 cm. 1927. The Penn Publishing Company.
--No, Virginia!. Smith, Wuanita (1866-), illus. LC 22-3700. 320 p. front., plates. 19 cm. 1922. The Penn Publishing Company.
--Now, Virginia!. Smith, Wuanita (1866-), illus. LC 22-22774. 6 p. l., 11-300 p. front., plates. 20 cm. 1922. The Penn Publishing Company.
--Oh, Virginia!. Smith, Wuanita (1866-), illus. LC 20-10730. 320 p. front., plates. 19 cm. (The Virginia Stories). 1920. The Penn Publishing Company.
--The Roly Poly Family. Price, Harriet Longstreet (1891-), illus. LC 24-17903. 208 p. front. 19 cm. 1924. The Penn Publishing Company.
--Rosemary for Remembrance. (The Outdoor Bks.). N.D. Penn.
--Why, Virginia!. Sweeney, Nora & Smith, Wuanita (1866-), illus. LC 24-5106. 7, 11-303 p. front., plates. 19 cm. 1924. The Penn Publishing Company.
--Yes, Virginia!. Smith, Wuanita (1866-), illus. LC 28-172761. 300 p. front., plates. 19 cm. 1928. The Penn Publishing Company.
Griffith, Helen Virginia (1934-)
--Alex and the Cat. 1st ed. Low, Joseph (1911-), illus. LC 81-11608. (Illus.). 63 p. 22cm. (A Greenwillow Read-Alone). c.1982. (ISBN 0-688-00420-2). (ISBN 0-688-00421-0). Greenwillow Books.
--Alex Remembers. Carrick, Donald (1929-), illus. LC 82-11913. p. cm. 32p. c.1983. (ISBN 0-688-01800-9). (ISBN 0-688-01801-7). Greenwillow Books.
--Foxy. LC 83-16392. 144p. (gr. 5-9). 1984. (ISBN 0-688-02567-6). Greenwillow.
--Mine Will, Said John. Batherman, Muriel (1926-), illus. LC 79-27886. (Illus.). 32 p. c.1980. (ISBN 0-688-80267-2). (ISBN 0-688-84267-4). Greenwillow Books.
--More Alex and the Cat. Carrick, Donald (1929-), illus. LC 83-1411. p. cm. 1983. (ISBN 0-688-02292-8). (ISBN 0-688-02293-6). Greenwillow Books.
--Nata. Tafuri, Nancy, illus. LC 85-727. (Illus.). 24 p. c.1985. (ISBN 0-688-04976-1). (ISBN 0-688-04977-X). Greenwillow Books.
Griffith, John W & Frey, Charles H
--Classics of Children's Literature. LC 80-18349. (Illus.). xviii, 957 p. 24cm. c.1981. (ISBN 0-02-347210-3). Macmillan.
Griffith, Leila Smith
--Boo and the Birds. LC 40-2318. 120 p. incl. illus., plates. 20 cm. 1940. Meador Publishing Company.
Griffith, Liewelyn Wyn (1884-), ed. see Mabinogion.
Griffith, Linda Hill, illus.
--Cinderella. (Illus.). 12p. (Pop-Up Bks.). (ps-3). N.D. (ISBN 0-8431-0952-1). Price Stern.
--Thumbelina. (Illus.). (Carousel Bks.). (ps-2). N.D. (ISBN 0-8431-0903-3). Price Stern.
Griffith, Liewelyn Wyn (1884-)
--Adventures of Pryderi: Taken from the Mabinogion. (gr. 3 up). 1962. Verry.
--The Wooden Spoon, 1 of 10 Vols. (My Own Library). c.1938. American Sunday-School Union.
Griffith, M. E
--Boys at Eastwick. LC 12-32856. 255 p. front., 2 pl. 18 cm. c.1876. Presbyterian Board of Publication.
Griffith, Susan M., Mrs. (1851-)
--The Elksville Girls, 1 of 60 vols. 2 p. l., 3-239 p. front., plates. 19 cm. (Crescent Lib.). c.1894. Set. American Baptist Publication Society.
--Little Jim and Hotel Douglas. LC 12-32854. 310 p. front., plates. 19 cm. c.1898. American Baptist Publication Society.
--My Pansy Bed. LC 12-32980. 76 p. incl. illus., 3 pl. 19 cm. 1904. The Cumberland Press.
Griffith, T. H.
--Dan's Crumbs. (Illus.). 216p. N.D. Sunday-School Publications.
Griffith, Valeria Winkler
--Jenny, the Fire Maker. 1st ed. Tomes, Jacqueline, illus. LC 63-9865. (Illus.). 158 p. 21cm. 1963. Lippincott.
--Mystery in Austria. Willett, Jillian, illus. LC 68-13232. (Illus.). 128 p. 22cm. 1968. (ISBN 0-200-71538-0). Abelard-Schuman.
--A Ride for Jenny. 1st ed. Tomes, Jacqueline, illus. LC 64-19050. 158 p. illus. 21 cm. 1964. Lippincott.
--Runaway. LC 74-132190. 128 p. 20cm. 1971. (ISBN 0-200-71756-1). Abelard-Schuman.
Griffith, William (1921-)
--Fantasies Two. Ward, Richard C., illus. LC 79-55742. p. cm. c.1980. (ISBN 0-89742-039-X). (ISBN 0-89742-038-1). Dawne-Leigh Publications.
Griffith, William (1921-) & Paris, John, eds.
--The Garden Book of Verse, 2 vols. in 1. LC 32-7228. Repr. of 1932 ed (Pub. by Morrow). (Granger Poetry Library). 1976. (ISBN 0-89609-019-1). Granger Bk.
Griffiths, Gordon Douglas (1910-1973)
--Abandoned. LC 74-18131. 96p. (gr. 4 up). 1975. (ISBN 0-695-80537-1). (ISBN 0-695-40537-3). Follett.
--Mattie: The Story of a Hedgehog. Adams, Norman, illus. LC 76-47240. (gr. 3-6). 1977. Delacorte.
Griffiths, Helen (1939-)
--Blackface Stallion. Ambrus, Victor G., pseud. (1935-), illus. Ambrus, Gyozo Laszlo. LC 80-15850. (Illus.). 156 p. 21cm. 1980. (ISBN 0-8234-0420-X). Holiday House.
--Dancing Horses. LC 81-6762. 151 p. 22cm. 1982, c.1981. (ISBN 0-8234-0437-4). Holiday House.
--The Dog at the Window. LC 84-3806. 128p. (gr. 4-7). 1984. (ISBN 0-8234-0527-3). Holiday.
--Greyhound. Ambrus, Victor G., pseud. (1935-), illus. Ambrus, Gyozo Laszlo. LC 66-12996. (Illus.). (gr. 5-8). 1964. (ISBN 0-385-04627-8). (ISBN 0-385-05810-1). Doubleday.
--The Greyhound. Ambrus, Victor G., pseud. (1935-), illus. Ambrus, Gyozo Laszlo. LC 66-12996. 180p. illus. 22cm. 1st U.S. edition. 1966, c.1964. Doubleday.
--Grip, a Dog Story. Hall, Douglas (1931-), illus. LC 78-6819. p. cm. 1978. (ISBN 0-8234-0335-1). Holiday House.
--Horse in the Clouds. Crowell, Pers (1910-), illus. LC 58-13066. 124p. illus. 21cm. 1st U.S. edition. 1958. Holt.
--Just a Dog. Ambrus, Victor G., pseud. (1935-), illus. Ambrus, Gyozo Laszlo. LC 74-19025. (Illus.). 159 p. 21cm. 1975, c.1974. (ISBN 0-8234-0251-7). Holiday House.
--The Last Summer: Spain 1936. Ambrus, Victor G., pseud. (1935-), illus. Ambrus, Gyozo Laszlo. LC 79-10469. (Illus.). 151 p. 21cm. 1979. (ISBN 0-8234-0361-0). Holiday House.
--Leon. Ambrus, Victor G., pseud. (1935-), illus. Ambrus, Gyozo Laszlo. LC 68-10602. (Illus.). (gr. 6). 1968. (ISBN 0-385-00357-9). Doubleday.
--Moshie Cat: The True Adventures of a Majorcan Kitten. Hughes, Shirley (1929-), illus. LC 70-122905. (Illus.). line drawings. 128p. 128p. 1st U.S. edition. (gr. 4-6). 1970. (ISBN 0-8234-0178-2). Holiday.
--The Mysterious Appearance of Agnes. Ambrus, Victor G., pseud. (1935-), illus. Ambrus, Gyozo Laszlo. LC 74-21793. p. cm. 1975. (ISBN 0-8234-0267-3). Holiday House.
--Rafa's Dog. LC 83-4384. 112p. (gr. 4-6). 1983. (ISBN 0-8234-0492-7). Holiday.
--Running Wild. Ambrus, Victor G., pseud. (1935-), illus. Ambrus, Gyozo Laszlo. LC 77-3814. (Illus.). 191 p. 21cm. 1977. (ISBN 0-8234-0309-2). Holiday House.
--Russian Blue. Ambrus, Victor G., pseud. (1935-), illus. Ambrus, Gyozo Laszlo. LC 73-78454. (Illus.). 150 p. 22cm. 1973. (ISBN 0-8234-0233-9). Holiday House.
--Stallion of the Sands. 1st American ed. LC 75-116343. 160 p. 22cm. 1970, c.1968. Lothrop, Lee & Shepard Co.
--Wild Heart. Ambrus, Victor G., pseud. (1935-), illus. Ambrus, Gyozo Laszlo. (Illus.). (gr. 5-8). 1964. Doubleday.
--The Wild Horse of Santander. Ambrus, Victor G., pseud. (1935-), illus. Ambrus, Gyozo Laszlo. (Illus.). 182 p. 22cm. 1967, c.1966. Doubleday. **Award: (CMA).**
Griffiths, Kitty Anna
--Come, Meet Abraham, God's Friend: The Story of Genesis 21-25. LC 76-54670. (Illus.). 95 p. 21cm. (Come, meet series). 1977. (ISBN 0-310-25201-6). Zondervan Pub. House.
--Come, Meet Abraham, the Pioneer: The Story of Genesis 12-20. LC 76-54844. (Illus.). 95 p. 21cm. (Come, meet series). 1977. (ISBN 0-310-25191-5). Zondervan Pub. House.
--Come, Meet Isaac: The Story of Genesis 25-28. LC 76-13173. (Illus.). 95 p. 21cm. (Come, meet series). 1977. (ISBN 0-310-25211-3). Zondervan Pub. House.
--Come, Meet Jacob, God's Prince: The Story of Genesis 32-36. Willy, illus. LC 78-16593. (Illus.). 95 p. 21cm. (Come, meet series). 1978. (ISBN 0-310-25281-4). Zondervan Pub. House.
--Come, Meet Jacob, the Grabbing Twin: The Story of Genesis 28-31. Willy, illus. LC 78-18458. (Illus.). 96 p. 21cm. (Come, meet series). 1978. (ISBN 0-310-25271-7). Zondervan Pub. House.
--Come, Meet Jesus, the Baby: The Story of Matthew 1 and Luke 1-2: 20. Willy, illus. LC 78-16703. (Illus.). 111 p. 21cm. (Come, meet series). 1978, c.1976. (ISBN 0-310-25241-5). Zondervan.
--Come, Meet Jesus, the Boy: The Story of Matthew 2, Luke 2: 21-52. Willy, illus. LC 78-16680. (Illus.). 96 p. 21cm. (Come, meet series). 1978, c.1976. (ISBN 0-310-25251-2). Zondervan Pub. House.
--Come, Meet Ruth: The Story of the Book of Ruth. Willy, illus. LC 78-16723. (Illus.). 95 p. 21cm. (Come, meet series). 1978, c.1976. (ISBN 0-310-25261-X). Zondervan Pub. House.
--In the Beginning. (Come Meet Ser). 1976. Zondervan.
--Isaac. (Come Meet Ser.). 1976. (ISBN 0-310-25211-3). Zondervan.
--Noah. (Come Meet Ser.). 1976. (ISBN 0-310-25181-8). Zondervan.
Griffiths, Margaret W.
--The House on the Fjord. (Three Star Bks.). N.D. Frederick Warne & Co.
Grigg, Marian Procter
--Cuddle Cat Kittens. N.D. George W Jacobs.
Griggs, G. P., ed. see Forester, Cecil Scott.
Griggs, William Charles, jt. ed. see Barnes, Annie Maria.
Grigs, Mary
--The Yellow Cat. Sale, Isabel & Sale, John Morton, illus. LC 37-271901. 110 p. illus. (part col.) 21 cm. 1937. H. Milford, Oxford University Press.
Grigson, Geoffrey Edward Harvey (1905-)
--The Cherry Tree. N.D. (ISBN 0-8149-0309-6). The Vanguard Press.
Grigson, Geoffrey Edward Harvey (1905-) & Grigson, Jane (1928-)
--More Shapes & Stories: A Book About Pictures. LC 67-20942. (Illus.). (gr. 8 up). 1967. (ISBN 0-8149-0310-X). Vanguard.
--Shapes & Stories: A Book About Pictures. LC 65-25262. (Illus.). (gr. 5 up). N.D. (ISBN 0-8149-0311-8). Vanguard.
Grigson, Jane, jt. auth. see Grigson, Geoffrey Edward Harvey.
Grill, Nannette, jt. auth. see Wali, Charonne.
Grill, Nannette L. (1935-) & Wali, Charonne
--Mister Abracadabra. (Illus.). (ps-5). 1971. Scarecrow Pubns.
--Mister Abracadabra in Pixieland. Crawford, Richard (1938-) & Mekelburg, David, illus. (Illus.). (ps-5). 1973. Scarecrow Pubns.
Grilley, Virginia
--The Puppy on Parade. Hoecker, Hazel, illus. LC 56-3455. unpaged. illus. 21cm. (Wonder books, 617). 1956. Wonder Books.
--A Shilling for Samuel. 1st ed. Grilley, Virginia, illus. LC 57-551202. 86p. illus. 22cm. c.1957. Little, Brown.

--German Household Tales. H.E.S., ed. LC 12-32879. 2 v. 18 cm. (Riverside literature series, no. 107-108). c.1897. Hougton, Mifflin and Company.
--German Popular Tales. Wehnert, Edward H., illus. (New Alta Lib.). N.D. Henry T. Coates & Co.
--The Glass Mountain. Hogrogian, Nonny (1932-), retold by. Hogrogian, Nonny (1932-), illus. LC 84-7848. (Illus.). 32 p. 29cm. c.1985. (ISBN 0-394-86724-6). (ISBN 0-394-96724-0). Knopf.
--Golden Bird, 1 of 4 Vols. (Illus.). (Grimm's Fairy Library). N.D. Set. James Miller.
--The Golden Bird. Fromm, Lilo (1928-), illus. Sadler, Richard, tr. from Ger. LC 73-101635. (Illus.). 31 p. 22cm. 1970. Doubleday.
--Golden Bird. Fromm, Lilo (1928-), illus. LC 73-101635. (Illus.). . 32p. 1st U.S. edition. Orig. Title: Goldene Vogel. (gr. 2-5). 1970. (ISBN 0-385-01276-4). (ISBN 0-385-03790-2). Doubleday.
--Golden Bird & Other Fairy Tales. Kredel, Fritz (1900-1973), illus. (Illus.). (gr. k-3). 1963. (ISBN 0-02-737280-4). Macmillan.
--Golden Bird, and Other Stories. (Illus.). N.D. James Miller.
--The Golden Bird and other Stories. Smith, Wuanita (1866-) & Shenton, Edward (1895-), illus. LC 23-6926. 116 p. col. front., plates (part col.) 20 cm. 1922. G. W. Jacobs & Company.
--The Golden Bird and Other Stories from Grimm's Household Tales. Andre, Richard, illus. Boldey, Ella, tr. from Ger. LC 44-11918. 1 p. l., 235-276, 136-138 p. col. front., illus. 26 1/2 x 21 1/2 cm. (On cover: Grimms fairy tale series). c.1890. McLoughlin Bros.
--The Golden Goose. Paterson, Diane R. Cole (1946-), illus. LC 80-29207. p. cm. 32p. c.1981. (ISBN 0-89375-476-5). (ISBN 0-89375-477-3). Troll Associates.
--The Golden Goose: A Grimms' Tale Retold. Bare, Arnold Edwin (1920-), illus. LC 47-9413. 23 p. col. illus. 21 cm. 1947. Houghton Mifflin Company.
--The Golden Goose: By the Brothers Grimm. Tenggren, Gustaf (1896-1970), illus. LC 54-14444. unpaged. illus. 21cm. (Little golden book, 200). 1954. Simon and Schuster.
--The Good-for-Nothings: A Story by the Brothers Grimm. Fischer, Hans Erich (1909-1958), illus. LC 57-656014. unpaged. illus. 19x31cm. 1st U.S. edition. 1957. Harcourt, Brace.
--The Goose Girl. Castaigne, Andre & Fisher, Harrison, illus. N.D. Bobbs-Merrill Company.
--The Goose Girl. Laszlo, Varvasovszky, illus. 32p. (Collection of Fairy Tales Ser.). 1983. (ISBN 0-87191-934-6). Childrens Bk Co.
--The Goose Girl, and Other Tales from Brothers Grimm. Nernan, Einar (1888-), illus. 5 p. l., 165 p. incl. illus., plates. col. front., col. plates. 17 cm. (The little library). 1929. The Macmillan Company.
--The Goose Girl: Creative's Collection of Fairy Tales. Redpath, Ann, ed. Varvasovszky, Laszlo, illus. 32p. N.D. (ISBN 0-87191-934-6). Creative Ed.
--Grimms. (Caxton Edition). N.D. Belford, Clarke & Co.
--Grimm's Animal Stories. Rae, John (1882-1963), illus. Crane, Lucy (1842-1885), tr. LC 11-25096. 23 x 23cm. 95p. 1911. Duffield & Co.
--Grimm's Best Stories. N.D. Thomas Nelson & Sons.
--Grimm's Best Stories. LC 3-11673. 19 cm. 128p. (Standard Literature Ser.: No. 55). 1903. University Publishing Co.
--Grimm's Fairy Library: Containing "Brave Little Tailor", "King of the Swans", "Golden Bird"and "The Three Brothers", 4 vols. (Illus.). N.D. James Miller.
--Grimm's Fairy Stories. Anderson, Anne, illus. N.D. Collins.
--Grimm's Fairy Stories. Gruelle, John Barton (1880-1938), illus. LC 22-18923. iv. 178 p. col. front., illus., col. pl. 24 cm. c.1922. Cupples and Leon Company.
--Grimm's Fairy Stories: Supplementary to First Reader. Hallburton, Margaret Winifred & Claxton, Philander Priestley (1862-), trs. LC 4710. 144 p. front., illus. 12 degree. 1900. B. F. Johnson Pub. Co.
--Grimm's Fairy Tales. (Famous Bks. for Young Americans). N.D. A. L. Burt Co.
--Grimm's Fairy Tales. (Illus.). (Burt's Young Folks's Library). N.D. A. L. Burt's Pubs.
--Grimm's Fairy Tales. Empire ed. 1905. American News Co.
--Grimm's Fairy Tales. N.D. Chanticleer Bks.
--Grimm's Fairy Tales. 207p. N.D. Charles E Merrill.
--Grimm's Fairy Tales. (Illus.). (The Favorite Lib.). N.D. DeWolfe, Fiske & Co.
--Grimm's Fairy Tales, Vol. I. (Illus.). N.D. Educational Publishing Company.
--Grimm's Fairy Tales. (The Roxburghe Classics). N.D. Estes & Lauriat's.
--Grimm's Fairy Tales. (Illus.). (Presentation Ser.). 1887. Frederick Warne & Co.
--Grimm's Fairy Tales. (Washington Square Classics Ser.). N.D. George W Jacobs.
--Grimms' Fairy Tales. (Illus.). 511p. (Colored Classics). N.D. George Routledge & Sons.
--Grimm's Fairy Tales. (The Children's Favorites). N.D. George W. Jacobs & Co.
--Grimm's Fairy Tales. (The Good Value bks). N.D. Grosset & Dunlap.
--Grimms' Fairy Tales. N.D. (ISBN 0-448-06009-4, Illustrated Junior Library). (ISBN 0-448-05909-6). 2.50(popular). (ISBN 0-448-05809-X). Grosset & Dunlap.
--Grimm's Fairy Tales, 12 vols. (Illus.). 511p. (Juvenile Classics Ser.). 1905. Set. H M Caldwell Co.
--Grimm's Fairy Tales. (Illus.). (Caldwell's Illustrated Library of Famous Books by Famouse Authors). N.D. H. M. Caldwell Co.
--Grimm's Fairy Tales. (Illus.). (Berkeley Lib.). N.D. H. M. Caldwell Co.
--Grimm's Fairy Tales. (Illus.). (Altemus' New Illustrated Young People's Library). N.D. Henry Altemus Company.
--Grimms Fairy Tales. (Illus.). (Children's Gift Ser.). N.D. Henry Altemus Company Publications.
--Grimms Fairy Tales. (Illus.). (Ever New Books for Young People). N.D. Henry Altemus Company Publications.
--Grimm's Fairy Tales. (Illus.). (Boys and Girls' Classics). N.D. Henry Altemus.
--Grimm's Fairy Tales. LC 64-5556. 63 p. illus. 60 mm. 1963. Hillside Press.
--Grimm's Fairy Tales, 1 of 64 vols. (Illus.). (Young America Library: No. 22). 1900. Set. Hurst & Co.
--Grimm's Fairy Tales. (Illus.). (Hurst's Presentation Ser.). 1900. Hurst and Company.
--Grimm's Fairy Tales. (Argyle Ser). N.D. Hurst & Company.
--Grimm's Fairy Tales. (Illus.). (Home Ser.). N.D. Hurst and Company.
--Grimm's Fairy Tales. (Illus.). (Hurst's Fairy Tale Ser.). N.D. Hurst and Company.
--Grimm's Fairy Tales. (Arlington Edition). (Illus.). N.D. Hurst and Company.
--Grimm's Fairy Tales. (Illus.). (One Syllable Ser.). N.D. Hurst and Company.
--Grimm's Fairy Tales. 196p. (St. Nicholas Ser.). N.D. Hurst & Co.
--Grimm's Fairy Tales. (Victoria Edition). 1882. J B Lippincott.
--Grimm's Fairy Tales. (Sunset Ser.). N.D. J. S. Ogilvie.
--Grimm's Fairy Tales. (Sears Juvenile Classics). N.D. J.H.Sears &Co.
--Grimm's Fairy Tales. (The Young People's Library). N.D. John C. Winston.
--Grimm's Fairy Tales. (Illus.). (New Oxford Ser). N.D. Set. Lovell, Coryell & Co.
--Grimm's Fairy Tales. (The Washington Square Classics). N.D. Macrae Smith.
--Grimms' Fairy Tales. (Illus.). (gr. 6-9). 1978. (ISBN 0-448-14942-7, G&D). Putnam Pub Group.
--Grimm's Fairy Tales. (Illus.). (Young People's Classics). N.D. R. F. Fenno & Co.
--Grimm's Fairy Tales, 1 of 26 Vols. (Illus.). (Warne's Popular Poets Ser.: No.8). N.D. R. Worthington.
--Grimm's Fairy Tales. (Illus.). 272p. (Windermere Classics Ser.). (gr. 3 up). 1972. (ISBN 0-528-87168-4). Rand.
--Grimm's Fairy Tales. (Twentieth Century Ser.). N.D. Rand, McNally & Co.'s.
--Grimm's Fairy Tales. (New Alpha Library). N.D. Rand, McNally & Co.'s.
--Grimm's Fairy Tales. (The Antique Library). N.D. Rand, McNally & Co.'s.
--Grimm's Fairy Tales. (The Advance Library Ser.: Vol. 107). N.D. Rand, McNally & Co.
--Grimm's Fairy Tales. (Illus.). (The Independent Library Ser.: Vol. 107). N.D. Rand, McNally & Co.
--Grimm's Fairy Tales. (Illus.). (The Junior Library Ser.: Vol. 6). N.D. Rand, McNally & Co.
--Grimm's Fairy Tales. (Illus.). (The Waldorf Lib.). N.D. T. Y. Crowell & Co.
--Grimm's Fairy Tales. (The New Astor Library of Prose). N.D. T. Y. Crowell & Co.
--Grimm's Fairy Tales. (Classic Ser.). N.D. World Publishing Co.
--Grimm's Fairy Tales. Abbott, Elenore Plaisted, ed. Abbott, Elenore Plaisted, illus. LC 20-179913. vii p., 1 l., 308 p. col. front., col. plates. 25 cm. 1920. C. Scribner's Sons.
--Grimm's Fairy Tales. Abbott, Elenore Plaisted, illus. (The Scribner Illustrated Classics). N.D. Charles Scribner's Sons.
--Grimm's Fairy Tales. Beeson, Ernest, tr. LC 25-793628. viii, 278 p., 1 l. incl. illus., plates. col. front., col. plates. 22 cm. 1924. George H. Doran Company.
--Grimm's Fairy Tales. Brundage, Frances, illus. LC 25-303282. 310 p. col. front., illus. 23 cm. (Lettered on cover: Companion series). c.1924. The Saalfield Publishing Company.
--Grimm's Fairy Tales. Combs, Lorraine, illus. LC 26-143251. 2 p. l., iii-iv, 244 p. col. front., illus. 25 cm. (Sears illustrated juveniles). c.1926. J. H. Sears & Company, Inc.
--Grimms' Fairy Tales. Crane, Fisher, illus. Crane, Lucy, tr. (Illus.). N.D. D. Lothrop Co.
--Grimm's Fairy Tales. Crane, Walter (1845-1915) & Wehnert, Edward H., illus. (Illus.). N.D. Donohue, Henneberry & Co.
--Grimm's Fairy Tales. Crane, Walter (1845-1915), illus. (Series of Books for the Young). N.D. MacMillan & Co.
--Grimm's Fairy Tales. New ed. Cruikshank, George (1792-1878), illus. N.D. Worthington's.
--Grimm's Fairy Tales. Dobbs, Rose, ed. Espenscheid, Gertrude Elliott, illus. LC 55-6063. unpaged. illus. 29cm. (gr. k-3). c.1955. (ISBN 0-394-80657-3). (ISBN 0-394-90657-8). Random House.
--Grimm's Fairy Tales. Folkard, Charles James (1878-1963), illus. (Children's Illustrated Classics). N.D. E. P. Dutton & Co.
--Grimms Fairy Tales. Grabianski, Janusz (1928-1976), illus. LC 62-6946. 348p. illus. 25cm. (Splendor book). 1962. Duell, Sloan and Pearce.
--Grimm's Fairy Tales. Complete ed. Gruelle, John Barton (1880-1938), illus. Hunt, Margaret Raine (1831-1912), tr. LC 14-18123. 6 p. l., 419 p. col. front., illus. col. plates. 25 cm. c.1914. Cupples and Leon Company.
--Grimm's Fairy Tales. New & Complete ed. Gruelle, John Barton (1880-1938) & Coussens, Penrhyn W (1873-), illus. Hunt, Margaret Raine (1831-1912), tr. from German. 1915. Cupples & Leon.
--Grimm's Fairy Tales. Hess, Erwin L., illus. LC 41-18350. 2 p. l., 228 p. illus. 21 cm. c.1941. Whitman Publishing Company.
--Grimm's Fairy Tales. Hunt, Margaret, tr. Sayers, F. C. (1786-1859) LC 68-10477. (Illus.). 53 full-color ils. 416p. (gr. 4 up). 1968. (ISBN 0-695-83515-7). Follett.
--Grimms' Fairy Tales. Kredel, Fritz (1900-1973), illus. Lucas, Alice & Crane, Lucy (1842-1882), trs. LC 46-5791. 4 p. l., 362, 1 p. col. front., illus., col. plates. 23 1/2 cm. (Illustrated junior library). 1945. Grosset & Dunlap.
--Grimm's Fairy Tales. Kredel, Fritz (1900-1973), illus. (Illustrated Junior Library). 1945. Grosset.
--Grimms' Fairy Tales. Kredel, Fritz (1900-1973), illus. N.D. (ISBN 0-448-05460-4). Grosset & Dunlap.
--Grimms' Fairy Tales. Kredel, Fritz (1900-1973), illus. N.D. Grosset & Dunlap.
--Grimms' Fairy Tales. Kredel, Fritz (1900-1973), illus. (Illus.). (gr. 4-9). N.D. (ISBN 0-448-11009-1, G&D). (ISBN 0-448-05460-4). (ISBN 0-448-06009-4). Putnam Pub Group.
--Grimm's Fairy Tales. Kredel, Fritz (1900-1973), illus. LC 37-391131. 400 p. illus., col. plates. 24 cm. c.1937. Stackpole Sons.
--Grimm's Fairy Tales. Lowe, Orton (1873-), ed. Prittie, Edwin John, illus. LC 25-213162. x, 310 p. col. front., illus., col. plates. 21 cm. (On cover: The Winston clear-type popular classics). c.1924. The John C. Winston Company.
--Grimm's Fairy Tales. Monsell, John Robert (1877-), illus. (Collins' Illustrated Pocket Classics). N.D. Collins.
--Grimms' Fairy Tales. Morel, Eve, adapted by. N.D. (ISBN 0-448-00315-5). Grosset & Dunlap.
--Grimms' Fairy Tales. Morel, Eve, ed. Carter, Roberta, illus. (Illus.). (Grow-up Books Ser.). (gr. k-3). 1962. (ISBN 0-448-02251-6, G&D). Putnam Pub Group.
--Grimm's Fairy Tales. Olcott, Frances Jenkins (1897-), ed. Sayers, Frances Clarke, frwd. by. LC 68-10477. (Illus.). 412 p. 24cm. 1968. Follet Pub. Co.
--Grimm's Fairy Tales. Olcott, Frances Jenkins, ed. Cramer, Rie, illus. LC 22-224658. 367 p. incl. col. front., illus. col. plates. 25 cm. 1922. The Penn Publishing Company.
--Grimm's Fairy Tales. O'Neill, Jean, illus. (Illus.). (Rainbow Classics). (gr. 4-6). 1947. (ISBN 0-529-02793-3). (ISBN 0-529-02794-1). World Pub.
--Grimm's Fairy Tales. Orr, Munro Scott (1874-), illus. 327 p. col. front., col. pl. 20 cm. (Golden books for children). 1917. D. McKay.
--Grimm's Fairy Tales. Pocock, Guy Noel (1880-), illus. LC 32-21264. v, 7-337 p. col. front., col. plates. 23 cm. 1930. Garden City Publishing Company, Inc.
--Grimm's Fairy Tales. Pratt, Mara Louise, Mrs., ed. Foster, Edith Francis, illus. LC 12-32863. 19cm. (Young Folk's Library of Choice Literature). 1892. Educational Publishing Co.
--Grimm's Fairy Tales. Prittie, Edwin John, illus. (The Children's Bookshelf). N.D. John C. Winston.
--Grimm's Fairy Tales. Prittie, Edwin John, illus. LC 22-10385. ix, 310 p. incl. col. front., illus. col. plates. 23 cm. c.1922. The John C. Winston Company.
--Grimm's Fairy Tales. Rackham, Arthur (1867-1939), illus. (Illus.). N.D. Doubleday, Page & Co.
--Grimm's Fairy Tales. Rackham, Arthur (1867-1939), illus. Lucas, Edgar, Mrs., tr. N.D. J.B. Lippincott.
--Grimm's Fairy Tales. Rackham, Arthur (1867-1939), illus. Lucas, Edgar, Mrs., tr. (Illus.). 232 p. 21cm. (Classics to grow on). 1966, c.1964. Parents' Magazine's Cultural Institute.
--Grimm's Fairy Tales. Remy, Jean S., retold by. Davis, J. Watson, illus. LC 1-15303. 92p. (Burt's Series of One Syllable Books). 1901. A. L. Burt Co.
--Grimm's Fairy Tales. Rich, Edwin Gile (1879-), ed. Orr, Munro Scott (1874-), illus. LC 36-36434. 4 p. l., 3-246 p. col. front., col. plates. 24 cm. 1931. Houghton Mifflin Company.
--Grimm's Fairy Tales. Rich, Edwin Gile (1879-), ed. LC 22-589. 4 p. l., 3-246 p. col. front., col. plates. 24 cm. c.1921. Small Maynard & Company.
--Grimm's Fairy Tales. Richardson, Peter, illus. Carter, Peter, tr. 272p. 1982. (ISBN 0-19-274529-8, Pub. by Oxford U Pr Childrens). Merrimack Pub Cir.
--Grimm's Fairy Tales. Roth, Arnold (1929-), illus. (gr. 3-5). 1963. Macmillan.
--Grimm's Fairy Tales. Scharl, Josef (1896-1954), illus. 1944. Pantheon Books.
--Grimm's Fairy Tales. Sowerby, Katherine Githa, retold by. Sowerby, Millicent, illus. (Illus.). 24 cm. 255p. 1910. Frederick A. Stokes.
--Grimm's Fairy Tales. Stratton, Helen, illus. N.D. Dodge Publishing Co.
--Grimm's Fairy Tales. Watson, Harry S., illus. LC 15-25682. 2 p. l., vii-x, 406 p. front., illus. 25 cm. 1894. The Cassell Publishing Co.
--Grimm's Fairy Tales. Weedon, L. L., tr. N.D. E P Dutton.
--Grimm's Fairy Tales. Weisgard, Leonard Joseph (1916-), illus. N.D. Doubleday.
--Grimm's Fairy Tales. Weisgard, Leonard Joseph (1916-), illus. LC 54-14471. 256p. illus. 22cm. 1954. Junior Deluxe Editions.
--Grimm's Fairy Tales. Wiltse, Sara Eliza (1849-), ed. King, Caroline S., illus. 2 v. illus. 18 cm. (On cover: Classics for children). 1894. Ginn & Company.
--Grimm's Fairy Tales. Wiltse, Sara Eliza (1849-), ed. LC 23-16992. 2 v. illus. (part col.) 18 cm. 1923. Ginn and Company.
--Grimm's Fairy Tales. Winter, Milo Kendall (1888-1956) & Snow, Dorothea Johnston (1909-), illus. N.D. Rand McNally & Co.
--Grimm's Fairy Tales. Young, Elsa Goldy, illus. LC 41-189028. 3 p. l., 9-253, 1 p. illus. (part col.) 27 cm. c.1941. Whitman Publishing Company.
--Grimm's Fairy Tales and Andersen's Fairy Tales: Two Books in One. N.D. World Publishing Co.
--Grimm's Fairy Tales and Stories, 1 of 6 vols. (Illus.). (Warne's Lansdowne Fairy Library Ser.). N.D. R. Worthington.
--Grimm's Fairy Tales and Stories. (Illus.). (Warne's Favorite Fairy Tales). N.D. Scribner, Welford & Armstrong.
--Grimm's Fairy Tales and Stories, 1 of 7 Vols. (Illus.). (Warne's Lansdowne Fairy Library). N.D. Scribner & Welford.
--Grimm's Fairy Tales: Classics for the Young. 1888. Worthington.
--Grimm's Fairy Tales in words of one syllable. Virginia, Aunt, retold by. LC 12-32874. 21cm. 162p. 1896. Hurst & Co.
--Grimm's Fairy Tales: Part I. Wiltse, Sara Eliza (1849-), ed. (Classics for Children). N.D. Ginn and Company.
--Grimm's Fairy Tales: Part II. Wiltse, Sara Eliza (1849-), ed. (Classics for Children). N.D. Ginn and Company.
--Grimm's Fairy Tales: Selected and Edited for Children in Their Third School Year. Fassett, James Hiram (1869-), ed. LC 4-28962. xi, 188 p. front., pl. 15 cm. (Macmillan's pocket American and English classics). 1904. The Macmillan Company.
--Grimms' Fairy Tales: Snow White and Other Stories. Goulden, Shirley, ed. Nardini, Sandro, illus. LC 57-484499. 60p. illus. 35cm. 1957. Grosset & Dunlap.

--Grimm's Fairy Tales: Stories and Tales of Elves, Goblins and Fairies. Rhead, Louis John (1857-1926), illus. LC 17-31071. 9 p. l., 443, 1 p. incl. front. (2 port.) illus. plates. 23 cm. 1917. Harper & Brothers.
--Grimm's Fairy Tales: The Household Stories. Crane, Lucy, tr. N.D. MacMillan.
--Grimm's Fairy Tales: Twenty Stories. Rackham, Arthur (1867-1939), illus. LC 78-7011. 1978. (ISBN 0-14-004908-8). Penguin Books.
--Grimm's Fairy Tales: Twenty Stories. Rackham, Arthur (1867-1939), illus. LC 73-6077. (Illus.). 127 p. 24cm. (Studio book). 1973. (ISBN 0-670-35532-1). Viking Press.
--Grimm's German Fairy Tales, 1 of 5 Vols. (Illus.). (Enchanting Library). N.D. Set. James Miller.
--Grimm's German Fairy Tales Selected. 1900. Maynard Merrill & Co.
--The Grimm's German Folk Tales. LC 59-5095. 674 p. 21cm. 1960. Southern Illinois University Press.
--Grimm's Goblins. Cruikshank, George (1792-1878), illus. LC 14-224471. 1 p. l., 111 p. col. plates. 20 cm. 1867. Ticknor & Fields.
--Grimm's Goblins. Cruikshank, George (1792-1878) & Wehnert, Edward H., illus. (Illus.). N.D. Worthington Company.
--Grimm's Golden Goose. Mikolaycak, Charles (1937-), illus. LC 69-17439. (Illus.). 32p. 1969. (ISBN 0-394-80710-3). (ISBN 0-394-90710-8). Random.
--Grimm's Hansel and Gretel. Bollinger-Savelli, Antonella, illus. LC 80-85054. (Illus.). 26 p. 23cm. 1981. (ISBN 0-19-520262-7). Oxford University Press.
--Grimm's Home Fairy Tales, 1 of 5 Vols. (Illus.). (Enchanting Library). N.D. Set. James Miller.
--Grimm's Home Stories, 1 of 3 Vols. (Illus.). (The Fairy Library). N.D. Set. George Routledge & Sons.
--Grimm's Household Fairy Tales. (Illus.). (The Fairy Library). N.D. A. L. Burt's Pubs.
--Grimm's Household Fairy Tales. (New Aldine Ser). N.D. International Book Co.
--Grimm's Household Fairy Tales. Andre, Richard, illus. Boldey, Ella, tr. from Ger. LC 12-32863. 2 p. l., 276 p. col. front., illus. 26 x 22 cm. c.1890. McLoughlin Bros.
--Grimm's Household Library: Containing "German Fairy Tales", "Fairy Tales and Legends", and "Home Fairy Tales", 3 vols. (Illus.). N.D. James Miller.
--Grimm's Household Stories. N.D. John C. Winston Co.
--Grimm's Household Stories. Alta ed. N.D. Porter & Coates.
--Grimm's Household Stories. Crane, Walter (1845-1915), illus. Crane, Lucy, tr. (Illus.). N.D. Worthington Company.
--Grimm's Household Stories. Monsell, John Robert (1877-), ed. Monsell, John Robert (1877-), illus. (Illus.). N.D. Cassell & Co.
--Grimm's Household Stories. Wehnert, Edward H., illus. N.D. George Routledge.
--Grimms' Household Tales. (Illus.). (The Cornell Series: No. 55). 1915. A L Burt & Co.
--Grimm's Household Tales, 1 of 2 vols. (The Excelsior Ser.: No. 13). N.D. Set. A. L. Burt's
--Grimm's Household Tales. (Twentieth Century Ser.). N.D. Rand, McNally & Co.'s.
--Grimm's Household Tales. (New Alpha Library). N.D. Rand, McNally & Co.'s.
--Grimm's Household Tales. (The Antique Library). N.D. Rand, McNally & Co.'s.
--Grimm's Household Tales. (The Advance Library Ser.: Vol. 108). N.D. Rand, McNally & Co.
--Grimm's Household Tales. (Illus.). (The Independent Library Ser.: Vol. 108). N.D. Rand, McNally & Co.
--Grimm's Household Tales. (Illus.). (The Junior Library Ser.: Vol. 7). N.D. Rand, McNally &
--Grimm's Household Tales,. Hunt, Margaret Raine (1831-1912), ed. LC 68-31090. 2 v. 22cm. 1968. Singing Tree Press.
--Grimm's Household Tales. Norris, E., ed. LC 6-41719. 134 p. 17 cm. c.1906. Educational Publishing Company.
--Grimm's Moore Tales. Sewell, Helen Moore (1896-1957) & Gekiere, Madeleine, illus. LC 54-12796. 142p. illus. 23cm. 1954. Oxford University Press.
--Grimm's Other Tales: A New Selection. Michaelis-Jena, Ruth & Ratcliff, Arthur, eds. Morgan, Gwenda, illus. Hansen, Wilhelm, tr. from Ger. LC 66-8573. 159p. illus. 22cm. 1966, c.1959. A. S. Barnes.
--Grimm's Popular Fairy Tales. (The Fairy Library). N.D. A. L. Burt Co.
--Grimm's Popular Tales. (Illus.). (The Cornell Series). 1915. A L Burt & Co.
--Grimm's Popular Tales. (The Manhattan Ser.). N.D. A. L. Burt's Pubs.
--Grimm's Popular Tales, 1 of 2 vols. (The Excelsior Ser.: No. 13). N.D. Set. A. L. Burt's Pubs.
--Grimm's Popular Tales. N.D. Belford, Clark & Co.
--Grimm's Popular Tales. (Standard Editions). N.D. Estes & Lauriat.
--Grimm's Popular Tales. N.D. John C. Winston Co.
--Grimm's Popular Tales and Household Stories. N.D. D. Appleton & Co.
--Grimm's Popular Tales and Household Stories. Wehnert, Edward H., illus. N.D. Porter & Coates.
--Grimm's Tales. (Illus.). 144p. (Primary School Library). N.D. Educational Publishing Company.
--Grimm's Tales, 1 of 74 Vols. (The Chandos Classics Ser.: No.25). N.D. R. Worthington.
--Grimm's Tales. Ruskin, John, ed. Cruikshank, George (1792-1878), illus. Taylor, Edgar, tr. Ruskin, John, intro. by. (Standard English and American Books). N.D. Estes & Lauriat's.
--Grimm's Tales and Stories, 1 of 8 vols. (New Translation). (Illus.). (Warne's Victoria Gift Books Ser.: No.3). N.D. R. Worthington.
--Grimm's Tales and Stories, 1 of 16 Vols. (Illus.). (Warne's Victoria Gift Books Ser.: No. 12). N.D. Scribner & Welford.
--Grimm's Tales for Children. (Illus.). N.D. George H. Doran.
--Grimm's Tales for Young & Old: The Complete Story. Manheim, Ralph (1907-), tr. LC 76-56318. 648p. (Anchor Folktale Library). (gr. up). 1983. (ISBN 0-385-18950-8, Anch.). Doubleday.
--Grimm's Tales for Young & Old: The Complete Stories. Manheim, Ralph (1907-), tr. LC 76-56318. 1977. Doubleday.
--Hans in Luck. Galdone, Paul (1914-), illus. LC 79-16154. (Illus.). 41 p. 24cm. 1980, c.1979. (ISBN 0-8193-1011-5). (ISBN 0-8193-1012-3). Parents Magazine Press.
--Hans in Luck. Hoffmann, Felix (1911-1975), illus. LC 74-18184. (Illus.). 24 p. 1st U.S. edition. 1975. (ISBN 0-689-50020-3). Atheneum.
--Hansel and Gretel. Adams, Adrienne (1906-), illus. Scribner, Charles, Jr. (1921-), tr. from Ger. LC 74-14080. (Illus.). 32 p. 27cm. c.1975. (ISBN 0-684-14400-X). Scribner.
--Hansel and Gretel. Brown, Kay (1943-), retold by. Embleton, Gerry, illus. LC 79-84829. (Illus.). 28 p. 31cm. (Derrydale Classic Fairy Tale Ser.). c.1979. (ISBN 0-517-28803-6). Derrydale Books.
--Hansel and Gretel. Browne, Anthony Edward Tudor (1946-), illus. LC 80-85287. (Illus.). 32 p. 25cm. 1981. (ISBN 0-531-04062-3). Julia MacRae Books.
--Hansel & Gretel. Browne, Anthony Edward Tudor (1946-), illus. (Illus.). 32p. (gr. k-3). 1982. (ISBN 0-531-04503-X, MacRae). Watts.
--Hansel and Gretel. Chappell, Warren (1904-), illus. 1944. Alfred A Knopf : distributed by Borzoi Books.
--Hansel and Gretel. Chorpenning, Charlotte Lee Barrows (1872-1955), adapted by. 1956. Coach House Press.
--Hansel & Gretel. Crawford, Elizabeth D. & Zwerger, Lisbeth, illus. (Illus.). 22p (Pub. by Wm. & Morrow). (gr. 1 up). 1983. (ISBN 0-907234-46-1, Pub. by Picture Bk Studio USA). Neugebauer Pr.
--Hansel and Gretel. Dugan, William J., illus. (A Golden Square Bk.). 1967. Golden Press.
--Hansel and Gretel. Galdone, Paul (1914-), illus. LC 82-9979. p. cm. 1982. (ISBN 0-07-022727-6). McGraw-Hill.
--Hansel and Gretel. Hayward, Linda, ed. Beckett, Sheilah (1913-), illus. LC 73-16856. (Illus.). 32 p. 21cm. 1974. (ISBN 0-394-82811-9). Random House.
--Hansel & Gretel. Jeffers, Susan, illus. LC 80-15079. (Illus.). 32p. (gr. k up). 1980. Dial Bks Young.
--Hansel & Gretel. Leopold, Celine, illus. LC 70-158863. (Illus.). color illus. 48p. (gr. k-3). 1971. (ISBN 0-8098-1183-9). Walck.
--Hansel & Gretel. Lobel, Arnold Stark (1933-), illus. LC 75-117296. (Illus.). 48 color ils. 48p. (gr. k-3). 1971. Delacorte.
--Hansel and Gretel. Mellon, Joseph, adapted by. Gilbert, Laura, illus. LC 78-72128. (Illus.). 32 p. 23cm. 1979. (ISBN 0-89799-108-7). (ISBN 0-89799-049-8). Dandelion Press.
--Hansel and Gretel. Pienkowski, Jan (1936-), illus. Walser, David, tr. LC 77-7332. p. cm. 1978. (ISBN 0-690-03818-6). Crowell.
--Hansel & Gretel. Pienkowski, Jan (1936-), illus. Walser, David, tr. LC 77-7332. (Illus.). (The Jan Pienkowski Fairy Tale Lib.). (gr. 1 up). 1978. (ISBN 0-690-03818-6, TYC-J). Har-Row.
--Hansel and Gretel. Nightingale, Sandy Ann, illus. LC 85-2222. (Illus.). 20 p. 31cm. (Knee-High Book). c.1985. (ISBN 0-394-87022-0). (ISBN 0-394-97022-5). Random House.
--Hansel and Gretel. Otto, Svend (1916-), illus. Bell, Anthea, tr. LC 82-83826. (Illus.). 27 p. 26cm. 1984. (ISBN 0-88332-291-9). Larousse.
--Hansel and Gretel. Pavel, Frances K. (1907-), adapted by. Kendrick, Alcy, illus. LC 60-14376. 58p. illus. 24cm. (Read it myself book). 1961. Holt, Rinehart and Winston.
--Hansel and Gretel. Rackham, Arthur (1867-1939), illus. N.D. E P Dutton.
--Hansel and Gretel. Wallner, John C. (1945-), illus. LC 85-6286. p. cm. c.1985. (ISBN 0-13-383654-1). Prentice-Hall.
--Hansel and Gretel. Wehr, Julian, illus. LC 44-6923. 26 p. col. illus. 19 x 20 cm. 1944. Grosset & Dunlap, Inc.
--Hansel and Gretel. Weihs, Erika (1917-), illus. LC 48-3503. 42 p. illus. (part col.) 21 cm. (The Little Golden Library: No. 17). 1945. Simon and Schuster.
--Hansel and Gretel. Wilkin, Eloise Burns (1904-), illus. LC 54-11350. unpaged. illus. 21cm. (Little golden book, 217). 1954. Simon and Schuster.
--Hansel & Gretel. Wilkin, Eloise Burns (1904-), illus. (Illus.). (gr. k-3). 1976. (ISBN 0-307-60419-5, Golden Pr). Western Pub.
--Hansel and Gretel. Wolpin, Harriet, ed. Wolpin, Harriet, illus. LC 47-18423. 82 p. incl. front., illus. (part col.) 25 1/2 cm. (On cover: Maxton books for little people). c.1946. Maxton Publishers, Inc.
--Hansel and Gretel. Zwerger, Lisbeth, illus. Crawford, Elizabeth D., tr. from Ger. LC 79-989. p. cm. 1979. (ISBN 0-688-22198-X). (ISBN 0-688-32198-4). Morrow. **Award: (ALA).**
--Hansel and Gretel: A Story of the Forest. Chappell, Warren (1904-), illus. 82 p. incl. col. front., col. illus. 19 1/2 x 25 cm. 1944. A. A. Knopf.
--Hansel & Gretel, the Seven Ravens, & the Little Red Cap. Crawford, Elizabeth D. & Zwerger, Lisbeth, illus. (Illus.). 66p (Pub. by Wm. & Morrow). (gr. 1 up). 1983. (ISBN 0-907234-49-6, Pub. by Picture Bk Studio USA). Neugebauer Pr.
--Hansel and Gretel with Benjy and Bubbles. Horowitz, Susan, adapted by. Razzi, James (1931-), illus. LC 77-28451. p. cm. (Read with Me Series). 1978. (ISBN 0-03-040246-8). Holt, Rinehart and Winston.
--Hansel and Grethel. Livings, Bess, illus. LC 37-176637. 32 p. col. illus. 17 cm. c.1937. Rand, McNally & Company.
--Hansel and Grethel: Adapted from the Story by Brothers Grimm. Rice, Alma, illus. LC 43-36151. 60 p. incl. col. front., illus. (part col.) 17 1/2 x 13 1/2 cm. (Little color classics). 1943. McLoughlin Brothers, Inc.
--Hansel & Grethel & Other Tales. Rackham, Arthur (1867-1939), illus. Lucas, Alice, tr. from Ger. LC 21-148522. x, 159, 1 p. illus., 20 mounted col. pl. (incl. front.) pl. 26 cm. (Half-title: Grimm's fairy tales). 1920. E. P. Dutton & Company.
--Hansel & Gretle. Felix, Monique, illus. 32p. (Collection of Fairy Tales Ser.). 1983. (ISBN 0-87191-935-4). Childrens Bk Co.
--Home Fairy Tales, 1 of 3 Vols. (Illus.). (Grimm's Fairy Library). N.D. Set. James Miller.
--Home Stories. N.D. George Routledge & Sons.
--Hop o' My Thumb's Wanderings and other Fairy Tales. (Illus.). N.D. E. P. Dutton & Co.
--The Horse, the Fox, and the Lion. Galdone, Paul (1914-), ed. Galdone, Paul (1914-), illus. LC 68-14085. (Illus.). 1 v. (unpaged. 1968. Seabury Press.
--The House in the Wood. Brooke, Leonard Leslie (1862-1940), illus. N.D. Frederick Warne & Co.
--The House in the Wood and Other Old Fairy Stories. Brooke, Leonard Leslie (1862-1940), illus. LC 10-36016. v, 1, 89, 1 p. col. front., illus., col. plates. 25 cm. 1910. F. Warne and Co.
--Household and Fairy Tales. Smith, Wuanita (1866-), illus. Lucas, Alice, et al., trs. LC 16-23527. 377 p. col. front., col. plates 20 cm. (On cover: The Washington square classics). 1916. G. W. Jacobs & Co.
--Household Stories. N.D. E P Dutton.
--Household Stories. LC 79-12246. p. cm. (Mayflower facsimile classics). 1979. (ISBN 0-8317-4582-7). Mayflower Books.
--Household Stories. LC 6-35944. (Illus.). 96p. 1906. McLoughlin Brothers.
--Household Stories. Crane, Walter (1845-1915), illus. Crane, Lucy (1842-1882), tr. LC 66-8283. (Illus.). x, 269 p. 23cm. 1966. McGraw-Hill.
--Household Stories. Crane, Walter (1845-1915), illus. (Illus.). N.D. (ISBN 0-8446-2167-6). Peter Smith Publisher, Inc.
--Household Stories. Crane, Walter (1845-1915), illus. Crane, Lucy (1842-1882), tr. from Ger. LC 24-260981. x, 269, 1 p. col. front., illus., plates. 20 cm. (The children's classics). 1923. The Macmillan Company.
--Household Stories. Kronheim & Co, illus. N.D. George Routledge & Sons.
--Household Stories. Wehnert, Edward H, illus. 1888. Porter & Coates.
--Household Stories from the Collection of the Brothers Grimm. Crane, Lucy, tr. 269p. 1886. (ISBN 0-486-21080-4). Dover Books.
--Household Stories: From the Collection of the Brothers Grimm. Crane, Walter (1845-1915), illus. Crane, Lucy (1842-1882), tr. LC 44-33932. 1 p. l., vii-x, 209, 1 p. illus. 17 1/2 cm. (On cover: Lovell's library). 1883. John W. Lovell Company.
--Household Stories from the Collection of the Brothers Grimm. Crane, Walter (1845-1915), illus. Crane, Lucy (1842-1882), tr. (Children's Classics). N.D. Macmillan.
--Household Stories from the Collection of the Brothers Grimm. Crane, Walter (1845-1915), illus. Crane, Lucy (1842-1862), tr. 342 p. front. 20 cm. N.D. T. Y. Crowell & Co.
--Household Stories from the Collection of the Brothers Grimm. Crane, Walter (1845-1915), illus. Crane, Lucy (1842-1882), tr. LC 66-8413. (Illus.). 24cm. x, 269p. (Legacy lib. facsim.). 1966. University Microfilms.
--Household Stories from the Collection of the Brothers Grimm. Troyer, Johannes (1902-), illus. Crane, Lucy (1842-1882), tr. from Ger. LC 54-13480. 260p. illus. 22cm. (New children's classics). 1954. Macmillan.
--Household Stories of the Brothers Grimm. Crane, Walter (1845-1915), illus. Crane, Lucy, tr. (Illus.). (gr. 3-9). 1886. Dover.
--Household Tales. xii, 343 p. illus. 18 cm. (Half-title: Everyman's library, ed. by Ernest Rhys. For young people). 1908. J. M. Dent & Co.
--Household Tales. Hoban, Russell Connell (1925-), intro. by. LC 79-64122. (gr. 3-9). 1979. (ISBN 0-8052-3721-6). (ISBN 0-8052-0633-7). Schocken.
--Household Tales, 2 Vols. Hunt, Margaret, ed. Hunt, Margaret, tr. from Ger. Lang, Andrew, intro. by. 1885. Scribner & Welford.
--How Six Men Got on in the World. Alderson, Brian W, tr. LC 81-40418. (Illus.). 28p. 1st U.S. edition. (Moonlight Editions Ser.). 1981. (ISBN 0-8052-3781-X, Moonlight Edns). Schocken.
--How the Moon Began: A Folk Tale from Grimm. Reeves, James (1909-), adapted by. Ardizzone, Edward Jeffrey Irving (1900-1979), illus. LC 72-169201. (Illus.). 42 p. 25cm. 1971. (ISBN 0-200-71862-2). Abelard-Schuman.
--Jorinda and Joringel. Adams, Adrienne (1906-), illus. Shub, Elizabeth, tr. from Ger. LC 68-12517. (Illus.). 1 v. (unpaged. 27cm. (gr. k-4). 1968. (ISBN 0-684-20841-5). Scribner. **Awards: (ALA); (BGH).**
--Jorinda and Joringel. Watts, Anna Bernadette (1942-), illus. LC 71-114218. (Illus.). 32 p. 32cm. 1970. World Pub. Co.
--The Juniper Tree, and Other Tales from Grimm. Segal, Lore Groszmann (1928-), selected by. Sendak, Maurice Bernard (1928-), illus. Jarrell, Randall (1914-1965), tr. LC 73-82698. (Illus.). 2 v. (332 p.). 19cm. 1973. (ISBN 0-374-18057-1). Farrar, Straus and Giroux. **Awards: (NYT).**
--The Juniper Tree, and Other Tales from Grimm. Segal, Lore Groszmann (1928-), ed. Sendak, Maurice Bernard (1928-), illus. LC 76-372143. (Illus.). 2 v. in 1 (332 p.). 18cm. (Noonday ; 534). 1976, c.1973. (ISBN 0-374-51358-9). Farrar, Straus and Giroux.
--King Grisly-Beard: A Tale from the Brothers Grimm. 1st ed. Sendak, Maurice Bernard (1928-), illus. Taylor, Edgar (1928-), tr. from Ger. LC 73-77911. (Illus.). 24 p. 23cm. 1973. Farrar, Straus & Giroux. **Awards: (NYT).**
--King Grisly-Beard: A Tale from the Brothers Grimm. Sendak, Maurice Bernard (1928-), illus. Taylor, Edgar (1793-1839), tr. from Ger. LC 78-4399. (Illus.). 24 p. 22cm. (Picture Puffin). 1978. (ISBN 0-14-050231-9). Puffin Books.
--King of the Swans, 1 of 4 Vols. (Illus.). (Grimm's Fairy Library). N.D. Set. James Miller.
--King of the Swans, and Other Stories. N.D. Lee & Shepard.
--King Thrushbeard. Hoffmann, Felix (1911-1975), illus. LC 74-128390. (Illus.). 32 p. 30cm. 1st U.S. edition. (gr. k-3). 1970. (ISBN 0-15-242940-9). Harcourt, Brace & World.
--King Wren, 1 of 6 Vols. (Illus.). (Grimm Library). N.D. Set. George Routledge & Sons.
--Little Brother and Little Sister. Cooney, Barbara (1917-), retold by. Cooney, Barbara (1917-), illus. LC 81-43058. p. cm. c.1982. (ISBN 0-385-14583-7). Doubleday.
--Little Brother and Little Sister and Other Tales by the Brothers Grimm. Rackham, Arthur (1867-1939), illus. 24 cm. 250p. 1917. Dodd Mead.
--Little Red-Cap. Blair, Susan B., illus. LC 63-12419. 1 v. (unpaged) col. illus. 24 cm. (Young owl book). 1964. Holt, Rinehart and Winston.
--Little Red-Cap. Blair, Susan B., illus. LC 63-12419. (Illus.). 41 p. 24cm. (Young owl book). 1964. Holt, Rinehart and Winston.

--The Little Red Cap. Crawford, Elizabeth D. & Zwerger, Lisbeth, illus. (Illus.). 22p. (gr. 1 up). 1983. (ISBN 0-907234-48-8, Pub. by Picture Bk Studio USA). Neugebauer Pr.
--Little Red Cap. Zwerger, LIsbeth, illus. Crawford, Elizabeth D., tr. from Ger. LC 82-14211. 1983. (ISBN 0-688-01715-0). (ISBN 0-688-01716-9). William Morrow. **Award: (NYT).**
--Little Red Riding Hood. N.D. Wilcox & Follett Co.
--Little Red Riding Hood. Galdone, Paul (1914-), adapted by. LC 74-6426. (Illus.). 32 p. 1974. (ISBN 0-07-022731-4). McGraw-Hill.
--Little Red Riding Hood. Mahan, Benton, illus. LC 80-27684. (Illus.). 32p. (gr. k-2). 1981. (ISBN 0-89375-488-9). (ISBN 0-89375-489-7). Troll Assocs.
--Little Red Riding-Hood. Mikolaycak, Charles (1937-), illus. LC 68-217968. 1 v. (unpaged) illus. pt. col.) 19cm. (Stardust bks.). 1968. C. R. Gibson.
--Little Red Riding Hood. Pincus, Harriet (1938-), illus. LC 68-11505. (Illus.). 32p. (ps-3). 1973. (ISBN 0-15-652850-9, VoyB). HarBraceJ.
--Little Red Riding Hood. 1st ed. Pincus, Harriet (1938-), illus. LC 68-11505. (Illus.). 1 v. (unpaged). 22cm. 1968. Harcourt, Brace & World.
--Little Red Riding Hood. Pincus, Harriet (1938-), illus. LC 85-27073. p. cm. (Voyager/HBJ book). 1985. (ISBN 0-15-652850-9). Harcourt Brace Jovanovich.
--Little Red Riding Hood. Watts, Anna Bernadette (1942-), illus. (Illus.). (gr. k-3). 1972. (ISBN 0-590-09186-7). Scholastic Inc.
--Little Red Riding Hood. Watts, Anna Bernadette (1942-), illus. LC 69-13141. (Illus.). 32 p. 33cm. 1st U.S. edition. (gr. k-3). 1969. World Pub. Co.
--Little Snow White and Other Fairy Tales. (Illus.). N.D. E. P. Dutton and Co.
--Little Snow-White and Other Grimm Fairy Tales. Stead, William Thomas (1849-), ed. Le Fanu, Brinsley, illus. LC 8-23091. 60 p. illus. 19 cm. (Children's Classics). 1908. The Penn Publishing Company.
--Little Table, Get Set. Despois, Pauline, adapted by. Bourre, Martine, illus. LC 79-19163. (Illus.). 19 p. 17cm. (Goodnight book). c.1980. (ISBN 0-394-84381-9). Knopf.
--The Luck Child. Chapman, Gaynor (1935-), illus. 1968. (ISBN 0-689-20128-1). Atheneum Publishers.
--The Magic Mirror: And Other Stories from Grimm's Household Tales. Andre, Richard, illus. Boldey, Ella, tr. LC 44-11914. 1 p. l., 1 37-281 p. col. front., illus. 26 1/2 x 21 1/2 cm. (On cover: Grimms fairy tale series). c.1890. McLoughlin Bros.
--More Tales from Grimm. Gag, Wanda (1893-1946), illus. Gag, Wanda (1893-1946), tr. from Ger. LC 47-11377. xiii, 257 p. illus. 9. 1947. Coward-McCann.
--More Tales from Grimm. Gag, Wanda (1893-1946), illus. Gag, Wanda (1893-1946), tr. LC 81-66879. (Illus.). xiii, 257 p. 21cm. 1981, c.1974. (ISBN 0-698-20534-0). Coward, McCann & Geoghegan.
--Mother Holly. Watts, Anna Bernadette (1942-), retold by. Watts, Anna Bernadette (1942-), tr. LC 77-185753. (Illus.). 32 p. 32cm. 1972. (ISBN 0-690-56363-9). Crowell.
--Mother Holly. Watts, Anna Bernadette (1942-), retold by. Watts, anna Bernadette (1942-), tr. LC 73-168998. (Illus.). 32 p. 33cm. 1972. (ISBN 0-19-279684-4). Oxford University Press.
--Mrs. Fox's Wedding. Corrin, Sara & Corrin, Stephen, eds. LeCain, Errol John (1941-), illus. 1980. Penguin.
--The Musicians of Bremen. LC 74-78599. (Illus.). N.D. (ISBN 0-88332-060-6). Larousse.
--The Musicians of Bremen. Miller, John Parr (1913-), illus. LC 54-2630. unpaged. illus. 21cm. (Little golden books, 189). 1954. Simon and Schuster.
--The Musicians of Bremen. Otto, Svend (1916-), illus. Rogers, Anne, tr. from Ger. LC 75-312012. (Illus.). 23 p. 26cm. 1974. (ISBN 0-88332-060-6). Larousse.
--The Musicians of Bremen. Rouke, Eve, ed. Ramirez, Pablo, illus. LC 66-14058. 1 v. (unpaged) col. illus. 24 cm. (Holly story book library). 1966. World Pub. Co.
--My Book of Hansel and Gretel. Nardini, Sandro, illus. LC 61-66500. unpaged.illus. 33cm. (Giant Maxton book). c.1960. Maxton Pub. Corp.
--My Book of Snow-White and the Seven Dwarfs. Nardini, Sandro, illus. LC 61-66501. unpaged. illus. 33cm. (Giant Maxton book). c.1960. Maxton Pub. Corp.
--The Old Goose Woman. Ramirez, Pablo, illus. LC 66-15631. (Illus.). 1 v. (unpaged). 24cm. (Holly story book library). 1966. World Pub. Co.
--Old Man & the Turnip. Morey, Sheenathea (1786-1859), ed. Mathieu, Dorothea, illus. (Illus.). (ps-3). 1965. (ISBN 0-695-46500-7). Follett.
--Old, Old Fairy Tales. N.D. Thomas Nelson & Sons.
--Poor Woodcutter & the Dove. LC 79-125037. (Illus.). color ils. 32p. (ps-3). 1970. (Sey Lawr). (Sey Lawr). Delacorte.
--Popular Fairy Tales. (Illus.). (Burt's Young Folks' Library). N.D. A. L. Burt's Pubs.
--Popular Stories. Cruikshank, George (1792-1878), illus. 19cm. 403p. 1937. Oxford University Press.
--Popular Tales. Wehnert, Edward H, illus. N.D. Porter & Coates.
--The Queen Bee. Davis, Allen, illus. 32p. (Collection of Fairy Tales Ser.). 1983. (ISBN 0-87191-939-7). Childrens Bk Co.
--Rapunzel. Ash, Jutta (1786-1859), illus. LC 81-13284. (Illus.). 27 p. 24cm. 1st U.S. edition. c.1982. (ISBN 0-03-061219-5). Holt, Rinehart and Winston.
--Rapunzel. Dodson, Bert, illus. LC 78-18066. (Illus.). 32 p. 24cm. c.1979. (ISBN 0-89375-135-9). Troll Associates.
--Rapunzel. Hague, Michael R., illus. 32p. (Collection of Fairy Tales Ser.). 1983. (ISBN 0-87191-936-2). Childrens Bk Co.
--Rapunzel. american ed. Hague, Michael R., illus. LC 83-71183. (Illus.). 31 p. 23cm. c.1984. (ISBN 0-87191-936-2). Creative Education.
--Rapunzel. Hoffmann, Felix (1911-1975), ed. Hoffmann, Felix (1911-1975), illus. LC 61-2865. (Illus.). (gr. k-3). 1961. (ISBN 0-15-265656-1, HJ). HarBraceJ.
--Rapunzel. Rogasky, Barbara, retold by. Hyman, Trina Schart (1939-), illus. LC 81-6419. (Illus.). 32p. (ps-3). 1982. (ISBN 0-8234-0454-4). Holiday. **Award: (ALA).**
--Rapunzel. Watts, Anna Bernadette (1942-), retold by. Watts, Anna Bernadette (1942-), illus. LC 75-8847. (Illus.). 28 p. 32cm. (ps-3). 1975. (ISBN 0-690-00979-8). (ISBN 0-690-00980-1). Crowell.
--Rapunzel: A Story by the Brothers Grimm. Hoffmann, Felix (1911-1975), illus. Sheppard, Katya, tr. LC 61-4533. unpaged. illus. 31cm. 1960. Oxford University Press.
--Rare Treasures from Grimm. Manheim, Ralph (1907-), ed. Blegvad, Erik (1923-), illus. LC 80-2350. (Illus.). x, 99 p. 27cm. c.1981. (ISBN 0-385-14548-9). Doubleday.
--Rumpelstiltskin. Ayer, Jacqueline (1930-), illus. LC 67-20165. (Illus.). 32 p. 26cm. (gr. k-3). 1967. (ISBN 0-15-269525-7). Harcourt, Brace & World.
--Rumpelstiltskin. Camp, Hamid H., contrib. by. (gr. k-3). N.D. (ISBN 0-590-04282-3). (ISBN 0-590-20601-X). Scholastic Inc.
--Rumpelstiltskin. Crane, Lucy (1842-1882), illus. LC 74-2139. (Illus.). 48p. (gr. k-3). 1974. (ISBN 0-590-07393-1, Four Winds). Scholastic Inc.
--Rumpelstiltskin. Hockerman, Dennis, illus. LC 78-18079. (Illus.). 32 p. 24cm. c.1979. (ISBN 0-89375-140-5). Troll Associates.
--Rumpelstiltskin. Stobbs, William (1914-), illus. LC 71-139859. (Illus.). ils., some in color. 32p. 1st U.S. edition. (gr. k-3). 1971. (ISBN 0-8098-1181-2). Walck.
--Rumpelstiltskin. Wallner, John C. (1945-), illus. LC 83-19100. (Illus.). 32p. 1984. (ISBN 0-13-783747-X). (ISBN 0-13-783747-X). P-H.
--Rumpelstiltskin: A Story from the Brothers Grimm. Stobbs, William (1914-), illus. LC 71-139859. (Illus.). 30 p. 24cm. 1971, c.1970. (ISBN 0-8098-1181-2). H. Z. Walck.
--Rumpelstiltskin: A Tale Told Long Ago by the Brothers Grimm. Tarvoc, Edith, retold by. Gorey, Edward St. John (1925-), illus. LC 74-2139. (Illus.). 48 p. 21cm. 1974, c.1973. Four Winds Press.
--Rumpelstiltskin: An Adaptation from Grimms' Fairy Tales. Jones, Patricia (1913-), adapted by. Balet, Jan Bernard (1913-), illus. LC 55-14302. (Illus.). 31 p. 24cm. (Concora book). c.1954. Rand McNally. **Award: (NYT).**
--The Secret Shoemakers, and Other Stories. Reeves, James (1909-), retold by. Ardizzone, Edward Jeffrey Irving (1900-1979), illus. LC 67-85136. (Illus.). 96 p. 22cm. 1966. Abelard-Schuman.
--Selected Tales. Luke, David (1921-), tr. LC 83-164476. (Penguin Classics). 1983. Penguin.
--The Seven Crows, 1 of 6 Vols. (Grimm Library). N.D. George Routledge & Sons.
--The Seven Ravens. LC 63-2602. unpaged. illus. 22 x 30 cm. 1963. Oxford University Press.
--The Seven Ravens. Crawford, Elizabeth D. & Zwerger, Lisbeth, illus. (Illus.). 22p (Pub. by Wm. & Morrow). (gr. 1 up). 1983. (ISBN 0-907234-47-X, Pub. by Picture Bk Studio USA). Neugebauer Pr.
--The Seven Ravens. Hoffmann, Felix (1911-1975), illus. LC 63-2506. (Illus.). 32 p. 1st U.S. edition. 1963. (ISBN 0-15-272920-8). Harcourt, Brace & World. **Award: (ALA).**
--The Seven Ravens. Zwerger, Lisbeth, illus. Crawford, Elizabeth, tr. from Ger. LC 80-25365. (Illus.). 24 p. 1981. (ISBN 0-688-00371-0). (ISBN 0-688-00372-9). Morrow.
--The Seven Ravens: A Grimm's Fairy Tale. Diamond, Donna (1950-), retold by. Diamond, Donna (1950-), illus. LC 77-14252. (Illus.). 32 p. 24cm. 1979. (ISBN 0-670-63557-X). Viking
--The Shepherd's Dream. Sprague, Rose Mueller, illus. Sprague, Mary A., tr. from Ger. LC 44-12294. 18 p., 1 l. col. front., illus., col. plates. 25 1/2 x 20 1/2 cm. 1893. L. Prang & Company.
--The Shoemaker and the Christmas Elves: A Folk Tale from Germany. Moncure, Jane Belk (1926-), retold by. Sommers, Linda, illus. LC 79-26617. p. cm. c.1980. (ISBN 0-89565-108-4). Child's World.
--The Shoemaker & the Elves. Adams, Adrienne (1906-), illus. Andrews, Wayne (1906-), tr. LC 60-12607. (Illus.). (gr. k-4). 1960. (ISBN 0-684-12982-5, ScribJ). (ISBN 0-684-12634-6, ScribJ). Scribner. **Award: (ALA).**
--The Shoes That Danced. Wolpin, Harriet, illus. LC 47-18422. 32 p. incl. front., illus. (part col.) 25 1/2 cm. (On cover: Maxton books for little people). c.1946. Maxton Publishers, Inc.
--Six Companions Find Their Fortune. Fromm, Lilo (1928-), illus. Sheppard, Katya, tr. LC 79-127216. (Illus.). 24 p. 29cm. (gr. 5-8). 1971, c.1969. (ISBN 0-385-02950-0). Doubleday.
--Six Fairy Tales from the Brothers Grimm. Hockney, David, illus. (Illus.). 52p. (ps-5). 1970. Box of Ten. (ISBN 0-902825-00-3). Petersburg Pr.
--Six Fairy Tales from the Brothers Grimm. Hockney, David, illus. LC 83-12193. 1983. (ISBN 0-902825-23-2). Petersburg Press.
--The Six Swans. (Grimm Library). N.D. Set. George Routledge & Sons.
--The Six Swans. Hospes, Adrie (1946-), illus. Hunt, Margaret Raine (1831-1912), tr. from Ger. LC 74-8580. (Illus.). 26 p. 29cm. 1974. (ISBN 0-07-030475-0). (ISBN 0-07-030476-9). McGraw-Hill.
--Sixty Fairy Tales of the Brothers Grimm. Rackham, Arthur (1867-1939), illus. Lucas, Alice, tr. Wilkins, Cary, frwd. by. LC 79-14513. (Illus.). x, 325 p., 20 leaves of plates. 26cm. 1979. Weathervane Books : Distributed by Crown Publishers.
--Sleeping Beauty. Hoffmann, Felix (1911-1975), adapted by. Hoffmann, Felix (1911-1975), illus. (Illus.). 32p. (gr. k-3). 1959. (ISBN 0-15-275672-8). HarBraceJ. **Award: (ALA).**
--The Sleeping Beauty. Hoffmann, Felix (1911-1975), illus. Collier, Peter, tr. LC 60-32772. unpaged. illus. 30cm. 1959. Oxford University Press. **Award: (ALA).**
--The Sleeping Beauty. Hutton, Warwick (1939-), retold by. Hutton, Warwick (1939-), illus. LC 78-64772. (Illus.). 32p. (gr. 1-9). 1979. (ISBN 0-689-50131-5, McElderry Bk). Atheneum.
--The Sleeping Beauty. 1st ed. Hyman, Trina Schart (1939-), adapted by. Hyman, Trina Schart (1939-), illus. LC 75-43769. p. cm. 1977, c.1976. (ISBN 0-316-38702-9). Little, Brown.
--Sleeping Beauty. Iizawa, Tadasu (1909-) & Hijikata, Shigemi (1915-), illus. LC 76-157672. (Illus.). 19 p. 29cm. 1971. (ISBN 0-448-04238-X). Grosset & Dunlap.
--The Sleeping Beauty. Pienkowski, Jan (1936-), illus. Walser, David, tr. LC 77-23338. p. cm. (Fairy Tale Library). 1978. (ISBN 0-690-03823-2). Crowell.
--The Sleeping Beauty. Schwartz, Lieselotte, illus. LC 74-108978. (Illus.). 32p. (ps-3). N.D. (ISBN 0-87592-047-0). Scroll Pr.
--The Sleeping Beauty and Other Tales. Brown, Wayne, illus. LC 72-79991. (Illus.). 224 p. 29cm. 1969. (ISBN 0-516-04247-5). Childrens Press.
--Snow White. N.D. Golden Press.
--Snow White. LC 75-1763. (Illus.). 24p. (gr. 2-5). 1975. (ISBN 0-88332-070-3). Larousse.
--Snow White. (Illus.). (Pop-up Fairy Tales Ser.,: No. 8). (gr. 1 up). N.D. Random.
--Snow White. Bell, Anthea, adapted by. Iwasaki, Chihiro (1918-1974), illus. Bell, Anthea, tr. LC 85-12158. (Illus.). 41 p. 29cm. c.1985. (ISBN 0-88708-012-X). Picture Book Studio USA.
--Snow White. Heins, Paul (1909-) & Hyman, Trina Schart (1939-), illus. LC 73-13585. (Illus.). (gr. k-3). 1979. (ISBN 0-316-35451-1, Pub. by Atlantic-Little Brown). (ISBN 0-316-35450-3). Little.
--Snow White. 1st ed. Hyman, Trina Schart (1939-), illus. Heins, Paul (1909-), tr. from Ger. LC 73-13585. (Illus.). 48 p. 23cm. 1974. (ISBN 0-316-35450-3). Little, Brown.
--Snow-White. Mellon, Joseph (1786-1859), adapted by. Read, Isobel, illus. LC 78-72127. (Illus.). 32 p. 23cm. 1979. (ISBN 0-89799-136-2). (ISBN 0-89799-048-X). Dandelion Press.
--Snow White. Miller, Doris R., pseud., ed. Mosesson, Gloria Rubin. Correas, Jose, illus. LC 65-247365. lv. (unpaged) col. illus. 24cm. (Holly story bk. lib.). c.1965. World.
--Snow White. Pienkowski, Jan (1936-), illus. Walser, David, tr. LC 77-23590. p. cm. (Fairy Tale Library). 1978. (ISBN 0-690-03820-8). Crowell.
--Snow White. Pienkowski, Jan (1936-), illus. Walser, David, tr. LC 77-23590. (The Jan Pienkowski Fairy Tale Library). (gr. 1 up). 1978. (ISBN 0-690-03820-8, TYC-J). Har-Row.
--Snow White. Smith, Wuanita (1866-) & Shenton, Edward (1895-), illus. LC 23-6927. 115 p. col. front., plates (part col.) 20 cm. c.1922. G. W. Jacobs & Company.
--Snow White. Watts, Anna Bernadette (1942-), illus. LC 82-20960. p. cm. 1983. (ISBN 0-571-12518-2). Faber and Faber.
--Snow White and Other Stories from Grimm. Cappe, Jeanne (1895-), ed. Huens, Jean Leon, illus. Ponsot, Marie Birmingham, tr. from Fr. LC 57-3756. unpaged. illus. 31cm. 1957. Grosset & Dunlap.
--Snow White and Rose Red. Adams, Adrienne (1906-), illus. LC 64-21290. (Illus.). 40 p. 26cm. 1964. Scribner.
--Snow-White and Rose-Red. Cooney, Barbara (1917-), illus. LC 66-7772. 47p. col. illus. 24cm. 1st U.S. edition. (gr. k-3). 1966, c.1965. Delacorte.
--Snow White & Rose Red. Grimm, Wilhelm Karl (1786-1859), illus. (Illus.). 48p. (Blackbird Bks). 1984. (ISBN 0-531-03756-8, Macrae). Watts.
--Snow White & Rose Red. Topor, Roland (1938-), illus. 32p. (Collection of Fairy Tales Ser.). 1983. (ISBN 0-87191-938-9). Childrens Bk
--Snow White and Rose Red. american ed. Topor, Roland (1938-), illus. LC 83-71185. (Illus.). 31 p. 23cm. c.1984. (ISBN 0-87191-938-9). Creative Education.
--Snow White and Red Rose. Wallner, John C. (1945-), illus. LC 84-4910. (Illus.). 24cm. 32p. (gr. k-3). 1984. (ISBN 0-13-815234-9). P-H.
--Snow White and Rose Red. Weren, James, illus. LC 78-18074. (Illus.). 32 p. 24cm. c.1979. (ISBN 0-89375-136-7). Troll Associates.
--Snow-White and Rose Red. Wolpin, Harriet, ed. Wolpin, Harriet, illus. LC 47-249027. 32 p. incl. front., illus. (part col.) 25 1/2 cm. (On cover: Maxton books for little people). c.1946. Maxton Publishers, Inc.
--Snow-White and Rose-Red: Another Story, About a Different Snow-White. Dunlap, Hope & Biers, Clarence, illus. LC 38-12741. 32 p. col. illus. 17 cm. c.1933. Rand McNally & Co.
--Snow White & the Seven Dwarfs. (Illus.). (gr. 3-8). N.D. (ISBN 0-685-11566-6). French & Eur.
--Snow White & The Seven Dwarfs. N.D. (ISBN 0-448-04221-5). Grosset & Dunlap Pub.
--Snow-White and the Seven Dwarfs. Burkert, Nancy Ekholm (1933-), illus. Jarrell, Randall (1914-1965), tr. LC 72-81489. (Illus.). 31 p. 32cm. 1972. (ISBN 0-374-37099-0). Farrar, Straus, and Giroux. **Awards: (ALA); (RCM).**
--Snow White and the Seven Dwarfs. Gag, Wanda (1893-1946), illus. Gag, Wanda (1893-1946), tr. LC 38-27575. 43 p. illus. 21 cm. c.1938. Coward-McCann, Inc. **Award: (RCM).**
--Snow White and the Seven Dwarfs. Littledale, Susan, ed. Jeffers, Susan, illus. LC 81-65910. p. cm. c.1981. (ISBN 0-590-07827-5). Four Winds Press.
--Snow White and the Seven Dwarfs. Otto, Svend (1916-), illus. Rogers, Anne, tr. from Ger. LC 75-1763. (Illus.). 23 p. 26cm. 1975. (ISBN 0-88332-070-3). Larousse.
--Snowdrop and other Tales. Rackham, Arthur (1867-1939), illus. N.D. E P Dutton.
--Stories from Grimm. (Illus.). (Stories Old and New Ser.). N.D. Caldwell.
--Stories from Grimm. (Illus.). 96p. (Fairy Tale Ser.). N.D. Cassell & Co.
--Stories from Grimm. N.D. Thomas Nelson
--Stories from Grimm. Banta-Benson, Alpha, ed. Dulin, James Harvey, illus. 32 p. illus. 18 cm. (On cover: The little classic series). 1922. A. Flanagan Company.
--Stories from Grimm. Benson, Alpha Banta, ed. Dulin, James Harvey, illus. LC 34-682. 32p. illus. 18cm. (The Little Classic Ser.). c.1922. A. Flanagan Co.
--Stories from Grimm: Told to the Children. Steedman, Amy, ed. LC 8-14768. vii, 116 p. 8 col. pl. (incl. front.) 15 cm. (Half-title: Told to the children series, ed. by Louey Chisholm). N.D. T. C. & E. C. Jack.
--The Once-Upon-a-Time Scratch and Sniff Book: Stories. Long, Ruthanna, adapted by. Wilkin, Eloise Burns (1904-), illus. LC 78-51144. (Illus.). 28 p. 24cm. (Golden scratch & Sniff book). c.1978. (ISBN 0-307-13525-X). Golden
--The Story of Hansel and Gretel. Serkin, Amalia, illus. LC 45-9191. 34, 1 p. illus. (part col.) 19 1/2 x 17 1/2 cm. (On cover: A Lothrop color storybook). 1945. Lothrop Lee & Shepard
--The Story of Snow-White and the Seven Dwarfs. Wegner, Fritz (1924-), illus. LC 73-5973. (Illus.). 48 p. 24cm. (Walck fairy tales with historical notes). 1973. (ISBN 0-8098-1208-8). H. Z. Walck.

--The Story of the Seven Ravens. Serkin, Amalia, illus. LC 46-8466. 35 p. illus. (part col.) 19 1/2 x 17 1/2 cm. (On cover: A Lothrop color storybook). 1946. Lothrop, Lee & Shepard Co., Inc.
--The Table, the Donkey & the Stick. (Illus.). (ps-3). 1976. (ISBN 0-07-022700-4, GB). (ISBN 0-07-022701-2). McGraw.
--The Table, the Donkey, and the Stick. Galdone, Paul (1914-), adapted by. Galdone, Paul (1914-), illus. LC 76-15559. (Illus.). 40 p. 27cm. c.1976. (ISBN 0-07-022700-4). McGraw Hill.
--Tales from Grimm. Gag, Wanda (1893-1946), illus. Gag, Wanda (1893-1946), tr. LC 36-28509. xiv p., 3 l., 3-237, 1 p. col. front., illus. 21 cm. c.1936. Coward-McCann, Inc.
--Tales from Grimm. Gag, Wanda (1893-1946), illus. Gag, Wanda, tr. from Ger. LC 81-66878. (Illus.). xiv, 237 p. 21cm. 1981, c.1964. (ISBN 0-698-20533-2). Coward, McCann & Geoghegan.
--Tales from Grimm. Gag, Wanda (1893-1946), tr. (Illus.). (gr. 3-6). 1936. (ISBN 0-8382-0840-1). Hale.
--Tales of Grimm and Andersen. Jacobi, Frederick, Jr. (1921-), ed. Auden, Wystan (1907-1973) LC 52-9545. 746p. 21cm. (Modern Library of the World's Best Books G76). 1952. Random House.
--Tenggren's The Giant with Three Golden Hairs. Tenggren, Gustaf (1896-1970), illus. LC 55-1633. unpaged. illus. 21cm. (Little golden book, 210). 1955. Simon and Schuster.
--Tenggren's The Golden Goose. Tenggren, Gustaf (1896-1970), illus. (Little Golden Book). 1956. Golden Press.
--The Three Brothers, and Other Stories. (Illus.). N.D. James Miller.
--Thorn Rose. LC 75-16835. (Illus.). 32 p. 1977, c.1975. (ISBN 0-02-737270-7). (ISBN 0-87888-086-0). Bradbury Press.
--The Three Brothers, 1 of 4 Vols. (Illus.). (Grimm's Fairy Library). N.D. Set. James Miller.
--Three Favorite Fairy Tales: Little Red Ridng Hood, Hansel and Gretel, Jack and the Beanstalk. Torchio, illus. LC 64-56264. 56 p. col. illus. 33 cm. (Big golden book). 1964. Golden Press.
--Three Feathers. Schmid, Eleonore (1939-), illus. 32p. (Collection of Fairy Tales Ser.). 1983. (ISBN 0-87191-941-9). Childrens Bk Co.
--Three Gay Tales from Grimm. Gag, Wanda (1893-1946), illus. Gag, Wanda (1893-1946), tr. (Illus.). (gr. k-4). 1943. (ISBN 0-698-30366-0). Coward.
--The Three Golden Hairs and Other Stories from Grimm's Household Tales. Andre, Richard, illus. Boldey, Ella, tr. from Ger. 1 p. l., 139-183 p. col. front., illus. 26 1/2 x 21 1/2 cm. (On cover: Grimms fairy tale series). c.1890. McLoughlin Bros.
--Three Grimms' Fairy Tales: The Fox & the Geese, The Magic Porridge Pot, The Silver Pennies, 3 bks. Watts, Anna Bernadette (1942-), illus. (Illus.). (gr. 4-8). 1981. Boxed set. (ISBN 0-316-32885-5). Little.
--Three Languages. Chermayeff, Ivan (1932-), illus. 32p. (Collection of Fairy Tales Ser.). 1983. (ISBN 0-87191-940-0). Childrens Bk Co.
--Three Tales. Watts, Anna Bernadette (1942-), retold by. Watts, Anna Bernadette (1942-), illus. LC 80-8101. (Illus.). 3 v. 15cm. 1980. (ISBN 0-316-32885-5). Little, Brown.
--Three Tales from Grimm: The Sleeping Beauty, the Frog Prince, and Mother Hulda. Schlotter, Brunhild, illus. LC 38-28955. 48 p. illus. (part col.) 23 cm. 1938. The Macmillan Company.
--Tom Thumb. Hoffmann, Felix (1911-1975), illus. LC 72-85915. 32p. (ps-3). 1973. (ISBN 0-689-30318-1, McElderry Bk). Atheneum. **Award: (ALA).**
--Tom Thumb. Mellon, Joseph (1785-1863), adapted by. Moffett, Robin, illus. LC 78-72130. (Illus.). 32 p. 23cm. c.1979. (ISBN 0-89799-140-0). (ISBN 0-89799-051-X). Dandelion Press.
--Tom Thumb: The Story by the Brothers Grimm. Hoffmann, Felix (1911-1975), illus. LC 72-85917. (Illus.). 32 p. 1st U.S. edition. 1973. Atheneum. **Award: (ALA).**
--The Traveling Musicians. Fischer, Hans Erich (1909-1958), ed. Fischer, Hans Erich (1909-1958), illus. LC 55-14877. (Illus.). 28 p. 32cm. 1955. Harcourt, Brace.
--The Traveling Musicians. Lowe, Edith May Kovar (1905-), ed. Windsor, Mary, pseud. Brackett, Esther M. (1920-), illus. Tingle, Dolli, pseud. LC 65-16158. 1 v. (unpaged) col. illus. 30 x 14 cm. (Read-aloud book). 1965. Follett Pub. Co.
--The Twelve Dancing Princesses. Beckett, Sheilah (1913-), illus. (Little Golden Book). 1954. Golden Press.
--The Twelve Dancing Princesses. Hockerman, Dennis, illus. LC 78-18077. (Illus.). 32 p. 24cm. c.1979. (ISBN 0-89375-139-1). Troll Associates.
--The Twelve Dancing Princesses. Le Cain, Errol John (1941-), illus. LC 79-308759. (Illus.). 32 p. 1978. Faber and Faber.
--The Twelve Dancing Princesses. Le Cain, Errol John (1941-), illus. LC 80-82883. (Illus.). 32 p. (Picture puffins). 1981, c.1978. (ISBN 0-14-050322-6). Puffin Books.
--The Twelve Dancing Princesses. Le Cain, Errol John (1941-), illus. LC 78-8578. p. cm. 1978. (ISBN 0-670-73358-X). Viking Press.
--The Twelve Dancing Princesses. Shulevitz, Uri (1935-), illus. Shub, Elizabeth, tr. from Ger. LC 66-7756. 1 v. (unpaged) col. illus. 23cm. 1966. Scribners.
--The Twelve Dancing Princesses. Werner, Jane (1915-), retold by. Beckett, Sheilah (1913-), illus. LC 55-119556. unpaged. illus. 21cm. (Little golden book, 194). c.1954. Simon and Schuster.
--The Two Brothers, 1 of 6 Vols. (Grimm Library). N.D. Set. George Routledge & Sons.
--The Valiant Little Tailor. Jauss, Anne Marie (1907-) illus. LC 67-16673. (Illus.). 48p. 1967 (ISBN 0-8178-3882-1). (ISBN 0-8178-3881-3). Harvey House.
--The Waifs of Bremen, and Other Tales from Grimm. (Illus.). (Stories Old and New Ser.). N.D. Caldwell.
--Wanda Gag's Jorinda and Joringel. Tomes, Margot Ladd (1917-), illus. Gag, Wanda (1893-1946), tr. LC 77-26680. (Illus.). 32 p. 18cm. 1978, c.1917. (ISBN 0-698-20110-9). Coward, McCann & Geoghegan.
--The Wolf and the Seven Kids. Craft, Kinuko Y., illus. LC 78-18076. (Illus.). 32 p. 24cm. c.1979. (ISBN 0-89375-138-3). Troll Associates.
--The Wolf and the Seven Kids. Obligado, Lilian Isabel (1931-), illus. LC 76-24172. (Illus.). 34 p. 21cm. (Random House pictureback). (best book club ever). c.1978. (ISBN 0-394-83742-8). (ISBN 0-394-83429-1). Random House.
--The Wolf and the Seven Little Goats. Miller, Doris R., pseud., ed. Mosesson, Gloria Rubin. Correas, Jose, illus. LC 65-247452. 1v. (unpaged) col. illus. 24cm. (Holly story bk lib). c.1965. World.
--Wolf & the Seven Little Kids. Hoffmann, Felix (1911-1975), ed. Hoffmann, Felix (1911-1975), illus. LC 59-16357. 32p. (gr. k-3). 1959. (ISBN 0-15-299108-5). HarBraceJ.
--The Wolf and the Seven Little Kids: A Story by the Brothers Grimm. Hoffmann, Felix (1911-1975), illus. LC 59-20400. unpaged. illus. 22x31cm. 1958. Oxford University Press.
--The Wren and the Bear. Buchert, Ilse, illus. Nesbitt, Alexander, tr. from Ger. LC 71-26308. (Illus.). 16 p. 22cm. 1971. Third & Elm Press.
--The Young Giant, 1 of 6 Vols. (Illus.). (Grimm Library). N.D. Set. George Routledge & Sons.

Grimm, Jakob Ludwig Karl (1785-1863) & Grimm, Wilhelm Karl (1786-1859), eds.
--German Popular Stories. Cruikshank, George, designed by. N.D. Scribner & Welford.
--German Popular Tales and Household Stories, 2 Vols. in 1. Wehnert, Edward H., illus. N.D. Porter and Coates.

Grimm, Wilhelm Karl, jt. auth. see Andersen, Hans Christian.

Grimm, Wilhelm Karl, jt. auth. see Grimm, Jakob Ludwig Karl.

Grimm, Wilhelm Karl, jt. auth. see Swift, Jonathan.

Grimm, Wilhelm Karl, jt. ed. see Grimm, Jakob Ludwig Karl.

Grimm Brothers, see Grimm, Jakob Ludwig Karl (1785-1863) & Grimm, Wilhelm Karl.

Grimshaw, Nigel Gilvoy (1925-)
--Bluntstone & the Wildkeepers. 152p. (gr. 5-7). 1978. (ISBN 0-571-10533-5). Faber & Faber.
--The Wildkeepers' Guest. 156p. (gr. 5-7). 1978. (ISBN 0-571-10899-7). Faber & Faber.

Gringhuis, Dirk, pseud., see Gringhuis, Richard H..

Gringhuis, Richard H. see Dirk, pseud.

Gringhuis, Richard H. see Gringhuis, Dirk, pseud.

Gringhuis, Richard H. (1918-1974)
--The Big Dig. Gringhuis, Dirk, pseud. Gringhuis, Richard H. (1918-1974), illus. Gringhuis, Dirk, pseud. 1962. Dial Press, Inc.
--Big Hunt: A Museum Exhibit Comes to Life. Gringhuis, Dirk, pseud. Gringhuis, Dirk, pseud. (Illus.). (gr. 4-6). 1962. Dial.
--The Eagle Pine. Gringhuis, Dirk, pseud. Gringhuis, Richard H. (1918-1974), illus. Gringhuis, Dirk, pseud. LC 58-7206. 181p. illus. 21cm. 1958. D. McKay Co.
--Giants, Dragons, & Gods: Constellations & Their Folklore. Gringhuis, Dirk, pseud. Gringhuis, Richard H. (1918-1974), illus. Gringhuis, Dirk, pseud. (Illus.). (gr. 3-6). 1968. (ISBN 0-696-61830-3). Hawthorn.
--Hope Haven: A Tale of a Dutch Boy and Girl Who Found a New Home in America. Gringhuis, Dirk, pseud. Gringhuis, Richard H. (1918-1974), illus. Gringhuis, Dirk, pseud. LC 47-30870. 132 p. illus. (part col.) 23 cm. 1947. W. B. Eerdmans Pub. Co.
--Lore of the Great Turtle. Gringhuis, Dirk, pseud. 96p. 1970. Mackinac Island State Park Comm.
--Mystery at Skull Castle. Gringhuis, Dirk, pseud. Gringhuis, Richard H. (1918-1974), illus. Gringhuis, Dirk, pseud. LC 64-16406. 1964. Reilly & Lee.
--Of Ships and Fish and Fisherman. Gringhuis, Dirk, pseud. Gringhuis, Richard H. (1918-1974), illus. Gringhuis, Dirk, pseud. LC 63-20349. 63 p. col. illus. 23 cm. (Our natural resources). 1963. A. Whitman.
--Saddle the Storm. Gringhuis, Dirk, pseud. (Illus.). (gr. 3-6). 1962. (ISBN 0-672-50473-1). Bobbs.
--Tulip Time. Gringhuis, Dirk, pseud. Gringhuis, Dirk, pseud. LC 51-3278. (Illus.). 30 p. 24cm. 1951. A. Whitman.
--The Young Voyageur. Gringhuis, Dirk, pseud. 202p. 1969. (ISBN 0-911872-34-5). Mackinac Island State Park Comm.
--The Young Voyageur. Gringhuis, Dirk, pseud. N.D. Whittlesey House.

Gringhuis, Richard H. (1918-1974), illus.
--The Mother Goose. Dirk, pseud. LC 47-2030. (Illus.). 29cm. 32p. 1946. Fideler Co.

Grinnell, George Bird (1849-1938)
--Beyond the Old Frontier. Bierhorst, John (1936-), ed. Parker, Robert Andrew (1927-), illus. N.D. Charles Scribner's Sons.
--Blackfeet Indian Stories. Wyeth, Newell Convers (1882-1945), illus. N.D. Charles Scribner's Sons.
--Blackfoot Lodge Tales. N.D. Charles Scribner's Sons.
--Blackfoot Lodge Tales: The Story of a Prairie People. 312p. 1962. University Of Nebraska Press.
--The Blue Jay & Other Stories. (Illus.). N.D. Harper & Brothers.
--Jack Among the Indians. Deming, Edwin Willard (1860-1942), illus. N.D. J. B. Lippincott Co.
--Jack Among the Indians: Or, A Boy's Summer on the Buffalo Plains. Deming, Edwin Willard (1860-1942), illus. LC 5966. 4 p. l., 301 p. front., plates. 19 cm. 1900. Frederick A. Stokes Company.
--Jack in the Rockies. Or, A Boy's Adventures with a Pack Train. N.D. J. B. Lippincott.
--Jack in the Rockies: Or, A Boy's Adventures with a Pack Train. Deming, Edwin Willard (1860-1942), illus. LC 4-26873. 272 p. front., 7 pl. 19 cm. 1904. Frederick A. Stokes Company.
--Jack the Young Canoeman. N.D. J. B. LIppincott Co.
--Jack, The Young Canoeman: An Eastern Boy's Voyage in a Chinook Canoe. Deming, Edwin Willard (1860-1942), illus. viii p., 1 l., 11-286 p. front., 7 pl. 20 cm. 1906. F. A. Stokes Company.
--Jack the Young Cowboy. N.D. J. B. Lippincott.
--Jack, the Young Cowboy: An Eastern Boy's Experience on a Western Round-Up. LC 13-17970. 5 p. l., 278 p. front., plates. 19 cm. 1913. Frederick A. Stokes Company.
--Jack, The Young Explorer: A Boy's Experiences in the Unknown Northwest. Cary, William M., illus. LC 8-24299. vi p., 3 l., 308 p. front., 6 pl. 20 cm. 1908. F. A. Stokes Company.
--Jack, the Young Ranchman: Or A Boy's Adventures in the Rockies. LC 99-407188. 4 p. l., 304 p. front., plates. 19 cm. 1899. F. A. Stokes Company.
--Jack the Young Ranchman: Or, a Boy's Adventures in the Rockies. N.D. J. B. Lippincott.
--Jack, the Young Trapper: An Eastern Boy's Fur Hunting in the Rocky Mountains. Stone, Walter King, illus. LC 7-29433. ix, 278 p. front., 3 pl. 20 cm. 1907. F. A. Stokes Company.
--Jack,the Young Ranchman: Or, A Boy's Adventures in the Rockies. Deming, Edwin Willard (1860-1942), illus. N.D. Frederick A. Strokes.
--Pawnee Hero Stories and Folk Tales. N.D. Charles Scribner's Sons.
--Pawnee Hero Stories and Folk-Tales. N.D. (ISBN 0-8446-2170-6). Peter Smith Publishing, Inc.
--Pawnee Hero Stories and Folk-Tales. Grinnell, George Bird (1849-1938), illus. 418p. 1961. University Of Nebraska Press.
--Trails of the Pathfinders. N.D. Charles Scribner's Sons.
--The Wolf Hunters. N.D. Charles Scribner's Sons.

Grinnell, George Bird (1849-1938) & Bierhorst, John (1936-), eds.
--The Whistling Skeleton: American Indian Tales of the Supernatural. Parker, Robert Andrew (1927-), illus. LC 81-69517. (Illus.). xi, 110 p. 24cm. c.1982 (Four Winds Press). (ISBN 0-590-07801-1). Scholastic Inc. **Award: (ALA).**

Grinstead, J E
--The Master Squatter. LC 27-7340. 188 p. 19 cm. (On cover: Western series, no. 13). 1927. Garden City Publishing Co., Inc.

Gripari, Pierre (1925-)
--Tales of the Rue Broca. McCully, Emily Arnold (1939-), illus. Grutman, Doriane, tr. LC 70-78282. (Illus.). 111 p. 22cm. 1969. Bobbs-Merrill.

Gripe, Maria Kristina (1923-)
--Elvis and His Friends. Gripe, Harald (1921-), illus. LC 75-8002. (Illus.). 214 p. 21cm. c.1976. (ISBN 0-440-02272-X). (ISBN 0-440-02273-8). Delacorte Press/S. Lawrence.
--Elvis and His Secret. Gripe, Harald (1921-), illus. LC 75-8000. (Illus.). 199 p. 21cm. c.1976. (ISBN 0-440-02282-7). Delacorte Press/Seymour Lawrence.
--The Glassblower's Children. Gripe, Harald (1921-), illus. La Farge, Sheila, tr. from Swedish. LC 73-949. (Illus.). 170 p. 21cm. 1973. Delacorte Press/Seymour Lawrence. **Award: (IBBY).**
--The Green Coat. LC 76-47235. 170 p. 22cm. c.1977. (ISBN 0-440-03232-6). (ISBN 0-440-03255-5). Delacorte Press/S. Lawrence.
--Hugo. 1st ed. Gripe, Harald (1921-), illus. Austin, Paul Britten, tr. from Swedish. LC 70-103057. (Illus.). 159 p. 21cm. 1970. Delacorte Press.
--Hugo and Josephine. 1st ed. Gripe, Harald (1921-), illus. Austin, Paul Britten, tr. from Swedish. LC 69-18438. (Illus.). 168 p. 21cm. 1969. Delacorte Press.
--In the Time of the Bells. Gripe, Harald (1921-), illus. LC 76-5594. p. cm. c.1976. (ISBN 0-440-04014-0). Delacorte Press/S. Lawrence.
--Josephine. Gripe, Harald (1921-), illus. (Illus.). 1970. (ISBN 0-440-03929-0). (ISBN 0-440-03930-4). Delacorte Press.
--Julia's House. Gripe, Harald (1921-), illus. Bothmer, Gerry, tr. from Swedish. LC 74-22632. p. cm. 1975. (ISBN 0-440-04413-8). Delacorte Press.
--The Land Beyond. Gripe, Harald (1921-), illus. La Farge, Sheila, tr. from Swedish. LC 73-18413. (Illus.). 214 p. 22cm. 1974. (ISBN 0-440-04645-9). Delacorte Press.
--The Night Daddy. Gripe, Harald (1921-), illus. Bothmer, Gerry, tr. from Swedish. LC 77-132365. (Illus.). 150 p. 21cm. 1971. Delacorte Press.
--Pappa Pellerin's Daughter. French, Kersti, tr. LC 66-15096. 156p. 21cm. 1st U.S. edition. 1966, c.1965. (ISBN 0-381-99803-7). John Day.

Grise, Jeannette, pseud., see Thomas, Jeannette Grise.

Grise, Jeannette, pseud. (1935-)
--Robert Benjamin and the Disappearing Act. Thomas, Jeannette Grise. 1st ed. Obschleger, Gail, illus. LC 80-19519. (Illus.). 155 p. 21cm. c.1980. (ISBN 0-664-32673-0). Westminster Press.
--Robert Benjamin and the Great Blue Dog Joke. Thomas, Jeannette Grise. Stein, Alex, illus. LC 78-17006. p. cm. c.1978. (ISBN 0-664-32637-4). Westminster Press.

Griset, Ernest
--The Funny Foxes and Their Feats at the Fair. Griset, Ernest, illus. Evans, Edmund, contrib. by. N.D. George Routledge & Sons.

Griset, Ernest, illus.
--Vikram and the Vampire: Or, Tales of Hindu Devilry. Burton, Richard Francis, Sir (1821-1890), tr. LC 78-94320. (Illus.). xxi, 243 p. 22cm. 1969. (ISBN 0-486-22057-5). Dover Publications.

Grishina-Givago, Nadejda J. (1884-)
--Gresha and His Clay Pig. Grishina-Givago, Nadejda J. (1884-), illus. LC 30-251912. 6 p. l., 138 p. col. front., illus. (part col.) 22 cm. 1930. Frederick A. Stokes Company.
--The Magic Squirrel. Grishina-Givago, Nadejda J. (1884-), illus. LC 34-30046. 142, 1 p. incl. col. front., illus., plates (part col.) 22 cm. 1934. Frederick A. Stokes Company.
--The Magic Squirrel. Grishina-Givago, Nadejda J. (1884-), illus. 1934. J. B. Lippincott.
--Peter Pea. Grishina-Givago, Nadejda J. (1884-), illus. LC 26-15747. 95, 1 p. incl. plates (part col.) 22 cm. 1926. Frederick A. Stokes Company.
--Peter Pea. Grishina-Givago, Nadeja J. (1884-), illus. N.D. J. B. Lippincott.
--Shorty. Grishina-Givago, Nadeja J. (1884-), illus. N.D. J. P. Lippincott.
--Shorty: A Nursery Tale from Far Away. Grishina-Givago, Nadejda J. (1884-), illus. LC 25-123. 14 x 19cm. 77p. 1924. Frederick A. Stokes.

--Sparrow House. Grishina-Givago, Nadejda J. (1884-), illus. N.D. J. B. Lippincott.
--Sparrow House: A Story in Twenty Pictures and Nineteen Chapters, Short and Long. Grishina-Givago, Nadejda J. (1884-), illus. LC 28-22371. 174, 1 p. incl. col. front., illus., col. plates. 22 cm. 1928. Frederick A. Stokes Company.
Griswold, Florence, Mrs., retold by see Jatakas.
Griswold, Frances Irene Burge Smith see Smith, F. B., pseud.
Griswold, Frances Irene Burge Smith (1826-1900)
--May: Or, Grandpapa's Pet. Smith, F. B., pseud, 1 of 5 Vols. (The May and Tom Library). N.D. Set. D Lothrop & Co.
--May: Or, Grandpapa's Pet. Smith, F. B., pseud. LC 47-36577. 2 p. l., 3-176 p. front., plates. 16 cm. (Her May and Tom stories). c.1869. Warren and Blakeslee.
Griswold, Hattie Tying (1840-1909)
--Waiting on Destiny: A Story for Girls. 314p. N.D. Universalist Publishing House.
Griswold, Latta (1876-1931)
--Deal Woods. LC 15-18816. 7 p. l., 284 p. front., illus. (map) plates. 20 cm. 1915. The Macmillan Company.
--Deering at Princeton: A Story of College Life. Caswell, Edward C., illus. LC 13-20848. 5 p. l., 380 p. front., plates. 20 cm. 1913. The Macmillan Company.
--Deering of Deal: Or, The Spirit of the School. LC 12-22315. 6 p. l., 317 p. front., plates, maps. 20 cm. 1912. The Macmillan Company.
--The Tides of Deal. LC 22-17223. 4 p. l., 279 p. front. 20 cm. 1922. The Macmillan Company.
--The Winds of Deal: A School Story. Harper, George, illus. LC 14-15185. 8 p. l., 320 p. incl. map. front., plates. 20 cm. 1914. The Macmillan Company.
--The Winds of Deal: A School Story. Harper, George, illus. 8 p. l., 320 p. incl. map. front., pl. 20 cm. 1923. The Macmillan Company.
Grize, Madeleine
--Valeriane ... Chatel, Ariane, illus. LC 60-123751. v. illus. 14cm. c.1960. F. Watts.
Groat, Diane De see De Groat, Diane.
Groat, Diane De see Flournoy, Valerie (1952-) & De Groat, Diane.
Groat, Florence De see Degroat, Florence.
Groat, Marion K. De see De Groot, Marion K.
Groch, Judith Goldstein (1929-)
--Play the Bach, Dear!. LC 77-76960. 191 p. 22cm. c.1978. (ISBN 0-385-13229-8). Doubleday.
Groelle, Marvin C., jt. auth. see Tudyman, Al.
Groen, Be Van Der
--Cobblestone Lane. Groen, Nora Van Der, illus. LC 48-1429. 32 p. col. illus. 24 cm. 1947. Pilgrim Press.
Groenhoff, Edwin L. (1924-)
--The Freshman. LC 83-71507. 1983. (ISBN 0-89636-110-1). Accent Books.
--Jerry's Summer. LC 75-18988. 112p. (Orig.). 1976. (ISBN 0-912692-83-9). Cook.
Grogan, William
--John Riffe of the Steelworkers. 1959. Coward-McCann Inc.
Groh, Lynn
--The Culper Spy Ringer. 1966. (ISBN 0-664-32447-9). Westminster Press.
Grohskopf, Bernice, compiled by see Shakespeare, William.
Grohskopf, Bernice (1921-)
--Blood & Roses. LC 78-14583. 256 p. 22cm. 1979. (ISBN 0-689-50101-3). Atheneum.
--Children in the Wind. LC 77-4758. 189 p. 22cm. 1977. (ISBN 0-689-30583-4). Atheneum.
--Notes on the Hauter Experiment: A Journey Through the Inner World of Evelyn B. Chestnut. LC 75-6749. (Illus.). 135 p. 22cm. 1975. (ISBN 0-689-30477-3). Atheneum.
--Shadow in the Sun. LC 74-19490. 182 p. 22cm. 1975. (ISBN 0-689-30448-X). Atheneum.
--Tell Me Your Dream. 191p. (Orig.). (gr. 7-12). 1981. (ISBN 0-590-30548-4). Scholastic Inc.
Grol, Lini Richards (1913-)
--The Bellfounder's Sons. Quackenbush, Robert Mead (1929-), illus. LC 73-137711. (Illus.). 31 p. 29cm. 1971. Bobbs-Merrill.
Groman, Gal
--Gertie McMichaels and the Odd Body Mystery. LC 74-26658. 224 p. 21cm. 1975. (ISBN 0-07-024945-8). (ISBN 0-07-024946-6). McGraw-Hill.
--Gertie McMichaels Finds Blood and Gore and Much Much More: A Stable Fable. LC 76-163844. 188 p. 22cm. 1971. (ISBN 0-07-024941-5). McGraw-Hill.
Gronbach, Phyllis M.
--Mr. Periwinkle Stories. (gr. 4-7). N.D. Carlton.
Gronoset, Dagfinn
--Anna. 1975. (ISBN 0-394-48986-1). Knopf.
Gronowicz, Antoni (1913-)
--Bolek. Gay, Zhenya (1906-1978), illus. McEwen, Jessie, tr. from Polish. LC 42-23223. vi, 240, 1 p. incl. front., illus., plates. 22 1/2 cm. 1942. T. Nelson and Sons.
--Four from the Old Town. Logan, Dwight, illus. Vetter, Joseph, tr. from Polish. LC 44-8098. 4 p. l., 149 p. illus. 20 1/2 cm. 1944. C. Scribner's Sons.
--The Piasts of Poland. (gr. 5-11). N.D. Charles Scibner's Sons.
Groom, Arthur William (1898-1964)
--Continent for Sale: A Story of the Louisiana Purchase. 1st ed. Bolden, Joseph, illus. LC 53-5330. 181p. illus. 22cm. (Winston adventure books). 1953. Winston.
--Young David. Azpelicueta, illus. (Illus.). (Young Biographies Ser). (gr. 6-10). N.D. Roy.
Groom, Gladys, jt. auth. see Grossman, Barney.
Groomer, Vera
--Dibe Yazhi. (ps). 1980. (ISBN 0-8127-0260-3). Review & Herald.
--Good Friends Again. 32p. (Come Unto Me Ser.: Year 2, Bk. 3). (ps). 1980. (ISBN 0-8127-0272-7). Review & Herald.
Grooms, Kathe, ed. see Masters, M.
Grosby, Ruth
--The Clue in the Camera. Laune, Paul Sidney (1899-), illus. LC 42-2895. vi p., 1 l., 214 p. incl. front. 20 cm. c.1942. Grossett & Dunlap.
--Mystery Across the Border. Laune, Paul Sidney (1899-), illus. LC 41-1238. vi p., 1 l., 242 p. incl. front. 20 cm. c.1941. Grossett & Dunlap.
--The Mystery at Mountain View. Laune, Paul Sidney (1899-), illus. LC 40-861241. iv p., 1 l., 243 p. incl. front. 20 cm. c.1940. Grossett & Dunlap.
--The Stolen Blueprints. Van Swearingen, E. C., illus. LC 39-110851. vi p., 1 l., 238 p. front. 20 cm. c.1939. Grossett & Dunlap.
Groseclose, Elgin Earl (1899-1983)
--The Scimitar of Saladin. Moyler, Alan, illus. LC 56-9359. 180p. illus. 21cm. 1956. Macmillan.
Groskreutz, Donna J.
--Spook & the Giant Ant. Glazer, Roberta L., illus. LC 79-64491. 1980. (ISBN 0-533-04298-4). Vantage.
Grosman, Ladislav (1921-)
--Bride. Urwin, Iris, tr. from Czech. LC 73-78666. (Illus.). . 120p. (gr. 7 up). 1970. (ISBN 0-385-00670-5). (ISBN 0-385-02192-5). Doubleday.
--Shop on Main Street. Ambrus, Victor G., pseud. (1935-), illus. Ambrus, Gyozo Laszlo. Urwin, Iris, tr. (Illus.). czech. 15 linecuts. 128p. (gr. 10 up). 1970. Doubleday.
Gross, Alan (1947-)
--The I Don't Want to Go to School Book. Venezia, Mike, illus. LC 81-17034. (Illus.). 31 p. 25cm. c.1982. (ISBN 0-516-03496-0). Childrens Press.
--What If the Teacher Calls on Me?. Venezia, Mike, illus. LC 79-18560. p. cm. c.1979. (ISBN 0-516-03671-8). Childrens Press.
Gross, Arthur William (1896-)
--Child's Garden of Bible Stories. N.D. Concordia Publishing House.
--Concordia Bible Story Book. LC 72-139512. (Illus.). 511 p. 27cm. 1971. (ISBN 0-570-03401-9). Concordia Pub. House.
Gross, Elizabeth Henry, ed.
--Once Upon a Time. LC 61-17990. 372 p. illus. 25 cm. (Collier's junior classics series). 1962. Crowell-Collier Pub. Co.
Gross, Gwen
--Knights of the Round Table. Green, Norman (1934-), illus. LC 85-2176. (Illus.). 109 p. 20cm. (Step-up Adventures). c.1985. Random House.
Gross, M.
--Eighteen Holes in My Head. N.D. McGraw-Hill.
Gross, Margaret Edith
--Sally Soapbubble and Her Silver Fish. LC 41-6235. 32 p. 20 cm. c.1940. Fortuny's.
Gross, Mark Stanislaus (1889-)
--Double-Eagles. 2d rev. ed. LC 23-8758. 5 p. l., 285 p. 20 cm. 1923. B. Herder Book Co.
--Haunted Hollow. LC 23-177677. 6 p. l., 3-291 p. 20 cm. 1924. B. Herder Book Co.
Gross, Mary Anne (1943-), ed.
--Ah, Man, You Found Me Again. Levins, Mike & Stevens, Jon Ellis, illus. LC 70-179148. (Illus.). x, 84 p. 27cm. 1972. (ISBN 0-8070-1532-6). (ISBN 0-8070-1533-4). Beacon Press.
Gross, Michael
--The Fable of the Fig Tree. Lazarevich, Mila (1942-), illus. LC 74-25972. (Illus.). 31 p. 23cm. 1975. (ISBN 0-8098-1228-2). H. Z. Walck.
Gross, Ruth Belov (1929-), retold by see Andersen, Hans Christian.
Gross, Ruth Belov (1929-)
--If You Were a Ballet Dancer. LC 79-3583. (Illus.). Repr. (Pub. by Scholastic). (gr. k-5). 1980. Dial Bks Young.
--If You Were a Ballet Dancer. (gr. 3). 1979. (ISBN 0-590-05746-4). Scholastic Inc.
--The Laugh Book. Jacobs, Leslie, illus. (Illus.). (gr. k-3). 1972. (ISBN 0-590-09250-2). Scholastic Inc.
--Money, Money, Money. Jacobs, Leslie, illus. (gr. k-3). 1976. (ISBN 0-590-09189-1). Scholastic Inc.
--What Is That Alligator Saying?. Hawkinson, John Samuel (1912-), illus. Orig. Title: Animal Communication. (gr. k-3). N.D. (ISBN 0-590-09386-X, Schol Trade Pap). Schol Bk Serv.
Gross, Ruth Belov (1929-), retold by.
--The Bremen Town Musicians. Kent, Jack, pseud. (1920-), illus. Kent, John Wellington. (Illus.). (gr. k-3). 1975. (ISBN 0-590-09894-2). (ISBN 0-590-20713-X). Scholastic Inc.
--The Girl Who Wouldn't Get Married. Kent, Jack, pseud. (1920-), illus. Kent, John Wellington. LC 83-1458. (Illus.). 1983. (ISBN 0-590-07908-5). (ISBN 0-590-07908-5). Four Winds Press.
--Hansel & Gretel. Tomes, Margot Ladd (1917-), illus. (Illus.). (gr. k-3). 1974. (ISBN 0-590-06125-9). (ISBN 0-590-20698-2). Scholastic Inc.
Gross, S. D.
--The Stolen Christmas Star. N.D. Carlton Press.
Gross, Sarah Chokla, ed. see Mattson, Olle.
Gross, Sarah Chokla (1906-1976), tr. see Cenac, Claude.
Gross, Sarah Chokla (1906-1976), tr. see Guillot, Rene.
Gross, Sarah Chokla (1906-1976), tr. see Perrault, Charles.
Gross, Sarah Chokla (1906-1976), ed.
--Every Child's Book of Verse. Cone, Marta, illus. LC 68-11709. (Illus.). xii, 302 p. 27cm. 1968. F. Watts.
Gross, Seymour, ed.
--The House of the Seven Gables. 1967. (ISBN 0-393-04287-1). (ISBN 0-393-09705-6). Norton & Co.
Gross, Seymour, ed. see Hawthorne, Nathaniel.
Gross, Theobald
--The Humming Top: Or, Debit and Credit in the Next World. Deluxe ed. Blashfield, Albert D., illus. Teuffel, Blanche Willis Howard Von (1847-1898), tr. LC 3-28580. 53 p., 1 l. incl. col. illus., 11 col. front. 18 cm. c.1903. Frederick A. Stokes Company.
Grossbart, Francine B.
--Big City. Grossbart, Francine B., illus. (Illus.). (gr. k-2). 1966. (ISBN 0-8382-1006-6). Hale.
--Big City. Grossbart, Francine B., illus. LC 66-5842. (Illus.). (ps-2). 1966. (ISBN 0-06-022124-0, HarpJ). Har-Row.
Grossberg, Rita, jt. auth. see Urquhart, John.
Grosscup, Clyde
--Pro Champion. LC 66-9667. 177p. illus. 22cm. (His Brad Carter ser.). 1966. Grosset.
--Pro Passer. LC 66-13086. (Illus.). 180 p. 22cm. (Brad Carter series). 1966. Grosset & Dunlap.
--Pro Rookie. LC 65-240500. 180p. 22cm. c.1965. Grosset.
--Throw the Bomb. (Illus.). 186 p. 22cm. 1967. Grosset & Dunlap.
--The Winning Spirit. LC 52-119125. 160p. illus. 20cm. (Barnes junior sports novel). c.1953. A.S. Barnes.
Grosser, Morton (1933-)
--The Snake Horn. 1st ed. Stone, David Karl (1922-), illus. LC 72-86938. (Illus.). 131 p. 22cm. 1973. Atheneum.
--The Snake Horn. Stone, David Karl (1922-), illus. LC 73-9678. (Illus.). 178 p. 25cm. 1973. (ISBN 0-8161-6126-7). G. K. Hall.
Grossman, Barney & Groom, Gladys
--Black Means ... Bible, Charles (1937-), illus. LC 78-126066. (Illus.). 63 p. 28cm. 1970. (ISBN 0-8090-3037-3). Hill & Wang.
Grossman, Larry, contrib. by see Blomquist, David.
Grossman, Mort (1933-)
--A Rage to Die. LC 73-3390. 185 p. 21cm. 1973. (ISBN 0-664-32531-9). Westminster Press.
--Summer Ends Too Soon. LC 75-20418. 159 p. 22cm. 1975. (ISBN 0-664-32580-7). Westminster Press.
Grossman, Rita, jt. auth. see Wylie, Harry Virgil.
Grossmith, George & Grossmith, Weedon
--The Diary of a Nobody. N.D. W. W. Norton & Inc.
Grossmith, Weedon, jt. auth. see Grossmith, George.
Grosvenor, Abbie Johnston, Mrs. (1865-)
--Strange Stories of the Great River: The Adventures of a Boy Explorer. LC 18-1149. 6 p. l., 194, 1 p. front., plates. 20 cm. 1918. Harper & Brothers.
--Strange Stories of the Great Valley: The Adventures of a Boy Pioneer. LC 17-12138. 7 p. l., 221, 1 p. front., plates, 19 cm. 1917. Harper & Brothers.
--Winged Moccasins: A Tale of the Adventurous Mound-Builders. Grosvenor, Ivan, illus. LC 33-4727. xi, 1 p., 1 l., 290, 1 p. front., illus. 20 cm. 1933. D. Appleton and Company.
Grosvenor, H. S., Mrs.
--The Brother's Choice. (Illus.). 228p. N.D. A. I. Bradley & Co.'s Pub.
--Captain Russell's Watchword: Or, I'll Try. (Illus.). 291p. N.D. A. I. Bradley & Co.'s Pub.
--The Old Red House. (Illus.). 388p. N.D. A. I. Bradley & Co.'s Pubs.
Grosvenor, Kali Diana (1960-)
--Poems by Kali. Halifax, Joan Squire (1942-) & Fletcher, Robert (1938-), photos by Kelley, William Melvin (1937-), intro. by. LC 77-101435. (Illus.). 62 p. 22cm. 1970. Doubleday.
Grote, William
--Fiddle, Flute, and the River. LC 67-24422. 180 p. 21cm. 1967. Meredith Press.
--J. P. and the Apaches. 1st ed. Waterhouse, Charles (1924-), illus. LC 67-14747. (Illus.). viii, 181 p. 21cm. 1967. Meredith Press.
Grote & Segur, Sophie Rostopchine (1799-1874)
--Grote and Segur's Two Great Retreats. (Classics for Children). N.D. Ginn and Company.
Groth, Eleanor
--Adventures in a Dishpan. Groth, Milt, illus. LC 36-17818. 31p. illus. part. col. 25cm. c.1936. Grosset & Dunlap.
Groth, John Henry, ed. see Wyss, Johann David Von.
Grousset, Paschal see Laurie, Andre, pseud.
Grousset, Paschal (1844-1909)
--The Crystal City. Laurie, Andre, pseud. Roux, G, illus. Smith, L. A., tr. from Fr. N.D. Dana Estes & Co.
--Schoolboy Days in France. Laurie, Andre, pseud. Robins, E. P., tr. LC 7-15451. 310 p. incl. 21 pl. front. 21 cm. c.1896. Estes and Lauriat.
--Schoolboy Days in Italy: Or, Tito, the Florentine. Laurie, Andre, pseud. Kendall, Laura E., tr. LC 7-15447. viii, 9-277 p. incl. illus., plates. front. 21 cm. c.1893. Estes and Lauriat.
--Schoolboy Days in Italy: Or, Tito the Florentine. Laurie, Andre, pseud. Roux, G, illus. Kendall, Laura E., tr. (College Life In All Countries Ser.). N.D. Educational Publishing Company.
--Schoolboy Days in Japan. Laurie, Andre, pseud. Kendall, Laura E., tr. LC 7-15448. viii, 9-270 p. incl. 22 pl. front. 21 cm. (Life in All Countries Ser.). c.1895. Estes and Lauriat.
--Schoolboy Days in Russia. Laurie, Andre, pseud. Kendall, Laura E., tr. LC 7-15449. 332 p. incl. front., 22 pl. 21 cm. c.1892. Estes and Lauriat.
--Schoolboy Days in Russia. Laurie, Andre, pseud. Roux, G., illus. Kendall, Laura E., tr. (College Life in all Countries). N.D. Educational Publishing Company.
Grout, Wesley G
--The Cat Nobody Wanted. 1st ed. LC 54-13138. 56p. illus. 21cm. 1955. Vantage Press.
Grove, Elizabeth
--The Mfums. Paton, Jane Elizabeth (1934-), illus. LC 67-13818. (Illus.). 95 p. 19cm. 1st U.S. edition. 1967. World Pub. Co.
--Wintercut. Stobbs, William (1914-), illus. (Illus.). (New Adventure Library). (gr. 5-9). 1957. (ISBN 0-685-21669-1). Verry.
Grove, Harriet Lee
--Where Pussies Grow. Lee, Ella Dolbear, illus. N.D. Methodist Book Concern.
Grove, Harriet Pyne
--The Adventurous Allens. LC 32-12019. 253 p. front. 20 cm. (Her The adventurous Allens series). c.1932. A. L. Burt Company.
--The Adventurous Allens Afloat. LC 32-12017. 248 p. front. 20 cm. (Her The adventurous Allens series). c.1932. A. L. Burt Company.
--The Adventurous Allens Find Mystery. LC 32-12018. 255 p. front. 20 cm. (Her The adventurous Allens series). c.1932. A. L. Burt Company.
--The Adventurous Allens Marooned. LC 32-120162. 251 p. front. 20 cm. (Her The adventurous Allens series). c.1932. A. L. Burt Company.
--The Adventurous Allens' Treasure Hunt. LC 33-11067. 256 p. front. 19 cm. (Her The adventurous Allens series). c.1933. A. L. Burt Company.
--Ann and the Jolly Six. LC 26-9755. 230 p. front. 20 cm. (Her Ann Sterling series). c.1926. A. L. Burt Company.
--Ann Crosses a Secret Trail. LC 26-11857. 234 p. front. 20 cm. (Her Ann Sterling series). c.1926. A. L. Burt Company.
--Ann Sterling. LC 26-91095. 223 p. front. 20 cm. (Her Ann Sterling series). c.1926. A. L. Burt Company.
--Ann's Ambitions. LC 27-10649. 233 p. front. 20 cm. (Her Ann Sterling series). c.1927. A. L. Burt Company.
--Ann's Search Rewarded. (The Ann Sterling Ser.). N.D. A L Burt Co.
--Ann's Sterling Heart. 224 p. front. 20 cm. (Her Ann Sterling series). c.1928. A. L. Burt Company.
--Betty Lee, Freshman. LC 31-12235. 254 p. front., 20 cm. (Her The Betty Lee series). c.1931. A. L. Burt Company.
--Betty Lee, Freshman. (Betty Lee Ser.). N.D. World Publishing Co.
--Betty Lee, Freshman and Betty Lee, Sophomore: Two Books in One. N.D. World Publishing Co.

--Raggedy Ann in Cookie Land. Gruelle, John Barton (1880-1938), illus. (Raggedy Ann Ser). (ps-3). N.D. (ISBN 0-672-50445-6). Bobbs.
--Raggedy Ann in Cookie Land. Gruelle, John Barton (1880-1938), illus. (Raggedy Ann Books). N.D. Johnny Gruelle Co.
--Raggedy Ann in the Deep Deep Woods. Gruelle, John Barton (1880-1938), illus. 1930. (ISBN 0-672-50446-4). Bobbs-Merrill.
--Raggedy Ann in the Deep, Deep Woods. Gruelle, John Barton (1880-1938), illus. LC 30-14108. 95 p. illus. (part col.) 24 cm. c.1930. The P. F. Volland Company.
--Raggedy Ann in the Garden. Gruelle, John Barton (1880-1938), illus. LC 41-9779. 61 p. incl. col. front., illus. (part col.) 17 cm. (The little color classics). c.1940. McLoughlin Bros., Inc.
--Raggedy Ann in the Garden. Gruelle, John Barton (1880-1938), illus. LC 43-16771. 44 p. incl. col. front., illus. (part col.) 23 x 19 cm. (On cover: Westfield classics). c.1943. McLoughlin Bros., Inc.
--Raggedy Ann in the Golden Meadow. Gruelle, John Barton (1880-1938), illus. LC 36-1741. 58 p. illus. (part col.) 33 cm. c.1935. Whitman Publishing Company.
--Raggedy Ann in the Magic Book. Gruelle, John Barton (1880-1938), illus. 1939. (ISBN 0-672-50453-7). Bobbs-Merill.
--Raggedy Ann in the Magic Book. Gruelle, John Barton (1880-1938), illus. LC 39-29964. 91 p. incl. col. front., illus. (part col.) 24 cm. c.1939. Johnny Gruelle Company.
--Raggedy Ann in the Snow White Castle. Gruelle, John Barton (1880-1938), illus. LC 46-8412. 95 p. incl. col. front., illus. (part col.) 23 1/2 cm. 1946. The Johnny Gruelle Company.
--Raggedy Ann in the Snow White Castle. Gruellle, John Barton (1880-1938), illus. 1946. (ISBN 0-672-50455-3). Bobbs-Merrill.
--Raggedy Ann Stories. Gruelle, John Barton (1880-1938), illus. 1918. (ISBN 0-672-50456-1). Bobbs-Merrill.
--Raggedy Ann Stories. Gruelle, John Barton (1880-1938), illus. LC 47-6753. 24cm. 95p. 1947. Johnny Gruelle Co.
--Raggedy Ann Stories. Gruelle, John Barton (1880-1938), illus. LC 31-19505. 95 p. col. illus. 23 cm. c.1918. P. F. Volland Company.
--Raggedy Ann's Adventure. Hays, Ethel, illus. LC 48-15984. 36 p. illus. (part col.) 21 cm. (Saalfield treasure book). 1947. Saalfield Pub. Co.
--Raggedy Ann's Alphabet Book. Gruelle, John Barton (1880-1938), illus. LC 37-17359. 38 p. col. illus. 19 cm. 1925. The P. F. Volland Company.
--Raggedy Ann's Lucky Pennies. Gruelle, John Barton (1880-1938), illus. 1932. (ISBN 0-672-50451-0). Bobbs-Merrill.
--Raggedy Ann's Lucky Pennies. Gruelle, John Barton (1880-1938), illus. LC 34-3542. 94 p. col. illus. 24 cm. c.1932. The P. F. Volland Company.
--Raggedy Ann's Magical Wishes. Gruelle, John Barton (1880-1938), illus. 1928. (ISBN 0-672-50452-9). Bobbs-Merrill.
--Raggedy Ann's Magical Wishes. Gruelle, John Barton (1880-1938), illus. LC 28-18329. 94 p. illus. (part col.) 24 cm. c.1928. P. F. Volland Company.
--Raggedy Ann's Merriest Christmas. Sinnickson, Tom, illus. LC 52-67080. unpaged. illus. 21cm. (Wonder books, 594). 1952. Wonder Books.
--Raggedy Ann's Mystery. Hays, Ethel, illus. LC 48-202889. 36 p. illus. (part col.) 21 cm. (Saalfield treasure book). 1947. Saalfield Pub. Co.
--Raggedy Ann's Secret. N.D (Wonder Books). Grosset & Dunlap.
--Raggedy Ann's Tea Party. Wilde, George A. & Wilde, Irma, illus. LC 54-327350. unpaged. illus. 21cm. (Wonder books 624). 1954. Wonder Books.
--Raggedy Ann's Very Own Fairy Stories. (Raggedy Ann Ser). (gr. 1-3). N.D. (ISBN 0-685-36675-8). Bobbs.
--Raggedy Ann's Wishing Pebble. (Raggedy Ann Books). N.D. Johnny Gruelle Co.
--Raggedy Ann's Wishing Pebble. Gruelle, John Barton (1880-1938), illus. (Raggedy Ann Ser.). (ps-3). N.D. (ISBN 0-672-50457-X). Bobbs.
--Raggedy Ann's Wishing Pebble. Gruelle, John Barton (1880-1938), illus. 96p. N.D. P. F. Volland Co.
--Raggedy Ann's Wishing Pebbles. 1925. (ISBN 0-672-50457-X). Bobbs-Merrill.
--Raggedy in the Deep, Deep Woods. (Raggedy Ann Books). N.D. Jonnny Gruelle Co.
--Wooden Willie. Gruelle, John Barton (1880-1938), illus. LC 27-23296. 95 p. col. illus. 24 cm. (Lettered on cover: Volland "Happy children books"). c.1927. The P. F. Volland Company.

Gruelle, John Barton (1880-1938) & Gooch, Thelma, illus.
--The All About Story Book. LC 29-13058. 20cm. 63p. 1929. Cupples & Leon Co.

Gruelle, Johnny see Gruelle, John Barton.

Gruelle, Justin C.
--A Mother Goose Parade. Gruelle, Justin C., illus. LC 29-14823. 31 p. col. illus. 30 cm. c.1929. The P. F. Vollani Co.

Gruelle, Prudence
--The Meadow Folk's Story Hour. Hatt, Nell, illus. LC 22-233482. vi p., 1 l., 101 p. col. illus. 19 cm. c.1921. The Gregg Publishing Company.

Gruenbaum, Hannah
--The Magic Carpet. Forst, Sigmund, illus. (Illus.). (ps-1). N.D. (ISBN 0-685-86206-2). Feldheim.

Gruenberg, Sidonie Matsner (1881-1974), ed.
--All Kinds of Courage: Stories About Boys and Girls of Yesterday and Today. 1st ed. Lewicki, James, illus. LC 62-15900. 428p. illus. 22cm. 1962. (ISBN 0-385-00270-X). Doubleday.
--Favorite Stories Old and New. Wiese, Kurt (1887-1974), illus. LC 42-36411. xvii, 372 p. illus. 23 1/2 cm. 1942. Doubleday, Doran & Company, Inc.
--Favorite Stories Old and New. rev and enl. ed. Wiese, Kurt (1887-1974), illus. LC 55-9012. 512p. illus. 22cm. 1955. Doubleday.
--Let's Hear a Story: Thirty Stories and Poems for Today's Boys and Girls. Wilson, Dagmar (1916-), illus. LC 61-6894. 160p. illus. (pt. col.) 29cm. c.1961. Doubleday.
--Let's Read a Story: Modern, Gay Stories for Boys and Girls. 1st ed. Parsons, Virginia, illus. LC 57-9852. 159p. illus. 27cm. 1957. Garden City Books.
--Let's Read More Stories. Wilson, Dagmar (1916-), illus. 27cm. 100p. 1960. (ISBN 0-385-02281-6). Doubleday and Company.
--More Favorite Storie Old and New for Boys and Girls. Rev. and enl. ed. Wiese, Kurt (1887-1974), illus. LC 60-12997. 510p. 1960, c.1948. Doubleday.
--More Favorite Stories Old and New for Boys and Girls. Floethe, Richard (1901-), illus. LC 48-9182. xvi. 399 p. illus. 24 cm. 1948. Doubleday.
--The Wonderful Story of How You Were Born. new rev. ed. Shimin, Symeon (1902-), illus. LC 71-920552. (Illus.). 1 v. (unpaged). (Zephyr Book). 1973. Doubleday.

Gruger, Heribert (1900-)
--The Sing Song Picture Book. Gruger, Johannes, illus. Gram-Swing, Betty, tr. LC 32-7514. 40 p. col. illus. 27 cm. 1931. J. B. Lippincott Company.

Grummond, Lena Young De see De Grummond, Lena Young & Delaune, Lynn De Grummond.

Grund, Josef Carl (1920-)
--Beyond the Bridge: A Novel. LC 68-12352. 143 p. 20cm. 1968. (ISBN 0-316-32992-4). Little, Brown.
--Never to Be Free: A Novel. Harrington, Lucile, tr. LC 79-91226. 202 p. 20cm. 1970. Little, Brown.
--You Have a Friend, Pietro. Schmischke, Kurt, illus. Mutch, Margaret, tr. from Ger. LC 65-15450. (Illus.). 145p. 1st U.S. edition. (A boy is caught in the backlash of a vendetta). (gr. 3-7). 1966. (ISBN 0-316-32995-9). Little.

Grundtvig, Svend Hersleb, 1824-1883 see Bay, Jens Christian.

Grundtvig, Svend Hersleb (1824-1883)
--Danish Fairy Tales. N.D. Four Seas.
--Danish Fairy Tales. Cramer, Jesse Grant (1890-), tr. LC 12-7643. 3 p. l., 5-122 p. 20 cm. c.1912. R. G. Badger.
--Danish Fairy Tales. Hein, Gustav, tr. 219, 1 p. col. front., plates 21 cm. 1914. Thomas Y. Crowell Company.
--Danish Fairy Tales. Van Heusen, Drew, illus. Cramer, Jesse Grant (1890-), tr. LC 72-91057. (Illus.). 115p. 28cm. 1972. (ISBN 0-486-22891-6). Dover Publications.
--Danish Fairy Tales. Van Heusen, Drew, illus. Cramer, Jesse Grant (1890-), tr. N.D. (ISBN 0-8446-4626-1). Peter Smith Publisher, Inc.
--Fairy Tales from Afar. Aldridge, Sydney F., illus. Mulley, Jane, tr. from Danish. LC 2-27947. 19cm. 302p. 1902. A. Wessels Co.
--More Danish Tales. Hatch, Mary Cottam (1912-1970), retold by. Edgun (1913-), illus. LC 49-100468. 237 p. illus. 21 cm. 1949. Harcourt, Brace.

Grundy, Solomon
--Stories I Tell Children. N.D. Carlton Press.

Grunzig, Curt
--Oscar the Model Maker. LC 39-16516. 187 p. incl. front., illus. (incl. plans) 21 cm. 1939. Meador Publishing Company.

Grussi, A. M.
--Three Indian Chiefs. N.D. A. L. Burt Co.

Grutman, Doriane, tr. see Gripari, Pierre.

Gruttner, Roswitha, illus.
--The Rabbit and the Turnip: A Chinese Fable. Sadler, Richard, tr. from Ger. LC 69-10288. (Illus.). 20 p. 24cm. 1968. Doubleday.

Guard, David (1934-)
--Dierdre: A Celtic Legend. Guard, Gretchen (1937-), illus. LC 80-6977. (Illus.). 22cm. 1981, c.1977. (ISBN 0-89742-047-0). Celestial Arts.
--Hale-Mano: A Legend of Hawaii. Sumile, Caridad, illus. LC 80-69773. (Illus.). 118p. (gr. 6). 1981. (ISBN 0-89742-048-9). Celestial Arts.

Guberlet, Muriel Lewin
--Hermie's Trailer House. Illman, Marjorie Kincaid, illus. N.D. Jaques Cattell Press.

Guck, Dorothy (1913-)
--Danger Rides the Forest. Waterhouse, Charles (1924-), illus. LC 68-30261. (Illus.). (gr. 6-8). 1968. (ISBN 0-8149-0312-6). Vanguard.

Guderjahn, Ernie L.
--A Children's Trilogy: Ali's Flying Rug, the Shadow Workers, & the Magic Cricket. (Orig.). (gr. 3 up). 1985. (ISBN 0-88734-504-2). Players Pr.

Gudmundson, Shirley M.
--The Hurricane: A Story of Children's Life in the West Indies. Shimin, Symeon (1902-), illus. LC 66-12909. 92p. illus. 23cm. (Venture bk). 1966. Braziller.
--The Turtle Net: A Story of Children's Life in the West Indies. Shimin, Symeon (1902-), illus. LC 65-193227. 94p. illus. 23cm. (Venture bk.). 1965. Braziller.

Gudrun see Almedingen, Martha Edith von.

Gue, Belle Willey
--The Adventurers. (Path Finders Tales). N.D. Four Seas.
--The Explorers. (Path Finders Tales). N.D. Four Seas.
--The Mountains. (Path Finders Tales). N.D. Four Seas.
--The Patriots. (Path Finders Tales). N.D. Four Seas.
--The Settlers. (Path Finders Tales). N.D. Four Seas.

Guerber, Helene A.
--Myths of Greece & Rome. (gr. 7 up). 1963. (ISBN 0-8277-0035-0). British Bk Ctr.

Guernsey, Clara F.
--Berty's Visit, Vol. 2. 62p. (The Leighton Children). N.D. Set. American Sunday-School Union.
--Boys of Eaglewood: Life at School. 406p. N.D. American Sunday-School Union.
--Elmira's Ambitions: or, Miss Ross and Her Career. 373p. N.D. American Sunday-School Union.
--The Ice Raft. N.D. Alfred Martien.
--The Mallory Girls: Or, The Wrong and the Right Way. (Illus.). 446p. N.D. American Sunday-School Union.
--The Merman and the Figure-Head. (Illus.). N.D. J B Lippincott.
--The New Boy. N.D. Alfred Martien.
--Oliver's Prisoner. N.D. Alfred Martien.
--The Plaid Pincushion, 1 of 6 Vols. (Beatitude Library Ser.). N.D. Set. T. Whittaker.
--The Shawnee Prisoner. (A Borderer's Story). N.D. American Sunday-School Union.
--Sibyl and the Sapphires: Or, Trading in Vanity Fair. 392p. N.D. American Sunday-School Union.
--The Silver Cup, 1 of 3. (The Silver Library). N.D. American Sunday-School Union.
--The Silver Library, 4 Vols. N.D. American Sunday-School Union.
--The Silver Rifle. N.D. American News Co.
--The Silver Rifle, 1 of 4 Vols. 256p. (The Schooner on the Beach Ser.: No.4). N.D. Set. American Sunday-School Union.

Guernsey, JoAnn Bren
--Five Summers. LC 82-9584. c.1983. (ISBN 0-89919-147-9). Clarion Books.
--Journey to an Unknown Father. LC 85-2685. p. cm. c.1985. (ISBN 0-89919-338-2). Clarion Books.

Guernsey, Lucy Ellen (1826-1899)
--Alice Fenton: Alone in the World. N.D. American Sunday-School Union.
--The Chevalier's Daughter. N.D. Thomas Whittaker.
--The Child's Treasure. N.D. Thomas Whittaker.
--Christmas at Cedar Hill: A Holiday Storybook. N.D. Thomas Whittaker.
--Cousin Deborah's Story: Or, The Great Plague, 1 of 3. (The Children of Stantoun Corbet Ser.). N.D. American Sunday-School Union.
--Ethel's Trials in Becoming a Missionary. N.D. American Sunday-School Union.
--The Fairchilds: Or Do What You Can, 1 of 5. (Nelly's Library). N.D. American Sunday-School Union.
--The Foster Sisters: Or, Lucy Corbet's Chronicles. N.D. Thomas Whittaker.
--The Heiress of McGregor: Or, Living for Self. N.D. American Sunday-School Union.
--The Hidden Treasure: A Tale of Troublous Times. N.D. Thomas Whittaker.
--Irish Amy: Or, The Child on the Street and on the Farm. N.D. The American Sunday-School Union.
--Kitty Maynard: Or, "To Obey Is Better Than Sacrifice.". LC 12-36047. 263 p. incl. front., plates. 16 cm. c.1857. American Sunday-School Union.
--Lady Betty's Governess: Or, The Corbet Chronicles, 1 of 3 Vols. (Lady Betty Library Ser.). N.D. Set. T. Whittaker.
--Lady Lucy's Secret: Or, The Gold Thimble, 1 of 3. (The Children of Stantoun Corbet Ser.). N.D. American Sunday-School Union.
--Lady Rosamond's Book, 1 of 3 Vols. (Lady Betty Library Ser). N.D. Set. T. Whittaker.
--The Langham Revels: The Fair Dame of Staunton. N.D. Alfred Martien.
--Lovedays History. N.D. Thomas Whittaker.
--Milly: Or, The Hidden Cross. LC 42-27119. 2 p. l., 3-136 p. 20 cm. 1866. Loring.
--The Mission-Box. (A Golden-Text Story). N.D. American Sunday-School Union.
--Nellie Grey: Or, Ups and Downs of Every-Day Life, and Their Lessons. N.D. American Sunday-School Union.
--Nellie West, From Ten to Twenty. N.D. American Sunday-School Union.
--Nelly: Or, The Best Inheritance. N.D. The American Sunday-School Union.
--Nelly's Library, 5 Vols. N.D. American Sunday-School Union.
--No Talent and Phil's Pansies. 169p. N.D. American Sunday-School Union.
--Oldham: Or, Beside All Waters. N.D. Thomas Whittaker.
--On the Mountain: or, Lost and Found, 1 of 5. (Nelly's Library). N.D. American Sunday-School Union.
--The Orphan Nieces. N.D. A. D. F. Randolph.
--Our Tabby and Her Travels. N.D. A. D. F. Randolph.
--Percy's Holidays. N.D. American Sunday-School Union.
--Red Plant. N.D. American Sunday-School Union.
--Rhoda's Education: Or, Too Much of a Good Thing. N.D. The American Sunday-School Union.
--The School Girls' Treasury: Or, Stories for Thoughtful Girls. N.D. T. Whittaker.
--The Schoolmate: Walking In The Light. N.D. Bradley & Woodruff.
--The Tame Turtle: Or, Geordie McGregor's Trouble. 199p. N.D. American Sunday-School Union.
--The Tattler: or, The History of Patty Steele. N.D. American Sunday-School Union.
--Upward and Onward. N.D. A. D. F. Randolph.
--Winifred: Or, After Many Days. N.D. T. Whittaker.
--Winifred: Or, After Many Days, 1 of 6 Vols. (Ferry-Boat Library Ser.). N.D. Set. T. Whittaker.
--Winifred: Or, After Many Days, 1 of 3 Vols. (Lady Betty Library Ser.). N.D. Set. T. Whittaker.

Guerrera, Jeannette Dion
--The Invisible Elf. LC 72-77555. (Illus.). 72 p. 22cm. 1972. (ISBN 0-912472-17-0). Miller Books.

Guerrero Rea, Jesus, tr. see Garcia, Richard.

Guerrier, Edith
--Wanderfolk in Wonderland. Brown, Edith, illus. N.D. Small, Maynard & Co.

Guest, Edgar Albert (1881-1959)
--Rhymes of Childhood. N.D. Reilly & Lee.

Guest, Elissa Haden
--The Handsome Man. LC 80-66247. p. cm. c.1980. (ISBN 0-590-07661-2). Four Winds Press.
--Over the Moon. 1986. (ISBN 0-688-04148-5, Morrow Junior Books). Morrow.

Guest, Gilbert
--The Adorable Sister Alicia: A Class-Room Etching. LC 25-277341. 157 p. 19 cm. 1925. Burkley Printing Company.

Guezenec, Alfred see Brehat, Alfred De, pseud.

Guggenmos, Josef, jt. auth. see Konopka, Ursula.

Guggenmos, Josef (1922-)
--Wonder-Fish from the Sea. Lucht, Irmgard, illus. Tresselt, Alvin R. (1916-), tr. LC 78-148165. (Illus.). color ils. 32p. (gr. k-3). 1971. (ISBN 0-8193-0483-2, Four Winds). (ISBN 0-8193-0484-0). Scholastic Inc.

Gugliotta, Bobette
--Katzimo, Mysterious Mesa. Bjorklund, Lorence F. (1913-1978), illus. LC 73-19084. (Illus.). 222 p. 22cm. 1974. (ISBN 0-396-06923-1). Dodd, Mead.

Guie, Heister Dean, ed. see Mourning Dove.

Guilbeau, Honore Cooke (1907-)
--Mrs. Magpie's Invention. Guilbeau, Honore Cooke (1907-), illus. LC 76-157420. (Illus.). 45 p. 24cm. 1971. (ISBN 0-201-09288-3). Young Scott Books.

Guild, Anne E. Gore (1826-1868)
--Grandmother Lee's Portfolio. Billings, Hammatt (1818-1874) & Andrew, John, illus. LC 80-492806. (Illus.). 74 p., 6 leaves of plates. 23cm. 1857. Whittemore, Niles, and Hall.

Guild, Caroline Snowden Whitmarsh, Mrs. (1827-1898), ed.
--Hymns and Rhymes for Home and School. LC 5-23992. vii, 152 p. 16 cm. 1875. Nichols and Hall.

Guilfoile, Elizabeth
--Have You Seen My Brother?. Stevens, Mary E. (1920-1966), illus. LC 62-15668. (Illus.). 29 p. 21cm. (The Follett beginning-to-read series). 1962. Follett Pub. Co.

--Spring Comes to the Forest. Cassinelli, Attilio, illus. LC 70-11083. (Illus.). 27 p. 20cm. (Little animal book). 1970. Doubleday.
--The Wonderful Ball. Cassinelli, Attilio, illus. LC 74-11084. (Illus.). 27 p. 20cm. (Little animal book). 1970. Doubleday.

Guoyi, Li
--A Boy & His Kitten. (Illus.). 16p. (Orig.). 1981. (ISBN 0-8351-0960-7). China Bks.

Gupta, Mallika C. see Ramakrishna, Swami.

Guptill, Elizabeth Frances Ephraim, Mrs., jt. auth. see Wormwood, Edyth M.

Guptill, Elizabeth Frances Ephraim, Mrs. (1870-)
--Growing the May Queen. N.D. March Brothers.
--Twelve Plays for Children, Humorous, Wise, and Otherwise. LC 17-8573. 160 p. 18 cm. c.1916. Beckley-Cardy Company.

Gur, Motta (1930-)
--Azeet, Paratrooper Dog. LC 72-2918. (Illus.). 131 p. 22cm. 1972. (ISBN 0-8407-6252-6). T. Nelson.

Guralsky, Jacob, tr. see Tolstoy, Leo Nikolaevich.

Gurley, Jayne
--The Birthday Wish. Truffin, Terry, ed. Masterson, Tom, illus. 24p. (Butterfly Books Ser.). (gr. 1-5). 1975. (ISBN 0-8007-0764-8). Revell.
--A Boy's Best Friend. Truffin, Terry, ed. Masterson, Tom, illus. 24p. (Butterfly Books Ser.). (gr. 1-5). 1975. (ISBN 0-8007-0765-6). Revell.
--A Day of Praise. Truffin, Terry, ed. Masterson, Tom, illus. 24p. (Butterfly Books Ser.). (gr. 1-5). 1975. (ISBN 0-8007-0763-X). Revell.
--A Mountaintop Adventure. Truffin, Terry, ed. Masterson, Tom, illus. 24p. (Butterfly Books Ser.). (gr. 1-5). 1975. (ISBN 0-8007-0766-4). Revell.
--On Thin Ice. Truffin, Terry, ed. Masterson, Tom, illus. LC 76-13412. (Illus.). 24 p. 18cm. (Butterfly books). c.1976. (ISBN 0-8007-0829-6). F. H. Revell Co.
--Someone Is Watching You. Truffin, Terry, ed. Masterson, Tom, illus. LC 76-13610. (Illus.). 24 p. 18cm. (Butterfly books). c.1976. Revell.

Gurner, Fred
--The Photographer and the Pony. Levy, Benjamin, illus. LC 72-88759. (Illus.). 32 p. 1973. Bobbs-Merrill.

Gurney, J. Eric (1910-)
--Gilbert. LC 63-21626. (Illus.). 63p. 24cm. 1963. Prentice-Hall.
--Eric Gurney's Pop-up Book of Dogs. Gurney, J. Eric (1910-), illus. LC 73-274. (Illus.). 20 p. 24cm. 1973. (ISBN 0-394-82634-5). Random House.

Gurney, Nancy Jack (1915-1973) & Gurney, J. Eric
--Impossible Dogs and Troublesome Cats. LC 73-957939. (Illus.). 95 p. 29cm. 1970. American Heritage Press.
--The King, the Mice and the Cheese. LC 65-21212. (Illus.). 63 p. 23cm. 1965. (ISBN 0-394-80039-7, Beginners Bks.). (ISBN 0-394-90039-1). Random House.
--The King, the Mice & the Cheese. Rivera, Carlos, tr. (Spanish Beginner Bks.). (gr. k-3). 1967. (ISBN 0-394-91600-X, Beginner Bks.). Random.

Gurney, J. Eric, jt. auth. see Gurney, Nancy Jack.

Gury, Jeremy
--The 'round and 'round Horse. Marsh, Reginald (1898-1954), illus. LC 43-17314. 47 p. incl. col. front., illus. (part col.) 21 x 26 cm. 1943. H. Holt and Company.
--The Wondrful World of Aunt Tuddy: From An Idea by Max Hess. Knight, Hilary (1926-), illus. LC 58-98778. unpaged. illus. 29cm. 1958. Random House.

Gury, Jeremy, jt. auth. see Marsh, Reginald.

Gusman, Annie, jt. auth. see Ricks, Charlotte Hall.

Gustafson, Anita
--Some Feet Have Noses: A Picture Essay. (gr. 5 up). 1982. (ISBN 0-688-00926-3). (ISBN 0-688-01154-3). Lothrop.

Gustafson, Anita, retold by.
--Monster Rolling Skull and Other Native American Tales. Stadler, John, illus. LC 79-7890. (Illus.). 90 p. 22cm. c.1980. (ISBN 0-690-04019-9). (ISBN 0-690-04020-2). Crowell.

Gustaitis, Rasa (1934-)
--Mixed-up Max. Wolf, Ann, illus. LC 68-13800. (Illus.). 30 p. 23cm. 1968. Follett Pub. Co.

Gustar, Susan Wakeling (1949-)
--When I Visit Daddy or Daddy Visits Me. Cramer, Vivien Whatmough, illus. LC 75-311739. (Illus.). 28 p. 21cm. 1973. S.N.

Gustason, Gerilee, jt. auth. see Wojcio, Michael D.

Gustavson, Harry (1914-)
--Up Goes the House. 40p. (gr. k-2). 1947. Oxford University Press.
--Up Goes the House: Adapted from a Story. Doremus, Robert (1913-), illus. LC 53-405169. unpaged. illus. 21cm. (Jolly books, 219). c.1953. Jolly Books.

Guterman, Norbert (1900-1984), tr. see Afanasev, Aleksandr Nikolaevich.

Guthridge, Sue Janet (1918-)
--Tom Edison, Boy Inventor. Graham, Betty, illus. LC 59-14003. 192p. illus. 20cm. (Chilhood of famous Americans). 1959. Bobbs, Merrill.
--Tom Edison, Boy Inventor. Wood, Wallace, illus. LC 47-2065. 200 p. illus. 19 1/2 cm. (The Childhood of famous Americans series). 1947. The Bobbs-Merrill Company.

Guthrie, Alfred Bertram, Jr. (1901-)
--Big It & Other Stories. 1960. HM.
--The Big Sky. (gr. 7-9). N.D. (ISBN 0-395-06790-1). HM.
--The Big Sky. Landau, Jacob (1917-), illus. 340p. N.D. William Sloane Associates.
--The Genuine Article. 1977. (ISBN 0-395-25361-6). HM.
--Once upon a Pond. 1st ed. Guthrie, Carol B., illus. LC 73-88505. (Illus.). 93p. 25cm. c.1973. (ISBN 0-87842-047-9). Mountain Press Pub.

Guthrie, Bass
--The Lucky Moores. (Illus.). N.D. (ISBN 0-8111-0540-7). The Naylor and Company.

Guthrie, Donna
--The Witch Who Lives Down the Hall. Schwartz, Amy (1954-), illus. LC 85-887. (Illus.). 32 p. 29cm. c.1985. (ISBN 0-15-298610-3). Harcourt Brace Jovanovich.

Guthrie, Kenneth Sylvan (1871-)
--Short Stories for Young Folks, and for Their Parents, Teachers, Friends, and Clergymen. gathered, tr. and arranged by kenneth sylvan guthrie;. Brauer, Katherine & Spreen, Meta, illus. LC 14-11527. 5 p. l., 138, 6, 45 (i. e. 55) p. front., illus. 20 cm. c.1914. Comparative Literature Press; Etc., Etc.

Guthrie, Thomas Anstey see Anstey, F., pseud.

Guthrie, Vee
--Animals from A to Z. LC 72-78647. (Illus.). 22p. 27cm. 1969. Van Nostrand Reinhold Co.

Gutman, Bill
--Jim Plunkett. LC 72-92926. (Illus.). 87 p. 21cm. (Thistle Book). 1973. (ISBN 0-448-21470-9). Grosset & Dunlap.
--My Father, the Coach," and Other Sports Stories. LC 75-42217. 190 21. c.1976. (ISBN 0-671-32786-0). (ISBN 0-671-32787-9). J. Messner.

Gutman, Naham (1899-1981)
--Path of the Orange Peels: Adventures in the Early Days of Tel Aviv. Gutman, Naham (1899-1981), illus. Segal, Nelly, tr. LC 79-52038. p. cm. 1979. (ISBN 0-396-07734-X). Dodd, Mead.

Gutridge, Rex
--Thunder Over Africa. Deakin, Cyril, illus. LC 58-9088. 223p. illus. 21cm. (The New Venture Library). 1958. Warne.

Gutteridge, Lindsay (1923-)
--Cold War in a Country Garden. 1971. (ISBN 0-399-10150-0). G. P. Putnam's Sons.
--Killer Pine. 1973. (ISBN 0-399-11129-8). G. P. Putnam's Sons.

Guy, Anne Welsh
--A Baby for Betsy. Pointer, Priscilla, illus. LC 57-13736. (Illus.). 31 p. 21cm. 1957. Abingdon Press.
--Cub Scout Donny. Crist, Richard Harrison, illus. LC 58-3325. 95p. illus. 22cm. 1958. (ISBN 0-687-10079-8). Abingdon Press.
--One Dozen Brownies. Kamen, Gloria (1923-), illus. LC 62-7864. 96p. illus. 22cm. 1962. Abingdon Press.
--William. (Illus.). (gr. 3-6). 1961. (ISBN 0-8382-0971-8). Hale.
--William. Crichlow, Ernest T. (1914-), illus. LC 61-12909. 124p. illus. 21cm. 1961. Dial Press.

Guy, M. M.
--Joe Doughty. (MacMillan Bks. for Boys & Girls). (gr. 7-9). N.D. MacMillan Bks.

Guy, Rosa Cuthbert (1928-)
--The Disappearance. LC 79-50672. 246 p. 22cm. c.1979. (ISBN 0-440-01189-2). Delacorte Press.
--Edith Jackson. LC 77-28098. 187 p. 24cm. 1978. (ISBN 0-670-28906-X). Viking Press.
--The Friends. LC 72-11068. 203 p. 22cm. 1973. Holt, Rinehart and Winston.
--Mirror of Her Own. LC 80-69448. 183 p. 22cm. c.1981. (ISBN 0-440-05513-X). Delacorte Press.
--New Guys Around the Block. LC 82-72818. 199 p. 22cm. c.1983. (ISBN 0-440-06005-2). Delacorte Press.
--Paris, Pee Wee, and Big Dog. Binch, Caroline, illus. LC 85-1654. (Illus.). 116 p. 22cm. c.1984. (ISBN 0-385-29407-7). Delacorte.
--Ruby. LC 76-2019. 192p. 1976. (ISBN 0-670-61023-2). Viking Pr.

Guy, Rosa Cuthbert (1928-), adapted by.
--Mother Crocodile: An Uncle Amadou Tale from Senegal. Steptoe, John Lewis (1950-), illus. LC 80-393. p. cm. 1980. (ISBN 0-440-06405-8). (ISBN 0-440-06406-6). Delacorte Press. **Awards: (CSKA); (ALA).**

Guyol, Louise Hubert
--The Funny House. Freret, Emily M., illus. LC 23-886. 4 p. l., 206 p. col. front., illus., plates. 19 cm. 1922. B. J. Brimmer Company.
--The Gallant Lallanes. King, Ruth, illus. LC 29-16078. 6 p. l., 251 1 p. incl. illus., plates col. front. 19 1/2 cm. 1929. Harper & Brothers.

Guyot, Jacqueline & Raynal, Francois
--Angela & Elton at Play. Hutchins, Roger, illus. (Illus.). 24p. (Woofits Ser.). 1982. (ISBN 0-8431-0980-7). Price Stern.
--Angela's House. Hutchins, Roger, illus. (Illus.). 24p. (Woofits Ser.). 1982. (ISBN 0-8431-0979-3). Price Stern.
--Flowers for Angela's Mother. Hutchins, Roger, illus. (Illus.). 24p. (Woofits Ser.). 1982. (ISBN 0-8431-0981-5). Price Stern.

Guyton, David E.
--Mother Berry of Blue Mountain. N.D. Broadman Press.

Guyton, Marion
--The Tiny Golden Whistle. N.D. Vantage Press.

Guzzo, Sandra E
--Fox and Heggie. Parkinson, Kathy, illus. LC 83-16672. p. cm. 1983. (ISBN 0-8075-2546-4). A. Whitman.

Gwen, Betty
--Jack London Stories of the Far North. 256p. Repr. (gr. 5 up). N.D (Schol Trade Pap). Schol Bk Serv.

Gwynne, Frederick Hubbard, jt. auth. see Addams, Charles Samuel.

Gwynne, Frederick Hubbard (1926-)
--Best in Show. Gwynne, Frederick Hubbard (1926-), illus. LC 58-11909. (Illus.). unpage. 26cm. 1958. Dutton.
--A Chocolate Moose for Dinner. 1 St. Ed. ed. Gwynne, Frederick Hubbard (1926-), illus. LC 76-4811. (Illus.). 47 p. 29cm. 1976. (ISBN 0-525-61545-8). Windmill Books.
--Ick's ABC. Gwynne, Frederick Hubbard (1926-), illus. LC 73-159155. (Illus.). 32 p. 1971. (ISBN 0-87807-040-0). (ISBN 0-87807-041-9). Windmill Books.
--The King Who Rained. Gwynne, Frederick Hubbard (1926-), illus. LC 74-130216. (Illus.). 40 p. 32cm. 1970. (ISBN 0-87807-008-7). Windmill Books.
--The Sixteen Hand Horse. Gwynne, Frederick Hubbard (1926-), illus. LC 79-13284. (Illus.). 48p. (gr. k-6). 1980. (ISBN 0-671-96100-4). Windmill Bks.
--The Story of Ick. Gwynne, Frederick Hubbard (1926-), illus. LC 78-148173. (Illus.). 48 p. 1971. (ISBN 0-87807-013-3). Windmill Books.

Gwynne, J. Harold
--Rainbow Book of Bible Stories. Savage, Steele (1900-), illus. LC 56-9264. (Illus.). 320p. (Rainbow Giants Ser). (gr. 4 up). 1956. (ISBN 0-529-04618-0). Collins Pubs.

Gyulnazaryan, Hadjak
--Little Arthur's Sun. Riordan, Jim & Solasko, Fainna, trs. 33p. 1983. (ISBN 0-8285-2580-3, Pub. by Raduga Pubs USSR). Imported Pubns.

H. De W. R
--Charity: Or, Nettie's Victories. LC 78-318176. (Illus.). 108 p., 2 leaves of plates. 18cm. 1866. Gen. Prot. Episc. S.S. Union and Church Book Society.

H, F. M.
--The War of the Wooden Soldiers. Wheeler, Willard & Wheeler, Marguerite L., illus. LC 42-47086. 76 p. illus. (part col.) 18 cm. (On cover: Dotty Dolly series). c.1915. Rand McNally & Co.

H. N. W. B.
--Belle Clement's Influence, 1 of 4 Vols. (The Good Hope Ser.). N.D. Set. Henry A Young & Co.
--Edith Withington, 1 of 4 Vols. (The Good Hope Ser.). N.D. Set. Henry A Young & Co.
--Lulu Reed's Pupil, 1 of 6 Vols. (The Good Hope Ser.). N.D. Set. Henry A Young & Co.
--Sophie's Letter Book, 1 of 4 Vols. (The Good Hope Ser.). N.D. Set. Henry A Young & Co.

H, S.
--The History of the Davenport Family: In Which Is Displayed a Striking Contrast Between Haughty Indolence and Healthy Activity, in the Characters of the Young Davenports, and Their Cousins, Sophia and Amelia Easy. Interspersed with Moral Reflections. LC 8-4785. 144 p. front., illus. 14 cm. 1798. Spotswood and Etheridge.

Haack, Bruce, contrib. by.
--The Witch's Vacation. (gr. k-3). N.D (Schol Trade Pap). Schol Bk Serv.

Haan, Gertrude
--The Christmas Heart. Gringhuis, Richard H. (1918-1974), illus. Gringhuis, Dirk, pseud. LC 57-14591. (Illus.). 24cm. 62p. 1957. International Publications.

Haan, Sheri Dunham
--Bible Stories in Rhyme and Rhythm. 63 p. 22cm. 1974. (ISBN 0-8010-4105-8). Baker Book House.
--A Child's Storybook of Bible People. Bentley, Martha, illus. LC 73-76202. (Illus.). 239 p. 24cm. 1973. (ISBN 0-8010-4077-9). Baker Book House.

Haar, Jaap Ter (1922-)
--Boris. Poortvliet, Rien, illus. Mearns, Martha, tr. from Dutch. LC 77-122770. (Illus.). 152 p. 21cm. 1970, c.1969. Delacorte Press.
--Boris. Poortvliet, Rien, illus. Mearns, Martha, tr. from Dutch. 1970. Delacorte.
--Danger on the Mountain. 1 st. American ed. Mussey, Barrows, tr. from Dutch. LC 60-12851. 186p. illus. 22cm. 1st U.S. edition. 1960. Duell, Sloan and Pearce.
--Duck Dutch. 1st ed. Van Looy, Rein, illus. Mussey, Barrows, tr. LC 62-8532. 89p. illus. 21cm. 1962. Duell, Sloan and Pearce.
--King Arthur. Poortvliet, Rien, illus. LC 77-74721. (Illus.). 159 p. 23cm. c.1973. (ISBN 0-8448-1053-3). Crane Russak.
--The World of Ben Lighthart. Mearns, Martha, tr. from Dutch. LC 76-47236. 123 p. 22cm. c.1977. (ISBN 0-440-09684-7). Delacorte Press/S. Lawrence.

Haarbeck, L
--The Wanderers: A Story of God's Loving Care. LC 27-23959. 128 p. illus. 17 1/2 cm. c.1927. Augustana Book Concern.

Haaren, John Henry (1855-1916), compiled by.
--Fairy Life. LC 20-17782. (Illus.). 19cm. 123p. (Golden Rod Bks.). 1896. University Publishing Co.
--Rhymes and Fables. LC 9-19086. (Illus.). 19cm. 96p. (Golden Rod Bks.). 1899. Newson & Co.

Haas, Ben
--Troubled Summer. 1966. E M Hale.

Haas, BenJamin Leopold (1926-1977)
--The Troubled Summer. LC 66-25289. 192 p. 22cm. 1966. Bobbs-Merrill.

Haas, Charlie (1952-) & Hunter, Tim (1947-)
--Over the Edge. LC 79-51728. (Illus.). 164 p., 16 leaves of plates. 18cm. (Black cat book ; B-426). 1979. (ISBN 0-394-17088-1). Grove Press.

Haas, Dorothy
--The Bears Upstairs. LC 78-54683. p. cm. c.1978. (ISBN 0-688-80169-2). (ISBN 0-688-84169-4). Greenwillow Books.
--Dorothy & the Seven-Leaf Clover. Rose, David S. (1947-), illus. LC 84-16080. (Illus.). 64p. (Brand-New Oz Adventures Ser.). (gr. 2-6). 1985. (ISBN 0-394-97037-3, BYR). (ISBN 0-394-87037-9). Random.
--Poppy and the Outdoors Cat. Apple, Margot, illus. LC 80-19140. p. cm. 1980. (ISBN 0-8075-6621-7). A. Whitman.
--Tink in a Tangle. Tucker, Kathleen, ed. Apple, Margot, illus. LC 83-16654. (Illus.). 128p. (gr. 2-5). 1984. (ISBN 0-8075-7952-1). A Whitman.

Haas, Dorothy, ed. see Wensell, Ulises.

Haas, Gordon
--The Spiritual Adventures of Courtney Flower. Rahkonen, Liisa, illus. LC 73-89372. 2 v. (chiefly col. illus. 21cm. c.1973. Haas Enterprises.

Haas, Irene (1929-)
--The Little Moon Theater. Haas, Irene (1929-), illus. LC 80-27476. p. cm. 1981. (ISBN 0-689-50201-X). Atheneum.
--The Maggie B. Haas, Irene (1929-), illus. LC 74-18183. (Illus.). 32 p. 1975. (ISBN 0-689-50021-1). Atheneum. **Award: (ALA).**

Haas, James Edward (1943-)
--Rainbow Songs. 40p. (Orig.). (gr. 1-8). 1975. (ISBN 0-8192-1201-6). Morehouse.

Haas, Jessie
--Keeping Barney. LC 81-7029. 152 p. 22cm. c.1982. (ISBN 0-688-00859-3). Greenwillow Books.
--Working Trot. LC 83-1696. p. cm. 1983. (ISBN 0-688-02384-3). Greenwillow Books.

Haas, Merle S. (1896-1985), tr. see Arabian Nights.

Haas, Merle S. (1896-1985), tr. see Brunhoff, Jean de.

Haas, Merle S., tr. see Brunhoff, Laurent De.

Haas, Merle S. (1896-1985), tr. see Du Genestoux, Magdeleine.

Haas, Patricia C.
--Swampfire. Robinson, Charles (1931-), illus. (Illus.). (gr. 4-6). 1975. (ISBN 0-590-09990-6, Schol Pap). Schol Bk Serv.

Habberton, John (1842-1921)
--Budge and Toddie. (The Good Value Books). N.D. Grosset & Dunlap.
--Helen's Babies. (Famous Bks. for Young Americans). N.D. A. L. Burt Co.
--Helen's Babies. N.D. Appleton Century Co.
--Helen's Babies. (The Good Value Books). N.D. Grosset & Dunlap.
--Helen's Babies. (Altemus' New Illustrated Young People's Library). N.D. Henry Altemus Company.
--Helen's Babies. (Illus.). (Little Men and Women Ser.). N.D. Henry Altemus Co.
--Helen's Babies. (Illus.). (Home Ser.). N.D. Hurst & Co.

Hadley, Arthur T., intro. by see Hughes, Thomas.
Hadley, Caroline
--Bible Stories for Young Children. N.D. J. B. Lippincott.
--Stories of Old: Bible Narratives for Children, Containing: Old Testament Series, New Testament Series, and Stories of the Apostles. N.D. Sheldon & Co.
Hadley, Eric & Hadley, Tessa
--Legends of Earth, Air, Fire, and Water. Waldman, Bryna, illus. LC 84-12089. (Illus.). 32 p. (Cambridge Books for Children). 1985. (ISBN 0-521-26311-5). Cambridge University Press.
--Legends of the Sun and Moon. Nesbitt, Jan, illus. LC 82-17720. p. cm. 1983. (ISBN 0-521-25227-X). Cambridge University Press.
Hadley, Harry L.
--Junior Detectives. 54p. N.D. T. S. Denison & Co.
--Never a Dull Moment. 46p. N.D. T. S. Denison & Co.

Hadley, Jay, jt. auth. see Wilson, Justin.

Hadley, Lee Irwin see Irwin, Hadley, pseud.

Hadley, Milton
--Beautiful Stories About Children: Or, Boys and Girls of Many Lands; Containing Full Descriptions of the Children and Youth of France, Norway, Italy...and Other Countries... v, 17-250 p. col. front., illus., plates (partly col.) 25 cm. 1903. National Publishing Company.

Hadley, Tessa, jt. auth. see Hadley, Eric.

Hadsell, Alice
--Mr. Punnymoon's Train. Phillips, Katherine L., illus. LC 51-6065. unpaged. illus. 21 cm. (Rand McNally book-elf book, 449). 1951. Rand McNally.
Hadsell, Virginia T.
--On the Go. Nestor, H., photos by. (Illus.). 51 photos. (Orig.). Repr. of 1966 ed. (gr. 2). N.D. (ISBN 0-912078-09-X). Glide.
Hadsell, Virginia T. & Newcom, Grethel C.
--Equal Start: A New School, a New Chance. Nestor, H., photos by. Sullivan, N. V., intro. by. (Illus.). 48 photos. 52p. (Orig.). (gr. 2). 1968. (ISBN 0-912078-10-3). Glide.
Hadtka, Myrtle Graham
--Georganne. LC 42-25435. 132 p. col. illus. 23 cm. 1942. The Wartburg Press.
Hadwin, Maria
--Sally Silverfur. LC 35-10044. 32p. illus. 20cm. 1935. Meador Pub, Co.
Haenigsen, Harry
--Penny. LC 53-9037. 158p. of illus. 20cm. 1953. Simon and Schuster.
Haertling, Peter see Hartling, Peter, pseud.
Haertling, Peter (1933-)
--Oma. Hartling, Peter, pseud. 1st ed. Ash, Jutta, illus. Bell, Anthea, tr. LC 76-58719. p. cm. c.1977. (ISBN 0-06-022237-9). (ISBN 0-06-022238-7). Harper & Row.
--Theo Runs Away. Hartling, Peter, pseud. Schmidt, W. & Schmidt, F., illus. Bell, Anthea, tr. 128p. 1981. (ISBN 0-905478-35-5, Pub. by Andersen-Hutchinson England). State Mutual Bk.

Haeseler, John, jt. auth. see Haeseler, Ruth, Mrs.

Haeseler, Ruth, Mrs. & Haeseler, John
--Shorty: The Story of a Little Chimpanzee. LC 26-135703. 63 p. illus. (incl. ports.) 17 x 15 1/2 cm. c.1936. Rand, McNally & Company.
Hafenrichter, Conrad, photos by.
--Nelly's Lucky Day. (Illus.). 24p. (Golden Little Photo Story Bks.). (ps). 1984. (ISBN 0-307-16030-0, Golden Pr). Western Pub.
--Tippy's Naughty Day. (Illus.). 24p. (Golden Little Photo Story Bks.). (ps). 1984. (ISBN 0-307-16031-9, Golden Pr). Western Pub.
Hafer, Flora Van Buren
--Captive Indian Boy. Lambo, Donald W. (1903-1966), illus. LC 63-10489. (Illus.). 154 p. 21cm. 1963. McKay.
Hafrey, Leigh, tr. see Korschunow, Irina.
Hagedorn, Hermann
--Eleven Who Dared. Parfit, Dorothea Hagedorn, adapted by. 144p. 1967. Four Winds Press.
--The Ten Dreams of Zach Peters. N.D. J. C. Winston Co.
Hageman-Shedd
--Children of Grizzly. N.D. World Book Co.
Hagemann, Gerard (1922-)
--Crossbearer to the Savages: A Story of Junipero Serra. LC 51-8882. (Illus.). 96p. 24cm. 1951. Dujaris Press.
Hagemeyer, Dora (1891-)
--Anne in the Periwinkle Patch. LC 46-3224. 4 p. l., 39 p., 1 l. 21 cm. 1945. The Carmel Pine Cone Press.
--The Periwinkle Patch: Rhymes for Little Children. LC 43-168820. 5 p. l., 49 p. 1 l. 20 1/2 cm. c.1942. The Carmel Pine Cone Press.
Hagen, Lyman B, ed. see Simon, Charlie May, Mrs.

Hager, Alice Marie Rogers (1894-1969)
--The Canvas Castle. Stevens, Mary E. (1920-1966), illus. LC 49-5953. 179 p. illus. 22 cm. 1949. J. Messner.
--Cathy Whitney, President's Daughter. LC 66-817619. 192p. 22cm. 1966. Messner.
--Dateline: Paris. LC 54-10586. 190p. 21cm. 1954. J. Messner.
--Janice, Airline Hostess. (gr. 7 up). 1948. Messner.
--Love's Golden Circle. LC 62-10202. 189p. 22cm. 1962. J. Messner.
--Washington Secretary. LC 58-10926. 192p. 21cm. 1958. J. Messner.
--The Wonderful Ice Cream Cart. Korach, Mimi (1922-), illus. LC 55-13619. 149p. illus. 21cm. 1955. Macmillan.
Hager, Betty
--Old Jake and the Pirate's Treasure. Dawkins, Ron, illus. LC 80-80606. (Illus.). 100 p. 23cm. c.1980. (ISBN 0-8178-0006-9). Harvey House.
Hager, Jean (1932-)
--The Secret of Riverside Farm. LC 71-110688. 156 p. 22cm. 1970. Steck-Vaughn Co.
--The Whispering House. LC 77-101565. iv, 181 p. 22cm. 1970. (ISBN 0-8114-7703-7). Steck-Vaughn Co.
Hager, Luther George (1885-) & Dearborn, Mary Hager, Mrs.
--The Adventures of Waddles. LC 36-601. 101 p. of illus. 23 1/2 cm. c.1935. Associated Authors.
Hagerup, Inger
--Helter Skelter. Aas, Tonje S., illus. Tate, Joan (1922-), tr. (Illus.). 32p. (ps-3). 1981. (ISBN 0-7207-1198-3, Pub. by Michael Joseph). Merrimack Pub Cir.
Hages, Clair Wallace (1887-)
--The Boy Allies on the North Sea Patrol: Or, Striking the First Blow at the German Fleet. LC 15-5819. 235 p. front. 19 1/2 cm. c.1915. A. L. Burt Company.
Haggard, Audrey
--Little Plays from the Greek Myths. LC 30-12133. 191, 1 p. incl. front., illus. 15 1/2 cm. (Half-title: The Kings treasuries of literature. General editor: Sir A. T. Quiller Couch). 1929. J. M. Dent & Sons Ltd.
Haggard, Henry Rider, Sir (1856-1925)
--Allan Quatermain. N.D. Norton & Co.
--Allan the Hunter: A Tale of Three Lions. (Illus.). N.D. Lothrop Publishing Company.
--Ayesha: The Return of She. N.D. W. W. Norton & Co.
--Ayesha: The Return of She. Greiffenhagen, Maurice, illus. LC 77-95555. (Illus.). 189 p. 24cm. 1978. (ISBN 0-486-23649-8). Dover Publications.
--Eric Brighteyes. Abridged. (Class Books of English Literature). N.D. Longmans, Green & Co.
--King Solomon's Mines. 320p. (Blackie Chosen Classics Ser.). (gr. 6 up). 1979. (ISBN 0-216-88516-7, Pub. by Blackie England). Hippocrene Bks.
--King Solomon's Mines. (Magnum Easy Eye Classic Ser). (gr. 7-10). N.D. Lancer.
--King Solomon's Mines. N.D. Norton & Co.
--King Solomon's Mines. 256p. (Puffin Classics Ser.). (gr. 3-7). 1983. (ISBN 0-14-035014-4, Puffin). Penguin.
--King Solomon's Mines. Bd. with She; Alan Quartermaine. (Illus.). (Children's Classics Ser.). 1979. (ISBN 0-7064-1062-9, Mayflower Bks). Smith Pubs.
--King Solomon's Mines. Jones, Betty Millsaps (1940-), retold by. D'Achille, Gino, illus. LC 82-3843. (Illus.). 95 p. 21cm. (Step-up Adventures). c.1982. (ISBN 0-394-95275-8). (ISBN 0-394-85275-3). Random House.
--King Solomon's Mines. West, M., adapted by. N.D. Longmans Green & Co.
--King Solomon's Mines. Whitear, A. R., illus. (Illus.). (Children's Illustrated Classics). (gr. 5-9). N.D. (ISBN 0-525-33234-0). Dutton.
--King Solomon's Mines, and Allan Quatermain. Kershner, Louise, adapted by. LC 56-14650. 336p. illus. 21cm. 1956. Globe Book Co.
--Nada the Lily. N.D. Norton & Co.
--She. N.D. W. W. Norton & Co.
--She. Greiffenhagen, Maurice & Kerr, Charles H. M, illus. LC 75-36065. (Illus.). xiii, 332 p. 22cm. c.1976. (ISBN 0-8055-1177-6). (ISBN 0-8055-0251-3). Hart Pub. Co.
--World-Famous King Solomon's Mines. Kramer, Frank, illus. LC 60-8668. 191p. illus. 20cm. (World-famous series, 204). 1960. Hart Pub. Co.
Hagler, Margaret
--Larry and the Freedom Man. Berson, Harold (1926-), illus. LC 59-13157. 175p. illus. 22cm. 1959. Lothrop, Lee & Shepard Co.
Hagon, Priscilla, pseud., see Allan, Mabel Esther.
Hagon, Priscilla, pseud. (1915-)
--Mystery of the Secret Square. Allan, Mabel Esther. Abel, Raymond (1911-), illus. (gr. 4-9). 1970. (ISBN 0-529-00787-8). World Pub.

Hague, Kathleen
--Alphabears: An ABC Book. Hague, Michael R., illus. LC 83-26476. (Illus.). 1984. (ISBN 0-03-062543-2). HR&W.
--The Legend of the Veery Bird. Hague, Michael R., illus. LC 84-19732. p. cm. 1985. (ISBN 0-15-243824-6). Harcourt Brace Jovanovich.
Hague, Kathleen & Hague, Michael R.
--East of the Sun and West of the Moon. Hague, Michael R., illus. LC 80-13499. (Illus.). 31 p. 26cm. c.1980. (ISBN 0-15-224702-5). (ISBN 0-15-224703-3). Harcourt Brace Jovanovich.
--The Man Who Kept House. Hague, Michael R., illus. LC 80-26258. (Illus.). 32 p. 26cm. c.1981. (ISBN 0-15-251698-0). Harcourt Brace Jovanovich.
Hague, Michael R., selected by.
--Mother Goose: A Collection of Classic Nursery Rhymes. Hague, Michael R., illus. LC 83-22559. (Illus.). viii, 61 p. 26cm. c.1984. Holt, Rinehart, and Winston.
Hague, Michael R., jt. auth. see Hague, Kathleen.
Hague, Michael R., ed. see Andersen, Hans Christian.
Hagy, Jeannie (1947-)
--And Then Mom Joined the Army. Stone, David Karl (1922-), illus. LC 75-25506. (Illus.). 143 p. 23cm. c.1976. (ISBN 0-687-01379-8). Abingdon Press.
Hahn, Bula
--Jet and the New Country. Arthur, Elizabeth, illus. LC 47-16957. 6 p. l., 11-248 p. incl. front., plates. 20 1/2 cm. 1946. Unity School of Christianity.
--Jet's Adventures. Arthur, Elizabeth, illus. LC 41-6040. 7 p. l., 11-232, 1 p. incl. front., illus., plates. 21 cm. 1940. Unity School of Christianity.
--Jet's Choice: The Story of a Group of Pioneer Boys and Girls. Forayth, Edith K., illus. 245 p. ill. 21 cm. N.D. Unity School of Christianity.
Hahn, Emily (1905-)
--Around the World with Nellie Bly. (Illus.). 1959. Houghton Mifflin.
--Francie. LC 54-8548. 237p. 20cm. (Starlight novels for modern girls). 1954, c.1951. Grosset & Dunlap.
--Francie. LC 51-10268. 237 p. 21cm. 1951. Watts.
--Francie Again. 216p. (gr. 8). 1953. Franklin Watts, Inc.
--Francie Again. (Starlight Novels). N.D. Grosset & Dunlap.
--Francie Comes Home. LC 56-7434. 247p. 21cm. 1956. Watts.
--June Finds a Way. LC 60-5582. 148p. 21cm. 1960. F. Watts.
Hahn, Frank G. see Noodles, pseud.
Hahn, Harriet
--The Plantain Season. 207p. 1976. (ISBN 0-393-08729-8). Norton.
Hahn, Julia Letheld
--Billy and Frisky Stories. N.D. Houghton Mifflin Co.
--The Story Way. N.D. Houghton Mifflin Co.
Hahn, Lena
--The Adventures of Baldwin, the Penguin. LC 63-15563. 1 v. (unpaged) col. illus. 22 cm. 1963. Putnam.
Hahn, Lotte K.
--The Unicorn Who Wanted to Be Seen. LC 60-12547. (Illus.). 1 v. (unpaged). 26cm. 1961. Warne.
Hahn, Mary Downing
--Daphne's Book. LC 83-7348. c.1983. (ISBN 0-89919-183-5). Clarion Books.
--The Jellyfish Season. LC 85-3759. 182 p. 22cm. c.1985. (ISBN 0-89919-344-7). Clarion Books.
--The Sara Summer. Sanderson, Ruth, illus. LC 79-12678. 152 p. 22cm. c.1979. (ISBN 0-8164-3238-4). Houghton Mifflin/Clarion Books.
--The Time of the Witch. LC 82-1195. 171 p. 22cm. c.1982. (ISBN 0-89919-115-0). Clarion Books.
Hahn, Phil, jt. auth. see Hanrahan, Jack.
Hahn, Phil & Hanrahan, Jack
--Beastly Rhymes. (Illus.). 48p. (gr. 1-4). 1966. (ISBN 0-448-05752-2). G&D.
--Show Me Book. Hanrahan, Jack, illus. (Illus.). 48p. (gr. 1-4). 1969. (ISBN 0-448-05754-9). (ISBN 0-448-02979-0). G&D.
Haig-Brown, Roderick Langmere (1908-1976)
--Ki-Yu: A Story of Panthers. Wiese, Kurt (1887-1974), illus. 1973. Houghton Mifflin Co.
--Mounted Police Patrol. LC 54-5758. 248 p. 21cm. (Morrow junior books). 1954. Morrow.
--Panther: The Story of a North American Mountain Lion. Stahl, Ben F., illus. LC 73-8843. (Illus.). viii, 210 p. 22cm. 1973, c.1934. (ISBN 0-395-17709-X). Houghton Mifflin.
--Saltwater Summer. N.D. E . M. Hale and Co.
--Saltwater Summer. LC 48-7698. 256 p. col. front. 21 cm. (Morrow junior books). 1948. W. Morrow.
--Silver: The Story of a Salmon. N.D. MacMillan.

--Starbuck Valley Winter. De Feo, Charles, illus. LC 43-14764. 4 p. l., 3-310 p. illus. 21 cm. 1943. W. Morrow & Company. **Award: (CLA).**
--The Whale People. Weiler, Mary, illus. LC 63-7234. (Illus.). 256 p. 22cm. 1963. Morrow. **Award: (CLA).**
Haigh, Richmond
--An Ethiopian Saga. LC 19-709686. x, 207 p. 19 1/2 cm. 1919. H. Holt and Company.
Haight, Ada Clementine Acker (1879-)
--Croton Waters. 1st ed. LC 51-13717. 121 p. 21 cm. 1951. Pageant Press.
Haight, Gordon Sherman (1901-), ed. see Eliot, George.

Haight, Margaret N., adapted by see Cooper, James Fenimore.
Hail, Maxine
--Myrtle the Turtle and Other Fables for Children: Best Loved Animal Tales in Rhyme. (Illus.). 1958. Exposition Press.
Haile, Ellen
--Hazel-Nut and Her Brothers. (Illus.). 256p. N.D. Cassell, Petter, Galpin.
--Hazel Nut Library. New ed. 1888. Set. Cassell & Co.
--Three Brown Boys and Other Happy Children. (Illus.). 228p. N.D. Cassell, Petter, Galpin.
--Two Gray Girls and Their Opposite Neighbors. (Illus.). 256p. N.D. Cassell, Petter, Galpin.
Hailmann, Eudora Lucas
--Song Games and Rhymes. N.D. Milton Bradley.
Haine, Hector Emanuel, jt. ed. see Grayson, M. H.
Haines, Alice Calhoun
--According to Grandma. (Illus.). N.D. Frederick A. Stokes.
--Cock-a-Doodle Hill: Being Further Chronicles of the Dudley Grahams. Day, Francis, illus. LC 9-23116. vi p. 1 l., 296 p. front., 3 pl. 19 cm. 1909. H. Holt and Comapny.
--Girls. Knipe, Emilie Benson, Mrs. (1870-1958), illus. 18 p. col. front 3 col pl. 31 1/2 x 25 1/2 cm. 1905. F. A. Stokes Company.
--Girls and Boys. Knipe, Emilie Benson, Mrs. (1870-1958), illus. LC 5-38072. 32 x 25cm. 34p. 1905. Frederick A. Stokes Co.
--Girls and Boys: Stories and Verses. (Illus.). 1910. Frederick A. Stokes.
--Indian Boys and Girls. Mar, Aliee & Deming, Edwin Willard (1860-1942), illus. LC 6-346390. (Illus.). 47, 1 p. incl. illus., plates. col. front., 3 col. pl. 26 x 20 1/2 cm. 1906. F. A. Stokes Company.
--Japanese Boys and Girls. Mar, Alice, illus. LC 5-37159. 32 x 26cm. 1905. Frederick A. Stokes Co.
--Japanese Child Life. Mar, Alice, illus. LC 5-37157. 32 x 25cm. 34p. 1905. Frederick A. Stokes Co.
--Little Folk of Brittany. Hunt, Esther, illus. LC 7-37268. 48 p. incl. illus., plates. col. front. 3 col. pl. 29 x 23 1/2 cm. 1907. F. A. Stokes Company.
--Little Japs at Home. Mar, Alice, illus. LC 5-37158. 32 x 26cm. 1905. Frederick A. Stokes Co.
--The Luck of the Dudley Grahams: As Related in Extracts from Elizabeth Graham's Diary. Day, Francis, illus. LC 7-32036. 2 p. l., 300 p. front., plates. 19 1/2 cm. 1907. H. Holt and Company.
--Partners for Fair. Avery, Faith, illus. LC 12-21140. vi p., 1 l., 232 p. front., plates. 19 /1/2 cm. 1919. H. Holt and Company.
--Pets. Rhead, Louis John (1857-1926), illus. LC 4-29367. 34cm. 33p. 1904. Frederick A. Stokes Co.
--What Grandma Says. Kilvert, Benjamin Sayre Cory (1879-), illus. LC 7-32005. 29.5 x 23 cm. 28p. 1907. Frederick A. Stokes.
--When Grandma was Little. Kilvert, Benjamin Sayre Cory (1879-), illus. LC 7-32179. 29.5 cm. 28p. 1907. Frederick A. Stokes.
Haines, Donal Hamilton (1886-)
--Blaine of the Backfield. LC 37-22963. 4 p. l., 3-281 p. front. 19 1/2 cm. c.1937. Farrar & Rinehart, Inc.
--Clearing the Seas: Or, The Last of the Warships. LC 15-19861. 3 p. l., 281, 1 p. front., plates. 19 1/2 cm. 1915. Harper & Brothers.
--David and Jonathan. LC 36-18964. 4 p. l., 3-298 p. front. 19 1/2 cm. 1936. Farrar & Rinehart, Inc.
--The Dragon-Flies: A Tale of the Flying Service. LC 19-15790. vi p., 1 l., 299, 1 p. front., plates. 19 1/2 cm. 1919. Houghton Mifflin Company.
--Fighting Blood: A Tale of Kitchener's Campaign in the Soudan. Thieme, A., illus. LC 27-18254. vi, 253 p. col. front. 19 1/2 cm. 1927. Houghton Mifflin Company.
--The Fortress: A Story of Hillton Academy. LC 45-372943. viii, 248 p. 19 1/2 cm. 1945. Farrar & Rinehart, Inc.
--Last Invasion. N.D. Harper & Brothers.
--Shadow on the Campus. LC 42-227164. 4 p. l., 3-278 p. front. 19 1/2 cm. 1942. Farrar & Rinehart, Inc.

--The Southpaw. Gould, Tod, illus. LC 31-29188. v, 272 p. front., pl. 21 cm. c.1931. Farrar & Rinehart, Incorporated.
--Team Play. LC 34-29550. 4 p. l., 3-308 p. front. 19 1/2 cm. c.1934. Farrar & Rinehart, Inc.
--Toss-up. LC 32-4343. v, 279 p. front. 21 cm. c.1932. Farrar & Rinehart, Incorporated.
--Triple Threat. LC 33-236757. 4 p. l., 3-278 p. front. 19 1/2 cm. c.1933. Farrar & Rinehart, Incorporated.

Haines, Francis
--Red Eagle and the Absaroka. Yost, Arthur Kenneth, illus. LC 60-5624. 191p. illus. 22cm. 1960. Caxton Printers.

Haines, Frank (0000-1963), adapted by see Mother Goose.

Haines, Frank, adapted by see Otto, Margaret Glover.

Haines, Jimmie (1940-)
--The Story of Billy Bug. Hobbs, Chris, illus. LC 40-7926. 62 p. incl. illus. (part col) col. pl. 26 1/2 x 21 cm. c.1939. American Features, Inc.

Haining, Peter (1940-), ed.
--The Clans of Darkness: Scottish Stories of Fantasy and Horror. N.D. (ISBN 0-8008-1621-8). Taplinger.
--Deadly Nightshade: Seventeen Strange Tales of the Dark. LC 77-92787. p. cm. 1978, c.1977. (ISBN 0-8008-2123-8). Taplinger Pub. Co.
--Gothic Tales of Terror: Classic Horror Stories From Great Britain and the United States. 1940. (ISBN 0-8008-3625-1). Taplinger.
--The Magic Valley Travellers: The Walsh Stories of Fantasy and Horror. 1940. (ISBN 0-8008-5047-5). Taplinger.
--Nightfrights: Occult Stories for All Ages. N.D. (ISBN 0-8008-5556-6). Taplinger.
--The Wild Night Company: Irish Stories of Fantasy and Horror. Bradbury, Ray Douglas (1920-), frwd. by. LC 70-147810. (gr. 8 up). N.D. (ISBN 0-8008-8335-7). Taplinger.

Hairston, Florence
--Nifty Nina, Ghetto Girl. 1979. (ISBN 0-533-03561-9). Vantage.

Hairston, William
--The World of Carlos. Ford, George Cephas, Jr., illus. (Illus.). 159 p. 21cm. 1968, c.1967. Putnam.

Haiz, Danah
--Jonah's Journey. Hechtkopf, Henry K. (1910-), illus. LC 72-268. (Illus.). 32 p. 31cm. 1973. (ISBN 0-8225-0362-X). Lerner Publications Co.

Hajj 'Abd al-Hayy al-Amin
--The Story of Noah. Sanders, Malika, illus. (Illus.). (Stories of the Prophets Ser.). 1980. (ISBN 0-935290-02-8). Iqra.

Hajnal, Gabriella
--The Prince & His Magic Horse. (Illus.). 110p. (gr. 3-7). N.D. Newbury Bks.

Hakansson, Gunvor
--Mr. Pomander. Runnstrom, Ake, illus. LC 60-14521. 84p. illus. 21cm. 1961, c.1960. Abelard-Schuman.
--The Pomanders of Little Chipping. Runnstrom, Ake, illus. Gombrich, Lisboth, tr. from Swedish. LC 63-703345. 92p. illus. 21cm. 1962. Abelard-Schuman.

Haker, Loren F.
--The Li'l Rascals: Tale of a Fish. Haker, Loren F., illus. (Illus.). 66p. (gr. 1-8). 1984. (ISBN 0-9609964-2-7). (ISBN 0-9609964-3-5). Haker Books.
--The Li'l Rascals: Timmy & the Bees. (Illus.). 56p. (gr. 1-8). 1984. (ISBN 0-9609964-0-0). (ISBN 0-9609964-1-9). Haker Books.

Hakes, Thomas L. & Thomas, Lynda K.
--A Little Poetry for Tiny People. 18p. 1984. (ISBN 0-915020-26-2). Bardic.

Hakluyt & Morley, Henry
--Voyager's Tales. N.D. Educational Publishing Company.

Halacy, Daniel Stephen, Jr. (1919-)
--Adventures of Ethan Strong. 1967. (ISBN 0-07-025542-3). (ISBN 0-07-025543-1). McGraw.
--Beyond Tomorrow. (Illus.). 1965. Macrae Smith Co.
--Copter Cowboy. LC 63-9449. 189 p. 21 cm. 1963. Chilton Books.
--Dive from the Sky. (gr. 7 up). 1967. (ISBN 0-07-025541-5). McGraw.
--Duster Pilot. 1st ed. LC 61-126912. 149p. 21cm. 1961. Chilton Co., Book Division.
--Ethan Strong: Strike and Fight Back. Guzzi, George, illus. (Illus.). 126 p. 22cm. 1968. McGraw-Hill.
--Ethan Strong: Watch by the Sea. Guzzi, George, illus. (gr. 5 up). 1969. (ISBN 0-07-025544-X). McGraw.
--High Challenge. LC 57-7886. 196 p. 21cm. 1957. Macmillan.
--High Challenge. LC 64-9551. 185 p. 20cm. (Acorn books, AB17). 1963, c.1957. Macmillan.
--Return from Luna. LC 69-12620. 181 p. 21cm. 1969. Norton.
--Robots Are Here. (gr. 5-8). N.D. (ISBN 0-448-02118-8). (ISBN 0-448-25914-1). G&D.
--The Robots are Here. 1965. Norton Company.
--Rocket Rescue. 191 p. 21cm. 1968. W. W. Norton.
--The Secret of the Cove. LC 74-86981. (Illus.). 155 p. 24cm. 1969. Lion Press.
--Sky on Free. LC 65-21464. 186 p. 21 cm. 1965. Macmillan.
--The Sky Trap. LC 75-12957. 124 p. 21cm. 1975. (ISBN 0-8407-6461-8). T. Nelson.
--Star for a Compass. LC 56-9360. 172 p. 21 cm. 1956. Macmillan.
--Surfer!. LC 65-11759. (Illus.). 217 p. 22cm. 1965. Macmillan.
--Whale Spotters. LC 58-6960. 202 p. 21 cm. 1958. Macmillan.

Halas, Frantisek, jt. auth. see Bradford, Barbara Taylor.

Halasz, Judit, tr. see Degh, Linda.

[illegible] ed. see [illegible] Stephen Townley.

Haldane, John Burdon Sanderson (1892-1964)
--My Friend Mr. Leakey. Rosoman, Leonard (1913-), illus. 1938. Harper & Bros.

Haldeman, Joe William (1943-)
--War Year. LC 77-182778. 122 p. 22cm. 1972. (ISBN 0-03-088595-7). (ISBN 0-03-088596-5). Holt, Rinehart and Winston.

Haldeman, Joe William (1943-), compiled by.
--Cosmic Laughter: Science Fiction for the Fun of It. LC 72-91652. 189 p. 22cm. 1974. (ISBN 0-03-006931-9). Holt, Rinehart and Winston.

Haldeman-Julius, Anna Marcet (1888-)
--Once Upon a Time: The Faerie Doings in Cedar Creek Valley. LC 17-1934. 122 p., 1 l., 26 cm. c.1916. Press of the Girard Job Shop.

Hale, Allean Lemmond (1914-)
--Remind Me to Live. 1960. Friendship Press.

Hale, Anne Gardner (1823-)
--The Closed Balcony. Hale, Lillian & Goss, John, illus. 5 p. l., 334 p. front., 9 pl. 19 1/2 cm. 1907. The C. M. Clark Publishing Co.
--Uncle Mark's Amaranths, 1 of 50 vols. (Illus.). 350p. (Sunday-School Lib: No. 14). N.D. Set. Lothrop Pub. Co.
--Uncle Mark's Amaranths, 1 of 4 vols. (The Amaranth Library). 1882. D Lothrop.

Hale, Arlene (1924-)
--Blossoms in the Wind. 1959. Holt, Rinehart and Winston.
--Ghost Town's Secret. LC 62-756412. 157p. illus. 21cm. 1962. Abelard-Schuman.
--The Impossible Love. 208p. (Orig.). (gr. 7 up). 1982. (ISBN 0-590-32360-1, Wildfire). Scholastic Inc.
--Lisa. 176p. (Orig.). (gr. 7 up). 1981. (ISBN 0-590-32001-7, Wildfire). Scholastic Inc.
--Listen to Your Heart. LC 62-10201. 190 p. 22cm. 1962. J. Messner.
--Nothing but a Stranger. 169 p. 23cm. 1966. Four Winds Press.

Hale, Beatrice (1883-)
--Little Allies: A Story of Four Children. Beard, Alice, illus. LC 18-17242. 6 p. l., 225 p. col. front., col. plates. 22 1/2 cm. c.1918. Frederick A. Stokes Company.

Hale, Dorelle Shivez
--Oney of Oregon. LC 54-12875. 122 p. 21cm. 1954. Pageant Press.

Hale, Edward Everett see Ingham, Col. Frederick, pseud.

Hale, Edward Everett (1822-1909), ed. see Arabian Nights.

Hale, Edward Everett, rev. by see Bulfinch, Thomas.

Hale, Edward Everett (1822-1900), ed. see Trimmer, Sarah Kirby, Mrs.

Hale, Edward Everett, ed. see Vernon, Thomas.

Hale, Edward Everett (1822-1909)
--Afloat and Ashore. LC 15-23108. 1 p. l., 5-31 p. 17 1/2 cm. (On cover: The young patriot series). 1891. Searle & Gorton.
--Boys' Heroes. (Illus.). N.D. Lothrop Publishing Co.
--Christmas in Narragansett: A Story. 293p. N.D. Funk & Wagnalls.
--Crusoe in New York and Other Tales. N.D. Messrs. Roberts Brothers.
--Four and Five: A Story of a Lend-a-Hand Club. LC 9-1852. 194 p. 17 1/2 cm. (His Ten times one series). 1891. Roberts Brothers.
--The Good Time Coming. 1875. Roberts Brothers.
--In His Name, 1 of 7 Vols, Vol. 1. 89p. (Tales For Travellers). N.D. Lockwood, Brooks & Co. for American Tract Society.
--In His Name. N.D. Roberts Brothers.
--The Lost Palace, and Other Stories, 1 of 7 Vols, Vol. 6. 88p. (Tales For Travellers). N.D. Lockwood, Brooks and Co. for American Tract Society.
--The Man Without a Country, 1 of 25 vols. (Illus.). (The Young of Heart Ser.: No. 9). N.D. Set. Dana Estes & Co.
--The Man Without a Country. (Illus.). (The Young Folks Lib.). N.D. H. M. Caldwell Co.
--The Man Without a Country. (Altemus' Wyncote Ser.). N.D. Henry Altemus Co.
--A Man Without a Country. N.D. Hurst & Co.
--The Man Without a Country. N.D. Little Brown & Co.
--The Man Without a Country. (gr. 7 up). N.D. Pyramid Pubns.
--The Man Without a Country. Bridgman, Lewis Jesse (1857-1931), illus. Tapper, Thomas, annotations by. (Cosy Corner Ser.). N.D. L. C. Page & Co.
--The Man Without a Country and Other Patriotic Stories. Foote, John McFarland (1883-), ed. Coleman, Ralph Pallen & Ferris, J. L. G., illus. LC 26-7840. xix, 266 p. incl. plates. col. front., col. plates. 21 cm. (The Winston clear-type popular classics). c.1925. The John C. Winston Company.
--The Man Without a Country & Other Stories. (Magnum Easy Eye Classic Ser). (gr. 8-10). N.D. [illegible]
--The Man Without Country. Fisher, Leonard Everett (1924-), illus. (Illus.). (Illustrated Editions). (gr. 7 up). 1960. (ISBN 0-531-01057-0). Watts.
--Mrs. Merriam's Scholars. A Story of the "Original Ten". LC 6-42374. v p., 1 l., 9-269 p. 18 cm. (His Ten times one series). 1904. Little, Brown, and Co.
--Mrs. Merriam's Scholars. A Story of the "Original Ten". LC 6-461866. v p., 1 l., 9-269 p. 17 cm. (Ten times one series). 1878. Roberts Brothers.
--Nicolette and Aucassin And Other Stories, 5 of 7, Vol. 5. 92p. (Tales For Travellers). N.D. Lockwood, Brooks & Co. for American Tract Society.
--Our New Crusade. 1875. Roberts Brothers.
--Spoons in a Wherry And Other Stories, 7 of 7, Vol.7. 96p. (Tales For Travellers). N.D. Lockwood, Brooks & Co. for American Tract Society.
--Stand and Wait and Other Stories, 3 of 7, Vol. 3. 74p. (Tales For Travellers: No. 3). N.D. Lockwood, Brooks & Co. for American Tract Society.
--A Tale of the Simplon, and Other Stories, 1 of 7 Vols, Vol. 4. 68p. (Tales For Travellers). N.D. Lockwood, Brooks & Co. for American Tract Society.
--Ten Times One Is Ten. Ingham, Col. Frederick, pseud, 1 of 7 Vols, Vol. 2. 68p. (Tales For Travellers). N.D. Lockwood, Brooks & Co. for American Tract Society.
--Ten Times One Is Ten: The Possible Reformation:. Ingham, Col. Frederick, pseud. vi p., 1 l., 9-148 p. 18 cm. 1871. Roberts Brothers.
--Ten Times One Is Ten: The Possible Reformation:. Ingham, Col. Frederick, pseud, Pt. 1-2. vi p., 2 l., 9-262 p. 17 1/2 cm. 1883. Roberts Brothers.
--Ten Times One Is Ten: The Possible Reformation:. Ingham, Col. Frederick, pseud, Pt. 1-2. LC 9-3030. 1 p. l., v-vi p., 2 l., 9-262 p. 17 1/2 cm. 1893. Roberts Brothers.

Hale, Edward Everett (1822-1909), intro. by.
--The Only True Mother Goose. (Illus.). Repr. of 1833 ed. 1905. Lee and Shepard Company.
--Stories of Adventure: Told by Adventurers. N.D. Messrs. Roberts Brothers.
--Stories of the Sea: Told by Sailors. N.D. Messrs. Roberts Brothers.
--Stories of War: Told by Sailors. N.D. Messrs. Roberts Brothers.

Hale, Edward Everett (1822-1909) & Hale, Susan (1833-1910)
--A Family Flight Around The Home. (The Family Flight Ser.). N.D. D. Lothrop Co.
--A Family Flight Over Egypt. (The Family Flight Ser.). N.D. D. Lothrop Co.
--A Family Flight Through France. (The Family Flight Ser.). N.D. D. Lothrop Co.
--A Family Flight Through Mexico. (The Family Flight Ser.). N.D. D. Lothrop Co.
--A Family Flight Through Spain. (The Family Flight Ser.). N.D. D. Lothrop Co.

Hale, Edward Everett (1822-1909) & Hawthorne, Nathaniel (1804-1864), eds.
--Greek Myths in English Dress. LC 2-7300. xii, 244 p. 17 1/2 cm. (Hawthorne classics). 1902. Globe School Book Co.

Hale, Edward Everett (1822-1909) & Hubbard, Elbert (1856-1915)
--Patriotic American Stories: Including The Man Without a Country. Foote, John McFarland (1883-), ed. Coleman, Ralph Pallen, et al., illus. LC 37-36394. xvi, 268 p. incl. plates. col. front., col. plates. 22 cm. c.1937. The John C. Winston Company.

Hale, Florence Maria, ed.
--Autumn Plays and Programs: A Collection of Entertainment Material for Classroom and Auditorium Use. LC 34-246386. 1 p. l., 7-81 p. illus. (incl. ports.) 27 1/2 cm. 1934. Educational Publishing Corporation.
--New Stories to Tell: More Story Telling Hour Stories for Primary Grades. LC 41-5696. 80 p. illus. 28 x 21 1/2 cm. 1941. Educational Publishing Corporation.
--Spring Plays and Programs: A Collection of Entertainment Material for Classroom and Auditorium Use. LC 34-41625. 80 p. illus. 27 1/2 cm. 1934. Educational Publishing Corporation.
--The Story Telling Hour: A Collection of One Hundred Fifty Short Stories for Primary Grades. LC 34-35837. 80 p. illus. 27 1/2 cm. 1934. Educational Publishing Corporation.

Hale, Gertrude Elisabeth
--Little Flower People. (Illus.). N.D. Ginn & Co.

Hale, Harry
--Jack Race, Air Scout: Or, Adventures in a War Aeroplane. (Illus.). (Jack Race Ser.). 1915. Harper & Brothers Trade-List.
--Jack Race at Boarding-School: Or, The Leader of Merrivale Academy. (Illus.). (Jack Race Ser.). 1915. Harper & Brothers Trade List.
--Jack Race on the Ranch: Or, The Triumphs of a Tenderfoot. (Illus.). (Jack Race Ser.). 1915. Harper & Brothers Trade-List.
--Jack Race, Speed King: Or, A Trip Across the Continent. (Illus.). (Jack Race Ser.). 1915. Harper & Brothers Trade-List.
--Jack Race's Baseball Nine: Or, Winning the Junior League Pennant. (Illus.). (Jack Race Ser.). 1915. Harper & Brothers Trade-List.

Hale, Irina (1932-)
Brown Bear in a Brown Chair. Hale, Irina (1932-), illus. LC 82-16244. p. cm. 1983. (ISBN 0-689-50267-2). Atheneum.
--Chocolate Mouse & Sugar Pig and How They Ran Away to Escape Being Eaten. LC 78-6132. (Illus.). 32p. (ps-4). 1979. (ISBN 0-689-50113-7, McElderry Bk). Atheneum.
--Donkey's Dreadful Day. Hale, Irina (1932-), illus. LC 81-10773. (Illus.). 32. 1982. Atheneum.

Hale, Janet Campbell (1947-)
--The Owl's Song. LC 73-11700. 160 p. 22cm. 1974. (ISBN 0-385-01944-0). (ISBN 0-385-01944-0). Doubleday.

Hale, Jeanne & Beust, Nora Ernestine (1888-), eds.
--Through Golden Windows. LC 58-5038. 10v. illus. 24cm. c.1958. E. M. Hale.

Hale, Jeanne & Leary, Bernice E., eds.
--Mostly Magic. N.D. E. M. Hale and Co.
--Wonderful Things Happen. N.D. E. M. Hale and Co.

Hale, Kathleen (1898-)
--Henrietta the Faithful Hen. 1967. (ISBN 0-04-823073-1). Allen Unwin.
--Henrietta, the Faithful Hen. Hale, Kathleen (1898-), illus. LC 51-11108. 24 x 32 cm. 32p. 1953. Coward-McCann, Inc.
--Henrietta's Magic Egg. 1973. (ISBN 0-04-823107-X). Allen Unwin.
--Manda. Hale, Kathleen (1898-), illus. LC 52-13314. (Illus.). 29 p. 26cm. 1953. Coward-McCann.
--Orlando Buys a Farm. Hale, Kathleen (1898-), illus. (Orlando Series). N.D. Transatlantic Arts.
--Orlando Goes to the Moon. Hale, Kathleen (1898-), illus. (Illus.). color ils. (gr. 1-4). 1969. (ISBN 0-7195-1818-0). Transatlantic.
--Orlando, His Silver Wedding. Hale, Kathleen (1898-), illus. (Orlando Series). N.D. Transatlantic Arts.
--Orlando Keeps A Dog. Hale, Kathleen (1898-), illus. (Orlando Series). N.D. Transatlantic Arts.
--Orlando, The Frisky Housewife. Hale, Kathleen (1898-), illus. (Orlando Series). N.D. Transatlantic Arts.
--Orlando, the Judge. (Illus.). (gr. 1-4). N.D. Transatlantic.
--Orlando, the Marmalade Cat: A Camping Holiday. Hale, Kathleen (1898-), illus. 1938. Scribner.
--Orlando the Marmalade Cat & the Water Cats. Hale, Kathleen (1898-), illus. LC 72-185736. (Illus.). 32p. 1st U.S. edition. (gr. k-3). 1979. (ISBN 0-224-00662-2, Pub. by Chatto Bodley Jonathan). Merrimack Pub Cir.
--Orlando the Marmalade Cat Buys a Farm. LC 48-7072. 32 p. col. illus. 37 cm. 1947 (Transatlantic Arts). Country Life.
--Orlando the Marmalade Cat Buys a Farm. Hale, Kathleen (1898-), illus. LC 45-1435. 32p. col. ill. 37cm. 1944 (Country Life). Transatlantic Arts.
--Orlando's Camping Holiday. Hale, Kathleen (1898-), illus. (Orlando Series). N.D. Transatlantic Arts.
--Orlando's Evening Out. (Illus.). (gr. 1-4). N.D. Transatlantic.
--Orlando's Home Life. Hale, Kathleen (1898-), illus. LC 51-11109. (Illus.). 29p. (A Harlequin Picture Bk.). 1951. Coward-McCann, Inc.
--Orlando's Home Life. Hale, Kathleen (1898-), illus. LC 43-6289. (Illus.). 30p. 18 x 22cm. (Puffin Picture Bks.). 1942. Penguin Books Limited.
--Orlando's Magic Carpet. (Illus.). (gr. 1-4). 1960. Transatlantic.
--Orlando's Seaside Holiday. (Illus.). N.D. Transatlantic Arts, Inc.

--Orlando's Trip Abroad. Hale, Kathleen (1898-), illus. (Orlando Series). N.D. Transatlantic Arts.

Hale, Linda Howe (1929-)

--The Glorious Christmas Soup Party. Hale, Linda Howe (1929-), illus. LC 62-15442. 40p. 1962. Viking Press.

Hale, Lucretia Peabody (1820-1900)

--The Complete Peterkin Papers. LC 60-9095. (Illus.). 302 p. 25cm. 1960. Houghton Mifflin.

--The Last of the Peterkins, with Others of Their Kin. 263p. N.D. Little,Brown & Co.

--The Last of the Peterkins, with Others of Their Kin. LC 12-32903. 4 p. l., 7-263 p. front., plates. 17 1/2 cm. 1886. Roberts Brothers.

--The Last of the Peterkins, with Others of Their Kin, and The Queen of the Red Chessmen. LC 65-24024. 167p. illus. 22cm. (T1468). 1965. Dover.

--The Peterkin Papers. LC 59-4351. 248p. illus. 20cm. (Looking glass library. 6). 1959. Looking Glass Library; Distributed by Random House.

--The Peterkin Papers. 1880. Osgood.

--The Peterkin Papers. 1960. Sharon.

--The Peterkin Papers. Brett, Harold Matthews (1880-), illus. LC 24-23175. 219 p. col. front., illus., col. plates. 22 cm. (Riverside bookshelf). 1924. Houghton Mifflin Company.

--The Peterkin Papers. Brett, Harold Matthews (1880-), illus. LC 64-15709. 210 p. 21cm. (Classics to grow on). 1966, c.1964. Parents' Magazine's Cultural Institute.

--The Peterkin Papers. Brett, Harold Matthews (1880-), illus. LC 13-338607. 2 p. l., 9-219 p. front., illus. 22 cm. 1887. Ticknor and Company.

--The Peterkin Papers. Keats, Ezra Jack (1916-1983), illus. LC 55-36727. 192p. illus. 22cm. 1955. Junior Deluxe Editions.

--The Peterkin Papers. Keats, Ezra Jack (1916-1983), illus. LC 66-8991. (Illus.). 219 p. 22cm. (Legacy library facsimile). 1966. Mich University Microfilms.

--The Queen of the Red Chessman. N.D. Happy Hour Library.

--Stories for Children, Containing Simple Lessons in Morals. 1892. Leach, Shewell and Sanborn.

--Stories from the Peterkin Papers. Weil, Lisl (1910-), illus. (Illus.). (gr. 4-6). 1972 (Starline). Schol Bk Serv.

Hale, Lucretia Peabody (1820-1900) & Whitman, Bernard, Mrs.

--Sunday School Stories. LC 44-27299. 18cm. 219p. 1889. Roberts Brothers.

--Sunday-School Stories for Little Children. N.D. Robert Brothers.

Hale, M. P.

--Amy & the Birds, and Other Stories. (Illus.). N.D. Methodist Bk Concern.

--An Orphan's Story: Or, Sketches of Some Friends Whom I Have Known. (Illus.). 242p. N.D. Methodist Bk Concern.

--Summer at Walnut Ridge, 1 of 25 vols. (Illus.). (Selected Bks for Sunday School: No. 21). N.D. Set. Methodist Bk Concern.

Hale, Nancy (1908-)

--The Night of the Hurricane. LC 77-15454. (gr. 6-10). 1978. (ISBN 0-698-20437-9, Coward). Putnam Pub Group.

Hale, Robert Beverly (1901-)

--Snowland. Ross, Larry (1943-), illus. LC 72-129270. (Illus.). 174 p. 24cm. 1971. Doubleday.

Hale, Sarah J., Mrs., selected by see Taylor, Jane.

Hale, Sarah Josepha Buell, Mrs. (1788-1879), ed. see Aikin, John.

Hale, Sarah Josepha Buell, Mrs. (1788-1879), ed. see Barbauld, Anna Letitia Aikin, Mrs.

Hale, Sarah Josepha Buell, Mrs. (1788-1879), ed. see Schmid, Christoph Von.

Hale, Sarah Josepha Buell, Mrs. (1788-1879)

--Aunt Mary's New Stories for Young People. LC 1-937. iv p., 1 l., 125 p. front. 16 cm. 1849. J. Munroe & Company.

--Mary Had a Little Lamb. De Paola, Tomie, pseud. (1934-), illus. De Paola, Thomas Anthony. LC 83-22369. (Illus.). 32p. (ps-3). 1984. (ISBN 0-8234-0509-5). (ISBN 0-8234-0519-2). Holiday. **Award: (ALA).**

Hale, Sarah Josepha Buell, Mrs. (1788-1879), ed.

--My Little Song Book: Adapted to Children and Youth. LC 28-9657. vii, 9-71 p. 15 cm. 1841. J. B. Dow.

--The School Song Book. Adapted to the Scenes of the School Room; Written for American Children and Youth. LC 26-17358. vii, 9-71 p. 15 1/2 cm. 1834. Allen & Ticknor.

Hale, Susan, jt. auth. see Hale, Edward Everett.

Hale, Susan (1833-1910)

--Inklings for Thinklings. LC 19-16028. 69 l. illus. 24 cm. 1919. Marshall Jones Company.

Hale, Thomas, jt. auth. see Westbrook, Bill.

Hales, A. G.

--A Fight for a Friend. (Illus.). N.D. Cassell & Co.

--Telegraph Dick. (Illus.). N.D. Cassell & Co.

Halewood, Constance

--The Dear Old Nursery Rhymes. N.D. Frederick Warne & Co.

Haley, Gail Einhart (1939-)

--The Abominable Swamp Man. 1st ed. Haley, Gail Einhart (1939-), illus. LC 75-6580. (Illus.). 48 p. 1975. (ISBN 0-670-10042-0). Viking Press.

--Birdsong. Haley, Gail Einhart (1939-), illus. LC 83-14372. 32p. (gr. k-3). 1984. (ISBN 0-517-55051-2). Crown.

--Go Away, Stay Away!. Haley, Gail Einhart (1939-), illus. LC 77-6759. (Illus.). 32 p. 1977. (ISBN 0-684-15272-X). Scribner.

--The Green Man. Haley, Gail Einhart (1939-), illus. LC 79-20490. (Illus.). 32 p. 1980, c.1979. (ISBN 0-684-16338-1). Scribner.

--Jack Jouett's Ride. (Illus., Pub. by Viking Pr). (Viking Seafarer Ser.). (gr. 1-4). 1976. (ISBN 0-670-05102-0, Puffin). Penguin.

--Jack Jouett's Ride. Haley, Gail Einhart (1939-), illus. (Illus.). 32p. (gr. k-3). 1973. (ISBN 0-670-40466-7). Viking Pr.

--My Kingdom for a Dragon. Haley, Gail Einhart (1939-), illus. LC 63-213. unpaged. illus. (part col.) 23 cm. 1962. Crozet Print Shop.

--Noah's Ark. Haley, Gail Einhart (1939-), illus. LC 75-134810. (Illus.). 30 p. 27cm. 1971. Atheneum.

--One, Two, Buckle My Shoe. Haley, Gail Einhart (1939-), illus. LC 64-14943. 63 col. illus. 29. (gr. k-3). 1964. Doubleday.

--The Post Office Cat. Haley, Gail Einhart (1939-), illus. LC 77-351233. (Illus.). 32 p. 1976. (ISBN 0-370-10758-6). Bodley Head. **Award: (KGM).**

--The Post Office Cat. Haley, Gail Einhart (1939-), illus. LC 76-8377. (Illus.). 30 p. c.1976. (ISBN 0-684-14653-3). Scribner.

--Round Stories about Our World. Haley, Gail Einhart (1939-), illus. 1966. Follet.

--Round Stories about Things that Grow. Haley, Gail Einhart (1939-), illus. 1966. Follet.

--Round Stories about Things That Live on Land and in Water, 2 Vols. Haley, Gail Einhart (1939-), illus. 1966. Follet.

--A Story, a Story: An African Tale Retold. Haley, Gail Einhart (1939-), illus. LC 69-18961. (Illus.). 4 color woodcuts. 36p. (gr. k-3). 1970. (ISBN 0-689-20511-2). Atheneum. **Awards: (RCM); (BGH).**

--A Story, a Story: An African Tale Retold. Haley, Gail Einhart (1939-), illus. 1976. (ISBN 0-689-70423-2, Aladdin). Atheneum.

--The Wonderful Magical World of Marguerite. Haley, Gail Einhart (1939-), illus. 1964. McGraw Hill.

Haley, Mary M.

--A Dornfield Summer. 302p. N.D. Little, Brown.

Haley, Patrick

--Wildflower & the Big Voice in the Sky. Kool, Jonna, illus. LC 82-82990. (Illus.). 44p. (gr. 3-4). 1982. (ISBN 0-9605738-1-X). East Eagle.

Halfyard, Lynda, jt. auth. see Rose, Karen.

Hal Hahn, Ida Marie Louise Sophie Friederike Gustava (1805-1880)

--Endoxia: A Picture of the Fifth Century. LC 6-46159. iv, 5-237 p. 19 1/2 cm. 1869. Lelly, Piet & Co.

Haliburton, Thomas Chandler

--The Clockmaker: The Sayings and Doings of Samuel Slick of Slickville. Darley, Felix Octavius Carr (1822-1888), illus. N.D. Hurd & Houghton.

Halick, Irene

--A Blackberry Named Patty. 1977. (ISBN 0-917726-12-X). Hunter Bks.

Halkett, Sarah Phelps Stokes & Pyle, Katharine

--The Elf King's Flowers. 79p. N.D. E P Dutton.

Halkin, Hillel, tr. see Orlev, Uri.

Hall, A. Oakey

--Old Whitey's Christmas Trot. (Illus.). 1882. Harper's Trade-List.

Hall, A. W., Mrs., ed.

--Icelandic Fairy Tales. Hall, A. W., Mrs., tr. (The Fairy Library). N.D. A. L. Burt Co.

--Icelandic Fairy Tales. Hall, A. W., Mrs., et al., trs. N.D. Frederick Warne & Co.

Hall, Adele (1910-)

--Beauty Queen. LC 57-11278. 189p. 22cm. 1957. J. Messner.

--Seashore Summer. LC 62-7310. 197p. 22cm. 1962. Harper.

Hall, Albert Neely (1883-)

--The Wonder Hill: Or, The Marvelous Rescue of Prince Lota. Hall, Norman P., illus. LC 14-29777. 271 p. col. front., illus., col. plates. 23 1/2 cm. c.1914. Rand, McNally & Company.

Hall, Alberta, jt. auth. see Baum, Lyman Frank.

Hall, Alice

--The Cat, the Dog, and the Dormouse. N.D. Barse & Co.

Hall, Amanda, adapted by.

--The Gossipy Wife. LC 83-15797. (Adapted from a Russian Folk Tale). 1984. (ISBN 0-911745-19-X). Blackie.

--The Gossipy Wife: Adapted from a Russian Folktale. (Illus.). 1984. Harper.

Hall, Andrew, pseud., see Hall, Anne.

Hall, Andrew

--Frost. 1967. G P Putman's Sons.

Hall, Andrew see Hall, Anne.

Hall, Anna Gertrude (1882-1967)

--Cyrus Holt and the Civil War. Morse, Dorothy Bayley (1906-1979), illus. LC 64-12644. 128 p. illus., music. 22 cm. 1964. Viking Press.

--Nansen. Artzybasheff, Boris Mikhailovich (1899-1965), illus. 176p. 1940. Viking Press. **Award: (JNM).**

Hall, Anna Maria (1800-1881)

--Annie Price: Or, Grandmamma's Sunshine, 1 of 103 vols. (The Pearl Library: No. 4). 1900. Hurst & Co.

--Cosmo's Visit to His Grandfather, 1 of 103 vols. (The Pearl Library: No. 15). 1900. Set. Hurst & Co.

--Dolly's Christmas Chickens, 1 of 103 vols. (The Pearl Library: No. 19). 1900. Set. Hurst & Co.

--Faithful Rover, 1 of 103 vols. (The Pearl Library: No. 22). 1900. Set. Hurst & Co.

--Fun & Work, 1 of 103 vols. (The Pearl Library: No. 28). 1900. Set. Hurst & Co.

--Happy Charlie, 1 of 103 vols. (The Pearl Library: No. 31). 1900. Set. Hurst & Co.

--Harry & His Pony, 1 of 103 vols. (The Pearl Library: No. 32). 1900. Set. Hurst & Co.

--Kitty's Victory, 1 of 103 vols. (The Pearl Library: No. 51). 1900. Set. Hurst & Co.

--Lost Spectacles, 1 of 103 vols. (The Pearl Library: No. 57). 1900. Set. Hurst & Co.

--Maggie & the Sparrows, 1 of 103 vols. (The Pearl Library: No. 59). 1900. Set. Hurst & Co.

--What Elsie Loved Best: Or, The Pet Rabbits, 1 of 103 vols. (The Pearl Library: No. 101). 1900. Set. Hurst & Co.

Hall, Anne see Hall, Andrew, pseud.

Hall, Anne

--Peeps Elliott & Family. Hall, Andrew, pseud. LC 50-6977. 248 p. 21 cm. 1950. Dodd, Mead.

Hall, Arlene Stevens, ed. see Egermeier, Elsie Emilie.

Hall, Arlene Stevens (1923-)

--Bible Story ABC Book. N.D. Warner Press.

Hall, Arthur Vine

--Poems of a South African: The Collected Verse of Arthur Vine Hall. LC 26-17818. xii, 267, 2 p. 19 1/2 cm. $3.0. 1926. Longmans, Green and Co., Ltd.

Hall, Avery (1936-)

--Twice Upon A Time. Korty-Lucas Films, illus. (Illus.). 48p. (gr. k up). 1982. (ISBN 0-671-46005-6). Messner.

Hall, Avery (1936-) & Korty, John Van Cleave

--Twice Upon a Time. (Illus.). 48p. 1983. (ISBN 0-671-45633-4, Little Simon). S&S.

Hall, Aylmer, pseud., see Hall, Norah E. L..

Hall, Aylmer, pseud. (1914-)

--Beware of Moonlight. Hall, Norah E. L.. LC 70-119357. 224 p. 21cm. 1970. T. Nelson.

--Colonel Bull's Inheritance. Hall, Norah E. L.. LC 69-19051. 250 p. 21cm. 1969, c.1968. Meredith Press.

--The Search for Lancelot's Sword. Hall, Norah E. L.. 1962. JUV. Criterion Books.

Hall, Bertha M

--The Happy-Thought Story Book. Young, Florence Liley, illus. LC 26-8191. 199 p. col. front., col. plates. 19 cm. c.1926. Lothrop, Lee & Shepard Co.

Hall, Bertha Parker

--Ducky Daddles and the Three Bears. LC 21-190758. 56 p., 1 l. incl. front., illus. 18 x 27 1/2 cm. 1921. E. P. Dutton & Company.

--Ducky Daddle's Party. LC 51-54227. 52 p. illus. 19 x 26 cm. 1918. Dutton.

--Henny and Penny. Farrell, Clements, illus. LC 22-21322. ix p., 1 l., 172 p. incl. front., illus., plates. 19 1/2 cm. c.1922. E. P. Dutton & Company.

Hall, Bill

--Fish Tale. Johnson, John Emil (1929-), illus. LC 67-1325. 1 v. (unpaged) col. illus. 25 cm. 1967. Norton.

--Whatever Happens to Baby Animals. Parsons, Virginia, illus. (Illus.). 64p. Repr. (gr. k-2). 1973. (ISBN 0-307-68001-0, Golden Pr). Western Pub.

--Whatever Happens to Baby Horses?. Parsons, Virginia, illus. LC 66-4011. 1 v. (unpaged) col. illus. 33 cm. 1965. Golden Press.

--Whatever Happens to Bear Cubs?. Parsons, Virginia, illus. (Illus.). 26 p. 33cm. (Big golden book). 1968. Golden Press.

--Whatever Happens to Kittens?. Parsons, Virginia, illus. LC 67-6919. (Illus.). 1 v. (unpaged. 33cm. (Big golden book). 1967. Golden Press.

--Whatever Happens to Puppies?. Parsons, Virginia, illus. (Illus.). 26 p. 33cm. (Big golden book). 1966, c.1965. Golden Press.

Hall, Bolton (1854-1938)

--Monkey Shines. Huntington, intro. by. Jones, Leon Foster, illus. N.D. Public Publishing Co.

--Monkey Shines: Little Stories for Little Children. Huntington, ed. Jones, Leon Foster, illus. LC 4-34503. N.D. Wessels & Bissell.

Hall, Brian Patrick (1935-)

--The Wizard of Maldoone. Waldman, Bryna, illus. LC 75-34844. (Illus.). 143 p. 23cm. c.1975. (ISBN 0-8091-0203-X). (ISBN 0-8091-1922-6). Paulist Press.

Hall, Brian Patrick (1935-) & Osburn, Joseph

--Nog's Vision. Griffin, Donna, illus. LC 73-85136. (Illus.). 140 p. 23cm. 1973. (ISBN 0-8091-0187-4). (ISBN 0-8091-1795-9). Paulist Press.

Hall, Carol, jt. auth. see Calloway, Northern J.

Hall, Caroline Davis, Mrs.

--The Dandelion Clock. LC 42-13426. 29 x 22 cm. 28p. 1942. Joan Comins.

Hall, Caryl, pseud., see Hansen, Caryl Hall.

Hall, Caryl, pseud. (1929-)

--Gold on Her Shoulder. Hansen, Caryl Hall. (gr. 7-11). 1964. (ISBN 0-308-80104-0). Funk & W.

--The Prettiest Politician. Hansen, Caryl Hall. LC 68-27997. 192 p. 22cm. 1968. Funk & Wagnalls.

Hall, Charles, Mrs.

--Kattie Summers: A Little Tale for Little Readers. N.D. Thomas Nelson and Sons.

Hall, Charles W.

--Adrift in the Ice-Fields, 1 of 3 vols. (Author of "Drifting Round the World."). (Illus.). (The Ice-Bound Ser.). 1882. Lee & Shepard.

--Adrift in the Ice Fields, 1 of 60 vols. (American Boys' Ser.: No. 1). 1900. Set. Lee & Shepard.

--Drifting Around the World: A Boy's Adventure by Sea and Land. (Author of "Adrift in the Ice-Fields" and "The Great Bonanza."). (Illus.). 1882. Lee & Shepard.

--Twice Taken: A Tale of Louisburg, 1 of 50 vols. (Illus.). (The Norwood Ser.: No. 16). 1900. Lee & Shepard.

Hall, Conrad

--Story of a Little Colored Coon. (Illus.). (The Little Ones' Library Ser.). N.D. Frederick A. Stokes Co.

Hall, Donald Andrew, Jr. (1928-)

--Andrew the Lion Farmer. 1959. (ISBN 0-8382-0040-0, Cadmus Books). E. M. Hale and Company.

--Andrew the Lion Farmer. Miller, Jane Judith (1925-), illus. LC 59-12551. unpaged. illus. 23x27cm. 1959. F. Watts.

--The Man Who Lived Alone. Azarian, Mary, illus. LC 84-47655. (Illus.). 36 p. 25cm. 1984. (ISBN 0-87923-538-1). D.R. Godine.

--Ox-Cart Man. Cooney, Barbara (1917-), illus. LC 83-8008. p. cm. 1983, c.1979. (ISBN 0-14-050441-9). Puffin Books.

--Ox-Cart Man. Cooney, Barbara (1917-), illus. LC 79-14466. (Illus.). 40 p. 1979. (ISBN 0-670-53328-9). Viking Press. **Awards: (RCM); (NYT); (ALA).**

--Riddle Rat. Gerberg, Mort, illus. LC 76-45306. (Illus.). 57 p. 25cm. c.1977. (ISBN 0-7232-6138-5). F. Warne.

Hall, Donald Andrew, Jr. (1928-), ed.

--Man & Boy: An Anthology. (Illus.). 224p. (gr. 9 up). 1968. (ISBN 0-531-01721-4). Watts.

--The Oxford Book of Children's Verse in America. LC 84-20755. xxxviii, 319 p. 23cm. 1985. (ISBN 0-19-503539-9). Oxford University Press.

--Poetry Sampler. (gr. 7 up). 1962. (ISBN 0-531-01725-7). Watts.

--Poetry Sampler. (Keith Jennison Large Type Bks). (gr. 6 up). N.D. (ISBN 0-531-00264-0). Watts.

Hall, Edith King

--Adventures in Toyland. (The Rugby Series for Boys and Girls). N.D. A. L. Burt Company.

--Adventures in Toyland. (Illus.). (The Little Women Ser.). N.D. A. L. Burt's Pubs.

--Adventures in Toyland. (Illus.). (Scribner-Blackie Series of Books for Young People). N.D. Charles Scribner's Sons.

--Adventures in Toyland. (Illus.). 164p. N.D. Hurst & Co.

--Adventures in Toyland: What the Marionette Told Molly. LC 5968. xii, 13-177 p. incl. front., illus. 17 cm. (Altemus' Young People's Library). (No. 35). c.1900. Henry Altemus Company.

Hall, Edna Anne

--Adventure at Table Mountain. LC 56-10490. 188p. illus. 22cm. 1956. Ariel Books.

Hall, Eliza Calvert

--Aunt Jane of Kentucky. N.D. Little, Brown & Co.

Hall, Elizabeth (1929-)

--Phoebe Snow. Holmes, Bea, illus. LC 68-29899. (Illus.). 140 p. 22cm. 1968. Houghton Mifflin.

--Stand up, Lucy. Krush, Beth (1918-) & Krush, Joe (1918-), illus. LC 73-142823. (Illus.). 188 p. 22cm. 1971. (ISBN 0-395-12365-8). Houghton Mifflin.

Hall, Elvajean (1910-), ed. see Pumphrey, Margaret Blanche.

Hall, Elvajean (1910-)

--Pilgrim Neighbors. 1964. E M Hale.

--Pilgrim Neighbors: More True Pilgrim Stories. Nielsen, Jon (1912-), illus. LC 64-16833. (Illus.). 175 p. 21cm. 1964. Rand McNally.

AUTHOR INDEX HALL, MARJORY

Hall, Elvajean (1910-), ed.
--Pilgrim Stories: From Margaret Pumphrey's Pilgrim Stories. Rev ed. Nielsen, Jon (1912-), illus. 176p. illus 21cm. (Merit bks.). 1968, c.1962. Houghton.
--Pilgrim Stories: From Margaret Pumphrey's Pilgrim Stories. Rev ed. Nielsen, Jon (1912-), illus. LC 62-804661. 176p. c.1962. Rand McNally.
Hall, Emily Catherine Dunham, Mrs. (1883-)
--Random Scenes for Nancy. LC 38-18530. 76 p. front. 19 1/2 cm. 1938. Meador Publishing Company.
Hall, Esther Greenacre
--Back to Buckeye. N.D. Random House.
--Back to Buckeye. Townsend, Lee (1895-), illus. LC 24-36561. 317 p. incl. 1 illus., plates. 19 1/2 cm. 1934. H. Smith & R. Haas.
--College on Horseback. Brown, Paul (1893-1958), illus. LC 33-24067. 319 p. front., plates. 19 1/2 cm. 1933. H. Smith & R. Haas.
--College on Horseback. Brown, Paul (1893-1958), illus. N.D. Random House.
--Haverhill Herald. De Aragon, J. M., illus. LC 38-31062. 286 p. incl. front., plates. 21 cm. c.1938. Random House.
--The Here-to-Yonder Girl. Bonte, Willard, illus. LC 32-463833. 5 p. l., 3-285 p. incl. plates front. 20 cm. 1932. The Macmillan Company.
--Mario and the Chuna: A Boy and a Bird of the Argentine. De Aragon, J. M., illus. LC 40-27606. 4 p. l., 3-61 p. col. illus. 24 1/2 cm. c.1940. Random House.
--Sharon's Career. Suba, Susanne (1913-), illus. LC 42-18667. 5 p. l., 267 p. illus. 21 cm. 1942. Random House.
--Up Creek and Down Creek. Braune, Anna Parker, illus. LC 36-29801. 236 p. front., plates. 20 cm. c.1936. Random House.
Hall, Felicia M., tr. see Kurtycz, Marcos & Garcia Kobeh, Ana.
Hall, Fergus
--Groundsel. (Illus.). 32p. (ps-4). 1983. (ISBN 0-224-01938-4, Pub by Jonathan Cape). Merrimack Pub Cir.
Hall, Florence Marion
--Flossy's Play-Days. LC 6-23160. 4 p. l., 11-238 p. front., 7 pl. 19 cm. c.1906. D. Estes & Company.
Hall, Frederic Aldin (1854-)
--Homeric Stories for Young Readers. LC 3-28840. 200 p. incl.front., illus. 19 cm. (Electric school readings). 1903. American Book Company.
Hall, Frederick Fairchild (1873-)
--Toggles: An Outdoor Boy. Copeland, Charles, illus. LC 18-20472. 256 p. front., plates. 20 1/2 cm. 1918. Lothrop, Lee & Shepard Co.
Hall, Gertrude Calvert
--The Nowadays Girls in the Adirondacks: Or, The Deserted Bungalow on Saranac Lake. Caswell, Edward C., illus. LC 15-18722. vi p., 2 l., 302 p. front., plates. 19 1/2 cm. $1.0. c.1915. Dodd, Mead & Company.
Hall, Gordon Langley, pseud., see Simmons, Dawn Langley.
Hall, Gordon Langley, pseud.
--Peter Jumping Horse at the Stampede. Simmons, Dawn Langley. Kent, Jennifer, illus. LC 62-16307. (Illus.). 141p. (gr. 4-6). 1962. (ISBN 0-03-035385-8). (ISBN 0-03-035530-3). HR&W.
Hall-Guest, Olga & Sando, Anne
--Fuzzy Wuzzy: Or, The Story of a Pet Raccoon. N.D. Bobbs-Merrill Co.
Hall, H. Tom
--The Golden Tombo. Hall, H. Tom, illus. LC 59-5216. (Illus.). unpaged. 28cm. 1959. Knopf.
Hall, Harriet S.
--The Bella and Her Crew. (Illus.). N.D. E & J B Young.
Hall, Henry Rushton
--Days Before History. (Illus.). (The Sunshine Library for Young People). N.D. Thomas Y. Crowell.
Hall, Howard B
--Evenings at Shadycroft. LC 12-32906. 168 p. front., illus. 20 cm. c.1897. American Baptist Publication Society.
Hall, Isaac Freeman, jt. ed. see Kent, Roland Grubb.
Hall, J.
--Buried Cities. 1964. MacMillan Co.
Hall, James A. (1936-)
--Aesop's Fables. Bradbury, Christopher, illus. LC 71-190282. (Illus.). 47 p. 30cm. 1972. CBS Records.
Hall, James Norman see Gravel, Fern, pseud.
Hall, James Norman, jt. auth. see Nordhoff, Charles Bernard.
Hall, James Norman (1887-1951)
--High Adventure. (Riverside Library). N.D. Houghton Mifflin Co.
--Mother Goose Land. Bacharach, Herman Ilfeld (1899-), illus. LC 30-24317. 4 p. l., 97 p. illus. 21 1/2 cm. 1930. Houghton Mifflin Company.
--The Tale of a Shipwreck. (Riverside Library). N.D. Houghton Mifflin Co.
Hall, James Phillip, jt. ed. see Brady, John Joseph.
Hall, Jarvis
--Across the Mesa. (The Outdoor Bks.). N.D. Penn.
--Through Mocking Bird Camp. (The Outdoor Bks.). N.D. Penn.
Hall, Jennie, jt. auth. see Gordon, Eva Lucretia.
Hall, Jennie (1875-1921)
--Four Old Greeks: Achilles, Herakles, Dionysos Alkestis. LC 3-17527. 224 p. incl. front., illus. 18 cm. c.1901. Rand, McNally & Co.
--Four Old Greeks: Achilles, Herakles, Dionysos, Alkestis. Perry, Raymond, illus. LC 32-7115. 228 p. incl. front., illus. 18 cm. c.1933. Rand, McNally & Company.
--Viking Tales. Lambdin, Victor R., illus. LC 2-20986. 207 p. incl. front. (map) illus. 18 cm. 1902. Rand, McNally & Co.
Hall, Jessie Helen Sims, Mrs., jt. auth. see Hall, William Franklin.
Hall, John
--Foundation Stones, for Young Builders. N.D. American Sunday-School Union.
Hall, John Leander (1875-)
--Country Tales for City Boys. 1 p. l., 5-109 p. front. (port.) col. pl. 24 cm. c.1935. J. L. Hall.
Hall, Katharine Hedges, jt. auth. see Barrows, Sarah Tracy.
Hall, Katy
Nothing but Soup. Taylor, Doug, illus. LC 77-359042. (Illus.). 32 p. 23cm. c.1976. (ISBN 0-695-80670-X). (ISBN 0-695-40670-1). Follett.
Hall, Katy & Eisenberg, Lisa (1949-)
--Fishy Riddles. (Illus.). 48p. (Dial Book for Young Readers Ser.). (ps-3). 1983. (ISBN 0-8037-2419-5). (ISBN 0-8037-2431-4). Dutton.
--Fishy Riddles. Taback, Simms, illus. 1983. Dial.
--A Gallery of Monsters. Mathieu, Joseph (1945-), illus. (Illus.). 64p. (gr. 2-5). 1981. (ISBN 0-394-84743-1). Random.
Hall, Kenneth Franklin (1926-)
--On the Trail of a Twin. Case, Bernard, illus. LC 66-11134. 127p. illus. 21cm. c.1966. Friendship.
Hall, Lynn (1937-)
--Barry: The Bravest Saint Bernard. Cohen, Gil, illus. LC 73-7557. (Illus.). 48p. (Famous Animal Stories Ser.). (gr. 2-5). 1973. (ISBN 0-8116-4852-4). Garrard.
--Bob: Watchdog of the River. Oughton, Taylor (1925-), illus. LC 73-13573. (Illus.). 45 p. 23cm. (Famous animal stories). 1974. (ISBN 0-8116-4853-2). Garrard Pub. Co.
--The Boy in the Off-White Hat. LC 84-13982. 112p. (gr. 5-7). 1984. (ISBN 0-684-18224-6, ScribJ). Scribner.
--Danza!. LC 81-8992. p. cm. 1981. (ISBN 0-684-17158-9). Scribner.
Denison's Daughter. LC 83-11521. 115 p. 22cm. c.1983. (ISBN 0-684-17955-5). Scribner's.
--The Disappearing Grandad. Jefferson, William H., illus. LC 80-18805. c.1981. (ISBN 0-695-41467-4). Follett Pub. Co.
--Dog of the Bondi Castle. LC 78-21646. 124 p. 23cm. c.1979. (ISBN 0-695-81255-6). (ISBN 0-695-41255-8). Follett Pub. Co.
--Dragon's Delight. Van Severen, Joe, illus. LC 80-15104. (Illus.). 109 p. 23cm. c.1981. (ISBN 0-695-41366-X). Follett Pub. Co.
--The Famous Battle of Bravery Creek. Vestal, Herman B., illus. LC 78-163176. (Illus.). 63 p. 24cm. 1972. (ISBN 0-8116-4253-4). Garrard Pub. Co.
--Flash: Dog of Old Egypt. Oughton, Taylor (1925-), illus. LC 73-6577. (Illus.). 48 p. 23cm. 1973. (ISBN 0-8116-4851-6). Garrard Pub. Co.
--Gently Touch the Milkweed. 127p. 18cm. 1977, c.1970. (ISBN 0-380-00982-X). Avon Books.
--Ghost of the Great River Inn. Davis, Allen, illus. LC 80-18585. p. cm. c.1981. (ISBN 0-695-41465-8). Follett Pub. Co.
--The Giver. LC 84-27676. 119 p. 22cm. c.1985. (ISBN 0-684-18312-9). Scribner.
--Half the Battle. LC 81-23285. 151 p. 22cm. c.1982. (ISBN 0-684-17348-4). Charles Scribner's Sons.
--The Haunting of the Green Bird. Cunningham, David (1938-), illus. LC 80-18499. p. cm. 1980, c.1981. (ISBN 0-695-41466-6). Follett Pub. Co.
--A Horse Called Dragon. Cellini, Joseph (1924-), illus. LC 71-121411. (Illus.). 96 p. 23cm. 1971. (ISBN 0-695-40134-3). Follett.
--The Horse Trader. LC 80-26533. 121 p. 22cm. 1981. (ISBN 0-684-16852-9). Scribner.
--Just One Friend. LC 85-40294. p. cm. 1985. (ISBN 0-684-18471-0). Scribner.
--The Leaving. LC 80-18636. p. cm. 1980. (ISBN 0-684-16716-6). Scribner. **Award: (BGH).**
--Lynn Hall's Dog Stories. Cellini, Joseph (1924-), illus. (Illus.). 1972. (ISBN 0-695-80321-2). (ISBN 0-695-40321-4). Follett Co.
--Megan's Mare. LC 83-3009. 56 p. 22cm. 1983. (ISBN 0-684-17874-5). Scribner.
--The Mysterious Moortown Bridge. Sanderson, Ruth, illus. LC 80-18808. p. cm. 1980, c.1981. (ISBN 0-695-41468-2). Follett Pub. Co.
--The Mystery of Plum Park Pony. Daniel, Alan (1939-), illus. LC 79-28125. (Illus.). 64 p. 23cm. (Garrard mystery book). c.1980. (ISBN 0-8116-6414-7). Garrard Pub. Co.
--The Mystery of Pony Hollow. Hutchinson, William Miller (1916-), illus. LC 81-6389. p. cm. (Garrard mystery book). 1982. (ISBN 0-8116-6416-3). Garrard Pub. Co.
--The Mystery of Pony Hollow. Sanderson, Ruth, illus. LC 78-8137. (Illus.). 64 p. 23cm. (Mystery book). c.1978. (ISBN 0-8116-6404-X). Garrard Pub. Co.
--The Mystery of the Caramel Cat. Sanderson, Ruth, illus. LC 80-22146. p. cm. (Garrard mystery book). 1981. Garrard Pub. Co.
--The Mystery of the Lost and Found Hound. Daniel, Alan (1939-), illus. LC 78-27502. (Illus.). 64 p. 23cm. (Garrard mystery book). c.1979. (ISBN 0-8116-6408-2). Garrard Pub. Co.
--The Mystery of the Schoolhouse Dog. Hutchinson, William Miller (1916-), illus. LC 78-12181. (Illus.). 64 p. 23cm. (Mystery book). c.1979. (ISBN 0-8116-6406-6). Garrard Pub. Co.
--The Mystery of the Stubborn Old Man. Vestal, Herman B, illus. LC 79-28287. p. cm. (Mystery book). 1980. (ISBN 0-8116-6413-9). Garrard Pub. Co.
--New Day for Dragon. Cellini, Joseph (1924-), illus. LC 74-83606. (Illus.). 123 p. 23cm. 1975. (ISBN 0-695-80515-0). (ISBN 0-695-40515-2). Follett Pub. Co.
--Owney: The Traveling Dog. Erickson, Barbara M., illus. LC 76-46292. (Illus.). 48 p. 23cm. (Famous animal stories). c.1977. (ISBN 0-8116-4860-5). Garrard Pub. Co.
--Ride a Wild Dream. Roth, George (1932-), illus. LC 69-15961. (Illus.). 160 p. 23cm. 1969. Follett Pub. Co.
--Riff, Remember. LC 73-81998. 107 p. 23cm. 1973. (ISBN 0-695-80413-8). (ISBN 0-695-80413-8). Follett.
--The Secret of Stonehouse. Cellini, Joseph (1924-), illus. LC 68-13796. 155 p. 23cm. (Merit mystery). 1968. Follett Pub. Co.
--Shadows. Cellini, Joseph (1924-), illus. LC 76-50324. (Illus.). 72 p. 23cm. c.1977. (ISBN 0-695-80741-2). (ISBN 0-695-40741-4). Follett Pub. Co.
--The Shy Ones. Elgaard, Greta, illus. 188 p. 23cm. 1967. Follett.
--The Siege of Silent Henry. LC 72-2789. 142 p. 23cm. 1972. (ISBN 0-695-80041-8). Follett Pub Co.
--The Something-Special Horse. Rabinowitz, Sandy (1954-), illus. LC 84-23636. (Illus.). 101 p. 22cm. c.1985. (ISBN 0-684-18343-9). Scribner.
--Sticks and Stones. LC 73-161553. 220 p. 23cm. 1972. (ISBN 0-695-80237-2). (ISBN 0-695-40237-4). Follett.
--Stray. Cellini, Joseph (1924-), illus. LC 73-90053. (Illus.). 95 p. 23cm. 1974. (ISBN 0-695-80442-1). Follett Pub. Co.
--Tin Can Tucker. LC 82-5891. 154 p. 22cm. c.1982. (ISBN 0-684-17623-8). Scribner.
--To Catch a Tartar. Cellini, Joseph (1924-), illus. LC 72-85582. (Illus.). 93 p. 23cm. 1973. (ISBN 0-695-80370-0). Follett.
--Too Near the Sun. new ed. Martin, Stefan (1936-), illus. LC 76-85939. (Illus.). frontispiece. 192p. (gr. 5 up). 1970. (ISBN 0-695-80069-8). (ISBN 0-695-40069-X). Follett.
--Troublemaker. Cellini, Joseph (1924-), illus. LC 74-78455. (Illus.). 96 p. 23cm. 1974. (ISBN 0-695-40479-2). (ISBN 0-695-80479-0). Follett Pub. Co.
--Uphill All the Way. LC 83-20202. 128p. (gr. 7 up). 1984. (ISBN 0-684-18066-9, ScribJ). Scribner.
--The Whispered Horse. LC 79-20096. 110 p. 23cm. c.1979. (ISBN 0-695-41263-9). Follett Pub. Co.
--Wild Mustang. Orig. Title: A Horse Called Dragon. (gr. 4-6). 1974. (ISBN 0-590-09393-2, Schol Trade Pap). Schol Bk Serv.
Hall, Lynn (1937-) & Cellini, Joseph
--Dragon Defiant. LC 76-19887. (Illus.). 96 p. 23cm. c.1977. (ISBN 0-695-80697-1). (ISBN 0-695-40697-3). Follett Pub. Co.
--Flowers of Anger. LC 76-2235. (Illus.). 128 p. 23cm. c.1976. (ISBN 0-695-80669-6). (ISBN 0-695-40669-8). Follett.
Hall, Lynn (1937-) & Mawicke, Tran
--Captain, Canada's Flying Pony. LC 75-6765. (Illus.). 48 p. 23cm. (Famous animal stories). c.1976. (ISBN 0-8116-4857-5). Garrard Pub. Co.
Hall, M.
--Icelandic Fairy Tales. Mason, Alfred Bishop (1851-1933), illus. 1910. Frederick Warne & Co.
--Quite Contrary: Dr. Mary Edwards Walker. (Young Reader's Book Ser.). N.D. (ISBN 0-308-80255-1). Funk & Wagnalls.
Hall, Mabel (1937-)
--The Skipping Hillies. Leland, Stanley F., illus. LC 34-31966. 143 p. incl. front., plates. 19 1/2 cm. c.1933. B. Humphries, Inc.
Hall, Madeline
--Giddy-Go-Round. Hall, Madeline, illus. (Illus.). N.D. Frederick Warne & Co.
--Miss Browne. Hall, Madeline, illus. 20p. N.D. E. P. Dutton & Co.
--Miss Browne: The Story of a Superior Mouse. Hall, Madeline, illus. LC 78-106900. (Illus.). 24 p. 25cm. c.1978. (ISBN 0-8055-1262-4). Hart Pub. Co.
--Nobody Knows: Mother Goose Jingles. Hall, Madeline, illus. (Illus.). N.D. Frederick Warne & Co.
Hall, Malcolm (1945-)
--Caricatures. Degen, Bruce, illus. LC 77-16631. (Illus.). 63 p. 23cm. (Break-of-day book). c.1978. (ISBN 0-698-30685-6). Coward, McCann & Geoghegan.
--Deadlines. Degen, Bruce, illus. LC 82-1457. p. cm. 1982. (ISBN 0-698-30739-9). Coward, McCann & Geoghegan.
--Derek Koogar Was a Star. Schick, Joel (1945-), illus. LC 75-331910. (Illus.). 57, 7 p. 23cm. (Break-of-day book). c.1975. (ISBN 0 698 30581 7). Coward, McCann & Geoghegan.
--The Electric Book. Schick, Joel (1945-), illus. LC 75-10454. (Illus.). 125 p. 22cm. c.1975. (ISBN 0-698-20339-9). (ISBN 0-698-30592-2). Coward, McCann & Geoghegan.
--Forecast. Degen, Bruce, illus. LC 77-1265. (Illus.). 63 p. 23cm. (Break-of-day book). c.1977. (ISBN 0-698-30666-X). Coward, McCann & Geoghegan.
--Forecast. Degen, Bruce, illus. 1977. Putnam.
--The Friends of Charlie Ant Bear. Wallner, Alexandra (1946-), illus. LC 79-4307. (Illus.). 60 p. 23cm. (Break-of-day book). c.1980. (ISBN 0-698-30711-9). Coward, McCann & Geoghegan.
--Headlines. Tripp, Wallace Whitney (1940-), illus. LC 72-85616. (Illus.). 64 p. 24cm. (Break-of-day book). 1973. (ISBN 0-698-20230-9). Coward, McCann & Geoghegan.
Hall, Malcolm (1945-) & De Paola, Tomie, pseud. (1934-)
--Edward, Benjamin, and Butter. De Paola, Thomas Anthony. LC 80-22238. (Illus.). 38 p. 23cm. (Break-of-day book). c.1981. (ISBN 0-698-30731-3). Coward, McCann & Geoghegan.
Hall, Margaret C
--The Teeterville Dinosaur. Hall, Margaret C., illus. LC 62-10875. (Illus.). 24 p. 22cm. (William-Frederick juvenile). 1962. William-Frederick Press.
Hall, Marjory (1908-)
--After a Fashion. Baker, Jean, illus. LC 44-2720. 2 p. l., 188 p. illus. 21 cm. 1944. Houghton Mifflin Company.
--Another Kind of Courage. 236 p. 21cm. 1967. Westminster Press.
--The April Ghost. LC 75-17932. 184, 3 p. 21cm. 1975. (ISBN 0-664-32578-5). Westminister Press.
--Beneath Another Sun. LC 77-110081. 188 p. 21cm. 1970. (ISBN 0-664-32472-X). Westminster Press.
--Bread and Butter. Baker, Jean, illus. LC 42-194327. 3 p. l., 213, 1 p. illus. 22 cm. 1942. Houghton Mifflin Company.
--Bright Red Ribbon. LC 61-6814. 246 p. 22cm. 1961. Funk & Wagnalls.
--The Carved Wooden Ring. LC 76-170114. 176 p. 21cm. 1972. (ISBN 0-664-32506-8). Westminster Press.
--Cathy and Her Castle. LC 57-6507. 213p. 22cm. 1957. Funk & Wagnalls.
--Clotheshorse. LC 66-12582. 214p. illus. 22cm. c.1966. Funk & Wagnalls.
--Copy Kate. Darby, Elinor, illus. LC 47-30716. 241 p. illus. 21 cm. 1947. Houghton Mifflin Co.
--Drumbeat on the Shore. LC 65-15620. 238 p. 21 cm. 1965. Westminster Press.
--Fanfare for Two. LC 63-8869. 218 p. 22 cm. 1963. Funk & Wagnalls.
--The Gold-Lined Box. 198 p. 22cm. 1968. Westminster Press.
--Greetings from Glenna. Barnes, Catherine J. (1918-), illus. LC 53-6979. 252p. illus. 22cm. 1953. Funk & Wagnalls.
--A Hatbox for Mimi. LC 60-6425. 248p. 22cm. 1960. Funk & Wagnalls Co.
--Hatful Of Gold. 1964. (ISBN 0-8382-0321-3, Cadmus Books). E. M. Hale and Company.
--A Hatful of Gold. LC 64-14866. 192 p. 21 cm. 1964. Westminster Press.
--Linda Clayton. Barnes, Catherine J. (1918-), illus. LC 51-12139. 243 p. illus. 22 cm. 1951. Sloane.
--Look at Me!. 192 p. 22cm. 1967. Funk & Wagnalls.
--The Magic Word. LC 59-74145. 206p. 21cm. 1959. Westminster Press.

--Mirror, Mirror. LC 56-8415. 188p. 21cm. 1956. Westminster Press.
--Model Child. Coffin, Winifred W., illus. LC 45-8462. 2 p. l., 211 p. front. 19 cm. 1945. Houghton Mifflin Company.
--Morning Glory. LC 56-777756. 215p. 22cm. 1956. Funk & Wagnalls.
--Mystery at Lions Gate. 125 p. 21cm. 1967. Funk & Wagnalls.
--Mystery at October House. LC 76-46565. 163 p. 21cm. c.1977. (ISBN 0-664-32606-4). Westminster Press.
--One Perfect Rose. LC 64-11122. 218 p. 22 cm. 1964. Funk & Wagnalls.
--Orchids for Anita. LC 54-6357. (Illus.). 250 p. 22cm. 1954. Funk & Wagnalls.
--The Other Girl. LC 73-18334. 185 p. 21cm. 1974. (ISBN 0-664-32542-4). Westminster Press.
--Paper Moon. LC 54-6362. (Illus.). 282 p. 22cm. 1954. Funk & Wagnalls.
--A Picnic for Judy. LC 55-5075. (Illus.). 274 p. 22cm. 1955. Funk & Wagnalls.
--Rita Rings a Bell. (gr. 7-11). 1962. Funk & W.
--Romance at Courtesy Bend. LC 58-7682. 192p. 21cm. 1959. Westminster Press.
--Saralee's Silver Spoon. Barnes, Catherine J. (1918-), illus. LC 52-9165. 306 p. illus. 22 cm. 1952. Sloane.
--See the Red Sky. LC 63-9970. 192 p. 21 cm. 1963. Westminster Press.
--The Seventh Star. LC 77-78482. 166, 1 p. 21cm. 1969. (ISBN 0-664-32451-7). Westminster Press.
--Star Island. LC 53-107907. 279p. 22cm. 1953. Funk & Wagnalls.
--Star Island Again. LC 55-11097. (Illus.). 224 p. 22cm. 1955. Funk & Wagnalls.
--Straw Hat Summer. LC 57-807058. 188p. 22cm. 1957. Westminster Press.
--Success in Reserve. Baker, Jean, illus. 2 p. l., 226, 1 p. illus. 22 cm. 1941. Houghton Mifflin Company.
--Three Stars for Star Island. LC 58-7281. 210 p. 22cm. 1958. Funk & Wagnalls.
--To Paris and Love. LC 62-115178. 202p. 21cm. 1962. Westminster Press.
--Tomorrow Is Another Day. LC 60-70372. 194p. 21cm. 1960. Westminster Press.
--The Treasure Tree. LC 66-136406. 234p. 22cm. 1966. Westminster.
--A Valentine for Vinnie. LC 65-11725. 249p. 22cm. c.1965. Funk & Wagnalls.
--Whirl of Fashion. LC 61-971860. 192p. 21cm. 1961. Westminster Press.
--The Whistle Stop Mystery. Korach, Mimi (1922-), illus. LC 69-12154. (Illus.). 127 p. 21cm. 1969. Funk & Wagnalls.
--White Collar Girl. LC 59-8086. 248p. 21cm. 1959. Funk and Wagnalls.
--A Year from Now. Draper, Judith, illus. LC 52-14039. (Illus.). 246 p. 22cm. 1952. Sloane.

Hall, Marquerite Radclyffe (1886-1943)
--Adam's Breed. LC 26-12289. 6 p. l., 379 p. 20 cm. 1926. Doubleday, Page & Company.

Hall, Mary Leora & Palmer, Sarah Elizabeth
--Story Plays for Little Children, with Music, Finger Plays, and Rhythms. LC 17-13505. 3 p. l., 5-89 p. col. front., illus. 24 x 20 cm. 1917. Lothrop, Lee & Shepard Co.

Hall, Maud R., jt. auth. see Yeatman, F. E.

Hall, Maud R., ed. see Yeatman, F. E.

Hall, May Emery
--Jan and Betje: A Story of Two Dutch Children. LC 16-26820. 122 p. illus. 17 cm. (Merrill's Story Bks.). c.1914. Charles E. Merrill Company.

Hall, Minerva Jones
--The Adventures of Mr. Scoodle-do and Brother Rabbit. new ed. Drucklieb, Herman L., illus. N.D. Dodd Mead & Co.
--Mr. Scoodle-Do and His Many Adventures. with an introduction letter by john martin. ed. Martin, John, intro. by. LC 27-21943. 105 p. front., illus., pl. 26 cm. c.1927. Dodd, Mead and Company.

Hall, N. M.
--Tales of Captains and Conquest. N.D. Ginn & Co.
--Tales of Pioneers and Kings. N.D. Ginn & Co.
--Tales of the Far-off Days. N.D. Ginn.

Hall, Nan & Children of the Fifth Grade, Pryor St. School
--Little Pitchers with Big Ears. LC 42-8147. (Illus.). 64p. 27cm. 1942. Garden City Publishing Co.

Hall, Nancy Christensen
--Macmillan Fairy Tale Alphabet Book. O'Brien, John (1953-), illus. LC 82-20905. (Illus.). 64p. 1983. (ISBN 0-02-741960-6). Macmillan.

Hall, Nancy Christensen, ed.
--The Platt & Munk Treasury of Stories for Children. LC 79-56868. (Illus.). 114 p. 30cm. 1981. (ISBN 0-448-47722-X). Platt & Munk.

Hall, Natalie Watson (1923-)
--Palace of Fun. Hall, Natalie Watson (1923-), illus. (Illus.). (gr. 2-5). 1965. (ISBN 0-670-53715-2). (ISBN 0-670-53716-0). Viking Pr.
--World in a City Block. Hall, Natalie Watson (1923-), illus. (Illus.). (gr. 1-5). 1960. (ISBN 0-670-78465-6). Viking Pr.
--Zig-Zag Zeppo. Hall, Natalie Watson (1923-), illus. 32p. 1961. Viking Press.

Hall, Norah E. L. see Hall, Aylmer, pseud.

Hall, Patricia, jt. auth. see Hillery, Mable.

Hall, Penelope Coker see Wilson, Penelope Coker, pseud.

Hall-Quest, Edna Olga Wilbourne, Mrs. (1899-) & Sando, Anne
--Fuzzy-Wuzzy: The Story of a Pet Raccoon. LC 41-16071. 4 p. l, 11-98. p. illus. 22 1/2 cm. c.1941. The Bobbs-Merrill Company.
--Powhatan and Captain Smith. 1957. Farrar, Straus and Cudahy, Inc.

Hall, Robin, jt. auth. see Hall, William Franklin.

Hall, Rosalys Haskell (1914-)
--Animals to Africa. Eichenberg, Fritz (1901-), illus. N.D. Holiday House.
--Baker's Man. Werth, Kurt (1896-), illus. LC 54-7297. unpaged. illus. 26cm. 1954. Lippincott.
--Bertie and Eddie. N.D. E. M. Hale and Co.
--Bertie and Eddie. Reed, Veronica, pseud. (1916-), illus. Sherman, Theresa. 120p. 1956. Henry Z. Walck, Inc., Publishers.
--Bertie and Eddie. Reed, Veronica, pseud. (1916-), illus. Sherman, Theresa. LC 56-800736. 115p. illus. 21cm. (Oxford books for boys and girls). 1956. Oxford University Press.
--The Bright and Shining Breadboard. Werth, Kurt (1896-), illus. LC 69-14329. (Illus.). 32 p. 26cm. 1969. Lothrop, Lee & Shepard.
--The Dog's Boy. Weiss, Emil (1896-1965), illus. LC 61-17688. (Illus.). 42 p. 23cm. 1962. Lothrop, Lee and Shepard.
--Green As Spring. 1st ed. Werth, Kurt (1896-), illus. LC 57-7089. 214p. 21cm. 1957. Longmans, Green.
--Green As Spring. Werth, Kurt (1896-), illus. (gr. 6-9). 1957. (ISBN 0-679-20066-5). McKay.
--Miranda's Dragon. Werth, Kurt (1896-), illus. LC 68-24343. (Illus.). 39 p. 26cm. 1968. McGraw-Hill.
--No Ducks for Dinner. 1953. E M Hale.
--No Ducks for Dinner. Werth, Kurt (1896-), illus. 48p. (Horn Books). 1953. Henry Z. Walck, Inc., Publishers.
--No Ducks for Dinner. Werth, Kurt (1896-), illus. 1953. Oxford University Press.
--Out of Provincetown. Malvern, Corinne (1905-1956), illus. LC 41-14709. 5 p. l., 3-296 p. incl. front., illus. 19 1/2 cm. N.D. Farrar & Rinehart, Inc.
--Seven for Saint Nicholas. 1st ed. Werth, Kurt (1896-), illus. LC 58-7531. 156p. illus. 22cm. 1958. Lippincott.
--The Tailor's Trick. Werth, Kurt (1896-), illus. 1955. J. B. Lippincott Co.
--The Three Beggar Kings: A Story of Christmas. Werth, Kurt (1896-), illus. LC 74-826. (Illus.). 36p. (gr. k-3). 1974. (ISBN 0-394-92114-3, BYR). Random.
--Young Fancy. (gr. 7-9). 1960. McKay.
--Young Fancy. 1st ed. Bolognese, Donald Alan (1934-), illus. LC 60-10211. 184p. illus. 21cm. 1960. Longmans, Green.

Hall, Rubylea Ray (1910-)
--Davey. LC 51-10885. (Illus.). 288 p. 21cm. 1951. Duell, Sloan and Pearce.
--Flamingo Prince. Shepherd, J. Clinton, illus. LC 54-11125. (Illus.). 313 p. 21cm. 1954. Duell, Sloan and Pearce.
--God has a Sense of Humor. 1960. Duell,Sloan and Pearce Pub.

Hall, Ruth
--The Golden Arrow. N.D. HHoughton Mifflin.

Hall, S. C., Mrs.
--Animal Sagacity. Weir, Harrison William (1824-1906), illus. (Partridge's Juveniles). N.D. George Routledge & Sons.
--Grace Huntley. (Golden Link Ser.). N.D. R. Worthington & Co.
--The Lucky Penny, and Other Tales. N.D. George Routledge & Sons.
--The Merchant's Daughter. (Golden Links Ser.). N.D. R. Worthington & Co.
--The Merchant's Daughter. 1875. Scribner, Welford, & Armstrong.

Hall, S. L.
--Years Ago: Or, Boys and Girls of Olden Times. 215p. N.D. Congregational Sunday-School and Publishing Society.

Hall, Samuel Carter, Mrs. (1800-1881)
--Chronicles of Cosy Nook. (The Cosy Nook Ser.). N.D. Thomas Nelson & Sons.
--Daddy Dacre's School. N.D. George Routledge & Sons.
--Daily Governess. (Golden Links Ser.). N.D. R. Worthington & Co.
--Daily Governess. (Illus.). 1875. Scribner, Welford & Armstrong.
--Daily Governess. (Golden Links Ser.). N.D. Scribner, Welford & Armstrong.
--Grace Huntly. (Illus.). 1875. Scribner, Welford & Armstrong.
--Grace Huntly. (Golden Links Ser.). N.D. Scribner, Welford & Armstrong.
--Grandmamma's Pockets. N.D. Thomas Whittaker.
--The Merchant's Daughter. (Golden Links Ser.). N.D. Scribner, Welford & Armstrong.
--Merchant's Daughter. (Warne's Star Ser.). N.D. Scribner & Welford.
--The Purse and Other Tales, 1 of 6 vols. (The Blue Bells Ser.). N.D. Hurst & Co.
--The Swan's Eggs. N.D. Thomas Whittaker.
--Turns of Fortune and Other Tales, 1 of 6 vols. (The Blue Bells Ser.). N.D. Hurst & Co.
--Uncle Sam's Money Box. N.D. Thomas Whittaker.
--The Whisperer. N.D. Thomas Whittaker.

Hall, Steven Leonard (1960-)
--Down Came the Sun. Steffan, illus. Hall, Mary A. LC 72-176097. (Illus.). 64p. (gr. 3 up). 1972. (ISBN 0-87929-010-2). Barlenmir.

Hall, Susan, jt. auth. see Adelman, Bor.

Hall, Teddy, jt. auth. see Carney, Don.

Hall, Theresa Oakey
--A Christmas Journey, 1 of 6 Vols. (Neighborly Love Library). N.D. Set. T. Whittaker.
--Christmas Journey and Other Stories. N.D. T. Whittaker.
--Little Miss Fancy: A Story for Little People. (Illus.). 207p. (Quarto Picture Books). 1876. Dodd, Mead & Co.
--Nuts for Christmas Cracking. (Illus.). 1888. Thomas Whittaker.

Hall, Tom
--The Fun and Fighting of the Rough Riders. (Illus.). N.D. Frederick A. Stokes.
--Heroes of the Revolution. N.D. Frederick A. Stokes.

Hall, William Franklin (1885-)
--Green Fire. LC 34-25532. 2 p. l., 211 p. front. 20 cm. (His Top notch detective stories). c.1934. Cupples & Leon Company.
--Hidden Danger. LC 34-25533. 2 p. l., 210 p. front. 20 cm. (His Top notch detective stories). c.1934. Cupples & Leon Company.
--The Shoelace Robin. Lawson, Robert (1892-1957), illus. 32p. 1945. Thomas Y. Crowell Co.
--Slow Vengeance. LC 34-25531. 2 p. l., 204 p. front. 20 cm. (His Top notch detective stories). c.1934. Cupples & Leon Company.
--Telltime the Rabbit. Steiner, Charlotte, illus. 28p. 1945. Thomas Y. Crowell Co.
--Telltime's Alphabet Book. LC 58-6606. 28p. 1958. Thomas Y. Crowell Co.
--Winkie's World. Duvoisin, Roger Antoine (1904-1980), illus. N.D. Doubleday.

Hall, William Franklin (1885-) & Hall, Jessie Helen Sims, Mrs. (1901-)
--My Dog Lucky. Hetherington, Mildred Lyon, illus. LC 40-35465. 189 p. col. illus. 20 cm. c.1940. Beckley-Cardy Company.
--Rod, the Sky Lad. Bilder, Arthur K., illus. LC 51-11331. 181 p. illus. 21 cm. 1951. Beckley-Cardy Co.

Hall, William Franklin (1885-) & Hall, Robin
--Telltime Goes A'counting. Steiner, Charlotte, illus. LC 56-13771. unpaged. illus. 21cm. c.1956. Crowell.

Hall, William Norman (1915-1974)
--Christmas Pony. Duvoisin, Roger Antoine (1904-1980), illus. LC 48-8237. 82 p. col. illus. 26 cm. 1948. A. A. Knopf.
--The Seven Little Elephants. Littlejohn, Fini R. (1914-), illus. LC 47-30908. 32 p. col. illus. 27 cm. c.1947. T. Y. Crowell Co.
--Walking Hat. 1st ed. Wiese, Kurt (1887-1974), illus. LC 50-6308. (Illus.). 82p. Repr. of 1950 ed. N.D. (ISBN 0-394-91820-7). Knopf.
--Watch the Kitten Grow. Carroll, Ruth Robinson, Mrs. (1899-), illus. LC 46-417010. 15 l. col. illus. 21 x 26 cm. c.1946. Thomas Y. Crowell Company.
--Watch the Pony Grow. Steiner, Charlotte, illus. LC 43-1374. 15 l. col. illus. 22 x 27 1/2 cm. c.1942. Thomas Y. Crowell Company.
--Watch the Puppy Grow. Carroll, Ruth Robinson, Mrs. (1899-), illus. LC 48-3294. 15 l. col. illus. 22 x 27 cm. 1945. T. Y. Crowell Co.

Hall, William Norman (1915-1974) & Steiner, Charlotte
--Stilty, the Deer Who Learned to Eat. LC 44-7924. 24 p. col. illus. 24 1/2 cm. 24p. c.1944. Thomas Y. Crowell Company.

Hall, Willis, jt. auth. see Waterhouse, Keith Spencer.

Hall, Willis (1929-)
--Kidnapped at Christmas: A Play for Children. (gr. 10). 1975. (ISBN 0-435-23368-8). Heinemann Ed.
--Kidnapped at Christmas: A Play for Children. Blake, Quentin (1932-), illus. LC 77-364215. (Illus.). 80 p. 19cm. 1975. (ISBN 0-573-05037-6). French.

Halladay, Anne M, Mrs.
--The Apple Tree House. Nicholas, Frank, illus. LC 57-6167. 125p. illus. 22cm. 1957. Friendship Press.
--Cuddle Bear. Wiese, Kurt (1887-1974), illus. LC 60-15681. (Illus.). 128p. 1960. Bethany Press.
--Cuddle Bear of Piney Forest. Livsey, Carmon V., illus. LC 30-18648. 127 p. incl. front., illus. 19 cm. c.1930. The Bethany Press.
--Cuddle Bear of Piney Forest. Wiese, Kurt (1887-1974), illus. LC 60-15681. 128p. illus. 21cm. 1960. Bethany Press.
--Davey in the Sand Hills. Martinez, Jean, illus. LC 51-7734. 126 p. illus. 21cm. 1951. Friendship Press.
--The Door Under the Eaves. LC 36-7259. 4 p. l, 232 p. col. front., illus. 19 cm. 1936. Harper & Brother.
--Little Black-Nosed Engine. Teichman, Dorothy, illus. (ps-2). 1964. (ISBN 0-8272-2110-X). Bethany Pr.
--New Friends for Pepe. Smalley, Janet (1893-), illus. LC 59-8629. unpaged. illus. 21cm. 1959. Bethany Press.
--The Pigtail Twins. LC 43-5774. 126 p., 1 l., incl. front., illus. 21 x 16 cm. 1943. Friendship Press.
--Secrets at White Owl. Warren, Betsy, pseud. (1916-), illus. Warren, Elizabeth Avery. LC 67-181359. vii, 87p. col. illus. 24cm. (gr. 3-4). 1967. (ISBN 0-8114-7641-3). Steck.
--Toshio and Tama: Children of New Japan. N.D. Friendship Press.
--Up and Down South America. Paflin, Roberta, pseud. (1903-), illus. Petty, Roberta Harris Pfafflin. LC 42-14741. 127 p. incl. front., illus. 19 1/2 cm. 1942. Friendship Press.

Halladay, Anne M, Mrs. & Cooper, Matlie Lula
--The Boy with the Busy Walk. Johnson, Iris Beatty, illus. LC 54-6192. 126p. illus. 21cm. 1954. Friendship Press.

Hallahan, William
--The Search for Joseph Tully. LC 74-1901. 288p. 1974. (ISBN 0-672-51997-6). Bobbs.

Hallam, Atlantis
--Star Ship on Saddle Mountain. LC 55-14991. 182p. 21cm. 1955. Macmillan.

Hallard, Peter J., pseud., see Catherall, Arthur.

Hallard, Peter J., pseud. (1906-)
--Barrier Reef Bandits. Catherall, Arthur. Marshall, Hugh, illus. LC 60-14136. (Illus.). 183. 22cm. (A Criterion Book for Young People). 1960. Criterion Books.

Hallburton, Margaret Winifred, tr. see Grimm, Jakob Ludwig Karl (1785-1863) & Grimm, Wilhelm Karl.

Hallenbeck, Cleve & Williams, Juanita H.
--Legends of the Spanish Southwest. N.D. Gale Reprint.

Haller, Danita Ross
--Not Just Any Ring. Ray, Deborah (1940-), illus. LC 81-14242. (Illus.). 48 p. c.1982. (ISBN 0-394-85082-3). Knopf.

Haller, Dorcas Woodbury, jt. auth. see Jensen, Virginia Allen.

Halleran, Eugene Edward (1905-)
--The Blazing Border. (Bull's-Eye Westerns). N.D. Macrae Smith Co.

Hallet, Richard
--The Rolling World. N.D. Houghton Mifflin Co.

Halliard, Jack
--Voyages and Adventures of Jack Halliard. LC 21-2690. viii, 9-142 p. incl. front., illus. 13 cm. c.1833. Russell, Odiorne, & Co.

Halliday, Brett, pseud. (1904-1977), ed. see Mystery Writers of America.

Hallin, Emily Watson
--Moya and the Flamingoes. Anderson, Rus, illus. LC 69-12953. (Illus.). 86 p. 21cm. 1969. D. McKay Co.

Hallin, Emily Watson & Buell, Robert Kingery
--Follow the Honey Bird. Toschik, Larry (1922-), illus. (Illus.). (gr. 5-7). 1967. (ISBN 0-679-20057-6). (ISBN 0-679-25049-2). McKay.
--Wild White Wings. Toschik, Larry (1922-), illus. LC 65-14135. (Illus.). (gr. 6-9). 1965. (ISBN 0-679-20246-3). McKay.

Hallinan, Patrick Kenneth (1944-)
--How Really Great to Walk This Way. Buckley, Jim, illus. LC 73-178496. (Illus.). 32p. (gr. k-3). 1972. (ISBN 0-516-03474-X). Childrens.
--Just Being Alone. Hallinan, Patrick Kenneth (1944-), illus. LC 76-8852. (Illus.). (ps-3). 1976. (ISBN 0-516-03516-9). Childrens.
--Just Open a Book. Hallinan, Patrick Kenneth (1944-), illus. LC 80-22099. (Illus.). 30 p. 25cm. c.1981. (ISBN 0-516-03521-5). Childrens Press.
--The Looking Book. Hallinan, Patrick Kenneth (1944-), illus. LC 73-6573. (Illus.). 45 p. 24cm. 1973. Childrens Press.
--That's What a Friend Is. Hallinan, Patrick Kenneth (1944-), illus. LC 76-27744. (Illus.). 28 p. 25cm. c.1977. (ISBN 0-516-03628-9). Childrens Press.
--We're Very Good Friends, My Brother and I. Hallinan, Patrick Kenneth (1944-), illus. LC 72-8371. (Illus.). 32 p. 25cm. 1973. (ISBN 0-516-03659-9). Childrens Press.
--Where's Michael?. LC 77-15952. (Illus.). 32p. (ps-3). 1978. (ISBN 0-516-03668-8). Childrens.

Hamilton, Bob (1931-)
--Gene Autry and the Redwood Pirates: An Original Story Featuring Gene Autry, Famous Motion Picture Star, As the Hero. authorized. Hess, Erwin L., illus. LC 46-996885. 2 p. l., 9-248 p. illus. 20 1/2 cm. 1946. Whitman Publishing Company.
--Gene Autry and the Thief River Outlaws: An Original Story Featuring Gene Autry, Famous Motion Picture Star, As the Hero. authorized. Muller, Daniel Cody (1889-), illus. LC 45-3094. 21cm. 249p. c.1944. Whitman Publishing Company.
Hamilton, C. J.
--The Story of Steady and Sure. 160p. N.D. Thomas Y Crowell Co.
Hamilton, Catherine
--A Tale for Little Girls. N.D. Catholic Publication Society.
Hamilton, Dorothy Drumm (1906-1983)
--Amanda Fair. Converse, James, illus. LC 80-25073. (Illus.). 115 p. 20cm. 1981. (ISBN 0-8361-1943-6). Herald Press.
--Anita's Choice. Moon, Ivan, illus. LC 70-131535. 22cm. 96p. 1971. Herald Press.
--Bittersweet Days. Graber, Esther Rose, illus. LC 77-18867. (Illus.). 123 p. 22cm. 1978. (ISBN 0-8361-1845-6). (ISBN 0-8361-1846-4). Herald Press.
--The Blue Caboose. Needler, Jerry, illus. LC 72-5474. (Illus.). 135 p. 23cm. 1973. (ISBN 0-8361-1695-X). Herald Press.
--Busboys at Big Bend. Fraley, Betty Baker, illus. LC 74-8689. (Illus.). 100 p. 22cm. 1974. (ISBN 0-8361-1744-1). Herald Press.
--Carlie's Pink Room. Graber, Esther Rose, illus. LC 83-26437. 1984. (ISBN 0-8361-3354-4). Herald Press.
--The Castle. Graber, Esther Rose, illus. LC 75-15599. (Illus.). 112 p. 23cm. 1975. (ISBN 0-8361-1775-1). (ISBN 0-8361-1776-X). Herald Press.
--Charco. Ponter, James J., illus. LC 74-153966. (Illus.). 126 p. 22cm. 1971. (ISBN 0-8361-1650-X). Herald Press.
--Christmas for Holly. Graber, Esther Rose, illus. LC 72-141831. (Illus.). 110 p. 22cm. 1971. (ISBN 0-8361-1635-6). Herald Press.
--Cricket. Van Demark, Paul, illus. LC 74-30421. (Illus.). 113 p. 22cm. 1975. (ISBN 0-8361-1760-3). (ISBN 0-8361-1761-1). Herald Press.
--The Eagle. LC 74-13069. 168p. 1974. (ISBN 0-8361-1748-4). Herald Pr.
--Eric's Discovery. Wind, Betty, illus. LC 79-18537. (Illus.). 111 p. 21cm. 1979. (ISBN 0-8361-1902-9). (ISBN 0-8361-1903-7). Herald Press.
--The Gift of a Home. Wallace, Edwin B., illus. LC 73-13989. (Illus.). 117 p. 21cm. 1974. (ISBN 0-8361-1727-1). Herald Press.
--Gina in-Between. Converse, James, illus. LC 81-13388. (Illus.). 122 p. 20cm. 1982. (ISBN 0-8361-1986-X). Herald Press.
--Holly's New Year. Graber, Esther Rose, illus. LC 81-4098. (Illus.). 127 p. 20cm. 1981. (ISBN 0-8361-1961-4). Herald Press.
--Jason. Ponter, James J., illus. LC 73-14813. (Illus.). 107 p. 21cm. 1974. (ISBN 0-8361-1728-X). Herald Press.
--Jim Musco. Ponter, James J., illus. LC 71-189563. (Illus.). 94 p. 21cm. 1972. (ISBN 0-8361-1668-2). Herald Press.
--Joel's Other Mother. Graber, Esther Rose, illus. LC 84-20508. 1984. (ISBN 0-8361-3355-2). Herald Press.
--Ken's Bright Room. Converse, James, illus. LC 82-23351. p. cm. 1982. (ISBN 0-8361-3327-7). (ISBN 0-8361-3328-5). Herald Press.
--Ken's Hideout. Converse, James, illus. LC 78-21269. (Illus.). 84 p. 22cm. 1979. (ISBN 0-8361-1880-4). (ISBN 0-8361-1881-2). Herald Press.
--Kerry. Graber, Esther Rose, illus. LC 72-4073. (Illus.). 112 p. 21cm. 1973. (ISBN 0-8361-1690-9). Herald Press.
--Last One Chosen. Converse, James, illus. LC 82-3150. (Illus.). 106 p. 20cm. 1982. (ISBN 0-8361-3306-4). Herald Press.
--Linda's Rain Tree. Moon, Ivan, illus. LC 75-16301. (Illus.). 118 p. 23cm. 1975. (ISBN 0-8361-1777-8). (ISBN 0-8361-1778-6). Herald Press.
--Mari's Mountain. Graber, Esther Rose, illus. LC 78-10620. p. cm. 1978. (ISBN 0-8361-1868-5). (ISBN 0-8361-1869-3). Herald Press.
--Mindy. Wallace, Edwin B., illus. LC 72-5098. (Illus.). 111 p. 23cm. 1973. (ISBN 0-8361-1692-5). Herald Press.
--Neva's Patchwork Pillow. Graber, Esther Rose, illus. LC 74-32009. (Illus.). 111 p. 22cm. 1975. (ISBN 0-8361-1758-1). (ISBN 0-8361-1759-X). Herald Press.
--The Quail. LC 73-7634. 152 p. 21cm. 1973. (ISBN 0-8361-1716-6). Herald Press.
--Rosalie. Unada, pseud. (1927-), illus. Gliewe, Unada Grace. LC 76-39961. (Illus.). 120 p. 22cm. 1977. (ISBN 0-8361-1806-5). (ISBN 0-8361-1807-3). Herald Press.
--Rosalie at Eleven. Gliewe, Unada Grace (1927-), illus. LC 80-18979. 112p. (gr. 3-8). 1980. (ISBN 0-8361-1931-2). Herald Pr.
--Scamp and the Blizzard Boys. Converse, James, illus. LC 79-23670. (Illus.). 78 p. 22cm. 1980. (ISBN 0-8361-1918-5). (ISBN 0-8361-1919-3). Herald Press.
--Straight Mark. Van Demark, Paul, illus. LC 76-26661. 22cm. 120p. 1976. (ISBN 0-8361-1341-1). (ISBN 0-8361-1342-X). Herald Press.
--Tony Savala. Ponter, James J., illus. LC 75-171537. (Illus.). 107 p. 22cm. 1972. (ISBN 0-8361-1664-X). Herald Press.
--Winter Caboose. Converse, James, illus. LC 83-10816. (Sequel to The Blue Caboose). (Illus.). 112p. (Orig.). (gr. 4-8). 1983. (ISBN 0-8361-3341-2). Herald Pr.
--Winter Girl. Eitzen, Allan (1928-), illus. LC 75-40344. (Illus.). 119 p. 22cm. 1976. (ISBN 0-8361-1787-5). (ISBN 0-8361-1788-3). Herald Press.
Hamilton, E. M.
--The General Peg Series, 6 Vols. 64p. N.D. Pilgrim Press.
Hamilton, E. M & Hamilton, Kate Waterman (1841-)
--Billy's Motto. LC 22-17333. 3 p. l., 5-68 p. front., pl. 17 1/2 cm. (Dotty series, no. 3). c.1894. Congregational Sunday-School and Publishing Society.
--Dot's Christmas. LC 22-17331. 72 p. front. pl. 17 1/2 cm. (Dotty series, no. 1). c.1894. Congregational Sunday-School and Publishing Society.
--Giving and Keeping. LC 22-17336. 81 p. front., pl. 17 1/2 cm. (Red book series). c.1891. Congregational Sunday-School and Publishing Society.
--How Billy Helped the Church. LC 22-17332. 3 p. l., 5-72 p. front., pl. 17 1/2 cm. (Dotty series, no. 4). c.1894. Congregational Sunday-School and Publishing Society.
--In Search of a Fortune. LC 22-173342. 3 p. l., 5-73 p. front., pl. 17 1/2 cm. (Dotty series, no. 6). c.1894. Congregational Sunday-School and Publishing Society.
--Tommy and Millie. LC 22-17338. 83 p. front. pl. 17 1/2 cm. (Red book series). c.1891. Congregational Sunday-School and Publishing Society.
Hamilton, Edith (1867-1963), ed.
--The Greek Way. 1930. Norton Company.
--Mythology. N.D. (ISBN 0-448-00093-8). Grosset & Dunlap.
--Mythology. (Keith Jennison Large Type Bks). (gr. 7 up). 1966. (ISBN 0-531-00246-2). Watts.
--Mythology. Savage, Steele (1900-), illus. (Illus.). (A book of Greek, Roman & Norse myths). (gr. 7 up). 1942. (ISBN 0-316-34114-2). Little.
--A Treasury of Edith Hamilton. LC 70-90989. (Illus.). 143 p. 22cm. 1969. (ISBN 0-393-04313-4). Norton.
Hamilton, Elaine (1937-)
--I'm a Lucky Dog: Jill, the Airedale. Keele, Norman, illus. LC 37-3152. (Illus.). 127p. 1937. David McKay Co.
Hamilton, Elizabeth Verner
--When Walls Are High. Peck, Laura, illus. LC 72-93195. (Illus.). vii, 151 p. 21cm. 1973, c.1972. Tradd Street Press.
Hamilton, Elizabeth (1945-)
--The C-Circus. Ladd, Michael, illus. LC 46-22497. 32 p. illus. 19 1/2 x 26 cm. 1946. Coward-McCann.
--Go West, Young Bear. Wiese, Kurt (1887-1974), illus. LC 48-2249. 94 p. illus. 25 c. 1948. Coward-McCann.
--The P-Zoo. Hurd, Peter (1904-1984), illus. Gag, Flavia, contrib. by. LC 45-35219. (Illus.). 32p. N.D. Coward-McCann.
Hamilton, Emily, jt. auth. see Hamilton, Morse.
Hamilton, Esme (1912-)
--Children at Moyinish. Gill, Margery Jean (1925-), illus. LC 60-5828. 159p. illus. 21cm. (Wonderful world book). 1960. Barnes.
--Rainbow and Speedy. Edwards, Lionel Dalhousie Robertson (1878-), illus. LC 59-12795. 160p. illus. 21cm. (Wonderful world book). 1959. Barnes.
--Speedy: The Story of an Irish Pony. William, Barbara Moray, illus. LC 59-12793. 202p. illus. 21cm. (Wonderful world book). 1959. Barnes.
--Starlight. Buchanan, Lilian, illus. LC 60-5829. 144p. illus. 20cm. (Wonderful world book). 1960. Barnes.
Hamilton, Gail, pseud., see Corcoran, Barbara.
Hamilton, Gail, pseud., see Dodge, Mary Abigail.
Hamilton, Gail (1833-1896)
--Child World: Part First. 1873. Shepard & Gill.
--Child World: Part Second. N.D. Shepard & Gill.
--Nursery Noonings. LC 13-20114. 17cm. 310p. 1875. Harper & Brothers.
Hamilton, Gail, pseud. (1911-)
--Love Comes to Eunice K. O'Herlihy. Corcoran, Barbara. 1st ed. LC 77-1580. 22cm. 131p. (gr. 5-8). 1977. (ISBN 0-689-30584-2). Atheneum.
--Titania's Lodestone. Corcoran, Barbara. LC 74-19491. 200 p. 22cm. 1975. (ISBN 0-689-30449-8). Atheneum.
Hamilton, George W.
--Finding Blodgett. N.D. Standard Publishing Co.
--Finding Blodgett. The Story of a Boy and His Dog. LC 7-4670. 1 p. l., 160 p. front., plates. 18 1/2 cm. c.1890. D. Lothrop Company.
Hamilton, J. A. G.
--Dick Layard: Or, A School-boy's Trial (Pub. by Society for Promoting Christian Knowledge). N.D. E. & J. B. Young & Co.
Hamilton, James Shelley
--Butt Chanler: Freshman. 5 p. l., 324 p., 1 l. col. front., 3 col. pl. 20 cm. 1908. D. Appleton and Company.
--The New Sophomore. LC 9-26954. 6 p. l., 296 p., 1 l. col. front., 3 col. pl. 20 cm. 1909. D. Appleton and Company.
Hamilton, John Ralph, jt. auth. see Christie, Don.
Hamilton, Kate Waterman, jt. auth. see Hamilton, E. M.
Hamilton, Kate Waterman (1841-)
--Chinks of Clannyford. LC 12-32893. 380 p. front., plates. 18 cm. c.1872. Presbyterian Board of Publications.
--Dick and His Cousins. LC 22-17335. 79 p. front., pl. 17 1/2 cm. (Red book series). c.1891. Congregational Sunday School and Publishing Society.
--Doctor Lincoln's Children. 207p. N.D. Pilgrims Press.
--Dolly's Guest. LC 22-17330. 51 p. front., pl. 17 1/2 cm. (Dotty series. no. 2). c.1894. Congregational Sunday-School and Publishing Society.
--The Hand with the Keys. LC 12-328836. 304 p. front., plates. 18 cm. c.1890. Presbyterian Board of Publications and Sabbath-School Work.
--Like a Story. 3 p. l., 5-62 p. front., pl. 17 1/2 cm. (Dotty series. no. 3). c.1894. Congregational Sunday-School and Publishing Society.
--Nellie's Red Book. LC 22-173373. 81 p. front., pl. 17 1/2 cm. (Red book series). c.1891. Congregational Sunday-School and Publishing Society.
--Nellie's Red Book Series, 6 Vols. (Illus.). N.D. Pilgrim Press.
--Odd and Even Stories, 6 Vols. (Illus.). N.D. Pilgrim Press.
--Old Portmanteau. LC 12-32937. 277 p. front., plates. 18 cm. c.1878. Presbyterian Board of Publication.
--Robin Hood and Another Hood, and Other Stories. (Illus.). N.D. D. Lothrop & Co.
--The Royal Service: Or, The King's Seal. LC 12-32884. 2 p. l., 192 p. front., plates. 19 cm. c.1887. Congregational Sunday-School and Publishing Society.
--Royal Service: Or, The/King's Seal, 1 of 10 vols. (The Boys' Bookshelf Library). N.D. Pilgrims Press.
--Tad's Telephone. (Illus.). (Play and Study Ser.). N.D. D. Lothrop Co.
--Tangles and Corners in Kezzie Driscoll's Life. LC 12-328819. 335 p. front., plates. 18 cm. c.1882. Presbyterian Board of Publication.
--Two and a Half. LC 22-173397. 75 p. front., pl. 17 1/2 cm. (Red book series). c.1891. Congregational Sunday-School and Publishing Society.
--Unity Dodge and Her Patterns. LC 12-32940. 336 p. front., plates. 18 cm. c.1883. Presbyterian Board of Publication.
--Vagabond and Victor: The Story of David Sheldon. LC 12-32938. 331 p. front., plates. 18 cm. 1880. Presbyterian Board of Publication.
--We Three. LC 12-32939. 270 p. front., plates. 18 cm. c.1877. Presbyterian Board of Publication.
--What Dollie and Robbie Did, 1 of 6 Vols. (Nellie's Red Book Ser.: Vol. 5). N.D. Set. Sunday-School Library.
--What Dolly and Robbie Did. LC 22-17340. 67 p. front., pl. 17 1/2 cm. (Red book series). c.1891. Congregational Sunday-School and Publishing Society.
Hamilton, Katharine Parr (1881-)
--The Purple Tree: A Group of Poems. Jessen, Bubi, illus. LC 53-39527. 79p. illus. 24cm. 1953. C. Hertzog.
Hamilton, Kay, pseud., see De Leeuw, Cateau Wilhelmina.
Hamilton, Lee David
--Adventures with Elsie, the Famous Cow. LC 64-19919. 63 p. illus., facsims., ports. 24 cm. 1964. Putnam.
Hamilton, Madeleine, tr. see Peterson, Hans.
Hamilton, Madelen C
--Where the Thunderbirds Dwell. LC 77-23383. p. cm. 1977. (ISBN 0-8024-3978-0). Moody Press.
Hamilton, Mary
--Our Games. N.D. Thomas Nelson and Sons.
Hamilton-Merritt, Jane
--Boonmee and the Lucky White Elephant. Phongsun, illus. LC 79-179552. (Illus.). 86 p. 24cm. 1972. (ISBN 0-684-12684-2). Scribner.
--Lahu Wildfire. Barkowsky, Gerd, illus. LC 72-1167. (Illus.). 144 p. 22cm. 1973. (ISBN 0-684-13251-6). Scribner.
--My First Days of School. Hamilton-Merritt, Jane, photos by. (Illus.). 32p. (New Feeling Bks.). (ps-k). 1982. (ISBN 0-671-44417-4, Little Simon). S&S.
--My First Days of School. LC 81-21361. p. cm. c.1982. (ISBN 0-671-44417-4). Simon & Schuster.
--My First Days of School. Hamilton-Merritt, Jane, photos by. 1982. Messner.
--Our New Baby. Hamilton-Merritt, Jane, photos by. LC 81-18469. (Illus.). 28 p. 24cm. c.1982. (ISBN 0-671-44416-6). Little Simon.
Hamilton, Mollie, pseud., see Kaye, Mary Margaret.
Hamilton, Mollie, pseud. (1909-)
--The Animals' Vacation: A Fable in Which Some Animals Take a Vacation and Discover Some Things About Themselves. Kaye, Mary Margaret. Hamilton, Mollie, pseud. (1909-), illus. Kaye, Mary Margaret. LC 64-157641. (Illus.). 45 p. 1964. New York Graphic Society.
Hamilton, Morris & Willoughby, Jane
--Tunes for Tiny Troubadours. Willoughby, Walter J., illus. 31p. (gr. 1-2). N.D. G P Putnam's Sons.
Hamilton, Morse (1943-)
--Big Sisters Are Bad Witches. Hafner, Marylin (1925-), illus. LC 79-24907. (Illus.). 33 p. 20cm. c.1981. (ISBN 0-688-80268-0). (ISBN 0-688-84268-2). Greenwillow Books.
Hamilton, Morse (1943-) & Hamilton, Emily
--My Name Is Emily. Oliver, Jenni (1947-), illus. LC 78-4537. (Illus.). 32 p. 26cm. c.1979. (ISBN 0-688-80181-1). (ISBN 0-688-84181-3). Greenwillow Books.
Hamilton-Paterson, James
--Hostage!. LC 79-25114. 187 p. 22cm. 1980, c.1978. (ISBN 0-529-05596-1). Collins.
--The House in the Waves. LC 76-103043. 157 p. 22cm. 1970. (ISBN 0-87599-171-8). S. G. Phillips.
Hamilton, Pearl & Hamilton, Vi
--Songs 'bout Animals 'n' Things, for Children: Words and Music. LC 43-173745. cover-title, 32 p. 30 1/2 cm. 1940. Paull-Pioneer Music Corporation.
Hamilton, Robert W., pseud., see Stratemeyer Syndicate.
Hamilton, Robert W., pseud.
--Belinda of the Red Cross. Stratemeyer Syndicate. Repr. of 1917 ed (Pub. by Sully & Kleinteich). N.D. World Publishing Co.
--Belinda of the Red Cross. Stratemeyer Syndicate. Scott, Arthur O., illus. Repr. of 1917 ed (Pub. by Sully & Kleinteich). 1918. A. L. Burt.
--Belinda of the Red Cross. Stratemeyer Syndicate. Scott, Arthur O., illus. 1917. Sully & Kleinteich.
Hamilton, Ron
--Alan & the Baron. Deal, Peggy B., illus. (Illus.). 50p. (Orig.). 1983. (ISBN 0-913072-54-0). Natl Assn Deaf.
Hamilton, Tressa
--Angels Bells. (Illus.). 30p. (Orig.). 1984. (ISBN 0-9613806-0-8). T Hamilton.
Hamilton, Vi, jt. auth. see Hamilton, Pearl.
Hamilton, Victoria
--McDuff in the Daffodils. Robb, Rochelle, illus. (Illus.). 44p. (Orig.). (gr. 4-12). 1974. (ISBN 0-939198-00-2). Blue Heron.
Hamilton, Virginia (1936-)
--Arilla Sun Down. LC 76-13180. 256p. (gr. 7 up). 1976. (ISBN 0-688-80058-0). (ISBN 0-688-84058-2). Greenwillow. **Award: (ALA).**
--Dustland. LC 79-19003. 180 p. 22cm. c.1980. (ISBN 0-688-80228-1). (ISBN 0-688-84228-3). Greenwillow Books.
--The Gathering. LC 80-12512. p. cm. c.1980. (ISBN 0-688-80269-9). (ISBN 0-688-84269-0). Greenwillow Books. **Award: (ALA).**
--The House of Dies Drear. Keith, Bros, illus. LC 84-19847. p. cm. 1984, c.1968. (ISBN 0-02-043520-7). Collier Books.
--The House of Dies Drear. Keith, Eros, illus. LC 68-23059. (Illus.). 246 p. 21cm. 1968. Macmillan. **Award: (ALA).**
--Jahdu. Pinkney, Jerry (1939-), illus. LC 79-16039. (Illus.). 55 p. 22cm. (Greenwillow read-alone). 1980. (ISBN 0-688-80246-X). (ISBN 0-688-84246-1). Greenwillow Books.
--Junius over Far. LC 84-48344. 288p. (Charlotte Zolotow Bk.). (gr. 7 up). 1985. (ISBN 0-06-022194-1). (ISBN 0-06-022195-X). HarpJ.
--Justice and Her Brothers. LC 78-54684. 217 p. 22cm. c.1978. (ISBN 0-688-80182-X). (ISBN 0-688-84182-1). Greenwillow Books.
--A Little Love. LC 84-1753. 192p. 1984. (ISBN 0-399-21046-6, Philomel). (ISBN 0-399-21046-6). Putnam Pub Group.
--M. C. Higgins, the Great. LC 76-1002. 400 p. 25cm. 1976, c.1974. (ISBN 0-8161-6356-1). G. K. Hall.

--At the Defense of Pittsburgh: Or, The Struggle to Save America's "Fighting Steel" Supply. (The Conquest of the United States Ser.). Henry Altemus Co.N.D. Henry Altemus Company.
--Bountyville Boys. LC 7-29725. vii, 335 p. col. front., 3 col. pl. 20 cm. 1907. D. Appleton and Company.
--Chuggins: The Youngest Hero with the Army. Claghorn, Joseph C., illus. LC 4-21726. ix p., 1 l., 13-96 p. incl. col. front., illus. 4 pl. 19 cm. (Altemus' Hollytree series). 1904. Henry Altemus Company.
--Dave Darrin After the Mine Layers: Or, Hitting the Enemy a Hard Naval Blow. LC 20-365. 251 p. incl. front., illus. 19 1/2 cm. (Lettered on cover: The Dave Darrin series). c.1919. Henry Altemus Company.
--Dave Darrin and the German Submarines: Or, Making a Clean-up of the Hun Sea Monsters. (Altemus' Dave Darrin Ser.). N.D. Henry Altemus Company.
--Dave Darrin at Vera Cruz: Or, Fighting with the U.S. Navy in Mexico. LC 14-9880. 256 p. incl. front., plates. 19 1/2 cm. (His The Dave Darrin series) $0.50). c.1914. Henry Altemus Company.
--Dave Darrin on Mediterranean Service: Or, With Dan Dalzell on European Duty. (Altemus' Dave Darrin Ser.). N.D. Henry Altemus Company.
--Dave Darrin on the Asiatic Station: Or, Winning Lieutenant's Commissions on the Admiral's Flagship. LC 19-17073. 251 p. incl. front., illus. 19 1/2 cm. c.1919. Henry Altemus Company.
--Dave Darrin's First Year at Annapolis: Or, Two Plebe Midshipmen at the U.S. Naval Academy. LC 10-30145. 19.5 cm. 253p. (Altemus' Annapolis Ser.). 1910. Henry Altemus Company.
--Dave Darrin's Fourth Year at Annapolis: Or, Headed for Graduation and the Big Cruise. LC 11-20882. 19.5 cm. 255p. (Altemus' Annapolis Series). 1911. Henry Altemus Company.
--Dave Darrin's Second Year at Annapolis: Or, Two Midshipmen as Naval Academy "Youngsters". LC 11-20821. 19.5 cm. 249p. (Altemus' Annapolis Ser.). 1911. Henry Altemus Company.
--Dave Darrin's South American Cruise: Or, Two Innocent Young Naval Tools of an Infamous Conspiracy. LC 19-15974. 255 p. incl. front. 19 1/2 cm. (Lettered on cover: The Dave Darrin series). c.1919. Henry Altemus Company.
--Dave Darrin's Third Year at Annapolis: Or, Leaders of the Second Class Midshipmen. LC 11-20883. 19.5 cm. 254p. (Altemus' Annapolis Series). 1911. Henry Altemus Company.
--Detective Johnson of New Orleans. (The Eureka Detective Stories). N.D. J. S. Oglivie Co.
--Dick Prescott's First Year at West Point: Or, Two Chums in the Cadet Gray. LC 10-29414. 19.5 cm. 255p. (Altemus' West Point Ser.). 1910. Henry Altemus Co.
--Dick Prescott's Fourth Year at West Point: Or, Ready to Drop the Gray for Soldier Straps. LC 11-20307. 19.5 cm. 252p. (Altemus' West Point Ser.). 1911. Henry Altemus Co.
--Dick Prescott's Second Year at West Point: Or, Finding the Glory of the Soldier's life. LC 11-30305. 19.5 cm. 253p. (Altemus' West Point Ser.). 1911. Henry Altemus Co.
--Dick Prescott's Third Year at West Point: Or, Standing Firm for Flag and Honor. LC 26-7501. 251 p. incl. front., plates. 19 1/2 cm. (His West Point series). 1911. Henry Altemus Company.
--The Grammar School Boys in Summer Athletics: Or, Dick & Co. Make Their Fame Secure. (The Grammar School Boys Ser.). N.D. Henry Altemus Company.
--The Grammar School Boys in the Woods: Or, Dick & Co. Trail Fun and Knowledge. (The Grammar School Boys Ser.). N.D. Henry Altemus Company.
--The Grammar School Boys of Gridley: Or, Dick & Co. Start Things Moving. (The Grammar School Boys Ser.). N.D. Henry Altemus Company.
--The Grammar School Boys Snowbound: Or, Dick & Co. at Winter Sports. (The Grammar School Boys Ser.). N.D. Henry Altemus Company.
--The High School Boy's Canoe Club: Or, Dick and Co.'s Rivals on Lake Pleasant. (High School Boy's Vacation Ser.). N.D. Henry Altemus Co.
--The High School Boys' Fishing Trip: Or, Dick & Co. in the Wilderness. LC 13-17957. 251 p. incl. front., plates. 19 1/2 cm. (His The high school vacation series). c.1913. Henry Altemus Company.
--High School Boys in Summer Camp: Or, The Dick Prescott Six Training for the Gridley Eleven. (High School Boys' Vacation Ser.). N.D. Henry Altemus Co.
--High School Boy's Training Hike: Or, Dick and Co. Making Themselves "Hard as Nails". (High School Boys' Vacation Ser.). N.D.
--The High School Captain of the Team: Or, Dick & Co. Leading the Athletic Vanguard. LC 11-1859. 19.5 cm. 246p. (The High School Boys Ser.). 1910. Henry Altemus Company.
--The High School Freshmen: Or, Dick & Co.'s First Year Pranks and Sports. LC 11-23304. 19.5 cm. 250p. (The High School Boys Series). 1910. Henry Altemus Company.
--The High School Left End: Or, Dick & Co. Grilling on the Football Gridiron. (The High School Boys Ser.). N.D. Henry Altemus Company.
--The High School Pitcher: Or, Dick & Co. on the Gridley Diamond. LC 11-23303. 19.5cm. 248p. (The High School Boys Ser.). 1910. Henry Altemus Company.
--His Evil Eye. (The Eureka Detective Stories). N.D. J. S. Ogilvie Co.
--In the Battle for New York: Or, Uncle Sam's Boys in the Desperate Struggle for the Metropolis. (The Conquest of the United States Ser.). N.D. Henry Altemus Company.
--Inspector Henderson: The Central Office Detective. (The Eureka Detective Stories). N.D. J. S. Ogilvie Co.
--The Invasion of the United States: Or, Uncle Sam's Boys at the Capture of Boston. LC 16-213946. 256 p. incl. front., illus. 19 1/2 cm. (His Conquest of the United States series, vol. I)). c.1916. Henry Altemus Company.
--Making the Last Stand for Old Glory: Or, Uncle Sam's Boys in the Last Frantic Drive. (The Conquest of the United States Ser.). N.D. Henry Altemus Company.
--The Motor Boat Club and the Wireless: Or, The Dot, Dash and Dare Cruise. LC 9-28035. 256 p. incl. front., plates. 19 1/2 cm. c.1909. H. Altemus Company.
--The Motor Boat Club at the Golden Gate: Or, A Thrilling Capture in the Great Fog. (The Motor Boat Club Ser.). N.D. Henry Altemus Co.
--The Motor Boat Club in Florida: Or, Laying the Ghost of Alligator Swamp. (The Motor Boat Club Ser.). N.D. Henry Altemus Co.
--The Motor Boat Club of the Kennebec: Or, The Secret of Smugglers' Island. LC 9-19189. 235 p. incl. front., plates. 19 1/2 cm. 20cm. 255p. c.1909. H. Altemus Company.
--The Motor Boat Club off Long Isalnd: Or, A Daring Marine Game at Racing Speed. LC 9-24895. 252 p. incl. front., plates. 19 1/2 cm. $1.0. c.1909. H. Altemus Ocmpany.
--The Motor Boat Club on the Great Lakes: Or, The Flying Dutchman of the Big Fresh Water. N.D. Henry Altemus Co.
--The Square Dollar Boys Wake up: Or, Fighting the Trolley Franchise Steal. LC 12-22319. 253 p. incl. front., plates. 19 1/2 cm. (His The square dollar boys series)). c.1912. Henry Altemus Company.
--The Motor Boat Club at Nantucket: Or, The Mystery of the Dunstan Heir. (The Motor Boat Club Ser.). N.D. Henry Altemus Co.
--Uncle Sam's Boys as Lieutenants: Or, Serving Old Glory as Line Officers. (The Boys of the Army Ser.). N.D. Henry Altemus Co.
--Uncle Sam's Boys as Sergeants: Or, Handling their First Real Commands. (The Boys of the Army Ser.). N.D. Henry Altemus Co.
--Uncle Sam's Boys in the Philippines: Or, Following the Flag Against the Moros. LC 12-17517. 254 p. incl. front., plates. 19 1/2 cm. (His The boys of the army series). c.1912. Henry Altemus Company.
--Uncle Sam's Boys in the Ranks: Or, Two Recruits in the United States Army. LC 10-26764. 20cm. 254p. (The Boys of the Army Ser.). 1910. Henry Altemus Co.
--Uncle Sam's Boys on Field Duty: Or, Winning Corporal's Chevrons. (The Boys of the Army Ser.). N.D. Henry Altemus Co.
--Uncle Sam's Boys on Their Mettle: Or, A Chance to Win Officers' Commissions. (The Boys of the Army Ser.). N.D. Henry Altemus Co.
--Uncle Sam's Boys Smash the Germans: Or, Helping the Allies Wind up the Great World War. (The Boys of the Army Ser.). N.D. Henry Altemus Co.
--Uncle Sam's Boys with Pershing: Or, Dick Prescott at Grips with the Boche. (The Boys of the Army Ser.). N.D. Henry Altemus Co.
--The Young Engineers in Arizona: Or, Laying Tracks on the Man-Killer Quicksand. LC 12-20639. 250 p. incl. front., plates. 19 1/2 cm. (His The Young engineers series)). c.1912. Henry Altemus Company.
--The Young Engineers in Colorado: Or, At Railroad Building in Earnest. LC 68-31142. 252 p. incl. front., plates. 19 1/2 cm. (His The young engineers series). c.1912. Henry Altemus Company.
--The Young Engineers in Mexico: Or, Fighting the Mine Swindlers. (The Young Engineers' Ser). N.D. Henry Altemus Co.
--The Young Engineers in Nevada: Or, Seeking Fortune on the Turn of a Pick. (The Young Engineers' Ser.). N.D. Henry Altemus Co.
--The Young Engineers on the Gulf: Or, The Dread Mystery of the Million-Dollar Breakwater. (The Young Engineers' Ser.). N.D. Henry Altemus Co.

Hancock, Lyn (1938-)
--There's A Seal in My Sleeping Bag. 1972. Brozoi Books.

Hancock, Mary A (1923-)
--Menace on the Mountain. Hall, H. Tom, illus. LC 68-31142. (Illus.). 175 p. 21cm. 1968. Macrae Smith.
--The Thundering Prairie. Hall, H. Tom, illus. LC 79-87990. (Illus.). 192 p. 21cm. 1969. Macrae Smith.

Hancock, Myrtle J. Marti see Marty, pseud.

Hancock, Rubye Kilgore
--Mount up with Wings. LC 56-427829. 153p. 20cm. 1956. Zondervan Pub. House.

Hancock, Sibyl (1940-)
--An Ark and a Rainbow: Noah and the Ark for Beginning Readers : Genesis 6-9 for Children. Cunningham, Aline, illus. LC 76-14924. (Illus.). 39 p. 23cm. (I can read a Bible story). c.1976. (ISBN 0-570-07309-X). Concordia Pub. House.
--The Blazing Hills. Cuffari, Richard (1925-1978), illus. LC 74-77594. (Illus.). 47 p. 23cm. (See and read book). c.1975. (ISBN 0-399-20422-9). (ISBN 0-399-60913-X). Putnam.
--Climbing up to Nowhere: The Tower of Babel for Beginning Readers : Genesis 10-11: 1-9 for Children. Cunningham, Aline, illus. LC 77-7210. (Illus.). 48 p. 22cm. (I can read a Bible story). c.1977. (ISBN 0-570-07322-7). (ISBN 0-570-07316-2). Concordia Pub. House.
--Freaky Francie. Shortall, Leonard W., illus. LC 79-15226. p. cm. c.1979. (ISBN 0-13-330563-5). Prentice-Hall.
--Mario's Mystery Machine. De Paola, Tomie, pseud. (1934-), illus. De Paola, Thomas Anthony. LC 72-163425. (Illus.). 48 p. 23cm. (See and read storybook). 1972. Putnam.
--Old Blue. Ingraham, Erick, illus. LC 79-9928. (Illus.). 46 p. 23cm. (See & read book). c.1980. (ISBN 0-399-61141-X). Putnam. **Award: (ALA).**

Hancock, Sibyl (1940-), adapted by.
--Esteban & the Ghost. Zimmer, Dirk, illus. LC 82-22125. (Original Author: Ralph Steele Boggs, 1901-). (Illus.). 32p. (Dial Book for Young Readers). (ps-3). 1983. (ISBN 0-8037-2443-8). (ISBN 0-8037-2443-8). (ISBN 0-8037-2411-X). Dutton. **Award: (ALA).**

Hand, David, jt. auth. see Martin, Nancy.

Hand, David (1900-)
--Martha Armstrong-Hand's Living Dolls: A Picture Story. Armstrong-Hand, Martha, illus. LC 84-159120. (Illus.). 60 p. c.1983. (ISBN 0-87588-199-8). Hobby House Press.

Hand, Desmond, jt. auth. see Robbie, Dorothy.

Handel, Joanna, ed. see St. John, Elizabeth.

Handel, Leo H.
--Dog Named Duke. (Illus.). (gr. 5-10). 1966. (ISBN 0-8382-1012-0). Hale.
--Dog Named Duke: True Stories of German Shepherds at Work with the Law. LC 66-10902. (Illus.). photos. (gr. 7-9). 1966. (ISBN 0-397-30860-4, JBL-J). Har-Row.
--A Dog Named Duke: True Stories of German Shepherds at Work with the Law. 166p. 1969. J. B. Lippincott Company.

Handford, Elizabeth R.
--The Mystery of the Smudged Postmark. 128p. (Preteen Ser.). (gr. 4-7). 1974. (ISBN 0-8024-3540-8). Moody.

Handford, Thomas W., ed.
--Tommy's First Speaker for Little Boys and Girls. LC 71-149104. 160 p. 21cm. (Granger index reprint series). 1971. (ISBN 0-8369-6229-X). Books for Libraries Press.

Handforth, Thomas Schofield (1897-1948)
--Faraway Meadow. Handforth, Thomas Schofield (1897-1948), illus. LC 39-32824. 30cm. 32p. 1939. Doubleday Doran Books.
--Mei Li. Handforth, Thomas Schofield (1897-1948), illus. LC 38-27994. (Illus.). 31cm. 52p. 1938. Doubleday Honor Books. **Award: (RCM).**
--Mei Li. Handforth, Thomas Schofield (1897-1948), illus. LC 38-27994. 52 p. illus. 31 cm. (Junior Books). 1963, c.1938. Doubleday, Doran & Company, Inc.

Hands, Lydia
--Golden Threads from an Ancient Loom. (Illus.). N.D. E P Dutton.

Handy, Alice, Mrs.
--Billy Whiskers and the Radio: Continuing the Famous Billy Whiskers Series. Brundage, Frances, illus. LC 28-13021. 3 p. l., 11-169 p. col. front., illus., col. plates. 23 1/2 cm. (The Billy Whiskers series v. 26). c.1927. The Saalfield Publishing Company.
--Billy Whiskers' Treasure Hunt: Continuing the Famous Billy Whiskers Series. Brundage, Frances, illus. LC 28-30548. 156 p. col. front., illus., col. plates. 22 1/2 cm. (The Billy Whiskers series, v. 30). c.1928. The Saalfield Publishing Company.

Hane, Setsuko, jt. auth. see Kijima, Hajime.

Haner, Ray Cass
--The Tales of Kiku. LC 59-27179. (Illus.). 24cm. 47p. 1958. Sandmar House.

Hanes, Charles
--William Shakespeare & His Plays. LC 68-10337. (Illus.). map. index. bibliog. app. ca. 192p. (Franklin Watts Biographies Ser.). (gr. 7 up). 1968. (ISBN 0-531-00923-8). Watts.

Hanes, DeWitt
--The Big Opportunity. LC 34-145409. 253 p. front. 19 cm. (Mystery and adventure series for boys). c.1934. A. L. Burt Company.

Haney, Germaine
--Christmas Frolics. 118p. N.D. T. S. Denison & Co Inc.
--Five Minute Plays for Children. 95p. N.D. Northwestern Press.
--Five Minute Plays for Children. 95p. N.D. T. S. Denison & Co Inc.
--Jolly Juvenile Readings. 95p. N.D. T. S. Denison.
--Practical Plays. 103p. N.D. Northwestern Press.
--Practical Plays. 103p. N.D. T. S. Denison & Co.
--Recital Readings for Children. 96p. N.D. T. S. Denison & Co Inc.
--Short Plays for Girls. 103p. N.D. T. S. Denison & Co.
--Short Selections for Little Tots. 96p. N.D. Northwestern Press.
--Short Selections for Little Tots. 96p. N.D. T. S. Denison & Co Inc.

Haney, Lynn, ed. see Semple, Lorenzo.

Haney, Lynn (1941-)
--I Am a Dancer. Curtis, Bruce, illus. (Illus.). 64p. (gr. 10 up). 1981. (ISBN 0-399-20724-4). (ISBN 0-399-20792-9). Putnam Pub Group.

Hanff, Helene
--Butch Elects a Mayor. Brown, Judith Gwyn (1933-), illus. LC 78-77784. (Illus.). 41 p. 1969. (ISBN 0-8193-0277-5). Parents' Magazine Press.
--Terrible Thomas. Siebel, Fritz (1913-), illus. LC 64-12812. 33 p. illus. (part col.) 30 cm. 1964. Harper & Row.

Hanford, Barbara
--Magic Table. (gr. 4-6). 1966. (ISBN 0-07-025986-0). McGraw.

Hanighen, Bernard David (1908-)
--Pan Ku. LC 53-22519. 14 x 18cm. c.1953. Winston.

Hank, Elsa see Marston, Elsa.

Hankey, Donald
--A Student in Arms. N.D. E P Dutton.

Hankey, John, ed. see John, Timothy.

Hankin, Cliff
--Rookie Running Back. Chauncy, Francis, illus. LC 68-57466. (Illus.). 191 p. 21cm. 1968. Vanguard Press.
--Tony's Two-Sport Spring. (gr. 7 up). 1970. (ISBN 0-8149-0682-6). Vanguard.

Hankins, Maude McGehee
--Daddy Gander. Cadie, Ve Elizabeth, illus. LC 28-18830. (Illus.). 19cm. 40p. (Sunny Bks.). 1928. P. F. Volland Co.
--Fermentations of Eliza. LC 16-213619. 2 p. l., 9-230 p. front., plates. 19 cm. c.1915. Thomas Y. Crowell Company.

Hanle, Zack & Hertz, Martin
--The Golden Ladle. N.D. Ziff-Davis.

Hanley, Amy Carr
--Towhead in Mexico. Manning, Kenneth, illus. LC 47-6866. 109 p. illus. 24 cm. 1947. Review and Herald Pub. Assn.

Hanley, Eve
--A Blazing Torch. Geer, Charles Hand (1922-), illus. LC 66-27703. (Illus.). 88 p. 22cm. 1967, c.1966. I. Washburn.
--The Enchanted Toby Jug. Unwin, Nora Spicer (1907-), illus. LC 65-11557. 134p. illus. 21cm. 1965, c.1964. Washburn Dist. McKay.
--Jane and the Nodding Mandarin. Linton, Anne, illus. LC 68-28274. (Illus.). 112 p. 21cm. 1968, c.1965. Weybright and Talley.
--New Song. Nebel, Gustave E., illus. LC 68-12863. (Illus.). 21cm. 110p. (gr. 5-9). 1967. Weybright.

Hanley, Georgia Eldredge
--The One-Eyed Fairies. LC 24-753349. 214 p. col. front., illus. 19 1/2 cm. c.1924. Lothrop, Lee & Shepard Co.

Hanley, Gerald
--Gilligan's Last Elephant. 272p. 1962. The World Publishing Company.

Hanley, May Carr
--Story Time. LC 52-18194. 96 p. illus. 21 cm. 1951. Southern Pub. Association.

Hanlon, Emily (1945-)
--Circle Home. LC 81-6171. 224p. (gr. 6-9). 1981. (ISBN 0-02-742640-8). Bradbury Pr.

--How a Horse Grew Hoarse on the Site Where He Sighted a Bare Bear: A Tale of Homonyms. Tomei, Lorna, illus. LC 75-26682. (Illus.). 32 p. c.1976. (ISBN 0-440-03832-4). (ISBN 0-440-03833-2). Delacorte Press.
--It's Too Late for Sorry. LC 78-4422. p. cm. 22cm. 222p. 1978. (ISBN 0-87888-136-0). Bradbury Press.
--Love Is No Excuse. LC 82-9580. 227 p. 22cm. c.1982. (ISBN 0-87888-204-9). Bradbury Press.
--The Swing. LC 78-26400. 209 p. 22cm. c.1979. (ISBN 0-87888-146-8). Bradbury Press.
--What If a Lion Eats Me and I Fall into a Hippopotamus' Mud Hole?. Grant, Alice Leigh (1947-), illus. LC 75-8007. p. cm. 1975. (ISBN 0-440-05950-X). (ISBN 0-440-05951-8). Delacorte Press.
--The Wing & the Flame. LC 80-13082. 160p. (gr. 7 up). 1980. (ISBN 0-02-742540-1). Bradbury Pr.

Hann, Florence Yates, adapted by see Rostand, Edmond Eugene Alexis.

Hann, Jacquie (1951-)
--Big Trouble. LC 78-1712. (Illus.). 39 p. 22cm. c.1978. (ISBN 0-590-07557-8). Four Winds Press.
--Crybaby. Hann, Jacquie (1951-), illus. LC 78-22035. (Illus.). 39 p. 17cm. c.1979. (ISBN 0-590-07609-4). Four Winds Press.
--Follow the Leader. LC 81-22172. (Illus.). 32 p. c.1982. (ISBN 0-517-54603-5). Crown Publishers.
--That Man Is Talking to His Toes. Hann, Jacquie (1951-), illus. LC 76-13496. (Illus.). 39 p. 24cm. c.1976. (ISBN 0-590-07456-3). Four Winds Press.
--Up Day, Down Day. Hann, Jacquie (1951-), illus. LC 77-15936. (Illus.). 32 p. 21cm. c.1978. (ISBN 0-590-07519-5). Four Winds Press.
--Up Day, Down Day. Hann, Jacquie (1951-), illus. 1978. Harper.
--Where's Mark?. Hann, Jacquie (1951-), illus. LC 76-54869. (Illus.). 39 p. 22cm. c.1977. (ISBN 0-590-07499-7). Four Winds Press.

Hann, Penelope
--Edward the Elephant. LeClaire, Dominique, illus. LC 82-181239. (Illus.). 28p. Orig. Title: Eduard, der Elefant. 1982. (ISBN 0-907234-04-6). Picture Bk Studio USA.

Hanna-Barbera Productions
--Huckberry Hound and His Friends. LC 62-53654. 60 p. illus. 32 cm. (Giant golden book). 1962. Golden Press.
--Yogi Bear and His Friends: Huckleberry Hound, Cindy Bear, Mr. Jinks, Pixie and Dixie, Boo Boo Bear. LC 62-1174. 61p. illus. 31cm. (Giant golden book). c.1961. Golden Press.

Hanna-Barbera Productions & Lewis, Jean
--The Flintstones Meet the Gruesomes. De Santis, George, illus. LC 65-1991. 1v. (unpaged) col. illus. 33cm. (Big Golden bk.). 1965. Golden.

Hanna-Barbera Productions & Memling, Carl (1918-1969)
--The Flintstones. LC 63-1579. unpaged. illus. 28 cm. (Big golden book). c.1962. Golden Press.

Hanna, Mary Carr (1905-)
--Cassie & Ike. LC 73-77900. 207 p. 23cm. 1973. (ISBN 0-910244-70-7). F. Blair.

Hanna, Paul R., jt. auth. see Barry, Mary E.

Hanna-Barbera Productions Hollywood, Calif, jt. auth. see Memling, Carl.

Hannaford, Pauline
--The Bomb-Scare Mystery. LC 72-93415. (Illus.). 110 p. 23cm. 1973. (ISBN 0-87076-882-4). Stanwix House.

Hannah, Annie L.
--Roy's Opportunity, 1 of 50 vols. 382p. (Library of Best Authors). 1905. American Tract Society.
--Roy's Opportunity: And How He Improved It... LC 12-32907. 381 p. front., plates. 19 cm. c.1892. American Tract Society.

Hannah, Harvey L.
--Benny and Buster Bug. LC 42-20812. 54 p. incl. front., illus. 23 cm. 1942. Dorrance and Company.
--Benny and Buster Bug and Pokey Snail. LC 47-12168. 63 p. illus. 24 cm. 1947. Dorrance.

Hannay, Allen
--Love and Other Natural Disasters. LC 81-23674. (Illus.). 241 p. 22cm. c.1982. (ISBN 0-316-34362-5). Little, Brown.

Hannon, Ruth
--Children's Bible Stories from the Old Testament. Giordano, Joe, illus. (Illus.). 1978. (ISBN 0-307-13740-6, Golden Pr). (ISBN 0-307-63740-9). Western Pub.
--Noah's Ark. Bracken, Carolyn, illus. LC 73-77490. (Illus.). 33 p. 28cm. 1973. Golden Press.

Hannum, Sara & Chase, John Terry, eds.
--To Play Man Number One. Schachner, Erwin, illus. LC 73-75518. (Illus.). woodcuts. 192p. (gr. 8 up). 1969. (ISBN 0-689-30016-6). Atheneum. **Award: (ALA).**
--The Wind Is Round. Bowen, Ron, illus. LC 79-115083. (Illus.). xiii, 100 p. 25cm. 1970. Atheneum.

Hannum, Sara & Reed, Gwendolyn Elizabeth (1932-), eds.
--Lean Out of the Window: An Anthology of Modern Poetry. Tischler, Ragna, illus. Johnson, Siddie Joe (1905-1977), intro. by. LC 65-10480. (Illus.). xiv, 112 p. 25cm. 1965. Atheneum. **Award: (ALA).**

Hanor, Mary
--Corky. LC 52-16448. unpaged. illus. 27 cm. 1951. Erle Press.
--Ebony. Hutchins, Gardner & Mlodock, Richard, illus. LC 52-67534. unpaged. illus. 27cm. 1952. Erle Press.

Hanrahan, Jack, jt. auth. see Hahn, Phil.

Hanrahan, Jack & Hahn, Phil
--Beastly Rhymes. Hanrahan, Jack, illus. LC 66-9321. (Illus.). 1 v. (unpaged. 22cm. (Laugh books). 1966. Wonder Books.
--The Show Me Book. Hanrahan, Jack, illus. LC 66-31221. (Illus.). 1 v. (unpaged. 22cm. (Laugh Books). 1966. Wonder Books.

Hanrahan, Mariellen
--My Little Book of Trains. Seward, James E., illus. (Illus.). (Tell-a-Tale Readers). (gr. k-3). 1979. (ISBN 0-307-68648-5, Whitman). Western Pub.
--Surprise at the Farm. Crawford, Mel (1925-), illus. (Illus.). 26p. (Golden Panorama Ser). (ps). 1975. (ISBN 0-307-11093-1, Golden Pr). Western Pub.

Hanrahan, Mariellen, ed. see Masters, M.

Hanrahan, Mariellen, et al., eds. see Masters, M.

Hans, Marcie
--How Many "Ers" Are You. 1st ed. Goldblatt, Burt, illus. LC 64-17116. (Illus.). 24cm. 32p. 1964. Bobbs-Merrill.

Hansberry, Lorraine Vivian (1930-1965)
--Raisin in the Sun. (gr. 4 up). 1969. (ISBN 0-394-40688-5). Random.

Hanscom, Beatrice, ed.
--The Child's Hansel and Gretel. Kirk, Maria Louise (1860-), illus. N.D. Frederick A. Stokes.

Hansell, Caroline
--The Kindergarten Children. (Illus.). N.D. White, Stokes & Allen.

Hansen, Agnes Camilla, tr. see Soya, Carl Erik Martin.

Hansen, Carla & Hansen, Vilh.
--Barnaby Bear Builds a Boat. LC 79-3902. (Illus.). 32 p. 26cm. c.1979. (ISBN 0-394-84247-2). Random House.
--Barnaby Bear Visits the Farm. LC 79-3903. (Illus.). 32 p. 26cm. c.1979. (ISBN 0-394-84248-0). Random House.

Hansen, Caryl Hall see Hall, Caryl, pseud.

Hansen, Joseph (1923-)
--Troublemaker. N.D. Harper & Row.

Hansen, Joyce
--The Gift-Giver. LC 80-12969. 118 p. 22cm. c.1980. (ISBN 0-395-29433-9). Houghton Mifflin/Clarion Books.
--Home Boy. 160p. (gr. 6 up). 1982. (ISBN 0-89919-114-2, Clarion). HM.
--Yellow Bird and Me. LC 85-484. p. cm. c.1985. (ISBN 0-89919-335-8). Clarion Books.

Hansen, L. F.
--Adventures of a Sea Rover. N.D. Bruce Humphries, Inc.

Hansen, Mary Lewis, jt. auth. see Drdek, Richard E.

Hansen, Vilh., jt. auth. see Hansen, Carla.

Hansen, Virginia (1912-)
--Anytime Stories for Kids. LC 85-12435. 32 p. 18cm. c.1985. (ISBN 0-8163-0620-6). Pacific Press Pub. Association.

Hansen, Wilhelm, tr. see Grimm, Jakob Ludwig Karl (1785-1863) & Grimm, Wilhelm Karl.

Hansjurgen Press
--The Adventures of the Black Hand Gang. LC 77-5950. 1977, c.1976. (ISBN 0-13-013938-6). Prentice-Hall.
--The Adventures of the Black Hand Gang. Littlewood, Barbara, ed. Littlewood, Barbara, illus. (Illus.). 128p. (gr. 3-7). 1983. (ISBN 0-13-013938-6, Pub. by Treehouse). (ISBN 0-13-014035-X). P-H.

Hanson, Alice, ed. see Disney, Walt, Productions.

Hanson, Alice Stuebe (1909-)
--Hello!. Fleur, Anne Elizabeth (1901-), illus. Sari, pseud. LC 55-44862. unpaged. illus. 22cm. (Cozy-corner book, 2425). c.1955. Whitman Pub. Co.

Hanson, Andrea, adapted by.
--The Adventures of Black Beauty, Beauty and Vicky. LC 83-21264. (Based on the Adventures of Black Beauty Television Series. Original Author: Anna Sewell, 1820-1878). c.1984. (ISBN 0-394-86383-6). Random House.

Hanson, Andrea, ed. see Sewell, Anna.

Hanson, B. Joan
--Teenage Rebel. 1970. (ISBN 0-87508-764-7). Chr Lit.

Hanson, Charles Henry
--Stories of Old Rome: The Wanderings of Aeneas & the Founding of Rome. (Illus.). N.D. Thomas Nelson & Sons.

Hanson, Eugene Kenneth (1930-)
--Little Star. Mickelson, Melva, illus. LC 60-14165. unpaged. illus. 22cm. 1960. Augsburg Pub. House.

Hanson, Harvey (1941-)
--Game Time. LC 75-4776. (Illus.). 87 p. 21cm. 1975. (ISBN 0-531-02831-3). F. Watts.

Hanson, Helen Patten
--Betty May. N.D. Abingdon Press.

Hanson, Joan, jt. auth. see Marsh, Jeri.

Hanson, Joan (1938-)
--Alfred Snood. LC 79-187560. (Illus.). 32 p. 19cm. 1972. (ISBN 0-399-20253-6). (ISBN 0-399-60765-X). Putnam.
--I Don't Like Timmy. LC 77-131863. (Illus.). 33 p. 1972. (ISBN 0-87614-028-2). Carolrhoda Books.
--I Don't Like Timmy. rev. ed. LC 75-309130. (Illus.). 36 p. 19cm. 1973. (ISBN 0-87614-026-6). Carolrhoda Books.
--I Won't Be Afraid. LC 74-9033. (Illus.). 32 p. 22cm. c.1974. (ISBN 0-87614-050-9). Carolrhoda Books.
--I'm Going to Run Away. Hanson, Joan (1938-), illus. LC 75-24621. (Illus.). 28 p. 29cm. 1976. (ISBN 0-8228-7576-4). Platt & Munk Publishers.
--Monster's Nose Was Cold. Hanson, Joan (1938-), illus. LC 73-131864. (Illus.). 23cm. 37p. (gr. k-3). 1971. (ISBN 0-87614-025-8). Carolrhoda Bks.

Hanson, Joseph E. (1894-1971)
--Grandfather Todd of Old Cape Cod. Porter, Jean Macdonald (1906-), illus. LC 59-5384. 64p. illus. 22cm. 1959. D. McKay Co.

Hanson, June Andrea (1941-)
--Summer of the Stallion. Singer, Gloria (1949-), illus. LC 78-24212. (Illus.). 108 p. 22cm. c.1979. (ISBN 0-02-742620-3). Macmillan.
--Winter of the Owl. LC 80-15966. 126 p. 22cm. c.1980. (ISBN 0-02-742530-4). Macmillan.

Hanson, Kitty
--Rebels in the Streets: The Story of New York's Girl Gangs. LC 64-17365. viii, 183 p. 22cm. 1964. Prentice-Hall.

Hanson, Lida
--Eric The Red. Hansen, Ernst, illus. N.D. Doubleday Doran Books.

Hanson, Lida Siboni, tr. see Michaelis, Karin.

Hanson, Margaret M.
--Carmelita. (Illus.). (gr. k-5). N.D. Vantage.

Hanson, Ruth Katie (1900-)
--Bird & Rocket Stories. 80p. 1960. Forum Publishing & Co.
--Children's Bird Stories. LC 58-14252. 65p. illus. 21cm. 1959. Meador Pub. Co.

Hansson, Ola
--Young Ofeg's Ditties. Egerton, George, tr. N.D. Messrs Roberts Brothers.

Hanthorn, Alice
--Billy Boy on the Farm. Norman, Vera Stone, illus. LC 29-29557. 20cm. 122p. 1929. B. H. Sanborn & Co.

Hantzig, Deborah
--A Visit to the Sesame Street Hospital. Mathieu, Joseph (1945-), illus. LC 84-17852. (Illus.). 32p. (Picturebacks Ser.). (ps-4). 1985. (ISBN 0-394-97062-4, BYR). (ISBN 0-394-87062-X). Random.

Hapgood, Charles Hutchins (1904-)
--Great Mysteries of the Earth. Eggers, Robert, illus. LC 60-6877. 72p. illus. 23cm. 1960. Putnam.

Hapgood, Elizabeth Reynolds, tr. see Shvarts, Evgenii Livovich.

Hapgood, Isabel F., tr. see Amicis, Edmondo de.

Hapgood, Isabel Flersome (1850-1922), tr. see Amicis, Edmondo De.

Hapgood, Isabel Florence (1850-1928), tr. see Amicis, Edmondo De.

Hapgood, Isabel Florence (1850-1928), tr. see Gogol, Nikolai Vasilevich.

Hapgood, Miranda & McCully, Emily Arnold (1939-)
--Martha's Mad Day. LC 77-3163. (Illus.). 32 p. 16cm. c.1977. (ISBN 0-517-52997-1). Crown Publishers.

Harbaugh, Henry (1817-1867), tr. see Hoffmann, Franz.

Harbaugh, Rose Oller
--Eddie Elephant Has a Party. Suba, Susanne (1913-), illus. LC 47-12169. 32 p. col. illus. 27 cm. 1947. Rand McNally.

Harbaugh, Thomas Chalmers (1849-)
--For Freedom's Cause: Or, On to Saratoga. LC 13-8940. 244. 19cm. (Boys of Liberty Library). 1913. D. McKay.
--The Young Captains: Or, Prisoners of the King. LC 13-8056. 233p. 19cm. (Boys of Liberty Library). 1913. D. McKay.

Harboe, Paul
--A Child's Story of Hans Christian Andersen. N.D. Duffield.

Harborough, Mark
--When Wolf Meets Wolf: A Scouting Story. N.D. Macmillan.

Harbour, Jefferson Lee (1857-1931)
--Marcia and the Major. (Illus.). (Crowell's Child Life Series.). 1915. T Y Crowell.
--Marcia and the Major. (Illus.). (The From Nine To Twelve Ser.). N.D. Thomas Y. Crowell & Co.
--Marcia and the Major. (The "Bimbi" Series of Children's Booklets). N.D. Thomas Y. Crowell.
--Marcia and the Major: A/Story of Life in the Rockies. LC 1-23030. 83p. 18cm. 1901. T. Y. Crowell.

Harcourt, Helen, pseud., see Warner, Helen Garnie.

Harcourt, Helen, pseud. (1846-)
--Bertram Raymond: Or, The Cruise of the Dolphin. Warner, Helen Garnie. N.D. Claxton,Remsen & Haffelfinger.

Harcourt, Helen, pseud. (1846-) & Mahon, Mary B.
--Southern Stories for Little Readers. Warner, Helen Garnie. LC 5-8661. (Illus.). 20cm. 154p. 1904. C. W. Bardeen.

Hard, Eleanor, tr. see Huld, Palle.

Hardaway, B. Touchstone (1930-)
--One Small Drum. LC 81-24115. p. cm. (Historical Fiction for the Young at Heart). 1982, c.1981. (ISBN 0-941186-00-8). Twin Oaks Co.

Hardcastle, Michael (1933-)
--Aim for the Flag. LC 69-10249. 192 p. 23cm. 1969, c.1967. (ISBN 0-695-40180-7). Follett Pub. Co.

Hardeman, Eva, jt. auth. see Lamport, Mary Frances.

Harden, E., tr. see Lorenzini, Carlo.

Hardendorff, Jeanne B.
--Sing Song Scuppernong. Chwast, Jacqueline (1932-), illus. LC 73-12399. (Illus.). 64p. (gr. k up). 1974. (ISBN 0-03-011986-3). HR&W.

Hardendorff, Jeanne B., retold by.
--The Bed Just So. Weil, Lisl (1910-), illus. LC 75-15462. (Illus.). 32 p. 16cm. c.1975. (ISBN 0-590-07349-4). Four Winds Press.
--The Frog's Saddle Horse: And Other Tales. Webber, Helen, illus. LC 68-10772. (Illus.). 157 p. 21cm. 1968. Lippincott.
--Just One More. Bolognese, Donald Alan (1934-), illus. LC 69-12002. (Illus.). 169 p. 21cm. 1969. Lippincott.
--Slip! Slop! Gobble!. McCully, Emily Arnold (1939-), illus. LC 76-117248. (Illus.). 32 p. 27cm. 1970. Lippincott.
--Tricky Peik, and Other Picture Tales. De Paola, Tomie, pseud. (1934-), illus. De paola, Thomas Anthony. LC 67-2695. (Illus.). 122 p. 21cm. 1967. Lippincott.
--Witches, Wit, and a Werewolf. Kubinyi, Laszlo (1937-), illus. LC 75-153516. (Illus.). 124 p. 21cm. 1971. Lippincott.

Hardendorff, Jeanne B., ed. see Domjan, Joseph Spiri.

Harder, Eleanor Loraine (1925-)
--Darius and the Dozer Bull. Stone, David Karl (1922-), illus. LC 72-147303. (Illus.). 111 p. 24cm. 1971. (ISBN 0-687-10270-7). Abingdon Press.

Harder, Janet
--Letters from Carrie. Schernerhorn, Bonney, illus. LC 80-83940. (Illus.). 152p. 1st U.S. edition. (gr. 6 up). 1980. (ISBN 0-932052-23-1). North Country.

Hardesty, Joseph A.
--Red and Me. LC 26-15507. 3 p. l., 3-94 p. illus. 23 cm. c.1926. Republic Print.

Hardesty, Vida A.
--The Turn-of-the-Century Party. Kahl, Steven, illus. LC 77-82129. (Illus.). (National History Ser.). (gr. 4 up). 1980. (ISBN 0-89482-001-X). (ISBN 0-89482-008-7). Stevenson Pr.

Hardie, Katherine Johnson
--A Very Special Day. Mill, Eleanor, illus. (Illus.). (gr. k). 1966. (ISBN 0-8042-2980-5). John Knox.

Hardin, Charline
--Tails, Tails, Tails, Tails, Tails. Brewer, Sally King (1947-), illus. LC 72-10317. (Illus.). 20 x 25cm. 39p. c.1972. Hall & McCreary Ci.

Harding, Caroline Hirst Brown, Mrs. & Harding, Samuel Bannister (1866-1927)
--Stories of Greek Gods, Heroes and Men: A Primer of the Mythology and History of the Greeks. LC 18-18824. vi, 195 p. front., plates. 18 cm. 1897. Scott, Foresman and Company.

Harding, Claud
--The Capture of the "Estrella". A Tale of the Slave Trade, 8 vols. (Illus.). 384p. (Books for Boys). 1905. Set. Cassell & Co.

Harding, Emily Grace
--Leoline: Or, Captured and Rescued. (Illus.). N.D. E. P. Dutton & Co.
--Robin's Promise. N.D. Potts & Co.

Harding, Emily J.
--Fairy Tales of the Slav Peasants and Herdsmen. Harding, Emily J., tr. (Illus.). N.D. Dodd, Mead & Co.
--Slav Fairy Tales. Harding, Emily J., illus. Harding, Emily J., tr. (The Fairy Library). N.D. A. L. Burt Co.

--A Letter from Father Christmas. N.D. Raphael Tuck & Sons.

Harding, Emily J., tr. see Chodzko, Aleksander Borejko.

Harding, Lee John (1937-)

--Misplaced Persons. LC 78-19824. 149 p. 21cm. c.1979. (ISBN 0-06-022216-6). (ISBN 0-06-022217-4). Harper & Row.

Harding, Lee John (1937-) & Schoenherr, John Carl (1935-)

--The Fallen Spaceman. LC 79-2006. p. cm. 1979, c.1980. (ISBN 0-06-022212-3). (ISBN 0-06-022213-1). Harper & Row.

Harding, Mary Van B., Mrs.

--The Amazing Adventures of the Kimpsies and Whiff. Northrop, Christine, illus. LC 40-31721. 112 p. front., illus. 19 1/2 cm. c.1940. Dorrance and Company.

Harding, Maude Burbank

--The Children's Own Book of Letters and Stories. 221p. 1926. Marshall Jones.

Harding, Newman

--Little Black Monkey. Millar, Harold Robert (1869-1939), illus. (Romance and Legend Series.). N.D. Dodge Publishing Co.

Harding, Samuel Bannister, jt. auth. see Harding, Caroline Hirst Brown, Mrs.

Hardt, Elaine

--Stories from Beyond the Double Rainbow. (Orig.). (gr. 1-8). 1982. (ISBN 0-932960-03-0). Thinking Caps.

Hardwick, Michael Drinkrow (1924-) & Hardwick, Mollie

--Game's Afoot. 102p. 1969. (ISBN 0-7195-1924-1). Intl Pubns Serv.

Hardwick, Mollie, jt. auth. see Hardwick, Michael Drinkrow.

Hardwick, Richard Holmes, Jr. (1923-)

--Flipper: The Mystery of the Black Schooner. Allen, Robert & Anderson, Al, illus. LC 67-1941. (Illus.). 190 p. 22cm. 1966. Whitman Pub. Co.

Hardwick, Sylvia, pseud., see Doherty, Ivy R. Duffy.

Hardwick, Sylvia, pseud. (1922-)

--Singing Tree & Laughing Waters. Doherty, Ivy R. Duffy. LC 71-101534. 18cm. 128p. (gr. 4-9). 1970. Pacific Pr Pub Assn.

Hardwicke, Bess & Hardwicke, Jennifer

--Punkin's Own Story or the Autobiography of Miss Punkin Jones. Cole, Charlotte, illus. (Illus.). (gr. k-5). 1977. (ISBN 0-682-48735-X). Exposition.

Hardwicke, Jennifer, jt. auth. see Hardwicke, Bess.

Hardy, Alice Dale, pseud., see Stratemeyer Syndicate.

Hardy, Alice Dale, pseud.

--The Flyaways and Cinderella. Stratemeyer Syndicate. Rogers, Walter S., illus. (Flyaways Ser.: No. 1). 1925. Grosset & Dunlap.

--The Flyaways and Goldilocks. Stratemeyer Syndicate. Rogers, Walter S., illus. (Flyaways Ser.: No. 3). 1925. Grosset & Dunlap.

--The Flyaways and Little Red Riding Hood. Stratemeyer Syndicate. Rogers, Walter S., illus. (Flyaways Ser.: No. 2). 1925. Grosset & Dunlap.

--The Riddle Club at Home: How the Club was Formed, What Riddles were Asked and How the Members Solved a Mystery. Stratemeyer Syndicate. Rogers, Walter S., illus. (The Riddle Club Ser.: No. 1). 1924. Grosset & Dunlap.

--The Riddle Club at Rocky Falls: How They Went up the River, What Adventures They Had in the Woods, and How They Solved the Mystery of the Deserted Hotel. Stratemeyer Syndicate. Rogers, Walter S., illus. LC 29-11016. 2 p. l., 244 p. front., plates. 19 1/2 cm. (The Riddle Club Ser.: No. 6). 1929. Grosset & Dunlap.

--The Riddle Club at Shadybrook: Why They Went There, What Happened on the Way and What Occurred during Their Absence from Home. Stratemeyer Syndicate. Rogers, Walter S., illus. (The Riddle Club Ser.: No. 5). 1926. Grosset & Dunlap.

--The Riddle Club at Sunrise Beach: How They Toured to the Shore, What Happened on the Sand and How They Solved the Mystery of Rattlesnake Island. Stratemeyer Syndicate. Rogers, Walter S., illus. LC 25-4772. 2 p. l., 246 p. front., plates. 19 1/2 cm. (The Riddle Club Ser.: No. 4). 1925. Grosset & Dunlap.

--The Riddle Club in Camp: How They Journeyed to the Lake, What Happened around the Campfire and How a Forgotten Name was Recalled. Stratemeyer Syndicate. Rogers, Walter S., illus. (The Riddle Club Ser.: No. 2). 1924. Grosset & Dunlap.

--The Riddle Club Through the Holidays: The Club and Its Doings, How the Riddles were Solved and What the Snowman Revealed. Stratemeyer Syndicate. Rogers, Walter S., illus. (The Riddle Club Ser.: No. 3). 1924. Grosset & Dunlap.

Hardy, Arthur Sherburne (1847-1940)

--Aurelie. Green, Elizabeth Shippen, illus. LC 12-21618. 3 p. l., 30, 1 p. col. front., illus., col. pl. 22 1/2 cm. 1912. Harper & Brothers.

Hardy, Arthur Steffens (1875-1940)

--Sea Stories for Wonder Eyes. (Illus.). 157p. N.D. Dana Estes and Company.

Hardy, E. Stuart, illus.

--Nursery Rhymes, 1 of 4 vols. (Little People's Story Box). N.D. Dutton.

Hardy, Elizabeth, ed. see Aesopus.

Hardy, James (1940-)

--Death in the Forest. LC 81-9652. p. cm. c.1981. (ISBN 0-939834-00-6). Northland Publishers.

Hardy, John M., ed. see Cooper, James Fenimore.

Hardy, Lucy

--The Fortunes of the Fairies (Pub. by Society for Promoting Christian Knowledge). N.D. E. & J. B. Young & Co.

Hardy, Marjorie (1888-)

--Surprise Stories, a first reader. Enders, Lucille & Breuer, Matilda, illus. 19cm. 140p. (The Child's Own Way Ser.). 1926. Wheeler Publishing Co.

--Wag and Puff. Enders, Lucille & Breuer, Matilda, illus. 19cm. 140p. (The Child's Own Way Ser.). 1926. Wheeler Publishing Co.

Hardy, Marjorie (1888-) & Teeters, Helen

--Best Stories (National Life). A Third Reader. Breuer, Matilda, illus. 3 p. l., 282 p. illus. (part col.) 19 cm. (child's own way series). 1927. Wheeler Publishing Company.

Hardy, Mary Earle, Mrs. (1846-)

--Columbus and Pepper: Or, The Little Folks from Science Town. LC 29-29546. 111 p. incl. front., illus. 21 cm. c.1929. A. Whitman & Co.

--Fairy Roads to Science-Town. N.D. Dodd, Mead & Co.

--The Girl of the Forest. Cady, Cora J., illus. LC 27-18544. 222 p. incl. col. front., illus. (part col.) 24 cm. (A just right book). c.1927. A. Whitman & Company.

--The Little King and the Princess True. Winter, Milo Kendall (1888-1956), illus. LC 12-16612. 21cm. 182p. 1912. Rand McNally & Co.

--Little Ta-wish: Indian Legends from Geyserland. Inukai, Kyohei, illus. LC 14-12467. 12cm. 154p. 1914. Rand McNally & Co.

--Nature's Wonder Lore: The Little King and the Princess True. Winter, Milo Kendall (1888-1956), illus. LC 13-23020. 2 p. l., 3-141 p. incl. front., illus., pl. 20 cm. c.1913. Rand, McNally & Company.

--Sea Stories for Wonder Eyes. 1904. Ginn.

--Three Singers. LC 27-35. 17cm. 127p. 1894. Press of Chapman.

Hardy, Robina F., see Gordon, Janet, pseud.

Hardy, Robina F.

--Arthur's Adventure, 1 of 12 vols. (Illus.). (The Home Sunshine Ser.: No.1). N.D. Set. Thos Nelson & Sons.

--Coral Necklace, 1 of 6 Vols. (Illus.). (Victory Ser.: No.1). N.D. Set. Thomas Nelson & Sons.

--Daisy Dingle, 1 of 12 vols. (Illus.). (The Home Sunshine Ser.: No.1). N.D. Set. Thos Nelson & Brothers.

--Dorothy's Venture, 1 of 6 Vols. (Illus.). (Victory Ser.: No.1). N.D. Set. Thos Nelson & Sons.

--Frieda's First Lesson, 1 of 6 Vols. (Illus.). (Way to Win Ser.: No.1). N.D. Set. Thos Nelson & Sons.

--The Ghost of Greythorn Manor, 1 of 6 vols. (Illus.). (Way to Win Ser.: No.1). N.D. Set. Thos Nelson & Sons.

--The Good Ship Rover, 1 of 12 vols. (Illus.). (The Home Sunshine Ser.: No.1). N.D. Set. Thos Nelson & Sons.

--Hannah's Home, 1 of 12 Vols. (Illus.). (The Home Sunshine Ser.: No.1). N.D. Set. Thos Nelson & Sons.

--Heedless Harry, 1 of 12 vols. (Illus.). (The Home Sunshine Ser.: No.1). N.D. Set. Thos Nelson & Sons.

--A Hero's Son, 1 of 12 vols. (Illus.). (The Home Sunshine Ser.: No.1). N.D. Set. Thos Nelson & Sons.

--Hilda's Fortune, 1 of 12 vols. (Illus.). (The Home Sunshine Ser.: No.1). N.D. Set. Thos Nelson & Sons.

--His Own Master, 1 of 6 Vols. (Illus.). (Way to Win Ser.). N.D. Thomas Nelson & Sons.

--Jacqueline. Gordon, Janet, pseud. 1 of 7 Vols (The Mossdale Ser.). N.D. Cassell, Petter, & Galpin.

--Jaqueline. Gordon, Janet. pseud. N.D. Nelson & Phillips.

--Kenneth's Charge, 1 of 6 vols. (Illus.). (Victory Ser.). N.D. Set. Thos Nelson & Sons.

--Kitty's Holiday, 1 of 12 vols. (Illus.). (Home Sunshine Ser.). N.D. Set. Thos Nelson & Sons.

--Launch of the Victory, 1 of 6 vols. (Illus.). (Way to Win Ser.). N.D. Set. Thos Nelson & Sons.

--The Little Lace Maker, 1 of 6 vols. (Illus.). (Way to Win Ser.). N.D. Set. Thos Nelson & Sons.

--The Lost Kite, 1 of 12 vols. (Illus.). (The Sunshine Ser.). N.D. Set. Thos Nelson & Sons.

--Magpie's Nest, 1 of 6 Vols. (Illus.). (Victory Ser.). N.D. Set. Thomas Nelson & Co.

--Matilda's Mirror, 1 of 12 vols. (Illus.). (The Home Sunshine Ser.). N.D. Set. Thos Nelson & Sons.

--Phemie's Fortune, 1 of 6 Vols. (Illus.). (Victory Ser.). N.D. Set. Thomas Nelson & Co.

--Polly Who was "Nobody's Child". N.D. E. & J. B. Young & Co.

--Rhoda's Victory, 1 of 6 vols. (Illus.). (Victory Ser.). N.D. Set. Thos Nelson & Sons.

--Tim's Basket, 1 of 6 Vols. (Illus.). (Way to Win Ser.). N.D. Set. Thomas Nelson & Sons.

--Violet's Promise, 1 of 12 vols. (Illus.). (The Home Sunshine Ser.). N.D. Set. Thos Nelson & Brothers.

--The Wishing-Well, 1 of 12 vols. (Illus.). (The Sunshine Ser.). N.D. Set. Thos Nelson & Sons.

Hardy, Shirley

--Adventures of Arnold. (gr. k). 1983. (ISBN 0-8062-2142-9). Carlton.

Hardy, Thomas (1840-1928)

--Far From the Madding Crowd. (Great Illustrated Classics). (gr. 9 up). 1968. (ISBN 0-396-05704-7). Dodd.

--Far from the Madding Crowd. (gr. 7-12). 1972 (Starline). School Bk Service.

--Jude the Obscure. (Magnum Easy Eye Classic Ser.). (gr. 9-12). N.D. Lancer.

--Our Exploits at West Poley. LC 72-191224. (Illus.). xii, 97 p. 21cm. 1970. Folcroft Press.

--Our Exploits at West Poley. Lamb, Lynton Harold (1907-1977), illus. LC 52-14501. 109 p. illus. 21 cm. 1952. Oxford University Press.

--Our Exploits at West Poley. Lawrence, John (1933-), illus. Purdy, Richard L., intro. by. LC 53-167142. xii, 97p. illus. 19cm. 1952. Oxford University Press.

--The Pinnacled Tower: Selected Poems. Leighton, Clare Veronica Hope (1899-), illus. LC 74-14836. xiii, 146 p. 22cm. 1975. (ISBN 0-02-742630-0). Macmillan.

--The Pinnacled Tower: Selected Poems of Thomas Hardy. Plotz, Helen Ratnoff (1913-), ed. Leighton, Clare Veronica Hope (1899-), illus. (Illus.). index. 160p. (gr. 7 up). 1975. (ISBN 0-02-742630-0). Macmillan.

--Return of the Native. (Great Illus. Classics). (gr. 9 up). N.D. (ISBN 0-396-03154-4). Dodd.

--The Return of the Native. (Magnum Easy Eye Classics). (gr. 9-12). N.D. Lancer.

--Return of the Native. (gr. 7-12). N.D (Starline). School Bk. Serv.

--Return of the Native. large type ed. (Keith Jennison Bks). (gr. 7 up). N.D. (ISBN 0-531-00272-1). Watts.

Hardy, Thomas (1840-1928) & Lawrence, John (1933-)

--Our Exploits at West Poley. LC 78-40518. 23cm. 77p. (Oxford illustrated classics). 1978. (ISBN 0-19-274527-1). Oxford University Press.

Hare, Christopher

--The Story of Bayard. Cole, Herbert, illus. N.D. E P Dutton.

Hare, Emily

--Little Blossom's Reward, 1 of 25 vols. (Illus.). (Mayflower Ser. for Girls: No. 14). 1900. Lee & Shepard.

Hare, Eric B. (1894-)

--Clever Queen. (gr. 4-9). N.D. Pacific Pr Pub Assn.

--Jungle Storyteller. (gr. 4-9). N.D. Review & Herald.

Hare, Humphrey, tr. see Druon, Maurice Samuel Roger Charles.

Hare, Lorraine

--Who Needs Her?. Hare, Lorraine, illus. LC 82-13899. p. cm. 1983. (ISBN 0-689-50268-0). Atheneum.

Hare, Norma Quarles (1924-)

--Mystery at Mouse House. Ormai, Stella, illus. LC 79-28254. (Illus.). 48 p. 23cm. (Mystery book). c.1980. (ISBN 0-8116-6412-0). Garrard Pub. Co.

--Who Is Root Beer?. Davidson, Rosalie (1921-), illus. LC 76-16015. (Illus.). 39 p. 23cm. c.1977. (ISBN 0-8116-4400-6). Garrard Pub. Co.

--Wish Upon a Birthday. Dawson, Diane, illus. LC 79-14596. (Illus.). 46 p. 23cm. (Imagination book). c.1979. (ISBN 0-8116-4418-9). Garrard Pub. Co.

Hare, Thomas Truxtun (1878-)

--A Graduate Coach. Boyer, Ralph L., illus. LC 11-284324. 369 p. front., plates. 20 cm. 1911. The Penn Publishing Company.

--A Junior in the Line. Boyer, Ralph L., illus. LC 9-28209. 347 p. front., 6 pl. 20 cm. 1909. The Penn Publishing Company.

--A Junior in the Line. Boyer, Ralph L., illus. LC 38-12749. 347 p. front., plates. 19 cm. 1925. The Penn Publishing Company.

--Kent of Malvern. Boyer, Ralph L., illus. LC 19-16355. 320 p. front., plates. 20 cm. 1919. The Penn Publishing Company.

--Making the Freshman Team. Boyer, Ralph L, illus. LC 7-30842. 333 p. incl. front. 7 pl. 20 cm. 1907. The Penn Publishing Company.

--Making the Freshman Team. Boyer, Ralph L., illus. LC 35-28577. 333 p. incl. front. 19 cm. 1928. The Penn Publishing Company.

--Philip Kent. Boyer, Ralph L., illus. LC 14-183013. 354 p. front., plates. 20 cm. 1914. The Penn Publishing Company.

--Philip Kent in the Lower School. Boyer, Ralph L., illus. LC 16-23361. 335 p. front., plates. 20 cm. 1916. The Penn Publishing Company.

--Philip Kent in the Upper School. Boyer, Ralph L., illus. LC 18-139021. 327 p. front., plates. 20 cm. 1918. The Penn Publishing Company.

--A Senior Quarter-Back. Boyer, Ralph L., illus. LC 38-6980. 5, 9-363 p. front. 19 cm. c.1938. The Penn Publishing Company.

--A Sophomore Half-Back. Boyer, Ralph L., illus. LC 8-23551. 343 p. front., 6 pl. 20 cm. 1908. The Penn Publishing Company.

--A Sophomore Half-Back. Boyer, Ralph L., illus. LC 36-10832. 244 p. front., plates. 19 cm. c.1936. The Penn Publishing Company.

Hare, Walter Ben

--The White Christmas and Other Christmas Plays. N.D. T. S. Denison.

Harewood, Maria Donata Stein Lascelles & Duncan, Ronald Frederick Henry (1914-1982), eds.

--Classical Songs for Children. Cosman, Milein, illus. Young, Percy Marshall, contrib. by. LC 64-22683. 263p. illus. 26cm. 1965, c.1964. Potter Dist. Crown.

Hargeaves, Roger

--Mr. Greedy. (The Mr. Bks.). 1980. (ISBN 0-8431-0817-7). Price Stern.

Hargis, Polly

--Sunday with Stevie. Smalley, Janet (1893-), illus. LC 56-3606. unpaged. illus. 22cm. c.1956. Broadman Press.

Hargrave, Carrie Guerphan

--Jean and Tom in Casablanca. 1st ed. Causer, Rufus, illus. LC 53-7666. 103p. illus. 21cm. 1953. Exposition Press.

Hargreaves, Roger

--Albert the Alphabetical Elephant. LC 81-84548. (Illus.). 30 p. 25cm. c.1982. (ISBN 0-448-12319-3). Grosset & Dunlap.

--Count Worm. Hargreaves, Roger, illus. LC 81-84547. (Illus.). 32p. (ps-1). 1982. (ISBN 0-448-12318-5, G&D). Putnam Pub Group.

--Grandfather Clock. LC 81-84549. (Illus.). 30 p. 25cm. c.1982. (ISBN 0-448-12320-7). Grosset & Dunlap.

--Hippo Leaves Home. Hargreaves, Roger, illus. LC 81-84546. (Illus.). 32p. (ps-1). 1982. (ISBN 0-448-12317-7, G&D). Putnam Pub Group.

--Hippo, Potto & Mouse. Hargreaves, Roger, illus. LC 81-84544. (Illus.). 32p. (ps-1). 1982. (ISBN 0-448-12315-0, G&D). Putnam Pub Group.

--Little Miss Bossy. Hargreaves, Roger, illus. (Illus.). 32p. (Little Miss Bks.). 1981. (ISBN 0-8431-0893-2). Price Stern.

--Little Miss Bossy Zoo Animals. Hargreaves, Roger, illus. (Illus.). 8p. (Little Miss Bks.). (ps-2). 1982. (ISBN 0-8431-0886-X). Price Stern.

--Little Miss Chatterbox. LC 85-8288. (Illus.). 32 p. c.1985. (ISBN 0-86592-933-5). Rourke Enterprises.

--Little Miss Helpful. Hargreaves, Roger, illus. (Illus.). 32p. 1st U.S. edition. (Little Miss Bks.). 1981. (ISBN 0-8431-0897-5). Price Stern.

--Little Miss Helpful's Visit to the Doctor. Hargreaves, Roger, illus. (Illus.). 8p. (Little Miss Bks.). (ps-2). 1982. (ISBN 0-8431-0887-8). Price Stern.

--Little Miss Late. Hargreaves, Roger, illus. (Illus.). 32p. 1st U.S. edition. (Little Miss Bks.). 1981. (ISBN 0-8431-0896-7). Price Stern.

--Little Miss Naughty. Hargreaves, Roger, illus. 32p. 1st U.S. edition. (Little Miss Bks.). 1981. (ISBN 0-8431-0889-4). Price Stern.

--Little Miss Naughty Nursery Rhymes. Hargreaves, Roger, illus. (Illus.). 8p. (Little Miss Bks.). (ps-2). 1982. (ISBN 0-8431-0868-1). Price Stern.

--Little Miss Neat. Hargreaves, Roger, illus. 32p. 1st U.S. edition. (Little Miss Bks.). 1981. (ISBN 0-8431-0894-0). Price Stern.

--Little Miss Scatterbrain. Hargreaves, Roger, illus. (Illus.). 32p. (Little Miss Bks.). 1981. (ISBN 0-8431-0891-6). Price Stern.

--Little Miss Splendid. Hargreaves, Roger, illus. (Illus.). 32p. (Little Miss Bks.). 1981. (ISBN 0-8431-0888-6). Price Stern.

--Little Miss Splendid Colors. Hargreaves, Roger, illus. (Illus.). 8p. (Little Miss Bks.). (ps-2). 1982. (ISBN 0-8431-0884-3). Price Stern.

--Little Miss Sunshine. Hargreaves, Roger, illus. (Illus.). 32p. (Little Miss Bks.). 1981. (ISBN 0-8431-0899-1). Price Stern.

--Little Miss Sunshine's Shapes. Hargreaves, Roger, illus. (Illus.). 8p. (Little Miss Bks.). (ps-2). 1982. (ISBN 0-8431-0885-1). Price Stern.

--Little Miss Tiny. Hargreaves, Roger, illus. (Illus.). 32p. (Little Miss Bks.). 1981. (ISBN 0-8431-0892-4). Price Stern.

--Little Miss Trouble. LC 81-12195. (Illus.). 32 p. 20cm. c.1981. (ISBN 0-86592-603-4). Rourke Enterprises.

--Little Miss Trouble. Hargreaves, Roger, illus. (Illus.). 32p. (Little Miss Bks.). 1981. (ISBN 0-8431-0890-8). Price Stern.
--Mouse Gets Caught. LC 81-84545. (Illus.). 30 p. 25cm. c.1982. (ISBN 0-448-12316-9). Grosset & Dunlap.
--The Mr. Bks. Incl. Mr. Silly. (ISBN 0-448-11686-3). (ISBN 0-448-13169-2); Mr. Bump. (ISBN 0-448-11687-1). (ISBN 0-448-13170-6); Mr. Tickle. (ISBN 0-448-11688-X). (ISBN 0-448-13171-4); Mr. Topsy-Turvy. (ISBN 0-448-11689-8). (ISBN 0-448-13172-2). (Illus.). 1st U.S. edition. Orig. Title: Mr. Series. (gr. k-3). 1974. G&D.
--Mr. Bounce. (The Mr. Bks.). 1980. (ISBN 0-8431-0809-6). Price Stern.
--Mr. Bounce's Numbers. Hargreaves, Roger, illus. (Illus.). 12p. (Mr. Men Bks.). 1981. (ISBN 0-8431-0873-8). Price Stern.
--Mr. Bump. LC 73-16665. (Illus.). 1 v. (unpaged). 16cm. 1974, c.1971. (ISBN 0-448-11687-1). Grosset & Dunlap.
--Mr. Busy. Hargreaves, Roger, illus. (Illus.). (Mr. Men Bks.). 1981. (ISBN 0-8431-0818-5). Price Stern.
--Mr. Chatterbox. (The Mr. Bks.). 1980. (ISBN 0-8431-0808-8). Price Stern.
--Mr. Chatterbox's Words. Hargreaves, Roger, illus. (Illus.). 12p. (Mr. Men Bks.). 1981. (ISBN 0-8431-0870-3). Price Stern.
--Mr. Clever. Hargreaves, Roger, illus. (Illus.). 32p. (Mr. Men Bks.). 1982. (ISBN 0-8431-1131-3). Price Stern.
--Mr. Clumsy. 32p. (Mr. Bks.). 1980. (ISBN 0-87191-817-X). Creative Ed.
--Mr. Daydream. Hargreaves, Roger, illus. (Illus.). 32p. (Mr. Men Bks.). 1982. (ISBN 0-8431-1127-5). Price Stern.
--Mr. Dizzy. Hargreaves, Roger, illus. (Illus.). 32p. (Mr. Men Bks.). 1982. (ISBN 0-8431-1132-1). Price Stern.
--Mr. Forgetful. (The Mr. Bks.). 1980. (ISBN 0-8431-0805-3). Price Stern.
--Mr. Forgetful Learns a Lesson. 48p. (ps-2). 1982. (ISBN 0-8431-0861-4). Price Stern.
--Mr. Funny. 32p. (Mr. Bks.). 1981. (ISBN 0-87191-908-7). Creative Ed.
--Mr. Funny at the Circus. Hargreaves, Roger, illus. (Illus.). 24p. (Mr. Men Bks.). (gr. k-3). 1982. (ISBN 0-8431-1100-3). Price Stern.
--Mr. Funny's T.V. Show. 12p. (Orig.). (Mr. Men & Little Miss Pop-Up Bks.). 1983. (ISBN 0-8431-0831-2). Price Stern.
--Mr. Fussy. (The Mr. Bks.). 1980. (ISBN 0-8431-0807-X). Price Stern.
--Mr. Greedy. 32p. (Mr. Bks.). 1980. (ISBN 0-87191-819-6). Creative Ed.
--Mr. Greedy Goes Shopping. LC 81-13758. (Illus.). 24 p. 22cm. (A Mr. Men Word Book). c.1981. (ISBN 0-86592-582-8). Rourke.
--Mr. Grumpy. 32p. (Mr. Bks.). 1980. (ISBN 0-87191-764-5). Creative Ed.
--Mr. Happy. (The Mr. Bks.). 1980. (ISBN 0-8431-0813-4). Price Stern.
--Mr. Happy Goes to the Beach. Hargreaves, Roger, illus. (Illus.). 24p. (Mr. Men Bks.). (gr. k-3). 1982. (ISBN 0-8431-1105-4). Price Stern.
--Mr. Impossible. Hargreaves, Roger, illus. (Illus.). (Mr. Men Bks.). 1981. (ISBN 0-8431-0819-3). Price Stern.
--Mr. Lazy. (The Mr. Bks.). 1980. (ISBN 0-8431-0806-1). Price Stern.
--Mr. Men at the Beach. 6p. (The Mr. Men Cloth Bks.). 1983. (ISBN 0-686-88649-6). Price Stern.
--Mr. Men Going Places. 6p. (The Mr. Men Cloth Bks.). 1983. (ISBN 0-686-88651-8). Price Stern.
--Mr. Men Indoors. 6p. (The Mr. Men Cloth Bks.). 1983. (ISBN 0-686-88650-X). Price Stern.
--Mr. Messy. (The Mr. Bks.). 1980. (ISBN 0-8431-0812-6). Price Stern.
--Mr. Messy Has a Party. 48p. (ps-2). 1982. (ISBN 0-8431-0862-2). Price Stern.
--Mr. Mischief. (The Mr. Bks.). 1980. (ISBN 0-8431-0802-9). Price Stern.
--Mr. Muddle. Hargreaves, Roger, illus. (Illus.). (Mr. Men Bks.). 1981. (ISBN 0-8431-0820-7). Price Stern.
--Mr. Muddle Goes to School. Hargreaves, Roger, illus. (Illus.). 24p. (Mr. Men Bks.). (gr. k-3). 1982. (ISBN 0-8431-1104-6). Price Stern.
--Mr. Nervous. Hargreaves, Roger, illus. (Illus.). 32p. (Mr. Men Bks.). N.D. (ISBN 0-8431-1128-3). Price Stern.
--Mr. Noisy. 32p. (Mr. Bks.). 1980. (ISBN 0-87191-762-9). Creative Ed.
--Mr. Noisy Goes to the Library. 48p. (ps-2). 1982. (ISBN 0-8431-0863-0). Price Stern.
--Mr. Nonsense. Hargreaves, Roger, illus. (Illus.). (Mr. Men Bks.). 1981. (ISBN 0-8431-0821-5). Price Stern.
--Mr. Nosey. (The Mr. Bks.). 1980. (ISBN 0-8431-0816-9). Price Stern.
--Mr. Nosey Follows His Nose. Hargreaves, Roger, illus. (Illus.). 24p. (Mr. Men Bks.). (gr. k-3). 1982. (ISBN 0-8431-1102-X). Price Stern.
--Mr. Quiet. (The Mr. Bks.). 1980. (ISBN 0-8431-0803-7). Price Stern.
--Mr. Rush. (Illus.). 32p. (ps-3). 1982. (ISBN 0-8431-0880-0). Price Stern.
--Mr. Silly. LC 73-16663. (Illus.). 1 v. (unpaged). 16cm. 1974, c.1972. (ISBN 0-448-11686-3). Grosset & Dunlap.
--Mr. Silly Joins the Circus. 48p. (ps-2). 1982. (ISBN 0-8431-0860-6). Price Stern.
--Mr. Silly on the Farm. Hargreaves, Roger, illus. 24p. (Mr. Men Bks.). (gr. k-3). 1982. (ISBN 0-8431-1106-2). Price Stern.
--Mr. Silly's Do's & Don't's. Hargreaves, Roger, illus. (Illus.). (Mr. Men Bks.). 1981. (ISBN 0-8431-0872-X). Price Stern.
--Mr. Silly's Rainy Day. 48p. 1st U.S. edition. (gr. 6-10). 1982. (ISBN 0-8431-0829-0). Price Stern.
--Mr. Skinny. Hargreaves, Roger, illus. (Illus.). (Mr. Men Bks.). 1981. (ISBN 0-8431-0822-3). Price Stern.
--Mr. Slow. (Illus.). 32p. (ps-3). 1982. (ISBN 0-8431-0881-9). Price Stern.
--Mr. Small. Hargreaves, Roger, illus. (Illus.). (Mr. Men Bks.). 1981. (ISBN 0-8431-0823-1). Price Stern.
--Mr. Small's Baby Animals. Hargreaves, Roger, illus. (Illus.). 12p. (Mr. Men Bks.). 1981. (ISBN 0-8431-0869-X). Price Stern.
--Mr. Sneeze. Hargreaves, Roger, illus. (Illus.). 32p. (Mr. Men Bks.). 1982. (ISBN 0-8431-1125-9). Price Stern.
--Mr. Snow. Hargreaves, Roger, illus. (Illus.). 32p. (Mr. Men Bks.). 1982. (ISBN 0-8431-1133-X). Price Stern.
--Mr. Stingy. Hargreaves, Roger, illus. (Illus.). 32p. (Mr. Men Bks.). 1982. (ISBN 0-8431-1130-5). Price Stern.
--Mr. Strong. (Illus.). 32p. (ps-3). 1982. (ISBN 0-8431-0877-0). Price Stern.
--Mr. Strong to the Rescue. Hargreaves, Roger, illus. 24p. (Mr. Men Bks.). (gr. k-3). 1982. (ISBN 0-8431-1101-1). Price Stern.
--Mr. Tall. Hargreaves, Roger, illus. (Illus.). 32p. (Mr. Men Bks.). 1982. (ISBN 0-8431-1126-7). Price Stern.
--Mr. Tickle. LC 73-16666. (Illus.). 1 v. (unpaged. 16cm. 1974. (ISBN 0-448-11688-X). Grosset & Dunlap.
--Mr. Tickle Goes Shopping. 48p. (ps-2). 1982. (ISBN 0-8431-0865-7). Price Stern.
--Mr. Tickle in the Park. Hargreaves, Roger, illus. (Illus.). 24p. (Mr. Men Bks.). (gr. k-3). 1982. (ISBN 0-8431-1103-8). Price Stern.
--Mr. Tickle's Toys. Hargreaves, Roger, illus. (Illus.). 12p. (Mr. Men Bks.). 1981. (ISBN 0-8431-0871-1). Price Stern.
--Mr. Topsy-Turvy. LC 73-16667. (Illus.). 1 v. (unpaged. 16cm. 1974, c.1972. (ISBN 0-448-11689-8). Grosset & Dunlap.
--Mr. Uppity. (Illus.). 32p. (ps-3). 1982. (ISBN 0-8431-0882-7). Price Stern.
--Mr. Worry. (The Mr. Bks.). 1980. (ISBN 0-8431-0800-2). Price Stern.
--Mr. Wrong. (Illus.). 32p. (ps-3). 1982. (ISBN 0-8431-0879-7). Price Stern.
--My Very Own Mr. Men Book. 32p. (Orig.). (My Very Own Mr. Men & Little Miss Bks.). 1983. (ISBN 0-8431-0866-5). Price Stern.
--Show & Tell. Hargreaves, Roger, illus. (Illus.). 48p. (Mr. Men & Little Miss Bks.). (ps-1). 1982. (ISBN 0-8431-1110-0). Price Stern.

Haring, C. H.
--The Buccaneers of the West Indies. N.D. E P Dutton.

Hark, Ann
--Island Treasure. Smalley, Janet (1893-), illus. LC 38-18600. 234 p. col. front., plates. 21 cm. c.1938. J. B. Lippincott Company.
--Market House Mystery. Bloch, Georgia, illus. LC 55-5058. (Illus.). 214 p. 22cm. 1955. Winston.
--The Phantom of the Forest. Morse, Dorothy Bayley (1906-1979), illus. LC 39-23983. 282 p. col. front., illus. 21 cm. c.1939. J. B. Lippincott Company.
--The Seminary's Secret. Brunner, F. Sands, illus. LC 36-185589. 309 p. col. front., plates. 21 cm. c.1936. J. B. Lippincott Company.
--Sugar Mill House: A Mystery Story for Girls. De Angeli, Marguerite Lofft, Mrs. (1889-), illus. LC 37-18108. 307 p. col. front., plates. 21 cm. c.1937. J. B. Lippincott Company.

Hark, Mildred see McQueen, Mildred Hark (1908-) & McQueen, Noel.

Hark, Mildred (1908-) & McQueen, Noel
--A Home for Penny. Spilka, Arnold (1917-), illus. LC 59-9794. 202p. illus. 21cm. 1959. Watts.
--Junior Plays for All Occasions: A Collection of Royalty-Free, One-Act Plays for Children. LC 78-6107. vii, 576 p. 22cm. 1969. Plays, Inc.
--Mary Lou and Johnny: An adventure in Seeing. Oughton, Taylor (1925-), illus. 226p. 1963. Franklin Watts.
--Mary Lou & Johnny: An Adventure in Seeing. Oughton, Taylor (1925-), illus. (Illus.). (gr. 4-6). 1963. (ISBN 0-531-01723-0). Watts.

Harker, James, tr. see Unnerstad, Edith Totterman.

Harker, Lizzie Allen, Mrs. (1863-)
--A Romance of the Nursery. rev & enl. ed. LC 9-25979. 410p. 20cm. 1909. C. Scribner's Sons.
--A Romance of the Nursery. Roberts, Katharine M., illus. LC 2-27516. 20cm. 333p. 1903. J. Lane.

Harkins, Philip (1912-)
--Argentine Road Race. LC 62-14365. 221p. illus. 21cm. 1962. Morrow.
--The Big Silver Bowl. LC 47-19424. 3 p. l., 218 p. 21 cm. 1947. W. Morrow & Company.
--Bomber Pilot. LC 44-401744. 2 p. l., 6-329 p. 21 cm. 1944. Harcourt, Brace and Company.
--Breakaway Back. LC 59-10548. 254p. 21cm. (Morrow junior books). 1959. Morrow.
--Center Ice. 1952. (ISBN 0-8382-0162-8, Cadmus Books). E. M. Hale and Company.
--Center Ice. LC 52-3949. 200 p. 21cm. 1952. Holiday House.
--Coast Guard, Ahoy!. LC 43-148162. 6 p. l., 3-229, 1 p. 21 cm. 1943. Harcourt, Brace and Company.
--The Day of the Drag Race. LC 60-117079. 223p. 22cm. (Morrow junior books). 1960. Morrow.
--Double Play. LC 51-12713. 249 p. 21cm. 1951. Holiday House.
--Fight Like a Falcon. LC 61-12351. 223p. 21cm. 1961. Morrow.
--Game, Carol Canning!. LC 58-8373. 221p. 21cm. (Morrow junior books). 1958. Morrow.
--Knockout. (Famous Sports Stories). N.D. Grosset & Dunlap.
--Knockout. LC 50-7143. 242 p. 21cm. 1950. Holiday House.
--Lightning on Ice. LC 46-252761. 4 p. l., 215 p. 20 1/2 cm. 1946. W. Morrow & Company.
--No Head for Soccer. LC 64-21159. 214 p. 21 cm. 1964. W. Morrow.
--Punt Formation. LC 49-9984. 253 p. 21 cm. (Morrow junior books). 1949. W. Morrow.
--Road Race. LC 53-8412. 276 p. 21cm. 1953. Crowell.
--Son of the Coach. (Famous Sports Stories). N.D. Grosset & Dunlap.
--Son of the Coach. LC 50-10228. 252 p. 21 cm. 1950. Holiday House.
--Southpaw from San Francisco. (Famous Sports Stories). N.D. Grosset & Dunlap.
--Southpaw from San Francisco. LC 48-8792. 247 p. 21 cm. (Morrow junior books). 1948. W. Morrow.
--Touchdown Twins. LC 47-652146. 22cm. 234p. (Morrow junior bks.). 1947. Wm. Morrow.
--Where the Shark Waits. LC 63-17103. 191 p. 21 cm. 1963. Morrow.
--Young Skin Diver. LC 56-848083. 188p. 21cm. (Morrow junior books). 1956. Morrow.

Harkness, Peter T
--Andy the Acrobat: Or, Out with the Greatest Show on Earth. LC 7-256629. 2 p. l., 9-233 p. front., plates. 19 cm. (On cover: The great show series). c.1907. Chatterton-Peck Company.
--Andy, the Acrobat: Or, With the Greatest Show on Earth. (The Enterprise Bks.). N.D. Grosset & Dunlap.

Harlan, Elizabeth
--Footfalls. LC 82-6727. 1982. (ISBN 0-689-50255-9). Atheneum.

Harlan, Esther
--The Story of a Little Beech Tree. Barnhart, H., illus. LC 5723. 52p. 1900. E. P. Dutton & Co.

Harlan, Ethel Andrews
--The Adventures of Little Man Coco. Frizzi, Tullius John, illus. LC 65-24218. 133 p. illus. 23 cm. 1966. Branden Press.

Harlan, Glen, pseud., see Cebulash, Mel.

Harlan, Glen, pseud. (1937-)
--Petey the Pup. Cebulash, Mel. Hogarth, William, illus. (Illus.). Orig. Title: Petey Wouldn't Bark. (gr. k-3). 1972. (ISBN 0-590-09310-X, Schol Trade Pap). Schol Bk Serv.

Harlan, Mary E.
--Tell Me a Story: Poems. LC 40-326401. 58 p. 22 cm. c.1939. Exposition Press.

Harland, Henry see Luska, Sidney, pseud.

Harland, Henry (1861-1905)
--Mademoiselle Miss & Other Stories. 192p. 1904. John Lane.

Harland, Marion, pseud., see Terhune, Mary Virginia Hawes.

Harlem Youth Group
--Let's Fly Away. 1985. (ISBN 0-8062-2446-0). Carlton.

Harler, Anne, pseud., see Van Steenwyk, Elizabeth Ann.

Harley, Dr.
--The Young Crusoe: Or, Adventures of a Shipwrecked Boy, 1 of 50 vols. (Illus.). (The Norwood Ser.: No. 17). N.D. Lee & Shepard.

Harley, Ruth, jt. auth. see Potter, Grace Elizabeth.

Harley, Ruth W. (1919-)
--Andy Churchmouse and the Pastor. Crawford, Mel (1925-), illus. LC 76-350101. (Illus.). 20 p. 21cm. c.1975. (ISBN 0-8378-8901-4). C. R. Gibson Co.
--Andy Churchmouse Tells About God's Rules. Crawford, Mel (1925-), illus. LC 76-150442. (Illus.). 20 p. 22cm. c.1976. (ISBN 0-8378-8903-0). C. R. Gibson Co.
--Andy Churchmouse Tells About Prayer. Crawford, Mel (1925-), illus. LC 76-350100. (Illus.). 20 p. 22cm. c.1975. (ISBN 0-8378-8902-2). C. R. Gibson Co.
--Andy Churchmouse, What Shall I Be?. Crawford, Mel (1925-), illus. LC 76-150443. (Illus.). 20 p. 21cm. c.1976. (ISBN 0-8378-8904-9). C. R. Gibson Co.
--Glenn L. Martin: Boy Conqueror of the Air. Doremus, Robert (1913-), illus. LC 67-17739. 200p. illus., 20cm. (Childhood of Famous Americans). 1967. Bobbs.
--Mini-Mysteries. Cooke, Dorothea, illus. LC 72-87193. 64p. illus. 18cm. c.1972. Xerox Education Publication.

Harley, Timothy
--Moon Lore. LC 79-99981. (Illus.). (gr. 9 up). 1970. (ISBN 0-8048-0749-3). C E Tuttle.

Harlow, Alvin Fay (1875-)
--Joel Chandler Harris: Plantation Story-Teller. N.D. Julian Messner, Inc.
--When Horses Pulled Boats: A Story of Early Canals. Lowell, Orson (1871-), illus. LC 36-4000. vi, 7-68 p. incl. front., illus. 20 cm. (Our changing world). 1936. T. Nelson and Sons.

Harlow, Alvin Fay (1875-) & Enslow, Ella
--Schoolhouse in the Foothills. Benton, Thomas Hart (1889-1975), illus. 1935. Simon and Schuster, Inc Publications.

Harlow, Joan Hiatt (1932-)
Shadow Bear. 1st ed. Arnosky, Jim (1946-), illus. LC 80-7507. (Illus.). 32 p. c.1981. (ISBN 0-385-15066-0). (ISBN 0-385-15067-9). Doubleday.

Harlow, Jules
--Lessons from Our Living Past. Weihs, Erika (1917-), illus. LC 72-2055. (Illus.). 128 p. 26cm. 1972. (ISBN 0-87441-085-1). Behrman House.

Harlow, Rex F.
--Tinkletoes and Other Stories. Briggs, Thomas, intro. by. LC 26-182785. 2 p. l., xi, 128 p. incl. col. illus. 20 cm. 1926. Harlow Publishing Co.

Harman, Fred, jt. auth. see Winterbotham, Russell Robert.

Harman, Humphrey
--African Samson. LC 66-818559. 220p. map. 21cm. 1966, c.1965. Viking.

Harman, Humphrey, ed.
--Tales Told Near a Crocodile: Stories from Nyanza. Ford, George Cephas, Jr., illus. LC 67-3307. (Illus.). 185 p. 22cm. 1st U.S. edition. 1967, c.1962. Viking Press.

Harmeling, Jean
--The Incredible Will of H. R. Heartman. LC 82-73656. 113. (A Crossway Youth Book). c.1983. (ISBN 0-89107-279-9). Crossway Books.

Harmer, Mabel (1894-)
--Lizzie, the Lost Toys Witch. Watson, Wendy Mcleod (1942-), illus. LC 73-108861. (Illus.). 30 p. 26cm. 1970. (ISBN 0-8255-4125-5). Macrae Smith.
--The Youngest Soldier. LC 53-39521. 263p. 20cm. 1953. Deseret Book Co.

Harmon, A. W.
--Base Hit. 1st ed. LC 79-117238. 21cm. 156p. (gr. 4-6). 1970. (ISBN 0-397-31113-3). Lippincott.

Harmon, Barbara
--Monday's Mouse. LC 70-28611. (Illus.). 24 p. 12cm. 1970. Children's Gallery Press.
--Thimbly Hill: A Day with the Tiny Folks Down in Tumpfee Wood. Harmon, Barbara, illus. LC 80-70013. (Illus.). 50 p. 31cm. c.1980. Children's Gallery Press.
--The Tumpfee Wood Acorn Book. Harmon, Barbara, illus. LC 77-82038. (Illus.). 18cm. 36p. c.1977. Children's Gallery Book.

Harmon, Lyn S. (1930-)
--Clyde's Clam Farm. Shortall, Leonard W., illus. LC 66-10898. 125 p. illus. 21 cm. 1966. Lippincott.
--Flight to Jewell Island. Kocsis, James C. (1936-), illus. Paul, James, pseud. LC 67-10346. (Illus.). 143 p. 21cm. 1967. Lippincott.

Harms, David, jt. auth. see Marshak, Samuil Iakovlevich.

Harnard, Lois
--Coco, the Monkey, 1 of 3. (Nanny's Christmas Bks.: No. 3). N.D. Claxton, Remsen & Haffelfinger.
--Velvet-Coat, the Cat, 1 of 3. (Nanny's Christmas Bks.: No. 2). N.D. Claxton,Remsen & Haffelfingers.

Harnard, Lois, tr. see Dumont, Melaine.

Harnden, Ruth Peabody
--Golly and the Gulls. 1962. (ISBN 0-8382-0297-7, Cadmus Books). E. M. Hale and Company.
--Golly and the Gulls. Guthrie, Vee, illus. LC 62-12251. (Illus.). 118 p. 23cm. 1962. Houghton Mifflin.

--The High Pasture. Guthrie, Vee, illus. LC 64-12278. 188 p. illus. 21 cm. 1964. Houghton Mifflin.
--Next Door. Friedman, Marvin (1930-), illus. LC 79-105247. (Illus.). 166 p. 22cm. 1970. Houghton Mifflin.
--Runaway Raft. Friedman, Marvin (1930-), illus. LC 68-28056. (Illus.). 155 p. 22cm. 1968. Houghton Mifflin.
--Summer's Turning. Gretzer, John, illus. LC 66-8668. 170p. illus. 22cm. 1966. Houghton.
--Trapped in the Ice. Orig. Title: Golly & the Gulls. (gr. 4-6). 1972 (Starline). Schol Bk Serv.
--Wonder Why. Livermore, Elaine, illus. LC 78-161652. (Illus.). 47 p. 22cm. 1971. (ISBN 0-395-12755-6). Houghton Mifflin.

Harner, Elizabeth F., jt. ed. see Kerr, Mildred Lewis.

Harner, S. H. & Neilson, Harry B.
--Whys and Other Whys: Or, Curious Creatures and their Tales. (Illus.). N.D. E. P. Dutton & Co.

Harnett, Cynthia Mary (1893-1981)
--The Cargo of the Madalena. Harnett, Cynthia Mary (1893-1981), illus. LC 83-24874. (Illus.). 235 p., 3 p. of plates. 23cm. 1984. (ISBN 0-8225-0890-7). Lerner.
--Caxton's Challenge. Harnett, Cynthia Mary (1893-1981), illus. LC 60-12900. 254p. illus. 22cm. 1960, c.1959. World Pub Co. **Awards: (ALA); (CMA).**
--The Drawbridge Gate. Harnett, Cynthia Mary (1893-1981), illus. LC 54-5743. (Illus.). 250 p. 21cm. 1954, c.1953. Putnam.
--The Great House. 174p. N.D. British Book Centre.
--The Great House. Harnett, Cynthia Mary (1893-1981), illus. LC 83-24880. (Illus.). 173 p. 23cm. 1984, c.1949. (ISBN 0-8225-0893-1). Lerner Publications Co.
--The Great House. Harnett, Cynthia Mary (1893-1981), illus. LC 68-15274. (Illus.). 190 p. 21cm. 1968. World Pub. Co.
--The Merchant's Mark. Harnett, Cynthia Mary (1893-1981), illus. LC 83-24879. (Illus.). 192p. (Cynthia Harnett's Adventure Novels Ser.). (gr. 5 up). 1984. (ISBN 0-8225-0891-5). Lerner Pubns.
--Nicholas and the Wool-Pack: An Adventure Story of the Middle Ages. Harnett, Cynthia Mary (1893-1981), illus. LC 53-6422. (Illus.). 181 p. 22cm. 1953. Putnam.
--The Sign of the Green Falcon. Harnett, Cynthia Mary (1893-1981), illus. LC 83-24831. (Illus.). 288p. (Cynthia Harnett's Adventure Novels Ser.). (gr. 5 up). 1984, c.1953. (ISBN 0-8225-0888-5). Lerner Pubns.
--Stars of Fortune. Harnett, Cynthia Mary (1893-1981), illus. LC 83-24836. (Illus.). 288p. (Cynthia Harnett's Adventure Novels Ser.). (gr. 5 up). 1984. (ISBN 0-8225-0892-3). Lerner Pubns.
--Stars of Fortune. 1st American ed. Harnett, Cynthia Mary (1893-1981), illus. LC 56-10269. (Illus.). 22cm. 256p. 1956, c.1953. Putnam.
--The Writing on the Hearth. Floyd, Gareth (1940-), illus. LC 83-23904. (Illus.). 299 p. 23cm. 1984. (ISBN 0-8225-0889-3). Lerner.
--The Writing on the Hearth. Floyd, Gareth (1940-), illus. LC 72-91400. (Illus.). 318 p. 22cm. 1973, c.1971. (ISBN 0-670-79119-9). Viking Press.

Harnishfeger, Lloyd
--Hunters of the Black Swamp. Overlie, George, illus. LC 70-128803. (Illus.). 93 p. 23cm. 1970, c.1971. (ISBN 0-8225-0701-3). Lerner Publications Co.
--Prisoner of the Mound Builders. Overlie, George, illus. LC 72-7655. (Illus.). 141 p. 23cm. 1973. (ISBN 0-8225-0754-4). Lerner Pub. Co.

Harnoncourt, Rene d'
--The Hole in the Wall. 1st ed. LC 31-28020. (Illus.). 21 x 28cm. 18p. 1931. A. A. Knopf.

Harold, Childe, pseud., see Field, Edward Salisbury.

Harold, Hal, pseud., see Foster, Harold Rudolf.

Harold, Margaret
--Daddy Is a Doctor. Gibso, Mary Richards, illus. (Illus.). (gr. 1-4). 1963. (ISBN 0-87167-123-9). Allied Fla.

Harowitz, Eugene (1930-)
--A Catch in the Breath. LC 68-10879. 237p. 1968. (ISBN 0-393-08554-6). Norton & Co.

Harper, Don, ed. see Carroll, Lewis.

Harper, Harry, jt. auth. see Grahame-White, Claude.

Harper, Irene Mason, Mrs.
--Chand of India. 128p. 1954. Friendship Press.
--Shera of the Punjab. Newton, Margaret, illus. LC 38-13931. vi p., 1 l., 120 p. incl. front., illus. 19 cm. c.1938. The Central Committee on the United Study of Foreign Missions.

Harper, Martha Rebecca Barnhart
--Bittersweet. 1964. David McKay Company Inc.
--Bittersweet. Best, Allena Champlin, Mrs. (1892-1974), illus. Berry, Erick, pseud. LC 48-5386. viii, 238 p. illus. 22 cm. 1948. Longmans, Green.
--Red Silk Pantalettes. Bowen, Betty Morgan (1921-), illus. LC 46-6029. x p., 1 l., 228 p. incl. front., illus. 21 cm. 1946. Longmans, Green and Co.
--Winter Wedding. 1st ed. LC 50-9248. viii, 266 p. 22 cm. 1950. Longmans, Green.
--Winter Wedding. (gr. 9 up). 1950. (ISBN 0-679-20253-6). McKay.

Harper, Theodore Acland (1871-)
--Allison's Girl. King, Ruth, illus. N.D. Viking Press.
--The Mushroom Boy. Clark, Florenz, illus. LC 24-17455. 6 p. l., 11-215 p. col. front., illus., plates (part col.) 22 cm. 1924. The Penn Publishing Company.
--Red Sky. Zaidenberg, Arthur, illus. N.D. The Viking Press.
--Seventeen Chimneys. Nadejen, Theodore, illus. N.D. Viking Press.
--Singing Feathers. Clark, Florenz, illus. LC 25-15672. 288 p. col. front., illus., col. plates. 23 cm. 1925. The Penn Publishing Company.

Harper, Theodore Acland (1871-) & Harper, Winifred
--Forgotten Gods. Rowland, Kate, illus. N.D. Doubleday Doran & Co.
--His Excellency and Peter. Wiese, Kurt (1887-1974), illus. LC 30-314912. vi, 313 p. col. front. 21 cm. 1930. Doubleday, Doran & Company, Inc.
--The Janitor's Cat. LC 27-18137. ix, 1 p., 1 l., 206, 1 p. front., illus. 20 cm. 1927. D. Appleton and Company.
--Kubrik the Outlaw. Reindel, Edna, illus. N.D. Doubleday Doran & Co.
--Siberian Gold. (Young Moderns Ser.). N.D. Doubleday Doran.
--Windy Island. Houser, Lowell, illus. LC 31-335531. x, 308 p. col. front., maps. 21 cm. 1931. Doubleday, Doran & Company, Inc.

Harper, Wilhelmina (1884-1973), selected by see Fillmore, Parker Hoysted.

Harper, Wilhelmina, jt. ed. see Lang, Andrew.

Harper, Wilhelmina (1884-1973), ed. see Youth's Companion.

Harper, Wilhelmina (1884-1973), ed.
--Around the Hearth Fire, Stories of Favorite Holidays Selected from the Youth's Companion. The, Youth's Companion Merwin, Decie (1894-1961), illus. LC 31-22437. viii, 326 p. illus. 21 cm. 1931. D. Appleton and Company.
--Brownie of the Circus and Other Stories of Today. Neville, Vera (1900-1978), illus. LC 41-19720. 107, 1 p. incl. col. front., illus. (part col.) 24 x 19 cm. c.1941. David McKay Company.
--Dog Show, a Selection of Favorite Dog Stories. Nichols, Marie C. (1905-), illus. LC 50-5662. 182 p. illus. 21 cm. 1950. Houghton Mifflin.
--Down in Dixie: Stories from the South Central States. 1st ed. Morse, Dorothy Bayley (1906-1979), illus. LC 48-4689. 245 p. illus. 21 cm. (Her Our States in story). 1948. E. P. Dutton.
--Easter Chimes: Stories for Easter & the Spring. New Rev.Ed. ed. Von Zitzewitz, Hoot, illus. (gr. 2 up). 1967. Dutton.
--Easter Chimes: Stories for Easter and the Spring Season. Jones, Wilfred J. (1888-), illus. LC 68-937689. 223, 1 p. incl. front., illus. 21 cm. 1959, c.1942. E. P. Dutton.
--Easter Chimes: Stories for Easter and the Spring Season. New Rev. Ed. ed. Von Zitzewitz, Hoot, illus. LC 64-106882. 253p. illus. 22cm. 1965. Dutton.
--Flying Hoofs: Stories of Horses. Brown, Paul (1893-1958), illus. LC 39-31192. 6 p., 2 l., 292 p. illus., 22 cm. 1939. Houghton Mifflin Company.
--For Love of Country: Stories of Young Patriots. Jones, Wilfred J. (1888-), illus. LC 42-17802. 5 p. l., 15-257 p. incl. front., illus. 21 cm. 1942. E. P. Dutton & Co., Inc.
--Ghosts & Goblins. New Rev. Ed. ed. Wiesner, William (1899-), illus. (Illus.). (gr. 2 up). 1965. Dutton.
--Ghosts and Goblins: Stories for Hallowe'en and Other Time. Jones, Wilfred J. (1888-), illus. LC 36-27389. 3 p. l., 9-271 p. front., illus. 20 cm. c.1936. E. P. Dutton & Co., Inc.
--The Girl of Tiptop and Other Stories. N.D. Little Brown & Co.
--The Gunniwolf. Wiesner, William (1899-), illus. LC 67-22387. (Illus.). 1 v. (unpaged. 25cm. 1967, c.1918. Dutton.
--The Gunniwolf and Other Merry Tales. Seredy, Kate (1899-1975), illus. LC 36-35050. 4 p. l., 7-103, 2 p. incl. col. front., illus., (part col.) 24 cm. c.1936. David McKay Company.
--Harvest Feast. rev. ed. Mars, Witold Tadeusz J. (1912-), illus. (Illus.). (gr. 5 up). 1967. Dutton.
--The Harvest Feast: Stories of Thanksgiving Yesterday and Today. Jones, Wilfred J. (1888-), illus. LC 38-21858. 308 p., 1 l. incl. front., illus. 20 cm. c.1938. E. P. Dutton & Co., Inc.
--The Harvest Feast: Stories of Thanksgiving Yesterday and Today. new, rev. ed. Mars, Witold Tadeusz J. (1912-), illus. LC 65-21282. (Illus.). 256p. 22cm. 1965. Dutton.
--A Little Book of Necessary Ballads. Evers, Helen Baker, illus. (Round Table Ser.). 1930. Harper & Bros.
--The Lonely Little Pig and Other Animal Tales. Neville, Vera (1900-1978), illus. LC 38-34129. 107, 9 p. incl. col. front., illus. (part col.) 24 cm. c.1938. David McKay Company.
--Merry Christmas to You. New rev. ed. Rocker, Fermin (1907-), illus. 1967. E.P. Dutton & Co.
--Merry Christmas to You: Stories for Christmas. rev ed. Jones, Wilfred J. (1888-), illus. LC 35-13822. 3 p. l., 5-276 p. incl. front., illus. 20 cm. c.1935. E. P. Dutton & Co., Inc.
--Merry Christmas to You: Stories for Christmas. New, Rev. ed. Rocker, Fermin (1907-), illus. LC 65-21283. (Illus.). 254p. 22cm. 1965. Dutton.
--More Story-Hour Favorites. LC 29-4998. xii, 295 p. 20 cm. c.1929. The Century Co.
--The Selfish Giant and Other Stories. Seredy, Kate (1899-1975), illus. LC 35-32766. 5 p. l., 9-86 p. col. front., col. plates. 24 cm. c.1935. David McKay Company.
--Story-Hour Favorites, Selected for Library, School, and Home Use. LC 18-17760. xii p., 2 l., 3-245 p. 19 cm. 1918. The Century Co.
--Stowaway and Other Stories for Boys. N.D. Little Brown & Co.
--Uncle Sam's Story Book: Adventures of Yesterday's Boys and Girls. Paull, Grace A. (1898-), illus. LC 44-47729. 144 p. incl. front., illus. (part col.) 24 x 19 cm. 1944. David McKay Company.
--Where the Redbird Flies: Stories from the Southeastern States. Avison, George F. (1885-), illus. LC 46-2487. 277 p. illus. 21 cm. (Her Our states in story). 1946. E. P. Dutton & Co., Inc.
--Wings of Courage and Other Stories for Girl Scouts. Morse, Dorothy Bayley (1906-1979), illus. LC 41-22364. xvi, 308 p. incl. front., illus. 21 cm. 1941. D. Appleton-Century Company, Incorporated.
--Yankee Yarns: Stories from the Northeastern States. Walker, Nedda, illus. LC 44-3605. 315 p. illus. 21 cm. (Her Our states in story). 1944. E. P. Dutton & Co., Inc.

Harper, Wilhelmina (1884-1973) & Hamilton, Aymer J.
--Pleasant Pathways. N.D. MacMillan.

Harper, Winifred, jt. auth. see Harper, Theodore Acland.

Harraden, Beatrice (1864-)
--At the Green Dragon, and Other Tales. (Illus.). (Marguerite Ser.). N.D. Weeks & Co.
--Little Rosebud, 1 of 25 Vols. (Illus.). (The Editha Ser.: No. 8). 1905. Set. H M Caldwell Co.
--Little Rosebud: Or, Things Will Take a Turn. (Illus.). (The Little Women Ser.). N.D. A. L. Burt's Pubs.
--Little Rosebud: Or, Things Will Take a Turn. LC 96-19. ix, 11-131 p. incl. illus., plates. front. 19 cm. (The young of heart series v. 12). c.1898. D. Estes & Company.
--New Book of the Fairies. N.D. E. P. Dutton & Co.
--Things Will Take a Turn. (Illus.). (Stories Old and New Ser.). N.D. Caldwell.
--Things Will Take a Turn. (Illus.). (Scribner-Blackie Series of books for young people). N.D. Charles Scribner's Sons.
--Things Will Take a Turn. (Illus.). (Boys' and Girls' Classics). N.D. Henry Altemus Co.
--The Umbrella Mender. (Illus.). (Marguerite Ser.). N.D. Weeks & Co.

Harrah, Michael
--First Offender. LC 79-21821. 186 p. 22cm. 1980. (ISBN 0-529-05540-6). Collins.

Harrald, Marilee
--The Mystery Man of Horseshoe Bend. Boorman, Linda, illus. LC 79-55320. (Illus.). 100 p. 20cm. (Winner book). (Horseshoe Bend Mystery Ser.). c.1980. (ISBN 0-88207-488-1). Victor Books.

Harranth, Wolf
--My Old Grandad. Oppermann-Dimov, Christina, illus. Carter, Peter, tr. (Illus.). 32p. (ps-3). 1984. (ISBN 0-19-279787-5, Pub. by Oxford U Pr Childrens). Merrimack Pub Cir.

Harrell, Nell Jenkins
--The Two Little Redstarts. 1st ed. Kirke, Jean, illus. LC 53-12641. (Illus.). 48p. 21cm. 1954, c.1953. Exposition Press.

Harrell, Sara Jeanne Gordon (1940-)
--Cottage by the Sea. Willman, Gordon, illus. LC 77-13518. (Illus.). 114 p. 23cm. (Bro-kee series). c.1978. (ISBN 0-570-07764-8). Concordia Pub. House.
--Semo. Cummins, James (1914-), illus. LC 76-30673. (Illus.). 48 p. 23cm. c.1977. (ISBN 0-570-03458-2). (ISBN 0-570-03459-0). Concordia Pub. House.
--Willowcat and the Chimney Sweep. 1st ed. Drath, Bill, illus. LC 80-81702. (Illus.). 31 p. 26cm. c.1980. (ISBN 0-931948-07-X). Peachtree Publishers.

Harries, Christie
--Cariboo Trail. 1st ed. LC 57-13892. 188p. 21cm. 1957. Longmans, Green.

Harriett, pseud., see Ginnings, Harriett Wilcoxen.

Harriett, pseud. (1905-), ed. see Frog He Would a-Wooing Go.

Harriett, pseud. (1905-)
--Animal ABC. Ginnings, Harriett Wilcoxen. Harriett, pseud. (1905-), illus. Ginnings, Harriett Wilcoxen. LC 49-5159. (Illus.). 17cm. 31p. (Tell-a-Tale Books). c.1949. Whitman Pub Co.
--Froggie Went A-Courtin'. (Illus.). (gr. k-3). 1967. (ISBN 0-8178-3762-0). Harvey.

Harrig, Frederick Harrison
--The Jingledom Series: New Rymes for Youngsters. LC 26-619. 22 1/2cm. c.1926. Harrig.

Harriman, E. E.
--Texas Men and Texas Cattle. LC 26-5893. 2 p. l., 188 p. 19 cm. 1926. Garden City Publishing Co., Inc.

Harriman, Edward
--Captain Capsize. Streeter, Sherry, illus. LC 81-66913. (Illus.). 31 p. 22cm. c.1981. Down East Books.
--Leroy the Lobster & Crabby Crab. (gr. 1-3). 1967. Down East.

Harriman, Marinell & Harriman, Robert
--A Myriad of Minstrels. Harriman, Marinell & Harriman, Robert, illus. (Illus.). 32p. (Orig.). N.D. Drollery Pr.

Harriman, Robert, jt. auth. see Harriman, Marinell.

Harriman, Susan S., Mrs., ed.
--Stories for Little Children. LC 21-1043. xxiii, 1 p., 1 l., 449, 1 p. col. front., illus., plates (part col.) 20 cm. (Half-title: The kindergarden children's hour, ed. by Lucy Wheelock ... v. 1). c.1920. Houghton Mifflin Company.

Harrington, Edwin
--Tamazine. Belevich, Alexis, illus. LC 82-80349. (Illus.). 160p. 1982. (ISBN 0-941066-02-9). Hillside Pr.

Harrington, Florence
--Georgie Merton: Or, Only a Girl. (Illus.). N.D. Thos Nelson & Sons.

Harrington, Helen & Pierson, Clara Dillingham
--Outwitting the Weasels: And New-Fangled Notions. LC 24-14147. 4 p. l., 3-139 p. diagrs. 20 cm. c.1924. E. P. Dutton & Company.

Harrington, Isis L., Mrs.
--The Eagles' Nest. Bennett, Richard Michael (1899-), illus. LC 30-213313. 5 p. l., 114 p. incl. illus., plates. front. 17 cm. (The little library). 1930. The Macmillan Company.
--Komoki of the Cliffs. LC 34-5295. 95 p. incl. col. front., illus. (part col.) 19 x 18 cm. c.1934. C. Scribner's Sons.
--Nah le Kah De, He Herds Sheep: The Story of a Navajo Boy. Beaujon, Louise, illus. LC 37-14927. 96 p. illus. 21 cm. 1937. E. P. Dutton & Company.

Harrington, John Walker (1868-)
--The Adventures of Admiral Frog. Price, Willard Bertram, illus. LC 2-22308. (Illus.). 49p. 22cm. 1902. R. H. Russell.
--The Jumping Kangaroo and the Apple Butter Cat. Conde, J. M., illus. LC 1-29053. 130 p. front., illus. 25 cm. 1900. McClure, Phillips.
--The King and Queen of Hearts. Conde, J. M., illus. N.D. McClure, Phillips & Co.

Harrington, Lucile, tr. see Grund, Josef Carl.

Harrington, Lyn Davis (1911-)
--Ootook, Young Eskimo Girl. LC 56-10030. 127p. illus. 24cm. 1956. Abelard-Schuman.
--Ootook, Young Eskimo Girl. 1962. E M Hale.
--Stormy Summer. Ilsley, Velma Elizabeth (1918-), illus. LC 56-5909. 190p. illus. 22cm. 1956. Abelard-Schuman.

Harrington, Mark Raymond (1882-1971)
--The Indians of New Jersey: Dickon Among the Lenapes. Ellsworth, Clarence (1885-), illus. LC 63-15519. 352 p. illus. 22 cm. 1963. Rutgers University Press.
--The Indians of New Jersey: Dickon Among the Lenape Indians. Ellsworth, Clarence (1885-), illus. LC 38-220199. xiii, 1 353 p. front., illus. (incl. plan) plates. 22 cm. c.1938. The John C. Winston Company.
--The Iroquois Trail: Dickon Among the Onondagas & Senecas. Perceval, Don Louis (1908-), illus. LC 64-8262. (Illus.). 215 p. illus., maps. 22 cm. (gr. 4-8). 1965. (ISBN 0-8135-0479-1). Rutgers U Pr.

Harrington, Mildred Priscilla (1886-), compiled by.
--Ring-A-Round. Bell, Corydon Whitten (1894-), illus. (Illus.). (gr. k-3). 1965. Macmillan.
--Ring-a-Round: A Collection of Verse for Boys and Girls. Bell, Corydon Whitten (1894-), illus. LC 30-28636. xvi, 250 p. col. front., illus., col. plates. 23 1/2 cm. 1930. The Macmillan Company.

--Uncle Remus. limited. Frost, Arthur Burdett (1851-1928), illus. LC 79-118395. (Illus.). 172 p., 1 leaf of plates. 22cm. (Collected stories of the world's greatest writers). (Collected Stories of the World's Greatest Writers.). 1979. Franklin Library.
--Uncle Remus. Frost, Arthur Burdett (1851-1928), illus. LC 65-14828. (Illus.). xx, 198 p. 21cm. (Schocken paperbacks, SB101). 1965. Schocken Books.
--Uncle Remus and Brer Rabbit. 1907. Stokes.
--Uncle Remus and Bre'r Rabbit. Conde, J. M., illus. N.D. Frederick A. Stokes.
--Uncle Remus and His Friends. LC 14-15739. xxxiv, 357, 1 p. front. (port.) plates. 20 cm. 1914. Houghton Mifflin Company.
--Uncle Remus & His Friends. Frost, Arthur Burdett (1851-1928), illus. N.D. Houghton Mifflin.
--Uncle Remus and His Friends: Old Plantation Stories, Songs, and Ballads, with Sketches of Negro Character. Frost, Arthur Burdett (1851-1928) & Vereck, Frank, illus. xv p., 2 l., 3-357 p. front., plates. 20 cm. 1892. Houghton, Mifflin and Company.
--Uncle Remus and the Little Boy. N.D. Dodd, Mead & Co.
--Uncle Remus and the Little Boy. LC 10-19619. xi, 1, 13-173, 1 p. incl. col. front., illus., col. plates. 22 cm. c.1910. Small, Maynard & Company.
--Uncle Remus: Being Legends of the Old Plantation. Eichenberg, Fritz (1901-), illus. LC 37-29161. 135, 1 p. incl. illus., plates. 25 cm. c.1937. The Peter Pauper Press.
--The Uncle Remus Book. Huber, Miriam Blanton (1889-), retold by. Frost, Arthur Burdett (1851-1928), illus. LC 35-17492. viii, 151 p. incl. front., illus. 20 cm. 1935. D. Appleton-Century Company, Incorporated.
--Uncle Remus: His Songs and His Saying. new and rev. ed. Frost, Arthur Burdett (1851-1928), illus. LC 4-104455. xxi p., 1 l., 265 p. illus., 11 pl (incl. front.) 20 cm. 1903. D. Appleton and Company.
--Uncle Remus: His Songs and His Sayings. N.D. Grosset & Dunlap.
--Uncle Remus: His Songs and His Sayings. Bright, M. Aline, ed. Frost, Arthur Burdett (1851-1928), illus. LC 31-18270. xxiii, 283 p. illus. 19 cm. (Half-title: Appleton modern literature series). c.1931. D. Appleton and Company.
--Uncle Remus: His Songs and His Sayings. Frost, Arthur Burdett (1851-1928) & Kemble, Edward Windsor (1861-1933), illus. LC 20-194328. xxii, 265 p. col. front., illus., plates. 26 cm. 1920. D. Appleton and Company.
--Uncle Remus: His Songs & His Sayings. Frost, Arthur Burdett (1851-1928), illus. Reissue of 1880 ed. 1921. Macrae Smith Co.
--Uncle Remus, His Songs and His Sayings. Hemenway, Robert E. (1941-), intro. by. LC 82-7482. p. cm. (Penguin American Library). 1982. (ISBN 0-14-039014-6). Penguin Books.
--Uncle Remus: His Songs and His Sayings. Moy, Seong (1921-), illus. Connelly, Marc, frwd. by. LC 58-657. xviii, 158p. illus. 25cm. 1957. For the Members of the Limited Editions Club.
--Uncle Remus: His Songs and His Sayings. Moy, Seong (1921-), illus. Connelly, Marc, frwd. by. LC 59-2765. 158p. illus. 25cm. c.1957. Heritage Press.
--Uncle Remus: His Songs and His Sayings: The Folklore of the Old Plantation. Church, Frederick S. & Moser, James H., illus. 1881. Appleton.
--Uncle Remus, His Songs and Sayings. Bright, M. Aline, ed. Frost, Arthur Burdett (1851-1928), illus. LC 31-18270. (Illus.). 283p. 18cm. (Appleton Modern Literature Ser.). 1931. D. Appleton and Company.
--Uncle Remus: His Songs and Sayings. new and rev. ed. Frost, Arthur Burdett (1851-1928), illus. LC 35-354349. xvi p., 2 l., 3-265 p. front., illus., plates. 20 cm. 1934. D. Appleton-Century Company Incorporated.
--Uncle Remus: His Songs and Sayings: The Folklore of the Old Plantation. Church, Frederick S. & Moser, James H., illus. LC 7-2896. (Illus.). 19cm. 231p. 1880. D. Appleton and Company.
--Uncle Remus Returns. Frost, Arthur Burdett (1851-1928) & Conde, J. M., illus. LC 18-16557. v, 1 p., 2 l., 174, 2 p. col. front., plates. 19 cm. 1918. Houghton Mifflin Company.
--Uncle Remus Stories. Shaw, Jane, retold by. Backhouse, G. W., illus. 64p. 1970. (ISBN 0-00-138187-3). Collins & World.
--Uncle Remus: Tales. Frost, Arthur Burdett (1851-1928), illus. LC 74-76980. (Illus.). xxviii, 206 p. 26cm. 1974. Beehive Press.
--Wally Wanderoon and His Story-Telling Machine. Moseley, Karl, illus. LC 3-22518. 4 p. l., 294 p. incl. 31 pl. front. 22 cm. 1903. McClure, Phillips & Co.
--Walt Disney's Uncle Remus Stories. Palmer, Marion (1898-), retold by. Dempster, Al, illus. Justice, Bill, adapted by. (Illus.). (gr. 3-5). 1964. (ISBN 0-307-15551-X, Golden Pr). (ISBN 0-307-65551-2). Western Pub.
--The Witch Wolf: An Uncle Remus Story. 1st ed. Dwiggins, W. A., illus. LC 54-49950. 30p. illus. 18cm. 1921. Bacon & Brown.
--The Wonderful Tar-Baby, Told by Uncle Remus: Retold for Little Children. Cunningham, Dellwyn, illus. LC 52-38422. unpaged. illus. 21 cm. (Wonder books, 581). 1952. Wonder Books.

Harris, Joel Chandler (1848-1908), ed.
--The Merry Maker. LC 55-2144. x, 316p. illus. (part col.) 21cm. (Young Folks Library: 2). c.1955. Auxiliary Educational League.

Harris, Joel Chandler (1848-1908) & Brown, Margaret Wise (1910-1952)
--Brer Rabbit & Brer Fox. Frost, Arthur Burdett (1851-1928), illus. (gr. 3 up). 1969. (ISBN 0-00-138188-1, Philomel). Putnam Pub Group.

Harris, Joel Chandler (1848-1908) & Harris, Esther La Rose (1854-)
--Uncle Remus Stories. Frost, Arthur Burdett (1851-1928), illus. LC 34-234634. 12 p. col. illus. 33 cm. c.1934. The Saalfield Publishing Company.

Harris, John see Hebden, Mark, pseud.

Harris, Julia Florida, tr. see Ispirescu, Petre.

Harris, Kilroy, jt. auth. see Harris, Leila.

Harris, Laura
--Away We Go. Flory, Jane Trescott (1917-), illus. LC 48-3621. 47 p. col. illus. 28 cm. 1945. Garden City Pub. Co.
--Freddie and the Fire Engine. Zaffo, George J., illus. N.D. Crown Publishers.
--The Happy Little Choo-Choo. Wehr, Julian, illus. LC 44-8655. 24 p. col. illus. 20 1/2 x 26 1/2 cm. 1944. Wm. Penn Publishing Corp.

Harris, Laura, ed. see Aesopus.

Harris, Laura & Zaffo, George J.
--Freddie and the Fire Engine. N.D. Lothrop Lee & Shepard.

Harris, Lavinia, pseud., see Johnson, Norma.

Harris, Lavinia
--Dreams & Memories. 192p. (Orig.). (gr. 7 up). 1982. (ISBN 0-590-32439-X, Windswept). Scholastic Inc.
--The Great Rip-Off. 240p. (gr. 7 up). 1984. (ISBN 0-590-33059-4, Point). Scholastic Inc.
--A Touch of Madness. Johnson, Norma. LC 85-2268. p. cm. c.1985. (ISBN 0-590-33057-8). Scholastic Inc.

Harris, Leila Gott, Mrs. & Harris, Walter Kilroy
--Blackfellow Bundi: A Native Australian Boy. Wiese, Kurt (1887-1974), illus. LC 39-30375. 62, 1 p. incl. col. front., illus. (part col.) 24 cm. 1939. A. Whitman & Co.
--The Lost Hole of Bingolla, a Story of the Australian Bush. Forrest, Will, illus. LC 42-21761. 207 p. illus. 21 1/2 cm. 1942. The Bobbs-Merrill Company.

Harris, Leila & Harris, Kilroy
--The Last Hole of Bingoola. Forrest, Will, illus. N.D. David McKay Co.
--The Lost Hole of Bingoola. N.D. Bobbs-Merrill Co.

Harris, Leon A., Jr. (1926-)
--The Great Diamond Robbery. Schindelman, Joseph (1923-), illus. LC 85-7965. p. cm. 1985. (ISBN 0-689-31188-5). Atheneum.
--The Great Picture Robbery. 1963. (ISBN 0-8382-0307-8, Cadmus Books). E. M. Hale and Company.
--The Great Picture Robbery. Schindelman, Joseph (1923-), illus. LC 63-10378. unpaged. illus. 19 x 22 cm. 1963. Atheneum. **Award: (NYT).**
--Maurice Goes to Sea. 1st ed. Schindelman, Joseph (1923-), illus. LC 68-16569. (Illus.). 1 v. (unpaged). 1968. W. W. Norton.
--The Moscow Circus School. (Illus.). 1970. (ISBN 0-689-20513-9). Atheneum Publishers.
--The Night Before Christmas, in Texas, That Is. Wohlberg, Meg (1905-), illus. LC 52-13635. unpaged. illus. 27 cm. N.D. Lothrop, Lee & Shepard.
--Night Before Christmas-in Texas, That Is. Wohlberg, Meg (1905-), illus. (Illus.). Repr. of 1952 ed. (gr. k-7). 1977. (ISBN 0-88289-175-8). Pelican.
--Russian Ballet School. (Illus.). photos. (gr. 3-7). 1970. (ISBN 0-689-20612-7). Atheneum.
--Yvette. Turkle, Brinton Cassaday (1915-), illus. LC 73-80969. (Illus.). 36 p. 27cm. 1970. McGraw-Hill.
--Yvette of the Opera Ballet. Turkle, Brinton Cassaday (1915-), illus. (Illus.). 40p. (gr. 2-5). 1970. (ISBN 0-07-026793-6). (ISBN 0-07-026794-4). McGraw.

Harris, Leonore
--Big Lonely Dog. Deets, Dorothy Allyn, illus. LC 43-51141. 41 p. col. illus. 21 cm. (On cover: Nursery books). 1943. Houghton Mifflin Company.

Harris, Lina Small & Harris, Valeria
--Tony and Toinette in the Tropics. Dornbusch, Margrette Oatway, illus. LC 39-23300. 90 p. col. front., illus. 24 cm. 1939. A Whitman & Co.

Harris, Linnie Sarah
--Bertha's Summer Boarders. (The Girl Chum Ser.). N.D. A. L. Burt Company.

Harris, Louise, jt. auth. see Harris, Norman Dyer.

Harris, Louise Dyer & Harris, Norman Dyer
--Flash: The Life Story of a Firefly. 1st ed. Kane, Henry Bugbee (1902-1971), illus. LC 66-10819. 57 p. col. illus. 21 cm. 1966. Little, Brown.
--Hummer and Buzz. N.D. E. M. Hale and Co.
--Hummer and Buzz. 1st ed. Candy, Robert (1920-), illus. LC 56-6763. 55p. illus. 21cm. 1956. Little, Brown.
--Little Red Newt. N.D. E. M. Hale & Co.
--Little Red Newt. 1st ed. Kane, Henry Bugbee (1902-1971), illus. LC 58-8668. 56p. illus. 21cm. 1958. Little, Brown.
--Slim Green. 1st ed. Candy, Robert (1920-), illus. LC 55-5190. 52p. illus. 21cm. 1955. Little, Brown.

Harris, Mabel Arundel, compiled by.
--Riddles and Laughter: A Book of Fun for Young Folks. 176p. 1928. George Sully & Co.

Harris, Marilyn (1931-)
--Bleeding Sorrow. LC 75-27418. 352p. 1976. (ISBN 0-399-11657-5). Putnam.
--The Peppersalt Land. LC 70-124189. 218 p. 22cm. 1970. Four Winds Press.
--The Runaway's Diary. LC 73-161021. 222 p. 22cm. 1971. Four Winds Press.

Harris, Mark Jonathan (1941-)
--Confessions of a Prime Time Kid. LC 84-20144. p. cm. 1985. (ISBN 0-688-03979-0). Lothrop, Lee & Shepard.
--The Last Run. LC 81-5110. 160 p. 22cm. c.1981. (ISBN 0-688-00634-5). (ISBN 0-688-00635-3). Lothrop, Lee & Shepard Books.
--With a Wave of the Wand. LC 79-18259. 191 p. 22cm. c.1980. (ISBN 0-688-41920-8). (ISBN 0-688-51920-2). Lothrop, Lee & Shephard Books.

Harris, Mark (1960-)
--The Doctor Who Technical Manual. LC 83-42868. p. cm. 1983. (ISBN 0-394-96214-1). (ISBN 0-394-86214-7). Random House.

Harris, Mary
--Jessica on Her Own. LC 78-427988. (Illus.). 21cm. 202p. (Faber Fanfare Ser.). 1978. (ISBN 0-571-08462-1). Faber & Faber.
--The Wolf. N.D. Sheed & Ward Inc.

Harris, Mary Craig
--Journeys of Johnny Jackrabbit. Harris, Mary Craig, illus. LC 22-20752. 4 p. l., 135, 1 p. front., plates. 19 cm. c.1921. The Bobbs-Merrill Company.

Harris, Mary Kathleen (1905-1966)
--The Bus Girls. Green, Eileen, illus. LC 68-6491. (Illus.). 21cm. 206p. N.D. Grosset & Dunlap.
--Emily and the Headmistress. N.D. Transatlantic Arts.
--Helena. (Illus.). N.D. Sheed & Ward.
--Henrietta of St. Hilary's. 1953. Staples Press.
--A Safe Lodging. Bolognese, Donald Alan (1934-), illus. LC 57-6053. 153p. illus. 20cm. 1957. Sheed & Ward.
--Seraphina. Rose, Sheila, illus. 196p. 1960. (ISBN 0-571-07012-4). Faber & Faber.
--Thomas. Roberts, Cliff, illus. LC 56-6134. unpaged. illus. 20cm. c.1956. Sheed & Ward.

Harris, May V.
--Carnival Time at Strobeck. Wiese, Kurt (1887-1974), illus. LC 38-31617. 62, 2 p. incl. col. front., illus. (part col.) 24 cm. 1938. A. Whitman & Co.

Harris, Miriam Coles (1834-1925), ed. see Monniot, Victorine.

Harris, Miriam Coles, Mrs. (1834-1925)
--Louie's Last Term. N.D. G W Carleton & Co.
--Louie's Last Term at St. Mary's. LC 11-16139. 239p. 19cm. 1871. C. Scribner & Company.
--Louie's Last Term at St. Mary's. LC 7-2905. 3 p. l., v-vi, 7-239 p. 18 cm. 1889. Houghton, Mifflin and Company.
--Roundhearts and Other Stories. Cresson, illus. LC 7-2911. 185 p. front., plates. 18 cm. 1871. C. Scribner & Company.
--Roundhearts and Other Stories. Cresson, illus. LC 7-2910. 4 p. l., 11-185 p. front., plates. 18 cm. 1867. Carleton;.

Harris, Norman Dyer, jt. auth. see Harris, Louise Dyer.

Harris, Norman Dyer (1920-) & Harris, Louise
--Slim Green. N.D. E. M. Hale & Co.

Harris, Peter
--Monkey & the Three Wizards. Foreman, Michael (1938-), illus. LC 76-57800. (Illus.). 40p. (gr. 2-4). 1977. (ISBN 0-87888-110-7). Bradbury Pr.

Harris, Peter David, tr. see Wu, Ch'Eng-En Ca.

Harris, Raymond
--Best Short Stories: Advanced Level. Burgoyne, Mari-Ann S., illus. (Illus.). 560p. (Orig.). (gr. 9 up). 1980. (ISBN 0-89061-234-X). (ISBN 0-89061-318-4). Jamestown Pubs.
--Best Short Stories, Middle Level. Lawrence, George & Watling, James, illus. (gr. 6-10). 1983. (ISBN 0-89061-322-2). (ISBN 0-89061-321-4). Jamestown Pubs.

Harris, Robie H.
--Don't Forget to Come Back. De Luna, Tony, illus. LC 78-3266. (Illus.). 40 p. 22cm. c.1978. (ISBN 0-394-83849-1). (ISBN 0-394-93849-6). Knopf : Distributed by Random House.
--Rosie's Double Dare. Harris, Robie H., illus. LC 79-26907. p. cm. (Capers). c.1980. (ISBN 0-394-84459-9). (ISBN 0-394-94459-3). Knopf.
--Rosie's Razzle Dazzle Deal. LC 81-2627. (Illus.). 121 p. 20cm. (Capers). c.1982. (ISBN 0-394-84975-2). (ISBN 0-394-94975-7). Knopf : Distributed by Random House.

Harris, Robie H. & Paterson, Diane (1946-)
--I Hate Kisses. Paterson, Diane R. Cole (1946-), illus. LC 79-18370. p. cm. c.1980. (ISBN 0-394-84324-X). (ISBN 0-394-94324-4). Knopf.

Harris, Robin
--Hello Kitty Sleeps Over. Gray, J. M. L., illus. LC 81-53045. (Illus.). 24 p. 17cm. c.1982. (ISBN 0-394-85154-4). Random House.
--My Melody's New Bike. Bracken, Carolyn, illus. LC 81-53046. (Illus.). 24 p. 17cm. c.1982. (ISBN 0-394-85153-6). Random House.

Harris, Rolf, ed.
--Friday Miracle & Other Stories. 1st U.S. edition. (gr. 1-6). 1970. (ISBN 0-14-030423-1, Puffin). Penguin.

Harris, Rosemary Jeanne (1923-)
--The Bright and Morning Star. LC 73-171566. x, 254 p. 21cm. 1972. Macmillan.
--The Child in the Bamboo Grove. Le Cain, Errol John (1941-), illus. LC 72-4064. (Illus.). 28 p. 26cm. 1971. (ISBN 0-87599-194-7). S. G. Phillips.
--The Flying Ship. Le Cain, Errol John (1941-), illus. (Illus.). 32p. (ps-5). 1975. (ISBN 0-571-10504-1). Faber & Faber.
--Janni's Stork. Wijngaard, Juan, illus. LC 83-15796. (Illus.). 32 p. 24cm. c.1982. (ISBN 0-911745-20-3). Bedrick/Blackie : Distributed by Harper & Row.
--The King's White Elephant. Le Cain, Errol John (1941-), illus. (Illus.). 32p. 1977. (ISBN 0-571-10302-2). (ISBN 0-571-11133-5). Faber & Faber.
--The Little Dog of Fo. Le Cain, Errol John (1941-), illus. LC 77-354183. (Illus.). 32p. (ps-5). 1976. (ISBN 0-571-10897-0). Faber & Faber.
--The Lotus and the Grail: Legends from East to West. Le Cain, Errol John (1941-), illus. LC 85-6778. p. cm. 1985. (ISBN 0-571-13536-6). Faber and Faber.
--The Moon in the Cloud. LC 71-99121. 192p. 1st U.S. edition. (gr. 7 up). 1970. Macmillan. **Award: (CMA).**
--The Seal-Singing. 280 p. 18cm. 1974, c.1971. Collier Books.
--The Seal Singing. LC 75-155265. 245p. 22cm. 1971. Macmillan.
--The Shadow on the Sun. LC 73-120716. x, 198 p. 21cm. 1970. The Macmillan Co.
--A Wicked Pack of Cards. 2nd ed. (gr. 5 up). N.D. (ISBN 0-571-10130-5, Pub. by Faber & Faber). Merrimack Pub Cir.
--Zed. 192p. 1984. (ISBN 0-571-11947-6). Faber & Faber.

Harris, Rosemary Jeanne (1923-), retold by.
--Beauty and the Beast. 1st ed. Le Cain, Errol John (1941-), illus. LC 79-7482. (Illus.). 32 p. 1980, c.1979. (ISBN 0-385-15482-8). Doubleday.
--Sea Magic and Other Stories of Enchantment. LC 73-8578. x, 178 p. 22cm. 1974. (ISBN 0-02-742650-5). Macmillan.

Harris, Sherwood
--Great Flying Adventures. (Illus.). 1973. (ISBN 0-394-82438-5). (ISBN 0-394-92438-X). Random House.

Harris, Thaddeus Mason (1768-1842), ed. see Oliver, N. W.

Harris, Theodore L., et al.
--Spacestone. (Keys to Reading Ser.). (gr. 6). 1975. Economy Co.
--Sunspinners. (Keys to Reading Ser.). (gr. 6). 1975. duplicating masters 20.16. (ISBN 0-87892-547-3). Economy Co.

Harris, Thomas
--Black Sunday. 1975. (ISBN 0-399-11443-2). G. P. Putnam's Sons.

Harris, Valeria, jt. auth. see Harris, Lina Small.

Harris, W. L., jt. auth. see Henry, William J.

Harris, Walter Kilroy, jt. auth. see Harris, Leila Gott, Mrs.

Harris, William T., ed. see Austin, Oscar Phelps.

Harris, William T., ed. see Kirk, E. B.

Harrison, et al.
--Chief Joseph. 35p. (gr. 1-9). 1981. Dormac.

AUTHOR INDEX HART, GWENDOLYN

Harrison, Ada M.
--The Doubling Rod. Price, Christine Hilda (1928-1980), illus. LC 58-6883. (Illus.). 192 p. 21cm. 1st U.S. edition. 1958. Harcourt, Brace.
Harrison, Ada M. & Austin, Robert
--Lucy's Village. Austin, Robert, illus. (Illus.). 1979. (ISBN 0-85967-524-6, Star & Eleph Bks). Green Tiger Pr.
Harrison, Amelia Williams see Compton, Margaret, pseud.
Harrison, Amelia Williams, Mrs. (1852-1903)
--American Indian Fairy Tales. Compton, Margaret, pseud. Bjorklund, Lorence F. (1913-1978), illus. LC 75-132623. (Illus.). 159 p. 24cm. 1971. (ISBN 0-396-06273-3). Dodd, Mead.
--Bockers and His Chum Peggy. Compton, Margaret, pseud. Rev ed. Betts, John Henderson, illus. LC 5003. 6, 9-218 p. front., plates. 20 cm. 1900. The Penn Publishing Company.
Harrison, Ann M.
--Pearls Are Made. Rev. ed. LC 58-7031. (Illus.). 135p. 21cm. 1958. Friendship Press.
--Pearls Are Made. Marguerite, Gayer, illus. LC 50-8256. 135 p. illus. 21 cm. 1950. Friendship Press.
Harrison, Burton see Harrison, Constance Cary Burton, Mrs.
Harrison, Carrol
--Fintu. (Illus.). (gr. 4-8). 1975. (ISBN 0-87482-076-6). Wake-Brook.
Harrison, Constance Cary Burton, Mrs. (1846-1920)
--Alice In Wonderland. Tenniel, John, Sir (1820-1914), illus. N.D. The De Witt Publishing House.
--Bric-a-Brac Stories. Crane, Walter (1845-1915), illus. N.D. Charles Scribner's Sons.
--The Old-Fashioned Fairy Book. Emmet, Rosina, illus. LC 11-6413. xxi, 343 p. incl. front., illus., plates. 16 cm. 1884. C. Scribner's Sons.
Harrison, Constance Cary (1846-1920)
--Crow's Nest, and Belhaven Tales. (Illus.). 210p. N.D. The Century Co.
Harrison, Crane Blossom
--The Odd One. 1st ed. Dauber, Elizabeth, illus. LC 58-8481. (Illus.). 269 p. 20cm. 1958. Little, Brown.
--Tomorrow for Patricia. 1st ed. Suba, Susanne (1913-), illus. LC 55-8092. 250p. illus. 20cm. 1955. Little, Brown.
Harrison, David Lee see Graham, Kennon, pseud.
Harrison, David Lee (1937-)
--The Book of Giant Stories. Fix, Philippe, illus. LC 79-148125. (Illus.). 44 p. 27cm. 1972. (ISBN 0-07-026858-4). American Heritage Press.
--The Boy with a Drum. Wilkin, Eloise Burns (1904-), illus. LC 71-154031. (Illus.). 25 p. 33cm. (Golden book favorite). 1971. Golden Press.
--Bugs Bunny in Escape from Noddington Castle. Graham, Kennon, pseud. Baker, Darrell, illus. LC 80-13646. p. cm. c.1980. (ISBN 0-307-10827-9). Western Pub. Co.
--The Case of Og, the Missing Frog. Warshaw, Jerry (1929-), illus. LC 72-3439. (Illus.). 62 p. 24cm. (Fledgling book). 1972. (ISBN 0-528-82634-4). (ISBN 0-528-82634-4). Rand McNally.
--The Circus Is in Town. Ross, Larry (1943-), illus. (Illus.). (Young Reader Ser.). (gr. k-3). 1979. (ISBN 0-307-60168-4, Golden Pr). Western Pub.
--Detective Bob and the Great Ape Escape. Delaney, Ned, pseud. (1951-), illus. Delaney, Thomas Nicholas III. LC 80-10584. (Illus.). 42 p. 24cm. c.1980. (ISBN 0-8193-1031-X). (ISBN 0-8193-1032-8). Parents Magazine Press.
--Little Turtle's Big Adventure. Miller, John Parr (1913-), illus. LC 70-87823. (Illus.). 36 p. 24cm. (Random House early bird book). 1969. Random House.
--Little Turtle's Big Adventure. Miller, John Parr (1913-), illus. LC 76-24166. (Illus.). 34 p. 21cm. (Best book club ever). (Random House pictureback). c.1978. (ISBN 0-394-83442-9). Random House.
--Little Turtle's Big Adventure. Miller, John Parr (1913-), illus. LC 83-13823. p. cm. (Random House Pictureback). 1985, c.1978. (ISBN 0-394-86345-3). (ISBN 0-394-96345-8). Random House.
--Monster! Monster!. Fry, Rosalind, illus. (Eager Readers Ser.). (gr. k-3). 1975. (ISBN 0-307-60808-5, Golden Pr). Western Pub.
--My Funny Bunny Phone Book. Butrick, Lyn M., illus. (Illus.). 14p. (Golden Play & Learn Bk.). (ps). 1980. (ISBN 0-307-10728-0, Golden Pr). Western Pub.
--Piggy Wiglet and the Great Adventure. Gray, Leslie, illus. LC 72-93773. (Illus.). 20 p. 32cm. 1973. Golden Press.
Harrison, David Lee (1937-), ed.
--Cinderella. Noel, Arlene, illus. (Illus.). 8p. of color ils. 20p. (gr. k-3). 1970. (ISBN 0-87529-033-7). Hallmark.
--Peter Pan. Brackman, Bob, illus. (Illus.). 8p. of color ils. 20p. (gr. k-3). 1970. (ISBN 0-87529-041-8). Hallmark.
Harrison, Deloris (1938-)
--Journey All Alone. LC 79-134854. 192p. (gr. 7 up). 1971. Dial.
Harrison, E.
--Offero, the Giant. (Folk Lore And Fairy Tales). N.D. MacMillan Bks.
--Secret Passage. (gr. 4 up). 1968. (ISBN 0-03-072840-1). HR&W.
Harrison, Edith Ogden, Mrs.
--Biblical Stories: Retold for Children. N.D. A. C. McClurg & Co.
--The Enchanted House and Other Fairy Stories. Richardson, Frederick (1862-1937), illus. 5 p. l., 9-126, 1 p. col. front., col. plates. 20 cm. 1915. A. C. McClurg & Company.
--The Flaming Sword: And Other Legends of the Earth and Sky. Perkins, Lucy Fitch, Mrs. (1865-1937), illus. LC 8-37065. 7 p. l., 13-133, 1 p. col. front., illus., 3 col. pl. 26 cm. 1908. A. C. McClurg & Co.
--The Glittering Festival. Wilson, Clara Powers, illus. LC 12-1476. 26cm. 176p. 1911. A.C. McClurg & Co.
--Ladder of Moonlight. Perkins, Lucy Fitch, Mrs. (1865-1937), illus. LC 9-26823. 20cm. 28p. (Biblical Stories Retold for Children). 1909. A. C. McClurg & Co.
--The Mocking-bird. Perkins, Lucy Fitch, Mrs. (1865-1937), illus. LC 9-26824. 20cm. 27p. (Biblical Stories Retold for Children). 1909. A. C. McClurg & Co.
--The Moon Princess. Perkins, Lucy Fitch, Mrs. (1865-1937), illus. N.D. A. C. McClurg & Co.
--Polar Star. Perkins, Lucy Fitch, Mrs. (1865-1937), illus. LC 9-26823. 20cm. 28p. (Biblical Stories Retold for Children). 1909. A. C. McClurg & Co.
--Prince Silverwings, and Other Fairy Tales. Perkins, Lucy Fitch, Mrs. (1865-1937), illus. LC 2-24328. 122, 1 p., 1 l. col. front., illus., col. plates. 26 x 20 cm. 1902. A. C. McClurg & Co.
--Princess Sayrane: A Romance of the Days of Prester John. Betts, Harold H., illus. LC 10-23314. 4 p. l., 313, 1 p. col. front., col. plates. 21 cm. 1910. A. C. McClurg & Co.
--The Star Fairies. Perkins, Lucy Fitch, Mrs. (1865-1937), illus. N.D. A. C. McClurg & Co.
Harrison, Elizabeth (1849-1927)
--In Story Land. 14th ed. LC 9-20914. viii, 9-192 p. 20 cm. c.1895. Central Publishing Company.
--In Story-Land. N.D. MacMillan.
--In Story-Land. LC 13-20117. viii, 9-186 p. 21 cm. 1895. The Sigma Publishing Co.
--In the Story World: Best Legends for Boys and Girls. Lupprian, Hildegard (1897-), illus. LC 31-9709. 204 p. incl. front., plates. 20 cm. c.1931. Milton Bradley Co.
--Misunderstood Children: Sketches Taken from Life. LC 10-1721. 3 p. l., 168 p. front. 19 cm. c.1910. Central Publishing Company.
Harrison, Ethel
--Prince Fearless and the Little Dwarf. Stewart, A. W., illus. LC 28-13252. 62 p., 1 l. incl. col. front. col. illus. 15 cm. c.1928. Henry Altemus Company.
Harrison, F. Bayford
--Brothers in Arms. (Illus.). (Scribner-Blackie Series of Books for Young People). N.D. Charles Scribner's Sons.
--The Theft of the Princes (Pub. by Society for Promoting Christian Knowledge). N.D. E. & J. B. Young & Co.
--Under Canvas (Pub. by Society for Promoting Christian Knowledge). N.D. E. & J. B Young & Co.
Harrison, Florence (1910-)
--In the Fairy Ring. Harrison, Florence (1910-), illus. (Illus.). N.D. Caldwell.
--Rhyme of a Run. (Illus.). N.D Dodge Publishing Co.
--The Rhyme of a Run, and Other Verse for Children. Harrison, Florence (1910-), illus. (Illus.). N.D. Caldwell.
Harrison, Frederick
--Sea Scouts Afloat: A Story of the Great War. N.D. Macmillan.
Harrison, G. B., jt. ed. see Granville-Barker, Harley.
Harrison, George Bagshawe (1894-), ed.
--More Tales from the Old Testament. Cox, E. A., illus. 182p. N.D. Thomas Nelson & Sons.
--The Wanderings of Ulysses. Kedwards, E. J., illus. LC 38-4427. ix p., 1 l., 13-144 p. incl. col. front., plates. 21 cm. (Horizon books). 1937. T. Nelson and Sons, Ltd.
Harrison, Gertude, Mrs.
--Listen, My Children: Poems for Boys and Girls. Samuelson, Val, illus. LC 40-349743. 3 p. l., 9-389, 9 p. col. plates. 23 cm. c.1940. H. Harrison.
Harrison, Gregory
--Posting Letters: Poems. Farmer, Peter, illus. LC 79-365551. (Illus.). 21cm. vi, 90p. 1968. Oxford Univ. Press.
--Turn Back for a Glove. Lebenson, Richard, illus. LC 75-10074. (Illus.). b & w ils. 96p. 1st U.S. edition. (gr. 8 up). 1970. (ISBN 0-8098-3086-8). Walck.
Harrison, Gregory, jt. auth. see Smith, Laurence.
Harrison, Harry Max, jt. auth. see Aldiss, Brian Wilson.
Harrison, Harry Max (1925-)
--The California Iceberg. Barry, James E., illus. LC 74-78109. (Illus.). 128 p. 22cm. 1975. (ISBN 0-8027-6194-1). Walker.
--The Men from P.I.G. and R.O.B.O.T. LC 77-22875. 141 p. 21cm. 1978, c.1974. (ISBN 0-689-30634-2). Atheneum.
--Spaceship Medic. LC 70-103750. 142 p. 22cm. 1970. Doubleday.
--The Stainless Steel Rat Saves the World. 1972. (ISBN 0-399-11047-X). G. P. Putnam's Sons.
--Star Smashers of the Galaxy Rangers. 1973. (ISBN 0-399-11186-7). G. P. Putnam's Sons.
--Tunnel Through the Deeps. 1972. (ISBN 0-399-10918-8). G. P. Putnam's Sons.
Harrison, Harry Max (1925-), ed.
--Science Fiction: Authors Choice. 1974. (ISBN 0-399-11188-3). G. P. Putnam's Sons.
--Science Fiction Reader. (Scribner School Paperback Ser.). (gr. 4-7). 1972. (ISBN [illegible], ScribC). Scribner.
--Worlds of Wonder: Sixteen Tales of Science Fiction. LC 76-78664. 264p. (gr. 9 up). 1969. (ISBN 0-385-07783-1). Doubleday.
Harrison, Harry Max (1925-) & Aldiss, Brian Wilson (1925-), eds.
--Best Science Fiction: 1972. 1973. (ISBN 0-399-11112-3). G. P. Putnam's Sons.
--Best Science Fiction: 1973. 1974. (ISBN 0-399-11301-0). G. P. Putnam's Sons.
Harrison, Hayford & Parker, Hershel, eds.
--Moby Dick. 1967. (ISBN 0-393-04284-7). (ISBN 0-393-09670-X). Norton & Co.
Harrison, Helen H.
--The Little Typewriter. LC 63-23440. (Illus.). 20cm. 15p. 1963. Naylor Co.
Harrison, Henry Syndor
--Angela's Business. N.D. Grosset & Dunlap.
Harrison, Herbert (1869-)
--A Lad of Kent. 1914. Macmillan.
Harrison, Jennie, pseud., see Tomkins, Jane Harrison.
Harrison, Jennie
--Little Boots. N.D. E. P. Dutton.
Harrison, John
--After-Dinner Stories. 200p. (Popular Handbooks). N.D. Penn Publication Ser.
Harrison, Mary Bennett
--By a Way They Knew Not: An Idyll of the First Century. Harrison, Mary Bennett, illus. LC 24-23804. 91, 1 p. front., illus. 20 cm. c.1924. Fleming H. Revell Company.
--Shining Windows. LC 25-17416. 20cm. 26p. 1925. Harrison & Hathaway.
Harrison, Mary ST. Leger Kingsley see Malet, Lucas, pseud.
Harrison, Michael
--In the Footsteps of Sherlock Holmes. 1960. Frederick Fell Inc.
Harrison, Michael & Stuart-Clark, Christopher, eds.
--Noah's Ark. (Illus.). 144p. 1st U.S. edition. (gr. 2-5). 1984. (ISBN 0-19-276047-5, Pub. by Oxford U Pr Childrens). Merrimack Pub Cir.
--The Oxford Book of Christmas Poems. (Illus.). 160p. 1984. (ISBN 0-19-276051-3, Pub. by Oxford U Pr Childrens). Merrimack Pub Cir.
Harrison, Mrs. Carter H. see Harrison, Edith Ogden, Mrs.
Harrison, Patricia
--With Warmth & Feeling. new ed. LC 74-2875. 28p. (gr. 9 up). 1974. (ISBN 0-8111-0534-2). Naylor.
Harrison, Sarah (1942-) & Wilks, Mike
--In Granny's Garden. LC 79-28585. (Illus.). 32 p. 29cm. c.1980. (ISBN 0-03-052441-5). Holt, Rinehart and Winston.
Harrison, Ted
--Children of the Yukon. LC 77-79543. (Illus.). (gr. 1-4). 1977. (ISBN 0-912766-83-2). Tundra Bks.
Harrison, Thad
--Westward to Adventure. Hoffman, H. Lawrence, illus. LC 60-6269. 159p. illus. 22cm. (Criterion book for young people). 1960. Criterion Books.
Harrison, Vincent
--The Jungle Joke Book. Coker, Paul, Jr., illus. LC 66-9094. (Illus.). 1 v. (unpaged. 22cm. (Laugh books). 1966. Wonder Books.
Harriss, Bernice Kelly (1894-)
--Santa on the Mantel. Spanfeller, James John (1930-), illus. LC 64-14274. 1964. Doubleday & Co.
Harrod, H. H.
--Nine Little Fairy Tales. (Folk Lore And Fairy Tales). N.D. MacMillan Bks.
Harrold, Blanche, Mrs., jt. auth. see Harrold, Orville.
Harrold, Orville (1878-) & Harrold, Blanche, Mrs. (1894-)
--Adventures of Nibble Bunny. LC 38-6765. 5 p. l., 100 numb. l. 25 m. c.1938. Suttonhouse.
Harrop, Beatrice
--Sing Hey Diddle Diddle: Sixty-Six Nursery Rhymes & Their Traditional Tunes. Francis, Frank & Cheese, Bernard, illus. (Illus.). 96p. (Orig.). (ps-3). 1984. (ISBN 0-7136-2334-9, Pub. by A & C Black UK). Sterling.
Harrower, Charles S., ed.
--Harry Lane, and Other Stories in Verse. N.D. Methodist Bk Concern.
Harrower, Mary Rachel (1906-)
--Plain Jane. Hale, Kathleen (1898-), illus. LC 29-8657. 5 p. l., 73 p. illus. 19 1/2 cm. 1929. Coward-McCann, Inc.
Harry
--Summer in Ashcroft. (Illus.). 1882. Harper's Trade-List.
Harry Moore Family
--Sad Dad. (Illus.). (ps). N.D. (ISBN 0-8170-0432-7). Judson.
Harry, Myriam
--The Little Daughter of Jerusalem. Allen, Phoebe, tr. 1918. E P Dutton.
Harry, Robert Reese, Sr.
--Elephant Boy of Burma. Kalmenoff, Matthew, illus. LC 60-10030. (Illus.). (gr. 5-8). 1960. (ISBN 0-394-91118-0). Random.
--Island Boy: A Story of Ancient Hawaii. Lonette, Reisie Dominee (1924-), illus. LC 56-9156. 209p. illus. 2icm. 1956. Lothrop, Lee & Shepard Co.
--Sea of Fire. Lonette, Reisie Dominee (1924-), illus. LC 58-107197. 223p. illus. 22cm. 1958. Lothrop. Lee and Shepard.
--Shark Boy: An Adventure in Ancient Hawaii. Lonette, Reisie Dominee (1924-), illus. LC 57-11653. (Illus.). 249 p. 22cm. 1957. Lothrop, Lee & Shepard Co.
Harshaw, Ruth Hetzel, Mrs. (1890-1968)
--The Council of the Gods. Kaissaroff, Nicolas, illus. LC 31-206602. xxii, 23-198 p. incl. front., illus., plates 24 cm. 1931. Thomas S. Rockwell Company.
--My Viking Book. Washburne, Carleton Wolsey (1889-), ed. Iannelli, Margaret, illus. LC 35-5971. 288 p. col. illus. 19 cm. c.1934. Rand, McNally & Company.
--Reindeer of the Waves. Washburne, Carleton Wolsey (1889-), ed. Iannelli, Margaret, illus. LC 34-24092. 288 p. col. illus. 22 cm. c.1934. Rand, McNally & Company.
Harste, Jerome C., jt. auth. see Goss, Janet L.
Harston, Ruth, et al. (1944-)
--Bradford and the Burglar. Harston, Ruth, et al. (1944-), illus. LC 75-179369. (Illus.). 48 p. 1972. (ISBN 0-201-09128-3). Young Scott Books.
Hart-Berry, Alice
--To School in the Spanish Main. N.D. Penguin Bks.
Hart, Bruce, jt. auth. see Moss, Jeffrey.
Hart, Carole, et al., eds. see Thomas, Marlo.
Hart, Carole (1943-)
--Delilah. Frascino, Edward, illus. LC 73-5483. (Illus.). 63 p. 22cm. 1973. (ISBN 0-06-022235-2). (ISBN 0-06-022235-2). Harper & Row.
Hart, Carolyn Gimpel (1936-)
--Danger: High Explosives!. LC 78-179087. 192p. (gr. 6 up). 1972. (ISBN 0-87131-043-0). M Evans.
--Dangerous Summer. LC 68-12394. 190 p. 22cm. 1968. Four Winds Press.
--No Easy Answers. LC 74-12289. (gr. 6-9). 1970. (ISBN 0-87131-078-3). M Evans.
--No Easy Answers. (gr. 7-12). 1972. (ISBN 0-590-09193-X, Schol Trade Pap). Schol Bk Serv.
--Rendezvous in Veracruz. LC 70-106593. (gr. 7 up). 1970. (ISBN 0-87131-088-0). M Evans.
--Secret of the Cellars. LC 64-23286. viii, 208p. (gr. 7-9). 1964. (ISBN 0-396-05070-0). Dodd.
--Spy Track. 192p. (gr. 5-8). 1970. M Evans.
Hart, Dick (1920-), illus.
--Fairy Tales from Andersen. N.D. L. B. Fischer.
Hart, Elsie
--The Travels of Mr. Trot. MacKnight, Ninon (1908-), illus. Ninon, pseud. LC 41-7941. 140 p. incl. illus., plates. 21 x 16 cm. c.1941. The Vanguard Press.
Hart, Eva Cruzen, jt. auth. see Reed, Myrtle.
Hart, Fanny Wheeler, Mrs.
--The Runaway: A Story for the Young. LC 36-29326. 3 p. l., 241, 1 p. front., plates 18 cm. 1872. Macmillan and Co.
Hart, Frank J
--The Speed Boy: A Story of the Big League. Copeland, Charles, illus. LC 38-890625. 5 p. l., 226 p. incl. front., illus. 24 cm. c.1938. Lakewood House.
Hart, Gwendolyn
--Takeo & the Wish. Hart, Gwendolyn, illus. LC 72-128640. (Illus.). 32p. (gr. 2-5). 1971. (ISBN 0-7232-1304-6). Warne.
Hart, Harold, jt. ed. see Strong, Joanna.
Hart, Hazel C., jt. ed. see Smith, Nila Banton.
Hart, Helen, pseud., see Lowe, Samuel Edward.
Hart, Horace Porter Biddle De see De Hart, Horace Porter Biddle.

Hart, Jane, compiled by.
--Singing Bee!. A Collection of Favorite Children's Songs. Lobel, Anita Kempler (1934-), illus. LC 82-15296. (Illus.). 160p. 1982. (ISBN 0-688-41975-5). Lothrop.
Hart, Jeanne McGahey
--Gloomy Erasmus. Shortall, Leonard W., illus. LC 57-743097. unpaged. illus. 21cm. 1957. Coward-McCann.
--Scareboy. Hart, Gerhardt, illus. LC 57-8067. (Illus.). (gr. 1-4). 1957. (ISBN 0-395-27660-8). Parnassus.
Hart, Johan
--Picture Tales from Holland. Phares, Frank E. & Phares, Margaret, illus. LC 35-27312. viii p., 1 l., 117 p. incl. illus., plates. 14 x 19 cm. 1935. Frederick A. Stokes Company.
--Picture Tales from Holland. Phares, Margaret, illus. N.D. J. B. Lippincott.
Hart, John G., tr. see Cramer, Marie.
Hart, Kingsley, tr. see Jansson, Tove.
Hart, Laverne
--Billy Bentson and His Family. Martin, Ron (1947-), illus. LC 81-65819. (Illus.). 32 p. 24cm. c.1981. (ISBN 0-8054-4270-7). Broadman Press.
--Billy Bentson, Helper. McPheeters, William N., illus. LC 78-102280. (Illus.). 31 p. 24cm. c.1977. (ISBN 0-8054-4237-5). Broadman Press.
--You May Wear Your Shoes in Church. Behrens, Paul R., illus. LC 81-66556. (Illus.). 32 p. 24cm. c.1981. (ISBN 0-8054-4275-8). Broadman Press.
Hart, Mrs.
--Clare Linton's Friend. N.D. Cassell & Co.
--Daisy's Dilemmas. N.D. Cassell & Co.
--Wrong from the First. N.D. Cassell & Co.
Hart, Nevada Lewis (1864-), ed.
--Pittypat and Tippytoe and Other Poems. Arthur, Rosalie, illus. LC 2-23751. 1 p. l., 7-64 p. illus. 16 x 13 cm. 1902. The Dodge Publishing Company.
Hart, Philip
--Adventures of a Patriot. LC 30-10810. vi, 7-256 p. front. 20 cm. (Mystery and adventure series for boys). c.1930. A. L. Burt Company.
--The Black Skimmer: A Story of Adventure and Mystery. LC 29-9875. 242 p. front. 20 cm. (Mystery and adventure series for boys). c.1929. A. L. Burt Company.
--The Flight of the Mystic Owls. LC 29-9721. 242 p. front. 20 cm. (Mystery and adventure series for boys). c.1929. A. L. Burt Company.
--The Forgotten Island. LC 35-8290. vi p., 1 l., 241 p. front. 21 cm. c.1935. A. L. Burt Company.
--The Golden Lure. LC 34-8053. 256 p. front. 20 cm. (Mystery and adventure series for boys). c.1934. A. L. Burt Company.
--The Midnight Canyon Mystery. LC 35-8291. vi p., 1 l., 9-250 p. 21 cm. c.1935. A. L. Burt Company.
--The Mysterious Trail. LC 34-14541. 256 p. front. 20 cm. (Mystery and adventure series for boys). c.1934. A. L. Burt Company.
--The Mystic Owls in Mystery. LC 35-8292. vi p., 1 l., 9-248 p. front. 21 cm. c.1935. A. L. Burt Company.
--The Strange Teepee. LC 31-12237. 252 p. front. 20 cm. (Mystery and adventure series for boys). c.1931. A. L. Burt Company.
--The Wreck of the Dauntless. LC 29-937145. 254 p. front. 20 cm. (Mystery and adventure series for boys). c.1929. A. L. Burt Company.
Hart, Stephanie (1949-)
--Is There Any Way Out of Sixth Grade?. LC 78-17388. p. cm. 1978. (ISBN 0-698-20445-X). Coward, McCann & Geoghegan.
Hart, Susanne (1927-)
--Spider's Tales. 16 drawings. 38p. (gr. 1-3). 1971. Tri-Ocean.
Hart, T. & Henn, W.
--Life Is No Yuk for the Yak. 371p. 1976. (ISBN 84-252-0611-1, French & Eur). French & Eur.
Hart, Tony
--Puppets & Moving Toys. (Illus.). 32p. 1st U.S. edition. (Tony Hart Fun Bks.). (gr. 1-4). 1984. (ISBN 0-7182-2951-7, Pub. by Kaye & Ward). David & Charles.
Hart, William Shakespeare see Bill Hart's Pinto Pony, pseud.
Hart, William Surrey (1870-1946)
--The Golden West Boys: "Injun" and "Whitey"; a Story of Adventure. Pancoast, Morris H., illus. LC 19-159675. xvi, 17-317 p. front., plates. 20 cm. (Boy's golden West series). c.1919. Britton Publishing Company.
--The Golden West Boys: Injun and Whitey Strike Out for Themselves. Cue, Harold, illus. LC 21-5270. v p., 1 l., 278 2 p. front., plates,. 20 cm. (Boy's golden West series). 1921. Houghton Mifflin Company.
--The Golden West Boys: Injun and Whitey to the Rescue. Cue, Harold, illus. LC 22-9360. v, 1 p., 2 l. 305 1 p. front., plates. 20 cm. (His Boy's golden West series). 1922. Houghton Mifflin Company.
--Injun & Whitey. N.D. Houghton Mifflin.
Harte, Bret see Harte, Francis Brett.
Harte, Bret, jt. auth. see Hawthorne, Nathaniel.
Harte, Francis Brett (1836-1902)
--The Luck of Roaring Camp & Other Stories. (Magnum Easy Eye Classic Ser.). (gr. 6-10). N.D. Lancer.
--The Luck of Roaring Camp & Other Stories: Includes; "The Outcast of Poker Flats", "Tennessee's Partner", "How Santa Claus Came to Simpson's Bar", and Other Popular Tales. Salomon, Louis, intro. by. 309p. (Great Illustrated Classics). 1961. Dodd, Mead & Co.
--Luck of Roaring Camp & Three Other Stories. Fisher, Leonard Everett (1924-), illus. (Illus.). scratchboard drawings. 96p. (gr. 7 up). 1968. (ISBN 0-531-01072-4). Watts.
--Luck of the Roaring Camp & Other Stories. (Riverside Library). (gr. 7 up). N.D. HM.
--Stories of the Early West: The Luck of Roaring Camp and Sixteen Other Exciting Tales. Clark, Walter Van Tilburg, frwd. by. (Illus.). (Great Writers Collection). (gr. 7 up). 1964. Platt.
Hartelius, Margaret A.
--The Birthday Trombone. Hartelius, Margaret A., illus. LC 76-14533. (Illus.). 48 p. c.1977. (ISBN 0-385-12292-6). (ISBN 0-385-12293-4). Doubleday.
--The Chicken's Child. Hartelius, Margaret A., illus. LC 74-18884. (Illus.). 39 p. 1975. (ISBN 0-385-07363-1). (ISBN 0-385-07370-4). Doubleday.
Hartell, John Anthony, illus.
--Over in the Meadow: An Old Nursery Song. LC 36-8270. 24 p. col. illus. 24 x 33 cm. 1936. Harper & Brothers.
Harter, Helen
--The Follett Picture-Story of Bread. LC 38-2424. 1 p. l., 40 p. illus. 21 x 17 cm. c.1936. Follett Publishing Company.
Harter, Helen & McIntire, Alta
--The Follett Picture-Story of Food. LC 38-2423. 1 p. l., 40 p. illus. 21 x 17 cm. c.1936. Follett Publishing Company.
Harter, Walter L.
--The Dog That Smiled. Walker, Charles W., illus. LC 65-20186. 102p. illus. 23cm. c.1965. Macmillan.
--Osceola's Head and Other American Ghost Stories. Waldman, Neil, illus. LC 73-13892. (Illus.). 71 p. 22cm. 1974. (ISBN 0-13-642991-2). Prentice-Hall.
--The Phantom Hand. Totten, Robert, illus. (Illus.). 128p. (gr. 4 up). 1976. (ISBN 0-13-661843-X, Pub. by Treehouse). P-H.
Hartland, Edwin Sidney (1848-1927), ed.
--English Fairy and Folk Tales. (Illus.). N.D. Charles Scribner's Sons.
--English Fairy and Other Folk Tales. LC 68-21772. 282p. Repr. of 1890 ed. 1968 (Gale Reprints). Singing Tree Press.
Hartley, C. H.
--Daniel Boone. (New Oxford Ser). N.D. Set. Lovell, Coryell & Co.
Hartley, Cecil, ed. see Aikin, John (1747-1822) & Barbauld, Anna Letitia Aikin, Mrs.
Hartley, Cecil, ed. see Day, Thomas.
Hartley, Emily, Mrs.
--Barley Loaves. LC 12-32959. 339p. N.D. American Sunday-School Union.
--Christmas with the Boys ... LC 12-32960. 201 p. incl. front. plates. 17 cm. c.1872. American Sunday-School Union.
--Christmas with the Girls ... LC 12-32961. 250 p. incl. front. plates. 18 cm. c.1875. American Sunday-School Union.
--Dora Kemper: Or, How the Bitter Was Made Sweet. LC 12-32962. 361 p. incl. front. plates. 18 cm. 1879. American Sunday-School Union.
--Odd Moments of the Willoughby Boys. LC 12-329575. 228 p. incl. front. plates. 17 cm. c.1879. American Sunday-School Union.
--Phil Derry: The Western Boy Who Became a Missionary. LC 12-34685. 1 p. l., 5-369 p. front., plates. 17 cm. c.1875. American Sunday-School Union.
--Records of "The Do-Without Society,". LC 12-32964. 272 p. incl. front. plates. 18 cm. 1879. American Sunday-School Union.
--Ruth Allerton: The Missionary's Daughter. LC 12-32963. 283 p. incl. front. plates. 17 cm. c.1871. American Sunday-School Union.
--Sandy Cameron: Or, The Way One Looks at It ... LC 12-329585. 267 p. incl. front. plates. 17 cm. c.1874. American Sunday-School Union.
Hartley, George Inness (1887-)
--Boy Hunters in Demerara. Sheperd, J. Clinton, illus. LC 21-16536. 5 p. l., 3-295 p. front., plates. 20 cm. 1921. The Century Co.
--The Last Parrakeet. Teague, Donald (1897-), illus. LC 23-12999. 5 p. l., 3-292 p. front., plates. 20 cm. 1923. The Century Co.
--The Lost Flamingos. Allen, Courtney, illus. LC 24-21815. 5 p. l., 3-319 p. front., plates. 20 cm. c.1924. The Century Co.
Hartling, Peter, pseud., see Haertling, Peter.
Hartman, Ann Kemp
--Adventure in the Everglades: An Indian Story. 1st ed. LC 54-11910. 94p. illus. 21cm. c.1955. Exposition Press.
Hartman, Emerson
--Daniel, the Hebrew Boy. LC 45-10323. 160 p. illus. 20 cm. 1945. The Wartburg Press.
--The Giant of the Sierras. LC 46-22687. 158 p. incl. front. (group port.) plates, facsim. 20 cm. 1945. Chapman & Grimes, Inc.
Hartman, Evert
--War Without Friends. Crampton, Patricia, tr. LC 82-10093. p. cm. 1982. (ISBN 0-517-54754-6). Crown Publishers.
Hartman, Gertrude (1876-1955)
--In Bible Days. Voute, Kathleen (1892-), illus. (Illus.). (gr. 7 up). 1948. Macmillan.
Hartman, Lou
--The Monstrous Leathern Man. 1st ed. Sagsoorian, Paul (1923-), illus. LC 78-115080. (Illus.). 185 p. 25cm. 1970. Atheneum.
Hartman, Mary E., jt. auth. see Dehnbostel, Nancy L.
Hartman, Zoe & Wansborough, Harold
--The Christmas Bazaar. N.D. T. S. Denison.
Hartmann, John
--A Deer in the Family. Nielson, Edith M., tr. N.D. E. P. Dutton & Co.
Hartmann, Lorice
--Who Will Fly with Butterfly?. (Illus.). (gr. k-3). 1978. (ISBN 0-912760-51-6). Valkyrie Hse.
Hartmann, Sven
--Jacob Extra. 1983. (ISBN 0-8120-2397-8). (ISBN 0-8120-2396-X). Barron.
Hartmann, Sven & Hartner, Thomas
--Jacob: Little Cat Tales. Bernard, Jack, ed. Macri, Angelika, tr. 80p. (gr. 1-6). 1980. (ISBN 0-8120-2290-4). (ISBN 0-8120-2297-1). Barron.
--Jacob, Little Cat Tales. Macri, Angelika, tr. LC 80-13668. (Illus.). 79 p. 28cm. 1981, c.1977. (ISBN 0-8120-2290-4). Barron's.
--Jacob Two: Me & My Human. Bernard, Jack F. (1930-), ed. Macri, Angelika, tr. 80p. (gr. k-6). 1981. (ISBN 0-8120-2391-9). (ISBN 0-8120-2392-7). Barron.
Hartner, Eva, pseud., see Twardowska, Emma Eve Henriette Von.
Hartner, Eva, pseud. (1845-1889)
--Pythia's Pupil. Twardowska, Emma Eve Henriette Von. (Illus.). (The Wellesley Series for Girls). N.D. A. L. Burt's Pubs.
--Pythia's Pupils: A Story for Young Girls. Twardowska, Emma Eve Henriette Von. Davis, J. W, Mrs., tr. from German. (Illus.). N.D. George Routledge.
--Pythia's Pupils: A Story of A School. Twardowska, Emma Eve Henriette Von. (The Rugby Ser.). N.D. A. L. Burt Company.
Hartner, Thomas, jt. auth. see Hartmann, Sven.
Hartog, Jan De see De Hartog, Jan.
Hartough, M. S.
--Marah: Stories for Little People, 1 of 4 Vols. Penney, L., ed. 72p. (The Never-Begin Series). N.D. Per set in box 3.00. National Temperance Society.
Hartsell, Lynn
--Pitch in & Play Fair. Sustendal, Pat, illus. (Illus.). 40p. (Huddles Ser.). (ps-3). N.D. (ISBN 0-910313-05-9). Parker Bro.
Hartshorn, Leon R.
--Inspiring Stories for Young Latter-Day Saints. LC 75-5178. viii, 268 p. 24cm. 1975. (ISBN 0-87747-547-4). Deseret Book Co.
Hartshorn, Nancy, pseud., see McPherson, M. E..
Hartshorne, Grace, ed.
--In the Sweetness of Childhood: Poems of Mother Love. LC 5727. 2 p. l., ix-xv p., 2 l., 11-172 p. front., plates. 19 cm. 1900. D. Estes & Company.
Hartson, Eleanore, jt. auth. see Adams, Phylliss.
Hartwell, John Anthony, illus.
--Over in the Meadow;. An Old Nursery Song. LC 36-3270. (Illus.). 24p. 24 x 33cm. 1936. Harper & Brothers.
Hartwell, Marjorie, jt. auth. see Dixon, Rachel Taft.
Hartwell, Marjorie (1951-)
--The Animals of the Friendly Farm. LC 46-18714. (Illus.). 28. 30 x 23cm. 1946. F. Watts, Inc.
--Animals of the Friendly Farm. LC 51-3716. (Illus.). 30p. N.D. Wilcox & Follett Co.
--Into The Ark. (Illus.). 27cm. 28p. 1945. Franklin Watts, Inc.
--Purrrt. Hartwell, Marjorie (1951-), illus. LC 53-16718. 16p. illus. 17cm. (Fuzzy wuzzy tell-a-tales). c.1952. Whitman Pub. Co.
Hartwell, Nancy, pseud., see Callahan, Claire Wallis.
Hartwick, Harry
--Farewell to the Farivox. Ohlsson, Ib (1935-), illus. LC 73-182115. (Illus.). 46 p. 24cm. 1972. Four Winds Press.
--The Runaway Ride of Old 88. 1st ed. Klapholz, Mel, illus. LC 76-129910. (Illus.). 57 p. 22cm. 1971. Little, Brown.
Hartz, Mina Frasa
--A Book for Us; Poems. LC 55-12515. 55p. 21cm. 1955. Pageant Press.
Hartzell, L. W., ed. see Appleton, Carolyn Ten Eyck.
Hartzler, Arlene & Gaeddert, John, eds.
--Children's Hymnary. LC 67-24327. (gr. k-7). 1967. (ISBN 0-87303-095-8). Faith & Life.
Harven, Emile De see De Harven, Emile.
Harvey, B. Norman
--Any Old Dollars, Mister?. 155p. 1964. Tri-Ocean Books.
Harvey, Bonnie C., jt. ed. see Phillips, Cheryl M.
Harvey, Bonnie C., ed. see Stirrup Associates, Inc.
Harvey, Catherine, tr. see Chetin, Helen.
Harvey, Edith Mary, jt. ed. see McLaren, Jane Minerva.
Harvey, Edith Mary & McLaren, Jane Minerva
--Hansel and Gretel: A Play for Little Children. N.D. Frederick A. Stokes Co.
Harvey, George Brinton McClellan (1864-)
--On Track and Diamond. LC 9-10040. xii p., 2 l., 200 p., 1 l. incl. front. 7 pl. 19 cm. (On verso of t.-p.: Harper's athletic series). 1909. Harper & Brothers.
Harvey, George Cockburn, jt. auth. see Defoe, Daniel.
Harvey, George Cockburn (1858-), ed. see Sewell, Anna.
Harvey, George Cockburn (1858-), ed.
--Robin Hood. Prittie, Edwin John, illus. LC 23-14088. 22cm. 352p. (The Children's Bookshelf). 1923. John C. Winston.
--Robin Hood. Prittie, Edwin John, illus. LC 57-12795. (Illus.). 278. 22cm. (The Children's Classics). 1957. Winston.
Harvey, James O. (1926-)
--Beyond the Gorge of Shadows. LC 65-22028. 224 p. 22 cm. 1965. Lothrop, Lee & Shepard Co.
Harvey, Jane B., Mrs.
--Billy's Scrapbook. Billings, Edna, illus. LC 41-3673. 43p. 27cm. 1941. The Caxton Printers Ltd.
Harvey, Lillian, jt. ed. see Newcomb, Frances Lynette Johnson.
Harvey, Lois F.
--Toyanuki's Rabbit: Story of a Paiute Boy. Eckart, Frances & Luhrs, Henry, illus. LC 64-19882. 62 p. col. illus. 24 cm. (Melmont look, read, learn). 1964. Melmont Publishers.
Harvey, Paul, jt. auth. see Frost, Erica.
Harvey, Paul, jt. auth. see Kim, Joy.
Harvey, S. J.
--Dolly's New Shoes. (Illus.). (Model Lib.: No. 4). N.D. Set. American Tract Society.
Harvey, Sarah A. B., Mrs. (1846-), tr. see Gautier, Judith.
Harvey, Sarah A. B., Mrs. (1843-), tr. see Normand, Charles.
Harvey, William (1796-1866), illus.
--Lane's Arabian Nights: The Thousand and One Nights Commonly Called the Arabian Nights' Entertainment, 3 Vols. Lane, Edward William (1801-1876), tr. from Arabic. (Illus.). (Standard English and American Bks). N.D. Estes & Lauriat's.
--Tales from the Thousand and One Nights. Dawood, Nessim Joseph (1927-), tr. LC 73-176480. (Illus.). 406 p. 19cm. (Penguin classics). 1973. (ISBN 0-14-044289-8). Penguin Books.
Harvitt, Helene Josephine, jt. auth. see Dlugo, Ethel F.
Harvitt, Helene Josephine, tr. see Brandenburg, Albert Jacques.
Harwick, B. L.
--The Frog Prints. LC 76-13840. (Illus.). 48p. (Fiction). (gr. k-2). 1976. (ISBN 0-8172-0152-1). Raintree Pubs.
Harwood, Henry David (1938-)
--Alert to Danger!. LC 70-90930. (Illus.). 151 p. 21cm. 1969. Roy Publishers.
Harwood, John
--Aladdin and His Wonderful Lamp. (Porpoise Bks.). N.D. Houghton Mifflin Co.
--Christmas Manger. (Illus.). (gr. 3-6). N.D. (ISBN 0-14-049103-1, Puffin). Penguin.
Harwood, John, illus.
--Puffin Rhymes. LC 46-3702. (Illus.). 18cm. 32p. (A Baby Puffin Bk.). 1944. Penguin Books, Limited.
Harwood, Pearl Augusta Bragdon (1903-)
--The Carnival with Mr. and Mrs. Bumba. Overlie, George, illus. LC 76-156360. (Illus.). 30 p. 24cm. (Mr. & Mrs. Bumba Bks.). 1971. (ISBN 0-8225-0128-7). Lerner Publications Co.
--Climbing a Mountain with Mr. and Mrs. Bumba. Overlie, George, illus. LC 70-156353. (Illus.). 30 p. 24cm. (Mr. & Mrs. Bumba Bks.). 1971. (ISBN 0-8225-0129-5). Lerner Publications Co.
--A Happy Halloween for Mr. and Mrs. Bumba. Overlie, George, illus. LC 73-156362. (Illus.). 30 p. 24cm. (Mr. & Mrs. Bumba Bks.). 1971. (ISBN 0-8225-0126-0). Lerner Publications Co.

Hatch, Mary Cottam (1912-1970), retold by.
--Thirteen Danish Tales. Edgun (1913-), illus. Bay, Jens Christian (1871-), tr. LC 49-10046. (Illus.). (gr. 3-6). 1949, c.1947. (ISBN 0-15-285683-8, HJ). HarBraceJ.
Hatch, Mary Cottam (1912-1970) & Bay, Jens Christian (1871-), eds.
--Thirteen Danish Tales. Edgun (1913-), illus. LC 47-30505. (Illus.). 21cm. 169p. 1947. Harcourt, Brace.
Hatch, May D
--Rhymes and Jingles for Little Speakers. LC 16-3088. 87 p. 17 cm. c.1889. The De Witt Publishing House.
Hatch, Palmer D.
--Kindergarten Jingles. Ostrander, Willie, illus. LC 15-23999. 51 p. col. illus. 24 cm. c.1886. Hard & Parsons.
Hatch, Richard Warren (1898-)
--All Aboard the Whale!. Simont, Marc (1915-), illus. LC 42-23669. 4 p. l., 216 p. illus. 21 cm. 1942. Dodd, Mead & Company.
--The Curious Lobster. Wakeman, Marion Freeman (1891-1953), illus. LC 37-24113. 5 p. l., 3-248 p. incl. front., illus., plates. 21 cm. c.1937. Harcourt, Brace and Company.
--The Curious Lobster's Island. LC 39-224437. x p. 1 l., 264 p. incl. illus., plates. col. front. 21 cm. 1939. Dodd, Mead and Company.
--The Fugitive. N.D. Dodd Mead & Co.
--The Lobster Books: The Curious Lobster and The Curious Lobster's Island. LC 51-11001. (Illus.). 347 p. 22cm. 1951, c.1939. Mifflin.
Hatcher, Charles
--What Shape Is It?. Adamson, Gareth (1925-1982), illus. LC 65-25480. 32p. illus. (pt. col.) 25cm. 1st U.S. edition. 1966, c.1963. Duell Dist. Meredith.
Hatcher, Josephine
--Bubble and the Circus. N.D. Transatlantic Arts, Inc.
Hathaway, Cynthia
--Two Bridgets. Doane, Pelagie (1906-1966), illus. LC 41-17580. (Illus.). 82p. 1941. Doubleday Doran & Co.
Hathaway, Harriet N.
--The Children's Chip Basket. (Illus.). 102p. N.D. American Tract Society.
Hathaway, Katharine Butler
--Mr. Muffet's Cat and Her Trip to Paris. Hatheway, Katherine Butler, illus. LC 34-35320. 5 p. l., 161 p. front., illus., plates. 21 1/2 cm. 1934. Harper & Brothers.
Hathaway, Lulu Bailey, jt. auth. see Heppe, Margaret.
Hathaway, Mary E. N.
--Johnny's Vacations. (Illus.). N.D. D. Lothrop Co.
Hathaway, Maurine, Mrs.
--Little Steps in Child Training. LC 21-8542. 23 1/2cm. 43p. c.1921. Elsie Lincoln Benedict Lecture Courses.
--Tinkle Bell Tales. LC 22-24596. (Illus.). 27 1/2cm. 32p. c.1922. Standard Pub.
Hatherell, William, illus.
--Sentimental Tommy. N.D. Charles Scribner's Sons.
Hatheway, Flora
--Arrow Creek Stories. (Indian Culture Ser.). (gr. 3-9). 1973. (ISBN 0-686-22294-6). MT Coun Indian.
--The Little People. (Indian Culture Ser.). (gr. 2-9). 1971. (ISBN 0-89992-034-9). MT Coun Indian.
--Old Man Coyote. (Indian Culture Ser.). (gr. 2-9). 1970. (ISBN 0-89992-008-X). MT Coun Indian.
Hatheway, Jan, pseud., see Neubauer, William Arthur.
Hatheway, Mary E. N
--Cats in Gloves Catch No Mice. LC 15-23975. 28 p. front., illus. 12 x 15 1/2 cm. c.1887. D. Lothrop Company.
Hatsley, Nivessa R.
--Growing Down with Mama. 1983. (ISBN 0-686-84440-8). Vantage.
Hatt, E. M., tr. see LeMarchand, Jacques.
Hatten, Joseph
--Captured By Cannibals. N.D. Pott & Co.
Hattie
--The Little Princess & Other Stories. N.D. Methodist Bk Concern.
Hattie, Kathryn
--When Noodlehead Went to The Fair. Watson, Wendy McLeod (1942-), illus. 48p. 1968. Parents' Magazine Press.
Hatton, Barbara
--Tales of the White Cockade. N.D. E. P. Dutton & Co.
Haubensak-Tellenback, Margrit
--The Story of Noah's Ark. Emhardt, Erna, illus. (Illus.). 1983. (ISBN 0-517-55050-4). Crown.
Haubiel, Charles (1894-) & Bradley, Fay
--Mother Goose Songs. Simplified. Ellender, Elizabeth & Beverley, Katherine, illus. LC 44-44455. 36 p. illus. 31 x 23 1/2 cm. (First Series). 1937. The Composers Press, Inc.
Haubiel, Charles (1894-) & Mother Goose
--Mother Goose Songs: First Series. Beverley, Katherine & Ellender, Elizabeth, illus. LC 44-44456. 31 p. illus. 31 x 23 1/2 cm. (First Series). 1935. The Composers Press, Inc.
Hauck, Louise Platt see Archer, Lane, pseud.
Hauck, Louise Platt, Mrs. (1883-1943)
--At Midnight: A Mystery Story for Girls. Morris, Beth Krebs, illus. LC 30-7789. 6 p. l., 11-290 p. front., illus., plates. 20 1/2 cm. c.1930. The Bobbs-Merrill Company.
--Cherry Pit. Morris, Beth Krebs, illus. LC 30-22024. 297 p. front., illus., plates. 19 1/2 cm. c.1930. The Bobbs-Merrill Company.
--The Gold Trail: How Two Boys Followed It in '49. Cue, Harold, illus. LC 29-8726. 256 p. front., plates. 19 1/2 cm. c.1929. Lothrop, Lee & Shepard Co.
--High Jinks Ranch. Snyder, Harold E., illus. LC 27-169151. 320 p. front., plates. 19 1/2 cm. 1927. The Penn Publishing Company.
--Lucky Shot: A Story of Bent's Fort. Archer, Lane, pseud. Cue, Harold, illus. LC 31-10355. 262 p. front., plates. 19 1/2 cm. c.1931. Lothrop, Lee & Shepard Co.
--Marise: A Story for Girls. Morris, Beth Krebs, illus. LC 29-16993. 296 p. front., illus., plates. 21 cm. c.1929. The Bobbs-Merrill Company.
--At Midnight. N.D. Grosset & Dunlap.
--Mystery Mansion. Archer, Lane, pseud. LC 31-29825. 304 p. front., plates. 19 1/2 cm. c.1931. The Penn Publishing Company.
--The Youngest Rider: A Story of the Pony Express. Harman, Fred (1902-1982), illus. LC 27-7928. 245 p. front., plates. 19 1/2 cm. c.1927. Lothrop, Lee & Shepard Co.
Hauer, Mary E.
--Esmerelda Witch & the Ebony Soldier. Smilowitz, Stuart, illus. (Illus.). 1977. (ISBN 0-533-03058-7). Vantage.
Hauff, Wilhelm, jt. auth. see Horwitz, Carolyn Norris.
Hauff, Wilhelm (1802-1827)
--Arabian Days' Entertainments. new ed. Hoppin, Augustus (1828-1896), illus. Curtis, Herbert Pelham, tr. from Ger. N.D. Houghton Mifflin.
--The Arabian Days' Entertainments. Hoppin, Augustus (1828-1896), illus. Curtis, Herbert Pelham, tr. N.D. James R Osgood and Company.
--The Big Book of Stories. Grabianski, Janusz (1928-1976), illus. LC 76-143400. (Illus.). 288 p. 25cm. (gr. 4-6). 1971, c.1970. (ISBN 0-531-01974-8). F. Watts.
--The Caravan. Silverman, Burton Philip (1928-), illus. LC 64-20688. (Illus.). xi, 220 p. 23cm. 1964. Crowell.
--The Cold Stone Heart. Sanderson, William, illus. Schalit, Michael, tr. LC 65-230159. 63p. illus. 23cm. c.1965. M. Schalit, Dover St.
--Dwarf Long-Nose. Sendak, Maurice Bernard (1928-), illus. Orgel, Doris, tr. LC 60-10031. (Illus.). 60 p. 24cm. 1960. Random House. **Award: (ALA).**
--Fairy Tales. (The Girls' Own Library). N.D. David McKay.
--Fairy Tales of Wilhelm Hauff. Schramm, Ulrik (1912-), illus. Bell, Anthea, tr. LC 69-11048. 223p. 1969. Abelard-Schuman.
--The Golden Treasury of Wonderful Fairy Tales: Stories Adapted from Marchenalmanach. Cremonini, illus. LC 61-16296. 154p. illus. 33cm. (Giant golden book, 620). 1961. Golden Press.
--Hauff's Fairy Tales. (Illus.). (St. Nicholas Series for Girls). N.D. International Book Co.
--Hauff's Fairy Tales. Pinkerton, E. Percy, tr. (Illus.). (American Classic Ser.). N.D. David Mc Kay.
--The Heart of Stone. 1964. MacMillan Co.
--A Heart of Stone. 1st ed. Thompson, Arthur R., illus. LC 66-324. 61 p. illus. 21 cm. 1966. Vantage Press.
--Monkey's Uncle. Orgel, Doris (1929-), ed. Miller, Mitchell (1947-), illus. LC 70-88784. (Illus.). (gr. 4 up). 1969. (ISBN 0-374-35016-7). FS&G.
--Tales. N.D. Harcourt Brace & Co.
--Tales of the Caravan Inn, and Place. Stowell, Edward L., tr. LC 22-14735. 397 p. illus. 19 cm. 1882. Jansen, McClurg & Company.
Haufrecht, Herbert, jt. ed. see Garson, Eugenia.
Haugaard, Erik Christian (1923-), ed. see Andersen, Hans Christian.
Haugaard, Erik Christian (1923-), tr. see Andersen, Hans Christian.
Haugaard, Erik Christian (1923-)
--A Boy's Will. Howell, Troy, illus. LC 83-83. (Illus.). 48p. (gr. 2-5). 1983. (ISBN 0-395-33227-3). HM.
--Chase Me, Catch Nobody!. LC 80-371. 209 p. 22cm. 1980. (ISBN 0-395-29208-5). Houghton Mifflin.
--Cromwell's Boy. LC 78-14392. p. cm. 1978. (ISBN 0-395-27203-3). Houghton Mifflin.
--Hakon of Rogen's Saga. Dillon, Leo (1933-) & Dillon, Diane (1933-), illus. (Illus.). 132 p. 21cm. (Sandpiper Book). 1973, c.1963. (ISBN 0-395-16037-5). Houghton.
--Leif the Unlucky. LC 82-1053. (Illus.). x, 206 p. 22cm. c.1982. (ISBN 0-395-32156-5). Houghton Mifflin.
--The Little Fishes. Johnson, Milton (1932-), illus. LC 67-14701. (Illus.). 214 p. 22cm. 1967. Houghton Mifflin. **Award: (BGH).**
--A Messenger for Parliament. LC 76-21737. 218 p. 22cm. 1976. (ISBN 0-395-24392-0). Houghton Mifflin.
--Orphans of the Wind. Johnson, Milton (1932-), illus. LC 66-17172. (Illus.). 22cm. 186p. (gr. 7 up). 1966. (ISBN 0-395-06805-3). HM.
--The Rider and His Horse. Dillon, Leo (1933-) & Dillon, Diane (1933-), illus. LC 68-29900. (Illus.). 243 p. 23cm. 1968. Houghton Mifflin.
--The Samurai's Tale. 256p. (gr. 7 up). 1984. (ISBN 0-395-34559-6). HM. **Award: (ALA).**
--A Slave's Tale. Dillon, Leo (1933-) & Dillon, Diane (1933-), illus. LC 65-12171. (Illus.). 217p. (gr. 7 up). 1965. (ISBN 0-395-06804-5). HM. **Award: (ALA).**
--Untold Tale. Dillon, Leo (1933-) & Dillon, Diane (1933-), illus. LC 74-135133. (Illus.). 208p. (gr. 5 up). 1971. (ISBN 0-395-12366-6). HM. **Award: (ALA).**
Haugaard, Kay
--China Boy. LC 71-141863. 223 p. 22cm. 1971. (ISBN 0-200-71763-4). Abelard-Schuman.
--Myeko's Gift. Ternei, Dora, illus. LC 66-317677. 160p. illus. 22cm. 1967, c.1966. Abelard.
Haugan, Randolph E., ed.
--Christmas. 72p. N.D. Augsburg Publishing House.
Hauge, Mary & Hauge, Carl, illus.
--Old MacDonald Had a Farm. (Illus.). 32p. (Golden Melody Bks.). (ps-1). 1983. (ISBN 0-307-12244-1, Golden Pr). Western Pub.
Hauge, Patricia A., jt. auth. see Green, Walter D.
Haugen, Tormod
--The Night Birds. (gr. 2-5). 1982. Delacorte.
Haughey, Betty Ellen
--Stephanie Lane: Editorial Secretary. LC 67-2870. 192 p. 21cm. (Career romance for young moderns). 1967. Messner.
Haughey, Paul S.
--Ringtail, and Other Stories. Provonsha, Clyde N., illus. LC 56-15681. 80p. illus. 24cm. 1955. Southern Pub. Association.
Haughton, Rosemary Luling (1927-)
--The Carpenter's Son. (gr. 5-8). 1967. (ISBN 0-02-743430-3). Macmillan.
Haugsrud, L. B.
--My Eight Other Lives: By Tiger Haugsrud As Dictated to L. B. Haugsrud. Haugsrud, L. B., illus. LC 57-12703. unpaged. illus. 28cm. (Denison's series of picture books). 1957. T. S. Denison.
Hauman, Doris, Mrs., jt. auth. see Hauman, George.
Hauman, George (1890-1961) & Hauman, Doris, Mrs. (1897-)
--Buttons: Six Gay Stories with Pictures. Hauman, George (1890-1961) & Hauman, Doris, Mrs. (1897-), illus. LC 36-7829. 64 p. incl. col. front., col. illus. 21 1/2 cm. 1936. The Macmillan Company.
--Happy Harbor: A Seashore Story. LC 38-6238. 60 p. incl. col. front., col. illus. 22 cm. 1938. The Macmillan Company.
--Puppies for Keep. N.D. MacMillan.
--Surprise for Timmy. Hauman, George (1890-1961) & Hauman, Doris, Mrs. (1897-), illus. LC 46-8408. 78, 1 p. incl. col. front., illus. (part col.) 21 cm. 1946. The Macmillan Company.
Haupt, Istar
--The Story of Stick-a-Nose-In. Haupt, Istar, illus. LC 61-10491. 1961. Little, Brown and Company.
Hauptmann, Gerhart Johann Robert (1862-1946)
--Parsival. Williams, Oakley, tr. LC 15-6367. 3 p. l., 117 p. 18 1/2 cm. 1915. The Macmillan Company.
Hauptmann, Tatjana
--Adeline Schlime. LC 80-82138. (Illus.). 32 p. 28cm. 1980. (ISBN 0-03-057979-1). Holt, Rinehart, and Winston.
--Day in the Life of Petronella Pig. (gr. 1-3). 1980. Holt.
--A Day in the Life of Petronella Pig. 1st Holt ed. LC 82-235207. (Illus.). 14 leaves. 1982, c.1978. (ISBN 0-03-057794-2). Holt, Rinehart and Winston.
--A Day in the Life of Petronella Pig. LC 79-3067. p. cm. 1980. (ISBN 0-8317-2150-2). Mayflower Books.
--Papa Pig Comes Home Again. Hauptmann, Tatjana, illus. LC 81-80743. (Illus.). 48p. (gr. k-3). 1981. (ISBN 0-03-059896-6). HR&W.
Haus, Felice
--Hello Kitty's Book of Seasons. Shine, Deborah, ed. Gray, J. M. L., illus. LC 83-62672. (Illus.). 24p. (Sniffy Bks.). (ps-1). 1984. (ISBN 0-394-86379-8, BYR). Random.
Hauser, Henrich
--The Folding Father. Gergely, Tibor (1900-1978), illus. Mussey, Barrows, tr. LC 42-7374. 24cm. 24p. N.D. Lothrop Lee & Shepard.
Hauser, Margaret Louise see Head, Gay, pseud.
Hausman, Gerald (1945-)
--Beth: The Little Girl of Pine Knoll. Totten, Bob, illus. LC 74-82228. (Illus.). 39 p. 21cm. c.1974. (ISBN 0-912846-08-9). Bookstore Press.
--The Boy with the Sun Tree Bow. Totten, Bob, illus. LC 73-91009. (Illus.). 47 p. 1973. (ISBN 0-912944-13-7). Berkshire Traveller Press.
--Sitting on the Blue-Eyed Bear: Navajo Myths & Legends. Hausman, Sidney, illus. LC 75-23920. (Illus.). 144p. (gr. 7 up). 1976. (ISBN 0-88208-061-X). Lawrence Hill.
Hausman, James
--Mystery at San Souci. LC 77-18520. (Illus.). 180 p. 22cm. 1978. (ISBN 0-689-30644-X). Atheneum.
Hausman, Suzanne, illus.
--Yes, Virginia. N.D. (ISBN 0-685-86235-6). Pubns Devl Co TX.
Hautzig, Deborah (1956-)
--The Handsomest Father. Batherman, Muriel (1926-), illus. LC 78-21277. (Illus.). 56p. (Greenwillow Read-Alone Bks). (gr. 1-3). 1979. (ISBN 0-688-80214-1). (ISBN 0-688-84214-3). Greenwillow.
--Happy Birthday, Little Witch. Brown, Marc Tolon (1946-), illus. LC 85-1796. (Illus.). 48 p. 24cm. (Step into reading. A step 2 book). c.1985. (ISBN 0-394-97365-8). (ISBN 0-394-87365-3). Random House.
--Hey, Dollface. LC 78-54685. 151 p. 22cm. c.1978. (ISBN 0-688-80170-6). (ISBN 0-688-84170-8). Greenwillow Books.
--Little Witch's Big Night. Brown, Marc Tolon (1946-), illus. LC 84-3309. 1984. (ISBN 0-394-86587-1). Random.
--Second Star to the Right. LC 81-1589. p. cm. c.1981. (ISBN 0-688-00498-9). (ISBN 0-688-00499-7). Greenwillow Books.
Hautzig, Deborah (1956-), ed.
--Big Bird Visits the Dodos. Mathieu, Joseph, contrib. by. LC 84-43051. (Based on the Movie Sesame Street Presents: Follow That Bird! By the Children's Television Workshop). (Illus.). 32 p. 21cm. 1985. (ISBN 0-394-87373-4). (ISBN 0-394-97373-9). Random House/Children's Television Workshop.
--The Christmas Story: Based on the Gospels According to St. Matthew & St. Luke. Beckett, Sheilah (1913-), illus. LC 83-60411. (Illus.). 24p. (ps-2). 1983. (ISBN 0-394-86124-8). Random.
--Follow That Bird. LC 84-43052. (Storybook Based on the Movie). (Illus.). 48p. (gr. 1-4). 1985. (ISBN 0-394-97225-2, BYR). (ISBN 0-394-87225-8). Random.
--Sesame Street Presents Follow That Bird!. LC 84-43052. (Storybook Based on the Movie). (Illus.). 42 p. 29cm. 1985. (ISBN 0-394-87225-8). (ISBN 0-394-97225-2). Random House : Children's Television Workshop.
--A Visit to the Sesame Street Hospital: Featuring Jim Henson's Sesame Street Muppets. Mathieu, Joseph (1945-), illus. LC 84-17852. (Illus.). 32 p. 21cm. (Random House pictureback). 1985. (ISBN 0-394-87062-X). (ISBN 0-394-97062-4). Random House/Children's Television Workshop.
--The Wizard of Oz. Smith, Joseph A. (1936-), illus. LC 83-13792. (Original Author: Lyman Frank Baum, 1856-1919). c.1984. (ISBN 0-394-85331-8). Random House.
Hautzig, Deborah (1956-) & Oechsli, Kelly (1918-), eds.
--Rumpelstiltskin. LC 79-64717. (Illus.). 48 p. 23cm. c.1979. (ISBN 0-394-62003-8). Random House.
Hautzig, Esther Rudomin (1930-), retold by see Peretz, Isaac Loeb.
Hautzig, Esther Rudomin (1930-), tr. see Peretz, Isaac Loeb.
Hautzig, Esther Rudomin (1930-)
--At Home: A Visit in Four Languages. Aliki, pseud. (1929-), illus. Brandenberg, Aliki Liacouras. LC 68-23063. (Illus.). full color ils. phonetic guides. glossary. russian alphabet. 32p. (gr. k-2). 1968. (ISBN 0-02-743470-2). Macmillan.
--The Endless Steppe: A Girl in Exile (Pub. by Crowell). (gr. 7-12). 1968. (ISBN 0-590-04445-1). Scholastic Inc.
--The Endless Steppe: Growing up in Siberia. LC 68-13582. (gr. 7 up). 1968. (ISBN 0-690-26371-6, TYC-J). Har-Row. **Award: (ALA).**
--A Gift for Mama. Diamond, Donna (1950-), illus. LC 80-24973. p. cm. 1981. (ISBN 0-670-33976-8). Viking Press. **Award: (ALA).**
--In the Park: An Excursion in Four Languages. Keats, Ezra Jack (1916-1983), illus. LC 68-10067. (Illus.). 30 color ils. 32p. (gr. 1-3). 1968. (ISBN 0-02-743450-8). Macmillan.
Hautzig, Esther Rudomin (1930-), ed.
--In School: Learning in Four Languages. Hogrogian, Nonny (1932-), illus. LC 69-18236. (Illus.). 36 p. 26cm. 1969. Macmillan.

--Piebald, King of Bronchos: The Biography of a Wild Horse. Copeland, Charles, illus. N.D. Macrae Smith.
--Redcoat: The Phantom Fox. Bull, Charles Livingston (1874-1932), illus. LC 27-258831. 8 p. l., 238 p. front., plates. 19 cm. c.1927. Milton Bradley Company.
--Roany: The Horse Who Smelled Smoke. Tyng, Griswold, illus. LC 37-12425. 4 p. l., 13-251 p. incl. front., plates. 19 1/2 cm. c.1935. Milton Bradley Company.
--Shaggycoat. Copeland, Charles, illus. LC 6-36434. 20cm. 273p. 1906. G. W. Jacobs & Co.
--Shaggycoat: The Biography of a Beaver. Copeland, Charles, illus. N.D. Macrae Smith.
--Shovelhorns: The Biography of a Moose. Copeland, Charles, illus. 270p. 1909. Macrae Smith.
--Silversheene, King of Sled Dogs. LC 43-157674. 2 p. l., ix-xvii, 1, 234 p. col. front. 19 cm. 1943. The Platt & Munk Co., Inc.
--Silversheene: King of Sled Dogs. Bull, Charles Livingston (1874-1932), illus. LC 24-8276. xvii, 234 p. front., plates. 19 cm. c.1924. Milton Bradley Company.
--Stories of the Good Greenwood. (Twentieth Century Ser.). 1905. Thomas Y. Crowell & Co.
--The Strange Adventures of Mr. Turtle. Gnos, Olga, illus. LC 44-603243. 176 p. illus. 21 cm. 1944. Harbinger House.
--Tenants of the Trees. Copeland, Charles, illus. N.D. Macrae Smith.
--Trails to Woods & Waters. Copeland, Charles, illus. N.D. Macrae Smith.
--Uncle Billy, the Curious Cobbler. N.D. Chapman & Grimes.
--Wanted a Mother. LC 22-21323. 4 p. l., 7-227 p. front., plates. 19 cm. c.1922. G. W. Jacobs & Co.
--The Way of the Wild. Copeland, Charles, illus. N.D. Macrae Smith.
--The White Czar: A Story of a Polar Bear. Bull, Charles Livingston (1874-1932), illus. LC 23-17368. 4 p. l., 7-202 p. front., plates. 19 cm. 1923. Milton Bradley Company.
--A Wilderness Dog: The Biography of a Gray Wolf. Copeland, Charles, illus. N.D. Macrae Smith.
--Wood & Water Friends. Copeland, Charles, illus. 1925. Macrae Smith.
--Wood and Water Friends. Copeland, Charles, illus. 1917. Thomas Y. Crowell Company.

Hawkes, Ellen & Manso, Peter (1940-)
--The Shadow of the Moth: A Novel of Espionage with Virginia Woolf. 272p. 1983. (ISBN 0-312-71414-9, Pub. by Mareu). St Martin.

Hawkes, Hester (1900-)
--Lee Po's Search. Petie, Haris, pseud. (1915-), illus. Petty, Roberta. LC 57-11720. (Illus.). unpaged. 23cm. 1958. Coward-McCann.
--Ning's Pony. N.D. E. M. Hale & Co.
--Ning's Pony. Wiese, Kurt (1887-1974), illus. LC 53-8392. unpaged. illus. 22cm. 1953. Coward-McCann.
--Tami's New House. Matsumoto, Betty, illus. LC 55-6889. (Illus.). unpaged. 23cm. 1955. Coward-McCann.
--Three Seeds. Wiese, Kurt (1887-1974), illus. LC 56-9955. unpaged. illus. 23cm. 1956. Coward-McCann.
--Wally's Burro. Bartell, George, illus. LC 62-13802. (Illus.). 27cm. 30p. 1962. Golden, Gate Junior Books.

Hawkes, Laura
--Favorite Christmas Stories. 64p. 1973. (ISBN 0-89036-015-4). Hawkes Publishing Inc.

Hawkesworth, tr.
--Fenelon's Adventures of Telemachus. N.D. D. Appleton & Co.

Hawkesworth, Jenny
--The Lonely Skyscraper. Schongut, Emanuel, illus. LC 79-6703. (Illus.). 30 p. 27cm. c.1980. (ISBN 0-385-15947-1). (ISBN 0-385-15948-X). Doubleday.

Hawkins
--Mysterious & Delicious. N.D. (ISBN 0-8277-4042-5). British Bk Ctr.

Hawkins, Anthony Hope see Hope, Anthony, pseud.

Hawkins, Chauncey Jeddie (1875-)
--Ned Brewster's Bear Hunt. Hawkins, Chauncey Jeddie (1875-), illus. LC 13-200308. 285p. (Ned Brewster Ser.). 1913. Little, Brown.
--Ned Brewster's Year in the Big Woods. Hawkins, Chauncey Jeddie (1875-), illus. LC 12-24683. (Illus.). 291p. 20cm. 1912. Little, Brown and Company.

Hawkins, Colin
--Pat the Cat. Hawkins, Colin, illus. LC 82-18104. p. cm. 1983. (ISBN 0-399-20957-3). Putnam.
--Take Away Monsters. Hawkins, Colin, illus. (Illus.). 12p. (A Pull-the-Tab Bk.). (ps-2). 1984. (ISBN 0-399-20962-X, Putnam). Putnam Pub Group.
--What Time Is It, Mr. Wolf?. LC 82-21571. p. cm. 1983. (ISBN 0-399-20959-X). Putnam.

Hawkins, Colin & Hawkins, Jacqui
--Boo! Who?. Hawkins, Colin & Hawkins, Jacqui, illus. LC 83-80071. (Illus.). 20p. (ps-1). 1983. (ISBN 0-03-063929-8). HR&W.
--Hush Now, Baby Bear. Hawkins, Colin & Hawkins, Jacqui, illus. LC 85-2440. p. cm. 1986, c.1985. (ISBN 0-394-87562-1). (ISBN 0-394-97562-6). Random House.
--Jen the Hen. Hawkins, Colin & Hawkins, Jacqui, illus. LC 84-42955. p. cm. (Flip-the-page rhyming book). 1985. (ISBN 0-399-21207-8). Putnam.
--Mig the Pig. Hawkins, Colin & Hawkins, Jacqui, illus. (Illus.). 20p. (A Flip-the-Page Rhyming Bk.). (gr. k-3). 1984. (ISBN 0-399-21061-X, Putnam). Putnam Pub Group.
--Old Mother Hubbard. Hawkins, Colin & Hawkins, Jacqui, illus. LC 84-18333. (Illus.). 20 p. 23cm. 1985, c.1984. (ISBN 0-399-21162-4). Putman.
--Snap! Snap!. Hawkins, Colin & Hawkins, Jacqui, illus. LC 84-9892. (Illus.). 32p. (ps-3). 1984. (ISBN 0-399-21163-2, Putnam). (ISBN 0-399-21184-5). Putnam Pub Group.

Hawkins, Helena Ann Quail (1905-)
--Androcles and the Lion: Retold from Apion. Negri, Rocco (1932-), illus. Apion LC 75-104301. (Illus.). 48 p. 1970. Coward-McCann.
--Aunt-Sitter. Turkle, Brinton Cassaday (1915-), illus. LC 58-3872. 36p. 1958. Holiday House.
--The Best Birthday. 1st ed. Sotomayor, Antonio (1902-), illus. LC 54-9839. 63p. illus. 24cm. (Junior books). 1954. Doubleday.
--Don't Run, Apple!. Cote, Phyllis N. (1921-), illus. LC 44-41884. 36 p. illus. 23 cm. 1944. Holiday House.
--Mark, Mark, Shut the Door!. 1st ed. Busoni, Rafaello (1900-1962), illus. LC 49-16173. 31 p. col. illus. 23 cm. (Beginning to read book). 1947. Holiday House.
--Mountain Courage. 1st ed. Buel, Hubert, illus. LC 57-10455. 143p. illus. 22cm. 1957. Doubleday.
--A Puppy for Keeps. Wiese, Kurt (1887-1974), illus. LC 43-513064. 28 p. illus. 23 cm. 1943. Holiday House.
--Too Many Dogs. Wiese, Kurt (1887-1974), illus. LC 46-7276. 57 p. illus. 21 1/2 x 16 1/2 cm. 1946. Holiday House.
--Who Wants An Apple. N.D. E. M. Hale & Co.
--Who Wants an Apple. Granahan, David & Granahan, Lolita, illus. LC 42-239540. 39 p. incl. front., illus. 22 cm. 1942. Holiday House.
--Who Wants an Apple. Granahan, David & Granahan, Lolita, illus. 40p. 1957. Holiday House.

Hawkins, Jacqui, jt. auth. see Hawkins, Colin.

Hawkins, Mark & Vallario, Jean
--A Lion Under Her Bed. Hawkins, Mark, illus. LC 77-18865. (Illus.). 32 p. 24cm. c.1978. (ISBN 0-03-040381-2). Holt, Rinehart and Winston.

Hawkins, May Anderson
--Philip Barton's Secret. (Illus.). N.D. Methodist Bk Concern.

Hawkins, Q., ed. see Stephens, James.

Hawkins, Quail see Hawkins, Helena Ann Quail.

Hawkins, Quail, jt. auth. see Von Hagen, Victor Wolfgang.

Hawkins, Robert A.
--Bible Songs for Children. N.D. E Fudge.

Hawkins, Seckatary, pseud., see Schulkers, Robert Franc.

Hawkins, Sheila (1905-)
--Appleby John: The Miller's Lad. Hawkins, Sheila (1905-), illus. LC 39-27799. 92, 1 p. illus. 28 x 26 cm. 1939. Harper & Brothers.
--Bruzzy Bear, and the Cabin Boy. 1st ed. Hawkins, Sheila (1905-), illus. LC 40-32219. (Illus.). 27 x 21cm. 32p. c.1940. Harper & Brothers.
--Ena--Meena--Mina--Mo--and Benjamin. Hawkins, Sheila (1905-), illus. LC 36-1434. 57, 1 p. illus. (part col.) 19 x 23 cm. 1935. F. Warne and Co., Ltd.
--Little Gray Colo: The Adventures of A Koala Bear. Hawkins, Sheila, illus. LC 39-13752. (Illus.). 41p. N.D. Grosset & Dunlap.
--Pepito. Hawkins, Sheila (1905-), illus. LC 40-27391. 84, 2 p. incl. col. front., illus. (part col.) 28 x 26 cm. 1940. Harper & Brothers.

Hawkins, Willis Brooks (1852-)
--Queerful Widget. Ta'Bois, J. Flora, illus. LC 21-102500. xi p., 1 l., 17-137 p. incl. front., illus. 21 cm. c.1920. Boni and Liveright.

Hawkinson, John Samuel, jt. auth. see Friskey, Margaret Richards.

Hawkinson, John Samuel (1912-)
--The Mouse That Fell off the Rainbow. Hawkinson, John Samuel (1912-), illus. LC 75-150802. (Illus.). 32 p. 1971. (ISBN 0-8075-5296-8). A. Whitman.
--The Old Stump. Hawkinson, John Samuel (1912-), illus. LC 65-23883. (Illus.). 19cm. (Self Starter Bks.). (ps-2). 1965. (ISBN 0-8075-5969-5). A Whitman.
--Our Wonderful Wayside. Hawkinson, John Samuel (1912-), illus. LC 66-16078. 40p. illus. (pt. col.) 24cm. 1966. A. Whitman.
--Robins and Rabbits. Hawkinson, John Samuel (1912-), illus. LC 60-13636. unpaged. illus. 24cm. 1960. A. Whitman.
--Where the Wild Apples Grow. Hawkinson, John Samuel (1912-), illus. LC 67-17418. (Illus.). 37 p. 24cm. 1967. A. Whitman.
--Who Lives There?. Hawkinson, John Samuel (1912-), illus. LC 79-115895. (Illus.). 40 p. 24cm. 1970. (ISBN 0-8075-9035-5). A. Whitman.

Hawkinson, John Samuel (1912-) & Hawkinson, Lucy Ozone (1924-1971)
--Little Boy Who Lives Up High. Hawkinson, John Samuel (1912-) & Hawkinson, Lucy Ozone (1924-1971), illus. LC 67-26515. (Illus.). (Self Starter Bks.). (ps-2). 1967. (ISBN 0-8075-4580-5). A Whitman.
--Little Boy Who Lives up High. Hawkinson, John Samuel (1912-) & Hawkinson, Lucy Ozone (1924-1971), illus. (Cadmus Bks.). (gr. k-2). 1967. (ISBN 0-8382-1062-7). Hale.
--Winter Tree Birds. Hawkinson, John Samuel (1912-) & Hawkinson, Lucy Ozone (1924-1971), illus. LC 56-7751. unpaged. illus. 23cm. 1956. Whitman.

Hawkinson, Lucy Ozone, jt. auth. see Hawkinson, John Samuel.

Hawkinson, Lucy Ozone (1924-1971)
--All in One Day. Hawkinson, Lucy Ozone (1924-1971), illus. (Illus.). (ps-1). 1966. (ISBN 0-8075-0280-4). A Whitman.
--All in One Day. Hawkinson, Lucy Ozone (1924-1971), illus. LC 55-7787. (Illus.). unpaged. 24cm. 1955. Whitman.
--Dance, Dance, Amy-Chan!. Hawkinson, Lucy Ozone (1924-1971), illus. LC 64-16369. 1 v. (unpaged) illus. (part col.) 24 cm. 1964. A. Whitman.
--Days I Like. Hawkinson, Lucy Ozone (1924-1971), illus. LC 65-23884. 1 v. (unpaged) illus. (part col.) 24 cm. 1965. A. Whitman.
--The New River Train. Hawkinson, Lucy Ozone (1924-1971), illus. LC 76-126438. (Illus.). 19cm. 32p. 1970. (ISBN 0-8075-7823-1). A.Whitman.
--Pockets. Hawkinson, Lucy Ozone (1924-1971), illus. LC 55-27084. unpaged. illus. 17cm. (Tell-a-tale books). c.1955. Whitman Pub. Co.
--Surprise!. Hawkinson, Lucy Ozone (1924-1971), illus. LC 56-11561. unpaged. illus. 21cm. (Rand McNally elf book, 562). c.1956. Rand McNally.

Hawley, Harriet Eunice
--The Little Tin Soldier. Low, Loretta, illus. 1915. Cupples & Leon.
--Timothy Toddlekin. Low, Loretta, illus. 1915. Cupples & Leon.
--A Woodland Party. Low, Loretta, illus. 1915. Cupples & Leon.

Hawley, Harriet Smith
--Bless You, Betsy: A Novel. LC 34-15797. 256 p. 19 1/2 cm. c.1934. R. D. Henkle.
--The Goose Girl of Nurnberg. Pogany, Willy (1882-1955), illus. LC 37-15602. 59 p. col. front., illus. 27 1/2 cm. 1936. Suttonhouse, Ltd.

Hawley, Hattie L., ed. see Dana, Richard Henry, Jr.

Hawley, Katharine, tr. see Celli, Rose.

Hawley, Katherine
--Here Are the Quittens. Bindrum, Elsie Spaney (1906-), illus. LC 35-870. 60 p. illus. 13 1/2 x 17 cm. c.1935. Whitman Publi; Hing Co.
--Stories of the Quin-Puplets. Smock, Nell Stolp, illus. LC 35-171. 1 p. l.,7-58, 2 p. front., illus. 16 cm. c.1935. Whitman Publishing Company.

Hawley, Mabel C., pseud., see Stratemeyer Syndicate.

Hawley, Mabel C., pseud.
--Four Little Blossoms and Their Winter Fun. Stratemeyer Syndicate. Repr. of 1920 ed (Pub. by George Sully & Co.). (Four Little Blossoms Ser.: No. 3). 1938. Saalfield Publishing Co.
--Four Little Blossoms and their Winter Fun. Stratemeyer Syndicate. Herbert, Robert Gaston, illus. Repr. of 1920 ed (Pub. by George Sully & Co). (Four Little Blossoms Ser.: No. 3). N.D. Cupples & Leon Co.
--Four Little Blossoms and Their Winter Fun. Stratemeyer Syndicate. Herbert, Robert Gaston, illus. 160p. (Four Little Blossoms Ser.: No. 3). 1920. George Sully & Co.
--Four Little Blossoms at Brookside Farm. Stratemeyer Syndicate. Herbert, Robert Gaston, illus. Repr. of 1920 ed (Pub. by George Sully & Co). (Four Little Blossoms Ser.: No. 1). N.D. Cupples & Leon Co.
--Four Little Blossoms at Brookside Farm. Stratemeyer Syndicate. Herbert, Robert Gaston, illus. 160p. (Four Little Blossoms Ser.: No. 1). 1920. George Sully & Co.
--Four Little Blossoms at Brookside Farm. Stratemeyer Syndicate. Herbert, Robert Gaston, illus. Repr. of 1920 ed (Pub. by George Sully & Co.). (Four Little Blossoms Ser.: No. 1). 1938. Saalfield Publishing Co.
--Four Little Blossoms at Oak Hill School. Stratemeyer Syndicate. Herbert, Robert Gaston, illus. Repr. of 1920 ed (Pub. by George Sully & Co). (Four Little Blossoms Ser.: No. 2). N.D. Cupples & Leon Co.
--Four Little Blossoms at Oak Hill School. Stratemeyer Syndicate. Herbert, Robert Gaston, illus. 160p. (Four Little Blossoms Ser.: No. 2). 1920. George Sully & Co.
--Four Little Blossoms at Oak Hill School. Stratemeyer Syndicate. Herbert, Robert Gaston, illus. Repr. of 1920 ed (Pub. by George Sully & Co). (Four Little Blossoms Ser.: No. 2). 1938. Saalfield Publishing Co.
--Four Little Blossoms at Sunrise Beach. Stratemeyer Syndicate. LC 29-11571. 180 p. incl. col. front. col. pl. 19 1/2 cm. (Four Little Blossoms Ser.: No. 6). 1929. Cupples & Leon Co.
--Four Little Blossoms at Sunrise Beach. Stratemeyer Syndicate. Repr. of 1929 ed (Pub. by George Sully & Co). (Four Little Blossoms Ser.: No. 6). N.D. Saalfield Publishing Co.
--Four Little Blossoms Indoors and Out. Stratemeyer Syndicate. LC 30-16935. 179 p. incl. col. front. col. pl. 19 1/2 cm. (Four Little Blossoms Ser.: No. 7). 1930. Cupples & Leon Co.
--Four Little Blossoms on Apple Tree Island. Stratemeyer Syndicate. Rogers, Walter S., illus. Repr. of 1921 ed (Pub. by George Sully & Co.). (Four Little Blossoms Ser.: No. 4). N.D. Cupples & Leon Co.
--Four Little Blossoms on Apple Tree Island. Stratemeyer Syndicate. Rogers, Walter S., illus. 160p. (Four Little Blossoms Ser.: No. 4). 1921. George Sully & Co.
--Four Little Blossoms on Appletree Island. Stratemeyer Syndicate. Repr. of 1921 ed (Pub. by George Sully & Co). (Four Little Blossoms Ser.: No. 4). 1938. Saalfield Publishing Co.
--Four Little Blossoms Through the Holidays. Stratemeyer Syndicate. Repr. of 1922 ed (Pub. by George Sully & Co). (Four Little Blossoms Ser.: No. 5). N.D. Cupples & Leon Co.
--Four Little Blossoms through the Holidays. Stratemeyer Syndicate. (Four Little Blossoms Ser.: No. 5). 1922. George Sully & Co.
--Four Little Blossoms through the Holidays. Stratemeyer Syndicate. Repr. of 1922 ed (Pub. by George Sully & Co). (Four Little Blossoms Ser.: No. 5). N.D. Saalfield Publishing Co.

Hawley, Mary Alice
--The Little Pony. Hartwell, Marjorie, illus. LC 52-65928. unpaged. illus. 17cm. (Tell-a-tale books). c.1952. Whitman Pub. Co.

Hawley, Zoa Grace
--A Boy Rides with Custer. LC 38-30605. 5 p. l., 3-295, 1 p. front. plates (incl. ports.) 20 cm. 1938. Little, Brown and Company.

Haworth, Clarence V (1875-)
--Indiana Supplement: Wayland's History Stories for Primary Grades. Wayland, John Walter, illus. LC 22-542. (1872 History Stories for Primary Grades). iii, 1, 59 p. illus. 18 1/2 cm. 1922. The Macmillan Company.

Haworth, Karen, jt. auth. see Severy, Richard.

Haworth, P.
--An Elizabethan Story Book. N.D. Longman, Green & Co.

Haworth, Paul Leland (1876-)
--Trailmakers of the Northwest. N.D. Harcourt Brace & Co.

Hawse, Alberta
--Vinegar Boy. LC 75-104817. 176 p. 22cm. 1970. Moody Press.

Hawthorne, Ben
--Bessie Bossie. Booth, Hollis C., illus. LC 39-19156. 24cm. 24p. N.D. Grosset & Dunlap.

Hawthorne, Dorothy
--A Wish for Lutie. 1st ed. Voute, Kathleen (1892-), illus. LC 55-8309. 117p. illus. 22cm. 1955. Longmans, Green.

Hawthorne, H.
--The Ox-Team Miracle. 1942. David McKay Company Inc.

Hawthorne, Hildegarde (1871-1952)
--Deedah's Wonderful Year. LC 27-21888. 3 p. l., 235, 1 p. front. 19 1/2 cm. 1927. D. Appleton and Company.
--Girls in Bookland. Adams, John Wolcott, illus. LC 17-291408. xii p., 1 l., 15-291 p. front., plates. 22 1/2 cm. c.1917. George H. Doran Company.
--Island Farm. 1926. Appleton Century Co.
--Lone Rider. Rodgers, Richard H. (1876-1953), illus. LC 33-23934. vii, 264 p. incl. front., illus., plates. 20 1/2 cm. 1933. Longmans, Green and Co.
--Makeshift Farm. LC 25-17345. 19 1/2cm. 246p. 1925. D. Appleton-Century Co.
--Maybe True Stories. Sichel, Harold M. (1881-), illus. LC 26-22999. 5 p. l., 3-186 p. incl. illus., plates. col. front. 19 1/2 cm. 1926. Duffield & Company.
--The Miniature's Secret. Birch, Reginald Bathurst (1856-1943), illus. LC 38-101979. x p., 1 l., 252 p. incl. front., illus. 21 1/2 cm. 1938. D. Appleton-Century Company, Incorporated.

--The Mystery at Star-C Ranch. LC 29-17284. 3 p. l., 232, 1 p. front. 19 1/2 cm. 1929. D. Appleton & Company.

--The Mystery in Navajo Canon. Block, La Verne Nelson, illus. LC 30-248481. 6 p. l., 3-225 p. front., illus., plates. 19 1/2 cm. c.1930. The Century Co.

--No Road Too Long. MacDonald, James, illus. LC 40-690230. vi p., 1 l.,261 p. illus. 22 cm. 1940. Longmans, Green and Co.

--On the Golden Trail. Tonsey, Sanford, illus. LC 36-27390. ix, 302 p. incl. front., illus., plates. 20 1/2 cm. 1936. Longmans, Green and Co.

--Riders of the Royal Road: A Tale of the Camino Real. Gincano, John, illus. LC 32-7615. 4 p. l., 276, 1 p. front. illus. 20 cm. 1932. D. Appleton & Company.

--Rising Thunder: The Story of Jack Jouett of Virginia. Barton, Loren, illus. LC 37-17504. viii p., 1 l., 272 p. illus. 20 1/2 cm. 1937. Longmans, Green and Co.

--Runaway. Sperry, Armstrong W. (1897-1976), illus. LC 41-517318. 4 p. l., 78, 1 p. incl. front., illus. 21 x 16 cm. (story parade adventure book). c.1941. Grossett & Dunlap.

--The Secret of Rancho del Sol: A Story of Old California. Thomas, Leslie D., illus. LC 31-5060. 4 p. l., 235, 1 p., 1 l. front., illus. 20 cm. 1931. D. Appleton and Company.

--The Shining Tree and other Christmas Stories. (gr. 7-11). 1941. A. A. Knopf.

--Tabitha of Lonely House: A Tale of Old Concord. Berger, William Merritt (1872-), illus. LC 34-332763. 2 p. l., vii-ix, 268 p. incl. front., illus. 19 1/2 cm. 1934. D. Appleton-Century Company, Incorporated.

--Wheels Toward the West. Rodgers, Richard H. (1876-1953), illus. LC 31-25223. ix p., 1 l., 243 p. incl. front., illus., plates. 20 1/2 cm. c.1931. Longmans, Green and Co.

Hawthorne, Hildegarde (1871-1952), ed.

--Arabian Nights. Sterrett, Virginia Frances (1900-), illus. N.D. Penn Publish Co.

--Story Parade: A Collection of Modern Stories for Boys and Girls. Key, Alexander Hill (1904-1979) & Milhous, Katherine (1894-1977), illus. LC 40-34869. xi p., 1, 379 p. illus. (incl. music) 23 1/2 cm. c.1940. The John C. Winston Company.

Hawthorne, J. R.

--The Pioneer of a Family: Or, Adventures of a Young Governess. (Illus.). 313p. 1884. A. I. Bradley & Co.'s Pubs.

Hawthorne, Julian (1846-1934)

--Rumpty Dudgets Tower. N.D. J. B. Lippincott.

--Rumpty-Dudget's Tower: A Fairy Tale. Hood, George W., illus. LC 24-22579. xiii, 72 p. col. front., illus., plates. 21 cm. 1924. Frederick A. Stokes Company.

Hawthorne, Julian (1846-1934) & Allen, Grant (1848-1899)

--Mayflower Tales. LC 3-21933. 19cm. 191p. (Mayflower Library: No. 6). 1892. J. A. Taylor and Co.

Hawthorne, Nathaniel, jt. ed. see Hale, Edward Everett.

Hawthorne, Nathaniel (1804-1864)

--The Birthmark & Other Stories. (gr. 7-12). 1972 (Starline). Schol Bk Serv.

--A Charlie Brown Christmas. N.D. New American Library.

--The Complete Greek Stories of Nathaniel Hawthorne: From the Wonder Book and Tanglewood Tales. Jones, Harold (1904-), illus. Lines, Kathleen, frwd. by. LC 63-14738. 352p. illus. 21cm. c.1963. (ISBN 0-531-01647-1). Watts.

--The Gentle Boy and Other Tales. (Riverside Literature Ser.). N.D. Houghton Mifflin Co.

--The Golden Apple, (Illus.). (The Editha Ser.: No. 10). 1905. Set. H M Caldwell Co.

--The Golden Touch. (Illus.). (Riverside Juvenile Classics). N.D. Houghton Mifflin Co.

--The Golden Touch. Galdone, Paul (1914-), illus. Eaton, Anne Thaxter (1881-1971), frwd. by. LC 59-10711. 61p. illus. 22cm. 1959. (ISBN 0-07-027318-9). Whittlesey House.

--The Gorgon's Head. (Illus.). (Riverside Juvenile Classics). N.D. Houghton Mifflin Co.

--Grandfather's Chair,   (The Rugby Ser.). 1905. Set. A L Burt Co.

--Grandfather's Chair. (Burt's Home Library). N.D. A L Burt Co.

--Grandfather's Chair. (Illus.). (Burt's Young Folks' Library). N.D. A. L. Burt's Pubs.

--Grandfather's Chair, No. 53. (The Cornell Ser.). N.D. A. L. Burt's Pubs.

--Grandfather's Chair. Household ed. N.D. Belford, Clarke & Co.

--Grandfather's Chair. N.D. Charles E. Merrill Co.

--Grandfather's Chair. (Illus.). (The Young Folks Lib.). N.D. H. M. Caldwell Co.

--Grandfather's Chair, 1 of 3 vols. (The Lakeside Series of Handy Volume Classics: No. 7). N.D. H. M. Caldwell Co.

--Grandfather's Chair. (Illus.) (The Empyreal Library of Handy Volume Classics). N.D. H. M. Caldwell & Co.

--Grandfather's Chair. (Illus.). 1905. Henry Altemus Co.

--Grandfather's Chair. (Altemus' New Illustrated Young People's Library). N.D. Henry Altemus Company.

--Grandfather's Chair. 1884. Houghton, Mifflin & Co.

--Grandfather's Chair. (Home Series for Girls). N.D. Hurst & Co.

--Grandfather's Chair, 1 of 24 vols. (Illus.). (Children's Favorite Classics). 1900. T. Y. Crowell & Co.

--Grandfather's Chair. (Illus.). (The Waldorf Lib.). N.D. T. Y. Crowell & Co.

--Grandfather's Chair. (The New Astor Library of Prose). N.D. T. Y. Crowell & Co.

--Grandfather's Chair. (Illus.). (Children's Classics). N.D. Thomas Y. Crowell & Co.

--Grandfather's Chair. (Handy Volume Classics). N.D. Thomas Y. Crowell & Co.

--Great Stone Face & Other Tales of the White Mountains. (Illus.). (gr. 7 up). N.D. (ISBN 0-395-07787-7). HM.

--Great Stone Face & Two Other Stories. Fisher, Leonard Everett (1924-), illus. (Illus.). (gr. 7 up). 1967. (ISBN 0-531-01068-6). Watts.

--Hawthorne's Little Daffydowndilly, and Other Stories. (Illus.). 96p. (Riverside Library Ser.: No. 29). N.D. Houghton, Mifflin and Company.

--Hawthorne's Short Stories. (Illus.). (Great Il. Classics). (gr. 9 up). 1962. (ISBN 0-396-04723-8). Dodd.

--Hawthorne's Tales of the White Hills, and Sketches: With Introduction. 96p. (Riverside Literature Ser: No. 40). N.D. Houghton, Mifflin and Company.

--Hawthorne's Tanglewood Tales, Pts. I & II. pron. vocab. 96p. (Riverside Library: Nos. 22-23). N.D. Houghton, Mifflin and Company.

--Hawthorne's Tanglewood Tales. School ed. Beggs, Robert Henry (1844-1914), ed. LC 7-13437. xi, 210 p. front. (port.) 14 1/2 cm. (Macmillan's Pocket American and English classics). 1907. The Macmillan Company.

--Hawthorne's Wonder Books for Boys and Girls. (Illus.). pron. vocab. 96p. (Riverside Literature Ser: Nos. 17-18). N.D. Nos. 17, 18 bound together. Houghton, Mifflin and Company.

--The House of Seven Gables. (Great Illustrated Classics). N.D. Dodd, Mead & Co.

--House of the Seven Gables. (Burt's Home Lib.). N. D. A L Burt's Pubs.

--The House of the Seven Gables. N.D. Brown Book company.

--House of the Seven Gables, No. 1. N.D. Educational Publishing Company.

--House of the Seven Gables, No. 2. N.D. Educational Publishing Company.

--The House of the Seven Gables. Handy Volume, Large Type ed. (Illus.). (Beauxarts Ser.). N.D. Henry Altemus.

--The House of the Seven Gables. (Illus.). (Library of Standard Authors). N.D. Henry Altemus.

--The House of the Seven Gables. (Cambridge Classics). N.D. Houghton Mifflin Co.

--The House of the Seven Gables. (Riverside Literature Ser.: 91). N.D. Houghton Mifflin Co.

--The House of the Seven Gables. (Illus.). (Hurst's Half Leather Classics). N.D. Hurst and Company.

--House of the Seven Gables. (Arlington Edition). (Illus.). N.D. Hurst and Company.

--House of Seven Gables. (New Pocket Classics). N.D. Macmillan.

--House of the Seven Gables. 404p. N.D. Oxford University Press.

--The House of the Seven Gables. 375p. N.D. Scott,Foresman & Co.

--The House of the Seven Gables. (Classic Ser.). N.D. World Publishing Co.

--The House of the Seven Gables. Angelo, Valenti (1897-), illus. N.D. Heritage Press.

--The House of the Seven Gables-. Grose, Helen Mason (1880-), illus. 1924. Houghton.

--The House of the Seven Gables. Gross, Seymour, ed. 1967. (ISBN 0-393-04287-1). (ISBN 0-393-09705-6). Norton & Co.

--The House of the Seven Gables, and The Snow-Image. (Riverside Edition). N.D. Houghton Mifflin Co.

--The Marble Faun. (Riverside Literature Ser.: 148). N.D. Houghton Mifflin Co.

--Mosses from an Old Manse. (Illus.). (American Classic Ser.). N.D. David McKay.

--Mosses from an Old Manse. (Illus.). (Boys' and Girls' Classics). N.D. Henry Altemus Co.

--Pandora's Box: The Paradise of Children. Galdone, Paul (1914-), illus. LC 67-3142. (Illus.). 58 p. 22cm. 1967. (ISBN 0-07-027318-9). McGraw-Hill.

--The Paradise of Children. (Illus.). (Riverside Juvenile Classics). N.D. Houghton Mifflin Co.

--The Pygmies, 25 vols. (Illus.). (The Editha Ser.: No. 14). 1905. Set. H M Caldwell Co.

--The Scarlet Letter. N.D. A L Burt Co.

--The Scarlet Letter. Empire ed. 1905. American News Co.

--The Scarlet Letter. N.D. Brown Book Company.

--Scarlet Letter. (Illus.). (Great Il. Classics). (gr. 9 up). 1979. Dodd.

--The Scarlet Letter. (Everyman's Library). N.D. E. P. Dutton & Co.

--The Scarlet Letter. (The People's Library). N.D. Funk & Wagnalls.

--The Scarlet Letter. (The Good Value Books). N.D. Grosset & Dunlap.

--The Scarlet Letter. (The Children's Favorite Ser.). N.D. Grosset & Dunlap.

--The Scarlet Letter. N.D. Hendricks House-Farrar, Straus.

--The Scarlet Letter. 1905. Henry Altemus Co.

--The Scarlet Letter. Cambridge Classics ed. 1900. Houghton Mifflin & Co.

--The Scarlet Letter. (Cambridge Classics Ser.). N.D. Houghton Mifflin.

--The Scarlet Letter. (Children's Library). N.D. Houghton Mifflin Co.

--The Scarlet Letter. Popular ed. (Illus.). N.D. Houghton Mifflin & Co.

--The Scarlet Letter, 1 of 300 vols. (The Hawthorne Library). 1900. Hurst & Co.

--The Scarlet Letter, 1 of 183 vols. Pocket ed. (The Universal Library). 1900. Hurst & Co.

--The Scarlet Letter. (Illus.). (The New Argyle Ser.). N.D. Hurst and Company.

--The Scarlet Letter. (Arlington Edition). (Illus.). (Arlington Edition). N.D. Hurst and Company.

--The Scarlet Letter. James R. Osgood.

--The Scarlet Letter. (8j). (Magnum Easy Eye Classic Ser.). (gr. 10 up). N.D. Lancer.

--Scarlet Letter. (Modern Reader's Ser.). N.D. Macmillan.

--The Scarlet Letter. N.D. Modern Library.

--The Scarlet Letter. 1966. (ISBN 0-393-09567-7) (ISBN 0-393-05318-0). Norton & Co.

--Scarlet Letter. 266p. N.D. Oxford University Press.

--The Scarlet Letter. (Illus.). N.D. Rand McNally & Co.

--The Scarlet Letter. (gr. 7 up). 1972. (ISBN 0-590-09075-5). Scholastic Inc.

--The Scarlet Letter. N.D. Thomas Nelson & Sons.

--Scarlet Letter. large type ed. (Keith Jennison Bks.). (gr. 6 up). N.D. (ISBN 0-531-00275-6). Watts.

--Scarlet Letter. large type ed. (Franklin Watts Classics). (gr. 7 up). N.D. (ISBN 0-531-00408-2). Watts.

--The Scarlet Letter. Bradley, Sculley & Beatty, Richmond Croom, eds. 1966. (ISBN 0-393-05318-0). (ISBN 0-393-09562-2). Norton & Co.

--The Scarlet Letter. Davenport, Basil, intro. by. (Illus.). N.D. Dodd, Mead & Co.

--The Scarlet Letter. Duggins, W. A., illus. N.D. Heritage Press.

--The Scarlet Letter. Holiday ed. Foote, Mary Hallock, Mrs. (1847-), illus. 1900. Houghton Mifflin & Co.

--The Scarlet Letter. Gordon, Frederick C., illus. N.D. Frederick Stokes Co.

--The Scarlet Letter. Hardy, E. S., illus. (Collins' Illustrated Pocket Classics). N.D. Collins.

--The Scarlet Letter. Salem ed. Lathrop, G. P., intro. by. 1900. Houghton Mifflin & Co.

--Scarlet Letter. Levin, Harry (1912-), ed. LC 60-2662. (gr. 9 up). 1960. (ISBN 0-395-05142-8, Riv. Ed.). HM.

--The Scarlet Letter. Sherman, Stuart P., ed. (Modern Students Library). N.D. Charles Scribner's Sons.

--The Scarlet Letter. Warren, Austin, ed. 251p. 1947. Rinehart & Co.

--The Scarlet Letter and Selected Prose Works. 432p. 1949. Farrar, Straus & Cudahy.

--The Scarlet Letter, and The Blithedale Romance. N.D. Houghton Mifflin Co.

--The Scarlet Letter and, the Blithedale Romance. (Riverside Edition). N.D. Houghton Mifflin Co.

--Selections from Twice Told Tales. N.D. MacMillan.

--Snow Image. Lathrop, Dorothy Pulis (1891-1980), illus. LC 30-31804. 1930. MacMillan.

--The Snow-Image: A Childish Miracle. Waterman, Marcus, illus. N.D. Houghton, Osgood & Co.

--Snow Image and Other Twice-Told Tales. (Standard Literature Ser.: No. 20). N.D. University Publishing Company.

--Stories of Classical Fables: A/Wonder Book for Boys and Girls. LC 8-19153. 134p. 24cm. 1908. Mcloughlin Bros.

--The Tale of King Midas and the Golden Touch. Eichenberg, Fritz (1901-), illus. LC 52-2815. (Illus.). 31cm. 47p. (The Evergreen Tales; Or, Tales for the Ageless). Orig. Title: The Golden Touch. 1952. Limited Editions Club.

--Tanglewood Tales, (The Rugby Ser. for Boys). 1905. Set. A L Burt Co.

--Tanglewood Tales. (Burt's Home Library). N.D. A L Burt Co.

--Tanglewood Tales, No. 152. (The Cornell Ser.). N.D. A. L. Burt's Pubs. Co.'s.

--Tanglewood Tales. N.D. Grosset & Dunlap.

--Tanglewood Tales. LC 98-357. 3 p. l., 5-251 p. front. (port.) plates. 16 cm. c.1898. H. Altemus.

--Tanglewood Tales. (Illus.). (Caldwell's Illustrated Library of Famous Books by Famous Authors). N.D. H. M. Caldwell Co.

--Tanglewood Tales. (Illus.). (Berkeley Lib.). N.D. H. M. Caldwell Co.

--Tanglewood Tales. (Illus.). (The Empyreal Library of Handy volume Classics). N.D. H. M. Caldwell Co.

--Tanglewood Tales, 1 of 2 vols. (Illus.). (The Calumet Ser.: No. 14). N.D. Set. H. M. Caldwell Co.

--Tanglewood Tales. (Illus.). (The Young Folks Lib.). N.D. H. M. Caldwell Co.

--Tanglewood Tales, 1 of 3 vols. (The Lakeside Series of Handy Volume Classics: No. 7). N.D. H. M. Caldwell Co.

--Tanglewood Tales. Handy Volume, Large Type ed. LC 7-37701. (Illus.). 16cm. 251p. (Petit-Trianon Ser.). 1897. Henry Altemus.

--Tanglewood Tales. (New Alta Lib.). N.D. Henry T. Coates & Co.

--Tanglewood Tales. Handy Volume, Large Type ed. (Illus.). (Beauxarts Ser.). N.D. Henry Altemus.

--Tanglewood Tales. (Illus.). 1900. Houghton Mifflin & Co.

--Tanglewood Tales, 1 of 64 vols. (Young America Library: No. 41). 1900. Set. Hurst & Co.

--Tanglewood Tales. (Illus.). (Alligator Classics). N.D. Hurst & Co.

--Tanglewood Tales. (Illus.). N.D. James R. Osgood and Company.

--Tanglewood Tales. (Sears Juvenile Library) N.D. J.H.Sears & Co.

--Tanglewood Tales. (Illus.). (Young People's Classics). N.D. R. F. Fenno & Co.

--Tanglewood Tales. The Advance Library Ser.: Vol. 303. N.D. Rand, McNally & Co.

--Tanglewood Tales. (Illus.). (The Independent Library Ser.: Vol. 303). N.D. Rand, McNally & Co.

--Tanglewood Tales, 1 of 24 vols. (Illus.). (Children's Favorite Classics). 1900. T. Y. Crowell & Co.

--Tanglewood Tales. (Illus.). (The Waldorf Lib.) N.D. T. Y. Crowell & Co.

--Tanglewood Tales. (The New Astor Library of Prose). N.D. T. Y. Crowell & Co.

--Tanglewood Tales. N.D. Williams Collins Sons & Company Ltd.

--Tanglewood Tales. (Classic Ser.). N.D. World Publishing Co.

--Tanglewood Tales. Beckett, Sheilah (1913-), illus. (Illus.). 247 p. 20cm. (Companion library). 1967. Grosset & Dunlap.

--Tanglewood Tales. Dulac, Edmund (1882-1953), illus. LC 19-7106. 5 p. l., 244, 1 p. 14 col. mounted pl. (incl. front.) 28 cm. 1919. Hodder and Stoughton.

--Tanglewood Tales. MacIntyre, Robert, ed. N.D. Thomas Nelson & Sons.

--Tanglewood Tales. Peat, Fern Bisel, Mrs. (1893-), illus. LC 30-13385. 4 p. l., 13-252 p. front., illus. 19 cm. (Half-title: Every child's library). c.1930. The Saalfield Publishing Company.

--Tanglewood Tales. Sterrett, Virginia Frances (1900-), illus. LC 22-1549. 4 p. l., 261 p. col. front., illus., col. plates. 28 1/2 cm. c.1921. The Penn Publishing Company.

--Tanglewood Tales. windermere ed. Winter, Milo Kendall (1888-1956), illus. LC 13-18737. 2 p. l., 3-283 p. col. front., plates (part col.) 23 1/2 cm. c.1913. Rand, McNally & Company.

--Tanglewood Tales for Girls and Boys: Being a Second Wonder-Book. 230, xi p. front. plates. 18 cm. (Riverside literature ser. no. 22-23). c.1887. Houghton, Mifflin Company.

--Tanglewood Tales for Girls and Boys: Being a Second Wonder-Book. LC 7-3770. iii, 264 p. col. front., plates. 17 1/2 cm. c.1897. T. Y. Crowell & Company.

--Tanglewood Tales for Girls and Boys: Being a Second Wonder-Book. xv, 180 p. pl. 21 cm. (His Works... Popular ed. New York 1902, v. 14). 1902. T. Y. Crowell & Company.

--Tanglewood Tales for Girls and Boys: Being a Second Wonderbook. LC 7-3779. 336 p. plates. 17 cm. 1853. Ticknor, Reed, and Fields.

--Tanglewood Tales for Girls and Boys: Being a Second Wonderbook. Edwards, George Wharton (1859-1950), illus. LC 4-30406. iv, 190 p. incl. illus., plates. front. 27 cm. 1887. Houghton, Mifflin and Company.

--Tanglewood Tales for Young and Old: Being a Second Wonder-Book. complete ed. LC 4717. 308 p. front. (port.) plates. 16 cm. c.1900. W. B. Conkey Company.

--The Scarlet Letter. Leisy, E. E., ed. 1929. The Ronald Press Co.

--The Three Golden Apples. (Illus.). (Riverside Juvenile Classics). N.D. Houghton Mifflin Co.

--Twice Told Tales, No. 169. (The Cornell Ser.). N.D. A L Burt's Pubs.

--Twice-Told Tales. N.D. Charles E. Merrill Co.

--Twice-Told Tales. (Everyman's Library). N.D. E. P. Dutton & Co.
--Twice-Told Tales, No. 1. N.D. Educational Publishing Company.
--Twice-Told Tales, No. 2. N.D. Educational Publishing Company.
--Twice Told Tales. (Illus.). (Berkeley Lib.). N.D. H. M. Caldwell Co.
--Twice Told Tales. (Illus.). (The Empyreal Library of Handy Volume Classics). N.D. H. M. Caldwell Co.
--Twice Told Tales. (Illus.). (The Exquisite Ser.). N.D. H. M. Caldwell Co.
--Twice Told Tales. (Illus.). (The Chateau Ser.). N.D. H. M. Caldwell Co.
--Twice Told Tales. (Illus.). (Boys' and Girls' Classics). N.D. Henry Altemus Co.
--Twice Told Tales. (Illus.). (Vademecum Ser.). N.D. Henry Altemus.
--Twice Told Tales. Handy Volume, Large Type ed. (Illus.). (Petit-Trianon Ser.). N.D. Henry Altemus.
--Twice Told Tales. Handy Volume, Large Type ed. (Illus.). (Beauxarts Ser.). N.D. Henry Altemus.
--Twice-Told Tales. (Riverside Edition). N.D. Houghton Mifflin Co.
--Twice-Told Tales. N.D. James R. Osgood.
--Twice Told Tales. (Magnum Easy Eye Classic Ser.). (gr. 9 up). N.D. Lancer.
--Twice Told Tales. (American Classic Ser.). 1891. McClurg.
--Twice Told Tales. (The Advance Library Ser.: Vol. 314). N.D. Rand, McNally & Co.
--Twice Told Tales. (Illus.). (The Independent Library Ser.: Vol. 314). N.D. Rand, McNally & Co.
--Twice-Told Tales. 554p. (The Lake English Classics). N.D. Scott Foresman & Co.
--Twice Told Tales, 1 of 88 vols. Birch Bark ed. (Handy Volume Classics). 1900. T. Y. Crowell & Co.
--Twice Told Tales, 1 of 88 vols. popular ed. (Handy Volume Classics). N.D. T. Y. Crowell & Co.
--Twice Told Tales. (Illus.). (The Waldorf Lib.). N.D. T. Y. Crowell & Co.
--Twice Told Tales. (The New Astor Library of Prose). N.D. T. Y. Crowell & Co.
--Twice Told Tales. N.D (Standard & Holiday Books). The American News Co.
--Twice Told Tales. (Standard Library). N.D. Thomas Y. Crowell & Co.
--Twice-Told Tales. (Standard Literature Ser.: No. 15). N.D. University Publishing Co.
--Two Tanglewood Tales: The Dragon's Teeth, The Mintaur. LC 99-2256. 1 p. l., 74 p. incl. illus. (port.) pl. 16 1/2 cm. (On cover: Maynard's English Classic Ser. no. 217). 1899. Maynard, Merrill & Co.
--The Whole History of Grandfather's Chair. Bates, Katherine Lee, intro. by. LC 2-20798. 244p. 1902. T. Y. Crowell & Co.
--A Wonder Book, (The Rugby Ser.). 1905. Set. A L Burt Co.
--A Wonder Book. (Burt's Home Lib.). N.D. A. L. Burt's Pubs.
--A Wonder Book. (Illus.). (The Little Men Ser.). N.D. A. L. Burt's Pubs.
--A Wonder Book. (The Cornell Ser.: No. 186). N.D. B. L. Burt's Pubs.
--Wonder Book. (Illus.). (The Alcazar Classics). N.D. Caldwell.
--The Wonder Book. (Illus.). (The Empyreal Library of Handy Volume Classics). N.D. H. M. Caldwell Co.
--Wonder Book. (Illus.). (The Calumet Ser.). N.D. Set. H. M. Caldwell Co.
--The Wonder Book. (Illus.). (The Young Folks Lib.). N.D. H. M. Caldwell.
--Wonder Book. (The Lakeside Series of Handy Volume Classics). N.D. Set. H. M. Caldwell Co.
--The Wonder Book. (Altemus' New Illustrated Young People's Library). N.D. Henry Altemus Company.
--Wonder Book. (Illus.). (Boys' and Girls' Classics). N.D. Henry Altemus Co.
--A Wonder Book. (Illus.). (Vademecum Ser.). N.D. Henry Altemus.
--A Wonder Book. Handy Volume, Large Type ed. (Illus.). (Petit-Trianon Ser.). N.D. Henry Altemus.
--A Wonder Book. Handy Volume, Large Type ed. (Illus.). (Beauxarts Ser.). N.D. Henry Altemus.
--Wonder Book. (Home Series for Girls). N.D. Hurst & Co.
--Wonder Book. (Sears Juvenile Classics). N.D. J.H.Sears & Co.
--A Wonder Book, 1 of 24 vols. (Illus.). (Children's Favorite Classics). 1900. T. Y. Crowell & Co.
--Wonder Book. (Illus.). (The Waldorf Lib.). N.D. T. Y. Crowell & Co.
--Wonder Book. (The New Astor Library of Prose). N.D. T. Y. Crowell & Co.
--Wonder Book. (Illus.). (Children's Favorite Classics). N.D. Thomas Y. Crowell.
--A Wonder Book. (Standard Literature Ser.: No.16). N.D. University Publishing Co.
--A Wonder Book. Abbott, Elenore Plaisted & Shenton, Edward (1895-), illus. LC 25-274668. 201 p. col. front. plates (part col.) 20 cm. (The Franklin classics). 1925. Macrae Smith Company.
--Wonder Book. Chuse, Anne, illus. LC 29-44618. 2 p. l., iii-vi, 232 p. col. front. 23 cm. (Sears illustrated juveniles). c.1928. J. H. Sears Company, Inc.
--A Wonder Book. Cuffari, Richard (1925-1978), illus. LC 67-24235. (Illus.). viii, 183 p. 20cm. (Companion library). 1967. Grosset & Dunlap.
--A Wonder Book. Fell, Herbert Granville, illus. LC 27-26600. 127, 1 p. col. front., col. plates. 18 1/2 cm. (Half-title: Tales for children from many lands). 1927. J. M. Dent & Sons, Lmited.
--A Wonder Book. Perkins, Lucy Fitch, Mrs. (1865-1937), illus. Perkins, Lucy Fitch (1865-1937), selected by. LC 8-23535. xii p., 1 l., 125 p. incl. col. front., illus. 11 col. pl. 25 1/2 cm. (Half-title: The dandelion classics for children). 1908. F. A. Stokes Company.
--A Wonder Book. Rackham, Arthur (1867-1939), illus. LC 32-212050. xi, 206, 1 p. incl. col. front., illus. col. plates 22 1/2 cm. N.D. Garden City Publishing Co., Inc.
--A Wonder Book. Rackham, Arthur (1867-1939), illus. LC 23-26056. 2 p. l., vii-xii, 206 p., 1 l. mounted front., illus., col. plates (part mounted) 24 cm. 1922. George H. Doran Company.
--A Wonder Book. Thorndike, Edward Lee (1874-), ed. Johnson, Robert Ward, illus. LC 35-2733. 5 p. l., 3-226 p. incl. front., illus. 19 1/2 cm. (Thorndike library). c.1935. D. Appleton-Century Company, Incorporated.
--A Wonder Book. Van Abbe, Salaman (1883-1955), illus. (Children's Illustrated Classics). 1949. Dutton.
--Wonder-Book. Wolfe, Lloyd E. (1852-), ed. LC 5-64878. xiii, 236 p. front. (port.) 14 1/2 cm. (Macmillan's pocket American and English classics). 1905. The Macmillan Company.
--The Wonder Book and Tanglewood Tales. N.D. E P Dutton.
--Wonder Book & Tanglewood Tales. (Washington Square Classics Ser.). N.D. George W Jacobs.
--A Wonder-Book, and Tanglewood Tales. LC 23-15173. 421 p. col. front., illus., col. plates. 22 cm. (Riverside bookshelf). 1923. Houghton Mifflin Company.
--A Wonder-Book & Tanglewood Tales. Holiday ed. (Illus.). N.D. Houghton Mifflin & Co.
--A Wonder Book and Tanglewood Tales. 6 p. l., 404 p. 17 1/2 cm. (Half-title: Everyman's library, ed. by Ernest Rhys. For young people). 1907. J. M. Dent & Co.
--A Wonder Book and Tanglewood Tales. (The Winston Clear-Type Popular Classics). N.D. John C. Winston.
--A Wonder-Book: And Tanglewood Tales. Abbott, Elenore Plaisted & Knipe, Helen Alden, illus. LC 11-25673. 437 p. col. front., col. plates. 20 cm. (On cover: The Washington square classics). 1911. G. W. Jacobs and Company.
--A Wonder Book, and Tanglewood Tales. Bowers, Fredson Thayer, ed. LC 77-150221. (Illus.). xi, 463 p. 25cm. (centenary edition of the works of Nathaniel Hawthorne, v. 7. Writings for children, 2). 1972. (ISBN 0-8142-0158-X). Ohio State University Press.
--A Wonder Book and Tanglewood Tales. Knipe, Helen Alden & Abbott, Elenore Plaisted, illus. LC 26-1392. 437 p. col. front., col. plates. 20 cm. (Lettered on cover: The Washington square classics). N.D. Macrae, Smith Company.
--A Wonder-Book and Tanglewood Tales. Reid, Stephen (1873-1934), illus. LC 34-283163. 6 p., 1 l., 11-356 p. incl. col. front. col. plates. 19 cm. (golden books). 1934. D. McKay.
--A Wonder Book and Tanglewood Tales. Richardson, Frederick (1862-1937), illus. Carpenter, Katherine G., intro. by. LC 30-202058. xvi p., 1 l., 403 p. col. front., illus., col. plates. 22 cm. c.1930. The John C. Winston Company.
--A Wonder Book and Tanglewood Tales. Tenggren, Gustaf (1896-1970), illus. 1923. Houghton.
--A Wonder Book and Tanglewood Tales for Girls and Boys. Parrish, Frederick Maxfield (1870-1966), illus. LC 34-28308. ix, 358 p. col. front., col. plates. 24 1/2 cm. 1934. (ISBN 0-396-00732-5). Dodd, Mead & Company.
--A Wonder Book and Tanglewood Tales for Girls and Boys. Parrish, Frederick Maxfield (1870-1966), illus. LC 10-239422. ix, 358 p. col. front., 9 col. pl. 25 cm. 1910. Duffield & Company.
--A Wonder Book and True Stories. (Illus.). (Caldwell's Illustrated Library of Famous Books by Famous Authors). N.D. H. M. Caldwell Co.
--A Wonder Book and True Stories. (Illus.). (Berkeley Lib.). N.D. H. M. Caldwell Co.
--Wonder Book for Boys and Girls. (Advance Ser.). N.D. Donohue, Henneberry & Co.
--A Wonder Book for Boys and Girls and Tanglewood Tales. Pyle, Howard (1853-1911), illus. LC 1-29739. 23cm. 515p. (Complete Writings of Nathaniel Hawthorne: Vol. 13). 1900. Houghton Mifflin & Co.
--The Wonder-Book for Girls & Boys. (Illus.). 1900. Houghton Mifflin & Co.
--The Wonder-Book for Girls and Boys. (Illus.). N.D. James R Osgood and Company.
--A Wonder Book for Girls and Boys. LC 7-3766. 3 p. l., v-x, 210 p. col. front., col. illus., 19 col. pl. 25 cm. 1893. Printed at the Riverside Press.
--A Wonder-Book for Girls and Boys. windermere ed. LC 13-18736. 2 p. l., 3-254 p. col. front., plates (part col.) 23 1/2 cm. c.1913. Rand, McNally & Company.
--A Wonder Book for Girls and Boys. LC 7-3763. vi, 233 p. col. front., plates. 17 cm. c.1896. T. Y. Crowell & Company.
--A Wonder-Book for Girls and Boys. LC 2-20806. 1 p. l., xviii, 159 p. front., pl. 21 cm. (Added t.-p.: The works of Nathaniel Hawthorne... Popular ed. v. 13). 1902. T. Y. Crowell & Company.
--A Wonder-Book for Girls and Boys. LC 7-3867. vi, 7-256 p. front., plates. 17 cm. 1852. Ticknor, Reed, and Fields.
--A Wonder Book for Girls and Boys. LC 7-3764. 121 p. 18 1/2 cm. (On cover: Standard literature series, no. 16). 1896. University Publishing Company.
--A Wonder Book for Girls and Boys. LC 4721. 259p. 16cm. 1900. W. B. Conkey.
--A Wonder-Book for Girls and Boys. Church, Frederick S., illus. LC 7-3767. 5 p. l., 3-150 p. front., illus. 26 1/2 cm. 1885. Houghton, Mifflin and Company.
--A Wonder-Book for Girls & Boys. Holiday ed. Church, Frederick S., illus. 1900. Houghton Mifflin & Co.
--A Wonder Book for Girls & Boys. Crane, Walter (1845-1915), illus. LC 75-300414. (Illus.). x, 210 p., 19 leaves of plates. 24cm. 1893, c.1892. Houghton, Mifflin.
--Wonder Book for Girls and Boys. Crane, Walter (1845-1915), illus. LC 4-17572. x, 210 p. col. front., col. illus., 18 col. pl. 28 1/2 cm. 1902. Houghton, Mifflin and Company.
--A Wonder-Book for Girls and Boys. Peat, Fern Bisel, Mrs. (1893-), illus. (Illus.). 23cm. iv, 234p. (Companion series). 1930. Saalfield Pub. Co.
--A Wonder-Book for Girls and Boys. Peat, Fern Bisel, Mrs. (1893-), illus. LC 29-130610. 234 p. incl. front. illus., plates. 19 cm. (Half-title: Every child's library). c.1929. The Saalfield Publishing Company.
--A Wonder Book for Girls and Boys: Comprising Stories of Classical Fables. iv p., 2 l., 290 p. front., plates. 19 cm. (On cover: Home library). N.D. A. L. Burt.
--Wonder Book Stories. (Illus.). (Every Boy's Library). N.D. Caldwell.
--Wonder Book Stories, (Illus.). (The Editha Ser.: No. 9). 1905. Set. H M Caldwell Co.
--A Wonder Book: Tanglewood Tales. LC 36-37038. x, 310 p. 17 1/2 cm. (Half-title: Everyman's library, ed. by Ernest Rhys. For young people. no. 5(). 1933. J. M. Dent & Sons, Ltd.
--A Wonder-Book, Tanglewood Tales, and Grandfather's Chair. (Riverside Edition). N.D. Houghton Mifflin Co.
--A Wonder Book: The Gorgon's Head, The Golden Touch, The Three Golden Apples. LC 7-3765. 96 p. illus. 17 cm. (On cover: Maynard's English classics, no. 168). c.1895. Maynard, Merrill & Co.
--Wonder Tales:. Pandora and the Mysterious Box; Midas, the King Who Turned Everything into Gold; Pegasus, the Winged Horse. Stead, William Thomas (1849-), ed. Le Fanu, Brinsley, illus. LC 8-23108. (Illus.). 62p. 18cm. 1908. The Penn Publishing Co.
--Wonderbook and Tanglewood Tales. (gr. 5-7). 1853, c.1972. Houghton Mifflin.
--A Wonderbook and Tanglewood Tales. Richardson, Frederick (1862-1937), illus. (The Children's Bookshelf). N.D. John C. Winston.
--A Wonderbook for Boys and Girls. Bates, Katherine Lee, intro. by. LC 2-20806. 21cm. 159p. (The Works of Nathaniel Hawthorne: Vol. 13). 1902. T. Y. Crowell & Co.
--Writings for Children. Charvat, William (1905-), ed. Ohio. State University Columbus. Ohio State Center for Textual Studies LC 74-162949. v. 25cm. (centenary edition of the works of Nathaniel Hawthorne, v. 6). N.D. Ohio State University Press.

Hawthorne, Nathaniel (1804-1864), retold by.
--Pegasus, the Winged Horse: A Greek Myth. Levit, Herschel (1912-), illus. Lowell, Robert Traill Spence, Jr., intro. by. LC 63-24867. 39p. col. illus. 34cm. (gr. 4-6). 1963. Macmillan.

Hawthorne, Nathaniel (1804-1864) & Harte, Bret (1836-1902)
--David Swan and Tennessee's Partner. Bumpass, F. L., ed. (Let's Read Stories: Book 4). N.D. McGraw-Hill Book Company.

Hawthorne, Nathaniel (1804-1864) & Trinidad, Angel
--The House of the Seven Gables. Farr, Naunerle, ed. Guitierez, Domy, illus. LC 77-79438. (Illus.). 62 p. 21cm. (Now age books illustrated). c.1977. (ISBN 0-88301-265-0). Pendulum Press.

Hawton, Hector (1901-)
--The Tower of Darkness. 1950. Roy Publishers.

Hawver, Adele (1892-)
--The Gypsy and the Prince. LC 56-197231. 57p. 24cm. 1955. Columbia's Pub. Co.

Haxton, Elaine
--Parrot in a Flame Tree. Haxton, Elaine, illus. LC 68-28956. (Illus.). 32p. (gr. k-3). 1971. St Martin.
--A Parrot in a Flame Tree: Adapted from a Medieval Christmas Carol. Haxton, Elaine, illus. LC 68-28956. (Illus.). unpaged. 1968. F. W. Cheshire.

Haxton, Jane
--Following the Trails at Camp Algonquin: A Story for Girls. Merrill, Frank Thayer (1848-), illus. LC 26-2455. 319 p. col. front. 19 1/2 cm. c.1925. W. A. Wilde Company.

Hay, Dean
--Now I Can Count. Hay, Dean, photos by. LC 68-20449. (Illus.). 55 p. 21cm. 1968. Lion Press.

Hay, Doddy
--Hit the Silk. LC 72-85004. 128 p. 22cm. 1968. (ISBN 0-87599-163-7). S. G. Phillips.

Hay, Ella H.
--Friendly Tales for Children. King, George A., illus. LC 35-190035. 64 p. col. front., illus. 24 cm. c.1935. Cupples & Leon Co.

Hay, George M.
--Samuel George Washington Jones Snake. 1st ed. Uroskie, Annette, illus. LC 80-70015. (Illus.). 30 p., 1 leaf of plates. 28cm. c.1980. (ISBN 0-938490-00-1). Abbincott Pub. Co.

Hay, Grace Trobaugh
--The K-House Mystery. Hoeflich, Sherman C., illus. LC 58-10694. 156p. illus. 21cm. c.1958. D. McKay Co.
--Seven Go to Eastcroft. Hoeflich, Sherman C., illus. LC 39-25705. 256 p. illus. 21 cm. c.1939. David McKay Company.

Hay, Ian (1876-1952)
--Happy-Go-Lucky. N.D. Grosset & Dunlap.
--The Liberry. (Riverside Library). N.D. Houghton Mifflin Co.
--The Willing Horse. N.D. Houghton Mifflin Co.

Hay, Kathleen
--Friendly House. Isham, Benjamin, illus. LC 42-21764. 125 p. incl. plates. 20 cm. 1942. The Wartburg Press.
--Golden Links. LC 32-23572. 76 p. incl. front. 17 1/2 cm. 1932. Augustana Book Concern.
--The Sweetest Story Told. 1931. Augustana Book Concern.

Hay, Keith, et al.
--Beaver's Way. Bourne, Russell & Lawrence, Bonnie S., eds. LC 73-83782. 32p. (Ranger Rick's Best Friends Ser.). (gr. 1-6). 1973. (ISBN 0-912186-06-2). Natl Wildlife.

Haycox, Ernest (1899-1950)
--The Border Trumpet. N.D. Pocket Bks, Inc.
--The Wild Bunch. LC 75-31606. p. cm. 1975, c.1943. (ISBN 0-89190-973-7). Rivercity Press.
--Winds of Rebellion. Kidwell, Carl (1910-), illus. 1964. JUV. Criterion Books.

Haycraft, Howard, jt. ed. see Beecroft, John William Richard.

Haycraft, Howard (1905-), ed. see Doyle, Arthur Conan, Sir.

Haycraft, Howard (1905-), ed.
--The Boys' Book of Great Detective Stories. LC 38-7471. viii p., 1 l., 315 p. 24 cm. 1938. Harper & Brothers.
--The Boys' Second Book of Great Detective Stories. LC 40-7099. viii p., 1 l., 352 p. 24 cm. c.1940. Harper & Brothers.

Haycraft, Margaret Scott
--Little Mother, 1 of 6 Vols. (Illus.). 96p. (The Young Folks Ser.). N.D. Set. F H Revell.
--Myrtle and Rue: A story for the Young, 1 of 12 Vols. (Illus.). 244p. (The Progress Ser.). N.D. Fleming H Revell.
--Rags and Rainbows, 1 vol. Juv ed. Macnab, P., illus. N.D. Cassell & Co.
--Sybil's Repentance: Or, A Dream of Good. (Illus.). N.D. Methodist Bk Concern.

Haycraft, Molly Costain (1911-)
--The Reluctant Queen. (gr. 7-9). 1962. (ISBN 0-397-00237-8). Lippincott.
--Too Near the Throne. (gr. 7-9). 1959. Lippincott.

Haycroft, Howard (1905-), ed. see Doyle, Arthur Conan, Sir.

Hayden, Gwendolen Lampshire, jt. auth. see Gischler, Pearl Clements.

Hayden, Gwendolen Lampshire (1904-)
--Boom Stick Bear. (gr. 7 up). N.D. Review & Herald.
--Mary Martha's Really-Truly Stories. Nye, Vernon Paul, illus. LC 47-421. v. col. illus. 21 cm. N.D. Review and Herald Pub. Assn.
--Pawnee Pony. (gr. 1-3). N.D. Review & Herald.
--Silver-Dollar Rosebush. Nye, Vernon Paul, illus. LC 79-142732. (Illus.). 128 p. 22cm. (Penguin series). 1971. Review and Herald Pub. Association.
--Skip, the Pioneer Boy. LC 67-19661. (Illus.). 104 p. 22cm. 1967. Denison.

Hayden, Gwendolen Lampshire (1904-) & Gischler, Pearl Clements
--Muslin Town: A Story About Gold Rush Days in Oregon. LC 47-177711. 70 p. illus 22 1/2 cm. 1947. Binfords & Mort.
--Thunder Hill. Dowling, Colista, illus. LC 48-3150. 74p. 1947. Binfords & Mort.

Hayden, Gwendolyn Lampshire, jt. auth. see Gischler, Pearl Clements.

Hayden, Robert Earl (1913-1980), compiled by.
--Kaleidoscope: Poems by American Negro Poets. Hayden, Robert Earl, intro. by. LC 67-18543. (Illus.). photos. 231p (Curriculum Related Bks.). (gr. 7-12). 1968. (ISBN 0-685-11837-1). Hal Brace).
--Selected Poems. 2nd ed. (Orig.). 1966. (ISBN 0-8079-0061-3). (ISBN 0-8079-0062-1). October.

Haydn, Hiram (1907-1973) & Cournos, John, eds.
--A World of Great Stories. 960p. 1947. Crown.

Haydon, Arthur Lincoln (1872-)
--The Book of Robin Hood: An Account of the Brave Deeds and Merry Pranks of the Famous Outlaw; Collected from Old Ballads, Chap-Books and Other Sources. Robinson, Thomas Heath (1869-1950), illus. LC 31-28121. xxiii, 263 p. col. front., col. plates. 21 1/2 cm. 1931. F. Warne & Co., Ltd.
--Kidnapped from Downways. N.D. Frederick Warne & Co.
--Manisty of the School-House. (The Crown Library for Boys & Girls). N.D. Frederick Warne & Co.
--The Secret of Tuff's Tower. (The Magnet Library). N.D. Frederick Warne & Co.
--The Skipper of the Team. (The Treasure Library). N.D. Frederick Warne & Co.
--Stand Fast Wymondham. (The Treasure Library). N.D. Frederick Warne & Co.

Hayens, E.
--Paris at Bay. (Illus.). N.D. Charles Scribner's Sons.

Hayens, Herbert (1861-)
--Jack Fraser's Adventures. (The Forward Ser.). N.D. William Collins Co.
--Red Caps of Lyons. N.D. Appleton Century Co.
--Under the Lone Star. (Illus.). (The Round Table Ser.). N.D. A. L. Burt's Pubs.
--Under the Lone Star: A Story of Revolution in Nicaragua. Stacey, W. S., illus. N.D. Thomas Nelson & Sons.
--Under the Lone Star: A Story of the Revolution in Nicaragua, (The Rugby Ser.). 1905. Set. A L Burt Co.

Hayes
--The Gift Horse. Orig. Title: The Carousel Horse. (gr. 4-5). 1980. (ISBN 0-590-30905-6). Scholastic Inc.

Hayes, A. A.
--Cast-Away in the Cold, 1 of 3 vols. (Illus.). (The Ice Bound Ser.). 1882. Lee & Shepard.

Hayes, Anna Hansen (1886-)
--The Adventures of Hedvig and Lollie. Orrin, Carl A., illus. LC 60-56268. 134p. illus. 22cm. 1961. Caxton Printers.

Hayes, Barbara (1944-)
--Ali Baba. Blasco, Jesus, illus. LC 84-11458. (Illus.). 23 p. 27cm. (Easy to read for little readers). (Classic Fairy Tales). c.1984. (ISBN 0-86592-227-6). Rourke Enterprises.
--Brer Rabbit. Livraghi, Virginio, illus. LC 84-11531. (Illus.). 23 p. 27cm. (Easy to read for little readers). (Classic Fairy Tales). c.1984. (ISBN 0-86592-228-4). Rourke Enterprises.
--Cinderlad. Lewis, Brian, illus. LC 84-11525. (Illus.). 23 p. 27cm. (Easy to read for little readers). (Classic Fairy Tales). c.1984. (ISBN 0-86592-196-2). Rourke Enterprises.
--Donkey Skin. Blasco, Jesus, illus. LC 84-11461. (Illus.). 23 p. 27cm. (Easy to read for little readers). (Classic Fairy Tales). c.1984. (ISBN 0-86592-226-8). Rourke Enterprises.
--The Enchanted Lion. Blasco, Jesus, illus. LC 84-11536. (Illus.). 23 p. 27cm. (Easy to read for little readers). (Classic Fairy Tales). c.1984. (ISBN 0-86592-197-0). Rourke Enterprises.
--Hansel & Gretel. Blasco, Jesus, illus. LC 84-11743. p. cm. (Easy to read for little readers). (Classic Fairy Tales). 1984. (ISBN 0-86592-232-2). Rourke Enterprises.
--Hop O' My Thumb. Embleton, G. A., illus. LC 84-16062. (Illus.). 23 p. 27cm. (Easy to read for little readers). (Classic Fairy Tales). c.1984. (ISBN 0-86592-234-9). Rourke Enterprises.

--The Lazy Princess. Colombi, Nino, illus. LC 84-17737. p. cm. (Easy to read for little readers). (Classic Fairy Tales). 1984. (ISBN 0-86592-229-2). Rourke Enterprises.
--The Magic Horse. Embleton, G. A, illus. LC 84-11459. (Illus.). 23 p. 27cm. (Easy to read for little readers). (Classic Fairy Tales). c.1984. (ISBN 0-86592-225-X). Rourke Enterprises.
--The Tailor Prince. Blasco, Jesus, illus. LC 84-17736. p. cm. (Easy to read for little readers). (Classic Fairy Tales). 1984. (ISBN 0-86592-233-0). Rourke Enterprises.
--The Three Soldiers. Embleton, Ronald, illus. LC 84-17742. p. cm. (Easy to read for little readers). (Classic Fairy Tales). 1984. (ISBN 0-86592-237-3). Rourke Enterprises.
--Thumbelina. LC 84-17734. p. cm. (Easy to read for little readers). (Classic Fairy Tales). 1984. (ISBN 0-86592-235-7). Rourke Enterprises.
--Tom Thumb. Coelho, Jorge, illus. LC 84-18034. (Illus.). 23 p. 27cm. (Easy to read for little readers). (Classic Fairy Tales). c.1984. (ISBN 0-86592-230-6). Rourke Enterprises.

Hayes, Charles N.
--Johnny Greenhorn. (gr. 4-7). 1970. Vantage.

Hayes, Clair Wallace see Drake, Ensign Robert L., pseud

Hayes, Clair Wallace, (1887-)
--The Boy Allies at Jutland: Or, The Greatest Naval Battle of History. Hayes, Clair Wallace. Drake, Robert L., pseud. (The Boy Allies with the Navy). N.D. A. L. Burt Co.
--The Boy Allies at Liege: Or, Through Lines of Steel. LC 15-4210. 256 p. 19 1/2 cm. c.1915. A. L. Burt Company.
--The Boy Allies at Verdun: Or, Saving France from the Enemy. (The Boy Allies with the Army). N.D. A. L. Burt Co.
--The Boy Allies in Great Peril: Or, with the Italian Army in the Alps. (The Boy Allies with the army). N.D. A. L. Burt Co.
--The Boy Allies in the Balkan Campaign: Or, The Struggle to Save a Nation. (The Boy Allies with the Army). N.D. A. L. Burt Co.
--The Boy Allies in the Baltic: Or, Through Fields of Ice to Aid the Czar. Drake, Robert L., pseud. (The Boy Allies with the Navy). N.D. A. L. Burt Co.
--The Boy Allies in the Trenches: Or, Midst Shot and Shell Along the Aisne. LC 20-15063. 236 p. front. 19 1/2 cm. c.1915. A. L. Burt Company.
--The Boy Allies on the Firing Line: Or, Twelve Days Battle Along the Maine. LC 20-19340. 250 p. front. 16 1/2 cm. c.1915. A. L. Burt Company.
--The Boy Allies on the Somme: Or, Courage and Bravery Rewarded. (The Boy Allies with the Army). N.D. A. L. Burt Co.
--The Boy Allies Under the Sea: Or, The Vanishing Submarine. Drake, Robert L., pseud. (The Boy Allies with the Navy). N.D. A. L. Burt Co.
--The Boy Allies Under the Stars and Stripes: Or, Leading the American Troops to the Firing Line. (The Boy Allies with the Army). N.D. A. L. Burt Co.
--The Boy Allies Under Two Flags: Or, Sweeping the Enemy from the Seas. Drake, Robert L., pseud. (The Boy Allies with the Navy). N.D. A. L. Burt Co.
--The Boy Allies with Haig in Flanders: Or, The Fighting Canadians of Vimy Ridge. (The Boy Allies with the Army). N.D. A. L. Burt Co.
--The Boy Allies with Marshal Foch: Or, The Closing Days of the Great World War. (The Boy Allies with the Army). N.D. A. L. Burt Co.
--The Boy Allies with Pershing in France: Or, Over the Top at Chateau Thierry. (The Boy Allies with the Army). N.D. A. L. Burt Co.
--The Boy Allies with the Cossacks: Or, A Wild Dash Over the Carpathians. (The Boy Allies With the Army). N.D. A. L. Burt Co.
--The Boy Allies with the Great Advance: Or, Driving the Enemy Through France and Belgium. (The Boy Allies with the Army). N.D. A. L. Burt Co.
--The Boy Allies With the Submarine D-Thirty-Two: Or, The Fall of the Russian Empire. Drake, Robert L., pseud. (The Boy Allies With the Navy). N.D. A. L. Burt Company.
--The Boy Allies with the Terror of the Seas: Or, The Last Shot of Submarine D-16:. Drake, Ensign Robert L., pseud. LC 52-50337. 253 p. illus. 20 cm. c.1915. A. L. Burt Co.
--The Boy Allies With the Victorious Fleets: Or, The Fall of the German Navy. Drake, Robert L., pseud. (The Boy Allies With the Navy). N.D. A. L. Burt Company.
--The Boy Allies With Uncle Sam's Cruisers: Or, Convoying the American Army Across the Atlantic. Drake, Robert L., pseud. (The Boy Allies With the Navy). N.D. A. L. Burt Company.

--The Boy Troopers Among the Wild Mountaineers. LC 22-10019. 240 p. front. 19 1/2 cm. (His The Boy Troopers Ser.). c.1922. A. L. Burt Company.
--The Boy Troopers in the Northwest. LC 22-10091. 240 p. front. 19 1/2 cm. (His Boy Troopers Ser.). c.1922. A. L. Burt Company.
--The Boy Troopers on Duty. (The Boy Troopers Ser.). N.D. A. L. Burt Co.
--The Boy Troopers on the Trail. LC 22-824110. 249 p. front. 19 1/2 cm. (His Boy TroopersSer.). c.1922. A. L. Burt Company.
--The Boys Allies with the Flying Squadron: Or, the Naval Raiders of the Great War. Drake, Robert L., pseud. (The Boy Allies with the Navy). N.D A. L. Burt Co.

Hayes, Courtenay
--(The Magnet Library). N.D. Frederick Warne & Co.
--Rover Ahoy. (The Magnet Library). N.D. Frederick Warne & Co.

Hayes, Elizabeth Le May
--Old Days in Groton. LC 55-39144. 78p. illus. 22cm. 1955. Groton Historical Society.

Hayes, Florence Sooy (1895-), adapted by see Spyri, Johanna Heusser.

Hayes, Florence Sooy (1895-)
--Alaskan Hunter. Wiese, Kurt (1887-1974), illus. LC 59-9723. (Illus.). 248 p. 22cm. 1959. Houghton Mifflin.
--The Boy in the Forty-Ninth Seat. Yamazaki, Sanae, illus. LC 63-14750. (Illus.). (gr. 3-5). 1963. (ISBN 0-394-80132-6). (ISBN 0-394-90132-0). Random.
--The Boy in the Rooftop School. Wong, Jeunyee (1920-), illus. LC 67-5470. (Illus.). 57 p. 24cm. (Gateway books). 1967. Random House.
--The Burro Tamer. Lee, Manning De Villeneuve (1894-1980), illus. LC 46-25277. 3 p. l., 3-299 p. illus. 21 cm. 1946. Random House.
--Chee and His Pony, the Story of a Navajo Boy. Moyers, William (1916-), illus. LC 50-5663. 262 p. illus. 21 cm. 1950. Houghton Mifflin.
--The Eskimo Hunter. Wiese, Kurt (1887-1974), illus. LC 45-790614. 6 p. l., 3-275 p. incl. col. front., illus. (1 col.) plates. 19 1/2 cm. 1945. Random House.
--The Good Luck Feather. Stein, Harve (1904-), illus. LC 57-12083. 204p. illus. 22cm. 1958. Houghton Mifflin.
--Hedi. (Illus.). N.D. Random House Inc.
--Hosh-Ki, the Navajo. Chase, Charlotte Anna, illus. LC 43-512402. 4 p. l., 3-250 p. illus. 22 cm. 1943. Random House.
--Joe-Pole, New American. Gringhuis, Richard H. (1918-1974), illus. Gringhuis, Dirk, pseud. LC 52-5909. 244 p. illus. 22 cm. 1952. Houghton Mifflin.
--Skid. Fax, Elton Clay (1909-), illus. LC 48-8307. 216 p. illus. 22 cm. 1948. Houghton Mifflin Co.

Hayes, Geoffrey (1947-)
--The Alligator & Uncle Tooth. Hayes, Geoffrey (1947-), illus. LC 76-21387. (Illus.). (gr. 3-5). 1977. (ISBN 0-06-022264-6, HarpJ). (ISBN 0-06-022265-4). Har-Row.
--Bear by Himself. Hayes, Geoffrey (1947-), illus. LC 76-2345. (Illus.). 32 p. 20cm. c.1976. (ISBN 0-06-022262-X). (ISBN 0-06-022263-8). Harper & Row.
--Beyond the Troll Bridge: A Fairy Tale. Hayes, Geoffrey (1947-), illus. LC 78-19833. p. cm. 1979. (ISBN 0-06-022268-9). (ISBN 0-06-022269-7). Harper & Row.
--Christmas in Puttyville. Hayes, Geoffrey (1947-), illus. LC 85-2009. (Illus.). 32 p. 17cm. c.1985. (ISBN 0-394-87286-X). (ISBN 0-394-97286-4). Random House.
--Elroy & the Witch's Child. Hayes, Geoffrey (1947-), illus. LC 81-48645. (Illus.). 32p. (gr. 1-4). 1982. (ISBN 0-06-022259-X, HarpJ). (ISBN 0-06-022258-1). Har-Row.
--The Mystery of the Pirate Ghost: An Otto & Uncle Tooth Adventure. Hayes, Geoffrey (1947-), illus. LC 84-18228. (Illus.). 48p. (Step into Reading Bks.). (gr. 2-3). 1985. (ISBN 0-394-97220-1, BYR). (ISBN 0-394-87220-7). Random.
--Patrick and Ted. Hayes, Geoffrey (1947-), illus. LC 83-18486. (Illus.). 32p. 1984. (ISBN 0-590-07902-6). (ISBN 0-590-07902-6). Four Winds Press.
--Patrick Buys a Coat. Hayes, Geoffrey (1947-), illus. LC 84-1659. (Illus.). 32 p. 14cm. c.1985. (ISBN 0-590-07928-X). Knopf : Distributed by Random House.
--Patrick Comes to Puttyville, and Other Stories. Hayes, Geoffrey (1947-), illus. LC 77-25668. (Illus.). 118 p. 21cm. c.1978. (ISBN 0-06-022266-2). (ISBN 0-06-022267-0). Harper & Row.
--Patrick Eats His Dinner. Hayes, Geoffrey (1947-), illus. LC 84-5924. (Illus.). 32 p. 14cm. c.1985. (ISBN 0-590-07929-8). Knopf : Distributed by Random House.
--Patrick Goes to Bed. Hayes, Geoffrey (1947-), illus. LC 84-6099. (Illus.). 32 p. 14cm. c.1985. (ISBN 0-590-07926-3). Knopf.

--Patrick Takes a Bath. Hayes, Geoffrey (1947-), illus. LC 84-1658. (Illus.). 32 p. 14cm. c.1985. (ISBN 0-590-07927-1). Knopf : Distributed by Random Press.
--The Secret Inside. Hayes, Geoffrey (1947-), illus. LC 79-8519. (Illus.). 32 p. 20cm. c.1980. (ISBN 0-06-022273-5). (ISBN 0-06-022274-3). Harper & Row.

Hayes, Gilmore
--Flappy, the Circus Seal. Dotterer, Lloyd J., illus. LC 42-24101. 40 p. incl. col. front., col. illus. 23 1/2 x 19 1/2 cm. 1942. The Platt & Munk Co., Inc.

Hayes, Helen (1900-) & Kennedy, Mary
--Star on Her Forehead. LC 49-11927. viii, 247 p. 21 cm. (Career books). 1949. Dodd, Mead.
--Star on Her Forehead. LC 60-2189. 18cm. 190p. 1067. 1949. Popular Library.

Hayes, Hiram Wallace (1858-)
--The Newspaper Game: How It Was Successfully Played by Two Enterprising Boys. Cue, Harold, illus. LC 27-19187. 348 p. front., plates. 19 1/2 cm. c.1927. Lothrop, Lee & Shepard Co.

Hayes, Hobart Vance
--The Adventure. Hayes, Hobart Vance, illus. LC 65-12102. 1 v. (unpaged) col. illus. 24 cm. 1965 Westminster Press

Hayes, Isaac I.
--Cast Away in the Cold, 1 of 60 vols. (American Boys' Ser.: No. 11). 1900. Set. Lee & Shepard.

Hayes, Joe, retold by.
--The Day It Snowed Tortillas: Tales from Spanish New Mexico. Jelinek-Thompson, Lucy, illus. LC 82-179464. (Illus.). 21cm. 63p. (Enchanting Land bks.). c.1982. Mariposa Books.

Hayes, John F. (1904-)
--Bugles in the Hills. Finley, Fred J., illus. LC 56-106874. 192p. illus. 22cm. 1956. J. Messner.
--The Dangerous Cove. Finley, Fred J., illus. LC 60-7049. 191 p. 22cm. 1960. Messner. **Award:** (CLA).
--A Land Divided. Finley, Fred J., illus. LC 53-8527. (Illus.). 207 p. 21cm. 1954. Westminster Press.

Hayes, Joseph (1918-)
--Coyote: Native American Folk Tales. Jelinek-Thompson, Lucy, illus. LC 83-190710. (Illus.). 77 p., 1 leaf of plates. c.1983. Mariposa Pub.

Hayes, Leona T.
--The Lost Treasures of Peep-Eye Cove: Short Fiction. Budahl, Lee, illus. LC 78-110134. (Illus.). 68 p. 24cm. (Western Carolina University heritage publication). (Series: Western Carolina University. Mountain Heritage Center.). (Western Carolina University heritage publication). (Mountain Heritage Day Ser.). c.1978. Western Carolina University Mountain Heritage Center.

Hayes, Marjorie
--Alice-Albert Elephant. Wiese, Kurt (1887-1974), illus. LC 38-295595. 4 p. l., 3-134, 1 p. front., illus. 23 1/2 cm. 1938. Little, Brown and Company.
--Green Peace. Lee, Manning De Villeneuve (1894-1980), illus. LC 45-35220. 5 p. l., 230 p. illus. 21 cm. 1945. J. B. Lippincott Company.
--The Little House on Runners. Hauman, George (1890-1961) & Hauman, Doris, Mrs. (1897-), illus. LC 39-448919. 8 p. l., 3-274 p. incl. front., illus., plates. 21 cm. 1939. Little, Brown and Company.
--The Little House on Wheels. Hauman, George (1890-1961) & Hauman, Doris, Mrs. (1897-), illus. LC 34-29563. xii, 285 p. incl. front., illus., plates. 21 cm. 1934. Little, Brown and Company.
--Robin and Company. 1st ed. Treidler, Adolph, illus. LC 52-5008. 159 p. illus. 25 cm. 1952. Little, Brown.
--Robin on the River. 1st ed. Treidler, Adolph, illus. LC 50-9907. 162 p. illus. 25 cm. 1950. Little, Brown.
--Wampum and Sixpence. Stephenson, Eunice Holmes, illus. LC 36-221853. xiv, 309 p., 1 l. incl. front., illus., plates. 21 cm. 1936. Little, Brown, and Company.
--Young Patriots. (Illus.). (Mistletoe Ser.). N.D. Dewolfe, Fiske & Co.
--The Young Patriots. Lawson, Marie Abrams (1894-1956), illus. LC 41-8539. 292 p., 2 l. incl. illus., plates. col. front. 21 cm. c.1941. J. B. Lippincott Company.

Hayes, Nins
--Granny's Birds. Staples, Jean, illus. LC 47-23971. 40 p. illus. 21cm. c.1947. Saalfield Pub. Co.

Hayes, Richard
--The Secret Army. LC 78-11302. 212 p. 22cm. 1979, c.1977. (ISBN 0-670-62839-5). Viking Press.

Hayes, Robert Priestley
--The Land of Laughter: Rhymes for Children. LC 17-1333. 20cm. 23p. 1902. W. A. Leonard.

Hayes, Sheila (1937-)
--The Carousel Horse. p. cm. c.1978. (ISBN 0-8407-6610-6). T. Nelson.

--Me and My Mona Lisa Smile. LC 80-29345. 116 p. 21cm. c.1981. (ISBN 0-525-66731-8). Elsevier/Nelson Books.
--No Autographs, Please. LC 84-13545. c.1984. (ISBN 0-525-67157-9). Dutton.
--Speaking of Snapdragons. LC 82-9901. 151 p. 22cm. c.1982. (ISBN 0-525-66785-7). Lodestar Books.
Hayes, Wanda
--Bible Stories Make Me Happy. Hook, Frances Arnold (1912-), illus. (Illus.). 24p. (A Happy Day Book). (gr. k-3). 1979. (ISBN 0-87239-352-6). Standard Pub.
--A Child's First Book of Bible Stories. Gambill, Henrietta (1912-), ed. LC 83-664. (Illus.). 128p. (ps). 1983. (ISBN 0-87239-659-2). Standard Pub.
--My Friends Make Me Happy. Hook, Frances Arnold (1912-), illus. (Illus.). 24p. (A Happy Day Book). (gr. k-3). 1979. (ISBN 0-87239-351-8). Standard Pub.
--Saying Thank You Makes Me Happy. Hook, Frances Arnold (1912-), illus. (Illus.). 24p. (A Happy Day Book). (gr. k-3). 1979. (ISBN 0-87239-353-4). Standard Pub.
Hayes, Will, jt. auth. see Young, W. Edward.
Hayes, Will (1910-)
--The Biggest Pig. Totten, Robert, illus. LC 58-9773. (Illus.). 30 p. 22cm. (Look, read, learn). 1958. Melmont Publishers.
--Good Times on Boats. Luhrs, Henry, illus. LC 62-7002. 47 p. illus. 24 cm. (Look, read, learn). 1963. Melmont Publishers.
Hayes, William Dimitt (1913-)
--Hold That Computer!. Frame, Paul (1913-), illus. LC 67-19005. (Illus.). 162 p. 22cm. 1968. Atheneum.
--How the True Facts Started in Simpsonville, and Other Tales of the West. 1st ed. Hayes, William Dimitt (1913-), illus. LC 72-75271. (Illus.). 94 p. 22cm. 1972. Atheneum.
--Johnny and the Tool Chest. 1st ed. Frame, Paul (1913-), illus. LC 64-19560. (Illus.). 93 p. 22cm. 1964. Atheneum.
--Johnny and the Tool Chest. Frame, Paul (1913-), illus. 1964. (ISBN 0-8382-0387-6, Cadmus Books). E. M. Hale And Company.
--The Monkey Tree. Hayes, William Dimitt (1913-), illus. LC 63-9681. unpaged. illus. 23 cm. c.1963. Putnam.
--Mystery at Squaw Peak. Koering, Ursula (1921-), illus. LC 65-15910. (Illus.). (gr. 3-7). 1965. (ISBN 0-689-20158-3). Atheneum.
--Project, Genius. 1st ed. Hayes, William Dimitt (1913-), illus. LC 62-15367. (Illus.). 22cm. 135p. (gr. 3-7). 1962. (ISBN 0-689-20152-4). (ISBN 0-689-20153-2). Atheneum.
--Project Scoop. 1st ed. Hayes, William Dimitt (1913-), illus. LC 66-5713. (Illus.). 154 p. 22cm. 1966. Atheneum.
--Project, Scoop. Hayes, William Dimitt (1913-), illus. (Illus.). (gr. 3-7). 1972. (ISBN 0-689-70305-8, Aladdin). Atheneum.
Hayes, William Dimmit, jt. auth. see Hitte, Kathryn.
Hayford, Harrison, ed. see Melville, Herman.
Hayllar, T. A. S, jt. auth. see Sadler, R. K.
Haymon, Sylvia
--Loyal Traitor: A Story of Khett's Rebellion. Collard, Derek, illus. (Illus.). (gr. 5 up). 1965. (ISBN 0-685-21317-X). Verry.
Hayne, Coe Smith (1875-)
--The God of Yotto: The Lost City; a Hopi Indian Story. Houy, Hartke, illus. LC 29-13624. 128 p. incl. illus., pl. 19 1/2 cm. c.1928. David C. Cook Publishing Company.
--Prisoners of Spirit Mountain: A Navajo Indian Story. LC 31-318514. 2 p. l., 7-110 p. incl. 1 illus., plates. 19 1/2 cm. c.1930. David C. Cook Publishing Co.
Hayne, Paul H.
--Legends and Lyrics. N.D. J. B. Lippincott.
Haynes, Ambrose
--Alpine Fugitives. 1974. (ISBN 0-87508-643-8). Chr Lit.
--Heroic Messenger. 1959. Christian Lit.
--Meet the Gunthers. (gr. 6-8). 1966. (ISBN 0-87508-721-3). Chr Lit.
Haynes, Barbara
--A Girl Named Sam. 124p. (Orig.). (gr. 7 up). 1980. (ISBN 0-590-31330-4, Schol Pap). Scholastic Inc.
Haynes, Bessie Doak & Haynes, Edgar
--The Grizzly Bear. N.D. University of Oklahoma Press.
--Sylvia Bear. Wood, Chuck, illus. (Illus.). 112p. (gr. k-3). 1971. (ISBN 0-8092-8487-1). Regnery.
Haynes, Betsy (1937-)
--The Against Taffy Sinclair Club. LC 76-22667. 125 p. 21cm. c.1976. (ISBN 0-8407-6501-0). T. Nelson.
--Cowslip. LC 72-13251. 139 p. 22cm. 1973. (ISBN 0-8407-6266-6). T. Nelson.
--The Ghost of Gravestone Hearth. LC 77-1978. (gr. 6 up). 1977. (ISBN 0-525-66544-7). Lodestar Bks.
--The Ghost of the Gravestone Hearth. LC 77-1978. 128 p. 21cm. c.1977. (ISBN 0-8407-6544-4). T. Nelson.
--The Shadows of Jeremy Pimm. LC 80-28920. 125 p. 22cm. c.1981. (ISBN 0-8253-0045-2). Beaufort Books.
--Slave Girl. Orig. Title: Cowslip. (gr. 4-6). 1974. (ISBN 0-590-06119-4, Starline). Schol Bk Serv.
--Spies on the Devil's Belt. LC 74-13187. p. cm. 1974. (ISBN 0-8407-6407-3). T. Nelson.
Haynes, Bob, jt. auth. see Ward, Nanda Weedon.
Haynes, Doris McGee
--Cowboy Matt and Belleza. Herrington, Roger, illus. LC 73-78022. (Illus.). 64 p. 23cm. (Cowboys of many races). 1973. Benefic Press.
Haynes, E. S.
--Personalia (Edward Thomas). 128p. Repr. of 1918 ed (Pub. by Selwyn & Blount). 1979. (ISBN 0-89987-352-9). Darby Bks.
Haynes, Edgar, jt. auth. see Haynes, Bessie Doak.
Haynes, Henry Louis (1956-) & Epstein, Len
--Squarehead and Me. 1st ed. Epstein, Len, illus. LC 79-25523. (Illus.). 143 p. 21cm. c.1980. (ISBN 0-664-32663-3). Westminster Press.
Haynes, Louise Marshall
--Through the Church Door. Fitts, Clara E. Atwood, illus. LC 25-114. 53, 1 p. illus. 23 1/2 cm. c.1924. Wright & Potter Printing Co.
Haynes, Lucius M. S., ed. see Defoe, Daniel.
Haynes, Mary
--Pot Belly Tales. 1st ed. Deraney, Michael J., illus. LC 81-12325. (Illus.). 74 p. 26cm. c.1982. (ISBN 0-688-00892-5). Lothrop, Lee & Shepard.
--Wordchanger. Nones, Eric Jon, illus. LC 83-773. p. cm. 1982. (ISBN 0-688-02273-1). Lothrop, Lee & Shepard Books.
Haynes, Muriel
--Our Electric World. Collins, Harold Dean, illus. LC 34-33284. vii p., 1 l. 11-67 p. illus. 19 1/2 cm. (Our changing world). 1934. T. Nelson and Sons.
Haynes, Nelma
--Panther Lick Creek. Moyers, William (1916-), illus. LC 74-99795. (Illus.). 157 p. 24cm. 1970. (ISBN 0-687-30012-6). Abingdon Press.
Hays, Anna Jane
--See No Evil, Hear No Evil, Smell No Evil. Mathieu, Joseph (1945-), illus. LC 72-2885. (Illus.). 28 p. 25cm. (Golden fragrance book). 1975. (ISBN 0-307-13541-1). Western Pub. Co.
Hays, Daniel, jt. auth. see Hays, Hoffman Reynolds.
Hays, Ethel, illus.
--My Favorite Story Book. LC 42-19351. 66 p. illus. (part col.) 30 1/2 x 25 1/2 cm. c.1942. The Saalfield Publishing Company.
Hays, Helen, Mrs.
--The Adventures of Prince Lazybones and Other Stories. LC 49-30239. 271 p. plates. 17 cm. (Harper's young people series). 1885. Harper.
--Castle Comfort: A Story for Children. (Whittaker's Bks). 1888. Thomas Whittaker.
--City Cousin. (Whittaker Select Bks.). 1888. Thomas Whittaker.
--A Domestic Heroine. (Whittaker's Select Bks). 1888. Thomas Whittaker.
--A Loving Sister. (Whittaker's Select Bks). 1888. Thomas Whittaker.
--The Princess Idleways: A Fairy Story. LC 12-34160. 2 p. l. 7-124 p. incl., plates. 16 1/2 x 13 cm. 1880. Harper & Brothers.
--Princess Lazybones. (Illus.). N.D. Harper & Brothers.
Hays, Hoffman Reynolds (1904-1980) & Hays, Daniel
--Charley Sang a Song. Shulevitz, Uri (1935-), illus. (Illus.). (gr. k-3). 1964. (ISBN 0-06-022261-1). Har-Row.
Hays, John Willis
--In Peril. N.D. D. Lothrop Co.
Hays, Margaret G.
--Kiddie Land. Wiederseim, Grace G., illus. N.D. George W. Jacobs & Co.
--Kiddie Rhymes. Wiederseim, Grace G., illus. N.D. George W. Jacobs & Co.
--The Turr'ble Tales of Kaptin Kiddo. Wiederseim, Grace G, illus. 30p. N.D. Edward Stern & Co.
Hays, S.
--Stories for Little Children. LC 21-2696. 2 pt. illus. 12 1/2 cm. 1812. Published by Johnson & Warner.
Hays, W. J. see Hays, Helen, Mrs.
Hays, Wilma Pitchford (1909-)
--The Apricot Tree. 1968. David McKay Company.
--The Apricot Tree. LC 68-28345. 152 p. 21cm. 1968. I. Washburn.
--The Burro That Ran Away. 1st ed. McClary, Nelson, illus. LC 72-77449. (Illus.). 42 p. 22cm. 1969. Little, Brown.
--Cape Cod Adventure. Jaeger, Elinor, illus. LC 64-17993. 94 p. illus. 22 cm. 1964. Coward-McCann.
--Christmas on the Mayflower. Duvoisin, Roger Antoine (1904-1980), illus. LC 56-9956. (Illus.). unpaged. 23cm. 1956. Coward-McCann.
--Circus Girl Without a Name. 1970. David McKay Company.
--Circus Girl Without a Name. Ferguson, William, illus. LC 71-102661. (Illus.). 115 p. 21cm. 1970. Washburn.
--Drummer Boy for Montcalm. Moyler, Alan, illus. LC 59-4620. (Illus.). 191 p. 21cm. 1959. Viking Press.
--Easter Fires. Burchard, Peter Duncan (1921-), illus. LC 59-144157. (Illus.). (gr. 3-5). 1960. (ISBN 0-698-30067-X). Coward.
--For Ma & Pa: On the Oregon Trail 1844. Burchard, Peter Duncan (1921-), illus. (Illus.). 64p. (gr. 3-6). 1972. (ISBN 0-698-30425-X, Coward). Putnam Pub Group.
--Fourth of July Raid. Burchard, Peter Duncan (1921-), illus. LC 59-5234. 64p. illus. 23cm. 1959. Coward-McCann.
--Fourth of July Raid. Burchard, Peter Duncan (1921-), illus. (Illus.). (gr. 4-6). 1963. (ISBN 0-698-30092-0). Coward.
--The French Are Coming: Colonial Williamsburg. Weisgard, Leonard Joseph (1916-), illus. LC 65-226812. xvi, 102p. illus. 24cm. c.1965. Holt.
--The Ghost at Penniman House. Krupinski, Loretta, illus. LC 78-78364. (Illus.). 61 p. 21cm. (Weekly reader books). c.1979. Xerox Education Publications.
--The Goose That Was a Watchdog. 1st ed. McClary, Nelson, illus. LC 67-17290. (Illus.). (A young weeder-goose in Mississippi proves her worth to a family whose livelihood is threatened). (gr. 1-3). 1967. (ISBN 0-316-35231-4). (ISBN 0-316-35240-3). Little.
--Highland Halloween. Burchard, Peter Duncan (1921-), illus. LC 62-10946. 64p. illus. 23cm. 1962. Coward-McCann.
--Little Hawaiian Horse. Dennis, Wesley (1903-1966), illus. LC 63-13460. (Illus.). 40p. (gr. 2-5). 1963. (ISBN 0-316-35241-1). Little.
--The Little Horse That Raced a Train. Dennis, Wesley (1903-1966), illus. LC 59-5281. (Illus.). 21cm. 31p. (gr. 1-3). 1959. (ISBN 0-316-35243-8). Little.
--Little Hurricane Happy. Dennis, Wesley (1903-1966), illus. LC 65-16845. 45p. illus. 21cm. c.1965. Little.
--Little Yellow Fur. Cuffari, Richard (1925-1978), illus. LC 72-89767. (Illus.). 48 p. 23cm. (Break-of-day book). 1973. (ISBN 0-698-30503-5). (ISBN 0-698-20250-3). (ISBN 0-698-20250-3). Coward, McCann & Geoghegan.
--The Long Blond Wig. Miller, Marilyn Jean (1925-), illus. LC 70-144023. (Illus.). 119 p. 21cm. 1971. I. Washburn.
--Mary's Star. Smith, Lawrence Beall (1909-), illus. LC 68-11960. (Illus., Orig.). (Young Readers Ser.). (gr. 4-7). 1968. (ISBN 0-910412-65-0). Williamsburg.
--Mary's Star: A Tale of Orphans in Virginia, 1781. Smith, Lawrence Beall (1909-), illus. (Illus.). 108 p. 24cm. 1968. Colonial Williamsburg; Distributed by Holt, Rinehart and Winston, New York.
--May Day for Samoset. Miller, Marilyn Jean (1925-), illus. LC 68-14317. (Illus.). 62 p. 23cm. 1968. Coward-McCann.
--Monsters and Oil Wells Don't Mix. Riswold, Gilbert, illus. LC 76-13783. (Illus.). 77 p. 24cm. (Weekly Reader Children's Book Club edition). c.1976. (ISBN 0-88375-213-1). Xerox Education Publications.
--Naughty Little Pilgrim. Miller, Marilyn Jean (1925-), illus. LC 77-82668. (Illus.). 48 p. 23cm. 1969. I. Washburn.
--Naugthy Little Pilgrim. (Illus.). 1969. David McKay Company.
--Noko, Captive of Columbus. Burchard, Peter Duncan (1921-), illus. LC 67-8572. (Illus.). 64 p. 23cm. 1967. Coward-McCann.
--The Open Gate, New Year's 1815. Tierney, Carolyn Cather, illus. LC 75-118120. (Illus.). 62 p. 23cm. 1970. (ISBN 0-698-30270-2). Coward-McCann.
--Patrick of Ireland. (Illus.). (gr. 3-6). 1970. (ISBN 0-698-30279-6). Coward.
--Pilgrim Thanksgiving. 1955. E M Hale.
--Pilgrim Thanksgiving. Weisgard, Leonard Joseph (1916-), illus. LC 55-107917. (Illus.). unpaged. 23cm. 1955. Coward-McCann.
--Pilgrims to the Rescue. Miller, Marilyn Jean (1925-), illus. LC 71-165009. (Illus.). 47 p. 23cm. 1971. I. Washburn.
--The Pup Who Became a Police Dog. 1st ed. Dennis, Wesley (1903-1966), illus. LC 62-12379. (Illus.). 44 p. 21cm. 1963. Little, Brown.
--The Scarlet Badge. Burchard, Peter Duncan (1921-), illus. LC 63-12613. (Illus.). 109 p. 24cm. 1963. Colonial Williamsburg; Distributed by Holt, Rinehart and Winston, New York.
--The Story of Valentine. Weisgard, Leonard Joseph (1916-), illus. LC 56-7142. (Illus.). 55 p. 23cm. 1956. Coward-McCann.
--Yellow Fur and Little Hawk. Cuffari, Richard (1925-1978), illus. LC 77-10712. p. cm. (Break-of-day book). 1978. (ISBN 0-698-30687-2). Coward, McCann & Geoghegan.
--Yellow Fur and Little Hawk. Rao, Anthony, illus. 1980. Putnam.
Hays, Wilma Pitchford (1909-) & Cox, Peter (1942-)
--Siege!. The Story of St. Augustine in 1702. LC 75-22276. (Illus.). 93 p. 27cm. c.1976. (ISBN 0-698-20357-7). Coward, McCann & Geoghegan.
Haystead, Ladd (1903-)
--Preacher's Kid. Gincano, John, illus. LC 42-24736. xiii, 216 p. incl. front., illus. 19 1/2 cm. 1942. G. P. Putnam's Sons.
Hayward, Enos Franklin (1866-)
--Kiddie Jingles for Boys and Girls. LC 48-30434. cover title, 1 l., 5-63 p. illus. 19 cm. 1932. Hayward Pub. Co.
Hayward, Linda
--The Curious Little Kitten. Swanson, Maggie, illus. LC 80-84779. (Illus.). 20 p. 24cm. (Golden storytime book). c.1982. (ISBN 0-307-11952-1). Golden Press.
--The Curious Little Kitten: Sniff Sniff Book. Swanson, Maggie, illus. (Illus.). 16p. (Little Golden Sniff It Bks.). (ps-k). 1983. (ISBN 0-307-13206-4, Golden Pr). Western Pub.
--The Curious Little Kitten's First Christmas. Swanson, Maggie, illus. LC 83-83293. (Illus.). 24 p. 15cm. (First little golden book). c.1984. (ISBN 0-307-10127-4). (ISBN 0-307-68151-3). Western Pub. Co.
--A Day in Life of Oscar the Grouch. Davis, Bill (1949-), illus. LC 81-83507. (Illus.). 32p. (Sesame Street Read-Aloud Bks.). (ps). 1982. (ISBN 0-307-11611-5, Golden Pr). (ISBN 0-307-61611-8). Western Pub.
--A Day in the Life of Oscar the Grouch: Featuring Jim Henson's Sesame Street Muppets. Davis, Bill (1949-), illus. LC 81-81630. (Illus.). 24 p. 27cm. c.1981. (ISBN 0-307-23138-0). Western Pub. Co. in Conjunction with Children's Television Workshop.
--Early Bird on Sesame Street: Featuring Jim Henson's Sesame Street Muppets. Leigh, Tom, illus. Children's Television Workshop LC 80-50848. (Illus.). 26 p. 26cm. c.1980. (ISBN 0-307-23116-X). Western Pub. Co. in Conjunction with Children's Television Workshop.
--The Sesame Street Storybook Alphabet: Featuring Jim Henson's Sesame Street Muppets. Cooke, Tom, illus. LC 79-91475. (Illus.). 27cm. 28p. (Children's Television Workshop). c.1980. Western Pub. Co.
--The Sesame Street Sun: Featuring Jim Hensons's Sesame Street Muppets. Kirk, Tim, illus. LC 80-84526. (Illus.). 26 p. 27cm. c.1981. (ISBN 0-307-23136-4). Western Pub. Co. in Conjunction with Children's Television Workshop.
--When You Were a Baby. Sanderson, Ruth, illus. LC 80-85029. (Illus.). 24 p. 21cm. (little golden book). c.1982. (ISBN 0-307-02099-1). Golden Press.
--Which One Doesn't Belong?. And Other Puzzles from Sesame Street : Featuring Jim Henson's Sesame Street Muppets. McSaparran, Kimberly A., illus. Children's Television Workshop LC 80-83290. (Illus.). 26 p. 26cm. c.1981. (ISBN 0-307-23127-5). Western Pub. Co. in Conjunction with Children's Television Workshop.
Hayward, Linda, ed. see Grimm, Jakob Ludwig Karl (1785-1863) & Grimm, Wilhelm Karl.
Hayward, Linda, ed. see Loof, Jan.
Hayward, Linda, tr. see Loof, Jan.
Hayward, Linda, tr. see Mayrocker, Friederike.
Hayward, Linda & Henson, Jim, pseud. (1936-)
--The Case of the Missing Duckie. Henson, James Maury. Swanson, Maggie, illus. LC 81-83508. (Illus.). 25 p. 27cm. (Sesame Street read-aloud book). c.1981. (ISBN 0-307-11609-3). (ISBN 0-307-61699-1). Western Pub. Co. in Conjunction with Children's Television Workshop.
--Sesame Seasons: Featuring Jim Henson's Sesame Street Muppets. Henson, James Maury. Brown, Richard Eric (1946-), illus. LC 80-84193. (Illus.). 61 p. 29cm. c.1981. (ISBN 0-307-15550-1). (ISBN 0-307-65550-4). Western Pub. Co.
--Twiddlebugs at Work: Featuring Jim Henson's Sesame Street Muppets. Henson, James Maury. Trivas, Irene, illus. LC 80-50850. (Illus.). 27cm. 26p. c.1980. (ISBN 0-307-23115-1). Western Pub. Co.
Hayward, Max, ed. see Chukovsky, Kornei Ivanovich.
Hayward, Mildred
--How Honey Bear Got His Name. Carroll, J. A., illus. LC 47-30702. 30 p. illus. (part col.) 24 cm. 1947. B. Humphries.

AUTHOR INDEX HEIDE, FLORENCE

Heath, Virginia & Fairfield, Frances
--Little Stories of Great Pictures. (Illus.). 32p. 1903. L. H. Nelson Co.
Heath, William L. (1924-)
--The Earthquake Man. 1st ed. LC 80-20270. p. cm. c.1980. (ISBN 0-8253-0008-8). Beaufort Books.
--Max the Great. Koda, Dorothy, illus. LC 76-44620. (Illus.). 88 p. 24cm. c.1977. (ISBN 0-8448-1038-X). Crane Russak.
--Most Valuable Player. Lawrence, Spencer, illus. LC 72-88168. (Illus.). 156 p. 21cm. 1973. (ISBN 0-15-255720-2). Harcourt Brace Jovanovich.
Heathers, Anne
--Four Puppies. Obligado, Lilian Isabel (1931-), illus. (ps-2). 1960. (ISBN 0-307-61405-0, Golden Pr). Western Pub.
Heathers, Anne & Frances, Esteban (1915-)
--Handful of Surprises. 1st ed. LC 61-6117. (Illus.). 28cm. (gr. k-3). 1961. (ISBN 0-15-233257-X). HarBraceJ.
--The Thread Soldier. LC 60-6210. (Illus.). unpaged. 18cm. c.1960. Harcourt, Brace.
Heaton, Ava
--Shu Shu Land & Other Stories. 1980. (ISBN 0-533-04582-7). Vantage.
Heaton, Hugh
--Albert, the Camel's Son. Sellen, H. E. M., illus. 44p. (gr. k-1). 1949. Oxford University Press.
--The Story of Madame Hen and Little Horace. Sellen, H. E. M., illus. 35p. (gr. k-1). 1948. Oxford University Press.
--The Story of Professor Porky. 36p. (gr. k-1). 1947. Oxford University Press.
Heaton, William
--The Story of Robin Hood, 1 of 4 vols. LC 14-22086. 2 p. l., vii-xii, 13-219 p. col. plates. 17 cm. (The True Crusoe Ser.). 1870. Cassell, Petter, and Galpin.
Heatter, Basil (1918-)
--Against Odds. LC 72-125141. (Illus.). 151 p. 21cm. (Ariel book). 1970. Farrar, Straus & Giroux.
--The Black Coast. 1967. Farrar, Straus And Giroux.
--Wreck Ashore!. LC 73-87210. 154 p. 21cm. (Ariel book). 1969. Farrar, Straus & Giroux.
Heaven, Constance (1911-)
--The Fires of Glenlochy. LC 75-44091. 240p. 1976. (ISBN 0-698-10726-8, Coward). Putnam Pub Group.
Heavey, Jean
--The Pastor's Dog. Blaisdell, Elinore (1904-), illus. LC 51-13720. 155 p. illus. 21 cm. 1951. Scribner.
Heavey, Regina & Stewart, Harriet L.
--Teen-Age Tales: Bks. A,B,C. 2d Ed. ed. 3v. (various p.) illus. (pt. col.) 23cm. 1966, c.1959. Heath.
Heavilin, Jay
--Fast Ball Pitcher. 1st ed. Kweskin, Sam, illus. LC 65-14017. 143 p. illus. 22 cm. (Signal book). 1965. Doubleday.
--Fear Rides High. 1st ed. Komoda, Kiyoaki (1937-), illus. LC 67-1805. (Illus.). 141 p. 22cm. (Doubleday signal book). 1967. Doubleday.
Heavilin, Jay, ed.
--Nonsense Book of Nonsense. (Illus.). (gr. 2 up). 1964. (ISBN 0-394-81427-4). (ISBN 0-394-91427-9). Random.
Hebb, David
--Cars in Pictures. LC 65-15816. (Illus.). 96 p. 27cm. (Visual industry series). 1965. Sterling Pub. Co.
Hebden, Mark, pseud., see Harris, John.
Hebden, Mark, pseud. (1916-)
--A Pride of Dolphins. Harris, John. LC 74-26710. 304p. 1975. (ISBN 0-15-174031-3). HarBraceJ.
Hecht, Ben (1893-1964)
--The Cat That Jumped Out of the Story. 1st ed. Bacon, Peggy, pseud. (1895-), illus. Bacon, Margaret Frances. LC 47-12371. 31 p. illus. (part col.) 21 cm. 1947. J. C. Winston Co.
--Treasury of Ben Hecht. N.D. Crown Pub Inc.
Hecht, Henri Joseph see Maik, Henri, pseud.
Hecht, Herbert T.
--Timely Tales. (Illus.). 47p. 1983. (ISBN 0-533-05574-1). Vantage.
Heck, Bessie Holland (1911-)
--Cactus Kevin. 1st ed. Bjorklund, Lorence F. (1913-1978), illus. LC 65-19711. 157 p. illus. 21 cm. 1965. World Pub. Co.
--Captain Pete. Cassell, Robert H., illus. LC 67-13823. 152p. illus. 21cm. 1967. World.
--Cave-in at Mason's Mine. Robinson, Charles (1931-), illus. LC 80-18637. p. cm. 1980. (ISBN 0-684-16718-2). Scribner.
--Golden Arrow. Robinson, Charles (1931-), illus. LC 81-4099. (Illus.). vii, 136 p. 22cm. c.1981. (ISBN 0-684-16882-0). Scribner.
--The Hopeful Years. Bjorklund, Lorence F. (1913-1978), illus. LC 64-20963. 185 p. illus. 21 cm. 1964. World Pub. Co.
--Millie. Stevens, Mary, illus. LC 61-14111. (Illus.). 185 p. 21cm. 1961. World Pub. Co.
--The Year at Doggy. Frame, Paul (1913-), illus. LC 66-13899. 156p. illus. 21cm. 1966. World.
Heck, Joseph
--Dinosaur Riddles. Hoffman, Sanford, illus. LC 82-6429. (Illus.). 126 p. 22cm. c.1982. (ISBN 0-671-45201-0). J. Messner.
--Dinosaur Riddles. Hoffman, Sanford, illus. LC 82-4889. p. cm. c.1982. (ISBN 0-671-45547-8). Wanderer Books.
Heckel, Inge, jt. auth. see Goldin, Diana.
Heckel, Pearl Bash
--From Ark to Zoo. LC 54-1208. unpaged. illus. 23cm. 1953. Comet Press Books.
Heckelmann, Charles Newman (1913-)
--Danger Rides the Range. LC 50-9642. 221 p. front. 20 cm. 1950. Cupples and Leon.
--Outlaw Valley. LC 50-9643. 221 p. front. 20 cm. 1950. Cupples and Leon Co.
Heckla
--Three of Us. [illegible] Co.
Heckman, Anna F.
--His Great Ambition. LC 12-34164. 317 p. front., plates. 19 1/2 cm. 1895. Presbyterian Board of Publication and Sabbath--School Work.
Heckmann, Herbert (1931-)
--A Boy Called Spoons. Janosch, pseud. (1931-), illus. Eckert, Horst. (gr. 2-6). 1975. (ISBN 0-8277-4490-0). British Bk Ctr.
Hectus, Carol
--Silver Visits the Attic. 1st. ed. (Illus.). 30 p. 21cm. 1974. (ISBN 0-533-00776-3). Vantage Press.
Hedderwick, Mairi (1939-)
--Katie Morag Delivers the Mail. Hedderwick, Mairi (1939-), illus. (Illus.). 32p. (gr. 3-6). 1984. (ISBN 0-370-30569-8, Pub. by the Bodley Head). Merrimack Pub Cir.
Heddle, Enid Moodie (1904-), ed.
--The Boomerang Book of Legendary Tales. Parker, Nancy Winslow (1930-), illus. LC 57-4959. 150p. illus. 23cm. 1957. Longmans, Green.
Hedges, Sid G. & Ruete, T.
--The African Heir. (The Star Library). N.D. Frederick Warne & Co.
Hedges, Ursula M. (1940-)
--Carol & Johnny Go to New Guinea. (gr. 1-3). N.D. Southern Pub.
--Down Under with Carol and Johnny. LC 77-180600. (Illus.). 127 p. 21cm. (Penguin series). 1973. Review and Herald Pub. Association.
Hedrick, Elinor, jt. auth. see Van Noy, Kathryne.
Heenan, Barry
--The Treasure Seekers: The Story of William Phips. LC 70-90058. (Illus.). 144 p. 25cm. 1969. T. S. Denison.
Heermans, Forbes (1856-)
--Thirteen: Stories of the Far West. LC 12-34680. 263 p. 18 1/2 cm. 1887. C. W. Bardeen.
Heesakkers, Wim
--My Little Brother. Heesakkers, Wim, illus. LC 85-1341. p. cm. 1985. (ISBN 0-8120-5643-4). Barron's.
Hefflefinger, Jane, jt. auth. see Hoffman, Elaine.
Hefflefinger, Jane & Hoffman, Elaine
--One Hundred Dresses at a Time. N.D. Elk Grove Press.
Heffron, Dorris (1944-)
--Crusty Crossed. LC 77-362015. 177 p. 21cm. 1976. (ISBN 0-333-19735-6). Macmillan.
--A Nice Fire and Some Moonpennies. LC 70-179721. 160 p. 22cm. 1972, c.1971. Atheneum.
Heflin, Mary L., ed. see Savage, Charles D.
Hefter, Richard see Rogers, Fred McFeely.
Hefter, Richard (1942-)
--An Animal Alphabet. Hefter, Richard (1942-), illus. LC 73-92606. (Illus.). 32 p. 24cm. 1974. (ISBN 0-88470-002-X). (ISBN 0-88470-002-X). Strawberry Books; Distributed by Larousse, New York.
--Babysitter Bears. Hefter, Richard (1942-), illus. LC 83-8205. p. cm. (Stickybear Bks.). c.1983. (ISBN 0-911787-08-9). Optimum Resource.
--Bears at Work. Hefter, Richard (1942-), illus. LC 83-2192. (Illus.). 32p. 1st U.S. edition. (Stickybear Bks.). (ps-1). 1983. (ISBN 0-911787-00-3). Optimum Res Inc.
--Bears Away from Home. Hefter, Richard (1942-), illus. LC 83-4149. (Illus.). (Stickybear Bks.). (gr. 3-6). 1983. (ISBN 0-911787-05-4). Optimum Res Inc.
--Fast Food. Hefter, Richard (1942-), illus. LC 83-6734. (Illus.). 36 p. 25cm. (Stickybear bk.). (Strawberry Library of First Learning). c.1983. (ISBN 0-911787-09-7). Optimum Resource.
--Goof-off Goose's Dinner Party. Hefter, Richard (1942-), illus. LC 82-80260. (Illus.). 20 p. 17cm. (A Random House Sniffy Bk.). c.1982. (ISBN 0-394-85399-7). Random House.
--Hippo Jogs for Health. Perle, Ruth Lerner, ed. Hefter, Richard (1942-), illus. LC 77-16320. (Illus.). 33 p. 25cm. (Sweet Pickles Ser.). c.1977. Holt, Rinehart and Winston.
--Jobs for Bears. Hefter, Richard (1942-), illus. LC 83-2197. (Illus.). 32p. 1st U.S. edition. (Stickybear Bks.). (ps-1). 1983. (ISBN 0-911787-02-X). Optimum Res Inc.
--Kiss Me, I'm Vulture. Hefter, Richard (1942-), illus. LC 78-16268. p. cm. (Sweet Pickles Ser.). 1979. (ISBN 0-03-042071-7). Holt, Rinehart and Winston.
--Lion Is Down in the Dumps. Perle, Ruth Lerner, ed. Hefter, Richard (1942-), illus. LC 77-7256. p. cm. (Sweet Pickles Ser.). 1977. (ISBN 0-03-021441-6). Holt, Rinehart, and Winston.
--Lots of Little Bears. Hefter, Richard (1942-), illus. LC 83-2184. (Illus.). 32p. 1st U.S. edition. (Stickybear Bks.). (ps-1). 1983. (ISBN 0-911787-04-6). Optimum Res Inc.
--Moody Moose Buttons. Perle, Ruth Lerner, ed. Hefter, Richard (1942-), illus. LC 77-7255. p. cm. (Sweet Pickles Ser.). 1977. (ISBN 0-03-021446-7). Holt, Rinehart and Winston
--Neat Feet. Hefter, Richard (1942-), illus. LC 83-8035. (Illus.). (Stickybear Bks.). (gr. 3-6). 1983. (ISBN 0-911787-07-0). Optimum Res Inc.
--No Kicks for Dog. Hefter, Richard (1942-), illus. LC 78-17009. (Illus.). 32 p. 25cm. (Sweet Pickles Ser.). c.1978. (ISBN 0-03-042011-3). Holt, Rinehart and Winston.
--A Noise in the Closet. Hefter, Richard (1942-), illus. LC 74-81377. (Illus.). 32 p. 24cm. 1974. (ISBN 0-88470-012-7). (ISBN 0-88470-013-5). Strawberry Books : Distributed by Larousse.
--One Bear, Two Bears: The Strawberry Number Book. Hefter, Richard (1942-), illus. 118p. 1980. (ISBN 0-07-027825-3). McGraw.
--One White Crocodile Smile. Hefter, Richard (1942-), illus. (Illus.). (Strawberry Books Ser.). 1977. (ISBN 0-448-14404-2, G&D). Putnam Pub Group.
--One White Crocodile Smile: A Number Book. Hefter, Richard (1942-), illus. LC 73-92607. (Illus.). 32 p. 24cm. 1974. (ISBN 0-88470-004-6). (ISBN 0-88470-004-6). Strawberry Books; Distributed by Larousse.
--Pig Thinks Pink. Perle, Ruth Lerner, ed. Hefter, Richard (1942-), illus. LC 78-9581. (Illus.). 32 p. 25cm. (Sweet Pickles Ser.). 1978. (ISBN 0-03-042051-2). Holt, Rinehart, and Winston.
--The Stickybear's Scary Night. Hefter, Richard (1942-), illus. LC 84-22749. (Illus.). 32 p. 21cm. c.1984. (ISBN 0-911787-41-0). Optimum Resource.
--Stork Spills the Beans. Perle, Ruth Lerner, ed. Hefter, Richard (1942-), illus. LC 76-44020. (Illus.). 32 p. 26cm. (Sweet Pickles Ser.). c.1977. (ISBN 0-03-018076-7). Holt, Rinehart and Winston.
--The Strawberry Book of Colors. Hefter, Richard (1942-), illus. LC 80-14610. p. cm. 1980, c.1975. (ISBN 0-07-027826-1). McGraw-Hill.
--The Strawberry Look Book. Hefter, Richard (1942-), illus. 120p. 1980. (ISBN 0-07-027824-5). McGraw.
--The Strawberry Word Book. Hefter, Richard (1942-), illus. LC 73-92605. (Illus.). 32 p. 24cm. 1974. (ISBN 0-88470-000-3). (ISBN 0-88470-000-3). Strawberry Books; Distributed by Larousse.
--Turtle Throws a Tantrum. Perle, Ruth Lerner, ed. Hefter, Richard (1942-), illus. LC 77-16319. (Illus.). 36 p. 25cm. (Sweet Pickles Ser.). c.1978. (ISBN 0-03-042061-X). Holt, Rinehart and Winston.
--Very Worried Walrus. Perle, ruth Lerner, ed. Hefter, Richard (1942-), illus. LC 76-43092. (Illus.). 32 p. 26cm. (Sweet Pickles Ser.). c.1977. (ISBN 0-03-018091-0). Holt, Rinehart and Winston.
--Watch Out!. Hefter, Richard (1942-), illus. LC 83-2190. 32p. 1st U.S. edition. (Stickybear Bks.). (ps-1). 1983. (ISBN 0-911787-03-8). Optimum Res Inc.
--Weekly Reader Books Presents Quick Lunch Munch. Perle, Ruth Lerner, ed. Hefter, Richard (1942-), illus. LC 81-7805. (Illus.). 36 p. 21cm. (Sweet Pickles). c.1981. (ISBN 0-937524-08-5). Euphrosyne.
--Weekly Reader Books Presents Robot S.P.3. Perle, Ruth Lerner, ed. Hefter, Richard (1942-), illus. LC 81-7759. (Illus.). 36 p. 21cm. (Sweet Pickles). c.1981. (ISBN 0-937524-09-3). Euphrosyne.
--Where Is the Bear?. Hefter, Richard (1942-), illus. LC 83-6296. p. cm. (Stickybear Books). c.1983. (ISBN 0-911787-06-2). Optimum Resources.
--Who Can Trust You, Kangaroo?. Hefter, Richard (1942-), illus. LC 78-16748. p. cm. (Sweet Pickles Ser.). 1979. (ISBN 0-03-042031-8). Holt, Rinehart and Winston.
--Xerus Won't Allow It. Perle, Ruth Lerner, ed. Hefter, Richard (1942-), illus. LC 77-16321. (Illus.). 32 p. 25cm. (Sweet Pickles Ser.). c.1978. (ISBN 0-03-042076-8). Holt, Rinehart and Winston.
--Yakety-Yak-Yak Yak. Perle, Ruth Lerner, ed. Hefter, Richard (1942-), illus. LC 77-7250. p. cm. (Sweet Pickles Ser.). 1977. (ISBN 0-03-021436-X). Holt, Rinehart, and Winston.
--Zip Goes Zebra. Perle, Ruth Lerner, ed. Hefter, Richard (1942-), illus. LC 76-44019. (Illus.). 32 p. 26cm. (Sweet Pickles Ser.). c.1977. (ISBN 0-03-018081-3). Holt, Rinehart and Winston.
Hefter, Richard (1942-), ed.
--Strawberry Mother Goose. new ed. Di Fiori, Lawrence, illus. LC 75-3808. (Illus.). 40p. (ps-1). 1975. (ISBN 0-88470-016-X, Pub by One Strawberry). (ISBN 0-88470-017-8). McGraw.
Hefter, Richard (1942-), illus.
--Speedy Delivery. LC 73-15437. 44p (Pub. by Small World Enterprises). (I Am, I Can, I Will Ser.). 1979. (ISBN 0-8331-0037-8). Hubbard Sci.
--Speedy Delivery: A Story from Mister Rogers' Neighbourhood. Muro, John, photos by. Moskof, Martin Stephen (1930-), designed by. LC 73-15437. (Illus.). 42 p. 22cm. (Mister Rogers' neighborhood library). c.1973. Small World Enterprises.
Hefter, Richard (1942-) & Moskof, Martin Stephen (1930-)
--Christopher's Parade. Hefter, Richard (1942-), illus. LC 72-394. (Illus.). 33 p. 29cm. 1972. (ISBN 0-8193-0586-3). (ISBN 0-8193-0587-1). Parents' Magazine Press.
--Everything: An Alphabet, Number, Reading, Counting & Color Identification Bk. Hefter, Richard (1942-), illus. LC 72-153656. (Illus.). color ils. 40p. (gr. k-2). 1971. (ISBN 0-8193-0488-3, Four Winds). (ISBN 0-8193-0489-1). Scholastic Inc.
--The Great Big Alphabet Picture Book with Lots of Words. Hefter, Richard (1942-), illus. LC 72-183030. (Illus.). 35 p. 32cm. 1972. (ISBN 0-448-02930-8). (ISBN 0-448-04436-6). Grosset & Dunlap.
Hegarty, Reginald Beaton (1906-1973)
--The Rope's End. Tripp, Wallace Whitney (1940-), illus. (Illus.). (gr. 4-6). 1965. (ISBN 0-395-06809-6). HM.
Hegel, Irma (1901-)
--Black Icicles. LC 41-278852. 61 p. 18 cm. c.1941. The Wartburg Press.
--Merry Christmas Was Her Name. LC 48-15196. 64 p. 19 cm. 1947. Wartburg Press.
--Something for Nothing. LC 41-278861. 64 p. 18 cm. c.1941. The Wartburg Press.
--The Thimble Farm Mystery. LC 43-16893. 64 p. 18 cm. 1943. The Wartburg Press.
Heggen, Thomas
--Mister Roberts. Bryant, Samuel Hanks, illus. (Keith Jennison Large Type Bks). (gr. 6 up). N.D. (ISBN 0-531-00237-3). Watts.
Hegner, Gladys M.
--The House Wren Family. Hartzell, William, illus. LC 56-11654. unpaged. illus. 20cm. 1956. Comet Press Books.
Hegwood, Mamie
--My Friend Fish. 1st ed. De Groat, Diane (1947-), illus. LC 75-5822. p. cm. 1975. Holt, Rinehart and Winston.
Heibert, A. W., et al., illus.
--The Friendly Playmate and Other Stories from Norway. Poulsson, Anne Emilie (1853-1939), tr. LC 31-24065. 133 p. col. front., illus. 21 c. c.1931. Lothrop, Lee & Shepard Co.
Heide, Florence Parry see Allen, Alex B, pseud.
Heide, Florence Parry (1919-)
--Alphabet Zoop. Mathews, Sally, illus. (Illus.). 1970. E.P. Dutton & Co.
--Alphabet Zoop. Mathews, Sally, illus. 64p. 1970. (ISBN 0-8415-2017-8). McCall Publishing Company.
--Banana Blitz. LC 82-48753. p. cm. c.1983. (ISBN 0-8234-0480-3). Holiday House.
--Banana Twist. LC 78-6818. 111 p. 21cm. c.1978. (ISBN 0-8234-0334-3). Holiday House. **Award: (ALA).**
--Benjamin Budge and Barnaby Ball. Matthews, Sally, illus. LC 68-15709. 1 v. (unpaged) col. illus. 21 x 24cm. c.1967. Four Winds.
--Benjamin Budge & Barnaby Ball. Matthews, Sally, illus. LC 68-15709. (Illus.). (gr. k-3). 1968, c.1967. (ISBN 0-590-07104-1, Four Winds). Schol Bk Serv.
--Benjamin Budge & Barnaby Ball. Matthews, Sally, illus. (Illus.). 32p. (gr. k-3). 1970. (ISBN 0-590-02353-5). (ISBN 0-590-04397-8). Scholastic Inc.
--Giants Are Very Brave People. Robinson, Charles (1931-), illus. LC 75-93857. (Illus.). 42 p. 27cm. 1970. Parents' Magazine Press.
--Growing Anyway Up. (gr. 5-7). 1976. Harper & Row.
--Growing Anyway up. 1st ed. LC 75-40033. 128 p. 21cm. c.1976. (ISBN 0-397-31657-7). Lippincott.
--The Key. 1st ed. Forberg, Ati, pseud. (1925-), illus. Forberg, Beate Gropius. LC 76-134813. (Illus.). 56 p. 22cm. 1971. Atheneum.
--Little One. Longtemps, Kenneth (1933-), illus. LC 70-112647. (Illus.). 2 color ils. 32p. (gr. k-3). N.D. (ISBN 0-87460-138-X). Lion Bks.
--Look! Look!. A Story Book. Nicklaus, Carol, illus. (Illus.). 1971. E.P. Dutton & Co.

--Look! Look! A Story Book. Nicklaus, Carol, illus. LC 76-142340. (Illus.). 32 p. 24cm. 1971. (ISBN 0-8415-2034-8). McCall Pub. Co.
--Maximilian Becomes Famous. Renfro, Ed, illus. LC 70-81922. (Illus.). 33 p. 26cm. 1969. Funk & Wagnalls.
--My Castle. Shimin, Symeon (1902-), illus. LC 68-54818. (Illus.). 46 p. 27cm. 1972. (ISBN 0-07-027863-6). McGraw-Hill.
--The Problem with Pulcifer. 1st ed. Glasser, Judith, illus. LC 81-48606. (Illus.). 54 p. 21cm. c.1982. (ISBN 0-397-32001-9). (ISBN 0-397-32002-7). Lippincott.
--Sebastian. Fraser, Betty M., pseud. (1928-), illus. Fraser, Elizabeth Marr. Van Clief, Sylvia Worth, contrib. by. LC 68-21121. (Illus.). 36 p. 26cm. 1968. Funk & Wagnalls.
--Secret Dreamer, Secret Dreams. (gr. 6-8). 1978. Harper & Row.
--Secret Dreamer, Secret Dreams. LC 78-8736. 95 p. 21cm. c.1978. (ISBN 0-397-31812-X). Lippincott.
--The Shrinking of Treehorn. Gorey, Edward St. John (1925-), illus. LC 78-151753. (Illus.). 63 p. 16cm. 1971. (ISBN 0-8234-0189-8). Holiday House. **Awards: (NYT); (ALA).**
--Some Things Are Scary. Osburn, illus. (Illus.). (gr. k-3). 1971. (ISBN 0-590-01619-9, Schol Pap). Schol Bk Serv.
--Sound of Sunshine, Sound of Rain. Longtemps, Kenneth (1933-), illus. LC 77-117555. (Illus.). 40 p. 24cm. 1970. Parents' Magazine Press.
--Tales for the Perfect Child. Chess, Victoria (1939-), illus. LC 84-5710. p. cm. 80p. 1985. (ISBN 0-688-03892-1). (ISBN 0-688-03893-X). Lothrop, Lee & Shepard Books.
--Time Flies!. Hafner, Marylin (1925-), illus. LC 84-47833. 1984. (ISBN 0-8234-0542-7). Holiday.
--Time's Up. 11 x 12 1/2. 148p. Repr. of 1982 ed (Pub. by Holiday House). (17 pt.). (gr. 4-6). N.D. Am Printing Hse.
--Time's Up!. Hafner, Marylin (1925-), illus. LC 81-13240. (Illus.). 119 p. 21cm. c.1982. (ISBN 0-8234-0441-2). Holiday House. **Award: (ALA).**
--Treehorn's Treasure. Gorey, Edward St. John (1925-), illus. LC 81-4043. p. cm. c.1981. (ISBN 0-8234-0425-0). Holiday House. **Award: (ALA).**
--Treehorn's Wish. Gorey, Edward St. John (1925-), illus. LC 83-6240. (Illus.). 64p. (ps-7). 1984. (ISBN 0-8234-0493-5). (ISBN 0-8234-0493-5). Holiday.
--The Wendy Puzzle. LC 82-80818. p. cm. c.1982. (ISBN 0-8234-0463-3). Holiday House.
--When the Sad One Comes to Stay. LC 75-9747. 74 p. 21cm. 1975. (ISBN 0-397-31651-8). Lippincott.
--Who Needs Me?. Mathews, Sally, illus. LC 71-159011. (Illus.). 32 p. 29cm. 1971. (ISBN 0-8066-1134-0). Augsburg Pub. House.

Heide, Florence Parry (1919-) & Heide, Roxanne
--Black Magic at Brillstone. Krush, Joe (1918-), illus. LC 81-487. p. cm. (Pilot books). 1981. (ISBN 0-8075-0782-2). A. Whitman.
--Body in the Brillstone Garage. Krush, Joe (1918-), illus. LC 79-18368. p. cm. (Pilot books). 1979. (ISBN 0-8075-0825-X). A. Whitman.
--The Body in the Brillstone Garage. Krush, Joe (1918-), illus. 1980. Whitman.
--Brillstone Break-in. Krush, Joe (1918-), illus. LC 77-2220. 127 p. 21cm. (Pilot book). c.1977. (ISBN 0-8075-0888-8). A. Whitman.
--The Face at the Brillstone Window. Krush, Joe (1918-), illus. LC 78-15060. p. cm. (Pilot books). 1978. (ISBN 0-8075-2216-3). A. Whitman.
--Fear at Brillstone. Krush, Joe (1918-), illus. LC 78-1307. 127 p. 21cm. (Pilot books). c.1978. (ISBN 0-8075-2304-6). A. Whitman.
--A Monster Is Coming! A Monster Is Coming!. Farrow, Rachi, illus. LC 80-10955. (Illus.). 32 p. 22cm. (Easy-read story book). 1980. (ISBN 0-531-03449-6). F. Watts.
--Mystery at Keyhole Carnival. Fleishman, Seymour (1918-), illus. LC 76-45426. p. cm. (Pilot books series). (A Spotlight Club Mystery). 1976. (ISBN 0-8075-5361-1). A. Whitman.
--Mystery at Southport Cinema. Fleishman, Seymour (1918-), illus. LC 78-1300. (Illus.). 128 p. 21cm. (Pilot books). (A Spotlight Club Mystery). c.1978. (ISBN 0-8075-5363-8). A. Whitman.
--Mystery of the Bewitched Bookmobile. Fleishman, Seymour (1918-), illus. LC 75-6763. (Illus.). 128 p. 21cm. (Pilot books). (A Spotlight Club Mystery). 1975. A. Whitman.
--Mystery of the Forgotten Island. Fleishman, Seymour (1918-), illus. LC 79-18367. p. cm. (Pilot books). 1979. (ISBN 0-8075-5376-X). A. Whitman.
--Mystery of the Lonely Lantern. Fleishman, Seymour (1918-), illus. LC 76-28537. p. cm. (Pilot books series). (A Spotlight Club Mystery). 1976. (ISBN 0-8075-5377-8). A. Whitman.
--Mystery of the Melting Snowman. Fleishman, Seymour (1918-), illus. LC 74-16333. (Illus.). 128 p. 21cm. (Their A Spotlight Club mystery). 1974. (ISBN 0-8075-5378-6). A. Whitman.
--Mystery of the Midnight Message. Fleishman, Seymour (1918-), illus. LC 77-14382. p. cm. (Pilot books). (A Spotlight Club Mystery). 1977. (ISBN 0-8075-5381-6). A. Whitman.
--Mystery of the Mummy's Mask. Fleishman, Seymour (1918-), illus. LC 78-31728. (Illus.). 127 p. 21cm. (Pilot books). (A Spotlight Club Mystery). c.1979. (ISBN 0-8075-5384-0). A. Whitman.
--Mystery of the Vanishing Visitor. Fleishman, Seymour (1918-), illus. LC 75-33634. (Illus.). 128 p. 21cm. (Spotlight Club mystery). c.1975. (ISBN 0-8075-5388-3). A. Whitman.
--Mystery on Danger Road. Fleishman, Seymour (1918-), illus. LC 83-1324. p. cm. 1983. (ISBN 0-8075-5396-4). A. Whitman.
--Time Bomb at Brillstone. LC 82-10863. p. cm. 1982. (ISBN 0-8075-7942-4). A. Whitman.

Heide, Florence Parry (1919-) & Van Clief, Sylvia Worth
--The Day It Snowed in Summer. Longtemps, Kenneth (1933-), illus. LC 68-13072. (Illus.). 32 p. 26cm. (Fun & frolic book). 1968. Funk & Wagnalls.
--Fables You Shouldn't Pay Any Attention To. LC 77-14253. (Illus.). 62 p. 24cm. c.1978. (ISBN 0-397-31782-4). Lippincott.
--The Hidden Box Mystery. Fleishman, Seymour (1918-), illus. LC 72-13351. (Illus.). 128 p. 21cm. (Pilot books series). (A Spotlight Club Mystery). 1973. (ISBN 0-8075-3270-3). A. Whitman.
--How Big Am I?. Suyeoka, George, illus. LC 68-10487. (Illus.). 32 p. 23cm. 1968. Follett Pub. Co.
--It Never Is Dark. Almquist, Don (1929-), illus. (Illus.). (Wonderland Picture Books). (ps-3). 1967. (ISBN 0-695-84390-7). (ISBN 0-695-44390-9). Follett.
--It Never Is Dark. Almquist, Don (1929-), illus. LC 67-21152. 32p. illus. (pt. col.) 22cm. 1968. Follett.
--Maximilian. Renfro, Ed, illus. LC 67-26040. (Illus.). 32 p. 26cm. 1967. Funk & Wagnalls.
--Mystery at MacAdoo Zoo. Fleishman, Seymour (1918-), illus. LC 73-7316. (Illus.). 127 p. 21cm. (Their A Spotlight Club mystery). 1973. (ISBN 0-8075-5358-1). Whitman.
--The Mystery of the Missing Suitcase. Fleishman, Seymour (1918-), illus. LC 72-83683. (Illus.). 127 p. 21cm. 1972. (ISBN 0-8075-5382-4). A. Whitman.
--Mystery of the Silver Tag. Fleishman, Seymour (1918-), illus. LC 75-188429. (Illus.). 128p. (Pilot Bks. - Spotlight Club Mysteries Ser.). (gr. 3-7). 1972. (ISBN 0-8075-5387-5). A Whitman.
--Mystery of the Whispering Voice. Fleishman, Seymour (1918-), illus. LC 74-8511. (Illus.). 127 p. 20cm. (Pilot books series). (A Spotlight Club Mystery). 1974. (ISBN 0-8075-5389-1). A. Whitman.
--The New Neighbor. Warshaw, Jerry (1929-), illus. LC 71-93805. (Illus.). 32 p. 23cm. 1970. Follett.
--Songs to Sing About Things You Think About. Schmidt, Rosalie Petrash, illus. LC 76-155016. (Illus.). color ils. 48p. (gr. 1-3). 1971. (ISBN 0-381-99798-7). John Day.
--That's What Friends Are For. Turkle, Brinton Cassaday (1915-), illus. LC 68-27267. (Illus.). 39 p. 1968. Four Winds Press.

Heide, Roxanne, jt. auth. see Heide, Florence Parry.

Heiderstadt, Dorothy (1907-)
--A Bow for Turtle. Ferguson, William, illus. LC 60-5668. 1960. David Mckay Company Inc.
--Indian Friends and Foes. (Illus.). 1958. David McKay Company.
--Jimmy Flies. Veise, Inger, illus. LC 30-245150. 95 p. col. illus. 16 cm. 1930. Frederick A. Stokes Company.
--Lois Says Aloha. Geer, Charles Hand (1922-), illus. LC 63-9629. 150 p. illus. 21 cm. 1963. Nelson.
--Marie Tanglehair. Koering, Ursula (1921-), illus. LC 65-11843. 120p. illus. 21cm. c.1965. McKay.
--More Indian Friends and Foes. (Illus.). 1963. David McKay Company.

Heidish, Marcy Moran (1947-)
--A Woman Called Moses: A Novel Based on the Life of Harriet Tubman. 1976. (ISBN 0-395-21535-8). HM.

Heifner, Fred
--Isaiah, Messenger for God. Johnston, Clifford, illus. LC 78-105150. (Illus.). 48 p. 24cm. (Biblearn series). c.1978. (ISBN 0-8054-4243-X). Broadman Press.

Heighway, Jane Alstine
--Outdoor Stories for Indoor Folk. Troth, Emma, illus. LC 17-172852. 4 p. l, 101, 1 p. front., plates. 19 cm. $0.7. c.1917. The Bobbs--Merrill Company.

Heilbroner, Joan Knapp (1922-)
--The Happy Birthday Present. Chalmers, Mary Eileen (1927-), illus. LC 61-12094. (Illus.). 5 7/8 x 8 1/2. 64p. (18 pt.). (I Can Read Bks.). (gr. k-3). 1961. (ISBN 0-06-022271-9). Har-Row. **Award: (ALA).**
--Robert the Rose Horse. Eastman, Philip Dey (1909-), illus. LC 62-9218. (Illus.). (gr. 1-2). 1962. (ISBN 0-394-80025-7). (ISBN 0-394-90025-1). Beginner.
--This Is the House Where Jack Lives. Aliki, pseud. (1929-), illus. Brandenberg, Aliki Liacouras. LC 62-7311. (Illus.). 5 7/8 x 8 1/2. 64p. (18 pt.). (I Can Read Bks.). (gr. k-3). 1962. (ISBN 0-06-022286-7). Har-Row.
--Tom the TV Cat. Murdocca, Salvatore, illus. LC 83-24600. (Illus.). 48 p. 24cm. (Step into reading. A Step 2 book). c.1984. (ISBN 0-394-86708-4). (ISBN 0-394-96708-9). Random House.

Heild, Mrs.
--Pet's Posy of Pictures and Short Stories. 180p. N.D. Cassell, Petter, & Galpin.
--Pet's Posy of Pictures and Stories, 1 of 6 vols. (Illus.). (Cosey Corner Ser. No. 2). N.D. Cassell, Peter, Galpin.

Heilman, Dan
--Daddy is an artist. Heilman, Dan, illus. LC 64-17215. 31cm. 34p. 1964. Allied Publications, Inc.

Heiman, Grover
--Jet Tanker. 1st Ed. LC 61-9047. 189p. 22cm. 1961. Holt, Rinehart and Winston.

Heiman, Grover George, Jr., jt. auth. see Montgomery, Rutherford George.

Heimburg, W., pseud., see Behrens, Bertha.

Heimburg, W., pseud.
--Christmas Stories. Behrens, Bertha. Davis, W. J., Mrs., tr. N.D. Frederick A Stokes Co.
--Christmas Stories. Behrens, Bertha. Davis, W. J., Mrs., tr. (Illus.). 1891. Worthington Co.

Heimeran, Ernst (1902-1955)
--The Story of the Coal-Black Horse. Braun-Fock, Beatrice, illus. LC 68-29535. (Illus.). 32 p. 29cm. 1968. Hart Pub. Co.
--The Story of the Coal-Black Horse. Heimeran, Ernst (1902-1955), illus. 48p. N.D. (ISBN 0-87460-177-0). (ISBN 0-87460-176-2). Lion Press.

Hein, Gustav, tr. see Grundtvig, Svend Hersleb.

Hein, Lucille Eleanor (1915-)
--From Sea to Shining Sea. Orfe, Joan, illus. LC 75-11839. (Illus.). 32 p. 25cm. c.1975. (ISBN 0-8170-0681-8). Judson Press.
--My Very Special Friend. Orfe, Joan, illus. LC 73-16790. (Illus.). 33 p. 25cm. 1974. (ISBN 0-8170-0618-4). Judson Press.
--Prayer Gifts for Christmas. Nelson, Carol, illus. LC 72-78557. (Illus.). 32 p. 1972. (ISBN 0-8066-1224-X). Augsburg Pub. House.
--A Tree I Can Call My Own. Orfe, Joan, illus. LC 78-6550. (Illus.). 29 p. 25cm. 1974. (ISBN 0-8170-0605-2). Judson Press.
--Walking in God's World. Orfe, Joan, illus. LC 72-75081. (Illus.). 27 p. 25cm. 1972. (ISBN 0-8170-0567-6). (ISBN 0-8170-0568-4). Judson Press.

Heine, Helme
--Friends. Heine, Helme, illus. LC 82-45313. (Illus.). 32p. (ps-3). 1982. (ISBN 0-689-50256-7, McElderry Bk). Atheneum.
--King Bounce the First. Heine, Helme, illus. LC 82-183495. (Illus.). 28p. 1st U.S. edition. 1982. (ISBN 0-907234-11-9, Pub. by Picture Bk Studio USA). Neugebauer Pr.
--Merry-Go-Round. Heine, Helme, illus. LC 80-65442. (Illus.). 26 p. 28cm. 1980. (ISBN 0-8120-5393-1). Barron's Educational Series Inc.
--The Most Wonderful Egg in the World. Heine, Helme, illus. LC 82-49350. p. cm. 1983. (ISBN 0-689-50280-X). Atheneum.
--Mr. Miller, the Dog. Heine, Helme, illus. LC 80-81298. (Illus.). 54 p. 21cm. 1st U.S. edition. 1980. (ISBN 0-689-50174-9). Atheneum. **Award: (NYT).**
--The Pigs' Wedding. Heine, Helme, illus. LC 78-57691. (Illus.). 26 p. 28cm. 1st U.S. edition. 1979, c.1978. (ISBN 0-689-50127-7). Atheneum.
--Superhare. Heine, Helme, illus. LC 79-84658. (gr. k-6). 1979. (ISBN 0-8120-5357-5). Barron.
--Three Little Friends:. The Alarm Clock. Heine, Helme, illus. 28p. 1985. (ISBN 0-689-71043-7). Atheneum McElderry.
--Three Little Friends:. The Racing Cart. Heine, Helme, illus. 28p. 1985. (ISBN 0-689-71045-3). Atheneum McElderry.
--Three Little Friends:. The Visitor. Heine, Helme, illus. 28p. 1985. (ISBN 0-689-71044-5). Atheneum McElderry.

Heinemann, Thea
--Stories of Jesus. Bolognese, Donald Alan (1934-), illus. Brooks, Walter, designed by. (Illus.). 223 p. 27cm. (Whitman library of giant books). 1968. Whitman Pub. Division, Western Pub. Co.

Heinlein, Robert Anson (1907-)
--Between Planets. Geary, Clifford N. (1916-), illus. (Illus.). 222 p. 21cm. 1951. Scribner.
--Beyond This Horizon. 1981. (ISBN 0-8398-2672-9, Gregg). G K Hall.
--Citizen of the Galaxy. (Illus.). (Hudson River Edition). (gr. 5-11). 1977. (ISBN 0-684-15364-5, ScribJ). Scribner.
--Farmer in the Sky. Geary, Clifford N. (1916-), illus. LC 50-14133. (Illus.). 216 p. 21cm. 1950. Scribner.
--Farnham's Freehold. 1964. (ISBN 0-399-10279-5). G. P. Putnam's Sons.
--Have Space Suit-Will Travel. LC 58-10638. 276p. illus. 21cm. 1958. (ISBN 0-684-12649-4). Scribner.
--I Will Fear No Evil. 1970. (ISBN 0-399-10460-7). G. P. Putnam's Sons.
--The Moon is a Harsh Mistress. 1966. (ISBN 0-399-10556-5). G. P. Putnam's Sons.
--Orphans of the Sky. 1964. (ISBN 0-399-10613-8). Putnam Pub Group.
--The Past Through Tomorrow: 'Future History' Stories. 667 p. 22cm. (His Future history series). 1967. Putnam.
--Podkayne of Mars: Her Life and Times. 1963. (ISBN 0-399-10642-1). Putnam Pub Group.
--Red Planet: A Colonial Boy on Mars. Geary, Clifford N. (1916-), illus. 211p. (gr. 4-10). 1949. Charles Scribner's Sons.
--Rocket Ship Galileo. Voter, Thomas W., illus. LC 47-6539. 212 p. illus. 21 cm. 1947. C. Scribner's Sons.
--The Rolling Stones. Geary, Clifford N. (1916-), illus. LC 52-13941. (Illus.). 276 p. 21cm. 1952. Scribner.
--Space Cadet. Geary, Clifford N. (1916-), illus. LC 48-4723. 242 p. illus. 21 cm. 1948. C. Scribner's Sons.
--The Star Beast. Geary, Clifford N. (1916-), illus. LC 54-9431. 282 p. 21cm. 1954. Scribner.
--Starman Jones. Geary, Clifford N. (1916-), illus. LC 53-12457. (Illus.). 305 p. 21cm. 1953. Scribner.
--Starship Troopers. 1960. (ISBN 0-399-20209-9). G. P. Putnam's Sons.
--Starship Troopers. LC 59-12950. 309 p. 21cm. 1959. Putnam.
--Stranger in a Strange Land. 1961. (ISBN 0-399-10772-X). G. P. Putnam's Sons.
--Time Enough for Love: The Lives of Lazarus Long. 1973. (ISBN 0-399-11151-4). G. P. Putnam's Sons.
--Time for the Stars. LC 56-9286. 244p. 21cm. 1956. Scribner.
--Tunnel in the Sky. (Illus.). (gr. 5-11). 1955. (ISBN 0-684-12402-5, ScribJ). Scribner.

Heinrich, Doris S.
--Red Is a Lollipop. Heinrich, Doris S., illus. (Illus.). (gr. 4-8). N.D. Vantage.

Heinrich, Judy
--Big Stories for Little Folk, 3 vols. Pitts, Mary F., illus. Incl. Vol. 1. Moses; Vol. 2. Jonah; Vol. 3. Noah. (Illus.). (gr. 1-3). 1968. Southern Pub.

Heinrichs, E.
--My Little Friends. 6 p. l., 71 p. incl. front., 2 pl., 34 port. 25 x 20 1/2 cm. c.1891. Reproduced and Printed by the Art Publishing Co.

Heins, Paul (1909-), tr. see Grimm, Jakob Ludwig Karl (1785-1863) & Grimm, Wilhelm Karl.

Heinsenfelt, Kathryn, retold by see Lorenzini, Carlo.

Heinz, Kurth
--Hello Sam. 32p. (Orig.). 1984. (ISBN 0-8431-1024-4). Price Stern.

Heisenfelt, Kathryn
--Ann Rutherford and the Key to Nightmare Hall: An Original Story Featuring Ann Rutherford, Famous Motion-Picture Player, As the Heroine. authorized. Vallely, Henry E., illus. LC 42-221721. 4 p. l., 18-246 p. illus. 20 1/2 cm. 1942. Whitman Publishing Company.
--Ann Sheridan and the Sign of the Sphinx: An Original Story Featuring Ann Sheridan, Famous Motion Picture Star, As the Heroine. authorized. Vallely, Henry E., illus. LC 43-22700. 3 p. l., 11-248 p. illus. 20 1/2 cm. 1943. Whitman Publishing Company.
--Betty Grable and the House of Cobwebs: An Original Story Featuring Betty Grable, Famous Motion Picture Star, As the Heroine. authorized. Meixner, Hedwig Jo, illus. LC 49-13590. 250 p. illus. 21 cm. 1947. Whitman Pub. Co.
--Betty Grable and the House with the Iron Shutters: An Original Story Featuring Betty Grable, Famous Motion Picture Star, As the Heroine. authorized. Vallely, Henry E., illus. LC 43-22701. 2 p. l., 9-252 p. illus. 20 1/2 cm. 1943. Whitman Publishing Company.

--Arctic Hunter. Helmericks, Bud, pseud. Kane, Henry Bugbee (1902-1971), illus. 1955. Little, Brown and Compnay.
--Oolak's Brother. Helmericks, Bud, pseud. Kane, Henry Bugbee (1902-1971), illus. LC 52-12628. (Illus.). 144 p. 24cm. 1953. Little, Brown.

Helmering, Doris Wild (1942-)
--I Have Two Families. Palmer, Heidi (1948-), illus. LC 80-22392. p. cm. c.1981. (ISBN 0-687-18507-6). Abingdon.

Helmering, Doris Wild (1942-) & Helmering, John William (1945-)
--We're Going to Have a Baby. Cassell, Robert H., illus. LC 77-24742. (Illus.). 32 p. 27cm. c.1978. (ISBN 0-687-44280-X). Abingdon.

Helmering, John William, jt. auth. see Helmering, Doris Wild.

Helmrath, Marilyn Olear & Bartlett, Janet La Spiza
--Bobby Bear and the Bees. Mankato, Marilou, illus. LC 64-25743. 27cm. 32p. (The Wonderful World of Childrens' Readers). 1964. Oddo Publishing Inc.
--Bobby Bear & the Bees. Marilue, pseud. (1931-), illus. Johnson, Marilue Carolyn. LC 68-56806. (Illus.). (Bobby Bear Ser.). (ps-1). 1968. (ISBN 0-87783-003-7). (ISBN 0-87783-177-7). Oddo.
--Bobby Bear Finds Maple Sugar. Marilue, pseud. (1931-), illus. Johnson, Marilue Carolyn. LC 68-56805. (Illus.). (Bobby Bear Ser.). (ps-1). 1968. (ISBN 0-87783-005-3). (ISBN 0-87783-178-5). Oddo.
--Bobby Bear Goes Fishing. Johnson, Marilue Carolyn (1931-), illus. LC 68-56807. 26cm. 32p. 1968. Oddo Publishing Inc.
--Bobby Bear Goes Fishing. Marilue, pseud. (1931-), illus. Johnson, Marilue Carolyn. LC 64-25741. (Illus.). 27cm. 32p. (The Wonderful World of Children's Books). 1964. Oddo Pub.
--Bobby Bear Goes Fishing. Marilue, pseud. (1931-), illus. Johnson, Marilue Carolyn. LC 68-56807. (Illus.). (Bobby Bear Ser.). (ps-1). 1968. (ISBN 0-87783-006-1). (ISBN 0-87783-179-3). Oddo.
--Bobby Bear Goes Fishing. Marilue, pseud. (1931-), illus. Johnson, Marilue Carolyn. (Illus.). (ps-1). 1978. (ISBN 0-89508-054-0). Rainbow Bks.
--Bobby Bear in the Spring. Marilue, pseud. (1931-), illus. Johnson, Marilue Carolyn. LC 64-25745. (Illus.). 27cm. 32p. (The Wonderful World of Children's Bks.). 1964. Oddo.
--Bobby Bear in the Spring. Marilue, pseud. (1931-), illus. Johnson, Marilue Carolyn. LC 68-56810. (Illus.). (Bobby Bear Ser.). (ps-1). 1968. (ISBN 0-87783-007-X). (ISBN 0-87783-180-7). Oddo.
--Bobby Bear Ser, 13 bks. (Five titles by Marilue, two titles by Kay D. Oana). (Illus.). (ps-1). N.D. Set. (ISBN 0-87783-163-7). (ISBN 0-87783-181-5). Oddo.
--Bobby Bear's Halloween. Marilue, pseud. (1931-), illus. Johnson, Marilue Carolyn. LC 64-25744. (Illus.). 32. 27cm. (The Wonderful World of Children). 1964. Oddo Pub.
--Bobby Bear's Halloween. Marilue, pseud. (1931-), illus. Johnson, Marilue Carolyn. LC 68-56808. (Illus.). (Bobby Bear Ser.). (ps-1). 1968. (ISBN 0-87783-004-5). (ISBN 0-87783-084-3). (ISBN 0-87783-183-1). Oddo.
--Bobby Bear's Rocket Ride. Marilue, pseud. (1931-), illus. Johnson, Marilue Carolyn. LC 64-25740. (Illus.). 32p. 27cm. (The Wonderful World of Children). 1964. Oddo.
--Bobby Bear's Rocket Ride. Marilue, pseud. (1931-), illus. Johnson, Marilue Carolyn. LC 68-56809. (Illus.). 32 p. 26cm. (Wonderful world of children's books). 1968. Oddo Publishing.

Helms, Elmer Ellsworth
--Forgotten Stories. N.D. Abingdon Press.

Helps, Racey (1913-1971)
--The Blow-Away Balloon. 1st ed. Helps, Racey (1913-1971), illus. LC 67-22755. (Illus.). 48 p. 18cm. 1967. Chilton Book Co.
--The Clean Sweep. Helps, Racey (1913-1971), illus. LC 67-22756. (Illus.). 48 p. 17cm. 1967. Chilton Book Co.
--Little Dilly's Party: A/Counting Story. LC 51-4403. (Illus.). 33cm. 260p. 1951. John Martin's House.
--Mr. Roley to the Rescue. Helps, Racey (1913-1971), illus. LC 66-7262. (Illus.). 1 v. (unpaged. 1966. Chilton Books.
--Pinny Takes a Bath. 1st ed. Helps, Racey (1913-1971), illus. LC 66-835399. 48p. illus. (pt. col.) 18cm. 1966. Chilton.
--Prickly Pie. 1st ed. Helps, Racey (1913-1971), illus. LC 68-21136. (Illus.). 46 p. 17cm. 1968. Chilton Book Co.
--Selina, the Circus Seal. 1st ed. Helps, Racey (1913-1971), illus. LC 67-22757. (Illus.). 48 p. 18cm. 1967. Chilton Book Co.
--Two from a Teapot. 1st ed. Helps, Racey (1913-1971), illus. LC 66-9517. (Illus.). 48 p. 18cm. 1966. Chilton Books.
--Two's Company. Helps, Racey (1913-1971), illus. LC 68-23362. (Illus.). 46 p. 17cm. 1968. Chilton Book Co.

Heltman, Harry Joseph., jt. ed. see Brown, Helen Ada.

Helton, Roy Addison (1886-)
--The Early Adventures of Peacham Grew. Shenton, Edward (1895-), illus. LC 25-6854. vii p., 1 l., 117 p. illus. 20 cm. 1925. The Penn Publishing Company.
--Jimmy Sharswood. Dunkelberger, Ralph, illus. 4 p. l., 7-290 p. front., illus. plates. 21 cm. 1924. The Penn Publishing Company.

Helweg, Marianne, tr. see Proysen, Alf.

Helweg, Marianne, tr. see Sandman Lilius, Irmelin.

Hemalata
--Dhruva. Chakravarty, Saila, illus. (Illus.). (gr. 1-8). 1979. (ISBN 0-89744-153-2). Auromere.
--Mahagiri. 7th ed. Biswas, Pulak, illus. (Illus.). 24p. (Orig.). (gr. k-3). N.D. (ISBN 0-89744-213-X, Pub. by Children's Bk Trust India). Auromere.

Hemalata, jt. auth. see Dutta, S.

Hembree, Lawrence, ed.
--Henny Penny. N.D. (ISBN 0-448-00759-2, Three-D Puppet Story Books). Grosset & Dunlap.

Hemenway, Robert E. (1941-), intro. by see Harris, Joel Chandler.

Hemery, Paul Arnold Valentine & Read, Nora
--Children's Action Songs. Steele, Marshall, illus. 36p. N.D. Funk & Wagnalls Co.

Heming, Arthur Henry Howard (1870-)
--The Living Forest. Heming, Arthur Henry Howard (1870-), illus. LC 25-19825. x p., 1 l., 268 p. col. front., col. plates. 21 cm. 1925. Doubleday, Page & Company.
--The Living Forest: Two Boys in the Canadian Woods. Heming, Arthur Henry Howard (1870-), illus. LC 35-7675. x p., 1 l., 268 p. front., plates. 20 1/2 cm. (Young moderns books). 1935. Doubleday, Doran & Company, Inc.

Heming, Jack
--Blue Wings. LC 46-40170. 256 p. col. front. 20 cm. 1938. F. Warne & Co., Ltd.

Hemmer, Jarl (1893-)
--A Fool of Faith. Lyon, Francis Hamilton (1885-), tr. from Swedish. LC 85-18074. 4 p. l., 3-336 p. 19 1/2 cm. c.1935. Liveright Publishing Corp.

Hemmings, Muriel
--Through a Needle's Eye. (Illus.). (Arch Bk.: No. 16). 1979. (ISBN 0-570-06125-3). Concordia.

Hemon, Louis (1880-1913)
--Maria Chapdelaine: A Tale of the Lake St. John Country. Blake, W. H., tr. LC 21-21094. 4 p. l., 8-288 p. 20 1/2 cm. 1921. The Macmillan Company.

Hemphill, Martha Locke (1904-1973)
--Christmas. LC 69-18147. (Illus.). (ps). N.D. (ISBN 0-8170-0421-1). Judson.

Hemrath, Marilyn Olear & Bartlett, Janet La Spiza
--Bobby Bear in the Spring. Johnson, Marilue Carolyn (1931-), illus. LC 64-25745. 27cm. 32p. N.D. Oddo Publishing Inc.

Hemschemeyer, Judith (1935-)
--Trudie & the Milch Cow. Grossman, Nancy S. (1940-), illus. LC 67-82927. (Illus.). 24cm. 59p. (gr. 2-5). 1967. (ISBN 0-394-81733-8). Random.

Hemsley, Harry
--Harry Hemsley's Stories for Children. Hemsley, Harry, illus. LC 38-380672. 127, 1 p. incl. illus., plates. 19cm. 1938. F. Warne & Co., Ltd.

Hemyng, Bracebridge
--Jack Harkaway and his Friends in Search of the Mountain of Gold, 1 of 8. (Frank Leslie's Boys' Library Ser.). N.D. American News Co.
--Jack Harkaway and the Secret of Wealth, 1 of 8. (Frank Leslie's Boys' Library Ser.). N.D. American News Co.
--Jack Harkaway in America, 1 of 8. (Frank Leslie's Boys' Library Ser.). N.D. American News Co.
--Jack Harkaway out West among the Indians, 1 of 8. (Frank Leslie's Boys' Library Ser.). N.D. American News Co.
--Red Dog, Blue Horse, and Ghost-that-Lies-in-the-Woods, 1 of 8. (Frank Leslie's Boys' Library Ser.). N.D. American News Co.

Hench, John, adapted by see Disney, Walt, Productions.

Hench, John & Dempster, Al, eds.
--Walt Disney's Peter Pan. Disney, Walt, Studio, illus. (Illus.). (Big Golden Bks.). (gr. k-3). 1952. (ISBN 0-307-10453-2, Golden Pr). Western Pub.

Henchel, Joseph
--Life with Uncle Charlie in Yorkville. N.D. Vantage Press Inc.

Hencke, Paul, jt. ed. see Trussell, Tait.

Henderley, Brooks, pseud., see Stratemeyer Syndicate.

Henderley, Brooks, pseud.
--The Y. M. C. A. Boys at Football: Or, Lively Doings On and Off the Gridiron. Stratemeyer Syndicate. Owen, Robert Emmett (1878-), illus. (The Y. M. C. A. Boys Ser.: No. 3). 1917. Cupples & Leon Co.
--The Y. M. C. A. Boys of Cliffwood: Or, The Struggle for the Holwell Prize. Stratemeyer Syndicate. Rogers, Walter S., illus. LC 17-220083. 2 p. l., 246 p. front., plates. 19 1/2 cm. (Y. M. C. A. Boys Ser.: No. 1). 1916. Cupples & Leon Co.
--The Y. M. C. A. Boys on Bass Island: Or, The Mystery of Russabaga Camp. Stratemeyer Syndicate. Owen, Robert Emmett (1878-), illus. LC 16-235910. 2 p. l., 246 p. front., plates. 19 1/2 cm. (Y. M. C. A. Boys Ser.: No. 2). 1916. Cupples & Leon Co.

Henderson, Alice Corbin, tr. see Andersen, Hans Christian.

Henderson, Anna R.
--Children of a Sunny Land. N.D. D. Lothrop Co.

Henderson, Bernard Lionel Kingston, jt. auth. see Calvert, C.

Henderson, Bernard Lionel Kingston & Jones, Stephen
--Wonder Tales of Ancient Wales. Williamson, Dorie, illus. N.D. Small,Maynard & Co.
--Wonder Tales of Old Tyrol. Rowlands, Constance E., illus. N.D. Frederick A. Stokes Co.

Henderson, Carrie W.
--Susy, that Third Little Pig. LC 55-8504. (Illus.). 23cm. 20p. 1955. Comet Press Books.

Henderson, Christine L.
--Thoughtful Petie's Adventures, and Other Poems. LC 40-2377. 42p. 19cm. (Verse Craft Ser.). 1939. Banner Press.

Henderson, Daniel MacIntyre (1880-)
--Boone of the Wilderness: A Tale of Pioneer Adventure and Achievement in "the Dark and Bloody Ground". LC 21-18478. iii p., 1 l., 207 p. front., plates. 21 1/2 cm. c.1921. E. P. Dutton & Company.
--Pirate Princes and Yankee Jacks: Setting Forth David Forsyth's Adventures in America's Battles on Sea and Desert with the Buccaneer Princes of Barbary, with an Account of a Search Under the Sands of the Sahara Desert for the Treasure Filled Tomb of Ancient Kings. LC 23-82731. xiv, 224 p. incl. plates. port., map. front. (port.) 21 cm. c.1923. E. P. Dutton & Company.

Henderson, Dion Winslow (1921-)
--The Waltons: The Bird Dog. LC 75-321032. 140 p. 20cm. 1975. (ISBN 0-307-01516-5). Western Pub. Co.
--The Wolf of Thunder Mountain: And Other Stories. LC 68-30927. (Illus.). 210 p. 20cm. 1970. Western Pub. Co.

Henderson, Doris & Henderson, Marion
--Stories for Bedtime. Henderson, Doris, illus. LC 52-1972. unpaged. illus. 21 cm. (Easy-to-read book, 4201). 1952. Saalfield Pub. Co.

Henderson, George C.
--The Cowpokes of Bitter Creek. LC 39-5218. 2 p. l., 7-257 p. 20 cm. c.1939. Phoenix Press.
--Whizz Fargo, Gunfighter. LC 37-201944. 256 p. 19 1/2 cm. c.1937. Phoenix Press.

Henderson, Gertrude, jt. auth. see Burrows, Edith Maie, Mrs.

Henderson, Gertrude (1872-)
--The Ring of the Nibelung. Tenggren, Gustaf (1896-1970), illus. LC 32-22532. ix p., 2 l., 217, 1 p. incl. illus. plates. col. front. 24 1/2 cm. 1932. A. A. Knopf.

Henderson, Harold Gould (1889-1974)
--Haiku in English. LC 67-16413. (Illus.). (gr. 9 up). 1967. (ISBN 0-8048-0228-9). C E Tuttle.

Henderson, Harold Gould (1889-1974), ed.
--Tales from the Japanese Storytellers: As Collected in Ho-Dan Zo. 1974. (ISBN 0-8048-1132-6). Charles E. Tuttle co.

Henderson, John (1915-)
--The Reachers. Case, Bernard, illus. LC 63-8679. 143 p. illus. 21 cm. c.1963. Friendship Press.

Henderson, LeGrand see LeGrand, pseud.

Henderson, LeGrand (1901-1965)
--The Amazing Adventures of Archie and the First Hot Dog. LeGrand, pseud. LC 64-14793. 1 v. (unpaged) col. illus. 25 cm. 1964. Abingdon Press.
--Are Dogs Better Than Cats?. LeGrand, pseud. Henderson, LeGrand (1901-1965), illus. LeGrand, pseud. LC 53-29435. unpaged. illus. 21cm. (Wonder books, 565). 1953. Wonder Books.
--Augustus and the Desert. LeGrand, pseud. Henderson, LeGrand (1901-1965), illus. LeGrand, pseud. LC 48-9040. 158 p. illus. (part col.) 26 cm. 1948. Bobbs-Merrill Co.
--Augustus and the Desert. LeGrand, pseud. Henderson, LeGrand (1901-1965), illus. LeGrand, pseud. LC 61-4924. 128p. illus. 26cm. (Augustus books, 6). 1961, c.1948. Grosset & Dunlap.
--Augustus and the Mountains. LeGrand, pseud. (The Augustus Series). N.D. Grosset & Dunlap.
--Augustus and the Mountains. LeGrand, pseud. LC 41-17949. 186 p. illus. (part col.) 26 cm. c.1941. The Bobbs-Merrill Company.
--Augustus and the River. LeGrand, pseud. LC 64-9040. 128 p. illus. 26 cm. (His The Augustus books, 1). 1964, c.1939. Grosset & Dunlap.
--Augustus and the River. LeGrand, pseud. LC 39-30184. 128 p. illus. 25 1/2 cm. c.1939. The Bobbs-Merrill Company.
--Augustus Drives a Jeep. LeGrand, pseud. Henderson, LeGrand (1901-1965), illus. LeGrand, pseud. LC 44-5034. 125 p. illus. (part col.) 26 cm. 1944. The Bobbs-Merrill Company.
--Augustus Flies. LeGrand, pseud. Henderson, LeGrand (1901-1965), illus. LeGrand, pseud. LC 44-882950. 133 p. illus. (part col.) 25 1/2 cm. 1944. The Bobbs-Merrill Company.
--Augustus Goes South. LeGrand, pseud. (The Augustus Series). N.D. Grosset & Dunlap.
--Augustus Goes South. LeGrand, pseud. LC 40-317228. 128 p. illus. (part col.) 26 cm. c.1940. The Bobbs-Merrill Company.
--Augustus Helps the Army. LeGrand, pseud. LC 43-7237. 180 p. illus. 26 cm. 1943. The Bobbs-Merrill Company.
--Augustus Helps the Marines. LeGrand, pseud. LC 43-14403. 134 p. illus. (part col.) 25 1/2 cm. 1943. The Bobbs-Merrill Company.
--Augustus Helps the Navy. LeGrand, pseud. (The Augustus Ser.). N.D. Grosset & Dunlap.
--Augustus Helps the Navy. LeGrand, pseud. LC 42-21966. 128 p. illus. (part col.) 25 1/2 cm. 1942. The Bobbs-Merrill Company.
--Augustus Hits the Road. LeGrand, pseud. Henderson, LeGrand (1901-1965), illus. LeGrand, pseud. LC 46-3857. 136 p. illus. (part col.) 25 1/2 cm. 1946. The Bobbs-Merrill Company.
--Augustus Rides the Border. LeGrand, pseud. Henderson, LeGrand (1901-1965), illus. LeGrand, pseud. 127p. illus. 26cm. (Augustus Bks., 5). 1961, c.1947. Grosset & Dunlap.
--Augustus Rides the Border. LeGrand, pseud. Henderson, LeGrand (1901-1965), illus. LeGrand, pseud. LC 47-3101. 134, 1 p. illus. (part col.) 26 cm. 1947. The Bobbs-Merrill Company.
--Augustus Saves a Ship. LeGrand, pseud. Henderson, LeGrand (1901-1965), illus. LeGrand, pseud. LC 45-415131. 136 p. illus. (part col.) 25 1/2 cm. 1945. The Bobbs-Merrill Company.
--Cap'n Dow & the Hole in the Doughnut. LeGrand, pseud. Henderson, LeGrand (1901-1965), illus. LeGrand, pseud. (gr. 1-4). N.D. (ISBN 0-687-04623-8). Abingdon.
--Cats for Kansas. LeGrand, pseud. Henderson, LeGrand (1901-1965), illus. Legrand, pseud. LC 48-8277. (Illus.). 38p. (gr. 1-5). 1948. (ISBN 0-687-04773-0). Abingdon.
--Glory Horn. LeGrand, pseud. Henderson, LeGrand (1901-1965), illus. LeGrand, pseud. LC 41-28299. 266 p. incl. front., illus., plates. 19 1/2 cm. c.1941. R.M. McBride & Company.
--Here Come the Perkinses!. LeGrand, pseud. Henderson, LeGrand (1901-1965), illus. LeGrand, pseud. LC 49-11203. N.D. Bobbs-Merrill Co.
--How Baseball Began in Brooklyn. LeGrand, pseud. LC 58-867. 58p. illus. 21cm. 1958. Abingdon Press.
--How Basketball Began. LeGrand, pseud. LC 62-11147. (Illus.). 63 p. 22cm. 1962. Abingdon Press.
--How Space Rockets Began. LeGrand, pseud. LC 60-5318. (Illus.). 64 p. 23cm. 1960. Abingdon Press.
--Matilda. LeGrand, pseud. Henderson, LeGrand (1901-1965), illus. LeGrand, pseud. LC 56-140648. (Illus.). 21cm. 63p. 1956. Abingdon Press.
--Mostly About Mutt. LeGrand, pseud. LC 38-35029. (Illus.). 27cm. 28p. 1938. Garden City Publishing Co.
--The Puppy Who Chased the Sun. LeGrand, pseud. Henderson, LeGrand (1901-1965), illus. LeGrand, pseud. LC 50-9290. (Illus.). 21cm. 44p. 1950. Wonder Books.
--Samson Catches a Mystery. LeGrand, pseud. Henderson, LeGrand (1901-1965), illus. LeGrand, pseud. LC 62-8140. 150p. illus. 22cm. 1962. Houghton Mifflin.
--Saturday for Samuel. Le Grand, pseud. Henderson, LeGrand (1901-1965), illus. LeGrand, pseud. LC 41-19420. (Illus.). 44p. 22 x 23cm. 1941. Greystone Press.
--Tom Benn & Blackbeard, the Pirate. LeGrand, pseud. Henderson, LeGrand (1901-1965), illus. LeGrand, pseud. LC 54-3053. 22cm. 63p. (gr. 3-5). 1954. (ISBN 0-687-42354-6). Abingdon.
--The Tomb of the Mayan King. LeGrand, pseud. Henderson, LeGrand (1901-1965), illus. LeGrand, pseud. LC 58-13067. 192p. illus. 22cm. 1958. Holt.
--What About Willie. LeGrand, pseud. LC 39-24926. (Illus.). 27cm. 28p. 1939. Garden City Publishing Co.

--When the Mississippi Was Wild. LeGrand, pseud. Henderson, LeGrand (1901-1965), illus. LeGrand, pseud. LC 52-3039. 25cm. (gr. 1-5). 1952. (ISBN 0-687-45074-8). Abingdon.
--Why Cowboys Sing, in Texas. LeGrand, pseud. LC 68-54909. (Illus.). 38 p. 25cm. (Merit books). 1969, c.1950. Houghton Mifflin.
--Why Cowboys Sing in Texas. LeGrand, pseud. Henderson, LeGrand (1901-1965), illus. LeGrand, pseud. LC 50-8727. (Illus.). 25 cm. 40p. (gr. 1-5). 1950. (ISBN 0-687-45424-7). Abingdon.

Henderson, Lima L.
--Resolute. Beistle, Mary Alice, illus. LC 40-32777. 64 p. illus. 21 1/2 x 18 cm. c.1940. David McKay Company.

Henderson, Lois
--The Blessing Deer. (gr. 4-9). 1980. (ISBN 0-89191-244-4). Cook.
--A Candle in the Dark. (Orig.). (gr. 5-9). 1983. (ISBN 0-89191-504-4). Cook.
--The Touch of the Golden Scepter. (gr. 5 up). 1981. (ISBN 0-89191-375-0). Cook.

Henderson, Loulie Richmond Stebbins, Mrs. (1886-)
--The Jolly Journey of Jack and Billy. N.D. The Reilly & Britton Co.
--The Magic Aeroplane: A Fairy Tale. Nelson, Emile A., illus. LC 45-22321. 96 p. col. front., illus., col. plates. 29 cm. 1911. The Reilly & Britton Co.
--The Magic Airplane: A Fairy Tale. Nelson, Emile A., illus. LC 29-14764. 96 p. col. front., illus., col. plates. 27 cm. c.1929. The Reilly & Lee Co.
--Visit to Santa Claus. (Illus.). N.D. The Reilly & Britton Co.

Henderson, Marion, jt. auth. see Henderson, Doris.

Henderson, Mrs.
--Asriel: or, the Crystal Cup, 1 of 7. (Sunday School Reward Ser.). N.D. Cassell, Petter, & Galpin.

Henderson, Nancy Wallace (1916-)
--Celebrate America: A Baker's Dozen of Plays. Frame, Paul (1913-), illus. LC 78-15169. (Illus.). 128 p. 22cm. c.1978. (ISBN 0-671-32907-3). J. Messner.
--Janet Climbs. Willman, Gordon, illus. LC 77-13271. (Illus.). 99 p. 23cm. (Bro-kee series). c.1978. (ISBN 0-570-07762-1). Concordia Pub. House.
--Walk Together: Five Plays on Human Rights. Sowell, Floyd (1929-), illus. LC 72-1423. (Illus.). 128p. 1st U.S. edition. (gr. 4 up). 1972. (ISBN 0-671-32538-8). Messner.

Henderson, Richard (1924-)
--First Sail for Skipper. Henderson, Richard (1924-), illus. LC 60-12002. 44p. illus. (part col.) 29cm. c.1960. Reilly & Lee.

Henderson, Rose
--Five Little Indians. Reid, James (1907-), illus. LC 31-22068. v. 78 p. col. front., illus. 21 1/2 cm. 1931. R. M. McBride & Company.

Henderson, William James (1855-1937)
--Afloat with the Flag. LC 12-341623. vi p., 1 l., 250 p. front., plates. 19 cm. 1895. Harper & Brothers.
--Folk Lore of the Northern Counties of England and the Borders. Baring-Gould, Sabine (1834-1924), suppls. by. Repr. of 1866 ed. 1973. (ISBN 0-87471-141-X). Rowman and Littlefield.
--The Last Cruise of the Mohawk: A Boy's Adventures in the Navy in the War of the Rebellion. Edwards, Harry C., illus. LC 12-34193. x p., 1 l., 278 p. front., plates. 19 cm. 1897. C. Scribner's Sons.
--Sea Yarns for Boys, Spun by an Old Salt. LC 12-34132. viii, 195 p. front., plates. 19cm. 1895. Harper & Brothers.
--Strange Stories of 1812. LC 7-18099. xi, 1 p. front., 7 pl. 18 1/2 cm. 1907. Harper & Brothers.

Hendra, Judith, ed.
--The Illustrated Treasury of Humor for Children. LC 79-91869. (Illus.). x, 244 p. 26cm. c.1980. (ISBN 0-448-16429-9). Grosset and Dunlap.

Hendrich, Paula Griffith (1928-)
--Baby in the Schoolroom. Wohlberg, Meg (1905-), illus. LC 61-11928. unpaged. illus. 25cm. 1962. Lothrop, Lee & Shepard.
--The Girl Who Slipped Through Time. LC 77-17947. 128 p. 22cm. c.1978. (ISBN 0-688-41836-8). (ISBN 0-688-51836-2). Lothrop, Lee & Shepard Co.
--Trudy's First Day at Camp. Adams, Adrienne (1906-), illus. LC 58-10720. (Illus.). unpaged. 26cm. 1959. Lothrop, Lee & Shepard.
--Who Says So?. Hyman, Trina Schart (1939-), illus. LC 73-13643. (Illus.). 176 p. 25cm. 1973, c.1972. (ISBN 0-8161-6150-X). G. K. Hall.
--Who Says So. Hyman, Trina Schart (1939-), illus. 1972. (ISBN 0-688-51481-2). William Morrow and Company.

Hendrick, Edward P.
--Copper Coleson's Ghost. Cue, Harold, illus. LC 30-23896. 5 p. l., 302 p. front., plates. 19 1/2 cm. c.1930. L. C. Page & Company.
--The Cruise of the Sally. Freeman, Dean, illus. LC 28-22772. 5 p. l., 325 p. front., plates. 19 1/2 cm. c.1930. L. C. Page & Company.
--The Seventh Scout. White, E. P., illus. LC 38-34543. 309 p. front., 1 illus., pl. 21 cm. c.1938. W. Wilde Company.

Hendrick, Helmut
--The Last Paradise. (Illus.). 160p. 1959. Chilton Books.

Hendricks, Stanley, compiled by.
--A Child's Rhymes: Best-Loved Verses for Children. Smith, Vivian (1933-), illus. LC 68-30513. (Illus.). 60p. 29cm. 1968. Hallmark Editions.

Hendrickson, Dorris Walsh (1910-)
--Breakneck Hill. Weil, Lisl (1910-), illus. LC 54-10095. (Illus.). 32 p. 26cm. 1954. Follett.

Hendrix, William F.
--Cruise of the Annie Lee: A Sequel to "The Great Bridge". LC 47-12523. 177 p. front. 21 cm. 1947. Benziger Bros.
--The Great Bridge: A Story for Boys. LC 37-31. viii, 9-229 p. front. 19 1/2 cm. 1936. Benziger Brothers.
--Harry Brown at Barchester. LC 30-310323. 254 p. front. 19 1/2 cm. 1930. Benziger Brothers.
--Red Halligan. LC 32-232815. 245 p. front. 19 1/2 cm. 1932. Benziger Brothers.
--That Boy, Joe Fox. LC 33-34614. 188 p. front. 19 cm. 1933. Benziger Brothers.

Hendryx, James Beardsley (1880-1963)
--Connie Morgan Hits the Trail. Walker, Ernest, illus. LC 29-17890. vi p., 1 l., 221 p. front. 20 1/2 cm. (windmill books). 1929. Doubleday, Doran & Company, Inc.
--Connie Morgan in Alaska. LC 16-21404. vi p., 1 l., 341 p. front., illus. 20 cm. 1916. G. P. Putnam's Sons.
--Connie Morgan in the Arctic. LC 36-8623. 5 p. l., 3-239 p. incl. front. 20 cm. c.1936. G. P. Putnam's Sons.
--Connie Morgan in the Cattle Country. Schoonover, Frank Earle (1877-1972), illus. LC 23-14480. 1923. G.P. Putnam's Sons.
--Connie Morgan in the Fur Country. LC 21-185874. 2 p. l., iii-vi p., 1 l., 312 p. front., plates. 20 cm. 1921. G. P. Putnam's Sons.
--Connie Morgan in the Lumber Camps. LC 19-157291. vi p., 1 l., 313 p. front., illus. 20 cm. 1919. G. P. Putnam's Sons.
--Connie Morgan with the Forest Rangers. LC 26-5479. v, 275 p. front., plates. 20 cm. 1925. G. P. Putnam's Sons.
--Connie Morgan with the Mounted. LC 18-21165. vi p., 1 l., 293 p. front., illus. 20 cm. 1918. G. P. Putnam's Sons.

Hengesbaugh, Jane
--I Live in So Many Places. Evans, Katherine Floyd (1901-1964), illus. LC 56-137476. unpaged illus. 25cm. c.1956. Childrens Press.

Hengler, Florence
--Little Miss Daphne, and Other Tales. Morton, Isabella, illus. LC 13-87557. 90 p. col. front., 1 illus., plates (part. col.) 21 1/2 cm. $1.0. c.1912. The Bookery.

Heniger, Alice Minnie Herts
--The Kingdom of the Child. N.D. E P Dutton.

Henius, Frank
--Songs and Games of the Americas. Fabres, Oscar (1900-), illus. LC 43-10968. 56 p. illus. (part col.) 26 cm. 1943. C. Scribner's Sons.

Henius, Frank, compiled by.
--Stories from the Americas. Politi, Leo (1908-), illus. Henius, Frank (1908-), tr. LC 44-7131. ix, 1 p., 1 l., 114 p., 1 l. illus. 24 1/2 cm. 1944. C. Scribner's Sons.

Henkel, Joyce R., ed.
--Calico Book of Homestead Verses. (Illus.). 1977. (ISBN 0-686-23385-9). Calico Papers.

Henkes, Kevin
--All Alone. LC 81-105. (Illus.). 32 p. 26cm. c.1981. (ISBN 0-688-00604-3). (ISBN 0-688-00605-1). Greenwillow Books.
--Bailey Goes Camping. LC 84-29027. (Illus.). 24 p. 22cm. c.1985. (ISBN 0-688-05701-2). (ISBN 0-688-05702-0). Greenwillow Books.
--Clean Enough. Henkes, Kevin, illus. LC 81-6386. (Illus.). 24 p. 21cm. c.1982. (ISBN 0-688-00828-3). (ISBN 0-688-00829-1). Greenwillow Books.
--Margaret & Taylor. 1st ed. Henkes, Kevin, illus. LC 82-21134. (Illus.). 64 p. 22cm. c.1983. (ISBN 0-688-01425-9). (ISBN 0-688-01426-7). Greenwillow.
--Return to Sender. Henkes, Kevin, illus. LC 83-16567. (Illus.). 5 3/8 x 8. 128p. (14 pt.). (gr. 3-5). 1984. (ISBN 0-688-02571-4). (ISBN 0-688-02573-0). Greenwillow.
--Something for Grandma. LC 82-9230. p. cm. c.1983. (ISBN 0-688-01425-9). (ISBN 0-688-01426-7). Greenwillow Books.

Henle, Mary Ellen
--The Fiddler Crab and the Sand Dollar. Smith, Barbara, illus. LC 50-7227. (Illus.). 23cm. 38p. N.D. Vanguard Press.

Henley, Bessie Stella Jones, Mrs. (1888-)
--The Little White Gnome: A Fairy Tale for Children and Grown Ups Who Still Believe In Fairies. LC 36-41. 3 p. l., 9-74 p. illus. 21 1/2 cm. c.1935. Pipp Brothers.

Henley, William Ernest (1849-1903)
--Lyra Heroica. Henley, William Ernest (1849-1903), ed. N.D. Charles Scribner's Sons.
--The Song of the Sword. N.D. Charles Scribner's Sons.

Henn, Shirley
--Adventures of Hooty Owl and His Friends. Henn, Shirley, illus. LC 55-9401. (Illus.). 21cm. 40p. 1955. Exposition Press.

Henn, W., jt. auth. see Hart, T.

Hennagin, Allie D.
--Third Daughter. LC 54-9874. (Illus.). 189 p. 21cm. 1954. Nelson.

Hennessey, Le Roy
--Mamie Whockety. N.D. Comet Press Books.

Hennessey, William A.
--Hoppy Toad Tales. LC 23-13500. 4 p. l., 7-46 p. illus. 20 cm. c.1923. The Christopher Publishing House.

Hennessy, Maurice N. & Sauter, Edwin Charles Scott, Jr. (1930-)
--A Crown for Thomas Peters. (gr. 6-8). N.D. Washburn.
--Sword of the Hausas. LC 64-200079. viii, 142p. map. 21cm. (Men of Africa, 2). c.1964. Dist. New York, McKay.
--Sword of the Hausas. LC 64-20007. viii, 142 p. map. 21 cm. (men of africa, 2. 1964. (ISBN 0-679-27066-3). I. Washburn.

Hennig, Helen Anderson
--Puppydog Tales for Sleepytime. LC 24-1296. 71 p. illus. 22 1/2 cm. c.1923. The Leader Press.

Henniker-Major, retold by see Poe, Edgar Allan.

Henninges, William T.
--The Block-House on the Shore. Ireland, Mary Eliza Haines, Mrs. (1834-1927), tr. from Ger. LC 19-12054. 256 p. front., illus., plates. 16 1/2 cm. c.1890. American Baptist Publication Society.

Henriksen, Hild
--Sea Hawk Calling!. Lundbergh, Holer, tr. from Norwegian. LC 62-834420. 157p. 21cm. 1st U.S. edition. 1962. Harcourt, Brace & World.

Henriod, Lorraine (1925-)
--Grandma's Wheelchair. Chevalier, Christa (1937-), illus. LC 81-12918. (Illus.). 32 p. 21cm. (Concept Bks.: Bk. 1). 1981, c.1982. (ISBN 0-8075-3035-2). A. Whitman.
--I Know a Zoo Keeper. Evans, Jane A., illus. (Illus.). 2-color drawings. 48p. (Community Helper Bks.). (gr. 1-3). 1969. (ISBN 0-399-60295-X). Putnam.
--Peter and the Desert. Klapholz, Mel, illus. LC 71-92808. (Illus.). 47 p. 23cm. (See and read beginning to read storybook). 1970. Putnam.
--The Rock Hunters. Frame, Paul (1913-), illus. LC 70-166988. (Illus.). 44 p. 23cm. (See and read beginning to read storybook). 1972. Putnam.

Henrioud, Charles see Matias, pseud.

Henrioud, Charles
--The Four Seasons. Les Quatre Saisons;. Matias, pseud. LC 61-8141. unpaged. illus. 23cm. 1961. H. Z. Walck.
--A Little Bird. Matias, pseud. LC 62-15021. unpaged. illus. 22cm. 1962. Orion Press.
--A Little Clown. Matias, pseud. LC 62-15022. unpaged. illus. 22cm. 1962. Orion Press.
--A Little Donkey. Un Petit Ane. Matias, pseud. LC 59-65469. unpaged. illus. 23cm. 1959. H. Z. Walck.
--A Little Elephant. Matias, pseud. LC 62-15080. unpaged. illus. 22cm. 1962. Orion Press.
--A Little Rabbit. Un Petit Lapin. Matias, pseud. LC 61-8142. unpaged. illus. 23cm. 1961. H. Z. Walck.
--Mr. Noah and the Animals. Matias, pseud. LC 60-16238. (Illus.). 23cm. 1960, c.1959. H. Z. Walck.

Henry, Arthur (1867-1934) & Henry, Maude Wood
--The Flight of a Pigeon, and Other Stories. Harts, Jessamy, illus. LC 44-31646. 3 p. l., 3-216 p., 1 l. illus. 18 1/2 cm. 1894. W. T. Squire.

Henry, Dorothy Mary
--Hardy Little Acorns. LC 72-83754. 172 p. 22cm. 1972. T. Gaus Sons.

Henry, George Alfred (1832-1902)
--By Pike and Dyke: A Tale of the Rise of the Dutch Republic. N.D. Charles Scribner's Sons.
--Cat of Bubastese: Or, A Story of Ancient Egypt. N.D. Charles Scribner's Sons.
--Redskin and Cowboy. N.D. Charles Scribner's Sons.
--With Lee in Virginia: A Story of the Civil War. N.D. Charles Scribner's Sons.
--With Wolfe in Canada: Or, the Winning of a Continent. N.D. Charles Scribner's Sons.

Henry, Gilbert
--Robin Hood. Crane, Walter (1845-1915), illus. N.D. Frederick A. Stokes.

Henry, Glenn E.
--The Christmas Owl. 48p. 1983. (ISBN 0-682-49928-5). Exposition.

Henry, Jan
--Tiger's Chance. 1st ed. Knight, Hilary (1926-), illus. LC 57-56104. 138p. illus. 22cm. 1957. Harcourt, Brace.
--Whaleman's World: A Novel. LC 72-119363. 174 p. 22cm. 1970. T. Nelson.

Henry, Joanne Landers (1927-)
--Elizabeth Blackwell, Girl Doctor. Doremus, Robert (1913-), illus. LC 61-15555. 200p. illus. 20cm. (Childhood of famous Americans). 1961. Bobbs-Merrill.
--George Eastman, Young Photographer. Rawson, Maurice, illus. LC 59-14005. 192p. illus. 20cm. (Childhood of famous Americans). c.1959. Bobbs-Merrill.

Henry, Louis
--The Boston Boy. N.D. Andrew F. Graves.
--Only Ask. N.D. Andrew F. Graves.

Henry, Marguerite, jt. auth. see True, Barbara.

Henry, Marguerite (1902-)
--Always Reddy. Dennis, Wesley (1903-1966), illus. LC 47-5835. 79 p. illus. 24 cm. 1947. Whittlesey House.
--Auno and Tauno: A Story of Finland. Blackwood, Gladys Rourke, illus. LC 40-27548. (Illus.). 26cm. 27p. 1940. Albert Whitman & Co.
--Benjamin West and His Cat Grimalkin. Dennis, Wesley (1903-1966), illus. LC 47-382031. 147 p. illus. 25 cm. 1947. The Bobbs-Merrill Company.
--Big Little Horse. Loughead, Robert, illus. (Illus.). (gr. 1 up). N.D. (ISBN 0-528-82443-0). (ISBN 0-528-82444-9). Rand.
--Black Gold. Dennis, Wesley (1903-1966), illus. LC 57-14557. 25cm. 172p. (gr. 4-9). 1957. (ISBN 0-528-82130-X). (ISBN 0-528-87688-0). Rand.
--Born to Trot. Dennis, Wesley (1903-1966), illus. LC 50-10271. (Illus.). 219 p. 25cm. 1950. Rand McNally.
--A Boy and a Dog. Thorne, Diana (1894-) & Foy, Ottilie, illus. LC 44-8300. (Illus.). 42p. 1944. Wilcox & Follett Co.
--Brighty of the Grand Canyon. Dennis, Wesley (1903-1966), illus. LC 53-7233. (Illus.). 222 p. 25cm. 1953. Rand McNally.
--Cinnabar: The One O'Clock Fox. Dennis, Wesley (1903-1966), illus. LC 56-11343. 154p. illus. 25cm. 1956. Rand McNally.
--Dear Readers & Riders. (Illus.). photos. 208p. (gr. 4 up). 1969. (ISBN 0-528-80162-7). Rand.
--Dilly Dally Sally. Blackwood, Gladys Rourke, illus. LC 40-81723. (Illus.). 16p. 1940. Saalfield.
--Five O'Clock Charlie. Dennis, Wesley (1903-1966), illus. LC 62-11987. (Illus.). unpage. 24cm. 1962. Rand McNally.
--Gaudenzia, Pride of the Palio. Ward, Lynd Kendall (1905-1985), illus. LC 60-8264. (Illus.). 237 p. 25cm. 1960. (ISBN 0-528-82030-3). Rand McNally.
--Geraldine Belinda. Blackwood, Gladys Rourke, illus. LC 42-25190. 301p. 1942. Platt & Munk Co.
--Justin Morgan Had a Horse. 1945. Rand McNally. **Award: (JNM).**
--Justin Morgan Had A Horse. N.D. Wilcox & Follett Co.
--Justin Morgan Had a Horse. Dennis, Wesley (1903-1966), illus. LC 54-8903. (Illus.). 169 p. 25cm. 1954. (ISBN 0-528-82255-1). (ISBN 0-528-87682-1). Rand McNally.
--King of the Wind. Dennis, Wesley (1903-1966), illus. LC 48-8773. (Illus.). 172, 3 p. 25cm. 1948. Rand McNally. **Award: (JNM).**
--The Little Fellow. Rudish, Rich, illus. LC 75-6828. (Illus.). 48 p. 24cm. 1975. (ISBN 0-528-82142-3). (ISBN 0-528-87147-1). Rand McNally.
--The Little Fellow. Thorne, Diana (1894-), illus. 1956. Holt, Reinhart and Winston.
--Little-or-Nothing from Nottingham. Dennis, Wesley (1903-1966), illus. LC 49-101430. 64 p. part col.) 15 x 24 cm. 1949. Whittlesey House.
--Misty of Chincoteague. Dennis, Wesley (1903-1966), illus. LC 47-11404. 173 p. illus. (part col.) 25 cm. 1947. Rand McNally. **Award: (JNM).**
--Misty, the Wonder Pony. McKinley, Clare, illus. LC 61-11902. unpaged. illus. 33cm. 1961, c.1956. Rand McNally.
--Misty, the Wonder Pony: By Misty, Herself. McKinley, Clare, illus. LC 56-8340. unpaged. illus. 21cm. (Rand McNally elf book, 536). c.1956. Rand McNally.
--Muley-Ears: Nobody's Dog. (Illus.). (gr. 2-4). 1959. (ISBN 0-8382-0560-7). Hale.
--Muley-Ears, Nobody's Dog. Dennis, Wesley (1903-1966), illus. LC 59-5359. (Illus.). unpaged. 26cm. 1959. Rand McNally.
--Mustang, Wild Spirit of the West. Lougheed, Robert, illus. LC 66-10876. (Illus.). 224p. (gr. 4-12). 1966. (ISBN 0-528-82327-2). (ISBN 0-528-87683-X). Rand.
--One Man's Horse. Dennis, Wesley (1903-1966), illus. LC 77-10080. (Illus.). 103, 1 p. 25cm. c.1977. (ISBN 0-528-82092-3). (ISBN 0-528-80057-4). Rand McNally.
--Our First Pony. Rudish, Rich, illus. LC 84-13409. (Illus.). 64 p. 24cm. c.1984. (ISBN 0-528-82129-6). Rand McNally.

--Peter Lundy and the Medicine Hat Stallion. Lougheed, Robert, illus. LC 77-83915. (Illus.). 230 p. 24cm. Orig. Title: San Domingo, the Medicine Hat Stallion. 1976, c.1972. (ISBN 0-528-87025-4). Rand McNally.

--A Pictorial Life Story of Misty. Dennis, Wesley (1903-1966), illus. LC 76-41864. p. cm. 1976. (ISBN 0-528-82210-1). (ISBN 0-528-80030-2). Rand McNally.

--Robert Fulton, Boy Craftsman. Dresser, Lawrence T., illus. LC 45-8648. 187 p. illus. (incl. facsims.) 19 1/2 cm. (Childhood of famous Americans series). 1945. The Bobbs-Merrill Company.

--Robert Fulton, Boy Craftsman. Patterson, Robert (1899-), illus. LC 62-100385. 200p. illus. 20cm. (Childhood of famous Americans). 1962. Bobbs-Merrill.

--San Domingo: The Medicine Hat Stallion. Lougheed, Robert, illus. LC 72-7416. (Illus.). 230 p. 26cm. 1972. (ISBN 0-528-82443-0). (ISBN 0-528-82443-0). Rand McNally.

--Sea Star: Orphan of Chincoteague. Dennis, Wesley (1903-1966), illus. LC 49-11474. 172 p. illus., map. 25 cm. 1949. Rand McNally.

--Stories from Around the World. 1974. Rand McNally.

--Stormy: Misty's Foal. Dennis, Wesley (1903-1966), illus. LC 63-13334. (Illus.). 25cm. 224p. (gr. 4-9). 1963. (ISBN 0-528-82083-4). (ISBN 0-528-87690-2). Rand.

--White Stallion of Lipizza. Dennis, Wesley (1903-1966), illus. LC 64-17445. 116p. illus. (pt. col.) 29cm. c.1964. (ISBN 0-528-82041-9). (ISBN 0-528-80154-6). Rand McNally.

--White Stallion of Lipizza. Dennis, Wesley (1903-1966), illus. LC 64-17445. (Illus.). 112p. (gr. 3-8). 1979. (ISBN 0-528-87050-5). Rand.

--The Wildest Horse Race in the World. Ward, Lynd Kendall (1905-1985), illus. LC 76-16072. (Illus.). 237 p. 24cm. Orig. Title: Gaudenzia, Pride of the Palio. N.D. (ISBN 0-528-82038-9). (ISBN 0-528-80032-9). (ISBN 0-528-87012-2). Rand McNally.

Henry, Mary H. see Benning, Howe, pseud.

Henry, Mary H.

--At Opening Doors. Benning, Howe, pseud. LC 99-4549. 351 p. front., plates. 19 cm. 1899. American Tract Society.

--The Benhurst Club. Benning, Howe, pseud. (Illus.). (The Wellesley Series for Girls). N.D. A. L. Burt.

--The Benhurst Club: A Girls' Story. Benning, Howe, pseud. (The Girl Chums Ser.). N.D. A. L. Burt Company.

--The Benhurst Club: Or, The Doings of Some Girls. Benning, Howe, pseud. LC 7-3028. 318 p. front., plates. 19 1/2 cm. 1897. Pilgrim Press.

--Essie's Journey. Benning, Howe, pseud. 130p. N.D. Congregational Sunday-School and Publilshing Society.

--Father's House. Benning, Howe, pseud. LC 11-150647. 278 p. front., plates. 17 1/2 cm. c.1880. American Tract Society.

--Father's House. Benning, Howe, pseud, 1 of 50 vols. 278p. 1905. American Tract Society.

--Finding Her Place. Benning, Howe, pseud. 368 p. front., plates. 19 cm. c.1883. American Tract Society.

--Finding Her Place. Benning, Howe, pseud, 1 of 50 vols. 368p. 1905. American Tract Society.

--Goshen Hill: Or, A Life's Broken Pieces. Benning, Howe, pseud. LC 7-30304. 319 p. front., plates. 19 cm. 319p. c.1895. American Tract Society.

--Grace Courtney: Or, Seeking the Shepard. Benning, Howe, pseud. LC 7-3032. 225p. 1871. I. P. Warren.

--Grandpa's Desk: Or, Who Wins. Benning, Howe, pseud. LC 7-3027. 96 p. front., plates. 22 cm. 96p. c.1896. American Tract Society.

--Grandpa's Desk: Or, Who Wins?. Benning, Howe, pseud. (Illus.). 96p. 1905. American Tract Society.

--Hester Lenox. Benning, Howe, pseud. 272p. 1877. American Tract Society.

--Hester Lenox. Benning, Howe, pseud. (Illus.). 272p. 1905. American Tract Society.

--Hope Reed's Upper Windows. Benning, Howe, pseud. LC 7-3026. 304 p. front., plates. 19 cm. c.1885. American Tract Society.

--Hope Reed's Upper Windows. Benning, Howe, pseud. (Illus.). 304p. 1905. American Tract Society.

--Jean's Opportunity. Benning, Howe, pseud. LC 99-421530. 339 p. front., pl. 19 1/2 cm. c.1899. The Union Press.

--Miss Charity's House. Benning, Howe, pseud. (The Girl Chum Ser.). N.D. A. L. Burt Company.

--Miss Charity's House. Benning, Howe, pseud. (Illus.). (The Wellesley Series for Girls). N.D. A. L. Burt.

--Miss Charity's House. Benning, Howe, pseud. LC 7-3025. 353 p. front., plates. 19 1/2 cm. c.1886. Congregational Sunday School and Publishing Society.

--Miss Charity's House. Benning, Howe, pseud. (Girls' Bookshelf Library). N.D. Pilgrims Press.

--Nix's Offerings. Benning, Howe, pseud. 400p. (Crowell's Sunday-School Library No. 6). N.D. T. Y. Crowell.

--Nix's Offerings. Benning, Howe, pseud. LC 7-3024. 400p. 17cm. 1873. Warren and Wyman.

--One Girl's Way Out. Benning, Howe, pseud. (Illus.). (The Wellesley Series for Girls). N.D. A. L. Burt.

--Opening Plain Paths. Benning, Howe, pseud. LC 7-3023. 336 p. front., plates. 19 cm. c.1881. American Tract Society.

--Opening Plain Paths. Benning, Howe, pseud, 1 of 50 vols. 336p. (Library of Best Authors). 1905. American Tract Society.

--Quiet Corners. Benning, Howe, pseud. LC 7-302223. 373 p. front., plates. 18 1/2 cm. c.1882. American Tract Society.

--Quiet Corners. Benning, Howe, pseud, 1 of 50 vols. 373p. (Library of Best Authors). 1905. American Tract Society.

--Ursula's Beginnings. Benning, Howe, pseud. LC 7-30210. 296 p. front., plates. 19 cm. c.1885. American Tract Society.

--Ursula's Beginnings. (Illus.). 296p. 1905. American Tract Society.

Henry, Maude Wood, jt. auth. see Henry, Arthur.

Henry, O., pseud., see Porter, William Sydney.

Henry, O., jt. auth. see Twain, Mark.

Henry, O., pseud. (1862-1910)

--A Gift from the Heart. Porter, William Sydney. Bumpass, F. L., ed. (Let's Read Stories: Book 2). N.D. (ISBN 0-07-008882-9). McGraw-Hill Book Company.

--The Gift of the Magi. Porter, William Sidney. Glaser, Byron, illus. LC 80-21844. (Illus.). 32 p. 23cm. (Creative classic series). c.1980. (ISBN 0-87191-775-0). Creative Education.

--The Gift of the Magi. Porter, William Sidney. rev. ed. Marshall, Rita, illus. 32p. (Christmas Stories Ser.). 1983. (ISBN 0-87191-954-0). Childrens Bk Co.

--Gift of the Magi & Five Other Stories. Porter, William Sydney. Rocker, Fermin (1907-), illus. (Illus.). (gr. 7 up). 1967. (ISBN 0-531-01067-8). Watts.

--Gift of the Magi: Creative's Christmas Stories. Porter, William Sidney. Redpath, Ann, ed. Marshall, Rita, illus. 32p. 1983. (ISBN 0-87191-954-0). Creative Ed.

--The Gifts & Other Stories. Porter, William Sidney. (Illus.). (Progressive English Readers Ser.). (gr. 3up). 1974. (ISBN 0-19-580574-7). Oxford U Pr.

--The Last Leaf. Porter, William Sidney. (Illus.). 32p. (Creative's Classics Ser.). (gr. 4-9). 1980. (ISBN 0-87191-774-2). Creative Ed.

--O. Henry Stories. Porter, William Sidney. (Great Writers Collection). (gr. 7 up). N.D. (ISBN 0-448-41105-9). Platt.

--O. Henry's Short Stories. Porter, William Sidney. (Magnum Easy Eye Classic Ser). (gr. 8-12). N.D. Lancer.

--The Ransom of Red Chief. Porter, William Sydney. (Thrushwood Bks.). N.D. Grosset & Dunlap.

--The Ransom of Red Chief. Porter, William Sidney. Glaser, Byron, illus. LC 80-21656. (Illus.). 40 p. 23cm. (Creative classic series). c.1980. (ISBN 0-87191-776-9). Creative Education.

--The Ransom of Red Chief and Cask of Wine. Porter, William Sydney. Bumpass, F. L., ed. (Let's Read Stories: Book 5). N.D. McGraw-Hill Book Company.

--Waifs and Strays. Porter, William Sydney. (Illus.). (The Brookside Library For Girls). N.D. CHeap Sunday-School Library.

Henry, R. & Pannell, L.

--Chuggety-Chug. N.D. Wilcox & Follett Co.

Henry, Rene

--Mary Lou. N.D. Frederick Warne & Co.

Henry, Sarah Ann

--The Little Book of Big Knock Knock Jokes. Ross, David (1949-), illus. LC 76-5529. (Illus.). 16cm. 32p. c.1977. Harvey House.

Henry, Sarepta Myrenda Irish, Mrs. (1839-1900)

--After the Truth. LC 7-3020. 286 p. 17 1/2 cm. 1874. Hitchcock and Walden.

--After the Truth. LC 7-3018. 345 p. 17 1/2 cm. 1877. Hitchcock and Walden.

--Afterward. A Sequel to "Beforehand.". LC 7-30167. 2 p. l., v, 3-568 p. front., pl. 19 1/2 cm. 1891. The National Temperance Society and Publication House.

--Beforehand. LC 7-3012. 529p. 19cm. 1888. The National Temperance Society and Publication House.

--Francis Raymond's Investment, or, The Cost of a Boy. LC 7-3017. 51 p. incl. illus., plates. front. 19 1/2 cm. 1889. Woman's Temperance Publication Association.

--Mabel's Work. A Sequel to The Voice of the Home. LC 7-3015. 468 p. incl. front. 17 1/2 cm. 1882. National Temperance Society and Publication House.

--One More Chance: Or, In Fallow. A Story of the Patience of God. LC 7-3664. 598 p. front. 17 1/2 cm. 1885. The National Temperance Society and Publication House.

--The Pledge and the Cross; a History of Our Pledge Roll. LC 7-3014. 256 p. incl. front. 17 1/2 cm. 1879. The National Temperance Society and Publication House.

--The Voice of the Home: Or, How Roy Went West, and How He Came Home Again. LC 7-3013. 405 p. 17 1/2 cm. 1882. National Temperance Society and Publication House.

Henry, Vera

--Ong, the Wild Gander. 1st ed. Rocker, Fermin (1907-), illus. LC 66-9730. (Illus.). 95 p. 22cm. 1966. Lippincott.

Henry, Will, pseud., see Allen, Henry Wilson.

Henry, Will, pseud. (1912-)

--The Day Fort Larking Fell: The Legend of the Last Great Indian Fight. Allen, Henry Wilson. 178p. (gr. 8 up). 1969. (ISBN 0-8019-5452-5). (ISBN 0-8019-5453-3). Chilton.

--Maheo's Children: The Legend of Little Dried River. Allen, Henry Wilson. LC 68-17165. (gr. 8 up). 1968. (ISBN 0-8019-5311-1). (ISBN 0-8019-5312-X). Chilton.

--Sons of the Western Frontier. Allen, Henry Wilson. (gr. 8 up). 1966. (ISBN 0-8019-5133-X). Chilton.

Henry, William J. & Harris, W. L.

--Hetty Porter: Or, God Knows Best. (Illus.). N.D. Methodist Bk Concern.

Henry Tall Bull & Weist, Tom

--Cheyenne Legends of Creation. (Indian Culture Ser.). (gr. 4-9). 1972. (ISBN 0-89992-025-X). MT Coun Indian.

--Grandfather & the Popping Machine. (Indian Culture Ser.). (gr. 2-12). 1970. (ISBN 0-89992-004-7). MT Coun Indian.

--Mista. (Indian Culture Ser.). (gr. 2-12). 1971. (ISBN 0-89992-011-X). MT Coun Indian.

--The Rolling Head: Cheyenne Tales. (Indian Culture Ser.). (gr. 3-9). 1971. (ISBN 0-89992-013-6). MT Coun Indian.

--The Spotted Horse. (Indian Culture Ser.). (gr. 2-10). 1970. (ISBN 0-89992-002-0). MT Coun Indian.

--The Turtle Went to War. (Indian Culture Ser.). (gr. 1-5). 1971. (ISBN 0-686-22283-0). MT Coun Indian.

--Veho. (Indian Culture Ser.). (gr. 2-6). 1971. (ISBN 0-89992-007-1). MT Coun Indian.

--The Winter Hunt. (Indian Culture Ser.). (gr. 3-9). 1971. (ISBN 0-89992-006-3). MT Coun Indian.

Henshaw, Helen (1876-1908)

--The Passing of the Word. LC 10-7171. 5 p. l., 3-360 p. 20 cm. 1910. The Torch Press.

Henson Associates

--Muppet Madness. Henson Associates, illus. LC 79-5269. (Illus., Orig.). (gr. 2-6). 1980. (ISBN 0-394-84393-2). Random.

Henson, Clyde E.

--Joseph Kirkland. N.D. Grosset & Dunlap.

Henson, Elsie Grant

--Secrets of Old Stormy. Harper, Arthur, illus. LC 48-7643. 168 p. illus. 21 cm. 1948. Broadman Press.

--Tom and Sally of Red Horse Creek. Picken, Henry Moore, illus. LC 53-9051. 185p. illus. 22cm. 1953. W. A. Wilde Co.

--The Winged Secret. LC 43-18198. 62 p. 18 cm. 1943. The Wartburg Press.

Henson, James Maury see Henson, Jim, pseud.

Henson, James Maury, jt. auth. see Damashek, Sandy.

Henson, James Maury, jt. auth. see Elliot, Dan.

Henson, James Maury see Howe, James (1946-) & Henson, Jim.

Henson, James Maury, jt. auth. see Stone, Jon.

Henson, James Maury, jt. auth. see Weiss, Ellen.

Henson, James Maury (1936-)

--Ernie & Bert Can- Can You?. Featuring Jim Henson's Sesame Street Muppets. Smollin, Michael J., illus. Children's Television Workshop LC 81-83696. (Illus.). 28 p. (Chunky book). c.1982. (ISBN 0-394-85150-1). Random House : CTW.

Henson, Jim, pseud., see Henson, James Maury.

Henson, Jim, pseud.

--The Count's Counting Book: Featuring Jim Henson's Muppets. Henson, James Maury. Cooke, Tom, illus. Penick, Ib, designed by. LC 79-56535. (Illus.). 14 p. 24cm. (CTW Sesame Street Pop-up: No. 14). c.1980. (ISBN 0-394-84436-X). Random House/Children's Television Workshop.

Henson, Jim, jt. auth. see Bruce, Sheilah B.

Henson, Jim, jt. auth. see Cooke, Tom.

Henson, Jim, jt. auth. see Ellsworth, Daisy.

Henson, Jim, jt. auth. see Gikow, Louise.

Henson, Jim, jt. auth. see Hayward, Linda.

Henson, Jim, jt. auth. see Howe, James.

Henson, Jim, jt. auth. see Korr, David.

Henson, Jim see Stone, Jon (1931-) & Henson, James Maury.

Henson, Jim, jt. auth. see Williams, Gregory.

Henstra, Friso (1928-)

--Mighty Mizzling Mouse. 1st ed. Henstra, Friso (1928-), illus. LC 82-48459. p. cm. c.1983. (ISBN 0-397-32003-5). (ISBN 0-397-32004-3). Lippincott.

--Mighty Mizzling Mouse & the Red Cabbage House. Henstra, Friso (1928-), illus. (Illus.). 1984. (ISBN 0-316-35778-2). (ISBN 0-316-35779-0). Little.

--Wait and See. Henstra, Friso (1928-), illus. LC 78-1020. (Illus.). 32 p. 24cm. c.1978. (ISBN 0-201-03077-2). Addison-Wesley Pub. Co.

Hentoff, Nathan Irving (1925-)

--The Day They Came to Arrest the Book: A Novel. LC 82-71100. p. cm. 160p. 1982. (ISBN 0-440-02039-5). Delacorte Press.

--Does This School Have Capital Punishment?. LC 80-68733. 170 p. 22cm. c.1981. (ISBN 0-440-02051-4). Delacorte Press.

--I'm Really Dragged but Nothing Gets Me Down. LC 68-29762. 127 p. 22cm. 1968. Simon & Schuster.

--In the Country of Ourselves. LC 78-163480. 128 p. 22cm. 1971. (ISBN 0-671-65197-8). Simon and Schuster.

--Jazz Country. LC 65-15557. 146 p. 22cm. 1965. Harper & Row. **Award: (ALA).**

--This School Is Driving Me Crazy: A Novel. LC 75-8003. p. cm. 160p. 1975. (ISBN 0-440-05287-4). Delacorte Press.

Henton, Gladys

--Oh Lord, I Wish I Was a Buzzard. Greenberg, Polly (1932-), ed. Aliki, pseud. (1929-), illus. Brandenberg, Aliki Liacouras. LC 68-24103. (Illus.). 1 v. (unpaged. 26cm. 1968. Macmillan.

Hentschel, Harriet L. (1922-), illus.

--Near the Friendly Meadows. LC 50-13848. 30 p. col. illus. 20 cm. (Friendly book, 1707). 1950. John Martin's House.

Henty, D. T., pseud., see Stratemeyer, Edward L..

Henty, D. T., pseud. (1862-1930)

--Malcolm, the Waterboy: Or, A Mystery of Old London. Stratemeyer, Edward L.. LC 6644. iv, 209 p. front., plates. 19 cm. 1900. The Mershon Company.

Henty, George Alfred (1832-1902)

--Among Malay Pirates. (Illus.). (The Henty Series for Boys). N.D. A. L. Burt's Pubs.

--Among Malay Pirates. (The Ideal Ser.). N.D. A. L. Burt's Pubs.

--Among Malay Pirates: A Story of Adventure and Peril. (Henty Series for Boys). 1910. Hurst & Co.

--Among Malay Pirates: A Tale of Adventure and Peril. LC 39-17476. iii, 274 p. front. 19 cm. 274p. N.D. M. A. Donohue & Company.

--Among the Malays. (Henty Bks). N.D. George M Hill Co.

--At Aboukir and Acre: A Story of Napoleon's Invasion of Egypt. Rainey, William R. I. (1852-1936), illus. LC 98-489. vi p., 2 l., 331 p. illus. (plans) 8 pl. (incl. front.) 19 cm. 1898. C. Scribner's Sons.

--At Aboukir and Acre: A/Story of Napoleon's Invasion of Egypt. Rainey, William R. I. (1852-1936), illus. LC 98-489. (Illus.). vi, 331. 19cm. 1898. C. Scribner's Sons.

--At Agincourt: A Tale of the White Hoods of Paris. Paget, Walter, illus. LC 12-34137. vi p., 2 l., 356 p. front., plates. 19 cm. 1896. C. Scribner's Sons.

--At the Point of the Bayonet: A Tale of the Mahratta War. Paget, Walter, illus. LC 1-23628. vi p. 2 l., 376 p. front., illus., plates. 19 cm. 1901. C. Scribner's Sons.

--Beric the Briton: A Story of the Roman Invasion. Parkinson, W., illus. LC 12-34147. 383 p. front., 11 pl. 19 cm. 1892. C. Scribner's Sons.

--Bonnie Prince Charlie, 1 of 5 vols. (George Alfred Henty's Wks.). N.D. Set. A. L. Burt's Pubs.

--Bonnie Prince Charlie. (Illus.). (The Henty Series for Boys). N.D. A. L. Burt's Pubs.

--Bonnie Prince Charlie. (The Ideal Ser.). N.D. A. L. Burt's Pubs.

--Bonnie Prince Charlie. Empire ed. 1905. American News Co.

--Bonnie Prince Charlie. (Illus.). N.D. British Book Centre Inc.

--Bonnie Prince Charlie. N.D. Charles Scribner's Sons'.

--Bonnie Prince Charlie, 1 of 64 vols. LC 39-17478. 19cm. 350p. (Young America Library: No. 8). 1900. Set. Hurst & Co.

--Bonnie Prince Charlie: A tale of Fontenoy & Culloden. 1900. George M Hill Co.

--Bonnie Prince Charlie: A Tale of Fontenoy and Culloden. vi (i. e. iv), 7-350 p. 19 cm. N.D. Hurst and Company.

--Bonnie Prince Charlie: A Tale of Fontenor and Culloden. (Illus.). (Henty Ser.). N.D. Hurst & Co.

--Bonnie Prince Charlie: A Tale of Fontenoy and Culloden. Browne, Gordon Frederick (1858-1932), illus. LC 39-17477. vi (i. e. iv), 7-350 p. front. 19 1/2 cm. N.D. A. L. Burt.

--Jack Archer: A Tale of the Crimea. LC 4-878. (Illus.). 19cm. 362p. (The Henty Series for Boys). N.D. A. L. Burt's Pubs.
--Jack Archer: A Tale of the Crimea. LC 14-18242. 2 p. l., 302 p. 8 pl. (incl. front.) 18 cm. 1892. C. E. Brown and Company.
--Jack Archer: A Tale of the Crimea. 1900. George M Hill Co.
--Jack Archer: A Tale of the Crimea, 1 of 64 vols. (Young America Library: No. 27). 1900. Set. Hurst & Co.
--Jack Archer: A Tale of the Crimea. (Illus.). N.D. Messrs. Roberts Brothers.
--Jack Archer: A Tales of the Crimea. (Illus.). (Henty Series for Boys). 1910. Hurst & Co.
--A Jacobite Exile: Being the Adventures of a Young Englishman in the Service of Charles XII of Sweden. Hardy, Paul (1862-), illus. LC 12-341437. 353 p. front., plates, double map. 19 cm. 1893. C. Scribner's Sons.
--A Knight of the White Cross: A Tale of the Siege of Rhodes. Peacock, Ralph, illus. LC 12-34138. 400 p. front., plates, plan. 19 cm. 1895. C. Scribner's Sons.
--The Lion of Saint Mark: A Story of Venice in the Fourteenth Century. (Illus.). (The Henty Series for Boys). N.D. A. L. Burt's Pubs.
--The Lion of St. Mark. (The Ideal Ser.). N.D. A. L. Burt's Pubs.
--Lion of St. Mark. Empire ed. 1905. American News Co.
--Lion of St. Mark. (Illus.). N.D. British Book Centre Inc.
--Lion of St. Mark. N.D. Charles Scribner's Sons'.
--The Lion of St. Mark. (Illus.). (Henty Series for Boys). 1910. Hurst & Co.
--The Lion of St. Mark: A Story of Venice in the Fourteenth Century. Browne, Gordon Frederick (1858-1932), illus. LC 39-17487. 362 p. plates. 19 cm. (His Fireside Henty series). N.D. M. A. Donohue & Co.
--The Lion of St. Mark: A Story of Venice in the Fourteenth Century. Browne, Gordon Frederick (1858-1932), illus. LC 39-17486. 362 p. front., plates. 19 cm. N.D. The F. M. Lupton Publishing Company.
--Lion of St. Mark: A Tale of Venice in the Fourteenth Century. 1900. George M Hill Co.
--The Lion of the North. (Illus.). (Henty Ser. for Boys). N.D. A. L. Burt's Publications.
--The Lion of the North. (The Ideal Ser.). N.D. A. L. Burt's Pubs.
--Lion of the North. Empire ed. 1905. American News Co.
--Lion of the North. N.D. Charles Scribner's Sons'.
--The Lion of the North. (Illus.). (Roundabout Lib.). N.D. Henry T. Coates & Co.
--The Lion of the North. (Illus.). (Henty Series for Boys). 1910. Hurst & Co.
--The Lion of The North. (Roundabout Library). N.D. John C. Winston Co.
--Lion of the North: A Tale of Gustavus Adolphus & the Wars of Religion. 1900. George M Hill Co.
--The Lion of the North: A Tale of the Times of Gustavus Adolphus and the Wars of Religion. LC 39-17488. 340 p. front., plates. 19 cm. N.D. The Mershon Company.
--The Lost Heir. (Illus.). (Henty Series for Boys). 1910. Hurst & Co.
--Maori and Settler. (The Ideal Ser.). N.D. A. L. Burt's Pubs.
--Maori and Settler. Empire ed. 1905. American News Co.
--Maori and Settler. N.D. Charles Scribner's Sons'.
--Maori and Settler: A Story of New Zealand War. (Illus.). (The Henty Series for Boys). N.D. A. L. Burt's Pubs.
--Maori and Settler: A Story of the New Zealand War. (Illus.). (Henty Ser.). N.D. Hurst & Co.
--Maori and Settler: A Story of the New Zealand War. Pearse, Alfred (1856-) illus. LC 39-17489. 4, v-vi, 322 p. front., plates, map. 19 cm. N.D. M. A. Donohue & Co.
--Maori & Settler: A Tale of the New Zealand War. 1900. George M Hill Co.
--A March on London: Being a Story of Wat Tyler's Insurrection. Margetson, W. H., illus. vi p., 2 l., 339 p. front., plates. 18 1/2 cm. 1897. C. Scribner's Sons.
--For Name and Fame: or, Through Afghan Passes. N.D. Charles Scribner's Sons'.
--No Surrender!. A Tale of the Rising in La Vendee. Wood, Stanley L. (1866-1928), illus. LC 99-4216. vi p., 2 l., 345 p. front., plates. 19 cm. 1899. C. Scribner's Sons.
--On the Irrawaddy: A Story of the First Burmese War. Overend, W. H., illus. LC 12-34136. vi p., 2 l., 315 p. front., plates. 19 cm. 1897. C. Scribner's Sons.
--One of the Twenty-Eighth, 1 of 5 vols. (George Alfred Henty's Wks.: No. 2). N.D. Set. A. L. Burt's Pubs.
--One of the Twenty-Eighth. (Illus.). (The Henty Series for Boys). N.D. A. L. Burt's Pubs.
--One of the Twenty-Eighth. (The Ideal Ser.). N.D. A. L. Burt's Pubs.
--One of the Twenty-Eighth. Empire ed. 1905. American News Co.
--One of the Twenty-Eighth. N.D. Charles Scribner's Sons.
--One of the Twenty Eighth: A Story of Waterloo. N.D. Charles Scribner's Sons'.
--One of the Twenty Eighth: A Tale of Waterloo. LC 39-17490. vi, 384 p. front. 19 cm. N.D. A. L. Burt.
--One of the Twenty Eighth: A Tale of Waterloo. (The Ideal Ser.). N.D. A. L. Burt.
--One of the Twenty Eighth: A Tale of Waterloo. 1900. George M Hill Co.
--One of the Twenty Eighth: A Tale of Waterloo. (Illus.). (Henty Ser.). N.D. Hurst & Co.
--Orange and Green. (Illus.). (The Henty Series for Boys). N.D. A. L. Burt's Pubs.
--Orange and Green. (The Ideal Ser.). N.D. A. L. Burt's Pubs.
--Orange and Green. Empire ed. 1905. American News Co.
--Orange and Green. (Illus.). (Roundabout Lib.). N.D. Henry T. Coates & Co.
--Orange and Green. (Roundabout Library). N.D. John C. Winston Co.
--Orange and Green: A Tale of the Boyne and Limerick. N.D. Charles Scribner's Sons.
--Orange and Green: A Tale of the Boyne and Limerick. LC 39-17491. vi, 295 p. front., plates. 19 cm. N.D. Geo. M. Hill Co.
--Orange & Green: A Tale of the Boyne & Limerick. 1900. George M Hill Co.
--Orange & Green: A Tale of the Boyne & Limerick, 1 of 64 vols. (Young America Library: No. 30). 1900. Set. Hurst & Co.
--Orange and Green: A Tale of the Boyne and Limerick. (Illus.). (Henty Series for Boys). N.D. Hurst & Co.
--Out on the Pampas. Empire ed. 1905. American News Co.
--Out on the Pampas. 1882. E P Dutton.
--Out on the Pampas: A Tale of South America. 1900. George M Hill Co.
--Out on the Pampas: A Tale of South America, 1 of 64 vols. (Young America Library: No. 31). 1900. Set. Hurst & Co.
--Out on the Pampas: A Tale of South America. (Illus.). (Henty Series for Boys). 1910. Hurst & Co.
--Out on the Pampas: Or, the Young Settlers. (Illus.). (The Henty Series for Boys). N.D. A. L. Burt's Pubs.
--Out on the Pampas: Or, The Young Settlers. (The Ideal Ser.). N.D. A. L. Burt's Pubs.
--Out with Garibaldi: A Story of the Liberation of Italy. Rainey, William R. I. (1852-1936), illus. LC 5058. 4 p. l., 346 p. front., plates, maps. 19 cm. 1900. C. Scribner's Sons.
--Pike and Dyke. Empire ed. 1905. American News Co.
--By Pyke and Dyke. N.D. Grosset & Dunlap.
--Redskin and Cow-Boy: A Tale of the Western Plains. Pearse, Alfred (1856-), illus. LC 12-34150. 384 p. front., plates. 19 cm. 1891. C. Scribner's Sons.
--Redskin and Cowboy. 256p. 1953. British Book Centre Inc.
--Redskin and Cowboy. Pearse, Alfred (1856-), illus. (Illus.). N.D. Grosset & Dunlap.
--Redskins and Colonists. (Henty Series for Boys). N.D. Hurst & Co.
--Redskins and Colonists: Or, A Boy's Adventures in the Early Days of Virginia. LC 5-36926. iv p., 1 l., 283 p. front., plates. 19 cm. 1905. Stitt Publishing Company.
--By Right of Conquest: or, With Cortez in Mexico. N.D. Charles Scribner's Sons'.
--A Roving Commission: Or, Through the Black Insurrection at Hayti. 1899. Charles Scribner's Sons.
--Rujub, the Juggler. (Illus.). (Henty Series for Boys). 1910. Hurst & Co.
--Rujub, the Juggler ... LC 1-12826. iv, 385 p. front. 12. 1901. The Mershon Co.
--By Sheer Pluck. N.D. Charles Scribner's Sons'.
--St. Bartholomew's Eve. (Illus.). 224p. N.D. British Book Centre Inc.
--St. Bartholomew's Eve: A/Tale of the Huguenot Wars. Draper, H. J., illus. LC 12-34129. (Illus.). 384p. 19cm. 1893. C. Scribner's Sons.
--St. George for England. (Illus.). (The Henty Series for boys). N.D. A. L. Burt's Pubs.
--St. George for England. Empire ed. 1905. American News Co.
--St. George for England. (Illus.). N.D. British Book Centre Inc.
--St. George for England. N.D. Charles Scribner's Sons'.
--St. George for England: A Tale of Cressy and Poitiers. (The Ideal Ser.). N.D. A. L. Burt.
--St. George for England: A Tale of Cressy & Poitiers. 1900. George M Hill Co.
--St. George for England: A Tale of Cressy and Poitiers. (Illus.). (Henty Series for Boys). N.D. Hurst & Co.
--St. George for England: A Tale of Cressy and Poitiers. Browne, Gordon Frederick (1858-1932), illus. LC 12-34173. iv p., 2 l., 9-352 p. front., plates. 19 cm. 1884. Blackie & Son, Limited.
--Sturdy & Strong. 1900. George M Hill Co.
--Sturdy and Strong: Or, How George Andrews Made His Way. (Illus.). (The Henty Series for Boys). N.D. A. L. Burt's Pubs.
--Sturdy and Strong: Or, How George Andrews Made His Way. (The Ideal Ser.). N.D. A. L. Burt's Pubs.
--Sturdy and Strong: Or, How George Andrew made His Way. (Illus.). (Henty Series for boys). 1910. Hurst & Co.
--Through Russian Snows. N.D. Charles Scribner's Sons'.
--Through the Fray. (Illus.). (The Henty Series for Boys). N.D. A. L. Burt's Pubs.
--Through the Fray. (The Ideal Ser.). N.D. A. L. Burt's Pubs.
--Through the Fray. Empire ed. 1905. American News Co.
--Through the Fray. N.D. Charles Scribner's Sons'.
--Through the Fray, 1 of 64 vols. (Young America Library: No. 42). 1900. Set. Hurst & Co.
--Through the Fray: A Story of the Laddite Riots. (Illus.). 1910. Hurst & Co.
--Through the Fray: A Story of the Luddite Riots. 1900. George M Hill Co.
--Through the Sikh War: A Tale of the Conquest of the Punjaub. Hurst, Hal, illus. LC 12-34135. 386 p. front., plates, double map. 19 cm. 1893. C. Scribner's Sons.
--Through Three Campaigns: A Story of Chitral, Tirah, and Ashanti. Paget, Walter, illus. LC 3-22809. ix, 373 p. front., 7 pl., 3 maps. 19 cm. 1903. C. Scribner's Sons.
--Through Three Campaigns: A Story of Chitral, Tirah and Ashanti. Paget, Walter, illus. (Illus.). N.D. Grosset & Dunlap.
--The Tiger of Mysore: A Story of the War with Tippoo Saib. Margetson, W. H., illus. LC 12-34145. 390 p. front., illus. (plans) plates, double map. 19 cm. 1895. C. Scribner's Sons.
--To Herat and Cabul: A Story of the First Afghan War. Sheldon, Charles M., illus. LC 1-23675. vi p., 2 l., 346 p. front., plates, fold. map. 19 cm. 1901. C. Scribner's Sons.
--The Treasure of the Incas: A Tale of Adventure in Peru. Paget, Walter, illus. LC 2-22472. ix, 340 p. front., pl., map. 19 cm. 1902. C. Scribner's Sons.
--The Treasure of the Incas: A Tale of Adventures in Peru. Paget, Walter, illus. (Illus.). N.D. Grosset & Dunlap.
--Treasures of the Incas. 256p. 1953. British Book Centre Inc.
--True to the Old Flag, 1 of 5 vols. (George Alfred Henty's Wks.). N.D. Set. A. L. Burt's Pubs.
--True to the Old Flag. (Illus.). (The Henty Series for Boys). N.D. A. L. Burt's Pubs.
--True to the Old Flag. (The Ideal Ser.). N.D. A. L. Burt's Pubs.
--True to the Old Flag. Empire ed. 1905. American News Co.
--True to the Old Flag. N.D. Charles Scribner's Sons'.
--True to the Old Flag. (Illus.). (Roundabout Lib.). N.D. Henry T. Coates & Co.
--True to the Old Flag, 1 of 64 vols. (Young America Library: No. 48). 1900. Set. Hurst & Co.
--True to the Old Flag. (Illus.). (Henty Series for Boys). 1910. Hurst & Co.
--True to the Old Flag: A Tale of Independence. LC 42-196867. vi, 482 p. front., illus. (map. plans) plates. 19 cm. N.D. A. L. Burt.
--True to the Old Flag: A Tale of the American War for Independence. 1900. George M Hill Co.
--True to the Old Flag: A Tale of the American War of Independence. Browne, Gordon Frederick (1858-1932), illus. LC 12-341707. vi, 2, 9-390 p. incl. front., illus. (map, plans) plates. 19 cm. N.D. Blackie & Son, Limited.
--Under Drake's Flag. (Illus.). (Henty Ser. for Boys). N.D. A. L. Burt's Publications.
--Under Drake's Flag, 1 of 5 vols. (George Alfred Henty's Wks.). N.D. Set. A. L. Burt's Pubs.
--Under Drake's Flag. (The Ideal Ser.). N.D. A. L. Burt's Pubs.
--Under Drake's Flag. Empire ed. 1905. American News Co.
--Under Drake's Flag. 256p. 1956. British Book Centre Inc.
--Under Drake's Flag. (Illus.). (Roundabout Lib.). N.D. Henry T. Coates & Co.
--Under Drake's Flag, 1 of 64 vols. (Young America Library: No. 52). 1900. Set. Hurst & Co.
--Under Drake's Flag. (Illus.). (Henty Series for Boys). 1910. Hurst & Co.
--Under Drake's Flag: A Tale of the Spanish Main. 1900. George M Hill Co.
--Under Drake's Flag: A Tale of the Spanish Main. Browne, Gordon Frederick (1858-1932), illus. LC 12-18729. iv, 331 p. front., plates. 19 1/2 cm. 1912. A. L. Burt Company.
--Under Drake's Flag: A Tale of the Spanish Main. Browne, Gordon Frederick (1858-1932), illus. LC 38-35036. iv, 331 p. front. 19 1/2 cm. N.D. A. L. Burt.
--Under Drake's Flag: A Tale of the Spanish Main. Browne, Gordon Frederick (1858-1932), illus. LC 4-17540. 368 p. incl. front. 11 pl. 19 1/2 cm. N.D. Blackie & Son, Limited.
--Under Drake's Flag: A Tale of the Spanish Main. Browne, Gordon Frederick (1858-1932), illus. LC 67-120459. (Illus.). 19cm. 356p. 1894. Scribner.
--Under Wellington's Command. 224p. N.D. British Book Centre Inc.
--Under Wellington's Command: A Tale of the Peninsular War. Paget, Walter, illus. LC 98-191. 1 p. l., v-vii p., 2 l., 386 p. illus. (plans) plates. 19 cm. 1898. C. Scribner's Sons.
--Under Wellington's Command: A Tale of the Peninsular War. Paget, Walter, illus. LC 33-7779. vii p., 2 l., 386 p. front., illus. (plans) plates. 19 1/2 cm. 1903. C. Scribner's Sons.
--When London Burned. 224p. N.D. British Book Centre Inc.
--When London Burned: A Story of Restoration Times and the Great Fire. Finnemore, J., illus. LC 12-34155. 403 p. front., plates. 19 cm. 1894. C. Scribner's Sons.
--Winning His Spurs. (Illus.). N.D. British Book Centre Inc.
--With Buller in Natal: Or, A Born Leader. Rainey, William R. I. (1852-1936), illus. 5 p. l., 370 p. 10 pl. (incl. front.) 19 cm. 1903. C. Scribner's Sons.
--With Clive in India. (Illus.). (Henty Ser. for Boys). N.D. A. L. Burt's Publications.
--With Clive in India. Empire ed. 1905. American News Co.
--With Clive in India. (Illus.). N.D. British Book Centre Inc.
--With Clive in India. Browne, Gordon Frederick (1858-1932), illus. LC 67-9150. (Illus.). 308p. (The Children's Favorite Ser.). N.D. Grosset & Dunlap.
--With Clive in India: or, the Beginnings of an Empire. N.D. Charles Scribner's Sons'.
--With Clive in India: Or, The Beginnings of an Empire. 1900. George M Hill Co.
--With Clive in India: Or, The Beginnings of an Empire. (Illus.). (Roundabout Lib.). N.D. Henry T. Coates & Co.
--With Clive in India: Or, The Beginnings of an Empire. LC 26-24703. vi p., 2 l., 7-378 p. incl. front. 19 cm. (Henty series for boys). N.D. Hurst & Company.
--With Clive in India: Or, The Beginnings of an Empire. LC 26-34703. (Illus.). 19cm. 378p. (Henty Series for Boys). N.D. Hurst & Co.
--With Clive in India: Or, The Beginnings of an Empire. (Roundabout Library). N.D. John C. Winston Co.
--With Clive in India: Or, The Beginnings of an Empire. empire ed. LC 48-40912. v, 336 p. 20 cm. N.D. New York Pub. Co.
--With Clive in India: Or, The Beginnings of an Empire. Browne, Gordon Frederick (1858-1932), illus. LC 41-42440. vii, 7-384 p. front., illus. (map) 19 cm. N.D. A. L. Burt.
--With Clive in India: Or, The Beginnings of an Empire. Browne, Gordon Frederick (1858-1932), illus. LC 39-17493. vii, 7-384 p. plates. 19 1/2 cm. N.D. A. L. Burt Company.
--With Clive in India: Or, The Beginnings of an Empire. Browne, Gordon Frederick (1858-1932), illus. LC 41-42140. 19cm. 384p. (The Ideal Ser.). N.D. A. L. Burt's Pubs.
--With Clive in India: Or, The Beginnings of an Empire. Browne, Gordon Frederick (1858-1932), illus. LC 44-25673. vi, 2, 9-382 p. front., plates, maps (1 double) 19 1/2 cm. 1887. Scribner and Welford.
--With Cochrane the Dauntless. 224p. 1957. British Book Centre Inc.
--With Cochrane the Dauntless: A Tale of the Exploits of Lord Cochrane in South American Waters. Margetson, W. H., illus. LC 12-34153. vi p., 2 l., 11-388 p. front., plates. 19 cm. 1896. C. Scribner's Sons.
--With Frederick the Great: A Story of the Seven Years' War. Paget, Walter, illus. LC 12-34139. vi p., 1 l., 2, 374 p. front., illus. (maps) plates. 18 1/2 cm. 1897. C. Scribner's Sons.
--With Kitchener in the Soudan: A/Story of Atbara and Omdurman. Rainey, William R. I. (1852-1936), illus. LC 2-22397. (Illus.). ix, 380. 19cm. 1902. C. Scribner's Sons.
--With Kitchener in the Soudan: A Story of Atbara and Omdurman. Rainey, William R. I. (1852-1936), illus. LC 39-17494. 1 p. l., v-ix, 380 p. front., plates, maps. 19 1/2 cm. 1905. C. Scribner's Sons.
--With Lee in Virginia. (Illus.). (Henty Ser. for Boys). N.D. A. L. Burt's Publications.
--With Lee in Virginia, 1 of 5 vols. (George Alfred Henty's Wks.). N.D. Set. A. L. Burt's Pubs.
--With Lee in Virginia. (The Ideal Ser.). N.D. A. L. Burt's Pubs.
--With Lee in Virginia. Empire ed. 1905. American News Co.
--With Lee in Virginia. (Illus.). 224p. N.D. British Book Centre Inc.

--Prisoners of the Sun. Remi, Georges. (Illus.). 62p. N.D. (ISBN 0-416-92620-7). (ISBN 0-416-77410-5). French & Eur.
--Prisoners of the Sun: The Adventure Tintin. Remi, Georges. Herge, pseud. (1907-1983), illus. Remi, Georges. 1975. Little Brown and Company.
--Red Rackham's Treasure. Remi, Georges. (Illus.). 62p. N.D. (ISBN 0-416-92540-5). (ISBN 0-416-80010-6). French & Eur.
--Red Rackham's Treasure. Remi, Georges. (The Adventures of Tintin). 1959. Golden Press.
--Red Rackham's Treasure. Remi, Georges. LC 73-21253. (Illus.). 64p. (Orig., Pub. by Casterman). (The Adventures of Tintin Ser.). 1974. (ISBN 0-316-35834-7, Pub. by Atlantic Monthly Pr). Little.
--The Red Sea Sharks. Remi, Georges. (Illus.). 62p. N.D. (ISBN 0-416-60570-2). (ISBN 0-416-24070-4). French & Eur.
--The Red Sea Sharks. Remi, Georges. (The Adventures of Tintin Ser). 1976. (ISBN 0-316-35848-7, Pub. by Atlantic Monthly Pr.). Little.
--The Secret of the Unicorn. Remi, Georges. (Illus.). 62p. N.D. (ISBN 0-416-92530-8). (ISBN 0-416-80020-3). French & Eur.
--The Secret of the Unicorn. Remi, Georges. (The Adventures of Tintin). 1959. Golden Press.
--The Secret of the Unicorn. Remi, Georges. LC 73-21250. (Illus.). 64p. (Orig., Pub. by Casterman). (The Adventures of Tintin Ser). 1974. (ISBN 0-316-35832-0, Pub. by Atlantic Monthly Pr). Little.
--The Seven Crystal Balls. Remi, Georges. (Illus.). 62p. (gr. 3-8). N.D. (ISBN 0-416-92610-X). (ISBN 0-416-78000-8). French & Eur.
--The Seven Crystal Balls: The Adventures of Tintin. Remi, Georges. Herge, pseud. (1907-1983), illus. Remi, Georges. 1975. Little Brown and Company.
--The Shooting Star. Remi, Georges. (Illus.). 62p. N.D. (ISBN 0-416-60580-X). (ISBN 0-416-24080-1). French & Eur.
--Tintin - the Blue Oranges. Remi, Georges. (Illus.). (gr. 3-8). N.D. French & Eur.
--Tintin & the Broken Ear. Remi, Georges. (Illus.). 62p. N.D. (ISBN 0-416-83450-7). (ISBN 0-416-57030-5). French & Eur.
--Tintin & the Golden Fleece. Remi, Georges. (gr. 3-8). N.D. (ISBN 0-685-11599-2). French & Eur.
--Tintin & the Lake of Sharks. Remi, Georges. (Illus.). 62p. N.D. (ISBN 0-416-78950-1). (ISBN 0-416-83630-5). French & Eur.
--Tintin & the Picaros. Remi, Georges. (Illus.). 62p. N.D. (ISBN 0-416-85170-3). (ISBN 0-416-57990-6). French & Eur.
--Tintin au Congo. Remi, Georges. (Illus.). (gr. 7-9). N.D. (ISBN 0-685-28415-8). French & Eur.
--Tintin in Tibet. Remi, Georges. (Illus.). 62p. N.D. (ISBN 0-416-92600-2). (ISBN 0-416-24090-9). French & Eur.
--Tintin in Tibet. Remi, Georges. LC 74-21621. (The Adventures of Tintin Ser). 1975. (ISBN 0-316-35839-8, Pub. by Atlantic Monthly Pr). Little.

Hering, Jeanie
--A Banished Monarch: and Other Stories, 1 of 7 vols. (The Magic Mirror Library). N.D. Cassell, Petter, Galpin.
--Golden Days. New ed. N.D. Cassel, Petter, & Galpin.
--Golden Days, 1 of 6 vols. (The Notable Library). N.D. Cassell, Petter, Galpin.
--Little Pickles. N.D. Cassell Petter & Galpin.

Herman, Agnes, jt. auth. see Herman, Erwin.

Herman, Arthur Ludwig (1930-), ed.
--India Folk Tales. Jarvis, Maggie, illus. LC 68-3340. (Illus.). 61 p. 20cm. 1968. Peter Pauper Press.

Herman, Ben (1927-)
--The Rhapsody in Blue of Mickey Klein. LC 80-28261. 143 p. 23cm. c.1981. (ISBN 0-916144-68-2). Stemmer House Publishers.

Herman, Charlotte, ed. see Wensell, Ulises.

Herman, Charlotte (1937-)
--The Big Cereal Gyp. Herman, Toni, illus. 1975. J. Philip O'Hara Inc.
--The Difference of Ari Stein. 1st ed. Shecter, Ben (1935-), illus. LC 75-25406. (Illus.). 150 p. 21cm. c.1976. (ISBN 0-06-022309-X). Harper & Row.
--Just We Three. Carpenter, Mia, illus. LC 72-13254. (Illus.). 118 p. 18cm. 1975, c.1973. New American Library.
--Millie Cooper, 3B. LC 84-25951. p. cm. c.1985. (ISBN 0-525-44157-3). Dutton.
--Millie Cooper, 3B. Cogancherry, Helen, illus. LC 85-43425. p. cm. 1986, c.1985. (ISBN 0-14-032072-5). Puffin Books.
--My Mother Didn't Kiss Me Good-Night. Durell, Ann, ed. Degen, Bruce, illus. LC 80-190. (Illus.). 32 p. 26cm. c.1980. Dutton.
--On the Way to the Movies. Dawson, Diane, illus. LC 79-19015. (Illus.). 32 p. 26cm. c.1980. (ISBN 0-525-36400-5). Dutton.
--Our Snowman Had Olive Eyes. LC 77-7143. p. cm. 1977. E. P. Dutton.
--String Bean. Funk, Thompson (1911-), illus. LC 74-186882. (Illus.). 48 p. 23cm. (Lead-off book). 1972. (ISBN 0-87955-104-6). (ISBN 0-87955-704-4). J. P. O'Hara.
--The Three of Us. Carpenter, Mia, illus. LC 72-18254. (Illus.). 24cm. 126p. 1973. (ISBN 0-87955-204-2). (ISBN 0-87955-804-0). J. Philip O'Hara.
--What Happened to Heather Hopkowitz?. LC 81-5111. p. cm. c.1981. (ISBN 0-525-42455-5). Dutton.
--You've Come a Long Way, Sybil Macintosh. LC 73-2258. (Illus.). Repr. (gr. 3-7). 1977. (ISBN 0-87955-207-7). (ISBN 0-87955-807-5). Lamplight Pub.
--You've come a Long Way Sybil Macintosh. Hyman, Trina Schart (1939-), illus. 1974. (ISBN 0-87955-207-7). J. Philip O'Hara Inc.

Herman, Emily
--Hubknuckles. Ray, Deborah, pseud. (1940-), illus. Kogan Ray, Deborah. LC 84-21355. (Illus.). 32 p. 23cm. c.1985. (ISBN 0-517-55646-4). Crown Publishers.

Herman, Erwin & Herman, Agnes
--The Yanov Torah. Kahn, Katherine Janns, illus. LC 85-5269. p. cm. 1985. (ISBN 0-930494-45-8). (ISBN 0-930494-46-6). Kar-Ben Copies.

Herman, Ethel A
--Roy's Cruise in Hawaiian Waters. LC 52-4490. 112 p. 22 cm. 1952. Vantage Press.

Herman, Harriet (1937-)
--The Forest Princess. Dwinell, Carole Petersen (1943-), illus. (Illus.). 1 v. (unpaged). 25cm. 1974. Over the Rainbow Press.
--Return of the Forest Princess. Dwinell, Carole Petersen (1943-), illus. LC 75-34177. p. cm. c.1975. Over the Rainbow Press.

Herman, Humphrey
--Men of Masaba. N.D. (ISBN 0-670-46892-4). Viking Press.

Herman, R. L. & Satterlee, Walter
--Cradle Songs of Many Nations. Satterlee, Walter, illus. N.D. Dodd, Mead & Co.

Herman, Victor J (1919-)
--Juanito's Railroad in the Sky. Herman, Victor J. (1919-), illus. LC 75-37460. (Illus.). 61 p. c.1976. (ISBN 0-307-15584-6). Golden Press.

Hermen, T. J.
--Mr. Shingles. 1962. Exposition Press.

Hermes, Patricia (1936-)
--Friends Are Like That. LC 83-18407. 128p. (gr. 4-6). 1984. (ISBN 0-15-229722-7, HJ). (ISBN 0-15-229722-7). HarBraceJ.
--Nobody's Fault?. LC 81-47532. p. cm. c.1981. (ISBN 0-15-257466-2). Harcourt Brace Jovanovich.
--A Solitary Secret. 1985. (ISBN 0-15-277190-5). Farrar Strauss.
--What If They Knew?. LC 79-90033. 121 p. 21cm. c.1980. (ISBN 0-15-295317-5). Harcourt Brace Jovanovich.
--Who Will Take Care of Me?. 1st ed. LC 82-48757. p. cm. c.1983. (ISBN 0-15-296265-4). Harcourt Brace Jovanovich.
--You Shouldn't Have to Say Good-Bye. 1st ed. LC 82-47933. 117 p. 21cm. c.1982. (ISBN 0-15-299944-2). Harcourt Brace Jovanovich.
--You Shouldn't Have to Say Good-bye. (gr. 5-8). 1982. Houghton Mifflin.

Hernandez, Felicia
--I Don't Know You but I Love You: Write Me a Letter. Bosserman, Lorelei, illus. (Illus.). (gr. 7-12). 1978. (ISBN 0-915288-36-2). Shameless Hussy.

Herndon, Betty Boulton (1908-)
--Adventures in Cactus Land. Herndon, Betty Boulton (1908-), illus. 1950. Caxton Publishers.
--Bill and the Clown Bird. Herndon, Betty Boulton (1908-), illus. LC 57-5249. 153p. illus. 22cm. 1957. Caxton Printers.

Herne, Bobbi
--Hippopotamus. Miller, Jeane H., illus. (Illus.). 2 color throughout. 32p. (Ready to Read Bks). (ps-2). 1969. (ISBN 0-448-02388-1). G&D.
--Poems about Everything. 48p. 1966. Pitman Publishing.

Herne, Niall
--The Cross of McKennor. (Illus.). N.D. E & J B Young.

Herodotus
--The Magic Loaves and Other Tales. Watkins, Hope Brister, adapted by. Minton, Harold, illus. LC 31-10522. 4 p. l., 192 p. incl. illus., plates. col. front. 16 1/2 cm. (The Little library). 1931. The Macmillan Company.
--Wonder Stories from Herodotus. Boden, George Harry & D'Almeida, William Barrington, eds. Fell, Herbert Granville, illus. LC 4-14088. 5 p. l., 3-163 p., 1 l. col. front., col. plates. 21 cm. 1900. Harper & Brothers.

Herold, Ann Bixby & De Larrea, Victoria
--The Helping Day. LC 79-4451. (Illus.). 32 p. 21cm. c.1980. (ISBN 0-698-20492-1). Coward, McCann & Geoghegan.

Heron, Frances Dunlap
--Betty Ann, Beginner: Lines from Her Diary. Craighead, Mauriece, illus. LC 30-13870. 128 p. illus. 20 cm. 1930. Bethany Press.
--The Busy Berrys. Shearer, Ted, illus. LC 50-4095. 126 p. illus. (part col.) 20 cm. 1950. Friendship Press.
--Kathy Ann, Kindergartner. Smalley, Janet (1893-), illus. (Illus.). 1955. (ISBN 0-687-20731-2). Abingdon.
--With My Whole Heart. Howe, Gertrude Herrick (1902-), illus. LC 50-10443. 50 p. illus. (part col.) 17 x 23 cm. (Children's hour library). 1950. Westminster Press.

Heron, Grace
--Fur and Feathers And a Few Other People. LC 33-440. 50 p. illus. 24 cm. (The checker series. no. 1). c.1932. R. F. Seymour.

Heron, Henrietta & Shonkweiler, James Harvey (1877-), eds.
--Pageants for the Year. LC 28-11738. 192 p. illus. (incl. music) 24 cm. c.1928. The Standard Publishing Company.

Heron, Michael, tr. see Castex, Pierre Georges.

Heron, Michael, tr. see Lindgren, Astrid Ericsson.

Heron, Michael, tr. see Sanchez-Silva, Jose Maria.

Heron, Virginia
--Pedro's Gift. Walstad, Chi Chi, illus. LC 79-119555. (Illus.). 29cm. 31p. (Third Grade Bk.). (gr. 3-4). N.D. Denison.

Heroy, Frances Louise
--Dollikin's Party and other Stories. LC 5-24171. (Illus.). 15cm. 68p. (The Juvenile Gems). 1905. Cupples & Leon.
--The Pug Family Entertains. LC 5-24172. (Illus.). 14cm. 70p. (The Juvenile Gems). 1905. Cupples & Leon.

Herr, Charlotte B.
--A Brownie Robinson Crusoe. White, Orrin A., illus. LC 20-17993. 6 p. l., 3-136 p. col. front., col. plates. 21 cm. 1920. Dodd, Mead and Company.

Herren, Janet M., jt. auth. see Morss, Willard N.

Herrick, Christine Terhune, Mrs. (1859-), ed. see Carroll, Lewis.

Herrick, Florence E., tr. see Dussauze, Alice.

Herrick, H. W.
--Alphabet of Country Scenes. (Uncle Sam's Picture Books). 1873. McLoughlin Bros.

Herrick, Richard, ed. see Dodgson, Charles Lutwidge.

Herring, Ann K., tr. see Kishida, Eriko.

Herring, Ann K., tr. see Tsutsui, Keisuke.

Herring, Ann King, jt. auth. see Bartoli, Jennifer.

Herring, Ann King, tr. see Otsuka, Yuzo.

Herring, Ann King (1923-), tr. see Takahashi, Hiroyuki.

Herring, Ann King (1918-), tr. see Tchaikovsky, Peter Ilich (1840-1893) & Hoffmann, Ernst Theodor Amadeus.

Herring, Elder Roosevelt
--Wide-Awake Rhymes. Carambella, Gladys, illus. LC 35-1933. 1 p. l., 5-60 p., 1 l. illus. 19 cm. c.1935. The Harter Publishing Company.

Herriot, James, pseud., see Wright, James Alfred.

Herriot, James, pseud. (1916-)
--Moses the Kitten. Wright, James Alfred. Barrett, Peter, illus. LC 84-50930. (Illus.). 32p. 1984. (ISBN 0-312-54905-9). St Martin.
--Only One Woof. Wright, James Alfred. Barrett, Peter, illus. (First Published in England in 1974). 32p. 1985. (ISBN 0-312-58583-7). St. Martin.

Herriott, Hallie Irene
--The Jungle Jingle Book. Herriott, Ruth Elizabeth, illus. LC 10-27629. (Illus.). 17 x 14cm. 50p. 1910. Carnation Press.

Herrmann, Frank (1927-)
--The Giant Alexander. Him, George (1900-1982), illus. (gr. k-4). 1965. (ISBN 0-07-028383-4). (ISBN 0-07-028384-2). McGraw.
--The Giant, Alexander. Him, George (1900-1982), illus. LC 65-16660. 32p. illus. (pt. col.) 28cm. 1965, c.1964. Whittlesey-McGraw.
--The Giant Alexander and Hannibal the Elephant. Him, George (1900-1982), illus. LC 74-172531. (Illus.). 32 p. 29cm. 1972. (ISBN 0-07-028372-9). McGraw-Hill.
--Giant Alexander & the Circus. Him, George (1900-1982), illus. LC 66-8645. (gr. k-3). 1966. (ISBN 0-07-028381-8). (ISBN 0-07-028382-6). McGraw.
--The Giant Alexander in America. Him, George (1900-1982), illus. LC 68-25215. (Illus.). 27 p. 28cm. 1968. McGraw-Hill.

Herrmann, Oscar, tr. see Homerus.

Herrmann, Reinhard
--Children's Bible Picture Books. 24p. (gr. 2-6). 1967. Augsburg.

Herrmanns, Ralph (1933-)
--The Car Named Julia. Herrmanns, Ralph (1933-), illus. MacMillan, Annabelle, pseud. (1922-), tr. from Swedish. Quick, Annabelle. LC 64-9841. 1v. (unpaged) col. illus. 22cm. 1964, c.1963. (ISBN 0-15-214580-X). Harcourt.
--In Search of the Abominable Snowman. LC 73-127114. (Illus.). 40p. (gr. 7 up). 1971. (ISBN 0-385-04501-8). Doubleday.
--Lee Lan Flies the Dragon Kite. MacMillan, Annabelle, pseud. (1922-), tr. from Swedish. Quick, Annabelle. LC 63-198067. (Illus.). unpaged. 30cm. 1962. (ISBN 0-15-267471-3). Harcourt, Brace & World.
--River Boy: Adventure on the Amazon. Tate, Joan (1922-), tr. from Swedish. LC 65-81522. 1v. (unpaged) col. illus., col. maps (on lining papers) 30cm. 1st U.S. edition. c.1965. Harcourt.

Herron, Edward Albert (1912-)
--The Big Country, a Story of Alaska. Mars, Witold Tadeusz J. (1912-), illus. LC 53-12194. (Illus.). 190 p. 21cm. (American heritage). 1953. Aladdin Books.
--The Return of the Alaskan: Mailboat in the Outpost. Langley, Gene, illus. LC 55-5883. (Illus.). 190 p. 21cm. (American heritage series). 1955. Aladdin Books.
--Signal Hill. 1st ed. Geary, Clifford N. (1916-), illus. LC 56-5278. 183p. illus. 22cm. 1956. Knopf.

Hersey, Heloise E., ed. see Browning, Robert.

Hersey, John Richard (1914-)
--A Bell For Adano. 1975. Borzoi Books.
--Bell for Adano. (gr. 10 up). 1944. (ISBN 0-394-41660-0). Knopf.
--Bell for Adano. (Keith Jennison Large Type Bks). (gr. 7 up). N.D. (ISBN 0-531-00160-1). Watts.
--The Conspiracy. 1972. Borzoi Books.
--My Petition for More Space. 1974. (ISBN 0-394-49466-0). Knopf.
--A Single Pebble. 1956. Borzoi Books.
--The Wall. 1950. Borzoi Books.

Hershaw, Fay McKeene
--Verse Along the Way. 1st ed. LC 54-11911. 21cm. 48p. 1954. Exposition Press.

Hershberger, Hazel Effie Kuhns see Allen, Hazel, pseud.

Hershberger, Hazel Effie Kuhns
--The Little Church on the Big Rock. Allen, Hazel, pseud. Duvoisin, Roger Antoine (1904-1980), illus. LC 58-6738. unpaged. illus. 21cm. 1958. Scribner.
--Up from the Sea Came an Island. Allen, Hazel, pseud. Miller, Marilyn Jean (1925-), illus. LC 60-633617. unpaged. illus. 21cm. 1962. Scribner.

Hershenburgh, Anne
--Animal Designs, No. 3 Coloring Book. 48p. 1984. (ISBN 0-8431-1014-7). Price Stern.

Hersholt, Jean, tr. see Andersen, Hans Christian.

Hersholt, Jean (1886-)
--Aladdin & the Wonderful Lamp. Kredel, Fritz (1900-1973), illus. LC 49-12617. 39 p. col. illus. 31 cm. (The Evergreen Tales: or, Tales for the Ageless). 1949. Limited Editions Club.

Hershon, Robert Richard (1914-)
--Little Red Wagon Painted Blue. Hershon, M., illus. 56p. N.D. Unicorn Press.

Hertel, Arthur
--The Impossible Isle. (Illus.). (gr. k-3). N.D. Vantage.

Herter, Jonina
--Eighty-Eight Kisses. LC 78-14048. p. cm. c.1977. (ISBN 0-932430-02-3). Boss Books.

Hertz, David
--Valdemar. LC 39-5771. (Illus.). 47p. 1938. Longmans Green and Co.

Hertz, Grete Janus (1915-)
--Hi, Daddy, Here I Am. Jensinius, Kirsten, illus. Gracza, Margaret Young (1928-), tr. LC 64-2541. (Illus.). 22cm. 31p. (Foreign Lands Bks). (gr. k-3). 1964. (ISBN 0-8225-0351-4). Lerner Pubns.
--Teddy. Duvoisin, Roger Antoine (1904-1980), illus. LC 64-14434. (Illus.). 1 v. (unpaged. 16cm. (Lothrop little book). 1964. Lothrop, Lee & Shepard Co.
--When Lena and Lisa Had Measles. Ware, Kay (1916-) & Sutherland, Lucille, eds. Leo-Hongell, Veronica, illus. LC 64-6442. (Illus.). 23cm. (The Read for Fun Ser.). 1964. Webster Division, McGraw-Hill.

Hertz, Martin, jt. auth. see Hanle, Zack.

Hertz, Ole
--Tobias Catches Trout. Hertz, Ole, illus. Tobias, Tobi (1938-), tr. from Danish. LC 83-27224. (Illus.). 32p. (gr. k-3). 1984. (ISBN 0-87614-263-3). Carolrhoda Bks.
--Tobias Goes Ice Fishing. Hertz, Ole, illus. Tobias, Tobi (1938-), tr. from Danish. LC 83-26356. (Illus.). 32p. (gr. k-3). 1984. (ISBN 0-87614-260-9). Carolrhoda Bks.
--Tobias Has a Birthday. Hertz, Ole, illus. Tobias, Tobi (1938-), tr. from Danish. LC 83-27287. (Illus.). 32p. (gr. k-3). 1984. (ISBN 0-87614-261-7). Carolrhoda Bks.

Hertzog, Rudolph
--The Story of Helga. Lewisohn, Adele, tr. N.D. E P Dutton.

Hervey, E. L.
--The Children of the Pear Garden. (Illus.). N.D. Scribner, Welford & Armstrong.
--The Rock Light, 1 of 22 Vols. (Illus.). (Warne's Home Circle Ser.). N.D. Scribner & Welford.

--Spice and the Devil's Cave. Ward, Lynd Kendall (1905-1985), illus. LC 30-20164. xi, 331 p. incl. front. illus. 20 cm. 1930. A. A. Knopf. **Award: (JNM).**
--The Sword of Roland Arnot. Strayer, Paul (1896-1970), illus. LC 39-7583. 5 p. l., 206 p. col. front., col. plates. 22 cm. 1939. Houghton Mifflin Company.
--Swords on the Sea. 1928. Alfred A. Knopf.
--With the Will to Go. 1960. David McKay Company Inc.
--With the Will to Go. 1st ed. Lambo, Donald W. (1903-1966), illus. LC 60-10212. 244p. illus. 21cm. 1960. Longmans, Green.

Hewett, Anita (1918-)
--The Bull Beneath the Walnut Tree, and Other Stories. Gobbato, Imero (1923-), illus. (Illus.). 155 p. 24cm. 1967, c.1966. McGraw-Hill.
--Dragon from the North. Fiammenghi, Gioia (1929-), illus. LC 64-8617. (gr. k-3). 1965. (ISBN 0-07-028504-7). (ISBN 0-07-028505-5). McGraw.
--Elephant Big and Elephant Little And Other Stories. Hough, Helen Charlotte Woodyatt (1924-), illus. LC 60-7647. 64p. illus. 21cm. (Wonderful world book). 1960. Barnes.
--A Hat for a Rhinoceros and Other Stories. Gill, Margery Jean (1925-), illus. LC 60-10197. (Illus.). 21cm. 80p. 1960. A. S. Barnes & Co.
--Koala Bear's Walkabout. Jauss, Anne Marie (1907-), illus. 1959. Sterling.
--Kola Bear's Walkabout. N.D. E . M. Hale and Co.
--The Laughing Bird. Jauss, Anne Marie (1907-), illus. LC 59-10874. (Illus.). 22cm. 32p. 1959. Sterling.
--The Little White Hen. Stobbs, William (1914-), illus. (gr. k-3). 1963. (ISBN 0-07-028503-9). McGraw.
--The Little Yellow Jungle Frogs And Otdher Stories. Hough, Helen Charlotte Woodyatt (1924-), illus. LC 60-7648. 78p. illus. 21cm. (Wonderful world book). 1960. Barnes.
--Mister Faksimily and the Tiger. Broomfield, Robert (1930-), illus. LC 69-10253. (Illus.). 30 p. 1969, c.1967. Follett.
--Mrs. Mopple's Washing Line. Broomfield, Robert (1930-), illus. LC 66-883020. 29p. col. illus. 19 x 26cm. 1st U.S. edition. 1966. (ISBN 0-07-028506-3). McGraw.
--Piccolo. Hart, Dick (1920-), illus. LC 61-8572. 89p. illus. 22cm. (Wonderful world book). 1961. Barnes.
--The Tale of the Turnip. Gill, Margery Jean (1925-), illus. LC 61-15388. (Illus.). (ps). 1961. (ISBN 0-07-028500-4). (ISBN 0-07-028501-2). Whittlesey House.
--Think, Mr. Platypus. Jauss, Anne Marie (1907-), illus. LC 58-12533. (Illus.). 23cm. 31p. 1958. Sterling.

Hewett, George Mattram Andrews
--The Open Air Boy. (Illus.). (The Boy's Own Authors Ser.). N.D. Dana Estes & Co.

Hewett, Hilda (1904-)
--Harriet and the Cherry Pie. Fligg, Kathryn L., illus. LC 64-21197. 224 p. illus. 22 cm. 1st U.S. edition. 1964. Lothrop, Lee & Shepard Co.

Hewett, Joan
--Fly Away Free. Hewett, Richard R., photos by. LC 80-50449. (Illus.). 32p. 1st U.S. edition. (gr. 2-5). 1981. (ISBN 0-8027-6402-9). (ISBN 0-8027-6403-7). Walker & Co.

Hewett, Joan & Hewett, Richard R.
--The Mouse and the Elephant. LC 77-7259. p. cm. c.1977. (ISBN 0-316-35966-1). Little, Brown.

Hewett, Richard R., jt. auth. see Hewett, Joan.

Hewins, Caroline Maria (1846-1926)
--A Mid-Century Child and Her Books. LC 69-16070. 136p. Repr. of 1926 ed. 1969 (Gale Reprints). Singing Tree Press.

Hewitt, Emma Churchman, Mrs. (1850-)
--Three Little Denvers. 20cm. 160p. (Lad and Lassie Series.). 1902. George W Jacobs.

Hewitt, Garnet, retold by.
--Ytek and the Arctic Orchid: An Inuit Legend. Woodall, Heather, illus. LC 79-56919. (Illus.). 38 p. 25cm. (gr. 6 up). c.1981. (ISBN 0-8149-0836-5). Vanguard Press. **Awards: (CCCL); (AFH).**

Hewitt, Ivy H.
--Bobbo Keeps Smiling. 30p. 1962. Pitman Publishing Corporation.
--Tales of a Little. 36p. 1962. Pitman Publishing Corporation.

Hewitt, Kathryn
--Two by Two: The Untold Story. Hewitt, Kathryn, illus. LC 84-4579. (Illus.). 32p. (ps-3). 1984. (ISBN 0-15-291801-9, HJ). HarBraceJ.

Hewitt, William
--Luke Barnicott, 1 vol. Juv ed. (Illus.). N.D. Cassell & Co.

Hewlett, Maurice
--The Light Heart. N.D. Henry Holt.

Hewson, Isabel Manning & Miller, Barbara (1902-)
--The Land of the Lost. Bailey, Olive, illus. LC 45-4450. 3 p. l., 5-60 p. col. illus. 26 cm. 1945. Whittlesey House, McGraw-Hill Book Company, Inc.

Hey, F., tr. see Specter, Otto.

Hey, Wilhelm (1789-1854)
--Picture Fables. new ed. Speckter, Otto (1807-1871) & Dalziel, George (1815-1902), illus. Dulcken, Henry William (1832-1894), tr. from Ger. LC 25-7697. viii p., 1 l., 101, 1 p. incl. front., illus. 21 cm. 1863. Routledge, Warne, and Routledge.

Heydekampf Bruhl, Edelgard Von see Kruss, James.

HeyDuck-Huth, Hilde (1929-)
--In the Forest. HeyDuck-Huth, Hilde (1929-), illus. 18p. N.D. Harcourt Brace Jovanovich.
--In the Village. Heyduck-Huth, Hilde (1929-), illus. LC 72-57808. (Illus.). Orig. Title: Thomas in Dorf. (ps-1). 1971. (ISBN 0-15-238751-X, HJ). HarBraceJ.
--The Red Spot. Heyduck-Huth, Hilde (1929-), illus. LC 80-506840. (Illus.). 26 p. 27cm. 1979. (ISBN 0-222-00725-7). Burke Books.
--When the Sun Shines. Heyduck-Huth, Hilde (1929-), illus. (Illus.). Orig. Title: Wenn die Sonne Scheint. (ps-1). 1971. (ISBN 0-15-295601-8). HarBraceJ.

Heyer, Georgette (1902-1974)
--Merely Murder ... LC 37-2768. 4 p. l., 303 p. 20 cm. N.D. Sundial Press, Inc.

Heyliger, William see Williams, Hawley, pseud.

Heyliger, William (1884-1955)
--Against Odds. LC 15-18821. 5 p. l., 309, 1 p. col. front., col. plates 20 cm. 1913. D. Appleton and Company.
--Backfield Comet. Richards, George Mather (1880-), illus. LC 24-29549. 3 p. l., 246 p. incl. illus., plates, front. 20 cm. 1934. D. Appleton-Century Company, Incorporated.
--Backfield Play. LC 38-21319. 20cm. 265p. N.D. D. Appleton-Century Co.
--Bartley, Freshman Pitcher. LC 11-28834. ix, 1, 234 p. 1 l. incl., plates. front. 20 cm. 1911. D. Appleton and Company.
--Bartley, Freshman Pitcher. (Every Boy's Library). 1911. Grosset & Dunlap.
--Batter Up!. Williams, Hawley, pseud. LC 12-22317. 5 p. l., 302, 1 p. col. front., col. plates. 20 cm. 1912. D. Appleton and Company.
--Bean Ball Bill And Other Stories. Salg, Bert N., illus. 213p. (Buddy Bks for Boys). c.1930. Grosset & Dunlap.
--The Big Leaguer. Salg, Bert N., illus. LC 36-407. 4 p. l., 15-250 p. 20 cm. c.1936. The Goldsmith Publishing Company.
--Bill Darrow's Victory. Salg, Bert N., illus. LC 30-12151. 3 p. l., 188 p. front., plates. 20 cm. c.1930. Grosset & Dunlap.
--Bucking the Line. LC 12-11158. ix, 260, 1 p. incl. illus., plates. front. 20 cm. 1912. D. Appleton and Company.
--The Builder of the Dam. LC 29-17318. 4 p. l., 229, 1 p. front. 20 cm. 1929. D. Appleton and Company.
--Captain Fair-and-Square. Clark, William Wallace, illus. LC 16-194264. 5 p. l., 312, 1 p. col. front., col. plates. 20 cm. 1916. D. Appleton and Company.
--The Captain of the Nine. LC 12-21761. 5 p. l., 280, 1 p. front., illus. 20 cm. 1912. D. Appleton and Company.
--The County Pennant. Clarke, William Wallace, illus. LC 17-242036. 5 p. l., 285, 1 p. col. front., col. plates. 20 cm. 1917. D. Appleton and Company.
--Dan's To-Morrow. LC 22-18092. 2 p. l, 255, 1 p. front. 20 cm. 1922. D. Appleton and Company.
--Detectives, Inc. A Mystery Story for Boys. LC 39-10518. 4 p. l., 13-246 p. 20 cm. c.1935. The Goldsmith Publishing Company.
--Dill Darrow's Victory. Salg, Bert N., illus. 188p. (Buddy Bks for Boys). c.1930. Grosset & Dunlap.
--Don Strong, American. LC 20-80365. 3 p. l., 268, 1 p. front. 20 cm. 1920. D. Appleton and Company.
--Don Strong of the Wolf Patrol. Rockwell, Norman Percevel (1894-1978), illus. LC 16-146384. 4 p. l., 296, 1 p. front., plates. 19 cm. c.1916. D. Appleton and Company.
--Don Strong of the Wolf Patrol. Rockwell, Norman Percevel (1894-1978), illus. 298p. c.1916. Grosset & Dunlap.
--Don Strong, Patrol Leader. Louderback, Walt, illus. 5 p. l., 287, 1 p. front., plates. 20 cm. 1918. D. Appleton and Company.
--Don Strong, Patrol Leader. Louderback, Walt, illus. (Every Boy's Library). N.D. Grosset & Dunlap.
--Dorset's Twister. LC 26-6258. 3 p. l., 241, 1 p. front. 20 cm. 1926. D. Appleton and Company.
--Fair Play!. Williams, Hawley, pseud. LC 15-18817. 5 p. l., 286, 1 p. col. front., col. plates. 20 cm. 1915. D. Appleton and Company.
--Fighting Blood. LC 39-10517. 4 p. l., 15-248 p. 19 cm. c.1936. The Goldsmith Publishing Company.
--The Fighting Captain, and Other Stories. LC 26-171105. 3 p. l., 265, 1 p. front. 20 cm. 1926. D. Appleton and Company.
--Fighting for Fairview. Clarke, William Wallace, illus. LC 18-20477. 4 p. l., 290, 1 p. col. front., col. plates. 19 cm. 1918. D. Appleton and Company.
--Five Yards to Go!. Williams, Hawley, pseud. LC 13-20393. 5 p. l., 290, 1 p. col. front., col. plates. 20 cm. 1913. D. Appleton and Company.
--The Gallant Crosby, a Baseball Story. McKell, James C., illus. LC 33-647277. 3 p. l., 257, 1 p. front., illus., 20 cm. 1933. D. Appleton and Company.
--Gasoline Jockey. Beebe, Robb (1891-), illus. LC 42-10025. 4 p. l., 257 p. front., illus., pl. 20 cm. 1942. D. Appleton-Century Company, Incorporated.
--Gridiron Glory. Richards, George Mather (1880-), illus. LC 40-30563. 4 p. l., 274 p. front., illus., 20 cm. 1940. D. Appleton-Century Company, Incorporated.
--High Benton. Williams, J. Scott, illus. LC 19-18838. 5 p. l., 316, 1 p. front., plates. 20 cm. 1919. D. Appleton and Company.
--High Benton, Worker. LC 21-12854. 3 p. l., 299, 1 p. col. front. 20 cm. 1921. D. Appleton and Company.
--Hot-Dog Partners. Hastings, Howard Livingston (1887-), illus. LC 31-132267. v, 196 p. front., plates. 20 cm. c.1931. Grosset & Dunlap.
--Jerry Hicks and His Gang. Salg, Bert N., illus. LC 29-11655. 3 p. l., 198 p. front., plates. 20 cm. c.1929. Grosset & Dunlap.
--Jerry Hicks, Explorer. Salg, Bert N., illus. LC 30-132362. v. 196 p. front., plates. 20 cm. c.1930. Grosset & Dunlap.
--Jerry Hicks, Ghost Hunter. Salg, Bert N., illus. LC 29-11654. 3 p. l., 196 p. front., plates. 20 cm. c.1929. Grosset & Dunlap.
--Johnny Bree. Warren, Ferdinand E., illus. LC 31-21313. 4 p. l., 233, 1 p. front., illus. 20 cm. 1931. D. Appleton and Company.
--Johnson of Lansing. Williams, Hawley, pseud. Avison, George F. (1885-), illus. LC 14-16205. 5 p. l., 332, 1 p. front., plates. 20 cm. 1914. D. Appleton and Company.
--The Loser's End. LC 37-6386. 3 p. l., 13-252 p. 20 cm. c.1937. The Goldsmith Publishing Co.
--The Macklin Brothers. LC 28-20340. 4 p. l., 234, 1 p. front. 20 cm. 1928. D. Appleton & Company.
--Making of Peter Cray. 1927. Appleton Century Co.
--The Mill in the Woods. Jones, Wilfred J. (1888-), illus. LC 36-19446. 4 p. l., 234 p. incl. illus., plates. front. 20 cm. 1936. D. Appleton-Century Company, Incorporated.
--Off Side. Varian, George, illus. LC 14-16212. 6 p. l., 300, 1 p. front., plates. 20 cm. (St. Mary's Ser.). 1914. D. Appleton and Company.
--Quarterback Hot-Head. Grubb, W. B., illus. LC 31-13219. 3 p. l., 247 p. front., plates. 20 cm. c.1931. Grosset & Dunlap.
--Quarterback Reckless. Williams, Hawley, pseud. LC 12-21921. 5 p. l., 239, 1 p. col. front., col. plates. 20 cm. 1912. D. Appleton and Company.
--Quinby and Son. LC 25-15846. 3 p. l., 239, 1 p. front. 20 cm. 1925. D. Appleton and Company.
--Ritchie of the News. Warren, Ferdinand E., illus. LC 33-215167. 3 p. l., 247, 1 p. front., illus. 20 cm. 1933. D. Appleton-Century Company, Incorporated.
--River Man. Jones, Wilfred J. (1888-), illus. LC 38-29555. 4 p. l., 240, 1 p. front., illus. 20 cm. 1938. D. Appleton-Century Company, Incorporated.
--S O S Radio Patrol. LC 42-8145. 5 p. l., 3-180 p. 21 cm. 1942. Dodd, Mead & Company.
--The Silver Run, a Story of the Sardine Industry. Richards, George Mather (1880-), illus. LC 34-8728. 3 p. l., 230 p. incl. illus., plates. front. 20 cm. 1934. D. Appleton-Century Company, Incorporated.
--Son of the Apple Valley. Beebe, Robb (1891-), illus. LC 40-4717. 5 p. l., 253 p. incl. front., illus., plates. 20 cm. 1940. D. Appleton-Century Company, Incorporated.
--The Spirit of the Leader. LC 28-13335. 4 p. l., 270, 1 p. front. 20 cm. 1923. D. Appleton and Company.
--Steve Merrill, Engineer. Richards, George Mather (1880-), illus. LC 35-131750. 3 p. l., 240 p. front., illus. 20 cm. 1935. D. Appleton-Century Company, Incorporated.
--Straight Ahead?. Williams, Hawley, pseud. LC 17-28658. 4 p. l., 3-270, 1 p. col. front., col. plates. 20 cm. 1917. D. Appleton and Company.
--Strike Three!. LC 13-20852. 5 p. l., 297, 1 p. col. front., col. plates. 20 cm. 1913. D. Appleton and Company.
--Top Lineman. Lusby, Scott, illus. 4 p. l., 198 p., 1 l. incl. front., illus. 19 1/2 cm. 1943. D. Appleton-Century Company, Incorporated.
--Wildcat. N.D. D. Appleton-Century Co.
--The Winning Hit. Williams, Hawley, pseud. LC 14-4306. 5 p. l., 281, 1 p. col. front., col. plates. 20 cm. 1914. D. Appleton and Company.
--You're on the Air. O'Keeffe, Neil, illus. LC 41-437771. 5 p. l., 262 p. incl. front., illus., plates. 20 cm. 1941. D. Appleton-Century Company, Incorporated.
--Yours Truly, Jerry Hicks. Salg, Bert N., illus. LC 29-11653. 3 p. l., 210 p. front., plates. 20 cm. c.1929. Grosset & Dunlap.

Heyman, Anita
--Exit from Home. LC 77-23323. 277 p. 22cm. c.1977. (ISBN 0-517-52903-3). Crown Publishers.
--Final Grades. LC 82-45997. 184 p. 22cm. 1983. (ISBN 0-396-08141-X). Dodd, Mead.

Heyman, Ken
--City Duck. LC 68-58455. (Illus.). 24 p. 29cm. (Carousel book). 1969. L. W. Singer Co.

Heyman, Ken & Mason, Michael
--Clyde of Africa. Heyman, Ken, photos by. LC 63-18825. (gr. k-3). 1963. Macmillan.

Heyman, William see Kramer, George, pseud.

Heymans, Annemie & Heymans, Margriet
--The Dolls' Party. LC 77-24831. (Illus.). 48 p. 22cm. 1971. Atheneum.

Heymans, Margriet
--Cats and Dolls. Heymans, Margriet, illus. LC 75-7542. (Illus.). 30 p. 22cm. 1976, c.1975. (ISBN 0-201-02909-X). Addison-Wesley Pub. Co.
--Pippin & Robber Grumblecroak's Big Baby. Heymans, Margriet, illus. (Illus.). 24p. (ps-2). 1974. (ISBN 0-201-02908-1, A-W Childrens). A-W.

Heymans, Margriet, jt. auth. see Heymans, Annemie.

Heyn, Jean
--The Tessie C. Price. Howell, Claude (1915-), illus. LC 79-9442. (Illus.). 210 p. 20cm. 1980, c.1979. (ISBN 0-89587-010-X). J. F. Blair.

Heyneman, Anne (1910-)
--The Whosit Book. Heyneman, Anne (1910-), illus. LC 41-17950. 26cm. 45p. 1941. Charles Scribner's Sons.
--William Wigglewhistle. Heyneman, Anne (1910-), illus. N.D. Charles Scribner's Sons.

Heyneman, Anne (1910-) & Kappel, H.
--The Happy Hippopotamus. LC 43-16588. (Illus.). 27cm. 32p. 1943. Charles Scribner's Sons.

Heyser, K., tr. see Zeller, Luise.

Heyward, Du Bose (1885-1940)
--The Country Bunny & the Little Gold Shoes: As Told to Jenifer. Flack, Marjorie (1897-1958), illus. LC 30-8350. (Illus.). 48p. (gr. k-3). 1939. (ISBN 0-395-15990-3). (ISBN 0-395-18557-2, Sandpiper). HM.
--The Country Bunny and the Little Gold Shoes: As Told to Jenifer. Flack, Marjorie (1897-1958), illus. LC 74-170316. (Illus.). 48 p. 23cm. (Sandpiper books). 1974, c.1939. (ISBN 0-395-18557-2). Houghton Mifflin.

Heyward, Zan
--Swampy and Babs in Okefenokee. LC 62-409938. 94p. illus. 24cm. 1962. Southern Junior Book Publishers.

Heywood, Abel, ed.
--Norwegian Fairy Tales. (Illus.). N.D. George Routledge & Sons.

Heywood, Elizabeth
--Grocer's Boy: The Young American Who Did Not want to be Extraordinary. (Illus.). N.D. Methodist Book Concern.

Heywood, John (1497-1580)
--Days of Sunshine, Days of Rain. Frye, Dean, ed. Duvoisin, Roger Antoine (1904-1980), illus. LC 64-241043. 32p. illus. (part col.) 26cm. (gr. 2-4). c.1965. (ISBN 0-07-022582-6). (ISBN 0-07-022583-4). McGraw.

Hezlep, William
--Cayman Duppy. (gr. 5 up). 1984. (ISBN 0-88734-403-8). Players Pr.

H. H. F
--Lame Bessie. (Fern Glen Ser.). N.D. D. Lothrop Co.

Hibbert, Christopher (1924-) & Thomas, Charles
--Search for King Arthur. LC 77-91594. (Illus.). 153p. (Horizon Caravel Bks). (gr. 6 up). 1969. (ISBN 0-06-022313-8, Dist. by Har-Row). (ISBN 0-06-022314-6, Dist. by Har-Row). Am Heritage.

Hibbert, Eleanor Burford see Carr, Philippa, pseud.

Hickey, Agnes MacCarthy
--Little Stories in Verse. LC 41-14787. 59 p. front., illus., port. 24 cm. c.1940. The Torch Press.

Hickey, David Harold
--Up Anchor, a Sea Story. LC 29-16244. 222 p. 20 cm. c.1929. The Abingdon Press.

Highwater, Jamake Mamake (1942-) & Scholder, Fritz (1937-)
--Anpao: An American Indian Odyssey. LC 77-9264. (Illus.). 256 p. 24cm. c.1977. (ISBN 0-397-31750-6). Lippincott. **Awards: (BGH); (JNM).**
Higonnet-Schnopper, Janet, ed.
--Tales from Atop a Russian Stove. Altschuler, Franz (1923-), illus. LC 70-188430. (Illus.). 160 p. 22cm. 1973. (ISBN 0-8075-7755-3). A. Whitman.
Hilbert, Peter Paul (1914-)
--Zoo on the First Floor. Shortall, Leonard W., illus. (Illus.). 159 p. 22cm. 1st U.S. edition. 1967. Coward-McCann.
Hildebrandt, Greg (1939-), compiled by.
--A Christmas Treasury. Hildebrandt, Greg (1939-), illus. LC 84-8798. (Illus.). 42 p. c.1984. (ISBN 0-88101-013-8). Unicorn Pub. House.
--Greg Hildebarndt's Favorite Fairy Tales. Hildebrandt, Greg (1939-), illus. (Illus.). 224p. (gr. 3 up). c.1984. (ISBN 0-671-50327-8, Little Simon). S&S.
--Greg Hildebrandt's Favorite Fairy Tales. Hildebrandt, Greg (1939-), illus. LC 84-10048. (Illus.). 218 p. 26cm. c.1984. (ISBN 0-671-50327-8). Little Simon.
Hildeburn, Mary Jane Reed, Mrs. (1821-1882)
--Bessie Lane's Mistake. Wealth Is Not Happiness. LC 12-35165. 330 p. front., 1 illus., plates. 17 cm. c.1865. Presbyterian Publication Committee.
--Fannie's Rule: Or, Better Than Gold. LC 45-30236. 72 p. front., pl. 15 cm. 1868. Presbyterian Publication Committee.
--Flora Morris' Choice: Or "Be Not Conformed to the World.". LC 12-34163. 320 p. front., plates. 18 cm. c.1867. Presbyterian Publication Committee.
--Three Cents: Or, Lettie's Way of Doing Good. LC 45-29165. 72 p. front., pl. 15 cm. 1863. Presbyterian Publication Committee.
Hildegarde, Hopkins, illus.
--Little Dog Who Forgot How to Bark and Other Stories. N.D. Grosset & Dunlap.
--Little Puppy Who Would Not Mind His Mother. N.D. Grosset & Dunlap.
Hildick, Edmund Wallace (1925-)
--The Active-Enzyme, Lemon-Freshened Junior High School Witch. Schweitzer, Iris, illus. LC 72-89316. (Illus.). 207 p. 22cm. 1973. (ISBN 0-385-05327-4). (ISBN 0-385-05327-4). Doubleday.
--Birdy and the Group. Rose, Richard (1933-), illus. LC 75-88177. (Illus.). 159 p. 22cm. 1969, c.1968. Stackpole Books.
--Birdy in Amsterdam. Rose, Richard (1933-), illus. LC 79-100346. (Illus.). 127 p. 22cm. 1971. (ISBN 0-8117-0247-2). Stackpole Books.
--Birdy Jones. Rose, Richard (1933-), illus. LC 79-88178. (Illus.). 140 p. 22cm. 1969, c.1963. Stackpole Books.
--Birdy Jones and the New York Heads. LC 73-8426. 196 p. 22cm. 1974. Doubleday.
--Birdy Swings North. Rose, Richard (1933-), illus. LC 75-100345. (Illus.). 127 p. 22cm. 1971. (ISBN 0-8117-0249-9). Stackpole Books.
--The Case of the Bashful Bank Robber. Weil, Lisl (1910-), illus. LC 80-24589. (Illus.). 138 p. 22cm. (McGurk mystery). c.1981. (ISBN 0-02-743870-8). Macmillan.
--The Case of the Condemned Cat. Weil, Lisl (1910-), illus. LC 75-14196. (Illus.). 106 p. 21cm. 1st U.S. edition. (McGurk mystery). 1975. (ISBN 0-02-743810-4). Macmillan.
--The Case of the Felon's Fiddle. Weil, Lisl (1910-), illus. LC 82-10078. p. cm. (A McGurk Mystery). 1982. (ISBN 0-02-743900-3). Macmillan Co.
--The Case of the Four Flying Fingers. Weil, Lisl (1910-), illus. LC 81-2517. (Illus.). 137 p. 22cm. (A McGurk Mystery). c.1981. (ISBN 0-02-743880-5). Macmillan.
--The Case of the Invisible Dog. Weil, Lisl (1910-), illus. LC 77-4466. (Illus.). 101p. (A McGurk Mystery). (gr. 3-6). 1977. (ISBN 0-02-743830-9). Macmillan.
--The Case of the Nervous Newsboy. Weil, Lisl (1910-), illus. LC 75-35873. (Illus.). 106 p. 22cm. (McGurk mystery). c.1976. (ISBN 0-02-743790-6). Macmillan.
--The Case of the Phantom Frog. Weil, Lisl (1910-), illus. LC 78-10836. (Illus.). 121 p. 22cm. (McGurk mystery). c.1979. (ISBN 0-02-743840-6). Macmillan.
--The Case of the Secret Scribbler. Weil, Lisl (1910-), illus. LC 78-2340. (Illus.). 106 p. 22cm. 1st U.S. edition. (McGurk mystery). 1978. (ISBN 0-02-743780-9). Macmillan.
--The Case of the Slingshot Sniper. Weil, Lisl (1910-), illus. LC 82-20913. (Illus.). 138 p. 22cm. (A McGurk Mystery Ser.). c.1983. (ISBN 0-02-743920-8). Macmillan Pub. Co.
--The Case of the Snowbound Spy. Weil, Lisl (1910-), illus. LC 80-12272. (Illus.). 132 p. 22cm. (McGurk mystery). c.1980. (ISBN 0-02-743860-0). Macmillan.
--The Case of the Treetop Treasure. Weil, Lisl (1910-), illus. LC 79-20747. (Illus.). 121 p. 22cm. (McGurk mystery). c.1980. (ISBN 0-02-743850-3). Macmillan.
--The Case of the Vanishing Ventriloquist: A McGurk Mystery. Parkinson, Kathy, illus. LC 84-21801. (Illus.). 138 p. 22cm. c.1985. (ISBN 0-02-743930-5). Macmillan.
--A Cat Called Amnesia. Biro, Val, pseud. (1921-), illus. Biro, Balint Stephen. LC 75-39807. (Illus.). 152 p. 22cm. c.1976. (ISBN 0-87250-248-1). D. White.
--Deadline for McGurk. Weil, Lisl (1910-), illus. LC 74-20616. (Illus.). 104 p. 21cm. (McGurk mystery). 1975. (ISBN 0-02-743800-7). Macmillan.
--The Doughnut Dropout. Komoda, Kiyoaki (1937-), illus. LC 70-180081. (Illus.). viii, 222 p. 22cm. 1972. Doubleday.
--The Dragon That Lived Under Manhattan. Berson, Harold (1926-), illus. LC 76-127522. (Illus.). 62 p. 24cm. 1970. Crown Publishers.
--The Ghost Squad and the Ghoul of Grunberg. LC 85-29350. p. cm. (Ghost Squad book). 1985, c.1986. (ISBN 0-525-44229-4). Dutton.
--The Ghost Squad and the Halloween Conspiracy. LC 85-6835. 176p. (Ghost Squad book). ((Series: Hildick, E. W. (Edmund Wallace), 1925-). (Ghost Squad book.). c.1985. (ISBN 0-525-44111-5). E.P. Dutton.
--The Ghost Squad Breaks Through. LC 84-3985. 1984. (ISBN 0-525-44097-6). Dutton.
--The Ghost Squad Flies Concorde. LC 85-1487. p. cm. (Ghost Squad book). (Ghost Squad book.). c.1985. (ISBN 0-525-44191-3). Dutton.
--The Great Rabbit Rip-off. Weil, Lisl (1910-), illus. LC 76-46296. (Illus.). 101 p. 22cm. (McGurk mystery). 1977, c.1976. (ISBN 0-02-743820-1). Macmillan.
--Here Comes Parren. Frankenberg, Robert Clinton (1911-), illus. LC 70-184016. (Illus.). 63 p. 21cm. 1972, c.1968. (ISBN 0-529-04668-7). (ISBN 0-529-04538-9). World Pub.
--Jaunty Jalopies. 1969. Berkley.
--Jim Starling and the Colonel. LC 68-21680. 190 p. 22cm. 1968, c.1960. Doubleday.
--Kids Commune. Liebman, Oscar (1919-), illus. LC 72-83991. (Illus.). 153 p. 22cm. 1973. (ISBN 0-87250-246-5). (ISBN 0-87250-246-5). D. White.
--Lemon Kelly. Stewart, Arvis L., illus. LC 68-14192. (Illus.). 162 p. 22cm. 1968. Doubleday.
--Louie's Lot. LC 68-10662. 146 p. 19cm. 1968, c.1965. D. White.
--Louie's Ransom. LC 77-21240. vi, 184 p. 22cm. c.1978. (ISBN 0-394-83458-5). (ISBN 0-394-93458-X). Knopf.
--Louie's Snowstorm. 1st ed. Schweitzer, Iris, illus. LC 73-20822. (Illus.). 198 p. 22cm. 1974. (ISBN 0-385-06452-7). (ISBN 0-385-06452-7). Doubleday.
--Louie's SOS. Schweitzer, Iris, illus. LC 75-116213. (Illus.). 187p. 22cm. 1968. Doubleday.
--Louie's SOS. Schweitzer, Iris, illus. LC 75-116213. (Illus.). 12 line art. 168p. 1st U.S. edition. (gr. 4-6). 1970. (ISBN 0-385-09013-7). (ISBN 0-385-09208-3). Doubleday.
--Manhattan Is Missing. Palmer, Janice, illus. LC 68-22475. (Illus.). 239 p. 22cm. 1969. Doubleday.
--McGurk Gets Good and Mad. Weil, Lisl (1910-), illus. LC 81-20698. (Illus.). 136 p. 22cm. (A McGurk Mystery). c.1982. (ISBN 0-02-743890-2). Macmillan.
--My Kid Sister. Schweitzer, Iris, illus. LC 72-155074. (Illus.). 64 p. 21cm. 1971. World Pub. Co.
--The Nose Knows. Gliewe, Unada Grace (1927-), illus. LC 72-94239. (Illus.). 112 p. 18cm. (Tempo books). (A McGurk Mystery). 1973. (ISBN 0-448-05721-2). Grosset & Dunlap.
--The Nose Knows: A McGurk Mystery. 128p. (gr. 3-6). 1974. (ISBN 0-448-05721-2, Tempo). G&D.
--The Prisoners of Gridling Gap: A Report: with Expert Comments from Doctor Ranulf Quitch. LC 79-144272. (Illus.). 232 p. 22cm. 1971. (ISBN 0-385-09237-7). Doubleday.
--The Questers. Chew, Ruth (1920-), illus. LC 72-106182. (Illus.). 145 p. 22cm. 1970. Hawthorn Books.
--The Secret Spenders. Nebel, Gustave E., illus. LC 74-147341. (Illus.). 175 p. 22cm. 1971. Crown Publishers.
--The Secret Winners. Nebel, Gustave E., illus. LC 74-113401. (Illus.). 159 p. 22cm. 1970. Crown Publishers.
--Time Explorers, Inc. Ohanian, Nancy, illus. LC 75-33094. (Illus.). 222 p. 22cm. c.1976. (ISBN 0-385-09986-X). Doubleday.
--Top Boy at Twisters Creek. Liebman, Oscar (1919-), illus. LC 75-90934. (Illus.). 151 p. 22cm. 1969. (ISBN 0-87250-238-4). (ISBN 0-87250-435-2). D. White.
--The Top-Flight Fully-Automated Junior High School Girl Detective. Schweitzer, Iris, illus. LC 76-42337. (Illus.). 195 p. 22cm. 1977. (ISBN 0-385-08259-2). (ISBN 0-385-08328-9). Doubleday.
Hildner, Victor G. (1807-1865)
--Joyfully Sing. (Concordia Music Education Ser,Bk. 1). (gr. k-2). 1961. Concordia.
--Sing in Harmony. (Illus.). (Music Education Series: Bk. 6). (gr. 6). 1968. Concordia.
Hildreth, Charles Lotin
--Oo: Adventures in Orbello Land. LC 19-2907. 316 p. incl. front., illus. 20 cm. c.1889. Belford Company.
Hildreth, Dolly, et al.
--The Money God. (Indian Culture Ser.). (gr. 6). 1972. (ISBN 0-89992-031-4). MT Coun Indian.
Hildreth, Gertrude
--At Play. N.D. John C. Winston.
--Fun in Story. N.D. John C. Winston.
--Going to School. N.D. John C. Winston.
--Good Stories. N.D. John C. Winston.
--I Know A Secret. N.D. John C. Winston.
--Mac and Muff. (Easy Growth in Reading Ser.). N.D. John C. Winston.
--Tom and Don. N.D. John C. Winston.
Hildreth, Richard
--Memoirs of a Fugitive: America's First Antislavery Novel. Ritchie, Barbara, adapted by. LC 74-140647. (gr. 6-9). 1971. (ISBN 0-690-52949-X). T Y Crowell.
Hilel, O.
--Kibbutz Adventure. LC 65-15711. photos. 32p. (gr. 2-5). 1964. (ISBN 0-7232-0359-8). (ISBN 0-7232-0360-1). Warne.
--A Kibbutz Adventure. Lotan, Joel, ed. Lotan, Joel, et al., photos by LC 63-19357. 1 v. (unpaged) illus. 29 cm. 1963. F. Warne.
Hilgartner, Beth
--Great Gorilla Grins: An Abundance of Animal Alliterations. Morrill, Leslie H, illus. LC 78-10364. (Illus.). 32 p. 26cm. c.1979. (ISBN 0-316-36235-2). Little, Brown.
--A Necklace of Fallen Stars. Hague, Michael R., illus. LC 79-14916. (Illus.). 209 p. 22cm. c.1979. (ISBN 0-316-36236-0). Little, Brown.
Hilker, Elmer Albert (1897-)
--Bre'r Fox Adventures ... Canada, Ouida, illus. LC 46-22728. v. illus. (part col.) 20 1/2 cm. N.D. Children's Press.
Hill, Agnes Leonard Scanland, Mrs. (1842-)
--Heights and Depths. LC 7-4749. 271 p. 19 cm. 1871. H. A. Summer.
Hill, Alonzo F.
--Our Boys in the Army. (Illus.). (St. Nicholas Series for Boys). N.D. International Book Co.
--White Rocks: Or, The Robbers' Den. (Illus.). (St. Nicholas Series for Boys). N.D. International Book Co.
Hill, Barbara Tinker
--Little Yellow Duck. 1st ed. Shook, Larry, illus. LC 76-5990. (Illus.). ca. 150 p. 28cm. c.1976. Hill.
Hill, Christopher (1950-)
--Tom Turtle. Hill, Tom (1922-), illus. LC 72-97339. (Illus.). 32 p. (Magic circle book). 1974. (ISBN 0-663-25464-7). Ginn.
Hill, Cuthbert William
--The Adventures of Jock and Jonathan. Denton, Phyllis, illus. LC 58-9086. (Illus.). 20cm. 1957. F. Warne.
Hill, Dave, pseud., see Hill, David Charles.
Hill, Dave, pseud. (1936-)
--The Boy Who Gave His Lunch Away. Hill, David Charles. 1967. Lutheran Publications.
--The Boy Who Gave His Lunch Away. Hill, David Charles. (Little Folks Bible Story Books). 1967. (ISBN 0-87162-077-4). Warner Press.
--The Most Wonderful King: Luke 19: 28-24: 43 and John 12: 12-20: 31 for Children. Hill, David Charles. Wind, Betty, illus. (Illus.). 32 p. 21cm. (Arch books). 1968. Concordia Pub. House.
--Ramon's World. Hill, David Charles. Eitzen, Allan (1928-), illus. LC 65-18235. 101 p. illus. 22 cm. 1965. Herald Press.
--Welfare Kid. Hill, David Charles. Eitzen, Allan (1928-), illus. LC 66-29536. 176p. illus. 22cm. 1966. (ISBN 0-8361-1541-4). Herald Pr.
Hill, David Charles see Hill, Dave, pseud.
Hill, Deborah, ed. see Spyri, Johanna Heusser.
Hill, Donna Marie (1921-)
--Eerie Animals: Seven Stories. 1st ed. LC 82-13755. (Illus.). 160 p. 25cm. 1983. (ISBN 0-689-30956-2). Atheneum.
--First Your Penny. LC 84-20459. 207 p. 22cm. 1985. (ISBN 0-689-31093-5). Atheneum.
--Mr. Peeknuff's Tiny People. Daniel, Alan (1939-), illus. LC 80-12271. (Illus.). 32 p. 26cm. 1981. (ISBN 0-689-30778-0). Atheneum.
--Ms. Glee Was Waiting. Dawson, Diane, illus. LC 77-21137. (Illus.). 32 p. 1978. (ISBN 0-689-30618-0). Atheneum.
--Not One More Day. Hill, Donna Marie (1921-), illus. LC 57-1582. (Illus.). 32 p. 1957. Viking Press.
Hill, Douglas Arthur, jt. ed. see Robinson, Gail.
Hill, Douglas Arthur (1935-)
--Alien Citadel. LC 83-17142. 150p. (gr. 7 up). 1984. (ISBN 0-689-50281-8, Argo). Atheneum.
--The Caves of Klydor. LC 84-20481. 118 p. 22cm. 1985. (ISBN 0-689-50320-2). Atheneum.
--Day of the Starwind. LC 81-3476. p. cm. 1981. (ISBN 0-689-50205-2). Atheneum.
--Deathwing Over Veynaa. LC 80-20262. 125 p. 22cm. (Argo book). 1981, c.1980. (ISBN 0-689-50192-7). Atheneum.
--Exiles of Colsec. LC 84-3043. 126p. (gr. 7 up). 1984. (ISBN 0-689-50315-6, Argo). Atheneum.
--Galactic Warlord. LC 79-22604. p. cm. (Argo book). 1980. (ISBN 0-689-50164-1). Atheneum.
--The Huntsman. LC 82-3959. p. cm. 144p. 1982. (ISBN 0-689-50240-0). Atheneum.
--Planet of the Warlord. LC 81-12841. 128 p. 22cm. 1982. (ISBN 0-689-50222-2). Atheneum.
--Warriors of the Wasteland. 1st ed. LC 82-13896. 130 p. 23cm. 1983. (ISBN 0-689-50269-9). Atheneum.
--Young Legionary. LC 83-2834. p. cm. 1983. (ISBN 0-689-50292-3). Atheneum.
Hill, E. V., Mrs.
--Bessie White. 149p. (The Star Lib.). N.D. American Tract Society.
Hill, Edwin C.
--The Iron Horse. N.D. Grosset & Dunlap.
Hill, Eileen, pseud., see Stack, Nicolette Meredith.
Hill, Eileen, pseud. (1896-)
--The Mystery of Glengary Castle. Stack, Nicolette Meredith. Haggander, Sylvia, illus. LC 67-1661. (Illus.). 190 p. 22cm. (Your Robin Kane library, 3). 1966. Whitman Pub. Co.
--The Mystery of the Blue Pelican. Stack, Nicolette Meredith. Haggander, Sylvia, illus. LC 67-2982. (Illus.). 190 p. 22cm. (Your Robin Kane library, 1). 1966. Whitman Pub. Co.
--The Mystery of the Phantom. Stack, Nicolette Meredith. Haggander, Sylvia, illus. LC 67-2583. (Illus.). 192 p. 22cm. (Your Robin Kane library, 2). 1966. Whitman Pub. Co.
Hill, Elizabeth
--Contraband Bonnets. LC 35-16581. 3 p. l., v-vii, 178 p., 1 l. front. (port.) 21 cm. 1935. The Bradford Press.
--My Wonderful Visit. Stevens, Beatrice (1876-), illus. LC 3-25201. vi p., 1 l., 270 p. front., 4 pl. 20 cm. 1903. C. Scribner's Sons.
--When Kitty Came to Portland. Stevens, Beatrice (1876-), illus. LC 33-29636. 7 p. l., 307, 1 p. front., illus., plates. 21 cm. 1933. The Bradford Press.
Hill, Elizabeth Bjork
--Elsa's Lullaby. 1953. Augustana Book.
Hill, Elizabeth Starr (1925-)
--Evan's Corner. 1st ed. Grossman, Nancy S. (1940-), illus. LC 67-279. (Illus.). 1 v. (unpaged. 24cm. c.1967. Holt, Rinehart and Winston.
--Ever-After Island. LC 76-56859. 119 p. 22cm. c.1977. (ISBN 0-525-29415-5). Dutton.
--Fangs Aren't Everything. Ross, Larry (1943-), illus. LC 84-18748. (Illus.). 84 p. 22cm. c.1985. (ISBN 0-525-44152-2). E.P. Dutton.
--Master Mike and the Miracle Maid. 1st ed. LC 67-17719. 110 p. 22cm. 1967. Holt, Rinehart and Winston.
--Pardon My Fangs. LC 68-11830. 78 p. 22cm. 1968, c.1969. Holt, Rinehart and Winston.
--The Window Tulip. Williams, Hubert, illus. LC 64-13624. 1v. (unpaged) illus. (pt. col.) 25cm. c.1964. F. Warne.
--The Wonderful Visit to Miss Liberty. 1st ed. Galdone, Paul (1914-), illus. LC 61-518470. unpaged. illus. 21 x 26cm. 1961. Holt, Rinehart and Winston.
Hill, Eric
--At Home. LC 82-60627. (Illus.). 14p. (Eric Hill's Baby Bear Bks.). (ps-k). 1983. (ISBN 0-394-85638-4). Random.
--Baby Bear's Bedtime. Schulman, Janet, ed. Hill, Eric, illus. LC 83-43133. (Illus.). 24p. (Eric Hill Baby Bear Storybooks). (ps-1). 1984. (ISBN 0-394-86572-3, BYR). (ISBN 0-394-96572-8). Random.
--Donde Esta Spot?. Hill, Eric, illus. (Illus.). (ps-2). 1983. (ISBN 0-399-21018-0, Putnam). Putnam Pub Group.
--Fairy Tales. 24p. (Orig.). (Peek-A-Book Ser.). 1985. (ISBN 0-8431-0919-X). Price Stern.
--Good Morning, Baby Bear. Schulman, Janet, ed. Hill, Eric, illus. LC 83-43135. (Illus.). 24p. (Eric Hill Baby Bear Storybooks). (gr. k-1). 1984. (ISBN 0-394-86571-5, BYR). (ISBN 0-394-96571-X). Random.
--Here's Spot!. Hill, Eric, illus. (Illus.). (ps-2). 1983. (ISBN 0-399-21021-0, Putnam). Putnam Pub Group.
--My Pets. LC 82-60625. (Illus.). 14p. (Eric Hill's Baby Bear Bks.). (ps). 1983. (ISBN 0-394-85637-6). Random.

--Surprise for Judy Jo: An Apple Market Street Story. Hill, Mabel Betsy (1877-), illus. LC 39-27730. 64 p. incl. front., illus. (part col.) 16 x 22 cm. 1939. Frederick A. Stokes Company, Inc.

Hill, Margaret Livingston

--Bible for Children. Slade, C. Arnold, illus. N.D. David McKay Co.

--The Children's Lamp. LC 32-17675. 52 p. illus. (part col.) 28 1/2 x 31 1/2 cm. c.1932. David McKay Company.

Hill, Margaret Ohler (1915-)

--The Extra-Special Room. Hill, Mabel Betsy (1877-), illus. LC 62-12387. 312 p. 20cm. 1962. Little, Brown.

--Goal in the Sky. 1st ed. Lee, Manning De Villeneuve, contrib. by. LC 53-7308. (Illus.). 20cm. 212p. (About a girl's training to be an airline hostess). (gr. 7-10). 1953. (ISBN 0-316-36333-2, Pub. by Atlantic Monthly Pr). Little.

--Hostess in the Sky. 1st ed. Lee, Manning De Villeneuve, contrib. by. LC 55-891. (Illus.). 20cm. 276p. (gr. 7-10). 1955. (ISBN 0-316-36334-0, Pub. by Atlantic Monthly Pr). Little.

--Really, Miss Hillsbro!. 1st ed. LC 60-9337. 233 p. 20cm. 1960. Little, Brown.

--Senior Hostess. 1st ed. Lee, Manning De Villeneuve, contrib. by. LC 58-6033. 276p. illus. 20cm. 1958. (ISBN 0-316-36336-7, Pub. by Atlantic Monthly Pr.). Little, Brown.

--Time to Quit Running. LC 76-100573. 191 p. 22cm. 1970. (ISBN 0-671-32229-X). J. Messner.

--Turn the Page, Wendy. LC 80-26784. 176 p. 23cm. c.1981. (ISBN 0-687-42700-2). Abingdon.

Hill, Marion, Mrs. (1870-)

--Harmony Hall: A Story for Girls. Edwards, Robert, illus. LC 11-256741. 4 p. l., 206 p. front., plates. 19 1/2 cm. $1.00. c.1911. Small, Maynard & Company.

Hill, Marjorie Yourd

--Look for the Stars. LC 56-570020. 244p. 21cm. c.1956. Crowell.

--The Secret of Avalon. LC 65-17651. 187p. illus. 21cm. c.1965. McGraw.

Hill, Mary L.

--My Dad's a Park Ranger. DeHart, Tom, illus. LC 77-3523. (Illus.). (Career Adventures Ser.). (gr. 2-4). 1978. (ISBN 0-516-07635-3, Elk Grove Bks). Childrens.

--My Dad's a Smokejumper. Hendricks, Donald (1932-), illus. LC 77-5127. (Illus.). 32p. (Career Adventures Ser.). (gr. 2-4). 1978. (ISBN 0-516-07636-1, Elk Grove Bks). Childrens.

Hill, Mavis A.

--The Edible Sea. N.D. (ISBN 0-498-01550-5). A. S. Barnes Company.

Hill, May, ed.

--The Child's Treasury ... LC 23-15037. 2 p. l., 3-384 p. illus. (part col.) 24 1/2 cm. (Foundation library). c.1923. Foundation Desk Company Incorporated.

--The Child's Treasury ... LC 32-11117. 2 p. l., 3-387 p. illus. (part col.) 24 1/2 cm. (Foundation library). c.1931. Foundation Desk Company, Incorporated.

Hill, Meredith

--The Silent Witness. 192p. (Orig.). (gr. 7 up). 1983. (ISBN 0-590-32552-3, Windswept). Scholastic Inc.

Hill, Miranda

--Cinderella. (Illus.). 48p. (The Little Folks Plays Ser.). 1905. Set. Cassell & Co.

--The Fairy Spinner and Out of Date or Not. N.D. Thomas Nelson and Sons.

--Rumpelstiltzkin and Dumpling: Two Plays. (Illus.). 48p. (The Little Folks Plays Ser.). 1905. Set. Cassell & Co.

Hill, Monica, pseud., see Watson, Jane Werner.

Hill, Monica, jt. auth. see Verral, Charles Spain.

Hill, Olive

--Our Cat: The Adventures of Mrs. Tabitha's Kittens. Simmons, Will, illus. LC 28-22385. 3 p. l., v-viii p., 1 l., 117 p. col. front., illus. 21 1/2 cm. 1928. Frederick A. Stokes Company.

Hill, Patty Smith, jt. ed. see Farquhar, Silas Edgar.

Hill, Patty Smith, ed. see Read, Helen S.

Hill, Patty Smith (1868-)

--Songs Stories for the Kindergarten. N.D. E. Steiger & Co.

Hill, Patty Smith (1868-) & Murray, Gretchen Ostrander, Mrs., eds.

--Favorites from Storyland. LC 37-37796. 1 p. l., 7-124 p. col. front., illus., col. plates. 35 cm. c.1937. Whitman Publishing Company.

Hill, Phyllis see Gant, Phyllis, pseud.

Hill, Ralph Nading (1917-)

--Robert Fulton and the Steamboat. (Illus.). 1954. Random House Inc.

--The Voyages of Brian Seaworthy. Boyajian, Robert A., illus. LC 75-154485. (Illus.). vii, 151 p. 24cm. c.1971. Vermont Life Magazine.

Hill, Randolph, Jr.

--Tom, the Ready. (Illus.). (The Boys' Home Ser.). N.D. A. L. Burt.

--Tom, the Ready: Or, Up From the Lowest. (The Rugby Seris for Boys and Girls). N.D. A. L. Burt Company.

--Tom, the Ready: Or, Up from the Lowest. (Illus.). (The Alger Series for Boys). N.D. A. L. Burt's Pubs.

--Tom, the Ready: Or, Up from the Lowest. (Wide Awake Boys Ser.). N.D. A. L. Burt.

Hill, Ruth Livingston (1898-)

--This Side of Tomorrow. N.D. Zondervan Publishing House.

Hill, Susan

--Go Away, Bad Dreams. Julian-Ottie, Vanessa, illus. LC 84-17759. (Illus.). 32p. (Pictureback Ser.). (ps-2). 1985. (ISBN 0-394-97222-8, BYR). (ISBN 0-394-87222-3). Random.

Hill, Virginia & Gondor, Emery I.

--Squirly: The Curly Pig. LC 42-117. 32 p. incl. front., illus. 26 cm. c.1941. Island Press.

Hill, W. M., pseud., see Dodd, Edward Howard.

Hill, Weldon, pseud., see Scott, William Ralph.

Hill, Weldon, pseud. (1918-)

--Jefferson McGraw: A Novel. Scott, William Ralph. 286 p. 18cm. 1973, c.1972. Curtis Books.

--Jefferson McGraw: A Novel. Scott, William Ralph. LC 75-151905. 248 p. 22cm. 1972. Morrow.

--One of The Casualties. Scott, William Ralph. N.D. Doubleday & Co.

Hill, William L

--Jackieboy in Rainbowland. Cory, Fanny Young, illus. LC 12-28709. 23cm. 84p. 1911. Rand McNally.

Hillary, Edmund, ed.

--Challenge of the Unknown. (Illus.). (gr. 7 up). 1958. (ISBN 0-525-27565-7). Dutton.

Hille-Brandts, Lene

--Guess What. Duckworth, Elisabeth, adapted by. Dumler, Doris, illus. (Illus.). 32p. (Easy Reading Picture Story Bks). (gr. k-3). 1966. (ISBN 0-516-03487-1). Childrens.

--If I Were ... Duckworth, Elisabeth, adapted by. Otto, Doris, illus. LC 69-19019. (Illus.). 31 p. 24cm. 1969. Childrens Press.

--If I Were. Otto, Doris, illus. (Illus.). 32p. (Easy Reading Picture Story Bks). Orig. Title: If I Were Very Small. (gr. k-3). 1969. (ISBN 0-516-03504-5). Childrens.

--The Little Black Hen. american ed. Koenig, Marion, ed. Heuck, Sigrid, illus. LC 68-31313. (Illus.). 31 p. 24cm. 1968, c.1967. Childrens Press.

Hillegas, Rose T., selected by see Mother Goose.

Hiller, B. B.

--Camp-Out on Danger Mountain. Tommasino, David, illus. (Illus.). 96p. (Orig.). (Twistaplot Ser.: No. 11). (gr. 7 up). 1984. (ISBN 0-590-33102-7). Scholastic Inc.

--The Fantastic Journey of the Space Shuttle Astra. Zimmerman, Jerry, illus. (Illus.). 64p. (Orig.). (Pick-a-Path Bks.). (gr. 2-6). 1984. (ISBN 0-590-32972-3). Scholastic Inc.

--The Karate Kid. 144p. (Orig.). (gr. 7 up). 1984. (ISBN 0-590-33306-2, Point). Scholastic Inc.

--The Secret of Thirteen. Dodson, Bert, illus. (Illus.). 64p. (Orig.). (Pick-a-Path Ser.). (gr. 2-4). 1984. (ISBN 0-590-33294-5). Scholastic Inc.

Hiller, Catherine (1946-)

--Abracatabby. De'Larrea, Victoria, illus. LC 80-10182. (Illus.). 62 p. 23cm. (Break-of-day book). c.1981. (ISBN 0-698-30727-5). Coward, McCann & Geoghegan.

--Argentaybee and the Boonie. Szekeres, Cyndy (1933-), illus. LC 77-15643. (Illus.). 32 p. 26cm. c.1979. (ISBN 0-698-20441-7). Coward, McCann & Geoghegan.

Hiller, Doris, pseud., see Nussbaum, Albert F..

Hiller, Doris, pseud. (1934-)

--Black Beach. Nuss baum, Albert F.. LC 78-15985. (Illus.). (Pacesetters Ser.). (gr. 4 up). 1978. (ISBN 0-516-02166-4). Childrens.

--Little Big Top. Nuss baum, Albert F.. LC 78-72328. (Illus.). (Pacesetters Ser.). (gr. 4 up). 1979. (ISBN 0-516-02186-9). Childrens.

Hillerich, Robert L., jt. auth. see Hamsa, Bobbie.

Hillerman, Tony (1925-)

--The Boy Who Made Dragonfly: A Zuni Myth. Kubinyi, Laszlo (1937-), illus. LC 72-76498. (Illus.). 86 p. 21cm. 1972. (ISBN 0-06-022311-1). Harper & Row.

Hillern, Wilhelmine von

--Only a Girl. Wister, A. L., tr. N.D. J. B. Lippincott Co.

Hillert, Margaret (1920-), retold by see The, Three Bears.

Hillert, Margaret (1920-)

--Away Go the Boats. Masheris, Robert, illus. LC 80-14519. (Illus.). 31 p. 21cm. (Follett just beginning-to-read book). c.1981. (ISBN 0-695-41454-2). (ISBN 0-695-31454-8). Follett.

--The Baby Bunny. Masheris, Robert, illus. LC 79-26415. (Illus.). 31 p. 21cm. (Follett just beginning-to-read book). c.1981. (ISBN 0-695-41352-X). Follett.

--The Ball Book. Brooks, Nan, illus. LC 80-23590. (Illus.). 31 p. 21cm. (Follett just beginning-to-read books). c.1982. (ISBN 0-695-41553-0). (ISBN 0-695-31553-6). Follett Pub. Co.

--The Birthday Car. Oechsli, Kelly (1918-), illus. LC 67-1286. (Illus.). 27 p. 21cm. (Follett just beginning-to-read series). 1966. Follett Pub. Co.

--The Boy and the Goats. Miyake, Yoshi, illus. LC 80-20840. p. cm. (Follett just beinning-to-read series). 1981. (ISBN 0-695-41545-X). (ISBN 0-695-31545-5). Follett Pub. Co.

--Cinderella at the Ball. LaSalle, Janet (1926-), illus. LC 75-85952. (Illus.). 31 p. 21cm. (Follett just beginning-to-read books). 1970. Follett Pub. Co.

--Circus Fun. Raphael, Elaine, pseud. (1933-), illus. Bolognese, Elaine Raphael Chionchio. LC 69-15968. (Illus.). 31 p. 21cm. (Her A Follett just beginning-to-read book). 1969. Follett Pub. Co.

--City Fun. Corey, Barbara, illus. LC 80-14564. (Illus.). 31 p. 21cm. (Her Follett just beginning-to-read books). c.1981. (ISBN 0-695-41457-7). (ISBN 0-695-31457-2). Follett.

--Come Play with Me. Craft, Kinuko Y., illus. LC 75-884. (Illus.). 31 p. 21cm. (Follett just beginning-to-read book of verse). c.1975. (ISBN 0-695-40587-X). (ISBN 0-695-30587-5). Follett Pub. Co.

--Come to School, Dear Dragon. Helton, David Kirby (1940-), illus. LC 83-22066. (Illus.). 31 p. 21cm. (Modern Curriculum Press Beginning to Read Series). c.1985. (ISBN 0-87895-878-9). (ISBN 0-87895-890-8). Modern Curriculum Press.

--The Cookie House. Craft, Kinuko Y., illus. LC 78-106128. (Illus.). 28 p., 1 leaf of plates. 21cm. (Follett just beginning-to-read book). c.1978. (ISBN 0-695-30880-7). Follett Pub. Co.

--The Cow That Got Her Wish. Stasiak, Krystyna, illus. LC 82-2366. (Illus.). 32 p. 21cm. c.1982. (ISBN 0-695-41672-3). (ISBN 0-695-31672-9). Follett.

--Farther Than Far. Fraser, Betty M., pseud. (1928-), illus. Fraser, Elizabeth Marr. LC 69-10258. (Illus.). 48p. (gr. 1-3). 1969. (ISBN 0-695-82500-3). (ISBN 0-695-42500-5). Follett.

--Four Good Friends. Stasiak, Krystyna, illus. LC 79-26083. (Illus.). 31 p. 21cm. (Follett just beginning-to-read book). 1980, c.1981. (ISBN 0-695-41356-2). (ISBN 0-695-31356-8). Follett Pub. Co.

--A Friend for Dear Dragon. Helton, David Kirby (1940-), illus. LC 83-22074. (Illus.). 31 p. 21cm. (Modern Curriculum Press Beginning to Read Series). c.1985. (ISBN 0-87895-881-9). (ISBN 0-87895-893-2). Modern Curriculum Press.

--Fun Days. Rogers, Joe, illus. LC 80-21419. (Illus.). 31 p. 21cm. (Follett just beginning-to-read books). c.1982. (ISBN 0-695-41546-8). (ISBN 0-695-31546-3). Follett Pub. Co.

--Funny Baby. Depper, Hertha, illus. LC 63-9617. (Illus.). (Just Beginning-to-Read Ser.). (ps). 1963. (ISBN 0-695-83300-6, Dist. by Caroline Hse). (ISBN 0-695-43300-8). (ISBN 0-695-33300-3). Modern Curr.

--The Funny Ride. Sumichrast, Jozef (1948-), illus. LC 80-20864. (Illus.). 31 p. 21cm. (Follett just beginning-to-read books). c.1982. (ISBN 0-695-41552-2). (ISBN 0-695-31552-8). Follett Pub. Co.

--Go to Sleep, Dear Dragon. Helton, David Kirby (1940-), illus. LC 83-22068. (Illus.). 31 p. 21cm. (Modern Curriculum Press Beginning to Read Series). c.1985. (ISBN 0-87895-880-0). (ISBN 0-87895-892-4). Modern Curriculum Press.

--Happy Birthday, Dear Dragon. Kock, Carl, illus. LC 77-156062. (Illus.). 31 p. 20cm. (Follett just beginning-to-read book). c.1977. (ISBN 0-695-30743-6). (ISBN 0-695-40743-0). Follett Pub. Co.

--Happy Birthday, Dear Dragon. Kock, Carl, illus. LC 81-71353. p. cm. (A Follett Just Beginning-to-Read Book). 1982, c.1977. (ISBN 0-695-40743-0). (ISBN 0-695-30743-6). Follett Pub. Co.

--Happy Easter, Dear Dragon. Kock, Carl, illus. LC 79-23814. (Illus.). 31 p. 21cm. (Follett just beginning-to-read book). c.1981. (ISBN 0-695-41363-5). Follett Pub. Co.

--Help for Dear Dragon. Helton, David Kirby (1940-), illus. LC 83-22073. (Illus.). 30 p. 21cm. (Modern Curriculum Press Beginning to Read Series). c.1985. (ISBN 0-87895-876-2). (ISBN 0-87895-888-6). Modern Curriculum Press.

--House for Little Red. Oechsli, Kelly (1918-), illus. LC 75-85953. (Illus.). four color ils. 32p. (Just Beginning-To-Read Ser.). (ps). 1970. (ISBN 0-695-40082-7, Dist. by Caroline Hse). (ISBN 0-695-30082-2). Modern Curr.

--I Like Things. Axeman, Lois, illus. LC 80-21409. (Illus.). 31 p. 21cm. (Follett just beginning-to-read book). c.1982. (ISBN 0-695-41554-9). (ISBN 0-695-31554-4). Follett Pub. Co.

--I Love You, Dear Dragon. Kock, Carl, illus. LC 79-23669. (Illus.). 31 p. 21cm. (Follett just beginning-to-read book). c.1981. (ISBN 0-695-41362-7). (ISBN 0-695-41362-7). Follett Pub. Co.

--I Need You, Dear Dragon. Helton, David Kirby (1940-), illus. LC 83-22069. (Illus.). 31 p. 21cm. (Modern Curriculum Press Beginning to Read Series). c.1985. (ISBN 0-87895-879-7). (ISBN 0-87895-891-6). Modern Curriculum Press.

--It's Circus Time, Dear Dragon. Helton, David Kirby (1940-), illus. LC 83-22070. (Illus.). 31 p. 21cm. (Modern Curriculum Press Beginning to Read Series). c.1985. (ISBN 0-87895-877-0). (ISBN 0-87895-889-4). Modern Curriculum Press.

--It's Halloween, Dear Dragon. Kock, Carl, illus. LC 79-23433. (Illus.). 31 p. 21cm. (Follett just beginning-to-read book). c.1981. (ISBN 0-695-41361-9). Follett.

--Let's Go, Dear Dragon. Kock, Carl, illus. LC 79-23672. (Illus.). 31 p. 21cm. (Follett just-beginning-to-read books). c.1981. (ISBN 0-695-41360-0). Follett Pub. Co.

--Let's Have a Play. Elzaurdia, Sharon, illus. LC 80-21437. (Illus.). 31 p. 21cm. (Follett just beginning-to-read book). c.1982. (ISBN 0-695-41544-1). (ISBN 0-695-31544-7). Follett Pub. Co.

--The Little Cookie. Charles, Donald, pseud. (1929-), illus. Meighan, Donald Charles. LC 79-23845. (Illus.). 31 p. 21cm. (Follett just beginning-to-read book). c.1981. (ISBN 0-695-41355-4). (ISBN 0-695-31355-X). Follett Pub. Co.

--The Little Cowboy and the Big Cowboy. Siculan, Daniel (1922-), illus. LC 80-14566. (Illus.). 31 p. 21cm. (Follett just beginning-to-read book). c.1981. (ISBN 0-695-41453-4). (ISBN 0-695-31453-X). Follett.

--Little Puff. Jordan, Sid, illus. LC 73-81993. (Illus.). 27 p. 21cm. (Follett just beginning-to-read book). 1973. (ISBN 0-695-80416-2). (ISBN 0-695-80416-2). Follett Pub. Co.

--Little Red Riding Hood. Connelly, Gwen, illus. LC 80-20983. (Illus.). 31 p. 21cm. (Follett just beginning-to-read books). c.1982. (ISBN 0-695-31543-9). Follett Pub. Co.

--The Little Runaway. Anderson, Irv, illus. LC 67-1287. (Illus.). 27 p. 21cm. (Follett just beginning-to-read series). 1966. Follett Pub. Co.

--The Magic Beans. Pekarsky, Mel, illus. LC 67-1288. (Illus.). 26 p. 21cm. (Follett just beginning-to-read series). 1966. Follett Pub. Co.

--The Magic Nutcracker. Iversen, Portia, illus. LC 80-13667. (Illus.). 31 p. 21cm. (Follett just-beginning-to read book). c.1981. (ISBN 0-695-41456-9). (ISBN 0-695-31456-4). Follett Pub. Co.

--Merry Christmas, Dear Dragon. Kock, Carl, illus. LC 79-26409. (Illus.). 31 p. 21cm. (Follett just beginning-to-read book). c.1981. (ISBN 0-695-41359-7). Follett Pub. Co.

--Not I, Not I. Magnuson, Diana, illus. LC 79-23847. (Illus.). 31 p. 21cm. (Follett just beginning-to-read books). c.1981. (ISBN 0-695-31353-3). (ISBN 0-695-41353-8). Follett Pub. Co.

--Pinocchio. Hamilton, Laurie, illus. (Illus.). 32p. (Just Beginning-to-Read Ser.). (gr. 1-6). 1981. (ISBN 0-695-41551-4, Dist. by Caroline Hse). (ISBN 0-695-31551-X). Modern Curr.

--Play Ball. Martin, Dick (1927-), illus. LC 78-106127. (Illus.). 31 p. 21cm. (Follett just beginning-to-read book). c.1978. (ISBN 0-695-30879-3). (ISBN 0-695-40879-8). Follett Pub. Co.

--The Purple Pussycat. Stasiak, Krystyna, illus. LC 80-14136. (Illus.). 31 p. 21cm. (Follett just beginning-to-read-book). c.1981. (ISBN 0-695-41455-0). (ISBN 0-695-31455-6). Follett Pub. Co.

--Run to the Rainbow. Corey, Barbara, illus. LC 79-23889. (Illus.). 31 p. 21cm. (Follett just beginning-to-read book). c.1981. (ISBN 0-695-41354-6). (ISBN 0-695-31354-1). Follett Pub. Co.

--The Sleepytime Book. Ruth, Rod (1912-), illus. (Illus.). 10p. (Golden Touch & Feel Book). (ps). 1975. (ISBN 0-307-12145-3, Golden Pr). Western Pub.

--The Snow Baby. Dauber, Elizabeth, illus. LC 69-15969. (Illus.). 31 p. 21cm. (Her A Follett just beginning-to-read book). 1969. Follett Pub. Co.

--Take a Walk, Johnny. Miyake, Yoshi, illus. LC 81-4044. (Illus.). 31 p. 21cm. c.1981. (ISBN 0-695-41625-1). (ISBN 0-695-31625-7). Follett.

AUTHOR INDEX HINGST, ADOLPHINE

--The Three Goats. Pekarsky, Mel, illus. LC 63-9616. (Illus.). 27p. 21cm. (The Follett Just Beginning to Read Ser.). 1963. Follett Pub. Co.
--Three Goats. Pekarsky, Mel, illus. (Illus.). (Just Beginning-to-Read Ser.). (ps). 1963. (ISBN 0-695-48720-5, Dist. by Caroline Hse). (ISBN 0-695-38720-0). Modern Curr.
--The Three Little Pigs. Wilde, Irma, illus. LC 63-9615. 27p. col. illus. 21cm. (The Follett Just Beginning-To-Read Ser.). 1963. Follett Pub. Co.
--Three Little Pigs. Wilde, Irma, illus. (Illus.). (Beginning-to-Read Bks). (ps). 1963. (ISBN 0-695-48730-2, Dist. by Caroline Hse). (ISBN 0-695-38730-8). Modern Curr.
--Tom Thumb. Hockerman, Dennis, illus. LC 80-20839. (Illus.). 31 p. 21cm. (Follett just beginning-to-read book). c.1982. (ISBN 0-695-41542-5). (ISBN 0-695-31542-0). Follett Pub. Co.
--Up, Up, and Away. Masheris, Robert, illus. LC 80-21403. (Illus.). 31 p. 21cm. (Follett just beginning-to-read books). c.1982. (ISBN 0-695-41541-7). (ISBN 0-695-31541-2). Follett Pub. Co.
--What Am I?. Elzaurdia, Sharon, illus. 32p. (Beginning-to-Read Ser.). 1980. (ISBN 0-695-41351-1, Dist. by Caroline Hse). (ISBN 0-695-31351-7). Modern Curr.
--What Is It?. Craft, Kinuko Y., illus. LC 78-106150. (Illus.). 27 p. 21cm. (Follett just beginning-to-read mystery in verse). c.1978. (ISBN 0-695-30882-3). (ISBN 0-695-40882-8). Follett Pub. Co.
--Who Goes to School?. Brooks, Nan, illus. LC 80-15009. (Illus.). 31 p. 21cm. (Follett just beginning-to-read book). c.1981. (ISBN 0-695-41458-5). (ISBN 0-695-31458-0). Follett.
--Why We Have Thanksgiving. Siculan, Daniel (1922-), illus. LC 80-21431. (Illus.). 31 p. 21cm. (Follett Just Beginning-to-Read Books). c.1982. (ISBN 0-695-41550-6). (ISBN 0-695-31550-1). Follett Pub. Co.
--The Witch Who Went for a Walk. Stasiak, Krystyna, illus. LC 80-21433. (Illus.). 32 p. 21cm. (Follett just beginning-to-read book) c.1982. (ISBN 0-695-41549-2). (ISBN 0-695-31549-8). Follett Pub. Co.
--The Yellow Boat. Young, Ed (1931-), illus. LC 67-1289. (Illus.). 27 p. 21cm. (Follett just beginning-to-read series). 1966. Follett Pub. Co.

Hillert, Margaret (1920-), adapted by.
--The Golden Goose. Santa, Monica, illus. LC 78-106115. (Illus.). 31 p. 21cm. (Follett just beginning-to-read book). c.1978. Follett Pub. Co.

Hillery, Mable & Hall, Patricia
--A Guide to the Use of Street-Folk-Musical Games in the Classroom: Vol. II, Chanting Games. Kendrick, John & May, Warren, illus. Freeman, Harold, Jr., intro. by. (Illus.). 76p. (Orig.). (Street-Folk-Musical Games Ser.: Vol. II). (gr. 2-6). 1981. (ISBN 0-939632-05-5). ILM.

Hilles, Helen Train, Mrs.
--Auction Today. 1st ed. Reed, Veronica, pseud. (1916-), illus. Sherman, Theresa. LC 55-11812. 90p. illus. 20cm. c.1956. (ISBN 0-397-30323-8). Lippincott.
--Cowboy Holiday. Townsend, Lee (1895-), illus. LC 33-7566. xi, 219 p. incl. front., illus., plates. 20 cm. 1933. The Macmillan Company.
--A Mile of Freedom. Thorne, Diana (1894-), illus. LC 32-12722. x p., 1 l., 248 p. incl. front., illus. 20 cm. 1932. The Macmillan Company.
--Moving Day. 1st ed. Tamburine, Jean (1930-), illus. 62p. illus. 20cm. 1954. Lippincott.
--Pierre Comes to P. S. 20. Barnum, Jay Hyde (1888-1962), illus. LC 52-9328. 64 p. illus. 22 cm. (Everyday adventure stories). 1952. J. Messner.
--Play Street. Gay, Zhenya (1906-1978), illus. LC 36-20246. 238 p. front., plates. 21 cm. c.1936. Random House.
--Rainbow on the Rhine. 1st ed. Werth, Kurt (1896-), illus. LC 59-5800. 91p. illus. 22cm. 1959. Lippincott.

Hilliard, A.
--Under the Black Eagle. (Illus.). (Scribner-Blackie Series of books for young people). N.D. Charles Scribner's Sons.

Hilliard, Susan E
--Simon the Snake. Mason, Alice Leedy, retold by. Hockerman, Dennis, illus. LC 84-23134. p. cm. (Teaching Tales). 1984. (ISBN 0-516-09126-3). Childrens Press.

Hillier, Caroline
--Winter's Tales for Children. Marshall, Hugh, illus. LC 65-25196. 200p. illus. 25cm. 1966, c.1965. Macmillan.
--Winter's Tales for Children. Marshall, Hugh, illus. LC 65-25196. v. illus. 25 cm. annual. 1965. St Martin's Press.

Hillig, Chuck
--The Magic King. Hesik, Blue, illus. (Illus.). 32p. (Orig.). (ps-2). 1984. (ISBN 0-913299-07-3). Stillpoint.

Hillis, Don W.
--Cuba's Miracle Lad, and Other Missionary Stories. LC 61-13671. 104p. 20cm. (Valor Ser.). 1961. Baker Book House.
--Stories of Love That Lasts. 80p. (gr. 9-12). 1980. (ISBN 0-89323-015-4). BMA Pr.

Hillman, Priscilla (1940-)
--A Merry-Mouse Book of Favorite Poems. LC 80-2551. (Illus.). 32 p. 27cm. 1981. (ISBN 0-385-17104-8). Doubleday.
--A Merry-Mouse Book of Months. LC 79-8021. (Illus.). 32 p. 27cm. c.1980. (ISBN 0-385-15594-8). (ISBN 0-385-15595-6). Doubleday.
--A Merry-Mouse Book of Nursery Rhymes. 1st ed. Hillman, Priscilla (1940-), illus. LC 80-2053. p. cm. c.1981. (ISBN 0-385-17102-1). Doubleday.
--A Merry-Mouse Christmas ABC. LC 79-6586. (Illus.). 32 p. 27cm. c.1980. (ISBN 0-385-15596-4). (ISBN 0-385-15597-2). Doubleday.
--The Merry-Mouse Schoolhouse. LC 81-43137. (Illus.). 32 p. 27cm. c.1982. (ISBN 0-385-17107-2). Doubleday.

Hillmann, Mary V
--In the Jersey Hills. LC 27-5948. v, 307 p. 20 1/2 cm. 1926. P. J. Kennedy& Sons.

Hillock, Elizabeth A.
--Ned Melbourne's Mission. N.D. Lothrop Pub. Co.

Hillock, Mabel
--A Dog's Life: The Story of Ring. LC 72-188542. (Illus.). 127p. 21cm. (Penguin Ser.). c.1972. Review and Herald Pub. Association.

Hillocks, George, ed.
--The Last Laugh. (gr. 10-12). 1976. (ISBN 0-590-10171-4, Schol Pap). Scholastic Inc.

Hills, C. Laura, ed.
--Flower Folk: A Book for Children. Pratt, M. Anna, illus. N.D. Frederick Stokes.

Hills, Nora Kathleen (1877-), tr. see Vimar, Nicolas Staniglas Auguste.

Hills, Verna
--Martin and Judy ... LC 45-583. v. illus., col. plates. 22 x 20 cm. 1944. The Beacon Press.
--Martin and Judy ... Fahs, Sophia Blanche Lyon (1876-1976), ed. LC 39-21147. v. illus. (part col.) col. plates. 22 x 20 cm. 1939. The Beacon Press, Inc.

Hills, Verna & Fahs, Sophia Blanche Lyon, Mrs. (1876-1978)
--Martin and Judy in Their Two Little Houses. Ingersoll, W. King, illus. LC 39-21147. v. illus. (part col.) col. plates. 22 x 20 cm. N.D. The Beacon Press, Inc.

Hillyard, Mary Dorothea (1886-)
--The Exciting Family. N.D. Barse & Co.
--The Exciting Family. Kovalesky, Dorathea & Kovalesky, Agnes, illus. LC 37-17807. 94 p. col. front., col. plates. 20 1/2 cm. 1936. Coward-McCann, Inc.

Hillyard, W. D.
--Peggy's Giant. N.D. Macmillan.

Hillyer, Virgil Mores (1875-1934)
--The Dark Secret. Jones, Mary Sherwood Wright, illus. LC 31-24681. xi, 367 p. incl. front., illus. 20 cm. $2.50. c.1931. The Century Co.

Hillyer, William Hurd (1880-)
--The Box of Daylight. Best, Allena Champlin, Mrs. (1892-1974), illus. Berry, Erick, pseud. LC 31-15936. 1 p. l., vii-xv, 1 179 p. front., illus. 21 cm. 1931. A. A. Knopf.

Hilmer
--Bedtime Mother Goose. (Illus.). 24p. (ps-3). 1982. (ISBN 0-307-61855-2). Western Pub.

Hilpert, Ruth Ewing, Mrs., ed. see Dodge, Mary Elizabeth Mapes, Mrs.

Hilton, Agnes A.
--Midsummer Madness. N.D. Mamillan.

Hilton, Bruce (1930-)
--My Brother is a Stranger. 128p. 1963. Friendship Press.

Hilton, Irene Pothus (1912-)
--Bluey from Down Under. Heugh, James, illus. 176p. illus. 21cm. 1962. Westminster Press.
--Bluey's Runaway Kangaroo. LC 63-7782. 184 p. illus. 22 cm. 1963. Westminster Press.
--Enemy in the Sky. Gretzer, John, illus. LC 64-10666. 175p. illus. 23cm. c.1964. Westminster.

Hilton, James (1900-1954)
--Good-Bye, Mr. Chips. (Illus.). (Mr. Hilton's classic story of an English schoolmaster). (gr. 7 up). 1935. (ISBN 0-316-36420-7, Pub. by Atlantic Monthly Pr). Little.
--Goodbye Mr. Chips. (Keith Jennison Large Type Bks). (gr. 9 up). 1966. (ISBN 0-531-00192-X). Watts.
--The Passionate year. LC 24 23737. 3 320p. 19 1/2cm. 1924. Little Brown & Co.

Hilton, William Atwood (1878-)
--Indian Animal Stories for Children. LC 56-12193. 71p. illus. 21cm. 1957, c.1956. Vantage Press.

Him, George, ed. see Cervantes Saavedra, Miguel de.

Himes, Vera C, adapted by see Topelius, Zakarias.

Himes, Vera Carole
--Ola and the Runaway Bread. Dewey, Katherine, illus. LC 32-22193. 64 p. incl. col. front., col. illus. 20 cm. c.1932. Thomas Y. Crowell Co.
--Pepi and the Golden Hawk: A Tale of Old Egypt. Dewey, Katherine, illus. LC 32-22194. 64 p. incl. col. front., illus. (part. col) 21 1/2 cm. c.1932. T. Y. Crowell Company.

Himler, Ann, jt. auth. see Himler, Ronald Norbert.

Himler, Ann (1946-)
--Waiting for Cherries. Bolognese, Donald Alan (1934-), illus. LC 75-25412. (Illus.). 24 p. 23cm. c.1976. (ISBN 0-06-022319-7). (ISBN 0-06-022320-0). Harper & Row.

Himler, Ronald Norbert (1937-)
--The Girl on the Yellow Giraffe. LC 76-3826. (Illus.). 32 p. 24cm. c.1976. (ISBN 0-06-022317-0). (ISBN 0-06-022318-9). Harper & Row.
Glad Day and Other Classical Poems for Children. Himler, Ronald Norbert (1937-), illus. LC 72-160336. (Illus.). 32 p. 1972. Putnam.
--Wake up, Jeremiah. LC 77-25679. (Illus.). 25 p. c.1979. (ISBN 0-06-022323-5). (ISBN 0-06-022324-3). Harper & Row.

Himler, Ronald Norbert (1937-) & Himler, Ann (1946-)
--Little Owl, Keeper of the Trees. LC 74-2615. (Illus.). 63 p. 23cm. 1974. (ISBN 0-06-022321-9). (ISBN 0-06-022322-7). Harper & Row.

Himmel, Roger J.
--Avoiding Litter. Manoni, Mary Hallahan (1924-), ed. Peters, Luther J. & Ross, Connie, illus. (Illus.). (The Adventures of the Lollipop Dragon Ser.). (gr. k-3). 1978. (ISBN 0-89290-045-8). Soc for Visual.
--Care of Property. new ed. Manoni, Mary Hallahan (1924-), ed. Peters, Luther J. & Ross, Connie, illus. (Illus.). (The Adventures of the Lollipop Dragon Ser.). (gr. k-3). 1978. (ISBN 0-89290-046-6). Soc for Visual.
--How the Lollipop Dragon Got His Name. new ed. Manoni, Mary Hallahan (1924-), ed. Peters, Luther J. & Ross, Connie, illus. LC 70-738042. (Illus.). (The Adventures of the Lollipop Dragon Ser.). (gr. k-3). 1978. (ISBN 0-89290-043-1). Soc for Visual.
--Kindness to Animals. Manoni, Mary Hallahan (1924-), ed. Peters, Luther J. & Ross, Connie, illus. (Illus.). (The Adventures of the Lollipop Dragon Ser.). (gr. k-3). 1978. (ISBN 0-89290-048-2). Soc for Visual.
--Lollipop Dragon Helps Santa. Manoni, Mary Hallahan (1924-), ed. Peters, Luther J. & Ross, Connie, illus. LC 75-739480. (Illus.). (The Adventures of the Lollipop Dragon Ser.). (gr. k-3). 1978. (ISBN 0-89290-037-7). Soc for Visual.
--Lollipop Dragon's First Halloween. Manoni, Mary Hallahan (1924-), ed. Peters, Luther J. & Ross, Connie, illus. (Illus.). (The Adventures of the Lollipop Dragon Ser.). (gr. k-3). 1978. (ISBN 0-89290-040-7). Soc for Visual.
--Lollipop Dragon's Valentine Party. new ed. Manoni, Mary Hallahan (1924-), ed. Peters, Luther J. & Ross, Connie, illus. LC 70-739484. (Illus.). (The Adventures of the Lollipop Dragon Ser.). (gr. k-3). 1978. (ISBN 0-89290-041-5). Soc for Visual.
--Mother's Day Surprise. new ed. Manoni, Mary Hallahan (1924-), ed. Peters, Luther J. & Ross, Connie, illus. LC 73-739485. (Illus.). (The Adventures of the Lollipop Dragon Ser.). (gr. k-3). 1978. (ISBN 0-89290-042-3). Soc for Visual.
--Taking Turns. Manoni, Mary Hallahan (1924-), ed. Peters, Luther J. & Ross, Connie, illus. (Illus.). (The Adventures of the Lollipop Dragon Ser.). (gr. k-3). 1978. (ISBN 0-89290-047-4). Soc for Visual.
--Thanksgiving in Tumtum. Manoni, Mary Hallahan (1924-), ed. Peters, Luther J. & Ross, Connie, illus. LC 79-739481. (Illus.). (The Adventures of the Lolipop Dragon Ser.). (gr. k-3). 1978. (ISBN 0-89290-038-5). Soc for Visual.
--Working Together. Manoni, Mary Hallahan (1924-), ed. Peters, Luther J. & Ross, Connie, illus. (Illus.). (The Adventures of the Lollipop Dragon Ser.). (gr. k-3). 1978. (ISBN 0-89290-044-X). Soc for Visual.

Himmel, Roger J. & Manoni, Mary Hallahan (1924-)
--The Big Easter Egg Hunt. new ed. Peters, Luther J. & Ross, Connie, illus. LC 72-739482. (Illus.). (The Adventures of the Lollipop Dragon Ser.) (gr. k-3). 1978. (ISBN 0-89290-039-3). Soc for Visual.

Himmelman, John
--Amanda and the Witch Switch: Story and Pictures. Himmelman, John, illus. LC 84-19515. (Illus.). 32 p. 24cm. 1985. (ISBN 0-670-11531-2). Viking Kestrel.
--Talestar the Lizard. Himmelman, John, illus. LC 81-68775. (Illus.). 32p. (ps-2). 1982. (ISBN 0-8037-8787-1). (ISBN 0-8037-8788-X). Dial Bks Young.
--Talester the Lizard. Himmelman, John, illus. LC 81-68775. (Illus.). 32 p. 21cm. (ps-2). c.1982. (ISBN 0-8037-8787-1). Dial Press.

Hinchman, Catharine Sellew see Sellew, Catharine Freeman.

Hinchman, Catharine Sellew (1922-)
--Torchlight. 1st ed. LC 60-9339. 215p. 21cm. 1960. Little, Brown.

Hinchman, Jane
--A Talent for Trouble. 1st ed. LC 66-15444. 162p. 2icm. 1966. Doubleday.

Hinckley, Helen see Jones, Helen Hinckley.

Hinckley, Marcia (1920-)
--Bumpy Jones and the Penny Pig: A Real Piggy-Bank Book. Guyther, Wayne, illus. LC 53-22438. unpaged. illus. 22x28cm. c.1953. M. T. Mathews Pub. Co.

Hinde, Cecilia & Hinde, Jean
--One Little Cat: A Number Book. (ps-1). 1962. Vorry.

Hinde, Jean, jt. auth. see Hinde, Cecilia.

Hindle, Thomas Clark (1876-1949)
--Gray: The Story of a Brave Dog. LC 58-7105. 189p. 20cm. 1953. Morrow.

Hindman, Darwin A.
--Eighteen-Hundred Riddles, Enigmas & Conundrums. 154p. (Orig.). (gr. 4 up). 1963. Dover.

Hinds, Margery
--Makpa: The Story of an Eskimo-Canadian Boy. Sneyd, Douglas, illus. LC 76-142158. (Illus.). 142 p. 23cm. 1971. (ISBN 0-7700-0342-7). Ryerson Press.

Hinds, Pat
--Kittens Need Someone to Love. Phillips, Alan, illus. (Illus.). (Look-Look Bks.). (ps). 1981. (ISBN 0-307-11865-7, Golden Pr). (ISBN 0-307-61865-X). Western Pub.

Hinds & Miller
--Tank McNamara. N.D (Tempo Books). Grosset & Dunlap.

Hine, Alfred Blakelee see Gibson, Josephine, pseud.

Hine, Alfred Blakelee see Kirtland, G B., pseud.

Hine, Alfred Blakelee (1915-)
--Where in the World Do You Live?. 1st ed. Alcorn, John (1935-), illus. LC 62-7728. unpaged. illus. 24cm. 1962. Harcourt, Brace & World.

Hine, Alfred Blakelee (1915-), ed.
--From Other Lands: Poetry That Makes History Live. LC 72-82404. 256p. (gr. 7 up). 1969. (ISBN 0-397-31073-0, JBL-J). Har-Row.
--This Land Is Mine: An Anthology of American Verse. Vosburgh, Leonard W. (1912-), illus. LC 65-13437. (Illus.). (gr. 7-9). 1965. (ISBN 0-397-30840-X). Lippincott.

Hine, H. G., illus.
--The House that Jack Built. N.D. (ISBN 0-85967-500-9). Green Tiger Pr.

Hine, James, Mrs.
--George Austin. LC 12-341671. 2 p. l., 3-228 p. front., plates. 18 1/2 cm. c.1885. American Baptist Publication Society.

Hine, Seslyn Joslin see Joslin, Sesyle.

Hine, Sesyle Joslin see Joslin, Sesyle.

Hines, Anna Grossnickle
--All by Myself. Hines, Anna Grossnickle, illus. LC 84-19882. (Illus.). 28 p. 21cm. c.1985. (ISBN 0-89919-293-9). Clarion Books.
--Bethany for Real. Hines, Anna Grossnickle, illus. LC 84-5927. (Illus.). 24 p. 24cm. c.1985. (ISBN 0-688-04008-X). (ISBN 0-688-04009-8). Greenwillow Books.
--Cassie Bowen Takes Witch Lessons. Owens, Gail, illus. LC 85-10302. p. cm. c.1985. (ISBN 0-525-44214-6). E.P. Dutton.
--Come to the Meadow. Hines, Anna Grossnickle, illus. LC 83-14408. (Illus.). 32p. (ps-3). 1984. (ISBN 0-89919-227-0, Clarion). Hm.
--Don't Worry, I'll Find You. Hines, Anna Grossnickle, illus. LC 85-16129. p. cm. 1986, c.1985. (ISBN 0-525-44228-6). Dutton.
--Maybe a Band-Aid Will Help. Hines, Anna Grossnickle, illus. LC 84-1533. (Illus.). 24p. (ps-1). 1984. (ISBN 0-525-44115-8). Dutton.
--Taste the Raindrops. Hines, Anna Grossnickle, illus. LC 82-9251. p. cm. c.1983. (ISBN 0-688-01422-4). (ISBN 0-688-01423-2). Greenwillow Books.

Hines, Marie, jt. auth. see Lederman, Janet.

Hines, William (1910-)
--The Camel Boy. McIlrath, James, illus. LC 78-60722. (Illus.). 74 p., 2 leaves of plates. 29cm. c.1978. (ISBN 0-87973-354-3). Our Sunday Visitor.

Hingst, Adolphine
--Rhymes and Songs for My Little Ones. (Illus.). N.D. Lothrop, Lee & Shepard Co's.

Hinize, Naomi A.
--Buried Treasure Waits For You. 1962. (ISBN 0-672-50529-0). Bobbs-Merill.

Hinkins, Virginia
--Gently Now. LC 62-19728. 21cm. 156p. 1963. McGraw-Hill Book Co.
--Stonewall's Courier: The Story of Charles Randolph and General Jackson. 21cm. 185p. (Young pioneer bk.: No. 78010). 1966, c.1959. McGraw.
--Stonewall's Courier: The Story of Charles Randolph and General Jackson. 1st ed. LC 59-8541. 185p. 21cm. 1959. Whittlesey House.

Hinkle, Thomas Clark (1876-1949)
--Barry: The Story of a Wolf Dog. 242 p. illus. 20 cm. 1961, c.1938. Grosset & Dunlap.
--Barry: The Story of a Wolf Dog. LC 38-6693. vi, 242 p. 19 1/2 cm. 1938. W. Morrow & Co.
--Bing: The Story of a Tramp Dog. LC 32-15435. viii, 9-224 p. 19 1/2 cm. 1932. W. Morrow & Co.
--Black Storm: A Horse of the Kansas Hills. LC 29-18212. xiii p., 3 l., 234 p. front., plates. 19 1/2 cm. 1929. W. Morrow & Company.
--Black Tiger: The Story of a Faithful Horse. 188 p. 22 cm. (Famous horse stories). 1962, c.1952. Grosset & Dunlap.
--Black Tiger: The Story of a Faithful Horse. LC 52-5933. 188 p. 20 cm. 1952. Morrow.
--Blackjack, a Ranch Dog. LC 46-5739. 224 p. 19cm. 1946. W. Morrow & Company.
--Blaze Face; the Story of a Horse. LC 47-5498. 191 p. 20 cm. 1947. W. Morrow.
--Buckskin: The Story of a Western Horse. 1939. William Morrow & Co.
--Bugle: A Dog of the Rockies. LC 29-4466. xiv p., 1 l,. 238, 1 p. 19 1/2 cm. 1929. W. Morrow & Company.
--Cinchfoot. (Famous Horse Stories). N.D. Grosset & Dunlap.
--Cinchfoot: The Story of a Range Horse. LC 38-201194. 253 p. 19 cm. 1938. W. Morrow & Co.
--Crazy Dog Curly. LC 37-16541. 5 p. l., 3-244 p. 19 1/2 cm. 1937. W. Morrow & Co.
--Dapple Gray. LC 50-7857. 192 p. 20cm. (Morrow junior books). 1950. Morrow.
--Doctor Rabbit & Big Horned Owl. Winter, Milo Kendall (1888-1956), illus. (The Greenwood Ser.). N.D. Rand McNally.
--Doctor Rabbit and Brushtail the Fox. LC 20-8022. 128 p. incl. front., illus. col. plates. 17 cm. (greenwood series). c.1919. Rand, McNally & Company.
--Doctor Rabbit and Grumpy Bear. LC 20-802322. 128 p. incl. front., illus. col. plates. 17 1/2 cm. (Greenwood Ser.). c.1919. Rand, McNally & Company.
--Doctor Rabbit and Ki-Yi Coyote. LC 19-828. ix, 1, 106 p. col. plates. 17 1/2 cm. (Greenwiid Ser.). c.1918. Rand, McNally & Company.
--Doctor Rabbit & Slinky the Black Wolf. Winter, Milo Kendall (1888-1956), illus. (The Greenwood Ser.). N.D. Rand McNally.
--Doctor Rabbit and Tom Wildcat. LC 20-802402. ix, 1, 95 p. incl. front., illus., col. plates 17 1/2 cm. (Greenwood Ser.). c.1918. Rand, McNally & Company.
--Dusty: The Story of a Wild Dog. LC 40-10378. 252 p. 19 1/2 cm. 1940. W. Morrow & Co.
--Gray: The Story of a Brave Dog. (Dog Stories). 1953. William Morrow & Co.
--Hurricane Pinto: The Story of an Outlaw Horse. LC 35-9701. 5 p. l., 3-257 p. 19 1/2 cm. N.D. W. Morrow & Company.
--Jolly White Tail. Beem, Frances M., illus. (The Greenwood Ser.). N.D. Rand McNally.
--Jube: The Story of a Trapper's Dog. LC 45-6470. 187 p. 19 cm. 1945. W. Morrow & Company.
--King: The Story of a Sheep Dog. LC 36-17725. vi, 238 p. 19 1/2 cm. 1936. W.Morrow & Co.
--Mustang. (Illus.). (gr. 4-6). 1956. G&D.
--Mustang: A Horse of the Old West. LC 42-16455. 4 p. l., 247 p. 19 1/2 cm. 1942. W. Morrow & Co.
--Old Nick and Bob: Two Dogs of the West. LC 41-11115. viii, 289 p. 19 1/2 cm. 1941. W. Morrow and Company.
--Ring Neck. LC 54-7625. 158p. 20cm. 1954. Morrow.
--Shag: The Story of a Dog. LC 31-217528. xiv p., 2 l., 19-254 p. incl. front., illus., plates. 19 1/2 cm. 1931. W. Morrow & Company.
--Shep: A Collie of the Old West. LC 43-7521. 224 p. 19 1/2 cm. 1943. W. Morrow & Co.
--Silver. (gr. 7-12). 1973 (Starline). Schol Bk Serv.
--Silver: The Story of a Wild Horse. LC 34-20805. viii p., 2 l., 245 p. 19 1/2 cm. 1934. W. Morrow & Co.
--Snowy Tail. Winter, Milo Kendall (1888-1956), illus. (The Greenwood Ser.). N.D. Rand McNAlly.
--Split-Ear: A Battling Coyote. Clarke, William Wallace, illus. LC 25-10725. 209 p. illus., col. pl. 19 1/2 cm. c.1925. Rand, McNally & Company.
--Tan: A Wild Dog. LC 51-12176. 191 p. 20 cm. 1951. Morrow.
--Tawny: A Dog of the Old West. LC 27-4090. 5 p. l., 238 p. 19 1/2 cm. 1927. W. Morrow & Company.
--Tiny Cottontail. Winter, Milo Kendall (1888-1956), illus. (The Greenwood Ser.). N.D. Rand McNally.
--Tomahawk, Fighting Horse of the Old West. LC 44-57187. 192 p. 19 1/2 cm. 1944. W. Morrow & Company.
--Tornado Boy: A Horse of the West. LC 30-22440. xiv p., 2 l., 19-252 p. incl. front. plates. 19 1/2 cm. 1930. W. Morrow & Company.
--Trueboy: The Story of a Great Dog. 235 p. 20 cm. (Famous Hinkle dog story). 1961, c.1956. Grosset & Dunlap.
--Trueboy: The Story of a Great Dog. LC 28-6116. ix p., 1 l., 13-236 p. 19 1/2 cm. 1928. W. Morrow & Company.
--Vic: A Dog of the Preiries. LC 49-100003. 192 p. 20 cm. 1949. W. Morrow.
--Waddy Rabbit. Winter, Milo Kendall (1888-1956), illus. (The Greenwood Ser.). N.D. Rand McNally.
--Wolf, a Range Dog. LC 48-3195. 192p. 20cm. 1948. W. Morrow.

Hinkley, James W.
--The Book of Vampires. Deas, Michael, illus. LC 78-24070. (Illus.). (Easy-Read Fact Bks.). (gr. 2-4). 1979. (ISBN 0-531-02276-5). Watts.

Hinojosa, Francisco
--The Old Lady Who Ate People: Frightening Stories. Maciel, Leonel, illus. LC 82-17247. (Illus.). (gr. k-3). 1984. (ISBN 0-316-54220-2). Little.

Hinshaw, David (1882-)
--Alli and the Wishing Rock. Edwards, Parker F., illus. LC 53-816505. 95p. illus. 22cm. 1953. Putnam.

Hinternhoff, John F
--Barry's Boys. 1st ed. Geary, Clifford N. (1916-), illus. LC 52-9043. 180 p. illus. 21 cm. 1952. Holt.
--Decatur of High Barbary. 1st ed. Geary, Clifford N. (1916-), illus. LC 55-105683. 221p. illus: 21cm. 1955. Holt.

Hinton, Howard
--My Comrades: Adventures in the Highlands and Legends of the Neutral Ground. LC 13-177426. 3-327 p. front., plates. 19 1/2 cm. 1874. Henry L. Hinton & Co.
--My Comrades: Or, School-Days at Mt. Pleasant (A Story of the Hudson, Including Traditions and Legends of the Hill-Country Bordering the East Bank of That Historic River). LC 9-28070. 4 p. l., 7-329 p. front., plates. 19 1/2 cm. 1909. Mount Pleasant Academy.

Hinton, Nigel (1941-)
--Collision Course. (gr. 6-9). 1977. Lodestar.
--Collision Course. LC 77-4030. 159 p. 21cm. c.1976. (ISBN 0-8407-6541-X). T. Nelson.
--Getting Free. LC 78-14833. p. cm. c.1978. (ISBN 0-8407-6615-7). T. Nelson.

Hinton, Susan Eloise
--The Outsiders. LC 67-136068. 188 p. 22cm. 1967. Viking Press.
--Rumble Fish. LC 75-8004. 122 p. 22cm. 1975. (ISBN 0-440-05919-4). Delacorte Press.
--Tex. LC 78-50448. 194 p. 22cm. c.1979. (ISBN 0-440-08641-8). Delacorte Press.
--That Was Then, This Is Now. LC 70-150116. 159 p. 22cm. 1971. (ISBN 0-670-69798-2). Viking Press.

Hintze, Naomi A
--Buried treasure awaits you. (Illus.). N.D. Bobbs-Merrill Co, Inc.
--Buried Treasure Waits For You. 1962. (ISBN 0-8382-0133-4, Cadmus Books). E. M. Hale and Company.

Hippel, Ursula Von see Von Hippel, Ursula.

Hipple, Theodore Wallace (1935-)
--Stories of Youth and Action. LC 76-43396. (Illus.). vii, 214 p. 24cm. (Allyn & Bacon literature series). c.1977. Allyn and Bacon.
--Tales of Mystery and Suspense. LC 76-43395. (Illus.). ix, 260 p. 24cm. (Allyn & Bacon literature Ser.). c.1977. Allyn and Bacon.

Hipple, Theodore Wallace (1935-), compiled by.
--Twentieth Century American Short Stories. LC 76-43398. viii. 215p. ill. 23cm. (The Allyn and Bacon Literature Ser.). c.1977. Allyn and Bacon.

Hipple, Theodore Wallace (1935-) & Wright, Robert Granger (1937-)
--The Worlds of Science Fiction. LC 78-66719. (Illus.). vii, 248 p. 24cm. (Allyn & Bacon literature Ser.). c.1979. Allyn and Bacon.

Hippopotamus, Eugene H., pseud., see Kraus, Robert.

Hippopotamus, Eugene H., pseud. (1925-)
--Hello Hippopotamus. Kraus, Robert. LC 69-16101. (Illus.). color ils. 32p. (gr. 1-5). 1969. (ISBN 0-671-66505-7, Juveniles). (ISBN 0-671-66506-5). S&S.

Hirawa, Jasuko
--Songs of the Sour Plum. Majima, Setsuko, illus. (Illus.). 1968. Weatherhill.

Hiroshi Minami
--Psychology of the Japanese People. LC 74-151439. (No. 36). 1970. East-West Center.

Hirsch, Audrey & Hirsch, Harvey
--A Home for Tandy. Hildebrandt, Tim (1939-) & Hildebrandt, Greg (1939-), illus. LC 79-145671. (Illus.). 32 p. 28cm. 1971. Platt & Munk.

Hirsch, Constance, tr. see Collin Delavaud, Marie Moreal De Brevans.

Hirsch, Constance, tr. see Deletaille, Albertine.

Hirsch, Constance, tr. see Simon, Romain (1915-) & Faucher, Paul.

Hirsch, Harvey, jt. auth. see Hirsch, Audrey.

Hirsch, Karen (1941-)
--My Sister. Inderieden, Nancy, illus. LC 77-74015. (Illus.). (gr. k-4). 1977. (ISBN 0-87614-091-6). Carolrhoda Bks.

Hirsch, Karen (1941-) & Esco, Jo
--Becky. LC 80-27619. p. cm. c.1981. (ISBN 0-87614-144-0). Carolrhoda Books.

Hirsch, Linda (1949-)
--The Sick Story. Wallner, John C (1945-), illus. LC 76-13138. (Illus.). 40 p. 23cm. c.1977. (ISBN 0-8038-6733-6). Hastings House.
--You're Going Out There a Kid, but You're Coming Back a Star!. Wallner, John C. (1945-), illus. (Illus.). 128p. (gr. 5 up). 1982. (ISBN 0-8038-8603-9). Hastings.

Hirsch, Phil (1926-)
--Behind the Ape Ball. (gr. 4-6). 1978. (ISBN 0-590-05360-4). Scholastic Inc.

Hirsch, Phil (1926-), ed.
--Great Untold Stories of World War Two. (gr. 7 up). N.D. Pyramid Pubns.
--More Kids Lib. (Orig.). 1974. (ISBN 0-515-03551-3). BJ Pub Group.
--One Hundred & One Hamburger Jokes. (gr. 4-6). 1978. (ISBN 0-590-11890-0). Scholastic Inc.
--Underwater. (Orig.). (gr. 6-10). N.D. Pyramid Pubns.

Hirschfeld, Burt (1923-)
--After the Alamo: The Story of the Mexican War. Martin, Barry, illus. LC 66-13998. 191p. illus. 22cm. c.1966. Messner.

Hirschfeld, Phyllis
--Color and Colors with George, Josie, and Me. McKie, Roy, illus. (Illus.). 23 p. (Take-along books). 1968. Random House.
--Sense and Senses with George, Josie, and Me. McKie, Roy, illus. LC 68-24473. (Illus.). 24 p. 17cm. (Take-along books). 1968. Random House.

Hirsh, Marilyn (1944-), adapted by see Jews.

Hirsh, Marilyn (1944-)
--Ben Goes into Business. Hirsh, Marilyn (1944-), illus. LC 72-92579. (Illus.). 32 p. 28cm. 1973. (ISBN 0-8234-0219-3). Holiday House.
--Deborah the Dybbuk: Ghost Story. Hirsh, Marilyn (1944-), illus. LC 78-2408. (Illus.). 40 p. c.1978. (ISBN 0-8234-0315-7). Holiday House.
--Elephants & the Mice: A Panchatantria Story. Hirsh, Marilyn (1944-), illus. 1970. World Pub.
--George and the Goblins. Hirsh, Marilyn (1944-), illus. (Illus.). 32p. 1972. Crown.
--Hannibal & His Thirty-Seven Elephants. Hirsh, Marilyn (1944-), illus. LC 77-590. (Illus.). 32p. (gr. 1-3). 1977. (ISBN 0-8234-0300-9). Holiday.
--The Hanukkah Story. Hirsh, Marilyn (1944-), illus. LC 77-22183. (Illus.). (gr. k-4). 1977. (ISBN 0-88482-756-9, Bonim Bks). Hebrew Pub.
--How the World Got Its Color. Hirsh, Marilyn (1944-), illus. LC 70-185088. (Illus.). (ps-2). 1972. Crown.
--I Love Hanukkah. Hirsh, Marilyn (1944-), illus. LC 84-497. (Illus.). 32p. (ps-3). 1984. (ISBN 0-8234-0525-7). (ISBN 0-8234-0525-7). Holiday.
--The Pink Suit. Hirsh, Marilyn (1944-), illus. LC 70-127518. (Illus.). 35 p. 29cm. 1970. Crown Publishers.
--Potato Pancakes All Around: A Hanukkah Tale. Hirsh, Marilyn (1944-), illus. LC 78-17927. p. cm. c.1978. (ISBN 0-88482-762-3). Bonim Books.
--Potato Pancakes All Around: A Hanukkah Tale. Hirsh, Marilyn (1944-), illus. 1978. Hebrew.
--Potato Pancakes All Around: A Hanukkah Tale. Hirsh, Marilyn (1944-), illus. LC 82-13113. (Illus.). 35 p. 24cm. 1982, c.1978. (ISBN 0-8276-0217-0). Jewish Publication Society of America.
--The Rabbi & the Twenty-Nine Witches. (gr. k-3). 1977. (ISBN 0-590-10315-6). Scholastic Inc.
--The Rabbi & the Twenty-Nine Witches. Hirsh, Marilyn (1944-), illus. LC 75-30710. (Illus.). 32p. (gr. k-3). 1981. (ISBN 0-8234-0270-3). Holiday.
--The Rabbi and the Twenty-Nine Witches: A Talmudic Legend. Hirsh, Marilyn (1944-), illus. LC 75-30710. (Illus.). 32 p. 24cm. c.1976. (ISBN 0-8234-0270-3). Holiday House.
--The Secret Dinosaur. Hirsh, Marilyn (1944-), illus. LC 79-1492. p. cm. c.1979. (ISBN 0-8234-0353-X). Holiday House.
--Where Is Yonkela?. Hirsh, Marilyn (1944-), illus. LC 70-88591. (Illus.). 32 p. 29cm. 1969. Crown Publishers.

Hirsh, Marilyn (1944-), adapted by.
--Captain Jiri and Rabbi Jacob. Hirsh, Marilyn (1944-), illus. LC 76-6114. (Illus.). 32 p. 25cm. c.1976. (ISBN 0-8234-0279-7). Holiday House.
--Could Anything Be Worse?. A Yiddish Tale. Hirsh, Marilyn (1944-), illus. LC 73-17364. (Illus.). 32 p. 28cm. 1974. (ISBN 0-8234-0239-8). Holiday House.
--The Elephants and the Mice: A Panchatantra Story. Hirsh, Marilyn (1944-), illus. LC 70-101838. (Illus.). 32 p. 1970. World Pub. Co.
--The Tower of Babel. Hirsh, Marilyn (1944-), illus. LC 80-21196. (Illus.). 32p. (ps-2). 1981. (ISBN 0-8234-0380-7). Holiday.

Hirsh, Marilyn (1944-) & Narayan, Maya
--Leela and the Watermelon. Hirsh, Marilyn (1944-), illus. LC 79-147345. (Illus.). 30 p. 29cm. 1971. Crown Publishers.

Hirshberg, Albert Simon (1909-1973)
--The Battery for Madison High. 1st ed. Galdone, Paul (1914-), illus. LC 55-5182. 245p. illus. 20cm. (Barry Drake baseball story). c.1955. Little, Brown.
--Varsity Double Play. 1st ed. Galdone, Paul (1914-), illus. LC 56-5924. 246p. illus. 20cm. (Barry Drake baseball story). 1956. Little, Brown.

Hischmann, Joan, ed. see Aesopus.

Hiser, Iona Seibert
--The Coyote. Roever, Joan Marilyn (1935-), illus. (Illus.). 29 p. 24cm. 1968. Steck-Vaughn Co.
--The Mountain Lion. Roever, Joan Marilyn (1935-), illus. LC 72-101561. (Illus.). 30 p. 24cm. 1970. Steck-Vaughn Co.

Hisey, Lehmann
--Sea Grist: A Personal Narrative of Five Months in the Merchant Marine. LC 22-8594. 5 p. l., 251 p. front., plates. 19 1/2 cm. c.1922. Post Printing & Binding Company.

Hislop, James
--Noah's Ark. N.D. Fleming H. Revell Co.
--Stories from the Old Testament. Brock, Henry Matthew (1875-1960), illus. N.D. Fleming H. Revell Co.
--Tell Me a Bible Story. Brock, Henry Matthew (1875-1960), illus. N.D. Fleming H. Revell Co.

Hiss, Tony (1941-)
--The Giant Panda Book. Hildebrandt, Greg (1939-) & Hildebrandt, Tim (1939-), illus. (Illus.). (gr. 1 up). 1973. (ISBN 0-307-63753-0, Golden Pr). Western Pub.

Hitchcock, Alfred Joseph (1899-1980), ed. see Marchesi, Steve.

Hitchcock, Alfred Joseph (1899-1980), ed.
--Alfred Hitchcock & the Three Investigators in the Mystery of the Laughing Shadow. (Illus.). (Three Investigators Ser.: No. 12). (gr. 4-7). 1969. (ISBN 0-394-81492-4, BYR). (ISBN 0-394-91492-9). (ISBN 0-394-83775-4). Random.
--Alfred Hitchcock Presents Stories Not for the Nervous. 1965. Random House INc.
--Alfred Hitchcock Presents: Stories to Be Read with the Doors Locked. 320p. 1975. (ISBN 0-394-49839-9, BYR). Random.
--Alfred Hitchcock's Daring Detectives. Shilstone, Arthur, illus. LC 76-79077. (Illus.). 208 p. 27cm. 1969. Random House.
--Alfred Hitchcock's Ghostly Gallery. (Illus.). 1962. (ISBN 0-394-81226-3, BYR). (ISBN 0-394-91226-8). Random.
--Alfred Hitchcock's Haunted Houseful. LC 84-15949. ix, 262 p. 20cm. (Alfred Hitchcock Story Collections for Young Readers). 1985, c.1961. (ISBN 0-394-87041-7). Random House.
--Alfred Hitchcock's Haunted Houseful. Banbery, Fred, illus. (Illus.). (gr. 4-9). 1961. (ISBN 0-394-81224-7, BYR). (ISBN 0-394-91224-1). Random.
--Alfred Hitchcock's Monster Museum. Mayan, Earl E., illus. (Illus.). 207 p. 27cm. 1965. Random House.
--Alfred Hitchcock's Monster Museum. Mayan, Earl E., illus. LC 81-13883. x, 213 p. 20cm. 1982. (ISBN 0-394-84899-3). Random House.
--Alfred Hitchcock's Sinister Spies. Spina, Paul, illus. (Illus.). (gr. 7-11). 1966. (ISBN 0-394-81564-5, BYR). (ISBN 0-394-91564-X). (ISBN 0-394-84901-9). Random.
--Alfred Hitchcock's Sinister Spies. Spina, Paul, illus. LC 67-147. (Illus.). 206 p. 27cm. 1966. Random House.
--Alfred Hitchcock's Solve-Them-Yourself Mysteries. Banbery, Fred, illus. (Illus.). (gr. 6-9). 1963. (ISBN 0-394-81242-5, BYR). (ISBN 0-394-91242-X). Random.
--Alfred Hitchcock's Spellbinders in Suspense. LC 81-12175. (Illus.). 224p. (gr. 5 up). 1982. (ISBN 0-394-84900-0). Random.
--Alfred Hitchcock's Spellbinders in Suspense. Isen, Harold, illus. (Illus.). (gr. 7-11). 1967. (ISBN 0-394-84900-0, BYR). (ISBN 0-394-91665-4). Random.

--What Happened When Jack & Daisy Tried to Fool the Tooth Fairies. (Illus.). (gr. k-3). 1972. (ISBN 0-590-08114-4). Scholastic Inc.
--What Happened When Jack and Daisy Tried to Fool the Tooth Fairies. Hoban, Lillian (1925-), illus. LC 66-290090. 1v. (unpaged) col. illus. 16x22cm. 1966, c.1965. Four Winds Pr. Dist. Scholastic.
Hoban, Russell Conwell (1925-) & Hoban, Lillian (1925-)
--London Men and English Men. Hoban, Lillian (1925-), illus. LC 62-8871. (Illus.). 32 p. 1962. Harper & Row.
--Save My Place. LC 67-15415. (Illus.). 32 p. 21cm. 1967. W. W. Norton.
--Some Snow Said Hello. LC 63-9089. (Illus.). 32 p. 1963. Harper & Row.
Hoban, Russell Conwell (1925-) & Selig, Sylvie (1942-)
--Crocodile & Pierrot. Selig, Sylvie (1942-), illus. (Illus.). (Encore Ser.). (gr. k-1). 1977. (ISBN 0-684-17375-1, ScribJ). Scribner.
--Crocodile & Pierrot: A See-the-Story Book. LC 77-73930. (Illus.). 24 p. 27cm. 1977. (ISBN 0-684-14901-X). Scribner.
--Ten What?. A Mystery Counting Book. LC 75-2747. (Illus.). 24 p. 27cm. 1975, c.1974. (ISBN 0-684-13400-4). Scribner.
Hoban, Tana
--Big Ones, Little Ones. Hoban, Tana, illus. (ps). 1976. Greenwillow.
--A Children's Zoo. LC 84-25318. (Illus.). 9 7/8 x 8. 24p. (32 pt.). (ps-1). 1985. (ISBN 0-688-05202-9). (ISBN 0-688-05204-5). Greenwillow.
--I Walk & Read. Hoban, Tana, illus. LC 83-14215. (Illus.). 9 7/8 x 8. 32p. (18 pt.). (ps-1). 1984. (ISBN 0-688-02575-7). (ISBN 0-688-02576-5). Greenwillow.
--Is It Red? Is It Yellow? Is It Blue?. Hoban, Tana, illus. LC 78-2549. (Illus.). 32p. (gr. k-3). 1978. (ISBN 0-688-80171-4). (ISBN 0-688-84171-6). Greenwillow. **Award: (ALA).**
--Is It Red? Is It Yellow? Is It Blue?. Hoban, Tana, illus. (ps-3). N.D. (ISBN 0-590-62009-6). Scholastic Inc.
--One Little Kitten. Hoban, Tana, illus. LC 78-31862. (Illus.). 24p. (gr. k-3). 1979. (ISBN 0-688-80222-2). (ISBN 0-688-84222-4). Greenwillow.
--One Little Kitten. Hoban, Tana, illus. (Illus.). 24p. (Orig.). (ps-3). 1981. (ISBN 0-590-30894-7, Schol Pap). Scholastic Inc.
--One, Two, Three. 1985. Greenwillow. **Award: (ALA).**
--Shapes, Shapes, Shapes. LC 85-17569. (Illus.). 9 7/8 x 8. 32p. (14 pt.). (ps-3). 1986. (ISBN 0-688-05832-9). (ISBN 0-688-05833-7). Greenwillow.
--Where Is It?. Hoban, Tana, illus. LC 73-8573. (Illus.). 32 p. 18cm. (ps). 1974. (ISBN 0-02-744070-2). Macmillan.
--Where Is It?. Hoban, Tana, illus. LC 77-25289. (Illus.). 32 p. 18cm. (Windmill paperback). c.1978. Windmill Books.
Hobart, George Vere (1867-1936)
--Li'l Verses for Li'l Fellers. (Harper's Selected Juveniles). N.D. Harper & Brothers.
--Li'l Verses for Li'l Fellers. Mars, Ethel (1876-) & Squire, Maud Hunt (1873-), illus. LC 3-25286. vii p., 1 l., 121, 2 p. incl. port. col. front., 15 pl. (7 col.) 26 1/2 cm. 1903. R. H. Russell.
Hobart-Hampden, Helene Langel, Mrs.
--The Secret Valley. LC 33-20980. 4 p. l., 271 p. front., plates. 20 cm. 1932. L. C. Page & Company.
Hobart, Lois Elaine
--Behind the Walls. LC 61-12963. 216 p. 22cm. 1961. Funk & Wagnalls.
--Elaine Forrest, Visiting Nurse. LC 59-7134. 192 p. 21cm. (Romance for young moderns). 1959. Messner.
--Katie and Her Camera. LC 55-9858. 190 p. 21cm. (Romance for young moderns). 1955. Messner.
--Laurie, Physical Therapist. LC 57-9746. 192p. 21cm. (Romance for young moderns). 1957. J. Messner.
--A Palette for Ingrid. LC 56-10449. 188p. 21cm. (Romance for young moderns). 1956. J. Messner.
--Strangers Among Us. LC 57-10584. 246 p. 22cm. 1957. Funk & Wagnalls.
--What Is a Whispery Secret?. Alexander, Martha G. (1920-), illus. LC 68-11663. (Illus.). 38 p. 21cm. 1968. Parents' Magazine Press.
Hobbie, Holly
--The Days of Holly Hobbie. Hobbie, Holly, illus. LC 76-56955. (Illus.). 18 p. 32cm. (Cricket book). c.1977. (ISBN 0-8228-6512-2). Platt & Munk.
--Holly Hobbie's Nursery Rhymes. Hobbie, Holly, illus. LC 78-100064. (Illus.). 32cm. 45p. (gr. k-2). 1977. (ISBN 0-448-47215-5). Platt.
--Holly Hobbie's Nursery Rhymes. Hobby, Holly, illus. LC 78-100064. (Illus.). 45 p. 32cm. c.1977. (ISBN 0-8228-7215-3). Ottenheimer Publishers.
--Holly Hobbie's Special Days. Hobbie, Holly, illus. LC 78-60676. (Illus.). 45 p. 31cm. c.1978. (ISBN 0-448-47218-X). (ISBN 0-448-13030-0). Ottenheimer Publishers.
--Holly Hobbie's Time Book. Hobbie, Holly, illus. LC 79-112436. (Illus.). 29cm. 28p. c.1979. Watertower Books.
--A Treasury of Holly Hobbie. Hobbie, Holly, illus. LC 79-117305. (Illus.). 60 p. 29cm. c.1979. (ISBN 0-528-82341-8). Rand McNally.
Hobbie, Holly, jt. auth. see Moore, Clement Clarke.
Hobbs, Barbara
--Alexander's Animals. LC 57-12077. (Illus.). 27cm. 80p. 1958. Houghton Mifflin.
--The Hungry Sea Monster. LC 59-5189. (Illus.). 25cm. 27p. 1959. Houghton Mifflin.
Hobbs, C. A.
--Boys of Princeville: Or, Temperance Reform in the Fifties. 152p. N.D. American Baptist Publication Society.
Hobbs, J.
--Between the Wickets. (MacMillan Bks. for Boys & Girls). (gr. 7-9). N.D. MacMillam Bks.
Hobbs, M., jt. auth. see Milligan, Spike.
Hobbs, Mabel
--Outdoor Plays for Boys and Girls. Sanford, A. P., ed. N.D. Dodd Mead & Co.
Hoben, Alice May
--Knights Old and New. LC 29-21392. vii p., 1 l., 197 p. illus. 19 1/2 cm. c.1929. D. Appleton and Company.
Hoberg, Marielis, pseud., see Robert, Mati.
Hoberman, Mary Ann (1930-)
--All My Shoes Come in Twos. Hoberman, Norman, illus. (Illus.). (gr. k up). 1957. (ISBN 0-316-36728-1). Little.
--Bugs: Poems. Chess, Victoria (1939-), illus. LC 76-8845. p. cm. 1976. (ISBN 0-670-19454-9). Viking Press.
--The Cozy Book. Chen, Tony (1929-), illus. (ps-3). 1982. Viking.
--The Cozy Book. Fraser, Betty M., pseud. (1928-), illus. Fraser, Elizabeth Marr. LC 80-10916. p. cm. 1980. (ISBN 0-670-24447-3). Viking Press.
--Hello & Good-By. Hoberman, Norman, illus. (Illus.). (gr. k-3). 1959. Little.
--A House is a House for Me. Fraser, Betty M., pseud. (1928-), illus. Fraser, Elizabeth Marr. LC 82-559. (Illus.). 46 p. 23cm. 1982. (ISBN 0-14-050394-3). Puffin Books.
--A House is a House for Me. 1st ed. Fraser, Betty M., pseud. (1928-), illus. Fraser, Elizabeth Marr. LC 77-15518. (Illus.). 48 p. 29cm. 1978. (ISBN 0-670-38016-4). Viking Press.
--A House is a House for Me. Fraser, Betty M., pseud. (1928-), illus. Fraser, Elizabeth Marr. 1982. Viking Press. **Award: (ABA).**
--How Do I Do. Hoberman, Norman, illus. 1958. Little, Brown.
--I Like Old Clothes. Chwast, Jacqueline (1932-), illus. LC 75-25967. (Illus.). 24 p. c.1976. (ISBN 0-394-83092-X). (ISBN 0-394-93092-4). Knopf : Distributed by Random House.
--A Little Book of Little Beasts. Parnall, Peter (1936-), illus. LC 72-88404. (Illus.). 48 p. 1973. (ISBN 0-671-65203-6). Simon and Schuster.
--The Looking Book. Joyner, Jerry (1938-), illus. 1973. Borzoi Books.
--The Looking Book. Joyner, Jerry (1938-), illus. LC 72-5272. (Illus.). 32 p. 22cm. 1973. (ISBN 0-394-82502-0). (ISBN 0-394-82502-0). Knopf; Distributed by Random House.
--Not Enough Beds for the Babies. Spyer, Helen, illus. LC 65-10590. 41p. col. illus. 22cm. c.1965. Little.
--Nuts To You and Nuts To Me. Solbert, Ronni, pseud. (1925-), illus. Solbert, Romaine G.. 1974. Brozoi Books.
--Nuts to You & Nuts to Me: An Alphabet of Poems. Solbert, Ronni, pseud. (1925-), illus. Solbert, Romaine G.. LC 74-734. (Illus.). 32 p. 1974. (ISBN 0-394-82742-2). (ISBN 0-394-82742-2). Knopf; Distributed by Random House.
--The Raucous Auk: A Menagerie of Poems. Low, Joseph (1911-), illus. LC 73-5140. (Illus.). 48 p. 26cm. 1973. Viking Press.
--What Jim Knew. Hoberman, Norman, illus. LC 63-13461. (Illus.). 22cm. 32p. 1963. Little Brown.
--Yellow Butter, Purple Jelly, Red Jam, Black Bread: Collected Poems. Bernstein, Chaya M., illus. LC 80-26555. 64p. 1981. (ISBN 0-670-79382-5). Viking Press.
--Yellow Butter Purple Jelly Red Jam Black Bread. Burstein, Chaya M., illus. (Illus.). 64p. (ps-3). 1981. (ISBN 0-670-79382-5). Viking Pr.
Hobrecker, Karl (1876-)
--Spin Top Spin and Rosmarie and Thyme. Eisgruber, Elsa, illus. LC 29-27529. 32p. col. illus. 27 1/2cm. 1929. Macmillan Co.
Hobson, George Cavey, jt. auth. see Linfield, Esther.
Hobson, Harriet Malone
--Jinks' Inside. LC 11-24399. 248 p. col. front., col. plates. 18 cm. $1.00. 1911. G. W. Jacobs & Company.
--Sis Within. LC 13-22097. xv, 351 p. 20 cm. $1.2. 1913. G. W. Jacobs & Company.
Hobson, Laura Keane Zametkin (1900-)
--A Dog of His Own. Miller, Jane Judith (1925-), illus. LC 41-4811. 40 p. col. illus. 19 x 23 cm. 1941. Viking Press.
--I'm Going to Have a Baby. Kirkham, May, illus. LC 67-10821. (Illus.). 44 p. 25cm. 1967. John Day Co.
Hobson, Loella M.
--Let's Read About Penny & Her Pets. (gr. 1-5). N.D. Carlton.
Hobson, Polly, pseud., see Evans, Julia Rendell.
Hobson, Polly, pseud. (1913-)
--Mystery House. Evans, Julia Rendell. (Illus.). (gr. 5-8). 1963. (ISBN 0-8382-0569-0). Hale.
--Mystery House. Evans, Julia Rendell. Lawrence, Judith Ann, illus. LC 64-19053. (Illus.). 21cm. 187p. (gr. 4-6). 1964. (ISBN 0-397-30773-X). Lippincott.
Hobson, Richmond Pearson (1870-)
--Buck Jones at Annapolis. LC 7-29590. vii, 370 p. col. front., 3 col. pl. 20 1/2 cm. 1907. D. Appleton and Company.
Hobson, Ruth A.
--Great Grandmother's Book: The Daisy. (Illus.). N.D. Caldwell.
Hobson, Sam B., pseud., see Linfield, Esther.
Hoburg, Maryanne Regal & Gray, Merrilee
--B.B. Bear, Basic Brown Bear. LC 78-62751. (Illus.). 31 p. 24cm. c.1978. HW, Inc.
Hobzek, Mildred T. (1919-)
--We Came a Marching, One, Two, Three. Du Bois, William Sherman Pene (1916-), illus. LC 78-7793. p. cm. c.1978. (ISBN 0-8193-0974-5). Parents' Magazine Press.
Hoch, Edward D. (1930-)
--Baffling Detective Cases. Duenewald, Doris, ed. LC 78-58885. (Illus.). (Inkpot Mini-Mysteries Ser.). (gr. 3-7). N.D. (ISBN 0-448-16370-5, G&D). Putnam Pub Group.
--Clues for Supersleuths. Duenewald, Doris (1930-), ed. Hoch, Edward D., illus. LC 78-58884. (Illus.). (Inkpot Mini-Mysteries Ser.). (gr. 3-7). 1978. (ISBN 0-448-16369-1, G&D). Putnam Pub Group.
--The Monkey's Clue & The Stolen Sapphire. Duenewald, Doris, ed. Ho, Tien, illus. LC 78-58882. (Illus.). (Inkpot Mini-Mysteries). (gr. 3-7). 1978. (ISBN 0-448-16367-5, G&D). Putnam Pub Group.
--The Monkey's Clue & The Stolen Sapphire: Two Mysteries for You to Solve! : Match Wits with Detective Tommy Preston. Duenewald, Doris, ed. HO, Tien, illus. LC 78-58882. (Illus.). 64 p. (p. 64 blank). 21cm. (Inkpot books). c.1978. (ISBN 0-448-16367-5). Grosset & Dunlap.
--Mysteries for Crime-Busters. Duenewald, Doris, ed. LC 78-58883. (Illus.). (Inkpot Mini-Mysteries Ser.). (gr. 3-7). 1978. (ISBN 0-448-16368-3, G&D). Putnam Pub Group.
Hochman, Baruch, tr. see Biber, Yehoash.
Hochman, Sandra (1936-)
--The Magic Convention. Shecter, Ben (1935-), illus. LC 75-118967. (Illus.). 32 p. 22cm. 1971. Doubleday.
Hochschild, Arlie Russell (1940-)
--Coleen the Question Girl. Ashby, Gail, illus. LC 74-1196. (Illus.). 32 p. 28cm. 1974. (ISBN 0-912670-12-6). The Feminist Press.
Hocker, Karla (1901-)
--The Three Times Lost Dog. Kuckei, Helge, illus. Aubry, Lynn, tr. from Ger. LC 67-19000. (Illus.). 120 p. 22cm. 1967. Atheneum.
Hockerman, Dennis, jt. auth. see Wold, Jo Anne.
Hocking, Silas Kitto (1850-1925)
--Chips. (The Welcome Library). N.D. Frederick Warner & Co.
--Chips, Joe, and Poor Mike. N.D. Frederick Warne & Co.
--Dick's Fairy: A Story of Good Nature. N.D. Frederick Warne & Co.
--Doctor Dick and Other Tales. N.D. Frederick Warne & Co.
--Poor Mike. (The Welcome Library). 1910. Frederick Warne & Co.
--Sea Waif. N.D. Frederick Warne & Co.
Hockridge, Derek, tr. see Peyo.
Hockridge, Derek, tr. see Peyo, pseud. & Delporte, Yvan.
Hodder, Edwin (1837-1904)
--Book-Stall Boy of Batherton. (Illus.). N.D. D. Lothrop Co.
--Bookstall Boy. (Illus.). (Child Life Ser.). N.D. D. Lothrop Co.
--Bookstall Boy. (Golden Lily Ser.). N.D. D. Lothrop Co.
--Bookstall Boy, 1 of 30 vols. (Illus.). (Morning Glory Ser). N.D. Lothrop Pub. Co.
--In Strange Quarters. (Illus.). 312p. N.D. A. I. Bradley & Co.'s Pub.
--The Junior Clerk: A Tale of City Life. (Illus.). N.D. Methodist Bk Concern.
--Siberian Exiles' Children: Or, Thrown on the World, 1 of 20 vols. Browne, Gordon Frederick (1858-1932), illus. 402p. (Selected Bks for Sunday School: No. 19). N.D. Set. Methodist Bk Concern.
Hodder-William, John Ernest, Sir (1876-1927), ed.
--The Children's Edition of the Pilgrim's Progress. (Illus.). (The New Line Upon Line Series.). N.D. George H Doran.
--Fifty-Two Bible Stories for Children. (Illus.). (The New Line Upon Line Series.). N.D. George H Doran & Co.
--The New Line Upon Line. Rev. ed. (Illus.). (The New Line Upon Line Series). N.D. George H Doran.
--The New Peep of Day. New & Rev. ed. (Illus.). (The New Line Upon Line Series). N.D. George H Doran.
--The New Precept Upon Precept. (Companion volume to "The New Peep of Day."). (Illus.). (The New Line Upon Line Series.). N.D. George H Doran.
Hodeir, Andre (1921-) & Ungerer, Tomi, pseud. (1931-)
--Cleopatra Goes Sledding. Ungerer, Jean Thomas. LC 67-28781. (Illus.). 32 p. 31cm. 1968, c.1967. Grove Press.
--Warwick's 3 Bottles. Ungerer, Jean Thomas. LC 67-1380. (Illus.). 32 p. 31cm. c.1966. Grove Press.
Hodel, Emilia
--This Way to the Circus. Bergmann, Franz, illus. LC 39-43870. 96 p. col. illus. 18 1/2 x 26 cm. c.1938. Hale, Cushman and Flint.
Hodgell, Patricia Christine (1951-)
--Dark of the Moon. LC 85-7454. p. cm. 1985. (ISBN 0-689-31171-0). Atheneum.

Hodges, Carl G. (1902-1964)
--Baxie Randall and the Blue Raiders. Clements, Kenneth, illus. LC 62-10024. 187p. illus. 22cm. 1962. (ISBN 0-672-50214-3). Bobbs-Merrill.
--Benjie Ream. LC 64-15668. 153 p. 21 cm. 1964. Bobbs-Merrill.
--Dobie Sturgis and the Dog Soldiers. Walker, Charles W., illus. LC 63-11652. 156 p. illus. 22 cm. 1963. Bobbs-Merrill.
--Land Rush. Martinez, John, illus. LC 65-24861. 152 p. illus., map. 22 cm. 1965. Duell, Sloan and Pearce.
--Land Rush. Martinez, John, illus. (Illus.). (gr. 4-7). 1965. (ISBN 0-696-67944-2). Hawthorn.
Hodges, Cyril Walter (1909-)
--The Marsh King. Hodges, Cyril Walter (1909-), illus. LC 67-3270. (Illus.). 253 p. 23cm. 1967. Coward-McCann.
--The Namesake. Hodges, Cyril Walter (1909-), illus. LC 64-13068. 269 p. illus. 23 cm. 1964. Coward-McCann. **Award: (ALA).**
--Plain Lane Christmas. Hodges, Cyril Walter (1909-), illus. LC 77-17233. (Illus.). 32 p. 26cm. 1978. (ISBN 0-698-20454-9). Coward, McCann & Geoghegan.
--Playhouse Tales. Hodges, Cyril Walter (1909-), illus. LC 72-94147. (Illus.). 168 p., 3 leaves of plates. 23cm. 1st U.S. edition. 1974. (ISBN 0-698-20268-6). Coward, McCann & Geoghegan.
--Sky High: The Story of a House That Flew. Hodges, Cyril Walter (1909-), illus. LC 47-11928. 112 p. illus. 22 cm. 1947. Coward-McCann.
Hodges, Elizabeth Jamison
--Free As a Frog. Giovanopoulos, Paul Arthur (1939-), illus. LC 73-88687. (Illus.). 23cm. 32p. (gr. k-3). 1969. (ISBN 0-201-02890-5, A-W Childrens). A-W. **Award: (NYT).**
--A Song for Gilgamesh. 1st ed. White, David Omar (1927-), illus. LC 70-115070. (Illus.). 178 p. 22cm. 1971. Atheneum.
--Three Princes of Serendip. Berg, Joan, pseud. (1942-), illus. Victor, Joan Berg. (Illus.). (gr. 4 up). 1964. (ISBN 0-689-20166-4). (ISBN 0-689-20167-2). Atheneum.
Hodges, Elizabeth Jamison, ed. see Armeno, Christoforo.
Hodges, Glen A.
--Lost Bear. 1st ed. Stone, David Karl (1922-), illus. LC 74-23883. (Illus.). 72 p. 22cm. 1975. (ISBN 0-525-34220-6). Dutton.
Hodges, M. Constance
--Alice in Danceland. Troxel, Rose, illus. Hodges, Del & Mavity, Dennis, photos by (Illus., Orig.). (Delarts Bks.). (gr. 3-8). 1979. Delcon.
Hodges, Margaret Moore, retold by see Ershov, Petr Pavlovich.
Hodges, Margaret Moore, adapted by see Hearn, Lafcadio.
Hodges, Margaret Moore (1911-)
--The Avenger. LC 82-10246. (Illus.). 178 p. 22cm. c.1982. (ISBN 0-684-17636-X). Scribner's.
--A Club Against Keats. Schreiter, Rick (1936-), illus. LC 62-10132. (Illus.). 64 p. 21cm. 1962. Dial Press.

--The Freewheeling of Joshua Cobb. Cuffari, Richard (1925-1978), illus. LC 74-11456. (Illus.). 108 p. 21cm. 1974. (ISBN 0-374-32464-6). Farrar, Straus and Giroux.
--The Hatching of Joshua Cobb. Mars, Witold Tadeusz J. (1912-), illus. LC 67-19880. (Illus.). 135 p. 21cm. 1967. Farrar, Straus & Giroux.
--The High Riders. LC 79-25177. 172 p. 22cm. c.1980. (ISBN 0-684-16456-6). Scribner.
--Hopkins of the Mayflower: Portrait of a Dissenter. LC 72-81485. (Illus.). appendix. bibl. index. 288p. (gr. 7 up). 1972. (ISBN 0-374-33324-6). FS&G.
--If You Had a Horse: Steeds of Myth and Legend. Van Steenburgh, D. Benjamin, illus. LC 84-14024. _____1. 1984. (ISBN 0-684-18220-3). Scribner.
--Knight Prisoner: The Tale of Sir Thomas Malory and King Arthur. LC 76-26693. 200p. (gr. 7 up). 1976. (ISBN 0-374-34269-5). FS&G.
--The Making of Joshua Cobb. Mars, Witold Tadeusz J. (1912-), illus. LC 71-149218. (Illus.). 169 p. 21cm. (Ariel book). 1971. (ISBN 0-374-34737-9). Farrar, Straus and Giroux.
--One Little Drum. Galdone, Paul (1914-), illus. LC 58-10521. (Illus.). 21cm. 63p. (gr. 2-4). 1958. (ISBN 0-695-46595-3). Follett.
--The Secret in the Woods. Brown, Judith Gwyn (1933-), illus. LC 63-16422. 64 p. illus. 23 cm. 1963. (ISBN 0-8037-7702-7). Dial Press.
--Secrets of the Woods. (Illus.). 184p. (The Wood Folk Ser.). N.D. Ginn & Co. Trade Dept.
--Sing Out, Charley!. Ilsley, Velma Elizabeth (1918-), illus. (Illus.). 93 p. 21cm. 1968. Farrar, Straus & Giroux.
--What's for Lunch, Charley?. Aliki, pseud (1929-), illus. Brandenberg, Aliki Liacouras. LC 61-12908. (Illus.). 72 p. 21cm. 1961. ial Press.

Hodges, Margaret Moore (1911-), retold by.
--Baldur and the Mistletoe: A Myth of the Vikings. 1st ed. Hoover, Gerry, illus. LC 73-608. (Illus.). 30 p. 24cm. (Her Myths of the world). 1973, c.1974. (ISBN 0-316-36787-7). Little, Brown.
--Constellation: A Shakespeare Anthology. LC 68-13677. (Index). (gr. 7 up). 1968. (ISBN 0-374-31485-3). FS&G.
--The Fire Bringer: A Paiute Indian Legend. 1st ed. Parnall, Peter (1936-), illus. LC 70-182247. (Illus.). 31 p. 24cm. 1972. Little, Brown. **Award: (ALA).**
--The Gorgon's Head: A Myth from the Isles of Greece. 1st ed. Mikolaycak, Charles (1937-), illus. LC 75-169009. (Illus.). 30 p. 24cm. (Her Myths of the world). 1972. (ISBN 0-316-36781-8). Little, Brown.
--The Other World: Myths of the Celts. Keith, Eros, illus. LC 72-94719. (Illus.). xv, 176 p. 21cm. 1973. (ISBN 0-374-35673-4). Farrar, Straus and Giroux.
--Persephone and the Springtime: A Greek Myth. Stewart, Arvis L., illus. LC 72-7492. (Illus.). 32 p. 24cm. (Her Myths of the world). 1973. (ISBN 0-316-36786-9). Little, Brown.
--Saint George and the Dragon: A Golden Legend. 1st ed. Hyman, Trina Schart (1939-), illus. LC 83-19980. (Original author: Edmund Spencer, 1552-1599). p. cm. c.1984. (ISBN 0-316-36789-3). Little, Brown. **Awards: (NYT); (RCM); (ALA).**
--Tell It Again: Great Tales from Around the World. Berg, Joan, pseud. (1942-), illus. Victor, Joan Berg. LC 63-9779. 127 p. illus. 25 cm. 1963. Dial Press.

Hodges, Turner, pseud., see Morehead, Albert Hodges.

Hodges, Turner, pseud. (1909-1966), ed.
--Bible Story Library. Morehead, Albert Hodges. (Illus.). (gr. 1 up). 1963. Bobbs.

Hodgetts, A. Brayley, ed. see Wyss, Johann David Von.

Hodgetts, Blake Christopher (1967-)
--Dream of the Dinosaurs. Hodgetts, Victoria, illus. LC 77-82949. (Illus.). 48 p. 32cm. c.1978. (ISBN 0-385-12138-5). (ISBN 0-385-12139-3). Doubleday.

Hodgetts, Edward Arthur Brayley (1859-), tr. see Wyss, Johann David Von.

Hodgetts, James Frederick
--The Champion of Odin. (Illus.). (Story Books for Boys). N.D. Cassell & Co.'s Pubs.
--Edwin, The Boy Outlaw: Or, The Dawn of Freedom in England. N.D. Thomas Whittaker.

Hodgkins, Mary Davenport Hutchinson, Mrs., ed.
--The Atlantic Treasury of Childhood Stories. Stevens, Beatrice (1876-), illus. LC 24-25186. 12 p. l., 3-408, 8 p. col. front., illus. 24 1/2 cm. c.1924. The Atlantic Monthly Press.

Hodgman, Ann
--Attack of the Mutants: A Thundercats Adventure. Mones, illus. LC 85-2015. (Adapted from the Teleplay by Julian P. Gardner). p. cm. 1985. (ISBN 0-394-87452-8). Random House.

Hodgson, Ila
--Bernadette's Busy Morning. Johnson, John Emil (1929-), illus. LC 68-11652. (Illus.). 41 p. 1968. Parents' Magazine Press.

Hodgson, Louise
--Geraldine Goes to a Restaurant. Ebbe, Jean L., illus. LC 68-21244. (Illus.). 1 v. 29cm. 36p. 1968. T. S. Denison.
--A Splendor of Sounds. Kleitz, Mary, illus. (Illus.). (Third Grade Bk. Ser.). (gr. 3-4). N.D. (ISBN 0-513-00416-5). Denison.

Hodnett, Edward (1901-), ed.
--Poems to Read Aloud. LC 67-2547. 390p. 1967. (ISBN 0-393-04292-8). Norton & Co.

Hodson, Violet
--Charlie Churchmouse. Koefler, Leatha, illus. (Illus.). 40p. (gr. k-4). 1976. (ISBN 0-87239-104-3). Standard Pub.

Hoefer, Amalie
--Little Rhymes and Jingles. (Illus.). 128p. (The Sunbeam Books). N.D. The Reilly & Britton Co.

Hoehling, Mary Duprey (1914-)
--Thaddeus Lowe: America's One-Man Air Corps, Born August 20, 1832, Died January 16, 1913. LC 58-7260. 189p. illus. 22cm. 1958. Messner.

Hoekstra, Ethel D
--Joy Cometh in the Morning: A Story for Boys. LC 24-24607. 126 p. incl. front., plates. 18 cm. c.1924. Augustana Book Concern.

Hoest, Bill (1954-)
--A Taste of Carrot. 1st ed. LC 67-29287. 1 v. (chiefly col. illus.) 11 x 16cm. 1967. Atheneum.

Hoest, William see Hoest, Bill.

Hofberg, Herman
--Swedish Fairy Tales. (Illus.). (Swedish Fairy Tales Ser.). N.D. W. B. Conkey Company.

Hofer, Andrea
--Child's Christ Tales. (Illus.). N.D. E. Steiger & Co.

Hofer, Mari Ruef
--Festival and Civic Plays from Greek and Roman Tales. LC 27-1690. 237 p. incl. front., illus. 19 cm. (Educational play-book series). c.1926. Beckley-Cardy Company.
--Festival and Civic Plays from Greek and Roman Tales. rev. ed. ... LC 31-32740. 237 p. incl. front. (port.) illus. 19 cm. (Educational play-book series). c.1931. Beckley-Cardy Company.

Hofer, Philip, ed. see Lear, Edward.

Hoff, Carol (1900-)
--Chris. Patterson, Robert (1899-), illus. LC 60-9368. 157p. 23cm. 1960. Follett Pub. Co.
--Four Friends. Ponter, James J., illus. (Illus.). (gr. 1-3). 1958. (ISBN 0-695-83140-2). Follett.
--Head to the West. Moyers, William (1916-), illus. LC 57-8281. 159p. illus. 25cm. 1957. Follett Pub. Co.
--Johnny Texas. Meyers, Robert William (1919-), illus. LC 50-7823. (Illus.). (gr. 4-6). 1950. (ISBN 0-695-84550-0). (ISBN 0-695-44550-2). Follett.
--Johnny Texas on the San Antonio Road: A Story. Sherwan, Earl (1917-), illus. LC 53-8722. (Illus.). 191 p. 25cm. 1953. (ISBN 0-695-44551-0). Wilcox and Follett.

Hoff, M.
--Christmas Cupboard. (Illus.). (Young Reader's Book Ser.). N.D. (ISBN 0-308-80058-3). Funk & Wagnalls.

Hoff, Sydney (1912-)
--Albert the Albatross. Hoff, Sydney (1912-), illus. LC 61-5767. (Illus.). (Early I Can Read Books). (gr. k-2). 1961. (ISBN 0-06-022445-2, HarpJ). (ISBN 0-06-022446-0). Har-Row.
--Amy's Dinosaur. Hoff, Sydney (1912-), illus. LC 74-4348. (Illus.). 48 p. 22cm. 1974. (ISBN 0-525-61521-0). Windmill Books.
--Barkley. Hoff, Sydney (1912-), illus. LC 75-6290. (Illus.). 5 7/8 x 8 1/2. 32p. (18 pt.). (Early I Can Read Bks.). (ps-3). 1975. (ISBN 0-06-022447-9). (ISBN 0-06-022448-7). Har-Row.
--Baseball Mouse. Hoff, Sydney (1912-), illus. LC 68-24515. (Illus.). 48 p. 23cm. 1969. Putnam.
--Chester. Hoff, Sydney (1912-), illus. LC 61-5768. (Illus.). 5 7/8 x 8 1/2. 64p. (18 pt.). (I Can Read Bks.). (gr. k-3). 1961. (ISBN 0-06-022456-8). Har-Row.
--Danny & the Dinosaur. Hoff, Sydney (1912-), illus. LC 58-7754. (Illus.). 5 7/8 x 8 1/2. 64p. (18 pt.). (I Can Read Bks.). (gr. k-3). 1958. (ISBN 0-06-022465-7). (ISBN 0-06-022466-5). (ISBN 0-06-444002-8). Har-Row.
--The Doggy Bag, 3 vol. set. Hoff, Sydney (1912-), illus. (Illus.). (ps up). 1981. (ISBN 0-671-43397-0). Windmill Bks.
--Eight Little Artists. Hoff, Sydney (1912-), illus. LC 54-10214. 27cm. 1954. Abelard-Schuman, Inc.
--Giants, and Other Plays for Kids. Hoff, Sydney (1912-), illus. LC 72-84838. 24cm. 1973. (ISBN 0-399-20266-8). (ISBN 0-399-20266-8). Putnam.
--Grizzwold. Hoff, Sydney (1912-), illus. LC 64-14366. (Illus.). (I Can Read Books). (gr. k-3). 1963. (ISBN 0-06-022481-9, HarpJ). Har-Row.
--Happy Birthday, Henrietta!. Hoff, Sydney (1912-), illus. LC 82-1064. (Illus.). 48p. (Imagination Ser.). (gr. k-4). 1983. (ISBN 0-8116-4423-5). Garrard.
--Henrietta, Circus Star. Hoff, Sydney (1912-), illus. LC 78-58524. (Illus.). 48 p. 23cm. (imagination book). c.1978. (ISBN 0-8116-4413-8). Garrard Pub. Co.
--Henrietta Goes to the Fair. Hoff, Sydney (1912-), illus. LC 78-22051. (Illus.). 48 p. 23cm. (Imagination Book). c.1979. (ISBN 0-8116-4416-2). Garrard Pub. Co.
--Henrietta Lays Some Eggs. Hoff, Sydney (1912-), illus. LC 76-44325. (Illus.). 43 p. 23cm. c.1977. (ISBN 0-8116-4406-5). Garrard Pub. Co.
--Henrietta, the Early Bird. Hoff, Sydney (1912-), illus. LC 77-21246. (Illus.). 48 p. 23cm (Imagination book). c.1978. (ISBN 0-8116-4410-3). Garrard Pub. Co.
--Henrietta's Fourth of July. Hoff, Sydney (1912-), illus. LC 81-2334. (Illus.). 48 p. 23cm. (Imagination book). c.1981. (ISBN 0-8116-4422-7). Garrard Pub. Co.
--Henrietta's Halloween. Hoff, Sydney (1912-), illus. LC 79-23729. (Illus.). 48 p. 23cm. (Imagination book). c.1980. (ISBN 0-8116-4421-9). Garrard Pub. Co.
--Henrietta's Vacation. Hoff, Sydney (1912-), illus. LC 85-12680. p. cm. 1985. (ISBN 0-8116-4424-3). Garrard Pub.
--Henrietta's Valentine's Day. Hoff, Sydney (1912-), illus. LC 85-12711. p. cm. 1985. (ISBN 0-8116-4425-1). Garrard.
--Herschel the Hero. Hoff, Sydney (1912-), illus. LC 69-14387. (Illus.). 45 p. 27cm. 1969. Putnam.
--The Horse in Harry's Room. Hoff, Sydney (1912-), illus. LC 71-104753. (Illus.). 5 7/8 x 8 1/2. 32p. (18 pt.). (Early I Can Read Bks.). (ps-3). 1970. (ISBN 0-06-022483-5). Har-Row.
--Ida, the Bareback Rider. Hoff, Sydney (1912-), illus. LC 71-172411. (Illus.). 31 p. 23cm. (see and read storybook). 1972. Putnam.
--Irving and Me. Hoff, Sydney (1912-), illus. LC 67-7749. 226 p. 22cm. 1967. Harper & Row.
--Jeffrey at Camp. Hoff, Sydney (1912-), illus. LC 68-24516. (Illus.). 48 p. 23cm. 1969, c.1968. Putnam.
--Jokes to Enjoy, Draw & Tell. new ed. Hoff, Sydney (1912-), illus. LC 73-88524. (Illus.). 96p. (gr. 3-6). 1974. (ISBN 0-399-60879-6). Putnam Pub Group.
--Julius. Hoff, Sydney (1912-), illus. LC 59-89711. (Illus.). 5 7/8 x 8 1/2. 64p. (18 pt.). (I Can Read Bks.). (gr. k-3). 1959. (ISBN 0-06-022491-6). Har-Row.
--Katy's Kitten. Hoff, Sydney (1912-), illus. 1975. Dutton.
Katy's Kitty. Three Kitty Stories. Hoff, Sydney (1912-), illus. LC 74-26657. (Illus.). 80 p. 15cm. 1975. (ISBN 0-525-61519-9). Windmill Books.
--Kip Van Wrinkle. Hoff, Sydney (1912-), illus. LC 73-83992. (Illus.). 31 p. 23cm. (see and read storybook). 1974. (ISBN 0-399-20378-8). (ISBN 0-399-20378-8). Putnam.
--Lengthy. Hoff, Sydney (1912-), illus. LC 64-10410. (Illus.). 48 p. 1964. Putnam.
--The Litter Knight. Hoff, Sydney (1912-), illus. LC 75-107291. (Illus.). 38 p. 1970. McGraw-Hill.
--Little Chief. Hoff, Sydney (1912-), illus. LC 61-12098. (Illus.). 23cm. 64p. (I Can Read Books). (gr. k-3). 1961. (ISBN 0-06-022500-9, HarpJ). (ISBN 0-06-022501-7). Har-Row.
--Little Red Riding Hood. Mikolaycak, Charles (1937-), illus. 1968. (ISBN 0-8378-1914-8). C. R. Gibson Company.
--The Littlest Leaguer. Hoff, Sydney (1912-), illus. LC 75-25782. (Illus.). 48 p. 22cm. c.1976. (ISBN 0-525-61536-9). Windmill Books.
--Mahatma. Hoff, Sydney (1912-), illus. LC 68-24517. (Illus.). 47 p. 24cm. 1969. Putnam.
--Merry Christmas, Henrietta!. Hoff, Sydney (1912-), illus. LC 79-19787. (Illus.). 48 p. 23cm. (Imagination book). c.1980. (ISBN 0-8116-4419-7). Garrard Pub. Co.
--Mrs. Switch. Hoff, Sydney (1912-), illus. LC 67-1378. (Illus.). 48 p. 24cm. c.1966. (ISBN 0-399-60480-4). Putnam.
--The Mule Who Struck It Rich. 1st ed. Hoff, Sydney (1912-), illus. LC 79-150050. (Illus.). 32 p. 20cm. 1971. Little, Brown.
--Muscles and Brains. Hoff, Sydney (1912-), illus. LC 40-32148. 64 p. illus. 21 1/2 x 17 cm. 1940. The Dial Press.
--My Aunt Rosie. Hoff, Sydney (1912-), illus. LC 72-76513. (Illus.). 32 p. 23cm. 1972. (ISBN 0-06-022503-3). Harper & Row.
--Ogluk the Eskimo. LC 60-10771. (Illus.). unpaged. 1960. Holt, Rinehart and Winston.
--Oliver. Hoff, Sydney (1912-), illus. LC 60-5779. (Illus.). 5 7/8 x 8 1/2. 64p. (18 pt.). (I Can Read Bks.). (gr. k-3). 1960. (ISBN 0-06-022516-5). Har-Row.
--Palace Bug. Hoff, Sydney (1912-), illus. LC 68-24519. (Illus.). 47 p. 24cm. (See and read beginning to read book). 1970. Putnam.
--Patty's Pet. Hoff, Sydney (1912-), illus. LC 55-8535. unpaged. illus. 27cm. 1955. Abelard-Schuman.
--Pedro and the Bananas. Hoff, Sydney (1912-), illus. LC 75-149330. (Illus.). 31 p. 23cm. (See and read beginning to read storybook). 1972. Putnam.
--Pete's Pup: Three Puppy Stories. Hoff, Sydney (1912-), illus. LC 74-26718. (Illus.). 80 p. 15cm. 1975. (ISBN 0-525-61507-5). Windmill Books.
--Roberto and the Bull. Hoff, Sydney (1912-), illus. LC 69-16255. (Illus.). 38 p. 1969. McGraw-Hill.
--Sammy the Seal. Hoff, Sydney (1912-), illus. LC 59-5316. (Illus.). 5 7/8 x 8 1/2. 64p. (18 pt.). (I Can Read Bks.). (gr. k-3). 1959. (ISBN 0-06-022526-2). (ISBN 0-06-444028-1). Har-Row.
--Santa's Moose. Hoff, Sydney (1912-), illus. LC 78-22483. (Illus.). 5 7/8 x 8 1/2. 32p. (18 pt.). (Early I Can Read Bks.). (ps-3). 1979. (ISBN 0-06-022505-X). (ISBN 0-06-022506-8). Har-Row.
--Siegfried, Dog of the Alps. Hoff, Sydney (1912-), illus. LC 79-122559. (Illus.). 33 p. 1970. Grosset & Dunlap.
--Slithers. Hoff, Sydney (1912-), illus. LC 68-24518. (Illus.). 47 p. 1968. Putnam.
--Slugger Sal's Slump. HOff, Sydney (1912-), illus. LC 78-26338. (Illus.). 48 p. 22cm. c.1979. (ISBN 0-525-61590-3). Windmill Books.
--Soft Skull Sam. Hoff, Sydney (1912-), illus. LC 80-24590. (Illus.). 32 p. 22cm. (Let me read book). c.1981. (ISBN 0-15-277062-3). (ISBN 0-15-277063-1). Harcourt Brace Jovanovich.
--Stanley. Hoff, Sydney (1912-), illus. LC 62-8873. (Illus.). 5 7/8 x 8 1/2. 64p. (18 pt.). (I Can Read Bks.). (gr. k-3). 1962. (ISBN 0-06-022536-X). (ISBN 0-06-444010-9). Har-Row.
--Stanley. Hoff, Sydney (1912-), illus. (Illus.). (I Can Read Bk.). 1978. (ISBN 0-06-444010-9, Trophy). Har-Row.
--Syd Hoff's Animal Jokes. Hoff, Sydney (1912-), illus. LC 84-48353. p. cm. 48p. c.1985. (ISBN 0-397-32116-3). (ISBN 0-397-32117-1). Lippincott.
--Syd Hoff's Best Jokes Ever. Hoff, Sydney (1912-), illus. LC 78-413. (Illus.). 64 p. 22cm. c.1978. (ISBN 0-399-61119-3). Putnam.
--Syd Hoff's Joke Book. Hoff, Sydney (1912-), illus. LC 75-170075. (Illus.). 63 p. 23cm. 1972. Putnam.
--Thunderhoof. Hoff, Sydney (1912-), illus. LC 75-129855. (Illus.). 5 7/8 x 8 1/2. 32p. (18 pt.). (Early I Can Read Bks.). (ps-3). 1971. (ISBN 0-06-022560-2). Har-Row.
--A Walk Past Ellen's House. Hoff, Sydney (1912-), illus. LC 72-11751. (Illus.). 32 p. 22cm. 1973. (ISBN 0-07-029175-6). (ISBN 0-07-029175-6). McGraw-Hill.
--Walpole. Hoff, Sydney (1912-), illus. LC 76-41514. (Illus.). 5 7/8 x 8 1/2. 32p. (18 pt.). (Early I Can Read Bks.). (ps-3). 1977. (ISBN 0-06-022543-2). (ISBN 0-06-022544-0). Har-Row.
--Wanda's Wand. Hoff, Sydney (1912-), illus. LC 68-1536. (Illus.). 25 p. 19cm. 1968. C. R. Gibson Co.
--When Will It Snow?. 1st ed. Chalmers, Mary Eileen (1927-), illus. LC 64-16657. (Illus.). 38 p. 17cm. 1971. (ISBN 0-06-022554-8). Harper & Row.
--Where's Prancer?. Hoff, Sydney (1912-), illus. LC 60-9450. (Illus.). unpaged. 28cm. 1960. Harper.
--Who Will Be My Friends?. Hoff, Sydney (1912-), illus. LC 60-14096. (Illus.). 5 7/8 x 8 1/2. 32p. (18 pt.). (Early I Can Read Bks.). (ps-3). 1960. (ISBN 0-06-022556-4). Har-Row.
--Wilfred the Lion. Hoff, Sydney (1912-), illus. LC 69-16913. (Illus.). 48 p. 23cm. 1970. Putnam.
--The Witch, the Cat, and the Baseball Bat. LC 68-12741. (Illus.). 41 p. 29cm. 1968. Grosset & Dunlap.

Hoff, Virginia
--Mr. Grabbit: The Rabbit. Charlie, illus. LC 53-233095. unpaged. illus. 17cm. (Tell-a-tale books). 1953, c.1952. Whitman Pub. Co.

Hoff, Virginia, jt. auth. see Steiner, Charlotte.

Hoffine, Lyla (1897-)
--Carol Blue Wing, What Is Your Pleasure?. LC 67-26863. 214 p. 21cm. 1967. D. McKay Co.
--The Eagle Feather Prize. Lonsbury, Earl, illus. LC 62-10754. 149p. illus. 21cm. 1962. McKay.
--Eagle Feather Prize. Lonsbury, Earl, illus. (Illus.). (gr. 4-6). 1962. McKay.
--Jennie's Mandan Bowl. 1960. David McKay Company Inc.
--Jennie's Mandan Bowl. 1st ed. Toschik, Larry (1922-), illus. LC 60-670473. 105p. illus. 21cm. 1960. Longmans, Green.
--Running Elk. 1st ed. Boodell, Patricia, illus. LC 57-8693. 108p. illus. 23cm. 1957. Bobbs-Merrill.
--Sioux Trail Adventure: Wi Sapa: Black Moon. LC 57-5245. (Illus.). 160 p. 22cm. 1957. Caxton Printers.

--White Buffalo: A Story of the Northwest Fur Trade. Furman, E. A., illus. LC 39-24451. xvi p., 1 l., 284 p. illus. 20 1/2 cm. 1939. Longmans, Green and Co.
--Wi Sapa: The Story of a Sioux Indian Boy. LC 36-20688. (Illus.). 161p. 1936. American Book Company.
Hoffman, Alice Spencer, retold by.
--As You Like It: Temple Shakespeare for Children. Curtis, Dora, illus. N.D. Dutton & Co.
--The Children's Shakespeare: Being Stories From The Plays With Illustrative Passages. Folkard, Charles James (1878-1963), illus. 1911. E P Dutton.
--Hamlet: Temple Shakespeare for Children. Wilson, Patten, illus. N.D. E P Dutton & Co.
--Henry V: Temple Shakespeare for Children. Curtis, Dora, illus. N.D. E P Dutton & Co.
--Julius Caesar: Temple Shakespeare for Children. Robinson, Thomas Heath (1869-1950), illus. N.D. E P Dutton & Co.
--King John: Temple Shakespeare for Children. Curtis, Dora, illus. N.D. E P Dutton & Co.
--Macbeth: Temple Shakespeare for Children. Robinson, Thomas Heath (1869-1950), illus. N.D. E P Dutton & Co.
--Merchant of Venice: Temple Shakespeare for Children. Curtis, Dora, illus. N.D. E P Dutton & Co.
--Midsummer's Night Dream: Temple Shakespeare for Children. Bell, Robert Anning, illus. N.D. E P Duttton & Co.
--Romeo and Juliet: Temple Shakespeare for Children. Curtis, Dora, illus. N.D. E P Dutton & Co.
--Tempest: Temple Shakespeare for Children. Crane, Walter (1845-1915), illus. N.D. E P Dutton & Co.
Hoffman, Beth Greiner
--Animal Gym. Gergely, Tibor (1900-1978), illus. LC 56-1861. unpaged. illus. 21cm. (Little golden book, 249). 1956. Simon and Schuster.
--Red Is for Apples. Bolognese, Donald Alan (1934-), illus. LC 67-272. 1 v. (unpaged) col. illus. 24 cm. 1966. (ISBN 0-394-91584-4). Random House.
Hoffman, Betsy
--Haunted Places. Ross, Tom, illus. (Illus.). 96p. (gr. 4 up). 1982. (ISBN 0-671-34005-0). Messner.
Hoffman, Elaine, jt. auth. see Hefflefinger, Jane.
Hoffman, Elaine (1922-) & Hefflefinger, Jane (1921-)
--Family Helpers. Irwin, Peggy, photos by. LC 55-1358. (Illus.). 23 p. (Look, read, learn). 1954. Melmont Publishers.
--More Friendly Helpers. Irwin, Peggy, photos by. LC 54-12601. (Illus.). 23 p. (Look, read, learn). 1954. Melmont Publishers.
--Our Friendly Helpers. LC 54-12107. (Illus.). 31 p. (Look, read, learn). 1954. Melmont Publishers.
Hoffman, Eleanor (1895-)
--Sierra Sally. Lundean, Louis, illus. Irwin, Peggy, photos by. LC 44-334363. 139 p. incl. front., illus. 21 cm. 1944. T. Nelson and Sons.
Hoffman, Elizabeth Parkinson (1921-)
--This House Is Haunted!. LC 77-10981. (Illus.). (Myth, Magic & Superstition). (gr. 4-5). 1977. (ISBN 0-8172-1033-4). Raintree Pubs.
Hoffman, Ernst Theodor Amadeus, jt. auth. see Dumas, Alexandre.
Hoffman, Florence K
--The Wanderings of Coco. (Illus.). 166p. N.D. Drexel Biddle's Pub.
Hoffman, Franz (1814-1882)
--Hartz Boys. (Fern Glen Ser.). N.D. D. Lothrop Co.
--The Parsonage of Libenau. Smith, Charles A. (1809-1879), tr. from Ger. LC 7-5899. 222p. 17cm. (The Fatherland Ser.). 1880. Lutheran Publication Society.
Hoffman, Franz (1814-1882) & Hoffman, Julius
--Little Things, the Germs of Greatness; & Floating on the Ice. LC 7-5908. 38p. 16cm. (American Youth's Library). 1872. Hoffman & Morwitz.
Hoffman, Gloria
--Home at Last. Hoffman, Gloria, illus. (gr. 3-7). 1951. David McKay Co.
--Primitivo and His Dog. LC 49-10293. 47 p. illus. 32 cm. 1949. E. P. Dutton.

Hoffman, Helen, jt. auth. see Hoffman, Ruth.

Hoffman, Henry, pseud., see Hoffmann-Donner, Heinrich.

Hoffman, Jo Ann S. (1942-)
--Martin's Invisible Invention. 1977. (ISBN 0-8170-0735-0). Judson.

Hoffman, Joan, ed. see Gregorich, Barbara.
Hoffman, Julius, jt. auth. see Hoffman, Franz.
Hoffman, Lola B.
--Meet the Allens. Lund, Herbert C., photos by. LC 55-16135. 158p. illus. 21cm. 1954. American Book Institute.
--Meet the Allens. Lund, Herbert C., photos by. LC 60-444209. 158p. illus. 21cm. 1960. Narcotics Education.
Hoffman, Mary Ann (1949-) & Sitler, Filomena (1949-)
--A New Adventure. Strok, Susan, illus. LC 81-11086. p. cm. c.1981. (ISBN 0-87021-513-2). Naval Institute Press.
--A Special Family. Strok, Susan, illus. LC 81-11087. p. cm. c.1981. (ISBN 0-87021-513-2). Naval Institute Press.
Hoffman, Maud Miller
--Nee-Na, the Wild Flower's Good Fairy. 1st ed. Hoffman, Maud Miller, illus. 38 p. illus. (part col.) 29 cm. 1949. William-Frederick Press.
Hoffman, Phyllis Miriam (1944-), ed. see Andersen, Hans Christian.
Hoffman, Phyllis Miriam (1944-)
--Steffie and Me. McCully, Emily Arnold (1939-), illus. LC 71-77951. (Illus.). 32 p. 1970. Harper & Row.
Hoffman, Rosekrans (1926-)
--Anna Banana. LC 75-2538. (Illus.). 40 p. 1975. (ISBN 0-394-83109-8). (ISBN 0-394-93109-2). Knopf : Distributed by Random House.
--Sister Sweet Ella. Hoffman, Rosekrans (1926-), illus. LC 81-11200. (Illus.). 32 p. 1982. (ISBN 0-688-00865-8). (ISBN 0-688-00866-6). Morrow.
Hoffman, Ruth (1900-) & Hoffman, Helen (1900-)
--Little Arab Ali. Hoffman, Ruth (1900-) & Hoffman, Helen (1900-), illus. LC 41-16806. 24cm. 47p. 1941. J. B. Lipincott.
Hoffman, Sam, pseud., see Davis, Samuel Hoffman.
Hoffman, Virginia
--Lucy Learns to Weave. 46p. 1970. (ISBN 0-89019-009-7). O'Sullivan Woodside & Co.

Hoffmann-Donner, Heinrich see Hoffmann, Henry, pseud.

Hoffmann-Donner, Heinrich (1809-1894)
--Cruel Frederick. Hoffman, Henry, pseud. (Slovenly Peter). N.D. John C Winston.
--The Cry Baby. Hoffmann, Henry, pseud. (Slovenly Peter). N.D. John C Winston.
--The Dirty Child. Hoffmann, Henry, pseud. (Slovenly Peter). N.D. John C Winston.
--Envious Minny. Hoffmann, Henry, pseud. (Slovenly Peter). N.D. John C winston.
--Fidgety Philip. Hoffmann-Donner, Heinrich. (Slovenly Peter). N.D. John C Winston.
--Flying Robert. Hoffmann, Henry, pseud. (Slovenly Peter). N.D. John C Winston.
--Frank the Liar. Hoffmann, Henry, pseud. (Slovenly Peter). N.D. John C Winston.
--The Inky Boys. Hoffmann, Hnery, pseud. (Slovenly Peter). N.D. John C Winston.
--Johnny Look-in-the-Air. Hoffmann, Henry, pseud. (Slovenly Peter). N.D. John C Winston.
--Lazy Charlotte. Hoffmann, Henry, pseud. (Slovenly Peter). N.D. John C Winston.
--Little Jacob. Hoffmann, Henry, pseud. (Slovenly Peter). N.D. John C Winston.
--Little Suck-a-Thumb. Hoffmann, Henry, pseud. (Slovenly Peter). N.D. John C Winston.
--Magic Lantern Struwwelpeter. Hoffmann, Henry, pseud. (Illus.). N.D. Frederick Warne & Co.
--Mountain-Bounder: Rollicking Rhymes and Pictures. Hoffmann, Henry, pseud. Prelutsky, Jack, tr. from Ger. The/Mountain-Bounder. LC 67-15050. (Illus.). 24cm. 1967. (ISBN 0-02-744170-9). Macmillan.
--Pauline & the Matches. Hoffmann, Henry, pseud. (Slovenly Peter). N.D. John C Winston.
--Peter Teeter Stories. Hoffmann, Henry, pseud. Garman, Raymond H. & Garman, Raymond H., illus. (H. L. Schwetzky added stories to the original book.). 1905. Thompson & Thomas.
--Romping Polly. Hoffmann, Henry, pseud. (Slovenly Peter). N.D. John C Winston.
--Slovenly Peter. Hoffmann, Henry, pseud. Kredel, Fritz (1900-1973), illus. (Harper Junior Classics). N.D. Harper & Bros.
--Slovenly Peter. 1st ed. Kredel, Fritz (1900-1973), illus. Twain, Mark, pseud. (1835-1910), tr. from Ger. Clemens, Samuel Langhorne. LC 35-14240. (Illus.). 34p. 23cm. 1935. The Marchbanks Press.
--Slovenly Peter and Other Delightful Stories. (Illus.). N.D. Thomas R. Knox & Co.
--Slovenly Peter: Cheerful Stories and Funny Pictures for Good Little Folks. Hoffmann, Henry, pseud. (Illus.). N.D. Porter and Coates.
--Slovenly Peter: Or, Cheerful Stories and Funny Pictures for Good Little Folks. Hoffmann, Henry, pseud. (Illus.). 26cm. 90p. N.D. J. C. Winston Co.
--Slovenly Peter, or Pretty Stories & Funny Pictures for Little Children. Hoffmann, Henry, pseud. LC 69-16176. (Illus.). 52p. Repr. of 1844 ed. (ps-3). 1969. (ISBN 0-8048-0033-2). C E Tuttle.
--Struwel Peter: A Picture Book for Boys and Girls. Hoffmann, Henry, pseud. LC 12-34472. 48 p. illus. (part col.) 28 x 22 cm. c.1904. McLoughlin Bros.
--Struwelpeter. Hoffmann, Henry, pseud. N.D. E. P. Dutton & Co.
--Struwelpeter. Hoffmann, Henry, pseud. 1967. (ISBN 0-88302-324-5, Peter Possum). Mulberry Pr.
--Struwelpeter: Merry Stories and Funny Pictures. Hoffmann, Henry, pseud. LC 62-5602. (Illus.). 27 cm. 24p. 1962. F. Warne.
--Struwwelpeter. Hoffmann, Henry, pseud. (Illus.). (gr. 1-5). 1909. (ISBN 0-7100-1534-8). Routledge & Kegan.
--Tom the Thief. Hoffmann, Henry, pseud. (Slovenly Peter Ser.). N.D. John C Winston.
--The Wild Huntsman. Hoffmann, Henry, pseud. (Slovenly Peter). N.D. John C Winston.
Hoffmann, Eleanor (1895-)
--A Cat of Paris. Gay, Zhenya (1906-1978), illus. LC 40-14676. ix p., 1 l., 145 p. illus. 21 1/2 cm. 1940. Frederick A. Stokes Company.
--A Cat of Paris. Gay, Zhenya (1906-1978), illus. N.D. J. B. Lippincott.
--The Charmstone. Grant, Campbell (1909-), illus. LC 64-23726. (Illus.). 23cm. 94p. 1964. McNally and Loftin.
--The Four Friends. Wiese, Kurt (1887-1974), illus. LC 47-300614. 105 p. illus. 22 cm. 1946, c.1943. Macmillan Co.
--The Lion of Barbary. Coggins, Jack Banham (1914-), illus. LC 47-30015. 2 p. l., 217 p. front. (map) illus. 20 1/2 cm. 1946. Holiday House.
--Melika and Her Donkey. KOS, pseud., illus. Dombrowski, Baroness. LC 37-23085. 6 p. l., 195 p. incl. front., illus. 19 cm. 1937. Frederick A. Stokes Company.
--Mischief in Fez. Eichenberg, Fritz (1901-), illus. LC 43-51143. 109, 1 p. col. front., illus. (part col.) 24 1/2 cm. 1943. Holiday House.
--The Mystery of the Lion Ring. Coggins, Jack Banham (1914-), illus. LC 52-13585. (Illus.). 245 p. 21cm. 1953. Dodd, Mead.
--Princess of the Channel Isles. Kreis, Hans, illus. LC 47-30419. 144 p. illus. 21 cm. 1947. T. Nelson.
--The Search for the Gold Fishhook. Wiese, Kurt (1887-1974), illus. LC 51-14164. (Illus.). 228 p. 21cm. 1951. Dodd, Mead.
--Summer at Horseshoe Ranch. McCann, Gerald (1916-), illus. LC 57-541620. 306p. illus. 21cm. 1957. Dodd, Mead.
--The Tall Stallion. Brown, Paul (1893-1958), illus. LC 50-13860. (Illus.). 180 p. 21cm. 1950. Dodd, Mead.
--The Travels of a Snail. Gay, Zhenya (1906-1978), illus. LC 39-11498. 6 p. l., 140, 1 p. front., illus. 21 1/2 cm. 1939. Frederick A. Stokes Company.
--Trouble at Sweet Springs Ranch. Stenbery, Algot, illus. LC 54-97815. 237p. illus. 21cm. 1954. Dodd, Mead.
--White Mare of the Black Tents. LC 49-48762. 214 p. 21 cm. 1949. Dodd, Mead.
Hoffmann, Ernst Theodor Amadeus, jt. auth. see Borska, Ilona.
Hoffmann, Ernst Theodor Amadeus, jt. auth. see Cooke, Donald Ewin.
Hoffmann, Ernst Theodor Amadeus, jt. auth. see Tchaikovsky, Peter Ilich.
Hoffmann, Ernst Theodor Amadeus, jt. auth. see Yamanushi, Toshiko.
Hoffmann, Ernst Theodor Amadeus (1776-1822)
--The Child from Far Away. Orgel, Doris (1929-), retold by. Eagle, Michael (1942-), illus. LC 12-74110347. (Illus.). 63p. (gr. 2-6). 1971. (ISBN 0-201-02883-2, Addisonian). A-W.
--Fairy Tales of Hoffmann. Watson, Marjorie R., ed. Phillipps, W. F., illus. (Illus.). (gr. 3-6). N.D. (ISBN 0-525-29574-7). Dutton.
--Nutcracker. Petisvka, E., ed. Berkova, Dagmar, illus. Kuthanova, Olga, tr. LC 68-10470. (Illus.). color ils. 72p. (Curtain Raiser Bks). (gr. 4-6). 1969. (ISBN 0-531-01754-0). Watts.
--The Nutcracker. Sendak, Maurice Bernard (1928-), illus. Manheim, Ralph (1907-), tr. (Illus.). 120p. 1984. (ISBN 0-517-55285-X). Crown. **Award: (NYT).**
--The Nutcracker. Zwerger, Lisbeth, illus. Bell, Anthea, tr. LC 83-8092. p. cm. (Picture Book Studio USA). 1983, c.1979. (ISBN 0-907234-33-X). Neugebauer Press USA.
--The Nutcracker. J ed. Zwerger, Lisbeth, illus. Bell, Anthea, tr. from Ger. LC 83-8092. (Illus.). 32p. Orig. Title: Knussknacker und Mause Koenig. c.1979. (ISBN 0-907234-33-X). Picture Bk Studio USA.
--The Nutcracker and Mouse-King. Saint Simon, Mrs., tr. from Ger. LC 7-6589. 138 p. front., plates. 16 1/2 cm. 1853. D. Appleton & Company.
--Nutcracker and Mouse-King: A Legend. Reinecke, Carl, ed. N.D. Lockwood, Brooks, and Co.
--The Nutcracker and the Mouse-King. Brock, Emma Lillian (1886-1974), illus. Encking, Louise F., tr. from Ger. LC 30-28191. 2 p. l., vii-xi, 1, 7-123 p. incl. col. front., illus. (part col.) 23 1/2 cm. c.1930. A. Whitman & Co.
--The Nutcracker and the Mouse King. Zwerger, Lisbeth, illus. Bell, Anthea, tr. 1983. Neugebauer.
--The Strange Child. Bell, Anthea, adapted by. Zwerger, Lisbeth, illus. Bell, Anthea, tr. LC 84-8404. 1984. (ISBN 0-907234-60-7). Neugebauer.
--Tales of Hoffmann. N.D. Dodd, Mead & Co.
--Weird Tales. Bealby, John Thomas (1858-), tr. from Ger. 20cm. 1923. C. Scribner's Sons.
Hoffmann, Felix (1911-1975), ed. see Grimm, Jakob Ludwig Karl (1785-1863) & Grimm, Wilhelm Karl.
Hoffmann, Felix (1911-1975)
--Dominic: A Good Action Always Has Its Reward. N.D. Pott, Young & Co.
--The Wolf & the Seven Little Kids. Hoffmann, Felix (1911-1975), illus. LC 59-16357. (Illus.). 32p. (ps-3). 1959. (ISBN 0-15-299108-5, HJ). HarBraceJ.
Hoffmann, Felix (1911-1975), retold by.
--A Boy Went Out to Gather Pears: An Old Verse with New Pictures. Hoffmann, Felix (1911-1975), illus. LC 66-7751. 1 v. (unpaged) col. illus. 10x23cm. 1st U.S. edition. 1966. Harcourt. **Awards: (NYT); (ALA).**
--The Story of Christmas. Hoffmann, Felix (1911-1975), illus. LC 75-6921. (Illus.). 32p. (gr. k up). 1975. (ISBN 0-689-50031-9, McElderry Bk). Atheneum. **Award: (ALA).**
Hoffmann, Franz (1814-1882)
--The Adventures of Leo Rembrandt. Steiner, Lewis Henry (1837-1892), tr. from Ger. LC 7-6014. iv, 5-241 p. front., plates. 17 cm. 1869. Reformed Church Publication Board.
--Alli: Or, Blessed are the Merciful for They Shall Obtain Mercy; A Story for My Young Friends. Croll, Philip C., tr. from Ger. 176 p. 17 cm. (On cover: The Fatherland series). c.1886. Lutheran Publication Society.
--Anton the Fisherman. Manderson, M. A., Mrs., tr. from Ger. LC 7-6015. viii, 9-172 p. plates. 17 1/2 cm. (Added t.-p.: The Fatherland series). 1870. Lutheran Board of Publication.
--Basil and Adelbert: Or, Each in His Own Way. Butcher, M. P., tr. from Ger. LC 7-601715. 144 p. front. 17 cm. (On cover: The Fatherland series). 1883. Lutheran Publication Society.
--Buried in the Snow. Manderson, M. A., Mrs., tr. from Ger. LC 7-60185. vii, 8-161 p. plates. 17 cm. (Added t.-p.: The Fatherland series). 1870. Lutheran Board of Publication.
--Christmas: A Story for My Friends. Harbaugh, Henry (1817-1867), tr. LC 7-6019. 3 p. l., 5-114 p. plates. 17 cm. (Added t.-p.: The Fatherland series). 1875. Lutheran Board of Publication.
--Climbing the Glacier. Walker, Katherine Kent Child (1833-), tr. from Ger. 131 p. 16 cm. 1865. A. D. F. Randolph.
--The Czar's Favorite: Or, Pride Goes Before a Fall. LC 7-6003. 232 p. front., plates. 16 cm. (ivy series. no. 2). 1878. J. A. Moore.
--Day in Capernaum. (Fatherland Series Library, No. 1.). N.D. Lutheran Publication.
--Dominic. Or, Bread Upon the Waters. Schively, Rebecca H., tr. from Ger. 246 p. plates. 17 cm. (Added t.-p.: The Fatherland series). 1870. Lutheran Board of Publication.
--The Emerald. (Series No. 5). (Fatherland Ser.). N.D. Claxton,Remsen & Haffelfinger.
--The Emerald. Conrad, H. D., tr. from Ger. LC 7-5919. 17cm. 156p. (Fatherland Series Library, No. 1.). 1883. Lutheran Publication.
--The Emigrants: A Tale of the Last Century. Conrad, H. D., Mrs., tr. from Ger. LC 7-5919. 1 p. l., 5-156 p. front., pl. 16 1/2 cm. c.1883. The American Sunday-School Union.
--Fritz: Or, Filial Obedience. Manderson, M. A., Mrs., tr. from Ger. LC 7-59186. vii, 9-125 p. pl. 17 1/2 cm. (Half-title: The Fatherland series). 1870. Lutheran Board of Publication.
--Geyer Walty: Or, Fidelity Rewarded. Manderson, M. A., Mrs., tr. from Ger. LC 7-5917. 2 p. l., vii, 8-196 p. plates. 17 cm. (On cover: The Fatherland series). 1870. Lutheran Board of Publication.
--God's Ways Are Wonderful: A Story for Children. Ireland, Mary Eliza Haines, Mrs. (1834-1927), tr. from Ger. LC 22-17729. 128 p. incl. front., pl. 18 cm. c.1922. Augustana Book Concern.
--The Gold-Seeker. Sheip, Levi C., tr. from Ger. LC 7-5916. 186 p. 17 cm. (On cover: The Fatherland series). 1883. Lutheran Publication Society.
--The Greek Slave. Brodfuhrer, J. C., tr. from Ger. LC 7-5915. 239 p. plates 17 cm. (Half-title: The Fatherland series). 1870. Lutheran Board of Publication.
--The Hartz Boys, 1 of 4 vols. (Illus.). (Hartz Boys Library). N.D. D. Lothrop & Co.
--The Hartz Boys. (Illus.). N.D. E. & J. B. Young & Co.

--Nicodemus and His Gran'pappy. Hogan, Inez (1895-), illus. LC 36-4003. 49 p. illus. (part col.) 19 1/2 cm. c.1936. E. P. Dutton & Co., Inc.
--Nicodemus and His Little Sister. Hogan, Inez (1895-), illus. LC 32-17792. 17cm. 47p. 1932. E. P. Dutton & Co.
--Nicodemus and His New Shoes. Hogan, Inez (1895-), illus. LC 38-1820. 49 p. col. illus. 19 1/2 cm. c.1937. E. P. Dutton & Co., Inc.
--Nicodemus and Petunia. LC 37-2944. 51 p. col. illus. 19 1/2 cm. c.1937. E. P. Dutton & Co., Inc.
--Nicodemus and the Gang. Hogan, Inez (1895-), illus. LC 39-2713. 53 p. illus. 19 1/2 cm. c.1939. E. P. Dutton & Co., Inc.
--Nicodemus and the Goose. Hogan, Inez (1895-), illus. LC 45-3443. 47 p. col. illus. 19 1/2 cm. 1945. E. P. Dutton & Co. Inc.
--Nicodemus and the Houn' Dog. Hogan, Inez (1895-), illus. LC 33-18660. 51 p. illus. 19 1/2 cm. c.1933. E. P. Dutton & Co., Inc.
--Nicodemus and the Little Black Pig. Hogan, Inez (1895-), illus. LC 34-17977. 61 p. col. illus. 19 1/2 cm. c.1934. E. P. Dutton & Co., Inc.
--Nicodemus and the Newborn Baby. Hogan, Inez (1895-), illus. LC 40-3667. 53 p. illus. 19 1/2 cm. c.1940. E. P. Dutton & Co., Inc.
--Nicodemus Helps Uncle Sam. Hogan, Inez (1895-), illus. LC 43-8950. 48 p. col. illus. 20 cm. 1943. E. P. Dutton & Co. Inc.
--Nicodemus Laughs. Hogan, Inez (1895-), illus. N.D. E. P. Dutton & Co.
--Nicodemus Runs Away. Hogan, INez (1895-), illus. LC 42-199366. 55p. col. illus. 20 cm. c.1942. E. P. Dutton & Co., Inc.
--A Party for Poodles. 1st ed. Hogan, Inez (1895-), illus. LC 52-8252. unpaged. illus. 27cm. 1952. Dutton.
--Racoon Twins. Hogan, Inez (1895-), illus. LC 46-5255. 49 p. illus. 20 1/2 cm. 1946. E. P. Dutton & Co., Inc.
--Read to Me About Charlie. Hogan, Inez (1895-), illus. LC 50-6044. (Illus.). 26cm. 43p. 1950. Dutton.
--Read to Me About Nono, the Baby Elephant. Hogan, Inez (1895-), illus. LC 47-4821. 2 l., 9-44 p. illus. 26 cm. 1947. E. P. Dutton.
--Read to Me About Peter Platypus. Hogan, Inez (1895-), illus. LC 48-58489. 45 p. illus. 25 cm. 1948. E. P. Dutton.
--Read to Me About the Littlest Cowboy. 1st ed. Hogan, Inez (1895-), illus. LC 51-9926. (Illus.). 45p. 26cm. 1951. Dutton.
--Runaway Toys. Hogan, Inez (1895-), illus. LC 50-9955. 23cm. 40p. 1950. E. P. Dutton & Co.
--Sandy, Skip and the Man in the Moon. Hogan, Inez (1895-), illus. LC 28-24749. 3 p. l., 1, 98, 2 p. illus. (part col.) 19 1/2 cm. c.1928. Macrae Smith Company.
--Twin Colts. Hogan, Inez (1895-), illus. LC 44-6371. 49 p. illus. 20 1/2 cm. 1944. (ISBN 0-525-41616-1). E. P. Dutton & Co. Inc.
--Twin Deer. Hogan, Inez (1895-), illus. LC 41-89609. 52 p. illus. 20 1/2 cm. c.1941. E. P. Dutton & Co., Inc.
--Twin Kids. Hogan, Inez (1895-), illus. LC 37-175108. 50 p. illus. 20 1/2 cm. c.1937. E. P. Dutton & Co., Inc.
--Twin Kittens. 1st ed. Hogan, Inez (1895-), illus. unpaged. illus. 21cm. 1958. Dutton.
--Twin Lambs. Hogan, Inez (1895-), illus. LC 51-11690. unpaged. illus. 21cm. 1951. Dutton.
--Twin Otters & The Indians. Hogan, Inez (1895-), illus. LC 62-7495. 21cm. 41p. 1962. E. P. Dutton & Co.
--Twin Puppies. 1st ed. Hogan, Inez (1895-), illus. unpaged. illus. 21cm. 1959. Dutton.
--Twin Seals. Hogan, Inez (1895-), illus. N.D. E. P. Dutton & Co.
--Upside Down Book, a Story for Little Boys. Hogan, Inez (1895-), illus. LC 55-5641. (Illus.). 26cm. 23p. 1955. Dutton.
--We Are a Family. Hogan, Inez (1895-), illus. LC 52-5292. 93p. illus. 26cm. 1952. Dutton.
--White Kitten and the Blue Plate. Hogan, Inez (1895-), illus. LC 30-19501. 21cm. 44p. N.D. MacMillan.
--World Round. Hogan, Inez (1895-), illus. LC 49-10294. 64 p. illus. 27 cm. 1949. E. P. Dutton.

Hogan, Kirk, jt. auth. see Hogan, Paula Z.

Hogan, Paula Z.
--I Hate Boys, I Hate Girls. Hockerman, Dennis, illus. LC 79-24056. (Illus.). 31 p. 24cm. c.1980. (ISBN 0-8172-1358-9). Raintree Publishers.
--Sometimes I Don't Like School. Ford, Pamela B., illus. LC 79-24055. (Illus.). 30 p. 24cm. c.1980. (ISBN 0-8172-1357-0). Raintree Childrens Books.
--Sometimes I Get So Mad. Shapiro, Karen, illus. LC 79-24057. (Illus.). 31 p. 24cm. c.1980. (ISBN 0-8172-1359-7). Raintree Childrens Books.
--Will Dad Ever Move Back Home?. Leder, Dora, illus. Muir, Martha F., intro. by. LC 79-24058. (Illus.). 31 p. 24cm. c.1980. (ISBN 0-8172-1356-2). Raintree Childrens Books.

Hogan, Paula Z & Hogan, Kirk
--The Hospital Scares Me. Thelen, Mary, illus. Wilson, Jerriann Myers, intro. by. LC 79-23886. (Illus.). 31 p. 24cm. c.1980. (ISBN 0-8172-1351-1). Raintree Childrens Books.

Hogan, Robert J.
--Howl at the Moon. Nicholas, Frank, illus. LC 53-6207. 202p. illus. 22cm. 1953. Houghton Mifflin Co.

Hogarth, C. J., jt. auth. see Thatcher, A.

Hogarth, Grace, ed. see Twain, Mark.

Hogarth, Grace Weston Allen see Gay, Amelia, pseud.

Hogarth, Grace Weston Allen (1905-)
--As a May Morning. 1st Ed. LC 58-5709. 190p. 22cm. 1958. Harcourt, Brace.
--The Funny Guy. (gr. 4-6). 1972 (Starline). Schol Bk Serv.
--The Funny Guy. 1st ed. Wegner, Fritz (1924-), illus. LC 55-5965. 230p. illus. 22cm. 1955. Harcourt, Brace.
--John's Journey. 1st ed. Unwin, Nora Spicer (1907-), illus. LC 52-6461. (Also Wrote under Pseudonyms: Amelia Gary; Allen Weston). 214p. illus. 21cm. 1952. Harcourt, Brace.
--A Sister for Helen. Marriott, Patricia (1920-), illus. LC 79-64313. (Illus.). 139 p. 21cm. 1976. (ISBN 0-233-96817-2). Andre Deutsch.

Hogarth, Peter & Clery, Val (1924-)
--Dragons. LC 79-4530. (Illus.). 1979. (ISBN 0-670-28176-X, Studio). Viking Pr.

Hoge, Dorothy
--The Black Heart of Indri. Domanska, Janina, illus. LC 66-12920. (Illus.). 1 v. (unpaged. 26cm. 1966. Scribner.

Hogeboom, A. E.
--Tales from the High Seas. Floethe, Richard (1901-), illus. N.D. Lothrop Bks.

Hogeboom, Amy (1891-)
--Ann Comes to New York. LC 44-476139. 3 p. l., 210 p. col. front. 21 cm. 1944. Lothrop, Lee & Shepard Company.
--Christopher Columbus and His Brothers. Hogeboom, Amy (1891-), illus. LC 51-7269. 188 p. illus. 22 cm. 1951. Lothrop, Lee & Shepard.
--Gay Kilties of Cape Breton. Hogeboom, Amy (1891-), illus. LC 41-10978. 190 p. illus. 21 cm. 1941. E. P. Dutton & Company, Inc.
--The Mysterious Valley: Adventures of Robert La Salle. Hogeboom, Amy (1891-), illus. LC 41-151971. 4 p. l., 244 p. illus. 21 cm. c.1941. Lothrop, Lee & Shepard Co.
--Treasure in Gaspesy. Hogeboom, Amy (1891-), illus. LC 39-20727. 4 p. l., 13-114, 1 p. incl. col. front., illus. (part col.) 18 x 24 cm. 1939. E. P. Dutton & Company, Inc.

Hogeboom, Amy (1891-), ed.
--The Boys' Book of the West. Bennett, Richard Michael (1899-), illus. LC 46-22918. vii, 419 p. illus. 21 1/2 cm. 1946. Lothrop, Lee and Shepard Company.

Hogg, Garry (1902-1976)
--In the Nick of Time. LC 59-9920. 160p. 21cm. 1958. Roy Publishers.
--They Did it the Hard Way: Seven Astounding Adventures. (Illus.). 1973. (ISBN 0-394-82602-7). Pantheon Books.

Hogg, M. G.
--Marian Temple's Work, and What Came of It. (Illus.). N.D. Publications of the Methodist Book Concern.

Hogins, James Burl
--Literature: Mythology and Folklore. LC 74-82303. (Illus.). iv, 122 p. 24cm. 1975, c.1974. (ISBN 0-574-17005-7). Science Research Associates.

Hogner, Dorothy Childs, Mrs.
--Barnyard Family. N.D. Oxford University Press.
--Barnyard Family. Hogner, Nils (1893-1970), illus. LC 66-84. (Illus.). 224p. (gr. 4-7). 1942. (ISBN 0-8098-2312-8). Walck.
--The Bible Story. Hogner, Nils (1893-1970), illus. 445p. 1943. Oxford University Press.
--Blue Swamp. Hogner, Nils (1893-1970), illus. LC 47-2543. 46 2 p. illus. (part col.) 23 x 20 cm. 1947. Oxford University Press.
--Daisy: A Farm Fable. Hogner, Nils (1893-1970), illus. 48p. 1949. Henry Z. Walck, Inc., Publishers.
--Daisy: A Farm Fable. Hogner, Nils (1893-1970), illus. LC 49-10086. 48 p. illus. 18 x 24 cm. (Oxford books for boys and girls). 1949. Oxford Univ. Press.
--The Dog Family. Hogner, Nils (1893-1970), illus. 1954. Oxford University Press.
--Don't Blame the Puffins. Hogner, Nils (1893-1970), illus. LC 40-5386. 50 1 p., 1 l. incl. col. front., illus. (part col.) plates. 19 1/2 x 17 cm. c.1940. Oxford University Press.
--Dusty's Return. Hogner, Nils (1893-1970), illus. LC 50-9120. 190 p. illus. 24 cm. 1950. Oxford University Press.
--The Education of a Burro. Hogner, Nils (1893-1970), illus. LC 36-17397. 56 1 p. illus. 22 1/2 cm. 1936. T. Nelson and Sons.
--Lady Bird. Hogner, Nils (1893-1970), illus. LC 38-27502. 18 1/2cm. 47p. 1938. Oxford University Press.
--Little Esther. LC 37-10695. 63 p. incl. front., illus. 22 cm. 1937. T. Nelson & Sons.
--Navajo Winter Nights. 180p. N.D. Thomas Nelson & Sons.
--Old Hank Weatherby. Hogner, Nils (1893-1970), illus. LC 39-8351. 70, 1 p. incl. front., illus. 28 1/2 cm. 1939. Oxford University Press.
--Pancho. Hogner, Nils (1893-1970), illus. LC 38-16756. 60 1 p. illus. 22 1/2 x 19 1/2 cm. 1938. T. Nelson and Sons.
--Reward for Brownie. Hogner, Nils (1893-1970), illus. LC 44-7472. 28 p. illus. 17 1/2 x 23 1/2 cm. 1944. Oxford University Press.
--Rufus. Hogner, Nils (1893-1970), illus. LC 55-5645. 70p. illus. 24cm. 1955. (ISBN 0-397-30308-4). Lippincott.
--Santa Fe Caravans. Hogner, Nils (1893-1970), illus. LC 37-529651. 65 p. illus. 19 1/2 cm. (Our changing world). 1937. T. Nelson and Sons.
--Snails. Hogner, Nils (1893-1970), illus. LC 58-9188. 81p. illus. 21cm. 1958. Crowell.
--Snowflake. Hogner, Nils (1893-1970), illus. LC 52-9431. 18cm. 30p. 1952. Oxford University Press.
--Snowflake: A Small but Tempting Christmas Story. Hogner, Nils (1893-1970), illus. 32p. 1952. Henry z. Walck, Inc., Publishers.
--Stormy, the First Mustang. Hogner, Nils (1893-1970), illus. LC 41-18355. ix p., 1 l., 13-151, 1 p. incl. front., illus., plates. 21 x 16 cm. c.1941. Oxford University Press.
--Unexpected Journey: The Story of a Dog. LC 45-8978. 3 p. l., 3-172 p. incl. front., illus. 21 cm. 1945. Creative Age Press, Inc.
--Water Beetles. Hogner, Nils (1893-1970), illus. LC 63-15089. (Illus.). 57 p. 21cm. 1963. Crowell.
--Water over the Dam. Hogner, Nils (1893-1970), illus. 256p. 1960. J. B. Lippincott Company.
--Wide River. Hogner, Nils (1893-1970), illus. LC 54-7130. 64p. illus. 21cm. 1954. (ISBN 0-397-30289-4). Lippincott.
--The Wild Little Honker. Hogner, Nils (1893-1970), illus. unpaged. illus. 17 x 20cm. 1959, c.1951. H. Z. Walck.
--The Wild Little Honker. Hogner, Nils (1893-1970), illus. 1951. Oxford University Press.
--Winky, King of the Garden. Hogner, Nils (1893-1970), illus. 32p. 1946. Henry Z. Walck, Inc., Publishers.
--Winky, King of the Garden. Hogner, Nils (1893-1970), illus. LC 48-3620. 32 p. col. illus. 23 cm. 1946. Oxford Univ. Press.

Hogner, Franz
--Can You See What I See?. 1974. (ISBN 0-685-50416-6). Scroll Pr.

Hogner, Nils (1893-1970)
--Boldy. Hogner, Nils (1893-1970), illus. LC 53-10641. unpaged. illus. 27cm. 1953. Abelard Press.
--The Devil Stallion. Hogner, Nils (1893-1970), illus. LC 67-2075. (Illus.). 60 p. 24cm. 1967. H. Z. Walck.
--Dynamite: The Wild Stallion. Hogner, Nils (1893-1970), illus. unpaged. illus. 23cm. c.1953. Aladdin Books.
--Dynamite, the Wild Stallion. Hogner, Nils (1893-1970), illus. N.D. E. P. Dutton & Co.
--Farm for Rent. Hogner, Nils (1893-1970), illus. LC 57-808275. unpaged. illus. 27cm. c.1958. Abelard-Schuman.
--Jean's Whale. Hogner, Nils (1893-1970), illus. LC 55-5066. unpaged. illus. 27cm. 1955. Abelard-Schuman.
--Jean's Whale. Hogner, Nils (1893-1970), illus. N.D. E. M. Hale & Co.
--Jimmy's First Roundup. Hogner, Nils (1893-1970), illus. LC 59-5388. unpaged. illus. 26cm. 1959. Abelard-Schuman.
--Jimmy's First Roundup. Hogner, Nils (1893-1970), illus. N.D. E. M. Hale and Co.
--The Lost Tugboat. Hogner, Nils (1893-1970), illus. LC 52-2572. (Illus.). unpaged. 28cm. 1952. Abelard Press.
--Molly the Black Mare. Hogner, Nils (1893-1970), illus. LC 62-9423. (Illus.). (gr. k-3). 1962. (ISBN 0-8098-1081-6). Walck.
--The Nosy Colt. Lebenson, Richard, illus. LC 72-10650. (Illus.). 30 p. 23cm. 1973. (ISBN 0-8098-1204-5). H. Z. Walck.
--Sad Eye, the Clown: A Circus Story. Hogner, Nils (1893-1970), illus. LC 56-5022. unpaged. illus. 27cm. 1956. Abelard-Schuman.
--Tanny. Hogner, Nils (1893-1970), illus. LC 60-6420. (Illus.). (gr. k-3). 1960. (ISBN 0-8098-1065-4). Walck.

Hogrogian, Nonny, jt. auth. see Kherdian, David.

Hogrogian, Nonny (1932-), retold by see Grimm, Jakob Ludwig Karl (1785-1863) & Grimm, Wilhelm Karl.

Hogrogian, Nonny (1932-)
--Apples. Hogrogian, Nonny (1932-), illus. LC 71-146626. (Illus.). 30 p. 1972. Macmillan.
--Billy Goat and His Well-Fed Friends. Hogrogian, Nonny (1932-), illus. LC 72-76497. (Illus.). 62 p. 23cm. (I can read book). 1972. (ISBN 0-06-022565-3). (ISBN 0-06-022565-3). Harper & Row.
--Carrot Cake. Hogrogian, Nonny (1932-), illus. LC 76-17628. (Illus.). 32 p. 22cm. (ps-3). c.1977. (ISBN 0-688-80061-0). (ISBN 0-688-84061-2). Greenwillow Books.
--The Contest. Hogrogian, Nonny (1932-), illus. LC 75-40389. p. cm. c.1976. (ISBN 0-688-80042-4). (ISBN 0-688-84042-6). Greenwillow Books. **Awards: (ALA); (RCM).**
--The Contest. Hogrogian, Nonny (1932-), illus. LC 72-92440. p. cm. 1974. (ISBN 0-02-744020-6). Macmillan.
--The Hermit and Harry and Me. Hogrogian, Nonny (1932-), illus. LC 76-183851. (Illus.). 32 p. 1972. Little, Brown.
--One Fine Day. Hogrogian, Nonny (1932-), illus. LC 75-119834. (Illus.). 32 p. 1974, c.1971. Collier Books.
--One Fine Day. Hogrogian, Nonny (1932-), illus. LC 75-119834. (Illus.). color ils. 32p. (gr. k-3). 1971. (ISBN 0-02-744000-1). Macmillan. **Award: (RCM).**

Hogrogian, Nonny (1932-), retold by.
--Cinderella. Hogrogian, Nonny (1932-), illus. LC 80-15394. (Original Authors: Jakob Ludwig Karl Grimm, 1785-1863 and Wilhelm Karl Grimm, 1786-1859). 1981. (ISBN 0-688-80299-0). (ISBN 0-688-84299-2). Greenwillow Books.

Hogrogian, Nonny (1932-), illus.
--One I Love, Two I Love And Other Loving Mother Goose Rhymes. LC 79-179047. (Illus.). 28 p. 19cm. 1972. (ISBN 0-525-36420-X). Dutton.
--Rooster Brother. LC 73-8090. (Illus.). 32 p. 1974. (ISBN 0-02-743990-9). Macmillan.
--The Story of Prince Ivan, the Firebird, and the Gray Wolf. Whitney, Thomas Porter (1917-), tr. from Russian. LC 68-12521. (Illus.). 32 p. 1968. Scribner. **Award: (ALA).**
--The Thirteen Days of Yule. Murray, Anthony, intro. by. LC 68-21606. (Illus.). 31 p. 21cm. 1968. Crowell. **Award: (ALA).**

Hogstrand, Olle
--The Debt. Blair, Alan, tr. 1973. (ISBN 0-394-49191-2). Pantheon Books.

Hogstrom, Daphne Doward
--My Big Book of Fingerplays: A Fun-To-Say Fun-To-Play Collection. Augustiny, Sally, illus. 1974. (ISBN 0-307-60500-0, Golden Pr). Western Pub.
--My Little Book of Farm Animals. Hauge, Carl & Hauge, Mary, illus. 24p. (Tell-a-Tale Reader). (ps-3). 1980. (ISBN 0-307-68490-3, Golden Pr). Western Pub.
--One Silver Second: A Fable for All Ages. Laite, Gordon (1925-), illus. LC 71-174641. (Illus.). 32 p. 25cm. 1972. (ISBN 0-528-82188-1). (ISBN 0-528-82189-X). Rand McNally.
--The Real Book of First Pictures. Wager, Justin, illus. LC 70-185175. (Illus.). 62 p. 29cm. 1972. (ISBN 0-528-82162-8). Rand McNally.

Hogue, Wilbur Owings
--Bob Clifton: African Planter. 1st ed. Wiese, Kurt (1887-1974), illus. LC 52-13067. 152p. illus. 21cm. 1953. Holt.
--Bob Clifton, Congo Crusader. 1st ed. Wiese, Kurt (1887-1974), illus. LC 51-13481. 152 p. illus. 21 cm. 1951. Holt.
--Bob Clifton: Elephant Hunter. Wiese, Kurt (1887-1974), illus. LC 49-2149. 151 p. illus. 21 cm. 1949. H. Holt.
--Bob Clifton: Jungle Traveler. Wiese, Kurt (1887-1974), illus. LC 50-9909. ix, 146 p. illus. 21 cm. 1950. Holt.

Hoguet, Susan Ramsay
--I Unpacked My Grandmother's Trunk. 1st ed. Hoguet, Susan Ramsay, illus. LC 83-1701. p. cm. c.1983. Dutton.

Hohler, Mrs. Edwin. see Hohler, Venetia Edwin.

Hohler, Venetia Edwin (1871-)
--The Green Toby Jug & the Princess Who Lived Opposite. (Illus.). N.D. Thomas Nelson & Sons.
--Peter: A christmas Story. LC 7-31482. v, 182 p. front., 5 pl. 19 1/2 cm. 1907. E. P. Dutton & Company.

Hohn, Hazel Stumper
--The King Who Could Not Smile: A Story with a Moral. Hampson, Denman, illus. LC 63-8177. unpaged, illus. 28 cm. 1963. Parents' Magazine Press.

Hohoff, Tay, pseud., see Torrey, Therese Von Hohoff.

Hohoff, Tay, pseud. (1898-1974)
--The Cat Who Wanted Out. Torrey, Therese Von Hohoff. Grom, Bogdan, illus. LC 59-6704. 32p. 1959. J. B. Lippincott.

Hoisington, May Folwell, Mrs., jt. auth. see Roy, Lillian Elizabeth Becker, Mrs.

Hoke, Helen, jt. auth. see Gill, Richard Cochran.

Hoke, Helen L. see Sterling, Helen, pseud.

Hoke, Helen L., Mrs. (1903-)
--The Big Dog and the Very Little Cat. Thorne, Diana (1894-), illus. LC 69-19295. (Illus.). 33 p. 28cm. 1969. Watts.

--The Biggest Family in the Town. Sterling, Helen, pseud. Locke, Vance, illus. LC 47-12111. 28 p. col. illus. 20 x 27 cm. c.1947. D. McKay.

--Doctor, the Puppy Who Learned. Thorne, Diana (1894-), illus. LC 44-8548. 18 p. col. illus. 22 1/2 x 22 cm. c.1944. J. Messner, Inc.

--Factory Kitty. Lees, Harry Hanson, illus. LC 49-9484. 34 p. col. illus. 29 cm. 1949. F. Watts.

--The Furry Bear. Tate, Sally, illus. LC 43-16226. 16 p. col. illus. 23 x 18 cm. c.1943. J. Messner, Inc.

--The Fuzzy Puppy. Hart, Dick (1920-), illus. LC 45-7531. 16 p. col. illus. 23 x 18 cm. c.1945. J. Messner, Inc.

--Grocery Kitty. Lees, Harry Hanson, illus. (gr. 1-4). 1946. Franklin Watts, Inc.

--Grocery Kitty. Lees, Harry Hanson, illus. LC 46-3564. 36 p. incl. col. front., col. illus. 28 x 28 1/2 cm. 1946. Reynal & Hitchcock.

--The Horse That Takes the Milk Around. Sterling, Helen, pseud. Hartwell, Marjorie, illus. LC 47-1332. 28 p. col. illus. 19 1/2 x 26 cm. c.1946. F. Watts, Inc.

--The Horse That Takes the Milk Around. Sterling, Helen, pseud. Hartwell, Marjorie, illus. LC 65-22599. 1v. (unpaged) col. illus. 20x27cm. 1965, c.1946. Watts.

--Little Choo Choo. Sterling, Helen, pseud. Budd, Denison M. (1898-), illus. LC 44-8035. 28 p. col. illus. 16 1/2 x 24 cm. c.1944. F. Watts, Inc.

--Little Moo and the Circus. Sterling, Helen, pseud. Lees, Harry Hanson, illus. LC 45-10687. 28 p. col. illus. 20 x 26 1/2 cm. c.1945. F. Watts, Inc.

--Major and and the Kitten. Thorne, Diana (1894-), illus. LC 41-17042. 36 p., 1 l. incl. front., illus. (part col.) 31 cm. c.1941. H. Holt and Company.

--Major and the Kitten. Thorne, Diana (1894-), illus. N.D. Franklin Watts, Inc.

--Mr. Sweeney. Wills, William, illus. N.D. Franklin Watts, Inc.

--Mr. Sweeney. Wills, William, illus. LC 40-14815. 76 p. illus. 27 1/2 x 21 cm. c.1940. H. Holt and Company.

--Mrs. Silk. Thorne, Diana (1894-), illus. LC 46-1555. 24 p. col. illus. 28 1/2 x 21 1/2 cm. c.1945. Veritas Press, Inc.

--Rags' Day. Thorne, Diana (1894-), illus. LC 46-25029. 21 p. col. illus. 28 1/2 x 21 1/2 cm. c.1945. Veritas Press, Inc.

--Riddle Giggles. Parkhouse, Tony, illus. LC 74-26364. (Illus.). 48 p. 23cm. 1975. (ISBN 0-531-02096-7). F. Watts.

--The Shaggy Pony. Hart, Dick (1920-), illus. LC 44-40380. 16 p. col. illus. 22 1/2 x 18 cm. c.1944. J. Messner, Inc.

--Shep and the Baby. Thorne, Diana (1894-), illus. LC 44-8549. 17 p. col. illus. 22 1/2 x 22 cm. c.1944. J. Messner, Inc.

--Spirits, Spooks, and Other Sinister Creatures. LC 83-21603. 1984. (ISBN 0-531-04769-5). F. Watts.

--Too Many Kittens. Lees, Harry Hanson, illus. LC 47-297910. 34 p. incl. col. front., col. illus. 28 1/2 x 22 cm. 1947. David McKay Company.

--Too Many Shoes and Stockings. Lees, Harry Hanson, illus. (gr. 4). N.D. David McKay Co.

Hoke, Helen L., Mrs. (1903-), ed.

--Big Book of Jokes. Erdoes, Richard (1912-), illus. LC 78-161837. (Illus.). 192p. (Big Bks). (gr. 4-6). 1971. (ISBN 0-531-01990-X). Watts.

--Big Book of Stories of Many Lands. (gr. 1-4). N.D. (ISBN 0-531-01847-4). Watts.

--A Chilling Collection. 1st ed. LC 79-18864. p. cm. c.1979. (ISBN 0-525-66662-1). Elsevier/Nelson Books.

--Creepies, Creepies, Creepies: A Covey of Quiver-and-Quaver Tales. Prosser, Bill, illus. LC 77-6289. xii,178 24. (Terrific triples). 1977. (ISBN 0-531-01323-5). F. Watts.

--Demonic, Dangerous & Deadly. 160p. (gr. 12 up). 1983. (ISBN 0-525-67141-2). Lodestar Bks.

--Demonic, Dangerous & Deadly: An Anthology. 1st ed. LC 82-17697. xiii, 143 p. 24cm. c.1983. (ISBN 0-525-67141-2). Dutton.

--Devils, Devils, Devils. Barker, Carol Minturn (1938-), illus. LC 75-38035. (Illus.). 216 p. 24cm. 1976. (ISBN 0-531-01140-2). Watts.

--Doctors, Doctors, Doctors. (gr. 7 up). N.D. (ISBN 0-531-01656-0). Watts.

--Dragons, Dragons, Dragons. Barker, Carol Minturn (1938-), illus. LC 74-182300. (Illus.). x, 240 p. 25cm. 1972. (ISBN 0-531-02036-3). F. Watts.

--Eerie, Weird & Wicked. LC 77-7252. (gr. 7 up). 1977. (ISBN 0-525-66554-4). Lodestar Bks.

--Eerie, Weird, and Wicked: An Anthology. Brychta, Alex (1956-), illus. LC 77-7252. p. cm. c.1977. (ISBN 0-8407-6554-1). T. Nelson.

--Fear! Fear! Fear!. Eckett, Sean, illus. LC 80-26909. (Illus.). 144 p. 24cm. 1981. (ISBN 0-531-04255-3). F. Watts.

--Ghastly, Ghoulish, Gripping Tales. LC 82-17619. 160 p. 24cm. 1983. (ISBN 0-531-04593-5). F. Watts.

--Ghostly, Grim & Gruesome. LC 76-54258. (gr. 6 up). 1977. (ISBN 0-525-66545-5). Lodestar Bks.

--Ghosts and Ghastlies. Prosser, Bill, illus. LC 76-13036. (Illus.). 181 p. 24cm. 1976. (ISBN 0-531-01210-7). F. Watts.

--Giants! Giants! Giants!. From Many Lands and Many Times. Lavis, Stephen, illus. LC 80-10599. (Illus.). 156 p. 24cm. (Terrific Triple). 1980. (ISBN 0-531-04172-7). F. Watts.

--Haunts, Haunts, Haunts. Keeping, Charles William James (1924-), illus. LC 76-56146. (Illus.). 191 p. 24cm. 1977. (ISBN 0-531-00098-1). F. Watts.

--Hoke's Jokes, Cartoons & Funny Things. Hill, Eric, illus. LC 74-7459. p. 1974, c.1973. (ISBN 0-531-02682-5). Watts.

--Horrors, Horrors, Horrors. Prosser, Bill, illus. LC 78-2350. (Illus.). xiii, 177 p. 24cm. 1978. (ISBN 0-531-02211-0). Watts.

--Jokes & Fun. Parkhouse, Tony, illus. LC 72-2403. (Illus.). 22cm. 48p. (gr. 1-4). 1973. (ISBN 0-531-02616-7). Watts.

--Jokes, Jests, and Jollies. Kelley, True Adelaide (1946-), illus. LC 72-80124. (Illus.). 31 p. (Magic circle book). c.1973. (ISBN 0-663-25494-9). Ginn.

--Jokes Jokes Jokes. Erdoes, Richard (1912-), illus. 1954. (ISBN 0-531-01704-4). Franklin Watts.

--The Little Riddle Book. Brychta, Jan, illus. LC 77-155081. (Illus.). 40 p. 22cm. c.1977. (ISBN 0-89332-008-0). Frank Book Corp.

--Monsters, Monsters, Monsters. Keeping, Charles William James (1924-), illus. LC 75-310343. (Illus.). 187 p. 24cm. 1974. (ISBN 0-85166-532-2). F. Watts.

--Monsters, Monsters, Monsters. Keeping, Charles William James (1924-), illus. LC 75-6045. (Illus.). 187 p. 23cm. 1975. (ISBN 0-531-02846-1). Watts.

--More Ghosts, Ghosts, Ghosts. LC 81-3048. x, 130 p. 24cm. 1981. (ISBN 0-531-04352-5). F. Watts.

--More Jokes Jokes Jokes. Erdoes, Richard (1912-), illus. 1965. (ISBN 0-531-01736-2). Franklin Watts.

--More Riddles, Riddles, Riddles. Haro, illus. LC 76-10696. (Illus.). 157 p. 24cm. 1976. (ISBN 0-531-00351-5). F. Watts.

--Mysterious, Menacing & Macabre. 160p. (gr. 7 up). 1981. (ISBN 0-525-66753-9). Lodestar Bks.

--Mysterious, Menacing & Macabre: An Anthology. LC 81-9738. 148 p. 24cm. c.1981. (ISBN 0-525-66753-9). Elsevier/Nelson Books.

--Nurses, Nurses, Nurses. (gr. 7 up). 1960. (ISBN 0-531-01753-2). Watts.

--Sinister, Strange, and Supernatural. LC 80-22717. p. cm. 1980. (ISBN 0-525-66703-2). Elsevier/Nelson Books.

--Spectres, Spooks and Shuddery Shades. Keeping, Charles William James (1924-), illus. LC 78-310518. (Illus.). 191 p. 24cm. 1977. (ISBN 0-85166-620-5). F. Watts.

--Spooks, Spooks, Spooks. Lohse, William R., illus. LC 66-10138. (Illus.). (Terrific Triple Titles Ser). (gr. 7 up). 1956. (ISBN 0-531-01797-4). Watts.

--Tales of Fear & Frightening Phenomena: An Anthology. LC 82-7299. 132 p. 24cm. c.1982. (ISBN 0-525-66789-X). E. P. Dutton.

--Tales of Fear & Frightening Phenomena. 160p. (gr. 7 up). 1982. (ISBN 0-525-66789-X). Lodestar Bks.

--Terrors, Terrors, Terrors. Prosser, Bill, illus. LC 79-16295. (Illus.). 191 p. 24cm. (Terrific triples). 1979. (ISBN 0-531-04093-3). F. Watts.

--Thrillers, Chillers & Killers. LC 79-4502. 1979. (ISBN 0-525-66633-8). Lodestar Bks.

--Uncanny Tales of Unearthly and Unexpected Horrors: An Anthology. 1st ed. LC 83-8911. xiii, 126 p. 24cm. c.1983. (ISBN 0-525-66919-1). Dutton.

--Venomous Tales of Villainy & Vengeance. 144p. (gr. 7 up). 1984. (ISBN 0-525-67158-7). Lodestar Bks.

--Weirdies, Weirdies, Weirdies. Keeping, Charles William James (1924-), illus. LC 73-14010. (Illus.). 244p. (Terrific Triple Titles Ser). (gr. 6 up). 1975. (ISBN 0-531-02683-3). Watts.

--Witches, Witches, Witches. Lohse, William R., illus. (Illus.). (Terrific Triple Titles Ser). (gr. 4-6). 1966. (ISBN 0-531-01823-7). Watts.

Hoke, Helen L., Mrs. (1903-) & Fox, Natalie

--The Woolly Lamb. Tate, Sally, illus. LC 42-20328. 16 p. col. illus. 23 1/2 cm. c.1942. J. Messner, Inc.

Hoke, Helen L., Mrs. (1903-) & Gill, Richard C.

--Paco Goes to the Fair: A Story of Far-away Ecuador. Gannett, Ruth Chrisman Arens (1896-1979), illus. 1940. Henry Holt & Co.

Hoke, Helen L., Mrs. (1903-) & Leeming, Joseph (1897-1968), eds.

--Jokes,Riddles, Puns. (Illus.). 786p. 1960. Franklin Watts, Inc.

Hoke, Helen L., Mrs. (1903-) & Randolph, Boris, eds.

--Puns, Puns, Puns. Nydorf, Seymour, illus. (Illus.). 256p. 1958. Franklin Watts, Inc.

Hoke, Helen L., Mrs. (1903-) & Teichner, Miriam

--The Fuzzy Kitten. Wohlberg, Meg (1905-), illus. LC 41-16072. 16 p. col. illus. 23 x 18 1/2 cm. c.1941. J. Messner, Inc.

Holabird, Katherine

--Angelina Ballerina. Craig, Helen, illus. LC 83-8233. (Illus.). (ps-2). 1983. (ISBN 0-517-55083-0). (ISBN 0-517-55083-0). C. N. Potter. Dist. by Crown.

--Angelina's Christmas. Craig, Helen, illus. LC 85-12389. (Illus.). 25 p. 1985. (ISBN 0-517-55823-8). C.N. Potter : Distributed by Crown Publishers.

--The Little Mouse One Two Three. Craig, Helen, illus. (Illus.). 32p. (The Little Mouse Learning Bks.). N.D. (ISBN 0-671-47732-3, Little Simon). S&S.

Holaday, Alice May Cusick, Mrs.

--On the Side Lines. LC 25-21766. 5 p. l., 3-295 p. front., plates. 19 1/2 cm. $1.7. c.1925. The Century Co.

Holaves, Sharon

--Pano the Train. Giannini, Jean, illus. (Illus.). 24p. (ps-3). 1975. (ISBN 0-307-60117-X, Golden Pr). Western Pub.

Holberg, Ruth Langland, Mrs. (1891-)

--At the Sign of the Golden Anchor. 1st ed. Castle, Jane, illus. LC 47-569942. x, 209 p. illus., map (on lining-papers) 22 cm. 1947. Doubleday.

--The Bells of Amsterdam. Holberg, Richard A. (1889-1942), illus. LC 40-30189. 96p. 1940. Thomas Y. Cromell Co.

--Captain John Smith: The Lad from Lincolnshire. Morgan, Ava Lisbeth, illus. LC 46-7875. 4 p. l., 181 p. incl. illus. 21 cm. 1946. Thomas Y. Crowell Company.

--The Catnip Man. Weil, Lisl (1910-), illus. LC 51-5491. 114 p. illus. 22 cm. 1951. Crowell.

--The Girl in the Witch House. Coe, Lloyd (1899-1976), illus. LC 66-833561. 127p. illus. 22cm. 1966. (ISBN 0-8038-2603-6). Hastings.

--Girl in the Witch House. Coe, Lloyd (1899-1976), illus. (Illus.). (gr. 4-6). 1966. (ISBN 0-8038-2603-6). Hastings.

--Gloucester Boy. Holberg, Richard A. (1889-1942), illus. LC 40-80684. 24cm. 48p. 1940. Doubleday Doran & Co.

--Hester & Timothy, Pioneers. Holberg, Richard A. (1889-1942), illus. LC 37-210298. 6 p. l., 128 p. incl. col. front., illus., plates (part col.) 23 1/2 cm. 1937. Doubleday, Doran & Company, Inc.

--Jill and the Applebird House. 1st ed. Komoda, Kiyoaki (1937-), illus. LC 68-10601. (Illus.). 161 p. 22cm. 1968. Doubleday.

--Kate and the Devil. Payne, Joan Balfour (1923-1973), illus. LC 67-30945. (Illus.). 96 p. 22cm. 1968. Hastings House.

--Luke and the Indians. Tolford, Joshua (1909-), illus. LC 70-85231. (Illus.). 94 p. 22cm. 1969. (ISBN 0-8038-4265-1). Hastings House.

--Marching to Jerusalem. Jones, Henrietta, illus. LC 43-16227. 3 p. l., 149 p., 1 l. col. front., illus. 23 1/2 cm. 1943. Thomas Y. Crowell Company.

--Michael and the Captain. James, Sandra, illus. LC 44-7925. 4 p. l., 114 p. incl. illus., plates. 24 cm. 1944. Thomas Y. Crowell Company.

--Mitty and Mr. Syrup. Holberg, Richard A. (1889-1942), illus. LC 35-27409. 32p. 1935. Doubleday Doran & Co.

--Mitty on Mr. Syrup's Farm. Holberg, Richard A. (1889-1942), illus. LC 36-27375. 32p. 1936. Doubleday Doran & Co.

--Not So Long Ago. Holberg, Richard A. (1889-1942), illus. LC 39-10759. 3 p. l., 131, 1 p. incl. front., illus. (part col.) 22 1/2 cm. 1939. Thomas Y. Crowell Company.

--Oh Susannah. Holberg, Richard A. (1889-1942), illus. LC 39-30376. 5 p. l., 108 p. incl. illus., plates (part col., 1 double) 23 1/2 cm. 1939. Doubleday, Doran & Company, Inc.

--Restless Johnny: The Story Johnny Appleseed. 210p. (gr. 5-9). 1950. Thomas Y. Crowell Co.

--Rowena Carey. Paull, Grace A. (1898-), illus. LC 49-8893. 242 p. illus. 21 cm. 1949. Doubleday.

--Rowena the Sailor. 1st ed. Paull, Grace A. (1898-), illus. LC 54-6786. 224p. illus. 22cm. 1954. Doubleday.

--The Smugglers of Sandy. N.D. E . M. Hale and Co.

--The Smugglers of Sandy Bay. 1st ed. Werth, Kurt (1896-), illus. LC 57-114235. 192p. illus. 22cm. 1957. Doubleday.

--Tabitha's Hill. 1st ed. Werth, Kurt (1896-), illus. LC 56-10763. 223p. illus. 22cm. 1956. Doubleday.

--Tam Morgan: The Liveliest Girl in Salem. 1st ed. Spier, Peter Edward (1927-), illus. LC 53-50464. 224p. illus. 21cm. 1953. Doubleday.

--Tansy for Short. 1st ed. Moment, John, illus. LC 51-12839. 208 p. illus. 21 cm. 1951. Doubleday.

--Three Birthday Wishes. Weil, Lisl (1910-), illus. LC 53-5088. 121p. illus. 21cm. 1953. Crowell.

--Tibby's Venture. Cote, Phyllis N. (1921-), illus. LC 43-51308. 3 p. l., 122 p. illus. 24 cm. 1943. Doubleday, Doran & Company, Inc.

--Tomboy Row. 1st ed. Paull, Grace A. (1898-), illus. LC 52-5762. 220 p. illus. 21 cm. 1952. Doubleday.

--Wee Brigit O'Toole ... Holberg, Richard A. (1889-1942), illus. LC 38-27995. 32 p. illus. (part col.) 23 cm. 1938. Doubleday, Doran & Company, Inc.

--Wendy's Private Life. 1st ed. Magagna, Anna Marie, illus. LC 59-12631. 187p. illus. 22cm. 1959. Doubleday.

--What Happened to Virgilia. 1st ed. Lonette, Reisie Dominee (1924-), illus. LC 63-18232. 168 p. illus. 22 cm. 1963. Doubleday.

--The Wonderful Voyage. Cote, Phyllis N. (1921-), illus. LC 45-10299. 208 p. illus. 23 1/2 cm. 1945. Doubleday, Doran & Company, Inc.

Holbrock, Mabel Kohler

--Sally, a Doll Story. (Illus.). 54 p. 21cm. 1974. (ISBN 0-533-01036-5). Vantage.

Holbrook, A. W.

--The Little Terror. N.D. J. S. Ogilvie Co.

Holbrook, David Kenneth (1923-), ed.

--Thieves and Angels: Dramatic Pieces for Use in Schools. Miles, Bernard, frwd. by. LC 62-53198. 205p. illus. 22cm. 1962. Cambridge University Press.

Holbrook, David Kenneth (1923-) & McKenzie, Christine, eds.

--The Honey of Man. (Illus.). 123p. (gr. 4 up). 1977. (ISBN 0-684-14701-7). Scribner.

Holbrook, Florence (1860-1932)

--Hiawatha Alphabet. Pohl, Hugo D., illus. LC 10-19183. 60p. (gr. 6-8). 1910. Rand McNally & Co.

--Northland Heroes: The Stories of Fridthof and Beowulf. LC 5-36928. x p., 2 l., 3-111, 2 p. incl. front., illus. 19 1/2 cm. c.1905. Houghton, Mifflin and Company.

--Northland Heroes: The Stories of Fridthjof and Beowulf. (Riverside Literature Ser.). N.D. Houghton Mifflin Co.

Holbrook, Ruth

--Cap'n Benny's Birdhouses. LC 38-34135. 1938. Doubleday Doran & Co.

--Katy's Quilt. LC 40-30565. 78 p. incl. col. front., illus. (part col.) 25 1/2 cm. 1940. Doubleday, Doran & Co., Inc.

Holbrook, Sabra, pseud., see Erickson, Sabra Rollins.

Holbrook, Sabra, pseud. (1912-)

--Bruno & Karen of Berlin. Erickson, Sabra Rollins. (gr. 4-6). 1967. (ISBN 0-531-01626-9). Watts.

--The Goat That Made a Boy Grow Big. Erickson, Sabra Rollins. Petie, Haris, pseud. (1915-), illus. Petty, Roberta. LC 65-10879. 95p. illus. 23cm. c.1965. Coward.

--Sir Tristan of All Time. Erickson, Sabra Rollins. Arno, Enrico (1913-1981), illus. LC 70-113771. 192p. (gr. 7 up). 1970. (ISBN 0-374-36963-1). FS&G.

Holbrook, Stewart Hall (1893-1964)

--Wild Bill Hickok Tames the West. Richardson, Ernest, illus. LC 52-7224. (Illus.). 179 p. 22cm. (Landmark books 25). 1952. Random House.

--Wyatt Earp, U.S. Marshal. Richardson, Ernest, illus. LC 56-8824. 180p. illus. 22cm. (Landmark books 67). 1956. Random House.

Holbrook, Vincent W.

--Santa's North Pole Circus. 1st ed. Lyons, Dave, illus. LC 55-12528. 57p. illus. 21cm. 1955. Pageant Press.

Holcomb, Helen Harriet Howe, Mrs. (1836-)

--Mabel's Summer in the Himalayas. LC 12-34418. 192 p. front., plates. 18 cm. c.1886. Presbyterian Board of Publication.

Holden, Edith & Stott, Rowena

--The Hedgehogs' Feast. 1978. (Windmill). Dutton.

Holden, Edward Singleton (1846-1914), ed.

--Stories from the Arabian Nights. LC 1075. 4 p. l., vii-xxi, 1 248 p. incl. front., illus., pl. 18 1/2 cm. (Half-title: Appletons' home reading books, ed. by W. T. Harris ... Division iv. Literature). 1900. D. Appleton and Company.

Holden, Elisabeth

--Nate and the Traveling Store. Coe, Lloyd (1899-1976), illus. LC 62-16496. 87p. illus. 22cm. 1962. (ISBN 0-8038-4990-7). Hastings House.

Holden, John

--The Rattlesnake God. Orbaan, Albert F. (1913-), illus. LC 59-5453. 190p. illus. 21cm. 1959. John Day Co.

Holden, Molly (1927-)

--The Unfinished Feud. Charlton, Michael Alan (1923-), illus. LC 70-129481. (Illus.). 136 p. 21cm. 1970. Hawthorn Books.

Holden, Philip

--Fawn: The First Year in the Life of a Red Deer in New Zealand. Oliver, Tony, illus. LC 77-357198. (Illus.). 128 p. 22cm. 1976. (ISBN 0-340-19321-2). Hodder & Stoughton.

Holder, Charles Frederick (1851-1915)

--A Frozen Dragon and Other Tales: A Story Book of Natural History for Boys and Girls. Beard, James Carter (1837-) & Beard, Daniel Carter (1859-1941), illus. LC 4-29430. vi, 285 p. illus. 21 1/2 x 18 1/2 cm. 1888. Dodd, Mead & Company.

--Treasure Divers. (Illus.). N.D. Dodd, Mead & Co.

Holder, Glenn, jt. ed. see Lapman, Maurice.

Holder, Glenn (1906-)

--Talking Totem Poles. LC 72-11256. (Illus.). bibl. index. 64p. (gr. 3-7). 1973. Dodd.

Holdich, L. H.

--Anton, the Peasant Boy, 1 of 8 Vols. (Illus.). (Meadowside Stories). N.D. Set. Publications of the Methodist Book Concern.

--The Book: A Story of the Mountains, 1 of 8 Vols. (Illus.). (Meadowside Stories). N.D. Set. Publications of the Methodist Book Concern.

--Faithful Lina: The Story of Three Swiss Orphans. (Meadowside Stories). N.D. Nelson & Phillips.

--Faithful Lina: The Story of Three Swiss Orphans, 1 of 8 Vols. (Illus.). (Meadowside Stories). N.D. Set. Publications of the Methodist Book Concern.

--Good Daughters: Or, The Seashore and the Cottage, 1 of 8 Vols. (Illus.). (Meadowside Stories). N.D. Set. Publications of the Methodist Book Concern.

--Katie and Her Mother: Or, The Widow's Trust, 1 of 8 Vols. (Illus.). (Meadowside Stories). N.D. Set. Publications of the Methodist Book Concern.

--Meadowside: Or, Aunt Grace and Dora, 1 of 8 Vols. (Illus.). (Meadowside Stories). N.D. Set. Publications of the Methodist Book Concern.

--Meadowside Stories, 1 of 100 vols. (Illus.). (Selected Bks for Sunday School: No. 5). N.D. Set. Methodist Bk Concern.

--Sally Grafton and Her Teacher, 1 of 8 Vols. (Illus.). (Meadowside Stories). N.D. Set. Publications of the Methodist Book Concern.

--Victor: Or, Paris Troubles and Province Roses, 1 of 8 Vols. (Illus.). (Meadowside Stories). N.D. Set. Publications of the Methodist Book Concern.

Holding, Carlisle B. (1849-1929)

--Cash!. Or, Number Nineteen. N.D. Methodist Bk Concern.

--The Colonel's Charge. A Companion Volume to "The Little Corporal.". LC 12-34419. 354 p. 19 cm. 1891. Cranston & Stowe.

--Her Ben: A Tale of Foyal Resolves. LC 12-34420. 357 p. 19 cm. 1889. Cranston & Stowe.

--The Little Corporal: Or, For One Hundred Days. LC 12-360617. 357 p. 19 cm. 1891. Cranston & Stowe.

--An Odd Fellow: A Tale of Today. LC 12-34421. 391 p. front., plates. 18 1/2 cm. 1895. Cranston & Curts.

--Reuben, a Prince in Disguise. LC 12-34422. 315 p. 19 cm. 1890. Hunt & Eaton.

--Reuben: A Prince in Disguise. N.D. Methodist Bk Concern.

Holding, Elisabeth Sanxay (1889-)

--Miss Kelly. Johnson, Margaret Sweet (1893-1964), illus. LC 47-30838. 125 p. illus. 23 cm. 1947. W. Morrow.

Holding, Elizabeth E.

--A Little Leaven: A Missionary Story. (Illus.). N.D. Methodist Bk Concern.

Holding, James Clark Carlisle Jr. see Carlisle, Clark, pseud.

Holding, James Clark Carlisle, Jr. (1907-)

--A Bottle of Pop. Lynch, Lorenzo (1932-), illus. LC 79-163424. (Illus.). 47 p. 23cm. (See and read beginning to read storybook). 1972. Putnam.

--Cato the Kiwi Bird. Smith, Lee (1925-), illus. LC 63-15558. unpaged. illus. 25 cm. 1963. Putnam.

--The King's Contest, and Other North African Tales. Keeping, Charles William James (1924-), illus. LC 64-12187. 125 p. illus. (part col.) 22 cm. 1964. Abelard-Schuman.

--The Lazy Little Zulu. (Illus.). (gr. 2-4). 1962. (ISBN 0-8382-0426-0). Hale.

--The Lazy Little Zulu. Aliki, pseud. (1929-), illus. Brandenberg, Aliki Liacouras. LC 62-84847. unpaged. illus. 26cm. 1962. Morrow.

--Mister Moonlight & Omar. (Illus.). (gr. 2-4). 1963. (ISBN 0-8382-0535-6). Hale.

--Mr. Moonlight and Omar. Aliki, pseud. (1929-), illus. Brandenberg, Aliki Liacouras. LC 63-7200. (Illus.). 32 p. 26cm. 1963. Morrow.

--The Mystery of Dolphin Inlet. LC 68-11001. 198 p. 21cm. 1968. Macmillan.

--The Mystery of the False Fingertips. LC 64-11832. iv, 250 p. 22 cm. 1964. Harper & Row.

--Poko and the Golden Demon. Keeping, Charles William James (1924-), illus. LC 67-19608. (Illus.). 22cm. 125p. 1968. Abelard-Schuman.

--The Robber of Featherbed Lane. Allen, Laura Jean, illus. LC 68-24520. (Illus.). 43 p. 23cm. 1970. Putnam.

--Sherlock on the Trail. Aliki, pseud. (1929-), illus. Brandenberg, Aliki Liacouras. LC 64-11559. 1 v. (unpaged) col. illus. 21 x 24 cm. 1964. Morrow.

--The Sky-Eater and Other South Sea Tales. Keeping, Charles William James (1924-), illus. LC 65-228207. 124 p. illus. (part col.) 22 cm. 1965. Abelard-Schuman.

--The Three Wishes of Hu. Haley, Gail Einhart (1939-), illus. LC 65-10874. 62p. illus. (pt. col.) 24cm. c.1965. (ISBN 0-399-60632-7). Putnam.

--Weekly Reader Children's Book Club Presents The Ugliest Dog in the World. Miller, Marilyn Jean (1925-), illus. LC 78-78365. (Illus.). 31 p. 23cm. (Weekly Reader Children's Book Club). c.1979. (ISBN 0-88375-219-0). Xerox Education Publications.

--Weekly Reader Children's Book Club Presents The Watchcat. Miller, Marilyn Jean (1925-), illus. LC 74-17695. (Illus.). 62 p. 23cm. 1975. (ISBN 0-88375-206-9). Xerox Weekly Reader Family Books.

Holdridge, Betty

--Island Boy. Lantz, Paul (1908-), illus. LC 42-16018. 110, 1 p. col. illus. 21 x 16 cm. 1942. Holiday House.

Holdsworth, William Curtis, illus.

--The Gingerbread Boy. LC 68-23751. (Illus.). 25 p. 1968. Farrar, Straus, and Giroux.

--The Little Red Hen. LC 76-85360. (Illus.). 32 p. 23cm. 1969. Farrar, Strauss & Giroux.

Holelson, Doug, jt. auth. see Krogman, Dane.

Holhler, E., Mrs.

--The Picture on the Stairs. N.D. E. & J. B Young & Co.

Holiday, Ensor

--Altair Design. (Illus.). (gr. 1 up). 1973. (ISBN 0-394-82548-9). Pantheon.

Holkeboer, Tena

--God's Bridge: Or, The Story of Jin-gi. N.D. E. P. Dutton & Co.

Holl, Adelaide, jt. ed. see Ringi, Kjell Arne Sorensen.

Holl, Adelaide Hinkle (1910-), retold by see Lehoczky, Gyorgy.

Holl, Adelaide Hinkle (1910-), retold by see Newth, Mette.

Holl, Adelaide Hinkle (1910-)

--Bedtime for Bears. Szekeres, Cyndy (1933-), illus. LC 72-10460. (Illus.). 40 p. 24cm. 1973. (ISBN 0-8116-6727-8). Garrard Pub. Co.

--Bright, Bright Morning. Howard, Rob, illus. LC 69-14540. (Illus.). 36 p. 1969. Lothrop, Lee & Shepard Co.

--Colors are Nice. Shortall, Leonard W., illus. LC 66-9447. (Illus.). 22cm. 1966, c.1962. Golden Press.

--First Adventures in Learning Program. LC 63-17546. 16 v. vol. illus. 21 x 27 cm. 1963. Golden Book Educational Services.

--Gus Gets the Message. Morrison, Bill (1935-), illus. LC 74-8179. (Illus.). 63 p. 23cm. 1974. (ISBN 0-8116-6973-4). Garrard Pub. Co.

--Have You Seen My Puppy. Veno, Joseph, illus. (Illus.). (Early Bird Bks.). (ps-1). 1968. (ISBN 0-394-81249-2, BYR). (ISBN 0-394-91249-7). Random.

--Hide-and-Seek ABC. Ames, Lee Judah (1921-), illus. LC 74-142081. (Illus.). 60 p. 32cm. 1971. Platt & Munk.

--If We Could Make Wishes. Pelikan, Judy, illus. LC 76-16113. (Illus.). 47 p. 23cm. c.1977. (ISBN 0-8116-4401-4). Garrard Pub. Co.

--Journey to the Sea. Sickles, Noel, illus. LC 68-55406. (Illus.). 32 p. (Carousel book). c.1968. L. W. Singer Co.

--Let's Count. McQueen, Lucinda, illus. LC 71-11564. 27cm. 32p. c.1976. (ISBN 0-201-02899-9). Addison-Wesley.

--Lisette. Duvoisin, Roger Antoine (1904-1980), illus. LC 61-17693. unpaged. illus. 30cm. c.1962. Lothrop, Lee & Shepard.

--The Long Birthday. Gold, Ethel, illus. LC 74-8103. (Illus.). 63 p. 23cm. 1974. (ISBN 0-8116-6974-2). Garrard Pub. Co.

--Magic Tales. Karch, Pat & Karch, Paul, illus. LC 64-23031. 128 p. col. illus. 24 cm. (Told-again tales from many lands). c.1964. C. E. Merrill Books.

--The Man Who Had No Dream. Ringi, Kjell Arne Soerensen (1939-), illus. LC 78-90293. 34 p. col. ill. 27cm. c.1959. Random House.

--Man Who Had No Dream. Ringi, Kjell Arne Sorensen (1939-), illus. (Illus.). (gr. k-4). 1970. (ISBN 0-394-90838-4, BYR). Random.

--Minnikin, Midgie, and Moppet: A Mouse Story. Hillman, Priscilla (1940-), illus. LC 76-54599. (Illus.). 47 p. 26cm. (Kid's paperback ; 12362). c.1977. (ISBN 0-307-12362-6). Golden Press.

--Moon Mouse. Szekeres, Cyndy (1933-), illus. LC 69-17437. (Illus.). 34 p. 1969. Random House.

--Moon Mouse. Szekeres, Cyndy (1933-), illus. LC 72-9561. (Illus.). 32 p. 1973, c.1969. (ISBN 0-394-82624-8). Random House.

--Most-of-the-Time Maxie: A Story. Knight, Hilary (1926-), illus. LC 74-164368. (Illus.). 32 p. 21cm. 1974. (ISBN 0-88375-202-6). Xerox Family Education Services.

--Mrs. McGarrity's Peppermint Sweater. Graboff, Abner (1919-), illus. LC 66-14609. 1 v. (unpaged) illus. (part col.) 21 x 27 cm. 1966. Lothrop, Lee & Shepard Co.

--My Father and I. 1973. (ISBN 0-531-02560-8). Franklin Watts.

--My Father and I. Ringi, Kjell Arne Sorensen (1939-), created by. Ringi, Kjell Arne Sorensen (1939-), illus. LC 78-185922. (Illus.). 30 p. 29cm. 1972. (ISBN 0-531-02560-8). Watts.

--My Weekly Reader Picture Word Book. Perry, Alfred (1929-), illus. LC 74-29212. (Illus.). 128 p. 31cm. 1975. (ISBN 0-88375-105-4). Xerox Education Publications.

--New Friends for the Saggy Baggy Elephant. Neely, Jan & Alvarado, Peter, illus. (Illus.). (gr. k-3). 1976. (ISBN 0-307-60131-5, Golden Pr). Western Pub.

--One Kitten for Kim. Madden, Donald B. (1927-), illus. LC 69-15799. (Illus.). 32 p. 24cm. 1969. Addison-Wesley Pub. Co.

--The Parade. Ringi, Kjell Arne Sorensen (1939-), illus. LC 72-3840. (Illus.). 32p. (gr. k-3). 1975. (ISBN 0-531-02605-1). Watts.

--Poky Little Puppy Follows His Nose Home. Miclat, Alex, illus. (Illus.). (gr. k-3). 1977. (ISBN 0-307-60030-0, Golden Pr). Western Pub.

--The Poky Little Puppy's First Christmas. Winship, Florence Sarah, illus. LC 72-96318. (Illus.). 20 p. 32cm. 1973. Golden Press.

--The Rain Puddle. Duvoisin, Roger Antoine (1904-1980), illus. LC 65-220260. 1v. (unpaged) col. illus. 20x26cm. c.1965. (ISBN 0-688-51096-5). Lothrop.

--A Real Kitten. Henderson, Doris & Henderson, Marion, illus. LC 65-45824. (Illus.). 32p. (Our Animal Story Books). 1962. Heath and Co.

--The Remarkable Egg. Duvoisin, Roger Antoine (1904-1980), illus. LC 68-24455. (Illus.). 1 v. (unpaged). 1968. Lothrop, Lee & Shepard Co.

--The Runaway Giant. Funai, Mamoru R. (1932-), illus. LC 67-2942. 1 v. (unpaged) col. illus. 26 cm. 1967. Lothrop, Lee & Shepard.

--The Runaway Hat. Hirsh, Marilyn (1944-), illus. LC 68-58306. (Illus.). 24 p. 29cm. (Carousel book). 1969. L. W. Singer.

--Sir Kevin of Devon. Weisgard, Leonard Joseph (1916-), illus. LC 63-16778. unpaged. illus. 31 cm. 1963. Lothrop, Lee and Shepard.

--Small Bear and the Secret Surprise. Tien, illus. LC 77-17204. (Illus.). 47 p. 23cm. (Small Bear adventures). c.1978. (ISBN 0-8116-4455-3). Garrard Pub. Co.

--Small Bear Builds a Playhouse. Szekeres, Cyndy (1933-), illus. LC 77-11640. (Illus.). 46 p. 23cm. (Small Bear adventures). c.1978. (ISBN 0-8116-4454-5). Garrard Pub. Co.

--Small Bear Solves a Mystery. Cauley, Lorinda Bryan (1951-), illus. LC 78-16727. (Illus.). 46 p. 23cm. (Her Small Bear adventures). c.1979. (ISBN 0-8116-4456-1). Garrard Pub. Co.

--Small Bear's Birthday Party. Grant, Alice Leigh (1947-), illus. LC 77-5630. (Illus.). 46 p. 23cm. c.1977. (ISBN 0-8116-4453-7). Garrard Pub. Co.

--Small Bear's Busy Day. Ulrich, George M, illus. LC 77-910. p. cm. 1977. (ISBN 0-8116-4452-9). Garrard Pub. Co.

--Small Bear's Name Hunt. Bargielski, Pat, illus. LC 76-56141. (Illus.). 46 p. 23cm. c.1977. (ISBN 0-8116-4451-0). Garrard Pub. Co.

--Sylvester, the Mouse with the Musical Cat. Bodecker, Nils Mogens (1922-), illus. LC 61-13295. (Illus.). 22cm. 31p. 1961. Golden Press.

--Sylvester: The Mouse with the Musical Ear. Bodecker, Niels Mogens (1922-), illus. (Illus.). 33cm. 32p. 1st U.S. edition. (gr. k-3). 1973. (ISBN 0-307-12503-3, Golden Pr). (ISBN 0-307-62059-X). Western Pub.

--Too Fat to Fly. Morrison, Bill (1935-), illus. LC 72-12849. (Illus.). 39 p. 23cm. 1973. (ISBN 0-8116-6731-6). Garrard Pub. Co.

--Wake up, Small Bear. Bargielski, Pat, illus. LC 76-44318. (Illus.). 48 p. 23cm. c.1977. (ISBN 0-8116-4450-2). Garrard Pub. Co.

--Zeke the Raccoon. Henderson, Doris & Henderson, Marion, illus. LC 64-14991. (Illus.). 32p. (Our Animal Story Books). 1962. Heath Co.

Holl, Kristi D.

--Cast a Single Shadow. LC 83-15888. p. cm. 128p. (Escapade). 1985. (ISBN 0-689-31380-2). Atheneum/Escapade.

--Footprints up My Back. LC 84-6176. (Illus.). 168p. (gr. 4-7). 1984. (ISBN 0-689-31070-6). Atheneum.

--Just Like a Real Family. LC 82-16239. p. cm. 1983. (ISBN 0-689-30970-8). Atheneum.

--Mystery by Mail. LC 83-6425. p. cm. (Escapade). 1983. (ISBN 0-689-31374-8). Atheneum.

--The Rose Beyond the Wall. LC 85-7948. vi, 153 p. 22cm. 1985. (ISBN 0-689-31150-8). Atheneum.

Holladay, Virginia

--Bantu Tales. 1st ed. Crane, Louise, ed. Negri, Rocco (1932-), illus. LC 79-102927. (Illus.). 95 p. 23cm. 1970. (ISBN 0-670-14798-2). Viking Press.

Holland, Alice & Moore, Clement Clarke (1779-1863)

--The Story of Santa Claus and Mrs. Claus and "The Night Before Christmas.". Desow, Lillian, illus. LC 46-21785. 32 p. col. illus. 25 1/2 cm. 1946. The Children's Company.

Holland, Arthur J.

--The Adventures of Bernie Ben. Shcottman, Tom, illus. (Illus.). (Parent Read Aloud Ser.). (gr. k-4). 1984. (ISBN 0-911491-05-8). Nassau Pr.

Holland, Barbara Adams (1925-)

--Creepy-Mouse Coming to Get You. LC 84-14202. 109 p. 22cm. c.1985. (ISBN 0-89919-329-3). Clarion Books.

--The Pony Problem. LC 76-56772. 122 p. 22cm. c.1977. (ISBN 0-525-37345-4). Dutton.

--Prisoners at the Kitchen Table. LC 79-11730. p. cm. c.1979. (ISBN 0-8164-3239-2). Seabury Press.

--Prisoners of the Kitchen Table. 1979. Houghton.

Holland, Cecelia Anastasia (1943-)

--Ghost on the Steppe. Cuffari, Richard (1925-1978), illus. LC 69-18956. (Illus.). 141 p. 25cm. 1969. Atheneum.

--The King's Road. Cuffari, Richard (1925-1978), illus. LC 74-115071. (Illus.). 151 p. 25cm. 1970. Atheneum.

Holland, Clella

--Babby. Hull, Merle, illus. (Illus.). (gr. k-3). N.D. Vantage.

Holland, David & Day, Will

--Secret of the Old Church. Willman, Gordon, illus. LC 77-13776. (Illus.). 103 p. 23cm. (Bro-kee series). c.1978. (ISBN 0-570-07763-X). Concordia Pub. House.

Holland, Isabelle (1920-)

--Abbie's God Book. McLaughlin, James (1948-), illus. LC 81-21845. p. cm. c.1982. (ISBN 0-664-32688-9). Westminster Press.

--Alan and the Animal Kingdom. LC 76-55371. 191 p. 21cm. c.1977. (ISBN 0-397-31745-X). Lippincott.

--Amanda's Choice. LC 71-101901. 152 p. 22cm. 1970. Lippincott.

--Cecily: A Novel. 189 p. 21cm. 1967. Lippincott.

--Dinah & the Fat Green Kingdom. LC 78-8612. (gr. 5-12). 1978. (ISBN 0-397-31818-9, JBL-J). Har-Row.

--Dinah and the Fat Green Kingdom. LC 78-8612. p. cm. c.1978. (ISBN 0-397-31818-9). Lippincott.

--The Empty House. 1983. Harper.

--The Empty House. 1st ed. LC 82-48464. p. cm. c.1983. (ISBN 0-397-32005-1). (ISBN 0-397-32006-X). Lippincott.

--God, Mrs. Muskrat, and Aunt Dot. Krush, Beth (1918-) & Krush, Joe (1918-), illus. LC 82-23794. (Illus.). 77 p. 22cm. c.1983. (ISBN 0-664-32703-6). Westminster Press.

--Heads You Win, Tails I Lose: A Novel. LC 73-5811. 159 p. 22cm. 1973. (ISBN 0-397-31380-2). Lippincott.

--Hitchhike. LC 77-7931. 157 p. 21cm. c.1977. (ISBN 0-397-31751-4). Lippincott.

--A Horse Named Peaceable. LC 82-204. (Illus.). 160p. (gr. 5 up). 1982. (ISBN 0-688-00534-9). Lothrop.

--The Island. LC 84-11176. 182 p. 22cm. c.1984. (ISBN 0-316-36993-4). Little, Brown.

--Journey for Three. Robinson, Charles (1931-), illus. LC 74-17382. (Illus.). 105 p. 22cm. 1975, c.1974. Houghton Mifflin.

--Journey for Three. Robinson, Charles (1931-), illus. LC 74-166180. (Illus.). 105 p. 22cm. 1974. (ISBN 0-88375-201-8). Xerox Family Education Services.

--Kevin's Hat. Lubin, Leonard B., illus. LC 83-14857. (Illus.). 32p. (gr. k-3). 1984. (ISBN 0-688-02358-4). (ISBN 0-688-02360-6). Lothrop.

--The Man Without a Face. LC 73-6830. 248 p. 25cm. 1973, c.1972. (ISBN 0-8161-6111-9). G. K. Hall.

--The Man Without a Face. (gr. 6-9). 1972. Harper & Row.

--The Man Without a Face. LC 71-37736. 159 p. 21cm. 1972. (ISBN 0-397-31286-5). (ISBN 0-397-31211-3). Lippincott.

--Now Is Not Too Late. LC 79-22610. 159 p. 22cm. c.1980. (ISBN 0-688-41937-2). (ISBN 0-688-51937-7). Lothrop, Lee & Shepard Books.

--Of Love and Death and Other Journeys. LC 74-30012. p. cm. 1975. (ISBN 0-397-31566-X). Lippincott.

Hollis, James, ed. see Pettit, Terry, et al.

Hollis, Marcia

--The Witch of Shakerag Hollow, and Other Sewanee Ghosts. Hollis, Marcia, illus. LC 73-80865. (Illus.). xii, 58 p. 23cm. 1973. University Press.

Hollister, C. Warren (1930-) & Pike, Judith

--The Moons of Meer. Lebenson, Richard, illus. LC 69-17912. (Illus.). 208 p. 24cm. 1969. (ISBN 0-8066-2408-6). H. Z. Walck.

Hollister, Mary Brewster, Mrs. (1891-)

--Beggars of Dreams. Wiese, Kurt, illus. LC 37-175017. 5 p. l., 234, 1 p. incl. front., illus., plates. 21 cm. 1937. Dodd, Mead & Company).

--Bright Sky Tomorrow. Wood, Esther, pseud. (1905-), illus. Brady, Esther Wood. LC 40-13525. 3 p. l., 122 p. illus. 19 1/2 cm. c.1940. Friendship Press.

--Dike Against the Sea. Wiese, Kurt, illus. LC 48-3012. (Illus.). 20cm. 126p. (China). 1948. Friendship Press.

--Kee-Kee and Company: A Story of American Children in China. Wiese, Kurt (1887-1974), illus. LC 38-32013. 5 p. l., 3-192 p. incl. illus., plates. 21 cm. 1938. Dodd, Mead & Company.

--Mulberry Village: A Story of Country Life in China. Wiese, Kurt (1887-1974), illus. LC 36-21828. vii, 287 p. incl. front., illus. 21 cm. 1933. Dodd, Mead & Company.

--Pagoda Anchorage: A Story of Tea Clipper Days in China. Ayer, Margaret (0000-1981), illus. LC 39-32442. vii, 268 p. incl. illus., plates. 21 cm. 1939. Dodd, Mead & Company.

--River Children: A Story of Boat Life in China. Wiese, Kurt (1887-1974), illus. LC 35-18424. 5 p. l., 246 p. incl. front., illus. plates. 20 1/2 cm. 1935. Dodd, Mead & Company.

--Trailer Town. Thompson, Marjorie, illus. LC 45-8980. 4 p. l., 119 p. illus. 20 cm. 1945. Friendship Press.

Holliston, Carol

--Wild Rose. (Sweet Violets Library of Choice Books for Young Ladies). 1875. George Routledge & Sons.

--Wild Rose, and Other Tales. (Illus.). (Trap to Catch a Sunbeam). N.D. George Routledge & Sons.

Hollman, Darrell

--The Adventures of Hezikiah Hare & Ernie Byrd. 1978. (ISBN 0-89274-091-4). Harrison Hse.

Hollmann, Clide Anne (1896-1966)

--The Eagle Feather. Moyers, William (1916-), illus. LC 63-16170. 152 p. illus. 22 cm. 1963. Hastings House Publishers.

--Partners on the Santa Fe Trail. LC 62-8219. 160p. 21cm. 1962. Westminster Press.

Hollmann, Clide Anne (1896-1966) & Plummer, Myrtes Marie (1898-)

--Jim Bridger: King of Scouts. LC 53-10296. 157p. illus. 22cm. c.1953. Vantage Press.

Hollmann, Clide John see Hollmann, Clide Anne.

Hollmann, Clide John see Hollmann, Clide Anne (1896-1966) & Plummer, Myrtes Marie.

Hollom, Dora, adapted by.

--Class-Room Plays from Great Novels. LC 32-3175. 190 p., 1 l. incl. front. (port.) 15 1/2 cm. (Half-title: The Kings treasuries of literature. General editor: Sir A. T.Quiller Couch). 1931. J. M. Dent & Sons Ltd,.

Holloway, Charles W.

--Little Tweet. Gehr, Mary, illus. LC 51-25842. (Illus.). 17cm. 32p. (Tell-a-Tale Bks.). 1952. Whitman.

Holloway, Emory see Holloway, Rufus Emory.

Holloway, Jane

--At Flower Farm. Kay, Gertrude Alice (1884-1939), illus. LC 9-22270. 71 p. col. front., illus. 3 col. pl. 28 1/2 cm. $1.0. 1909. E. Stern & Co, Inc.

--Moses P. Pickles and Others. (Illus.). 98p. N.D. Barse and Hopkins.

--Moses P. Pickles and Others. 98p. N.D. Edward Stern & Co.

Holloway, Ronald

--Z is For Zagreb. N.D. (ISBN 0-498-01123-2). A. S. Barnes Company.

Holloway, Rufus Emory (1885-1977)

--Janice in Tomorrow-Land. LC 36-9228. vi, 208 p. illus. 19 1/2 cm. c.1936. American Book Company.

Holloway, Teresa Bragunier (1906-)

--Governor's Girl. LC 62-5526. 221 p. 20 cm. c.1961. Avalon Books.

--Heart's Haven. LC 55-13900. 253p. 21cm. 1955. Avalon Books.

--Rosemary King: Government Girl. LC 57-8722. 224p. 20cm. 1957. Avalon Books.

--Terry's Television Career. LC 57-12685. 222p. 21cm. 1957. Avalon Books.

Hollowell, Lillian, ed.

--A Book of Children's Literature. N.D. Farrar & Rinehart.

--A Book of Children's Literature. 3d Ed. LC 66-10189. xi, 580p. illus. 26cm. c.1966. Holt.

Hollowood, Jane

--Maggie & the Birthday Surprise. Hollowood, Jane, illus. (Illus.). (gr. k-6). N.D. Merry Thoughts.

--Maggie & the Chickens. Hollowood, Jane, illus. (Illus.). (gr. k-6). N.D. Merry Thoughts.

--Maggie in the Snow. Hollowood, Jane, illus. (Illus.). (gr. k-6). N.D. Merry Thoughts.

Holly, J. Hunter, pseud., see Holly, Joan Carol.

Holly, J. Hunter, pseud. (1932-) & Malzberg, Barry N.

--Graduated Robot & Other Stories. Holly, Joan Carol. Elwood, Roger (1943-), ed. Groenjes, Kathleen, illus. LC 73-21477. (Il!us.). 48p. (Science Fiction Bks.). (gr. 4-8). 1974. (ISBN 0-8225-0956-3). Lerner Pubns.

Holly, Joan Carol see Holly, J. Hunter, pseud.

Holly, S. B., Mrs. & Aunt Funny (1822-1894)

--Teresa's Book. LC 42-26900. 128 p. incl. front.,illus. 12 1/2 cm. (Twelve little sisters 8). 1881. D. & J. Sadlier & Co.

Hollyer, Belinda

--David & Goliath. Baxter, Leon, illus. LC 84-50452. (Illus.). 24p. (Bible Stories Ser.). (gr. 3 up). 1984. (ISBN 0-382-06940-4). (ISBN 0-382-06791-6). Silver.

--Jonah & the Great Fish. Baxter, Leon, illus. LC 84-50451. (Illus.). 24p. (Bible Stories Ser.). (gr. 3 up). 1984. (ISBN 0-382-06792-4). (ISBN 0-382-06941-2). Silver.

--Noah & the Ark. Baxter, Leon, illus. LC 84-50450. (Illus.). 24p. (Bible Stories Ser.). (gr. 3 up). 1984. (ISBN 0-382-06793-2). (ISBN 0-382-06942-0). Silver.

Hollyn, Lynn

--Lynn Hollyn's Christmas Toyland. Anzalone, Lori, illus. LC 85-5212. p. cm. 1985. (ISBN 0-394-87631-8). (ISBN 0-394-97631-2). Knopf.

Holm, Anne see Holm, Else Anne Lise.

Holm, Else Anne Lise (1922-)

--North to Freedom. (gr. 6-8). 1984. Peter Smith.

--North to Freedom. Kingsland, Leslie William (1912-), tr. LC 65-12612. 190 p. 21cm. 1965. Harcourt, Brace & World. **Award: (ALA).**

--North to Freedom. Kingsland, Leslie William (1912-), tr. LC 73-12928. 190 p. 19cm. (Voyager book, AVB 82). 1974, c.1965. (ISBN 0-15-666100-4). Harcourt Brace Jovanovich.

--Peter. Kingsland, Leslie William (1912-), tr. LC 67-17153. (gr. 7 up). 1968. (ISBN 0-15-261065-0). HarBraceJ.

Holm, Hannebo, pseud., see Tenfjord, Johanne Marie Giaever.

Holm, Hannebo

--Beauty Queen. LC 61-15711. 159 p. 21cm. 1962, c.1961. Abelard-Schuman.

Holm, John R.

--C Minus. Holm, John R., illus. (O.s.i.). (gr. 7-9). 1972 (Starline). Schol Bk Serv.

Holm, Mayling Mack

--A Forest Christmas. LC 76-58696. (Illus.). 32 p. 31cm. c.1977. (ISBN 0-06-022572-6). (ISBN 0-06-022573-4). Harper & Row.

Holm, Miriam Lorimer

--Youth. N.D. Augustana Book Concern.

Holman, Arthur

--My Dog Rex. 207p. N.D. Funk & Wagnalls.

Holman, Felice (1919-)

--At the Top of My Voice and Other Poems. N.D (W. W. Norton Juveniles For Children). Grosset & Dunlap Pub.

--At the Top of My Voice and Other Poems. 1st ed. Gorey, Edward St. John (1925-), illus. LC 75-36056. (Illus.). 55p. 21cm. 1976, c.1970. (ISBN 0-684-14562-6). Charles Scribner's Sons.

--At the Top of My Voice And Other Poems. Gorey, Edward St. John (1925-), illus. LC 68-22728. (Illus.). 55 p. 21cm. 1970. W. W. Norton.

--The Blackmail Machine. De Larrea, Victoria, illus. LC 68-11002. (Illus.). 182 p. 21cm. 1967, c.1968. Macmillan.

--The Cricket Winter. N.D. Grosset & Dunlap.

--The Cricket Winter. 1st ed. Pinto, Ralph, illus. (Illus.). 107 p. 21cm. 1967. W. W. Norton.

--Elisabeth and the Marsh Mystery. Blegvad, Erik (1923-), illus. LC 66-11105. 50 p. illus. 22 cm. 1966. Macmillan.

--Elisabeth & the Marsh Mystery. Blegvad, Erik (1923-), illus. LC 66-11105. (Illus.). 64p. (gr. k-3). 1974. (ISBN 0-02-043660-2, Collier). Macmillan.

--Elisabeth, the Bird Watcher. Blegvad, Erik (1923-), illus. LC 63-16362. (Illus.). 43 p. 23cm. 1963. Macmillan.

--Elisabeth, the Treasure Hunter. Blegvad, Erik (1923-), illus. LC 64-12538. 41 p. illus. 23 cm. 1964. Macmillan.

--The Escape of the Giant Hogstalk. Shecter, Ben (1935-), illus. LC 72-1169. (Illus.). 94 p. 21cm. 1974. (ISBN 0-684-13174-9). Scribner.

--The Future of Hooper Toote. Wilson, Gahan (1930-), illus. LC 77-180757. (Illus.). 138 p. 22cm. 1972. (ISBN 0-684-12688-5). Scribner.

--The Holiday Rat & the Utmost Mouse. 1st ed. Tripp, Wallace Whitney (1940-), illus. LC 79-81911. (Norton Juvenile Ser). (gr. 2-6). 1969. (ISBN 0-448-21368-0). (ISBN 0-448-26139-1). G&D.

--The Holiday Rat and the Utmost Mouse. Tripp, Wallace Whitney (1940-), illus. LC 79-81911. (Illus.). 79 p. 21cm. 1969. Norton.

--I Hear You Smiling. Kubinyi, Laszlo (1937-), illus. (Illus.). (Encore Edition). (gr. 4-6). 1973. (ISBN 0-684-15840-X). Scribner.

--I Hear You Smiling, and Other Poems. Kubinyi, Laszlo (1937-), illus. LC 72-7122. (Illus.). 62 p. 21cm. 1973. (ISBN 0-684-13512-4). Scribner.

--Professor Diggins' Dragons. Ohlsson, Ib (1935-), illus. Valen, Nanine Elisabeth. (1950-), contrib. by. LC 66-16103. 133p., music (2p.) illus. 21cm. c.1966. Macmillan.

--Professor Diggins' Dragons. Ohlsson, Ib (1935-), illus. (Illus.). (gr. 4-6). 1967. Macmillan.

--Professor Diggins' Dragons. Ohlsson, Ib (1935-), illus. LC 66-16103. (Illus.). 144p. (gr. 3-7). 1974. (ISBN 0-02-043680-7, Collier). Macmillan.

--Silently, the Cat, and Miss Theodosia. Dinnerstein, Harvey (1928-), illus. LC 65-15188. 58p. illus. 23cm. c.1965. Macmillan.

--Slake's Limbo. LC 74-11675. 117 p. 22cm. 1974. (ISBN 0-684-13926-X). Scribner.

--Solomon's Search. Richter, Mischa (1910-), illus. LC 73-127733. (Illus.). 58 p. 24cm. 1970. Grosset & Dunlap.

--The Song in My Head. Spanfeller, James John (1930-), illus. LC 84-23573. (Illus.). 62 p. 21cm. c.1985. (ISBN 0-684-18295-5). Scribner.

--Victoria's Castle. Hoban, Lillian (1925-), illus. LC 66-10784. 40p. col. illus. 26cm. 1966. Norton.

--The Wild Children. LC 85-3541. 149 p. 20cm. 1985, c.1983. (ISBN 0-14-031930-1). Puffin Books.

--The Wild Children. LC 83-8974. 151 p. 22cm. c.1983. (ISBN 0-684-17970-9). Scribner.

--The Witch on the Corner. 1st ed. Lobel, Arnold Stark (1933-), illus. LC 66-8359. (Illus.). 89 p. 24cm. 1966. Norton.

--A Year to Grow. McCully, Emily Arnold (1939-), illus. LC 68-27636. (Illus.). 100 p. 21cm. 1968. Norton.

Holman, Felice (1919-) & Valen, Nanine Elisabeth (1950-)

--The Drac: French Tales of Dragons and Demons. Walker, Stephen (1951-), illus. LC 75-4029. (Illus.). ix, 84 p. 21cm. c.1975. (ISBN 0-684-14334-8). Scribner.

Holman-Hunt, Diana

--My Grandmothers and I. 1961. Norton & Co.

Holmberg, Ake (1907-)

--Margaret's Story. Bothmer, Gerry, tr. LC 61-7698. 190p. 21cm. 1961. Viking Press.

Holme, Bryan (1913-), ed. see Grimm, Jakob Ludwig Karl (1785-1863) & Grimm, Wilhelm Karl.

Holme, Bryan (1913-), ed.

--Fairy Tales of Hans Christian Andersen. Nielsen, Kay Rasmus (1886-1957), illus. (Illus.). 156p. 1981. (ISBN 0-670-30557-X, Studio). Viking Pr.

--Tales from Times Past. LC 77-4665. (Illus.). 175 p. 24cm. (Studio book). 1977. (ISBN 0-670-69159-3). Viking Press.

Holmes, Agnes Kennedy, compiled by.

--Songs Children Sing. 1954. Broadman Press.

--Story Hour Songs. N.D. Broadman Press.

Holmes, Alfred I, ed.

--The Cute Sayings of Our Little Ones, and Poems of Childhood. 350 p. 18 1/2 cm. 1889. The Author.

Holmes, Barbara Ware

--Charlotte Cheetham, Master of Disaster. Himmelman, John, illus. LC 85-42617. (Illus.). 117 p. 22cm. c.1985. (ISBN 0-06-022587-4). (ISBN 0-06-022588-2). Harper & Row.

Holmes, Burnham (1942-)

--The Mysterious Ghosts of Flight Four Hundred One. LC 78-21852. (Unsolved Mysteries of the World Ser.). N.D. (ISBN 0-686-79596-2). Silver.

Holmes, Darryl, ed. see Keel-Williams, Mildred.

Holmes, Efner Tudor (1949-)

--Amy's Goose. Tudor, Tasha (1915-), illus. LC 77-3027. (Illus.). 32 p. c.1977. (ISBN 0-690-03800-3). (ISBN 0-690-03801-1). Crowell.

--Carrie's Gift. Tudor, Tasha (1915-), illus. LC 78-8452. p. cm. c.1978. (ISBN 0-529-05428-0). (ISBN 0-529-05429-9). CollinsWorld.

--Carrie's Gift. Tudor, Tasha (1915-), illus. 1978. Putnam.

--The Christmas Cat. Tudor, Tasha (1915-), illus. LC 76-14802. (Tasha Tudor is the lagal name change for Starling Burgess.). p. cm. 1976. (ISBN 0-690-01267-5). Crowell.

Holmes, F. Morell

--The Children of the Court, and Two Little Waifs, 1 of 6 vols. (Illus.). 230p. (The Evening Hour Library). N.D. Cassell, Petter, Galpin.

--The Children of the Court: And Two Little Waifs, 1 vol. (Illus.). 230p. N.D. Cassell & Co.

--Hugh Melville's Quest: A Boy's Adventures in the Days of the Armada. Boucher, W (0000-1906), illus. (Illus.). N.D. J. B. Lippincott.

--Jack Marston's Anchor, 1 vol. Juv ed. Macnab, P., illus. N.D. Cassell & Co.

Holmes, F. Ratcliffe

--The Secret People: Adventure in Africa. Best, Allena Champlin, Mrs. (1892-1974), illus. Berry, Erick, pseud. LC 28-8641. 6 p. l., 258 p. col. front. 21 cm. 1928. Doubleday, Doran & Company, Inc.

Holmes, Keith D.

--Songs of the Maggodee. Eames, Sarah S., illus. (Illus.). 95p. (Orig.). 1982. (ISBN 0-9608250-0-2). Educ Serv Pub.

Holmes, Lillian

--Little Sir Galahad. LC 4-34933. (Illus.). 17cm. 61p. 1904. D. C. Cook.

Holmes, Lora L., jt. auth. see Gaynor, Jessie Love Smith, Mrs.

Holmes, Mabel Dodge (1883-), ed. see Swift, Jonathan.

Holmes, Mabel Dodge, ed. see Wyss, Johann David Von.

Holmes, Marion

--Jungle Prize. 1955. Friendship Press.

Holmes, Marjorie, adapted by see Cooper, James Fenimore.

Holmes, Marjorie (1910-)

--Cherry Blossom Princess. LC 60-5124. 188p. 21cm. c.1960. Westminster Press.

--Follow Your Dream. LC 61-5484460. 188p. 21cm. 1961. Westminster Press.

--Love Is a Hopscotch Thing. LC 63-8060. 192 p. 21 cm. 1963. Westminster Press.

--Saturday Night. LC 59-508384. 203p. 21cm. 1959. Westminster Press.

--Senior Trip. LC 62-719650. 192p. 21cm. 1962. Westminster Press.

Holmes, Mary Jane Hawes, Mrs. (1828-1907)

--The Christmas Font. A Story for Young Folks. LC 7-6005. 2 p. l., 9067 p. front., plates 14 1/2 cm. 1868. G.W. Carleton.

--Christmas Stories. 1885. G. W. Carleton & Co.

--Dora Deane. (Illus.). N.D. J. S. Ogilvie.

--Ethelyn's Mistake; or, The Home in the West: A Novel. LC 1-18494. 330 p. 12. 1869. Carleton.

--Maggie Miller: or, Old Hagar's Secret. (Illus.). (Knickerbocker Classics). N.D. Hurst & Co.

--Red-Bird: A Brown Cottage Story. LC 7-600405. 2 p. l., vii-viii, 9-107 p. front.,plates. 15 cm. 1890. G. W. Carleton & Co.

--Redbirds Christmas Storeis. (Illus.). N.D. G. W. Carleton.

Holmes, Oliver Wendell (1809-1894)

--Autocrat of the Breakfast-Table. (Riverside Literature Ser.). N.D. Houghton Mifflin Ser.

--The Deacon's Masterpiece: Or, The Wonderful One-Hoss Shay. Galdone, Paul (1914-), illus. LC 65-22595. 32p. illus. (pt. col.) 26cm. c.1965. (ISBN 0-07-029615-4). McGraw.

--Grandmother's Story of Bunker Hill. McVickar, H. W., illus. N.D. White, Stokes & Allen.

--Grandmother's Story of Bunker Hill Battle, and Other Poems. (Riverside Literature Ser.). N.D. Houghton Mifflin Co.

--Grandmother's Story of Bunker Hill Battle. LC 12-34365. 18cm. 96p. (Riverside Literature Ser.: No. 6). 1891. Houghton, Mifflin And Co.

--Grandmother's Story of Bunker Hill Battle. LC 3-13797. (Illus.). 18cm. 96p. (The Riverside School Library). 1903. Houghton Mifflin & Co.

--The Professor at the Breakfast-Table. (Cambridge Classics). N.D. Houghton Mifflin Co.

--The School-Boy. N.D. Houghton, Mifflin And Co.

Holmes, Ruth Vickery

--Model Theatre Plays. LC 40-358526. 61 p. 19 cm. c.1940. S. French.

--Short Plays for Small People. LC 38-377921. 178 p. diagr. 18 1/2 cm. c.1938. S. French.

Holmes, Thomas K., pseud., see Stratemeyer Syndicate.

Holmes, Thomas K., pseud.

--The Heart of Canyon Pass. Stratemeyer Syndicate. Repr. of 1921 ed (Pub. by George Sully & Co). N.D. A. L. Burt.

--The Heart of Canyon Pass. Stratemeyer Syndicate. 1921. George Sully & Co.

--The Man from Tall Timber. Stratemeyer Syndicate. Repr. of 1919 ed (Pub. by George Sully & Co). 1922. A. L. Burt.

--The Man from Tall Timber. Stratemeyer Syndicate. 1919. George Sully & Co.

Holmes, Thomas W. & Holmes, Blanche Fisher, illus.

--The Real Book of Nursery Tales. Storeis of the Three Little Pigs, Henny Penny, the Three Bears, Little Red Ridinghood and the Three Little Kittens. LC 50-14286. 57 p. col. illus. 31 cm. 1950. Garden City Pub. Co.

Holmes, William Kersley (1882-), tr. see Andersen, Hans Christian.

Holmes, William Kersley (1882-), tr. see Rosenfeld, Friedrich.

Holmgren, Virginia Cunningham see Cunningham, Virginia.

Holmgren, Virginia Cunningham (1909-)

--The Adventures of Brother Cat. McIlrath, James, illus. LC 79-84533. (Illus.). 46 p. 24cm. c.1979. (ISBN 0-87973-356-X). Our Sunday Visitor.

--Stories from the Odyssey. Lang, Jeanie & Chisholm, Louey (1872-), eds. Robinson, William Heath (1872-1944), illus. LC 8-6084. 4 p. l., 118 p. col. front., 7 col. pl. 15 x 12 cm. (Half-title: Told to the children series). N.D. T. C. & E. C. Jack.

--The Story of the Iliad. Condensed. Church, Alfred John (1829-1912), retold by. Blaisdell, Albert Franklin (1847-), illus. LC 12-31411. 64 p. 17 cm. (English classic series. no. 59). c.1886. Clark & Maynard.

--The Story of the Iliad. Church, Alfred John (1829-1912), retold by. Flaxman, John (1755-1826), illus. xii, 314 p. 16 col. pl. 19 cm. 1902. The Macmillan Company.

--The Story of the Iliad: Or, The Siege of Troy. Flaxman, John (1755-1826), illus. LC 13-18246. 346 p. illus. 19 1/2cm. (Classic Stories Ser. for Boys and Girls). 1890. The Penn Publishing Company.

--The Story of the Odyssey. Church, Alfred John (1829-1912), retold by. Flaxman, John (1755-1826), illus. LC 4-14081. vii, 306 p. 16 col. pl. 19 cm. 1891. Macmillan and Co.

--The Story of the Odyssey. Church, Alfred John (1829-1912), retold by. LC 5-960432. xiii, 232 p. incl. front. (port.) 15 cm. (Macmillan's pocket American and English classics). 1905. The Macmillan Company.

--The Story of the Odyssey: Or, The Adventures of Ulysses. LC 19-390324. 370 p. incl. plates. front. 19cm. (Classic Stories Ser.for Boys and Girls). 1892. The Penn Publishing Company.

--The Story of Ulysses for Boys and Girls. LC 26-22501. 3 p. l., iii-xv, 6-154, viii p. illus. 19 cm. 1923. Public School Publishing Co.

--The Toils and Travels of Odysseus. Center, Stella Stewart, ed. Pease, Cyril Arthington (1868-), tr. LC 27-3026. viii, 2, 428 p. front., illus. (incl. map) plates. 17 cm. (Academy classics for junior high schools). c.1926. Allyn and Bacon.

--The Toils & Travels of Odysseus. Pape, Frank Cheyne (1878-), illus. Pease, Cyril Arthington (1868-), tr. LC 18-26481. xvii, 340 p. incl. front., plates. fold. map. 21 cm. N.D. Frederick A. Stokes Company.

--The Trojan Horse. Reeves, James (1909-), retold by. Turska, Krystyna Zofia (1933-), illus. LC 68-29697. (Illus.). 32 p. 29cm. 1969, c.1968. F. Watts.

--The Trojan War. Witt, Karl (1815-1891), retold by. Younghusband, Frances, tr. v p., 1 l., 102 p. 18 cm. 1900. Longmans, Green, and Co.

Homerus, jt. auth. see Church, Alfred John.

Homerus, jt. auth. see Clarke, Michael.

Homerus, jt. auth. see Colum, Padraic.

Homerus, jt. auth. see Cullen, James J.

Homerus, jt. auth. see Gale, Agnes Spofford Cook, Mrs.

Homerus, jt. auth. see Perry, Walter Copland.

Homerus see White, Anne Terry.

Homerus & Church, Alfred John (1829-1912)

--The Iliad and the Odyssey of Homer. Karlin, Eugene (1918-), illus. LC 64-21760. (Illus.). 277 p. 24cm. (Macmillan classics, 26). 1964. Macmillan.

Homespun, Sophia, pseud., see Mannouth, E. H..

Homespun, Sophia, pseud.

--Blue-Eyed Jimmie: Or, The Good Boy. Mannouth, E. H.. (Illus.). (Child Life Ser.). N.D. D. Lothrop Co.

--Blue-Eyed Jimmy: The Good Boy. Mannouth, E. H., 1 of 5 vols. (Homespun Library). N.D. D. Lothrop & co.

--Homespun Library: Containing "Blue-Eyed Jimmy, or The Good Boy," "Ruthie Shaw, or The Good Girl," "Johnny Jones, or The Bad Boy," etc. Mannouth, E. H., 5 vols. N.D. Set. D. Lothrop & Co.

--Johnny Jones: Or, The Bad Boy. Mannouth, E. H., 1 of 5 vols. (Illus.). (Homespun Library). N.D. D. Lothrop Co.

--Johnny Jones: Or, The Bad Boy. Mannouth, E. H.. (Child Life Ser.). N.D. D. Lothrop & Co.

--Much Fruit. Mannouth, E. H., 1 of 5 vols. (Illus.). (Homespun Library). N.D. D. Lothrop & Co.

--Much Fruit. Mannouth, E. H.. (Child Life Ser.). N.D. D. Lothrop & Co.

--Nettie Nesmith: Or, The Bad Girl. Mannouth, E. H., 1 of 5 vols. (Illus.). (Homespun Library). N.D. D. Lothrop Co.

--Nettie Nesmith: The Bad Girl. Mannouth, E. H.. 1870. D. Lothrop & Co.

--Ruthie Shaw: Or, the Good Girl. Mannouth, E. H., 1 of 5 vols. (Illus.). (Homespun Library). N.D. D. Lothrop & Co.

--Ruthie Shaw: Or, The Good Girl. Mannouth, E. H.. (Illus.). (Child Life Ser.). N.D. Lothrop Pub. Co.

Homola, Priscilla

--The Willow Whistle. Lewin, Ted (1935-), illus. LC 83-11698. (Illus.). 109 p. 21cm. c.1983. (ISBN 0-396-08207-6). Dodd, Mead.

Honegger-Lavater, Warja

--The Cricket and the Ant. (Folded Story Ser.). 1964. George Wittenborn Inc.

--Extra-Ordinary Lemuel. 1964. George Wittenborn Inc.

--The Good Intention Is Blue. 1964. George Wittenborn Inc.

--Lucky Jack. (Ger). (gr. 3-7). 1967. (ISBN 0-87663-055-7). Universe.

--Match. 1964. George Wittenborn Inc.

--Night and Day and Night. 1964. George Wittenborn Inc.

--Party. 1964. George Wittenborn Inc.

--The Ugly Duckling. (Ger). (gr. 3-7). 1967. (ISBN 0-87663-056-5). Universe.

Honeycutt, Natalie

--Invisible Lissa. Rutherford, Jenny, illus. LC 84-20466. 168 p. 22cm. c.1985. (ISBN 0-02-744360-4). Bradbury Press.

Honeyman, Arthur

--Sam and His Cart. De Waide, Michael, illus. LC 80-36714. p. cm. 1980. (ISBN 0-88436-793-2). EMC Pub. Co.

--Sam and His Cart. De Waide, Michael, illus. LC 78-100794. (Illus.). 56 p. 24cm. c.1977. Wheel Press.

Hong, Edna Hatlestad (1913-)

--Bright Valley of Love. LC 75-22723. 160p. 1979. (ISBN 0-8066-1700-4). Augsburg.

Hong, Edna Hatlestad (1913-) & Hong, Howard (1912-)

--Muskego Boy. Mero, Lee, illus. LC 43-6281. 3 p. l., 96 p. illus. (part col.) 29 1/2 x 23 cm. 1943. Augsburg Publishing House.

Hong, Howard, jt. auth. see Hong, Edna Hatlestad.

Honig, Donald (1931-)

--Breaking In. Powers, Bill (1931-), illus. LC 73-9547. (Illus.). 48p. (gr. 3 up). 1973. (ISBN 0-531-02658-2). Watts.

--Coming Back. Powers, Bill (1931-), illus. (Illus.). 48p. (gr. 3 up). 1974. (ISBN 0-531-02661-2). (ISBN 0-531-02369-9). Watts.

--Dynamite!. LC 71-108011. 144 p. 22cm. 1971. Putnam.

--An End of Innocence. LC 72-75013. (Illus.). 128 p. 21cm. 1972. (ISBN 0-399-20254-4). (ISBN 0-399-60768-4). Putnam.

--Fury on Skates. LC 74-8333. p. 1974. (ISBN 0-590-07353-2). Four Winds Press.

--Going the Distance. Powers, Bill (1931-), illus. LC 73-11403. p. (Target book). 1974. (ISBN 0-531-02679-5). Educational Services.

--Hurry Home. Irvin, Fred M (1914-), illus. LC 75-9923. (Illus.). 32 p. 22cm. c.1976. (ISBN 0-201-02975-8). Addison-Wesley.

--In the Days of the Cowboy. (Illus.). 1970. (ISBN 0-394-80484-8). (ISBN 0-394-90484-2). Random House.

--Jed McLane and Storm Cloud. Savitt, Al, illus. LC 67-25353. (Illus.). 140 p. 22cm. 1968. McGraw-Hill.

--Jed McLane and the Stranger. Savitt, Al, illus. LC 75-85159. (Illus.). 158 p. 21cm. 1969. McGraw-Hill.

--Johnny Lee. 1971. E.P. Dutton & Co.

--Johnny Lee. LC 75-135440. 115 p. 21cm. 1971. (ISBN 0-8415-2023-2). McCall Pub. Co.

--The Journal of One Davey Wyatt. Fink, Sam (1916-), illus. LC 74-171901. (Illus.). 122 p. 22cm. 1972. (ISBN 0-531-02040-1). Watts.

--Playing for Keeps. Powers, Bill (1931-), illus. LC 73-9543. (Illus.). 47 p. (Target book). 1974. (ISBN 0-531-02659-0). Educational Services.

--The Professional. Powers, Bill (1931-), illus. LC 73-9545. 48p. (gr. 3 up). 1974. (ISBN 0-531-02660-4). Watts.

--Running Harder. Powers, Bill (1931-), illus. (Illus.). 48p. (Target Bks.). (gr. 3 up). 1976. (ISBN 0-531-01184-4). Watts.

--Way to Go, Teddy. LC 72-8494. 147 p. 21cm. 1973. (ISBN 0-531-02604-3). F. Watts.

--Winter Always Comes. LC 76-54874. 135 p. 22cm. c.1977. (ISBN 0-590-07452-0). Four Winds Press.

Honness, Elizabeth Hoffman, Mrs. (1904-)

--Belinda Balloon and the Big Wind. Doane, Pelagie (1906-1966), illus. LC 40-11021. (Illus.). 23cm. 32p. N.D. Grosset & Dunlap.

--Did You Ever?. Doane, Pelagie (1906-1966), illus. LC 40-31949. 30 p. col. illus. 23 x 21 cm. c.1940. Oxford University Press.

--The Fight of Fancy. 44p. 1941. Oxford University Press.

--The Great Gold Piece Mystery. Wilkin, Eloise Burns (1904-), illus. LC 61-493159. 192p. illus. 21cm. 1960, c.1944. Lippincott.

--The Great Gold Piece Mystery. Wilkin, Eloise Burns (1904-), illus. LC 44-7836. 3 p. l., 122 p. incl. front., illus. 21 cm. 1944. Oxford University Press.

--Mystery at the Doll Hospital. 1st ed. Ilsley, Velma Elizabeth (1918-), illus. LC 55-7985. 183p. illus. 22cm. 1955. (ISBN 0-397-31604-6). Lippincott.

--Mystery at the Villa Caprice. 1st ed. Frame, Paul (1913-), illus. LC 76-82405. (Illus.). 174 p. 22cm. 1969. Lippincott.

--Mystery in the Square Tower. LC 57-10325. 155 p. illus. 21 cm. 1957. Lippincott.

--Mystery of the Auction Trunk. 1st ed. Morse, Dorothy Bayley (1906-1979), illus. LC 56-9270. 191p. illus. 21cm. 1956. (ISBN 0-397-30337-8). Lippincott.

--Mystery of the Diamond Necklace. 1st ed. Merwin, Decie (1894-1961), illus. LC 54-7295. 1954. Lippincott.

--Mystery of the Hidden Face. LC 63-18500. 154 p. illus. 21 cm. 1963. Lippincott.

--Mystery of the Maya Jade. Frame, Paul (1913-), illus. 1971. Harper.

--Mystery of the Maya Jade. Frame, Paul (1913-), illus. LC 75-141454. (Illus.). 176 p. 21cm. 1971. Lippincott.

--Mystery of the Pirate's Ghost. 1st ed. Krush, Joe (1918-) & Krush, Beth (1918-), illus. LC 66-9581. (Illus.). 160 p. 21cm. 1966. Lippincott.

--Mystery of the Secret Message. Krush, Joe (1918-) & Krush, Beth (1918-), illus. LC 61-14637. (Illus.). 188 p. 21cm. 1961. Lippincott.

--Mystery of the Wooden Indian. 1st ed. Morse, Dorothy Bayley (1906-1979), illus. LC 58-868158. 188p. illus. 21cm. 1958. (ISBN 0-397-30428-5). Lippincott.

--Sammy Squirrel Goes to Town. Doane, Pelagie (1906-1966), illus. LC 37-14282. 54, 1 p. incl. front., illus., plates. 23 cm. 1937. T. Nelson and Sons.

--The Spy at Tory Hole. Distler, Pamela, illus. LC 75-43446. p. cm. (Bicentennial Historiettes Ser.). 1975. (ISBN 0-915892-03-0). Regional Center for Educational Training.

--The Tail of the Sorry Sorrel Horse. Doane, Pelagie (1906-1966), illus. LC 36-17480. (Illus.). 17 x 22cm. 48p. 1936. T. Nelson & Sons.

Honour, Alan

--Cave Riches. N.D. McGraw-Hill.

--Man Who Could Read Stones: The Champollion & the Rosetta Stone. Aviles, Anthony, illus. (Illus.). (gr. 8 up). 1966. Hawthorn.

Honsinger, Welthy

--Travels of Kin and Chin Chu: The Korean Twins. N.D. Abingdon Press.

--Travels of Mona and Mani: The Indian Twins. N.D. Abingdon Press.

--Travels of Tan and Taro: The Japanese Twins. N.D. Abingdon Press.

--Travels of Wen Chi and Wen Bao: The Chinese Twins. N.D. Abingdon Press.

Hood, Basil Charles Willett (1864-1917) & Johnson, Richard (1573-1659)

--Saint George of England. Appleton, Honor C., illus. LC 22-794. 185, 1 p. col. front., col. plates. 19 cm. 1920. J. B. Lippincott Company.

Hood, Christopher, jt. auth. see Hood, Jasper.

Hood, E.

--A Head of Police. N.D. Doubleday Doran & Co.

Hood, Edwin Paxton (1820-1885)

--Blind Amos and his Velvet Principles. N.D. Alfred Martien.

--Bye-path Meadow, 1 of 4 vols. (Shell Cove Ser.). N.D. D. Lothrop & Co.

Hood, Flora Mae (1898-)

--The Longest Beard in the World. Luhrs, Henry, illus. LC 62-13800. (Illus.). 24cm. 47p. 1962. Golden, Gate Junior Books.

--One Luminaria for Antonio: A Story of New Mexico. Kirn, Ann Minette (1910-), illus. LC 67-1013. (Illus.). 23cm. 46p. (See & Read Storybooks Ser). (gr. 1-3). 1966. (ISBN 0-399-60498-7). Putnam.

--Pink Puppy. Spanfeller, James John (1930-), illus. LC 66-14325. (Illus.). 47 p. 26cm. 1967, c.1966. Putnam.

--Something for the Medicine Man. Dranko, Robert, illus. LC 62-7001. (Illus.). 22cm. 47p. (Look, Read, Learn). 1962. Melmont Publishers.

Hood, Flora Mae (1898-), ed.

--The Turquoise Horse: Prose & Poetry of the American Indian. Reifsnyder, Marylou, illus. LC 72-81586. (Illus.). 32 p. 1972. (ISBN 0-399-60744-7). Putnam.

Hood, Flora Mae (1898-) & Gerson, Thomas Isaac (1906-)

--Uncle Sam. 1963. (ISBN 0-672-50553-3). Bobbs-Merrill.

Hood, Jane Reynolds, jt. auth. see Hood, Thomas.

Hood, Jasper & Hood, Christopher

--Contact with Maldonia. (Illus.). 176p. (gr. 3-6). 1983. (ISBN 0-434-94327-4, Pub. by W Heinemann). David & Charles.

Hood, John Edward (1924-)

--Guardians of the Forest. 1st Amer. ed. LC 63-10971. 21cm. 192p. 1962, c.1961. Putnam.

Hood, Margaret Graham

--Tales of Discovery: On the Pacific Slope. LC 98-160. vi, 7-172 p. incl. illus., plates. col. front. 18 cm. (Western series of readers. Ed. by H. Wagner ... v. 4). 1898. The Whitaker & Ray Company (Incorporated.

Hood, Mary G.

--For Girls and the Mothers of Girls. N.D. Bobbs-Merrill Company.

Hood, Mary L

--The Pranks of Two Jolly Goblins. Daley, Rena A. & Moore, Isabel, illus. LC 28-21405. 4 p. l., 7-127, 1 p. incl. front., illus., plates. 18 1/2 cm. 1928. A. Flanagan Company.

Hood, Thomas (1835-1874), tr. see L'Epine, Ernest Louis Victor Jules.

Hood, Thomas (1799-1845)

--Fairy Land. Hood, Thomas, Jr. (1835-1874), illus. N.D. E P Dutton.

Hood, Thomas, Jr. (1835-1874)

--Faithless Nelly Gray. Seaver, Robert, illus. N.D. Houghton Mifflin.

--From Nowhere to the North Pole. 1875. George Routledge & Sons.

--Old Fashioned Fairy Tales: Retold from the Poetic Version of Tom Hood. Washburne, Marion Foster, Mrs. (1863-), retold by. Webb, Margaret Ely, illus. LC 9-25753. 102 p. col. illus., col. plates. 23 1/2 cm. $1.25. c.1909. Rand, McNally and Co.

--Petsetilla's Posy: A Fairy Tale for Young and Old. Barnard, Frederick (1847-1896) & Dalziel, George (1815-1902), illus. LC 44-303097. 2 p. l., 156 p. front., illus. 18 x 14 cm. 1871. G. Routledge and Sons.

Hood, Thomas (1799-1845) & Hood, Jane Reynolds (1794-1846)

--Fairy Land, or, Recreation for the Rising Generation. Hood, Thomas, Jr. (1835-1874), illus. LC 44-30628. xv, 173 p. incl. front., plates. 17 1/2 cm. 1882. Griffith & Farran.

Hood, Tom (1835-1974), tr. see L'Epine, Ernest Louis Victor Jules.

Hoofnagle, Keith Lundy (1941-)

--The Story of Linda Lookout. Hoofnagle, Keith Lundy (1941-), illus. (Illus.). (gr. 4 up). N.D. (ISBN 0-911010-95-5). Naturegraph.

Hoogstraal, Harry (1917-) & Martinson, Melvin (1889-)

--Insects and Their Stories. Mohr, Carl Otto (1902-), illus. LC 41-51779. c p. l., 3-144 p. illus. 20 x 24 1/2 cm. 1941. Thomas Y. Crowell Company.

Hook, Frances Arnold (1912-), illus.

--My Book of Bible Stories. (Illus.). (gr. k-2). 1964. (ISBN 0-87239-240-6). Standard Pub.

Hook, George E.

--Coyote Country. (gr. 4-9). 1962. (ISBN 0-87315-007-4). Golden Bell.

Hook, Martha (1936-)

--Little Ones Listen to God. Boren, Tinka, illus. LC 72-156256. (Illus.). 127 p. 22cm. 1971. Zondervan Pub. House.

Hook, Richard, jt. auth. see Windrow, Martin.

Hook, Theodore

--Cousin Geoffrey. N.D. George Routledge & Sons.

--Cousin William. N.D. George Routledge & Sons.

Hooke, Hilda M.

--Thunder in the Mountains: Legends of Canada. Bice, Clare (1909-1976), illus. (Illus.). (gr. 5-7). 1947. (ISBN 0-19-540043-7). Oxford U Pr.

Hooke, Nina Warner (1907-)

--The Starveling. Maxey, Betty, illus. LC 68-29956. (Illus.). 125 p. 21cm. 1st U.S. edition. 1968, c.1967. John Day Co.

Hooker, B., jt. auth. see Carter, E.

Hooker, Brian, jt. auth. see Hastings, Wells Southworth.

Hooker, Fanny see Hoven, Erniest, pseud.

Hooker, Fanny

--The Man with Two Shadows. Hoven, Erniest, pseud. LC 7-25763. 17cm. 203p. (Ohio Ser.). 1869. A. D. F. Randolph & Co.

--Turning Points: Or, The Boys of Dr. Starbrook's School. LC 12-344171. 2 p. l., 3-396 p. front., plates. 18 1/2 cm. c.1888. American Baptist Publication Society.

Hooker, Forrestine Cooper, Mrs. (1867-1932)

--Civilizing Cricket: A Story for Girls. Crump, Leslie (1894-), illus. LC 27-24342. viii p., 1 l., 306 p. col. front. 20 1/2 cm. 1927. Doubleday, Page & Company.

--Civilizing Cricket, a Story for Girls. Crump, Leslie (1894-), illus. LC 38-23551. (Illus.). 306p. 20cm. (Young Moderns Bookshelf). 1938. The Sun Dial Press.

--Cricket: A Little Girl of the Old West. LC 25-20407. x p., 1 l., 344 p. col. front. 21 cm. 1925. Doubleday, Page & Company.

--The Garden of the Lost Key. Hader, Elmer Stanley (1889-1973), illus. LC 29-22143. xiv p., 1 l., 288 p. col. front. 21 cm. 1929. Doubleday, Doran & Company, Inc.

--Just George. Grant, George, illus. LC 26-23681. viii p., 1 l., 315 p. col. front. 21 cm. 1926. Doubleday, Page & Company.

--The Little House on the Desert. Grosvenor, Thelma Cudlipp, illus. LC 24-9997. 3 p. l., 220 p. col. front. 20 1/2 cm. 1924. Doubleday, Page & Company.

--Prince Jan, St. Bernard. Hunt, Lynn Bogue, illus. LC 46-22425. 3 p. l., 186 p. incl. front., plates. 20 1/2 cm. (Young moderns). 1946. Doubleday & Co., Inc.

AUTHOR INDEX HOPE, LAURA

--Prince Jan, St Bernard: How a Dog from the Land of Snow Made Good in the Land of No Snow. LC 37-24124. 7 p. l., 186 p. incl. col. front., plates. 20 1/2 cm. (Young modern bookshelf). 1937. The Sun Dial Press, Inc.
--Prince Jan., St. Bernard: How a Dog from the Land of Snow Made Good in the Land of No Snow. Hunt, Lynn Bogue, illus. LC 21-17576. 6 p. l., 186 p., 1 l. incl. front., plates. 19 1/2 cm. 1921. And Toronto, Doubleday, Page & Company.
--Star: The Story of an Indian Pony. LC 64-13860. 168 p. illus. 24 cm. 1964. Doubleday.
--Star: The Story of an Indian Pony. (Young Moderns Ser.). (gr. 2-6). N.D. Doubleday Doran
--Star: The Story of an Indian Pony. Bull, Charles Livingston (1874-1932), illus. Miles, Nelson A., intro. by. LC 22-23384. xi p., 1 l., 191 p. col. front. 20 1/2 cm. 1922. Doubleday, Page & Company.
--Star: The Story of an Indian Pony. Bull, Charles Livingston (1874-1932), illus. Miles, Nelson A., intro. by. LC 37-22648. xi p., 1 l., 191 p. front. 20 1/2 cm. (Young moderns bookshelf). 1937. The Sun Dial Press, Inc.
--Star: The Story of an Indian Pony. Christensen, Christina F., illus. LC 46-8613. xi p., 1 l., 191 p. 20 1/2 cm. (Young moderns). 1946. Doubleday & Co., Inc.

Hooker, Le Roy
--Me An' Teddy, by Me. Carqueville, Will, illus. LC 6-22314. 87 p. incl. col. front., col. illus. 21 x 16 cm. c.1906. W. B. Conkey Company.

Hooker, Mary Ann, Mrs. (1796 1838)
--The Seasons. LC 15-21867. 105 p. front. 15 cm. c.1840. American Sunday School Union.

Hooker, Ruth (1920-)
--At Grandma and Grandpa's House. Rosner, Ruth, illus. LC 85-15547. p. cm. 1986. (ISBN 0-8075-0477-7). A. Whitman.
--Gertrude Kioppenberg (private). Kamen, Gloria (1923-), illus. LC 75-87306. (Illus.). 24cm. 96p. 1970. Abingdon Press.
--Gertrude Kloppenberg II. Kamen, Gloria (1923-), illus. LC 73-19712. (Illus.). 112 p. 24cm. 1974. (ISBN 0-687-14097-8). Abingdon Press.
--Kennaquhair. Michini, Albert, illus. LC 76-4799. (Illus.). 159 p. 21cm. c.1976. (ISBN 0-687-20794-0). Abingdon.

Hooker, Ruth (1920-) & Smith, Carole
--The Kidnapping of Anna. Armstrong, George Douglas (1927-), illus. LC 78-32051. (Illus.). 128 p. 21cm. (Pilot books). c.1979. (ISBN 0-8075-4176-1). A. Whitman.
--The Pelican Mystery. Armstrong, George Douglas (1927-), illus. LC 77-7330. (Illus.). 128 p. 22cm. (Pilot books). c.1977. (ISBN 0-8075-6395-1). A. Whitman.

Hooker, Yvonne
--Round in a Circle. Michelini, Carlo A., illus. (Illus.). (ps-1). 1983. (ISBN 0-448-01455-6, G&D). Putnam Pub Group.

Hooks, Arah
--Mr. Nosey. Goetz, Esther Becker (1907-), illus. LC 48-3536. 31 p. illus. part col. 26 cm. 1945. D. Appleton-Century Co.

Hooks, William H, jt. auth. see Reit, Seymour.

Hooks, William H. (1921-)
--Circle of Fire. LC 82-3982. 144p. (gr. 5-9). 1982. (ISBN 0-689-50241-9, McElderry Bk). Atheneum.
--Crossing the Line. LC 78-3269. 1978. (ISBN 0-394-83938-2). Knopf.
--Doug Meets the Nutcracker. Spanfeller, James John (1930-), illus. LC 77-75042. (Illus.). 80 p. 23cm. c.1977. (ISBN 0-7232-6146-6). F. Warne.
--Maria's Cave. Juhasz, Victor, illus. LC 76-40908. (Illus.). 21cm. 60p. (Science Discovery Bks.). (gr. 3-5). 1977. (ISBN 0-698-20403-4, Pub. by Coward). (ISBN 0-698-30648-1). Putnam Pub Group.
--Mean Jake and the Devils. Zimmer, Dirk, illus. LC 81-65846. p. cm. c.1981. (ISBN 0-8037-5563-5). (ISBN 0-8037-5564-3). Dial Press.
--The Mystery on Bleeker Street. Natti, Susanna (1948-), illus. LC 79-28288. (Illus.). 128p. (Capers Ser.). (gr. 3-6). 1980. (ISBN 0-394-94431-3). (ISBN 0-394-84431-9). Knopf.
--The Mystery on Liberty Street. Detrich, Susan, illus. LC 82-2010. (Illus.). 114 p. 20cm. (Capers). c.1982. (ISBN 0-394-95240-5). (ISBN 0-394-85240-0). Knopf : Distributed by Random House.
--The Seventeen Gerbils of Class Four A. Schick, Joel, illus. LC 75-28000. 24cm. 62p. c.1976. (ISBN 0-698-20369-0). (ISBN 0-698-30621-X). Coward, McCann & Geoghegan.
--Three Rounds with Rabbit. McLaughlin, Lissa, illus. LC 83-14876. (Illus.). 32p. (ps-1). 1984. (ISBN 0-688-02363-0). (ISBN 0-688-02364-9). Lothrop.

Hooper, Bayard
--Christmas Secrets. Meryman, Hope, illus. LC 61-16250. (Illus.). 21cm. 32p. (gr. k-3). 1961. (ISBN 0-394-81023-6). (ISBN 0-394-91023-0). Pantheon.

Hooper, Byrd, pseud., see St. Clair, Byrd Hooper.

Hooper, Byrd, pseud. (1905-1976)
--Beef for Beauregard!. St. Clair, Byrd Hooper. Geer, Charles Hand (1922-), illus. LC 59-766958. 218p. 21cm. 1959. Putnam.

Hooper, Cyrus Lauron
--Johnny Goes a-Hunting. Rankin, Hugh, illus. LC 25-18187. 200 p. incl. col. front., col. illus. 20 cm. c.1925. Rand, McNally & Company.

Hooper, Jane Winnard
--Arbell. Godwin, James, illus. N.D. George Routledge & Sons.
--Arbell's School Days. N.D. Nichols & Halls.

Hooper, John Simpson (1905-)
--The Circus Boat. reprint ed. Pont, Charles Ernest (1898-), illus. LC 83-72422. (Illus.). 45 p. 23cm. 1984, c.1983. (ISBN 0-89272-179-0). Down East Books.
--The Circus Boat. Pont, Charles Ernest (1898-), illus. LC 39-19010. 47p. incl. col. ill. 22 1/2cm. 1939. Stephen Daye Press.

Hooper, John Simpson (1905-) & Bede, Regina
--Johnny Jump Up. LC 42-10632. (Illus.). 22cm. 48p. N.D. Macmillan.

Hooper, Lucille L
--The Patent-Leather Thumping Shoes. Norling, Ernest Ralph (1892-), illus. LC 55-7976. 220p. illus. 22cm. 1955. Caxton Printers.

Hooper, Muriel
--Company at the Mill. (Illus.). (gr. 2-6). N.D. Transatlantic.
--The Company at the Mill. Kennedy, Richard (1910-), illus. LC 64-57900. 151p. illus. 21cm. 1964, c.1963. Faber and Faber.

Hooper, Patrick
--Muster Up!. By Paddy Hooper. Phillips, Jim, illus. LC 66-1555. 123p. illus. 23cm. 1966, c.1965. Angus & Robertson.

Hooper, Roberta Anderson
--The Bible story in verse. 1963. Exposition Press.

Hooper, Washington Wells (1853-)
--Phil Sidney: Or, A Rich Boy's Trials; Jim Dexter; or, Handsome Is As Handsome Docs. LC 3-25213. 356 p. front. (port.) 5 pl. 19 1/2 cm. 1903. The Brooklyn Eagle Press.
--That Minister's Boy: Or, Was He as Black as They Painted Him?. Gunnison, Herbert F., intro. by. LC 2-19723. 19cm. 256p. 1902. Eagle Press.

Hoopes, Lyn Littlefield
--Daddy's Coming Home. Degen, Bruce, illus. LC 83-47693. (Illus.). 32p. (Charlotte Zolotow Bk.). (ps-2). 1984. (ISBN 0-06-022568-8). (ISBN 0-06-022569-6). HarpJ.
--Nana. Zeldich, Arieh (1949-), illus. LC 81-47110. p. cm. 1981. (ISBN 0-06-022574-2). (ISBN 0-06-022575-0). Harper & Row.
--When I Was Little. Sewall, Marcia (1935-), illus. 1983. Dutton.

Hoopes, Margaret Campbell
--The Fairyland Story Book. Willis, Bess Goe & Gallagher, J. L., illus. LC 31-17282. 60 p. 1 l. incl. col. front., col. illus. 25 cm. c.1930. Henry Altemus Company.
--The Little Folks Animal Story Book. Willis, Bess Goe & Roach, William A., illus. LC 30-18299. 2 p. l., 9-62 p., 1 l. col. front., col. illus. 24 1/2 cm. c.1930. Henry Altemus Company.

Hoose, William H. Van see Van Hoose, William H.

Hoosier, A. H. E & Whitehead, Edwin Kirby (1861-)
--The Farm Animals on Strike. LC 23-13501. 160 p. illus. 19 cm. 1923. A. Flanagan Company.

Hoover, Helen Drusilla Blackburn (1910-1984)
--Animals Near and Far. Shimin, Symeon (1902-), illus. LC 68-21089. (Illus.). 64 p. 24cm. 1970. Parents' Magazine Press.
--The Great Wolf and the Good Woodsman. Mikolaycak, Charles (1937-), illus. LC 67-18463. (Illus.). 48 p. 1967. Parents' Magazine Press.

Hoover, Helen Mary (1935-)
--Another Heaven, Another Earth. LC 81-2622. p. cm. 1981. (ISBN 0-670-12883-X). Viking Press.
--The Bell Tree. LC 82-2827. 180p. 1st U.S. edition. (gr. 5 up). 1982. (ISBN 0-670-15600-0). Viking Pr.
--Children of Morrow. LC 72-87080. 229 p. 22cm. 1973. Four Winds Press.
--Children of Morrow. LC 84-23728. 229 p. 18cm. 1985. (ISBN 0-14-031873-9). Puffin Books.
--The Delikon. LC 76-54271. 148 p. 24cm. 1977. (ISBN 0-670-26681-7). Viking Press.
--The Lion's Cub. LC 74-8594. (Illus.). 211, 2 p. 21cm. 1974. (ISBN 0-590-07375-3). Four Winds Press.
--The Lost Star. LC 78-25718. 150 p. 24cm. 1979. (ISBN 0-670-44129-5). Viking Press.
--The Rains of Eridan. 139 p. 18cm. 1979, c.1977. (ISBN 0-380-41871-1). Avon Books.
--The Rains of Eridan. LC 77-23533. p. cm. 1977. Viking Press.
--Return to Earth: A Novel of the Future. LC 79-18846. 172 p. 24cm. 1980. (ISBN 0-670-59593-4). Viking Press.
--The Shepherd Moon. LC 83-16784. 180p. (gr. 7 up). 1984. (ISBN 0-670-63977-X, Viking Kestrel). Viking.
--This Time of Darkness. LC 84-17942. 161 p. 19cm. 1985, c.1980. (ISBN 0-14-031872-0). Puffin Books.
--This Time of Darkness. LC 80-15923. 161 p. 23cm. 1980. (ISBN 0-670-50026-7). Viking Press.
--Treasures of Morrow. LC 75-28098. 171 p. 22cm. c.1976. (ISBN 0-590-17420-7). Four Winds Press.

Hoover, Lathard
--The Aircraft Boys And the Phantom Airplane. Hastings, Howard Livingston (1887-), illus. LC 32-6315. v, 7-216 p. incl. front. 19 cm. c.1932. Henry Altemus Company.
--Camp Fire Boys in African Jungles. LC 30-10000. 20cm. 252p. (The Camp Fire Boys Ser.). 1930. A L Burt Co.
--The Camp-Fire Boys in Australian Gold Fields. LC 33-12724. 19cm. 251p. (Camp-Fire Boys Ser.). 1932. A. L Burt Company.
--The Camp-Fire Boys In Borneo. LC 30-12295. 19cm. 254p. (Camp-Fire Boys Ser.). 1930. A. L. Burt Company.
--The Camp-Fire Boys in the Brazilian Widerness. LC 29-110197. 255 p. front. 19 1/2 cm. (His Camp-fire boys series). c.1929. A. L. Burt Company.
--The Camp-Fire Boys in the Philippines. LC 30-116249. 256 p. front. 19 1/2 cm. (His Camp-fire boys series). c.1930. A. L. Burt Company.
--Camp Fire Boys in the South Seas. LC 29-11018. 20cm. 227p. (The Camp Fire Boys Ser.). N.D. A L Burt Co.
--The Camp-Fire Boys' Treasure Quest. 256 p. front. 19 1/2 cm. (His Camp-fire boys series). c.1929. A. L. Burt Company.

Hoover, Opal C.
--Roads to Everywhere. 105p. (gr. 4-6). 1959. (ISBN 0-87178-748-2). Brethren.

Hoover, Roseanna, tr. see Bolliger, Max.

Hoover, Roseanna, tr. see Kubler, Arthur.

Hoover, Roseanna (1944-), tr. see Kyber, Manfred.

Hoover, Roseanna, tr. see Scharen, Beatrix.

Hope, A. R.
--Adventures of Two Runaways. (MacMillan Bks. for Boys & Girls). (gr. 7-9). N.D. MacMillan Bks.
--The Adventures of Lazybones. (True Or Might-Be-True Stories). N.D. MacMillan Bks.

Hope, Anne
--Percy Pig, House Painter. Hammond, Elizabeth, illus. LC 58-11766. unpaged. illus. 14x19cm. 1958. Warne.
--Umphy Elephant, Window Cleaner. Hammond, Elizabeth, illus. LC 58-9084. unpaged. illus. 14x19cm. 1958. F. Warne.

Hope, Anthony, pseud., see Hawkins, Anthony Hope.

Hope, Anthony, Sir, pseud. (1863-1933)
--The Heart of Princess Osra. Hawkins, Anthony Hope. 250p. Repr. of 1896 ed. N.D. (ISBN 0-89966-477-6). Buccaneer Bks.
--The Prisoner of Zenda. Hawkins, Anthony Hope. N.D. Grosset & Dunlap.
--The Prisoner of Zenda. Hawkins, Anthony Hope. (Looking Glass Library). (gr. 3 up). 1961. (ISBN 0-394-80475-9). (ISBN 0-394-90475-3). Random.
--The Prisoner of Zenda. Hawkins, Anthony Hope. Godfrey, Michael, illus. (Illus.). (Children's Illustrated Classics). 1962. E.P. Dutton & Co.
--The Prisoner of Zenda and Rupert of Hentzau: Ruritainia Complete. Hawkins, Anthony Hope. Gibson, Charles Dana (1867-1944), illus. (Illus.). 395 p. 21cm. 1961. Dover Publications.
--Rupert of Hentzau. Hawkins, Anthony Hope. (Illus.). 251p. 1st U.S. edition. Repr. of 1963 ed. (Childrens Illustrated Classics Ser). 1970. (ISBN 0-460-05057-5, Pub. by J. M. Dent England). Biblio Dist.
--Rupert of Hentzau. Hawkins, Anthony Hope. Godfrey, Michael, illus. (Illus.). (Children's Illustrated Classics). (gr. 7 up). 1963. (ISBN 0-525-38761-7). Dutton.
--The Prisoner Zenda. Hawkins, Anthony Hope. Godfrey, Michael, illus. (Illus.). (Children's Illustrated Classics). (gr. 7 up). 1955. (ISBN 0-525-37827-8). Dutton.

Hope, Ascott R., pseud., see Moncrieff, Ascott Robert Hope.

Hope, Ascott R., pseud. (1846-1927)
--Boys' Own Stories. Moncrieff, Ascott Robert Hope. N.D. J. B. Lippincott Co.
--The Day After the Holidays. Moncrieff, Ascott Robert Hope. Phiz, pseud. (1815-1882), illus. Browne, Hablot Knight. N.D. D. Appleton & Co.
--Homespun Stories. Moncrieff, Ascott Robert Hope. (Illus.). N.D. D. Appleton and Co.
--My Schoolboy Friends. Moncrieff, Ascott Robert Hope. N.D. R. Worthington.
--The Parish Clerk. Moncrieff, Ascott Robert Hope. N.D. E. & J. B .Young & Co.
--Seven Wish Scholars. Moncrieff, Ascott Robert Hope. (Illus.). (Scribner-Blackie Series of books for young people). N.D. Charles Scribner's Sons.
--Stories of a Old Renoun. Moncrieff, Ascott Robert Hope. (Illus.). (Scribner-Blackie Series of Books for young people). N.D. Charles Scribner's Sons.
--Young Travellers' Tales. Moncrieff, Ascott Robert Hope. (Illus.). (Scribner-Blackie Series of books for young people). N.D. Charles Scribner's Sons.

Hope, Carolyn
--Dorothy, and Other Stories. (Illus.). N.D. E & J B Young.

Hope, Christopher David Tully, jt. auth. see Menuhin, Yehudi.

Hope, Christopher David Tully (1944-)
--The Dragon Wore Pink. Barrett, Angela, illus. LC 85-7964. (Illus.). 32 p. 28cm. c.1985. (ISBN 0-689-31175-3). Atheneum

Hope, Daring, pseud., see Johnson, Anna.

Hope, Essex, Mrs.
--Garry: The Story of a Dog. Brien, Stanislaus, illus. LC 38-560476. 5 p. l., 3-152 p. incl. front., illus., plates. 21 cm. c.1938. Harcourt, Brace and Company.

Hope, F. T. L.
--The Three Homes. 400p. N.D. Cassell, Petter, & Galpin.
--The Three Homes. 390p. N.D. E. P. Dutton.

Hope, Laura Lee, pseud., see Stratemeyer Syndicate.

Hope, Laura Lee, pseud.
--The Blue Poodle Mystery. Stratemeyer Syndicate. Singer, Gloria (1949-), illus. LC 79-24909. (A Pre Nancy Drew/Hardy Boys Mystery Book). 127 p. 19cm. (The Bobbsey Twins (1980-) Ser.: Vol. 1). c.1980. (ISBN 0-671-95546-2). (ISBN 0-671-95554-3). Wanderer Books.
--The Blythe Girls: Helen, Margy and Rose; or, Facing the Great World. Stratemeyer Syndicate. Gooch, Thelma, illus. LC 25-9816. iv, 214 p. front., plates. 19 1/2 cm. (The Blythe Girls Bks.: No. 1). c.1925. Grosset & Dunlap.
--The Blythe Girls: Helen, Margy and Rose; or, Facing the Great World. Stratemeyer Syndicate. Gooch, Thelma, illus. Repr. of 1925 ed (Pub. by Grosset & Dunlap). (The Blythe Girls Bks.: No. 1). N.D. Whitman Publishing Co.
--The Blythe Girls: Helen's Strange Boarder; or, The Girl from Bronx Park. Stratemeyer Syndicate. Gooch, Thelma, illus. Repr. of 1925 ed (Pub. by Grosset & Dunlap). (The Blythe Girls Bks.: No. 4). N.D. Whitman Publishing Co.
--The Blythe Girls: Helen's Strange Border; or, The Girl from Bronx Park. Stratemeyer Syndicate. Gooch, Thelma, illus. (The Blythe Girls Bks.: No. 4). 1925. Grosset & Dunlap.
--The Blythe Girls: Helen's Wonderful Mistake; or, The Mysterious Necklace. Stratemeyer Syndicate. Gooch, Thelma, illus. LC 32-12753. 2 p. l., 195 p. front., plates. 19 1/2 cm. (The Blythe Girls Bks.: No. 12). c.1932. Grosset & Dunlap.
--The Blythe Girls: Margy's Mysterious Visitor; or, Guarding the Pepper Fortune. Stratemeyer Syndicate. Gooch, Thelma, illus. LC 30-12304. iv, 208 p. front., plates. 19 1/2 cm. (The Blythe Girls Bks.: No. 10). c.1930. Grosset & Dunlap.
--The Blythe Girls: Margy's Queer Inheritance; or, The Worth of a Name. Stratemeyer Syndicate. Gooch, Thelma, illus. LC 25-9817. iv, 214 p. front., plates. 19 1/2 cm. (The Blythe Girls Bks.: No. 2). c.1925. Grosset & Dunlap.
--The Blythe Girls: Margy's Queer Inheritance; or, The Worth of a Name. Stratemeyer Syndicate. Gooch, Thelma, illus. Repr. of 1925 ed (Pub. by Grosset & Dunlap). (The Blythe Girls Bks.: No. 2). N.D. Whitman Publishing Co.
--The Blythe Girls: Margy's Secret Mission; or, Exciting Days at Shadymore. Stratemeyer Syndicate. Gooch, Thelma, illus. (The Blythe Girls Bks.: No. 6). 1926. Grosset & Dunlap.
--The Blythe Girls: Rose's Great Problem; or, Face to Face with a Crisis. Stratemeyer Syndicate. Gooch, Thelma, illus. LC 25-981530. iv, 214 p. front., plates. 19 1/2 cm. (The Blythe Girls Bks.: No. 3). c.1925. Grosset & Dunlap.
--The Blythe Girls: Rose's Great Problem; or, Face to Face with a Crisis. Stratemeyer Syndicate. Gooch, Thelma, illus. Repr. of 1925 ed (Pub. by Grosset & Dunlap). (The Blythe Girls Bks.: No. 3). N.D. Whitman Publishing Co.

--The Blythe Girls: Rose's Hidden Talent. Stratemeyer Syndicate. Gooch, Thelma, illus. LC 31-13101. iv, 192 p. front., plates. 19 1/2 cm. (The Blythe Girls Bks.: No. 11). c.1931. Grosset & Dunlap.
--The Blythe Girls: Rose's Odd Discovery; or, The Search for Irene Conroy. Stratemeyer Syndicate. Gooch, Thelma, illus. (The Blythe Girls Bks.: No. 7). 1927. Grosset & Dunlap.
--The Blythe Girls: Snowbound in Camp; or, The Mystery at Elk Lodge. Stratemeyer Syndicate. Gooch, Thelma, illus. iv, 210 p. front., plates. 19 1/2 cm. (The Blythe Girls Bks.: No. 9). c.1929. Grosset & Dunlap.
--The Blythe Girls: The Disappearance of Helen, or, The Art Shop Mystery. Stratemeyer Syndicate. Gooch, Thelma, illus. LC 28-126550. iv, 210 p. front., plates. 19 1/2 cm. (The Blythe Girls Bks.: No. 8). c.1928. Grosset & Dunlap.
--The Blythe Girls: Three on a Vacation; or, The Mystery at Peach Farm. Stratemeyer Syndicate. Gooch, Thelma, illus. (The Blythe Girls Bks.: No. 5). 1925. Grosset & Dunlap.
--The Bobbsey Twins. Stratemeyer Syndicate. rev. ed. LC 50-6959. (Published without the subtitle). (Illus.). x, 176 p. front. 20 cm. (The Bobbsey Twins Ser.: Vol. 1). 1950. Grosset & Dunlap.
--The Bobbsey Twins' Adventure in the Country. Stratemeyer Syndicate. rev. ed. LC 61-19145. (Illus.). 179 p. 20cm. (The Bobbsey Twins Ser.: Vol. 2). Orig. Title: The Bobbsey Twins in the Country. 1961. Grosset & Dunlap.
--The Bobbsey Twins' Adventure in Washington. Stratemeyer Syndicate. rev. ed. LC 63-6277. (Illus.). vii, 174 p. illus. 20 cm. (The Bobbsey Twins Ser.: Vol. 12). Orig. Title: The Bobbsey Twins in Washington. 1963. Grosset & Dunlap.
--The Bobbsey Twins' Adventures with Baby May. Stratemeyer Syndicate. rev. ed. LC 68-12753. (Illus.). 173 p. 20cm. (The Bobbsey Twins Ser.: Vol. 17). Orig. Title: The Bobbsey Twins and Baby May. 1968. Grosset & Dunlap.
--The Bobbsey Twins and Baby May. Stratemeyer Syndicate. Rogers, Walter S., illus. (The Bobbsey Twins Ser.: Vol. 17). 1924. Grosset & Dunlap.
--The Bobbsey Twins and Dr. Funnybone's Secret. Stratemeyer Syndicate. (Illus.). 196p. (The Bobbsey Twins Ser.: Vol. 65). 1972. Grosset & Dunlap.
--The Bobbsey Twins and the Big River Mystery. Stratemeyer Syndicate. LC 63-1129. (Illus.). 176 p. illus. 20 cm. (The Bobbsey Twins Ser.: Vol. 56). 1963. Grosset & Dunlap.
--The Bobbsey Twins and the Cedar Camp Mystery. Stratemeyer Syndicate. rev. ed. Adams, Harriet Stratemeyer (1894-1982), rev. by. LC 67-24237. (Illus.). 176 p. 20cm. (The Bobbsey Twins Ser.: Vol. 14). Orig. Title: The Bobbsey Twins at Cedar Camp. 1967. Grosset & Dunlap.
--The Bobbsey Twins and the Circus Surprise. Stratemeyer Syndicate. rev. ed. LC 61-65811. (Illus.). 183p. illus. 20cm. (The Bobbsey Twins Ser.: Vol. 25). Orig. Title: The Bobbsey Twins at the Circus. c.1960. Grosset & Dunlap.
--The Bobbsey Twins and the Coral Turtle Mystery. Stratemeyer Syndicate. LC 78-57928. (Illus.). 20cm. 179p. (The Bobbsey Twins Ser.: Vol. 72). c.1979. (ISBN 0-448-08072-9). Grosset & Dunlap.
--The Bobbsey Twins and the County Fair Mystery. Stratemeyer Syndicate. rev. ed. LC 61-65812. (Illus.). 182p. illus. 20cm. (The Bobbsey Twins Ser.: Vol. 15). Orig. Title: The Bobbsey Twins at the County Fair. c.1960. Grosset & Dunlap.
--The Bobbsey Twins and the Doodlebug Mystery. Stratemeyer Syndicate. LC 69-16138. (Illus.). 176 p. 20cm. (The Bobbsey Twins Ser.: Vol. 62). 1969. Grosset & Dunlap.
--The Bobbsey Twins and the Flying Clown. Stratemeyer Syndicate. LC 73-16661. (Illus.). 181 p. 20cm. (The Bobbsey Twins Ser.: Vol. 67). c.1974. Grosset & Dunlap.
--The Bobbsey Twins and the Four-Leaf Clover Mystery. Stratemeyer Syndicate. rev. ed. LC 68-29948. (Illus.). 176 p. 20cm. (The Bobbsey Twins Ser.: Vol. 19). Orig. Title: The Bobbsey Twins at Cloverbank. 1968. Grosset & Dunlap.
--The Bobbsey Twins and the Goldfish Mystery. Stratemeyer Syndicate. LC 62-133545. (Illus.). 175p. illus. 20cm. (The Bobbsey Twins Ser.: Vol. 55). 1962. Grosset & Dunlap.
--The Bobbsey Twins and the Greek Hat Mystery. Stratemeyer Syndicate. LC 64-1715. (Illus.). vii, 176 p. illus. 20 cm. (The Bobbsey Twins Ser.: Vol. 57). 1964. Grosset & Dunlap.
--The Bobbsey Twins and the Horseshoe Riddle. Stratemeyer Syndicate. LC 53-2321. (Written for the Stratemeyer Syndicate by Harriet Stratemeyer Adams, 1894-1982, under the pseudonym, Laura Lee Hope). (Illus.). 181p. illus. 20cm. (The Bobbsey Twins Ser.: Vol. 46). 1953. Grosset & Dunlap.
--The Bobbsey Twins and the Mystery at Snow Lodge. Stratemeyer Syndicate. rev. ed. LC 60-36952. (Illus.). 179p. illus. 20cm. (The Bobbsey Twins Ser.: Vol. 5). Orig. Title: The Bobbsey Twins at Snow Lodge. 1960. Grosset & Dunlap.
--The Bobbsey Twins and the Play House Secret. Stratemeyer Syndicate. rev. ed. LC 68-29947. (Illus.). 174 p. 20cm. (The Bobbsey Twins Ser.: Vol. 18). Orig. Title: The Bobbsey Twins Keeping House. 1968. Grosset & Dunlap.
--The Bobbsey Twins and the Secret of Candy Castle. Stratemeyer Syndicate. LC 68-12752. (Illus.). 175 p. 20cm. (The Bobbsey Twins Ser.: Vol. 61). 1968. Grosset & Dunlap.
--The Bobbsey Twins and the Smoky Mountain Mystery. Stratemeyer Syndicate. LC 76-22808. (Illus.). 180 p. 20cm. (The Bobbsey Twins Ser.: Vol. 70). c.1977. (ISBN 0-448-08070-2). Grosset & Dunlap.
--The Bobbsey Twins and the Tagalong Giraffe. Stratemeyer Syndicate. LC 72-92932. (Illus.). 180 p. 20cm. (The Bobbsey Twins Ser.: Vol. 66). 1973. Grosset & Dunlap.
--The Bobbsey Twins and the Talking Fox Mystery. Stratemeyer Syndicate. LC 79-106307. (Illus.). 175 p. 20cm. (The Bobbsey Twins Ser.: Vol. 63). 1970. Grosset & Dunlap.
--The Bobbsey Twins and Their Camel Adventure. Stratemeyer Syndicate. LC 66-13816. (Illus.). 177 p. illus. 20 cm. (The Bobbsey Twins Ser.: Vol. 59). 1966. Grosset & Dunlap.
--The Bobbsey Twins and Their Schoolmates. Stratemeyer Syndicate. LC 28-6311. (Illus.). 2 p. l., 244 p. front., plates. 19 1/2 cm. (The Bobbsey Twins Ser.: Vol. 21). c.1928. Grosset & Dunlap.
--The Bobbsey Twins at Big Bear Pond. Stratemeyer Syndicate. LC 54-8465. (Written for the Stratemeyer Syndicate by Harriet Stratemeyer Adams, 1894-1982, under the pseudonym, Laura Lee Hope). (Illus.). 184p. 20cm. (The Bobbsey Twins Ser.: Vol. 47). 1953. Grosset & Dunlap.
--The Bobbsey Twins at Cedar Camp. Stratemeyer Syndicate. Rogers, Walter S., illus. (The Bobbsey Twins Ser.: Vol. 14). 1921. Grosset & Dunlap.
--The Bobbsey Twins at Cherry Corners. Stratemeyer Syndicate. (Illus.). (The Bobbsey Twins Ser.: Vol. 20). 1927. Grosset & Dunlap.
--The Bobbsey Twins at Cloverbank. Stratemeyer Syndicate. (Illus.). (The Bobbsey Twins Ser.: Vol. 19). 1926. Grosset & Dunlap.
--The Bobbsey Twins at Home. Stratemeyer Syndicate. Rogers, Walter S., illus. (The Bobbsey Twins Ser.: Vol. 8). 1916. Grosset & Dunlap.
--The Bobbsey Twins at Indian Hollow. Stratemeyer Syndicate. Schubert, Marie (1890-), illus. LC 40-793026. (Written for the Stratemeyer Syndicate by Harriet Stratemeyer Adams, 1894-1982, under the pseudonym, Laura Lee Hope). 2 p. l., 214 p. front., pl. 19 1/2 cm. (The Bobbsey Twins Ser.: Vol. 33). c.1940. Grosset & Dunlap.
--The Bobbsey Twins at Lighthouse Point. Stratemeyer Syndicate. Schubert, Marie (1890-), illus. LC 39-114090. 2 p. l., 216 p. front., pl. 19 1/2 cm. (The Bobbsey Twins Ser.: Vol. 32). c.1939. Grosset & Dunlap.
--The Bobbsey Twins at London Tower. Stratemeyer Syndicate. LC 59-16082. (Illus.). 182p. illus. 20cm. (The Bobbsey Twins Ser.: Vol. 52). 1959. Grosset & Dunlap.
--The Bobbsey Twins at Meadow Brook. Stratemeyer Syndicate. (Illus.). (The Bobbsey Twins Ser.: Vol. 7). 1915. Grosset & Dunlap.
--The Bobbsey Twins at Mystery Mansion. Stratemeyer Syndicate. (Written for the Stratemeyer Syndicate by Harriet Stratemeyer Adams, 1894-1982, under the pseudonym, Laura Lee Hope). (Illus.). (The Bobbsey Twins Ser.: Vol. 38). (gr. 1-4). 1945. (ISBN 0-448-08038-9). Grosset & Dunlap.
--The Bobbsey Twins at Pilgrim Rock. Stratemeyer Syndicate. LC 57-13577. (Illus.). 182p. illus. 20cm. (The Bobbsey Twins Ser.: Vol. 50). 1957, c.1956. Grosset & Dunlap.
--The Bobbsey Twins at School. Stratemeyer Syndicate. LC 43-44549. (Illus.). 2 p. l., 216 p. front., plates. 19 1/2 cm. (The Bobbsey Twins Ser.: Vol. 4). c.1913. Grosset & Dunlap.
--The Bobbsey Twins at Snow Lodge. Stratemeyer Syndicate. (Illus.). (The Bobbsey Twins Ser.: Vol. 5). 1913. Grosset & Dunlap.
--The Bobbsey Twins at Spruce Lake. Stratemeyer Syndicate. Rogers, Walter S., illus. LC 30-2686. 2 p. l., 242 p. front., plates. 19 1/2 cm. (The Bobbsey Twins Ser.: Vol. 23). c.1930. Grosset & Dunlap.
--The Bobbsey Twins at Sugar Maple Hill. Stratemeyer Syndicate. LC 46-18010. (Written for the Stratemeyer Syndicate by Harriet Stratemeyer Adams, 1894-1982, under the pseudonym, Laura Lee Hope). (Illus.). 4 p. l., 210 p. incl. front. 19 1/2 cm. (The Bobbsey Twins Ser.: Vol. 39). 1946. Grosset & Dunlap.
--The Bobbsey Twins at the Circus. Stratemeyer Syndicate. Schubert, Marie (1890-), illus. LC 32-127520. 2 p. l., 250 p. front., plates. 19 1/2 cm. (The Bobbsey Twins Ser.: Vol. 25). c.1932. Grosset & Dunlap.
--The Bobbsey Twins at the County Fair. Stratemeyer Syndicate. Rogers, Walter S., illus. (The Bobbsey Twins Ser.: Vol. 15). 1922. Grosset & Dunlap.
--The Bobbsey Twins at the Ice Carnival. Stratemeyer Syndicate. Schubert, Marie (1890-), illus. LC 41-10149. 3 p. l., 216 p. incl. front. pl. 19 1/2 cm. (The Bobbsey Twins Ser.: Vol. 34). c.1941. Grosset & Dunlap.
--The Bobbsey Twins at the Seashore. Stratemeyer Syndicate. Repr. (The Bobbsey Twins Ser.: Vol. 3). 1940. Goldsmith Publishing Co.
--The Bobbsey Twins at the Seashore. Stratemeyer Syndicate. rev. ed. LC 50-6960. (Illus.). x, 179 p. front. 20 cm. (The Bobbsey Twins Ser.: Vol. 3). 1950. Grosset & Dunlap.
--The Bobbsey Twins at the Seashore. Stratemeyer Syndicate. LC 79-88913. (Illus.). 186 p. 20cm. (The Bobbsey Twins Ser.: Vol. 3). c.1979. (ISBN 0-671-95681-7). (ISBN 0-671-95521-7). Wanderer Books.
--The Bobbsey Twins at the Seashore. Stratemeyer Syndicate. Miller, Martha E., illus. 2 p. l., 11-251, 1 p. front., illus. 20 1/2 cm. Repr. (The Bobbsey Twins Ser.: Vol. 3). c.1940. The Saalfield Publishing Company.
--The Bobbsey Twins at the Seashore. Stratemeyer Syndicate. Nuttall, Charles, illus. LC 7-30433. iii, 211 p. front., plates. 17 cm. (The Bobbsey Twins Ser.: Vol. 3). c.1907. Chatterton-Peck Company.
--The Bobbsey Twins at the Seashore. Stratemeyer Syndicate. Nuttall, Charles, illus. Repr. of 1907 ed (Pub. by Chatterton-Peck Co). (The Bobbsey Twins Ser.: Vol. 3). 1908. Grosset & Dunlap.
--The Bobbsey Twins at the Seashore. Stratemeyer Syndicate. Scott, Janet Laura, illus. LC 50-12510. 216 p. illus. 21 cm. Repr. (The Bobbsey Twins Ser.: Vol. 3). 1950. Whitman Publishing Co.
--The Bobbsey Twins at the Seashore. Stratemeyer Syndicate. Scott, Janet Laura, illus. LC 54-438013. 282p. illus. 20cm. Repr. (The Bobbsey Twins Ser.: Vol. 3). 1954. Whitman Publishing Co.
--The Bobbsey Twins at Whitesail Harbor. Stratemeyer Syndicate. LC 52-10245. (Written for the Stratemeyer Syndicate by Harriet Stratemeyer Adams, 1894-1982, under the pseudonym, Laura Lee Hope). (Illus.). 177 p. illus. 20 cm. (The Bobbsey Twins Ser.: Vol. 45). 1952. Grosset & Dunlap.
--The Bobbsey Twins at Windmill Cottage. Stratemeyer Syndicate. Schubert, Marie (1890-), illus. LC 38-10329. (Illus.). 2 p. l., 215 p. front., pl. 19 1/2 cm. (The Bobbsey Twins Ser.: Vol. 31). c.1938. Grosset & Dunlap.
--The Bobbsey Twins' Big Adventure at Home. Stratemeyer Syndicate. rev. ed. LC 61-658130. (Illus.). 176p. illus. 20cm. (The Bobbsey Twins Ser.: Vol. 8). Orig. Title: The Bobbsey Twins at Home. c.1960. Grosset & Dunlap.
--The Bobbsey Twins Camping Out. Stratemeyer Syndicate. (Illus.). (The Bobbsey Twins Ser.: Vol. 16). 1923. Grosset & Dunlap.
--The Bobbsey Twins Camping Out. Stratemeyer Syndicate. rev. ed. LC 62-404576. (Illus.). 184p. illus. 20cm. (The Bobbsey Twins Ser.: Vol. 16). c.1955. Grosset & Dunlap.
--The Bobbsey Twins' Forest Adventure. Stratemeyer Syndicate. LC 58-145866. (Illus.). 182p. illus. 20cm. (The Bobbsey Twins Ser.: Vol. 51). 1958, c.1957. Grosset & Dunlap.
--The Bobbsey Twins in a Great City. Stratemeyer Syndicate. Rogers, Walter S., illus. (The Bobbsey Twins Ser.: Vol. 9). 1917. Grosset & Dunlap.
--The Bobbsey Twins in a Radio Play. Stratemeyer Syndicate. Schubert, Marie (1890-), illus. LC 37-814977. 2 p. l., 212 p. front., plates. 19 1/2 cm. (The Bobbsey Twins Ser.: Vol. 30). c.1937. Grosset & Dunlap.
--The Bobbsey Twins in a TV Mystery Show. Stratemeyer Syndicate. LC 77-76127. (Illus.). 179 p. 20cm. (The Bobbsey Twins Ser.: Vol. 71). c.1978. (ISBN 0-448-08071-0). Grosset & Dunlap.
--The Bobbsey Twins in Echo Valley. Stratemeyer Syndicate. Schubert, Marie (1890-), illus. LC 43-81770. (Written for the Stratemeyer Syndicate by Harriet Stratemeyer Adams, 1894-1982, under the pseudonym, Laura Lee Hope). 3 p. l., 210 p. incl. front. 19 1/2 cm. (The Bobbsey Twins Ser.: Vol. 36). 1943. Grosset & Dunlap.
--The Bobbsey Twins in Eskimo Land. Stratemeyer Syndicate. Schubert, Marie (1890-), illus. LC 36-10343. 2 p. l., 218 p. front. 19 1/2 cm. (The Bobbsey Twins Ser.: Vol. 29). c.1936. Grosset & Dunlap.
--The Bobbsey Twins in Mexico. Stratemeyer Syndicate. LC 47-22178. (Written for the Stratemeyer Syndicate by Harriet Stratemeyer Adams, 1894-1982, under the pseudonym, Laura Lee Hope). (Illus.). v p., 1 l., 212 p. incl. front. 19 1/2 cm. (The Bobbsey Twins Ser.: Vol. 40). 1947. Grosset & Dunlap.
--The Bobbsey Twins in Rainbow Valley. Stratemeyer Syndicate. LC 50-4002. (Written for the Stratemeyer Syndicate by Harriet Stratemeyer Adams, 1894-1982, under the pseudonym, Laura Lee Hope). (Illus.). viii, 180 p. 20 cm. (The Bobbsey Twins Ser.: Vol. 43). 1950. Grosset & Dunlap.
--The Bobbsey Twins in the Country. Stratemeyer Syndicate. Repr. (The Bobbsey Twins Ser.: Vol. 2). 1940. Goldsmith Publishing Co.
--The Bobbsey Twins in the Country. Stratemeyer Syndicate. rev. ed. LC 50-6961. (Illus.). x, 178 p. front. 20 cm. (The Bobbsey Twins Ser.: Vol. 2). 1950. Grosset & Dunlap.
--The Bobbsey Twins in the Country. Stratemeyer Syndicate. LC 79-88911. (Illus.). 215 p. 20cm. (The Bobbsey Twins Ser.: Vol. 2). c.1979. (ISBN 0-671-95673-6). (ISBN 0-671-95521-7). Wanderer Books.
--The Bobbsey Twins in the Country. Stratemeyer Syndicate. Miller, Martha E., illus. LC 40-10454. 2 p. l., 11-252 p. front., illus. 20 1/2 cm. Repr. (The Bobbsey Twins Ser.: Vol. 2). c.1940. The Saalfield Publishing Company.
--The Bobbsey Twins in the Country. Stratemeyer Syndicate. Nuttall, Charles, illus. LC 7-23464. iii, 242 p. front., plates. 17 cm. Repr. of 1904 ed (Pub. by Mershon Co). (The Bobbsey Twins Ser.: Vol. 2). c.1907. Chatterton-Peck Company.
--The Bobbsey Twins in the Country. Stratemeyer Syndicate. Nuttall, Charles, illus. LC 29-2739. iii, 242 p. front., plates. 19 1/2 cm. Repr. of 1904 ed (Pub. by Mershon Co). (The Bobbsey Twins Ser.: Vol. 2). 1908. Grosset & Dunlap.
--The Bobbsey Twins in the Country. Stratemeyer Syndicate. Nuttall, Charles, illus. (The Bobbsey Twins Ser.: Vol. 2). 1904. The Mershon Co.
--The Bobbsey Twins in the Country. Stratemeyer Syndicate. Scott, Janet Laura, illus. LC 50-12511. 216 p. illus. 21 cm. Repr. (The Bobbsey Twins Ser.: Vol. 2). 1950. Whitman Publishing Co.
--The Bobbsey Twins in the Country. Stratemeyer Syndicate. Scott, Janet Laura, illus. LC 54-438501. 282p. illus. 20cm. Repr. (The Bobbsey Twins Ser.: Vol. 2). 1954. Whitman Publishing Co.
--The Bobbsey Twins in the Great West. Stratemeyer Syndicate. Rogers, Walter S., illus. (The Bobbsey Twins Ser.: Vol. 13). 1920. Grosset & Dunlap.
--The Bobbsey Twins in the Land of Cotton. Stratemeyer Syndicate. Schubert, Marie (1890-), illus. LC 42-134244. (Written for the Stratemeyer Syndicate by Harriet Stratemeyer Adams, 1894-1982, under the pseudonym, Laura Lee Hope). v, 216 p. incl. front. 19 1/2 cm. (The Bobbsey Twins Ser.: Vol. 35). 1942. Grosset & Dunlap.
--The Bobbsey Twins in the Mystery Cave. Stratemeyer Syndicate. LC 60-346581. (Illus.). 181p. illus. 20cm. (The Bobbsey Twins Ser.: Vol. 53). 1960. Grosset & Dunlap.
--The Bobbsey Twins in Tulip Land. Stratemeyer Syndicate. LC 49-4080. (Written for the Stratemeyer Syndicate by Harriet Stratemeyer Adams, 1894-1982, under the pseudonym, Laura Lee Hope). (Illus.). viii, 210 p. front. 20 cm. (The Bobbsey Twins Ser.: Vol. 42). 1949. Grosset & Dunlap.
--The Bobbsey Twins in Volcano Land. Stratemeyer Syndicate. LC 61-172534. (Illus.). 180p. illus. 20cm. (The Bobbsey Twins Ser.: Vol. 54). 1961. Grosset & Dunlap.
--The Bobbsey Twins in Washington. Stratemeyer Syndicate. Rogers, Walter S., illus. LC 38-5610. 2 p. l., 244 p. front. 19 1/2 cm. (The Bobbsey Twins Ser.: Vol. 12). 1919. Grosset & Dunlap.
--The Bobbsey Twins Keeping House. Stratemeyer Syndicate. (Illus.). (The Bobbsey Twins Ser.: Vol. 18). 1925. Grosset & Dunlap.
--The Bobbsey Twins' Mystery at Cherry Corners. Stratemeyer Syndicate. rev. ed. LC 72-144072. (Illus.). 178 p. 20cm. (The Bobbsey Twins Ser.: Vol. 20). Orig. Title: The Bobbsey Twins at Cherry Corners. 1971. Grosset & Dunlap.
--The Bobbsey Twins' Mystery at Meadowbrook. Stratemeyer Syndicate. rev. ed. LC 63-6278. (Illus.). vii, 177 p. illus. 20 cm. (The Bobbsey Twins Ser.: Vol. 7). Orig. Title: The Bobbsey Twins at Meadow Brook. 1963. Grosset & Dunlap.
--The Bobbsey Twins' Mystery at School. Stratemeyer Syndicate. rev. ed. LC 62-523054. (Illus.). 176p. illus. 20cm. (The Bobbsey Twins Ser.: Vol. 4). Orig. Title: The Bobbsey Twins at School. 1962. Grosset & Dunlap.

--The Bobbsey Twins' Mystery of the King's Puppet. Stratemeyer Syndicate. LC 67-13652. (Illus.). 177p. illus. 20cm. (The Bobbsey Twins Ser.: Vol. 60). 1967. Grosset & Dunlap.
--The Bobbsey Twins' Mystery on the Deep Blue Sea. Stratemeyer Syndicate. rev. ed. LC 65-18449. (Illus.). 177p. illus. 20cm. (The Bobbsey Twins Ser.: Vol. 11). Orig. Title: The Bobbsey Twins on the Deep Blue Sea. c.1965. Grosset.
--The Bobbsey Twins of Lakeport. Stratemeyer Syndicate. rev. ed. LC 61-191445. (Illus.). 178p. illus. 20cm. (The Bobbsey Twins Ser.: Vol. 1). Orig. Title: The Bobbsey Twins; Or, Merry Days Indoors and Out. 1961. Grosset & Dunlap.
--The Bobbsey Twins on a Bicycle Trip. Stratemeyer Syndicate. (Written for the Stratemeyer Syndicate by Harriet Stratemeyer Adams, 1894-1982, under the pseudonym, Laura Lee Hope). (Illus.). (The Bobbsey Twins Ser.: Vol. 48). 1954. Grosset & Dunlap.
--The Bobbsey Twins on a Houseboat. Stratemeyer Syndicate. LC 29-150. (Illus.). 2 p. l., 244 p. front., plates. 19 cm. (The Bobbsey Twins Ser.: Vol. 6). c.1915. Grosset & Dunlap.
--The Bobbsey Twins on a Houseboat. Stratemeyer Syndicate. rev. ed. Adams, Harriet Stratemeyer (1894-1982), rev. by. LC 62-518480. (Illus.). 184p. illus. 20cm. (The Bobbsey Twins Ser.: Vol. 6). c.1955. Grosset & Dunlap.
--The Bobbsey Twins on a Ranch. Stratemeyer Syndicate. Schubert, Marie (1890-), illus. 2 p. l., 206 p. front., plates. 19 1/2 cm. (The Bobbsey Twins Ser.: Vol. 28). c.1935. Grosset & Dunlap.
--The Bobbsey Twins on an Airplane Trip. Stratemeyer Syndicate. Braley, Margaret Temple, illus. LC 33-7087. 2 p. l., 246 p. front., pl. 19 1/2 cm. (The Bobbsey Twins Ser.: Vol. 26). c.1933. Grosset & Dunlap.
--The Bobbsey Twins on Blueberry Island. Stratemeyer Syndicate. rev. ed. LC 59-319061. (Illus.). 181p. illus. 20cm. (The Bobbsey Twins Ser.: Vol. 10). 1959. Grosset & Dunlap.
--The Bobbsey Twins on Blueberry Island. Stratemeyer Syndicate. Rogers, Walter S., illus. (The Bobbsey Twins Ser.: Vol. 10). 1917. Grosset & Dunlap.
--The Bobbsey Twins on the Deep Blue Sea. Stratemeyer Syndicate. Rogers, Walter S., illus. (The Bobbsey Twins Ser.: Vol. 11). 1918. Grosset & Dunlap.
--The Bobbsey Twins on the Pony Trail. Stratemeyer Syndicate. Schubert, Marie (1890-), illus. LC 45-271. (Written for the Stratemeyer Syndicate by Harriet Stratemeyer Adams, 1894-1982, under the pseudonym, Laura Lee Hope). 4 p. l., 213 p. incl. front. 19 1/2 cm. (The Bobbsey Twins Ser.: Vol. 37). 1944. Grosset & Dunlap.
--The Bobbsey Twins on the Sun-Moon Cruise. Stratemeyer Syndicate. LC 74-10460. (Illus.). 180 p. 20cm. (The Bobbsey Twins Ser.: Vol. 68). c.1975. (ISBN 0-448-08068-0). Grosset & Dunlap.
--The Bobbsey Twins: Or, Merry Days Indoors and Out. Stratemeyer Syndicate. (Illus.). Repr. of 1904 ed (Pub. by Mershon Co). (The Bobbsey Twins Ser.: Vol. 1). 1907. Chatterton-Peck Co.
--The Bobbsey Twins: Or, Merry Days Indoors and Out. Stratemeyer Syndicate. Repr. (The Bobbsey Twins Ser.: Vol. 1). 1940. Goldsmith Publishing Co.
--The Bobbsey Twins: Or, Merry Days Indoors and Out. Stratemeyer Syndicate. (Illus.). Repr. of 1904 ed (Pub. by Mershon Co). (The Bobbsey Twins Ser.: Vol. 1). 1908. Grosset & Dunlap.
--The Bobbsey Twins: Or, Merry Days Indoors and Out. Stratemeyer Syndicate. LC 4-32325. (Illus.). iii, 197 p. front., plates. 17 cm. (The Bobbsey Twins Ser.: Vol. 1). c.1904. The Mershon Company.
--The Bobbsey Twins: Or, Merry Days Indoors and Out. Stratemeyer Syndicate. LC 79-88910. (Illus.). 181 p. 20cm. (The Bobbsey Twins Ser.: Vol. 1). c.1979. (ISBN 0-671-95665-5). (ISBN 0-671-95521-7). Wanderer Books.
--The Bobbsey Twins: Or, Merry Days Indoors and Out. Stratemeyer Syndicate. Miller, Martha E., illus. LC 40-10458. 3 p. l., 13-247 p. front., illus. 20 1/2 cm. Repr. (The Bobbsey Twins Ser.: Vol. 1). c.1940. The Saalfield Publishing Company.
--The Bobbsey Twins: Or, Merry Days Indoors and Out. Stratemeyer Syndicate. rev. & enl. ed. Rogers, Walter S., illus. (The Bobbsey Twins Ser.: Vol. 1). 1928. Grosset & Dunlap.
--The Bobbsey Twins: Or, Merry Days Indoors and Out. Stratemeyer Syndicate. Scott, Janet Laura, illus. LC 50-12512. 216 p. illus. 21 cm. Repr. (The Bobbsey Twins Ser.: Vol. 1). 1950. Whitman Publishing Co.
--The Bobbsey Twins: Or, Merry Days Indoors and Out. Stratemeyer Syndicate. Scott, Janet Laura, illus. Repr. (The Bobbsey Twins Ser.: Vol. 1). 1954. Whitman Publishing Co.
--The Bobbsey Twins' Own Little Ferryboat. Stratemeyer Syndicate. LC 56-136407. (Illus.). 184p. illus. 20cm. (The Bobbsey Twins Ser.: Vol. 49). 1956. Grosset & Dunlap.
--The Bobbsey Twins' Own Little Railroad. Stratemeyer Syndicate. LC 51-4228. (Written for the Stratemeyer Syndicate by Harriet Stratemeyer Adams, 1894-1982, under the pseudonym, Laura Lee Hope). (Illus.). viii, 178 p. illus. 20 cm. (The Bobbsey Twins Ser.: Vol. 44). 1951. Grosset & Dunlap.
--The Bobbsey Twins' Search for the Green Rooster. Stratemeyer Syndicate. LC 65 13773. (Illus.). 177 p. illus. 20 cm. (The Bobbsey Twins Ser.: Vol. 58). 1965. Grosset & Dunlap.
--The Bobbsey Twins' Search in the Great City. Stratemeyer Syndicate. rev. ed. LC 61-658149. (Illus.). 182p. illus. 20cm. (The Bobbsey Twins Ser.: Vol. 9). Orig. Title: The Bobbsey Twins in a Great City. c.1960. Grosset & Dunlap.
--The Bobbsey Twins' Secret at the Seashore. Stratemeyer Syndicate. rev. ed. (Illus.). (The Bobbsey Twins Ser.: Vol. 2). Orig. Title: The Bobbsey Twins at the Seashore. 1962. Grosset & Dunlap.
--The Bobbsey Twins: Seventy Fifth Anniversary Commemorative Editions. Stratemeyer Syndicate, 3 vols. Incl. The Bobbsey Twins: Or, Merry Days Indoors and Out. (ISBN 0-671-95665-5); The Bobbsey Twins at the Seashore. (ISBN 0-671-95681-7); The Bobbsey Twins in the Country. (ISBN 0-671-95673-6). (Original Texts and Illustrations of the first three volumes). (Illus.). 1979. Set. (ISBN 0-671-95521-7). Wanderer Bks.
--The Bobbsey Twins Solve a Mystery. Stratemeyer Syndicate. Schubert, Marie (1890-), illus. LC 34-3290. 2 p. l., 218 p. front., plates. 19 cm. (The Bobbsey Twins Ser.: Vol. 27). c.1934. Grosset & Dunlap.
--The Bobbsey Twins' Toy Shop. Stratemeyer Syndicate. (Written for the Stratemeyer Syndicate by Harriet Stratemeyer Adams, 1894-1982, under the pseudonym, Laura Lee Hope). (Illus.). (The Bobbsey Twins Ser.: Vol. 41). (gr. 1-5). 1948. Grosset & Dunlap.
--The Bobbsey Twins Treasure Hunting. Stratemeyer Syndicate. Rogers, Walter S., illus. LC 29-11652. 2 p. l., 244 p. front., plates. 19 1/2 cm. (The Bobbsey Twins Ser.: Vol. 22). c.1929. Grosset & Dunlap.
--The Bobbsey Twins' Visit to the Great West. Stratemeyer Syndicate. rev. ed. LC 66-7102. (Illus.). 174p. illus. 20cm. (The Bobbsey Twins Ser.: Vol. 13). Orig. Title: The Bobbsey Twins in the Great West. 1966. Grosset.
--The Bobbsey Twins' Wonderful Secret. Stratemeyer Syndicate. Rogers, Walter S., illus. LC 31-12249. 2 p. l., 246 p. front., plates. 19 1/2 cm. (The Bobbsey Twins Ser.: Vol. 24). c.1931. Grosset & Dunlap.
--The Bobbsey Twins' Wonderful Winter Secret. Stratemeyer Syndicate. rev. ed. LC 78-304004. (Illus.). vii, 179 p. 20cm. (The Bobbsey Twins Ser.: Vol. 24). Orig. Title: The Bobbsey Twins' Wonderful Secret. c.1962. (ISBN 0-448-08024-9). Grosset & Dunlap.
--Bunny Brown and His Sister Sue. Stratemeyer Syndicate. Nosworthy, Florence England, illus. (The Bunny Brown Ser.: No. 1). 1916. Grosset & Dunlap.
--Bunny Brown and His Sister Sue and Their Shetland Pony. Stratemeyer Syndicate. Gooch, Thelma, illus. (The Bunny Brown Ser.: No. 8). 1916. Grosset & Dunlap.
--Bunny Brown and His Sister Sue and Their Trick Dog. Stratemeyer Syndicate. Rogers, Walter S., illus. (The Bunny Brown Ser.: No. 13). 1923. Grosset & Dunlap.
--Bunny Brown and His Sister Sue at a Sugar Camp. Stratemeyer Syndicate. Rogers, Walter S., illus. (The Bunny Brown Ser.: No. 14). 1924. Grosset & Dunlap.
--Bunny Brown and His Sister Sue at Aunt Lu's City Home. Stratemeyer Syndicate. Nosworthy, Florence England, illus. (The Brown Bunny Ser.: No. 5). 1916. Grosset & Dunlap.
--Bunny Brown and His Sister Sue at Berry Hill. Stratemeyer Syndicate. Rogers, Walter S., illus. LC 29-109572. 2 p. l., 246 p. front., plates. 19 1/2 cm. (The Bunny Brown Ser.: No. 18). c.1929. Grosset & Dunlap.
--Bunny Brown and His Sister Sue at Camp Rest-a-While. Stratemeyer Syndicate. Nosworthy, Florence England, illus. (The Brown Bunny Ser.: No. 4). 1916. Grosset & Dunlap.
--Bunny Brown and His Sister Sue at Christmas Tree Cove. Stratemeyer Syndicate. Rogers, Walter S., illus. (The Bunny Brown Ser.: No. 10). 1920. Grosset & Dunlap.
--Bunny Brown and His Sister Sue at Shore Acres. Stratemeyer Syndicate. Rogers, Walter S., illus. LC 28-132255. 2 p. l., 248 p. front., plates. 19 1/2 cm. (The Bunny Brown Ser.: No. 17). c.1928. Grosset & Dunlap.
--Bunny Brown and His Sister Sue at Sky Top. Stratemeyer Syndicate. Rogers, Walter S., illus. LC 30-123025. 2 p. l., 244 p. front., plates. 19 1/2 cm. (The Bunny Brown Ser.: No. 19). c.1930. Grosset & Dunlap.
--Bunny Brown and His Sister Sue at the Summer Carnival. Stratemeyer Syndicate. Rogers, Walter S., illus. LC 31-122508. 2 p. l., 243 p. front., plates. 19 1/2 cm. (The Bunny Brown Ser.: No. 20). c.1931. Grosset & Dunlap.
--Bunny Brown and His Sister Sue Giving a Show. Stratemeyer Syndicate. Rogers, Walter S., illus. (The Brown Bunny Ser.: No. 9). 1919. Grosset & Dunlap.
--Bunny Brown and His Sister Sue in the Big Woods. Stratemeyer Syndicate. Nosworthy, Florence England, illus. (The Bunny Brown Ser.: No. 6). 1917. Grosset & Dunlap.
--Bunny Brown and His Sister Sue in the Sunny South. Stratemeyer Syndicate. Rogers, Walter S., illus. (The Bunny Brown Ser.: No. 11). 1921. Grosset & Dunlap.
--Bunny Brown and His Sister Sue Keeping Store. Stratemeyer Syndicate. Rogers, Walter S., illus. (The Bunny Brown Ser.: No. 12). 1922. Grosset & Dunlap.
--Bunny Brown and His Sister Sue on an Auto Tour. Stratemeyer Syndicate. Nosworthy, Florence England, illus. (The Bunny Brown Ser.: No. 7). 1917. Grosset & Dunlap.
--Bunny Brown and His Sister Sue on Grandpa's Farm. Stratemeyer Syndicate. Nosworthy, Florence England, illus. (The Bunny Brown Ser.: No. 2). 1916. Grosset & Dunlap.
--Bunny Brown and His Sister Sue on Jack Frost Island. Stratemeyer Syndicate. Rogers, Walter S., illus. (The Bunny Brown Ser.: No. 16). 1927. Grosset & Dunlap.
--Bunny Brown and His Sister Sue on the Rolling Ocean. Stratemeyer Syndicate. Rogers, Walter S., illus. LC 25-9818. 20cm. 246p. (The Bunny Brown Ser.: No. 15). 1925. Grosset & Dunlap.
--Bunny Brown and His Sister Sue Playing Circus. Stratemeyer Syndicate. Nosworthy, Florence England, illus. (The Bunny Brown Ser.: No. 3). 1916. Grosset & Dunlap.
--The Camp Fire Mystery. Stratemeyer Syndicate. Speirs, John, illus. LC 81-24090. 126 p. 20cm. (The Bobbsey Twins (1980-) Ser.: Vol. 6). c.1982. (ISBN 0-671-43374-1). (ISBN 0-671-43373-3). Wanderer Books.
--Double Trouble. Stratemeyer Syndicate. Speirs, John, illus. LC 82-11061. p. cm. (The Bobbsey Twins (1980-) Ser.: Vol. 7). c.1982. (ISBN 0-671-43384-1). (ISBN 0-671-43383-X). Wanderer Books.
--The Dune Buggy Mystery. Stratemeyer Syndicate. Sanderson, Ruth, illus. LC 80-22265. (A Pre Nancy Drew/Hardy Boys Mystery Book). 109 p. 20cm. (The Bobbsey Twins (1980-) Ser.: Vol. 3). c.1981. (ISBN 0-671-42293-6). (ISBN 0-671-42294-4). Wanderer Books.
--The Freedom Bell Mystery. Stratemeyer Syndicate. LC 75-17386. (Illus.). 180 p. 20cm. (The Bobbsey Twins Ser.: Vol. 69). 1977, c.1976. (ISBN 0-448-08069-9). Grosset & Dunlap.
--The Ghost in the Computer. Stratemeyer Syndicate. Barish, Wendy, ed. Speirs, John, illus. LC 83-23303. 128p. (The Bobbsey Twins Ser.: Vol. 10). 1984. (ISBN 0-671-43591-4). Wanderer Bks.
--The Haunted House Mystery. Stratemeyer Syndicate. Arico, Diane, ed. Speirs, John, illus. 128p. (The Bobbsey Twins (1980-) Ser.: Vol. 12). (gr. 7-10). 1985. (ISBN 0-671-54996-0). Wanderer Bks.
--Laura Lee Hope's The Bobbsey Twins. Stratemeyer Syndicate. rev. ed. Kline, Bennett, retold by. Vallely, Henry E., illus. LC 40-327785. ("Retold in 96 pages"). 1 p. l., 7-94 p. front., illus. (part col.) 17 x 14 cm. (The Bobbsey Twins Ser.: Vol. 1). Orig. Title: The Bobbsey Twins; Or, Merry Days Indoors and Out. c.1940. Whitman Publishing Company.
--Meet the Bobbsey Twins. Stratemeyer Syndicate. Dillon, Corinne Boyd, illus. LC 54-327366. unpaged. illus. 21cm. (Wonder Books: No. 623). Orig. Title: The Bobbsey Twins; Or, Merry Days Indoors and Out. c.1954. Wonder Books.
--The Missing Pony Mystery. Stratemeyer Syndicate. Sanderson, Ruth, illus. LC 80-25802. (A Pre Nancy Drew/Hardy Boys Mystery Book). 112 p. 20cm. (The Bobbsey Twins (1980-) Ser.: Vol. 4). c.1981. (ISBN 0-671-42295-2). (ISBN 0-671-42296-0). Wanderer Books.
--The Moving Picture Girls at Oak Farm: Or, Queer Happenings While Taking Rural Plays. Stratemeyer Syndicate. Repr. of 1914 ed (Pub. by Grosset & Dunlap). (The Moving Picture Girls Ser.: Vol. 2). N.D. Goldsmith Publishing Co.
--The Moving Picture Girls at Oak Farm: Or, Queer Happenings While Taking Rural Plays. Stratemeyer Syndicate. Rogers, Walter S., illus. (The Moving Picture Girls Ser.: Vol. 2). 1914. Grosset & Dunlap.
--The Moving Picture Girls at Oak Farm: Or, Queer Happenings While Taking Rural Plays. Stratemeyer Syndicate. Rogers, Walter S., illus. Repr. of 1914 ed (Pub. by Grosset & Dunlap). (The Moving Picture Girls Ser.: Vol. 2). N.D. World Syndicate Publishing Co.
--The Moving Picture Girls at Rocky Ranch: Or, Great Days Among the Cowboys. Stratemeyer Syndicate. Rogers, Walter S., illus. (The Moving Picture Girls Ser.: Vol. 5). 1914. Grosset & Dunlap.
--The Moving Picture Girls at Rocky Ranch: Or, Great Days Among the Cowboys. Stratemeyer Syndicate. Rogers, Walter S., illus. Repr. of 1914 ed (Pub. by Grosset & Dunlap). (The Moving Picture Girls Ser.: Vol. 5). N.D. World Syndicate Publishing Co.
--The Moving Picture Girls at Sea: Or, A Pictured Shipwreck That Became Real. Stratemeyer Syndicate. Rogers, Walter S., illus. (The Moving Picture Girl Ser.: Vol. 6). 1915. Grosset & Dunlap.
--The Moving Picture Girls at Sea: Or, A Pictured Shipwreck that Became Real. Stratemeyer Syndicate. Rogers, Walter S., illus. Repr. of 1915 ed (Pub. by Grosset & Dunlap). (The Moving Picture Girls Ser.: Vol. 6). N.D. World Syndicate Publishing Co.
--The Moving Picture Girls in War Plays: Or, The Sham Battles at Oak Farm. Stratemeyer Syndicate. Rogers, Walter S., illus. (The Moving Picture Girls Ser.: Vol. 7). 1916. Grosset & Dunlap.
--The Moving Picture Girls in War Plays: Or, The Sham Battles at Oak Farm. Stratemeyer Syndicate. Rogers, Walter S., illus. Repr. of 1916 ed (Pub. by Grosset & Dunlap). (The Moving Picture Girls Ser.: Vol. 7). N.D. World Syndicate Publishing Co.
--The Moving Picture Girls: Or, First Appearances in Photo Dramas. Stratemeyer Syndicate. Rogers, Walter S., illus. (The Moving Picture Girls Ser.: Vol. 1). 1914. Grosset & Dunlap.
--The Moving Picture Girls: Or, First Appearances in Photo Dramas. Stratemeyer Syndicate. Rogers, Walter S., illus. Repr. of 1914 ed (Pub. by Grosset & Dunlap). (The Moving Picture Girls Ser.: Vol. 1). N.D. World Syndicate Publishing Co.
--The Moving Picture Girls Snowbound: Or, The Proof on the Film. Stratemeyer Syndicate. Repr. of 1914 ed (Pub. by Grosset & Dunlap). (The Moving Picture Girls Ser.: Vol. 3). N.D. Goldsmith Publishing Co.
--The Moving Picture Girls Snowbound: Or, The Proof on the Film. Stratemeyer Syndicate. Rogers, Walter S., illus. (The Moving Picture Girls Ser.: Vol. 3). 1914. Grosset & Dunlap.
--The Moving Picture Girls Snowbound: Or, The Proof on the Film. Stratemeyer Syndicate. Rogers, Walter S., illus. Repr. of 1914 ed (Pub. by Grosset & Dunlap). (The Moving Picture Girls Ser.: Vol. 3). N.D. World Syndicate Publishing Co.
--The Moving Picture Girls Under the Palms: Or, Lost in the Wilds of Florida. Stratemeyer Syndicate. Repr. of 1914 ed (Pub. by Grosset & Dunlap). (The Moving Picture Girls Ser.: Vol. 4). N.D. Goldsmith Publishing Co.
--The Moving Picture Girls Under the Palms: Or, Lost in the Wilds of Florida. Stratemeyer Syndicate. Rogers, Walter S., illus. (The Moving Picture Girls Ser.: Vol. 4). 1914. Grosset & Dunlap.
--The Moving Picture Girls Under the Palms: Or, Lost in the Wilds of Florida. Stratemeyer Syndicate. Rogers, Walter S., illus. Repr. of 1914 ed (Pub. by Grosset & Dunlap). (The Moving Picture Girls Ser.: Vol. 4). N.D. World Syndicate Publishing Co.
--The Music Box Mystery. Stratemeyer Syndicate. Barish, Wendy, ed. Speirs, John, illus. (A Pre Nancy Drew/Hardy Boys Mystery Book). 128p. (The Bobbsey Twins (1980-) Ser.: Vol. 9). (gr. 2-5). 1983. (ISBN 0-671-43588-4). (ISBN 0-671-43589-2). Wanderer Bks.
--The Mystery of the Hindu Temple. Stratemeyer Syndicate. LC 85-7201. p. cm. (The Bobbsey Twins (1980-) Ser.: Vol. 13). c.1985. (ISBN 0-671-55499-9). Wanderer Books.
--Mystery of the Laughing Dinosaur. Stratemeyer Syndicate. Barish, Wendy, ed. Speirs, John, illus. 128p. (The Bobbsey Twins (1980-) Ser.: Vol. 8). (gr. 8-12). 1983. (ISBN 0-671-43586-8). (ISBN 0-671-43587-6). Wanderer Bks.
--The Outdoor Girls Along the Coast: Or, The Cruise of the Motor Boat Liberty. Stratemeyer Syndicate. Rogers, Walter S., illus. (The Outdoor Girls Ser.: No. 16). 1926. Grosset & Dunlap.

--The Outdoor Girls Around the Campfire: Or, The Old Maid of the Mountains. Stratemeyer Syndicate. Rogers, Walter S., illus. (The Outdoor Girls Ser.: No. 13). 1923. Grosset & Dunlap.

--The Outdoor Girls at Bluff Point: Or, A Wreck and a Rescue. Stratemeyer Syndicate. Rogers, Walter S., illus. (The Outdoor Girls Ser.: No. 10). N.D. Grosset & Dunlap.

--The Outdoor Girls at Cedar Ridge: Or, The Mystery of the Old Windmill. Stratemeyer Syndicate. Repr. of 1931 ed (Pub. by Grosset & Dunlap). (The Outdoor Girls Ser.: No. 21). N.D. Whitman Publishing Co.

--The Outdoor Girls at Cedar Ridge: Or, The Mystery of the Old Windmill. Stratemeyer Syndicate. Rogers, Walter S., illus. LC 31-132201. 2 p. l., 214 p. front., plates. 19 1/2 cm. (The Outdoor Girls Ser.: No. 21). c.1931. Grosset & Dunlap.

--The Outdoor Girls at Foaming Falls: Or, Robina of Red Kennels. Stratemeyer Syndicate. Rogers, Walter S., illus. LC 25-9819. 2 p. l., 212 p. front. 19 1/2 cm. (The Outdoor Girls Ser.: No. 15). c.1925. Grosset & Dunlap.

--The Outdoor Girls at New Moon Ranch: Or, Riding with the Cowboys. Stratemeyer Syndicate. Rogers, Walter S., illus. LC 28-631222. 2 p. l., 212 p. front., plates. 19 1/2 cm. (The Outdoor Girls Ser.: No. 18). c.1928. Grosset & Dunlap.

--The Outdoor Girls at Ocean View: Or, The Box that was Found in the Sand. Stratemeyer Syndicate. Rogers, Walter S., illus. (The Outdoor Girls Ser.: No. 6). 1915. Grosset & Dunlap.

--The Outdoor Girls at Rainbow Lake: Or, The Stirring Cruise of the Motor Boat Gem. Stratemeyer Syndicate. (Illus.). (The Outdoor Girls Ser.: No. 2). 1913. Grosset & Dunlap.

--The Outdoor Girls at Spring Hill Farm: Or, The Ghost of the Old Milk House. Stratemeyer Syndicate. Rogers, Walter S., illus. (The Outdoor Girls Ser.: No. 17). 1927. Grosset & Dunlap.

--The Outdoor Girls at the Hostess House: Or, Doing Their Best for The Soldiers. Stratemeyer Syndicate. Owen, Robert Emmett (1878-), illus. (The Outdoor Girls Ser.: No. 9). 1919. Grosset & Dunlap.

--The Outdoor Girls at Wild Rose Lodge: Or, The Hermit of Moonlight Falls. Stratemeyer Syndicate. Rogers, Walter S., illus. (The Outdoor Girls Ser.: No. 11). 1921. Grosset & Dunlap.

--The Outdoor Girls In a Motor Car: Or, The Haunted Mansion of Shadow Valley. Stratemeyer Syndicate. LC 26-7499. (Illus.). 2 p. l., 212 p. front., plates 19 1/2 cm. (The Outdoor Girls Ser.: No. 3). c.1913. Grosset & Dunlap.

--The Outdoor Girls in a Winter Camp: Or, Glorious Days on Skates and Iceboats. Stratemeyer Syndicate. (Illus.). (The Outdoor Girls Ser.: No. 4). 1913. Grosset & Dunlap.

--The Outdoor Girls in Army Service: Or, Doing Their Bit for the Soldier Boys. Stratemeyer Syndicate. Rogers, Walter S., illus. (The Outdoor Girls Ser.: No. 8). 1918. Grosset & Dunlap.

--The Outdoor Girls in Desert Valley: Or, Strange Happenings in a Cowboy Camp. Stratemeyer Syndicate. Braley, Margaret Temple, illus. LC 33-124201. 2 p. l., 212 p. front., plates. 19 1/2 cm. (The Outdoor Girls Ser.: No. 23). c.1933. Grosset & Dunlap.

--The Outdoor Girls in Florida: Or, Wintering in the Sunny South. Stratemeyer Syndicate. (Illus.). (The Outdoor Girls Ser.: No. 5). 1913. Grosset & Dunlap.

--The Outdoor Girls in the Air: Or, Saving the Stolen Invention. Stratemeyer Syndicate. Repr. of 1932 ed (Pub. by Grosset & Dunlap). (The Outdoor Girls Ser.: No. 22). N.D. Whitman Publishing Co.

--The Outdoor Girls in the Air: Or, Saving the Stolen Invention. Stratemeyer Syndicate. Braley, Margaret Temple, illus. LC 32-12751. 2 p. l., 213 p. front., plates. 19 1/2 cm. (The Outdoor Girls Ser.: No. 22). c.1932. Grosset & Dunlap.

--The Outdoor Girls in the Saddle: Or, The Girl Miner of Gold Run. Stratemeyer Syndicate. Rogers, Walter S., illus. (The Outdoor Girls Ser.: No. 12). 1922. Grosset & Dunlap.

--The Outdoor Girls of Deepdale: Or, Camping and Tramping for Fun and Health. Stratemeyer Syndicate. (Illus.). (The Outdoor Girls Ser.: No. 1). 1913. Grosset & Dunlap.

--The Outdoor Girls on a Canoe Trip: Or, The Secret of the Brown Mill. Stratemeyer Syndicate. Repr. of 1930 ed (Pub. by Grosset & Dunlap). (The Outdoor Girls Ser.: No. 20). N.D. Whitman Publishing Co.

--The Outdoor Girls on a Canoe Trip: Or, The Secret of the Brown Mill. Stratemeyer Syndicate. Rogers, Walter S., illus. LC 30-12303. iv, 212 p. front., plates. 19 1/2 cm. (The Outdoor Girls Ser.: Vol. 20). c.1930. Grosset & Dunlap.

--The Outdoor Girls on a Hike: Or, The Mystery of the Deserted Airplane. Stratemeyer Syndicate. Repr. of 1929 ed (Pub. by Grosset & Dunlap). (The Outdoor Girls Ser.: No. 19). N.D. Whitman Publishing Co.

--The Outdoor Girls on a Hike: Or, The Mystery of the Deserted Airplane. Stratemeyer Syndicate. Rogers, Walter S., illus. LC 29-10961. iv, 236 p. front., plates. 19 1/2 cm. (The Outdoor Girls Ser.: No. 19). c.1929. Grosset & Dunlap.

--The Outdoor Girls on Cape Cod: Or, Sally Ann of Lighthouse Rock. Stratemeyer Syndicate. Rogers, Walter S., illus. (The Outdoor Girls Ser.: No. 14). 1924. Grosset & Dunlap.

--The Outdoor Girls on Pine Island: Or, A Cave and What it Contained. Stratemeyer Syndicate. Rogers, Walter S., illus. (The Outdoor Girls Ser.: No. 7). 1916. Grosset & Dunlap.

--The Red, White, and Blue Mystery. Stratemeyer Syndicate. LC 79-144071. (Illus.). 178 p. 20cm. (The Bobbsey Twins Ser.: Vol. 64). 1971. (ISBN 0-448-08064-8). Grosset & Dunlap.

--The Rose Parade Mystery. Stratemeyer Syndicate. Sanderson, Ruth, illus. LC 81-11575. p. cm. (The Bobbsey Twins (1980-) Ser.: Vol. 5). c.1981. (ISBN 0-671-43372-5). (ISBN 0-671-43371-7). Wanderer Books.

--The Scarecrow Mystery. Stratemeyer Syndicate. Barish, Wendy, ed. Speirs, John, illus. 128p. (The Bobbsey Twins (1980-) Ser.: Vol. 11). (gr. 2-5). 1984. (ISBN 0-671-53238-3). Wanderer Bks.

--The Secret in the Pirate's Cave. Stratemeyer Syndicate. Sanderson, Ruth, illus. LC 80-15070. (A Pre Nancy Drew/Hardy Boys Mystery Book). 124 p. 20cm. (The Bobbsey Twins (1980-) Ser.: Vol. 2). c.1980. (ISBN 0-671-41118-7). (ISBN 0-671-41113-6). Wanderer Books.

--Six Little Bunkers. Stratemeyer Syndicate. (A Four-in-one reprint from The Six Little Bunkers Series). (Illus.). Repr. 1933. Grosset & Dunlap.

--Six Little Bunkers at Aunt Jo's. Stratemeyer Syndicate. Owen, Robert Emmett (1878-), illus. (The Six Little Bunkers Ser.: No. 2). 1918. Grosset & Dunlap.

--Six Little Bunkers at Captain Ben's. Stratemeyer Syndicate. Owen, Robert Emmett (1878-), illus. (The Six Little Bunkers Ser.: No. 6). 1920. Grosset & Dunlap.

--Six Little Bunkers at Cousin Tom's. Stratemeyer Syndicate. Owen, Robert Emmett (1878-), illus. (The Six Little Bunkers Ser.: No. 3). 1918. Grosset & Dunlap.

--Six Little Bunkers at Cowboy Jack's. Stratemeyer Syndicate. Rogers, Walter S., illus. LC 29-27402. 2 p. l., 246 p. front., plates. 19 1/2 cm. (The Six Little Bunkers Ser.: No. 7). 1921. Grosset & Dunlap.

--Six Little Bunkers at Farmer Joel's. Stratemeyer Syndicate. Rogers, Walter S., illus. (The Six Little Bunkers Ser.: No. 9). 1923. Grosset & Dunlap.

--Six Little Bunkers at Grandma Bell's. Stratemeyer Syndicate. Owen, Robert Emmett (1878-), illus. (The Six Little Bunkers Ser.: No. 1). 1918. Grosset & Dunlap.

--Six Little Bunkers at Grandpa Ford's. Stratemeyer Syndicate. Owen, Robert Emmett (1878-), illus. LC 29-3268. iv, 248 p. col. front., plates. 19 1/2 cm. (The Six Little Bunkers Ser.: No. 4). 1918. Grosset & Dunlap.

--Six Little Bunkers at Happy Jim's. Stratemeyer Syndicate. Rogers, Walter S., illus. LC 28-12652. iv, 248 p. col. front., plates. 19 1/2 cm. (The Six Little Bunkers Ser.: No. 12). c.1928. Grosset & Dunlap.

--Six Little Bunkers at Indian John's. Stratemeyer Syndicate. Rogers, Walter S., illus. LC 25-9820. 2 p. l., 246 p. front., plates 19 1/2 cm. (The Six Little Bunkers Ser.: No. 11). c.1925. Grosset & Dunlap.

--Six Little Bunkers at Lighthouse Nell's. Stratemeyer Syndicate. Rogers, Walter S., illus. LC 30-13238. iv, 242 p. col. front., plates. 19 1/2 cm. (The Six Little Bunkers Ser.: No. 14). c.1930. Grosset & Dunlap.

--Six Little Bunkers at Mammy June's. Stratemeyer Syndicate. Rogers, Walter S., illus. (The Six Little Bunkers Ser.: No. 8). 1922. Grosset & Dunlap.

--Six Little Bunkers at Miller Ned's. Stratemeyer Syndicate. Rogers, Walter S., illus. (The Six Little Bunkers Ser.: No. 10). 1924. Grosset & Dunlap.

--Six Little Bunkers at Skipper Bob's. Stratemeyer Syndicate. Rogers, Walter S., illus. LC 29-109623. iv, 246 p. col. front., plates. 19 1/2 cm. (The Six Little Bunkers Ser.: No. 13). c.1929. Grosset & Dunlap.

--Six Little Bunkers at Uncle Fred's. Stratemeyer Syndicate. Owen, Robert Emmett (1878-), illus. (The Six Little Bunkers Ser.: No. 5). 1918. Grosset & Dunlap.

--The Story of a Bold Tin Soldier. Stratemeyer Syndicate. Smith, Harry L., illus. LC 20-175289. 3 p. l., 120 p. front., plates. 18 1/2 cm. (Make-Believe Stories: No. 4). c.1920. Grosset & Dunlap.

--The Story of a Calico Clown. Stratemeyer Syndicate. Smith, Harry L., illus. LC 20-155097. 3 p. l., 118 p. front., plates. 18 1/2 cm. (Make-Believe Stories: No. 7). c.1920. Grosset & Dunlap.

--The Story of a Candy Rabbit. Stratemeyer Syndicate. Smith, Harry L., illus. LC 20-155107. 3 p. l., 120 p. front., plates. 18 1/2 cm. (Make-Believe Stories: No. 5). c.1920. Grosset & Dunlap.

--The Story of a China Cat. Stratemeyer Syndicate. Smith, Harry L., illus. (Make-Believe Stories: No. 9). 1921. Grosset & Dunlap.

--The Story of a Lamb on Wheels. Stratemeyer Syndicate. Smith, Harry L., illus. LC 20-175292. 3 p. l., 120 p. front., plates. 18 1/2 cm. (Make-Believe Stories: No. 3). c.1920. Grosset & Dunlap.

--The Story of a Monkey on a Stick. Stratemeyer Syndicate. Smith, Harry L., illus. 3 p. l., 120 p. front., plates. 18 1/2 cm. (Make-Believe Stories: No. 6). c.1920. Grosset & Dunlap.

--The Story of a Nodding Donkey. Stratemeyer Syndicate. Smith, Harry L., illus. (Make-Believe Stories: No. 8). 1921. Grosset & Dunlap.

--The Story of a Plush Bear. Stratemeyer Syndicate. Smith, Harry L., illus. (Make-Believe Stories: No. 10). 1921. Grosset & Dunlap.

--The Story of a Sawdust Doll. Stratemeyer Syndicate. Smith, Harry L., illus. LC 20-155121. 3 p. l., 120 p. front., plates. 18 1/2 cm. (Make-Believe Stories: No. 1). c.1920. Grosset & Dunlap.

--The Story of a Stuffed Elephant. Stratemeyer Syndicate. Smith, Harry L., illus. (Make-Believe Stories: No. 11). 1922. Grosset & Dunlap.

--The Story of a White Rocking Horse. Stratemeyer Syndicate. Smith, Harry L., illus. LC 20-155130. 3 p. l., 120 p. front., plates. 18 1/2 cm. (Make-Believe Stories: No. 2). c.1920. Grosset & Dunlap.

--The Story of a Woolly Dog. Stratemeyer Syndicate. Smith, Harry L., illus. (Make-Believe Stories: No. 12). 1923. Grosset & Dunlap.

Hope, Mrs.

--Changed Scenes: Or, The Castle & the Cottage. N.D. Thos Nelson & Sons.

Hope-Simpson, Jacynth (1930-)

--Black Madonna. LC 76-376888. 4, 124 p. 23cm. 1976. (ISBN 0-434-94318-5). Heinemann.

--Black Madonna. LC 76-27315. 1390p. 21 cm. c.1976. (ISBN 0-8407-6516-9). T. Nelson.

--A Cavalcade of Witches. Turska, Krystyna Zofia (1933-), illus. LC 67-11. (Illus.). 225 p. 26cm. 1st U.S. edition. 1967, c.1966. H. Z. Walck.

--The Curse of the Dragon's Gold: European Myths and Legends. 1st ed. Longoni, Alberto, illus. LC 69-15165. (Illus.). ix, 180 p. 24cm. 1969. Doubleday.

--The Edge of the World. Warner, Peter (1939-), illus. LC 66-131299. 94p. illus. 22cm. 1st U.S. edition. 1966, c.1965. Coward.

--The Great Fire. Marriott, Patricia (1920-), illus. LC 62-14211. 128p. 21cm. 1962, c.1961. Dutton.

--The Unknown Island. LC 70-75793. 192 p. 22cm. 1969, c.1968. Coward-McCann.

--Who Knows?. Twelve Unsolved Mysteries. LC 76-3612. 160p. 1st U.S. edition. (gr. 6 up). 1976. (ISBN 0-525-66484-X). Elsevier-Nelson.

Hope, Stanton

--Smugglers' Gallows. Aldin, Cecil Charles Windsor (1870-1935) & Matthews, R. G., illus. LC 38-443142. viii p., 1 l., 11-209 p. col. front., illus., plates. 21 1/2 cm. 1937. C. Scribner's Sons.

Hope, Winifred Ayres

--Friends in Bookland. N.D. Macmillan.

Hopf, Alice Lightner see Lightner, A. M., pseud.

Hopf, Alice Lightner see Lightner, A. M., pseud.

Hopf, Alice Lightner (1904-)

--Biography of a Rhino. Lightner, A. M., pseud. new ed. (Illus.). (Nature Biography Ser.). (gr. 3-5). 1972. (ISBN 0-399-60745-5). Putnam.

--The Day of the Drones. Lightner, A. M., pseud. LC 69-12618. 255 p. 21cm. 1969. Norton.

--Gods or Demons?. Lightner, A. M., pseud. LC 73-81172. 208 p. 22cm. (gr. 5-10). 1973. (ISBN 0-590-07314-1). Four Winds Press.

--The Space Gypsies. Lightner, A. M., pseud. LC 74-7483. v, 216 p. 21cm. 1974. (ISBN 0-07-037835-5). McGraw-Hill.

--Star Circus. Lightner, A. M., pseud. LC 77-8489. p. cm. c.1977. (ISBN 0-525-39890-2). Dutton.

--Star Dog. Lightner, A. M, pseud. LC 72-8989. 179 p. 21cm. 1973. (ISBN 0-07-037840-1). McGraw-Hill.

--The Thursday Toads. Lightner, A. M., pseud. LC 73-167494. 189 p. 22cm. 1971. (ISBN 0-07-037833-9). McGraw-Hill.

--The Walking Zoo of Darwin Dingle. Lightner, A. M., pseud. Cuffari, Richard (1925-1978), illus. LC 75-77778. (Illus.). 156 p. 22cm. 1969. Putnam.

Hopka, Erich, tr. see Wiemer, Rudolf Otto.

Hopkins, Annette Brown

--The Knight of the Lion. (Everychild's Ser.). N.D. Macmillan.

Hopkins, Annette Brown (1879-), adapted by see Chrestien De Troyes.

Hopkins, Caleb

--Story of Frank... LC 15-231031. 180 p. illus. 15 cm. (His School library of useful and general knowledge. vol. II). 1832. M'Elrath & Bangs.

Hopkins, Clark see Lee, Roy, pseud.

Hopkins, Clark (1895-1976)

--Cyrus Hunts the Cougar. Lee, Roy, pseud. 1st ed. Rowand, Phyllis (1915-), illus. LC 54-510627. 115p. illus. 22cm. 1954. Little, Brown.

--Indians, Fire Engines, and Rabbit. Lee, Roy, pseud. Rowand, Phyllis (1915-), illus. LC 51-7288. 125 p. illus. 21 cm. 1951. Little, Brown.

Hopkins, Emma Stelter (1870-), tr. see Spyri, Johanna Heusser.

Hopkins, George

--Ralph's Possession, 1 of 50 vols. (Young People's Library: No. 31). N.D. Set. Lothrop Publishing Co.

Hopkins, Gerard, tr. see Baudouy, Michel Aime.

Hopkins, Gerard, tr. see Bosco, Henri.

Hopkins, Henry Clayton

--The Moon-Boat And Other Verse. Clayton, W. Philip Vinton, illus. LC 18-15624. 27 p. col. illus. 28 1/2 cm. c.1918. D. McKay.

Hopkins, Hildegarde L., illus.

--The Little Dog Who Forgot How to Bark: The Little Boy Who Found His Fortune, Why the Monkey Still Has a Tail. LC 46-21743. 40 p. illus. (part col.) 25 x 19 cm. 1946. Wonder Books.

Hopkins, Isabel Thompson, Miss

--Arrow Head Light. LC 12-34681. 366 p. front., plates. 19 cm. (Sunday-Hour Lib.). c.1887. American Tract Society.

--The Blue Badge Boys. 384p. (The Golden Rod Lib). 1881. American Tract Society.

--The Blue Badge Boys, 1 of 50 vols. 384p. (Library of Best Authors). 1905. American Tract Society.

--Christmas at the Beeches. 170p. N.D. Hurd & Houghton for American Tract Society.

--Christmas at the Beeches. 170p. (Cozy House Stories). N.D. Lockwood, Brooks, & Co. for American Tract Society.

--Cozy-House Tales. 163p. N.D. Hurd & Houghton for American Tract Society.

--Cozy-House Tales. 163p. N.D. Lockwood, Brooks, & Co. for American Tract Society.

--Endeavor Chris. 401p. N.D. Pilgrim Press.

--Floy Lindsley and Her Friends. LC 12-34416. (Illus.). 17cm. 296p. 1875. American Tract Society.

--The Good Time Girls, 1 of 50 vols. LC 12-34414. 472p. (Library of Best Authors). 1884. Set. American Tract Society.

--Harry Fenimore's Principles. LC 12-34413. (Illus.). 17cm. 296p. 1877. American Tract Society.

--Judge Havisham's Will, 1 of 50 vols. LC 12-344122. 19cm. 311p. (Library of Best Authors). 1888. Set. American Tract Society.

--Ready and Willing. LC 12-34425. 17cm. 333p. N.D. American Tract Society.

--Ruthie's Venture. (Illus.). 336p. 1876. American Tract Society.

--Tall Chestnuts of Vandyke, 1 of 50 vols. LC 12-34424. 18 1/2cm. 395p. (Library of Best Authors). 1886. Set. American Tract Society.

--Up to the Mark, 1 of 50 vols. LC 12-34423. 18 1/2cm. 372p. (Library of Best Authors). 1883. Set. American Tract Society.

Hopkins, J. H.

--The Three Kings of Orient: A Christmas Carol. (Illus.). N.D. Hurd & Houghton.

Hopkins, L. P., Mrs., jt. auth. see Davis, Caroline E. Kelly, Mrs.

Hopkins, Lee B. (1938-), selected by see Behn, Harry.

Hopkins, Lee Bennett (1938-), ed. see Hughes, James Langston.

Hopkins, Lee Bennett, selected by see Sandburg, Carl August.

Hopkins, Lee Bennett (1938-)

--A-Haunting We Will Go: Ghostly Stories and Poems. Rosenberry, Vera, illus. LC 76-45449. (Illus.). 128 p. 24cm. c.1977. (ISBN 0-8075-3356-4). A Whitman.

--Charlie's World: A Book of Poems. Robinson, Charles (1931-), illus. LC 72-75884. (Illus.). 43 p. 1972. (ISBN 0-672-51706-X). Bobbs-Merrill.

--City Talk. Arenella, Roy (1939-), photos by. LC 74-102801. (Illus.). 46 p. 24cm. 1970. Knopf.

Horgan, Paul (1903-)
--Men of Arms. Horgan, Paul (1903-), illus. N.D. David McKay Co.
--Toby and the Night-time. Smith, Lawrence Beall (1909-), illus. LC 63-9074. 71 p. illus. 24 cm. 1963. Ariel Books.
--Toby & the Nighttime. Smith, Lawrence Beall (1909-), illus. (Illus.). (gr. 1-5). 1963. FS&G.
--Whitewater. LC 76-122830. 320p. 337p. (gr. 8 up). 1970. (ISBN 0-374-28970-0). FS&G.
Horio, Seishi
--The Monkey & the Crab. Murakami, Tsutomu, illus. Ooka, D. T., tr. from Japanese. (Illus.). 32p. (Japanese Fairy Tale Ser.). 1985. (ISBN 0-89346-246-2). Heian Intl.
Horler, Hans
--Kel of the Ancient River. Roschl, Kurt, illus. McGavin, Moyra, tr. from Ger. LC 63-9060. 190 p. illus. 22 cm. 1963, c.1962. Warne.
Horler, Sydney
--Miss Mystery. 1935. Little, Brown & Co.
--The Prince of Plunder. 1934. Little, Brown & Co.
Hormann, Toni
--Onions, Onions. Stanley, Diane (1943-), illus. LC 79-7837. (Illus.). 32 p. 24cm. c.1981. (ISBN 0-690-04056-3). (ISBN 0-690-04057-1). Crowell.
Hormann, Toni, jt. auth. see Kroll, Steven.
Horn, Alfred Aloysius & Lewis, Ethelreda, Mrs.
--The Boys' Trader Horn: The Adventures of a Boy Trader on the Ivory Coast and in the African Jungle. Kempton, Kenneth Payson. (1891-), ed. LC 28-29966. 7 p. l., 218 p. plates. 21 cm. 1928. Simon and Schuster.
Horn, Axel
--Only Us! Only Us!. Horn, Axel, illus. LC 74-150057. (Illus.). 48 p. 1971. Little, Brown.
--You Can Be Taller. Ehrenberg, Myron, photos by. Horn, Axel, designed by. LC 70-189264. (Illus.). 32 p. 23cm. 1974. (ISBN 0-316-37322-2). Little, Brown.
Horn, Geoffrey & Cavanaugh, Arthur, eds.
--Bible Stories for Children. Stewart, Arvis L, illus. LC 79-27811. (Illus.). xiii, 317 p. 29cm. c.1980. MacMillan.
Horn, Gladys M.
--Benny the Bus. Vaughan, Eileen Fox, illus. LC 50-34659. (Illus.). 17cm. 32p. (Tell-a-Tale Bks.). 1950. Whitman.
--Bounce: The Story of a Kitten. Wohlberg, Meg. (1905-), illus. LC 41-21725. 32 p. illus. (part col.) 22 1/2 x 20 cm. c.1941. The John C. Winston Company.
--Cradle Rhymes. Rachel, illus. LC 49-5077. 32 p. col. illus. 17 cm. (Tell-a-tale books). 1949. Whitman Pub. Co.
--Franky, the Fuzzy Goat. Suzanne, illus. LC 51-25619. (Illus.). 16p. 17cm. (Fuzzy Wuzzy Tell-a-Tales). 1951. Whitman Publishing Co.
--Fuzzy Joe Bear. Berry, Anne Scheu, illus. LC 54-37053. unpaged. illus. 17cm. (Fuzzy wuzzy tell-a-tales). c.1954. Whitman Pub. Co.
--Hi! Cowboy. Williams, Ben, illus. LC 50-34273. (Illus.). 17cm. 32p. (Tell-a-Tale Bk.). 1950. Whitman.
--A Horse for Henry. Helweg, Hans H. (1917-), illus. LC 52-4206. unpaged. illus. 21 cm. (Cozy-corner book). 1952. Whitman Pub. Co.
--Pitty Pat, the Fuzzy Cat. Winship, Florence Sarah, illus. LC 54-37051. unpaged. illus. 17cm. (Fuzzy wuzzy book). 1954. Whitman Pub. Co.
--Somebody Forgot. Stang, Judy, pseud. (1921-1977), illus. Stang, Judit. LC 54-35677. (Illus.). 17cm. (Tell-a-Tale Bks.). 1954. Whitman Pub. Co.
--Sunny, Honey, and Funny. Lesko, Zillah, illus. LC 51-25620. (Illus.). 16p. 17cm. (Fuzzy Wuzzy Tell-a-Tales). 1951. Whitman Pub. Co.
--Who Said It?. Depper, Hertha, illus. LC 54-33173. (Illus.). 21cm. (A Cozy-Corner Bk.). 1954. Whitman Pub. Co.
Horn, Madeline Darrough, Mrs.
--Dannie: A Tale of the Galveston Hurricane of 1900. LC 52-11253. 118 p. illus. 22 cm. 1952. Naylor Co.
--Farm on the Hill. Wood, Grant (1892-1942), illus. LC 36-8013. viii p., 2 l., 3-78 p. col. front., col. plates. 24 1/2 cm. 1936. C. Scribner's Sons.
--Log Cabin Family. McCray, Francis, illus. LC 39-30529. 95 p. col. plates. 24 1/2 cm. c.1939. C. Scribner's Sons.
--The New Home. Stein, Harve (1904-), illus. LC 62-9288. (Illus.). (gr. 2-6). 1962. (ISBN 0-684-20854-7). Scribner.
Horn, Max, jt. auth. see Wohlberg, Meg.
Horn, William Van see Van Horn, William.
Horn, Yvonne Michie
--Sing for Your Supper: Earning Your Living As a Singer. LC 79-87519. p. cm. c.1979. (ISBN 0-15-274959-4). Harcourt Brace Jovanovich.
Horna, Luis De see De Horna, Luis.
Hornady, William T.
--Tales from Nature's Wonderlands. N.D. Charles Scribner's Sons.
Hornback, Florence M.
--Kianga. (Illus.). (gr. 1-3). 1948. St Anthony.
Hornby, George Arthur (1911-)
--The City Dog and the Country Cat. Yeakey, Carol, illus. LC 46-263973. 32 p. col. illus. 23 x 21 cm. c.1945. The Domesday Press, Inc., Random House, Distributors.
--Poems for Children and Other People. Cybis Inc, illus. LC 75-35971. (Illus.). 108 p. 29cm. c.1975. (ISBN 0-517-11731-2). Crown Publishers.
--Through Many-Colored Glasses: The Child's World in Verse and Song. Kohs, Marion R., illus. LC 45-820583. 2 p. l., 7-62 p. illus. (part col.) 31 1/2 cm. 1945. The Domesday Press, Inc.
Hornby, George Arthur (1911-) & Hofrichter, Allen, eds.
--The Long-Ago Book. Kramer, Florian (1908-), illus. LC 45-264. 32 p. col., illus. 15 1/2 x 45 1/2 cm. N.D. L. B. Fischer Publishing Corp.; Sole Distributors: J. L. Schilling Co.
Horne, Catherine
--Word Weaving: A Storytelling Workbook. LC 80-54094. 136p. (gr. k-6). 1980. (ISBN 0-936434-03-1). Zellerbach F F.
Horne, Richard Henry, jt. auth. see Elwes, Alfred.
Horne, Richard Henry (1803-1884)
--The Good-Natured Bear: A Story for Children of All Ages. Hummel, Lisl, illus. LC 27-184587. xvi, 159 p. incl. front., illus., plates. 16 1/2cm. (Half-title: The little library). 1927. The Macmillan Company.
--King Penguin: A Legend of the South Sea Isles. Daugherty, James Henry (1889-1974), illus. Fox, Frances Margaret (1870-), intro. by. LC 25-149681. xvi p., 1 l., 95 p. incl. illus., plates. col. front., col. plates. 17cm. the little library. 1925. The Macmillan Company.
--Memoirs of a London Doll. new ed. Fisher, Margery Tuner (1913-), ed. Gillies, Margaret & Smith, Richard S., illus. LC 68-18475. (Illus.). 19 line drawings. bibl. footnotes. 176p. 1st U.S. edition. (gr. 3-5). 1968. (ISBN 0-02-744540-2). Macmillan.
Horner, Althea Jane (1926-)
--Little Big Girl. Rosamilia, Patricia, illus. LC 81-20164. p. cm. 1982. (ISBN 0-89885-098-3). Human Sciences Press.
Horner, Letta D.
--Nanette. N.D. Pageant Press, Inc.
Hornibrook, Isabel Katherine (1859-)
--Ann of Seacrest High. LC 25-2658. 4 p. l., 222 p. front., plates. 19 1/2cm. c.1924. David McKay Company.
--Camp and Trail: A Story of the Maine Woods. Barnes, George Foster, illus. 2 p. l., 3-365 p. front., plates. 19 1/2cm. 1897. Lothrop Publishing Company.
--Camp Fire Girls and Mt. Greylock. Goss, John, illus. LC 18-1223. 5 p. l., 347 p. col. front., col. plates. 19 1/2cm. 1917. Lothrop, Lee & Shepard Co.
--Camp Fire Girls in War and Peace. Goss, John, illus. LC 20-362223. vii, 292 p. col. front., col. plates. 19 1/2cm. c.1919. Lothrop, Lee & Shepard Co.
--Coxswain Drake of the Seascouts. N.D. Little Brown & Co.
--Drake and the Adventurers' Cup. Gallagher, Sears (1869-1955), illus. LC 22-9361. x p., 2 l., 3-309 p. incl. front. plates. 19 1/2 cm. $1.75. 1922. Little, Brown and Company.
--Drake of Troop One. Gallagher, Sears (1869-1955), illus. LC 16-21970. 5 p. l., 321 p. front., plates. 19 1/2 cm. 1916. Little, Brown, and Company.
--From Keel to Kite: How Oakley Rose Became a Naval Architect. Smith, Frank Vining, illus. LC 8-31470. 5 p. l., 511 p. front., 6 pl. 19 1/2 cm. $1.50. 1908. Lothrop, Lee & Shepard Co.
--Girls of the Morning-Glory Camp Fire. Goss, John, illus. LC 16-12238. 6 p. l., 321 p. front., plates. 19 1/2cm. c.1916. Lothrop, Lee & Shepard Co.
--Heroes of Air and Sea. LC 13-25609. 63 p. illus. 17 1/2 cm. $0.12. c.1913. David C. Cook Publishing Co.
--Pemrose Lorry, Camp Fire Girl. Rollins, Nana Bickford, illus. LC 21-173717. 6 p. l., 300 p., 1 l. front., plates. 19 1/2 cm. $1.75. 1921. Little, Brown, and Company.
--Pemrose Lorry, Radio Amateur. Rollins, Nana Bickford, illus. LC 23-798117. viii p., 1 l., 311 p. front., plates. 19 1/2cm. 1923. Little, Brown, and Company.
--Pemrose Lorry, Sky Sailor. Rollins, Nana Bickford, illus. LC 24-289562. vi p., 1 l., 325 p. front., plates. 19 1/2cm. 1924. Little, Brown, and Company.
--Pemrose Lorry, Torchbearer. Rollins, Nana Bickford, illus. LC 26-103193. vi p., 1 l., 281 p. front., plates. 19 1/2cm. 1926. Little, Brown, and Company.
--Romee Ann, Junior. Davis, Emma Earlenbaugh, illus. LC 27-110278. 3 p. l., 236 p. front., plates. 19 1/2cm. c.1926. David McKay Company.
--Romee Ann, Sophomore. Davis, Emma Earlenbaugh, illus. LC 25-19905. v p., 1 l., 196 p. front., plates. 19 1/2cm. c.1925. David McKay Company.
--Scout Drake in War Time. Gallagher, Sears (1869-1955), illus. LC 18-185402. 5 p. l., 305 p. front., plates. 19 1/2cm. 1918. Little, Brown, and Company.
--A Scout of to-Day. LC 13-15169. 6 p. l., 290 p., 1 l. col. front., plates. 19 1/2 cm. $1.00. 1913. Houghton Mifflin Company.
--Tuke. N.D. Thos Nelson & Sons.
Horning, Pat
--Discovery on a Summer-Ripe Day, and Other Stories from Listen Magazine. LC 78-24510. p. cm. 1979. Review and Herald Publishing Association.
Hornnes, Esther, jt. auth. see Magos, Eunice.
Hornstein, J G
--Caravan Tales. N.D. Frederick A Stokes.
Hornung, Ernest William (1866-1921)
--Young Blood. LC 12-343900. vii, 320 p. 19 cm. 1898. C. Scribner's Sons.
Hornyansky, Michael, jt. ed. see Barbeau, Charles Marius.
Hornyansky, Michael, retold by see Barbeau, Marius.
Horowitz, Abraham, jt. auth. see Fidell, Jeanette.
Horowitz, Anthony (1955-)
--The Devil's Door-Bell. LC 83-8587. 158 p. 22cm. 1st U.S. edition. 1984, c.1983. (ISBN 0-03-063813-5). Holt, Rinehart and Winston.
--The Night of the Scorpion. LC 84-25518. 159 p. 23cm. 1st U.S. edition. 1984. (ISBN 0-448-47751-3). Pacer Books.
--The Sinister Secret of Frederick K. Bower. Woodgate, John, illus. LC 80-17312. p. cm. 1980. (ISBN 0-531-09570-3). D. Elliott : Distributed by F. Watts.
Horowitz, Caroline see Crawford, Jack B., pseud.
Horowitz, Caroline see French, Marion N., pseud.
Horowitz, Caroline see Jollison, Marion, pseud.
Horowitz, Caroline see Lansing, Jane K., pseud.
Horowitz, Caroline see Strong, Joanna, pseud.
Horowitz, Caroline see Winters, Mary K., pseud.
Horowitz, Caroline (1909-)
--Alphabet Zoo. Lansing, Jane K., pseud. Davidson, Ruby & Weihs, Erika (1917-), illus. LC 64-24876. 1965. Hart Pub. Co.
--The Ask-Me Book of Best-Loved Fairy Tales. Winters, Mary K., pseud. Flory, Jane Trescott (1917-), illus. LC 50-3999. 96 p. col. illus. 22 cm. (Happy hour books). 1950. Hart.
--Being Nice is Lots of Fun. Lansing, Jane K., pseud. Myers, Bernice, illus. 72p. N.D. (ISBN 0-87460-153-3). (ISBN 0-87460-152-5). Lion Press.
--Favorite Folktales and Fables for Boys and Girls. Strong, Joanna, pseud. Whatley, Hubert, illus. LC 50-2777. 96 p. col. illus. 22 cm. (Happy hour books). 1950. Hart Pub. Co.
--Legends Children Love. Strong, Joanna, pseud. Whatley, Hubert, illus. LC 50-6071. 96 p. col. illus. 22 cm. (Happy hour books). 1950. Hart Pub. Co.
--Myths and Legends of the Ages. French, Marion N., pseud. rev. ed. Davis, Bette J. (1923-), illus. LC 57-141516. 319p. illus. 25cm. 1957, c.1956. Hart Pub. Co.
--The Roly-Poly Policeman. Lansing, Jane K., pseud. Weihs, Erika (1917-), illus. LC 64-248792. 25p. col. illus. 32cm. c.1965. Hart.
--Sing a Song of Manners. Jollison, Marion, pseud. Myers, Bernice, illus. LC 52-14493. 63 p. illus. 25 cm. 1952. Hart Publications.
--A Treasury of Good Night Stories. Barreaux, Adolphe, illus. LC 49-1546. 180 p. col. illus. 23 cm. c.1948. Hart Pub. Co.
--A Treasury of Good Night Stories. rev. ed. Barreaux, Adolphe, illus. LC 53-9275. 189p. illus. 23cm. 1952, c.1948. Hart Pub. Co.
--Wild West Show. Crawford, Jack B., pseud. King, Robin, pseud. (1919-), illus. Raleigh-King, Robin Victor Lethbridge. LC 51-5441. 192 p. illus. 27 cm. 1951. Hart Pub. Co.
Horowitz, Caroline (1909-) & Leonard, Tom B. (1908-), eds.
--Big Book of Laughs for Boys & Girls. Strong, Joanna, pseud. LC 49-10681. 192 p. illus. (part col.) 28 cm. 1949. Hart. Pub. Co.
--A Treasury of the World's Great Myths and Legends for Boys and Girls. Strong, Joanna, pseud. Whatley, Hubert, illus. LC 51-12383. 319 p. illus. 24 cm. 1951. Hart Pub. Co.
Horowitz, Eugene (1930-)
--Mr. Jack and the Greenstalks. LC 79-90979. 384p. 1970. (ISBN 0-393-08593-7). Norton & Co.
Horowitz, Harold Hart see Thompson, Jeff, pseud.
Horowitz, Harold Hart (1903-), ed.
--Jolly Jokes and Jingles for Boys and Girls. Thompson, Jeff, pseud. Bley, Hy, illus. LC 50-2776. 96 p. col. illus. 22 cm. (Happy hour books). 1950. Hart Pub. Co.
Horowitz, Susan, adapted by.
--Cinderella with Benjy & Bubbles. Razzi, James (1931-), illus. LC 77-17679. (Read with Me Ser.). 1978. (ISBN 0-03-040236-0). HR&W.
--Jack and the Beanstalk, with Benjy and Bubbles. Razzi, James (1931-), illus. LC 77-17681. p. cm. (Read with Me Series). 1978. (ISBN 0-03-040241-7). Holt, Rinehart, and Winston.
--Snow White & the Seven Dwarfs with Benjy & Bubbles. LC 77-176880. (Illus.). (Read with Me Ser.). (gr. k-3). 1978. (ISBN 0-03-040231-X). HR&W.
Horowitz, Susan, ed. see Grimm, Jakob Ludwig Karl.
Horowitz, Susan, adapted by see Grimm, Jakob Ludwig Karl (1785-1863) & Grimm, Wilhelm Karl.
Horowitz, Susan & Perle, Ruth Lerner, eds.
--Little Red Riding Hood with Benjy and Bubbles. Maestro, Giulio (1942-), illus. LC 78-55627. p. cm. (Read with Me Series). 1979. (ISBN 0-03-044961-8). Holt, Rinehart and Winston.
--Rumpelstilskin with Benjy & Bubbles. Maestro, Giulio (1942-), illus. LC 78-55628. (Illus.). (Read with Me Ser.). (gr. k-3). 1979. (ISBN 0-03-044956-1). HR&W.
Horry & Weems
--Life of Marion. (Illus.). (St. Nicholas Series for Boys). N.D. International Book Co.
Horseman, Elaine
--Hubble's Bubble. Sergeant, John, illus. LC 64-207862. (Illus.). 220 p. 21cm. 1964. Norton.
--Hubbles' Treasure Hunt. (Norton Juvenile Ser). (gr. 4-6). N.D. (ISBN 0-448-25881-1). G&D.
--The Hubbles' Treasure Hunt. Sergeant, John, illus. LC 66-117731. 174p. illus. 21cm. 1966, c.1965. Norton.
Horsfall, Carra Elisabeth Hunting
--Bluebirds Seven: Paintings. Horsfall, Robert Bruce (1869-1948), illus. Audubon Society of Portland, Oregon LC 78-51360. (Illus.). 66 p. 27cm. 1978. (ISBN 0-931686-03-2). Audubon Society of Portland, Oregon.
Horsfall, Magdalene
--The Fairy Latchkey. (Illus.). 1910. R. F. Fenno & Co.
Horsfall, Robert Bruce (1869-1948), illus.
--Stories by Seasons. N.D. Marshall Jones Co.
Horsley, Reginald
--Blue Ballon. (Illus.). N.D. E. P. Dutton & Co.
Horst, Brian Van Der see Van Der Horst, Brian.
Horta, Dorothy
--Dondi & Other Stories. (gr. 4-7). N.D. Carlton.
Horton, Edith Kendall, Mrs., jt. auth. see Russell, Dorothy Kendall, Mrs.
Horton, Elizabeth, jt. auth. see Wilhoite, Mariel.
Horton, Jean
--The Playful Little Dog. N.D. Grosset & Dunlap.
Horton, Millard C
--Joan of the Everglades. LC 22-19058. 1 p. l., 7-235 p. 20 1/2 cm. c.1922. E. W. Allen & Co.
Horton, Robert Forman (1855-)
--The Hero of Heroes. Clark, James, illus. LC 11-18249. 22cm. 326p. 1911. Fleming H. Revell Co.
Horvat, Dilwyn
--Operation Titan. LC 84-71417. 128p (Pub. by Lion Pub). (gr. 9-12). 1984. (ISBN 0-89107-322-1, Crossway Bks). Good News.
Horvath, Betty F (1927-)
--Be Nice to Josephine. Porter, Patricia Grant, illus. LC 70-117178. (Illus.). 48 p. 27cm. 1970. (ISBN 0-531-01939-X). Watts.
--The Cheerful Quiet. Stover, Jo Ann (1931-), illus. LC 75-77238. (Illus.). 39 p. 27cm. 1969. F. Watts.
--Hooray for Jasper. Rocker, Fermin (1907-), illus. LC 66-15292. (Illus.). 1 v. (unpaged. 27cm. 1966. F. Watts.
--Jasper and the Hero Business. Bolognese, Donald Alan (1934-), illus. LC 77-6712. (Illus.). 32 p. 22cm. (Easy-read story book). 1977. (ISBN 0-531-01317-0). F. Watts.
--Jasper Makes Music. 1967. (ISBN 0-8382-1061-9, Cadmus Books). E. M. Hale and Company.
--Jasper Makes Music. Rocker, Fermin (1907-), illus. LC 67-319. (Illus.). 1 v. (unpaged. 27cm. 1967. F. Watts.
--Not Enough Indians. Lewin, Ted (1935-), illus. LC 73-132068. (Illus.). 47 p. 26cm. 1971. (ISBN 0-531-01968-3). F. Watts.
--Small Paul and the Bully of Morgan Court. Perl, Susan (1922-1983), illus. LC 79-125132. (Illus.). 24 p. 23cm. (Magic circle book). 1971. Ginn.
--Will the Real Tommy Wilson Please Stand up. Robinson, Charles (1931-), illus. LC 69-15880. (Illus.). 38 p. 27cm. 1969. F. Watts.
Horwich, Frances Rappaport (1908-), ed.
--Miss Frances of Ding Dong School Selects Stories and Poems to Enjoy. Jackson, Polly, pseud. (1918-), illus. Jackson, Pauline. LC 61-11226. 128p. col. illus. 29cm. c.1962. Doubleday.

--The Russian Grandmother's Wonder Tales. Bends, W. T., illus. LC 6-32363. xvii p., 1 l., 348 p. front., 7 pl. 20 cm. 1906. C. Scribner's Sons.

House, Boyce

--As I Was Saying. (Illus.). (gr. 7 up). 1957. (ISBN 0-8111-0007-3). Naylor.

House, Charles Albert (1916-)

--The Biggest Mouse in the World. 1st ed. Hamberger, John F. (1934-), illus. LC 68-10715. (Illus.). 42 p. 26cm. 1968. W. W. Norton.

--The Friendly Woods. De Larrea, Victoria, illus. LC 73-76456. 19 cm. 96p. c.1973. Four Winds Press.

--The Lonesome Egg. (gr. k-3). N.D. (ISBN 0-448-26087-5). G&D.

--The Lonesome Egg. 1st ed. Langner, Nola (1930-), illus. LC 67-18684. 40p. col. illus. 26cm. 1968. Norton.

--The World at Christmas. LC 68-56623. (Illus.). 183 p. 25cm. 1969. Bruce Pub. Co.

House, Edward Howard (1836-1901)

--The Midnight Warning, and Other Stories. LC 12-34429. 3 p. l., ix-x, 299 p. front., illus. plates. 19 cm. 1892. Harper & Brothers.

The, House That Jack Built

--The House That Jack Built, and Other Favorite Jingles. Anderson, Robert Lindberg & Bradford, John Carroll, illus. LC 63-9401. 1 v. (unpaged) illus. (part col.) 21 cm. (Harlan Quist book). 1964. Dell Publ. Col.

House, Wanda Rogers

--Peter Goes to School. Doremus, Hal W., illus. LC 53-29591. unpaged. illus. 21cm. (Wonder books, 600). 1953. Wonder Books.

Household, Geoffrey Edward West (1900-)

--Doom's Caravan. LC 79-143705. (gr. 8 up). 1971. (ISBN 0-316-37431-8, Pub. by Atlantic Monthly Pr.). Little.

--Escape into Daylight. LC 76-10162. (Illus.). 138 p. 22cm. c.1976. (ISBN 0-316-37436-9). Little, Brown.

--Prisoner of the Indies. Chappell, Warren (1904-), illus. (Illus.). (gr. 7 up). 1968. (ISBN 0-316-37423-7, Pub. by Atlantic Monthly Pr). Little.

--Red Anger. 1975. (ISBN 0-316-37435-0, Pub. by Atlantic Monthly Pr.). Little.

--The Spanish Cave. Pitz, Henry Clarence (1895-1976), illus. LC 36-20849. 5 p. l., 3-202 p. incl. illus., plates. front. 21 cm. 1936. Little, Brown, and Company.

Housekeeper, M. R. (1838-)

--Face the Lions. Eckman, F. A., illus. LC 5-39586. ix p., 1 l., 13-174 p. incl. front. 3 pl. 18 cm. (Cherrycroft Ser.). c.1905. H. Altemus Company.

--Face the Lions, 1 of 21 vols. Eckman, F. A., illus. (Illus.). (Boys & Girls Booklovers Ser.: No. 18). 1905. Set. Henry Altemus Co.

Houselander, Frances Caryll (1901-1954)

--Inside the Ark & Other Stories. (Illus.). (gr. 3-7). 1956. (ISBN 0-8362-0383-6). Guild Bks.

--Inside the Ark, and Other Stories. George, Renee (1924-), illus. LC 56-9532. 144p. illus. 20cm. 1956. Sheed & Ward.

--Terrible Farmer Timson, and Other Stories. George, Renee (1924-), illus. LC 57-10190. 152p. illus. 20cm. 1957. Sheed & Ward.

Housman, Alfred Edward (1859-1936)

--A Shoreshire Lad. N.D. David McKay Co.

--A Shropshire Lad. 92p. 1946. Thomas Y. Crowell Co.

Housman, Laurence (1865-), ed. see Arabian Nights.

Housman, Laurence (1865-1959), retold by see Sindbad the Sailor.

Housman, Laurence (1865-1959)

--Cotton-Wooleena. Binks, Robert (1926-), illus. LC 79-157429. (Illus.). 58 p. 22cm. 1974, c.1967. (ISBN 0-385-05673-7). (ISBN 0-385-05673-7). Doubleday.

--A Doorway in Fairyland. LC 23-88293. 3 p. l., 11-219, 1 p. incl. front., plates. 21 cm. 1923. Harcourt, Brace & Company.

--A Farm in Fairyland. LC 74-171660. (Illus.). 160 p. 20cm. 1894. Dodd, Mead.

--The Field of Clover. Housman, Clemence, illus. LC 68-30802. (Illus.). 148 p. 21cm. 1968. Dover Publications.

--The Field of Clover. Housman, Clemence, illus. LC 42-26897. 5 p. l., 3-148 p., 1 l. front, plates. 20 cm. 1902. John Lane.

--Moonshine & Clover. Housman, Clemence, illus. LC 23-10502. 3 p. l., 11 219, 1 p. incl. front., plates. 21 cm. 1923. Harcourt, Brace & Company.

--The Rat-Catcher's Daughter. Greene, Ellin (1927-), selected by. Noonan, Julia (1946-), illus. LC 73-75436. (Illus.). (gr. 4-7). 1974. (ISBN 0-689-30420-X, McElderry Bk). Atheneum.

--Turn Again Tales. Housman, Laurence (1865-1959), illus. LC 31-14068. vii, 1 280 p. enl. mounted front, illus., col. mounted plates. 25 cm. 1930. H. Holt and Company.

--What O'Clock Tales. N.D. Frederick A. Stokes.

Housman, Laurence (1865-1959), retold by.

--Ali Baba: And Other Stories from the Arabian Nights. Dulac, Edmund (1882-1953), illus. N.D. George H Doran & Co.

--Arabian Nights: Five Stories from the Arabian Nights. Dulac, Edmund (1882-1953), illus. N.D. Charles Scribner's Sons.

--The Magic Horse: And Other Stories from the Arabian Nights. Dulac, Edmund (1882-1953), illus. N.D. George H Doran & Co.

--Puss in Boots. (Roundabout Ser.). N.D. D. Dppleton & Co.

--Stories from the Arabian Nights. Dulac, Edmund (1882-1953), illus. LC 32-21561. xxii p., 1 l., 27-205 p. incl. col. front., illus., col. plates. 22 1/2 cm. N.D. Garden City Publishing Co., Inc.

--Stories from the Arabian Nights. Dulac, Edmund (1882-1953), illus. LC 23-26784. xxiii p., 1 l., 27-237 p. inc. col. mounted front., 13 col. mounted pl. 23 1/2 cm. 1923. George H. Doran Company.

--Story of the Seven Young Gosling. (Illus.). (Scribner-Blackie Series of books for young people). N.D. Charles Scribner's Sons.

Housman, Louise

--On Stage!. N.D. Harper & Bros.

Housman, Louise & Koehler, Edward T.

--Footlights up!. Practical Plays for Boys and Girls. Koehler, Edward T., illus. LC 35-4395. x p., 1 l., 220 p. incl. front., illus. 19 cm. 1935. Harper & Brothers.

Houston, Alma

--Nuki. Houston, James Archibald (1921-), illus. LC 52-13724. (Illus.). 150 p. 21cm. 1953. Lippincott.

Houston, D.

--Villains. 1980. (ISBN 0-931064-21-X). Starlog.

Houston, Edwin James (1847-1914)

--At School in the Cannibal Islands. LC 9-23810. 412 p. front., illus., 4 pl. 21 cm. (Half-title: The Pacific series, no. iv). 1909. The Griffith & Rowland Press.

--The Boy Electrician: Or, The Secret Society of the Jolly Philosophers. McKernan, Frank, illus. LC 7-36998. 326 p. front., 10 pl. 20 cm. 1907. J. B. Lippincott Company.

--The Boy Electricians As Detectives. McKernan, Frank, illus. LC 12-23062. 313 1 p. front., plates. 20 cm. 1912. J. B. Lippincott Company.

--The Boy Geologist at School and in Camp. Pullinger, Herbert, illus. LC 7-36229. 320 p. incl. front., plates. 19 cm. c.1907. H. Altemus Company.

--Cast Away at the North Pole. LC 7-23530. 382 p. front., 3 pl. 19 1/2 cm. (His The "North Pole" series). c.1907. The J. C. Winston Co.

--A Chip of the Old Block: Or, At the Bottom of the Ladder. Taylor, H. Weston, illus. LC 10-21604. 363 p. front., illus., plates. 20 1/2 cm. (Half-title: The young mineralogist series, I). 1910. The Griffith & Rowland Press.

--The Discovery of the North Pole. LC 7-23532. 377 p. front., 3 pl. 19 1/2 cm. (His The "North Pole" series). c.1907. The J. C. Winston Co.

--Five Months on a Derelict: Or, Adventures on a Floating Wreck in the Pacific. LC 8-20577. 360 p. front., plates, maps. 20 1/2 cm. (Half-title: The Pacific series, no. 1). 1908. The Griffith & Rowland Press.

--In Captivity in the Pacific: Or, In the Land of the Breadfruit Tree. LC 9-552218. 422 p. front. 4 pl. 20 1/2 cm. (Half-title: The Pacific series, no. III). 1909. The Griffith & Rowland Press.

--The Jaws of Death: Or, In and Around the Canons of the Colorado. Taylor, H. Weston, illus. LC 11-9897. 395 p. front., illus., diagrs. map. 20 1/2 cm. (Half-title: The young mineralogist series III) 1911. The Griffith & Rowland Press.

--The Land of Drought: Or, Across the Great American Desert. LC 10-28167. 355 p. front., plates, map. 20 1/2 cm. (Half-title: The young mineralogist series II). c.1910. The Griffith & Rowland Press.

--The Land of Ice and Snow: Or, Adventures in Alaska. LC 12-24243. 412 p. front. illus. plates, fold. map. 20 1/2 cm. (His The young mineralogist series .IV). 1912. The Griffith & Rowland Press.

--Once a Volcano: Or, Adventures Among the Extinct Volcanoes of the United States. LC 12-11405. 374 p. front., plates. 20 1/2 cm. (Half-title: The young mineralogist series V) 1912. The Griffith & Rowland Press.

--Our Boy Scouts in Camp. Houston, Edwin James (1847-1914), illus. LC 12-17662. 330 p. col. front., plates. 20 cm. c.1912. D. McKay.

--The Search for the North Pole. LC 7-23531. 383 p. front., 3 pl. map. 19 1/2 cm. (His The "North Pole" series). c.1907. The J. C. Winston Co.

--Wrecked on a Coral Island. Houston, Edwin James (1847-1914), illus. LC 9-1582. 416 p. front., illus., 4 pl. 20 1/2 cm. (Half-title: The Pacific series, no. II). 1908. The Griffith & Rowland Press.

--The Yellow Magnet: Or, Attracted by Gold. Taylor, H. Weston, illus. LC 11-29083. 376 p. front., plates, map. 20 1/2 cm. (His The young mineralogist series)). 1911. The Griffith & Rowland Press.

--The Young Prospector: Or, The Search for the Lost Gold Mine. Stecher, William Frederick (1864-), illus. LC 6-43785. 400 p. front. 4 pl. 20 cm. c.1906. W. A. Wilde Company.

Houston, James Archibald (1921-)

--Akavak: An Eskimo Journey. Houston, James Archibald (1921-), illus. LC 68-26426. (Illus.). 75 p. 21cm. 1968. Harcourt, Brace & World. **Award: (ALA).**

--Black Diamonds: A Search for Arctic Treasure. Houston, James Archibald (1921-), illus. LC 81-10868. (Illus.). 170 p. 22cm. 1982. (ISBN 0-689-50223-0). Atheneum.

--Eagle Mask: A West Coast Indian Tale. 1st ed. Houston, James Archibald (1921-), illus. LC 66-5951. 63 p. illus. 22 cm. 1966. Harcourt, Brace & World.

--Frozen Fire. Houston, James Archibald (1921-), illus. LC 77-6366. (Illus.). 160p. (gr. 7 up). 1977. (ISBN 0-689-50083-1, McElderry Bk). Atheneum.

--Frozen Fire. Houston, James Archibald (1921-), illus. (gr. 7 up). N.D. (ISBN 0-689-70489-5, Aladdin). Atheneum.

--Ghost Paddle: A Northwest Coast Indian Tale. Houston, James Archibald (1921-), illus. LC 72-76364. (Illus.). 55 p. 22cm. 1972. (ISBN 0-15-230760-5). Harcourt Brace Jovanovich.

--Ice Swords: An Undersea Adventure. Houston, James Archibald (1921-), illus. LC 85-7328. (Illus.). 149 p. 22cm. 1985. (ISBN 0-689-50333-4). Atheneum.

--Kiviok's Magic Journey: An Eskimo Legend. Houston, James Archibald (1921-), illus. LC 73-75435. (Illus.). 40 p. 27cm. 1973. (ISBN 0-689-30419-6). Atheneum.

--Long Claws. Houston, James Archibald (1921-), illus. LC 81-3478. (Illus.). 32p. (gr. 4-7). 1981. (ISBN 0-689-50206-0, McElderry Bk). Atheneum.

--River Runners: A Tale of Hardship and Bravery. Houston, James Archibald (1921-), illus. LC 79-14337. p. cm. 1979. (ISBN 0-689-50151-X). Atheneum. **Award: (CLA).**

--Tiktaliktak: An Eskimo Legend. 1st ed. Houston, James Archibald (1921-), illus. LC 65-21696. (Illus.). 63 p. 21cm. 1965. (ISBN 0-15-287745-2). Harcourt, Brace & World. **Award: (CLA).**

--The White Archer: An Eskimo Legend. 1st ed. Houston, James Archibald (1921-), illus. LC 67-17154. (Illus.). 95 p. 22cm. 1967. Harcourt, Brace & World. **Award: (CLA).**

--The White Archer: An Eskimo Legend. 1st ed. Houston, James Archibald (1921-), illus. LC 79-14458. p. cm. (Voyager/HBJ book). 1979, c.1967. (ISBN 0-15-696224-1). Harcourt Brace Jovanovich.

--The White Dawn: An Eskimo Tale. Houston, James Archibald (1921-), illus. 275p. N.D. Harcourt Brace Jovanovich.

--Wolf Run: A Caribou Eskimo Tale. Houston, James Archibald (1921-), illus. LC 78-140778. (Illus.). 52, 11 p. 22cm. 1971. (ISBN 0-15-299104-2). Harcourt Brace Jovanovich.

Houston, James Archibald (1921-), ed.

--Songs of the Dream People: Chants & Images from the Indians & Eskimos of North America. Houston, James Archibald (1921-), illus. LC 72-77130. (gr. 4 up). 1972. (ISBN 0-689-30306-8, McElderry Bk). Atheneum.

Houston, Joan (1928-)

--Crofton Meadows. LC 61-14529. 242p. 21cm. 1961. Crowell.

--Horse Show Hurdles. Brown, Paul (1893-1958), illus. LC 58-5592. 243p. illus. 21cm. c.1957. Crowell.

--Jump-Shy. Brown, Paul (1893-1958), illus. LC 56-5701. (Illus.). 261 p. 21cm. 1956. Crowell.

Houston, John (1935-)

--The Bright Yellow Rope. Fitch, Winnie, illus. LC 73-4769. (Illus.). 33 p. 24cm. 1973. (ISBN 0-201-02995-2). Addison-Wesley.

--The Meddybemps Fair. Fitch, Winnie, illus. LC 72-7462. (Illus.). 40 p. 24cm. 1973. (ISBN 0-201-02991-X). Addison-Wesley.

--A Mouse in My House. Fitch, Winnie, illus. LC 79-164405. (Illus.). 33 p. 24cm. 1972. Addison-Wesley.

--A Room Full of Animals. Fitch, Winnie, illus. LC 73-4814. (Illus.). 33 p. 24cm. 1973. Addison-Wesley.

Houston, Ralph (1908-)

--White Jade. Seldon, Reeda, illus. LC 51-22599. 20 cm. 21p. 1950. Great Pyramid Press.

Hovde, Jeanne

--Bobcat!. 1978. (ISBN 0-89191-112-X). Cook.

--A Horse Named Cinnamon. 132p. (Pennypincher Bks.). (gr. 3-6). 1982. (ISBN 0-89191-714-4). Cook.

--Winter of the White-Tail Buck. Hauge, Carl, illus. LC 75-36698. (Illus.). 143 p. 18cm. c.1976. (ISBN 0-912692-88-X). D. C. Cook Pub. Co.

Hovde, Jeanne & Zimmerman, Marjorie

--Danger in the Forest: Three Novels of Adventure. LC 81-17256. (Illus.). 378 p. 19cm. (Chariot Books). c.1981. (ISBN 0-89191-533-8). D.C. Cook Pub. Co.

Hovde, Louise, ed.

--The Cradle Book of Verse: An Anthology of Baby Poetry. LC 72-2997. (Illus.). 301 p. 22cm. (Granger index reprint series). 1972, c.1927. (ISBN 0-8369-8244-4). Books for Libraries Press.

--The Cradle Book of Verse: An Anthology of Baby Poetry. LC 27-5031. xvi p., 1 l., 21-301 p. col. front. 22 cm. c.1927. George H. Doran Company.

--The Cradle Book of Verse: An Anthology of Baby Poetry. LC 78-74818. 301 p. 20cm. (Granger Poetry Library). 1979. (ISBN 0-89609-137-6). Granger Book Co.

Hovell, Lucille A. Peterson see Temkin, Sara Anne Schlossberg (1913-) & Hovell, Lucy A.

Hovell, Lucy A., jt. auth. see Temkin, Sara Anne Schlossberg.

Hovelsrud, Joyce & Chaffe, Beatrice

--Mr. Crinkle's Magic Spring. (Children's Theatre Playscript & Music Ser.). 1969. (ISBN 0-88020-041-3). Coach Hse.

Hoven, Erniest, pseud., see Hooker, Fanny.

Hover, M.

--Here Comes Santa Claus. Santoro, Christopher, illus. (Illus.). 14p. (Golden Sturdy Shape Bks.). (ps). 1982. (ISBN 0-307-12267-0, Golden Pr). Western Pub.

Hover, M. A. & Fletcher, Evelyn

--Nice Stories. (Illus.). 96p. 1900. Thomas Nelson & Sons.

How, Louis

--Nursery Rhymes of New York City. Bischoff, Ilse Marthe (1903-), illus. N.D. Alfred A Knopf.

--Nursery Rhymes of New York City. Bischoff, Ilse Marthe (1903-), illus. N.D. Harbor Press.

How, Ruth Winifred

--Adventures at Friendly Farm. Moment, John, illus. LC 52-635. 218 p. illus. 21 cm. 1952. Coward-McCann.

--The Friendly Farm. Moment, John, illus. LC 51-10273. 212 p. illus. 21 cm. 1951. Coward-McCann.

Howard, Alan (1922-)

--Nativity Stories. Forczek, Lesczek (1946-), illus. LC 79-20746. (Illus.). 95 p. 24cm. c.1980. (ISBN 0-89742-027-6). (ISBN 0-89742-026-8). Dawne-Leigh Publications.

Howard, Alan (1922-), illus.

--David & Goliath. (Illus.). 1977. (ISBN 0-571-08413-3). Faber & Faber.

Howard, Alice C, Mrs., ed. see Floyd, Silas Xavier.

Howard, Alice Woodbury, Mrs.

--Ching-Li and the Dragons. Ward, Lynd Kendall (1905-1985), illus. LC 31-32087. 3 p. l., 55 p., 1 l. col. illus.26 x 22 cm. 1931. The Macmillan Company.

--The Princess Runs Away: A Story of Egypt in 1900 B.C. Howard, John T., illus. LC 34-3142. 4 p. l., 106 p. col. front., illus. 19 1/2 cm. 1934. The Macmillan Company.

--Sokar and the Crocodile: A Fairy Story of Egypt. Kybinyi, Coleman, illus. LC 28-218048. 4 p. l., 58, v, 2 p. incl. illus., plates. col. front., plates (part col.) 21 cm. 1928. The Macmillan Company.

Howard, C. B., Mrs.

--The Do Society". Or, The Three Cousins. LC 12-344928. 217 p. 16 1/2 cm. 1888. Southern Methodist Publishing House.

Howard, Charlotte

--Ding-a-Ling Book. Miller, John Parr (1913-), illus. (A Danny Doo-It Bk.). 1970. Golden Press.

Howard, Clifford (1868-)

--What Happened at Olenberg. Nelson, Emile A., illus. LC 11-28744. (Illus.). 204p. 20cm. 1911. The Reilly & Britton Co.

Howard, Coralie, pseud., see Cogswell, Coralie Norris.

Howard, Coralie, pseud. (1930-), ed.

--The First Book of Short Verse. Cogswell, Coralie Norris. Funai, Mamoru R. (1932-), illus. LC 64-17783. viii, 125 p. illus. 23 cm. 1964. Watts.

--Lyric Poems. Cogswell, Coralie Norris. Fowler, Mel, illus. LC 68-10684. (Illus.). woodcuts.index. refs. 128p. (gr. 7 up). 1968. (ISBN 0-531-01073-2). Watts.

Howard, Elizabeth, pseud., see Mizner, Elizabeth Howard.

Howard, Elizabeth, pseud. (1907-)

--Adventure for Alison. Mizner, Elizabeth Howard. LC 42-24668. 4 p. l., 216 p. 20 1/2 cm. 1942. Lothrop, Lee & Shepard Co.

--Candle in the Night. Mizner, Elizabeth Howard. (gr. 7 up). 1952. Morrow.

--The Courage of Bethea. Mizner, Elizabeth Howard. LC 59-9582. 255 p. 21cm. (Morrow junior books). 1959. Morrow.
--Dorinda. Mizner, Elizabeth Howard. Weisgard, Leonard Joseph (1916-), illus. LC 44-3686. 5 p. l., 303 p incl. plates, 21 c. 1944. Lothrop, Lee & Shepard Co.
--A Girl of the North Country. Mizner, Elizabeth Howard. LC 57-51102. 222p. 21cm. (Morrow junior books). 1957. Morrow.
--North Winds Blow Free. Mizner, Elizabeth Howard. Darling, Louis, Jr. (1916-1970), illus. LC 49-4521. 192 p. front. 21 cm. morrow junior books. 1949. W. Morrow.
--Out of Step with the Dancers. Mizner, Elizabeth Howard. LC 77-25928. 222 p. 22cm. 1978. (ISBN 0-688-32141-0). Morrow.
--Peddler's Girl. Mizner, Elizabeth Howard. Darling, Louis, Jr. (1916-1970), illus. (Illus.). (gr. 7 up). 1951. Morrow.
--The Road Lies West. Mizner, Elizabeth Howard. (gr. 7 up). 1955. William Morrow & Co.
--Sabina. Mizner, Elizabeth Howard. Suba, Susanne (1913-), illus. LC 41-21287. 4 p. l., 269 p. illus. 21 cm. c.1941. Lothrop, Lee & Shepard Company.
--A Star to Follow. Mizner, Elizabeth Howard. LC 51-5078. 222 p. 21cm. 1951. Morrow.
--Summer Under Sail. Mizner, Elizabeth Howard. LC 47-19423. 4 p. l., 3-213 p. 21 cm. 1947. W. Morrow & Co.
--Verity's Voyage. Mizner, Elizabeth Howard. LC 64-21160. 221 p. 21 cm. 1964. W. Morrow.
--Wilderness Venture. Mizner, Elizabeth Howard. LC 73-4991. 190 p. 21cm. 1973. (ISBN 0-688-20074-5). (ISBN 0-688-20074-5). Morrow.
--Winter on Her Own. Mizner, Elizabeth Howard. LC 68-16625. 219 p. 21cm. 1968. W. Morrow.

Howard, Ellen
--Circle of Giving. LC 83-15631. 96p. (gr. 3-7). 1984. (ISBN 0-689-31027-7). Atheneum.
--When Daylight Comes. LC 85-7963. xiii, 210 p. 22cm. 1985. (ISBN 0-689-31133-8). Atheneum.

Howard, Elva
--Knights of Slumberland: Lessons in Simple Knowledge for the Children. Howard, Elva, illus. LC 54-38656. 70p. illus. 25cm. 1954. White Wing Pub. House & Press.

Howard, F. Martin
--The Porpoise of Pirate Bay. Ward, Lynd Kendall (1905-1985), illus. LC 38-28957. 152 p. incl. illus., plates. 24 1/2 cm. c.1938. Random House.

Howard, Frank Ward (1872-), ed.
--Banbury Cross Stories. LC 9-30449. 123 p. incl. front., illus. 17 cm. (Merrill's story books)). c.1909. C. E. Merrill Co.
--Dick Whittington. (Illus.). (The Cinderella Series.). N.D. George H Doran.
--Dick Whittington, 1 of 64 Vols. (Illus.). (Aunt Louisa's London Toy Books Ser.: No.15). N.D. Scribner & Welford.
--Dick Whittington and other Stories. LC 9-30448. 167 p. incl. front., illus., pl. 17 cm. (Merrill's story books). c.1909. C. E. Merrill Co.

Howard-Gibbon, Amelia Frances (1826-1874)
--An Illustrated Comic Alphabet. Howard-Gibbon, Amelia Frances (1826-1874), illus. LC 67-2074. (Illus.). 1 v. (unpaged). 26cm. 1967, c.1966. H. Z. Walck.
--An Illustrated Comic Alphabet. Howard-Gibbon, Amelia Frances (1826-1874), illus. LC 67-95741. (Illus.). 31 p. 26cm. 1967. Oxford U.P.

Howard, Harriet Shriver
--If You Had a Pony. Rosenthal, Susan, photos by. LC 65-14487. 39p. illus. 26cm. 1965. Harper.

Howard, Helen Littler (1909-)
--Hannah's Sod House. Smith, Barbara, illus. LC 47-5389. 211 p. illus. 24 cm. 1947. Caxton Printers.

Howard, J. H.
--Baby. Howard, J. H., illus. (Uncle Sam's Picture Books). 1873. McLoughlin Bros.
--Pocahontas. Howard, J. H., illus. (Uncle Sam's Big Picture Books). 1873. McLoughlin Bros.
--Putnam. Howard, J. H., illus. (Uncle Sam's Big Picture Books). 1873. McLoughlin Bros.

Howard, J. H., illus.
--Rhymes and Jingles for Little Children. cover-title, 16 p. col. illus. 25 x 20 cm. c.1866. McLoughlin Brothers.

Howard, Jane R (1935-)
--When I'm Sleepy. Cherry, Lynne (1952-), illus. LC 84-25895. (Illus.). 24 p. 27cm. c.1985. (ISBN 0-525-44204-9). Dutton.

Howard, Janet
--Counting Katie. Cotton, De Forest, illus. LC 47-216. 40 p. col. illus. 20 1/2 x 17 cm. 1946. Lothrop, Lee & Shepard Co.
--Jumpy, the Kangaroo. Duvoisin, Roger Antoine (1904-1980), illus. LC 44-7921. 41 p. col. illus. 17 x 16 cm. 1944. Lothrop, Lee & Shepard Co.

Howard, Jean G
--Of Mice and Mice. Howard, Jean G., illus. LC 78-50486. (Illus.). 48 p. c.1978. (ISBN 0-930954-03-3). (ISBN 0-930954-04-1). Tidal Press.
--Tuk, the Timid: The Story of a Sea Otter. Howard, Jean G., illus. LC 84-50217. (Illus.). 80p. (Orig.). (gr. 3 up). 1984. (ISBN 0-930954-20-3). Tidal Pr.

Howard, Joan, pseud., see Gordon, Patricia.

Howard, Joan
--Light In The Tower. N.D. E. M. Hale & Co.
--Quillenback for Fire Chief. MacKenzie, Garry (1921-), illus. 49p. 1951. Henry Z. Walck, Inc.
--Quillenback for Fire Chief. MacKenzie, Garry (1921-), illus. LC 51-13251. 1951. Oxford University Press.
--Story of Mark Twain. McKay, Donald A. (1893-), illus. (Illus.). (gr. 4-6). N.D. (ISBN 0-448-05623-2, Sign). G&D.
--The Thirteenth is Magic. Adams, Adrienne (1906-), illus. (Illus.). 169p. (gr. 3-6). 1950. Lothrop.

Howard, John
--Backyard Mystery. (Illus.). (gr. 2-3). 1972. (ISBN 0-89375-046-8). Troll Assocs.

Howard, Katherine
--Little Bunny Follows His Nose. Miller, John Parr (1913-), illus. LC 75-140422. (Illus.). 30 p. 24cm. (Golden fragrance book). 1971. Golden Press.
--Max, the Nosey Bear. Miller, John Parr (1913-), illus. LC 72-75833. (Illus.). 26 p. 25cm. (Golden fragrance book). 1972. Golden Press.

Howard, Laura Katherine
--Along Childhood's Road. N.D. Pageant Press INC.

Howard, Lin, illus.
--Baby Talk. (Illus.). 14p. (Pillow Pals Ser.). (ps). 1984. (ISBN 0-448-41201-2, G&D). Putnam Pub Group.

Howard, Lisa
--On Stage, Miss Douglas. Schary, Dore, intro. by. LC 60-12449. 190 p. 21cm. (Career romance for young moderns). 1960. Messner.

Howard, Lloyd Leonard
--Adventures of Tidly and Hildy. Howard, Lloyd Leonard, illus. N.D. Vantage Press, Inc.

Howard, Lonny
--The Child Queen Who Changed the World for Children. 1981. (ISBN 0-533-04893-1). Vantage.

Howard, Margaret
--You Know You're Really in Love When ....You Know It's Time to Break up When. (Illus.). 80p. (Orig.). 1981. (ISBN 0-590-31786-5, Schol Pap). Scholastic Inc.

Howard, Marion, Miss
--Fred's Hard Fight, 1 of 4 Vols. (Silver Lake Ser.). N.D. National Temperance Society.

Howard, Mary, pseud., see Mussi, Mary.

Howard, Mary, pseud. (1907-)
--Sixpence in Her Shoe. Mussi, Mary. LC 54-7491. 224p. 20cm. 1954. Arcadia House.

Howard, Matthew V.
--Blink, the Patchwork Bunny. Moline, Earl Warren, Jr., illus. (Illus.). (Kindergarten Read-to Bks.). (gr. k-2). N.D. Denison.
--Nancy & Sue in a Stew at the Zoo. Moline, Earl Warren, Jr., illus. LC 68-21563. (Illus.). 1 v. (unpaged. 29cm. 1968. Denison.

Howard, Matthew V. & Moline, Earl W.
--Nancy and the Unhappy Lion. LC 58-13722. 26cm. 32p. 1958. T. S. Denison & Co Inc.

Howard, Mattie H
--A Mother's Influence: Or, The Beauty of Religion. A Story for the Young. LC 12-34411. 143 p. 16 1/2 cm. 1886. Southern Methodist Publishing House.

Howard, Max & Mercie, Tina
--People Papers. Mercie, Tina, illus. LC 77-355697. (Illus.). 32 p. 26cm. c.1974. (ISBN 0-8252-0112-8). (ISBN 0-8252-0113-6). H. Quist.
--People Papers. Mercie, Tina, illus. (Illus.). 32p. (Harlin Quist Bks). (gr. 2-5). 1975. (ISBN 0-8252-6167-8). Quist.

Howard, Moses Leon see Nagenda, Musa, pseud.

Howard, Moses Leon (1928-)
--The Human Mandolin. Morrow, Barbara, illus. LC 74-3122. (Illus.). 32 p. 1974. (ISBN 0-03-012961-3). Holt, Rinehart and Winston.
--The Ostrich Chase. Seuling, Barbara (1937-), illus. LC 73-17372. (Illus.). 118 p. 22cm. 1974. (ISBN 0-03-012096-9). Holt, Rinehart and Winston.

Howard, Nancy
--Three Billys Go to Town. Johnson, John Emil (1929-), illus. LC 67-5009. (Illus.). 1 v. (unpaged). 1967. Parents' Magazine Press.

Howard, Nina
--Barber, Barber, Shave a Pig. Rayl, Eleanor, illus. 16p. (ps-k). 1981. (ISBN 0-917206-13-4). Children Learn Ctr.

Howard, Oliver Otis (1830-1909)
--Donald's School Days. Shute, A. Burnham, illus. LC 99-2113. 369p. 1899. Lee & Shepard.
--Famous Indian Chiefs I Have Known. Varian, George, illus. LC 8-24369. x, 364 p. incl. plates, ports. front. 20 cm. 1908. The Century Co.
--Henry in the War: Or, The Model Volunteer. Shute, A. Burnham, illus. LC 99-1981. xi, 245 p. front., plates. 19 cm. 1899. Lee and Shepard.

Howard, Pauline Stoddard
--The W. Chuck Family. Drucklieb, Herman, illus. LC 20-19296. 108 p. front., illus. 26 1/2 cm. c.1920. John Martin's House, Inc.

Howard, Pearl A.
--A Special Guest for Mr. & Mrs. Bumba. (Mr. Bumba Bks.). (gr. k-3). 1983. (ISBN 0-8225-0123-6). Lerner Pubns.

Howard, Rex Zedrick (1889-)
--Steve Scott and the Hidden City: A Mystery Story for Boys. LC 49-9091. 87 p. 18 cm. 1948. Moody Press.

Howard, Richard (1929-), tr. see Brunhoff, Laurent de.

Howard, Richard, tr. see Perrault, Charles.

Howard, Sidney, pseud., see Ray, Anna Chapin.

Howard, Vanessa
--A Screaming Whisper. Pinderhughes, J., photos by. LC 79-182781. (Illus.). 80p. (gr. 7-12). 1972. (ISBN 0-03-088366-0). HR&W.

Howard, Velma Swanston, Mrs. (1868-), ed. see Lagerlof, Selma Ottiliana Lovisa.

Howard, Velma Swanston, Mrs. (1868-), tr. see Lagerlof, Selma Ottiliana Lovisa.

Howard, Vernon Linwood (1918-)
--Acts for Comedy Shows: How to Perform and Write Them. Anderson, Doug, illus. LC 64-24675. (Illus.). 128 p. 21cm. 1964. Sterling Pub. Co.
--California Ho!. 1950. Christian Lit.
--Grand Canyon Mystery. 1952. Christian Lit.
--Humorous Monologues. 128p. (gr. 2 up). 1973. (ISBN 0-8069-7002-2). (ISBN 0-8069-7003-0). Sterling.
--Monologues for Teens. (gr. 8 up). 1957. (ISBN 0-8069-7000-6). Sterling.
--Pantomimes, Charades & Skits. rev. ed. LC 59-12983. (Illus.). index. 124p. (gr. 4 up). 1974. (ISBN 0-8069-7004-9). (ISBN 0-8069-7005-7). Sterling.
--Puppet & Pantomime Plays. (gr. 5 up). 1962. (ISBN 0-8069-7008-1). (ISBN 0-8069-7009-X). Sterling.
--Quick Comedy Skits. Howard, Vernon Linwood (1918-), illus. LC 62-50945. 59 p. illus. 20 cm. 1959, c.1955. Zondervan Pub. House.
--Short Plays for All-Boy Casts: Thirty Royalty-Free Comedies and Skits. LC 54-10967. 186p. 21cm. 1954. Plays.
--Short Plays from the Great Classics: For Young Actors and Actresses. Shizu, illus. LC 60-103839. 123p. illus. 21cm. c.1960. Sterling Pub. Co.
--Yankee Saddle. 1948. Christian Lit.

Howard-Vyse, George & Preston, Chloe, illus.
--The Peek-A-Boos among the Bunnies. N.D. George H Doran.

Howard, Walter Scott, illus.
--Old Father Gander: Or,The Better Half of Mother Goose. (Rhymes, Chimes and Jingles). 89p. Repr. (Gift Book Ser.). 1900. L. C. Page & Co.

Howard, Wilbur K
--Fracture Zone. Escourido, Joseph, illus. LC 62-7851. 127p. illus: 21cm. 1962. Friendship Press.

Howard, Willis Blanche
--A Battle and a Boy: An Interesting Book for Boys. N.D. Frederick Stokes Co.

Howard, Winifred
--Out of the Everywhere. Montgomery, Elizabeth, illus. LC 30-10017. 77, 1 p. illus. 19 1/2 cm. 1929. Oxford University Press.

Howarth, David Armine (1912-)
--Waterloo: Day of Battle. (Illus.). 1968. (ISBN 0-689-10138-4). Atheneum Publishers.

Howarth, J. R.
--The Trials of Lulu and Leander. N.D. Frederick A. Stokes.

Howarth, Matt (1954-)
--Changes: A Psycho-Visual Novel. LC 78-14397. p. cm. c.1978. (ISBN 0-89471-051-6). (ISBN 0-89471-050-8). Running Press.

Howe, Benning
--Opening Doors. 351p. N.D. American Tract Co.

Howe, Betty
--Peter Pig and His Airplane Trip. Howe, Betty, illus. LC 43-3617. 60 p. incl. front., illus. (part col.) 17 1/2 x 13 1/2 cm. (Little color classics). 1943. McLoughlin Brothers, Inc.
--The Pig Whose Tail Would Not Curl. Howe, Betty, illus. LC 42-25561. (Illus.). 26p. 22 x 30cm. 1942. McLoughlin Bros.

Howe, Caroline Walton
--Counting Penguins. Howe, Caroline Walton, illus. LC 82-48860. (Illus.). 32p. (ps-1). 1983. (ISBN 0-06-022618-8, HarpJ). (ISBN 0-06-022619-6). Har-Row.
--Teddy Bear's Band. Howe, Caroline WAlton, illus. LC 79-14464. p. cm. 1979. Windmill Books.
--Teddy Bear's Bird & Beast Band. Howe, Caroline Walton, illus. LC 79-14464. (Illus.). 32p. (ps-3). 1980. (ISBN 0-671-96116-0). Windmill Bks.

Howe, D. H.
--The Stone Junk & Other Stories of East Asia. (Illus.). (Oxford Progressive English Readers Ser.). (gr. k-6). 1972. (ISBN 0-19-638225-4). Oxford U Pr.

Howe, De Lancey
--The Star of Umbria. LC 28-19752. 5 p. l., 3-149 p. front. (port.) illus., map. 21 cm. c.1928. Thomas Fleet Company.

Howe, Deborah (1946-1978) & Howe, James (1946-)
--Bunnicula: A Rabbit Tale of Mystery. Daniel, Alan (1939-), illus. LC 78-11472. (Illus.). xii, 98 p. 22cm. 1979. (ISBN 0-689-30700-1). Atheneum. **Award: (ALA).**
--Teddy Bear's Scrapbook. Rose, David S. (1947-), illus. LC 79-22794. (Illus.). 72 p. 23cm. 1980. (ISBN 0-689-30746-2). Atheneum.

Howe, Dorothy
--Around the Year with the Little Bennetts. LC 9-16982. (Illus.). 18cm. 127p. 1907. Educational Publishing Co.

Howe, Edgar Watson (1854-)
--A Moonlight Boy. LC 12-36055. 342 p. incl. front. (port.) 19 cm. 1886. Ticknor and Company.

Howe, Emmy
--Rennie the Fish. LC 72-1858. (Illus.). 32 p. 1972. (ISBN 0-442-23555-0). Van Nostrand Reinhold.

Howe, Fanny
--Race of the Radical. LC 85-40445. 150 p. 22cm. 1985. (ISBN 0-670-80557-2). Viking Kestrel.

Howe, Irving (1920-) & Greenberg, Eliezer (1896-1977), eds.
--Yiddish Stories, Old and New. LC 74-8116. 128 p. 22cm. 1974. (ISBN 0-8234-0246-0). Holiday House.

Howe, James, jt. auth. see Howe, Deborah.

Howe, James (1946-)
--The Celery Stalks at Midnight. Morrill, Leslie H., illus. LC 83-2665. p. cm. 1983. (ISBN 0-689-30987-2). Atheneum.
--The Day the Teacher Went Bananas. Hoban, Lillian (1925-), illus. LC 84-1536. (Illus.). 32p. (ps-2). 1984. (ISBN 0-525-44107-7). Dutton.
--How The Ewoks Saved the Trees: An Old Ewok Legend. Velez, Walter, illus. LC 83-13708. (Illus.). 48p. (Return of the Jedi Ser.). (gr. k-3). 1984. (ISBN 0-394-86129-9, BYR). (ISBN 0-394-96129-3). Random.
--Howliday Inn. Munsinger, Lynn (1951-), illus. LC 81-10886. (Illus.). vii, 195 p. 22cm. 1982. (ISBN 0-689-30846-9). Atheneum.
--Mister Tinker in Oz. Rose, David S. (1947-), illus. LC 84-16105. (Illus.). 64 p. 20cm. c.1985. (ISBN 0-394-87038-7). Random House.
--Morgan's Zoo. Morrill, Leslie H., illus. LC 84-6325. (Illus.). 192p. (gr. 3-7). 1984. (ISBN 0-689-31046-3). Atheneum.
--A Night Without Stars. LC 82-16278. p. cm. 1983. (ISBN 0-689-30957-0). Atheneum.
--What Eric Knew: A Sebastian Barth Mystery. LC 85-7418. 138 p. 22cm. (Sebastian Barth Mysteries: Bk.1). 1985. (ISBN 0-689-31159-1). Atheneum.

Howe, James (1946-) & Henson, Jim (1936-)
--The Case of the Missing Mother: Starring Jim Henson's Muppets. Cleaver, William, illus. LC 82-13287. p. cm. 1983. (ISBN 0-394-85729-1). Muppet Press.

Howe, James (1946-) & Starr, Leonard
--Annie Joins the Circus. Shortall, Leonard W., illus. LC 82-3769. (Illus.). 62 p. 20cm. c.1982. (ISBN 0-394-85364-4). (ISBN 0-394-95364-9). Random House.

Howe, Jane Moore
--Amelia Earhart, Kansas Girl. 1st ed. Laune, Paul Sidney (1899-), illus. LC 50-6741. 196 p. illus. 20 cm. (Childhood of famous Americans series). 1950. Bobbs-Merrill.
--Amelia Earhart, Kansas Girl. Morrow, Gray, illus. LC 62-9246. 200p. illus. 20cm. (Childhood of famous Americans). c.1961. Bobbs-Merrill.

Howe, Janet Rogers
--Benjamin Big. Ruth, Rod (1912-), illus. LC 58-5189. 21cm. 128p. 1958. The Westminister Press.
--Curly. Bobrizky, George, illus. LC 56-6333. 84p. illus. 24cm. 1956. Lothrop, Lee & Shepard Co.
--The Mystery of the Marmalade Cat. Blaker, Clay, illus. LC 69-12908. (Illus.). 192 p. 22cm. 1969. (ISBN 0-664-32439-8). Westminster Press.
--Samuel Small's Secret Society. Hall, H. Tom, illus. LC 60-7631. 21cm. 100p. 1960. The Westminister Press.
--Secret of Castle Balou. 1964. E M Hale.
--The Secret of Castle Balou. 1st ed. Hall, H. Tom, illus. LC 64-10031. 155 p. illus. 21 cm. c.1964. Westminster Press.

--Star: An Irish Wolfhound. Ruth, Rod (1912-), illus. LC 59-5849. 160p. illus. 21cm. 1959. Westminster Press.
--Thunder and Jerry. LC 49-11121. 212 p. illus. 22 cm. 1949. Lothrop, Lee & Shepard Co.
--Trinket. Smalley, Janet (1893-), illus. LC 61-10624. (Illus.). 21cm. 157p. (gr. 1-6). 1961. (ISBN 0-664-32264-6). Westminster.

Howe, Katherine Mallett (1898-)
--Miss Muffett! Miss Muffett!. Howe, Katherine Mallett (1898-), illus. LC 48-16379. 32 p. col. illus. 29 cm. 1947, c.1946. J. Martin's House.

Howe, Laura Elizabeth see Richards, Laura Elizabeth Howe, Mrs.

Howe, Margaret, pseud., see Brucker, Margaretta.

Howe, Norma
--God, the Universe and Hot Fudge Sundaes. LC 83-26548. 182 p. 22cm. 1984. (ISBN 0-395-35483-8). Houghton Mifflin.

Howell, Alvin, jt. auth. see Benjamin, Bezaleel Solomon.

Howell, B. Florence
--The Coral Bracelet, and Other Sketches. N.D. M. E. Church.

Howell, Carrie Macknet
--Susie's Three Christmas Days. LC 26-23674. 48 p. incl. plates. 21 cm. c.1926. The Christopher Publishing House.

Howell, Lynn & Howell, Richard
--Winifred's New Bed. Howell, Lynn & Howell, Richard, illus. LC 85-5237. (Illus.). 26 p. 1st U.S. edition. c.1985. (ISBN 0-394-87772-1). Knopf : Distributed by Random House.

Howell, Margaret
--I Can Keep a Secret. Greer, Terence (1929-), illus. (Illus.). (gr. k-3). 1974 (Schol Trade Pap). Schol Bk Serv.
--The Mouse Who Wanted to Be a Man. Wilkinson, Barry, illus. LC 73-178595. (Illus.). 30 p. 22cm. (Minnow book). 1973. (ISBN 0-582-16474-5). Longman Young Books.

Howell, Mary Hubbard
--Dorothy and Her Ships. LC 12-34493. 203 p. incl. front. 2 pl. 19 cm. 1895. The American Sunday-School Union.
--Through the Winter. LC 9-12080. 20 cm. 399p. 1909. The American Sunday-School Union.

Howell, Michael & Ford, Peter
--The Elephant Man: Retold for Children. Geary, Robert, illus. (Illus.). (gr. 2-8). 1984. (ISBN 0-8052-8160-6, Pub. by Allison & Busby England). Schocken.

Howell, Richard, jt. auth. see Howell, Lynn.

Howell, Ruth Rea
--A Crack in the Pavement. 1st ed. Strong, Arline, illus. LC 76-98612. (Illus.). 48 p. 25cm. 1970. Atheneum.
--Everything Changes. (Illus.). 64 p. 24cm. 1968. Atheneum.

Howell, Virginia (1910-)
--Who Likes The Dark?. N.D. E. M. Hale & Co.
--Who Likes the Dark?. Thompson, Marjorie, illus. LC 46-25039. 40 p. illus. (part col.) 23 cm. c.1945. Howell, Soskin.
--Who Likes the Dark?. Thompson, Marjorie, illus. (gr. k-3). N.D. Lothrop Bks.

Howells, Mildred, ed. see Howells, William Dean.

Howells, Mildred (1872-)
--The Woman Who Lived in Holland. Holdsworth, William Curtis, illus. LC 72-93787. (Illus.). 32 p. 23cm. 1973. (ISBN 0-374-38460-6). Farrar, Straus and Giroux.

Howells, William Dean (1837-1920)
--A Boy's Town. LC 75-131748. (Illus.). vi, 247 p. 22cm. (Deacribed for "Harper's Young People".). 1972. (ISBN 0-403-00635-X). Scholarly Press.
--A Boy's Town: Described for "Harper Young People". LC 78-98764. (Illus.). vi, 247 p. 23cm. 1970. (ISBN 0-8371-2804-8). Greenwood Press.
--A Boy's Town: Described for "Harper's Young People,". LC 9-17. vi, 247 p. front., 22 pl. 19 1/2 cm. 1890. Harper & Brothers.
--A Chance Aquaintance. 1873. James R. Osgood.
--Christmas Every Day. Richards, Harriet Roosevelt, illus. LC 9-3052. 30cm. 22p. 1908. Harper & Brothers.
--Christmas Every Day, and Other Stories Told for Children. LC 76-9896. (Illus.). 150 p. 20cm. 1976. (ISBN 0-8486-0204-8). Core Collection Books.
--Christmas Every Day,and Other Stories Told for Children. 4 p. l., 3-150 p. incl. illus., plates. front. 19 cm. 1893. Harper & Brothers.
--The Flight of Pony Baker: A Boy's Town Story. LC 4-17809. v, 222, 1 p. front., 7 pl. 19 cm. 1908. Harper & Brothers.
--The Howells Story Book. ed. Burt, Mary Elizabeth (1850-1918) & Howells, Mildred (1872-), eds. Howells, Mildred, Miss (1872-), illus. LC 50657. 5 p. l., vii-xiii, 161 p. front. (port.) illus., plates. 18 1/2 cm. (Scribner's series of school reading). 1900. C. Scribner's Sons.
--The Rise of Silas Lapham. (Illus.). (Great Il. Classics). (gr. 9 up). 1964. (ISBN 0-396-05042-5). Dodd.
--The Sleeping-Car and The Parlor-Car. (Riverside Literature Ser.). N.D. Houghton Mifflin Co.

Howes, Barbara (1914-) & Smith, Gregory Jay, eds.
--The Sea-Green Horse: A Collection of Short Stories. LC 73-89589. notes. 288p. (gr. 7-12). 1970. (ISBN 0-02-744610-7). Macmillan.

Howes, Edith Annie
--Fairy Rings. Watkins, Frank, illus. N.D. Funk & Wagnalls.
--The Long Bright Land: Fairy Tales from Southern Seas. Lathrop, Dorothy Pulis (1891-1980), illus. LC 29-18883. xiv, 207 p. incl. illus., plates. col. front. 21 1/2 cm. 1929. Little, Brown, and Company.
--Maoriland Fairy Tales. N.D. Frederick Warne & Co.
--Rainbow Children. N.D. Funk & Wagnalls.
--Sandals of Pearl. Chalmers, Audrey (1899-1957), illus. LC 28-20905. x, 246 p. incl. mounted col. front. plates. 21 cm. 1928. W. Morrow & Company.
--The Sun's Babies. Watkins, Frank, illus. LC 14-4180. xii, 236 p. col. front., col. plates. 21 1/2 cm. 1913. Cassell and Company, Ltd.
--The Sun's Babies. Watkins, Frank, illus. N.D. Funk & Wagnalls.

Howes, Isaiah C.
--Jane, Be Good!. Barus, Jane Garey, intro. by. LC 28-22792. xi p., 1 l. 154 p., 1 l. illus. 18 x 14 cm. 1928. The Macmillan Company.

Howitt
--Charming Stories. N.D. Hurst & Company.

Howitt, Mary Botham, Mrs. (1799-1888)
--Alice Franklin, 14 Vols. (Series of Popular Juvenile Works). N.D. D. Appleton & Co.
--Baldwin's Fables, 1 of 4. (Our Cousin's Library). N.D. Collins & Bro.
--Bright Days. (Illus.). N.D. D. Lothrop & Co.
--The Children's Year in a Happy Home. ed. Poulsson, Anne Emilie (1853-1939) & Young, Florence Liley, illus. LC 27-22477. 240 p. col. front., col. plates. 20 cm. c.1927. Lothrop, Lee & Shepard Co.
--Dick and the Angel. N.D. D. Lothrop & Co.
--Fireside Tales. N.D. Roberts Bros.
--Gabriel of Wichnor Wood. (Our Cousin's Library). N.D. Collins & Brother's Publications.
--Hope On, Hope Ever, 1 of 14 Vols. (Series of Popular Juvenile Works: Vol. 2). N.D. D. Appleton & Co.
--John Oriel's Start in Life. (Young Folks Series, Number Three). N.D. Fleming H Revell Co.
--John Oriel's Start in Life. N.D. Thomas Whittaker.
--Lillieslea: or, Lost and Found. Absolon, illus. N.D. George Routledge & Sons.
--Little Coin, Much Care, 3 of 14 Vol. LC 79-10072. 16cm. 171p. (Series of Popular Juvenile Works: Vol. 3). 1855. D. Appleton & Co.
--The Little Peacemakers. Juv ed. (Illus.). N.D. Cassell & Co.
--Love and Money, 1 of 14 Vol. (Series of Popular Juvenile Works: Vol. 4). N.D. D. Appleton & Co.
--Mabel on Midsummer Day: A Story of the Olden Time. Hinds, Helen Marie, illus. LC 15-24000. 14 p., 12 l. plates. 20 1/2 x 25 1/2 cm. 1881. J. R. Osgood and Company.
--Mary Howitt's Tales for All Season. (Victoria Edition). 1882. J B Lippincott.
--Mary Howitt's Treasury of Old Favorite Tales. (The A.L.O.E. Ser.). N.D. The American News Co.
--Mary Leeson. (The Claremont Library). N.D. American News Co.
--Mid-Summer Day: A Tale of the Olden Time. Poe, Lucy Arnold, illus. 16 p. col. front., col. plates. 28 cm. c.1931. R. G. Badger.
--My Own Story, 1 of 14 Vols. (Series of Popular Juvenile Works: Vol. 5). N.D. D. Appleton & Co.
--My Uncle, 1 of 14 Vols. (Series of Popular Juvenile Works: Vol. 6). N.D. D. Appleton & Co.
--My Uncle the Clockmaker. (The Welcome Library). 1910. Frederick Warne & Co.
--No Sense Like Common Sense, 1 of 14 Vols. (Series of Popular Juvenile Works: Vol. 7). N.D. D. Appleton & Co.
--Our Cousins in Ohio. (Our Cousin's Library). N.D. Collins & Brother's Publications.
--Parley's Animals. (Our Cousin's Library). N.D. Collins & Brother's Publications.
--Peter Parley's Fable of The Spider and Fly. LC 24-9821. 13 p. col. front., illus. 13 cm. 1830. Carter and Hendee.
--Pictures for the Young. Howitt, Mary Botham, Mrs. (1799-1888), illus. (Illus.). N.D. D. Lothrop & Co.
--Sowing and Reaping: Or, What Will Come of It, 1 of 14 vols. LC 26-6595. 3 p. l, 170 p. front. (port.) 15 cm. (Series of Popular Juvenile Works: Vol. 8). 1851. D. Appleton & Company.
--Steadfast Gabriel. N.D. Thomas Wittaker.
--Story of a Genius, 1 of 14 Vols. (Series of Popular Juvenile Works: Vol. 9). N.D. D. Appleton & Co.
--The Story of a Happy Home: Or, The Children's Year and How They Spent It. N.D. Thomas Nelson and Sons.
--Strive and Thrive, 1 of 14 Vols. (Series of Popular Juvenile Works: Vol. 10). N.D. D. Appleton & Co.
--Tales in Verses. (Illus.). 1882. Harper.
--Two Apprentices, 1 of 14 Vols. (Series of Popular Juvenile Works: Vol. 11). N.D. D. Appleton & Co.
--The Two Apprentices. (The Welcome Library). 1910. Frederick Warne & Co.
--Which is Wiser, 1 of 14 Vols. (Series of Popular Juvenile Works: Vol. 12). N.D. D. Appleton & Co.
--Who is Greatest, 1 of 14 Vols. (Series of Popular Juvenile Works: Vol. 13). N.D. D. Appleton & Co.
--Work and Wages: Tales for the People and Their Children, 1 of 14 vols. (Mary Howitt's Ser.: Vol. 13). 1843. D. Appleton & Co.

Howitt, William (1792-1879)
--Boy's Adventures in the Wilds of Australia: Or, Herbert's Note-Book. Harvey, William (1796-1866), illus. N.D. George Routledge & Sons.
--A Boy's Adventures in the Wilds of Australia. N.D. James R. Osgood.
--A Country Book for the Field, the Forest, and the Fireside, 1 of 3 Vols. (Illus.). (The Fireside Stories Library). N.D. Set. George Routledge & Sons.
--Jack o' the Mill, 1 of 3 Vols. (Illus.). (The Fireside Stories Library). N.D. Set. George Routledge & Sons.

Howker, Janni
--Badger on the Barge and Other Stories. LC 84-10293. 208p. (gr. 5-9). c.1984. (ISBN 0-688-04215-5). Greenwillow. **Awards: (IRA); (ALA).**
--The Nature of the Beast. 1985. Greenwillow. **Award: (ALA).**

Howland, Avia C.
--Tales of Old Times in Rhode Island: An Ancient Book Now Republished. Wood, Martha C., ed. Wood, Martha C., illus. LC 4-16413. 158 p. front., illus., plates. 20 1/2 x 18 cm. 1903. G. Rice & Sons.

Howland, Ethel
--Scarey-Ann (the Wooden Doll) and the Cookie Man. Eulalie, pseud. (1896-), illus. Banks, Eulalie M.. LC 33-19705. 3 p. l, 9-100, 1 p. illus. (part col.) 23 cm. c.1932. Suttonhouse.

Howles, Edith Annie
--The Band Played Murder. LC 46-217452. 4 p. l., 243 p. 19 1/2 cm. 1946. M.S. Mill Co., Inc.

Howliston, Mary H.
--Cat-Tails and Other Tales. Howliston, Mary H., illus. LC 99-5429. 187 1 p. illus. 19 1/2 cm. 1899. A. Flanagan.

Hows, John A., illus.
--Christmas Carol: "Christ Was Born on Christmas Day". N.D. Hurd & Houghton.

Hoxie, Bertha Davidson
--Christmas in Denmark: Hilda's Wish. (Illus.). (Christmas in Many Lands Ser.). N.D. Dana Estes & Co.

Hoxie, Evelyn
--Little Folks Stories and Story Plays. Weaver, Thomas Bryan, illus. Bugbee, Willis Newton (1870-) 95 p. illus. 19 cm. (The Bushel O' Fun Series). c.1927. The Willis N.Bugbee Co.

Hoxie, Jane Lincoln (1863-)
--A Kindergarten Story Book. LC 6-18837. viii p., 1 l, 119 p. front. 20 cm. 1906. M. Bradley Company.

Hoyer, M. A.
--Missing Monkey. (Illus.). N.D. E. P. Dutton & Co.

Hoyland, John
--The Ivy Garland. Vicary, Richard, illus. 1983. Schocken.

Hoyland, Rosemary Jean (1929-)
--Ethelbert: The Tale of a Tiger. Hoyland, Rosemary Jean (1929-), illus. LC 55-8943. (Illus.). (gr. k-3). 1955. Knopf.

Hoyle, Fred (1915-) & Hoyle, Geoffrey (1942-)
--Into Deepest Space. LC 74-4859. 224p. 1974. (ISBN 0-06-011984-5, HarpT). Har-Row.

Hoyle, Geoffrey, jt. auth. see Hoyle, Fred.

Hoyle, Zoe
--The Peek-A-Boos Desert Island. Preston, Chloe, illus. N.D. George H Doran & Co.

Hoyt, Charles A.
--The Claim-Jumpers. Parsons, Priscilla B., illus. LC 27-21012. xi, 218 p. front., plates. 19 1/2 cm. c.1927. The Century Co.
--Prairie Treasure. Phares, Frank E., illus. LC 26-5017. xiv, 280 p. front., plates. 19 cm. $1.7. c.1926. The Century Co.

Hoyt, Deristhe Levinte
--Barbara's Heritage: Or, Young Americans Among the Old Italian Masters. LC 99-4926. 358 p. front., illus., 7 pl. 19 1/2 cm. c.1899. W. A. Wilde Company.

Hoyt, Edwin P.
--The Mutiny on the Globe. LC 75-5779. 224p. 1975. (ISBN 0-394-49365-6). Random.

Hoyt, Elisabeth, ed.
--After School. Bruce, Josephine, illus. LC 13-26559. 96 p. incl. front., illus. (part col.) 19 1/2 cm. (Happy hour ser.). c.1913. W. A. Wilde Company.
--The Doll's Story Book. (Illus.). (Happy Hour Ser.). 1910. W. A. Wilde Co.
--Little Chum Club. LC 10-28496. (Illus.). 20 x 16cm. 96p. (Happy Hour Ser.). N.D. W. A. Wilde Co.
--Little Folks in the Country. (Illus.). (Happy Hour Ser.). 1910. W. A. Wilde Co.
--Little Stories for Little People. Bruce, Charlotte, illus. (Illus.). (Happy Hour Ser.). N.D. W. A. Wilde Co.
--Play Days. LC 9-27957. (Illus.). 20cm. 96p. (Happy Hour Ser.). 1909. W. A. Wilde Co.
--Santa Claus' Dolls. LC 11-29955. (Illus.). 20cm. 96p. (Happy Hour Ser.). 1911. W. A. Wilde Co.
--Some Little Cooks and What They Did. Hoyt, Elisabeth, illus. LC 13-6896. 96 p. incl. col. front., illus. (part col.) 19 1/2 cm. (Happy Hour Ser.). c.1912. W. A. Wilde Company.

Hoyt, Helen P.
--Aloha, Susan!. 1 st. ed. LC 61-9517. 22cm. 167p. 1961. Doubleday.
--The Jeweled Cross. LC 64-16237. 189 p. 22 cm. 1964. Doubleday.

Hoyt, Hildegarde
--Little Blacknose. N.D. E. M. Hale and co.

Hoyt, J. K., tr. see Verne, Jules.

Hoyt, Jeanette Ralston Chase, Mrs. (1847-)
--Janet and Her Friends. Hoyt, Jeanette Ralston Chase, Mrs. (1847-), illus. LC 32-195400. 83 p. illus. 25 cm. c.1876. D. Appleton & Co.

Hoyt, R
--Legends of the Springtime. Hoyt, R., illus. LC 2-17231. 106 p. incl. illus., plates. 18 cm. (On cover: Educational juvenile series). c.1899. Educational Publishing Company.

Hoyt, Vance Joseph (1889-)
--Bar-Rac: The Biography of a Raccoon. Hoyt, Vance Joseph (1889-), illus. LC 31-10077. 111 p. front., plates. 21 1/2 cm. c.1931. Lothrop, Lee & Shepard Co.
--Malibu: A Nature Story. Bull, Charles Livingston (1874-1932), illus. LC 31-240649. 272 p. front., plates. 22 1/2 cm. c.1931. Lothrop, Lee & Shepard Co.
--Sequoia, a Nature Story. A Nature Story. 272 p. front., plates. 21 cm. Orig. Title: Malibu. 1935. Grosset & Dunlap.
--Silver Boy: The Gray Fox of Topanga. Bull, Charles Livingston (1874-1932), illus. LC 29-191926. 265 p. front., plates. 22 1/2 cm. c.1929. Lothrop, Lee & Shepard Co.
--Song Dog: The Story of a Coyote. Shenton, Edward (1895-), photos by. LC 39-30687. xi, 228 p. col. front., illus. 22 1/2 cm. c.1939. The John C. Winston Company.
--Zorra: The Biography of a Gray Fox. Hoyt, Vance Joseph (1889-), illus. LC 33-245403. 125 p. front., plates, ports. 21 1/2 cm. c.1933. Lothrop, Lee & Shepard Co.

Hricko, M. Gabriel
--Cyril a Metod Hovoria Slovensky. Cyril and Method Speak Slovak. LC 72-195774. (Illus.). 179 p. 24cm. (Slovak language course). 1971. First Catholic Slovak Union.

Hrolfs Saga Kraka, jt. auth. see Collin, Hedvig.

Hsiao, Ellen
--A Chinese Year. Hsiao, Ellen, illus. LC 70-106591. (Illus.). 64p. (Two World Bks.). (gr. 4 up). 1970. (ISBN 0-87131-095-3). M Evans.

Hsiao, Jen & Huang, Cheng
--Capture the Old Bald Eagle: Story. Kan, Wu-Yen, illus. LC 78-102591. (Illus.). 59 p. 25cm. 1977. Foreign Languages Press.

Hsieh, Tehyi, Dr. (1884-)
--Chinese Picked Tales for Children. LC 48-1368. 57 p. illus. 23 cm. 1948. Chinese Service Bureau.
--Chinese Village Folk Tales. N.D. Bruce Humphries, Inc.
--Our Little Manchurian Cousin. Owl, illus. Yih, Koliang, frwd. by. LC 33-13644. x p., 3 l., 106 p., 1 l. col. front., illus. (map) plates. 19 1/2 cm. (little cousin series). c.1933. L. C. Page & Company.

Hsiung, Shikh-i (1902-), tr. see Wang Pao-Chuan.

Hsiung, Thelma
--The Adventures of Little Brother. Hsiung, Thelma, illus. LC 64-12739. 1964. Abelard-Schuman.

AUTHOR INDEX HUELSBERG, ENID

Htin Aung, U (1909-) & Trager, Helen Gibson (1910-)
--A Kingdom Lost for a Drop of Honey, and Other Burmese Folktales. Pau Oo Thet, U., illus. LC 68-11653. (Illus.). 96 p. 23cm. 1968. Parents' Magazine Press.
Huang, Cheng, jt. auth. see Hsiao, Jen.
Hubbard, Alice & Babbitt, Adeline, eds.
--The Golden Flute: An Anthology of Poetry for Young Children. LC 32-10417. (gr. k-3). 1932. (ISBN 0-381-97020-5). John Day.
Hubbard, Allen, ed. see Disney, Walt, Productions.
Hubbard, Carson Margaret
--Boss Chombale. N.D. E . M. Hale and Co.
Hubbard, Clara Beeson
--Merry Songs and Games: For the Use of the Kindergarten. 2 pt. in 1 v. 30 x 22 1/2 cm. c.1901. Pub. for the Author by Dulmer & Weber.
Hubbard, Della
--Buzz, the Famous Burro. (gr. 1-6). N.D. (ISBN 0-8181-0252-7). Pageant-Poseidon.
Hubbard, Dexter
--The Journal of Elizabeth Smith. Book, William, illus. LC 76-356309. (Illus.). 68 p. 21cm. 1975. Lancelot Press.
Hubbard, Donald Lee (1929-)
The Dragon Comes to Admela, Another Book About Admela and Its Royal Family. Charles, Donald, pseud. (1929-), illus. Meighan, Donald Charles. LC 67-20697. (Illus.). 40 p. 23cm. 1967. Reilly and Lee Co.
--Dragons, Dragons: A Story. Charles, Donald, pseud. (1929-), illus. Meighan, Donald Charles. LC 67-3024. (Illus.). 26 p. 23cm. 1967. Reilly and Lee Co.
Hubbard, Elbert, jt. auth. see Hale, Edward Everett.
Hubbard, Eleanore Mineah
--Citizenship Plays: A Dramatic Reader for Upper Grades. LC 22-3043. vi, 344 p. 19 1/2 cm. c.1922. B. H. Sanborn & Co.
--Peter Piper's Playmates: The Eleanore Mineah Hubbard Edition. Hubbard, Eleanore Mineah, illus. LC 30-28750. 61 p. incl. front., illus. 23 cm. c.1930. A. Whitman & Co.
--Plays on the Old World Backgrounds of American History: A Dramatic Reader for Middle and Upper Grades. Hubbard, Eleanore Mineah, illus. LC 35-13203. x, 277 p. col. front., illus. 19 1/2 cm. 1935. B. H. Sanborn & Co.
Hubbard, Fran (1924-)
--A Day with Tupi: An Authentic Story of an Indian Boy in California's Mountains. Vella, Ed, illus. 1v. (unpaged) illus. 28cm. 1966. Ginn.
Hubbard, Freeman Henry (1894-)
--The Roundhouse Cat, and Other Railroad Animals. Wiese, Kurt (1887-1974), illus. LC 51-10523. 124 p. illus. 22 cm. 1951. Whittlesey House.
--The Train That Never Came Back, and Other Railroad Stories. Wiese, Kurt (1887-1974), illus. LC 52-9453. 127 p. illus. 22 cm. 1952. Whittlesey House.
--Vinnie Ream and Mr. Lincoln. LC 49-11038. (Illus.). 271p. 21cm. 1949. Whittlesey House.
Hubbard, Freeman Henry (1894-) & Farley, Leonard V
--Great days of the Circus. 1962. Harper & Row Publishers.
Hubbard, Howell Mary
--On the Way Home. LC 12-34494. 19 cm. 390p. 1882. The American Sunday School Unin.
Hubbard, Inez
--Danny. Edgell, Kyle, illus. LC 84-62082. (Illus.). 48p. (Orig.). (gr. k-3). 1984. (ISBN 0-931571-00-6). Lifetime Pr.
Hubbard, Irene & Soderstrom, Lori
--Primarily Me. (gr. k-3). 1976. (ISBN 0-916456-09-9). Good Apple.
Hubbard, Joan, pseud., see Jackson, Kathryn.
Hubbard, Lindley Murray
--An Express of 'Seventy-Six: A Chronicle of the Town of York in the War for Independence. Beales, I. B., illus. 3 p. l., iii, xi-xii p., 1 l., 340 p., 1 l. front., 4 pl. 20 1/2 cm. 1906. Little, Brown, and Company.
Hubbard, Margaret Ann (1909-)
--The Blue Gonfalon. 1st ed. Miller, Shane (1907-), illus. LC 60-8873. 187p. illus. 22cm. (Clarion books). 1960. Doubleday.
--Captain Juniper. LC 47-122104. 257 p. map (on lining-papers) 22 cm. 1947. Macmillan Co.
--Crosswind Canyon. LC 50-10366. 195 p. 22 cm. 1950. Macmillan.
--A Crown for Carly. Elgin, Jill, illus. LC 55-14748. 207p. illus. 21cm. 1955. Macmillan.
--Flight of the Swan: A Novel Based on the Life of Hans Christian Andersen. LC 47-174. 5 p. l., 310 p. illus. 20 1/2 cm. 1946. The Bruce Publishing Company.
--Halloran's Hill. LC 53-126592. 248p. 22cm. 1953. Macmillan.
--The Hickory Limb. Morse, Dorothy Bayley (1906-1979), illus. LC 42-21071. 5 p. l., 291 p. incl. front. 21 cm. 1942. The Macmillan Company.
--Little Whirlwind. Morse, Dorothy Bayley (1906-1979), illus. LC 40-6696. 4 p. l., 291, 1 p. incl. front., illus. 21 cm. 1940. The Macmillan Company.
--Lone Boy. LC 43-11459. 5 p. l., 9-259 p. incl. front. 21 cm. 1943. The Macmillan Company.
--Pennyweather Luck. LC 48-11366. 243 p. 22 cm. 1948. Macmillan Co.
--The Road to the King's Mountain. LC 63-17459. 184 p. illus., map (on lining papers) 22 cm. 1963. Doubleday.
--Seraphina Todd. Lee, Manning De Villeneuve (1894-1980), illus. LC 41-5700. 308 p. illus. 21 cm. 1941. The Macmillan Company.
--St. Louis & the Last Crusade. (Illus.). (gr. 4-10). 1958 (Vision). FS&G.
--Thunderhead Mountain. LC 52-12583. 204 p. 22cm. 1952. Macmillan.
--The Trouble on Shake-Rag Creek. 1st ed. Cather, Carolyn, illus. LC 67-17276. (Illus.). 166 p. 22cm. 1967. Doubleday.
Hubbard, Margaret Carson
--Boss Chombale. Spier, Peter Edward (1927-), illus. LC 57-6568. 183p. illus. 21cm. c.1957. Crowell.
Hubbard, Ralph
--Queer Person. Von Schmidt, Harold (1896-1982), illus. LC 30-21954. 7 p. l., 336 p. front., double plates. 20 1/2 cm. 1930. Doubleday, Doran & Company, Inc. **Award: (JNM).**
--Queer Person. Von Schmidt, Harold (1896-1982), illus. LC 78-52836. (Illus.). 336 p., 8 leaves of plates. 21cm. 1978. (ISBN 0-9601652-0-7). Theodore Roosevelt Nature and History Association.
--The Wolf Song. Kihn, W. Langdon, illus. LC 35-16782. 5 p. l., 287 p. incl. 1 illus., plates. front. 20 1/2 cm. 1935. Doubleday, Doran & Company, Inc.
--The Wolf Song. Kihn, W. Langdon, illus. LC 78-52830. (Illus.). 287 p. 21cm. 1978. (ISBN 0-9601652-1-5). Theodore Roosevelt Nature and History Association.
Hubbell, Harriet Weed (1909-)
--Cannons Over Niagara. LC 54-698461. 192p. 22cm. 1954. Westminster Press.
--The Captain's Secret. Smith, Edward John, illus. LC 55-5877. (Illus.). 192 p. 22cm. 1955. Westminster Press.
--The Friendship Tree. LC 62-15984. 217p. 22cm. 1962. T. Nelson.
--Moonpenny Lane. LC 61-6805. 184p. 22cm. 1961. T. Nelson.
--Surprise Summer. LC 58-5480. 175p. 21cm. 1958. Westminster Press.
Hubbell, Mrs. Rose Strong, Mrs., jt. auth. see Christie, Catherine Allison, Mrs.
Hubbell, Patricia (1928-)
--The Apple Vendor's Fair. Maas, Julie, illus. LC 63-10368. 53 p. illus. 22 cm. 1963. Atheneum.
--Catch Me a Wind. 1st ed. Trommler, Susan, illus. LC 68-12239. (Illus.). 52 p. 22cm. 1968. Atheneum.
--Eight A. M. Shadows. Maas, Julie, illus. LC 65-21718. (Illus.). (gr. 2-7). 1965. (ISBN 0-689-20184-2). Atheneum.
Hubbell-Plummer, Beatrice
--Little Homespun Songs and Verses Woven from Thoughts of Children: Words and Music. Russell, Mary La Fetra, illus. LC 21-12877. 104 p. incl. col. front., col. plates. 30 1/2 x 23 1/2 cm. c.1920. Frederick A. Stokes Company.
Hubbell, Rose Strong, Mrs.
--If I Could Fly: Stories in Free Verse for Children. Gaze, Harold, illus. LC 17-29877. vii p., 1 l., 113 p. col. front., col. plates. 23 1/2 cm. 1917. G. P. Putnam's Sons.
Huber, Anne L
--The Nursery Rattle: For Little Folks. Faber, Hermann, illus. LC 17-1335. 136 p. incl. col. front., col. plates. 20 1/2 x 15 1/2 cm. 1873. Claxton, Remsen & Haffelfinger.
--The Nursery Rattle. For Little Folks. Faber, Hermann, illus. LC 16-3084. 136 p. incl. col. front., col. plates. 20 x 15 1/2 cm. 1875. J. B. Lippincott & Co.
Huber, Maureen
--Cherry Cobbler. 1976. (ISBN 0-686-15735-4). Rod & Staff.
Huber, Miriam Blanton (1889-), retold by see Harris, Joel Chandler.
Huber, Miriam Blanton, Mrs. (1889-), ed.
--Story and Verse for Children. rev. ed. Ward, Lynd Kendall (1905-1985), illus. LC 55-3727. 812p. illus. 26cm. 1955. Macmillan.
--Story and Verse for Children. 3d ed. Ward, Lynd Kendall (1905-1985), illus. LC 65-15190. (Illus.). xxxi, 878 p. 26cm. 1965. Macmillan.
--Story and Verses for Children. Artzybasheff, Boris Mikhailovic (1899-1965), illus. LC 40-10342. (Illus.). 25cm. 857p. N.D. Macmillan Co.
Huber, Miriam Blanton, Mrs. (1889-) & Bruner, Herbert Bascom (1892-1974), eds.
--Children's Poetry. v. 19 cm. c.1925. Rand, McNally & Company.
--The Poetry Book. Hartwell, Marjorie, illus. LC 27-1305. 9 v. col. fronts., illus. 19 cm. c.1926. Rand, McNally & Company.
--The Poetry Book: Vol. 4. Hartwell, Marjorie, illus. LC 79-51968. (Illus.). Repr. of 1926 ed (Pub. by Rand). (Granger Poetry Library). (gr. 4). 1980. (ISBN 0-89609-183-X). Granger Bk.
Huber, Ursula
--Nock Family Circus. Piatti, Celestino (1922-), illus. LC 67-19003. (Illus.). (ps-4). 1968. (ISBN 0-689-20336-5). Atheneum.
Huberman, Edward (1900-), tr. see Robles, Antonio.
Hubert, Amelia
--Sweet Dreams for Sally. Cooke, Tom, illus. LC 82-22332. p. cm. c.1982. (ISBN 0-910313-01-6). Parker Bros.
Hubert, Sr. & Julitta, Sr.
--Our Little King. N.D. Bruce Publication Co.
Hubka, Betty Josephine Morgan (1924-)
--Bernie. Hubka, Betty Josephine Morgan (1924-), illus. LC 62-115018. (Illus.). (gr. k-3). 1962. (ISBN 0-8114-7502-6). Steck-V.
--Octavius. Hubka, Betty Josephine Morgan (1924-), illus. LC 63-13013. (Illus.). 48 p. 24cm. 1963. (ISBN 0-8114-7541-7). Steck Co.
--Stubborn As a Mule. Hubka, Betty Josephine Morgan (1924-), illus. LC 67-15877. 32p. col. illus. 24cm. 1967. Steck.
--Where Is the Bear?. Crawford, Mel (1925-), illus. (A Young Reader Ser.). (gr. k-3). 1979. (ISBN 0-307-60204-4, Golden Pr). Western Pub.
Hubler, Richard Gibson see Gibson, Harry Clark.
Hubley, Faith Elliot, jt. auth. see Hubley, John.
Hubley, Faith Elliot (1924-), created by see Swados, Elizabeth.
Hubley, Faith Elliot (1924-) & Hubley, John (1914-1977)
--The Hat. 1st ed. Hubley, Faith Elliot (1924-) & Hubley, John (1914-1977), illus. LC 74-1197. (Illus.). 48 p. 1974. Harcourt Brace Jovanovich.
Hubley, John, jt. auth. see Hubley, Faith Elliot.
Hubley, John (1914-1977) & Hubley, Faith Elliot (1924-)
--Dig!. A Journey Under the Earth's Crust. Hubley, John (1914-1977) & Hubley, Faith Elliot (1924-), illus. LC 72-88169. (Illus.). 61 p. 1973. (ISBN 0-15-223490-X). Harcourt Brace Jovanovich.
Hubner, Carol K.
--The Haunted Shul. Kramer, Devorah, illus. (Judaica Youth Series: Devorah Doresh Mysteries). (gr. 3-8). 1979. (ISBN 0-910818-14-2). (ISBN 0-910818-45-2). Judaica Pr.
--The Silent Shofar. Forst, Sigmund, illus. (Devora Doresh Mysteries). (gr. 3 up). N.D. Judaica Pr.
--The Tattered Tallis. Kramer, Devorah, illus. (Illus.). 128p. (Judaica Youth Series: Devorah Doresh Mysteries). (gr. 3-8). 1979. (ISBN 0-910818-19-3). (ISBN 0-686-77614-3). Judaica Pr.
--The Twisted Menorah. (Deborah Donesh Mysteries). (gr. 3-8). 1981. (ISBN 0-910818-41-X). (ISBN 0-910818-42-8). Judaica Pr.
--The Whispering Mezuzah. Kramer, Devorah, illus. (Illus.). (Judaica Youth Series: Devorah Doresh Mysteries). 1979. (ISBN 0-910818-18-5). (ISBN 0-686-64802-1). Judaica Pr.
Hubp, Loretta B.
--Que Sera - What Can It Be?. Vasiliu, Mircea (1920-), illus. LC 69-10828. (Illus.). line drawings. 64p. (gr. 3 up). 1970. (ISBN 0-381-99779-0). John Day.
Huddleson, Maude Connell
--Fairy Secrets: Or, The Birth of Thought. Huddleson, Maude Connell, illus. LC 43-15844. 2 p. l., 9-59, 1 p. incl. mounted col. front., illus. (part col.) 29 x 22 cm. 1943. W. F. Lewis, Times-Mirror Press.
Huddy, Delia (1934-)
--How Edward Saved St. George. Hall, Dorothy & Hall, Douglas (1931-), illus. LC 67-19768. (Illus.). 1 v. (unpaged. 24cm. 1st U.S. edition. 1967, c.1966. Delacorte Press.
--The Humboldt Effect. LC 82-9212. p. cm. c.1982. (ISBN 0-688-01526-3). Greenwillow Books.
--Tale of the Crooked Crab. LC 80-83010. (Julia MacRae Blackbird Bks.). (gr. k-3). 1981. (ISBN 0-531-04283-9). Watts.
--Time Piper. LC 78-24339. 247 p. 22cm. 1979, c.1976. (ISBN 0-688-80212-5). (ISBN 0-688-84212-7). Greenwillow Books.
Hudelson, Kenneth
--Fountains of Joy: Children's Bible Songs. 32p. (gr. 2-6). 1971. Star Bible.
Hudleston, Claire Alexander
--Buzz and Splash. Wilmot, Natalie Clairborne, illus. LC 32-22708. (Illus.). 20p. 21 x 32cm. 1932. Handcraft Press.
Hudlow, Jean
--Eric Plants a Garden. Hudlow, Jean, illus. LC 79-150803. (Illus.). 40 p. 24cm. 1971. (ISBN 0-8075-2136-1). A. Whitman.
Hudnut, Selma
--A Horse of Her Own. Anderson, Rus, illus. LC 63-20491. 1963. Van Nostrand.
--Irish Hurdles. Nall, Wallace, illus. LC 66-27520. (Illus.). vii, 161 p. 21cm. 1966. Van Nostrand.
--The Redhead and the Roan. Savitt, Sam (1917-), illus. LC 65-170397. vii, 182p. illus. 21cm. c.1965. Van Nostrand.
Hudson, ed. see Shakespeare, William.
Hudson, Alma
--Peter Rabbit and the Fairies. (Peter Rabbit Ser.). N.D. Cupples & Leon Co.
--Peter Rabbit at the Circus. (Peter Rabbit Ser.). N.D. Cupples & Leon Co.
--Peter Rabbit in Mother Goose Land. (Peter Rabbit Ser.). N.D. Cupples & Leon Co.
Hudson, Anne & Daniels, Neil
--Ozzie: An Odyssey of Love. Daniels, Neil, illus. (Illus.). 72p. (Orig.). (gr. 1-6). 1983. (ISBN 0-940258-10-2). Kripalu Pubns.
Hudson, Derek Rommel see Dickens, Charles John Huffam.
Hudson, Eleanor
--The Care Bears Help Out. Gray, J. M. L., illus. LC 82-61596. (Illus.). 32p. (Care Bear Mini-Storybooks). (gr. 1-6). 1982. (ISBN 0-394-85842-5). Random.
--A Whale of a Rescue. Gerver, Jane, ed. Paris, Pat, illus. LC 82-61014. (Illus.). 32p. (Sea World Mini-Storybooks). (gr. 1-5). 1983. (ISBN 0-394-85642-2). Random.
Hudson, Jan
--Sweetgrass. 1983. Tree Frog. **Award: (CLA).**
Hudson, Leafy
--The Lost Buzzer-the Haunted Meadow. Kennedy, Timothy, illus. (Illus.). 24p. (Orig.). (Buzzy Byron Bumblebee Story Ser.: No. 1). (ps-4). 1982. (ISBN 0-910219-03-6). Little People.
Hudson, Patric
--Circus Alphabet. Hudson, Patric, illus. LC 55-22541. unpaged. ill. 17cm. (Tell-a-Tale Book). 1955, c.1954. Whitman Pub.
Hudson, Robert
--Beyond the Dragon Temple. (Illus.). N.D. Sully and Kleinteich.
Hudson, Theresa Barna, jt. auth. see Knight, Vick Ralph, Jr.
Hudson, William Henry (1841-1922)
--The Disappointed Squirrel: And Other Stories from "The Book of a Naturalist". Kirmse, Marguerite (1885-1954), illus. LC 25-21605. 143, 1 p. incl. col. mounted front., illus., col. mounted plates. 23 1/. c.1925. George H. Doran Company.
Green Mansions. (Magnum Easy Eye Classic Ser.). (gr. 8-12). N.D. Lancer.
--Green Mansions. (gr. 7-12). 1972 (Starline). Schol Bk Serv.
--Green Mansions. (Keith Jennison Large Type Bks). (gr. 7 up). N.D. (ISBN 0-531-00196-2). Watts.
--Green Mansions. Teale, Edwin Way (1899-1980), intro. by. (Illus.). (Great Il. Classics). (gr. 9 up). N.D. (ISBN 0-396-03096-3). Dodd.
--A Little Boy Lost. Lathrop, Dorothy Pulis (1891-1980), illus. 187 p. col. front., illus., col. plates. 28 1/2 cm. 1920. A. A. Knopf.
--A Little Boy Lost. Lathrop, Dorothy Pulis (1891-1980), illus. LC 38-27798. 187 p. incl. col. front., illus., plates (part col.) 25 cm. 1939. A. A. Knopf.
--A Little Boy Lost. McCormick, Arthur David (1860-), illus. LC 18-18543. 222 p. incl. front., illus., plates. 21 cm. 1918. A. A. Knopf.
--A Little Boy Lost. McCormick, Arthur David (1860-), illus. 1958. Knopf.
--A Little Boy Lost, Together with the Poems of W. H. Hudson. LC 72-184152. ix, 200 p. 23cm. (collected works of W. H. Hudson). 1968. AMS Press.
--Tales of the Gauchos. Coatsworth, Elizabeth Jane (1893-), ed. Pitz, Henry Clarence (1895-1976), illus. LC 46-891. 5 p. l., 251, 2 p. col. illus., col. plates (part double) 23 1/2 cm. (Borzoi books for young people). 1946. A. A. Knopf.
--Tales of the Pampas. 1917. Alfred A. Knopf.
--Tales of the Pampas. 1939. Alfred A. Knopf.
Hudson, Wilson Mathis (1907-) & Maxwell, Allen
--The Golden log. 174p. 1962. Texas Folklore Society Publications.
Huebel, Russ
--The Big Bad Wolf in Texas. Espinosa, Tony, illus. (Illus.). 48p. (Orig.). 1983. (ISBN 0-9611604-2-X). C Del Grullo.
Huebsch, Alfhild Lamm, Mrs. (1887-), tr. see Geijerstam, Gustaf Af.
Hueffer, Ford Madox see Ford, Ford Madox, pseud.
Huelsberg, Enid L.
--Sometimes of Children. (gr. k-2). 1976. (ISBN 0-89039-172-6). Ann Arbor FL.

Huemer, Dick, ed. see Disney, Walt, Productions.
Huemer, Richard Martin, jt. auth. see Grant, Joseph Clarence.
Huemer, Richard Martin (1898-), adapted by see Disney, Walt, Productions.
Huens, Jean Leon & Ivanovsky, Elizabeth, illus.
--Once Upon a Time Stories. Ponsot, Marie Birmingham, tr. (Illus.). (gr. 1-5). 1945. (ISBN 0-448-00336-8). G&D.
Huerlimann, Bettina, tr. see Furrer, Juerg.
Huerlimann, Ruth see Hurley, William James, Jr.
Huerlimann, Ruth see Hurlimann, Ruth.
Hueston, Ethel Powelson, Mrs. (1887-)
--Eve to the Rescue. Summers, Dudley Gloyme, illus. N.D. Bobbs-Merrill Co.
--Leave It to Doris. (Growing Literature Ser.). N.D. Grosset & Dunlap.
--Leave It to Doris. King, W. B., illus. N.D. Bobbs-Merrill Co.
--Little Lady Comb: A Story of the Dressing-Table. LC 21-19074. 95, 1 p. front., plates. 19 cm. 1921. The Bobbs-Merrill Company.
--Prudence of the Parsonage. N.D. Grosset & Dunlap.
--Prudence of the Parsonage. Brown, Arthur William, illus. N.D. Bobbs-Merrill Co.
--Prudence Says So. N.D. Bobbs-Merrill Co.
--Prudence Says So. (The Prudence Bks.). N.D. Grosset & Dunlap.
--Sunny Slopes. N.D. Grosset & Dunlap.
--Sunny Slopes. Brown, Arthur William, illus. N.D. Bobbs-Merrill Co.
Huey, Maud Morrison
--Marjorie Moxie: Her Experiences. Hallock, Ruth Mary (1876-), illus. LC 10-22534. 2 p. l., 362 p. col. front., plates. 20 cm. 1910. Rand, McNally & Company.
Huff, Afton A. Walker (1928-)
--The Silent Message. 186 p. 22cm. 1970. Steck-Vaughn Co.
Huff, Barbara A., jt. auth. see Graham, Helen Holland.
Huff, Betty Tracy
--Teen-Age Comedies for the Amateur Stage. N.D. (ISBN 0-8238-0029-6). Plays, Inc.
Huff, Charlotte Evelyn
--The Love That Transformed: An Easter Story of Long, Long Ago. LC 19-9097. 58 p., 1 l. incl. front. 18 1/2 cm. c.1919. C. L. Huff.
--Loves Makes Everything Come Right: A Christmas Story for Chidren. LC 18-4823. 16cm. 39p. c.1917. E. A. Wright.
Huff, Darrell (1913-)
--The Dog That Came True. Moran, Constance Oehler (1898-) & Thorne, Diana (1894-), illus. LC 46-3163. 59 p. illus. 26 cm. 1946. Whittlesey-House, McGraw-Hill Book Company, Inc.

Huff, Elizabeth Willis De see De Huff, Elizabeth Willis, Mrs.

Huff, Roderick Remmele (1920-)
--The Blue Racer. Shortall, Leonard W., illus. LC 66-6994. 159p. illus. 21cm. 1966. (ISBN 0-525-26766-2). Dutton.
--Bugle Boy. Shortall, Leonard W., illus. LC 59-5317. (Illus.). 117 p. 22cm. 1959. Harper.
--Chip. Greenwald, Sheila, pseud. (1934-), illus. Green, Sheila Ellen. LC 58-5299. 184p. illus. 22cm. 1958. Harper.
Huff, Russell J. (1936-), ed.
--Beware the Red Baron, and other Stories: s. LC 68-24199. 93 p. 22cm. 1968. Dujarie Press.
--The Special Type, and Other Stories. LC 68-23383. 94 p. 22cm. 1968. Dujarie Press.
Huff, William
--Little Mook, and Other Fairy Tales. N.D. Putman & Sons.
Huffard, Grace Thompson, Mrs. (1892-)
--When Rebels Rode. 1st ed. Lonette, Reisie Dominee (1924-), illus. LC 63-11665. 171 p. illus. 22 cm. 1963. Bobbs-Merrill.
Huffard, Grace Thompson, Mrs. (1892-) & Carlisle, Laura Mae, Mrs., eds.
--My Poetry Book: An Anthology of Modern Verse for Boys and Girls. Pogany, Willy (1882-1955), illus. LC 34-28463. xxii, 504 p. incl. plates (part col.) col. front. 22 1/2 cm. c.1934. The John C. Winston Company.
--My Poetry Book: An Anthology of Modern Verse for Boys and Girls. rev. ed. Pogany, Willy (1882-1955), illus. De Angeli, Marguerite Lofft, Mrs. (1899-), intro. by. LC 56-109242. (Illus.). 504 p. 22cm. 1956. Winston.
Huffman, Maxine Fish, retold by.
--Tico Tales: Costa Rican Folk Tales. 1st ed. Muller, Rose Marie Castro, illus. LC 63-23752. 63 p. illus., coat of arms 22 cm. c.1963. Exposition Press.
Hufford, Lois G
--Shakespeare in Tale & Verse. N.D. Macmillan.
Hugessen
--Puss-Cat Mew & Other New Fairy Stories. (Illus.). N.D. Harper & Brothers.
Hugessen, Edward Hugessen Knatchbull see Brabourne, Edward Hugessen Knatchbull-Hugessen.
Huggins, Alice Margaret (1891-1971)
--Fragrant Jade. Kimball, Marybelle, illus. LC 49-1573. 86 p. col. illus. 24 cm. c.1948. Broadman Press.
--The Red Chair Waits. Wong, Jeanyee (1920-), illus. (Illus.). (gr. 4-6). 1948. (ISBN 0-664-32047-3). Westminster.
Huggins, Alice Margaret (1891-1971) & Robinson, Hugh Laughlin
--Spend Your Heart. (gr. 7-10). 1965. (ISBN 0-664-32344-8). Westminster.
--Wan-Fu: Ten Thousand Happiness. 1957. David McKay Company Inc.
--Wan-Fu: Ten Thousand Happinesses. Moynihan, Roberta, illus. Ballou, Earle Hoit, contrib. by. LC 57-8358. 186p. 21cm. 1957. Longmans, Green.
Huggins, Edward, as told by.
--Blue and Green Wonders, and Other Latvian Tales. Wood, Owen, illus. LC 75-163482. (Illus.). 128 p. 22cm. 1971. (ISBN 0-671-65199-4). Simon and Schuster.
Huggins, Susan, jt. auth. see Dayton, Laura.
Huggler, Thomas E.
--Westwind Woods. Caulfield, James, illus. East, Ben, frwd. by. LC 78-106385. (Illus.). 132 p. 23cm. c.1978. Michigan United Conservation Clubs.
Hughes, Arthur, et al. (1832-1915), illus.
--Little Ben Bute. 1882. J B Lippincott.
Hughes, Arthur, jt. auth. see Rossetti, Christina Georgina.
Hughes, Arthur (1832-1915)
--At the Back of the North Wind. (Illus.). N.D. George Routledge & Sons.
--Gutta-Percha Willie. (Illus.). N.D. George Routledge & Sons.
Hughes, Arthur (1832-1915), illus.
--The Princess and the Goblin. (Illus.). N.D. George Routledge & Sons.
Hughes, Avah Willyn, jt. ed. see Coffin, Rebecca Jane.
Hughes, Avah Willyn, jt. ed. see Fenner, Phyllis Reid.
Hughes, Brenda
--New Guinea Folk Tales. N.D. Roy Pub.
Hughes, Cledwyn (1920-)
--The King Who Lived on Jelly, & Other Stories. Foreman, Michael (1938-), illus. (Illus.). (gr. 3-7). 1961. (ISBN 0-685-21278-5). Verry.
Hughes, Dean (1943-)
--As Wide As the River. LC 80-14646. 150p. 1980. Deseret Bk.
--Facing the Enemy. LC 82-12810. (Illus.). 143 p., 2 p. of plates. 24cm. c.1982. (ISBN 0-87747-928-3). Deseret Book Co.
--Honestly, Myron. Weston, Martha, illus. LC 81-8083. p. cm. 1982. (ISBN 0-689-30881-7). Atheneum.
--Millie Willenheimer and the Chestnut Corporation. 1st ed. LC 82-13758. 136 p. 22cm. 1983. (ISBN 0-689-30958-9). Atheneum.
--Nutty and the Case of the Mastermind Thief: Featuring William Bilks, Boy Genius. LC 84-20486. 146 p. 21cm. 1985. (ISBN 0-689-31094-3). Atheneum.
--Nutty and the Case of the Ski-Slope Spy: Featuring William Bilks, Boy Genius. LC 85-7962. 123 p. 22cm. 1985. (ISBN 0-689-31126-5). Atheneum.
--Nutty for President. 1st ed. Sims, Blanche, illus. LC 80-36719. (Illus.). 147 p. 22cm. 1981. (ISBN 0-689-30812-4). Atheneum.
--Switching Tracks. LC 82-3899. 180p. (gr. 5-9). 1982. (ISBN 0-689-30923-6). Atheneum.
--Under the Same Stars. (gr. 7-12). 1979. Deseret Bk.
Hughes, Ethel McNeal (1880-)
--The Treasure Hunt. LC 52-6302. 219 p. 21 cm. 1951. Island Press.
Hughes, Francis Peter Maze see Hughes, Peter.
Hughes, Francis Peter Maze (1921-)
--Baron Brandy's Boots. Rose, Gerald Hembdon Seymour (1935-), illus. LC 67-3696. (Illus.). 1 v. (unpaged. 26cm. 1966. Abelard-Schuman.
--The King Who Loved Candy. Rose, Gerald Hembdon Seymour (1935-), illus. LC 64-13725. (Illus.). 1 v. (unpaged). 1964. Abelard-Schuman.
Hughes, Harold F
--Legendary Heroes of Ireland. LC 22-14454. 161 p. plates. 20 cm. 1922. Harr Wagner Publishing Co.
--The Valley of the Yokuts. LC 40-36109. xi p., 1 l., 144 p. incl. front., illus. 22 cm. c.1940. Lymanhouse.
Hughes, Helen Glintz (1928-)
--The Zoopie Zats. Jones, Jacki, illus. LC 76-128609. (Illus.). 28 p. 29cm. 1971, c.1969. Platt & Munk.
Hughes, James, jt. auth. see Carpenter, John Allan.
Hughes, James Langston (1902-1967)
--Black Misery. Arouni, illus. 1969. Eriksson.
--Don't You Turn Back: Poems. Hopkins, Lee Bennett (1938-), ed. Grifalconi, Ann (1929-), illus. LC 78-82549. (Illus.). 78 p. 24cm. 1969. Knopf. **Award: (ALA).**
--Dream Keeper. Sewell, Helen Moore (1896-1957), illus. (Illus.). (gr. 7-11). 1932. (ISBN 0-394-91096-6). Knopf.
--Fields of Wonder. 1947. Knopf.
--Selected Poems of Langston Hughes. 1959. Knopf.
--Simple's Uncle Sam. (Keith Jennison Large Type Bks). (gr. 6 up). N.D. (ISBN 0-531-00282-9). Watts.
Hughes, James Langston (1902-1967), ed.
--The Best Short Stories by Negro Writers. (An anthology from 1899 to the present). (gr. 8 up). 1967. (ISBN 0-316-38032-6). (ISBN 0-316-38031-8). Little.
Hughes, Janet Herron
--The Frosty Filly. Mazoujian, Charles J., illus. LC 61-16674. 207p. illus. 21cm. 1961. C. S. Hammond.
Hughes, Jean Gordon
--Ditta's Tree. Willett, Mary, illus. LC 76-2547. (Illus.). 104 p. 19cm. (Puffin books, PS57). 1968. Penguin Books.
Hughes, John
--Mask of Evil. McWilliams, Alden, illus. LC 83-83354. (Illus.). (Golden Super Adventure Bks.). (gr. k-5). 1984. (ISBN 0-307-11370-1, Golden Bks). Western Pub.
Hughes, John Cledwyn see Hughes, Cledwyn.
Hughes, Kate Elizabeth Duval, Mrs.
--The Fair Maid of Connaught and Other Tales for Catholic Youth. LC 12-34409. 178 p. 16 1/2 cm. 1889. P. J. Kenedy.
Hughes, Kate Elizabeth Duval, Mrs., adapted by.
--The Little Pearls: Or, Gems of Virtue. Hughes, Kate Elizabeth Duval, Mrs., tr. from Fr. LC 12-36252. 2 p. l., 118 p. 19 1/2 cm. 1877. P. O'Shea.
Hughes, Langston, jt. auth. see Bontemps, Arna Wendell.
Hughes, Langston see Hughes, James Langston.
Hughes, Lilian B.
--Off the Reel: Stories. 1900. Massachusetts New-Church Union.
Hughes, Madeleine
--Why Carlo Wore a Bonnet. Seidler, Rosalie, illus. LC 67-22585. (Illus.). 1 v. (unpaged. 26cm. 1967. Lothrop, Lee & Shepard Co.
Hughes, Margie S.
--Annetta: Or, the Story of a Life. 282p. N.D. Nelson & Phillips.
Hughes, Monica (1925-)
--Beyond the Dark River. LC 80-36726. p. cm. 1981. (ISBN 0-689-30811-6). Atheneum.
--Crisis on Conshelf Ten. LC 76-25204. 143 p. 23cm. 1977, c.1975. (ISBN 0-689-30555-9). Atheneum.
--Devil on My Back. LC 84-21657. p. cm. 1985. (ISBN 0-689-31095-1). Atheneum.
--The Guardian of Isis. LC 81-10837. 140 p. 22cm. 1982. (ISBN 0-689-30902-3). Atheneum. **Award: (CCCL).**
--Hunter in the Dark. LC 82-13807. p. cm. 1983. (ISBN 0-689-30959-7). Atheneum. **Award: (CCCL).**
--The Isis Pedlar. LC 83-2630. p. cm. 1983. (ISBN 0-689-30988-0). Atheneum.
--Keeper of the Isis Light. LC 81-1340. p. cm. 1981. (ISBN 0-689-30847-7). Atheneum.
--Ring-Rise, Ring-Set. 144p. (Julia MacRae Bks.). (gr. 7). 1982. (ISBN 0-531-04433-5, MacRae). Watts.
Hughes, Mrs.
--The Two Schools: A Moral Tale. N.D. Catholic Publication Society.
Hughes, Paul (1916-)
--Jeff. LC 53-9558. 251 p. 21cm. 1953. J. Day Co.
Hughes, Peter see Hughes, Francis Peter Maze.
Hughes, Peter (1921-)
--Baron Brandy's Boots. Rose, Gerald Hembdon Seymour (1935-), illus. (Illus.). 64p. 1964. Abelard-Schuman Press.
--The Emperor's Oblong Pancake. Rose, Gerald Hembdon Seymour (1935-), illus. 64p. 1962. Obelard-Schumann.
Hughes, Richard Arthur Warren (1900-1976)
--Don't Blame Me!. Eichenberg, Fritz (1901-), illus. LC 40-31724. 4 p. l., 3-159 p. incl. illus., plates. 21 cm. 1940. Harper & Brothers.
--Gertrude & the Mermaid. Claveloux, Nicole, illus. (Illus.). 32p. (gr. k up). N.D. Quist.
--Gertrude's Child. Claveloux, Nicole, illus. LC 74-80273. (Illus.). 32 p. 1975, c.1974. (ISBN 0-8252-0119-5). (ISBN 0-8252-0120-9). Harlin Quist.
--Gertrude's Child. Schreiter, Rick (1936-), illus. LC 66-7978. 1 v. (unpaged) illus. 22 cm. 1966. Harlin Qust: Distributed by Crown Publishers, New York.
--High Wind in Jamaica: Or the Innocent Voyage. (Keith Jennison Large Type Bks). (gr. 6 up). N.D. (ISBN 0-531-00201-2). Watts.
--The Spider's Palace. Charlton, George, illus. (Illus.). (Looking Glass Library No. 23). (gr. 3 up). 1960. (ISBN 0-394-80473-2). Random.
--The Spider's Palace and Other Stories. Charlton, George, illus. LC 32-6437. vii, 163, 1 p. incl. illus., plates. col. front., col. plates. 21 cm. 1932. Harper & Brothers.
--The Wonder-Dog: The Collected Children's Stories of Richard Hughes. Maitland, Antony Jasper (1935-), illus. LC 77-1977. (Illus.). 180 p. 22cm. c.1977. (ISBN 0-688-80099-8). (ISBN 0-688-84099-X). Greenwillow Books.
Hughes, Riley (1914-1981)
--Frontier Bishop. 1959. Bruce Pub Co.
Hughes, Rosalind, ed.
--Let's Enjoy Poetry: An Anthology of Children's Verse for Grades IV, V, and VI with Suggestions for Teaching. LC 63-23611. 298 p. c.1961. Houghton Mifflin.
Hughes, Rosalind & Edwards, G. N., eds.
--Let's Enjoy Poetry: An Anthology of Children's Verse for Kindergarten, Grades I, II, and III, with Suggestions for Teaching. xxix, 278p. 22cm. 1958. Houghton Mifflin.
Hughes, Rupert (1872-)
--The Dozen from Lakerim. Relyea, Charles M., illus. LC 99-4927. 7 p. l., 223 p. incl. front., plates. 19 1/2 cm. 1899. The Century Co.
--The Fairy Detective. Chase, Rhoda Campbell, illus. LC 19-14699. c.1919. Harper & Brothers.
--The Lakerim Athletic Club. Relyea, Charles M., illus. LC 98-604000002. 290p. 1898. The Century Co.
--The Lakerim Cruise. Relyea, Charles M., illus. LC 10-24300. 5 p. l., 3-248 p. incl. plates. front. 20 cm. 1910. The Century Co.
--War of the Mayan King: A Story of Yucatan. 1st ed. Smith, Edward John, illus. LC 52-9816. 168 p. illus. 22 cm. (Winston adventure books). 1952. Winston.

Hughes, Serge, tr. see Manzi, Alberto.

Hughes, Shirley (1929-)
--Alfie Gets in First. Hughes, Shirley (1929-), illus. LC 81-8427. (Illus.). 32 p. 21cm. 1st U.S. edition. 1982, c.1981. (ISBN 0-688-00848-8). (ISBN 0-688-00849-6). Lothrop, Lee & Shepard Books. **Award: (ALA).**
--Alfie Gives a Hand. Hughes, Shirley (1929-), illus. LC 83-14883. (Illus.). 32p. 1984. (ISBN 0-688-02386-X). (ISBN 0-688-02387-8). Lothrop. **Award: (ALA).**
--Alfie's Feet. Hughes, Shirley (1929-), illus. LC 82-13012. p. cm. 1983, c.1982. (ISBN 0-688-01660-X). Lothrop, Lee & Shepard Books. **Award: (ALA).**
--Bathwater's Hot. Hughes, Shirley (1929-), illus. LC 84-14389. p. cm. 1985. (ISBN 0-688-04202-3). Lothrop, Lee & Shepard Books. **Award: (ALA).**
--Charlie Moon & the Big Bonanza Bust-Up. Hughes, Shirley (1929-), illus. (Illus.). 128p. (gr. 3-8). 1984. (ISBN 0-370-30918-9, Pub. by the Bodley Head). Merrimack Pub Cir.
--Chips and Jessie. Hughes, Shirley (1929-), illus. LC 85-23892. p. cm. c.1985. (ISBN 0-688-06402-7). Lothrop, Lee & Shepard.
--David and Dog. LC 77-27070. p. cm. 1978, c.1977. (ISBN 0-13-197301-0). Prentice-Hall.
--An Evening at Alfie's. Hughes, Shirley (1929-), illus. LC 84-11297. (Illus.). 32 p. 21cm. c.1984. (ISBN 0-688-04122-1). (ISBN 0-688-04123-X). Lothrop, Lee & Shephard Books. **Award: (ALA).**
--George, the Babysitter. Hughes, Shirley (1929-), illus. LC 77-4833. p. cm. 1977, c.1975. (ISBN 0-13-352682-8). Prentice-Hall.
--George the Babysitter. Hughes, Shirley (1929-), illus. (Illus.). 28p. 25cm. 1980, c.1975. (ISBN 0-13-352674-7). Prentice-Hall.
--Haunted House. LC 77-26814. p. cm. 1978, c.1977. Prentice-Hall.
--Lucy & Tom at the Seaside. 1976. (Pub. by Gollancz England). David & Charles.
--Lucy & Tom Go to School. 1973. (Pub. by Gollancz England). David & Charles.
--Lucy & Tom's Day. 1960. (Pub. by Gollancz England). David & Charles.
--Lucy and Tom's Day. Hughes, Shirley (1929-), illus. LC 60-50372. 28cm. 32p. (Young Scott Books). 1960. W. R. Scott.
--Moving Molly. Hughes, Shirley (1929-), illus. LC 78-16732. p. cm. 1st U.S. edition. 1979, c.1978. (ISBN 0-13-604587-1). Prentice-Hall.
--Noisy. LC 84-12632. p. cm. 1985. (ISBN 0-688-04203-1). Lothrop, Lee & Shepard Books. **Award: (ALA).**
--Stories for Nine-Year-Olds and Other Young Readers. Corrin, Sara (1929-) & Corrin, Stephen, eds. LC 79-670371. (Illus.). 159 p. (gr. 2-5). 1979. (ISBN 0-571-11409-1). Faber and Faber.
--Up and up. LC 79-22081. p. cm. 1979. (ISBN 0-13-938266-6). Prentice-Hall.
--When We Went to the Park. LC 84-12624. p. cm. 1985. (ISBN 0-688-04204-X). Lothrop, Lee & Shepard Books. **Award: (ALA).**

AUTHOR INDEX HUGHES, THOMAS

Hughes, Ted (1930-)
--Earth-Owl & Other Moon-People. (Illus.). 46p. (gr. 2-6). 1963. (ISBN 0-571-05627-X). Faber & Faber.
--The Earth-Owl and Other Moon-People. Brandt, R. A., illus. 1964. Atheneum.
--How the Whale Became & Other Stories. Schreiter, Rick (1936-), illus. LC 64-19570. (Illus.). (gr. 2-7). 1964. (ISBN 0-689-20185-0). (ISBN 0-689-20186-9). Atheneum.
--The Iron Giant: A Story in Five Nights. Nadler, Robert (1934-), illus. LC 68-24326. (Illus.). 56 p. 24cm. 1968. Harper & Row.
--Meet My Folks. Lazarevich, Mila (1942-), illus. LC 73-1753. (Illus.). 40 p. 1973. (ISBN 0-672-51797-3). Bobbs-Merrill.
--Nessie the Monster. Pyk, Jan (1934-), illus. LC [illegible] (Illus.). [illegible] (ISBN 0-672-51798-1). Bobbs-Merrill.
--What Is the Truth?. A Farmyard Fable for the Young. Lloyd, R. J., illus. LC 85-117493. (Illus.). 127 p. 1984. (ISBN 0-571-13155-7). Faber.
Hughes, Ted (1930-), ed.
--Moon-Whales and Other Moon Poems. Baskin, Leonard (1922-), illus. LC 76-6168. p. cm. 1976. (ISBN 0-670-48864-X). Viking Press. **Award: (ALA)**
--Poetry Is. LC 70-110216. xvi, 101 p. 22cm. 1970, c.1967. Doubleday.
--Season Songs. Baskin, Leonard (1922-), illus. (Illus.). 80p. (gr. 7 up). 1975. (ISBN 0-670-62725-9). Viking Pr. **Award: (ALA).**
--The Tiger's Bones, and Other Plays for Children. 1st ed. Cober, Alan Edwin (1935-), illus. LC 73-5150. (Illus.). 141 p. 22cm. 1974. (ISBN 0-670-71263-9). Viking Press.
--With Fairest Flowers While Summer Lasts: Poems from Shakespeare. LC 76-144274. 120p. (Paperback Ser.). (gr. 7 up). 1971. (ISBN 0-385-06930-8). (ISBN 0-385-06154-4). Doubleday.
Hughes, Thomas (1822-1896)
--Brown and Arthur: An Episode from "Tom Brown's School Days". Chalmers, Anna Maria Hickman Otis Mead, Mrs. (1809-1891), ed. LC 7-540439. xvi, 17-184 p. 17 1/2 cm. 1861. West & Johnston.
--Hughes' Tom Brown's School-Days. Lillard, Walter Huston (1881-), ed. LC 13-180051. xxxi, 1, 383 p. incl. front. port. 18 cm. (Half-title: English readings for schools. General editor: W. L. Cross). 1913. H. Holt and Company.
--Hughes's Tom Brown at Rugby. Robinson, ed. (Classics for Children). N.D. Ginn and Company.
--School Days At Oxford. N.D. Harper & Brothers.
--School Days at Rugby. LC 24-22237. viii, 409 p. 18 cm. 1857. Ticknor and Fields.
--School Days at Rugby. author's ed. LC 7-54111. viii, 405 p. 18 cm. 1861. Ticknor and Fields.
--School Days at Rugby. LC 24-22238. viii, 405 p. front. (port.) 18 cm. 1863. Ticknor and Fields.
--Tom Brown. N.D. Hurst & Company.
--Tom Brown at Oxford. (The Rugby Ser.). 1905. Set. A L Burt Co.
--Tom Brown at Oxford. (Illus.). (Burt's Home Library). 1915. A L Burt & Co.
--Tom Brown at Oxford. (The Excelsior Ser.). N.D. Set. A. L. Burt's Pubs.
--Tom Brown at Oxford, 1 of 110 vols. (The Manhattan Ser.). N.D. A. L. Burt's Pubs.
--Tom Brown at Oxford, No. 163. (The Cornell Ser.). N.D. A. L. Burt's Pubs.
--Tom Brown At Oxford. N.D. American News Company.
--Tom Brown at Oxford. N.D. Belford, Clarke & Co.
--Tom Brown at Oxford, Nos.46-47. (Lakeside Library Ser.). N.D. Donnelley, Loyd & Co.
--Tom Brown at Oxford. (The Roxburghe Classics). N.D. Estes & Lauriat's.
--Tom Brown at Oxford. (Illus.). (Famous Books for Boys Ser.). 1905. Set. H M Caldwell Co.
--Tom Brown at Oxford. (Illus.). (Caldwell's Illustrated Library of Famous Books by Famous Authors). N.D. H. M. Caldwell Co.
--Tom Brown at Oxford, 1 of 2 vols. (Illus.). (Athenaeum Lib.). N.D. Set. H. M. Caldwell Co.
--Tom Brown at Oxford. (Illus.). (Berkeley Lib.). N.D. H M Caldwell Co.
--Tom Brown at Oxford. (New Alta Lib.). N.D. Henry T. Coates & Co.
--Tom Brown at Oxford. (Illus.). N.D. Houghton, Mifflin & Co.
--Tom Brown at Oxford, 1 of 64 vols. (Young America Library: No. 43). 1900. Set. Hurst & Co.
--Tom Brown at Oxford. (Argyle Ser). N.D. Hurst & Company.
--Tom Brown at Oxford. (Illus.). (Almonte Library). N.D. Hurst and Company.
--Tom Brown at Oxford. (Illus.). (The New Argyle Ser.). N.D. Hurst and Company.
--Tom Brown at Oxford, 2 Vols, Vol. II. N.D. International Book Co.
--Tom Brown at Oxford. N.D. James R. Osgood.
--Tom Brown at Oxford. (Illus.). N.D. John E. Potter & Co.
--Tom Brown at Oxford. N.D. Lovell, Coryell & Co.
--Tom Brown at Oxford. (Illus.). (Series of Works of Fiction). N.D. Macmillan & Co.
--Tom Brown at Oxford. (Illus.). N.D. MacMillan.
--Tom Brown at Oxford, 1 of 8 vols. (Illus.). (Macmillan's Dollar and a Half Series of Books for the Young). N.D. Macmillan & Co.
--Tom Brown at Oxford. Alta ed. (Illus.). N.D. Porter & Coates.
--Tom Brown at Oxford. (The Advance Library Ser.: Vol. 311). N.D. Rand, McNally & Co.
--Tom Brown at Oxford. (Illus.). (The Independent Library Ser.: Vol. 311). N.D. Rand, McNally & Co.
--Tom Brown at Oxford. (Illus.). (The Tudor Library Ser.: Vol. 15). N.D. Rand, McNally & Co.
--Tom Brown at Oxford, 1 of 2 vols. Somerset ed. (Illus.). N.D. Set. T. Y. Crowell & Co.
--Tom Brown at Oxford. (Illus.). (The Waldorf Lib.). N.D. T. Y. Crowell & Co.
--Tom Brown at Oxford. (The New Astor Library of Prose). N.D. T. Y. Crowell & Co.
--Tom Brown at Oxford. (Nelson Classic). N.D. Thomas Nelson & Sons.
--Tom Brown at Oxford. (Crowell's New Illustrated Library). N.D. Thomas Y. Crowell & Co.
--Tom Brown at Rugby, No.7. (Lakeside Library Ser.). N.D. Donnelley, Loyd & Co.
--Tom Brown at Rugby. (Illus.). N.D. Estes & Lauriat.
--Tom Brown at Rugby, (Illus.). (Famous Books for Boys Ser.). 1905. Set. H M Caldwell Co.
--Tom Brown at Rugby. (Illus.). (Caldwell's Illustrated Library of Famous Books by Famous Authors). N.D. H. M. Caldwell Co.
--Tom Brown at Rugby, 1 of 2 vols. (Atheneum Lib.). N.D. Set. H. M. Caldwell Co.
--Tom Brown at Rugby. (Illus.). (Berkeley Lib.). N.D. H. M. Caldwell.
--Tom Brown at Rugby. N.D. J. B. Lippincott.
--Tom Brown at Rugby. N.D. Thomas Y. Crowell & Co.
--Tom Brown of Oxford. N.D. MacMillan.
--Tom Brown's at Oxford. (Illus.). (Young American Library). N.D. Hurst and Company.
--Tom Brown's at Oxford. (Standard Library). N.D. Thomas Crowell & Co.
--Tom Brown's School Days, (The Rugby Ser.). 1905. Set. A L Burt Co.
--Tom Brown's School Days. (Illus.). (Burt's Home Library). 1915. A L Burt & Co.
--Tom Brown's School Days. N.D. A. L. Burt Co.
--Tom Brown's School Days (The Manhattan Ser.). N.D. A. L. Burt's Pubs.
--Tom Brown's School Days. (The Excelsior Ser.). N.D. Set. A. L. Burt's Pubs.
--Tom Brown's School Days, No. 164. (The Cornell Ser.). N.D. A. L. Burt's Pubs.
--Tom Brown's School Days. Empire ed. 1905. American News Co.
--Tom Brown's School Days, 1 Vols. (The Excelsior Edition). N.D. American News Company.
--Tom Brown's School Days. N.D. Dodd Mead & Co.
--Tom Brown's School Days. 325p. (School Library: No. 3). N.D. Educational Publishing Company.
--Tom Brown's School Days. (The Roxburghe Classics). N.D. Estes & Lauriat's.
--Tom Brown's School-Days. (Classics for Children). N.D. Ginn.
--Tom Brown's School Days. (The Good Value Books). N.D. Grosset & Dunlap.
--Tom Brown's School Days. LC 7-5406. 2 p. l., 3-352 p. front. (port.) 15 cm. 1895. H. Altemus.
--Tom Brown's School Days. 1905. Henry Altemus Co.
--Tom Brown's School Days. (English Readings Ser.). N.D. Henry Holt.
--Tom Brown's School Days. (Illus.). (Boys' and Girls' Classics). N.D. Henry Altemus Co.
--Tom Brown's School Days. (Illus.). (Petit-Trainon Ser.). N.D. Henry Altemus Co.
--Tom Brown's School Days. (Illus.). (Beauxarts Ser.). N.D. Henry Altemus Co.
--Tom Brown's School Days. (Illus.). (Vademecum Ser.). N.D. Henry T. Altemus.
--Tom Brown's School Days. xxiv p., 1 l., 364 p. 20 cm. (Riverside literature series no. 85). c.1895. Houghton, Mifflin and Company.
--Tom Brown's School Days. LC 31-8214. xxvi, 375 p. illus. (map) 19 cm. (Riverside literature series). c.1931. Houghton Mifflin Company.
--Tom Brown's School Days. (Cambridge Classics). N.D. Houghton Mifflin Co.
--Tom Brown's School Days, 1 of 64 vols. (Young America Library: No. 44). 1900. Set. Hurst & Co.
--Tom Brown's School Days, 1 of 183 vols. Pocket ed. (The Universal Library). 1900. Hurst & Co.
--Tom Brown's School Days. 6th ed. LC 49-421287. xx, 357 p. illus., port. 19 cm. N.D. Hurst.
--Tom Brown's School Days. (Argyle Ser). N.D. Hurst & Company.
--Tom Brown's School Days. (Illus.). (Young American Library). N.D. Hurst and Company.
--Tom Brown's School Days. (Illus.). (Almonte Library). N.D. Hurst and Company.
--Tom Brown's School Days. (Illus.). (The New Argyle Ser.). N.D. Hurst and Company.
--Tom Brown's School Days. (Illus.). (Hurst's Presentation Ser.). N.D. Hurst and Company.
--Tom Brown's School Days. (Illus.). (Arlington Edition). N.D. Hurst and Company.
--Tom Brown's School Days. (New Aldine Ser). N.D. International Book Co.
--Tom Brown's School Days, Vol. I. N.D. International Book Co.
--Tom Brown's School Days. (The Sunset Ser.). N.D. J. S. Ogilvie Publishing Co.
--Tom Brown's School Days. LC 7-54082. cover-title, 9-298 p. 18 1/2 cm. (Lovell's library. v. 2, no. 61). 1883. J. W. Lovell Company.
--Tom Brown's School Days. (Sears Juvenile Classics). N.D. J.H.Sears & Co.
--Tom Brown's School Days. (Illus.). N.D. John E. Potter & Co.
--Tom Brown's School Days. (The Young People's Library). N.D. John C. Winston.
--Tom Brown's School Days. N.D. Laird & Lee's.
--Tom Brown's School Days. Abridged. (Class Books of English Literature). N.D. Longmans, Green & Co.
--Tom Brown's School Days. N.D. Lovell, Coryell & Co.
--Tom Brown's School Days. (The Washington Square Classics). N.D. Macrae Smith.
--Tom Brown's School Days. (The Nelson Classics). N.D. Nelson Bks.
--Tom Brown's School days. N.D. Norton & Co.
--Tom Brown's School Days. N.D. Oxford University Press--American.
--Tom Brown's School Days. (Illus.). N.D. R. F. Fenno & Co.
--Tom Brown's School Days. (The Advance Library Ser.: Vol. 312). N.D. Rand, McNally & Co.
--Tom Brown's School Days. (Illus.). (The Independent Library Ser.: Vol. 312). N.D. Rand, McNally & Co.
--Tom Brown's School Days. (Lake English Classics). N.D. Scott Foresman & Co.
--Tom Brown's School Days, 1 of 2 vols. Somerset ed. (Illus.). 21cm. 369p. 1890. Set. T. Y. Crowell & Co.
--Tom Brown's School Days. (Illus.). (The Waldorf Lib.). N.D. T. Y. Crowell & Co.
--Tom Brown's School Days. (The New Astor Library of Prose). N.D. T. Y. Crowell & Co.
--Tom Brown's School Days, 1 of 67 vols. (The Westminster Series of Poetry and Prose). N.D. T. Y. Crowell & Co.
--Tom Brown's School Days. LC 43-40129. xii, 13-269 p. 19 cm. N.D. The F. M. Lupton Publishing Company.
--Tom Brown's School Days. (The Luxembourg Illustrated Library). N.D. Thoms Y. Crowell Company.
--Tom Brown's School Days. (Standard Library). N.D. Thomas Y. Crowell & Co.
--Tom Brown's School Days. (Classic Ser.). N.D. World Publishing Co.
--Tom Brown's School Days. Ashe, E. M., illus. LC 3-17909. 21cm. 415p. (Library for Young People). 1903. P. F. Collier & Son.
--Tom Brown's School Days. Bradby, Henry Christopher (1868-), ed. Thomson, Hugh (1860-1920), illus. LC 18-13644. xi, 442 p. incl. front., illus. 19 cm. c.1918. Ginn and Company.
--Tom Brown's School Days. Bradby, Henry Christopher (1868-), ed. Thomson, Hugh (1860-1920), illus. LC 20-14761. xi, 412 p. incl. col. front., illus., col. pl. 21 cm. c.1920. L. Philips.
--Tom Brown's School Days. Caldecott, Randolph (1846-1886), illus. 1888. Porter & Coates.
--Tom Brown's School Days. De Mille, Alan Bertram (1873-), ed. LC 14-12288. 3 p. l., 13-422 p. front (map) 17 cm. (Lake English classics). c.1914. Scott, Foresman and Company.
--Tom Brown's School-Days. De Mille, Alban Bertram (1873-), ed. LC 1-295084. xvi p., 1 l., 339 p. col. front. 22 cm. 1900. Dodd, Mead and Company.
--Tom Brown's School Days. De Mille, Alban Bertram (1873-), ed. LC 20-7725. 4 p. l., 13-433 p. 1 illus. (map) 17 cm. (Half-title: The Lake English classics, general editor, L. T. Damon...). c.1920. Scott, Foresman and Company.
--Tom Brown's School Days. Gosling, Thomas Warrington (1872-), ed. LC 17-9349. 302 p. front. (port.) 1 illus. 17 cm. (Eclectic English classics). c.1917. American Book Company.
--Tom Brown's School Days. Gosling, Thomas Warrington, ed. LC 17-9349. 17cm. 302p. 1917 (Standard and Holiday Books). The American News Co.
--Tom Brown's School Days. Hadley, Arthur T., intro. by. Ashe, E. M., illus. LC 4-17295. (Illus.). 312p. 19cm. (Library for Young People). 1902. Macmillan and Co. Limited.
--Tom Brown's School Days. Hall, Sydney Prior & Hughes, Arthur (1832-1915), illus. LC 7-15445. 1 p. l., 62 p. illus. (incl. port.) 29 1/2 cm. (Harper's Franklin square library. no. 237). 1882. Harper & Brothers.
--Tom Brown's School Days. Hall, Sydney Prior & Hughes, Arthur (1832-1915), illus. LC 7-5409. xx p., 1 l., 376 p. front., illus., 16 pl. 19 cm. 1881. Macmillan and Co.
--Tom Brown's School Days. [illegible], illus. 369p. N.D. Thomas Y. Crowell Co.
--Tom Brown's School Days. Pierce, Winthrop H., illus. N.D. Thomas Y. Crowell & Co.'s Catalogue.
--Tom Brown's School Days. Pierce, Winthrop H., illus. (Crowell's New Illustrated Library). N.D. Thomas Y. Crowell & Co.
--Tom Brown's School-Days. Rhead, Louis John (1857-1926) & Schoonover, Frank Earle (1877-1972), illus. LC 11-27504. xxiv, 1, 375 p. incl. illus., plates. front. 23 1/2 cm. c.1911. Harper & Brothers.
--Tom Brown's School Days. Rhys, Ernest, ed. (Illus.). 18cm. 336p. (Everyman's Library for Young People). 1906. E. P. Dutton & Co.
--Tom Brown's School Days. Strang, Herbert, ed. (Illus.). (Herbert Strang's Library). N.D. George H. Doran.
--Tom Brown's School Days. Sullivan, E. T., illus. (Pocket Classics). N.D. Macmillan Co.
--Tom Brown's School Days. Tarrant, Percy, illus. LC 23-27440. 311, 1 p. col. front., col. plates. 20 cm. (Half-title: The Washington square classics). 1923. G. W. Jacobs and Company.
--Tom Brown's School Days. Thomas, Charles Swain, ed. LC 8-28986. xxx p., 1 l., 296 p. front. 15 cm. (Macmillan's pocket American and English classics). 1908. The Macmillan Company.
--Tom Brown's School Days and"Tom Brown at Oxford, 2 Vols. in 1. (Illus.). N.D. Harper & Brothers' Trade-List.
--Tom Brown's School Days at Rugby. (Popular Standard Editions). N.D. Belford, Clarke & Co.
--Tom Brown's School Days at Rugby. New ed. (Illus.). 1900. Henry T. Coates & Co.
--Tom Brown's School Days at Rugby. (New Alta Lib.). N.D. Henry T. Coates & Co.
--Tom Brown's School-Days At Rugby. (Illus.). N.D. Houghton, Mifflin And Co.
--Tom Brown's School days at Rugby. New ed. (Illus.). N.D. Houghton, Mifflin & Co's Trade List.
--Tom Brown's School-Days at Rugby. (Illus.). N.D. James R Osgood and Company.
--Tom Brown's School Days at Rugby. (New International Library). N.D. John C. Winston Co.
--Tom Brown's School Days at Rugby. (New Acorn Library). N.D. John C. Winston & Co.
--Tom Brown's School Days at Rugby. New ed. Caldecott, Randolph (1846-1886), illus. (Illus.). N.D. Porter & Coates.
--Tom Brown's School Days: By an Old Boy. LC 31-8214. 18cm. 375p. 1931. Houghton Mifflin.
--Tom Brown's School Days: By an Old Boy. (Golden Treasury). N.D. Macmillan & co.
--Tom Brown's Schooldays. LC 41-40537. 302 p. 18 1/2 cm. (Half-title: The people's library. 13). 1907. Cassell and Company, Ltd.
--Tom Brown's SchoolDays. (Illus.). (Famous Books for Boys). N.D. H. M. Caldwell Co.
--Tom Brown's Schooldays. LC 72-190375. 288 p. 18cm. (Puffin books). 1971. (ISBN 0-14-030534-3). Penguin.
--Tom Brown's SchoolDays. (Illus.). N.D. White, Stokes & Allen.
--Tom Brown's Schooldays. (Illus.). N.D. William Collins Sons & Company Ltd.
--Tom Brown's Schooldays. Newbolt, Henry, ed. (The Nelson Classics). N.D. Thomas Nelson & Sons.
--Tom Brown's Schooldays. Van Abbe, Salaman (1883-1955), illus. LC 52-8383. (Illus.). 340p. 21 cm. (Children's illustrated classics). 1951. Dent.
--Tom Brown's Schooldays. Van Abbe, Salaman (1883-1955), illus. (Children's Illus. Classics). 1949. Dutton.
--Tom Brown's SchoolDays. Von Abbe, Salaman (1883-1955), illus. (Illus.). (Children's Illustrated Classics). 1951. E.P. Dutton & Co.
--Tom Brown's Schooldays: By an Old Boy. People's_Ed. ed. (Illus.). N.D. MacMillan.
--Tom Brown's Schooldays: By an Old Boy. Cheap Ed. ed. Hughes, Arthur (1832-1915) & Hall, Sydney Prior, illus. N.D. MacMillan.
--TomBrown's School Days. (Illus.). (The Junior Library Ser.: Vol. 16). N.D. Rand, McNally & Co.

--The Boy Who Had No Birthday. Wright, Cameron, illus. LC 35-16045. 5 p. l., 259 p. front., illus. 21 cm. 1935. Frederick A. Stokes Company.
--The Boy Who Had No Birthday. Wright, Cameron, illus. 1935. J. B. Lippincott.
--Corn-Belt Billy. Wiese, Kurt (1887-1974), illus. LC 42-6765. 28 p. incl. col. front., illus. (part col.) 25 x 21 cm. (story parade picture book). 1942. Grosset & Dunlap.
--Cristy at Skippinghills. 1st ed. Ilsley, Velma Elizabeth (1918-), illus. LC 58-10136. (Illus.). 22cm. 139p. (gr. 4-6). 1958. (ISBN 0-397-30403-X). Lippincott.
--Cupola House. 1st ed. Unwin, Nora Spicer (1907-), illus. LC 61-6060. 126p. illus. 22cm. 1961. Lippincott.
--The Double Birthday Present. Blaisdell, Elinore (1904-), illus. LC 47-4067. 21cm. 52p. 1948. J. B. Lippincott.
--Have You Seen Tom Thumb?. Eichenberg, Fritz (1901-), illus. 1942. J. B. Lippincott. **Award: (JNM).**
--John of Pudding Lane. Funk, Clotilde Embree, illus. LC 41-15027. x p., 1 l., 161 p. incl. front., illus. 21 1/2 cm. c.1941. Frederick A. Stokes Company.
--John of Pudding Lane. Funk, Clotilde Embree, illus. N.D. J. B. Lippincott.
--Johnny-up and Johnny-Down. Berson, Harold (1926-), illus. LC 62-9329. 93p. illus. 21cm. 1962. Lippincott.
--Ladycake Farm. Funk, Clotilde Embree, illus. LC 52-5107. (Illus.). 126 p. 21cm. 1952. Lippincott.
--The Little Girl With Seven Names. 1964. (ISBN 0-8382-0450-3, Cadmus Books). E. M. Hale And Company.
--Little Girl with Seven Names. Paull, Grace A. (1898-), illus. LC 36-20142. 3 p. l., 63, 1 p. illus. 21 1/2 cm. 1936. Frederick A. Stokes Company.
--Little Girl with Seven Names. Paull, Grace A. (1898-), illus. 1934. J. B. Lippincott.
--Little Grey Gown. Bischoff, Ilse Marthe (1903-), illus. LC 39-27733. 4 p. l., 168 p. illus. 21 cm. 1939. Frederick A. Stokes Company.
--Little Grey Gown. Bischoff, Ilse Marthe (1903-), illus. 1939. J. B. Lippincott.
--Lucinda: A Little Girl of Eighteen-Sixty. Wright, Cameron, illus. LC 34-29565. ix p., 1 l., 233 1 p. illus. 21 cm. 1934. Frederick A. Stokes Company.
--Lucinda: A Little Girl of Eighteen-Sixty. Wright, Cameron, illus. 1934. J. B. Lippincott.
--Matilda's Buttons. 1st ed. Blaisdell, Elinore (1904-), illus. LC 48-8043. 132 p. illus. 21 cm. 1948. J.B. Lippincott Co.
--Michel's Island. Seredy, Kate (1899-1975), illus. LC 40-30716. xll, 265p. 1 p. incl. front., illus., plates. 23 1/2cm. 1940. Frederick A. Stokes Company.
--Michel's Island. Seredy, Kate (1899-1975), illus. N.D. J. B. Lippincott.
--Miss Jellytot's Visit. 1st ed. Ilsley, Velma Elizabeth (1918-), illus. LC 55-564710. (Illus.). 26p. (gr. 4-6). 1955. (ISBN 0-397-30305-X). Lippincott.
--The Peddler's Clock. Jones, Elizabeth Orton (1910-), illus. LC 43-8182. 21 1/2cm. 28p. (Parade Picture Book). 1943. Grosset and Dunlap.
--Peter Piper's Pickled Peppers. Milhous, Katherine (1894-1977), illus. LC 42-36063. 61, 1 p. incl. illus., col. plates. 16 cm. 1942. Frederick A. Stokes Company.
--Sibby Botherbox. Collison, Marjory, illus. LC 45-7910. 174 p., 1 l. illus. 24 cm. 1945. J. B. Lippincott Company.
--Singing Among Strangers. Gibian, Irene, illus. LC 54-7128. (Illus.). 213 p. 21cm. 1954. Lippincott.
--The Sixty-Ninety Grandchild. Blaisdell, Elinore (1904-), illus. 1951. J. B. Lippincott.
--The Sixty-Ninth Grandchild. Blaisdell, Elinore (1904-), illus. LC 51-11168. 68 p. illus. 22 cm. 1951. Lippincott.
--Stars for Cristy. 1st ed. Ilsley, Velma Elizabeth (1918-), illus. LC 56-10725. (Illus.). 141 p. 22cm. 1956. Lippincott.
--Such a Kind World. Potter, Edna, illus. LC 47-2862. 23cm. 28p. (Parade Picture Book). 1947. Grosset and Dunlap.
--Susan, Beware!. Boyle, Mildred, illus. LC 37-28755. xi, 243 p. illus. 21 cm. 1937. Frederick A. Stokes Company.
--Susan, Beware!. Boyle, Mildred, illus. N.D. J. B. Lippincott.
--The Wonderful Baker. Paull, Grace A. (1898-), illus. LC 50-5869. 22cm. 47p. 1950. J. B. Lippincott Co.
--Young Man of the House. Slobodkin, Louis (1903-1975), illus. LC 44-4874. ix, 170, 1 p. incl. illus., plates. 21 1/2 cm. 1944. J. B. Lippincott Company.

Hunt, Madeline Bonavia
--Aunt Tabitha's Waifs, 1 of 7 vols. (Author of "Little Hinges."). (The Young Folks' Library). N.D. Cassell, Petter, Galpin.
--History of Five Little Pitchers Who Had Very Large Ears, 1 of 6 vols. (Illus.). (The Little Pitcher Library). N.D. Cassell, Petter, Galpin.
--Little Empress Joan, 1 of 6 vols. (Illus.). (The Notable Library). N.D. Cassell, Petter, Galpin.
--Little Hinges. Edwards, Mary Ellen, illus. (Author of "Brave Little Heart."). N.D. Cassell, Petter, Galpin.
--Maid Marjory, 1 of 7 vols. (Author of "Little Hinges."). (Illus.). (The Young Folks' Library). N.D. Cassell, Petter, Galpin.
--Margaret's Enemy. Juv ed. (Illus.). 268p. N.D. Cassell & Co.
--Through Trial to Triumph: Or, The Royal Way. (Illus.). 256p. (The Crown and Crown Ser.). N.D. Cassell & Co.'s Pubs.

Hunt, Margaret, ed. see Grimm, Jakob Ludwig Karl (1785-1863) & Grimm, Wilhelm Karl.

Hunt, Margaret, tr. see Grimm, Jakob Ludwig Karl (1785-1863) & Grimm, Wilhelm Karl.

Hunt, Margaret Raine (1831-1912), ed. see Grimm, Jakob Ludwig Karl (1785-1863) & Grimm, Wilhelm Karl.

Hunt, Margaret Raine (1831-1912), tr. see Grimm, Jakob Ludwig Karl (1785-1863) & Grimm, Wilhelm Karl.

Hunt, Marigold
--Hester and the Gnomes. Charlot, Jean (1898-1979), illus. LC 55-8902. 124p. illus. 21cm. 1955. Whittlesey House.
--St. Patrick's Summer. N.D. Sheed & Ward, Inc.

Hunt, Maxine
--The General's Daughter. LC 60-7048. 191p. 22cm. 1960. Messner.
--That Girl Pat. LC 63-11798. 212 p. 21 cm. 1963. Macmillan.

Hunt, Patricia Joan
--Bible Stories. McBride, Angus, illus. LC 81-14198. p. cm. c.1981. (ISBN 0-517-36051-9). Crescent Books : Distributed by Crown Publishers.

Hunt, Regina Victoria
--Bright Banners. Benson, Andrew, illus. LC 56-9644. 132p. illus. 22cm. (Catholic treasury books). 1956. Bruce Pub. Co.
--A Candle for Our Lady. Hunt, Regina Victoria, illus. LC 55-9763. 119p. illus. 22cm. (Catholic treasury books). 1955. Bruce Pub. Co.

Hunt, Robert
--The Accident & Derring-Do. McKissack, Vernon, illus. LC 76-730163. (Illus.). (Tales of Winnie the Witch Book Cassettes). (gr. k). 1978. (ISBN 0-89290-024-5). Soc for Visual.
--Beishung The Giant Panda. Dunnington, Tom, illus. LC 74-735891. (Illus.). (Wildlife Stories). (gr. 2-5). 1978. (ISBN 0-89290-032-6). Soc for Visual.
--Bossy, Boring Maurice the Beast. McKissack, Vernon, illus. LC 76-730161. (Illus.). (Tales of Winnie the Witch Book Cassette). (gr. k). 1978. (ISBN 0-89290-022-9). Soc for Visual.
--Buffy The Sea Otter. Teason, James G., illus. LC 74-735892. (Illus.). (Wildlife Stories). (gr. 2-5). 1978. (ISBN 0-89290-033-4). Soc for Visual.
--Coco & Chacha The Coatis. Dunnington, Tom, illus. LC 74-735893. (Illus.). (Wildlife Stories). (gr. 2-5). 1978. (ISBN 0-89290-034-2). Soc for Visual.
--Curly & Simba Twin African Lions. McBarron, H. Charles, illus. LC 74-735890. (Illus.). (Wildlife Stories). (gr. 2-5). 1978. (ISBN 0-89290-031-8). Soc for Visual.
--Glu the Emperor Penguin. Producciones Ancora, illus. LC 72-736442. (Illus.). 16p. (Adventures of Wild Animals Book). (gr. 2-5). 1978. (ISBN 0-89290-027-X). Soc for Visual.
--The Glut's Peanut Butter Pie. McKissack, Vernon, illus. LC 76-730160. (Illus.). (Tales of Winnie the Witch Book Cassettes). (gr. k). 1978. (ISBN 0-89290-021-0). Soc for Visual.
--Jamboo the African Elephant. Producciones Ancora, illus. LC 72-736441. (Illus.). (Adventures of Wild Animals Book). (gr. 2-5). 1978. (ISBN 0-89290-026-1). Soc for Visual.
--Kiboko the African Hippo. Producciones Ancora, illus. LC 72-736443. (Illus.). (Adventures of Wild Animals Book). (gr. 2-5). 1978. (ISBN 0-89290-028-8). Soc for Visual.
--Koolah The White Koala. Teason, James G., illus. LC 74-735895. (Illus.). (Wildlife Stories Book). (gr. 2-5). 1978. (ISBN 0-89290-036-9). Soc for Visual.
--The Lake Murkwood Monster. McKissack, Vernon, illus. LC 76-730159. (Illus.). (Tales of Winnie the Witch Book Cassettes). (gr. k). 1978. (ISBN 0-89290-020-2). Soc for Visual.
--Lucifer & Bully Balderdash. McKissack, Vernon, illus. LC 76-730158. (Illus.). (Tales of Winnie the Witch Book Cassettes). (gr. k). 1978. (ISBN 0-89290-019-9). Soc for Visual.
--The Magic Words. McKissack, Vernon, illus. LC 76-730162. (Illus.). (Tales of Winnie the Witch Book Cassettes). 1978. (ISBN 0-89290-023-7). Soc for Visual.
--Marsu the Red Kangaroo. Producciones Ancora, illus. LC 72-736444. (Illus.). (Adventures of Wild Animals Book). (gr. 2-5). 1978. (ISBN 0-89290-029-6). Soc for Visual.
--Windy The Snow Goose. Burridge, Marge Opitz, illus. LC 74-735894. (Illus.). (Wildlife Stories). (gr. 2-5). 1978. (ISBN 0-89290-035-0). Soc for Visual.

Hunt, Robert Booher (1906-)
--Coppertop. Manget, Jeanne C., illus. LC 57-7431. unpaged. illus. 23cm. 1957. Coward-McCann.

Hunt, Roderick
--The Oxford Christmas Book for Children. (Illus.). 160p. 1982. (ISBN 0-19-278104-9, Pub. by Oxford U Pr Childrens). Merrimack Pub Cir.

Hunt, Sara Keables, Mrs.
--Arthur & Bessie in Egypt. (Illus.). (Selected Bks for Sunday School). N.D. Set. Methodist Bk Concern.
--Yusuf in Egypt. 220p. N.D. American Tract Society.

Hunt, Violet Brooke (0000-1910)
--The Life Story of a Cat. N.D. Macmillan.
--Prisoners of the Tower. (Illus.). N.D. E. P. Dutton & Co.

Hunt, W. Ben
--The Golden Book of Crafts & Hobbies. 1957. Golden Press.

Hunt, Wolf Robe (1898-)
--The Dancing Horses of Acoma. Rushmore, Helen (1898-), illus. 160p. 1963. The World Publishing Co.

Hunt & Draper
--Ghost Trails to Ghost Towns. N.D. The Swallow Press.

Hunter
--Peculiar Triumph of Professor Branestawn. (gr. 3-6). 1974 (Puffin). Penguin.

Hunter, Cora Work
--The Little Strawman. Hunter, Cora Work, illus. LC 14-3250. 63 p. col. front., illus., col. plates. 23 1/2 cm. c.1914. Rand, McNally & Company.

Hunter, E. A.
--Wiscasset Stories. (Illus.). 256p. 1905. American Tract Society.

Hunter, E. A., jt. auth. see Noble, Annette Lucile.

Hunter, Edith Fisher (1919-)
--The Family Finds Out. Ware, Charlotte, illus. Fahs, Sophia Lyons, pref. by. LC 52-6318. 150 p. illus. 28 cm. 1951. Beacon Press.
--Sue Ellen. Holmes, Bea, illus. LC 77-90274. (Illus.). 170 p. 23cm. 1969. Houghton Mifflin.

Hunter, Eileen
--Tales of Waybeyond. Baynes, Pauline Diana (1922-), illus. LC 79-64184. (Illus.). 87 p. 22cm. 1979. (ISBN 0-233-97084-3). A. Deutsch.

Hunter, Eleanor Augusta (1855-)
--Some Friends of Mine. Hunter, Eleanor Augusta, illus. LC 15-2598. 159 p. front., illus., plates. 19 cm. 1889. Hunt & Eaton.
--Some Friends of Mine. Hunter, Eleanor Augusta, illus. (Illus.). N.D. Methodist Bk Concern.

Hunter, Evan see McBain, Ed, pseud.

Hunter, Evan (1926-)
--Every Little Crook and Nanny. N.D. New Americans Library.
--Find the Feathered Serpent. LC 79-9914. xi, 207 p. 22cm. (Gregg Press science fiction series). 1979, c.1952. (ISBN 0-8398-2519-6). Gregg Press.
--Find the Feathered Serpent. (Winston Science Fiction Ser.). 1952. John C. Winston Co.
--Happy New Year, Herbie and Other Stories. 1963. Simon and Schuster, Inc Publications.
--Me and Mr. Stenner. 1976. Harper.
--Me and Mr. Stenner. LC 76-24810. 157 p. 21cm. c.1976. (ISBN 0-397-31689-5). Lippincott.
--The Remarkable Harry. Hunter, Ted & Hunter, Mark, illus. LC 61-6390. 48p. 1961. Abelard-Schuman.
--The Wonderful Button. Blake, Quentin (1932-), illus. LC 61-13321. unpaged. illus. 26cm. c.1961. Abelard-Schuman.

Hunter, Fern, ed. see The, Children's Friend.

Hunter, Hiram
--Which One Are You?. A Conscience Book for Little Folks. Hunter, Hiram, illus. LC 51-52462. 77 p. col. illus. 20 x 25 cm. 1918. Little Folks Pub. Co.

Hunter, Iris
--In Toyland: Being the Tale of the Missing Wooden Soldiers and Their Brave Captain. Gaba, illus. LC 28-28942. 64 p. col., illus. 24 cm. 1928. The Children's Press.

Hunter, James Hogg (1890-)
--The Mystery of Mar Saba. N.D. Zondervan Publishing.
--Uncle Jim's Stories from Nature's Wonderland. Hunter, James Hogg (1890-), illus. LC 54-20970. 71p. illus. 20cm. 1953. Zondervan Pub. House.

Hunter, John (1891-)
--The White Phantom. Hunter, John (1891-), illus. LC 35-1941. 3 p. l., 11-323 p. col. front., illus. 19 1/2 cm. 1935. H. Smith and R. Haas.

Hunter, Julius & Gomez, Ronald
--Absurd Alphabedtime Stories. LC 76-22534. (Illus.). 32 p. c.1976. (ISBN 0-8272-0012-9). Bethany Press.

Hunter, Kay
--Bimbo and His Jacket. Gincano, John, illus. LC 35-11478. (Illus.). 23 x 27 1/2cm. 31p. 1935. Gabriel Sons & Co.

Hunter, Kay, jt. auth. see Gincano, John Anthony.

Hunter, Kristin Eggleston (1931-)
--Boss Cat. Franklin, Harold, illus. LC 73-162786. 12cm. 58p. 1971. (ISBN 0-684-12491-2). Charles Scribner's Sons.
--Guests in the Promised Land: Stories. LC 72-9036. 133 p. 22cm. 1973. (ISBN 0-684-13227-3). Scribner.
--Lou in the Limelight. LC 81-9264. p. cm. 1981. (ISBN 0-684-16880-4). Scribner.
--The Pool Table War. 1971. Houghton Mifflin.
--The Soul Brothers and Sister Lou. LC 68-29365. 248 p. 22cm. 1968. Scribner.
--Uncle Daniel and the Raccoon. 1972. Houghton Mifflin.

Hunter, Maude W.
--Music Within the Wall. (Illus.). (gr. 1-4). 1964. (ISBN 0-682-42049-2). Exposition.

Hunter, mollie see McIlwraith, Maureen Mollie Hunter McVeigh.

Hunter, Mollie (1922-)
--Ferlie. Cellini, Joseph (1924-), illus. LC 68-27998. (Illus.). 128p. (gr. 3-7). 1968. (ISBN 0-308-80056-7). Funk & W.
--A Furl of Fairy Wind. Gammell, Stephen, illus. LC 76-58732. (Illus.). (gr. 2-5). 1977. (ISBN 0-06-022674-9, HarpJ). (ISBN 0-06-022675-7). Har-Row.
--Ghosts of Glencoe. LC 69-12154. (Illus.). maps. photos. 192p. (gr. 6-8). 1969. (ISBN 0-308-80243-8). Funk & W.
--The Haunted Mountain. Kubinyi, Laszlo (1937-), illus. LC 77-183164. (Illus.). 175p. (gr. 5 up). 1972. (ISBN 0-06-022667-6, HarpJ). Har-Row. **Award: (ALA).**
--The Haunted Mountain. Kubinyi, Laszlo (1937-), illus. LC 77-183164. (Illus.). 144p (Pub. by Har-Row). (Story of Suspense). (gr. 5 up). 1973. (ISBN 0-06-440041-7, Trophy). Har-Row.
--Hold on to Love. LC 83-47695. c.1984. (ISBN 0-06-022687-0). Harper & Row.
--The Knight of the Golden Plain. 1st ed. Simont, Marc (1915-), illus. LC 82-47747. p. cm. c.1983. (ISBN 0-06-022685-4). (ISBN 0-06-022686-2). Harper & Row.
--Lothian Run. 224p. (gr. 7 up). 1970. (ISBN 0-308-80256-X). Funk & W.
--A Pistol in Greenyards. 191 p. 22cm. 1968, c.1965. (ISBN 0-308-80229-2). Funk & Wagnalls.
--Pistols in Greenyards. 192p. (gr. 7-11). 1968. (ISBN 0-308-80229-2). Funk & W.
--The Smartest Man in Ireland. Keeping, Charles William James (1924-), illus. LC 65-19342. 95p. illus. 21cm. 1965, c.1963. (ISBN 0-308-80019-2). Funk & Wagnalls.
--The Spanish Letters. LC 67-3029. 192 p. 22cm. 1967, c.1964. (ISBN 0-308-80214-4). Funk & Wagnalls.
--A Stranger Came Ashore. LC 75-10814. 192p. (Story of Suspense Ser.). (gr. 5 up). 1975. (ISBN 0-06-022652-8, HarpJ). Har-Row. **Awards: (ALA); (BGH).**
--Thomas & the Warlock. Cellini, Joseph (1924-), illus. (Illus.). (gr. 3-7). 1967. (ISBN 0-308-80043-5). Funk & W.
--The Three-Day Enchantment. Simont, Marc (1915-), illus. LC 84-48350. p. cm. (Knight of the Golden Plain book). ((Series: Hunter, Mollie, 1922-). (Knight of the Golden Plain book.). c.1985. (ISBN 0-06-022691-9). (ISBN 0-06-022693-5). Harper & Row.
--Walking Stones. Hyman, Trina Schart (1939-), illus. (Illus.). (Story of Suspense Ser.). (gr. 4 up). 1970. (ISBN 0-06-022664-1, HarpJ). Har-Row.
--The Wicked One: A Story of Suspense. LC 76-41515. 136p. (gr. 5-8). 1980. (ISBN 0-06-440117-0, Trophy). Har-Row.
--You Never Knew Her As I Did!. LC 81-47114. p. cm. c.1981. (ISBN 0-06-022678-1). (ISBN 0-06-022679-X). Harper & Row.

Hunter, Norman George Lorimer (1899-)
--The Best of Branestawm. LC 81-670197. (Illus.). 254 p. 22cm. 1981. (ISBN 0-370-30362-8). Bodley Head.
--Count Bakwerdz on the Carpet & Other Incredible Stories. Cole, Babette, illus. (Illus.). 126p. (gr. 4-9). 1981. (ISBN 0-370-30161-7, Pub. by Chatto-Bodley-Jonathan). Merrimack Pub Cir.
--Dribblesome Teapots & Other Incredible Stories. (gr. 3). 1971. (ISBN 0-14-030490-8, Puffin). Penguin.
--The Frantic Phantom, and Other Incredible Stories. Spence, Geraldine (1931-), illus. LC 77-353398. (Illus.). 96 p. 19cm. (Puffin books). 1976. (ISBN 0-14-030798-2). Puffin Books.

Hurd, Edith Thacher, Mrs. (1910-) & Hurd, Clement (1908-)
--The Cat from Telegraph Hill. (Illus.). 32 p. 25cm. 1955. Lothrop, Lee & Shephard Co.
--Johnny Littlejohn. LC 57-11647. unpaged. illus. 15x22cm. 1957. Lothrop, Lee & Shepard.
--Mr. Charlie, the Fireman's Friend. LC 58-5978. (Illus.). 31 p. 23cm. 1958. Lippincott.
--Mr. Charlie's Camping Trip. LC 57-5802. (Illus.). 32 p. 22cm. 1957. Lippincott.
--Mr. Charlie's Chicken House. LC 55-5106. unpaged. illus. 22cm. c.1955. Lippincott.
--Mr. Charlie's Farm. 1960. E. M. Hale & Co.
--Mr. Charlie's Pet Shop. LC 59-6702. (Illus.). 32 p. 23cm. 1959. Lippincott.
--Nino and His Fish. LC 54-8907. (Illus.). 34 p. 25cm. 1954. Lothrop, Lee & Shepard Co.
--Sky High. N.D. Lothrop Lee & Shepard.
--Somebody's House. LC 53-6891. 28cm. 42p. N.D. Lothrop, Lee & Shepard.

Hurd, Edith Thacher, Mrs. (1910-) & Hurd, Thacher (1949-)
--Little Dog, Dreaming. Hurd, Clement (1908-), illus. LC 67-4068. (Illus.). 1 v. (unpaged. 1967. Harper & Row.

Hurd, Edith Thacher, Mrs. (1910-) & McCully, Emily Arnold (1939-)
--The Black Dog Who Went into the Woods. LC 79-2000. (Illus.). 32 p. 23cm. c.1980. (ISBN 0-06-022683-8). (ISBN 0-06-022684-6). Harper & Row.

Hurd/Edith Thacher & Brown, Margaret Wise see Sage, Juniper, pseud.

Hurd, Margaret
--The Bennett Twins. (Every Boy's and Every Girl's Ser.). N.D. The Macmillan Co.

Hurd, Marian Kent & Wilson, Jean B
--When she Came Home from College. N.D. Houghton Mifflin Co.

Hurd, Michael John (1928-)
--Sailor's Songs & Shanties. Miller, John Parr (1913-), illus. (Illus.). (gr. 4-7). 1965. (ISBN 0-8098-2036-6). Walck.

Hurd, Thacher, jt. auth. see Hurd, Edith Thacher, Mrs.

Hurd, Thacher (1949-)
--Axle the Freeway Cat. Hurd, Thacher (1949-), illus. LC 80-8432. p. cm. c.1981. (ISBN 0-06-022697-8). (ISBN 0-06-022698-6). Harper & Row.
--Hobo Dog. Hurd, Thacher (1949-), illus. (Illus.). 32p. (Orig.). (ps-3). 1981. (ISBN 0-590-31283-9). Scholastic Inc.
--Mama Don't Allow. Hurd, Thacher (1949-), illus. LC 83-47703. (Illus.). 40p. (ps-3). 1984. (ISBN 0-06-022689-7). (ISBN 0-06-022690-0). HarpJ. **Award: (BGH).**
--Mystery on the Docks. 1st ed. Hurd, Thacher (1949-), illus. LC 82-48261. p. cm. c.1983. (ISBN 0-06-022701-X). (ISBN 0-06-022702-8). Harper & Row.
--The Old Chair. Hurd, Thacher (1949-), illus. LC 77-1581. (Illus.). 32 p. 17cm. c.1978. (ISBN 0-688-80104-8). (ISBN 0-688-84104-X). Greenwillow Books.
--The Quiet Evening. Hurd, Thacher (1949-), illus. LC 78-2797. (Illus.). 30 p. c.1978. (ISBN 0-688-80166-8). (ISBN 0-688-84166-X). Greenwillow Books.

Hurdy, John M., ed. see Cooper, James Fenimore.

Hurlbert, Delpha, jt. auth. see Egan, Evelyn.

Hurlbut, Jesse Lyman (1843-), ed. see Cooper, James Fenimore.

Hurlbut, Jesse Lyman (1843-1930), ed.
--Beautiful Bible Stories for Children. (The Standard Ser.). N.D. John C. Winston.
--Bible Stories Everyone Should Know. Leinweber, Robert, et al., illus. N.D. (ISBN 0-448-02871-9). Grosset & Dunlap.
--Child's Own Book of Bible Stories. (Illus.). (The Golden Days' Ser.). N.D. John C. Winston & Co.
--Stories About Children of All Nations Every Child Can Read. LC 8-29614. 4 p. l., 289 p. front., plates. 20 cm. (Lettered on cover: Every child's library). c.1908. The John C. Winston Co.

Hurlbut, Phillip R
--Jeraboam and the Amazing Spaghetti Mountain. Renfroe, Dan, illus. LC 79-90933. (Illus.). vii, 123 p. 20cm. 1979. Entertainment Factory.

Hurlbutt, Isabelle B
--Little Heiskell. Conover, Alida Van R., illus. LC 28-19746. 3 p. l., 59 p. incl. col. front., col. illus., col. plates. 20 cm. c.1928. E. P. Dutton & Company.

Hurley, Beatrice Jane Davis & Sartorius, Ina Craig, Mrs. (1892-)
--School Boys of Long Ago ... Rodd, Henry, Jr., illus. LC 95-15911. 2 v. fronts., illus. 20 cm. (Our changing world). 1935. T. Nelson and Sons.

Hurley, Jane, jt. auth. see Hurley, William James, Jr.

Hurley, Max
--Psi Patrol: Max's Book. LC 85-8328. p. cm. c.1985. (ISBN 0-590-33203-1). Scholastic Inc.

Hurley, Richard J., ed.
--Beyond Belief. (gr. 7-12). 1973. (ISBN 0-590-01455-2, Schol Pap). Scholastic Inc.

Hurley, William James, Jr. (1924-)
--Dan Frontier and the Wagon Train. (Dan Frontier Series). N.D. Benefic Press.
--Dan Frontier Goes Hunting. N.D. Robert Bentley Inc.
--Dan Frontier Scouts with the Army. Boyd, Jack (1952-), illus. LC 62-11393. (Illus.). 128 p. 23cm. (His Dan Frontier series). 1962. Benefic Press.
--Dan Frontier, Sheriff. Boyd, Jack (1952-), illus. LC 60-6583. (Illus.). 128 p. 23cm. (His Dan Frontier series). 1960. Benefic Press.
--Dan Frontier With The Indians. (Dan Frontier Series). N.D. Benefic Press.
--Peter and the Rocket Ship. N.D. Benefic Press.

Hurley, William James, Jr. (1924-) & Hurley, Jane
--Dan Frontier Goes to Congress. Rohrer, George, illus. LC 64-19184. (Illus.). 160 p. 22cm. (His Dan Frontier series). 1964. Benefic Press.

Hurlimann, Bettina (1909-)
--Barry;. The/Story of a Brave St. Bernard. Nussbaumer, Paul Edmund (1934-), illus. Crawford, Elizabeth D., tr. LC 68-3304. (Illus.). 1 v. (unpaged. 1968, c.1967. Harcourt, Brace & World.
--William Tell and His Son. Nussbaumer, Paul Edmund (1934-), illus. Crawford, Elizabeth D., tr. from Ger. LC 67-3888. 1 v. (unpaged) illus. (part col.) 23 x 32 cm. 1967, c.1965. Harcourt, Brace & World.

Hurlimann, Ruth (1939-), retold by see Grimm, Jakob Ludwig Karl & Grimm, Wilhelm Karl.

Hurlimann, Ruth (1939-)
--The Mouse with the Daisy Hat. Hurlimann, Ruth (1939-), illus. LC 78-138980. (Illus.). 30 p. 24cm. 1971. (ISBN 0-87250-245-7). D. White.

Hurlimann, Ruth (1939-), retold by.
--The Proud White Cat. Hurlimann, Ruth (1939-), illus. Bell, Anthea, tr. LC 76-51807. (Illus.). 32 p. 1977. (ISBN 0-688-22095-9). (ISBN 0-688-32095-3). Morrow.

Hurlong, Lena F
--Adventures of Jaboti on the Amazon. Lord, John Vernon (1939-), illus. LC 68-13227. (Illus.). 125 p. 22cm. 1968. (ISBN 0-200-71534-8). Abelard-Schuman.

Hurmence, Belinda
--A Girl Called Boy. LC 80-28066. p. cm. c.1981. (ISBN 0-395-31022-9). Houghton Mifflin/Clarion Books.
--Tancy. LC 83-19035. 224p. (gr. 6 up). 1984. (ISBN 0-89919-228-9, Clarion). HM.
--Tough Tiffany. LC 79-6979. 166 p. 22cm. c.1980. (ISBN 0-385-15082-2). (ISBN 0-385-15083-0). Doubleday. **Award: (ALA).**

Hurst, Fannie (1889-1968)
--Anitra's Dance. Hurst, Fannie (1889-1968), illus. LC 34-5900. 3 p. l., 385 p. illus. (music) 22 cm. 1934. Harper & Brothers.

Hurst, Irene
--One, Two, Three, Four and Many More: Stories. Hurst, Irene, illus. LC 57-9827. 56p. illus. 21cm. (Bookland juvenile). 1957. Comet Press Books.

Hurt, Freda Mary Elizabeth (1911-)
--Benny and the Dolphin. Jackson, A. J., illus. LC 68-26892. (Illus.). 128 p. 21cm. 1968. Roy Publishers.
--Caravan Cat. Langley, Nina Scott, illus. LC 64-19926. (Illus.). 21cm. 122p. (gr. k-3). 1964. Roy.
--Crab Island. Jackson, A. J., illus. LC 66-11192. 135p. illus. 21cm. 1966, c.1965. Roy.
--Mr. Twink and the Jungle Garden. Langley, Nina Scott, illus. LC 61-122942. 122p. illus. 20cm. 1960. Roy Publishers.
--Mr. Twink and the Pirates. Langley, Nina Scott, illus. LC 59-13394. 127p. ill. 19cm. 1959. Roy Pub.

Hurwitz, Claudine see Claudine, pseud.

Hurwitz, Claudine
--Rabash. Claudine, pseud. Hurwitz, Claudine, illus. Claudine, pseud. LC 65-20491. 1v. (unpaged) col. illus. 26cm. c.1965. Macmillan.

Hurwitz, Johanna (1937-)
--The Adventures of Ali Baba Bernstein. Owens, Gail, illus. LC 84-27387. (Illus.). 82 p. 22cm. c.1985. (ISBN 0-688-04161-2). Morrow.
--Aldo Applesauce. Wallner, John C (1945-), illus. LC 79-16200. (Illus.). 127 p. 21cm. 1979. (ISBN 0-688-22199-8). (ISBN 0-688-32199-2). Morrow.
--Aldo Ice Cream. Wallner, John C (1945-), illus. LC 80-24371. (Illus.). 124 p. 21cm. 1981. (ISBN 0-688-00375-3). (ISBN 0-688-00376-1). Morrow.
--Ali Baba Bernstein. 96p. N.D. (ISBN 0-688-04157-4, Morrow Junior Books). (ISBN 0-688-04158-2). Morrow.
--All About Aldo. 96p. (gr. 3-7). 1981. (ISBN 0-590-31314-2, Schol Pap). Scholastic Inc.
--Baseball Fever. Cruz, Raymond (1933-), illus. LC 81-5633. p. cm. 1981. (ISBN 0-688-00710-4). (ISBN 0-688-00711-2). Morrow.
--Busybody Nora. Jeschke, Susan (1942-), illus. LC 75-25921. (Illus.). 64 p. 21cm. 1976. (ISBN 0-688-22057-6). (ISBN 0-688-32057-0). Morrow.
--DeDe Takes Charge!. De Groat, Diane (1947-), illus. LC 84-9085. (Illus.). 128p. (gr. 3-7). 1984. (ISBN 0-688-03853-0, Morrow Junior Books). (ISBN 0-688-03853-0). Morrow.
--Hot & Cold Summer. Owens, Gail, illus. LC 83-19336. (gr. 4-7). 1984. (ISBN 0-688-02746-6). (ISBN 0-688-02746-6). Morrow.
--Much Ado About Aldo. Wallner, John C (1945-), illus. LC 78-5434. (Illus.). 95 p. 21cm. 1978. (ISBN 0-688-22160-2). (ISBN 0-688-32160-7). Morrow.
--New Neighbors for Nora. 1st ed. Jeschke, Susan (1942-), illus. LC 78-12631. (Illus.). 78 p. 21cm. 1979. (ISBN 0-688-22173-4). Morrow. **Award: (ALA).**
--Rip-Roaring Russell. Hoban, Lillian (1925-), illus. LC 83-1019. p. cm. 1983. (ISBN 0-688-02347-9). (ISBN 0-688-02348-7). Morrow. **Award: (ALA).**
--Russell Rides Again. Hoban, Lillian (1925-), illus. LC 85-7287. p. cm. 1985. (ISBN 0-688-04628-2). (ISBN 0-688-04629-0). W. Morrow.
--Tough-Luck Karen. De Groat, Diane (1947-), illus. LC 82-6443. (Illus.). 156 p. 21cm. 1982. (ISBN 0-688-01485-2). William Morrow.
--What Goes up, Must Come Down. (gr. 4-6). N.D. (ISBN 0-590-05782-0, Schol Pap). Scholastic Inc.
--What Goes up Must Come down. Fetz, Ingrid (1915-), illus. (Illus.). 128p. (gr. 3-6). 1983. (ISBN 0-590-32777-1, Apple Paperbacks). Scholastic Inc.

Hurwitz, Johanna (1937-) & Fetz, Ingrid (1915-)
--Once I Was a Plum Tree. LC 79-23518. (Illus.). 160 p. 21cm. 1980. (ISBN 0-688-22223-4). (ISBN 0-688-32223-9). Morrow.

Hurwitz, Johanna (1937-) & Johnson, Pamela, illus.
--The Rabbi's Girls. LC 82-2102. (Illus.). 158 p. 21cm. 1982. (ISBN 0-688-01089-X). Morrow. **Award: (ALA).**

Hurwood, Bernhardt J. (1926-)
--Eerie Tales of Terror & Dread. (gr. 7-12). 1974. (ISBN 0-590-02457-4, Schol Pap). Scholastic Inc.
--Ghosts, Ghouls & Other Horrors. 144p. Repr. (gr. 5 up). 1974 (Starbright). Schol Bk Serv.
--Haunted Houses. (gr. 7-9). 1972. (ISBN 0-590-03448-0). Scholastic Inc.
--Haunted Houses. 128p. (gr. 5 up). 1974 (Starbright). Schol Bk Serv.
--Strange Curses. (gr. 7-12). 1975. (ISBN 0-590-10154-4). Scholastic Inc.
--Vampires, Werewolves & Other Demons. (gr. 7-9). 1972. (ISBN 0-590-09384-3, Schol Pap). Scholastic Inc.

Hurwood, Bernhardt J. (1926-), ed.
--Ghosts, Ghouls & Other Horrors. (gr. 7-9). 1972. (ISBN 0-590-09168-9, Schol Pap). Scholastic Inc.

Husband, A. P.
--The Roosevelt Bears Visit Llanerch: An Account of Their Possible Experiences on Such a Trip. LC 8-19166. 39p. 19 x 26cm. 1908. St. Andrews Men's Club.

Huse, Harriet Pinckney, Mrs.
--Rolands Squires. (Illus.). N.D. William R. Jenkins.

Huse, Marylinn
--Eddie's Absolutely Incredible Birthday and Treasure Hunt. Jenkyns, Chris (1924-), illus. LC 72-93097. (Illus.). 45 p. 27cm. 1973. (ISBN 0-378-60635-2). Ward Ritchie Press.

Hussong, Clara
--The Golden Picture Book of Nature Walks: Animals and Plants to See on Walks Through Fields and Woods, Around Ponds and Marshes, and Along Streams; How to Enjoy a Hike in Each of the Four Seasons. Hartwell, Marjorie, illus. LC 61-2552. 57p. illus. 29cm. (Fun-to-learn golden books, FL-13). c.1961. Golden Press.

Husted, Helen McLanahan, Mrs.
--Timothy Taylor, Ambassador of Goodwill: The Story of an English Boy. Mireur, A., illus. LC 41-4026. 63 p. illus. 20 cm. c.1941. Coward-McCann, Inc.

Husted, Mary Irving
--Cunning-Cunning and His Merry Comrades. Husted, Mary Irving, illus. LC 32-25735. 24cm. 48p. N.D. Lothrop Lee & Shepard Co.

Huston, Anne
--The Cat Across the Way. Ilsley, Velma Elizabeth (1918-), illus. LC 68-24732. (Illus.). 128 p. 21cm. 1968. Seabury Press.
--Ollie's Go-Kart. James, Harold Laymont (1929-), illus. LC 76-146654. (Illus.). 143 p. 22cm. 1971. Seabury Press.

Huston, Anne & Yolen, Jane Hyatt (1939-)
--Trust a City Kid. Kocsis, James C. (1936-), illus. Paul, James, pseud. LC 66-8284. (Illus.). 192 p. 22cm. 1966. Lothrop, Lee & Shepard Co.

Hutchens, Paul (1902-1977)
--Adventure in an Indian Cemetery: A Sugar Creek Gang Story. LC 48-15385. 71 p. 21 cm. 1947. Van Kampen Press.
--Blue Cow at Sugar Creek. LC 54-7336. 90p. 21cm. 1953. Van Kampen Press.
--Further Adventures of the Sugar Creek Gang. LC 40-30961. 88 p. 20 cm. 1940. Wm. B. Eerdmans Publishing Company.
--The Green Tent Mystery at Sugar Creek. LC 51-123. 93 p. 21 cm. 1950. Van Kampen Press.
--The Haunted House at Sugar Creek: A Sugar Creek Gang Story. LC 49-9485. 76 p. 21 cm. 1949. Van Kampen Press.
--It All Began with Jeanie. 128p. 1965. Moody.
--Killer Bear. (Sugar Creek Gang Ser.). N.D. (ISBN 0-686-13766-3). Believers Bkshelf.
--Lost Campers. (Sugar Creek Gang Ser.). N.D. (ISBN 0-686-13772-8). Believers Bkshelf.
--Lost in a Sugar Creek Blizzard: A Sugar Creek Gang Story. LC 50-2915. 68 p. 21 cm. 1950. Van Kampen Press.
--Mystery at Sugar Creek. LC 43-114652. 4 p. l., 7-88 p. 20 cm. 1943. Wm. B. Eerdmans Publishing Co.
--A New Sugar Creek Mystery. LC 46-20741. 88 p. 20 cm. 1946. Wm. B. Eerdmans Publishing Company.
--North Woods Manhunt: A Sugar Creek Gang Story. LC 49-1248. 80 p. 21 cm. (His New Sugar Creek gang series, no. 4). 1948. Van Kampen Press.
--Old Stranger's Secret at Sugar Creek. LC 58-15209. 96p. 21cm. 1957. Scripture Press, Book Division.
--One Stormy Day at Sugar Creek. LC 46-1110. 88 p. 20 cm. 1946. Wm. B. Serdmans Publishing Company.
--Palm Tree Manhunt. (Sugar Creek Gang Ser.). N.D. (ISBN 0-686-13769-8). Believers Bkshelf.
--Shenanigans at Sugar Creek. LC 47-334811. 87 p. 20 cm. 1947. Wm. B. Eerdmans Publishing Company.
--The Sugar Creek Gang: A Story for Boys. LC 39-300736. 96 p. 20 cm. 1939. Wm. B. Eerdmans Publishing Company.
--The Sugar Creek Gang & Blue Cow. Hutchens, Paul (1902-1977), illus. (Illus.). 128p. (Pre-Teen Bks). (gr. 3-7). 1971. (ISBN 0-8024-4822-4). Moody.
--The Sugar Creek Gang & Screams in the Night. (gr. 3-7). 1967. (ISBN 0-8024-4812-7). Moody.
--Sugar Creek Gang & the Battle of the Bees. 128p. (gr. 3-7). 1972. (ISBN 0-8024-4830-5). Moody.
--The Sugar Creek Gang & the Brown Box Mystery. (gr. 3-7). 1970. (ISBN 0-8024-4834-8). Moody.
--The Sugar Creek Gang & the Bull Fighter. (gr. 3-7). N.D. (ISBN 0-8024-4820-8). Moody.
--The Sugar Creek Gang & the Cemetery Vandals. 128p. (gr. 3-7). 1972. (ISBN 0-8024-4829-1). Moody.
--The Sugar Creek Gang and The Chicago Adventure. (gr. 3-7). 1968. (ISBN 0-8024-4805-4). Moody.
--The Sugar Creek Gang & the Colorado Kidnapping. (gr. 3-7). 1970. (ISBN 0-8024-4827-5). Moody.
--The Sugar Creek Gang & The Ghost Dog. (gr. 3-7). 1968. (ISBN 0-8024-4832-1). Moody.
--The Sugar Creek Gang & the Green Tent Mystery. (gr. 3-7). N.D. (ISBN 0-8024-4819-4). Moody.
--The Sugar Creek Gang & the Haunted House. (gr. 3-7). 1967. (ISBN 0-8024-4816-X). Moody.
--The Sugar Creek Gang & the Indian Cemetary. (gr. 3-7). 1970. (ISBN 0-8024-4813-5). Moody.
--The Sugar Creek Gang & the Killer Bear. (gr. 3-7). N.D. (ISBN 0-8024-4802-X). Moody.
--The Sugar Creek Gang & the Killer Cat. (gr. 3-7). 1966. (ISBN 0-8024-4825-9). Moody.
--The Sugar Creek Gang & the Lost Campers. (gr. 3-7). 1968. (ISBN 0-8024-4804-6). Moody.
--The Sugar Creek Gang & the Lost in the Blizzard. (gr. 3-7). 1970. (ISBN 0-8024-4817-8). Moody.
--The Sugar Creek Gang & the Mystery Cave. (gr. 3-7). 1966. (ISBN 0-8024-4807-0). Moody.
--The Sugar Creek Gang & the Mystery Thief. (gr. 3-7). N.D. (ISBN 0-8024-4809-7). Moody.
--The Sugar Creek Gang & the Palm Tree Manhunt. (gr. 3-7). 1969. (ISBN 0-8024-4808-9). Moody.
--The Sugar Creek Gang & the Runaway Rescue. 96p. (gr. 3-7). 1973. (ISBN 0-8024-4828-3). Moody.
--The Sugar Creek Gang & the Secret Hideout. (gr. 3-7). 1968. (ISBN 0-8024-4806-2). Moody.

--Mopsa the Fairy. LC 75-32172. (Illus.). x, 248 p., 8 leaves of plates. 19cm. (Classics of Children's Literature, 1621-1932). 1977. (ISBN 0-8240-2284-X). Garland Pub.

--Mopsa, the Fairy. N.D. George Routledge & Sons.

--Mopsa, the Fairy. (Lippincott Juniors). N.D. J. B. Lippincott.

--Mopsa, the Fairy. xii, 208 p. illus., plates. 17 cm. (Half-title: Everyman's library. For young people no. 619). N.D. J. M. Dent & Sons, Ltd.

--Mopsa, the Fairy. LC 4-21559. 4 p. l., 244 p., 1 l. front., plates. 19 cm. 1901. Little, Brown, and Company.

--Mopsa the Fairy. (Illus.). 1882. Roberts Brothers.

--Mopsa, the Fairy. LC 1-15268. 4 p. l., 228 p. col. front., plates. 17 cm. 1901. T. Y. Crowell & Co.

--Mopsa, the Fairy. (Illus.). (Children's Classics). N.D. Thomas Y. Crowell & Co.

--Mopsa the Fairy. (Hsandy Volume Classics). N.D. Thomas Y. Crowell & Co.

--Mopsa, the Fairy. Curtis, Dora & Stanley, Diana (1909-), illus. LC 64-1964. xii, 142 p. illus. (part col.) 22 cm. 1964. J. M. Dent; New York, Dutton.

--Mopsa, the Fairy. Kirk, Maria Louise (1860-), illus. LC 10-213341. 253 p., 1 l. col. front., illus., 9 col. pl. 21 cm. 1910. J. B. Lippincott Company.

--Mopsa the Fairy. Lathrop, Dorothy Pulis (1891-1980), illus. LC 27-23022. 6 p. l., 259 p. incl. illus., plates. col. front. 22 cm. 1927. Harper and Brothers.

--Mopsa the Fairy. Walker, Dugald Stewart (1888-1937), illus. LC 27-19974. xi, 258 p., 1 l. incl. illus., plates. col. front. 20 cm. (The Macmillan children's classics). 1927. The Macmillan Company.

--Poor Matt: Or, The Clouded Intellect. N.D. Robert Brothers.

--The Shepherd Lady, and Other Poems. (Illus.). N.D. Robert Brothers.

--A Sister's Bye Hours. New ed. N.D. E & J B Young.

--A Sister's Bye Hours. N.D. George Routledge & Sons.

--Stories Told to a Child. N.D. George Routledge & Sons.

--Stories Told to a Child. (Illus.). (The Boys' and Girls' Books). N.D. Little, Brown and Company.

--Stories Told to a Child. (First and Second Series). N.D. Messrs. Roberts Brothers.

--Three Fairy Tales. Dole, Charles Fletcher (1845-1927), ed. Ripley, A. J., illus. LC 1-30595. viii, 56 p. incl. front., illus. 20 cm. (On cover: Heath's home and school classes). 1901. D. C. Heath & Co.

--To the Land of Fair Delight: Three Victorian Tales of the Imagination. Streatfeild, Noel, intro. by. LC 60-13018. 583 p. illus. 21 cm. 1960. F. Watts.

--Wonder Box Tales. (Illus.). (Editha Ser.). N.D. Caldwell.

--Wonder Box Tales. (Illus.). (Children Hour Series.). N.D. Dodge Publishing Co.

--Wonder-Box Tales. Horne, Diantha W., illus. LC 2-17229. 97 p. incl. front. plates. 19 cm. (The young of heart series, 35). 1902. D. Estes & Company.

Inger, Nan see Ostman, Nan Inger.

Inger, Nan (1820-1897)

--Katie & Nan. Nordenskjold, Birgitta (1919-), illus. MacMillan, Annabelle, pseud. (1922-), tr. Quick, Annabelle. LC 65-21697. (Illus.). (gr. 2-4). 1965. (ISBN 0-15-242118-1). HarBraceJ.

--Katie & Nan Go to Sea. Zetterlund, Eva, illus. MacMillan, Annabelle, pseud. (1922-), tr. Quick, Annabelle. LC 66-23288. (Illus.). (gr. 3-6). 1966. (ISBN 0-15-242120-3). HarBraceJ.

Ingersoll, Ernest (1852-1946)

--The Bear Family. (Christmas Hearth Library). N.D. D. Lothrop & Co.

--The Bear Family: With Other Stories in Natural History, 1 of 5 vols. (Good Fortune Library). N.D. Set. Lothrop Publishing Co.

--Birds in Legend, Fable, and Folklore. LC 68-26576. 292p. Repr. of 1923 ed. 1968 (Gale Reprints). Singing Tree Press.

--Dragons and Dragon Lore. N.D. Brewer & Warren Inc.

--Dragons and Dragon Lore. Osborn, Henry Fairfield, illus. LC 68-26577. 202p. Repr. of 1928 ed. 1968 (Gale Reprints). Singing Tree Press.

--Eight Secrets. LC 6-42426. ix, 338 p. front., 5 pl. 20 cm. 1906. The Macmillan Company.

--The Ice Queen. LC 4-16140. 17cm. 25p. 1885. Harper & Brothers.

--An Island in the Air: A Story of Singular Adventures in the Mesa Country. (Illus.). N.D. Grosset & Dunlap.

--Old Ocean. (Reading Union Library). N.D. D. Lothrop Co.

--The Raisin Creek Exploring Club. LC 19-14348. vi p., 1 l., 289, 1 p. illus., diagr. 20 cm. 1919. D. Appleton and Company.

Ingersoll, Frances

--Peter Gets His Wish. Ingersoll, Frances, illus. LC 48-16127. 32 p. col. illus. 21 cm. (Bonnie book). 1947. J. Martin's House.

Ingersoll, Robert

--Bug in a Rug. Seidle, Katherine, illus. LC 64-25330. 1 v (unpaged) 67 p. illus. (part col.) 24 cm. 1964. Dorrance.

Ingham, Clara Cogswell, Mrs.

--Howdy-Do. Dowling, Colista, illus. 24p. N.D. Binfords & Mort.

--Howdy-Do. Dowling, Colista, illus. LC 41-22148. (Illus.). 22p. 25cm. 1941. Metropolitan Press.

Ingham, Col. Frederick, pseud., see Hale, Edward Everett.

Ingle, Annie

--Alph & Ralph. Nicklaus, Carol, illus. (Illus.). (gr. 1-4). 1980. (Gingerbread). Dutton.

--The Little Ballerina. Tien, illus. LC 85-2239. p. cm. c.1985. (ISBN 0-394-87115-4). (ISBN 0-394-97115-9). Random House.

--Nosy Norman. Rosenberg, Amye, illus. (Illus.). (ps-3). 1980. (Gingerbread). Dutton.

Ingles, James Wesley

--Test of Valor. 1953. Westminster Press.

Inglis, Alexander James, jt. auth. see Baker, Charles McCoy.

Inglis, Ernest John D'Oyly (1899-)

--Chokra. Tresilian, Cecil Stuart (1891-), illus. LC 58-1071. 247p. illus. 21cm. 1957. Macmillan.

--Chokra and Tags. Tresilian, Cecil Stuart (1891-), illus. LC 58-4035. 202p. illus. 21cm. 1958. Macmillan.

Ingoglia, Gina

--Benji & the Tornado. Schaare, Barbara, illus. (Illus.). 24p. (Golden Look-Look Bks.). (ps-3). 1982. (ISBN 0-307-61871-4, Golden Pr). (ISBN 0-307-11871-1). Western Pub.

--The Biskitts in Double Trouble. Costanza, John, illus. LC 84-246089. (Illus.). 24 p. 20cm. (Little Golden books). c.1984. (ISBN 0-307-01119-4). Golden Press.

--Joe Camp's Benji: Fastest Dog in the West. Willis, Werner, illus. (Illus.). (A Big Picture Bk.). (ps-k). 1979. (ISBN 0-307-10826-0, Golden Pr). (ISBN 0-307-60826-3). Western Pub.

--Rainbow Brite Gets Rescued. LC 84-82180. (Illus.). 40 p. 29cm. c.1984. (ISBN 0-307-16004-1). (ISBN 0-307-66004-4). Golden Book.

Ingoglia, Gina, adapted by.

--Aurora Presents Don Bluth Productions' The Secret of Nimh: Mrs. Brisby and the Magic Stone. Nicklaus, Carol, illus. LC 81-86144. (Illus.). 24 p. 22cm. c.1982. (ISBN 0-307-60191-9). (ISBN 0-307-01108-9). Golden Press.

Ingoglia, Gina & Camp, Joe

--Joe Camp's Benji, Fastest Dog in the West. Willis, Werner, illus. LC 79-10477. (Illus.). 18 p. 32cm. 1979, c.1978. Golden Press.

Ingoldsby, Thomas, pseud., see Barham, Richard Harris.

Ingoldsby, Thomas (1788-1845)

--Ingoldsby Legends: Or, Mirth or Marvels. Rackham, Arthur (1867-1939), illus. 1898. E P Dutton.

--Misadventures at Margate. Barham, Richard Harris. Jessop, Ernest M., illus. N.D. E & J B Young.

Ingpen, Roger, ed.

--One Thousand Poems for Children. Betts, Ethel Franklin, illus. N.D. Macrae Smith.

--One Thousand Poems for Children: A Choice of the Best Verse Old and New. LC 3-21968. viii, 446 p. 21 cm. 1903. G. W. Jacobs & Co.

--One Thousand Poems for Children: A Choice of the Best Verse Old and New. rev. and enl. ed. LC 20-19453. xxvii p., 1 l., 11-549 p. 22 cm. c.1920. G. W. Jacobs & Company.

--One Thousand Poems for Children: A Choice of the Best Verse Old and New. rev. and enl. ed. Betts, Ethel Franklin, illus. LC 23-15170. xxviii p., 2 l., 11-563 p. col. front., col. plates. 25 cm. c.1923. G. W. Jacobs and Company.

Ingraham, Corinne (1887-)

--Cottontail and the Wishing Fairy And Other Stories. Walker, Dugald Stewart (1888-1937), illus. 39p. (The Wishing Fairy and her Animal Friends Ser.). 1921. Brentano's.

--The Peacock and the Wishing Fairy And Other Stories. Walker, Dugald Stewart (1888-1937), illus. 45p. (The Wishing Fairy and Her Animal Friends Ser.). 1921. Brentano's.

--The Wishing-Fairy's Animal Friends. Walker, Dugald Stewart (1888-1937), illus. LC 21-18236. 140, 1 p. col. front. illus., col. plates. 25 cm. c.1921. Brentano's.

--The Zebra and the Wishing Fairy And Other Stories. Walker, Dugald Stewart (1888-1937), illus. 45p. (The Wishing Fairy and Her Animal Friends Ser.). 1921. Brentanos.

Ingram, Eleanor M.

--The Flying Mercury. Frederick, Edmund, illus. N.D. Bobbs-Merrill Co.

--The Game and the Candle. Johnson, P. D., illus. N.D. Bobbs-Merrill Co.

--Stanton Wins. Frederick, Edmund, illus. N.D. Bobbs-Merrill Co.

Ingram, John H. (1849-1916), tr. see Caballero, Fernan.

Ingram, Jule

--Ski-Hi. Masarachia, Toni, illus. LC 32-2349. (Illus.). 26p. 23cm. 1931. Hoffman Press.

Ingram, Kristen J.

--Bible Stories for the Church Year. Russell, Joseph P., ed. (Orig.). 1984. (ISBN 0-8164-2627-9). Seabury.

Ingram, Thomas Henry see Ingram, Tom, pseud.

Ingram, Tom, pseud., see Ingram, Thomas Henry.

Ingram, Tom, pseud. (1924-)

--Garranane. Ingram, Thomas Henry. Geldart, Bill, illus. LC 73-188833. (Illus.). 191 p. 22cm. 1st U.S. edition. 1972, c.1971. (ISBN 0-87888-044-5). Bradbury Press.

--The Night Rider. Ingram, Thomas Henry. LC 74-29010. 192p. (gr. 6-8). 1975. (ISBN 0-87888-082-8). Bradbury Pr.

Inkiow, Janakier Dimiter (1932-)

--Me and Clara and Baldwin the Pony. 1st ed. Reiner, Gertraud & Reiner, Walter, illus. McGuire, Paula, tr. from Ger. LC 79-21820. (Illus.). 82 p. 20cm. (A Me-and-Clara Storybook). c.1980. (ISBN 0-394-84434-3). (ISBN 0-394-94434-8). Pantheon Books.

--Me and Clara and Casimir the Cat. 1st ed. Reiner, Gertraud & Reiner, Walter, illus. McGuire, Paula, tr. from Ger. LC 78-31316. (Illus.). 77 p. c.1979. (ISBN 0-394-94124-1). Pantheon Books.

--Me and Clara and Snuffy the Dog. 1st ed. Reiner, Gertraud & Reiner, Walter, illus. McGuire, Paula, tr. from Ger. LC 79-21959. (Illus.). 76 p. 20cm. (A Me-and-Clara Storybook). 1980. (ISBN 0-394-84433-5). (ISBN 0-394-94433-X). Pantheon Books.

--Me and My Sister Clara. 1st ed. Reiner, Gertraud & Reiner, Walter, illus. McGuire, Paula, tr. from Ger. LC 78-31310. (Illus.). 84 p. 20cm. c.1979. (ISBN 0-394-84123-9). (ISBN 0-394-94123-3). Pantheon Books.

Inkpen, Mick, jt. auth. see Butterworth, Nick.

Inkslinger, John Rogers

--Paul Bunyan in the Army. N.D. Binfords & Mort.

Inman, Escott see Inman, Herbert Escott.

Inman, Henry Escott (1837-1899)

--The Ranch on the Oxhide: A Story of Boys' and Girls' Life on the Frontier. xiii, 297 p. front., pl. 20 cm. 1923. The Macmillan Company; Etc., Etc.

Inman, Herbert Escott (1837-1899)

--Buffalo Jones' Adventures on the Plains. (Illus.). N.D. (ISBN 0-8446-0721-5). Peter Smith Publisher, Inc.

--David Chester's Motto: Honor Bright. (Illus.). 1910. Frederick Warne & Co.

--The Delahoydes: Boy Life on the Old Santa Fe Trail. LC 3-20452. 283 p. front., plates. 20 cm. 1899. Crane & Company.

--The Did of Didn't Think: A Fairy Tale for Thoughtless Children. (Illus.). N.D. Frederick Warne & Co.

--Gobbo Bobo: The Two-Eyed Griffin. (Illus.). (Warne's Fairy Library). 1910. Frederick Warne & Co.

--The Nidding Nod of Once-Upon-a-Time: A Companion Volume to the Pattypats. Mason, Ernold A., illus. LC 3-25400. xii, 13-309 p. front., illus., plates. 20 cm. c.1902. Rand, McNally & Company.

--The One Eyed Griffin. (Illus.). N.D. Frederick Warne & Co.

--The Ranch on the Oxhide. (Every Boy's Library). 1923. Grosset & Dunlap.

--The Ranch on the Oxhide: A Story of Boys' and Girls' Life on the Frontier. xiii, 297 p. front., plates. 20 cm. 1898. The Macmillan Company.

--The Saga of Jarl the Neatherd: A Fairy Story of Another Land and Time. LC 6-750. (Illus.). 352p. 20cm. 1905. Rand, McNally & Co.

Innes, Elsie

--The Elfin Oak of Kensington Gardens. Innes, Ivor, illus. N.D. Frederick Warnes & Co.

Innes, Hammond, pseud., see Hammond-Innes, Ralph.

Innes, Hammond, pseud. (1913-)

--Levkas Man. Hammond-Innes, Ralph. 1971. (ISBN 0-394-41862-X). Borzoi Book.

--The Strode Venturer. Hammond-Innes, Ralph. Innes, Hammond, pseud. (1913-), illus. Hammond-Innes, Ralph. 1965. Borzoi Books.

--The Wreck of the Mary Deare. Hammond-Innes, Ralph. 1956. Borzoi Books.

Innes, Luna May

--Our Little Boer Cousin. Goss, John, illus. LC 15-18913. ix p., 2 l., 140 p col. front., col. plates. 20 cm. (On verso of half-title:The little cousin series). 1915. The Page Company.

--Our Little Danish Cousin. Otis, Elizabeth, illus. LC 12-14710. viii p., 1 l., 2, 154 p. col. front., illus. (map) col. plates. 20 cm. (The little cousin series). 1912. L. C. Page & Company.

--Our Little South African Cousin. Goss, John, illus. LC 24-15199. ix p., 2 l., 140 p col. front., col. plates. 20 cm. (The little cousin series). 1923. L. C. Page & Company, Incorporated.

Innes, Ralph Hammond see Hammond, Ralph, pseud.

Innes, Ralph Hammond (1913-)

--Cocos Gold. Hammond, Ralph, pseud. LC 50-7103. 266 p. front. 21 cm. 1st U.S. edition. 1950. Harper.

--Cruise of Danger. Hammond, Ralph, pseud. LC 54-6431. 201p. 22cm. 1954, c.1952. Westminster Press.

Innis, Charles L.

--The Stowaway Kittens. N.D. Pageant Press Inc.

Innis, Pauline B. Coleman (1918-)

--Ernestine: Or, the Pig in the Potting Shed. Evans, Timothy, illus. LC 63-20428. 121 p. ill. 22cm. 1963. R. B. Luce.

--Ernestine, the Pig in the Potting Shed. 1963. David McKay Company Inc.

--The Ice Bird: A Christmas Legend. Dennis, Wesley (1903-1966), illus. LC 65-25828. 1v. (unpaged) illus. 26cm. c.1965. McKay.

--The Wild Swans Fly. LC 64-24576. viii, 149 p. illus. 21 cm. 1964. D. McKay Co.

--Wind of the Pampas. Lambo, Donald W. (1903-1966), illus. LC 67-24420. 215 p. 21cm. 1967. D. McKay Co.

Innis, Pauline B. Coleman (1918-) & Archibald, Joseph

--Hurricane Fighters. (gr. 9 up). 1962. McKay.

Innocenti, Roberto, jt. auth. see Gallaz, Christopher.

Inoue, Yukitoshi see Yuki, pseud.

Insight, James, pseud., see Coleman, Robert William Alfred.

Insight, James, pseud. (1916-)

--Country Parson. Coleman, Robert William Alfred. (gr. 9 up). 1964. (ISBN 0-8119-0026-6). Fell.

Institute of Pacific Relations. American Council, jt. auth. see Greenbie, Sydney.

International Kindergarten Union. Literature Committee

--Told Under the Green Umbrella: Old Stories for New Children. Gilkison, Grace, Mrs., illus. LC 30-281892. x p., 1 l., 188 p., 1 l. incl. illus., plates, col. front, col. plates. 24 cm. 1930. The Macmillan Company.

Intervisual

--Tron Pop-up Book. (Illus.). 16p. (ps-3). 1982. (ISBN 0-671-44851-X, Pub. by Simon Says). S&S.

Intrator, Mira, tr. see Daniel-Rops, Henry.

Inui, T.

--Village of Snowy Herons. (Illus.). 18p. N.D. International Pub.

Inyart, Gene (1927-)

--Jenny. Grossman, Nancy S. (1940-), illus. LC 66-183017. 166p. illus. 21cm. c.1966. Watts.

--Orange October. De Larrea, Victoria, illus. LC 68-22142. (Illus.). 114 p. 22cm. 1968. F. Watts.

--Susan & Martin. Gaulke, Gloria, illus. LC 65-117472. viii, 130p. illus. 21cm. (gr. 4-6). c.1965. (ISBN 0-531-01806-7). Watts.

--Tent Under the Spider Tree. Beech, Carol, illus. LC 59-11485. (Illus.). 143 p. 21cm. 1959. Watts.

Ionesco, Eugene (1912-)

--Conte..., one: Contes Numero 1 (Pour Enfants de Moins de Trois Ans). (Illus.). 26p. 1976. (ISBN 0-686-54189-8). French & Eur.

--Conte..., two: Contes Numero 2 (Pour Enfants de Moins de Trois Ans). (Illus.). 18p. 1976. (ISBN 0-686-54190-1). French & Eur.

--Story Number Four. Claveloux, Nicole, illus. Vaughan, Ciba, tr. from Fr. LC 72-78352. (Illus.). 24p. (Harlin Quist Bks). (gr. 2-5). 1973. (ISBN 0-8252-0110-1). Quist.

--Story Number One: For Children Under Three Years of Age. Delessert, Etienne (1941-), illus. Towle, Calvin K., tr. from Fr. LC 68-18199. (Illus.). 32 p. 29cm. 1968. (ISBN 0-531-04020-8). (ISBN 0-531-05020-3). H. Quist; Distributed by Crown Publishers. **Award: (NYT).**

--Story Number Three. Vaughan, Oiba, tr. (Illus.). (gr. k up). N.D. (ISBN 0-531-04007-0). (ISBN 0-531-05007-6). Quist.

--Story Number Three: For Children Over Three Years of Age. Corentin, Philippe, illus. Vaughn, Ciba, tr. from Fr. LC 74-141522. (Illus.). 31 p. 29cm. 1971. (ISBN 0-8252-0065-2). (ISBN 0-8252-0066-0). H. Quist.

--Story Number Two: For children under Three Years of Age. Delessert, Etienne (1941-), illus. N.D. Crown Publishers.

Iongh, Anna M. De see De Iongh, Anna M.

Iosa, Ann, ed.

--Witches. Iosa, Ann, illus. LC 80-84447. (Illus.). 39 p. 31cm. c.1981. (ISBN 0-448-42002-3). Platt & Munk.

Ioseliani, O.

--Bacho & Gocha. 24p. 1975. (ISBN 0-8285-1104-7, Pub. by Progress Pubs USSR). Imported Pubns.

--Rip Van Winkle. Cooke, Edna W. & Darley, Felix Octavius Carr (1822-1888), illus. LC 23-17206. 20cm. 69p. (The Children's Classics). 1923. J. B. Lippincott Co.
--Rip Van Winkle. Gallagher, Sears (1869-1955), illus. Ball, Francis Kingsley, intro. by. LC 23-17673. 19cm. 242p. 1923. Ginn & Co.
--Rip Van Winkle. Gant, Elizabeth & Gant, Katherine, eds. Aloise, Frank E., illus. LC 69-10614. (Illus.). 39 p. 29cm. 1969. Abingdon Press.
--Rip Van Winkle. Graef, Robert A., illus. LC 41-221471. 60 p. incl. col. front., illus. (part col.) 17 x 13 1/2 cm. (The little color classics). c.1941. McLoughlin Bros., Inc.
--Rip Van Winkle. Perard, Victor Semon (1870-1957), illus. N.D. Frederick A. Stokes.
--Rip Van Winkle. Perard, Victor Semon (1870-1957), illus. N.D. J. B. Lippincott.
--Rip Van Winkle. Rackham, Arthur (1867-1939), illus. 26cm. 61p. 1910. Doubleday, Page & Co.
--Rip Van Winkle. Rackham, Arthur (1867-1939), illus. LC 67-19272. (Illus.). xiv, 64 p. 24cm. 1967. Lippincott.
--Rip Van Winkle. Wehr, Julian, illus. LC 45-4833. (Illus.). 22p. 22 x 18cm. 1945. S. Daye, Inc.
--Rip Van Winkle. Wyeth, Newell Convers (1882-1945), illus. 26cm. 86p. 1921. David McKay Co.
--Rip Van Winkle: A Legend of the Hudson. LC 31-352272. 1 p. l., 7-230 p. front., illus. 17 cm. (Altemus' young people's library). 1900. Henry Altemus Company.
--Rip Van Winkle: A Tale of the Hudson. Brundage, Frances, illus. LC 27-186152. 3 p. l., 11-92 p. col. front., illus. 20 cm. (John Newbery series). c.1927. The Saalfield Publishing Company.
--Rip Van Winkle and Christmas Eve. (Illus.). (Gem Series of Gift Bks.). N.D. E. P. Dutton & Co.
--Rip Van Winkle and other American Essays. LC 7-9496. 18cm. 99p. (The Riverside Literature Ser.: No. 5). 1891. Houghton Mifflin & Co.
--Rip Van Winkle and Other Sketches. (Classics for Children). N.D. Ginn & co.
--Rip Van Winkle & Other Stories. Suba, Susanne (1913-), illus. (Illus.). (gr. 4-7). N.D. (ISBN 0-385-00699-3). Doubleday.
--Rip Van Winkle and Sleepy Hollow. LC 7-19468. 14cm. 128p. (The Nutshell Library). 1907. Old Greek Press.
--Rip Van Winkle and The Legend of Sleepy Hollow. N.D. David McKay Co.
--Rip Van Winkle and the Legend of Sleepy Hollow. 152p. Repr. 1974. (ISBN 0-912882-09-3). Sleepy Hollow Restorations.
--Rip Van Winkle and the Legend of Sleepy Hallow. Boughton, George Henry (1834-1905), illus. (Pocket Classics). N.D. Macmillan Co.
--Rip Van Winkle and The Legend of Sleepy Hollow. Boughton, George Henry (1834-1905), illus. LC 79-22226. p. cm. (Facsimile Classics Series). 1980. Mayflower Books.
--Rip Van Winkle and the Legend of Sleepy Hollow. Boughton, George Henry (1834-1905), illus. 1980. Smith.
--Rip Van Winkle and The Legend of Sleepy Hollow. Cooke, Edna W. & Darley, Felix Octavius Carr (1822-1888), illus. LC 25-26122. 21cm. 148p. (Lippincott Juniors). 1924. J. B. Lippincott.
--Rip Van Winkle and The Legend of Sleepy Hollow. Fitz, John, Jr., illus. Weekes, Blanche Ethel, intro. by. LC 28-14271. 21cm. 106p. (The Winston large-type Classics for Little Folks). 1928. John C. Winston Co.
--Rip Van Winkle, and The Legend of Sleepy Hollow. Jefferson, Joseph, intro. by. 149p. (Thumb-Nail Ser.). N.D. Century Co.
--Rip Van Winkle and the Legend of Sleepy Hollow. Levine, David (1926-), illus. 1963. MacMillan.
--Rip Van Winkle, and the Legend of Sleepy Hollow. Pape, Eric (1870-), illus. LC 25-21157. 19cm. 183p. (The Macmillan Children's Classics). 1925. Macmillan Co.
--Rip Van Winkle, The Legend of Sleepy Hallow and other Tales. N.D. (ISBN 0-448-05482-5, Companion Library). Grosset & Dunlap.
--Rip Van Winkle, the Legend of Sleepy Hollow & Other Tales. Clark, R. C., illus. (Illus.). (Companion Lib.). (gr. 6 up). N.D. (ISBN 0-448-05482-5, G&D). Putnam Pub Group.
--Rip Van Winkle: The Legend of Sleepy Hollow. Pulliam, Roy Avron (1913-) & Darby, Oscar Nolan, eds. Rice, Elizabeth (1913-), illus. LC 50-14208. 64 p. illus. 22 cm. (Treasure book). 1949. Steck Co.
--Selections from the Sketch Book. (gr. 7 up). N.D. Pyramid Pubns.
--The Sketch-Book. 568p. (Merrill's English Texts). N.D. Charles E Merrill.
--The Sketch Book. (Heath's English Classics Ser.). N.D. D C Heath.
--The Sketch-Book. (Riverside Edition). N.D. G. P. Putnam's Sons.
--The Sketch Book. (Classics for Children). N.D. Ginn.
--The Sketch Book. N.D. Longmans,Green & Co.
--The Sketch Book. N.D. Silver, Burdett.
--Stories and Legends. (Illus.). (Putnam's Knickerbocker Ser.). N.D. G. P. Putnam's Sons.
--Tales from the Alhambra. Brock, Charles Edmond (1870-1938), illus. N.D. Houghton Mifflin.
--Tales From Washington Irving's Alhambra. Cheney, Leila H., ed. N.D. J.B. Lippincott.
--Tales of a Traveller. (Burt's Home Library). N.D. A L Burt Co.
--Tales of a Traveller. (Riverside Edition). N.D. G. P. Putnam's Sons.
--Tales of a Traveller. N.D. Longmans,Green & Co.
--Tales of a Traveller. 559p. (The Lake English Classics). N.D. Scott Foresman & Co.
--Tales of a Traveller. (The Navarre Ser.). N.D. Thomas Y. Crowell & Co.
--Tales of a Traveller. Carpenter, George Rice, illus. (Longmans' English Classics: No.1). 1895. Longmans Green & Co.
--Tales of Alhambra. Dixon, Arthur A & Brock, Henry Matthew (1875-1960), illus. (Raphael House Library). N.D. David McKay.
--Tales of the Alhambra. Goldston, Robert Conroy (1927-), ed. Stephane, illus. LC 62-19333. (Illus.). 153 p. 24cm. 1962. Bobbs-Merrill.
--Tales of Washington Irving's Alhambra. Cheney, Leila H., ed. Hood, George W., illus. 120 p. 4 col. pl. (incl. front.) 19 1/2 cm. (The children's classics). c.1917. J. B. Lippincott Company.
--Washington Irving's Ichabod Crane and the Headless Horseman. York, Carol Beach (1928-), ed. Uehlinger, Diana, illus. LC 79-66323. (Illus.). 48 p. 23cm. (Folk Tales of America). c.1980. (ISBN 0-89375-316-5). (ISBN 0-89375-315-7). Troll Associates.
--Washington Irving's "Rip Van Winkle". York, Carol Beach (1928-), ed. Craft, Kinuko Y., illus. LC 79-66314. (Illus.). 46 p. 23cm. (Folk Tales of America). c.1980. (ISBN 0-89375-300-9). Troll Associates.
--Washington Irving's Tales of the Supernatural. Wagenknecht, Edward Charles (1900-), ed. Alley, R. W., illus. LC 80-29313. (Illus.). 307p. (gr. 6 up). 1982. (ISBN 0-916144-64-X). (ISBN 0-916144-65-8). Stemmer Hse.

Irving, William
--The North Woods: An Adventure Story for Boys. D'Emo, Leon, illus. LC 33-136396. vi, 177 p. illus. 20 cm. 1933. G. P. Putnam's Sons.

Irwin
--Young Bess. 1966. (ISBN 0-15-699824-6, VoyB). HarBraceJ.

Irwin, Annabelle Bowen, jt. auth. see Irwin, Hadley.

Irwin, Annabelle Bowen (1915-)
--One Bite at a Time. Allen, Nena, illus. LC 72-8493. (Illus.). 116 p. 21cm. 1973. (ISBN 0-531-02603-5). F. Watts.

Irwin, Annabelle Bowen (1915-) & Reida, Bernice (1915-)
--Moon of the Red Strawberry. LC 72-85163. 105 p. 22cm. c.1977. (ISBN 0-87695-159-0). Aurora Publishers.

Irwin, Bernice Piilani, Mrs.
--In Menehune Land. LC 36-17945. 134, 2 p. incl. illus., plates. front. 24 cm. 1936. Printed by the Printshop Co., Ltd.

Irwin, Constance Erick see Frick, C. H., pseud.

Irwin, Constance H. Frick (1913-)
--The Comeback Guy. LC 61-6115. 180 p. 22 cm. 1961. Harcourt, Brace & World.
--Five Against the Odds. LC 55-8676. 210 p. 21 cm. 1965. Harcourt, Brace.
--Jonathan D. Werth, Kurt (1896-), illus. LC 58-14494. unpaged. illus. 26cm. 1959. Lothrop, Lee and Shepard.
--Patch. LC 57-6559. 188 p. 22 cm. 1957. Harcourt, Brace.
--Strange Footprints on the Land. LC 78-19519. (Illus.). 192p. (gr. 7 up). 1980. (ISBN 0-06-022772-9, HarpJ). (ISBN 0-06-022773-7). Har-Row.
--Tourney Team. LC 54-8572. 215 p. 21 cm. 1954. Harcourt, Brace.

Irwin, Florence (1869-)
--In Santa Claus' House. Bickford, Nana French, illus. LC 17-28329. xi, 198 p. col. front., col. plates. 19 1/2 cm. 1917. Little, Brown, and Company.

Irwin, Grace (1891-)
--Almost Fifteen. Irwin, Mary Grace (1891-), illus. LC 38-19638. 5 p. l., 15-255 p. front., illus. 20 1/2 cm. 1938. Lothrop, Lee and Shepard Company.
--Brown-Eyed Susan. Irwin, Mary Grace (1891-), illus. LC 17-9254. 4 p. l., 103 p. front., illus. 17 1/2 cm. 1917. The Little Book Publisher.
--The Happy Tower. Irwin, Mary Grace (1891-), illus. LC 40-8614. 5 pl l., 13-305 p. incl. front., illus. 20 1/2 cm. 1940. Lothrop, Lee and Shepard Company.
--Little Miss Redhead. Irwin, Mary Grace (1891-), illus. LC 36-19833. 5 p. l., 13-241 p. incl. front., illus. 20 1/2 cm. 1936. Lothrop, Lee and Shepard Company.
--Peter & Cynthia. Irwin, Mary Grace (1891-), illus. LC 41-6801. 3 p. l., 272 p. illus. 20 1/2 cm. c.1941. Lothrop, Lee and Shepard Company.

Irwin, Hadley, pseud., see Hadley, Lee Irwin.

Irwin, Hadley, pseud. (1934-) & Irwin, Annabelle Bowen (1915-)
--Bring to a Boil and Separate. Hadley, Lee Irwin. LC 79-23090. (Hadley Irwin is the joint pseud of Lee Irwin Hadley (1934); and Annabelle Bowen Irwin (19150). 123 p. 22cm. 1980. (ISBN 0-689-50156-0). Atheneum.
--I Be Somebody. Hadley, Lee Irwin. LC 84-490. (Hadley Irwin is the joint pseud of Lee Irwin Hadley (1934); and Annabelle Bowen Irwin (1915)). 180p. (gr. 4-7). 1984. (ISBN 0-689-50308-3, McElderry Bk). Atheneum.
--The Lilith Summer. Hadley, Lee. LC 78-24379. (Hadley Irwin is the joint pseud of Lee Irwin Hadley (1934); and Annabelle Bowen Irwin (1915)). 109 p. 24cm. c.1979. (ISBN 0-912670-52-5). Feminist Press.
--Moon and Me. Hadley, Lee Irwin. LC 80-24052. (Hadley Irwin is the joint pseud of Lee Irwin Hadley (1934); and Annabelle Bowen Irwin (1915)). 150 p. 22cm. 1981. (ISBN 0-689-50194-3). Atheneum.
--We Are Mesquakie, We Are One. Hadley, Lee Irwin. LC 80-19000. (Hadley Irwin is the joint pseud of Lee Irwin Hadley (1934); and Annabelle Bowen Irwin (1915)) (Illus.). 115 p. 24cm. c.1980. (ISBN 0-912670-85-1). Feminist Press.
--What About Grandma?. Hadley, Lee Herwin. LC 81-10809. (Hadley Irwin is the joint pseud of Lee Irwin Hadley (1934); and Annabelle Bowen Irwin (1915)). 165 p. 22cm. 1982. (ISBN 0-689-50224-9). Atheneum.

Irwin, Inez Haynes, Mrs. (1873-1970)
--Maida's Little Cabins. LC 47-11160. 212 p. illus., maps (on lining-papers) 20 cm. 1947. Grosset & Dunlap.
--Maida's Little Camp. LC 40-6809. viii p., 1 l., 213 p. incl. front. 19 1/2 cm. c.1940. Grosset & Dunlap.
--Maida's Little Farm. LC 53-1369. 180p. 20cm. 1953. Grosset & Dunlap.
--Maida's Little Farm. (The Maida Ser.). N.D. Grosset & Dunlap.
--Maida's Little Hospital. LC 52-8138. 179 p. 20 cm. (The Maida Ser). 1952. Grosset & Dunlap.
--Maida's Little House. LC 21-21096. 4 p. l., 7-264 p. front. 19 1/2 cm. (The Maida Ser.). 1921. B. W. Huebsch, Inc.
--Maida's Little House. N.D. Grosset & Dunlap.
--Maida's Little House. 264p. N.D. Viking Press.
--Maida's Little House Party. LC 54-1194. 177p. illus. 20cm. (The Maida Ser.). 1954. Grosset & Dunlap.
--Maida's Little Houseboat. LC 43-81780. vii p., 1 l., 207 p. incl. front. plan. 19 1/2 cm. 1943. Grosset & Dunlap.
--Maida's Little Island. LC 39-124361. 251 p. front., map. 19 1/2 cm. (The Maida Ser.). c.1939. Grosset & Dunlap.
--Maida's Little Lighthouse. LC 51-7735. 176 p. illus. 20 cm. (The Maida Ser.). 1951. Grosset & Dunlap.
--Maida's Little School. (The Maida Ser.). N.D. Grosset & Dunlap.
--Maida's Little School. LC 26-154271. 246 p. col. front. 19 1/2 cm. 1926. The Viking Press.
--Maida's Little Shop. (The Maida Ser.). N.D. Grosset & Dunlap.
--Maida's Little Shop. 246p. (The Maida Ser.). N.D. Viking Press.
--Maida's Little Shop. Heubsch, Gertrude, illus. LC 10-71734. 294 p. front. 19 1/2 cm. 1910. B. W. Huebsch.
--Maida's Little Theater. LC 46-207420. vii p., 1 l., 211 p. incl. front. 19 1/2 cm. 1946. Grosset & Dunlap.
--Maida's Little Treasure Hunt. 182p. illus. 20cm. (Her The Maida books 15). c.1955. Grosset & Dunlap.
--Maida's Little Village. LC 42-178394. vii p., 1 l., 205 p. incl. front. 19 1/2 cm. 1942. Grosset & Dunlap.
--Maida's Little Zoo. LC 49-1720. ix, 207 p. front. 20 cm. 1949. Grosset & Dunlap.

Irwin, Kathleen
--Fury. Crawford, Mel (1925-), illus. LC 57-13728. unpaged. illus. 21cm. (Little golden book, 286). 1957. Simon and Schuster.

Irwin, Louise Godfrey
--Mystery of the Grey Oak Inn: A Story for Boys. LC 12-23209. 5 p. l., 317 p. front., plates. 19 1/2 cm. 1912. Moffat, Yard and Company.
--The Secret of Old Thunder-Head. Perard, Victor Semon (1870-1957), illus. LC 9-286089. 4 p. l., 290 p. front., 4 pl. 19 1/2 cm. 1909. H. Holt and Company.

Irwin, Mary Grace (1891-)
--Under Summer Skies. Irwin, Mary Grace (1891-), illus. LC 37-191583. 243 p. incl. front., illus., plates. 20 1/2 cm. 1937. Lothrop, Lee and Shepard Company.

Irwin, Peggy Louise
--The Curious Kittens. LC 55-7640. (Illus.). unpaged. 29cm. 1955. A. A. Wyn.

Irwin, Violet Mary, jt. auth. see Stefansson, Vilhjalmur.

Irwin, Violet Mary (1881-)
--The Shaman's Revenge. Grier, Geoffrey, illus. LC 25-16606. (Based on the Arctic Diaries of Vilhjalmur Stefansson). (Illus.). 236p. 19cm. 1925. Macmillan Company.
--The Short Sword. Best, Allena Champlin, Mrs. (1892-1974), illus. Berry, Erick, pseud. LC 28-22465. 5 p. l., 249 p. front., 1 illus. 19 1/2 cm. 1928. The Macmillan Company.

Isaac, Ella M.
--Skunklets. Striplin, Clara M. & Miller, Ada L., eds. Ayres, Robert T., illus. LC 48-28215. 93 p. illus. 21 cm. 1948. Southern Pub. Assn.

Isaac, Joanne (1934-)
--Amanda: A Little Girl Who Did Not Want to Have Her Hair Combed. Isaac, Joanne (1934-), illus. LC 68-23766. (Illus.). 38 p. 21cm. 1968. (ISBN 0-8225-0267-4). Lerner Publications Co.
--Tom Thumb's Alphabet. Isaac, Joanne (1934-), illus. LC 79-92826. (Illus.). 32 p. 32cm. 1970. Putnam.

Isaacs, Abram Samuel (1852-)
--School Days in Home Town. LC 28-12812. 162 p. 20 cm. 1928. The Jewish Publication Society of America.
--Step by Step. N.D. Harlem Book Co.
--The Young Champion. N.D. Harlem Book Co.

Isaacs, Jorge (1837-1895)
--Maria: A South American Romance. Ogden, Rollo (1856-), tr. Janvier, Thomas A., intro. by. LC 4-16890. xi p., 2 l., 902 p. 18 cm. 1890. Harper & Brothers.

Isaacson, Yvonne
--The Littlest Rabbit. Talarczyk, June, illus. LC 67-24771. (Illus.). 32 p. 29cm. 1968. T. S. Denison.

Isadora, Rachel
--Ben's Trumpet. Isadora, Rachel, illus. LC 78-12885. (Illus.). 32 p. c.1979. (ISBN 0-688-80194-3). (ISBN 0-688-84194-5). Greenwillow Books. **Awards: (ALA); (BGH); (RCM).**
--City Seen from A to Z. Isadora, Rachel, illus. LC 82-11966. (Illus.). 8 x9 7/8. 32p. (28 pt.). 1983. (ISBN 0-688-01802-5). (ISBN 0-688-01803-3). Greenwillow.
--I Hear. Isadora, Rachel, illus. LC 84-6103. (Illus.). 32 p. 22cm. c.1985. (ISBN 0-688-04061-6). (ISBN 0-688-04062-4). Greenwillow Books.
--I See. Isadora, Rachel, illus. LC 84-6104. (Illus.). 32 p. 22cm. c.1985. (ISBN 0-688-04059-4). (ISBN 0-688-04060-8). Greenwillow Books.
--I Touch. Isadora, Rachel, illus. LC 84-13673. (Illus.). 32 p. 21cm. c.1985. (ISBN 0-688-04255-4). (ISBN 0-688-04256-2). Greenwillow Books.
--Jesse & Abe. Isadora, Rachel, illus. LC 80-15584. (Illus.). 32 p. 26cm. c.1981. (ISBN 0-688-80302-4). (ISBN 0-688-84302-6). Greenwillow Books.
--Max. Isadora, Rachel, illus. LC 84-7649. (Reading Rainbow Book). 1984, c.1976. (ISBN 0-02-043800-1). Collier Books.
--Max. Isadora, Rachel, illus. LC 76-9088. p. cm. 24cm. 32p. c.1976. (ISBN 0-02-747450-X). Macmillan. **Award: (ALA).**
--My Ballet Class. LC 79-16297. (Illus.). 32 p. 26cm. c.1980. (ISBN 0-688-80253-2). (ISBN 0-688-84253-4). Greenwillow Books.
--No, Agatha!. LC 79-26734. (Illus.). 32 p. 26cm. c.1980. (ISBN 0-688-80274-5). (ISBN 0-688-84274-7). Greenwillow Books.
--Opening Night. Isadora, Rachel, illus. LC 83-20791. (Illus.). 8 x 9 7/8. 32p. (14 pt.). (gr. k-3). 1984. (ISBN 0-688-02726-1). (ISBN 0-688-02727-X). Greenwillow.
--The Pirates of Bedford Street. LC 84-25904. p. cm. 1985. (ISBN 0-688-04033-0). (ISBN 0-688-04034-9). Greenwillow Books.
--The Potters' Kitchen. LC 76-47666. (Illus.). 32 p. 26cm. c.1977. (ISBN 0-688-80089-0). (ISBN 0-688-84089-2). Greenwillow Books.
--Willaby. Isadora, Rachel, illus. LC 77-4469. (Illus.). 32 p. c.1977. (ISBN 0-02-747460-7). Macmillan.

Isadora, Rachel, retold by.
--The Nutcracker. Isadora, Rachel, illus. LC 81-6042. (Illus.). 32 p. 26cm. c.1981. (ISBN 0-02-747470-4). Macmillan.

Isadora, Rachel, jt. auth. see Maiorano, Robert.

Isasi, Mirim Erena & Denny, Melcena Burns
--White Stars of Freedom. Wiese, Kurt (1887-1974), illus. LC 42-23978. 5 p. l., 17-308 p. col. front., illus., plates (part col.) 23 1/2 cm. 1942. A. Whitman & Company.

Jackson, Alice F., retold by see Kingsley, Charles.
Jackson, Alice F., retold by see Scott, Walter, Sir.
Jackson, Bennett B. & Deming, Norma H.
--Thrift and Success. 266p. N.D. Century Co.
Jackson, Brian (1933-1983), ed. see Jefferies, Richard.
Jackson, Byron, jt. auth. see Garfield, Robert.
Jackson, Byron, jt. auth. see Jackson, Kathryn.
Jackson, C. V.
--Playing at Work. (Illus.). (gr. 2-6). N.D. (ISBN 0-7195-0708-1). Transatlantic.
Jackson, Caary Paul see Jackson, O. B., pseud.
Jackson, Caary Paul see Paulson, Jack, pseud.
Jackson, Caary Paul (1902-)
--Barney of the Babe Ruth League. Hamilton, William, illus. LC 54-5615. (Illus.). 148 p. 21cm. 1954. Crowell.
--Basketball Clown. Jackson, O. B., pseud. Henneberger, Robert G. (1921-), illus. LC 56-10319. (Illus.). 160 p. 21cm. 1956. Whittlesey House.
--Beginner Under the Backboards. Butterfield, Ned (1917-), illus. LC 74-13428. (Illus.). 124 p. 21cm. 1974. (ISBN 0-8038-0762-7). Hastings House.
--Big Play in the Small League. Kramer, Frank, illus. LC 67-29994. (Illus.). 93 p. 22cm. 1968. Hastings House.
--Bud Baker: College Pitcher. Kramer, Frank, illus. LC 74-103056. (Illus.). 128 p. 22cm. 1970. Hastings House.
--Bud Baker: High School Pitcher. Kramer, Frank, illus. LC 67-15342. (Illus.). 125 p. 22cm. 1967. Hastings House.
--Bud Baker: Racing Swimmer. Kramer, Frank, illus. LC 62-10084. 128p. illus. 22cm. 1962. (ISBN 0-8038-0714-7). Hastings House.
--Bud Baker: T Quarterback. Kramer, Frank, illus. LC 60-10583. 157p. illus. 22cm. 1960. Hastings House.
--Bud Plays Junior High Basketball. Kramer, Frank, illus. (Illus.). Orig. Title: Bud Plays Senior High Basketball. (gr. 6-9). 1957. (ISBN 0-8038-0715-5). Hastings.
--Bud Plays Junior High Basketball. Kramer, Frank, illus. LC 59-108465. 178p. illus. 22cm. 1959. (ISBN 0-8038-0712-0). Hastings House.
--Bud Plays Junior High Football. Tolford, Joshua (1909-), illus. LC 57-107363. 157p. illus. 22cm. 1957. Hastings House.
--Bud Plays Senior High Basketball. Kramer, Frank, illus. LC 64-19078. 118p. illus. 22cm. 1964. Hastings House.
--Bullpen Bargain. Kramer, Frank, illus. LC 61-7199. (Illus.). 157 p. 22cm. 1961. Hastings House.
--Buzzy Plays Midget League Football. Royt, Kevin, illus. LC 56-9865. (Illus.). 112 p. 23cm. 1956. Follett Pub. Co.
--Chris Plays Small Fry Football. Kramer, Frank, illus. LC 63-16167. 123 p. illus. 22 cm. 1963. Hastings House.
--Clown at Second Base. LC 52-6721. 250 p. 21cm. 1952. Crowell.
--Dub, Halfback. LC 52-8654. 184 p. 21cm. 1952. Crowell.
--Eric and Dud's Football Bargain. Butterfield, Ned (1917-), illus. LC 72-4259. (Illus.). 127 p. 22cm. 1972. (ISBN 0-8038-1911-0). Hastings House.
--Fifth Inning Fade-Out. Torbert, Floyd James (1922-), illus. LC 73-39117. (Illus.). 124 p. 22cm. 1972. (ISBN 0-8038-2287-1). Hastings House.
--Freshman Forward. Jackson, O. B., pseud. Henneberger, Robert G. (1921-), illus. LC 58-59663. 100p. illus. 21cm. 1959. Whittlesey House.
--Fullback in the Large Fry League. Kramer, Frank, illus. LC 65-19074. 125p. illus. 22cm. c.1965. Hastings.
--Giant in the Midget League. Klinger, Charles, illus. LC 53-8414. 90p. illus. 21cm. 1953. Crowell.
--Halfback!. LC 70-170631. (Illus.). 127 p. 22cm. 1971. (ISBN 0-8038-2649-4). Hastings House.
--Hall of Fame Flankerback. Kramer, Frank, illus. LC 68-21868. (Illus.). 126 p. 22cm. 1968. Hastings House.
--Haunted Halfback. LC 69-10269. 125 p. 23cm. 1969. Follett Pub. Co.
--High School Backstop. Jackson, O. B., pseud. Henneberger, Robert G. (1921-), illus. LC 62-21572. 160 p. illus. 21 cm. 1963. Whittlesey House.
--Hillbilly Pitcher. Jackson, O. B., pseud. Henneberger, Robert G. (1921-), illus. LC 56-7559. 168p. (gr. 6 up). 1956. (ISBN 0-07-032099-3). (ISBN 0-07-032090-X). McGraw.
--The Jamesville Jets. Galdone, Paul (1914-), illus. LC 59-10271. (Illus.). 143 p. 23cm. 1959. (ISBN 0-695-44532-4). Follett Pub. Co.
--Junior High Freestyle Swimmer. Kramer, Frank, illus. LC 65-23199. 128 p. illus. 22 cm. 1965. Hastings House.
--Little League Tournament. Geer, Charles Hand (1922-), illus. LC 58-14480. 117p. illus. 22cm. c.1959. (ISBN 0-8038-4241-4). Hastings House.
--Little Leaguer's First Uniform. Klinger, Charles, illus. LC 52-7861. (Illus.). 99 p. 21cm. 1952. Crowell.
--Little Major Leaguer. Kramer, Frank, illus. LC 62-22121. (Illus.). 119 p. 22cm. 1963. Hastings House.
--Match Point. LC 56-5107. 188p. 21cm. c.1956. Westminster Press.
--Midget League Catcher. LC 66-16536. 139 p. 22 cm. 1966. Follett Pub. Co.
--Minor League Shortstop. Kramer, Frank, illus. LC 64-8122. 128 p. illus. 22 cm. 1965. Hastings House.
--No Talent Letterman. Walker, Charles W., illus. LC 66-16051. 127 p. illus. 21 cm. 1966. McGraw-Hill Book.
--Pass Receiver. Butterfield, Ned (1917-), illus. LC 76-124618. (Illus.). 127 p. 22cm. 1970. Hastings House.
--Pee Wee Cook of the Midget League. Kramer, Frank, illus. LC 64-13481. (Illus.). 123 p. 22cm. 1964. Hastings House.
--Pennant Stretch Drive. Kramer, Frank, illus. LC 69-17518. 126 p. 22cm. 1969. Hastings House.
--Pro Football Rookie. Kramer, Frank, illus. LC 62-16193. 126p. illus. 22cm. 1962. Hastings House.
--Pro Hockey Comeback. Kramer, Frank, illus. LC 61-11989. 148p. illus. 22cm. 1961. Hastings House.
--Puck Grabber. Henneberger, Robert G. (1921-), illus. LC 57-12583. 160p. illus. 21cm. 1957. Whittlesey House.
--Rookie Catcher with the Atlanta Braves. Chauncy, Francis, illus. LC 66-11901. 159 p. illus 21 cm. c.1966. (ISBN 0-8038-6304-7). Hastings.
--Rookie First Baseman. LC 50-8512. vi, 266 p. 21cm. 1950. Crowell.
--Rose Bowl All-American. LC 49-11716. viii, 245 p. 21 cm. 1949. Crowell.
--Rose Bowl Line Backer. LC 51-12881. 184 p. 21cm. 1951. Crowell.
--Rose Bowl Pro. LC 79-125002. 143p. 22cm. c.1970. (ISBN 0-8038-6313-6). Hastings House.
--Second Time Around Rookie. LC 68-17648. 157 p. 22cm. 1968. Hastings House.
--The Short guard. Henneberger, Robert G. (1921-), illus. LC 61-14355. 156p. illus. 21cm. 1961. Whittlesey House.
--Short Guard. Jackson, O. B., pseud. Henneberger, Robert G. (1921-), illus. (gr. 6 up). 1961. (ISBN 0-07-032092-6). McGraw.
--Shorty at Shortstop. Royt, Kevin, illus. LC 51-7237. 153 p. illus. 23 cm. 1951. Wilcox & Follett.
--Shorty at the State Tournament. Royt, Kevin, illus. LC 55-7495. (Illus.). 159 p. 23cm. 1955. Follett Pub. Co.
--Shorty Carries the Ball. Boehl, Jackie, illus. LC 52-14346. (Illus.). 153 p. 23cm. 1952. Wilcox and Follett Co.
--Shorty Makes First Team. Royt, Kevin, illus. LC 50-8019. (Illus.). 160 p. 23cm. 1950. Wilcox and Follett.
--Side Line Victory. Hamilton, William, illus. LC 57-5093. 185p. illus. 21cm. 1957. Westminster Press.
--Spice's Football. Shortall, Leonard W., illus. LC 55-58361. 90p. illus. 21cm. c.1955. Crowell.
--Squeeze Play. LC 50-6178. 207 p. 21cm. 1950. Crowell.
--Star Kicker. Jackson, O. B., pseud. Henneberger, Robert G. (1921-), illus. LC 55-8286. (Illus.). 160 p. 21cm. 1955. Whittlesey House.
--Stepladder Steve Plays Basketball. Kramer, Frank, illus. LC 68-31693. (Illus.). 126 p. 22cm. 1969. Hastings House.
--Stock Car Racer. LC 57-11034. (Illus.). 224 p. 23cm. 1957. Follet Pub. Co.
--Stretch Smith Makes a Basket. LC 49-2205. vii, 194 p. 21 cm. 1949. T. Y. Crowell Co.
--Super Modified Driver. Torbert, Floyd James (1922-), illus. LC 64-22506. 164 p. illus. 22 cm. 1964. Hastings House.
--Three-and-Two Pitcher. LC 51-935. 206 p. 21cm. 1951. Crowell.
--Tim The Football Nut. Kramer, Frank, illus. LC 67-21843. (Illus.). 120 p. 22cm. 1967. Hastings House.
--Tom Mosely,. Midget Leaguer. Butterfield, Ned (1917-), illus. LC 74-137765. (Illus.). 128 p. 22cm. 1971. (ISBN 0-8038-7107-4). Hastings House.
--Tommy: Soap Box Derby Champion. Torbert, Floyd James (1922-), illus. LC 63-12298. 94 p. illus. 22 cm. 1963. Hastings House.
--Tournament Forward. LC 48-7998. 179 p. 21 cm. 1948. T. Y. Crowell Co.
--Tournament Forward. 179p. 1948. Thomas Y. Crowell.
--Triple Play. LC 52-6722. 193 p. 21cm. 1952. Crowell.
--Two Boys and a Soap Box Derby. Martin, Roger, illus. LC 58-9010. (Illus.). 118 p. 22cm. 1958. Hastings House.
--Uniform for Harry. Goldsborough, June (1923-), illus. (Illus.). (gr. 2-4). 1962. (ISBN 0-695-89005-0). Follett.
--World Series Rookie. Ricketts, Ralph E., illus. LC 59-145463. 148p. illus. 22cm. 1960. Hastings House.
Jackson, Charles Tenney (1874-)
--The Call to the Colors. Clarke, William Wallace, illus. LC 18-1146. vii, 323, 1 p. front., plates. 20 cm. 1918. D. Appleton and Company.
--Jimmy May in the Fighting Line. Clarke, William Wallace, illus. LC 18-22893. vii, 314, 1 p. front., plate. 1918. D. Appleton and Company.
Jackson, Charlotte E. Cobden, Mrs. (1902-)
--Mercy Hicks. Burbank, Addison Bushnell (1895-), illus. LC 49-48771. 241 p. illus. 21 cm. 1949. Dodd, Mead.
--Roger and the Fishes. Wiese, Kurt (1887-1974), illus. LC 43-11957. 4 p. l., 76 p. illus. (part col.) 25 1/2 cm. 1943. Dodd, Mead & Company.
--Round the Afternoon. Weisgard, Leonard Joseph (1916-), illus. LC 46-8668. 63 p. incl. col. front., illus. (part col.) 25 cm. 1946. Dodd, Mead and Company.
--Sarah Deborah's Day. Simont, Marc (1915-), illus. LC 41-18613. 5 p. l., 74 p. incl. col. front., illus. (part col.) 26 cm. 1941. Dodd, Mead & Company.
--Tito, the Pig of Guatemala. Wiese, Kurt (1887-1974), illus. LC 40-6446. 73p. 25cm. 1940. Dodd, Mead and Co.
Jackson, Cherry R.
--Agate Eyes. Morbiim, illus. (Illus., Orig.). 1978. (ISBN 0-9605208-1-3). Sea Urchin.
Jackson, Chrystal M.
--Christmas in Ladybug Village. LC 74-190372. (Illus.). 32 p. 14cm. 1974. Creative House.
--Wendy and the Gypsies. Jackson, Chrystal M., illus. LC 77-88708. (Illus.). 40 p. 27cm. 1970. F. Warne.
Jackson, David
--The Way to the Zoo. (Illus.). 128p. N.D. (ISBN 0-19-276045-9). Oxford U Pr.
Jackson, Donald, jt. auth. see Perry, Shauneille.
Jackson, Dorothy Virginia Steinhauer (1924-)
--Bold Venture: A Novel. LC 52-7462. 245 p. 21cm. 1952. Lippincott.
--Rising Star. LC 55-9504. 181 p. 22cm. 1955. Lippincott.
Jackson, Edgar Newman
--Green Mountain Hero: Based on the Events in the Life of Solomon Story, Eldest Son of Ann Story, Known in History As 'The Mother of the Green Mountain Boys'. Jackson, James O., illus. LC 61-10734. (Based on the Events in the Life of Solomon Story, Eldest Son of Ann Story, Known in History As "The Mother of the Green Mountain Boys'.). 192p. illus. 21cm. 1961. (ISBN 0-8313-0070-1). Lantern Press.
Jackson, Elizabeth Rhodes
--Beacon Hill Children: Or, Chronicles of the Corey Family. Dee, as told by. Cato, Deane, illus. LC 47-18424. 6 p. l., 218 p. front., plates. 20 cm. 1947. L. C. Page & Company.
--Its Your Fairy Tale You Know. LC 23-896. 5 p. l., 116 p. illus., plates. 23 cm. 1922. B. J. Brimmer Company.
Jackson, Elizabeth Rhodes, retold by.
--Alice in Wonderland. 1973. (ISBN 0-435-23465-X). Heinemann Ed.
Jackson, Ellen B. (1943-)
--The Bear in the Bathtub. Apple, Margot, illus. LC 80-26535. p. cm. c.1981. (ISBN 0-201-04701-2). Addison-Wesley.
--The Bear in the Bathtub. Apple, Margot, illus. LC 84-40744. p. cm. 1985, c.1981. (ISBN 0-201-04701-2). Lippincott.
--The Grumpus Under the Rug. Gustafson, Scott, illus. LC 81-4045. (Illus.). 31 p. 21cm. c.1981. (ISBN 0-695-41626-X). (ISBN 0-695-31626-5). Follett Pub. Co.
Jackson, Eva E (1858-)
--Stories for the Twilight for Young People. LC 12-13483. 153 p. incl. front., illus. plates. 21 cm. 1912. W. B. Rose.
Jackson, Gabrielle Emilie Snow, Mrs. (1861-)
--The Adventures of Tommy Postoffice: The True Story of a Cat. LC 10-20384. 230 p. incl. front., illus. 20 cm. c.1910. E. P. Dutton and Company.
--The Adventures of Tommy Postoffice: The True Story of a Cat. LC 5-33619. 137 p. front., illus. 19 1/2cm. 1905. A. C. McClurg & Co.
--Another Year with Denise and Ned Toodles. (Illus.). (Little Men and Women Ser.). N.D. Henry Altemus Co.
--Another Year with Denise Ned and Toodles, 1 of 21 vols. Relyea, Charles M., illus. LC 5-15694. (Boys & Girls Booklovers Ser.: No. 9). 1904. Set. Henry Altemus Co.
--Big Jack, and other True Stories for Horses. LC 3-22521. 20cm. 181p. 1903. J F Taylor & Co.
--Big Jack, and other True Stories of Horses. N.D. D. Appleton & Co.
--A Blue Grass Beauty. LC 3-27516. ix p., 1 l., 13-130 p. incl. front., pl. 20 cm. (Altemus good times series). c.1903. H. Altemus Company.
--By Love's Sweet Rule: A Story for Girls. LC 6-14554. viii, 9-320 p. front., 3 pl. 20 cm. 1906. The J. C. Winston Company.
--Caps and Capers. (Illus.). (Little Men and Women Ser.). N.D. Henry Altemus & Co.
--Caps and Capers: A Story of Boarding-School Life. Relyea, Charles M., illus. LC 1-24976. 1901. Henry Altemus Company.
--Captain Polly, an Annapolis Co-Ed. LC 11-27804. 5 p. l., 350 p. front. plates. 21 cm. c.1911. E. P. Dutton & Company.
--Captain Polly of Annapolis. LC 10-24302. v p. l l, 280 p. front., pl. 21cm. c.1910. E. P. Dutton.
--The Colburn Prize. N.D. Appleton and Co.
--The Colburn Prize. LC 1-273910. 1 p. l., 120 p. front., plates. 20 cm. 1901. J. F. Taylor & Company.
--Denise and Ned Toodles: A True Story. Relyea, Charles M., illus. LC 98-497. ix p. 1 l. 224 p. incl. illus. plates. front. 20 cm. 1898. The Century Co.
--A Dixie School Girl. LC 14-3174. 239 p. incl. front., plates. 20 cm. c.1913. M. A. Donohue & Co.
--Doughnuts and Diplomas. Relyea, Charles M., illus. LC 2-26346. xiii, 15-352 p. incl. front. plates. 19 cm. c.1902. H. Altemus Company.
--Hope's Messenger. LC 14-3175. 319 p. col. front., col. plates. 20 cm. c.1913. M. A. Donohue & Company.
--The Joy of Piney Hill. Relyea, Charles M., illus. LC 7-295895. ix, 239 p. col. front., 3 col. pl. 20 cm. 1907. D. Appleton and Company.
--Little Comrade, the Story of a Cat, and Other Animal Stories. N.D. D. Appleton and Company.
--Little Comrade: The Story of a Cat, and Other Animal Stories. LC 3-22813. 192 p. front. 20 cm. 1903. J. F. Taylor & Company.
--Little Miss Cricket. LC 5-30271. ix, 249 p. col. front., 3 col. pl. 20 cm. 1905. D. Appleton and Company.
--Little Miss Cricket at School. 1908. D. Appleton & Co.
--Little Miss Cricket's New Home. LC 7-29588. ix, 256 p. col. front., 3 col. pl. 20 cm. 1907. D. Appleton and Company.
--Little Miss Sunshine. N.D. D. Appleton and Company.
--Little Miss Sunshine. LC 2-25165. 418 p. front., plates. 20 cm. 1902. J. F. Taylor & Company.
--Peggy Stewart. LC 11-27652. vii, 302 p. col. front. 20 cm. 1911. The Macmillan Company.
--Peggy Stewart at Home. N.D. The Macmillan Co.
--Peggy Stewart at School. Beard, Alice, illus. LC 12-24620. ix, 333 p. front., plates. 20 cm. 1912. The Macmillan Company.
--Peggy Stewart: Debutante. N.D. G.P. Putnam's Sons.
--Peggy Stewart,. Navy Girl, at Home. LC 20-213364. vii, 302 p. col. front. 20 cm. 1920. G. P. Putnam's Sons.
--Peggy Stewart,. Navy Girl, at School. LC 21-4905. vii, 333 p. 20 cm. 1921. G. P. Putnam's Sons.
--Peterkin. Parrish, Frederick Maxfield (1870-1966), illus. LC 12-21619. 5 p. l., 9-75 p. col. front. 25 cm. 1912. Duffield and Company.
--Pretty Polly Perkins. 293p. 1915. The Century Co.
--Pretty Polly Perkins. Relyea, Charles M., illus. LC 5749. viii p., 2 l., 298 p. incl. plates. front., 20 cm. 1900. The Century Co.
--Silverheels. LC 17-30276. 148 p. front., plates. 20 cm. c.1917. George H. Doran Company.
--Sunlight and Shadow. LC 6-32354. 5 p. l., 241 p. col. front. 3 col. pl. 20 cm. 1906. D. Appleton and Company.
--Three Graces. Relyea, Charles M., illus. LC 3-22821. vii p., 1 l., 251 p. front., 3 pl. 21 cm. 1903. D. Appleton and Company.
--Three Graces at College: Sequeal to Three Graces. Relyea, Charles M., illus. 20cm. 271p. 1904. D. Appleton and Company.
--Three Little Women: A Story for Girls. LC 8-330071. 317 p. incl. front. 3 pl. 20 cm. c.1908. The J. C. Winston Company.
--Three Little Women as Wives. (The New "Three Little Women" Series for Girls). N.D. John C. Winston.
--Three Little Women at Work. (The New "Three Little Women" Series for Girls). 1909. John C. Winston.
--Three Little Women's Success. (The New "Three Little Women" Series for Girls). 1910. John C. Winston.
--Wee Winkles. (Illus.). N.D. Harper & Brothers.

AUTHOR INDEX JACKSON, KAY

--Wee Winkles & Her Friends. Robinson, Rachael, illus. LC 7-30868. 5 p. l., 154 p., 1 l. front. 7 pl. 21 cm. 1907. Harper & Brothers.
--Wee Winkles & Snowball. Hart, Mary Theresa, illus. LC 6-36633. 5 p. l., 146, 1 p. front., 7 pl. 21 cm. 1906. Harper & Brothers.
--Wee Winkles & Wideawake. Hart, Mary Theresa, illus. LC 5-334977. 4 p. l., 152, 1 p. front., 7 pl. 21 cm. 1905. Harper & Brothers.
--Wee Winkles at the Mountains. Robinson, Rachael, illus. 1908. Harper & Brothers.

Jackson, George
--The Adventures of the Jackson Kids. Sanz, Juan C., illus. (Illus.). 80p. (Orig.). (gr. 3-6). 1983. (ISBN 0-913211-00-1). G D Jackson.

Jackson, George L.
--Daddy, Tell Me a Story. Palmgren, Mildred & Thomas, Walter, illus. LC 62-19047. 111p. illus. 22cm. 1962. Pioneer Pub. Co.

Jackson, George Russell
--Ambergris Island: Or, The New El Dorado. LC 7-9474. 1 p. l., v-viii, 9-236 p. 18 cm. 1882. W. A. Evans & Bro.

Jackson, Helen Maria Fiske Hunt, Mrs. (1831-1885)
--Bits of Talk: In Verse and Prose, for Young Folks. LC 4-268644. vi, 7-244 p., 1 l. front. 18 cm. 1904. Little, Brown and Company.
--Bits of Talk: In Verse and Prose, for Young Folks. LC 21-415134. 244 p. incl. front. plates. 15 cm. 1876. Roberts Brothers.
--Cat Stories: Containing Letters fron a Cat" "Mammy Tittleback and Her Family" "The Hunter Cats of Connorloau". LC 4-17810. 3v. in 1 front., plates. 19 cm. 1898. Roberts Brothers.
--The Hunter Cats of Connorloa. 85p. (Cat Stories). N.D. Little, Brown.
--The Hunter Cats of Connorloa. LC 7-10809. 2 p. l., 9-156 p. front., plates. 19 x 15 cm. 1884. Roberts Brothers.
--Letters from a Cat: Pub. by Her Mistress for the Benefit of All Cats and the Amusement of Little Children. Ledyard, Addie, illus. LC 7-10808. 89 p. front., plates. 20 x 15 cm. 1879. Roberts Brothers.
--Letters from a Cat: Published by Her Mistress for the Benefit of All Cats and the Amusement of Little Children. Ledyard, Addie, illus. LC 7-33907. 89 p. incl. front. plates. 19 cm. 1906. Little, Brown, and Company.
--Mammy Tittleback and Her Family. 101p. (Cat Stories). N.D. Little,Brown & Co.
--Mammy Tittleback and Her Family: A True Story of Seventeen Cats. Ledyard, Addie, illus. LC 7-10807. 101 p. front., plates. 19 x 15 cm. 1881. Roberts Brothers.
--Nelly's Silver Mine. (Beacon Hill Bookshelf). N.D. Little, Brown & Co.
--Nelly's Silver Mine: A Story of Colorado Life. LC 75-32183. (Illus.). x, 379 p., 3 leaves of plates. 19cm. (Classics of Children's Literature, 1621-1932). 1976, c.1878. (ISBN 0-8240-2295-5). Garland Pub.
--Nelly's Silver Mine. A Story of Colorado Life. LC 6-28453. 379 p. front., plates. 19 cm. 1906. Little, Brown, and Company.
--Nelly's Silver Mine. A Story of Colorado Life. LC 4-16141. 379 p. front., 3 pl. 18 cm. 1878. Roberts Brothers.
--Nelly's Silver Mine: A Story of Colorado Life. Richards, Harriet Roosevelt, illus. LC 10-24180. 332 p. col. front. pl. 22 1/2cm. c.1910. Little Brown & Co.
--Nelly's Silver Mine: A Story of Colorado Life. Richards, Harriet Roosevelt, illus. LC 24-26906. 4 p. l., 332 p. col. front., col. plates. 23 cm. (Beacon Hill bookshelf). 1924. Little, Brown, and Company.
--Nelly's Silver Mine. A Story of Early Colorado. 1974. The Abbotsford Publishing Company.
--Pansy Billings and Popsy: Two Stories of Girl Life. LC 7-10806. 107 p. front., pl. 20 cm. c.1898. Lothrop Publishing Company.
--Ramona. abr. ed. (gr. 7 up). 1974. (ISBN 0-590-03298-4, Schol Pap). Scholastic Inc.
--Ramona. Stoops, Herbert Morton, illus. N.D. Little Brown & Co.
--Ramona. New ed. Wyeth, Newell Convers (1882-1945), illus. (Illus.). Repr. of 1884 ed. (Wyeth ed). (gr. 6 up). 1939. (ISBN 0-316-45467-2). Little.

Jackson, Holbrook, ed. see Lear, Edward.

Jackson, Jacqueline (1928-)
--Chicken Ten Thousand. Morrow, Barbara, illus. LC 68-15558. (Illus.). 31 p. 1968. Little, Brown.
--The Ghost Boat. 1st ed. Jackson, Jacqueline (1928-), illus. LC 69-11783. (Illus.). 148 p. 21cm. 1969. Little, Brown.
--Julie's Secret Sloth. Henneberger, Robert G. (1921-), illus. LC 53-7311. (Illus.). 186 p. 21cm. 1953. Little, Brown.
--Missing Melinda. 1st ed. Burns, Irene, illus. LC 67-19800. 142 p. 23cm. 1967. Little, Brown.
--The Orchestra Mice. Morrow, Robert (1917-), illus. LC 74-102103. (Illus.). 29 p. 1970. Reilly & Lee Books.
--The Paleface Redskins. 1st ed. Jackson, Jacqueline (1928-), illus. LC 58-8485. (Illus.). 275 p. 22cm. 1958. Little, Brown.
--Spring Song. 1st ed. Jackson, Sumner A., ed. Morrow, Barbara, illus. LC 73-79052. (Illus.). 31 p. 26cm. 1968, c.1969. (ISBN 0-87338-040-1). Kent State University Press.
--The Taste of Spruce Gum. 1st ed. Obligado, Lilian Isabel (1931-), illus. LC 66-11004. 212 p. illus. 22 cm. 1966. Little Brown. **Award: (ALA).**

Jackson, Jacqueline (1928-) & Perlmutter, William
--The Endless Pavement. Cuffari, Richard (1925-1978), illus. LC 73-7130. (Illus.). 45 p. 23cm. 1973. (ISBN 0-8164-3105-1). Seabury Press.

Jackson, James William
--A Lost Letter: Or, The Triumph of Patience. LC 9-14413. 2 p. l., 181 p. 20 cm. c.1909. The Standard Publishing Co.

Jackson, Janet
--Who Will Milk My Cow?. Johnson, Audean, illus. LC 64-20349. (Illus.). 29 p. 21cm. (Follett beginning-to-read books). 1964. (ISBN 0-695-89325-4). (ISBN 0-695-49325-6). Follett Pub. Co.

Jackson, Jeannette (1939-) & Jackson, Leon (1942-)
--The Land of Never Ever Say: A Legend. LC 85-23895. p. cm. c.1985. (ISBN 0-935757-00-7). JKL Publishers.

Jackson, Jesse (1908-1983)
--Anchor Man. Spiegel, Doris (1901-), illus. LC 47-11000015. (Illus.). 21cm. 142p. (gr. 5 up). 1947. (ISBN 0-06-022780-X, HarpJ). Har-Row.
--Call Me Charley. (The American Negro 0200494xx). N.D. Friendship Press.
--Call Me Charley. Large-type ed. Spiegel, Doris (1901-), illus. LC 68-1375. (Illus.). 183 p. 29cm. 1945. Harper & Row.
--Call Me Charley. Spiegel, Doris (1901-), illus. LC 45-9807. 5 p. l., 156 p. incl. plates. 21 cm. 1945. Harper & Brothers.
--Charley Starts from Scratch. LC 58-9779. 152 p. 22cm. 1958. Harper.
--The Fourteenth Cadillac. 1st ed. LC 73-180082. vi, 184 p. 22cm. 1972. (ISBN 0-385-08602-4). (ISBN 0-385-08602-4). Doubleday.
--Room for Randy. Nicholas, Frank, illus. LC 57-6164. 136p. illus. 22cm. 1957. Friendship Pr.
--The Sickest Don't Always Die the Quickest. LC 79-131083. 185 p. 22cm. 1971. Doubleday.
--Tessie. James, Harold Laymont (1929-), illus. LC 67-20586. (Illus.). 243p. 22cm. 1968. Har-Row.

Jackson, Kathryn see Garfield, Robert, pseud.

Jackson, Kathryn see Hubbard, Joan, pseud.

Jackson, Kathryn, et al. (1907-)
--My Nursery Tale Book. Scarry, Richard McClure (1919-), illus. (Illus.). (gr. k-3). 1964 (Golden Pr). Western Pub.

Jackson, Kathryn (1907-)
--The Animals' Merry Christmas. Scarry, Richard McClure (1919-), illus. (Little Golden Book). 1958. Golden Press.
--The Animals' Merry Christmas. Scarry, Richard McClure (1919-), illus. LC 72-189455. 68p. col. illus. 31cm. 1972. Golden Press.
--The Animals' Merry Christmas. Scarry, Richard McClure (1919-), illus. LC 50-10262. 96p. (Giant Golden Book: 556). 1950. Simon and Schuster.
--The Animals' Merry Christmas. Scarry, Richard McClure (1919-), illus. (Illus.). 72p. (ps-3). 1950. (ISBN 0-307-63773-5, Golden Pr). (ISBN 0-307-13773-2). Western Pub.
--Around the World with Kao Koala. Benvenuti, G., illus. LC 73-78210. (Illus.). 141 p. 29cm. 1974. (ISBN 0-307-66817-7). Golden Press.
--The Around-the-Year Storybook. Miller, John Parr (1913-), illus. LC 74-154825. (Illus.). 91 p. 31cm. (Giant golden book). 1971. Golden Press.
--The Boss of the Barnyard and Other Barnyard Stories. Scarry, Richard McClure (1919-), illus. (Golden Story Book). 1949. Golden Press.
--The Boss of the Barnyard, and Other Barnyard Stories. Hubbard, Joan, pseud. Scarry, Richard McClure (1919-), illus. LC 49-48822. 124 p. col. illus. 18cm. (A Golden Story Book: 4). 1949. Simon and Schuster.
--The Circus ABC. Miller, John Parr (1913-), illus. LC 55-14341. unpaged. illus. 21cm. (Little Golden Library). 1955. Simon & Schuster.
--The Golden Bedtime Book: Three Hundred and Sixty-Six Original Stories and Poems, One for Every Day of the Year. Scarry, Richard McClure (1919-), illus. LC 55-38521. 236p. illus. 28cm. (Big golden book, 752). 1955. Simon and Schuster.
--Golden Book of Three Hundred Sixty-Five Stories. Scarry, Richard McClure (1919-), illus. 1955. (ISBN 0-307-15557-9, Golden Pr). (ISBN 0-307-65575-X). Western Pub.
--The Golden Circus. Provensen, Alice (1918-) & Provensen, Martin (1916-), illus. LC 50-12199. 29cm. 28p. (Fuzzy Golden Bk.: 444). 1950. Simon and Schuster.
--The Golden Picture Book of School Days: Easy-to-Read Stories and Things to Do. La Mont, Violet, illus. LC 54-14446. 64p. illus. 29cm. (Fun-to-learn golden book, FL-3). 1954. Simon and Schuster.
--A Golden Play Book of Dolls and Toys. Miloche, Hilda & Kane, Wilma, illus. LC 53-1660. 88p. illus. 28cm. (Golden play book, P-3). 1953. Simon and Schuster.
--The Golden Storytime Book of Bedtime Tales. Scarry, Richard McClure (1919-), illus. 1957. Golden Press.
--The Hedgehog's Christmas. Rosenberg, Amye, illus. (Illus.). 16p. (Little Golden Sniff It Bks.). (ps). N.D. (ISBN 0-307-13205-6, Golden Pr). (ISBN 0-307-63205-9). Western Pub.
--The Hedgehogs' Christmas Tree. Rosenberg, Amye, illus. LC 81-84153. (Illus.). 12 p. 22cm. (Little Golden sniff it book). c.1982. (ISBN 0-307-13205-6). Golden Press.
--Here Comes the Parade. Scarry, Richard McClure (1919-), illus. LC 51-13055. unpaged. illus. 21 cm. (Little golden library, 143). 1951. Simon and Schuster.
--The Little Eskimo. Weisgard, Leonard Joseph (1916-), illus. LC 52-10807. unpaged. illus. 21 cm. (Little golden library, 155). 1952. Simon and Schuster.
--Nurse Nancy. Malvern, Corinne (1905-1956), illus. LC 53-8157. unpaged. illus. 21cm. (Little golden library, 154). 1952. Simon and Schuster.
--Pantaloon. Weisgard, Leonard Joseph (1916-), illus. LC 51-11263. unpaged. illus. 21 cm. (Little golden library, 114). 1951. Simon and Schuster.
--The Santa Claus Book: Forty-Three Christmas Stories and Poems. Jackson, Kathryn (1907-), ed. Worcester, Retta, illus. LC 52-12983. 128 p. illus. 28 cm. (Big gloden book, 568). 1952. Simon and Schuster.
--The Story of Christmas with Its Own Advent Calendar. Napoli, Augie, illus. (ps-3). 1973. (ISBN 0-307-15782-2, Golden Pr). Western Pub.
--Tawny Scrawny Lion. Tenggren, Gustaf (1896-1970), illus. LC 52-8697. unpaged. illus. 21 cm. (Little golden library, 138). 1952. (ISBN 0-307-60138-2). Simon and Schuster.
--Tawny, Scrawny Lion. Tenggren, Gustaf (1896-1970), illus. (Illus.). (ps-3). 1952. (ISBN 0-307-60138-2, Golden Pr). Western Pub.
--Wheels. Weisgard, Leonard Joseph (1916-), illus. LC 52-8698. unpaged. illus. 21 cm. (Little golden library, 141). 1952. Simon and Schuster.

Jackson, Kathryn (1907-) & Jackson, Byron (1899-1949)
--African Adventure. N.D. Golden Press.
--Animal Babies. Werber, Adele, illus. LC 47-11889. 42 p. illus. (part col) 21cm. (Little Golden Library, 39). 1947. Simon & Schuster.
--The Big Elephant. Rojankovsky, Feodor Stepanovich (1891-1970), illus. LC 49-11929. 34cm. 30p. (Big Golden Book). 1949. Simon and Schuster.
--The Big Elephant. Rojankovsky, Feodor Stepanovich (1891-1970), illus. (Illus.). 32p. (ps-1). 1974. (ISBN 0-307-62064-6, Golden Pr). Western Pub.
--Big Farmer Big. Rojankovsky, Feodor Stepanovich (1891-1970), illus. LC 49-134. 60, p. col. illus. 32x14cm. 1948. Simon and Schuster.
--Big Farmer Big and Little Farmer Little. Rojankovsky, Feodor Stepanovich (1891-1970), illus. 1948. Simon & Schuster.
--Brave Cowboy Bill. Scarry, Richard McClure (1919-), illus. 1950. Simon & Schuster.
--Busy Timmy. Goldsborough, June (1923-), illus. LC 80-85030. (Illus.). 24 p. 16cm. (First little golden book). c.1982. (ISBN 0-307-10114-2). Golden Press.
--Busy Timmy. Wilkin, Eloise Burns (1904-), illus. LC 48-7820. 21cm. 28p. (The Little Golden Library: No. 50). 1948. Simon and Schuster.
--The Cat Who Went to Sea,and Other Cat Stories. Battaglia, Aurelius (1910-), illus. LC 50-4975. 124 p. col. illus. 19 cm. (Golden story book, 16). 1950. Simon and Schuster.
--Christopher and the Columbus. Gergely, Tibor (1900-1978), illus. LC 51-13056. unpaged. illus. 21 cm. (Little golden library, 103). 1951. Simon and Schuster.
--Circus Stories. LC 49-488940. 18cm. 124p. (A golden story book, 8). (A Golden Story Book: 8). 1949. Simon and Schuster.
--Cowboys and Indians. Tenggren, Gustaf (1896-1970), illus. 1948. Simon & Schuster.
--A Day at the Beach. Malvern, Corinne (1905-1956), illus. LC 51-11262. unpaged. illus. 21 cm. (Little golden library, 110). 1951. Simon and Schuster.
--Duck and His Friends. Scarry, Richard McClure (1919-), illus. LC 50-5794. 20cm. 28p. (Little Golden Book: 81). 1950. Simon and Schuster.
--Duck & His Friends. Scarry, Richard McClure (1919-), illus. (ps-2). 1949. (ISBN 0-307-60081-5, Golden Pr). Western Pub.
--Farm Stories. Tenggren, Gustaf (1896-1970), illus. LC 46-25058. 2 p. l., 9-91, 1 p. illus. (part col.) 33 x 26 cm. (On cover: A Giant golden book). 1946. Simon and Schuster.
--The Golden Treasure Books: Thirty-Four Stories of Fun and Adventure. De Witt, Cornelius Hugh, et al. (1905-), illus. LC 51-8267. 192 p. illus. 28 cm. (Big golden book, 560). 1951. Simon and Schuster.
--Jerry at School. Malvern, Corinne (1905-1956), illus. LC 50-10645. 20cm. 41p. (Little golden book, 94). (Little Golden Library). 1950. Simon & Schuster.
--Kathryn and Byron Jackson's The Big Elephant. Rojankovsky, Feodor Stepanovich (1891-1970), illus. LC 73-77491. (Illus.). 25 p. 30cm. 1973, c.1949. Golden Press.
--Katie the Kitten. Morrill, Leslie H., illus. LC 81-83003. (Illus.). 24 p. 15cm. (First little golden book). c.1982. (ISBN 0-307-10124-X). Golden Press.
--Katie the Kitten. Provensen, Alice (1918-) & Provensen, Martin (1916-), illus. LC 49-8895. 21cm. 28p. (The Little golden library, 75). (The Little Golden Library: 75). 1949. Simon and Schuster.
--Let's Go Fishing. Scarry, Richard McClure (1919-), illus. LC 50-5795. 7 l. col. illus. 22 x 23cm. (A Golden Toy Book). c.1949. Simon & Schuster.
--Little Galoshes. Miller, John Parr (1913-), illus. LC 49-11453. 30cm. 42p. (The Little Golden Library: 68). 1949. Simon and Schuster.
--The Little Trapper. Tenggren, Gustaf (1896-1970), illus. LC 50-6271. 21cm. 41p. (Little Golden Book: 79). 1950. Simon and Schuster.
--Little Yip Yip andHis Bark. Gergely, Tibor (1900-1978), illus. LC 50-7825. 21cm. 42p. (Little Golden Library). 1950. Simon and Shuster.
--More Farmyard Tales. Tenggren, Gustaf (1896-1970), illus. LC 70-856130. (Illus.). 13cm. 189p. (Gold star library). 1970. (ISBN 0-601-07389-4). Hamlyn.
--Mouse's House. Scarry, Richard McClure (1919-), illus. LC 49-833711. 1949. Simon and Schuster.
--My Nursery Tale Book. 1974. (ISBN 0-307-62066-2, Golden Pr). Western Pub.
--My Toy Box. Wilkin, Eloise Burns (1904-), illus. LC 52-30356. unpaged. illus. 21 cm. (See-saw book, 1). 1952. Simon and Schuster.
--Off to School. Malvern, Corinne (1905-1956) & Lamont, Violet, illus. (Giant Little Golden Book). 1958. Golden Press.
--The Party Pig. Scarry, Richard McClure (1919-), illus. LC 54-2629. unpaged. illus. 21cm. (little golden books, 191. 1954. Simon and Schuster.
--Pirates, Ships and Sailors. Tenggren, Gustaf (1896-1970), illus. LC 50-12200. 93 p. col. illus. 34 cm. (Giant golden book, 601). 1950. Simon and Schuster.
--The Rabbit Who Had Four Lucky Feet. Jackson, Kathryn (1907-) & Jackson, Byron (1899-1949), illus. LC 42-24670. 17 p. illus. (part col.) 26 1/2 x 23 1/2 cm. 1942. Simon and Schuster.
--Rob Whitlock, a Pioneer Boy in Old Ohio. De Witt, Cornelius Hugh (1905-), illus. LC 52-16446. 78 p. illus. 19 cm. (Sandpiper books). 1951. Simon and Schuster.
--The Saggy Baggy Elephant. Tenggren, Gustaf (1896-1970), illus. LC 70-143791. (Illus.). 34 p. 33cm. 1971, c.1952. Golden Press.
--The Saggy Baggy Elephant. Tenggren, Gustaf (1896-1970), illus. LC 47-5467. 42 p. illus. (part col.) 21 cm. (little golden library, 36). 1947. Simon and Schuster.
--Tenggren's Cowboys and Indians. Tenggren, Gustaf (1896-1970), illus. LC 79-1907. (Illus.). 96 p. 34cm. (Giant golden book). 1968. Golden Press.
--Tenggren's Cowboys and Indians. Tenggren, Gustaf (1896-1970), illus. LC 48-853125. 33cm. 96p. (giant golden book, 600). (Series: Giant golden books). (A Giant Golden Book). 1948. Simon and Schuster.
--Tenggren's Farm Stories. Tenggren, Gustaf (1896-1970), illus. 1945. Simon & Schuster.
--Tenggren's Farm Stories. Tenggren, Gustaf (1896-1970), illus. (Giant Golden Book: 711). 1946. Simon and Schuster.
--Tenggren's Pirates, Ships, and Sailors. Tenggren, Gustaf (1896-1970), illus. LC 75-156297. (Illus.). 60 p. 31cm. (Big golden book). 1971, c.1950. Golden Press.
--Tenggren's Saggy Baggy Elephant & Tawny Scrawny Lion. new ed. Tenggren, Gustaf (1896-1970), illus. 36p. 1st U.S. edition. (ps-4). 1971. (ISBN 0-307-12039-2, Golden Pr). Western Pub.

Jackson, Kay
--Billy & the Boys. Schor, Narca, illus. (Illus.). 1978. (ISBN 0-685-33041-9). Vantage.

Jackson, Kim
--First Day of School. Goodman, John, illus. LC 84-8631. (Illus.). 32p. (Giant First Start Reader Ser.). (gr. k-2). 1985. (ISBN 0-8167-0359-0). (ISBN 0-8167-0439-2). Troll Assocs.
Jackson, Leon, jt. auth. see Jackson, Jeannette.
Jackson, Leroy Freeman (1881-)
--The Animal Show. Grider, Dorothy (1915-), illus. (Illus.). (ps-k). N.D. (ISBN 0-528-88822-6). Rand.
--Animal Show and Other Peter Patter Rhymes. 1965. (ISBN 0-8382-0048-6, Hale Giant Books). E. M. Hale and Company.
--The Animal Show And Other Peter Patter Rhymes. Grider, Dorothy (1915-), illus. LC 67-4787. 1v. (unpaged) col. illus. 33cm. (Rand McNally giant bk.). c.1965. Rand McNally.
--Billy Be Nimble. (The Uncle Owl Ser.). N.D. Rand McNally.
--Billy Bumpkins. (The Uncle Owl Ser.). N.D. Rand McNally.
--Hinky Pinky. (The Uncle Owl Ser.). N.D. Rand McNAlly.
--The Jolly Jingle Book. McKinley, Clare, illus. LC 51-31793. unpaged. illus. 17 cm. (Rand McNally book-elf junior, 667). 1951. Rand McNally.
--The Jolly Jingle Picture Book. Eger, Ruth Caroline, illus. LC 38-1049. 96 p. incl. col. front., illus. (part col.) 31 cm. 1937. Rand, McNally & Company.
--Peter Patter Book: Rimes for Children. LC 32-25168. 224 p. incl. col. front., illus. (part. col.) 20 cm. c.1932. Rand McNally & Company.
--The Peter Patter Book: Rimes for Children. Wright, Blanche Fisher (1878-), illus. LC 19-260258. 110 p. incl. col. front., col. illus. 31 cm. (On verso of half-title: Classics new and old for children). c.1918. Rand, McNally & Co.
--The Peter Patter Book: Rimes for Children. Wright, Blanche Fisher (1878-), illus. LC 25-24374. 215 p. incl. col. front., illus. (part col.) 22 cm. c.1925. Rand, McNally & Company.
--Pink Lemonade & Other Peter Patter Rhymes. (Illus.). (gr. k-2). 1965. (ISBN 0-8382-0660-3). Hale.
--Pink Lemonade And Other Peter Patter Rhymes. Grider, Dorothy (1915-), illus. LC 66-14019. iv. (unpaged) col. illus. 23cm. (Rand McNally, giant bk.). 1966, c.1965. Rand McNally.
--Pink Lemonade & Other Stories. Grider, Dorothy (1915-), illus. (Illus.). (ps-k). 1966. (ISBN 0-528-88813-7). Rand.
--Playtime Rhymes. Eger, Ruth Caroline, illus. N.D. G.P. Putnam's Sons.
--Rimskittle's Book. Eger, Ruth Caroline, illus. LC 26-15413. 110 p. incl. col. front., illus. (part col.) 31 cm. (Classics new and old for children). c.1926. Rand, McNally & Company.
Jackson, Linda
--Petey. Buck, Dorothy, illus. LC 42-22145. 2 p. l., 56 p., 1 l. incl. col. front., col. illus. 22 x 18 1/2 cm. 1942. Harcourt, Brace and Company.
Jackson, Lora Ziesel, Mrs.
--Around the Clock: A Story About Telling Time. Martin, Miles J., photos by. LC 37-36392. 56 p. illus. 26 cm. c.1937. Grosset & Dunlap.
Jackson, Louise Allen (1937-)
--Grandpa Had a Windmill, Grandma Had a Churn. Ancona, George (1929-), photos by. LC 77-23313. (Illus.). 32 p. c.1977. (ISBN 0-8193-0873-0). Parents' Magazine Press.
--Over on the River. Ancona, George (1929-), photos by. LC 79-23262. (Illus.). 36 p. c.1980. (ISBN 0-688-41945-3). (ISBN 0-688-51945-8). Lothrop, Lee & Shepard Books.
Jackson, Lucie E.
--The Abbey on the Moor. (Illus.). 1900. Thomas Nelson & Sons.
--Feadora's Failure. Macfarlane, J., illus. LC 7-22917. 2 p. l., 9-253 p. front., plates. 20 cm. c.1907. D. McKay.
Jackson, Mary Coleman
--Climb to the Crow's Nest. D'Adamo, Anthony, illus. LC 57-11024. (Illus.). 80 p. 21cm. 1957. (ISBN 0-695-41430-5). Follett Pub. Co.

Jackson, Maud Cies (1885-)
--The Code of Bar-Q Ranch. LC 48-1242. 94 p. 18 cm. 1945, c.1946. Wartburg Press.
--Joe Clown's Trix. Schminke, Arthur F., illus. LC 55-19321. 83p. illus. 20cm. 1954. Wartburg Press.
--Plays and Recitations for Tots: For the First Grade and Preschool Ages. LC 39-6979. 115 p. 18 cm. c.1938. T. S. Denison.

Jackson, Myrtle Cook
--The Butternut Tree. LC 70-125920. (Illus.). 64 p. 21cm. 1970. Christopher Pub. House.

Jackson, O. B., pseud., see Jackson, Caary Paul.

Jackson, O. B., pseud. (1902-)
--Basketball Comes to North Island. Jackson, Caary Paul. Geer, Charles Hand (1922-), illus. LC 63-18543. 128 p. illus. 21 cm. 1963. McGraw-Hill.
--Southpaw in the Mighty Mite League. Jackson, Caary Paul. Geer, Charles Hand (1922-), illus. LC 65-255449. 128p. illus. 21cm. c.1965. Whittlesey-McGraw.

Jackson, Peter
--The Penny Puppy and Other Dog Stories. Battaglia, Aurelius (1910-), illus. (Golden Story Book). 1949. Golden Press.
--The Penny Puppy and Other Dog Stories. Battaglia, Aurelius (1910-), illus. (Golden Story Book). 1949. Simon and Schuster.
Jackson, Phyllis Wynn
--Victorian Cinderella: The Story of Harriet Beecher Stowe. Means, Elliott, illus. LC 48-6479. 296 p. illus. 21 cm. 1947. Holiday House.
Jackson, Richard Webber (1935-)
--Douglas Saves the Day. Lomoda, Beverly, illus. LC 64-14035. 32 p. col. illus. 24 x 31cm. 1964. Macmillan.
--A Year Is a Window. Blegvad, Erik (1923-), illus. LC 62-15921. unpaged. illus. 19 cm. (A Sense and nonsense book). 1963. Doubleday.
Jackson, Robert Blake (1926-)
--Classic Cars. LC 73-7530. (Illus.). 64p. (gr. 4-6). 1974. (ISBN 0-8098-2094-3). Walck.
Jackson, Sally, pseud., see Kellogg, Jean Defrees.
Jackson, Sally, pseud. (1916-1978)
--Is This Your Dog. Kellogg, Jean Defrees. Martin, Dick (1927-), illus. (Illus.). (ps-3). 1962. Reilly & Lee.
--Littlest Skater. Kellogg, Jean Defrees. Martin, Dick (1927-), illus. (Illus.). (ps-3). 1961. Reilly & Lee.
--The Littlest Star. Kellogg, Jean Defrees. Martin, Dick (1927-), illus. 32p. 1961. Reilly & Lee Company.
Jackson, Shirley (1919-1965)
--The Bad Children: A Play in One Act for Bad Children. LC 60-23482. 36p. illus. 18cm. 1959. Dramatic Pub. Co.
--Famous Sally. Slackman, Charles B. (1934-), illus. LC 66-9518. (Illus.). 46 p. 22cm. 1966. Harlin Quist; Distributed by Crown Publishers.
--Life Among the Savages. 24p. (gr. 7-12). 1969 (StarLine). Schol Bk Serv.
--Nine Magic Wishes. 1963. MacMillan Co.
--Nine Magic Wishes. Fox, Lorraine (1922-1976), illus. LC 63-8302. 43 p. illus. 30cm. 1963. Crowell-Collier Press.
--Raising Demons. 320p. (gr. 7-12). 1969 (StarLine). Schol Bk Serv.
Jackson, Stanley
--Tony's Railway Gift. N.D. Frederick Warne & Co.
Jackson, Sumner A., ed. see Jackson, Jacqueline.
Jackson, Thomas
--Stories About Animals. (Illus.). 253p. N.D. Cassell, Petter, Galpin.
Jacob, Helen Pierce (1927-)
--The Diary of the Strawbridge Place. LC 77-22713. 159 p. 22cm. 1978. (ISBN 0-689-30619-9). Atheneum.
--A Garland for Gandhi. Sader, Lillian, illus. LC 68-21993. (Illus.). 47 p. 27cm. 1968. Parnassus Press.
--The Secret of the Strawbridge Place. 1st ed. Delaney, Antoinette, illus. LC 75-23199. (Illus.). 211 p. 22cm. 1976. (ISBN 0-689-30504-4). Atheneum.
Jacob, Piers Anthony Dillingham see Anthony, Piers, pseud.
Jacobi, Elizabeth P.
--The Adventures of Andris. Benedek, Kata, illus. LC 29-18263. 7 p. l., 124, 1 p. incl. illus., pl. col. front. 23 cm. 1929. The Macmillan Company.
Jacobi, Frederick, Jr. (1921-), ed. see Grimm, Jakob Ludwig Karl (1785-1863) & Grimm, Wilhelm Karl.
Jacobs, A. Gertrude, compiled by.
--The Chinese-American Song and Game Book. Chao, Shih-Chen & Hsu, Ching-Yi, illus. Mather, Richard, contrib. by. LC 44-598. 96 p. incl. front. (port.) illus. (part col.) 23 x 20 cm. 1944. A. S. Barnes and Company, Inc.
Jacobs, Alice M.
--Knights of the Wing. N.D. D. Appleton-Century Co.
--Leonard: The Kangaroo Who Had a Hearing Aid. 1983. (ISBN 0-8062-1889-4). Carlton.
Jacobs, Allan Duane (1934-) & Jacobs, Leland Blair (1907-)
--Behind the Circus Tent. Baltzer, Hans (1900-), illus. LC 67-157033. (Illus.). 1 v. (unpaged). 1967. Lerner.
Jacobs, Allan Duane (1934-) & Jacobs, Leland Blair (1907-), eds.
--Arithmetic in Verse and Rhyme. Oechsli, Kelly (1918-), illus. LC 76-141256. (Illus.). 63 p. 24cm. (A Reading shelf book). 1971. (ISBN 0-8116-4109-0). Garrard Pub. Co.
--Sports and Games in Verse and Rhyme. DeLara, George, illus. LC 74-18274. (Illus.). 64 p. 24cm. 1975. (ISBN 0-8116-4118-X). Garrard Pub. Co.
Jacobs, Anita
--Where Has Deedie Wooster Been All These Years?. A Novel. LC 81-65493. p. cm. 224p. 1981. (ISBN 0-440-09461-5). Delacorte Press.
Jacobs, Beth
--Look to the Mountains. LC 63-16794. 192 p; 21 cm. 1963. J. Messner.
Jacobs, Caroline Elliott Hoogs, Mrs. (1835-1916) & Richards, Lela Horn, Mrs. (1870-)
--Blue Bonnet in Boston: Or, Boarding-School Days at Miss North's. Goss, John, illus. LC 14-145459. 4 p. l., 386 p. front., plates. 20 cm. (Blue Bonnet series). 1914. The Page Company.
--Blue Bonnet Keeps House: Or, The New Home in the East. Goss, John, illus. LC 16-7663. 4 p. l., 346 p. front., plates. 20 cm. (Blue Bonnet series). 1916. The Page Company.
--Blue Bonnet's Ranch Party. Goss, John, illus. LC 12-16851. 4 p. l., 305 p. front., plates. 20 cm. 1912. L. C. Page & Company.
--Joan's California Summer. LC 17-30039. 308 p. front., plates. 20 cm. c.1917. G. W. Jacobs & Co.
--Joan's California Summer. (The Joan Bks.). N.D. Macrae Smith.

Jacobs, Caroline Emilia see Elliott, Emilia, pseud.

Jacobs, Caroline Emilia (1872-1909)
--Bab's Christmas at Stanhope. Elliot, Emilia, pseud. (Illus.). (The Cosy Corner Ser.). N.D. The Page Company.
--A Christmas Promise. Elliott, Emilia, pseud. Bruce, Josephine, illus. LC 16-954900. 4 p. l., 60 p. front., plates. 19 cm. (cosy corner series). 1915. The Page Company.
--The Christmas Surprise Party. Elliot, Emilia, pseud. (Illus.). (The Cosy Corner Ser.). N.D. The Page Company.
--Joan of Juniper Inn. Elliott, Emilia, pseud. LC 7-27610. 395 p. front., 4 pl. 21 cm. 1907. G. W. Jacobs & Company.
--Joan of Juniper Inn. Elliott, Emilia, pseud. (The Joan Bks.). N.D. Macrae Smith.
--Joan's Jolly Vacation. Elliott, Emilia, pseud. LC 9-26955. 335 p. front., 4 pl. 20 cm. 1909. G. W. Jacobs & Company.
--Joan's Jolly Vacation. Elliott, Emilia, pseud. (The Joan Bks.). N.D. Macrae Smith.
--Patricia. Elliott, Emilia, pseud. LC 10-163275. 5 p. l., 3-168 p. 21 cm. 1910. G. W. Jacobs & Co.
--Patricia. Elliott, Emilia, pseud. (The Joan Bks.). N.D. Macrae Smith.
--The S. W. F. Club. Elliott, Emilia, pseud. LC 12-19326. 5 p. l., 3-251 p. front., plates. 20 cm. 1912. G. W. Jacobs & Co.
--S. W. F. Club. Elliott, Emilia, pseud. (The Joan Bks.). N.D. Macrae Smith.
--A Texas Blue Bonnet. Elliott, Emilia, pseud. Goss, John, illus. LC 10-25218. 4 p. l., 421 p. front., plates. 20 cm. 1910. L. C. Page & Company.
Jacobs, Dee (1934-)
--Laura's Gift. Karlsson, Kris, illus. LC 81-117033. (Illus.). 58 p. 24cm. c.1980. (ISBN 0-938628-01-1). (ISBN 0-938628-00-3). Oriel Press.
Jacobs, Don (1946-)
--Happy Exercise: An Adventure into a Fit World. Speidel, Sandy, illus. LC 80-23547. (Illus.). 47 p. 26cm. c.1981. (ISBN 0-89037-170-9). Anderson World.
Jacobs, Emma Atkins (1885-)
--Chance to Belong. Liebman, Oscar (1919-), illus. LC 53-8967. (Illus.). 214p. (gr. 7-9). 1953. (ISBN 0-03-065255-3). HR&W.
--Far West Summer. Doremus, Robert (1913-), illus. LC 49-111541. 213 p. front 21cm. 1949. Aladdin Books.
--For Each a Dream. 1st ed. Ilsley, Velma Elizabeth (1918-), illus. LC 58-6515. (Illus.). 189 p. 21cm. 1958. Holt.
--The Secret Spring: A Mystery Romance for Young People. Ayer, Margaret (0000-1981), illus. LC 44-47005. 4 p. l., 3-234 p. col. front., illus. 22 cm. 1944. The John C. Winston Company.
--Smooth Sailing. 1st ed. Allen, Courtney, illus. LC 54-10386. (Illus.). 214 p. 21cm. 1954. Holt.
--Trailer Trio. Doane, Pelagie (1906-1966), illus. LC 42-23551. 4 p. l., 280 p. col. front., illus. 22 1/2 cm. 1942. The John C. Winston Company.
--Vicki's Mysterious Friend. Maclaughlin, Jean, illus. LC 47-11802. xi, 210 p. illus. 22 cm. 1947. J. C. Winston Co.
Jacobs, Flora Gill (1918-)
--The Doll House Mystery. Gruen, Chuck, illus. LC 58-7003. (Illus.). 96 p. 20cm. 1958. Coward-McCann.
--The Haunted Birdhouse. Lonette, Reisie Dominee (1924-), illus. LC 78-105575. (Illus.). 87 p. 20cm. 1970. Coward-McCann.
--The Toy Shop Mystery. Sofia, pseud. (1926-), illus. Zeiger, Sophia. LC 60-6883. (Illus.). 96 p. 20cm. 1960. Coward-McCann.
Jacobs, Frances E
--Finger Plays and Action Rhymes. Owen, Lura & Owen, Courtney, photos by LC 41-18892. 5 p. l., 53 p. illus. 19 x 26 cm. c.1941. Lothrop, Lee and Shepard Company.
Jacobs, Francine (1935-)
--The King's Ditch: A Hawaiian Tale. Pinkney, Jerry (1939-), illus. LC 71-127947. (Illus.). 48 p. 24cm. 1971. (ISBN 0-698-30209-5). Coward, McCann & Geoghegan.
--The Legs of the Moon. Negri, Rocco (1932-), illus. LC 74-132592. (Illus.). 48 p. 1971. Coward, McCann & Geoghegan.
--Supersaurus. Tyler, D. D., illus. (Illus.). 48p. 1982. (ISBN 0-399-61150-9). Putnam Pub Group.
Jacobs, Frank
--Alvin Steadfast on Vernacular Island. Gorey, Edward St. John (1925-), illus. LC 65-23967. 64p. c.1965. Dial.
--Alvin Steadfast on Vernacular Island. Gorey, Edward St. John (1925-), illus. LC 78-20692. (Illus.). 64 p. 23cm. 1979. (ISBN 0-8008-0173-3). (ISBN 0-8008-0174-1). Taplinger Pub. Co.
Jacobs, Helen Hull (1908-)
--Adventure in Bluejeans. LC 47-11471. 216 p. 21 cm. 1947. Dodd, Mead.
--Courage to Conquer. LC 67-26157. viii, 208 p. 21cm. 1967. Dodd, Mead.
--Judy: Tennis Ace. LC 51-11033. 212 p. 21 cm. 1951. Dodd, Mead.
--Laurel for Judy. LC 45-7530. 4 p. l., 211 p. 19 cm. 1945. Dodd, Mead & Company.
--Proudly She Serves!. The Realistic Story of a Tennis Champion Who Becomes a Wave. LC 53-5470. 214p. 21cm. (Career books). 1953. Dodd, Mead.
--The Tennis Machine. LC 76-176118. 220 p. 22cm. 1972. (ISBN 0-684-12687-7). Scribner.
Jacobs, Howard (1908-), ed. see Trosclair.
Jacobs, James Vernon (1898-)
--Everyday Stories. LC 43-147745. 192 p. illus. 20 cm. 1943. The Standard Publishing Company.
--Junior Stories for Today. LC 37-4379. 171 p. illus. 20 cm. c.1937. The Standard Publishing Company.
Jacobs, Joseph, jt. auth. see Peppe, Rodney Darrell.
Jacobs, Joseph (1854-1916), ed. see Aesopus.
Jacobs, Joseph (1854-1916), ed. see Batten, John Dickson.
Jacobs, Joseph (1854-1916), ed. see Cole, Henry, Sir.
Jacobs, Joseph, jt. ed. see Haviland, Virginia.
Jacobs, Joseph, jt. ed. see Stern, Simon.
Jacobs, Joseph, jt. ed. see Stobbs, William.
Jacobs, Joseph (1854-1916), ed.
--The Book of Wonder Voyages. Batten, John Dickson (1860-1932), illus. xii p., 1 l., 230 p. front., illus. 21 cm. 1919. G. P. Putnam's Sons.
--The Book of Wonder Voyages. Batten, John Dickson (1860-1932), illus. xii p., 1 l., 230p. front., illus. 21cm. 1967. Putnam.
--The Book of Wonder Voyages. Batten, John Dickson (1860-1932), illus. LC 18-8478. xii, 224 p. front., illus., plates. 23 cm. 1896. The Macmillan Company.
--The Book of Wonder Voyages. Batten, John Dickson (1860-1932), illus. LC 67-30376. (Illus.). viii, 224 p. 22cm. (Legacy library facsimile). 1967. University Microfilms.
--The Buried Moon. Jeffers, Susan, illus. LC 75-86637. (Illus.). 31 p. 26cm. 1969. Bradbury Press.
--Celtic Fairy Tales. (Illus.). N.D. Penn Publishing Co.
--Celtic Fairy Tales. N.D. Roy Pub.
--Celtic Fairy Tales. Batten, John Dickson (1860-1932), illus. xii p., 1 l., 328 p. front., illus., plates. 19 cm. 1899. A. L. Burt Company.
--Celtic Fairy Tales. Batten, John Dickson (1860-1932), illus. (The Fairy Library). N.D. A. L. Burt Co.
--Celtic Fairy Tales. Batten, John Dickson (1860-1932), illus. (Illus.). xiv, 267 p. 22cm. 1968. Dover Publications.
--Celtic Fairy Tales. Batten, John Dickson (1860-1932), illus. LC 23-265865. 5 p. l., v-xii p., 1 l., 291 p. incl. front., illus. 21 cm. (The fairy library. 3). N.D. G. P. Putnam's Sons.
--Celtic Fairy Tales. Batten, John Dickson (1860-1932), illus. xiv, 267p. illus. 22cm. (Dover bk., T1826 rebound). 1968. (ISBN 0-8446-2302-4). Peter Smith.
--Celtic Folk & Fairy Tales. Batten, John Dickson (1860-1932), illus. (Illus.). (gr. 3-6). 1905. (ISBN 0-399-20029-0). Putnam.
--Coo-My-Dove, My Dear. Sewall, Marcia (1935-), illus. LC 76-4467. (Illus.). 32 p. 27cm. 1976. (ISBN 0-689-30543-5). Atheneum.
--The Crock of Gold: A Picture Book. Stobbs, William (1914-), illus. LC 70-149499. (Illus.). 28 p. 1971. (ISBN 0-695-80213-5). Follett Pub. Co.

--English Fairy Tales. (Illus.). N.D. (ISBN 0-8446-2303-2). Peter Smith Publisher, Inc.
--English Fairy Tales. Batten, John Dickson (1860-1932), illus. (The Fairy Library). N.D. A. L. Burt Co.
--English Fairy Tales. Batten, John Dickson (1860-1932), illus. LC 67-19703. (Illus.). xii, 261 p. 22cm. 1967. Dover Publications.
--English Fairy Tales. 3d ed., rev. Batten, John Dickson (1860-1932), illus. LC 4-10446. xiv p., 1 l., 261 p. front., illus., 7 pl. 22 cm. 1902. G. P. Putnam's Sons; Etc., Etc.
--English Fairy Tales. Batten, John Dickson (1860-1932), illus. LC 38-276922. 3 p. l., 296 p. col. front., illus. 22 cm. 1932. Grosset & Dunlap.
--English Fairy Tales. Batten, John Dickson (1860-1932), illus. xi, 261p. illus. 22cm. (Dover bk. rebound). 1968. Peter Smith.
--English Fairy Tales. 3d, rev. ed. Batten, John Dickson (1860-1932), illus. LC 67-15749. (Illus.). 277 p. 21cm. 1967. Schocken Books.
--English Fairy Tales. Gill, Margery Jean (1925-), illus. LC 76-25040. (Illus.). 159 p. 19cm. (Puffin books, PS466). 1970. (ISBN 0-14-030466-5). Penguin.
--English Folk & Fairy Tales. Batten, John Dickson (1860-1932), illus. (Illus.). (gr. 3-6). 1904. (ISBN 0-399-20045-2). Putnam.
--Europa's Fairy Book. Batten, John Dickson (1860-1932), illus. LC 16-2959. xv, 264 p. incl. illus. plates. front. 21 cm. 1916. G. P. Putnam's Sons.
--Europa's Fairy Tales. Batten, John Dickson (1860-1932), illus. N.D. G. P. Putnam's Sons.
--European Folk and Fairy Tales. Batten, John Dickson (1860-1932), illus. LC 67-24160. xv, 264 p. illus. 21 cm. 1967, c.1916. Putnam.
--Gaelic Fairy Tales. N.D. Putman & Sons.
--Guleesh: A Picture Story from Ireland. Stobbs, William (1914-), illus. LC 77-165545. (Illus.). 32 p. 27cm. 1972, c.1971. (ISBN 0-695-80036-1). (ISBN 0-695-40036-3). Follett Pub. Co.
--Henny Penny. Stobbs, William (1914-), illus. (Illus.). color ils. 32p. 1st U.S. edition. (Picture Book Ser). (ps-3). 1970. (ISBN 0-695-40112-2). Follett.
--Hereafter This. Galdone, Paul (1914-), illus. LC 72-12677. (Illus.). 32 p. 1973. (ISBN 0-07-022690-3). (ISBN 0-07-022690-3). McGraw-Hill.
--Hudden and Dudden and Donald O'Neary. Burn, Doris (1923-), illus. LC 68-18825. (Illus.). 48 p. 27cm. 1968. Coward-McCann.
--Indian Fairy Tales. LC 4-10447. xiv p., 1 l., 255 p. front., illus., 8 pl. 22 cm. N.D. G. P. Putnam's Sons.
--Indian Fairy Tales. (Illus.). N.D. (ISBN 0-8446-0723-1). Peter Smith Publisher, Inc.
--Indian Fairy Tales. Batten, John Dickson (1860-1932), illus. (The Fairy Library). N.D. A. L. Burt Co.
--Indian Fairy Tales. Batten, John Dickson (1860-1932), illus. LC 68-55534. (Illus.). xiv, 255 p. 22cm. 1969. Dover Publications.
--Indian Folk & Fairy Tales. Batten, John Dickson (1860-1932), illus. (Illus.). (gr. 3-6). 1925. (ISBN 0-399-20100-9). Putnam.
--Jack and the Beanstalk. Gill, Margery Jean (1925-), illus. LC 74-5477. (Illus.). 32 p. 24cm. 1975. (ISBN 0-8098-1221-5). H. Z. Walck.
--Jack the Giant-Killer. Wegner, Fritz (1924-), illus. LC 70-158866. (Illus.). 45 p. 24cm. 1971, c.1970. (ISBN 0-8098-1185-5). H. Z. Walck.
--Johnny-Cake. Brock, Emma Lillian (1886-1974), illus. LC 33-27398. 32p. illus. 20x20cm. 1933. Putnam.
--Johnny-Cake. Stobbs, William (1914-), illus. LC 72-9959. (Illus.). 28 p. 1973, c.1972. (ISBN 0-670-40826-3). Viking Press.
--Joseph Jacobs' the Story of the Three Little Pigs. 1st ed. Cauley, Lorinda Bryan (1951-), illus. LC 79-28422. (Illus.). 32 p. 24cm. 1980. (ISBN 0-399-20733-3). (ISBN 0-399-20732-5). Putnam.
--King of the Cats: A Ghost Story. Galdone, Paul (1914-), illus. LC 79-16659. p. cm. 1980. (ISBN 0-8164-3010-1). Seabury Press.
--King of the Cats: A Ghost Story. Galdone, Paul (1914-) & Galdone, Paul (1914-), illus. LC 79-16659. (Illus.). 32p. (ps-3). 1980. (ISBN 0-395-29030-9, Clarion). HM.
--Lazy Jack. Wilkinson, Barry, illus. (Illus.). color ils. 32p. (ps-3). 1970. (ISBN 0-529-00802-5). (ISBN 0-529-00803-3). Collins-World.
--Lazy Jack: A Picture Book. Wilkinson, Barry, illus. LC 72-89499. (Illus.). 26 p. 1st U.S. edition. 1970, c.1969. World Pub. Co.
--The Magpie's Nest: A Picture Book. Stobbs, William (1914-), illus. LC 74-131903. (Illus.). 28 p. 1970. (ISBN 0-695-80210-0). Follett Pub. Co.
--Master of All Masters. Rockwell, Anne F. (1934-), illus. LC 76-183031. (Illus.). 31 p. (Thistle book). 1972. (ISBN 0-448-21433-4). (ISBN 0-448-21433-4). Grosset & Dunlap.
--Molly Whuppie: An Old English Fairy Tale. Doane, Pelagie (1906-1966), illus. LC 39-27805. 46 p. illus. (part col.) 23 cm. 1939. Oxford University Press.
--More Celtic Fairy Tales. Batten, John Dickson (1860-1932), illus. LC 67-242249. x, 234p. illus. 22cm. 1968. Dover.
--More Celtic Fairy Tales. Batten, John Dickson (1860-1932), illus. LC 4-10448. xii p., 1 l., 234 p. front., illus., 7 pl. 22 cm. 1902. G. P. Putnam's Sons; Etc., Etc.
--More English Fairy Tales. LC 23-108144. 4 p. l., v-xiii, 268 p. incl. front., illus., pl. 20 cm. 1922. G. Putnam's Sons.
--More English Fairy Tales. Batten, John Dickson (1860-1932), illus. LC 67-27547. (Illus.). xii, 243 p. 22cm. 1967. Dover Publications.
--More English Fairy Tales. Batten, John Dickson (1860-1932), illus. xii, 243p. illus. 22cm. (Rebound ed. of Unabridged & unaltered repubn. by Dover of the work orig. pub. . . . in 1894). 1968. (ISBN 0-8446-2305-9). P. Smith.
--More English Fairy Tales. Batten, John Dickson (1860-1932), illus. LC 68-9566. (Illus.). xii, 243 p. 21cm. 1968. Schocken Books.
--More English Folk & Fairy Tales. Batten, John Dickson (1860-1932), illus. (Illus.). (gr. 3-6). 1904. (ISBN 0-399-20172-6). Putnam.
--The Most Delectable History of Reynard the Fox. Calderon, William Frank (1865-1943), illus. Rieff, Phillip, contrib. by. LC 67-15750. xi, 244p. illus. 20cm. (Schocken paperbacks). 1967. Schocken.
--Munachar & Manachar: An Irish Story. Rockwell, Anne F. (1934-), illus. LC 70-127605. (Illus.). 33 p. 1970. Crowell.
--The Pied Piper, and Other Fairy Tales. Hill, James (1914-), illus. 1963. Macmillan.
--Pied Piper & Other Fairy Tales. Hill, James (1914-), illus. (Illus.). (gr. k-3). 1968. (ISBN 0-02-747520-4). Macmillan.
--The Pied Piper and other Tales. Hill, James (1914-), illus. 1963. MacMillan Co.
--Reynard the Fox. (Burt's Home Lib.). N.D. A. L. Burt's Pubs.
--Reynard the Fox. (Illus.). (The Rugby Series for Boys). N.D. A. L. Burt's Pubs.
--The Stars in the Sky: A Scottish Tale. Amtmann, Airdrie, illus. LC 78-11718. p. cm. 1978. (ISBN 0-374-37229-2). Farrar, Straus, and Giroux.
--The Three Sillies & Other Stories. 1967. (ISBN 0-88302-355-5, Peter Possum). Mulberry Pr.
--Tom Tit Tot: An English Folk Tale. Ness, Evaline Michelow, Mrs. (1911-), illus. LC 65-14769. 32p. col. illus. 26cm. c.1965. (ISBN 0-684-20899-7). Scribners. **Awards: (ALA); (RCM).**

Jacobs, Joseph (1854-1916) & Galdone, Paul (1914-), eds.
--The Three Sillies. Galdone, Paul (1914-), illus. LC 80-22197. p. cm. 1981. (ISBN 0-395-30172-6). Clarion Books/Houghton Mifflin.

Jacobs, Joseph (1854-1916) & Turnbull, E. Lucia, eds.
--Celtic Fairy Tales. N.D. Dufour.

Jacobs, Leland Blair, jt. auth. see Jacobs, Allan Duane.

Jacobs, Leland Blair, jt. ed. see Jacobs, Allan Duane.

Jacobs, Leland Blair (1907-)
--Alphabet of Girls. 1st ed. Johnson, John Emil (1929-), illus. LC 69-11810. (Illus.). 40 p. 23cm. 1969. Holt, Rinehart and Winston.
--April Fool!. Cunette, Lou, illus. LC 72-10677. (Illus.). 39 p. 24cm. 1973. (ISBN 0-8116-6728-6). Garrard Pub. Co.
--Good Night: Mr Beetle. Riswold, Gilbert, illus. LC 63-8838. unpaged. illus. 17 x 24 cm. (Little owl book). c.1963. Holt, Rinehart and Winston.
--I Don't, I Do. Carlings, Frank, illus. LC 79-155570. (Illus.). 40 p. 24cm. 1971. (ISBN 0-8116-6705-7). Garrard Pub. Co.
--Is Somewhere Always Far Away?. Johnson, John Emil (1929-), illus. LC 67-10738. (Illus.). 48 p. 1967. Holt, Rinehart and Winston.
--Just Around the Corner. 1st ed. Johnson, John Emil (1929-), illus. LC 64-11626. (Illus.). 41 p. 1964. Holt, Rinehart and Winston.
--Monkey & the Bee. Oechsli, Kelly (1918-), illus. (Golden Beginning Readers). (ps-2). 1969. (ISBN 0-307-61158-2, Golden Pr). Western Pub.
--Old Lucy Lindy. Renfro, Ed, illus. LC 64-12964. 1 v. (unpaged) col. illus. 29cm. (A Young Owl Book). 1964. Holt, Rinehart and Winston.
--What Would You Do?. Carlings, Frank, illus. LC 72-1772. (Illus.). 63 p. 24cm. 1972. (ISBN 0-8116-6963-7). Garrard Pub. Co.

Jacobs, Leland Blair (1907-), ed.
--All About Me: Verses I Can Read. Depper, Hertha, illus. LC 73-155566. (Illus.). 39 p. 23cm. 1971. (ISBN 0-8116-6701-4). Garrard Pub. Co.
--Animal Antics in Limerick Land. Malsberg, Edward, illus. LC 79-151137. (Illus.). 63 p. 24cm. 1971. (ISBN 0-8116-4111-2). Garrard Pub. Co.
--Belling the Cat and Other Stories. Berson, Harold (1926-), illus. LC 61-3071. 22cm. 31p. (Golden Beginning Reader). 1960. Golden Press.
--Delight in Number. Komoda, Kiyoaki (1937-), illus. LC 64-16155. (Illus.). 26. 29cm. (A Young Owl Bk.). 1964. Holt, Rinehart and Winston.
--Funny Bone Ticklers in Verse and Rhyme. Malsberg, Edward, illus. LC 73-3178. (Illus.). 62 p. 24cm. 1973. (ISBN 0-8116-4115-5). Garrard Pub. Co.
--Funny Folks in Limerick Land. Burns, Raymond Howard (1924-), illus. LC 78-142066. (Illus.). 62 p. 24cm. 1971. (ISBN 0-8116-4110-4). Garrard Pub. Co.
--Hello, People!. Malsberg, Edward, illus. LC 72-77469. (Illus.). 63 p. 23cm. 1972. (ISBN 0-8116-6952-1). Garrard Pub. Co.
--Hello, Pleasant Places!. Oechsli, Kelly (1918-), illus. LC 72-77470. (Illus.). 64 p. 23cm. 1972. (ISBN 0-8116-6951-3). Garrard Pub. Co.
--Hello, Year!. Aloise, Frank E., illus. LC 72-77468. (Illus.). 63 p. 23cm. 1972. (ISBN 0-8116-6954-8). Garrard Pub. Co.
--Holiday Happenings in Limerick Land. Malsberg, Edward, illus. LC 72-76327. (Illus.). 64 p. 24cm. 1972. (ISBN 0-8116-4112-0). Garrard Pub. Co.
--Playtime in the City. Oechsli, Kelly (1918-), illus. LC 70-155565. (Illus.). 39 p. 24cm. 1971. (ISBN 0-8116-6700-6). Garrard Pub. Co.
--Poems About Fur and Feather Friends. Aloise, Frank E., illus. LC 79-157847. (Illus.). 40 p. 24cm. 1971. (ISBN 0-8116-6713-8). Garrard Pub. Co.
--Poetry for Autumn. Nagel, Stina (1918-), illus. LC 68-16160. (Illus.). 64 p. 25cm. 1968. Garrard Pub. Co.
--Poetry for Bird Watchers. Schroeder, Ted (1931-1973), illus. LC 70-101303. (Illus.). 64 p. 24cm. 1970. Garrard Pub. Co.
--Poetry for Chuckles and Grins. De Paola, Tomie, pseud. (1934-), illus. De Paola, Thomas Anthony. LC 68-16162. (Illus.). 64 p. 25cm. 1968. Garrard Pub. Co.
--Poetry for Space Enthusiasts. Aloise, Frank E., illus. LC 70-139785. (Illus.). 64 p. 24cm. 1971. (ISBN 0-8116-4108-2). Garrard Pub. Co.
--Poetry for Summer. Stover, Jo Ann (1931-), illus. LC 76-114183. (Illus.). 64 p. 24cm. (Reading shelf book). 1970. Garrard Pub. Co.
--Poetry for Winter. Oechsli, Kelly (1918-), illus. LC 68-16161. (Illus.). 64 p. 24cm. 1970. Garrard Pub. Co.
--Poetry of Witches, Elves, and Goblins. Aloise, Frank E., illus. LC 70-99767. (Illus.). 63 p. 24cm. (Reading shelf book). 1970. Garrard Pub. Co.
--The Read-It-Yourself Storybook. LC 77-154823. (Illus.). 214 p. 28cm. (Deluxe golden book). 1971. Golden Press.
--The Stupid Lion, and Other Stories. Stuecklin, Karl W., illus. LC 68-54982. (Illus.). 32 p. 29cm. (Carousel book). 1969. L. W. Singer Co.

Jacobs, Leland Blair (1907-) & Lucey, Marilyn
--Teeny-Tiny. LC 75-6550. (Illus.). 32 p. 23cm. 1976. (ISBN 0-8116-6070-2). Garrard Pub. Co.

Jacobs, Leland Blair (1907-) & Nohelty, Sally, eds.
--Poetry for Young Scientists. Young, Ed (1931-), illus. LC 64-15427. 1v. (unpaged) col. illus. 24cm. (Young owl bk.). 1964. Holt.

Jacobs, Leland Blair (1907-) & Turner, Jo Jasper, eds.
--Happiness Hill. LC 66-5513. 192p. col. illus. 24cm. (Treasury of lit. readers: Banner ed.). 1966. Merrill.

Jacobs, Linda C. (1943-)
--A Candle, a Feather, a Wooden Spoon. Wright, Kathleen Mary, illus. LC 74-23770. p. cm. (Her Really me!). 1974. (ISBN 0-88436-151-9). (ISBN 0-88436-150-0). EMC Corp.
--Checkmate Julie. Wright, Kathleen Mary, illus. LC 74-23756. p. cm. (Her Really me!). 1974. (ISBN 0-88436-155-1). (ISBN 0-88436-154-3). EMC Corp.
--Ellen the Expert. Snyder, Paul (1923-), illus. LC 73-19715. (Illus.). 38 p. 24cm. (Her Winners all). 1974. (ISBN 0-88436-076-8). (ISBN 0-88436-076-8). EMC Corp.
--Everyone's Watching Tammy. Wright, Kathleen Mary, illus. LC 74-23759. 23cm. 34p. (Her Really me!). 1974. (ISBN 0-88436-153-5). (ISBN 0-88436-152-7). EMC Corp.
--For One-or for All. Snyder, Paul (1923-), illus. LC 73-19713. (Illus.). 38 p. 24cm. (Her Winners all). 1974. (ISBN 0-88436-082-2). (ISBN 0-88436-083-0). EMC Corp.
--Go for Six. Snyder, Paul (1923-), illus. LC 73-19714. (Illus.). 38 p. 24cm. (Her Winners all). 1974. (ISBN 0-88436-078-4). (ISBN 0-88436-078-4). EMC Corp.
--In Tennis, Love Means Nothing. Snyder, Paul (1923-), illus. LC 73-19701. (Illus.). 38 p. 24cm. (Her Winners all). 1974. (ISBN 0-88436-080-6). (ISBN 0-88436-080-6). EMC Corp.
--Will the Real Jeannie Murphy Please Stand Up. Wright, Kathleen Mary, illus. LC 74-23758. 23cm. 34p. (Her Really me!). 1974. (ISBN 0-88436-157-8). (ISBN 0-88436-156-X). EMC Corp.

Jacobs, Louis, Jr. (1921-)
--Cyra-Nose, the Sea Elephant. Jacobs, Louis, Jr. (1921-), illus. LC 72-10185. (Illus.). glossary. 48p. (gr. 2-4). 1973. (ISBN 0-516-07621-3, Elk Grove Bks). Childrens.
--Duncan The Dolphin. Jacobs, Louis, Jr. (1921-), illus. LC 66-16938. 32p illus. 26cm. c.1966. (ISBN [illegible]). Follett.
--The Shapes of Our Land. (Illus.). (gr. 1 up). 1970. (ISBN 0-399-60579-7). Putnam.

Jacobs, W. W.
--Night Watches. 256p. (Century Seafarers). (gr. 6). 1984. (ISBN 0-7126-0335-2). Hippocrene Bks.

Jacobs, William Jay
--Mother, Aunt Susan and Me: The First Fight for Women's Rights. LC 78-25715. (Illus.). 61 p. 24cm. c.1979. (ISBN 0-698-20480-8). Coward, McCann & Geoghegan.

Jacobs, William Wymark (1863-1943)
--The Monkey's Paw. Richardson, I. M, adapted by. Lawn, John, illus. LC 81-19824. (Illus.). 32 p. 24cm. (Famous Tales of Suspense). (gr. 5-9). c.1982. (ISBN 0-89375-628-8). (ISBN 0-89375-629-6). Troll Associates.

Jacobsen, Betty
--Girl Before the Mast. N.D. Charles Scribner's Sons.

Jacobsen, Jacqueline
--The Alligator in My Back Yard. N.D. Carlton Press.

Jacobsen, Sybil Victoria Sutton-Vane (1899-)
--The Black Whippet. Grahame Johnstone, Anne & Grahame Johnstone, Janet, illus. LC 57-59281. 192p. illus. 21cm. 1957. Viking Press.

Jacobsen, Virginia Budd, Mrs. & Daines, Lyman Luther (1883-)
--The Adventures of Jimmy Microbe. Russon, Kay, illus. LC 39-1542. 94 p. illus. 21 cm. c.1937. The Reilly & Lee Co.
--Hitch-Hiking with Jimmy Microbe. 92p. N.D. Reilly & Lee.

Jacobson, Ethel
--Curious Cats. Harrison, Florence (1910-), photos by. LC 68-29038. (Illus.). 64 p. 27cm. 1969. Funk & Wagnalls.

Jacobson, Harold S
--For the Freedom of the Mohawk. Rodgers, Richard H. (1876-1953), illus. LC 31-23202. 320 p. incl. front., illus. 20 cm. 1931. E. P. Dutton & Company, Inc.

Jacobson, Helen
--The First Book of Legendary Beings. Zacks, Lewis, illus. LC 62-7381. 53p. illus. 23cm. 1962. F. Watts.
--The First Book of Mythical Beasts. LC 74-501030. (Illus.). 23cm. 69p. (The First Book Series). 1970. (ISBN 0-85166-043-6). Franklin Watts Ltd.
--The First Book of Mythical Beasts. Zacks, Lewis, illus. LC 60-9387. 69p. illus. (part col.) 23cm. (First books, 128). c.1960. Watts.

Jacobson, Jane
--City, Sing for Me: A Country Child Moves to the City. Rowen, Amy, illus. LC 77-11130. (Illus.). 36 p. 24cm. c.1978. (ISBN 0-87705-358-8). Human Sciences Press.

Jacobson, Millie Bock
--For the Story Hour. LC 29-18416. 98 p. incl. illus., plates. 18 cm. c.1929. Augsburg Publishing House.

Jacobson, V. H.
--Prairie Grove Tales. N.D. Carlton Press.

Jacobson, Viola E., jt. auth. see Lowe, Samuel Edward.

Jacoby, Edith A
--Little Stories for Little People. LC 65-17337. 50 p. 23cm. (William-Frederick juvenile). 1967. William-Frederick Press.

Jacot, Michael (1924-)
--The Last Butterfly. LC 73-16803. 224p. 1974. (ISBN 0-672-51926-7). Bobbs.

Jaeger, Charles De see De Jaeger, Charles.

Jaeger, Cyril Karel Stuart (1912-)
--The Bull That Was Terrifico. Cam, pseud. (1913-), illus. Campbell, Barbara Mary. 1955. Dufour Editions.
--The Bull That Was Terrifico. Cam, pseud. (1913-), illus. Campbell, Barbara Mary. LC 56-10214. unpaged. illus. 23cm. 1st U.S. edition. 1956, c.1955. J. Day Co.
--The Bull That Was Terrifico. Cam, pseud. (1913-), illus. Campbell, Barbara Mary. unpaged. illus. 23cm. 1965. Putnam.
--The Little Banditta. Cam, pseud. (1913-), illus. Campbell, Barbara Mary. 95p. 1957. Dufour Editions.

--The Little Banditta. Cam, pseud. (1913-), illus. Campbell, Barbara Mary. LC 64-9213. 1 v. (unpaged) illus. 23cm. 1964, c.1957. Putnam.
--Niccolo. Fellin, Peter, illus. LC 61-8570. (Illus.). 59 p. illus. 22cm. (Wonderful world book). 1961, c.1959. A. S. Barnes & Company, Inc.
--Pinook. LC 64-9211. 95p. illus. (pt. col.) 23cm. 1964, c.1960. Putnam.

Jaeger, Ina C., ed. see Duras, Marguerite.

Jafa, Manorama
--The Donkey on the Bridge. Bhusan, Reboti, illus. (Illus.). 24p. (Orig.). (gr. k-3). 1980. (ISBN 0-89744-209-1, Pub. by Children's Bk Trust India). Auromere.

Jaffe, Dan (1933-) & Wheeler, Sylvia, eds.
--For Kids-by Kids. 1977. (ISBN 0-933532-13-X). BkMk.

Jaffe, Grace, jt. auth. see Goldman, Phyllis W.

Jaffe, Jennifer
--My Special Father & Me. Selser, Diana, photos by. (Illus.). 48p. (gr. 1-8). 1981. (ISBN 0-915288-43-5). Shameless Hussy.

Jaffe, Rona (1932-)
--Last of the Wizards. Blegvad, Erik (1923-), illus. (Illus.). (gr. k-3). 1961. S&S.

Jaffee, Allan
--Funny Jokes & Foxy Riddles. Jaffee, Allan, illus. 80p. (Orig.). (gr. 7-9). 1968 (Golden Pr). Western Pub.
--Ghastly Jokes. Jaffee, Allan, illus. LC 76-27263. (Illus.). 80 p. 28cm. 1977, c.1976. (ISBN 0-448-12870-5). (ISBN 0-448-13412-8). Grosset & Dunlap.
--The Mad Book of Magic. Jaffee, Allan, illus. N.D. New American Library.
--Witty Jokes & Wild Riddles. Jaffee, Allan, illus. (Illus.). 89p. 1st U.S. edition. (Golden Paperbacks Ser). (gr. 7-9). 1970 (Golden Pr). Western Pub.

Jaffrey, Madhur
--Seasons of Splendor: Tales, Myths & Legends of India. Foreman, Michael (1938-), illus. LC 84-24585. (Illus.). 128 p. 28cm. c.1985. (ISBN 0-689-31141-9). Atheneum.

Jagdfeld, G., jt. auth. see Gernet, Nina Vladimirovna.

Jagendorf, Moritz Adolf, jt. ed. see Clark, Barrett Harper.

Jagendorf, Moritz Adolf (1888-1981)
--Fairyland and Footlights: Five Children's Plays. Haweis, Stephen, illus. LC 25-22588. xiii, 162 p., 1 l. incl. plates. 20 cm. c.1925. Brentano's.
--Folk Stories of the Old South. N.D. (ISBN 0-8149-0000-3). Vanguard Press.
--Folk Stories of the South. Parks, Michael, illus. 1973. Vanguard.
--In the Days of the Han. Neumann, Erwin R. F., illus. LC 36-23523. 5 p. l., 168 p. illus., plates (part col.; part double) 24 cm. 1936. Sutton-House, Ltd.
--The Marvelous Adventures of Johnny Darling. Simon, Howard (1903-1979), illus. 1949. Vanguard Press.
--The Merry Men of Gotham. Miller, Shane (1907-), illus. LC 51-9500. 150p. illus. 21cm. 1950. (ISBN 0-8149-0333-9). Vanguard Press.
--New England Bean-Pot: American Folk Stories to Read and to Tell. McKay, Donald A. (1895-), illus. Botkin, Benjamin Adolf (1901-1975), intro. by. LC 48-9145. xviii, 272p. illus. 22cm. 1948. Vanguard Press.
--Noodlehead Stories from Around the World. Miller, Shane (1907-), illus. LC 57-12266. 302p. illus. 22cm. c.1957. (ISBN 0-8149-0329-0). Vanguard Press.
--Pantomimes for the Children's Theatre. 239p. 1926. Brentano's.
--Penny Puppets, Penny Theatre & Penny Plays. Clark, Fletcher, illus. (Illus.). (gr. 4-9). 1941. (ISBN 0-8238-0071-7). Plays.
--The Priceless Cats: And Other Italian Folk Stories. Fiammenghi, Gioia (1929-), illus. LC 56-120396. 158p. illus. 22cm. 1956. (ISBN 0-8149-0336-3). Vanguard Press.
--Sand in the Bag And Other Folk Stories of Ohio, Indiana, and Illinois. Moment, John, illus. LC 52-11125. (Illus.). 192 p. 22cm. 1952. (ISBN 0-8149-0332-0). Vanguard Press.
--Tales from the First Americans. Endewelt, Jack, illus. LC 78-56057. (Illus.). 96 p. 25cm. (The World Folktale Library). c.1979. (ISBN 0-382-03347-7). Silver Burdett Co.
--Tales of Mystery. Liebman, Oscar (1919-), illus. LC 78-56056. (Illus.). 96 p. 25cm. (The World Folktale Library). c.1979. (ISBN 0-382-03356-6). Silver Burdett Co.
--Tyll Ulenspiegel's Merry Pranks. Eichenberg, Fritz (1901-), illus. LC 38-9511. (Illus.). 188p. (gr. 5-6). 1938. (ISBN 0-8149-0337-1). Vanguard.
--Upstate, Downstate: Folk Stories of the Middle Atlantic States. Simon, Howard (1903-1979), illus. N.D. The Vanguard Press.

Jagendorf, Moritz Adolf (1888-1981), compiled by.
--Nine Short Plays: Written for Young People to Stage. Bufano, Remo, contrib. by. LC 28-25644. xv p., 21., 3-206p. illus. 22cm. 1928. The Macmillan Company.
--One-Act Plays for Young Folks. Shute, James, illus. LC 24-28252. xxix, 220 p., 1 l illus., plates, 20 cm. c.1924. Brentano's.
--One-Act Plays for Young Folks. Shute, James, illus. LC 77-89723. (Illus.). xxix, 220 p., 12 leaves of plates. 20cm. (One-Act Plays in Reprint). 1977. (ISBN 0-8486-2028-3). Core Collection Books.
--Twenty-Five Non-Royalty Plays for Children. LC 42-22429. ix p., 1 l., 317p. 21cm. 1942. Greenberg.
--Twenty Non-Royalty One-Act Ghost Plays. LC 44-4811. 4p. l., 280p. 21cm. 1944. Greenberg.

Jagendorf, Moritz Adolf (1888-1981) & Boggs, Ralph Steele (1901-), eds.
--King of the Mountains: A Treasury of Latin-American Folk Stories. Carybe, illus. LC 60-15073. (Illus.). 313p. (gr. 4-8). 1960. (ISBN 0-8149-0338-X). Vanguard.

Jagendorf, Moritz Adolf (1888-1981) & Lazare, June, eds.
--The Ghost of Peg-Leg Peter And Other Stories of Old New York & Songs of Old New York. Lipinski deOrlov, Lino Sigismondo (1908-), illus. Lipinski, Lino S., pseud. LC 65-17371. 125p. illus. 24cm. 1966. Vanguard.

Jagendorf, Moritz Adolf (1888-1981) & Schrottky, Oleda, eds.
--Plays for Club, School and Camp for Boys and Girls from 8 to 14. Mantell, Charlotte, illus. LC 36-367923. xiv, 135 p. illus. 19 cm. 1935. S. French.

Jagendorf, Moritz Adolf (1888-1981) & Tillhagen, Carl Herman (1906-), eds.
--The Gypsies' Fiddle, and Other Gypsy Tales. Helweg, Hans H. (1917-), illus. LC 56-789113. 186p. illus. 22cm. 1956. Vanguard Press.

Jagendorf, Moritz Adolf (1888-1981) & Weng, Virginia, eds.
--The Magic Boat and Other Chinese Folk Tales. (gr. 4-7). 1980. Vanguard.

Jahn, Mary Lee
--Deedo and Fawny. LC 40-32783. 32 p. col. illus. 23 x 31 cm. c.1940. Oxford University Press.
--Yelly. LC 41-18356. 32 p. col. illus. 23 x 31 cm. c.1941. Oxford University Press.

J. A. K, pseud., see Williams, Annie Bowles.

Jakatas
--More Jataka Tales. Babbit, Ellen C., retold by. Young, Ellsworth, illus. LC 22-9163. 6 p. l., 3-94 p. illus. 21 cm. 1922. The Century Co.

Jakes, John William (1932-)
--Secrets of Stardeep. LC 71-85391. 192 p. 21cm. 1969. Westminster Press.
--The Texans Ride North: The Story of the Cattle Trails. 1st ed. Edrop, Arthur, illus. LC 52-8964. 184 p. illus. 22 cm. (Winston adventure books). 1952. Winston.
--Time Gate. LC 72-175546. 174 p. 21cm. 1972. (ISBN 0-664-32510-6). Westminster Press.

Jalbert, Louise
--The Radish & the Shoe. (Illus.). 40p. (Orig.). (Star & Elephant Ser.). 1984. (ISBN 0-88138-023-7, Pub. by Envelope Bks). Green Tiger Pr.

James, A. W., tr. see Nyblom, Helena Augusta Roed.

James, Bessie Williams Rowland, Mrs. (1895-1974)
--The Happy Animals of Atagahi. Lohse, William R., illus. LC 35-16588. 260 p. incl. col. front., col. illus. 24 cm. c.1935. The Bobbs-Merrill Company.

James, Captain Lew, pseud., see Stratemeyer, Edward L..

James, Captain Lew, pseud. (1862-1930)
--The Collis Express Robbers: Or, Hunting Down Two Desperate Criminals. Stratemeyer, Edward L.. (Log Cabin Library: No. 193). 1892. Street & Smith.
--Cool Dan, the Sport: Or, The Crack Shot of Creede. Stratemeyer, Edward L.. (Log Cabin Library: No. 180). 1892. Street & Smith.
--Cool Dan the Sport's Contest: Or, Fighting the Creede Combination. Stratemeyer, Edward L.. (Log Cabin Library: No. 210). 1893. Street & Smith.
--Cool Dan the Sport's Wonderful Nerve: Or, The Madman's Matchless Mine. Stratemeyer, Edward L.. (Log Cabin Library: No. 190). 1892. Street & Smith.
--Crazy Bob, the Terror of Creede: Or, Cool Dan the Sport again to the Front. Stratemeyer, Edward L.. (Log Cabin Library: No. 186). 1892. Street & Smith.
--Ouray Jack, the Go-It-Lively Sport: Or, A Winner from the Start. Stratemeyer, Edward L.. (Log Cabin Library: No. 211). 1893. Street & Smith.
--Straight Flush Lou, the Man from Denver: Or, Playing for a Triple Stake. Stratemeyer, Edward L.. (Log Cabin Library: No. 217). 1893. Street & Smith.
--Two Old Sports: Or, Pards in Every Deal. Stratemeyer, Edward L.. (Log Cabin Library: No. 213). 1893. Street & Smith.

James, Chester Le Roy (1912-)
--Talking Letters. LC 47-194308. cover-title, 56 p. col. illus. 27 1/2 cm. c.1946. Litho-Central Printing Service.

James, E. B.
--Dangerous Holiday. 164p. 1963. Tri-Ocean Books.

James, Elizabeth, jt. auth. see Barkin, Carol.

James, Emily
--The Chipmunks in Alvin the Angel. Cole, Corny, illus. LC 84-17983. p. cm. 1985. (ISBN 0-394-87206-1). Random House.

James, Florence, jt. auth. see Cusack, Ellen Dymphna.

James, Florence Alice Price Mrs. see Warden, Florence, pseud.

James, Frederick, pseud., see Eckrich, James Frederick.

James, G.
--Green Willow and Other Fairy Tales. (Folk Lore and Fairy Tales). (MacMillan Bks. For Boys & Girls). (gr. 4-6). N.D. MacMillan Bks.

James, Gail Elder
--Fredia Skunk Takes Her Children Adventuring: A Story for Children. LC 51-4227. 63 p. illus. 23 cm. 1951. Exposition Press.

James, George Payne Rainford (1801-1860)
--Forest Days. Jackson, Alice F., retold by. (Illus.). (Classics Retold to Children). N.D. George W. Jacobs & Co.

James, Grace
--Green Willow & Other Fairy Tales. Goble, Warwick, illus. N.D. Macmillan.

James, Grace, jt. auth. see Hearn, Lafcadio.

James, Harry Clebourne (1896-1978)
--A Day With Honau: A Hopi Indian Boy. 1959. (ISBN 0-516-08050-4). Melmont Publishers.
--A Day with Honau: A Hopi Indian Boy. Perceval, Don Louis (1908-), illus. LC 57-13620. 31 p. illus. 21 x 23cm. 1957. Melmont Pub.
--A Day with Poli: A Hopi Indian Girl. Perceval, Don Louis (1908-), illus. LC 57-13621. 31 p. 21 x 23 cm. 1957. Melmont Pub.
--Grizzly Adams. Eckart, Frances, illus. LC 63-9705. (Illus.). 127 p. 22cm. (Frontiers of America). 1963. (ISBN 0-516-03329-8). Childrens Press.
--Ovada: An Indian Boy of the Grand Canyon. Perceval, Don Louis, illus. LC 68-30702. (Illus.). 46 p. 27cm. 1969. Ward Ritchie Press.

James, Hartwell, ed.
--The Enchanted Castle: A Book of Fairy Tales from Flowerland. Neill, John Rea (1878-1943), illus. LC 6-33583. x p., 1 l., 13-123 p. incl. front., illus., plates. 19 cm. (Altemus' fairy tales series). c.1906. H. Altemus Company.
--The Jeweled Sea: A Book of Chinese Fairy Tales. Neill, John Rea (1878-1943), illus. LC 6-34048. x p., 1 l., 13-102 p., 1 l. incl. front., illus., plates. 18 1/2 cm. (Altemus' fairy tales series). c.1906. Henry Altemus Company.

James, Henry (1843-1916)
--The Jolly Corner. Rocker, Fermin (1907-), illus. Bd. with The Real Thing. (Illus.). 96p. (gr. 7up). 1958. (ISBN 0-531-01069-4). Watts.
--Turn of the Screw. (Keith Jennison Large Type Bks). (gr. 6 up). N.D. (ISBN 0-531-00298-5). Watts.
--The Turn of the Screw. Stewart, Diana, adapted by. Shaw, Charles (1941-), illus. LC 81-5217. (Illus.). 48p. (Raintree Short Classics). (gr. 4 up). 1981. (ISBN 0-8172-1672-3). Raintree Pubs.
--The Turn of the Screw. Stewart, Diana, adapted by. Shaw, Charles (1941-), illus. LC 81-5217. (Illus.). 48p. (Raintree Short Classics Ser.). (gr. 4-12). 1983. (ISBN 0-8172-2027-5). Raintree Pubs.
--The Turn of the Screw & Daisy Miller. (Magnum Easy Eye Classic Ser). (gr. 8 up). N.D. Lancer.
--The Turn of the Screw & Other Stories. (gr. 7-12). 1972 (Starline). Schol Bk Serv.

James, Josephine, pseud., see Sterne, Emma Gelders.

James, Josephine, pseud. (1894-) & Lindsay, Barbara
--An Affair of the Heart. Sterne, Emma Gelders. Klimley, Stanley, illus. LC 65-18995. (Josephine James is the joint pseud of Emma Gelders Sterne (1894-) and Barbara Lindsey). 187 p. illus. 20 cm. (Kathy Martin story, 11). 1965. Golden Press.
--African Adventure. Sterne, Emma Gelders. Klimley, Stanley, illus. LC 65-18918. (Josephine James is the joint pseud of Emma Gelders Sterne (1894-) and Barbara Lindsey). 187 p. illus. 20 cm. (Kathy Martin story, 13). 1965. Golden Press.
--Assignment in Alaska. Sterne, Emma Gelders. Plummer, William Kirtman, illus. LC 62-9847. (Josephine James in the joint pseud of Emma Gelders Sterne (1894) And Barbara Lindsay). 184p. illus. 20cm. (Their A Kathy Martin story, 5). c.1961. Golden Press.
--A Cap for Kathy. Sterne, Emma Gelders. Firnic, John, illus. LC 59-459415. (Josephine James is the joint pseud of Emma Gelders Sterne (1894-) and Barbara Lindsey). 188p. illus. 21cm. (A Kathy Martin Story). 1959. Golden Press.
--Courage in Crisis. Sterne, Emma Gelders. Plummer, William Kirtman, illus. LC 64-18534. (Josephine James is the joint pseud of Emma Gelders Sterne (1894) and Barbara Lindsay). (A Kathy Martin Story). 1964. Golden Press.
--Junior Nurse. Sterne, Emma Gelders. Plummer, William Kirtman, illus. LC 60-51322. (Josephine James is the joint pseud of emma Gelders Sterne (1894) and Barbara Lindsay). 188p. illus. 20cm. (Their A Kathy Martin story, 2). 1960. Golden Press.
--Off-Duty Nurse. Sterne, Emma Gelders. Plummer, William Kirtman, illus. LC 64-18585. (Josephine James is the joint pseud of Emma Gelders Sterne (1894) and Barbara Lindsay). 20cm. 186p. (A Kathy Martin Story). 1964. Golden Press.
--The Patient in Two-Zero-Two. Sterne, Emma Gelders. Plummer, William Kirtman, illus. LC 61-9902. (Josephine James is the joint pseud of Emma Gelders Sterne (1894) and Barbara Lindsay). 20cm. 186p. 1961. Golden Press.
--Peace Corps Nurse. Klimley, Stanley, illus. LC 65-189949. (Josephine James is the joint pseud of Emma Gelders Sterne (1894-) and Barbara Lindsey). 188p. illus. 20cm. (Kathy Martin story, 12). c.1965. Golden.
--Private Nurse. Sterne, Emma Gelders. Plummer, William Kirtman, illus. LC 62-9846. (Josephine James is the joint pseud of Emma Gleders Sterne (1894) and Barbara Lindsay). 185p. illus. 20cm. (Their A Kathy Martin story, 6). 1962. Golden Press.
--Private Nurse. Sterne, Emma Gelders. Plummer, William Kirtman, illus. (Josephine James is the joint pseud of Emma Gelders Sterne (1894-) and Barbara Lindsay). (A Kathy Martin Story). 1962. Golden Press.
--Search for an Island. Sterne, Emma Gelders. Plummer, William Kirtman, illus. LC 63-9382. (Josephine James is the joint pseud of Emma gleders Sterne (1894) and Barbara Lindsay). 186 p. illus. 20 cm. (Their A Kathy Martin story, 7). 1963. Golden Press.
--Senior Nurse. Sterne, Emma Gelders. Plummer, William Kirtman, illus. LC 60-513234. (Josephine James is the joint pseud of lEmma Gelders Sterne (1894) and Barbara Lindsay). 188p. illus. 20cm. (Their A Kathy Martin story, 3). 1960. Golden Press.
--Sierra Adventure. Sterne, Emma Gelders. Plummer, William Kirtman, illus. LC 64-18535. (Josephine James is the joint pseud of Emma Gelders Sterne (1894) and Barbara Lindsay). 20cm. 164p. (A Kathy Martin Storty). 1964. Golden Press.

James, M. R., ed.
--Favorite Tales of Hans Andersen. (Faber Fanfares Ser). 1978. (ISBN 0-571-11151-3). Faber & Faber.

James, M. R., tr. see Andersen, Hans Christian.

James, Martha, pseud., see Doyle, Martha Claire Macgowan.

James, Matthew, pseud., see Lucey, James Dennis.

James, Matthew, pseud. (1923-)
--The Adventures of Davy West. Lucey, James Dennis. 1st ed. Grossman, Nancy S. (1940-), illus. LC 65-15760. 154 p. illus. 22 cm. 1965. Doubleday.

James, Montague Rhodes, jt. auth. see Andersen, Hans Christian.

James, Montague Rhodes (1862-1936), tr. see Andersen, Hans Christian.

James, Montague Rhodes (1862-1936), tr. see Andersen, Hans Christian (1805-1875) & James, Montague Rhodes.

James, Neill
--White Reindeer. Baldridge, Cyrus LeRoy (1889-), illus. LC 40-30717. 4 p. l., 157 p. illus. 21 cm. 1940. C. Scribner's Sons.

James, Norma Wood
--Bittersweet Year. 1961. (ISBN 0-679-20024-X). David McKay Company.
--Bittersweet Year. LC 61-13102. 208 p. 21cm. 1961. Longmans, Green.
--Dawn at Lexington. 1st ed. Walker, Nedda, illus. LC 57-10526. 216p. illus. 21cm. 1957. Longmans, Green.
--Young Doctor of New Amsterdam. 1st ed. Dowling, Victor J. (1906-), illus. LC 58-8686. (Illus.). 215 p. 21cm. 1958. Longmans, Green.

James, Simon
--Across the Great Divide. (gr. 4-6). 1979. (ISBN 0-590-11799-8). Scholastic Inc.

James, T. G.
--Myths & Legends of Ancient Egypt. Zappler, Georg, ed. Melling, Brian, illus. LC 73-136363. (Illus.). 105 color ils. bibl. index. 162p. 1st U.S. edition. (All-Color Guides Ser). (gr. 5 up). 1971. (ISBN 0-448-00866-1). G&D.

--Moominsummer Madness. LC 61-8872. (Illus.). 163 p. 21cm. 1961. H.Z. Walck.
--Moominvalley in November. Jansson, Tove (1914-), illus. Hart, Kingsley, tr. LC 74-158867. (Illus.). ils. 160p. (gr. 4-7). 1971. (ISBN 0-8098-2416-7). Walck.
--The Summer Book. Teal, Thomas, tr. 1975. (ISBN 0-394-49249-8). Pantheon Books.
--Tales from Moominvalley. Jansson, Tove (1914-), illus. LC 64-22550. (Illus.). (gr. 4-7). 1964. (ISBN 0-8098-2371-3). Walck.
--Who Will Comfort Toffle. Jansson, Tove (1914-), illus. Hart, Kingsley, tr. LC 68-29031. (Illus.). eight color ils. 32p. 1st U.S. edition. (gr. k-3). 1969. (ISBN 0-8098-1149-9). Walck.

Janvier, Emma N., Mrs.
--Agnes Morton's Trial, & the Young Governess, 1 of 25 vols. (Selected Bks for School Library: The/Avondale Library). N.D. Set. Methodist Bk Concern.
--Agnes Morton's Trial: Or, The Lost Diamonds. 1873. Nelson & Phillips.
--Fernwood: Or, Hattie's Birth-Day Visit. LC 12-32174. 204 p. incl. front. plates. 17 cm. c.1871. American Sunday-School Union.
--Forgiveness: Or, The Story of Margaret Lisle ... LC 12-828254. 1 p. l., 5-212 p. front., pl. 17 cm. c.1870. American Sunday-School Union.
--Marion and Jessie: Or, Children's Influence. LC 12-34619. 210 p., front., plates. 17 cm. 1870. Hitchcock and Walden.
--Marion and Jessie: Or, Children's Influence. 210p. N.D. Nelson & Phillips.
--Our Western Home. N.D. American Sunday-School Union.
--The Young Governess. 1873. Nelson & Phillips.

Janvier, Margaret Thomson see Vandegrift, Margaret, pseud.

Janvier, Margaret Thomson (1845-)
--The Dead Doll, and Other Verses. Vandergrift, Margaret, pseud. LC 12-34617. (Illus.). 169p. 22cm. 1889. Ticknor and Company.

Janvier, Thomas Allibone (1849-1913)
--The Aztec Treasure House. Kutcher, Ben (1895-), illus. (Harper's Junior Classics). (gr. 7). N.D. Haper & Bros.
--In the Aztec Treasure House. Faulkner, Nancy, ed. LC 61-16995. 228p. illus. 26cm. (Companion book series). 1961. Walker.

Janzarik, Hilde
--The Lively Adventures of a Burly Woodcutter: A Pintsized Inventor, Two Pretty Pastry Cooks, and a Gang of Desperate Criminals. Flora, Paul, illus. Ignatowicz, Nina & Monjo, J. N., trs. LC 66-6989. 79 . i3lus. 29c4. 1966. Harper.

Japp, Darsie, tr. see Supervielle, Jules.

Japrisot, Sebastien
--Trap for Cinderella. (Crime Monthly Ser). 1979. (ISBN 0-14-005364-6). Penguin.

Jaques, Bertha E
--The Story of Shep. LC 12-25537. 105 p. incl. plates. front. 21 cm. 1912. T. Rubovits, Printer.

Jaques, Faith (1923-)
--Kidnap in Willowbank Wood. (Illus.). 40p. 1st U.S. edition. (ps-2). 1983. (ISBN 0-434-94442-4, Pub. by W. Heinemann England). David & Charles.
--Tilly's House. Jaques, Faith (1923-), illus. LC 78-31105. p. cm. 1979. (ISBN 0-689-50138-2). Atheneum. **Award: (NYT).**
--Tilly's Rescue. LC 80-14419. p. cm. 1980. (ISBN 0-689-50175-7). Atheneum.
--Tilly's Rescue. Jaques, Faith (1923-), illus. 1981. Atheneum.

Jaques, Faith (1923-), illus.
--A Peck of Pepper. 28p. 1978. (ISBN 0-7011-5043-2, Pub. by Chatto Bodley Jonathan). Merrimack Pub Cir.

Jaques, Florence Page (1890-1972)
--There Once Was a Puffin, and Other Nonsense Verses. 1st ed. Jaques, Francis Lee (1887-1969), illus. LC 56-13284. unpaged. illus. 20cm. 1956. Wake-Brook House.

Jaquith, Priscilla & Emrich, Duncan Black MacDonald, eds.
--Bo Rabbit Smart for True: Folktales from the Gullah. Young, Ed (1931-), illus. (Original Author: Albert Henry Stoddard, 1872-1954). (Illus.). 64p. (gr. 6-12). 1981. (ISBN 0-399-20793-7, Philomel). (ISBN 0-399-61179-7). Putnam Pub Group. **Award: (ALA).**

Jarden, Mary Louise (1908-)
--The Young Brontes, Charlotte and Emily, Branwell and Anne. Sewell, Helen Moore (1896-1957), illus. LC 38-27965. 279 p. illus. 22 cm. 1938. The Viking Press.

Jardin, Judy Du see Du Jardin, Rosamond Neal (1902-1963) & Du Jardin, Judy.

Jardin, Luis (1901-)
--The Armadillo and the Monkey. Jardin, Luis (1901-), illus. Cimino, Maria, tr. 48p. N.D. Coward-McCann.

Jardin, Rosamond Neal Du see Du Jardin, Rosamond Neal.

Jardine, Maggie
--I Need. (gr. k-1). N.D. G&D.
--I Need. 24p. 1965. Pitman Publishing.

Jarnagin, Dorothy Greve (1884-)
--Gipsy Fortunes: A Novel for Girls. LC 28-12658. ix, 326 p. front., plates. 20 cm. c.1928. The Century Co.
--Mardee Gray's Choice. Stecher, William Frederick (1864-), illus. LC 23-13486. 5 p. l., 300 p., 1 l. front., plates. 20 cm. 1923. Little, Brown, and Company.

Jaroch, Francis Anthony Randy (1947-) & Jaroch, J. Chipp
--The Adventures of the Sneeky Sneekers, the Tornado. Axeman, Lois, illus. LC 77-4844. p. cm. 1977. (ISBN 0-516-03405-7). Childrens Press.
--The Ghost of Gleason Mansion. Axeman, Lois, illus. LC 77-16419. p. cm. (Adventures of the Sneeky Sneekers). c.1978. (ISBN 0-516-03472-3). Children's Press.
--Washout at Liberty Valley. Axeman, Lois, illus. LC 78-5466. p. cm. (Adventures of the Sneeky Sneekers). 1978. (ISBN 0-516-03407-3). Childrens Press.

Jaroch, J. Chipp, jt. auth. see Jaroch, Francis Anthony Randy.

Jaroch, Mike, jt. auth. see Jaroch, Francis Anthony Randy.

Jaros, R., jt. auth. see Kates, H. E.

Jarratt, Elizabeth Ann (1895-)
--Smart Mr. Tim. Smock, Nell Stolp, illus. LC 49-980889. 24 p. col. illus. 19 x 22 cm. c.1949. Abingdon-Cokesbury Press.

Jarrell, Mary Von Schrader (1914-)
--The Knee-Baby. 1st ed. Shimin, Symeon (1902-), illus. LC 73-75295. (Illus.). 32 p. 24cm. 1973. (ISBN 0-374-34246-6). Farrar, Straus and Giroux.

Jarrell, Randall, tr. see Bechstein, Ludwig.

Jarrell, Randall (1914-1965), tr. see Grimm, Jakob Ludwig Karl (1785-1863) & Grimm, Wilhelm Karl.

Jarrell, Randall (1914-1965)
--The Animal Family. Sendak, Maurice Bernard (1928-), illus. LC 65-206595. (Illus.). 179 p. 18cm. 1965. Pantheon Books. **Awards: (NYT); (ALA); (JNM).**
--A Bat Is Born, from The Bat-Poet. 1st ed. Schoenherr, John Carl (1935-), illus. LC 77-653. (Illus.). 31 p. 1977, c.1964. (ISBN 0-385-12223-3). Doubleday.
--The Bat-Poet. Sendak, Maurice Bernard (1928-), illus. LC 64-16812. 23cm. 42p. 1964. MacMillan Co. **Award: (NYT).**
--The Bat-Poet. Sendak, Maurice Bernard (1928-), illus. LC 76-17823. (Illus.). 42 p. 23cm. 1976, c.1964. (ISBN 0-02-043910-5, Collier Bks.). MacMillan.
--Fly by Night. Sendak, Maurice Bernard (1928-), illus. LC 76-27313. (Illus.). 30 p. 21cm. 1976. (ISBN 0-374-32348-8). Farrar, Straus and Giroux. **Award: (NYT).**
--The Gingerbread Rabbit. 1st ed. Williams, Garth Montgomery (1912-), illus. LC 63-16364. 55 p. illus. 23 cm. 1964. Macmillan.
--The Gingerbread Rabbit. Williams, Garth Montgomery (1912-), illus. 1972. Macmillan.

Jarunkova, Klara
--Don't Cry for Me. Thelmer, George, tr. from Slovak. LC 68-12392. 287 p. 22cm. 1968. Four Winds Press.

Jarvis, Charles, tr. see Cervantes Saavedra, Miguel de.

Jarvis, Josephine, tr. see Froebel, Friedrich Wilhelm August.

Jarvis, Sally Melcher
--The Biggest Splash. 32p. 1965. Pitman Publishing.
--The Elephant Bell. 32p. 1965. Pitman Publishing.
--Fried Onions & Marshmallows, and Other Little Plays for Little People. Luke, Franklin, illus. LC 68-21080. (Illus.). 60 p. 1968. (ISBN 0-8193-0334-8). Parents' Magazine Press.

Jasner, W. K., pseud., see Watson, Jane Werner.

Jasner, W. K., pseud. (1915-)
--Which Is the Witch?. Watson, Jane Werner. Chess, Victoria (1939-), illus. LC 78-11757. (Illus.). (I Am Reading Bks.). (gr. 2-4). 1979. (ISBN 0-394-83978-1). (ISBN 0-394-93978-6). Pantheon.

Jason, Leon
--Grandy Goose. N.D (Wonder Books). Grosset & Dunlap.
--Heckle & Jeckle. N.D (Wonder Books). Grosset & Dunlap.
--Heckle and Jeckle's Visit to the Farm. (Wonder Books). N.D. Grosset & Dunlap Pub.
--Sparkie: No School Today. Jason, Leon, illus. LC 55-35943. (A Story and Game Book, Based on the Radio Program, "No School Today".). unpaged. illus. 21cm. (Treasure Bks.). 1955. Treasure Books.

Jason, Leon, jt. auth. see Sutton, Felix.

Jaszi, Jean Yourd
--Everybody Has Two Eyes. Foster, Marian Curtis, illus. Mariana, pseud. LC 56-11404. (Illus.). 24cm. 1956. Lothrop, Lee & Shepard.

Jatakas
--Hindu Fairy Tales Retold for Children. Griswold, Florence, Mrs., retold by. Bridgman, Lewis Jesse (1857-1931), illus. LC 18-17188. 213 p. col. front., illus., plates. 20 cm. 1918. Lothrop, Lee & Shepard Co.
--Jataka Tales. Babbitt, Ellen C., retold by. Young, Ellsworth, illus. LC 12-40653. xiii, 92 p. illus. 20 cm. 1912. The Century Co.
--Jataka Tales Out of Old India. Aspinwall, Marguerite, retold by. Hall, Arnold, illus. LC 27-19306. xii, 239 p. incl. plates, front. 21 cm. 1927. G. P. Putnam's Sons.
--Twenty Jataka Tales. Inayat, Noor, retold by. Le Mair, Henriette Willebeek (1889-1966), illus. LC 39-7582. 138 p. front., plates. 23 cm. c.1939. David McKay Company.

Jatakas see Rockwell, Anne F.

Jaufre Provencal Romance
--Geoffrey the Knight: A Tale of Chivalry of the Days of King Arthur. Dore, Louis Christophe Paul Gustave (1832-1883), illus. LC 42-33510. 215 p. incl. front., illus., plates. 19 cm. 1869. T. Nelson and Sons.
--Jaufry the Knight and the Fair Brunissende. Ives, Vernon, tr. LC 36-27175. 5 p. l., 124 p. illus. 20 cm. 1935. Holiday House.

Jauss, Anne Marie, tr. see Lowe, Patricia Tracy.

Jauss, Anne Marie (1907-)
--The Pasture. LC 68-19614. (Illus.). 83 p. 24cm. 1968. D. McKay Co.
--The River's Journey. N.D. E. M. Hale and Co.
--The River's Journey. LC 57-5863. 48p. illus. 19x23cm. 1957. Lippincott.

Jauss, Anne Marie (1907-), selected by.
--Legends of Saints and Beasts. 1st ed. Jauss, Anne Marie (1907-), illus. LC 54-9271. unpaged. illus. 22cm. 1954. Aladdin Books.
--Legends of Saints and Beasts. Jauss, Anne Marie (1907-), illus. N.D. E. P. Dutton & Co.

Javal, Lily Leon-Levy
--Fortune's Caravan. Field, Rachel Lyman (1894-1942), adapted by. Salcedo, Maggie, illus. Saunders, Marion, tr. LC 33-32415. 120 p. illus. (part col.) 21 cm. 1933. W. Morrow & Company.

Jay, Edith Katharine Spicer see Prescott, E. Livingston, pseud.

Jay, Edith Katharine Spicer
--A Small, Small Child. Prescott, E. Livingston, pseud. (Illus.). (Goldenrod Library Ser.). 1905. L. C. Page & Co.
--A Small, Small Child. Prescott, E. Livingston, pseud. McCormick, Arthur David (1860-), illus. N.D. George Routledge & Sons.
--A Small Small Child. McCormick, Arthur David (1860-), illus. LC 1-18545. 3 p. l., 68 p. incl. illus., plates. front. 19 cm. (On cover: Cosy corner series). 1901. L. C. Page & Company.

Jay, Gladys (1902-)
--The Magic Hen. 28p. (Paine's Popular Plays). 1931. Pain Publishing Co.
--The Twins in Fruitland. Regina & Ludwig, illus. LC 30-28879. 160 p. incl. col. front., col. illus. 20 cm. 1929. Beckley-Cardy Company.

Jay, Griffin
--Mr. X. LC 37-4540. 5 p. l., 261 p. 20 cm. 1937. C. Scribner's Sons.

Jay, Mae Foster
--The Girl of the Mesa: A Story. Cue, Harold, illus. LC 30-9325. 300 p. front. 20 cm. c.1929. W. A. Wilde Company.
--Green Needles. N.D. W. A. Wilde Co.
--High on a Hill. Cue, Harold, illus. 1934. W. A. Wilde Co.
--Morning's at Seven. N.D. W. A. Wilde Co.
--The Orchard Fence. Burkard, Albert M., illus. 1935. W. A. Wilde.
--Rag-House Tales. LC 28-8586. 184 p. front., illus., plates. 20 cm. c.1927. W. A. Wilde Company.
--The Shell. Cue, Harold, illus. N.D. W. A. Wilde Co.
--The Sleigh Bell Trail. Cue, Harold, illus. N.D. W. A. Wilde Co.
--Tad. Cue, Harold, illus. LC 30-31192. 7, 11-294 p. incl. front. 20 cm. c.1930. W. A. Wilde Company.

Jay, Ruth Ingrid see Johnson, Ruth I.

Jay, Ruth Ingrid (1920-)
--Joy Sparton & Her Problem Twin. Johnson, Ruth I. (gr. 5-8). 1963. (ISBN 0-8024-4404-0). Moody.
--Joy Sparton & the Money Mix-Up. Johnson, Ruth I. (gr. 5-8). 1960. (ISBN 0-8024-4403-2). Moody.
--Joy Sparton & the Mystery in Room Seven. Johnson, Ruth I. 128p. (Orig.). (gr. 5-8). 1974. (ISBN 0-8024-4405-9). Moody.
--Joy Sparton & the Vacation Mix-Up. Johnson, Ruth I. (gr. 5-8). 1959. (ISBN 0-8024-4402-4). Moody.
--Joy Sparton of Parsonage Hill. Johnson, Ruth I., (gr. 5-8). 1958. (ISBN 0-8024-4401-6). Moody.

Jay, Ruth J.
--Mary Slessor: White Queen of the Cannibals. (Orig.). 1985. (ISBN 0-8024-0464-2). Moody.

Jay, W. M. L.
--Holden With the Chords. (Illus.). (The Girl's Own Favorite Ser.). N.D. E. P. Dutton & Co.

Jayanti, Amber
--Silas and the Mad-Sad People. Beier, Ellen, illus. LC 80-83882. (Illus.). 31 p. 22cm. c.1981. (ISBN 0-938678-08-6). (ISBN 0-938678-08-6). New Seed Press.

Jayme, William North (1925-) & Cook, Roderick (1939-)
--William North Jayme and Roderick Cook's Know Your Toes: And Other Things to Know. Einsel, Walter (1926-) & Einsel, Naiad, illus. LC 63-19901. 1 v. illus. 30 cm. 1963. C. N. Potter.

Jayne, Lieutenant R. H., pseud., see Ellis, Edward Sylvester.

Jayne, Mitchell F
--The Forest in the Wind. Hoban, Lillian (1925-), illus. LC 66-18285. 150p. illus. 22cm. c.1966. (ISBN 0-672-50283-6). Bobbs.

Jaynes, Ruth M (1899-)
--Benny's Four Hats. Mandlin, Harvey, photos by. LC 67-26370. 1 v. (unpaged) col. illus. 21 x 23 cm. (Bowmar early childhood series). 1967. Bowmar Pub. Corp.
--The Biggest House. Rupp, Jacques, illus. LC 67-31188. (Illus.). 31 p. (Bowmar Early Childhood Ser.). 1968. Bowmar Pub. Co.
--A Box Tied with a Red Ribbon. Mandlin, Harvey, photos by. LC 68-17034. (Illus.). 27 p. (Bowmar early childhood series). 1968. Bowmar Pub. Corp.
--Do You Know What ...?. Mandlin, Harvey, photos by. LC 67-31189. 1 v. (chiefly col. illus.) 21 x 23 cm. (Bowmar early childhood series). c.1967. Bowmar Pub. Corp.
--Friends! Friends! Friends!. Mandlin, Harvey, photos by. LC 67-26371. (Illus.). 27 p. (Bowmar early childhood series). 1967. Bowmar Pub. Corp.
--Melinda's Christmas Stocking. Curry, Nancy, ed. Mandlin, Harvey, photos by. LC 68-17031. (Early Childhood Ser.). 1967. (ISBN 0-8372-0265-5). Bowmar-Noble.
--Melinda's Christmas Stocking. George, Richard, illus. LC 68-17031. (Illus.). 31 p. (Bowmar Early Childhood Ser.). 1968. Bowmar Pub. Corp.
--My Tricycle and I. Mandlin, Harvey, photos by. LC 68-17027. (Illus.). 28 p. (Bowmar early childhood series). 1968. Bowmar Pub. Corp.
--Tell Me Please! What's That?. Curry, Nancy, ed. Mandlin, Harvey, photos by. LC 68-17028. (Illus.). 27 p. (Bowmar early childhood series). 1968. Bowmar Pub. Co.
--That's What It Is. Curry, Nancy, ed. Mandlin, Harvey, photos by. LC 67-31543. (Early Childhood Ser.). (ps-3). 1967. (ISBN 0-8372-0250-7). Bowmar-Noble.
--That's What It Is!. Mandlin, Harvey, photos by. LC 67-31543. (Illus.). 1 v. (unpaged. (Bowmar early childhood series). 1968. Bowmar Pub. Corp.
--Three Baby Chicks. Curry, Nancy, ed. Mandlin, Harvey, photos by. LC 67-31190. 1 v. (unpaged) col. illus. 21 x 23cm. (Bowmar early childhood ser.). c.1967. Bowmar-Noble.
--Watch Me Indoors. Curry, Nancy, ed. Mandlin, Harvey, photos by. LC 67-31476. (Early Childhood Ser.). (ps-3). 1967. (ISBN 0-8372-0249-3). Bowmar-Noble.
--Watch Me Outdoors. Mandlin, Harvey, photos by. LC 67-25574. (Illus.). 1 v. (unpaged. (Bowmar Early Childhood Ser.). 1967. Bowmar-Noble.
--What Is a Birthday Child?. Curry, Nancy, ed. Mandlin, Harvey, photos by. LC 67-27125. 27 p. (chiefly col. illus. (Bowmar early childhood series). 1967. Bowmar-Noble.
--Where Is Whiffen?. Curry, Nancy, ed. Mandlin, Harvey, photos by. LC 67-27126. 1 v. (unpaged) col. illus. 21 x 23 cm. (Bowmar Early Childhood Ser.). 1967. Bowmar-Noble.
--Yo Ho & Kim. (gr. 1-4). N.D. (ISBN 0-87505-319-X, Pub. by Lawrence). Borden.
--Yo Ho & Kim at Sea. (gr. 1-4). N.D. (ISBN 0-87505-320-3, Pub. by Lawrence). Borden.

J. C. G, retold by see Wyss, Johann David Von.

Jean, Priscilla
--Pattie Round & Wally Square. (gr. k-3). N.D. G&D.
--Pattie Round and Wally Square. LC 64-23768. (Illus.). 24p. 21cm. (An Astor Bk.). 1965. I. Oblensky.
--Pattie Round & Wally Square. Jean, Priscilla, illus. (Illus.). (gr. k-3). 1965. (ISBN 0-8392-3048-6). Astor-Honor.
--Pattie Round & Wally Square. Obolensky. LC 64-23768. 24 p. col. illus. 21 cm. (Astor bk.). c.1965. World.

Jefferds, J. A.
--Lame Willie. 128p. N.D. Hurd & Houghton for American Tract Society.
--Lame Willie. 128p. (Young Hero Stories). N.D. Lockwood, Brooks, & Co. for American Tract Society.

--The Little Governor in Fableland. Farnsworth, Ethel N., illus. LC 7-31416. 3 p. l., 3-104 p. col. front., illus., plates (part col.) 20 x 10 cm. (Christmas Stocking Ser.). 1907. F. A. Stokes Company.
--More Bunny Stories for Young People. Barnes, Culmer, illus. LC 6252. 4 p. l., 7-195 p. incl. illus., plates. front. 21 x 18 cm. c.1900. Frederick A. Stokes Company.
--Snuggy Bedtime Stories. Upjohn, Anna Milo, illus. LC 6-30933. 2 p. l., 3-126 p. illus., 8 col. pl. (incl. front.) 20 x 10 cm. (Christmas Stocking Ser.). 1906. F. A. Stokes Company.
--Tiny's Christmas Fairy. LC 17-1849. 19p. 14cm. 1895. A. W. Carter.
--What Happened to the Little Chicks. (Illus.). (Grandmother Goose Stories). N.D. Small, Maynard & Co.

Jewett, Sarah Orne (1849-1909)
--Betty Leicester: A Story for Girls. 287p. 1890. Houghton Mifflin.
--Betty Leicester: A Story for Girls. Stevens, Beatrice (1876-), illus. LC 29-9723. xii, 1, 273, 1 p. col. front., illus., col. plates. 21 cm. 1929. Houghton Mifflin Company.
--Betty Leicester's Christmas. LC 4-17811. 3 p. l., 68 p. 1 l. front., 3 pl. 20 cm. 1899. Houghton, Mifflin and Company.
--Country of the Pointed Firs. (gr. 7 up). N.D. (ISBN 0-448-26098-0). G&D.
--The Country of the Pointed Firs. 269p. (Riverside Literature Ser.). 1910. Houghton Mifflin Co.
--Country of the Pointed Firs. (Keith Jennison Large Type Bks). (gr. 7 up). N.D. (ISBN 0-531-00177-6). Watts.
--Katy's Birthday. LC 8-1677. 149 p. front., illus., plates. 19 cm. (Peace Island Ser.). c.1883. D. Lothrop and Company.
--The King of Folly Island and Other People. 339p. 1888. Houghton Mifflin Co.
--Play Day Stories. Shute, Katharine H., ed. LC 14-5043. xxvii, 102 p. front. (port.) pl. 18 cm. (The Riverside Literature Series). c.1914. Houghton Mifflin Company.
--Play Days. A Book of Stories for Children. LC 7-9733. 213 p. 18 cm. 1878. Houghton, Osgood and Company.
--Play Days: A Book of Stories for Children. LC 6-37922. 213 p. 18 x 14 cm. c.1906. Houghton, Mifflin and Company.
--Play-Days: A Book of Stories for Girls. 213p. Repr. of 1878 ed. 1906. Houghton Mifflin.
--The Queen's Twin and Other Stories. 232p. 1899. Houghton Mifflin Co.
--Stories & Poems for Children. 1900. Houghton Mifflin & Co.
--Stories and Tales, 5. 1910. Houghton Mifflin Co.
--White Heron. Cooney, Barbara (1917-), illus. LC 63-12651. (Illus.). 24cm. 34p. (gr. 4-6). 1963. (ISBN 0-690-88570-9). (ISBN 0-690-88571-7). T Y Crowell.
--A White Heron, The Night Before Thanksgiving, and Other Stories and Tales. (Riverside Literature Ser.). N.D. Houghton Mifflin Co.

Jewett, Sophic (1861-1909), tr. see Amicis, Edmondo De.

Jewett, Sophie, tr. see Amicis, Edmondo De.

Jewett, Xisra H.
--Little Rhymes for Little Minds. N.D. Bruce Humphries.

Jewish, Theological Seminary of America. Melton Research Cernter, jt. auth. see Newman, Shirley.

Jews
--One Little Goat: A Passover Song. Hirsh, Marilyn (1944-), adapted by. Hirsh, Marilyn (1944-), illus. LC 78-24354. (Illus.). 32 p. c.1979. (ISBN 0-8234-0345-9). Holiday House.

Jews--Hist.--B. C. 586-A. D. 70--Fiction
--Omar: Designed to Illustrate the Jewish History, from B. C. 63, to the Birth of Christ ... LC 7-23684. 252 p. incl. front. 16 cm. c.1835. American Sunday-School Union.

Jezard, Alison (1919-)
--Albert. Schroeder, Ted (1931-1973), illus. LC 72-119860. (Illus.). 57 p. 22cm. 1970. Prentice-Hall.
--Albert & Henry. 1970. (Pub. by Gollancz England). David & Charles.
--Albert & Tum Tum. 1973. (Pub. by Gollancz England). David & Charles.
--Albert Goes Treasure Hunting. 1980. (Pub. by Gollancz England). David & Charles.
--Albert Goes Trekking. 1976. (Pub. by Gollancz England). David & Charles.
--Albert in Scotland. 1969. (Pub. by Gollancz England). David & Charles.
--Albert on the Farm. 1979. (Pub. by Gollancz England). David & Charles.
--Albert Police Bear. 1975. (Pub. by Gollancz England). David & Charles.
--Albert up the River. 1971. (Pub. by Gollancz England). David & Charles.
--Albert's Christmas. 1970. (Pub. by Gollancz England). David & Charles.
--Albert's Circus. 1977. (Pub. by Gollancz England). David & Charles.

Jhabvala, Ruth Prawer (1927-)
--Travelers. LC 72-9765. 247 p. 22cm. 1973. (ISBN 0-06-012193-9). Harper & Row.
--Travelers. 246p. (Perennial Library). 1977. (ISBN 0-06-080432-7). Harper & Row.

Jiandgong, Zhu
--A Crown for the Polite Elephant. Jianguo, Du, illus. (Illus.). 22p. (ps-2). 1983. (ISBN 0-8351-1244-6). China Bks.

Jiler, John (1946-)
--Wild Berry Moon. Harris, Susan Yard, illus. LC 82-6071. p. cm. c.1982. (ISBN 0-688-01530-1). (ISBN 0-688-01531-X). Greenwillow Books.

Jimenez-Landi, Antonio
--The Treasure of the Muleteer, and Other Spanish Tales. Sowell, Floyd (1929-), illus. Blackburn, Paul, tr. LC 73-11690. (Illus.). 14 p. 25cm. 1974. (ISBN 0-385-08027-1). (ISBN 0-385-08027-1). Doubleday.

Jimmerson, J. W.
--Little David & Mr. Grunt. (gr. k-3). N.D. Carlton.

Jippensha, Ikku
--Shank's Mare. 1960. (ISBN 0-8048-0524-5). Charles E. Tuttle Co.

J. L. E, tr. see Kokhanovsky.

Joan, Natalie
--Ameliaranne and the Big Treasure. Pearse, Susan Beatrice, illus. LC 33-493. 62 p. incl. (part col.) col. pl. 21 cm. 1932. David McKay Company.
--Ameliaranne in Town. Pearse, Susan Beatrice, illus. LC 30-20871. 63 p. incl. col. front., illus. (part col.) 21 cm. c.1930. David McKay Company.
--Biddy the Fugitive. N.D. George Sully & Co.
--Cozy Time Tales. N.D. Thomas Nelson & Sons.
--Lie Down Stories. Anderson, Anne, illus. N.D. Dodge Pub. Co.

Joan, Natalie, jt. auth. see Sowerby, Katherine Githa.

Joan, Natalie & Sowerby, Githa
--The Glad Book. authorized. Sowerby, Millicent, illus. LC 35-287285. 29 p. col. front., illus. (part col.) 22 cm. c.1935. Artists and Writers Guild, Inc.

Joannes see Kelsey, Alice Geer.

J. O. C. New York, H. Holt and Co., jt. auth. see Dyer, Walter Alden.

Joe, Jeanne
--Ying-Ying: Pieces of a Childhood. Caigoy, Faustino, illus. (Illus.). 112p. (Orig.). (gr. 4 up). 1982. (ISBN 0-934788-02-2). E-W Pub Co.

Joerns, Consuelo
--The Foggy Rescue. Joerns, Consuelo, illus. LC 80-11375. (Illus.). 40 p. 20cm. (gr. k-3). c.1980. (ISBN 0-590-07744-9). Four Winds Press.
--The Forgotten Bear. Joerns, Consuelo, illus. LC 78-1546. (Illus.). 440 p. 19cm. c.1978. (ISBN 0-590-07560-8). Four Winds Press.
--The Lost & Found House. LC 79-11030. p. cm. c.1979. (ISBN 0-590-07627-2). Four Winds Press.
--The Midnight Castle. LC 82-24923. (Illus.). 40p. (gr. k-3). 1983. (ISBN 0-688-02090-9). (ISBN 0-688-02091-7). Lothrop.
--Oliver's Escape. Joerns, Conselo, illus. LC 81-1904. (Illus.). 40 p. 24cm. c.1981. (ISBN 0-590-07817-8). Four Winds Press.

Joffe, Rona
--The Last of the Wizards. Blegvad, Erik (1923-), illus. 1961. Simon and Schuster.

Joffo, Joseph
--A Bag of Marbles. LC 74-11132. 304p. 1974. (ISBN 0-395-19392-3). HM.

Johansen, Carol, jt. auth. see Cotter, Paulette.

Johansen, Margaret Alison, Mrs.
--Hawk of Hawk Clan. O'Brian, William, illus. LC 41-17951. viii, 280 p. incl. illus., plates. 20 cm. 1941. Longmans, Green and Co.

Johansen, Margaret Alison, Mrs., jt. auth. see Lide, Alice Alison, Mrs.

Johl, Janet Pagter, Mrs.
--Wilhelmina: A Little Dutch Girl. Lane, Rosalie L., illus. LC 41-196389. 3 p. l., 5-121 p. col. front., illus., col. plates. 26 cm. c.1941. The Greystone Press.

John, Betty
--Seloe: The Story of a Fur Seal. 1st ed. Nonnast, Marie (1924-), illus. LC 55-8246. (Illus.). 185 p. 22cm. 1955. World Pub. Co.

John, Elizabeth Beaman see St. John, Elizabeth, pseud.

John, Eugenie see Marlitt, E., pseud.

John, Hughes
--Bob the Super Clerk. (Illus.). 40p. (People Working Today Ser.). (gr. 7-12). 1975. (ISBN 0-915510-01-4). Janus Bks.
--Janet the Hospital Helper. (Illus.). 40p. (People Working Today Ser). 1975. (ISBN 0-915510-02-2). Janus Bks.
--Jester the Bellhop. (Illus.). 40p. (People Working Today Ser). (gr. 7-12). 1975. (ISBN 0-915510-05-7). Janus Bks.

John, Joseph (1924-)
--Three Cheers for Tomorrow. Howard, Brother Bernar, illus. LC 53-39589. 109 p. illus. 24cm. 1953. Dujarie Press.

John Martin's Book
--The Be Better Book: Or, The Best B's for Bairns. LC 24-22942. 120 p. illus. 26 cm. c.1924. John Martin's Book House.
--Stories for Little Men & Women. LC 29-13037. 184 p. incl. front., illus. (part col.) 26 cm. c.1929. The Platt & Munk Co. Inc.
--Tell Me a Story. LC 32-15193. 184 p. col. front., illus. 26 cm. c.1932. The Platt & Munk Co., Inc.

John, Naomi
--Roadrunner. 1st ed. McLeod, Emilie Warren, ed. Parnall, Peter (1936-) & Parnall, Virginia, illus. LC 80-10213. (Illus.). 32 p. c.1980. Dutton.

John the Giant-Killer Esq
--A New Riddle Book. (Forgotten Children's Books). N.D. Charles Scribner's Sons.

John, Timothy
--A Great Song Book. Hankey, John, ed. Ungerer, Tomi, pseud. (1931-), illus. Ungerer, Jean Thomas. (gr. 1 up). 1978. Doubleday. **Awards: (NYT); (ALA).**

John, Timothy & Hankey, John, eds.
--The Great Story Book. Ungerer, Tomi, pseud. (1931-), illus. Ungerer, Jean Thomas. (Illus.). (gr. 1 up). 1978. (ISBN 0-385-13328-6). Doubleday.

John, V. P.
--She Sell Seashells. N.D. (ISBN 0-308-70346-4). Funk & Wagnalls.

Johnathan, pseud., see Stein, Monte.

Johns, C. A.
--Pictures and Stories for Little Children. 1874. Pott, Young, & Co.

Johns, Cecil Starr
--The Fairies' Annual, Presented. LC 19-2556. viii, 180 p., 1 l. incl. illus., plates. 16 col. pl. (incl. front.) 26 cm. N.D. John Lane.

Johns, Richard A
--Return to Heroism. LC 69-12784. 127 p. 20cm. 1969. Broadman Press.

Johns, Rowland (1882-)
--Jock, The King's Pony. Brown, Paul (1893-1958), illus. LC 36-8266. 3 p. l., 11-60 p. front., illus. 22 cm. c.1936. E. P. Dutton and Company, Inc.

Johns, Sylvia K.
--Granny and Me. N.D. Carlton Press Inc.
--Granny and Me. LC 57-7017. (Illus.). 30p. 21cm. (A Bookland Juvenile). 1957. Comet Press Books.

Johns, William Earle (1893-1968)
--Adventure Bound. Relf, Douglas, illus. LC 55-2926. 118p. illus. 19cm. (Panther library). 1955. T. Nelson.

Johnson, A E, pseud., see Johnson, Annabell Jones.

Johnson, A E, Mrs., pseud. (1921-)
--Clarence and Corinne: Or, God's Way. Johnson, Annabell Jones. LC 12-34755. 2 p. l., 3-187 p. front., plates. 19 cm. c.1890. American Baptist Publication Society.
--The Hazeley Family. Johnson, Annebell Jones. LC 12-34754. 2 p. l., 3-191 p. front., plates. 19 cm. c.1894. American Baptist Publication Society.

Johnson, A. E., pseud. (1921-) & Johnson, Edgar Raymond (1912-)
--Blues I Can Whistle. Johnson, Annabell Jones. LC 78-81698. (A. E. Johnson Joint pseud. for Annabell Jones Johnson and Edgar Raymond Johnson). 256p. (gr. 9 up). 1969. (ISBN 0-590-17162-3, Four Winds). Schol Bk Serv.

Johnson, Addie
--Funny Fat Fairy. 1979. (ISBN 0-533-03966-5). Vantage.

Johnson, Albert
--Conquest In Burma. 1963. Friendship Press.

Johnson, Alexander L
--Oasis for Lucy. LC 56-93455. 248p. 21cm. 1956. Dodd, Mead.

Johnson, Alfred Edwin (1879-), tr. see Perrault, Charles, et al.

Johnson, Alfred Edwin, et al. (1879-), trs. see Perrault, Charles.

Johnson, Alfred Spencer
--Six Short French Plays for the Use of Preparatory Schools. LC 18-76750. vii, 96 p. incl. front., illus 17 cm. 1910. Longmans, Green, and Co.

Johnson, Alice Cheney
--Arabella's New House. Banfield, V. M., illus. LC 67-24775. (Illus.). 48 p. 21cm. 1967. Dorrance.

Johnson, Alice M
--Sinbad, the Gorilla. LC 51-38086. unpaged. illus. 24 cm. 1951. Pacific Press Pub. Association.

Johnson, Allan L
--Hot Rod Reporter. LC 61-69847. 152p. 21cm. 1961. Duell, Sloan and Pearce.
--Mystery of Skull Canyon. Kinstler, Everett Raymond (1926-), illus. (Illus.). (gr. 5-8). 1960. (ISBN 0-696-72497-9). Hawthorn.

Johnson, Alma D (1915-)
--Sunflower Petals: Children's Stories All Through the Year. LC 54-38446. 51p. 20cm. 1954. Story Book Press.

Johnson, Alvin
--The Battle of the Wild Turkey. 1961. Atheneum.

Johnson, Ann Donegan
--The Value of Love: The Story of Johnny Appleseed. Pileggi, Stephen, illus. LC 79-31873. (Illus.). (The Value Tales Ser.). (gr. k-6). 1979. (ISBN 0-916392-35-X, Dist. by Oak Tree Pubns). Value Comm.
--The Value of Self-Discipline: The Story of Alexander Graham Bell. Pileggi, Stephen, illus. LC 85-7986. (Illus.). 62 p. 26cm. (ValueTales). c.1985. (ISBN 0-7172-8176-0). Value Communications.

Johnson, Anna see Daring, Hope, pseud.

Johnson, Anna (1860-)
--Agnes Grant's Education. Daring, Hope, pseud. (Bks. for Camp Fire Girls). N.D. Abingdon Press.
--Agnes Grant's Education. Daring, Hope, pseud. LC 2-22475. 320 p. 19 cm. 1902. Jennings & Pye.
--Agnes Grant's Education. Daring, Hope, pseud. N.D. Methodist Book Concern.
--An Abundant Harvest. Daring, Hope, pseud. LC 4-23728. 281 p. 19 1/2cm. 1904. Eaton & Mains, New York; Jennings & Graham, Cincinnati.
--An Abundant Harvest. Daring, Hope, pseud. N.D. Methodist Book Concern.
--Entering into His Own. Daring, Hope, pseud. LC 3-20891. 3 p. l., 279p. front. pl. 19 1/2cm. 1903. American Tract Society.
--The Furniture People. Daring, Hope, pseud. LC 3-21296. 116 p. front., 5 pl. 19 cm. 1903. G. W. Jacobs & Co.
--Hopscotch Valley ... Daring, Hope, pseud. LC 45-20693. v. illus. 23 1/2 cm. N.D. The Deseret News Press.
--Madeline, the Island Girl. Hope, Daring, pseud. (Bks. for Camp Fire Girls). N.D. Abingdon Pres.
--Madeline, the Island Girl. Hope, Daring, pseud. LC 6-13937. 282 p. 4pl. 19cm. c.1906. Eaton & Mains, New York, Jenning & Graham, Cincinatti.
--Rainbow Trails. LC 41-27324. 41p. 20cm. 1941. The Caxton Printers, Ltd.
--The Woods in the Home. Daring, Hope, pseud. Fisher, Elizabeth M., illus. LC 27-17416. 116 p. incl. col. front., col. illus. 19 cm. (A "Just right" book). c.1927. A. Withman & Company.

Johnson, Annabell Jones see Johnson, A. E., pseud.

Johnson, Annabell Jones (1921-)
--As a Speckled Bird. Johnson, A. E., pseud. 1956. Crowell.

Johnson, Annabell Jones (1921-) & Johnson, Edgar Raymond (1912-)
--An Alien Music. LC 82-70417. 192p. (gr. 7 up). 1982. (ISBN 0-590-07842-9, Four Winds). Scholastic Inc.
--The Bearcat. LC 60-9458. 22cm. 231p. (gr. 7 up). 1960. (ISBN 0-06-022836-9, HarpJ). Har-Row. **Award: (ALA).**
--The Big Rock Candy. 1957. Crowell.
--Black Symbol. Saunders, Brian, illus. LC 58-9780. (gr. 7 up). 1959. (ISBN 0-06-022846-6, HarpJ). Har-Row.
--The Burning Glass. LC 66-798166. 244p. 22cm. 1966. (ISBN 0-06-022851-2). Harper.
--Count Me Gone. LC 68-16147. 188 p. 21cm. 1968. Simon & Schuster.
--The Danger Quotient. LC 83-48439. 216 p. 22cm. c.1984. (ISBN 0-06-022852-0). (ISBN 0-06-022853-9). Harper & Row.
--Finders, Keepers. LC 80-69994. (Illus.). vii, 119 p. 22cm. c.1981. (ISBN 0-590-07790-2). Four Winds Press.
--A Golden Touch. LC 63-10592. 230 p. 22cm. 1963. Harper & Row. **Award: (ALA).**
--The Grizzly. Riswold, Gilbert, illus. LC 64-11831. (Illus.). 160 p. 22cm. 1964. Harper & Row. **Award: (ALA).**
--The Last Knife. LC 71-144786. 192 p. 22cm. 1971. (ISBN 0-671-65166-8). Simon and Schuster.
--Peculiar Magic. 1965. E M Hale.
--Peculiar Magic. Ward, Lynd Kendall (1905-1985), illus. LC 65-22508. (Illus.). 22cm. 246p. (gr. 4-6). 1965. (ISBN 0-395-06843-6). HM.
--Pickpocket Run. LC 61-12087. 185 p. 22cm. 1961. Harper.
--Prisoner of PSI. 149p. 1985. (ISBN 0-689-31132-X). Atheneum.
--The Rescued Heart. LC 61-9335. 199 p. 22cm. 1961. Harper.
--Torrie. Falconer, Pearl, illus. LC 59-8973. 217 p. 22cm. 1960. Harper. **Award: (ALA).**
--Wilderness Bride. LC 62-12603. 232 p. 22cm. 1962. Harper & Row. **Award: (ALA).**

Johnson, Annie Fellows, Mrs. (1863-1931)
--Big Brother. Secker, A. M., illus. (Cosy Corner Ser.). N.D. L. C. Page & Co.
--Flips "Islands of Providence". Bonsall, E. F., illus. (Cosy Corner Ser.). N.D. L. C. Page & Co.
--The Little Man in Motley. Waite, Emily B., illus. (Cosy Corner Ser.). N.D. L. C. Page & Co.
Johnson, Artis
--Oliver Wants a Pony. (gr. 2-4). 1978. (ISBN 0-682-49028-8). Exposition.
Johnson, Audean, illus.
--Soft as a Kitten. (Illus.). 14p. (Random House Touch-Me Bks.). (ps). 1982. (ISBN 0-394-85517-5). Random.
Johnson, Audrey Pike (1915-)
--Little Lies. 160p. (Orig.). (gr. 7 up). 1984. (ISBN 0-590-33492-1, Wildfire). Scholastic Inc.
--The Pet Show. Hillinger, Edith, illus. LC 74-162048. (Illus.). 24 p. 26cm. (Magic circle book). 1972. (ISBN 0-663-22967-7). Ginn.
--Sisters. 160p. (Orig.). (gr. 7 up). 1982. (ISBN 0-590-32183-8, Wishing Star). Scholastic Inc.
Johnson, August Wisdom (1898-)
--Tell Us About Texas. Benton, Lynn Walcott, illus. LC 36-5940. 7 p. l., 115 p., incl. front., illus., 2 col. pl. 23 cm. 1935. Tardy Publishing Company, Incorporated.
--Wagon Yard. Bywaters, Jerry, illus. LC 40-83792. 3 p. l., 201 p. front., illus. 24 cm. c.1938. W. T. Tardy.
Johnson, Barbara Greenough
--The Big Fish. N.D. E. M. Hale & Co.
--The Big Fish. 1st ed. Means, Mary Greenough, illus. LC 59-7350. (Illus.). 43 p. 26cm. 1959. Little, Brown.
Johnson, Barney
--Thunder of the Sierras. LC 31-115. 264 p. plates. 20 cm. 1930. Trade Service Publishing Co.
Johnson, Burdetta Faye see Beebe, Burdetta Faye.
Johnson, Burdetta Faye Beebe (1920-)
--Assateague Deer. Johnson, James Ralph (1922-), illus. LC 65-14126. (Illus.). 150 p. 21cm. 1965. D. McKay Co.
--Chestnut Cub. Johnson, James Ralph (1922-), illus. LC 63-16694. 153 p. illus. 21 cm. 1963. (ISBN 0-679-25030-1). D. McKay Co.
--Coyote, Come Home. Toschik, Larry (1922-), illus. LC 65-10488. (Illus.). 143 p. 21cm. 1963. D. McKay Co.
--Coyote for Keeps. Johnson, James Ralph (1922-), illus. LC 65-14478. (Illus.). 160 p. 23cm. 1965. Follett Pub. Co.
--Little Dickens, Jaguar Cub. Johnson, James Ralph (1922-), illus. LC 74-102651. (Illus.). 133 p. 21cm. 1970. (ISBN 0-679-20096-7). McKay.
--Little Red. Johnson, James Ralph (1922-), illus. LC 66-16939. (Illus.). 160 p. 22cm. 1966. Follett Pub. Co.
--Ocelot. Johnson, James Ralph (1922-), illus. LC 66-77667. 151p. illus. 22cm. 1966. McKay.
--Run, Light Buck, Run!. The Adventurous Life of a Lone Pronghorn and a Man on Arizona's Paria Plateau. Toschik, Larry (1922-), illus. LC 62-10749. 122p. illus. 21cm. (gr. 6-10). 1962. D. McKay Co.
--Yucatan Monkey. Johnson, James Ralph (1922-), illus. LC 67-20202. (Illus.). 146 p. 21cm. 1967. (ISBN 0-679-25184-7). D. McKay Co.
Johnson, Burges, jt. auth. see Mayhew, Ralph.
Johnson, Burges (1877-1963), ed.
--Childhood. Hunter, Cecilia Bull & Ogden, Caroline, illus. LC 12-24448. 44p. 30 x 24cm. 1912. Thomas Y. Crowell Company.
--A Little Book of Necessary Nonsense. (Round Table Ser.). N.D. Harper & Bros.
--More Necessary Nonsense. (Round Table Ser.). N.D. Harper & Bros.
--Rhymes of Little Boys. N.D. Putnam's Trade List.
--Rhymes of Little Boys. (Illus.). 1905. Thomas Y. Crowell & Co.
Johnson, Caesar, ed.
--Memories of Home. Besunder, Marvin, illus. LC 78-91818. (Illus.). 84 p. 21cm. 1970. C. R. Gibson Co.
Johnson, Charles F., ed. see Coffin, Charles Carleton.
Johnson, Charles Frederick
--Steve Fletcher, U. S. Marine: A Story of Recruit Training in the Marine Corps. 1st ed. Grimley, Oliver, illus. LC 57-10195. 176p. illus. 22cm. 1957. Winston.
Johnson, Clare I.
--The Golden Trail. N.D. Augustena Book Concern.
Johnson, Clarke, Mrs.
--Earning Her Way: A Story for Girls. Waugh, Ida, illus. (Illus.). (Keystone Ser.). N.D. Penn Publishing Co.
--Earning Her Way to College: A Story for Girls. Waugh, Ida, illus. LC 3891. 373 p. front., plates. 19 cm. (College girl's stories). 1900. The Penn Publishing Company.
--Her College Days: A Story for Girls. Waugh, Ida, illus. LC 12-347531. 1 p. l., 5-336 p. front., plates. 19 cm. (College Girl's Stories). 1896. The Penn Publishing Company.
Johnson, Clifton (1865-), ed. see Abbott, Jacob.
Johnson, Clifton, ed. see Cervantes Saavedra, Miguel de.
Johnson, Clifton, retold by see Day, Thomas.
Johnson, Clifton (1865-), ed. see Dodgson, Charles Lutwidge.
Johnson, Clifton (1865-), retold by see Edgeworth, Maria.
Johnson, Clifton (1865-), ed. see Malory, Thomas, Sir.
Johnson, Clifton (1865-1940), ed. see Mother Goose.
Johnson, Clifton (1865-), adapted by see Reynard the Fox. English & Von Goethe, Johann Wolfgang.
Johnson, Clifton (1865-1940)
--Babes in the Wood. (Illus.). N.D. E. P. Dutton & Co.
--The Babes in the Wood. Smith, Harry L., illus. (Bedtime Wonder Tales). N.D. Cupples & Leon Co.
--The Babes in the Wood. Smith, Harry L., illus. LC 20-6890. 128 p. col. front., col. plates. 18 cm. (Bedtime wonder tales). c.1919. The Macaulay Company.
--Battleground Adventures. (Illus.). N.D. Houston Mifflin Co.
--Cinderella. Smith, Harry L., illus. LC 19-17058. 128 p. col. front., col. plates. 18 cm. (Bedtime wonder tales). c.1919. The Macaulay Company.
--The Farmer's Boy. Johnson, Clifton (1865-1940), illus. (Illus.). 1905. Appleton and Co.
--The Fox and the Little Red Hen. Smith, Harry L., illus. LC 20-6892. 128 p. col. front., col. plates. 18 cm. (Bedtime wonder tales). c.1919. The Macaulay Company.
--Golden Hair and the Three Bears. Smith, Harry L., illus. (Bedtime Wonder Tales). N.D. Cupples & Leon Co.
--Golden Hair and the Three Bears. Smith, Harry L., illus. LC 20-689112. 128 p. col. front., col. plates. 18 cm. (Bedtime wonder tales). c.1919. The Macaulay Company.
--Hop-O'-My-Thumb. Smith, Harry L., illus. LC 20-1682. 128 p. col. front., col. plates. 19 cm. (Bedtime wonder tales). c.1919. The Macaulay Company.
--Jack and the Beanstalk. Smith, Harry L., illus. (Bedtime Wonder Tales). N.D. Cupples & Leon Co.
--Jack and the Beanstalk. Smith, Harry L., illus. LC 19-17057. 128 p. col. front., col. plates. 18 cm. (Bedtime wonder tales). c.1919. The Macaulay Company.
--Little Red Riding Hood. Smith, Harry L., illus. (Children's Popular Library). N.D. Cupples & Leon Co.
--Little Red Ridinghood. Smith, Harry L., illus. LC 19-17056. 128 p. col. front., col. plates. 18 cm. (Bedtime wonder tales). c.1919. The Macaulay Company.
--The Pied Piper. Smith, Harry L., illus. (Bedtime Wonder Tales). N.D. Cupples & Leon Co.
--Puss in Boots. Smith, Harry L., illus. (Bedtime Wonder Tales). N.D. Cupples & Leon Co.
--Puss in Boots. Smith, Harry L., illus. LC 19-170556. 128 p. col. front., col. plates. 18 cm. (Bedtime wonder tales). c.1919. The Macaulay Company.
--Robin Hood ... Bonte, Willard, illus. LC 10-24203. xiv, 293 p. col. front., plates. 20 cm. (Half-title: Golden books for children, ed. by C. Johnson). 1910. The Baker & Taylor Company.
--Sailing for Gold. Reid, James (1907-), illus. LC 38-6757. 4 p. l., 3-264 p. incl. front., illus. 20 cm. c.1938. G. P. Putnam's Sons.
--The Seasons: Being Four Conversation Between John Simons and Jane Smith. Johnson, Clifton (1865-1940), illus. LC 14-22469. 18 p. ill. 15 cm. 1893. Bryant Print.
--The Sleeping Beauty. Smith, Harry L., illus. (Bedtime Wonder Tales). N.D. Cupples & Leon Co.
--St. George and the Dragon. Smith, Harry L., illus. (Bedtime Wonder Tales). N.D. Cupples & Leon Co.
--The Story of Chicken-Licken. Smith, Harry L., illus. (Bedtime Wonder Tales). N.D. Cupples & Leon Co.
--The Story of Chicken-Licken. Smith, Harry L., illus. LC 19-170540. 128 p. col. front., col. plates. 18 cm. (Bedtime wonder tales). c.1919. The Macaulay Company.
--The Story of Johny-Cake. Thomson, Rodney, illus. N.D. Dodge.
--The Tale of a Black Cat. Nankivell, Frank A., illus. N.D. Dodge.
--Tom Thumb. Smith, Harry L., illus. (Bedtime Wonder Tales). N.D. Cupples & Leon Co.
--Waste Not, Want Not Stories. LC 5-38491. 260 p. illus. 19 cm. (On cover: Eclectic readings). c.1905. American Book Company.
Johnson, Clifton (1865-1940), ed.
--The Arabian Nights. Emerson, Caspar & D'Emo, Leon, illus. (Illus.). N.D. Baker & Taylor Co.
--The Arabian Nights' Entertainments. LC 4-26248. ix, 258 p. front., illus. (map) 15 cm. (Macmillan's pocket American and English classics). 1904. The Macmillan Company.
--The Birch-Tree Fairy Book: Favorite Fairy Tales. Bonte, Willard, illus. LC 6-40590. xiv p., 1 l., 346 p., 1 l. incl. front., illus., plates. 21 cm. 1906. Little, Brown, & Company.
--Bluebeard. Smith, Harry L., illus. (Bedtime Wonder Tales). N.D. Cupples & Leon Co.
--A Book of Fairy-Tale Bears: Selections from Favorite Folk-Lore Stories. Nankivell, Frank A., illus. LC 13-20748. vi p., 2 l., 3-184 p. col. front., col. plates. 18 cm. 1913. Houghton Mifflin Company.
--A Book of Fairy-Tale Foxes: Selections from Favorite Folk-Lore Stories. Nankivell, Frank A., illus. LC 14-13124. vi p., 2 l., 3-224 p., 1 l. col. front., col. plates. 18 cm. (Bedtime fairy-tale series, ed. by C. Johnson). 1914. Houghton Mifflin Company.
--The Brave Tin Soldier. Smith, Harry L., illus. (Bedtime Wonder Tales). N.D. Cupples & Leon Co.
--Cinderella. Smith, Harry L., illus. (Bedtime Wonder Tales). N.D. Cupples & Leon Co.
--The Elm-Tree Fairy Book: Favorite Fairy Tales. Hiller, Lejaren A., illus. LC 8-37186. 2 p. l., vii-xiii, 338 p., 1 l. incl. front., illus., plates. 21 cm. 1908. Little, Brown, & Company.
--The Fir-Tree Fairy Book: Favorite Fairy Tales. Popini, Alexander, illus. LC 12-25994. xii, 333, 1 p. incl. front., illus., plates. col. plates. 21 cm. 1912. Little, Brown, & Company.
--The Fox and the Little Red Hen. Smith, Harry L., illus. (Bedtime Wonder Tales). N.D. Cupples & Leon Co.
--Hop-O'-My-Thumb. Smith, Harry L., illus. (Bedtime Wonder Tales). N.D. Cupples & Leon Co.
--King Arthur and the Knights of the Round Table. N.D. Macmillan.
--Little Folks' Book of Verse. Bassett, Mary Robertson, illus. LC 11-27151. xviii, 232 p. col. front., plates. 20 cm. (Half-title: Golden books for children). 1911. The Baker & Taylor Company.
--Little Red Riding-Hood. Smith, Harry L., illus. (Bedtime Wonder Tales). N.D. Cupples & Leon Co.
--Mother Goose Rhymes. Knowles, Machan, illus. LC 11-2993. (Illus.). 199p. 20cm. 1911. The Baker & Taylor Company.
--The Oak-Tree Fairy Book. (Illus.). N.D. (ISBN 0-8446-2334-2). Peter Smith Publisher, Inc.
--The Oak-Tree Fairy Book: Favorite Fairy Tales. Bonte, Willard, illus. LC 68-28407. (Illus.). xvi, 365 p. 21cm. 1968. Dover Publications.
--The Oak-Tree Fairy Book: Favorite Fairy Tales. Bonte, Willard, illus. LC 5-35594. xvi p., 1 l. 365 p. incl. front., illus., plates. 21 cm. 1905. Little, Brown, and Company.
--Poems My Children Love Best of All. Bassett, Mary Robertson & Hammell, Will, illus. LC 18-26262. 4 p. l., 256 p. col. front., col. plates 21 cm. 1917. L. A. Noble.
Johnson, Constance Fuller Wheeler, Mrs. (1879-)
--The Carter Children in France. Camp, Leslie, illus. LC 27-24200. 187 p. incl. front. ill. pl. 20 1/2cm. 1927. Dodd Mead & Co.
--Mary in California. LC 22-19477. viii p., 2 l., 242 p. col. front., plates. 20 cm. 1922. The Macmillan Company.
--Mary in New Mexico. LC 21-191985. 7 p. l., 209 p. front., plates. 20 cm. 1921. The Macmillan Company.
--When Mother Lets Us Keep Pets. N.D. Dodd Mead & Co.
Johnson, Crockett, pseud., see Leisk, David Johnson.
Johnson, Crockett, jt. auth. see Krauss, Ruth Ida.
Johnson, Crockett, pseud. (1906-1975)
--Harold's Fairy Tale: Further Adventures with the Purple Crayon. Leisk, David Johnson. LC 56-8147. (Illus.). 64 p. 16cm. c.1956. Harper.
Johnson, Dana William (1945-)
--The Willow Flute: A North Country Tale. Johnson, Dana William (1945-), illus. LC 74-13183. (Illus.). 48 p. 21cm. 1975. (ISBN 0-316-46756-1). Little, Brown.
Johnson, Dana William (1945-), adapted by.
--Jack and the Beanstalk. Johnson, Dana William (1945-), illus. LC 76-3527. (Illus.). 46 p. 26cm. c.1976. Little, Brown.
Johnson, Donna Kay (1935-)
--Brighteyes. Johnson, Donna Kay (1935-), illus. LC 78-4353. (Illus.). (gr. 1 up). 1978. (ISBN 0-03-044651-1). HR&W.
Johnson, Doris (1922-)
--Cloud of Summer. Mars, Witold Tadeusz J. (1912-), illus. (Illus.). (gr. 1-3). 1967. (ISBN 0-695-41434-8). Follett.
--Su An. Weisgard, Leonard Joseph (1916-), illus. LC 68-13787. (Illus.). 30 p. 20cm. 1968. Follett Pub. Co.
Johnson, Dorothy Ann
--Little Koala Bear. Johnson, Dorothy Ann, illus. LC 37-12227. 34 p. illus. 26cm. 1937. Saalfield Pub, Co.
Johnson, Dorothy Marie (1905-)
--All the Buffalo Returning. LC 78-22425. (gr. 10 up). 1979. Dodd.
--Buffalo Woman. LC 76-53436. (gr. 10 up). 1977. Dodd.
--Farewell to Troy. Miret, Gil, illus. LC 64-21955. 214 p. illus. 22 cm. 1964. Houghton Mifflin.
--Flame on the Frontier: Short Stories of Pioneer Women. LC 67-4788. 141 p. 21cm. 1967. Dodd, Mead.
--Short Stories of Pioneering Women: Short Stories of Pioneering Women. (gr. 9 up). 1967. (ISBN 0-396-05555-9). Dodd.
--Witch Princess. Cather, Carolyn, illus. LC 67-23308. (Illus.). photos. (gr. 7 up). 1967. (ISBN 0-395-06844-4). HM.
Johnson, E.
--The Judge's Pets. N.D. Hurd & Houghton.
Johnson, E. K., illus.
--Puss in Boots. (Illus.). N.D. White, Stokes & Allen.
Johnson, E. Ned, pseud., see Johnson, Enid.
Johnson, Edgar Raymond, jt. auth. see Johnson, A. E.
Johnson, Edgar Raymond, jt. auth. see Johnson, Annabell Jones.
Johnson, Edith L
--Log Cabin Children. Downer, Marion (1892-1971), illus. LC 42-134232. 5 p. l., 191 p. illus. 21 cm. 1942. Lothrop, Lee & Shepard Co.
Johnson, Edna, ed.
--Anthology of Children's Literature. 4th ed. Eichenberg, Fritz (1901-), illus. LC 59-16179. (Illus.). 1239 p. 25cm. 1959. Houghton Mifflin.
--Anthology of Children's Literature. 5th ed. Wyeth, Newell Convers (1882-1945), illus. LC 76-20869. (Illus.). xxxvi, 1180 p., 4 leaves of plates. 25cm. c.1977. (ISBN 0-395-24554-0). Houghton Mifflin.
Johnson, Edna & Scott, Carrie Emma (1874-1943), eds.
--Anthology of Children's Literature. LC 35-1392. xxvii, p., 2 l., 3-914 p. 25 cm. c.1935. Houghton Mifflin Company.
--Anthology of Children's Literature. 2d ed. LC 48-725013. xiv, 1114 p. illus. 25 cm. 1948. Houghton, Mifflin Co.
--Anthology of Children's Literature. 3d ed. Wyeth, Newell Convers (1882-1945) & Eichenberg, Fritz (1902-), illus. LC 40-33745. xxix p., 2 l., 917 p. col. plates. 26 cm. 1940. Houghton Mifflin Company.
Johnson, Edna & Sickels, Evelyn Ray (1895-), eds.
--Anthology of Children's Literature. 4th ed. Eichenberg, Fritz (1901-), illus. LC 72-129203. (Illus.). xxxviii, 1289 p. 25cm. 1970. Houghton Mifflin.
Johnson, Edwin A.
--The Live Boy: Or, Charlie's Letters. (Illus.). N.D. Methodist Book Concern.
--Peter Thatsall. N.D. Vantage Press.
Johnson, Eleanor Murdoch, jt. ed. see Nolen, Barbara.
Johnson, Eleanor Noyes
--Armitage Hall. LC 65-13119. 135 p. 22cm. 1965. Macmillan.
--Buffington Castle. 1st ed. Geer, Charles Hand (1922-), illus. LC 62-8530. 149p. illus. 21cm. 1962. Duell, Sloan and Pearce.
--Mountaintop Summer. Case, Bernard, illus. LC 59-5866. 164p. illus. 21cm. 1959. Broadman Press.
--Mrs Perley's People. N.D. (ISBN 0-664-32477-0). Westminster Press.
Johnson, Elinor M
--The Plant Hunters. Stewart, Arvis L., illus. LC 79-80504. (Illus.). 107 p. 21cm. 1969. Addison-Wesley.
Johnson, Elizabeth Goodwin
--Peter Pother, Junior. Masterson, Dorothy Goodwin, illus. LC 51-8662. 60 p. illus. 22 cm. 1951. Vantage Press.
Johnson, Elizabeth Harrover
--Almost Cousins. Case, Bernard, illus. LC 61-127565. 147p. illus. 21cm. 1961. Washburn.
--Christy Finds a Rider. Savitt, Sam (1917-), illus. LC 65-21601. (Illus.). 89 p. 20cm. 1965. I. Washburn.
--Horse Show Fever. Walker, Charles W., illus. LC 62-18467. 135p. illus. 21cm. 1962. Washburn.
--Horse Show Fever. Walker, Charles W., illus. (Illus.). (gr. 4-6). 1963. (ISBN 0-679-27027-2). Washburn.
--The Mysterious Trunk. N.D. David McKay Company Inc.
--The Mysterious Trunk. Voute, Kathleen (1892-), illus. LC 60-13321. (Illus.). 21cm. 153p. (gr. 4-6). 1960. (ISBN 0-679-27040-X). Washburn.

AUTHOR INDEX JOHNSON, MARGARET

--The Old Quarry Fox Hunt. Savitt, Sam (1917-), illus. LC 64-21321. vi, 125 p. illus. 21 cm. 1964. I. Washburn.
--The Pony That Didn't Grow. Lewis, Richard William (1933-1966), illus. LC 63-16689. (Illus.). 62 p. 20cm. 1963. I. Washburn.

Johnson, Elizabeth (1911-)
--All in Free but Janey. Hyman, Trina Schart (1939-), illus. LC 68-15556. (Illus.). 31 p. 25cm. 1968. Little, Brown. **Award: (BGH).**
--Break a Magic Circle. Hyman, Trina Schart (1939-), illus. LC 70-129911. (Illus.). 70 p. 23cm. 1971. Little, Brown.
--The Little Knight. Solbert, Romaine (1925-), tr. Solbert, Ronni, pseud. LC 57-8042. 56p. illus. 24cm. 1957. Brown.
--The Little Knight. Solbert, Ronni, pseud. (1925-), illus. Solbert, Romaine G. LC 57-8042. (Illus.). (gr. 2-4). 1957. (ISBN 0-316-46767-7). Little.
--No Magic, Thank You. 1st ed. Price, Garrett W. (1896-1979), illus. LC 64-13979. 55 p. illus. 22 cm. 1964. Little, Brown.
--Stuck with Luck. 1st ed. Hyman, Trina Schart (1939-), illus. LC 67-1754. (Illus.). 88 p. 22cm. 1967. Little, Brown.
--The Three-in-One Prince. Solbert, Romaine G. (1925-), illus. Solbert, Ronni, pseud. LC 61-5318. (Illus.). 58 p. 24cm. 1961. Little, Brown.

Johnson, Elmer S.
--At Least Once. 1983. (ISBN 0-533-05566-0). Vantage.

Johnson, Emilie Fendall, see Johnson, Emillie Louise Dickey.

Johnson, Emillie Louise Dickey see Johnson, Emilie Fendall.

Johnson, Emillie Louise Dickey (1892-)
--The Umbrella Bird, and Other Verses. Johnson, Emilie Fendall, Malcher, Lucretia, illus. LC 40-6334. (Illus.). 83p. 25cm. 1939. Falmouth Book House.

Johnson, Emily Rhoads
--Spring & the Shadow Man. Geiger, Paul, illus. LC 84-1675. 160p. (gr. 4 up). 1984. (ISBN 0-396-08330-7). (ISBN 0-396-08330-7). Dodd.

Johnson, Enid see Johnson, E. Ned, pseud.

Johnson, Enid, jt. auth. see Peck, Anne Merriman.

Johnson, Enid (1892-)
--Big Bright Land. Peck, Anne Merriman (1884-), illus. LC 54-855382. 264p. illus. 20cm. (Starlight novels for modern girls). 1954, c.1947. Grosset & Dunlap.
--Big Bright Land. Peck, Anne Merriman (1884-), illus. LC 47-2101. 22cm. 264p. 1947. Messner.
--Cochise, Great Apache Chief. Bjorklund, Lorence F. (1913-1978), illus. LC 53-10505. (Illus.). 180 p. 22cm. 1953. J. Messner.
--Cowgirl Kate. McCarthy, Frank, illus. 1950. Jullian Messner, Inc.
--Cross-Country Bus Ride. Zansky, Louis, illus. LC 53-10506. 62p. illus. 22cm. (Everyday adventure story). 1953. J. Messner.
--Garbage Dump Treasure. rev. ed. Koering, Ursula (1921-), illus. LC 64-16787. (Illus.). 63 p. 21cm. (New everyday adventure story). 1964. Melmont Publishers.
--Ho for California!. Peck, Anne Merriman (1884-), illus. LC 39-20772. 5 p. l., 3-243 p. incl. front., illus. 21 cm. 1939. Harper & Brothers.
--Jerry's Treasure Hunt. Koering, Ursula (1921-), illus. LC 51-13236. 64 p. illus. 22 cm. (Everyday adventure story). 1951. Messner.
--Nancy Runs the Bookmobile. LC 56-6790. 189p. 21cm. (Romance for young moderns). 1956. Messner.
--Natalie. Wallower, Lucille (1910-), illus. LC 38-32617. 5 p. l., 17-287 p. incl. illus., plates. col. front., col. pl. 28 cm. 1938. A. Whitman & Co.
--The Right Job for Judith. LC 51-12797. 184 p. 21 cm. (Romance for young moderns). 1951. Messner.
--Runaway Balboa. Peck, Anne Merriman (1884-), illus. LC 38-12121. 26cm. 41p. 1938. Harper & Bros.
--Second Chance. LC 58-11489. 190 p. 22cm. 1958. Messner.
--The Three J's. Fleur, Anne Elizabeth (1901-), illus. Sari, pseud. LC 52-9332. 63 p. illus. 22 cm. (Everyday adventure story). 1952. Messner.
--Tommy and the Orange-Lemon Tree. Peck, Anne Merriman (1884-), illus. LC 53-7384. 63p. illus. 22cm. (Everyday adventure story). 1953. J. Messner.
--Wyatt Earp, Gunfighting Marshal. Johnson, E. Ned, pseud. Bjorklund, Lorence F. (1913-1978), illus. LC 56-6789. 192p. illus. 22cm. 1956. J. Messner.

Johnson, Enid (1892-) & Johnson, Margaret
--Mystery of the Seven Murals. 1940. Random House.
--Sally's Real Estate Venture. LC 54-6769. 190p. 21cm. (Romance for young moderns). 1954. J. Messner.

Johnson, Eric Warner (1918-)
--Escape into the Zoo. Goldsborough, June (1923-), illus. LC 70-151471. (Illus.). 64p. (gr. k-3). 1971. (ISBN 0-397-31174-5). (ISBN 0-397-31175-3). Lippincott.
--The Stolen Ruler. Goldsborough, June (1923-), illus. LC 72-117239. (Illus.). 64 p. 21cm. 1970. Lippincott.

Johnson, Ethel B.
--Animal Stories the Indians Told. 1927. Alfred A. Knopf.
--Monte & the Coons. (gr. k-3). 1978. (ISBN 0-682-48978-6). Exposition.

Johnson, Eugene Harper
--Almost Cousins. 1961. David Mckay Company Inc.
--Christy Finds A Rider. 1965. David McKay Company Inc.
--Kenny. 1st ed. Johnson, Eugene Harper, illus. LC 57-5749. 190p. illus. 21cm. 1957. Holt.
--The Old Quarry Fox Hunt. N.D. David McKay Company Inc.
--The Pony That Didn't Grow. 1964. David McKay Company Inc.

Johnson, Eva J.
--Woozie. N.D. (ISBN 0-8062-2269-7). Carlton.

Johnson, Evelyne (1932-)
The Elephant's Ball. Tien, illus. LC 76-51743. (Illus.). 37 p. 22cm. c.1977. (ISBN 0-07-032614-2). (ISBN 0-07-032615-0). McGraw-Hill.

Johnson, Evelyne (1932-), retold by.
--The Cow in the Kitchen: A Folk Tale. Rao, Anthony, illus. LC 82-23987. (Illus.). 18 p. 21cm. c.1983. (ISBN 0-671-46086-2). Little Simon.

Johnson, F. Roy
--Supernaturals Among Carolina Folk & Their Neighbors. Mizelle, Judy G., illus. (Illus.). bibl. footnotes. index. 256p. (gr. 8-12). 1974. (ISBN 0-930230-25-6). Johnson NC.

Johnson, Fred (1908-)
--The Foxes. LC 73-83781. (Illus.). 32 p. 27cm. (Ranger Rick's best friends). 1973. (ISBN 0-912186-04-6). National Wildlife Federation.
--Jim Boy. Molloy, Eideen, illus. (Illus.). 1977. (ISBN 0-533-02902-3). Vantage.

Johnson, Frederica
--Brighter Tomorrow. LC 57-11280. 170p. 21cm. c.1957. Pageant Press.

Johnson, Gail E.
--Phantom Horse of Collister's Fields. (Indian Culture Ser.). (gr. 4-12). 1974. (ISBN 0-89992-062-4). MT Coun Indian.

Johnson, George M.
--Peace River Justice. (Western Stories for Boys). N.D. Grosset & Dunlap.
--Riders of the Trail. (Western Stories for Boys). N.D. Grosset & Dunlap.
--Trouble Ranch. (Western Stories for Boys). N.D. Grosset & Dunlap.

Johnson, Gladys O
--Jimmie, the Youngest Errand Boy. Talarczyk, June, illus. LC 66-30583. (Illus.). 32 p. 29cm. 1967. T. S. Denison.

Johnson, Grace Cecelia Tracy
--Courage Wins. 1st ed. Burchard, Peter Duncan (1921-), illus. LC 54-582953. 222p. illus. 21cm. 1954. Dutton.

Johnson, Grace Cecelia Tracy & Johnson, Harold Nels
--The Broken Rosary. LC 59-9082. 191p. 22cm. 1959. Bruce Pub. Co.
--A Hand Raised at Gettysburg. LC 55-103936. 122p. illus. 22cm. (Catholic treasury books). 1955. Bruce Pub. Co.
--Kay Ann. LC 51-9928. 221 p. 21 cm. 1951. Whittlesey House.
--Roman Collar Detective. LC 53-2668. 184p. 22cm. 1953. Bruce Pub. Co.

Johnson, Gyneth
--How the Donkeys Came to Haiti. Benedetto, Angelo Di, illus. LC 48-7727. 86 p. illus. 23 cm. 1949. Devin-Adair Co.

Johnson, Hammel
--The House of Many Stairways. LC 28-2514. v, 1 p., 1 l., 237, 1 p. front. 20 cm. 1928. D. Appleton and Company.
--Priscilla of Prydehurst. LC 27-5422. 3 p. l., 246, 1 p. front. 20 cm. 1927. D. Appleton and Company.
--Prydehurst. LC 26-149831. 3 p. l., 234, 1 p. front. 20 cm. 1926. D. Appleton and Company.

Johnson, Hannah Lyons
--From Seed to Jack-O-Lantern. Dorn, Daniel, illus. LC 74-6458. (Illus.). 40p. (gr. k-4). 1974. (ISBN 0-688-51644-0). Lothrop.
--Hello, Small Sparrow. Chen, Tony (1929-), illus. LC 74-135298. (Illus.). 33 p. 22cm. 1971. Lothrop, Lee & Shepard Co.
--Hello Small Sparrow. Chen, Tony (1929-), illus. 1970. (ISBN 0-688-40979-2). William Morrow and Company.
--Lets Make Jam. Dorn, Daniel, illus. 1975. (ISBN 0-688-41682-9). William Morrow and Company.

Johnson, Hannah More
--First the Blade. LC 12-34752. 270 p. front., plates. 18 cm. c.1883. Presbyterian Board of Publication.

Johnson, Harold Nels, jt. auth. see Johnson, Grace Cecelia Tracy.

Johnson, Harriet
--Honolulu Zoo Riddles. Thompson, Judi, illus. (Illus.). 1974. (ISBN 0-914916-07-6). Topgallant.
--Kinji Goes Fishing. Summers, Leo, illus. LC 67-5988. (Illus.). 1 v. (unpaged. 29cm. (Carousel book). 1967. L. W. Singer Co.

Johnson, Harvey L., tr. see Altamirano, Ignacio Manuel.

Johnson, Hedvig
--Love Helps You Grow. Paris, Pat & Shackelford, Jeanie, illus. LC 83-27315. (Illus.). 44 p. 29cm. (Rose-Petal Place Ser.). (ps-3). c.1984. (ISBN 0-910313-58-X). Parker Bros.

Johnson, Helen Kendrick (1844-1917), ed.
--Illustrated Poems and Songs for Young People. LC 6-35047. 307, 1, xv p. incl. front., illus., plates. 22 x 18 cm. 1884. G. Routledge and Sons.
--Poems for Childhood. (Illus.). 316p. N.D. Monarch Book Company
--Roddy's Ideal. (Illus.). (Roddy Ser.). N.D. Set. G P Putnam's Sons.
--Roddy's Realities. 1875. G. P. Putnam's Sons.
--Roddy's Romance. (Illus.). (Roddy Ser.). N.D. Set. G P Putnam's Sons.

Johnson, Helen Lossing, Mrs., jt. auth. see Johnson, Margaret Sweet.

Johnson, Hugh Samuel (1882-)
--Williams of West Point. LC 8-28984. viii p., 1 l., 292 p., 1 l. col. front., 3 col. pl. 20 cm. 1908. D. Appleton and Company.
--Williams of West Point. (Every Boy's Library). N.D. Grosset & Dunlap.

Johnson, Humphrey (1925-1976)
--The Perilous Journey. 1st ed. Johnson, Iris Beatty, illus. LC 57-11685. 144p. illus. 21cm. 1957. Holt.

Johnson, Irma Bolan (1903-)
--The Goodenough Poultry Farm. Krieger, Carol, illus. (Illus.). 34 p. 24cm. 1967. Elk Grove Press.
--March of the Harvest. N.D. Elk Grove Press.

Johnson, Jack, jt. auth. see Johnson, Laura.

Johnson, James Ralph (1922-)
--Big Cypress Buck. Johnson, James Ralph (1922-), illus. LC 57-11031. (Illus.). 25cm. 128p. (gr. 5 up). 1957. (ISBN 0-695-40760-0). Follett.
--Blackie, the Gorilla. Johnson, James Ralph (1922-), illus. LC 68-29567. (Illus.). ils. bibl. 160p. (gr. 6-9). 1968. (ISBN 0-679-20026-6). McKay.
--Camels West. Johnson, James Ralph (1922-), illus. LC 64-19409. 154 p. illus. 21 cm. 1964. D. McKay Co.
--Everglades Adventure. LC 71-102653. (Illus.). 176 p. 21cm. 1970. McKay.
--Lost on Hawk Mountain. Johnson, James Ralph (1922-), illus. LC 54-10103. (Illus.). 23cm. 187p. (gr. 5 up). 1954. (ISBN 0-695-45390-4). Follett.
--Moses' Band of Chimpanzees. Johnson, James Ralph (1922-), illus. LC 69-12951. (Illus.). 149 p. 21cm. 1969. D. McKay Co.
--Mountain Bobcat. Sherwan, Earl (1917-), illus. LC 53-10602. (Illus.). 160 p. 23cm. 1953. Wilcox and Follett Co.
--Pepper: A Puerto Rican Mongoose. Johnson, James Ralph (1922-), illus. LC 67-25324. (Illus.). 137 p. 21cm. 1967. D. McKay Co.
--Ringtail. Johnson, James Ralph (1922-), illus. LC 68-14120. (Illus.). 170 p. 21cm. 1968. D. McKay Co.
--Utah Lion. Johnson, James Ralph (1922-), illus. LC 62-156708. (Illus.). 160 p. 23cm. 1962. Follett Pub. Co.
--Wild Venture. Johnson, James Ralph (1922-), illus. LC 61-8813. (Illus.). 176 p. 24cm. 1961. Follett Pub. Co.
--The Wolf Cub. Johnson, James Ralph (1922-), illus. LC 66-12913. 152 p. illus. 21 cm. 1966. D. McKay Co.

Johnson, James Weldon (1871-1934) & Rosamund, J.
--Lift Every Voice & Sing. Thompson, Mozelle (1926-), illus. b & w ils. 32p. (gr. 4 up). 1970. (ISBN 0-8015-4536-6). Hawthorn. **Award: (NYT).**

Johnson, Jan
--The Secret Task of Nurse Cavell: A Story About Edith Cavell. LC 77-86604. (Illus.). (Stories About Christian Heroes). (gr. 1-5). 1977. (ISBN 0-03-041661-2). Winston Pr.

Johnson, Jan, jt. auth. see Johnson, Ron L.

Johnson, Jane (1951-)
--Bertie on the Beach. LC 81-2299. (Illus.). 32 p. 26cm. 1981. (ISBN 0-590-07822-4). Four Winds Press.
--A Book of Nursery Riddles. LC 84-15677. (Illus.). 32 p. 22cm. 1985, c.1984. (ISBN 0-395-37766-8). Houghton Mifflin.
--Today I Thought I'd Run Away. LC 84-25920. (Illus.). 31 p. 26cm. c.1985. (ISBN 0-525-44193-X). Dutton.

Johnson, Jill, illus.
--Tell About Tales. LC 50-3120. 33cm. 86p. 1949. Garden City Publishing Co.

Johnson, John Emil (1929-)
--The Me Book. Johnson, John Emil (1929-), illus. LC 79-62042. (Illus.). (Cloth Bks.). (ps). 1979. (ISBN 0-394-84243-X, BYR). Random.
--My School Book. LC 79-63898. (Illus.). 21 p. 16cm. c.1979. (ISBN 0-394-84293-6). Random House.

Johnson, John Norton, jt. auth. see Krohn, Gretchen.

Johnson, Johnile Curry see Carey, Michael, pseud.

Johnson, Johnile Curry
--Sunspur. Carey, Michael, pseud. LC 54-8141. 117p. 21cm. 1954. Pageant Press.

Johnson, Joseph
--The Master's Likeness: A School. (Illus.). N.D. Thomas Whittaker.

Johnson, Josephine Winslow (1910-)
--Paulina: The Story of an Apple-Butter Pot. Johnson, Josephine Winslow (1910-), illus. LC 39-33012. 3 p. l., 3-56, 1 p. illus. 16 x 24 cm. 1939. Simon and Schuster.
--The Sorcerer's Son and Other Stories. 1965. Simon and Schuster, Inc Publications.

Johnson, June Lathrop (1904-)
--The Peek-a-Boo Circus. LC 30-292. 33 p. col. front., illus. 20 1/2cm. c.1929. McLoughlin Bros, Inc.
--The Peek-a-Boos Among the Bunnies. LC 30-293. 47 p. incl. col. front., illus. col. pl. 20 1/2cm. c.1929. McLoughlin Bros, Inc.
--The Peek-a-Boos at School. LC 30-294. 53 p. col. front., illus. (part col.) col. pl. 21 cm. c.1929. McLoughlin Bros., Inc.

Johnson, L.
--Willy Nil and The Sleeping Lesson. N.D. Carlton Press.

Johnson, La Verne Bravo (1925-)
--Night Noises. Alexander, Martha G. (1920-), illus. LC 68-21075. (Illus.). 41 p. 24cm. 1968. Parents' Magazine Press.

Johnson, Laura Rinkle
--The Teddy Bear A-B-C. Sanford, Margaret Landers, illus. LC 7-34586. (Illus.). 22cm. 55p. 1907. Caldwell.

Johnson, Laura & Johnson, Jack
--The Leaky Whale. N.D. Houghton Mifflin Co.

Johnson, Lillian Hartman, Mrs.
--The First Christmas Gift. LC 8-36782. 22cm. 96p. 1908. Myers Printing Co.

Johnson, Lissa H.
--Runaway Dreams. LC 84-29826. (Galaxy Ser.). (gr. 7-11). 1985. (ISBN 0-8307-1027-2). Regal.

Johnson, Lois Smith (1894-)
--Christmas Stories Round the World. Stone, David Karl (1922-), illus. LC 71-110365. (Illus.). 103 p. 29cm. 1970. Rand McNally.

Johnson, Lois Walfrid (1936-)
--Aaron's Christmas Donkey. Roberts, Jim, illus. LC 74-79364. (Illus.). 32 p. 1974. (ISBN 0-8066-1425-0). Augsburg Pub. House.

Johnson, Louise (1916-)
--Malunda. Durose, Edward, illus. LC 81-15441. (Illus.). 48 p. 23cm. (Carolrhoda on my own books). c.1982. (ISBN 0-87614-177-7). Carolrhoda Books.
--Outpost Encounters: Nature Stories. LC 79-92927. (Illus.). 75 p. 22cm. c.1980. (ISBN 0-89002-081-7). (ISBN 0-89002-082-5). Northwoods Press.

Johnson, Lucie M.
--The Tree House. (gr. 4-7). N.D. Carlton.

Johnson, M.
--Miralda. N.D. Benziger Brothers.

Johnson, M. O., Mrs.
--Carrie Ellsworth: Or, Seed Sowing, 1 of 20 vols. New ed. (Illus.). 350p. (Sunday-School Lib: No. 13). 1895. Set. Lothrop Pub.
--Elms Homestead. N.D. J B Lippincott.

Johnson, Mabel
--Escape from Scrooby. (gr. 7 up). 1975. (ISBN 0-9600838-2-0). M Johnson.
--The Foolish Little Mouse. McGuire, Linda, illus. (Illus.). (gr. 5 up). 1978. (ISBN 0-9600838-3-9). M Johnson.
--Sweet Little Alice. McGuire, Linda, illus. (Illus.). (gr. 5 up). 1978. (ISBN 0-9600838-4-7). M Johnson.

Johnson, Mabel Hubbard
--Jean and Jerry's Vacation. Jones, Wilfred J. (1888-), illus. LC 31-895676. 192 p. incl. col. front., col. illus. 20 cm. c.1931. American Book Company.

Johnson, Margaret
--The Procession of the Zodiac. Twelve Month-Poems. McDermott, Jessie, illus. LC 15-23985. 52 p., 2 l, incl. front., plates. 19 x 24 cm. c.1885. D. Lothrop and Company.

Johnson, Margaret, jt. auth. see Foster, Edith Francis.

Johnson, Margaret, jt. auth. see Johnson, Enid.

Johnson, Margaret Sweet (1893-1964)
--Briar: A Collie. Johnson, Margaret Sweet (1893-1964), illus. LC 52-5064. (Illus.). 21cm. 92p. (gr. 4-6). 1952. Morrow.
--Bright Flash. Johnson, Margaret Sweet (1893-1964), illus. LC 61-5270. (Illus.). 21cm. 64p. (ps-1). 1961. (ISBN 0-688-31123-7). Morrow.
--Gavin: A Scottish Deerhound. Johnson, Margaret Sweet (1893-1964), illus. LC 60-5242. 95p. illus. 21cm. 1960. Morrow.
--Gay: A Shetland Sheepdog. Johnson, Margaret Sweet (1893-1964), illus. LC 48-6431. 96 p. illus. 22 cm. 1948. W. Morrow.
--Gray Shadow. Johnson, Margaret Sweet (1893-1964), illus. LC 64-10059. 64 p. illus. 21 cm. 1964. Morrow.
--Jamie: A Basset Hound. Johnson, Margaret Sweet (1893-1964), illus. LC 59-50190. 64p. illus. 21cm. 1959. (ISBN 0-688-31667-0). Morrow.
--Kelpie: A Shetland Pony. Johnson, Margaret Sweet (1893-1964), illus. LC 62-715519. 64p. illus. 21cm. 1962. Morrow.
--Lance of Oak Valley. Johnson, Margaret Sweet (1893-1964), illus. LC 63-7201. 64 p. illus. 21 cm. 1963. Morrow.
--Larry of Snowy Ridge. Johnson, Margaret Sweet (1893-1964), illus. LC 56-5145. 93p. illus. 21cm. 1956. Morrow.
--Megan,. A Welsh Corgi. Johnson, Margaret Sweet (1893-1964), illus. LC 57-50735. 62p. illus. 21cm. 1957. Morrow.
--Randy and the Queen of Sheba. Johnson, Margaret Sweet (1893-1964), illus. LC 51-9358. 63 p. illus. 21 cm. 1951. Morrow.
--Red Joker. Johnson, Margaret Sweet (1893-1964), illus. LC 50-5827. (Illus.). 95 p. 22cm. (Morrow junior books). 1950. Morrow.
--Rex of the Coast Patrol. Johnson, Helen Lossing, Mrs. (1865-1946) & Johnson, Helen Lossing, Mrs. (1865-1946), illus. LC 44-36787. 4 p. l., 3-95 p. illus. 22 x 18 cm. 1944. Harcourt, Brace and Company.
--Runaway Puppy. Johnson, Helen Lossing, Mrs. (1865-1946) & Johnson, Helen Lossing, Mrs. (1865-1946), illus. LC 42-6281. 3 p. l., 3-86, 2 p. illus. 22 x 18 cm. 1942. Harcourt, Brace and Company.
--Sam and the Inkspot. Johnson, Margaret Sweet (1893-1964), illus. LC 52-12117. (Illus.). 62 p. 21cm. (Morrow junior books). 1953. Morrow.
--Silver Dawn. Johnson, Margaret Sweet (1893-1964), illus. LC 58-5141. 80p. illus. 21cm. 1958. (ISBN 0-688-21670-6). W. Morrow.
--Snowshoe Paws. Johnson, Margaret Sweet (1893-1964), illus. LC 49-7846. 62 p. illus. 21 cm. (Morrow junior books). 1949. W. Morrow.
--Stowaway Cat. Johnson, Margaret Sweet (1893-1964), illus. LC 55-5310. 62p. illus. 21cm. 1955. W. Morrow.
--Wilderness Pup. Johnson, Margaret Sweet (1893-1964), illus. LC 54-5186. (Illus.). 21cm. 94p. 1954. Wm. Morrow.

Johnson, Margaret Sweet (1893-1964) & Johnson, Helen Lossing, Mrs. (1865-1946)
--Barney of the North. Johnson, Helen Lossing, Mrs. (1865-1946) & Johnson, Margaret Sweet (1893-1964), illus. LC 39-276659. 3 p. l., 3-114 p. front., illus. 24 cm. c.1939. Harcourt, Brace and Company.
--Black Bruce. Johnson, Helen Lossing, Mrs. (1865-1946) & Johnson, Margaret Sweet (1893-1964), illus. LC 38-27594. 4 p. l., 3-153, 1 p. incl. front., illus., plates, maps. 24 cm. c.1938. Harcourt, Brace and Company.
--Carlo,. The/Hound Who Thought He Was a Calf. Johnson, Margaret Sweet (1893-1964) & Johnson, Helen Lossing, Mrs. (1865-1946), illus. LC 41-40283. 3 p. l., 3-86, 1 p. col. illus. 22 x 18 cm. c.1941. Harcourt, Brace and Company.
--Derry: The Wolfhound. Johnson, Margaret Sweet (1893-1964) & Johnson, Helen Lossing, Mrs. (1865-1946), illus. LC 43-51226. 3 p. l., 3-74, 1 p. illus. 22 x 18 cm. 1943. Harcourt, Brace and Company.
--Dixie Dobie: A Sable Island Pony. Johnson, Margaret Sweet (1893-1964) & Johnson, Helen Lossing, Mrs. (1865-1946), illus. LC 45-283620. 3 p. l., 3-90 p. front., illus. 22 x 17 1/2 cm. 1945. Harcourt, Brace and Company.
--Joey and Patches: A Story of Two Kittens. Johnson, Margaret Sweet (1893-1964), illus. LC 47-30141. 70 p. illus. 21 x 17 cm. 1947. W. Morrow and Company.
--Rolf: An Elkhound of Norway. Johnson, Helen Lossing, Mrs. (1865-1946) & Johnson, Margaret Sweet (1893-1964), illus. LC 41-15466. 3 p. l., 3-106 p. front., illus. (incl. map) 25 x 19 cm. c.1941. Harcourt, Brace and Company.
--Sir Lancelot and Scamp. Johnson, Margaret Sweet (1893-1964) & Johnson, Helen Lossing, Mrs. (1865-1946), illus. LC 45-8115. 78 p. illus. 21 x 17 cm. 1945. Harcourt, Brace and Company.
--The Smallest Puppy. Johnson, Margaret Sweet (1893-1964) & Johnson, Helen Lossing, Mrs. (1865-1946), illus. LC 40-27272. 4 p. l., 3-88, 1 p. illus. 22 x 18 cm. c.1940. Harcourt, Brace and Company.
--A Spaniel of Old Plymouth. Johnson, Margaret Sweet (1893-1964) & Johnson, Helen Lossing, Mrs. (1865-1946), illus. LC 37-285161. 4 p. l., 3-161 p. incl. front., illus, plates. 24 cm. c.1937. Harcourt, Brace and Company.
--Stablemates: The Story of Dick and Daisy. Johnson, Margaret Sweet (1893-1964) & Johnson, Helen Lossing, Mrs. (1865-1946), illus. LC 42-217633. 3 p. l., 3-104 p. illus. 22 x 18 cm. 1942. Harcourt, Brace and Company.
--The Story of Rickey. Johnson, Margaret Sweet (1893-1964) & Johnson, Helen Lossing, Mrs. (1865-1946), illus. LC 39-4590. 3 p. l., 3-88, 1 p. illus. 22 cm. c.1939. Harcourt, Brace and Company.
--Tally-Ho. Johnson, Margaret Sweet (1893-1964), illus. LC 36-274332. 4 p. l., 3-120 p. incl. front., plates, illus., 25 cm. c.1936. Harcourt, Brace and Company.
--Tim: A Dog of the Mountains. Johnson, Margaret Sweet (1893-1964) & Johnson, Helen Lossing, Mrs. (1865-1946), illus. LC 40-307223. 3 p. l., 3-112 p. front. illus. 24 x 19 cm. c.1940. Harcourt, Brace and Company.
--Vicki: A Guide Dog. Johnson, Margaret Sweet (1893-1964) & Johnson, Helen Lossing, Mrs. (1865-1946), illus. LC 46-3688. 3 p. l., 3-87 p. front., illus. 22 x 17 cm. 1946. Harcourt, Brace and Company.

Johnson, Margaret (1860-)
--Alice's Alphabet. N.D. J. B. Lippincott.
--A Bunch of Keys. Walcott, Jessie McDermott, illus. 1903. E P Dutton.
--Dorothea's Double. Caswell, Edward C., illus. LC 26-16361. ix, 230 p. front. illus. (map) plates. 20 cm. c.1926. The Century Co.
--Polly and the Wishing Ring. Pogany, Willy (1882-1955), illus. LC 18-195742. vi p., 1 l., 123 p. col. front. 20 cm. (Half-title: The opening door series). 1918. The Macmillan Company.
--What Did the Black Cat Do. (Illus.). (Rebus Books for Little Folks). N.D. Dana Estes and Company.
--What O'Clock Jingles. Johnson, Margaret (1860-), illus. LC 17-1850. 23cm. 30p. 1887. D. Lothrop Co.
--Where Was the Little White Dog. Johnson, Margaret (1860-), illus. (Illus.). (Rebus Books for Little Folks). N.D. Dana Estes and Company.

Johnson, Margie L.
--Mini Verses. Rahmas, Sigrid, ed. Proper, Churchill, illus. 32p. (gr. k-3). 1971. Story House.
--The Money Tree. Rahmas, Sigrid, ed. Proper, Churchill, illus. 22p. (gr. k-3). 1971. Story House.

Johnson, Margie L., jt. auth. see Johnson, Mary E.

Johnson, Marilue Carolyn see Marilue, pseud.

Johnson, Marilue Carolyn (1931-)
--Bobby Bear's Christmas. LC 77-83628. (Illus.). (ps-2). 1978. (ISBN 0-89508-021-4). Rainbow Bks.
--Bobby Bear's Christmas. Marilue, pseud. (1931-), illus. Johnson, Marilue Carolyn. LC 77-83628. (Illus.). 32 p. 24cm. c.1978. (ISBN 0-87783-143-2). Oddo Pub.
--Bobby Bear's New Home. Johnson, Marilue Carolyn (1931-), illus. (Illus.). (ps-1). 1978. (ISBN 0-89508-053-2). Rainbow Bks.

Johnson, Marilyn Carolyn see Marilue, pseud.

Johnson, Marjorie Guinn
--Book of Mormon Stories for Little Children. LC 76-3991. (Illus.). 96 p. (p. 95-96 blank). 22cm. 1977, c.1976. (ISBN 0-88290-063-3). Horizon Publishers.

Johnson, Marjorie R.
--Chinatown Stories. Johnson, Amy B., illus. 87p. 1900. Dodge Publishing Co.

Johnson, Martha, pseud., see Lansing, Elisabeth Carleton Hubbard.

Johnson, Martha P & Schroeder, Howard
--Mystery at Winter Lodge. Furan Illustrators, illus. LC 81-3303. p. cm. (Roundup). c.1981. (ISBN 0-89686-152-X). (ISBN 0-08-968616-0). Crestwood House.

Johnson, Martha (1907-)
--Ann Bartlett at Bataan. 334p. 1943. Thomas Y. Crowell Co.
--Ann Bartlett in the South Pacific. 334p. 1943. Thomas Y. Crowell Co.
--Ann Bartlett, Navy Nurse. Rose, Richard (1933-), illus. 321p. 1941. Thomas Y. Crowell Co.
--Ann Bartlett Returns to the Philippines. 256p. 1945. Thomas Y. Crowell Co.
--Sandra Mitchell Stands By. 208p. 1944. Thomas Y. Crowell Co.

Johnson, Martin
--Cannibal-Land. (Riverside Library). N.D. Houghton Mifflin Co.

Johnson, Mary E.
--The Adventures of Maggie & Her Teddy Bear. Johnson, Margie, illus. 1984. (ISBN 0-318-01304-5). Animal Cracker.
--The Falcon & the Dragon. Robson, Deborah, illus. LC 76-150818. (Illus.). 32 p. 31cm. c.1976. (ISBN 0-914742-10-8). Woolman Press.

Johnson, Mary E. & Johnson, Margie L.
--Baby Bigfoot. (ps-3). 1977. (ISBN 0-686-21383-1). Animal Cracker.

Johnson, Mary Parke
--The Keris Emerald. Bryan, Brigitte, illus. LC 70-106535. (Illus.). 32 p. 21cm. 1970. Scribner.

Johnson, Mary Thomson
--Popular Plays. 135p. N.D. Northwestern Press.
--Popular Plays. 135p. N.D. T. S. Denison & Co.

Johnson, Maud
--Christy's Choice. (Orig.). (gr. 7 up). 1982. (ISBN 0-590-32387-3, Wildfire). Scholastic Inc.
--Christy's Love. 176p. (Orig.). (gr. 7 up). 1984. (ISBN 0-590-33096-9, Wildfire). Scholastic Inc.
--A Kiss for Tomorrow. 176p. (Orig.). (gr. 7 up). 1981. (ISBN 0-590-31571-4, Wildfire). Scholastic Inc.
--Warm in Winter, Cold in Summer. (gr. 7 up). 1978. (ISBN 0-590-11913-3). Scholastic Inc.
--The World of Christy, 4 bks. Incl. I'm Christy; Christy's Choice; Christy's Love; Christy's Senior Year. (Orig.). (gr. 11 up). 1984. Boxed Set. (ISBN 0-590-00661-4, Wildfire). Scholastic Inc.

Johnson, Merle De Vore (1874-1935), ed. see Pyle, Howard.

Johnson, Mildred D
--Wait! Skates. Dunnington, Tom, illus. LC 82-22228. p. cm. (Rookie Reader). 1983. (ISBN 0-516-02039-0). Childrens Press.

Johnson, Norma see Harris, Lavinia, pseud.

Johnson, Olive McClintic
--Bunky's Book: Or, Tell it Again Stories. LC 55-7619. 24cm. 62p. 1955. Pageant Press, Inc.

Johnson, Olive McClintic & Chute, Mary
--Little Tejas, Child of the Twilight. Lore, B. J. & Hamilton, T. G., illus. LC 38-18279. 256 p. col. front., illus. 20 cm. c.1937. The Economy Company.

Johnson, Osa Helen Leighty (1894-1953)
--Jungle Babies. Flinsch, Margaret, illus. LC 30-22872. vii, 169 p incl. illus., plates. 23 cm. 1930. G. P. Putnam's Sons.
--Jungle Pets. LC 32-32161. 215 p. front., plates, ports. 23 cm. 1932. G. P. Putnam's Sons.
--Osa Johnson's Jungle Friends. 200p. 1939. J. B. Lippincott.
--Pantaloons: Adventures of a Baby Elephant. Jansson, Arthur August (1890-), illus. LC 41-22154. 1 p. l., 7-56 p. illus. (part col.) 29 x 23 cm. c.1941. Random House.
--Snowball: Adventures of a Young Gorilla. Jansson, Arthur August (1890-), illus. LC 42-25586. 51, 1 p. illus. (part col.) 28 1/2 x 23 cm. 1942. Random House.
--Tarnish,. The/True Story of a Lion Cub. Jansson, Arthur August (1890-), illus. LC 44-510485. 2 p. l., 59 p. col. illus. 23 1/2 x 18 1/2 cm. 1944. Wilcox & Follett Co.

Johnson, Owen McMahon (1878-)
--The Humming Bird. LC 10-12100. 6 p. l., 3-86 p. front., plates. 19 cm. 1910. The Baker & Taylor Company.
--Lawrenceville Stories. LC 67-25392. (gr. 5 up). 1967. (ISBN 0-671-41074-1). S&S.
--The Prodigious Hickey. N.D. Grosset & Dunlap.
--The Prodigious Hickey. N.D. Little Brown & Co.
--Skippy Bedelle. N.D. Gosset & Dunlap.
--Skippy Bedelle. N.D. Little Brown & Co.
--Stover at Yale. N.D. Little Brown & Co.
--The Tenessee Shad. N.D. Little Brown & Co.
--The Tennessee Shad. N.D. Grosset & Dunlap.
--The Varmint. N.D. Grosset & Dunlap.
--The Varmint. N.D. Little Brown & Co.
--The Varmint. LC 10-152367. 396 p. front., plates. 20 cm. (His Lawrenceville stories). 1910. The Baker & Taylor Company.
--Virtuous Wives. LC 18-15781. xii p., 2 l., 3-352 p. front., plates. 20 cm. 1918. Little, Brown, and Company.

Johnson, Pamela, jt. auth. see Zimelman, Nathan.

Johnson, Pat & Osborne, Walter
--Horse Named Kelso. Reeves, Richard S., illus. DuPont, R. C., Mrs., intro. by. (Illus.). 5 ils. 96p. (gr. 5 up). 1970. (ISBN 0-308-80072-9). Funk & W.

Johnson, Phyllis, jt. auth. see Brown, Vinson.

Johnson, Preston P. see Preston, John, pseud.

Johnson, Preston P. (1880-)
--Saucer Ears in the Ozarks. Preston, John, pseud. LC 43-16006. (Story Based on the Author's experience in the Ozark Moutains). 300 p. front., pl. 20cm. 1943. Caxton Printers, Ltd.

Johnson, Priscilla A.
--King Quincy and the Candy Canes. Kauper, Jean Dorion, illus. LC 64-7592. 31 p. col. ill. 24cm. c.1964. E. C. Seale.

Johnson, Reginald Brimley (1867-), ed. see Rands, William Brighty.

Johnson, Richard, jt. auth. see Hood, Basil Charles Willett.

Johnson, Richard (1573-1659)
--Saint George and the Dragon. Dalgliesch, Alice (1893-), ed. Maloy, Lois (1902-), illus. LC 41-5506. 24 x 20cm. 30p. 1941. Charles Scribner's Sons.

Johnson, Richard & Darton, Frederick Joseph Harvey
--The Seven Champions of Christendom. Ault, Norman (1880-1950), illus. LC 15-261379. xiv, 415 1 p. incl. plates. col. front. 21 cm. 1913. F. A. Stokes.

Johnson, Richard (1573-1659) & Kingston, William Henry Giles (1814-1880)
--Saint George & the Dragon. Shenton, Edward (1895-), illus. LC 50-1665. 75 p. col. illus. 31 cm. (Evergreen tales; or, Tales for the ageless). 1949. Limited Editions Club.

Johnson, Robert Elliott, jt. auth. see Anderson, Anita Melva.

Johnson, Ron L & Johnson, Jan
--Stolen Moments. Coopes, Jenny, illus. LC 77-369000. (Illus.). 104 p. c.1976. (ISBN 0-471-02383-3). J. Wiley.

Johnson, Rossiter (1840-1931)
--The End of a Rainbow: An American Story. LC 12-34745. vi p., 1 l., 344 p. front., illus., plates. 19 cm. 1892. C. Scribner's Sons.
--The Hero of Manila. (Young Heroes of Our Navy). N.D. D. Appleton & Co.
--Phaeton Rogers: A Novel of Boy Life. LC 4-16143. vi p., 1 l., 344 p. incl. front., illus., plates. 19 cm. 1881. C. Scribner's Sons.
--Two Fortune-Seekers, And Other Stories. LC 18-17308. 345 p. incl. front., illus. plates. 18 cm. 1876. D. Lothrop & Co.

Johnson, Russ
--Trail of the Golden Feather. 1963. Macmillan Company.
--Trail of the Moaning Ghost. 1963. Macmillan Company.

Johnson, Ruth I., see Jay, Ruth Ingrid.

Johnson, Ryerson see Johnson, Walter Ryerson.

Johnson, Sally Patrick, ed.
--Harper Book of Princes. Domanska, Janina, illus. LC 64-16647. (Illus.). (ps-3). 1964. (ISBN 0-06-023031-2). Har-Row.
--The Princesses: Sixteen Stories about Princesses. Montresor, Beni (1926-), illus. LC 62-14318. (Illus.). 23 cm. 318p. (ps-3). 1962. (ISBN 0-06-023041-X, HarpJ). Har-Row. **Award: (NYT).**

Johnson, Samuel Lawrence (1909-1978)
--Captain Ducky & Other Children's Sermons. LC 76-4913. 125 p. 19cm. c.1976. (ISBN 0-687-04630-0). Abingdon.
--The Cross-Eyed Bear. 1980. Abingdon.
--The Mouse's Tale. 1978. Abingdon.
--The Pig's Brother and other Children's Sermons. LC 79-97577. 128 p. 20cm. 1970. (ISBN 0-687-31423-2). Abingdon Press.
--The Squirrel's Bank Account. LC 79-186827. (gr. 1-5). 1972. (ISBN 0-687-39268-3). Abingdon.

Johnson, Samuel (1709-1784)
--The Idler And The Adventurer. Bate, W. J. & Bullitt, John M., eds. 516p. 1963. Yale.
--Rasselas. (Classics for Children). N.D. Ginn.
--Rasselas. (Cabinet Library). 1873. Leavitt & Allen Bros.
--Rasselas Prince of Abyssina: A Tale, 1 of 4 Vols. (Illus.). (Classical Library Ser.: Vol. 2). N.D. Set. James Miller.

Johnson, Shirley King (1927-)
--A Dog Named Chip. LC 63-17748. 118 p. 21 cm. 1963. Zondervan Pub. House.

Johnson, Siddie Joe (1905-1977)
--Cat Hotel. Holland, Janice (1913-1962), illus. LC 55-5757. (Illus.). 132 p. 21cm. 1955. Longmans, Green.
--Cathy. Baker, Mary (1897-), illus. LC 45-35059. ix, 146 p. incl. illus., plates. 20 cm. 1945. Green and Co.
--Debby. 1940. David McKay Company Inc.
--Debby. MacKnight, Ninon (1908-), illus. Ninon, pseud. LC 40-139744. ix, 213 p. incl. front., illus., plates. 21 cm. 1940. Longmans, Green and Co.
--Feather in My Hand. McGee, Barbara J. (1943-), illus. LC 67-2751. (Illus.). 24cm. 47p. (gr. 2-7). 1967. (ISBN 0-689-20193-1). (ISBN 0-689-20195-8). Atheneum.
--Joe and Andy Want a Boat. Jeffries, Lucille & Maples, Barbara, illus. LC 51-13252. 1951. Steck Co.
--A Month of Christmases. 1st ed. Moon, Henrietta Jones, illus. LC 52-8517. 132 p. illus. 22 cm. 1952. Longmans, Green.
--New Town in Texas. Ayer, Margaret (0000-1981), illus. LC 42-21563. xi p., 1 l., 301 p. incl. front., illus., plates. 21 x 16 cm. 1942. Longmans, Green and Co.
--Rabbit Fires. LC 51-2840. 24cm. 32p. 1951. Highland Press.
--Susan's Year. Peck, Anne Merriman (1884-), illus. LC 48-3590. 168 p. illus. 22 cm. 1948. Longmans, Green.

Johnson, Spencer (1938-)
--The Value of Curiosity: The Story of Christopher Columbus. Pileggi, Stephen, illus. LC 77-11032. (Illus.). (ValueTales Ser). (gr. k-6). N.D. (ISBN 0-916392-13-9, Dist. by Oak Tree Pubns.). Value Comm.
Johnson, Susan C.
--Little Moon & the Sacred Oak. (gr. 1-6). 1970. Vantage.
Johnson, Sylvia A.
--Downy the Duckling. Hammarberg, Dyan, tr. LC 76-1289. (Illus.). 24p. (The Animal Friends Bks). (gr. k-4). 1976. (ISBN 0-87614-063-0). Carolrhoda Bks.
--Penelope the Tortoise. Hammarberg, Dyan, tr. from Fr. LC 76-3411. (Illus.). 24p. (The Animal Friends Bks). (gr. k-4). 1976. (ISBN 0-87614-077-X). Carolrhoda Bks.
--Penny & Pete the Lambs. Hammarberg, Dyan, tr. from Fr. LC 76-3434. (Illus.). 24p. (The Animal Friends Bks). (gr. k-4). 1976. (ISBN 0-87614-067-3). Carolrhoda Bks.
Johnson, Theodore, et al. (1891-)
--Easy Plays for Teen Girls. LC 39-6981. 3 p. l., 3-118 p. diagr. 19 cm. c.1938. Fitzgerald Publishing Corporation.
Johnson, Victor, ed. see Goodman, Robert B. & Spicer, Robert A.
Johnson, Virginia Wales (1849-)
--The Catskill Fairies. Fredericks, Alfred, illus. 4 p. l., 11-163 p. incl. front., illus., 6 pl. 23 cm. 1876. Harper & Brothers.
Johnson, Virginia Weisel (1910-)
--The Calderwood Secret. N.D. Harper & Bros.
--The Cedars of Charlo. Rosier, Lydia, illus. LC 75-85132. (Illus.). 192 p. 22cm. 1969. W. Morrow.
--The Cricket's Friends. 219p. (The Kettle Club Ser.). N.D. Lockwood, Brooks & Co.
--Grandfather's Pocket-Book. 212p. (The Kettle Club Ser.). N.D. Lockwood, Brooks & Co.
--Jack's Kite, 1 of 4. (Doll's Club Ser.). N.D. Claxton, Remsen, & Haffelfinger.
--Jo's Doll, 1 of 4. (Doll's Club Ser.). N.D. Claxton, Remsen, & Haffelfinger.
--Joseph the Jew. N.D. Harper & Bros.
--Katy's Christmas, 1 of 4. (Doll's Club Ser.). N.D. Claxton, Remsen, & Haffelfinger.
--The Kettle Club: Christmas Tales for Children. 159p. (The Kettle Club Ser.). N.D. Lockwood, Brooks & Co.
--The Kettle's Birth-Day Party. 193p. (The Kettle Club Ser.). N.D. Lockwood, Brooks & Co.
--Patty's Pranks, 1 of 4. (Doll's Club Ser.). N.D. Claxton, Remsen, & Haffelfinger.
--A Sack of Gold. N.D. Harper & Bros.
Johnson, W. Branch (1893-)
--Folk Tales of Brittany. Johnson, W. Branch (1893-), illus. N.D. Frederick A. Stokes.
--Folk Tales of Provence. Johnson, W. Branch (1893-), illus. N.D. Frederick A. Stokes Co.
Johnson, Walter Ryerson (1901-)
--Gozo's Wonderful Kite. N.D. E. M. Hale & Co.
--Gozo's Wonderful Kite. Lignell, Lois (1911-), illus. (Illus.). 58 p. 21cm. 1951. Crowell.
--I Like Dinosaurs. Sherwood, Blanche A., illus. LC 76-160022. (Illus.). (gr. k-2). 1971. (ISBN 0-8382-1091-0). Hale.
--Let's Play Dinosaur. Alexander, Frank, ed. Lignell, Lois (1911-), illus. LC 78-56500. (Illus.). (gr. 3-8). 1978. (ISBN 0-915256-06-1). Front Row.
--Let's Walk Up the Wall. Cellini, Eva, illus. LC 67-3393. (Illus.). 21 x 24cm. 48p. (gr. k-3). 1967. (ISBN 0-8234-0067-0). Holiday.
--Let's Walk up the Wall. Cellini, Eva, illus. (gr. k-3). 1978. (ISBN 0-590-05383-3). Scholastic Inc.
--The Monkey and the Wild, Wild Wind. Lignell, Lois (1911-), illus. LC 61-15421. unpaged. illus. 26cm. c.1961. Abelard-Schuman.
--Mouse & the Moon. (Illus.). (gr. k-2). 1968. (ISBN 0-8382-0553-4). Hale.
--Susi Did It. Eagle, Michael (1942-), illus. LC 72-77628. (Illus.). 31 p. 23cm. (Magic circle book). c.1973. (ISBN 0-663-25498-1). Ginn.
--The Trail of the Deadly Image. 1st ed. Whittingham, William, illus. LC 62-20795. 186 p. illus. 18 cm. (His A Bob Blake adventure). 1963. Collier Books.
--The Trail of the Golden Feather. 1st ed. Whittingham, William, illus. LC 62-21182. 158 p. illus. 18 cm. (His A Bob Blake adventure). 1963. Collier Books.
--The Trail of the Moaning Ghost. 1st ed. Whittingham, William, illus. LC 62-21183. 186 p. illus. 18 cm. (His A Bob Blake adventure). 1963. Collier Books.
--The Trail of the Witchwood Treasure. Whittingham, William, illus. LC 62-21184. 191 p. illus. 18 cm. (His A Bob Blake adventure). 1963. Collier Books.
Johnson, Ward
--Ben's New Buddy. Cooke, Tom, illus. LC 83-22145. (A Tale From the Care Bears). c.1984. (ISBN 0-910313-16-4). Parker Bros.
--Caring Is What Counts. Cooke, Tom, illus. LC 83-2394. p. cm. c.1983. (ISBN 0-910313-05-9). Parker Bros.
--Koosas for the Kids. LC 85-491. p. cm. (Cabbage Patch Kids). c.1985. (ISBN 0-910313-90-3). Parker Bros.
Johnson, Winifred McNally (1905-)
--Footlight Fever. LC 63-8061. 21cm. 192p. (gr. 7-10). 1963. (ISBN 0-664-32298-0). Westminster.
--Londi. LC 62-7186. 176p. 21cm. 1962. Westminster Press.
--Senior Panic. LC 64-10550. 191 p. 21 cm. 1964. Westminster Press.
--The Stained Glass House. LC 65-24903. 175p. 22cm. c.1965. Macrae.
Johnston
--King Arthur, His Knights & Their Ladies. (gr. 7-12). 1980. (ISBN 0-590-30007-5, Schol Pap). Scholastic Inc.
Johnston, Annie Fellows, jt. auth. see Richards, Laura Elizabeth Howe, Mrs.
Johnston, Annie Fellows, Mrs. (1863-1931)
--Aunt 'Liza's Hero. Taylor, W. L., et al., illus. (Cosy Corner Ser.). N.D. L. C. Page & Co.
--Aunt Liza's Hero. Taylor, W. L., illus. (Cosy Corner Ser.). N.D. L. C. Page & Co.
--Big Brother. LC 7-10533. 3 p. l., 58 p. front., illus. 19 cm. (On cover: Cosy corner series). 1894. J. Knight Company.
--Big Brother. Merrill, Frank Thayer (1848-), illus. LC 7-26597. 4 p. l., 91 p. col. front., illus., 7 col. pl. 20 cm. 1907. L. C. Page & Company.
--Cicely, and Other Stories. Gallagher, Sears (1869-1955), illus. LC 2-17555. 137 p. incl. illus., plates front. 19 cm. (Cosy corner series). 1903. L. C. Page & Company.
Flip's "Islands of Providence". Bonsall, E. F., illus. LC 3-20576. 3 p. l., 11-180 p. incl. 7 pl. front. 20 cm. 1901. L. C. Page & Company.
--For Pierre's Sake and Other Stories. Chapman, Billie, illus. LC 34-37089. vi p., 3 l., 3-200 p. front., illus. 20 cm. c.1934. L. C. Page & Company.
--The Gate of the Giant Scissors. Barry, Etheldred Breeze (1870-), illus. LC 98-124. (Illus.). 187p. 1898. L. C. Page & Co.
--Georgina of the Rainbows. LC 16-17421. viii, 2, 11-348 p. col. front., illus., plates. 20 cm. c.1916. Britton Publishing Company.
--Georgina of the Rainbows. LC 20-16157. x p., 2 l., 11-348 p. illus., plates. 20 cm. 1920. D. Appleton and Company.
--Georgina of the Rainbows. N.D. Grosset & Dunlap.
--Georgina of the Rainbows. Martin, George Madden (1866-1946), illus. Rice, Alice Caldwell Hegan (1870-1942), intro. by. N.D. L. C. Page.
--Georgina's Service Stars. N.D. Grosset & Dunlap.
--Georgina's Service Stars. Rice, Alice Caldwell Hegan (1870-1942), intro. by. N.D. Page Co.
--The Giant Scissors, 41. Barry, Etheldred Breeze (1870-), illus. (Cosy Corner Ser.). N.D. L. C. Page & Co.
--The Giant Scissors. Merrill, Frank Thayer (1848-), illus. LC 6-29772. 4 p. l., 201 p. col. front., illus., 7 col. pl. 20 cm. 1906. L. C. Page & Company.
--In the Desert of Waiting. (Illus.). (The Johnston Jewel Ser.). N.D. L. C. Page.
--The Jester's Sword. (The Johnston Jewel Ser.). N.D. L. C. Page.
--Joel, a Boy of Galilee. (Illus.). (The Sterling Library). N.D. A. L. Chatterton Co.
--Joel: A Boy of Galilee. new ed. Bridgman, Lewis Jesse (1857-1931), illus. LC 4-16173. (Illus.). 4 p. l., 253 p. front., 7 pl. 20 cm. 1904. L. C. Page & Company.
--Joel: A Boy of Galilee. Searles, Victor A., illus. LC 7-10534. 2 p. l., 253 p. front., 9 pl. 20 cm. 1895. Roberts Brothers.
--Keeping Tryst: A Tale of King Arthur's Time. LC 6-19000. 2 p. l., 62 p. front. 18 cm. 1906. L. C. Page & Company.
--The Land of the Little Colonel. (The Little Colonel Ser.). N.D. L. C. Page.
--The Legend of the Bleeding-Heart. LC 7-250767. 3 p. l., 41 p. front. 18 cm. 1907. L. C. Page & Company.
--The Legend of the Bleeding Heart. 16mocm. (The Johnston Jewel Ser.). N.D. L. C. Page.
--The Little Colonel. N.D. Grosset & Dunlap.
--The Little Colonel. Special holiday ed. (Illus.). N.D. L. C. Page & Co.
--The Little Colonel. Barry, Etheldred Breeze (1870-), illus. LC 7-10535. 4 p. l., 102 p. front., illus. 19 cm. (On cover: Cosy corner series). 1896. J. Knight Company.
--The Little Colonel. Barry, Etheldred Breeze (1870-), illus. (Cosy Corner Ser.). N.D. L. C. Page & Co.
--The Little Colonel. Brett, Harold Matthews (1880-), illus. LC 4-33220. 4 p. l., 145 p. illus., 8 col. pl. (incl. front.) 20 cm. 1905. L. C. Page & Company.
--The Little Colonel at Boarding-School. Barry, Etheldred Breeze (1870-), illus. LC 3-17914. 306 p. front., 7 pl. 21 cm. 1904. L. C. Page & Company.
--The Little Colonel at Boarding-School. Barry, Etheldred Breeze (1870-), illus. LC 20-15611. 306 p. front., plates. 20 cm. 1919. The Page Company.
--Little Colonel Doll Book. (The Little Colonel Ser.). N.D. The Page Co.
--The Little Colonel in Arizona. Barry, Etheldred Breeze (1870-), illus. LC 4-24492. 4 p. l., 313 p. front., 7 pl. 21 cm. 1905. L. C. Page & Company.
--The Little Colonel in Arizona. Barry, Etheldred Breeze (1870-), illus. LC 20-15613. 4 p. l., 313 p. front., plates. 20 cm. 1919. The Page Company.
--The Little Colonel: Maid of Honor. Barry, Etheldred Breeze (1870-), illus. LC 6-37197. 4 p. l., 295 p. front., 7 pl. 21 cm. 1906. L. C. Page & Company.
--The Little Colonel: Maid of Honor. Barry, Etheldred Breeze (1870-), illus. LC 20-15619. 4 p. l., 295 p. front., plates. 20 cm. 1920. The Page Company.
--The Little Colonel Stories. Barry, Etheldred Breeze (1870-), illus. 4 p. l., 192 p. front., illus. 20 cm. (Cosy Corner Ser.). 1904. L. C. Page & Company.
--The Little Colonel Stories. Barry, Etheldred Breeze (1870-), illus. LC 20-15615. 6 p. l., 114 p., 2 l., 11-187 p., 2 l., 11-192, incl. front., illus., plates. 20 cm. 1919. The Page Company.
--The Little Colonel Stories: First Series. N.D. (ISBN 0-89201-070-3). Zenger Pub.
--The Little Colonel Stories: Second Series. (The Little Colonel Ser.). N.D. Page Co.
--The Little Colonel Stories. Second Series. Cue, Harold, illus. LC 31-2909. vii p., 4 l., 5-276 p. front., plates. 20 cm. (Her The Little Colonel series). c.1931. L. C. Page & Company.
--The Little Colonel's Christmas Vacation. Barry, Etheldred Breeze (1870-), illus. LC 5-33311. 4 p. l., 333 p. front., 7 pl. 21 cm. 1906. L. C. Page & Company.
--The Little Colonel's Christmas Vacation. Barry, Etheldred Breeze (1870-), illus. LC 20-15612. 4 p. l., 333 p. front., plates. 20 cm. 1919. The Page Company.
--The Little Colonel's Chum: Mary Ware. N.D. (ISBN 0-89201-036-3). Zenger Pub.
--The Little Colonel's Good Times Book. (The Little Colonel Ser.). N.D. The Page Co.
--The Little Colonel's Hero. Barry, Etheldred Breeze (1870-), illus. Fellows-Bacon, Albion, contrib. by. LC 2-24250. 274 p. front., plates. 20 cm. 1903. L. C. Page and Company.
--The Little Colonel's Holidays. Bridgman, Lewis Jesse (1857-1931), illus. LC 1-25663. 232 p. front., pl. 20 cm. 1901. L. C. Page and Company.
--The Little Colonel's House Party. Barry, Etheldred Breeze (1870-), illus. (Gift Book Series for Boys and Girls). N.D. L. C. Page & Co.
--The Little Colonel's House Party. Meynelle, Louis, illus. LC 6653. 4 p. l., 11-264 p. front., 7 pl. 20 cm. 1901. L. C. Page and Company.
--The Little Colonel's House Party. Meynelle, Louis, illus. LC 20-15614. 4 p. l., 264 p. front., plates. 20 cm. 1919. The Page Company.
--The Little Colonel's Knight Comes Riding. Barry, Etheldred Breeze (1870-), illus. LC 7-33204. 4 p. l., 318 p. front., 7 pl. 21 cm. 1907. L. C. Page & Company.
--The Little Colonel's Knight Comes Riding. Barry, Etheldred Breeze (1870-), illus. LC 17-6104. 4 p. l., 318 p. front., plates. 20 cm. 1916. The Page Company.
--The Little Colonial, Maid of Honor. (The Little Colonel Ser.). N.D. L. C. Page.
--The Little Man in Motley. Waite, Emily B., illus. (Cosy Corner Ser.). N.D. L. C. Page & Co.
--The Mary Ware Doll Book. (The Little Colonel Ser.). N.D. The Page Co.
--Mary Ware in Texas. Merrill, Frank Thayer (1848-), illus. LC 19-23674. 20cm. 385p. (The Little Colonel Ser.). 1910. L. C. Page.
--Mary Ware, the Little Colonel's Chum. Barry, Etheldred Breeze (1870-), illus. LC 8-30930. ix p., 1 l., 305 p. front., 7 pl. 21 cm. 1908. L. C. Page & Company.
--Mary Ware's Promised Land. Goss, John, illus. LC 12-23920. 6 p. l., 317 p. front., plates. 20 cm. (Her The Little Colonel series). 1912. L. C. Page & Company.
--Mildred's Inheritance. (Illus.). (The Cosy Corner Ser.). N.D. The Page Company.
--Mildred's Inheritance: Just Her Way; Ann's Own Way. Horne, Diantha W., illus. LC 6-19002. 5 p. l., 74 p. incl. illus., plates. front. 19 cm. (On cover: Cosy corner series). 1906. L. C. Page & Company.
--Miss Santa Claus of the Pullman. Birch, Reginald Bathurst (1856-1943), illus. N.D. L. C. Page.
--Miss Santa Claws of the Pullman. Birch, Reginald Bathurst (1856-1943), illus. 160p. N.D. Century Co.
--Ole Mammy's Torment. Johnston, Mary G. & Sacker, Amy M., illus. LC 7-10536. 5 p. l., 118 p. incl. front., illus., plates. 19 cm. (On cover: Cosy corner series). 1897. L. C. Page and Company.
--Pigwiggen: His Dashing Career. N.D. Transatlantic Arts.
--The Quilt that Jack Built. Barry, Ethelred Breeze (1870-), illus. (Cosy Corner Ser.). N.D. L. C. Page & Co.
--The Quilt That Jack Built: How He Won the Bicycle. Barry, Etheldred Breeze (1870-), illus. LC 4-30592. 5 p. l., 56 p. incl. illus., plates. front. 19 cm. (On cover: Cosy corner series). 1905. L. C. Page & Company.
--The Rescue of the Princess Winsome: A Fairy Play for Old and Young. (The Johnston Jewel Ser.). N.D. L. C. Page.
--The Road of the Loving Heart. Bromhall, Winifred, illus. LC 22-20460. 76, 1 p. incl. front., illus. 20 cm. 1922. The Page Company.
--The Story of Dago. Barry, Etheldred Breeze (1870-), illus. LC 19-93. 6 p. l., 103 p. incl. front., illus., plates. 12 degree. (On cover: Cosy corner series). 1900. L. C. Page & Company.
--The Story of the Red Cross As Told to the Little Colonel. Goss, John, illus. LC 18-209366. 5 p. l., 85 p. front., plates. 20 cm. 1918. The Page Company.
--The Three Weavers: A Fairy Tale for Fathers and Mothers as Well as for their Daughters. (The Johnston Jewel Ser.). N.D. L. C. Page.
--Two Little Knights of Kentucky. Barry, Etheldred Breeze (1870-), illus. (Cosy Corner Ser.). N.D. L. C. Page & Co.
--Two Little Knights of Kentucky Who Were the "Little Colonel's" Neighbours. Barry, Etheldred Breeze (1870-), illus. LC 99-4934. 192 p. incl. illus., plates. front. 19 cm. (On cover: Cosy corner series). 1899. L. C. Page and Company.
--Two Little Knights of Kentucky Who Were the Little Colonel's Neighbours. illustrated holiday. Brett, Harold Matthews (1880-), illus. LC 5-33649. 5 p. l., 203 p. 8 col. pl. (incl. front.) 20 cm. 1906, c.1905. L. C. Page & Company.
Johnston, Annie Fellows, Mrs. (1863-1931) & Bacon, Albion Fellows (1865-)
--Songs Ysame. N.D. L. C. Page & Co.
Johnston, Brenda see McCluskey, John.
Johnston, Brenda, jt. auth. see Pruitt, Pamela.
Johnston, Catherine D.
--I Hear the Day. Mark, Joseph, illus. (Illus.). (gr. 2-3). 1977. (ISBN 0-914562-04-5). (ISBN 0-914562-05-3). Merriam-Eddy.
Johnston, Charles Haven Ladd (1877-1943)
--Our Little Viking Cousin of Long Ago, Being the Story of Biarne Herjulfson, a Boy of Norway. Packard, H. W., illus. LC 16-140404. ix p., 2 l., 134 p. col. front., plates. 20 cm. (Little Cousins of Long Ago Series). 1916. The Page Company.
Johnston, Dorothy Grunbock (1915-)
--Cathy and Carl and the Sea Horse Mystery. LC 58-15372. 96p. 21cm. 1957. Scripture Press.
--Cathy and Carl Captured. LC 54-14342. 108p. 21cm. 1954. Scripture Press.
--Cathy and Carl Join the Gold Rush. LC 55-2073. 94p. 21cm. 1955. Scripture Press.
--Cathy and Carl of the Covered Wagon. LC 54-14341. 104p. 21cm. 1954. Scripture Press.
--Cathy and Carl Shipwrecked. LC 56-58196. 95p. 21cm. 1956. Scripture Press.
--Four Teens: How Dan and His Pals Solve Teen-Age Tangles God's Way. LC 56-58213. 125p. illus. 21cm. 1956. Scripture Press.
--Ginger and the Glacier Express. LC 53-308821. 104p. 21cm. 1953. Van Kampen Press.
--Ginger and the Turkey Raiders. LC 52-31746. 80 p. 20 cm. 1952. Van Kampen Press.
--Ginger and the Witch Doctor. LC 56-16392. 76p. 21cm. 1955. Scripture Press, Book Division.
--Ginger at Dogfish Bay. LC 49-50162. 92 p. 20 cm. 1949. Van Kampen Press.
--Ginger in Alaska. LC 51-12156. 91 p. 20cm. 1951. Van Kampen Press.
--Ginger in the Jungles. LC 55-30071. 92p. 20cm. c.1954. Van Kampen Press.
--Hey, Mom. 128p. (gr. 9 up). 1972. (ISBN 0-8024-0129-5). Moody.
--Pete & Penny Know & Grow. 128p. (gr. 1-6). 1972. (ISBN 0-8024-1652-7). Moody.
--Pete and Penny Live and Learn. LC 63-15994. 159 p. illus. 23 cm. 1963. Scripture Press Publications.
--Pete & Penny Play & Pray. 128p. (gr. 1-6). 1972. (ISBN 0-8024-1651-9). Moody.
--Pete & Penny Think & Thank. 128p. (gr. 1-6). 1972. (ISBN 0-8024-1653-5). Moody.
--Pounding Hooves. Crowell, Pers (1910-), illus. LC 75-18645. (Illus.). 254 p. 18cm. c.1976. (ISBN 0-912692-77-4). D. C. Cook Pub. Co.
--Stop, Look, Listen. (Illus.). 24p. (Orig.). (gr. k-2). 1977. (ISBN 0-87239-273-2). Standard Pub.

Johnston, Eileen (1908-)
--Jamie and the Dump Truck. LC 43-14800. 40p. (gr. k-1). 1943. Harper & Bros.
--Jamie and the Fire Engine. Elliott, Miss, illus. LC 40-30190. (Illus.). 40p. (gr. k-1). 1940. Harper & Bros.
--Jamie and the Little Rubber Boat. Cassal, Lys, illus. LC 51-11659. 46p. 1951. Harper & Brothers.
--Jamie and the Tired Train. Edwards, Ora, illus. LC 46-22549. 40p. (gr. k-1). 1946. Harper & Bros.
Johnston, Emma Louisa (1863-) & Barnum, Madalene Demarest (1874-)
--A Book of Plays for Little Actors. LC 7-37031. 171 p. illus. 17 cm. c.1907. American Book Company.
Johnston, Emma M., Miss, jt. auth. see Boyd, E. E., Mrs.
Johnston, Hugh Anthony Stephen see Sturton, Hugh, pseud.
Johnston, Ida Lee
--The Bluebird House and Other Stories for Boys and Girls. LC 28-21896. 89 p. incl. illus., pl. 18 cm. c.1928. Augustana Book Concern.
--The King's Image and Other Stories for Young People. LC 28-21898. 94 p. illus. 18 cm. c.1992. Augustana Book Concern.
--The Lost Slipper and Other Stories for Little Folks. LC 28-218998. 96 p. illus. 18 cm. c.1928. Augustana Book Concern.
Johnston, Isabel McElheny
--The Jeweled Toad. 211 p. incl. col. front., col. illus. col. plates. 24 cm. c.1907. The Bobbs-Merrill Company.
Johnston, Joe
--The Adventures of Teebo: A Tale of Magic & Suspense. Johnston, Joe, illus. LC 83-24686. (Illus.). 48p. (Return of the Jedi Ser.). (gr. 2-7). 1984. (ISBN 0-394-96568-X, BYR). (ISBN 0-394-86568-5). Random.
Johnston, Johanna (1914-1982), abridged by see Stevenson, Robert Louis.
Johnston, Johanna, retold by see Wyss, Johann David Von.
Johnston, Johanna (1914-1982)
--All Kinds of Kings in Fact & Legend. Karmiller, Murry, illus. (gr. 4-6). N.D. (ISBN 0-448-26145-6). G&D.
--A Birthday for General Washington. Burgeson, Marjorie, illus. LC 75-38545. (Illus.). 32p. (Holiday Play Books). (gr. k-4). 1976. (ISBN 0-516-08881-5, Golden Gate). Childrens.
--Close Your Eyes. Wilson, Dagmar (1916-), illus. LC 60-11448. unpaged. illus. 27cm. c.1960. Dodd, Mead.
--Edie Changes Her Mind. Galdone, Paul (1914-), illus. LC 64-10419. (Illus.). 48 p. 27cm. 1964. Putnam.
--Great Gravity the Cat. 1st ed. Wiese, Kurt (1887-1974), illus. LC 58-535561. 66p. illus. 23cm. (Borzoi books for young people). 1958. Knopf.
--The Indians & the Strangers. Negri, Rocco (1932-), illus. LC 72-1447. (Illus.). (gr. 2-5). 1972. Dodd.
--Kings, Lovers & Fools. 126p. (Orig.). 1981. (ISBN 0-590-30954-4, Schol Pap). Scholastic Inc.
--Penguin's Way. 1962. E M Hale.
--Penguin's Way. 1st ed. Weisgard, Leonard Joseph (1916-), illus. LC 62-7070. unpaged. illus. 25cm. c.1962. Doubleday.
--Speak up, Edie!. Galdone, Paul (1914-), illus. LC 73-82025. (Illus.). 45 p. 27cm. 1974. (ISBN 0-399-20374-5). (ISBN 0-399-20374-5). Putnam.
--Special Bravery. Grifalconi, Ann (1929-), illus. LC 67-20777. app. 96p. (Junior Bks). (gr. 1-8). 1970. (ISBN 0-8152-0518-X). Apollo Eds.
--Stories of the Norsemen. 1st ed. Mars, Witold Tadeusz J. (1912-), illus. LC 58-8641. 88p. illus. 32cm. 1959. Garden City Books.
--Sugarplum. Bileck, Marvin (1920-), illus. (Illus.). 40 p. 1955. Knopf.
--Sugarplum & Snowball. Bordigoni, Idelette, illus. LC 68-11166. (Illus.). 1 v. (unpaged. 22cm. 1968. Knopf.
--Supposings. Sayers, Rudy, illus. (Illus.). 32 p. 27cm. 1967. Holiday House.
--That's Right Edie. Galdone, Paul (1914-), illus. (Illus.). (gr. 1-2). 1967. (ISBN 0-399-60627-0). Putnam Pub Group.
--Whale's Way. Weisgard, Leonard Joseph (1916-), illus. LC 65-103516. 21x 28cm. N.D. Doubleday.
Johnston, Johanna (1914-1982), retold by.
--The Story of The Barber of Seville. Rossini, Gioachino Antonio (1792-1868) Perl, Susan (1922-1983), illus. Metropolitan Opera Guild LC 65-25611. 61p. illus. (pt. col.) 27cm. c.1966. (ISBN 0-399-60038-8). Putnam.
Johnston, Julia H.
--Who Was It?. N.D. Richard G. Badger.
Johnston, K. M., compiled by.
--Almond Blossom. N.D. Frederick Warne & Co.
Johnston, Louisa Mae
--The Bible Story Hour. Magagna, Anna Marie, illus. LC 74-9831. p. cm. 1974, c.1975. Standard Educational Corp.
--Mystery Hotel. Royt, Kevin, illus. LC 64-16370. 128 p. illus. 21 cm. 1964. A. Whitman.
Johnston, Louisa & Bristle, Mable C.
--A Monkey in the Family. Axeman, Lois, illus. LC 73-188431. (Illus.). 128p. (gr. 3-7). 1972. (ISBN 0-8075-5256-9). A Whitman.
Johnston, Lynn Beverley (1947-)
--Is This "One of Those Days," Daddy?. Johnston, Lynn Beverley (1947-), illus. LC 82-72417. (Illus.). 128p. (gr. 5 up). 1982. (ISBN 0-8362-1197-9). Andrews & McMeel.
Johnston, Marion
--The Snow House. Downer, Marion (1892-1971), illus. N.D. E. P. Dutton & Co.
Johnston, Mary Anne (1936-)
--Sing Me a Song. Magine, John (1921-), illus. LC 76-57727. (Illus.). 32 p. c.1977. (ISBN 0-913778-81-8). Child's World.
Johnston, Minton Coyne (1900-)
--How the Littlest Cherub Was Late for Christmas. McDonald, Ralph J., illus. LC 67-8150. (Illus.). 32 p. 21cm. 1967. Abingdon Press.
Johnston, Norma
--The Bridge Between. LC 66-7935. 223 p. 22cm. 1966. Funk & Wagnalls.
--The Crucible Year. LC 78-12173. (gr. 7 up). 1979. (ISBN 0-689-30683-0). Atheneum.
--The Days of the Dragon's Seed. LC 81-10786. xi, 194 p. 22cm. 1982. (ISBN 0-689-30882-5). Atheneum.
--Gabriel's Girl. LC 83-2631. p. cm. 1983. (ISBN 0-689-30989-9). Atheneum.
--Glory in the Flower. LC 73-84830. 198 p. 22cm. 1974. Atheneum.
--If You Love Me, Let Me Go. LC 78-6711. 162 p. 24cm. 1978. (ISBN 0-689-30655-5). Atheneum.
--The Keeping Days. LC 73-78727. 233 p. 22cm. 1973. Atheneum.
--A Mustard Seed of Magic. LC 77-1214. p. cm. 1977. (ISBN 0-689-30587-7). Atheneum.
--Myself and I. LC 80-21855. 210 p. 22cm. 1981. (ISBN 0-689-30814-0). Atheneum.
--A Nice Girl Like You. LC 79-22586. 222 p. 22cm. 1980. Atheneum.
--Of Time and of Seasons. LC 75-9748. 282 p. 24cm. 1975. (ISBN 0-689-30479-X). Atheneum.
--Pride of Lions. LC 79-12463. p. cm. 1979. (ISBN 0-689-30711-X). Atheneum.
--Ready or Not. LC 65-117267. 243p. 22cm. c.1965. Funk & Wagnalls.
--The Sanctuary Tree. LC 76-40406. 219 p. 24cm. 1977. (ISBN 0-689-30568-0). Atheneum.
--Strangers Dark and Gold. LC 74-19463. (Illus.). 240 p. 25cm. 1975. (ISBN 0-689-30451-X). Atheneum.
--A Striving After Wind. LC 76-4473. 250 p. 24cm. 1976. (ISBN 0-689-30540-0). Atheneum.
--The Swallow's Song. LC 77-21239. 192 p. 25cm. 1978. (ISBN 0-689-30632-6). Atheneum.
--Timewarp Summer. LC 82-16240. p. cm. 1983. (ISBN 0-689-30960-0). Atheneum.
--The Wider Heart. LC 64-11123. 243 p. 22 cm. 1964. Funk & Wagnalls.
--The Wishing Star. LC 63-8871. 243 p. 22 cm. 1963. Funk & Wagnalls.
Johnston, Ralph E.
--Old Tangle Eye. Moyers, William (1916-), illus. LC 54-9045. (Illus.). 178 p. 22cm. 1954. Houghton Mifflin.
--Old Tangle Eye. Moyers, William (1916-), illus. LC 66-22543. 179p. illus. 22cm. 1966. Houghton.
--Stagecoach Trail. LC 39-232974. viii, 213 p. illus., double plates. 21 cm. 1939. Thomas Y. Crowell Company.
Johnston, Rhod O.
--Iyabo of Nigeria. Samuel, A. Nupo, illus. (Illus.). (gr. 5-12). 1973. (ISBN 0-914522-01-9). Alpha Iota.
Johnston, Sue Mildred Lee (1900-)
--Sonny. LC 33-17943. 168 p. 19 cm. 1933. Benziger Brothers.
Johnston, Susan T. see Johnston, Tony, pseud.
Johnston, Susan T. (1942-)
--The Adventures of Mole & Troll. Johnston, Tony, pseud. Tripp, Wallace Whitney (1940-), illus. LC 70-179023. (Illus.). 61 p. 23cm. 1972. (ISBN 0-399-20271-4). (ISBN 0-399-60747-1). Putnam.
--Fig Tale. Johnston, Tony, pseud. Maestro, Giulio (1942-), illus. LC 74-79673. (Illus.). 32 p. 27cm. 1974. (ISBN 0-399-60908-3). (ISBN 0-399-20417-2). Putnam.
--Five Little Foxes in the Snow. Johnston, Tony, pseud. Szekeres, Cyndy (1933-), illus. LC 76-50579. 21cm. 25p. 1977. (ISBN 0-399-20557-8). Putnam.
--Four Scary Stories. Johnston, Tony, pseud. Tomes, Margot Ladd (1917-), illus. 1980. Putnam.
--Mole and Troll Trim the Tree. Johnston, Tony, pseud. Tripp, Wallace Whitney (1940-), illus. LC 73-82024. (Illus.). 32 p. 23cm. 1974. (ISBN 0-399-60909-1). Putnam.
--Odd Jobs and Friends. Johnston, Tony, pseud. De Paola, Tomie, pseud. (1934-), illus. De Paola, Thomas Anthony. LC 82-511. p. cm. (A See & Read Book). c.1982. (ISBN 0-399-61204-1). Putnam.
--The Quilt Story. Johnston, Tony, pseud. De Paola, Tomie, pseud. (1934-), illus. De Paola, Thomas Anthony. LC 84-18212. p. cm. c.1984. Putnam.
--The Vanishing Pumpkin. Johnston, Tony, pseud. De Paola, Tomie, pseud. (1934-), illus. De Paola, Thomas Anthony. LC 83-3122. (Illus.). (gr. k-4). 1983. (ISBN 0-399-20991-3, Putnam). (ISBN 0-399-20991-3). Putnam Pub Group.
--The Witch's Hat. Johnston, Tony, pseud. Tomes, Margot Ladd (1917-), illus. LC 84-9948. (Illus.). p. cm. 32p. c.1984. (ISBN 0-399-21010-5). Putnam Pub. Group.
Johnston, Susan T. (1942-) & De Paola, Tomie, pseud. (1934-)
--Four Scary Stories. Johnston, Tony, pseud. De Paola, Thomas Anthony. LC 77-13027. (Illus.). 32 p. 27cm. c.1978. (ISBN 0-399-20614-0). Putnam.
--Odd Jobs. Johnston, Tony, pseud. De Paola, Thomas Anthony. LC 76-39794. 23cm. 47p. (See and Read Storybook). c.1977. (ISBN 0-399-61048-0). Putnam.
Johnston, Susan T. (1942-) & Stanley, Diane (1943-)
--Little Mouse Nibbling. Johnston, Tony, pseud. LC 78-24265. (Illus.). 32 p. 20cm. c.1979. (ISBN 0-399-20673-6). Putnam.
Johnston, Susan T. (1942-) & Szekeres, Cyndy (1933-)
--Happy Birthday, Mole & Troll. Johnston, Tony, pseud. LC 78-25717. (Illus.). 63 p. 23cm. (See and read storybook). c.1979. (ISBN 0-399-61137-1). Putnam.
--Night Noises and Other Mole and Troll Stories. Johnston, Tony, pseud. LC 76-3653. (Illus.). 63 p. 23cm. (See and read book). c.1977. (ISBN 0-399-61016-2). Putnam.
Johnston, Thomas
--The Fight for Arkenvald. 1st ed. Walworth, Jane Armstrong, illus. LC 75-185581. (Illus.). 150 p. 22cm. 1973. Doubleday.
Johnston, Tony, pseud., see Johnston, Susan T..
Johnston, Wesley J.
--The House that Jack Built. N.D. Publications of the Methodist Book Concern.
Johnston, William Andrew (1871-)
--Limpy. (Growing Literature Ser.). N.D. Grosset & Dunlap.
--Limpy: The Boy Who Felt Neglected. Brown, Arthur William, illus. LC 17-7454. 5 p. l., 334 p. front., plates. 20 cm. 1917. Little, Brown, and Company.
--Room Two Hundred & Twenty-Two: Have You Heard About Kelley, No. 6. (gr. 7 up). 1973 (Tempo). G&D.
--Soul City Downstairs. (gr. 5 up). N.D. Pyramid Pubns.
Johnston, William T.
--Bill Johnston's Second Joy Book. Fox, Fontaine (1884-1964), illus. N.D. D. Appleton & Co.
Johnston, William (1924-)
--Animal Stories. Aloise, Frank E. & Goldsborough, June (1923-), illus. Brooks, Walter, designed by. LC 68-11118. (Illus.). 223 p. 27cm. (Whitman Library of Giant Books). 1968. Whitman Pub. Division, Western Pub. Co.
--Bugs Bunny Party Pest. Anderson, Al & McKimson, Thomas, illus. (Illus.). (Tell-a-Tale Readers). (gr. k-3). 1978. (ISBN 0-307-68607-8, Whitman). Western Pub.
--Dr. Kildare: The Magic Key. Authorized. Anderson, Al & Jason Art Studio, illus. LC 64-5029. 210 p. col. illus. 20 cm. 1964. Whitman Pub. Co.
Johnstone, Anne Grahame, jt. auth. see Johnstone, Janet Grahame.
Johnstone, C. T.
--The Young Emigrants. (Illus.). N.D. Thomas Nelson & Sons.
Johnstone, D. L.
--The Brotherhood of the Coast. (Illus.). N.D. Thomas Whittaker.
--The Land of the Golden Plume. N.D. Thomas Whittaker.
Johnstone, Janet Grahame & Johnstone, Anne Grahame
--Book of Fairy Tales. (Illus.). (ps-3). N.D. (ISBN 0-685-24612-4). Merry Thoughts.
--Gift Book of Fairy Tales. (Illus.). (ps-3). N.D. Merry Thoughts.
--Gift Book of Nursery Rhymes. (Illus.). (ps-3). N.D. Merry Thoughts.
--New Gift Book of Nursery Rhymes. (ps-3). N.D. (ISBN 0-685-27822-0). Borden.
--New Gift Book of Nursery Rhymes. (Illus.). (ps-3). N.D. Merry Thoughts.
--Puppy Dog Rhymes. Johnstone, Janet Grahame & Johnstone, Anne Grahame, illus. (Illus.). (ps-3). N.D. Merry Thoughts.
--Pussy Cat Rhymes. Johnstone, Janet Grahame & Johnstone, Anne Grahame, illus. (Illus.). (ps-3). N.D. Merry Thoughts.
Johnstone, Kathleen Yerger (1906-)
--Sea Treasure. (Illus.). 1957. Houghton Mifflin
Johnstone, Mrs.
--The Diversions of Hollycot: Or, The Mother's Art of Thinking, 1 of 4 vols. (Hollycot Library Ser.). N.D. Set. T. Whittaker.
Johnstone, Muriel
--The Magic Key. Holland, Sylvia, illus. LC 53-253805. unpaged. illus. 21cm. (Jolly books, 206). 1952. Avon Pub. Co.
Johnstone, Parker
--The Turtle Speaks. N.D. Vantage Press.
Johnstone, Paul
--Escape from Attila. Phelan, Joseph A., illus. LC 68-15244. (Illus.). 143 p. 22cm. 1969. Criterion Books.
Johnstone, Sally, ed.
--Sam & Company. Johnstone, Sally, illus. LC 82-83034. (Illus.). 32p. (Orig.). (ps). 1982. (ISBN 0-914766-87-2). IWP Pub.
John the Giant-Killer
--A New Riddle Book. (Teur, A. W.). (Illus.). N.D. Distributed by Charles Scribner's Sons.
Johonnot, James (1823-1888)
--Friends in Feathers and Fur, and Other Neighbors. 140p. 1885. Appleton & Co.
Jokai, Moritz (1825-1904) & Lermontov, Mikhail Iurevich (1814-1841)
--The Golden Fairy Book. 19cm. 320p. 1894. A. L. Burt Co.
--The Golden Fairy Book. Millar, Harold Robert (1869-1939), illus. N.D. D. Appleton and Co.
Jollison, Marion, pseud., see Horowitz, Caroline.
Jolly, Erin see Kelley, Sally, pseud.
Jolly, Erin
--Summer Growing Time. Kelley, Sally, pseud. 1st ed. Mackay, Donald A. (1895-), illus. LC 77-165249. (Illus.). 125 p. 22cm. 1971. (ISBN 0-670-68172-5). (ISBN 0-670-68173-3). Viking Press.
Jolly, Stephen, tr. see Capek, Josef.
Joly, Janet, Mrs., ed. see Bishop, Claire Huchet, Mrs.
Jonas, Ann (1919-)
--Holes & Peeks. Jonas, Ann (1919-), illus. LC 83-14128. (Illus.). 7 3/8 x 8. 24p. (20 pt.). (ps-1). 1984. (ISBN 0-688-02537-4). (ISBN 0-688-02538-2). Greenwillow. **Award: (ALA).**
--Now We Can Go. LC 85-12614. (Illus.). 7 3/8 x 8. 24p. (24 pt.). (ps-1). 1986. (ISBN 0-688-04802-1). (ISBN 0-688-04803-X). Greenwillow.
--The Quilt. Jonas, Ann (1919-), illus. LC 83-25385. (Illus.). 8 x 9 7/8. 32p. (24 pt.). (ps-1). 1984. (ISBN 0-688-03825-5). (ISBN 0-688-03826-3). Greenwillow. **Award: (ALA).**
--Round Trip. 1st ed. Jonas, Ann (1919-), illus. LC 82-12026. (Illus.). 32 p. 26cm. c.1983. (ISBN 0-688-01772-X). (ISBN 0-688-01781-9). Greenwillow Books. **Awards: (NYT); (ALA).**
--The Trek. Jonas, Ann (1919-), illus. LC 84-25962. (Illus.). 8 x 9 7/8. 32p. (14 pt.). (gr. k-3). 1985. (ISBN 0-688-04799-8). (ISBN 0-688-04800-5). Greenwillow.
--Two Bear Cubs. Jonas, Ann (1919-), illus. LC 82-2860. (Illus.). 28 p. 21cm. c.1982. (ISBN 0-688-01407-0). (ISBN 0-688-01408-9). Greenwillow Books.
--When You Were a Baby. LC 81-12800. (Illus.). 28 p. 22cm. c.1982. (ISBN 0-688-00863-1). (ISBN 0-688-00864-X). Greenwillow Books.
Jonas, Nita
--The Little Golden Book of Dogs. Gergely, Tibor (1900-1978), illus. Reissue of 1956 ed. (Little Golden Book). 1959. Golden Press.
--The Little Golden Book of Dogs. Gergely, Tibor (1900-1978), illus. LC 52-11752. (Illus.). 21cm. (The Little Golden Library). 1952. Simon and Schuster.
--Wild & Woolly Animal Book. Maxey, Dale, illus. LC 61-7873. (Illus.). 33cm. (gr. k-2). 1961. (ISBN 0-394-90688-8, BYR). Random.
Jonas, Nita, ed.
--Puppy Dog Tales. Maxey, Dale (1927-), illus. LC 63-7809. (Illus.). 33cm. 25p. (gr. k-2). 1964. (ISBN 0-394-80752-9). (ISBN 0-394-90752-3). Random.
Jonathan, Norton Hughes
--Dan Hyland, Police Reporter. LC 36-416. 5 p. l., 15-250 p. 20 cm. c.1936. The Goldsmith Publishing Company.
Jones, A. C.
--Four Little Sixes. N.D. Pott & Co.
Jones, Adrienne (1915-)
--Another Place, Another Spring. LC 74-163167. (Illus.). 285 p. 22cm. 1971. (ISBN 0-395-12757-2). Houghton Mifflin.
--The Beckoner. LC 79-1715. 243 p. 22cm. c.1980. (ISBN 0-06-023059-2). (ISBN 0-06-023060-6). Harper & Row.
--The Hawks of Chelney. Gammell, Stephen, illus. LC 77-11855. (Illus.). 245 p. 22cm. c.1978. (ISBN 0-06-023057-6). (ISBN 0-06-023058-4). Harper & Row. **Award: (ALA).**
--A Matter of Spunk. LC 82-47710. c.1983. (ISBN 0-06-023053-3). Harper & Row.

Jones, Mabel Cronise
--Dolly's College Experience. LC 9-28696. 3 p. l., 276 p. front., 7 pl. 20 cm. 1909. The C. M. Clark Publishing Company.
Jones, McClure
--Cast Down the Stars. LC 78-4277. p. cm. 24cm. 186p. c.1978. (ISBN 0-03-042501-8). Holt, Rinehart and Winston.
--Fix-up Service. LC 84-25370. p. cm. 1985. (ISBN 0-399-21132-2). Pacer Books.
Jones, Manley H.
--Christmas is Coming. Becker, Charlotte (1906-), illus. LC 39-28986. 1939. Houghton Mifflin Co.
Jones, Mary Alice (1898-)
--Bible Stories for Little Children. N.D. Thomas Nelson & Sons.
--Bible Stories for Little Children. Lee, Manning De Villeneuve (1894-1980), illus. LC 74-1245. (Illus.). 113 p. 29cm. N.D. Rand McNally.
--Bible Stories: God at Work with Man. Armstrong, Tom, illus. LC 72-13486. (Illus.). 80p. (gr. 1-4). 1973. (ISBN 0-687-03384-5). Abingdon.
--Bible Stories: God at Work with Man. Armstrong, Tom, illus. LC 72-13486. (Illus.). 77 p. 27cm. 1973. Abingdon Press.
--The Bible Story of the Creation. Holland, Janice (1913-1962), illus. LC 47-606. 38, 1 p. col. illus. 21 x 16 cm. 1946. Rand McNally & Company.
--The Bible Story of the Creation. Patton, Lucia, illus. 64 p. illus. (part col.) 17 x 14 cm. c.1941. Rand McNally & Company.
--The Bible Story of the Creation. Stone, David Karl (1922-), illus. LC 67-21608. (Illus.). 44 p. 24cm. 1967. Rand McNally.
--Favorite Prayers & Stories. (Illus.). (ps-3). 1966. (ISBN 0-528-82964-5). Rand.
--Favorite Stories of Jesus. (Illus.). 112p. (Rand McNally "Favorite" Ser.). (ps-2). 1981. (ISBN 0-528-82313-2). Rand.
--God's Plan for Growing Things. Wilde, Irma, illus. LC 65-13185. 1 v. (unpaged) col. illus. 27 cm. 1965, c.1964. Rand McNally.
--Old Testament Stories. Ropp, Charles, illus. N.D. Rand McNally & Co.
--Robert and the Rainbow and Other Stories. Henderson, Leslie, illus. LC 26-11852. 64 p. illus., col. plates. 31 cm. (Cokesbury character series for boys and girls). c.1926. Cokesbury Press.
--The Story of Joseph. (ps-k). 1966. (ISBN 0-528-88865-X). Rand.
--Tell Me About Christmas. Cooper, Marjorie (1910-), illus. LC 58-8955. 71p. illus. 27cm. 1958. Rand McNally.
--Tell Me About the Bible. Doane, Pelagie (1906-1966), illus. (gr. 1-5). 1945. (ISBN 0-528-82582-8). Rand.
--Winter Is Coming and Other Stories. LC 25-9825. vi, 176 p. 20 cm. 1925. Cokesbury Press.
Jones, Mary M
--The Adventures of Bunny Boy. LC 40-9820. 83 p. illus. 20 cm. c.1940. House of Field, Inc.
Jones, Mary Voell, jt. auth. see Knoche, Norma R.
Jones, May Farinholt (1868-)
--Keep-Well Stories for Little Folks. Wright, Pauline, Miss, illus. LC 16-23406. viii, 140 p. col. illus. 20 cm. 1916. J. B. Lippincott Company.
Jones, Maynard see Jones, Nard, pseud.
Jones, Maynard (1904-1972)
--West, Young Man!. Jones, Nard, pseud. Edwards, Howard (1904-), illus. LC 37-157808. 6 p. l., 3-204 p., 1 l. incl. plates. 21 cm. c.1937. Metropolitan Press.
Jones, Maynard (1904-1972) & Gose, J. Gordon
--West, Young Man. Jones, Nard, pseud. 220p. N.D. Binfords & Mort.
Jones, Michael P., ed.
--Andorff the Energy Ant's Coloring Book. abr. ed. (Illus.). 34p. 1984. (ISBN 0-89904-071-3). (ISBN 0-89904-072-1). Crumb Elbow Pub.
Jones, Mrs.
--Little Talks With Little People, 1 of 6 vols. (Illus.). (Cosey Corner Ser.: No. 2). N.D. Cassell, Petter, Galpin.
--Stories of the Olden Time, 1 of 6 vols. (Illus.). (The Golden Library). N.D. Cassell, Petter, Galpin.
Jones, Nard, pseud., see Jones, Maynard.
Jones, O., tr. see Brunhoff, Laurent de.
Jones, Olive
--In the Troll Wood. Bauer, John Albert (1882-1918), illus. LC 77-18419. p. cm. 1978. (ISBN 0-458-93240-X). Methuen.
Jones, Olive, retold by.
--Aladdin. Crespi, Francesca, illus. LC 83-23972. (Illus.). 28 p. 11cm. 1984. (ISBN 0-8037-0079-2). Dial Books for Young Readers.
--Hansel and Gretel. Crespi, Francesca, illus. LC 83-23907. (Illus.). 28 p. 11cm. 1984. (ISBN 0-8037-0079-2). Dial Books for Young Readers.
--Jack and the Beanstalk. Crespi, Francesca, illus. LC 83-23909. (Illus.). 28 p. 10cm. 1984. (ISBN 0-8037-0079-2). Dial Books for Young Readers.
--A Little Box of Fairy Tales, 4 bks. Crespi, Francesca, illus. (Illus.). 28p. (Dial Book for Young Readers). (ps-3). 1983. (ISBN 0-8037-4765-9). Dutton.
--Rapunzel. Crespi, Francesca, illus. LC 83-23913. (Illus.). 28 p. 11cm. 1984. (ISBN 0-8037-0079-2). Dial Books for Young Readers.
Jones, Olive, ed. see Blackmore, Richard Doddridge.
Jones, Olive, ed. see Cervantes Saavedra, Miguel de.
Jones, Olive, adapted by see Kruse, Max.
Jones, Olive, tr. see Rettich, Margret.
Jones, Patricia (1913-), adapted by see Grimm, Jakob Ludwig Karl (1785-1863) & Grimm, Wilhelm Karl.
Jones, Penelope (1938-)
--Holding Together. LC 80-27101. 173 p. 22cm. c.1981. (ISBN 0-87888-177-8). Bradbury Press.
--I Didn't Want to Be Nice. Orlando, Rosalie, illus. LC 76-57907. 24cm. 32p. c.1977. (ISBN 0-87888-111-5). Bradbury Press.
--I'm Not Moving!. Aitken, Amy (1952-), illus. LC 79-13062. (Illus.). 32 p. 24cm. c.1980. (ISBN 0-87888-156-5). Bradbury Press.
--The Stealing Thing. LC 82-22653. p. cm. 1983. (ISBN 0-87888-211-1). Bradbury Press.
Jones, Peter (1934-)
--Rebel in the Night. LC 75-121814. 185, 1 p. 24cm. 1971. Dial Press.
Jones, R. G., jt. auth. see Weimer, T.
Jones, R. & Colby, J. Rose, eds.
--Eliot's Silas Marner. N.D. D. Appleton-Century Co.
Jones, Raymond F., et al. (1915-)
--Future Kin: Eight Science Fiction Stories. Elwood, Roger (1943-), compiled by. LC 73-21158. (Illus.). 192p. (gr. 7-9). 1974. (ISBN 0-385-05488-2). (ISBN 0-385-08913-9). Doubleday.
Jones, Raymond F. (1915-)
--Moonbase One. (Criterion Books). 1972. (ISBN 0-200-71853-3). Abelard-Schuman.
--Moonbase One. LC 71-160108. 144 p. 22cm. 1971. (ISBN 0-200-71853-3). Criterion Books.
--Planet of Light. Schomburg, Alex, illus. LC 53-7339. 211p. 22cm. (Science fiction). 1953. Winston.
--Son of the Stars. (Winston Science Fiction Ser.). 1952. Holt, Rinehart and Winston.
--The World of Weather. Preston, William, illus. LC 61-66747. 90p. illus. 24cm. (Whitman badger book). 1961. Whitman Pub. Co.
--The Year When Stardust Fell. Schomburg, Alex & Heugh, James, illus. LC 58-5676. 203p. 22cm. 1958. Winston.
Jones, Rebecca Castaldi (1947-)
--Angie and Me. LC 81-4367. 113 p. 22cm. c.1981. Macmillan.
--The Biggest, Meanest, Ugliest Dog in the Whole Wide World. Watson, Wendy McLeod (1942-), illus. LC 82-6612. p. cm. c.1982. (ISBN 0-02-747800-9). Macmillan.
--Madeline and the Great (Old) Escape Artist. 1st ed. LC 83-11630. p. cm. c.1983. (ISBN 0-525-44074-7). Dutton.
Jones, Richard, jt. ed. see Baker, Franklin T.
Jones, Rimsky
--Mouse Margaret. Jones, Rimsky, illus. (Illus.). (gr. 2-5). 1976. (ISBN 0-932220-01-0). Broken Whisker.
Jones, Rimsky, illus.
--Roland of the Hills. (Illus.). 1977. (ISBN 0-685-76959-3). Broken Whisker.
Jones, Robinson Godfrey (1871-)
--Playtime Stories. Dunlop, Agnes Mary Robertson (0000-1982), ed. LC 21-19406. 112 p. col. illus. 19 cm. c.1921. American Book Company.
Jones, Ruth Fosdick
--Boy of the Pyramids: A Mystery of Ancient Egypt. Morse, Dorothy Bayley (1906-1979), illus. LC 52-5854. (Illus.). 140 p. 22cm. 1952. (ISBN 0-394-90977-1). Random House.
--Escape to Freedom. Morse, Dorothy Bayley (1906-1979), illus. (Illus.). 21cm. 236p. (gr. 5-9). 1958. (ISBN 0-394-91126-1). Random.
Jones, Sarah Clark
--Little Miss Weezy's Brother. (Penn Shirley Books). N.D. Lothrop, Lee & Shepard.
--Little Miss Weezy's Sister. (Penn Shirley Books). N.D. Lothrop, Lee & Shepard.
Jones, Sarah J
--Downward: Or, The New Distillery. LC 7-11684. 224 p. incl. front. pl. 19 cm. c.1883. The American Sunday-School Union.
--Godfrey Brenz: A Tale of Persecution. LC 7-11686. v, 7-208 p. 20 cm. 1894. The American Sunday-School Union.
--None Other Name: Or, The Blacksmith of Minnaberg. A Story of the Reformation. LC 7-11685. 2 p. l., 7-232 p. 20 cm. 1893. American Sunday-School Union.
--Rest or Unrest. A Story of the Parisian Sabbath in America. LC 7-11687. 260 p. 19 cm. 1888. Phillips & Hunt.
--Struggling Upward. LC 7-11688. 279 p. incl. front. pl. 19 cm. c.1883. The American Sunday-School Union.
--Words and Ways: Or, What They Said, and What Came of It. LC 7-11689. 302 p. 19 cm. 1885. Phillips & Hunt.
Jones, Stanley Howard (1906-)
--The Call of the Lapwing. Marriott, Patricia (1920-), illus. LC 63-10361. 159 p. illus. 22cm. 1963, c.1961. Duell, Sloan & Pearce.
Jones, Stephen, jt. auth. see Henderson, Bernard Lionel Kingston.
Jones, Terry (1942-)
--Fairy Tales. Foreman, Michael (1938-), illus. LC 81-23227. p. cm. 1st U.S. edition. 1982, c.1981. (ISBN 0-8052-3807-7). Schocken Books.
--The Saga of Erik the Viking: A Story for Bill. Foreman, Michael (1938-), illus. LC 83-7420. p. cm. 128p. 1st U.S. edition. 1983. (ISBN 0-8052-3876-X). Schocken Books.
Jones, Thelma H.
--The Road to San Luis Rey. LC 73-87882. (Illus.). (gr. 7-12). 1974. (ISBN 0-912472-18-9). Miller Bks.
Jones, Theodoric, ed.
--Great Story-Poems. LC 65-246883. 191p. illus. 23cm. (Sunrise lib.). 1966. Hart.
Jones, Thomas Firth (1934-)
--Rebel Gold. LC 75-9812. 158 p. 21cm. 1975. (ISBN 0-664-32571-8). Westminster Press.
Jones, Thomas Orton (1916-) & Jones, Elizabeth Orton (1910-)
--Minnie the Mermaid. Jones, Elizabeth Orton (1910-), illus. 48p. 1939. Oxford University Press.
Jones, Toeckey
--Go Well, Stay Well. LC 79-3603. p. cm. 1980, c.1979. (ISBN 0-06-023061-4). (ISBN 0-06-023062-2). Harper & Row.
Jones, Vera R.
--Stories of Jesus. 1983. (ISBN 0-8062-2242-5). Carlton.
Jones, Viola May
--Peter and Gretchen of Old Nuremberg. Sewell, Helen Moore (1896-1957), illus. LC 35-9328. 96 p. illus. (part col.) 26 cm. 1935. A. Whitman & Co.
Jones, Virginia M.
--The Predicament of Gregory Gray. Gidionsen, Rosemary, illus. LC 66-1016. 1 v. (unpaged) col. illus. 22 cm. 1965. Bethany Press.
--Sweet William. 1959. Exposition Press.
Jones, Weyman B. (1928-)
--Edge of Two Worlds. Kocsis, James C. (1936-), illus. Paul, James, pseud. LC 68-15256. (Illus.). 143 p. 21cm. 1968. Dial Press. **Award: (ALA).**
--The Talking Leaf. Johnson, Eugene Harper, illus. LC 65-239667. 95p. illus. 21cm. c.1965. Dial.
Jones, Wilfrid
--Epic of Kings. N.D. MacMillan.
Jones, William Edward (1921-)
--Going to School. LC 68-56811. (Illus.). (ps-1). 1968. (ISBN 0-87783-015-0). Oddo.
Jones, William Edward (1921-) & Goldberg, Minerva J.
--Going to Kindergarten. Wallner, Shirley J., illus. LC 65-27621. 32p. col. illus., ports. 26cm. 1966, c.1965. Oddo.
--Going to Kindergarten. Wallner, Shirley J., illus. LC 68-56811. (Illus.). 32 p. col. illus. parts. 26cm. (ps-k). N.D. Oddo.
Jones, Willis Knapp (1895-)
--The Hammon Twins. Humphreys, Donald S., illus. LC 26-14914. vii p., 2 l., 3-339 p. front., plates. 11 cm. 1926. The Century Co.
Jones Vernon, Vernon Stanley (1874-1936), adapted by see Aesopus.
Jong, David Cornel De see De Jong, David Cornel.
Jong, Dola De see De Jong, Dola.
Jong, Meindert De see De Jong, Meindert.
Jonge, Joanne De see De Jonge, Joanne.
Jonk, Clarence (1906-)
--Jimmy, a Little Pup. Berta, Hugh, illus. LC 59-14649. unpaged. illus. 29cm. 1959. T. S. Denison.
--Ma Poos and the Fabulous Whimplegoose. Minick, Newell R., illus. LC 59-146512. unpaged. illus. 29cm. 1959. T. S. Denison.
--Old Angus, the Unhappy Baker. Minick, Newell R., illus. LC 59-14650. (Illus.). 29cm. (Second Grade Bk.). (gr. 2-3). 1959. Denison.
--Whimsies: Poems for All Ages. Smith, Richard, illus. LC 75-190693. (Illus.). (gr. k up). 1972. (ISBN 0-8283-1359-8). Branden.
Jonsen, George, retold by.
--Favorite Tales of Monsters and Trolls. O'Brien, John (1953-), illus. LC 76-24182. (Illus.). 32 p. 21cm. (Random House pictureback). c.1977. (ISBN 0-394-83477-1). Random House.
Jonson, Marian
--The Beauty of the Dreaming Wood. 1973. (ISBN 0-85343-510-3). Coach Hse.
--The Cricket on the Hearth. (Children's Theatre Playscript Ser.). 1957. (ISBN 0-88020-023-5). Coach Hse.
--Greensleeves' Magic. (Children's Theatre Playscript Ser.). 1954. (ISBN 0-88020-000-6). Coach Hse.
--Snow White & the Seven Dwarfs. (Children's Theatre Playscript Ser.). 1957. (ISBN 0-88020-057-X). Coach Hse.
--Timblewit & Other Plays. 1973. (ISBN 0-85343-508-1). Coach Hse.
--Timblewit and Other Plays: Timblewit, Island of the Winds and The Beauty of the Dreaming Wood. LC 74-165276. (Illus.). 56 p. 22cm. 1973. (ISBN 0-85343-508-1). J. B. Miller.
Jonsson, Runer
--Viki Viking. Karlsson, Ewert (1918-), illus. Rogers, Birgit & Love, Patricia Tracy, trs. from Ger. LC 68-14688. (Illus.). 143 p. 20cm. 1st U.S. edition. 1968. World Pub. Co.
Joos, Dorothy Heslop
--The Golden Prince. Wells, Rhea (1891-), illus. LC 28-22725. 6 p. l., 3-129, 1 p. incl. illus., plates. col. front. 27 cm. 1928. Duffield and Company.
Joosse, Barbara Monnot (1949-)
--Fourth of July. McCully, Emily Arnold (1939-), illus. LC 82-17301. (Illus.). 40 p. 1985. (ISBN 0-394-85195-1). (ISBN 0-394-95195-6). Knopf Books for Young Readers.
--Spiders in the Fruit Cellar. Chorao, Ann McKay Sproat (1936-), illus. LC 82-4694. p. cm. 1983. (ISBN 0-394-85327-X). Knopf Books for Young Readers.
--The Thinking Place. Chorao, Ann McKay Sproat (1936-), illus. LC 81-515. (Illus.). 36 p. 18cm. c.1982. (ISBN 0-394-84908-6). (ISBN 0-394-94908-0). Knopf : Distributed by Random House.
Jope-Slade, Christine
--St. David Walks Again. Custis, Eleanor Parke, illus. LC 28-242712. 7 p. l., 130 p. incl. front., plates. 18 cm. 1928. Harper & Brothers.
Jopp, Regina, tr. see Parma, Clemens.
Jordan, Alton, ed. see Barber, Phyllis.
Jordan, Alton, ed. see Burke, Suzanne.
Jordan, Alton, ed. see Reese, Bob.
Jordan, Alton, ed. see Reese, Nancy.
Jordan, Alton, ed. see Reese, Ron.
Jordan, Alton, ed. see Selman, LaRue.
Jordan, Alton, ed. see Shebar, Sharon Sigmond (1945-) & Schoder, Judy.
Jordan, Alton, ed. see Smith, Glenna C.
Jordan, Alton, ed. see Stoddard, Darrell.
Jordan, Alton, ed. see Willoughby, Alana.
Jordan, Alton, ed. see Winder, Jack.
Jordan, Ben
--Dirt-Track Twister. LC 67-24428. 160p. (gr. 7 up). 1967. (ISBN 0-696-58060-8). Hawthorn.
--Dirt-Track Twister: A Teen-Age Novel. LC 67-94428. 154 p. 21cm. 154p. 1967. Meredith Press.
--Leatherjackets. LC 63-16830. 154 p. illus. 21 cm. 1963. Duell, Sloan and Pearce.
--Sky Jumpers: A Novel About Free Fall Parachuting. LC 65-13739. 191 p. 22cm. 1965. J. Day Co.
Jordan, Charlotte Brewster, Mrs.
--Tuckaway House. LC 37-22826. 2 p. l., vii-ix p., 1 l., 313 p. col. front., illus., plates. 21 cm. (Young moderns bookshelf). 1937. The Sun Dial Press, Inc.
--Tuckaway House. Norcross, Grace & Oehler, Bernice Olivia (1881-), illus. LC 26-18321. 2 p. l., vii-ix p., 1 l., 313 p. col. front., illus., plates. 21 cm. 1926. Doubleday, Page & Company.
--The Tuckaway Twins. Norcross, Grace, illus. LC 28-218257. viii p., 1 l., 301 p. col. front., illus. 21 cm. 1928. Doubleday, Doran & Company, Inc.
Jordan, David Starr, Dr., intro. by see Miller, Joaquin.
Jordan, David Starr (1851-1931)
--The Book of Knight and Barbara: Being a Series of Stories Told to Children. LC 99-5517. viii, 265 p. front., illus., plates. 21 cm. 1899. D. Appleton and Company.
--Eric's Book of Beasts Done in Water-Colors and Accompanied with Appropriate Jingles. LC 12-143954. v p., 1 l., 112, 3 p. front., illus. 20 cm. c.1912. P. Elder and Company.
--Matka and Kotik: A Tale of the Mist-Islands. LC 7-11691. 68 p., 1 l. front., illus., plates, map. 22 cm. 1897. The Whitaker & Ray Company (Incorporated.
Jordan, E. T.
--Dark Time Fun. N.D. Carlton Press.
--Flickle's Rain Games. N.D. Carlton Press.
Jordan, Elizabeth Garver (1867-1947)
--May Iverson: Her Book. (Girls' Library). 1904. Harper & Bros.
--May Iverson Tackles Life. (Girls' Library). 1912. Harper & Bros.
--May Iverson's Career. (Girls' Library). 1914. Harper & Bros.
--The Trap. LC 37-14573. 3 p. l., 308 p. 20 cm. 1937. D. Appleton-Century Company, Incorporated.

AUTHOR INDEX JUDD, FRANCES

Jordan, Gene
--White Beauty. LC 56-19239. 85p. illus. 21cm. 1955. Me., Falmouth Pub. House.
Jordan, Hope Dahle (1905-)
--The Fortune Cake. LC 76-156920. 160 p. 22cm. 1972. Lothrop, Lee & Shepard Co.
--Haunted Summer. LC 67-15713. 158 p. 22cm. 1967. Lothrop, Lee and Shepard.
--Stranger in Their Midst. LC 74-5189. 160 p. 22cm. 1974. (ISBN 0-688-41649-7). (ISBN 0-688-41649-7). Lothrop, Lee & Shepard.
--Supermarket Sleuth. LC 76-81755. 128 p. 22cm. 1969. Lothrop, Lee & Shepard.
--Take Me to My Friend. (gr. 7 up). 1962. Lothrop.
--Talk About the Tarchers. LC 67-22587. 128 p. 21cm. 1968. Lothrop, Lee & Shepard Co.
Jordan, Jael Michal (1949-)
--August Fourth. (Illus.). 1975. (ISBN 0-87466-070-X). Parnassus Press.
Jordan, June Meyer (1936-)
--His Own Where. LC 71-146283. (gr. 7 up). 1971. (ISBN 0-690-38133-6, TYC-J). Har-Row.
--Kimako's Story. Burford, Kay, illus. LC 81-2894. (Illus.). 42 p. 21cm. 1981. (ISBN 0-395-31601-0). Houghton Mifflin.
--New Life,. Cruz, Raymond (1933-), illus. LC 73-9755. (Illus.). 52 p. 24cm. 1975. (ISBN 0-690-00211-4). (ISBN 0-690-00212-2). Crowell. **Award: (ALA).**
--New Life. Cruz, Raymond (1933-), illus. LC 73-9755. (Illus.). 64p. (gr. 3-5). 1975. (ISBN 0-690-00212-2, TYC-J). Har-Row.
--New Life, New Room. Dron, Ed, illus. 1973. Crowell.
--Who Look at Me. LC 69-13641. (Illus.). 97 p. 22cm. 1969. Crowell. **Award: (ALA).**
Jordan, June Meyer (1936-) & Bush, Terri, eds.
--The Voice of the Children. LC 77-119095. (Illus.). 101 p. 22cm. 1970. Holt, Rinehart and Winston.
Jordan, Kate
--The Happifats and the Grouch. N.D. E P Dutton.
--Trouble-the-House. LC 21-20883. 3 p. l., 306 p., 1 l. 20 cm. 1921. Little, Brown, and Company.
Jordan, Margaret E.
--Happy Hearts and Pleasant Faces. Burke, Bridget Ellen, Mrs. (1850-), intro. by. LC 15-23430. (Illus.). 48p. 21cm. (Educational Series for Homes and Schools). 1897. Rosary Publication Company.
Jordan, Marie Anne
--Mother's Rhymes for Story Times. Jordan, Marie Anne (1901-), illus. LC 30-24319. 78, 2 p. incl. col. front., col. illus. 25 cm. c.1930. Lothrop, Lee and Shepard Co.
Jordan, Mildred Anne (1901-)
--I Won't," Said the King: Or, The Purple Flannel Underwear. Duvoisin, Roger Antoine (1904-1980), illus. LC 45-8327. 4 p. l., 103, 1 p. incl. front., illus. col. plates. 21 x 16 1/2 cm. 1945. A. A. Knopf.
--Proud to Be Amish. Mars, Witold Tadeusz J. (1912-), illus. LC 68-26801. (Illus.). 144 p. 22cm. 1968. Crown Publishers.
--The Shoo-Fly Pie. Pitz, Henry Clarence (1895-1976), illus. LC 44-4324. 3 p. l., 118 p., 1 l. illus., col. plates (2 double) 23 1/2 cm. 1944. A. A. Knopf.
Jordan, Myra J. & Grant, Roy E.
--Floppy Rabbit: An Easter Musical. (Illus.). 30p. (Orig.). (ps-1). 1980. (ISBN 0-914562-09-6). Merriam-Eddy.
--Santa's Problem. (Illus.). 30p. (Orig.). (ps-1). 1980. (ISBN 0-914562-08-8). Merriam-Eddy.
Jordan, Myrtle L., ed.
--Alice in Wonderland. N.D. Bruce Humphries.
--An Irish Song. N.D. Bruce Humphries.
Jordan, Philip Dillon (1903-)
--The Burro Benedicto, and Other Folktales and Legends of Mexico. Powers, Richard M. Gorman (1921-), illus. LC 60-6884. 92p. illus. 27cm. 1960. Coward-McCann.
--Fiddlefoot Jones of the North Woods. Helweg, Hans H. (1917-), illus. LC 57-7687. (Illus.). 21cm. 209p. (gr. 4-7). 1957. (ISBN 0-8149-0340-1). Vanguard.
Jordan, Susan, illus.
--Little Red Riding Hood. LC 34-31803. (Illus.). 19 x 21cm. 48p. 1934. Whitman Publishing Co.
Jordan, Tina
--Isha The Magic Doll. N.D. Vantage Press Inc.
--A Visit to the Eagles' Nest. Jordan, Debra, illus. (Illus.). 20p. (gr. 3-5). 1980. (ISBN 0-938574-00-0). Cherubim.
Jorgensen, Dan
--Sky Hook. LC 85-14983. 128 p. 18cm. c.1985. (ISBN 0-89191-682-2). Chariot Books.
Jorgensen, Ida M., jt. ed. see Ketchum, Agnes Taylor.
Jorgensen, Mary Venn see Adrian, Mary, pseud.
Jorgensen, Nels Leroy
--The Balloon Boys. Moore, Samuel Taylor (1893-1974) & Weldon, Dan, illus. LC 26-15066. 2 p. l., 301 p. front., illus., plates. 20 cm. c.1926. Harcourt, Brace and Company.
--Dave Palmer's Diamond Mystery: A Tale of the Little League. LC 55-168857. 221p. illus. 20cm. c.1954. Cupples and Leon Co.
--Smoke Jumpers. Kidwell, Carl (1910-), illus. LC 54-13048. 190p. illus. 21cm. c.1954. Bouregy & Curl.
Jorgensen, Olive H.
--A Pocketful of Poems. Counts, Kathy, illus. LC 75-42819. (Illus.). 48p. (Pocketful Books Ser). (ps-3). 1976. (ISBN 0-570-03452-3). Concordia.
Jorgenson, Rusty
--Tales the Peacock Might Have Told. LC 73-153587. (Illus.). 67 p. 19cm. 1972. Full Circle Press.
Joscelyn, Archie L. (1899-)
--Cheyenne Justice. LC 55-309054. 254p. 21cm. 1955. Avalon Books.
--Eric Hearle, Detective. N.D. World Publishing Co.
--Prisoner's Valley. LC 35-12680. 3 p. l., 9-247 p. 20 cm. c.1935. The World Syndicate Publishing Company.
Joselma, Sr.
--The Littlest Brother. Rembert, M., Sr., illus. LC 55-9387. 45 p. illus. 21cm. (Herald Books, No. 5). c.1955. Franciscan Herald Press.
Joseph, Alfred Ward
--Sondo, a Liberian Boy. Magnie, Bernice, illus. LC 36-15966. 32 p. incl. front. illus. 25cm. c.1936. A. Whitman & Co.
Joseph, Helen Haiman, Mrs.
--Ali Baba, and Other Plays for Young People or Puppets. LC 27-23021. 4 p. l., 3-150, 4 p. incl. front., illus. (incl. music) 20 cm. c.1927. Harcourt, Brace and Company.
--Little Mr. Clown: The Adventures of a Marionette. LC 32-28839. xvi, 190 p. incl. front., illus., plates. 20 cm. c.1932. Harcourt, Brace and Company.
Joseph, Michael, jt. ed. see Drew, Elizabeth A.
Joseph, Stephen M. (1938-)
--The People Zoo. Price, George (1901-), illus. LC 74-159158. (Illus.). 32 p. 29cm. 1971. (ISBN 0-87807-034-6). (ISBN 0-87807-035-4). Windmill Books.
Joseph, Stephen M. (1938-), ed.
--The Me Nobody Knows. 144p. N.D. World Publishing Company.
Joshi, Jagadish, jt. auth. see Davidar, E. R.
Josika, Nicholas
--King Matthias & the Beggar Boy. Gaye, Selina, adapted by. (Illus.). N.D. Thomas Nelson & Sons.
Joslin, Sarah Proctor, Mrs.
--The Major Stories. LC 6-44367. (Illus.). 63p. 20 x 16cm. 1906. W. B. Clarke.
Joslin, Sesyle (1929-)
--Baby Elephant & the Secret Wishes. Weisgard, Leonard Joseph (1916-), illus. LC 62-14244. (Illus.). 19cm. (gr. k-3). 1962. (ISBN 0-15-205156-2, HJ). HarBraceJ.
--Baby Elephant Goes to China. Weisgard, Leonard Joseph, illus. LC 63-15401. 1 v. (unpaged) col. illus. 19 cm. 1963. Harcourt, Brace & World.
--Baby Elephant's Baby Book. Weisgard, Leonard Joseph (1916-), illus. LC 64-17086. (Illus.). 19cm. 48p. (ps-1). 1964. (ISBN 0-15-205138-4). (ISBN 0-15-205139-2). HarBraceJ.
--Baby Elephant's Trunk. Weisgard, Leonard Joseph (1916-), illus. LC 61-10110. (Illus.). unpaged. 19cm. 1961. Harcourt, Brace & World. **Award: (ALA).**
--Brave Baby Elephant. Weisgard, Leonard Joseph (1916-), illus. LC 60-10245. (Illus.). (ps-1). 1960. (ISBN 0-15-211598-6, HJ). HarBraceJ.
--Doctor George Owl. Weil, Lisl (1910-), illus. LC 76-98517. (Illus.). 45 p. 27cm. 1970. Houghton-Mifflin.
--The Gentle Savages. LC 79-14611. p. cm. 1979. (ISBN 0-689-50147-1). Atheneum.
--Last Summer's Smugglers. 1st ed. Joslin, Sesyle (1929-), illus. LC 72-88170. (Illus.). 144 p. 21cm. 1973. (ISBN 0-15-243620-0). Harcourt, Brace, Jovanovich.
--The Night They Stole the Alphabet. Arno, Enrico (1913-1981), illus. LC 68-11501. (Illus.). 190 p. 21cm. 190p. 1968. Harcourt, Brace & World.
--Pinkety, Pinkety: A Practical Guide to Wishing. Roselli, Luciana, illus. LC 66-12589. 1v. (unpaged) illus. 19x23cm. c.1966. Harcourt.
--Please Share That Peanut!. Taback, Simms, illus. LC 65-12613. (A Prosperous Pageant in Fourteen Acts, Concerned with the Exquisite Joys and Extraordinary Adventures of Young Ladies and Gentlemen Engaged in the Pleasurable Practice of Sharing.). 1v. (unpaged) illus. 23cm. c.1965. Harcourt. **Award: (NYT).**
--Senor Baby Elephant, the Pirate. Weisgard, Leonard Joseph (1916-), illus. LC 62-7729. (Illus.). unpaged. 19cm. 1962. Harcourt, Brace & World.
--The Spy Lady and the Muffin Man. 1st ed. Joslin, Sesyle (1929-), illus. LC 74-137757. (Illus.). 188 p. 21cm. 1971. (ISBN 0-15-278182-X). Harcourt Brace Jovanovich.
--There Is a Bull on My Balcony. Barry, Katharina Watjen (1936-), illus. LC 66-11202. (Illus.). (gr. 1-6). 1966. (ISBN 0-15-285057-0, HJ). HarBraceJ.
--What Do You Say, Dear?. Sendak, Maurice Bernard (1928-), illus. (ps-3). 1980. (ISBN 0-590-01625-3). Scholastic Inc.
Joslin, Stu
--The Woble Stories. 1981. (ISBN 0-8062-1777-4). Carlton.
Joslyn, Dorothy
--Nature Stories. Vivienne, pseud. (1889-1982), illus. Entwistle, Florence Vivienne. LC 47-25850. 52 p. illus. (part col.) 17 cm. (Story hour series). c.1947. Whitman Pub. Co.
Joslyn, Marcellus N. (1901-)
--Huck Jones: A Novel of a Pre-Teenage Boy. 1st ed. LC 57-14227. 274p. 21cm. 1957. Exposition Press.
Josselyn, C. R., Mrs.
--The South Shore: Or, "As the Twig Is Bent the Tree Is Inclined.". LC 12-36156. 4 p. l., 7-216 p. 19 cm. 1881. I. Bradley & Co.
--South Shore: Or, As the Twig is Bent the Tree is Inclined. N.D. Universalist Publishing House.
Joutsen, Britta-Lisa
--Lingonberries in the Snow. Saris, Anthony, illus. LC 67-21159. (Illus.). 190 p. 23cm. 1968. Follett Pub. Co.
Jowett, Margaret
--A Cry of Players. Scott, Asgeir, illus. LC 63-16201. 164 p. illus. 23cm. 1963, c.1961. Roy Publishers.
Joy, Charles Rhind (1885-), ed.
--Young People of the West Indies: Their Stories in Their Own Words. LC 64-22645. x, 208p. map. 21cm. c.1964. Duell Dist. Meredith.
--Young People of West Africa: Their Stories in Their Own Words. LC 61-15817. 206 p. 21cm. 1961. Duell, Sloan and Pearce.
Joy, Jane Ellis
--Golden Years. N.D. Standard Publishing Co.
Joy, Margaret
--Allotment Lane School Again. Allen, Rowena, illus. LC 84-28781. (Illus.). 110 p. 21cm. 1985. (ISBN 0-571-13563-3). Faber and Faber.
--Gran's Dragon. Ling, Maggie, illus. LC 80-670087. (Illus.). 96 p. 21cm. 1980. (ISBN 0-571-11520-9). Faber and Faber.
--Hairy and Slug. Allen, Rowena, illus. LC 83-11667. p. cm. 1983. (ISBN 0-571-13107-7). Faber and Faber.
--Monday Magic. Allen, Rowena, illus. LC 82-7420. p. cm. 1982. (ISBN 0-571-11924-7). Faber and Faber.
--Tales from Allotment Lane School. Allen, Rowena, illus. LC 83-5517. (Illus.). 112p. (gr. k-3). 1983. (ISBN 0-571-11992-1). Faber & Faber.
Joyce, Carolyn
--The Magic Donkey. Prestopino, Gregorio, illus. LC 76-153910. (Illus.). 16 p. 24cm. (Magic circle book). 1972. (ISBN 0-663-22979-0). Ginn.
Joyce, Deborah
--Irresistible Love. 192p. (Orig.). (gr. 10-12). 1985. (ISBN 0-310-46612-1, Pub. by Serenade-Serenata). Zondervan.
Joyce, Irma
--Lonesome Sam. Engelhardt, Nick, illus. LC 72-2800. (Illus.). 20 p. 16cm. (Downy book). 1972. (ISBN 0-528-82446-5). Rand McNally.
--Never Talk to Strangers. Buckett, George (1936-), illus. (gr. 4 up). 1970. (ISBN 0-307-10876-7, Golden Pr). (ISBN 0-307-60876-X). Western Pub.
Joyce, James Anthony Aloysius (1882-1941)
--An Encounter. Higashi, Sandra, illus. LC 82-73337. (Illus.). 32 p. 23cm. (Creative classic series). c.1982. (ISBN 0-87191-896-X). Creative Education.
--The Boarding House. Higashi, Sandra, illus. LC 82-73338. (Illus.). 32 p. 23cm. (Creative classic series). c.1982. (ISBN 0-87191-895-1). Creative Education.
--The Cat and the Devil. Blachon, illus. LC 81-40419. p. cm. (Moonlight editions). 1981. (ISBN 0-8052-3782-8). Schocken Books.
--The Cat and the Devil. Erdoes, Richard (1912-), illus. LC 64-23896. (Illus.). 48 p. 24cm. 1964. Dodd, Mead.
Joyce, Jewel
--The Blue Dragon. 1st ed. Kilgore, Al, illus. LC 53-126877. 114p. illus. 21cm. 1953. Pageant Press.
Joyce, Joy
--Me & More Shadows. Treadway, Jerry, ed. Ross, Ray, intro. by. (Illus.). 62p. (gr. 1-6). 1981. (ISBN 0-9605984-1-3). Joy-Co.
Joyce, Robert
--The Stray Child. LC 34-18530. 25cm. 38p. 1934. E. P. Dutton & Co.
Joyce, William
--George Shrinks. LC 83-47697. (Illus.). 32 p. c.1985. (ISBN 0-06-023070-3). (ISBN 0-06-023071-1). Harper & Row.
Joyner, Jerry, jt. auth. see Charlip, Remy.
Jubelier, Ruth
--About Jack's Dental Checkup. Johnson, James David (1920-1973), illus. LC 59-10857. (Illus.). 24cm. 30p. (Look, read, learn.). (gr. k-3). 1959. (ISBN 0-516-08110-1). Melmont.
--About Jill's Checkup. (Illus.). (gr. k-3). 1957. (ISBN 0-516-08111-X). Melmont.
Juchen, Aurel von
--The Holy Night: The Story of the First Christmas. Piatti, Celestino (1922-), illus. Schaeffer, Cornelia, tr. from German. LC 68-9774. (Illus.). 29p. 22 x 31cm. 1968. Atheneum.
Jucker, Sita (1921-)
--Squaps, the Moonling: A Picture-Book. Jucker, Sita (1921-), illus. Gollob, Barbara Kowal, tr. from Ger. LC 75-75521. (Illus.). 27 p. 1969. Atheneum.
Juda, Lyon (1923-)
--The Wise Old Man. LC 64-1119. 1964. Nelson.
Judah, Aaron (1923-)
--The Careless Cuckoos. N.D. Transatlantic Arts.
--Clown on Fire. 211 p. 21cm. 1967, c.1965. Dial Press.
--God and Mr. Sourpuss. Kennedy, Richard (1910-), illus. LC 60-10200. 53p. illus. 22cm. (Wonderful world book). 1960, c.1959. Barnes.
--The Pot of Gold,. Peake, Mervyn Lawrence (1911-1968), illus. LC 60-101002. 62p. illus. 22cm. (Wonderful world book). 1960, c.1959. Barnes.
--Tommy With A Hole In His Shoe. N.D. Transatlantic Arts.
Judd, Denis Nan (1938-)
--Return to Treasure Island. LC 78-61014. (Illus.). 209 p. 23cm. 1979, c.1978. (ISBN 0-312-67912-2). St. Martin's Press.
Judd, Frances K, pseud., see Stratemeyer Syndicate.
Judd, Frances K, pseud.
--Beneath the Crimson Briar Bush. Stratemeyer Syndicate. Furman, illus. LC 37-36092. iv, 206 p. front. 20 cm. (Kay Tracey Mystery Stories: Vol. 8). 1937. Cupples & Leon Co.
--The Crimson Briar Bush. Stratemeyer Syndicate. LC 52-1291. (Illus.). 206 p. illus. 20 cm. Repr. of 1937 ed (Pub. by Cupples & Leon Co). (Kay Tracey Mystery Stories: Vol. 12). 1952. Garden City Books.
--The Crimson Brier Bush. Stratemeyer Syndicate. Repr. of 1937 ed (Pub. by Cupples & Leon Co). (Kay Tracey Mystery Stories: Vol. 7). N.D. Books, Inc.
--The Double Disguise. Stratemeyer Syndicate. Repr. of 1941 ed (Pub. by Cupples & Leon Co). (Kay Tracey Mystery Stories: Vol. 14). N.D. Books, Inc.
--The Double Disguise. Stratemeyer Syndicate. LC 41-12691. (Illus.). vi, 212 p. front. 20 cm. (Kay Tracey Mystery Stories: Vol. 16). 1941. Cupples & Leon Co.
--The Double Disguise. Stratemeyer Syndicate. LC 52-1290. (Illus.). 212 p. illus. 20 cm. Repr. of 1941 ed (Pub. by Cupples & Leon Co). (Kay Tracey Mystery Stories: Vol. 7). 1952. Garden City Books.
--The Double Disguise. Stratemeyer Syndicate. Repr. of 1941 ed (Pub. by Cupples & Leon Co.). (Kay Tracey Mystery Stories: Vol. 4). 1978. Lamplight Publishing Inc.
--The Forbidden Tower. Stratemeyer Syndicate. LC 40-63056. (Illus.). iv, 212 p. front. 20 cm. (Kay Tracey Mystery Stories: Vol. 13). 1940. Cupples & Leon Co.
--The Green Cameo Mystery. Stratemeyer Syndicate. Repr. of 1936 ed (Pub. by Cupples & Leon Co). (Kay Tracey Mystery Stories: Vol. 11). N.D. Books, Inc.
--The Green Cameo Mystery. Stratemeyer Syndicate. LC 53-496919. (Illus.). 188p. illus. 20cm. Repr. of 1936 ed (Pub. by Cupples & Leon Co). (Kay Tracey Mystery Stories: Vol. 13). 1952. Garden City Books.
--The Green Cameo Mystery. Stratemeyer Syndicate. Repr. of 1936 ed (Pub. by Cupples & Leon Co). (Kay Tracey Mystery Stories: Vol. 6). 1978. Lamplight Publishing Inc.
--The Green Cameo Mystery. Stratemeyer Syndicate. Furman, illus. LC 36-17704. iv, 211 p. front. 20 cm. (Kay Tracey Mystery Stories: Vol. 6). 1936. Cupples & Leon Co.
--In the Sunken Garden. Stratemeyer Syndicate. Repr. of 1939 ed (Pub. by Cupples & Leon Co). (Kay Tracey Mystery Stories: Vol. 2). N.D. Books, Inc.
--In the Sunken Garden. Stratemeyer Syndicate. LC 39-186574. (Illus.). iv, 210 p. front. 20 cm. (Kay Tracey Mystery Stories: Vol. 12). 1939. Cupples & Leon Co.

--In the Sunken Garden. Stratemeyer Syndicate. LC 51-7123. (Illus.). 210 p. illus. 20 cm. Repr. of 1939 ed (Pub. by Cupples & Leon Co). (Kay Tracey Mystery Stories: Vol. 4). 1951. Garden City Books.
--In the Sunken Garden. Stratemeyer Syndicate. Repr. of 1939 ed (Pub. by Cupples & Leon Co). (Kay Tracey Mystery Stories: Vol. 3). 1978. Lamplight Publishing Inc.
--The Lone Footprint. Stratemeyer Syndicate. Repr. of 1941 ed (Pub. by Cupples & Leon Co). (Kay Tracey Mystery Stories: Vol. 15). N.D. Books, Inc.
--The Lone Footprint. Stratemeyer Syndicate. LC 41-680269. (Illus.). iv, 209 p front. 20 cm. (Kay Tracey Mystery Stories: Vol. 15). 1941. Cupples & Leon Co.
--The Lone Footprint. Stratemeyer Syndicate. LC 52-1308. (Illus.). 209 p. illus. 20 cm. Repr. of 1941 ed (Pub. by Cupples & Leon Co). (Kay Tracey Mystery Stories: Vol. 10). 1952. Garden City Books.
--The Mansion of Secrets. Stratemeyer Syndicate. Repr. of 1942 ed (Pub. by Cupples & Leon Co). (Kay Tracey Mystery Stories: Vol. 3). N.D. Books, Inc.
--The Mansion of Secrets. Stratemeyer Syndicate. LC 42-13425. (Illus.). iv, 208 p. front. 20 cm. (Kay Tracey Mystery Stories: Vol. 17). 1942. Cupples & Leon Co.
--The Mansion of Secrets. Stratemeyer Syndicate. LC 51-7126. (Illus.). 208 p. illus. 20 cm. Repr. of 1942 ed (Pub. by Cupples & Leon Co). (Kay Tracey Mystery Stories: Vol. 1). 1951. Garden City Books.
--The Mansion of Secrets. Stratemeyer Syndicate. Repr. of 1942 ed (Pub. by Cupples & Leon Co). (Kay Tracey Mystery Stories: Vol. 1). 1978. Lamplight Publishing Inc.
--The Message in the Sand Dunes. Stratemeyer Syndicate. Repr. of 1938 ed (Pub. by Cupples & Leon Co). (Kay Tracey Mystery Stories: Vol. 8). N.D. Books, Inc.
--The Message in the Sand Dunes. Stratemeyer Syndicate. LC 52-1289. (Illus.). 204 p. illus. 20 cm. Repr. of 1938 ed (Pub. by Cupples & Leon Co). (Kay Tracey Mystery Stories: Vol. 11). 1952. Garden City Books.
--The Message in the Sand Dunes. Stratemeyer Syndicate. Repr. of 1938 ed (Pub. by Cupples & Leon Co). (Kay Tracey Mystery Stories: Vol. 5). 1978. Lamplight Publishing Inc.
--The Message in the Sand Dunes. Stratemeyer Syndicate. Furman, illus. LC 38-17274. 204p. (Kay Tracey Mystery Stories: Vol. 9). 1938. Cupples & Leon Co.
--The Murmuring Portrait. Stratemeyer Syndicate. Repr. of 1938 ed (Pub. by Cupples & Leon Co). (Kay Tracey Mystery Stories: Vol. 9). N.D. Books, Inc.
--The Murmuring Portrait. Stratemeyer Syndicate. LC 52-1288. (Illus.). 204 p. illus. 20 cm. Repr. of 1938 ed (Pub. by Cupples & Leon Co). (Kay Tracey Mystery Stories: Vol. 9). 1952. Garden City Books.
--The Murmuring Portrait. Stratemeyer Syndicate. Furman, illus. LC 38-17275. iv, 204 p. front. 20 cm. (Kay Tracey Mystery Stories: Vol. 10). 1938. Cupples & Leon Co.
--The Mysterious Neighbors. Stratemeyer Syndicate. Repr. of 1942 ed (Pub. by Cupples & Leon Co). (Kay Tracey Mystery Stories: Vol. 6). N.D. Books, Inc.
--The Mysterious Neighbors. Stratemeyer Syndicate. LC 42-21055. (Illus.). iv, 200 p. front. 20 cm. (Kay Tracey Mystery Stories: Vol. 18). 1942. Cupples & Leon Co.
--The Mysterious Neighbors. Stratemeyer Syndicate. LC 51-8308. (Illus.). 209 p. illus. 20 cm. Repr. of 1942 ed (Pub. by Cupples & Leon Co). (Kay Tracey Mystery Stories: Vol. 5). 1951. Garden City Books.
--The Mystery of the Swaying Curtains. Stratemeyer Syndicate. Furman, illus. LC 35-18692. iv, 208 p. front. 20 cm. (Kay Tracey Mystery Stories: Vol. 3). 1935. Cupples & Leon Co.
--The Sacred Feather. Stratemeyer Syndicate. LC 56-18911. (Illus.). 211p. illus. 20cm. Repr. of 1940 ed (Pub. by Cupples & Leon Co). (Kay Tracey Mystery Stories: Vol. 2). 1951. Books, Inc.
--The Sacred Feather. Stratemeyer Syndicate. Repr. of 1940 ed (Pub. by Cupples & Leon Co). (Kay Tracey Mystery Stories: Vol. 1). N.D. Books, Inc.
--The Sacred Feather. Stratemeyer Syndicate. LC 40-10375. (Illus.). iv, 211 p. front. 20 cm. (Kay Tracey Mystery Stories: Vol. 14). 1940. Cupples & Leon Co.
--The Sacred Feather. Stratemeyer Syndicate. LC 51-7124. (Illus.). 211p. 20cm. (Kay Tracey Mystery Ser.). 1951. Garden City Books.
--The Secret at the Windmill. Stratemeyer Syndicate. Repr. of 1937 ed (Pub. by Cupples & Leon Co). (Kay Tracey Mystery Stories: Vol. 10). N.D. Books, Inc.
--The Secret at the Windmill. Stratemeyer Syndicate. LC 52-1307. (Illus.). 203 p. illus. 20 cm. Repr. of 1937 ed (Pub. by Cupples & Leon Co). (Kay Tracey Mystery Stories: Vol. 8). 1952. Garden City Books.
--The Secret at the Windmill. Stratemeyer Syndicate. Furman, illus. LC 37-360913. iv, 203 p. front. 20 cm. (Kay Tracey Mystery Stories: Vol. 7). 1937. Cupples & Leon Co.
--The Secret of the Red Scarf. Stratemeyer Syndicate. Repr. of 1934 ed (Pub. by Cupples & Leon Co). (Kay Tracey Mystery Stories: Vol. 13). N.D. Books, Inc.
--The Secret of the Red Scarf. Stratemeyer Syndicate. LC 53-4039. (Illus.). 192p. 20cm. Repr. of 1934 ed (Pub. by Cupples & Leon Co). (Kay Tracey Mystery Stories: Vol. 15). 1953. Garden City Books.
--The Secret of the Red Scarf. Stratemeyer Syndicate. Furman, illus. LC 34-259103. iv, 206 p. front. 20 cm. (Kay Tracey Mystery Stories: Vol. 1). 1934. Cupples & Leon Co.
--The Shadow on the Door. Stratemeyer Syndicate. Furman, illus. LC 35-186915. iv, 204 p. front. 20 cm. (Kay Tracey Mystery Stories: Vol. 4). 1935. Cupples & Leon Co.
--The Six-Fingered Glove Mystery. Stratemeyer Syndicate. Repr. of 1936 ed (Pub. by Cupples & Leon Co). (Kay Tracey Mystery Stories: Vol. 4). N.D. Books, Inc.
--The Six Fingered Glove Mystery. Stratemeyer Syndicate. LC 51-7124. (Illus.). 203 p. illus. 20 cm. Repr. of 1936 ed (Pub. by Cupples & Leon Co). (Kay Tracey Mystery Stories: Vol. 3). 1951. Garden City Books.
--The Six-Fingered Glove Mystery. Stratemeyer Syndicate. Repr. of 1938 ed (Pub. by Cupples & Leon Co). (Kay Tracey Mystery Stories: Vol. 2). 1978. Lamplight Publishing Inc.
--The Six Fingered Glove Mystery. Stratemeyer Syndicate. Furman, illus. LC 36-177131. iv, 203 p. front. 20 cm. (Kay Tracey Mystery Stories: Vol. 5). 1936. Cupples & Leon Co.
--The Strange Echo. Stratemeyer Syndicate. Repr. of 1934 ed (Pub. by Cupples & Leon Co). (Kay Tracey Mystery Stories: Vol. 12). N.D. Books, Inc.
--The Strange Echo. Stratemeyer Syndicate. LC 53-1785. (Illus.). 192p. illus. 20cm. Repr. of 1934 ed (Pub. by Cupples & Leon Co). (Kay Tracey Mystery Stories: Vol. 14). 1953. Garden City Books.
--The Strange Echo. Stratemeyer Syndicate. Furman, illus. LC 34-25911. iv, 206 p. front. 20 cm. (Kay Tracey Mystery Stories: Vol. 2). 1934. Cupples & Leon Co.
--When the Key Turned. Stratemeyer Syndicate. Repr. of 1939 ed (Pub. by Cupples & Leon Co). (Kay Tracey Mystery Stories: Vol. 5). N.D. Books, Inc.
--When the Key Turned. Stratemeyer Syndicate. LC 39-11050. (Illus.). iv, 204 p. front. 20 cm. (Kay Tracey Mystery Stories: Vol. 11). 1939. Cupples & Leon Co.
--When the Key Turned. Stratemeyer Syndicate. LC 51-8258. (Illus.). 204 p. illus. 20 cm. Repr. of 1939 ed (Pub. by Cupples & Leon Co). (Kay Tracey Mystery Stories: Vol. 6). 1951. Garden City Books.

Judd, Mary Catherine

--The A-B-C Book of Birds for Children: Large or Small. LC 1-27476. 60 p. col. illus., col. pl. 27 cm. 1902. A. W. Mumford.

Judd, Mary Catherine, retold by.

--Classic Myths. MacDonall, Angus, illus. LC 2-5205. 1 p. l., 204 p. incl. illus., pl. 19 cm. 1901. Rand-McNally & Co.
--Classic Myths. Greek, German and Scandinavian. LC 21-18307. 2 p. l., 3-94 p. front., plates. 19 cm. (School education helps, v. 1). 1894. School Education Company.
--Wigwam Stories. (Illus.). 278p. N.D. Dana Estes and Company.
--Wigwam Stories. (Illus.). 278p. N.D. Ginn & Co.

Judson, Clara Ingram, Mrs. (1879-1960)

--Alice Ann. Foster, John M., illus. LC 28-18113. 300 p. front., plates. 20 cm. c.1928. Barse & Co.
--Bed Time Tales. LC 15-1047. v. illus. 15 x 26 cm. N.D. The Adams Newspaper Service.
--Billy Robin and His Neighbors. LC 19-160347. 3 p. l., 11-76 p. incl. col. front., illus. (part col.) 20 cm. c.1917. Rand, McNally & Company.
--Bruce Carries the Flag. LC 57-8278. 198 p. 23cm. 1957. Follett.
--The Camp at Gravel Point. LC 21-193906. 4 p. l., 266 p., 1 l. front., plates. 20 cm. 1921. Houghton Mifflin Company.
--Favorite Christmas Carols. N.D. Follett Co.
--Flower Fairies. Enright, Maginel Wright, illus. LC 16-6078. 6 p. l., 3-93 p. incl. col. front., illus., col. plates. 24 cm. c.1915. Rand, McNally & Company.
--Foxy Squirrel in the Garden. Beem, Frances M., illus. N.D. Rand McNally.
--Garden Adventures in Winter. Beem, Frances M., illus. N.D. Rand McNally.
--Garden Adventures of Tommy Tittlemouse. Beem, Frances M., illus. LC 23-5152. 64 p. incl. col. front., illus. (part col.) 20 cm. c.1922. Rand, McNally & Company.
--Good-Night Stories. Wilson, Clara Powers, illus. LC 16-22922. 4 p. l., 131 p. illus. 18 cm. 1916. A. C. McClurg & Co.
--Green Ginger Jar. Brown, Paul (1893-1958), illus. LC 49-10169. (Illus.). 210p. (gr. 4-6). 1949. (ISBN 0-395-06847-9). HM.
--In Scotland. (Mary Jane Ser.). (gr. 1-4). N.D. Grosset & Dunlap.
--Jerry & Jean "Detecters". Gregory, Dorothy Lake, illus. N.D. Rand McNally.
--Lost Violin. Bradfield, Margaret, illus. Bd. with They Came from Bohemia. (Illus.). (gr. 4-6). 1958. (ISBN 0-695-45415-3). Follett.
--The Lost Violin: They Came from Bohemia. Bradfield, Margaret & Polseno, Jo, illus. LC 58-8976. 204p. illus. 23cm. 1958, c.1947. Follett Pub. Co.
--The Lost Violin: They Came from Bohemia. Bradfield, Margaret, illus. LC 47-307212. viii, 204 p. illus. 22 cm. 1947. Houghton Mifflin Co.
--Mary Jane at School. (The Mary Jane Ser.). N.D. Barse & Hopkins.
--Mary Jane Down South. (The Mary Jane Ser.). N.D. Barse & Hopkins.
--Mary Jane Down South. (Mary Jane Ser.). (gr. 1-4). N.D. Grosset & Dunlap.
--Mary Jane: Her Book. (The Mary Jane Ser.). N.D. Barse & Hopkins.
--Mary Jane: Her Book. (gr. 1-4). N.D. Grosset & Dunlap.
--Mary Jane: Her Visit. (The Mary Jane Ser.). N.D. Barse & Hopkins.
--Mary Jane: Her Visit. (Mary Jane Ser.). (gr. 1-4). N.D. Grosset & Dunlap.
--Mary Jane in Canada. Wrenn, Charles L., illus. LC 24-15754. 208 p. incl. front., plates. 20 cm. (Her Mary Jane series). c.1924. Barse & Hopkins.
--Mary Jane in England. (Mary Jane Ser.). (gr. 1-4). N.D. Grosset & Dunlap.
--Mary Jane in England. Wrenn, Charles L., illus. LC 28-11322. 216 p. incl. front., plates. 20 cm. (Her Mary Jane series). c.1928. Barse & Co.
--Mary Jane in France. (Mary Jane Ser.). (gr. 1-4). N.D. Grosset & Dunlap.
--Mary Jane in France. Wrenn, Charles L., illus. LC 30-9322. 209 p. incl. front., plates. 20 cm. (Her Mary Jane series). c.1930. Barse & Co.
--Mary Jane in Italy. (Mary Jane Ser.). (gr. 1-4). N.D. Grosset & Dunlap.
--Mary Jane in Italy. Schubert, Marie (1890-), illus. LC 33-32817. 208 p. incl. front., plates. 20 cm. (Her Mary Jane series). c.1933. Grosset & Dunlap.
--Mary Jane in New England. (The Mary Jane Ser.). N.D. Barse & Hopkins.
--Mary Jane in New England. (Mary Jane Ser.). (gr. 1-4). N.D. Grosset & Dunlap.
--Mary Jane in Scotland. Wrenn, Charles L., illus. LC 29-922381. 216 p. incl. plates, map. front. 20 cm. 1929. Barse & Co.
--Mary Jane in Spain. (Mary Jane Ser.). N.D. Grosset & Dunlap.
--Mary Jane in Spain. Schubert, Marie (1890-), illus. LC 37-2170. 236 p. incl. front., plates. 20 cm. c.1937. Grosset & Dunlap.
--Mary Jane in Switzerland. LC 31-12240. 213 p. incl. plates. front. 20 cm. (Her Mary Jane series). c.1931. Barse & Co.
--Mary Jane in Switzerland. (Mary Jane Ser.). (gr. 1-4). N.D. Grosset& Dunlap.
--Mary Jane's City Home. (The Mary Jane Ser.). N.D. Barse & Hopkins.
--Mary Jane's City Home. (The Mary Jane Ser.). (gr. 1-4). N.D. Grosset & Dunlap.
--Mary Jane's Country Home. (The Mary Jane Ser.). N.D. Barse & Hopkins.
--Mary Jane's Country Home. (Mary Jane Series). (gr. 1-4). N.D. Grosset & Dunlap.
--Mary Jane's Friends in Holland. (Mary Jane Ser.). N.D. Grosset & Dunlap.
--Mary Jane's Friends in Holland. Foster, Genevieve Stump (1893-1979), illus. LC 39-19900. 213 p. front., pl. 20 cm. c.1939. Grosset & Dunlap.
--Mary Jane's Kindergarten. (Mary Jane Ser.). (gr. 1-4). N.D. Grosset & Dunlap.
--Mary Jane's Kindergarten: Sequel to Mary Jane--Her Visit. White, Frances, illus. LC 18-12212. 215 p. incl. front., plates. 20 cm. (Her The Mary Jane series). c.1918. Barse & Hopkins.
--Mary Jane's Summer Fun. (The Mary Jane Ser.). 1925. Barse & Hopkins.
--Mary Jane's Summer Fun. (Mary Jane Ser.). (gr. 1-4). N.D. Grosset & Dunlap.
--Mary Jane's Summer Fun. Wrenn, Charles L., illus. LC 25-10973. 4 p. l., 13-213 p. incl. plates. front. 20 cm. (Her Mary Jane series). c.1925. Barse & Hopkins.
--Mary Jane's Vacation. (The Mary Jane Ser.). N.D. Barse & Co.
--Mary Jane's Winter Sports. (The Mary Jane Ser.). N.D. Barse & Co.
--Michael's Victory. 192 p. 23cm. 1957, c.1946. Follett.
--Michael's Victory. Wexler, Elmer, illus. LC 46-7313. 4 p. l., 192 p. plates. 21 cm. 1946. Houghton Mifflin Company.
--The Mighty Soo. N.D. Wilcox & Follett Co.
--Mr. Justice Holmes. (Illus.). 1956. Follett Pub Co. **Award: (JNM).**
--People Who Come to Our House. Peters, Marjorie, illus. LC 40-10456. 48 p. illus. (part col.) 26 cm. c.1940. Rand McNally & Company.
--People Who Work in the Country and in the City. Ward, Keith, illus. LC 43-4558. 94 p., 1 l. illus. (part col.) 26 x 20 cm. 1943. Rand McNally & Company.
--People Who Work Near Our House. Ward, Keith, illus. LC 42-9901. 48 p. illus. (part col.) 26 cm. 1942. Rand McNally & Company.
--Petar's Treasure: They Came from Dalmatia. Koering, Ursula (1921-), illus. LC 58-8975. (Illus.). 186 p. 23cm. 1958, c.1945. Follett.
--Petar's Treasure: They came from Dalmatia. Koering, Ursula (1921-), illus. LC 45-8890. 3 p. l.,186 p. plates. 21 1/2 cm. 1945. Houghton Mifflin Company.
--Pierre's Lucky Pouch. Lenski, Lois (1893-1974), illus. LC 57-8277. 245p. illus. 23cm. 1957. Follett Pub. Co.
--Pioneer Girl: The Early Life of Frances Willard. Foster, Genevieve Stump (1893-1979), illus. LC 39-27137. 80 p. illus. 22 cm. c.1939. Rand McNally & Company.
--Play Days. Dailey, Arthur, photos by. LC 37-1018. 39 p. illus. 22 cm. c.1937. Grosset & Dunlap.
--Railway Engineer: The Story of George Stephenson. Simon, Eric M., illus. LC 41-51991. 4 p. l., 171 p. incl. illus., plates. 22 cm. c.1941. C. Scribner's Sons.
--Reaper Man. N.D. Houghton Mifflin Co.
--Sod-House Winter. Caswell, Edward C., illus. (Illus.). 213 p. 23cm. 1957, c.1942. Follet.
--Summertime. Jackson, Polly, pseud. (1918-), illus. Jackson, Pauline. LC 49-416. (Illus.). 44p. 24cm. 1948. Broadman Press.
--They Came from France. Lenski, Lois (1893-1974), illus. LC 43-117447. vii, 1 p., 1 l., 245, 1 p. incl. front., illus. 22 cm. 1943. Houghton Mifflin Company.
--They Came from Scotland. Reardon, Mary A., illus. LC 44-8197. 4 p. l., 198 p. col. front., plates. 21 cm. 1944. Houghton Mifflin Company.
--They Came from Sweden. Caswell, Edward C., illus. LC 42-21304. vii, 1 p., 1 l., 213, 1 p. incl. front., illus. 22 cm. 1942. Houghton Mifflin Company.
--Vacation. (Mary Jane Ser.). (gr. 1-4). N.D. Grosset & Dunlap.
--Virginia Lee. Wrenn, Charles L., illus. LC 26-13045. N.D. Barse & Hopkins.
--Virginia Lee's Bicycle Club. N.D. Grosset & Dunlap.
--Winter Sports. (Mary Jane Ser.). (gr. 1-4). N.D. Grosset & Dunlap.

Judson, Edward Zane Carroll (1823-1886)

--Buffalo Bill and His Adventures in the West. LC 74-15731. (Illus.). 314 p. 23cm. (Popular Culture in America). 1974, c.1886. (ISBN 0-405-06366-0). Arno Press.

Judson, Emily Chubbuck, Mrs. (1817-1854)

--The Great Secret: Or, How to Be Happy. 3d ed. LC 24-16669. 1 p. l., v-vi, 7-256 p. 16 cm. 1848. L. Colby and Company.

Judson, Jeanne see Hancock, Frances Dean, pseud.

Judson, Jeanne see Hancock, Frances Dean, pseud.

Judson, Jeanne (1890-)

--A Blue Ribbon for Alice. LC 57-126803. 224p. 20cm. 1957. Avalon Books.
--Lady Guide. LC 54-8725. 256 p. 21cm. 1954. Avalon Books.
--Summer Cruise. Hancock, Frances Dean, pseud. LC 58-12504. 221p. 21cm. 1958. Avalon Books.
--Susan Brown. Hanocock, Frances Dean, pseud. LC 56-13507. 224p. 21cm. 1956. Avalon Books.

Judson, Katharine Berry

--Myths and Legends of California and Old Southwest. N.D. A. C. McClurg.
--Myths and Legends of the Mississippi Valley and the Great Lakes. N.D. A. C. McClurg.
--Old Crow and His Friends: Animal Adventures Based Upon Indian Myths. Bull, Charles Livingston (1874-1932), illus. LC 18-18502. viii p., 1 l., 202 p., 1 l. front., plates. 21 cm. 1918. Little, Brown, and Company.
--Old Crow Stories. Bull, Charles Livingston (1874-1932), illus. LC 17-24075. 4 p. l., 163 p. front., plates. 22 cm. 1917. Little, Brown, and Company.

Juergens, Mary

--The Wonder Book of Bible Stories. N.D. Wonder Books.

Juergens, Mary, adapted by.
--The Big Book of Favorite Bible Stories. N.D. Grosset & Dunlap.
Juhl, Jerry
--The Big Orange Thing. Martin, Charles E. (1910-), illus. LC 79-86638. (Illus.). 30 p. 27cm. 1969. Bradbury Press.
Jukes, Mavis
--Blackberries in the Dark. Allen, Thomas Burt (1928-), illus. LC 85-4259. p. cm. 1985. (ISBN 0-394-87599-0). (ISBN 0-394-97599-5). Knopf. **Award: (ALA).**
--Like Jake and Me. Bloom, Lloyd, illus. LC 83-8380. (Illus.). 32 p. 27cm. c.1984. (ISBN 0-394-85608-2). (ISBN 0-394-95608-7). Knopf : Distributed by Random House. **Awards: (DCII), (JPM), (ALA).**
--No One Is Going to Nashville. Bloom, Lloyd, illus. LC 82-18901. (Illus.). 48p. (gr. 2-5). 1983. (ISBN 0-394-95609-5). (ISBN 0-394-85609-0). Knopf.
Jules, Mark
--The Ant and the Marshallow. (Illus.). 29 p. 21cm. 1974. (ISBN 0-533-00985-5). Vantage Press.
Julian, Faye
--A Magic Christmas! A Play for Children in One Act. (Illus.). 28p. 1st U.S. edition. (gr. k-12). 1983. (ISBN 0-88680-121-4). I E Clark.
Julian, Lee
--Dally. Clement, Charles (1921-), illus. LC 51-8911. unpaged. illus. 17 cm. (Tell-a-tale books). N.D. Whitman Pub. Co.
Julian, Nancy R. (1923-)
--Miss Pickett's Secret. Cooke, Donald Ewin (1916-), illus. LC 52-5481. (Illus.). 74p. (gr. k-4). 1952. (ISBN 0-03-035780-2). HR&W.
--The Peculiar Miss Pickett. Cooke, Donald Ewin (1916-), illus. (Illus., Pub. by Winston). (gr. 4-6). 1972. (ISBN 0-590-00489-1, Schol Pap). Schol Bk Serv.
--The Peculiar Miss Pickett. 1st ed. Cooke, Donald Ewin (1916-), illus. LC 51-3762. 73 p. illus. 22 cm. 1951. Winston.
Julien, Louis Marie (1850-), adapted by.
--Lives of Two Cats. Allen, C. E., illus. Richards, M. B., tr. from Fr. LC 1-149. (Original Story by Pierre Loti.). (Illus.). 92p. 12cm. 1900. The Riverside Press.
Juline, Ruth Bishop, pseud., see Ritchie, Ruth.
Julita, M., Sr.
--The Poor Little Rich Man. Vianney, M. John, Sr., illus. LC 57-65. unpaged. illus. 21cm. (Christian Child's Stories, 11). 1956. Bruce Pub. Co.
Julitta, Sr., jt. auth. see Hubert, Sr.
Juliusburger, Susanna
--Beginnings. 153 p. 18cm. (Berkley Medallion Book). 1976, c.1974. (ISBN 0-425-03051-2). Berkley Publishing Corp.
--Beginnings. LC 74-83009. 191 p. 22cm. 1974. (ISBN 0-698-10646-6). Coward McCann & Geoghegan.
Jump, Margaret & Agnew, Edith
--Edge of the Village. 1959. Friendship Press.
Jund, Trinedad
--Among Them: A Miniature Verse Cyclopedia for Young People About Real and Fictional Notables. LC 56-12678. 131p. 21cm. 1957. Exposition Press.
June, Caroline Silver, pseud., see Smith, Laura Rountree.
June, Larry & Alger, Joseph
--The Shadow's Holiday. June, Larry, illus. LC 32-5597. 43 p. illus. 24 cm. c.1931. Farrar and Rinehart Incorporated.
Junior, B., pseud., see Beimdieck, John F..
Junior, B., pseud.
--Everybody's Friend: Or, Rhymes and Not Rhymes. Beimdieck, John F.. LC 20-13744. 20cm. 196p. 1873. St. Louis Book and News Co.
Junior High School Principals Association of New York City
--Moments of Enchantment. Patri, Angelo (1876-), illus. LC 42-7216. 72 p. illus. (part col.; incl. music) 36 cm. 1941. Duenewald Printing Corporation.
Junkermann, Katharine Eggleston
--Little Jumping Joan: A Mother Goose Comedy. LC 7-42463. 76 p. incl. front. (port.) illus. 23 c 20 cm. 1907. The Mc Cormick Press.
Junne, I. K., ed.
--Floating Clouds, Floating Dreams: Favorite Asian Folktales. LC 73-15349. viii, 134 p. 25cm. 1974. (ISBN 0-385-05204-9). (ISBN 0-385-05204-9). Doubleday.
Junne, I. K & Selig, Sylvie
--Long, Broad, and Sharpsight: A Slovak Folktale. LC 76-101432. (Illus.). 31 p. 25cm. c.1971. Doubleday.
Jupo, Frank J. (1904-)
--Adventure of Light. 1958. (ISBN 0-8382-0012-5, Cadmus Books). E. M. Hale and Company.
--The Adventure of Light. N.D. Prentice-Hall.
--Atu, the Silent One. Jupo, Frank J. (1904-), illus. LC 67-8763. (Illus.). 1 v. (unpaged. 32p. 1967. Holiday House.
--Count Carrot. Jupo, Frank J. (1904-), illus. LC 66-3350. 1v. (unpaged) col. illus. 24cm. c.1966. Holiday House.
--A Day Around the World. Jupo, Frank J. (1904-), illus. (Illus.). 32p. 1968. Abelard-Schuman Press.
--The Day It Happened: Stories of Nine Eventful Days Long Ago When Something Important Happened for the First Time. Jupo, Frank J. (1904-), illus. LC 58-6730. 63p. illus. 24cm. 1958. Macmillan.
--Hinkeldinkl. Jupo, Frank J. (1904-), illus. LC 55-14969. unpaged. illus. 26cm. 1955. Macmillan.
--The Mailbox Takes a Holiday. Jupo, Frank J. (1904-), illus. LC 53-12471. unpaged. illus. 21cm. c.1953. Macmillan.
--Sports, Sports Everywhere. Jupo, Frank J. (1904-), illus. 64p. illus. 24cm. 1962. Dodd, Mead.
--The Story of the Three R's. N.D. Prentice-Hall.
--The Sweetest Story Ever Told. Jupo, Frank J. (1904-), illus. LC 56-7705. unpaged. illus. 22cm. 1956. Sterling Pub. Co.
--To Carry & to Keep. Jupo, Frank J. (1904-), illus. LC 75-5543. (Illus.). (gr. 1-4). 1976. Dodd.
--Up the Trail and Down the Street. Jupo, Frank J. (1904-), illus. LC 56-11192. unpaged. illus. 27cm. 1956. Macmillan.
--Walls, Gates, and Avenues: The Story of the Town. Jupo, Frank J. (1904-), illus. LC 64-10252. 64 p. illus. 22 cm. 1964. Prentice-Hall.
--The Wishing Shoe. Jupo, Frank J. (1904-), illus. LC 54-5241. 95p. illus. 21cm. 1955. Abelard-Schuman.
Jurich, Jeff
--Guess How High I Jumped to Kiss the Laughing Moon's Nose?, 2 vols. (Illus.). 50p. (Orig.). (Star & Elephant Ser.). 1984. (ISBN 0-88138-024-5, Pub. by Envelope Bks). Green Tiger Pr.
Jurie, Jeri & Fahs, Anita
--Bizzy Bubbles, Santa's Littlest Elf. LC 77-82535. (Illus.). 30 p. 28cm. c.1977. Al Fresco Enterprise.
Just, Ward Swift (1927-)
--A Soldier of the Revolution. LC 76-112990. 224p. (gr. 6 up). 1970. (ISBN 0-394-44608-9). Knopf.
Juster, Norton (1929-)
--Alberic the Wise, and Other Journeys. Gnoli, Domenico (1933-), illus. LC 65-230065. 67p. illus. 29cm. c.1965. Pantheon. **Award: (NYT).**
--Otter Nonsense. Carle, Eric (1929-), illus. (Illus.). 64p. 1982. (ISBN 0-399-20932-8, Philomel). (ISBN 0-399-20931-X). Putnam Pub Group.
--The Phantom Tollbooth. Feiffer, Jules (1929-), illus. LC 61-13202. (Illus.). 255 p. 24cm. 1961. Epstein & Carroll; Distributed by Random House.
--Phantom Tollbooth. Feiffer, Jules (1929-), illus. 1961. Random.
Justice, Bill, ed. see Disney, Walt, Studio.
Justus, May (1898-)
--At the Foot of Windy Low. Dudley, Carrie, illus. LC 30-15096. 80 p. incl. col. front., illus. (part col.) col. plates. 21 cm. 1930. The P. F. Volland Company.
--Banjo Billy and Mr. Bones. Chisholm, Christine, illus. LC 44-9334. 63, 1 p. incl. col. front., illus. (part col.) 23 1/2 cm. 1944. A. Whitman & Company.
--Barney, Bring Your Banjo. 1st ed. Tamburine, Jean (1930-), illus. LC 59-7572. 61p. illus. 22cm. 1959. Holt.
--Betty Lou of Big Log Mountain. Gephart, Starr, illus. LC 28-8513. 4 p. l., 243 p. col. front. 22 cm. 1928. Doubleday, Doran & Company, Inc.
--Betty Lou of Big Log Mountain. Gephart, Starr, illus. LC 37-22650. 5 p. l., 243 p. col. front. 21 cm. (Young moderns bookshelf). 1937. The Sun Dial Press, Inc.
--Big Log Mountain. 1st ed. Tamburine, Jean (1930-), illus. LC 58-6511. 184p. illus. 21cm. 1958. Holt.
--Bluebird, Fly Up!. Finger, Helen, illus. LC 43-8209. 187 p. incl. front., illus. 21 cm. 1943. J. B. Lippincott Company.
--Cabin on Kettle Creek. Finger, Helen, illus. LC 41-22952. 7 p. l., 177 p. incl. front., illus., plates. 21 cm. c.1941. J. B. Lippincott Company.
--Children of the Great Smoky Mountains. 1st ed. Henneberger, Robert G. (1921-), illus. LC 52-7798. 158 p. illus. 21 cm. 1952. Dutton.
--The Complete Peddler's Pack: Games, Songs, Rhymes, and Riddles from Mountain Folklore. Tamburine, Jean (1930-), illus. LC 66-14774. (Illus.). xii, 87p. 24cm. 1967. University of Tennessee Press.
--Dixie Decides. Watson, Aldren Auld (1917-), illus. LC 42-20990. 295 p. illus. 21 cm. 1942. Random House.
--Eben and the Rattlesnake. Wilde, Carol (1938-), illus. LC 69-11772. (Illus.). 48 p. 23cm. (Reading shelf book). 1969. Garrard Pub. Co.
--Fiddle Away. Best, Allena Champlin, Mrs. (1892-1974), illus. Berry, Erick, pseud. LC 42-6766. (Illus.). 28p. 21 x 21cm. (A Story Parade Picture Bk.). 1942. Grosset & Dunlop.
--Fiddler's Fair. Chisholm, Christine, illus. LC 48-3619. (Illus.). 30p. 24cm. 1945. A. Whitman.
--Fun for Hunkydory. D'Avignon, Sue, illus. (Illus.). 24p. (gr. k-3). 1976. (ISBN 0-307-60521-3, Golden Pr). Western Pub.
--Gabby Gaffer. Dudley, Carrie, illus. LC 29-18019. 3 p. l., 180 p. illus., col. plates. 21 cm. (Lettered on cover: The Volland Inglenook series). c.1929. The P. F. Volland Company.
--Gabby Gaffer. Jansons, Inese, illus. LC 74-23498. (Illus.). 106 p. 22cm. 1975. (ISBN 0-87518-087-6). Dillon Press.
--Gabby Gaffer's New Shoes. Cox, Merle T., illus. LC 36-169. 4 p. l., 93 p. illus., col. plates. 24 cm. c.1935. Suttonhouse, Ltd.
Here Comes Mary Ellen. Finger, Helen, illus. LC 40-8615. 140 p. incl. illus., plates. col. front. 21 cm. c.1940. J. B. Lippincott Company.
--Holidays in No-End Hollow. Berger, Vivian, illus. LC 72-114182. (Illus.). 63 p. 24cm. (Reading shelf book). 1970. Garrard Pub. Co.
--Honey Jane. Smith, Charles, illus. LC 35-20113. 6 p. l., 202 p. col. front., illus., col. plates, 21 cm. 1935. Doubleday, Doran & Company, Inc.
--The House in No-End Hollow. Best, Allena Champlin, Mrs. (1892-1974), illus. Berry, Erick, pseud. LC 38-27999. x p., 1 l., 286 p. col. front., illus. 21 cm. 1938. Doubleday, Doran & Co., Inc.
--Hurrah for Jerry Jake. Chisholm, Christine, illus. LC 46-404. 62, 2 p. incl. col. front., illus. (part col.) 23 1/2 cm. 1945. A. Whitman & Company.
--It Happened in No-End Hollow. Korach, Mimi (1922-), illus. LC 68-20801. (Illus.). 48 p. 23cm. (Reading shelf book). 1969, c.1968. Garrard Pub. Co.
--Jerry Jake Carries on. Chisholm, Christine, illus. LC 43-109088. 62, 2 p. incl. col. front., illus. (part col.) 23 1/2 cm. 1943. A. Whitman & Company.
--Jumping Jack. Wallner, Shirley J., illus. LC 73-87803. (Illus.). 30 p. 25cm. c.1974. (ISBN 0-87783-123-8). (ISBN 0-87783-124-6). Oddo Pub.
--Jumping Johnny and Skedaddle. Henneberger, Robert G. (1921-), illus. LC 59-20403. 96p. illus. 23cm. 1958. Row, Peterson.
--Jumping Johnny Outwits Skedaddle. Burns, Raymond Howard (1924-), illus. LC 72-151990. (Illus.). 62 p. 24cm. (Reading shelf book). (American Folk Tales). 1971. (ISBN 0-8116-4028-0). Garrard Pub. Co.
--Lester and His Hound Pup. Payne, Joan Balfour (1923-1973), illus. LC 59-14550. (Illus.). 45 p. 26cm. 1960. Hastings House.
--Let's Play and Sing. Dugan, William J., illus. 1958. Broadman Press.
--Little Red Rooster Learns to Crow. Evans, Katherine Floyd (1901-1964), illus. LC 54-10942. unpaged. illus. 25cm. 1954. A. Whitman.
--Lizzie. Chisholm, Christine, illus. LC 44-388286. 62, 2 p. incl. col. front., illus. (part col.) 23 1/2 cm. 1944. A. Whitman & Company.
--Luck for Little Lihu. 1st ed. Chapman, Frederick Trench (1887-), illus. LC 50-9647. (Illus.). 112 p. 20cm. 1950. Aladdin Books.
--Luck for Little Lihu. Chapman, Frederick Trench (1887-), illus. N.D. E. P. Dutton & Co.
--Lucky Penny. 1st ed. Chapman, Frederick Trench (1887-), illus. LC 51-3814. 80 p. illus. 20 cm. 1951. Aladdin Books.
--The Mail Wagon Mystery. Patton, Lucia, illus. LC 40-141972. 5 p. l., 17-210 p. incl. illus., plates. col. front., col. pl. 23 cm. 1940. A. Whitman & Company.
--Mary Ellen. LC 48-15981. 93 p. illus. 23 cm. 1947. Broadman Press.
--Mr. Songcatcher and Company. 1st ed. Simon, Howard (1903-1979), illus. LC 40-276061. 7 p. l., 237 p. incl. front., illus., plates. 21 cm. 1940. Doubleday Doran & Co., Inc.
--Nancy of Apple Tree Hill. Patton, Lucia, illus. LC 42-225794. 5 p. l., 17-257 p. col. front., plates (1 col.) illus. 23 cm. 1942. A. Whitman & Company.
--Near-Side-and-Far. Mallon, Grace, illus. LC 37-12219. 5 p. l., 15-148 p. incl. illus., plates (1 col.) 21 cm. c.1936. Suttonhouse, Ltd.
--A New Home for Billy. Payne, Joan Balfour (1923-1973), illus. LC 66-8333. (Illus.). 24cm. 53p. (gr. 2-4). 1966. (ISBN 0-8038-5002-6). Hastings.
--The Other Side of the Mountain. Pugh, Mabel (1891-), illus. LC 31-280257. 5 p. l., 149, 1 p. incl. illus., plates. col. front. 20 cm. 1931. Doubleday, Doran & Company, Inc.
--The Other Side of the Mountain. Williams, Berkeley, Jr., illus. LC 58-6294. 143p. illus. 22cm. 1957. Hastings House.
--Peddler's Park. 1st ed. Tamburine, Jean (1930-), illus. LC 57-5745. 95p. illus. 25cm. 1957. Holt.
--Peter Pocket: A Little Boy of the Cumberland Mountains. Pugh, Mabel (1891-), illus. LC 27-19188. 7 p. l., 127, p. incl. illus., plates. col. front. 20 cm. 1927. Doubleday, Page, & Company.
--Peter Pocket and His Pickle Pup. Tamburine, Jean (1930-), illus. LC 53-8968. (Illus.). 141 p. 20cm. 1953. Holt.
--Peter Pocket's Book, 1. (gr. 5). N.D. Doubleday Doran.
--Peter Pocket's Books: Including Peter Pocket and Peter Pocket's Luck. Pugh, Mabel (1891-), illus. LC 34-5405. 7 p. l., 127, 2, 118 p. incl. illus., plates. col. front. 20 cm. 1934. Doubleday, Doran & Company, Inc.
--Peter Pocket's Luck. 1st ed. Pugh, Mabel (1891-), illus. LC 30-21942. 7 p. l., 118 p. incl. illus., plates. col. front. 20 cm. 1930. Doubleday, Doran & Company, Inc.
--The Right House for Rowdy. Tamburine, Jean (1930-), illus. LC 60-823596. 62p. illus. 21cm. 1960. Holt, Rinehart and Winston.
--Sammy. Chisholm, Christine, illus. LC 46-57427. 47 p. illus. (part col.) 24 x 20 1/2 cm. 1946. A. Whitman & Company.
--Smoky Mountain Sampler: Stories. Tamburine, Jean (1930-), illus. LC 62-11148. 127p. illus. 22cm. 1962. Abingdon.
--Step Along and Jerry Jake. Chisholm, Christine, illus. LC 42-18154. 62, 2 p. incl. col. front., illus. (part col.) 24 cm. 1942. A. Whitman & Company.
--Surprise for Perky Pup. Korach, Mimi (1922-), illus. LC 74-155569. (Illus.). 39 p. 23cm. 1971. (ISBN 0-8116-6704-9). Garrard Pub. Co.
--Surprise for Peter Pocket. Tamburine, Jean (1930-), illus. LC 55-5892. (Illus.). 20cm. 101p. (gr. 4-6). 1955. (ISBN 0-03-032080-1). HR&W.
--Susie. Chisholm, Christine, illus. LC 48-902. 46 p. illus. (part col.) music. 24 cm. 1947. A. Whitman.
--Tale of a Pig. Aloise, Frank E., illus. LC 63-7971. (Illus.). unpaged. 1963. Abingdon.
--Tales from Near-Side and Far. Vestal, Herman B., illus. LC 70-95350. (Illus.). 63 p. 24cm. 1970. Garrard Pub. Co.
--Then Came Mister Billy Barker. Payne, Joan Balfour (1923-1973), illus. LC 58-12897. (Illus.). 44p. (gr. 2-4). 1959. (ISBN 0-8038-7059-0). Hastings.
--Toby Has a Dog. Tousey, Thomas Sanford, illus. LC 49-503216. 28 p. illus. (part col.) 25 cm. 1949. Whitman.
--Use Your Head, Hildy. Tamburine, Jean (1930-), illus. LC 56-6229. (Illus.). 95p. (gr. 2-5). 1956. (ISBN 0-03-066390-3). HR&W.
--Whoopee, Hunkydory-. Vaughan, Eileen Fox, illus. LC 53-23308. unpaged. illus. 17cm. (Tell-a-tale books). 1953, c.1952. Whitman Pub. Co.
--Winds A'Blowing. Tamburine, Jean (1930-), illus. LC 61-7048. (Illus.). 79 p. 21cm. 1961. Abingdon Press.
--You're Sure Silly, Billy!. Vestal, Herman B., illus. LC 72-1077. (Illus.). 63 p. 23cm. 1972. (ISBN 0-8116-6958-0). Garrard Pub. Co.
Justus, May (1898-) & Payne, Joan Balfour (1923-1973)
--New Boy in School. LC 62-22122. (Illus.). 56 p. 24cm. 1963. Hastings House.
Juta, Jan (1895-)
--Look Out for the Ostriches!. Tales of South Africa. Pitz, Henry Clarence (1895-1976), illus. (gr. 7-11). N.D. A. A. Knopf.
Juvenal
--The Satires of Juvenal. Humphries, George Rolfe (1894-1969), tr. LC 58-12213. 192p. (Midland Bks.-Indiana University Greek & Latin Classics: No. 20). 1958. (ISBN 0-253-20020-2). Ind U Pr.
J. W. C., pseud., see Colby, James W..
J. W. C., pseud.
--Mary M'Neill: Or, The Word Remembered. A Tale of Humble Life. Colby, James W.. 1873. Leavitt & Allen Bros.
J. W. D., ed. see Scudder, Joseph, Mrs.
Jynch, Miriam
--Girl in the Shadows. 160p. (Orig.). (gr. 7 up). 1982. (ISBN 0-590-32283-4, Windswept). Scholastic Inc.
Jyotirmayi-Devi, jt. auth. see Yogesvara Dasa.
K. M.
--Annie and Pierre: Or, Our Father's Letters. N.D. Thomas Whittaker.
--Easter Day. N.D. Thomas Whittaker.
--Edith Leigh's Prayer Book. N.D. Thomas Whittaker.

Kaatz, Evelyn
--Motorcycle Road Racer. LC 77-22153. p. cm. c.1977. (ISBN 0-316-47750-8). Little, Brown.
--Race Car Driver. LC 79-14766. (Illus.). 55 p. 25cm. c.1979. (ISBN 0-316-47751-6). Little, Brown.
--Soccer!. How One Player Made the Pros. LC 80-26783. (Illus.). 71 p. 24cm. c.1981. (ISBN 0-316-47752-4). Little, Brown.
Kabakov, I., tr. see Zubkov, Boris.
Kabalevsky, Dmitri
--Joey the Clown: The Comedians. Watanabe, Saburo, illus. (Pictorial Fantasia Ser). (gr. 3-6). 1969. Silver.
Kabotie, Fred, jt. auth. see Kennard, Edward Allan.
Kabus, Dieter (1941-)
--The Secret Treasure. LC 85-8744. p. cm. (Castle mystery series). 1985. (ISBN 0-89840-097-X). Here's Life Publishers.
Kachel, Limana
--Homer Littlebird's Rabbit: Cheyenne Indian Story for Children. 32p. (ps-2). 1983. (ISBN 0-89992-084-5). MT Coun Indian.
Kadar, Livia, illus.
--The Polish Fairy Book. Byrde, Elsie, tr. LC 26-26142. 231, 1 p., col. front., col. plates. 21 cm. 1925. Frederick A. Stokes Company.
Kaemmerling, Effie Barnhurst (1870-)
--Once There Was a Prince. Day, Maurice (1892-), illus. LC 28-22142. 6 p. l., 3-302 p., 1 l. incl. illus., plates. col. front. 21 cm. 1928. Little, Brown, and Company.
Kafaroff, Bruce
--Deadwood Gulch. LC 41-10470. 5 p. l., 3-343, 1 p. 20 cm. 1941. A. A. Knopf.
Kaff, F.
--Monster for a Day: Or, The Monster in Gregory's Pajamas. Cushman, Doug, illus. LC 79-1866. (Illus.). 20 p. 32cm. c.1979. (ISBN 0-525-69002-6). (ISBN 0-525-69003-4). Gingerbread House.
Kafka, Sherry (1937-)
--Big Enough. Kuskin, Karla Seidman (1932-), illus. LC 73-92811. (Illus.). 32 p. 19cm. 1970. Putnam.
--I Need a Friend. Keith, Eros, illus. LC 74-133924. (Illus.). 30 p. 19cm. 1971. Putnam.
Kagay, Daniel Martin
--Eastside Boys. LC 9-27743. 2 p. l., 3-213 p. 20 cm. 1909. The Roxburgh Publishing Company, Incorporated.
Kagran Corporation
--Howdy Doody and the Monkey Tale. LC 53-24256. unpaged. illus. 17cm. (Tell-a-tale books). 1953. Whitman Pub. Co.
--Howdy Doody's Clarabell and Pesky Peanut. Featuring the Famous Star of the Television Show, Howdy Doody. Authorized. LC 54-21760. unpaged. illus. 17cm. (Tell-a-tale books, 934). 1954, c.1953. Whitman Pub. Co.
--Howdy Doody's Island Adventure: Featuring the Famous Star of the Television Show, Howdy Doody. Authorized. Gribbroek, Robert, illus. LC 56-178856. unpaged. illus. 22cm. (Cozy-corner book, 2410). c.1955. Whitman Pub. Co.
Kahl, Ann Hammel (1929-)
--Francis Discovers the World. 1962. David McKay Company Inc.
--Francis Discovers the World. LC 62-18477. unpaged. illus. 18x22cm. 1962. R. B. Luce.
--Trouble is a Cat. (Illus.). 1963. David McKay Company Co.
--Trouble Is a Cat. LC 63-10495. unpaged. illus. 18 x 22 cm. 1963. R. B. Luce.
Kahl, Virginia, jt. auth. see Vacheron, Edith.
Kahl, Virginia (1919-)
--Away Went Wolfgang!. Kahl, Virginia (1919-), illus. LC 54-7246. (Illus.). 32p. c.1954. Scribner.
--The Baron's Booty. Kahl, Virginia (1919-), illus. LC 63-10389. unpaged. illus. 1963. Scribner.
--Droopsi. Kahl, Virginia (1919-), illus. LC 58-6741. unpaged. illus. 26cm. c.1958. Scribner.
--Duchess Bakes a Cake. Encore ed. Kahl, Virginia (1919-), illus. LC 55-14215. (Illus.). (gr. k-3). 1955. (ISBN 0-684-12313-4, ScribJ). (ISBN 0-684-17410-3, ScribJ). Scribner.
--Giants, Indeed!. Kahl, Virginia (1919-), illus. LC 73-14401. (Illus.). 32 p. 27cm. 1974. Scribner.
--Gunhilde and the Halloween Spell. Kahl, Virginia (1919-), illus. LC 75-4055. (Illus.). 32 p. 26cm. c.1975. (ISBN 0-684-14335-6). Scribner.
--Gunhilde's Christmas Booke. Kahl, Virginia (1919-), illus. LC 72-1170. (Illus.). 32 p. 27cm. 1972. (ISBN 0-684-13011-4). Scribner.
--Habits of Rabbits. Kahl, Virginia (1919-), illus. LC 57-6077. (Illus.). (gr. k-3). 1957. (ISBN 0-684-12349-5). Scribner.
--How Do You Hide a Monster?. LC 73-143926. (Illus.). 32 p. 27cm. 1971. (ISBN 0-684-12318-5). Scribner.
--How Many Dragons Are Behind the Door?. Kahl, Virginia (1919-), illus. LC 76-57961. (Illus.). 32 p. 26cm. c.1977. (ISBN 0-684-14906-0). Scribner.
--Maxie. Kahl, Virginia (1919-), illus. LC 56-13810. (Illus.). unpaged. c.1956. Scribner.
--Perfect Pancake. Kahl, Virginia (1919-), illus. LC 60-7178. (Illus.). (gr. k-3). 1960. (ISBN 0-684-92305-X, ScribJ). Scribner.
--Plum Pudding for Christmas. Kahl, Virginia (1919-), illus. LC 56-9283. (Illus.). (gr. k-3). 1956. (ISBN 0-684-12427-0, ScribJ). Scribner.
--Small White Cat. LC 78-31278. (Illus.). 32 p. c.1979. (ISBN 0-684-16097-8). Scribner.
--Whose Cat Is That?. Kahl, Virginia (1919-), illus. (Illus.). 32p. (gr. k-2). 1979. (ISBN 0-684-16097-8, ScribJ). Scribner.
Kahler, Woodland (1895-)
--Giant Dwarf. N.D. Liveright Pulbications.
Kahmann, Mable Chesley, Mrs. (1901-)
--Carmen, Silent Partner. Sperry, Armstrong W. (1897-1976), illus. LC 34-38324. 3 p. l., 249 p. incl. front., illus. 20 cm. 1934. Dodd, Mead & Company.
--Felita. LC 32-26356. 6 p. l., 291 p. incl. illus., plates. col. front. 20 cm. 1932. Doubleday, Doran & Company, Inc.
--Felita. LC 39-24302. 6 p. l., 291 p. incl. illus., plates. 21 cm. (Young moderns bookshelf). 1939. The Sun Dial Press, Inc.
--Gypsy Goes to College. Baldridge, Cyrus LeRoy (1889-), illus. LC 41-101503. 5 p. l., 3-341 p. illus. 22 cm. c.1941. Random House.
--Gypsy Luck. Brazelton, Julian, illus. LC 37-29381. 230 p. illus. 21 cm. c.1937. J. Messner, Inc.
--Gypsy Luck. Brazelton, Julian, illus. 214p. Reissue of 1937 ed. 1949. Messner.
--Gypsy Melody. LC 49-11040. 21cm. 313p. 1949. Random House.
--Jasper, the Gypsy Dog. Wiese, Kurt (1887-1974), illus. LC 38-33561. 93 p. illus. 23 cm. c.1938. J. Messner, Inc.
--Lupe and the Senorita. Reeves, Norman, illus. LC 38-13403. 5 p. l., 3-276 p. illus. 21 cm. c.1938. Random House.
--Raquel: A Girl of Puerto Rico. LC 36-28510. 349 p. incl. front., illus. 21 cm. c.1936. Random House.
--Sinfi and the Little Gypsy Goat. Mora, F. Luis, illus. LC 40-72903. 5 p. l., 3-70 p. col. illus. 26 cm. c.1940. Random House.
--Tara. Mora, F. Luis, illus. 268 p. incl. front., illus., plates. 22 cm. 1935. H. Smith & R. Haas.
--Tara, Daughter of the Gypsies. 1st ed. Mora, F. Luis, illus. LC 35-25379. 288p. incl. front., 21 1/2cm. 1935. H. Smith & R. Haas.
--Tara, Daughter of the Gypsies. Mora, F. Luis, illus. N.D. Random House.
--XDY and the Soap Box Derby. Cunette, Louis, illus. LC 41-14771. 5 p. l., 3-201 p. illus. 20 cm. c.1941. Random House.
Kahn, Agnes Keesler
--Let's Play Stage: A Series of Children's Stories. LC 42-17424. v. 18 cm. c.1942. Rainbow Productions.
Kahn, Joan (1914-)
--Ladies and Gentlemen, Said the Ringmaster. Kahn, Joan (1914-), illus. 1938. Alfred A. Knopf.
--Seesaw. Bonsall, Crosby Barbara Newell (1921-), illus. LC 64-19716. (Illus.). 16cm. 24p. (ps-1). 1964. (ISBN 0-06-023081-9, HarpJ). Har-Row.
--To Meet Miss Long. LC 43-2942. 250 p. 21 cm. 1943. J. B. Lippincott Company.
Kahn, Joan (1914-), selected by.
--Handle with Care: Frightening Stories. LC 85-2764. xii, 209 p. 24cm. c.1985. (ISBN 0-688-04663-0). Greenwillow Books.
--Some Things Weird & Wicked: 12 Stories to Chill Your Bones. Cober, Alan Edwin (1935-), illus. LC 75-35855. (Illus.). x, 243p. (gr. 6 up). 1976. (ISBN 0-394-83244-2). Pantheon.
--Something Dark and Dangerous. 1973. Harper & Row.
--Some Things Dark and Dangerous. Kahn, Joan (1914-), ed. 1970. (ISBN 0-06-023082-7). Harper and Row.
--Something Fierce and Fatal. 1971. Harper & Row Pub.
--Something Strange and Sinster. 1973. Harper & Row Pub.
Kahn, Joan (1914-) & Bridgeman, Elizabeth (1921-)
--You Can't Catch Me. Kahn, Joan (1914-), illus. LC 76-9213. (Illus.). 24 p. 19cm. c.1976. (ISBN 0-06-023088-6). (ISBN 0-06-023089-4). Harper & Row.
Kahn, Joan (1914-) & Darrow, Whitney, Jr. (1909-)
--Hi, Jock, Run Around the Block. Kahn, Joan (1914-), illus. LC 77-11847. (Illus.). 24 p. 21cm. c.1978. (ISBN 0-06-023078-9). (ISBN 0-06-023079-7). Harper & Row.
Kahn, Peggy
--The Care Bears and the Kid Who Said "I Can't!". LC 85-2152. p. cm. c.1985. (ISBN 0-394-87503-6). (ISBN 0-394-97503-0). Random House.
--The Care Bears & the New Baby. Blake, Robert, illus. LC 82-61961. (Illus.). 32p. (Care Bear Mini-Storybooks). (gr. 1-6). 1983. (ISBN 0-394-85845-X). Random.
--The Care Bears' Book of ABC's. LC 82-18538. p. cm. c.1983. (ISBN 0-394-95808-X). Random House.
--The Care Bears' Book of Colors. Katz, Bobbi (1933-), ed. Barto, Bobbi, illus. LC 83-62102. (Illus.). 14p. (Care Bear Cuddle Bks.). (ps-1). 1984. (ISBN 0-394-86444-1, BYR). Random.
--The Care Bears Help Santa. Fleming, Denise, illus. LC 84-3385. (Illus.). 40p. (Care Bear Bks.). (ps-3). 1984. (ISBN 0-394-86807-2, BYR). (ISBN 0-394-96807-7, BYR). Random.
--The Care Bears' Up & Down. Katz, Bobbi (1933-), ed. Bracken, Carolyn, illus. LC 83-62009. (Illus.). 14p. (Care Bear Cuddle Bks.). (ps-1). 1985. (ISBN 0-394-86445-X, BYR). Random.
--The Handy Girls Can Fix It!. Jensen, Enola, illus. LC 83-21086. (Illus.). 32p. (Handy Girls Bks.). (ps-5). 1984. (ISBN 0-394-86252-X, BYR). (ISBN 0-394-86252-X). Random.
Kahn, Peggy, adapted by.
--The Care Bears' Night Before Christmas. Kamm, Diane, illus. LC 85-42532. (Based on the Story by Clement Clark Moore,). p. cm. c.1985. (ISBN 0-394-87502-8). (ISBN 0-394-97502-2). Random House.
Kahn, Ruth E.
--My Daddy Abc's. Foster, Celeste K., illus. LC 77-81601. (Illus.). 31 p. 29cm. 1969. T. S. Denison.
Kahn, Ruth Stiles Gannett see Gannett, Ruth Stiles.
Kaigh-Eustace, Edyth, Mrs.
--Jungle Babies. Bransom, Paul (1885-) & Nelson, Don, illus. Roosevelt, Kermit (1885-), frwd. by. LC 30-21633. 255, 1 p. illus., col. plates. 24 cm. c.1930. Rand, McNally & Company.
Kaine, George S.
--Phil Granger's Triumph. (Illus.). N.D. James A. Moore.
Kaine, George S., et al.
--Pearl Library: Containing "Margaret, or The Pearl", "The Angels' Song", "Lady Mary", and "Phil Granger's Triumph", 4 vols. N.D. Set. James A. Moore.
Kaiser, Joanne
--I Want to Be a Bird. LC 64-21805. (Illus.). 64 p. 24cm. (Read-by-yourself books). N.D. Houghton Mifflin.
--To Catch a Worm. Titleman, Lynn, illus. LC 69-17519. (Illus.). 48 p. 24cm. (Read-by-yourself books). 1969. Houghton Mifflin.
Kaiser, Judith B.
--Quick-Line Stories for Young Children. 1975. (ISBN 0-916406-12-1). Accent Bks.
Kaiulani, jt. auth. see Roes, Carol.
Kakacek, Gen., jt. auth. see Dolim, Mary Nuzum.
Kalan, Robert
--Blue Sea. 1st ed. Crews, Donald, illus. LC 78-18396. (Illus.). 24 p. c.1979. (ISBN 0-688-80184-6). (ISBN 0-688-84184-8). Greenwillow Books. **Award: (ALA).**
--Jump, Frog, Jump!. Barton, Byron (1930-), illus. LC 81-1401. p. cm. c.1981. (ISBN 0-688-80271-0). (ISBN 0-688-84271-2). Greenwillow Books.
--Rain. Crews, Donald, illus. LC 77-25312. (Illus.). 24p. (gr. k-3). 1978. (ISBN 0-688-80139-0). (ISBN 0-688-84139-2). Greenwillow.
Kalashnikoff, Nicholas (1888-1961)
--The Defender. Louden, Claire & Louden, George, illus. LC 51-12840. 136 p. illus. 22 cm. 1951. Scribner. **Award: (JNM).**
--Jumper, the Life of a Siberian Horse. Shenton, Edward (1895-), illus. LC 44-89627. 5 p. l., 5-224 p. illus. 21 cm. 1944. C. Scribner's Sons.
--My Friend Yakub. Rojankovsky, Feodor Stepanovich (1891-1970), illus. LC 53-12459. (Illus.). 249 p. 21cm. 1953. Scribner.
--Toyon: A Dog of the North and His People. 1st ed. Marokvia, Artur F. (1909-), illus. LC 50-9470. 246 p. illus. 22 cm. 1950. Harper.
Kalb, Jonah (1926-)
--The Goof That Won the Pennant. Kossin, Sandy (1926-), illus. LC 76-21678. (Illus.). 103 p. 22cm. 1976. (ISBN 0-395-24834-5). Houghton Mifflin.
--The Kids' Candidate. Kossin, Sandy (1926-), illus. LC 75-17027. (Illus.). 140 p. 22cm. 1975. (ISBN 0-395-21893-4). Houghton Mifflin.
Kalbaugh, Osborne Beale see Beale, John, pseud.
Kalbaugh, Osborne Beale (1891-)
--The Wind Whispers to Tubby. Beale, John, pseud. Perdue, Margaret, illus. LC 41-9411. (Music by Paris Harwood Bartley, 1894). (Illus.). 44p. 28cm. 1940. National Publishing Co.
Kaler, James Otis see Kaler, James, pseud.
Kaler, James Otis see Otis, James, pseud.
Kaler, James Otis (1848-1912)
--Aboard the Hylow. Otis, James, pseud. N.D. E. P. Dutton & Co.
--Aboard the Hylow on Sable Island Bank. Otis, James, pseud. LC 7-28976. v, 352 p. front., 4 pl. 22 cm. 1907. E. P. Dutton and Company.
--Across the Delaware: A Boy's Story of the Battle of Trenton in 1777. Otis, James, pseud. Davis, J. Watson, illus. LC 3-11672. 19cm. 347p. 1903. A. L. Burt.
--Across the Range, and Other Stories. Otis, James, pseud. LC 14-16946. 4 p. l., 178, 1 p. front., plates. 18 cm. 1914. Harper & Brothers.
--Admiral J. of Spurwink. Otis, James, pseud. LC 12-34743. 305 p. front., plates. 20 cm. c.1896. A. I. Bradley & Co.
--Admiral J. of Spurwink. Otis, James, pseud. (Young American Library). N.D. Hurst & Co.
--Adventures in Mexico. Otis, James, pseud. (Illus.). (James Otis Series.). 1915. A L Burt & Co.
--Adventures in Mexico. Otis, James, pseud. (The Rugby Series for Boys and Girls). N.D. A. L. Burt Company.
--The Aeroplane at Silver Fox Farm. Otis, James, pseud. Copeland, Charles, illus. LC 11-20818. 3 p. l., 360 p. front., plates. 21 cm. c.1911. Thomas Y. Crowell Company.
--Afloat in Freedom's Cause: The Story of Two Boys in the War of 1812. Otis, James, pseud. Davis, J. Watson, illus. LC 8-8300. 2 p. l., iii-iv, 343 p. front., 5 pl. 20 cm. c.1908. A. L. Burt Company.
--Airship Cruising from Silver Fox Farm. Otis, James, pseud. (Crowell's American Boy and Girl Library). N.D. Thomas Y. Crowell Company.
--An Amateur Fireman. Otis, James, pseud. LC 21-8685. v, 324 p. front., plates. 21 cm. 1898. E. P. Dutton & Company.
--An Amateur Fireman. Otis, James, pseud. LC 8-972. v, 324 p. front., 8 pl. 21 cm. 1904. E. P. Dutton & Company.
--Among the Fur Traders. Otis, James, pseud. Merrill, Frank Thayer (1848-), illus. (Historical Stories for Boys). N.D. Penn Publishing Co.
--Among the Fur Traders. Otis, James, pseud. Merrill, Frank Thayer (1848-), illus. LC 6-15426. 382 p. front., 6 pl. 20 cm. 1906. The Penn Publishing Company.
--Amos Dunkel, Oarsman: A Story of the Whale Boat Navy of 1776. Otis, James, pseud. Davis, J. Watson, illus. LC 1-12834. viii, 370 p. front., plates. 20 cm. 1901. A. L. Burt.
--Andy's Ward. Otis, James, pseud. (Vacation Ser.). N.D. Grosset & Dunlap.
--Andy's Ward: Or, the International Museum. Otis, James, pseud. LC 12-34742. iv, 7-358 p. front., plates. 19 cm. (Adventure Stories Ser.). 1895. The Penn Publishing Company.
--The Armed Ship America: Or, When We Sailed from Salem. Otis, James, pseud, 1 of 3 vols. Kennedy, J. W. Ferguson, illus. (The Privateers of 1812 Ser.: No. 3). 1900. Set. Dana Estes & Co.
--At the Siege of Detroit. Otis, James, pseud. Davis, J. Watson, illus. LC 4-10542. 19cm. 353p. 1904. A. L. Burt Co.
--At the Siege of Havana. Otis, James, pseud. (Illus.). (The Continental Ser.). N.D. A. L. Burt's Pubs.
--At the Siege of Havana: The Experience of Three Boys Serving Under Israel Putnam in 1762. Otis, James, pseud. 358p. 1899. A. L. Burt Co.
--At the Siege of Quebec. Carter, F. A., illus. LC 12-34741. 362 p. incl. front. 4 pl. 19 cm. (Historical Stories Ser. for Boys and Girls). 1897. The Penn Publishing Company.
--Aunt Hannah. Otis, James, pseud. (Illus.). (Sunshine Library). 1915. Thomas Y Crowel.
--Aunt Hannah and Seth. Otis, James, pseud. LC 4285. 3 p. l., 109 p. front. 20 cm. (Sunshine library). c.1900. T. Y. Crowell & Co.
--Beach Boy Joe. Otis, James, pseud. (The Boys Own Library). N.D. David McKay.
--Boston Boys of Seventeen-Seventy Five: Or, When We Besieged Boston. Otis, James, pseud, 1 of 11 vols. Bridgman, Lewis Jesse (1857-1931), illus. (Stories of American History Ser.: No. 1). 1900. Dana Estes & Co.
--The Boy Captain. Otis, James, pseud. (Illus.). (The Boy's Own Authors Ser.). N.D. Dana Estes & Co.
--The Boy Captain: Or, From Forecastle to Cabin. Otis, James, pseud, 1 of 6 vols. Barnes, George Foster, illus. LC 12-34740. 4 p. l., 290 p. front., 7 pl. 21 cm. (Jenny Wren Ser.). c.1896. Set. Estes and Lauriat.
--Boy Scouts in a Lumber Camp. Otis, James, pseud. (Crowell's Boy Scout Library). 1915. T Y Crowell.
--Boy Scouts in a Lumber Camp. Otis, James, pseud. Copeland, Charles, illus. LC 13-17409. 3 p. l., 335 p. front., plates. 19 cm. c.1913. Thomas Y. Crowell Company.
--Boy Scouts in the Maine Woods. Otis, James, pseud. (Illus.). (Crowell's Boy Scout Library). 1915. T Y Crowell.
--Boy Scouts in the Maine Woods. Otis, James, pseud. Copeland, Charles, illus. LC 11-199853. 3 p. l., 283 p. front., plates. 20 cm. c.1911. Thomas Y. Crowell Company.

--The Minute Boys of New York City. Otis, James, pseud. Bridgman, Lewis Jesse (1857-1931), illus. LC 9-20282. 327 p. front., 7 pl. 20 cm. 1909. D. Estes & Company.
--The Minute Boys of Philadelphia. Otis, James, pseud. (The Minute Boys Ser.). N.D. Page Co.
--The Minute Boys of Philadelphia. Otis, James, pseud. Bridgman, Lewis Jesse (1857-1931), illus. LC 11-18460. 315 p. incl. front. plates. 20 cm. c.1911. D. Estes and Company.
--The Minute Boys of South Carolina. Otis, James, pseud. (The Minute Boys Ser.). N.D. Page Co.
--The Minute Boys of South Carolina: A Story of "How We Boys Aided Marion, the Swamp Fox". Otis, James, pseud. Kennedy, J. W. Ferguson, illus. LC 7-25053. ix p., 2 l., 11-359 p. front., 7 pl. 20 cm. c.1907. D. Estes & Company.
--The Minute Boys of the Green Mountains. Otis, James, pseud. (The Minute Boys Ser.). N.D. Page Co.
--The Minute Boys of the Green Mountains. Otis, James, pseud. Shute, A. Burnham, illus. LC 4-19641. 350 p. front., 7 pl. 20 cm. 1904. D. Estes & Company.
--The Minute Boys of the Mohawk Valley. Otis, James, pseud. Shute, A. Burnham, illus. LC 5-17287. viii p., 2 l., 11-365 p. front., 7 pl. 20 cm. c.1905. D. Estes & Company.
--The Minute Boys of the Wyoming Valley. Otis, James, pseud. (The Minute Boys Ser.). N.D. Page Co.
--The Minute Boys of the Wyoming Valley. Otis, James, pseud. Shute, A. Burnham, illus. LC 6-17005. x p., 2 l., 11-367 p. front., 7 pl. 20 cm. c.1906. D. Estes & Company.
--The Minute Boys of York Town. Otis, James, pseud. (The Minute Boys Ser.). N.D. Page Co.
--The Minute Boys of York Town. Otis, James, pseud. Bridgman, Lewis Jesse (1857-1931), illus. LC 12-15150. 348 p. incl. front. plates. 20 cm. c.1912. D. Estes & Company.
--Morgan, the Jersey Spy. Otis, James, pseud. (Illus.). (The Young Patriot Ser.). N.D. A. L. Burt's Pubs.
--Morgan the Jersey Spy: A Story of the Siege of Yorktown in 1781. Otis, James, pseud. Davis, J. Watson, illus. LC 99-58. ix p., 2 l., 220 p. front., plates. 19 cm. (Young patriot series). c.1898. A. L. Burt.
--Mr. Stubb's Brother. Otis, James, pseud. N.D. Grosset & Dunlap.
--Mr. Stubb's Brother. Otis, James, pseud. (Harper's Young People's Ser.). N.D. Harper & Bros.
--Mr. Stubbs's Brother. Otis, James, pseud. Rogers, W. A., illus. LC 13-33880. 283 p. incl. front., plates. 17 cm. 1883. Harper & Brothers.
--Mr. Stubbs's Brother. Otis, James, pseud. Rogers, W. A., illus. LC 4-17527. 283 p. incl. front., 20 pl. 18 cm. 1903. Harper & Brothers.
--The Navy Boys at the Siege of Havana: Being the Experience of Three Boys Serving Under Israel Putnam in 1762. Kaler, James, pseud. (The Navy Boys Ser.). N.D. A. L. Burt Company.
--The Navy Boys' Cruise on the Pickering: A Boy's Story of Privateering in 1780. Otis, James, pseud. (The Navy Boys Ser.). N.D. A. L. Burt Company.
--The Navy Boys' Cruise With Paul Jones: A Boy's Story of a Cruise With the Great Commodore in 1776. Otis, James, pseud. (The Navy Boys Ser.). N.D. A. L. Burt Company.
--The Navy Boys in New York Bay: A Story of Three Boys Who Took Command of "The Laughing Mary." The First Vessel of the American Navy. Otis, James, pseud. (The Navy Boys Ser.). N.D. A. L. Burt Company.
--The Navy Boys on Lake Ontario: The/Story of Two Boys and Their Adventures in the War of 1812. Otis, James, pseud. (The Navy Boys Ser.). N.D. A. L. Burt Company.
--The Navy Boys On Long Island Sound: A Boy's Story of the Whaleboat Navy of 1776. Otis, James, pseud. (The Navy Boys Ser.). N.D. A.L. Burt Company.
--The Navy Boys With Grant at Vicksburg: A Boy's Story of the Siege at Vicksburg. Otis, James, pseud. (The Navy Boys Ser.). N.D. A. L. Burt Company.
--Neal, the Miller: A Son of Liberty. Otis, James, pseud. LC 12-34829. 89 p. incl. front., illus., plates. 20 cm. (On cover: Stories of American history by James Otis). 1895. Estes and Lauriat.
--Neal the Miller: A Son of Liberty. Otis, James, pseud. Bridgman, Lewis Jesse (1857-1931), illus. (Illus.). (The Stories of American History Ser.). N.D. Dana Estes & Co.
--Neal the Miller: A Son of Liberty. Otis, James, pseud. Bridgman, Lewis Jesse (1857-1931), illus. (Stories of American History). N.D. Estes & Lauriat's.
--Off Santiago with Sampson. Otis, James, pseud. LC 99-4745. 109 p. incl. front., illus., plates. 20 cm. (On verso of half-title: "Stories of American history" series, no. 2). 1899. D. Estes & Company.
--Old Ben: The Friend of Toby Tyler and Mr. Stubbs' Brother. Otis, James, pseud. Noble-Ives, Sarah, illus. LC 11-25556. 3 p. l., 187. 1 p. l illus., col. plates. 20 cm. 1911. Harper & Brothers.
--On Schedule Time. Otis, James, pseud. LC 12-34828. 1 p. l., 131 p. front., 2 pl. 19 cm. c.1896. T. Whittaker.
--On the Kentucky Frontier: A Story of the Fighting Pioneers of the West. Otis, James, pseud. Davis, J. Watson, illus. LC 4062. iv, 266 p. illus. 19 cm. (Young patriot series). 1900. Burt.
--Our Children's Songs. Otis, James, pseud. 1882. Harper's Trade-List.
--Our Uncle the Major: A Story of New York in 1765. Otis, James, pseud. LC 1-12835. (Illus.). 102p. (The Sunshine Library for Young People). 1901. Thomas Y. Crowell.
--The Princess and Joe Potter. Otis, James, pseud. (Stories of Newsboy Life). N.D. L. C. Page.
--The Princess and Joe Potter. Otis, James, pseud. N.D. Page Co.
--The Princess & Joe Potter. Otis, James, pseud. Oakley, Violet, illus. (Jenny Wren Ser.: New Vol.). N.D. Dana Estes & Co.
--The Princess and Joe Potter. Otis, James, pseud. Oakley, Violet, illus. 249p. 1898. Estes & Lauriat.
--Raising the "Pearl". Otis, James, pseud. N.D. Grosset & Dunlap.
--Raising the "Pearl". Otis, James, pseud. LC 12-34837. 300 p. incl. front., plates. 17 x 13 cm. (On verso of t.-p.: Harper's young people series). 1884. Harper & Brothers.
--Ralph Gurney's Oil Speculation. Otis, James, pseud. (Illus.). (James Otis Series.). 1915. A L Burt & Co.
--Ralph Gurney's Oil Speculation. Otis, James, pseud. (The Rugby Series for Boys and Girls). N.D. A. L. Burt Company.
--Reels and Spindles. Otis, James, pseud. New ed. 369p. N.D. W. A. Wilde Co.
--Reuben Green's Adventures at Yale. Otis, James, pseud. (The Boys Own Library). N.D. David McKay.
--Reuben Green's Adventures at Yale. Otis, James, pseud, 39 vols. (Illus.). (Famous Books for Boys Ser.: No. 25). 1905. Set. H M Caldwell Co.
--Reuben Green's Adventures at Yale. Otis, James, pseud. LC 2-18789. 1 p. l., ii, 7-255 p. 19 cm. 1902. Street & Smith.
--The Roaring Lions: Or, The Famous Club of Ashbury. Otis, James, pseud. LC 13-20582. 3 p. l., 178, 1 p. front. 18 cm. 1913. Harper & Brothers.
--Roy Barton's Adventures. Otis, James, pseud. (Illus.). (James Otis Series.). 1915. A L Burt & Co.
--A Runaway Brig. Otis, James, pseud. (Illus.). (James Otis Series.). 1915. A L Burt & Co.
--A Runaway Brig. Otis, James, pseud. (Illus.). (The Boys' Home Ser.). N.D. A. L. Burt.
--A Runaway Brig. Otis, James, pseud. (Illus.). (The Alger Series for Boys). N.D. A. L. Burt's Pubs.
--A Runaway Brig. Otis, James, pseud, 1 of 3 vols. (The Castaway Ser.). N.D. Set. A. L. Burt's Pubs.
--A Runaway Brig: Or, An Accidental Cruise. Otis, James, pseud. LC 12-34826. 288 p. incl. front., illus. 20 cm. (On cover: Boy's home library. v. 1, no. 16). c.1888. A. L. Burt.
--Sarah Dillard's Ride. Otis, James, pseud. (Illus.). vi p. 1 l., 267p. pl. 12cm. (The Young Patriot Ser.). 1899. A. L. Burt's Pubs.
--Sarah Dillard's Ride: A Story of the Carolinas in 1780. Otis, James, pseud. Davis, J. Watson, illus. LC 98-81. 4 p. l., 222 p. front., 5 pl. 19 cm. (Lettered on cover: Young patriot series). 1898. A. L. Burt.
--The Sarah Jane, Dicky Dalton, Captain: A Story of Tugboating in Portland Harbor. Otis, James, pseud. Kennedy, J. W. Ferguson, illus. LC 9-20281. 338 p. incl. front. 7 pl. 22 cm. (business venture series). c.1909. D. Estes & Company.
--The Sarah Jane: Dicky Dalton, Captain (A Story of Tugboating in Portland Harbour). Otis, James, pseud. Kennedy, J. W. Ferguson, illus. (The American Boy's Library). N.D. L. C. Page & Co.
--Search for the Silver City. Otis, James, pseud. (Illus.). (James Otis Series.). 1915. A L Burt & Co.
--The Search for the Silver City. Otis, James, pseud. (Illus.). (The Alger Series for Boys). N.D. A. L. Burt's Pubs.
--Search for the Silver City. Otis, James, pseud, 1 of 3 vols. (The Treasure-Finders Ser.). N.D. Set. A. L. Burt's Pubs.
--The Search for the Silver City. A Tale of Adventure in Yucatan. Otis, James, pseud. LC 12-34825. xi, 323 p. incl. front., 1 illus. 19 cm. c.1893. A. L. Burt.
--The Secret Chart. Otis, James, pseud. (The Boys Own Library). N.D. David McKay.
--A Short Cruise. Otis, James, pseud. LC 12-34824. 101 p. incl. front. 20 cm. c.1896. T. Y. Crowell & Company.
--A Short Cruise. Otis, James, pseud. (Illus.). (Sunshine Library for Young). N.D. T. Y. Crowell & Co.
--Short Cruise. Otis, James, pseud. (Illus.). (Sunshine Library). 1915. Thomas Y Crowell.
--The Signal Boys of '75: A Tale of the Siege of Boston. Otis, James, pseud. LC 12-34823. 99 p. incl. front., illus., plates. 20 cm. (On cover: Stories of American history by James Otis). 1897. Estes and Lauriat.
--Silent Pete: Or, the Stowaways. Otis, James, pseud. LC 12-34817. 17cm. 192p. 1886. Harper & Brothers.
--A Son of the Revolution. Otis, James, pseud. 301p. N.D. W. A. Wilde Co.
--The Spies With the Regulators: The Story of How the Boys Assisted the Carolina Patriots to Drive the British from that State. Otis, James, pseud. (The Boy Spies Ser.). N.D. A. L. Burt.
--Stephen of Philadelphia. Otis, James, pseud. LC 10-13919. (Illus.). 19cm. 166p. 1910. American Book Co.
--The Stockton Boys' Adventures. Otis, James, pseud. (The Rugby Series for Boys and Girls). N.D. A. L. Burt Company.
--A Struggle for Freedom. Otis, James, pseud. Davis, J. Watson, illus. LC 9-18369. 20cm. 370p. 1909. A. L. Burt Co.
--Teddy and Carrots: Or, Two Merchants of Newspaper Row. Otis, James, pseud. Rogers, W. A., illus. (No. 4). N.D. Dana Estes and Company.
--Teddy and Carrots: Two Merchants of Newspaper Row. Otis, Jamse, pseud. (Stories of Newsboy Life). N.D. L. C. Page.
--Teddy and Carrots: Two Merchants of Newspaper Now. Otis, James, pseud. Rogers, W. A., illus. LC 12-34818. vi p., 2 l., 22-225 p. incl. front., illus., plates. 21 cm. c.1896. Estes and Lauriat.
--Telegraph Tom's Venture. Otis, James, pseud. (Illus.). N.D. Caldwell.
--Tim And Tip. Otis, James, pseud. (Illus.). (Harper's Young People Ser.). N.D. Harper & Brothers.
--Tim and Tip: Or, The Adventures of a Boy and a Dog. Otis, James, pseud. Rogers, W. A., illus. LC 12-34819. 179 p. incl. front., plates. 17 cm. 1883. Harper & Brothers.
--Toby Tyler. Otis, James, pseud. 152p. Repr. 1981. (ISBN 0-89966-363-X). Buccaneer Bks.
--Toby Tyler. Otis, James, pseud. (Illus.). (gr. 4-6). N.D. (ISBN 0-448-05483-3). G&D.
--Toby Tyler. Otis, James, pseud. 188p. Repr. 1981. (ISBN 0-89967-037-7). Harmony & Co.
--Toby Tyler. Otis, James, pseud. (The Winston Clear-Type Popular Classics). N.D. John C. Winston.
--Toby Tyler. Otis, James, pseud. (Companion Library Ser.). (gr. 4-8). N.D. (ISBN 0-448-05483-3, G&D). Putnam Pub Group.
--Toby Tyler. Otis, James, pseud. abr. ed. (gr. 4-6). 1972. (ISBN 0-590-02061-7, Schol Trade Pap). Schol Bk Serv.
--Toby Tyler. Otis, James, pseud. (Classic Ser.). N.D. World Publishing Co.
--Toby Tyler. Otis, James, pseud. Glanzman, Louis S. (1922-), illus. (Illus.). (Rainbow Classic). (gr. 4-6). 1947. World Pub.
--Toby Tyler. Otis, James, pseud. Rodgers, Richard H. (1876-1953), illus. (Harper Junior Classics). N.D. Harper & Bros.
--Toby Tyler. Otis, James, pseud. Shinn, Everett (1876-1953), illus. Shinn, Everett (1876-1953), intro. by. (The Children's Bookshelf). N.D. John C. Winston.
--Toby Tyler: Or, Ten Weeks with a Circus. Otis, James, pseud. 1923. Buccaneer.
--Toby Tyler: Or, Ten Weeks With a Circus. Otis. James, pseud. (Illus.). (Harper's Young People Ser.). N.D. Harper & Brothers.
--Toby Tyler: Or, Ten Weeks with a Circus. Otis, James, pseud. LC 75-32185. Repr. of 1881 ed. (Classics of Children's Literature, 1621-1932: Vol. 48). 1977. (ISBN 0-8240-2297-1). Garland Pub.
--Toby Tyler: Or, Ten Weeks With a Circus. Otis, James, pseud. Becker, May Lamberton (1873-1958), intro. by. Glanzman, Louis S. (1922-), illus. LC 47-11722. (Illus.). 239p. 22cm. (Rainbow Classics). 1947. World Pub.
--Toby Tyler: Or, Ten Weeks with a Circus. Otis, James, pseud. Rodgers, Richard H. (1876-1953), illus. LC 30-253825. xvii p., 1 l., 251, 1 p. col. front., illus., col. plates. 24 cm. c.1930. Harper & Brothers.
--Toby Tyler: Or, Ten Weeks with a Circus. Otis, James, pseud. Rogers, W. A., illus. LC 4-16144. 265 p. incl. plates. front. 17 x 14 cm. 1881. Harper & Brothers.
--Toby Tyler: Or, Ten Weeks with a Circus. Otis, James, pseud. Rogers, W. A., illus. LC 6-34051. 265 p. incl. front., illus. 18 cm. 1902. Harper & Brothers.
--Toby Tyler: Or Ten Weeks with a Circus. Otis, James, pseud. Rogers, W. A., illus. LC 20-194387. xxi, 1 p. 1 l., 251, 1 p. front., plates. 20 cm. c.1920. Harper & Brothers.
--Toby Tyler: Or, Ten Weeks with a Circus. Otis, James, pseud. Shinn, Everett (1876-1953), illus. LC 37-21142. xi, 212 p. col. front., illus., col. plates. 22 cm. c.1937. The John C. Winston Company.
--Toby Tyler: Or, Ten Weeks with a Circus. Otis, James, pseud. Weisgard, Leonard Joseph (1916-), illus. LC 58-1093. 223p. illus. 22cm. 1958. Junior Deluxe Editions.
--Toby Tyler: Or, Ten Weeks with a Circus. Otis, James, pseud. Wilson, George, illus. LC 67-24233. (Illus.). 183 p. 20cm. (Companion library). 1967. Grosset & Dunlap.
--Toby Tyler: Or, Ten Weeks With the a Circus. Otis, James, pseud. LC 9-9471. 265p. 18cm. (Harper Young People Ser.). 1909. Harper & Bros.
--Tom Dexter Goes to School. Otis, James, pseud. (The Vacation Ser.). N.D. Penn.
--Tom Dexter Goes to School. Otis, James, pseud. (Adventure Stories for Boys). N.D. Penn.
--Tom Dexter Goes to School. Otis, James, pseud. (The Outdoor Bks.). N.D. Penn Publishing Co.
--Tom Dexter Goes to School. Otis, James, pseud. (Illus.). (The Little People's Ser.). N.D. Penn Publishing Co.
--Tom Haven with the White Squadron. Otis, James, pseud. (The Boys Own Library). N.D. David McKay.
--A Tory Plot. Otis, James, pseud. (Illus.). (The Young Patriot Ser.). N.D. A. L. Burt's Pubs.
--A Tory Plot: A Story of the Attempt to Kill General Washington in 1776. Otis, James, pseud. Davis, J. Watson, illus. LC 99-4243. vi p., 1 l., 265 p. front., plates. 19 cm. (Young patriot series). c.1899. A. L. Burt.
--Traitor's Escape. Otis, James, pseud. (Illus.). (The Young Patriot Ser.). N.D. A. L. Burt's Pubs.
--A Traitor's Escape. Otis, James, pseud. White, George G., illus. 277p. (Young Patriot Ser.). 1899. A. L. Burt Co.
--A Traitor's Escape. A Story of the Attempt to Seize Benedict Arnold After He Had Fled to New York. Otis, James, pseud. LC 13-33878. 1 p. l., 234 p. front., plates, port. 19 cm. (On cover: Young patriot series). 1898. A. L. Burt.
--Trapping in the Tropics. Otis, James, pseud. (Illus.). (James Otis Series.). 1915. A L Burt & Co.
--Trapping in the Tropics. Otis, James, pseud. (The Rugby Series for Boys and Girls). N.D. A. L. Burt Company.
--The Treasure-Finder Series. Otis, James, pseud, 3 vols. N.D. Set. A. L. Burt's Pubs.
--The Treasure Finders. Otis, James, pseud. (Illus.). (James Otis Series.). 1915. A L Burt & Co.
--The Treasure Finders. Otis, James, pseud. (The Rugby Seris for Boys and Girls). N.D. A. L. Burt Company.
--Treasure of Cocos Island. Otis, James, pseud. (The Rugby Series for Boys and Girls). N.D. A. L. Burt Company.
--The Treasure of Cocos Island. Otis, James, pseud. Davis, J. Watson, illus. LC 2-18742. 20cm. 352p. 1902. A. L. Burt Co.
--Treasure of Cross Island. Otis, James, pseud. (Illus.). (James Otis Series.). 1915. A L Burt & Co.
--Two Stowaways. Otis, James, pseud. (Illus.). (Crowell's Young People Ser.). N.D. Thomas Y. Crowell.
--Two Stowaways Aboard the Ellen Maria. Otis, James, pseud. LC 8-23097. 3 p. l., 232 p. front., 3 pl. 19 cm. c.1908. T. Y., Crowell & Co.
--Under the Liberty Tree: A Story of the "Boston Massacre". Otis, James, pseud. LC 12-34820. 115 p. incl. illus., plates. front. 20 cm. (On cover: Stories of American history in James Otis). 1896. Estes and Laurial.
--Under the Liberty Tree: A Story of the Boston Massacre. Otis, James, pseud. Bridgman, Lewis Jesse (1857-1931), illus. (Illus.). (The Stories of American History Ser.). N.D. Dana Estes & Co.
--Unprovoked Mutiny. Otis, James, pseud. (The Boys Own Library). N.D. David McKay.
--An Unprovoked Mutiny. Otis, James, pseud, 39 vols. (Illus.). (Famous Books for Boys Ser.: No. 22). 1905. Set. H M Caldwell Co.
--Wan Lun and Dandy. Otis, James, pseud. Davis, J. Watson, illus. LC 2-18742. 20cm. 252p. 1902. A. L. Burt Co.
--Wan Lun and Dandy: The Story of a Chinese Boy and a Dog. Otis, James, pseud, 36 vols. (Illus.). (St. Nicholas Ser.). 1905. Set. A L Burt Co.
--Wan Lun and Dandy: The Story of a Chinese Boy and a Dog. Otis, James, pseud. (Illus.). (The Wellesley Series for Girls). N.D. A. L. Burt.

Kaplan, Boche, jt. auth. see Roche, A. K.
Kaplan, Boche (1926-)
--The Clever Turtle. Roche, A. K., pseud., adapted by Abisch, Roslyn Kroop. Roche, A. K., pseud. & Kaplan, Boche, illus. Abisch, Roslyn Kroop. LC 69-14809. (A.K. Roche is joint pseudonym for Roslyn Kroop Abisch and Boche Kaplan). (Illus.). 32 p. 1969. Prentice-Hall.
--The Onion Maidens. Roche, A. K, pseud., adapted by Abisch, Roslyn Kroop. Roche, A. K., pseud. & Kaplan, Boche, illus. Abisch, Roslyn Kroop. LC 68-19036. (A.K. Roche is joint pseudonym for Roslyn Kroop Abisch and Boche Kaplan). (Illus.). 32 p. 1968. Prentice-Hall.
--The Pumpkin Heads. Roche, A. K, pseud., adapted by Abisch, Roslyn Kroop. Roche, A. K., pseud. & Kaplan, Boche (1926-), illus. Abisch, Roslyn Kroop. LC 68-13005. (A.K. Roche is joint pseudonym for Roslyn Kroop Abisch and Boche Kaplan, 1926-). (Illus.). 32 p. 1968. Prentice-Hall.

Kaplan, Howard S.
--The Dragon from the Bronx. Kaplan, Howard S., illus. LC 68-15059. (Illus.). 72 p. 1968. Putnam.

Kaplan, Irma, retold by see Hylten-Cavallius, Gunnar Olof.

Kaplan, Irma (1900-), retold by.
--Fairy Tales from Sweden. 1955. Dufour.
--Fairy Tales from Sweden. Calder, Carol, illus. (Illus.). (gr. 5 up). 1967. (ISBN 0-695-42450-5). Follett.
Kaplan, Jean Caryl Korn see Caryl, Jean, pseud.
Kaplan, Sidney E., tr. see Schiller, Johann Christoph Friedrich Von.
Kaplow, Robert
--Alex Icicle: A Romance in Ten Torrid Chapters. LC 84-10740. 192p. (gr. 5-9). 1984. (ISBN 0-395-36230-X). (ISBN 0-395-36230-X). HM.
--Two in the City. LC 78-31649. 146 p. 22cm. 1979. (ISBN 0-395-27813-9). Houghton Mifflin.
Kapp, Paul
--A Cat Came Fiddling. N.D. E. M. Hale & Co.
--A Cat Came Fiddling & Other Rhymes of Childhood. Haas, Irene (1929-), illus. (Illus.). (gr. k-3). 1956. (ISBN 0-15-215178-8). (ISBN 0-15-215179-6). HarBraceJ.
--Cock-A-Doodle Doo, Cock-A-Doodle Dandy. Lobel, Anita Kempler (1934-), illus. LC 65-22243. (Illus.). (gr. k-3). 1965. (ISBN 0-06-022388-X, HarpJ). Har-Row.
--Cock-a-Doodle-Doo, Cock-a-Doodle-Dandy. Lobel, Anita Kempler (1934-), illus. LC 65-22243. vii, 70p. illus. 29cm. c.1966. Harper.
Kappel, H., jt. auth. see Heyneman, Anne.
Kapral, Joan
--Little Lost Bee. Mlodock, Richard, illus. LC 72-1466. (Illus.). 28 p. 25cm. 1972. (ISBN 0-516-03536-3). Childrens Press.
Karaliichev, Angel (1902-)
--The World of Tales. Alexiera, Marguerite, ed. Gonalov, Ivan, illus. Dimitrova, Lyumila, et al., trs. from Bulgarian LC 66-2238. 298p. col. illus. 20cm. 1965. Foreign Langs. Pr.
Karasz, Ilonka (1896-1981)
--Christmas Calendar: The Days Before Christmas. LC 51-13254. unpaged. illus. 37 cm. 1951. Harper.
--Twelve Days of Christmas. Karasz, Ilonka (1896-1981), illus. LC 49-11875. (Illus.). (gr. 3-6). 1949. (ISBN 0-06-023090-8, HarpJ). (ISBN 0-06-023091-6). Har-Row.
Karayev, V.
--A White Sail Gleams. 79p. 1973. (ISBN 0-8285-1267-1, Pub. by Progress Pubs USSR). Imported Pubns.
Karazin, Nikolai Nikolnevich (1842-1908)
--Cranes Flying South. Bock, Vera, illus. Pokrovskaia, Magdalina, tr. LC 31-26864. 5 p. l., 235 p. incl. illus., plates. 21 cm. 1931. Junior Literary Guild.
Karff, Joan M
--The Adventures of Adam. Yale, Patti, illus. LC 68-26395. (Illus.). 55 p. 24cm. 1970. Whitehall Co.
Karig, Captain Walter
--Hungry Crawford, Legionnaire. Karig, Captain Walter, illus. LC 29-20975. xi p., 1 l., 15-320 p. incl. front., pl. 19 1/2cm. 1929. I. Washburn.
Karim, M.
--Golden Eagle Village. 127p. 1975. (ISBN 0-8285-1154-3, Pub. by Progress Pubs USSR). Imported Pubns.

Kark, Nina Mary Mabey see Bawden, Nina, pseud.

Karl, Jean Edna (1927-)
--Beloved Benjamin Is Waiting. LC 77-25286. 150 p. 22cm. c.1978. (ISBN 0-525-26372-1). Dutton.
--But We Are Not of Earth. LC 80-21849. 170 p. 22cm. c.1981. (ISBN 0-525-27342-5). Dutton.
--The Turning Place: Stories of a Future Past. LC 75-33669. 213 p. 22cm. c.1976. (ISBN 0-525-41573-4). Dutton. **Award: (ALA).**
Karl, Terry (1947-) & Dolgin, Gail
--Children of the Dragon: A Story of the People of Viet Nam. Reimer, Nina, illus. LC 74-11455. (Illus.). 48 p. 26cm. 1974. (ISBN 0-914750-00-3). Peoples Press.
Karlin, Nurit
--The Blue Frog. LC 82-18355. p. cm. 1983. (ISBN 0-698-20577-4). Coward, McCann.
--The Tooth Witch. Karlin, Nurit, illus. LC 84-48495. (Illus.). 32p. (ps-2). 1985. (ISBN 0-397-32119-8). (ISBN 0-397-32120-1). Lipp Jr Bks.
--A Train for the King. LC 82-18356. p. cm. 1983, c.1982. (ISBN 0-698-20578-2). Coward, McCann.
--Witch Switch. LC 84-48495. p. cm. c.1985. (ISBN 0-397-32119-8). (ISBN 0-397-32120-1). Lippincott.
Karlin, Nurit, jt. auth. see Cleveland, David.
Karlovich, Helen, jt. auth. see Delach, Mary K.
Karman, Janice, jt. auth. see Bagdasarian, Ross.
Karman, Janice & Bagdasarian, Ross
--Alvin Goes Wild. Cole, Corny, illus. LC 83-62052. (Illus.). 32p. (Chipmunks Mini-Storybooks Ser.). (gr. 1-5). 1984. (ISBN 0-394-86384-4, BYR). Random.
--The Chipmunk Story. Barto, Renzo, illus. LC 83-60760. (Illus.). 32p. (Chipmunks Mini-Storybks.). (ps-4). 1983. (ISBN 0-394-86188-4). Random.
--The Chipmunks' Cruise. Fanelli, Jenny, ed. LC 83-62052. (Illus.). 32p. (Chipmunks Mini-Storybooks). (gr. 1-5). 1984. (ISBN 0-394-86384-4, BYR). Random.
--A Mother for the Chipmunks. Stine, Megan & Stine, H. William, eds. Cole, Neil & Cole, Corny, illus. LC 84-18051. p. cm. c.1985. (ISBN 0-394-87150-2). Random House.
--The TV Chipmunks. Wildman, George, illus. LC 83-60759. (Illus.). 32p. (Chipmunks Mini-Story-Bks.). (ps-4). 1983. (ISBN 0-394-86189-2). Random.
Karman, Janice & Leigh, Amy
--The Chipmunks in Alvin's Big Ideas: A Treasury of Chipmunk Stories. Williams, A. O., illus. LC 84-18122. p. cm. 1985. (ISBN 0-394-87203-7). Random House.
Karmiller, Murry
--All Kinds of Kings in Fact and Legend, from Hammurabi to Louis XIV. 1st ed. Johnston, Johanna (1914-1982), illus. LC 73-89826. (Illus.). 197 p. 26cm. 1970. Norton.
Karney, Beulah Mullen
--Keepers of the Bell. LC 61-8280. 190p. 21cm. 1961. John Day Co.
--The Listening One. LC 62-14899. 191p. (The Daughters of Valor Bks.). 1962. John Day & Co.
--Wild Imp. LC 60-8728. 191p. 21cm. 1960. J. Day Co.
Karnovsky, B. N. S.
--Romper Room Bedtime Story Book. Williams, A. O., illus. LC 82-46039. (Illus.). 32p. (ps-k). 1984. (ISBN 0-385-18310-0). (ISBN 0-385-18310-0). Doubleday.
Karolyi, Erna M
--A Summer to Remember. Karolyi, Erna M., illus. LC 49-76937. 128 p. illus. 21 cm. 1949. Whittlesey House.
Karp, Laura
--Opposites. LC 77-155078. (Illus.). 18 p. 1971. World Pub. Co.
Karp, Naomi J (1926-)
--Nothing Rhymes with April. 1st ed. Johnson, Pamela, illus. LC 73-17938. (Illus.). 125 p. 21cm. 1974. (ISBN 0-15-257579-0). Harcourt Brace Jovanovich.
--The Turning Point. LC 76-12987. 154 p. 21cm. c.1976. (ISBN 0-15-291238-X). Harcourt Brace Jovanovich.
Karpeles, M., ed.
--Folk Songs of Europe. 1957. Dufour.
Karrik, Valerian Vil'iamovich (1869-1942)
--Animal Picture Tales from Russia. Karrik, Valerian Vil'iamovich (1869-1942), illus. LC 30-27813. 4 p. l., 3-00 p. illus. 26 cm. 1930. Frederick A. Stokes Company.
--More Russian Picture Tales. Karrik, Valerian Vil'iamovich (1869-1942), illus. Forbes, Nevill (1883-1929), tr. LC 76-114246. (Illus.). 116 p. 1970. (ISBN 0-486-22599-2). Dover Publications.
--More Russian Picture Tales. Karrik, Valerian Vil'iamovich (1869-1942), illus. Forbes, Nevill (1883-1929), tr. LC 21-653. 3 p. l., 116 p. illus. 14 x 19 cm. c.1920. Frederick A. Stokes Company.
--Picture Tales from the Russian. new ed. Karrik, Valerian Vil'iamovich (1869-1942), illus. LC 67-7973. 77 p. illus. (part col.) 21 cm. 1964. B. Blackwell.
--Picture Tales from the Russian. Karrik, Valerian Vil'iamovich (1869-1942), illus. LC 64-21414. 77p. illus. 21cm. 1966. Dufour.
--Picture Tales from the Russian. Karrik, Valerian Vil'iamovich (1869-1942), illus. Forbes, Nevill (1883-1929), tr. 2 p. l., 119 p. illus. 14 x 19 cm. 1920. F. A. Stokes Co.
--Still More Russian Picture Tales. N.D. J. B. Lippincott.
--Still More Russian Picture Tales. Karrik, Valerian Vil'iamovich (1869-1942), illus. Forbes, Nevill (1883-1929), tr. LC 70-114247. (Illus.). 119 p. Repr. of 1915 ed. 1970. (ISBN 0-486-22601-8). Dover Publications.
--Still More Russian Picture Tales. Karrik, Valerian Vil'iamovich (1869-1942), illus. Forbes, Nevill (1883-1929), tr. LC 22-11383. 3 p. l., 119 p. illus. 14 cm. c.1922. Frederick A. Stokes Company.
--Tales of Wise & Foolish Animals. Karrik, Valerian Vil'iamovich (1869-1942), illus. LC 69-17674. (Illus.). 74 drawings. 97p. (gr. k-4). 1969. Dover.
--Valery Carrick's Picture Folk-Tales. Karrik, Valerian Vil'iamovich (1869-1942), illus. LC 26-27496. 3 p. l., 90 p. illus. 26 cm. 1926. Frederick A. Stokes Company.
--Valery Carrick's Picture Folktales. Karrik, Valerian Vil'iamovich (1869-1942), illus. (Illus.). (gr. 3 up). 1967. (ISBN 0-486-21824-4). Dover.
--Valery Carrick's Tales of Wise and Foolish Animals. Karrik, Valerian Vil'iamovich (1869-1942), illus. LC 69-17674. (Illus.). 96 p. 24cm. 1969. Dover Publications.
--Valery Carrick's Tales of Wise and Foolish Animals. Karrik, Valerian Vil'iamovich (1869-1942), illus. LC 28-204242. 3 p. l., 96, 1 p. illus. 27 cm. 1928. Frederick A. Stokes Company.
Karroff, K. K. de, pseud., see Cummins, Kundry.
Karsavina, Jean Faterson (1908-)
--Reunion in Poland. Ward, Lynd Kendall (1905-1985), illus. LC 45-9834. 126 p., 1 l. illus. 22 cm. (Young world books). 1945. International Publishers.
--Tree by the Waters. LC 48-2897. 189 p. 22 cm. (Young World Books). 1948. International Publishers.
Karsten, Eleanor Daggett
--Saturday Magic. Maloy, Lois (1902-), illus. LC 38-21553. 119 p. col. front., illus. 20 cm. 1938. C. Scribner's Sons.

Karsunke, Yaak (1934-), tr. see Blech, Dietlind.

Kase-Baker, Judith, retold by.
--The Emperor's New Clothes. 1978. (ISBN 0-87602-125-9). Anchorage.
--Snow White & the Seven Dwarfs. 1984. (ISBN 0-87602-256-5). Anchorage.
Kase, Charles Robert, ed.
--Stories for Creative Acting: Stories Recommended and Used Successfully by Leading Creative Dramatics Directors and Teachers. Davenport, Gilbert Boyd, illus. LC 61-65896. 269p. illus. 22cm. 1961. French.
Kaser, Arthur LeRoy (1890-1956)
--The Fall of Humpty Dumpty: A Mother Goose Travesty. LC 74-194707. 21 p. 18cm. (Paine's popular plays). c.1937. Paine Pub. Co.
Kaser, Arthur LeRoy (1890-1956), ed.
--Bedtime Stories for Wide-Awake Children. LC 39-22041. 72 p. incl. col. front. col. illus. 31 cm. c.1939. McLoughlin Brothers, Inc.
--Poems for the Children's Hour. Pointer, Priscilla, illus. LC 39-225831. 1 p. l., vii-viii, 9-61 p. col. front., illus. (part col.) 17 cm. (On cover: The little color classics). c.1939. McLoughlin Brothers, Inc.
--Sunshine Story Book. LC 39-22042. 72 p. incl. col. front., illus. (part col.) 31 cm. c.1939. McLoughlin Brothers, Inc.
Kasius, Cora
--Nancy Clark: Social Worker. LC 49-487721. x 246 p. 21 cm. (Dodd, Mead career books). 1949. Dodd, Mead.
Kasper, Ray C.
--And What Is Woman & Other Poems. rev. ed. Kasper, Betty, illus. LC 81-66794. (Illus.). 64p. (gr. 7 up). 1981. (ISBN 0-939988-00-3). Chameleon.
--Pardon Me, Don't I Know You?. 86p. (Orig.). 1981. (ISBN 0-686-31158-2). Chameleon.
Kasper, Vancy
--Always Ask for a Transfer. Priestley, Glenn, illus. LC 85-27725. p. cm. (Schoolhouse novels). 1986, c.1984. (ISBN 0-8086-0313-2). Schoolhouse Press.
Kasraii, Siavoosh
--After Winter in Our Village. (Illus.). (gr. 7-9). 1968. (ISBN 0-685-82804-2). Intl Bk Ctr.
Kassian, Olena
--Flip the Dolphin Saves the Day. Kassian, Olena, illus. LC 83-83289. (Illus.). 24p. (Look-Look Bks.). (ps-2). 1984. (ISBN 0-307-12476-2, Golden Bks). Western Pub.
--Slip the Otter Finds a Home. Kassian, Olena, illus. LC 83-83286. (Illus.). 24p. (Golden Look-Look Bks). (ps-3). 1984. (ISBN 0-307-12475-4, Golden Bks). Western Pub.
Kassil, Lev Abramovich (1905-)
--The Black Book & Schwambrania. 253p. 1978. (ISBN 0-8285-1109-8, Pub. by Progress Pubs USSR). Imported Pubns.
--Brother of the Hero. LC 68-16107. (Illus.). 118 p. 22cm. (Venture book). 1968. G. Braziller.
--Once in a Lifetime. White, Anne Terry (1896-), tr. LC 76-101712. 192p. (gr. 3-7). 1970. (ISBN 0-385-05605-2). (ISBN 0-385-03178-5). Doubleday.
Kassirer, Norma
--The Doll Snatchers. MacKay, Donald A. (1895-), illus. LC 69-13085. (Illus.). 176 p. 22cm. 1969. Viking Press.
--Magic Elizabeth. Krush, Joe (1918-), illus. LC 66-11910. 173 p. illus. 22 cm. 1966. Viking Press.
Kasson, Gracia & Tschantre, E., Jr.
--Tin Tan Tales. N.D. Dutton.
--Tin Tans at Play. N.D. Dutton.
Kastner, Erich (1899-1974), retold by see Cervantes Saavedra, Miguel de.
Kastner, Erich (1899-1974), retold by see Munchausen.
Kastner, Erich (1899-1974)
--The Animal Conference. Trier, Walter (1890-1951), illus. Schauener, Zita de, tr. LC 53-7550. (Based on an Idea by Jella Lepman). (Illus.). 29cm. 1949. D. McKay.
--The Animal's Conference. Trier, Walter (1890-1951), illus. (gr. 5-9). 1953. David McKay Co.
--Annaluise and Anton: A Story for Children. Trier, Walter (1890-1951), illus. Sutton, Eric, tr. LC 33-12423. xi, 211 p. incl. illus., plates. col. front. 21 cm. 1933. Dodd, Mead & Company.
--Emil and the Detectives: A Story for Children. Trier, Walter (1890-1951), illus. Massee, May, tr. LC 30-24339. xi, 224 p. incl. plates (part col.) col. pl. 21 cm. (gr. 2-6). 1930. Doubleday, Doran & Company, Inc.
--Emil and the Three Twins: Another Book About Emil and the Detectives. Brooks, Cyrus Harry (1890-), tr. from Ger. LC 61-100715. 251p. illus. 21cm. 1961. F. Watts.
--Lisa and Lottie. De Larrea, victoria, illus. Brooks, Cyrus, tr. LC 69-11545. (Illus.). 136 p. 22cm. 1969. Knopf.
--Lisa and Lottie. Trier, Walter (1890-1951), illus. Brooks, Cyrus (1890-), tr. LC 51-11635. vi, 136 p. illus. 21 cm. 1st U.S. edition. 1951. Little, Brown.
--The Little Man. Schreiter, Rick (1936-), illus. Kirkup, James, tr. from Ger. LC 67-2072. 183 p. illus. 24 cm. c.1966. Knopf. **Award: (MLB).**

--Little Man & the Big Thief. Mack, Stanley (1935-), illus. Kirkup, James, tr. LC 77-108452. line drawings. 192p. 24cm. 162p. (gr. 2 up). 1969. (ISBN 0-394-91446-5). Knopf.
--The Thirty-Fifth of May: Or, Conrad's Ride to the South Seas. Trier, Walter (1890-1951), illus. Brooks, Cyrus Harry (1890-), tr. LC 34-1050. 192 p. incl. illus., plates. 21 cm. 1934. Dodd, Mead & Company.
--The Thirty-Fifth of May: Or, Conrad's Ride to the South Seas. Trier, Walter (1890-1951), illus. LC 61-10072. 192p. illus. 21cm. 1961. Watts.
Kastner, Erich (1899-1974), retold by.
--Puss in Boots. Trier, Walter (1890-1951), illus. Winston, Richard (1917-1979) & Winston, Clara, trs. LC 57-11504. 66p. illus. 27cm. (Harlequin books). 1957. J. Messner.
--Till Eulenspiegel, the Clown. Trier, Walter (1890-1951), illus. Winston, Clare & Winston, Richard (1917-1979), trs. LC 57-11505. 70p. illus. 27cm. (Harlequin books). 1957. Messner.
Kastner, John (1948-)
--Superman and the Dinosaurs. Kaster, John (1948-), illus. LC 80-18180. p. cm. c.1980. (ISBN 0-201-03901-X). Addison-Wesley.
Kasuya, Masahiro (1937-)
--The Beginning of the World. LC 81-3582. p. cm. 1982, c.1981. (ISBN 0-687-02765-9). Abingdon.
--The Tiniest Christmas Star. Schell, Mildred, adapted by. LC 79-116818. 24. 1979. (ISBN 0-8170-0822-5). Judson.
--The Way Christmas Came. Schell, Mildred, ed. Funakoshi, Chieko, tr. N.D. (ISBN 0-8170-0593-5). Judson Press.
Katchen, Carole (1944-)
--I Was a Lonely Teen-Ager. (Illus.). (gr. 7-12). 1972 (Starline). Schol Bk Serv.
Kates, H. E. & Jaros, R.
--Once Upon an Egg. (gr. 4-7). N.D. Carlton.
Katibah, Habeeb Ibrahim
--Other Arabian Nights. Berger, William Merritt (1872-), illus. LC 28-22607. xvii p., 3-266 p. col. plates. 21 cm. 1928. C. Scribner's Sons.
Kato, N
--Children's Stories from Japanese Fairy Tales and Legends. Vredenburg, Deric Walcott (1860-), ed. Theaker, Harry G., illus. LC 26-16425. 134 p. col. front., illus., col. plates. 25 cm. (The Raphael house library of gift books). N.D. R. Tuck & Sons, Ltd.

--A House Full of Echoes. LC 81-4094. 168 p. 24cm. 1981. (ISBN 0-517-54422-9). Crown Publishers.
--In Face of Danger. LC 77-21949. 219 p. 24cm. 1977, c.1976. (ISBN 0-517-53119-4). Crown Publishers.
--In Place of Katia. REv ed. Domanska, Janina, illus. LC 62-18282. 224 p. illus. 21 cm. 1963. Scribner.
--Masha. LC 68-27705. (Illus.). 280 p. 22cm. 1968. Lothrop, Lee & Shepard Co.
--One Small Clue. LC 82-5057. vi, 121 p. 24cm. c.1982. (ISBN 0-517-54615-9). Crown.
--The Youngest Lady in Waiting. LC 70-155009. 279 p. 21cm. 1971. John Day Co.

Kay, Ormonde De see De Kay, Ormonde, Jr.

Kay, Phyllis Charline Bockhold & Kay, Kenneth (1915-)
--The Magic Dolls. 1st ed. Kay, Elizabeth, illus. LC 76-42916. (Illus.). 170 p. 22cm. c.1976. (ISBN 0-912760-27-3). Valkyrie Press.

Kay, Ross
--Air Scout: An American Boy's Adventures When the Big War in Europe Began. Wrenn, Thomas N., illus. LC 14-19691. 252 p. front., plates. 21 cm. (His The big war series). c.1914. Barse & Hopkins.
--Battling on the Somme. Wrenn, Charles L., illus. LC 17-25748. 252 p. incl. front. plates. 20 cm. (His The big war series). c.1917. Barse & Hopkins.
--Dodging the North Sea Mines: The Adventures of an American Boy. Angell, Clare, illus. LC 15-7588. 249 p. front., plates. 21 cm. (His The big war series). c.1915. Barse & Hopkins.
--Fighting in France. Wrenn, Charles L., illus. LC 16-14722. 4 p. l., 11-243 p. front., plates. 21 cm. (His The big war series). c.1916. Barse & Hopkins.
--The Go Ahead Boys and Simon's Mine. (The Go Ahead Boys). N.D. Barse & Hopkins.
--The Go Ahead Boys and the Mysterious Old House. (The Go Ahead Boys). N.D. Barse & Hopkins.
--The Go Ahead Boys and the Racing Motor Boat. (The Go Ahead Boys). N.D. Barse & Hopkins.
--The Go Ahead Boys and the Treasure Cave. (The Go Ahead Boys). N.D. Barse & Hopkins.
--The Go Ahead Boys in the Island Camp. (The Go Ahead Boys). N.D. Barse & Hopkins.
--The Go Ahead Boys on Smugglers' Island. (The Go Ahead Boys). N.D. Barse & Hopkins.
--The Search for the Spy: The Adventures of an American Boy at the Outbreak of the War. Angell, Clare, illus. LC 14-19692. 253 p. front., plates. 21 cm. (His The big war series). c.1914. Barse & Hopkins.
--With Joffre on the Battle Line: The Adventures of an American Boy in the Trenches. Angell, Clare, illus. LC 15-7587. 249 p. incl. front. plates. 21 cm. (His The big war series). c.1915. Barse & Hopkins.
--With Pershing at the Front: America's Soldiers in the Trenches. Wrenn, Charles L., illus. LC 18-20099. 246 p. front., plates. 20 cm. (His The big war series). c.1918. Barse & Hopkins.

Kaye, Danny (1913-), ed.
--Around the World Story Book. LC 60-15897. 216p. col. illus. 29cm. c.1960. Random House.
--Danny Kaye's Stories from Many Lands. LC 60-16510. 33p. illus. 29cm. c.1960. Random House.
--Stories from Faraway Places. LC 60-10024. 33p. col. illus. 29cm. c.1960. Random House.

Kaye, Geraldine Hughesdon (1925-)
--Children of the Turnpike. Floyd, Gareth (1940-), illus. LC 77-364202. 152 p. 22cm. 1976. (ISBN 0-340-19544-4). Hodder and Stoughton.
--The Day After Yesterday. Ambrus, Glenys, illus. LC 80-70378. (Illus.). 93 p. 21cm. 1981. (ISBN 0-233-97344-3). A. Deutsch.
--Good-Bye, Ruby Red. Lawrie, Robin, illus. LC 75-40400. (Illus.). 24 p. 21cm. (Stepping stones). 1976, c.1974. (ISBN 0-516-03580-0). Childrens Press.
--Great Day in Ghana: Kwasi Goes to Town. Herbst, Valerie, illus. (Illus.). 32 p. 23cm. 1962. Abelard-Schuman.
--Joanna All Alone. Dinsdale, Mary (1920-), illus. LC 75-19065. 22cm. 127p. 1975. (ISBN 0-8407-6474-X). T. Nelson.
--Koto and the Lagoon. Stubbs, Joanna, illus. LC 71-80703. (Illus.). 128 p. 22cm. 1969, c.1967. Funk & Wagnalls.
--A Nail, a Stick, and a Lid. american ed. Birch, Linda, illus. LC 75-40345. (Illus.). 24 p. 21cm. (Stepping stones). 1976, c.1975. (ISBN 0-516-03587-8). Childrens Press.
--The Rotten Old Car. Wood, Leslie (1920-), illus. LC 75-42106. (Illus.). 24 p. 21cm. (Stepping stones). 1976, c.1973. (ISBN 0-516-03590-8). Childrens Press.
--The Sea Monkey: A Picture Story from Malaysia. Galsworthy, John Gay, illus. LC 68-14680. 32p. col. illus. 26cm. 1968. World Pub.
--The Sea Monkey: A Picture Story from Malaysia. Galsworthy, John Gay, illus. LC 68-14680. (Illus.). color ils. 32p. (Picture Story Book from Around the World Series). (gr. k-3). 1968. World Pub.
--The Tail of the Siamese Cat. Williams, Ferelith Eccles (1920-), illus. LC 67-13920. 55p. col. illus. 18cm. (Salamander bks.). 1967, c.1966. Nelson.
--Tim and the Red Indian Head-Dress. Dinan, Carolyn, illus. LC 75-41377. (Illus.). 24 p. 21cm. (Stepping stones). 1976, c.1973. (ISBN 0-516-03594-0). Childrens Press.
--Where Is Fred?. Cole, Michael, illus. LC 76-51273. (Illus.). 24 p. 21cm. (Stepping stones). 1977, c.1976. (ISBN 0-516-03598-3). Childrens Press.
--The Yellow Pom-Pom Hat. Palmer, Margaret, illus. LC 75-40401. (Illus.). 24 p. 21cm. (Stepping stones). 1976, c.1974. (ISBN 0-516-03595-9). Childrens Press.

Kaye, M., jt. auth. see Davis, S.

Kaye, Marilyn (1949-)
--Will You Cross Me?. Delaney, Ned, pseud. (1951-), illus. Delaney, Thomas Nicholas III. LC 84-47633. (Illus.). 32p. (Early I Can Read Bk.). (gr. k-3). c.1985. (ISBN 0-06-023102-5). (ISBN 0-06-023103-3). HarpJ.

Kaye, Mary Margaret see Hamilton, Mollie, pseud.

Kaye, Mary Margaret (1911-)
--The Ordinary Princess. Kaye, Mary Margaret (1911-), illus. LC 82-46036. (Illus.). 128p. (gr. 4-8). 1984. (ISBN 0-385-17855-7). (ISBN 0-385-17855-7). Doubleday.

Kaye, Sally, ed. see Knudsen, Eric A.

Kaye-Smith, Sheila
--Selina. LC 35-19671. 5 p. l., 304 p. 21 cm. 1935. Harper & Brothers.
--Summer Holiday. LC 32-12204. 5 p. l., 293 p. 20 cm. 1932. Harper & Brothers.

Kayser, Rita
--I'm Glad I'm Not an Alligator. Mahany, Patricia, ed. LC 82-62732. (Illus.). 24p. (Happy Day Bks.). (ps-2). 1983. (ISBN 0-87239-636-3). Standard Pub.

Kazakov, Yuri Pavlovich (1927-)
--Arcturus the Hunting Hound, and Other Stories. Holland, Bradford, illus. White, Anne Terry, tr. from Russian. LC 68-14186. (Illus.). 119 p. 24cm. 1968. Doubleday.

Kazama, Yasuo, jt. auth. see Grove-Merritt, Edgar C.

Keable, R.
--African Scout Stories. N.D. Macmillan.

Keal, William
--Great Spy Stories. (gr. 7 up). N.D. Soccer.

Kean, Edward (1924-)
--Howdy Doody and Clarabell. Seiden, Art, illus. LC 52-6594. unpaged. illus. 21 cm. (Little golden library, 121). 1951. Simon and Schuster.
--Howdy Doody and His Magic Hat. Seiden, Art, illus. LC 54-2153. (Based on the UPA Cartoon). (Illus.). unpaged. 21cm. (A Little Golden Book: No.184). 1954. Simon and Schuster.
--Howdy Doody and Mr. Bluster. Marge, Elias, illus. LC 54-149627. unpaged. illus. 20cm. (Little golden book, 204). 1954. Simon and Schuster.
--Howdy Doody and Santa Claus. Seiden, Art, illus. LC 55-412062. unpaged. illus. 21cm. (Little golden book, 237). 1955. Simon and Schuster.
--Howdy Doody and the Princess. Seiden, Art, illus. LC 52-4278. unpaged. illus. 21 cm. (Little golden library, 135). 1952. Simon and Schuster.
--Howdy Doody in Funland. Seiden, Art, illus. LC 53-435055. unpaged. illus. 21cm. (Little golden book, 172). 1953. Simon and Schuster.
--Howdy Doody in the Wild West. Seiden, Art, illus. LC 52-9899. unpaged. illus. 28 cm. (Big golden book, 475). 1952. Simon and Schuster.
--Howdy Doody's Birthday. Gormley, Dan & Dauber, Liz, illus. (Little Golden Library). 1950. Simon & Schuster.
--Howdy Doody's Circus. Gormley, Dan & Dauber, Liz, illus. LC 50-11852. (Illus.). 21cm. 28p. (Little Golden Book: 99). 1950. Simon and Schuster.
--Howdy Doody's Lucky Trip. McNaught, Harry, illus. LC 53-3481. unpaged. illus. 21cm. (Little golden library, 171). 1953. Simon and Schuster.
--It's Howdy Doody Time. Seiden, Art, illus. LC 55-1612. unpaged. illus. 21cm. (Little golden library, 223). 1955. Simon and Schuster.
--Surprise for Howdy Doody. Featuring the Famous Star of the Television Show, Howdy Doody. Authorized. LC 52-15074. unpaged. illus. 17 cm. (Tell-a-tale books, 882-15). 1951. Whitman Pub. Co.

Kean, Will
--Whosis and Whatsis: A Story About a Little Boy Who Was Very, Very Fond of Strawberry Shortcake. Kean, Will, illus. LC 35-7522. 206 p. illus. 20 cm. c.1935. Dorrance & Co., Inc.

Keane, Bil (1922-)
--Channel Chuckles. Keane, Bil (1922-), illus. (Illus.). (gr. 7-9). 1972 (Starline). Schol Bk Serv.
--The Family Circus Treasury. LC 77-10310. (Illus.). 1977. (ISBN 0-8362-0734-3). (ISBN 0-8362-0735-1). Andrews & McMeel.
--More Channel Chuckles. (Illus.). (gr. 7-9). 1972 (Schol Trade Pap). Schol Bk Serv.
--Sunday with The Family Circus. N.D. (ISBN 0-8170-0364-9). Judson Press.

Keane, Thomas J
--Lubbers Afloat. Rigney, Francis Joseph (1882-), illus. West, James E., frwd. by. LC 32-30787. ix p., 1 l., 242 p. incl. front., illus. 19 cm. 1932. Dodd, Mead & Company.

Kearney, Paul William (1896-)
--Dan, the Young Fireman. LC 31-21895. 5 p. l., 196 p. front., plates. 20 cm. c.1931. J. Cape & H. Smith.

Kearns, Frank
--Rin Tin Tin: One of the Family. Authorized. Armstrong, Samuel, illus. LC 54-154875. unpaged. illus. 22cm. (Cozy-corner book). c.1953. Whitman Pub. Co.

Kearton, Cherry (1871-1940)
--My Animal Friendships: The/Adventures of Timmy the Rat, Chuey the Cheetah, Robin Parker the Mongoose, Mr. Penguin, Jane the Elephant and Mrs. Spider. Kearton, Cherry (1871-1940), photos by. LC 28-29507. 124p. 1928. Arrowsmith.
--My Animal Friendships: The Adventures of Timmy the Rat, Chuey the Cheetah, Robin Parker the Mongoose, Mr. Penguin, Jane the Elephant and Mrs. Spider. Kearton, Cherry (1871-1940), photos by. 1929. Dodd Mead & Co.
--My Dog Simba: The Adventures of a Fox-terrier Who Fought a Lion in Africa. Kearton, Cherry (1871-1940), photos by. LC 27-2887. 127p. 1926. Arrowsmith.
--My Dog Simba: The Adventures of a Fox-Terrier Who Fought a Lion in Africa. Kearton, Cherry (1871-1940), photos by. LC 27-4084. xi p., 1 l., 105 p. front., plates. 19 cm. 1927. Dodd, Mead and Company.
--My Friend Toto. N.D. Dodd Mead & Co.
--My Happy Chimpanzee. N.D. Dodd Mead & Co.

Kearton, Grace, jt. auth. see Kearton, Richard.

Kearton, Richard (1862-1928)
--The Adventures of Cock Robin and His Mate. N.D. Funk & Wagnalls Co.
--The Adventures of Cock Robin and His Mate. Kearton, Cherry (1871-1940) & Kearton, Richard (1862-1928), photos by LC 14-3245. xvi, 240 p. incl. front., illus. 20 cm. 1909. Cassell and Company, Limited.
--The Fairyland of Living Things. Kearton, Cherry (1871-1940), photos by. (Illus.). N.D. Cassell & Co.
--Strange Adventures in Dicky-Bird Land. 207p. N.D. Funk & Wagnalls Co.
--Strange Adventures in Dicky-Bird Land. Kearton, Cherry (1871-1940), illus. Kearton, Cherry (1871-1940), photos by. LC 14-1217. (Illus.). 195p. 1901. Cassell and Company.

Kearton, Richard (1862-1928) & Kearton, Grace
--The Adventures of Jack Rabbit. 256p. N.D. Funk & Wagnalls Co.
--The Adventures of Jack Rabbit. xii, 248 p., col. front., illus., plates. 20 cm. 1911. Cassell and Company, Ltd.

Keary, Annie (1825-1879)
--The Magic Valley: Or, Patient Antoine. (Series of Books for the Young). 1877. MacMillan & Co.
--Sidney Grey: A Tale of School Life. LC 42-18460. viii, 9-358 p. incl. front. plates. 17 cm. N.D. General Protestant Episcopal Sunday School Union and Church Book Society.
--Sidney Grey: A Tale of School Life. N.D. Thomas Whittaker.
--A York and a Lancaster Rose, 1 of 8 vols. (Macmillan's Dollar and a Half Series of Books for the Young). N.D. Macmillan & Co.

Keary, Annie (1825-1879) & Keary, Eliza, eds.
--Heroes of Asgard. (Series of Books for the Young). N.D. MacMillan & Co.
--The Heroes of Asgard: Tales from Scandinavian Mythology, 1 of 8 vols. (Illus.). (Macmillan's Dollar Series of Popular Books for the Young). N.D. Macmillan & Co.
--The Heroes of Asgard: Tales from Scandinavian Mythology. Brock, Charles Edmond (1870-1938) & Brock, C. E., illus. LC 76-9898. (Illus.). 23cm. viii, 222p. (Children's Literature Reprint). 1976. Core Collection Books.
--The Heroes of Asgard: Tales from Scandinavian Mythology. LC 4-31062. xx p., 1 l., 221 p. front. 15 cm. (Macmillan's pocket American and English classics). 1904. The Macmillan Company.
--Little Wanderlin and Other Fairy Tales. (Series of Works for the Young). N.D. Macmillan & Co.

Keary, Eliza, jt. ed. see Keary, Annie.

Keary, Henry, Mrs.
--Bob and Her Winkles. (The Welcome Library). N.D. Frederick Warne & Co.
--Deb. (The Welcome Library). N.D. Frederick Warne & Co.
--Grandfather's Sixpence. (Illus.). 128p. (The Steadfast Ser.). N.D. Fleming H. Revell Co.
--Rod's First Venture. (The Welcome Library). N.D. Frederick Warne & Co.

Keary, Mary
--Hetty: Fresh Watercresses. (Round the Globe Library). N.D. Scribner, Welford & Armstrong.
--Phillis Phil: Or, Alone in the World. (Illus.). N.D. Scribner, Welford & Armstrong.
--Sam: Or, A Good Name. N.D. Scribner, Welford & Armstrong.

Keast, Winifred
--What Happened to Duchess's Pups?. (Illus.). 92p. (Orig.). (gr. 7 up). 1984. (ISBN 0-9613847-0-0). (ISBN 0-9613847-1-9). W Keast.

Keat, O. Eliphaz, tr. see Dumas, Alexandre (1802-1870) & Hoffman, Ernst Theodor Amadeus.

Keating, Joni
--Is There Room for Me?. (gr. 3-8). 1981. (ISBN 0-86653-020-7). Good Apple.

Keating, Lawrence A. see Thomas, Harlan C, pseud.

Keating, Lawrence A (1903-1966)
--Ace Rebounder. LC 64-16348. 192 p. 21 cm. 1964. Westminster Press.
--The Comeback Year. LC 66-16553. 189 p. 21cm. 1966. Westminster Press.
--False Start. LC 55-8201. 192p. 21cm. 1955. Westminster Press.
--Freshman Backstop. LC 57-893953. 182p. 21cm. 1957. Westminster Press.
--The Highview Mystery. LC 44-3474. 222 p. 19 1/2 cm. 1944. J. Messner, Inc.
--Junior Miler. LC 58-7700. 206p. 21cm. 1958. Westminster Press.
--Kid Brother. LC 56-7101. 188p. 21cm. 1956. Westminster Press.
--Red Ryder and the Adventures at Chimney Rock. Thomas, Harlan C., pseud. LC 46-7935. (Based on the Famous Newspaper Strip by Fred Harman). (Illus.). 249p. 20cm. 1946. Whitman Publishing Co.
--Riding the Range. (Western Stories for Boys). N.D. Grosset & Dunlap.
--Runner-up. LC 61-5483. 202 p. 21cm. 1961. Westminster Press.
--Senior Challenge. LC 59-9321. 208p. 21cm. 1959. Westminster Press.
--Wrong Way Neelen. LC 63-7928. 204 p. 21 cm. 1963. Westminister Press.

Keating, Leo Bernard, (1915-)
--The Horse That Won the Civil War. Keating, Bern, pseud. LC 64-10411. 157 p. map. 21 cm. 1964. Putnam.

Keating, Norman Connolly
--Mr. Chu. Bryson, Bernarda (1905-1977), illus. LC 64-11766. 34p. illus. (pt. col.) 20cm. c.1965. (ISBN 0-02-749460-8). Macmillan.

Keatley, John H (1907-)
--Annapolis Plebe. LC 57-11051. 174p. illus. 21cm. c.1957. Duell, Sloan and Pearce.

Keats, Emma, jt. auth. see Sampson, Emma Speed, Mrs.

Keats, Ezra Jack see Hutchins, Pat, et al.

Keats, Ezra Jack (1916-1983)
--Apt. Three. Keats, Ezra Jack (1916-1983), illus. LC 78-123135. (Illus.). 38 p. 1971. Macmillan.
--Apt. Three. Keats, Ezra Jack (1916-1983), illus. (Illus.). 32p. (gr. k-4). 1983. (ISBN 0-02-749510-8). Macmillan.
--Clementina's Cactus. Keats, Ezra Jack (1916-1983), illus. LC 82-2630. (Illus.). 32p. (ps-2). 1982. (ISBN 0-670-22517-7). Viking Pr.
--Dreams. Keats, Ezra Jack (1916-1983), illus. LC 77-16122. (Illus.). 32 p. 26cm. 1978, c.1974. (ISBN 0-02-044060-X). Collier Books.
--Dreams. Keats, Ezra Jack (1916-1983), illus. LC 73-15857. (Illus.). 28 p. 26cm. 1974. (ISBN 0-02-749610-4). Macmillan.
--Goggles. Keats, Ezra Jack (1916-1983), illus. LC 70-78081. (Illus.). 32 p. 1969. Macmillan.
Awards: (ALA); (RCM).
--Hi, Cat!. Keats, Ezra Jack (1916-1983), illus. 1969. Macmillan.
--Hi, Cat!. Keats, Ezra Jack (1916-1983), illus. LC 71-102968. (Illus.). 35 p. 1970. Macmillan.
Award: (BGH).
--Jennie's Hat. Keats, Ezra Jack (1916-1983), illus. LC 66-15683. (Illus.). 1 v. (unpaged. 1966. Harper & Row.
--John Henry: An American Legend. Keats, Ezra Jack (1916-1983), illus. (Illus.). (gr. k-3). 1965. (ISBN 0-394-91302-7). Pantheon.
--Kitten for a Day. LC 81-69518. (Illus.). 32 p. 26cm. 1982, c.1974. (ISBN 0-590-07813-5). Four Winds Press.
--Kitten for a Day. Keats, Ezra Jack (1916-1983), illus. LC 73-23057. (Illus.). 32 p. 26cm. 1974. (ISBN 0-531-02714-7). Watts.

--A Letter to Amy. Keats, Ezra Jack (1916-1983), illus. LC 68-24329. (Illus.). 36 p. 1968. Harper & Row.

--Louie. Keats, Ezra Jack (1916-1983), illus. LC 75-6766. (Illus.). 34 p. 1975. (ISBN 0-688-80002-5). (ISBN 0-688-84002-7). Greenwillow Books.

--Louie. Keats, Ezra Jack (1916-1983), illus. 1983. Greenwillow.

--Louie's Search. Keats, Ezra jack (1916-1983), illus. LC 80-10176. (Illus.). 33 p. c.1980. (ISBN 0-590-07743-0). Four Winds Press.

--Louie's Search. Keats, Ezra Jack (1916-1983), illus. LC 85-16128. p. cm. 1985, c.1980. (ISBN 0-02-749700-3). Four Winds Press.

--Maggie and the Pirate. Keats, Ezra Jack (1916-1983), illus. LC 78-23834. p. cm. [illegible] Press.

--Pet Show!. Keats, Ezra Jack (1916-1983), illus. LC 73-156843. (Illus.). 36 p. 1974, c.1972. Collier Books.

--Pet Show!. Keats, Ezra Jack (1916-1983), illus. LC 78-317338. (Illus.). 36 p. 1972. Macmillan.

--Peter's Chair. Keats, Ezra Jack (1916-1983), illus. LC 67-4816. (Illus.). 1v. unpaged. 21 x 24cm. 1967. Harper & Row.

--Pssst! Doggie. Keats, Ezra Jack (1916-1983), illus. LC 72-8642. (Illus.). 32 p. 27cm. 1973. (ISBN 0-531-02598-5). F. Watts.

--Regards to the Man in the Moon. Keats, Ezra Jack (1916-1983), illus. LC 85-10940. p. cm. 1985, c.1981. (ISBN 0-02-044130-4). Collier Books.

--Regards to the Man in the Moon. Keats, Ezra Jack (1916-1983), illus. LC 84-29464. p. cm. 1985, c.1981. (ISBN 0-02-749340-7). Four Winds Press.

--Skates!. Keats, Ezra Jack (1916-1983), illus. LC 73-6707. (Illus.). 32 p. 27cm. 1973. F. Watts.

--Skates!. Keats, Ezra Jack (1916-1983), illus. LC 80-70119. (Illus.). 32 p. 26cm. 1981, c.1973. (ISBN 0-590-07812-7). Four Winds Press.

--The Snowy Day. Keats, Ezra Jack (1916-1983), illus. LC 76-28805. p. cm. (Puffin books). 1976, c.1962. (ISBN 0-670-65400-0). Penguin Books.

--The Snowy Day. Keats, Ezra Jack (1916-1983), illus. LC 62-15441. (Illus.). 32 p. 1962. Viking Press. **Awards: (RCM); (ALA).**

--The Trip. Keats, Ezra Jack (1916-1983), illus. LC 77-24907. (Illus.). 36 p. 22 x 25cm. c.1978. (ISBN 0-688-80123-4). (ISBN 0-688-84123-6). Greenwillow Books.

--Whistle for Willie. LC 76-50644. p. cm. 1977. (ISBN 0-14-050202-5). Puffin Books.

--Whistle for Willie. Keats, Ezra Jack (1916-1983), illus. LC 64-13595. (Illus.). 33 p. 1964. Viking Press. **Award: (ALA).**

Keats, Ezra Jack (1916-1983) & Cherr, Pat

--My Dog Is Lost. Keats, Ezra Jack (1916-1983), illus. LC 60-11548. (Illus.). 48p. (gr. k-3). 1960. (ISBN 0-690-56691-3). (ISBN 0-690-56692-1). T Y Crowell.

Keats, John (1795-1821)

--The Naughty Boy: A Poem. Keats, Ezra Jack (1916-1983), illus. LC 65-13353. 31p. illus. (pt. col.) 18cm. c.1965. (ISBN 0-670-50516-1). Viking.

Keats, Mark (1905-)

--Sancho & His Stubborn Mule. Eichenberg, Fritz (1901-), illus. LC 44-40117. 41 p. col. illus. 13 1/2 x 17 cm. 1944. W. R. Scott, Inc.

--Sancho, Pronto, and the Engineer: Sancho, Pronto, y el Ingeniero. Cervantes, Alex, illus. Carrera, Paul, tr. LC 76-13008. p. cm. 1976. (ISBN 0-87917-053-0). B. Ethridge-Books.

Kectum, Jean

--Stick-In-The-Mud. N.D. E. M. Hale & Co.

Kedabra, Abby, ed.

--Nine Witch Tales. 112p. (gr. 4-6). 1970. (ISBN 0-590-02553-8, Schol Trade Pap). Schol Bk Serv.

Kedron, Jane, tr. see Seidler, Barbara.

Keech, Emily

--Dandy the Decoy. Campion, Emily, illus. LC 46-20791. (Illus.). 32p. 18 x 25cm. 1946. Rinehart and Company.

Keech, Lilian Sue

--Tommykin's Adventures. Albert, Virginia, illus. LC 23-6271. 110 p., 1 l. col. front., illus., col. plates. 20 cm. c.1923. Dorrance.

Keech, Roy A

--Ruth Visits Margot, a Little French Girl. Carter, Helene (1887-1960), illus. LC 34-37985. 207 p. incl. front. (map) col. illus., col. plates. 24 cm. 1934. A. Whitman & Co.

Keech, Roy A & MacKay, J. S

--Children Sing in New Mexico. Bugbee, H. D., illus. LC 41-233862. 32 p. incl. front., illus. 23 cm. 1941. The Clarendon Press.

Keefe, Betty

--Fingerpuppets, Fingerplays & Holidays. (Illus.). 106p. (ps-3). 1984. (ISBN 0-938594-30-3). Spec Lit Pr.

Keegan, Terry

--The Heavy Horse. N.D. (ISBN 0-498-01472-X). A. S. Barnes Company.

Keel-Williams, Mildred

--Legacies of a Shopping Bag Lady: Poems of Life. Holmes, Darryl, ed. George, Anthony & Washington, Ruby, photos by Harewood, Lasana K., frwd. by. LC 84-62520. (Illus.). 72p. (Orig.). (gr. 5-12). 1984. (ISBN 0-9614084-1-3). Mus Fed Ink.

Keele, Luqman & Pinkwater, Daniel Manus (1941-)

--Java Jack. LC 79-7892. (Illus.). 152 p., 1 leaf of plates. 21cm. c.1980. (ISBN 0-690-03995-6). (ISBN 0-690-03996-4). Crowell.

Keeler, Charles Augustus (1871-)

--Elfin Songs of Sunland. 3rd ed. Keeler, Louise, illus. LC 14-14256. (Illus.). 115p. 23cm. 1914. G. P. Putnam's Sons.

--Elfin Songs of Sunland. 4th ed. Keeler, Louise, [illegible] cm. c.1920. Live Oak Publishing Company.

Keeler, David Burr

--Memoirs of Simple Simon. Vandevort, C. S., illus. LC 1-25746. (Illus.). 56p. 28 x 23cm. 1901. R. H. Russell.

Keeler, Irene

--A Thingumajig Christmas. (Illus.). (gr. k-4). 1982. (ISBN 0-516-09157-3). Childrens.

Keeler, Katherine Southwick (1887-)

--Apple Rush. LC 44-830617. 32 p. col. illus. 26 cm. 1944. T. Nelson and Sons.

--Autumn Comes to Meadow Brook Farm. LC 48-721676. 39 p. illus (part col.) 26 cm. 1948. T. Nelson.

--Bronco Bill's Circus. LC 40-14198. 48 p. illus. 22 x 17 cm. 1940. T. Nelson and Sons.

Children's Zoo. LC 42-3782. 40 p. col. illus. 23 x 19 cm. 1942. T. Nelson and Sons.

Dog Days. LC 44-631125. 39 p. illus. (part col.) 23 x 19 1/2 cm. 1944. T. Nelson and Sons.

--In the Country. LC 53-8848. unpaged. illus. 28cm. 1953. Abelard Press.

--A Party for Hoppy. LC 40-141997. 48 p. illus. 22 x 18 cm. 1940. T. Nelson and Sons.

--Spring Comes to Meadow Brook Farm. LC 46-250344. 39, 1 p. col. illus. 26 cm. 1946. Etc. T. Nelson & Sons.

--Summer Comes to Meadow Brook Farm. LC 47-2896. 38, 2 p. col. illus. 26 x 19 1/2 cm. 1947. T. Nelson & Sons.

--Today with Dede. LC 39-20779. 48 p. illus. 22 cm. 1939. T. Nelson and Sons.

--Today with Tommy. LC 39-211461. 48 p. illus. 22 cm. 1939. T. Nelson and Sons.

--Winter Comes to Meadow Brook Farm. LC 49-100296. 40 p. illus. (part col.)26 cm. 1949. T. Nelson.

Keelor, Katharine Louise (1886-)

--Little Fox: The Story of an Indian Boy. LC 32-10338. 5 p. l., 3-121 p., 1 l. front., illus. 18 cm. (gr. k-3). 1932. (ISBN 0-02-749520-5). The Macmillan Company.

Keely, Harry Harris (1904-) & Price, Christine Hilda (1928-1980), eds.

--The City of the Dagger and Other Tales from Burma. Price, Christine Hilda (1928-1980), illus. LC 70-161066. (Illus.). 208 p. 23cm. 1971. F. Warne.

--The City of the Dagger, and Other Tales from Burma. Price, Christine Hilda (1928-1980), illus. LC 73-175030. (Illus.). 208 p. 23cm. 1972. (ISBN 0-7232-1473-5). F. Warne.

Keenan, Martha (1927-)

--The Mannerly Adventures of Little Mouse. Shardin, Meri, illus. LC 76-41397. (Illus.). 32 p. c.1977. (ISBN 0-517-52615-8). Crown Publishers.

Keene, Carolyn, pseud., see Adams, Harriet Stratemeyer.

Keene, Carolyn, jt. auth. see Dixon, Franklin W.

Keene, Carolyn, pseud. (1894-1982)

--The Bluebeard Room. Adams, Harriet Stratemeyer. Frame, Paul (1913-), illus. LC 85-11441. p. cm. (The Nancy Drew Mystery Stories: Vol. 77). c.1985. Wanderer Books.

--The Broken Anchor. Adams, Harriet Stratemeyer. Frame, Paul (1913-), illus. LC 82-21947. (Illus.). 189 p. 20cm. (The Nancy Drew Mystery Stories: Vol. 70). c.1983. (ISBN 0-671-46462-0). (ISBN 0-671-46461-2). Wanderer Books.

--The Bungalow Mystery. Adams, Harriet Stratemeyer. rev. ed. LC 61-65835. (Illus.). 180p. illus. 20cm. (The Nancy Drew Mystery Stories: Vol. 3). 1960. Grosset & Dunlap.

--The Bungalow Mystery. Adams, Harriet Stratemeyer. Tandy, Russell H., illus. LC 30-12386. iv, 204 p. front., plates. 20 cm. (The Nancy Drew Mystery Stories: Vol. 3). c.1930. Grosset & Dunlap.

--By the Light of the Study Lamp. Adams, Harriet Stratemeyer. Rev 2 ed. Warren, Ferdinand E., illus. LC 34-1234. 2 p. l., iii-iv, 215 p. front., plates. 20 cm. (The Dana Girls Mystery Stories: Vol. 1). c.1934. Grosset & Dunlap.

--Captive Witness. Adams, Harriet Stratemeyer. Frame, Paul (1913-), illus. LC 81-11414. p. cm. (The Nancy Drew Mystery Stories: Vol. 64). c.1981. (ISBN 0-671-42360-6). (ISBN 0-671-42361-4). Wanderer Books.

--The Circle of Footprints. Adams, Harriet Stratemeyer. rev. ed. Warren, Ferdinand E., illus. LC 37-2169. v, 216 p. front. 20 cm. (The Dana Girls Mystery Stories: Vol. 6). c.1937. Grosset & Dunlap.

--Clue in the Ancient Disguise. Adams, Harriet Stratemeyer. Frame, Paul (1913-), illus. LC 82-15966. p. cm. (The Nancy Drew Mystery Stories: Vol. 69). c.1982. (ISBN 0-671-45553-2). (ISBN 0-671-45552-4). Wanderer Books.

--The Clue in the Cobweb. Adams, Harriet Stratemeyer. Warren, Ferdinand E., illus. LC 39-10636. v p., 1 l., 213 p. front. 20 cm. (The Dana Girls Mystery Stories: Vol. 8). c.1939. Grosset & Dunlap.

--The Clue in the Crossword Cipher. Adams, Harriet Stratemeyer. LC 67-3330. (Illus.). 177 p. 20cm. (The Nancy Drew Mystery Stories: Vol. 44). 1967. Grosset & Dunlap.

--The Clue in the Crumbling Wall. Adams, Harriet Stratemeyer. rev. ed. LC 73-2182. (Illus.). 181 p. 20cm. (The Nancy Drew Mystery Stories: Vol. 22). 1973. (ISBN 0-448-09522-X). Grosset & Dunlap.

--The Clue in the Crumbling Wall. Adams, Harriet Stratemeyer. Tandy, Russell H., illus. LC 44-40384. v, 217 p. incl. front. 19 1/2 cm. (The Nancy Drew Mystery Stories: Vol. 22). 1945. Grosset & Dunlap.

--The Clue in the Diary. Adams, Harriet Stratemeyer. rev. ed. LC 62-52095. (Illus.). 174 p. 20cm. (The Nancy Drew Mystery Stories: Vol. 7). 1962. Grosset & Dunlap.

--The Clue in the Diary. Adams, Harriet Stratemeyer. Tandy, Russell H., illus. LC 32-2020. iv, 202 p. front., plates. 20 cm. (The Nancy Drew Mystery Stories: Vol. 7). c.1932. Grosset & Dunlap.

--The Clue in the Ivy. Adams, Harriet Stratemeyer. LC 52-10247. 211 p. illus. 20 cm. (The Dana Girls Mystery Stories: Vol. 14). 1952. Grosset & Dunlap.

--The Clue in the Jewel Box. Adams, Harriet Stratemeyer. rev. ed. LC 72-77109. (Illus.). 181 p. 20cm. (The Nancy Drew Mystery Stories: Vol. 20). 1972, c.1943. (ISBN 0-448-09520-3). Grosset & Dunlap.

--The Clue in the Jewel Box. Adams, Harriet Stratemeyer. Tandy, Russell H., illus. LC 43-1145. vi, p., 1 l., 216 p. incl. front. 19 1/2 cm. (The Nancy Drew Mystery Stories: Vol. 20). 1943. Grosset & Dunlap.

--The Clue in the Old Album. Adams, Harriet Stratemeyer. LC 47-16695. vi, 218 p. incl. front. 19 1/2 cm. (The Nancy Drew Mystery Stories: Vol. 24). 1947. Grosset & Dunlap.

--The Clue in the Old Album. Adams, Harriet Stratemeyer. rev. ed. LC 77-76129. (Illus.). 180 p. 20cm. (The Nancy Drew Mystery Stories: Vol. 24). c.1977. (ISBN 0-448-09524-6). Grosset & Dunlap.

--The Clue in the Old Stagecoach. Adams, Harriet Stratemeyer. LC 60-383. (Illus.). 180 p. 20cm. (The Nancy Drew Mystery Stories: Vol. 37). 1960. Grosset & Dunlap.

--The Clue of the Black Flower. Adams, Harriet Stratemeyer. LC 56-4976. 210p. illus. 20cm. (The Dana Girls Mystery Stories: Vol. 18). 1956. Grosset & Dunlap.

--The Clue of the Black Keys. Adams, Harriet Stratemeyer. (Illus.). (The Nancy Drew Mystery Stories: Vol. 28). 1951. Grosset & Dunlap.

--The Clue of the Black Keys. Adams, Harriet Stratemeyer. rev. ed. (Illus.). 174 p. 20cm. (The Nancy Drew Mystery Stories: Vol. 28). 1968. Grosset & Dunlap.

--The Clue of the Black Keys. Adams, Harriet Stratemeyer. Bolian, Polly (1925-), illus. LC 60-3779. 191p. illus. 22cm. (The Nancy Drew Mystery Stories: Vol. 28). 1960. Grosset & Dunlap.

--The Clue of the Broken Locket. Adams, Harriet Stratemeyer. rev. ed. LC 65-13789. (Illus.). 178 p. 20cm. (The Nancy Drew Mystery Stories: Vol. 11). 1965. Grosset & Dunlap.

--The Clue of the Broken Locket. Adams, Harriet Stratemeyer. Tandy, Russell H., illus. LC 34-23088. iv, 219 p. front., plates. 20 cm. (The Nancy Drew Mystery Stories: Vol. 11). c.1934. Grosset & Dunlap.

--The Clue of the Dancing Puppet. Adams, Harriet Stratemeyer. LC 62-898. (Illus.). 177 p. 20cm. (The Nancy Drew Mystery Stories: Vol. 39). 1962. Grosset & Dunlap.

--The Clue of the Leaning Chimney. Adams, Harriet Stratemeyer. LC 49-118548. viii, 212 p. illus. 20 cm. (The Nancy Drew Mystery Stories: Vol. 26). 1949. Grosset & Dunlap.

--The Clue of the Leaning Chimney. Adams, Harriet Stratemeyer. rev. ed. (Illus.). 176 p. 20cm. (The Nancy Drew Mystery Stories: Vol. 26). 1967. Grosset & Dunlap.

--The Clue of the Rusty Key. Adams, Harriet Stratemeyer. Warren, Ferdinand E., illus. LC 42-12308. v, 216 p. front. 20 cm. (The Dana Girls Mystery Stories: Vol. 11). 1942. Grosset & Dunlap.

--The Clue of the Tapping Heels. Adams, Harriet Stratemeyer. rev. ed. LC 71-86679. (Illus.). 176 p. 20cm. (The Nancy Drew Mystery Stories: Vol. 16). 1969. Grosset & Dunlap.

--The Clue of the Tapping Heels. Adams, Harriet Stratemeyer. Tandy, Russell H., illus. LC 39-1749. iv, 214 p. front. 20 cm. (The Nancy Drew Mystery Stories: Vol. 16). c.1939. Grosset & Dunlap.

--The Clue of the Velvet Mask. Adams, Harriet Stratemeyer. LC 53-5952. 211p. illus. 23cm. (The Nancy Drew Mystery Stories: Vol. 30). 1953. Grosset & Dunlap.

--The Clue of the Velvet Mask. Adams, Harriet Stratemeyer. rev. ed. LC 69-14266. (Illus.). 177 p. 20cm. (The Nancy Drew Mystery Stories: Vol. 30). 1969. Grosset & Dunlap.

--The Clue of the Velvet Mask. Adams, Harriet Stratemeyer. Bolian, Polly (1925-), illus. LC 59-342223. 192p. illus. 22cm. (The Nancy Drew Mystery Stories: Vol. 30). 1959. Grosset & Dunlap.

--The Clue of the Whistling Bagpipes. Adams, Harriet Stratemeyer. LC 64-1675. (Illus.). 177 p. 20cm. (The Nancy Drew Mystery Stories: Vol. 41). 1964. Grosset & Dunlap.

--The Crooked Banister. Adams, Harriet Stratemeyer. LC 77-130336. (Illus.). 179 p. 20cm. (The Nancy Drew Mystery Stories: Vol. 48). 1971. (ISBN 0-448-09548-3). Grosset & Dunlap.

--The Curious Coronation. Adams, Harriet Stratemeyer. LC 75-1581. (Illus.). 20cm. 179p. (The Dana Girls Mystery Stories: Vol. 14). 1976. (ISBN 0-448-09094-5). Grosset & Dunlap.

--Dana Girls Mystery Stories. Adams, Harriet Stratemeyer. LC 78-640914. (No. 1). c.1972. Grosset & Dunlap.

--The Double Jinx Mystery. Adams, Harriet Stratemeyer. LC 72-90826. (Illus.). 180 p. 20cm. (The Nancy Drew Mystery Stories: Vol. 50). 1973. (ISBN 0-448-09550-5). Grosset & Dunlap.

--The Elusive Heiress. Adams, Harriet Stratemeyer. Frame, Paul (1913-), illus. LC 81-19805. 206 p. 20cm. (The Nancy Drew Mystery Stories: Vol. 68). c.1982. (ISBN 0-671-44555-3). (ISBN 0-671-44553-7). Wanderer Books.

--The Emerald-Eyed Cat. Adams, Harriet Stratemeyer. Frame, Paul (1913-), illus. (The Nancy Drew Mystery Stories: Vol. 75). 1984. (ISBN 0-671-49740-5, Juveniles). (ISBN 0-671-49739-1). Wanderer Books.

--The Emerald-Eyed Cat. Adams, Harriet Stratemeyer. Frame, Paul (1913-), illus. LC 84-5232. (Illus.). (Nancy Drew Mystery Stories: No. 75). c.1984. (ISBN 0-671-49740-5). Wanderer Books.

--Enemy Watch. Adams, Harriet Stratemeyer. Frame, Paul (1913-), illus. LC 83-19836. p. cm. (The Nancy Drew Mystery Stories: Vol. 73). c.1984. (ISBN 0-671-49736-7). (ISBN 0-671-49735-9). Wanderer Books.

--The Eskimo's Secret. Adams, Harriet Stratemeyer. Frame, Paul (1913-), illus. LC 84-20936. 174 p. 20cm. (The Nancy Drew Mystery Stories: Vol. 76). c.1985. (ISBN 0-671-55047-0). (ISBN 0-671-55046-2). Wanderer Books.

--The Flying Saucer Mystery. Adams, Harriet Stratemeyer. Sanderson, Ruth, illus. LC 79-24954. p. cm. (The Nancy Drew Mystery Stories: Vol. 58). c.1980. (ISBN 0-671-95514-4). (ISBN 0-671-95601-9). Wanderer Books.

--The Ghost in the Gallery. Adams, Harriet Stratemeyer. LC 56-19039. (Illus.). 209 p. 20cm. (The Dana Girls Mystery Stories: Vol. 17). 1955. Grosset & Dunlap.

--The Ghost in the Gallery. Adams, Harriet Stratemeyer. LC 76-381494. (Originally published as Vol. 17). (Illus.). 180 p. 20cm. Reissue of 1955 ed. (The Dana Girls Mystery Stories: Vol. 13). 1975. (ISBN 0-448-09093-7). Grosset & Dunlap.

--The Ghost of Blackwood Hall. Adams, Harriet Stratemeyer. LC 48-5433. vi. 216 p. front. 20 cm. (The Nancy Drew Mystery Stories: Vol. 25). 1948. Grosset & Dunlap.

--The Ghost of Blackwood Hall. Adams, Harriet Stratemeyer. rev. ed. LC 67-20844. 178 p. illus. 20 cm. (The Nancy Drew Mystery Stories: Vol. 25). 1967. Grosset & Dunlap.

--Ghosts in the Gallery. Adams, Harriet Stratemeyer. LC 74-10467. (Illus.). 196p. (Dana Girls Ser.: Vol. 13). (gr. 4-7). 1975. (ISBN 0-448-09093-7, G&D). Putnam Pub Group.

--The Greek Symbol Mystery. Adams, Harriet Stratemeyer. Sanderson, Ruth, illus. LC 80-39778. 171 p. 19cm. (The Nancy Drew Mystery Stories: Vol. 60). c.1981. (ISBN 0-671-42297-9). (ISBN 0-671-42298-7). Wanderer Books.

--The Haunted Bridge. Adams, Harriet Stratemeyer. rev. ed. LC 72-77110. (Illus.). 180 p. 20cm. (The Nancy Drew Mystery Stories: Vol. 15). 1972. (ISBN 0-448-09515-7). Grosset & Dunlap.
--The Haunted Bridge. Adams, Harriet Stratemeyer. Tandy, Russell H., illus. LC 38-1042. 2 p. l., 220 p. front. 20 cm. (The Nancy Drew Mystery Stories: Vol. 15). c.1937. Grosset & Dunlap.
--The Haunted Carousel. Adams, Harriet Stratemeyer. Frame, Paul (1913-), illus. LC 83-6998. p. cm. (The Nancy Drew Mystery Stories: Vol. 72). c.1983. (ISBN 0-671-47554-1). (ISBN 0-671-47555-X). Wanderer Books.
--The Haunted Lagoon. Adams, Harriet Stratemeyer. LC 59-4256. 182p. illus. 20cm. (The Dana Girls Mystery Stories: Vol. 21). 1959. Grosset & Dunlap.
--The Haunted Lagoon. Adams, Harriet Stratemeyer. LC 72-90828. (Originally published as Vol. 21). (Illus.). 182 p. 20cm. Reissue of 1959 ed. (The Dana Girls Mystery Stories: Vol. 8). c.1973. (ISBN 0-448-09088-0). Grosset & Dunlap.
--The Haunted Showboat. Adams, Harriet Stratemeyer. LC 58-460. (Illus.). 184 p. 20cm. (The Nancy Drew Mystery Stories: Vol. 35). 1958, c.1957. Grosset & Dunlap.
--The Haunted Showboat. Adams, Harriet Stratemeyer. Bolian, Polly (1925-), illus. (The Nancy Drew Mystery Stories: Vol. 35). 1959. Grosset & Dunlap.
--The Hidden Staircase. Adams, Harriet Stratemeyer. rev. ed. LC 59-2537. (Illus.). 182 p. 20cm. (The Nancy Drew Mystery Stories: Vol. 2). 1959. Grosset & Dunlap.
--The Hidden Staircase. Adams, Harriet Stratemeyer. Bolian, Polly (1925-), illus. LC 60-2241. 186p. illus. 22cm. (The Nancy Drew Mystery Stories: Vol. 2). 1960. Grosset & Dunlap.
--The Hidden Staircase. Adams, Harriet Stratemeyer. Tandy, Russell H., illus. LC 30-12385. iv, 206 p. front., plates. 20 cm. (The Nancy Drew Mystery Stories: Vol. 2). c.1930. Grosset & Dunlap.
--The Hidden Window Mystery. Adams, Harriet Stratemeyer. LC 57-13578. (Illus.). 214 p. 20cm. (The Nancy Drew Mystery Stories: Vol. 34). 1957, c.1956. Grosset & Dunlap.
--The Hidden Window Mystery. Adams, Harriet Stratemeyer. rev. ed. LC 75-1582. (Illus.). 179 p. 20cm. (The Nancy Drew Mystery Stories: Vol. 34). c.1975. (ISBN 0-448-19534-8). Grosset & Dunlap.
--The Hidden Window Mystery. Adams, Harriet Stratemeyer. Bolian, Polly (1925-), illus. (The Nancy Drew Mystery Stories: Vol. 34). 1959. Grosset & Dunlap.
--The Hundred-Year Mystery. Adams, Harriet Stratemeyer. LC 76-14299. (Illus.). 180 p. 20cm. (The Dana Girls Mystery Stories: Vol. 15). c.1977. (ISBN 0-448-09095-3). Grosset & Dunlap.
--In the Shadow of the Tower. Adams, Harriet Stratemeyer. Rev 2 ed. Warren, Ferdinand E, illus. LC 34-1308. vi, 217 p. front., plates. 20 cm. (The Dana Girls Mystery Stories: Vol. 3). c.1934. Grosset & Dunlap.
--The Invisible Intruder. Adams, Harriet Stratemeyer. LC 69-12166. (Illus.). 175 p. 20cm. (The Nancy Drew Mystery Stories: Vol. 46). 1969. Grosset & Dunlap.
--The Kachina Doll Mystery. Adams, Harriet Stratemeyer. Sanderson, Ruth, illus. LC 81-11381. p. cm. (The Nancy Drew Mystery Stories: Vol. 62). c.1981. (ISBN 0-671-42346-0). (ISBN 0-671-42347-9). Wanderer Books.
--The Message in the Hollow Oak. Adams, Harriet Stratemeyer. rev. ed. LC 78-181844. (Illus.). 181 p. 20cm. (The Nancy Drew Mystery Stories: Vol. 12). 1972. (ISBN 0-448-09512-2). Grosset & Dunlap.
--The Message in the Hollow Oak. Adams, Harriet Stratemeyer. Tandy, Russell H., illus. LC 35-16901. iv, 218 p. front., plates. 20 cm. (The Nancy Drew Mystery Stories: Vol. 12). c.1935. Grosset & Dunlap.
--The Moonstone Castle Mystery. Adams, Harriet Stratemeyer. LC 63-1033. (Illus.). 178 p. 20cm. (The Nancy Drew Mystery Stories: Vol. 40). 1963. Grosset & Dunlap.
--Mountain-Peak Mystery. Adams, Harriet Stratemeyer. LC 77-76133. 180 p. 20cm. (The Dana Girls Mystery Stories: Vol. 16). c.1978. (ISBN 0-448-09096-1). Grosset & Dunlap.
--The Mysterious Fireplace. Adams, Harriet Stratemeyer. Warren, Ferdinand E., illus. LC 41-769635. v, 217 p. incl. front. 20 cm. (The Dana Girls Mystery Stories: Vol. 10). c.1941. Grosset & Dunlap.
--The Mysterious Image. Adams, Harriet Stratemeyer. Frame, Paul (1913-), illus. LC 83-16898. (Illus.). 192p. (The Nancy Drew Mystery Stories: Vol. 74). (gr. 4-7). 1984. (ISBN 0-671-49738-3). (ISBN 0-671-49737-5). Wanderer Bks.
--The Mysterious Mannequin. Adams, Harriet Stratemeyer. LC 77-100115. (Illus.). 178 p. 20cm. (The Nancy Drew Mystery Stories: Vol. 47). 1970. Grosset & Dunlap.
--The Mystery at Lilac Inn. Adams, Harriet Stratemeyer. rev. ed. LC 61-65834. (Illus.). 180 p. 20cm. (The Nancy Drew Mystery Stories: Vol. 4). 1961. Grosset & Dunlap.
--The Mystery at Lilac Inn. Adams, Harriet Stratemeyer. Tandy, Russell H., illus. LC 30-29250. iv, 200 p. front., plates. 20 cm. (The Nancy Drew Mystery Stories: Vol. 4). c.1930. Grosset & Dunlap.
--The Mystery at the Crossroads. Adams, Harriet Stratemeyer. LC 54-103980. 214p. illus. 20cm. (The Dana Girls Mystery Stories: Vol. 16). 1954. Grosset & Dunlap.
--The Mystery at the Moss Covered Mansion. Adams, Harriet Stratemeyer. rev. ed. LC 77-155244. (Illus.). 177 p. 20cm. (The Nancy Drew Mystery Stories: Vol. 18). 1971. (ISBN 0-448-09518-1). Grosset & Dunlap.
--The Mystery at the Moss-Covered Mansion. Adams, Harriet Stratemeyer. Tandy, Russell H., illus. LC 41-309. v p., 1 l., 215 p. incl. front. 20 cm. (The Nancy Drew Mystery Stories: Vol. 18). c.1941. Grosset & Dunlap.
--The Mystery at the Ski Jump. Adams, Harriet Stratemeyer. rev. ed. LC 68-21716. (Illus.). 176 p. 20cm. (The Nancy Drew Mystery Stories: Vol. 29). 1968. Grosset & Dunlap.
--The Mystery at the Ski Jump. Adams, Harriet Stratemeyer. Bolian, Polly (1925-), illus. LC 60-367123. 190p. illus. 22cm. (The Nancy Drew Mystery Stories: Vol. 29). 1960. Grosset & Dunlap.
--The Mystery of Crocodile Island. Adams, Harriet Stratemeyer. LC 77-76128. (Illus.). 180 p. 20cm. (The Nancy Drew Mystery Stories: Vol. 55). c.1978. (ISBN 0-448-09555-6). Grosset & Dunlap.
--The Mystery of the Bamboo Bird. Adams, Harriet Stratemeyer. LC 60-517733. 182p. illus. 20cm. (The Dana Girls Mystery Stories: Vol. 22). 1960. Grosset & Dunlap.
--The Mystery of the Bamboo Bird. Adams, Harriet Stratemeyer. LC 73-815. (Originally Published as Vol. 22). (Illus.). 182 p. 20cm. Reissue of 1960 ed. (The Dana Girls Mystery Stories: Vol. 9). 1973. (ISBN 0-448-09089-9). Grosset & Dunlap.
--The Mystery of the Brass Bound Trunk. Adams, Harriet Stratemeyer. rev. ed. LC 76-8371. (Illus.). 20cm. 180p. (The Nancy Drew Mystery Stories: Vol. 17). 1976. Grosset & Dunlap.
--The Mystery of the Brass Bound Trunk. Adams, Harriet Stratemeyer. Tandy, Russell H., illus. LC 40-47167. iv, 220 p. front. 20 cm. (The Nancy Drew Mystery Stories: Vol. 17). c.1940. Grosset & Dunlap.
--The Mystery of the Fire Dragon. Adams, Harriet Stratemeyer. LC 61-1112. (Illus.). 182 p. 20cm. (The Nancy Drew Mystery Stories: Vol. 38). 1961. Grosset & Dunlap.
--The Mystery of the Glowing Eye. Adams, Harriet Stratemeyer. LC 73-13372. (Illus.). 181 p. 20cm. (The Nancy Drew Mystery Stories: Vol. 51). 1974. (ISBN 0-448-09551-3). Grosset & Dunlap.
--The Mystery of the Ivory Charm. Adams, Harriet Stratemeyer. rev. ed. LC 74-3868. (Illus.). 179 p. 20cm. (The Nancy Drew Mystery Stories: Vol. 13). c.1974. (ISBN 0-448-09513-0). (ISBN 0-448-19513-5). Grosset & Dunlap.
--The Mystery of the Ivory Charm. Adams, Harriet Stratemeyer. Tandy, Russell H., illus. LC 36-19025. iv, 216 p. front. 20 cm. (The Nancy Drew Mystery Stories: Vol. 13). c.1936. Grosset & Dunlap.
--The Mystery of the Locked Room. Adams, Harriet Stratemeyer. Warren, Ferdinand E., illus. LC 38-183850. v, 218 p. front. 20 cm. (The Dana Girls Mystery Stories: Vol. 7). 1938. Grosset & Dunlap.
--Mystery of the Lost Dogs. Adams, Harriet Stratemeyer. O'Sullivan, Tom, illus. LC 77-75664. (Illus.). 61 p. 28cm. (Nancy Drew Picture Bks.: No. 1). c.1977. (ISBN 0-448-14900-1). Grosset & Dunlap.
--The Mystery of the Ninety-Nine Steps. Adams, Harriet Stratemeyer. LC 66-11318. 176p. illus. 20cm. (The Nancy Drew Mystery Stories: Vol. 43). c.1966. Grosset & Dunlap.
--The Mystery of the Ski Jump. Adams, Harriet Stratemeyer. LC 52-7170. 212 p. illus. 20 cm. (The Nancy Drew Mystery Stories: Vol. 29). 1952. Grosset & Dunlap.
--The Mystery of the Stone Tiger. Adams, Harriet Stratemeyer. LC 63-18957. 175 p. illus. 20 cm. (The Dana Girls Mystery Stories: Vol. 25). 1963. Grosset & Dunlap.
--The Mystery of the Stone Tiger. Adams, Harriet Stratemeyer. LC 77-180990. (Originally published as Vol. 25). (Illus.). 175 p. 20cm. Reissue of 1963 ed. (The Dana Girls Mystery Stories: Vol. 1). 1972. (ISBN 0-448-09081-3). Grosset & Dunlap.
--The Mystery of the Tolling Bell. Adams, Harriet Stratemeyer. rev. ed. LC 73-2183. (Illus.). 181 p. 20cm. (The Nancy Drew Mystery Stories: Vol. 23). 1973. (ISBN 0-448-09523-8). Grosset & Dunlap.
--The Mystery of the Tolling Bell. Adams, Harriet Stratemeyer. Tandy, Russell H., illus. LC 46-2010. vi p., 1 l., 213 p. incl. front. 19 cm. (The Nancy Drew Mystery Stories: Vol. 23). 1946. Grosset & Dunlap.
--The Mystery of the Wax Queen. Adams, Harriet Stratemeyer. LC 67-3470. (Illus.). 176 p. 20cm. (The Dana Girls Mystery Stories: Vol. 28). 1966. Grosset & Dunlap.
--The Mystery of the Wax Queen. Adams, Harriet Stratemeyer. LC 78-180993. (Originally published as Vol. 28). (Illus.). 176 p. 20cm. Reissue of 1966 ed. (The Dana Girls Mystery Stories: Vol. 4). c.1972. (ISBN 0-448-09084-8). Grosset & Dunlap.
--The Mystery of the Winged Lion. Adams, Harriet Stratemeyer. Frame, Paul (1913-), illus. LC 81-23967. (Illus.). 206 p. 19cm. (The Nancy Drew Mystery Stories: Vol. 65). c.1982. (ISBN 0-671-42370-3). (ISBN 0-671-42371-1). Wanderer Books.
--Nancy Drew Book of Hidden Clues. Adams, Harriet Stratemeyer. LC 80-19087. p. cm. 1980. (ISBN 0-671-95713-9). Wanderer Books.
--Nancy Drew Ghost Stories. Adams, Harriet Stratemeyer. Frame, Paul (1913-), illus. LC 82-20016. (Illus.). 160 p. 19cm. (The Nancy Drew Mystery Stories). c.1983. (ISBN 0-671-46466-3). (ISBN 0-671-46468-X). Wanderer Books.
--Nancy Drew Ghost Stories II. Adams, Harriet Stratemeyer. Arico, Diane, ed. Frame, Paul (1913-), illus. (Illus.). 160p. (Orig.). (The Nancy Drew Mystery Stories). (gr. 8-12). N.D. (ISBN 0-671-55075-6). (ISBN 0-671-55070-5). Wanderer Bks.
--Nancy Drew Gift Set. Adams, Harriet Stratemeyer, 3 vols. N.D. Boxed Set. (ISBN 0-317-12425-0). Wanderer Bks.
--Nancy Drew Mystery Stories. Adams, Harriet Stratemeyer. LC 78-642178. (Illus.). 20cm. c.1930. Grosset & Dunlap.
--The Nancy Drew Sleuth Book: Clues to Good Sleuthing. Adams, Harriet Stratemeyer. LC 78-58209. (Illus.). 152 p. 21cm. c.1979. (ISBN 0-448-15459-5). (ISBN 0-448-13600-7). Grosset & Dunlap.
--Nancy's Mysterious Letter. Adams, Harriet Stratemeyer. rev. ed. LC 68-15295. (Illus.). 174 p. 20cm. (The Nancy Drew Mystery Stories: Vol. 8). 1968. Grosset & Dunlap.
--Nancy's Mysterious Letter. Adams, Harriet Stratemeyer. Tandy, Russell H., illus. LC 32-12763. iv, 209 p. front., plates. 20 cm. (The Nancy Drew Mystery Stories: Vol. 8). c.1932. Grosset & Dunlap.
--The Password to Larkspur Lane. Adams, Harriet Stratemeyer. rev. ed. (Illus.). (The Nancy Drew Mystery Stories: Vol. 10). 1960. Grosset & Dunlap.
--The Password to Larkspur Lane. Adams, Harriet Stratemeyer. Tandy, Russell H., illus. LC 33-30727. iv, 220 p. front., plates. 20 cm. (The Nancy Drew Mystery Stories: Vol. 10). c.1933. Grosset & Dunlap.
--The Phantom of Pine Hill. Adams, Harriet Stratemeyer. LC 65-13774. 176p. illus. 20cm. (The Nancy Drew Mystery Stories: Vol. 42). c.1965. Grosset.
--The Phantom of Venice. Adams, Harriet Stratemeyer. Frame, Paul (1913-), illus. LC 85-11442. p. cm. (The Nancy Drew Mystery Stories: Vol. 78). c.1985. (ISBN 0-671-49745-6). (ISBN 0-671-49746-4). Wanderer Books.
--The Phantom Surfer. Adams, Harriet Stratemeyer. LC 68-29945. (Illus.). 175 p. 20cm. (The Dana Girls Mystery Stories: Vol. 30). 1968. Grosset & Dunlap.
--The Phantom Surfer. Adams, Harriet Stratemeyer. LC 71-181845. (Originally published as Vol. 30). (Illus.). 175 p. 20cm. Reissue of 1968 ed. (The Dana Girls Mystery Stories: Vol. 6). c.1972. (ISBN 0-448-09086-4). Grosset & Dunlap.
--The Portrait in the Sand. Adams, Harriet Stratemeyer. Warren, Ferdinand E., illus. LC 43-690720. v, 216 p. incl. front 19 1/2 cm. (The Dana Girls Mystery Stories: Vol. 12). c.1943. Grosset & Dunlap.
--The Quest of the Missing Map. Adams, Harriet Stratemeyer. rev. ed. LC 70-86692. (Illus.). 178 p. 20cm. (The Nancy Drew Mystery Stories: Vol. 19). 1969. Grosset & Dunlap.
--The Quest of the Missing Map. Adams, Harriet Stratemeyer. Tandy, Russell H., illus. LC 41-27887. vi p., 1 l., 213 p. incl. front. 20 cm. (The Nancy Drew Mystery Stories: Vol. 19). c.1942. Grosset & Dunlap.
--Race Against Time. Adams, Harriet Stratemeyer. Frame, Paul (1913-), illus. LC 81-21918. (Illus.). 206 p. 19cm. (The Nancy Drew Mystery Stories: Vol. 66). c.1982. (ISBN 0-671-42372-X). (ISBN 0-671-42373-8). Wanderer Books.
--The Riddle of the Frozen Fountain. Adams, Harriet Stratemeyer. 173 p. illus. 20 cm. (The Dana Girls Mystery Stories: Vol. 26). 1964. Grosset & Dunlap.
--The Riddle of the Frozen Fountain. Adams, Harriet Stratemeyer. LC 70-180991. (Originally published as Vol. 26). (Illus.). 173 p. 20cm. Reissue of 1964 ed. (The Dana Girls Mystery Stories: Vol. 2). c.1972. (ISBN 0-448-09082-1). Grosset & Dunlap.
--The Ringmaster's Secret. Adams, Harriet Stratemeyer. LC 54-8554. (Illus.). 214 p. 20cm. (The Nancy Drew Mystery Stories: Vol. 31). 1953. Grosset & Dunlap.
--The Ringmaster's Secret. Adams, Harriet Stratemeyer. rev. ed. LC 74-3867. (Illus.). 178 p. 20cm. (The Nancy Drew Mystery Stories: Vol. 31). c.1974. (ISBN 0-448-19531-3). Grosset & Dunlap.
--The Ringmaster's Secret. Adams, Harriet Stratemeyer. Bolian, Polly (1925-), illus. LC 59-384836. 192p. illus. 22cm. (The Nancy Drew Mystery Stories: Vol. 31). 1959. Grosset & Dunlap.
--The Scarlet Slipper Mystery. Adams, Harriet Stratemeyer. LC 55-106280. 214p. illus. 20cm. (The Nancy Drew Mystery Stories: Vol.32). c.1954. Grosset & Dunlap.
--The Scarlet Slipper Mystery. Adams, Harriet Stratemeyer. rev. ed. LC 74-3869. (Illus.). 179 p. 20cm. (The Nancy Drew Mystery Stories: Vol. 32). c.1974. (ISBN 0-448-09532-7). (ISBN 0-448-19532-1). Grosset & Dunlap.
--The Scarlet Slipper Mystery. Adams, Harriet Stratemeyer. Bolian, Polly (1925-), illus. LC 59-431623. 190p. illus. 22cm. (The Nancy Drew Mystery Stories: Vol. 32). 1959. Grosset & Dunlap.
--The Secret at Lone Tree Cottage. Adams, Harriet Stratemeyer. Rev 2 ed. Warren, Ferdinand E., illus. LC 34-1307. 3 p. l., 218 p. front., plates. 20 cm. (The Dana Girls Mystery Stories: Vol. 2). c.1934. Grosset & Dunlap.
--The Secret at Shadow Ranch. Adams, Harriet Stratemeyer. Tandy, Russell H., illus. LC 31-3099. iv, 208 p. front., plates. 20 cm. (The Nancy Drew Mystery Stories: Vol. 5). c.1931. Grosset & Dunlap.
--Secret at the Gatehouse. Adams, Harriet Stratemeyer. Warren, Ferdinand E., illus. LC 40-7291. vii, 216 p. incl. front. 20 cm. (The Dana Girls Mystery Stories: Vol. 9). c.1940. Grosset & Dunlap.
--The Secret at the Hermitage. Adams, Harriet Stratemeyer. Warren, Ferdinand E., illus. LC 36-1047. v, 218 p. front. 20 cm. (The Dana Girls Mystery Stories: Vol. 5). c.1936. Grosset & Dunlap.
--The Secret in the Old Attic. Adams, Harriet Stratemeyer. rev. ed. LC 78-100118. (Illus.). 177 p. 20cm. (The Nancy Drew Mystery Stories: Vol. 21). 1970. Grosset & Dunlap.
--The Secret in the Old Attic. Adams, Harriet Stratemeyer. Tandy, Russell H., illus. LC 43-22855. v. p., 1 l., 216 p. incl. front. 19 1/2 cm. (The Nancy Drew Mystery Stories: Vol. 21). 1944. Grosset & Dunlap.
--The Secret in the Old Lace. Adams, Harriet Stratemeyer. Sanderson, Ruth, illus. LC 80-17778. (Illus.). 167 p. 19cm. (The Nancy Drew Mystery Stories: Vol. 59). c.1980. (ISBN 0-671-41119-5). (ISBN 0-671-41114-4). Wanderer Books.
--The Secret in the Old Well. Adams, Harriet Stratemeyer. Tandy, Russell H., illus. LC 44-4357. v, 1, 215 p. incl. front. 19 1/2 cm. (The Dana Girls Mystery Stories: Vol. 13). 1944. Grosset & Dunlap.
--The Secret of Lost Lake. Adams, Harriet Stratemeyer. LC 63-1093. 174 p. illus. 20 cm. (The Dana Girls Mystery Stories: Vol. 24). 1963. Grosset & Dunlap.
--The Secret of Lost Lake. Adams, Harriet Stratemeyer. LC 73-13370. (Originally published as Vol. 24). (Illus.). 174 p. 20cm. Reissue of 1963 ed. (The Dana Girls Mystery Stories: Vol. 11). c.1974. (ISBN 0-448-09091-0). Grosset & Dunlap.
--The Secret of Mirror Bay. Adams, Harriet Stratemeyer. LC 75-180995. (Illus.). 178 p. 20cm. (The Nancy Drew Mystery Stories: Vol. 49). 1972. (ISBN 0-448-09549-1). Grosset & Dunlap.
--The Secret of Red Gate Farm. Adams, Harriet Stratemeyer. rev. ed. LC 61-66627. (Illus.). 178 p. 20cm. (The Nancy Drew Mystery Stories: Vol. 6). 1961. Grosset & Dunlap.
--The Secret of Red Gate Farm. Adams, Harriet Stratemeyer. Tandy, Russell H., illus. LC 31-21182. iv, 208 p. front., plates. 20 cm. (The Nancy Drew Mystery Stories: Vol. 6). c.1931. Grosset & Dunlap.
--The Secret of Shadow Ranch. Adams, Harriet Stratemeyer. rev. ed. LC 65-20039. (Illus.). 175 p. 20cm. (The Nancy Drew Mystery Stories: Vol. 5). Orig. Title: The Secret at Shadow Ranch. 1965. Grosset & Dunlap.

Keith, Eros
--Bedita's Bad Day. Keith, Eros, illus. LC 71-161278. (Illus.). color ils. 32p. (ps-2). 1971. (ISBN 0-87888-036-4). Bradbury Pr.
--The Biggest Noise. Keith, Eros, illus. (Illus.). (gr. k-3). N.D (HarpJ). Har-Row.
--In the Land of Enchantment: A Panorama of Fairy Tales. LC 75-654436. (Illus.). (ps-3). 1972. (ISBN 0-02-749640-6). Bradbury Pr.
--Nancy's Backyard. LC 69-10211. (Illus.). 32 p. 1973. (ISBN 0-06-023122-X). (ISBN 0-06-023123-8). Harper & Row.
--Rrra-Ah. Eros, Keith, illus. LC 78-93086. (Illus.). 32 p. 29cm. 1969. Bradbury Press.
--Small Lot. Keith, Eros, illus. LC 68-9054. (Illus.). 32p. (ps-2). 1968. (ISBN 0-87888-001-1). Bradbury Pr.
Keith, Frank H.
--The Turn Me Around Book. N.D. Carlton Press.
Keith, Frederick W
--Danger in the Everglades. Werth, Kurt (1896-), illus. LC 57-5625. 223p. illus. 22cm. 1957. Abelard-Schuman.
--The Sunken Island. LC 61-154422. 216p. 22cm. 1961. Lothrop, Lee & Shepard.
Keith, Harold Verne (1903-)
--The Bluejay Boarders. Berson, Harold (1926-), illus. LC 79-187938. (Illus.). xi, 224 p. 21cm. 1972. (ISBN 0-690-14922-0). (ISBN 0-690-14923-9). Crowell.
--Brief Garland. LC 73-140644. 307 p. 21cm. 1971. (ISBN 0-690-15969-2). Crowell.
--Go, Red, Go!. 1st ed. Glattauer, Ned, illus. LC 70-38749. (Illus.). 96 p. 21cm. 1972. (ISBN 0-8407-6217-8). T. Nelson.
--Komantcia. LC 65-14901. 299p. 21cm. c.1965. Crowell.
--The Obstinate Land. LC 77-1826. 214 p. 24cm. c.1977. (ISBN 0-690-01319-1). Crowell.
--A Pair of Captains. Woodbury, Mabel Jones, illus. LC 51-12917. 160 p. illus. 21 cm. 1951. Crowell.
--Rifles for Watie. (gr. 6-9). 1957. Harper & Row.
--Rifles for Watie. Burchard, Peter Duncan (1921-), illus. LC 57-10280. (Illus.). 332 p. 21cm. 1957. Crowell. **Awards: (JNM); (ALA).**
--The Runt of Rogers School. LC 79-141455. 125 p. 21cm. 1971. Lippincott.
--Shotgun Shaw: A Baseball Story. Woodbury, Mabel Jones, illus. LC 49-11984. 163 p. illus. 21 cm. 1949. Crowell.
--Susy's Scoundrel. Schoenherr, John Carl (1935-), illus. LC 74-1052. (Illus.). 209 p. 21cm. 1974. (ISBN 0-690-00496-6). Crowell.
Keith, James
--The Scuba Buccaneers. Parker, Nancy Winslow (1930-), illus. LC 66-19157. 164p. illus., map. 23cm. 1966. Angus and Robertson.
--The Scuba Buccaneers. Parker, Nancy Winslow (1930-), illus. LC 68-16326. (Illus.). 164 p. 23cm. 1968, c.1966. Roy Publishers.
Keith, Linton J.
--Follet Picture-Stories of Industry: Coal. LC 38-927. 40p. illus. 21cm. c.1937. Follett Pub.
--Follett Picture-Stories of Industry: Wood. LC 38-928. 40p. illus. 21cm. c.1937. Follett.
Keith, Marian, pseud., see MacGregor, Mary Esther Miller.
Keith, Marian, pseud.
--Duncan Polite. N.D. George H Doran.
--The End of the Rainbow. N.D. George H Doran.
--Treasure Valley. N.D. George H Doran.
Keithley, Maud Mattox
--Packy Climbs Pike's Peak. LC 41-25431. 110 p. incl. front., illus. 24 cm. c.1941. Abingdon-Cokesbury Press.
Kelen, Emery (1896-1978)
--Calling Dr. Owl. Kelen, Emery (1896-1978), illus. LC 45-4372. 48 p. incl. col. front., illus. (part col.) 28 cm. 1945. The Hyperion Press, Distributed by Duell, Sloan and Pearce.
--Food for the Valley. Kelen, Emery (1896-1978), illus. LC 64-24912. 59 p. illus. (part col.) 27 cm. 1964. Lothrop, Lee and Shepard.
--The Valley of Trust. Rev ed. Kelen, Emery (1896-1978), illus. LC 62-16572. 61 p. illus. 27 cm. 1962. Lothrop, Lee and Shepard.
--Yussuf the Ostrich. Kelen, Emery (1896-1978), illus. LC 44-383. 50 p. illus. (part col.) 28 cm. 1943. Hyperion Press; Distributed by Putnam.
Kellam, Ian
--The First Summer Year. Jacques, Robin (1920-), illus. LC 73-22445. (Illus.). viii, 275 p. 24cm. 1974, c.1972. (ISBN 0-690-00464-8). Crowell.
--The First Summer Year. Jacques, Robin (1920-), illus. LC 74-189403. (Illus.). 5, 274 p. 23cm. 1972. (ISBN 0-19-271343-4). Oxford University Press.
Kelland, Clarence Budington, jt. auth. see Barbour, Ralph Henry.
Kelland, Clarence Budington (1881-1964)
--Catty Atkins. LC 20-1213. 4 p. l., 326, 1 p. front., plates. 20 cm. c.1920. Harper & Brothers.
--Catty Atkins, Bandmaster. LC 24-18904. 4 p. l., 263 p. front., plates. 20 cm. 1924. Harper & Brothers.
--Catty Atkins, Financier. LC 23-894004. 4 p. l., 247 p. front., plates. 20 cm. 1923. Harper & Brothers.
--Catty Atkins, Riverman. LC 21-130641. 4 p. l., 258, 1 p. front., plates. 20 cm. c.1921. Harper & Brothers.
--Catty Atkins, Sailorman. LC 22-993341. 4 p. l., 229, 1 p. front., plates. 20 cm. 1922. Harper & Brothers.
--Into His Own: The Story of an Airedale. LC 15-9833. 18cm. 1915. David McKay.
--Mark Tidd. (The Mark Tidd Stories). N.D. Grosset & Dunlap.
--Mark Tidd. (Harper's Selected Juveniles). N.D. Harper & Brothers.
--Mark Tidd, Editor. (The Mark Tidd Stories). N.D. Grosset & Dunlap.
--Mark Tidd, Editor. LC 17-30119. 286p. (Harpers Selected Juveniles). 1917. Harper & Brothers.
--Mark Tidd: His Adventures and Strategies. Clarke, William Wallace, illus. LC 13-21742. 316, 1 p. front., plates. 19 cm. 1913. Harper & Brothers.
--Mark Tidd in Business. (The Mark Tidd Stories). N.D. Grosset & Dunlap.
--Mark Tidd in Business. LC 15-17978. 271p. (Harper's Selected Juveniles). 1915. Harper & Brothers.
--Mark Tidd in Egypt. (The Mark Tidd Stories). N.D. Grosset & Dunlap.
--Mark Tidd in Egypt. LC 26-15963. 4 p. l., 237 p. front., plates. 20 cm. c.1926. Harper & Brothers.
--Mark Tidd in Italy. (The Mark Tidd Stories). N.D. Grosset & Dunlap.
--Mark Tidd in Italy. LC 25-17280. 4 p. l., 264 p. front., plates. 20 cm. c.1925. Harper & Brothers.
--Mark Tidd in Sicily. (The Mark Tidd Stories). N.D. Grosset & Dunlap.
--Mark Tidd in Sicily. LC 28-24268. 4 p. l., 208 p. front., plates. 20 cm. 1928. Harper & Brothers.
--Mark Tidd in the Backwoods. (The Mark Tidd Stories). N.D. Grosset & Dunlap.
--Mark Tidd in the Backwoods. LC 14-15187. 3 p. l., 281, 1 p. front., plates. 20 cm. 1914. Harper & Brothers.
--Mark Tidd, Manufacturer. (The Mark Tidd Stories). N.D. Grosset & Dunlap.
--Mark Tidd, Manufacturer. LC 18-18744. 4 p. l., 3-256, 1 p. front., plates. 20 cm. 1918. Harper & Brothers.
--Mark Tidd's Citadel. (The Mark Tidd Stories). N.D. Grosset & Dunlap.
--Mark Tidd's Citadel. LC 16-225923. 3 p. l., 279, 1 p. front., illus. (map) plates (1 double) 20 cm. 1916. Harper & Brothers.
Kellar, Paul H.
--The Three Black Lambs. N.D. Meador Publishing Co.
Keller, Arthur I., illus.
--The Millionaire Baby. N.D. Bobbs-Merrill Company.
Keller, Beverly Lou
--The Bee Sneeze. Paterson, Diane R. Cole (1946-), illus. p. cm. 1982. (ISBN 0-698-30740-2). Coward, McCann & Geoghegan.
--The Beetle Bush. Simont, Marc (1915-), illus. LC 75-28180. (Illus.). 63 p. 23cm. (Break-of-day book). c.1976. (ISBN 0-698-20366-6). Coward, McCann & Geoghegan.
--Don't Throw Another One, Dover!. Chwast, Jacqueline (1932-), illus. LC 76-14813. 63p. (A Breal-of-Day Bk.). 1976. (ISBN 0-698-30638-4). Coward, McCann & Geoghegan.
--Fiona's Bee. Paterson, Diane R. Cole (1946-), illus. LC 75-7560. (Illus.). 44p. (Break-of-Day Bk.). (gr. 1-4). 1975. (ISBN 0-698-30595-7, Coward). Putnam Pub Group.
--Fiona's Flea. Paterson, Diane R. Cole (1946-), illus. LC 80-16853. (Illus.). 62 p. 22cm. (Break-of-day book). c.1981. (ISBN 0-698-30719-4). Coward, McCann & Geoghegan.
--A Garden of Love to Share. Paris, Pat & Posey, Pam, illus. LC 83-25146. (Illus.). 44 p. 28cm. (Rose-Petal Place). c.1984. (ISBN 0-910313-49-0). Parker Bro.
--The Genuine, Ingenious, Thrift Shop Genie, Clarrisa Mae Bean & Me. Davidson, Raymond (1926-), illus. LC 77-24050. (Illus.). 62 p. 23cm. c.1977. (ISBN 0-698-20433-6). Coward, McCann & Geoghegan.
--My Awful Cousin Norbert. Lewis, Bobby (1944-), illus. LC 81-6068. (Illus.). 60 p. 22cm. c.1982. (ISBN 0-688-00742-2). (ISBN 0-688-00743-0). Lothrop, Lee & Shepard.
--No Beasts! No Children!. 1st ed. LC 82-14011. 127 p. 22cm. c.1983. (ISBN 0-688-01678-2). Lothrop, Lee & Shepard Books.
--Pimm's Place. LC 77-27053. (Illus.). 63 p. 22cm. (Break-of-day books). c.1978. (ISBN 0-698-30689-9). Coward, McCann & Geoghegan.
--Rosebud, with Fangs. 128p. (gr. 4-6). 1985. (ISBN 0-688-03747-X). Lothrop.
--The Sea Watch. LC 80-70000. 128p. (gr. 3-7). 1981. (ISBN 0-590-07703-1, Four Winds). Scholastic Inc. **Award: (ALA).**
--A Small, Elderly Dragon. Langner, Nola (1930-), illus. LC 83-13632. p. cm. 1984. (ISBN 0-688-02553-6). Lothrop, Lee & Shepard.
--When Mother Got the Flu. Chambliss, Maxie, illus. (Illus.). 64p. (gr. 1-4). 1984. (ISBN 0-698-30743-7, Coward). Putnam Pub Group.
Keller, Beverly Lou see Harwick, B. L.

Keller, Charles, jt. auth. see Glovach, Linda.

Keller, Charles (1942-), ed.
--Astronauts. Cumings, Art, illus. LC 84-18204. p. cm. c.1984. (ISBN 0-13-049909-9). Prentice-Hall.
--Ballpoint Bananas and Other Jokes for Kids. Barrios, David, illus. LC 72-7338. (Illus.). 96 p. 22cm. 1973. (ISBN 0-13-055350-6). Prentice-Hall.
--Daffynitions. Fitzgerald, F. A., illus. LC 75-34280. 96p. 1976. (ISBN 0-13-196584-0). Prentice Hall.
--Giggle Puss: Pet Jokes for Kids. Coker, Paul, Jr., illus. LC 76-44837. 1977. (ISBN 0-13-356295-6). Prentice Hall.
--Glory, Glory, How Peculiar. McCrady, Lady (1951-), illus. LC 76-10171. (Illus.). 1976. (ISBN 0-13-357392-3). P-H.
--Going Bananas. Wilson, Roger Burdett (1947-), illus. LC 74-20906. (Illus.). 96 p. 22cm. 1975. (ISBN 0-13-357772-4). Prentice-Hall.
--Grime Doesn't Pay: Law and Order Jokes. Kent, Jack, pseud. (1920-), illus. Kent, John Wellington. LC 83-22894. 1984. (ISBN 0-13-365503-2). Prentice.
--Growing up Laughing: Humorists Look at American Youth. (Illus.). (gr. 5 up). 1981. (ISBN 0-13-367870-9). P-H.
--Laugh Lines. Randall, Christine, illus. LC 73-13979. (Illus.). 64 p. 18cm. 1974. (ISBN 0-13-526038-8). Prentice-Hall.
--Laughing: A Historical Selection of American Humor. LC 76-46321. (Illus.). (gr. 7 up). 1977. (ISBN 0-13-525790-5). P-H.
--Llama Beans. Nolan, Dennis (1945-), illus. LC 78-14553. (Illus.). 44 p. 22cm. c.1979. (ISBN 0-13-539122-9). Prentice-Hall.
--More Ballpoint Bananas. Shortall, Leonard W, illus. LC 77-5356. p. cm. c.1977. (ISBN 0-13-600981-6). Prentice-Hall.
--News Breaks. Cooper, Michael (1943-), illus. LC 80-19573. (Illus.). 64 p. 24cm. c.1980. (ISBN 0-13-620583-6). Prentice-Hall.
--Norma Lee I Don't Knock on Doors: Knock, Knock Jokes. Galdone, Paul (1914-), illus. LC 82-21549. (Illus.). 48 p. 24cm. c.1983. (ISBN 0-13-623587-5). Prentice-Hall.
--Oh Brother!. Frascino, Edward, illus. 1982. Prentice.
--Ohm on the Range: Robot and Computer Jokes. Cumings, Art, illus. LC 19-82007668. 1982. (ISBN 0-13-633552-7). Prentice Hall.
--Punch Lines. McWilliams, V. G, illus. LC 75-11621. (Illus.). 47 p. 24cm. 1975. Prentice-Hall.
--Rememeber the a la Mode: Riddles and Puns. Lorenz, Lee, illus. LC 83-13832. p. cm. c.1983. (ISBN 0-13-773358-5). Prentice-Hall.
--School Daze. Weissman, Sam Q, illus. LC 78-7970. 48p. (gr. 2-5). c.1978. (ISBN 0-13-793620-6). Prentice-Hall.
--Smokey the Shark, and Other Fishy Tales. Lorenz, Lee, illus. LC 80-25813. (Illus.). 48 p. 24cm. c.1981. (ISBN 0-13-814707-8). Prentice-Hall.
--The Star-Spangled Banana and Other Revolutionary Riddles. Baker, Richard, ed. De Paola, Tomie, pseud. (1934-), illus. De Paola, Thomas Anthony. LC 74-594. (Illus.). 64 p. 22cm. 1974. (ISBN 0-13-842971-5). Prentice-Hall.
--Still Going Bananas. Barrios, David, illus. 1982. Prentice.
--Swine Lake: Music & Dance Riddles. Filling, Gregory, illus. LC 85-6380. (Illus.). 48 p. 24cm. c.1985. (ISBN 0-13-879743-9). Prentice-Hall.
--Too Funny for Words: Gesture Jokes for Children. Anderson, Stephen, illus. LC 73-4694. 1973. (ISBN 0-13-925057-3). Prentice Hall.
--What's the Score: Sports Jokes. Mack, Stanley (1935-), illus. LC 81-10575. p. cm. c.1981. (ISBN 0-13-955021-6). Prentice-Hall.
--What's up, Doc?. Doctor & Dentist Jokes. Kessler, Leonard P. (1921-), illus. LC 84-6821. (Illus.). 64p. (gr. 3-7). 1984. (ISBN 0-13-954967-6). P-H.
--The Wizard of Gauze. Mahood, Kenneth (1930-), illus. LC 79-15105. p. cm. c.1979. (ISBN 0-13-961615-2). Prentice-Hall.

Keller, Charles (1942-) & Glovach, Linda (1947-), ed.
--Little Witch Presents a Monster Joke Book. (Illus.). 40p. (ps-4). 1983. (ISBN 0-13-537811-7, Pub. by Treehouse). P-H.
Keller, Dick & Keller, Irene
--The Thingumajig Christmas. (Illus.). 48p. (Good Friends Ser.). (gr. k-6). 1982. (ISBN 0-8249-8045-X). Ideals.
Keller, Dorothy H.
--The Hen Who Couldn't Say When. (gr. 2-4). N.D. Carlton.
Keller, Frances Ruth (1911-)
--The Contented Little Pussy Cat. Werber, Adele & Laslo, Doris, illus. LC 50-3443. (52) p. col. illus. 26 cm. 1949. Platt & Munk.
--The Curious Little Owl. Werber, Adele & Laslo, Doris, illus. LC 57-140918. unpaged. illus. 26cm. 1957. Platt & Munk.
Keller, Gottfried (1819-1890)
--The Fat of the Cat, and Other Stories. Sallak, Albert, illus. Untermeyer, Louis (1885-1977), tr. LC 25-17344. 7 p. l., 13-283 p. incl. illus., plates. plates (part col.) 21 cm. c.1925. Harcourt, Brace and Company.
Keller, Holly
--Cromwell's Glasses. Keller, Holly, illus. LC 81-6644. (Illus.). 32 p. c.1982. (ISBN 0-688-00834-8). (ISBN 0-688-00835-6). Greenwillow Books.
--Geraldine's Blanket. Keller, Holly, illus. LC 83-14062. (Illus.). 7 3/8 x 8. 32p. (16 pt.). (ps-1). 1984. (ISBN 0-688-02539-0). (ISBN 0-688-02540-4). (ISBN 0-688-02540-4). Greenwillow.
--Henry's Fourth of July. Keller, Holly, illus. LC 84-13707. (Illus.). 7 3/8 x 8. 32p. (18 pt.). (ps-1). c.1985. (ISBN 0-688-04012-8). (ISBN 0-688-04013-6). Greenwillow.
--Ten Sleepy Sheep. LC 83-1477. p. cm. 1983. (ISBN 0-688-02306-1). (ISBN 0-688-02307-X). Greenwillow Books.
--Too Big. Keller, Holly, illus. LC 82-15653. (Illus.). 7 3/8 x 8. 32p. (18 pt.). (gr. k-3). 1983. (ISBN 0-688-01998-6). (ISBN 0-688-01999-4). Greenwillow.
--When Francie Was Sick. LC 84-25970. (Illus.). 7 3/8 x 8. 24p. (14 pt.). (ps-1). 1985. (ISBN 0-688-05433-1). (ISBN 0-688-05434-X). Greenwillow.
--Will It Rain?. Keller, Holly, illus. LC 83-25423. (Illus.). 24p. (ps-1). 1984. (ISBN 0-688-03839-5). (ISBN 0-688-03840-9). Greenwillow.
Keller, Irene
--Benjamin Rabbit and the Stranger Danger. Keller, Dick, illus. LC 84-28673. (Illus.). 29 p. 27cm. c.1985. (ISBN 0-396-08655-1). Dodd, Mead.
--Kenny the Kitty. (Illus.). 16p. 1983. (ISBN 0-516-09117-4). Childrens.
--Kenny the Kitty. Keller, Dick, illus. (Illus.). 16p. (Orig.). (gr. k-6). 1982. (ISBN 0-8249-8989-9). Ideals.
--The Thingumajig Book of Do's and Don'ts. Keller, Dick, illus. LC 83-213608. (Illus.). 28 p. 29cm. c.1983. (ISBN 0-8249-8050-6). Ideals Pub. Corp.
--The Thingumajig Book of Manners. Keller, Dick, illus. LC 81-132832. (Illus.). 28 p. 29cm. c.1981. (ISBN 0-8249-8010-7). Ideals Pub. Corp.
Keller, Irene, jt. auth. see Keller, Dick.
Keller, J. B.
--The Affecting Story of Poor Cock Robin. cover-title, 2, 3-15 p. col. illus. 19 cm. 1852. J. B. Keller.
--The Comical Boys. 15 p. col. illus. 19 cm. (Keller, J. B. & W. L. Colored toy books). c.1852. J. B. Keller.
--The Comical Story of Master Nobody. 3-15 p. col. illus. 19 cm. (Keller, J. B. & W. L. Colored toy books). c.1852. J. B. Keller.
--Lady Golightly and Her Cousins, the Grasshoppers: Or, Make Hay While the Sun Shine !. LC 43-31965. 8 numb. l. col. illus. 27 cm. (J. B. Keller's ... Colored toy books). N.D. J. B. Keller.
Keller, John G
--Krispin's Fair. 1st ed. Emberley, Edward Randolph (1931-), illus. LC 76-3537. (Illus.). 32 p. c.1976. (ISBN 0-316-48652-3). Little, Brown.
Keller, Martha (1902-)
--The War Whoop of the Wily Iroquois. Powers, Richard M. Gorman (1921-), illus. LC 54-6318. unpaged. illus. 23cm. c.1954. Coward-McCann.
Keller, Robert S., jt. ed. see Glassmacher, W. J.
Keller, Victor
--The Scary Woods. Pelavin, Cheryl (1946-), illus. LC 77-142536. (Illus.). 31 p. 26cm. 1971. Four Winds Press.
Kellerhals-Stewart, Heather
--Muktu, the Backward Muskox. Muntean, Karen, illus. LC 77-364290. (Illus.). 32 p. c.1975. K.E.S.
Kellersberger, Julia Lake Skinner (1897-)
--The Salt Baby: Stories for Children and for Those Who Once Were Children. LC 46-231. 93 p. 19 1/2 cm. 1945. Fleming H. Revell Company.

Kelley, Anne
--Daisy's Discovery. Salih, Metin, illus. LC 85-9200. (Illus.). 29 p. 22cm. 1985. (ISBN 0-8120-5676-0). Barron's.
Kelley, C. E.
--Christmas Story. N.D. Henry Hoyt.
Kelley, Eliza J., ed. see Jefferies, Richard.
Kelley, Emily
--April Fools' Day. Nobens, C. A., illus. LC 82-23559. (Illus.). 56 p. 23cm. (Carolrhoda On My Own Books). c.1983. (ISBN 0-87614-218-8). Carolrhoda Books.
Kelley, Ethel M
--When I was Little. Squire, Maud Hunt (1873-), illus. LC 15-10077. (Illus.). 20cm. 96p. 1915. Rand McNally.
Kelley, Evelyn Owens
--Seeded Furrows: A Dramatic Historical Novel About the Reconstruction Period of the Civil War. LC 57-4801. 285p. 24cm. 1957. College Pub. Co.
Kelley, F. Beverly
--Denver Brown & the Traveling Town. (ps-3). 1966. (ISBN 0-682-44027-2). Exposition.
--Elmer Keith's Big Game Hunting. 1952. Little, Brown.
Kathleen Visits the Fair. 1952. Little, Brown & Co.
Kelley, J. Ellinor
--Ewin LLoyd: Or, How We All Got On. (Illus.). N.D. Pott & Co.
Kelley, Jay G.
--The Boy Mineral Collectors. 1900. J B Lippincott
Kelley, Leo Patrick (1928-)
Backward in Time. LC 79-51079. (Illus.). 64p (Space Police Bks.). (gr. 4 up). 1980. (ISBN 0-516-02231-8). Childrens.
--Backward in Time. Hofheimer, Steven, illus. LC 79-51079. (Illus.). 57 p., 2 leaves of plates. 18cm. (His A space police book). (Pacemaker book). c.1979. (ISBN 0-8224-6380-6). Fearon Pitman Publishers.
--Dead Moon. LC 78-68228. (Illus.). 64p. (Galaxy Five Ser.). (gr. 4 up). 1980. (ISBN 0-516-02251-2). Childrens.
--Death Sentence. Hofheimer, Steven, illus. LC 79-51081. (Illus.). 64p. (Space Police Bks.). (gr. 4 up). 1980. (ISBN 0-516-02232-6). Childrens.
--Death Sentence. Hofheimer, Steven, illus. LC 79-51081. (Illus.), 58 p., 2 leaves of plates. 18cm. (His A space police book). (Pacemaker book). c.1979. (ISBN 0-8224-6382-2). Fearon Pitman Publishers.
--Earth Two. Hofheimer, Steven, illus. LC 79-51077. (Illus.). 59 p., 2 leaves of plates. 18cm. (pacemaker book). c.1979. (ISBN 0-8224-6379-2). Fearon Pitman Publishers.
--Good-Bye to Earth. LC 78-68226. (Illus.). 64p. (Galaxy Five Ser.). (gr. 4 up). 1980. (ISBN 0-516-02252-0). Childrens.
--King of the Stars. Guidice, Rick, illus. LC 78-68231. (Illus.). 59 p. 18cm. (Pacemaker book). (The Galaxy 5 Ser.). c.1979. (ISBN 0-8224-3206-4). Fearon Pitman Publishers.
--Night of Fire & Blood. LC 78-72325. (Illus.). (Pacesetters Ser.). (gr. 4 up). 1979. (ISBN 0-516-02187-7). Childrens.
--On the Red World. (Illus.). 60 p. 18cm. (Pacemaker book). (The Galaxy 5 Ser.). 1980, c.1979. Fearon Pitman Publishers.
--Prison Satellite. Hofheimer, Steven, illus. LC 79-51075. (Illus.). 59 p., 2 leaves of plates. 18cm. (Pacemaker book). ((His A space police book). c.1979. (ISBN 0-516-02234-2). (ISBN 0-8224-6377-6). Fearon Pitman Publishers.
--Space Police, 6 bks. (gr. 7 up). 1979. (ISBN 0-8224-6376-8). Pitman Learning.
--Star Gold. LC 78-72333. (Illus.). 60 p. 18cm. (Pacemaker bestellers book). c.1979. (ISBN 0-8224-5369-X). Fearon Pitman Publishers.
--Sunworld. LC 79-51080. (Illus.). 64p. (Space Police Bks.). (gr. 4 up). 1980. (ISBN 0-516-02235-0). Childrens.
--The Time Trap. (Illus.). (Pacesetters Ser.). (gr. 4 up). 1978. (ISBN 0-516-02160-5). Childrens.
--Vacation in Space. Guidice, Rick, illus. LC 78-68232. (Illus.). 60 p. 18cm. (Pacemaker book). (The Galaxy 5 Ser.). 1980, c.1979. (ISBN 0-8224-3203-X). Fearon Pitman Publishers.
--Where No Sun Shines. LC 78-68229. (Illus.). 60 p. 18cm. (Pacemaker book). (The Galaxy 5 Ser.). 1980, c.1979. (ISBN 0-8224-3205-6). Fearon Pitman Publishers.
--Worlds Apart. LC 79-51079. (Illus.). 64p. (Space Police Bks.). (gr. 4 up). 1980. (ISBN 0-516-02236-9). Childrens.
--Worlds Apart. Hofheimer, Steven, illus. LC 79-51076. (Illus.). 59 p., 2 leaves of plates. 18cm. (His A space police book). (Pacemaker book). c.1979. (ISBN 0-8224-6378-4). Fearon Pitman Publishers.
Kelley, Leo Patrick (1928-), ed.
--Fantasy: The Literature of the Marvelous. LC 73-11015. vi, 305 p. 23cm. (Patterns in literary art). 1973, c.1974. (ISBN 0-07-033502-8). McGraw-Hill.
--The Supernatural in Fiction. 23cm. 313p. 1973. (ISBN 0-07-033497-8). McGraw-Hill.
--Themes in Science Fiction: A Journey Into Wonder. 23 cm. 428p. 1972. (ISBN 0-07-033504-4). Webster Division, McGraw-Hill.
Kelley, Martha Rose see Kelly, Marty.
Kelley, Orly, ed. see Berry, Joy Wilt.
Kelley, Robert Fulton
--Press Box. (Dodd, Mead Career Bks.). N.D. Dodd, Mead & Co.
Kelley, Robert Fulton, ed.
--The Junior Sports Anthology. Mullin, Willard (1902-1978), illus. LC 45-7243. 368 p. illus. 21 cm. 1945. Howell, Soskin.
Kelley, Sally, pseud., see Jolly, Erin.
Kelley, Sally, pseud.
--Trouble with Explosives. Jolly, Erin. LC 75-33609. (Illus.). 117 p. 22cm. c.1976. (ISBN 0-87888-094-1). Bradbury Press.
Kelley, Sam
--The Adventures of Walter M. Duffle Duff. MacKenzie, Garry (1921-), illus. LC 52-13045. 79 p. illus. 21 cm. 1952. Lothrop, Lee & Shepard.
Kelley, True Adelaide (1946-)
--Buggly Bear's Hiccup Cure. LC 81-16903. (Illus.). 38 p. 23cm. 1982. (ISBN 0-8193-1081-6). (ISBN 0-8193-1082-4). Parents Magazine Press.
--A Valentine for Fuzzboom. Kelley, True Adelaide (1946-), illus. LC 80-24284. (Illus.). 23 p. 17cm. (gr. k-2). 1981. (ISBN 0-395-30446-6). Houghton Mifflin.
Kelley, True Adelaide (1946-) & Lindblom, Steven Winther (1946-)
--The Mouses' Terrible Christmas. LC 78-6995. (Illus.). 63 p. 22cm. (Fun-to-read book). c.1978. (ISBN 0-688-41856-2). (ISBN 0-688-51856-7). Lothrop, Lee & Shepard.
--The Mouses' Terrible Halloween. LC 79-26980. (Illus.). 47 p. 22cm. c.1980. (ISBN 0-688-41950-X). (ISBN 0-688-51950-4). Lothrop, Lee & Shepard Books.
Kelley, Ying, jt. ed. see Peterson, Gayle.
Kelling, Furn L. (1914-)
--Listen to the Night. Turner, Mariel Wilhoite, illus. LC 57-6328. unpaged. illus. 22cm. c.1957. Broadman Press.
--This Is My Family. LC 63-9757. unpaged. illus. 21 cm. 1963. Broadman Press.
Kellock, Harold (1879-)
--Down in the Grass. Wiese, Kurt (1887-1974), illus. LC 29-802249. viii p., 1 l., 247 p. incl., illus., plates. col. front., plates. 20 cm. 1929. Coward-McCann, Inc.
Kellog, Caroline
Stories from the Life of Jesus: Told for Little Children. Speakman, Harold, illus. N.D. Bobbs-Merrill Company.
Kellogg, Charlotte Hoffman, Mrs.
--The Girl Who Ruled a Kingdom. Pruszynska, Aniela (1888-), illus. LC 38-21859. x, 154 p. incl. front., illus. 20 cm. 1938. D. Appleton-Century Company, Incorporated.
Kellogg, Charlotte Hoffman, Mrs., jt. auth. see Kellogg, Vernon Lyman.
Kellogg, Elijah, jt. auth. see Adams, William Taylor.
Kellogg, Elijah (1813-1901)
--The Ark of Elm Island. (Elm Island Stories). N.D. Colby and Rich.
--The Ark of Elm Island, 1 of 6 Vols. (Illus.). 288p. (Elm Island Stories). 1882. Lee & Shepard.
--The Ark of Elm Island. LC 98-366. 3 p. l., 5-288 p. front., plates. 18 cm. (His Elm Island stores. v. 3). 1897. Lee and Shepard.
--Ark of Elm Island, 1 of 60 vols. (American Boys' Ser.: No. 3). 1900. Set. Lee & Shepard.
--The Ark of Elm Island. LC 11-20308. 228p. 19cm. (Elm Island Stories). 1910. Lee & Shepard.
--Arthur Brown, the Young Captain. (Pleasant Cove Ser.). N.D. Colby and Rich.
--Arthur Brown, the Young Captain. LC 31-16200. 3 p. l., 5-288 p. front., plates. 18 cm. (Pleasant cove series. v. 1). 1871. Lee and Shepard.
--Arthur Brown, the Young Captain. LC 99-188. 288 p. front., plates. 19 cm. (pleasant cove series. v. 1). 1898. Lee and Shepard.
--Arthur Brown the Young Captain, 1 of 60 vols. (American Boys' Ser.: No. 4). 1900. Set. Lee & Shepard.
--Arthur Brown, the Young Captive. (Illus.). 288p. N.D. Lee & Shepard.
--Black Rifle's Mission: Or, On the Trail, 1 of 6 vols. (Illus.). (Forest Glen Ser.). 1882. Lee & Shepard.
--The Boy Farmers of Elm Island. (Elm Island Stories). N.D. Colby and Rich.
--The Boy Farmers of Elm Island, 1 of 6 Vols. (Illus.). (Elm Island Stories). 1882. Lee & Shepard.
--The Boy Farmers of Elm Island. 300 p. front., plates. 19 cm. (Added t.-p.: Elm Island stories). (Star Ser.). 1897. Lee and Shepard.
--The Boy Farmers of Elm Island, 1 of 60 vols. (American Boys' Ser.: No. 6). 1900. Set. Lee & Shepard.
--The Boy Farmers of Elm Island. LC 11-20309. 300 p. incl. front. plates. 19 cm. (His Elm Island stories). 1910. Lothrop, Lee & Shepard Co.
--Brought to the Front: Or, The Young Defenders. 1900. Set. Lee & Shepard.
--Brought to the Front: Or, The Young Defenders. LC 3-19670. 320 p. incl. front. plates. 19 cm. (His Forest Glen series v. 3). c.1903. Lee and Shepard.
--Burying the Hatchet: Or, the Young Brave of the Delawares. LC 50-47129. 336 p. plates. 18 cm. (His The forest glen series). c.1878. Lee and Shepard.
--Burying the Hatchet: Or, The Young Brave of the Delawares, 1 of 6 vols. (Forest Glen Ser.). 1882. Set. Lee & Shepard.
--Burying the Hatchet: Or, The Young Brave of the Delawares, 1 of 60 vols. (American Boys' Ser.: No. 10). 1900. Set. Lee & Shepard.
--Burying the Hatchet: or, the Young Braves of the Delawares. LC 6-34678. 336 p. incl. front. plates. 19 cm. (His The forest glen series). c.1906. Lothrop, Lee & Shepard Co.
--Charlie Bell, 1 of 6 Vols. (Elm Island Stories). N.D. Colby and Rich.
--Charlie Bell, 1 of 6 vols. (Illus.). 325p. (Elm Island Stories). 1882. Lee & Shepard.
--Charlie Bell, the Waif of Elm Island. LC 12-34896. 2 p. l., 3-325 p. front., plates. 19 cm. (Added t.-p.: Elm island stories. By Rev. Elijah Kellogg. no. 2). c.1896. Lee and Shepard.
--Charlie Bell the Waif of Elm Island, 1 of 60 vols. (American Boys' Ser.: No. 12). 1900. Set. Lee & Shepard.
--Child of the Island Glen. (Pleasant Cove Ser.). N.D. Colby and Rich.
--The Child of the Island Glen, 1 of 6 vols. (Pleasant Cove Ser.). 1882. Set. Lee & Shepard.
--The Child of the Island Glen. LC 6413. 336 p. incl. front. 19 cm. (pleasant cove series. v. 4). 1900. Lee and Shepard.
--Child of the Island Glen, 1 of 60 vols. (American Boys' Ser.: No. 13). 1900. Set. Lee & Shepard.
--Child of the Island Glen. (Illus.). N.D. Lee & Shepard.
--The Cruise of the Casco. (Pleasant Cove Ser.). N.D. Colby and Rich.
--The Cruise of the Casco. LC 12-31399. (Illus.). 18cm. 288p. (The Pleasant Cove Ser.). 1872. Lee & Shepard.
--The Cruise of the Casco. (Illus.). 326p. (The Pleasant Cove Ser.: Vol. 3). 1899. Lee & Shepard.
--Cruise of the Casco, 1 of 60 vols. (American Boys' Ser.: No. 15). 1900. Set. Lee & Shepard.
--Elm Island Stories, 6 vols. (Illus.). 1882. Set. Lee & Shepard.
--The Fisher Boys of Pleasant Cove. LC 21-13940. 3 p. l., 5-336 p. front., plates. 17 cm. (Added t.-p.: Pleasant Cove series). 1874. Lee and Shepard.
--The Fisher Boys of Pleasant Cove, 1 of 6 vols. (Pleasant Cove Ser.). 1882. Set. Lee & Shepard.
--Fisher Boys of Pleasant Cove, 1 of 60 vols. (Illus.). (American Boys' Ser.: No. 17). 1900. Lee & Shepard.
--The Fisher Boys of Pleasant Cove. LC 2-22398. 336 p. incl. front. pl. 19 cm. (His Pleasant Cove series). 1902. Lee and Shepard.
--Forest Glen: Or, the Mohawk's Friendship. LC 41-27441. 335 p. front., 2 pl. 18 cm. (Added t.-p.: The Forest glen series). c.1877. Lee and Shepard.
--Forest Glen: Or, The Mohawk's Friendship, 1 of 6 vols. (Forest Glen Ser.). 1882. Set. Lee & Shepard.
--Forest Glen: Or, The Mohawk's Friendship, 1 of 60 vols. (Illus.). (American Boys' Ser.: No. 18). 1900. Lee & Shepard.
--Forest Glen: Or, The Mohawk's Friendship. (Illus.). 335p. (American Boy's Ser.). (Forest Glen Ser.: Vol. 5). 1905. Lothrop,Lee & Shepard.
--Forest Glen Series, 6 vols. (Illus.). 1882. Set. Lee & Shepard.
--Good Old Times, 1 of 60 vols. (Illus.). (American Boys' Ser.: No. 19). 1900. Lee & Shepard.
--Good Old Times: Or, Grandfather's Struggle for A Homestead, 1 of 4 vols. (Good Old Times Ser.). 1882. Set. Lee & Shepard.
--Good Old Times: Or, the Grandfather's Struggle for a Homestead. LC 5-33627. 1 p. l., 5-280 p. plates. 19 cm. (On cover: American boy's series 19). c.1905. Lothrop, Lee & Shepard Co.
--The Hard Scrabble of Elm Island. LC 98-368. 18cm. 320p. (Elm Island Stories: Vol. 6). 1898. Lee & Shepard.
--The Hardscrabble of Elm Island, 1 of 6 Vols. (Elm Island Stories). N.D. Colby and Rich.
--The Hardscrabble of Elm Island, 1 of 6 vols. 320p. (Elm Island Stories). 1882. Lee & Shepard.
--Hardscrabble of Elm Island, 1 of 60 vols. (Illus.). (American Boys' Ser.: No. 20). 1900. Lee & Shepard.
--John Godsoe's Legacy. LC 22-16040. 304 p. front., plates. 17 cm. (His Pleasant cover series. v. 5). 1873. Lee and Shepard.
--John Godsoe's Legacy, 1 0f 6 vols. (Pleasant Cove Ser.). 1882. Set. Lee & Shepard.
--John Godsoe's Legacy, 1 of 60 vols. (Illus.). (American Boys' Ser.: No. 24). 1900. Lee & Shepard.
--John Godsoe's Legacy. LC 1-21988. 1 p. l., 5-304 p. 3 pl. (incl. front.) 19 cm. (pleasant cove series). 1901. Lee and Shepard.
--Lion Ben of Elm Island, 1 of 6. (Elm Island Stories). N.D. Colby and Rich.
--Lion Ben of Elm Island, 1 of 6 vols. (Illus.). (Elm Island Stories). 1882. Lee & Shepard.
--Lion Ben of Elm Island. LC 12-34897. 265 p. front., plates. 19 cm. (Added t.-p.: Elm Island stories. By Rev. Elijah Kellogg. no. 1). c.1896. Lee and Shepard.
--Lion Ben of Elm Island, 1 of 60 vols. (Illus.). (American Boys' Ser.: No. 26). 1900. Lee & Shepard.
--Little Pitchers. (Illus.). (Flaxie Frizzle Stories: 6 vols). N.D. Lee and Shepard.
--The Live Oak Boys: Or, The Adventures of Richard Constable. (Illus.). (Good Old Time Ser.). 1882. Lee & Shepard.
--The Live Oak Boys: Or, the Adventures of Richard Constable Afloat and Ashore. LC 11-22627. 356 p. front., plates. 18 cm. (On cover: Good old times series). 1883. Lee and Shepard.
--Live Oak Boys: Or, The Adventures of Richard Constable Afloat & Ashore, 1 of 60 vols. (Illus.). (American Boys' Ser.: No. 28). 1900. Lee & Shepard.
--The Mission of Black Rifle: Or, On The Trail, 1 of 6 vols. (American Boys' Ser.: No. 30). 1876. Set. Lee & Shepard.
--Mission of Black Rifle: Or, On the Trail, 1 of 60 vols. (Illus.). (American Boys' Ser.: No. 30). 1900. Lee & Shepard.
--The Mission of Black Rifle: Or, on the Trail. 316p. (Forest Glen Ser.). 1876. Lothrop,Lee & Shepard.
--Pleasant Cove Series, 6 vols. (Illus.). 1882. Set. Lee & Shepard.
--The Sophomores of Radcliffe: Or, James Trafton and His Boston Friends. (Whispering Pine Ser.). N.D. Colby and Rich.
--Sophomores of Radcliffe: Or, James Trafton and His Bosom Friends. LC 12-31400. 18cm. 281p. (The Whispering Pine Ser.). 1872. Lee & Shepard.
--The Sophomores of Radcliffe: Or, James Trafton and His Bosom Friends. LC 5-9659. (Illus.). 19cm. 281p. (The Whispering Pine Ser.). 1899. Lee & Shepard.
--Sophomores of Radcliffe: Or, James Trafton & His Boston Friends, 1 of 60 vols. (Illus.). (American Boys' Ser.: No. 34). 1900. Lee & Shepard.
--Sowed by the Wind: Or, The Poor Boy's Fortune, 1 of 60 vols. (Illus.). (American Boys' Ser.: No. 35). 1900. Lee & Shepard.
--Sowed by the Wind: Or, The Poor Boy's Fortune. LC 2-22395. (Illus.). 282p. (American Boy's Ser., No. 35). (Forest Glen Ser.: Vol. 1). 1902. Lee & Shepard.
--The Spark of Genius: Or, The College Life of James Trafton. (Whispering Pine Ser.). N.D. Colby and Rich.
--Spark of Genius: Or, the College Life of James Trafton. LC 99-4244. 272 p. front., plates. 19 cm. (whispering pine series). 1899. Lee and Shepard.
--Spark of Genius: Or, The College Life of James Trafton, 1 of 60 vols. (Illus.). (American Boys' Ser.: No. 36). 1900. Lee & Shepard.
--A Spark of Genius: Or, The College Life of of James Trafton, 1 0f 6 vols. (Whispering Pine Ser.). 1882. Set. Lee & Shepard.
--A Stout Heart: Or, The Student from Over the Sea. (Illus.). (The Whispering Pine Ser.). 1901. Lee & Shepard.
--Stout Heart: Or, The Student from Over the Sea, 1 of 60 vols. LC 2-11148. (Illus.). 19cm. 224p. (Whispering Pine Series: No. 37). 1901. Lee & Shepard.
--A Strong Arm and a Mother's Blessing. LC 12-34899. 1 p. l., 5-297 p. front., plates. 18 cm. (His Good old times series). 1881. Lee and Shepard.
--A Strong Arm and a Mother's Blessing, 1 of 4 vols. (Good Old Times Ser.). 1882. Set. Lee & Shepard.
--Strong Arm & a Mother's Blessing, 1 of 60 vols. (Illus.). (American Boys' Ser.: No. 38). 1900. Lee & Shepard.
--The Turning of the Tide: Or, Radcliffe Rich and His Patients. (Whispering Pine Ser.). 1873. Lee & Shepard.

--Turning of the Tide: Or, Radcliffe Rich & His Patients, 1 of 60 vols. (Illus.). (American Boys' Ser.: No. 41). 1900. Lee & Shepard.
--The Turning of the Tide: Or, Radcliffe Rich and His Patients. LC 1-20328. 288p. (The Whispering Pine Ser.). 1901. Lee & Shepard.
--The Unseen Hand: Or, James Renfew and His Boy Helpers. LC 12-34898. 2 p. l., 3-5, 9-328 p. front., plates. 18 cm. (His Good old times series). 1882. Lee and Shepard.
--Unseen Hand: Or, James Renfew & His Boy Helpers, 1 of 60 vols. (Illus.). (American Boys' Ser.: No. 42). 1900. Lee & Shepard.
--The Whispering Pine: Or, The Graduates of Radcliffe Hall. (Whispering Pine Ser.). N.D. Colby and Rich.
--The Whispering Pine: Or, The Graduates of Radcliffe, 1 of 6 vols. (Whispering Pine Ser.). 1882. Set. Lee & Shepard.
--The Whispering Pine: Or, the Graduates of Radcliffe Hall. LC 2838. 300 p. front., plates. 19 cm. (whispering pine series). 1900. Lee and Shepard.
--Whispering Pine: Or, The Graduates of Radcliffe, 1 of 60 vols. (Illus.). (American Boys' Ser.: No. 44). 1900. Lee & Shepard.
--Whispering Pine Ser, 6 vols. (Illus.). 1882. Lee & Shepard.
--Winning His Spurs: Or, Henry Morton's First Trial. (Whispering Pine Ser.). N.D. Colby and Rich.
--Winning His Spurs: Or, Henry Morton's First Trial. LC 14-193421. 253 p. front., plates. 18 cm. (His Whispering pine series). 1873. Lee and Shepard.
--Winning His Spurs: Or, Henry Morton's First Trail. LC 4-35656. 253 p. front., plates. 19 cm. (His Whispering pine series). 1899. Lee and Shepard.
--Winning His Spurs: Or, Henry Morton's First Trial, 1 of 60 vols. (Illus.). (American Boys' Ser.: No. 45). 1900. Lee & Shepard.
--Winning his Spurs: Or, Henry Morton's First Trial. LC 9-17448. 19cm. 253p. (The Whispering Pine Ser.). 1900. Lee & Shepard.
--Wolf Run: Or, The Boys of the Wilderness. (Illus.). 292p. (Forest Glen Ser.: Vol. 2). 1903. Lee & Shepard.
--The Young Deliverers. LC 3-14983. 20cm. 292p. N.D. Colby and Rich.
--The Young Deliverers of Pleasant Cove. LC 38-350594. 3 p. l., 5-304 p. front., plates. 18 cm. (His Pleasant cove series. no. 2). 1873. Lee and Shepard.
--The Young Deliverers of Pleasant Cove, 1 of 6 vols. (Pleasant Cove Ser.). 1882. Set. Lee & Shepard.
--The Young Deliverers of Pleasant Cove. LC 99-1568. 304 p. front., plates. 19 cm. (Added t.-p.: The Pleasant Cove series v. 2). 1899. Lee and Shepard.
--Young Deliverers of Pleasant Cove, 1 of 60 vols. (Illus.). (American Boys' Ser.: No. 48). 1900. Lee & Shepard.
--The Young Shipbuilders of Elm Island. (Elm Island Stories). N.D. Colby and Rich.
--The Young Shipbuilders of Elm Island, 1 of 6 vols. (Elm Island Stories). 1882. Lee & Shepard.
--The Young Shipbuilders of Elm Island. LC 98-66. 304p. (Elm Island Stories). 1898. Lee & Shepard.
--Young Shipbuilders of Elm Island, 1 of 60 vols. (Illus.). (American Boys' Ser.: No. 49). 1900. Lee & Shepard.

Kellogg, Frank Eugene (1854-)
--The Boy Duck Hunters. Kennedy, J. W. Ferguson, illus. LC 3895. 265p. 1900. Dana Estes & Co.
--The Boy Fisherman. LC 4-28420. 20cm. 288p. 1904. Saalfield Publishing Co.
--Flip Flap Fables. Grant, Louis F., illus. (Illus.). N.D. G. W. Dillingham.
--Four Boys on the Mississippi. (Illus.). (The Boy's Own Authors Ser.). N.D. Dana Estes & Co.
--Four Boys on the Mississippi: Or, The Cruise of the Greased Lightning. Dunton, W. Herbert, illus. LC 3-28602. 20cm. 319p. 1903. Saalfield Publishing Co.
--Young Duck-Shooters in Camp. LC 10-28332. (Illus.). 338p. 1910. Frederick A. Stokes.
--The Young Express Agent. Kennedy, J. W. Ferguson, illus. LC 6-17870. 328 p. front., 7 pl. 20 cm. c.1906. D. Estes & Company.

Kellogg, Jean Defrees see Jackson, Sally, pseud.

Kellogg, Jean Defrees (1916-1978), ed. see Baum, Lyman Frank.

Kellogg, Jean Defrees (1916-1978)
--Hans and the Winged Horse. Crowell, Pers (1910-), illus. LC 64-14606. 1 v. (unpaged) illus. (part col.) 24 cm. 1964. Reilly & Lee.
--Here We Go. Jackson, Sally, pseud. Garris, Normaand Dan, illus. LC 62-7259. (Illus.). 26cm. (ps-3). 1961. Reilly & Lee.
--Is This Your Dog?. Martin, Dick (1927-), illus. LC 62-16800. (Illus.). unpaged. 29cm. 1962. Reilly & Lee.
--The Littlest Skater: The Story of Jimmy One-Skate. Jackson, Sally, pseud. Martin, Dick (1927-), illus. LC 61-10746. unpaged. illus. 29cm. 1961. Reilly & Lee Co.
--The Littlest Star: A Story About Ballet. Jackson, Sally, pseud. Martin, Dick (1927-), illus. LC 61-7937. (Illus.). 31p. 29cm. (The Easy to Read Picture Book Ser.). 1961. Reilly & Lee Co.
--The Rod and the Rose. LC 64-20522. (Illus.). 171 p. 21cm. 1964. Reilly & Lee.

Kellogg, Marion George, jt. auth. see Bolenius, Emma Miller.

Kellogg, Marion George, ed. see Mother Goose.

Kellogg, Mary G.
--Doing Things & Happenings. Rytter, Peggy, illus. LC 80-80271. (Illus.). 90p. (gr. 1-6). 1979. (ISBN 0-9603972-0-5). (ISBN 0-9603972-1-3). Bks by Kellogg.

Kellogg, Steven (1941-)
--Can I Keep Him?. Kellogg, Steven, illus. LC 72-142453. (Illus.). unpaged. 27cm. 32p. (Pied piper book). 1971. (ISBN 0-8037-1305-3). Dial Press.
--Chicken Little. Kellogg, Steven (1941-), illus. LC 84-25519. (Illus.). 32 p. 29cm. c.1985. (ISBN 0-688-05690-3). (ISBN 0-688-05691-1). W. Morrow.
--The Island of the Skog. LC 73-6019. (Illus.). (A Pied Piper Book). (gr. k-3). 1976. Dial Bks Young.
--The Island of the Skog. Kellogg, Steven (1941-), illus. LC 73-6019. (Illus.). 32p. (ps-3). 1973. Dial Bks Young.
--Much Bigger Than Martin. Kellogg, Steven (1941-), illus. LC 75-27599. (Illus.). 32 p. 29cm. c.1976. (ISBN 0-8037-5809-X). (ISBN 0-8037-5810-3). Dial Press.
--The Mysterious Tadpole. Kellogg, Steven (1941-), illus. LC 77-71517. p. cm. 28cm. 32p. (ps-3). c.1977. (ISBN 0-8037-6245-3). (ISBN 0-8037-6246-1). Dial Press.
--The Mystery Beast of Ostergeest. Kellogg, Steven (1941-), illus. LC 79-158730. 32p. (ps-3). 1971. (Pied Piper). Dial Bks Young.
--The Mystery of the Flying Orange Pumpkin. LC 80-11748. (Illus.). 32 p. 17cm. c.1980. (ISBN 0-440-76115-8). (ISBN 0-440-76116-6). Dial Press.
--The Mystery of the Flying Orange Pumpkin. Kellogg, Steven (1941-), illus. LC 80-11748. (Illus.). 32p. (Dial Book for Young Readers Ser.). (ps-2). 1983. (ISBN 0-8037-0019-9). Dutton.
--The Mystery of the Magic Green Ball. Kellogg, Steven (1941-), illus. LC 78-51322. 17cm. 32p. c.1978. (ISBN 0-8037-6214-3). (ISBN 0-8037-6215-1). Dial Press.
--The Mystery of the Missing Red Mitten. Kellogg, Steven (1941-), illus. LC 73-15439. (Illus.). 32 p. 17cm. 1974. (ISBN 0-8037-6195-3). (ISBN 0-8037-6194-5). Dial Press.
--The Mystery of the Stolen Blue Paint. Kellogg, Steven (1941-), illus. p. cm. c.1982. Dial Press.
--The Orchard Cat. LC 73-181788. (Illus.). 39 p. 24cm. 1972. Dial Press.
--The Orchard Cat. Kellogg, Steven (1941-), illus. (Illus.). 40p. (Pied Piper Bks). (ps-3). 1983. (ISBN 0-8037-6481-2). Dial Bks Young.
--Pinkerton, Behave!. Kellogg, Steven (1941-), illus. LC 78-31794. (Illus.). 32 p. 28cm. c.1979. (ISBN 0-8037-6575-4). Dial Press.
--Pinkerton, Behave!. Kellogg, Steven (1941-), illus. (Illus.). 32p. (Pied Piper Bks.). (gr. k-3). 1982. (ISBN 0-8037-7250-5). Dial Bks Young.
--Ralph's Secret Weapon. Kellogg, Steven (1941-), illus. LC 82-22115. 1983. (ISBN 0-8037-7086-3). (ISBN 0-8037-7087-1). Dial Bks. for Young Readers.
--Ralph's Secret Weapons. (Illus.). (Dial Book for Young Readers). 1983. (ISBN 0-8037-7086-3). (ISBN 0-8037-7087-1). Dutton.
--A Rose for Pinkerton. Kellogg, Steven (1941-), illus. LC 81-65848. p. cm. (Dial Books for Young Readers). c.1981. (ISBN 0-8037-7502-4). (ISBN 0-8037-7503-2). Dial Press.
--Tallyho, Pinkerton!. Kellogg, Steven (1941-), illus. LC 82-70198. (Illus.). 32p. (ps-3). 1982. (ISBN 0-8037-8731-6). (ISBN 0-8037-8743-X). Dial Bks Young.
--The Wicked Kings of Bloon. Kellogg, Steven (1941-), illus. LC 72-117499. (Illus.). 32 p. 22cm. 1970. (ISBN 0-13-959403-5). Prentice-Hall.
--Won't Somebody Play with Me?. Kellogg, Steven (1941-), illus. LC 72-708. (Illus.). 32 p. 1972. Dial Press.

Kellogg, Steven (1941-), adapted by.
--Paul Bunyan. Kellogg, Steven (1941-), illus. LC 83-26684. (Illus.). 40p. 1984. (ISBN 0-688-03849-2, Morrow Junior Books). (ISBN 0-688-03850-6). Morrow.
--There Was an Old Woman. LC 80-15293. p. cm. 1980, c.1974. (ISBN 0-590-07779-1). Four Winds Press.
--There Was an Old Woman. Kellogg, Steven (1941-), illus. LC 73-13584. (Illus.). 41 p. 1974. (ISBN 0-8193-0715-7). (ISBN 0-8193-0716-5). Parents' Magazine Press. **Award: (NYT).**

Kellogg, Vernon Lyman (1867-1937), ed. see Bertelli, Luigi.

Kellogg, Vernon Lyman (1867-1937)
--Insect Stories. Shimada, Sekko & Lanktree, Maud, illus. LC 8-21773. vi p., 2 l., 3-298 p., 1 l. illus., plates. 21 cm. (American nature series. Group v. Diversions from nature). 1908. H. Holt and Company.
--Insect Stories. Rev. ed. Wellman, Mary & Lanktree, Maud, illus. LC 23-15272. viii p., 2 l., 3-298 p., 1 l. illus., plates. 20 cm. 1923. D. Appleton and Company.

Kellogg, Vernon Lyman (1867-1937) & Kellogg, Charlotte Hoffman, Mrs.
--Nuova; or, The New Bee: A Story for Children of Five to Fifty. Winter, Milo Kendall (1888-1956), illus. LC 20-176033. 7 p. l., 150 p., 1 l. col. front., plates. 23 cm. c.1920. Houghton Mifflin Company.

Kellogg, Warren F.
--Hunting in the Jungle. (Illus.). N.D. Dana Estes and Company.

Kelly, Bernadine Creswell
--Colonists & Caravans: Return to Santa Fe and The Name Day of Dona Clara. Thiele, Leo P., illus. LC 51-2040. 62 p. illus. 20 cm. 1950. University Pub. Co.
--Lujan Returns. Thiele, Leo P., illus. LC 51-2041. 63 p. illus. 20 cm. 1950. University Pub. Co.
--Tales for a Tenderfoot. Thiele, Leo P., illus. LC 51-2042. 64 p. illus. 20 cm. 1950. University Pub. Co.
--Trail Riders. Thiele, Leo P., illus. LC 51-2044. 63 p. illus. 20 cm. 1950. University Pub. Co.

Kelly, Charlotte M
--Those Terrible Trents. LC 49-415. 136 p. 21 cm. 1948. Ave Maria Press.

Kelly, Donald see Berg, Jean Horton.

Kelly, Donna
--The Clock Book. O'Sullivan, Tom, illus. (Illus.). (A Golden Book for Early Childhood Ser.). (gr. k-3). 1979. (ISBN 0-307-68962-X, Golden Pr). Western Pub.

Kelly, Donna, ed.
--The Wizard of Oz. Barto, Renzo, illus. (Illus.). (gr. k-2). 1976. (ISBN 0-307-68906-9, Golden Pr). Western Pub.

Kelly, Eric Philbrook (1884-1960)
--The Amazing Journey of David Ingram. 1949. J. B. Lippincott Co.
--At the Sign of the Golden Compass: A Tale of the Printing House of Christopher Plantin in Antwerp, 1576. Lufkin, Raymond H. (1897-), illus. LC 38-27802. 6 p. l., 194, 1 p. illus. 22 cm. 1938. The Macmillan Company.
--The Blacksmith of Vilno. Pruszynska, Aniela (1888-), illus. N.D. MacMillan.
--The Christmas Nightingale: Three Christmas Stories from Poland. De Angeli, Marguerite Lofft, Mrs. (1889-), illus. LC 32-24676. 6 p. l., 3-73, 1 p. front., illus. 21 cm. 1932. The Macmillan Company.
--From Star to Star: A Story of Krakow in 1493. Lee, Manning De Villeneuve (1894-1980), illus. LC 44-8026. x p., 1 l., 239 p. illus. 21 cm. 1944. J. B. Lippincott Company.
--Golden Star of Halich. Pruszynska, Aniela (1888-), illus. N.D. MacMillan.
--The Hand in the Picture. Lorentowicz, Irena (1910-), illus. 1947. J. B. Lippincott Co.
--In Clean Hay. Petersham, Maud Sylvia Fuller, Mrs. (1890-1971) & Petersham, Miska (1889-1960), illus. LC 53-12989. (Illus.). 31 p. 21cm. 1953. Macmillan.
--On the Staked Plain: El Llano Estacado. Stein, Harve (1904-), illus. LC 40-7102. 6 p. l., 250 p. incl. front., illus. 22 cm. 1940. The Macmillan Company.
--Three Sides of Agiochook: A Tale of the New England Frontier in 1775. Appleton, Le Roy, illus. LC 35-18693. 5 p. l., 211 p. front., illus. 21 cm. 1935. The Macmillan Company.
--Treasure Mountain. Lufkin, Raymond H. (1897-), illus. LC 37-24269. 5 p. l., 211 p. illus. 22 cm. 1937. The Macmillan Company.
--The Trumpeter of Krakow. new ed. Domanska, Janina, illus. Bechtel, Louis Seaman, frwd. by. LC 66-16712. (Illus.). x, 208 p. 25cm. 1966. Macmillan.
--The Trumpeter of Krakow. Pruszynska, Aniela (1888-), illus. LC 28-21739. 23cm. 218p. (MacMillan Bks. for Boys & Girls). (gr. 7-9). 1928. MacMillan Bks. **Award: (JNM).**
--The Trumpeter of Krakow. Pruszynska, Aniela (1888-), illus. LC 66-16712. 242 p. 18cm. (Collier Books). 1973, c.1956. MacMillan.

Kelly, Eric Philbrook (1884-1960), ed.
--Polish Legends and Tales. LC 78-162625. (Illus.). 93 p. 23cm. 1971. Polish Publication Society of America.

Kelly, Gerald A
--The Four Knights. LC 32-320. 5 p. l., 227 p. front., plates. 20 cm. c.1931. The Bruce Publishing Company.
--Terry Donovan. LC 31-529. 4 p. l., 231 p. front., plates. 20 cm. c.1930. The Bruce Publishing Company.

Kelly, Gerald A & Sharkey, Donald C. (1912-)
--Mickey O'Brien. LC 54-7736. 127p. illus. 22cm. 1954. Bruce Pub. Co.

Kelly, Jeffrey (1946-)
--Tramp Steamer and the Silver Bullet. LC 84-15668. 192p. (gr. 5-9). 1984. (ISBN 0-395-36632-1). (ISBN 0-395-36632-1). HM.

Kelly, Jim (1943-)
--Little Chick of Cricklewick. Kerr, Coral, illus. LC 77-5949. p. cm. (His Cricklewick books). 1977. (ISBN 0-912588-42-X). Brooke House.
--The Little Neighbor. Payne, Sally, illus. (Small Star Stories). 1975. MacMillan Publishing company.
--Neighbors. Payne, Sally, illus. LC 73-157950. (Illus.). 31 p. 32cm. 1972. Scarecrow Publications.
--Neighbors: Small Star Stories. Payne, Sally, illus. 1975. MacMillan Publishing Company.
--The Secret Hole. Payne, Sally, illus. 1975. MacMillan Publishing Company.
--Star Flowers: Small Star Stories. Payne, Sally, illus. 1975. MacMillan Publishing Company.
--A Trip to Ask Island. Kerr, Coral, illus. LC 77-5846. p. cm. (His Cricklewick books). 1977. (ISBN 0-912588-40-3). Brooke House.
--Wads and Gina's Songbook. Payne, Sally, illus. 1975. MacMillan Publishing Company.

Kelly, John M., Jr. (1919-)
--Folk Songs Hawaii Sings. (Illus.). (gr. 3 up). 1963. (ISBN 0-8048-0192-4). C E Tuttle.

Kelly, M. A. B.
--Leaves From Nature's Story-Book, Vol. I. (Illus.). (Thirty Volume School Library). N.D. Educational Publishing Company.
--Leaves From Nature's Story-Book, Vol.s I-III. (Illus.). N.D. Educational Publishing Company.

Kelly, Margaret Ricaud (1910-)
--Jack and the Flying Saucer, and Other Children's Stories. (Illus.). 44 p. 21cm. 1973. (ISBN 0-533-00565-5). Vantage.

Kelly, Martha Rose see Kelly, Marty, pseud.

Kelly, Marty, pseud., see Kelly, Martha Rose.

Kelly, Marty, pseud. (1914-)
--Green-up: The Story of a Buffalo. Kelly, Martha Rose. Goldsborough, June (1923-), illus. LC 71-117366. (Illus.). 61 p. 22cm. 1971. (ISBN 0-07-033878-7). American Heritage Press.
--Green-up: The Story of a Buffalo. Goldsborough, June (1923-), illus. (Illus.). (gr. 5-7). 1971. McGraw.
--The House on Deer Track Trail. Kelly, Martha Rose. Himler, Ronald Norbert (1937-), illus. LC 75-41455. (Illus.). 58 p. 21cm. c.1976. (ISBN 0-07-033886-8). (ISBN 0-07-033887-6). McGraw-Hill.

Kelly, Midge
--The Adventures of Dwinkle. LC 40-862029. 156 p. incl. front., illus. 22 cm. c.1940. Fortuny's.

Kelly, Ralph, pseud., see Geis, Darlene Stern.

Kelly, Raymond Ransome (1882-)
--Me and Andy: A Boy and a Dog Story. Papadopoulos, Electra & Wuerfel, Lillian B., illus. LC 38-33211. 2 p. l., 164 p. col. front., illus., col. plates. 22 cm. 1938. A. Whitman & Co.
--Me and Andy: A Boy and Dog Story. Papadopoulos, Electra, illus. LC 28-9060. 2 p. l., 164 p. col. front., illus., col. plates. 20 cm. 1928. Laidlaw Brothers.
--O-Go the Beaver. Wiese, Kurt (1887-1974), illus. LC 34-37987. 148 p. incl. illus., col. plates. 22 cm. 1934. A. Whitman & Co.

Kelly, Regina Zimmerman, Mrs. (1898-)
--Beaver Trail. Junge, Carl, illus. LC 53-9769. 237p. 23cm. 1955. Lothrop, Lee & Shepard.
--Chicago: Big-Shouldered City. Aloise, Frank E., illus. LC 62-16396. 158p. illus. 21cm. 1962. Reilly & Lee.
--Henry Clay: Statesman and Patriot. Walker, Charles W., illus. LC 60-6697. 191p. col. illus. (Piper bks.). c.1960. Houghton Mifflin.
--King Richard's Squire: A Tale of Chaucer's England. Hamilton, Russell, illus. LC 37-77170. 272 p. incl. front., illus., geneal. tab. 21 cm. c.1937. Thomas Y. Crowell Company.
--New Orleans: Queen of the River. Aloise, Frank E., illus. LC 63-19038. 176p. illus., geneal. table. 21cm. c.1963. Reilly & Lee.
--One Flag, One Land. Kemp, Wendy, illus. LC 67-14662. (Illus.). 21cm. 115p. (gr. 4-8). 1967. Reilly & Lee.
--Young Geoffrey Chaucer: His Boyhood Adventures, His Student Days at Oxford, His Romantic Training As a Page at Court. Chappell, Warren (1904-), illus. LC 52-10144. 170 p. illus. 22 cm. 1952. Lothrop, Lee and Shepard.

Kelly, Robert (1935-)
--How Do I Make up My Mind, Lord?. Story Devotions for Boys. Maakestad, Tom, illus. LC 82-70948. (Illus.). 110 p. 20cm. (Young Readers). c.1982. (ISBN 0-8066-1923-6). Augsburg Pub. House.

Kelly, Rosalie Ruth
--Addie's Year. LC 80-26566. 155 p. 22cm. c.1981. (ISBN 0-8253-0028-2). Beaufort Books.
--The Great Toozy Takeover. LC 74-21084. 127 p. 21cm. 1975. (ISBN 0-399-20452-0). Putnam.
Kelly, Walter Crawford (1913-1973)
--Can't. LC 77-84918. (Illus.). 28 p. 19cm. 1969. Lancelot Press.
--I Go Pogo. LC 52-12552. 190 p. illus. 20 cm. 1952. Simon and Schuster.
--The Incompleat Pogo. 1954. Simon & Schuster.
--The Pogo Papers. 1953. Simon & Schuster.
--Pogo Peek-A-Book. 1955. Simon & Schuster.
--Pogo's Stepmother Goose. 1954. Simon & Schuster.
--Pot Luck Pogo. 1955. Simon & Schuster.
--Prehysterical Pogo: (in Pandemonia). LC 67-17886. (Illus.). 22cm. 176p. 1967. Simon and Schuster.
--The Return of Pogo. 1965. Simon and Schuster, Inc Publications.
--Songs of the Pogo. (Illus.). 1956. Simon and Schuster, Inc.
--Ten Ever Lovin Blue Eyed Years with Pogo. 1959. Simon and Schuster, Inc.
--Uncle Pogo So-So Stories. 1953. Simon & Schuster.
--Walt Kelly's No. LC 70-84919. (Illus.). 28 p. 19cm. 1969. Lancelot Press.

Kelly, William Roswell (1891-) & Brogan, Helen M., eds.
--Poems for the Grades. Byrne, Annette, illus. Colum, Padraic (1881-1972), intro. by. LC 41-3446. 8 v. illus. 20 1/2 cm. 1939. W. H. Sadlier Inc.
Kelman, Janet Harvey, ed.
--Stories from Chaucer: Told to Children. Robinson, William Heath (1872-1944), illus. xi, 114 p. 8 col. pl. (incl. front.) 15 cm. (Half-title: Told to the children series). 1905. E. P. Dutton & Co.
Kelsey, Alice Geer (1896-)
--Adventures With The Bible. 128p. 1960. Friendship press.
--Big Family. Terrel, Mary Field, Mrs., illus. LC 50-10446. 49 p. illus. (part col.) 17 x 23 cm 1950. Westminster Press.
--Blueberry Acres and Other Stories. Finger, Helen, illus. LC 49-48926. 127 p. illus (part col.) 20 cm. 1949. Friendship Press.
--I Give You My Colt. Torrey, Helen (1901-), illus. 1956. David McKay Company Inc.
--I Give You My Colt. 1st ed. Torrey, Helen (1901-), illus. LC 56-9218. 160p. illus. 22cm. 1956. Longmans.
--Land of the Morning: Ten Stories from the Philippines. Hutchinson, William Miller (1916-), illus. LC 67-31368. 125p. illus., music. 19cm. 1968. (ISBN 0-685-11651-4). Friendship.
--Many Hands In Many Lands. 128p. 1953. Friendship Press.
--Mingo for the Merry-Go-Round. Smalley, Janet (1893-) & McLevy, Jeanne, illus. LC 48-6770. 128 p. illus. 20 cm. 1948. Friendship Press.
--More Stories for Junior Worship. LC 48-1312. 160 p. 20 cm. 1948. Abingdon-Cokesbury Press.
--Once the Hodja. 1943. E M Hale.
--Once the Hodja. Dobias, Frank (1902-), illus. 1943. David McKay Company Inc.
--Once the Hodja. Dobias, Frank (1902-), illus. LC 43-18205. xiii p., 1 l., 170 p. illus. 19 1/2 cm. 1943. Longmans, Green and Co.
--Once the Mullah. Werth, Kurt (1896-), illus. LC 54-825978. (Illus.). 137 p. 20cm. 1954. Longmans, Green.
--Racing the Red Sail. 1st ed. Morse, Dorothy Bayley (1906-1979) & Bayley, Robert, illus. LC 47-30645. xii, 140 p. illus. 22 cm. 1947. Longmans, Green.
--Ricardo's White Horse. 1st ed. Hopkins, Joseph W., illus. LC 48-7444. 179p. illus. 22cm. 1948. Longmans, Green & Co.
--Seven-Minute Stories for Church and Home. LC 58-5399. 128p. illus. 20cm. 1958. Abingdon Press.
--Stories for Growing. LC 55-8611. 126p. 20cm. 1955. Abingdon Press.
--Stories of Yesterday and Today for Juniors. LC 61-5194. 127p. illus. 20cm. 1961. Abingdon Press.
--The Teakwood Pulpit and Other Stories for Junior Worship. LC 50-9346. 159 p. 20 cm. 1950. Abingdon-Cokesbury Press.
--The Thirty Gilt Pennies. Laite, Gordon (1925-), illus. Joannes LC 68-15402. (Illus.). 64 p. 25cm. 1968. Abingdon Press.
--Tino & the Typhoon. (Illus.). (gr. 4-7). 1958. (ISBN 0-8382-0877-0). Hale.
--Tino and the Typhoon. Kashiwagi, Isami (1925-), illus. LC 58-12281. 151p. 1958. David McKay Company Inc.
Kelsey, Alice Geer (1896-) & Johnson, Cecile Ryden, illus.
--New Flags Flying. LC 64-1103. 127p. illus. 19cm. 1964. Friendship Press.
Kelsey, Dick, jt. ed. see Bedford, Annie North.
Kelsey, Dick, ed. see Disney, Walter Elias.
Kelsey, Dick, adapted by see Disney, Walt, Productions.
Kelsey, Joan Marshall see Grant, Joan Marshall, pseud.
Kelsey, Lella B., ed. see Gale, Zona.
Kelsey, Richard I., ed. see Disney, Walt, Productions.
Kelsey, Richard I., ed. see Disney, Walt, Studio.
Kelsey, Richmond I
--Goodenough Gismo. Kelsey, Richmond I., illus. LC 48-6062. 38 p. col. illus. 22 x 24 cm. 1948. Houghton Mifflin Co.
Kelsey, Vera
--Maria Rosa. Portinari, Candido (1903-1962), illus. 1942. Doubleday Doran & Co.
--Tomorrow is for You!. Minnesota, 1857. Tillenius, Clarence, illus. LC 53-12264. (Illus.). 247 p. 21cm. (Strength of the Union). 1953. Scribner.
Kelshaw, Terence
--The Daring Rabbit. 1978. (ISBN 0-8423-7817-0). Tyndale.
--The Foolish Rabbit. 1978. (ISBN 0-8423-5125-6). Tyndale.
--Rabbit in Danger. 1978. (ISBN 0-8423-0070-8). Tyndale.
--Rabbits to the Rescue. 1978. (ISBN 0-8423-7140-0). Tyndale.
Kemis, Ethel
--Holiday Songs. LC 43-7684. 38 p. 20 cm. 1941. McLaughlin & Reilly Co.
Kemp, Eleanor
--Bible Stories Retold for Children. 1925. Adelphi Co.
Kemp, Gene (1926-)
--Charlie Lewis' Plays for Time. Julian-Ottie, Vanessa, illus. LC 83-25297. (Illus.). 21cm. 132p. 1984. (ISBN 0-571-13248-0). (ISBN 0-571-13248-0). Faber and Faber.
--Christmas with Tamworth Pig. Dinan, Carolyn, illus. LC 78-300034. (Illus.). 93 p. 21cm. 1977. (ISBN 0-571-11117-3). Faber.
--The Clock Tower Ghost. Dinan, Carolyn, illus. LC 82-670031. (Illus.). 89 p. 20cm. 1981. (ISBN 0-571-11767-8). Faber and Faber.
--Gowie Corby Plays Chicken. LC 80-670082. 136 p. 21cm. 1979. (ISBN 0-571-11405-9). Faber and Faber.
--Gowie Corby Plays Chicken. 1980. Faber.
--Jason Bodger and the Priory Ghost. LC 85-4444. 140 p. 21cm. 1985. (ISBN 0-571-13645-1). Faber and Faber.
--No Place Like. LC 83-8901. p. cm. 1983. (ISBN 0-571-13153-0). Faber and Faber.
--The Prime of Tamworth Pig. Dinan, Carolyn, illus. (Illus.). 112p. (Fanfares Ser.). (ps-4). 1979. (ISBN 0-571-11335-4). Faber & Faber.
--Tamworth Pig & the Litter. Dinan, Carolyn, illus. LC 75-330636. (Illus.). 94p. (gr. 2-5). 1975. (ISBN 0-571-10743-5). Faber & Faber.
--Tamworth Pig Saves the Trees. (Illus.). 104p. (Fanfares Ser.). (ps-4). 1980. (ISBN 0-571-11493-8). Faber & Faber.
--Tamworth Pig Saves the Trees. Dinan, Carolyn, illus. LC 73-168777. (Illus.). 104p. (gr. 2-5). 1973. (ISBN 0-571-10115-1). Faber & Faber.
--The Turbulent Term of Tyke Tiler. Dinan, Carolyn, illus. LC 77-36255. (Illus.). 118p. (gr. 5-8). 1977. (ISBN 0-571-10966-7). Faber & Faber. **Award: (CMA).**
--The Well. Fouracre, Chantal, illus. LC 84-13538. 1984. (ISBN 0-571-13284-7). (ISBN 0-571-13284-7). Faber And Faber.
Kemp, Gene (1926-), ed.
--Ducks and Dragons: Poems for Children. Dinan, Carolyn, illus. LC 80-670271. (Illus.). 3-124 p. 21cm. 1980. (ISBN 0-571-11523-3). Faber & Faber.
Kemp, Moira
--Firebird: A Traditional Russian Fairy Tale. Kemp, Moira, illus. LC 83-11570. (Illus.). 32p. (gr. 2-5). 1984. (ISBN 0-87923-486-5). (ISBN 0-87923-486-5). Godine.
Kempadoo, Manghanita
--Letters of Thanks. Oxenbury, Helen (1938-), illus. LC 72-86943. (Illus.). 32 p. 19cm. 1969. Simon & Schuster.
Kempner, Carol
--Nicholas. LC 68-18333. (Illus.). 1 v. 29cm. 25p. 1968. Simon & Schuster.
Kempster, Aquila (1864-)
--The Mark. LC 3-27964. 4 p. l., 374 p. col. front., 3 col. pl. 21 cm. 1903. Doubleday, Page and Co.
Kempton, Jean Welch see Welch, Jean Louise, pseud.

Kempton, Kenneth Payson. (1891-), ed. see Horn, Alfred Aloysius & Lewis, Ethelreda, Mrs.

Kempton, Kenneth Payson (1891-)
--The Boy's Trader Horn. 1928. Golden Press.
--Dragon's Thunder. Jones, Wilfred J. (1888-), illus. LC 31-29494. 5 p. l., 3-239 p. col. front., illus. 21 cm. 1931. Little, Brown, and Company.
--Loot of the Flying Dragon. Jones, Wilfred J. (1888-), illus. LC 30-2054. viii p., 2 l., 3-269 p. col. front., illus. 22 cm. 1930. Little, Brown, and Company.
--The Luck of the Blue Macaw. Lee, Manning De Villeneuve (1894-1980), illus. LC 28-22959. 252 p. front., plates. 20 cm. 1928. I. Washburn.
--Phantom Gold. Varian, George, illus. LC 22-17725. 6 p. l., 3-224 p. front., plates. 19 cm. 1922. The Century Co.
--Red Eagle Island. Avison, George F. (1885-), illus. LC 25-176962. xix, 408 p. front., plates. 20 cm. c.1925. The Century Co.
--Seagoing Jock. LC 26-14911. xi, 375 p. front., plates. 20 cm. c.1926. The Century Co.
Kendal, Wallis (1937-)
--Just Gin. Ohlsson, Ib (1935-), illus. LC 72-91405. (Illus.). 159 p. 22cm. 1973. (ISBN 0-670-41095-0). Viking Press.
Kendall, Carol Seeger (1917-)
--The Big Splash. Obligado, Lilian Isabel (1931-), illus. LC 60-2135. 217p. illus. 21cm. 1960. Viking Press.
--The Firelings. Bond, Felicia, illus. LC 81-8096. (Illus.). 251 p. 22cm. 1982. (ISBN 0-689-50226-5). Atheneum.
--The Gammage Cup. Blegvad, Erik (1923-), illus. LC 59-8953. (Illus.). 20cm. 221p. (Voyager bk.: AVB43). 1966, c.1959. Harcourt. **Award: (JNM).**
--The Other Side of the Tunnel. Buchanan, Lilian, illus. LC 57-9475. 192p. illus. 21cm. 1957. Abelard Schuman.
--The Whisper of Glocken. Gobbato, Imero (1923-), illus. LC 65-21690. (Illus.). 256 p. 21cm. 1965. Harcourt, Brace & World.
Kendall, Carol Seeger (1917-) & Li, Yao-Wen (1924-)
--Sweet and Sour: Tales from China. LC 78-24349. (Illus.). 111 p. 22cm. 1979. (ISBN 0-8164-3228-7). Seabury Press.
Kendall, E. D., Mrs.
--The Judge's Sons, 1 of 3 vols. (Illus.). (Kendall's Bks.). N.D. D. Lothrop & Co.
--Kendall's Books: Containing: "Judge's Sons" "Master and Pupil" "The Stanifords of Staniford's Folly", 3 vols. N.D. D. Lothrop Co.
--Master and Pupil, 1 of 3 vols. (Illus.). (Kendall's Bks.). N.D. D Lothrop.
--Stanifords of Staniford's Folly, 1 of 6 vols. (Illus.). (The Staniford Ser.). N.D. D. Lothrop & Co.
Kendall, E. D., Mrs., et al.
--New Five Hundred Dollar Prize Series, Part Second: Containing "Lute Falconer," "The Judge's Sons," "Susy's Spectacles," "Trifles," etc, 7 vols. N.D. Set. D. Lothrop & Co.
Kendall, E. D., Mrs. & Leslie, Emma
--Interesting and Instructive Library for Boys: Containing "Shell Cove," "The Stanifords", "Percy Raydon", etc, 12 vols. N.D. Set-. D. Lothrop & Co.
Kendall, Edward Augustus
--Keeper's Travels in Search of His Master. 87, 2 p. front. 24 degree. 1808. Johnson and Warner.
Kendall, Joan
--The Story of Samuel. (Very First Bible Stories Ser.). (gr. k-4). 1984. (ISBN 0-87162-271-8). Warner Pr.
Kendall, John
--Dungeon of Darkness. LC 83-91421. 80p. (Fantasy Forest Adventures Ser.). (gr. 2-5). 1984. (ISBN 0-394-72459-3). Random.
--Under Dragon's Wing. Grainger, Sam, illus. LC 83-91423. 160p. (Endless Quest Bks.). (gr. 5up). 1984. (ISBN 0-394-72464-X). Random.
--Under Dragon's Wing. Grainger, Sam, illus. LC 83-91423. (Illus.). 157 p. 18cm. (Endless Quest Book ; #15). (Dungeons & dragons adventure book). c.1984. (ISBN 0-88038-076-4). TSR.

Kendall, Lace, pseud., see Stoutenburg, Adrien Pearl.

Kendall, Laura E., tr. see Grousset, Paschal.

Kendall, Oswald

--The Voyage of the Martin Connor. Teague, Donald (1897-), illus. LC 31-31333. 4 p. l., 312 p. col. front., plates (part col.) 22 cm. (Riverside bookshelf). 1931. Houghton Mifflin Company.
Kendall, Patricia, jt. auth. see Stevens, Alden Gifford.
Kendrick, Dennis, retold by.
--The Three Billy Goats Gruff. random house student book program ed. Kendrick, Dennis, illus. LC 79-65376. (Illus.). 32 p. c.1979. (ISBN 0-394-62044-5). Random House.
Kendrick, Dennis, jt. auth. see McCrady, Lady.
Kendrick, Mitch, jt. auth. see Wingate, Gifford W.
Kendrick, Vane, jt. auth. see Payson, Frances.
Keneally, Thomas Michael (1935-)
--Ned Kelly and the City of the Bees. Ryan, Stephen, illus. LC 80-66217. p. cm. 1981, c.1978. (ISBN 0-87923-338-9). (ISBN 0-87923-386-9). D. R. Godine.
Keneyer, Natlee Peoples (1907-) & Montgomery, Rutherford George (1896-)
--A Horse for Claudia and Dennis. LC 58-10441. 153p. illus. 21cm. 1958. Duell, Sloan and Pearce.
Keng Keng
--The Stuck-Up Kitty. Chiang Cheng-An & Wu Tai-Sheng, illus. (Illus.). 38p. 1st U.S. edition. (gr. 6-10). 1979. (ISBN 0-8351-0693-4). (ISBN 0-8351-0694-2). China Bks.
Kenkins, Sara Lucile see Sargent, Joan, pseud.
Kenkins, Sara Lucile (1905-)
--Holiday House. Sargent, Joan, pseud. LC 60-2326. 224p. 21cm. 1960. Avalon Books.
Kenlon, J.
--Fourteen Years a Sailor. N.D. Doubleday Doran & Co.
Kenly, Julie Closson
--Children of a Star. N.D. D. Appleton-Century Co.
--Cities of Wax. N.D. D. Appleton-Century Co.
--Green Magic. N.D. Appleton-Century-Crofts.
--Little Lives. N.D. D. Appleton-Century Co.
--Voices from the Grass. N.D. D. Appleton-Century Co.
--Wild Wings. N.D. D. Appleton-Century Co.
Kennard, Edward Allan (1907-) & Kabotie, Fred
--Field Mouse Goes to War: Tusan Homichi Tuwvota. Kabotie, Fred (1900-), illus. LC 80-455126. (Illus.). 76 p. 1944. Education Division, U.S. Indian Service.
Kennedy, A. E.
--My Animal Story Book. N.D. Dodge Pub. Co.
Kennedy, Celia Mary
--Pinafore Poems. Crowninshield, Laura H., illus. LC 25-8500. 4 p. l., 60 p. illus., plates. 24 cm. 1924. G. Wahr.
Kennedy, Daisy Ellen
--The Mysterious Legend of Spot. N.D. Carlton Press Inc.
Kennedy, Dorothy Mintzlaff, jt. ed. see Kennedy, X. J.
Kennedy, Florence M
--Polar Boy: Being the Story of Arklio, a Little Eskimo Boy Who Lives in Greenland. Madsen, Eleanora, illus. LC 38-18528. 2 p. l., 11-91, 1 p. col. front., illus. (part col.) 28 cm. c.1938. The Saalfield Publishing Company.
Kennedy, Foster
--The Disappearance of Mr. Allan. (gr. 4-6). 1977. (ISBN 0-590-11841-2, Schol Pap). Scholastic Inc.
Kennedy, Grace (1782-1825)
--Anna Ross. 4th American ed. LC 56-51692. 144p. 13cm. 1832. Printed by Chapman & Flagler for G. Hunt.
--Anna Ross. N.D. Robert Carter & Brothers.
--Anna Ross, Philip Colville, Jessy Allan, 1 of 3, Vol. 1. (Grace Kennedy's Stories). N.D. Alfred Martien.
--Jessy Allan. N.D. Robert Carter & Brothers.
--Jessy Allan, the Lame Girl, 1 of 103 vols. (The Pearl Library: No. 41). 1900. Set. Hurst & Co.
Kennedy, Howard Angus (1861-)
--The New World Fairy Book. Millar, Harold Robert (1869-1939), illus. LC 5-7732. xii, 354 p. incl. front., illus., plates, 21 cm. 1904. J. M. Dent & Co.
--The Red Man's Wonder Book. Cumine, George L., illus. LC 31-19280. xvi, 366 p. incl. front., illus. 20 cm. c.1931. E. P. Dutton & Co., Inc.
Kennedy, James Henry (1849-1934)
--Surprise Island, the Pirate of the Sycamore Tree. LC 15-21438. 5 p. l., 3-103, 1 p. incl. front., plates. 19 cm. 1915. Harper & Brothers.
Kennedy, Janet
--The Things I Can Do. Kennedy, Janet, illus. LC 52-1971. unpaged. illus. 21cm. (An Easy to-Read Book). c.1952. Saalfield Pub. Co.
Kennedy, Jean Wilson
--The Nunga Punga & the Booch. Burgess, Anne (1942-), illus. LC 74-24420. (Illus.). 91p. (Encore Edition). (gr. 2-6). 1975. (ISBN 0-684-14217-1, ScribJ). Scribner.
Kennedy, Jerome Richard (1932-)
--Amy's Eyes. Egielski, Richard (1952-), illus. LC 82-48841. (Illus.). 437 p., 2 p. of plates. 24cm. c.1985. (ISBN 0-06-023219-6). (ISBN 0-06-023220-X). Harper & Row.
--The Blue Stone. Himler, Ronald Norbert (1937-), illus. LC 76-9035. (Illus.). 93 p. 23cm. c.1976. (ISBN 0-8234-0283-5). Holiday House. **Award: (ALA).**
--The Boxcar at the Center of the Universe. Kronen, Jeff, illus. LC 81-47718. (Illus.). 89 p. 24cm. c.1982. (ISBN 0-06-023186-6). (ISBN 0-06-023187-4). Harper & Row.
--Come Again in the Spring. Sewall, Marcia (1935-), illus. LC 76-3830. (Illus.). 47 p. c.1976. (ISBN 0-06-023128-9). (ISBN 0-06-023129-7). Harper & Row.

--The Contests at Cowlick. Simont, Marc (1915-), illus. LC 74-23566. (Illus.). 48 p. 22cm. 1975. (ISBN 0-316-48863-1). Little, Brown.
--Crazy in Love. 1st ed. Sewall, Marcia (1935-), illus. LC 80-189. (Illus.). 57 p. 22cm. (Unicorn book). c.1980. (ISBN 0-525-28364-1). E. P. Dutton.
--The Dark Princess. Diamond, Donna (1950-), illus. LC 78-1548. (Illus.). 32 p. 24cm. c.1978. (ISBN 0-8234-0329-7). Holiday House. **Award: (ALA).**
--Delta Baby & Two Sea Songs. Dabcovich, Lydia & Mikolaycak, Charles (1937-), illus. LC 78-6895. (Illus.). 32 p. 25cm. c.1979. (ISBN 0-201-03598-7). Addison-Wesley.
--Inside My Feet: The Story of a Giant. Himler, Ronald Norbert (1937-), illus. LC 78-19479. p. cm. c.1979. (ISBN 0-06-023118-1). (ISBN 0-06-023119-X). Harper & Row.
--The Leprechaun's Story. 1st ed. Sewall, Marcia (1935-), illus. LC 79-11410. (Illus.). 40 p. (Unicorn book). c.1979. (ISBN 0-525-33472-6). Dutton.
--The Lost Kingdom of Karnica. Shulevitz, Uri (1935-), illus. LC 78-32052. (Illus.). 32 p. 26cm. c.1979. (ISBN 0-684-16164-8). Sierra Club Books/Scribner's.
--The Mouse God. 1st ed. Harvard, Stephen (1948-), illus. LC 78-11731. (Illus.). 32 p. 24cm. c.1979. (ISBN 0-316-48904-2). Little, Brown.
--Oliver Hyde's Dishcloth Concert. 1st ed. Parker, Robert Andrew (1927-), illus. LC 76-15980. (Illus.). 47 p. c.1977. (ISBN 0-316-48179-3). Little Brown.
--The Parrot and the Thief. Sewall, Marcia (1935-), illus. LC 74-11460. (Illus.). 30 p. 22cm. 1974. (ISBN 0-316-48862-3). Little, Brown.
--The Porcelain Man. 1st ed. Sewall, Marcia (1935-), illus. LC 75-25783. (Illus.). 30 p. c.1976. (ISBN 0-316-48901-8). Little, Brown.
--The Rise and Fall of Ben Gizzard. 1st ed. Sewall, Marcia (1935-), illus. LC 78-1816. (Illus.). 41 p. 22cm. c.1978. (ISBN 0-316-48903-4). Little, Brown.
--The Rise and Fall of Ben Gizzard. 1st ed. Sewall, Marcia (1935-), illus. LC 78-1816. (Illus.). 41p. 22cm. (An Atlantic Monthly Press Bk.). c.1978. (ISBN 0-316-48903-4). Little, Brown.
--Song of the Horse. 1st ed. Sewall, Marcia (1935-), illus. LC 81-5043. p. cm. (Unicorn book). c.1981. (ISBN 0-525-39679-9). Dutton. **Award: (ALA).**

Kennedy, Jimmy (1903-1984)
--Teddy Bears' Picnic. Sampson, Barbara, illus. (Illus.). (Dinosaur Ser.). (ps-1). 1978. (ISBN 0-85122-067-3, Pub. by Dino Pub). Merrimack Pub Cir.

Kennedy, Joseph Charles see Kennedy, X. J., pseud.

Kennedy, Leonard, jt. auth. see Bamman, Henry A.

Kennedy, Marian
--The Story of Cooky. Reichman, Edith, illus. LC 44-6677. 61 p. illus. (part col.) 17 cm. 1944. Rand McNally & Company.

Kennedy, Marie De Lourdes (1882-)
--Adorable Jack. LC 22-14352. 206 p. incl. front., illus. 19 cm. 1922. Cleveland, J. W. Winterich.
--Willie Frank of Stedley. LC 24-10216. 1 p. l., 5-6, 203 p. 20 cm. c.1919. P. J. Kennedy & Sons.

Kennedy, Mary
--Come and See Me. Alexander, Martha G. (1920-), illus. LC 66-5810. 1 v. (unpaged) col. illus. 19 cm. 1966. Harper & Row.
--The Glass Ring. Glass, Andrew, illus. LC 78-72143. (Illus.). (gr. 1-5). N.D. Dandelion Pr.
--Jenny. Adams, Adrienne (1906-), illus. LC 53-6748. 153p. illus. 23cm. 1954. Lothrop, Lee and Shepard.
--Jenny, Sam & the Invisible Hildegard. Adams, Adrienne (1906-), illus. (gr. k-3). 1977. (ISBN 0-590-10403-9, Schol Pap). Schol Bk Serv.
--River Secret: A Mystery of Florida. LC 41-160671. v p., 1 l., 206 p. col. front. 21 cm. 1941. Dodd, Mead & Company.
--Violets Are Blue. Stone, Helen (1904-), illus. LC 51-9930. 154 p. illus. 21 cm. 1951. Lothrop, Lee & Shepard Co.
--When the Owl Called. Goldsborough, June (1923-), illus. LC 78-73530. (Illus.). (gr. 2-5). N.D. Dandelion Pr.
--Wings. Stren, Patti, illus. (Illus.). 32p. 1980. (ISBN 0-590-31286-3, Schol Pap). Scholastic Inc.

Kennedy, Mary, jt. auth. see Hayes, Helen.

Kennedy, Mary-Lou
--Bill S: Shakespeare for Kids. (Illus.). 82p. (Tomorrow's Books for Today's Children). 1983. (ISBN 0-935326-10-3). Gallopade Pub Group.

Kennedy, Mary & Taylor, Deems (1885-1966)
--A Surprise to the Children. Dowd, James H., illus. LC 33-32771. x p., 1 l., 88 p. incl col front., illus. plates (part col.; 1 double) 20 cm. 1933. Doubleday, Doran & Company, Inc.

Kennedy, Mildred
--The Forest Beyond the Woodlands: A Fairy Tale. LC 21-20297. 152 p. illus., plates. 21 cm. 1921. A. A. Knopf.

Kennedy, Patrick (1801-1873), narrated by.
--Legendary Fictions of the Irish Celt. N.D. Gale Reprint.

Kennedy, Richard see Kennedy, Jerome Richard.

Kennedy, Sara Beaumont Cannon, Mrs.
--Told in a Little Boy's Pocket. N.D. Dodd, Mead & Co.
--Told in a Little Boy's Pocket. LC 8-24463. 4 p. l., 128 p., 1 l. col. front., illus., col. pl. 20 cm. 1908. Moffat, Yard & Company.

Kennedy, Sarah & Simon, John O., eds.
--A Raindrop Has to Do Her Work. 72p. (Orig.). (gr. k-12). 1979. (ISBN 0-917744-29-2). Aldebaran Rev.

Kennedy, Stephanie
--Hey, Didi Darling. LC 83-12774. 1983. (ISBN 0-395-34555-3). Houghton.

Kennedy, T. A, ed.
--The Illustrated Treasury of Fairy Tales. LC 82-81327. (Illus.). 191 p. 26cm. c.1982. (ISBN 0-448-16578-3). Grosset & Dunlap.

Kennedy, William Joseph (1923-)
--Bobbys' and Timmys' Visit to Rosie, the Elephant at the Portland Zoo. LC 54-30494. unpaged. illus. 21cm. c.1954. Locale Books.

Kennedy, X. J., pseud., see Kennedy, Joseph Charles.

Kennedy, X. J, pseud. (1929-)
--Did Adam Name the Vinegarroon?. Kennedy, Joseph Charles. Selig, Heidi Johanna, illus. LC 80-83964. (Illus.). 51 p. 26cm. 1982. (ISBN 0-87923-357-5). D.R. Godine.
--The Forgetful Wishing Well: Poems for Young People. Kennedy, Joseph Charles. Incisa, Monica, illus. LC 84-45977. (Illus.). 88 p. 22cm. 1985. (ISBN 0-689-50317-2). Atheneum. **Award: (ALA).**
--One Winter Night in August, and Other Nonsense Jingles. Kennedy, Joseph Charles. 1st ed. McPhail, Michael David (1940-), illus. LC 74-18185. (Illus.). 58 p. 22cm. 1975. (ISBN 0-689-50022-X). Atheneum.
--The Owlstone Crown. Kennedy, Joseph Charles. 1st ed. Chessare, Michele (1921-), illus. LC 81-3513. (Illus.). 209 p. 22cm. 1983. (ISBN 0-689-50207-9). Atheneum.
--The Phantom Ice Cream Man: More Nonsense Verse. Kennedy, Joseph Charles. McPhail, Michael David (1940-), illus. LC 78-23681. (Illus.). 56 p. 22cm. 1979. (ISBN 0-689-50134-X). (ISBN 0-689-50132-3). Atheneum.

Kennedy, X. J., pseud. (1929-) & Kennedy, Dorothy Mintzlaff, eds.
--Knock at a Star: A Child's Introduction to Poetry. Kennedy, Joseph Charles. 1st ed. Weinhaus, Karen Ann, illus. LC 82-7328. (Illus.). xii, 148 p. 22cm. c.1982. (ISBN 0-316-48853-4). Little, Brown.

Kennell, Ruth Epperson (1893-1977)
--Adventure in Russia: The Ghost of Kirghizia. Wonsetler, John Charles (1900-), illus. LC 47-31398. 196 p. illus., map. 22 cm. 1947. J. Messner.
--Comrade One-Crutch. Perts, Michael, illus. LC 32-25853. ix p., 1 l., 286 p. incl. illus., plates. pl. 22 cm. 1932. Harper & Brothers.
--The Secret Farmyard. Gotlieb, Jules, illus. LC 56-8989. 223p. illus. 22cm. 1956. (ISBN 0-200-72020-1). Abelard-Schuman.
--That Boy Nikolka and Other Tales of Soviet Children. LC 45-512331. 67 p. illus. 23 cm. 1945. Russian War Relief, Inc.
--Vanya of the Streets. Perts, Michael, illus. LC 31-23965. ix p., 1 l., 208 p. front., illus. 22 cm. 1931. Harper & Brothers.

Kennemore, Tim
--Changing Times. LC 84-13505. 192p. (gr. 6 up). 1984. (ISBN 0-571-13285-5). Faber & Faber.
--The Fortunate Few. LC 82-1461. 111 p. 22cm. 1st U.S. edition. 1982, c.1981. (ISBN 0-698-20555-3). Coward, McGann & Geoghegan.
--Here Tomorrow, Gone Today. LC 83-5524. p. cm. 1983. (ISBN 0-571-13011-9). Faber and Faber.
--Wall of Words. 173p. (gr. 5-8). 1983. (ISBN 0-571-11856-9). Faber & Faber.

Kennerson, Vern
--Love Stories for Children. Falk, Cathy Kennerson, illus. (gr. 4-9). 1977. (ISBN 0-682-48788-0). Exposition.

Kennett, John, retold by.
--Around the World in Eighty Days. (gr. 3 up). 1977. (ISBN 0-8277-5374-8). British Bk Ctr.
--Ben-Hur. (gr. 3 up). 1977. (ISBN 0-8277-5375-6). British Bk Ctr.
--The Count of Monte Cristo. (gr. 3 up). 1977. (ISBN 0-8277-5376-4). British Bk Ctr.
--Dr. Jekyll & Mr. Hyde. (gr. 3 up). 1977. (ISBN 0-8277-5377-2). British Bk Ctr.
--Journey to the Centre of the Earth. (gr. 3 up). 1977. (ISBN 0-8277-5379-9). British Bk Ctr.
--Oliver Twist. (gr. 3 up). 1977. (ISBN 0-8277-5380-2). British Bk Ctr.
--White Fang. (gr. 3 up). 1977. (ISBN 0-8277-5384-5). British Bk Ctr.

Kennett, John, retold by see Bronte, Charlotte.

Kenney, Arthur W. & Kenney, Stephen C.
--Charles Hampton: Research Chemist. LC 42-50418. 252p. (Dodd, Mead Career Bks.). 1942. Dodd, Mead & Co.

Kenney, Darrell L.
--Curly, the Promised Puppy. Munson, Harold W. (1920-), illus. LC 60-101048. unpaged. illus. 24cm. 1960. Pacific Press Pub. Association.

Kenney, Harriet
--Little Windjammer. Gordon, Isabel (1916-), illus. LC 72-81711. (Illus.). 62 p. 25cm. 1969. Dutton.

Kenney, Minnie E. see Paull, Minnie E. Kenney, Mrs.

Kenney, Pegeen
--The Farm Alphabet Party. McFall, Christie (1918-), illus. LC 46-22506. 52 p. illus., (part col.) 24 1/2 cm. 1946. The World Publishing Company.
--Games Around the Year. Wythe, Barbara, illus. LC 50-4797. (Animated by Abe Schenk). 20p. col. illus. 24cm. 1950. Garden City Pub.
--The Little Theatre. Herric, Pru, illus. LC 50-4798. (Animated by Abe Schenk). 20p. col. illus. 24cm. 1950. Garden City Pub.

Kenney, Stephen C., jt. auth. see Kenney, Arthur W.

Kenniston, Ida
--Prince Rudolf's Quest: Being a Story of the Strange Adventures of a Young Prince of the Olden Time. LC 12-19327. v, 150 p. front. 21 cm. 1912. The American Humane Education Society.

Kenniston, Ken
--The Man Who Loved Birds: A Fable for Children. Kenniston, Ken, illus. LC 62-17256. unpaged. illus. 21x26cm. 1962. (ISBN 0-8178-3412-5). Harvey House.

Kennon, Graham
--Woodsy Owl & the Trail Bikers. McSavage, Frank, illus. (Illus.). 24p. (gr. k-3). 1976. (ISBN 0-307-60107-2, Golden Pr). Western Pub.

Kenny, Ellsworth Newcomb see Newcomb, Ellsworth, pseud.

Kenny, Herbert Andrew (1912-)
--Alistare Owl. Tinkelman, Murray (1933-), illus. LC 78-77934. (Illus.). 80 p. 24cm. 1969. Harper & Row.
--Dear Dolphin. Oechsli, Kelly (1918-), illus. LC 67-20214. (Illus.). 174 p. 24cm. 1967. Random House.

Kenny, Kathryn
--The Hudson River Mystery. (Trixie Belden Mystery Stories). (gr. 3 up). 1979. (ISBN 0-307-61599-5, Golden Pr). (ISBN 0-307-21599-7). Western Pub.
--Mysterious Code. (Trixie Belden Mystery Stories Ser.). (gr. 4 up). 1977. (ISBN 0-307-61540-5, Golden Pr). (ISBN 0-307-21540-7). Western Pub.
--Mysterious Visitor. (Trixie Belden Mystery Stories Ser.). (gr. 4 up). 1977. (ISBN 0-307-61532-4, Golden Pr). (ISBN 0-307-21532-6). Western Pub.
--Mystery at Bob White Cave. (Trixie Belden Mystery Stories Ser.). (gr. 4 up). 1977. (ISBN 0-307-61586-3, Golden Pr). (ISBN 0-307-21586-5). Western Pub.
--Mystery at Mead's Mountain. (Trixie Belden Mystery Stories). (gr. 4 up). 1978. (ISBN 0-307-61593-6, Golden Pr). (ISBN 0-307-21593-8). Western Pub.
--Mystery at Saratoga. (Trixie Belden Mystery Stories Ser.). (gr. 5-9). 1979. (ISBN 0-307-61595-2, Golden Pr). (ISBN 0-307-21595-4). Western Pub.
--Mystery in Arizona. (Trixie Belden Mystery Stories Ser.). (gr. 4 up). 1977. (ISBN 0-307-61533-2, Golden Pr). (ISBN 0-307-21533-4). Western Pub.
--Mystery of Old Telegraph Road. (Trixie Belden Mystery Stories Ser.). (gr. 4 up). 1978. (ISBN 0-307-61591-X, Golden Pr). (ISBN 0-307-21591-1). Western Pub.
--The Mystery of the Antique Doll, No. 36. Spence, Jim, illus. LC 83-83352. (Illus.). 200p. (Trixie Belden Mysteries Ser.). (gr. 3-8). 1984. (ISBN 0-307-21559-8, Golden Bks). Western Pub.
--Mystery of the Blinking Eye. (Trixie Belden Mystery Stories Ser.). (gr. 4 up). 1977. (ISBN 0-307-61587-1, Golden Pr). (ISBN 0-307-21587-3). Western Pub.
--Mystery of the Castaway Children. (Trixie Belden Mystery Stories Ser.). (gr. 4 up). 1978. (ISBN 0-307-61592-8, Golden Pr). (ISBN 0-307-21592-X). Western Pub.
--Mystery of the Emeralds. (Trixie Belden Mystery Stories Ser.). (gr. 4 up). 1977. (ISBN 0-307-61522-7, Golden Pr). (ISBN 0-307-21522-9). Western Pub.
--The Mystery of the Ghostly Galleon. (Trixie Belden Ser.). (gr. 5-9). 1979. (ISBN 0-307-61598-7, Golden Pr). (ISBN 0-307-21598-9). Western Pub.
--The Mystery of the Headless Horseman. (Trixie Belden Ser.). (gr. 5-9). 1979. (ISBN 0-307-61597-9, Golden Pr). (ISBN 0-307-21597-0). Western Pub.
--The Mystery of the Memorial Day Fire, No. 35. Spence, Jim, illus. LC 83-83351. (Illus.). 200p. (Trixie Belden Mysteries Ser.). (gr. 3-8). 1984. (ISBN 0-307-21558-X, Golden Bks). Western Pub.
--Mystery of the Missing Heiress. (Trixie Belden Mystery Stories Ser.). (gr. 4 up). 1977. (ISBN 0-307-61542-1, Golden Pr). (ISBN 0-307-21542-3). Western Pub.
--Mystery of the Phantom Grasshopper. (Trixie Belden Mystery Stories Ser.). (gr. 4 up). 1977. (ISBN 0-307-61589-8, Golden Pr). (ISBN 0-307-21589-X). Western Pub.
--Mystery of the Queen's Necklace. (Trixie Belden Ser.). (gr. 5-9). 1979. (ISBN 0-307-61594-4, Golden Pr). (ISBN 0-307-21594-6). Western Pub.
--Mystery of the Uninvited Guest. (Trixie Belden Mystery Stories Ser.). (gr. 4 up). 1977. (ISBN 0-307-61588-X, Golden Pr). (ISBN 0-307-21588-1). Western Pub.
--Mystery off Glen Road. (Trixie Belden Mystery Stories Ser.). (gr. 4 up). 1977. (ISBN 0-307-61534-0, Golden Pr). (ISBN 0-307-21534-2). Western Pub.
--Mystery on Cobbett's Island. (Trixie Belden Mystery Stories Ser.). (gr. 4 up). 1977. (ISBN 0-307-61521-9, Golden Pr). (ISBN 0-307-21521-0). Western Pub.
--Mystery on the Mississippi. (Trixie Belden Mystery Stories Ser.). (gr. 4 up). 1977. (ISBN 0-307-61523-5, Golden Pr). (ISBN 0-307-21523-7). Western Pub.
--The Sasquatch Mystery. (Trixie Belden Ser.). (gr. 5-9). 1979. (ISBN 0-307-61596-0, Golden Pr). (ISBN 0-307-21596-2). Western Pub.
--Secret of the Mansion. (Trixie Belden Mystery Stories Ser.). (gr. 4 up). 1977. (ISBN 0-307-61524-3, Golden Pr). (ISBN 0-307-21524-5). Western Pub.
--Secret of the Unseen Treasure. (Trixie Belden Mystery Stories Ser.). (gr. 4 up). 1977. (ISBN 0-307-61590-1, Golden Pr). (ISBN 0-307-21590-3). Western Pub.
--Trixie Belden and the Marshland Mystery. Frame, Paul (1913-), illus. LC 68-680. 254 p. col. illus. 22 cm. (Your Trixie Belden library, 10). 1967. Golden Press.
--Trixie Belden and the Mysterious Code. Petie, Haris, pseud. (1915-) & Frame, Paul (1913-), illus. Petty, Roberta. LC 67-1940. 252 p. col. illus. 22 cm. (Your Trixie Belden library, 7). c.1966. Whitman Pub. Co.
--Trixie Belden Gift Set, 3 bks. (gr. 9 up). 1980. (ISBN 0-307-13623-X, Golden Pr). Western Pub.

Kenny, Kevin, pseud., see Krull, Kathleen.

Kenny, Kevin, pseud. (1952-) & Krull, Helen
--Sometimes My Mom Drinks Too Much. Krull, Kathleen. Cogancherry, Helen, illus. LC 80-14515. (Illus.). 31 p. 24cm. c.1980. (ISBN 0-8172-1366-X). Raintree Childrens Books.

Kenoyer, Natlee Peoples (1907-)
--Claudia's Five-Dollar Horse. 1st ed. Kinstler, Everett Raymond (1926-), illus. LC 59-9378. 194p. illus. 21cm. 1960. Duell, Sloan and Pearce.
--The Moon God's Daughter. Lape, Pranas (1921-), illus. LC 74-84476. (Illus.). 200 p., 1 leaf of plates. 22cm. 1974. (ISBN 0-87141-037-0). Manyland Books.
--Three Children and a Firehorse. Wiskur, Darrell D., illus. LC 68-55949. (Illus.). 144 p. 23cm. 1969. Bethany Press.

Kent, Alexander, pseud., see Reeman, Douglas Edward.

Kent, Alexander, pseud. (1924-)
--Midshipman Bolitho and the Avenger. Reeman, Douglas Edward. LC 78-9127. 143 p. 21cm. 1978. (ISBN 0-399-20652-3). Putnam.
--Richard Bolitho, Midshipman. Reeman, Douglas Edward. LC 76-4921. 158 p. 21cm. 1976, c.1975. (ISBN 0-399-20514-4). Putnam.

Kent, Barbara
--The House by the River: A Novel. Davis, Warren B. (1838-), illus. (Bound with the Children's Crusade by Frederick Whittaker 1838). 2 p. l., 7-328 p. illus. 20 cm. (Ledger library. no. 123). (The Choice Ser.: No. 123). 1895. R. Bonner's Sons.

Kent, David
--The Desert People. (Illus.). 32p. (Explorer Bible Stories Ser.). (gr. 3-5). 1982. (ISBN 0-531-09190-2, Warwick). Watts.
--Escape from Egypt. (Illus.). 32p. (Explorer Bible Stories Ser.). (gr. 3-5). 1982. (ISBN 0-531-09191-0, Warwick). Watts.
--The Kings of Israel. (Illus.). 32p. (Explorer Bible Stories). (gr. 3-5). 1982. (ISBN 0-531-09192-9, Warwick). Watts.

--Two Young Inventors: The Story of the Flying Boat. Picknell, George W., illus. LC 4-21997. (Illus.). 19cm. 312p. 1905. Lee and Shepard Company.
--Young Heroes of Wire & Rail. N.D. Lothrop,Lee & Shepard.
Kerr, Anne Judith (1923-)
--Mog in the Dark. (Illus.). 48p. (gr. k up). 1984. (ISBN 0-88332-373-7). Larousse.
--Mog, the Forgetful Cat. Kerr, Anne-Judith (1923-), illus. LC 75-174598. (Illus.). 42 p. 27cm. 1972, c.1970. (ISBN 0-8193-0544-8). (ISBN 0-8193-0545-6). Parents' Magazine Press.
--Mog's Christmas. Kerr, Anne Judith (1923-), illus. LC 77-78121. (Illus.). 32 p. 27cm. 1976. (ISBN 0-529-05376-4). Collins.
--Mog's Christmas. Kerr, Anne Judith (1923-), illus. LC 77-78121. (Illus.). 1st U.S. edition. (ps-3). 1977. (ISBN 0-529-05376-4, Philomel). Putnam Pub Group.
--The Other Way Round. LC 75-4254. 256 p. 22cm. 1975. (ISBN 0-698-20335-6). Coward, McCann & Geoghegan.
--A Small Person Far Away. Kerr, Anne Judith (1923-), illus. LC 78-13195. (gr. 6-8). 1979. (ISBN 0-698-20472-7, Coward). Putnam Pub Group.
--The Tiger Who Came to Tea. Keer, Anne Judith (1923-), illus. LC 68-18541. (Illus.). 32 p. 27cm. 1968. Coward-McCann.
--When Hitler Stole Pink Rabbit. Kerr, Anne-Judith (1923-), illus. LC 71-185765. (Illus.). 191 p. 22cm. 1972, c.1971. Coward, McCann & Geoghegan. **Award: (ALA).**
--When Willy Went to the Wedding. Kerr, Anne-Judith (1923-), illus. LC 72-8027. (Illus.). 41 p. 27cm. 1973, c.1972. (ISBN 0-8193-0658-4). (ISBN 0-8193-0658-4). Parents' Magazine Press.
Kerr, Annie Barclay (1873-)
--So Gracious Is the Time. Voute, Kathleen (1892-), illus. LC 38-33406. 6 p. l., 3-90 p. illus. 21 cm. c.1938. The Womans Press.
Kerr, Estelle M
--The Town Crier of Gevrey. LC 30-973638. 9 p. l., 129 p. 1 l. incl. illus., plates. front. 22 1/2 cm. 1930. The Macmillan Company.
Kerr, Frances Morse & Fidelman, Gertrude
--Holiday Times for Terry and Cherry: Stories for Children. Mandel, Saul, illus. LC 51-13958. 79 p. illus. 23 cm. 1951. Exposition Press.
Kerr, Helen V
--Grave Allegra. LC 75-102662. 121 p. 21cm. 1970. Ives Washburn.
--Helga's Magic. Wennerstrom, Genia Katherine (1930-), illus. Genia, pseud. LC 71-120954. (Illus.). 87 p. 21cm. 1970. Washburn.
Kerr, James Lennox see Dawlish, Peter, pseud.
Kerr, James Lennox (1899-1963)
--Aztec Gold. Dawlish, Peter, pseud. Jobson, Patrick (1919-), illus. LC 52-2509. 270p. illus. 19cm. 1951. Oxford University Press.
--MacClellan's Lake. Sharp, Roy, illus. LC 52-2510. 229p. illus. 24cm. 1951. Oxford University Press.
Kerr, James Stolee (1928-)
--Billy's Lost Smile. 16p. (Orig.). (ps-3). 1961. (ISBN 0-8066-9265-0). Augsburg.
--Dandy, the Dime. Mathews, S. Schofer, illus. LC 60-101786. unpaged. illus. 29cm. 1960. (ISBN 0-513-00317-7). T. S. Denison.
Kerr, Jessica (1901-)
--Shakespeare's Flowers. Dowden, Anne Ophelia (1907-), illus. LC 68-13585. (Illus.). color ils. index. 96p. (gr. 7 up). 1969. (ISBN 0-690-73163-9, TYC-J). Har-Row.
Kerr, Judith see Kerr, Anne Judith.
Kerr, Laura Nowak (1904-)
--The Girl Who Ran for President. N.D. Nelson Bks.
--Julie with Wings. LC 60-6426. 186p. illus. 22cm. 1960. Funk & Wagnalls Co.

Kerr, M. E, pseud., see Meaker, Marijane.
Kerr, M. E, pseud. (1927-)
--Dinky Hocker Shoots Smack. Meaker, Marijane. LC 73-4264. 242 p. 25cm. 1973, c.1972. G. K. Hall.
--Dinky Hocker Shoots Smack. Meaker, Marijane. LC 72-80366. 198 p. 22cm. 1972. (ISBN 0-06-023150-5). (ISBN 0-06-023150-5). Harper & Row. **Award: (ALA).**
--Gentlehands. Meager, Marijane. LC 77-11860. 183 p. 22cm. c.1978. (ISBN 0-06-023176-9). (ISBN 0-06-023177-7). Harper & Row.
--Him She Loves?. Meaker, Marijane. LC 83-48818. c.1984. (ISBN 0-06-023238-2). Harper & Row.
--I Stay Near You. Meaker, Marijane. LC 84-48342. 192p. (Charlotte Zolotow Bk.). (gr. 7 up). 1985. (ISBN 0-06-023104-1). (ISBN 0-06-023105-X). HarpJ.
--If I Love You, Am I Trapped Forever?. Meaker, Marijane. LC 73-20305. 258 p. 24cm. 1974, c.1973. (ISBN 0-8161-6173-9). G. K. Hall.
--If I Love You, Am I Trapped Forever?. Meaker, Marijane. LC 72-9860. 177 p. 22cm. 1973. (ISBN 0-06-023148-3). (ISBN 0-06-023149-1). Harper & Row.
--I'll Love You When You're More Like Me. Meaker, Marijane. LC 76-58709. 183 p. 22cm. c.1977. (ISBN 0-06-023136-X). (ISBN 0-06-023137-8). Harper & Row.
--Is That You, Miss Blue?. Meaker, Marijane. LC 74-2627. 170 p. 22cm. 1975. (ISBN 0-06-023144-0). (ISBN 0-06-023145-9). Harper & Row. **Award: (ALA).**
--Little Little. Meaker, Marijane. LC 80-8454. 183 p. 22cm. c.1981. (ISBN 0-06-023184-X). (ISBN 0-06-023185-8). Harper & Row. **Award: (ALA).**
--Love Is a Missing Person. Meaker, Marijane. LC 75-6299. 164 p. 22cm. c.1975. (ISBN 0-06-023161-0). (ISBN 0-06-023162-9). Harper & Row.
--The Son of Someone Famous. Meaker, Marijane. LC 73-14338. 226 p. 22cm. 1974. (ISBN 0-06-023146-7). (ISBN 0-06-023146-7). Harper & Row.
--The Son of Someone Famous. Meaker, Marijane. 1979. Harper.
--What I Really Think of You. Meaker, Marijane. LC 81-47735. p. cm. c.1982. (ISBN 0-06-023188-2). (ISBN 0-06-023189-0). Harper & Row.
Kerr, Michael
--Angela, the Lazy Princess. Kerr, Michael, illus. (Illus.). (gr. k-2). 1967. (ISBN 0-679-20013-4). McKay.
Kerr, Mildred Lewis & Harner, Elizabeth F., eds.
--Giants and Fairies. Tiedemann, Berthold & Evars, Ray, Jr., illus. LC 47-1329. 128 p. illus. 21 1/2 cm. 1946. Charles E. Merrill Co., Inc.
Kerr, Mildred Lewis & Ross, Frances, eds.
--First Fairy Tales. Sherwood Jones, Mary & Evans, Ray, Jr., illus. LC 47-19010. 1946. Charles E. Merrill Co.
Kerr, Pearl
--Happy Birthday. Orfe, Joan, illus. LC 69-18155. (Illus.). 21cm. 24p. (ps). 1969. (ISBN 0-8170-0430-0). Judson.
Kerr, Phyllis Forbes
--Bumble Cat: How She Came to Be. Kerr, Phyllis Forbes, illus. LC 85-11737. (Illus.). 32 p. 25cm. c.1985. Houghton Mifflin.
Kerr, Sue Felt
--Hello--Goodbye. LC 60-7135. unpaged. illus. 22 x 27 cm. 1960. Doubleday.
--Here Comes Weezie. Kerr, Sue Felt, illus. LC 67-26516. (Illus.). 24cm. 1967. A. Whitman.
--Weezie Goes to School. LC 74-91738. (Illus.). 32 p. 24cm. 1969. A. Whitman.
Kerr, Sue Felt see Felt, Sue.
Kerr, William J
--Zany Zoo Animal Rhymes. 1st Ed ed. Dahl, Carl G., illus. LC 55-102977. unpaged. illus. 21cm. 1955. Exposition Press.
Kerry, Lois, pseud., see Duncan, Lois Steinmetz.
Kerry, Lois, pseud. (1934-)
--Love Song for Joyce. Duncan, Lois Steinmetz. LC 58-11365. 244p. 22cm. 1958. Funk & Wagnalls.
--A Promise for Joyce. Duncan, Lois Steinmetz. LC 59-10892. 214p. 22cm. 1959. Funk & Wagnalls.
Kershaw, Patricia
--Terror for Three. 18cm. 226p. 1973. Zondervan.
--Trapped in the Old Cabin. LC 79-17213. 208 p. 21cm. (Pathfinder Ser.). 1980, c.1973. (ISBN 0-310-37861-3). Zondervan Pub. House.
--Trapped in the Old Cabin. Munger, Nancy, illus. LC 79-17213. (Illus.). 208p. (The Pathfinder Ser.). 1980. (ISBN 0-310-37861-3). Zondervan.
--A Truckload of Trouble. LC 79-19085. 207 p. 21cm. (Pathfinders Series: No. 8). c.1980. (ISBN 0-310-37881-8). Zondervan Pub. House.
Kershner, Louise, adapted by see Haggard, Henry Rider, Sir.
Ker Wilson, Barbara, jt. auth. see Fontannza, Luciennec.
Ker Wilson, Barbara (1929-)
--Ann & Peter in London. (gr. 7 up). N.D. Soccer.
--Ann and Peter in London. Toothill, Ilse & Toothill, Harry, illus. LC 66-950. 144p. illus. 20cm. (Kennedys abroad). 1966, c.1965. F. Muller.

--The Biscuit-Tin Family. 1st American ed. Dick, Astra Lacis, illus. LC 67-31581. (Illus.). 190p. 21cm. 1968, c.1967. World Pub. Co.

--The Geography Lesson. MacDonald, Gregory (1951-), illus. LC 79-110336. (Illus.). 32 p. 22cm. 1977. Seal Press.

--In the Shadow of Vesuvius. LC 65-197137. 191p. illus. 21cm. c.1965. World.

--The Lovely Summer. Hoffer, Marina, illus. LC 60-13666. (Illus.). 192 p. 21cm. 1960. Dodd, Mead.
--Path-Through-the-Woods. 1958. S G Phillips.
--Path-Through-the-Woods. Stewart, Charles William (1915-), illus. LC 58-9624. (Illus.). 182 p. 22cm. (Criterion book for young people). 1958. Criterion Books.
Ker Wilson, Barbara (1929-), retold by.
--Animal Folk Tales. Hanak, Mirko, illus. LC 70-141635. (Illus.). 140 p. 29cm. 1971, c.1968. Grosset & Dunlap.
--Fairy Tale of England. Goodall, John Strickland (1908-), illus. (Fairy Tales of Many Lands). N.D. E. P. Dutton & Co.
--Fairy Tales of England. Goodall, John Strickland (1908-), illus. LC 60-51317. unpaged. illus. 21 cm. c.1960. Dutton.
--Fairy Tales of France. Mclaren, William, illus. LC 60-51318. unpaged. illus. 21 cm. c.1960. Cassell.
--Fairy Tales of France. McLaren, William, illus. LC 60-51318. unpaged. illus. 21. (Fairy Tales of Many Lands). 1960. E. P. Dutton & Co.
--Fairy Tales of Germany. Mittelmann, Gertrude, illus. LC 60-933. unpaged. illus. 21 cm. c.1959. Cassell.
--Fairy Tales of Germany. Mittelmann, Gertrude, illus. LC 60-933. unpaged. illus. 21. (Fairy Tales of Many Lands). 1959. E. P. Dutton & Co.
--Fairy Tales of India. Mackensie, Rene, illus. LC 60-51315. unpaged. illus. 21. (Fairy Tales of Many Lands). 1960. E. P. Dutton & Co.
--Fairy Tales of Ireland. Miller, George W., illus. LC 60-934. unpaged. illus. 21 cm. c.1959. Cassell.
--Fairy Tales of Ireland. Miller, George W., illus. LC 60-934. unpaged. illus. 21. (Fairy Tales of Many Lands). 1959. E. P. Dutton & Co.
--Fairy Tales of Mexico. Miller, George W., illus. LC 60-51316. unpaged. illus. 21 cm. c.1960. Cassell.
--Fairy Tales of Mexico. Miller, George W., illus. LC 60-51316. unpaged. illus. 21. (Fairy Tales of Many Lands). 1960. E. P. Dutton & Co.
--Fairy Tales of Persia. Miller, George W., illus. LC 61-65151. unpaged. illus. 21 cm. c.1961. Dutton.
--Fairy Tales of Russia. Athram, Jacqueline, illus. LC 60-935. unpaged. illus. 21 cm. c.1959. Cassell.
--Fairy Tales of Russia. Athram, Jacqueline, illus. LC 60-935. unpaged. illus. 21. (Fairy Tales of Many Lands). 1959. E. P. Dutton & Co.
--Greek Fairy Tales. Toothill, Harry, illus. (Illus.). vi, 229 p. 23cm. (World fairy tale collections). 1968, c.1966. Follett Pub. Co.

--Scottish Folk-Tales and Legends. Kiddell-Monroe, Joan (1908-), illus. LC 55-14279. 207p. illus. 23cm. (Oxford myths and legends). 1954. Oxford University Press.

--Scottish Folk-Tales and Legends. Kiddell-Monroe, Joan (1908-), illus. LC 67-29286. (Illus.). xi, 207 p. 23cm. (Myths and legends series). N.D. Walck.

Ker Wilson, Barbara (1929-) & Bates, Daisy (1861-1951)
--Tales Told to Kabbarli. Thomas, Harold, illus. LC 72-79797. (Illus.). 101 p. 25cm. 1972. (ISBN 0-517-50073-6). Crown Publishers.
Kescel, Joseph Thomas (1874-)
--The Adventures of Dal Hamilton--Prospector: Or, Hustling for Pay Dirt. LC 21-7808. 260 p. front. 20 cm. c.1920. W. A. Wilde Company.
Kessel, Joseph Elie (1899-1979)
--The Lion. 1959. Borzoi Books.
--Lion. Johnson, Eugene Harper, illus. (Illus.). (gr. 6-9). 1962. (ISBN 0-394-81335-9). (ISBN 0-394-91335-3). Knopf.
Kessel, Joyce Karen (1937-)
--Halloween. Carlson, Nancy Lee (1953-), illus. LC 80-15890. (Illus.). 48p. (Carolrhoda on My Own Bks.). (gr. k-3). 1980. (ISBN 0-87614-132-7). Carolrhoda Bks.
--Valentine's Day. Ritz, Karen, illus. LC 81-3842. (Illus.). 48p. (Carolrhoda on My Own Bks.). (gr. k-3). 1981. (ISBN 0-87614-166-1). Carolrhoda Bks.
Kesselman, Wendy Ann
--Angelita. Holt, Norma, illus. LC 71-126067. (Illus.). 72 p. 27cm. 1970. (ISBN 0-8090-2662-7). Hill and Wang.
--Emma. Cooney, Barbara (1917-), illus. LC 77-15161. (Illus.). 32 p. c.1980. (ISBN 0-385-13461-4). (ISBN 0-385-13462-2). Doubleday.
--Flick. 1st ed. LC 80-8435. p. cm. c.1983. (ISBN 0-06-023182-3). (ISBN 0-06-023183-1). Harper & Row.
--Franz Tovey and the Rare Animals. Holt, Norma & Schmid, Eleonore, illus. LC 68-18196. 32 p. (chiefly illus). 27cm. 1968. H. Quist.
--Joey. Holt, Norma, illus. LC 72-83434. (Illus.). 61 p. 29cm. 1972. (ISBN 0-88208-005-9). L. Hill.
--Slash: An Aligator's Story. Weisbecker, Philippe, photos by. LC 75-141533. (Illus.). 32 p. 29cm. 1971. (ISBN 0-8252-0045-8). (ISBN 0-8252-0046-6). H. Quist.
--There's a Train Going by My Window. Chen, Tony (1929-), illus. LC 80-625. p. cm. 1981. (ISBN 0-385-15670-7). Doubleday.
--There's a Train Going By My Window. Chen, Tony (1929-), illus. 1982. Doubleday.
--Time for Jody. Dumas, Gerald J. (1930-), illus. LC 75-6295. (Illus.). 40 p. c.1975. Harper & Row.
Kessler, Ethel (1921-) & Kessler, Leonard P. (1921-)
--All Aboard the Train. Kessler, Leonard P. (1921-), illus. LC 64-11547. (Illus.). 42 p. 1964. Doubleday.
--All for Fall. Kessler, Leonard P. (1921-), illus. LC 74-2249. (Illus.). 32 p. 24cm. 1974. (ISBN 0-8193-0735-1). (ISBN 0-8193-0736-X). Parents' Magazine Press.
--Are You Square?. Kessler, Leonard P. (1921-), illus. LC 66-16596. 1v. (unpaged) col. illus. 21 x 28cm. N.D. Doubleday.
--Baby-Sitter, Duck. Kessler, Leonard P. (1921-), illus. LC 80-21857. (Illus.). 32 p. 23cm. (Begin to read with Duck and Pig). c.1981. (ISBN 0-8116-7552-1). Garrard Pub. Co.
--The Big Fight. Kessler, Leonard P. (1921-), illus. LC 80-17244. (Illus.). 32 p. 23cm. (Begin to read with Duck and Pig). c.1981. (ISBN 0-8116-7550-5). Garrard Pub. Co.
--Big Red Bus. Kessler, Leonard P. (1921-), illus. LC 57-8090. (Illus.). 1 v. (unpaged). 26cm. (Junior books.). (gr. k-2). c.1957. Doubleday. **Award: (NYT).**
--Church, Crunch. Kessler, Leonard P. (1921-), illus. LC 55-900804. unpaged. illus. 21x23cm. (Junior books). c.1955. Doubleday.
--The Day Daddy Stayed Home. Kessler, Leonard P. (1921-), illus. LC 59-5898. (Illus.). unpaged. 25cm. (Junior books). c.1959. Doubleday.
--Do Baby Bears Sit in Chairs?. What Animals Do. 1st ed. Kessler, Leonard P. (1921-), illus. LC 61-11141. (Illus.). 1961. (ISBN 0-385-08693-8, Zephyr). Doubleday.
--Grandpa Witch and the Magic Doobelator. Kessler, Leonard P. (1921-), illus. LC 81-5980. p. cm. (Ready-to-Read). c.1981. (ISBN 0-02-750210-4). Macmillan.
--Kim and Me. Kessler, Leonard P. (1921-), illus. LC 60-6942. unpaged. illus. 21 x 24cm. c.1960. Doubleday, Junior Books.
--Night Story. Kessler, Leonard P. (1921-), illus. LC 80-24626. (Illus.). 48 p. 23cm. (Ready-to-read). c.1981. (ISBN 0-02-750220-1). Macmillan.
--Our Tooth Story: A Tale of Twenty Teeth. Kessler, Leonard P. (1921-), illus. LC 74-175308. (Illus.). 46 p. 23cm. 1972. (ISBN 0-396-06472-8). Dodd, Mead.
--Peek-a-Boo. Kessler, Leonard P. (1921-), illus. LC 56-8234. unpaged. illus. 25cm. (Junior Books). c.1956. Doubleday.
--Pig's New Hat. Kessler, Leonard P. (1921-), illus. LC 80-17373. (Illus.). 32 p. 23cm. (Begin to read with Duck and Pig). c.1981. (ISBN 0-8116-7551-3). Garrard Pub. Co.
--Pig's Orange House. Kessler, Leonard P. (1921-), illus. LC 80-24222. (Illus.). 32 p. 23cm. (Begin to read with Duck and Pig). c.1981. (ISBN 0-8116-7553-X). Garrard Pub. Co.
--Plink, Plink!. Goes the Water in My Sink. Kessler, Leonard P. (1921-), illus. LC 54-8916. (Illus.). unpaged. (Junior books). c.1954. Doubleday.
--Slush, Slush!. Kessler, Leonard P. (1921-), illus. LC 73-4445. (Illus.). 34 p. 24cm. 1973. (ISBN 0-8193-0675-4). (ISBN 0-8193-0675-4). Parents' Magazine Press.
--Splish Splash. Kessler, Leonard P. (1921-), illus. LC 72-8137. (Illus.). 32 p. 24cm. 1973. (ISBN 0-8193-0654-1). Parents' Magazine Press.
--The Sweeneys from 9D. Kessler, Leonard P. (1921-), illus. LC 84-20156. (Illus.). 56 p. 23cm. (Ready-to-Read). c.1985. (ISBN 0-02-750230-9). Macmillan.
--Time to Play, Time to Sleep. Kessler, Leonard P. (1921-), illus. LC 80-13663. p. cm. 1981. (ISBN 0-8116-6082-6). Garrard.
--What Do You Play on a Summer Day?. Kessler, Leonard P. (1921-), illus. LC 76-18095. p. cm. 32p. 1977. (ISBN 0-8193-0866-8). (ISBN 0-8193-0867-6). Parents' Magazine Press.
--What's Inside the Box?. Kessler, Leonard P. (1921-), illus. LC 76-2523. (Illus.). 48 p. 24cm. c.1976. (ISBN 0-396-07328-X). Dodd, Mead.
Kessler, Jascha, tr. see Olujic, Grozdana.
Kessler, Leonard P., jt. auth. see Kessler, Ethel.
Kessler, Leonard P., jt. auth. see Pape, Donna Lugg.
Kessler, Leonard P. (1921-)
--Aqui Viene el Ponchado. Kessler, Leonard P. (1921-), illus. Belpre, Pura, tr. LC 69-14451. (Illus.). 5 7/8 x 8 1/2. 64p. (18 pt.). (Spanish I Can Read Bks.). (gr. 2-3). 1969. (ISBN 0-06-023154-8). Har-Row.
--Are We Lost, Daddy?. Kessler, Leonard P. (1921-), illus. (Illus.). 45 p. 24cm. 1967. Grosset & Dunlap.
--The Big Mile Race. 1st ed. Kessler, Leonard P. (1921-), illus. LC 82-9274. (Illus.). 46 p. 22cm. (Greenwillow read-alone). c.1983. (ISBN 0-688-01420-8). (ISBN 0-688-01421-6). Greenwillow Books.

--The Big Mile Race. Kessler, Leonard P. (1921-), illus. LC 82-9274. (Illus.). 6 14 x 8 3/8. 48p. (16 pt.). (gr. 1-3). 1983. (ISBN 0-688-01420-8). (ISBN 0-688-01421-6). Greenwillow.
--Did You Ever Hear a Klunk Say Please?. Kessler, Leonard P. (1921-), illus. LC 67-2305. (Illus.). 52 p. 19cm. 1967. Dodd, Mead.
--Do You Have Any Carrots?. Pierson, Lori, illus. LC 78-23708. (Illus.). 32 p. 23cm. c.1979. (ISBN 0-8116-6074-5). Garrard Pub. Co.
--Duck on a Truck. Kessler, Leonard P. (1921-), illus. (Easy Readers). (gr. 1-2). 1961. Wonder.
--The Forgetful Pirate. Kessler, Leonard P. (1921-), illus. LC 74-5026. (Illus.). 63 p. 23cm. 1974. (ISBN 0-8116-6972-6). Garrard Pub. Co.
--Here Comes the Strikeout. Kessler, Leonard P. (1921-), illus. LC 65-10728. (Illus.). 5 7/8 x 8 1/2. 64p. (18 pt.). (Sports I Can Read Bks.). (gr. k-3). 1965. (ISBN 0-06-023155-6). (ISBN 0-06-023156-4). (ISBN 0-06-444011-7). Har-Row.
--Hey Diddle Diddle. Kessler, Leonard P. (1921-), illus. LC 79-18966. (Illus.). 31 p. 23cm. (Young Mother Goose Books). c.1980. Garrard Pub. Co.
--Hickory Dickory Dock. Cushman, Doug, illus. LC 79-18775. (Illus.). 32 p. 23cm. (Young Mother Goose Books). c.1980. (ISBN 0-8116-7400-2). Garrard Pub. Co.
--How Old Is Old?. Kessler, Leonard P. (1921-), illus. LC 67-170659. 45p. col. illus. 25cm. (Sci. parade bk.). 1967. Harvey House.
--Kick, Pass, and Run. Kessler, Leonard P. (1921-), illus. LC 66-18656. (Illus.). 64 p. 23cm. (Sports I can read book). 1966. Harper & Row.
--Last One in Is a Rotten Egg. Kessler, Leonard P. (1921-), illus. LC 69-10209. (Illus.). 5 7/8 x 8 1/2. 64p. (18 pt.). (Sports I Can Read Bks.). (gr. k-3). 1969. (ISBN 0-06-023158-0). Har-Row.
--Last One in Is a Rotten Egg. Kessler, Leonard P. (1921-), illus. LC 69-10209. (Illus.). 64 p. 23cm. (Sports I can read book). 1969. Harper & Row.
--Mister Pine's Mixed-up Signs. Kessler, Leonard P. (1921-), illus. (Easy Readers Ser.). (gr. k-3). N.D. Wonder.
--The Mother Goose Game. Paris, Pat, illus. LC 79-18989. (Illus.). 31 p. 23cm. (Young Mother Goose Books). c.1980. (ISBN 0-8116-7402-9). Garrard Pub. Co.
--Mr. Pine's Mixed-up Signs. Kessler, Leonard P. (1921-), illus. LC 61-65991. 61p. illus. 22cm. 1961. Grosset & Dunlap.
--Mr. Pine's Purple House. Kessler, Leonard P. (1921-), illus. LC 65-14734. (Illus.). 22cm. 61p. (Wonder bks. easy reader: No. 5936). 1965. Grosset.
--Mr. Pine's Storybook. Kessler, Leonard P. (1921-), illus. LC 82-200938. (Illus.). 41 p. 26cm. c.1982. (ISBN 0-448-12036-4). Grosset & Dunlap.
--Mrs. Pine Takes a Trip. Kessler, Leonard P. (1921-), illus. LC 66-14286. 1 v. (unpaged) col. illus. 24 cm. 1966. (ISBN 0-448-02853-0). Grosset & Dunlap.
--Old Turtle's Baseball Stories. Kessler, Leonard P. (1921-), illus. LC 81-6390. (Illus.). 55 p. 22cm. (Greenwillow read-alone). c.1982. (ISBN 0-688-00723-6). (ISBN 0-688-00724-4). Greenwillow Books.
--Old Turtle's Riddle & Joke Book. Kessler, Leonard P. (1921-), illus. LC 85-12565. (Illus.). 6 1/4 x 8 3/8. 48p. (16 pt.). (Read-Alone Bks.). (gr. 1-4). 1986. (ISBN 0-688-05953-8). (ISBN 0-688-05954-6). Greenwillow.
--Old Turtle's Winter Games. Kessler, Leonard P. (1921-), illus. LC 83-1435. p. cm. 1983. (ISBN 0-688-02309-6). (ISBN 0-688-02310-X). Greenwillow Books.
--On Your Mark, Get Set, Go!. The First All-Animal Olympics. Kessler, Leonard P. (1921-), illus. LC 72-76516. (Illus.). 63 p. 23cm. (Sports I can read book). 1972. (ISBN 0-06-023152-1). (ISBN 0-06-023152-1). Harper & Row.
--Paint Me a Picture, Mr. Pine. Kuzich, John, illus. LC 77-162046. (Illus.). 31 p. 23cm. (Magic circle book). 1972. (ISBN 0-663-22965-0). Ginn.
--The Pirates' Adventure on Spooky Island. Kessler, Leonard P. (1921-), illus. LC 78-12379. (Illus.). 48 p. 23cm. (Imagination book). c.1979. (ISBN 0-8116-4414-6). Garrard Pub. Co.
--Riddles That Rhyme for Halloween Time. Kessler, Leonard P. (1921-), illus. LC 77-13140. (Illus.). 48 p. 23cm. (Imagination book). c.1978. (ISBN 0-448-01812-8). Garrard Pub. Co.
--The Sad Tale of the Careless Klunks. Kessler, Leonard P. (1921-), illus. LC 65-11931. 1v. (unpaged) col. illus. 19cm. c.1965. Dodd.
--The Silly Mother Hubbard. Cushman, Doug, illus. LC 79-18776. (Illus.). 32 p. 23cm. (Young Mother Goose Books). c.1980. (ISBN 0-8116-7401-0). Garrard Pub. Co.
--Soup for the King: A Fable. Kessler, Leonard P. (1921-), illus. LC 68-26151. (Illus.). 40 p. 29cm. 1969. Grosset & Dunlap.
--Super Bowl. Kessler, Leonard P. (1921-), illus. LC 80-10171. (Illus.). 53 p. 22cm. (Greenwillow read-alone). c.1980. (ISBN 0-688-84270-4). (ISBN 0-688-80270-2). Greenwillow Books.
--A Tale of Two Bicycles: Safety on Your Bike. Kessler, Leonard P. (1921-), illus. LC 72-116345. (Illus.). 40 p. 24cm. 1971. Lothrop, Lee & Shepard Co.
--Tricks for Treats on Halloween. Easton, Tom, illus. LC 78-21942. (Illus.). 32 p. 23cm. c.1979. (ISBN 0-8116-6075-3). Garrard Pub. Co.
--The Worst Team Ever. Kessler, Leonard P. (1921-), illus. LC 84-25883. (Illus.). 48 p. 22cm. (Greenwillow read-alone). c.1985. (ISBN 0-688-04234-1). (ISBN 0-688-04235-X). Greenwillow Books.
--The Worst Team Ever. Kessler, Leonard P. (1921-), illus. LC 84-25883. (Illus.). 6 1/4 x 8 3/8. 48p. (16 pt.). (Read-Alone Bks.). (gr. 1-4). 1985. (ISBN 0-688-04234-1). (ISBN 0-688-04235-X). Greenwillow.

Kessler, Ramon Wilke, compiled by.
--The Right to Solo: A Collection of the Best Airplane Stories for Boys and Girls. 1st ed. Knight, Clayton (1891-1969), illus. LC 31-23200. 20cm. 218p. 1931. E. P. Dutton & Co. Inc.
--Treasure Trove of Pirate Stories: A Collection of Best Pirate Stories for Young People. Scott, Arthur O., illus. LC 30-11612. 10 p. l., 3-276, 1 p. incl. front., illus., plates. 21 cm. 1930. D. Appleton and Company.

Kester, Ellen Skinner
--The Climbing Rope. Willman, Gordon, illus. LC 77-13306. (Illus.). 127 p. 23cm. (Bro-kee series). c.1978. Concordia Pub. House.

Kester, Max
--Ambush. Kenney, John, illus. (Illus.). (gr. 4-5). N.D. (ISBN 0-7214-0205-4). Merry Thoughts.
--Silver Arrow. Kenney, John, illus. (Illus.). (gr. 4-5). N.D. (ISBN 0-7214-0204-6). Merry Thoughts.

Kesteven, G. R., pseud., see Crosher, G. R..

Kesteven, G. R., pseud.
--The Awakening Water. Crosher, G. R.. (gr. 4-8). 1979. (ISBN 0 8038 0471 7). Hastings.
--The Pale Invaders. Crosher, G. R.. LC 75-305052. 192p. (gr. 6-9). 1976. (ISBN 0-689-30505-2). Atheneum.

Kestner, Jack
--Fire Tower. LC 60-12749. 214p. illus. 22cm. 1960. Funk and Wagnalls.
--Police Beat. LC 59-108964. 217p. 22cm. 1959. Funk and Wagnalls Co.

Keston, Margaret
--Only a Lad. N.D. E. & J. B. Young & Co.

Ketcham, Hank, pseud., see Ketcham, Henry King.

Ketcham, Hank, jt. ed. see Memling, Carl.

Ketcham, Hank, pseud. (1920-)
--Dennis the Menace & the Bible Kids. Ketcham, Henry King, 6 vols. Incl. No. 1. Jesus. Ketcham, Henry King. (ISBN 0-87680-794-5); No. 2. Moses. Ketcham, Henry King. (ISBN 0-87680-795-3); No. 3. David. Ketcham, Henry King. (ISBN 0-87680-796-1); No. 4. Joseph. Ketcham, Henry King; No. 5. Women of the Bible. (ISBN 0-87680-798-8); No. 6. More About Jesus. (ISBN 0-87680-799-6). 1977. Word Bks.

Ketcham, Henry King see Ketcham, Hank, pseud.

Ketchum, Agnes Taylor & Jorgensen, Ida M., eds.
--Kindergarten Gems. N.D. Christian Publication Company.
--Kindergarten Gems: A Collection of Stories and Rhymes for Little Folks. (Illus.). N.D. E. Steiger & Co.

Ketchum, Irma A & Rice, Anna L
--Our First Story Reader. N.D. Charles Scribner's Sons.

Ketchum, Jean (1926-)
--Stick-in-the-Mud: A Tale of a Village, a Custom, and a Little Boy. LC 53-7806. unpaged. illus. 20cm. (Young Scott books). 1953. W. R. Scott.

Ketchum, Lynne, jt. auth. see Beaudry, Jo.

Ketchum, Philip (1902-)
--The Great Axe Bretwalda. LC 55-8099. 220 p. 22cm. 1955. Little, Brown.

Kethcham, Henry
--Oriental Fairy Tales. (The Fairy Library). N.D. A. L. Burt Co.

Keto, Emma (1907-)
--Little Tee-Hee's Big Day. LC 36-17532. 30 p. col. illus. 16 cm. c.1936. Grosset & Dunlap, Inc.
--Ting-Ling and Mee-Too. LC 37-771875. 37 p. col. illus. 21 cm. c.1937. Grosset & Dunlap, Inc.
--Tonto and Pronto. LC 38-18604. 32 p. col. illus. 21 cm. c.1938. Grosset & Dunlap.

Kettelwell, John, ed. see Aladdin.

Kettle, Jocelyn
--The Athelsons. 1972. (ISBN 0-399-10955-2). G. P. Putnam's Sons.
--A Gift of Onyx. 1974. (ISBN 0-399-11189-1). G. P. Putnam's Sons.

Kettlewell, John
--Alladin. 1928. Alfred A. Knopf.

Keun, Irmgard (1909-)
--After Midnight. Clough, James, illus. LC 38-8825. 4 p. l., 3-233, 2 p. 19 1/2 cm. 1938. A. A. Knopf.

Keussen, Gudrun & Ars Edition Staff
--This Is How We Live in the Country. Keussen, Gudrun, illus. (Illus.). 18p. 1st U.S. edition. (ps-2). 1983. (ISBN 0-86724-025-3). Ars Edition.
--This Is How We Live in the Town. Keussen, Gudrun, illus. (Illus.). 18p. 1st U.S. edition. (ps-2). 1983. (ISBN 0-86724-026-1). Ars Edition.

Key, Alexander Hill (1904-1979)
--Bolts, a Robot Dog. Key, Alexander Hill (1904-1979), illus. LC 66-100208. 172p. illus. 23cm. c.1966. (ISBN 0-664-32361-8). Westminster.
--Cherokee Boy. LC 57-5122. 176p. 21cm. 1957. Westminster Press.
--Escape to Witch Mountain. Wisdom, Leon B., illus. (Illus.). 172 p. 21cm. 1968. Westminster Press.
--Flight to the Lonesome Place. LC 78-133889. 192 p. 21cm. 1971. Westminster Press.
--The Forgotten Door. (Illus.). (gr. 6-10). 1965. (ISBN 0-8382-0264-0). Hale.
--The Forgotten Door. (gr. 4-6). 1968. (ISBN 0-590-08534-4). Scholastic Inc.
--The Forgotten Door. LC 65-10170. 124p. (gr. 7 up). 1965. (ISBN 0-664-32342-1). Westminster.
--The Golden Enemy. LC 69-14200. 176 p. 21cm. 1969. Westminster Press.
--The Incredible Tide. LC 70-100952. 159 p. 21cm. 1970. Westminster Press.
Jagger, the Dog from Elsewhere. LC 76-12626. 126 p. 21cm. c.1976. (ISBN 0-664-32596-3). Westminster Press.
--Liberty or Death: The Narrative of William Dunbar, Partisan. 1st ed. Key, Alexander Hill (1904-1979), illus. LC 36-8382. xi p., 1 l., 224p. incl. front., illus. pl. 201/2cm. 1936. Harper Brothers.
--The Magic Meadow. LC 74-19194. (gr. 4-7). 1975. (ISBN 0-664-32561-0). Westminster.
--Mystery of the Sassafras Chair. Segal, Louis, illus. LC 67-3333. (Illus.). 156 p. 23cm. 1967. Westminster Press.
--The Preposterous Adventures of Swimmer. LC 73-7945. 128 p. 21cm. 1973. (ISBN 0-664-32537-8). Westminster Press.
--The Red Eagle: Being the Adventurous Tale of Two Young Flyers. Key, Alexander Hill (1904-1979), illus. LC 30-8367. (Gift Juveniles). 1935. A. L. Burt Co.
--Rivets & Sprockets. (Illus.). (gr. 3-5). 1964. (ISBN 0-8382-0706-5). Hale.
--Rivets & Sprockets. large type ed. Key, Alexander Hill (1904-1979), illus. LC 64-10077. (Illus.). 22cm. 100p. (gr. 1-6). 1964. (ISBN 0-664-32321-9). Westminster.
--Sprockets: A Little Robot. large type ed. Key, Alexander Hill (1904-1979), illus. LC 63-7075. (Illus.). 23cm. 144p. (gr. 3-6). 1963. (ISBN 0-664-32289-1). Westminster.
--The Strange White Doves. (Illus.). (gr. 4 up). 1972. (ISBN 0-664-32508-4). Westminster.
--The Sword of Aradel. LC 76-54893. 144 p. 21cm. c.1977. (ISBN 0-664-32609-9). Westminster Press.

Key, Alexander Hill (1904-1979) & Marmorstein, Malcolm
--Return from Witch Mountain. LC 77-26992. 144 p. 21cm. c.1978. (ISBN 0-664-32630-7). Westminster Press.

Key, Francis Scott (1779-1843)
--The Star-Spangled Banner. 1st ed. Spier, Peter Edward (1927-), illus. LC 73-79712. (Illus.). 52 p. 32cm. 1973. (ISBN 0-385-09458-2). (ISBN 0-385-09458-2). Doubleday.

Key, Ted see Key, Theodore.

Key, Theodore (1912-)
--The Biggest Dog in the World. 1st ed. Key, Theodore (1912-), illus. LC 60-12297. 44p. illus. 23cm. 1960. Dutton.
--Diz and Liz. Key, Theodore (1912-), illus. (gr. 6 up). N.D. (ISBN 0-448-05750-6). G&D.
--Hazel Power. Key, Theodore (1912-), illus. (Illus.). (gr. 3-7). 1971. Curtis.
--Ms Hazel. Key, Theodore (1912-), illus. (Orig.). (gr. 3-7). 1972. Curtis.
--Right on Hazel. Key, Theodore (1912-), illus. (Illus.). (gr. 3-7). 1972. Curtis.
--So'm I. Owen, Frank, illus. LC 54-8850. 67p. illus. 27cm. 1954. Dutton.
--Ted Key's Diz and Liz. Key, Theodore (1912-), illus. LC 67-191. (Illus.). 1 v. (unpaged). 22cm. (Laugh books). 1966. Wonder Books.

Keyes, Angela M.
--Stories and Story-Telling. LC 11-14714. 20cm. 286p. 1911. D. Appleton and Company.

Keyes, Frances Parkinson Wheeler, Mrs. (1885-1970)
--The Happy Wanderer. N.D. Jullian Messner, Inc.
--Kilmeny of the Orchard. N.D. Grosset & Dunlap.
--Once on Esplanade: A Cycle Between Two Creole Weddings. Burbank, Addison Bushnell (1895-), illus. LC 47-11240. xv, 202p. illus. 21cm. 1947. Dodd, Mead.

Keyes, Mary Willard
--Juniper Green. Boyd, Frank (1893-), illus. LC 29-16245. 4 p. l., 294 p. incl. plates. col. front. 19 1/2 cm. 1929. Longmans, Green and Co.
--Peacock Farm. N.D. Grosset & Dunlap.
--The Peacock Farm. Doane, Pelagie (1906-1966), illus. LC 34-29566. 3 p. l., 280 p. incl. illus., plates. front. 20 1/2 cm. 1934. Longmans, Green and Co.
--Toplofty. N.D. Grosset & Dunlap.
--Toplofty. Doane, Pelagie (1906-1966), illus. LC 31-25262. v p., 1 l., 270 p. incl. illus., plates. 20 cm. 1931. Longmans, Green and Co.

Keyser, Leander Sylvester (1856-)
--Bobby Redstart and Other Bird Stories. LC 3-4418. 125 p. 19 1/2 cm. (Twentieth century classics and school readings. no. 16). 1901. Crane & Company.
--Our Bird Comrades. N.D. Rand McNally.

Keyser, Marcia
--Roger on His Own. Dawson, Diane, illus. LC 82-5002. (Illus.). 32 p. c.1982. (ISBN 0-517-54476-8). Crown Publishers.

Keyser, Sarah, pseud., see McGuire, Leslie Sarah.

Keyser, Sarah, adapted by see Kruss, James.

Keyser, Sarah, pseud. (1945-)
--Greg Finds an Egg. McGuire, Leslie Sarah. Forster, Herta, illus. LC 77-166203. (Illus.). 16p. (ps-1). 1972. Platt.

Keyworth, Thomas
--A Long Delay. (Illus.). (The Home and Enterprise Library Ser.). N.D. Frederick Warne & Co.

Kha, Dang Manh
--In the Land of Small Dragon: A Vietnamese Folk Tale. Clark, Ann Nolan (1896-), as told to. Chen, Tony (1929-), illus. LC 78-26233. (Illus.). 40 p. 26cm. 1979. (ISBN 0-670-39697-4). Viking Press.

Khachatriants, Iakov Samsonovich, ed.
--Armenian Folk Tales. Saryan, Martyros, illus. Orloff, Nicholas W. (1895-), tr. LC 46-11818. (Illus.). 141p. 24cm. 1946. Colonial House.

Khan, Hassina (1951-)
--Tariq Learns to Swim. Athalye, Bal (1934-), illus. (Illus.). 32p. 1st U.S. edition. 1983. (ISBN 0-370-30530-2, Pub. by the Bodley Head). Merrimack Pub Cir.

Khan, Mary C. Inayat see Inayat Khan, Mary C.

Kharms, Daniil (1905-1942)
--Across the Stream. Ginsburg, Mirra (1919-), retold by. Tafuri, Nancy, illus. LC 81-20306. p. cm. c.1982. (ISBN 0-688-01204-3). (ISBN 0-688-01206-X). Greenwillow Books. **Award: (ALA).**

Khemvichanuvat, Cherdchai
--The Poor Lizard. Rodriguez, Gloria F., ed. Chang, Phillip, illus. Pinta, Thanom, tr. (Illus.). (gr. k-3). 1979. (ISBN 0-686-26621-8, Pub. by New Day Pub). Cellar.

Kherdian, David (1931-)
--The Animal. Hogrogian, Nonny (1932-), illus. LC 83-22268. (Illus.). 40p. (gr. k up). 1984. (ISBN 0-394-95597-8). (ISBN 0-394-85597-3). Knopf.
--Beyond Two Rivers. LC 81-1915. 118 p. 22cm. c.1981. (ISBN 0-688-00567-5). Greenwillow Books.
--It Started with Old Man Bean. LC 79-18372. 217 p. 22cm. c.1980. (ISBN 0-688-80247-8). (ISBN 0-688-84247-X). Greenwillow Books.
--The Mystery of the Diamond in the Wood. Geiger, Paul, illus. LC 83-272. (Illus.). 95 p. 22cm. c.1983. (ISBN 0-394-85603-1). Knopf.
--Poems Here and Now. Hogrogian, Nonny (1932-), illus. LC 75-37586. (Illus.). 64 p. 22cm. c.1976. (ISBN 0-688-80024-6). (ISBN 0-688-84024-8). Greenwillow Books.
--Right Now. Hogrogian, Nonny (1932-), illus. LC 82-21185. (Illus.). 36p. (ps-1). 1983. (ISBN 0-394-95596-X). (ISBN 0-394-85596-5). Knopf.
--The Road from Home: The Story of an Armenian Girl. 1979. Greenwillow. **Award: (JNM).**

--Odie Seeks a Friend. Wiese, Kurt (1887-1974), illus. LC 34-41992. 32 p. illus. 17 1/2 x 25 cm. c.1934. Coward-McCann, Inc.
--Our Dogs. Wessel, Charles W., illus. LC 37-20201. 28 p. illus. 24 cm. c.1937. The Harter Publishing Company.
--Peter and the Frog's Eye. Chace, Lynwood M., photos by. LC 36-31221. 81 p. illus. 22 x 28 1/2 cm. c.1936. The Junior Literary Guild and Grosset & Dunlap.

King, Kay
--Shanta, Sunil and the Cobra. Jackson, Penelope, illus. LC 68-20808. (Illus.). 32 p. 25cm. 1968. (ISBN 0-200-71527-5). Abelard-Schuman.

King, Larry L.
--That Terrible Night Santa Got Lost in the Woods. Oliphant, Patrick Bruce (1935-), illus. (Illus.). 29p. 1981. (ISBN 0-88426-060-7). Encino Pr.

King, Leon, tr. see Pitt, Giordano.

King, Linda
--The Case Files of Harwood Vanderpaw, P. I. 64p. (Orig.). (Beaucoup to Do Ser.). 1983. (ISBN 0-8431-0793-6). Price Stern.
--Fussylocks Versus Middletown Junior High. 64p. (Orig.). (Beaucoup to Do Ser.). 1983. (ISBN 0-8431-0791-X). Price Stern.
--Movies, TV, & Bob the Hairy Troll. 64p. (Orig.). (Beaucoup to Do Ser.). 1983. (ISBN 0-8431-0792-8). Price Stern.

King, Lise, jt. auth. see Greinke, Pamylle.

King, Loretta (1913-)
--The Purple Sea Horse, and Other Stories. Swanson, Judy, illus. LC 79-56712. p. cm. 1980, c.1979. (ISBN 0-934104-02-6). Woodland Pub. Co.

King, Marian
--ABC Game Book. LC 27-21122. 56 p. illus. 30 cm. 1927. W. Morrow and Company, Inc.
--Amnon: A Lad of Palestine. Enright, Elizabeth (1909-1968), illus. LC 31-293112. 4 p. l., 96 p. col. front., illus. (incl. music) col. plates. 21 cm. 1931. Houghton Mifflin Company.
--A Boy of Poland. Bowden, Dorothy C., illus. LC 34-379841. ix, 1 p., 2 l., 15-128 p. incl. col. front., illus. col. plates. 22 1/2 cm. 1934. A. Whitman & Co.
--A Boy of Poland. Wilson, Eleanore Hubbard, Mrs., illus. LC 34-37984. (Illus.). 128p. 22cm. (A Junior Press Bk.). 1934. A. Whitman & Co.
--The Dutch Mother Goose. Bowden, Dorothy C., illus. LC 30-29259. 127 p. incl. col. front., col. illus. 18 1/2 cm. 1930. A. Flanagan Company.
--The Golden Cat Head and Other Tales of Holland. Wilson, Eleanore Hubbard, illus. LC 33-33455. 109 p. incl. col. front., illus., col. plates. 22 1/2 cm. c.1933. A. Whitman & Co.
--It Happened in England. LC 39-29605. 4 p. l., 17-134, 2 p. col. front., illus. (part col.) pl. 24 cm. 1939. A. Whitman & Co.
--Kees. Enright, Elizabeth (1909-1968), illus. LC 30-25298. 79 p. col. illus. 26 cm. 1930. Harper and Brothers.
--Kees and Kleintje. Enright, Elizabeth (1909-1968), illus. LC 34-5687. 79, 1 p. col. illus. 26 1/2 cm. c.1934. A. Whitman & Co.
--Mico and Piccolino. Darwin, Beatrice, illus. LC 70-93522. (Illus.). 45 p. 21cm. 1972. (ISBN 0-8178-4911-4). (ISBN 0-8178-4911-4). Harvey House.
--Piccolino. Smock, Nell Stolp, illus. LC 39-135449. 32, 1 p. incl. col. front., illus. (part col.) 24 cm. 1939. A. Whitman & Co.
--Sean and Sheela. LC 37-23773. 1 p. l., 9-134, 1 p. col. front., illus. (part col.) 23 1/2 cm. 1937. A. Whitman & Co.
--Skeeta: A Wire Haired Fox-Terrier. Bowden, Dorothy C., illus. LC 33-33267. 94 p. illus. (part col.) 20 cm. 1933. A. Whitman & Co.
--The Star of Bethlehem. Koering, Ursula (1921-), illus. (Illus.). 37 p. 27cm. 1968. Harvey House.

King, Marie B., jt. auth. see Gordon, Margery.

King, Martha Bennett
--Bean Blossom Hill. Balet, Jan Bernard (1913-), illus. LC 58-836. (Illus.). 36p. 25cm. (Slottle Library Bks.). 1958, c.1957. Rand McNally.
--Papa Pompino. N.D. Rand McNally.
--The Snow Queen & the Goblin. (Children's Theatre Playscript Ser.). 1956. (ISBN 0-88020-056-1). Coach Hse.
--Space Harp. (Children's Theatre Playscript Ser.). 1969. (ISBN 0-88020-058-8). Coach Hse.
--The Witch's Lullaby. (Children's Theatre Playscript Ser.). 1955. (ISBN 0-88020-073-1). Coach Hse.

King, Martha C
--The Magic Whistle. Koering, Ursula (1921-), illus. LC 69-12912. (Illus.). 115 p. 21cm. 1969. Washburn.
--Smugglers' Island. Kidwell, Carl (1910-), illus. LC 79-102663. (Illus.). 110 p. 21cm. 1970. I. Washburn.
--Third Chair Drummer. Anderson, Rus, illus. LC 70-124493. (Illus.). vii, 120 p. 21cm. 1970. I. Washburn.

King, Mary B.
--Yankee Doodle Comes to Town. rev. ed. (Children's Theatre Playscript Ser.). 1975. (ISBN 0-88020-064-2). Coach Hse.

King, Mona Reed
--Patsy Ann: Her Happy Times. LC 35-14572. 62 p. illus. 17 cm. c.1935. Rand, McNally & Company.

King, Myra
--Tales Out of School. LC 13-15166. 77 p. col. front., illus. 19 x 16 cm. 1911. The Bolton Printing Company, Inc.

King, Patricia (1930-)
--Mabel, the Whale. Evans, Katherine Floyd (1901-1964), illus. LC 58-7296. (Illus.). 27 p. 21cm. (Follett beginning to read series). 1958. Follett Pub. Co.

King, Pauline
--Paper Doll Poems. LC 12-34962. 66 p. illus. 17 x 22 cm. 1896. The Century Co.

King, Regina
--The Treasure of Andor: A Robo Force Adventure. Fernando, illus. LC 84-62070. (Illus.). 32p. (Robo Force Mini-Storybks.). (ps-3). 1985. (ISBN 0-394-87174-X, BYR). Random.

King, Robin, pseud., see Raleigh-King, Robin Victor Lethbridge.

King, Robin, pseud. (1919-)
--The Angry Book: My ABC of Mean Things. Raleigh-King, Robin Victor Lethbridge. LC 62-19194. unpaged. illus 19x26cm. 1962. Norton.
--Burrito. Raleigh-King, Robin Victor Lethbridge. N.D. E. M. Hale & Co.
--Burrito. Raleigh-King, Robin Victor Lethbridge. 1 st. ed. King, Robin, pseud. (1919-), illus. Raleigh-King, Robin Victor Lethbridge. LC 56-5260. 63p. illus. 23cm. 1956. Dutton.
--Burrito. Raleigh-King, Robin Victor Lethbridge. King, Robin, pseud. (1919-), illus. Raleigh-King, Robin Victor Letheridge. LC 56-5260. 63p. illus. 23cm. 1956. Dutton.
--Hundl is a Dog. Raleigh-King, Robin Victor Lethbridge. N.D. E. M. Hale & Co.
--Hundl Is a Dog. Raleigh-King, Robin Victor Lethbridge. 1 st. ed. King, Robin, pseud. (1919-), illus. Raleigh-King, Robin Victor Lethbridge. LC 56-828723. 60p. illus. 22cm. 1956. Dutton.
--Hundl Is a Dog. Raleigh-King, Robin Victor Lethbridge. King, Robin, pseud. (1919-), illus. Raleigh-King, Robin Victor Lethbridge. LC 56-8287. 60p. illus. 22cm. 1956. Dutton.
--Just the Right Size. Raleigh-King, Robin Victor Lethbridge. King, Billie Morley (1925-), illus. LC 57-897658. 45p. illus. 23cm. 1957. Dutton.
--The Wondrous Egg of Abou. Raleigh-King, Robin Victor Lethbridge. King, Robin, pseud. (1919-), illus. Raleigh-King, Robin Victor Lethbridge. LC 57-7601. 60p. illus. 23cm. 1957. Dutton.

King, Robin, pseud. (1919-) & King, Billie Morley (1925-)
--The Biggest Hat in the World. Raleigh-King, Robin Victor Lethbridge. LC 59-5839. unpaged. illus. 22cm. 1959. Dutton.

King, Rose E.
--Runaways. (gr. 8 up). 1984. (ISBN 0-8062-2358-8). Carlton.

King, Ruth
--Amanda, Amelia, and Abigail. King, Ruth, illus. LC 53-8205. unpaged. illus. 23cm. 1953. Abelard Press.
--Nana: The Parlor Boarder. LC 54-5240. unpaged illus 23cm. 1954. Abelard-Schuman.
--Nana: The Parlor Boarder. (Illus.). 56p. 1954. Abelard-Schuman.
--Susie. LC 52-10248. unpaged. illus. 23 cm. 1952. Abelard Press.

King, Sara S., jt. auth. see Driggs, Howard Roscoe.

King-Smith, Dick (1922-)
--Babe: The Gallant Pig. Rayner, Mary (1933-), illus. LC 84-11429. p. cm. 1985, c.1983. (ISBN 0-517-55556-5). Crown. **Awards: (BGH); (ALA).**
--The Fox-Busters. 1978. (Pub. by Gollancz England). David & Charles.
--Magnus Powermouse. Rayner, Mary (1933-), illus. LC 83-48435. (Illus.). 128p. (gr. 5 up). 1984, c.1982. (ISBN 0-06-023231-5, HarpJ). (ISBN 0-06-023232-3). Har-Row.
--The Mouse Butcher. Apple, Margot, illus. LC 81-70656. (Illus.). viii, 132 p. 22cm. 1982. (ISBN 0-670-49145-4). Viking Press.
--Pigs Might Fly: A Novel. Rayner, Mary (1933-), illus. LC 81-11525. (Illus.). 158 p. 22cm. 1982. (ISBN 0-670-55506-1). Viking Press. **Award: (ALA).**
--The Sheep-Pig. Rayner, Mary (1933-), illus. LC 85-110385. (Illus.). 118 p. 21cm. 1984. (ISBN 0-575-03375-4). V. Gollancz.

King-Coit School, jt. auth. see Coit, Dorothy.

Kingdon, Jill
--Dizzy Dinosaur Gets Lost & Found. Eiser, Eric, illus. (Illus.). 32p. (Dizzy Dinosaur Ser.). (gr. 3-5). N.D. (ISBN 0-8326-2626-0). Delair.

Kingery, Nelle Ogg, Mrs.
--Poems for Girls and Boys. LC 40-1707. 48 p. 19 1/2 cm. c.1939. Wetzel Publishing Co., Inc.

Kinglsey, Emily Perl, jt. auth. see Sesame Street.

Kingman, Lee, pseud., see Natti, Marylee Kingman.

Kingman, Lee, pseud. (1919-)
--The Best Christmas. Natti, Marylee Kingman. Cooney, Barbara (1917-), illus. LC 49-483286. 95 p. illus. 20 cm. 1949. Doubleday.
--Break a Leg, Betsy Maybe!. Natti, Marylee Kingman. LC 76-20501. 245 p. 22cm. 1976. (ISBN 0-395-24741-1). Houghton Mifflin.
--Escape from the Evil Prophecy. Natti, Marylee Kingman. Cuffari, Richard (1925-1978), illus. LC 73-7902. (Illus.). 188 p. 22cm. 1973. (ISBN 0-395-17515-1). Houghton Mifflin.
--Flivver, the Heroic Horse. Natti, Marylee Kingman. 1st ed. Blegvad, Erik (1923-), illus. LC 58-7158. 75p. illus. 25cm. 1958. Doubleday.
--Georgina and the Dragon. Natti, Marylee Kingman. Shortall, Leonard W., illus. LC 70-184249. (Illus.). 105 p. 22cm. 1972. (ISBN 0-395-13730-6). Houghton Mifflin.
--Head Over Wheels. Natti, Marylee Kingman. LC 78-15650. p. cm. 1978. (ISBN 0-395-27202-5). Houghton Mifflin.
--House of the Blue Horse. Natti, Marylee Kingman. LC 60-13536. 237p. 22cm. 1960. Doubleday.
--Ilenka. Natti, Marylee Kingman. N.D. Houghton Mifflin Co.
--Ilenka. Natti, Marylee Kingman. Bare, Arnold Edwin (1920-), illus. LC 45-6104. 48 p. col. illus. 28 1/2 x 23 1/2 cm. 1945. Junior Literary Guild.
--Kathy and the Mysterious Statue. Natti, Marylee Kingman. 1st ed. Porter, Jean MacDonald (1906-), illus. LC 53-9143. 250p. illus. 21cm. 1953. Doubleday.
--The Magic Christmas Tree. Natti, Marylee Kingman. Bettina, pseud. (1903-), illus. Ehrlich, Bettina Bauer. LC 56-8650. 48p. illus. 25cm. 1956. Ariel Books.
--The Meeting Post: A Story of Lapland. Natti, Marylee Kingman. Asmussen, Des, illus. LC 73-139105. (Illus.). (Stories from Many Lands Ser). (gr. 2-5). 1972. (ISBN 0-690-52976-7, TYC-J). Har-Row.
--Mikko's Fortune. Natti, Marylee Kingman. N.D. E. M. Hale & Co.
--Mikko's Fortune. Natti, Marylee Kingman. Bare, Arnold Edwin (1920-), illus. 48p. 1955. Farrar, Straus and Cudahy, Inc.
--The Peter Pan Bag. Natti, Marylee Kingman. LC 78-98520. 219 p. 23cm. 1970. Houghton Mifflin.
--Peter's Long Walk. Natti, Marylee Kingman. Cooney, Barbara (1917-), illus. (gr. k-3). 1953. Doubleday.
--Peter's Pony. Natti, Marylee Kingman. Lasell, Fen, pseud. (1919-), illus. Calvert, Elinor H.. LC 63-7362. unpaged. illus. 21 x 27 cm. 1963. Doubleday.
--Phillipe's Hill. Natti, Marylee Kingman. Woodward, Hildegard (1898-), illus. 1950. Doubleday & Co.
--Pierre Pigeon. Natti, Marylee Kingman. Bare, Arnold Edwin (1920-), illus. 1943. Houghton Mifflin. **Award: (RCM).**
--Pierre Pigeon. Natti, Marylee Kingman. Bare, Arnold Edwin (1920-), illus. LC 43-18425. 48 p. col. illus. 28 1/2 x 23 1/2 cm. 1943. The Junior Literary Guild.
--Private Eyes: Adventures with the Saturday Gang. Natti, Marylee Kingman. 1st ed. Silverman, Burton Philip (1928-), illus. LC 64-11706. (Illus.). 192 p. 22cm. 1964. Doubleday.
--The Quarry Adventure. Natti, Marylee Kingman. 1st ed. Cooney, Barbara (1917-), illus. LC 51-13670. 209 p. illus. 21 cm. 1951. Doubleday.
--The Refiner's Fire. Natti, Marylee Kingman. LC 81-6313. p. cm. 1981. (ISBN 0-395-31606-5). Houghton Mifflin.
--The Rocky Summer. Natti, Marylee Kingman. Cooney, Barbara (1917-), illus. LC 48-783349. 209 p. illus. 22 cm. 1948. Houghton Mifflin Co.
--The Saturday Gang. Natti, Marylee Kingman. Silverman, Burton Philip (1928-), illus. LC 61-12541. 192p. illus. 22cm. 1961. Doubleday.
--Saturday Gang. Natti, Marylee Kingman. Silverman, Burton Philip (1928-), illus. LC 61-12541. (Illus.). 23 linecuts. 192p. Repr. (Zephyr Bk Ser). (gr. 3-7). 1971. (ISBN 0-385-08681-4). Doubleday.
--Saturday Gang. Natti, Marylee Kingman. 1st ed. Silverman, Burton Philip (1928-), illus. (Illus.). (gr. 5-8). 1961. (ISBN 0-8382-0723-5). Hale.
--The Secret Journey of the Silver Reindeer. Natti, Marylee Kingman. Ward, Lynd Kendall (1905-1985), illus. LC 68-12736. (Illus.). 93 p. 24cm. 1968. Doubleday.
--Sheep Ahoy. Natti, Marylee Kingman. Weil, Lisl (1910-), illus. LC 63-7326. 63 p. illus. 21 cm. (gr. 4-6). 1963. (ISBN 0-395-06863-0). (ISBN 0-395-06864-9). Houghton Mifflin.
--The Village Band Mystery. Natti, Marylee Kingman. 1st ed. Blegvad, Erik (1923-), illus. LC 56-9396. 256p. illus. 22cm. 1956. Doubleday.
--The Year of the Raccoon. Natti, Marylee Kingman. LC 66-8341. 246p. 22cm. 1966. Houghton. **Award: (ALA).**

Kingsbury, Alison Mason (1898-)
--The Adventures of Phunsi. LC 46-7279. 4 p. l., 3-88 p. incl. front., illus. 22 x 19 cm. 1946. G. P. Putnam's Sons.

Kingsbury, Carl Louis
--The Spring on the Hillside. LC 7-263436. 62 p. illus. 17 1/2 cm. c.1907. D. C. Cook Publishing Company.

Kingsbury, Helen Ovington
--All Aboard for Wonderland. Kay, Gertrude Alice (1884-1939), illus. LC 18-1718. 6 p. l., 190 p. col. front., illus., col. plates. 22 1/2 cm. 1917. Moffat, Yard and Company.

Kingsbury, Ruth Foote
--Lookout Tower. Norling, Ernest Ralph (1892-), illus. LC 56-7262. (Illus.). 254 p. 22cm. 1957. Caxton Printers.

Kingsland, L. W., tr. see Brodtkorb, Reidar.

Kingsland, Leslie William (1912-), tr. see Andersen, Hans Christian.

Kingsland, Leslie William (1912-), tr. see Holm, Else Anne Lise.

Kingsland, Leslie William (1912-), tr. see Kaudsen, Paul E.

Kingsland, Leslie William (1912-), tr. see Kullman, Harry.

Kingsley, jt. auth. see Cross.

Kingsley, Charles (1819-1875), ed. see Brock, Henry Matthew.

Kingsley, Charles (1819-1875)
--Charles Kingsley's Works: Containing: Alton Locke; Hereward; Two Years Ago; Heroes, and Poems; Hypatia; Yeast; Westward Ho; Water Babies, and Lady Why, Madame How, 8 vols. N.D. Set. Set. Lovella, Coryell & Co.
--Christmas Day. (Illus.). N.D. D. Lothrop Co.
--Glaucus: Or, The Wonderers of the Seashore. (Illus.). N.D. MacMillian.
--Greek Fairy Tales. (The New Children's Classics). N.D. Macmillan.
--Greek Heroes: Fairy Tales for My Children. (Burt's Home Library). N.D. A L Burt Co.
--Hereward the Wake. Jackson, Alice F., retold by. (Illus.). (Classics Retold to Children). N.D. George W. Jacobs & Co.
--The Heroes. N.D. Longmans Green & Co.
--The Heroes. (The Road In Storyland). N.D. Platt & Munk Co.
--The Heroes. N.D. Small,Maynard & Co.
--The Heroes. Kiddell-Monroe, Joan (1908-), illus. LC 63-4140. (Illus.). 22cm. 210p. (Children's Illustrated Classics). 1963. E.P. Dutton & Co.
--Heroes. King, Jessie, illus. N.D. E P Dutton.
--The Heroes. King, Ron, illus. LC 74-2316. (Illus.). 215 p. 29cm. (Educator classic library, 10). 1968. Classic Press.
--The Heroes. Robinson, Thomas Heath (1869-1950), illus. N.D. E P Dutton.
--The Heroes: Greek Fairy Tales. Bock, Vera, illus. LC 54-14649. 193p. illus. 22cm. (New children's classics). 1954. Macmillan.
--The Heroes: Greek Fairy Tales For My Children. Flint, W. Russell, illus. N.D. Hale Cushman & Flint.
--Heroes: Or, Fairy Tales for My Children. (Illus.). (The Rugby Ser.). N.D. A. L. Burt.
--The Heroes: Or, Greek Fairy Tales. Davie, Howard, illus. LC 27-25791. 4 p. l., 9-22 p., 2 l., 25-312 p. col. front., col. plates. 19 1/2 cm. (Newbery classics). 1927. David McKay Company.
--The Heroes: Or, Greek Fairy Tales. Davie, Howard, illus. (Raphael House Library). N.D. David McKay.
--Heroes: Or, Greek Fairy Tales for My Children. (Illus.). (The Little Men Ser.). N.D. A. L. Burt's Pubs.
--Heroes: Or, Greek Fairy Tales for My Children. (Illus.). N.D. A. L. Chatterton Co.
--The Heroes: Or, Greek Fairy Tales for My Children. LC 7-12796. 3 p. l., 5-208 p. front. (port.) 19 cm. 1895. H. Altemus.
--Heroes: Or, Greek Fairy Tales for My Children. (Illus.). (The Young Folks Lib.). N.D. H. M. Caldwell Co.
--Heroes: Or, Greek Fairy Tales for My Children. (Illus.). (The Exquisite Ser.). N.D. H. M. Caldwell Co.
--Heroes: Or, Greek Fairy Tales for My Children. (The Lakeside Series of Handy Volume Classics). N.D. H. M. Caldwell Co.
--Heroes: Or, Greek Fairy Tales for My Children. (Illus.). (The Chateau Ser.). N.D. H. M. Caldwell Co.
--Heroes: Or, Greek Fairy Tales for My Children. (Illus.). (Vademecum Ser.). N.D. Henry Altemus.
--Heroes: Or, Greek Fairy Tales for My Children. Handy Volume, Large Type ed. (Illus.). (Petit-Trianon Ser.). N.D. Henry Altemus.
--The Heroes: Or, Greek Fairy Tales for My Children. LC 4-20113. xviii p., 2 l., 218 p. illus. 19 1/2 cm. 1889. Macmillan and Co.
--Heroes: Or, Greek Fairy Tales for My Children. (Illus.). N.D. Putman.

--The Great Cookie Thief. Smollin, Michael J., illus. (Illus.). (Sesame Street Shape Bks.). (ps-3). 1977. (ISBN 0-307-68877-1, Golden Pr). Western Pub.
--I Can Do It Myself. Brown, Richard Eric (1946-), illus. (Illus.). 32p. (Sesame Street Read-Aloud Storybooks). (ps). 1981. (ISBN 0-307-11604-2, Golden Pr). (ISBN 0-307-61604-5). Western Pub.
--I Like School. Herbert, Tom, illus. (Illus.). 32p. (Sesame Street Read-Aloud Bks.). (ps). 1981. (ISBN 0-307-11602-6, Golden Pr). (ISBN 0-307-61602-9). Western Pub.
--The Sesame Street Circus of Opposites: Featuring Jim Henson's Sesame Street Muppets. Stevenson, Nancy W., illus. LC 81-81632. (Illus.). 28 p. 26cm. c.1981. (ISBN 0-307-23141-0). Western Pub. Co.
--The Sesame Street One, Two, Three Story Book. Mathieu, Joseph (1945-), illus. Random House, New York & Children's Television Workshop LC 73-2768. (Illus.). 63 p. 29cm. 1973. (ISBN 0-394-82694-9). (ISBN 0-394-82694-9). Random House.
--The Sesame Street Pet Show: Featuring Jim Henson's Sesame Street Muppets. Chartier, Normand (1945-), illus. Children's Television Workshop LC 79-91474. (Illus.). 26 p. 27cm. c.1980. (ISBN 0-307-23102-X). Western Pub. Co. : Children's Television Workshop.
--The Sesame Street Players Present the Little Red Hen. Cooke, Tom, illus. (Illus.). 32p. (Sesame Street Read-Aloud Bks.). (ps). 1982. (ISBN 0-307-11607-7, Golden Pr). (ISBN 0-307-61607-X). Western Pub.

Kingsley, Florence Morse, Mrs. (1859-1937)
--Kindly Light. Nagel, Eva M., illus. LC 4-10079. 16cm. 112p. 1904. H. Altemus Co.
--Under the Stars. LC 3-27913. (Illus.). 20cm. 106p. (Altemus' Good Times Ser.). 1903. H. Altemus Co.
--Wings and Fetters. N.D. Grosset & Dunlap.
--Wings and Fetters: A Story for Girls. Birch, Reginald Bathurst (1856-1943), illus. LC 2-27423. 19cm. 298p. 1902. H. Altemus Co.
--Wings & Fetters: A Story for Girls. New ed. Birch, Reginald Bathurst (1856-1943), illus. 1905. Henry Altemus Co.

Kingsley, H., jt. auth. see Yonge, Charlotte Mary.

Kingsley, Helen
--Ready for School?. LC 57-59557. 22 x 28cm. 32p. 1957. Greenwich Book Publishers.

Kingsley, Henry, ed. see Defoe, Daniel.

Kingsley, Henry (1830-1878)
--The Boy in Grey. (Illus.). N.D. George Routledge & Sons.
--Boy in Grey & Other Stories. N.D. Longmans,Green & Co.
--The Lost Child. (Little Classics). N.D. James R Osgood & Co.
--The Lost Child. Frolich, Lorenz, illus. N.D. R. Worthington & Co.
--The Mystery of the Island, 1 of 11 vols. (Popular Bks for Boys). 1900. Set. J B Lippincott.

Kingsley, Winola Bevier
--The Kindergarten Way. LC 63-18192. 31 p. 20 cm. 1963. Dorrance.

Kingston, F. C.
--The Young Middy. (Illus.). (Life-Boat Ser). N.D. Lee & Shepard.

Kingston, Jeremy Henry Spencer (1931-)
--The Bird Who Saved the Jungle. Rose, Gerald Hembdon Seymour (1935-), illus. (Illus.). 32p. 1977. (ISBN 0-571-10303-0). (ISBN 0-571-11130-0). Faber & Faber.
--The Dustbin Who Wanted to Be a General. Rose, Gerald Hembdon Seymour (1935-), illus. (Illus.). (ps-5). N.D. (ISBN 0-571-09517-8). Faber & Faber.

Kingston, May
--Bertha Gordon Series, 10 Vols. (Illus.). N.D. Pilgrim Press.

Kingston, William Henry Giles, et al. (1814-1880)
--Holiday Library for Young People: Containing "Sailing Orders", "Ben's Boyhood", "The Young Whaler", etc, 12 vols. N.D. Set. D. Lothrop & Co.
--Home Library for Boys and Girls: Containing "Home Sunshine", "Alice Benson's Trials", "The Log House", etc, 12 vols. N.D. Set. D. Lothrop & Co.
--Home Sunshine Ser. Containing "Home Sunshine," "Alice Benson's Trials," "Grace's Visit" etc. N.D. D. Lothrop & Co.
--Our Girls Holiday Library: Containing "Home Sunshine," "Alice Benson's Trials," "Grace's Visits," etc, 6 vols. (Illus.). N.D. D. Lothrop & Co.

Kingston, William Henry Giles, jt. auth. see Johnson, Richard.

Kingston, William Henry Giles, ed. see Wyss, Johann David Von.

Kingston, William Henry Giles (1814-1880), tr. see Verne, Jules.

Kingston, William Henry Giles (1814-1880)
--Adrift in a Boat. N.D. Claxton, Remsen & Haffelfinger.
--Adrift in a Boat. (The Bedford Library). 1891. Frederick Warne.
--Adrift in a Boat. (The Star Library). N.D. Frederick Warne & Co.
--Adrift in a Boat and Washed Ashore. (Illus.). (Warne's Home Circle Library). N.D. Frederick Warne & Co.
--Adrift in a Boat and Washed Ashore. (Illus.). (The Home and Enterprise Library Ser.). N.D. Frederick Warne & Co.
--Adrift in a Boat and Washed Ashore, 1 of 8 vols. (Illus.). (Excelsior Gift Books Ser.: Vol. 3). N.D. R. Worthington.
--Adrift in a Boat and Washed Ashore, 1 of 16 Vols. (Illus.). (Warne's Victoria Gift Books Ser.: Vol. 5). N.D. Scribner & Welford.
--Adrift in a Boat and Washed Ashore, 1 of 16 Vols. (Illus.). (Warne's Incident and Adventure Library: Vol. 1). N.D. Scribner & Welford.
--Adventures Among the Indians. (Caxton Edition). N.D. Belford, Clarke & Co.
--Adventures in Africa. (Illus.). N.D. George Routledge.
--Adventures in the Far East. (Illus.). N.D. George Routledge & Sons.
--Adventures of Dick Onslow Among the Red Indians, 1 of 4 Vols. (Illus.). (Boy Crusader Library). N.D. E & J B Young.
--The Adventures of Dick Onslow Among the Red Indians. N.D. Pott, Young & Co.
--The Adventures of Dick Onslow Among the Redskins, 1 of 50 vols. (Illus.). (The Norwood Ser.: No. 26). 1900. Lee & Shepard.
--The Adventures of Dick Onslow Among the Redskins. (The Popular Library). N.D. The American News Co.
--Afar in the Forest. (Illus.). N.D. Thomas Nelson & Sons.
--The African Trader. (The Kingston Library of Adventure). N.D. George Routledge & Sons.
--The African Trader. (The Kingston Library). N.D. Pott, Young & Co.
--The African Trader: Or, The Adventures of Harry Bayford. N.D. Pott, Young & Co.
--Alone on an Island. N.D. George Routledge & Sons.
--Among the Redskins: Or, Over the Rocky Mountains, 1 of 7 vols. (Illus.). (The Magic Mirror Library). N.D. Cassell, Petter, Galpin.
--An Adventure in the Far West. (Famous Books for Boys). N.D. H. M. Caldwell Co.
--Antony Waymouth;. Or, The Gentlemen Adventures. LC 53-53029. (Illus.). 294. 18cm. (The Life-boat Ser.). N.D. Lee and Shepard.
--Archibald Hughson. (The Kingston Library of Adventure). N.D. George Routledge & Sons.
--Archibald Hughson. (The Kingston Library). N.D. Pott, Young & Co.
--At the South Pole. Third ed. N.D. Cassell Petter & Galpin.
--At the South Pole: Or, the Adventures of Richard Pengelley, Mariner, 1 of 3. (The Ocean Library). N.D. Cassell, Petter, & Galpin.
--The Brothers. N.D. George Routledge & Sons.
--Charlie Laurel: A Story of Adventure by Sea and Land. N.D. Thomas Nelson & Sons.
--Charlie Laurel: A Story of Sea Life, 1 of 8 vols. (Illus.). (Kingston Ser.). N.D. D Lothrop.
--Dick Cheveley. (St. Nicholas Series for Boys). N.D. International Book Company.
--Dick Cheveley: His Adventures and Misadventures. new ed. 1887. S. Low, Marston, Searle & Rivington.
--Dick Onslow Among the Red Indian, 1 of 5 Vols. (Dick Onslow Series). N.D. Thomas Whittaker.
--Dick Onslow Among the Red Skins. N.D. Wm. F. Gill & Co.
--Digby Heathcote: Or, The Early Days of a Country Gentleman's Son and Heir. Weir, Harrison William (1824-1906), illus. N.D. George Routledge & Sons.
--Earnest Bracebridge. (Illus.). (Famous Books for Boys). N.D. H. M. Caldwell Co.
--Earnest Bracebridge: School-Boy Days. (The Boy's Library of Adventure). N.D. Pott, Young, & Co.
--Ernest Bracebridge: Or, Schoolboy Days, 1 of 5 Vols. (Dick Onslow Series.). N.D. Thomas Whittaker.
--The Ferryman of Brill, and Other Stories, 1 of 7 vols. (Illus.). (The Magic Mirror Library). N.D. Cassell, Petter, Galpin.
--The Fisher Boy: Or, Micheal Penguyne. (Illus.). N.D. Lothrop Pub Co.
--The Fortunes of the Ranger and Crusader. (The Illuminated Ser.). N.D. The American News Co.
--The Fortunes of the Ranger and Crusader: A Tale of Ships. (The Boys Library of Adventure). N.D. Pott, Young, & Co.
--Fred Markham in Russia. (Illus.). 1882. Harper's Trade-List.
--Fred Markham in Russia: Or, The Boy Travellers in the Land of the Czar. Londells, R. T., illus. LC 41-31403. 320 p. front., plates. 18 1/2 cm. N.D. E. P. Dutton & Co.
--From Powder Monkey to Admiral, 39 vols. (Illus.). (Famous Books for Boys Ser.: No. 8). 1905. Set. H M Caldwell Co.
--From Powder Monkey to Admiral. (Illus.). (St. Nicholas Series for Boys). N.D. International Book Co.
--The Frontier Fort: Or, Stirring Times in the Northwest Territory of British America (Pub. by Society for Promoting Christian Knowledge). N.D. E. & J. B Young & Co.
--Hendricks the Hunter: A Tale of Zululand. (Illus.). (New Kingston Library). 1882. A. C. Armstrong.
--Hendricks the Hunter: A Tale of Zululand. (Illus.). (St. Nicholas Series for Boys). N.D. International Book Co.
--The Heroic Wife: Or, The Wanderers on the Amazon. Petherick, H. W., illus. LC 41-31404. ix, 1 p., 1 l., 13-172 p. incl. front., plates. 16 1/2 cm. N.D. E. P. Dutton.
--The Heroic Wife: Or, The Wanderous on the Amazon, 1 of 6 vols. (Illus.). (Lucy's Campaign Library). N.D. E P Dutton.
--The Heroic Wife: or, Wanderers on the Amazon. 1875. Pott, Young & Co.
--Hurrican Hurry: Or, the Adventures of a Naval Officer Afloat and Ashore. 472p. 1875. Pott, Young & Co.
--Hurricane Hurry: Or, The Adventures of a Naval Officer during the American War of Independence. (Illus.). N.D. E. P. Dutton & co.
--Hurricane Hurry: The Adventures of a Naval Officer. N.D. Estes and Lauriat's Publications.
--In New Granada: Or, Heroes and Patriots, a Tale for Boys. LC 44-39846. xi, 1, 13 368 p. incl. front., plates. 19 cm. (On cover: Daring adventure library). 1884. T. Nelson and Sons.
--In the Eastern Seas. (The Adventure Library). N.D. Thomas Nelson & Sons.
--In the Eastern Seas: Or, The Regions of the Bird of Paradise, a Tale for Boys. LC 44-43121. ix, 13-608 p. incl. illus., plates. front. 19 cm. 1884. T. Nelson and Sons.
--In the Forest: A Tale of Settler-Life in North America. LC 74-178018. (Illus.). xii, 393 p. 19cm. 1880. T. Nelson.
--In the Rocky Mountains: A Tale of Adventure. LC 44-23382. xi, 13, 334 p. incl. front., plates. 18 cm. 1878. T. Nelson and Sons.
--In the Wilds of Africa. (The Adventure Library). N.D. Thomas Nelson & Sons.
--In the Wilds of Florida. A Tale of Warfare and Hunting. LC 24-11868. ix, 2, 10-461 p. incl. front., illus., plates. 19 1/2 cm. 1880. T. Nelson and Sons.
--The Ivory Trader. N.D. George Routledge & Sons.
--James Braithwaite, the Supercargo. (Illus.). (St. Nicholas Series for Boys). N.D. International Book Co.
--James Braithwaite the Supercargo: The Story of His Adventures Ashore and Afloat. LC 8-11004. xii, 266 p. front., 7 pl. 18 1/2 cm. 1883. A. C. Armstrong & Son.
--James McLaren. (The Kingston Library). N.D. Pott, Young & Co.
--Janet McLaren, the Faithful Nurse. (The Kingston Library). N.D. American News Co.
--John Deane, of Nottingham: His Adventures and Exploits. (Illus.). N.D. E. P. Dutton & Co.
--Kingston Ser. Containing "Voyage of the Steadfast", "Charley Laurel", "Virginia", "Little Ben Hadden", "Young Whaler", "Fisher Boy", etc, 8 vols. N.D. Set. D. Lothrop & Co.
--The Lily of Leyden. (Illus.). N.D. E & J B Young.
--Little Ben Hadden: Do Right Whatever Comes of It. N.D. D. Lothrop & Co.
--Little Peter, the Ship Boy. (Illus.). N.D. D. Lothrop & Co.
--The Log House, 1 of 6 vols. (Home Sunshine Ser.). N.D. D. Lothrop & Co.
--Log House by the Lake, 1 of 30 vols. (Illus.). (Morning Glory Ser). N.D. Lothrop Pub. Co.
--The Log House by the Lake: A Tale of Canada. (Illus.). (Golden Lilly Ser.). N.D. D. Lothrop Co.
--The Log House by the Lake: A Tale of Canada. (Illus.). N.D. E. & J. B. Young & Co.
--Manco, the Peruvian Chief: Or, An Englishman's Adventures in the Country of the Incas. (Illus.). (The Boy's Own Favorite Ser.). N.D. E. P. Dutton & Co.
--Manco, the Peruvian Chief: Or, An Englishman's Adventures in the Country of the Incas, 1 of 4 Vols. (Illus.). (Ocean Tales). N.D. Set. Pott, Young & Co.
--Manco the Peruvian Chief: Or, An Englishman's Adventures in the Country of the Incas. (The Forward Ser.). N.D. William Collins Co.
--Manco: the Peruvian Chief: Or, An Englishman's Adventures in the Country of the Incas. Schmolze, Karl Heinrich (1826-1859), illus. LC 41-31405. xi, 371 p. front., plates. 18 1/2 cm. N.D. E. P. Dutton & Co.
--Mary Leddiard. (The Kingston Library of Adventure). N.D. George Routledge & Sons.
--Mary Leddiard: A Tale of the Pacific. (The Kingston Library). N.D. American News Co.
--Mate of the Lily (Pub. by Society for Promoting Whristian Knowledge). N.D. E. & J. B. Young & Co.
--Millicent Courtenay's Diary: or, The Experiences of a Young Lady At Home and Abroad. N.D. George Routledge & Sons.
--The Missing Ship. (Illus.). (The Boy's Own Favorite Ser.). N.D. E. P. Dutton & Co.
--Mountain Moggy: or, The Stoning of Witch. (Illus.). N.D. E & J B Young.
--My First Voyage to Southern Seas. (The Pioneer Library). N.D. Thomas Nelson & Sons.
--My First Voyage to Southern Seas. A Book for Boys. LC 41-32452. vii, 1, 9-448 p. incl. front., illus., pl. 19 cm. (On cover: Daring adventure library). 1884. T. Nelson and Sons.
--My First Voyage to Southern Seas: A Book for Boys. vii, 1, 9-448 p. incl. front., illus. 19 cm. (On cover: The Kingston library for boys). 1887. T. Nelson and Sons.
--Off to Sea: Or, the Adventures Jovial Jack Junker on His Road to Fame, 1 of 4 Vols. (Album Library: No. 3). N.D. Colby and Rich.
--Off to Sea: or, The Adventures of Jovial Jack Junker on his Road to Fame, 1 of 4. 224p. (The True Crusoe Ser.). N.D. Cassell,Petter, & Galp in.
--Off to Sea: Or, The Adventures of Jovial Jack Junker on His Road to Fame, 1 of 4 Vols. (Illus.). 224p. (The Album Library Ser.). N.D. Lee & Shepard.
--Old Jack. (The Pioneer Library). N.D. Thomas Nelson & Sons.
--Old Jack: A Tale for Boys. LC 41-31406. viii, 9-507 p. front., illus. 19 cm. (On cover: Daring adventure library). 1884. T. Nelson and Sons.
--On the Banks of the Amazon: Or, A Boy's Journal of His Adventures in the Tropical Wilds of South America. (Illus.). N.D. Thomas Nelson and Sons.
--Owen Hartley: A Tale of Land and Sea, 1 of 4 Vols. (Illus.). (Tales of Heroes). N.D. Set. Pott, Young & Co.
--Paddy Finn: Or, The Adventures of a Midshipmen Afloat and Ashore. LC 44-46351. vii, 430 p., 1 l. front., plates. 19 cm. 1883. Griffith and Farran.
--Paul Gerrard, the Cabin Boy. N.D. George Routledge & Sons.
--Peter the Ship Boy, 1 of 8 vols. (Illus.). (Kingston Ser.). N.D. D. Lothrop Co.
--Peter the Whaler. (Illus.). 18cm. 389p. 1861. Crosby, Nichols, Lee & Co.
--Peter the Whaler. 18cm. 337p. (Everyman's Library). 1906. E. P. Dutton & Co.
--Peter the Whaler. (Illus.). (The Boy's Own Favorite Ser.). N.D. E. P. Dutton & Co.
--Peter the Whaler. (Illus.). (Famous Books for Boys: No. 24). 1905. Set. H M Caldwell Co.
--Peter the Whaler. (Illus.). (St. Nicholas Series for Boys). N.D. International Book Co.
--Peter the Whaler: Adventures in Arctic Regions. N.D. Nichols & Hall.
--Peter Trawl: The Adventures of a Whaler Round the World. (Illus.). (New Kingston Library). 1882. A. C. Armstrong.
--Peter Trawl: The Adventures of a Whaler Round the World. (Illus.). (St. Nicholas Series for Boys). N.D. International Book Co.
--Ralph and Dick, 1 of 8 vols. (Illus.). (Kingston Ser.). N.D. D. Lothrop Co.
--Ralph Clavering. N.D. E. P. Dutton.
--Ralph Clavering. N.D. Scribner, Welford & Armstrong.
--The Ranger and Crusader Ships, 1 of 5 Vols. (Dick Onslow Series.). N.D. Thomas Whittaker.
--Roger Kyffyn's Ward. N.D. George Routledge & Sons.
--Roger Willoughby. N.D. Pott & Co.
--Ronald Morton. N.D. George Routledge & Sons.
--Ronald Morton: Or,The Fire-Ship. (Illus.). N.D. E & J B Young.
--Round the World: A Tale for Boys. N.D. Nichols & Hall.
--Salt Water: Sea Life and Adventures. N.D. Nichols & Hall.
--Salt Water Tales. N.D. Set. Nichols & Halls.
--Salt Water: The Sea Life and Adventures of Neil D'Arcy, the Midshipman. Anelay, Henry, illus. LC 42-44499. 2 p. l., 371 p. front., plates. 19 1/2 cm. (On cover: The boy's own favourite series). N.D. Griffith and Farran.
--School-Boy Days. (Illus.). N.D. Lee & Shepard.
--The School Friends. N.D. George Routledge & Sons.
--The School Friends, and Other Tales. N.D. George Routledge & Sons.
--Schoolboy Days. (Jutland Ser.). N.D. Colby and Rich.
--Schoolboy Days, 1 of 4 vols. (Illus.). 344p. (Jutland Ser.). 1882. Lee & Shepard.
--The Settlers: A/Tale of Virginia. 1875. Pott, Young & Co.

--How the Camel Got His Hump: A 'Just So' Story. Weihs, Erika (1917-), illus. LC 55-11971. unpaged illus. 21cm. (Rand McNally Eif book, 52). c.1955. Rand McNally.
--How the Elephant Got Its Trunk, and, Cinderella. Ferrero, Elisabetta & Millet, Claude, illus. LC 84-18662. p. cm. c.1985. (ISBN 0-88110-252-0). Educational Development Corp.
--How the Leopard Got His Spots. Rojankovsky, Feodor Stepanovich (1891-1970), illus. LC 42-21075. 28 p. illus. (part col.) 24 cm. (His Just so stories series). 1942. Garden City Publishing Company, Inc.
--How the Leopard Got His Spots & Other Stories. (Peter Possum Paperbacks Ser). 1967. (ISBN 0-531-05124-2). Watts.
--How the Leopard Got Its Spots. Weisgard, Leonard Joseph (1916-), illus. 1972. Walker.
--How the Rhinoceros Got His Skin. Rojankovsky, Feodor Stepanovich (1891-1970), illus. LC 42-21076. 31 p. illus. (part col.) 24 cm. (His Just so stories series). 1942. Garden City Publishing Co., Inc.
--How the Rhinoceros Got His Skin. Weisgard, Leonard Joseph (1916-), illus. LC 73-76356. (Illus.). 32 p. 27cm. 1974. (ISBN 0-8027-6149-6). (ISBN 0-8027-6149-6). Walker.
--How the Rhinoceros Got His Skin: A 'Just So' Story;. Weihs, Erika (1917-), illus. LC 56-8342. unpaged. illus. 21cm. (Rand McNally eif book, 540). 1956. Rand McNally.
--How the Whale Got His Throat. Madden, Donald B. (1927-), illus. LC 77-164714. (Illus.). 32 p. 24cm. (His Just so stories series). 1972. (ISBN 0-201-03712-2). Addison-Wesley.
--The Illustrated Book of Kipling's Educational Stories for Children & Teenagers. (Illus.). 265p. Repr. of 1898 ed. 1984. (ISBN 0-89901-146-2). Found Class Reprints.
--Indian Tales. N.D. Dodge.
--Indian Tales. Bridgman, Lewis Jesse, et al. (1857-1931), illus. N.D. H. M. Caldwell & Co.
--The Jungle Book. LC 80-2243. 408p. (Fatback Ser.). (gr. 6-8). 1981. Doubleday.
--The Jungle Book. (Illus.). 303p. 1894. The Century Co.
--The Jungle Book. Dempster, William, illus. (Illus.). 217p. (Fun to Read Classics Series). (gr. 5 up). 1968. (ISBN 0-516-04231-9). Childrens.
--The Jungle Book. Dempster, William, illus. LC 74-166304. (Illus.). 217 p. 29cm. (Educator classic library, 5). c.1968. Classic Press.
--The Jungle Book. Eichenberg, Fritz (1901-), illus. (Illus.). (gr. 4-6). 1950. (ISBN 0-448-06014-0, G&D). (ISBN 0-448-11014-8, G&D). (ISBN 0-448-05464-7, G&D). Putnam Pub Group.
--Jungle Book. Kipling, Joseph Rudyard, et al. (1865-1936), illus. (Illus.). (gr. 7-11). N.D. (ISBN 0-385-07345-3). Doubleday.
--The Jungle Book. Wiese, Kurt (1887-1974), illus. N.D. Doubleday & Co.
--The Jungle Book. Wilson, Maurice Charles John (1914-), illus. LC 83-27181. 1984. (ISBN 0-8052-3906-5). Schocken Books.
--The Jungle Books. LC 80-2243. p. cm. 1981. (ISBN 0-385-15975-7). Doubleday.
--The Jungle Books. Fadiman, Clifton Paul (1904-), afterword by. 1964. MacMillan Co.
--The Jungle Books, 2. Watson, Aldren Auld (1917-), illus. Doubleday, Nelson, intro. by. 1948. Doubleday & Co.
--Just So Stories. LC 12-24463. 3 p. l., 249, 1 p. col. front., illus., plates (part col.) 25 1/2 cm. 1912. Doubleday, Page & Company.
--Just So Stories. LC 41-42441. 3 p. l., 249 p. incl. illus., plates. col. front., col. plates. 24 cm. 1922. Doubleday, Page & Company.
--Just So Stories. school ed. LC 38-9734. 4 p. l., 3-240 p. incl. front., 1 illus., plates. 19 1/2 cm. 1935. Doubleday, Doran & Company, Inc.
--Just So Stories. LC 46-20643. 4 p. l., 3-249 p. incl. illus., plates, map. 20 1/2 cm. 1946. Doubleday & Company, Inc.
--Just So Stories. Anniversary ed. LC 79-170932. 112p. (gr. 2-5). 1972. Doubleday.
--Just So Stories. Ambrus, Victor G., pseud. (1935-), illus. Ambrus, Gyozo Laszlo. LC 82-5400. (Illus.). 64 p. 29cm. c.1982. (ISBN 0-528-82422-8). R. McNally.
--Just So Stories. anniversary ed. Delessert, Etienne (1941-), illus. LC 79-170932. (Illus.). 111 p. 32cm. 1972. Doubleday. **Award: (NYT).**
--Just So Stories. Gleeson, Joseph M., illus. LC 12-24463. (Illus.). 249p. 25cm. 1912. Doubleday, Page & Company.
--Just So Stories. Gleeson, Joseph M., illus. 1946. Doubleday.
--Just So Stories. Harris, Aurand (1915-), ed. 1971. Anchorage Press.
--Just So Stories. Kipling, Joseph Rudyard (1865-1936), illus. (Illus.). N.D. (ISBN 0-385-07351-8). Doubleday and Company.
--Just So Stories. Mayan, Earl E., illus. (Illus.). 155 p. 20cm. (Companion library of classics). 1965. Grosset & Dunlap.
--Just So Stories. Mordvinoff, Nicolas (1911-1973), illus. Nicolas, pseud. LC 52-12166. 84 p. illus. 29 cm. 1952. Garden City Books.
--Just So Stories for Little Children. LC 79-22584. p. cm. (Facsimile Classics Series). 1980, c.1902. (ISBN 0-8317-5296-3). Mayflower Books.
--Just So Stories for Little Children. LC 78-23639. (Illus.). 210 p. 24cm. 1978. (ISBN 0-517-26655-5). Weathervane Books : Distributed by Crown Publishers.
--Just So Stories for Little Children. Kipling, Joseph Rudyard (1865-1936), illus. LC 83-25221. p. cm. 1983. (ISBN 0-517-43631-0). Chatham River Press.
--Just So Stories for Little Children. large type ed. Kipling, Joseph Rudyard (1865-1936), illus. LC 68-2893. (Illus.). 249 p. 29cm. N.D. F. Watts.
--Just So Stories for Little Children. Kipling, Joseph Rudyard (1865-1936), illus. LC 46-38954. 4 p. l., 3-249 p., 1 l. incl. illus., plates, map. 19 1/2 cm. 1914. Pub. by Doubleday, Page & Company for Review of Reviews Co.
--Just So Stories for Little Children. Kipling, Joseph Rudyard (1865-1936), illus. Read, Herbert Edward (1893-1968), intro. by. LC 65-27041. xii, 247p. illus. 21cm. c.1965. Schocken.
--Just So Stories for Little Children. Stalky & Co. LC 52-52926. 292, 247 p. illus. 21 cm. (Mandalay edition of the works of Rudyard Kipling). 1925. Doubleday, Page.
--Kim. (Kipling Library Edition). N.D. Doubleday & Co.
--Kim. N.D. The Modern Library.
--Kim. Innes, Michael, pseud. (1906-), intro. by Stewart, John Innes MacKintosh. (Great Illustrated Classics). N.D. Dodd, Mead & Co.
--Kim. Kipling, Joseph Rudyard (1865-1936), illus. LC 1-25039. (gr. 11 up). N.D. Doubleday.
--King Arthur and His Knights of the Round Table. popular ed. N.D. (ISBN 0-448-05816-2). Grosset & Dunlap.
--Kipling: A Selection of His Stories & Poems, 2 vols. Beecroft, John William Richard (1902-1966), ed. LC 56-6647. (Illus.). 1956. Doubleday.
--The Kipling Birthday Books. Kipling, Joseph Rudyard (1865-1936), illus. 4x6cm. 250p. N.D. Doubleday, Page & Co.
--Kipling Boy Stories. (Illus.). (The Junior Library Ser.: Vol. 10). N.D. Rand, McNally & Co.
--The Kipling Reader for Elementary Grades. N.D. D. Appleton & Co.
--The Kipling Reader for Upper Grades. N.D. D. Appleton & Co.
--Kipling Stories. (Great Writers Collection). (gr. 7 up). 1960. Platt.
--Kipling Stories and Poems Every Child Should Know. (Riverside Literature Ser. No. 257: Bk. 1). N.D. Houghton Mifflin Co.
--Kipling Stories and Poems Every Child Should Know. (Riverside Literature Ser. No. 258: Bk. 2). N.D. Houghton Mifflin Co.
--Kipling Stories and Poems Every Child Should Know. Burt, Mary Elizabeth (1850-1918) & Chapin, Wallace T., eds. Gleeson, Joseph M., illus. (The Every Child Should Know Ser.). N.D. Doubleday, Page & Co.
--Kipling Stories and Poems Every Child Should Know. Wiese, Kurt (1887-1974) & Gleeson, J. M., illus. LC 38-347971. xv p., 1 l., 19-246 p. col. front., illus. 23 cm. 1938. Garden City Publishing Co., Inc.
--Kipling Stories & Proverbs Every Child Should Know. N.D. Houghton Mifflin.
--Kipling Stories Every Child Should Know. Burt, Mary Elizabeth (1850-1918) & Chapin, Wallace T., eds. LC 40-4097. xvii, 298 p. col. front., illus. 19 1/2 cm. (What every child should know library. 2d ser.). 1939. Doubleday, Doran & Co., Inc., for the Parents' Institute, Inc.
--Kipling Stories: Twenty-Eight Exciting Tales. 502 p. 21cm. (Platt & Munk great writers collection). 1960. Platt & Munk.
--Kipling's Boy Stories. St. John, J Allen, illus. (The New Junior Library). N.D. Rand McNally.
--Kipling's Boy Stories. St. John, J. Allen, illus. 451p. (gr. 7-8). N.D. Rand McNally & Co.
--Kipling's Boys Stories. (Illus.). (Six to Sixteen Ser.). N.D. Caldwell.
--Kipling's Boy's Stories, 6 vols. (Illus.). N.D. H. M. Caldwell Co.
--Kipling's Stories and Poems. (Famous Bks. for Young Americans). N.D. A. L. Burt Co.
--Kipling's Stories for Boys. Hastings, Howard Livingston (1887-), illus. LC 31-19571. 5 p. l., 499 p. col. front., plates. 21 1/2 cm. c.1931. Cupples & Leon Company.
--Kipling's Stories for Children. N.D. Grosset & Dunlap.
--Kipling's Stories for Children. Osborne, Lloyd, illus. 3 p. l., 3-241 p. col. front., illus. 25 cm. (Sears illustrated juveniles). c.1928. J. H. Sears & Company, Inc.
--Kipling's Stories of India. Strayer, Paul (1896-1970), illus. N.D. Rand McNally & Co.
--Land and Sea Tales for Boys and Girls. LC 23-17162. ix p., 1 l., 322 p. 20 1/2 cm. 1923. Doubleday, Page & Company.
--Land and Sea Tales: For Scouts and Scout Masters. Lee, Manning De Villeneuve (1894-1980), illus. LC 37-23537. ix p., 1 l., 322 p. front. 20 1/2 cm. (Young moderns bookshelf). 1937. The Sun Dial Press, Inc.
--Land and Sea Tales for Scouts and Scoutmasters. (Windmill Bks.). N.D. Doubleday Doran & Co.
--The Light that Failed. (Illus.). (The Chateau Ser.). N.D. H. M. Caldwell Co.
--The Maltese Cat: A Polo Game of the Nineties. Edwards, Lionel Dalhousie Robertson (1878-), illus. LC 37-1530. 91 p. col. front., illus., col. plates. 21 cm. 1936. Doubleday, Doran & Company, Inc.
--The Man Who Would Be King. (gr. 7 up). 1977. (ISBN 0-590-10278-8). Schol Bk Serv.
--The Miracle of Purun Bhagat. LC 85-26956. p. cm. c.1985. (ISBN 0-88682-052-9). Creative Education, Inc.
--The Miracle of the Mountain. Leach, Aroline Arnett Beecher, adapted by. Baum, Willi (1931-), illus. LC 69-15801. (Illus.). 48 p. 24cm. 1969. Addison-Wesley.
--Mowgli, the Jungle Boy. Bartlett, William, illus. (Illus.). (gr. 4-6). N.D. G&D.
--The New Illustrated Just So Stories. (gr. 1-7). N.D. Doubleday.
--New Illustrated Just-So Stories. Nicolas, photos by. N.D. Garden City Books.
--Out of India. N.D. G. W. Dillingham Co.
--Phantoms & Fantasies. Silverman, Burton Philip (1928-), illus. LC 65-17269. (Illus.). (gr. 6-8). N.D. (ISBN 0-385-02709-5). Doubleday.
--Plain Tales From the Hills. N.D. A. L. Burt Co.
--Plain Tales from the Hills, 1 of 10 vols. (Illus.). (Choice Works of Rudyard Kipling). N.D. H. M. Caldwell & Co.
--Poems and Ballads. N.D. Dodge.
--Puck of Pook's Hill. Millar, Harold Robert (1869-1939), illus. N.D. Doubleday Page & Co.
--Puck of Pook's Hill. Rackham, Arthur (1867-1939), illus. (Illus.). 4 plates. (gr. 3-7). 1968. (ISBN 0-486-21880-5). Dover.
--Rewards and Fairies. Craig, Frank, illus. N.D. Doubleday Page & Co.
--Rikki-Tikki-Tavi. (Illus.). (ps-3). 1982. (ISBN 0-516-09223-5). Childrens.
--Rikki-Tikki-Tavi & the White Seal. 1967. (ISBN 0-88302-357-1, Peter Possum). Mulberry Pr.
--The Rudyard Kipling Storybook. (Thrushwood Bks.). N.D. Grosset & Dunlap.
--The Second Jungle Book. (gr. 7-11). 1923. Doubleday.
--The Second Jungle Book. Kipling, Joseph Rudyard (1865-1936), illus. (Illus.). 325p. N.D. The Century Co.
--Selected Stories From Rudyard Kipling. N.D. Doubleday Doran & Co.
--Selections from Just-So Stories. (Illus.). (gr. k-4). 1975. (ISBN 0-590-09846-2, Schol Pap). Schol Bk Serv.
--The Seven Seas. N.D. (ISBN 0-87821-113-6). Milford House Inc.
--Soldier Stories. N.D. Doubleday Doran & Co.
--Soldiers Three. (Illus.). (The Young Folks Library). N.D. Caldwell.
--Songs for Youth. N.D. Doubleday Doran & Co.
--Stalky & Co. (Kipling Library Edition). N.D. Doubleday & Co.
--Tales from The Jungle Book. McKinley, Robin, ed. Smith, Joseph A. (1936-), illus. LC 84-11724. p. cm. (Looking glass library book). 1985. (ISBN 0-394-86940-0). (ISBN 0-394-96940-5). Random House.
--Tales of India. Strayer, Paul (1896-1970), illus. (Windermere Ser.). N.D. G.P. Putnam's Sons.
--Tales of Kipling. (Classic Ser.). N.D. World Publishing Co.
--Teem: A Treasure Hunter. Kirmse, Marguerite (1885-1954), illus. LC 38-39435. 3 p. l., 46 p. front. 19 1/2 cm. 1938. Doubleday, Doran & Company, Inc.
--Ten Nights in a Bar-Room. (Illus.). (Vademecum Ser.). N.D. Henry Altemus.
--Thy Servant a Dog: Told by Boots. Kirmse, Marguerite (1885-1954), illus. LC 30-33156. 5 p. l., 3-95 p. front., plates. 20 1/2 cm. 1930. Doubleday, Doran & Company, Inc.
--The Two Jungle Books. N.D. Doubleday Doran & Co.
--Two Tales. N.D. (ISBN 0-8283-1460-8). Branden Press.
--Under the Deodars, the Phantom Rickshaw, and Wee Willie Winkie, 1 of 6 vols. New & Rev. ed. 1900. Doubleday Page & Co.
--Walt Disney's the Jungle Book. LC 74-3407. p. cm. (Disney's wonderful world of reading, 20). 1974. (ISBN 0-394-82560-8). (ISBN 0-394-92560-2). Random House.
--Walt Disney's The Jungle Book. LC 80-22776. p. cm. c.1980. (ISBN 0-517-54324-9). (ISBN 0-517-54328-1). Harmony Books.
--Wee Willie Winkie, 1 of 64 vols. (Young America Library: No. 54). 1900. Set. Hurst & Co.
--The White Seal. (Illus.). (ps-3). 1982. (ISBN 0-516-09224-3). Childrens.
--The White Seal. Jones, Chuck, ed. (Illus.). 48p. (gr. k-6). 1982. (ISBN 0-8249-8042-5). Ideals.

Kipling, Joseph Rudyard (1865-1936) & Chamberlain, Sarah
--How the Rhinoceros Got His Wrinkled Skin. LC 80-516603. (Illus.). 21 p. 19cm. 1976. Chamberlain Press.

Kipling, Rudyard see Kipling, Joseph Rudyard.

Kippax, Janet (1926-)
--The Gypsy. zonderavian ed. LC 78-24363. 90 p. 20cm. (Pathfinder Ser.). 1979, c.1972. (ISBN 0-310-37811-7). Zondervan Pub. House.

Kirby, Alfred F. P
--Green Island: A Tale for Youth. N.D. P. J. Kenedy.
--The Green Island: A Tale for Youth. LC 25-23744. 195 p. 15 1/2 cm. 1871. Kelly, Piet and Company.

Kirby, Anastasia Joan
--A Dream of Christmas Eve. Robson, Janet (1902-), illus. 22p. illus. 15 x 24cm. 1937. Saint Anthony Guild Press.

Kirby, Douglas J (1929-)
--The Silver Wood. Williams, Jenny (1939-), illus. LC 67-23543. (Illus.). 32 p. 26cm. 1st U.S. edition. 1967, c.1966. Four Winds Press.

Kirby, Elizabeth, jt. auth. see Gregg, Mary Kirby, Mrs.

Kirby, Elizabeth, jt. auth. see Kirby, Mary.

Kirby, Jean, pseud., see McDonnell, Virginia Bleecher.

Kirby, Jean, pseud. (1917-)
--Olympic Duty. McDonnell, Virginia Bleecher. 2nd ed (Pub. by Whitman). (Griffon Ser). (gr. 7 up). 1969 (Golden Pr). Western Pub.

Kirby, Mansfield
--The Secret of Thut-Mouse III: Or, Basil Beaudesert's Revenge. Post, Mance, illus. 64p. 1985. (ISBN 0-374-36677-2). FS&G.

Kirby, Mary see Gregg, Mary Kirby, Mrs. (1817-1893) & Kirby, Elizabeth.

Kirby, Mary & Kirby, Elizabeth
--Aunt Martha's Corner Cupboard. (Altemus' New Illustrated Young People's Library). N.D. Henry Altemus Company.
--Aunt Martha's Corner Cupboard. Wilford, Carol, ed. Breuer, Matilda, illus. N.D. A. Whitman & Co.

Kirby, Susan E
--Ike and Porker. LC 83-8507. 145 p. 22cm. 1983. (ISBN 0-395-34556-1). Houghton Mifflin.

Kirby, William Forsell (1844-1912), tr.
--The New Arabian Nights. Select Tales, Not Included by Galland or Lane. xi, 390 p. front., plates. 20 1/2 cm. 1883. J. B. Lippincott & Co.

Kircher, Harry B
--Diddledee Dog, the Dirt Digger. LC 68-57271. (Illus.). 19 p. 23cm. 1968. Interstate Printers & Publishers.

Kirchgessner, Maria (1908-)
--High Challenge. LC 62-7730. 287 p. 22cm. 1962. Harcourt, Brace & World.

Kirchhoff, Art
--The Porcupine Storybook. Kirchhoff, Art, illus. LC 75-310610. (Illus.). 47 p. 26cm. (Porcupine books). 1974. (ISBN 0-570-06994-7). Concordia Pub. House.

Kirchner, Clemens
--Sea Dogs & Tramps. Robinson, Charles (1931-), illus. LC 68-24525. (Illus.). 128p. (gr. 3-5). 1968. (ISBN 0-399-60564-9). Putnam.

Kirk, Barbara
--Grandpa, Me and Our House in the Tree. LC 78-9564. p. cm. c.1978. (ISBN 0-02-750750-5). Macmillan.

Kirk, Dolly W., jt. auth. see Greene, Frances Nimmo.

Kirk, E. B.
--The Story of Oliver Twist. Harris, William T., ed. (Appleton's Home Reading Books). N.D. D. Appleton & Co.

Kirk, Ellen Warner Olney, Mrs. (1842-)
--Dorothy and Her Friends. LC 99-5274. 4 p. l., 351, 1 p. front., plates. 18 1/2 cm. 1899. Houghton, Mifflin and Company.
--Dorothy Deane: A Children's Story. LC 98-896. 4 p. l., 325, 1 p. front., 5 pl. 18 cm. 1898. Houghton, Mifflin and Company.

Kirk, Maria Louise (1860-), tr. see Spyri, Johanna Heusser.

Kirk, Maria Louise (1860-), illus.
--Favorite Rhymes of Mother Goose. (Illus.). 128p. N.D. Cupples & Leon.

Kirk, Mildred
--A Different Kind of Birthday. Kirk, Isaac D., illus. 1980. (ISBN 0-533-03565-1). Vantage.

Kirk, Richard E.
--The Lightning and the Rainbow. LC 62-15820. 32 p. illus. 29cm. c.1962. Follett Pub. Co.

--Boomerang Hunter. Mars, Witold Tadeusz J. (1912-), illus. (Illus.). 172 p. 21cm. 1960. Holiday House.
--Buckskin Brigade. Ray, Ralph (1920-1952), illus. (Illus.). 310p. (gr. 7-11). 1947. (ISBN 0-8234-0014-X). Holiday.
--Chip, the Dam Builder. Ray, Ralph (1920-1952), illus. LC 50-10186. (Illus.). 233 p. 20cm. 1950. Holiday House.
--Coyote Song. MacLean, Robert (1926-), illus. LC 68-27820. (Illus.). xii, 174 p. 22cm. 1969. Dodd, Mead.
--Cracker Barrel Trouble Shooter. LC 54-5259. 213p. 21cm. 1954. Dodd, Mead.
--Dave and His Dog, Mulligan. Savitt, Sam (1917-), illus. LC 66-15715. 148 p. illus. 24 cm. 1966. Dodd, Mead.
--Desert Dog. Savitt, Sam (1917-), illus. LC 56-14250. 200p. 21cm. 1956. Holiday House.
--Double Challenge. Kenyon, Chris A., illus. LC 57-523321. 178p. 21cm. 1957. (ISBN 0-396-03915-4). Dodd, Mead.
--The Duck-Footed Hound. Simont, Marc (1915-), illus. LC 60-9160. 184p. illus. 21cm. 1960. Crowell.
--Fawn in the Forest & Other Wild Animal Stories. Savitt, Sam (1917-), illus. LC 62-20210. (Illus.). 21cm. 168p. (gr. 7-9). 1962. (ISBN 0-396-04712-2). Dodd.
--Fire-Hunter. Palazzo, Tony (1905-1970), illus. LC 51-12734. (Illus.). 217 p. 21cm. 1951. Holiday House.
--Forest Patrol. Palazzo, Tony (1905-1970), illus. LC 42-111. 298 p. illus. 21 cm. c.1941. Holiday House.
--Furious Moose of the Wilderness. Kunstler, Morton (1927-), illus. LC 65-11810. 149p. illus. 21cm. c.1965. (ISBN 0-396-05133-2). Dodd.
--Haunt Fox. 1954. (ISBN 0-8382-0324-8, Cadmus Books). E. M. Hale and Company.
--Haunt Fox. Rounds, Glen Harold (1906-), illus. LC 54-9569. 220p. illus. 20cm. 1954. (ISBN 0-8234-0040-9). Holiday House.
--Hi Jolly. Rossi, Kendall, illus. LC 59-619777. 183p. illus. 21cm. 1959. Dodd, Mead.
--Hidden Trail. Darling, Louis, Jr. (1916-1970), illus. LC 62-2067. (Illus.). 188 p. 21cm. 1962. Holiday House.
--Hound Dog and Other Yarns. Brown, Paul (1893-1958), illus. 1958. Dodd Mead.
--Irish Red. (gr. 4-6). 1955. (ISBN 0-448-00928-5). G&D.
--Irish Red. (Illus.). 224p. (gr. 7 up). 1951. (ISBN 0-8234-0060-3). Holiday.
--Irish Red. (gr. 6-9). N.D (StarLine). Schol Bk Serv.
--Irish Red, Son of Big Red. 224 p. 21cm. 1961, c.1951. Grosset & Dunlap.
--Irish Red, Son of Big Red. LC 51-3090. 224 p. 21cm. 1951. (ISBN 0-8234-0060-3). Holiday House.
--Kalak of the Ice. Kuhn, Bob, illus. LC 49-9043. 201 p. illus. 20 cm. 1949. Holiday House.
--The Land is Bright. 1958. Dodd Mead.
--Lion Hound. 1961. (ISBN 0-8382-0440-6, Cadmus Books). E. M. Hale And Company.
--Lion Hound. Landau, Jacob (1917-), illus. LC 55-13591. (Illus.). 216 p. 21cm. 1955. Holiday House.
--The Lost Wagon. Orbaan, Albert F. (1913-), illus. 1955. Dodd Mead.
--My Father's Collie. Simont, Marc (1915-), illus. 1960. Dodd Mead.
--A Nose for Trouble. LC 49-11129. 250 p. 21 cm. 1949. Holiday House.
--Outlaw Red: Son of Big Red. (Illus.). 230p. (gr. 6-10). N.D. (ISBN 0-448-00932-3). G&D.
--Outlaw Red: Son of Big Red. LC 53-12624. 230p. 21cm. 1953. Holiday House.
--Outlaw Red: Son of Big Red. 156p. (gr. 4-9). 1970 (Schol Trade Pap). Schol Bk Serv.
--Rebel Siege. Wilson, Charles Banks (1918-), illus. (Illus.). 252p. (gr. 7 up). 1943. (ISBN 0-8234-0092-1). Holiday.
--Rebel Siege. Wilson, Charles Banks (1918-), illus. 252p. Reissue of 1943 ed. 1953. Holiday House.
--Rescue Dog of the High Pass. N.D. E . M. Hale and Co.
--Rescue Dog of the High Pass. Shenton, Edward (1895-), illus. (Illus.). 158 p. 21cm. 1958. Dodd, Mead.
--Snow Dog. Landau, Jacob (1917-), illus. (Illus.). 236 p. 21cm. (Famous dog stories). 1961, c.1948. Grosset & Dunlap.
--Snow Dog. Landau, Jacob (1917-), illus. LC 48-888590. 236 p. illus. 21 cm. 1948. Holiday House.
--The Spell of the White Sturgeon. Voorhies, Stephen J., illus. LC 53-6314. 197 p. 21cm. 1953. Dodd, Mead.
--Stormy. Darling, Louis, Jr. (1916-1970), illus. LC 59-16199. (Illus.). 190 p. 21cm. 1959. Holiday House.
--The Story of Geronimo. Wilson, Charles Banks (1918-), illus. (Illus.). 179 p. 22cm. (Signature books, 44). 1958. Grosset & Dunlap.
--Swamp Cat. (Illus.). (gr. 6 up). 1957. (ISBN 0-8382-0830-4). Hale.
--Swamp Cat. Shenton, Edward (1895-), illus. LC 57-10167. 175p. illus. 21cm. 1957. (ISBN 0-396-03982-0). Dodd, Mead.
--Tigre. Kinstler, Everett Raymond (1926-), illus. 181p. 1961. Dodd, Mead & Co.
--Trading Jeff and His Dog. LC 56-52467. 181p. 21cm. 1956. Dodd, Mead.
--Trailing Trouble. LC 52-3944. 219 p. 21cm. 1952. Holiday House.
--Two Dogs and a Horse. Savitt, Sam (1917-), illus. LC 64-9853. 94 p. illus. 24 cm. 1964. Dodd, Mead.
--Ulysses and His Woodland Zoo. Rossi, Kendall, illus. 185p. illus. 21cm. 1960. Dodd, Mead.
--We Were There at the Oklahoma Land Run. Kenyon, Chris A., illus. (Illus.). 182 p. 24cm. (We were there books, 12). 1957. Grosset & Dunlap.
--Wild Trek. 1950. E M Hale.
--Wild Trek. 253 p. 21cm. 1950. Holiday House.
--Wildlife Cameraman. 218p. (gr. 7 up). 1957. (ISBN 0-8234-0149-9). Holiday.
--Wildlife Cameraman. Savitt, Sam (1917-), illus. LC 57-10851. 218p. illus. 21cm. 1957. (ISBN 0-8234-0149-9). Holiday House.
--Wolf Brother. 1957. E M Hale.
--Wolf Brother. Wilson, Charles Banks (1918-), illus. (Illus.). 189 p. 21cm. 1957. Holiday House.

Kjellstrand, A. W. (1864-), tr. see Janson, Betty.

Klaber, Florence W.

--Joseph: The Story of Twelve Brothers. (gr. 2-4). 1941. (ISBN 0-8070-1936-4). (ISBN 0-8070-1937-2). Beacon Pr.

Klaber, Kurt see Held, Kurt, pseud.

Klaber, Kurt

--The Outsiders of Uskoken Castle. Held, Kurt, pseud. Aubry, Lynn, tr. LC 67-15385. 353 p. 22cm. 1967. Doubleday.

Klaperman, Libby Mindlin (1921-1982)

--Bible Stories from the Old Testament. (gr. 1-5). N.D. (ISBN 0-448-00316-3). G&D.
--A Different Girl. Zanazania, Adrina, illus. (Illus.). 12 line. 160p. (gr. 5-9). 1969. (ISBN 0-87460-127-4). Lion Bks.
--The Dreidel Who Wouldn't Spin. N.D. Behrnan House Inc.
--The Five Brothers Maccabee: A Novel for Young Readers Based on the Story of Chanukah. LC 72-82699. 176 p. 22cm. (Sabra books). 1969. Funk and Wagnalls.

Klapholz, Yisroel Y.

--Stories of Elijah the Prophet. Nadav, Avigail, tr. (gr. 7 up). N.D. Feldheim.
--Tales of the Baal Shem Tov. Weinbach, S., tr. (gr. 7 up). N.D. Feldheim.

Klapp, William H., rev. by see Bulfinch, Thomas.

Klass, David

--The Atami Dragons. LC 84-14052. vii, 134 p. 22cm. c.1984. (ISBN 0-684-18223-8). Scribner.

Klass, Philipl William, jt. ed. see Anderson, Poul William.

Klass, Sheila Solomon (1927-)

--Alive & Starting Over. LC 83-14182. 137 p. 22cm. c.1983. (ISBN 0-684-17987-3). Scribner's.
--The Bennington Stitch. LC 85-40291. 133 p. 22cm. c.1985. (ISBN 0-684-18436-2). C. Scribner's.
--Nobody Knows Me in Miami. LC 81-1922. 149 p. 22cm. c.1981. (ISBN 0-684-16851-0). Scribner.
--To See My Mother Dance. LC 81-14424. p. cm. 1981. (ISBN 0-684-17227-5). Scribner.

Klatte, Esther

--Woodsy Talk. N.D. Carlton Press.

Klaue, Lola Shelton see Shelton, Lola.

Klausler, Alfred Paul (1910-)

--The Midnight Lion: Gustavus Adolphus, Soldier of God. LC 57-9723. 140p. 21cm. 1957. Augsburg Pub. House.

Klausner, Abraham J. (1915-)

--Child's Story & Prayer Book. 1976. (ISBN 0-8109-4550-9). Abrams.

Klavas, Ann Alexander

--The Stories Behind Famous American Sayings. 62 p. 21cm. (Bookland juvenile). 1965. Carlton Press.

Klaveness, Jan O'Donnell

--Ghost Island. LC 84-42979. 220 p. 21cm. c.1985. (ISBN 0-02-750740-8). Macmillan.
--The Griffin Legacy. LC 83-9353. p. cm. c.1983. (ISBN 0-02-750760-2). Macmillan.

Klaw, Barbara Van Doren see Gale, Martin, pseud.

Klaw, Barbara Van Doren (1920-)

--Joan and Michael: A Story of Today. Gale, Martin, pseud. LC 41-5301. 201 p. 22 cm. 1941. The Viking Press.
--One Summer: A Story. Gale, Martin, pseud. Van Doren, Margaret (1917-), illus. LC 36-27467. (Illus.). vii, 182 p. incl. illus., plates. 22 cm. 1936. The Viking Press.
--One Winter. Gale, Martin, pseud. Van Doren, Margaret (1917-), illus. LC 38-24737. 204 p. illus. 22 cm. 1938. Viking Press.
--A Pony Named Nubbin: A Story. Gale, Martin, pseud. Van Doren, Margaret (1917-), illus. LC 39-297257. 73, 1 p. col. illus. 27 cm. 1939. The Viking Press.

Klebe, Charles Eugene see Klebe, Gene, pseud.

Klebe, Gene, pseud., see Klebe, Charles Eugene.

Klebe, Gene, pseud. (1907-) & Ernst, Margot Klebe

--Penguin Family. Klebe, Charles Eugene. LC 67-14806. 45p. col. illus. 19x24cm. 1968, c.1967. Putnam.

Kleberger, Ilse (1921-)

--Grandmother Oma. Tripp, Wallace Whitney (1940-), illus. LC 67-2715. (Illus.). 124 p. 22cm. 1st U.S. edition. 1967, c.1966. Atheneum.
--Traveling with Oma. Behrens, Hans, illus. LC 73-98614. (Illus.). 150 p. 22cm. 1970, c.1969. Atheneum.

Klebsch, Mary Roberts (1886-) & Klebsch, Ralph Edward (1925-)

--Rob Roy, Detective: The Story of a Collie. LC 47-242163. iv, 63 p. illus. 19 1/2 cm. 1946. Argus Publishing Company.

Klebsch, Ralph Edward, jt. auth. see Klebsch, Mary Roberts.

Kleckner, Emma Robinson

--In the Misty Realm of Fable. Dean, Eva, illus. LC 1-30331. 3 p., l., 13-148 p., 1 l. illus., 2 port. (incl. front.) 20 cm. 1900. R. R. Donnelley & Sons Company.

Klein, Arthur Luce, adapted by see Perrault, Charles.

Klein, Bert Howard

--Once Upon a Pony: A Children's 'Poetale.'. LC 55-12518. 118p. illus. 24cm. c.1955. Pageant Press.

Klein, Earl, adapted by see Disney, Walt, Productions.

Klein, Gerda Weissman (1924-)

--The Blue Rose. 1st ed. Holt, Norma, illus. LC 74-9383. (Illus.). 64 p. 24cm. 1974. (ISBN 0-88208-047-4). (ISBN 0-88208-048-2). L. Hill.

Klein, H. Arthur, ed. see Busch, Wilhelm.

Klein, Howard Kenneth (1931-)

--My Best Friends Are Dinosaurs: Verse. Windrow, Patricia, illus. LC 65-12263. 28p. illus. 24cm. c.1965. (ISBN 0-679-20122-X). McKay.

Klein, Leonore Glotzer (1916-)

--Brave Daniel. Fischetti, John R. (1916-1980), illus. 32p. (gr. k-3). 1969. (ISBN 0-590-08020-2). Scholastic Inc.
--Brave Daniel: The Story of a Brave Boy. Kessler, Leonard P. (1921-), illus. LC 58-552416. unpaged. illus. 22cm. c.1958. Scott.
--D Is for Rover. Quackenbush, Robert Mead (1929-), illus. (Illus.). color ils. 48p. (gr. k-3). 1970. (ISBN 0-8178-4662-X). Harvey.
--Guess What?. N.D. Wonder Books.
--The Happy Surprise. N.D. Wonder Books.
--How Old is Old?. Kessler, Leonard P. (1921-), illus. LC 67-17065. (Illus.). 45p. 25cm. (A Science Parade Bk.). 1967. Harvey House.
--Huit Enfants et Un Bebe - Eight Children & One Baby. Foreman, Michael (1938-), illus. (Illus.). (Picture Book). (gr. k-3). 1966. (ISBN 0-200-00019-5). Abelard.
--Just Like You. Walters, Audrey (1929-), illus. LC 68-10696. (Illus.). 37 p. 1968. Harvey House.
--Mud, Mud, Mud. Wiggins, George, illus. LC 62-147736. (Illus.). (gr. k-3). 1962. (ISBN 0-394-91431-7). Knopf.
--Only One Ant. Robinson, Charles (1931-), illus. LC 76-146295. (Illus.). 34 p. 24cm. 1971. (ISBN 0-8038-5362-9). Hasting House.
--Picnics and Parades. Chwast, Jacqueline (1932-), illus. LC 76-8663. (Illus.). 32 p. c.1976. (ISBN 0-394-93290-0). (ISBN 0-394-83290-6). Knopf : Distributed by Random House.
--Runaway John. Warner, Sunny B., illus. LC 63-14422. (Illus.). 1 v. (unpaged. 26cm. 1963. Knopf.
--Silly Sam. Weiss, Harvey (1922-), illus. (Illus.). (gr. k-3). 1971. (ISBN 0-590-08757-6). (ISBN 0-590-20744-X). Scholastic Inc.
--Tom and the Small Ant. Sherman, Harriet, illus. LC 65-21568. 1v. (unpaged) col. illus. 29cm. c.1965. (ISBN 0-394-91759-6). Knopf.
--Too Many Parents. Tinkelman, Murray (1933-), illus. 1968. Borzoi Books.
--Too Many Parents. Tinkelman, Murray (1933-), illus. LC 67-18587. (Illus.). 48 p. 22cm. 1969. Knopf.
--What Would You Do If. LC 56-542067. unpaged. illus. 20cm. (Young Scott books). 1956. Scott.

Klein, Leonore Glotzer (1916-) & Bass, Saul

--Henri's Walk to Paris. LC 62-51665. (Illus.). unpaged. 29cm. (Young Scott books). 1962. W. R. Scott.

Klein, Margaret A.

--The Step-Ladder. 1893. A. S. Barnes & Co.

Klein, Monica

--Backyard Basketball Super Star. Langner, Nola (1930-), illus. LC 80-22113. (Illus.). 44 p. 24cm. (I am reading book). c.1981. (ISBN 0-394-94521-2). Pantheon Books.

Klein, Norma (1938-)

--Angel Face. LC 83-21657. 208 p. 228p. (gr. 7 up). 1984. (ISBN 0-670-12517-2, Viking Kestrel). Viking.
--Bizou: A Novel. LC 83-6932. p. cm. 1983. (ISBN 0-670-17053-4). Viking Press.
--Blue Trees, Red Sky. Porter, Patricia Grant, illus. LC 75-2545. (Illus.). 57 p. 22cm. 1975. (ISBN 0-394-83108-X). (ISBN 0-394-93108-4). Pantheon Books.
--Breaking Up. LC 80-10953. 224p. 1980. (ISBN 0-394-84445-9). (ISBN 0-394-94445-3). Pantheon.
--The Cheerleader: A Young Adult Novel. LC 85-224. p. cm. 1985. (ISBN 0-394-87577-X). (ISBN 0-394-97577-4). Knopf.
--Confessions of an Only Child. Cuffari, Richard (1925-1978), illus. LC 73-14750. (Illus.). 93 p. 23cm. 1974. (ISBN 0-394-82766-X). (ISBN 0-394-82766-X). Pantheon Books.
--Dinosaur's Housewarming Party. Marshall, James (1942-), illus. LC 74-80321. (Illus.). 39 p. 23cm. 1974. (ISBN 0-517-51692-6). Crown Publishers.
--Girls Can Be Anything. Doty, Roy (1922-), illus. LC 72-85258. (Illus.). 32 p. 22cm. 1973. (ISBN 0-525-30662-5). Dutton.
--Give and Take. LC 84-40714. 169 p. 22cm. 1985. (ISBN 0-670-80651-X). Viking.
--Hiding. LC 76-17592. 128p. 1976. (ISBN 0-590-07435-0, Four Winds). Scholastic Inc.
--A Honey of a Chimp. LC 79-20951. (gr. 3-7). 1980. (ISBN 0-394-84412-2). (ISBN 0-394-94412-7). Pantheon.
--If I Had My Way. Cruz, Raymond (1933-), illus. LC 73-1711. (Illus.). 30 p. 1974. (ISBN 0-394-82654-X). (ISBN 0-394-82654-X). Pantheon Books.
--It's Not What You Expect. LC 72-7626. xii, 128 p. 22cm. 1973. (ISBN 0-394-82604-3). (ISBN 0-394-82604-3). Pantheon Books.
--It's Okay If You Don't Love Me. (gr. 7 up). N.D. (ISBN 0-8037-4053-0). Dial Bks Young.
--Love Is One of the Choices. LC 78-51323. 1978. Dial Bks Young.
--Mom, the Wolf Man, and Me. LC 73-4249. 147 p. 25cm. 1973, c.1972. (ISBN 0-8161-6099-6). G. K. Hall.
--Mom, the Wolf Man, and Me. LC 72-260. x, 128 p. 22cm. 1972. (ISBN 0-394-82470-9). (ISBN 0-394-92470-3). Pantheon Books.
--Naomi in the Middle. Grant, Alice Leigh (1947-), illus. LC 74-2878. (Illus.). 53 p. 22cm. 1974. (ISBN 0-8037-6080-9). (ISBN 0-8037-6080-9). Dial Press.
--Robbie and the Leap Year Blues. LC 81-65852. p. cm. 1981. (ISBN 0-8037-7437-0). Dial Press.
--Snapshots. LC 84-7115. (gr. 7 up). 1984. (ISBN 0-8037-0129-2). Dial Bks Young.
--Taking Sides. LC 74-972. 156 p. 22cm. 1974. (ISBN 0-394-82822-4). (ISBN 0-394-82822-4). Pantheon Books.
--Tomboy. LC 78-4337. p. cm. c.1978. (ISBN 0-590-07521-7). Four Winds Press.
--A Train for Jane. 1st ed. Schottland, Miriam, illus. LC 74-11764. (Illus.). 30 p. 28cm. 1974. (ISBN 0-912670-34-7). Feminist Press.
--Visiting Pamela. LC 78-72203. (Illus.). 32 p. 25cm. c.1979. (ISBN 0-8037-9307-3). (ISBN 0-8037-9308-1). Dial Press.
--What It's All About. LC 75-10015. 146 p. 22cm. 1975. (ISBN 0-8037-5028-5). Dial Press.

Klein, Robert

--Thing. Lester, Alison, illus. (Illus.). 32p. (gr. 3-5). 1983. (ISBN 0-19-554330-0, Pub by Oxford U Pr Childrens). Merrimack Pub Cir.

Klein, Robin

--Hating Alison Ashley. LC 85-40448. p. cm. 1985. (ISBN 0-14-031672-8). Puffin Books.
--Penny Pollard's Diary. James, Ann, illus. (Illus.). 56p. (gr. 3-7). 1984. (ISBN 0-19-554415-3, Pub. by Oxford U Pr Childrens). Merrimack Pub Cir.

Klein, Ruthie

--Birdie That Fell Flat on His Face. (gr. k-2). N.D. Carlton.

Klein, Sara Guss (1911-)

--Juan & Juanita. (Illus.). 1956. (ISBN 0-685-11650-6). (ISBN 0-377-68861-4). Friendship Pr.
--Juan and Juanita. Escourido, Joseph, illus. LC 56-9249. unpaged--illus.--21cm. 1956. Friendship Press.
--The Little Seeds that Grew. Stone, Jacqueline C., illus. LC 50-9215. (Illus.). 34p. 18cm. (Children's Hour Library). 1950. Westminster Press.

Klein, Stanley (1930-)

--The Final Mystery. LC 70-180084. 96p. (gr. 3-5). 1974. Doubleday.

--We Were There with the Lafayette Escadrille. Knight, Clayton (1891-1969), illus. LC 61-1803. 182p. illus. 22cm. (We were there books, 33). 1961. Grosset & Dunlap.

Knight, Damon Francis (1922-), ed.

--Beyond Tomorrow: Ten Science Fiction Adventures. (gr. 7 up). N.D. (ISBN 0-06-023181-5, HarpJ). Har-Row.

--Dimension X: Five Science Fiction Novellas. LC 71-122940. 351 p. 22cm. 1970. (ISBN 0-671-65129-3). Simon and Schuster.

--One Hundred Years of Science Fiction. LC 68-28913. (gr. 7 up). 1968. (ISBN 0-671-20077-1). S&S.

--Orbit Fifteen. LC 74-1890. 224p. 1974. (ISBN 0-06-012439-3, HarpT). Har-Row.

--Tomorrow and Tomorrow: Ten Tales of the Future. LC 73-2152. (gr. 7 up). 1973. (ISBN 0-671-65210-9, Juveniles). S&S.

--Worlds to Come: Nine Science Fiction Adventures. xii, 337 p. 22cm. 1967. Harper & Row.

Knight, David Carpenter (1925-)

--Galaxies, Islands in Space. (Illus.). (gr. 4-6). 1979. (ISBN 0-688-22180-7). (ISBN 0-688-32180-1). Morrow.

--The Haunted Souvenir Warehouse. LC 77-76251. (gr. 3-7). 1978. Doubleday.

--The Moving Coffins: Ghosts and Hauntings Around the World. Waldman, Neil, illus. LC 83-9447. p. cm. c.1983. (ISBN 0-13-604645-2). Prentice-Hall.

--Poltergeists: Hauntings & the Haunted. Kubinyi, Laszlo (1937-), illus. LC 72-2449. (Illus.). 160p. (gr. 5-9). 1972. (ISBN 0-397-31488-4). (ISBN 0-397-31416-7). Lippincott.

--Science ABC. Schrotter, Gustav, illus. LC 62-7418. unpaged. illus. 11 x 15cm. 1962. F. Watts.

Knight, Eric Mowbray (1897-1943)

--Lassie Come Home. N.D. (ISBN 0-531-00219-5). Franklin Watts.

--Lassie Come Home. Baldridge, Cyrus LeRoy (1889-), illus. 1940. Holt.

--Lassie Come Home. Bolognese, Donald Alan (1934-), illus. 1940. Holt.

--Lassie Come-Home. rev. ed. Bolognese, Donald Alan (1934-), illus. LC 79-155826. (Illus.). 230 p. 24cm. 1971, c.1940. (ISBN 0-03-080227-X). (ISBN 0-03-080228-8). Holt, Rinehart and Winston.

--Lassie Come-Home. Helweg, Hans H. (1917-), illus. Sutton, Felix, abridged by. LC 54-855539. unpaged. illus. 34cm. (Big treasure books). c.1954. Grosset & Dunlap.

--Lassie Come-Home. Kirmse, Marguerite (1885-1954), illus. LC 78-3570. p. cm. 1978, c.1940. (ISBN 0-03-044101-3). Holt, Rinehart, and Winston.

--Lassie Come-Home. Kirmse, Marguerite (1885-1954), illus. LC 40-117081. vii, 248 p. col. front., illus. 23 cm. c.1940. The John C. Winston Company.

--Lassie Come-Home. Obligado, Lilian Isabel (1931-), illus. LC 64-2713. 221 p. illus. (part col.) 22 cm. 1964. Junior Deluxe Editions.

--Lassie Come-Home: A Picture Adapation of the Famous Story. Sutton, Felix (1910-), abridged by. Helweg, Hans H. (1917-), illus. LC 57-14075. (Illus.). 29cm. 61p. 1957. Grosset & Dunlap.

Knight, Francis Edgar see Knight, Frank, pseud.

Knight, Frank, pseud., see Knight, Francis Edgar.

Knight, Frank, pseud. (1905-)

--The Bluenose Pirate: A Story for Boys and Girls. Knight, Francis Edgar. Jobson, Patrick (1919-), illus. LC 56-14310. 257p. illus. 21cm. 1956. Macmillan.

--Captain Cook and the Voyage of the Endeavor. Knight, Francis Edgar. 1970. Nelson Junior Books.

--Clemency Draper. Knight, Francis Edgar. Stobbs, William (1914-), illus. LC 63-14996. 221 p. illus. 21 cm. 1963. Macmillan.

--Clemency Draper. Knight, Francis Edgar. Stobbs, William (1914-), illus. 1963. St Martin's Press.

--Clippers to China, a Junior Novel. Knight, Francis Edgar. Jobson, Patrick (1919-), illus. LC 55-12611. 268 p. illus. 21 cm. 21cm. 268p. 1955. St. Martin's Press.

--Family on the Tide. Knight, Francis Edgar. Whittam, Geoffrey William (1916-), illus. 1956. St Martin's Press.

--Family on the Tide: A Junior Novel for Girls. Knight, Francis Edgar. Whittam, Geoffrey William (1916-), illus. LC 56-139450. 273p. illus. 21cm. 1956. Macmillan.

--The Golden Monkey. Knight, Francis Edgar. Goodall, John Strickland (1908-), illus. LC 53-11884. (Illus.). 21cm. 195p. 1953. Macmillan.

--The Last of Lallow's: A Novel for Girls and Boys. Knight, Francis Edgar. Stobbs, William (1914-), illus. LC 61-19805. 222 p. illus. 21 cm. 1961. Macmillan.

--The Last of Lallow's: A Novel for Girls and Boys. Knight, Francis Edgar. Stobbs, William (1914-), illus. LC 61-198059. 222p. illus. c.1961. St. Martin's.

--Olaf's Sword. Knight, Francis Edgar. Sier, Andrew, illus. LC 71-76150. (Illus.). 47 p. 23cm. (Long-ago children series). 1970, c.1969. F. Watts.

--The Partick Steamboat: A Story for Boys and Girls. Knight, Francis Edgar. Jobson, Patrick (1919-), illus. LC 59-16025. v. 185p. illus. 21cm. 1958. St. Martin's Press.

--Please Keep Off The Mud. Knight, Francis Edgar. Jobson, Patrick (1919-), illus. 1957. St Martin's Press.

--Please Keep off the Mud: A Story for Girls and Boys. Knight, Francis Edgar. Jobson, Patrick (1919-), illus. LC 57-3175. 264p. illus. 20cm. 1957. Macmillan.

--Remember Vera Cruz!. Knight, Francis Edgar. Gorin, H. J., illus. LC 66-9536. 184 p. illus. 22 cm. 1966. Dial Press.

--The Sea Chest: Stories of Adventure at Sea. Knight, Francis Edgar. Riley, William, illus. LC 64-18260. 206 p. illus. 23 cm. 1964. Platt & Munk.

--Shadows on the Mud. Knight, Francis Edgar. Jobson, Patrick (1919-), illus. LC 61-170. 222 p. illus. 21 cm. 1960. Macmillan.

--Shadows on the Mud. Knight, Francis Edgar. Jobson, Patrick (1919-), illus. 1960. St Martin's Press.

--The Slaver's Apprentice: A Novel for Boys and Girls. Knight, Francis Edgar. Jobson, Patrick (1919-), illus. LC 61-3797. 247 p. illus. 21 cm. 1961. St. Martin's Press.

--Stories of Famous Sea Adventures. Knight, Francis Edgar. Nickless, Will (1902-), illus. (Illus.). (gr. 5-9). 1967. (ISBN 0-664-32399-5). Westminster.

--Stories of Famous Ships. Knight, Francis Edgar. Nickless, Will (1902-), illus. (Illus.). (gr. 4-7). 1966. (ISBN 0-664-32386-3). Westminster.

--Voyage to Bengal: A Junior Novel. Knight, Francis Edgar. Jobson, Patrick (1919-), illus. LC 54-4895. 265 p. illus. 21 cm. 1954. Macmillan.

Knight, George, ed. see Laster, Jim.

Knight, Hester

--The Donkey Derby. Millais, Raoul, illus. LC 65-15123. 144p. illus. 21cm. 1st U.S. edition. 1965, c.1963. Duell Dist. Meredith.

Knight, Hilary (1926-)

--Christmas Nutshell Library. LC 63-18904. 4 v. col. illus. 11 cm. c.1963. Harper & Row.

--Cinderella. Knight, Hilary (1926-), illus. LC 80-18660. (Illus.). 32p. (Picturebacks Ser.). (ps-2). 1982. (ISBN 0-394-93759-7). (ISBN 0-394-83759-2). Random.

--The Circus Is Coming: A Picture Parade Starring 240 Performers in 20 Scenes. LC 78-68425. (Illus.). 44 p. 27cm. c.1978. (ISBN 0-307-13737-6). Golden Press.

--Firefly in a Fir Tree. Knight, Hilary (1926-), illus. (Illus.). (ps-3). 1963. (ISBN 0-06-023190-4, HarpJ). Har-Row.

--Hilary Knight's ABC. Knight, Hilary (1926-), illus. 1962. Golden Press.

--Hilary Knight's Cinderella. LC 80-18660. (Illus.). 32 p. 21cm. (Random House pictureback). 1981, c.1978. (ISBN 0-394-83760-6). (ISBN 0-394-83759-2). (ISBN 0-394-93759-7). Random House.

--Hilary Knight's Mother Goose. Knight, Hilary (1926-), illus. 1962. Golden Press.

--Hilary Knight's the Twelve Days of Christmas. Knight, Hilary (1926-), illus. LC 81-2599. (Illus.). 34p. (ps up). 1981. (ISBN 0-02-750870-6). Macmillan.

--The Night Before Christmas. Knight, Hilary (1926-), illus. LC 65-7285. (Illus.). (ps-3). 1963. (ISBN 0-06-023195-5, HarpJ). Har-Row.

--Sylvia, the Sloth: A Round-About Story. Knight, Hilary (1926-), illus. LC 76-77947. 19cm. 32p. 1969. (ISBN 0-06-023202-1). Harper & Row.

--Where's Wallace?. Knight, Hilary (1926-), illus. LC 64-19717. (Illus.). 40 p. 24cm. 1964. Harper & Row.

Knight, Hilary (1926-) & Lear, Edward (1812-1888)

--Hilary Knight's The Owl and the Pussy-Cat. LC 83-9844. (Based on the Poem by Edward Lear). (Illus.). 32 p. 27cm. c.1983. (ISBN 0-02-750900-1). Macmillan.

Knight, James Arthur (1905-)

--He Sailed With Blackbeard. Jobson, Patrick (1919-), illus. 1958. St. Martin's Press.

--Mudlarks and Mysteries. Jobson, Patrick (1919-), illus. 1955. St. Martin's Press.

Knight, John, jt. ed. see Abranz, Alfred.

Knight, Katharine Sturges, jt. auth. see Knight, Clayton.

Knight, M. Forster (1901-)

--Mr. Tittlewit's Holiday. Knight, M. Forster (1901-), illus. LC 40-13978. 153, 2 p. col. front., illus. 22 cm. c.1940. J. B. Lippincott Company.

--The Return of Sandypaws. Knight, M. Forster (1901-), illus. LC 42-17224. 151 p. col. front., illus. 19 cm. 1942. J. B. Lippincott Company.

Knight, Marjorie

--Alexander's Birthday. Simon, Howard (1903-1979), illus. LC 40-12420. 120 p. incl. illus., col., plates 22 1/2 cm. 1940. E. P. Dutton & Company.

--Alexander's Christmas Eve. Simon, Howard (1903-1979), illus. LC 38-19926. 92, 1 p. incl. illus., col., plates. col. front. 22 1/2 cm. 1938. E. P. Dutton & Company , Inc.

--Alexander's Vacation. Simon, Howard (1903-1979), illus. LC 43-14781. 105, 1 p. incl. col. front., illus., col. plates. 22 cm. 1943. E. P. Dutton & Co., Inc.

--The Doll House at World's End. Knight, Clinton, illus. LC 36-15930. 119 p. incl. front., illus. 23 cm. c.1936. E. P. Dutton & Co., Inc.

--Humphrey, the Pig. Knight, Clinton, illus. LC 37-163793. 44, 1 p. illus. 21 cm. c.1937. E. P. Dutton & Co., Inc.

--The Japanese Garden: Or, The Four White Pebbles. Knight, Clinton, illus. LC 34-17243. 171 p. incl. front., illus., plates. 21 cm. c.1934. E. P. Dutton & Co., Inc.

--The Land of Lost Handkerchiefs. 1st ed. Fry, Rosalie Kingsmill (1911-), illus. LC 52-8244. 92p. illus. 23cm. 1954. Dutton.

Knight, Mary (1899-)

--The Fox That Wanted Nine Golden Tails. Bryan, Brigitte, illus. LC 69-10500. (Illus.). 94 p. 17cm. 1968, c.1969. Macmillan.

Knight, Max (1909-), tr. see Morgenstern, Christian.

Knight, Maxwell B., jt. auth. see Lasky, Kathryn.

Knight, Mrs.

--The Rocket. 118p. N.D. American Tract Society.

Knight, Peter

--Shadow on Skjarling. Stobbs, William (1914-), illus. LC 64-10453. (Illus.). 21cm. 153p. (gr. 5-8). 1964. (ISBN 0-698-20125-6). Coward McCann.

Knight, Ruth Adams (1898-1974)

--Brave Companions. Ward, Lynd Kendall (1905-1985), illus. LC 45-35198. 4 p. l., 215 p. col. front. 20 1/2 cm. 1945. Doubleday, Doran & Company, Inc.

--Day After Tomorrow. LC 52-10127. 219 p. 21 cm. 1952. Doubleday.

--First the Lightning. LC 55-10509. 224p. 22cm. 1955. Doubleday.

--A Friend in the Dark. Dennis, Morgan (1891-1960), illus. N.D. Grosset & Dunlap.

--Halfway to Heaven. (Illus.). (gr. 8-12). 1952. (ISBN 0-07-035110-4). McGraw.

--Halfway to Heaven, the Story of the St. Bernard. Dennis, Wesley (1903-1966), illus. LC 52-10848. 184 p. illus. 21 cm. 1952. Whittlesey House.

--It Might Be You. LC 49-105672. 206 p. 20 cm. 1949. Doubleday.

--The Land Beyond: A Story of the Children's Crusade. Dennis, Wesley (1903-1966), illus. LC 54-8814. 218p. illus. 21cm. 1954. Whittlesey House.

--Luck of the Irish. LC 51-12476. 242 p. 21 cm. 1951. Doubleday.

--Queen of Roses. LC 59-13975. 215p. 22cm. 1959. Doubleday.

--Search for the Galleon's Gold!. Stenbery, Algot, illus. LC 56-10320. 191p. illus. 21cm. 1956. Whittlesey House.

--Top of the Mountain. LC 53-99964. 222p. 21cm. 1953. Doubleday.

--Valiant Comrades: A Story of Our Dogs of War. LC 43-16552. ix p., 2 l., 238 p. 20 1/2 cm. 1943. Doubleday, Doran & Company, Inc.

--Word of Honor: A Story About Thoroughbreds. LC 64-14105. 250 p. 22 cm. 1964. Ariel Books.

Knight, Vick Ralph, Jr. (1928-)

--Earle the Squirrel. Stern, Ellen J., illus. LC 73-90550. (Illus.). 46 p. 27cm. c.1974. (ISBN 0-378-60263-2). Ward Ritchie Press.

Knight, Vick Ralph, Jr. (1928-) & Hudson, Theresa Barna

--The Night the Crayons Talked. Hudson, Theresa Barna, illus. LC 74-78585. (Illus.). 38 p. 27cm. c.1974. (ISBN 0-378-62726-0). W. Ritchie Press.

Knights, Roger (1944-)

--The Alphabets Go Shopping. LC 82-12273. p. cm. 1982. (ISBN 0-86592-806-1). Rourke Corp.

--The Alphabets Go to a Party. LC 82-12276. p. cm. 1982. (ISBN 0-86592-804-5). Rourke Corp.

--The Alphabets Go to the Circus. LC 82-12274. p. cm. 1982. (ISBN 0-86592-808-8). Rourke Corp.

--The Alphabets Go to the Park. Klimo, Kate, ed. Knights, Roger (1944-), illus. (Illus.). 32p. 1st U.S. edition. (Lettermen Ser.). (ps-3). 1982. (ISBN 0-671-45039-5, Little Simon). S&S.

--The Alphabets in the Garden. LC 82-12269. p. cm. 1982. (ISBN 0-86592-811-8). Rourke Corp.

--The Alphabets on the Farm. Klimo, Kate, ed. Knights, Roger (1944-), illus. (Illus.). 32p. 1st U.S. edition. (Lettermen Ser.). (ps-3). 1982. (ISBN 0-671-45040-9, Little Simon). S&S.

Knipe, Alden Arthur see Uncle Herbert, pseud.

Knipe, Alden Arthur, jt. auth. see Knipe, Emilie Benson, Mrs.

Knipe, Alden Arthur (1870-1950)

--Bunny Plays the Game. LC 25-17625. 4 p. l., 295 p. front., plates. 20 cm. 1925. Harper & Brothers.

--Captain of the Eleven. (Illus.). (Home Circle Series for Boys). N.D. American Tract Society.

--Captain of the Eleven. LC 10-21026. 4 p. l., 269, 1 p. front., 3 pl. 20 cm. 1910. Harper & Brothers.

--The Last Lap. LC 11-241152. 4 p. l., 340 p., 1 l. front., plates. 20 cm. 1911. Harper & Brothers.

--Remember Rhymes. Knipe, Emilie Benson, Mrs. (1870-1958), illus. LC 15-2294. 80 p. illus., col. plates. 20 cm. c.1914. Hearst's International Library Co.

--Remember Rhymes. Uncle Herbert, pseud. Knipe, Emilie Benson, Mrs. (1870-1958), illus. N.D. Penn.

Knipe, Delia

--The Playmate: A Picture and Story Book for Boys and Girls. LC 79-323134. (Illus.). 335 p., 1 leaf of plates. 21cm. c.1878. J. B. Lippincott.

Knipe, Emilie Benson, Mrs. (1870-1958)

--Diantha's Quest: A Tale of the Argonauts of '49. Knipe, Alden Arthur (1870-1950), illus. LC 21-185854. 4 p. l., 295 p. front., plates. 20 cm. 1921. The Macmillan Company.

Knipe, Emilie Benson, Mrs. (1870-1958) & Knipe, Alden Arthur (1870-1950)

--Beatrice of Denewood. Relyea, Charles M., illus. LC 13-21024. (Sequel to "The Lucky Sixpence"). 6 p. l., 3-437 p. incl. front., illus., plates. 20 cm. 1913. The Century Co.

--A Continental Dollar. Knipe, Emilie Benson, Mrs. (1870-1958), illus. LC 23-12966. 5 p. l., 3-372 p. front., plates. 21 cm. 1923. The Century Co.

--Little Miss Fales. Rogers, Frances (1888-1974), illus. LC 10-9256. 3 p. l., 225, 1 p. col. front. 20 cm. 1910. Harper & Brothers.

--Lost--a Brother. Pitz, Henry Clarence (1895-1976), illus. 5 p. l., 239 p. incl. plates. col. front. 20 cm. 1928. The Macmillan Company.

--The Lost Little Lady. Knipe, Emilie Benson, Mrs. (1870-1958), illus. LC 17-25247. 6 p. l., 3-410 p. incl. front., plates. 20 cm. 1917. The Century Co.

--The Luck of Denewood. Knipe, Emilie Benson, Mrs. (1870-1958), illus. LC 21-16535. 5 p., 3-359 p. front., plates. 20 cm. 1921. The Century Co.

--The Lucky Sixpence. Becher, Arthur E., illus. LC 12-22556. 5 p. l., 3-408 p. incl. plates, front. 20 cm. 1912. The Century Co.

--A Maid of Old Manhattan. Knipe, Emilie Benson, Mrs. (1870-1958), illus. LC 17-24856. 4 p. l., 292 p. front., plates. 20 cm. 1917. The Macmillan Company.

--The Missing Pearls: Little Miss Fales Goes West. LC 11-266127. 4 p. l., 286, 1 p. front., plates. 20 cm. 1911. Harper & Brothers.

--Now and Then. Knipe, Emilie Benson, Mrs. (1870-1958), illus. LC 25-179352. 5 p. l., 3-150 p. incl. front., illus. 20 cm. c.1925. The Century Co.

--A Patriot Maid, and Other Stories. Berger, William Merritt (1872-), illus. LC 28-21826. 5 p. l., 3-220 p. incl. front., illus. 20 cm. 1928. The Century Co.

--The Pirate's Ward. De Angeli, Marguerite Lofft, Mrs. (1889-), illus. LC 29-22805. 6 p. l., 267 p. incl. plates. front. 20 cm. 1929. The Macmillan Company.

--Polly Trotter, Patriot. Knipe, Emilie Benson, Mrs. (1870-1958), illus. LC 16-22754. 4 p. l., 303 p. front., plates. 20 cm. 1916. The Macmillan Company.

--The Treasure House. Ayer, Margaret (0000-1981), illus. LC 30-22901. vii, 300 p. front., plates. 20 cm. c.1930. The Century Co.

--The Treasure-Trove. Schroeder, Louis, illus. LC 27-196407. v, 330 p. front., plates. 20 cm. c.1927. The Century Co.

Knippel, Dolores

--Poems for the Very Young Child. Ellsworth, Mary, illus. 2 p. l., 9-123, 2 p. front., illus. 19 cm. c.1932. Whitman Publishing Co.

Knittle, Jessie Mahn

--The Circus Train, Verses. Dorcas, Couri, illus. LC 49-4086. 32 p. col. illus. 17cm. (Tell-a-tale books, 800). c.1948. Whitman Pub. Co.

--The Truck that Stopped at Village Small. Dorcas, Couri, illus. LC 51-25621. 32 p. col. ill. 17cm. (Tell-a-tale books, 813). c.1951. Whitman.

Knobel, Elizabeth

--When Little Thoughts Go Rhyming. Enright, Maginel Wright, illus. N.D. Rand McNally.

Knobler, Susan
--The Tadpole & the Frog. LC 74-83422. (Illus.). 32p. (Books Without Words Ser.). (ps-4). 1974. (ISBN 0-8178-5302-2). Harvey.
Knoche, Norma R & Jones, Mary Voell (1933-)
--What Do Mothers Do?. Tsambon, Athena, illus. LC 67-1939. (Illus.). 24 p. 30cm. (Whitman Small World Library BK.). c.1966. Whitman Pub. Co.
Knoche, Vikki
--Keith and the Cactus Patch. LC 81-1084. p. cm. 1981. (ISBN 0-8163-0426-2). Pacific Press.
Knoepfel & Farber
--Look! I'm Growing Up. Mahany, Patricia, ed. LC 82-62735. (Illus.). 24p. (Happy Day Bks.). (ps-2). 1983. (ISBN 0-87239-639-8). Standard Pub.
Knoepfle, John (1923-)
--Dogs & Cats & Things Like That Poems. Galdone, Paul (1914-), photos by. LC 79-160710. (Illus.). color ils. 40p. (gr. k-3). 1971. (ISBN 0-07-035125-2). (ISBN 0-07-035126-0). McGraw.
--Our Street Feels Good: Poems for Children. Unsworth, Bonnie D., illus. LC 76-39001. (Illus.). 48 p. 22cm. 1972. (ISBN 0-07-035128-7). McGraw-Hill.
Knoop, Faith Yingling (1896-)
--Kuni of the Cherokees. Augur, Monroe Ruth, illus. LC 57-31007. 230p. illus. 20cm. 1957. Harlow Pub. Corp.
--Lars and the Luck Stone. Moment, John, illus. LC 50-9394. (Illus.). 182 p. 21cm. 1950. Harcourt, Brace.
Knope, Teri
--The Adventures of Little Bird. (Illus.). 128p. (gr. 2-6). N.D. (ISBN 0-9613495-0-6). Images Ink.
Knott, Bill, pseud., see Knott, William Cecil Jr..
Knott, Bill, pseud. (1927-)
--Danger at Half-Moon Lake. Knott, William Cecil Jr.. Harlan, Jerry, illus. LC 68-12985. (Illus.). 134 p. 22cm. 1968. Steck-Vaughn Co.
--The Dwarf on Black Mountain. Knott, William Cecil Jr.. Smith, Ben, illus. LC 67-20462. (Illus.). vii, 160 p. 22cm. 1967. Steck-Vaughn Co.
--Fullback Fury. LC 72-1369. 136 p. 22cm. 1972. (ISBN 0-8114-7747-9). Steck-Vaughn Co.
--Journey Across the Third Planet. Knott, William Cecil Jr.. LC 79-80082. 160 p. 21cm. 1969. Chilton Book Co.
--Junk Pitcher. Knott, William Cecil Jr.. LC 63-9613. 224 p. 21 cm. 1963. (ISBN 0-8114-7638-3). Follett Pub. Co.
--Night Pursuit. Knott, William Cecil Jr.. Williams, Beaumont H., illus. LC 66-7534 172p. illus. 22cm. 1966. Steck.
--The Secret of the Old Brownstone. Knott, William Cecil Jr.. Nuhn, John, illus. LC 68-28366. (Illus.). 131 p. 22cm. 1969. Steck-Vaughn Co.
--The Serpent of Pirate Cove. Knott, William Cecil Jr.. LC 70-139288. 151 p. 22cm. 1971. (ISBN 0-8114-7719-3). Steck-Vaughn Co.
--The Taylor Street Irregulars. Knott, William Cecil Jr.. LC 70-101566. (Illus.). v, 115 p. 22cm. 1970. (ISBN 0-8114-7702-9). Steck-Vaughn Co.
Knott, William Cecil Jr. see Carol, Bill J, pseud.
Knott, William Cecil Jr. see Knott, Bill, pseud.
Knott, William Cecil, Jr. (1927-)
--Blocking Back. LC 74-9702. 156 p. 22cm. 1974. (ISBN 0-8114-7765-7). Steck-Vaughn Co.
--Double-Play Ball. LC 72-8651. 158 p. 22cm. 1973. (ISBN 0-8114-7754-1). Steck-Vaughn Co.
--Flare Pass. LC 73-8723. 174 p. 22cm. 1973. (ISBN 0-8114-7758-4). Steck-Vaughn Co.
--High Fly to Center. LC 70-176067. 141 p. 22cm. 1972. (ISBN 0-8114-7737-1). Steck-Vaughn Co.
--Lefty Finds a Catcher. LC 68-11224. 141 p. 21cm. 1968. Steck-Vaughn Co.
--Lefty's Long Throw. LC 67-1510. 156 p. 22cm. 1967. Steck-Vaughn Co.
--Sandy Plays Third. Caroll, Bill J., pseud. LC 70-108154. 160p. (gr. 5-6). 1970. (ISBN 0-8114-7706-1). Steck-V.
--Single to Center. LC 73-21921. 152 p. 22cm. 1974. (ISBN 0-8114-7763-0). Steck-Vaughn.
--Stop That Pass. LC 75-110689. 125 p. 22cm. 1970. Steck-Vaughn.
Knott, Irma
--This Thing Called Love. LC 61-14797. 160 p. 21cm. 1961. Follett Pub. Co.
Knotts, Howard Clayton, Jr., jt. auth. see Bunting, Anne Evelyn.
Knotts, Howard Clayton, Jr. (1922-)
--Follow the Brook. Knotts, Howard Clayton, Jr. (1922-), illus. LC 74-2607. (Illus.). 31 p. 22cm. 1975. (ISBN 0-06-023169-6). (ISBN 0-06-023168-8). Harper & Row.
--Great-Grandfather, the Baby, and Me. Knotts, Howard Clayton, Jr. (1922-), illus. LC 78-2940. (Illus.). 30 p. 21cm. 1978. (ISBN 0-689-30656-3). Atheneum.
--The Lost Christmas. Knotts, Howard Clayton, Jr. (1922-), illus. LC 78-1903. (Illus.). 32 p. 22cm. (Let me read book). c.1978. (ISBN 0-15-249361-1). (ISBN 0-15-653648-X). Harcourt Brace Jovanovich.
--The Summer Cat. Knotts, Howard Clayton, Jr. (1922-), illus. LC 79-9610. (Illus.). 32 p. 19cm. c.1981. (ISBN 0-06-023178-5). (ISBN 0-06-023179-3). Harper & Row.
--The Winter Cat. Knotts, Howard Clayton, Jr. (1922-), illus. LC 72-76525. (Illus.). 32 p. 19cm. 1972. (ISBN 0-06-023166-1). (ISBN 0-06-023167-X). Harper & Row.
Knotts, Howard, Jr., jt. auth. see Bunting, Anne Evelyn.
Knowles, Andrew
--The Crossroad Children's Bible. (Illus.). 448p. (gr. 4-8). 1981. Crossroad NY.
Knowles, Anne (1933-)
--The Halcyon Island. LC 80-7909. p. cm. 1981. c.1980. (ISBN 0-06-023203-X). (ISBN 0-06-023204-8). Harper & Row.
--Under the Shadow. LC 82-48857. 121 p. 21cm. 1st U.S. edition. c.1983. (ISBN 0-06-023221-8). (ISBN 0-06-023222-6). Harper & Row.
Knowles, E. J., ed.
--Christmas Chimes. (Illus.). N.D. Methodist Book Concern.
Knowles, Frederic Lawrence (1869-1905)
--The Story of Little Paul. Davidson, Bertha G., illus. N.D. Dana Estes and Company.
--The Story of Little Peter. (Illus.). N.D. Dana Estes and Company.
Knowles, James, Sir, compiled by.
--King Arthur and His Knights. Rhead, Louis John (1857-1926) & Schoonover, Frank Earle (1877-1972), illus. (Rhead's Illustrated Juveniles). N.D. Harper & Bros.
--Legends of King Arthur. (Illus.). (gr. 4-7). 1958. (ISBN 0-7232-0256-7). Warne.
--The Legends of King Arthur and His Knights. (The Albion Library). N.D. Frederick Warne & Co.
Knowles, John (1926-)
--Separate Peace. (gr. 9 up). 1960. (ISBN 0-02-564840-3). (ISBN 0-02-489390-0). Macmillan.
Knowles, Mabel Winifred see Wynne, May, pseud.
Knowles, Mabel Winifred (1875-)
--Angela Goes to School. Wynne, May, pseud. LC 29-20016. 253 p. front. 20 cm. c.1929. The World Syndicate Publishing Company.
--Kits at Clinton Court School. Wynne, May, pseud. (The Albion Library). N.D. Frederick Warne & Co.
--Little Sallie Mandy's Christmas Present. Wynne, May, pseud. Willis, Bess Goe, illus. LC 29-6443. 60 p., 1 l. incl. col. illus. 15 cm. (Altemus' wee books for wee folks.). c.1929. Henry Altemus Company.
--The Masked Rider. Wynne, May, pseud. Beck, Peggy Paver, illus. LC 31-30513. 4 p. l., 256 p. illus., pl. 20 cm. 1931. Laidlaw Brothers.
--Patient Pat Joins the Circus. Wynne, May, pseud. Willis, Bess Goe, illus. LC 31-24074. 60 p. 1 l. incl. col. front., col. illus. 15 cm. (Altemus' wee books for wee folks). c.1931. Henry Altemus Company.
--Peter Rabbit and Big Black Crows. Wynne, May, pseud. Willis, Bess Goe, illus. LC 32-665. 58 p., 1 l. incl. col. illus. 14 cm. (Altemus' Peter Rabbit series)). c.1931. Henry Altemus Company.
Knowles, Tillie M. S
--Sue and Mindy Find a New Friend. Barber, Dick, illus. LC 73-86469. (Illus.). 22 p. 23cm. 1973. (ISBN 0-87716-047-3). Moore Pub. Co.
Knowles, Wendell
--Sweet Skunks & Sneaky Butter. LC 79-92619. N.D. (ISBN 0-686-29415-7). Heritage Kansas.
Knowlton, Don (1892-)
--Brick House Stories. LC 36-9561. 8 p. l., 112 p. front., pl. 25cm. 1936. Gates Press.
Knowlton, Fanny Snow, ed.
--Nature Songs for Children. LC 12-34997. 111 p. 28 cm. 1898. Milton Bradley Company.
Knowlton, William (1927-)
--Beneath Hawaiian Seas. 1st ed. Bolian, Polly (1925-), illus. LC 62-14771. 144p. illus. 22cm. 1962. (ISBN 0-394-90940-2). Knopf.
--The Boastful Fisherman. Carle, Eric (1929-), illus. LC 74-84569. (Illus.). 34 p. 1970. Knopf.
--Sea Monster. Damrosch, Helen, pseud. (1893-1976), illus. Tee-Van, Helen Damrosch. 1959. Borzoi Books.
Knox, Elizabeth Edwards
--Animal Lines. Knox, Elizabeth Edwards, illus. LC 64-17217. ix, 83 p. illus. 22 cm. 1964. Naylor Co.
Knox, Esther Melbourne
--The Flags of Dawn. Lawson, Marie Abrams (1894-1956), illus. LC 44-2812. 5 p. l., 3-298 p. incl. front., plates. 20 cm. 1944. Little, Brown and Company.
--Swift Flies the Falcon: A Story of the First Crusade. King, Ruth, illus. LC 39-9648. vii, 245 p., 1 l. illus. 23 cm. c.1939. The John C. Winston Company.
Knox, Eva (1905-) & Best, Allena Champlin (1892-1974)
--Mr. Jones and Mr. Finnigan. Berry, Erick, pseud. LC 42-13305. 23cm. 32p. 1941. Oxford Univ. Press.
Knox, Evans
--The Story Of Su-Su. N.D. E. M. Hale & Co.
Knox, Gary, jt. auth. see Silberman, Joel.
Knox, Jessie Juliet Daily, Mrs.
--Little Almond Blossoms: A Book of Chinese Stories for Children. LC 4-27987. 5 p. l., 246 p., 1 l. front., 14 pl. 20 cm. 1904. Little, Brown, and Company.
Knox, Joann
--The Midnight Miracle. (Junior Adventure Series). 1973. (ISBN 0-88243-775-5). Gospel Pub.
--A New Home for Rhoda. (Junior Adventure Series). 1973. (ISBN 0-88243-771-2). Gospel Pub.
--Seven Days at Jericho & Rachel Meets the Healer. (Junior Adventure Ser.). 1973. (ISBN 0-88243-774-7). Gospel Pub.
--Shipwrecked. (Junior Adventure Series). 1973. (ISBN 0-88243-773-9). Gospel Pub.
--Tamar & the Desert Adventure. (Junior Adventure Series). 1973. (ISBN 0-88243-770-4). Gospel Pub.
--The War Without Fighting & the Oil That Multiplied. (Junior Adventure Series). 1973. (ISBN 0-88243-772-0). Gospel Pub.
Knox, Jolyne, jt. auth. see McGill-Franzen, Anne.
Knox, Kathleen
--Captain Eva: The Story of a Naughty Girl. N.D. E. & J. B. Young & Co.
--Cornertown Chronicles. N.D. E P Dutton.
--Fairy Gifts: or, a Wallet of Wonders. Greenaway, Kate (1846-1901), illus. 1875. Pott, Young & Co.
--Father Time's Story Book, 1 of 6 vols. (Illus.). (Happy Holidays Library). N.D. E P Dutton.
--Seven Birthdays: Or, The Children of Fortune:. (A Fairy Chronicle). (Illus.). N.D. E & J B Young.
--Seven Birthdays: Or, The Children of Fortune:. (A Fairy Chronicle). (Illus.). N.D. E. P. Dutton & Co.
Knox, Margaret (1924-)
--Betsey's Bee Tree. Partridge, Pat (1945-), illus. LC 80-19142. p. cm. c.1980. (ISBN 0-88319-055-9). Shoal Creek Publishers.
Knox, Margaret (1924-) & Lutkenhaus, Anna M.
--The Rainy Day Book for Boys and Girls. N.D. Appleton Century Co.
Knox, Ned
--So May You Find the Year. LC 37-22495. (A Book of Verses for and About Children, Together with the Child's Relationship to the Legal Holidays, Commemorative and Festive Days, of the National Year). x p., 1 l., 13-96 p. 21 cm. c.1937. The Christopher Publishing House.
Knox, Olive Elsie
--Black Falcon. Tillenius, Clarence, illus. LC 55-14471. 21cm. 192p. 1955. Bouregy& Curl.
--Little Giant (Miss-Top-Ashish). The/Story of Henry Kelsey. Tillenius, Clarence, illus. LC 54-13187. 186p. illus. 21cm. c.1954. Bouregy & Curl.
Knox, Rose Bell (1879-)
--The Boys and Sally Down on a Plantation. Lee, Manning De Villeneuve (1894-1980), illus. LC 30-26830. viii p., 2 l., 276 p. incl. illus., plates. col. front. 21 cm. 1930. Doubleday, Doran & Company, Inc.
--Cousins' Luck in the Louisiana Bayou Country. Lee, Manning de Villeneuve (1894-1980), illus. LC 40-33455. xiv p., 2 l., 258 p. illus. 21 cm. 1940. The Macmillan Company.
--Footlights Afloat. Couse, E. P., illus. LC 37-24275. xiii, 300 p. illus. 21 cm. 1937. Doubleday, Doran & Company, Incorporated.
--Gray Caps. Lee, Manning de Villeneuve (1894-1980), illus. LC 32-25732. x p., 2 l., 3-304 p. col. front., illus., plates. 21 cm. 1932. Doubleday, Doran & Company, Inc.
--Marty and Company on a California Farm. Iverd, Eugene, illus. LC 46-766211. x, 3-280 p. illus. 20 1/2 cm. (Young moderns). 1946. Doubleday & Co., Inc.
--Marty and Company on a Carolina Farm. Iverd, Eugene, illus. LC 33-27397. 5 p. l., ix-x, 280 p. col. front. illus. 21 cm. 1933. Doubleday, Doran & Company, Inc.
--Marty and Company on a Carolina Farm. Iverd, Eugene, illus. LC 43-13629. x, 3-280 p. illus. 20 1/2 cm. (Young moderns bookshelf). 1942. The Sun Dial Press.
--Miss Jimmy Deane and What Happened at Pleasant Meadows. Lee, Manning de Villeneuve (1894-1980), illus. LC 31-24446. xiv, 230 p. incl. illus., plates. col. front. 21 cm. 1931. Doubleday, Doran & Company, Incorporated.
--Miss Jimmy Deane and What Happened at Pleasant Meadows. Lee, Manning De Villeneuve (1894-1980), illus. LC 46-7649. x, 230 p. incl. illus., plates. 20 1/2 cm. (Young moderns). 1946. Doubleday & Co., Inc.
--Patsy's Progress. LC 35-27316. x, 273 p. col. front. 20 cm. 1935. Dodd, Mead & Company.
--The Step-Twins. Richman, Hilda, illus. LC 38-25515. xv p., 1 l., 233 p. incl. front., illus. 21 cm. 1938. Doubleday, Doran & Co., Inc.
Knox, Thomas Wallace, jt. auth. see Butterworth, Hezekiah.
Knox, Thomas Wallace (1835-1896)
--The Boy Travelers in Australia. N.D. Harper & Brothers.
--The Boy Travelers in Ceylon and India. N.D. Harper & Brothers.
--The Boy Travelers in Mexico. N.D. Harper & Brothers.
--The Boy Travelers in Northern Europe. N.D. Harper & Brothers.
--The Boy Travelers in South America. N.D. Harper & Brothers.
--Dog Stories and Dog Lore, 1 vol. N.D. Cassell & Co.
--John Boyd's Adventures: Merchant Sailor, Man-of-Warsman, Privateersman, Pirate and Algerine Slave. LC 21-12977. vi p., 1 l., 303 p. front., plates. 20 cm. 1893. D. Appleton and Company.
--The Land of the Kangaroo. 318p. 1910. W. A. Wilde Co.
--The Land of the Kangaroo: Adventures of Two Youths in a Journey of the Great Island Continent. Burgess, H., illus. LC 12-36033. 318 p. front., plates. 20 cm. (On cover: Travel-adventures series). c.1896. W. A. Wilde & Company.
--The Lost Army. LC 12-36037. iv, 5-296 p. front., plates. 20 cm. c.1894. The Merriam Company.
--The Talking Handkerchief, and Other Stories. (Illus.). N.D. Merriam Company.
--The Talking Handkerchief: And other Stories. Garnsey, John Henderson, illus. LC 12-360342. viii, 9-314 p. incl. front., illus., plates. 19 cm. c.1893. The Price-McGill Company.
--Teetotaler Dick: His Adventures, Temptations, and Triumphs. A Temperance Story. LC 21-12978. 2 p. l., 3-418 p. front., plates. 20 cm. c.1890. Ward & Drummond.
--The Young Nimrods around the World: A Book for Boys. 326 p. ill. 23 x 17cm. 1882. Harper Bros.
--The Young Nimrods in North America: A Book for Boys. LC 21-8683. 299 p. incl. front., illus. 23 cm. (His Hunting adventures on land and sea, pt. 1). 1881. Harper & Brothers.
--The Young Nimrods in North America: A Book for Boys. LC 9-10026. 299 p. incl. front., illus. 24 cm. (His Hunting Adventures on Land and Sea, Pt. 1). c.1909. Harper & Brothers.
Knox-Wagner, Elaine
--An Apartment's No Place for a Kid. Pate, Rodney, illus. LC 85-634. (Illus.). 32 p. 24cm. 1985. (ISBN 0-8075-0373-8). A. Whitman.
--My Grandpa Retired Today. Robinson, Charles (1931-), illus. LC 82-1935. (Illus.). 32 p. 24cm. 1982. (ISBN 0-8075-5334-4). A. Whitman.
--The Oldest Kid. Owens, Gail, illus. LC 81-294. (Illus.). 32 p. 24cm. (Concept books/level 1). 1981. (ISBN 0-8075-5986-5). A. Whitman.
Knox-Wagner, Elaine, jt. auth. see Delton, Judy.
Knudsen, Eric A.
--Spooky Stuffs. Kaye, Sally, ed. LC 74-80510. (Illus.). (gr. 1-7). 1974. (ISBN 0-89610-012-X). Island Her.
Knudsen, Krestine
--The Old Country Dolls. LC 29-19829. 79 p. illus. 21 cm. 1928. Krestine Knudsen.
Knudsen, Lynne
--Lullabies from Around the World. Tomes, Jacqueline, illus. (Illus.). (ps-3). 1967. (ISBN 0-695-45430-7). Follett.
Knudson, R. R., pseud., see Knudson, Rozanne.
Knudson, R. R., pseud. (1932-)
--Fox Running. Knudson, Rozanne. Koehn, Ilse (1929-), illus. LC 75-6294. (Illus.). 182 p. 21cm. c.1975. (ISBN 0-06-023211-0). (ISBN 0-06-023212-9). Harper & Row.
--Jesus Song. Knudson, Rozanne. Schick, Joel (1945-), illus. LC 73-1067. (Illus.). 24cm. 186p. (gr. 5-9). 1973. Delacorte.
--Rinehart Lifts. Knudson, Rozanne. LC 80-66825. 87 p. 22cm. c.1980. (ISBN 0-374-36294-7). Farrar, Straus, Giroux.
--Speed. Knudson, Rozanne. Eber, Linda, illus. LC 82-21009. (Illus.). 80p. (gr. 2 up). 1983. (ISBN 0-525-44052-6, Skinny Bk). (ISBN 0-525-44052-6). Dutton.
--You Are the Rain. Knudson, Rozanne. LC 73-15397. (Illus.). 22cm. 134p. 1974. (ISBN 0-440-08759-7). Delacorte Press.

--Zan Hagen's Marathon. Knudson, Rozanne. LC 84-47842. (Illus.). 183 p. 22cm. 1984. (ISBN 0-374-38811-3). Farrar, Straus & Giroux.
--Zanballer. Knudson, Rozanne. LC 72-1386. (Illus.). 166 p. 24cm. 1972. Delacorte Press.
--Zanbanger. Knudson, Rozanne. LC 75-25416. 162 p. 21cm. c.1977. (ISBN 0-06-023213-7). (ISBN 0-06-023214-5). Harper & Row.
--Zanboomer. Knudson, Rozanne. LC 77-11831. p. cm. c.1978. (ISBN 0-06-023217-X). (ISBN 0-06-023218-8). Harper & Row.

Knudson, Rozanne see Knudson, R. R., pseud.

Knutsson, Gosta Lars August (1908-)
--Pigge Lunke. Henschen, Helga, illus. Berzins, Helga, tr. LC 61-7918. (Music by Lar-Erik Larson). 90p. illus. 24cm. 1961. Bobbs-Merrill.

Knutt, Frigida
--The Snow Angel: A Tale of Life-Land and Dream-Land. LC 24-20463. 3 p. l., 5-261 p. front., plates. 17 cm. 1867. J. Miller.

Kobayashi, Kenzo (1926-)
--Two Little Ducks. english ed. Kobayashi, Kenzo (1926-), illus. LC 82-18786. p. cm. (Picture Book Studio Series). c.1983. (ISBN 0-907234-07-0). Neugebauer Press USA : Distributed by Alphabet Press.

Kobayashi, Masako Matsuno see Matsui, Tadashi.

Kobayashi, Masako Matsuno see Matsuno, Masako.

Kobrin, Janet, jt. auth. see Bernstein, Margery.

Kobrin, Janet & Bernstein, Margery
--The Summer Maker. Burgess, Anne (1942-), illus. LC 76-14875. p. cm. 1976. (ISBN 0-684-14716-5). Scribner.

Koch, Beverly, tr. see Asturias, Miguel Angel.

Koch, Claudia
--Kite in the Sea. (gr. 7-12). 1976. (ISBN 0-590-02082-X, Schol Trade Pap). Schol Bk Serv.
--When You Find Out Who You Are. (gr. 7-12). 1977. (ISBN 0-590-05422-8, Schol Pap). Scholastic Inc.

Koch, Dorothy Clarke (1924-)
--Gone Is My Goose. Lee, Doris Emrick (1905-1983), illus. LC 56-58072. unpaged. illus. 24cm. c.1956. Holiday House.
--I Play At The Beach. Rojankovsky, Feodor Stepanovich (1891-1970), illus. N.D. E. M. Hale & Co.
--I Play at the Beach. Rojankovsky, Feodor Stepanovich (1891-1970), illus. LC 55-14412. unpaged. illus. 24cm. c.1955. (ISBN 0-8234-0057-3). Holiday House.
--Let It Rain. Stone, Helen (1904-), illus. LC 59-16188. unpaged. illus. 26cm. 1959. Holiday House.
--Monkeys Are Funny That Way. Freeman, Don (1908-1978), illus. LC 62-6838. unpaged. illus. 27cm. (beginning-to-read book). c.1962. Holiday House.
--Up the Big Mountain. Hawkinson, Lucy Ozone (1924-1971) & Hawkinson, John Samuel (1912-), illus. LC 64-7107. (Illus.). 26cm. 35p. (gr. k-3). 1964. (ISBN 0-8234-0124-3). Holiday House.
--When The Cows Got Out. N.D. E. M. Hale & Co.
--When the Cows Got Out. Lantz, Paul (1908-), illus. LC 58-3774. (Illus.). 33 p. 23cm. (Beginning-to-read book). 1958. (ISBN 0-8234-0135-9). Holiday House.

Koch, Elers
--The High Trail. Cram, L. D. (1898-), illus. 180p. 1953. Caxton Publishers.

Koch, Frieda Redfield see Redfield, Fern, pseud.

Koch, Frieda Redfield
--The Red-Winged Goose and Other Indian Tales. Redfield, Fern, pseud. LC 40-9523. 5 p. l., 138 p. 20 cm. c.1940. Co-Operative Publishing Co.

Koch, Hellen L.
--Lady, Our Black Lady. 1985. (ISBN 0-8062-2462-2). Carlton.

Koch, John
--Hair-Raising Tales of Weston R. Sodbuster, Indian Scout. (Illus.). (gr. 1-3). 1967. (ISBN 0-8382-0310-8). Hale.
--Knight Named Rodney. (Illus.). (gr. 1-3). 1967. (ISBN 0-8382-0414-7). Hale.
--Peeky, the Curious Elf. (Illus.). (gr. k-2). 1967. (ISBN 0-8382-0639-5). Hale.
--Where Did You Come From. 1967. (ISBN 0-8382-0036-2, Hale House Books). E. M. Hale and company.

Koch, Katharine (1898-)
--Katie Meets Buffalo Bill. Paull, Grace A. (1898-), illus. LC 47-306337. 28 p. illus. (part col.) 23 cm. (Story parade picture book). 1947. Grosset & Dunlap.

Koch, Kenneth (1925-) & Farrell, Kate, eds.
--Talking to the Sun: An Illustrated Anthology of Poems for Young People. Metropolitan Museum of Art (New York, N.Y.) LC 85-15428. (Illus.). 112 p. 25cm. c.1985. (ISBN 0-87099-436-0). Metropolitan Museum of Art : Holt, Rinehart, and Winston.

Koch, Ron
--Goodbye Grandpa. Wallerstedt, Don, illus. LC 74-14183. (Illus.). 96 p. 20cm. 1975. (ISBN 0-8066-1465-X). Augsburg Pub. House.

Koch, Rosalie
--Holly and Mistletoe. Tales. Trauermantel, tr. from Ger. LC 27-734423. 2 p. l., 249 p. 17 cm. 1863. Crosby and Nichols.

Koch, Tom
--Tournament Trail. LC 50-6392. 185 p. 22 cm. 1950. Lothrop, Lee & Shepard.

Kochos, Mary George
--Thursday's Child. Kochos, Mary, illus. LC 55-11409. 112p. illus. 24cm. 1955. Creative Enterprises.

Koci, Mari M.
--Katakumba: The Story of an African Parrot. 1978. (ISBN 0-533-03099-4). Vantage.

Koci, Marta
--Blackie and Marie. Koci, Marta, illus. LC 80-24972. (Illus.). 32 p. 32cm. 1981. (ISBN 0-688-00217-X). (ISBN 0-688-00236-6). Morrow.
--Blackie & Marie. Koci, Marta, illus. LC 84-25520. (Illus.). 26 p. 29cm. 1985, c.1981. (ISBN 0-907234-73-9). Picture Book Studio USA : Distributed by Alphabet Press.
--Ivan, Divan, and Zariman. Koci, Marta, illus. LC 76-25196. (Illus.). 29 p. 1977, c.1973. (ISBN 0-8193-0893-5). (ISBN 0-8193-0894-3). Parents' Magazine Press.
--Katie's Kitten. Koci, Marta, illus. LC 82-60893. (Illus.). 28p. 1982. (ISBN 0-907234-21-6, Pub. by Picture Bk Stuido USA). Neugebauer Pr.

Kock, Carl
--Lady Bug. Kock, Carl, illus. LC 74-93803. (Illus.). 26 p. 21cm. 1970. Follett Pub. Co.

Koconda-Brons, Angela
--The Six Swans. Koconda-Brons, Angela, illus. (Illus.). 37p. (Orig.). (gr. 1-3). 1974. (ISBN 0-88010-069-9, Pub. by Steinerbooks). Anthroposophic.

Koconda-Brons, Angela, adapted by.
--Jorinda & Joringel. Kolonda-Brons, Angela, illus. (Illus.). 17p. (gr. 2-3). 1981. (ISBN 0-88010-052-4, Pub. by Verlag Walter Keller Switzerland). Anthroposophic.
--Jorinda & Joringel: Large Print. Koconda-Brons, Angela, illus. (Illus.). 17p. (gr. k-3). 1983. (ISBN 0-88010-089-3, Pub. by Walter Keller Switzerland). Anthroposophic.

Koehler, Alvin, jt. auth. see Koehler, Cynthia Iliff.

Koehler-Broman, Mela & Smith, Ingrid
--When Grandma Was a Little Girl. N.D. Duell, Sloan & Pearce.

Koehler, Cynthia Iliff & Koehler, Alvin
--Kittens and Puppies, Horses and Rabbits, and Insects, Turtles and Birds. LC 17-86675. 153 p. col. illus. 20cm. 1969. Grosset & Dunlap.

Koehler, Edward T., jt. auth. see Housman, Louise.

Koehler, William R (1914-) & Disney, Walt, Productions
--The Wonderful World of Disney Animals. Disney, Walt, Studio, photos by. LC 79-12333. (Illus.). 252 p. 26cm. c.1979. (ISBN 0-87605-810-1). Howell Book House.

Koehn, Ilse (1929-)
--Tilla. LC 81-2217. 240 p. 22cm. c.1981. (ISBN 0-688-00650-7). (ISBN 0-688-00651-5). Greenwillow Books.

Koeing, George
--Ghost of Gold Rush. (Illus.). 72p. 1968. La Siesta Press.

Koelling, Caryl
--Molly Mouse Goes Shopping. Acosta, Karen, illus. (Illus.). 22p. (Surprise Bks). (ps). 1982. (ISBN 0-8431-0628-X). Price Stern.
--Silly Stories Mix & Match. Andrus, Carroll, illus. LC 79-90789. (Illus.). (Mix & Match Bks.). (ps-2). 1980. Delacorte.

Koenig, Alma Johanna
--Gudrun. Bell, Anthea, tr. (Illus.). 187 p., 1 leaf of plates. 22cm. c.1979. (ISBN 0-688-41899-6). (ISBN 0-688-51900-8). (ISBN 0-688-51900-8). Lothrop, Lee, & Shepard Books.

Koenig, F.
--Jean Bart, 1 of 7 vols. (Premium Library: No. 1). 1891. Set. McCauley & Kilner.

Koenig, John
--B. Benny Bumpkin. (ps-3). N.D. Dghtrs St Paul.
--The Blown-Around Room. (Illus.). (ps-3). N.D. Dghtrs St Paul.
--The Boy Who Thought God Was Hiding. (Illus.). (ps-3). N.D. Dghtrs St Paul.
--Christmas Looking. (ps-3). N.D. Dghtrs St Paul.
--Grampy O'Shea Tells a Story. (Illus.). (ps-3). N.D. Dghtrs St Paul.
--Mean Until. (Illus.). (ps-3). N.D. Dghtrs St Paul.
--Peter Patrick Pancake. (Orig.). (ps-3). N.D. Dghtrs St Paul.
--Ricky Becomes Brave. (ps-3). 1970. Dghtrs St Paul.
--Visit to Heaven. (Illus.). (ps-3). N.D. Dghtrs St Paul.

Koenig, Marion
--Princess Kalina & the Hedgehog. Duntze, Dorothee, illus. (Illus.). 22p. 1981. (ISBN 0-571-11844-5). Faber & Faber.

Koenig, Marion, adapted by.
--The Tale of Fancy Nancy: A Spanish Folk Tale. Ensikat, Klaus, illus. 1978. Chatto. **Award: (NYT).**

Koenig, Marion, adapted by see Bianki, Vitalii Valentinovich.

Koenig, Marion, adapted by see Geelhaar, Anne.

Koenig, Marion, ed. see Hille-Brandts, Lene.

Koenig, Marion, adapted by see Mikhalkov, Sergei Vladimirovich.

Koenig, Marion, retold by see Nickl, Peter.

Koenig, Marion, tr. see Bolliger, Max.

Koenig, Marion, tr. see Paehr, Gunhild.

Koenig, Marion, tr. see Roels, Iliane.

Koenig, Marion, tr. see Rosenfeld, Friedrich.

Koenig, Marion, tr. see Ruck-Pauquet, Gina.

Koenig, Norma E.
--The Runaway Heart. (Orig.). (gr. 4-6). 1981. (ISBN 0-377-00112-0). Friend Pr.

Koenig, Richard
--The Seven Special Cats. 1 st. ed. Bacon, Peggy, pseud. (1895-), illus. Bacon, Margaret Frances. LC 61-6677. 57p. illus. 24cm. 1961. World Pub. Co.

Koenigsberg, Patricia Lakin
--Fig Boot's Happy Day. Gatie, John, illus. LC 83-22081. (Illus.). 40p. (Baby Strawberry Shortcake Ser.). (ps-3). 1984. (ISBN 0-910313-22-9). (ISBN 0-910313-22-9). Parker Bro.

Koenner, Alfred (1921-)
--The Peacock's Wedding. Ensikat, Klaus, illus. (Illus.). 26p. 1978. (ISBN 0-7011-5019-X, Pub. by Chatto Bodley Jonathan). Merrimack Pub Cir.

Koepke, Edith
--Jumbo. (gr. k-5). N.D. Carlton.

Koerner, Wolfgang (1937-)
--The Green Frontier. Crampton, Patricia, tr. from Ger. LC 77-24517. (gr. 7 up). 1977. (ISBN 0-688-22124-6). (ISBN 0-688-32124-0). Morrow.

Koester, Sharon Smith
--Where Are You Going Today?. Koester, Sharon Smith, illus. LC 57-7638. unpaged (chiefly illus.) 25cm. 1957. A. Whitman.

Koester, Sharon Smith, illus.
--Little Red Riding Hood. (Disney Little Golden Book). 1959. Golden Press.

Koff, Richard Myram (1926-)
--Christopher. Reinertson, Barbara, illus. LC 81-65885. p. cm. 1981. (ISBN 0-89742-050-0). Celestial Arts.

Koffler, Camilla see Ylla, pseud.

Koffler, Camilla, jt. auth. see Brown, Margaret Wise.

Koffler, Camilla, jt. auth. see Tucci, Niccolo.

Koffler, Camilla (0000-1955)
--Big and Little. Ylla, pseud. N.D. Charles Scribner's Sons.
--Two Little Bears. Ylla, pseud. Koffler, Camilla (0000-1955), illus. Ylla, pseud. LC 54-8963. (Illus.). 29cm. (ps-1). 1954. (ISBN 0-06-026811-5, HarpJ). Har-Row.
--Two Little Bears. Ylla, pseud. new ed. Koffler, Camilla (0000-1955), illus. Ylla, pseud. (Illus.). (ps-3). 1976. (ISBN 0-06-443016-2, Trophy). Har-Row.

Koffler, Camilla (0000-1955) & Bonsall, Crosby Barbara Newell (1921-)
--Here's Jellybean Breilly. Ylla, pseud. Newell, Crosby, pseud. Bouchage, Luc, illus. Rado, Charles, contrib. by. LC 67-2938. 1 v. (chiefly illus.) 30 cm. 1966. Harper & Row.
--Whose Eye Am I?. Ylla, pseud. Newell, Crosby, pseud. Koffler, Camilla (0000-1955), photos by. Ylla, pseud. Bouchage, Luc, designed by. LC 68-24336. (Illus.). 1 v. (unpaged). 30cm. 1968. (ISBN 0-06-020564-4). Harper & Row.

Koffler, Camilla (0000-1955) & Brown, Margaret Wise (1910-1952)
--The Sleepy Little Lion. Ylla, pseud. Koffler, Camilla (0000-1955), photos by. Ylla, pseud. LC 47-11482. 31 p. illus. 30 cm. c.1947. Harper.
--They All Saw It. Ylla, pseud. Koffler, Camilla (0000-1955), photos by. Ylla, pseud. LC 44-570775. 31 p. illus. 30 x 23 cm. c.1944. Harper & Brothers.

Koffler, Camilla (0000-1955) & Gregor, Arthur S (1923-)
--The Little Elephant. Ylla, pseud. Koffler, Camilla (0000-1955), illus. Ylla, pseud. Bouchage, Luc, designed by. LC 56-8140. unpaged. illus. 30cm. c.1956. (ISBN 0-06-026771-2). Harper. **Award: (NYT).**

Kofsky, Cynthia & Whittaker, Daphne
--Simba, the Baby Lion, and Other Stories and Poems for Kenya Children. LC 78-980390. (Illus.). 24cm. 28p. N.D. Kofsky.

Kogan Ray, Deborah see Gogol, Nikolai Vasilevich.

Kogan Ray, Deborah see Ray, Deborah.

Koger, Earl, Sr.
--Jocko: A Legend of the American Revolution. Miller, Don (1923-), illus. LC 75-34920. (Illus.). 32 p. 24cm. c.1976. (ISBN 0-13-510040-2). Prentice-Hall.

Koglin, Anna E
--The House That Jackson Built. Norman, Vera Stone, illus. LC 30-16890. 123 p. col. front., illus. 17 cm. c.1930. The Warner Press.

Kohan, Frances H & Weil, Truda T.
--Eagle in the Valley. Evans, Katherine Floyd (1901-1964), illus. LC 51-2315. (Illus.). 160 p. 22cm. 1951. Childrens Press.

Kohaus, Hannah More, Mrs., adapted by.
--A Collection of Poems for Youths and Children. LC 12-34965. (Especially Adapted for Sabbath School Concerts, MissionBands, and Christmas Festivals.). 1 p. l., 13 p. 23 cm. c.1886. A. E. Davis & Co.

Kohen, Apy
--Beauty & the Beast. Hague, Michael R., illus. (Illus.). 1980. (ISBN 0-914676-39-3, Star & Eleph Bks). (ISBN 0-914676-47-4). Green Tiger Pr.

Kohl, Dieter
--Noah. Steinmann, Friedel, illus. Lambregtse, Cornelius, tr. from Ger. (Illus.). (gr. 7 up). 1979. (ISBN 0-8028-1801-3). Eerdmans.

Kohl, Erica, jt. auth. see Kohl, Herbert R.

Kohl, Herbert R. (1937-) & Cruz, Victor Hernandez (1949-), eds.
--Stuff: A Collection of Poems, Visions & Imaginative Happenings from Young Writers in Schools-Opened & Closed. Chappell, Sean & Crowder, Phillip, illus. LC 77-124286. (Illus.). xiv, 122 p. 22cm. 1970. World.

Kohl, Herbert R (1937-) & Kohl, Erica
--Where Is Emmett Gold?. A Solve-It-Yourself Mystery. LC 84-20104. p. cm. c.1984. (ISBN 0-316-50133-6). (ISBN 0-316-50134-4). Little, Brown.

Kohl, Herbert (1937-) & Kohl, Judith
--The View from the Oak. Bayless, Roger, illus. LC 76-57680. (Illus.). (gr. 10 up). 1977. (ISBN 0-684-15016-6, ScribJ). (ISBN 0-684-15017-4, ScribJ). Scribner. **Awards: (NBA).**

Kohl, Judith, jt. auth. see Kohl, Herbert.

Kohl, Marguerite & Young, Frederica
--Jokes for Children. 1st ed. Patterson, Robert (1899-), illus. LC 63-11056. (Illus.). 116 p. 22cm. 1963. Hill and Wang.
--More Jokes for Children. Patterson, Robert (1899-), illus. 1966. E M Hale.
--More Jokes for Children. 1st ed. Patterson, Robert (1899-), illus. LC 66-15894. 111 p. illus. 22 cm. 1966. (ISBN 0-8090-1520-X). Hill and Wang.

Kohlap, Gay
--David: Boy of the High Country. 1976. (ISBN 0-8002-0148-5). Intl Pubns Serv.
--David: Boy of the High Country. Kohlap, George, illus. (Illus.). 100 photos. 66p. (gr. 1-3). 1969. Tri-Ocean.

Kohler, Christine (1953-)
--Jesus Makes Me Well. Neely, Keith R. (1943-), illus. LC 84-23095. (Illus.). 24 p. 26cm. (Growing up Christian Series). c.1985. (ISBN 0-570-04113-9). Concordia Pub. House.
--My Friend Is Moving. Neely, Keith R. (1943-), illus. LC 84-23062. (Illus.). 24 p. 26cm. (Growing up Christian Series). c.1985. (ISBN 0-570-04116-3). Concordia Pub. House.

Kohler, Julilly House (1908-1976)
--The Boy Who Stole the Elephant. 1st ed. Ames, Lee Judah (1921-), illus. LC 52-8162. 89 p. illus. 21 cm. 1952. (ISBN 0-394-90979-8). Knopf.
--Collins and His Rabbit. rev. ed. Blevin, illus. LC 69-14688. (Illus.). 30 p. 25cm. 1969. Childrens Press.
--Crazy As You Look. 1st ed. Ames, Lee Judah (1921-), illus. LC 54-5302. (Illus.). 120 p. 21cm. 1954. Knopf.
--Daniel in the Cub Scout Den. Powers, Richard M. Gorman (1921-), illus. N.D. E. P. Dutton & Co.
--Daniel in the Cub Scout Den. 1st ed. Powers, Richard M. Gorman (1921-), illus. LC 51-3813. 192 p. illus. 21 cm. 1951. Aladdin Books.
--Farmer Collins. Engelbrecht, Trientja (1925-), illus. LC 47-20366. 36 p. illus. (part col.) 20 x 17cm. (Story-book science series). 1947. Childrens Press, Inc.
--Football Trees. Adams, Pauline Batchelder (1897-), illus. LC 47-20230. 36p. illus. (part col.) 20 x 17cm. (Story-book Science Series). 1947. Childrens Press, Inc.
--Friend to All: A Girl Scout Story. Ames, Lee Judah (1921-), illus. N.D. E. P. Dutton & Co.
--Friend to All. Ames, Lee Judah (1921-), illus. LC 54-9274. 214p. illus. 22cm. 1954. Aladdin Books.
--Harmony Ahead. 1st ed. Burchard, Peter Duncan (1921-), illus. LC 52-12503. 188 p. illus. 22 cm. 1952. Aladdin Books.
--Razzberry Jamboree. Pitz, Henry Clarence (1895-1976), illus. LC 57-6570. 180p. illus. 21cm. 1957. Crowell.
--The Sun Shines Bright. Ames, Lee Judah (1921-), illus. LC 56-779670. 207p. illus. 21cm. 1956. Crowell.

Korman, Justine
--Inspector Gadget in the Case of the Mixed-Up Scientist. Gantz, David, illus. (Illus.). 24p. (Golden Look-Look Bks.). (ps-3). 1985. (ISBN 0-307-11789-8, Pub. by Golden Bks). Western Pub.

Kormos, Istvan
--It All Started with the Big Green Fish. Reich, Karoly, illus. Ribianszky, Alexandra, tr. from Hungarian. (Illus.). 23p. 1979. (ISBN 963-13-0543-0). Intl Pubns Serv.
--It All Started with the Big Green Fish. Reich, Karoly, illus. Ribianszky, Alexandra, tr. (Illus.). 24p. (ps-1). N.D. (ISBN 0-686-65441-2). Newbury Bks Inc.
--The Painted Kitten. (ps-1). N.D. (ISBN 0-686-65439-0). Newbury Bks Inc.

Korr, David
--ABC Toy Chest: Featuring Jim Henson's Sesame Street Muppets. Stevenson, Nancy W., illus. Children's Television Workshop LC 80-84192. (Illus.). 25 p. 27cm. c.1981. (ISBN 0-307-23129-1). Western Pub. Co. in Conjunctions with Children's Television Workshop.
--Cookie Monster and the Cookie Tree: Featuring Jim Henson's Muppets. Mathieu, Joseph (1945-), illus. Children's Television Workshop LC 79-10796. (Illus.). 24 p. 32cm. 1979, c.1977. (ISBN 0-307-60821-2). (ISBN 0-307-10821-X). Western Pub. Co.
--The Day the Count Stopped Counting: Featuring Jim Henson's Muppets. Smollin, Michael J., illus. Children's Television Workshop LC 77-73879. (Illus.). 46 p. 26cm. (Kid's paperback). c.1977. (ISBN 0-307-12358-8). Western Pub. Co.
--The Sesame Street Book of Nonsense: Featuring Jim Henson's Sesame Street Muppets. Cooke, Tom, illus. Children's Television Workshop LC 81-83453. (Illus.). 26 p. 26cm. (Sesame Street read-aloud book). 1982, c.1980. (ISBN 0-307-11612-3). (ISBN 0-307-61612-6). Western Pub. Co. in Conjunction with Children's Television Workshop.

Korr, David & Henson, Jim, pseud. (1936-)
--Prairie Dawn's Upside-Down Poem & Other Nonsense from Sesame Street: Featuring Jim Henson's Sesame Street Muppets. Henson, James Maury. Cooke, Tom, illus. LC 80-84191. (Illus.). 25 p. 26cm. c.1981. (ISBN 0-307-23130-5). Western Pub. Co., in Conjunction with Children's Television Workshop.

Korschunow, Irina
--The Foundling Fox. Michl, Reinhard, illus. Skofield, James, tr. from Ger. LC 84-47631. (Illus.). 48p. Orig. Title: Der Findefuchs. (gr. k-3). 1984. (ISBN 0-06-023243-9). (ISBN 0-06-023244-7). HarpJ.
--A Night in Distant Motion. Hafrey, Leigh, tr. from German. LC 81-47352. 112p. 1st U.S. edition. (gr. 7 up). 1983. (ISBN 0-87923-399-0). (ISBN 0-87923-399-0). Godine.
--Piebald Pup. (gr. k-3). N.D. G&D.
--Piebald Pup. Oberlander, Gerhard, illus. (Illus.). (gr. k-3). 1959. (ISBN 0-8392-3026-5). Astor-Honor.
--The Piebald Pup. Rev ed. Oberlander, Gerhard, illus. Murphy, Martha, tr. from Ger. unpaged. illus. 30 cm. (an astor book. 1959. McDowell, Obolensky.
--Who Killed Christopher?. LC 79-14432. p. cm. 1979. Collins.

Korshak, Jack
--The Strange Story of Oliver Jones. Borja, Corinne (1929-), illus. LC 66-24063. (Illus.). 1 v. (unpaged. 24cm. 1966. Mid-America Pub. Co.

Korsmeyer, Lavinia Bray, Mrs.
--Curiosity Cottage: The Adventures of David Benjamin Abercrombie. LC 30-10251. 143 p. incl. front. 21 cm. c.1930. The Christopher Publishing House.

Korson, George Gershon (1899-), ed. see Emrich, Marion Vallat.

Kort, Kees De, illus.
--What the Bible Tells Us: A Series for Young Children. Incl. Jesus Is Born. (ISBN 0-8066-1576-1, 10-3520); Jesus at the Wedding. (ISBN 0-8066-1577-X, 10-3490); The Good Samaritan. (ISBN 0-8066-1578-8, 10-2815); Jesus Is Alive. (ISBN 0-8066-1579-6, 10-3518). (Illus.). (gr. 1-4). 1977. Augsburg.

Kort, Kees De see De Kort, Kees.

Kortrecht, Augusta
--A Dixie Rose. Brown, Ethel Pennewill0174, illus. LC 10-216018. 284 p., 1 l., col. front. 20 cm. 1910. J. B. Lippincott Company.

Kortschak, Kate, tr. see Van Hille, C. Gaerthe.

Kortum, Jeanie
--Ghost Vision. Stermer, Dugald (1936-), illus. 1983. Pantheon.
--Ghost Vision. Stermer, Dugald (1936-), illus. LC 83-4706. (Illus.). 143 p. c.1983. (ISBN 0-394-86190-6). Sierra Club.

Korty, Carol (1937-)
--Plays from African Folktales. Cain, Sandra, illus. LC 74-24418. (With Ideas for Acting, Dance, Costumes, and Music). (Illus.). 128 p. 24cm. 1975. (ISBN 0-684-14199-X). Scribner.
--Silly Soup: Ten Zany Plays, with Songs and Ideas for Making Them Your Own. Cope, Jamie, photos by. LC 77-23102. (Illus.). vii, 148 p. 24cm. c.1977. (ISBN 0-684-15171-5). Scribner.

Korty, John Van Cleave, jt. auth. see Hall, Avery.

Korwin-Rodziszewski, Audrey, tr. see Konwicki, Tadeusz.

Korwin-Rodziszewski, George, tr. see Konwicki, Tadeusz.

Korzeniowski, Josef Teodor Konrad Walecz see Conrad, Joseph, pseud.

K. O. S, pseud., see Dombrowski Zu Papros und Krusvic, Kathe Schonberger Von.

Kosanke, Martha
--Indian Romances of the Western Frontier. 1st ed. Coombies, Gren, illus. LC 54-12288. 205p. illus. 21cm. c.1954. Exposition Press.

Kosava, Maria & Stanovsky, Vladislav, eds.
--African Tales of Magic and Mystery. Teisig, Karel, illus. Kuthanova, Olga, tr. from Czech. LC 70-20276. 191 p. col. illus. 29cm. 1970. Hamlyn, New York.
--African Tales of Magic and Mystery. Teisig, Olga, illus. Kuthanova, Olga, tr. from Czech. LC 75-653437. 191 p. col. illus. 29cm. 1975. (ISBN 0-600-01660-9). Hamlyn, New York.

Koshland, Ellen (1947-)
--The Magic Lollipop. 1st ed. Koshland, Ellen, illus. LC 73-149481. (Illus.). 43 p. 1971. (ISBN 0-394-92163-1). Knopf.

Kosht, Jean Berry (1879-)
--Canaries at Work and Play. LC 47-668. 102 p. incl. front., illus. 21 1/2cm. 1946. Wetzel Pub Co.

Kossak-Szczucka, Z.
--Troubles of a Gnome. (Folk Lore And Fairy Tales). N.D. MacMillan Bks.

Kossoff, David (1919-)
--Bible Stories. Barclay, William (1907-1978), frwd. by. 235 p. 18cm. 1973, c.1968. Warner Paperback Lib.
--Bible Stories. D'Achille, Gino, illus. Barclay, William, frwd. by. LC 69-18396. (Illus.). 285 p. 26cm. 1969, c.1968. Follett.

Koste, Virginia G.
--The Trial of Tom Sawyer. 1978. (ISBN 0-87602-213-1). Anchorage.
--The Wonderful Wizard of Oz. 60p. (Children's Theatre Playscript Ser.). (gr. 3-7). 1982. (ISBN 0-88020-106-1). Coach Hse.

Kostka, Matthew
--Climb to the Top. 1st ed. Micale, Albert (1913-), illus. LC 62-14787. (Illus.). 142 p. 22cm. (Signal book). 1962. Doubleday.

Kostman, Samuel
--Women of Valor. LC 77-12348. (Illus.). xii, 178 p. 22cm. 1978. (ISBN 0-8239-0425-3). Richards Rosen Press.

Kotler, Irma M
--Stories and Poems You Can Read to Your Grandchildren. Corsillo, George, illus. LC 74-25051. (Illus.). 62 p. 23cm. c.1974. (ISBN 0-914302-03-5). Prince Communications.

Kotowska, Monika (1942-)
--Bridge to the Other Side. Wojciechowska, Maia Teresa (1927-), tr. from Pol. LC 75-116264. (Illus.). . 168p. (gr. 7 up). 1970. (ISBN 0-385-03412-1). Doubleday.

Kotrba, Danella G.
--God's Helper. 32p. (Come Unto Me Ser.: Year 2, Bk. 1). (ps). 1980. (ISBN 0-8127-0211-5). Review & Herald.

Kotta, Susan, tr. see Bonzon, Paul-Jacques.

Kottmeyer, William, et al. (1910-)
--Fables and Folktales. LC 72-1253. (Illus.). 256 p. 25cm. 1973. (ISBN 0-07-033974-0). Webster Division, McGraw-Hill.

Kottmeyer, William, ed. see Dickens, Charles John Huffam.

Kottmeyer, William, ed. see Doyle, Arthur Conan, Sir.

Kottmeyer, William, ed. see Dumas, Alexandre.

Kottmeyer, William (1910-), ed. see Malory, Thomas, Sir.

Kottmeyer, William (1910-), adapted by see Munroe, Kirk.

Kottmeyer, William, ed. see Poe, Edgar Allan.

Kottmeyer, William (1910-), adapted by see Pyle, Howard.

Kottmeyer, William, ed. see Scott, Walter, Sir.

Kottmeyer, William (1910-), adapted by see Wallace, Lewis.

Kottmeyer, William (1910-)
--The Trojan War. Kottmeyer, William (1910-), illus. LC 52-32479. 122 p. illus. 21 cm. (Junior everyreaders). 1952. Webster Pub. Co.

Kottmeyer, William (1910-), ed.
--The Robin Hood Stories. LC 52-10360. 24cm. 153p. 1952. Webster Publishing Co.

Kotz, Kathleen Murphy
--Five Favorite Folk Plays. LC 46-348. (For the Primary Grades, As Dramatized). 82 p. 20 1/2 cm. c.1945. Row, Peterson and Company.

Kotzwinkle, William (1938-)
--The Ants Who Took Away Time. 1st ed. Servello, Joe (1932-), illus. LC 78-17833. p. cm. 1978, c.1977. (ISBN 0-385-12367-1). (ISBN 0-385-12368-X). Doubleday.
--The Day the Gang Got Rich. 1st ed. Servello, Joe (1932-), illus. LC 76-123019. (Illus.). 29 p. 1970. Viking Press.
--Dream of Dark Harbor. 1st ed. Servello, Joe (1932-), illus. LC 78-1244. (Illus.). 46 p. 25cm. c.1979. (ISBN 0-385-12486-4). (ISBN 0-385-12487-2). Doubleday.
--Elephant Boy: A Story of the Stone Age. Servello, Joe (1932-), illus. LC 71-106400. (Illus.). 43 p. 29cm. 1970. (ISBN 0-399-20936-0). Farrar, Straus and Giroux.
--The Extra Terrestrial Storybook. Servello, Joe (1932-), illus. 1982. (ISBN 0-399-20936-0). Putnam Pub Group.
--The Firemen. Servello, Joe (1932-), illus. LC 69-15706. (Illus.). 39 p. 1969. Pantheon Books.
--The Leopard's Tooth. Servello, Joe (1932-), illus. LC 75-25504. (Illus.). 95 p. 24cm. c.1976. (ISBN 0-8164-3162-0). Seabury Press.
--The Nap Master. 1st ed. Servello, Joe (1932-), illus. LC 78-12178. (Illus.). 32 p. c.1979. Harcourt Brace Jovanovich.
--The Oldest Man and Other Timeless Stories. Servello, Joe (1932-), illus. LC 77-153980. (Illus.). 66 p. 22cm. 1971. (ISBN 0-394-92288-3). Pantheon Books.
--The Ship That Came Down the Gutter. Servello, Joe (1932-), illus. LC 75-117454. (Illus.). 23 p. 21cm. 1970. Pantheon Books.
--The Supreme, Superb, Exalted and Delightful, One and Only Magic Building. 1st ed. Servello, Joe (1932-), illus. LC 72-96500. (Illus.). 40 p. 1973. (ISBN 0-374-37303-5). Farrar, Straus and Giroux.
--Trouble in Bugland: A Collection of Inspector Mantis Mysteries. Servello, Joe (1932-), illus. LC 82-49338. (Illus.). 160p. 1983. (ISBN 0-87923-472-5). (ISBN 0-87923-472-5). Godine.
--Up the Alley with Jack and Joe. Servello, Joe (1932-), illus. LC 74-2127. (Illus.). 62 p. 23cm. (Ready-to-read). 1974. (ISBN 0-02-750940-0). Macmillan.

Kotzwinkle, William (1938-) & Mathison, Melissa
--E.T. The Extra-Terrestrial Storybook. Mercer, Charles Edward (1917-), adapted by. LC 82-7530. p. cm. c.1982. (ISBN 0-399-20936-0). Putnam.

Kousbroek, H. R., tr. see Feder-Tal, Karah.

Kouts, Anne (1945-)
--Kenny's Rat. 1st ed. Fraser, Betty M., pseud. (1928-), illus. Fraser, Elizabeth Marr. LC 76-123018. (Illus.). 32 p. 23cm. 1970. Viking Press.

Kouzel, Daisy, adapted by.
--The Cuckoo's Reward: A Folk Tale from Mexico in Spanish and English Cuento Popular De Mexico En Espanol E Ingles. 1st ed. Thollander, Earl Gustave (1922-), illus. LC 75-46534. (Illus.). 32 p. c.1977. (ISBN 0-385-09513-9). (ISBN 0-385-09510-4). Doubleday.

Kovacs, Deborah
--Frazzle's Fantastic Day: Featuring Jim Henson's Sesame Street Muppets. Brown, Richard Eric (1946-), illus. LC 80-83289. (Illus.). 26 p. 27cm. c.1980. (ISBN 0-307-23123-2). Western Pub. Co. in Conjunction with Children's Television Workshop.
--When Is Saturday?. Featuring Jim Henson's Sesame Street Muppets. Brown, Richard Eric (1946-), illus. Children's Television Workshop LC 81-80469. (Illus.). 26 p. 27cm. c.1981. (ISBN 0-307-23137-2). Western Pub. Co. in Conjunction with Children's Television Workshop.

Kovacs, Deborah, ed.
--City Cat. Najaka, Marlies Merk, illus. LC 80-15958. p. cm. c.1980. McGraw-Hill.
--Country Cat. Najaka, Marlies Merk, illus. LC 80-15956. p. cm. c.1980. (ISBN 0-07-045859-6). McGraw-Hill.

Kovalik, Nada, jt. auth. see Kovalik, Vladimir.

Kovalik, Vladimir (1928-) & Kovalik, Nada (1926-)
--Undersea World of Tomorrow. Solonevich, George (1915-), tr. LC 69-12365. 51 p. illus. 22cm. 1969. Prentice-Hall.

Kovalskaia, Olga Nesterovna, ed. see Ershov, Petr Pavlovich.

Kovalskaia, Olga Nesterovna (1876) & Putnam
--Long Legs, Big Mouth, Burning Eyes. Chase, Rhoda Campbell & Cugat, Albert, illus. N.D. Milton Bradley Co.

Kovalskii, Kazimir Adolfovich, ed. see Ershov, Petr Pavlovich.

Kovar, Edith May. see Lowe, Edith May Kovar

Kovar, Edith May see Windsor, Mary, pseud.

Kovar, Edith May, jt. ed. see Barker, Cicely Mary.

Kovar, Edith May (1905-), as told by.
--Cinderella: A Fairy Story. Windsor, Mary, pseud. Bennett, Juanita C., illus. LC 35-21955. 22 p. col. illus. 33 cm. c.1935. Whitman Publishing Company.
--Fairy Gold and Other Stories. Windsor, Mary, pseud. Windsor, Mary (1905-), photos by. LC 31-25643. 1 p. l., 7-37, 1 p. illus., col. plates. 32 x 27 cm. c.1931. Whitman Publishing Company.
--The Little King and Other Fairy Tales. Windsor, Mary, pseud. Kovar, Edith May (1905-), illus. Windsor, Mary, pseud. LC 34-405054. 1 p. l., 5-30 p. illus. (part col.) 31 cm. c.1934. Whitman Publishing Co.
--The Sleeping Beauty. Windsor, Mary, pseud. Fleur, Anne Elizabeth (1901-), illus. Sari, pseud. (Illus.). 16p. 24cm. 1939. Grosset and Dunlap.

Koven, Reginald De see Field, Eugene (1850-1895) & De Koven, Reginald.

Kovend, James De see De Kovend, James.

Koziakin, Vladimir, jt. auth. see Phillips, Louis.

Kozikowski, Renate
--Sophie's Hideaway. Kozikowski, Renate, illus. LC 83-47504. (Illus.). 16p. (ps-1). 1983. (ISBN 0-06-023208-0, HarpJ). Har-Row.
--Titus Bear Goes to Bed. Kozikowski, Renate, illus. LC 83-48184. (Illus.). 14p. (ps). 1984. (ISBN 0-06-023224-2, HarpJ). Har-Row.
--Titus Bear Goes to School. Kozikowski, Renate, illus. LC 83-48185. (Illus.). 14p. (ps). 1984. (ISBN 0-06-023226-9, HarpJ). Har-Row.
--Titus Bear Goes to the Beach. Kozikowski, Renate, illus. LC 83-48183. (Illus.). 14p. (ps). 1984. (ISBN 0-06-023223-4, HarpJ). Har-Row.
--Titus Bear Goes to Town. Kozikowski, Renate, illus. LC 83-48186. (Illus.). 14 p. 15cm. 1984. (ISBN 0-06-023227-7). Harper & Row.

Kozisek, Josef (1861-)
--A Forest Story. Murphy, Helen, ed. Mates, Rudolf (1881-), illus. Szalatnay, Rafael D. (1884-), tr. LC 29-23122. 58 p. incl. col. front., col. illus. 27 cm. 1929. The Macmillan Company.
--The Magic Flutes. Mates, Rudolf (1881-), illus. Winlow, Clara Vostrovsky, Mrs. (1876-), tr. LC 29-27451. 56 p. col. illus. 25 x 32 cm. 1929. Longmans, Green and Co.

Kozlenko, William (1917-), ed.
--One Hundred Non-Royalty One-Act Plays. LC 41-51635. 6 p. l., 15-802 p. 24 cm. c.1940. Greenberg.

Kozloff, Arielle P
--Perry Grin's Travels. Edwards, Christine E., illus. Cleveland Museum of Art LC 82-105958. (Illus.). 32 p. c.1981. Cleveland Museum of Art.

Kozol, Jonathan (1936-)
--The Night is Dark and I Am Far From Home. 1975. Houghton Mifflin company.

Kraemer, Lillian Rosa
--Nicholas Basset: Who Learned Good Bathroom Manners. 1st ed. Biller, Alan, illus. LC 65-6944. 58 p. col. illus. 23 cm. 1965. Exposition Press.
--The Wheelchair Adventures of Jeannie and the Wallpaper Children. 1st ed. Drown, Eleanor J., illus. LC 55-5719. 150p. illus. 21cm. (Banner book). 1955. Exposition Press.

Kraenzel, Margaret Powell see Blue, Wallace, pseud.

Kraenzel, Margaret Powell (1899-)
--The Persian Donkey Bead. Fellin, Peter, illus. LC 60-102010. 107p. illus. 21cm. (Wonderful world book). 1960. Barnes.
--Rain Cloud, the Wild Mustang. Crowell, Pers (1910-), illus. LC 62-11066. (Illus.). 144 p. 22cm. 1962. Lothrop, Lee & Shepard.

Kraft, Irma
--The Power of Purim and Other Plays. N.D. Harlem Book Co.

Kraft, Ruth
--Spot and Scot. Baumgarten, Fritz, illus. Miller, Joseph, tr. LC 78-123151. (Illus.). 28 p. 1970. Miller Books.

Krag, Martha Ann & Reynolds, Florence Krag
--A Book of Nursery Rhymes. (Illus.). N.D. Bowen-Merrill Pub.
--Martha-Jane: Nursery Nonsense. Keep, Virginia, illus. LC 12-34969. (Illus.). 27cm. 24p. 1905. Bobbs-Merrill Co.

Kragg-Pederson, Geraldine
--The Melforts Go to Sea. Duncan, Gregor, illus. N.D. Holiday House.

Krahn, Fernando (1935-)
--Amanda and the Mysterious Carpet. Krahn, Fernando (1935-), illus. LC 84-14201. (Illus.). 32 p. 20cm. c.1985. (ISBN 0-89919-258-0). Clarion Books.
--April Fools. Krahn, Fernando (1935-), illus. LC 73-16279. 32 p. of illus. (part col. 1974. (ISBN 0-525-25825-6). Dutton.
--Arthur's Adventure in the Abandoned House. Krahn, Fernando (1935-), illus. LC 80-22249. (Illus.). 32 p. (gr. 1-3). c.1981. (ISBN 0-525-25945-7). Dutton.

--The Biggest Christmas Tree on Earth. Krahn, Fernando (1935-), illus. LC 78-9824. (Illus.). 32 p. 19cm. c.1978. (ISBN 0-316-50309-6). Little, Brown.
--Catch That Cat!. Krahn, Fernando (1935-), illus. LC 77-20820. (Illus.). 32 p. 18cm. c.1978. (ISBN 0-525-27555-X). Dutton.
--The Creepy Thing. Krahn, Fernando (1935-), illus. LC 81-18148. (Illus.). 32 p. 20cm. c.1982. (ISBN 0-89919-099-5). Clarion Books.
--The Family Minus. Krahn, Fernando (1935-), illus. LC 76-18093. (Illus.). 32 p. c.1977. (ISBN 0-8193-0860-9). (ISBN 0-8193-0861-7). Parents' Magazine Press.
--The Family Minus's Summer House. Krahn, Fernando (1935-), illus. LC 78-23717. p. cm. 1979. (ISBN 0-8193-0991-5). (ISBN [illegible]). Parents' Magazine Press.
--A Flying Saucer Full of Spaghetti. Krahn, Fernando (1935-), illus. LC 75-116883. (Illus.). 29 p. 1970. Dutton.
--A Funny Friend from Heaven. Krahn, Fernando (1935-), illus. (gr. 1-3). 1977. Harper.
--A Funny Friend from Heaven. Krahn, Fernando (1935-), illus. LC 77-3549. (Illus.). 40 p. 26cm. c.1977. (ISBN 0-397-31760-3). Lippincott.
--The Great Ape: Being the True Version of the Famous Saga of Adventure and Friendship. LC 78-9053. (Illus.). 40 p. 1978. (ISBN 0-670-34840-6). Viking Press.
--The Great Ape: Being the True Version of the Famous Saga of Adventure and Friendship. Krahn, Fernando (1935-), illus. LC 80-17379. (Illus.). 40 p. 1980, c.1978. (ISBN 0 14-005744-7). Penguin Books.
--Gustavus and Stop. Krahn, Fernando (1935-), illus. LC 60 13364. (Illus.). 40 p. 25cm. 1969. Dutton.
--Here Comes Alex Pumpernickel!. Krahn, Fernando (1935-), illus. LC 80-25531. (Illus.). 32 p. c.1981. (ISBN 0-316-50311-8). Little, Brown.
--Hildegarde & Maximillian. Krahn, Fernando (1935-), illus. LC 79-87170. (Illus.). 19cm. 41p. (ps-3). 1969. (ISBN 0-440-03634-8, Sey Lawr). (ISBN 0-440-03635-6, Sey Lawr). Delacorte Press.
--How Santa Claus Had a Long and Difficult Journey Delivering His Presents. Krahn, Fernando (1935-), illus. LC 72-122769. 28 l. (chiefly illus. 1970. Delacorte Press.
--Journeys of Sebastian: With an Appreciation by Alastair Reid. Krahn, Fernando (1935-), illus. LC 68-26131. 121 p. (chiefly illus. (part col.) 1968. (ISBN 0-440-04286-0). Delacorte Press.
--Little Love Story. LC 76-12427. p. cm. c.1976. (ISBN 0-397-31700-X). Lippincott.
--Mr. Top. Krahn, Fernando (1935-), illus. LC 83-1001. (Illus.). 32 p. 24cm. 1983. (ISBN 0-688-02368-1). Morrow.
--The Mystery of the Giant Footprints. Krahn, Fernando (1935-), illus. LC 76-50033. (Illus.). 32 p. 18cm. (ps-1). c.1977. (ISBN 0-525-35595-2). Dutton.
--Robot-Bot-Bot. Krahn, Fernando (1935-), illus. LC 78-21959. (ps-1). 1979. Dutton.
--Sebastian and the Mushroom. Krahn, Fernando (1935-), illus. LC 75-32918. (Illus.). 24 p. 16cm. c.1976. (ISBN 0-440-07694-3). (ISBN 0-440-07695-1). Delacorte Press/S. Lawrence.
--The Secret in the Dungeon. Krahn, Fernando (1935-), illus. LC 82-9595. p. cm. c.1982. (ISBN 0-89919-148-7). Clarion Books.
--The Self-Made Snowman. Krahn, Fernando (1935-), illus. LC 74-551. 32 p. (chiefly illus. 1974. (ISBN 0-397-31472-8). Lippincott.
--Sleep Tight, Alex Pumpernickel. Krahn, Fernando (1935-), illus. LC 81-20745. p. cm. 1982. (ISBN 0-316-50312-6). Little, Brown.
--Uncle Timothy's Traviata. Krahn, Fernando (1935-), illus. LC 67-19776. (Illus.). 1 v. (unpaged. 1967. Delacorte Press.
--What Is a Man?. Krahn, Fernando (1935-), illus. LC 77-182238. (Illus.). 62 p. 22cm. 1972. Delacorte Press.
--Who's Seen the Scissors?. Krahn, Fernando (1935-), illus. LC 74-26857. (Illus.). 32 p. (ps-1). 1975. Dutton.

Krahn, Fernando (1935-) & Krahn, Maria De La Luz
--The First Peko-Neko Bird. Krahn, Fernando (1935-), illus. LC 74-84140. (Illus.). 46 p. 23cm. 1969. Simon and Schuster.
--The Life of Numbers. Krahn, Fernando (1935-), illus. LC 70-107271. (Illus.). 47 p. 1970. Simon and Schuster.

Krahn, Maria De La Luz, jt. auth. see Krahn, Fernando.

Krakemisides, Baron
--The Careless Chicken. Neilson, Harry B., illus. LC 26-2090. 47, 1 p. incl. col. front., illus. (part col.) 19 x 19 cm. 1924. F. Warne & Co., Ltd.

Kral, Brian
--Ransom of Red Chief. (Orig.). 1980. (ISBN 0-87602-227-1). Anchorage.

Kralenke, Robert W.
--Stand Like Stars: Four Case Histories from the Edgar Cayce Readings. 28p. (Orig.). 1st U.S. edition. 1970. (ISBN 0-87604-039-3). ARE Pr.

Kramer, ed.
--Ghostly Hand & Other Haunting Stories. (gr. 4-6). 1974. (ISBN 0-590-03044-2, Schol Pap). Schol Bk Serv.

Kramer, Aaron (1921-), ed.
--On Freedom's Side: An Anthology of American Poems of Protest. (gr. 7up). 1972. (ISBN 0-02-750950-8). Macmillan.

Kramer, Ann
--Ten Exciting Minutes. Lawyer, Cindy & Parmerter, Sue, illus. LC 74-11345. (Illus.). 36 p. 21cm. 1974. (ISBN 0-914912-00-3). Kramer Pub.

Kramer, Bettina Leonard (1918-)
--Cave Men of the Old Stone Age. Kramer, Harold V., illus. LC 56-13661. unpaged. illus. 22 x 26cm. 1955. Melmont Pub.

Kramer, Caroline, retold by
--Read-Aloud Nursery Tales. Erickson, Phoebe (1907-), illus. LC 57-7524. 63p. illus. 29cm. c.1957. (ISBN 0-394-80673-5). Random House.

Kramer, George, pseud., see Heyman, William.

Kramer, George, pseud. (1912-1971)
--Kid Battery. Heyman, William. Gregori, Leon (1919-), illus. LC 68-15061. (Illus.). 128 p. 21cm. 1968. Putnam.
The Left Hander. Heyman, William. Frame, Paul (1913-), illus. LC 61 16000. 155 p. illus. 21 cm. 1964. Putnam.

Kramer, Helen
--Caught Between. 1955. Friendship Press.

Kramer, Janice
--Christmas ABC Book. Pallarito, Don, illus. LC 65-22699. 1 v. (unpaged) col. illus. 26 cm. 1965. Concordia Pub. House.
--Donkey Daniel in Bethlehem. Kramer, Janice, illus. (Illus.). 32 full-color. 32p. (Orig.). (Arch Bks: Set 7). (ps-4). 1970. (ISBN 0-570-06053-2). Concordia.
--Donkey Daniel in Bethlehem. Kramer, Janice, illus. 1970. Lutheran Publications.
--Good Samaritan. Mathews, Sally, illus. LC 63-23369. (Illus.). (Arch Bks: Set 1). 1964. (ISBN 0-570-06000-1). Concordia.
--The Princess and the Baby. Kramer, Janice, illus. 1969. Lutheran Publications.
--The Rich Fool. Matthews, Sally, illus. LC 62-11615. unpaged. illus. 21cm. (Lantern books). c.1962. (ISBN 0-570-06004-4). Concordia Pub. House.
--Sir Abner & His Grape Pickers. Kramer, Janice, illus. (Illus.). 32 full color. 32p. (Orig.). (Arch Bks.: Set 7). (ps-4). 1970. (ISBN 0-570-06051-6). Concordia.
--Sir Abner and His Grape Pickers. Kramer, Janice, illus. 1970. Lutheran Publications.
--Unforgiving Servant. Mathews, Sally, illus. (Illus.). (Arch Bks: Set 5). (gr. 5). 1968. (ISBN 0-570-06035 4). Concordia.

Kramer, Kay
--Danny's Angel. Kramer, Kay, illus. LC 80-65656. (Illus.). 63 p. 21cm. c.1980. (ISBN 0-87793-203-4). Ave Maria Press.

Kramer, Mark
--Mother Walter and the Pig Tragedy. 1972. Borzoi Books.

Kramer, Nora (1896-1984), ed.
--The Cozy Hour Storybook. Weisgard, Leonard Joseph (1916-), illus. LC 60-5853. 63p. illus. 29cm. 1960. (ISBN 0-394-80705-7). Random House.
--The Grandma Moses Storybook. Moses, Anna Mary Robertson (1860-1961), illus. LC 61-7875. (With a Biographical Sketch of Grandma Moses, by Otto Kalir). 141p. illus. 33cm. 1961. Random House.
--Grimms' Fairy Tales. Repr. (Starbright Editions). (gr. 4-6). 1973. Schol Bk Serv.
--Nora Kramer's Storybook for Threes and Fours. N.D. Julian Messner, Inc.
--Storybook. Krush, Joe (1918-) & Krush, Beth (1918-), illus. LC 55-9860. 160p. illus. 24cm. 1955. Gilbert Press; Distributed by J. Messner.
--Storybook: The 2d Nora Kramer Storybook. Krush, Joe (1918-) & Krush, Beth (1918-), illus. LC 56-11468. 128p. illus. 25cm. 1956. Gilbert Press; Distributed by J. Messner.

Kramer, Walter Smith
--Treasure at Bar X. McCann, Gerald (1916-), illus. LC 55-10602. 140p. illus. 21cm. 1955. Dodd, Mead.

Kramer, William Albert (1900-) & Schmieding, Alfred (1888-), eds.
--Treasury of Christian Literature. LC 50-13968. vii. 508 p. illus. 23cm. 1949. Concordia Pub. House.

Kramnick, Isaac, ed. see Day, Thomas.

Kramon, Florence (1920-)
--Eugene and the New Baby. Bracke, Charles, illus. LC 67-19807. (Illus.). 31 p. 26cm. 1967. Follett.
--Eugene and the Policeman. Bracke, Charles, illus. LC 67-19811. (Illus.). 31 p. 26cm. 1967. Follett.
--Eugene, Pack a Grip. Bracke, Charles, illus. LC 67-19809. (Illus.). 31 p. 26cm. 1967. Follett.
--Hippolito and Eugene G. Bracke, Charles, illus. LC 67-19812. (Illus.). 31 p. 26cm. 1967. Follett.
--Nobody Looks at Eugene. Bracke, Charles, illus. LC 67-19808. (Illus.). 31 p. 26cm. 1967. Follett.
--Wallpaper for Eugene's Room. Bracke, Charles, illus. LC 67-19810. 31p. col. illus. 26cm. 1967. Follett.

Krantz, Hazel Newman (1920-)
--Freestyle for Michael. Geer, Charles Hand (1922-), illus. LC 64-16255. 159 p. illus. 22 cm. 1964. Vanguard Press.
--One Hundred Pounds of Popcorn. Geer, Charles Hand (1922-), illus. LC 61-15479. 126p. illus. 22cm. 1961. Vanguard Press.
--The Secret Raft. Geer, Charles Hand (1922-), illus. LC 65-17372. 190 p. illus., map (on lining paper) 22 cm. 1965. Vanguard Press.
--Tippy. LC 68-14335. 221 p. 22cm. 1968. Vanguard Press.

Krantz, Leif
--The Children in the Jungle. Loefgren, Ulf (1931-), illus. Risom, Ole, tr. LC 61-11089. unpaged. illus. 27cm. 1961. Golden Press.

Krantz, Leif & Lofgren, Ulf
--Children in the Water. LC 67-2710. (Illus.). 32 p. 29cm. 1967. Childrens Press.

Kranzler, George see Kranzler, George Gershon.

Kranzler, George Gershon (1916-)
--An Unusual Seder. N.D. P Shalom Publication Inc.
--At B.A.T.T. LC 80-132702. 156 p. 23cm. 1978. Merkos L'inyonei Chinuch.
--The Averted Threat. N.D. P Shalom Publications.
--Carpets from Baghdad. 16p. N.D. P Shalom Publications Inc.
--The Faded Mezzuazah. N.D. P Shalom Publication Inc.
--The Golden Shames. 8p. N.D. P Shalomk Publications Inc.
--The Golden Shoes, and Other Stories. Kleinman, Zalman, illus. LC 63-1981. (Illus.). 195 p. 23cm. c.1960. P. Feldheim.
--The Leather Boots. N.D. P Shalom Publication Inc.
--Selichoth Night. N.D. P Shalom Publication Inc.
--The Silver Matzoth. N.D. P Shalom Publication Inc.
--The Silver Mezzuzah. N.D. P Shalom Publication Inc.
--The Smithy of Burgwald. N.D. P Shalom Publication Inc.
--Yoshko the Dumbbell. (gr. 4-9). 1969. (ISBN 0-87306-126-8). Feldheim.

Kranzler, Gershon see Kranzler, George Gershon.

Krapesh, Patti, adapted by see Dickens, Charles John Huffam.

Krapohl, Kern, tr. see Ivo, Ledo.

Krapp, George Philip (1872-1934)
--Ben Bidwell: A Tale of the Old Frontier. Von Saltza, Phillip, illus. LC 27-5599. vii, 1, 312 p. illus. 19 cm. (His American Life Series). c.1927. Rand, McNally & Company.
--Fanton Farm: A Story of Country Life. Von Saltza, Phillip, illus. LC 27-12302. vii, 1, 178 p. illus. 19 cm. (His American Life Series). c.1927. Rand, McNally & Company.
--Inland Oceans: A Tale of the Great Lakes. Von Saltza, Phillip, illus. LC 27-12303. vii, 1, 178 p. illus., 19 cm. (His American Life Series). c.1927. Rand, McNally & Company.
--Kipwillie: A Story of City Life. Von Saltza, Phillip, illus. LC 27-123041. vii, 1, 166 p. illus. 19 cm. (His American life series). c.1927. Rand, McNally & Company.
--The Kitchen Porch. Grosvenor, Thelma Cudlipp, illus. LC 23-135661. 165 p. col. front., illus., col. plates. 21 cm. 1923. A. A. Knopf.
--Sixty Years Ago: A Tale of the Civil War. Von Saltza, Phillip, illus. LC 27-12371. vii, 1, 178 p. illus. 19 cm. (His American Life Series). c.1927. Rand, McNally & Company.
--Tales of True Knights. Pitz, Henry Clarence (1895-1976), illus. LC 21-15890. xvi p., 3 l. 3-317 p. front., plates. 20 cm. 1921. The Century Co.
--Tongo: A Tale of the Great Plains. Von Saltza, Phillip, illus. LC 27-13659. viii, 174 p. illus., pl. 18 cm. (His American Life Series). c.1927. Rand McNally & Company.

Krappe, Alexander H., tr. see Grimm, Jakob Ludwig Karl (1785-1863) & Grimm, Wilhelm Karl.

Krasilovsky, Jessica
--The Boy Who Spoke Chinese. Krasilovsky, Jessica, illus. LC 77-177280. (Illus.). 33 p. 20cm. 1972. Doubleday.

Krasilovsky, Phyllis (1926-)
--Benny's Flag. Mars, Witold Tadeusz J. (1912-), illus. LC 60-5801. (Illus.). unpaged. 26cm. 1960. World Pub. Co.
--The Cow Who Fell in the Canal. 1st ed. Spier, Peter Edward (1927-), illus. LC 56-8236. unpaged. illus. 22x27cm. c.1957. (ISBN 0-385-08096-4). Doubleday.
--The First Tulips in Holland. 1st ed. Schindler, Steven D., illus. LC 81-43109. (Illus.). 32 p. 34cm. c.1982. (ISBN 0-385-17463-2). Doubleday.
--The Girl Who Was a Cowboy. 1st ed. Szekeres, Cyndy (1933-), illus. LC 64-15863. (Illus.). 31 p. 20cm. 1965. Doubleday.
--L. C. Is the Greatest. LC 74-34345. 129 p. 21cm. 1975. (ISBN 0-8407-6422-7). T. Nelson.
--The Man Who Cooked for Himself. Funai, Mamoru R. (1932-), illus. LC 81-16904. (Illus.). 42 p. 22cm. c.1981. (ISBN 0-8193-1075-1). (ISBN 0-8193-1076-X). Parents Magazine Press.
--The Man Who Didn't Wash His Dishes. 1st ed. Cooney, Barbara (1917-), illus. LC 50-8726. (Illus.). 33 p. 26cm. (Junior books). 1950. Doubleday.
--The Man Who Entered a Contest. 1st ed. Salzman, Yuri, illus. LC 79-3112. (Illus.). 64 p. 24cm. (Reading-on-my-own book). c.1980. (ISBN 0-385-13351-0). (ISBN 0-385-13352-9). Doubleday.
--The Man Who Tried to Save Time. Sewall, Marcia (1935-), illus. LC 77-74304. (Illus.). 64 p. 24cm. (Reading-on-my-own book). c.1979. (ISBN 0-385-12999-8). Doubleday.
The Popular Girls Club. Hyman, Trina Schart (1939-), illus. LC 72-80190. (Illus.). 47 p. 22cm. 1972. (ISBN 0-671-65196-X). Simon and Schuster.
--Scaredy Cat. MacKnight, Ninon (1908-), illus. Ninon, pseud. LC 59-5985. 23cm. (gr. k-2). 1959. (ISBN 0-02-750930-3). Macmillan.
--The Shy Little Girl. Hyman, Trina Schart (1939-), illus. LC 73-98519. (Illus.). 31 p. 24cm. 1970. Houghton Mifflin.
--Susan Sometimes. Giventer, Abbi, illus. LC 62-17335. (Illus.). 31 p. 19cm. 1962. Macmillan.
--The Very Little Boy. MacKnight, Ninon (1908-), illus. Ninon, pseud. LC 62-7276. (Illus.). unpaged. 23cm. 1962. Doubleday.
--Very Little Girl. MacKnight, Ninon (1908-), illus. Ninon, pseud. LC 53-5289. 23cm. (gr. k-1). 1953. Doubleday.
--The Very Tall Little Girl. 1st ed. Cole, Olivia H. H., illus. LC 69-15207. (Illus.). 30 p. 20cm. 1969. Doubleday.

Kraska, Edie
--Toys & Tales from Grandmother's Attic. (gr. 5 up). 1979. (ISBN 0-395-27807-4). (ISBN 0-395-28582-8). HM.

Kraske, Robert
--America the Beautiful: Stories of Patriotic Songs. LC 73-183845. (Illus.). 96p. (American Democracy Ser.). (gr. 3-6). 1972. (ISBN 0-8116-6506-2). Garrard.
--The Sea Robbers. LC 77 76139. 147 p. 21cm. c.1977. (ISBN 0-15-271170-8). Harcourt Brace Jovanovich.
--The Twelve Million Dollar Note. (gr. 4-6). 1979. (ISBN 0-590-12110-3, Schol Pap). Scholastic Inc.

Krasnov, Petr Nikolaevich (1869-)
--Yermak the Conqueror. Siegel, William (1905-), illus. Ruhl, Zinaida, Mrs. & Ruhl, Arthur Brown (1876-), trs. LC 30-27714. xi, 206 p., 1 l. incl. col. front. illus., plates. 24 cm. c.1930. Duffield and Company.

Kratz, Marilyn
--The Garden Book. Talarczyk, June, illus. LC 77-79596. 28 p. illus. (part col.) 18 x 23cm. c.1969. T. S. Denison.
--Whose Garden?. Edelson, Wendy, illus. LC 76-10047. (Illus.). 32 p. 17cm. c.1976. (ISBN 0-8178-5502-5). Harvey House.

Kraus, Bruce R. (1954-)
--According to Mork: The World As Mork Sees It. LC 80-23175. p. cm. c.1980. (ISBN 0-671-41486-0). Wanderer Books.
--Encyclopedia Galactica. LC 79-4649. p. cm. c.1979. (ISBN 0-525-61039-1). Windmill Books.

Kraus, Joanna Halpert (1937-)
--The Ice Wolf. 1967. New Plays.
--Mean to Be Free. 1968. New Plays.
--Vasalisa. 1973. New Plays.

Kraus, Pam, ed.
--A Treasury of Windmill Books: Selections from Twenty One of the Best-Loved Windmill Books. Windmill Books LC 81-12998. p. cm. 1981. (ISBN 0-671-44406-9). Windmill Books : Simon & Schuster.

Kraus, Pam, jt. auth. see Kraus, Robert.

Kraus, Pam, ed. see Gruelle, John Barton.

Kraus, Robert see Hippopotamus, Eugene H., pseud.

Kraus, Robert see Tubby, I. M., pseud.

Kraus, Robert, jt. auth. see Eicke, Edna.

Kraus, Robert, jt. auth. see Partch, Virgil Franklin, II.

Kraus, Robert (1925-), ed. see Smith, Dennis.

Kraus, Robert (1925-)
--All the Mice Came. Kraus, Robert (1925-), illus. LC 55-8589. unpaged. illus. 20 x 26 cm. 1967, c.1955. Harper.

Krieger, David L

--Too Many Stones. Krieger, David L., illus. LC 71-120946. (Illus.). 47 p. 26cm. 1970. Young Scott Books.

Kringle, Kriss

--Christmas Rhymes and Stories. LC 17-1328. (Illus.). 25cm. N.D. White, Stokes & Allen.

--Mother Goose Christmas. Satterlee, Walter, illus. (Illus.). N.D. White, Stokes & Allen.

Krinsley, Jeanette

--The Cow Went Over the Mountain. Rojankovsky, Feodor Stepanovich (1891-1970), illus. (Illus.). (ps-2). 1963. (ISBN 0-307-60576-0, Golden Pr). Western Pub.

Kripke, Dorothy Karp

--Debbie in Dreamland. Giacalone, Bill, illus. (gr. 2-5). 1960. (ISBN 0-685-06929-X). Bloch.

--Debbie in Dreamland: Her Holiday Adventures. Giacalone, Bill, illus. LC 60-165888. 54p. col. illus. 25cm. c.1960. National Women's League of the United Synagogue of America.

Kriskovic, Josip

--Milan and His Runaway Uncle. Kicevac-Popovic, Bosiljka, illus. Heppell, Muriel, tr. LC 73-102379. (Illus.). 128 p. 22cm. (Stackpole window books). 1970. Stackpole Books.

Kristensen, Evald Tang, 1843-1929 see Bay, Jens Christian.

Kristof, Jane (1932-)

--Steal Away Home. Harris, Aurand (1915-), adapted by. 1972. Anchorage Press.

--Steal Away Home. 1st ed. Mars, Witold Tadeusz J. (1912-), illus. LC 78-84168. (Illus.). 127 p. 22cm. 1969. Bobbs-Merrill.

Kristoffersen, Eva Margaret Stiegelmeyer (1901-)

--A Bee in Her Bonnet. Sewell, Helen Moore (1896-1957), illus. LC 44-4721. 4 p. l., 168 p. incl. front., illus. 20 1/2 cm. 1944. Thomas Y. Crowell Company.

--Cyclone Goes a-Viking: A Story of Norway. Rev ed. Collin, Hedvig, illus. LC 39-22931. 92, 2 p. incl. col. front., illus. (part col.) 24 cm. ("Junior press books."). 1939. A. Whitman & Co.

--Hans Christian of Elsinore. Rev ed. Collin, Hedvig, illus. LC 37-23779. 80 p. illus. (part col.) 26 cm. ("Junior press books."). 1937. A. Whitman & Co.

--The Merry Matchmakers: A Story of Sweden. Collin, Hedvig, illus. LC 40-32144. 95 p. col. front., illus. (incl. music, part col.) 24 x 19 cm. 1940. A. Whitman & Co.

Kritz, Reuven

--Little Sister. N.D. Vantage Press Inc.

Krivin, Felix

--Greatgrandmother Universe. Romadin, M, illus. Yankovsky, Eugene, tr. from Rus. (Illus.). (ps-3). 1983. (ISBN 0-8285-2431-9, Pub. by Malysh Pubs USSR). Imported Pubns.

Krock, Helen L, illus.

--Honey Bunny and Her Friends. LC 52-1975. unpaged. illus. 21 cm. (Easy-to-read book, 4206). 1952. Saalfield Pub. Co.

Krockover, Gerald H. & Krockover, Sharon D.

--Uncle Bill's Ice Cream Shop. 1978. (ISBN 0-533-03191-5). Vantage.

Krockover, Sharon D., jt. auth. see Krockover, Gerald H.

Kroeber, Theodora Kracaw (1897-1979)

--A Green Christmas. Larrecq, John Maurice (1926-1980), illus. LC 67-263042. 1v. (unpaged) col. illus. 20 x 21 cm. 1967. Parnassus Pr.

Kroeber, Theodora Kracaw (1897-1979) & Tait, Douglas (1944-)

--Carrousel. LC 77-2003. (Illus.). 91 p. 22cm. 1977. (ISBN 0-689-30589-3). Atheneum.

Kroeker, Kate F.

--New Fairy Tales from Brentano. Gould, F. Carruthers, illus. 1905. A C Armstrong & Sons.

Kroeker, Kate F., tr. see Brentano, Clemens Maria.

Kroft, Helen D.

--The Adventures of the Grey Cats. LC 55-1531. 23cm. 30p. 1954. Comet Press Books.

Krogman, Dane & Holelson, Doug

--Skeleton Boy: The Nuclear Hero. (Illus.). 80p. 1982. (ISBN 0-910519-00-5). Daneco Pubns.

Krohn, Gretchen & Johnson, John Norton

--The Scales of the Silver Fish. Haring, Mary Whitson, illus. LC 28-21572. 214, 1 p. front., plates. 21 cm. c.1928. The Bobbs-Merrill Company.

Krohn, Josephine Elliott, Mrs.

--Old King Cole. Mackay, Constance D'arey, intro. by. LC 25-10874. xiv p., 1 l., 17-208 p. 20 cm. (On cover: The Drama league junior play series). c.1925. George H. Doran Company.

Krohn, Julius Leopold Frederik, jt. auth. see Topelius, Zakarias.

Krohn, W. O.

--Little Farmers. (Illus.). 128p. (The Sunbeam Books). N.D. The Reilly & Britton Co.

Kroll, Edite, tr. see Davidson, Sandra Calder.

Kroll, Edite, tr. see Richter, Hans Peter.

Kroll, Edite, tr. see Ruck-Pauquet, Gina.

Kroll, Edite, tr. see Waechter, Friedrich Karl & Eilert, Bernd.

Kroll, Francis Lynde (1904-1973)

--Top Hand. Abel, Raymond (1911-), illus. LC 65-12131. 120 p. 21 cm. 1965. D. McKay Co.

--Young Crow Raider. Geer, Charles Hand (1922-), illus. LC 57-13579. 187p. illus. 20cm. (Young heroes library). c.1954. Grosset & Dunlap.

--Young Crow Raider. Geer, Charles Hand (1922-), illus. LC 54-10746. 187p. illus. 21cm. (Young heroes library). 1954. Lantern Press.

--Young Medicine Man. Geer, Charles Hand (1922-), illus. LC 56-7625. 189p. illus. 22cm. (Young heroes library). 1956. Lantern Press.

--Young Sand Hills Cowboy. Geer, Charles Hand (1922-), illus. (Young Heroes Library). N.D. Grosset & Dunlap.

--Young Sand Hills Cowboy. Geer, Charles Hand (1922-), illus. LC 53-55432. 189p. illus. 21cm. 1953. (ISBN 0-8313-0073-6). Lantern Press.

--Young Sioux Warrior. Geer, Charles Hand (1922-), illus. (Young Heroes Library). N.D. Grosset & Dunlap.

--Young Sioux Warrior. Geer, Charles Hand (1922-), illus. LC 52-9192. 189 p. illus. 21 cm. 1952. (ISBN 0-8313-0074-4). Lantern Press.

Kroll, Harry Harrison (1888-)

--Summer Gold. LC 55-8088. 176p. 22cm. 1955. Westminster Press.

Kroll, Steven (1941-)

--Amanda and the Giggling Ghost. Gackenbach, Dick, illus. LC 79-28379. (Illus.). 40 p. c.1980. (ISBN 0-8234-0408-0). Holiday House.

--Are You Pirates?. 1st ed. Hafner, Marylin (1925-), illus. LC 80-27621. (Illus.). 45 p. c.1982. (ISBN 0-394-83936-6). (ISBN 0-394-93936-0). Pantheon Books.

--The Big Bunny and the Easter Eggs. 1st ed. Stevens, Janet, illus. LC 81-11613. (Illus.). 32 p. 24cm. c.1982. (ISBN 0-8234-0436-6). Holiday House.

--The Biggest Pumpkin Ever. Bassett, Jeni Crisler, illus. LC 83-18492. (Illus.). 32p. (ps-3). 1984. (ISBN 0-8234-0505-2). (ISBN 0-8234-0505-2). Holiday.

--Breaking Camp. LC 85-42956. 169 p. 22cm. c.1985. (ISBN 0-02-751170-7). Macmillan.

--The Candy Witch. Hafner, Marylin (1925-), illus. LC 79-10141. (Illus.). 32 p. 22cm. c.1979. (ISBN 0-8234-0359-9). Holiday House.

--Fat Magic. De Paola, Tomie, pseud. (1934-), illus. De Paola, Thomas Anthony. 25cm. 323p. c.1978. (ISBN 0-8234-0327-0). Holiday House.

--Friday the Thirteenth. Gackenbach, Dick, illus. LC 80-28769. (Illus.). 32p. (gr. k-3). 1981. (ISBN 0-8234-0392-0). Holiday.

--Giant Journey. Chorao, Ann McKay Sproat (1936-), illus. LC 80-20512. (Illus.). 32 p. c.1981. (ISBN 0-8234-0381-5). Holiday House.

--The Goat Parade. Kirk, Tim, illus. LC 82-10604. (Illus.). 40 p. 23cm. c.1982. (ISBN 0-8193-1099-9). Parents Magazine Press.

--The Hand-Me-Down Doll. 1st ed. Ness, Evaline Michelow, Mrs. (1911-), illus. LC 83-4394. (Illus.). 32p. (gr. k-3). 1983. (ISBN 0-8234-0495-1). Holiday.

--Happy Mother's Day. Hafner, Marylin (1925-), illus. LC 83-18498. (Illus.). 32 p. 24cm. c.1985. (ISBN 0-8234-0504-4). Holiday House.

--If I Could Be My Grandmother. McCrady, Lady (1951-), illus. LC 77-4321. (Illus.). 32 p. c.1977. (ISBN 0-394-83554-9). (ISBN 0-394-93554-3). Pantheon Books.

--Is Milton Missing?. Gackenbach, Dick, illus. LC 75-4586. (Illus.). 32p. (ps-3). 1975. (ISBN 0-8234-0261-4). Holiday.

--Loose Tooth. Tusa, Tricia, illus. LC 83-49008. (Illus.). 32p. (ps-3). 1984. (ISBN 0-8234-0518-4). (ISBN 0-8234-0518-4). Holiday.

--Monster Birthday. Kendrick, Dennis, illus. LC 79-16203. (Illus.). 32 p. 23cm. c.1980. (ISBN 0-8234-0369-6). Holiday House.

--Mrs. Claus's Crazy Christmas. Wallner, John C. (1945-), illus. LC 84-25218. (Illus.). 32 p. 21cm. c.1985. Holiday House.

--One Tough Turkey. Wallner, John C. (1945-), illus. LC 82-2925. (Illus.). 32p. (ps-3). 1982. (ISBN 0-8234-0457-9). Holiday.

--Otto. Delaney, Ned, pseud. (1951-), illus. Delaney, Thomas Nicholas III. LC 82-19042. p. cm. 1983. (ISBN 0-8193-1105-7). (ISBN 0-8193-1106-5). Parents Magazine Press.

--Pigs in the House. Kirk, Tim, illus. LC 83-13310. (Illus.). 48p. (ps-2). 1983. (ISBN 0-8193-1111-1). Parents.

--Santa's Crash-Bang Christmas. De Paola, Tomie, pseud. (1934-), illus. De Paola, Thomas Anthony. 26cm. 32p. 1978. (ISBN 0-8234-0302-5). Holiday House.

--Sleepy Ida and Other Nonsense Poems. Chwast, Seymour (1931-), illus. LC 76-43101. (Illus.). 29 p. 21cm. c.1977. (ISBN 0-394-83252-3). (ISBN 0-394-93252-8). Pantheon Books.

--Space Cats. Henstra, Friso (1928-), illus. LC 78-15164. (Illus.). 48 p. 21cm. c.1979. (ISBN 0-8234-0339-4). Holiday House.

--T. J. Folger, Thief. Morrison, Bill (1935-), illus. LC 77-24575. (Illus.). 40 p. 21cm. c.1978. (ISBN 0-8234-0313-0). Holiday House.

--Take It Easy!. LC 82-20937. 144p. (gr. 7 up). 1983. (ISBN 0-590-07833-X, Four Winds). (ISBN 0-590-07833-X). Scholastic Inc.

--Toot! Toot!. Rockwell, Anne F. (1934-), illus. LC 82-9356. p. cm. c.1983. (ISBN 0-8234-0471-4). Holiday House.

--The Tyrannosaurus Game. De Paola, Tomie, pseud. (1934-), illus. De Paola, Thomas Anthony. LC 75-37078. (Illus.). 39 p. 20cm. c.1976. (ISBN 0-8234-0275-4). Holiday House.

--Woof, Woof!. Rubel, Nicole (1953-), illus. LC 82-9776. (Illus.). 32 p. c.1982. (ISBN 0-8037-9448-7). (ISBN 0-8037-9449-5). Dial Press.

Kroll, Steven (1941-) & Hormann, Toni

--Dirty Feet. LC 80-17570. (Illus.). 46 p. 24cm. c.1980. (ISBN 0-8193-1035-2). (ISBN 0-8193-1036-0). Parents Magazine Press.

Kroll, Steven (1941-) & Oechsli, Kelly (1918-)

--Gobbledygook. LC 76-41789. (Illus.). 32 p. 23cm. c.1977. (ISBN 0-8234-0293-2). Holiday House.

Kromer, Helen

--Caught Between. (gr. 9 up). 1955. Friend Pr.

Kronberg, Ruthild, jt. auth. see Ulmer, Louise.

Kronberg, Ruthilde

--Sungari. Schultz, Wendy, illus. (Illus.). 33p. N.D. (ISBN 0-86629-038-9). Sunrise MO.

Kronheim & Co

--Pussy's Picture Book. LC 76-376987. (Illus.). 113 p. 19cm. N.D. Routledge.

Kronheim & Co, illus.

--Aladdin. (Illus.). (Routledge's Threepenny Toy Bks.). N.D. George Routledge & Sons.

--Blue-Beard. (Illus.). (Routledge's Threepenny Toy Bks.). N.D. George Routledge & Sons.

--Childhood's Favorites. (Illus.). (Aunt Louisa Quarto Toy Books). N.D. Worthington & Company.

--Children's Gift. (Illus.). (Aunt Louisa Quarto Toy Books). N.D. Worthington Company.

--Cinderella, 1 of 4 vols. (Aunt Louisa's London Toy Books Ser.). N.D. R. Worthington.

--Colored Album for Children. (Illus.). N.D. George Routledge & Sons.

--Famous Horses and Dogs. (Illus.). (Aunt Louisa Quarto Toy Books). N.D. Worthington Company.

--Forty Thieves. (Illus.). (Routledge's Threepenny Toy Bks.). N.D. George Routledge & Sons.

--Jack the Giant-Killer. (Illus.). (Routledge's Threepenny Toy Bks.). N.D. George Routledge & Sons.

--Little Bo-Peep, 1 of 4 Vols. (Aunt Louisa's London Toy Books Ser.). N.D. R. Worthington.

--National Nursery Album. N.D. R. Worthington.

--Old Mother Hubbard, 1 of 4 Vols. (Aunt Louisa's London Toy Books Ser.). N.D. R. Wohrtington.

--Old Tales for the Young. LC 32-29781. 1 p. l., 391, 1 p. col. front., 5 col. pl. 17 cm. N.D. G. Routledge and Sons.

--Our Favorites. (Illus.). (Aunt Louisa Quarto Toy Books). N.D. Worthington Company.

--Red Riding Hood, 1 of 4 Vols. (Aunt Louisa's London Toy Books Ser.). N.D. R. Wohrtington.

--Sleeping Beauty. (Illus.). (Routledge's Threepenny Toy Bks.). N.D. George Routledge & Sons.

--Tom Thumb. (Illus.). (Routledge's Threepenny Toy Bks.). N.D. George Routledge & Sons.

--Welcome Guest. (Illus.). (Aunt Louisa Quarto Toy Books). N.D. Worthington Company.

Kronheim & Co & Dalziel, Edward (1817-1905), illus.

--Jack Horner's Picture Book. (Illus.). N.D. George Routledge & Sons.

Kronheim & Co. & Leighton Bros., illus.

--Aesop's Fables. (Routledge's New Toy-Bks.). N.D. George Routledge & Sons.

--Aladdin. (Routledge's New Toy-Bks.). N.D. George Routledge & Sons.

--Alphabet of Fairy Tales. (Routledge's New Toy-Bks.). N.D. George Routledge & Sons.

--The Babes in the Wood. (Routledge's New Toy-Bks.). N.D. George Routledge & Sons.

--Baby. (Routledge's New Toy-Bks.). N.D. George Routledge & Sons.

--Beauty and the Beast. (Routledge's New Toy-Bks.). N.D. George Routledge & Sons.

--The Cat's Tea Party. (Illus.). (Routledge's New Toy-Books). N.D. George Routledge & Sons.

--Cinderella. (Routledge's New Toy-Bks.). N.D. George Routledge & Sons.

--Cock-Sparrow. (Routledge's New Toy-Bks.). N.D. George Routledge & Sons.

--Dash and the Ducklings. (Routledge's New Toy-Bks.). N.D. George Routledge & Sons.

--Dog's Dinner Party. (Routledge's New Toy-Bks.). N.D. George Routledge & Sons.

--The Fair One with the Golden Locks. (Routledge's New Toy-Bks.). N.D. George Routledge & Sons.

--The Five Little Pigs. (Routledge's New Toy-Bks.). N.D. George Routledge & Sons.

--The Frog Prince. (Routledge's New Toy-Bks.). N.D. George Routledge & Sons.

--Gingerbread. (Routledge's New Toy-Bks.). N.D. George Routledge & Sons.

--Goody Two-Shoes. (Routledge's New Toy-Bks.). N.D. George Routledge & Sons.

--Henny Penny. (Routledge's New Toy-Bks.). N.D. George Routledge & Sons.

--History of Tom Thumb. (Routledge's New Toy-Bks.). N.D. George Routledge & Sons.

--Jack and the Bean-Stalk. (Routledge's New Toy-Bks.). N.D. George Routledge & Sons.

--Jack the Giant-Killer. (Routledge's New Toy-Bks.). N.D. George Routledge & Sons.

--The Lion's Reception. (Routledge's New Toy-Bks.). N.D. George Routledge & Sons.

--Little Ann and Her Mamma. (Routledge's New Toy-Bks.). N.D. George Routledge & Sons.

--Little Dog Trusty. (Routledge's New Toy-Bks.). N.D. George Routledge & Sons.

--Little Red Riding Hood. (Routledge's New Toy-Bks.). N.D. George Routledge & Sons.

--Mother Hubbard and Cock Robin. (Routledge's New Toy-Bks.). N.D. George Routledge & Sons.

--My Mother. (Routledge's New Toy-Bks.). N.D. George Routledge & Sons.

--New Tale of a Tub. (Routledge's New Toy-Bks.). N.D. George Routledge & Sons.

--Old Nursery Rhymes with Old Tunes. (Routledge's New Toy-Bks.). N.D. George Routledge & Sons.

--Peacock at Home. (Routledge's New Toy-Bks.). N.D. George Routledge & Sons.

--The Pet Lamb. (Routledge's New Toy-Bks.). N.D. George Routledge & Sons.

--Puss in Boots. (Routledge's New Toy-Bks.). N.D. George Routledge & Sons.

--Queer Characters. (Routledge's New Toy-Bks.). N.D. George Routledge & Sons.

--Reynard the Fox. (Routledge's New Toy-Bks.). N.D. George Routledge & Sons.

--The Robin's Christmas Song. (Routledge's New Toy-Bks.). N.D. George Routledge & Sons.

--Robinson Crusoe. (Routledge's New Toy-Bks.). N.D. George Routledge & Sons.

--The Sleeping Beauty in the Wood. (Routledge's New Toy-Bks.). N.D. George Routledge & Sons.

--The Three Bears. (Routledge's New Toy-Bks.). N.D. George Routledge & Sons.

--The Three Kittens. (Routledge's New Toy-Bks.). N.D. George Routledge & Sons.

--Tittums and Fido. (Routledge's New Toy-Bks.). N.D. George Routledge & Sons.

--The Ugly Duckling. (Routledge's New Toy-Bks.). N.D. George Routledge & Sons.

--The White Cat. (Routledge's New Toy-Bks.). N.D. George Routledge & Sons.

--The Yellow Dwarf. (Routledge's New Toy-Bks.). N.D. George Routledge & Sons.

Kronzek, Allan Z.

--The Secrets of Alkazar: A Book of Magic. Huffman, Tom, illus. LC 80-11436. (Illus.). 128p. (gr. 7 up). 1980. (ISBN 0-590-07425-3, Four Winds). Scholastic Inc.

Kropp, Paul Stephan (1948-)

--Baby, Baby. Gulland, Sandra, ed. Collins, Heather, illus. LC 82-12931. p. cm. (Encounters Ser.). c.1983. (ISBN 0-88436-962-5). EMC Pub.

--Burn Out. Gulland, Sandra, ed. Collins, Heather, illus. LC 81-5357. p. cm. (Encounters Ser.). 1981. (ISBN 0-88436-815-7). EMC Pub.

--Dead on. Collins, Heather, illus. LC 81-7871. p. cm. (Encounters series.). (Encounters Ser.). 1981. (ISBN 0-88436-816-5). EMC Pub.

--Dirt Bike. Gulland, Sandra, ed. Collins, Heather, illus. LC 81-5367. p. cm. (Encounters Ser.). 1981. (ISBN 0-88436-817-3). EMC Pub.

--Dope Deal. Collins, Heather LC 81-9766. p. cm. (Encounters Ser.). 1982. (ISBN 0-88436-818-1). EMC Pub.

--Fair Play. Gulland, Sandra, ed. Collins, Heather, illus. LC 81-5366. p. cm. (Encounters Ser.). 1981. (ISBN 0-88436-819-X). EMC Pub.

--Gang War. Gulland, Sandra, ed. McCusker, Paul, illus. LC 82-12928. p. cm. (Encounters Ser.). c.1983. (ISBN 0-88436-963-3). EMC Pub.

--Hot Cars. Collins, Heather, illus. LC 81-5358. p. cm. (Encounters Ser.). 1981. (ISBN 0-88436-820-3). EMC Pub.

--No Way. Gulland, Sandra, ed. Collins, Heather, illus. LC 81-5557. p. cm. (Encounters Ser.). 1981. (ISBN 0-88436-820-3). EMC Pub.

--Runaway. Collins, Heather, illus. LC 81-5356. p. cm. (Encounters Ser.). 1981. (ISBN 0-88436-822-X). EMC Pub.

--Snow Ghost. Gulland, Sandra, ed. Summers, Mark, illus. LC 82-12930. p. cm. (Encounters Ser.). c.1983. (ISBN 0-88436-964-1). EMC Pub.

--Wild One. Gulland, Sandra, ed. LC 82-12929. p. cm. (Encounters Ser.). c.1983. EMC Pub.

--Wilted: A Novel. LC 79-4592. 111 p. 22cm. c.1980. (ISBN 0-698-20493-X). Coward, McCann & Geoghegan.

Kroupa, Melanie, ed. see Callen, Larry.

Kroupa, Melanie, ed. see Garland, Sarah.

--Dr. Dick. Siebel, Fritz (1913-), illus. LC 61-12076. 63 p.illus. 19 cm. 1962. (ISBN 0-06-023506-3). Harper.
--Gas Station Gus. Domanska, Janina, illus. LC 61-12075. 63 p. illus. 19 cm. 1962. Harper.
--Junket Is Nice. Kunhardt, Dorothy Meserve, Mrs. (1901-1979), illus. LC 33-24081. 63 p. col. illus. 18 x 26 cm. c.1933. Harcourt, Brace and Company.
--Kitty's New Doll. McQueen, Lucinda, illus. LC 82-83786. (Illus.). 20 p. 24cm. (A Golden Storytime Book). c.1984. (ISBN 0-307-61965-6). (ISBN 0-307-11965-3). Golden Book.
--Little Ones. Wiese, Kurt (1887-1974), illus. LC 35-21956. 78, 1 p. col. illus. 26 cm. 1935. The Viking Press.
--Little Peewee: Or, Now Open the Box. Miller, John Parr (1913-), illus. LC 48-6657. 21cm. 42p. (Little golden library, 52). N.D. Simon and Schuster.
--Little Peewee, the Circus Dog. Miller, John Parr (1913-), illus. (Little Golden Book: 52). 1948. Simon and Schuster.
--Lucky Mrs. Ticklefeather. Rev ed. Miller, John Parr (1913-), illus. LC 35-15460. 63 p. col. illus. 18 x 26 cm. c.1935. Harcourt, Brace and Company.
--Lucky Mrs. Ticklefeather. Miller, John Parr (1913-), illus. LC 51-13830. unpaged. illus. 21 cm. (Little golden library, 122). 1951. Simon and Schuster.
--Lucky Mrs. Ticklefeather and Other Funny Stories. Williams, Garth Montgomery (1912-) & Miller, John Parr, illus. 72p. (ps-2). 1973. (ISBN 0-307-15781-4, Golden Pr). (ISBN 0-307-65781-7). Western Pub.
--Lucky Mrs. Ticklefeather and Other Funny Stories: The Best of Dorothy Kunhardt. Kunhardt, Dorothy Meserve, Mrs. (1901-1979), illus. LC 73-76966. (Illus.). 69 p. 31cm. 1973. Golden Press.
--More Please. Kunhardt, Dorothy Meserve, Mrs. (1901-1979), illus. 1946. Simon and Shuster.
--Now Open the Box. Kunhardt, Dorothy Meserve, Mrs. (1901-1979), illus. LC 34-314443. 61 p. col. illus. 18 x 26 cm. c.1934. Harcourt, Brace and Company.
--Once There Was A Little Boy. Sewell, Helen Moore (1896-1957), illus. N.D. Viking Press.
--Pat the Bunny. Kunhardt, Dorothy Meserve, Mrs. (1901-1979), illus. LC 40-33936. (Illus.). 14cm. 18p. 1940. Simon and Shuster.
--Pat the Bunny. Kunhardt, Dorothy Meserve, Mrs. (1901-1979), illus. (Illus.). (A Golden Touch & Feel Bk). (gr. k-3). 1962. (ISBN 0-307-12000-7, Golden Pr). Western Pub.
--Pudding Is Nice. Kunhardt, Dorothy Meserve, Mrs. (1901-1979), illus. LC 75-19948. 64p. Orig. Title: Junket Is Nice. (gr. 1 up). 1975. (ISBN 0-912846-18-6). (ISBN 0-912846-12-7). Bookstore Pr.
--Rennet Dessert Is Nice. Kunhardt, Dorothy Meserve, Mrs. (1901-1979), illus. LC 49-348042. 63 p. col. illus. 15 x 21 cm. c.1947. Forbes Lithograph Mfg. Co.
--The Telephone Book. Kunhardt, Dorothy Meserve, Mrs. (1901-1979), illus. 1942. Simon and Shuster.
--Tickle the Pig. Kunhardt, Dorothy Meserve, Mrs. (1901-1979), illus. 1965. Golden Press.
--Tiny Animal Stories. Williams, Garth Montgomery (1912-), illus. (Tiny Golden Book). 1948. Simon and Schuster.
--Tiny Golden Library. Williams, Garth Montgomery (1912-), illus. (Illus.). 24p. ea. (Tiny Golden Library Series). (gr. k-3). 1968. (ISBN 0-307-15582-X, Golden Pr). Western Pub.
--Tiny Golden Library: A Dozen Animal Nonsense Tales. Williams, Garth Montgomery (1912-), illus. (Illus.). 24p. (gr. 4-8). 1980. (ISBN 0-307-13618-3, Golden Pr). Western Pub.
--Tiny Nonsense Stories. Williams, Garth Montgomery (1912-), illus. (Tiny Golden Book). 1949. Simon and Schuster.
--Wise Old Aard-Vark. Kunhardt, Dorothy Meserve, Mrs. (1901-1979), illus. LC 36-307084. 62, 1 p. illus. 18 x 26 cm. 1936. The Viking Press.

Kunhardt, Edith T.
--Martha's House. Bracken, Carolyn, illus. LC 81-83005. (Illus.). 24 p. 16cm. (First little golden books). c.1982. (ISBN 0-307-10120-7). (ISBN 0-307-68120-3). Golden Press.
--The Mouse Family's New Home. Dawson, Diane, illus. LC 81-81325. (Illus.). 12 p. 21cm. (Little golden sniff it book). c.1981. (ISBN 0-307-13204-8). Golden Press.
--Mrs. Brisby's Remembering Game: The Secret of NIMH. Chandler, Jean (1927-), illus. (Illus.). 16p. (Little Golden Sniff It Bks.). (gr. 2-5). N.D. (ISBN 0-307-13209-9, Golden Pr). Western Pub.
--The Race to Pearl Peak: A Popeye Adventure. Campana, Manny, illus. (Illus.). 24p. (Golden Look-Look Bks.). (ps-2). 1982. (ISBN 0-307-61873-0, Golden Pr). (ISBN 0-307-11873-8). Western Pub.

Kunhardt, Philip Bradish, Jr. (1928-)
--Hats Make You Happy. LC 57-11536. unpaged. illus. 22cm. c.1957. Sterling Pub. Co.

Kunic, Debbie
--Cats & Kittens Coloring Album. Warner, Rita, illus. (Illus.). text. 32p. 1977. (ISBN 0-912300-80-9). Troubador Pr.

Kunnas, Mauri
--The Nighttime Book. Kunnas, Mauri, illus. 1985. Crown Pub.
--Santa Claus and His Elves. Kunnas, Tarja & Kunnas, Mauri, illus. LC 82-6043. (Illus.). 48 p. 30cm. c.1982. (ISBN 0-517-54781-3). Harmony Books.

Kunnas, Mauri & Kunnas, Tarja
--Santa Claus and His Elves. Kunnas, Mauri & Kunnas, Tarja, illus. LC 85-466. p. cm. 1985. (ISBN 0-517-55818-1). Crown Publishers.

Kunnas, Tarja, jt. auth. see Kunnas, Mauri.

Kunos, Ignacz (1862-1945), compiled by.
--Forty-four Turkish Fairy Tales. Pogany, Willy (1882-1955), illus. Kunos, Ignacz (1882-), tr. 25cm. 362p. 1914. T. Y. Crowell Co.
--Turkish Fairy and Folk Tales. Bain, tr. (Illus.). N.D. (ISBN 0-8446-0751-7). Peter Smith Publisher, Inc.
--Turkish Fairy Tales and Folk Tales. Levetus, Celia, illus. LC 76-80991. (Illus.). x, 275 p. 22cm. 1969. (ISBN 0-486-22344-2). Dover Publications.

Kuntz, Bob
--Stories You Can Tell. LC 76-58607. viii, 71 p. 22cm. c.1977. Discipleship Resources.

Kuntze, E. J.
--The Mystic Bell: A Wonder Book for Young People. N.D. G. P. Putnam's Sons.

Kunz, Edith F., tr. see Spyri, Johanna Heusser.

Kupfer, Grace Harriet (1873-)
--Stories of Long Ago in a New Dress. LC 12-34971. 177 p. incl. plates. front. 19 cm. 1897. D. C. Heath & Co.

Kuratomi, Chizuko (1939-)
--Mister Bear & the Robbers. Kakimoto, Kozo (1915-), illus. 32p. (gr. 1). 1972. Dial.
--Mister Bear Goes to Sea. Kakimoto, Kozo (1915-), illus. LC 77-88113. (Illus.). jap. 24 ils., 6 in color. 24p. Repr. of 1967 ed (Pub. by Shiko-Sha Co. Ltd). (ps-2). 1970. (ISBN 0-8170-0445-9). Judson.
--Mister Bear in the Air. Kakimoto, Kozo (1915-), illus. LC 71-116728. (gr. k-3). 1971. (ISBN 0-8170-0484-X). Judson.
--Mister Bear's Trumpet. Kakimoto, Kozo (1915-), illus. Jensh, Barbara L., adapted by. LC 78-116727. 24 color ils. 24p. 1st U.S. edition. 1970. (ISBN 0-8170-0483-1). Judson.
--Mr. Bear and the Robbers. Kakimoto, Kozo (1915-), illus. LC 72-710. (Illus.). 24 p. 25cm. 1973, c.1970. (ISBN 0-8037-5881-2). (ISBN 0-8037-5882-0). Dial Press.
--Mr. Bear and the Robbers. Kakimoto, Kozo (1915-), illus. (Illus.). 32p. 1975. (ISBN 0-8037-5881-2). (ISBN 0-8037-5882-0). Dial Press.
--Mr. Bear in the Air. Kakimoto, Kozo (1915-), illus. LC 71-116728. 28 p. (chiefly col. illus. 25cm. 1970. (ISBN 0-8170-0484-X). Judson Press.
--Mr. Bear's Trumpet. Jensh, Barbara, adapted by. Kakimoto, Kozo (1915-), illus. LC 78-116727. (Illus.). 28 p. 1970, c.1969. Judson Press.
--Mr. Bear's Trumpet. Kakimoto, Kozo (1915-), illus. (gr. k-3). 1975. (ISBN 0-8170-0690-7). Judson.

Kurelek, William (1927-1977)
--Lumberjack. Kurelek, William (1927-1977), illus. LC 74-9377. (Illus.). 48p. (gr. 1 up). 1974. (ISBN 0-395-19922-0). HM. **Award: (NYT).**
--A Prairie Boy's Summer. Kurelek, William (1927-1977), illus. LC 74-32137. 48p. (gr. 5 up). 1975. (ISBN 0-395-20280-9). HM.
--A Prairie Boy's Winter. Kurelek, William (1927-1977), illus. LC 73-8913. (Illus.). 48p. (gr. k-3). 1973. (ISBN 0-395-17708-1). HM. **Awards: (NYT); (BGH).**

Kurkul, Edward (1916-)
--Tiger in the Lake. Petie, Haris, pseud. (1915-), illus. Petty, Roberta. LC 68-11183. (Illus.). 32 p. 24cm. 1968. Lantern Press.

Kurt, Brother & Antonius, Brother
--Friar Among Savages:. Father Luis Caner. Lynch, Donald, illus. LC 58-13115. (Illus.). 176p. 22cm. (Banner Books). 1958. Benziger Bros.

Kurtycz, Marcos & Garcia Kobeh, Ana, eds.
--Tigers & Opossums: Animal legends. Kurtycz, Marcos, illus. Hall, Felicia M., tr. LC 82-17949. (Illus.). (gr. k-3). 1984. (ISBN 0-316-50718-0). (ISBN 0-316-50718-0). Little.

Kusan, Ivan (1933-)
--Koko and the Ghosts. Galdone, Paul (1914-), illus. LC 66-11203. 215 p. illus. 21 cm. 1st U.S. edition. 1966. Harcourt, Brace & World.
--The Myster of Green Hill. Adler, Kermit, illus. Petrovich, Michael B., tr. (gr. 4-6). 1966. Harcourt & Brace.
--The Mystery of Green Hill. Adler, Kermit, illus. Petrovich, Michael B., tr. LC 62-8743. (Illus.). 189 p. 21cm. 1st U.S. edition. 1962. Harcourt, Brace & World.
--The Mystery of the Stolen Painting. Robinson, Charles (1870-1937), illus. Willen, Drenka (1931-), tr. from Serbo-Croatian. LC 74-24324. (Illus.). 256 p. 21cm. 1st U.S. edition. 1975. (ISBN 0-15-243353-8). Harcourt Brace Jovanovich.

Kuse, James A., ed.
--Bunny Tales. rev. ed. (Illus.). (ps-3). 1979. (ISBN 0-89542-451-7). Ideals.

Kuse, James A., ed. see Jones, Jo.

Kuse, James A., ed. see Wiersum, Beverly.

Kuse, James & Luedtke, Ralph D., eds.
--Once Upon a Rhyme. (ps). 1978. (ISBN 0-89542-055-4). Ideals.

Kushida, Magoichi (1915-), ed. see Tchaikovsky, Peter Ilich (1840-1893) & Hoffmann, Ernst Theodor Amadeus.

Kushner, Donn
--The Violin Maker's Gift. Panton, Doug, illus. 11 x 12 1/2. 88p. Repr. of 1981 ed (Pub. by Farrar). (16 pt.). (gr. 5-6). N.D. Am Printing Hse.
--The Violin-Maker's Gift. Panton, Doug, illus. LC 81-19406. (Illus.). 74 p. 23cm. 1st U.S. edition. 1982, c.1981. (ISBN 0-374-38155-0). Farrar, Straus, Giroux. **Award: (CLA).**

Kuskin, Karla Seidman (1932-)
--ABCDEFGHIJKLMNOPQRSTUVWXYZ. Kuskin, Karla Seidman (1932-), illus. LC 63-14365. unpaged. illus. 14 cm. 1963. Harper & Row.
--Alexander Soames: His Poems. Kuskin, Karla Seidman (1932-), illus. LC 62-16416. unpaged. illus. 23cm. c.1962. Harper & Row.
--All Sizes of Noises. Kuskin, Karla Seidman (1932-), illus. (Illus.). (gr. k-3). 1962. (ISBN 0-06-023561-6). Har-Row.
--The Animals and the Ark. Kuskin, Karla Seidman (1932-), illus. LC 58-7753. unpaged. illus. 18x25cm. 1958. Harper.
--Any Me I Want to Be. Kuskin, Karla Seidman (1932-), illus. LC 77-105485. (Illus.). 64p. (gr. 1-4). 1972. (ISBN 0-06-023616-7, HarpJ). Har-Row.
--Any Me I Want to Be: Poems. Kuskin, Karla Seidman (1932-), illus. LC 77-105485. (Illus.). 30 (i.e. 64) p. 24cm. 1972. (ISBN 0-06-023615-9). (ISBN 0-06-023616-7). Harper & Row.
--The Bear Who Saw the Spring. Kuskin, Karla Seidman (1932-), illus. LC 60-11195. unpaged. illus. 28cm. 1961. Harper.
--A Boy Had a Mother Who Bought Him a Hat. Kuskin, Karla Seidman (1932-), illus. LC 76-12092. (Illus.). 32 p. 24cm. 1976. (ISBN 0-395-24740-3). Houghton Mifflin.
--Dogs and Dragons, Trees and Dreams: A Collection of Poems. Kuskin, Karla Seidman (1932-), illus. LC 79-2814. p. cm. c.1980. (ISBN 0-06-023543-8). (ISBN 0-06-023544-6). Harper & Row. **Award: (ALA).**
--Herbert Hated Being Small. Kuskin, Karla Seidman (1932-), illus. LC 77-25029. p. cm. 1978. (ISBN 0-395-26462-6). Houghton Mifflin.
--In the Flaky Frosty Morning. Kuskin, Karla Seidman (1932-), illus. LC 69-14446. (Illus.). 26 p. 21cm. 1969. Harper & Row.
--In the Middle of the Trees. Kuskin, Karla Seidman (1932-), illus. LC 58-5291. (Illus.). 38 p. 30cm. 1958. Harper. **Award: (ALA).**
--James & The Rain. Kuskin, Karla Seidman (1932-), illus. N.D. E. M. Hale & Co.
--James and the Rain. Kuskin, Karla Seidman (1932-), illus. LC 57-6851. illus, 23cm. 22cm. 48p. 1957. Harper.
--Just Like Everyone Else. Kuskin, Karla Seidman (1932-), illus. LC 59-5320. (Illus.). 32 p. 16cm. 1959. Harper.
--Just Like Everyone Else. Kuskin, Karla Seidman (1932-), illus. 1982. Harper.
--Near the Window Tree: Poems and Notes. Kuskin, Karla Seidman (1932-), illus. LC 74-20394. (Illus.). 63 p. 21cm. 1975. (ISBN 0-06-023539-X). (ISBN 0-06-023540-3). Harper & Row.
--Night Again. Kuskin, Karla Seidman (1932-), illus. LC 80-14400. (Illus.). 32 p. 19cm. c.1981. (ISBN 0-316-50721-0). Little, Brown.
--The Philharmonic Gets Dressed. 1st ed. Simont, Marc (1915-), illus. LC 81-48658. p. cm. c.1982. (ISBN 0-06-023622-1). (ISBN 0-06-023623-X). Harper & Row. **Award: (ALA).**
--Roar and More. Kuskin, Karla Seidman (1932-), illus. LC 56-813885. unpaged. illus. 18x22cm. 1956. Harper.
--The Rose on My Cake. (Illus.). 42 p. 27cm. 1964. Harper & Row.
--Sand and Snow. Kuskin, Karla Seidman (1932-), illus. (Illus.). 32 p. 1965. Harper & Row.
--Something Sleeping in the Hall: Poems. Kuskin, Karla Seidman (1932-), illus. LC 82-47721. (Illus.). 64 p. 23cm. (An I Can Read Book). c.1985. (ISBN 0-06-023633-7). (ISBN 0-06-023634-5). Harper & Row.
--Square As a House. Kuskin, Karla Seidman (1932-), illus. LC 60-5783. unpaged. illus. 21x24cm. 1960. Harper.
--The Walk the Mouse Girls Took. Kuskin, Karla Seidman (1932-), illus. LC 67-4152. (Illus.). 32 p. 24cm. 1967. Harper & Row.
--Watson, the Smartest Dog in the U. S. A. Kuskin, Karla Seidman (1932-), illus. LC 68-10370. (Illus.). 32 p. 1968. Harper & Row.
--What Did You Bring Me?. Kuskin, Karla Seidman (1932-), illus. LC 72-76503. (Illus.). 39 p. 24cm. 1973. (ISBN 0-06-023652-3). (ISBN 0-06-023652-3). Harper & Row.
--Which Horse Is William?. Kuskin, Karla Seidman (1932-), illus. LC 59-8974. (Illus.). 24cm. 32p. 1959. Harper.

Kussi, Peter, tr. see Prochawska, Jan.

Kuthanova, Olga, tr. see Hoffmann, Ernst Theodor Amadeus.

Kuthanova, Olga, tr. see Kosava, Maria & Stanovsky, Vladislav.

Kuttner, Henry see Edmonds, Paul, pseud.

Kutzer, Ernst, jt. auth. see Sixtus, Albert.

Kutzer, Ernst (1880-)
--Tallie, Tillie, and Tag: One Little Girl, One Little Doll, and One Little Dog. LC 33-2414. 35 p. illus. (part col.) 16 x 21 cm. 1932. A. Whitman & Company.

Kuwabara, Minoru
--Cut and Paste. 48p. 1962. Astor Books.

Kuzma, Kay (1941-) & Lee, Elfred
--The Kim, Kari, and Kevin Storybook. LC 78-61115. (Illus.). 126 p. 23cm. c.1979. (ISBN 0-8163-0239-1). Pacific Press Pub. Association.

Kvale, Velma Ruth (1898-)
--Tobuk, Reindeer Herder. LC 68-18117. (Illus.). 112 p. 25cm. 1968. T. S. Denison.

Kwapil, Marie J., jt. auth. see Alvarez, Juan.

Kwitz, Mary DeBall
--Little Chick's Breakfast. LC 82-48259. (Illus.). 5 7/8 x 8 1/2. (18 pt.). (Early I Can Read Bks.). (ps-3). 1983. (ISBN 0-06-023674-4). (ISBN 0-06-023675-2). Har-Row.
--Little Chick's Story. Szekeres, Cyndy (1933-), illus. LC 77-11841. (Illus.). 32 p. 22cm. (Early I can read book). c.1978. (ISBN 0-06-023664-7). (ISBN 0-06-023666-3). Harper & Row.
--Mouse at Home. LC 65-22879. 32p. col. illus. 15cm. c.1966. Harper.
--Rabbits' Search for a Little House. Cauley, Lorinda Bryan (1951-), illus. LC 76-45432. (Illus.). p. cm. 24cm. 32p. c.1977. (ISBN 0-517-52867-3). Crown Publishers.
--The Secret World. LC 71-85951. (Illus.). 32 p. 22cm. 1971. (ISBN 0-695-80088-4). Follett.
--When It Rains. Kwitz, Mary DeBall, illus. LC 73-90049. (Illus.). 29 p. 23cm. 1974. (ISBN 0-695-80411-1). (ISBN 0-695-80411-1). Follett.
--Whose Baby?. (Illus.). (Golden Touch & Feel Bks.). 1978. (ISBN 0-307-12151-8, Golden Pr). Western Pub.

Kwolek, Constance (1933-)
--Loner. LC 78-117610. 143 p. 22cm. (Doubleday signal books). 1970. Doubleday.

Kyber, Manfred (1880-1933)
--The Little Slipperman. Laimgruber, Monika (1946-), illus. LC 72-89336. (Illus.). 24p. (gr. k-4). 1973. (ISBN 0-87592-031-4). Scroll Pr.
--The Mouseball. Oberhansli, Trudi, pseud. (1944-), illus. Schlapbach-Oberhansli, Trudi. Hoover, Roseanna (1944-), tr. LC 69-13536. (Illus.). 20 p. 31cm. 1st U.S. edition. 1969. Atheneum.
--The Three Candles of Little Veronica. 2nd ed. Guarducci, Iris, illus. Reinhardt, Rosamond, tr. from Ger. LC 75-1960. (Illus.). 192p. 1975. (ISBN 0-914614-04-5). (ISBN 0-914614-05-3). Waldorf Pr.
--The Three Candles of Little Veronica: The Story of a Child's Soul in This World & the Other. Guarducci, Iris, illus. Reinhardt, Rosamund, tr. from Ger. Reinhardt, Rosamond, intro. by. (Illus.). 192p. (gr. 9 up). 1972. (ISBN 0-914614-00-2). Waldorf Pr.

Kyle, Anne Dempster (1896-)
--The Apprentice of Florence. Best, Allena Champlin, Mrs. (1892-1974), illus. Berry, Erick, pseud. LC 33-298053. xii, 276 p. incl. front., illus. 21 cm. 1933. Houghton Mifflin Company. **Award: (JNM).**
--Crusaders' Gold: A Story for Girls. LC 28-24273. 4 p. l., 284 p. col. front., illus. 19 1/2 cm. 1928. Houghton Mifflin Company.
--Prince of the Pale Mountains. Barney, Maginel Wright, Mrs. (1881-1966), illus. LC 29-23886. viii p., 1 l., 250 p. col. front., illus. 21 cm. 1929. Houghton Mifflin Company.
--Red Sky Over Rome. De Angeli, Marguerite Lofft, Mrs. (1889-), illus. LC 38-27868. 5 p. l., 260 p. front., plates. 22 cm. 1938. Houghton Mifflin Company.

Kyle, Elisabeth, pseud., see Dunlop, Agnes Mary Robertson.

Kyle, Elisabeth, pseud. (0000-1982)
--The Captain's House. Dunlop, Agnes Mary Robertson. LC 53-5880. 245p. illus. 22cm. 1953, c.1952. Houghton Mifflin.

--Fables: A Selection. Moriarty, L. M., footnotes by. (Primary Ser.). N.D. MacMillan.
--Fables Choisies. 1900. Henry Holt & Co.
--Fables of La Fontaine. Baudoin, Simonne, illus. Ponsot, Marie, tr. from Fr. LC 57-13971. unpaged. illus. 31cm. N.D. Grosset & Dunlap.
--The Fables of La Fontaine. Duke, Francis, tr. 1965. University Press Of Virginia.
--Fables of La Fontaine. Grandville, Jean Ignace Isidore Gerard (1803-1847), illus. Wright, Elizur, Jr. (1804-1885), tr. from Fr. LC 11-19439. 19cm. 1860. Derby & Jackson.
--The Fables of La Fontaine. 1st ed. Helle, Andre (1871-), illus. Brown, Margaret Wise (1910-), tr. 39p. col., illus. 28 x 22cm. 1940. Harper & Brothers.
--Fontaine Fables. LC 35-21954. 48p. illus. (part col.) 32cm. 1934. Whitman Publishing Co.
--Fontaine Fables. Smith, ed. N.D. Longmans, Green & Co.
--A Hundred Fables of La Fontaine. Billinghurst, Percy J. (1859-1932), illus. N.D. John Lane Co.
--A Hundred Fables of LaFontaine. Billinghurst, Percy J. (1859-1932), illus. N.D. Dodd Mead & Co.
--La Fontaine: A Present for the Young. LC 11-19441. 16cm. 108p. 1839. Weeks, Jordan & Co.
--La Fontaine's Fables. (The Children's Favorites). 1915. George W. Jacobs & Co.
--La Fontaine's Fables. (Illus.). (The Young Folks Lib.). N.D. H. M. Caldwell Co.
--La Fontaine's Fables. (Illus.). (The Exquisite Ser.). N.D. H. M. Caldwell Co.
--La Fontaine's Fables. (Illus.). (The Chateau Ser.). N.D. H. M. Caldwell Co.
--La Fontaine's Fables. (Library of Fables). 1873. Leavitt & Allen Bros.
--La Fontaine's Fables. (Illus.). N.D. Thomas Nelson & Sons.
--La Fontaine's Fables. Grandville, Jean Ignace Isidore Gerard (1803-1847), illus. Wright, Elizur, Jr., tr. from Fr. N.D. James Miller.
--La Fontaine's Fables. Thornbury, Walter, tr. N.D. Hurst & Co.
--The Lion and the Rat: A Fable. Wildsmith, Brian Lawrence (1930-), illus. LC 63-13300. (Illus.). 32 p. 29cm. 1963. F. Watts. **Award: (ALA).**
--The Miller, the Boy, and the Donkey. Wildsmith, Brian Lawrence (1930-), illus. N.D. Oxford.
--The North Wind & the Sun. Wildsmith, Brian Lawrence (1930-), illus. LC 64-13872. (Illus.). (gr. k-3). 1964. (ISBN 0-531-01536-X). Watts. **Award: (ALA).**
--The Rich Man and the Shoe-Maker: A Fable. Wildsmith, Brian Lawrence (1930-), illus. LC 80-511463. (Illus.). 28 p. 28cm. 1979. (ISBN 0-19-272104-6). Oxford University Press.
--The Rich Man and the Shoe-Maker: A Fable. Wildsmith, Brian Lawrence (1930-), illus. LC 65-20551. 1v. (unpaged) col. illus. 29cm. 1966, c.1965. Watts. **Award: (ALA).**
--Select Fables From. De Monvel, Boutet R., illus. Wright, Elizur, Jr., tr. N.D. E. & J. B. Young & Co.
--The Original Fables of La Fontaine. Tilney, Frederick Colin, illus. Tilney, Frederick Colin, tr. LC 19-15909. 19cm. 126p. (Tales for Children of Many Lands). 1913. E. P. Dutton & Co.
--The Turtle and the Two Ducks: Animal Fables. Plante, Patricia & Bergman, David (1950-), eds. Rockwell, Anne F. (1934-), illus. LC 81-47409. (Illus.). 32 p. c.1981. (ISBN 0-690-04148-9). (ISBN 0-690-04147-0). Crowell.
--The Turtle and the Two Ducks: Animal Fables Retold from La Fontaine. 1st ed. Plante, Patricia & Bergman, David (1950-), eds. Rockwell, Anne F (1934-), illus. LC 80-12682. p. cm. c.1980. (ISBN 0-416-00701-5). Methuen.

La Fontaine, Jean De (1621-1695) & Aesopus
--Fontaine's Fables: With Which Are Included Aesop's Fables. Rich, Edwin Gile (1879-), adapted by. LC 23-3786. viii, 133 p. col. front., col. plates. 24 cm. c.1922. Small, Maynard & Company.
--The Tortoise and the Hare. Smith, Doris Susan (1949-), illus. Sperber, Ann, tr. LC 78-12525. (Illus.). 21 p. 16cm. (Goodnight book). 1979. (ISBN 0-394-84102-6). Knopf : Distributed by Random House.

La Fontaine, Jean De (1621-1695) & Gay, John
--The Book of Fables: Including Fables by La Fontaine, John Gay, Robert Dodsley, Christian Gellert, Gotthold Lessing, Claris De Florian, Ivan Kriloff, and Others. Nickless, Will (1902-), illus. LC 63-16208. 160 p. illus. (part col.) 22 cm. 1963, c.1962. Warne.

La Fountaine, George (1934-)
--Two Minute Warning. LC 74-16642. 256p. 1975. (ISBN 0-698-10633-4, Coward). Putnam Pub Group.

Lage, Ida De see DeLage, Ida.

Lagercrantz, Rose Elsa (1947-)
--Tulla's Summer. McCrady, Lady (1951-), illus. Blecher, George & Thygreen-Blecher, Lone, trs. from Swedish LC 76-46786. (Illus.). 121 p. 21cm. 1st U.S. edition. 1977. (ISBN 0-15-291095-6). Harcourt Brace Jovanovich.

Lagerlof, Selma Ottiliana Lovisa (1858-1940)
--Further Adventures of Nils. Heiberg, Astri Welham, illus. Howard, Velma Swanston, Mrs. (1868-), tr. from Swedish. LC 11-240985. 6 p. l., 3-339 p. front., plates. 20 cm. 1911. Doubleday, Page & Company.
--Further Adventures of Nils. Heiberg, Astri Welam, illus. Howard, Velma Swanston, Mrs. (1868-), tr. 5 p. l., 3-339, 1 p. front. 20 cm. 1920. Doubleday, Page & Company.
--Liliecrona's Home. Barwell, Anna, tr. 1940. E P Dutton.
--The Wonderful Adventures of Nils. (Marbacks Edition). N.D. Doubleday Doran & Co.
--Wonderful Adventures of Nils. (Thrushwood Bks.). N.D. Grosset & Dunlap.
--The Wonderful Adventures of Nils. Aurell, Tage & Aurell, Kathrine, eds. Malmberg, Hans, illus. Oldenburg, Richard E., tr. LC 68-1274. (Illus.). 1 v. (unpaged). 30cm. 1967. Doubleday.
--The Wonderful Adventures of Nils. Baumhauer, Hans (1913-), illus. Howard, Velma Swanston, Mrs. (1868-), tr. from Swedish. LC 47-31397. 539 p. illus., map (on lining-papers) 24 cm. 1947. Pantheon.
--The Wonderful Adventures of Nils. Howard, Velma Swanston, Mrs. (1868-), ed. Frye, Mary Hamilton, illus. Howard, Velma Swanston, Mrs. (1868-), tr. from Swedish. LC 13-26099. xv, 263, 1 p. col. front., col. plates. 24 cm. 1913. Doubleday, Page & Company.
--The Wonderful Adventures of Nils. Howard, Velma Swanston, Mrs. (1868-), tr. LC 39-12112. xiii, 1 p., 3 l., 3-430 p. front., illus., plates. 22 cm. 1938. Doubleday, Doran & Company, Inc.
--The Wonderful Adventures of Nils: From the Swedish of Selma Lagerlof. Howard, Velma Swanston, Mrs. (1868-), tr. LC 43-39501. xiii, 1 p., 3 l., 3-430 p. front., illus., plates. 20 1/2 cm. c.1907. Grosset & Dunlap.

Lago, Florence M.
--How Chooko Got to America. LC 54-8368. 50 p. illus. 23cm. 1955, c.1951. Vantage Press.

Laguna, Frederica Anuis De see De Laguna, Frederica Annis.

Lahey, Nicholas J., tr. see Vandersteen, Willy.

Lahey, Thomas Aquinas (1886-)
--King of the Pygmies. Dart, Eleanor, illus. LC 44-46349. vii p., 1 l., 289, 1 p. illus. 22 1/2 cm. 1944. St. Anthony Guild Press.
--Twisted Trails. LC 35-15743. 243 p. 20 cm. c.1935. The Ave Maria Press.

Lahr, Georgiana L.
--Friendly Fairy Tales. 1970. (ISBN 0-685-20881-8). Vantage.
--Happy Holiday Plays. (Illus.). (gr. 3-8). 1971. (ISBN 0-685-28668-1). Vantage.
--Impie. N.D. Vantage Press.
--Merry Holiday Plays. 1979. (ISBN 0-533-03674-7). Vantage.

La Iglesia, Maria Elena De see De La Iglesia, Maria Elena.

Laing, Frederick (1905-)
--Ask Me If I Love You Now. Orig. Title: The Bride Wore Braids. (gr. 9-12). 1972 (Starline). Schol Bk Serv.
--The Bride Wore Braids. LC 68-27274. 192 p. 22cm. 1968. Four Winds Press.
--A Question of Pride. LC 67-23544. 128 p. 20cm. 1967. Four Winds Press.
--Tales from Scandinavia. Dillon, Leo (1933-) & Dillon, Diane (1933-), illus. LC 78-56060. (Illus.). 96 p. 25cm. (The World Folktale Library). c.1979. (ISBN 0-382-03355-8). Silver Burdett Co.
--Why Heimdall Blew His Horn: Tales of the Norse Gods. Dillon, Leo (1933-) & Dillon, Diane (1933-), illus. LC 68-26672. (Illus.). 96 p. 25cm. (Folk literature around the world). 1969. Silver Burdett Co.

Laing, John
--One Cool Cat. 56p. 1984. (ISBN 0-413-54220-3, Pub. by Eyre Methuen England). Methuen Inc.

Laird, Donivee Martin
--The Three Little Hawaiian Pigs and the Magic Shark. Jossem, Carol, illus. LC 81-67047. (Illus.). 37 p. 24cm. 1982. (ISBN 0-940350-03-3). Barnaby Books.
--Will Wai Kula & the Three Mongooses. Jossem, Carol, illus. (Illus.). 44p. (gr. k-3). 1983. (ISBN 0-940350-04-1). Barnaby Bks.

Laird, Freda
--Pat Presents Pearle Harbor and Other Stories. N.D. Vantage Press.

Laird, Helene (1905-)
--The Lombardy Children. Burchard, Peter Duncan (1921-), illus. LC 52-8440. 209 p. illus. 21 cm. 1st U.S. edition. 1952. World Pub. Co.
--Nancy Gets a Job. LC 51-10160. 224 p. 21 cm. 1951. World Pub. Co.
--Nancy Goes to College. 223p. 1950. The World Publishing Company.
--Nancy Keeps House. 190p. 1947. The World Publishing Co.

Laird, Jean Elouise (1930-)
--The Alphabet Zoo. Furan, Barbara Howell, illus. LC 74-190264. (Illus.). 32 p. 25cm. 1972. (ISBN 0-87783-053-3). Oddo Pub.
--Lost in the Department Store. Spiegel, Lawrence M., illus. LC 63-21158. 1 v. (unpaged) col. illus. 29 cm. 1964. Denison.
--The Plump Ballerina. LC 76-119557. (Illus.). 31 p. 29cm. 1970. T. S. Denison.

Laird, Rowena
--Stuffy. Laird, Rowena, illus. LC 45-7198. 32 p. col. illus. 26 1/2 x 21 1/2 cm. 1945. W. Morrow and Company.

Laird, Sally
--The Three Bears and Goldilocks. Phelan, Winnie Fitch, illus. LC 63-91654. 1v (unpaged) col. illus. 22 cm. c.1964. Dell Pub. Co.

Laite, Gordon (1925-), illus.
--Cinderella & Snow White & Rose Red. (Illus.). 24p. (gr. k-3). 1976. (ISBN 0-307-69052-0, Golden Pr). Western Pub.
--Cinderella Paper Dolls. (Little Golden Book). 1960. Golden Press.

Lake, Edna
--The Mystery of Tower House. (The Magnet Library). N.D. Frederick Warne & Co.

Lake, Edward John
--A Book of Animals for Children. (Illus.). 1910. Rand McNally & Co.
--A Book of Birds for Children. (Illus.). N.D. Rand McNally & Co.
--Pictures of Birds and Animals with Merry Rhymes. (Illus.). 1910. Rand McNally & Co.

Lake, Harry J (1920-)
--Jorj, "the Enchanted Dragon,". LC 41-18905. 32 p. illus. 15 x 12 cm. 1941. The Unicorn Publishing Company.

Lakeman, Mary
--Faith's festivals. N.D. Lee & Shepard.
--Pretty Lucy Merwin. (Illus.). (Our Girls' Prize Library). N.D. Lee & Shepard.
--Pretty Lucy Merwyn, 1 of 30 vols. (American Girls' Ser.: No. 15). 1900. Set. Lee & Shepard.
--Ruth Eliot's Dream. (Young Folks' Library). 1882. Lee & Shepard.
--Ruth Eliot's Dream, 1 of 30 vols. (American Girls' Ser.: No. 19). 1900. Set. Lee & Shepard.

Lakin, Pat
--Don't Touch My Room. Brewster, Patience, illus. LC 84-10063. (Illus.). 32 p. 24cm. c.1985. (ISBN 0-316-51230-3). Little, Brown.

Laklan, Carli see Clarke, John, pseud.

Laklan, Carli (1907-), abridged by see Collins, Wilkie.

Laklan, Carli (1907-)
--Migrant Girl. LC 77-130675. 144 p. 21cm. 1970. McGraw-Hill.
--Nancy Kimball, Nurse's Aide. 1st ed. Barron, John N., illus. LC 62-8397. (Illus.). 142 p. 22cm. (Signal book). 1962. Doubleday.
--Nurse in Training. 1st ed. Barron, John N., illus. LC 65-15667. (Illus.). 144 p. 22cm. (Signal book). 1965. (ISBN 0-385-05816-0). Doubleday.
--Second Year Nurse: Nancy Kimball at City Hospital. 1st ed. Guzzi, George, illus. LC 67-1410. (Illus.). 144 p. 22cm. (Doubleday signal books). 1967. Doubleday.
--Ski Bum. LC 73-6664. 137 p. 21cm. 1973. McGraw-Hill.
--Sudden Iron. Clarke, John, pseud. LC 69-17181. 193 p. 21cm. 1969. McGraw-Hill.
--Surf with Me. LC 67-24956. 160 p. 21cm. 1967. McGraw-Hill.
--Two Girls in New York. Frame, Paul (1913-), illus. (Illus.). 143 p. 22cm. (Signal book). 1964. Doubleday.

Lakritz, Esther Himmelman (1928-)
--Randy Visits the Doctor. Quinn, Sidney, illus. LC 61-5063. unpaged. illus. 21cm. c.1962. (ISBN 0-8054-4119-0). Broadman Press.

Lalicki, Barbara, compiled by.
--If There Were Dreams to Sell. Tomes, Margot Ladd (1917-), illus. LC 84-907. (Illus.). 32p. 1984. (ISBN 0-688-03821-2). (ISBN 0-688-03822-0). Lothrop. **Award: (NYT).**

Lalli, Judy (1949-)
--At Least I'm Getting Better: Poems for Kids and Other People. Mason-Fry, Douglas L. (1950-), illus. LC 81-6529. p. cm. c.1981. (ISBN 0-915166-49-6). Impact Publishers.

Lalo, Laurent
--David and Goliath. (Illus.). 24p. 1st U.S. edition. (gr. 1-6). 1983. (ISBN 0-88070-044-0). Multnomah.
--John the Baptist. (Illus.). 24p. 1st U.S. edition. (gr. 1-6). 1983. (ISBN 0-88070-045-9). Multnomah.
--The Miraculous Catch. (Illus.). 24p. 1st U.S. edition. (gr. 1-6). 1984. (ISBN 0-88070-046-7). Multnomah.

Lam, Roger
--The Cuckoo Clock Adventure. Gibb, George, ed. Sweetman, Daniel, illus. LC 82-99848. (Illus., Orig.). (gr. 5-12). 1983. (ISBN 0-943310-01-6). Six Pr.

Lamaitre, Odon-Jerome & Chauire, Yvette
--The Dance. N.D. (ISBN 0-8120-5127-0). Barron.

Lamar, Ashton, pseud., see Sayler, Harry Lincoln.

Lamar, Ashton, pseud. (1863-)
--Battling the Big Horn: Or, The Aeroplane in the Rockies. Sayler, Harry Lincoln. (The Famous Aeroplane Boys Ser.). N.D. The Reilly & Britton Co.
--The Boy Aeronaut's Club: Or, Flying for Fun. Sayler, Harry Lincoln. Riesenberg, S. H. & Gunn, W. L., illus. (The Aeroplane Boys Ser.). N.D. Reilly & Britton Co.
--The Boy Aeronaut's Grit: Or, The Aeroplane Express. Sayler, Harry Lincoln. Riesenberg, S. H. & Gunn, W. L., illus. (The Boy Aeroplane Ser.). N.D. Reilly & Britton Co.
--The Stolen Aeroplane: Or, How Bud Wilson Made Good. Sayler, Harry Lincoln. Gunn, M. G., illus. (The Aeroplane Boys Ser.). N.D. Reilly & Britton Co.
--When Scout Meets Scout: Or, The Aeroplane Spy. Sayler, Harry Lincoln. (Aeroplane Boys Ser.). N.D. The Reilly & Britton Co.

LaMarche, Jim, jt. auth. see Crofford, Emily Ardell.

La Mare, Colin De see De La Mare, Colin.

La Mare, Walter John de see De La Mare, Walter John.

La Mare, Walter John de see Jack and the Beanstalk.

La Mare, Walter John de see Child Study Association of America.

La Mare, Walter John de see De La Mare, Walter John.

LaMay, Jack D.
--Shelley and the Animals. 1983. (ISBN 0-686-84432-7). Vantage.

Lamb, Bertram John see Uncle Dick, pseud.

Lamb, Bertram John (1887-)
--Pip, Squeak, and Wilfred: Their "Luvly" Adventures. Uncle Dick, pseud. Payne, A. B., illus. LC 21-18527. 62 p. illus. 16 x 24 cm. c.1921. E. P. Dutton & Company.

Lamb, Cecil
--Flowers for Filbert. Lamb, Cecil, illus. LC 51-21209. 32 p. illus.(part col). 21cm. (A Cozy Corner Book). 1951. Whitman.

Lamb, Charles, jt. auth. see Edgeworth, Maria.

Lamb, Charles, jt. auth. see Lamb, Mary Ann.

Lamb, Charles, jt. auth. see Shakespeare, William.

Lamb, Charles (1775-1834), ed. see Homerus.

Lamb, Charles, ed. see Shakespeare, William.

Lamb, Charles (1775-1834)
--Adventures of Ulysses. (Harper's School Classics). N.D. American Book Co.
--Adventures of Ulysses. N.D. Longmans Green & Co.
--The Adventures of Ulysses. 154p. N.D. Platt & Munk Co.
--Beauty and the Beast. N.D. Thomas Yoseloff Pub.
--Beauty and the Beast: A Poem. Lang, Andrew (1844-1912), illus. (Illus.). N.D. Scribner & Welford's.
--Captain Christie's Granddaughter. (Illus.). N.D. Methodist Bk Concern.
--Dream Children. (Little Classics). N.D. James R Osgood & Co.
--Lamb's Tales from Shakespeare, 1 of 22 Vols. (Illus.). (Warne's Home Circle Ser.: No. 22). N.D. Scribner & Welford.
--Tales from Shakespeare, 12 vols. (Illus.). 400p. (Juvenile Classics Ser.). 1905. Set. H M Caldwell Co.
--Tales from Shakespeare. (Illus.). (The Empyreal Library of Handy Volume Classics). N.D. H. M. Caldwell Co.
--Tales from Shakespeare. (Illus.). (Boys' and Girls' Classics). N.D. Henry Altemus Co.
--Tales from Shakespeare. (Illus.). (Vademecum Ser.). N.D. Henry Altemus.
--Tales from Shakespeare. Handy Volume, Large Type ed. (Illus.). (Petit-Trianon Ser.). N.D. Henry Altemus.
--Tales from Shakespeare. (Illus.). (Children's Home Library). 1915. T Y Crowell.
--Tales from Shakespeare. Globe ed. Ainger, Alfred, ed. (Golden Treasury Ser.). N.D. MacMillian.
--Tales from Shakespeare. Godwin, Frank (1889-), illus. LC 2-21113. 1 p. l., viii-ix, vii-x. 194 p. col. front., illus. 18 cm. (Altemus' young people's library). 1901. H. Altemus Company.
--Tales from Shakespeare. Lamb, Mary Ann (1764-1847), ed. Elliot, Elizabeth Shippen Green, illus. (Illus.). 1922. David McKay Co.
--Tales from Shakespeare: Comedies. Rolfe, ed. N.D. American Book Co.
--Tales from Shakespeare: Tragedies. Rolfe, ed. N.D. American Book Co.

Lamb, Charles (1775-1834), adapted by.
--The Adventures of Ulysses. LC 12-36039. vii 109, 1 p. 18 cm. (On cover: Classics for children). 1886. Ginn & Company.

--Hi, Neighbor. LC 68-30828. 159 p. 21cm. 1968. E. P. Dutton.
--High Hurdles. LC 55-7126. 191p. illus. 21cm. 1955. Dutton.
--High Hurdles. (gr. 7-11). 1960. G&D.
--Introducing Parri. LC 62-14702. 189 p. 21cm. 1962. Dutton.
--Just Jenifer. LC 56-58401. 187p. 21cm. (Famous Janet Lambert books for Girls). 1956, c.1945. Grosset & Dunlap.
--Just Jenifer. Paflin, Roberta, pseud. (1903-), illus. Petty, Roberta Harris Pfaflin. LC 45-609816. 187 p. illus. 19 1/2 cm. 1945. E. P. Dutton & Company, Inc.
--Little Miss Atlas. LC 49-11006. 190 p. 20 cm. 1949. E. P. Dutton.
--Little Miss Atlas. LC 59-42545. 190p. 21cm. (Famous Janet Lambert books for girls 14). 1959, c.1949. Grosset & Dunlap.
--Love Taps Gently. LC 55-11081. 191p. 21cm. 1955. Dutton.
--Love to Spare. LC 67-2659. 155 p. 21cm. 1967. Dutton.
--Miss America. LC 51-13042. 189 p. illus. 21 cm. 1951. Dutton.
--Miss Tippy. LC 48-463449. 192 p. 20 cm. 1948. E. P. Dutton.
--Miss Tippy. N.D. Grosset & Dunlap.
--My Davy. LC 68-18349. 159 p. 21cm. 1968. Dutton.
--Myself and I. LC 57-12755. 188 p. 21cm. 1957. Dutton.
--Myself and I. LC 61-4917. 188p. 21cm. 1961, c.1957. Grosset & Dunlap.
--The Odd Ones. LC 78-81718. 155 p. 21cm. 1969. Dutton.
--On Her Own. LC 64-21704. 160 p. 22 cm. 1964. Dutton.
--One for the Money. LC 46-5412. 188 p. 21 cm. 1946. E. P. Dutton & Co., Inc.
--One For the Money: A Candy Kane Story. (Janet Lambert Books For Girls). N.D. Grosset & Dunlap.
--Practically Perfect. LC 47-18226. 192 p. 19 1/2 cm. 1947. E. P. Dutton & Company, Inc.
--Practically Perfect: A Penny Parrish Story. (Janet Lambert Books For Girls). N.D. Grosset & Dunlap.
--The Precious Days. LC 57-7545. 192p. 21cm. 1957. Dutton.
--Rainbow After Rain. LC 53-5212. (Illus.). 190 p. 22cm. 1953. Dutton.
--Rainbow After Rain. N.D. (ISBN 0-448-02625-2). Grosset & Dunlap.
--The Reluctant Heart. LC 50-14556. 192 p. 20 cm. 1950. Dutton.
--The Reluctant Heart. LC 61-4918. 192p. 21cm. 1960, c.1950. Grosset & Dunlap.
--A Song in Their Hearts. LC 56-8225. 191p. 22cm. 1956. Dutton.
--Spring Fever. LC 60-11867. 178p. 21cm. 1960. Dutton.
--Stagestruck Parri. LC 66-7401. 157p.21cm. 1966. Dutton.
--Star Dream. LC 51-10528. 190 p. 21 cm. 1951. Dutton.
--Star Dream. 190p. 21cm. 1960, c.1951. Grosset & Dunlap.
--Star Spangled Summer. LC 56-58534. 256p. illus. 21cm. (Famous Janet Lambert books for girls). 1956, c.1941. Grosset & Dunlap.
--Star-Spangled Summer. James, Sandra, illus. LC 41-1239. 281 p. illus. 21 cm. 1941. E. P. Dutton & Company, Inc.
--The Stars Hang High. LC 60-601125. 189p. 21cm. 1960. Dutton.
--Summer for Seven. LC 52-11164. (Illus.). 190 p. 21cm. 1952. Dutton.
--Summer Madness. LC 62-7833. 155p. 21cm. 1962. Dutton.
--Sweet As Sugar. LC 67-20127. 160 p. 21cm. 1967. Dutton.
--That's My Girl. LC 64-10691. 190 p. 21 cm. 1964. Dutton.
--Treasure Trouble. LC 49-815106. 189 p. 20 cm. 1949. E. P. Dutton.
--Treasure Trouble: A Tippy Parrish Story. (Janet Lambert Books For Girls). N.D. Grosset & Dunlap.
--Triple Trouble. LC 65-121819. 159p. 21cm. (Her Cinda Hollister bks.). c.1965. Dutton.
--Up Goes the Curtain. LC 46-2484. 189 p. 21 cm. 1946. E. P. Dutton & Co., Inc.
--Up Goes the Curtain: A Penny Parrish Story. (Janet Lambert Books For Girls). N.D. Grosset & Dunlap.
--Wedding Bells. LC 61-124630. 192p. 21cm. 1961. (ISBN 0-525-42353-2). Dutton.
--Welcome Home, Mrs. Jordon. LC 53-10330. 192p. 21cm. 1953. Dutton.
--We're Going Steady. LC 58-524311. 182p. 21cm. 1958. Dutton.
--Where the Heart Is. LC 48-67216. 192 p. 20 cm. 1948. E. P. Dutton.
--Where The Heart Is. N.D. Grosset & Dunlap.
--Whoa, Matilda!. LC 56-58574. 183p. 21cm. (Famous Janet Lambert books for girls). 1956, c.1944. Grosset & Dunlap.
--Whoa, Matilda!. Raflin, Roberta, illus. LC 44-5435. 183 p. 21 cm. 1944. E. P. Dutton & Co., Inc.

Lambert, Linda
--The Bee That Could Never Be Killed. (Illus.). (Little Book Ser). (gr. k-6). 1974. (ISBN 0-89409-005-4). Childrens Art.

Lambert, Mary, tr. see Reggiani, Renee.

Lambert, Regina
--Valerie's Adventure at Crystal Lake. LC 80-23892. p. cm. c.1980. (ISBN 0-8024-3937-3). Moody Press.
--Valerie's Adventure at Last Chance Mine. LC 82-2107. p. cm. c.1982. (ISBN 0-8024-3938-1). Moody Press.
--Valerie's Adventure on Slide Mountain. (Orig.). (Valerie Adventure Ser). (gr. 7-9). 1983. (ISBN 0-8024-0320-4). Moody.
--Valerie's Wilderness Adventure. LC 78-9027. 127 p. 17cm. c.1978. (ISBN 0-8024-3936-5). Moody Press.

Lambert, Richard Stanton (1894-)
--Franklin Of The Arctic. 1949. (ISBN 0-8382-0267-5, Cadmus Books). E. M. Hale and Company.
--Mutiny in the Bay: Henry Hudson's Last Voyage. Rosenthal, Joseph J. (1911-), illus. LC 63-14995. 160 p. illus. 22 cm. (Great stories of Canada, 27). 1963. St Martin's Press.
--North for Adventure. Mould, Vernon, illus. LC 53-294343. 208p. illus. 21cm. 1952. McClelland and Stewart.
--Redcoat Sailor: The Adventures of Sir Howard Douglas. Dingle, Adrian, illus. 160p. illus. 22cm. (Great Stories of Canada). 1956. St. Martin's Press.
--Redcoat Sailor, the Adventures of Sir Howard Douglas. Dingle, Adrian, illus. LC 57-714. 160p. illus. 22cm. (Great stories of Canada). 1956. St. Martin's Press.

Lambert, Saul (1928-)
--Mrs. Poggi's Holiday. Lambert, Saul (1928-), illus. LC 69-17440. (Illus.). 40p. (gr. k-3). 1969. (ISBN 0-394-90835-X). Random.

Lambertson, Floyd Wesley (1891-)
--World Over Stories: For Junior Boys and Girls. LC 30-141971. 160 p. front. 21 cm. c.1930. The Abingdon Press.

Lambie, Laurie Jo
--Daisy Discovers Dance. LC 73-2871. (Illus.). 32 p. 1974, c.1973. (ISBN 0-381-99636-0). John Day Co.

Lambie, Nat
--Where Continents Meet. LC 79-135283. (Illus.). photos. 64p. (gr. 9-12). 1972. (ISBN 0-381-99765-0). John Day.

Lamblin, Pierre
--Jacques Rogy and the Little Detectives. 1st ed. Selig, Sylvie (1942-), illus. LC 70-78744. (Illus.). 185 p. 22cm. 1969. Doubleday.

Lamborn, Florence, tr. see Lindgren, Astrid Ericsson.

Lambregtse, Cornelius, tr. see Kohl, Dieter.

Lamburn, Richmal Crompton see Crompton, Richmal, pseud.

Lamburn, Richmal Crompton (1890-1969)
--William and the Pop Singers. Crompton, Richmal, pseud. Ford, Henry Justice (1860-1941), illus. LC 66-4657. 190p. illus. 20cm. 1966, c.1965. G. Newnes.
--William's Treasure Trove. Crompton, Richmal, pseud. N.D. Transatlantic Arts Inc.

Lam Chan Quan, tr. see Nielsen, Kay (1923-) & Nielsen, Jon.

Lame Deer, et al.
--The Sound of Flutes and Other Indian Legends. Erdoes, Richard, ed. Goble, Paul (1933-), illus. LC 76-8660. (Illus.). 129 p. 21cm. c.1976. (ISBN 0-394-83181-0). (ISBN 0-394-93181-5). Pantheon Books. **Award: (ALA).**

Lamers, Mary McGuire (1908-)
--Cottage on the Curve. LC 46-57335. 222 p. illus. 20 1/2 cm. 1945. The Bruce Publishing Company.
--The Secret of Springhill. LC 48-384648. 215 p. illus. 21 cm. 1948. Bruce Pub. Co.

Lamers, Mary McGuire (1908-) & Lamers, William Mathias (1900-)
--Star Spangled Stories. N.D. Bruce Publishing Co.

Lamers, William Mathias, jt. auth. see Lamers, Mary McGuire.

Lamers, William Mathias (1900-)
--Bill and His Friends. LC 34-41986. ix, 230 p. front., plates. 21 cm. c.1934. The Bruce Publishing Company.
--Joe McGuire, Freshman. LC 33-4781. 4 p. l., 206 p. front., pl. 20 cm. c.1932. The Bruce Publishing Company.
--Ned Haskins. LC 32-869681. 4 p. l., 171 p. front., illus. 19 cm. 1932. Benziger Brothers.
--Thundermaker. 1959. Bruce Publishing Company.

Lamkey, Rosemary
--The Lonely Dwarf. Lamkey, Rosemary, illus. LC 39-32608. 49, 1 p. illus. (part col.) 21 cm. c.1939. H. Holt and Company.
--Skittles. Lamkey, Rosemary, illus. LC 40-33526. 52, 1 p. illus. (part col.) 21 x 17 cm. c.1940. H. Holt and Company.

Lammers, Ann Conrad, tr. see Steiner, Jorg.

Lamont, Bette
--Island Time. 1st ed. Turkle, Brinton Cassaday (1915-), illus. LC 75-26998. (Illus.). 46 p. c.1976. (ISBN 0-397-31568-6). Lippincott.

Lamont, Dorothy
--Malcolm & Grigio in the Land of the Light. 1984. (ISBN 0-533-05999-2). Vantage.

Lamont, Priscilla, retold by.
--The Troublesome Pig: A Nursery Tale. Lamont, Priscilla, illus. LC 84-7717. (Illus.). 32 p. 25cm. 1985, c.1983. (ISBN 0-517-55546-8). Crown Publishers.

Lamont, Violet, illus.
--Mother Goose. (Giant Little Golden Bk.). 1957. Golden Press.

LaMore, Gregory S. (1954-)
--Now I Understand. Ensing-Keelean, Jan, illus. LC 85-20639. p. cm. 1985. (ISBN 0-930323-13-0). Gallaudet College Press.

Lamorisse, Albert Emmanuel (1922-1970)
--The Red Balloon. LC 57-9229. (Illus.). unpaged. 32cm. 1957. Doubleday. **Award: (NYT).**
--The Red Balloon. Lamorisse, Albert Emmanuel (1922-1972), photos by. 1956. Doubleday.
--Trip in a Balloon. Lamorisse, Claude & Duparc, Alain, photos by LC 67-7156. (Illus.). (gr. 3-5). N.D. (ISBN 0-385-07908-7). Doubleday.

Lamorisse, Albert Emmanuel (1922-1972) & Prevert, Jaques Henri Marie (1900-1972)
--Bim, the Little Donkey. Lamorisse, Albert Emmanuel (1922-1972), photos by. Swados, Betty & Swados, Harvey (1920-1972), trs. from Fr LC 72-77396. (Illus.). 48p. (gr. k-2). 1973. (ISBN 0-385-09400-0). (ISBN 0-385-08113-8). Doubleday.

La Motte-Fouque, Friedrich Heinrich Karl (1777-1843)
--The Magic Ring, 1 of 5 Vols. (Illus.). (Fouque's Stories of Chivalry and Romance). N.D. Set. George Routledge & Sons.
--Romantic Fiction: A New Book for the Young. N.D. George Routledge.

L'Amour, Louis see Burns, Tex, pseud.

Lamp, Dana & Lamp, Ginger
--Quest For The Lost City. N.D. Grosset & Dunlap.

Lamp, Ginger, jt. auth. see Lamp, Dana.

Lampeduse, Giuseppe Di see Di Lampedusa, Giuseppe.

Lampel, Rusia
--That Summer with Ora. LC 67-11285. 159 p. 22cm. 1967. F. Watts.

Lampell, Millard (1919-)
--The Pig with One Nostril. 1st ed. Parnall, Peter (1936-), illus. LC 72-76184. (Illus.). 48 p. 1975. (ISBN 0-385-07082-9). (ISBN 0-385-07082-9). (ISBN 0-385-07082-9). Doubleday.

Lampen, Dudley
--The Queen of the Extinct Volcano. N.D. E. & J. B Young & Co.

Lampert, Diane, jt. auth. see Farrow, Peter.

Lampert, Emily
--A Little Touch of Monster. Chess, Victoria (1939-), illus. LC 85-26847. p. cm. c.1985. (ISBN 0-87113-022-X). Atlantic Monthly Press.
--The Unusual Jam Adventure. 1st ed. Oliver, Jenni (1947-), illus. LC 77-15642. (Illus.). 32 p. 22cm. c.1978. (ISBN 0-316-51295-8). Little, Brown.

Lamperti, Noelle
--Noelle's Brown Book. 1st ed. Dingman, Beth, illus. LC 79-89574. (Illus.). 28 p. c.1979. (ISBN 0-934678-03-0). New Victoria Publishers.

Lamplugh, Lois (1921-)
--Midsummer Mountains. Stobbs, William (1914-), illus. (Illus.). (gr. 3-7). 1961. (ISBN 0-685-21340-4). Verry.
--Pigeongram Puzzle. Stobbs, William (1914-), illus. (gr. 3-7). 1960. (ISBN 0-685-21416-8). Verry.
--Vagabonds' Castle. Stobbs, William (1914-), illus. (New Adventure Library Ser). (gr. 3-7). 1965. (ISBN 0-685-21641-1). Verry.

Lampman, Ben Hur (1886-)
--Here Comes Somebody. Blaine, Mahlon, illus. N.D. Binfords & Mort.
--Here Comes Somebody. Blaine, Mahlon, illus. LC 35-9335. 7 p. l., 3-275 p. incl. front., illus., plates. 23 cm. 1935. Metropolitan Press.

Lampman, Evelyn Sibley see Bronson, Lynn, pseud.

Lampman, Evelyn Sibley (1907-1980)
--The Bandit of Mok Hill. 1st ed. Friedman, Marvin (1930-), illus. LC 69-12188. (Illus.). 254 p. 22cm. 1969. Doubleday.
--Bargain Bride. LC 76-46567. 180 p. 22cm. 1977. (ISBN 0-689-50075-0). Atheneum.
--The Bounces of Cynthian'. Paull, Grace A. (1898-), illus. (Illus.). 21 cm. 200p. 1950. Doubleday & Co.
--Captain Apple's Ghost. 1st ed. Macknight, Ninon (1908-), illus. Ninon, pseud. LC 52-10126. (Illus.). 249 p. 21cm. 1952. Doubleday.
--Cayuse Courage. LC 76-94333. 192 p. 22cm. 1970. Harcourt, Brace & World.
--The City Under the Back Steps. 1st ed. Valintcourt, Honore, illus. LC 60-13539. 210p. illus. 22cm. 1960. Doubleday.
--Crazy Creek. 1st ed. Paull, Grace A. (1898-), illus. LC 48-8275. 213 p. illus. 21 cm. 1948. N. Y., Doubleday.
--Elder Brother. 1st ed. Bennett, Richard Michael (1899-), illus. LC 51-12887. (Illus.). 217 p. 21cm. 1951. Doubleday.
--Go up the Road. 1st ed. Robinson, Charles (1931-), illus. LC 79-190556. (Illus.). 187 p. 22cm. 1972. (ISBN 0-689-20583-X). Atheneum.
--Go Up the Road. Robinson, Charles (1931-), illus. LC 73-9853. (Illus.). 230 p. 24cm. 1973, c.1972. (ISBN 0-8161-6130-5). G. K. Hall.
--Half-Breed. 1st ed. Grifalconi, Ann (1929-), illus. LC 67-15374. 263p. illus. 22cm. 1967. (ISBN 0-385-08636-9). Doubleday.
--Mrs. Updaisy. (Illus.). (gr. 4-7). 1963. (ISBN 0-8382-0526-7). Hale.
--Mrs. Updaisy. Szekeres, Cyndy (1933-), illus. LC 63-12881. 1963. Doubleday.
--Navaho Sister. 1st ed. Lantz, Paul (1908-), illus. LC 56-9058. 189p. illus. 22cm. 1956. (ISBN 0-385-07588-X). Doubleday.
--Once Upon the Little Big Horn. Gretzer, John, illus. LC 78-113855. (Illus.). 159 p. 21cm. 1971. (ISBN 0-690-59540-9). Crowell.
--Popular Girl. Bronson, Lynn, pseud. LC 57-6704. 191p. 22cm. (gr. 7-11). 1957. Doubleday.
--The Potlatch Family. LC 75-28328. 135 p. 22cm. 1976. (ISBN 0-689-50039-4). Atheneum.
--Princess of Fort Vancouver. 1st ed. Gorsline, Douglas Warner (1913-1985), illus. LC 62-7656. 282p. illus. 22cm. 1962. Doubleday.
--Rattlesnake Cave. 1st ed. Johnson, Pamela, illus. LC 72-85918. 185 p. 22cm. 1974. (ISBN 0-689-30429-3). Atheneum.
--Rock Hounds. Spilka, Arnold (1917-), illus. LC 58-9661. 213p. illus. 22cm. 1958. Doubleday.
--Rusty's Space Ship. 1st ed. Krigstein, Bernard (1919-), illus. LC 57-10458. 240p. illus. 22cm. 1957. (ISBN 0-385-07688-6). Doubleday.
--The Shy Stegosaurus of Cricket Creek. Buel, Hubert, illus. LC 55-9233. 218p. illus. 22cm. 1955. (ISBN 0-385-07490-5). Doubleday.
--Shy Stegosaurus of Indian Springs. Galdone, Paul (1914-), illus. LC 62-15899. (Illus.). (gr. 5-8). 1962. (ISBN 0-385-02393-6). Doubleday.
--Special Year. 1st ed. Genia, pseud. (1930-), illus. Wennerstrom, Genia Katherine. LC 59-13102. 213p. illus. 22cm. 1959. (ISBN 0-385-07822-6). Doubleday.
--Squaw Man's Son. LC 77-17503. (Illus.). 172 p. 22cm. 1978. (ISBN 0-689-50102-1). Atheneum.
--Temple of the Sun: A Boy Fights for Montezuma. 1st ed. Rethi, Lili (1894-), illus. LC 64-16239. 229 p. illus. 22 cm. 1964. Doubleday.
--Three Knocks on the Wall. LC 79-23264. 182 p. 22cm. 1980. (ISBN 0-689-50167-6). Atheneum.
--The Tilted Sombrero. Cruz, Raymond (1933-), illus. LC 66-15445. 264 p. illus. 22 cm. 1966. Doubleday.
--Treasure Mountain. 1st ed. Bennett, Richard Michael (1899-), illus. LC 49-10164. 207 p. illus. 21 cm. 1949. Doubleday.
--Tree Wagon. 1st ed. Frankenberg, Robert Clinton (1911-), illus. LC 53-9138. 253p. illus. 21cm. (gr. 5-8). 1953. Doubleday.
--Wheels West: The Story of Tabitha Brown. Walker, Gil, illus. LC 65-13103. 226p. illus. 22cm. c.1965. Doubleday.
--White Captives. LC 74-18187. 181 p. 22cm. 1975. (ISBN 0-689-50023-8). Atheneum.
--Witch Doctor's Son. 1st ed. Bennett, Richard Michael (1899-), illus. LC 54-10765. (Illus.). 249 p. 22cm. 1954. Doubleday.
--The Year of Small Shadow. LC 73-152694. 190 p. 20cm. 1971. (ISBN 0-15-299815-2). Harcourt Brace Jovanovich.

Lamport, Mary Frances & Hardeman, Eva
--Jerry Giraffe's Short Journey. Hardeman, Eva, illus. LC 77-99129. (Illus.). 32 p. 21cm. c.1977. Ginny's Copying Service.

Lamprey, Louise, jt. auth. see Klenova, Varia.

Lamprey, Louise, jt. ed. see Chadwick, Mara Louise Pratt, Mrs.

Lamprey, Louise (1869-1951)
--Children of Ancient Britain. Petersham, Maud Sylvia Fuller, Mrs. (1890-1971) & Petersham, Miska (1889-1960), illus. LC 22-2638. (Illus.). 18cm. xi, 222p. Orig. Title: Long Ago People. 1921. Little, Brown and Company.
--Children of Ancient Egypt. Freeman, Margaret (1893-), illus. LC 26-12051. (Illus.). 19cm. viii, 267p. Orig. Title: Long Ago in Egypt. 1926. Little, Brown and Company.

--Children of Ancient Rome. Hart-Hubon, Edna F., illus. LC 22-199743. xiv, 262 p. incl. illus., plates. front. 20 cm. 1922. Little, Brown, and Company.
--Days of the Leaders. Sturtevant, Wallis H., illus. LC 25-17064. xv, 357 p. col. front., illus. (incl. maps) col. plates. 21 cm. (Great days in American history series). 1925. Frederick A. Stokes Company.
--In the Days of the Guild. Hatt, Mabel K. & Gardiner, Florence, illus. ix, 291 p. col. front., illus., col. plates. 23 cm. c.1918. Frederick A. Stokes Company.
--Long Ago in Egypt. Freeman, Margaret (1893-), illus. LC 26-5755. viii, 267 p. col. front., illus. 19 cm. 1926. Little, Brown, and Company.
--Long Ago in Gaul. Freeman, Margaret (1893-), illus. xv, 320 p. incl. illus., plates. col. front. 20 cm. 1927. Little, Brown, and Company.
--Long-Ago People: How They Lived in Britain Before History Began. Petersham, Maud Sylvia Fuller, Mrs. (1890-1971) & Petersham, Miska (1889-1960), illus. LC 21-19479. xi, 226 p. front., illus., plates. 19 cm. 1921. Little, Brown, and Company.
--Masters of the Guild. Curtis, Elizabeth & Choate, Florence, illus. LC 20-18171. vi, 2 p., 1 l., 240 p. col. front., plates (part col.) 23 cm. c.1920. Frederick A. Stokes Company.
--The Tomahawk Trail. Good, Stafford C. (1890-), illus. LC 34-34009. vii, xi-xv p., 1 l., 313 p. col. mounted front., col. plates. 21 cm. 1934. Frederick A. Stokes Company.
--The Treasure Valley. Freeman, Margaret (1893-), illus. LC 28-21507. xl, 1 p., 1 l., 337 p. incl. illus., plates. col. front., col. plates. 21 cm. c.1928. W. Morrow & Company.
--Wonder Tales of Architecture. Peck, A. Gladys, illus. LC 27-184839. xiv, 273 p. incl. illus., plates. col. front., col. plates. 22 cm. 1927. Frederick A. Stokes Company.

Lamson, Sally (1917-)
--Letters to George. LC 75-20956. (Illus.). 40 p. 29cm. c.1975. (ISBN 0-87133-054-7). Franklin Pub. Co.

Lancaster, Bruce (1896-1963)
--Guns in the Forest. (A young readers' edition of the author's GUNS OF BURGOYNE). (gr. 7-10). 1952. (ISBN 0-316-51343-1, Pub. by Atlantic Monthly Pr). Little.

Lancaster, Clay (1917-)
--Michiko: Or, Mrs. Belmont's Brownstone on Brooklyn Heights. Lancaster, Clay (1917-), illus. LC 65-25469. 59p. illus. 27cm. c.1965. Tuttle.
--The Periwinkle Steamboat. Lancaster, Clay (1917-), illus. LC 61-89468. 54p. illus. 24cm. 1961. Viking Press.

Lancaster, F. Hewes (1871-)
--Rainbow Boy. Walsh, Haidee Zack, illus. LC 26-16051. 255 p. incl. col. front., col. illus., col. plates. 24 cm. c.1926. A. Whitman & Co.

Lancaster, Flo
--Flip-Flap: The Great Oojah. Maybank, Thomas, illus. LC 56-51690. 80p. illus. (part col.) 19cm. (The Twilight Series for Little Folk: No. 1). 1920. James A. McCann Co.

Lancaster, William Joseph Cosens see Collinghood, Harry, pseud.

Lancaster, William Joseph Cosens (1851-1922)
--Blue and Grey, a Story of the American Civil War. Collinghood, Harry, pseud. LC 8-34814. 4 p. l., 317, 1 p. col. front., 3 col. pl. 19 cm. 1908. Cassell and Company, Limited.
--Pirate Island: A Story of the Southern Pacific. Collinghood, Harry, pseud. LC 20-19319. 188 p. incl. front., 2 pl. 16 cm. (Cover-title: Leather clad tales of adventure and romance. no. 4). 1890. F. F. Lovell & Company.

Lancer, Jack, pseud., see Stratemeyer Syndicate.

Lancer, Jack, pseud.
--Ace of Shadows. Stratemeyer Syndicate. LC 68-15285. (Illus.). (Christopher Cool T.E.E.N. Agent Ser.: Vol. 4). 1968. Grosset & Dunlap.
--Department of Danger. Stratemeyer Syndicate. LC 67-23798. 176 p. 20cm. (Christopher Cool T.E.E.N. Agent Ser.: Vol. 3). 1967. Grosset & Dunlap.
--Heads You Lose. Stratemeyer Syndicate. LC 68-24657. (Illus.). 176 p. 20cm. (Christopher Cool T.E.E.N. Agent Ser.: Vol. 5). 1968. (ISBN 0-448-07905-4). Grosset & Dunlap.
--Mission: Moonfire. Stratemeyer Syndicate. LC 67-23797. (Illus.). 176 p. 20cm. (Christopher Cool T.E.E.N. Agent Ser.: Vol. 2). 1967. (ISBN 0-448-07902-X). Grosset & Dunlap.
--Trial by Fury. Stratemeyer Syndicate. LC 69-17268. (Illus.). 176 p. 20cm. (Christopher Cool T.E.E.N. Agent Ser.: Vol. 6). 1969. Grosset & Dunlap.
--X Marks the Spy. Stratemeyer Syndicate. LC 67-23796. (Illus.). 176 p. 20cm. (Christopher Cool T.E.E.N. Agent Ser.: Vol. 1). 1967. Grosset & Dunlap.

Lancewood, Lawrence, pseud., see Wise, Daniel.

Lancewood, Lawrence, pseud. (1813-1898)
--Cousin Clara: Or, The Mislaid Jewels. Wise, Daniel. (The Lindendale Stories). 1868. Henry A. Young.
--Cousin Clara: Or, The Mislaid Jewels. Wise, Daniel, 1 of 5 vols. (Illus.). (Lindendale Stories Ser.: Vol. 4). N.D. Set. Methodist Bk Concern.
--Louis Sinclair: Or, The Silver Prize Medals. Wise, Daniel. (The Lindendale Stories). N.D. Henry A. Young.
--Louis Sinclair: Or, The Silver Prize Medals. Wise, Daniel, 1 of 5 vols. (Illus.). (Lindendale Stories Ser.: Vol. 3). N.D. Set. Methodist Bk Concern.
--Nellie Warren: Or, The Lost Watch. Wise, Daniel. (The Lindendale Stories). N.D. Henry A. Young.
--Nellie Warren: Or, The Lost Watch. Wise, Daniel, 1 of 5 vols. (Illus.). (Lindendale Stories Ser.: Vol. 2). N.D. Set. Methodist Bk Concern.
--Peter Clinton. Wise, Daniel. (The Lindendale Stories). 1869. Henry A. Young.
--Peter Clinton: The Story of a Boy. Wise, Daniel, 1 of 5 vols. (Illus.). (Lindendale Stories Ser.: Vol. 5). N.D. Set. Methodist Bk Concern.
--Sidney De Grey: Or, The Rival School Boys. Wise, Daniel. (The Lindendale Stories). N.D. Henry A. Young.
--Sidney DeGrey: Or, The Rival School-boys. Wise, Daniel, 1 of 5 vols. (Illus.). (Lindendale Stories Ser.: Vol. 1). N.D. Set. Methodist Bk Concern.

Lancey, Floy Winks De see DeLancey, Floy Winks.

Lancourt, Saul & Carlyle, Marguerite
--Robin Hood. Beckett, Sheilah (1913-), illus. LC 41-1547. 36 p. illus. (part col.; incl. music) 25 cm. c.1940. Garden City Publishing Co., Inc.

Lancourt, Saul & Rimskii-Korsakov, Nikolai Andreevich (1844-1908)
The Dumble Dee Prince. Beckett, Sheilah (1913-), illus. LC 41-1546. 36 p. illus. (part col.) 25 cm. c.1940. Garden City Publishing Co., Inc.

Land, Andrew (1844-1912)
--Tales of Troy and Greece. Bawden, Edward (1903-), illus. (gr. 5-8). 1978. Faber.

Land, Charles
--Calling Earth. Purcell, Darryle, illus. LC 78-70804. (Illus.). 56 p. 24cm. c.1978. (ISBN 0-87191-684-3). Creative Education.
--Once Upon a Garden Hose. O'Leary, Franklin J. (1922-), illus. LC 67-17330. (Illus.). 32 p. 27cm. 1967. (ISBN 0-8114-7543-3). Steck-Vaughn Co.

Land, Jane, pseud., see Borland, Kathryn Kilby.

Landa, Gertrude see Aunt Naomi, pseud.

Landa, Gertrude
--Jewish Fairy Tales and Fables. Aunt Naomi, pseud. (gr. 3-7). N.D. Feldheim.
--Jewish Fairy Tales and Fables. Aunt Naomi, pseud. Marks, J. & Strelett, E., illus. LC 15-14526. 169 p. illus. 20 cm. 1915. Bloch Publishing Company.
--Jewish Fairy Tales and Fables. Aunt Naomi, pseud. Strellett, E. & Marks, J., illus. 169 1 p. incl. illus. 20 cm. 1908. Bloch Publishing Co.
--Jewish Fairy Tales and Legends. Aunt Naomi, pseud. Aronson, Sol, illus. LC 19-8999. 294 p. incl. front., illus. 19 cm. 1919. Bloch Publishing Co.

Landau, Jane
--Bess' Happy Year. LC 25-758. 6 p. l., 3-308 p. col. front., plates. 20 cm. c.1924. The Cornhill Publishing Company.

Landau, Terry, jt. auth. see Berger, Judith.

Landeck, Beatrice (1904-), ed.
--Echoes of Africa in Folk Songs of the Americas. 2nd rev. ed. Dobkin, Alexander (1908-1975), illus. (Illus.). drawings. (gr. 9 up). 1969. (ISBN 0-679-50020-0). McKay.
--More Songs to Grow On. Martin, David Stone (1913-), illus. (Illus.). (gr. k-3). 1954. (ISBN 0-688-02110-7). Morrow.

--Songs to Grow on: A Collection of American Folk Songs for Children. Martin, David Stone (1913-), illus. LC 50-14154. (Assembled with Explanatory Text and Rhythm Band Arrangements; Piano Settings by Florence White). 125 p. illus. 29 cm. N.D. E. B. Marks Music Corp.

Lander, Sarah West, jt. auth. see Keil, Johnann Georg.

Lander, Sarah West (1810-1872), tr. from Ger.
--Fairy Bells, and What They Tolled Us. LC 28-3373. 1 p. l., 5-204 p. front., plates. 17 cm. 1868. H. B. Fuller.
--Fairy Bells, and What They Tolled Us. (Illus.). N.D. Hurst & Co.
--Fairy Bells and What They Tolled Us. New ed. N.D. Lockwood, Brooks & Co.

Landers, Judith
--Timothy & the King's Ship "Liberty". Petree, Ruth A., illus. (Illus.). 30p. (Orig.). (gr. 1-4). 1974. (ISBN 0-917012-62-3). RI Pubns Soc.

Landers, Vernette
--Impy. (Illus.). 46 p. 22cm. 1974. Vantage.

Landes, William-Alan
--Aladdin N' His Magic Lamp. rev. ed. 52p. (Wondrawhopper Ser.). (gr. 3-12). 1985. (ISBN 0-88734-102-0). (ISBN 0-88734-003-2). Players Pr.
--Alice n' Wonderland. (Orig.). (Wondrawhopper Ser.). (gr. 3 up). 1985. (ISBN 0-88734-112-8). Players Pr.
--Jack N' the Beanstalk. rev. ed. (Wondrawhopper Ser.). (gr. 3-12). 1985. (ISBN 0-88734-101-2). (ISBN 0-88734-001-6). Players Pr.
--Jack N' the Beanstalk: Music & Lyrics. rev. ed. (Wondrawhopper Ser.). (gr. 3-12). 1985. (ISBN 0-88734-000-8). Players Pr.
--Peter n' the Wolf. rev. ed. (Wondrawhopper Ser.). (gr. 3-12). 1985. (ISBN 0-88734-106-3). (ISBN 0-88734-013-X). Players Pr.
--Pyramus & Thisbe. rev. ed. (gr. 3 up). 1985. (ISBN 0-88734-103-9). Players Pr.
--Rhyme Tyme. rev. ed. (Wondrawhopper Ser.). (gr. 3-12). 1985. (ISBN 0-88734-108-X). Players Pr.
--Rumpelstiltskin. rev. ed. 52p. (Wondrawhopper Ser.). (gr. 3-12). 1985. (ISBN 0-88734-104-7). (ISBN 0-88734-005-9). Players Pr.

Landes, William-Alan & Lasky, Mark A.
--Grandpa's Bedtime Story. rev. ed. (gr. 3-12). 1985. (ISBN 0-88734-505-0). Players Pr.

Landes, William-Alan & Rizzo, Jeff
--Rumpelstiltskin: Music & Lyrics. rev. ed. (Wondrawhopper Ser.). (gr. 3-12). 1985. (ISBN 0-88734-004-0). Players Pr.

Landes, William-Alan & Standish, Marilyn
--The Wizard of Oz. rev. ed. (Wondrawhopper Ser.). (gr. 3-12). 1985. (ISBN 0-88734-105-5). (ISBN 0-88734-011-3). Players Pr.

Landin, Harold W.
--Daniel Boone. N.D. J. B. Lippincott.

Landin, Les (1923-)
--About Atoms for Junior. Landin, Les (1923-), illus. LC 61-5009. (Illus.). 31 p. 24cm. (Look, read, learn). 1961. Melmont Publishers.

Landis, James David
--Daddy's Girl. LC 83-18966. 1984. (ISBN 0-688-02763-6). Morrow.
--The Sisters Impossible. LC 78-32148. 171 p. 22cm. c.1979. (ISBN 0-394-84190-5). (ISBN 0-394-94190-X). Knopf : Distributed by Random House.

Landis, Mary M.
--The Coon Tree Summer: Merry Brook Farm Story. 1978. (ISBN 0-686-22987-8). Rod & Staff.
--The Missing Popcorn & Other Stories. (gr. 3-6). 1976. (ISBN 0-686-15480-0). Rod & Staff.
--Trouble at Windy Acres. (gr. 5-10). 1976. (ISBN 0-686-15486-X). Rod & Staff.

Landman, Isaac
--Stories of the Prophets. (gr. 7-10). N.D. UAHC.

Landon, Margaret Dorothea Mortenson (1903-)
--Anna and the King. Ayer, Margaret (0000-1981), illus. 256p. (gr. 7-11). 1947. John Day Bks.
--Anna & the King of Siam. Ayer, Margaret (0000-1981), illus. (Illus.). 1944. (ISBN 0-381-98136-3, JD-T). Har-Row.

Landru, Hortense Parker
--Sled Dogs of Alaska. LC 53-9603. 184 p. 21cm. 1953. Dodd, Mead & Co.

Landry, Anne
--Come Dance with Me: A Book and a Record. Landry, Anne, illus. Walberg, Betty, contrib. by. LC 64-21091. (Music by Betty Walberg). 58 p. col. illus. 29 cm. and phonodisc (2 s. 10 in 33 1/3 rpm. microgroove) in pocket. 1964. J. H. Heineman.

Landry, Tom
--The Ballad of Tont Lala. (Illus.). 32p. (gr. k-8). N.D. (ISBN 0-931108-11-X). Little Cajun.

Landsdown, Brenda
--Galumph. 1963. (ISBN 0-8382-0280-2, Cadmus Books). E. M. Hale and Company.

Landshoff, Ursula, jt. auth. see Jameson, Cynthia.

Landshoff, Ursula (1908-)
--Cats Are Good Company. LC 77-25648. (Illus.). 5 7/8 x 8 1/2. (18 pt.). (I Can Read Bks.). (gr. k-3). 1983. Har-Row.
--Daisy & Doodle. Landshoff, Ursula (1908-), illus. LC 74-86634. (Illus.). 28 drawings with color overlays. 32p. 1st U.S. edition. (ps-1). 1969. (ISBN 0-87888-013-5). Bradbury Pr.
--Daisy and the Stormy Night. Landshoff, Ursula (1908-), illus. LC 77-122738. (Illus.). 32 p. 1970. Bradbury Press.
--Okay, Good Dog. Landshoff, Ursula (1908-), illus. LC 77-25648. (Illus.). 5 7/8 x 8 1/2. 64p. (18 pt.). (I Can Read Bks.). (gr. k-3). 1978. (ISBN 0-06-023672-8). (ISBN 0-06-023673-6). Har-Row.

Landsman, Sandy
--The Gadget Factor. LC 83-15690. 180p. (gr. 4-8). 1984. (ISBN 0-689-31014-5). Atheneum.

Lane
--Princess. (gr. 4-6). 1980. (ISBN 0-590-30383-X). Scholastic Inc.

Lane, Andrew P.
--Helping the Birds With Their Bees. N.D. Vantage Press.

Lane, Ann
--Penny Visits England. N.D. Carlton Press Inc.

Lane, Anna Eichberg see King, Anna Eichberg, pseud.

Lane, Anna Eichberg, Mrs., tr. see Kirschner, Lula.

Lane, Bertha Palmer
--Lad and Other Story Plays. Lane, Rosamond, illus. 6p. 1.,3-188p.front., illus., plates 21.5 cm. c.1926. Woman's Press.

Lane, Blaise
--Mark Twain: Adventure in Old Nevada. 1st ed. Johnson, Eugene Harper, illus. LC 56-5481. 191p. illus. 21cm. (American heritage series). 1956. Aladdin Books.

Lane, Carl Daniel (1899-)
--Black Tide. LC 66-255586. 155p. illus. 28cm. 1966. LargePrint Pubns.
--Black Tide. Lane, Carl Daniel (1899-), illus. LC 52-5013. (Illus.). 221 p. 20cm. 1952. Little, Brown.
--The Fire Raft. LC 51-4411. x, 210 p. 20cm. 1951. Little, Brown.
--Mystery Trail. Lane, Carl Daniel (1899-), illus. LC 51-13627. (Illus.). 231 p. 20cm. 1951. Little, Brown.
--River Dragon. LC 48-11934. 105 p. illus. 22 cm. 1948. Little, Brown.
--Treasure Cave. 1st ed. Lane, Carl Daniel (1899-), illus. LC 50-4967. x, 283 p. illus., maps, 20 cm. 1950. Little, Brown.

Lane, Carol Morris (1930-), ed.
--The Happy Hour Story Book. Urbanowich, Evelyn & Weihs, Erika (1917-), illus. LC 55-3884. 160p. illus. 29cm. c.1955. Hart Book Co.

Lane, Carolyn (1926-)
--Echoes in an Empty Room and Other Supernatural Tales. LC 80-20278. 158 p. 22cm. c.1980. (ISBN 0-03-057477-3). Holt, Rinehart and Winston.
--Ghost Island. Lane, Carolyn (1926-), illus. LC 84-28859. (Illus.). 148 p. 22cm. 1985. (ISBN 0-395-38207-6). Houghton Mifflin.
--Turnabout Night at the Zoo. Van Sciver, Ruth (1915-), illus. LC 74-127377. (Illus.). 96 p. 23cm. 1971. (ISBN 0-687-42692-8). Abingdon Press.
--Uncle Max and the Sea Lion. 1st ed. Gobbato, Imero (1923-), illus. LC 75-98277. (Illus.). 104 p. 20cm. 1970. Bobbs-Merrill.
--The Voices of Greenwillow Pond. Tripp, Wallace Whitney (1940-), illus. LC 72-75606. (Illus.). 45 p. 1972. (ISBN 0-395-13897-3). Houghton Mifflin.
--The Winnemah Spirit. Shortall, Leonard W., illus. LC 74-30158. (Illus.). 119 p. 22cm. 1975. (ISBN 0-395-20490-9). Houghton-Mifflin.

Lane, Edward William (1801-1876), tr. see Alcott, Frances Jenkins.

Lane, Edward William (1801-1876), tr. see Arabian Nights.

Lane, Edward William (1801-1876), tr. see Holland, Rupert Sargent.

Lane, Edward William (1801-1876), tr. see Lane-Poole, Stanley.

Lane, Edward William (1801-1876), tr. see Olcott, Frances Jenkins.

Lane, Edward William (1801-1876), tr. see Taylor, Bayard.

Lane, Edward William (1801-1876), ed.

--Arabian Nights. Lane's ed. Harvey, William (1796-1866), illus. N.D. Charles Scribner's Sons.

--Arabian Nights' Entertainments: Or, The Thousand and One Nights. (Author of "The Manners and Customs of Modern Egyptians."). (Illus.). (Lane's Popular Edition). N.D. J Fagan.

--Arabian Nights' Entertainments: Or, The Thousand and One Nights, 2 vols. Lane, Edward William (1801-1876), illus. Lane, Edward William (1801-1876), tr. N.D. James Miller.

--Arabian Nights' Entertainments: Or, The Thousand and One Nights. Revised. (Illus.). 1900. David McKay.

--The Arabian Nights' Entertainments: Or, The Thousand and One Nights. LC 28-6675. xiv, 1260 p. col. front. 23 1/2 cm. 1927. The Pickwick Publishers, Inc.

--Arabian Nights' Entertainments: Or, the Thousand and One Nights. (Illus.). (Lane's Standard Edition). N.D. William T. Amies.

Lane, Elizabeth Baldwin (1908-)
--Review Boy. LC 57-9767. 104p. 21cm. 1957. Pageant Press.

Lane, Estella Hitchcock, Mrs.
--Come True Land Stories. LC 29-126528. 142 p. illus. 20 cm. c.1929. The Pilgrim Press.
--The Giant Who Liked Chocolate Cake. Hearon, Dorothy, illus. x p., 1 l., 170 p. illus. 20 cm. 1939. Harper & Brothers.

Lane, Frederick A.
--The First Admiral. 1st ed. Chapman, Frederick Trench (1887-), illus. LC 53-12186. 177p. illus. 21cm. (American heritage). 1953. Aladdin Books.
--A Flag for Lafitte: Story of the Battle of New Orleans. 1st ed. Vosburgh, Leonard W. (1912-), illus. LC 54-6150. 191p. illus. 21cm. (American heritage series). 1954. Aladdin Books.

--The Greatest Adventure: A Story of Jack London. 1st ed. Quinn, Sidney, illus. LC 54-6151. 192p. illus. 21cm. (American heritage series). 1954. Aladdin Books.
--The Magnificent Mariner: An Early Story of John Paul Jones. 1st ed. Chapman, Frederick Trench (1887-), illus. LC 53-12168. 192p. illus. 21cm. (American heritage). 1953. Aladdin Books.
--Nat Harkins, Privateersman. 1st ed. Schule, Clifford H., illus. LC 56-6230. 218p. illus. 21cm. 1956. Holt.
--Patrol to the Kimberleys. 1955. E M Hale.
--Patrol to the Kimberleys. LC 55-7315. 218p. illus. 21cm. (Lodestar books). 1955. Prentice-Hall.
--Westward the Eagle. 1st ed. Johnson, Eugene Harper, illus. LC 55-5893. 224p. illus. 21cm. 1955. Holt.

Lane, Jerry
--In the Zoo. Drawson, Blair (1943-), illus. LC 73-81591. (Illus.). 24 p. (Magic circle book). 1974. (ISBN 0-663-25462-0). Ginn.
--Run!. Snyder, Joel, illus. LC 73-75066. (Illus.). 16 p. 20cm. (Magic circle book). 1974. (ISBN 0-663-25447-7). Ginn.

Lane, John Veasey (1861-)
--Marching with Morgan: How Donald Lovell Became a Soldier of the Revolution. Goss, John, illus. LC 9-16370. 6 p. l., 364 p. front., 5 pl. 21 cm. 1909. L. C. Page & Company.
--Rodney, the Ranger: With Daniel Morgan on Trail and Battlefield. Goss, John, illus. LC 11-165657. viii p., 1 l., 297 p. front., plates. 21 cm. 1911. L. C. Page & Company.

Lane, Julie
--The Life and Adventures of Santa Claus. Hokie, illus. LC 32-82766. 3 p. l., 144 p. incl. front., illus. 29 cm. c.1932. Santa Claus Publishing Co.
--The Life & Legends of Santa Claus. Hokie, illus. LC 84-2741. (Illus.). p. cm. 160p. (gr. 3-6). 1984, c.1983. (ISBN 0-917057-00-7). Tonnis.

Lane, Laura M
--A Character: A Story for Girls. (Illus.). N.D. E & J B Young.
--Ella's Mistake. (Illus.). N.D. E & J B Young.

Lane, Margaret
--The Fish: The Story of the Stickleback. Butler, John, illus. (Illus.). 32p. (Pied Piper Bks). (gr. k-4). 1983. (ISBN 0-8037-2603-1). Dial Bks Young.
--The Frog. Butler, John, illus. LC 81-5545. (Illus.). 32p. (ps-4). 1982. Dial Bks Young.
--The Spider. Firth, Barbara, illus. LC 82-71354. (Illus.). 32p. (ps-4). 1982. (ISBN 0-8037-8303-5). (ISBN 0-8037-8308-6). Dial Bks Young.
--The Spider. Firth, Barbara, illus. LC 82-71354. (Illus.). 32p. (Dial Book for Young Readers Ser.). (ps-4). 1983. (ISBN 0-8037-8308-6). Dutton.
--The Squirrel. Lilly, Kenneth, illus. (Illus.). 32p. (Pied Piper Bks.). (gr. k-3). 1982. (ISBN 0-8037-8330-2). Dial Bks Young.

Lane, Martha Allan Luther (1862-), retold by.
--The Arabian Nights' Entertainments: Stories from The Thousand and One Nights Told for Young People. Winckler, Ruby, illus. LC 15-10078. x, 2, 364 p. illus. 18 cm. $0.5. c.1915. Ginn and Company.
--Stories for Children. (Eclectic School Readings). N.D. American Book Company.

Lane, Martha Allen Luther, jt. auth. see Seeley, Eva Brunell.

Lane, Neola Tracy
--Get Along, Mules. 1st ed. Low, Vaike, illus. LC 61-6067. 155p. illus. 21cm. 1961. (ISBN 0-397-30546-X). Lippincott.
--Grasshopper Year. 1st ed. Morse, Dorothy Bayley (1906-1979), illus. LC 60-7619. 149p. illus. 21cm. 1960. Lippincott.
--A Kiss Is for Keeps. LC 64-11449. 160 p. 21 cm. 1964. Lippincott.
--Secret of the Silver Spoons. 1 st ed. Stone, David Karl (1922-), illus. LC 63-11661. (Illus.). 126 p. 22cm. 1963. Bobbs-Merrill.

Lane, Pauline C., tr. see Volkmann, Richard von.
Lane-Poole, Stanley (1843-1931), ed.
--The Arabian Nights' Entertainment, 4. (Bohn's Popular Library: No.4). N.D. Harcourt Brace & Co.
--Best Selections from the Arabian Nights Entertainments. Harvey, William (1796-1866), illus. Lane, Edward William (1801-1876), tr. LC 77-371321. (Illus.). xvii, 462 p. 21cm. c.1976. (ISBN 0-8055-1171-7). (ISBN 0-8055-0244-0). Hart Pub. Co.
--Stories from the Thousand and One Nights: The Arabian Nights' Entertainments. Lane, Edward William (1801-1876), tr. LC 9-28190. 1 p. l., 460 p. front., pl. 22 1/2 cm. (Harvard classics, ed. by C. W. Eliot. xvi). c.1909. P. F. Collier & Son.

Lane, Rose W. (1887-1968), ed. see Wilder, Laura Ingalls, Mrs.

Lane, Rose Wilder (1887-1968)
--Let the Hurricane Roar. (gr. 9 up). 1933. McKay.

Lane, Veda A
--We Live in Montana. LC 53-647422. 62p. 23cm. 1953. Vantage Press.
Lane, William C., Mrs.
--Tower Legends. 152p. N.D. Beacon Press Inc.

Lanes, Selma Gordon see Gordon, Selma, pseud.
Lanes, Selma Gordon (1929-), ed.
--A Child's First Book of Nursery Tales. Szekeres, Cyndy (1933-), illus. LC 82-83144. 48p. 1983. (ISBN 0-307-15577-3, Golden Pr). Western Pub.
Lanfair, Harriet
--Smudgy. Lanfair, Harriet, illus. LC 46-7272. 32 p. col. illus. 28 1/2 x 22 cm. 1946. Murray & Gee, Incorporated.
Lang, Andrew (1844-1912), ed. see Arabian Nights.
Lang, Andrew, ed. see Homerus.
Lang, Andrew (1844-1912), ed. see Lang, Leonora Blanche.
Lang, Andrew (1844-1912), ed. see Little Red Riding Hood.
Lang, Andrew (1844-1912), ed. see Perrault, Charles.
Lang, Andrew (1844-1912), retold by see Titeurington, Jean.
Lang, Andrew (1844-1912), retold by.
--The Adventures of Odysseus. Kiddell-Monroe, Joan (1908-), illus. LC 62-52233. xii, 179p. illus., col. plates, map. 22cm. (Children's illus. classics.). 1962. Dent.
--The Adventures of Odysseus. Kiddell-Monroe, Joan (1908-), illus. LC 62-52253. (Illus.). (Children's Illustrated Classics). (gr. 5-9). 1962. (ISBN 0-525-25056-5). Dutton.
--Aladdin. Le Cain, Errol John (1941-), illus. 32p. (gr. k-3). 1983. (ISBN 0-14-050389-7, Puffin). Penguin.
--Aladdin and the Wonderful Lamp. Ford, Henry Justice (1860-1941) & Jacomb-Hood, George Percy (1857-1929), illus. 19cm. 259p. 1906. Longmans, Green & Co.
--Aladdin and the Wonderful Lamp. Le Cain, Errol John (1941-), illus. LC 81-4861. p. cm. 1981. (ISBN 0-670-11146-5). Viking Press.
--Aladdin and the Wonderful Lamp. Lubin, Leonard B., illus. 1982. Delacorte.
--Aladdin and the Wonderland Lamp, etc. (Fairy Books Ser.). N.D. Longmans Green & Co.
--The Animal Story Book. Ford, Henry Justice (1860-1941), illus. 1896. Longman.
--Animal Story Book. Ford, Henry Justice (1860-1941), illus. (Illus.). 400p. 1904. Longmans,Green & Co.
--Arabian Nights. (Lang Fairy Bks.). N.D. Longmans Green & Co.
--Arabian Nights. Dempster, William, illus. LC 70-2508. (Illus.). 217 p. 29cm. (Educator classic library, 8). 1968. Classic Press.
--The Arabian Nights Entertainments. LC 96-830. xvi, 424 p. incl. front., illus., plates. 18 1/2 cm. 1898. Longmans, Green and Co.
--The Arabian Nights Entertainments. LC 4-17294. xvi, 424 p. incl. front., illus., plates. 19 cm. 1902. Longmans, Green, and Co.
--The Arabian Nights Entertainments. Ford, Henry Justice (1860-1941), illus. LC 69-17098. (Illus.). xvi, 424 p. 22cm. 1969. Dover Publications.
--Beauty and the Beast, and Other Stories. Ford, Henry Justice (1860-1941), illus. 254p. (Fairy Book Ser.). 1910. Longmans Green & Co.
--The Blue Fairy Book. (The Fairy Library). N.D. A L. Burt Co.
--Blue Fairy Book. N.D. Set. A. L. Burt's Pubs.
--The Blue Fairy Book. (The Lang Fairy Bks). N.D. Grosset & Dunlap.
--The Blue Fairy Book. (The Good Value Bks). N.D. Grosset & Dunlap.
--Blue Fairy Book. (Illus.). N.D. Hurst & Co.
--The Blue Fairy Book. (The Winston Clear-Type Popular Classics). N.D. John C. Winston.
--The Blue Fairy Book. (The Washington Square Classics). N.D. Macrae Smith Co.
--The Blue Fairy Book. Ford, Henry Justice, et al. (1860-1941), illus. (Illus.). (Lang's Fairy Library). N.D. Caldwell.
--Blue Fairy Book. Ford, Henry Justice (1860-1941), illus. (Illus.). (Lang's Fairy Library). N.D. Dodge Publishing Co.
--The Blue Fairy Book. Ford, Henry Justice (1860-1941) & Jacomb-Hood, George Percy (1857-1929), illus. LC 65-25707. 390p. illus. 22cm. (T1437). 1965. Dover.
--The Blue Fairy Book. Ford, Henry Justice (1860-1941) & Jacomb-Hood, George Percy (1857-1929), illus. (Illus.). 390p. (Lang Fairy Bks.). 1901. Longmans Green & Co.
--The Blue Fairy Book. Ford, Henry Justice (1860-1941) & Jacomb-Hood, George Percy (1857-1929), illus. LC 5-18484. 5 p. l., 390 p. front., illus., 7 pl. 19 cm. 1903. Longmans, Green, and Co.
--The Blue Fairy Book. New ed. Ford, Henry Justice (1860-1941) & Jacomb-Hood, George Percy (1857-1929), illus. LC 20-613742. 2 v. col. fronts., illus., plates. 19 cm. 1920. Longmans, Green and Co.
--The Blue Fairy Book. Ford, Henry Justice (1860-1941) & Jacomb-Hood, George Percy (1857-1929), illus. LC 29-18355. xi, 475 p. col. front., illus., col. plates. 21 cm. 1929. Longman's Green and Co.
--The Blue Fairy Book. Ford, Henry Justice (1860-1941) & Jacomb-Hood, George Percy (1857-1929), illus. LC 66-7946. 390p. illus. 23cm. 1966. McGraw.
--The Blue Fairy Book. Godwin, Frank (1889-), illus. LC 34-28315. 3 p. l., 341 p. col. front., col. plates. 19 cm. (golden books). 1934. D. McKay.
--The Blue Fairy Book. Godwin, Frank (1889-), illus. LC 27-26986. 3 p. l., 341 p. col. front., col. plates. 20 cm. (Newbery classics). 1927. David McKay Company.
--Blue Fairy Book. Kutcher, Ben (1895-), illus. Davis, Mary Gould, frwd. by. LC 48-10139. xii, 372 p. illus. (part col.) 21 cm. 1948. Longmans, Green.
--The Blue Fairy Book. Lee, Manning De Villeneuve (1894-1980), illus. LC 26-27497. 428 p. col. front., plates (part col.) 22 cm. 1926. Macrae Smith Company.
--The Blue Fairy Book. Lonette, Reisie Dominee (1924-), illus. (Illus.). 445 p. 20cm. (Looking glass library, 2). 1959. Looking Glass Library; Distributed by Random House.
--The Blue Fairy Book. Richardson, Frederick (1862-1937), illus. Holmes, Mabel Dodge (1883-), intro. by. LC 30-20194. xi, 396 p. col. front., illus., col. plates. 22 cm. c.1930. The John C. Winston Company.
--The Blue Fairy Book: Selected Tales from the Collection. Spanfeller, James John (1930-), illus. LC 74-2951. (Illus.). 256 p. 22cm. 1969. Junior Deluxe Editions.
--Blue Parrot, and Other Stories. (Fairy Book Ser.). N.D. Longmans Green & Co.
--The Blue Poetry Book. Ford, Henry Justice (1860-1941) & Speed, Lancelot (1860-1931), illus. LC 77-80375. (Illus.). xx, 351 p. 21cm. (Granger index reprint series). 1969. (ISBN 0-8369-6080-7). Books for Libraries Press.
--The Blue Poetry Book. Ford, Henry Justice (1860-1941) & Speed, Lancelot (1860-1931), illus. LC 5-40976. xx, 351 p. incl. illus., plates. front.27 cm. 1891. Longmans, Green and Co.
--The Blue Poetry Book. Ford, Henry Justice (1860-1941) & Speed, Lancelot (1860-1931), illus. LC 67-28167. (Illus.). xx, 351 p. 22cm. (Legacy library facsimile). 1967. University Microfilms.
--The Book of Romance. Ford, Henry Justice (1860-1941), illus. LC 4-4635. xiv, 384 p. incl. illus., plates. col. front., col. plates. 19 cm. 1902. Longmans, Green, and Co.
--Brown Fairy Book. N.D. Dover.
--Brown Fairy Book. (Lang Fairy Bks.). N.D. Longmans Green & Co.
--The Brown Fairy Book. Ford, Henry Justice (1860-1941), illus. LC 65-25708. xiii, 350p. illus. 22cm. (T1438). 1965. Dover.
--The Brown Fairy Book. Ford, Henry Justice (1860-1941), illus. LC 4-25384. 350p. 1904. Longmans, Green & Co.
--The Brown Fairy Book. Ford, Henry Justice (1860-1941), illus. LC 13-9360. xii, 350 p. incl. illus., plates. 8 col. pl. (incl. front.) 19 cm. 1910. Longmans, Green and Co.
--The Brown Fairy Book. Ford, Henry Justice (1860-1941), illus. xiii, 350p. illus. 23cm. 1966. McGraw.
--The Brown Fairy Book. Ford, Henry Justice (1860-1941), illus. LC 66-8773. (Illus.). xiii, 350 p. 23cm. 1966. McGraw-Hill.
--Cats and Mice. (Heritage Story Bks.). N.D. Longmans, Green & Co.
--Cinderella. N.D. Longmans, Green & Co.
--Cinderella: Or, The Little Glass Slipper. Ford, Henry Justice (1860-1941) & Jacomb-Hood, George Percy (1857-1929), illus. 19cm. 104p. 1907. Longmans, Green & Co.
--Crimson Fairy Book. (Lang Fairy Bks.). N.D. Longmans Green & Co.
--The Crimson Fairy Book. Ford, Henry Justice (1860-1941), illus. LC 67-17988. (Illus.). xi, 371 p. 22cm. 1967. Dover Publications.
--The Crimson Fairy Book. Ford, Henry Justice (1860-1941), illus. LC 3-25717. xi, 371 p. incl. illus., plates. 8 col. pl. (incl. front.) 19 cm. 1903. Longmans, Green, and Co.
--The Crimson Fairy Book. Ford, Henry Justice (1860-1941), illus. LC 20-19585. xi, 371 p. incl. illus. 8 col. pl. 19 cm. 1919. Longmans, Green & Co.
--The Crimson Fairy Book. Ford, Henry Justice (1860-1941), illus. N.D. (ISBN 0-8446-0753-3). Peter Smith Publisher, Inc.
--Crimson Fairy Book. Kutcher, Ben (1895-), illus. Davis, Mary Gould, frwd. by. LC 47-11855. xii, 233 p. illus. (part col.) 21 cm. 1947. Longmans, Green.
--Dick Whittington, and Other Stories: Based on the Tales in "The Blue Fairy Book,". Ford, Henry Justice (1860-1941) & Jacomb-Hood, George Percy (1857-1929), illus. LC 5-16634. v, 148 p. front., illus. 19 cm. 1905. Longmans, Green, and Co.
--Elf Maiden, and Other Stories. Ford, Henry Justice (1860-1941), illus. 196p. (Fairy Book Ser.). 1906. Longmans Green & Co.
--Fairy Nurse, and Other Stories. (Fairy Book Ser.). N.D. Longmans Green & Co.
--Forty Thieves, and Other Stories. (Fairy Tale Ser.). N.D. Longsmans Green & Co.
--Giants and Dwarfs. (Heritage Story Bks.). N.D. Longmans Green & Co.
--The Gold of Fairnilee. Lemann, E. A. & Scott, T., illus. 1888. Longman.
--Golden Mermaid, and Other Stories. Ford, Henry Justice (1860-1941), illus. col. front,. 19cm. 196p. (Fairy Book Ser.). 1906. Longmans Green & Co.
--The Green Fairy Book. (The Fairy Library). N.D. A. L. Burt Co.
--Green Fairy Book, 1 of 4 vols. (Andrew Lang's Works). N.D. Set. A. L. Burt's Pubs.
--The Green Fairy Book. N.D. Airmount Classics.
--The Green Fairy Book. (The Lang Fairy Bks.). N.D. Grosset & Dunlap.
--Green Fairy Book. (Illus.). N.D. Hurst & Co.
--Green Fairy Book. 1978. Viking.
--The Green Fairy Book. Ford, Henry Justice (1860-1941), illus. (Illus.). (Lang's Fairy Library). N.D. Caldwell.
--Green Fairy Book. Ford, Henry Justice (1860-1941), illus. (Lang's Fairy Book). N.D. Dodge Publishing Co.
--The Green Fairy Book. Ford, Henry Justice (1860-1941), illus. LC 65-25709. xi, 366 p. illus. 22 cm. 1965. Dover Publications.
--The Green Fairy Book. 5th impression. ed. Ford, Henry Justice (1860-1941), illus. LC 1-13898. xi p., 1 l., 366 p. incl. front., illus., plates. 19 cm. 1899. Longmans, Green, and Co.
--The Green Fairy Book. authorized crown. Ford, Henry Justice (1860-1941), illus. LC 29-18356. xvi, 420 p. col. front., illus., col. plates. 21 cm. 1929. Longmans, Green and Co.
--The Green Fairy Book. Ford, Henry Justice (1860-1941), illus. LC 66-7831. xi, 366p. illus. 23cm. 1966. McGraw.
--The Green Fairy Book. Ford, Henry Justice (1860-1941), illus. N.D. (ISBN 0-8446-5056-0). Peter Smith Publisher, Inc.
--Green Fairy Book. Gregory, Dorothy Lake, illus. Davis, Mary Gould, frwd. by. LC 48-9075. xvii, 355 p. illus. (part col.) 21 cm. 1948. Longmans, Green.
--The Green Fairy Book. Harbour, Jennie, illus. LC 34-28314. 2 p. l., iii-v p., 2 l., 296 p. col. front., col. plates. 19 cm. (golden books). 1934. D. McKay.
--The Green Fairy Book. Harbour, Jennie, illus. LC 27-26987. 2 p. l., iii-v p., 2 l., 298 p. col. front., col. plates. 20 cm. (Newbery classics). 1927. David McKay Company.
--The Green Fairy Book. Lonette, Reisie Dominee (1924-), illus. LC 60-11941. 470p. illus. 20cm. (Looking glass library, 20). 1960. Looking Glass Library; Distributed by Random House.
--The Grey Fairy Book. Ford, Henry Justice (1860-1941), illus. LC 67-17983. xii, 387p. illus. 22cm. 1967. Dover.
--The Grey Fairy Book. Ford, Henry Justice (1860-1941), illus. LC 6419. xii, 387 p. incl. front., illus., pl. 19 cm. 1900. Longmans, Green and Co.
--The Grey Fairy Book. Ford, Henry Justice (1860-1941), illus. xii, 387p. illus. 22cm. (Dover bk. rebound). 1968. (ISBN 0-8446-2424-1). P. Smith.
--The History of Jack the Giant-killer. Ford, Henry Justice (1860-1941), illus. 19cm. 120p. (Fairy Tale Bks.). 1908. Longman's, Green & Co.
--The History of Whittington. Ford, Henry Justice (1860-1941) & Jacomb-Hood, George Percy (1857-1929), illus. 19cm. 168p. (Fairy Tale Bks.). 1907. Longman's, Green & Co.
--In Fairyland. Doyle, Richard (1824-1883), illus. Wilkins, Cary, frwd. by. LC 79-16656. (Illus.). 61 p. 29cm. 1979. (ISBN 0-517-29353-6). Derrydale Books.
--The Invisible Prince and Other Stories. Ford, Henry Justice (1860-1941), illus. LC 12-157471. 190 p. incl. illus., plates. col. front 19 cm. (Fairy Book Ser.). 1910. Longmans, Green, and Co.
--Jack, the Giant Killer. N.D. Longmans, green & Co.
--King Arthur & the Knights of the Round Table. (Peter Possum Paperbacks Ser). 1967. (ISBN 0-531-05102-1). Watts.
--King Arthur: Tales of the Round Table. Ford, Henry Justice (1860-1941), illus. LC 67-26996. (Illus.). viii, 174 p. 21cm. 1967. (ISBN 0-8052-0196-3). Schocken Books.
--King of the Waterfalls, and Other Stories. (Fairy Book Ser.). N.D. Longmans Green & Co.

LaPietra, Mary (1929-)
--Aram Finds the Master. LeHew, Ronald M, illus. LC 74-82022. (Illus.). 25, 6 p. 18cm. (David C. Cook rainbow series). 1975, c.1974. (ISBN 0-912692-46-4). D. C. Cook Pub. Co.
--Innkeeper for a King. LeHew, Ronald M., illus. LC 74-75542. (Illus.). 27 p. 18cm. (David C. Cook Rainbow series). 1974. (ISBN 0-912692-42-1). D. C. Cook Pub. Co.
--The Shawl of Waiting. Kohn, Arnold, illus. LC 75-18924. (Illus.). 118 p. 18cm. c.1976. (ISBN 0-912692-82-0). D. C. Cook Pub. Co.
--Three Dreams in Bethlehem. LeHew, Ronald M, illus. LC 74-25298. (Illus.). 29 p. 18cm. (David C. Cook Rainbow Series). c.1975. (ISBN 0-912692-53-7). D. C. Cook Pub. Co.
--A Tomahawk for Christmas. Kohn, Arnold, illus. LC 76-11478. (Illus.). 117 p. 18cm. (Her A Chappie Creek adventure). c.1976. (ISBN 0-89191-052-2). D. C. Cook Pub. Co.
Lapman, Maurice & Holder, Glenn, eds.
--Robin Hood. LC 52-10962. (Illus.). 294p. 21cm. 1952. Globe Book Company.
Lapointe, Claude, jt. auth. see Colvin, Andrew.
LaPointe, Savinien (1811-)
--Faerie Gold for Young and Old. Chorley, Henry F., tr. N.D. George Routledge & Sons.
Lapp, Eleanor J (1936-)
--The Blueberry Bears. Apple, Margot, illus. LC 83-1319. p. cm. 1983. (ISBN 0-8075-0796-2). Albert Whitman.
--Duane, the Collector. Westerberg, Christine (1950-), illus. LC 75-31943. p. cm. c.1976. (ISBN 0-201-04155-3). Addison-Wesley.
--Hey, Elephant!. Richards, John Paul, illus. LC 73-102099. (Illus.). 32 p. 1970. (ISBN 0-8114-7704-5). Steck-Vaughn Co.
--In the Morning Mist. Cunningham, David (1938-), illus. LC 77-28442. (Illus.). 32 p. 19cm. c.1978. (ISBN 0-8075-3634-2). A. Whitman.
--The Mice Came in Early This Year. Cunningham, David (1938-), illus. LC 76-45629. p. cm. 1976. (ISBN 0-8075-5111-2). A. Whitman.
Lapp, Marguerite Harrington
--The House that Moved. Brackett, Douglas Roger, illus. LC 73-178733. 48 p. col. illus. 21cm. c.1971. H. Stewart.
Lappa, Katherine T
--Rob and Robins. McCaffery, Janet, illus. LC 61-5719. (Illus.). 48p. 1961. G P Putman's Sons.
LaPrade, Becky, jt. auth. see LaPrade, Kerby E.
La Prade, Ernest
--Alice in Orchestralia. Snell, Carroll C., illus. Damrosch, Walter, frwd. by. 8 p. l., 171 p. front., illus. 20 cm. 1925. Doubleday, Page & Company.
LaPrade, Kerby E. & LaPrade, Becky
--Sleepy Alligator Finds a Bed. Hauptfleisch, Olivia, illus. (Illus.). (gr. 5 up). 1977. (ISBN 0-533-02880-9). Vantage.
Lapsley, Susan
--I Am Adopted. Charlton, Michael Alan (1923-), illus. LC 74-22852. (Illus.). 26 p. 1975, c.1974. (ISBN 0-87888-075-5). Bradbury Press.
--I Am Adopted. Charlton, Michael Alan (1923-), illus. 1975. Merrimack.
Laqueur, Alys, illus.
--Fuzzy Mittens for Three Little Kittens. LC 51-25622. (Illus.). 17cm. 16p. (Fuzzy Wuzzy Tell-a-Tales). 1951. Whitman Pub. Co.
La Ramee, Marie Louise de see De La Ramee, Marie Louise.
Larcom, Lucy (1824-1893)
--Childhood Songs. (Illus.). N.D. Houghton Mifflin.
--Childhood Songs. LC 11-30744. xiv, 15-202 p. incl. front., illus., plates. 20 cm. 1875. J. R. Osgood and Company.
--Childhood Songs: Poems. LC 78-102394. (Illus.). 202 p. 20cm. 1978. (ISBN 0-89609-069-8). Granger Book Co.
Lareuse, Jean
--Devils in the Castle. LC 79-692. (Illus.). 32 p. 26cm. c.1979. (ISBN 0-684-16100-1). Scribner.
Large, Dorothy Mabel (1891-)
--The Kind Companion. Lamb, Mildred R. & Coates, George, illus. LC 38-4432. 158 p. incl. plates. col. front. 21 cm. 1937. Frederick A. Stokes Company.
Large, Jean Henry, Mrs.
--Nancy Goes Camping. Edey, Frederick, Mrs., frwd. by. LC 31-5071. 4 p. l., 215, 1 p. front., 1 illus. 20 cm. 1931. D. Appleton and Company.
--Nancy Goes Girl Scouting. Hoover, Herbert, Mrs., intro. by. LC 30-25157. vi p., 1 l., 9-189 p. front. 20 cm. 1930. D. Appleton and Company.
--Nancy Goes Girl Scouting. Hoover, Herbert, Mrs., intro. by. LC 27-24579. vi p., 1 l., 9-189 p. front. 20 cm. c.1927. George H. Doran Company.
--Nancy's Lone Girl Scouts. Hoffman, William H., Mrs., frwd. by. LC 30-12300. vii, 189, 1 p. front., 1 illus. (music) 20 cm. 1930. D. Appleton and Company.
Large, Laura Antoinette Stevers, Mrs. (1887-)
--Famous Children of Storybook Land. LC 26-195423. 222 p. col. front., illus., plates, ports. 20 cm. c.1925. W. A. Wilde Company.
--Old Stories for Young Readers. Dixon, Rachel Taft & Hartwell, Marjorie, illus. LC 16-23139. x p., 1 l., 223 p. front., illus. 18 cm. (Everychild's Series). 1916. The Macmillan Company.
--A Visit to the Farm. (Everychild's Ser). N.D. Macmillan.
Large, Margaret
--The Kind Companion. N.D. J. B. Lippincott.
Larkin, Alice T.
--Zachary Goes Groundfishing on the Trawler Lucille B. Williams, Abby, illus. LC 81-66265. (Illus.). 48p. (gr. 4-6). 1982. Down East.
Larkin, Howard C., illus.
--Lost in the Desert: And Other Stories from Primary Treasure. LC 72-78432. (Illus.). 64 p. 19cm. 1972. (ISBN 0-685-42928-8). Pacific Press Pub. Association.
Larminie, William, ed.
--West Irish Folk-Tales and Romances. Larminie, William, tr. N.D. Gale Reprint.
--West Irish Folk-Tales and Romances. Larminie, William, tr. 258p. Repr. of 1893 ed. 1973. (ISBN 0-87471-155-X). Rowman and Littlefield.
Larmoth, Jeanine, ed. see Couratin, Patrick.
Larmoth, Jeanine, adapted by see Galeron, Henri.
Larned, Anne Murray
--There Was a Time. LC 16-14835. 30 p. 19cm. 1916. R. G. Badger.
Larned, Augusta (1835-)
--Country Stories, 1 of 3 vols. (Illus.). (Home Story Ser., No. 1.). N.D. Set. Methodist Bk Concern.
--Country Stories, 1 of 3 Vols. (Home Story Ser., No. 1). N.D. Set. Nelson & Phillips.
--Fireside Stories, 1 of 3 vols. (Home Story Ser., No. 2.). N.D. Set. Methodist Bk Concern.
--Fireside Stories, 1 of 3 Vols. (Home Story Ser., No. 2). N.D. Set. Nelson & Phillips.
--Holiday Stories, 1 of 3 vols. (Home Story Ser., No. 1.). N.D. Set. Methodist Bk Concern.
--Holiday Stories, 1 of 3 Vols. (Home Story Ser., No. 1). N.D. Set. Nelson & Phillips.
--Home Story Series, No. 1, 3 vols. N.D. Set. Methodist Bk Concern.
--Home Story Series, No. 2, 3 vols. N.D. Set. Methodist Bk Concern.
--Old Tales retold from Grecian Mythology in Talks Around the Fire. 498p. 1876. Nelson & Phillips.
--Old Tales Retold from Grecian Mythology in Talks Around the Fire. (Illus.). N.D. Publications of the Methodist Book Concern.
--Stories for Leisure Hours, 1 of 3 vols. (Home Story Ser., No. 1.). N.D. Set. Methodist Bk Concern.
--Stories for Leisure Hours, 1 of 3 Vols. (Home Story Ser., No. 1). N.D. Set. Nelson & Phillips.
--Stories for Little People, 1 of 3 vols. (Home Story Ser., No. 2.). N.D. Set. Methodist Bk Concern.
--Stories for Little People, 1 of 3 Vols. (Home Story Ser., No. 2). N.D. Set. Nelson & Phillips.
--Tales from the Norse Grandmother: The Elder Edda. N.D. Publications of the Methodist Book Concern.
--Tales from the Norse Grandmother (the Elder Edda). LC 20-16545. 432. 19cm. 1881. Walden & Stowe.
--Vacation Stories, 1 of 3 vols. (Illus.). (Home Story Ser., No. 2.). N.D. Methodist Bk Concern.
--Vacation Stories, 1 of 3 Vols. (Home Story Ser., No. 2). N.D. Set. Nelson & Phillips.
Larned, William Trowbridge, retold by.
--American Indian Fairy Tales. Rae, John (1882-1963), illus. N.D. A. L. Burt Co.
--Fairy Tales From France. Rae, John (1882-1963), illus. N.D. A. L. Burt Co.
--Fairy-Tales from France. Rae, John (1882-1963), illus. LC 20-12954. 93 p. col. illus. 24 cm. c.1920. P. F. Volland Company.
Larned, William Trowbridge & La Fontaine, Jean De (1621-1695), eds.
--Reynard the Fox and Other Fables. Rae, John (1882-1963), illus. LC 25-223972. 94 p. col. illus. 23 cm. N.D. The P. F. Volland Company.
Larnen, Brendan & Lomask, Milton Nachman (1909-)
--St. Thomas Aquinas and the Preaching Beggars. Fisher, Leonard Everett (1924-), illus. LC 57-850511. 190p. illus. 22cm. (Vision books, 25). 1957. Farrar, Straus & Cudahy.
La Roche, Mazo De see De La Roche, Mazo.
Larom, Henry V. (1903-1975)
--Bronco Charlie, Rider of the Pony Express. LC 51-12232. (Illus.). (gr. 2-4). 1951. (ISBN 0-07-036466-4). McGraw.
--Mountain Pony. (Famous Horse Stories). N.D. Grosset & Dunlap.
--Mountain Pony (Pub. by McGraw). (gr. 7-12). 1972 (Starline). Schol Bk Serv.
--Mountain Pony. N.D. Whittlesey House.
--Mountain Pony. Santee, Ross (1889-1965), illus. (Illus.). (gr. 4-6). N.D. (ISBN 0-448-02284-2). G&D.
--Mountain Pony and the Elkhorn Mystery. N.D. Grosset & Dunlap.
--Mountain Pony and the Elkhorn Mystery. Santee, Ross (1889-1965), illus. LC 50-10399. 222 p. illus. 21 cm. 1950. Whittlesey House.
--Mountain Pony and the Pinto Colt. (Famous Horse Stories). N.D. Grosset & Dunlap.
--Mountain Pony and the Pinto Colt. Santee, Ross (1889-1965), illus. LC 47-12093. 202 p. illus. 21 cm. 1947. Whittlesey House.
--Mountain Pony and the Rodeo Mystery. (Famous Horse Stories). N.D. Grosset & Dunlap.
--Mountain Pony and the Rodeo Mystery. Santee, Ross (1889-1965), illus. LC 49-559463. 228 p. illus., map (on lining-papers) 21 cm. 1949. Whittlesey House.
--Ride Like an Indian. Dennis, Wesley (1903-1966), illus. (gr. 4-6). 1958. (ISBN 0-07-078013-7). (ISBN 0-07-036454-0). McGraw.
--Ride Like an Indian!. 1st ed. Dennis, Wesley (1903-1966), illus. LC 58-6688. 140p. illus. 24cm. 1958. Whittlesey House.
Larrabeiti, Michael De see De Larrabeiti, Michael.
Larranaga, Robert O. (1940-)
--The King's Shadow. Greenwald, Joe, illus. LC 73-84093. (Illus.). 32 p. 1970. (ISBN 0-87614-004-5). Carolrhoda Books.
--Sniffles. Seitz, Patricia, illus. LC 72-7662. (Illus.). 32 p. 27cm. 1973. (ISBN 0-87614-040-1). Carolrhoda Books.
Larrea, Victoria de see Herold, Ann Bixby & De Larrea, Victoria.
Larrick, Nancy G., jt. ed. see Martignoni, Margaret E.
Larrick, Nancy (1910-)
--Color ABC. Martin, Rene (0000-1977), illus. LC 59-14420. unpaged. illus. 32cm. 1959. Platt & Munk.
--I Heard a Scream in the Street. LC 79-122820. (Illus.). 141 p. 21cm. 1970. M. Evans, and Distributed in Association with Lippincott, Philadelphia.
--Piper, Pipe That Song Again!. Poems for Boys and Girls. Oechsli, Kelly (1918-), illus. LC 65-10494. (Illus.). vii, 85 p. 24cm. 1965. (ISBN 0-394-91508-9). Random House.
--Poetry for Holidays. Oechsli, Kelly (1918-), illus. LC 66-10724. 64p. col. illus. 24cm. (Holiday bks.). c.1966. (ISBN 0-8116-4100-7). Garrard.
--The Wheels of the Bus Go Round and Round. 1972. (ISBN 0-516-08871-8). Childrens Press.
Larrick, Nancy (1910-), selected by.
--Bring Me All of Your Dreams: Poems. Mulvehill, Larry, illus. LC 79-26892. (Illus.). 110 p. 21cm. c.1980. (ISBN 0-87131-313-8). M. Evans.
--Crazy to Be Alive in Such a Strange World: Poems About People. Crosby, Alexander L. (1906-1980), illus. LC 76-49667. (Illus.). 192p. (gr. 5 up). 1977. (ISBN 0-87131-225-5). M Evans.
--Green Is Like a Meadow of Grass: An Anthology of Children's Pleasure in Poetry. Lehigh University,Bethlehem, Pa. School of Education Oechsli, Kelly (1918-), illus. LC 68-16159. (Illus.). 64 p. 1968. (ISBN 0-8116-4103-1). Garrard Pub. Co.
--More Poetry for Holidays. Berson, Harold (1926-), illus. LC 73-6806. (Illus.). 64 p. 24cm. 1973. (ISBN 0-8116-4116-3). Garrard Pub. Co.
--On City Streets: An Anthology of Poetry. 1st ed. Sagarin, David, photos by. LC 68-30505. (Illus.). 158 p. 21cm. 1968. Distributed in Association with Lippincott.
--Piping Down the Valleys Wild: Poetry for the Young of All Ages. Raskin, Ellen (1928-1984), illus. LC 67-19762. (Illus.). 16 drawings. 288p. (gr. 3-6). 1968. (ISBN 0-440-06923-8). Delacorte.
--Piping Down the Valleys Wild: Poetry for the Young of All Ages. Raskin, Ellen (1928-1984), illus. LC 68-27742. p. cm. 1985, c.1968. (ISBN 0-385-29429-8). Delacorte Press.
--Room for me and a Mountain Lion: Poetry of Open Space. LC 73-87710. (Illus.). 192p. 1974. (ISBN 0-87131-124-0). M. Evans & Company.
--Tambourines! Tambourines to Glory!. Prayers & Poems. LC 81-23158. 122p. (gr. 2-8). 1982. (ISBN 0-664-32689-7). Westminster.
--When the Dark Comes Dancing: A Bedtime Poetry Book. Wallner, John C. (1945-), illus. (ps-2). 1983. Putnam.
--When the Dark Comes Dancing: The Bedtime Poetry Book. Wallner, John C. (1945-), illus. LC 81-428. p. cm. 1981. (ISBN 0-399-20807-0). Philomel Books. **Award: (ALA).**
Larrieu, Odette, tr. see Reynard the Fox. English.
Larrimore, Lida, pseud., see Thomas, Lida Larrimore Turner.
Larris, Ann
--People Are Like Lollipops. LC 73-141408. (Illus.). 30 p. 1971. (ISBN 0-8234-0185-5). Holiday House.
Larsen, Bent Axel
--Jungle Journey and Other Stories. LC 76-7856. 95 p. 22cm. (Destiny book). c.1977. Pacific Press Pub. Association.
--The Schoolhouse Burned Twice. Nye, Vernon Paul, illus. LC 67-27707. (Illus.). 93 p. 22cm. (Panda book, P-110). 1968. Pacific Press Pub. Association.
Larsen, Blanche Ida see Rene, Blanche, pseud.
Larsen, Blanche Ida
--A Pony Cart of Verse. Rene, Blanche, pseud. LC 50-30610. 46 p. 22cm. N.D. Trovillion Private Press.
Larsen, Carl
--Lena: Or, The Stark Family, 1 of 25 vols. (Selected Bks for Sunday School). N.D. Set. Methodist Bk Concern.
Larsen, Chris, jt. auth. see Kolbrek, Loyal.
Larsen, Hanne
--Don't Forget Tom. LC 77-20953. (Illus.). (John Day Bk.). (gr. k-4). 1978. (ISBN 0-381-99554-2, TYC-J). T Y Crowell.
Larsen, Svend, ed. see Andersen, Hans Christian.
Larson, Bill
--Let's Go to Animal Town: A Book About Things That Go!. Hildebrandt, Tim (1939-) & Hildebrandt, Greg (1939-), illus. (Illus.). 26p. (Golden Panorama Ser). (ps). 1975. (ISBN 0-307-11092-3, Golden Pr). Western Pub.
Larson, C. E & Haskin, Richard A
--The Adventures of Goofus the Gopher: Goofus Wakes up. LC 76-381224. (Illus.). 19 p. 31cm. 1975. S.N.
Larson, Charles Raymond, ed. see Thurman, Wallace.
Larson, Freda
--Glad Lee, the Cross-Eyed Bear. LC 51-11437. 39p. illus. 23cm. 1951. Exposition Press.
Larson, Glen A. & Thurston, Robert Donald (1936-)
--The Battlestar Galactica Story Book. Mercer, Charles, adapted by. LC 79-198. (Illus.). 1979. (ISBN 0-399-20683-3). Putnam Pub Group.
Larson, Irene
--Mack's Treasure Mound. (Illus., Orig.). (gr. 3-4). 1979. (ISBN 0-912760-96-6). Valkyrie Hse.
Larson, Jane
--The Queen of Hats. 1st U.S. edition. 1979. (ISBN 0-533-03851-0). Vantage.
Larson, Jean Russell (1930-)
--The Glass Mountain & Other Arabian Tales. Cooke, Donald Ewin (1916-), illus. LC 71-38918. (Illus.). 112p. (gr. 4 up). 1971. (ISBN 0-8255-5190-0). (ISBN 0-8255-5191-9). Macrae.
--Jack Tar. Mayer, Mercer (1943-), illus. LC 72-87983. (Illus.). 76 p. 22cm. 1970. (ISBN 0-8255-5200-1). M. Smith Co.
--Palace in Bagdad: Seven Tales from Arabia. Yamaguchi, Marianne Illenberger (1936-), illus. LC 66-18186. 94p. illus. 26cm. c.1966. (ISBN 0-684-82159-1). Scribners.
--The Silkspinners. Shulevitz, Uri (1935-), illus. LC 67-23688. (Illus.). 93 p. 24cm. 1967. Scribner.
Larson, Mildred H., ed.
--Stories By O. Henry. 128p. 1973. (ISBN 0-87789-077-3). English Language Services.
Larson, William Herbert (1938-), ed.
--Seven Great Detective Stories. Lowenbein, Michael, illus. LC 79-112039. (Illus.). 210 p. 20cm. c.1979. (ISBN 0-307-21627-6). Golden Press.
--Seven Great Detective Stories. Lowenbein, Michael, illus. LC 68-25323. (Illus.). 210 p. 20cm. (Whitman classics). 1968. Whitman Pub. Division, Western Pub. Co.
Larssen, Pedar
--Landlubber. Wood, Worden, illus. LC 40-33281. 3 p. l., 151 p. illus. 22 cm. 1940. The Macmillan Company.
--Offshore Gold. Wood, Worden, illus. LC 41-147722. 3 p. l., 174 p. illus. 22 cm. 1941. The Macmillan Company.
Larsson, Gosta (1898-)
--The Wonderful Boat. Case, Bernard, illus. LC 57-6003. 219p. illus. 22cm. c.1957. Lothrop, Lee & Shepard Co.
Larsson, Karl, jt. auth. see Flack, Marjorie.
La Rue, Mabel Guinnip, Mrs.
--In Animal Land. Petersham, Maud Sylvia Fuller, Mrs. (1890-1971) & Petersham, Miska (1889-1960), illus. (Illus.). 157p. (True Or Might-Be-True Stories). 1924. MacMillan Bks.
--The Billy Bang Book. Petersham, Maud Sylvia Fuller, Mrs. (1890-1971) & Petersham, Miska (1889-1960), illus. 174p. (Folk Lore & Fairy Tales). (gr. 4-6). 1927. MacMillan Bks.
--Cats for the Tooseys. Wiese, Kurt (1887-1974), illus. LC 39-316864. 40 p. illus. 31 cm. 1939. T. Nelson and Sons.

--The Littlest Mouse. Lathrop, Dorothy Pulis (1891-1980), illus. LC 55-13732. 32p. illus. 21cm. 1955. Macmillan.
--The Lost Merry-Go-Round. LC 34-35692. 1934. MacMillan.
--Presents for Lupe. Lathrop, Dorothy Pulis (1891-1980), illus. LC 40-33937. 40 p. col. illus. 26 x 22 cm. 1940. The Macmillan Company.
--Puffy and the Seven Leaf Clover. Lathrop, Dorothy Pulis (1891-1980), illus. LC 54-8881. 1954. Macmillan.
--Puppies for Keeps. Lathrop, Dorothy Pulis (1891-1980), illus. LC 43-14001. 1943. Macmillan.
--Skittle Skattle Monkey. Lathrop, Dorothy Pulis (1891-1980), illus. LC 45-11419. (Illus.). 22 1/2cm. 48p. 1945. Macmillan.
--The Snail Who Ran. N.D. J. B. Lippincott.
--The Snail Who Ran. Lathrop, Dorothy Pulis (1891-1980), illus. LC 34-29543. 57, 1 p. incl. illus., plates. col. front. 16 cm. 1934. Frederick A. Stokes Company.
--Who Goes There?. Lathrop, Dorothy Pulis (1891-1980), illus. LC 35-20899. 41 p. illus. 21 x 25 cm. 1935. The Macmillan Company.

Lathrop, Dorothy West (1892-1974)

--Black River Captive. Logan, Dwight, illus. LC 46-6303. ix, 307 p. double plates, double map. 21 cm. 1946. Random House.
--Dogsled Danger. Powers, Richard M. Gorman (1921-), illus. LC 56-5449. 247p. illus. 21cm. 1956. (ISBN 0-394-81086-4). Random House.
--Juneau: The Sleigh Dog. N.D. Grosset & Dunlap.
--Juneau, The Sleigh Dog. Wiese, Kurt (1887-1974), illus. LC 42-11049. x p., 1 l., 13-279 p. illus. 21 cm. 1942. Random House.
--Keep the Wagons Moving. Duer, Douglas, illus. LC 49-631. 337 p. illus., fold. map. 21 cm. 1949. Random House.
--Monkey Ahoy!. Walker, Nedda, illus. LC 43-51161. 3 p. l., 9-233 p. illus. 21 cm. 1943. Random House.
--Northern Trail Adventure. LC 44-5433. 3 p. l., 217 p. 21 cm. 1944. Random House.
--River Circus. Dodge, Dick (1918-1974), illus. LC 53-6285. 252p. illus. 21cm. 1953. (ISBN 0-394-81549-1). Random House.
--Unwilling Pirate. Cirlin, Edgar, illus. LC 51-13111. 277 p. illus. 21 cm. 1951. (ISBN 0-394-91789-8). Random House.

Lathrop, George Parsons (1851-1898)

--Behind Time. Herford, Oliver (1863-1935), illus. LC 13-20108. 4 p. l., 5-198 p. front., plates. 18 cm. 1886. Cassell & Company, Limited.
--Behind Time. Herford, Oliver (1863-1935), illus. LC 44-36608. 4 p.l., 5-198 p. front., plates. 19 cm. 1895. The Cassell Publishing Co.

Lathrop, Gilbert A

--Mystery Rides the Rails. LC 37-582698. 4 p. l., 13-252 p. 20 cm. c.1937. The Goldsmith Publishing Company.
--Whispering Rails. LC 36-412. 3 p. l., 11-252 p. 20 cm. c.1936. The Goldsmith Publishing Company.

Lathrop, H. B., ed. see Malory, Thomas, Sir.

Lathrop, Rose Hawthorne, et al. (1851-1926)

--One Cent, 1 of 4 vols. (Illus.). (Winter Sunshine Ser.). N.D. D Lothrop.

Lathrop, Rose Hawthorne (1851-1926)

--Little Luckie. (Christmas Hearth Library). N.D. D. Lothrop & Co.
--Little Luckie: And Other Stories, 1 of 5 vols. (Illus.). (Good Fortune Library). N.D. Set. Lothrop Publishing Co.

Lathrop, West see Lathrop, Dorothy West.

Latimer, John (1937-)

--The King's Rock. LC 69-14774. 183 p. 21cm. 1969. Meredith Press.
--The Last Pharaoh. LC 71-119360. 128 p. 21cm. 1970. (ISBN 0-8407-6044-2). T. Nelson.

Latimer, Rebecca H

--Susie and Leyla: Teen-Agers in Turkey. LC 68-29302. 206 p. 22cm. 1968. (ISBN 0-672-50523-1). Bobbs-Merrill.

Latini, Angela

--Za, the Truffle Boy. 1st ed. Dell'Orco, Pino, illus. Colquhoun, Archibald (1912-1964), tr. from Ital. LC 61-10077. 128p. ill. 22cm. 1961, c.1960. F. Watts.

La Torre, Lillian De see De La Torre, Lillian.

Latourette, Jane

--Jon and the Little Lost Lamb: Luke 15: 1-7 for Children. Mathews, Sally & Wind, Betty, illus. LC 63-23144. 1 v. (unpaged) col. illus. 21 cm. (Arch Books). 1965. Concordia Pub. House.
--The Story of Noah's Ark. Mathews, Sally, illus. LC 63-23144. 35 p. 21cm. c.1965. Concordia Pub. House.

Latrobe, Carroll

--Digby the Only Dog. N.D. E. M. Hale & Co.

Latsha, Mabel (1906-)

--Don's California Canary. LC 80-15421. (Illus.). 112 p. 21cm. c.1980. Review and Herald Pub. Association.

Latshaw, George

--Pinocchio. (Children's Theatre Playscript, Puppet Playscript Ser.). 1959. (ISBN 0-88020-044-8). Coach Hse.

Latta, Richard (1946-)

--This Little Pig Had a Riddle. Fay, Anne, ed. Munsinger, Lynn (1951-), illus. (Illus.). 32p. (gr. 1-5). 1984. (ISBN 0-8075-7893-2). A Whitman.

Lattimore

--Which Way, Black Cat?. (gr. 3-5). 1980. (ISBN 0-590-30040-7, Schol Pap). Scholastic Inc.

Lattimore, Eleanor Frances (1904-)

--Adam's Key. Tiegreen, Alan, illus. LC 76-13013. p. cm. c.1976. (ISBN 0-688-22089-4). (ISBN 0-688-32089-9). Morrow.
--Bayou Boy. Lattimore, Eleanor Frances (1904-), illus. LC 46-252589. 127, 1 p. incl. front., illus., plates. 23 cm. 1946. W. Morrow and Company.
--Beachcomber Boy. Lattimore, Eleanor Frances (1904-), illus. LC 60-50807. 124p. illus. 21cm. 1960. W. Morrow.
--Bells for a Chinese Donkey. Lattimore, Eleanor Frances (1904-), illus. LC 51-4137. 126 p. illus. 22 cm. 1951. Morrow.
--Bird Song. Lattimore, Eleanor Frances (1904-), illus. LC 68-19034. (Illus.). 127 p. 21cm. 1968. Morrow.
--The Bittern's Nest. Lattimore, Eleanor Frances (1904-), illus. LC 62-7719. (Illus.). 127 p. 21cm. 1962. Morrow.
--The Bus Trip. Lattimore, Eleanor Frances (1904-), illus. LC 65-12868. (Illus.). 125 p. 21cm. 1965. W. Morrow.
--The Chinese Daughter. Lattimore, Eleanor Frances (1904-), illus. LC 60-5721. (Illus.). 125 p. 21cm. (Morrow junior books). 1960. Morrow.
--Christopher and His Turtle. Lattimore, Eleanor Frances (1904-), illus. LC 50-8513. 126 p. illus. 21 cm. 1950. Morrow.
--The Clever Cat. Lattimore, Eleanor Frances (1904-), illus. LC 36-19168. 6 p. l., 3-113 p. incl. front., illus., plates. 20 cm. c.1936. Harcourt, Brace and Company.
--Cousin Melinda. Lattimore, Eleanor Frances (1904-), illus. LC 61-972650. 128p. illus. 21cm. 1961. Morrow.
--Davy of the Everglades. Lattimore, Eleanor Frances (1904-), illus. LC 49-7851. 127 p. illus. 21 cm. 1949. W. Morrow.
--Deborah's White Winter. Lattimore, Eleanor Frances (1904-), illus. LC 49-4522. 124 p. illus. 21 cm. morrow junior books. 1949. W. Morrow.
--Diana in the China Shop. Lattimore, Eleanor Frances (1904-), illus. LC 55-5092. (Illus.). 128 p. 21cm. (Morrow junior books). 1955. Morrow.
--Fair Bay. Lattimore, Eleanor Frances (1904-), illus. LC 58-5364. 123p. illus. 21cm. 1958. Morrow.
--Felicia. Lattimore, Eleanor Frances (1904-), illus. LC 64-10132. 128 p. illus. 21 cm. 1964. Morrow.
--The Fig Tree. Lattimore, Eleanor Frances (1904-), illus. LC 51-185. 126 p. illus. 21 cm. 1951. Morrow.
--First Grade. Lattimore, Eleanor Frances (1904-), illus. LC 44-747151. 4 p. l., 3-147 p. incl. illus., plates. 19 1/2 cm. 1944. Harcourt, Brace and Company.
--The Fisherman's Son. Lattimore, Eleanor Frances (1904-), illus. LC 59-5020. (Illus.). 128 p. 21cm. (Morrow junior books). 1959. Morrow.
--The Girl on the Deer. Lattimore, Eleanor Frances (1904-), illus. LC 77-79096. (Illus.). 126 p. 21cm. 1969. Morrow.
--Happiness for Kimi. Lattimore, Eleanor Frances (1904-), illus. LC 58-5019. 126p. illus. 21cm. 1958. W. Morrow.
--Holly in the Snow. Lattimore, Eleanor Frances (1904-), illus. LC 54-5002. (Illus.). 125 p. 21cm. (Morrow junior books). 1954. Morrow.
--Indigo Hill. Lattimore, Eleanor Frances (1904-), illus. LC 50-214. (Illus.). 128 p. 21cm. (Morrow junior books). 1950. Morrow.
--Janetta's Magnet. Lattimore, Eleanor Frances (1904-), illus. LC 63-7140. (Illus.). 126 p. 21cm. 1963. Morrow.
--Jasper. Lattimore, Eleanor Frances (1904-), illus. LC 53-6657. (Illus.). 128 p. 21cm. (Morrow junior books). 1953. Morrow.
--Jeremy's Isle. Lattimore, Eleanor Frances (1904-), illus. LC 47-31079. (Illus.). 23cm. 123p. (Morrow Junior Books). 1947. Morrow.
--Jerry and the Pusa. Lattimore, Eleanor Frances (1904-), illus. LC 32-23875. 4 p. l., 3-197, 1 p. incl. illus., plates. front. 23 cm. c.1932. Harcourt, Brace and Company.
--Jonny. Lattimore, Eleanor Frances (1904-), illus. LC 39-27737. 4 p. l., 3-100, 1 p. front., illus. 22 cm. c.1939. Harcourt, Brace and Company.
--The Journey of Ching Lai. Lattimore, Eleanor Frances (1904-), illus. LC 57-7184. 126p. illus. 21cm. 1957. Morrow.
--Junior. Lattimore, Eleanor Frances (1904-), illus. (Illus.). (gr. 2-5). 1938. (ISBN 0-15-241491-6). HarBraceJ.
--Junior: A Colored Boy of Charleston. Lattimore, Eleanor Frances (1904-), illus. LC 38-27598. 6 p. l., 3-129, 1 p. incl. front., illus., plates. 28 cm. c.1938. Harcourt, Brace and Company.
--Laurie and Company. Lattimore, Eleanor Frances (1904-), illus. LC 62-7074. (Illus.). 128 p. 21cm. 1962. Morrow.
--Little Pear. Lattimore, Eleanor Frances (1904-), illus. LC 31-22069. (Illus.). (gr. k-3). 1968. (ISBN 0-15-652799-5, VoyB). HarBraceJ.
--Little Pear and His Friends. Lattimore, Eleanor Frances (1904-), illus. LC 34-27286. 4 p. l., 3-178, 1 p. incl. illus., plates. front. 28 cm. c.1934. Brace and Company.
--Little Pear and the Rabbits. Lattimore, Eleanor Frances (1904-), illus. LC 56-7857. 125p. illus. 23cm. 1956. (ISBN 0-688-21715-X). Morrow.
--Little Pear: The Story of a Little Chinese Boy. Lattimore, Eleanor Frances (1904-), illus. LC 31-220692. 3 p., l., 3-144 p. incl. illus., plates. front. 23 cm. c.1931. Harcourt, Brace and Company.
--The Little Tumbler. Lattimore, Eleanor Frances (1904-), illus. LC 63-8801. (Illus.). 128 p. 21cm. 1963. Morrow.
--Lively Victoria. Lattimore, Eleanor Frances (1904-), illus. LC 52-5934. 128 p. illus. 21 cm. 1952. Morrow.
--The Lost Leopard. Lattimore, Eleanor Frances (1904-), illus. LC 35-15312. c.1935. Harcourt, Brace and Company.
--The Mexican Bird. Lattimore, Eleanor Frances (1904-), illus. LC 65-10261. 123 p. illus. 21 cm. 1965. Morrow.
--Molly in the Middle. Lattimore, Eleanor Frances (1904-), illus. LC 56-6739. 127p. illus. 21cm. 1956. Morrow.
--The Monkey of Crofton. Lattimore, Eleanor Frances (1904-), illus. LC 57-506256. 127p. illus. 21cm. 1957. Morrow.
--More About Little Pear. Lattimore, Eleanor Frances (1904-), illus. LC 71-151939. (Illus.). 125 p. 21cm. 1971. W. Morrow.
--Peachblossom. Lattimore, Eleanor Frances (1904-), illus. LC 43-51224. 5 p. l., 3-96 p. incl. front., illus., plates. 22 1/2 cm. 1943. Harcourt, Brace and Company.
--Proudfoot's Way. 1st ed. Darwin, Beatrice, illus. LC 77-20057. (Illus.). 128 p. 21cm. 1978. (ISBN 0-688-22145-9). (ISBN 0-688-32145-3). Morrow.
--The Questions of Lifu: A Story of China. Lattimore, Eleanor Frances (1904-), illus. LC 42-362769. v, 104 p., 1 l. incl. col. front., col. illus., col. plates. 23 cm. 1942. Harcourt, Brace and Company.
--The Search for Christina. Lattimore, Eleanor Frances (1904-), illus. LC 66-6346. 128p. illus. 21cm. (Morrow junior bks.). c.1966. Morrow.
--The Seven Crowns. Lattimore, Eleanor Frances (1904-), illus. LC 33-24657. xii, 189 p. incl. front., illus., plates. 20 cm. c.1933. Harcourt, Brace and Company.
--A Smiling Face. Lattimore, Eleanor Frances (1904-), illus. LC 73-4925. (Illus.). 126 p. 21cm. 1973. Morrow.
--Storm on the Island. Lattimore, Eleanor Frances (1904-), illus. LC 42-36067. 5 p. l., 3-181 p. incl. front., illus., plates. 20 cm. 1942. Harcourt, Brace and Company.
--The Story of Lee Ling. Lattimore, Eleanor Frances (1904-), illus. LC 40-27609. 5 p. l., 3-114 p. incl. front., illus., plates. 23 cm. c.1940. Harcourt, Brace and Company.
--The Taming of Tiger. Lattimore, Eleanor Frances (1904-), illus. LC 74-34321. (Illus.). 127 p. 22cm. 1975. (ISBN 0-688-22031-2). (ISBN 0-688-32031-7). Morrow.
--The Three Firecrackers. Lattimore, Eleanor Frances (1904-), illus. LC 76-123148. (Illus.). 126 p. 21cm. 1970. W. Morrow.
--Three Little Chinese Girls. Lattimore, Eleanor Frances (1904-), illus. LC 48-76957. 128 p. illus. 22 cm. 1948. W. Morrow.
--The Two Helens. Lattimore, Eleanor Frances (1904-), illus. LC 67-19243. (Illus.). 128 p. 21cm. 1967. Morrow.
--Willow Tree Village. Lattimore, Eleanor Frances (1904-), illus. LC 55-7897. (Illus.). 128 p. 21cm. (Morrow junior books). 1955. Morrow.
--The Wonderful Glass House. Lattimore, Eleanor Frances (1904-), illus. LC 61-5212. (Illus.). 125 p. 21cm. (Morrow junior books). 1961. Morrow.
--Wu, the Gatekeeper's Son. Lattimore, Eleanor Frances (1904-), illus. LC 52-121188. 128p. illus. 21cm. 1953. Morrow.
--The Youngest Artist. Lattimore, Eleanor Frances (1904-), illus. LC 59-6594. 126p. illus. 21cm. 1959. Morrow.

Lattimore, Florence Larrabee

--Alice and Jumbo. LC 56-11390. 185p. illus. 26cm. 1956. Pageant Press.

Lattin, Anne, pseud., see Cole, Lois Dwight.

Lattin, Anne, pseud. (1903-1979)

--Peter Liked to Draw. Cole, Lois Dwight. Powers, Richard M. Gorman (1921-), illus. LC 53-10601. unpaged. illus. 32cm. c.1953. Wilcox and Follett Co.
--Peter's Policeman. Cole, Lois Dwight. Elliott, Gertrude, illus. (Illus.). 29 p. 21cm. (Follett Beginning to Read Ser.). 1958. Follett Pub. Co.
--Peter's Policeman. Cole, Lois Dwight. Espenscheid, Gertrude Elliott, illus. (Illus.). (gr. 2-4). 1958. (ISBN 0-695-46939-8). Follett.
--Sparky's Fireman. Cole, Lois Dwight. Frenck, Hal, illus. (Illus.). 29 p. 21cm. (Follett Beginning-to-Read Bks.). 1968. Follett.
--Sparky's Fireman. Cole, Lois Dwight. Frenck, Hal, illus. LC 68-13790. (Illus.). 32p. (Beginning-To-Read Ser). (gr. 2-4). 1968. (ISBN 0-695-48224-6). Follett.

Lattin, Harriet Stacey Pratt (1898-)

--Brick and the Abacus. (Illus.). (gr. 5 up). 1977. (ISBN 0-533-02556-7). Vantage.
--The Peasant Boy Who Became Pope: Story of Gerbert. LC 51-9799. xi, 179 p. ill. 19cm. (Story Biography Series, 3). 1951. H. Schuman.

Lau, Josephine Sanger see Sanger, Frances, pseud.

Lau, Josephine Sanger (1889-1974)

--Beggar Boy of Galilee. Hogg, Frederick, illus. LC 46-7637. 192 p. incl. illus., plates. 21 1/2 cm. 1946. Abingdon-Cokesbury Press.
--Cheeky: A Prairie Dog. Wiese, Kurt (1887-1974), illus. LC 37-9725. 62, 2 p. incl. col. front., illus. (part col.) 24 cm. 1937. A. Whitman & Company.
--The Silver Teapot. Sanger, Frances, pseud. Koering, Ursula (1921-), illus. LC 48-7965. 187 p. illus. 20 cm. 1948. Westminster Press.
--Slave Boy in Judea. Farris, Joseph G., illus. LC 53-7571. 188p. illus. 22cm. 1953. Abingdon-Cokesbury Press.
--The Story of Joseph. Godwin, Stephani & Godwin, Edward Fell (1912-), illus. LC 50-6479. 192 p. illus. 22 cm. 1950. Abingdon-Cokesbury Press.
--The Wooden Mug. Sanger, Frances, pseud. LC 50-9223. (Illus.). 187 p. 21cm. 1950. Westminster Press.

Lauber, Patricia Grace (1924-)

--Adventure at Black Rock Cave. (Gateway Ser.: No. 7). (gr. 3-5). 1959. (ISBN 0-394-90107-X, BYR). Random.
--Adventure at Black Rock Cave. Shortall, Leonard W., illus. LC 59-8474. (Illus.). 65 p. 24cm. 1959. (ISBN 0-394-90197-5). Random House.
--Champ: Gallant Collie. Shortall, Leonard W., illus. LC 60-10027. (Illus.). (Gateway Ser.: No. 18). (gr. 3-7). 1960. (ISBN 0-394-80118-0, BYR). (ISBN 0-394-90118-5). Random.
--Clarence & the Burglar. Galdone, Paul (1914-), illus. (Illus.). 48p. (Break-of-Day Bk.). (gr. 1-3). 1973. (ISBN 0-698-30489-6, Coward). Putnam Pub Group.
--Clarence and the Cat: Adapted from a Chapter in Clarence the TV Dog. Galdone, Paul (1914-), illus. LC 77-1276. (Adapted from a Chapter in Clearence the TV Dog). (Illus.). 64 p. 23cm. (Break-of-day book). c.1977. (ISBN 0-698-30667-8). Coward, McCann & Geoghegan.
--Clarence Goes to Town. Shortall, Leonard W., illus. LC 57-121992. 126p. illus. 22cm. 1957. Coward-McCann.
--Clarence Goes to Town. Shortall, Leonard W., illus. LC 67-23117. (Illus.). 117 p. 24cm. 1967, c.1957. Random House.
--Clarence Takes a Vacation. (gr. 4-6). 1978. (ISBN 0-590-05362-0). Scholastic Inc.
--Clarence the TV dog. N.D. E . M. Hale and co.
--Clarence, the TV Dog. Shortall, Leonard W., illus. LC 55-10787. (Illus.). 128 p. 22cm. 1955. Coward-McCann.
--Clarence the TV Dog. Shortall, Leonard W., illus. (Illus.). 128 p. 22cm. 1965. Coward-McCann.
--Clarence Turns Sea Dog. Shortall, Leonard W., illus. LC 59-1141. (Illus.). 124 p. 22cm. 1959. Coward-McCann.
--Clarence Turns Sea Dog. Shortall, Leonard W., illus. LC 65-22647. 124p. illus. 24cm. (Gateway bks.). 1965, c.1959. Random.
--Found, One Orange-Brown Horse. Shortall, Leonard W., illus. LC 57-7529. (Gateway Ser.: No. 2). (gr. 1-4). N.D. (ISBN 0-394-82173-4, BYR). Random.
--Our Friend the Forest: A Conservation Story. Jauss, Anne Marie (1907-), illus. LC 59-12567. (Illus.). 61 p. 27cm. 1959. Doubleday.
--Penguins on Parade. Howland, Douglas, illus. LC 57-12200. 62p. illus. 24cm. 1958. Coward-McCann.
--Rufus, the Red-Necked Hornbill. Cameron, Polly (1928-), illus. LC 58-13326. unpaged. illus. 27cm. 1958. Coward-McCann.
--Runaway Flea Circus. LC 58-6201. (Illus.). (Gateway Ser.: No. 3). (gr. 2-4). 1958. (ISBN 0-394-80103-2). (ISBN 0-394-90103-7). Random.
--Tales Mummies Tell. 1985. Crowell. **Award: (ALA).**

Lauber, Patricia Grace (1924-) & Chalmers, Mary Eileen (1927-)
--Home at Last!. A Young Cat's Tale. LC 79-28403. (Illus.). 47 p. 19cm. (gr. 2-4). c.1980. (ISBN 0-698-20507-3). Coward, McCann & Geoghegan.
Lauder, M Genevieve
--Plays for Grade and High School Children: Three One-Act Historical Dramatizations. Hynes, Harry G., frwd. by. LC 56-10974. 112p. 21cm. 1956. Exposition Press.
Lauder, Margaret Kyle
--Keepsakes: Poems. LC 76-53398. (Illus.). xxi, 198 p. 23cm. 1977. (ISBN 0-87012-270-3). McClain Print. Co..
Laudermilk, Pat, jt. auth. see Frederick, Vera M.
Laufer, Calvin Welss (1874-), ed. see Presbyterian Church in the U. S. A.
Lauter, David
--The Nothing in Between. LC 72-187479. (Illus.). 1 v. 16cm. 1972. Carnegie-Mellon University.
Laufer, Eva
--Young Folk of the Americas. Laufer, Thomas, illus. LC 45-4149. 50 p. illus. (part col., incl. map) 29 1/2 cm. 1945. Arco Publishing Company.
Laugesen, Mary Eakin (1906-)
--The Chrisamat Tree. Mars, Witold Tadeusz J. (1912-), illus. LC 73-118815. (Illus.). 40 p. 1970. Bobbs-Merrill.
Laughlin, Elsie M
--The West That Was. 1 st. ed. LC 57-4655. (A Novel of the Opening of the Dakotas). 309p. 21cm. 1957. Exposition Press.
Laughlin, Florence Young (1910-)
--Four to Get Ready!. Pucci, Albert John (1920-), illus. LC 68-4813. (Illus.). 28 p. 32cm. (Whitman giant tell-a-tale book). 1968. Western Pub. Co.
--The Horse from Topolo: A Mystery Story. Werner, Barbara, illus. LC 66-9622. (Illus.). 191 p. 21cm. 1966. Macrae Smith.
--The Little Leftover Witch. Greenwald, Sheila, pseud. (1934-), illus. Green, Sheila Ellen. LC 60-118153. (Illus.). 107 p. 20cm. 1960. Macmillan.
--Mystery Mountain. Werner, Barbara, illus. LC 64-19135. 156 p. illus. 22 cm. 1964. Macrae Smith Co.
--The Mystery of the McGilley Mansion. Oliver, Jane, pseud., illus. Rees, Helen Christina Easson Evans. LC 63-11678. 160 p. illus. 22 cm. 1963. Lothrop, Lee & Shepard Co.
--Sally's Lost Shoe and Other Stories. Salter, Florence, illus. LC 44-6745. 62 p. illus. (part col.) 17 cm. 1944. Rand McNally & Company.
--The Seventh Cousin. Greenwald, Sheila, pseud. (1934-), illus. Green, Sheila Ellen. LC 66-10163. 160p. illus. 22cm. c.1966. (ISBN 0-02-754540-7). Macmillan.
--Skyrockets for the President. Roth, George (1932-), illus. (Illus.). 64p. (gr. 2-5). 1973. (ISBN 0-528-82550-X). Rand.
Laughlin, Johnny
--A Study of Boyhood. (Illus.). N.D. Bobbs-Merrill Pub.
Laumer, Keith
--Relief's Ransom. 1971. (ISBN 0-399-10691-X). Putnam.
Laune, Paul Sidney (1899-)
--Mustang Roundup. Laune, Paul Sidney (1899-), illus. LC 64-12619. 154p. illus. 23cm. c.1964. Holt.
--The Thirsty Pony. Laune, Paul Sidney (1899-), illus. LC 40-31802. (Illus.). 24p. 1940. Grosset & Dunlap.
Laurel, Alicia Bay (1949-)
--Happy Day Cried the Rainbow Lady, Full of Light. (Illus.). 32p. 1972. (ISBN 0-06-065298-5, HarpR). Har-Row.
--Sylvie Sunflower. (Illus.). 32p. 1972. (ISBN 0-06-065299-3, HarpR). Har-Row.
Lauren, Ford see Ford, Julia Lauren.
Laurence
--Robert and the Statue of Liberty. Laurence, illus. LC 68-10709. (Illus.). 32 p. 1968. Bobbs-Merrill.
--Seymourina. Laurence, illus. LC 77-78281. (Illus.). 32 p. 1970. Bobbs-Merrill.
--A Village in Normandy. 1st ed. Laurence, illus. LC 67-20456. 1v. (unpaged) col. illus. 22x29cm. 1968. Bobbs.
Laurence, Alfred D
--Homer Pickle, the Greatest: His Stirring Adventures and Incredible Feats. Lee, Robert J. (1921-), illus. LC 70-154055. 138 p. 21cm. 1971. Platt & Munk.
Laurence, Ester Hauser (1935-)
--B-9, the Hungry Metal Eater. Bradford, Ron, illus. LC 72-3436. (Illus.). 62 p. 24cm. (Fledgling book). 1972. (ISBN 0-528-82632-8). (ISBN 0-528-82632-8). Rand McNally.
--We're off to Catch a Dragon. Brown, Cornelia, illus. LC 69-16943. (Illus.). 31 p. 29cm. 1969. Abingdon Press.
Laurence, Hugh
--Tales of an Old Yew Tree. (Illus.). (Stories Old and New Ser.). N.D. Caldwell.
Laurence, Isabelle
--Spy in Williamsburg. (Illus.). (gr. 4-6). 1955. (ISBN 0-528-87646-5). Rand.
Laurence, Johnnie, pseud., see Biers, Clarence.
Laurence, Johnnie, pseud.
--Dipsy Donkey. Biers, Clarence. Laurence, Johnnie, pseud., illus. Biers, Clarence. LC 48-101379. 32 p. col. illus. 17 cm. (Tell-a-tale books). c.1948. Whitman Pub. Co.
Laurence, Margaret
--A Bird in the House. 1970. Borzoi Press.
--The Christmas Birthday Story. Lucas, Helen, illus. LC 79-27159. p. cm. c.1980. (ISBN 0-394-84361-4). (ISBN 0-394-94361-9). Knopf.
--Jason's Quest. Torell, Staffan, illus. LC 78-106138. (Illus.). 211 p. 24cm. 1970. Knopf.
Laurgaard, Rachel Kelley
--Betty Reed's Doll. Michaels, Elizabeth Sykes, illus. LC 56-503865. 149p. illus. 22cm. 1956. Caxton Printers.
Laurie, Andre, pseud., see Grousset, Paschal.
Laurie, Annie
--The Little Boy Who Lived On the Hill. New ed. Swinnertop, James, illus. N.D. Desmond Fitzgerald Inc. Distributed by Warne & Co.
--The Little Boy Who Lived on the Hill. Swinnertop, James, illus. N.D. Doxey's Pubs.
Laurie, Rona & Potter, Helen Beatrix (1866-1943)
--Children's Plays from Beatrix Potter. LC 80-146465. (Illus.). 93 p. 24cm. 1980. (ISBN 0-7232-2488-9). F. Warne.
Laurin, Anne, pseud., see McLaurin, Anne.
Laurin, Anne, pseud. (1953-)
--Little Things. McLaurin, Anne. 1st ed. Sewall, Marcia (1935-), illus. LC 77-23868. (Illus.). 31 p. 1978. (ISBN 0-689-30633-7). Atheneum. **Award: (ALA).**
--Perfect Crane. McLaurin, Anne. Mikolaycak, Charles (1937-), illus. LC 80-7912. (Illus.). 32 p. 22cm. 1981. (ISBN 0-06-023743-0). (ISBN 0-06-023744-9). Harper & Row.
Lauring, Palle
--The Stone Daggers. 1st American ed. Olsen, Ib Spang (1921-), illus. Herberg, Ruth M., tr. from Danish. Fairservis, Walter A., Jr., intro. by. LC 64-11767. 160 p. illus. 21 cm. c.1964. MacMillan.
Lauritzen, Elizabeth Moyes (1909-)
--Shushma. Tsinajinie, Andy, illus. LC 64-15393. 188p. 1964. Caxton Printers, Ltd.
Lauritzen, Jonreed (1902-)
--Blood, Banners, and Wild Boars. Tales of Early Spain. 1st ed. Miret, Gil, illus. LC 67-1935. (Illus.). 151 p. 21cm. 1967. Little, Brown.
--Colonel Anza's Impossible Journey. Savage, Steele (1900-), illus. (Illus.). (Sagas of the West Ser). (gr. 7-10). 1966. (ISBN 0-399-60101-5). Putnam.
--The Glitter Eyed Wouser. N.D. E . M. Hale and Co.
--The Glitter- Eyed Wouser. 1st ed. Von Schmidt, Eric (1931-), illus. LC 60-9342. 238p. illus. 21cm. 1960. Brown.
--The Legend of Billy Bluesage. Chavez, Edward, illus. LC 61-9285. (Illus.). 217 p. 22cm. 1961. Little, Brown. **Award: (ALA).**
--The Ordeal of the Young Hunter. 1st ed. Denetsosie, Hoke, illus. LC 54-8313. 246p. illus. 21cm. 1954. (ISBN 0-316-51640-6). Little, Brown.
--Treasure of the High Country. 1st ed. Von Schmidt, Eric (1931-), illus. LC 59-5282. 210p. illus. 21cm. 1959. Little, Brown.
--The Young Mustangers. 1st ed. Lantz, Paul (1908-), illus. LC 57-8043. 240p. illus. 22cm. 1957. Little, Brown.
Laux, Dorothy (1920-)
--Did I Do That?. Eitzen, Allan (1928-), illus. LC 70-113215. (Illus.). 47 p. 23cm. 1970. Broadman Press.
Lavaivre, Noelle
--One Moonless Night. Lavaivre, Noelle, illus. LC 64-21768. (Illus.). (Juv.). (gr. k-3). 1964. (ISBN 0-8076-0272-8). Braziller.
La Valette, Andree De see De La Valette, Andree.
LaVanture, Pauline
--So, Indian Legend About the Blue Bonnett. LaVanture, Pauline, illus. LC 42-200. 27 p. col. illus. 22cm. 1941. Naylor Co.
La Varre, Andre, jt. auth. see La Varre, William.
La Varre, William & La Varre, Andre
--Johnny-Round-the-World. N.D. Simon & Schuster.
Lavater, Johann Caspar (1741-1801)
--The Little Keepsake: Selected in Part from the Writings of the Celebrated J. C. Lavater. LC 15-18031. 96 p. front., plates. 12 cm. 1843. S. Colman.
Lavell, Edith, Mrs.
--The Girl Scouts at Camp. (The Girl Scout Ser.). N.D. A. L. Burt Co.
--The Girl Scouts at Miss Allen's School. LC 22-9664. 241 p. front. 20 cm. (Her Girl scout series). c.1922. A. L. Burt Company.
--The Girl Scouts' Canoe Trip. (The Girl Scout Ser.). N.D. A. L. Burt Co.
--The Girl Scouts' Captain. LC 25-6164. 242 p. front. 20 cm. (Her Girl scouts series). c.1925. A. L. Burt Company.
--The Girl Scouts' Director. LC 25-6163. 253 p. front. 20 cm. (Her Girl scouts series). c.1925. A. L. Burt Company.
--The Girl Scouts' Good Turn. (The Girl Scout Ser.). N.D. A. L. Burt Co.
--The Girl Scouts' Motor Trip. LC 24-7955. 256 p. front. 20 cm. (Her Girl scouts series). c.1924. A. L. Burt Company.
--The Girl Scouts on the Ranch. LC 23-9689. 249 p. front. 20 c. (Her Girl scouts series). c.1923. A. L. Burt Company.
--The Girl Scouts' Vacation Adventures. LC 24-7954. 248 p. front. 20 cm. (Her Girl scouts series). c.1924. A. L. Burt Company.
--The Girl Scouts's Rivals. (The Girl Scout Ser.) N.D. A. L. Burt Co.
--Linda Carlton, Air Pilot. LC 31-13221. 246 p. front. 20 cm. (Her Linda Carlton series). c.1931. A. L. Burt Company.
--Linda Carlton's Hollywood Flight. LC 33-11068. 256 p. front. 19 cm. (Her Linda Carlton series). c.1933. A. L. Burt Company.
--Linda Carlton's Island Adventures. LC 31-13224. 287 p. front. 20 cm. (Her Linda Carlton series). c.1931. A. L. Burt Company.
--Linda Carlton's Ocean Flight. LC 31-132223. 283 p. front. 20 cm. (Her Linda Carlton series). c.1931. A. L. Burt Company.
--Linda Carlton's Perilous Summer. LC 32-127234. 247 p. front. 19 cm. (Her Linda Carlton series). c.1932. A. L. Burt Company.
--The Mystery at Dark Cedars. LC 35-8371. 254 p. front. 21 cm. (Her Mary Lou series). c.1935. A. L. Burt Company.
--The Mystery of the Fires. LC 35-837071. 250 p. front. 21 cm. (Her Mary Lou series). c.1935. A. L. Burt Company.
--The Mystery of the Secret Band. LC 35-8372. 254 p. front. 21 cm. (Her Mary Lou series). c.1935. A. L. Burt Company.
Lavelle, E.
--The Man Who Was Chosen. N.D. McGraw-Hill.
Lavender, David Sievert (1910-)
--Golden Trek. LC 48-7964. 265 p. 21 cm. 1948. Westminister Press.
--Mike Maroney Raider. LC 45-199. 5 p. l., 242 p. incl. front., plates. 21 cm. 1945. The Westminster Press.
--Trouble at Tamarack. LC 43-5801. 256 p. incl. front., illus., plates. 21 cm. 1943. The Westminster Press.
La Vergue, George Harrison De see De La Vergne, George Harrison.
Laverty, Maura
--Gold of Glanaree. Bowen, Betty Morgan (1921-), illus. LC 45-9069. 192 p. incl. front., illus. 21 cm. 1945. Longmans, Green and Co., Inc.
Lavin, Mary (1912-)
--Collected Stories. (Illus.). 1971. Houghton Mifflin Company.
--A Likely Story. LC 68-75105. 21cm. v, 34p. (The New Dolmen Chapbooks: No. 3). 1967. Dolmen P.
--A Likely Story. Unwin, Nora Spicer (1907-), illus. LC 57-11095. 78p. illus. 21cm. 1957. Macmillan.
--The Second-Best Children in the World. Ardizzone, Edward Jeffrey Irving (1900-1979), illus. LC 70-135132. (Illus.). 47 p. 26cm. 1972. (ISBN 0-395-13896-5). Houghton Mifflin.
Lavington, Margaret
--Cackles and Lays. Urquhart, Helen, illus. LC 18-10863. 4 p. l., 75, 1 p. illus., 4 col. pl. (incl. front.) 18 cm. 1918. John Lane.
Lavis, Stephen, illus.
--One Thousand One Arabian Nights. (Illus.). 256p. 1982. (ISBN 0-19-274530-1, Pub. by Oxford U Pr Childrens). Merrimack Pub Cir.
Lavitt, Edward, jt. ed. see McDowell, Robert Eugene.
Lavitt, Edward & McDowell, Robert Eugene (1928-), eds.
--In the Beginning ... Creation Stories for Young People. Borer, Alan, illus. LC 73-83166. (Illus.). ix, 166 p. 22cm. c.1973. (ISBN 0-89388-096-5). Odarkai Books.
Lavolle, L. N
--Captain Nuno. Rev. ed. Schwarz, Hans, illus. Kirkup, James, tr. from Fr. LC 63-11677. (Illus.). 128 p. 22cm. 1963. Lothrop, Lee and Shepard.
--Jade Gate. Rousseau, P., illus. Shelley, Hugh, tr. LC 64-10980. (Illus.). (gr. 7 up). 1963. Abelard.
--Jade Gate. Rousseau, P., illus. (Illus.). (gr. 6-12). 1963. (ISBN 0-8382-0375-2). Hale.
--The Key to the Desert. Daynie, J., illus. Shelley, Hugh, tr. from French. 159p. illus. 21cm. 1962. Abelard-Schuman.
--The Lost lake. Daynie, J., illus. Shelley, Hugh, tr. LC 61-15710. 21cm. 159p. 1962, c.1961. Abelard-Schuman.
--Nhoti, son of India. Lequeret, J. P., illus. Shelley, Hugh, tr. 146p. illus. 21cm. 1961, c.1960. Abelard-Schuman.
--The Silent House. Daynie, J., illus. Shelley, Hugh, tr. from Fr. LC 65-11384. 159p. illus. 20cm. 1965, c.1964. Abelard.
Lavranyov, B.
--The Courageous Heart. 28p. 1978. (ISBN 0-8285-1127-6, Pub. by Progress Pubs USSR). Imported Pubns.
Law, Carol Russell
--The Case of the Weird Street Firebug: A Mystery for the Mail-Order Detective. LC 79-26906. p. cm. (Capers). c.1980. (ISBN 0-394-84480-7). (ISBN 0-394-94480-1). Knopf.
Law, Frederick H., ed. see Stevenson, Robert Louis.
Law, Frederick Houk, ed. see Kipling, Joseph Rudyard.
Law, Joy, tr. see Spyri, Johanna Heusser.
Law, Katherine
--Hiccup Hippo. Renfro, Ed, illus. LC 67-5987. (Illus.). 32 p. 29cm. (Carousel book). 1967. L. W. Singer Co.
Law, Katheryn
--Salish Folk Tales. (Indian Culture Ser.). (gr. 2-8). 1972. (ISBN 0-89992-028-4). MT Coun Indian.
--Tales from the Bitterfoot Valley. (Indian Culture Ser.). (gr. 1-4). 1971. (ISBN 0-89992-014-4). MT Coun Indian.
La Wall, Irene, pseud., see Dornblaster, Irene La Wall.
La Wall, Irene, pseud.
--Land That I Love: The Escape of a Nazi Youth. Dornblaster, Irene La Wall. LC 45-4454. 93 p. 19 1/2 cm. 1945. The Wartburg Press.
Lawhead, Stephen R.
--The Sword & the Flame. LC 83-73341. 348p. (Dragon King Trilogy Ser.: Bk. III). 1984. (ISBN 0-89107-310-8, Crossway Bks). Good News.
Lawhead, Terry
--The Ferry Story. Richards, Paula, illus. LC 78-16743. (Illus.). 66 p. c.1978. (ISBN 0-914718-33-9). Pacific Search Press.
Lawler, Ann
--The Substitute. Parker, Nancy Winslow (1930-), illus. LC 77-23303. (Illus.). 33 p. 20cm. c.1977. (ISBN 0-8193-0902-8). (ISBN 0-8193-0903-6). Parents' Magazine Press.
Lawler, Pat
--My Brother's Place. LC 78-3288. p. cm. 1978. (ISBN 0-394-83846-7). (ISBN 0-394-93846-1). Pantheon.
--What about Me?. 176p. (Orig.). (gr. 7 up). 1982. (ISBN 0-590-32172-2, Wishing Star). Scholastic Inc.
Lawley, Clare D.
--Todd Puff-Tail of Toddington Manor. Lawley, K. G., illus. (Illus.). 48p. (gr. 2 up). 1978. Dorrance.
Lawlis, Merritt, ed. see Dekker, Thomas.
Lawlor, Laurie
--Addie Across the Prairie. Owens, Gail, illus. LC 85-15548. p. cm. 1986. (ISBN 0-8075-0165-4). A. Whitman.
Lawrence, Ann Margaret (1942-)
--The Good Little Devil. 1978. Macmillan.
--The Half-Brothers. LC 73-7392. 172 p. 22cm. 1973. (ISBN 0-8098-2425-6). H. Z. Walck.
--Mr. Fox. 1979. Macmillan.
--Oggy & the Holiday. (Illus.). 1979. (Pub. by Gollancz England). David & Charles.
--Tom Ass: Or, The Second Gift. Lazarevich, Mila (1942-), illus. 1973. (ISBN 0-8098-2424-8). David McKay Company.
--Tom Ass: Or, The Second Gift. Lazarevich, Mila (1942-), illus. LC 72-10653. (Illus.). 132 p. 24cm. 1973, c.1972. (ISBN 0-8098-2424-8). H. Z. Walck.
--The Travels of Oggy. (Illus.). 1973. (Pub. by Gollancz England). David & Charles.
Lawrence, Anne, pseud., see Fideler, Nancy B..
Lawrence, Betty
--Let's Play a Game, and Other Tales. LC 37-15601. 44p. 20cm. 1936. The Christopher Publishing House.
Lawrence, Bonnie S., ed. see Hay, Keith, et al.
Lawrence, Chester Henry (1887-)
--Santa Claus in Toyland. Lawrence, Chester Henry (1887-), illus. LC 15-8152. 96 p. incl. illus., plates. col. front., col. plates. 28 cm. c.1915. The Reilly & Britton Co.
Lawrence, Christopher George Holman see Lynn, Escott, pseud.
Lawrence, Clara Louise
--The Sea Witch and Other Stories and Poems for Children. LC 32-33420. 5-63 p. col. front. 29 cm. c.1932. Print. by Los Gatos Print Shop.
Lawrence, Cynthia
--Barbie Solves a Mystery. Smith, Clyde, illus. LC 63-18557. 181 p. illus. 22 cm. 1963. Random House.
--Barbie's New York Summer. Smith, Clyde, illus. LC 62-143000. 179p. illus. 21cm. 1962. (ISBN 0-394-80980-7). Random House.
Lawrence, Cynthia & Maybee, Bette Lou
--Barbie and Ken. Smith, Clyde, illus. LC 63-18556. 186 p. illus. 22 cm. 1963. Random House.

--Barbie, Midge & Ken. Patterson, Robert (1899-), illus. LC 64-20865. (Illus.). (gr. 5-9). 1964. (ISBN 0-394-80980-7). Random.

--Here's Barbie. Smith, Clyde, illus. LC 62-14299. 186p. illus. 21cm. 1962. Random House.

Lawrence, David Herbert (1885-1930)

--Birds, Beasts, and the Third Thing: Poems. Provensen, Alice (1918-) & Provensen, Martin (1916-), eds. Provensen, Alice (1918-) & Provensen, Martin (1916-), illus. Hall, Donald, intro. by. LC 81-70405. (Illus.). 40 p. 26cm. c.1982. (ISBN 0-670-16779-7). Viking Press. **Award: (ALA).**

--The Prussian Officer. 56p. (Creative's Classics Ser.). (gr. 1-7). 1982. (ISBN 0-87191-892-7). Creative Ed.

--The Rocking Horse Winner. 40p. (Creative's Classics Ser.). (gr. 1-7). 1982. (ISBN 0-87191-893-5). Creative Ed.

--You Touched Me. Higashi, Sandra, illus. LC 82-73340. (Illus.). 48 p. 23cm. c.1982. (ISBN 0-87191-894-3). Creative Education, Inc.

Lawrence, Harriet

--First There Was Adam. Geer, Charles Hand (1922-), illus. LC 65-24863. 90p. illus. 21cm. c.1965. Duell Dist. Meredith.

--H. Philip Birdsong's ESP. Huffaker, Sandy (1943-), illus. LC 69-14568. (Illus.). 303 p. 25cm. 1969. W. R. Scott.

Lawrence, Isabelle Wentworth

--Drumbeats in Williamsburg: A Story of Washington, Lafayette and Yorktown. Lee, Manning de Villeneuve (1894-1980), illus. LC 65-22219. 224 p. illus. 21 cm. 1965. (ISBN 0-528-82086-9). Rand McNally.

--The Gift of the Golden Cup: A Tale of Rome and Pirates. 1st ed. John, Charles V., illus. LC 46-3772. 286 p. incl. front., illus. 21 cm. 1946. The Bobbs-Merrill Company.

--The Night Watch: Adventure with Rembrandt. Lee, Manning de Villeneuve (1894-1980), illus. LC 52-7502. (Illus.). 272 p. 21cm. 1952. Rand McNally.

--Niko, Sculptor's Apprentice. Marokvia, Artur F. (1909-), illus. LC 56-14203. 184p. illus. 21cm. 1956. Viking Press.

--A Spy in Williamsburg. Lee, Manning De Villeneuve (1894-1980), illus. LC 55-6953. (Illus.). 224 p. 21cm. 1955. (ISBN 0-528-80105-8). Rand McNally.

--Theft of the Golden Ring. (gr. 4-8). 1960. (ISBN 0-672-50533-9). Bobbs.

--The Theft of the Golden Ring: A Tale of Rome and Treasure. John, Charles V., illus. LC 48-6472. 309 p. illus., map (on lining-papers) 21 cm. 1948. Bobbs-Merrill Co.

--Two for the Show: A Story of Shakespeare's England. 1 ed. LC 49-11280. 283 p. illus. 21 cm. 1949. Bobbs-Merrill Co.

--West to Danger. LC 64-25324. 207p. 22cm. 1964. Bobbs-Merrill.

Lawrence, Jacob (1917-)

--Harriet and the Promised Land. Lawrence, Jacob (1917-), illus. LC 68-25752. (Illus.). 1 v. (unpaged. 32cm. 1968 (Windmill Bks.). Simon & Schuster. **Award: (NYT).**

--Harriet and the Promised Land. Lawrence, Jacob (1917-), illus. (Illus.). 1968. Simon and Schuster Inx.

Lawrence, James Duncan (1918-)

--Barnaby's Bells. Lowenbein, Michael, illus. LC 65-131201. 186p. illus. 21cm. c.1965. Macmillan.

--Binky Brothers and the Fearless Four. Kessler, Leonard P. (1921-), illus. LC 75-77936. (Illus.). 64 p. 23cm. (I can read mystery). 1970. Harper & Row.

--Binky Brothers, Detectives. Kessler, Leonard P. (1921-), illus. LC 68-10374. (Illus.). 5 7/8 x 8 1/2. 64p. (18 pt.). (I Can Read Mysteries Ser.). (gr. k-3). 1968. (ISBN 0-06-023759-7) (ISBN 0-06-444003-6) Har-Row.

--Binky Brothers, Detectives. Kessler, Leonard P. (1921-), illus. LC 68-10374. (Illus.). 60 p. 23cm. (I can read mystery). 1968. (ISBN 0-06-023759-7). (ISBN 0-06-444003-6). Harper & Row.

--Binky Brothers, Detectives. Kessler, Leonard P. (1921-), illus. (Illus.). 60p. 22cm. (Harper Trophy I Can Read Book). 1978, c.1968. (ISBN 0-06-444003-6). Harper & Row.

--Davy Crockett and the Indian Secret: Adventures of a Boy Pioneer. LC 56-227263. 173p. illus. 21cm. 1955. Books, Inc.

Lawrence, Jerome (1915-)

--Oscar, the Ostrich. David, Mark, illus. LC 40-5634. 79 p. illus. 22 x 19 cm. 1940. Random House, Inc.

Lawrence, John, jt. auth. see Hardy, Thomas.

Lawrence, John, jt. ed. see Macfarlane, Iris.

Lawrence, John (1933-)

--The Giant of Grabbist. Lawrence, John (1933-), illus. LC 68-9035. (Illus.). 32 p. 28cm. 1969. D. White.

--Pope Leo's Elephant. LC 74-82765. (Illus.). 32 p. 19cm. 1970, c.1969. World Pub. Co.

--Rabbit & Pork Rhyming Talk. LC 75-6891. (Illus.). 48p. (gr. 1 up). 1975. (ISBN 0-690-00973-9, TYC-J). Har-Row.

Lawrence, John (1933-), retold by.

--The King of the Peacocks. Lawrence, John (1933-), illus. LC 79-126976. (Illus.). 32 p. 28cm. 1st U.S. edition. 1971, c.1970. (ISBN 0-690-47390-7). Crowell.

Lawrence, Josephine (1890-1978)

--The Adventures of Elizabeth Ann. Gooch, Thelma, illus. LC 28-701752. 215 p. incl. front., plates. 20 cm. c.1923. Barse & Hopkins.

--The Berry Patch. Gooch, Thelma, illus. LC 25-11484. 4 p. l., 312 p. col. front., plates. 20 cm. c.1925. Cupples & Leon Company.

--Brother and Sister. (The Brother and Sister). N.D. Cupples & Leon Co.

--Brother and Sister at Bayport. (The Brother and Sister Ser.). N.D. Cupples & Leon Co.

--Brother and Sister Keep House. (The Brother and Sister Ser.). N.D. Cupples & Leon Co.

--Brother & Sister's Holidays. (The Brother & Sister Ser.). N.D. Cupples & Leon Co.

--Brother and Sister's Schooldays. (The Brother and Sister Ser.). N.D. Cupples & Leon Co.

--Brother and Sister's Vacation. (The Brother and Sister Ser.). N.D. Cupples & Leon Co.

--Christine. Gooch, Thelma, illus. LC 30-16808. 5 p. l., 296 p. front., plates. 20 cm. c.1930. Cupples & Leon Company.

--The Dollville Railroad. Claghorn, Joseph C., illus. LC 28-18244. 48 p. incl. col. front., col. plates. 14 cm. (Her Toyland series, no. 8). c.1928. Barse & Co.

--Eagle Feather, the Laughing Indian. Claghorn, Joseph C., illus. LC 28-18241. 48p. 14cm. (Toyland Ser.). 1928. Barse & Co.

--Elizabeth Ann and Doris. Foster, John M., illus. LC 25-10307. 211 p. incl. plates. front. 20 cm. c.1928. Barse & Hopkins.

--Elizabeth Ann and Uncle Doctor. (The Elizabeth Ann Ser.). N.D. Barse & Co.

--Elizabeth Ann at Maple Spring. Gooch, Thelma, illus. LC 23-7637. 2 p. l., 9-219 p. incl. plates. front. 20 cm. c.1923. Barse & Hopkins.

--Elizabeth Ann's Borrowed Grandma. (The Elizabeth Ann Ser.). N.D. Barse & Co.

--Elizabeth Ann's Houseboat. Foster, John M., illus. LC 29-11746. 3 p. l., 11-214 p. incl. plates. front. 20 cm. (Her Elizabeth Ann series). c.1929. Barse & Co.

--Elizabeth Ann's Six Cousins. (The Elizabeth Ann Ser.). N.D. Barse & Hopkins.

--Elizabeth Ann's Spring Vacation. (The Elizabeth Ann SEr.). N.D. Barse & Co.

--Flying Cloud and His Rocking Horse. Claghorn, Joseph C., illus. LC 28-182406. 48 p. incl. col. front., col. plates. 14 cm. (Her Toyland series, no. 9). c.1928. Barse & Co.

--Glenna. Gooch, Thelma, illus. LC 29-11402. 5 p. l., 304 p. front., plates. 20 cm. c.1929. Cupples & Leon Company.

--Holland Kiddies. (Kiddie Wonder Ser.). N.D. Cupples & Leon Co.

--The Jolly Holly Berrys. Claghorn, Joseph C., illus. LC 28-18121. 48 p. incl. col. front., col. plates. 14 cm. (Her Toyland series, no. 6). c.1928. Barse & Co.

--Josephine Lawrence Stories for Girls: Three Complete Books in One Volume ... Gooch, Thelma, illus. LC 39-32383. 3 p. l., 310 p., 2 l., 312 p., 2 l., 308 p. front. 21 cm. c.1939. Cupples & Leon Company.

--Kiddie Fairy Tales. (Kiddie Wonder Ser.). N.D. Cupples & Leon Co.

--Kiddie Farmers. (Kiddie Wonder Ser.). N.D. Cupples & Leon Co.

--Kiddies Frolics. (Kiddie Wonder Ser.). N.D. Cupples & Leon Co.

--Kiddies In the Country. (Kiddie Wonder Ser.). N.D. Cupples & Leon Co.

--Kiddies Nursery Rhymes. (Kiddie Wonder Ser.). N.D. Cupples & Leon Co.

--Linda Lane. Wrenn, Charles L., illus. LC 25-10308. 3 p. l., 11-247 p. incl. plates. front 20 cm. c.1925. Barse & Hopkins.

--Linda Lane Experiments. (Linda Lane Ser.). N.D. Barse & Co.

--Linda Lane Helps Out. Wrenn, Charles L., illus. LC 25-10976. 3p. l., 11-248 p. incl. plates. front. 20 cm. c.1925. Barse & Hopkins.

--Linda Lane's Big Sister. Foster, John M., illus. LC 29-134710. 241 p. incl. plates. front. 20 cm. (Her Linda Lane series). c.1929. Barse & Co.

--Linda Lane's Problems. FOster, John M., illus. LC 28-14006. 3p. (Linda Lane Ser.). 1928. Barse & Co.

--Man in the Moon Stories Told Over the Radio-Phone. Gruelle, John Barton (1880-1938), illus. N.D. Cupples & Leon Co.

--Mother Goose and Her Kiddies. (Kiddie Wonder Ser.). N.D. Cupples & Leon Co.

--Mr White Helps Santa Claus. Claghorn, Joseph C., illus. LC 28-1824. 48 p. incl. col. front., col. plates. 14 cm. (Her Toyland series, no. 5). c.1928. Barse & Co.

--Next Door Neighbors. Burd, Clara Miller, illus. LC 26-18318. 4 p. l., 311 p. front., plates. 20 cm. c.1926. Cupples & Leon Company.

--Perry and Polly's Pictures. LC 28-142328. 62 p. incl. col. front., col. illus. 21 cm. c.1928. Barse & Co.

--The Policeman Cat. Claghorn, Joseph C., illus. LC 28-185821. 48 p. incl. col. front., col. plates. 14 cm. (Her Toyland series, no. 2). 1928. Barse & Co.

--Rainbow Hill. Gooch, Thelma, illus. LC 24-14876. 4 p. l., 312 p. front., plates. 20 cm. c.1924. Cupples & Leon Company.

--Red Arrow: A Warrior. Claghorn, Joseph C., illus. LC 28-181201. 48 p. incl. col. front., col. plates. 14 cm. (Her Toyland series, no. 7). c.1928. Barse & Co.

--Rosemary. Gooch, Thelma, illus. LC 2-17728. 4 p. l., 310 p. front., plates. 20 cm. c.1922. Cupples & Leon Company.

--Rosemary and the Princess. (Josephine Lawrence Books). N.D. Cupples & Leon Co.

--The Toys' Christmas Party. Claghorn, Joseph C., illus. LC 28-18243. 48 p. incl. col. front., col. plates. 14 cm. (Her Toyland series, no. 4). c.1928. Barse & Co.

--The Two Little Fellows. (The Two Little Fellows Ser.). N.D. Barse & Co.

--The Two Little Fellows Go Visiting. (The Two Little Fellows Ser.). N.D. Barse & Co.

--The Two Little Fellows in April. Foster, John M., illus. LC 29-11580. 216 p. incl. plates. front. 20 cm. (Her two little Fellows series). c.1929. Barse & Co.

--The Two Little Fellows' Secret. Foster, John M., illus. LC 28-11976. 213 p. incl. plates. front. 20 cm. (Her Two little fellows series). c.1928. Barse & Co.

--The Two Little Fellows Start School. (The Two Little Fellows Ser.). N.D. Barse & Co.

--The Unhappy Paper Doll. Claghorn, Joseph C., illus. LC 28-18583. 48 p. incl. col. front., col. plates. 14 cm. (Her Toyland series, no. 1). c.1928. Barse & Co.

--Wind's in the West. (Novels for Teen Age Girls). N.D. Platt & Munk.

--Wind's in the West. Tandy, Russell H., illus. LC 31-14180. vi p., 2 l., 305 p. front., plates. 20 cm. c.1931. Cupples & Leon Company.

Lawrence, Judith

--A Goat for Carlo. Dauber, Elizabeth, illus. LC 79-161028. (Illus.). 40 p. 23cm. 1971. (ISBN 0-8116-6709-X). Garrard Pub. Co.

Lawrence, Katharine D.

--The Fairy Dream. Pancoast, Charles W., illus. 129 p. front. 19 cm. 1901. Bonnell, Silver & Co.

Lawrence, Kathryn (1939-)

--The Purryfurs and the Meandering Path. LC 85-11942. p. cm. c.1985. (ISBN 0-934555-00-1). Sea Tree Press.

Lawrence, Leslie, ed. see Ames, Lee Judah.

Lawrence, Leslie, ed. see Kinsman, Barbara.

Lawrence, Leslie, ed. see Temko, Florence.

Lawrence, Louise (1943-)

--Calling B for Butterfly. LC 81-48648. 224p. (gr. 5 up). 1982. (ISBN 0-06-023749-X, HarpJ). (ISBN 0-06-023750-3). Har-Row.

--Cat Call. LC 78-22476. 214 p. 22cm. c.1980. (ISBN 0-06-023753-8). (ISBN 0-06-023754-6). Harper & Row.

--Children of the Dust. LC 85-42618. 183 p. 24cm. c.1985. (ISBN 0-06-023738-4). (ISBN 0-06-023739-2). Harper & Row.

--The Dram Road. 1st ed. LC 83-47601. p. cm. c.1983. (ISBN 0-06-023747-3). (ISBN 0-06-023748-1). Harper & Row.

--The Earth Witch. LC 80-8431. 214 p. 21cm. c.1981. (ISBN 0-06-023751-1). (ISBN 0-06-023752-X). Harper & Row.

--Good-Bye, Butterfly. LC 81-48648. p. cm. c.1982. (ISBN 0-06-023749-X). (ISBN 0-06-023750-3). Harper & Row.

--The Power of Stars. 192p (Pub. by Har-Row). (gr. 7 up). 1973. (ISBN 0-06-440043-3, Trophy). Har-Row.

--The Power of Stars: A Story of Suspense. LC 72-76519. 184 p. 21cm. 1972. (ISBN 0-06-023766-X). (ISBN 0-06-023766-X). Harper & Row.

--Sing and Scatter Daisies. LC 76-21393. 236 p. 21cm. c.1977. (ISBN 0-06-023772-4). (ISBN 0-06-023773-2). Harper & Row.

--Star Lord. LC 77-25674. 170 p. 21cm. c.1978. (ISBN 0-06-023776-7). (ISBN 0-06-023777-5). Harper & Row.

--The Wyndcliffe: A Story of Suspense. LC 74-20393. 183 p. 21cm. 1975, c.1974. (ISBN 0-06-023768-6). Harper & Row.

Lawrence, Margaret Dix, Mrs. (1885-)

--Rosemary for Remembrance. LC 41-23279. 132 p. incl. front. (port.) illus. 26 cm. 1941. The Brookville Press.

Lawrence, Margaret Oliver Woods, Mrs. (1813-1901), ed.

--Fading Flowers. LC 28-7672. xiv, 288 p. pl. 19 cm. 1860. J. E. Tilton and Company.

Lawrence, Marjorie Kahl

--Fairy Smoke: Children's Poems. (Illus.). 87 p. 21cm. 1974. (ISBN 0-682-47898-9). Exposition Press.

--Mother Goose for the Animals' Children: Inverses. 1st. ed. (Illus.). 94 p. 22cm. 1974. (ISBN 0-682-47885-7). Exposition.

Lawrence, Marjorie Kahl, selected by.

--A Beginning Book of Poems. 118p. illus. (pt. col.) 24cm. 1967. Addison.

--An Invitation to Poetry. LC 67-31891. 145 p. illus. (part col.) 24 cm. 1967. Addison-Wesley Pub. Co.

Lawrence, Merloyd, tr. see Sandberg, Karin Inger (1930-) & Sandberg, Lasse E. M.

Lawrence, Mildred Elwood (1907-)

--Along Comes Spring. LC 58-8732. 192p. 21cm. 1958. Harcourt, Brace.

--Crissy at the Wheel. 1st ed. Bileck, Marvin (1920-), illus. LC 52-6904. 200 p. illus. 21 cm. 1952. (ISBN 0-15-220906-9). Harcourt, Brace.

--Dreamboats for Trudy. 1st ed. Frankenberg, Robert Clinton (1911-), illus. LC 54-8573. 183p. illus. 21cm. 1954. Harcourt, Brace.

--Drums in My Heart. LC 64-17086. 192 p. 21cm. 1964. Harcourt, Brace & World.

--Forever and Always. LC 61-10111. 191 p. 21cm. 1961. Harcourt, Brace & World.

--Gateway to the Sun. LC 76-124843. 190 p. 21cm. 1970. (ISBN 0-15-230590-4). Harcourt Brace Jovanovich.

--Girl on Witches' Hill. 1st ed. LC 63-16034. 190 p. 21cm. 1963. Harcourt, Brace and World.

--Good Morning, My Heart. LC 57-9052. 191 p. 22cm. 1957. Harcourt, Brace.

--The Homemade Year. 1st ed. Suba, Susanne (1913-), illus. LC 50-9124. (Illus.). 217 p. 21cm. 1950. Harcourt, Brace.

--Indigo Magic. Liebman, Oscar (1919-), illus. N.D. E . M. Hale and Co.

--Indigo Magic. 1st ed. Liebman, Oscar (1919-), illus. LC 56-8353. 184p. illus. 22cm. 1956. Harcourt, Brace.

--Inside the Gate. LC 68-25187. 192 p. 20cm. 1968. Harcourt, Brace & World.

--Island Secret. 1st ed. Galdone, Paul (1914-), illus. LC 55-7611. 175p. illus. 21cm. 1955. Harcourt, Brace.

--No Slipper for Cinderella. LC 65-17990. 192p. 21cm. 1965. Harcourt.

--Once at the Weary Why. LC 76-84773. 189 p. 21cm. 1969. Harcourt, Brace & World.

--One Hundred White Horses. 1st ed. Liebman, Oscar (1919-), illus. LC 53-78663. 176p. illus. 21cm. 1953. (ISBN 0-15-258675-X). Harcourt, Brace.

--Peachtree Island. Stevens, Mary, illus. LC 48-9018. 244p. (gr. 3-7). 1948. (ISBN 0-15-260107-4). HarBraceJ.

--Peachtree Island. Stevens, Mary, illus. LC 48-9018. (Illus.). 21cm. 224p. (Voyager bk.: AVB27). 1966, c.1948. (ISBN 0-15-671560-0). Harcourt.

--The Questing Heart. LC 59-8954. 191 p. 21cm. 1959. Harcourt, Brace.

--Reach for the Dream. LC 67-18867. 192 p. 21cm. 1967. Harcourt, Brace & World.

--Sand in Her Shoes. 1st ed. Chastain, Madye Lee (1908-), illus. LC 49-10407. 211 p. illus. 21 cm. 1949. Harcourt, Brace.

--The Shining Moment. LC 60-10759. 187 p. 21cm. 1960. Harcourt, Brace.

--Starry Answer. LC 62-15627. 189 p. 21cm. 1962. Harcourt, Brace & World.

--Susan's Bears. N.D. Grosset & Dunlap.

--Tallie. 1st ed. Galdone, Paul (1914-), illus. LC 51-11740. (Illus.). 213 p. 21cm. 1951. Harcourt, Brace.

--Touchmark. Hollinger, Deanne, illus. LC 75-11579. (Illus.). 184 p. 21cm. 1975. (ISBN 0-15-289603-1). Harcourt Brace Jovanovich.

--Treasure and the Song. 1966. E M Hale.

--The Treasure and the Song. LC 66-5508. 192p. 21cm. c.1966. Harcourt.

--Walk a Rocky Road. LC 73-161387. 187 p. 21cm. 1971. (ISBN 0-15-294505-9). Harcourt Brace Jovanovich.

Lawrence, Robert Means (1847-1935)

--The Magic of the Horse-shoe with Other Folk-lore Notes. LC 68-22034. 344p. Repr. of 1898 ed. 1968 (Gale Reprints). Singing Tree Press.

Lawrence, Rosamond Napier, Lady (1878-)

--Letters to Patty. Lawrence, Rosamond Napier, illus. LC 11-28080. 153 p. illus. 20 cm. N.D. Doran.

Lawrence, S. J.

--Aquarius Ahoy!. 160p. (The Zodiac Club Ser.). (gr. 7 up). 1985. (ISBN 0-399-21222-1). Putnam Pub Group.

Lawrence, Una Roberts, Mrs. (1893-)

--Just Around the Corner Tales: Home Mission Stories for Boys and Girls. Wolf, Cleo Adele, illus. LC 27-1350. 166 p. incl. front., illus., plates. 19cm. c.1926. Home Mission Board of the Southern Baptist Convention.

Lawrie, Margaret, ed.

--Myths and Legends of The Torres Strait. N.D. (ISBN 0-8008-5464-0). Taplinger.

Lawrie, Robert Wheeler

--Chuffy. Brouwer, Jack, illus. LC 51-37091. unpaged. illus. 27 cm. (Story hour book). 1959. Fideler Co.

Lawrie, Robin

--Ready for Take-off. (Illus.). (gr. 5 up). 1973. (ISBN 0-394-82549-7). Pantheon.

Leader, Evelyn Barbara Blackburn see Castle, Frances, pseud.
Leadley, Valera
--The Adventures of Little-Hop. 1984. (ISBN 0-8062-2338-3). Carlton.
Leaf, Anne Sellers, illus.
--The House that Jack Built. LC 62-12368. (Illus.). 32cm. 1962, c.1959. Rand McNally.
--Little Boy Blue and Other Nursery Rhymes. LC 56-12103. unpaged. illus. 22cm. (Rand McNally elf book, 555). c.1956. Rand McNally.
--Princess and the Pea. 1965. (ISBN 0-8382-0660-3, Hale Giant Books). E. M. Hale and Co.
Leaf, Munro see Leaf, Wilbur Munro.
Leaf, VaDonna Jean (1929-)
--Robbie and the Stolen Minibike. LC 77-78849. (Illus.). 180 p. 22cm. c.1978. (ISBN 0-88419-127-3). Creation House.
--Willie Wilson's Wonderful Watermelon. Inderieden, Nancy, illus. LC 72-7665. (Illus.). 32 p. 27cm. 1974. (ISBN 0-87614-042-8). Carolrhoda Books.
Leaf, Walter (1852-1927)
--Little Poems from the Greek, First Series. N.D. Robert M McBride.
Leaf, Wilbur Munro see Calvert, John, pseud.
Leaf, Wilbur Munro (1905-1976)
--Aesop's Fables. Lawson, Robert (1892-1957), illus. N.D. Heritage Press.
--Boo, Who Used to Be Scared of the Dark. Hunter, Frances Tipton, illus. LC 48-11365. 40 p. illus. (part col.) 29 cm. c.1948. Random House.
--Fair Play. Leaf, Wilbur Munro (1905-1976), illus. LC 39-27738. 94 p. 1 l. illus. 26 cm. 1939. Frederick A. Stokes Company.
--Flock of Watchbirds. Leaf, Wilbur Munro (1905-1976), illus. 1946. J B Lippincott Company.
--Fly Away, Watchbird. Leaf, Wilbur Munro (1905-1976), illus. N.D. J. B. Lippincott.
--Gordon the Goat. Leaf, Wilbur Munro (1905-1976), illus. LC 44-9910. 46, 2 p. illus. (part col.) 21 x 16 cm. 1944. J. B. Lippincott Company.
--John Henry Davis. Leaf, Wilbur Munro (1905-1976), illus. LC 40-30567. 2 p. l., 56, 1 p. illus. (part col.) 22 cm. 1940. Frederick A. Stokes Company.
--Manners Can Be Fun. Leaf, Wilbur Munro (1905-1976), illus. 48p. 1958. J. B. Lippincott.
--Noddle. Leaf, Wilbur Munro (1905-1976), illus. N.D. Frederick A. Stokes.
--Noodle. Bemelmans, Ludwig (1898-1962), illus. LC 69-17252. (Illus.). 48 p. 1969, c.1937. Four Winds Press.
--Noodle. Bemelmans, Ludwig (1898-1962), illus. 48p. illus. 20 1/2 x 20cm. 1937. Frederick A. Stokes.
--Noodle. Leaf, Wilbur Munro (1905-1976), illus. N.D. J. B. Lippincott.
--Robert Francis Weatherbee. Leaf, Wilbur Munro (1905-1976), illus. LC 35-16201. 75 p. illus. (part col.) 16 cm. 1935. Frederick A. Stokes Company.
--Robert Francis Weatherbee. Leaf, Wilbur Munro (1905-1976), illus. N.D. J. B. Lippincott.
--Safety Can Be Fun. Leaf, Wilbur Munro (1905-1976), illus. LC 38-27652. 49 p. illus. (part col.) 26 cm. 1938. Frederick A. Stokes Company.
--Safety can be Fun. Leaf, Wilbur Munro (1905-1976), illus. LC 38-27652. 49p. illus. part. col. 26cm. 1938. Frederick A. Stokes.
--Safety Can Be Fun. new, rev. ed. Leaf, Wilbur Munro (1905-1976), illus. (Illus.). 63 p. 26cm. 1961. Lippincott.
--Sam and the Superdroop. Leaf, Wilbur Munro (1905-1976), illus. LC 48-10140. 122 p. illus. 21 cm. 1948. Viking Press.
--The Story of Ferdinand. Lawson, Robert (1892-1957), illus. LC 38-9624. (Illus.). 70 p. 21cm. 1938. The Viking Press.
--The Story of Ferdinand. Lawson, Robert (1892-1957), illus. LC 36-19452. (Illus.). 21cm. 81p. (gr. k-4). 1936. Viking.
--The Story of Simpson and Sampson. Lawson, Robert (1892-1957), illus. LC 41-23709. 61 p. illus. 26 x 22 cm. 1941. The Viking Press.
--Three and 30 Watchbirds. Leaf, Wilbur Munro (1905-1976), illus. N.D. J. B. Lippincott.
--Three Promises to You. Leaf, Wilbur Munro (1905-1976), illus. 48p. 1959. J. B. Lippincott.
--Turnabout. Leaf, Wilbur Munro (1905-1976), illus. LC 67-24973. (Illus.). 1 v. (unpaged. 22cm. 1967. Lippincott.
--The Watchbirds. Leaf, Wilbur Munro (1905-1976), illus. N.D. Frederick A. Stokes.
--The Watchbirds. Leaf, Wilbur Munro (1905-1976), illus. N.D. J. B. Lippincott.
--Wee Gillis. Lawson, Robert (1892-1957), illus. LC 84-26510. (Illus.). 71 p. 26cm. 1985, c.1938. (ISBN 0-14-050535-0). Puffin Books.
--Wee Gillis. Lawson, Robert (1892-1957), illus. LC 38-27870. (Illus.). 71 p. 26cm. 1938. The Viking Press. **Award: (RCM).**
--Wee Gillis. Lawson, Robert (1892-1957), illus. 1959. Viking.
--Who Cares I Do. Leaf, Wilbur Munro (1905-1976), illus. 40p. 1971. J. B. Lippincott company.
--The Wishing Pool. Leaf, Wilbur Munro (1905-1976), illus. LC 60-12913. 63p. illus. 23cm. 1960. Lippincott.
Leahy, Jack Thomas (1930-)
--Shadow on the Waters. 1960. Borzoi.
Leahy, Walter Thomas (1858-)
--Clarence Belmont: Or, A Lad of Honor. LC 12-36131. 288 p. 20 cm. (On cover: Catholic library). c.1894. H. L. Kilner & Co.
Leake, Mary Jane
--Herbie Changed His Mind. LC 63-7092. 96 p. illus. (part col.) 24 cm. (Read-by-yourself books). 1963. Houghton Mifflin.
Leale, John, Sir (1892-)
--The Saint and the Boy, and Twenty other Stories for Children. Sillince, illus. LC 58-7055. 106p. illus. 20cm. 1958. Roy Publishers.
Leamy, Edmund (1848-1904)
--The Fairy Minstrel of Glenmalure, and Other Stories for Children. LC 31-26064. 5 p. l., 13-92 p. 20 cm. 1930. D. FitzGerald, Inc.
--The Fairy Minstrel of Glenmalure, and Other Stories for Children. Bennett, Richard Michael (1899-), illus. LC 39-689. 5 p. l., 13-92 p. incl. front., illus. 20 cm. 1937. Longmans, Green and Co.
--The Fairy Minstrel of Glenmalure, and Other Stories for Children. Casseau, Vera, illus. LC 76-9901. (Illus.). 92 p., 3 leaves of plates. 20cm. (Children's literature reprint series). 1976. (ISBN 0-8486-0210-2). Core Collection Books.
--The Fairy Minstrel of Glenmalure, and Other Stories for Children. Casseau, Vera, illus. LC 13-22447. 92 p. col. front., col. plates. 20 cm. c.1913. Desmond FitzGerald, Inc.
--The Golden Spears, and Other Fairy Tales. LC 38-276532. ix, 169 p. 20 cm. 1938. Longmans, Green and Co.
--The Golden Spears and Other Fairy Tales. Turner, Corinne, illus. LC 76-9902. (Illus.). xv, 180 p. 20cm. (Children's Literature Reprint Series). 1976. (ISBN 0-8486-0211-0). Core Collection Books.
--The Golden Spears and Other Fairy Tales. Turner, Corinne, illus. LC 31-26065. xi, 180 p. front., plates. 20 cm. 1930. D. FitzGerald, Inc.
--Irish Fairy Stories for Children. 82p. (Orig.). (gr. 6-9). 1979. (ISBN 0-85342-602-3, Pub. by Mercier Pr Ireland). Irish Bk Ctr.
--Irish Fairy Tales. LC 78-33690. 18cm. 126p. 1978. (ISBN 0-85342-561-2, Pub. by Mercier Pr Ireland). Mercier Press Limited.
Leander, Ed, pseud., see Richelson, Geraldine.
Leander, Ed, pseud. (1922-)
--Here's Looking at You!. Richelson, Geraldine. Gaudriault, Monique, et al., illus. LC 73-80925. (Illus.). 32p. (Harlin Quist Bks). (gr. 2-5). N.D. (ISBN 0-8252-3747-5). Quist.
--Q is for Crazy. Richelson, Geraldine. Sumichrast, Jozef (1948-), illus. LC 77-73523. 30p. col. ill. 19cm. c.1977. (ISBN 0-8252-7512-1). Harlin Quist.
--What's the Big Idea?. Richelson, Geraldine. LC 74-80269. (Illus.). 32 p. 19cm. 1975. (ISBN 0-8252-0126-8). (ISBN 0-8252-0125-X). Harlin Quist : Distributed by Dial/Delacorte Sales.
Leander, Ed, pseud. (1922-) & Diot, Alain
--Crazy Days. Richelson, Geraldine. Keleck, illus. LC 75-30313. (Illus.). 32 p. 18cm. 1975. (ISBN 0-8252-0139-X). H. Quist : Distributed by Dial/Delacorte Sales.
Leander, Richard, pseud., see Volkmann, Richard von.
Leander, Richard, pseud. (1830-1889)
--Fantastic Stories. Volkmann, Richard Von. Fraser-Tytler, M., illus. Granville, Paulina T., tr. N.D. George Routledge & Sons.
--The Rusted Knight. Volkmann, Richard von. Landaberger, Marte, illus. Prentice, William Kelly (1871-), tr. from Ger. 135 p. illus. 28.5 cm. c.1938. B Humprhries.
Lear
--Aunt Atta: Or, the Long Vacation. (Illus.). N.D. E & J B Young.
Lear, Edward, jt. auth. see Knight, Hilary.
Lear, Edward (1812-1888)
--ABC. Lear, Edward (1812-1888), illus. LC 64-66410. 1v. (unpaged) illus. 26cm. c.1965. McGraw.
--The Book of Nonsense. N.D. Frederick Warne & Co.
--The Book of Nonsense. (Illus.). N.D. James Miler.
--The Book of Nonsense. (The Treasury Series for Children). N.D. Thomas Y. Crowell Co.
--The Book of Nonsense. Cruikshank, George (1792-1878), pref. by. Cruikshank, George (1792-1878), illus. Greene, David & Ries, Vera LC 75-32161. p. cm. (Classics of Children's Literature, 1621-1932). 1977. (ISBN 0-8240-2275-0). Garland Pub.
--The Book of Nonsense. Lear, Edward (1812-1888), illus. N.D. Thomas Y Crowell Co.
--A Book of Nonsense. Lear, Edward (1812-1888), illus. 1980. Viking.
--The Book of Nonsense and More Nonsense. N.D. Frederick Warne & Co.
--A Book of Nonsense Verse, Prose & Pictures. N.D. E. P. Dutton & Co.
--Calico Pie. N.D. Frederick Warne & Co.
--Calico Pie and Other Nonsense. Maxey, Dale (1927-), illus. LC 69-12135. (Illus.). 31 p. col. illus. 29 cm. (ps-3). 1969. (ISBN 0-695-81010-3). (ISBN 0-695-41010-5). Follett.
--The Complete Nonsense. Jackson, Holbrook, ed. Lear, Edward (1812-1888), illus. 1951. Dover.
--Complete Nonsense. Lear, Edward (1812-1888), illus. Jackson, Helen Maria Fiske Hunt, Mrs. (1831-1885), intro. by. (Illus.). (gr. 4-6). N.D. Dover.
--Complete Nonsense Book. Lear, Edward (1812-1888), illus. 1943. Dodd.
--Complete Nonsense Book. Strachey, Lady, ed. (gr. 4-6). 1961. (ISBN 0-396-00886-0). Dodd.
--The Complete Nonsense Book. Strachey, Lady, ed. 1912. Duffield.
--The Courtship of the Yonghy-Bonghy-Bo and the New Vestments. Maddison, Kevin W., illus. LC 79-14309. p. cm. (Studio book). 1979. (ISBN 0-670-24428-7). Viking Press.
--The Dog with a Luminous Nose. Gorey, Edward St. John (1925-), illus. LC 69-14571. (Illus.). 46 p. 1969. Young Scott Books.
--The Dog with a Luminous Nose. Gorey, Edward St. John (1925-), illus. LC 69-14571. (Illus.). 40p. 16 x 24cm. 46p. (ps-1). 1969. (ISBN 0-201-09173-9, A-W Childrens). Young Scott Books. **Award: (NYT).**
--The Duck and the Kangaroo. N.D. Frederick Warne & Co.
--The Duck and the Kangaroo and Other Nonsense Rhymes. Ward, John Stephen Keith (1938-), illus. LC 32-31874. 56 p. illus. (part col.) 17 cm. c.1932. Western Printing and Lithographing Co.
--An Edward Lear Alphabet. Newsom, Carol, illus. LC 82-10037. p. cm. 1983. (ISBN 0-688-00964-6). (ISBN 0-688-00965-4). Lothrop, Lee & Shepard Books.
--Edward Lear's Nonsense Books. (Companion Library Ser.). (gr. 5-10). N.D. (ISBN 0-685-78331-6). G&D.
--Edward Lear's Nonsense Books. Lear, Edward (1812-1888), illus. (Illus.). (gr. 2-6). 1967. (ISBN 0-448-05484-1). G&D.
--The Four Little Children Who Went Around the World. Lobel, Arnold Stark (1933-), illus. LC 68-10068. (Illus.). 44 p. 23cm. 1968. Macmillan.
--The History of the 7 Families of the Lake Pipple-Popple: And The Story of the 4 Little Children Who Went Round the World. LC 68-28354. (Illus.). 48 p. 26cm. 1968. Walker.
--How Pleasant to Know Mr. Lear!. LC 82-80822. (Illus.). 96p. 1982. (ISBN 0-8234-0462-5). Holiday.
--Incidents in the Life of My Uncle Arly. Maxey, Dale (1927-), illus. LC 78-90155. 31 p. (chiefly col. illus. 29cm. 1970, c.1969. Follett.
--The Jumblies. Gorey, Edward St. John (1925-), illus. LC 68-15341. (Illus.). 1 v. (unpaged. 1968. Young Scott Books.
--The Jumblies and Other Nonsense Verses. Brooke, Leonard Leslie (1862-1940), illus. N.D. Frederick Warne & Co.
--The Lear Omnibus. Megroz, M. L., ed. Lear, Edward (1812-1888), illus. 1938. Nelson.
--Lear's Book of Nonsense, 1 of 19 Vols. (Illus.). (Aunt Louisa's Choice Books Ser.: No. 19). N.D. Scribner & Welford.
--Lear's Nonsense Omnibus. (Illus.). (gr. 3-6). 1943. (ISBN 0-7232-0585-X). Warne.
--Lear's Nonsense Songs. (Illus.). (gr. 4-7). 1907. (ISBN 0-7232-0582-5). Warne.
--Lear's Nonsense Verses. LC 67-23805. 1 v. (unpaged) illus. (part col.) 29 cm. 1967. Grosset & Dunlap.
--Limericks: Verses. Ehlert, Lois Jane (1934-), illus. LC 65-22152. 1 v. (unpaged) col. illus. 30 cm. 1965. World Pub. Co.
--More Nonsense. N.D. Frederick Warne & Co.
--The New Vestments. LC 79-318130. (Illus.). 7 p. (on double leaves). 20cm. 1978. Chamberlain Press.
--The New Vestments. Lobel, Arnold Stark (1933-), illus. LC 75-104336. (Illus.). 32 p. 24cm. 1970. Bradbury Press.
--The Nonsense ABC's. Endres, Helen Elise & Bonfils, Robert, illus. LC 56-11562. unpaged. illus. 22cm. (Rand McNally elf book, 550). c.1956. Rand McNally.
--A Nonsense Alphabet. Scarry, Richard McClure (1919-), illus. LC 62-7188. (Illus.). unpaged. 20cm. 1962. Doubleday.
--Nonsense Book. 1st ed. Palazzo, Tony (1905-1970), selected by. Palazzo, Tony (1905-1970), illus. LC 56-734556. 80p. illus. 32cm. 1956. Garden City Books.
--Nonsense Books. (Illus.). (With all the original illustrations). (gr. 4-6). 1888. (ISBN 0-316-51829-8). Little.
--Nonsense Books: Nonsense Songs, Stories, Nonsense Pictures, Laughable Lyrics. N.D. Robert Brothers.
--Nonsense Botany and Alphabets, etc. New ed. N.D. Frederick Warne & Co.
--Nonsense Songs. (Illus.). N.D. Little Brown & Co.
--Nonsense Songs. N.D. Roberts Brothers.
--Nonsense Songs. Brooke, Leonard Leslie (1862-1940), illus. (Illus.). 1910. Frederick Warne & Co.
--Nonsense Songs. Glass, Dudley, contrib. by. N.D. Frederick Warne & Co.
--Nonsense Songs and Stories. Strachey, Edward, illus. N.D. Frederick Warne & Co.
--Nonsense Songs, etc. N.D. The Peter Pauper Press.
--Nonsense Songs, Stories, Botany. N.D. Robert Brothers.
--Nonsense Songs, Stories, Botany and Alphabets. N.D. James R. Osgood.
--Nonsense Stories and Alphabets. N.D. Frederick Warne & Co.
--The Nonsense Verse of Edward Lear. Lear, Edward (1812-1888), illus. 1984. Harmony.
--The Nutcrackers and the Sugar-Tongs. 1st ed. Sewall, Marcia (1935-), illus. LC 77-12696. (Illus.). 32 p. 27cm. c.1978. (ISBN 0-316-78181-9). Little, Brown. **Award: (NYT).**
--The Owl & the Pussy Cat. N.D. Frederick Warne & Co.
--The Owl and the Pussy-Cat. Cooney, Barbara (1917-), illus. LC 69-15759. (Illus.). 26 p. 22cm. 1969. Little, Brown.
--The Owl and the Pussy Cat. King, Harold (1945-), illus. LC 74-81667. (Illus.). 24 p. 18cm. (Stuff and nonsense books). 1974. (ISBN 0-7232-1810-2). F. Warne.
--The Owl and the Pussy-Cat. Masha, pseud. (1909-), illus. Stern, Marie Simchow. LC 64-5498. 1 v. (unpaged) col. illus. 22 cm. (Big golden book). 1964. Golden Press.
--The Owl and the Pussy Cat. Stevens, Janet, illus. LC 82-12092. p. cm. c.1983. (ISBN 0-8234-0474-9). Holiday House.
--The Owl & the Pussy-Cat & Other Nonsense. Wood, Owen, illus. LC 78-11651. (Illus.). 42 p. 30cm. (Studio book). 1979. (ISBN 0-670-53314-9). Viking Press.
--The Owl and the Pussy-Cat: Nonsense. Maxey, Dale (1927-), illus. LC 76-90543. (Illus.). 31 p. 29cm. 1970, c.1969. Follett.
--The Owl and the Pussycat. Cauley, Lorinda Bryan (1951-), illus. LC 84-24897. p. cm. 1985. (ISBN 0-399-21254-X). (ISBN 0-399-21253-1). Putnam.
--The Owl and the Pussycat. Cooney, Barbara (1917-), illus. 1969. Little.
--The Owl and the Pussycat. Du Bois, William Sherman Pene (1916-), illus. LC 62-7071. (Illus.). 1962, c.1961. (ISBN 0-385-00077-4). Doubleday and Company.
--The Owl and the Pussycat. Fulton, Gwen, illus. LC 77-77869. 24 p. 25 cm. 1st U.S. edition. 1977. (ISBN 0-689-30609-1). Atheneum.
--The Owl & the Pussycat & Other Verses. (Peter Possum Paperbacks Ser). 1967. (ISBN 0-531-05119-6). Watts.
--The Pelican Chorus. Berson, Harold (1926-), illus. LC 67-5382. (Illus.). 1 v. (unpaged. 24cm. 1967. Parents' Magazine Press.
--The Pelican Chorus & Other Nonsense Verses. Brooke, Leonard Leslie (1862-1940), illus. 1907. Frederick Warne & Co.
--The Pobble Who Has No Toes. Maddison, Kevin W., illus. LC 77-24913. 1978. (ISBN 0-670-56168-1, Studio). Viking Pr.
--The Pobble Who Has No Toes. Maxey, Dale (1927-), illus. LC 69-12136. (Illus.). (ps-3). 1969. (ISBN 0-695-87143-9). (ISBN 0-695-47143-0). Follett.
--The Quangle Wangle's Hat. Oxenbury, Helen (1938-), illus. LC 70-79141. (Illus.). 32 p. 29cm. 1970. Watts. **Award: (KGM).**
--The Story of the Four Little Children Who Went Round the World. Mack, Stanley (1935-), illus. (Illus.). 32 p. 29cm. 1967. H. Quist; Distributed by Crown Publishers.
--Teapots and Quails and Other New Nonsense. Davidson, Angus & Hofer, Philip, eds. Lear, Edward (1812-1888), illus. 1953. Harvard University Press.
--Two Laughable Lyrics: The Pobble Who Has No Toes, The Quangle Wangle's Hat. Galdone, Paul (1914-), illus. LC 66-14329. 1v. (unpaged) col. illus. 24cm. c.1966. Putnam.
--The Two Old Bachelors. Galdone, Paul (1914-), illus. LC 62-15745. 1962. (ISBN 0-07-036940-2). McGraw-Hill Book Company.
--The Two Old Bachelors. Galdone, Paul (1914-), illus. LC 62-15745. (Illus.). unpaged. 26cm. 1962. Whittlesey House.
--Whizz!. Domanska, Janina, illus. LC 72-81065. (Illus.). 33 p. 1973. Macmillan.

--Jelly Belly: Original Nursery Rhymes. Wijngaard, Juan, illus. LC 84-45915. p. cm. 1985. (ISBN 0-911745-94-7). (ISBN 0-87226-001-1). Bedrick.
--Nicholas Knock. Newfeld, Frank (1928-), illus. LC 76-27324. (Illus.). (gr. 3-7). 1977. (ISBN 0-395-24910-4). HM.
--Nicholas Knock and Other People. Newfeld, Frank (1928-), illus. LC 76-27324. p. cm. 1976, c.1974. (ISBN 0-395-24910-4). Houghton Mifflin.

Lee, Dennis Benyon (1939-) & Newfeld, Frank (1928-)
--Garbage Delight: Poems. LC 78-14836. p. cm. c.1978. (ISBN 0-395-27201-7). Houghton Mifflin. **Award: (CLA).**

Lee, Edgar, jt. auth. see Bulfinch, Thomas.

Lee, Edgar, ed. see Sewell, Anna.

Lee, Edward Edson see Edwards, Leo, pseud.

Lee, Edward Edson (1884-1944)
--Andy Blake. Edwards, Leo, pseud. Salg, Bert N., illus. LC 28-12698. vi, 280, 1 p. front., plates. 20 cm. (His Andy Blake series). 1928. Grosset & Dunlap.
--Andy Blake and the Pot of Gold. Edwards, Leo, pseud. Salg, Bert N., illus. LC 30-13874. xix, 228 p. front., plates. 20 cm. (His Andy Blake series). 1930. Grosset & Dunlap.
--Andy Blake in Advertising. Edwards, Leo, pseud. Salg, Bert N., illus. LC 22-18098. 3 p. l., 280, 1 p. front. 19 1/2 cm. 1922. D. Appleton and Company.
--Andy Blake's Comet Coaster. Edwards, Leo, pseud. Salg, Bert N., illus. LC 28-12699. xi p., 1 l., 247 p. incl. front. plates 19 1/2 cm. (His Andy Blake series). c.1928. Grosset & Dunlap.
--Andy Blake's Secret Service. Edwards, Leo, pseud. Salg, Bert N., illus. LC 29-10959. xiii, 1 p., 1 l., 237 p. front., plates. 20 cm. (His Andy Blake series.). 1929. Grossett & Dunlap.
--Caveman. Edwards, Leo, pseud. (The Jerry Todd Bks.). N.D. Grosset & Dunlap.
--The Flying Flapdoodle. Edwards, Leo, pseud. (The Jerry Todd Bks.). N.D. Grosset & Dunlap.
--The Hidden Dwarf. Edwards, Leo, pseud. LC 39-107615. v, 218 p. front. 19 1/2 cm. (His Poppy Ott detective stories). c.1939. Grosset & Dunlap.
--Hits the Trail. Edwards, Leo, pseud. (The Poppy Ott Bks.). N.D. Grosset & Dunlap.
--Jerry Todd and the Bob-Tailed Elephant. Edwards, Leo, pseud. Salg, Bert N., illus. LC 29-10219. xii p., 1 l., 235 p. front., illus., plates. 20 cm. (His Jerry Todd series). 1929. Grosset & Dunlap.
--Jerry Todd and the Buffalo Bill Bathtub. Edwards, Leo, pseud. Salg, Bert N., illus. LC 36-4198. vii, 232 p. front., plates. 20 cm. (His Jerry Todd series). 1936. Grosset & Dunlap.
--Jerry Todd and the Flying Flapdoodle. Edwards, Leo, pseud. Salg, Bert N., illus. LC 34-2425. vii, 244 p. front., plates. 20 cm. (His Jerry Todd series.). 1934. Grosset & Dunlap.
--Jerry Todd and the Oak Island Treasure. Edwards, Leo, pseud. (The Jerry Todd Bks.). 1924. Grosset & Dunlap.
--Jerry Todd and the Purring Egg. Edwards, Leo, pseud. (The Jerry Todd Bks.). N.D. Grosset & Dunlap.
--Jerry Todd and the Rose-Colored Cat. Edwards, Leo, pseud. (The Jerry Todd Bks.). 1924. Grosset & Dunlap.
--Jerry Todd & the Talking Frog. Edwards, Leo, pseud. (The Jerry Todd Bks.). 1924. Grosset & Dunlap.
--Jerry Todd and the Whispering Mummy. Edwards, Leo, pseud. Salg, Bert N., illus. LC 38-23775. xi p., 1 l., 235 p. front., plates. 19 1/2 cm. (His Jerry Todd series). c.1924. Grosset & Dunlap.
--Jerry Todd, Caveman. Edwards, Leo, pseud. Salg, Bert N., illus. LC 32-2130. xxv, 258 p. front., illus., plates. 20 cm. 1932. Grosset & Dunlap.
--Jerry Todd, Editor-in-Grief. Edwards, Leo, pseud. Salg, Bert N., illus. LC 30-13237. xxi, 1, 246 p. front., plates. 19 1/2 cm. (His Jerry Todd series). c.1930. Grosset & Dunlap.
--Jerry Todd In The Whispering Cave. Edwards, Leo, pseud. (The Jerry Todd Bks). N.D. Grosset & Dunlap.
--Jerry Todd, Pirate. Edwards, Leo, pseud. Salg, Bert N., illus. LC 28-18117. xv, 254 p. front., 1 illus., plates.20 cm. (His Jerry Todd series). 1928. Grosset & Dunlap.
--Jerry Todd's Cuckoo Camp. Edwards, Leo, pseud. Bacharach, Herman Ilfeld (1899-), illus. LC 40-7524. vii, 1, 216 p. front. 20 cm. (His Jerry Todd series). 1940. Grosset & Dunlap.
--Jerry Todd's Poodle Parlor. Edwards, Leo, pseud. Sheldon, Myrtle, illus. LC 38-19933. vii, 1 203 p. front., plates. 20 cm. (His Jerry Todd series). 1938. Grosset & Dunlap.
--Jerry Todd's Up the Ladder Club. Edwards, Leo, pseud. (The Jerry Todd Bks.). N.D. Grosset & Dunlap.
--Jerry Todd's Up-the-Ladder Club. Edwards, Leo, pseud. Sheldon, Myrtle, illus. LC 37-11006. vii p. 1 1., 235 p. front., illus., plates. 20 cm. (His Jerry Todd series). 1937. Grosset & Dunlap.
--The Monkey's Paw. Edwards, Leo, pseud. LC 38-10328. v, 214 p. front. 20 cm. (His Poppy Ott detective stories). 1938. Grosset & Dunlap.
--Poppy Ott & Co., Inferior Decorators. Edwards, Leo, pseud. LC 37-294154. vii, 210 p. front., plates. 19 1/2 cm. c.1937. Grosset & Dunlap.
--Poppy Ott & Co. Inferior Decorators. Edwards, Leo, pseud. Salg, Bert N., illus. LC 37-2941. vii, 210 p. front., plates. 20 cm. 1937. Grosset & Dunlap.
--Poppy Ott and the Freckled Goldfish. Edwards, Leo, pseud. Salg, Bert N., illus. LC 28-6306. viii p., 1 l., 269 p. front., illus., plates. 20 cm. (His Poppy Ott books). 1828. Grosset & Dunlap.
--Poppy Ott and the Galloping Snails. Edwards, Leo, pseud. (The Poppy Ott Bks). N.D. Grosset & Dunlap.
--Poppy Ott and the Hidden Dwarf. Edwards, Leo, pseud. (The Poppy Ott Bks.). N.D. Grosset & Dunlap.
--Poppy Ott and the Monkey's Paw. Edwards, Leo, pseud. (The Poppy Ott Bks.). N.D. Grosset & Dunlap.
--Poppy Ott and the Pedigreed Pickles. Edwards, Leo, pseud. (The Poppy Ott Bks). N.D. Grosset & Dunlap.
--Poppy Ott and the Prancing Pancake. Edwards, Leo, pseud. Salg, Bert N., illus. LC 31-1925. xxi, 298 p. front., plates. 20 cm. (His Poppy Ott books). c.1930. Grosset & Dunlap.
--Poppy Ott and the Seven League Stilts. Edwards, Leo, pseud. (The Poppy Ott Bks). N.D. Grosset & Dunlap.
--Poppy Ott and the Tittering Totem. Edwards, Leo, pseud. Salg, Bert N., illus. LC 29-5231. xv p., 1 l., 241 p. front., illus., plates. 20 cm. (His Poppy Ott books). 1929. Grosset & Dunlap.
--Poppy Ott Hits the Trial. Edwards, Leo, pseud. Salg, Bert N., illus. LC 33-1250. vii, 220 p. front., plates. 20 cm. (His Poppy Ott books). 1933. Grosset & Dunlap.
--Trigger Berg and His Seven Hundred Mouse Traps. Edwards, Leo, pseud. Salg, Bert N., illus. LC 30-2688. vii, 1, 242 p. front., plates. 20 cm. (His The Trigger Berg series). 1930. Grosset & Dunlap.
--Trigger Berg and the Cockeyed Ghost. Edwards, Leo, pseud. Salg, Bert N., illus. LC 33-9402. vii, 246 p. front., plates. 20 cm. (His The Trigger Berg series). 1933. Grosset & Dunlap.
--Trigger Berg and the Sacred Pig. Edwards, Leo, pseud. Salg, Bert N., illus. LC 31-3690. vii, 1, 246 p. front., plates. 20 cm. (His The Trigger Berg series). 1931. Grosset & Dunlap.
--Trigger Berg and the Treasure Tree. Edwards, Leo, pseud. Salg, Bert N., illus. LC 30-2689. vii, 1, 188 p. front., plates. 20 cm. (His The Trigger Berg series). 1930. Grosset & Dunlap.
--Tuffy Bean and the Lost Fortune. Edwards, Leo, pseud. Salg, Bert N., illus. LC 32-13937. vii, 1, 224 p. fronts., illus. 20 cm. (His Tuffy Bean series). 1932. Grosset & Dunlap.
--Tuffy Bean at Funny-Bone Farm. Edwards, Leo, pseud. Salg, Bert N., illus. LC 31-14065. 4 p. 1,, 225 p. front., illus. 20 cm. (His Tuffy Bean series). 1931. Grosset & Dunlap.
--Tuffy Bean's One-Ring Circus. Edwards, Leo, pseud. Salg, Bert N., illus. LC 31-14064. 4 p. 1., 238 p. front., illus. 20 cm. (His Tuffy Bean series). 1931. Grosset & Dunlap.
--Tuffy Bean's Puppy Days. Edwards, Leo, pseud. Salg, Bert N., illus. LC 31-14063. 4 p. 1., 238 p. front., illus. 20 cm. (His Tuffy Bean series). 1931. Grosset & Dunlap.

Lee, Elfred, jt. auth. see Kuzma, Kay.

Lee, Elisabeth
--All Summer to Play. Pyle, Katharine, contrib. by. LC 26-153740. 227 p. col. front. 20 1/2 cm. 1926. John Murphy Company.

Lee, Ella Dolbear
--Jean Mary in Virginia. LC 31-13230. 248 p. front. 19 1/2 cm. (Her Jean Mary series). c.1931. A. L. Burt Company.
--Jean Mary in Virginia. (Jean Mary Ser.). N.D. World Publishing Co.
--Jean Mary Solves the Mystery. LC 33-110691. 256 p. front. 19 cm. (Her Jean Mary series). c.1933. A. L. Burt Company.
--Jean Mary Solves the Mystery. (Jean Mary Ser.). N.D. World Publishing Co.
--Jean Mary's Adventures. LC 31-132286. 243 p. front. 19 1/2 cm. (Her Jean Mary series). c.1931. A. L. Burt Company.
--Jean Mary's Adventures. (Jean Mary Ser.). N.D. World Publishing Co.
--Jean Mary's Adventures and Jean Mary's Summer Mystery: Two Books in One, 2 Bks. in 1. N.D. World Publishing Co.
--Jean Mary's Romance. LC 31-132312. 243 p. front. 19 1/2 cm. (Her Jean Mary series). c.1931. A. L. Burt Company.
--Jean Mary's Romance. (Jean Mary Ser.). N.D. World Publishing Co.
--Jean Mary's Summer Mystery. LC 31-13229. 240 p. front. 19 1/2 cm. (Her Jean Mary series). c.1931. A. L. Burt Company.
--Jean Mary's Summer Mystery. (Jean Mary Ser.). N.D. World Publishing Co.

Lee, Ettie, adapted by.
--Silas Marner. Eadie, Eleanor Osborn, illus. LC 28-21372. (Original Author: Marian Evans (George Eliot, pseud), 1819-1880). xiii, 1, 119 p. illus. 19 1/2 cm. 1928. The Macmillan Company.

Lee, F. H., ed.
--Folk Tales of All Nations. 1000p. N.D. Coward McCann.

Lee, Fleming see Blitch, Fleming Lee, pseud.

Lee, Frances
--Laying the Keel, 1 of 20 vols. (Illus.). 178p. (Selected Bks for Sunday School: No. 22). N.D. Set. Methodist Bk Concern.

Lee, Frances, jt. auth. see Locke, Una.

Lee, Frank
--Bedtime Stories of the Saints, Bk. 1. rev ed. (Illus.). 96p. (ps-5). 1974. (ISBN 0-89243-003-6). Liguori Pubns.
--Bedtime Stories of the Saints, Bk. 2. 64p. (Orig.). (ps-4). 1980. (ISBN 0-89243-126-1). Liguori Pubns.

Lee, Frank Mrs. see Lee, Mary Chappell.

Lee, H. Alton (1939-)
--Seven Feet Four and Growing. LC 77-13923. 93 p. 21cm. c.1978. (ISBN 0-664-32623-4). Westminster Press.

Lee, Harper see Lee, Nelle Harper.

Lee, Harry H., illus.
--Jim Bridger, Mountain Boy. LC 55-108962. 188p. illus. 20cm. (Childhood of famous Americans series). 1955. Bobbs-Merrill.

Lee, Holme, pseud., see Parr, Harriet.

Lee, Holme, pseud. (1828-1900)
--Her Title of Honor. Parr, Harriet. (Illus.). (The Girl's Own Favorite Ser.). N.D. E. P. Dutton & Co.
--Holme Lee Fairy Tales. Parr, Harriet, 1 of 6 Vols. (Illus.). (Warne's Lansdowne Fairy Library: No. 4). N.D. R. Worthington.
--Legends from Fairy-Land. Parr, Harriet. N.D. Scribner, Welford & Armstrong.
--My Dog Match. Parr, Harriet. (Golden Link Ser.). N.D. R. Worthington & Co.
--My dog Match. Parr, Harriet, 1 of 16 Vols. (Illus.). (Warne's Incident and Adventure Library: No. 16). N.D. Scribner & Welford.
--Poor Match. Parr, Harriet. N.D. E. P. Dutton.
--Tuflongbo and Little Content, Their Adventures in the Enchanted Forest. Parr, Harriet. (Illus.). N.D. R. Worthington.
--Tuflongbo and Little Content: Their Wonderful Adventures in the Enchanted Forest. Parr, Harriet. (Illus.). N.D. Scribner, Welford & Armstrong.
--Tuflongbo's Life and Adventures, and How His Shoes Got Worn Out. Parr, Harriet. (Illus.). N.D. Scribner, Welford & Armstrong.

Lee, James (1886-) & Carey, James Thomas (1854-)
--Family Robinson of Italy. N.D. Small,Maynard & Co.
--The Italian Family Robinson. LC 23-6695. 3 p. l., 197 p. illus. 19 1/2 cm. c.1916. D. C. Heath and Company.

Lee, Jeanne M, retold by.
--Legend of the Li River: An Ancient Chinese Tale. Lee, Jeanne M., illus. LC 83-79. p. cm. c.1983. (ISBN 0-03-063523-3). Holt, Rinehart, and Winston.
--Legend of the Milky Way. 1st ed. Lee, Jeanne M., illus. LC 81-6906. (Illus.). 32 p. 22cm. c.1982. (ISBN 0-03-060439-7). Holt, Rinehart, and Winston.
--Toad Is the Uncle of Heaven: A Vietnamese Folk Tale. Lee, Jeanne M., illus. LC 85-5639. (Illus.). 32 p. 22cm. c.1985. Holt, Rinehart and Winston.

Lee, Jenny
--A Fish Tale. LC 79-25751. (Illus.). 48 p. 31cm. c.1980. (ISBN 0-915828-17-0). Sufism Reoriented.

Lee, Jessica, jt. auth. see Crespi, Pachita.

Lee, Joan
--Watch for the Clouds. Floherty, John Joseph, Jr. (1892-1964), illus. LC 65-24969. 46p. illus. 25cm. (Sci. parade bk.). c.1966. Harvey House.

Lee, John B.
--Joe Orphan, Seedling. 64p. 1984. (ISBN 0-89962-335-2). Todd & Honeywell.

Lee, John Darrell (1931-)
--The Ninth Man. LC 75-14989. 300p. 1976. (ISBN 0-385-11261-0). Doubleday.

Lee, John Robert, jt. auth. see Lee, Susan Dye.

Lee, Josephine (1921-)
--The Fabulous Manticora. LC 75-25784. 186 p. 21cm. 1976, c.1973. (ISBN 0-381-99619-0). John Day Co.
--Joy Is Not Herself. Marriott, Patricia (1920-), illus. LC 63-7898. (Illus.). 154 p. 21cm. 1st U.S. edition. 1963, c.1962. Harcourt, Brace & World.

Lee, Julian, pseud., see Latham, Jean Lee.

Lee, Julian, pseud. (1902-), adapted by see Dickens, Charles John Huffam.

Lee, Julian, ed. see Tallman, Jane.

Lee, Julian, Mrs., pseud. (1902-) & Clark, Ann Nolan
--Thanksgiving Programs for the Lower Grades. Latham, Jean Lee. 1937. Dramatic Publishing Company.

Lee, Julian, pseud. (1902-)
--Another Washington. Latham, Jean Lee. 1931. Dramatic Publishing Company.
--Big Brother Barges In. Latham, Jean Lee. 1940. Dramatic Publishing Company.
--Christmas for All. Latham, Jean Lee. 1932. Dramatic Publishing Company.
--A Fiance for Fanny. Latham, Jean Lee. 1931. Dramatic Publishing Company.
--The Ghost of Lone Cabin. Latham, Jean Lee. 1940. Dramatic Publishing Company.
--He Landed from London. Latham, Jean Lee. 1935. Dramatic Publishing Company.
--I Will! I Won't!. Latham, Jean Lee. 1931. Dramatic Publishing Company.
--Just for Justin. Latham, Jean Lee. 1932. Dramatic Publishing Company.
--Keeping Kitty's Dates. Latham, Jean Lee. 1931. Dramatic Publishing Company.
--Lincoln Yesterday and Today. Latham, Jean Lee. 1933. Dramatic Publishing Company.
--Tiny Jim. Latham, Jean Lee. 1933. Dramatic Publishing Company.
--Washington for All. Latham, Jean Lee. 1931. Dramatic Publishing Company.

Lee, Julian, pseud. (1902-) & Clark, Ann Nolan, Mrs. (1896-)
--Christmas Programs for the Lower Grades. Latham, Jean Lee. 1937. Dramatic Publishing Company.

Lee, Julian, pseud. (1902-) & Wilburr, Harriete
--The Children's Book. Latham, Jean Lee. 1933. Dramatic Publishing Company.

Lee, Laura (1916-)
--Come Sing with Me: A Collection of Illustrated Songs for the Home, Kindergarten and Primary Grades. Lee, Nata, illus. Goodman, Ruth, contrib. by. LC 50-12301. 61 p. illus. 29 cm. 1950. Boston Music Co.

Lee, Laurance
--The Snake God's Treasure. LC 35-19271. viii, 221 p. incl. front. 20 cm. c.1935. R. M. McBride & Company.

Lee, Laurel
--Barnaby Frost. Adler, Dennis, illus. LC 78-66195. (Illus.). 60 p. 24cm. 1980, c.1979. (ISBN 0-8423-0117-8). Tyndale House Publishers.
--Barnaby Frost Plants a Seed. Adler, Dennis, illus. LC 80-50521. (Illus.). 32 p. 24cm. c.1980. (ISBN 0-8423-0118-6). Tyndale House Publishers.

Lee, Lawrent, pseud., see Waltner, Erma.

Lee, Lawrent, pseud. & Waltner, Vera
--Adventures of the Seven Spartans. Waltner, Erma. McCurdy, Florence, illus. (Lee Lawrent is the joint Pseud. of Erma and Vera Waltner). N.D. Unity School of Christianity.

Lee, Leila
--Wee-Wee Songs for Our Little Pets. (Illus.). N.D. A. C. Armstrong & Son.
--Wee-Wee Songs for our Little Pets. (Illus.). N.D. Albert Mason.

Lee, Manfred Bennington, jt. auth. see Queen, Ellery, Jr.

Lee, Marian (1946-)
--The Missing Room & Other Mysteries to Solve. Crombie, Steven, illus. LC 83-26142. (Illus.). 48p. (From the Casebook of J. P. Landers, Master Detective Ser.). (gr. 4-7). 1984. (ISBN 0-516-01994-5). Childrens.
--Solve a Mystery: From the Casebook of J. P. Landers, Master Detective, Bk. 1. LC 82-9712. (Illus.). (gr. 4 up). 1982. (ISBN 0-516-01991-0). Childrens.
--Solve a Mystery: From the Casebook of J. P. Landers, Master Detective, Bk. 2. LC 82-9712. (Illus.). (gr. 4 up). 1982. (ISBN 0-516-01992-9). Childrens.
--Solve a Mystery: From the Casebook of J. P. Landers, Master Detective, Bk. 3. LC 82-9712. (Illus.). (gr. 4 up). 1982. (ISBN 0-516-01993-7). Childrens.

Lee, Mary B.
--Lucien Guglieri. N.D. Methodist Book Concern.

Lee, Mary Chappell (1849-)
--The Double D's. LC 14-22557. 4 p. l., 212 p. front., plates. 20 cm. $1.0. c.1914. The Pilgrim Press.
--Garret Grain. 336p. N.D. Pilgrim Press.
--Garret Grain. 336p. N.D. Sunday-School Library.
--Garret Grain: Or, The House Blessed. LC 7-13139. 6, 9-336 p. incl. pl. front., pl. 19 1/2 cm. c.1894. Congregational Sunday-School and Publishing Society.
--Little Boom Number One. 20cm. 255p. 1902. Pilgrim Press.
--Redmond of the Seventh; or, The Boys of Ninety. LC 7-13140. 3 p. l., 5-290 p. front., plates. 20 cm. c.1897. The Pilgrim Press.

--Daddy's Sword. 1915. Hodder and Stoughton.
--A Daughter of the Sea. 1902. Crowell.
--Eric's Good News. LC 7-13141. 47 p. incl. front., illus. 18 1/2 cm. c.1896. F. H. Revell Company.
--Eric's Good News. (Illus.). (The Kingship Ser.). N.D. Fleming H Revell.
--Four Gates. 1912. Cassell.
--Heather's Mistress. 1901. Crowell.
--His Big Opportunity. Cowell, Sydney, illus. (Illus.). 12cm. 193p. 1898. Fleming H. Revell Co.
--Jill's Red Bag. LC 3-9631. 2 p. l., 220 p. 20 cm. 1903. F. H. Revell Company.
--Legend-Led. LC 99-24288. 3 p. l., 240 p. 18 1/2 cm. 1899. Dodd, Mead and Company.
--The Little Discoverers. Johnston, M. D., illus. LC 24-30780. 192 p. col. front., illus. 19 cm. 7/. 1924. H. Milford.
--The Little Discoverers. Norcross, Grace, illus. LC 25-153863. 205 p. front., plates. 19 1/2 cm. 1925. The Penn Publishing Company.
--The Odd One. Lathbury, Mary Artemisia (1841-1913), illus. LC 7-13143. 141, 1 p. incl. front. 21 1/2 cm. 1897. F. H. Revell Company.
--Olive Tracy. 1901. Dodd Mead.
--Probable Sons. LC 7-13144. 20cm. 120p. (The Jessica Ser.). 1896. Fleming H. Revell.
--Probable Sons. (The Dolphin Ser.). 1897. Fleming H. Revell Co.
--Probable Sons. (Illus.). N.D. Rand, McNally & Co's.
--A Puzzling Pair. Lance, Eveline, illus. 8cm. 144p. 1898. Fleming H. Revell Co.
--Roses. Cowell, Sydney, illus. 266 p. incl. front. plates. 19 1/2 cm. c.1899. W. B. Ketcham.
--Teddy's Button. LC 7-13145. 119 p. incl. plates. front. 19 1/2 cm. 1896. F. H. Revell Company.
--Teddy's Button. Lance, Eveline, illus. N.D. Rand, McNally & Co.'s.
--A Thoughtless Seven. (Illus.). 1898. Fleming H. Revell Co.
--A Thoughtless Seven. (Illus.). N.D. Rand, McNally & Co's.
--Two Tramps. (Illus.). 1903. Fleming H. Revell Co.
--What the Wind Did. 19cm. 65p. (The Kingship Ser.). 1899. Fleming H. Revell Co.

LeFevre, Felicite, pseud., see Smith-Masters, Margaret Melville.

Lefevre, Felicite M. (1869-)
--Soldier Boy. Rev ed. Sarg, Tony, pseud. (1882-1942), illus. Sarg, Anthony Frederick. LC 26-10570. 64 p. col. illus. 19 1/2 cm. 1926. Greenberg, Inc.

Lefevre, Felicite M. (1869-), retold by.
--Cock, the Mouse & the Little Red Hen. (Illus.). (gr. 1-3). 1947. (ISBN 0-8255-5276-1). Macrae.
--Cock, the Mouse & the Little Red Hen. Sarg, Tony, pseud. (1882-1942), illus. Sarg, Anthony Frederick. (Illus.). Repr. of 1907 ed. (gr. 1-5). 1959. (ISBN 0-212-35873-1). Dufour.
--The Cock, the Mouse and the Little Red Hen. Sarg, Tony, pseud. (1882-1942), illus. Sarg, Anthony Frederick. N.D. Macrae Smith Co.
--The Cock, the Mouse and the Little Red Hen: An Old Tale. J. L. G, illus. LC 20-205511. 64 p. incl. col. front., col. illus. 14 1/2 cm. c.1920. Henry Altemus Company.
--The Cock, the Mouse and the Little Red Hen: An Old Tale. Sarg, Tony, pseud. (1882-1942), illus. Sarg, Anthony Frederick. 4 p. l., 12-102, 1 p. 24 col. illus. 20 cm. 1907. G. W. Jacobs & Company.

LeFevre, G. L.
--Favorite Bible Stories. Sparks, Judith, ed. 16p. (Orig.). (Bible Quiz 'N Tattletotals Ser.). (gr. 3-6). 1982. (ISBN 0-87239-578-2). Standard Pub.
--Parables & Miracles of Jesus. Sparks, Judith, ed. 16p. (Orig.). (Bible Quiz 'N Tattletotals Ser.). (gr. 3-6). 1982. (ISBN 0-87239-580-4). Standard Pub.
--Stories from Acts. Sparks, Judith, ed. 16p. (Orig.). (Bible Quiz 'N Tattletotals Ser.). (gr. 3-6). 1982. (ISBN 0-87239-581-2). Standard Pub.

Le Fevre, Laura Zenobia see Bird, Zenobia, pseud.

Lefferts, Sara Tawney
--The Christmas Letter. (Illus.). (The One Family Series.). 1915. Cupples & Leon.
--Mr. Cinnamon Bear. Bacquet, Louise, illus. LC 7-29006. 47p. col. front. 15 col. pl. 16 1/2 x 14 1/2cm. c.1907. F. A. Bassette Co.
--Mr. Cinnamon Bear. Smith, Wuanita (1866-), illus. (The One Family Series.). 1915. Cupples & Leon.
--The Pansy Wedding. Smith, Wuanita (1866-), illus. (Illus.). (The One Family Series.). 1915. Cupples & Leon.
--A Patriotic Jubilee. Smith, Wuanita (1866-), illus. (Illus.). (The One Family Series.). 1915. Cupples & Leon.

Lefferts, Sara Tawney, selected by.
--Land of Play. Kirk, Maria Louise (1860-) & Nosworthy, Florence England, illus. (Illus.). 128p. c.1911. Cupples & Leon Co.

Le Fleming, Christopher, jt. auth. see Potter, Helen Beatrix.

Lefler, Irene Whitney (1917-)
--Bessie Bee. Myers, Bill (1940-), illus. LC 72-86321. (Illus.). 106 p. 21cm. (Crown book). 1972. (ISBN 0-8127-0062-7). Southern Pub. Association.

Lefreve, Felicite, pseud., see Smith-Masters, Margaret Melville.

Lefroy, Ella Napier
--By the Gail Water (Pub. by Society for Promoting Christian Knowledge). N.D. E. & J. B. Young & Co.

Leftwich, Joseph (1892-1983), tr. see Schachnowitz, Selig.

Le Gallienne, Eva, tr. see Andersen, Hans Christian.

Le Gallienne, Eva (1899-), tr. see Ewald, Carl.

Le Gallienne, Eva (1899-)
--Flossie and Bossie. 1st ed. Williams, Garth Montgomery (1912-), illus. LC 49-11812. x, 210 p. illus. 22 cm. 1949. Harper.

Legaspi, Pilar F.
--Enchanted Pond. (gr. 6-8). 1971. Vantage.

Legere, Terri (1953-)
--Adventure in Glide's Garden. Mackie, Sheila, illus. LC 80-462899. (Illus.). 90 p. 22cm. 1978. (ISBN 0-85362-174-8). Oriel Press.
--Adventure in Glide's Garden. Mackie, Sheila, illus. (Illus.). 92p. (gr. 2-7). N.D. (ISBN 0-85362-174-8, Oriel). Routledge & Kegan.

Legh, Mary H. Cornwall
--Little Orphans: The Story of Trudchen and Darling. (Illus.). N.D. Thomas Nelson & Sons.
--My Dog Plato: His Adventures and Impressions. (Illus.). (The Little Men Ser.). N.D. A. L. Burt's Pubs.
--My Dog Plato: His Adventures Impressions. (The Rugby Series for Boys and Girls). N.D. A. L. Burt Company.

Legh, Richmond (1772-1827)
--The Dairyman's Daughter, 1 of 15 vols. (Selected Bks for Sunday School: The/Ludlow Library). N.D. Set. Methodist Bk Concern.

LeGrand, pseud., see Henderson, LeGrand.

Legrand, Michel (1932-) & Mendoza, George (1934-)
--Michel's Mixed-up Musical Bird. DePatie-Freleng Enterprises, illus. LC 77-15448. (Illus.). 1978. (ISBN 0-672-52396-5). Bobbs.

Le Guin, Ursula Kroeber (1929-)
--The Beginning Place. 1980. Harper.
--The Farthest Shore. Garraty, Gail, illus. LC 72-75273. (Illus.). 25cm. 223p. (gr. 5 up). 1972. (ISBN 0-689-30054-9). Atheneum. **Awards: (NBA).**
--Leese Webster. Brunsman, Jim, illus. LC 79-10424. p. cm. 1979. (ISBN 0-689-30715-2). Atheneum.
--Solomon Leviathan's Nine Hundred Thirty-First Trip Around the World. Austin, Alicia, illus. (Illus.). 40p. Repr. of 1976 ed. (Adventures in Kroy Ser.: No. 2). 1983. (ISBN 0-941826-03-1). Cheap St.
--The Tombs of Atuan. Garraty, Gail, illus. LC 70-154753. (Illus.). 163 p. 25cm. 1971. Atheneum. **Awards: (ALA); (JNM).**
--Very Far Away from Anywhere Else. LC 76-4472. 89 p. 22cm. 1976. (ISBN 0-689-30525-7). Atheneum. **Award: (ALA).**
--The Wind's Twelve Quarters. LC 75-6372. 312p. 1975. (ISBN 0-06-012562-4, HarpT). Har-Row.
--A Wizard of Earthsea. LC 72-183280. (Illus.). 205 p. 18cm. (Puffin books). 1971. (ISBN 0-14-030477-0). Penguin.
--A Wizard of Earthsea. Robbins, Ruth (1917-), illus. LC 68-21992. (Illus.). 23cm. 205p (Pub. by Parnassus). (gr. 5 up). 1968. (ISBN 0-395-27653-5). HM. **Awards: (BGH); (ALA).**

Legum, Margaret Ronay
--Mailbox, Quailbox. Shetterly, Robert, illus. LC 85-7960. (Illus.). 55 p. 23cm. 1985. (ISBN 0-689-31136-2). Atheneum.

Leher, Lore
--A Letter Goes to Sea. Krist-Schulz, Hetty, illus. LC 73-108908. (Illus.). 27 p. 26cm. 1st U.S. edition. 1970. (ISBN 0-8178-0474-9). Harvey House.

Le Hew, Ronald M., illus.
--Mother Goose. (Illus.). 26p. (Golden Panorama Ser). (ps). 1975. (ISBN 0-307-11091-5, Golden Pr). Western Pub.

Lehigh University,Bethlehem, Pa. School of Education see Larrick, Nancy.

Lehman, Agnes C
--Betje and Jan: A Story of Volendam. LC 32-305091. x p., 1 l., 113 p. incl. illus., plates. col. front., col. plates. 19 1/2 cm. c.1932. Coward-McCann, Inc.
--The Flahertys of Aran. Lehman, Agnes C., illus. LC 39-303742. viii p., 1 l., 212 p. incl. illus., plates. 21 cm. 1939. Dodd, Mead & Company.
--Milly and Her Village: A Story of Rhens on the Rhine. Lehman, Agnes C., illus. LC 31-29833. 5 p. l., 89 p. front., illus. 22 1/2 cm. 1931. The Macmillan Company.

Lehman, Anna
--Old and New Bohemian Tales: Original Stories. Bergmann, Walter, illus. LC 26-10548. 178 p. col. front., illus. 22 cm. c.1926. M. A. Donohue & Company.
--Story Hour with Aunt Anna: Original Stories. Lange, Walter, illus. LC 24-229564. 160 p. illus., col. plates. 19 cm. 1924. The York Printing Co.

Lehman, Dorothy Pierce (1883-)
--Sandy. Brown, Marion Frances (1896-), illus. LC 43-1293. 32 p., 1 l. col. illus. 23 x 27 1/2 cm. 1942. Dorrance & Company, Inc..

Lehman, H. S., Mrs.
--Aunt Marian's Parables. LC 29-109654. 4 p. l., 5-236 p. 19 1/2 cm. c.1928. The Biola Book Room, Bible Institute of Los Angeles.

Lehman, Louis Paul
--The Little White Bible That Grew. LC 56-25009. unpaged. illus. 21cm. (Zondervan stori-picture book). 1955. Zondervan Pub. House.

Lehman, Mary Wolf
--The Adventures of the Golden Twins and Other Stories. Zimmerman, L. H., illus. LC 52-11902. 58p. illus. 23cm. 1953. Vantage Press.

Lehmann, Hildegaard
--Tizz in Texas. Bialk, Elisa, pseud. (1912-), illus. Krautter, Elisa Bialk. LC 66-11618. 95p. illus. 24cm. c.1966. Childrens.

Lehmann, Linda (1906-)
--Better Than a Princess. LC 78-2370. 95 p. 21cm. c.1978. (ISBN 0-8407-6590-8). T. Nelson.
--Tilli's New World. 1st ed. LC 81-5396. 154 p. 21cm. c.1981. (ISBN 0-525-66748-2). Elsevier/Nelson Books.

Lehmann, Marcus (1831-1890)
--The Family y Aguilar: A Story of Jewish Heroism During the Spanish Inquisition. Breuer, Jacob, adapted by. LC 58-59896. 284p. 20cm. 1958. P. Feldheim.

Lehmer, Derrick Norman (1868-1938)
--Just the Two of Us: Verses for Boys and Girls. LC 43-4376. 71 p. illus. (incl. mounted port.) 20 x 16 cm. 1942. The Gillick Press.

Lehn, Cornelia (1920-)
--God Keeps His Promise: A Bible Story Book for Young Children. Darwin, Beatrice, illus. LC 76-90377. (gr. k-4). 1970. (ISBN 0-87303-291-8). Faith & Life.
--I Heard Good News Today. Schlegel, Ralph A., illus. Oyer, Lora S., intro. by. LC 83-80401. (Illus.). 148p. (gr. 1-6). 1983. (ISBN 0-87303-073-7). Faith & Life.
--The Sun & the Wind. Regier, Robert, illus. (Illus.). 32p. 1983. (ISBN 0-87303-072-9). Faith & Life.

Lehoczky, Gyorgy
--The Wonderful Tree: A Story of the Seasons. Holl, Adelaide Hinkle (1910-), retold by. Lehoczky, Gyorgy, illus. LC 74-75177. (Illus.). 28 p. 1974. Golden Press.

Lehr, Delores (1920-)
--The Tender Age. LC 60-15230. 205 p. 22cm. 1961. Lothrop, Lee and Shepard Co.
--Turnabout Summer. LC 65-13102. 192 p. 22cm. 1965. Doubleday.

Lehrman, Emily, tr. see Nagishkin, Dmitrii.

Lehrman, Robert
--Juggling. LC 81-48654. p. cm. c.1982. (ISBN 0-06-023818-6). (ISBN 0-06-023819-4). Harper & Row.

Leiber, Fritz Reuter, Jr. (1910-)
--In the Beginning. Austin, Alicia, illus. (Illus.). 40p. Repr. 1983. (ISBN 0-941826-01-5). (ISBN 0-941826-02-3). Cheap St.

Leibovitch, Kitty
--The Secret of the Lion of Venice. Barrer-Russell, Gertrude (1921-), illus. LC 76-121797. (Illus.). 132 p. 21cm. 1970. Young Scott Books.

Leichman, Seymour (1933-)
--The Boy Who Could Sing Pictures. Leichman, Seymour (1933-), illus. LC 68-18947. (Illus.). 59 p. 27cm. 1968. Doubleday.
--Freddie the Pigeon: A Tale of the Secret Service. 1st ed. Leichman, Seymour (1933-), illus. LC 73-162621. (Illus.). 169 p. 22cm. 1972. (ISBN 0-385-06454-3). (ISBN 0-385-02621-8). Doubleday.
--Rumpelstiltskin. Leichman, Seymour (1933-), illus. LC 76-24180. (Illus.). 32 p. 21cm. (Random House pictureback). (Best book club ever). c.1977. (ISBN 0-394-83479-8). Random House.
--Shaggy Dogs & Spotty Dogs & Shaggy & Spotty Dogs. 1st ed. Leichman, Seymour (1933-), illus. LC 73-75322. (Illus.). 32 p. 1973. (ISBN 0-15-278020-3). Harcourt Brace Jovanovich.
--The Wicked Wizard & the Wicked Witch. Leichman, Seymour (1933-), illus. LC 72-76365. (Illus.). 32 p. 27cm. 1972. (ISBN 0-15-296455-X). Harcourt Brace Jovanovich.

Leigh, Amy, adapted by.
--Alvin's Big Ideas: A Treasury of Chipmunk Stories. Williams, A. O., illus. LC 84-18122. (Illus.). 32p. (gr. k-3). 1985. (ISBN 0-394-87203-7, BYR). Random.

Leigh, Amy, jt. auth. see Karman, Janice.

Leigh, Bill
--The Far Side of Fear. LC 77-17770. 154 p. 22cm. 1978, c.1977. (ISBN 0-670-30789-0). Viking Press.
--The Mortal. Spenser, Roy, illus. (gr. 2-5). 1976. (ISBN 0-8277-4740-3). British Bk Ctr.

Leigh, Frances
--The Lost Boy. LC 76-23445. 112 p. 22cm. 1976. (ISBN 0-525-34221-4). Dutton.

Leigh, Fry
--Shreds and Patches. N.D. E. P. Dutton & Co.

Leigh, Lady
--Tommy's Tiny Tales. (Illus.). (Children's Library.). N.D. Frederick A. Stokes.

Leigh, Oretta
--Aloysius Sebastian Mozart Mouse. DeLacre, Lulu, illus. LC 83-13473. (Illus.). 32p. (gr. k-2). 1984. (ISBN 0-671-47791-9, Simon & Schuster). (ISBN 0-671-49773-1). Messner.
--The Merry-Go-Round. 1st. ed. Shoemaker, Kathryn E., illus. LC 84-15731. (Illus.). 32 p. 22cm. c.1985. (ISBN 0-8234-0544-3). Holiday House.

Leigh, Roberta
--Sara and Hoppity. Wilson, Marion, illus. LC 60-12859. 25cm. 36p. 1960. Eriksson-Taplinger Company, Inc.
--Sara and Hoppity Make New Friends. Wilson, Marion, illus. LC 60-12860. 38 illus. 25. 1960. Eriksson-Taplinger Company, Inc.
--Tomahawk. Mellersh, Sally, illus. LC 61-5856. (Illus.). 20cm. 87p. 1961, c.1960. Eriksson-Taplinger.
--Tomahawk and the Animals of the Wild. Mellersh, Sally, illus. LC 62-7701. 125 p. illus. 20 cm. 1st U.S. edition. 1962, c.1961. P. S. Eriksson.
--Tomahawk and the River of Gold. Mellersh, Sally, illus. LC 61-5857. (Illus.). 20cm. 96p. 1961, c.1960. Eriksson-Taplinger.
--Torchy and the Magic Beam. Barton, Patricia, illus. LC 60-12861. 38p. illus. 26cm. 1960. Ericksson-Taplinger.
--Torchy in Topsy Turvy Land. Barton, Patricia, illus. LC 60-12862. 26cm. 39p. 1960. Eriksson-Taplinger company, Inc.
--Torcy and the Magic Beam. N.D. Eriksson-Taplinger Company , Inc.

Leigh, Victoria
--Rustle of Spring. LC 67-19297. (Illus.). 63 p. 22cm. 1967. F. Warne.

Leight, Edward, jt. auth. see Moore, Nancy.

Leighton, Celestine
--Ann Takes a Trip into the Land of Magic. (gr. 2-4). N.D. Carlton.

Leighton, Clare Veronica Hope (1899-)
--The Musial Box. 1st ed. Leighton, Clare Veronica Hope (1899-), illus. LC 32-28840. (Illus.). 22 x 27 1/2cm. 32p. c.1932. Longmans, Green & Co.
--The Wood that Came Back. Leighton, Clare Veronica Hope (1899-), illus. LC 35-28729. 20 x 26 1/2cm. 32p. c.1935. Artists and Writers Guild.

Leighton, John Jay
--Robert Royalton. LC 28-30771. (The Veteran's Son, Who Fought His Own Battles with the Power of Inspiration and Courted the Woman He Loved in a Locomotive Cab and on the Banks of the Wabash). xii, 334 p. front., illus., plates. 19 1/2 cm. c.1928. The Rochester Press.

Leighton, Margaret Carver, Mrs. (1896-)
--Bride of Glory: The Story of Elizabeth Bacon Custer. LC 62-14499. 212p. 22cm. c.1962. Ariel Bks. Dist. Farrar.
--The Canyon Castaways. LC 66-7107. 150 p. 22cm. 1966. Farrar, Straus and Giroux.
--Comanche of The Seventh. 216p. (Ariel Bks.). 1957. Farrar, Straus & Giroux.
--Comanche of the Seventh. Means, Elliott, illus. LC 57-5767. 206 p. illus. 22 cm. 1957. Ariel Books.
--A Hole in the Hedge. LC 68-13678. 180 p. 22cm. 1968. Farrar, Straus and Giroux.
--Journey for a Princess. LC 60-12639. 216p. illus., map, 22cm. c.1960. Ariel Books Dist. Farrar, Straus and Cudahy.
--Judith of France. Pitz, Henry Clarence (1895-1976), illus. LC 48-5436. 281 p. illus. 22 cm. 1948. Houghton Mifflin Co.
--The Other Island. LC 71-158964. 183 p. 21cm. 1971. (ISBN 0-374-35671-8). Farrar, Straus & Giroux.
--The Secret of Bucky Moran. 1st ed. Thomson, Mary Leighton, illus. LC 52-9053. 216 p. illus. 22 cm. 1952. Ariel Books.
--Secret of Smuggler's Cove. (Illus.). (gr. 5-7). 1959. (ISBN 0-8382-0739-1). Hale.
--The Secret of Smugglers' Cove. Thomson, Mary Leighton, illus. LC 59-644818. 143p. illus. 22cm. 1959. Ariel Books.

--Christmas Carols for Young Children. Le Mair, Henriette Willebeek (1889-1966), illus. (Illus.). N.D. (ISBN 0-914676-34-2, Star & Elephant Bk). Green Tiger.
--Curly Locks: Traditional Nursery Rhymes. Le Mair, Henriette Willebeek (1889-1966), illus. (Illus.). Repr. of 1911 ed. 1978. (ISBN 0-85249-340-1, Star & Eleph Bks). Green Tiger Pr.
--Dickory Dickory Dock. Le Mair, Henriette Willebeek (1889-1966), illus. (Illus.). Repr. of 1911 ed. 1978. (ISBN 0-85249-339-8, Star & Elephant). Green Tiger.
--Four & Twenty Tailors. Le Mair, Henriette Willibeek (1889-1966), illus. (Illus.). Repr. of 1911 ed. 1978. (ISBN 0-85249-341-X, Star & Eleph Bks). Green Tiger Pr.
--Grannie's Little Rhyme Book. Le Mair, Henriette Willebeek (1899-1966), illus. (Le Mair Nursery Rhyme Ser.). N.D. David McKay.
--The Mullberry Bush. Le Mair, Henriete Willebeek (1889-1966), illus. (Illus.). Repr. of 1911 ed. 1978. (ISBN 0-85249-338-X, Star & Eleph Bks). Green Tiger Pr.
--Our Old Nursery Rhymes. Le Mair, Henriette Willebeek (1889-1966), illus. (Illus.). 64p. 1975. (ISBN 0-915112-05-1). Seattle Bk.

Le Mair, Henriette Willebeek (1889-1966), illus.
--Old Dutch Nursery Rhymes. Elkin, Rosie Helen (1895-), tr. N.D. David McKay.

Leman, Martin
--Ten Cats & Their Tales. Leman, Martin, illus. LC 82-6050. (Illus.). 24p. (gr. k-3). 1982. (ISBN 0-03-062176-3). HR&W.
--Twelve Cats for Christmas. 1983. Merrimack. **Award: (NYT).**

LeMarchand, Jacques (1908-)
--The Adventures of Ulysses. Francois, Andre (1915-), illus. Hatt, E. M., tr. LC 59-12204. (Illus.). unpaged illus. 31 cm. (A Criterion book for young people). 1960. JUV. Criterion Books. **Award: (NYT).**

Lemcke, H. J. H., tr. see Hoffmann, Franz.

Lemerise, Bruce
--Sheldon's Lunch. LC 80-10449. p. cm. 1980. (ISBN 0-8193-1025-5). (ISBN 0-8193-1026-3). Parents Magazine Press.

Lemieux, Michele
--What's That Noise?. Lemieux, Michele, illus. LC 84-16631. (Illus.). 32p. (Morrow Junior Bks.). (ps-1). 1985. (ISBN 0-688-04139-6, Morrow Junior Books). (ISBN 0-688-04140-X). Morrow.

Lemish, Jane, jt. auth. see Lemish, John.

Lemish, John (1921-) & Lemish, Jane
--Jeff Carson, Young Geologist. LC 60-8076. 211p. 21cm. (Dodd, Mead career books). 1960. Dodd, Mead.

Lemke, Horst (1922-)
--One Times One. LC 69-13206. (Illus.). 32p. 1969, c.1968. Watts.
--Places and Faces: A Picture Book. Lemke, Horst (1922-), illus. LC 78-160446. (Illus.). 31 p. 28cm. 1971. Scroll Press.

Lemke, Horst (1922-) & Bond, Susan McDonald (1937-)
--Ride with Me Through ABC. Lemke, Horst (1922-), illus. LC 67-19376. (Illus.). 1 v. (unpaged. 24cm. 1968. Scroll Press.

Lemke, Stefan & Lemke-Pricken, Marie-Luise
--The Creation. LC 76-11268. (Illus.). 20 p. 19cm. 1976. (ISBN 0-8006-1575-1). Fortress Press.
--Jonah. LC 76-11275. (Illus.). 20 p. 19cm. 1976. (ISBN 0-8006-1577-8). Fortress Press.
--Noah's Ark. LC 76-11269. (Illus.). 20 p. 19cm. 1976. (ISBN 0-8006-1576-X). Fortress Press.

Lemke-Pricken, Marie-Luise, jt. auth. see Lemke, Stefan.

Lemmer, Madeline
--Behind the Singing Gate. LC 58-145271. 73p. illus. 21cm. 1958, c.1957. Vantage Press.

Lemoine, Georges, illus.
--The Christmas Story According to St. Luke. 32p. (Christmas Stories Ser.). 1983. (ISBN 0-87191-957-5). Childrens Bk Co.

Lemon, Adele Marie (1901-)
--The Magic Wishbone. Carter, Charlotte Anne, illus. LC 64-56402. 94 p. illus. 22 cm. 1964. Lawrence Pub. Co.

Lemon, Betty (1911-1977)
--Teton Christmas Tales. Berrey, Phoebe, illus. LC 79-126522. (Illus.). 45 p., 1 leaf of plates. 29cm. c.1979. (ISBN 0-933160-07-0). Teton Bookshop.

Lemon, Mark (1809-1870)
--The Christmas Hamper. 1875. George Routledge & Sons.
--The Enchanted Doll. Bd. with Tinykin's Transformations. Repr. of 1869 ed. LC 75-32163. (Illus.). Repr. of 1849 ed. (Classics of Children's Literature, 1621-1932: Vol. 27). 1977. (ISBN 0-8240-2276-9). Garland Pub.
--The Enchanted Doll. Doyle, Richard (1824-1883), illus. N.D. E J B Young & Co.
--The Enchanted Doll and Tinykin's Transformations. LC 75-32163. (Illus.). viii, 77, 183 p. 19cm. (Classics of Children's Literature, 1621-1932). 1976. (ISBN 0-8240-2276-9). Garland Pub.

Lemp, Louise
--The Potter and the Little Greek Maid. Lemp, Louise, illus. LC 58-89. (Illus.). 26cm. 32p. 1958. Viking Press.

Lenard, Alexander, tr. see Milne, Alan Alexander.

Lenard, Yvone
--Elan. 1979. (ISBN 0-03-045961-3). HR&W.

Lencek, Helen, jt. tr. see Dekker, Jan.

Lencek, Helen, tr. see Kavcic, Vladimir.

Lender, Charles Franklin
--Down the Ohio with Clark. Ogg, Oscar John (1908-1971), illus. LC 37-17514. viii, 278 p. incl. front., illus. 21 cm. c.1937. Thomas Y. Crowell Company.
--Pirates on the Ohio: A Tale of the Brig St. Clair and the Indomitable Commodore Whipple. Avison, George F. (1885-), illus. LC 47-4659. 5 l., 9-196 p. illus. 21 cm. 1947. Howell, Soskin.
--With Wayne at Fallen Timbers. Schaare, C. Richard, illus. LC 41-12729. vi, 249 p. front., plates. 21 cm. c.1941. Cupples & Leon Company.

L'Engle, Madeleine (1918-)
--And Both Were Young. LC 82-72751. 241 p. 22cm. c.1983. (ISBN 0-440-00264-8). Delacorte Press.
--And Both Were Young. N.D. Lothrop Bks.
--The Anti-Muffins. Ortiz, Gloria, illus. LC 80-21425. (Illus.). 48 p. 24cm. (The Education of the Public and the Public School). c.1980. (ISBN 0-8298-0415-3). Pilgrim Press.
--The Arm of the Starfish. LC 65-10919. 243p 22cm. c.1965. Ariel Bks. Dist.Farrar.
--Camilla. LC 81-65494. p. cm. 1981. (ISBN 0-440-01020-9). Delacorte Press.
--Camilla. LC 65-21416. 282 p. 21cm. 1965. T. Y. Crowell Co.
--Camilla Dickinson, a Novel. LC 51-3595. 245 p. 21cm. 1951. Simon and Schuster.
--Dance in the Desert. 1st ed. Shimin, Symeon (1902-), illus. LC 68-29465. (Illus.). 55 p. 22cm. 1969. Farrar, Straus & Giroux.
--Dragons in the Waters. LC 76-2477. 293 p. 21cm. c.1976. (ISBN 0-374-31868-9). Farrar, Straus, Giroux.
--A House Like a Lotus. LC 84-48471. 307 p. 22cm. 1984. (ISBN 0-374-33385-8). Farrar, Straus, Giroux.
--Journey with Jonah. Fisher, Leonard Everett (1924-), illus. (gr. 7 up). 1967. (ISBN 0-374-33927-9). FS&G.
--Lines Scribbled on an Envelope & Other Poems. LC 71-85367. (gr. 7 up). 1969. (ISBN 0-374-34488-4). FS&G.
--Meet the Austins. LC 60-972676. 191p. illus. 20cm. c.1960. Vanguard Press. **Award: (ALA).**
--The Moon by Night. LC 63-9072. 218 p. 22cm. 1963. Ariel Books.
--The Other Side of the Sun. 344p. 1971. (ISBN 0-374-22805-1). FS&G.
--Prelude. LC 68-56600. 189 p. 21cm. 1968. Vanguard Press.
--A Ring of Endless Light. LC 79-27679. 324 p. 22cm. c.1980. (ISBN 0-374-36299-8). Farrar, Straus, Giroux. **Award: (ALA).**
--The Small Rain. New ed. L'Engle, Madeleine, intro. by. 371p. Repr. of 1945 ed. N.D. FS&G.
--The Small Rain. rev. ed. L'Engle, Madeleine (1918-) 168p. (gr. 7 up). 1968. Vanguard.
--The Summer of the Great-Grandmother. (Illus.). 245p. 1974. (ISBN 0-374-27174-7). Farrar, Straus and Giroux.
--A Swiftly Tilting Planet. LC 78-9648. 278 p. 22cm. c.1978. (ISBN 0-374-37362-0). Farrar, Straus and Giroux.
--The Time Trilogy: A Wrinkle in Time; A Wind in the Door; A Swiftly Tilting Planet, 3 vols. (gr. 4 up). 1979. Boxed Set. (ISBN 0-374-37592-5). FS&G.
--The Twenty-Four Days Before Christmas. Inga, illus. LC 64-22125. (Illus.). 56 p. 24cm. 1964. Ariel Books.
--The Twenty-Four Days Before Christmas: An Austin Family Story. DeVelasco, Joe E., illus. LC 84-5540. c.1984. (ISBN 0-87788-843-4). H. Shaw Publishers.
--A Wind in the Door. LC 73-75176. 211 p. 22cm. 1973. (ISBN 0-374-38443-6). Farrar, Straus and Giroux.
--A Wrinkle in Time. LC 62-7203. 211 p. 22cm. 1962. Ariel Books. **Awards: (JNM); (ALA).**
--The Young Unicorns. LC 68-13682. 245 p. 22cm. (Ariel book). 1968. Farrar, Straus and Giroux.

Lengstrand, Rolf
--A Horse Astray in Stockholm. Svenonius, Arthur, photos by. Seidler, Lotte, tr. LC 65-25945. (Illus.). 1 v. (unpaged. 23cm. 1965. Lerner Publications Co.

Lengstrand, Rolf & Rolen, Pierre L.
--The Long Pony Race. Svenonius, Arthur, photos by. Turner, Marianne, tr. LC 66-13782. 84p. illus. 27cm. 1966. Knopf.
--The Long Pony Trek. Blomquist, Lennart, photos by. Turner, Marianne, tr. LC 67-15806. (Illus.). 82 p. 26cm. 1968. Knopf.

Lenk, Margarete Klee, Mrs. (1841-)
--The Cotter's Son. N.D. Augustana Book Concern.
--The Cross and the Crescent. N.D. Augustana Book Concern.
--The House of Enchantment. N.D. Augustana Book Concern.
--In the Service of the Prince of Peace. N.D. Augustana Book Concern.
--Patrick's First Christmas and Other Stories for Children. LC 22-1071. 134 p. front. 17.5 cm. c.1921. Augustana Book Concern.
--The Winning of Willie. N.D. Augustana Book Concern.

Lennox, Mary
--Let's Pretend. Eulalie, pseud. (1896-), illus. Banks, Eulalie M.. LC 35-179. (Verses for Children). 16 p. illus. 19cm. c.1935. Farallon Press.
--The Wishing Tree. Eulalie, pseud. (1896-), illus. Banks, Eulalie M.. LC 35-28730. 2 p. l., 59 p. incl. front., illus. 19 1/2 cm. c.1935. The Farallon Press.

Lenotre, Therese
--The Mystery of Dog Flip. Eichenberg, Fritz (1901-), illus. Chamoud, Simone (1904-), tr. from Fr. 4 p. l., 190 p. illus. 21 cm. 1939. Frederick A. Stokes Company.
--The Mystery of Dog Flip. Eichenberg, Fritz (1901-), illus. Chamoud, Simone (1904-), tr. N.D. J. B. Lippincott.

Lenski, Lois, et al. (1893-1974)
--Christmas Comes to Blueberry Corners, and Other Christmas Stories for Children. Lenski, Lois (1893-1974), illus. LC 75-2837. (Illus.). 32p. (ps-4). 1975. (ISBN 0-8066-1483-8). Augsburg.

Lenski, Lois (1893-1974)
--Alphabet People. Lenski, Lois (1893-1974), illus. LC 28-23146. 4 p. l., 104 p. illus. (part col.) 24 cm. 1928. Harper & Brothers.
--Animals For Me. Lenski, Lois (1893-1974), illus. 1941. (ISBN 0-8098-1007-7). David McKay Company.
--Animals for Me. Lenski, Lois (1893-1974), illus. LC 59-12486. 1 v. (unpaged) col. illus. 13 x 15 cm. N.D. H. Z. Walck.
--Animals for Me. Lenski, Lois (1893-1974), illus. (Illus.). 48 p. N.D. H. Z. Walck.
--Animals for Me. Lenski, Lois (1893-1974), illus. LC 42-16501. 48 p. illus. (part col.) 13 x 15 cm. c.1941. Oxford University Press.
--Arabella and Her Aunts. Lenski, Lois (1893-1974), illus. LC 32-29502. 4 p. l., 115 p. incl. plates (part col.) col. front. 16 cm. 1932. Frederick A. Stokes Co.
--Arabella and Her Aunts. Lenski, Lois (1893-1974), illus. N.D. J. B. Lippincott.
--At Our House. Lenski, Lois (1893-1974), illus. LC 59-9667. (Illus.). (Read & Sing Bks). (gr. k-3). 1959. (ISBN 0-8098-1062-X). Walck.
--Bayou Suzette. Lenski, Lois (1893-1974), illus. LC 43-15172. 12, 2, 207, 2 p. incl. front., illus. (incl. map) 22 1/2 cm. 1943. Frederick A. Stokes Co.
--Bayou Suzette. Lenski, Lois (1893-1974), illus. N.D. J. B. Lippincott.
--Benny and His Penny. Lenski, Lois (1893-1974), illus. LC 31-23199. 32 p. col. illus. 20 x 29 cm. 1931. A. A. Knopf.
--Berries in the Scoop: A Cape Cod Cranberry Story. Lenski, Lois (1893-1974), illus. LC 56-6560. (Illus.). 124 p. 21cm. (Her Roundabout America). 1956. Lippincott.
--Big Little Davy. Lenski, Lois (1893-1974), illus. 1956. (ISBN 0-8098-1045-X). David McKay Company.
--Big Little Davy. Lenski, Lois (1893-1974), illus. 1956. Henry Z. Walck Inc.
--Big Little Davy. Lenski, Lois (1893-1974), illus. LC 56-9781. (Illus.). 48 p. (Oxford books for boys and girls). 1956. Oxford University Press.
--Blue Ridge Billy. 1st ed. Lenski, Lois (1893-1974), illus. LC 46-6400. xvi, 2, 203 p. illus. (incl. map) 22 cm. 1946. J. B. Lippincott Company.
--Blueberry Corners. Lenski, Lois (1893-1974), illus. LC 40-30539. xiv, 209 p. incl. front., illus. 22 1/2 cm. 1940. Frederick A. Stokes Co.
--Blueberry Corners. Lenski, Lois (1893-1974), illus. (gr. 4-6). 1940. (ISBN 0-397-30067-0). Lippincott.
--Boom Town Boy. 1st ed. Lenski, Lois (1893-1974), illus. LC 48-2379. xiii. 177 p. illus., map. 23 cm. (Regional Stories Ser.). 1948. (ISBN 0-397-30141-3). J. B. Lippincott Co.
--Bound Girl of Cobble Hill. Lenski, Lois (1893-1974), illus. (gr. 7-9). 1939. (ISBN 0-397-30055-7). Lippincott.
--Bound Girl of Cooble Hill. 1st ed. Lenski, Lois (1893-1974), illus. LC 38-27872. viii p., 1 l., 291, 1 p. illus. 21 cm. 1938. Frederick A. Stokes Co.
--City Poems. Lenski, Lois (1893-1974), illus. 1971. (ISBN 0-8098-2414-0). David McKay Company.
--City Poems. Lenski, Lois (1893-1974), illus. LC 70-119569. (Illus.). x, 118 p. 24cm. 1971. (ISBN 0-8098-2414-0). H. Z. Walck.
--Coal Camp Girl. Lenski, Lois (1893-1974), illus. LC 59-123560. (Illus.). 173 p. 23cm. 1959. Lippincott.
--Corn-Farm Boy. Lenski, Lois (1893-1974), illus. LC 54-84856. 179 p. illus. 22 cm. 1954. Lippincott.
--Cotton in My Sack. 1st ed. Lenski, Lois (1893-1974), illus. LC 49-3884. xii, 190 p. illus. 23 cm. 1949. (ISBN 0-397-30158-8). J. B. Lippincott Co.
--Cowboy Small. Lenski, Lois (1893-1974), illus. 1949. (ISBN 0-8098-2414-0). David McKay Company.
--Cowboy Small. Lenski, Lois (1893-1974), illus. LC 60-12094. (Illus.). 48 p. 19cm. 1960, c.1949. H.Z. Walck.
--Cowboy Small. Lenski, Lois (1893-1974), illus. LC 49-8493. 48 p. col. illus. 19 cm. 1949. Oxford Univ. Press.
--Cowboy Small. Lenski, Lois (1893-1974), illus. 46p. 1949. Walck.
--Davy and His Dog. Lenski, Lois (1893-1974), illus. LC 58-14241. (Illus.). 38 p. (Davy book). 1957. H. Z. Walck.
--Davy and His Dog. Lenski, Lois (1893-1974), illus. LC 57-11639. (Illus.). 38 p. (Davy book). 1957. Oxford University Press.
--Davy Goes Places. Lenski, Lois (1893-1974), illus. LC 61-12887. (Illus.). 46 p. (Davy book). 1961. H. Z. Walck.
--Davy's Day. Lenski, Lois (1893-1974), illus. LC 59-152312. unpaged. illus. 13x15cm. 1959, c.1943. H. Z. Walck.
--Davy's Day. Lenski, Lois (1893-1974), illus. LC 43-17034. 48 p. col. illus. 12 1/2 x 14 1/2 cm. 1943. Oxford University Press.
--Debbie and Her Dolls. Lenski, Lois (1893-1974), illus. LC 79-100705. (Illus.). 48 p. (A Debbie book). 1970. H. Z. Walck.
--Debbie & Her Family. Lenski, Lois (1893-1974), illus. LC 77-82676. (Illus.). 15cm. 46p. (Debbie Bks). (gr. k-3). 1969. (ISBN 0-8098-1156-1). Walck.
--Debbie and Her Grandma. Lenski, Lois (1893-1974), illus. LC 67-8148. 48p. col. illus. 13x15cm. (Her A Debbie bk.). 1967. H. Z. Walck.
--Debbie and Her Pets. Lenski, Lois (1893-1974), illus. LC 71-158869. (Illus.). 48 p. (Her A Debbie book). 1971. (ISBN 0-8098-1186-3). H. Z. Walck.
--Debbie Goes to Nursery School. Lenski, Lois (1893-1974), illus. LC 72-100706. (Illus.). 48 p. (A Debbie book). 1970. H. Z. Walck.
--Debbie Herself. Lenski, Lois (1893-1974), illus. LC 70-82677. (Illus.). 46 p. (Her A Debbie book). 1969. H Z. Walck.
--Deer Valley Girl. 1st ed. Lenski, Lois (1893-1974), illus. LC 68-10773. (Illus.). 145 p. 22cm. 1968. Lippincott.
--A Dog Came to School. Lenski, Lois (1893-1974), illus. (Illus.). 46 p. (Davy book). 1955. H. Z. Walck.
--A Dog Came to School. Lenski, Lois (1893-1974), illus. LC 55-10777. (Illus.). 13 x 15cm. 46p. (Oxford Books for Boys and Girls). 1955. Oxford University Press.
--The Easter Rabbit's Parade. Lenski, Lois (1893-1974), illus. LC 36-6660. 31 p. col. illus. 25 cm. c.1936. Oxford University Press.
--Flood Friday. Lenski, Lois (1893-1974), illus. LC 56-9901. 98 p. illus. 23 cm. (Regional Stories Ser.). 1956. (ISBN 0-397-30328-9). Lippincott.
--Forgetful Tommy. Lenski, Lois (1893-1974), illus. 1943. Greenacres Press.
--A Going to the Westward. Lenski, Lois (1893-1974), illus. LC 37-22818. xii p., 1 l., 369, 1 p. illus. 21 cm. 1937. Frederick A. Stokes Company.
--A Going to The Westward. Lenski, Lois (1893-1974), illus. (Regional Ser.). N.D. J. B. Lippincott.
--Gooseberry Garden. Lenski, Lois (1893-1974), illus. LC 34-32736. 32 p. col. illus. 17 x 22 cm. 1934. (ISBN 0-397-30367-X). Harper and Brothers.
--Grandmother Tippytoe. Lenski, Lois (1893-1974), illus. LC 31-23679. 6 p. l., 104 p. col. front., illus., col. plates. 23 1/2 cm. 1931. Frederick A. Stokes Co.
--Grandmother Tippytoe. Lenski, Lois (1893-1974), illus. N.D. J. B. Lippincott.
--High-Rise-Secret. 1st ed. Lenski, Lois (1893-1974), illus. LC 66-8133. (Illus.). 152 p. 21cm. (Roundabout America series). 1966. Lippincott.
--Houseboat Girl. X ed. Lenski, Lois (1893-1974), illus. LC 57-10330. (Illus.). 23cm. 175p. (Regional Stories Ser.). (gr. 4-6). 1957. (ISBN 0-397-30366-1). Lippincott.
--I Like Winter. LC 50-9862. 48p. col. illus. 13 x 14cm. 1950. Oxford University Press.
--I Like Winter. Lenski, Lois (1893-1974), illus. LC 60-13184. (Illus.). 48 p. 13 x 14cm. 1960, c.1950. H. Z. Walck.

--Second-Season Jinx. LC 52-13723. 216 p. 21cm. 1953. Lippincott.
--Stretch Bolton Comes Back. LC 57-13371. 192p. 21cm. 1958. Lippincott.
--Stretch Bolton: Mister Shortstop. LC 62-9340. 192 p. 21 cm. 1963. Lippincott.
--Stretch Bolton's Rookies. 192p. 1934. J. B. Lippincott.
--Stretch Bolton's Rookies. 01662168x. 1st ed. LC 61-797671. 190p. 21cm. 1961. Lippincott.
--Victory Pass. 1950. J. B. Lippincott.

Leonard, Constance Brink (1923-)
--Aground. LC 84-1470. 160p. (gr. 7 up). 1984. (ISBN 0-396-08329-3). (ISBN 0-396-08329-3). Dodd.
--The Marina Mystery. LC 80-2781. 160p. (gr. 8 up). 1981. Dodd.
--Shadow of a Ghost. (gr. 8 up). 1978. Dodd.
--Stowaway. LC 82-45996. p. cm. 1983. (ISBN 0-396-08144-4). Dodd, Mead.

Leonard, Edward
--The Silver Prince. LC 20-18660. 3 p. l., 269, 1 p. front. 19 1/2 cm. 1920. D. Appleton and Company.
--Tuck Simms, Forty-Niner. LC 29-11091. 3 p. l., 208 p. front., plates. 19 1/2 cm. c.1929. Grosset & Dunlap.
--Tuck Simms: Forty Niner. (Buddy Bks for Boys). N.D. Grosset & Dunlap.

Leonard, Jack
--The Fat Town and the Little Town. Laune, Paul Sidney (1899-), illus. LC 33-25674. 32 p. incl. front., illus. 19 1/2 x 20 cm. c.1933. G. P. Putnam's Sons.

Leonard, Julie
--Children's Songs from the Hillsides. LC 28-7674. 3 p. l., v-vii, 9-155 p. illus. 18 cm. 1865. E. P. Dutton and Company.

Leonard, Lawrence
--Horn of Mortal Danger. 192p. (gr. 3-7). 1982. (ISBN 0-531-04365-7, MacRae). Watts.

Leonard, Marcia, compiled by.
--Cricket's Jokes, Riddles and other Stuff. Grandits, John, illus. LC 77-3164. 64p. ill. 24cm. c.1977. (ISBN 0-394-83545-X). (ISBN 0-394-93545-4). Random House.

Leonard, Mary Finley (1862-)
--Candle and the Cat. LC 1-12839. (Illus.). vi, 88p. (The Sunshine Library for Young People). 1901. Thomas Y. Crowell.
--Christmas Tree House. LC 13-21477. 21 cm. 286p. (Crowell's American Boy and Girl Library). 1913. Thomas Y. Crowell Company.
--Everyday Susan. (Crowell's American Boy and Girl Library). N.D. Thomas Y. Crowell Company.
--Everyday Susan: A Story for Girls. Herr, Laetitia, illus. LC 12-21727. 2 p. l., vii-ix, 370 p. front., plates. 20 1/2 cm. c.1912. Thomas Y. Crowell Company.
--Half a Dozen Thinking Caps. LC 4289. 4 p. l., 80 p. front. 19 1/2 cm. (Added t.-p.: Sunshine Library). c.1900. T. Y. Crowell & Co.
--How the Two Ends Met. Falls, Charles Buckles (1874-1960), illus. (Illus.). (The Twentieth Century Juveniles). N.D. Thomas Y. Crowell.
--How the Two Ends Met: A Story of our Square. LC 3-19078. 20cm. 97p. 1903. T. Y. Crowell & Co.
--It All Came True. LC 4-18605. (Illus.). 20cm. 141p. 1904. T. Y. Crowell & Co.
--It All Came True. (Illus.). (Twentieth Century Ser.). 1905. Thomas Y. Crowell & Co.
--The Little Red Chimney: Being the Love Story of a Candy Man. Gassaway, Katharine, illus. LC 14-14805. (Illus.). 18 1/2cm. 164p. 1914. Duffield & Co.
--Mr. Pat's Little Girl: A Story of the Arden Foresters. Emerson, C. Chase, illus. LC 2-211034. 322 p. incl. front. pl. 20 cm. 1902. W. A. Wilde Company.
--On Hyacinth Hill. (Illus.). 262p. 1910. W. A. Wilde Co.
--On Hyacinth Hill: A Story. Copeland, Charles, illus. LC 4-24569. 262 p. front., 3 pl. 19 1/2 cm. 1904. W. A. Wilde Company.
--The Pleasant Street Partnership: A Neighborhood Story. Merrill, Frank Thayer (1848-), illus. LC 3-23432. 269 p. front., 3 pl. 19 1/2 cm. 1903. W. A. Wilde Company.
--The Pleasant Street Partnership: A Story. (Illus.). 269p. 1910. W. A. Wilde Co.
--The Spectacle Man. (Illus.). 266p. 1910. W. A. Wilde Co.
--The Spectacle Man: A Story of the Missing Bridge. Merrill, Frank Thayer (1848-), illus. 266 p. front., plates. 19 cm. c.1901. W. A. Wilde Company.
--The Story of the Big Front Door. LC 7-13146. iv, 258 p. front., plates, 20 cm. c.1898. T. Y. Crowell & Company.
--Story of the Big Front Door. (Illus.). (Twentieth Century Ser.). 1905. Thomas Y. Crowell & Co.
--Susan Grows Up. LC 14-13852. (Illus.). 20cm. 307p. 1914. T. Y. Crowell.
--The Ways of Jane: A Story with Which the Wise and Prudent Have No Concern. LC 17-8350. 18 cm. 268p. 1917. Duffield & Co.

Leonard, Mayme Rolf, Mrs. (1876-), ed.
--The Children's Hour: A Week-Day Project for Church Schools. LC 39-5563. 183 p. 21 1/2 cm. c.1929. The Standard Publishing Company.

Leonard, Nellie Mabel (1875-)
--Grand-Daddy Whiskers, M.D. LC 20-6447. 3 p. l., 9-104 p. illus. 19 1/2 cm. c.1919. Thomas Y. Crowell Company.
--Grandfather Whiskers, M. D: A Graymouse Story. Cooney, Barbara (1917-), illus. LC 52-13130. 216 p. illus. 20 cm. 1953. Crowell.
--The Graymouse Family. LC 17-1361. 1 p. l., 7-100 p. illus. 19 1/2 cm. c.1916. Thomas Y. Crowell Company.
--The Graymouse Family. Cooney, Barbara (1917-), illus. LC 50-13512. (Illus.). 209 p. 20cm. 1950. Crowell.
--Limpy Toes' Attic Home. N.D. Thomas Y. Crowell Company.
--Uncle Squeaky's Country Store. N.D. Thomas Y. Crowell Company.
--Uncle Squeaky's Vacation. N.D. Thomas Y. Crowell Company.

Leonard, Robert Maynard, ed.
--Poems on Children. LC 15-9127. 128 p. 17 cm. (Oxford garlands). 1914. H. Milford.

Leonard, Tom B., jt. ed. see Horowitz, Caroline.

Leonard, William Ellery, ed.
--Beowulf. Ward, Lynd Kendall (1905-1985), illus. Leonard, William Ellery, tr. 138p. N.D. Heritage Press.

Leonard, William Ellery, ed. see Aesopus.

Leonardo Da Vinci (1452-1519) & Grant, Davidno
--Leonardo Da Vinci's Fantastic Animals. Saviozzi, Adriana (1928-), illus. LC 77-372984. (Illus.). 4-93 p. 29cm. 1976. (ISBN 0-00-138137-7). Collins.

Leoning, Grover (1912-), ed. see Sutton, Felix.

Le Paillot, Jean
--Caroline and the King's Hunt. Florence, pseud., illus. Wabbes, Maria. LC 72-673. 28 p. 27cm. 1972. (ISBN 0-8193-0604-5). (ISBN 0-8193-0605-3). Parents' Magazine Press.
--Caroline at the King's Ball. Florence, pseud., illus. Wabbes, Maria. LC 75-183378. 28 col. illus. 27cm. 1972. (ISBN 0-8193-0551-0). (ISBN 0-8193-0552-9). Parents' Magazine Press.
--Caroline's Green Tongue. Florence, pseud., illus. Wabbes, Maria. De Caroline & Saunders, Rubie, trs. LC 72-6070. p. 1973. (ISBN 0-8193-0632-0). (ISBN 0-8193-0633-9). Parents' Magazine Press.
--Caroline's Moving Day. Florence, pseud., illus. Wabbes, Maria. LC 72-12921. p. 1973. (ISBN 0-8193-0673-8). (ISBN 0-8193-0673-8). Parents' Magazine Press.

LePere, Jean M., jt. auth. see Durr, William Kirtley.

L'Epine, Ernest Louis Victor Jules (1826-1893)
--The Fortress of Fear. Dore, Louis Christophe Paul Gustave (1832-1883), illus. Hood, Tom (1835-1974), tr. from French. LC 55-2147. 110p. illus. 24cm. c.1953. Story Classics.
--The Legend of Croquemitaine, and the Chivalric Times of Charlemagne. Dore, Louis Christophe Paul Gustave (1832-1883) & Dore, Gustave, illus. Hood, Thomas (1835-1874), tr. from Fr. LC 20-21249. x p. 1 l., 259 p. incl. front., illus., plates. 32 1/2 cm. 1866. Cassell, Petter, and Galpin.

Le Pla, Fannie M
--Little Nature Verses. LC 30-22728. 88 p. illus. 20 1/2 cm. c.1930. The Christopher Publishing House.

Le Pla, Lillie (1894-)
--The Secret of the Wood. (The Magnet Library). N.D. Frederick Warne & Co.
--The Secret Shore. N.D. Frederick Warne & Co.
--Tangletrees. Forbes, Margaret, illus. LC 29-13899. ix, 11-197 p. incl. front., illus. 19 cm. 1928. T. Nelson and Sons.

Leppard, Lois Gladys
--Mandie & the Cherokee Legend. 144p. (Orig.). (Mandie Ser.: No. 2). (gr. 4-7). 1983. (ISBN 0-87123-321-5). Bethany Hse.
--Mandie & the Forbidden Attic. 144p. (Orig.). (gr. 4-7). 1985. Bethany Hse.
--Mandie & the Ghost Bandits. 128p. (Orig.). (Mandie Ser.). (gr. 5-7). 1984. (ISBN 0-87123-442-4). Bethany Hse.
--Mandie and the Secret Tunnel. LC 82-74053. 141 p. 18cm. (Mandie book ; 1). ((Series: Leppard, Lois Gladys.). (Mandie book ; 1.). c.1983. (ISBN 0-87123-320-7). Bethany House Publishers.

Lepping, Carola, tr. see Cavin, Ruth Brodie.

Le Prince De Beaumont, jt. auth. see Perrault, Charles.

Le Prince De Beaumont, Marie, jt. auth. see Wahl, Jan.

Le Prince De Beaumont, Marie (1711-1780)
--Beauty and the Beast. Ducornet, Erica (1943-), illus. Muir, Percival Horace (1894-1979), tr. from Fr. LC 68-12435. (Illus.). 47 p. 24cm. 1968. (ISBN 0-394-90948-8). Knopf.
--Beauty and the Beast. Goode, Diane (1949-), illus. LC 76-57884. (Illus.). 31 p. 27cm. c.1978. (ISBN 0-02-726400-9). (ISBN 0-87888-119-0). Bradbury Press.
--Beauty and the Beast. Legrand, Edy (1893-), illus. Muir, Percival Horace (1894-1979), tr. from Fr. LC 50-17009. 45 p. col. illus. 31 cm. (Evergreen Tales; or, Tales for the Ageless). 1949. Limited Editions Club.

Le Rat, illus.
--The Fables of La Fontaine, 2 vols. Wright, Elizur, Jr., tr. from French. Dam, E., designed by. (Illus.). (Exquisite Ser.). N.D. Per set. Estes & Lauriat's.

Lerch, Harold H.
--Numbers in the Land of Hand. Sharpe, Anne, illus. LC 66-11151. 56p. illus. 26cm. 1966. Southern Illinois University Press.

Lerch, Marilyn, jt. auth. see Siddiqui, Ashraf Hossain.

Lermont, Lorentz
--Ups and Downs: Or, The Lost Treasure Restored. LC 22-5140. 150 p. 3 col. pl. (incl. front.) 17 cm. c.1852. The Author.

Lermont, Lorentz, tr. from Ger.
--My Play is Study: A/Book for Children. LC 22-5158. 111p. 20cm. 1852. J.K. Simon.

Lermontov, Mikhail Iurevich, jt. auth. see Jokai, Moritz.

Lerner, Marguerite Rush (1924-)
--Dear Little Mumps Child. Overlie, George, illus. LC 59-15145. (Illus.). unpaged. 26cm. c.1959. Medical Books for Children.
--Doctors Tools. Overlie, George, illus. LC 59-15484. unpaged. illus. 26cm. 1959. Medical Books for Children.
--Lefty: The Story of Left-Handedness. Andre, Rov, illus. LC 60-14007. (Illus.). 32 p. 27cm. 1960. Medical Books for Children.
--Michael Gets the Measles. Overlie, George, illus. LC 59-13630. (Illus.). 27cm. (Medical Bks for Children). (gr. k-6). 1959. (ISBN 0-8225-0001-9). Medical Books for Children.
--Michael Gets the Measles. Overlie, George, illus. LC 59-13630. unpaged. illus. 27cm. c.1959. Medical Books for Children.
--Peter Gets the Chickenpox. Overlie, George, illus. LC 59-15144. (Illus.). unpaged. 26cm. c.1959. Medical Books for Children.
--Red Man, White Man, African Chief: The Story of Skin Color. Overlie, George, illus. LC 60-14005. (Illus.). unpaged. 26cm. 1960. Medical Books For Children.

Lerner, Sharon Ruth (1925-), ed. see Sesame Street.

Lerner, Sharon Ruth (1938-1982)
--Big Bird Says-. A Game to Read and Play : Featuring Jim Henson's Sesame Street Muppets. Mathieu, Joseph (1945-), illus. LC 85-1959. (Illus.). 31 p. 24cm. (Step into reading. A Step 1 book). c.1985. (ISBN 0-394-87499-4). (ISBN 0-394-97499-9). Random House : Children's Television Workshop.
--Follow the Monsters!. Featuring Jim Henson's Sesame Street Muppets. Cooke, Tom, illus. LC 84-18031. (Illus.). 30 p. 23cm. (Step into Reading Book. A Step 1 Book). 1985. (ISBN 0-394-87126-X). (ISBN 0-394-97126-4). Random House.
--I Picked a Flower. Lerner, Sharon (1938-1982), illus. LC 67-15699. 31p. col. illus. 27cm. 1967. Lerner.
--Nitty-Gritty Rhyming Riddle Book. Ross, Larry (1943-), illus. (Illus.). (Electric Company Ser.). (gr. 1-5). 1973. (ISBN 0-307-64823-0, Golden Pr). Western Pub.
--Who Will Wake up Spring?. (Illus.). 30 p. 24cm. 1967. Lerner Publications Co.

Lerner, Sharon Ruth (1938-1982) & Cerf, Christopher Bennett (1941-)
--The Prisoner of Vega. Swanson, Robert, illus. LC 77-70858. (Illus.). 41 p. 23cm. c.1977. (ISBN 0-394-93576-4). Random House.

Lerner, Sharon Ruth (1938-1982) & Frith, Michael (1925-), eds.
--Big Bird's Busy Book: Featuring Jim Henson's Muppets. Crawford, Mel, et al. (1925-), illus. Rowan, Charles (1933-), photos by. Children's Television Workshop LC 74-5521. 31cm. 96p. 1975. (ISBN 0-394-82904-2). Random House.

Lerner, Sharon Ruth (1938-1982) & Mathieu, Joseph
--Big Bird's Copycat Day: Featuring Jim Henson's Sesame Street Muppets. LC 84-6869. (Illus.). 32 p. 24cm. (Step into reading. A step 1 book). c.1984. (ISBN 0-394-86912-5). (ISBN 0-394-96912-X). Random House : Children's Television Workshop.

Leroe, Ellen W. (1949-)
--Confessions of a Teenage TV Addict. LC 83-8987. 160p. (gr. 7 up). 1983. (ISBN 0-525-66909-4). Lodestar Bks.
--The Plot Against the Pom-Pom Queen. LC 84-21153. 134 p. 22cm. c.1985. (ISBN 0-525-67161-7). Dutton.
--Robot Romance. LC 84-48349. 192p. (gr. 6-9). 1985. (ISBN 0-06-023746-5). (ISBN 0-06-023745-7). HarpJ.

Le Row, Caroline Bigelow (1843-)
--Duxberry Doings. (Illus.). (The Pilgrim Endeavor Library). N.D. Pilgrims Press.
--Duxberry Doings: A New England Story. (The Girl Chums Ser.). N.D. A. L. Burt Co.
--Duxberry Doings: A New England Story. (Illus.). (The Wellesley Series for Girls). N.D. A. L. Burt.
--A Fortunate Failure, 1 of 20 vols. New ed. (Illus.). 350p. (Sunday-School Lib: No. 13). 1895. Set. Lothrop Pub. Co.

Leroy, Amelie Claire see Stuart, Esme, pseud.

LeRoy, Gen
--Bridget. LC 72-11240. (Illus.). 149 p. 22cm. 1973. (ISBN 0-06-023793-7). (ISBN 0-06-023793-7). Harper & Row.
--Cold Feet. LC 77-25642. 217 p. 22cm. c.1979. (ISBN 0-06-023778-3). (ISBN 0-06-023779-1). Harper & Row.
--Emma's Dilemma. LC 75-6293. 123 p. 21cm. c.1975. (ISBN 0-06-023788-0). (ISBN 0-06-023789-9). Harper & Row.
--Hotheads. LC 76-41519. 249 p. 22cm. c.1977. (ISBN 0-06-023786-4). (ISBN 0-06-023787-2). Harper & Row.

LeRoy, Gen & Higginbottom, Jeffery Winslow (1945-)
--Billy's Shoes. LC 81-3774. (Illus.). 44 p. 22cm. c.1981. (ISBN 0-07-037201-2). McGraw-Hill.
--Lucky Stiff!. LC 80-27421. (Illus.). 42 p. 22cm. c.1981. (ISBN 0-07-037203-9). McGraw-Hill.

Le Roy, Kate Warner & Livingstone, Mabel
--Flower Fair, and Other Poems. LC 43-7682. 1 p. l., 22 p. illus. 26 1/2 x 26 1/2 cm. c.1941. Musette Publishers.

Le Roy, Kate Warner & Seymour, Harriet Ayer
--Fifty Little Songs. LC 43-7683. 2 p. l., 23 p. 31 x 27 cm. c.1941. Musette Publishers.

LeRoy, Marcel
--Land of the Niamoo. 1955. Associated Booksellers.

Lerrigo, Charles Henry (1872-)
--The Boy Scout Treasure Hunters: Or, The Lost Treasure of Buffalo Hollow. Wrenn, Charles L., illus. LC 17-22091. 247 p. front., plates. 20 cm. (On verso of t.-p.: The Boy Scout Life Series). 1917. Barse & Hopkins.
--The Boy Scouts of Round Table Patrol. (The Boy Scout Life Ser.). N.D. Barse & Co.
--The Boy Scouts of Round Table Patrol. Newman, George A., illus. LC 24-214027. 5 p. l., 252 p. front., plates. 19 1/2 cm. 1924. Little, Brown, and Company.
--Boy Scouts on Special Service. Newman, George A., illus. LC 22-18471. 4 p. l., 268 p., 1 l. front., plates. 19 1/2 cm. $1.7. 1922. Little, Brown, and Company.
--The Boy Scouts to the Rescue. Wrenn, Charles L., illus. LC 21-11637. 231 p. incl. front. plates. 20 cm. (On verso of t.-p.: The Boy Scout Life Series). c.1920. Barse & Hopkins.
--The Castle of Cheer. LC 16-823020. 304 p. front., pl. 20 1/2 cm. c.1916. Fleming H. Revell Company.
--The Merry Men of Robin Hood Patrol. N.D. Barse & CO.
--A Son of John Brown. Lowell, Harold, illus. LC 37-16377. 265 p. incl. front., plates. 20 cm. 1937. T. Nelson and Sons.

Lerrigo, Peter H. J. (1875-)
--Anita: A/Tale of the Philippines. LC 25-11315. 20cm. 268p. 1925. Judson press.

LeSage, A. R.
--Adventures of Gil Blas. (Burt's Home Library). N.D. A L Burt Co.
--Adventures of Gil Blas. (The Lotus Library of Continental Masterpieces). N.D. Brentano's.

LeShan, Eda J. (1922-)
--What's the Matter with Me?. (gr. 7-12). 1976. (ISBN 0-590-10162-5, Schol Pap). Scholastic Inc.

LeSieg, Theo., pseud., see Geisel, Theodor Seuss.

LeSieg, Theo., pseud., see Geisel, Theodore Seuss.

LeSieg, Theo., pseud. (1904-)
--Come Over to My House. Geisel, Theodore Seuss. Erdoes, Richard (1912-), illus. LC 66-10686. (Illus.). 24. 63p. (gr. k-3). 1966. (ISBN 0-394-80044-3). (ISBN 0-394-90044-8). Beginner.
--Hooper Humperdink . . .?. Not Him!. Geisel, Theodor Seuss. Martin, Charles E. (1910-), illus. LC 76-747. (Illus.). (Bright & Early Bk.: No. 22). (ps-1). 1976. (ISBN 0-394-83286-8, BYR). (ISBN 0-394-93286-2). Random.
--In a People House. Geisel, Theodor Seuss. LC 75-37406. (Illus.). 24cm. 28p. (Bright & Early Bk: No. 12). (ps-1). 1972. (ISBN 0-394-82395-8, BYR). (ISBN 0-394-92395-2). Random.

Levin, Ali (1893-)
--The Three Tall-Tale Tellers. Rodin, David, pseud. Lichenstein, I., illus. Burstein, Abraham, tr. LC 52-11891. 102p. illus. 23cm. 1952. Vantage Press.
Levin, Beatrice
--Indian Myths from the Southeast. (Indian Culture Ser.). (gr. 4-12). 1974. (ISBN 0-89992-071-3). MT Coun Indian.
--John Hawk: White Man, Black Man, Indian Chief. Davenport, May, illus. LC 81-71904. (Illus.). 160p. (Orig.). 1st U.S. edition. (gr. 7-12). 1982. (ISBN 0-943864-03-8). (ISBN 0-943864-02-X). Davenport.
Levin, Betty (1927-)
--A Binding Spell. LC 84-8087. 179 p. 23cm. c.1984. (ISBN 0-525-67151-X). E. P. Dutton.
--The Forespoken. LC 76-15575. 282 p. 22cm. c.1976. (ISBN 0-02-756400-2). MacMillan.
--A Griffon's Nest. LC 74-23497. 346 p. 22cm. 1975. (ISBN 0-02-757350-8). Macmillan.
--The Keeping-Room. LC 80-23931. 247 p. 22cm. c.1981. (ISBN 0-688-80300-8). (ISBN 0-688-84300-X). Greenwillow Books.
--Landfall. LC 79-12421. 198 p. 22cm. 1979. (ISBN 0-689-50148-X). Atheneum.
--Put on My Crown. LC 84-28845. 182 p. 22cm. c.1985. (ISBN 0-525-67163-3). Lodestar Books.
--The Sword of Culann. LC 73-583. 280 p. 22cm. 1973. (ISBN 0-02-757340-0). Macmillan.
--The Zoo Conspiracy. Parry, Marian (1924-), illus. LC 73-1218. (Illus.). 123 p. 22cm. 1973. (ISBN 0-8038-8811-2). Hastings House.
Levin, Deana, jt. auth. see Baltermants, Dmitrii Nikolaevich.
Levin, Harry (1912-), ed. see Hawthorne, Nathaniel.
Levin, Jane Whitbread (1914-)
--Star of Danger. LC 66-69237. 160p. map. 21cm. (gr. 7 up). 1966. (ISBN 0-15-279380-1). Harcourt.
Levin, Marcia Lauter Obrasky see Martin, Marcia, pseud.
Levin, Marcia Lauter Obrasky (1918-), retold by see Sewell, Anna.
Levin, Marcia Lauter Obrasky (1918-)
--How the Clown Got His Smile. Martin, Marcia, pseud. Rev 2 ed. Hull, John (1919-), illus. LC 52-6681. unpaged. illus. 21 cm. (Wonder books, 566). c.1951. Wonder Books.
--Johnny Grows up. Martin, Marcia, pseud. Cummings, Alison, illus. LC 54-27002. unpaged. illus. 21 cm. (Wonder books, 618). 1954. Wonder Books.
--Let's Take a Ride. Martin, Marcia, pseud. Wilde, George A., illus. LC 53-29433. unpaged. illus. 20 cm. (Treasure books, 862). 1953. Treasure Books.
--A Little Cowboy's Christmas. Martin, Marcia, pseud. rev. 3 ed. Dert, Eleanor, illus. LC 51-38085. unpaged. illus. 21 cm. (Wonder books, 570). 1951. Wonder Books.
--The Merry Mailman. Martin, Marcia, pseud. Rev 2 ed. Wood, Ruth, illus. LC 53-40519. unpaged. illus. 21 cm. (Treasure books, 865). 1953. Treasure Books.
--The Merry Mailman Around the World. Martin, Marcia, pseud. Wood, Ruth, illus. LC 55-35944. unpaged. illus. 21 cm. (Treasure books, 892). 1955. Treasure Books.
--Peter Pan. Martin, Marcia, pseud. Derwinski, Beatrice, illus. LC 52-42175. (A Retelling of the Story, Peter and Wendy. Originally by Sir James Mathew). unpaged. illus. 21 cm. (Wonder Books, 597) "A...retelling of the...story, Peter and Wendy...by J. M. Barrie."). 1952. Wonder Books.
--Sonny the Bunny. Martin, Marcia, pseud. Seiden, Art, illus. LC 52-8223. unpaged. illus. 21 cm. (Wonder books, 591). 1952. Wonder Books.
--Tom Corbett's Wonder Book of Space. Martin, Marcia, pseud. Vaughn, Frank E., illus. LC 53-29588. unpaged. illus. 21 cm. (Wonder books, 603). 1953. Wonder Books.
Levin, Marcia Obrasky see Martin, Marcia, pseud.
Levin, Marcia Obrasky (1918-), adapted by see Carroll, Lewis.
Levin, Meyer (1905-)
--If I Forgot Thee, a Picture Story of Modern Palestine. Goldman, P. & Alexander, Sasha, photos by LC 47-11955. 26cm. 143p. 1947. Viking Press.
Levin, Yehuda Harry (1907-)
--Miriam Comes Home: A Story of Our Israel Cousins. Levin, Ruth, illus. McGrath, Earl J., frwd. by. LC 53-9499. 163p. illus. 22cm. 1953. L. C. Page.
Levine, Abby, ed. see Brown, Drollene.
Levine, Abby, ed. see Sinclair, Tom.
Levine, Abby & Levine, Sarah
--Sometimes I Wish I Were Mindy. Sims, Blanche, illus. LC 85-15549. p. cm. 1986. (ISBN 0-8075-7542-9). A. Whitman & Co.
Levine, Betty Krasne (1933-)
--The Great Burgerland Disaster. LC 80-36713. 104 p. 22cm. 1981, c.1980. (ISBN 0-689-30815-9). Atheneum.
--Hawk High. Jefferson, Louise E, illus. LC 79-22668. (Illus.). 104 p. 22cm. 1980. (ISBN 0-689-30748-9). Atheneum.
--Hex House. Marshall, Daniel, illus. LC 73-5485. (Illus.). 157 p. 22cm. 1973. (ISBN 0-06-023801-1). (ISBN 0-06-023802-X). Harper & Row.
Levine, Caroline Anne (1942-)
--Knockout Knock Knocks. Maestro, Giulio (1942-), illus. 1978. Dutton.
--The Silly Kid Joke Book. Maestro, Giulio (1942-), illus. LC 82-17727. p. cm. c.1983. (ISBN 0-525-44039-9). Dutton.
--Silly School Riddles and Other Classroom Crack-Ups. Munsinger, Lynn (1951-), illus. LC 84-17300. (Illus.). 32 p. 22cm. 1984. (ISBN 0-8075-7359-0). A. Whitman.
Levine, David (1926-), selected by.
--The Fables of Aesop. Levine, David (1926-), illus. Gregory, Patrick & Gregory, Justina, trs. (Illus.). 108p. 1984. (ISBN 0-87645-074-5, Pub. by Gambit). (ISBN 0-87645-116-4). Harvard Common Pr.
Levine, Edna Sarah
--Little Nemo in Slumberland. McCay, Winsor (1869-1934), illus. LC 41-19426. 63 p. illus. (part col.) 17 x 14 cm. c.1941. Rand McNally & Company.
Levine, Edna Simon
--Lisa & Her Soundless World. Kamen, Gloria (1923-), illus. LC 73-14819. (Illus.). 32p. (ps-3). 1974. (ISBN 0-87705-104-6). Human Sci Pr.
--Lisa and Her Soundless World. Kamen, Gloria (1923-), illus. (gr. 3-5). 1984. Human Sciences.
Levine, Joan Goldman
--A Bedtime Story. 1st ed. Owens, Gail, illus. LC 74-23715. (Illus.). 32 p. 19 x 24cm. 1975. (ISBN 0-525-26290-3). Dutton.
--The Santa Claus Mystery. 1st ed. Owens, Gail, illus. LC 75-6565. (Illus.). 39 p. 23cm. 1975. (ISBN 0-525-38795-1). Dutton.
Levine, Joel
--The Zonk who wanted a Friend. N.D. Vantage Press Inc .
Levine, Milton, jt. auth. see Seligmann, Jean.
Levine, Milton I. & Seligmann, Jean H.
--A Baby is Born. Wilin, Eloise, illus. 1962. Golden Press.
Levine, Rhoda
--Arthur. 1st ed. Aison, Everett, illus. LC 62-736921. unpaged. illus. 24c26cm. 1962. Atheneum.
--Harrison Loved His Umbrella. Kuskin, Karla Seidman (1932-), illus. LC 64-11896. 18cm. 46p. 1964. (ISBN 0-689-20523-6). (ISBN 0-689-20225-3). Atheneum Publishers.
--He Was There from the Day We Moved in. Gorey, Edward St. John (1925-), illus. LC 68-18197. (Illus.). 24 p. 20cm. 1969, c.1968. Harlin Quist.
--Herbert Situation. Ross, Larry (1943-), illus. (gr. k up). N.D. (ISBN 0-531-04024-0). (ISBN 0-531-05024-6). Quist.
--Quiet Story. 1st ed. Richards, Rosalie, illus. LC 69-10548. unpaged. illus. 16 cm. 1963. Atheneum.
--Three ladies beside the sea. Gorey, Edward St. John (1925-), illus. LC 63-10370. 19 x 22cm. 34p. 1963. Atheneum.
Levine, Sarah, jt. auth. see Levine, Abby.
Levine, Suarti & Stuart-Fox, David, eds.
--Favourite Stories from Bali. (Favourite Stories Ser.). 1978. (ISBN 0-686-60354-0). Heinemann Ed.
Levine-Provost, Gail, jt. auth. see Provost, Gary.
Levinger, Elma C. Ehrlich, Mrs. (1887-1958)
--Beautiful Garden & Other Bible Tales. Robinson, Jessie Berkowitz, illus. (Illus.). (gr. 3-5). N.D. (ISBN 0-8197-0253-6). Bloch.
--Benjamin's Book About His Family. Wiese, Kurt (1887-1974), illus. LC 33-11089. x p., 1 l., 269 p. col. front., illus. 20 1/2 cm. 1933. Doubleday, Doran & Company, Inc.
--The Golden Door: Stories of the Jews Who Had a Part in the Making of America. Fiedler, Israel A., illus. LC 47-22180. xii, 204 p. illus. 21 cm. 1947. Bloch Publishing Company.
--More Stories of the New Land. LC 39-12536. (Illus.). 19cm. vii, 165p. 1938. Bloch Publishing Co.
--The New Land, Stories of Jews who had a part in the Making of Our Country. LC 20-10306. 19cm. 175p. 1920. Bloch publishing company.
--Pilgrims to Palestine: And Other Stories. LC 40-100831. x, 274 p., 1 l. plates. 19 cm. 1940. The Jewish Publication Socity of America.
--Playmates in Egypt: And Other Stories. LC 20-21482. 130 p. 19 1/2 cm. 1920. The Jewish Publication Society of America.
--Tales of Old and New. LC 26-15183. 247 p. 19 cm. 1926. Bloch Publishing Company, Inc.
--Think and Thank. N.D. Harlem Book Co.
Levinson, Marilyn
--And Don't Bring Jeremy. De Groat, Diane (1947-), illus. LC 84-22484. (Illus.). 122 p. 22cm. c.1985. (ISBN 0-03-002999-6). Holt, Rinehart, and Winston.
Levinson, Nancy Smiler (1938-)
--Make a Wish. 144p. (Orig.). (gr. 7 up). 1982. (ISBN 0-590-32444-6, Wildfire). Scholastic Inc.
--The Ruthie Greene Show. LC 85-13096. p. cm. c.1985. (ISBN 0-525-67172-2). Dutton.
--Silent Fear. Schroeder, Howard, ed. Hanson, Tracye, illus. LC 81-3301. p. cm. (Roundup). c.1981. (ISBN 0-89686-154-6). (ISBN 0-89686-162-7). Crestwood House.
--World of Her Own. library ed. Feller, Gene, illus. LC 80-81791. (Illus.). 122 p., 1 leaf of plates. 22cm. c.1981. (ISBN 0-8178-0014-X). Harvey House.
Levinson, Riki
--Watch the Stars Come Out. Goode, Diane (1949-), illus. LC 84-28672. (Illus.). 32 p. 29cm. c.1985. (ISBN 0-525-44205-7). Dutton. **Award: (ALA).**
Levitin, Sonia (1934-)
--All the Cats in the World. 1st ed. Robinson, Charles (1931-), illus. LC 81-20036. p. cm. c.1982. (ISBN 0-15-202396-8). Harcourt Brace Jovanovich.
--Beyond Another Door. Heimdahl, Ralph (1909-) & Lorencz, William, illus. LC 76-41184. 174 p. 22cm. 1977. (ISBN 0-689-30569-9). Atheneum.
--The Fisherman and the Bird. Livingston, Francis, illus. LC 81-18840. (Illus.). 41 p. 26cm. 1982. (ISBN 0-395-31860-2). Parnassus Press.
--Jason and the Money Tree. 1st ed. Porter, Patricia Grant, illus. LC 73-17939. (Illus.). 121 p. 21cm. 1974. (ISBN 0-15-239820-1). Harcourt Brace Jovanovich.
--Journey to America. Robinson, Charles (1931-), illus. LC 70-98616. (Illus.). 150 p. 22cm. (Aladdin Book, A27). 1973, c.1970. Atheneum.
--The Mark of Conte. 1st ed. Negron, Bill, illus. LC 75-23041. (Illus.). 226 p. 23cm. 1976. (ISBN 0-689-30506-0). Atheneum.
--The No-Return Trail. LC 77-88964. 154 p. 21cm. c.1978. (ISBN 0-15-257545-6). Harcourt Brace Jovanovich.
--Nobody Stole the Pie. 1st ed. Krahn, Fernando (1935-), illus. LC 79-90032. (Illus.). 32 p. 26cm. (Voyager/HJB book). c.1980. (ISBN 0-15-257469-7). (ISBN 0-15-665959-X). Harcourt Brace Jovanovich.
--Rita, the Weekend Rat. 1st ed. Shortall, Leonard W., illus. LC 73-134815. (Illus.). 124 p. 22cm. 1971. Atheneum.
--Roanoke: A Novel of the Lost Colony. Gretzer, John, illus. LC 73-76323. (Illus.). 213 p. 25cm. 1973. (ISBN 0-689-30114-6). Atheneum.
--A Single Speckled Egg. Larrecq, John Maurice (1926-1980), illus. LC 75-4189. (Illus.). 34 p. 27cm. c.1976. (ISBN 0-87466-074-2). (ISBN 0-87466-075-0). Parnassus Press.
--Smile Like a Plastic Daisy. LC 83-15616. 192p. (gr. 8 up). 1984. (ISBN 0-689-31024-2). ATheneum.
--A Sound to Remember. 1st ed. Lisowski, Gabriel (1946-), illus. LC 79-87522. (Illus.). 31 p. 26cm. c.1979. (ISBN 0-15-277248-0). Harcourt Brace Jovanovich.
--Who Owns the Moon?. Larrecq, John Maurice (1926-1980), illus. LC 73-77124. (Illus.). 27cm. 34p (Pub. by Parnassus). (ps-3). 1973. (ISBN 0-395-27657-8). (ISBN 0-87466-005-X). (ISBN 0-395-27656-X). HM. **Award: (ALA).**
--The Year of Sweet Senior Insanity. 11 x 12 1/2. 208p. Repr. of 1982 ed (Pub. by Atheneum). (15 pt.). (gr. 8-9). N.D. Am Printing Hse.
--The Year of Sweet Senior Insanity. LC 81-8081. 192 p. 22cm. 1982. (ISBN 0-689-30883-3). Atheneum.
Levitt, Betsy Ratner
--Baldy the Eagle. Melanson, Donya, illus. LC 75-138505. (Illus.). 28 p. 22cm. 1971. (ISBN 0-8059-1520-6). Dorrance.
Levitt, Harry
--Goodness Gracious: The Story of a Very Special Whale. 1st ed. Patina, Maureen, illus. LC 80-52245. (Illus.). 60 p. 23cm. 1980. (ISBN 0-934588-02-3). Ranger Associates.
Levitt, Saul (1911-1977)
--Jim Thorpe, All American. (Orig.). 1980. (ISBN 0-87602-237-9). Anchorage.
Levoy, Myron
--Alan and Naomi. LC 76-41522. 192 p. 22cm. c.1977. (ISBN 0-06-023799-6). (ISBN 0-06-023800-3). Harper & Row. **Award: (BGH).**
--The Hanukkah of Great-Uncle Otto. Ruff, Donna, illus. LC 84-12635. (Illus.). 48 p. 24cm. c.1984. (ISBN 0-8276-0242-1). Jewish Publication Society of America.
--Penny Tunes and Princesses. 1st ed. Keats, Ezra Jack (1916-1983), illus. LC 72-76517. (Illus.). 31 p. 27cm. 1972. (ISBN 0-06-023797-X). (ISBN 0-06-023797-X). Harper & Row.
--A Shadow Like a Leopard. LC 79-2812. 184 p. 22cm. c.1981. (ISBN 0-06-023816-X). (ISBN 0-06-023817-8). Harper & Row.
--Three Friends. LC 83-47713. c.1984. (ISBN 0-06-023826-7). Harper & Row.
--The Witch of Fourth Street, and Other Stories. 1st ed. Lisowski, Gabriel (1946-), illus. LC 74-183174. (Illus.). 110 p. 22cm. 1972. (ISBN 0-06-023795-3). (ISBN 0-06-023796-1). Harper & Row.
Levy, Elizabeth (1942-)
--The Bride. LC 84-43013. (Illus.). 60 p. 29cm. (Movie Storybooks). c.1985. (ISBN 0-394-97371-2). (ISBN 0-394-87371-8). Random House.
--Come Out Smiling. LC 80-68734. 186 p. 22cm. c.1981. (ISBN 0-440-01378-X). Delacorte Press.
--The Computer That Said Steal Me. LC 83-5509. p. cm. 1983. (ISBN 0-590-07860-7). Four Winds Press.
--The Dani Trap. LC 84-9025. 144p. (gr. 5 up). 1984. (ISBN 0-688-03867-0, Morrow Junior Books). Morrow.
--A Different Twist. 128p. (Orig.). (gr. 4-6). 1984. (ISBN 0-590-33229-5, Apple Paperbacks). Scholastic Inc.
--Dracula Is a Pain in the Neck. 1st ed. Gerstein, Mordicai, illus. LC 82-47707. p. cm. c.1983. (ISBN 0-06-023822-4). (ISBN 0-06-023823-2). Harper & Row.
--Father Murphy's First Miracle. LC 82-20516. p. cm. c.1983. (ISBN 0-394-85810-7). Random House.
--Frankenstein Moved in on the Fourth Floor. 1st ed. Gerstein, Mordicai, illus. LC 78-19830. (Illus.). 57 p. 24cm. c.1979. (ISBN 0-06-023810-0). (ISBN 0-06-023811-9). Harper & Row.
--Lizzie Lies a Lot. Wallner, John C (1945-), illus. LC 75-32914. p. cm. c.1976. (ISBN 0-440-04919-9). (ISBN 0-440-04920-2). Delacorte Press.
--Nice Little Girls. Gerstein, Mordicai, illus. LC 73-15394. (Illus.). 48 p. 26cm. 1974. (ISBN 0-440-06207-1). (ISBN 0-440-06128-8). Delacorte Press.
--Running Out of Magic with Houdini. LC 80-28427. p. cm. c.1981. (ISBN 0-394-94685-5). (ISBN 0-394-84685-0). Knopf : Distributed by Random House.
--Running Out of Time. Mars, Witold Tadeusz J. (1912-), illus. LC 79-28064. (Illus.). 121 p. 20cm. (Capers). c.1980. (ISBN 0-394-84422-X). (ISBN 0-394-94422-4). Knopf : Distributed by Random House.
--The Shadow Nose. Gerstein, Mordicai, illus. LC 83-7925. (Illus.). 55 p. 24cm. 1983. (ISBN 0-688-02410-6). (ISBN 0-688-02411-4). Morrow.
--Something Queer at the Ballpark. Gerstein, Mordicai, illus. LC 74-16332. (gr. 1-3). 1979. Delacorte.
--Something Queer at the Ballpark: A Mystery. Gerstein, Mordicai, illus. LC 74-16332. (Illus.). 48 p. 26cm. 1975. (ISBN 0-440-05992-5). (ISBN 0-440-05993-3). Delacorte Press.
--Something Queer at the Haunted School. Gerstein, Mordicai, illus. LC 81-1940. (Illus.). 46 p. 28cm. 1982. (ISBN 0-440-08349-4). (ISBN 0-440-08355-9). Delacorte Press.
--Something Queer at the Lemonade Stand. Gerstein, Mordicai, illus. LC 81-69666. (Illus.). 47 p. 28cm. 1982. (ISBN 0-440-07859-8). (ISBN 0-440-07878-4). Delacorte Press.
--Something Queer at the Library. Gerstein, Mordicai, illus. LC 76-49906. (Illus.). (gr. 1-3). 1979. Delacorte.
--Something Queer at the Library: A Mystery. Gerstein, Mordicai, illus. LC 76-49906. (Illus.). 47 p. 27cm. c.1977. (ISBN 0-440-08127-0). (ISBN 0-440-08128-9). Delacorte Press.
--Something Queer Is Going on. Gerstein, Mordicai, illus. LC 72-7959. 27cm. 48p. (ps-3). 1973. Delacorte.
--Something Queer Is Going on: A Mystery. Gerstein, Mordicai, illus. LC 72-7959. (Illus.). 48p. (gr. 1-4). 1973. Delacorte.
--Something Queer on Vacation. Gerstein, Mordicai, illus. LC 78-72858. (gr. 1-3). 1980. Delacorte.
--Something Queer on Vacation: A Mystery. Gerstein, Mordicai, illus. LC 78-72858. (Illus.). 48 p. 26cm. c.1980. (ISBN 0-440-08346-X). (ISBN 0-440-08347-8). Delacorte Press.
--The Tryouts. Hann, Jacquie (1951-), illus. LC 78-22125. (Illus.). 102 p. 22cm. c.1979. (ISBN 0-590-07487-3). Four Winds Press.
Levy, Elizabeth (1942-), adapted by.
--Return of the Jedi. (Illus.). 72p. (Step-Up Movie Adventures Ser.). (gr. 1-3). 1983. (ISBN 0-394-86117-5). (ISBN 0-394-96117-X). Random.
Levy, Harry (1905-)
--The Bombero: Tales from Latin America. Simon, Howard (1903-1979), illus. LC 43-15649. 5 p. l., 3-86, 1 p., 1 l. incl. col. front., illus. col. plates. 21 cm. 1943. A. A. Knopf.
--The Burro That Learned to Dance. Simon, Howard (1903-1979), illus. 47 p. illus. (part col.) 17 x 22 1/2 cm. 1942. A. A. Knopf.
--The Dog That Wanted to Whistle. Simon, Howard (1903-1979), illus. LC 41-722146. 31 p. illus. 21 x 17 1/2 cm. 1940. Lothrop, Lee & Shepard Co.

Lewis, Hugh

--The Gladiators' Revolt: A Story of the Uprising of the Slaves in Italy in 73 B.C. LC 33-32923. 3 p. l., 3-315 p. illus. (map) 19 1/2 cm. c.1933. H. Holt and Company.

Lewis, Janet (1899-)

--The Friendly Adventures of Ollie Ostrich. Turpin, Fay, illus. N.D. Doubleday Page & Co.

--Keiko's Bubble. 1st ed. Mizumura, Kazue, illus. LC 61-126061. 62p. illus. 25cm. 1961. Doubleday.

Lewis, Jean, jt. auth. see Hanna-Barbera Productions.

Lewis, Jean, ed. see Fornatora, Nancy.

Lewis, Jean (1924-)

--Alvin and the Chipmunks and the Deep Sea Blues. (Illus.). 1966. Whitman Publishing.

--Bamm-Bamm and Pebbles Flintstone. (Illus.). 1963. Artist & Writer's Press.

--Benji the Detective. Goldsborough, June (1923-), illus. (Illus.). (Tell-a-Tale Readers). (gr. k-3). N.D. (ISBN 0-307-68640-X, Whitman). Western Pub.

--Benjie, the Detective. (Illus.). 1978. Western Publishing.

--Boo Boo Bear and the V. I. V. (Illus.). 1965. Whitman Publishing.

--Bugs Bunny: Too Many Carrots. Alvarado, Peter, illus. (Illus.). 24p. (ps-4). 1977. (ISBN 0-307-60145-5, Golden Pr). Western Pub.

--Bullwinkle's Casserole. (Illus.). 1975. Western Publishing.

--Doctor Leo's Pet Patients. Madden, Donald B. (1927-), illus. LC 71-142982. (Illus.). 47 p. 25cm. 1971. American Heritage Press.

--The Flintstones at the Circus. (Illus.). 1963. Whitman Publishing.

--The Flintstone's Picnic Panic. (Illus.). 1965. Whitman Publishing.

--Frankenstein Junior and the Devilish Double. (Illus.). 1968. Whitman Publishing.

--Gumby and Pokey to the Rescue. (Illus.). 1969. Western Publishing.

--Hong Kong Phooey and the Fortune Cookie Caper. (Illus.). 1975. Western Publishing.

--Hoppity Hooper vs. Skippity Snooper. authorized. De Santis, George, illus. LC 66-9065. (Illus.). 1 v. (unpaged. 16cm. (Tell-a-tale books). 1966. Whitman Pub. Co.

--Hot Dog. (Silver Library). N.D. (ISBN 0-448-04095-6). Grosset & Dunlap.

--Jane and the Mandarin's Secret. 1st ed. Burns, Howard M., illus. LC 77-98185. (Illus.). 72 p. 23cm. 1970. Hawthorn Books.

--Kathi and Hash San and the Case of Measles. Collins, Muriel & Collins, Jim (1934-), illus. LC 72-3438. (Illus.). 62 p. 24cm. (Fledgling book). 1972. (ISBN 0-528-82630-1). (ISBN 0-528-82631-X). Rand McNally.

--Lassie and the Busy Morning. (Illus.). 1973. Western Publishing.

--Mickey Mouse and the Pet Show. (Illus.). 1976. Western Publishing.

--Mumbley to the Rescue. (Illus.). 1977. Western Publishing.

--Nancy and Sluggo and the Big Surprise. (Illus.). 1974. Western Publishing.

--The Road Runner and the Birds Watchers. (Illus.). 1968. Whitman Publishing.

--Santa's Runaway Elf. (Illus.). 1977. Western Publishing.

--Scooby Doo and the Haunted Dog House. (Illus.). 1975. Western Publishing.

--Scooby Doo and the Mystery Monster. (Illus.). 1975. Western Publishing.

--Scooby Doo and the Pirate Treasure. (Illus.). 1974. Western Publishing.

--The Sleeping Tree Mystery. (Illus.). 1975. Western Publishing.

--The Teddy Bear Clan from Evergreen Woods. Goldsborough, June (1923-), illus. (ps-2). 1983. (ISBN 0-448-47495-6, G&D). Putnam Pub Group.

--Tom and Jerry Scairdy Cat. (Illus.). 1969. Whitman Publishing.

--Tom and Jerry Under the Big Top. (Illus.). 1969. Whitman Publishing.

--Touche Turtle and the Fire Dog. (Illus.). 1963. Whitman Publishing.

--Wacky Witch and the Mystery of the King's Gold. (Illus.). 1973. Western Publishing.

--Wacky Witch and the Royal Birthday. (Illus.). 1971. Western Publishing.

Lewis, Jean (1924-), adapted by.

--The Absent-Minded Professor. (Illus.). 1968. Golden Press.

--Chitty Chitty Bang Bang. (Original Author: Ian Fleming, 1908-1964). (Illus.). 1968. GOlden Press.

--The Jungle Book. Disney, Walt, Studio, illus. LC 67-7258. (Original Author: Rudyard Kipling (1865-1936)). (Illus.). 25 p. 33cm. (Big golden book). 1967. Golden Press.

--Swiss Family Robinson. (Original Author: Johann David Wyss, 1743-1818). (Illus.). 1961. Artist and Writers Press.

--The Tortoise and the Hare. (Illus.). 1963. Whitman Publishing.

Lewis, Jocelyn

--The Adventures of Dorothy. Stone, Seymour M., illus. LC 3-27317. 19cm. 189p. 1903. The Outlook company.

Lewis, Judith Mary see Berrisford, Judith Mary, pseud.

Lewis, K. D.

--Flowers of Fate. (For the Little Tots). N.D. Paul Elder & Company Catalogue.

Lewis, La Rae M.

--Sardar & the King. Parr, Janice C., illus. LC 79-57207. (Illus.). 110p. (Orig.). (gr. k-7). 1980. (ISBN 0-934400-08-3). Landmark Bks.

Lewis, Laura

--Child's Garden of Verses. Crichlow, Ernest T. (1914-), illus. N.D. Pilot Pub Corp.

--Enter In. 1st ed. Crichlow, Ernest T. (1914-), illus. LC 59-12922. 31p. illus. 21cm. 1959. Pilot Pub. Corp.

Lewis, Lorna

--Puppy and the Cat. Dawson, Lucy, illus. LC 40-11710. 4 p. l., 44 p., 1 l. incl. front., illus. 22 1/2 x 21 cm. c.1940. Grosset & Dunlap.

Lewis, Luevester

--Jackie. 1st ed. Jolly, Cheryl, illus. LC 74-187913. (Illus.). 32 p. 14 x 22cm. 1970. Third World Press.

Lewis, Marjorie (1929-)

--The Boy Who Would Be a Hero. Dabcovich, Lydia, illus. LC 81-15147. (Illus.). 32 p. c.1982. (ISBN 0-698-20546-4). Coward, McCann & Geoghegan.

--Ernie and the Mile Long Muffler. Apple, Margot, illus. LC 82-1458. p. cm. c.1982. (ISBN 0-698-20557-X). Coward, McCann & Geoghegan.

--Wrongway Applebaum. Apple, Margot, illus. LC 84-3242. (Illus.). 64p. (gr. 3-6). 1984. (ISBN 0-698-20610-X, Coward). Putnam Pub Group.

Lewis, Mary

--The Foxfire King. Lewis, Richard William (1933-1966), illus. LC 66-142405. 1v. (unpaged) illus. 24cm. c.1966. Washburn.

--Halloween Kangaroo. (Illus.). 1964. David McKay Company Inc.

--The Halloween Kangaroo. Lewis, Richard William (1933-1966), illus. LC 64-19652. (Illus.). 1 v. (unpaged. 24cm. 1964. Washburn.

--Joey and the Fawn. Hall, H. Tom, illus. LC 67-14372. (Illus.). 32 p. 26cm. 1967. I. Washburn.

--Olle and the Wild Geese. (Illus.). 1964. David McKay Company Inc.

--Olle and the Wild Geese. Lewis, Richard William (1933-1966), illus. LC 64-12515. (Illus.). 144 p. 21cm. 1964. Washburn.

Lewis, Mary Christianna Milne see Brand, Christianna, pseud.

Lewis, Mary Christianna Milne (1907-)

--Danger Unlimited. Brand, Christianna, pseud. LC 48-10102. 184 p. 21 cm. (Junior Red badge mysteries). 1948. Dodd, Mead.

--Nurse Matilda. Brand, Christianna, pseud. Ardiozzone, Edward Jeffrey Irving (1900-1979), illus. LC 64-21702. 127 p. illus. 18 cm. 1st U.S. edition. 1964. Dutton.

--Nurse Matilda. Brand, Christianna, pseud. Ardizzone, Edward Jeffrey Irving (1900-1979), illus. 1980. (ISBN 0-8398-2604-4, Gregg). G K Hall.

--Nurse Matilda. Brand, Christianna, pseud. Ardizzone, Edward Jeffrey Irving (1900-1979), illus. Holtze, Sally Holmes, intro. by. LC 79-18085. (Illus.). 11, 127 p. 21cm. (Gregg Press Children's Literature Series). 1980, c.1964. (ISBN 0-8398-2604-4). Gregg Press.

--Nurse Matilda Goes to Hospital. Brand, Christianna, pseud. Ardizzone, Edward Jeffrey Irving (1900-1979), illus. 1974. Dutton.

--Nurse Matilda Goes to Town. Brand, Christianna, pseud. 1st ed. Ardizzone, Edward Jeffrey Irving (1900-1979), illus. LC 68-13416. (Illus.). 128 p. 18cm. 1968, c.1967. Dutton.

--Nurse Matilda Goes to Town. Brand, Christianna, pseud. Ardizzone, Edward Jeffrey Irving (1900-1979), illus. (Illus.). (gr. 2-5). 1968. (ISBN 0-525-36211-8). (ISBN 0-525-36212-6). Dutton.

Lewis, Mary Christianna Milne (1907-), ed.

--Naughty Children: An Anthology. Brand, Christianna, pseud. 1st ed. Ardizzone, Edward Jeffrey Irving (1900-1979), illus. LC 62-18692. 314 p. illus. 23 cm. 1st U.S. edition. 1963. Dutton.

Lewis, Mary R

--At the Zoo. LC 27-180597. 96 p. incl. col. front., col. illus. 15 1/2 cm. 1927. T. Nelson and Sons.

Lewis, Mildred D. see DeWitt, James, pseud.

Lewis, Mildred D (1912-)

--The Honorable Sword. Ghikas, Panos (1923-), illus. LC 60-9093. 179p. illus. 21cm. 1960. (ISBN 0-395-06886-X). Houghton, Mifflin.

Lewis, Milton

--David White, Crime Reporter. LC 58-9901. 235p. 21cm. (Dodd, Mead career books). 1958. Dodd, Mead.

Lewis, Mortimer Reis (1908-)

--Freddie. LC 54-41578. 63p. illus. 19cm. c.1954. R. Rosen Associates.

Lewis, Naomi

--The Butterfly Collector. Testa, Fulvio, illus. LC 78-26023. p. cm. 1979, c.1978. Prentice-Hall.

--Puffin. King, Deborah, illus. LC 83-23864. (Illus.). 32p. (gr. k-3). 1984. (ISBN 0-688-03783-6). (ISBN 0-688-03784-4). Lothrop.

Lewis, Naomi, ed.

--The Silent Playmate: A Collection of Doll Stories. Jones, Harold (1904-), illus. LC 80-27477. p. cm. 1st U.S. edition. 1981, c.1979. (ISBN 0-02-758590-5). Macmillan.

--The Snow Queen. Bogdanovic, Toma (1937-), illus. LC 68-17218. (Original Author: Hans Christian Andersen). (Illus.). 1 v. (unpaged). 1968, c.1967. Scroll Press.

--The Snow Queen. LeCain, Errol John (1941-), illus. LC 78-10462. (Original Author: Hans Christian Andersen). (Illus.). 32 p. 32cm. 1st U.S. edition. 1979. (ISBN 0-670-65378-0). Viking Press.

--Story of Aladdin. Wilkinson, Barry, illus. LC 75-133296. (Illus.). color ils. 48p. 24cm. 46p. 1st U.S. edition. (gr. k-3). 1970. (ISBN 0-8098-1177-4). Walck.

Lewis, Naomi, jt. auth. see Andersen, Hans Christian.

Lewis, Naomi, intro. by see Andersen, Hans Christian.

Lewis, Naomi, ed. see Bronte, Emily Jane.

Lewis, Naomi & Ross, Tony

--Hare & Badger go to Town. 32p. N.D. (ISBN 0-905478-94-0, Pub. by Andersen-Hutchinson England). State Mutual Bk.

Lewis, Oscar, ed. see Thompson, Harlan H.

Lewis, Ray

--Two Men Round the Moon. (Illus.). 48p. (gr. 1-5). 1974. (ISBN 0-682-47930-6). Exposition.

Lewis, Richard (1935-), ed. see Tagore, Rabindranath, Sir.

Lewis, Richard William (1933-1966)

--Summer Adventure. Lewis, Richard William (1933-1966), illus. LC 62-13325. (Illus.). 23cm. 105p. (gr. 2-6). 1962. (ISBN 0-06-023806-2). Har-Row.

Lewis, Richard (1935-), ed.

--I Breathe a New Song: Poems of the Eskimo. Oonark, illus. 1971. Simon.

--In a Spring Garden. Keats, Ezra Jack (1916-1983), illus. (Illus.). (gr. 4 up). 1965. Dial Bks Young.

--Journeys: Prose by Children of the English-Speaking World. LC 70-87882. (Illus.). 215 p. 21cm. 1969. Simon and Schuster.

--Luminous Landscape: Chinese Art & Poetry. LC 79-7691. (Illus.). 64p. (gr. 5 up). 1981. Doubleday.

--Miracles: Poems by Children of the English-Speaking World. LC 66-20248. (Illus.). 215 p. 21cm. 1966. Simon and Schuster. **Award: (ALA).**

--Miracles: Poems by Children of the English-Speaking World. LC 81-5639. (Illus.). 214 p. 20cm. (Fireside book). 1981, c.1966. (ISBN 0-671-42797-0). Simon and Schuster.

--The Moment of Wonder: A Collection of Chinese & Japanese Poetry. (Illus.). (gr. 7 up). 1963. (ISBN 0-8037-5788-3). Dial. **Award: (ALA).**

--Muse of the Round Sky: Lyric Poetry of Ancient Greece. Barnstone, Willis (1927-), tr. LC 79-84136. (Illus.). photos. biographical notes. index. 128p. (gr. 3-12). 1969. (ISBN 0-671-65075-0, Juveniles). S&S.

--Of This World: A Poet's Life in Poetry. Buttfield, Helen, photos by. LC 68-28739. (Illus.). photos. 96p. (gr. 7-12). 1968. Dial.

--Out of the Earth I Sing: Poetry and Songs of Primitive Peoples of the World. 1968. Norton.

--Still Waters of the Air: Poems by Three Modern Spanish Poets. Stewart, Arvis L., illus. (Eng & Span). (Illus.). 30 photos. 96p. (gr. 9 up). 1970. Dial.

--There Are Two Lives. LC 72-123242. (Illus.). 96 p. 21cm. 1970. (ISBN 0-671-65141-2). Simon and Schuster.

--There Are Two Lives: Poems by Children of Japan. Kimura, Haruna, tr. LC 72-123242. (Illus.). 21cm. 96p. 1970. (ISBN 0-671-65141-2, Juveniles). (ISBN 0-671-65142-0). S&S.

--The Way of Silence: The Prose & Poetry of Basho. 112p. (gr. 8 up). 1970. Dial Bks Young.

--The Wind and the Rain: Children's Poems. Buttfield, Helen, photos by. LC 68-18331. (Illus.). 44 p. 31cm. 1968. Simon & Schuster.

Lewis, Shari (1934-)

--Dear Shari. LC 63-20056. 1 v. (unpaged) illus. 22 cm. 1963. Stein and Day.

--Impossible, Unless You Know How. Clarke, Victoria, illus. LC 79-2357. p. cm. (Kids-only club). 1979. (ISBN 0-03-049681-0). (ISBN 0-03-049686-1). Holt, Rinehart and Winston.

--The Kids-Only Club Book. LC 76-10507. (Illus.). 290p. (gr. 1-6). 1976. (ISBN 0-87477-054-8). (ISBN 0-87477-072-6). J P Tarcher.

--Spooky Stuff. (Illus.). (Kids-Only Club Books). (gr. 3-6). 1979. (ISBN 0-03-049671-3). (ISBN 0-03-049676-4). HR&W.

--The Tell It-Make It Book. Boze, Calvin, illus. LC 72-86656. (Illus.). vii, 113 p. 17 x 25cm. 1972. (ISBN 0-87477-003-3). J. P. Tarcher; Distributed by Hawthorn Books.

Lewis, Shari (1934-) & O'Kun, Lan

--One-Minute Bedtime Stories. 1st ed. Cumings, Art, illus. LC 79-8024. (Illus.). 47 p. 27cm. (Doubleday Balloon Books). c.1982. (ISBN 0-385-15292-2). Doubleday.

Lewis, Shari (1934-) & Reinach, Jacquelyn

--The Headstart Book of Be Nimble & Be Quick. Salisbury, Kent & Zanazanian, Adrina, illus. LC 68-28842. (Illus.). 59 p. 27cm. 1968. McGraw-Hill.

Lewis, Sinclair see Graham, Tom, pseud.

Lewis, Sinclair (1885-1951)

--Arrowsmith. LC 25-78. (Modern Classic Ser.). (gr. 10 up). 1949. (ISBN 0-15-108216-2). HarBraceJ.

--Hike and the Aeroplane. Graham, Tom, pseud. Hutchins, Arthur, illus. LC 12-17967. 4 p. l., 275 p. col. front., col. plates. 19 1/2 cm. 1912. Frederick A. Stokes Company.

--Main Street. LC 20-18934. (Modern Classic Ser.). (gr. 10 up). 1950. (ISBN 0-15-155547-8). HarBraceJ.

Lewis, Thomas Parker (1936-)

--Call for Mr. Sniff. Woldin, Beth Weiner (1955-), illus. LC 79-2679. (Illus.). 62 p. 23cm. (I can read mystery). c.1981. (ISBN 0-06-023814-3). (ISBN 0-06-023815-1). Harper & Row.

--Clipper Ship. Sandin, Joan (1942-), illus. LC 77-11858. (Illus.). 63 p. 22cm. (I can read history book). c.1978. (ISBN 0-06-023808-9). (ISBN 0-06-023809-7). Harper & Row.

--The Dragon Kite. 1st ed. Le Cain, Errol John (1941-), illus. LC 72-76578. (Illus.). 64 p. 24cm. 1973, c.1974. (ISBN 0-03-091961-4). Holt, Rinehart and Winston.

--Hill of Fire. Sandin, Joan (1942-), illus. LC 70-121802. (Illus.). 63 p. 23cm. (I can read history book). 1971. (ISBN 0-06-023804-6). (ISBN 0-06-444040-0). Harper & Row.

--Mr. Sniff and the Motel Mystery. Weiner, Beth Lee, illus. LC 82-47729. (Illus.). 64 p. 23cm. (An I Can Read Book). (gr. k-3). c.1984. (ISBN 0-06-023824-0). (ISBN 0-06-023825-9). Harper & Row.

Lewis, William Franklin (1912-) & Corchia, Alfred J.

--Kerry, the Fire Engine Dog. Grider, Dorothy (1915-), illus. LC 49-10171. 21cm. 83p. (A Rand McNally book-elf book). 1949. Rand McNally & Co.

Lewisohn, Adele, tr. see Hertzog, Rudolph.

Lewiton, Mina see Simon, Mina Lewiton.

Lewiton, Mina (1904-1970)

--A Cup of Courage. LC 48-9662. 244 p. 21 cm. (Youth today series). 1948. D. McKay Co.

--Divided Heart. Simon, Howard (1903-1979), illus. (Illus.). (gr. 7-11). N.D. (ISBN 0-679-25037-9). McKay.

--Elizabeth and the Young Stranger. 1961. David McKay Company Inc.

--Elizabeth & the Young Stranger. (Illus.). (gr. 6 up). 1961. (ISBN 0-8382-0226-8). Hale.

--Elizabeth & the Young Stranger. (gr. 9-12). N.D. McKay.

--Humphrey on the Town. Simon, Howard (1903-1979), illus. LC 67-19767. (Illus.). 16 drawings. 96p. (gr. 2-6). 1971. Delacorte.

--Rachel. Simon, Howard (1903-1979), illus. (Illus.). (gr. 4-6). 1954. (ISBN 0-531-01908-X). Watts.

--Rachel and Herman. N.D. E . M. Hale and Co.

--Rachel & Herman. Simon, Howard (1903-1979), illus. (Illus.). (gr. 4-6). 1966. (ISBN 0-531-01774-5). Watts.

--That Bad Carlos. Simon, Howard (1903-1979), illus. LC 64-12972. (Illus.). (gr. 2-6). 1964. (ISBN 0-06-023846-1, HarpJ). Har-Row.

--Young Girl Going Out of the Door. LC 68-27740. 224p. 21cm. (gr. 7 up). 1969. Delacorte.

Lewiton, Mind see Simon, Mina Lewiton.

Lewitt, Jan (1907-)

--The Vegetabull. LC 56-6360. (Illus.). unpage. 28cm. 1956. Harcourt, Brace.

Lexau, Joan M. see Nodset, Joan L., pseud.

Lexau, Joan M

--Archimedes Takes a Bath. Murdocca, Salvatore, illus. LC 69-11084. (Illus.). 56 p. 23cm. 1969. Crowell.

--Becky & the Bookworm. Brooks, Andrea, illus. LC 78-73526. (Illus.). (gr. 2-5). N.D. Dandelion Pr.

--Benjie. 1964. (ISBN 0-8382-0068-0, Cadmus Books). E. M. Hale and Company.

--Benjie. Bolognese, Donald Alan (1934-), illus. LC 64-12294. (Illus.). 38 p. 19 x 26cm. 1964. Dial Press.

--Benjie on His Own. Bolognese, Donald Alan (1934-), illus. LC 72-102830. (Illus.). 38 p. 19 x 26cm. 1970. Dial Press.

--Cathy Is Company. Aliki, pseud. (1929-), illus. Brandenburg, Aliki Liacouras. LC 61-12907. 22cm. (gr. k-3). 1961. Dial.

--The Christmas Secret. Bolognese, Donald Alan (1934-), illus. (Illus.). (gr. k-3). 1973. (ISBN 0-590-04202-5, Schol Pap). Scholastic Inc.

--School Daze. Repr. (Starbright Editions). (gr. 4-6). 1973. Schol Bk Serv.

Liebers, Ruth (1910-)

--Time for Breakfast. 32p. 1965. Pitman Publishing.

Liebers, Ruth (1910-) & Rothenberg, Lillian (1922-)

--Hector Goes to School. Stinemetz, Morgan, illus. LC 63-7972. (Illus.). (gr. k-3). 1963. (ISBN 0-687-16792-2). Abingdon.

--Stevie Finds A Way. N.D. E. M. Hale & Co.

--Stevie Finds a Way. Doremus, Robert (1913-), illus. N.D. Abingdon Press.

Lieberthal, Jules M

--Muggsy: The Make Believe Puppy. Neebe, William, illus. LC 56-8339. unpaged. illus. 21cm. (Rand McNally elf book, 537). c.1956. Rand McNally.

--Slowpoke: The Lazy Little Puppy. Neebe, William, illus. LC 57-825139. unpaged. illus. 21cm. (Rand McNally elf book, 582). c.1957. Rand McNally.

--Snoopy, the Nosey Little Puppy. Neebe, William, illus. LC 55-10120. unpaged illus. 21cm. (Rand McNally elf book, 509). c.1955. Rand McNally.

Lieblich, Irene, jt. auth. see Singer, Isaac Bashevis.

Liebman, Arthur (1926-), compiled by.

--Classic Crime Stories. 274p. (Masterworks of Mystery Ser.). (gr. 7-12). 1975. (ISBN 0-8239-0310-9). (ISBN 0-686-67135-X). Rosen Group.

--Science Fiction: Creators and Pioneers. LC 78-31599. p. cm. (Science Fiction Ser.). 1979. (ISBN 0-8239-0493-8). Richards Rosen Press.

--Science Fiction: The Best of Yesterday. LC 80-12746. 211 p. 22cm. (Worlds of science fiction). (Series: Worlds of Science Fiction.). 1980. R. Rosen Press.

--Tales of Espionage & Intrigue. 274p. (Masterworks of Mystery Ser). (gr. 7-12). 1976. (ISBN 0-8239-0311-7). (ISBN 0-685-66609-3). Rosen Group.

--Tales of Horror & the Supernatural. LC 73-94058. 22cm. 274p. (Masterworks of Mystery Ser.). (gr. 7-12). 1975. (ISBN 0-8239-0299-4). (ISBN 0-686-67049-3). Rosen Group.

--Thirteen Classic Detective Stories. LC 73-84994. 192p. (Masterworks of Mystery Ser.). (gr. 7-12). 1974. (ISBN 0-8239-0290-0). (ISBN 0-686-66890-1). Rosen Group.

Liebow, Gina

--Juanito of the Tower. Liebow, Harold, photos by. LC 67-805. 64p. illus. 26cm. 1966. McGraw.

--Pierre and the Challenge: A French Family Story. LC 67-20176. 62 p. 26cm. 1967. McGraw-Hill.

Lief, Luise K.

--Scott & Todd & the Soccer Gang. Lief, Luise K., illus. (Illus.). 160p. (gr. 2-7). 1980. (ISBN 0-935808-01-9). Magic Carpet.

Liefde, Jacob De see De Liefde, Jacob.

Liefde, John De see De Liefde, John.

Lientz, Thelma

--The Black Box. LC 29-11021. 249 p. front. 20 cm. (Mystery and adventure series for girls). c.1929. A. L. Burt Company.

--Kay and the Secret Code. LC 30-116230. 254 p. front. 20 cm. (Mystery and adventure series for girls). c.1930. A. L. Burt Company.

Liers, Emil Ernest (1890-)

--A Beaver's Story. Sherin, Ray, illus. LC 58-14708. 192p. illus. 22cm. 1958. Viking Press.

--A Black Bear's Story. Sherin, Ray, illus. LC 62-9629. 192p. illus. 22cm. 1962. (ISBN 0-670-17058-5). Viking Press.

--A Mink's Story. LC 78-10374. 126 p. 17cm. (Orion). c.1979. Southern Pub. Association.

--Otter's Story. Palazzo, Tony (1905-1970), illus. (Illus.). (gr. 4-6). 1953. (ISBN 0-670-52976-1). (ISBN 0-670-52976-1). Viking Pr.

Liesching, F. F.

--Through Peril to Fortune, 1 of 7 vols. (Illus.). (The Young Folks' Library). N.D. Cassell, Petter, Galpin.

Liffring, Joan Louise (1929-)

--Dee and Curtis on a Dairy Farm. Liffring, Joan Louise (1929-), photos by. LC 57-11025. 64p. illus. 26cm. (Farm life series). 1957. (ISBN 0-695-42065-8). Follett Pub. Co.

--Jim and Alan on a Cotton Farm. Liffring, Joan Louise (1929-), photos by. LC 59-10274. 64p. illus. 26cm. (Farm life series). 1959. (ISBN 0-695-44541-3). Follett Pub. Co.

--Mike and Dick on a Washington Apple Farm. Liffring, Joan Louise (1929-), photos by. LC 62-13557. 64p. illus. 27cm. (Farm life series). 1962. Follett Pub. Co.

--Ray and Stevie on a Corn Belt Farm. Liffring, Joan Louise Louise (1929-), photos by. LC 56-7450. 63p. illus. 27cm. 1956. (ISBN 0-695-47490-1). Follett Pub. Co.

Lifschultz, Burton Benjamin, tr. see Geijerstam, Gustaf Af.

Lifschultz, Burton Benjamin, tr. see Sand, George.

Lifton, Betty Jean (1926-)

--The Cock and the Ghost Cat. 1st ed. Akino, Fuku (1908-), illus. LC 65-21709. (Illus.). 32 p. 25cm. 1965. Atheneum. **Award: (ALA).**

--The Dwarf Pine Tree. 1st ed. Akino, Fuku (1908-), illus. LC 63-9299. (Illus.). 37 p. 25cm. 1963. Atheneum. **Award: (ALA).**

--Good Night, Orange Monster. 1st ed. Szekeres, Cyndy (1933-), illus. LC 72-75275. (Illus.). 46 p. 24cm. 1972. Atheneum.

--I'm Still Me. LC 80-24372. 243 p. 22cm. c.1981. (ISBN 0-394-84783-0). Knopf : Distributed by Random House.

--Jaguar, My Twin. Leggett, Ann, illus. LC 76-4475. (Illus.). x, 114 p. 22cm. 1976. Atheneum.

--Joji and the Amanojaku. 1st ed. Mitsui, Eiichi (1920-), illus. LC 65-11009. (Illus.). 1 v. (umpaged. 26cm. 1965. Norton.

--Joji and the Dragon. Mitsui, Eiichi (1920-), illus. LC 57-7185. (Illus.). 64 p. 27cm. (Morrow junior books). 1957. Morrow.

--Joji and the Fog. Mitsui, Eiichi (1920-), illus. LC 59-5049. 1959. (ISBN 0-8382-0389-2, Cadmus Books). E. M. Hale And Company.

--Joji and the Fog. Mitsui, Eiichi (1920-), illus. LC 59-5049. unpaged. illus. 26cm. 1959. Morrow.

--Kap and the Wicked Monkey. Mitsui, Eiichi (1920-), illus. LC 68-15751. (Illus.). 1 v. (unpaged. 26cm. 1968. Norton.

--Kap, the Kappa. Mitsui, Eiichi (1920-), illus. LC 60-5008. (Illus.). unpaged. 26cm. 1960. Morrow.

--The Many Lives of Chio and Goro. 1st ed. Segawa, Yasuo (1932-), illus. LC 68-1786. (Illus.). 1 v. (unpaged. 26cm. 1968. W. W. Norton.

--Mogo, the Mynah. Scott, Anne, illus. LC 58-666971. unpaged. illus. 28cm. (Morrow junior books). 1958. Morrow.

--The Mud Snail Son. 1st ed. Akino, Fuku (1908-), illus. LC 77-134816. 38p. illus. (part. col. 25cm. 1971. Athenuem.

--The One-Legged Ghost. 1st ed. Akino, Fuku (1908-), illus. LC 68-18450. (Illus.). 39 p. 25cm. 1968. Atheneum.

--Return To Hiroshima. Hosoe, Eikoh (1933-), illus. 1970. (ISBN 0-689-20525-2). Atheneum Publishers.

--The Rice-Cake Rabbit. Mitsui, Eiichi (1920-), illus. LC 65-18040. 1v. (unpaged) illus. 26cm. c.1966. Norton.

--The Secret Seller. Holt, Norma & Delessert, Etienne (1941-), illus. LC 67-18674. (Illus.). 43 p. 26cm. 1968. W. W. Norton.

--The Silver Crane. Kubinyi, Laszlo (1937-), illus. LC 79-142156. (Illus.). 121 p. 20cm. 1971. Seabury Press.

--Taka-Chan & I. (gr. k-3). N.D. (ISBN 0-448-26048-4). G&D.

--Taka-Chan and I: A Dog's Journey to Japan, by Runcible. 1st ed. Hosoe, Eikoh (1933-), photos by. LC 67-9539. (Illus.). 62 p. 29cm. 1967. Norton.

Liger-Belair, Edgard

--Gigi and Gogo. Sa, Luiz, illus. LC 43-16439. 1, 15, 15 p. col. illus. 16 x 22 1/2 cm. c.1943. Reynal & Hitchcock.

Liggett, Thomas (1918-)

--The Hollow. LC 58-3773. (Illus.). 237 p. 22cm. 1958. Holiday House.

--Pigeon, Fly Home!. Simont, Marc (1915-), illus. LC 56-13887. 189p. illus. 21cm. 1956. Holiday House.

Light Brooklyn, New York, N.Y.

--Light Stories for Children. LC 82-100109. 192 p. 22cm. 1980. Lightbooks : Distributor, Z. Berman Books : Judaica Book Agency Distributor.

--Light Stories for Teenage Boys. LC 82-100100. 252 p. 22cm. 1980. Lightbooks : Distributor, Z. Berman Books.

Lightfoot, Gordon

--The Pony Man. Delessert, Etienne (1941-), illus. LC 71-184374. (Illus.). 32 p. 24cm. 1972. (ISBN 0-06-126325-7). (ISBN 0-06-126325-7). Harper's Magazine Press.

Lightner, A. M., pseud., see Hopf, Alice Lightner.

Lightner, A. M., pseud. (1904-)

--Day of the Drones. Hopf, Alice Lightner. (gr. 7 up). N.D. (ISBN 0-448-26107-3). G&D.

--Doctor to the Galaxy. Hopf, Alice Lightner. LC 65-11008. 175p. 21cm. c.1965. Norton.

--The Galactic Troubadours. Hopf, Alice Lightner. LC 65-180412. 237p. 21cm. c.1965. Norton.

--The Planet Poachers. Hopf, Alice Lightner. LC 65-10864. 184p. illus. 21cm. c.1965. Putnam.

--The Rock of Three Planets. Hopf, Alice Lightner. McMains, Denny, illus. LC 63-15559. (Illus.). 157 p. 21cm. 1963. Putnam.

--The Space Ark. Hopf, Alice Lightner. McMains, Denny, illus. LC 68-11363. (Illus.). 190 p. 21cm. 1968. Putnam.

--The Space Olympics. Hopf, Alice Lightner. LC 67-18676. 211 p. 21cm. 1967. Norton.

--The Space Plague. Hopf, Alice Lightner. LC 66-11771. 156p. 21cm. c.1966. Norton.

--Star Dog. Hopf, Alice Lightner. 208p. (gr. 4-6). 1983. (ISBN 0-590-31777-6). Scholastic Inc.

--Thursday Toads. Hopf, Alice Lightner. 160p. (gr. 7 up). 1971. (ISBN 0-07-037834-7). McGraw.

--Walking Zoo of Darwin Dingle. Hopf, Alice Lightner. Cuffari, Richard (1925-1978), illus. (Illus.). 160p. (gr. 5-8). 1969. (ISBN 0-399-20224-2). Putnam.

--Wild Traveler: The Story of a Coyote. Hopf, Alice Lightner. Summers, Leo, illus. LC 67-1412. (Illus.). 174 p. 21cm. 1967. Norton.

Lignell, Lois (1911-)

--Three Japanese Mice and Their Whiskers. Princehorn, Betz, illus. LC 34-33120. 32 p. illus. 21 x 28 1/2cm. 1934. Farrar & Rinehart, Inc.

Likhanov, Albert

--The Maze. 288p. 1977. (ISBN 0-8285-1206-X, Pub. by Progress Pubs USSR). Imported Pubns.

--Shadows Across the Sun. Lourie, Richard, tr. from Rus. LC 80-8440. 128p. 1st U.S. edition. (gr. 7 up). 1983. (ISBN 0-06-023868-2, HarpJ). (ISBN 0-06-023869-0). Har-Row.

Liles, Alice V.

--The Orphans. (gr. 2-4). N.D. Carlton.

Liley, Helen Margaret Irwin, jt. auth. see Day, Beth Feagles.

Lilius, Irmelin S.

--The Goldmaker's House. Ionicus, illus. LC 79-2104. (gr. 5 up). 1980. (Sey Lawr). Delacorte.

--Horses of the Night. Ionicus, illus. LC 79-2105. (gr. 5 up). 1980. (Sey Lawr). Delacorte.

Liljencrantz, Ottilia Adelina (1876-)

--The Scrape That Jack Built. LC 7-18993. 248 p. front., plates. 19 cm. 1896. A. C. McClurg and Company.

Lillard, Walter Huston (1881-), ed. see Hughes, Thomas.

Lillegard, Dee

--Where Is It?. Hillerich, Robert L. & Sharp, Gene (1923-), illus. LC 84-7005. (Illus.). 31 p. 19cm. (A Rookie Reader). c.1984. (ISBN 0-516-02065-X). Childrens Press.

Lillie, Amy Morris

--The Book of Three Festivals: Stories for Christmas, Easter and Thanksgiving. 1st ed. MacDonald, James, illus. LC 48-5874. 189 p. illus. 22 cm. 1948. E. P. Dutton.

--Everybody's Island. 1st ed. Morse, Dorothy Bayley (1906-1979), illus. LC 52-7795. 182 p. illus. 21 cm. 1952. Dutton.

--Judith: Daughter of Jericho. Walker, Nedda, illus. LC 51-6022. 21cm. 1951. Dutton.

--Nathan: Boy of Capernaum. Walker, Nedda, illus. LC 45-2840. xii, 13-192 p. col. front., illus., col. plates (1 double) 22 1/2 cm. 1945. E. P. Dutton & Co., Inc.

--Run the Good Race. Savage, Steele (1900-), illus. N.D. (ISBN 0-687-36653-4). Abingdon Press.

--Stephen: Boy of the Mountain. Walker, Nedda, illus. LC 47-1530. 189 p. col. front., illus. 23 cm. 1947. E. P. Dutton & Co., Inc.

Lillie, C. J.

--Little Bird Red and Little Bird Blue. Macquoid, Thomas Robert (1820-1912), illus. N.D. George Routledge & Sons.

--Little Plays for Little Folk. (Illus.). N.D. Goerge Routledge & Sons.

Lillie, Lucy Cecil White, Mrs. (1855-1908)

--Alison's Adventures. (Roundabout Library). (Honest Endeavor Library). N.D. John C. Winston Co.

--Alison's Adventures. N.D. John C. Winston.

--Alison's Adventures: Or, The Broderick Estate. LC 7-18992. (Illus.). (Roundabout Lib.). (Honest Endeavore Ser.). N.D. Henry T. Coates & Co.

--The Colonel Money. (Illus.). (Harper's Young People Series.). N.D. Harper & Brothers.

--Elinor Beldon. N.D. John C. Winston.

--Esther's Fortune, 1 of 3 vols. (Illus.). (Roundabout Lib.). (Millbrook Lib.). N.D. Set. Henry T. Coates & Co.

--Esther's Fortune, 1 of 4 vols. (Roundabout Library). (Milbrook Library). N.D. John C. Winston Co.

--Esther's Fortune: A Story for Girls. LC 7-18991. 408 p. front., 3 pl. 20 cm. c.1889. Porter & Coates.

--The False Witness. (Harper's Young People Ser.). N.D. Harper & Brothers.

--A Family Dilemma. (Illus.). (Roundabout Lib.). (Honest Endeavor Ser.). N.D. Henry T. Coates & Co.

--The Family Dilemma. (Roundabout Library). (Honest Endeavor Library). N.D. John E. Winston Co.

--A Family Dilemma: A Story for Girls. LC 7-18990. 2 p. l., 314 p. front., plates, 20 cm. (On cover: Honest endeavor series). c.1894. Porter & Coates.

--For Honor's Sake, 1 of 4 vols. (Roundabout Library). (Millbrook Library). N.D. John C. Winston Co.

--For Honor's Sake: A Sequel to "The Squire's Daughter". LC 7-189894. iv, 5-450 p. front., plates. 20 cm. (On cover: Millbrook library). (Roundabout Lib.). c.1891. Porter & Coates.

--Girl's Ordeal. N.D. John C. Winston.

--Helen Glenn: Or, My mother's enemy, 1 of 4 vols. (Milbrook Library). N.D. John C. Winston Co.

--Helen Glenn: Or, My Mother's Enemy. A Story for Girls, 1 of 4 vols. 2 p. l., iii-iv, 320 p. front., plates. 19 cm., (On cover: Millbrook library). (Roundabout Lib.). c.1891. Porter & Coates.

--The Household of Glen Holly. LC 7-18794. viii, 368 p. incl. plates. front. 17 cm. (On cover: Harper's young people series). 1888. Harper & Brothers.

--Joe's Opportunity. N.D. Harper & Bros.

--Jo's Opportunity. LC 7-18795. 3 p. l., 5-175 p., front., plates. 17 cm. (On cover: Harper's young people series). 1886. Harper & Brothers.

--Mildred's Bargain. (Illus.). (Harper's Young People Ser.). N.D. Harper & Brothers.

--Mildred's Bargain and Other Stories. LC 7-19384. 231 p. incl. plates. front. 17 cm. (On cover: Harper's young people series). 1883. Harper & Brothers.

--Music And Musicians. (Illus.). (Harper's Young People Ser.). N.D. Harper & Brothers.

--My Mother's Enemy. A Story for Girls. LC 7-18796. iv p., 1 l., 5-272 p. front., plates. 20 cm. c.1887. Porter & Coates.

--Nan. LC 7-18797. 202 p. incl. front. plates. 17 cm. (On cover: Harper's young people series). 1883. Harper & Brothers.

--Phil and the Baby. (Illus.). N.D. Harper & Brothers.

--Prudence. (Illus.). N.D. Harper & Brothers.

--Rolf House. LC 7-18987. viii, 266 p. incl. front. plates. 17 cm. (On cover: Harper's young people series). 1886. Harper & Brothers.

--Ruth Endicott's Way. (Roundabout Library). (Honest Endeavor Library). N.D. John C. Winston Co.

--Ruth Endicott's Way: Or, Hargrave's Mission. (Illus.). (Honest Endeavor Ser.). N.D. Set. Henry T. Coates & Co.

--The Squire's Daughter, 1 of 4 vols. (Roundabout Library). (Milbrook Library). N.D. John C. Winston Co.

--The Squire's Daughter. A Story for Girls, 1 of 4 vols. LC 7-18988. (On Cover: Millibrook Library). (Roundabout Lib.). c.1891. Porter & Coates.

Lillie, Patricia

--One Very, Very Quiet Afternoon. LC 85-782. (Illus.). 7 1/2 x 9. 24p. (24 pt.). (ps-1). 1986. (ISBN 0-688-04322-4). (ISBN 0-688-04323-2). Greenwillow.

Lillington, Kenneth James (1916-)

--Isabel's Double. LC 83-25317. 128p. (gr. 6 up). 1984. (ISBN 0-571-13197-2). (ISBN 0-571-13197-2). Faber & Faber.

--Selkie. LC 85-1448. 145 p. 21cm. 1985. (ISBN 0-571-13421-1). Faber and Faber.

--Young Man of Morning. 176p. 1st U.S. edition. (gr. 6-9). 1979. (ISBN 0-571-11421-0). Faber & Faber.

Lilly, Jean

--A Hundred Tuftys. Gergely, Tibor (1900-1978), illus. LC 40-13278. 26cm. 32p. 1940. E. P. Dutton & Co.

Lim, Genny

--Wings for Lai Ho. Ja, Andrea, illus. Lew, Gordon, tr. (Illus.). 48p. (Orig.). (gr. 5-8). 1982. (ISBN 0-934788-01-4). E-W Pub Co.

Lim, Sing

--West Coast Chinese Boy. Lim, Sing, illus. (Illus.). 64p. (gr. 6-12). 1979. (ISBN 0-88776-121-6). Tundra Bks.

Limbach, Russell T. (1904-)

--But Once a Year. Limbach, Russell T. (1904-), illus. LC 41-21175. 32 p. illus. 17cm. (American Artists Group Gift Books: No. 8). N.D. American Artists Group, Inc.

Limited Editions Club Inc., New York see Lorenzini, Carlo.

Limited Editions Club, Inc., New York see Yeats, William Butler.

Limmer, Hans, jt. auth. see Wiegman, Lies.

Limmer, Hans (1926-)

--My Donkey Benjamin. Osbeck, Lennart, photos by. Cleary, Timothy, tr. LC 70-80428. (Illus.). 48 p. 24cm. (Terra magica children's book). 1969. (ISBN 0-8090-2147-1). Hill and Wang.

--My Kangaroo Phoebe. Wiegman, Lies, photos by. LC 76-113099. (Illus.). photos. (gr. 2-6). 1970. (ISBN 0-8090-2149-8, Terra Magica). Hill & Wang.

Limpscomb, George Dewey (1898-)

--Tales from the Land of Simba. Worden, Felice, illus. LC 61-8575. 90p. illus. 22cm. (A Wonderful World Bk.). 1961. Barnes.

Limpus, Aitken

--The Sea Lord: Francis Drake. Berger, William, illus. LC 32-10343. ix p., 1 l., 272 p., 1 l. incl. front., illus., plates. 21 cm. 1932. The Macmillan Company.

AUTHOR INDEX LINDMAN, MAJ

Lin, Adet (1923-)
--Milky Way, and Other Chinese Folk Tales. Arno, Enrico (1913-1981), illus. (Illus.). (gr. 4-6). N.D. (ISBN 0-15-254200-0). HarBraceJ.
--The Milky Way, and Other Fairy Tales. Arno, Enrico (1913-1981), illus. 92p. 1961. Hartcourt Brace & World Inc.
Lin, Beth
--Mother Goose goes to War. Rethi, Lili (1894-), illus. 1962. Exposition Press.
Linam, Gail
--Angie's New Friends. Martin, Ron (1947-), illus. LC 80-113631. (Illus.). 32 p. 24cm. (gr. k-3). c.1980. (ISBN 0-8054-4261-8). Broadman Press.
--Kind Doctor, Missionary Friend. LC 81-66555. (gr. 1-3). 1981. (ISBN 0-8054-4274-X). Broadman
Linch, Elizabeth Johanna see Linch, Jo, pseud.
Linch, Elizabeth Johanna
--Samson. Linch, Jo, pseud. Linch, Elizabeth Johanna, illus. Linch, Jo, pseud. LC 62-13311. (Illus.). 46 p. 1964. Harper & Row.
Linch, Jo, pseud., see Linch, Elizabeth Johanna.
Lincoln, Andrew Carey
--Motorcycle Chums in New England: Or, The Mt. Holyoke Adventure. LC 13-234. 228&p. incl. front. 20 cm. c.1912. M. A. Donohue & Co.
--Motorcycle Chums in the Land of the Sky: Or, Thrilling Adventures on the Carolina Border. LC 13-320343. 230 p. incl. front. 20 cm. c.1912. M. A. Donohue & Co.
--Motorcycle Chums in Yellowstone Park: Or, Lending a Helping Hand. LC 53-54072. 240 p. front. 29cm. c.1913. M. A. Donohue.
--Motorcycle Chums on the Santa Fe Trail: Or, The Key to the Indian Treasure Cave. LC 13-233. 234 p. incl. front. 20 cm. c.1912. M. A. Donohue & Company.
--Motorcycle Chums Stormbound: Or, The Strange Adventures of a Road Chase. LC 14-10729. 256 p. incl. front. 20 cm. c.1914. M. A. Donohue & Company.
Lincoln, Edith Maas (1891-1977)
--Little Folks Fairy Tales. N.D. E P Dutton.
Lincoln, John Willard (1875-)
--The Young Home Steaders. (Seal Ser.). N.D. D. Lothrop Co.
--Young Homesteaders, 1 of 4 vols. (Rocky Fork Library). 1882. D Lothrop.
--The Young Homesteaders: A Story of How Two Boys Made a Home in the West. Copeland, Charles, illus. LC 14-111. iv, 2 409 p. col. front. 20 cm. c.1913. W. A. Wilde Company.
Lincoln, Joseph C.
--Cap'n Dan's Daughter. 1921. A. L. Burt Co.
--Cap'n Earl. 1921. A. L. Burt Co.
--Cap'n Warren's Wards. 1921. A. L. Burt Co.
Lincoln, Reuben
--Pecker, the Super-Bird: Or, The Cave of Delight. Chant, Marie, illus. LC 52-30874. 149 p. illus. 26 cm. 1951. Serjeants Press.
Lincoln, Victoria (1904-1981)
--Everyhow Remarkable. Jeffers, Susan, illus. LC 67-14420. 1 v. (unpaged) illus. 22 cm. 30p. 1967. Crowell-Collier Press.
Lind, Betty
--I Am Thing. (gr. k-2). N.D. Carlton.
Lind, Levi Robert (1906-), ed.
--Latin Poetry in Verse Translation. LC 57-59176. (gr. 9 up). 1957. (ISBN 0-395-05118-5, RivEd). HM.
Linday, Ryllis Elizabeth Paine (1919-)
--Look at Me. Derwinski, Beatrice, illus. LC 60-5029. (Illus.). (ps). 1960. (ISBN 0-8054-4117-4). (ISBN 0-8054-4116-6). Broadman.
--Now I Am Two. Teichman, Dorothy, illus. LC 63-9756. unpaged. illus. 21 cm. 1963. Broadman Press.
Lindberg, Maja
--Karl's Journey to the Moon. Lindberg, Maja, illus. Andrews, Siri, tr. LC 28-26081. 28 p. 1 l., col. illus. 29cm. 1927. Harper & Bros.
Lindbergh, Anne Morrow Spencer (1906-)
--Bailey's Window. Craft, Kinuko Y., illus. LC 83-18360. (Illus.). 132p. (gr. 4-6). 1984. (ISBN 0-15-205642-4, HJ). (ISBN 0-15-205642-4). HarBraceJ.
--Nobody's Orphan. 1st ed. LC 83-8499. 147 p. 22cm. c.1983. (ISBN 0-15-257468-9). Harcourt Brace Jovanovich.
--The People in Pineapple Place. LC 82-47935. p. cm. c.1982. (ISBN 0-15-260517-7). Harcourt Brace Jovanovich.
--The Worry Week. Hewitt, Kathryn, illus. LC 84-19299. p. cm. c.1985. (ISBN 0-15-299675-3). Harcourt Brace Jovanovich.
Lindbergh, Holgin, tr. see Olenius, Elsa.
Lindblom, Steven Winther, jt. auth. see Kelley, True Adelaide.
Lindblom, Steven Winther (1946-)
--Let's Give Kitty a Bath!. Kelley, True Adelaide (1946-), illus. LC 81-19068. (Illus.). 32 p. 17cm. c.1982. (ISBN 0-201-10712-0). Addison-Wesley.
--Let's Give Kitty a Bath!. Kelley, True Adelaide (1946-), illus. LC 84-46023. p. cm. 1985, c.1982. (ISBN 0-201-10712-0). Crowell.
Lindbloom, James A.
--Make the Morning. Lindbloom, Nancy, illus. (Illus.). (gr. k-6). 1977. (ISBN 0-89409-007-0). Childrens Art.
Linde, Freda
--Toto and the Aardvark. Giovanopoulos, Paul Arthur (1939-), illus. Berends, Polly Berrien (1939-) & Berends, Jan, trs. from Afrikaans LC 69-15890. (Illus.). 59 p. 25cm. 1969. Doubleday.
Linde, Gunnel (1924-)
--Bicycles Don't Grow on Trees. Svend, Otto Sorenson (1916-), illus. Crampton, Patricia, tr. LC 84-230690. (Illus.). 134 p. 23cm. 1984. (ISBN 0-460-06144-5). J.M. Dent.
--Chimney-Top Lane. Wikland, Ilon (1930-), illus. McKinnon, Lise Somme, tr. from Swedish. LC 65-21700. 21cm. 160p. 1965. (ISBN 0-15-217416-8). Hardcourt Brace Jovanovich.
--The Invisible League and the Royal Ghost. Palmquist, Eric, illus. Parker, Anne, tr. LC 77-125129. (Illus.). 188 p. 21cm. 1st U.S. edition. 1970. (ISBN 0-15-238832-X). Harcourt Brace Jovanovich.
--Pony Surprise. Kennedy, Richard (1910-), illus. Parker, Anne, tr. from Swedish. LC 68-15424. (Illus.). 130 p. 21cm. 1st U.S. edition. 1968. Harcourt, Brace & World
--Trust in the Unexpected. Svend, Otto Sorenson (1916-), illus. Crampton, Patricia, tr. LC 83-73165. (Illus.). 134 p. 23cm. 1984 (McElderry Bk). (ISBN 0-689-50300-8). Atheneum.
--The White Stone. Gobbato, Imero (1923-), illus. Winston, Richard & Winston, Clara, trs. from Swedish LC 66-742104. 185p. illus. 21cm. 1st U.S. edition. 1966. (ISBN 0-15-295910-6). Harcourt. **Award: (ALA).**
Lindegren, Signe, Mrs.
--Ingrid's Holidays. Neville, Vera (1900-1978), illus. Schleef, Caroline, tr. LC 32-11563. 4 p. l., 238 p. front., illus. 20 cm. 1932. The Macmillan Company.
Linder, Enid, ed. see Potter, Helen Beatrix.
Linder, Remo E, jt. auth. see Finst, Rudy.
Linderman, Frank Bird (1868-1938)
--How It Came About Stories. Boog, Carle Michel, illus. LC 21-15946. viii p., 3 l., 3-221 p. col. front., illus., col. plates. 21 cm. 1921. C. Scribner's Sons.
--Indian Lodge-Fire Stories. N.D. Charles Scribner's Sons.
--Indian Old-Man Stories. Russell, Charles M., illus. N.D. Charles Scribner's Sons'.
--Indian Why Stories. Russell, Charles M., illus. N.D. Charles Scribner's Sons'.
--Kootenai Why Stories. Bull, Charles Livingston (1874-1932), illus. N.D. Charles Scribner's Sons'.
--Stumpy. Stoops, Herbert Morton, illus. LC 33-5477. (Illus.). 3p.p., 3-147, 1p. c.1933. The John Day Company.
Lindgren, Astrid, jt. auth. see Riwkin-Brick, Anna.
Lindgren, Astrid Ericsson, jt. auth. see Riwkin-Brick, Anna.
Lindgren, Astrid Ericsson (1907-), adapted by see Forsslund, Karl Erik.
Lindgren, Astrid Ericsson (1907-)
--Bill Bergson and the White Rose Rescue. Freeman, Don (1908-1978), illus. Lamborn, Florence, tr. from Swedish. LC 65-13358. 215p. illus. 21cm. (gr. 5-8). 1965. (ISBN 0-670-16592-1). Viking.
--Bill Bergson Lives Dangerously. Freeman, Don (1908-1978), illus. Antoine, Herbert, tr. from Swedish. LC 54-4337. 214p. illus. 21cm. 1954. Viking Press.
--Bill Bergson, Master Detective. Glanzman, Louis S. (1922-), illus. Antoine, Herbert, tr. from Swedish. LC 52-12922. (Illus.). 200p. (gr. 4-6). 1952. (ISBN 0-670-16660-X). Viking Pr.
--Bill Bergson, Master Detective. Glanzman, Louis S. (1922-), illus. LC 52-12922. (Illus.). 200p. (gr. 4-6). 1968. (ISBN 0-670-05008-3, Seafarer). Viking Pr.
--Brenda Brave Helps Grandmother. Ware, Kay & Sutherland, Lucille, eds. Wikland, Ilon (1930-), illus. LC 61-68453. unpaged. illus. 23cm. (Read for fun series). c.1961. Wester Pub. Co.
--The Brothers Lionheart. Lambert, James Kenton (1940-), illus. LC 85-573. (Illus.). 183 p. 20cm. 1985, c.1975. (ISBN 0-14-031955-7). Puffin Books.
--The Brothers Lionheart. Lambert, James Kenton (1940-), illus. LC 75-2228. p. cm. 1975. The Viking Press.
--The Children of Noisy Village. Wikland, Ilon (1930-), illus. Lamborn, Florence, tr. LC 62-18694. (Illus.). 124 p. 22cm. 1962. Viking Press.
--The Children on Troublemaker Street. Wikland, Ilon (1930-), illus. Lamborn, Florence (1930-), tr. LC 64-11768. (Illus.). 29cm. 30p. 1964. Macmillan.
--Christmas in Noisy Village. 1981. Penguin.
--Christmas in Noisy Village. Wikland, Ilon (1930-), illus. LC 64-21473. (Illus.). 30 p. 1964. Viking Press.
--Christmas in the Stable. Wiberg, Harald Albin (1908-), illus. LC 62-14449. unpaged. illus. 22x28cm. 1962. (ISBN 0-698-30042-4). Coward-McCann.
--Christmas in the Stable. new ed. Wiberg, Harald Albin (1908-), illus. LC 62-14449. (Illus.). (gr. k-2). 1979. (ISBN 0-698-20489-1, Coward). Putnam Pub Group.
--Dirk Lives in Holland. Riwkin-Brick, Anna (1908-), illus. (gr. 1-3). 1963. Macmillan.
--Emil and Piggy Beast. Berg, Bjorn (1923-), illus. Heron, Michael, tr. from Fr. LC 72-91228. (Illus.). 191 p. 23cm. 1973. (ISBN 0-695-80356-5). (ISBN 0-695-80356-5). Follett Pub. Co.
--Emil in the Soup Tureen. Berg, Bjorn (1923-), illus. LC 79-93795. (Illus.). 126 p. 23cm. 1970. (ISBN 0-695-42210-3). Follett.
--Emil's Pranks. Berg, Bjorn (1923-), illus. LC 75-118959. (Illus.). 128 p. 23cm. 1971. (ISBN 0-695-80158-9). Follett Pub. Co.
--Happy Times in Noisy Village. Wikland, Ilon (1930-), illus. Lamborn, Florence, tr. (Illus.). (gr. 1-5). 1963. (ISBN 0-670-36119-4). (ISBN 0-670-36120-8). Viking Pr.
--I Want a Brother or Sister. Wikland, Ilon (1930-), illus. LC 81-142965. (Illus.). 29 p. 27cm. 1981. (ISBN 0-15-239387-0). Harcourt Brace Jovanovich.
--Karlsson-on-the-Roof. Pyk, Jan (1934-), illus. Turner, Marianne, tr. LC 76-162670. (Illus.). 127 p. 24cm. 1971. (ISBN 0-670-41176-0). (ISBN 0-670-41177-9). Viking Press.
--Lotta on Troublemaker Street. Brinckloe, Julie Lorraine (1950-), illus. Bothmer, Gerry, tr. from Swedish. LC 63-10406. (Illus.). 57 p. 23cm. 1963. Macmillan.
--Lotta on Troublemaker Street. Brinckloe, Julie Lorraine (1950-), illus. LC 83-25619. (Illus.). 57 p. 23cm. 1984, c.1963. (ISBN 0-02-759040-2). Macmillan.
--Marko Lives in Yugoslavia. Riwkin-Brick, Anna, photos by. (Illus.). (gr. 1-2). 1963. Macmillan.
--Mio, My Son. Wikland, Ilon (1930-), illus. Turner, Marianne, tr. from Swedish. LC 56-14361. 179p. illus. 22cm. 1956. (ISBN 0-670-47740-0). Viking Press.
--Mischievous Meg. Domanska, Janina, illus. LC 85-575. (Illus.). 139 p. 20cm. 1985, c.1962. (ISBN 0-14-031954-9). Puffin Books.
--Mischievous Meg. Domanska, Janina, illus. Bothmer, Gerry, tr. LC 62-9925. (Illus.). 139 p. 21cm. 1962. Viking Press.
--My Swedish Cousins. Riwkin-Brick, Anna (1908-), photos by. LC 60-1549. 22cm. 1960. Macmillan.
--Of Course Polly Can Do Almost Everything. Wikland, Ilon (1930-), illus. LC 79-126912. (Illus.). 30 p. 29cm. 1978, c.1977. (ISBN 0-695-80967-9). Follett Pub. Co.
--Of Course Polly Can Ride a Bike. Wikland, Ilon (1930-), illus. LC 72-190774. (Illus.). 32 p. 29cm. 1972. (ISBN 0-695-80349-2). (ISBN 0-695-80349-2). Follett.
--Pippi Gift Set, 3 vols. N.D. Boxed Set. (ISBN 0-317-12419-6, Puffin). Penguin.
--Pippi Goes on Board. Glanzman, Louis S. (1922-), illus. LC 76-54740. p. cm. 1977, c.1957. (ISBN 0-14-030959-4). Puffin Books.
--Pippi Goes on Board. Glanzman, Louis S. (1922-), illus. Lamborn, Florence, tr. from Swedish. LC 57-4316. 140p. illus. 21cm. 1957. Viking Press.
--Pippi in the South Seas. Glanzman, Louis S. (1922-), illus. LC 76-54802. p. cm. 1977. (ISBN 0-14-030958-6). Puffin Books.
--Pippi in the South Seas. Glanzman, Louis S. (1922-), illus. Bothmer, Gerry, tr. LC 59-4758. (Illus.). 126 p. 21cm. 1959. Viking Press.
--Pippi Longstocking. Glanzman, Louis S. (1922-), illus. LC 77-1374. p. cm. 1977. (ISBN 0-14-030957-8). Puffin Books.
--Pippi Longstocking. Glanzman, Louis S. (1922-), illus. Lamborn, Florence (1922-), tr. from Swedish. LC 50-10396. (Illus.). 158 p. 21cm. 1950. Viking Press.
--Pippi on the Run. Gyberg, Bo-Erik, illus. LC 75-31944. p. cm. 1976. (ISBN 0-670-55751-X). Viking Press.
--Rasmus and the Vagabond. Palmquist, Eric, illus. Bothmer, Gerry, tr. LC 60-1908. (Illus.). 192 p. 22cm. 1960. Viking Press.
--Ronia, the Robber's Daughter. Crompton, Patricia, tr. LC 82-60081. 176 p. 24cm. 1st U.S. edition. 1983. (ISBN 0-670-60640-5). Viking Press. **Awards: (MLB); (ALA).**
--Ronia, the Robber's Daughter. Lindgren, Astrid Ericsson (1907-), illus. LC 84-11848. 176 p. 20cm. 1985, c.1983. (ISBN 0-14-031720-1). Puffin Books.
--The Runaway Sleigh Ride. Wikland, Ilon (1930-), illus. LC 83-23347. (Illus.). 33 p. 29cm. 1984. (ISBN 0-670-40454-3). Viking Press.
--Seacrow Island. Hales, Robert, illus. Ramsden, Evelyn, tr. LC 71-85872. (Illus.). 22cm. 287p. 1st U.S. edition. (gr. 7 up). 1969, c.1968. (ISBN 0-670-62591-4). (ISBN 0-670-62592-2). Viking Pr.
--Sia Lives on Kilimanjaro. LC 59-16282. unpaged. illus. 22cm. 1959. Macmillan.
--Skrallan and the Pirates. Deler, Sven-Eric & Hallgren, Stig, illus. Read, Albert & Sapieha, Christine, trs. LC 73-7344. (Illus.). 48 p. 32cm. 1969, c.1967. Doubleday.
--Springtime in Noisy Village. Wikland, Ilon (1930-), illus. LC 66-156486. 28p. col. illus. 23x29cm. 1966. Viking.
--The Tomten: Adapted by Astrid Lingren from a poem by Viktor Rydberg. Wiberg, Harald Albin (1908-), illus. LC 61-10658. (Illus.). unpaged. 1961. Coward-McCann.
Lindgren, Barbro
--Hilding's Summer. Tusan, Stan (1936-), illus. MacMillan, Annabelle, pseud. (1922-), tr. from Swedish. Quick, Annabelle. LC 67-1972. (Illus.). 138 p. 22cm. 1967. Macmillan.
--[illegible] illus. Carlson, Susan, tr. from Sewdish. LC 77-369041. (Illus.). 26 p. 17cm. 1976. Clamshell Press.
--Sam's Ball. Eriksson, Eva, illus. (Illus.). 31 p. 17cm. 1983. (ISBN 0-688-02359-2). Morrow.
--Sam's Bath. Eriksson, Eva, illus. LC 83-724. (Illus.). 31 p. 17cm. 1983. (ISBN 0-688-02362-2). Morrow. **Award: (ALA).**
--Sam's Car. Eriksson, Eva, illus. LC 82-3437. (Illus.). 32p. Orig. Title: Max Bil. (gr. k-3). 1982. (ISBN 0-688-0126[illegible]). Morrow.
--Sam's Cookie. Eriksson, Eva, illus. LC 82-3419. (Illus.). 32p. Orig. Title: Max Kaka. (gr. k-3). 1982. (ISBN 0-688-01267-1). Morrow.
--Sam's Lamp. Eriksson, Eva, illus. LC 83-743. (Illus.). 31 p. 17cm. 1983. (ISBN 0-688-02356-8). Morrow.
--Sam's Teddy Bear. Eriksson, Eva, illus. LC 82-3418. (Illus.). 32p. (gr. k-3). 1982. (ISBN 0-688-01270-1). Morrow.
--The Wild Baby. Prelutsky, Jack, adapted by. Eriksson, Eva, illus. LC 81-2151. (Illus.). 24 p. 26cm. c.1981. (ISBN 0-688-00600-0). (ISBN 0-688-00601-9). Greenwillow Books.
--The Wild Baby Goes to Sea. Eriksson, Eva, illus. Prelutsky, Jack, tr. from Swedish. LC 82-15623. p. cm. c.1983. (ISBN 0-688-01960-9). (ISBN 0-688-01961-7). Greenwillow Books.
Lindley, Alice, Mrs.
--The Story of the Little Round Man. Angela, illus. LC 79-63277. (Illus.). 72 p. 1979. (ISBN 0-7232-2185-5). F. Warne.
Lindman, Maj, Mrs.
--Dear Little Deer. LC 53-10029. (Illus.). 27 p. 26cm. 1953. A. Whitman.
--Fire Eye: The Story of a Boy and His Horse. Lindman, Maj, Mrs., illus. LC 48-2380. 32 p. illus. (part col.) 21 x 26 cm. 1948. A. Whitman.
--Flicka, Ricka, Dicka and a Little Dog. LC 48-3307. 27 p. col. illus. 26 cm. 1946. A. Whitman.
--Flicka, Ricka, Dicka and the Big Red Hen. LC 60-13639. 26cm. 1960. A. Whitman.
--Flicka, Ricka, Dicka and the Girl Next Door. LC 40-10779. 27 p. illus. (part col.) 26 cm. 1940. A. Whitman & Co.
--Flicka, Ricka, Dicka and the New Dotted Dresses. LC 39-17419. 26 p. illus. (part col.) 26 cm. 1939. A. Whitman & Co.
--Flicka, Ricka, Dicka & The New Dotted Dresses. N.D. E. M. Hale & Co.
--Flicka, Ricka, Dicka and the Strawberries. LC 44-3052. 27 p. col. illus. 25 1/2 x 21 cm. 1944. A. Whitman & Company.
--Flicka, Ricka, Dicka and the Three Kittens. LC 41-17581. 27 p. illus. (part col.) 26 x 21 cm. 1941. A. Whitman & Co.
--Flicka, Ricka, Dicka and Their New Friend. LC 42-22574. 27 p. illus. (part col.) 25 x 21 cm. 1942. A. Whitman & Company.
--Flicka, Ricka, Dicka & Their New Skates. Lindman, Maj, Mrs., illus. LC 51-284. (Illus.). (gr. k-2). 1950. (ISBN 0-8075-2488-3). A Whitman.
--Flicka, Ricka, Dicka Bake a Cake. Lindman, Maj, Mrs., illus. 1955. Albert Whitman & Co.
--Flicka, Ricka, Dicka Go to Market. LC 58-9950. 26cm. 1958. A. Whitman.
--Holiday Time. LC 52-8929. unpaged. illus. 26 cm. 1952. Whitman.
--Little Folks' Life of Jesus. Lindman, Maj, Mrs., illus. N.D. Albert Whitman & Co.
--Sailboat Time. LC 51-14171. (Illus.). 27 p. 26cm. 1951. A. Whitman.
--Snipp, Snapp, Snurr and the Big Farm. LC 47-378157. 27 p. illus. (part col.) 25 x 20 1/2 cm. 1946. A. Whitman & Company.
--Snipp, Snapp, Snurr & The Big Surprise. N.D. E. M. Hale & Co.
--Snipp, Snapp, Snurr & the Big Surprise. Lindman, Maj, Mrs., illus. LC 37-35180. (Illus.). (gr. k-2). 1937. (ISBN 0-8075-7503-8). A Whitman.
--Snipp, Snapp, Snurr, and the Buttered Bread. LC 34-37832. 23 p. illus. (part col.) 26 cm. 1934. A. Whitman & Co.
--Snipp, Snapp, Snurr and the Gingerbread. LC 33-5936. 23 p. col. illus. 25 cm. 1932. A. Whitman & Company.

--Snipp, Snapp, Snurr and the Gingerbread. LC 36-32643. 23 p. illus. (part col.) 25 cm. 1936. A. Whitman & Company.
--Snipp, Snapp, Snurr & The Gingerbread. N.D. E. M. Hale & Co.
--Snipp, Snapp, Snurr and the Magic Horse. 47 p. col. illus. 24 cm. 1933. The Junior Literary Guild and Albert Whitman & Company.
--Snipp, Snapp, Snurr & The Red Shoes. N.D. E. M. Hale & Co.
--Snipp, Snapp, Snurr & the Red Shoes. Lindman, Maj, Mrs., illus. LC 32-2696. (Illus.). (gr. k-2). N.D. (ISBN 0-8075-7509-7). A Whitman.
--Snipp, Snapp, Snurr, and the Reindeer. LC 57-11745. (Illus.). 27 p. 26cm. 1957. A. Whitman.
--Snipp, Snapp, Snurr and the Seven Dogs. LC 59-14391. (Illus.). 27 p. 26cm. 1959. A. Whitman.
--Snipp, Snapp, Snurr and the Yellow Sled. LC 36-27391. 27 p. illus. (part col.) 26 cm. 1936. A. Whitman & Co.
--Snipp, Snapp, Snurr & The Yellow Sled. N.D. E. M. Hale & Co.
--Snipp, Snapp, Snurr Learn to Swim. LC 54-9945. (Illus.). unpaged. 26cm. 1954. A. Whitman.
--Snowboot, Son of Fire Eye. Lindman, Maj, Mrs., illus. LC 50-8391. (Illus.). 26 p. 1950. Whitman.

Lindop, Audrey Erskine (1920-)
--The Adventures of the Wuffle. Stobbs, William (1914-), illus. LC 68-17192. (Illus.). 126 p. 24cm. 1968, c.1966. McGraw-Hill.

Lindop, Edmund (1925-)
--The Dazzling Twenties. 1970. (ISBN 0-531-01840-7). Franklin Watts Single Titles.
--George Washington and the First Balloon Flight: A Story. Carlson, Jane, illus. LC 64-7716. 1 v. (unpaged) illus. (part col.) 24cm. 1964. A. Whitman.
--Hubert, the Traveling Hippopotamus. Carlson, Jane, illus. LC 61-10189. 26cm. 28p. 1961. Little, Brown and Company.
--Jumbo, King of Elephants. Carlson, Jane, illus. LC 59-7354. 30p. illus. (part col.) 27cm. (ps-3). c.1960. (ISBN 0-316-52656-8). Little, Brown.
--Pelorus Jack, Dolphin Pilot. Carlson, Jane, illus. LC 64-13982. (Illus.). (gr. k-3). 1964. (ISBN 0-316-52642-8). Little.
--War Eagle. Carlson, Jane, illus. LC 66-110075. 32p. col. illus. 26cm. c.1966. Little.

Lindquist, Jennie Dorothea (1899-1977)
--The Crystal Tree. Chalmers, Mary Eileen (1927-), illus. LC 64-16658. (Illus.). 297 p. 21cm. 1966. Harper & Row.
--The Golden Name Day. Williams, Garth Montgomery (1912-), illus. LC 55-8823. (Illus.). 247 p. 21cm. 1955. Harper. **Awards: (ALA); (JNM).**
--The Golden Name Day. Williams, Garth Montgomery (1912-), illus. LC 72-172060. (Illus.). 247 p. 20cm. (Harper trophy book, J24). 1966, c.1955. (ISBN 0-06-440024-7). Harper & Row.
--The Little Silver House. Williams, Garth Montgomery (1912-), illus. LC 59-8975. 213p. illus. 21cm. 1959. (ISBN 0-06-023891-7). Harper.

Lindquist, Kathleen, adapted by.
--CB: The/Three Bears. 1969. Golden Press.

Lindquist, Willis, jt. auth. see Disney, Walter Elias.

Lindquist, Willis, as told by see Disney, Walter Elias.

Lindquist, Willis, adapted by see Pyle, Howard.

Lindquist, Willis (1908-)
--Burma Boy. N.D. E. M. Hale and Co.
--Burma Boy. Mordvinoff, Nicolas (1911-1973), illus. Nicolas, pseud. LC 53-8017. 93p. illus. 22cm. 1953. Whittlesey House. **Award: (ALA).**
--Call of the White Fox. Hutchison, P. A., illus. LC 56-133964. 192p. illus. 21cm. c.1957. Whittlesey House.
--Folktales from Many Lands. Laite, Gordon (1925-), illus. LC 71-79223. (Illus.). 47 p. 29cm. (Carousel book). 1969. L. W. Singer Co.
--Haji of the Elephants. Miller, Don (1923-), illus. LC 76-4804. (Illus.). 147 p. 21cm. c.1976. (ISBN 0-07-037892-4). McGraw-Hill.
--The Red Drum's Warning. Johnson, Eugene Harper, illus. LC 58-11184. 128p. illus. 21cm. 1958. (ISBN 0-07-037897-5). Whittlesey House.

Lindquist, Willis (1908-), adapted by.
--Ben-Hur. Cooper, Mario (1905-), illus. (An abridgement of the novel by Lew Wallace). (A Golden Picture Classic). 1956. Golden Press.
--The Merry Adventures of Robin Hood. Lynch, Donald, illus. (Abridgements of Stories by Howard Pyle). (A Golden Picture Classic). 1957. Golden Press.

Lindsay
--The Violet Apple and the Witch. N.D. Chicago Reveiw Press Books.

Lindsay, Ann & Cohen, Aaron
--Cat Who Could Not Purr. 32p. (ps-2). 1971. (ISBN 0-685-00830-4). Impress Hse.

Lindsay, Barbara
--Captain Kangaroo's Surprise Party. Schmidt, Edwin, illus. (Little Golden Book). 1958. Golden Press.
--Fun at my House. March, Jane, illus. N.D. E. P. Dutton & Co.
--The Toy Show Surprise. Anderson, Doug, illus. LC 55-10370. unpaged. illus. 22cm. 1955. Sterling Pub Co.

Lindsay, Barbara, jt. auth. see James, Josephine.

Lindsay, Barbara, jt. ed. see Sterne, Emma Gelders, Mrs.

Lindsay, Gillian
--The Toffee Apple Tree. Duchesne, Janet (1930-), illus. (Illus.). 48p. 1st U.S. edition. (gr. 2-5). 1984. (ISBN 0-241-10985-X, Pub. by Hamish Hamilton England). David & Charles.

Lindsay, Jeanne Warren (1929-)
--Do I Have a Daddy?. A Story About a Single-Parent Child with Special Section for Single Mothers and Fathers. Warr, DeeDee Upton, illus. LC 82-81645. (Illus.). 44 p. c.1982. (ISBN 0-930934-10-5). Morning Glory Press.

Lindsay, Maud McKnight (1874-)
--The Amazing Adventures of Ali. Berger, William Merritt (1872-), illus. LC 31-31936. 166 p. col. front., col. plates 20 1/2 cm. c.1931. Lothrop, Lee & Shepard Co.
--Bobby and the Big Road. Young, Florence Liley, illus. LC 20-26565. (Illus.). 112p. c.1920. Lothrop, Lee & Shepard Co.
--The Choosing Book. Young, Florence Liley, illus. LC 28-22730. 5 p. l., 13-177 p. col. front., illus., col. plates. 19 cm. c.1928. Lothrop, Lee & Shepard Co.
--Fun on Children's Street. Downer, Marion (1892-1971), illus. 1941. Lothrop Lee & Shepard.
--Jock Barefoot. Linton, Jane, illus. LC 39-25439. x, 13-177 p. incl. front., illus. 23 cm. 1939. Lothrop, Lee and Shepard Company.
--Little Missy. Young, Florence Liley, illus. LC 22-3714. 188 p. col. front., col. plates. 19 x 17 cm. c.1922. Lee & Shepard Co.
--More Mother Stories. N.D. Distributed by Baker & Taylor.
--More Mother Stories. Sanborn, F. C. & Railton, Fanny, Mrs., illus. 183 p. front., 19 pl. 19 cm. 1905. Milton Bradley Company.
--Mother Stories. N.D. Distributed by Baker & Taylor.
--Mother Stories. Noble-Ives, Sarah, illus. LC 1-30112. 4 p. l., 182 p. plates. 19 cm. 1900. M. Bradley Company.
--Mother Stories and More Mother Stories. Howe, Gertrude Herrick (1902-), illus. 192p. 1947. Platt & Munk Co.
--Posey and the Peddler. Credle, Liley, illus. LC 38-19252. x p., 1 l., 11-186 p. incl. front., illus. 21 cm. 1938. Lothrop, Lee and Shepard Company.
--Silverfoot. Young, Florence Liley, illus. LC 25-26025. 223 p. col. front., col. plates. 19 cm. c.1924. Lothrop, Lee & Shepard Co.
--A Story Garden for Little Children. N.D. Lothrop Lee & Shepard.
--The Story-Teller. Young, Florence Liley, illus. 1915. Lothrop, Lee and Shepard Co.Ccp.
--The Storyland Tree. Hill, Mimi Clare & Draper, Kayren, illus. LC 33-24194. 159 p. incl. illus., plates. col. front. 19 cm. c.1933. Lothrop, Lee & Shepard Co.
--The Toy Shop. Young, Florence Liley, illus. LC 26-163647. 158 p. incl. illus., plates. col. front 19 cm. c.1926. Lothrop, Lee & Shepard Co.

Lindsay, Maud McKnight (1874-) & Poulsson, Emilie (1853-1939)
--The Joyous Guests. Berger, William Merritt (1872-), illus. LC 21-21201. 208&p. col. front., col. plates. 23 cm. 1921. Lothrop, Lee & Shepard Co.
--The Joyous Travelers. Berger, William Merritt (1872-), illus. LC 19-9661. 157 p. col. front., illus. (incl. music) 23 cm. c.1919. Lothrop, Lee & Shepard Co.

Lindsay, Nicholas Vachel (1879-1931)
--Johnny Appleseed. (Children's Classics Ser.). N.D. Macmillan.
--Johnny Appleseed & Other Poems. 129p. Repr. 1981. (ISBN 0-89966-365-6). Buccaneer Bks.
--Johnny Appleseed & Other Poems. 138p. 1981. (ISBN 0-89967-039-3). Harmony & Co.
--Johnny Appleseed and Other Poems. Richards, George Mather (1880-), illus. (Illus.). (gr. 5-8). 1928. Macmillan.
--Springfield Town is Butterfly Town: And Other Poems for Children. LC 74-79063. (Illus.). 72 p. 24cm. 1969. (ISBN 0-87338-041-X). Kent State University Press.

Lindsay, Norman Alfred William (1879-1969)
--The Magic Pudding: Being the Adventures of Bunyip Bluegum and His Friends Bill Barnacle and Sam Sawnoff. Lindsay, Norman Alfred William (1879-1969), illus. LC 76-362988. 1936. Farrar & Rinehart.
--Saturdee". Lindsay, Norman Alfred William (1879-1969), illus. LC 75-41175. (Illus.). vii, 277 p. 19cm. 1976. (ISBN 0-404-14716-X). AMS Press.

Lindsay, Philip (1906-)
--The Knights at Bay. LC 61-16997. 112p. illus. 26cm. (Companion book series). 1961. Walker.
--The Knights at Bay. Ogg, Oscar John (1908-1971), illus. LC 35-6537. viii p., 1 l., 11-222, 1 p. incl. illus., plates, map. 22 cm. (Tales of action. no. 1). c.1935. Loring & Mussey.

Lindsay, Walter (1870-)
--This Wooden Pig Went with Dora. Reid, James (1907-), illus. LC 30-295696. 4 p. l., 78 p. col. front., illus., col. plates. 24 cm. 1930. R. M. McBride & Company.

Lindsey, David L, jt. auth. see Whitehead, Barbara.

Lindsey, H. L.
--Little African Book. N.D. Carlton.

Lindskoog, Kathryn Ann (1934-) & Stevenson, Robert Louis (1850-1894)
--A Child's Garden of Christian Verses. LC 83-9534. (Illus.). 158 p. 22cm. c.1983. (ISBN 0-8307-0890-1). Regal Books.

Lindvall, Ella K.
--The Lost Son & Other Stories. Rowe, Gavin, illus. (Illus.). (People of the Bible Ser.). 1984. (ISBN 0-8024-0399-9). Moody.
--Read Aloud Bible Stories. LC 82-2114. (Illus.). v. 1. 28cm. c.1982. (ISBN 0-8024-7163-3). Moody Press.

Line, David
--Soldier and Me. LC 65-21018. 181p. 22cm. c.1965. Harper.
--Soldier and Me. large type ed. 181 p. 29cm. N.D. Harper & Row.

Lineaweaver, Marion McLennan (1911-)
--Jimmy and the Spy. 1st ed. Meyers, Robert William (1919-), illus. LC 51-9962. 180 p. illus. 21 cm. 1951. Bobbs-Merrill.
--The Wildfire. Fabry, Alois, Jr., illus. LC 53-10798. 187 p. 22cm. 1953. Funk & Wagnalls.

Lines, Kathleen, retold by.
--Agib and the Honey Cakes. Wilkinson, Barry, illus. LC 72-3208. (Illus.). 48 p. 24cm. (Walck fairy tales with historical notes). 1972. (ISBN 0-8098-1198-7). H. Z. Walck.
--Dick Whittington. Ardizzone, Edward Jeffrey Irving (1900-1979), illus. LC 75-126975. (Illus.). 42 p. 24cm. 1970. (ISBN 0-8098-1172-3). H. Z. Walck.
--The Faber Book of Magical Tales. Howard, Alan (1922-), illus. LC 85-4437. (Illus.). 176 p. 22cm. 1985. (ISBN 0-571-13648-6). Faber and Faber.
--The Faber Storybook. Howard, Alan (1922-), illus. (Illus.). (ps-5). 1972. (ISBN 0-571-10176-3). Faber & Faber.
--Faber Storybook. Howard, Alan (1922-), illus. (gr. k-3). 1967. (ISBN 0-571-04359-3). Transatlantic.
--The Haunted and the Haunters: Tales of Ghosts and Other Apparitions. LC 75-20361. x, 275 p. 22cm. 1975. (ISBN 0-374-32900-1). Farrar, Straus, Giroux.
--House of the Nighmare & Other Eerie Tales. LC 68-23749. 256p. 256p. 1st U.S. edition. (gr. 7 up). 1968. (ISBN 0-374-33432-3). FS&G.
--Lavender's Blue. Jones, Harold (1904-), illus. (Illus.). 180p. (ps-3). 1982. (ISBN 0-19-279537-6, Pub. by Oxford U Pr Childrens). Merrimack Pub Cir.
--Lavender's Blue: A Book of Nursery Rhymes. Jones, Harold (1904-), illus. LC 54-9816. 180p. illus. 26cm. 1954. (ISBN 0-531-01707-9). F. Watts. **Awards: (ALA); (CMA).**
--Lavender's Blue: A Book of Nursery Rhymes. Jones, Harold (1904-), illus. LC 54-9816. 180p. illus. 26cm. 1956. F. Watts.
--Nursery Stories. Jones, Harold (1904-), illus. LC 61-16020. 127p. col. illus. 26cm. 1961, c.1960. F. Watts.
--Nursery Stories. Jones, Harold (1904-), illus. (Illus.). (gr. k-3). 1960. (ISBN 0-531-01752-4). Watts.
--Once in Royal David's City. Jones, Harold (1904-), illus. (Illus.). 1956. Franklin Watts, Inc.
--Poems and Pictures. Montgomerie, Norah Mary (1913-), illus. LC 59-5244. 63p. illus. 26cm. c.1959. Abelard-Schuman.
--A Ring of Tales. Jones, Harold (1904-), illus. LC 59-667859. 239p. illus. 21cm. 1959, c.1958. Watts.
--Tales of Magic & Enchantment. Howard, Alan (1922-), illus. (gr. 4-6). 1967. (ISBN 0-571-06852-9). Transatlantic.

Lines, Kathleen, ed. see Defoe, Daniel.

Lines, Kathleen, jt. ed. see Lang, Andrew.

Lines, Kathleen, selected by see Uttley, Alison, Mrs.

Linevski, A.
--An Old Tale Carved Out of Stone. Polushkin, Maria, tr. from Rus. LC 72-92386. 256p. 1st U.S. edition. (gr. 7 up). 1973. Crown. **Awards: (MLB); (ALA).**

Linfield, Esther see Hobson, Sam B., pseud.

Linfield, Esther, tr. see Linfield, Esther & Hobson, George Cavey.

Linfield, Esther & Hobson, George Cavey (1890-1945)
--The Lion of the Kalahari. Hobson, Sam B., pseud. Linfield, Esther & Linfield, Esther, trs. from Afrikaans LC 76-3432. p. cm. c.1976. (ISBN 0-688-80049-1). (ISBN 0-688-84049-3). Greenwillow Books.

Linford, Marilyn, jt. auth. see Linford, Richard.

Linford, Richard & Linford, Marilyn
--I Hope They Call Me on a Mission Too. Young, Julie, illus. (ps-5). 1984. (ISBN 0-87747-991-7). Deseret Bk.

Ling, Yuriko
--A Little Tiny Bell and Other Stories. LC 81-117534. (Illus.). 50 p. 26cm. N.D. Y. Ling.

Lingard, Joan (1932-)
--Across the Barricades. LC 72-8915. 159 p. 23cm. 1973. (ISBN 0-8407-6280-1). T. Nelson.
--The Clearance. LC 74-1289. 160 p. 23cm. 1974. (ISBN 0-8407-6400-6). Nelson.
--The File on Fraulein Berg. LC 80-10447. p. cm. c.1980. (ISBN 0-525-66684-2). Elsevier/Nelson Books.
--Hostages to Fortune. LC 76-49646. 158 p. 21cm. c.1977. (ISBN 0-8407-6539-8). T. Nelson.
--Into Exile. LC 73-6549. 175 p. 22cm. 1973. (ISBN 0-8407-6324-7). T. Nelson.
--No Place for Love. (gr. 7-12). 1976. (ISBN 0-590-10142-0, Schol Trade Pap). Schol Bk Serv.
--Odd Girl Out. LC 79-4672. 187 p. 21cm. 1979, c.1978. Elsevier/Nelson Books.
--The Pilgrimage. LC 77-367996. 159 p. 23cm. 1976. (ISBN 0-241-89399-2). Hamilton.
--The Pilgrimage. LC 76-40902. p. cm. c.1976. (ISBN 0-8407-6500-2). T. Nelson.
--A Proper Place. LC 75-6591. 158 p. 21cm. 1975. (ISBN 0-8407-6425-1). T. Nelson.
--The Resettling. LC 75-35985. 166 p. 21cm. c.1975. (ISBN 0-8407-6485-5). T. Nelson.
--The Reunion. LC 78-2793. 159 p. 21cm. c.1978. (ISBN 0-8407-6592-4). T. Nelson.
--Snake Among the Sunflowers. LC 77-10706. p. cm. c.1977. (ISBN 0-8407-6570-3). T. Nelson.
--Strangers in the House. 1st ed. LC 83-1714. p. cm. 1983, c.1981. (ISBN 0-525-66912-4). E.P. Dutton.
--The Twelfth Day of July: A Novel of Modern Ireland. LC 72-1454. 158 p. 23cm. 1972. (ISBN 0-8407-6254-2). T. Nelson.

Lings, Albert A.
--Story of the Divine Child. (Illus.). N.D. Benziger.

Lingstrom, F. & Bird, M.
--Andy Pandy. N.D. Transatlantic Arts.

Lingstrom, Freda
--Richard's Wheel. Gurbutt, Barry, illus. LC 62-21657. 156p. illus. 21cm. 1963, c.1961. Roy Publishers.

Link, Margaret Schevill
--In the Garden of the Home God: A Retelling of a Navajo Tale. LC 44-205487. 25 p. incl. col. front., col. illus. 26 x 20 1/2 cm. 1943. Hazel Dreis Editions.

Link, Martin A., jt. ed. see Blood, Charles Lewis.

Link, Phoebe Forrest
--Small? Tall? Not at All!. Walstad, Chi Chi, illus. LC 72-88721. (Illus.). 32 p. 1973. (ISBN 0-513-01297-4). Denison.

Link, Ruth (1923-)
--A House Full of Mice. Dombret, Marianne, illus. LC 71-115073. (Illus.). 106 p. 20cm. 1970. Atheneum.

Link, Sheila, jt. auth. see Dixon, Franklin W.

Linker, Maud
--I am Sambo. LC 60-42192. 64p. illus. 24cm. 1960. Katydid Pub. Co.
--I Am Timbuctoo. LC 63-5993. 93 p. illus. 24cm. 1963. Katydid Pub. Co.

Linker, Robert, tr. see Butts, M.

Linker, Robert, tr. see Ogier le Danois & De Paris, Raimbert.

Linker, White Robert, tr. see Chrestien De Troyes.

Linklater, Andro
--Amazing Maisie and the Cold Porridge Brigade. Carey, Joanna, illus. LC 78-11118. 1979. (ISBN 0-394-84009-7). (ISBN 0-394-94009-1). Pantheon Books.

Linklater, Eric Robert Russell K. (1899-1974)
--The Pirates of the Deep Green Sea. Reeves, William, illus. LC 49-5189. 1949. Macmillan.
--The Wind on the Moon. Bentley, Nicolas Clerihew (1907-1978), illus. LC 44-40381. 4 p l., 323 p. illus. 19 1/2 cm. 1944. The Macmillan Company. **Award: (CMA).**

Linkletter, Arthur Gordon (1912-)
--Kids Sure Rite Funny!. A Child's Garden of Misinformation. Darrow, Whitney, Jr. (1909-), illus. LC 62-16685. (Illus.). 238 p. 22cm. 1962. B. Geis Associates; Distributed by Random House.

Links, Marty
--Candy Canes: A Holiday Treat. 1st ed. LC 70-163506. 63 p. illus. 19cm. c.1971. (ISBN 0-03-086736-3). Holt, Rinehart, Winston.

--Stories of Many Lands. Greenwood, Grace, pseud. (Illus.). (St. Nicholas Series for Girls). N.D. International Book Co.
--Stories of Many Lands. Greenwood, Grace, pseud, 1 of 9 vol. set. (Illus.). (Grace Greenwood's Stories for Children). N.D. International Book Co.
--Stories of Many Lands. Greenwood, Grace, pseud. LC 7-15864. viii, 206 p. plates. 17 c. 1867. Ticknor and Fields.
--Stories of My Childhood. Greenwood, Grace, pseud. (Illus.). (St. Nicholas Series for Girls). N.D. International Book Co.
--Stories of My Childhood and Other Tales. Greenwood, Grace, pseud. new, rev. ed. Klepper, Max F., illus. LC 7-18791. 2 p. l., 7-249 p. front., plates. 21 cm. c.1890. United States Book Company, Successors to J. W. Lovell Company.

Lippman, Peter J. (1936-)
--Amazing Travels of Ingrid Our Turtle. Lippman, Peter J. (1936-), illus. (Illus.). (ps-2). 1973. (ISBN 0-307-12500-9, Golden Pr). (ISBN 0-307-62050-6). Western Pub.
--Animals! Animals!. Lippman, Peter J. (1936-), illus. (Illus.). (gr. k-4). 1976. (ISBN 0-307-16808-5, Golden Pr). (ISBN 0-307-66808-8). Western Pub.
--Archibald: Or, I Was Very Shy. LC 75-6751. (Illus.). 32 p. 26cm. 1975. (ISBN 0-525-61531-8). Windmill Books.
--Busy Trains. Lippman, Peter J. (1936-), illus. LC 77-86145. (Illus.). 32p. (Picturebacks Ser.). (ps-3). 1981. (ISBN 0-394-93748-1). (ISBN 0-394-83748-7). Random.
--Busy Wheels. (Illus.). (A Pictureback Book). 1973. (ISBN 0-394-82706-6). Random House.
--From Here to There. Lippman, Peter J. (1936-), illus. LC 75-19947. (Illus.). 48p. (gr. 1 up). 1975. (ISBN 0-912846-11-9). Bookstore Pr.
--The Great Escape: Or, The Sewer Story. Lippman, Peter J. (1936-), illus. LC 73-76288. (Illus.). 45 p. 31cm. 1973. (ISBN 0-307-63575-9). Golden Press.
--Ingrid Our Turtle. Lippman, Peter J. (1936-), illus. LC 72-77847. (Illus.). 24 p. 33cm. 1973. Golden Press.
--The Know-It-Alls Go to Sea. Lippman, Peter J. (1936-), illus. LC 81-43430. (Illus.). 28 p. 16cm. c.1982. (ISBN 0-385-17396-2). Doubleday.
--The Know-It-Alls Help Out. Lippman, Peter J. (1936-), illus. LC 81-43431. (Illus.). 28 p. 16cm. c.1982. (ISBN 0-385-17397-0). Doubleday.
--The Know-It-Alls Mind the Store. Lippman, Peter J. (1936-), illus. LC 81-43432. (Illus.). 28 p. 16cm. c.1982. (ISBN 0-385-17399-7). Doubleday.
--The Know-It-Alls Take a Winter Vacation. Lippman, Peter J. (1936-), illus. LC 81-43433. (Illus.). 28 p. 16cm. (Doubleday Balloon Books). c.1982. (ISBN 0-385-17398-9). Doubleday.
--The Little Riddle Book. LC 71-187297. (Illus.). 65 p. 1972. (ISBN 0-06-023909-3). (ISBN 0-06-023910-7). Harper & Row.
--Mix or Match Mysteries: Carstairs Cat Solves Millions of Cases!. Lippman, Peter J. (1936-), illus. LC 82-61988. (Illus.). 9p. (ps-3). 1983. (ISBN 0-394-85809-3). Random.
--The Mix or Match Storybook: 2,097,152 Silly Stories. Gantz, David, illus. LC 73-18934. (Illus.). 9p. 1974. (ISBN 0-394-82808-9, BYR). Random.
--New at the Zoo. Lippman, Peter J. (1936-), illus. LC 79-77945. (Illus.). 31 p. 1969. Harper & Row.
--Plunkety Plunk. Lippman, Peter J. (1936-), illus. LC 63-16476. (Illus.). unpaged. 26cm. 1963. Ariel Books. **Award: (NYT).**

Lippmann, Julie Mathilde (1864-)
--Dearie, Dot and the Dog. Winner, Margaret F., illus. (Illus.). (The Little People's Ser.). N.D. Penn Publishing Co.
--Dearie, Dot and the Dog. Winner, Margaret F., illus. LC 3-14266. 194 p. front., plates. 20 cm. (Sunbeam Ser. For Young People). 1903. The Penn Publishing Company.
--Del's Debt, 1 of 21 vols. (Illus.). (Boys & Girls Booklovers Ser.: No. 19). 1905. Set. Henry Altemus Co.
--Del's Debt. (Illus.). (Illustrated Cherrycroft Ser.). N.D. Henry Altemus Co.
--Del's Debt. Bennett, Virginia, illus. 1 p. l., 283 p. incl. plates. front. 18 cm. c.1905. H. Altemus Company.
--Dorothy Day. Waugh, Ida, illus. (Keystone Ser.). N.D. Penn Publishing Co.
--Dorothy Day: A Story for Girls. Waugh, Ida, illus. 325 p. front., plates. 19 cm. 1898. The Penn Publishing Company.
--Dreamland. Betts, Anna Whelan, illus. (Illus.). (The Little People's Ser.). N.D. Penn Publishing Co.
--Dreamland. Betts, Anna Whelan, illus. LC 1-18529. 211 p. front., plates 20 cm. (Sunbeam Ser. for Young People). 1901. The Penn Publishing Company.
--Every-Day Girls. LC 4-25094. 4 p. l., 249 p. col. front., 3 col. pl. 20 cm. 1904. D. Appleton and Company.
--Every-Day Girls. (The Girls' Own Library). N.D. David McKay.
--Everyday Girls. (Illus.). 1905. D Appleton and Co.
--The Governess. Chickering, Charles R., illus. LC 16-15153. 370 p. front., plates. 20 cm. 1916. The Penn Publishing Company.
--The Interlopers. (Stories for Girls 9 to 16). N.D. Penn.
--Jock O' Dreams. McDermott, Jessie, illus. N.D. Robert Brotherts.
--Martha and Cupid. N.D. Grosset & Dunlap.
--Martha By-the-Day. N.D. Grosset & Dunlap.
--Miss Wildfire. Waugh, Ida, illus. (Keystone Ser.). N.D. Penn Publishing Co.
--Miss Wildfire: A Story for Girls. Waugh, Ida, illus. LC 12-18790. 370 p. front., plates. 19 cm. 1897. The Penn Publishing Company.
--Sweet P's. LC 2-19995. 192 p. front., plates. 20 cm. (Sunbeam Ser. For Young People). 1902. The Penn Publishing Company.
--Sweet P'S. Waugh, Ida, illus. (Illus.). (The Little People's Ser.). N.D. Penn Publishing Co.

Lips, Julius Ernst (1895-)
--Tents in the Wilderness. Wiese, Kurt (1887-1974), illus. N.D. J. B. Lippincontt.
--Tents in the Wilderness: The Story of a Labrador Indian Boy. Wiese, Kurt (1887-1974), illus. LC 42-22147. 297 p. incl. front., illus., plates. 21 cm. 1942. Frederick A. Stokes Company.

Lipscomb, George Dewey (1898-)
--Tales from the Land of Simba. Worden, Felice, illus. LC 46-859919. 96 p. illus. 24 cm. 1946. The Beechhurst Press.

Lipscomb, Marie Lauve
--The Lost Treasure. LC 59-16805. 118p. 21cm. 1959. Zondervan Pub. House.

Lipsett, Ella Partridge
--A Summer in the Apple Tree Inn. Wellman, Mary, illus. LC 6-10655. 4 p. l., 247 p. 4 pl. 19 cm. 1906. H. Holt and Company.

Lipson, Greta
--Fact, Fantasy, Folklore. (gr. 3-12). 1977. (ISBN 0-916456-11-0). Good Apple.
--It's a Special Day. Swanson, Wallace & Kropa, Susan, illus. (gr. k-4). 1978. (ISBN 0-916456-25-0). Good Apple.

Lipsyte, Robert Michael (1938-)
--The Contender. LC 67-19683. 182 p. 22cm. 1967. Harper & Row.
--Jock & Jill. 160p. (gr. 7 up). 1983. (ISBN 0-590-32862-X). Scholastic Inc.
--Jock and Jill: A Novel. LC 81-47723. 153 p. 21cm. (A Charlotte Zolotow Bk.). c.1982. (ISBN 0-06-023899-2). (ISBN 0-06-023900-X). Harper & Row.
--One Fat Summer. LC 76-49746. 152 p. 22cm. c.1977. (ISBN 0-06-023895-X). (ISBN 0-06-023896-8). Harper & Row.
--Summer Rules: A Novel. LC 79-2816. 150 p. 22cm. c.1981. (ISBN 0-06-023897-6). (ISBN 0-06-023898-4). Harper & Row.
--The Summerboy: A Novel. 1st ed. LC 82-47578. 153 p. 22cm. c.1982. (ISBN 0-06-023888-7). (ISBN 0-06-023889-5). Harper & Row.

Liquori, Sal
--Psi Patrol: Sal's Book. LC 84-14154. 148 p. 18cm. (Point). 1985, c.1984. (ISBN 0-590-33201-5). Scholastic Inc.

Lisetor, Scott, jt. auth. see Shirley, Scott.

Lisker, Sonia O. (1933-)
--The Attic Witch. Lisker, Sonia O. (1933-), illus. LC 73-76453. 48 p. of col. illus. 22cm. 1973. Four Winds Press.
--I Am. Linker, Sonia O. (1933-), illus. LC 73-10409. (Illus.). 32 p. 19cm. 1973. (ISBN 0-8038-3387-3). Hastings House Publishers.
--I Can Be. Lisker, Sonia O. (1933-), illus. LC 72-4243. (Illus.). 32 p. 19cm. 1972. (ISBN 0-8038-3383-0). Hastings House.
--I Used to. Lisker, Sonia O. (1933-), illus. LC 76-54810. (Illus.). 32 p. 21cm. c.1977. (ISBN 0-590-07469-5). Four Winds Press.
--Lost. Lisker, Sonia O. (1933-), illus. LC 74-22281. (Illus.). 48 p. 26cm. 1975. (ISBN 0-15-249363-8). Harcourt Brace Jovanovich.

Lisker, Sonia O. (1933-) & Dean, Leigh
--Two Special Cards. Lisker, Sonia O. (1933-), illus. LC 75-35609. (Illus.). 48 p. 21cm. c.1976. Harcourt Brace Jovanovich.

Lisker, Tom (1928-)
--Mysterious Castle Builders. LC 78-21886. (Unsolved Mysteries of the World Ser.). N.D. (ISBN 0-89547-074-8). Silver.
--The Mystery of Robin Hood. LC 79-18396. (Unsolved Mysteries of the World Ser.). N.D. (ISBN 0-89547-079-9). Silver.
--The Mystery of Robin Hood: Fact or Fantasy?. Whitehead, Samuel B, illus. LC 79-18396. (Illus.). 48 p. 24cm. c.1979. (ISBN 0-89547-079-9). C.P.I.
--Tall Tales: American Myths. LC 77-11104. (Illus.). 48 p. 24cm. c.1977. (ISBN 0-8172-1039-3). Contemporary Perspectives.

Lisle, Clifton
--Hobnails & Heather. Newman, Ernest, illus. N.D. Harcourt Brace & Co.
--Lenape Trails. Esley, Joan, illus. LC 28-22314. 6 p. l., 3-310 p. front., plates. 20 cm. c.1928. Harcourt, Brace and Company.
--Saddle Bags. Dennis, Morgan (1891-1960), illus. LC 28-12164. (Illus.). 5p. l., 278 p. 1923. Harcourt, Brace and Co.
--Sandy Flash: The Highwayman of Castle Rock. LC 22-232589. 3 p. l., 281 p. front., plates. 19 cm. c.1922. Harcourt, Brace and Company.
--The Treasure of the Chateau. Siegel, William (1905-), illus. LC 29-189286. 5 p. l., 3-279 p. incl. front., plates. 20 cm. c.1929. Harcourt, Brace and Company.

Lisle, Eric
--Under Honour's Flag. (The Albion Library). N.D. Frederick Warne & Co.

Lisle, Janet Taylor
--The Dancing Cats of Applesap. Shefts, Joelle, illus. LC 83-15696. (Illus.). 176p. (gr. 5-6). 1984. (ISBN 0-02-759140-9). Bradbury Pr.
--Sirens and S.P.I.E.S. LC 84-21518. 169 p. 22cm. c.1985. (ISBN 0-02-759150-6). Bradbury Press. **Award: (ALA).**

Lisle, Ruth J.
--Chickens Don't Turn to Dust. (Illus.). (gr. 2-5). 1968. (ISBN 0-8059-0175-2). Dorrance.

Lisle, Seward D., pseud., see Ellis, Edward Sylvester.

Lisowski, Gabriel (1946-)
--The Invitations. Lisowski, Gabriel (1946-), illus. (ps). 1980. (ISBN 0-03-051016-3). HR&W.
--Miss Piggy. Lisowski, Gabriel (1946-), illus. LC 77-2888. (Illus.). 32 p. c.1977. (ISBN 0-03-019471-7). Holt, Rinehart and Winston.
--On the Little Hearth: Words and Music for the Popular Yiddish Classic, Oifn Pripitchik. Lisowski, Gabriel (1946-), illus. LC 78-4270. (Illus.). 24 p. 24cm. c.1978. (ISBN 0-03-039931-9). Holt, Rinehart, Winston.
--Roncalli's Magnificent Circus. Lisowski, Gabriel (1946-), illus. LC 79-8430. (Illus.). 32 p. 29cm. c.1980. (ISBN 0-385-14856-9). (ISBN 0-385-14857-7). Doubleday.

Lisowski, Gabriel (1946-), adapted by.
--How Tevye Became a Milkman. LC 76-8226. (Abapted from a Story by Shalom Rabinowitz). p. cm. c.1976. (ISBN 0-03-016636-5). Holt, Rinehart, and Winston.

Liss, Howard, jt. auth. see Tittle, Yelberton Abraham.

Liss, Howard (1922-)
--Asgeir of Iceland. Lippmann, Ingeborg, illus. LC 74-123560. (Illus.). 64 p. 23cm. 1970. J. Messner.
--The Giant Book of Strange but True Sports Stories. Mathieu, Joseph (1945-), illus. LC 76-8132. p. cm. 1976. (ISBN 0-394-83287-6). (ISBN 0-394-93287-0). Random House.

List, Erna C.
--Freddie Visits Earth. Macrae, Ruth K., illus. LC 62-18871. 31p. illus. 20cm. 1962. Dorrance.

List, Ilka Katherine (1935-)
--Grandma's Beach Surprise. Sanderson, Ruth, illus. LC 75-712. (Illus.). 47 p. 20cm. c.1975. (ISBN 0-399-60958-X). Putnam.

Lista, J. G., tr. see Amicis, Edmondo de.

Lister, Marion Mazer
--Big Brother and Little Brother. Rosenberg, Edna Mazer, illus. LC 48-3537. 28 p. col. illus. 20 cm. 1946. Rinehart.

Lister, R., retold by.
--Bedtime Stories. Serkin, Amalia, illus. Wagner, Soltan, photos by. LC 49-17374. 21 p. col. illus. 27cm. (A Chanticleer Junior Book). 1948. Chanticleer Press.

Litchfield, Ada Bassett (1916-)
--A Button in Her Ear. Rubin, Caroline, ed. Mill, Eleanor, illus. LC 75-28390. (Illus.). 32p. (Concept Bks.). (gr. 2-4). 1976. (ISBN 0-8075-0987-6). A Whitman.
--A Cane in Her Hand. Mill, Eleanor, illus. LC 77-14255. p. cm. (Concept book). 1977. (ISBN 0-8075-1056-4). A. Whitman.
--Captain Hook, That's Me. Lisker, Sonia O. (1933-), illus. LC 82-70495. (Illus.). 32p. (gr. 2-6). 1982. (ISBN 0-8027-6445-2). (ISBN 0-8027-6446-0). Walker & Co.
--The Good-Morning Book. Hartshorn, Ruth M. (1928-), illus. LC 66-12930. 32p. col. illus. 24cm. c.1966. Steck.
--The Good-Night, Sleep-Tight Book. 1969. (ISBN 0-8114-7651-0). Steck-Vaughn Company.
--The Good Night, Sleep Tight Book. Hartshorn, Ruth M. (1928-), illus. LC 69-11091. (Illus.). 32 p. 24cm. 1969. Steck-Vaughn Co.
--I Can. Can You?. Hartshorn, Ruth M. (1928-), illus. LC 70-110690. (Illus.). 32 p. 24cm. 1971. (ISBN 0-8114-7710-X). Steck-Vaughn Co.
--It's Going to Rain. Hartshorn, Ruth M. (1928-), illus. LC 80-12732. p. cm. 1980. (ISBN 0-689-30779-9). Atheneum.
--Making Room for Uncle Joe. Owens, Gail, illus. LC 83-17036. (Illus.). 30 p. 24cm. 1984. (ISBN 0-8075-4952-5). A. Whitman.
--The Wonderful, Wonderful Book. Hartshorn, Ruth M. (1928-), illus. LC 68-11217. (Illus.). 32 p. 23cm. 1968. Steck-Vaughn Co.
--Words in Our Hands. Cogancherry, Helen, illus. LC 79-28402. p. cm. (Concept book/level 2). 1980. A. Whitman.

Litchfield, Grace Denio (1849-)
--Little He and She. (Illus.). N.D. Lothrop Lee & Shepard Co.

Litchfield, Mary Elizabeth (1854-)
--The Nine Worlds: Stories from Norse Mythology. LC 12-362066. vi p., 1 l., 163 p. front., pl., diagrs. 19 cm. 1890. Ginn & Company.

Litgen, Kurt
--Two Against the Arctic: The Story of a Restless Life Between Greenland and Alaska. McHugh, Isabel & McHugh, Florence, trs. from Ger. 239p. illus. 22cm. 1957. Pantheon.

Litowinsky, Olga
--The High Voyage. LC 77-24893. p. cm. 1977. (ISBN 0-670-37155-6). Viking Press.

Littell, Margaret
--The Campus Medal. LC 31-3180. 96 p. incl. plates. 20 cm. c.1930. David C. Cook Publishing Co.

Littell, Robert (1937-)
--Gaston's Ghastly Green Thumb. 1st ed. Wende, Philip (1939-), illus. LC 79-87083. (Illus.). 31 p. 26cm. 1969. Cowles.
--Left and Right with Lion and Ryan. Wende, Philip (1939-), illus. LC 76-87077. (Illus.). 31 p. 25cm. 1969. Cowles Book Co.

Litten, Frederic Nelson (1885-1951)
--Air Mission to Algiers. LC 43-15502. xii p., 1 l., 274 p. 21 cm. 1943. Dodd, Mead & Company.
--Air Trails North. LC 39-25956. viii p., 1 l., 236 p. 21 cm. 1939. Dodd, Mead & Company.
--Airmen of the Amazon. LC 42-23862. viii, 280 p. 21 cm. 1942. Dodd, Mead & Company.
--Brooks of the Valley Airways. Elven, Sven, illus. LC 31-83288. v, 1 p., 1 l., 280, 1 p. front., illus. 20 cm. 1931. D. Appleton and Company.
--The Kingdom of Flying Men: A Story of Air Cargo. LC 46-71797. 5 p. l., 9-247 p. 21 cm. 1946. The Westminster Press.
--Pilot of the High Andes. LC 41-18123. viii p., 1 l., 298 p. 21 cm. 1941. Dodd, Mead & Company.
--Pilot of the High Sierras. LC 37-30400. viii p., 1 l., 350 p. 21 cm. 1937. Dodd, Mead & Company.
--Pilot of the North Country: A Johnny Caruthers Flying Story. LC 38-32615. viii p., 1 l., 244 p. 21 cm. 1938. Dodd, Mead & Company.
--Rendezvous on Mindanao. LC 45-10322. x, 237 p. 19 cm. 1945. Dodd, Mead & Company.
--Rhodes of the Flying Cadets. LC 29-19880. 5 p. l., 251, 1 p. front. 20 cm. 1929. D. Appleton and Company.
--Rhodes of the Leathernecks. LC 35-19983. vi p., 1 l., 376 p. front. 20 cm. 1935. Dodd, Mead & Company.
--Rhodes of the 94th. Knight, Clayton (1891-1969), illus. LC 33-220447. 306 p. front., plates. 20 cm. c.1933. Sears Publishing Company, Inc.
--Sinister Island Squadron. LC 44-9747. x p., 1 l., 251 p. 19 cm. 1944. Dodd, Mead & Company.
--Sun-Up on the Range. Henning, Albin, illus. LC 30-298251. 5 p. l., 263, 1 p. front., illus. 20 cm. 1930. D. Appleton and Company.
--Transatlantic Pilot,. LC 40-34112. viii p., 1l., 307p. 21cm. 1940. Dodd, Mead & Company.
--Treasure Bayou. LC 49-11234. 223 p. 22 cm. 1949. Westminster Press.

Littke, Lael J. (1929-)
--Cave-in!. Dunnington, Tom, illus. LC 80-28189. p. cm. (Prime time adventures). 1981. (ISBN 0-516-02102-8). Childrens Press.
--Trish for President. LC 84-4587. 160p. (gr. 7 up). 1984. (ISBN 0-15-290512-X, HJ). (ISBN 0-15-290512-X). HarBraceJ.

Little, Archibald
--The Rat's Plaint. (Illus.). N.D. Charles Scribner's Sons.

Little, Caroline Frances
--Little Winter-Green. LC 7-19393. iv, 98 p. front., 2 pl. 19 cm. (The "little heroine" series). c.1896. T. Whittaker.

Little, Eleanor Ann
--A Birthday Present for Janmie. Little, Eleanor Ann, illus. LC 54-9531. 31 p. illus. 22cm. c.1954. Comet Press Books.

Little, Flora Jean (1932-)
--From Anna. Sandin, Joan (1942-), illus. LC 72-76505. (Illus.). 201 p. 21cm. 1972. (ISBN 0-06-023911-5). (ISBN 0-06-023911-5). Harper & Row.
--Home from Far. Lazare, Gerald John (1927-), illus. LC 65-11473. (Illus.). 145p. (Another poignant story about a different sort of handicap). (gr. 5 up). 1965. (ISBN 0-316-52792-0). Little.
--Kate. LC 70-148419. 162 p. 20cm. (Trophy Book, J37). 1972, c.1971. (ISBN 0-06-440037-9). Harper.
--Listen for the Singing. LC 76-58323. 215 p. 22cm. c.1977. (ISBN 0-525-33705-9). Dutton. **Award: (CCCL).**

--A Crazy Flight, and Other Poems. Spanfeller, James John (1930-), illus. LC 69-13775. (Illus.). 47 p. 21cm. 1969. Harcourt, Brace & World.
--Four Way Stop, and Other Poems. Spanfeller, James John (1930-), illus. LC 75-28068. (Illus.). 40 p. 21cm. 1976. (ISBN 0-689-50040-8). Atheneum.
--Happy Birthday!. 1st ed. Blegvad, Erik (1923-), illus. LC 64-11492. (Illus.). 32 p. 18cm. 1964. Harcourt, Brace & World.
--I'm Hiding. 1st ed. Blegvad, Erik (1923-), illus. LC 61-6119. (Illus.). (gr. k-2). 1961. (ISBN 0-15-238090-6, HJ). HarBraceJ.
--I'm Not Me. 1st ed. Blegvad, Erik (1923-), illus. LC 63-7899. (Illus.). unpaged. 18cm. 1963. Harcourt, Brace & World.
--I'm Waiting. Blegvad, Erik (1923-), illus. LC 66-12590. (Illus.). 32p. (gr. k-3). 1966. (ISBN 0-15-238211-9). HarBraceJ.
--A Lollygag of Limericks. Low, Joseph (1911-), illus. LC 77-18060. (Illus.). 44 p. 1978. (ISBN 0-689-50104-8). Atheneum.
--The Malibu and Other Poems. Spanfeller, James John (1930-), illus. LC 72-190557. (Illus.). 44 p. 21cm. 1972. Atheneum.
--Monkey Puzzle & Other Poems. Frasconi, Antonio (1919-), illus. LC 84-3050. (Illus.). 64p. (gr. 7 up). 1984. (ISBN 0-689-50310-5, McElderry Bk). Atheneum.
--Moon & a Star & Other Poems. Shahn, Judith, illus. LC 65-14115. (Illus.). 48p. (gr. 3-5). 1965. (ISBN 0-15-255330-4). HarBraceJ.
--No Way of Knowing: Dallas Poems. Giovanni, Nikki, intro. by. LC 80-14584. 64p. (gr. 5 up). 1980. (ISBN 0-689-50179-X, McElderry Bk). Atheneum.
--O Frabjous Day: Poetry for Holidays and Special Occasions. LC 76-28510. xi, 205 p. 22cm. 1977. (ISBN 0-689-50076-9). Atheneum.
--O Sliver of Liver: Together with Other Triolets, Cinquains, Haiku, Verses, and a Dash of Poems. Van Rynbach, Iris, illus. LC 78-21190. (Illus.). 42 p. 21cm. 1979. (ISBN 0-689-50133-1). Atheneum.
--Old Mrs. Twindlytart & Other Rhymes. Arno, Enrico (1913-1981), illus. (Illus.). (gr. k-3). 1967. (ISBN 0-15-257770-X). (ISBN 0-15-257771-8). HarBraceJ.
--Old Mrs. Twindlytart: Poems. 1st ed. Arno, Enrico (1913-1981), illus. LC 67-2794. (Illus.). 48 p. 22cm. 1967. Harcourt, Brace & World.
--Poems of Christmas. LC 80-13627. p. cm. 1980. (ISBN 0-689-50180-3). Atheneum.
--See What I Found. 1st ed. Blegvad, Erik (1923-), illus. LC 62-8744. (Illus.). 18cm. 1962. Harcourt, Brace & World.
--Sky Songs. Fisher, Leonard Everett (1924-), illus. LC 83-12955. (Illus.). 32p. (ps-3). 1984. (ISBN 0-8234-0502-8). (ISBN 0-8234-0502-8). Holiday.
--The Way Things Are, and Other Poems. 1st ed. Oliver, Jenni (1947-), illus. LC 74-76275. (Illus.). 40 p. 21cm. (gr. 5 up). 1974. (ISBN 0-689-50008-4, McElderry Bk). Atheneum.
--Whispers: And Other Poems. 1st ed. Chwast, Jacqueline (1932-), illus. LC 58-57112. (Illus.). 48 p. 18cm. (gr. 1-4). 1958. (ISBN 0-15-295707-3). Harcourt, Brace.
--Why Am I Grown So Cold?. Poems of the Unknowable. LC 82-6646. xxi, 269 p. 22cm. 1982. (ISBN 0-689-50242-7). Atheneum.
--Wide Awake, & Other Poems. Chwast, Jacqueline (1932-), illus. LC 59-5629. (Illus.). (gr. 1-4). 1959. (ISBN 0-15-296602-1). HarBraceJ.
--Worlds I Know and Other Poems. Arnold, Tim, illus. LC 85-7344. p. cm. 1985. (ISBN 0-689-50332-6). Atheneum.

Livingston, Myra Cohn (1926-), selected by.
--Christmas Poems. Hyman, Trina Schart (1939-), illus. LC 83-18559. (Illus.). c.1984. (ISBN 0-8234-0508-7). Holiday House. **Award: (ALA).**
--Easter Poems. Wallner, John C. (1945-), illus. LC 84-15866. (Illus.). 32p. (gr. k-3). 1985. (ISBN 0-8234-0546-X). Holiday.
--Listen, Children, Listen: An Anthology of Poems for the Very Young. Hyman, Trina Schart (1939-), illus. LC 70-167836. (Illus.). 96 p. 19cm. 1972. (ISBN 0-15-245570-1). Harcourt Brace Jovanovich.
--One Little Room, an Everywhere: Poems of Love. Frasconi, Antonio (1919-), illus. LC 75-8859. (Illus.). 152p. (gr. 7 up). 1975. (ISBN 0-689-50032-7, McElderry Bk). Atheneum.
--Speak Roughly to Your Little Boy: A Collection of Parodies and Burlesques, Together with the Original Poems, Chosen and Annotated for Young People. Low, Joseph (1911-), illus. LC 71-140779. (Illus.). xi, 180 p. 22cm. 1971. (ISBN 0-15-277859-4). Harcourt Brace Jovanovich.
--Thanksgiving Poems. Gammell, Stephen, illus. LC 85-762. (Illus.). 32 p. 24cm. c.1985. (ISBN 0-8234-0570-2). Holiday House.
--A Tune Beyond Us: A Collection of Poetry. Spanfeller, James John (1930-), illus. LC 68-11502. (gr. 6 up). 1968. (ISBN 0-15-291098-0, HJ). HarBraceJ. **Award: (ALA).**
--What a Wonderful Bird the Frog Are: An Assortment of Humorous Poetry-Verse. LC 72-88171. (gr. 5-9). 1973. (ISBN 0-15-295400-7, HJ). HarBraceJ.

Livingston, Richard Roland
--The Hunkendunkens. Pincus, Harriet (1938-), illus. LC 68-25188. (Illus.). 36 p. 1968. Harcourt, Brace & World.

Livingston, Robert, pseud., see Scaife, Roger Livingston.

Livingston, Rosa Ackerman
--Turkey Feathers: Tales of Old Bergen County. LC 63-15381. 166 p. illus. 24 cm. 1963. Phillip-Campbell Press.

Livingstone, Cora Luetta (1874-)
--Glimpses of Pioneer Life for Little Folks ... LC 4-18494. 166 p. col. front., illus., col. pl. 19 cm. 1904. A. Flanagan Company.

Livingstone, Mabel, jt. auth. see Le Roy, Kate Warner.

Livingstone, Malcolm
--Eric and the Mad Inventor. Sheridan, John, illus. LC 79-7322. (Illus.). 32 p. 28cm. 1979. (ISBN 0-672-52609-3). Bobbs-Merrill Co.

Livius, Titus., jt. auth. see Church, Alfred John.

Livne, Zvi (1891-)
--The Children of the Cave: A Tale of Israel and of Rome. Ambrus, Victor G., pseud. (1935-), illus. Ambrus, Gyozo Laszlo. LC 70-491976. (Illus.). 22cm. v, 168p. 1969. Oxford Univ. Press.
--Children of the Cave: A Tale of Israel and of Rome. Raphael, Sipora, tr. LC 70-100707. 224p. 1st U.S. edition. (gr. 8 up). 1970. (ISBN 0-8098-3087-6). Walck.

Livoni, Cathy (1956-)
--Element of Time. 1st ed. LC 82-48761. 182 p. 22cm. c.1983. (ISBN 0-15-225369-6). Harcourt Brace Jovanovich.

Livsey, Rosemary E, ed.
--A. B, C. Go!. LC 61-17989. 400p. illus. 25cm. (Collier's junior classics series). 1962. Crowell-Collier Pub. Co.

Llerena, Aquirre Carlos Antonio (1952-)
--The Fair at Kanta: A Story from Peru. LC 75-6764. p. cm. 1975. (ISBN 0-03-014766-2). Holt, Rinehart and Winston.
--Sticks, Stones. LC 76-44201. (Illus.). 32 p. 24cm. c.1977. (ISBN 0-03-018246-8). Holt, Rinehart and Winston.

Llewellen, E. L.
--The Deserted Mill and Potter Party. N.D. Andrew F. Graves.

Llewellyn, David William Alun see Taffy, pseud.

LLewellyn, E. E.
--The Dove's Nest, 1 of 25 vols. (Illus.). (New Primary Lib.: No. 15). N.D. A. I. Bradley & Co.'s Pubs.
--Fido and Frank, 1 of 25 vols. (Illus.). (New Primary Lib.: No. 15). N.D. Set. A. I. Bradley & Co.'s Pubs.
--Piety And Pride. N.D. Bradley & Woodruff.
--Uncle John, 1 of 25 vols. (Illus.). (New Primary Lib.: No. 15). N.D. A. I. Bradley & Co.'s Pubs.
--A Visit to the Woods, 1 of 36 vols. (Illus.). (New Primary Lib.: No. 15). N.D. Set. A. I. Bradley & Co.'s Pubs.

Llewellyn, H.
--Custer's Last Charge: or the Raven of Death. (Champion Stories). 1877. C. T. DeWitt.
--Grizzly Gulch: or, Squatting Bear's Last Bullet. (Champion Stories). 1877. C. T. DeWitt.
--Ojibbeway Joe: or, Red Eagle's Last Fight. (Champion Stories). 1877. C. T. Dewitt.

Llewellyn, Lloyd Richard Dafydd see Llewellyn, Richard, pseud.

Llewellyn, Megan
--The Eagle of Gwernabwy: Tales from Wales. Bryant, David (1938-), illus. LC 77-79865. (Illus.). 48 p. 21cm. (The Pergamon English Library). 1970. Pergamon Press.
--The Stray Cow: Tales from Wales. Usbourne, Karen, illus. LC 73-99942. (Illus.). 46 p. 21cm. (The Pergamon English Library). 1970. (ISBN 0-08-015697-5). Pergamon Press.

Llewellyn, Richard, pseud., see Llewellyn, Lloyd Richard Dafydd.

Llewellyn, Richard, pseud. (1906-)
--How Green Was My Valley. Llewellyn, Lloyd Richard Dafydd. (gr. 9 up). 1941. (ISBN 0-02-573430-X). (ISBN 0-02-022550-4). Macmillan.

--The Witch of Merthyn: A Tale of Smuggling in the Time of Scarlet Capes and the Red Tricorne. Llewellyn Lloyd, Richard D. LC 54-7669. 253p. illus. 22cm. (Cavalcade books). 1954. Doubleday.

Llewelyn, G. Michael
--Holiday Adventure. N.D. Transatlantic Arts, Inc.

Llimona, Mercedes
--The Seasons with Strawberry Shortcake. Llimona, Mercedes, illus. LC 80-50180. (Illus.). 14 p. 20cm. c.1980. (ISBN 0-394-84569-2). Random House.
--Strawberry Shortcake's Favorite Mother Goose Rhymes. Llimona, Mercedes, illus. LC 82-5204. p. cm. 1983. (ISBN 0-394-95431-9). Random House.

Lloyd
--Lloyd's Literature for Little Folks. N.D. Sower, Potts & Co.

Lloyd, David (1945-)
--Silly Games. Cross, Peter, illus. LC 84-27697. (Illus.). 25 p. 17cm. (Dinosaur Days). 1985. (ISBN 0-394-87380-7). Random House.
--The Terrible Thing. Cross, Peter, illus. LC 84-27702. (Illus.). 25 p. 17cm. (Dinosaur Days). 1985. (ISBN 0-394-87381-5). Random House.
--Today I Saw a Hippopotamus. Tomblin, Gill, illus. LC 84-27694. p. cm. 1985. (ISBN 0-394-87492-7). (ISBN 0-394-97492-1). Random House.
--Today I Was a Pirate. Tomblin, Gill, illus. LC 85-1816. p. cm. 1985. (ISBN 0-394-87491-9). (ISBN 0-394-97491-3). Random House.

Lloyd, Davide, intro. by see Voake, Charlotte.

Lloyd, Elizabeth (1848-1917)
--The Old Red School-House. A Temperance Story for Teachers and Pupils. LC 7-10395. 127 p. front., illus. 18 cm. 1895. Friends' Book Association of Philadelphia.

Lloyd, Ernest, ed.
--Animal Heroes. LC 46-22075. 160 p. illus. 20 1/2 cm. 1946. Pacific Press Publishing Assn.
--Our Dog Friends. LC 67-31684. 64p. (ps-3). 1950. Pacific Pr Pub Assn.
--Prayer Stories for Boys and Girls. LC 48-623824. 96 p. illus. 23 cm. 1948. Pacific Press Pub. Assn.
--Stories of Clever Dogs: Old Stories and New. Chavarria, Luis, illus. LC 24-4559. 92 p. incl. front., illus. 20 cm. c.1924. Review and Herald Publishing Assn.

Lloyd, ErnestGould Harmon, ed. see White, Allen Gould.

Lloyd, Errol (1943-)
--Nandy's Bedtime. (Illus.). 32p. (ps). 1982. (ISBN 0-370-30395-4, Pub by The Bodley Head). Merrimack Pub Cir.
--Nini at Carnival. LC 78-4776. (Illus.). 26 p. 1979, c.1978. (ISBN 0-690-03891-7). (ISBN 0-690-03892-5). Crowell.
--Nini at Carnival. (Illus.). 1979. Harper.

Lloyd, Evelyn
--Big Bird's Birthday Party: Sesame Street. Bradfield, Roger (1924-), illus. (Illus.). (Golden Play & Learn Bk). (ps-2). 1973. (ISBN 0-307-10744-2, Golden Pr). Western Pub.

Lloyd, Francis V. (1908-)
--Forward to Teach. Gretzer, John, illus. LC 67-2964. (Illus.). x, 172 p. 21cm. 1967. Little, Brown.

Lloyd, Freeman
--A B C of Dogs. Thorne, Diana (1894-), illus. LC 38-18281. 44 p. illus. (part col.) 20 cm. c.1938. Rand McNally & Company.

Lloyd, Hugh
--Among the River Pirates. Fogel, Seymour, illus. LC 34-6276. vi, 7-197 p. front. 20 cm. (His Skippy Dare mystery stories). c.1934. Grosset & Dunlap.
--The Clue at Skeleton Rocks. Salg, Bert N., illus. LC 32-13241. vi, 276 p. front., plates. 20 cm. (His Hal Keen mystery stories). c.1931. Grosset & Dunlap.
--The Copperhead Trail Mystery. Salg, Bert N., illus. LC 31-12243. vi, 218 p. front., plates. 20 cm. (His Hal Keen mystery stories). c.1931. Grosset & Dunlap.
--The Doom of Stark House. Salg, Bert N., illus. LC 33-3288. vi, 238 p. front., plates. 20 cm. (His Hal Keen mystery stories). c.1933. Grosset & Dunlap.
--Held for Ransom. Fogel, Seymour, illus. LC 34-6278. vi, 7-221 p. front. 20 cm. (His Skippy Dare mystery stories). c.1934. Grosset & Dunlap.
--The Hermit of Gordon's Creek. Salg, Bert N., illus. LC 31-12242. vi, 237 p. front., plates. 20 cm. (His Hal Keen mystery stories). c.1931. Grosset & Dunlap.
--Kidnapped in the Jungle. Salg, Bert N., illus. LC 31-12241. vi, 244 p. front., pl. 20 cm. (His Hal Keen mystery stories). c.1931. Grosset & Dunlap.
--The Lonesome Swamp Mystery. Salg, Bert N., illus. LC 32-2021. vi, 264 p. front., plates. 20 cm. (His Hal Keen mystery stories). c.1932. Grosset & Dunlap.
--The Lost Mine of the Amazon. Salg, Bert N., illus. LC 33-24531. vi, 212 p. front., plates. 20 cm. (His Hal Keen mystery stories). c.1933. Grosset & Dunlap.
--The Mysterious Arab. Salg, Bert N., illus. LC 31-22802. vi, 237 p. front., plates. 20 cm. (His Hal Keen mystery stories). c.1931. Grosset & Dunlap.
--The Mystery at Dark Star Ranch. LC 34-322087. vi, 240 p. front., plates. 20 cm. (His Hal Keene mystery stories). c.1934. Grosset & Dunlap.
--Prisoners in Devil's Bog. Fogel, Seymour, illus. LC 34-6277. vi, 212 p. front. 20 cm. (His Skippy Dare mystery stories). c.1934. Grosset & Dunlap.
--The Smugglers' Secret. Salg, Bert N., illus. LC 31-21183. vi, 249 p. front., plates. 20 cm. (His Hal Keen mystery stories). c.1931. Grosset & Dunlap.

Lloyd, Jeremy
--The Woodland Gospels According to Captain Beaky and His Band. Percy, Graham, illus. Archbishop of Canterbury, frwd. by. LC 83-20790. (Illus.). 62 p. 30cm. 1984. (ISBN 0-571-13211-1). (ISBN 0-571-13270-7). Faber and Faber.

Lloyd, John Uri (1849-1936)
--Etidorpha. N.D. Dodd Mead & Co.
--Stringtown on the Pike. N.D. Dodd Mead & Co.

Lloyd, Margaret
--Seven Dwarfs. (gr. k-2). N.D. Carlton.

Lloyd, Marion
--Penny and Peter of the Island. Tait, Agnes (1897-), illus. LC 41-18352. 62 p. col. illus. 28 cm. c.1941. J. Messner, Inc.

Lloyd, Mary Edna
--Glad Easter Day. Goldsborough, June (1923-), illus. (gr. k-1). 1961. (ISBN 0-687-14765-4). Abingdon.
--Jesus, the Children's Friend. Paull, Grace A. (1898-), illus. LC 55-14816. unpaged. illus. 21cm. c.1955. Abingdon Press.
--Jesus, the Little New Baby. Paull, Grace A. (1898-), illus. N.D. Abingdon Press.

Lloyd, Mary Norris (1908-)
--Billy Hunts the Unicorn. Papish, Robin Lloyd, illus. LC 64-19080. (Illus.). 26cm. 61p. (gr. 4-6). 1964. (ISBN 0-8038-0686-8). Hastings.
--The Desperate Dragons. Payne, Joan Balfour (1923-1973), illus. LC 59-11252. 61p. illus. 26cm. 1960. Hastings House.
--Katie and the Catastrophe. Sirdofsky, Sam, illus. (Illus.). 74 p. 22cm. 1968. Reilly & Lee.
--The Village that Allah Forgot: A Story of Modern Tunisia. Piechocki, Ed, illus. LC 72-8190. (Illus.). 128 p. 21cm. 1973. (ISBN 0-8038-7746-3). Hastings House.

Lloyd, Megan
--Chicken Tricks. 1st ed. Lloyd, Megan, illus. LC 82-48846. p. cm. c.1983. (ISBN 0-06-023984-0). (ISBN 0-06-023985-9). Harper & Row.

Lloyd, Noel, jt. auth. see Palmer, Geoffrey.

Lloyd, Noel, jt. ed. see Palmer, Geoffrey.

Lloyd, Norman, jt. auth. see Boni, Margaret Bradford.

Lloyd, Norman (1909-1980)
--The New Golden Song Book. Blair, Mary Robinson (1911-), illus. (Giant Golden Book). 1955. Golden Press.

Lloyd, Pamela
--Ikerchat and Sarah. Lloyd, Pamela, illus. LC 60-12004. (Illus.). 32p. 1960. Reily & Lee and Company.
--Samuel, the Ambitious Flea. Lloyd, Pamela, illus. LC 61-5568. (Illus.). 31p. 21cm. 1961. Reilly & Lee.

Lloyd, Rawson
--The Easter-Story. (Children's Picture Bible). (gr. 4-6). 1981. (ISBN 0-86020-515-0, Usborne-Hayes). (ISBN 0-88110-096-X). (ISBN 0-86020-520-7). EDC.
--Stories Jesus Told. (Children's Picture Bible Ser.). (gr. 4-6). 1982. (ISBN 0-86020-516-9, Usborne-Hayes). (ISBN 0-88110-097-8). (ISBN 0-86020-521-5). EDC.

Lloyd, Robert (1864-)
--The Treasure of Shag Rock. Downey, Frank, illus. N.D. Lothrop Lee & Shepard Co.

Lloyd, Trevor
--Sky Highways. N.D. Houghton Mifflin Co.

Lloyd Webber, Andrew (1948-) & Rice, Tim
--Joseph and the Amazing Technicolor Dreamcoat. Blake, Quentin (1932-), illus. LC 81-23722. (Illus.). 41 p. 29cm. c.1982. (ISBN 0-03-061517-8). Holt, Rinehart, and Winston.

Lobagola
--African Folk Tales. N.D. Alfred A. Knopf.
--Folk Tales of a Savage. 1930. Alfred A. Knopf.

Loban, Walter & Watkins, Lillian, eds.
--Best in Children's Literature. Incl. Sense & Nonsense. (ISBN 0-8372-1936-1). (ISBN 0-8372-1942-6); Ocean Capers. (ISBN 0-8372-1933-7). (ISBN 0-8372-1939-6); Never Never Land. (ISBN 0-8372-1934-5); Myths & Legends Around the World. (ISBN 0-8372-1932-9). (ISBN 0-8372-1938-8). (Ser. 4). (gr. k-4). N.D. Bowmar-Noble.
--Best in Children's Literature. Incl. Funny Bones. (ISBN 0-8372-0932-3); Friendly Dragons. (ISBN 0-8372-0937-4); Ecology. (ISBN 0-8372-0941-2). (ISBN 0-8372-1056-9); Folktales from Other Lands. (ISBN 0-8372-1011-9). (Ser. 3). (gr. k-4). N.D. Bowmar-Noble.

Lobb, Frances, tr. see Bruckner, Karl.

Lobb, Frances, tr. see De Cesco, Federica.
Lobdell, Helen (1919-)
--Captain Bacon's Rebellion. LC 59-8241. 192p. 22cm. 1959. Macrae Smith Co.
--The Fort in the Forest. Bjorklund, Lorence F. (1913-1978), illus. LC 63-15286. 218 p. illus. 22 cm. 1963. Houghton Mifflin.
--Golden Conquest. Fleishman, Seymour (1918-), illus. LC 53-6208. 277p. illus. 22cm. 1953. Houghton Mifflin.
--The King's Snare. Hodges, Cyril Walter (1909-), illus. LC 55-52179. 218p. illus. 22cm. 1955. Houghton Mifflin.
--Prisoner of Taos. LC 72-95139. 256p. 1st U.S. edition. (gr. 7 up). 1970. Abelard.
--Thread of Victory: A Story of Reform in Britain's Cotton Mills. LC 63-15882. 152 p. 21 cm. 1963. D. McKay.
Lobe, Mira
--The Grandma in the Apple Tree. Brown, Judith Gwyn (1933-), illus. Orgel, Doris (1929-), tr. LC 75-127972. (Illus.). 96 p. 24cm. 1970. (ISBN 0-07-038212-3). McGraw-Hill.
--The Snowman Who Went for a Walk. Opgenoorth, Winifried, illus. LC 83-27298. (Illus.). 32p. (ps-2). 1984. (ISBN 0-688-03865-4, Morrow Junior Books). (ISBN 0-688-03866-2). Morrow.
--The Zoo Breaks Out. Weigel, Suzanne, illus. Dale, Norman, tr. from Ger. LC 60-7603. (Illus.). 1960. A. S. Barnes & Co.
Lobel, Adrianne
--A Small Sheep in a Pear Tree. LC 76-58721. p. cm. c.1977. (ISBN 0-06-023952-2). (ISBN 0-06-023953-0). Harper & Row.
Lobel, Anita Kempler (1934-)
--A Birthday for the Princess. Lobel, Anita Kempler (1934-), illus. LC 73-5487. (Illus.). 46 p. 26cm. 1973. (ISBN 0-06-023943-3). (ISBN 0-06-023943-3). Harper & Row.
--King Rooster, Queen Hen. Lobel, Anita Kempler (1934-), illus. LC 75-9787. (Illus.). 48 p. 22cm. (Greenwillow read-alone). 1975. (ISBN 0-688-80008-4). (ISBN 0-688-84008-6). Greenwillow Books. **Award: (ALA).**
--King Rooster, Queen Hen. Lobel, Anita Kempler (1934-), illus. LC 74-19037. p. cm. (Ready-to-read). 1975. (ISBN 0-02-759250-2). Macmillan.
--The Pancake. Lobel, Anita Kempler (1934-), illus. LC 77-24970. (Illus.). 48 p. 22cm. (Greenwillow Read-alone). c.1978. (ISBN 0-688-80125-0). (ISBN 0-688-84125-2). Greenwillow Books.
--Potatoes, Potatoes. Lobel, Anita Kempler (1934-), illus. LC 67-16231. (Illus.). 40 p. 1967. Harper & Row.
--The Seamstress of Salzburg. Lobel, Anita Kempler (1934-), illus. LC 75-85037. (Illus.). 49 p. 1970. Harper & Row.
--The Straw Maid. Lobel, Anita Kempler (1934-), illus. LC 81-6325. (Illus.). 7 x 9. 56p. (16 pt.). (gr. 1-3). 1983. (ISBN 0-688-00344-3). (ISBN 0-688-00330-3). Greenwillow.
--Sven's Bridge. Lobel, Anita Kempler (1934-), illus. LC 65-14491. (Illus.). v. (unpaged). 1965. Harper & Row. **Award: (NYT).**
--The Troll Music. Lobel, Anita Kempler (1934-), illus. LC 66-7117. (Illus.). (Picture Bk.). (ps-3). 1966. (ISBN 0-06-023929-8, HarpJ). Har-Row.
--Under a Mushroom. Lobel, Anita Kempler (1934-), illus. LC 75-121806. (Illus.). 40 p. 1970. Harper & Row.
--The Wishing Penny, and Other Stories. Lobel, Anita Kempler (1934-), illus. LC 67-5204. (Illus.). 69 p. 24cm. 1967. Parents' Magazine Press.
Lobel, Arnold Stark (1933-)
--The Bears of the Air. Lobel, Arnold Stark (1933-), illus. LC 65-14634. 1 v. (unpaged) illus. 25 cm. 1965. Harper & Row.
--The Book of Pigericks. 1st ed. Lobel, Arnold Stark (1933-), illus. LC 82-47730. p. cm. c.1983. (ISBN 0-06-023982-4). (ISBN 0-06-023983-2). Harper & Row. **Award: (ALA).**
--Days with Frog and Toad. Lobel, Arnold Stark (1933-), illus. LC 78-21786. 64p. (I can read book). c.1979. (ISBN 0-06-023963-8). (ISBN 0-06-023964-6). Harper & Row. **Award: (ALA).**
--Fables. Lobel, Arnold Stark (1933-), illus. LC 79-2004. (Illus.). 40 p. 30cm. c.1980. (ISBN 0-06-023973-5). (ISBN 0-06-023974-3). Harper & Row. **Awards: (RCM); (ALA).**
--Frog & Toad All Year. Lobel, Arnold Stark (1933-), illus. LC 76-2343. (Illus.). 5 7/8 x 8 1/2. 64p. (18 pt.). (I Can Read Bks.). (gr. k-3). 1976. (ISBN 0-06-023950-6). (ISBN 0-06-023951-4). Har-Row.
--Frog and Toad All Year. Lobel, Arnold Stark (1933-), illus. LC 76-2343. (Illus.). 64 p. 23cm. (I can read book). c.1976. (ISBN 0-06-023950-6). (ISBN 0-06-023951-4). Harper & Row. **Award: (ALA).**
--Frog and Toad Are Friends. Lobel, Arnold Stark (1933-), illus. LC 73-105492. (Illus.). 64 p. 22cm. (I can read book). 1970. Harper & Row. **Award: (RCM).**
--Frog and Toad are Friends. Lobel, Arnold Stark (1933-), illus. LC 73-105492. (Illus.). 64p. (I Can Read Books). 1979. (ISBN 0-06-444020-6, Trophy). Harper & Row.
--The Frog & Toad Coloring Book. Lobel, Arnold Stark (1933-), illus. (Illus.). 32p. (ps-3). 1981. (ISBN 0-06-023978-6, HarpJ). Har-Row.
--Frog & Toad Together. Lobel, Arnold Stark (1933-), illus. LC 73-183163. (Illus.). 5 7/8 x 8 1/2. 64p. (18 pt.). (I Can Read Bks.). (gr. k-3). 1972. (ISBN 0-06-023959-X). (ISBN 0-06-023960-3). (ISBN 0-06-444021-4). Har-Row.
--Frog and Toad Together. Lobel, Arnold Stark (1933-), illus. LC 73-183163. (Illus.). 64 p. 23cm. (I can read book). 1972. (ISBN 0-06-023959-X). Harper & Row. **Awards: (ALA); (NYT).**
--Giant John. Lobel, Arnold Stark (1933-), illus. 1964. (ISBN 0-8382-0284-5, Cadmus Books). E. M. Hale and Company.
--Giant John. Lobel, Arnold Stark (1933-), illus. LC 64-16639. (Illus.). 32 p. 28cm. 1964. Harper & Row.
--Grasshopper on the Road. LC 77-25653. (Illus.). 62 p. 23cm. (I can read book). c.1978. (ISBN 0-06-023961-1). (ISBN 0-06-023962-X). Harper & Row. **Award: (ALA).**
--The Great Blueness and Other Predicaments. Lobel, Arnold Stark (1933-), illus. LC 68-24323. (Illus.). 32 p. 28cm. 1968. Harper & Row.
--Gregory Griggs and Other Nursery Rhyme People. Lobel, Arnold Stark (1933-), illus. LC 77-22209. (Illus.). 47 p. c.1978. (ISBN 0-688-80128-5). (ISBN 0-688-84128-7). Greenwillow Books. **Award. (ALA).**
--A Holiday for Mister Muster. Lobel, Arnold Stark (1933-), illus. LC 63-15323. unpaged. illus. 20 x 26 cm. 1963. Harper & Row. **Award: (NYT).**
--A Holiday for Mr. Muster. Lobel, Arnold Stark (1933-), illus. (gr. 2-3). 1980. (ISBN 0-590-38088-5). (ISBN 0-590-24003-X). Scholastic Inc.
--How the Rooster Saved the Day. Lobel, Anita Kempler (1934-), illus. LC 76-17602. (Illus.). 32 p. c.1977. (ISBN 0-688-80063-7). (ISBN 0-688-80063-7). Greenwillow Books.
--How the Rooster Saved the Day. Lobel, Anita Kempler (1934-), illus. LC 79-565. (Illus.). 32 p. 1979, c.1977. (ISBN 0-14-050309-9). Puffin Books.
--The Ice-Cream Cone Coot, and Other Rare Birds. Lobel, Arnold Stark (1933-), illus. LC 80-15290. p. cm. 1980, c.1971. Four Winds Press.
--The Ice-Cream Cone Coot, and Other Rare Birds. Lobel, Arnold Stark (1933-), illus. LC 78-136994. (Illus.). 40 p. 26cm. 1971. (ISBN 0-8193-0443-3). Parents' Magazine Press.
--Lucille. Lobel, Arnold Stark (1933-), illus. LC 64-11616. (Illus.). 64 p. 22cm. (I can read book). 1964. (ISBN 0-06-023966-2). Harper & Row.
--The Man Who Took the Indoors Out. Lobel, Arnold Stark (1933-), illus. LC 74-2618. (Illus.). 32 p. 24cm. 1974. (ISBN 0-06-023946-8). (ISBN 0-06-023947-6). Harper & Row. **Award: (NYT).**
--Martha, the Movie Mouse. Lobel, Arnold Stark (1933-), illus. LC 66-18654. 1 v. (unpaged) col. illus. 20 cm. 1966. Harper & Row.
--Ming Lo Moves the Mountain. Lobel, Arnold Stark (1933-), illus. LC 81-13327. (Illus.). 32 p. c.1982. (ISBN 0-688-00610-8). (ISBN 0-688-00611-6). Greenwillow Books. **Award: (ALA).**
--Mouse Soup. Lobel, Arnold Stark (1933-), illus. LC 76-41517. (Illus.). 5 7/8 x 8 1/2. 64p. (18 pt.). (I Can Read Bks.). (gr. k-3). 1977. (ISBN 0-06-023967-0). (ISBN 0-06-023968-9). (ISBN 0-06-444041-9). Har-Row.
--Mouse Soup. Lobel, Arnold Stark (1933-), illus. LC 76-41517. (Illus.). 63 p. 22cm. (I can read book). c.1977. (ISBN 0-06-023967-0). (ISBN 0-06-023968-9). Harper & Row.
--Mouse Tales. Lobel, Arnold Stark (1933-), illus. LC 72-76511. (Illus.). 61 p. 23cm. (I can read book). 1972. (ISBN 0-06-023941-7). (ISBN 0-06-023942-5). Harper & Row.
--On Market Street. Lobel, Anita Kempler (1934-), illus. LC 80-21418. (Illus.). 40 p. 26cm. c.1981. (ISBN 0-688-80309-1). (ISBN 0-688-84309-3). Greenwillow Books. **Awards: (NYT); (ALA); (BGH); (RCM).**
--On the Day Peter Stuyvesant Sailed into Town. Lobel, Arnold Stark (1933-), illus. LC 75-148420. (Illus.). 39 p. 1971. (ISBN 0-06-023972-7). Harper & Row. **Award: (ALA).**
--Owl at Home. Lobel, Arnold Stark (1933-), illus. LC 74-2630. (Illus.). 64 p. 23cm. (I can read book). c.1975. (ISBN 0-06-023948-4). (ISBN 0-06-023949-2). Harper & Row. **Award: (ALA).**
--Prince Bertram the Bad. Lobel, Arnold Stark (1933-), illus. LC 63-8471. (Illus.). 32 p. 29cm. 1963. Harper & Row.
--The Rose in My Garden. Lobel, Anita Kempler (1934-), illus. LC 83-14097. (Illus.). 8 x 9 7/8. 40p. (14 pt.). (gr. k-3). 1984. (ISBN 0-688-02586-2). (ISBN 0-688-02587-0). Greenwillow.
--Small Pig. Lobel, Arnold Stark (1933-), illus. LC 69-10213. (Illus.). 5 7/8 x 8 1/2. 64p. (18 pt.). (I Can Read Bks.). (gr. k-3). 1969. (ISBN 0-06-023932-8). Har-Row.
--Uncle Elephant. Lobel, Arnold Stark (1933-), illus. (Illus.). 5 7/8 x 8 1/2. (18 pt.). (I Can Read Bks.). (ps-3). 1982. (ISBN 0-06-023979-4). (ISBN 0-06-023980-8). Har-Row.
--Uncle Elephant. Lobel, Arnold Stark (1933-), illus. LC 80-8944. p. cm. (I can read book). c.1981. (ISBN 0-06-023979-4). (ISBN 0-06-023980-8). Harper & Row. **Award: (ALA).**
--Whiskers and Rhymes. Lobel, Arnold Stark (1933-), illus. LC 83-25424. c.1984. (ISBN 0-688-03835-2). Greenwillow Books.
--A Zoo for Mister Muster. Lobel, Arnold Stark (1933-), illus. LC 62-7313. (Illus.). unpaged. 1962. Harper.
Loberg, Mary Alice (1943-)
--I Wish You Bluebirds. Conklin, Marilyn, illus. LC 76-110229. (Illus.). 48 p. 10cm. (Hallmark editions). 1970. (ISBN 0-87529-097-3). Hallmark Cards.
LoBianco, Joseph R.
--What Happened to the Donkey After Christmas?. Gaber, Susan, illus. (Illus.). (gr. k-5). 1979. (ISBN 0-682-49212-4). Exposition.
Lobingier, Elizabeth Erwin Miller, Mrs. (1889-)
--Ship East--Ship West. Lobingier, Elizabeth Erwin Miller, Mrs. (1889-), illus. LC 37-36389. 4 p. l., 87 p. incl. front., illus. 24 cm. c.1937. Friendship Press.
Lobsenz, Amelia Freitag
--Kay Everett Calls CQ. LC 51-10459. 213 p. illus. 22cm. 1951. Vanguard Press.
--Kay Everett Works DX. LC 52-11122. 176 p. 22cm. 1952. Vanguard Press.
Loch, Joice Mary Nan Kivell see Nankivell, Joice Mary.
Lochak, Michele (1936-)
--Suzette and Nicholas and the Sunijudi Circus. Ichikawa, Satomi (1939-), illus. LC 79-28649. (Illus.). 29 p. 29cm. 1st U.S. edition. 1980, c.1979. Philomel Books.
Lochak, Michele (1936-) & Mangin, Marie-France
--Suzette & Nicholas & the Sunijudi Circus. Ichikawa, Satomi (1939-), illus. (Illus.). 32p. (gr. 4-8). 1981. (ISBN 0-399-20750-3, Philomel). (ISBN 0-399-61160-6). Putnam Pub Group.
Lock, Alma S.
--The Campbell Kids at Home. N.D. Rand McNally & Co.
--The Campbell Kids Have a Party. N.D. Rand McNally & Co.
Lockard, William
--The C. S. S. Virginia Merrimack: Or, Billy & The Ironclad. (Illus.). 176p. (gr. 5 up). 1972. (ISBN 0-682-47604-8). Exposition.
Locke, Angela
--Mr. Mullett Owns a Cloud. (Illus.). 128p. 1st U.S. edition. 1983. (ISBN 0-7011-2639-6, Pub. by Chatto & Windus). Merrimack Pub Cir.
Locke, Brent
--Mystery of the Hidden Cat. Tomes, Jacqueline, illus. LC 57-12202. 255p. illus. 20cm. 1957. Coward-McCann.
--Mystery of the Vanishing Jaguar. Burchard, Peter Duncan (1921-), illus. LC 60-6892. 222p. 21cm. 1960. Coward-McCann.
Locke, Charles Edward
--The First Christmas Story. N.D. Dodge.
Locke, Clinton W., pseud., see Stratemeyer Syndicate.
Locke, Clinton W., pseud.
--Who Closed the Door: Or, Perry Pierce and the Old Storehouse Mystery. Stratemeyer Syndicate. Repr. of 1931 ed (Pub. by Henry Altemus Co). (Perry Pierce Mystery Stories: No. 1). N.D. Goldsmith Publishing Co.
--Who Closed the Door: Or, Perry Pierce and the Old Storehouse Mystery. Stratemeyer Syndicate. Repr. of 1931 ed (Pub. by Henry Altemus Co). (Perry Pierce Mystery Stories: No. 1). N.D. M. A. Donohue & Co.
--Who Closed the Door: Or, Perry Pierce and the Old Storehouse Mystery. Stratemeyer Syndicate. Tandy, Russell H., illus. LC 31-15550. iv, 5-212 p. front., plates. 20 cm. (Perry Pierce Mystery Stories: No. 1). 1931. Henry Altemus Co.
--Who Hid the Key: Or, Perry Pierce Tracing Counterfeit Money. Stratemeyer Syndicate. Tandy, Russell H., illus. LC 32-21439. iv, 5-212 p. front., plates. 20 cm. (Perry Pierce Mystery Stories: No. 3). 1932. Henry Altemus Co.
--Who Hid the Key: Or, Perry Pierce Tracing the Counterfeit Money. Stratemeyer Syndicate. Repr. of 1932 ed (Pub. by Henry Altemus Co). (Perry Pierce Mystery Stories: No. 3). N.D. Goldsmith Publishing Co.
--Who Hid the Key: Or, Perry Pierce Tracing the Counterfeit Money. Stratemeyer Syndicate. Repr. of 1932 ed (Pub. by Henry Altemus Co). (Perry Pierce Mystery Stories: No. 3). N.D. M. A. Donohue & Co.
--Who Opened the Safe: Or, Perry Pierce and the Secret Cipher Mystery. Stratemeyer Syndicate. Repr. of 1931 ed (Pub. by Henry Altemus Co). (Perry Pierce Mystery Stories: No. 2). N.D. Goldsmith Publishing Co.
--Who Opened the Safe: Or, Perry Pierce and the Secret Cipher Mystery. Stratemeyer Syndicate. Repr. of 1931 ed (Pub. by Henry Altemus Co). (Perry Pierce Mystery Stories: No. 2). N.D. M. A. Donohue & Co.
--Who Opened the Safe: Or, Perry Pierce and the Secret Cipher Mystery. Stratemeyer Syndicate. Tandy, Russell H., illus. LC 31-18069. iv, 5-216 p. front., plates. 20 cm. (Perry Pierce Mystery Stories: No. 2). 1931. Henry Altemus Co.
--Who Took the Papers: Or, Perry Pierce Gathering the Printed Clues. Stratemeyer Syndicate. Repr. of 1934 ed (Pub. by Henry Altemus Co). (Perry Pierce Mystery Stories: No. 4). N.D. Goldsmith Publishing Co.
--Who Took the Papers: Or, Perry Pierce Gathering the Printed Clues. Stratemeyer Syndicate. Repr. of 1934 ed (Pub. by Henry Altemus Co). (Perry Pierce Mystery Stories: No. 4). N.D. M. A. Donohue & Co.
--Who Took the Papers: Or, Perry Pierce Gathering the Printed Clues. Stratemeyer Syndicate. Stevens, C. C., illus. LC 39-105158. 2 p. l., 7-222 p. front., plates. 21 cm. (Perry Pierce Mystery Stories: No. 4). 1934. Henry Altemus Co.
Locke, Edith Raymond
--Red Door. Goodman, Ann O. R., illus. LC 65-20821. (Illus.). (gr. k-3). 1965. (ISBN 0-8149-0353-3). Vanguard.
Locke, Elsie (1912-)
--The Runaway Settlers: An Historical Novel. 1st ed. Maitland, Antony Jasper (1935-), illus. LC 66-13266. (Illus.). 190 p. 22cm. 1966. Dutton.
Locke, Mary
--Mimi Goes to New Orleans. 12p. 1971. (ISBN 0-911116-94-X). Pelican Publishing Company Inc.
Locke, Reynolds
--Mayday Seven Forty Seven. LC 73-91850. 288p. 1974. (ISBN 0-8128-1674-9). Stein & Day.

Locke, Una & Lee, Frances
--Holiday Tales. 217p. N.D. Hurd & Houghton for American Tract Society.
--Holiday Tales. 217p. (Pleasant-grove Ser.). N.D. Lockwood, Brooks, & Co. for American Tract Society.

Locke, William J.
--A Christmas Mystery: The Story of the Three Wise Men. Campbell, Blendon, illus. N.D. John Lane.
--Far-Away Stories. N.D. John Lane.
--The Fortunate Youth. N.D. Grosset & Dunlap.
--The Fortunate Youth. N.D. John Lane.
--The Glory of Clementia. N.D. John Lane.
--Jaffery. N.D. John Lane.
--The Joyous Adventures of Aristide Pujol. N.D. John Lane.
--Simon the Jester. N.D. John Lane.
--Stella Maris. N.D. John Lane.
--Viviette. Crawford, Earl Stetson, illus. N.D. John Lane.
Locker, Arthur, pseud., see Forbes, J. H..
Locker, Arthur, pseud.
--On a Coral Reef: The Story of a Runaway Trip to Sea. Forbes, J. H., 1 of 4. (The True Crusoe Ser.). N.D. Cassell, Petter, & Galpin.
Locker, Frederick
--What the Blackbird Said: A Story in four Chirps. Caldecott, Randolph (1846-1886), illus. (Illus.). N.D. George Routledge.
Locker, Thomas (1937-)
--The Mare on the Hill. Locker, Thomas (1937-), illus. LC 85-1684. p. cm. 1985. (ISBN 0-8037-0207-8). (ISBN 0-8037-0208-6). Dial Books for Young Readers.
--Where the River Begins. Locker, Thomas (1937-), illus. LC 84-1709. (Illus.). 1984. (ISBN 0-8037-0089-X). Dial Books. **Award: (NYT).**
Lockerbie, Jeanette W. Honeyman
--On Your Mark. LC 63-15748. 104 p. 22 cm. c.1963. Zondervan Pub. House.
--Return of the Rebel. N.D. Zondervan Publishing House.
Lockett, Sharon
--No Moccasins Today. LC 77-123116. 134 p. 21cm. 1970. Nelson.
Lockhart, J. C.
--Mysteries of the Sea: A Book of Strange Tales. (Nautilus Library). N.D. Frederick A. Stokes Co.
Lockhart, James L
--Porkey: An Arkansas Razorback. Lockhart, James L., illus. LC 39-23298. 64 p. illus. 23 cm. 1939. A. Whitman & Co.

Lockley, Ronald
--Seal-Woman. LC 75-11114. 192p. 1975. (ISBN 0-87888-087-9). Bradbury Pr.
Locklin, Anne Littlefield
--Tidewater Tales. Busoni, Rafaello (1900-1962), illus. LC 42-24040. 2 p. l., 7-222 p. illus. 21 cm. 1942. The Viking Press.
Lockling, Lydia Waldo
--Adventures of Polly and Gilbert in the Capitol City. N.D. The Mosher Books.
Lockridge, Frances Louise Davis (0000-1963)
--The Proud Cat. Lockridge, Richard (1898-1982) & Blaisdell, Elinore (1904-), illus. LC 51-11172. 94 p. illus. 22 cm. 1951. Lippincott.
Lockridge, Frances Louise Davis (0000-1963) & Lockridge, Richard (1898-1982)
--Burnt Offering. 189p. 1955. J. B. Lippincott.
--The Cat who Rode Cows. Bacon, Peggy, pseud. (1895-), illus. Bacon, Margaret Frances. LC 55-7988. 36 p. illus. 21cm. 1955. Lippincott.
--The Lucky Cat. Gay, Zhenya (1906-1978), illus. LC 52-12909. 89p. illus. 22cm. 1953. Lippincott.
--The Nameless Cat. Bacon, Peggy, pseud. (1895-), illus. Bacon, Margaret Frances. LC 53-12836. 78p. illus. 22cm. 1954. Lippincott.
Lockridge, Richard, jt. auth. see Lockridge, Frances Louise Davis.
Lockwood, Eleanor Stanley
--Chum, Judith Anne. Marasco, Frank, illus. LC 39-23299. 262 p. incl. front., plates. 20 cm. c.1939. The Bruce Publishing Company.
Lockwood, Hazel
--The Golden Book of Birds. Rojankovsky, Feodor Stepanovich (1891-1970), illus. LC 43-13706. 42 p. illus. 20 x 17cm. 1943. Simon & Schuster.
Lockwood, Ingersoll (1841-)
--Baron Trump's Marvellous Underground Journey. (Illus.). 1900. Lee & Shepard.
--Baron Trump's Marvellous Underground Journey. Johnson, Charles Howard, illus. LC 44-35373. xiv, p., 1 l., 235 p. incl. front., plates. 21 cm. 1893. Lee and Shepard.
--Extraordinary Experiments of Little Captain Doppelkop on the Shore of Bubbleland. Johnson, Clifton (1865-1940), illus. 1900. Lee & Shepard.
--The Travels & Adventures of Little Baron Trump & His Wonderful Dog Bulger. Edwards, George Wharton (1859-1950), illus. 1900. Lee & Shepard.
--Wonderful Deeds and Doings of Little Giant Boab and His Talking Raven Tabib. Johnson, Clifton (1865-1940), illus. LC 44-366101. 302 p. incl. front., illus. 21 1/2 cm. 1891. Lee and Shepard.
--Wonderful Deeds & Doings of Little Giant Boab & His Talking Raven Tabib. Johnson, Clifton (1865-1940), illus. 1900. Lee & Shepard.
Lockwood, Judy
--Ballerina: A Paper Doll Story Book. Lockwood, Judy, illus. (Big Golden Book). 1960. Golden Press.
Lockwood, Myna
--Beckoning Star: A Story of Old Texas. Lockwood, Myna, illus. LC 43-5781. 242 p. incl. front., illus. 21 cm. 1943. E. P. Dutton and Company, Inc.
--Delecta Ann: The Circuit Rider's Duaghter. Lockwood, Myna, illus. LC 41-3675. 335 p. incl. front., illus. 21 cm. 1941. E. P. Dutton and Company, Inc.
--Free River: A Story of Old New Orleans. Lockwood, Myna, illus. LC 42-16135. 255 p. incl. front., illus. 21 cm. 1942. E. P. Dutton and Company, Inc.
--Happy-Go-Hoppy. Vasiliu, Mircea (1920-), illus. LC 76-169919. (Illus.). 27 p. 33cm. 1971, c.1972. Golden Press.
--Indian Chief: The Story of Keoduk. 320p. 1943. Oxford University Press.
--Lo and Behold!. Lockwood, Myna, illus. LC 45-1873. 213 p. illus. 21 cm. 1945. Oxford University Press.
--Macaroni, an American Tune. Lockwood, Myna, illus. LC 39-25145. 44, 2 p. illus. (part col.) 22 cm. c.1939. Oxford University Press.
--The Mysterious Box. Lockwood, Myna, illus. LC 41-18619. 47, 1 p. illus. (part col.) 22 x 19 cm. c.1941. Oxford University Press.
--Up with Your Banner. Lockwood, Myna, illus. LC 45-6795. 256 p. illus. 19 1/2 cm. 1945. E. P. Dutton and Company, Inc.
--The Violin Detectives. Lockwood, Myna, illus. LC 40-32437. 48 p. col. illus. 22 x 19 cm. c.1940. Oxford University Press.
Lockwood, Peggy
--Tales for Tots. Belliveau, Gloria, illus. (Illus.). 63 p. 22cm. 1974. Vantage.
Lockwood, Sara Elizabeth (Husted) (1854-) see Lorenzini, Carlo.
Lockyer, Lisa
--Child's Influence: Or, Kathleen and Her Great Uncle. 198p. N.D. E. P. Dutton.
Lodge, Bernard, jt. auth. see Roffey, Maureen.
Lodge, Henry Cabot (1850-1924), ed.
--Selected Popular Tales. Third Series. LC 44-35886. 74 p. front., illus., plates. 20 1/2 cm. 1881. G. A. Smith and Company.
Lodge, Margaret Beatrice
--A Fairy to Stay. Watson, A. H., illus. LC 30-9228. 159 p. col. front., plates. 22 cm. 1929. Oxford University Press.
Lodge, Sydney Johnston
--Skeeter McCoy: A Tale of American Boarding School Life. LC 19-9098. 283, 1 p. incl. front. plates. 23 cm. c.1919. Printed by E. H. De Camp.
Lodi, Maria
--Charlotte Morel. 1969. (ISBN 0-399-10131-4). G. P. Putnam's Sons.
Loeb, Elinor G. & Nathan, Adele Gutman
--Let's Play Garden. Fanchette, illus. LC 36-18142. (Story Idea Originated by Nadine L. Rand). (Illus.). 12p. 23 x 27cm. 1936. Grosset & Dunlop.
Loeb, Marjorie
--Checkers. Kumme, Walter, illus. LC 46-1789. 31 p. illus. 26 x 21cm. c.1946. K. Miles.
Loeffler, Gisella, jt. auth. see Bianco, Margery Williams, Mrs.
Loefgren, Ulf (1931-)
--The Boy Who Ate More Than the Giant and Other Swedish Folktales. Loefgren, Ulf (1931-), illus. La Fargue, Sheila, tr. from Swedish. LC 78-8653. (Illus.). 32 p. 22cm. (A Storycraft Book). 1978. (ISBN 0-529-05450-7). (ISBN 0-529-05451-5). Collins.
--The Color Trumpet. Loefgren, Ulf (1931-), illus. 24p. 1974. (ISBN 0-201-04312-2). Addision-Wesley.
--Felix Forgetful. Loefgren, Ulf (1931-), illus. Sjoberg, Leif (1931-) & Sandberg-Diment, Erik, trs. LC 69-19816. (Illus.). 134 p. 22cm. 1969. Delacorte Press.
--One Two Three. Loefgren, Ulf (1931-), illus. 24p. 1974. (ISBN 0-201-04316-5). Addison-Wesley.
--The Traffic Stopper That Became a Grandmother Visitor. Loefgren, Ulf (1931-), illus. LC 73-8441. (Illus.). 24p. (Learning with Fun Ser). (ps-2). 1974. (ISBN 0-201-04318-1, A-W Childrens). A-W.
--What Ever You Want. 1st american ed. Loefgren, Ulf (1931-), illus. Pyk, Ann (1934-), tr. LC 70-166985. (Illus.). 32 p. 1972. Putnam.
--The Wonderful Tree. Loefgren, Ulf (1931-), illus. LC 79-101997. (Illus.). 32 p. 1970. Delacorte Press.
Loelling, Carol
--Whose House Is This?. (Surprise Bk). (ps-4). 1978. (ISBN 0-8431-0444-9). Price Stern.
Loening, Grover Cleveland (1888-)
--The Conquering Wing. 1st ed. LC 79-111380. 173 p. 21cm. 1970. Chilton Book Co.
Loeper, John Joseph (1929-)
--Away We Go!. LC 81-8045. (Illus.). 64p. (gr. 4-6). 1982. (ISBN 0-689-30884-1). Atheneum.
--Galloping Gertrude: By Motorcar in 1908. LC 79-21974. (Illus.). 66, 1 p. 24cm. (gr. 4-6). 1980. (ISBN 0-689-30749-7). Atheneum.
--The Golden Dragon: By Clipper Ship Around the Horn. LC 78-5085. (Illus.). 61, 4 p. 24cm. 1978. (ISBN 0-689-30658-X). Atheneum.
--The House on Spruce Street. LC 82-1821. (Illus.). 96p. (gr. 4-6). 1982. (ISBN 0-689-30929-5). Atheneum.
Loewen, Jean
--Loren Boys Escape Red China. 40p. N.D. Zondervan Publishing House.
--Loren Boys Turn Detective. 40p. N.D. Zondervan Publishing House.
Loew's Incorporated, jt. auth. see Archer, Peter.
Lofgren, Ulf, jt. auth. see Krantz, Leif.
Loftie, J. W.
--A Ride in Egypt. New ed. (Illus.). N.D. MacMillian.
Loftin, Tee, ed. see Zarambouka, Sofia.
Loftin, Tee, tr. see Zarambouka, Sofia.
Lofting, Hugh John (1886-1947), ed. see Perkins, Al.
Lofting, Hugh John (1886-1947)
--Doctor Dolittle: A Treasury. LC 67-19270. vii, 246 p. illus. 26 cm. 1967. Lippincott.
--Doctor Dolittle and the Green Canary. Lofting, Hugh John (1886-1947), illus. LC 50-14375. xi, 276 p. illus. 21 cm. 1950. Lippincott.
--Doctor Dolittle & the Pirates. Perkins, Albert Rogers (1904-1975), ed. Wende, Philip (1939-), illus. LC 68-14483. 4 color ils. (ps-3). 1968. (ISBN 0-394-80049-4). (ISBN 0-394-90049-9). Beginner.
--Doctor Dolittle and the Secret Lake. 1st ed. Lofting, Hugh John (1886-1947), illus. LC 48-8401. xii, 306 p. illus. 21 cm. 1948. J. B. Lippincott Co.
--Doctor Dolittle Circus. Lofting, Hugh John (1886-1947), illus. LC 68-6818. 1952. J. B. Lippincott.
--Doctor Dolittle in the Moon. Lofting, Hugh John (1886-1947), illus. LC 28-22386. x p., 1 l., 307 p. incl. plates. col. front 21 cm. 1928. Frederick A. Stokes Co.
--Doctor Dolittle in the Moon. Lofting, Hugh John (1886-1947), illus. LC 65-6817. x, 307 p. illus. 21 cm. c.1956. Lippincott.
--Doctor Dolittle in the Moon. Lofting, Hugh John (1886-1947), illus. LC 73-367131. (Illus.). 19cm. 169p. (Puffin bks.: PS 370). 1968. Penguin.
--Doctor Dolittle's Birthday Book. Lofting, Hugh John (1886-1947), illus. LC 68-8923. (Illus.). 224p. (gr. 4-6). 1968. (ISBN 0-397-30996-1, JBL-J). Har-Row.
--Doctor Dolittle's Caravan. Lofting, Hugh John (1886-1947), illus. LC 26-18089. ix p., 1 l., 342 p. col. front., illus. 22 cm. 1926. Frederick A. Stokes Co.
--Doctor Dolittle's Caravan. Lofting, Hugh John (1886-1947), illus. N.D. J. B. Lippincott.
--Doctor Dolittle's Circus. Lofting, Hugh John (1886-1947), illus. LC 24-24604. x p., 1 l., 379 p. front., illus. 21 cm. c.1924. Frederick A. Stokes Co.
--Doctor Dolittle's Circus. Lofting, Hugh John (1886-1947), illus. LC 65-6818. x, 379 p. illus. 22 cm. c.1952. Lippincott.
--Doctor Dolittle's Garden. Lofting, Hugh John (1886-1947), illus. LC 27-23200. viii, 327 p. col. front., illus. 21 cm. c.1927. Frederick A. Stokes Co.
--Doctor Dolittle's Garden. Lofting, Hugh John (1886-1947), illus. LC 66-34862. viii, 327 p. illus. 22 cm. 1955, c.1927. Lippincott.
--Doctor Dolittle's Post Office. Lofting, Hugh John (1886-1947), illus. LC 23-129620. x p., 1 l., 359 p. col. front., illus. 21 cm. c.1923. F. A. Stokes Co.
--Doctor Dolittle's Post Office. Lofting, Hugh John (1886-1947), illus. 1923. J. B. Lippincott Co.
--Doctor Dolittle's Post Office. Lofting, Hugh John (1886-1947), illus. LC 66-2022. x, 359 p. illus. 21 cm. (Stokes book). N.D. Lippincott.
--Doctor Dolittle's Puddleby Adventures. Lofting, Hugh John (1886-1947), illus. LC 52-7457. 241 p. illus. 21 cm. 1952. Lippincott.
--Doctor Dolittle's Return. Lofting, Hugh John (1886-1947), illus. LC 33-307216. viii p., 2 l., 273 p. incl. 1 illus., plates. col. front. 21 cm. 1933. Fred A. Stokes of.
--Doctor Dolittle's Zoo. Lofting, Hugh John (1886-1947), illus. LC 25-20167. xi p., 1 l., 338 p. incl. illus., plates. col. front. 21 cm. c.1925. Fred A. Stokes Co.
--Doctor Dolittle's Zoo. Lofting, Hugh John (1886-1947), illus. (Illus.). (gr. 4-6). 1925. (ISBN 0-397-30009-3, JBL-J). Har-Row.
--Doctor Dolittle's Zoo. Lofting, Hugh John (1886-1947), illus. LC 66-40945. xi, 338 p. illus. 21 cm. 1953, c.1925. Lippincott.
--Dr. Dolittle's Garden. N.D. Grosset & Dunlap.
--Dr. Dolittle's Return. Lofting, Hugh John (1886-1947), illus. N.D. Frederick A. Stokes.
--Dr. Dolittle's Return. Lofting, Hugh John (1886-1947), illus. N.D. J. B. Lippincott.
--Gub-Gub's Book. Lofting, Hugh John (1886-1947), illus. N.D. J. B. Lippincott.
--Gub Gub's Book: An Encyclopedia of Food ... LC 32-29908. 6 p. l., 3-185 p. incl. plates. col. front., col. pl. 20 cm. c.1932. Frederick A. Stokes Co.
--Hugh Lofting's Doctor Dolittle and the Pirates. Perkins, Albert Rogers (1904-1975), adapted by. Wende, Philip (1939-), illus. LC 68-14483. (Illus.). 61 p. 24cm. 1968. Beginner Books.
--Noisy Nora. Lofting, Hugh John (1886-1947), illus. LC 29-13473. 53 p. incl. front., illus. (part col.) pl. 16 cm. c.1929. F. A. Stokes Co.
--Porridge Poetry. LC 24-28245. 94, 1 p. incl. illus. (part col.) plates (part col.) 14 x 19 cm. c.1924. F. A. Stokes Co.
--The Story of Doctor Dolittle. 1920. J. B. Lippincott Co.
--Story of Doctor Dolittle. Lofting, Hugh John (1886-1947), illus. (Illus.). (gr. 4-6). 1920. (ISBN 0-397-30000-X, JBL-J). Har-Row.
--The Story of Doctor Dolittle: Being the History of His Peculiar Life at Home and Astonishing Adventures in Foreign Parts; Never Before Printed. Lofting, Hugh John (1886-1947), illus. LC 20-189250. 6 p. l., 180 p. col. front., illus., plates. 21 cm. 1920. Frederick A. Stokes Company.
--The Story of Doctor Dolittle: Being the History of His Peculiar Life at Home and Astonishing Adventures in Foreign Parts; Never Before Printed. Lofting, Hugh John (1886-1947), illus. LC 40-4714. xii p., 3 l., 180 p. incl. front., illus., pl. 19 cm. 1938. Frederick A. Stokes Company.
--The Story of Doctor Dolittle: Being the History of His Peculiar Life at Home and Astonishing Adventures in Foreign Parts; Never Before Printed. Lofting, Hugh John (1886-1947), illus. Walpole, Hugh, intro. by. LC 57-3087. xvi, 172p. illus. 20cm. 1956, c.1948. Lippincott.
--The Story of Mrs Tubbs. Lofting, Hugh John (1886-1947), illus. LC 23-13420. 91, 3 p. incl. front., plates (part col.) 14 cm. c.1923. Fred A. Stokes Co.
--The Story of Mrs. Tubbs. Lofting, Hugh John (1886-1947), illus. LC 68-10777. (Illus.). 1 v. 53p. 1968, c.1923. Lippincott.
--Tommy, Tilly and Mrs. Tubbs. Lofting, Hugh John (1886-1947), illus. LC 36-246825. 3 p. l., 119, 2 p. incl. plates. col. front. 14 x 19 cm. c.1936. F. A. Stokes Co.
--Tommy, Tilly and Mrs. Tubbs. Lofting, Hugh John (1886-1947), illus. LC 37-32450. 4 p. l., 78, 3 p. incl. col. front., illus., plates (part col.) 14 x 20 cm. c.1937. F. A. Stokes Co.
--Tommy, Tilly and Mrs. Tubbs. Lofting, Hugh John (1886-1947), illus. N.D. J. B. Lippincott.
--Travels of Doctor Dolittle in English & French. Perkins, Albert Rogers (1904-1975), ed. Wende, Philip (1939-), illus. Vallier, Jean, tr. (Illus.). 4 color ils. 1st U.S. edition. (French Beginner Books). (gr. 1-6). 1968. (ISBN 0-394-90175-4). Beginner.
--Travels of Doctor Dolittle in English & Spanish. Perkins, Albert Rogers (1904-1975), ed. Wende, Philip (1939-), illus. Rivera, Carlos, tr. (Illus.). 4 color ils. 1st U.S. edition. (Spanish Beginner Books). (gr. 1-6). 1968. (ISBN 0-394-91579-8). Beginner.
--The Twilight of Magic. N.D. Grosset & Dunlap.
--The Twilight of Magic. Lenski, Lois (1893-1974), illus. LC 30-29904. vi p., 1 l., 303 p. col. front., illus. 21 cm. 1930. Frederick A. Stokes Co.
--The Twilight of Magic. Lenski, Lois (1893-1974), illus. LC 67-17092. (Illus.). 303 p. 22cm. 1967. Lippincott.
--The Voyages of Doctor Dolittle. Lofting, Hugh John (1886-1947), illus. LC 22-20686. ix p., 2 l., 364 p. col. front., illus., col. pl. 21 cm. 1922. Fred A. Stokes Co. **Award: (JNM).**
--The Voyages of Doctor Dolittle. Lofting, Hugh John (1886-1947), illus. LC 64-2997. ix, 364 p. illus. 21 cm. c.1950. Lippincott.
Lofting, Hugh John (1886-1947) & Perkins, Albert Rogers (1904-1975), eds.
--Hugh Lofting's Travels of Doctor Dolittle. Wende, Philip (1939-), illus. LC 67-25853. (Illus.). 63 p. 24cm. 1967. Beginner Books.
Lofting, Lynne
--Squawky and Bawky. Peirce, Waldo (1884-1970), illus. LC 39-30329. 16 p. col. illus. 32 cm. c.1939. C. Scribner's Sons.
Lofts, Norah Robinson (1904-1983)
--The Maude Reed Tale. Grahame Johnstone, Anne & Grahame Johnstone, Janet, illus. LC 73-1228. (Illus.). 246 p. 25cm. 1973, c.1972. (ISBN 0-8161-6085-6). G. K. Hall.
--The Maude Reed Tale. Grahame Johnstone, Anne & Grahame Johnstone, Janet, illus. LC 72-4117. (Illus.). 174 p. 22cm. 1972. (ISBN 0-8407-6248-8). T. Nelson.
--Rupert Hatton's Story. Grahame Johnstone, Anne & Grahame Johnstone, Janet, illus. LC 72-13459. (Illus.). 135 p. 22cm. 1st U.S. edition. 1973. (ISBN 0-8407-6286-0). T. Nelson.
Loftus-Price, Henry James (1896-)
--The Mystery of the Silver Dart. Wardel, Raymond C., illus. LC 31-14062. 3 p. l., 221 p. incl. plates. col. front. 20 cm. 1931. The Mohawk Press.
Logan, Dwight
--Pete, the Great Magician. LC 48-6238. 56 p. col. illus. 15 x 20cm. (gr. 1-3). 1948. Charles Scribner's Sons.
Logan, E.
--Lily and Mr Ginger. N.D. E J B Young & Co.
Logan, John Burton (1923-), adapted by.
--Tom Savage: A Boy of Early Virginia. Siculan, Daniel (1922-), illus. LC 62-11694. unpaged. illus. 29cm. (Encyclopaedia Britannica true-to-life books). 1962. Encyclopaedia Britannica Press; Distributed in association with Meredith Press.
Logan, Lloyd
--Boys and Girls of Ridgeway. LC 26-17611. 180 p. front., plates. 18 cm. c.1926. Augustana Book Concern.
Logan, Marshall
--The World's Famous Fairy Tales. 320p. (The Famous "Retold" Series for Boys and Girls). N.D. John C. Winston.
Logan, Nora
--Jungle Adventure. Gothard, David, illus. 64p. (Orig.). (Pick-a-Path Bks.). (gr. 3-6). 1984. (ISBN 0-590-33050-0). Scholastic Inc.
Logie, Sarah E Chester, Mrs.
--Out of the Fold ... LC 12-36243. 240 p. front., plates. 17 cm. c.1882. American Tract Society.
Logue, Christopher (1926-), compiled by.
--The Children's Book of Comic Verse. Tidy, Bill, illus. (Illus.). 160p. 1st U.S. edition. 1980. (Pub. by Batsford England). David & Charles.
--Ode to the Dodo: Poems 1953-1978. 176p. 1983. (ISBN 0-224-01892-2, Pub by Jonathan Cape). (ISBN 0-224-01893-0). Merrimack Pub Cir.
--Puss in Boots. Bayley, Nicola (1935-), illus. LC 76-11679. (Illus.). (ps-3). 1977. (ISBN 0-688-86002-8). Greenwillow.
Logue, Christopher (1926-) & Anderson, Wayne (1946-)
--The Magic Circus. LC 78-24761. (Illus.). 32 p. 28cm. (Studio book). 1979. (ISBN 0-670-44809-5). Viking Press.

AUTHOR INDEX LONG, HELEN

--Ratsmagic. LC 76-379467. (Illus.). 30 p. 28cm. 1976. (ISBN 0-224-01227-4). Cape.
--Ratsmagic. LC 76-4891. p. cm. 1976. (ISBN 0-394-83300-7). (ISBN 0-394-93300-1). Pantheon Books.

Lohan, Maria, jt. ed. see Lohan, Robert.

Lohan, Robert & Lohan, Maria, eds.
--A New Christmas Treasury: With More Stories for Reading Aloud. LC 54-12862. (gr. 1-5). N.D. (ISBN 0-8044-2536-1, Stephen Daye Pr). Ungar.

Lohan, Robert & Lohn, Maria, eds.
--Christmas Tales for Reading Aloud. 3rd enl. ed. LC 66-10811. (gr. 1-5). N.D. (ISBN 0-8044-2534-5, Pub. by Stephen Daye Pr). Ungar.

Lohmeyer, Julius (1835-1903) & Schanz, Frieda
--Prince Fridolin's Courtship. Kleinmichel, Julius illus. Clifton, Sidney, tr. LC 17-1696. 40 p. col. illus. 24 x 27 1/2cm. 1888. Sackett & Wilhelms.

Lohn, Maria, jt. ed. see Lohan, Robert.

Lohse, Charlotte & Seaton, Judith
--The Mysterious Continent. N.D. Bobbs-Merrill Co.

Loiseaux, Louis Marie Auguste, tr. see Segur, Sophie Rostopchine, Mrs.

Loisy, Jeanne (1913-)
--Don Tiburcio's Secret. Estachy, Francoise, illus. Kirkup, James, tr. LC 60-11489. 144p. 1960, c.1959. Pantheon Books.
--Pim and the Caves of Coscorron. Daure, Philippe, illus. Emerson, Joyce, tr. from Fr. LC 63-15479. (Illus.). 181 p. 22cm. 1963. Pantheon Books.

Loken, Anna Belle
--The Colt from the Dark Forest. Bolognese, Donald Alan (1934-), illus. LC 58-144992. 127p. illus. 22cm. 1959. Lothrop, Lee & Shepard.
--Maku. Reader, Sarah, illus. LC 67-22588. (Illus.). 64 p. 24cm. 1968. Lothrop, Lee & Shepard.
--No Hurdle Too High. LC 61-11923. 159p. 22cm. 1961. Lothrop, Lee and Shepard.

Loken, Anna Belle & Loken, Hjalmar J.
--When the Sun Danced. Bennett, Richard Michael (1899-), illus. LC 53-6747. (Illus.). 180 p. 22cm. 1954. Lothrop, Lee & Shepard.

Loken, Hjalmar J., jt. auth. see Loken, Anna Belle.

Lokvig, Tor & Murphy, Chuck
--Star Trek, the Motion Picture: The Pop-up Book. LC 80-111852. (Illus.). 13 p. 25cm. 1980. (ISBN 0-671-95536-5). Wanderer Books.

Lolmaugh, Nellie H.
--The Little Pink House: A Story in Verse for Children. 1st ed. Otteson, Madalene, illus. LC 55-9404. unpaged. illus. 24cm. 1955. Exposition Press.

Lomas, Steve, pseud., see Brennan, Joseph Lomas.

Lomask, Milton Nachman, jt. auth. see Larnen, Brendan.

Lomask, Milton Nachman (1909-)
--Assignment to the Council. 1st ed. Baker, Hugh, illus. LC 65-19938. 187 p. illus. 22 cm. 1966. Doubleday.
--Beauty & the Traitor: The Story of Mrs. Benedict Arnold. (gr. 7-10). 1967. (ISBN 0-8255-5400-4). Macrae.
--A Bird in the Hand. Neville, Ray, illus. LC 64-22861. v, 119 p. illus. 21 cm. 1964. Bruce Pub. Co.
--Cross Among the Tomahawks. 1st ed. Orbaan, Albert F. (1913-), illus. LC 61-138061. 192p. (Clarion bks.). c.1961. Doubleday.
--The Cure of Ars: The Priest Whot Outalked the Devil, Vol. 36. Troyer, Johannes (1902-), illus. 190p. (Vision Book). 1958. Farrar,Straus and Cudahy, Inc.
--The Secret of Grandfather's Diary. Mars, Witold Tadeusz J. (1912-), illus. LC 58-5321. 181p. illus. 22cm. 1958. Ariel Books.
--The Secret of the Marmalade Cat. Cassel, Lili, pseud. (1924-), illus. Wronker, Lili Cassel. LC 60-12638. 178p. illus. 22cm. 1960. Ariel Books.
--The Secret of the One-Eyed Moose. Mars, Witold Tadeusz J. (1912-), illus. LC 61-11321. 187p. illus. 22cm. 1961. Ariel Books.
--Ship's Boy with Magellan. 1st ed. Plummer, William KIrtman, illus. LC 60-12306. 185p. illus., endpaper map 22cm. (Clarion books). c.1960. Doubleday.
--The Spirit of Seventeen Eighty-Seven: The Making of Our Constitution. 224p. (gr. 4 up). N.D. (ISBN 0-374-37149-0). FS&G.
--St. Augustine & His Search for Faith, Vol. 21. Troyer, Johannes (1902-), illus. (Illus.). (gr. 4-8). 1957. (ISBN 0-374-80192-4, Vision). FS&G.

Lomasney, Eileen
--My Book of Happiness: The Beatitudes for Children. Hausner, Alice, illus. LC 76-3616. p. cm. c.1976. (ISBN 0-570-03455-8). Concordia Pub. House.
--Timmy Greenthumb. LC 82-72646. 32p. (Orig.). (gr. 3-6). 1983. (ISBN 0-8066-1953-8). Augsburg.

Lomax, Alan (1915-)
--Harriet and Her Harmonium: An American Adventure with Thirteen Folk Songs from the Lomax Collection. Binder, Pearl, pseud. (1904-), illus. Elwyn-Jones, Pearl Binder. Gill, Robert, contrib. by. LC 59-127884. unpaged. illus. 29cm. N.D. Barnes.
--Mister Jelly Roll. N.D. Grosset & Dunlap.

Lomax, Alan (1915-) & Lomax, John Avery (1872-1948), eds.
--American Ballads & Folk Songs. (gr. 7 up). 1934. (ISBN 0-02-574150-0). Macmillan.
--Best Loved American Folk Songs. (gr. 7-9). N.D. (ISBN 0-448-01460-2). G&D.
--Cowboy Songs & Other Frontier Ballads. (gr. 7 up). 1966. (ISBN 0-02-574210-8). Macmillan.

Lomax, John Avery, jt. ed. see Lomax, Alan.

Lombard, Charles W.
--Tiger Slayer. LC 39-138862. 9, 13-209 p. 21 cm. 1939. Meador Publishing Company.

Lombardo, Kathleen
--Macaroni. Szekeres, Cyndy (1933-), illus. LC 68-23659. (Illus.). 1 v. (unpaged. 1968. Random House.

Lombardo, Mary A
--The Really Red School House. Lombardo, Mary A., illus. LC 72-88597. (Illus.). 25 p. 22cm. 1969. Dorrance.

Lombroso Carrara, Paola
--The Adventures of Chicchi. Herbert, Robert Gaston, illus. Curtis, Mary Ellen Wood & Aspinwall, Marguerite, trs. LC 27-22161. vii, 166 p. col. front., illus., col. plates. 26 cm. 1927. G. P. Putnam's Sons.

Lombroso, Irena K., tr. see Garretto.

Lomen, Helen, jt. auth. see Flack, Marjorie.

Lomeo, Angelo, jt. auth. see Bullaty, Sonja.

London, Carolyn (1918-)
--Cat-Alog. London, Carolyn (1918-), illus. (Illus.). 128p. (Children's Bks). (gr. 5 up). 1971. (ISBN 0-8024-1120-7). Moody.
--Olu's Lions. London, Carolyn (1918-), illus. N.D. (ISBN 0-686-13761-2). Believers Bkshelf.
--Olu's Lions. London, Carolyn (1918-), illus. (Illus.). 128p. (Children's Bks). (gr. 5 up). 1971. (ISBN 0-8024-1610-1). Moody.
--Rat Catcher's Son. London, Carolyn (1918-), illus. N.D. (ISBN 0-686-13763-9). Believers Bkshelf.
--The Rat-Catcher's Son & Other Stories. London, Carolyn (1918-), illus. (Illus.). 128p. (Children's Bks). (gr. 3-7). 1971. (ISBN 0-8024-1710-8). Moody.
--Twins Solve a Fire Mystery. (gr. 4-8). 1975. (ISBN 0-8024-1799-X). Moody.
--Twins Solve the Mystery of the Missing Money. LC 77-4470. p. cm. c.1977. (ISBN 0-8024-1798-1). Moody Press.
--Zarga's Shadow. 1st ed. Wilson, George, illus. LC 66 17036. 149 p. 21 cm. 1966. Duell, Sloan and Pearce.

London, Jack (1876-1916)
--The Adventures of Captain Grief. 190p. 1954. The World Publishing Co.
--Brown Wolf and Other Jack London Stories. Mathiews, Franklin K., ed. (Every Boy's Library). N.D. Grosset & Dunlap.
--Brown Wolf: And Other Jack London Stories. Mathiews, Franklin K., selected by. LC 21-380. 3 p. l., 312 p. front. 20 cm. 1920. The Macmillan Company.
--Brown Wolf & Other Stories. (gr. 7-10). 1963. (ISBN 0-02-044270-X). Macmillan.
--The Call of the Wild. (Illus.). N.D. Dial Press Inc.
--The Call of the Wild. (Growing Literature Ser.). N.D. Grosset & Dunlap.
--The Call of the Wild. (Every Boy's Library). N.D. Grosset & Dunlap.
--The Call of the Wild. (Thrushwood Bks.). N.D. Grosset & Dunlap.
--The Call of the Wild. 1963. MacMillan Publishing Company.
--The Call of the Wild. King, Ron & Irwin, Don, illus. LC 76-2930. (Illus.). 217 p. 29cm. (Educator classic library, 11). 1968. Classic Press.
--The Call of the Wild. Nordlich, Lillian, adapted by. Barberis, Juan Carlos, illus. LC 79-24464. (Illus.). 48 p. 24cm. c.1980. (ISBN 0-8172-1656-1). Raintree Publishers.
--The Call of the Wild. Pickard, Charles, illus. LC 68-114638. 7 113p. 4 plates, illus. (incl. 2 col.) 22cm. (Children's illus. classics). 1968. Dent.
--The Call of the Wild. Price, Olive, adapted by. Allen, Douglas, illus. LC 62-20699. 59p. illus. 22cm. c.1961. Grosset & Dunlap.
--The Call of the Wild. Terhune, Albert Payson (1872-1942), ed. (Famous Dog Stories). N.D. Grosset & Dunlap.
--Call of the Wild. Todd, Robert, illus. 1962. Macmillan.
--The Call of the Wild and Other Stories. N.D. (ISBN 0-448-05827-8). Grosset & Dunlap.
--Call of the Wild and Other Stories. N.D. Macmillan.
--The Call of the Wild and Other Stories. LC 80-54135. (Illus.). iv, 242, 42 p. 18cm. (A Silver Classic). 1981, c.1982. (ISBN 0-382-03434-1). Silver Burdett Co.
--The Call of The Wild & Other Stories. Solomon, Louis, intro. by. (Great Illustrated Classics). 1960. Dodd, Mead & Co.
--The Call of the Wild: And Other Stories. Tsugami, Kyuzo, illus. LC 65-21851. (Illus.). 186 p. 24cm. (Illustrated junior library). 1965. Grosset & Dunlap.
--The Call of the Wild, and Other Stories. Tsugami, Kyuzo, illus. LC 81-210995. (Illus.). 188 p., 9 leaves of plates. 21cm. (Illustrated Junior Library). 1981. (ISBN 0-448-11027-X). Grosset & Dunlap.
--The Cruise of the Dazzler. N.D. Appleton Century Co.
--The Cruise of the Dazzler. (Every Boy's Library). N.D. Grosset & Dunlap.
--The Cruise of the Dazzler. Burns, J. M., illus. 250p. 1902. The Century Co.
--The Cruise of the Snark. 1928. Macmillan Company.
--A Daughter of the Snows. N.D. J.B. Lippincott.
--Dutch Courage and Other Stories. LC 22-19053. xii p., 2 l., 180 p. front. (port.) plates. 20 cm. 1922. The Macmillan Company.
--The Iron Heel. 1958. MacMillan Company.
--Jack London in the High School Aegis. Sisson, James E., ed. Lttell, Katherine, pref. by. (Illus.). 125p. (Orig.). (gr. 7-12). 1980. (ISBN 0-932458-01-7). Star Rover.
--Jack London Stories. (Great Writers Collection). (gr. 7 up). 1960. (ISBN 0-448-41103-2). Platt.
--Jack London Stories. (gr. 3 up). 1978. (ISBN 0-448-41103-2, G&D). Putnam Pub Group.
--Jack London's Stories for Boys. N.D. Cupples & Leon.
--Jack London's Stories of the North. Owen, Betty, ed. (gr. 7-12). 1973 (Schol Trade Pap). Schol Bk Serv.
--Martin Eden. 1957. MacMillan Publishing Company.
--Mutiny of the Elsinore. N.D. Macmillan.
--The Sea Wolf. N.D. Grosset & Dunlap.
--The Sea Wolf. (Magnum Easy Eye Classic Ser). (gr. 7 up). N.D. Lancer.
--Sea-Wolf. Large Type ed. 366p. 1937. Macmillan Company.
--The Sea-Wolf. 1937. MacMillan Publishing Company.
--The Selected Works. 453 p. 21cm. (Classics to grow on). 1966, c.1964. Parents' Magazine's Cultural Institute.
--Short Stories of Jack London. N.D. (ISBN 0-308-90045-6). Funk & Wagnalls.
--Star Rover. Fisher, Leonard Everett (1924-), illus. (gr. 7 up). 1963. (ISBN 0-02-759550-1). Macmillan.
--Stories of Hawaii. (gr. 7-9). 1965. Hawthorn.
--Tales of the Fish Patrol. (Every Boy's and Every Girl's Ser.). N.D. The Macmillan Co.
--To Build a Fire. Glaser, Byron, illus. LC 80-21856. (Illus.). 48 p. 23cm. (Creative classic series). c.1980. (ISBN 0-87191-769-6). Creative Education.
--White Fang. N.D. (ISBN 0-531-00303-5). Franklin Watts.
--White Fang. (Growing Literature Ser.). N.D. Grosset & Dunlap.
--White Fang. (Thrushwood Bks.). N.D. Grosset & Dunlap.
--White Fang. 1935. MacMillan Publishing Company.
--White Fang. LC 85-42971. p. cm. (Puffin classics). 1985. (ISBN 0-14-035045-4). Puffin Books.
--White Fang. Cole, Dick, illus. LC 70-110031. (Illus.). 224 p. 29cm. 1970, c.1969. (ISBN 0-516-04216-5). Childrens Press.
--White Fang. Terhune, Albert Payson (1872-1942), ed. (Famous Dog Stories). N.D. Grosset & Dunlap.
--White Fang & Other Stories. Adams, A. K., intro. by. 308p. (Great Illustrated Classics Ser.). 1963. Dodd & Mead Co.

London, Jane, pseud., see Geis, Darlene Stern.

London, Jane, pseud.
--The Musical Toy Parade. Geis, Darlene Stern. Setterberg, Carl, illus. LC 55-2229. (Illus.). unpaged. 21cm. (Magic talking books, T-6). 1955. J. C. Winston Co.

Lonergan, Joy
--Brian's Secret Errand. 1st ed. Szekeres, Cyndy (1933-), illus. LC 69-10045. (Illus.). 40 p. 27cm. 1969. Doubleday.
--A Pretend ABC. Murray, Irene (1935-), illus. LC 61-9743. unpaged. illus. 19cm. 1962. F. Watts.
--There You Are. Smith, Lawrence Beall (1909-), illus. LC 62-121406. unpaged. illus. 23cm. c.1962. F. Watts.
--When My Father Was a Little Boy. Polseno, Jo, illus. LC 61-517759. unpaged. illus. 19cm. c.1961. F. Watts.
--When My Mother Was a Little Girl. Galati, Veronica, illus. LC 61-5178. unpaged. illus. 19cm. c.1961. F. Watts.

Lonette, Reisie Dominee (1924-) see Child Study Association of America.

Long, Claudia & Glasser, Judy
--Albert's Story. Long, Claudia & Glasser, Judy, illus. LC 77-72614. (Illus.). 30 p. c.1978. (ISBN 0-440-00080-7). Delacorte Press.

Long, Dorothy, tr. see Radau, Hanns.

Long, Earlene R. (1938-)
--Gone Fishing. Brown, Richard Eric (1946-), illus. LC 83-23558. (Illus.). 32p. (ps-3). 1984. (ISBN 0-395-35570-2). HM.

Long, Earlene R. (1938-) & Slavin, Neal
--Johnny's Egg. Mikolaycak, Charles (1937-), illus. LC 79-21248. (Illus.). 30 p. 22cm. c.1980. (ISBN 0-201-04153-7). Addison-Wesley.

Long, Ellesley Waldo (1895-)
--Ricardo of the Lion Heart. Abbott, Jacob Bates (1803-1879), illus. LC 40-752738. 304 p. front., illus., plates 20 cm. c1910. The Penn Publishing Company.

Long, Eula Lee Kennedy (1902-)
--Chocolate, from Mayan to modern. 1st ed. Long, Eula Lee Kennedy (1902-), illus. LC 50-12768. ix, 207 p. illus.(part col.). 1950. Aladdin Books.
--Faraway Holiday. Long, Eula Lee Kennedy (1902-), illus. LC 47-31098. 63 p. illus. 22 cm. 1947. W. Morrow.
--Pirate's Doll: The Story of the China Poblana. Long, Eula Lee Kennedy (1902-), illus. LC 56-527146. (Illus.). (gr. 1-4). 1956. (ISBN 0-394-81507-6). Knopf.

Long, Frances M.
--The Mystery of Devil's Gully. (Illus.). (gr. 4-8). N.D. Vantage.

Long, Grayce E.
--Tiny Tunes. Blunt, Betty Bacon, illus. 32p. 1946. John Day Books.

Long, H. K.
--Square Sails and Spice Islands. N.D. Longmans Green & Co.
--Without Valour. N.D. Longmans Green & Co.

Long, Helen Beecher, pseud., see Stratemeyer Syndicate.

Long, Helen Beecher, pseud.
--The Girl He Left Behind. Stratemeyer Syndicate. Owen, Robert Emmett (1878-), illus. 1918. George Sully & Co.
--How Janice Day Won. Stratemeyer Syndicate. Repr. of 1916 ed (Pub. by Sully & Kleinteich). (Do Something Ser.: No. 3). 1919. George Sully & Co.
--How Janice Day Won. Stratemeyer Syndicate. Repr. of 1916 ed (Pub. by Sully & Kleinteich). (Do Something Ser.: No. 4). N.D. Goldsmith Publishing Co.
--How Janice Day Won. Stratemeyer Syndicate. Repr. of 1916 ed (Pub. by Sully & Kleinteich). (Do Something Ser.: No. 4). N.D. Saalfield Publishing Co.
--How Janice Day Won. Stratemeyer Syndicate. Turner, Corinne, illus. LC 16-192197. vi p., 1 l., 310 p. front., plates. 20 cm. (Do Something Ser.: No. 3). 1916. Sully & Kleinteich.
--Janice Day at Poketown. Stratemeyer Syndicate. Repr. of 1916 ed (Pub. by Sully & Kleinteich). (Do Something Ser.: No. 1). 1919. George Sully & Co.
--Janice Day at Poketown. Stratemeyer Syndicate. Repr. of 1915 ed (Pub. by Sully & Kleinteich). (Do Something Ser.: No. 2). N.D. Goldsmith Publishing Co.
--Janice Day at Poketown. Stratemeyer Syndicate. Repr. of 1914 ed (Pub. by Sully & Kleinteich). (Do Something Ser.: No. 2). N.D. Saalfield Publishing Co.
--Janice Day at Poketown. Stratemeyer Syndicate. Rogers, Walter S., illus. LC 14-16762. vii, 308 p. front., plates. 20 cm. (Do Something Ser.: No. 1). 1914. Sully & Kleinteich.
--Janice Day at Poketown. Stratemeyer Syndicate. Rogers, Walter S., illus. Repr. of 1914 ed (Pub. by Sully & Kleinteich). (Do Something Ser.: No. 1). N.D. The Christian Herald.
--Janice Day, The Young Homemaker. Stratemeyer Syndicate. Repr. of 1919 ed (Pub. by George Sully & Co). (Do Something Ser.: No. 1). N.D. Goldsmith Publishing Co.
--Janice Day, the Young Homemaker. Stratemeyer Syndicate. Repr. of 1919 ed (Pub. by George Sully & Co). (Do Something Ser.: No. 1). N.D. Saalfield Publishing Co.
--Janice Day, the Young Homemaker. Stratemeyer Syndicate. Turner, Corinne, illus. LC 20-1217. viii p., 1 l., 307 p. incl. front. plates. 20 cm. (Do Something Ser.: No. 5). 1919. George Sully & Co.
--The Mission of Janice Day. Stratemeyer Syndicate. Repr. of 1917 ed (Pub. by Sully & Kleinteich). (Do Something Ser.: No. 4). 1919. George Sully & Co.
--The Mission of Janice Day. Stratemeyer Syndicate. Repr. of 1917 ed (Pub. by SUlly & Kleinteich). (Do Something Ser.: No. 5). N.D. Goldsmith Publishing Co.
--The Mission of Janice Day. Stratemeyer Syndicate. Repr. of 1917 ed (Pub. by Sully & Kleinteich). (Do Something Ser.: No. 5). N.D. Saalfield Publishing Co.

--The Mission of Janice Day. Stratemeyer Syndicate. Turner, Corinne, illus. LC 17-10670. vi p., 1 l., 310 p. front., plates. 20 cm. (Do Something Ser.: No. 4). 1917. Sully & Kleinteich.
--The Testing of Janice Day. Stratemeyer Syndicate. Repr. of 1915 ed (Pub. by Sully & Kleinteich). (Do Something Ser.: No. 2). 1919. George Sully & Co.
--The Testing of Janice Day. Stratemeyer Syndicate. Repr. of 1916 ed (Pub. by Sully & Kleinteich). (Do Something Ser.: No. 3). N.D. Goldsmith Publishing Co.
--The Testing of Janice Day. Stratemeyer Syndicate. Repr. of 1915 ed (Pub. by Sully & Kleinteich). (Do Something Ser.: No. 3). N.D. Saalfield Publishing Co.
--The Testing of Janice Day. Stratemeyer Syndicate. Turner, Corinne, illus. LC 15-19473. xii, 310 p. front., plates. 19 1/2 cm. (Do Something Ser.: No. 2). 1915. Sully & Kleinteich.

Long, Helena, tr. see Bumgartner, Alexander (1841-1910) & B.A.V.

Long, Helena, tr. see Spillmann, Joseph.

Long, Helena, Miss, tr. see Spillmann, Joseph.

Long, James, jt. auth. see Patterson, Nancy-Lou.

Long, John Cuthbert (1892-)
--Maryland Adventure: A Story of the Battle of the Severn. 1st ed. Camana, Joseph C., illus. LC 55-6453. 180p. illus. 22cm. (Winston adventure books). 1956. Winston.
--Soldier for the King: A Story of Amherst in America. 1st ed. Nofer, Frank, illus. LC 54-5065. 182p. illus. 22cm. (Winston adventure books). 1954. Winston.

Long, John Luther (1861-1927)
--Little Miss Joy-Sing: How She Became the Beautiful Pine-Tree in the Garden of Prince of Don't-Care-What. Miller, W. R. S., photos by. LC 4-24493. ix p., 1 l., 13-148 p., 1 l. front., illus., 7 pl. 18 cm. 1904. H. Altemus Company.
--The Prince of Illusion. 304p. N.D. The Century Co.

Long, Judith Elaine see Long, Judy, pseud.

Long, Judy, pseud., see Long, Judith Elaine.

Long, Judy, pseud. (1953-)
--Volunteer Spring. Long, Judith Elaine. LC 75-38365. 126 p. 21cm. c.1976. (ISBN 0-396-07304-2). Dodd, Mead.

Long, Laura Mooney (1892-1967)
--David Farragut: Boy Midshipman. Laune, Paul Sidney (1899-), illus. LC 50-9960. 192 p. illus. 20 cm. (Childhood of famous Americans series). 1950. Bobbs-Merrill.
--David Farragut: Boy Midshipman. Pious, Robert, illus. LC 62-16596. 200 p. col. illus. 20cm. (Childhood of famous Amers.). 1963, c.1950. Bobbs.
--Douglas MacArthur: Young Protector. Morrow, Gray, illus. LC 65-14815. 200 p. col. illus. 20 cm. (Childhood of famous Americans) Bibl.). c.1965. Bobbs.
--George Dewey, Vermont Boy. Doremus, Robert (1913-), illus. LC 62-16622. 200 p. illus. 20 cm. (Childhood of famous Americans). 1963. Bobbs-Merrill.
--George Dewey: Vermont Boy. Lees, Harry Hanson, illus. LC 52-5821. 184 p. illus. 20 cm. (Childhood of famous Americans series). 1952. Bobbs-Merrill.
--Hannah Courageous. Caswell, Edward C., illus. LC 39-277404. x, 246 p. illus. 23 cm. 1939. Longmans, Green and Co.
--Joseph, Slave and Prince. LC 55-7413. 126p. illus. 20cm. (Heroes of God series). 1955. Association Press.
--Oliver Hazard Perry, Boy of the Sea. Fiorentino, Al, illus. LC 62-16605. 200 p. illus. 20 cm. (Childhood of famous Americans). 1962. Bobbs-Merrill.
--Oliver Hazard Perry, Boy of the Sea. Laune, Paul Sidney (1899-), illus. LC 49-10598. 192 p. illus. 20 cm. (Childhood of famous Americans Series). 1949. Bobbs-Merrill Co.
--Singing Sisters. LC 41-51898. vii p., 1 l., 260 p. illus. 22 cm. 1941. Longmans, Green and Co.
--Without Valour. Caswell, Edward C., illus. LC 40-13975. viii p., 1 l., 244 p. illus. 22 cm. 1940. Longmans Green and Co.

Long, Lucile, pseud., see Brandt, Lucile Long Strayer.

Long, Lucile, pseud. (1900-)
--Anna Elizabeth - Seventeen. Brandt, Lucile Long Strayer. 1978. (ISBN 0-87178-041-0). Brethren.
--Anna Elizabeth, a Dunker Maid of 1748. Brandt, Lucile Long Strayer. Goughnour, Inez, illus. LC 43-8533. 125 p. illus. 20 cm. 1942. Brethren Publishing House.

Long, Mae Van Norman
--The Wonder Woman. (The Outdoor Bks.). N.D. Penn.

Long, Manning, jt. auth. see Coffin, Lewis.

Long, Marguerite Thomson & Racette, Dora Fanchon
--Skipper Dee Skee. Piaget, Helen W. & Wilde, Florence R. A., illus. LC 30-23406. xvi p., 1 l., 9-138 p. incl. col. fron., illus., col. plates. 22 cm. c.1930. The Macaulay Company.

Long, Nina Payne
--My Talking Parakeet: And Other Stories for Children. 58p. 24cm. c.1958. Pageant Press.

Long, Nona (1916-) & Long, Sumner Arthur (1921-)
--The Adventures of Gaylor the Sailor. Long, Sumner Arthur (1921-), illus. 52 p. illus. 28cm. 1948. Venture Press.

Long, Olive M
--The Lollipops: The Adventures of the Lollipop Children. Long, Olive M., illus. LC 2-8127. 28 p. illus. 16 x 22 cm. 1901. R. H. Russell.

Long, Philip S.
--Ranch Boy Hunter. Hofmeister, Jane, ed. Engstrom, Ted, illus. (Illus.). (gr. 5 up). 1977. (ISBN 0-918292-03-4). Griggs Print.

Long, Ruthanna
--A Basketful of Kittens. Renfro, Ed, illus. LC 70-160208. (Illus.). 48 p. 31cm. 1972. Golden Press.
--The Great Monster Contest. Hildebrandt, Greg (1939-) & Hildebrandt, Tim (1939-), illus. LC 76-52896. (Illus.). 48 p. 26cm. (Kid's paperback). c.1977. (ISBN 0-307-12363-4). Golden Press.
--The Runaway Circus. Beylon, Catherine M., illus. LC 73-77488. (Illus.). 34 p. 28cm. 1973. Golden Press.
--Tales of Sesame Gulch. Cooke, Tom, illus. Children's Television Workshop LC 77-73878. (Illus.). 47 p. 26cm. (Kid's paperback). c.1977. (ISBN 0-307-12357-X). Western Pub. Co.
--Ten Little Chipmunks. Goldsborough, June (1923-), illus. (Illus.). 22p. (Golden Sturdy Happy Bk). (gr. 2-5). 1971. (ISBN 0-307-12135-6, Golden Pr). Western Pub.
--Tiny Bear & His New Sled. Allen, Joan, illus. (Illus.). (Golden Beginning Readers). (ps-2). 1969. (ISBN 0-307-61159-0, Golden Pr). Western Pub.
--Tiny Bear Goes to the Fair. Allen, Joan, illus. LC 72-5485. (Illus.). 30 p. 24cm. (Golden beginning reader). 1969. Golden Press.
--Witches, Ghosts, and Goblins: A Spooky Search for Miranda's Cat. Durand, Paul, illus. LC 72-93996. (Illus.). 141 p. 29cm. 1974. (ISBN 0-307-61818-8). Golden Press.

Long, Ruthanna, adapted by see Grimm, Jakob Ludwig Karl (1785-1863)

Long, Sherry, jt. auth. see Blocksma, Mary.

Long, Sherry, jt. auth. see Costigan, Shirleyann.

Long, Sumner Arthur, jt. auth. see Long, Nona.

Long, William
--Woodfolk Comedies. N.D. Harper & Bros.

Long, William Joseph (1867-), ed. see Dodgson, Charles Lutwidge.

Longanecker, Georgia
--Howdy Out There!. Phonics Fun. Longanecker, Georgia, illus. LC 76-62681. (Illus.). 63 p. c.1977. (ISBN 0-9601126-1-8). Longanecker Books.

Longden, H. W. D.
--Ways of the Veld Dwellers. Longden, H. W. D. & Pinner, Erna, illus. N.D. Frederick Warne & Co.

Longfellow, Henry Wadsworth (1807-1882), tr. see Schottenfels, Getrude Ruth.

Longfellow, Henry Wadsworth (1807-1882)
--The Adventures of Hiawatha. Voight, Virginia Frances (1909-), adapted by. Laite, Gordon (1925-), illus. LC 68-20802. (Illus.). 47 p. 23cm. (Reading Shelf Bks.). (American Folktales). 1969. Garrard Pub. Co.
--The Children's Hour, and Other Poems. (Illus.). Notes. 96p. (Riverside Literature Ser: No. 11). N.D. Nos 11 & 63 bound together in linen. Houghton, Mifflin and Company.
--The Children's Longfellow: Retold Stories of the Poems and Ballads of Longfellow. (Illus.). (The Children's Own Series.). N.D. George H Doran & Co.
--The Children's Own Longfellow. 1908. Houghton.
--The Children's Own Longfellow. LC 66-1138. (Illus.). 103 p. 21cm. 1920. Houghton Mifflin.
--Christmas Bells. (Illus.). (Finesse Classics). N.D. Barse and Hopkins.
--Christmas Bells. (Illus.). (Christmas Classics). N.D. Barse and Hopkins.
--Christmas Bells. (Silk Vellum and Ooze covers). (Illus.). (Golden Thoughts Ser.). N.D. Barse and Hopkins.
--Complete Poetic & Dramatic Works. Scudder, Horace Elisha (1838-1902), ed. (Cambridge Editions). (gr. 7 up). N.D. HM.
--Courtship of Miles Standish. (Burt's Home Library). N.D. A L Burt Co.
--The Courtship of Miles Standish. N.D. David McKay Co.
--The Courtship of Miles Standish. (Remarque Edition of Literary Masterpieces). N.D. Dodge.
--The Courtship of Miles Standish. Good Value ed. N.D. Grosset & Dunlap.
--The Courtship of Miles Standish. 97p. (Riverside Literature Ser: No. 2). N.D. Houghton, Mifflin and Company.
--The Courtship of Miles Standish. (Dramatized, for Private Theatricals in Schools and Families. With Portrait). 96p. (No. 3). N.D. Houghton, Mifflin and Company.
--Courtship of Miles Standish. N.D. Thomas Y Crowell Co.
--The Courtship of Miles Standish. Christy, Howard Chandler (1873-1952), illus. N.D. Bobbs-Merrill Co.
--The Courtship of Myles Standish. Wyeth, Newell Convers (1882-1945), illus. N.D. Houghton Mifflin Co.
--The Coutship of Miles Standish. Eaton, M. A., ed. N.D. Educational Publishing Company.
--Easter Joys. Rhead, Louis John (1857-1926), illus. N.D. Dodge.
--Evangeline. (Traymore Ser.). N.D. Barse & Hopkins.
--Evangeline. (Illus.). (Biltmore Ser.). N.D. Barse and Hopkins.
--Evangeline. (Illus.). (Blenheim Ser.). N.D. Barse and Hopkins.
--Evangeline. N.D. David McKay Co.
--Evangeline. (The Good Value Books). N.D. Grosset & Dunlap.
--Evangeline. N.D. Grosset & Dunlap.
--Evangeline. (Illus.). (The Exquisite Ser.). N.D. H. M. Caldwell Co.
--Evangeline. (Illus.). (The Chateau Ser.). N.D. H. M. Caldwell Co.
--Evangeline, 1 of 3 vols. (The Lakeside Ser.). N.D. H. M. Caldwell Co.
--Evangeline. (Illus.). (The Empyreal Library of Handy Volume Classics). N.D. H. M. Calwell & Co.
--Evangeline. (Illus.). (Vademecum Ser.). N.D. Henry Altemus.
--Evangeline. (Illus.). (Petit-Trianon Ser.). N.D. Henry Altemus.
--Evangeline. Handy Volume, Large Type ed. (Illus.). (Beauxarts Ser.). N.D. Henry Altemus.
--Evangeline. 96p. (Riverside Literature Ser: No. 1). N.D. Houghton, Mifflin and Company.
--Evangeline. (Illus.). (Hurst's Half Leather Classics). N.D. Hurst and Company.
--Evangeline. (Illus.). (Arlington Edition). N.D. Hurst and Company.
--Evangeline. N.D. James R. Osgood.
--Evangeline, 1 of 56 vols. (Illus.). (The Colonial Lib.). 1900. T. Y Crowell & Co.
--Evangeline, 1 of 16 vols. (Illus.). (The Copley Ser.). 1900. T. Y. Crowell & Co.
--Evangeline, 1 of 88 vols. Birch Bark ed. (Handy Volume Classics). 1900. T. Y. Crowell & Co.
--Evangeline, 1 of 56 vols. (Illus.). (The Faience Lib.). N.D. T. Y. Crowell & Co.
--Evangeline, 1 of 67 vols. Gilt Edge ed. N.D. T. Y. Crowell & Co.
--Evangeline, 1 of 45 vols. Woodbine ed. N.D. T. Y. Crowell & Co.
--Evangeline, 1 of 52 vols. Abbotsford ed. N.D. Thomas Y. Crowell & Co.
--Evangeline. Christy, Howard Chandler (1873-1952), illus. N.D. Bobbs-Merrill Co.
--Evangeline. Eaton, M. A., ed. N.D. Educational Publishing Company.
--The First Book Edition of Paul Revere's Ride. Fisher, Leonard Everett (1924-), illus. 1963. Watts.
--The Golden Legend, Nos. 25, 26. Bent, S. A. 96p. (Riverside Literature Ser: Nos. 25-26). N.D. Houghton, Mifflin and Company.
--Hiawatha. (Burt's Home Lib.). N.D. A. L. Burt's Pubs.
--Hiawatha. (Embassy Ser.). N.D. Barse & Hopkins.
--Hiawatha. (Traymore Ser.). N.D. Barse & Hopkins.
--Hiawatha. (Ardsley Ser.). N.D. Barse & Hopkins.
--Hiawatha. (Illus.). (Essex Ser.). N.D. Barse and Hopkins.
--Hiawatha. (Illus.). (Biltmore Ser.). N.D. Barse and Hopkins.
--Hiawatha. (Illus.). (Regis Ser.). N.D. Barse and Hopkins.
--Hiawatha. (Illus.). (Savoy Ser.). N.D. Barse and Hopkins.
--Hiawatha. (Illus.). (New Retlaw Ser.). N.D. Barse and Hopkins.
--Hiawatha. (Illus.). (New Relyea Classics). N.D. Barse and Hopkins.
--Hiawatha. (Illus.). (New Drexel Ser.). N.D. Barse and Hopkins.
--Hiawatha. (Illus.). (Aberdeen Ser.). N.D. Barsse and Hopkins.
--Hiawatha. (Illus.). (Blackstone Ser.). N.D. Barse and Hopkins.
--Hiawatha. (Illus.). (Blenheim Ser.). N.D. Barse and Hopkins.
--Hiawatha. (Illus.). (The Young Folks Library). N.D. Caldwell.
--Hiawatha. (Illus.). 32p. (A Dial Book for Young Readers Ser.). (gr. k up). 1983. (ISBN 0-8037-0013-X). (ISBN 0-8037-0004-0). Dutton.
--Hiawatha. N.D. Educational Publising Company.
--Hiawatha. N.D. Garden City Publishing City.
--Hiawatha. (The Good Value Books). N.D. Grosset & Dunlap.
--Hiawatha. (Illus.). (The Empyreal Library of Handy Classics). N.D. H. M. Caldwell Co.
--Hiawatha. (Illus.). (The Exquisite Ser.). N.D. H. M. Caldwell Co.
--Hiawatha. (Illus.). (The Chateau Ser.). N.D. Set. H. M. Caldwell Co.
--Hiawatha. (Illus.). (Little Men and Women Ser.). N.D. Henry Altemus & Co.
--Hiawatha. (Illus.). (Hurst's Half Leather Classics). N.D. Hurst and Company.
--Hiawatha. (Illus.). (The New Argyle Ser.). N.D. Hurst and Company.
--Hiawatha, 1 of 56 vols. (Illus.). (The Colonial Lib.). 1900. T. Y. Cowell & Co.
--Hiawatha, 1 of 16 vols. (Illus.). (The Copley Ser.). 1900. T. Y. Crowell & Co.
--Hiawatha. N.D. (Abbotsford Edition) .60. T. Y. Crowell & Co.
--Hiawatha, 1 of 88 vols. popular ed. (Handy Volume Classics). N.D. T. Y. Crowell & Co.
--Hiawatha, 1 of 88 vols. Oak Leaf ed. (Handy Volume Classics). N.D. T. Y. Crowell & Co.
--Hiawatha, 1 of 56 vols. (Illus.). (The Faience Lib.). N.D. T. Y. Crowell & Co.
--Hiawatha, 1 of 52 vols. Abbotsford ed. notes. N.D. T. Y. Crowell & Co.
--Hiawatha. Gladstone ed. (Illus.). notes. N.D. T. Y. Crowell & Co.
--Hiawatha, 1 of 45 vols. Woodbine ed. notes. N.D. T. Y. Crowell & Co.
--Hiawatha, 1 of 67 vols. Gilt Edge ed. Notes. N.D. T. Y.Crowell & Co.
--Hiawatha. (Choice Literary Masterpieces). N.D. Thomas Y Crowell Co.
--Hiawatha. Astor ed. notes. (Crowell's Poets). N.D. Thomas Y. Crowell & Co.
--Hiawatha. (Classic Ser.). N.D. World Publishing Co.
--Hiawatha. Jeffers, Susan, illus. 1983. Dial.
--Hiawatha. Molan, Christine, illus. LC 83-26972. (Raintree Stories). 1984. (ISBN 0-8172-2106-9). Raintree Children's Books.
--Hiawatha. Molan, Christine, illus. LC 85-28856. p. cm. (Great Tales from Long Ago). 1986, c.1985. (ISBN 1-550-01026-3). Torstar Books.
--Hiawatha: Retold After Longfellow's Poem. Serkin, Amalia, illus. LC 49-1997. 20 p. col. illus. 27 cm. (Chanticleer Junior Bk.). 1948. Chanticleer Press.
--Hiawatha's Childhood: From "The Song of Hiawatha". Semel, Jeffrey, illus. LC 78-72099. (Illus.). 31 p. 23cm. 1979. (ISBN 0-89799-109-5). (ISBN 0-89799-054-4). Dandelion Press.
--Hiawatha's Childhood: From "The Song of Hiawatha". Stoops, Herbert Morton, illus. LC 41-22781. 15 p. illus. (part col.) 27 x 27 cm. c.1941. Garden City Publishing Co., Inc.
--Hyperion. (Altemus' New Vademecum Ser.). N.D. Henry Altemus Co.
--Kavanagh. (Altemus' New Vademecum Series). N.D. Henry Altemus Co.
--Longfellow's Poems: The Poetical Works of Henry Wadsworth Longfellow. 488p. Repr. of 1884 ed (Pub. by Houghton, Mifflin & Co). (gr. 9-12). 1981. (ISBN 0-86649-026-4). Twentieth Century.
--A Moosehead Journal, My Garden Acquaintance and A Good Word for Winter. (Riverside Literature Ser.). N.D. Houghton Mifflin Co.
--My Uncle my Cure, 1 of 88 vols. popular ed. (Handy Volume Classics). N.D. T. Y. Crowell & Co.
--Paul Revere's Ride. (Illus.). (Windmill Books). 1973. (ISBN 0-87807-050-8). Abelard-Schuman.
--Paul Revere's Ride. Brewster, Lynn, illus. LC 78-72097. (Illus.). 30 p. 23cm. 1979. (ISBN 0-89799-131-1). (ISBN 0-89799-053-6). Dandelion Press.
--Paul Revere's Ride. Galdone, Paul (1914-), illus. (Illus.). 32p. 1963. Thomas Y. Crowell Company.
--Paul Revere's Ride. Parker, Nancy Winslow (1930-), illus. LC 84-4139. (Illus.). 7 x 9. 48p. (20 pt.). 1985. (ISBN 0-688-04014-4). (ISBN 0-688-04015-2). Greenwillow.
--Poems of Henry W. Longfellow. Fuller, Edmund, ed. Ross, John (1921-) & Ross, Clare Romano (1922-), illus. LC 67-10072. (Poets Ser). (gr. 6 up). 1967. (ISBN 0-690-64075-7). T Y Crowell.
--Prue and I, 1 of 56 vols. (Illus.). (The Colonial Lib.). 1900. T. Y. Crowell & Co.
--Skeleton in Armor. Kennedy, Paul Edward (1929-), illus. (Illus.). (gr. 4-7). 1967. (ISBN 0-13-812735-2). P-H.
--The Skeleton in Armor. Kennedy, Paul Edward (1929-), illus. LC 63-14680. 31 p. illus. (part col.) 24 cm. 1963. Prentice-Hall.

--Today's Special: Z.A.P. and Zoe. Jenkins, Jean, illus. LC 84-9661. (Illus.). 150 p. 52cm. c.1984. (ISBN 0-02-761440-9). Macmillan.

Lord, Beman (1924-)

--Bats and Balls. Spilka, Arnold (1917-), illus. LC 62-14057. (Illus.). 57 p. 21cm. 1962. H. Z. Walck.

--The Day the Spaceship Landed. Berson, Harold (1926-), illus. LC 67-19926. (Illus.). 63 p. 21cm. 1967. H. Z. Walck.

--Guards for Matt. Spilka, Arnold (1917-), illus. LC 61-12885. (Illus.). 64 p. 21cm. 1961. H. Z. Walck.

--A Monster's Visit. Bolognese, Donald Alan (1934-), illus. LC 67-5172. (Illus.). 1 v. (unpaged. 20cm. 1967. H. Z. Walck.

--Mystery Guest at Left End. Spilka, Arnold (1917-), illus. LC 64-21119. (Illus.). 62 p. 21cm. 1964. H. Z. Walck.

--Mystery Player at Left End. Spilka, Arnold (1917-), illus. 48p. Orig. Title: Mystery Guest at Left End. (gr. 4-6). 1969. (ISBN 0-590-08075-X, Schol Pap). Schol Bk Serv.

--On the Banks of the Hudson: A View of Its History & Folklore. Negri, Rocco (1932-), illus. LC 75-142451. (Illus.). color ils. 64p. (gr. 4-7). 1971. (ISBN 0-8098-2075-7). Walck.

--Our New Baby's ABC. Ilsley, Velma Elizabeth (1918-), illus. 1964. (ISBN 0-8098-1100-6). David McKay Company.

--Our New Baby's ABC. Ilsley, Velma Elizabeth (1918-), illus. LC 64-14101. 1 v. (chiefly col. illus.) 24 cm. 1964. H. Z. Walck.

--The Perfect Pitch. Berson, Harold (1926-), illus. LC 65-23255. 54p. illus. 21cm. c.1965. Walck.

--The Perfect Pitch. Spilka, Arnold (1917-), illus. LC 80-24624. p. cm. (Gregg Press Children's Literature Series). 1981, c.1965. Gregg Press.

--Quarter backs Aim. Spilka, Arnold (1917-), illus. 1968. (ISBN 0-8098-2904-5). David McKay Company.

--Quarterback's Aim. Spilka, Arnold (1917-), illus. LC 60-9799. (Illus.). 60 p. 21cm. 1960. H. Z. Walck.

--Rough Ice. Spilka, Arnold (1917-), illus. LC 63-17190. (Illus.). 64 p. 21cm. 1963. H. Z. Walck.

--Shot-Put Challenge. Berson, Harold (1926-), illus. 1972. (ISBN 0-8098-2911-8). David McKay Company.

--Shot-Put Challenge. Berson, Harold (1926-), illus. LC 69-17904. (Illus.). 63 p. 21cm. 1969. H. Z. Walck.

--Shrimp's Soccer Goal. Berson, Harold (1926-), illus. LC 79-119571. (Illus.). 62 p. 21cm. 1970. (ISBN 0-8098-2070-6). H. Z. Walck.

--The Spaceship Returns. Berson, Harold (1926-), illus. LC 70-100708. (Illus.). 62 p. 21cm. 1970. H. Z. Walck.

--Trouble with Francis. (Illus.). (gr. 3-5). 1958. (ISBN 0-8382-0899-1). Hale.

--The Trouble with Francis. Spilka, Arnold (1917-), illus. LC 58-10297. (Illus.). 54 p. 21cm. 1958. (ISBN 0-8098-2008-0). H. Z. Walck.

Lord, Beman (1924-), ed.

--The Days of the Week. Erhard, Walter (1920-), illus. LC 68-11229. (Illus.). 32 p. 18cm. 1968. H. Z. Walck.

Lord, Bette Bao (1938-)

--In the Year of the Boar and Jackie Robinson. 1st ed. Simont, Marc (1915-), illus. LC 83-48440. (Illus.). 169p. c.1984. (ISBN 0-06-024003-2). (ISBN 0-06-024004-0). Harper & Row. **Award: (ALA).**

Lord, Doreen Mildred Douglas see Lord, Douglas, pseud.

Lord, Doreen Mildred Douglas (1904-)

--Kiwi Jane. Lord, Douglas, pseud. Hawkins, Sheila (1905-), illus. N.D. Transatlantic Arts.

Lord, Douglas, pseud., see Lord, Doreen Mildred Douglas.

Lord, John Vernon (1939-)

--Mr. Mead and His Garden: Verses. Lord, John Vernon (1939-), illus. LC 74-20766. (Illus.). 32 p. 27cm. 1975, c.1974. (ISBN 0-395-20278-7). Houghton Mifflin.

--The Runaway Roller Skate. Lord, John Vernon (1939-), illus. LC 73-22053. (Illus.). 32 p. 1974, c.1973. (ISBN 0-395-18514-9). Houghton Mifflin.

Lord, John Vernon (1939-) & Burroway, Janet Gay (1926-)

--The Giant Jam Sandwich. Lord, John Vernon (1939-), illus. LC 72-13578. (Illus.). 32 p. 1973, c.1972. (ISBN 0-395-16033-2). Houghton Mifflin.

Lord, John Vernon (1939-) & Maschler, Fay

--Miserable Aunt Bertha. Lord, John Vernon (1939-), illus. LC 80-670116. (Illus.). 32 p. 27cm. 1980. (ISBN 0-224-01613-X). J. Cape.

Lord, Katharine

--The Little Playbook. LC 20-9125. 4 p. l., 3-153 p. 21 cm. 1920. Duffield and Company.

--Plays for School and Camp. LC 22-11463. xvi, 224 p., 1 l. 21 cm. 1922. Little, Brown, and Company.

Lord, Nancy, pseud., see Titus, Eve.

Lord, Nancy, pseud. (1922-)

--My Dog & I. Titus, Eve. N.D. E. M. Hale & Co.

--My Dog & I. Titus, Eve. Galdone, Paul (1914-), illus. LC 57-12904. (Illus.). (gr. k-2). 1958. (ISBN 0-07-038741-9). McGraw.

Lord, William Sinclair (1863-1925)

--Blue and Gold and Other Verses. N.D. Fleming H. Revell Co.

--Jingle and Jangle, and Other Verses for and about Children. 56p. 1899. Fleming H. Revell Co.

--The Rock-a-Bye Book and a Bag of Dreams: Children's Lyrics. LC 5-27155. viii, 54 p. 20 cm. c.1905. Fleming H. Revell Company.

Loree, Kate Lambie (1920-)

--Pails and Snails. Walters, Audrey (1929-), illus. LC 67-2662. (Illus.). 37 p. 1967. Harvey House.

Loree, Sharron

--The Sunshine Family and the Pony. Loree, Sharron, illus. LC 71-171859. (Illus.). 48 p. c.1972. (ISBN 0-8164-3066-7). Seabury Press.

Lorentowicz, Irena (1910-)

--What's in the Trunk?. Lorentowicz, Irena (1910-), illus. LC 46-22119. 28 p. col. illus. 26 x 21 cm. 1946. Roy Publishers.

Lorentowicz, Irena (1910-), ed.

--Lullaby: Why the Pussy-Cat Washes Himself So Often ; A Folklore. Lorentowicz, Irena (1910-), illus. Bernhard, Josephine Butkowska, Mrs., tr. from Pol. LC 44-5854. 26 p. illus. (part col.) 21 1/2 x 26 1/2 cm. c.1944. Roy Publishers.

Lorentzen, Karin (1939-)

--Lanky Longlegs. Tate, Joan (1922-), tr. from Norwegian. LC 82-72246. (Illus.). 90 p. 23cm. 1st U.S. edition. 1983, c.1982. (ISBN 0-689-50260-5). Atheneum.

Lorenz, Clarissa

--Junket to Japan. 1960. Little, Brown and Company.

Lorenz, Eleanor

--Jerry Journeyed to Jericho. N.D. Carlton Press Inc.

Lorenz, Ellen Jane (1907-), ed.

--Bible Sing-a-Story. Hitton, Kathryn, illus. (Illus.). 40p. (gr. k-3). 1976. (ISBN 0-87239-076-4). Standard Pub.

--Playtime Songs: A Collection of Short Rote Songs for Small Children. LC 43-43341. 32 p. 26 1/2 cm. c.1937. Lorenz Publishing Co.

Lorenz, Lee

--Big Gus and Little Gus. Lorenz, Lee, illus. LC 81-20956. (Illus.). 32 p. c.1982. (ISBN 0-13-077875-3). Prentice-Hall.

--The Feathered Ogre. Lorenz, Lee, illus. LC 81-7369. p. cm. c.1981. (ISBN 0-13-308304-7). Prentice-Hall.

--Hugo and the Spacedog. Lorenz, Lee, illus. LC 82-22960. (Illus.). 32 p. c.1983. (ISBN 0-13-444497-3). Prentice-Hall.

--Pinchpenny John. Lorenz, Lee, illus. LC 80-25999. (Illus.). 32 p. 29cm. c.1981. (ISBN 0-13-676254-9). Prentice-Hall.

--Scornful Simkin. Lorenz, Lee, illus. (Illus.). 30p. (Orig.). (gr. k-3). 1982. (ISBN 0-13-796730-6, Pub. by Treehouse). P-H.

--A Weekend in the Country. Lorenz, Lee, illus. LC 84-22881. (Illus.). 32 p. 27cm. c.1985. (ISBN 0-13-947961-9). Prentice-Hall.

Lorenz, Lee, retold by see Chaucer, Geoffrey.

Lorenzini, Carlo see Collodi, Carlo, pseud.

Lorenzini, Carlo, jt. auth. see Disney, Walt, Productions.

Lorenzini, Carlo, jt. auth. see Mayer, Marianna.

Lorenzini, Carlo (1826-1890)

--Adventures Every Child Should Know: The Marvellous Adventures of Pinocchio. Collodi, Carlo, pseud. Burt, Mary Elizabeth (1850-1918), ed. Chamberlin, Emily Hall, illus. Caprani, Augustus G., tr. LC 9-4295. xx, 241 p. col. front., 7 col. pl. 19 cm. 1909. Doubleday, Page & Company.

--Adventures of Pinocchio. Collodi, Carlo, pseud. N.D. Blue Ribbon Books Inc.

--The Adventures of Pinocchio. Collodi, Carlo, pseud. (Riverside Literature Ser.). N.D. Houghton Mifflin Co.

--Adventures of Pinocchio. Collodi, Carlo, pseud. 224p. (Magnum Easy Eye Classic Ser). (gr. 5-8). 1968. Lancer.

--Adventures of Pinocchio. Collodi, Carlo, pseud. (gr. 4-6). 1978. (ISBN 0-590-05357-4). Scholastic Inc.

--The Adventures of Pinocchio. Collodi, Carlo, pseud. (Illus.). 256p. (Orig.). (Bambi Classics Ser.). 1981. (ISBN 0-89531-069-4). Sharon Pubns.

--The Adventures of Pinocchio. Collodi, Carlo, pseud. Bacharach, Herman Ilfeld (1899-), illus. Sweet, May McDaniel, Mrs. (1865-), tr. LC 27-20372. vii, 1 p., 2 l., 212, 1 p. col. front., illus., col. plates. 23 cm. (Riverside bookshelf). 1927. Houghton Mifflin Company.

--The Adventures of Pinocchio. Collodi, Carlo, pseud. Beare, Cornelia, ed. Bacharach, Herman Ilfeld (1899-), illus. Sweet, May McDaniel, Mrs. (1865-), tr. LC 29-10183. vii 1 p., 1 l., 215, 1 p. front., illus., plates. 20 cm. (Riverside literature series). c.1929. Houghton Mifflin Company.

--The Adventures of Pinocchio. Collodi, Carlo, pseud. Cramp, Walter Samuel (1867-), tr. Lockwood, Sara Elizabeth (Husted) (1854-) Copeland, Charles, illus. LC 4-22857. vi, 212 p. incl. front., illus. 18 cm. (Once Upon a Time Ser.). 1904. Ginn and Company.

--The Adventures of Pinocchio. Collodi, Carlo, pseud. Einsel, Naiad, illus. Della Chiesa, Carolyn M. (1887-), tr. LC 63-14841. vi, 192 p. illus. (part col.) 24 cm. (Macmillan classics, 20). 1963. (ISBN 0-02-722840-1). Macmillan.

--The Adventures of Pinocchio. Collodi, Carlo, pseud. Friend, Esther, illus. LC 39-22582. 254 p. col., front., illus., col. plates. 24 cm. c.1939. Rand McNally & Company.

--The Adventures of Pinocchio. Collodi, Carlo, pseud. Goulden, Shirley, retold by. Maraja, pseud., illus. Maraja, Libico. LC 63-16842. 126 p. illus. 32cm. 1963. Duell Sloan & Pearce.

--The Adventures of Pinocchio. Collodi, Carlo, pseud. Goulden, Shirley, retold by. Maraja, pseud., illus. Maraja, Libico. LC 57-4835. 126p. illus. 35cm. 1957. Grosset & Dunlap.

--Adventures of Pinocchio. Collodi, Carlo, pseud. Kredel, Fritz (1900-1973), illus. Murray, Mary Alice (1900-1973), tr. LC 46-2699. (Illus.). (gr. 4-6). 1946. (ISBN 0-448-05801-4, G&D). (ISBN 0-448-05471-X). (ISBN 0-448-06001-9). Putnam Pub Group.

--The Adventures of Pinocchio. Collodi, Carlo, pseud. Leone, Mariano, illus. Murray, Mary Alice, tr. LC 65-171898. 192p. illus. 20cm. (Companion lib. of classics). 1965. Grosset.

--The Adventures of Pinocchio. Collodi, Carlo, pseud. Liddell, Mary, illus. Patri, Angelo (1896-), tr. LC 30-24232. xiii p., 1 l., 280, 1 p. incl. illus., plates. col. front. 20 1/2 cm. 1930. Doubleday, Doran and Company, Inc.

--The Adventures of Pinocchio. Collodi, Carlo, pseud. MacDonald, Roberta, illus. LC 55-4273. 223p. illus. 22cm. 1955. Junior Deluxe Editions.

--Adventures of Pinocchio. Collodi, Carlo, pseud. Morris, Neil (1905-1962) & Baber, Frank, retold by. (Illus.). 96p. (gr. 3-6). 1982. (ISBN 0-528-82071-0). Rand.

--The Adventures of Pinocchio. Collodi, Carlo, pseud. Mozley, Charles (1915-), illus. McIntyre, Jane, tr. LC 59-11159. 224p. illus. 23cm. (Around the world treasures: Italy). 1959. F. Watts.

--The Adventures of Pinocchio. Collodi, Carlo, pseud. Mussino, Attilio (1878-1954), illus. LC 51-10553. vii, 206 p. illus. 22 cm. (New children's classics). 1951. Macmillan.

--Adventures of Pinocchio. Collodi, Carlo, pseud. rev. ed. Mussino, Attilio (1878-1954), illus. Della Chiesa, Carolyn M., tr. Cimino, M., intro. by. LC 25-26908. (Illus.). 288 color ils. 320p. 1969. (ISBN 0-02-722820-7). Macmillan.

--The Adventures of Pinocchio. Collodi, Carlo, pseud. Mussino, Attilio (1878-1954), illus. Della Chiesa, Carolyn M. (1887-), tr. from Ital. LC 73-5662. (Illus.). 309 p. 30cm. 1969. Macmillan.

--The Adventures of Pinocchio. Collodi, Carlo, pseud. Mussino, Attilio (1878-1954), illus. Della Chiesa, Carolyn M. (1887-), tr. (Illus.). (gr. 3-5). 1972. (ISBN 0-02-042740-9, Collier). Macmillan.

--The Adventures of Pinocchio. Collodi, Carlo, pseud. 3d ed. Mussino, Attilio (1878-1954), illus. Della Chiesa, Carolyn M. (1887-), tr. LC 25-26908. (Illus.). 5 p. 30cm. 1925. The Macmillan Company.

--The Adventures of Pinocchio. Collodi, Carlo, pseud. Mussino, Attilio (1878-1954), illus. Della Chiesa, Carolyn M. (1887-), tr. LC 27-24302. xv p., 1 l., 220 p. col. front., illus., col. plates. 19 1/2 cm. (Macmillan children's classics). 1927. The Macmillan Company.

--The Adventures of Pinocchio. Collodi, Carlo, pseud. Safford, Mary Joanna, tr. (Illus.). N.D. Sully and Kleinteich.

--The Adventures of Pinocchio: Tale of a Puppet. Collodi, Carlo, pseud. Howell, Troy, illus. Rosenthal, M. L., tr. LC 83-801. (Illus.). 256p. (gr. 3 up). 1983. (ISBN 0-688-02267-7). Lothrop.

--The Animated Pinocchio. Collodi, Carlo, pseud. Merrill, Marion, illus. LC 46-597. 26 p. col. illus. 20 x 22 1/2cm. 1945. Cima Pub. Co.

--Beppo: Or, The Little Rose-Colored Monkey. Collodi, Carlo, pseud. Cramp, Walter Samuel (1867-), tr. LC 7-42013. 2 p. l., 125 p. front., illus., 2 pl. 18 cm. 1907. Small, Maynard & Company.

--Carlo Collodi's Famous Story Pinocchio. Collodi, Carlo, pseud. Andreas, Evelyn, adapted by. Seiden, Art, illus. LC 54-18561. unpaged. illus. 21cm. (Wonder books, 615). 1954. Wonder Books.

--Carlo Collodi's Pinocchio. Collodi, Carlo, pseud. Abrams, Michael D, adapted by. Gantz, David, illus. LC 68-8913. (Illus.). 62 p. 1968. Lancelot Press.

--My Book of Pinocchio. Lupatelli, Anthony, illus. Lupatelli, pseud. LC 62-11765. unpaged. illus. 33cm. (A Giant Maxton Book). 1962, c.1961. Maxton Pub. Corp.

--Pinnocchio. Collodi, Carlo, pseud. Richardson, Frederick (1862-1937), illus. N.D. John C. Winston Co.

--Pinocchio. Collodi, Carlo, pseud. (Illus.). 1st U.S. edition. Repr. of 1972 ed. (Childrens Illustrated Classics Ser.). 1975. (ISBN 0-460-06923-3, Pub. by J. M. Dent England). Biblio Dist.

--Pinocchio. Collodi, Carlo, pseud. (Illus.). (gr. 3-8). N.D. (ISBN 0-685-11495-3). French & Eur.

--Pinocchio. Collodi, Carlo, pseud. (Thrushwood Bks.). N.D. Grosset & Dunlap.

--Pinocchio. Collodi, Carlo, pseud. (Twilight Ser.). N.D. Harper & Bros.

--Pinocchio. Collodi, Carlo, pseud. (Illus.). 22p. (The Gakken Picture Story Ser.). (gr. k-7). 1972. (ISBN 0-87040-192-0). Japan Pubns.

--Pinocchio. Collodi, Carlo, pseud. (The Winston Clear-Type Popular Classics). N.D. John C. Winston.

--Pinocchio. Collodi, Carlo, pseud. (Classic Ser.). N.D. World Publishing Co.

--Pinocchio. Collodi, Carlo, pseud. Brown, Kay (1943-), retold by. Embleton, Gerry, illus. LC 79-13751. p. cm. (Derrydale Fairy Tale Library). 1979. (ISBN 0-517-28809-5). Derrydale Books.

--Pinocchio. Collodi, Carlo, pseud. Brundage, Frances, illus. LC 25-3061. xii p., 1 l., 15-247 p. col. front., illus. 24 cm. (On cover: Mayflower series). c.1924. The Saalfield Publishing Co.

--Pinocchio. Collodi, Carlo, pseud. Carruth, Jane, retold by. Embleton, Elisabeth, illus. 32p. (Illustrated Classics Ser.). 1972. (ISBN 0-529-04798-5). (ISBN 0-529-04799-3). Collins & World.

--Pinocchio. Collodi, Carlo, pseud. Chaffee, Allen, ed. Lenski, Lois (1893-1974), illus. LC 47-222. (Illus.). (ps-3). 1946. (ISBN 0-394-80671-9). (ISBN 0-394-90671-3). Random.

--Pinocchio. Collodi, Carlo, pseud. Dempster, William, illus. Walker, Joseph, tr. LC 73-2478. (Illus.). 215 p. 29cm. (Educator classic library, 3). 1968. Classic Press.

--Pinocchio. Collodi, Carlo, pseud. Fiammenghi, Gioia (1929-), illus. LC 75-303207. (Illus.). 231 p. 20cm. (Puffin books). 1974. (ISBN 0-14-030230-1). Penguin Books.

--Pinocchio. Collodi, Carlo, pseud. Floethe, Richard (1901-), illus. (Illus.). (Rainbow Classics). (gr. k-3). N.D. (ISBN 0-529-02861-1). World Pub.

--Pinocchio. Collodi, Carlo, pseud. Folkard, Charles James (1878-1963), illus. 194p. 1964. Parent's magazine Press.

--Pinocchio. Collodi, Carlo, pseud. Friend, Esther, illus. LC 30-31. 128 p. illus. 17 cm. c.1938. Rand, McNally & Company.

--Pinocchio. Collodi, Carlo, pseud. Harden, E., tr. 1974. (ISBN 0-14-030230-1, Puffin). Penguin.

--Pinocchio. Collodi, Carlo, pseud. Iizawa, Tadasu (1909-) & Hijikata, Shigemi (1915-), illus. LC 77-157675. (Illus.). 20 p. 29cm. 1971. (ISBN 0-448-04274-6). Grosset & Dunlap.

--Pinocchio. Collodi, Carlo, pseud. Irwin, Don, illus. (Illus.). (Fun to Read Classics Ser). (gr. 5 up). 1968. (ISBN 0-516-04233-5). Childrens.

--Pinocchio. Collodi, Carlo, pseud. Miller, Albert G., ed. (Illus.). (Pop-up Classics Ser No. 2). (gr. k-3). 1968. (ISBN 0-394-81489-4). Random.

--Pinocchio. Collodi, Carlo, pseud. Mozley, Charles (1915-), illus. (Illus.). (Keith Jennison Large Type Bks). (gr. 5 up). 1967. (ISBN 0-531-00261-6). Watts.

--Pinocchio. Collodi, Carlo, pseud. Murray, Mary Alice, tr. x p., 1 l., 11-258 p. front., illus. 7 col. pl. 20 cm. (Half-title: The golden books for children). 1918. D. McKay.

--Pinocchio. Collodi, Carlo, pseud. Petersham, Maud Sylvia Fuller, Mrs. (1890-1971) & Petersham, Miska (1889-1960), illus. LC 32-18244. ix p., 2 l., 3-323 p. col. front., col. plates. 23 cm. c.1932. Garden City Publishing Co., Inc.

--Pinocchio. Collodi, Carlo, pseud. Piper, Watty (1870-1945), ed. Sarg, Tony, pseud. (1882-1942), illus. Sarg, Anthony Frederick. LC 40-29655. 1 p. l., 5-122 p. illus., col. plates. 28 x 22 cm. c.1940. The Platt & Munk Co., Inc.

--Pinocchio. Collodi, Carlo, pseud. Rouke, Eve, retold by. Correas, Jose, illus. LC 65-24746. 1 v. (unpaged) col. illus. 24 cm. (Holly story book library). 1965. World Pub. Co.

--Pinocchio. Collodi, Carlo, pseud. Rule, Christopher, illus. LC 26-14323. 2 p. l., iii-vi, 236 p. col. front., illus. 25 cm. (Sears illustrated juveniles). 1926. J. H. Sears & Company, Inc.

Lothrop, ed.
--Lothrop's Annual of Prose and Poetry. (Illus.). N.D. Lothrop Pub. Co.

Lothrop, Amy, pseud., see Warner, Anna Bartlett.

Lothrop, Harriet Mulford Stone see Sidney, Margaret, pseud.

Lothrop, Harriet Mulford Stone, Mrs., jt. auth. see Fitzgerald, Scott F.

Lothrop, Harriet Mulford Stone, Mrs. (1844-1924)
--An Adirondack Cabin: A Family Story Telling of Journeyings by Lake and Mountain, and Idyllic Days in the Heart of the Wilderness. Sidney, Margaret, pseud. Lothrop, Harriet Mulford Stone, Mrs. (1844-1924), illus. Sydney, Margaret, pseud. LC 12-36311. 4 p. l., 432 p. incl. front., illus., plates. 22 cm. c.1890. D. Lothrop Company.
--The Adventures of Joel Pepper. Sidney, Margaret, pseud. N.D. Grosset & Dunlap.
--The Adventures of Joel Pepper. Sidney, Margaret, pseud. Becher, Arthur E., illus. LC 38-3242. vi, 9-461 p. incl. plates. col. front. 20 cm. 1937. Houghton Mifflin Company.
--The Adventures of Joel Pepper. Sidney, Margaret, pseud. Gallagher, Sears (1869-1955), illus. (The Famous Pepper Books). 1900. Lothrop, Lee & Shepard.
--Ballad of the Lost Hare. Sidney, Margaret, pseud. LC 16-1245. cover-title, 13 l. col. plates 23 x 33 cm. c.1882. D. Lothrop & Co.
--Ben Pepper. Sidney, Margaret, pseud. N.D. Grosset & Dunlap.
--Ben Pepper. Sidney, Margaret, pseud. Becher, Arthur E., illus. LC 38-1812. 2 p. l., 3-6, 9-474 p. col. front. 20 cm. 1937. Houghton Mifflin Company.
--Ben Pepper. Sidney, Margaret, pseud. Wireman, Eugenie M., illus. LC 5-28012. 474 p. front., 5 pl. 20 cm. 1905. Lothrop Publishing Company.
--Dilly and the Captain. Sidney, Margaret, pseud, 1 of 3 vols. Hassam, F. Childe (1859-1935), illus. LC 20-231602. 1 p. l., 11-228 p. incl. illus., plates. 19 cm. (Fun and Fancy Library). c.1887. D. Lothrop Company.
--Five Little Grown up. Sidney, Margaret, pseud. N.D. Grosset & Dunlap.
--The Five Little Peppers. Sidney, Margaret, pseud. 320p. Repr. 1980. (ISBN 0-89967-015-6). Harmony & Co.
--Five Little Peppers. Sidney, Margaret, pseud. Magagna, Anna Marie, illus. Fadiman, Clifton (1904-), afterword by. LC 62-18398. 290p. illus. 24cm. (Macmillan classics, 33). 1962. Macmillan.
--Five Little Peppers. Sidney, Margaret, pseud. Weber, Nettie, illus. Becker, May Lamberton, intro. by. LC 50-11367. 256 p. illus. part col. 22 cm. (Rainbow classics). 1950. (ISBN 0-529-02843-3). World Pub. Co.
--Five Little Peppers Abroad. Sidney, Margaret, pseud. N.D. Grosset & Dunlap.
--Five Little Peppers Abroad. Sidney, Margaret, pseud. Becher, Arthur E., illus. LC 37-15462. 5 p. l., 9-449 p. col. front. 20 cm. 1937. Houghton Mifflin Company.
--Five Little Peppers Abroad. Sidney, Margaret, pseud. Cory, Fanny Young, illus. LC 2-15206. 449 p. front. pl. 20 cm. 1902. Lothrop Publishing Company.
--Five Little Peppers and How They Grew: A World-Famous Classic Simply Told. Sidney, Margaret, pseud. McLaughlin, Jean & Middlebrooks, Janilee, illus. LC 59-13679. 120p. illus. 21cm. (Pixie books). 1953. Winston.
--The Five Little Peppers & How They Grew. Sidney, Margaret, pseud. 302p. Repr. 1981. (ISBN 0-89966-340-0). Buccaneer Bks.
--Five Little Peppers: And How They Grew. Sidney, Margaret, pseud. LC 13-2077. 410 p. incl. illus., plates. front. 19 cm. 1881. D. Lothrop and Company.
--Five Little Peppers and How They Grew. Sidney, Margaret, pseud. LC 76-25845. p. cm. 1976. (ISBN 0-688-41775-2). Morrow.
--Five Little Peppers and How They Grew. Sidney, Margaret, pseud. (Read-Aloud Bks.). (gr. k-3). N.D. Wonder.
--Five Little Peppers and How They Grew. Sidney, Margaret, pseud. (Classic Ser.). N.D. World Publishing Co.
--Five Little Peppers and How They Grew. Sidney, Margaret, pseud. Cooney, Barbara (1917-), illus. LC 54-144682. 320p. illus. 22cm. 1954. Junior Deluxe Editions.
--Five Little Peppers & How They Grew. Sidney, Margaret, pseud. Darling, Richard Lewis (1925-), intro. by. LC 76-25845. (Illus.). (gr. 4 up). 1976, c.1880. (ISBN 0-688-41775-2). Lothrop.
--Five Little Peppers and How They Grew. Sidney, Margaret, pseud. Fleur, Anne Elizabeth (1901-), illus. Sari, pseud. LC 55-3819. 284p. illus. 21cm. (Whitman famous classics, 1609). 1955. Whitman Pub. Co.
--Five Little Peppers: And How They Grew. Sidney, Margaret, pseud. Giguere, George, illus. LC 36-35615. 384 p. col. front., plates (part col.) 22 cm. (Riverside bookshelf). 1936. Houghton Mifflin Company.
--Five Little Peppers: And How They Grew. Sidney, Margaret, pseud. Rev. ed. Heyer, Herman, illus. LC 3-32792. viii p., 1 l., 11-427 p. incl. front. 7 pl. 20 cm. 1903. Lothrop Publishing Company.
--Five Little Peppers: And How They Grew. Sidney, Margaret, pseud. Lohman, Fred D., illus. LC 38-178247. 3 p. l., 13-253 p. col. front., illus., pl. 21 cm. c.1938. The Saalfield Publishing Company.
--Five Little Peppers and How They Grew. Sidney, Margaret, pseud. Lonette, Reisie Dominee (1924-), illus. LC 63-6894. viii, 273 p. illus. 20 cm. (Companion library) "5459."). 1963. Grosset & Dunlap.
--Five Little Peppers and How they Grew. Sidney, Margaret, pseud. Musil, Rosemary Gabbert, adapted by. (Dramatized from Margaret Sidney's Story by Rosemary Gabbert Musil). (Illus.). 60p. c.1940. Children's Theatre Press.
--The Five Little Peppers and How They Grew. Sidney, Margaret, pseud. Unabridged. O'Sullivan, Tom, illus. LC 65-11918. 254p. col. illus. 22cm. (Whitman classics lib. 2709). c.1965. Whitman Pub.
--Five Little Peppers and How They Grew. Sidney, Margaret, pseud. Paflin, Roberta, pseud. (1903-), illus. Petty, Roberta Harris Pfafflin. LC 51-8261. 237 p. illus. 21 cm. 1951. Whitman Pub. Co.
--Five Little Peppers and How They Grew. Sidney, Margaret, pseud. Pitz, Henry Clarence (1895-1976), illus. N.D. Grosset & Dunlap.
--Five Little Peppers & How They Grew. Sidney, Margaret, pseud. Price, Olive, adapted by. Nankivel, Claudine, illus. N.D. Grosset & Dunlap.
--Five Little Peppers and How They Grew. Sidney, Margaret, pseud. See, Carolyn, illus. LC 75-32184. p. cm. (Classics of Children's Literature ; 1621-1932). 1976, c.1880. (ISBN 0-8240-2296-3). Garland Pub.
--Five Little Peppers & How They Grew. Sidney, Margaret, pseud. Deluxe ed. Sharp, William (1900-), illus. LC 48-11833. 310 p. illus. (part col.) 24 cm. (Illustrated junior library). 1948. Grosset & Dunlap.
--Five Little Peppers & How They Grew. Sidney, Margaret, pseud. Popular ed. Sharp, William (1900-), illus. LC 48-11831. (Illus.). 275. (gr. 4-6). N.D. (ISBN 0-448-05808-1, G&D). (ISBN 0-448-05459-0). (ISBN 0-448-06008-6). pap. 4.95. (ISBN 0-448-11008-3). Putnam Pub Group.
--Five Little Peppers & How they Grew. Sidney, Margaret, pseud. Special ed. Sharp, William (1900-), illus. LC 48-11832. (Illus.). 310. (Grow-up Books Ser.). (gr. 4-6). N.D. (ISBN 0-448-02239-7, G&D). Putnam Pub Group.
--Five Little Peppers & Their Friends. Sidney, Margaret, pseud. N.D. Grosset & Dunlap.
--Five Little Peppers: And Their Friends. Sidney, Margaret, pseud. Becher, Arthur E., illus. LC 38-181478. 3 p. l., 5-6, 9-471 p. col. front. 20 cm. 1937. Houghton Mifflin Company.
--Five Little Peppers: And Their Friends. Sidney, Margaret, pseud. Wireman, Eugenie M., illus. LC 4-29788. 1 p. l., 471 p. front., 7 pl. 20 cm. 1904. Lothrop Publishing Company.
--Five Little Peppers at School. Sidney, Margaret, pseud. Becher, Arthur E., illus. LC 37-15464. 2 p. l., 3-458 p. col. front., 20 cm. 1937. Houghton Mifflin Company.
--Five Little Peppers at School. Sidney, Margaret, pseud. Heyer, Herman, illus. LC 3-27969. 453 p. front., 7 pl. 20 cm. 1903. Lothrop Publishing Company.
--Five Little Peppers Grown up. Sidney, Margaret, pseud. 334p. Repr. 1981. (ISBN 0-89966-341-9). Buccaneer Bks.
--Five Little Peppers Grown Up. Sidney, Margaret, pseud. Becher, Arthur E., illus. LC 37-15468. vi p., 1 l., 11-479 p. col. front. 20 cm. 1937. Houghton Mifflin Company.
--Five Little Peppers Grown Up: A Sequel to Five Little Peppers Midway. Sidney, Margaret, pseud. Mente, illus. LC 9-323107. 5 p. l., 9-527 p. incl. illus., plates. front. 19 cm. c.1892. D. Lothrop Company.
--Five Little Peppers Grown Up: A Sequel to Five Little Peppers Midway. Sidney, Margaret, pseud. Mente, illus. LC 44-2465. 5 p. l., 9-527 p. incl. illus., plates. front. 19 1/2 cm. 1904. Lothrop Publishing Company.
--Five Little Peppers in the Little Brown House. Sidney, Margaret, pseud. N.D. Grosset & Dunlap.
--Five Little Peppers in the Little Brown House. Sidney, Margaret, pseud. Becher, Arthur E., illus. LC 38-181319. 2 p. l., iii-v, 434 p. col. front. 20 cm. 1937. Houghton Mifflin Company.
--Five Little Peppers in the Little Brown House. Sidney, Margaret, pseud. Heyer, Herman, illus. LC 7-28450. vii, 434 p. front., 7 pl. 20 cm. 1907. Lothrop, Lee & Shepard Co.
--Five Little Peppers Midway. Sidney, Margaret, pseud. N.D. Grosset & Dunlap.
--Five Little Peppers Midway. Sidney, Margaret, pseud. Becher, Arthur E., illus. LC 37-15596. 4 p. l., 11-426 p. col. front. 20 cm. 1937. Houghton Mifflin Company.
--The Five Little Peppers Midway. Sidney, Margaret, pseud. Unabridged. O'Sullivan, Tom & Goldsborough, June (1923-), illus. LC 65-11919. 254 p. col. illus. 22 cm. (Whitman classics library). 1965. Whitman Pub. Co.
--Five Little Peppers Midway. Sidney, Margaret, pseud. Taylor, W. L., illus. LC 12-37038. (Sequel to Five Little Peppers and How They Grew). 512 p. incl. illus., plates front. 18 cm. c.1890. D. Lothrop Company.
--Five Little Peppers Midway. Sidney, Margaret, pseud. Taylor, W. L., illus. LC 12-36312. (A Sequel to Five Little Peppers and How They Grew). 2 p. l., 3-512 p. incl. illus., plates. front., 19 cm. 1893. D. Lothrop Company.
--The Gingham Bag: The Tale of an Heirloom. Sidney, Margaret, pseud. Brooks, Amy (0000-1931), illus. LC 12-36314. 369 p. incl. front. plates. 20 cm. c.1896. Lothrop Publishing Company.
--The Golden West as Seen by the Ridgway Club. Sidney, Margaret, pseud. (Illus.). N.D. Lothrop Publishing Co.
--Half Year at Bronckton. Sidney, Margaret, pseud. LC 12-36321. vi, 7-350 p. incl. front. 2 pl. 19 cm. c.1881. D. Lothrop & Company.
--Hester, and Other New England Stories. Sidney, Margaret, pseud. (Margaret Sidney Popular Library). N.D. Lothrop, Lee & Shepard.
--How They Went to Europe. LC 12-36313. 150 p. incl. front., illus., plates. 18 cm. c.1884. D. Lothrop and Company.
--How Tom and Dorothy Made and Kept a Christian Home. Sidney, Margaret, pseud. N.D. D. Lothrop Co.
--The Kaleidoscope. Sidney, Margaret, pseud. LC 12-363221. 129 p. front. 19 cm. c.1892. D. Lothrop Company.
--A Little Maid of Boston Town. Sidney, Margaret, pseud. Merrill, Frank Thayer (1848-), illus. N.D. Lothrop, Lee & Shepard.
--A Little Maid of Concord Town: A Romance of the American Revolution. Sidney, Margaret, pseud. Merrill, Frank Thayer (1848-), illus. 2 p. l., 3-405 p. front., plates. 19 cm. c.1900. Lothrop Publishing Company.
--Little Paul and the Frisbie School. Sidney, Margaret, pseud. LC 12-36320. 206 p. incl. front. plates. 19 cm. 1893. D. Lothrop Company.
--The Little Red Shop. Sidney, Margaret, pseud. LC 12-363193. 225 p. incl. front. 2 pl. 19 cm. c.1889. D. Lothrop Company.
--A New Departure for Girls. Sidney, Margaret, pseud. Hassam, F. Childe (1859-1935), illus. LC 12-36318. 4 p. l., 7-97 p. incl. illus., plates. front. 20 cm. c.1886. D. Lothrop and Company.
--The Old Town Pump: A Story of East and West. Sidney, Margaret, pseud. Barnes, Hiram Putnam, illus. LC 12-36445. 386 p. incl. front., plates. 19 cm. 1895. Lothrop Publishing Co.
--Our Davie Pepper. Sidney, Margaret, pseud. N.D. Grosset & Dunlap.
--Our Davie Pepper. Sidney, Margaret, pseud. Becher, Arthur E., illus. LC 38-1815. 3 p. l., v-vi, 492 p. col. front. 20 cm. 1937. Houghton Mifflin Company.
--Our Davie Pepper. Sidney, Margaret, pseud. Stephens, Alice Barber (1858-1932), illus. LC 16-205878. vi p., 1 l., 492 p. front., plates. 20 cm. 1916. Lothrop, Lee & Shepard Co.
--Our Town: Dedicated to All Members of the Y. P. S. C. E. Sidney, Margaret, pseud. LC 12-363171. 381 p. front., pl. 19 cm. c.1889. D. Lothrop Company.
--Phronsie Pepper. Sidney, Margaret, pseud. N.D. Grosset & Dunlap.
--Phronsie Pepper: The Youngest of the "Five Little Peppers". Sidney, Margaret, pseud. Becher, Arthur E., illus. LC 37-155952. ix, 3, 9-427 p. incl. illus., plates. col. front. 20 cm. 1937. Houghton Mifflin Company.
--Phronsie Pepper: The Youngest of the "Five Little Peppers". Sidney, Margaret, pseud. McDermott, Jessie, illus. LC 9-19671. ix, 437 p. incl. front., illus., plates. 20 cm. 1897. Lothrop, Lee & Shepard Co.
--Phronsie Pepper: The Youngest of the "Five Little Peppers". Sidney, Margaret, pseud. McDermott, Jessie, illus. LC 44-257934. ix, 437 p. incl. front., illus., plates. 19 1/2 cm. 1904. Lothrop Publishing Company.
--Polly. Sidney, Margaret, pseud. Johnson, Margaret (1860-), illus. N.D. D. Lothrop Co.
--Polly and the Children. Sidney, Margaret, pseud, 1 of 6 vols. (Little Wanderer Ser.). N.D. Set. D. Lothrop Co.
--Polly Pepper's Book. Sidney, Margaret, pseud. N.D. Grosset & Dunlap.
--Polly Pepper's Book. Sidney, Margaret, pseud. N.D. Houghton Mifflin.
--Ringing Words: And Other Sketches. Sidney, Margaret, pseud. LC 22-14782. 2 p., 7-98 p. incl. front., illus., plates, port. 17 cm. c.1885. D. Lothrop and Company.
--Rob: A Story for Boys. Sidney, Margaret, pseud. LC 12-36316. 245 p. front., 2 pl. 19 cm. c.1891. D. Lothrop Company.
--Sally, Mrs. Tubbs. Sidney, Margaret, pseud. N.D. Lothrop, Lee & Shepard.
--So As by Fire. Sidney, Margaret, pseud. LC 28-484718. vi, 7-253 p. incl. front. plates. 19 cm. c.1881. D. Lothrop and Company.
--So As by Fire. Sidney, Margaret, pseud. LC 12-36324. vi, 7-253 p. incl. front. pl. 18 cm. (On cover: Young folk's library, no. 17). 1885. D. Lothrop and Comapny.
--So As by Fire. Sidney, Margaret, pseud. (Margaret Sidney Popular Library). N.D. Lothrop, Lee & Shepard.
--St. George and the Dragon: A Story of Boy Life, and Kensington, Junior. Sidney, Margaret, pseud. LC 12-36315. 175 p. front., plates. 18 cm. c.1888. D. Lothrop Company.
--The Stories Polly Pepper Told to the Five Little Peppers in the Little Brown House. Sidney, Margaret, pseud. Becher, Arthur E., illus. LC 38-1816. 469 p. col. front., illus. 20 cm. 1937. Houghton Mifflin Company.
--The Stories Polly Pepper Told to the Five Little Peppers in the Little Brown House. Sidney, Margaret, pseud. McDermott, Jessie & Barry, Etheldred Breeze (1870-), illus. LC 99-1999. 3 p. l., 3-469 p. front., illus. 19 cm. c.1899. Lothrop Publishing Company.
--Tom and Dorothy. Sidney, Margaret, pseud. (Margaret Sidney Popular Library). N.D. Lothrop, Lee & Shepard.
--Tressy's Christmas. Sidney, Margaret, pseud, 1 of 4 vols. LC 28-4846. (Illus.). 20cm. 400p. (Winter Sunshine Ser.). 1880. D. Lothrop & Co.
--Two Little Friends in Norway. Sidney, Margaret, pseud. Heyer, Herman, illus. LC 6-34797. ix, 431 p. front., 7 pl. 20 cm. (Two little friends series). c.1906. Lothrop, Lee & Shepard Co.
--Two Modern Little Princes: And Other Stories. Sidney, Margret, pseud. LC 12-36323. 2 p. l., 7-207 p. incl. front., plates. 18 cm. c.1886. Lothrop and Company.
--What The Seven Did. Sidney, Margaret, pseud. Champney, Wells G., illus. N.D. D. Lothrop & Co.
--Whittier with the Children. Sidney, Margaret, pseud. N.D. Lothrop, Lee & Shepard.
--Who Told It to Me. Sidney, Margaret, pseud. Hassam, F. Childe (1859-1935), illus. N.D. Lothrop Publishing Company.
--Young Folks' Cyclopaedia of Stories... Sidney, Margaret, pseud. LC 15-12475. 638 p. front., illus. 25 cm. c.1885. D. Lothrop and Company.

Lothrop, Harriet Mulford Stone, Mrs. (1844-1924), ed.
--Lullabies and Jingles. Sidney, Margaret, pseud. LC 16-3081. 32 p. col. front., illus., col. plates 26 cm. 1893. D. Lothrop Company.

Lothrop, Matthew Henry (1851-), ed.
--Delightful Days: Illustrated Stories of American Life and Adventure. LC 22-14566. 249 p. front., illus., plates. 24 x 20 cm. c.1883. D. Lothrop and Company.
--The Poet and the Children: Carefully Selected Poems from the Works of the Best and Most Popular Writers for Children. Champ, pseud. (1843-1903) & Humphrey, L. B., Miss, illus. Champney, James Wells. LC 11-30745. xiv, 242 p. incl. front., illus., plates, port. 25 x 19 cm. 1882. D. Lothrop and Company.

Loti, Pierre, pseud., see Viand, Louis Marie Julien.

Loti, Pierre, pseud. (1850-1923)
--An Iceland Fisherman. Viand, Louis Marie Julien. Chapman, Frederick Trench (1887-), illus. Endore, Gamuel Gay (1900-1970), tr. (gr. 7). 1946. A. A. Knopf.
--Iceland Fisherman. Viand, Louis Marie Julien. (The Rugby Series for Boys and Girls). N.D. A. L. Burt Company.
--Lives of Two Cats. Viand, Louis Marie Julien. (Illus.). (Editha Ser.). N.D. Caldwell.
--Lives of Two Cats. Viand, Louis Marie Julien. Allen, C. E., illus. Richards, Mary B., tr. from Fr. LC 2-16929. 3 p. l., 3-92 p. front., plates. 19 cm. (The young of heart series, 32). 1902. D. Estes & Company.
--Lives of Two Cats. Viand, Louis Marie Julien. Richards, Mary B., tr. from Fr. (Children Hour Series.). N.D. Dodge Publishing Co.

Lottman, Eileen (1927-)
--Summersea. LC 75-10468. 256p. 1975. (ISBN 0-698-10684-9). Coward.

Louden, Adelaide Bolton
--Black Douglas. Cook, Gladys Emerson, illus. LC 57-11533. 124p. illus. 21cm. 1957. Sterling Pub. Co.
Louden, Claire & Louden, George
--Far into the Night: A Story of Bali. Louden, Claire & Louden, George, illus. LC 55-14965. unpaged. illus. 26cm. c.1955. Scribner.
--Rain in the Wind. Louden, Claire & Louden, George, illus. N.D. E. M. Hale and Co.
--Rain in the Winds: A Story of India. Louden, Claire & Louden, George, illus. LC 53-127555. unpaged. illus. 26cm. c.1953. Scribner.
Louden, George, jt. auth. see Louden, Claire.
Louden, Leo, jt. auth. see Orgill, Michael Thomas.
Loughead, Flora Haines Apponyi, Mrs. (1855-)
--The Abandoned Claim. LC 12-36325. iv, 330 p. 18 cm. 1891. Houghton, Mifflin and Company.
Loughlin, Burren & Flood, L. L.
--Bright-Wits: Prince of Mogadore. Loughlin, Burrem & Flood, L. L., illus. LC 9-24942. 3 p. l., v-vii, 63 p. illus., plates (partly double) 23 cm. c.1909. H. M. Caldwell Co.
Louie, Ai-Ling, retold by.
--Yeh-Shen: A Cinderella Story from China. Young, Ed (1931-), illus. LC 80-11716. (Illus.). 31 p. 27cm. c.1982. (ISBN 0-399-20900-X). Philomel Books. **Award: (ALA).**
Louis, Louise
--Honeybee Cousin. Peck, Terry, illus. (Illus.). 88p. (gr. 4-11). 1979. (ISBN 0-941242-01-3). Pen-Art.
--Twin Playlets for Children: Mr. Wishing Match & Community Sing, 2 bks. (gr. 4-11). 1979. (ISBN 0-941242-09-9). Pen-Art.
Lounsberry, Alice
--Frank and Bessie's Forester. Kirk, Maria Louise (1860-) & Stone, Walter King, illus. LC 12-20636. 4 p. l., 191 p. col. front., plates. 20 cm. 1912. Frederick A. Stokes Company.
Lounsberry, Lionel
--Cadet Kit Carey. (The Boys' Own Library). N.D. David McKay.
--Capt. Carey, of the Gallant 7th: Or, Fighting the Indians at Pine Ridge. LC 99-2001. 187 p. 18 cm. (On cover: Medal library. no. 6). 1899. Street & Smith.
--Captain Carey of the Gallant Seventh: Or, Fighting the Indians at Pine Ridge. (Boys Own Library). N.D. David McKay.
--Centre-board Jim: Or, The Secret of the Sargasso Sea. 210p. (Medal Library: No. 27). 1899. Street & Smith.
--Kit Carey's Protege. (The Boys Own Library). N.D. David McKay.
--Lieut. Carey's Luck. (The Boys' Own Library). N.D. David McKay.
--Midshipman Merrill. (Lieutenant Lionel Lounsberry). 18cm. 198p. (Medal Library: No. 15). 1899. Street & Smith.
--Out With Commodore Decatur: Or, The Brave Boys of 1812. (The Boys Own Library). N.D. David McKay.
--Out with Commodore Decatur: Or, The Brave Boys of 1812. LC 2-16917. 19cm. 248p. (Boys of Liberty Ser.). 1902. Street & Smith.
--Randy the Pilot: Or, Perils of the Great Lakes. (The Boys Own Library). N.D. David McKay.
--Randy the Pilot: Or, Perils of the Great Lakes. LC 2-19269. 19cm. 248p. 1902. Street & Smith.
--Rob Ranger the Young Ranchman: Or, Going it Alone at Lost River. (The Rob Ranger Ser.). N.D. David McKay.
--Rob Ranger's Cowboy Days: Or, The Young Hunter of the Big Horn. (Rob Ranger Ser.). N.D. David McKay.
--Rob Ranger's Mine: Or, The Boy Who Got There. (The Rob Ranger Ser.). N.D. David McKay.
--Tom Truxton's Ocean Trip: Or, The Island of Palms. LC 3-17007. 19cm. 287p. (Boy's Own Library). 1903. Street & Smith.
--Tom Truxton's School Days: Or, Fun and Mystery at Pickle Academy. (The Boys Own Ser.). N.D. David McKay.
--Tom Truxton's School Days: Or, Fun and Mystery at Pickle Academy. LC 1-17006. 19cm. 285p. (Boy's Own Library). 1903. Street & Smith.
--The Treasure of the Golden Crater. (The Boys Own Library). N.D. David McKay.
--The Treasure of the Golden Crater. LC 2-18931. 19cm. 248p. 1902. Street & Smith.
--Won at West Point: Or, An army Cadet in School and Camp, 39 vols. (Illus.). (Famous books for Boys Ser.: No. 30). 1905. Set. H M Caldwell Co.
--Won at West Point: Or, An Army Cadet in School and Camp. 227p. (Medal Library: No. 21). 1899. Street & Smith.
--Won at West Point: Or, Army Cadet in School and Camp. N.D. David McKay.
Lounsbury, Athea, jt. auth. see Wells, Maie Lounsbury.
Lounsbury, Kathryn
--White Angel Kitty. Koski, Barbara, illus. LC 55-12369. unpaged. ill. 15 x 22cm. c.1955. Comet Press Books.
Loup, Jean Jacques
--The Architect. LC 77-85228. (Illus.). 1978. (ISBN 0-8120-5200-5). Barron.
--Patatrac. LC 77-85229. (Illus.). (Juvenile Ser.). (gr. k-6). 1977. (ISBN 0-8120-5203-X). Barron.
Lourie, Richard, tr. see Korczak, Janusz.
Lourie, Richard, tr. see Likhanov, Albert.
Lourie, Richard (1940-), tr. see Sevela, Efraim.
Lourie, Richard, tr. see Shulevitz, Uri.
Lousada, Audrey
--Poachers in the Serengeti. Tresilian, Cecil Stuart (1891-), illus. LC 68-13994. (Illus.). 159 p. 24cm. 1968, c.1965. Walker.
Louv's
--Animals I Like. Guertik, Helene, illus. LC 38-9622. 32 p. illus. (part col.) 21 x 21 cm. (On cover: A Pere Castor book). c.1935. Artists and Writers Guild, Inc.
Louws, Cornelius, tr. see Bartels, Lambert.
Lovato, Rebecca
--Carlos at the Fiesta. Cardona, Consuelo M., tr. LC 76-42856. (gr. 6-12). 1976. (ISBN 0-89430-000-8). Relos Verdes.
Love, Adelaide (1889-1973)
--The Slender Singing Tree. N.D. Dodd, Mead & Co.
Love, E. Ray
--The Lost Trail. Love, E. Ray, illus. LC 56-6003. 107p. illus. 21cm. 1956. Bruce Humphries.
Love, Edwin M.
--Rocking Island. Love, Edwin M., illus. LC 27-4315. 5 p. l., 182 p. col. front., plates (part col.) 24 cm. c.1927. T. Nelson & Sons.
Love, Katheine, jt. ed. see Fillmore, Parker Hoysted.
Love, Katherine, jt. ed. see Fillmore, Parker Hoysted.
Love, Katherine Isabel (1907-), ed.
--April Showers: Poems. MacKenzie, Garry (1921-), illus. LC 48-5984. 46 p. col. illus. 12 cm. 1948. T. Y. Crowell Co.
--A Little Laughter. Lorraine, Walter Henry (1929-), illus. LC 57-10283. (Illus.). 114 p. 21cm. 1957. Crowell. **Award: (ALA).**
--A Pocketful of Rhymes. Jones, Henrietta, illus. LC 46-7716. x, 134 p. illus. 21 cm. 1946. Thomas Y. Crowell Company.
Love, Margaret
--An Explorer for an Aunt. Einzig, Susan (1922-), illus. LC 67-3602. (Illus.). 158 p. 23cm. (Merit mystery, 2347). 1967, c.1960. Follett Pub. Co.
Love, Patricia Tracy, tr. see Jonsson, Runer.
Love, Rose Leary
--Nebraska and His Granny. Haygood, Preston, illus. LC 37-2457. 5 p. l., 6. p. illus. 20 cm. 1936. Tuskegee Institute Press.
Love, Rose Leary, ed.
--A Collection of Folklore for Children in Elementary School and at Home. LC 64-2852. 83p. illus. 21cm. c.1964. Vantage.
Love, Sandra Weller (1940-)
--But What About Me?. 1st ed. Sandin, Joan (1942-), illus. LC 75-40403. (Illus.). 151 p. 21cm. c.1976. (ISBN 0-15-249900-8). Harcourt Brace Jovanovich.
--Crossing Over. LC 81-2613. 155 p. 22cm. c.1981. (ISBN 0-688-41984-4). (ISBN 0-688-51984-9). Lothrop, Lee & Shepard Books.
--Dive for the Sun. LC 82-11716. 209 p. 22cm. 1982. (ISBN 0-395-32864-0). Houghton Mifflin.
--Melissa's Medley. LC 77-88965. 137 p. 21cm. c.1978. (ISBN 0-15-253166-1). Harcourt Brace Jovanovich.
Love, Stewart A. & Cumming, William D.
--Girls' Plays for Reading and Recording. N.D. (ISBN 0-8238-0037-7). Plays, Inc.
Lovejoy, Bahija Fattuhi, jt. ed. see Cohen, Barbara.
Lovejoy, Bahija Fattuhi (1914-)
--Two Boys of Baghdad. Lovejoy, Bahija Fattuhi (1914-), illus. LC 74-133628. (Illus.). 128p. (gr. 2-6). 1972. (ISBN 0-688-41479-6). (ISBN 0-688-51478-2). Lothrop.
Lovejoy, Jack
--The Rebel Witch. Brown, Judith Gwyn (1933-), illus. LC 78-18378. p. cm. c.1978. (ISBN 0-688-41868-6). (ISBN 0-688-51868-0). Lothrop, Lee & Shepard.
Lovejoy, Mary Isabella (1894-), ed.
--Nature in Verse: A Poetry Reader for Children. LC 78-73490. (Illus.). xiv, 305 p. 20cm. (Granger Poetry Library). 1979. (ISBN 0-89609-116-3). Granger Book Co.
Lovelace, Delos Wheeler, et al. (1894-1967)
--The Illustrated King Kong. LC 76-27268. (gr. 3-6). 1976. (ISBN 0-448-12787-3, Pretzel Pr). G&D.
Lovelace, Delos Wheeler, jt. auth. see Conaway, Judith.
Lovelace, Delos Wheeler, jt. auth. see Lovelace, Maud Hart, Mrs.
Lovelace, Delos Wheeler (1894-1967)
--King Kong. LC 76-27267. (Illus.). Repr. of 1932 ed. (gr. 4-9). 1976. (ISBN 0-448-12788-1). G&D.
--King Kong: A Picture Book. Powers, Richard M. Gorman (1921-), illus. Wallace, Edgar (1875-1932) & Cooper, Merian C, concept by. LC 76-27269. (Illus.). 48 p. 28cm. (Elephant books). c.1976. (ISBN 0-448-12789-X). Grosset & Dunlap.
--That Dodger Horse. Geary, Clifford N. (1916-), illus. LC 56-9497. (gr. 5-9). 1956. (ISBN 0-690-81186-1). T Y Crowell.
Lovelace, Maud Hart, Mrs. (1892-1980)
--Betsy and Joe: A Betsy-Tracy High School Story. Neville, Vera (1900-1978), illus. LC 48-8096. 256. (gr. 5-11). 1948. (ISBN 0-690-13378-2, TYC-J). Har-Row.
--Betsy and Tacy Go Downtown. 186p. 1943. Scholastic.
--Betsy and Tacy Go Downtown. Lenski, Lois (1893-1974), illus. LC 79-110884. (Illus.). 180 p. 20cm. (Harper trophy book). 1979, c.1943. (ISBN 0-06-440098-0). Harper & Row.
--Betsy and the Great World. Neville, Vera (1900-1978), illus. LC 52-8657. 1952. (ISBN 0-690-13591-2). Thomas T. Crowell.
--Betsy in Spite of Herself. Neville, Vera (1900-1978), illus. LC 46-119956. x p., 2 l., 272 p. illus. 21 cm. 1946. (ISBN 0-690-13662-5). Thomas Y. Crowell Company.
--Betsy-Tacy. Lenski, Lois (1893-1974), illus. LC 40-30965. 5 p. l., 112, 1 p. front., illus. 23 cm. 1940. (ISBN 0-690-13804-0). (ISBN 0-690-13805-9). Thomas Y. Crowell Company.
--Betsy-Tacy. Lenski, Lois (1893-1974), illus. (Illus.). 113 p. 21cm. 1974, c.1968. Thomas Y Crowell.
--Betsy-Tacy and Tib. Lenski, Lois (1893-1974), illus. 128p. 19cm. (Harper Trophy Book). 1979, c.1969. (ISBN 0-06-440097-2). Harper & Row.
--Betsy-Tacy and Tib. Lenski, Lois (1893-1974), illus. LC 41-18714. 5 p. l., 127, 2 p. front., illus. 23 cm. 1941. (ISBN 0-690-13875-X). (ISBN 0-690-13876-8). Thomas Y. Crowell Company.
--Betsy-Tacy and Tib. Lenski, Lois (1893-1974), illus. LC 41-18714. (Illus.). 128 p. 21cm. (Crowell Crocodile). 1974, c.1969. (ISBN 0-690-00632-2). Thomas Y. Crowell.
--Betsy-Tacy Books, 6 vols. N.D. Boxed Set. (ISBN 0-317-12416-1, Trophy). HarpJ.
--Betsy Was a Junior: A Betsy-Tacy High School Story. Neville, Vera (1900-1978), illus. LC 46-11995. (gr. 5-11). 1947. (ISBN 0-690-13946-2, TYC-J). Har-Row.
--Betsy Was a Junior: A Betsy-Tacy High School Story. Neville, Vera (1900-1978), illus. LC 47-11043. vii, 248 p. illus. 21 cm. 1947. (ISBN 0-690-13946-2). T. Y. Crowell Co.
--Betsy's Wedding. Neville, Vera (1900-1978), illus. LC 55-11108. 241 p. illus. 21cm. (gr. 5-11). 1955. (ISBN 0-690-13733-8, TYC-J). Har-Row.
--Carney's House Party: A Deep Valley Story. Neville, Vera (1900-1978), illus. LC 49-10403. viii, 239 p. illus. 21 cm. 1949. T. Y. Crowell Co.
--Down Town: A Betsy-Tacy Story. Lenski, Lois (1893-1974), illus. LC 43-512645. 5 p. l., 180 p. illus. 23 cm. 1943. (ISBN 0-690-13449-5). (ISBN 0-690-13450-9). Thomas Y. Crowell Company.
--Emily of Deep Valley. Neville, Vera (1900-1978), illus. LC 50-9461. (Illus.). x, 257 p. 21cm. 1950. Crowell.
--Heaven to Betsy. Neville, Vera (1900-1978), illus. 268 p. 18cm. 1980, c.1979. (ISBN 0-06-440110-3). Harper & Row.
--Heaven to Betsy: A Betsy-Tacy High School Story. Neville, Vera (1900-1978), illus. LC 45-9806. (Illus.). ix, 268 p. 21cm. 1945. (ISBN 0-690-37449-6). Thomas Y. Crowell Company.
--Over the Big Hill: A Betsy-Tacy Story. Lenski, Lois (1893-1974), illus. LC 42-23557. 5 p. l., 171 p. illus. 23 cm. 1942. (ISBN 0-690-13520-3). (ISBN 0-690-13521-1). Thomas Y. Crowell Company.
--The Trees Kneel at Christmas. Howe, Gertrude Herrick (1902-), illus. LC 51-6802. 127 p. illus. 20 cm. 1951. Crowell.
--The Tune Is In the Tree. Wilkin, Eloise Burns (1904-), illus. LC 50-6908. 177p. (gr. 1-5). 1950. Thomas Y. Crowell Co.
--The Valentine Box. Fetz, Ingrid (1915-), illus. LC 66-14942. 1 v. (unpaged) illus. 22 cm. 1966. Crowell.
--What Cabrillo Found: The Story of Juan Rodriguez Cabrillo. Galdone, Paul (1914-), illus. LC 58-8119. 180p. illus. 21cm. 1958. Crowell.
--Winona's Pony Cart. Neville, Vera (1900-1978), illus. LC 53-841719. 117p. illus. 21cm. 1953. Crowell.
Lovelace, Maud Hart, Mrs. (1892-1980) & Lovelace, Delos Wheeler (1894-1967)
--The Golden Wedge. Chase, Charlotte Anna, illus. 160p. 1942. Thomas Y. Crowell Co.
Loveland, Nicole
--Boogins Gets a Basket. (Illus.). 32p. (ps-2). 1984. (ISBN 0-917107-00-4). Cat-Tales Pr.
--Boogins' Rainy Day. Stebbins, Pat, illus. (Illus.). (ps-3). 1985. (ISBN 0-917107-02-0). Cat Tales Pr.
Loveland, Seymour
--Illustrated Bible Story Bk. New Testament. Winter, Milo Kendall (1888-1956), illus. N.D. Rand McNally & Co.
--Illustrated Bible Story Book. Winter, Milo Kendall (1888-1956), illus. N.D. G.P. Putnam's Sons.
Loveland, Seymour & Meyer, Edith Paterson (1895-)
--The Illustrated Bible Story Bk. One-Volume Edition. Meyer, Milo, illus. N.D. Rand McNally & Co.
Loveless, William A.
--Beating Wings. Baerg, Harry John (1909-), illus. LC 64-17654. 96 p. illus. 22 cm. 1964. Review and Herald Pub. Association.
Lovell, D. A.
--The Strange Adventures Of Emma. N.D. Transatlantic Arts.
Lovell, Isabel
--Stories in Stone from the Roman Forum. N.D. Macmillan.
Lovell, Josephine
--Antelope: A Navaho Indian Boy. (Indian Library). N.D. Platt & Munk.
--Eight Little Indians. LC 37-14932. 96 p. illus. (part col.) 21 cm. c.1936. The Platt & Munk Co., Inc.
--Gray Bird: A Little Plains Indian. (Indian Library). N.D. Platt & Munk.
--Leaping Trout: A Little Iroquois Boy. (Indian Library). N.D. Platt & Munk.
--Micco: A Seminole Indian Boy. (Indian Library). N.D. Platt & Munk.
--Morning Star: A Pueblo Girl. (Indian Library). N.D. Platt & Munk.
--Nigalek: A Little Eskimo Boy. (Indian Library). N.D. Platt & Munk.
--Watlala: An Indian of the Northwest. (Indian Library). N.D. Platt & Munk.
--Winona: A Prairie Indian Girl. (Indian Library). N.D. Platt & Munk.
Lovell, Lucile
--Andy. Nagel, Eva M., illus. (The Vacation Ser.). N.D. Penn.
--Andy. Nagel, Eva M., illus. (Illus.). (The Little People's Ser.). N.D. Penn Publishing Co.
--The Walcott Twins. Waugh, Ida, illus. (Illus.). (The Little People's Ser.). N.D. Penn Publishing Co.
--The Walcott Twins. Waugh, Ida, illus. LC 4070. 211 p. front., plates. 20 cm. (Sunbeam Ser. for Young People). 1900. The Penn Publishing Company.
Lovelock, Yann, jt. ed. see Hekmat, Forough-es-Saltaneh.
Loveman, Leonora (0000-1924)
--Revolt: A Story of Adventure. LC 26-12245. 204 p. 20 cm. 1926. H. Vinal.
Lover, Samuel (1797-1868)
--Handy Andy. (Warne's Crown Library). N.D. Frederick Warne.
--Handy Andy. N.D. Hurst & Co.
--Handy Andy. (Beacon Library of Fiction Classics). N.D. Little Brown & Co.
--Handy Andy. (Atlantic Library). N.D. Rand,McNally & Co.'s.
--Handy Andy. (Twentieth Century Ser.). N.D. Randy,McNally & Co.'s.
--Handy Andy. (New Alpha Library). N.D. Rand, McNally & Co.'s.
--Handy Andy. (The Antique Library). N.D. Rand, McNally & Co's.
--Irish Legends, No.123. (Seaside Library Ser.). N.D. George Munro: Dist. by American News Co.
--Irish Stories and Legends. (Royal Library of Choice Books). N.D. Ward Lock & Bowden.
--Legends and Stories of Ireland. N.D. P. J. Kenedy.
Lovett, Howard Meriwether
--Grandmother Stories from the Land of Used to Be. LC 74-2413. (Illus.). 254 p. 22cm. 1974, c.1913. (ISBN 0-87152-173-3). Reprint Co.
Lovett, Lois
--Little Lost Kitten. Maxey, Dale (1927-), illus. LC 62-899280. unpaged. illus. 33cm. c.1962. (ISBN 0-394-80664-6). Random House.
Lovett, Margaret Rose (1915-)
--The Great and Terrible Quest. LC 67-17993. 187 p. 21cm. 1967. Holt, Rinehart and Winston.
--Jonathan. LC 72-78088. 205 p. 22cm. 1972. (ISBN 0-525-32805-X). E. P. Dutton.
Lovoos, Janice
--Design is a Dandelion. 1966. (ISBN 0-87464-030-X). (ISBN 0-87464-031-8). Golden Gate Junior Books.
Low
--Joshua Hawsepipe's Adventures. N.D. George Routledge & Sons.
Low, Alice, jt. auth. see Mc Naughton, Colin.
Low, Alice, jt. auth. see Stone, Bernard.

Low, Alice (1926-)
--All Around the Farm. Swanson, Maggie, illus. LC 83-62379. c.1984. (ISBN 0-394-85955-3). Random House.
--All Through the Town. Fleming, Denise, illus. LC 83-62378. c.1984. (ISBN 0-394-85954-5). Random House.
--At Jasper's House and Other Stories. LC 68-24563. 168 p. 22cm. 1968. (ISBN 0-394-91293-4). Pantheon Books.
--David's Windows. De Paola, Tomie, pseud. (1934-), illus. De Paola, Thomas Anthony. LC 73-88525. (Illus.). 32 p. 20cm. 1974. (ISBN 0-399-20393-1). (ISBN 0-399-20393-1). Putnam.
--A Day of Your Own: Your Birthday. Boys'Edition ed. McKie, Roy, illus. LC 64-18121. 1 v. (unpaged) col. illus. 15cm. (Mail-me Books). 1964. Random House.
--A Day of Your Own: Your Birthday. Girls'Edition ed. Weil, Lisl (1910-), illus. LC 64-14234. 1 v. (unpaged) col. illus. 13cm. (Mail Me Books). 1964. Random House.
--Genie and the Witch's Spells. McCrady, Lady (1951-), illus. LC 81-15619. (Illus.). 107 p. 20cm. (Capers). c.1982. (ISBN 0-394-95173-5). (ISBN 0-394-85173-0). Knopf.
--Grandmas and Grandpas. Wilson, Dagmar (1916-), illus. LC 62-8995. unpaged. illus. 32cm. 1962. Random House.
--Herbert's Treasure. De Larrea, Victoria, illus. LC 76-125386. (Illus.). 48 p. 21cm. 1971. Putnam.
--Kallie's Corner. LC 66-12457. (Illus.). 246 p. 22cm. 1966. Pantheon Books.
--Open up My Suitcase. Malvern, Corinne (1905-1956), illus. LC 54-3746. unpaged. illus. 21cm. (Little golden book, 207). 1954. Simon and Schuster.
--Out of My Window. Jackson, Polly, pseud. (1918-), illus. Jackson, Pauline. LC 55-139037. unpaged. illus. 21cm. (Little golden book, 245). 1955. Simon and Schuster.
--Summer. McKie, Roy, illus. LC 63-15628. 61 p. col. illus. 24 cm. 1963. Beginner Books.
--The Witch Who Was Afraid of Witches. Gundersheimer, Karen, illus. LC 78-5856. (Illus.). 40 p. 24cm. c.1978. (ISBN 0-394-83718-5). (ISBN 0-394-93718-X). Pantheon Books.
--Witches' Holiday. Walton, Tony, illus. LC 73-153971. (Illus.). 30 p. 26cm. 1971. (ISBN 0-394-92165-8). Pantheon Books.
Low, Alice (1926-), adapted by.
--If Dinosaurs Were Cats & Dogs. McNaughton, Colin, illus. (Illus.). 32p. (gr. k-3). 1981. (ISBN 0-590-07826-7, Four Winds). Scholastic Inc.
Low, Archibald Montgomery (1888-)
--Tick-Tock. LC 46-314623. 259 p. illus. 21 cm. 1946. R. M. McBride & Company.
Low, Charles Rathbone (1837-1918)
--The Adventures of Joshua Hawsepipe. N.D. George Routledge & Sons.
--Captain Cook's Voyages. 1875. George Routledge & Sons.
--The Letter of Marque, and other Tales. 1875. George Routledge & Sons.
--The Man-o'-Wars's Bell. N.D. George Routledge & Sons.
--Tales of Naval Adventure. N.D. George Routledge & Sons.
--Tales of Old Ocean. (Warne's Home Circle Library). N.D. Frederick Warne & Co.
--Tales of Old Ocean. 1875. Scribner, Welford & Armstrong.
--Tales of Old Ocean, 11 of 15 Vols. (Illus.). (Warne's Daring Deeds Library). N.D. Scribner & Welford.
Low, Elizabeth Hammond (1898-)
--High Harvest. Gorsline, Douglas Warner (1913-1985), illus. LC 48-8370. 288 p. illus. 21 cm. 1948. Harcourt, Brace.
--Hold Fast the Dream. N.D (Tempo Books). Grosset & Dunlap.
--Hold Fast the Dream. LC 55-5238. 245 p. 21cm. 1955. Harcourt, Brace.
--Mouse, Mouse, Go Out of My House. Solbert, Ronni, pseud. (1925-), illus. Solbert, Romaine G.. (Illus.). (gr. k-3). 1958. (ISBN 0-316-53372-6). Little.
--Mouse,Mouse, Go Out of My House. 1958. E M Hale.
--Snug in the Snow. Solbert, Ronni, pseud. (1925-), illus. Solbert, Romaine G.. (Illus.). (gr. 1-3). 1963. (ISBN 0-316-53376-9). Little.
Low, Ivy, tr. see Rozanov, Sergei Grigor Evich.
Low, Joseph, jt. auth. see Mother Goose.
Low, Joseph (1911-)
--Adam's Book of Odd Creatures: Verse. 1st ed. Low, Joseph (1911-), illus. LC 62-8029. unpaged. illus. 22 x 26cm. 1962. Atheneum.
--Beastly Riddles: Fishy, Flighty, and Buggy, Too. Low, Joseph (1911-), illus. LC 83-856. p. cm. c.1983. (ISBN 0-02-761380-1). Macmillan.
--Benny Rabbit and the Owl. Low, Joseph (1911-), illus. LC 77-4125. (Illus.). 56 p. 23cm. (Greenwillow read-alone). c.1978. (ISBN 0-688-80117-X). (ISBN 0-688-84117-1). Greenwillow Books.
--Boo to a Goose. 1st ed. Low, Joseph (1911-), illus. LC 74-18188. (Illus.). 40 p. 24cm. 1975. (ISBN 0-689-50009-2). Atheneum.
--The Christmas Grump. Low, Joseph (1911-), illus. LC 77-3903. p. cm. 1977. (ISBN 0-689-50092-0). Atheneum.
--The Devil Himself. Low, Joseph (1911-), illus. LC 77-17772. (Illus.). 40 p. 22cm. c.1978. (ISBN 0-07-038795-8). McGraw-Hill.
--Don't Drag Your Feet. Low, Joseph (1911-), illus. LC 82-13898. p. cm. 1983. (ISBN 0-689-50271-0). Atheneum.
--Five Men Under One Umbrella: And Other Ready-to-Read Riddles. Low, Joseph (1911-), illus. LC 74-20615. (Illus.). 63 p. 22cm. (Ready-to-read). 1975. (ISBN 0-02-761460-3). Macmillan.
--Little Though I Be. Low, Joseph (1911-), illus. LC 75-42195. (Illus.). 40 p. 27cm. c.1976. (ISBN 0-07-038842-3). (ISBN 0-07-038843-1). McGraw-Hill. **Award: (NYT).**
--A Mad Wet Hen and Other Riddles. Low, Joseph (1911-), illus. LC 76-44329. (Illus.). 55 p. 22cm. (Greenwillow read-alone books). c.1977. (ISBN 0-688-80082-3). (ISBN 0-688-84082-5). Greenwillow Books.
--Mice Twice. Low, Joseph (1911-), illus. LC 79-23274. p. cm. 1980. (ISBN 0-689-50157-9). Atheneum. **Awards: (ALA); (RCM).**
--My Dog, Your Dog. Low, Joseph (1911-), illus. LC 77-12032. (Illus.). 32 p. c.1978. (ISBN 0-02-761400-X). Macmillan.
--Smiling Duke. Low, Joseph (1911-), illus. LC 63-14522. 30 p. col. illus. 22 x 25 cm. 1963. Houghton Mifflin.
--There Was a Wise Crow. Low, Joseph (1911-), illus. LC 76-86254. (Illus.). 32 p. 1969. Follett Pub. Co.
--Trust Reba. Low, Joseph (1911-), illus. LC 73-17418. (Illus.). 40 p. 22cm. 1974. McGraw-Hill.
--What If ... ?. Fourteen Encounters-Some Frightful, Some Frivolous-That Might Happen to Anyone. Low, Joseph (1911-), illus. LC 76-12465. (Illus.). 32 p. 25cm. 1976. (ISBN 0-689-50064-5). Atheneum.
Low, Ruth Irma (1896-)
--The Adventures of Bunny Bob-Tail. Stout, Les (1898-), illus. LC 35-6772. viii p., 1 l., 134 p. incl. front., plates. 20 cm. 1935. Lothrop, Lee and Shepard Company.
--Adventures of Bunny Bobtail. N.D. Small,Maynard & Co.
--In Story-Land. Low, Ruth Irma (1896-), illus. LC 20-17011. 4 p. l., 175 p. col. front., plates. 20 cm. c.1920. Small, Maynard and Company.
--In Storyland. Woodward, Hildegard (1898-), illus. LC 35-6766. 5 p. l., 175 p. front., illus. 21 cm. 1935. Lothrop, Lee and Shepard Company.
--Maureen O'Day: A Story for Juveniles. LC 33-34617. 131, 1 p. front. 19 cm. 1933. Benziger Brothers.
--Maureen O'Day at Glengarif: A Story for Juveniles. LC 34-116613. 131, 1 p. front. 19 cm. 1934. Benziger Brothers.
--Maureen O'Day: Songbird. 3 p. l., 122 p. col. front., col. plates. 19 cm. 1940. Benziger Brothers, Inc.
--Peggy Moran. LC 31-31663. 127, 1 p. front. 19 cm. 1931. Benziger Brothers.
--Plays for Primary Grades. 96p. N.D. Northwestern Press.
--Ragamuffin. LC 30-100931. 126, 1 p. front. 19 cm. 1930. Benziger Brothers.
--The Raggy Bears. N.D. Small,Maynard & Co.
Low, Vaike
--Drip and Drop: From the Clouds and Back. LC 64-24396. 1v. (unpaged) col. illus. 21cm. c.1964. J. H. Heineman.
Lowe, Bess Chase (1897-)
--Honey Bunny. Emerson, Rosemary, illus. LC 49-4738. 27 p. illus. (part col.) 24 cm. c.1949. Bellevue Books.

Lowe, Edith May Kovar see Windsor, Mary, pseud.
Lowe, Edith May Kovar (1905-), retold by see Barrie, James Matthew, Sir.

Lowe, Edith May Kovar (1905-), ed. see Grimm, Jakob Ludwig Karl (1785-1863) & Grimm, Wilhelm Karl.
Lowe, Edith May Kovar see Kovar, Edith May.
Lowe, Edith May Kovar (1905-), adapted by see The, Three Bears.

Lowe, Edith May Kovar (1905-)
--A to Z: Alphabet Picture Book. Darien, Elsie, illus. LC 66-15392. 30 p. col. illus. 30 x 14cm. (A Read-aloud Book). 1966. Follett Pub. Co.
--Animal Parade. Windsor, Mary, pseud. Fleur, Anne Elizabeth (1901-), illus. Sari, pseud. LC 51-27549. 24 p. illus. (part col.) 20cm. (A Bountie Book). 1951. S. Lowe Co.
--The Boy Jesus: A Story of the Boyhood of Christ. Windsor, Mary, pseud. LC 34-2041. 28 p. illus. 26 cm. c.1933. Whitman.
--Bunnies: A Polka Dot Book. Windsor, Mary, pseud. Pollard, Nancy D. (1925-), illus. N.D. Garden City Publishing Co.
--Cookie the Rabbit. Windsor, Mary, pseud. Eckart, Frances, illus. LC 50-7086. 24 p. col. illus. 31 x 15 cm. 1949. Garden City Pub. Co.
--The Donkey Named Will and Other Stories. Windsor, Mary, pseud. Stearns, Sharon (1912-) & Kippy, illus. N.D. Garden City Publishing Co.
--The Donkey Named Will: And Other Stories. Windsor, Mary, pseud. Stearns, Sharon (1912-) & Kippy, illus. LC 49-1064. 36 p. col. illus. 25 cm. 1948. John Martin's House.
--Fairy Gold: And Other Stories. Windsor, Mary, pseud. LC 31-25643. 1 p. l., 7-37, 1 p. illus., col. plates. 32 x 26 1/2 cm. 1931. Whitman Publishing Company.
--The Flip Flap Book. Windsor, Mary, pseud. Hentschel, Harriet L. (1922-), illus. LC 50-14750. 54 p. (on 7 fold. leaves) col illus. 27 cm. c.1950. Garden City Pub. Co.
--Fluffy is Lost. Windsor, Mary, pseud. Howe, Katherine Mallett (1898-), illus. LC 50-13859. 20 p. col. illus. 20cm. (Friendly Book, 1712). 1950. John Martin's House.
--Friendly Farm. Windsor, Mary, pseud. Margie, illus. LC 49-1249. 25 p. col. illus. 32 cm. 1948. John Martin's House.
--How Jacky Bunny came to Parson's Wood. Carbe, Nino (1909-), illus. 30 p. col. ill. 20cm. (Friendly Book, 1709). 1950. John Martin's House.
--The Life of a Chicken. Windsor, Mary, pseud. Woodruff, Claude W., illus. LC 34-40509. 56 p. illus. 14 cm. c.1934. Whitman.
--The Life of a Cow. Windsor, Mary, pseud. Woodruff, Claude W., illus. LC 34-40510. 56 p. illus. 14 cm. c.1934. Whitman.
--The Little Bear Who Wanted Friends. Windsor, Mary, pseud. Eckart, Frances, illus. LC 49-10599. 24 p. col. illus. 32 x 15 cm. 1949. Garden City Pub. Co.
--The Little Bear Who Wanted Friends: A Story. Windsor, Mary, pseud. Eckart, Frances, illus. LC 62-16896. 35 p. illus. 29 x 14cm. (A Read-aloud Book). 1962. Follett Pub, Co.
--The Little Brown Hen: And The Squirrel's Name Is Bundle of Tricks. Windsor, Mary, pseud. LC 50-7087. 40 p. illus. (part col.) 23 cm. (Double story book). 1949. Garden City Pub. Co.
--Little Friends from Many Lands. Windsor, Mary, pseud. Best, Roy, illus. LC 35-21949. 20 p. col. illus. 33 cm. c.1935. Whitman.
--The Little King: And Other Fairy Tales. Windsor, Mary, pseud. LC 34-40505. 30 p. illus. (part col.) 31 cm. 1934. Whitman.
--The Little Town on the Hill. Windsor, Mary, pseud. LC 49-1574. 28 p. col. illus. 21 cm. (Bonnie book). 1948. John Martin's House.
--The Magic Sprinkling Can. Windsor, Mary, pseud. Wosmek, Frances (1917-), illus. N.D. Garden City Publishing Co.
--Mr. Gallagher's Donkey. Windsor, Mary, pseud. Darien, Elsie, illus. LC 51-4406. 28 p. col. illus. 29cm. c.1950. Garden City Pub.
--On Christmas Day in the Morning. Windsor, Mary, pseud. LC 43-34443. 20 p. col. illus. 25 cm. c.1939. Whitman.
--Pets. Windsor, Mary, pseud. Watson, Joseph, Mrs., illus. LC 51-46665. 56 p. illus. 14 x 17 cm. 1935. Whitman.
--The Story of Willie the Donkey. Windsor, Mary, pseud. Darien, Elsie, illus. LC 51-27550. 24 p. col. illus. 20cm. (A Bonnie Story Puzzle Book). 1950. S. Lowe Co.
--Throughout the Day. Windsor, Mary, pseud. Wosmek, Frances (1917-), illus. LC 50-2903. 28 p. col. illus. 22 cm. (Bonnie book). 1949. John Martin's House.
--Ticker and Tocker. Windsor, Mary, pseud. LC 50-7088. ("The First Years" story by Richard Stephen). 40 p. illus. (part col.) 23 cm. (Double story book). 1949. Garden City Pub. Co.
--The Wee Kitten. Champion, Hope Loring (1913-), illus. LC 50-13854. 30 p. col. illus. 20mc. (Friendly book, 1705). 1950. John Martin's House.
--Where Things Come from: An Explanation Book. Windsor, Mary, pseud. LC 49-7845. 29 p. col. illus. 32 cm. (Chanticleer junior book). c.1948. Chanticleer Press.
--Would You Like to Know Peter. Windsor, Mary, pseud. Best, Roy, illus. LC 35-37276. 47 p. illus. (part col.) 17 cm. c.1935. Whitman.
Lowe, Edith May Kovar (1905-), ed.
--Happi-Time Story Book. Windsor, Mary, pseud. LC 42-14598. 3 p. l., 5-316, 3 p. col. front., illus. (part col.) col. plates 24 cm. c.1941. Sears, Roebuck & Co.
--Three, Four, Shut the Door: Favorite Counting Rhymes. Windsor, Mary, pseud. Kral, Lu, illus. LC 54-31861. unpaged. illus. 20cm. (Bonnie book, 4290). 1952. S. Lowe Co.
Lowe, Florence (1896-)
--Somebody Else's Shoes. Morse, Dorothy Bayley (1906-1979), illus. LC 48-1513. 153 p. illus. 22 cm. 1948. Rinehart.
Lowe, Harry William
--African Animal Stories. Baerg, Harry John (1909-), illus. LC 53-16406. 176p. illus. 20cm. 1952. Southern Pub. Association.
Lowe, Orton, ed. see Dodge, Mary Elizabeth Mapes, Mrs.
Lowe, Orton (1873-), ed. see Grimm, Jakob Ludwig Karl (1785-1863) & Grimm, Wilhelm Karl.
Lowe, Orton (1873-), ed.
--The Arabian Nights. LC 26-21302. xv, 3-257 p. col. front., illus., col. plates. 21 cm. (On cover: The Winston clear-type popular classics). c.1924. The John C. Winston Company.
Lowe, Patrica (1876-1942), tr. see Pushkin, Alexander sergeyevich.
Lowe, Patricia, tr. see Lowe, Patricia Tracy.
Lowe, Patricia Tracy
--The Different Ones. LC 64-25316. 153p. 22cm. 22cm. 1965, c.1964. Bobbs.
--Different Ones. 1964. (ISBN 0-8382-0203-9, Cadmus Books). E. M. Hale.
--The Runt. Waldman, Neil, illus. LC 83-24045. (Illus.). 64p. 1984. (ISBN 0-89845-278-3). (ISBN 0-89845-279-1). Caedmon.
Lowe, Patricia Tracy, retold by.
--The Little Horse of Seven Colors: And Other Portuguese Folk Tales. Jauss, Anne Marie (1907-), illus. Jauss, Anne Marie, tr. from Portuguese. LC 76-101842. (Illus.). 122 p. 22cm. 1970. World Pub. Co.
--The Tale of Czar Saltan: Or, The Prince and the Swan Princess. Bilibin, Ivan Iakovlevich (1876-1942), illus. Lowe, Patricia, tr. LC 75-5655. (Original Author: Alexander Sergeyevich Pushkin, 1799-1837). (Illus.). 20 p. 1975. (ISBN 0-690-00792-2). Crowell.
--The Tale of the Golden Cockerel. Bilibin, Ivan Iakovlevich (1876-1942), illus. Lowe, Patricia Tracy, tr. LC 75-4623. (Original Author: Alexander Sergeyevich Pushkin, 1799-1837). (Illus.). 19 p. 24 x 30cm. 1975. (ISBN 0-690-00790-6). Crowell.
Lowe, Patricia Tracy, ed. see Greenaway, Kate (1846-1901) & Moore, Anne Carroll.
Lowe, Samuel Edward see Hart, Helen, pseud.
Lowe, Samuel Edward (1884-)
--In the Court of King Arthur. O'Keeffe, Neil, illus. LC 20-4280. 223, 1 p. col. front., col. plates. 23 cm. c.1918. Western Ptg. and Litho. Co.
--Little Rabbit. Hart, Helen, pseud. Livings, Bess, illus. LC 34-42878. 48 p. illus. 22 cm. c.1934. Whitman Publishing Co.
Lowe, Samuel Edward (1884-) & Jacobson, Viola E.
--Fifty Famous Stories. O'Keeffe, Neil, illus. LC 22-1069. 256 p. col. front., illus., col. plates. 23 cm. c.1920. Whitman Publishing Co.
Lowe, Stephanie, jt. auth. see Wong, Kat.
Lowe, Viola Ruth (1908-), ed. see Alcott, Louisa May.
Lowe, Viola Ruth (1908-)
--Sammy Goes Around the World. LC 34-40674. 58, 1 p. illus. 22 x 20 cm. c.1934. Whitman Publishing Company.
Lowe, Viola Ruth (1908-), compiled by.
--Three-Hundred and Sixty-Five Bedtime Stories. LC 38-32856. (Illus.). 378p. 29cm. 1938. Whitman Publishing Co.
Lowe Corporation, jt. auth. see Field, Eugene.
Lowell, Anna Cabot Jackson, Mrs. (1819-1874)
--Posies for Children. A Book of Verse. LC 17-9682. viii, 9-192 p. 16 cm. 1871. Roberts Brothers.
--Posies for Children: A Book of Verse. (Illus.). 1882. Robert Brothers.
Lowell, Anna Cabot Jackson, Mrs. (1819-1874), ed.
--Poetry for Home and School. Selected by the Author of the "Theory of Teaching," and "Edward's First Lessons in Grammar.". LC 12-4280. xii, 13-360 p. 18 cm. 1843. S. G. Simpkins.
Lowell, Daniel Ozro Smith (1851-)
--Jason's Quest. Reed, Charles W., illus. LC 4-5461. xi, 1, 228 p. front., illus., plates. 17 cm. 1893. Leach, Shewell & Sanborn.
--Jason's Quest. Reed, Charles W., illus. 1905. Lee and Shepard Company.
Lowell, John Paul
--The Two Boys. LC 3-18175. 222 p. front. 19 cm. 1903. The Editor Publishing Co.
Lowell, Juliet (1901-)
--Dear Folks. Brown, William Ferdinand (1928-), illus. 116p. illus. 21cm. 1960. Putnam.
Lowenfels, Walter (1897-1976), ed.
--The Writing on the Wall: One Hundred Eight American Poems of Protest. LC 69-12187. (Illus.). 192p. (gr. 9 up). 1969. (ISBN 0-385-04838-6). (ISBN 0-385-01744-8). Doubleday.
Lowenstein, Edna & Thompson, Ethel C. S.
--The Wig-Wags Go to the Circus. LC 30-15405. 32 p. col. illus. 20 x 20 cm. 1929. The Regensteiner Corporation.
Lower, Edward
--Froggie's Suit and Other Stories. LC 52-13208. 23cm. 32p. 1953. Vantage Press Books.

AUTHOR INDEX LUCERO, FAUSTINA

Lower, Thelma & Cogswell, Frederick, eds.
--The Enchanted Land: Canadian Poetry for Young Readers. 1967. Gage.
Lowery, Lawrence F.
--Animals Two by Two. Amundsen, Richard E., illus. (Illus.). 32p. 1st U.S. edition. (Golden Science Readers Ser). (gr. 1-3). 1970. (ISBN 0-307-11214-4, Golden Pr). Western Pub.
--Larry's Racing Machine. new ed. Loehle, Richard, illus. 32p. 1st U.S. edition. (Golden Science Readers Ser). (gr. 1-3). 1970. (ISBN 0-307-11218-7, Golden Pr). Western Pub.
--Peter and the Rocks. Goldsborough, June (1923-), illus. (A Golden Science Reader Bk.). 1969. Golden Press.
--Peter and the Rocks. Goldsborough, June (1923-), illus. LC 69-20251. (Illus.). 32 p. 24cm. (His An I wonder why reader). 1969. (ISBN 0-03-081177-5). Holt, Rinehart and Winston.
--Soft As a Bunny. Renfro, Ed, illus. (Illus.). color ils. 32p. (Golden Science Readers). (gr. 3-6). 1969. (ISBN 0-307-11204-7, Golden Pr). Western Pub.
Lowery, Ritchie
--Six Silver Spoons. 1971. Harper & Row.
Lowey, Warren G.
--An Indian Tale of Old Long Island. 61p. (gr. 3-8). 1957. (ISBN 0-912954-00-0). Edmond Pub Co.
--Little fox Indian Boy. 64p. 1972. (ISBN 0-912954-02-7). Edmond Publishing Company.
Lowis, Geoffery
--Ruthless Roger's School For Pirates. N.D. Transatlantic Arts.
Lowitz, Anson, jt. auth. see Lowitz, Sadyebeth Heath.
Lowitz, Anson C., jt. auth. see Lowitz, Sadyebeth Heath.
Lowitz, Sadyebeth Heath (1901-1969) & Lowitz, Anson C. (1901-1978)
--Barefoot Abe. Lowitz, Anson C. (1901-1978), illus. (The Really Truly Stories). N.D. Grosset & Dunlap.
--Cruise of Mr. Christopher Columbus. Lowitz, Anson C. (1901-1978), illus. (The Really Truly Stories). N.D. Grosset & Dunlap.
--General George the Great. (The Really Truly Stories). N.D. Grosset & Dunlap.
--The Magic Fountain. LC 35-7529. 60 p. illus. (part col.) 19 x 22 cm. (The Really True Stories). c.1935. Grosset & Dunlap.
--Mr. Key's Song. LC 37-14733. 56 p. illus. (part col.) 19 x 22 cm. (The Really True Stories). c.1937. Grosset & Dunlap.
--The Pilgrim's Party. (The Really Truly Stories). N.D. Grosset & Dunlap.
--The Pilgrims' Party. rev. ed. Lowitz, Anson C. (1901-1978), illus. LC 68-708. 1 v. (unpaged) illus. 19 x 22 cm. (The Really True Stories). 1967, c.1931. Lerner Publications Co.
--The Pilgrims Party. Lowitz, Anson C. (1901-1978), illus. LC 31-241363. 75 p. illus. (part col.) 19 x 23 cm. (The Really True Stories). 1931. R. R. Smith, Inc.
--The Pilgrims' Party. Lowitz, Anson C. (1901-1978), illus. LC 64-136774. 73 p. illus. 19 x 23 cm. (The Really True Stories). 1964, c.1959. Stein and Day.
--Tom Edison Finds Out. Lowitz, Anson C. (1901-1978), illus. LC 40-30568. 48 p. illus. (part col.) 19 x 22 cm. (The Really True Stories). c.1940. Grosset & Dunlap.
Lowndes, Cecilia Selby
--A Bunch of Roses: And their Thorns. N.D. E. & J. B. Young & Co.
--Dandy (Pub. by Society for Promoting Christian Knowledge). N.D. E. & J. B. Young & Co.
--Dandy. (A New Ser.). N.D. E. & J. B. Young & Co.
--Enid's Victory (Pub. by Society for Promoting Christine Knowledge). N.D. E. & J. B. Young & Co.
--Four Peas in a Pod (Pub. by Society for Promoting Christian Knowledge). N.D. E. & J. B. Young & co.
--A Heart of Gold (Pub. by Society for Promoting Christian Knowledge). N.D. E. & J. B. Young & Co.
--A High Resolve. (Illus.). N.D. E & J B Young.
--Lena Graham. (Illus.). (The Home and Enterprise Library Ser.). N.D. Frederick Warne & Co.
--Linford Green. (Illus.). (Warne's Home Circle Library). N.D. Frederick Warne & Co.
--Linford Green. (Illus.). (The Home and Enterprise Library Ser.). N.D. Frederick Warne & Co.
--Miss Hope's Niece. N.D. Thomas Whittaker.
--New Honours. (Illus.). (The Home and Enterprise Library Ser.). N.D. Frederick Warne & Co.
--Nina's Visit. (Illus.). N.D. Society for Promoting Christian Knowledge.
--Ray's Discovery (Pub. by Society for Promoting Christian Knowledge). N.D. E. & J. B. Young & Co.
Lowndes, Marion
--Ghosts that Still Walk. N.D. Alfred A. Knopf.
Lowndes, Robert W.
--Mystery of the Third Mine. (Winston Science Fiction Sers.). 1953. Holt, Rinehart and Winston.
--Mystery of the Third Mine. LC 52-12901. 201p. (gr. 7-9). 1952. (ISBN 0-03-034015-2). HR&W.
Lownsbery, Eloise, jt. auth. see Singh, Reginald Lal.
Lownsbery, Eloise (1888-)
--The Boy Knight of Reims. Wolcott, Elizabeth Tyler, illus. LC 27-22155. 6 p. l., 332 p. col. front., illus., col. plates 21 cm. 1927. Houghton Mifflin Company.
--A Camel for a Throne. Wolcott, Elizabeth Tyler, illus. LC 41-7315. 6 p. l., 305 p., 1 l. illus. 22 cm. 1941. Houghton Mifflin Company.
--Lighting the Torch. Wolcott, Elizabeth Tyler, illus. LC 34-27254. xv, 335 p. incl. front., illus. 21 cm. 1934. Longmans, Green and Company.
--Marta the Doll. Werten, Marya, illus. LC 46-7311. ix, 118 p. incl. col. front., col. illus., col. plates 21 cm. 1946. Longmans, Green and Co.
--Out of the Flame. Wolcott, Elizabeth Tyler, illus. LC 31-25969. xiii, 352 p. incl. front., illus. 20 cm. 1931. Longmans, Green and Co. **Award: (JNM).**
Lowrey, Janette Sebring (1892-)
--The Bird. Merida, Carlos (1898-), illus. LC 47-31244. 32 p. col. illus. 27 cm. 1947. Harper.
--A Day in the Jungle. Gergely, Tibor (1900-1978), illus. LC 44-4502. 42 p. illus. (part col.) 20 x 17 cm. (On cover: The Little golden library. 18). 1943. Artists & Writers Guild, Inc., Simon & Schuster, Distributors.
--In the Morning of the World. Gay, Zhenya (1906-1978), illus. LC 44-9745. xxii p., 1 l., 168 p. illus. 21 1/2 cm. 1944. Harper & Brothers.
--The Lavender Cat. Busoni, Rafaello (1900-1962), illus. LC 44-9704. ix, 180 p. incl. illus., plates. 21 cm. 1944. Harper & Brothers.
--Love, Bid Me Welcome. LC 64-19713. 249 p. geneal. table. 21 cm. 1964. Harper & Row.
--Margaret. LC 50-10613. (gr. 9 up). 1950. (ISBN 0-06-024035-0, HarpJ). Har-Row.
--Mr Heff and Mr Ho. N.D. E. M. Hale and Co.
--Mr. Heff and Mr. Ho. Bacon, Peggy, pseud. (1895-), illus. Bacon, Margaret Frances. 1952. Harper & Brothers.
--The Poky Little Puppy. Tenggren, Gustaf (1896-1970), illus. LC 63-6588. unpaged. illus. 35 cm. (Big golden book in full color). c.1942. Golden Press.
--The Poky Little Puppy. Tenggren, Gustaf (1896-1970), illus. Reissue of 1956 ed. (Little Golden Book). N.D. Golden Press.
--The Poky Little Puppy. Tenggren, Gustaf (1896-1970), illus. LC 42-24234. 42 p. illus. (part col.) 20 1/2 x 17 1/2 cm. (On cover: The Little golden library. 8). 1942. Simon and Schuster, Inc.
--Poky Little Puppy. Tenggren, Gustaf (1896-1970), illus. (Illus.). (ps-1). 1973. (ISBN 0-307-68941-7, Golden Pr). Western Pub.
--Rings on Her Fingers. Holland, Janice (1913-1962), illus. LC 41-2553. 4 p. l., 192 p. incl. col. front., illus. (part col.) 23 x 17 cm. c.1941. Harper & Brothers.
--Six Silver Spoons. Quackenbush, Robert Mead (1929-), illus. LC 77-105469. (Illus.). 64p. (I Can Read History Books). (ps-2). 1971. (ISBN 0-06-024037-7, HarpJ). Har-Row.
--Tap-a-Tan!. Masha, pseud. (1909-), illus. Stern, Marie Simchow. LC 42-36209. 4 p. l., 98 p. incl. col. front., illus. (part col.) 21 x 17 cm. 1942. Harper & Brothers.
--A Woods Story. N.D. Harper & Bros.
Lowrey, Perrin Holmes (1923-)
--The Great Speckled Bird. Gerrard, Paula, illus. (Illus.). 230p. 1964. Reilly & Lee.
Lowry, Goodrich
--Streetcar Man: Tom Lowry & the Twin City Rapid Transit Company. LC 79-2584. (Illus.). (Adult & Young Adult Bks.). (gr. 7 up). 1979. (ISBN 0-8225-0764-1). Lerner Pubns.
Lowry, Henry Dawson (1869-1906)
--Make Believe. Robinson, Charles (1870-1937), illus. LC 44-48099. 1, 3-7, 9-161 (i.e. 160) numb. l., 1 l. incl. front., illus., plates. 14 1/2 cm. 1896. John Lane.
Lowry, James W.
--In the Whale's Belly & Other Martyr Stories. (Illus.). 1981. (ISBN 0-87813-513-8). Christian Light.
Lowry, Lois (1937-)
--Anastasia Again!. De Groat, Diane (1947-), illus. LC 81-6466. p. cm. 1981. (ISBN 0-395-31147-0). Houghton Mifflin.
--Anastasia, Ask Your Analyst. DeGroat, Diane (1947-), illus. LC 83-26687. 160p. (gr. 3-6). 1984. (ISBN 0-395-36011-0). HM.
--Anastasia at Your Service. De Groat, Diane (1947-), illus. LC 82-9231. p. cm. 1982. (ISBN 0-395-32865-9). Houghton Mifflin.
--Anastasia Krupnik. De Groat, Diane (1947-), illus. LC 79-18625. p. cm. 1979. (ISBN 0-395-28629-8). Houghton Mifflin. **Award: (ALA).**
--Anastasia on Her Own. Lowry, Lois (1937-), illus. LC 84-22432. (Illus.). 131 p. 22cm. 1985. (ISBN 0-395-38133-9). Houghton Mifflin.
--Autumn Street. LC 80-376. 188 p. 22cm. 1980. (ISBN 0-395-27812-0). Houghton Mifflin. **Award: (ALA).**
--Find a Stranger, Say Goodbye. LC 78-1024. 187 p. 22cm. 1978. (ISBN 0-395-26459-6). Houghton Mifflin.
--The One Hundredth Thing About Caroline. LC 83-12629. p. cm. 1983. (ISBN 0-395-34829-3). Houghton Mifflin. **Award: (ALA).**
--A Summer to Die. Oliver, Jenni (1947-), illus. LC 77-83. (Illus.). 154 p. 22cm. 1977. (ISBN 0-395-25338-1). Houghton Mifflin. **Awards: (IRA).**
--Switcharound. Lowry, Lois (1937-), illus. LC 85-14576. (Illus.). 118 p. 22cm. 1985. (ISBN 0-395-39536-4). Houghton Mifflin.
--Taking Care of Terrific. LC 82-23331. 168 p. 22cm. 1983. (ISBN 0-395-34070-5). Houghton Mifflin.
--Us and Uncle Fraud. LC 84-12783. 148 p. 22cm. 1984. (ISBN 0-395-36633-X). Houghton Mifflin.
Lowther, George Francis (1913-1975)
--Tom Mix and the Mystery of the Flaming Warrior. LC 48-11345. 169 p. illus. 21 cm. 1947. D. X. McMullen Co.
Lowther, George Francis (1913-1975) & Siegel, Jerry (1914-)
--Superman. Shuster, Joe (1914-), illus. LC 80-105150. (Illus.). x p., p. 3-215. 21cm. (Kassel classic). c.1979. Kassel Books.
--Superman. Shuster, Joe (1914-), illus. LC 42-25581. x, 3-215 p. incl. front., illus., col. plates. 23 1/2 cm. 1942. Random House.
Lowy, Edith, jt. auth. see Steinhorn, Harriet.
Loxton, Polly, jt. auth. see Biesele, Megan.
Luanoff, Pierre
--Maya. (Madison Square Press Books). N.D. (ISBN 0-448-02020-3). Grosset & Dunlap.
Lubell, Cecil, jt. auth. see Lubell, Winifred A. Millus.
Lubell, Winifred, jt. auth. see Williams, Jay.
Lubell, Winifred A. Milius (1914-) & Lubell, Cecil (1914-)
--Green is for Growing. Lubell, Winifred A. Milius (1914-), illus. 1964. (ISBN 0-8382-0307-8, Cadmus Books). E. M. Hale and Company.
--Green Is for Growing. Lubell, Winifred A. Milius (1914-), illus. LC 64-103377. (Illus.). 64 p. 24cm. 1964. Rand McNally. **Award: (ALA).**
--In a Running Brook. Lubell, Winifred A. Milius (1914-), illus. (Illus.). 63 p. 24cm. 1968. Rand McNally.
--Rosalie, the Bird Market Turtle. Lubell, Winifred A. Milius (1914-), illus. (Illus.). (gr. 3-5). 1962. (ISBN 0-8382-0710-3). Hale.
--Rosalie: The Bird Market Turtle. Lubell, Winifred A. Milius (1914-), illus. LC 62-126481. unpaged. illus. 24cm. c.1962. Rand McNally.
--Tall Grass Zoo. Lubell, Winifred A. Milius (1914-), illus. 1960. E M Hale.
--The Tall Grass Zoo. Lubell, Winifred A. Milius (1914-), illus. LC 60-5694. unpaged. illus. 24cm. 1960. Rand McNally.
--Up A Tree. N.D. E. M. Hale & Co.
--Up a Tree. Lubell, Winifred A. Milius (1914-), illus. LC 61-6840. unpaged. illus. 27cm. 1961. Rand McNally.
Lubin, Leonard B., adapted by.
--Aladdin & His Wonderful Lamp. Lubin, Leonard B., illus. Burton, Richard Francis, Sir, tr. from Arabic. LC 82-70308. (Illus.). 48p. (gr. 1-4). 1982. (ISBN 0-440-00302-4). (ISBN 0-440-00304-0). Delacorte.
Lubin, Leonard B., illus.
--This Little Pig: A Mother Goose Favorite. LC 84-10021. (Illus.). 32 p. 26cm. 1985. (ISBN 0-688-04088-8). (ISBN 0-688-04089-6). Lothrop, Lee, & Shepard Books.
Lubin, Leonard B., adapted by see Aulnoy, Marie Catherine Jumelle de Berneville.
Luca, Angelo Michael see De Luca, Angelo Michael (1912-) & Giuliano, William.
Lucas, Alice, tr. see Andersen, Hans Christian.
Lucas, Alice, tr. see Grimm, Jakob Ludwig Karl (1785-1863) & Grimm, Wilhelm Karl.
Lucas, Alice, et al., trs. see Grimm, Jakob Ludwig Karl (1785-1863) & Grimm, Wilhelm Karl.
Lucas, Alice, Mrs., tr. see Andersen, Hans Christian.
Lucas, Annie
--Wenzel's Inheritance: Or, Faithful unto Death. N.D. Thomas Nelson & Sons.
Lucas, Carolyn Parcells (1894-)
--Rhymes for Robin. Lucas, Carolyn Parcells (1894-), illus. LC 55-16136. 72p. illus. 29cm. 1954. William Lyon Phelps Foundations.
Lucas, Christopher
--Tiki and the Dolphin: The Adventures of a Boy in Tahiti. LC 74-76441. x, 161 p. 21cm. 1974. (ISBN 0-8149-0741-5). Vanguard Press.
Lucas, E. V., selected by see Edgeworth, Maria (1767-1849) & Abbott, Jacob.
Lucas, Edgar, Mrs., tr. see Andersen, Hans Christian.
Lucas, Edgar, Mrs., tr. see Grimm, Jakob Ludwig Karl (1785-1863) & Grimm, Wilhelm Karl.
Lucas, Edward Verrall (1868-1938), ed. see Taylor, Jane, et al.
Lucas, Edward Verrall (1868-1938)
--Anne's Terrible Good Nature. N.D. Macmillan.
--A Book of Children's Verse. N.D. George H Doran.
--Book of Shops. Bedford, Francis Donkin (1864-1950), illus. N.D. E. P. Dutton & Co.
--A Book of Verses for Children. N.D. Henry Holt.
--The Flamp: The Ameliorator, and The Schoolboy's Apprentice. Crane, Olive, illus. LC 27-10054. 5 p. l., 3-144, 1 p. col. front., illus., col. plates. 20 cm. 1927. Frederick A. Stokes Company.
--Four and Twenty Toilers. Bedford, Francis Donkin (1864-1950), illus. LC 31-26969. 55 p. incl. col. illus., col. pl. 24 cm. N.D. McDevitt-Wilson's Inc.
--Piccalili. Farmiloe, Edith, illus. (Illus.). N.D. E. P. Dutton and Co.
--Playtime & Company: A Book for Children. Shepard, Ernest Howard (1879-1976), illus. LC 25-23614. viii, 9-93 p., 1 l. incl. front., illus. 24 cm. c.1925. George H. Doran Company.
--The Slowcoach. N.D. Macmillan.
Lucas, Edward Verrall (1868-1938), ed.
--Another Book of Verses for Children. Bedford, Francis Donkin (1864-1950), illus. LC 7-32337. xix, 431 p. incl. col. front., illus. 22 cm. 1907. The Macmillan Company.
--A Book of Verses for Children. LC 71-121927. xii, 304 p. 21cm. (Granger Index reprint series). 1970. Books for Libraries Press.
--Forgotten Tales of Long Ago. Bedford, Francis Donkin (1864-1950), illus. LC 7-35046. xviii, 424, 1 p. incl. illus., plates. front. 21 cm. 1906. Wells-Gardner-Darton & Co. Ltd.
--Old Fashioned Tales. (Illus.). (Fine Art Juveniles Ser.). N.D. Frederick A. Stokes Co.
Lucas, Edward Verrall (1868-1938) & Smith, H. O.
--A Cat Book. (Illus.). (Dumpy Books for Children Ser.). N.D. Frederick A. Stokes Co.
Lucas, Eric
--Corky: Stories & Pictures. Lucas, Eric, illus. LC 39-1035. 63 p. illus. 23 cm. c.1938. International Publishers.
--Swamp for Brigade: Adventures with General Francis Marion's Guerillas. Brazelton, Julian, illus. LC 45-9571. 128 p. illus. 22 cm. (Young world books). 1945. International Publishers.
--Voyage Thirteen. Wells, James L., illus. LC 47-3548. 128 p. incl. front., illus. 22 cm. (Young world books). 1946. International Publishers.
Lucas, George, jt. auth. see Martin, Les.
Lucas, George, jt. auth. see Weinberg, Larry.
Lucas, George (1944-)
--Star Wars. Weinberg, Larry, adapted by. LC 84-18151. (Illus.). 72p. (Step-Up Movie Adventure Ser.). (ps-5). 1985. (ISBN 0-394-96869-7, BYR). (ISBN 0-394-86869-2). Random.
Lucas, George (1944-) & Richelson, Geraldine
--The Star Wars Storybook. LC 77-90196. (Based on the Film by George Lucas). (Illus.). 60 p. 29cm. c.1978. (ISBN 0-394-83785-1). (ISBN 0-394-93785-6). Random House.
Lucas, George (1944-) & Steneman, Shep
--The Empire Strikes Back Storybook. LC 79-5463. (Based on the Film by George Lucas). p. cm. 1980. (ISBN 0-394-84414-9, BYR). (ISBN 0-394-94414-3). Random House.
Lucas, Jannette May (1885-)
--The Big Brewster Family: A Story of Plymouth in 1623. Hill, Mabel Betsy (1877-), illus. LC 46-8273. x, 165 p. illus. 21 cm. 1946. J. B. Lippincott Company.
Luce, Celia Geneva Larsen, jt. auth. see Luce, Willard Ray.
Luce, Willard Ray (1914-)
--Jerry Lindsey, Explorer to the San Juan. Collett, Farrell R., illus. LC 58-373766. 83p. illus. 24cm. 1958. Deseret Book Co.
--The Red Stallion. Collett, Farrell R., illus. LC 61-315165. 110p. illus. 24cm. 1961. Deseret Book Co.
Luce, Willard Ray (1914-) & Luce, Celia Geneva Larsen (1914-)
--Timmy and the Golden Spike. LC 63-3489. 74 p. illus. 24 cm. 1963. Deseret Book Co.
Lucero, Faustina H.
--Little Indians' ABC. Pearson, Jeanne, illus. (Illus.). 32p. (gr. k-2). 1974. Oddo.
Lucey, James Dennis see James, Matthew, pseud.
Lucey, Marilyn, jt. auth. see Jacobs, Leland Blair.

Lucia, Rose
--Peter and Polly in Autumn. LC 19-3496. 176 p. incl. col. front., illus. (port col.) 19 cm. c.1918. American Book Company.
--Peter and Polly in Spring. 176 p. illus. (part col.) 19 cm. c.1915. American Book Company.
--Peter and Polly in Winter. 100 p. illus. (part col.) 19 cm. c.1914. American Book Company.
Luckcock, Janet
--Vimala the Rebel. Armour-Chelu, Ian, illus. LC 68-13144. 118 p. illus. 20 cm. c.1964. Roy Publishers.
Luckenbach, William Henry (1828-1896), ed.
--Song Stories for Little People. LC 11-30743. 300 p. 19 1/2 cm. 1890. Funk & Wagnalls.
Luckett, Karen Beth (1944-)
--Short Stories for Boys & Girls. Meyd, Orella S., illus. (Illus.). (gr. k-4). 1971. (ISBN 0-682-47293-X). Exposition.
Luckhardt, Mildred Madeleine Corell (1898-)
--Bat Boy of the Giants. N.D. The Westminster Press.
--The Bells Ring Out. Walker, Nedda, illus. LC 50-7204. 50 p. illus. (part col.) 17 x 23 cm. 1950. Westminster Press.
--Brother Francis & the Christmas Surprise. (Illus.). 32p. (Orig.). 1983. (ISBN 0-8091-6549-X). Paulist Pr.
--Coast Guard to the Rescue. Wonsetler, John Charles (1900-), illus. LC 53-74432. 61p. illus. 22cm. (As Everyday adventure story). 1953. J. Messner.
--Funny Stories to Read or Tell. McDonald, Ralph J., illus. LC 73-5984. (Illus.). 160 p. 25cm. 1974. (ISBN 0-687-13869-8). Abingdon Press.
--Good King Wenceslas. Laite, Gordon (1925-), illus. LC 64-10150. 112 p. col. illus. 23 cm. 1964. Abingdon Press.
--Merrily We Roll Along. Stein, Harve (1904-), illus. LC 52-9338. (Illus.). 64 p. 22cm. (Everyday adventure stories). 1952. Messner.
--Mr. Pupsy. LC 41-27892. 96 p. 18 cm. 1941. The Wartburg Press.
--Spooky Tales About Witches, Ghosts, Goblins, Demons, and Such. McDonald, Ralph J., illus. LC 79-171049. (Illus.). 223 p. 25cm. 1972. (ISBN 0-687-39256-X). Abingdon Press.
--Spring World, Awake: Stories, Poems, and Essays. McDonald, Ralph J., illus. LC 71-83705. (Illus.). 352 p. 25cm. 1970. Abingdon Press.
--Story of St. Nicholas. Laite, Gordon (1925-), illus. (Illus.). (gr. 3-6). N.D. (ISBN 0-687-39728-6). Abingdon.
--Thanksgiving-Feast & Festival. McDonald, Ralph J., illus. (Illus.). (gr. 4 up). 1966. (ISBN 0-687-41404-0). Abingdon.
Luckhardt, Mildred Madeleine Corell (1898-), compiled by.
--Brave Journey: Launching of the United States. Armstrong, Tom, illus. LC 74-34273. (Illus.). 208p. (gr. 3-7). 1975. (ISBN 0-687-03965-7). Abingdon.
--Christmas Comes Once More. Dotzenko, Grisha, illus. (Illus.). (gr. 3-7). 1962. (ISBN 0-687-07804-0). Abingdon.
Luckmann, Helmut
--Aida. Luckmann, Helmut, illus. LC 76-106159. (Illus.). 47 p. 29cm. (Curtain-raiser book). 1970. (ISBN 0-531-01928-4). F. Watts.
Lucretia, Hosie, jt. auth. see Baskin, Leonard.
Lucy, pseud., see MacDonald, Lucy.
Ludd, Bettye, ed.
--The Three Little Pigs. Pritzen, Barbara, illus. (ps-1). 1973. (ISBN 0-307-68972-7, Golden Pr). Western Pub.
Luderer, Lynn Marie
--The Toad Intruder. DeGroat, Diane (1947-), illus. LC 81-13397. (Illus.). 46 p. 24cm. 1982. Houghton Mifflin.
Ludgin, Earle
--The Timid Giant, and the Boy Who Was Not Afraid. Riedel, Boris, illus. LC 28-28941. 64 p. col. illus. 24 cm. 1928. The Children's Press.
Ludins, Ryah
--The Wonder Rock: An Indian Myth. Ludins, Ryah, illus. LC 31-29420. 40 p. illus. 18 x 23 cm. 1931. Coward-McCann, Inc.
Ludium, Stuart
--Willie & the Yank. (Illus.). (gr. 7-9). 1975. (ISBN 0-590-08603-0, Schol Trade Pap). Schol Bk Serv.
Ludlow, Fitz Hugh (1836-1870) & U. S. Sanitary Commission
--Cinderella. Dramatized from the Original Fairy Tale, for the Children's Performance During the New-York Sanitary Fair, in Behalf of the Sanitary Commission. LC 10-101698. 1 p. l., 32 p. 21 cm. 1864. J. A. Gray & Green, Printers.
Ludlow, Margaret
--The Trouble with Timothy. 1st ed. Cooke, Tom, illus. LC 82-18912. p. cm. c.1982. (ISBN 0-910313-00-8). Parker Brothers.
Ludlow, Park
--Nick Hardy. (Red Shanty Ser.). 1873. Henry A. Young.
--The Red Shanty Boys: Or, Pictures of New-England School-Life Thirty Years ago. N.D. Henry A. Young.
Ludlum, Jean Kate
--Was He Wise?. LC 12-36418. 306 p. 19 cm. 1887. Phillips & Hunt.
Ludman, Barbara
--The Strays. LC 76-19046. 149 p. 21cm. c.1976. (ISBN 0-8407-6503-7). T. Nelson.
Ludmann, Oscar Henri (1900-)
--Hansi the Stork. Brock, Emma Lillian (1886-1974), illus. LC 32-30028. 62 p. illus. (part col.) 18 x 22 cm. 1932. A. Whitman.
Ludwig, Charles Skelton (1918-)
--The Adventures of Juma. LC 44-8307. iii p., 1 l., 7-98 p. 19 1/2 cm. 1944. The Warner Press.
--Cannibal Country. LC 48-361269. 119 p. 20 cm. 1948. Warner Press.
--Leopard Glue. LC 47-197897. 135 p. 19 1/2 cm. 1946. The Warner Press.
--Man-Eaters and Masai Spears: A Missionary Adventure Story. LC 54-166619. 69p. illus. 21cm. 1953. Scripture Press.
--Man-Eater's Claw: A Missionary Adventure Story. LC 58-15371. 67p. 21cm. 1957. Scripture Press, Book Division.
--Man-Eaters Don't Knock: A Missionary Adventure Story. 68p. illus. 21cm. 1953. Scripture Press.
--Man-Eaters Don't Laugh: A Missionary Adventure Story. LC 56-163904. 67p. 21cm. 1955. Scripture Press.
--Radio Pals Fight the Flood. LC 53-13421. 87p. 20cm. 1953. Van Kampen Press.
--Radio Pals in the Flaming Forest. 72p. 20cm. 1955. Zondervan Publishing House.
--Radio Pals in the Hands of the Mau Mau. LC 55-270809. 88p. 20cm. 1955, c.1954. Van Kampen Press.
--Radio Pals Marooned. LC 52-1486. 80 p. 20 cm. 1952. Van Kampen Press.
--Radio Pals on Bar T Ranch. LC 53-9084. 82p. 20cm. 1953. Van Kampen Press.
--Witch Doctor's Holiday. N.D. Warner Press.
Ludwig, Lyndell
--The Shoemaker's Gift. LC 82-73196. (Illus.). 50p. (Children's Ser.). 1983. (ISBN 0-916870-53-7). Creative Arts Bk.
--Ts'ao Chung Weighs an Elephant. LC 82-73197. (Illus.). 50p. (Orig.). (Children's Ser.). 1983. (ISBN 0-916870-52-9). Creative Arts Bk.
Ludwig, Nancy
--Christmas Puppets Plays & Art Project Puppets. Fowler, Christopher, illus. (Illus.). 32p. (Stick-Out-Your-Neck Ser.). (gr. k-3). 1983. (ISBN 0-88724-045-3). Carson-Dellos.
Ludwig & Bernal
--California Story & Coloring Book. (Illus.). 32p. (Orig.). N.D. (ISBN 0-930504-01-1). Polaris Pr.
Lueders, Edward, jt. ed. see Dunning, Arthur Stephen.
Lueders, Edward, jt. ed. see Dunning, Arthur Stephen, Jr.
Lueders, Edward George (1923-) & St. John, Primus, eds.
--Zero Makes Me Hungry: A Collection of Poems for Today. Reuter-Pacyna, John, illus. LC 75-33543. (Illus.). 144p. (gr. 7 up). 1976. (ISBN 0-688-41745-0). (ISBN 0-688-51745-5). Lothrop. **Award: (ALA).**
Luedtke, Ralph D., jt. ed. see Kuse, James.
Luenn, Nancy
--The Dragon Kite. 1st ed. Hague, Michael R., illus. LC 81-11709. (Illus.). 32 p. 21cm. c.1982. Harcourt Brace Jovanovich.
--The Ugly Princess. Wiesner, David, illus. LC 81-1403. (Illus.). 27 p. 24cm. c.1981. (ISBN 0-316-53560-5). Little, Brown.
Lugard, Flora Louisa Shaw see Shaw, Flora L., pseud.
Lugard, Flora Louisa Shaw, Lady (1852-1929)
--Castle Blair: A Story of Youthful Days. Varian, George, illus. LC 23-13002. 3 p. l., 341 p. front., plates. 21 cm. 1923. Little, Brown, and Company.
--Castle Blair: A Story of Youthful Days. Whitney, H. & Whitney, I., illus. LC 3-707. ix, 306 p., 1 l. incl. front., illus. 20 cm. 1902. D. C. Heath & Co.
Lugard, Flora Luisa Shaw see Shaw, Flora L., Lady.
Luger, Harriett Mandelay (1914-)
--Chasing Trouble. DeGroat, Diane (1947-), illus. LC 75-43902. (Illus.). 119 p. 24cm. c.1976. (ISBN 0-670-21291-1). Viking Press.
--The Elephant Tree. 1st ed. McIntosh, Jon, illus. LC 77-16416. 115 p. 22cm. 1978. (ISBN 0-670-29173-0). Viking Press.
--The Last Stronghold: A Story of the Modoc Indian War, 1872-1873. LC 72-5305. (Illus.). 223 p. 22cm. 1972. (ISBN 0-201-09296-4). Young Scott Books.
--Lauren. LC 79-12713. p. cm. 1979. (ISBN 0-670-42002-6). Viking Press.
--The Un-Dudding of Roger Judd. LC 82-50362. p. cm. 1983. (ISBN 0-670-73886-7). Viking Press.
Luginbuhl, Edna
--The Red Wool Man. Sharpe, Caroline (1947-), illus. LC 76-141859. (Illus.). 46 p. 26cm. 1971. (ISBN 0-200-71757-X). Abelard-Schuman.
Luibheid, Colm
--All the Green Gold. (Illus.). map. 160p. (Young Readers Ser). (gr. 7 up). 1970. Praeger.
Luis, Earlene W (1929-) & Millar, Barbara Finn (1924-)
--Listen, Lissa!. A Candy Striper Meets the Biggest Challenge. LC 68-27821. 144 p. 21cm. (gr. 8up). 1968. Dodd, Mead.
--Wheels for Ginny's Chariot. LC 66-13852. 205p. 21cm. c.1966. (ISBN 0-396-05287-8). Dodd.
--Wheels for Ginny's Chariot. (Illus.). (gr. 6-10). 1966. (ISBN 0-8382-1042-2). Hale.
Lukan, Karl
--Mountain Adventures. 1 st. ed. (Illus.). 128 p. 26cm. (Internation Library). 1972. (ISBN 0-531-02110-6). Franklin Watts.
Luke, David (1921-), tr. see Grimm, Jakob Ludwig Karl (1785-1863) & Grimm, Wilhelm Karl.
Luke, Mary M. (1919-)
--The Nonsuch Lure. LC 76-12605. 288p. 1976. (ISBN 0-698-10750-0, Coward). Putnam Pub Group.
Luke, Melinda (1955-)
--The Astrosniks and the Quasar Caper. Jacquet, Jean-Pierre, illus. LC 83-19282. 32p. 1984. (ISBN 0-394-86392-5). Random House.
--The Baby Ewoks' Picnic Surprise. Paris, Pat, illus. LC 83-62249. (Illus.). 32 p. 13cm. c.1984. (ISBN 0-394-86353-4). Random House.
--Casey & the Dolphins: A Snork Adventure. Wildman, George, illus. LC 84-60487. (Illus.). 32p. (Snork Mini-Storybks.). (ps-3). 1984. (ISBN 0-394-86814-5, Pub. by BYR). Random.
--My Little Pony & the Mystery Chase. Beylon, Catherine M., illus. LC 84-17723. (Illus.). 32p. (My Little Pony Mini-Storybooks Ser.). (ps-3). 1985. (ISBN 0-394-87106-5, BYR). Random.
--My Little Pony at the Country Fair. Lisman, Sharon & Herrera, Julio (1929-), illus. LC 84-60333. (Illus.). 32 p. 13cm. c.1984. (ISBN 0-394-86811-0). Random House.
--My Little Pony Under the Big Top. Bracken, Carolyn, illus. LC 85-42536. p. cm. 1985. (ISBN 0-394-87385-8). Random House.
--Spike and the Magic Shoes. Beylon, Catherine M., illus. LC 84-18218. p. cm. c.1985. (ISBN 0-394-87107-3). Random House.
--Wicket Finds a Way: An Ewok Adventure. Paris, Pat, illus. LC 83-62252. (Illus.). 32 p. 3cm. c.1984. (ISBN 0-394-86356-9). Random House.
Lukesova, Milena
--Julian in the Autumn Woods. Kudlacek, Jan (1928-), illus. LC 77-2157. p. cm. c.1977. (ISBN 0-03-021151-4). Holt/Rinehart/Winston.
--The Little Girl and the Rain. Kudlacek, Jan (1928-), illus. LC 77-1090. p. cm. c.1978. (ISBN 0-03-021146-8). Holt, Rinehart and Winston.
Lukiyanenko, Maria, jt. auth. see Rudchenko, Ivan.
Luling, Elizabeth & Thompson, Sylvia Elizabeth Afiola (1902-)
--Do Not Disturb: The Adventures of M'm and Teddy. Salter, George, illus. LC 37-20436. 98, 2 p. incl. col. front., col. illus. 16 1/2 cm. c.1937. Oxford University Press.
Lull, Margaret Young
--Blue Mountain. Esley, Joan, illus. LC 31-20306. viii p., 1 l., 253 p. col. front., illus. 19 cm. 1931. Harper & Brothers.
--Face West. Best, Allena Champlin, Mrs. (1892-1974), illus. Berry, Erick, pseud. LC 36-18971. 6 p. l., 231 p. incl. illus., plates. col. front. 19 cm. 1936. Harper & Brothers.
--Golden River. King, Ruth, illus. LC 30-185571. ix p., 1 l., 297 p. incl. illus., plates. col. front. 19 1/2 cm. 1930. Harper & Brothers.
Lum, Bertha
--Gods,Ghosts & Goblins: Weird Legends of the Far East. N.D. J.B. Lippincott.
Lum, Peter, pseud., see Crowe, Bettina Lum.
Lum, Peter, pseud. (1911-), retold by
--Fabulous Beasts. Crowe, Bettina Lum. Jauss, Anne Marie (1907-), illus. 1951. Pantheon Books Inc.
--Fairy Tales of China. Crowe, Bettina Lum. Miller, George W., illus. LC 60-943. unpaged. illus. 21cm. c.1959. Cassell.
--Fairy Tales of China. Crowe, Bettina Lum. Miller, George W., illus. (Fairy Tales of Many Lands). N.D. E. P. DUtton & Co.
--Italian Fairy Tales. Crowe, Bettina Lum. Toothhill, Harry & Toothhill, Ilse, illus. LC 67-21171. 193p. illus. 23cm. 1967, c.1963. Follett.
--Italian Fairy Tales. Crowe, Bettina Lum. Toothill, Harry & Toothill, Ilse, illus. (Illus.). Drawings. (World Fairy Tale Ser). (gr. 4-7). N.D. (ISBN 0-695-44395-X). Follett.
--Stars in Our Heaven. Crowe, Bettina Lum. Jauss, Anne Marie (1907-), illus. (Illus.). 1948. (ISBN 0-394-91675-1). Pantheon.
Lumbers, Eugene
--I, Smocker. Goodall, Robin, illus. LC 72-178239. (Illus.). 118 p. 22cm. 1971. Macmillan.
Lu Meng
--Three Precious Pearls. Fang Jun, illus. (Illus.). 19p. (Orig.). (gr. 3-6). 1983. (ISBN 0-8351-1253-5). China Bks.
Lumiansky, R. M., tr. see Chaucer, Geoffrey.
Lummis, Charles Fletcher (1859-1928)
--The Enchanted Burro. Corwin, C. A., illus. 5x7 1/2cm. 277p. N.D. Doubleday, Page & Co.
--The Gold Fish of Gran Chimu. (Illus.). 349p. N.D. The Century Co.
--The Man Who Married the Moon. Edwards, George Wharton (1859-1950), illus. 239p. N.D. The Century Co.
--A New Mexico David. Lummis, Charles Fletcher (1859-1928), illus. N.D. Charles Scribner's Sons.
--Pueblo Indian Folk-Lore Stories. Edwards, George Wharton (1859-1950), illus. (Illus.). 257p. Orig. Title: The Man Who Married the Moon. N.D. Century Co.
--Pueblo Indian Folk-Stories. N.D. Appleton Century Co.
Lumn, Peter, jt. auth. see Norris, Faith.
Lund, Doris Herold (1919-)
--Attic of the Wind. Forberg, Ati, pseud. (1925-), illus. Forberg, Beate Gropius. LC 65-18657. 1v. (unpaged) col. illus. 26cm. c.1966. Parents' Mag. Pr. Sch. & Lib. Ed. Dist. Chicago, Childrens.
--Did You Ever?. Hampson, Denman, illus. LC 64-19768. 1v. (unpaged) col. illus. 20x26cm. c.1965. Parents' Mag.
--Did You Ever. Hampson, Denman, illus. LC 64-19768. (Illus.). (gr. k-2). 1965. (ISBN 0-8193-0088-8, Four Winds). (ISBN 0-8193-0089-6). Scholastic Inc.
--Did You Ever Dream?. Luke, Franklin, illus. LC 72-81194. (Illus.). 40 p. 1969. Parents' Magazine Press.
--I Wonder What's Under. McCaffery, Janet, illus. LC 70-117556. (Illus.). 43 p. 1970. (ISBN 0-8193-0426-3). Parents' Magazine Press.
--The Paint-Box Sea. Shimin, Symeon (1902-), illus. LC 72-7260. (Illus.). 32 p. 27cm. 1973. (ISBN 0-07-039097-5). (ISBN 0-07-039097-5). McGraw-Hill.
--You Ought to See Herbert's House. Kellogg, Steven (1941-), illus. LC 77-185690. (Illus.). 32 p. 27cm. 1973. F. Watts.
Lund, Jane & Menlove, Nancy
--Take a Giant Step: Fourteen Original Fables for Today's Children. Lund, Jane, illus. LC 68-21500. (Illus.). 60 p. 29cm. 1968. Deseret Book Co.
Lund, Velma
--School Picnic of Long Ago. Nair, Christina, illus. (Illus.). (gr. 5 up). 1977. (ISBN 0-533-02771-3). Vantage.
Lundberg, Holger, tr. see Unnerstad, Edith Totterman.
Lundbergh, Holer, tr. see Henriksen, Hild.
Lundbergh, Holger, tr. see Hallqvist, Britt G.
Lundbergh, Holger, tr. see Nyblom, Helena Augusta Roed.
Lundborg, Florence, designed by.
--The Lark Book Two, Nos. 13-24. N.D. Doxey's Pubs.
Lundeberg, Olav K
--The Enchanted Valley: A Story and Legend of Christmas in Telemark in the Old Time. Thorpe, Eldrid, illus. LC 37-38599. 5 p. l., 3-108, 1 p. illus. 22 1/2 cm. c.1937. Augsburg Publishing House.
Lundell, Margo
--The Get Along Gang & the Big Bully. Baker, Darrell, illus. (Illus.). 32p. (Orig.). (Get Along Gang Ser.). (ps-2). 1984. (ISBN 0-590-33188-4). Scholastic Inc.
Lundgren, Max (1937-)
--Matt's Grandfather. Hald, Fibben, illus. LC 71-186797. (Illus.). 23 p. 1972. Putnam.
Lundgren, Sue
--The Great Big Funny Book. Lundgren, Sue, illus. LC 74-21515. (Illus.). 71 p. 32cm. (Child guidance book). 1975. (ISBN 0-8228-7380-X). Platt & Munk.
--Knee Slappers & Rib Ticklers. Zimmerman, Jerry, illus. LC 78-66935. (Illus.). (Pandabacks). (gr. 1-5). N.D. (ISBN 0-448-49612-7). Platt.
Lundy, Jo Evalin
--The Challengers: Oregon in the 1840's. 1st ed. Nicholas, Frank, illus. LC 53-12189. (Illus.). 192 p. 21cm. (American heritage). 1953. Aladdin Books.
--Seek the Dark Gold. Best, Allena Champlin, Mrs. (1892-1974), ed. Berry, Erick, pseud. Shenton, Edward (1895-), illus. (Land of the Free Ser.). N.D. John C. Winston Co.
--Tidewater Valley. Ayer, Margaret (0000-1981), illus. N.D. John C. Winson Co.

--The First Disciples, Miracle at Cana, the Well at Samaria, Riot at Nazareth, the Great Catch, Bk. 18. (Illus.). 16p. (Bible Story Cartoons Ser.). (gr. 1-5). 1978. (ISBN 0-87239-298-8). Standard Pub.
--From Rehoboam to Joash, Jonah, Amos the Prophet. LC 80-17529. (Illus.). (Bible Story Cartoons Ser.). 1977. (ISBN 0-87239-293-7). Standard Pub.
--Gideon & His Three Hundred , the Mighty Samson. (Illus.). (Bible Story Cartoons Ser.). 1976. (ISBN 0-87239-288-0). Standard Pub.
--The Great Healer, Sermon on the Mount, a Roman's Faith, the Road to Nain, a Sermon for Simon, Bk. 19. Lynch, Norman E., illus. (Illus.). 16p. (Bible Story Cartoons Ser.). 1978. (ISBN 0-87239-299-6). Standard Pub.
--Isaac's Wells, the Perils of Jacob. (Illus.). (Bible Story Cartoons Ser.). 1976. (ISBN 0-87239-283-X). Standard Pub.
--Isaiah, Micah, Josiah, Jeremiah. (Illus.). (Bible Story Cartoons Ser.). 1977. (ISBN 0-87239-294-5). Standard Pub.
--Joseph & His Brothers. (Illus.). (Bible Story Cartoons Ser.). 1976. (ISBN 0-87239-284-8). Standard Pub.
--Joshua, God's Great General, the Early Judges. (Illus.). (Bible Story Cartoons Ser.). 1976. (ISBN 0-87239-287-2). Standard Pub.
--The Last Supper, Death on the Cross, the Final Triumph, Bk. 23. Lynch, Norman E., illus. (Illus.). 16p. (Bible Story Cartoons Ser.). (gr. 1-5). 1978. (ISBN 0-87239-303-8). Standard Pub.
--Moses in Egypt. (Illus.). (Bible Story Cartoons Ser.). 1976. (ISBN 0-87239-285-6). Standard Pub.
--Moses in the Wilds. (Illus.). (Bible Story Cartoons Ser.). 1976. (ISBN 0-87239-286-4). Standard Pub.
--Perilous Journey, Jairus' Daughter, the Feeding of 5000, Fear in the Night, Miracles on the Mountain, Bk. 20. Lynch, Norman E., illus. (Illus.). 16p. (Bible Story Cartoons Ser.). (gr. 1-5). 1978. (ISBN 0-87239-300-3). Standard Pub.
--Perils of Daniel. (Illus.). (Bible Story Cartoons Ser.). 1977. (ISBN 0-87239-295-3). Standard Pub.
--Perils of David, Wisdom of Solomon. (Illus.). (Bible Story Cartoons Ser.). 1977. (ISBN 0-87239-291-0). Standard Pub.
--Return from Exile, Esther Saves Her People, Nehemiah. (Illus.). (Bible Story Cartoons Ser.). 1977. (ISBN 0-87239-296-1). Standard Pub.
--The Sinful Woman, the Blind Man, the Good Samaritan, Mary, Martha, & Lazarus, Stories Jesus Told, Bk. 21. Lynch, Norman E., illus. (Illus.). 16p. (Bible Story Cartoons Ser.). (gr. 1-5). 1978. (ISBN 0-87239-301-1). Standard Pub.
--Story of David, Saul & Jonathan. (Illus.). (Bible Story Cartoons Ser.). 1977. (ISBN 0-87239-290-2). Standard Pub.
--Story of Ruth, Samuel & Saul. (Illus.). (Bible Story Cartoons Ser.). 1977. (ISBN 0-87239-289-9). Standard Pub.
--Ten Sick Men, the Beggar at Jericho, the Triumphal Entry, More Stories Jesus Told, Bk. 22. Lynch, Norman E., illus. (Illus.). 16p. (Bible Story Cartoons Ser.). (gr. 1-5). 1978. (ISBN 0-87239-302-X). Standard Pub.
--The Tower of Babel, Abraham, Isaac, Rebekah. (Illus.). (Bible Story Cartoons Ser.). 1976. (ISBN 0-87239-282-1). Standard Pub.

Lynch, Patricia Nora (1898-1972)
--Brogeen and the Bronze Lizard: 1st ed. Vestal, Herman B., illus. LC 77-99123. (Illus.). ix, 180 p. 21cm. 1970. Macmillan.
--Brogeen and the Little Wind: A Brogeen Story. Sanders, Beryl, illus. LC 62-18445. 158 p. illus. 21cm. 1963, c.1962. Roy Publishers.
--Brogeen Follows the Magic Tune. Pinto, Ralph, illus. LC 68-24105. (Illus.). ix, 165 p. 22cm. 1st U.S. edition. 1968. Macmillan.
--The Donkey Goes Visiting: The Story of an Island Holiday. Altendorf, George, illus. LC 36-15927. 6 p. l., 229 p., col. front., illus., plates (part col.) 19 1/2 cm. c.1936. E. P. Dutton & Co., Inc.
--Fiddler's Quest. Morton-Sale, Isobel (1904-), illus. LC 43-6646. ix, 309 p. col. front., illus. 20 1/2 cm. 1943. E. P. Dutton and Company, Inc.
--Grania of Castle O'Hara. Rivers, Elizabeth, illus. LC 52-8720. 208 p. illus. 20 cm. 1952. L. C. Page.
--The Grey Goose of Kilnevin. Keating, John, illus. LC 40-12858. 5 p. l., 285 p. col. front., illus. 19 1/2 cm. 1940. E. P. Dutton & Co., Inc.
--King of the Tinkers. Lloyd, Katharine C., illus. LC 38-29630. ix, 240, 1 p. col. front., illus., col. plates. 20 cm. 1938. E. P. Dutton & Company, Inc.
--Knights of God: Tales and Legends of the Irish Saints. Ambrus, Victor G., pseud. (1935-), illus. Ambrus, Gyozo Laszlo. LC 69-11811. (Illus.). xix, 219 p. 24cm. 1969. Holt, Rinehart and Winston.
--Shane Comes to Dublin. Fortnum, Peggy, pseud. (1919-), illus. Nutall-Smith, Margaret Emily Noel. 186p. illus. 22cm. (Criterion book for young people). 1958. Criterion Books.
--Shane Comes to Dublin. Fortnum, Peggy, pseud. (1919-), illus. Nutall-Smith, Margaret Emily Noel. LC 58-5902. (Illus.). (gr. 4-7). 1958. (ISBN 0-87599-070-3). S G Phillips.
--The Turf-Cutter's Donkey: An Irish Story of Mystery and Adventure. Yeats, Jack Butler (1871-1957), illus. LC 35-10745. viii, 245 p. incl. col. front., plates. col. plates. 19 1/2 cm. 1935. E. P. Dutton & Co., Inc.
--The Turf-Cutter's Donkey Kicks up His Heels. Bromhall, Winifred, illus. LC 39-12106. 246 p. incl. front., illus., plates. 19 1/2 cm. 1939. E. P. Dutton & Co., Inc.

Lynch-Watson, Janet (1936-)
--The Shadow Puppet Book. LC 79-65069. (Illus.). (gr. 3 up). 1979. (ISBN 0-8069-7030-8). (ISBN 0-8069-7031-6). Sterling.

Lynde, Elmer
--Mabel: Or, Tiny Stories for Tiny People. 92p. N.D. American Tract Society.

Lynde, Francis (1856-)
--Blind Man's Buff. LC 28-12083. 3 p. l., 324 p. 19 1/2 cm. 1928. C. Scibner's Sons.
--The Cruise of the Cuttlefish. LC 25-16604. 4 p. l., 284 p. front., plates. 19 1/2 cm. 1925. C. Scribner's Sons.
--Dick and Larry, Freshmen. Avison, George F. (1885-), illus. LC 22-19302. 4 p. l., 192 p. front., plates. 19 cm. 1922. C. Scribner's Sons.
--The Donovan Chance. Fogarty, Thomas (1873-), illus. LC 21-145492. 4 p. l., 215 p. front., plates. 19 cm. 1921. C. Scribner's Sons.
--The Fight on Standing Stone. N.D. Charles Scribner's Sons'.
--The Flight of the Gray Goose. LC 27-214062. 5 p. l., 3-215 p. col. front., plates. 19 1/2 cm. (Scribner series for young people). 1927. C. Scribner's Sons.
--The Girl a Horse and a Dog. N.D. Charles Scribner's Sons.
--The Golden Spider. LC 23-12402. 5 p. l., 210 p. front., plates. 19 cm. (His The Dick and Larry series). 1923. C. Scribner's Sons.
--The Master of Appleby. De Thulstrup, T., illus. N.D. Bobbs-Merrill Co.
--Pirates' Hope. N.D. Charles Scribner's Sons'.
--The Tenderfoots. N.D. Charles Scribner's Sons'.

Lyndon
--Margaret: A Story of Life in a Prairie Home. N.D. Charles Scribner's Sons.

Lynds, Dennis see Arden, William, pseud.

Lynds, Dennis see West, Nick, pseud.

Lynds, Dennis (1924-)
--Alfred Hitchcock and the Three Investigators in The Secret of the Crooked Cat. LC 80-19143. 168 p. 20cm. (Alfred Hitchcock and the Three Investigators Series ; 13). 1981, c.1970. (ISBN 0-394-84677-X). Random House.
--Mystery of the Blue Condor. Ulrich, George M., illus. LC 72-86212. (Illus.). 63 p. 23cm. (Magic circle book). c.1973. (ISBN 0-663-25489-2). Ginn.

Lynn, Claire
--A Cave Is a Deep Dark Hole. 48p. (gr. 8-12). 1978. (ISBN 0-89323-012-X). BMA Pr.

Lynn, Claire, jt. ed. see Ellis, Joyce K.

Lynn, Elizabeth A. (1946-)
--The Silver Horse. LC 84-108609. c.1984. (ISBN 0-312-94405-5). Bluejay.

Lynn, Escott, pseud., see Lawrence, Christopher George Holman.

Lynn, Escott, pseud. (1866-1950)
--Comrades Ever!. Lawrence, Christopher George Holman. Tarrant, Percy, illus. LC 23-6846. 351, 1 p. front., plates. 19 cm. 1921. J. B. Lippincott Company.
--Rebels of the Green Cockade. Lawrence, Christopher George Holman. N.D. J.B. Lippincott.
--Robin Hood & His Merry Men. Lawrence, Christopher George Holman. N.D. J.B. Lippincott.

Lynn, Eva
--Nests of Stories. N.D. Set. Congregational Sunday-School and Publishing Society.

Lynn, Godfrey
--Captain Kitty. Webbe, Elizabeth, illus. LC 51-31794. unpaged. illus. 17cm. c.1951. Rand McNally.
--Henrietta's Ride. Webbe, Elizabeth, illus. N.D. Rand McNally & Co.

Lynn, Gordon
--The Golden book of Camping & Camp Crafts. Barth, Ernest Kurt, illus. 1959. Golden Press.

Lynn, Haney (1941-) & Foster, Alan Dean (1946-)
--The Last Starfighter Storybook. LC 84-4924. (Illus.). 64p. 1984. (ISBN 0-399-21078-4, Putnam). (ISBN 0-399-21079-2). Putnam Pub Group.

Lynn, Margaret
--The Land of Promise. Hoskins, Gayle, illus. LC 27-7670. 4 p. l., 3-280 p. front., plates. 19 1/2 cm. 1927. Little, Brown, and Company.

Lynn, Patricia, pseud., see Watts, Mabel Pizzey.

Lynn, Patricia, pseud. (1906-)
--Around and About Buttercup Farm. Watts, Mabel Pizzey. Kane, Wilma & Miloche, Hilda, illus. LC 52-16194. unpaged. illus. 17 cm. (Tell-a-tale books). c.1951. Whitman Pub. Co.
--Farm ABC. Watts, Mabel Pizzey. Michell, Gladys Turley, illus. LC 55-17929. unpaged. illus. 17cm. (Tell-a-tale books, 965). c.1954. Whitman Pub. Co.
--Getting Ready for Roddy. Watts, Mabel Pizzey. Helweg, Hans H. (1917-), illus. LC 56-26169. unpaged. illus. 17cm. (Tell-a-tale books, 2530). c.1955. Whitman Pub. Co.

Lynn, Ruth Nadelman (1948-)
--Ester: The Story of a Small Ghost. Wagner, R. M., ed. Lynn, Ruth Nadelman (1948-), illus. LC 81-69693. (Illus.). 28p. 1981. (ISBN 0-941674-00-2). Woodcock Pr.

Lynnde, Elmer
--Daphne Stories. Lyon, David, illus. (Six books in a box.). 1879. American Tract Society.

Lyon, David
--The Brave Little Computer. Alley, R. W, illus. LC 85-166570. (Illus.). 42 p. ("A Little Simon book"). c.1984. (ISBN 0-671-52455-0). Simon & Schuster.
--The Runaway Duck. LC 84-5677. (Illus.). 33 p. 26cm. c.1985. (ISBN 0-688-04002-0). (ISBN 0-688-04003-9). Lothrop, Lee, & Shepard.

Lyon, Elinor (1921-)
--Cathie Runs Wild. Elgaard, Greta, illus. (Illus.). 155 p. 22cm. 1968, c.1960. Follett Pub. Co.
--The Dream Hunters. Dinsdale, Mary (1920-), illus. LC 67-3604. (Illus.). 150 p. 23cm. (Merit mystery, 2097). 1967, c.1966. Follett Pub. Co.
--Echo Valley. Dinsdale, Mary (1920-), illus. LC 67-3603. (Illus.). 144 p. 23cm. (Merit mystery, 2145). 1967, c.1965. Follett Pub. Co.
--Green Grow the Rushes. Byfield, Graham, illus. (Illus.). 153 p. 23cm. (Merit mystery, 3485). 1967, c.1964. Follett Pub. Co.
--Hilary's Island. Werth, Kurt (1896-), illus. LC 50-6627. 248 p. 20 cm. c.1949. Coward-McCann.
--The House in Hiding: A Mystery. LC 51-8072. 218 p. illus. 20 cm. c.1950. Coward-McCann.
--Rider's Rock. Carpenter, Mia, illus. LC 68-10497. (Illus.). 224 p. 23cm. (Merit mystery). 1968, c.1958. Follett Pub. Co.
--Run Away Home. Price, Christine Hilda (1928-1980), illus. LC 53-3219. (Illus.). 192 p. 21cm. 1953. Viking Press.
--The Secret of Hermit's Bay. Lazare, Gerald John (1927-), illus. LC 67-21172. (Illus.). 159 p. 23cm. (Merit mysteries). 1967, c.1962. (ISBN 0-695-47834-6). Follett.
--Strangers at the Door. Dinsdale, Mary (1920-), illus. LC 69-10255. (Illus.). 191 p. 23cm. (Merit mystery). 1969, c.1967. (ISBN 0-695-48363-3). (ISBN 0-695-88363-1). Follett Pub. Co.
--The Wishing Pool. Dinsdale, Mary (1920-), illus. LC 72-1895. (Illus.). 86 p. 22cm. 1972. (ISBN 0-8407-6250-X). (ISBN 0-8407-6250-X). T. Nelson.
--Wishing Water Gate. LC 49-10493. 212 p. illus., map. 20 cm. 1949. Coward-McCann.

Lyon, Francis Hamilton (1885-), tr. see Hemmer, Jarl.

Lyon, George Ella (1949-)
--Father Time and the Day Boxes. Parker, Robert Andrew (1927-), illus. LC 85-4132. p. cm. 1985. (ISBN 0-02-761370-4). Bradbury Press.

Lyon, Jene
--Our Sun and the Worlds Around It: Planets, Moons, Comets, and Other Wonders of the Solar System. Solenewitsch, George, illus. LC 57-4288. 56p. illus. 29cm. (Fun-to-learn golden book, FL-9). c.1957. Simon and Schuster.

Lyon, Jessica, pseud., see De Leeuw, Cateau Wilhelmina.

Lyon, Kennedy
--The Vagabond Scouts: The Adventures of Duncan Dunn. Cue, Harold, illus. (Bks. of Boy Scouts). N.D. L. C. Page.

Lyon-Villiger, Kati
--Wonderland Stories. 35p. (Orig.). (gr. 6). 1981. (ISBN 0-89260-183-3). Hwong Pub.

Lyons, Barbara Baldwin (1912-)
--Maui Mischievous Hero. 32p. 1969. (ISBN 0-912180-07-2). The Petroglyph Press.

Lyons, Barbara Baldwin (1912-), retold by.
--Fire and Water, and Other Hawaiian Legends. Rice, Betty, illus. LC 72-88932. (Illus.). 91 p. 24cm. 1973. (ISBN 0-8048-1092-3). C. E. Tuttle Co.

Lyons, Dorothy Marawee (1907-)
--Blue Smoke. 1st ed. Dennis, Wesley (1903-1966), illus. LC 53-7867. (Illus.). 244 p. 22cm. (Voyager book, AVB 53). 1953. (ISBN 0-15-613275-3). Harcourt, Brace.
--Bluegrass Champion. Dennis, Wesley (1903-1966), illus. (Illus.). (gr. 4-6). N.D. (ISBN 0-448-02271-0). G&D.
--Bright Wampum. Dennis, Wesley (1903-1966), illus. LC 58-9747. (Illus.). 190 p. 22cm. 1958. Harcourt, Brace.
--Copper Khan. 1st ed. Dennis, Wesley (1903-1966), illus. LC 50-9398. (Illus.). vi, 232 p. 21cm. 1950. Harcourt, Brace.
--Dark Sunshine. 1st ed. Dennis, Wesley (1903-1966), illus. LC 51-11741. 244 p. illus. 21 cm. (Voyager book, AVB 9). 1951. (ISBN 0-15-623936-1). Harcourt, Brace.
--Golden Sovereign. Dennis, Wesley (1903-1966), illus. LC 46-6304. iv, 259 p. incl. illus., plates. 20 1/2 cm. 1946. Harcourt, Brace and Company.
--Harlequin Hullabaloo. 1st ed. Dennis, Wesley (1903-1966), illus. LC 49-5257. vi, 264 p. illus. 21 cm. 1949. Harcourt, Brace.
--Java Jive. LC 55-8679. 214p. illus. 21cm. 1955. Harcourt, Brace.
--Midnight Moon. Nims, W. C., illus. LC 41-15462. 4 p. l., 3-276 p. incl. plates. front. 22 cm. c.1941. Harcourt, Brace and Company.
--Pedigree Unknown. LC 73-5242. 172 p. 21cm. 1973. (ISBN 0-15-260170-8). Harcourt Brace Jovanovich.
--Red Embers. Dennis, Wesley (1903-1966), illus. LC 48-8369. (Illus.). (gr. 7-9). N.D. (ISBN 0-15-266014-3, HJ). HarBraceJ.
--Silver Birch. Taylor, Joan, illus. LC 39-237516. x, 308 p. incl. front., illus., plates. 22 cm. c.1939. Harcourt, Brace and Company.
--Smoke Rings. LC 60-11011. (Illus.). 222 p. 21cm. 1960. Harcourt, Brace.

Lyons, Grant
--Tales the People Tell in Mexico. Antal, Andrew, illus. LC 72-1424. (Illus.). 94 p. 23cm. 1972. (ISBN 0-671-32533-7). J. Messner.

Lyons, John H.
--Stories of Our American Patriotic Songs. Landau, Jacob (1917-), illus. LC 42-24375. (Illus.). (gr. 5-12). N.D. (ISBN 0-8149-0354-1). Vanguard.

Lyons, Kennedy, pseud., see Strong, Paschal Neilson.

Lyons, Mary Frances
--The Town Clock, and Other New Lyrics for Children. LC 37-4461. 47, 1 p. 19 1/2 cm. c.1934. B. Humphries, Inc.

Lyons, Nellie, jt. ed. see Sheldon, William Denley.

Lyons, Oren
--Dog Story. Lyons, Oren, illus. LC 72-92581. (Illus.). 32 p. 22cm. 1973. (ISBN 0-8234-0218-5). Holiday House.

Lyrienne, Richard De see De Lyrienne, Richard.

Lys, Christian, pseud., see Brebner, Percy.

Lys, Christian, pseud.
--Mr Quixley of the GateHouse. Brebner, Percy. (Illus.). N.D. Frederick Warne & Co.

Lysaker, Gene see Grey, Jane, pseud.

Lystad, Mary Hanemann (1928-)
--Halloween Parade. Szekeres, Cyndy (1933-), illus. LC 73-76129. (Illus.). 32 p. 1973. (ISBN 0-399-20358-3). (ISBN 0-399-20358-3). Putnam.
--James the Jaguar. Szekeres, Cyndy (1933-), illus. LC 76-187562. (Illus.). 30 p. 1972. (ISBN 0-399-60750-1). Putnam.
--Jennifer Takes Over P.S. 94. Cruz, Raymond (1933-), illus. LC 79-166990. (Illus.). 30 p. 1972. Putnam.
--Millicent the Monster. Chess, Victoria (1939-), illus. LC 68-18200. (Illus.). 32p. Repr. (Harlin Quist Bks). (gr. 2-5). 1973. (ISBN 0-8252-0105-5). Dial.
--Millicent the Monster. Chess, Victoria (1939-), illus. LC 68-18200. (Illus.). 1 v. (unpaged. 20cm. 1968. H. Quist.
--That New Boy. McCully, Emily Arnold (1939-), illus. LC 72-92384. (Illus.). 32 p. 1973. (ISBN 0-517-50259-3). Crown Publishers.

Lyster, A. A.
--Bryan and Katie. (Illus.). (Girls' Gem Library). N.D. Publication of E. P. Dutton & Co.

Lyster, Annette
--Alone in Crowds. (Illus.). N.D. E & J B Young.
--The Boy Who Never Lost a Chance. (Illus.). (The Steadfast Ser.). N.D. Fleming H Revell.
--Chryssie's Hero. (Illus.). N.D. E & J B Young.
--Daddy's Right Hand (Pub. by Society for Promoting Christian Knowledge). N.D. E. &. J. B. Young & Co.
--Dora and Nora: Or, Dreaming and Doing. N.D. E. & J. B. Young & Co.
--Fan's Silken String. (Illus.). N.D. E & J B Young.
--The Fortunes of Peggy Treherne. N.D. Thomas Whittaker.
--Janet's Boys (Pub. by Society for Promoting Christian Knowledge). N.D. E. & J. B. Young & Co.

McAlpine, William, jt. ed. see McAlpine, Helen.

MacAlvay, Nora Tully

--Beauty & the Beast. (Children's Theatre Playscript Ser.). 1955. (ISBN 0-88020-019-7). Coach Hse.

--Cathie and the Paddy Boy. MacAlvay, Nora Tully, illus. LC 62-962799. 192p. illus. 22cm. 1962. Viking Press.

--Cathie Stuart. MacAlvay, Nora Tully, illus. LC 57-14045. 159p. illus. 22cm. 1957. Viking Press.

--Cathy Stuart. N.D. E . M. Hale and Co.

MacAlvay, Nora Tully, jt. auth. see Chorpenning, Charlotte Lee Barrows.

McAnulla, Jan, jt. auth. see Bertail, Inez.

Macari, Mario, Jr., jt. auth. see Charette, Beverly R.

MacArthur, David Wilson (1903-)

--Traders North. Stobbs, William (1914-), illus. LC 51-11071. 246 p. illus. 22 cm. 1st U.S. edition. 1952, c.1951. Knopf.

Macarthur-Onslow, Annette Rosemary (1933-)

--Minnie. Macarthur-Onslow, Annette Rosemary (1933-), illus. (Illus.). 64p. (gr. 3 up). 1972. (ISBN 0-528-82278-0). Rand.

--Uhu. LC 74-97782. (Illus.). 54 p. 29cm. 1970, c.1969. Knopf.

MacArthur, Ruth Alberta Brown, Mrs. (1881-)

--Daisy: A Book for Girls. LC 19-15734. 3 p. l., 292 p. col. plates (incl. front.) 20 1/2 cm. c.1919. Thomas Y. Crowell Company.

--The Gingerbread House. Longstreet, Harriet Price, illus. N.D. Penn.

--Little Mother. McConnell, Emlen, illus. LC 16-14842. 338 p. col. front., plates. 22 cm. 1916. The Penn Publishing Company.

McAssey, Mary Walfrieda, jt. auth. see Strickland, Catherine Patricia O'Malley.

Macaulay

--Lays of Ancient Rome. (Illus.). (Boys' and Girls' Classics). N.D. Henry Altemus.

Macaulay, Charles Raymond (1871-)

--Fantasma Land. Rev ed. Macaulay, Charles Raymond (1871-), illus. LC 4-9960. 5 p. l., 204 p. front., illus. 20 1/2 cm. 1904. The Bobbs-Merrill Company.

Macaulay, David Alexander (1946-)

--Baaa. Macaulay, David Alexander (1946-), illus. LC 85-2316. (Illus.). 61. 1985. (ISBN 0-395-38948-8). Houghton Mifflin.

--Underground. Macaulay, David Alexander (1946-), illus. (Illus.). 112p. 1983. (ISBN 0-395-34065-9). HM. **Award: (ALA).**

Macaulay, Fannie Caldwell see Little, Frances, pseud.

McAulay, Sara

--In Search of the Petroglyph. LC 78-9290. (Illus.). 170 p. c.1978. (ISBN 0-698-20470-0). Coward, McCann & Geoghegan.

Macauley, Charles Raymond, jt. auth. see Bangs, John Kendrick.

Macauley, James

--Grey Hawk. (Illus.). (St. Nicholas Series for Boys). N.D. International Book Co.

McAuliffe, Jim

--Three Mile House. LC 78-5473. (Illus.). (Pacesetters Ser.). (gr. 4 up). 1978. (ISBN 0-516-02159-1). Childrens.

McAvoy, Katherine T.

--Seymore Snake & Friends: Complete Program. (gr. 3-6). 1981. (ISBN 0-86703-030-5). Opportunities Learn.

--Seymore Snake & Friends: Shadra O'Shay. (gr. 3-6). 1981. (ISBN 0-86703-035-6). Opportunities Learn.

--Seymore Snake & Friends: Theodore Throughly. (gr. 3-6). 1981. (ISBN 0-86703-036-4). Opportunities Learn.

McAvoy, T. J., ed.

--Readings and Recitations for Children, 16 vols. (Ideal Ser.: No. 1). 1905. Set. Bobbs-Merrill Co.

McBain, Ed, pseud., see Hunter, Evan.

McBain, Ed, pseud. (1926-)

--Jack & the Beanstalk. Hunter, Evan. 1984. (ISBN 0-03-062197-6). HR&W.

McBain, Rhoda

--The Bandana Bunny. Crandall, C. Leslie, illus. LC 49-8102. 26 p. col. illus. 26 cm. c.1949. Hollow-Tree House.

--Buzzita. Crandall, C. Leslie, illus. LC 48-21643. 23 p. col. illus. 27 cm. 1948. Hollow Tree House.

MacBeth, George Mann (1932-)

--Jonah and the Lord. Gordon, Margaret (1939-), illus. LC 72-80320. (Illus.). 31 p. 1970. (ISBN 0-03-081612-2). Holt.

--Noah's Journey. Gordon, Margaret (1939-), illus. LC 66-19659. (Illus.). 1 v. (unpaged. 1966. Viking Press.

McBride, Claude D.

--Cyrock. Walmsley, Bertha, illus. (Illus.). 1978. (ISBN 0-682-49147-0). Exposition.

McBride, H. Elliott

--McBride's Latest Dialogues: A Collection of Dialogues, Parlor Dramas, Colloquies, and Amateur Plays Designed for the Use of Young People in Schools. Rogers, Richard, illus. LC 13-18413. 176 p. 19 1/2 cm. (On cover: Fireside series, no. 90). c.1889. J. S. Ogilvie.

McBride, James Lloyd (1882-)

--Golden Glacier. LC 32-24671. vi p., 1 l., 244 p. col. front. 20 1/2 cm. 1932. Doubleday, Doran & Company, Inc.

--The Smoky Valley Claim. Dreany, E. Joseph, illus. LC 49-7261. 260 p. illus. 24 cm. 1948. Caxton Printers.

McBride, Mary Margaret (1899-1976)

--The Growing up of Mary Elizabeth. Bjorklund, Lorence F. (1913-1978), illus. LC 67-1017. (Illus.). 175 p. 24cm. 1966. Dodd, Mead.

--Tune in for Elizabeth: Career Story of a Radio Interviewer. LC 45-10360. 4 p. l., 191 p. 20 1/2 cm. 1945. Dodd, Mead & Company.

McBride, Robert A.

--The Cat That Went Woof. Taylor, Arthur Raymond (1936-), illus. LC 66-10051. 1v. (unpaged) illus. (pt. col.) 24cm. c.1966. Westminster.

McBride, Vaughn, jt. auth. see Sexton, Nancy N.

McBrier, Page

--Oliver and the Lucky Duck. Sims, Blanche, illus. LC 85-8417. p. cm. c.1985. (ISBN 0-8167-0541-0). (ISBN 0-8167-0542-9). Troll Associates.

--Oliver's Lucky Day. Sims, Blanche, illus. LC 85-8437. p. cm. c.1985. (ISBN 0-8167-0538-0). (ISBN 0-8167-0537-2). Troll Associates.

McBrier, Willie Bernice

--Fun for You. 60p. (gr. k-1). N.D. Associated Publishers.

McBrown, Gertrude Parthenia

--The Picture-Poetry Book. LC 36-4191. x, 73 p. incl. front., illus. 22 cm. 1935. The Associated Publishers, Inc.

McBurney, Laressa Cox

--Doctor Charles Wife. (Illus.). N.D. (ISBN 0-8111-0582-2). The Naylor Company.

McCabe, Inger

--Week in Henry's World: El Barrio. McCabe, Inger, illus. LC 78-146609. (Illus.). 45 photos. 48p. (Face to Face Bks.). (gr. k-2). 1971. (ISBN 0-685-00338-8, CCPr). (ISBN 0-02-765380-3, CCPr). Macmillan.

McCabe, Lee

--T-Shirt Tourists. LC 55-5862. 170 p. 21cm. 1955. Dodd, Mead.

McCabe, Lee & Fagan, Norbert

--I'll Take Cappy. Jones, Lois Mailou, illus. LC 48-8408. 160 p. illus. 21 cm. 1948. Whittlesey House.

MacCabe, Lorin, jt. auth. see MacCabe, Naomi.

MacCabe, Naomi (1905-) & MacCabe, Lorin (1904-1949)

--Cable Car Joey. LC 49-9965. 61 p. col. illus. 26 cm. 1949. Stanford Univ. Press.

McCabe, Olivia

--The Rose Fairies. Dunlap, Hope, illus. LC 11-19005. (Illus.). 150p. 23cm. 1911. Rand, McNally & Co.

McCaffery, Janet

--The Swamp Witch. McCaffery, Janet, illus. LC 70-90764. (Illus.). 32 p. 26cm. 1970. W. Morrow.

--The Swamp Witch. McCaffery, Janet, illus. 1973. (ISBN 0-688-21648-X). William Morrow and Company.

McCaffery, M. J. A.

--The Worst Boy in the School. N.D. G. W. Dillingham Co.

McCaffery, William A.

--How to Watch a Parade. McCaffery, William A., illus. (Illus.). (ps-1). 1959. (ISBN 0-06-024116-0). Har-Row.

McCaffrey, Anne (1926-)

--Dragondrums. 1979. Antheum.

--Dragonsinger. LC 76-40988. (Illus.). 264 p. 24cm. 1977. (ISBN 0-689-30570-2). Atheneum.

--A Time When, Being a Tale of Young Lord Jaxom, His White Dragon, Ruth and Various Fire-Lizards. LC 76-356969. (Illus.). 20cm. 76p. c.1975. (ISBN 0-915368-07-2). Nesfa Press.

McCaffrey, Anne (1926-) & Lydecker, Laura

--Dragonsong. LC 75-30530. (Illus.). 202 p. 24cm. 1976. (ISBN 0-689-30507-9). Atheneum. **Award: (ALA).**

McCaffrey, Mary

--My Brother Ange. 1st ed. Saldutti, Denise, illus. LC 81-43887. (Illus.). 86 p. 21cm. c.1982. (ISBN 0-690-04194-2). (ISBN 0-690-04195-0). Crowell.

--My Brother Ange. Saldutti, Denise, illus. (gr. 3-6). 1982. Harper & Row.

McCaig, Robert J.

--That Nester Kid. Papin, Joseph (1914-), illus. LC 61-13375. 191p. illus. 21cm. 1961. Scribner.

McCain, Murray

--The Boy Who Walked off the Page. 1st ed. Smith, Alvin (1933-), illus. LC 69-13369. (Illus.). 47 p. 27cm. 1969. Dutton.

McCaleb, Walter Flavius (1873-1967)

--Bigfoot Wallace. LC 57-20962. 121p. illus. 20cm. c.1956. Naylor Co.

--Ring: A Frontier Dog. Megargee, Edwin, illus. LC 22-71324. xv, 189 p. col. front., illus., plates. 23 cm. 1921. Prentice-Hall, Inc.

McCall, Adeline Denham (1900-)

--Timothy's Tunes. LC 44-1222. vii, 1, 79 p. illus. (part col.) 22 x 28 cm. 1943. The Boston Music Company.

McCall, Barbara

--The Alley Oop Fun Book. Wildman, George & Williams, Bill, illus. (Happy House Bks). (gr. 3-7). N.D. (ISBN 0-394-84785-7). Random.

--Johnny Wonder's Wonderful Book. Wildman, George, illus. (Illus.). (Happy House Bks). (gr. 3-7). N.D. (ISBN 0-394-84786-5). Random.

--The Nancy & Sluggo Fun Book. Wildman, George, illus. (Illus.). (Happy House Bks.). (gr. 3-7). N.D. (ISBN 0-394-84789-X). Random.

--The Three Investigator's Book of Mystery Puzzles. Rao, Anthony, illus. (Illus.). 64p. (The Three Investigators Mystery Ser.). (gr. 3-7). 1982. (ISBN 0-394-85107-2). Random.

McCall, Edith Sansom (1911-)

--Adventures of the American Colonies. Rogers, Carol, illus. LC 61-1547. 125p. illus. (Her Frontiers of America: Supplementary readers in American history). 1961, c.1960. Grosset.

--Bucky Button. LC 53-13309. (Illus.). 48 p. 21cm. (Her The Button books). 1953. Beckley-Cardy.

--Bucky Button. (Button Family Adventures). N.D. Benefic Press.

--Butternut Bill and His Friends. Wiskur, Darrell D., illus. (Illus.). 64 p. 23cm. (Her Butternut Bill series). 1968. Benefic Press.

--Butternut Bill and the Train. Wiskur, Darrell D., illus. LC 71-87128. (Illus.). 64 p. 23cm. (Butternut Bill series). 1969. Benefic Press.

--Buttons and Mr. Pete. N.D. Benefic Press.

--The Buttons and the Boy Scouts. LC 58-14819. (Illus.). 96 p. 21cm. (Her The Button books). 1958. Benefic Press.

--Buttons and the Little League. N.D. Benefic Press.

--The Buttons and the Pet Parade. LC 54-13324. (Illus.). 62 p. 21cm. (Her The Button books). 1955, c.1954. Beckley-Cardy Co.

--The Buttons and the Pet Parade. (Button Family Adventures). N.D. Benefic Press.

--Buttons and the Whirlybird. N.D. Benefic Press.

--The Buttons at the Farm. LC 55-14669. (Illus.). 64 p. 21cm. (Her The Button books). 1955. Beckley-Cardy Co.

--Buttons at the Farm. N.D. Benefic Press.

--The Buttons at the Soap Box Derby. Boyd, Jack (1952-), illus. LC 57-13732. 96p. illus. 21cm. (Her The Button Books). 1957. Benefic Press.

--The Buttons at the Zoo. (Button Family Adventures). N.D. Benefic Press.

--Buttons at the Zoo. N.D. Robert Bentley.

--The Buttons Go Camping. Boyd, Jack (1952-), illus. LC 57-8079. 96p. illus. 21cm. (Her The Button books). 1956. Benefic Press.

--Buttons See Things That Go. (Button Family Adventure Ser.). (gr. k-2). 1960. Benefic.

--Buttons take a Boat Ride. N.D. Benefic Press.

--The Buttons Take a Boat Ride. Boyd, Jack (1952-), illus. LC 57-2424. 64p. illus. 21cm. (Her The Button books). 1957. Benefic Press.

--Cumberland Gap and Trails West. Rogers, Carol, illus. LC 61-10102. x. 126p. (Frontiers of America). 1961. Children's Press.

--Explorers in a New World. Borja, Robert (1923-), illus. LC 60-6675. 123p. illus., map. 22cm. (Her Frontiers of America). c.1960. Childrens Press.

--Explorers in a New World. Borja, Robert (1923-), illus. LC 60-6675. (Illus.). 128p. (Frontiers of America Ser.). (gr. 3-10). 1980. (ISBN 0-516-03318-2). Childrens.

--Gold Rush Adventures. Eckart, Frances, illus. LC 62-9530. 127 (incl. covre) illus. 22cm. (Her Frontiers of America). 1962. Children Press.

--Gold Rush Adventures. Eckart, Frances, illus. LC 62-9530. (Illus.). 128p. (Frontiers of America Ser.). (gr. 3-10). 1980. (ISBN 0-516-03328-X). Childrens.

--Heroes of American Explorations. Borja, Robert (1923-), illus. 123p. illus. (Her Frontiers of America). 1961, c.1960. Grosset.

--Heroes of the Western Outposts. Tanis, William, illus. LC 60-1155. 126p. illus., map. 22cm. (Her Frontiers of America). (gr. 3-8). c.1960. (ISBN 0-516-03331-X). Childrens Press.

--Heroes of Western Outposts. Tanis, William, illus. LC 60-11155. (Illus.). 128p. (Frontiers of America Ser.). (gr. 3-10). 1980. (ISBN 0-516-03331-X). Childrens.

--Hunters Blaze the Trails. Rogers, Carol, illus. LC 59-3666. 125p. illus. 22cm. (Frontiers of America). 1959. Childrens Press.

--Hunters Blaze the Trails. Rogers, Carol, illus. LC 59-3666. (Illus.). 128p. (Frontiers of America Ser.). (gr. 3-10). 1980. (ISBN 0-516-03332-8). Childrens.

--Iron Horses and the Men Who Rode Them. Rogers, Carol, illus. LC 61-1549. (Illus.). 125p. 22cm. (Frontiers of America). Orig. Title: Men on Iron Horses. 1960. Grosset & Dunlop.

--Log Fort Adventures. Rogers, Carol, illus. LC 58-325766. 125p. illus. 22cm. (Frontiers of America). 1958. (ISBN 0-516-03344-1). Childrens Press.

--Mail Riders. 1965. Childrens Press, Inc.

--Mail Riders. Eckart, Frances, illus. LC 61-10103. (Illus.). 128p. (Frontiers of America Ser.). (gr. 3-10). 1980. (ISBN 0-516-03347-6). Childrens.

--Mail Riders: Paul Revere to the Pony Express. Eckart, Frances, illus. LC 61-10103. (Illus.). 125p. 22cm. (Frontiers of America). 1961. Childrens Press.

--Men on Iron Horses. Rogers, Carol, illus. LC 60-676. (Illus.). 125p. 22cm. (Frontiers of America). 1960. Childrens Press.

--Message from the Mountains. LC 85-3142. (Illus.). xi, 122 p., 1 leaf of plates. 22cm. (Walker's American History Series for Young People). c.1985. (ISBN 0-8027-6582-3). Walker.

--Pioneer Show Folk. Rogers, Carol, illus. (Illus.). (gr. 3-8). 1963. (ISBN 0-516-03359-X). Childrens.

--Pioneer Traders. Palm, Felix, illus. LC 64-19885. (Illus.). 127p. 21cm. (Frontiers of America). 1964. Childrens Press.

--Pioneering on the Plains. Rogers, Carol, illus. LC 62-15638. 127p. illus. 22cm. (Her Frontiers of America). 1962. (ISBN 0-516-03358-1). Childrens Press.

--Pioneering on the Plains. Rogers, Carol, illus. LC 62-15638. (Illus.). 128p. (Frontiers of America Ser.). (gr. 3-10). 1980. (ISBN 0-516-03358-1). Childrens.

--Pioneers on Early Waterways: Davy Crockett to Mark Twain. Rogers, Carol, illus. LC 61-101049. 127p. illus. 22cm. (Her Frontiers of America). 1961. Childrens Press.

--Settlers on a Strange Shore. Rogers, Carol, illus. LC 60-111541. 125p. illus., map. 22cm. (Her Frontiers of America). c.1960. Childrens Press.

--Settlers on a Strange Shore. Rogers, Carol, illus. LC 60-11154. (Illus.). 128p. (Frontiers of America Ser.). (gr. 3-10). 1980. (ISBN 0-516-03367-0). Childrens.

--Steamboats to the West. LC 59-3665. 123p. illus. 22cm. (Frontiers of America). 1959. Childrens Press.

--Stories of American Steamboats. Borja, Robert (1923-), illus. LC 61-1723. (Illus.). 123p. 21cm. (Frontiers of America). Orig. Title: Steamboats to the West. N.D. Grosset & Dunlop.

--Wagons Over the Mountains. Rogers, Carol, illus. LC 61-10101. 123p. illus. 22cm. (Her Frontiers of America). 1961. Childrens Press.

--Wagons Over the Mountains. Rogers, Carol, illus. LC 61-10101. (Illus.). 128p. (Frontiers of America Ser.). (gr. 3-10). 1980. (ISBN 0-516-03376-X). Childrens.

McCall, Irma

--Danger Zone. Orig. Title: Perilous Journeys. (gr. 7-9). 1972 (Starline). Schol Bk Serv.

McCall, Oswald W. S.

--The Stringing of the Bow. N.D. Abingdon Press.

McCall, Virginia Nielsen see Nielsen, Virginia, pseud.

McCall, Virginia Nielsen (1909-)

--Adassa and Her Hen. Koering, Ursula (1921-), illus. LC 76-136006. (Illus.). 79 p. 22cm. 1971. D. McKay Co.

--Kimo and Madame Pele: The Story of a Volcanic Eruption. Koering, Ursula (1921-), illus. LC 66-8458. (Illus.). 117 p. 22cm. 1966. D. McKay Co.

--The Mystery of Secret Town. LC 69-13783. vi, 184 p. 21cm. 1969. D. McKay Co.

--Navy Nurse. LC 68-14940. 191 p. 21cm. (Career romance for young moderns). 1968. Messner.

--The Road to the Valley. Earle, Vana (1917-), illus. LC 61-6107. (Illus.). 152p. 21cm. 1961. D. McKay Co.

--The Whistling Wind. LC 63-16696. 152p. 21cm. 1964. D. McKay Co.

McCall, Yvonne Holloway

--The Angry King. Roberts, Jim, illus. (Arch Books: No. 4). (gr. k-2). 1977. (ISBN 0-570-06110-5). Concordia.

--Braggy King of Babylon. (Arch Bks: Set 6). 1969. (ISBN 0-570-06042-7). Concordia.

--The Prince & the Promise. (Illus.). (Arch Bk Ser.: No. 15). (gr. k-3). 1978. (ISBN 0-570-06117-2). Concordia.

--Samir's Midnight Friend: How God Answers Prayer. (Illus.). color ils. 32p. (Orig.). (Arch Bks: Set 8). (ps-4). 1971. (ISBN 0-570-06059-1). Concordia.

--The Story of Barabbas. (Illus.). (Arch Bk.: No. 16). 1979. (ISBN 0-570-06126-1). Concordia.

--The Wicked Trick. (Illus.). 32p. (Arch Bks.: No. 9). (ps-4). 1972. (ISBN 0-570-06068-0). Concordia.

McCall, Yvonne Holloway & Roberts, Jim

--The Angry King: 1 Samuel 18-2 Samuel 5 for Children. LC 76-27365. p. cm. (Arch books ; ser. 14). c.1976. (ISBN 0-570-06110-5). Concordia Pub. House.

McCallen, A. J.

--Listen!. Themes from the Bible Retold for Children. Williams, Ferelith Eccles (1920-), illus. (Illus.). 190p. Repr. of 1976 ed (Pub. by Collins). 1981. (ISBN 0-89283-106-5). Servant.

--Praise!. Songs & Poems from the Bible Retold for Children. (Illus.). 100p. Repr. of 1976 ed (Pub. by Collins). 1981. (ISBN 0-89283-107-3). Servant.

--Praise!. Songs & Poems from the Bible Retold for Children. Williams, Ferelith Eccles (1920-), illus. (Illus.). 96p. (gr. 3 up). 1980. (ISBN 0-529-05738-7). Collins Pubs.

McCallum, George P

--Visitor from Another Planet and Other Plays. Teacher's Ed ed. LC 82-2299. (Illus.). xvi, 167 p. 23cm. 1982. (ISBN 0-19-503167-9). Oxford University Press.

McCampbell, Marie Gertrude, Mrs.

--The Pointsettia: A Christmas Legend. LC 30-1260. viii, 11p. 19cm. 1929. J. J. Little and Ives Company.

McCandless, Hugh Douglas (1907-)

--The Christmas Manger. Little, Mary E. (1912-), illus. 1962. Charles Scribner's Sons.

McCandless, Yvonne

--The Big Indian, How He Came to Go to the Other World. LC 27-15079. 61 p. incl. col. front., illus. (part col.) 23 1/2 cm. ("A just right book"). c.1927. A. Whitman & Co.

McCandlish, Edward Gerstell (1887-)

--The Bunny Tots at the Seashore. McCandlish, Edward Gerstell (1887-), illus. LC 28-10434. 2 p. l., 3-98 p. col. front., illus. 20 1/2 cm. (His Bunny tots' stories). c.1928. A. L. Burt Company.

--The Bunny Tots' Circus Book. McCandlish, Edward Gerstell (1887-), illus. LC 28-101183. 2 p. l., 3-103 p. col. front., illus. 20 1/2 cm. (His Bunny tots' stories). c.1928. A. L. Burt Company.

--The Bunny Tots' Games and Amusements. McCandlish, Edward Gerstell (1887-), illus. LC 28-10121. 3 p. l., 3-104 p. col. front., illus., pl. 21 1/2 cm. (His Bunny tots' stories). c.1928. A. L. Burt Company.

--The Bunny Tots' Rainy Day Book. McCandlish, Edward Gerstell (1887-), illus. LC 28-10117. 2 p. l., 3-103 p. col. front., illus. 20 1/2 cm. (His Bunny tots' stories). c.1928. A. L. Burt Company.

--The Bunny Tots' Snow Book. McCandlish, Edward Gerstell (1887-), illus. LC 28-101201. 2 p. l., 3-100 p. col. front., illus. 20 1/2 cm. (His Bunny tots' stories). c.1928. A. L. Burt Company.

--The Bunny Tots' Window Book. McCandlish, Edward Gerstell (1887-), illus. LC 28-101191. 3 p. l., 3-107 p. col. front., illus. 20 1/2 cm. (His Bunny tots' stories). c.1928. A. L. Burt Company.

McCann, Rebecca

--The Annabel Books. LC 18-7407. 2 v. col. illus. 13 1/2 cm. 1918. Doubleday, Page & Company.

--Children's Cheerful Cherub. Bonner, Mary Graham (1890-1974), ed. LC 32-24059. 63 p. col. illus. 18 1/2 cm. c.1932. Covici, Friede.

McCannon, Dindga

--Peaches. McCannon, Dindga, illus. (Illus.). 96p. (gr. 4 up). 1974. (ISBN 0-688-41658-6). (ISBN 0-688-51658-0). Lothrop.

--Wilhemina Jones, Future Star: A Novel. LC 79-53602. 202 p. 22cm. c.1980. (ISBN 0-440-09857-2). Delacorte Press.

McCarley, Laura

--Welcome to No Man's Valley. Godfrey, Elsa, illus. LC 81-50717. p. cm. 1981. (ISBN 0-394-84878-0). Random House.

Maccarone, Grace, jt. auth. see Weyn, Suzanne.

Maccarone, Grace & Weyn, Suzanne

--The Little Winner. Clarke, Bob, illus. (Illus.). 32p. (Orig.). (Little Mini Bks.). (ps-3). 1984. (ISBN 0-590-33153-1). Scholastic Inc.

--The Littles Move In. Clarke, Bob, illus. (Illus.). 32p. (Orig.). (Littles Mini Bks.). (ps-3). 1984. (ISBN 0-590-33152-3). Scholastic Inc.

McCarrick, Elizabeth, jt. auth. see Adams, Florence.

McCarroll, Marion Clyde, jt. auth. see Farnam, Suzanne Silveruys.

McCarter, Margaret Hill

--Cuddy's Baby. (Sunflower Ser.). N.D. A. C. McClurg.

McCarthy, Agnes (1933-)

--The Impossibles. 1st ed. Gainsford, illus. LC 68-10188. 108 p. 22cm. 1968. Doubleday.

--Room Ten. Ohlsson, Ib (1935-), illus. LC 66-8826. 71p. illus. 22cm. 1966. Doubleday.

--Room Ten. 1st ed. Ohlsson, Ib (1935-), illus. LC 66-10727. (Illus.). 11 linecuts. 72p. (Zephyr Bk Ser). (ps-5). 1971. (ISBN 0-385-08810-8). Doubleday.

MacCarthy, D. & Guiness, B. W.

--Story of a Nutcracker. N.D. W. S. Heinman.

McCarthy, Eugene Joseph (1916-)

--Mr. Raccoon and His Friends. Ecklund, James, illus. LC 77-20506. (Illus.). 119 p. 24cm. c.1977. (ISBN 0-915864-17-7). Acacdemy Press.

McCarthy, Frances Boyle

--A Peek Through My Window. N.D. Vantage Press.

McCarthy, Gerald (1947-)

--War Story: Vietnam War Poems. LC 77-23320. p. cm. (Crossing Press series of new poets). c.1977. (ISBN 0-912278-87-0). (ISBN 0-912278-86-2). Crossing Press.

MacCarthy, Josephine

--In the Air. Publisher's Photo Service, photos by. LC 35-174. (Illus.). 62p. 16cm. 1935. Whitman Publishing.

--Noah's Ark, with Stories. LC 35-17241. 50 p. col. illus. 31 1/2 cm. c.1935. Whitman Publishing Company.

McCarthy, Margery Sybil see Colman, Margery, pseud.

McCarthy, Mary

--Lydia Longley: The First American Nun. Lawn, John, illus. 192p. (Vision Bk.: No. 29). 1958. Farrar, Straus & Giroux.

McCarthy, Patricia, ed. see Arnold, Joanne M.

McCarthy, Patricia, ed. see Bacon, Jo A.

McCarthy, Patricia, ed. see Schwach, Howard.

McCarthy, Patricia, ed. see Townsend, Marvin.

McCarthy, Ruth

--Katie and the Smallest Bear. Boon, Emilie, illus. LC 85-9791. p. cm. 1st U.S. edition. c.1985. (ISBN 0-394-87855-8). (ISBN 0-394-97855-2). Knopf : Distributed by Random House.

McCarthy, T. J.

--Daddy's Darling. N.D. (ISBN 0-8283-1491-8). Branden Press.

McCartney, Dorothy W.

--Lemmus Lemmus And Other Poems. N.D. (ISBN 0-8283-1487-X). Branden Press.

McCarty, Edward Clayton (1901-) & McCarty, Sara Sloane, Mrs. (1905-)

--Star Bright, and Four Other Short Plays for the Teens. LC 38-34195. vi, 169 p. diagrs. 21 cm. c.1938. Row, Peterson & Company.

M'Carty, J. Hendrickson

--Inside the Gates. N.D. Methodist Book Concern.

McCarty, Rega Kramer (1904-)

--Brenda Becomes a Buyer. LC 60-12447. 191p. 22cm. (Career romance for young moderns). 1960. J. Messner.

--Lorna Evans, Social Worker. LC 61-13826. 192 p. 21cm. (Career romance for young moderns). 1961. Messner.

McCarty, Sara Sloane, Mrs., jt. auth. see McCarty, Edward Clayton.

McCarty, Toni

--The Skull in the Snow, and Other Folktales. Coville, Katherine (1939-), illus. LC 80-68730. (Illus.). vii, 87 p. 24cm. c.1981. (ISBN 0-440-08028-2). (ISBN 0-440-08030-4). Delacorte Press.

McCasland, Dave

--The Culture Trap. (gr. 9-12). 1982. (ISBN 0-88207-191-2). Victor Bks.

McCaslin, Nellie (1914-)

--Little Snow Girl. (Children's Theatre Playscript Ser.). 1963. (ISBN 0-88020-037-5). Coach Hse.

--The Rabbit Who Wanted Red Wings. (Children's Theatre Playscript Ser.). 1963. (ISBN 0-88020-045-6). Coach Hse.

--Theatre for Young Audiences. LC 77-17710. (Illus.). x, 182 p. 25cm. c.1978. (ISBN 0-582-28011-7). Longman.

McCaughwean, Genildine

--One Thousand & One Arabian Nights. (Oxford Illustrated Classics Ser.). N.D. (ISBN 0-318-01962-0, Pub. by Oxford U Pr Childrens). Merrimack Pub Cir.

MacCauley, Billy Ray

--Cinderella: An Original Version. LC 76-383891. (Illus.). 55 p. 42cm. c.1976. (ISBN 0-916378-07-1). Oasis Press : Distributed by Publishing Services.

McCauley, Mary Weaver, Mrs., jt. auth. see Cuddy, Lucy Alsanson, Mrs.

McCauseland, Eric & McCauseland, Marjorie Musgrave

--Bugs, Bunty!. LC 35-4530. (Illus.). 28p. 22cm. 1934. Suttonhouse Publishers.

McCauseland, Marjorie Musgrave, jt. auth. see McCauseland, Eric.

McCaw, Mabel Niedermeyer (1899-)

--I Know What Love Is. Hoecker, Hazel, illus. (Illus.). 32 p. 21cm. 1968, c.1967. Broadman Press.

--My Friend Next Door. Gibson, Mary Richards, illus. LC 68-26111. (Illus.). 32 p. 21cm. 1968. Bethany Press.

--Orange Juice for Terry. Teichman, Dorothy, illus. LC 62-7101. (Illus.). (ps). 1962. (ISBN 0-8054-4122-0). (ISBN 0-686-66385-3). Broadman.

--Orange Juice for Terry. Teichman, Dorothy, illus. LC 62-7101. unpaged. illus. 21cm. c.1962. Broadman Press.

--Our Happy Family. Pointer, Priscilla, illus. LC 58-9107. unpaged. illus. 22cm. c.1958. Bethany Press.

McCay, Winsor Silas (1869-1934)

--Dreams of the Rarebit Fiend. N.D. Frederick A. Stokes Co.

--Little Sammy Sneeze. (Illus.). N.D. Frederick A. Stokes Co.

MacClain, George, jt. auth. see Ames, Lee Judah.

McClain, Jane

--Mug & the Brown Cow. 30p. (Orig.). (gr. 1up). 1983. (ISBN 0-8024-0271-2). Moody.

McClain, Mary, illus.

--Hansel & Gretel. 10p. (Carousel Bks.). (ps-2). N.D. (ISBN 0-8431-0901-7). Price Stern.

McClarren, J. K.

--Mexican Assignment. (gr. 7-11). 1957. Funk & W.

McClary, Jane Stevenson see McIlvaine, Jane.

McClausland, Clare, jt. auth. see Jewett, Frances

McCleary, Cornelia Walter

--The Celestial Circus. LC 21-7882. xii p., 1 l., 89 p. front., illus. 22 1/2 cm. c.1920. The Cornhill Company.

McCleary, Fione

--American Songs for Children. Palmer, Winthrop Bushnell, Mrs., ed. Cady, Walter Harrison (1877-1970), illus. LC 31-28053. 5 p. l., 61, 3 p. illus., pl. 23 x 29 cm. 1931. The Macmillan Company.

McCleery, William Thomas (1911-)

--Wolf Story. 1st ed. Chappell, Warren (1904-), illus. LC 47-30394. 4 l., 3-82 p. illus. 20 cm. 1947. A. A. Knopf.

--Wolf Story. Chappell, Warren (1904-), illus. 1961. Simon and Schuster.

McClellan, Jack, et al. (1912-)

--Where Is Home. (Illus.). drawings 156p. 1st U.S. edition. (Citizens All Ser). (gr. 4-6). 1970. HM.

McClellan, Jack & Black, Millard H. (1912-)

--A Blind Man Can!. Lewin, Ted (1935-), illus. LC 68-264. (Illus.). 124 p. 25cm. (Citizens all series). 1968. Houghton Mifflin.

--Up, Out, and Over!. Lewin, Ted (1935-), illus. LC 76-5573. (Illus.). 156 p. 25cm. (Citizens all series). 1969. Houghton Mifflin.

McClelland, Herbert L.

--Secret Flower of Rantan. LC 82-71949. (Illus.). 60p. (Rantan Stories: No. 1). (gr. k-5). 1982. (ISBN 0-943864-10-0). Davenport.

McClelland, Hugh

--The Bold Bad Buccaneers. LC 68-15439. 59p. col. lilus. 21x26cm. 1968. Macmillan.

--The Magic Lassoo. McClelland, Hugh, illus. LC 63-7473. (Illus.). 24cm. 1963. St. Martin's Press.

McClelland, Mary Greenway (1853-1895)

--Sam. Nagel, Eva M., illus. LC 6-41720. 1 p. l., vii-ix p., 1 l., 13-146 p. incl. illus., plates. front. 18 1/2 cm. 1906. Henry Altemus Company.

McClenathan, Louise

--The Easter Pig. Hoffman, Rosekrans (1926-), illus. LC 82-2249. (Illus.). 36 p. 1982. (ISBN 0-688-01445-3). (ISBN 0-688-01446-1). Morrow.

--My Mother Sends Her Wisdom. 1st ed. Hoffman, Rosekrans (1926-), illus. LC 79-164. (Illus.). 32 p. 1979. (ISBN 0-688-22193-9). (ISBN 0-688-32193-3). Morrow.

McClendon, Marie Millicent Dancy, Mrs. (1900-)

--Mystery Camp. Rev ed. Martin, P. L., illus. LC 26-5386. 7 p. l., 306 p. front., plates. 19 1/2 cm. c.1926. L. C. Page & Company.

--Secrets Inside. Rev ed. Freeman, Dean, illus. LC 28-256271. 5 p. l., 315 p. front., plates. 19 1/2 cm. 1928. L. C. Page & Company.

McClintock, Gray

--Itinerants of the Timber Lands. LC 34-5167. 285, 1 p. 19 1/2 cm. c.1934. Thomas Y. Crowell Company.

McClintock, Inez Bertail see Bertail, Inez.

McClintock, Letitia

--Cottagers of Glencarren, 1 of 25 vols. (Illus.). (Selected Bks for Sunday School: No. 24). N.D. Set. Methodist Bk Concern.

--A Little Candle, and Other Stories. N.D. Thomas Nelson & Sons.

McClintock, Marshall see Duncan, Gregory, pseud.

McClintock, Marshall see McClintock, Mike, pseud.

McClintock, Mike, pseud., see McClintock, Marshall.

McClintock, Mike, pseud. (1906-1967)

--David & the Giant. McClintock, Marshall. Siebel, Fritz (1913-), illus. LC 60-11196. (Illus.). (I Can Read Books). (gr. k-3). 1960. (ISBN 0-06-024126-8, HarpJ). (ISBN 0-06-024125-X). Har-Row.

--A Fly Went by. McClintock, Marshall. Siebel, Fritz (1913-), illus. LC 58-9018. (Illus.). 62 p. 24cm. (Beginner books, 3). 1958. Beginner Books; Distributed by Random House.

--Stop That Ball!. McClintock, Marshall. Siebel, Fritz (1913-), illus. LC 59-9741. (Illus.). 62 p. 24cm. (Beginner books B-10). c.1959. Beginner Books; Distributed by Random House.

--What Have I Got. McClintock, Marshall. Kessler, Leonard P. (1921-), illus. LC 60-11197. (Illus.). (Early I Can Read Books). (gr. k-2). 1961. (ISBN 0-06-024141-1, HarpJ). Har-Row.

McClintock, Theodore (1902-1971), tr. see Neumann, Rudolf.

McClintock, Theodore (1902-1971), tr. see Wimmer, Hedwig

McClinton, Leon (1933-)

--Cross-Country Runner. LC 73-15934. 217 p. 22cm. 1974. (ISBN 0-525-28375-7). Dutton.

McCloskey, John Robert (1914-1969)

--Blueberries for Sal. McCloskey, John Robert (1914-1969), illus. LC 48-4955. 54 p. illus. 23 x 29 cm. 1948. Viking Press. **Award: (RCM).**

--Burt Dow, Deep-Water Man: A Tale of the Sea in the Classic Tradition. McCloskey, John Robert (1914-1969), illus. (Illus.). 61 p. 30cm. 1963. Viking Press.

--Centerburg Tales. McCloskey, John Robert (1914-1969), illus. LC 77-21458. p. cm. 1977, c.1951. (ISBN 0-14-031072-X). Puffin Books.

--Centerburg Tales. McCloskey, John Robert (1914-1969), illus. LC 51-10675. 190 p. 24cm. 1951. Viking Press.

--Homer Price. LC 76-39988. p. cm. (Puffin books). 1976, c.1943. (ISBN 0-14-030927-6). Penguin Books.

--Homer Price. McCloskey, John Robert (1914-1969), illus. LC 43-16001. (Illus.). 149 p. 24cm. 1943. The Viking Press.

--Lentil. McCloskey, John Robert (1914-1969), illus. LC 77-26192. (Illus.). 61 p. 23cm. (Picture puffin). 1978, c.1940. (ISBN 0-14-050287-4). Puffin Books.

--Lentil. McCloskey, John Robert (1914-1969), illus. LC 40-8617. (Illus.). 61 p. 31cm. 1940. The Viking Press.

--Make Way for Ducklings. 67p. illus. 31x24cm. 1959. The Viking Press.

--Make Way for Ducklings. McCloskey, John Robert (1914-1969), illus. LC 41-51868. 67 p. illus. 31 x 23 1/2 cm. 1941. The Viking Press. **Award: (RCM).**

--One Morning in Maine. McCloskey, John Robert (1914-1969), illus. 1952. Viking. **Award: (RCM).**

--Time of Wonder. McCloskey, John Robert (1914-1969), illus. LC 76-54741. (Illus.). 64p. (gr. k-3). 1977, c.1957. (ISBN 0-14-050201-7, Puffin). Penguin.

--Time of Wonder. McCloskey, John Robert (1914-1969), illus. LC 57-14197. 63p. illus. 31cm. 1957. Viking Press. **Awards: (RCM); (ALA).**

MacCloud, Malcolm

--A Gift of Mirrovax. LC 81-1399. p. cm. 1981. (ISBN 0-689-30849-3). Atheneum.

--The Tera Beyond. LC 80-36728. (Illus.). 190 p. 22cm. (Argo book). 1981. (ISBN 0-689-30817-5). Atheneum.

McCloy, Helen Worell Clarkson (1904-)

--The Deadly Truth. LC 41-8172. 4 p. l., 3-278 p. 19 1/2 cm. 1941. W. Morrow and Company.

McClung, Robert Marshall (1916-)

--Black Jack, Last of the Big Alligators. Sandford, Lloyd, illus. LC 67-20983. (Illus.). 63 p. 22cm. 1967. Morrow.

--Blaze: The Story of a Striped Skunk. McClung, Robert Marshall (1916-), illus. LC 76-76982. (Illus.). 48 p. 22cm. 1969. Morrow.

--Bufo: The Story of a Toad. McClung, Robert Marshall (1916-), illus. LC 54-6258. (Illus.). 40 p. 22cm. 1954. Morrow.

--Buzztail: The Story of a Rattlesnake. McClung, Robert Marshall (1916-), illus. LC 58-514271. (Illus.). 64 p. 22cm. (Morrow junior books). 1958. W. Morrow.

--Green Darner: The Story of a Dragonfly. McClung, Robert Marshall (1916-), illus. LC 56-7623. (Illus.). 48 p. 22cm. (Morrow junior books). 1956. Morrow.

--Honker: The Story of a Wild Goose. Hines, Robert W., illus. LC 65-104422. (Illus.). 63 p. 22cm. 1965. Morrow.

--Horseshoe Crab. McClung, Robert Marshall (1916-), illus. (Illus.). 48 p. 22cm. 1967. W. Morrow.

--Ladybug. McClung, Robert Marshall (1916-), illus. LC 66-14752. (Illus.). 22cm. 48p. (gr. k-3). 1966. (ISBN 0-688-35010-0). (ISBN 0-688-35009-7). Morrow.

--Leaper: The Story of an Atlantic Salmon. McClung, Robert Marshall (1916-), illus. LC 57-5120. 61p. illus. 22cm. (Morrow junior books). (gr. 3-6). 1957. (ISBN 0-688-31529-1). Morrow.

--Little Burma. Stubblefield, Hord, illus. LC 58-8003. 256p. illus. 21cm. 1958. Morrow.

--Luna: The Story of a Moth. McClung, Robert Marshall (1916-), illus. LC 57-8561. 45p. 22cm. (Morrow Junior Books). 1957. Morrow.

--Major, the Story of a Black Bear. 64p. 1956. Morrow.

--Major: The Story of a Black Bear. McClung, Robert Marshall (1916-), illus. (Illus.). (gr. 4-6). 1956. (ISBN 0-688-31506-2). Morrow.

--Major: The Story of a Black Bear. McClung, Robert Marshall (1916-), illus. LC 56-5182. 64p. illus. 22cm. (gr. 4-6). 1956. (ISBN 0-688-31506-2). W. Morrow.

--Mighty Bears. (Illus.). (Gateway Ser: No. 41). (gr. 2-4). 1967. (ISBN 0-394-90141-X, BYR). Random.

--Otus: The Story of a Screech Owl. Sandford, Lloyd, illus. LC 59-7932. (Illus.). 47 p. 22cm. (Morrow junior books). 1959. Morrow.

--Possum. McClung, Robert Marshall (1916-), illus. (Illus.). 47 p. 22cm. 1963. Morrow.

--Redbird: The Story of a Cardinal. McClung, Robert Marshall (1916-), illus. LC 68-14805. (Illus.). 21cm. 47p. 1968. W. Morrow.

--Ruby Throat: The Story of a Humming Bird. McClung, Robert Marshall (1916-), illus. LC 50-4796. (Illus.). 48 p. 22cm. (Morrow junior books). 1950. Morrow.

--Samson, Last of the California Grizzlies. Hines, Robert W., illus. (Illus.). 96p. (gr. 3-7). 1973. (ISBN 0-688-21935-7). (ISBN 0-688-31935-1). Morrow.

--Scoop, Last of the Brown Pelicans. Sandford, Lloyd & McClung, Robert Marshall (1916-), illus. LC 70-168474. (Illus.). 63 p. 22cm. 1972. Morrow.

--Screamer, Last of the Eastern Panthers. Sandford, Lloyd, illus. LC 64-10508. (Illus.). 64 p. 22cm. 1964. W. Morrow.

--Shag. Darling, Louis, Jr. (1916-1970), illus. LC 60-6512. 96p. illus. 22cm. 1960. Morrow.

--Shag, Last of the Plains Buffalo. Darling, Louis, Jr. (1916-1970), illus. (Illus.). (gr. 3-7). 1960. (ISBN 0-688-31800-2). Morrow.

--Sphinx: The Story of a Caterpillar. McClung, Robert Marshall (1916-), illus. LC 49-100067. 48 p. illus. (part col.) 22 cm. (Morrow junior books). 1949. W. Morrow.

--Spike: The Story of a Whitetail Deer. McClung, Robert Marshall (1916-), illus. LC 52-5936. 63 p. illus. 22 cm. (Morrow junior books). 1952. Morrow.

--Spotted Salamander. McClung, Robert Marshall (1916-), illus. (Illus.). 47 p. 22cm. 1964. W. Morrow.

--Stripe: The Story of a Chipmunk. McClung, Robert Marshall (1916-), illus. LC 51-11438. (Illus.). 48 p. 22cm. (Morrow junior books). 1951. Morrow.

--Thor, Last of the Sperm Whales. Hines, Robert W., illus. LC 71-134485. (Illus.). 62 p. 22cm. 1971. Morrow.

--Tiger: The Story of a Swallowtail Butterfly. McClung, Robert Marshall (1916-), illus. (Illus.). 44 p. 22cm. (Morrow junior books). 1953. Morrow.

--Vulcan: The Story of a Bald Eagle. Sandford, Lloyd, illus. LC 55-6912. (Illus.). 63 p. 22cm. 1955. Morrow.

--Whitefoot: The Story of a Wood Mouse. McClung, Robert Marshall (1916-), illus. LC 61-11219. (Illus.). 22cm. 48p. (gr. 1-5). 1961. Morrow.

--Whooping Crane. Sandford, Lloyd, illus. LC 59-5137. (Illus.). 63 p. 22cm. (Morrow junior books). 1959. Morrow.

--Wings in the Woods. McClung, Robert Marshall (1916-), illus. LC 48-7694. 251 p. illus. 21 cm. 1948. W. Morrow.

McClure, Gillian Mary (1948-)

--Fly Home McDoo. McClure, Gillian Mary (1948-), illus. LC 79-64312. (Illus.). 32 p. 26cm. 1979. (ISBN 0-233-97108-4). Deutsch.

--Prickly Pig. McClure, Gillian Mary (1948-), illus. (Illus.). (ps-1). 1980. (ISBN 0-233-96780-X). Andre Deutsch.

McClure, James Gore King (1848-)

--Grandfather Tells Some More Stories by Request ... LC 28-7171. 3 p. l., 117 p. 19 1/2 cm. c.1928. R. R. Donnelley & Sons Co.

--Grandfather Tells Some Stories As a Pastime ... LC 27-1313. 3 p. l., 72 p., 1 l. 19 cm. c.1926. Printed by R. R. Donnelley & Sons Co.

McCluskey, John, ed.

--Stories from Black History: Nine Stories, 5 vols. Incl. Mr. Impossible. Gaines, Edith (gr. 5 up). (ISBN 0-913678-12-0, 205); Can You Count, 2 vols in 1. Ceasor, Frank G., Sr. (gr. 5 up). (ISBN 0-913678-11-2, 204); Little Jess and the Circus"Forty Acre", 2 Vols in 1. Shepard, Mary ("Little Jess and the Circus" bound with "Forty Acres"). (gr. 5 up). (ISBN 0-913678-10-4, 203); Jubilee Day "Wildfire", 2 Vols in 1. Gaines, Edith & Smith, Martha ("Jubilee Day" bound with "Wildfire"). (gr. 5 up). (ISBN 0-913678-09-0); Henry Box Brown "Struggle for Freedom", 2 Vols in 1. Pruitt, Pamela & Johnston, Brenda ("Henry Box Brown" bound with "Struggle for Freedom"). (gr. 5 up). (ISBN 0-913678-08-2, 201). (Illus., Orig.). (Series 2). 1975. (ISBN 0-913678-07-4). New Day Pr.

MacColl, Ewan

--Dawn of Love. (gr. 7 up). 1978. (ISBN 0-685-47064-4, Schol Pap). Schol Bk Serv.

McConathy, Osbourne

--Favorite Songs from Shakespeare. N.D. Silver,Burdett & Co.

McConnell, Dorothy F

--Uncle Sam's Family. Peirson, Katharine, illus. LC 24-28674. 5 p. l, 13-125 p. illus. 19 cm. c.1924. Coucil of Women for Home Missions and Missionary Education Movement.

McConnell, James Douglas Rutherford (1915-)

--The Gunshot Grand Prix. LC 73-90296. 184 p. 22cm. 1974, c.1972. Bradbury Press.

--Killer on the Track. 1st ed. LC 73-94114. 190 p. 22cm. (gr. 6-8). 1974, c.1973. (ISBN 0-87888-070-4). Bradbury Press.

--Rally to the Death. LC 75-891. (Illus.). 166 p. 22cm. (Checkered flag series). 1975, c.1974. (ISBN 0-87888-084-4). Bradbury Press.

McConnell, Jane Tompkins (1898-)

--The Beaver Twins. Comstock, Enos Benjamin (1879-1945), illus. LC 40-31355. vii, 112 p. illus. 21 1/2 x 16 cm. 1940. Frederick A. Stokes Company.

--The Beaver Twins. Comstock, Enos Benjamin (1879-1945), illus. 1940. J. B. Lippincott Co.

--The Black Bear Twins. 1st ed. Wiese, Kurt (1887-1974), illus. LC 52-7460. 112p. illus. 22cm. 1952. Lippincott.

--Moo-Wee, the Musk-Ox. Rev ed. Wiese, Kurt (1887-1974), illus. LC 38-29560. xi, 103p. illus. 22cm. 1938. F. A. Stokes Co.

--The Other Twins. 1st ed. Wiese, Kurt (1887-1974), illus. LC 55-7992. 120p. illus. 22cm. 1955. Lippincott.

--The Porcupine Twins. 1st ed. Wiese, Kurt (1887-1974), illus. LC 54-7129. 120p. illus. 22cm. 1954. Lippincott.

--The Red Squirrel Twins. 1st ed. Wiese, Kurt (1887-1974), illus. LC 50-14874. 123p. illus. 22cm. 1950. Lippincott.

--The Reindeer Twins. 1st ed. Wiese, Kurt (1887-1974), illus. LC 56-9268. 125p. illus. 22cm. 1956. Lippincott.

--Two Pennies Overboard: A Story of Nantucket Island. 1st ed. Norton, Natalie, illus. LC 48-3293. 175 p. illus., map. 21 cm. 1948. J. B. Lippincott Co.

McConnell, Margaret

--Bobo the Barrage Balloon. Gergely, Tibor (1900-1978), illus. LC 43-9928. 1, 36, 4 p. col. front., illus. (part col.) 25 cm. c.1943. Lothrop, Lee & Shepard Co.

McConnell, William (1833-1867)

--Pippins & Pies: Or, Sketches Out of School. Being the Adventures and Misadventures of Master Frank Pickleberry During That Month He Was Home for the Holidays. McConnell, William, illus. LC 42-33509. 2 p. l., 186 p. front., illus., plates. 17 1/2 cm. 1855. G. Routledge & Co.

McCook, Henry Christopher (1837-1911)

--Old Farm Fairies. (Illus.). N.D. Fords, Howard, & Hulbert.

--Old Farm Fairies. Beard, Daniel Carter, et al. (1859-1941), illus. (Illus.). 432p. N.D. George W. Jacobs & Co.

--Old Farm Fairies: A Summer Campaign in Brownie-Land, Against King Cobweaver's Pixies. A Story for Young People. LC 12-36412. xxxvi, 302 p. illus. 19 cm. 1895. G. W. Jacobs & Co.

McCord, David Thompson Watson (1897-)

--All Day Long. Kane, Henry Bugbee (1902-1971), illus. (Illus.). (Fifty new verses to delight readers of all ages). (gr. 5 up). 1966. (ISBN 0-316-55508-8). Little.

--All Day Long: Fifty Rhymes of the Never Was and Always Is. 1st ed. Kane, Henry Bugbee (1902-1971), illus. LC 66-17688. xii, 104p. illus. 21cm. 1966. Little.

--Away & Ago. Morrill, Leslie H., illus. (Illus.). 96p. (gr. 4 up). 1975. (ISBN 0-316-55513-4). Little.

--Away and Ago: Rhymes of the Never Was and Always Is. 1st ed. Morrill, Leslie H., illus. LC 74-14642. (Illus.). xii, 83 p. 21cm. 1974. (ISBN 0-316-55513-4). Little, Brown.

--Every Time I Climb a Tree. 1st ed. Simont, Marc (1915-), illus. LC 67-25611. (Illus.). 1 v. (unpaged. 27cm. 1967. Little, Brown.

--Far & Few. Kane, Henry Bugbee (1902-1971), illus. (Illus.). (Fifty-odd poems-the kind children like to hear & say). (gr. 3 up). 1952. (ISBN 0-316-55502-9). Little.

--Far and Few: Rhymes of the Never Was and Always Is. LC 52-8336. 90 p. illus. 21 cm. 1952. Little,Brown.

--For Me to Say. Kane, Henry Bugbee (1902-1971), illus. (Illus.). (gr. 5 up). 1970. (ISBN 0-316-55511-8). Little.

--For Me to Say: Rhymes of the Never Was and Always Is. 1st ed. Kane, Henry Bugbee (1902-1971), illus. LC 76-122534. (Illus.). x, 100 p. 21cm. 1970. Little, Brown.

--One at a Time: Collected Poems for the Young. Kane, Henry Bugbee (1902-1971), illus. (Illus.). (gr. 4 up). 1977. (ISBN 0-316-55516-9). Little.

--One at a Time: His Collected Poems for the Young. Kane, Henry Bugbee (1902-1971), illus. 1977. Little.

--Pen, Paper and Poem. 1973. Holt Rinehart.

--Speak Up: More Rhymes of the Never Was and Always Is. 1st ed. Simont, Marc (1915-), illus. LC 80-15260. p. cm. c.1980. (ISBN 0-316-55517-7). Little, Brown.

--The Star in the Pail. Simont, Marc (1915-), illus. (Illus.). 48p. (gr. 1-3). 1975. (ISBN 0-316-55515-0). Little.

--The Star in the Pail: Poems. 1st ed. Simont, Marc (1915-), illus. LC 75-15605. p. cm. 1975. (ISBN 0-316-55515-0). Little, Brown.

--Take Sky. Kane, Henry Bugbee (1902-1971), illus. (Illus.). (gr. 4 up). 1962. (ISBN 0-316-55509-6). Little.

--Take Sky: More Rhymes of the Never Was and Always Is. LC 62-12392. (Illus.). 107 p. 21cm. 1962. Little, Brown.

McCord, Jean (1924-)

--Bitter Is the Hawk's Path. LC 71-154756. 149 p. 22cm. 1971. Atheneum.

--Deep Where the Octopi Lie. LC 68-18451. 192p. (gr. 7 up). 1968. (ISBN 0-689-20255-5). (ISBN 0-689-20256-3). Atheneum.

--Turkeylegs Thompson. LC 78-12174. 242 p. 22cm. 1979. (ISBN 0-689-30686-5). Atheneum.

McCorkle, Lutie Andrews, Mrs.

--Old Time Stories of the Old North State. LC 3-4198. vi, 159 p. front. (map) illus. 18 1/2 cm. 1903. D. C. Heath & Co.

--Old Time Stories of the Old North State. LC 21-22325. vi, 163 p. front., illus., map. 19 cm. N.D. D. C. Heath & Co.

McCorkle, Ruth, ed.

--The Alaskan Ten-Footed Bear, and Other Legends. Walluk, Wilbur, illus. LC 58-12559. (Illus.). 39 p. 23cm. 1958. R.D. Seal.

McCormack, John E.

--Rabbit Travels. Cherry, Lynne (1952-), illus. LC 83-14075. (Illus.). 24p. (Unicorn Bk.). (ps-3). 1984. (ISBN 0-525-44087-9). (ISBN 0-525-44087-9). Dutton.

McCormack, John E & Oliver, Jenni

--Rabbit Tales. LC 79-20089. (Illus.). 40 p. (Unicorn book). c.1980. (ISBN 0-525-38005-1). Dutton.

McCormack, Marie Elizabeth

--Growing Gains. N.D. Pageant Press Inc.

McCormick, Alma Heflin

--Merry Makes a Choice. LC 49-1259. 243 p. illus. 20 cm. 1949. Little, Brown.

McCormick, Brooks, pseud., see Adams, William Taylor.

McCormick, Brooks, pseud. (1822-1897)

--The Giant Islanders. Adams, William Taylor. (The Boys Own Library). N.D. David McKay.

--How He Won. Adams, William Taylor. (The Boys Own Library). N.D. David McKay.

--How He Won. Adams, William Taylor. 18cm. 238p. (Medal Library: No. 62). 1900. Street & Smith.

--Nature's Young Nobleman. Adams, William Taylor. (The Boys Own Library). N.D. David McKay.

--Nature's Young Nobleman. Adams, William Taylor. (Illus.). (St. Nicholas Series for Boys). N.D. International Book Co.

--Rival Battalions. Adams, William Taylor. (The Boys Own Library). N.D. David McKay.

--The Rival battalions. Adams, William Taylor. LC 1-29254. 18cm. 300p. (Medal Library: No. 79). 1900. Street & Smith.

McCormick, Dell J., jt. auth. see Malcolmson, Anne Burnett, Mrs.

McCormick, Dell J. (1892-1949)

--Paul Bunyan Swings His Axe. 1960. Caxton.

--Paul Bunyan Swings His Axe. N.D. E. M. Hale and Co.

--Paul Bunyan Swings His Axe. McCormick, Dell J. (1892-1949), illus. LC 36-33409. 111 p. incl. col., front., illus. 23 1/2 cm. 1936. The Caxton Printers, Ltd.

--Tall Timber Tales: More Paul Bunyan Stories. Livesley, Lorna, illus. LC 39-20778. 155 p. incl. col. front., illus., plates. 23 1/2 cm. 1939. The Caxton Printers, Ltd.

McCormick, Edith Joan (1934-), tr. see Nygaard, Jakob Johannes Bech.

McCormick, Edith Joan (1934-), tr. see Winterfeld, Henry.

McCormick, Jo M.

--Etti-Cat, the Courtesy Cat. (Illus.). (ps-3). 1965. (ISBN 0-8038-1886-6). Hastings.

McCormick, Leander James (1888-), tr. see McCormick, Renee De Fontarce.

McCormick, Renee De Fontarce (1899-)

--Little Coquette: The Story of a French Girlhood. Suba, Susanne (1913-), illus. McCormick, Leander James (1888-), tr. LC 44-6129. 5 p. l., 3-295 p. front., plates. 20 1/2 cm. 1944. Houghton Mifflin Company.

McCormick, Rose Matthew

--My Care and Share Book: An Around-the-World Picture Story. LC 74-98408. 47 p. (chiefly illus. 28cm. 1969. Maryknoll/Friendship Press.

McCormick, Theodore

--Dangerous Rescue. LC 64-17431. (Illus.). 184 p. 22cm. 1964. Funk & Wagnalls.

McCormick, Wilfred F. (1903-)

--The Automatic Strike: A Rocky McCune Baseball Story. LC 60-5154. 173p. illus. 21cm. N.D. D. McKay Co.

--Bases Loaded. (gr. 4-8). 1957. (ISBN 0-448-08406-6). G&D.

--Bases Loaded: A Bronc Burnett Story. LC 57-13580. 182p. 20cm. c.1950. Grosset & Dunlap.

--Bases Loaded: A Bronc Burnett Story. LC 50-6310. 182 p. 20 cm. 1950. Putnam.

--The Big Ninth. (The Bronc Burnett Ser.). N.D. Grosset & Dunlap.

--The Big Ninth. LC 58-10207. 188p. 20cm. 1958. Putnam.

--The Bigger Game: A Rock McCune Football Story. LC 58-106935. 178p. illus. 21cm. c.1958. D. McKay Co.

--Bluffer. (gr. 4-8). N.D. (ISBN 0-448-08414-7). G&D.

--The Bluffer: A Bronc Burnett Baseball Story. LC 61-8518. 151p. 20cm. 1961. D. McKay Co.

--The Captive Coach: A Rocky McCune Story. LC 56-9974. 179p. 21cm. 1956. D. McKay Co.

--Double Steal. 1961. David McKay Company Co.

--Eagle Scout. (The Bronc Burnett Ser.). N.D. Grosset & Dunlap.

--Eagle Scout: A Bronc Burnett Story. LC 52-5268. 183 p. 20 cm. N.D. Putnam.

--Fielder's Choice. (gr. 4-8). 1956. (ISBN 0-448-08403-1). G&D.

--Fielder's Choice: A Bronc Burnett Story. LC 49-1569. 180 p. 20 cm. 1949. G. P. Putnam's Sons.

--First and Ten: A Dyke Redman Story. LC 52-9843. 184 p. 20cm. 1952. Putnam.

--The Five Man Break: A Rocky McCune Basketball Story. LC 62-174453. 177p. 21cm. 1962. D. McKay Co.

--Five Yards to Glory: A Rocky McCune Football Story. LC 59-90584. 180p. illus. 21cm. 1959. D. McKay Co.

--Flying Tackle. (Famous Sports Stories). N.D. Grosset & Dunlap.

--Flying Tackle. (The Bronc Burnett Ser.). N.D. Grosset & Dunlap.

--Flying Tackle: A Bronc Burnett Story. LC 49-10447. 184 p. diagrs. 20 cm. 1949. G. P. Putnam's Sons.

--Fullback in the Rough. Shortall, Leonard W., illus. LC 72-89543. (Illus.). v, 185 p. 22cm. 1969. Prentice-Hall.

--Go-Ahead Runner. (gr. 4-8). N.D. (ISBN 0-448-08422-8). G&D.

--Go-Ahead Runner. (gr. 7-9). 1965. McKay.

--The Go-Ahead Runner: A Bronc Burnett Story. 181p. 20cm. (8422). 1966, c.1965. Grosset.

--The Go-Ahead Runner: A Bronc Burnett Story. LC 65-13496. 181p. 20cm. c.1965. McKay.

--Grand-Slam Homer. (gr. 4-8). 1958. (ISBN 0-448-08407-4). G&D.

--Grand-Slam Homer: A Bronc Burnett Story. LC 51-3561. 183 p. 20 cm. 1951. Putnam.

--Home-Run Harvest: A Rocky McCune Baseball Story. LC 62-776805. 179p. illus. 21cm. 1962. D. McKay Co.

--The Hot Corner: A Rocky McCune Baseball Story. LC 58-8464. 175p. 21cm. c.1958. D. McKay Co.

--The Incomplete Pitcher: A Bronc Burnett and Rocky McCune Story. LC 66-29904. 180 p. 20cm. 1967. Bobbs-Merrill.

--The Last Put-Out. LC 60-563. 192p. 20cm. 1960. Putnam.

--Legion Tourney. (gr. 4-8). 1956. (ISBN 0-448-08402-3). G&D.

--Legion Tourney: A Bronc Burnett Story. LC 48-406649. 180 p. 20 cm. 1948. G. P. Putnam's Sons.

--Man in Motion. LC 61-10609. 177p. 21cm. (A Bronc Burnett Series Story). 1961. D. McKay.

--Man in Motion: A Bronc Burnett Story. LC 61-13467. 177p. 20cm. 1961. D. McKay Co.
--The Man on the Bench: A Rocky McCune Story. LC 55-106092. 181p. 21cm. 1955. D. McKay Co.
--No Place for Heroes: A Bronc Burnett and Rocky McCune Story. LC 66-22581. 182p. 20cm. 1966. (ISBN 0-672-50405-7). Bobbs.
--Once a Slugger. 176p. 20cm. (Bronc Burnett baseball story). 1965, c.1963. Grosset.
--One Bounce Too Many: A Bronc Burnett and Rocky McCune Story. LC 67-18654. 181p. 20cm. 1967. Bobbs.
--One O'Clock Hitter. (gr. 4-8). N.D. (ISBN 0-448-08412-0). G&D.
--One O'clock Hitter: A Bronc Burnett Story. 183p. 20cm. 1960. D. McKay Co.
--Phantom Shortstop. (gr. 7-12). 1962. McKay.
--The Play for One: A Rocky McCune Basketball Story. LC 61-134684. 181p. illus. 21cm. 1961. D. McKay Co.
--The Pro Toughback. 1st ed. LC 64-29649. 180 p. 21 cm. 1964. Duell Sloan & Pearce.
--The Proud Champions: A Rocky McCune Baseball Story. LC 59-5117. 176p. illus. 21cm. 1959. D. McKay Co.
--Quick Kick. (The Bronc Burnett Ser.). N.D. Grosset & Dunlap.
--Quick Kick: A Bronc Burnett Story. LC 51-13801. (Illus.). 20cm. 183p. 1951. Putnam.
--Rambling Halfback. (The Bronc Burnett Ser.). N.D. Grosset & Dunlap.
--Rambling Halfback: A Bronc Burnett Story. LC 50-9866. 20cm. 184p. 1950. Putnam.
--Rebel with a Glove: A Bronc Brunette Story LC 64-11423. 148p. (gr. 4-8). c.1961. (ISBN 0-448-08417-1). G&D.
--Rebel with a Glove: A Bronc Burnett Baseball Story. LC 62-7767. 148p. 20cm. (His Sports series: Bronc Burnett books). 1962. D. McKay Co.
--The Right End Option. LC 64-18236. 181 p. 20cm. 1964. David McKay Company Inc.
--The Right-End Option: A Bronc Burnett Story. 180p. illus. 20cm. 1965, c.1964. Grosset.
--Rookie on First. (Illus.). (Sports Shelf Ser). (gr. 5 up). 1967. (ISBN 0-399-60548-7). Putnam.
--Rookie on First. Loh, George, illus. LC 67-13579. 217p. illus. 21cm. 1967. Putnam.
--Rough Stuff. 1963. David McKay Company Inc.
--Rough Stuff. 146 p. 20cm. (gr. 4-8). 1964. (ISBN 0-448-08418-X). G&D.
--Seven in Front: A Bronc Burnett Story. LC 65-23831. 179p. 20cm. c.1965. McKay.
--Seven in Front: A Bronc Burnett Story. vii, 179p. 20cm. 1966, c.1965. Grosset.
--Starmaker. 1st ed. LC 61-11076. 160 p. 22cm. 1963. R. Speller.
--Stranger in the Backfield: A Bronc Burnett Story. LC 60-11851. 168p. illus. 20cm. 1960. D. McKay Co.
--Tall at the Plate: A Bronc Burnett Story. LC 66-18603. 188p. 20cm. c.1966. (ISBN 0-672-50526-6). Bobbs.
--Three-Two Pitch. (gr. 4-8). 1956. (ISBN 0-448-08401-5). G&D.
--The Three-Two Pitch: A Bronc Burnett Story. LC 48-616644. 186 p. 20 cm. 1948. G. P. Putnam's Sons.
--The Throwing Catcher. (gr. 4-8). N.D. (ISBN 0-448-08420-1). G&D.
--Throwing Catcher: A Bronc Burnett Baseball Story. LC 64-12368. vii, 179 p. 20cm. (gr. 6-8). 1964. McKay.
--The Throwing Catcher: A Bronc Burnett Story. LC 65-10096. 177p. 20cm. 1965, c.1964. Grosset.
--Too Late to Quit: A Bronc Burnett Story. LC 62-18463. 176p. 20cm. 1962. David McKay Co.
--Too Many Forwards: A Rocky McCune Basketball Story. LC 60-11850. 180p. illus. 21cm. 1960. D. McKay Co.
--Touchdown for the Enemy. Chauncy, Francis, illus. LC 65-25446. 217p. illus. 21cm. c.1965. Putnam.
--Two-One-Two Attack. (gr. 10 up). 1963. (ISBN 0-679-20223-4). McKay.
--Wild on the Bases: A Rocky McCune Baseball Story. LC 65-16273. vii, 152p. illus. 21cm. c.1965. Duell Dist. Meredith.

MacCouillard, Grace
--The Making of Little Hippo. 1975. (ISBN 0-399-11406-8). G. P. Putnam's Sons.

McCourt, Edward Alexander (1907-1972)
--Revolt in the West: The Story of the Real Rebellion. Ferguson, Jack, illus. LC 59-161101. 159p. illus. 22cm. (Great stories of Canada, 17). 1958. St. Martin's Press.

McCowan, Hervey Smith
--Trail a Boy Travels and other Stories. N.D. Association Press.

McCoy, Elin
--The Incredible Year-Round Playbook. Trivas, Irene, illus. LC 78-55909. (Illus.). 1979. (ISBN 0-394-83564-6, BYR). (ISBN 0-394-93564-0). Random.

McCoy, Iola Fuller see Fuller, Iola, pseud.

McCoy, Joseph Jerome (1917-)
--Lords of the sky. (Illus.). N.D. Bobbs-Merrill Co, Inc.
--Shadows Over the Land. LC 77-111212. 160p. (gr. 5 up). 1970. (ISBN 0-8164-3061-6, Clarion). HM.

McCoy, Neely
--Jupie and the Wise Old Owl. McCoy, Neely, illus. LC 31-9627. 5 p. l., 95, 1 p. incl. illus., plates. col. front., col. plates. 22 1/2 cm. 1931. The Macmillan Company.
--Jupie Follows his Tale. McCoy, Neely, illus. LC 28-14277. 5 p. l., 106 p., 1 l. incl. plates. illus. col. front., col. plates. 22 1/2 cm. 1928. The Macmillan Company.
--The Tale of the Good Cat Jupie. McCoy, Neely, illus. LC 26-16727. xvi p., 3 l., 99 p. incl. illus. plates. col. front. col. plates. 22 1/2 cm. 1926. The Macmillan Company.

McCoy, Patrick Terrance
--Kiltie McCoy. N.D. Bobbs-Merrill Co.

McCoy, Paul S.
--Modern Comedies for Teen-Agers. (gr. 7 up). 1962. (ISBN 0-8238-0039-3). Plays.

McCoy, Samuel Duff (1882-1964)
--The Mystery at Pickle Point. Tate, Sally, illus. LC 47-7784. 172 p. illus. 21 cm. (His A J.J. Jenks Jr. mystery.). 1948. J. B. Lippincott Co.
--Mystery at Robbers' Rock. Tate, Sally, illus. (Illus.). (gr. 4-6). 1950. (ISBN 0-397-30172-3). Lippincott.

McCracken, Blair
--Joey's Secret. Snyder, Joel, illus. LC 72-77625. (Illus.). 46 p. 22cm. (Magic circle book). c.1973. (ISBN 0-663-25490-6). Ginn.

McCracken, Elizabeth (1876-), ed. see Yonge, Charlotte Mary.

McCracken, Elizabeth (1876-), ed.
--To Mother: An Anthology of Mother Verse. Wiggin, Kate Douglas Smith (1856-1923), intro. by. LC 17-13752. (Illus.). Repr. of 1917 ed (Pub. by Houghton). (Granger Poetry Library). 1976. (ISBN 0-89609-051-5). Granger Bk.

McCracken, Harold (1894-)
--The Biggest Bear on Earth. Bransom, Paul (1885-), illus. 1943. J. B. Lippincott Co.
--Caribou Traveler. 1st ed. Ruth, Rod (1912-), illus. LC 49-11182. ix, 204 p. illus., map. 21 cm. 1949. J. B. Lippincott Co.
--The Flaming Bear. LC 51-11173. 222 p. illus. 21 cm. 1951. Lippincott.
--The Great White Buffalo. Schuyler, Remington (1884-1955), illus. LC 46-7680. xiv, 268 p. incl. front., illus. 22 cm. 1946. J. B. Lippincott Company.
--Iglaome: The Lone Hunter. Couse, W. P., illus. LC 30-106127. ix, 248 p. incl. front. plates. 19 1/2 cm. $1.7. c.1930. The Century Company.
--The Last of the Sea Otters. Bransom, Paul (1885-), illus. N.D. J. B. Lippincott.
--Pirate of the North. Tonk, Ernest, illus. LC 53-8914. 213p. illus. 21cm. (gr. 7-9). 1953. Lippincott.
--Sentinel of the Snow Peaks: A Story of the Alaskan Wild. Comstock, Enos Benjamin (1879-1945), illus. LC 45-8210. 151 p. incl. illus., plates. 21 1/2 cm. 1945. J. B. Lippincott Company.
--Son of the Walrus King. Hunt, Lynn Bogue, illus. LC 44-74120. x, 128, 1 p. incl. illus., plates. col. front. 26 cm. 1944. J. B. Lippincott Company.
--Toughy: Bulldog in the Arctic. Burger, Carl Victor (1888-1967), illus. N.D. J. B. Lippincott.

McCracken, Russell
--The Elegant Elephant. Suba, Susanne (1913-), illus. LC 44-9748. 28, 4 p. illus. (part col.) 26 cm. (Slottie library). 1944. Rand McNally & Company.
--The Gentle Giraffe. Suba, Susanne (1913-), illus. LC 46-2488. 31, 1 p. illus. (part col.) 26 cm. (Slottie library). c.1945. Rand McNally & Company.
--Mystery of Carmen the Cow. Suba, Susanne (1913-), illus. LC 47-292. 31, 1, illus. (part col.) 26. (Slottie library). 1946. Garden City Publishing Co.
--The Mystery of Carmen the Cow. Suba, Susanne (1913-), illus. LC 47-292. 31, 1 p. illus. (part col.) 26 cm. (Slottie library). 1946. Rand McNally & Company.
--The Sound of Sleigh Bells. Phillips, Louis, illus. LC 51-3028. unpaged. illus. 20 cm. 1951. Farrar, Straus, and Young.

McCrady, Elizabeth F.
--Abdul of Arabia. 1937. Platt & Munk.
--Children of Foreign Lands. LC 38-194041. 96 p. illus. (part col.) 21 cm. c.1937. The Platt & Munk Co., Inc.
--Ching Ling and Ting Ling of China. 1937. Platt & Munk.
--Chula of Siam. LC 33-33673. 11 p. ill. (part col.). 1937. Platt & Munk.
--Kala of Hawaii. LC 37-33674. 11 p. illus. (part col.) 20 1/2 cm. 1937. The Platt & Muck Co., Inc.
--Maria and Carlos of Spain. 1937. Platt & Munk.
--Matsu and Taro of Japan. 1937. Platt & Munk.
--Wilhelmina of Holland. LC 37-33678. 11 p. illus. (part col.) 20 1/2 cm. 1937. The Platt & Munk Co., Inc.

McCrady, Lady (1951-)
--Junior's Tune. LC 80-348. (Illus.). 32 p. c.1980. (ISBN 0-8234-0411-0). Holiday House.
--Mildred and the Mummy. LC 79-17902. (Illus.). 32 p. 25cm. c.1980. (ISBN 0-8234-0372-6). Holiday House.
--Miss Kiss and the Nasty Beast. McCrady, Lady (1951-), illus. LC 79-10002. p. cm. c.1979. (ISBN 0-8234-0355-6). Holiday House.
--The Witch's Pig: A Cornish Folktale. Wilkins, Mary Huiskamp. McCrady, Lady, illus. LC 76-27321. (Illus.). 32 p. 26cm. 1977. (ISBN 0-688-22092-4). (ISBN 0-688-32092-9). Morrow.

McCrady, Lady (1951-), ed.
--Grasshopper to the Rescue: A Georgian Story. McCrady, Lady (1951-), illus. Carey, Bonnie, tr. from Rus. LC 78-11824. (Illus.). 32 p. 26cm. 1979. (ISBN 0-688-22172-6). (ISBN 0-688-32172-0). Morrow.

McCrady, Lady (1951-) & Kendrick, Dennis
--The Perfect Ride. LC 80-25612. (Illus.). 44 p. 22cm. c.1981. (ISBN 0-8193-1051-4). Parents Magazine Press.

McCrae, Ruth D
--A Present for Molly. McCrae, Ruth D., illus. LC 49-11861. 59 p. illus. (part col.) 21 cm. 1949. Aladdin Books.

McCraith, L M
--Irish Heroines. N.D. Longmans,Green & Co.

McCravey, E
--King Jack. LC 48-11524. 59 p. 23 cm. 1947. Exposition Press.

McCraw, Louise Harrison (1893-1975)
--As the Snow on the High Hills. 198p. (Orig.). 1979. (ISBN 0-89323-001-4). BMA Pr.

McCrea, Eleanor
--Abba Kadaba. LC 42-20794. 24 p. illus. 16 x 13 1/2 cm. 1942. Press of McManus-Troup.

McCrea, James Craig, Jr. (1920-) & McCrea, Ruth Pirman (1921-)
--The Birds. X ed. LC 66-12849. 1 v. (unpaged) col. illus. 24. 1966. (ISBN 0-689-20259-8). Atheneum Publishers.
--King's Procession. 1963. (ISBN 0-8382-0408-2, Cadmus Books). E. M. Hale And Company.
--King's Procession. McCrea, James Craig, Jr. (1920-) & McCrea, Ruth Pirman (1921-), illus. (Illus.). (ps-3). 1963. (ISBN 0-689-20262-8). Atheneum.
--The Magic Tree. 1 v. (unpaged) col. illus. 24cm. c.1965. Atheneum.
--Magic Tree. (Illus.). (gr. 1-3). 1965. (ISBN 0-8382-0495-3). Hale.
--Magic Tree. McCrea, James Craig, Jr. (1920-) & McCrea, Ruth Pirman (1921-), illus. (Illus.). (ps-3). 1965. (ISBN 0-689-20263-6). (ISBN 0-689-20264-4). Atheneum.
--Story of Olaf. McCrea, James Craig, Jr. (1920-) & McCrea, Ruth Pirman (1921-), illus. (Illus.). (gr. k-3). 1964. (ISBN 0-689-20265-2). (ISBN 0-689-20266-0). Atheneum.

McCrea, Lilian, ed.
--Stories to Play in the Infant School. LC 57-285596. 159p. illus. 19cm. 1956. Oxford University Press.
--Stories to Tell in the Nursery School. 175 p. illus. 19 cm. 1950. Oxford University Press.

McCrea, Lilian & Twinn, Michael
--By the Stream: A Nature Story. Hook, Richard, illus. LC 73-152575. (Illus.). 38 p. (Origami story book). 1972. (ISBN 0-528-82677-8). Rand McNally.

McCrea, Mary, jt. ed. see Fenner, Phyllis Reid.

McCrea, Ruth Pirman, jt. auth. see McCrea, James Craig, Jr.

McCready, Thomas Leighton
--Adventures of a Beagle. Tudor, Tasha (1915-), illus. LC 59-621115. unpaged. illus. 21cm. 1959. Ariel Books.
--Adventures of a Beagle. Tudor, Tasha (1915-), illus. (Illus.). (gr. k-3). 1959. FS&G.
--Biggity Bantam. Tudor, Tasha (1915-), illus. LC 54-5202. (Illus.). 49 p. 21cm. 1954. Ariel Books.
--Increase Rabbit. Tudor, Tasha (1915-), illus. LC 57-963459. unpaged. illus. 21cm. 1958. Ariel Books.
--Mr. Stubbs. Tudor, Tasha (1915-), illus. LC 56-9445. (Illus.). 21cm. 48p. 1956. Ariel Books.
--Pekin White. Tudor, Tasha (1915-), illus. LC 55-6684. (Illus.). 49 p. 21cm. 1955. Ariel Books.

McCreary, Tressie Fern
--Bob's Red Letter Days. LC 34-2148. 134 p. illus. 19 cm. c.1934. The Warner Press.

MacCrimmon, Bruce
--The Magic Fingers. MacCrimmon, Bruce, illus. LC 68-5242. (Illus.). 32 p. 24cm. 1965. E. M. Hale.

McCrindell, Rachel, Miss
--The Convent. N.D. Robert Carter & Brothers.
--School Girl in France. N.D. Robert Carter & Brothers.

McCrody, Elizabeth F.
--Olga of Norway. LC 37-336773. 11 p. illus. (part col.) 20 1/2 cm. 1937. The Platt & Munk Co., Inc.

McCue, Dick
--Bunny's Numbers. McCue, Lisa, illus. LC 85-132571. (Illus.). 11 p. 16cm. c.1984. (ISBN 0-671-50944-6). Little Simon.

McCue, Lillian Bueno see De La Torre, Lillian, pseud.

McCue, Lisa, illus.
--Ducky's Seasons. (Illus.). (Animal Shape Board Bks.). (ps-2). 1983. (ISBN 0-671-45491-9, Little Simon). S&S.
--Froggie's Treasure. (Illus.). (Animal Shape Board Bks.). (ps-2). 1983. (ISBN 0-671-45488-9, Little Simon). S&S.
--Kitty's Colors. (Illus.). (Animal Shape Board Bks.). (ps-2). 1983. (ISBN 0-671-45489-7, Little Simon). S&S.
--Teddy Dresses. (Illus.). (Animal Shape Board Bks.). 1983. (ISBN 0-671-45490-0, Little Simon). S&S.
--They Call Boober Fraggle. (Illus.). 48p. (Fraggle Rock Bk.). (gr. 1-4). 1983. (ISBN 0-03-068677-6). HR&W.

McCullers, Lula Carson (1917-1967)
--Sweet As a Pickle & Clean As a Pig. (gr. 10 up). 1964. (ISBN 0-395-06906-8). HM.

McCulloch, Derek Ivor Breashur (1897-1967), ed.
Every Child's Pilgrim's Progress. (Illus.). (gr. 3-9). 1957. (ISBN 0-8042-1944-3). John Knox.

McCulloch, J. H., pseud., see Rawlings, James R..

McCulloch, J. H., pseud.
--The Splendid Renegade. Rawlings, James R.. N.D. Grosset & Dunlap.

McCulloch, Margaret Neher
--Second Year Nurse. 1st ed. Guzzi, George, illus. LC 57-5556. 189p. 22cm. 1957. Westminster Press.

McCulloch, Robert W. (1868-1946)
--Come, Jack!. Coburn, Duncan, illus. LC 46-3587. 5 p. l., 202, 1 p. col. plates. 20 cm. 1946. Houghton Mifflin Company.
--Polly Kent Rides West, in the Days of '49. Hargens, Charles, Jr. (1893-), illus. 1940. John C. Winston.

McCullough, Frances Monson (1938-), ed.
--Earth, Air, Fire & Water. (gr. 6-8). 1971. (ISBN 0-698-20037-3, Coward). Putnam Pub Group.
--Earth, Air, Fire & Water: A Collection of Over One Hundred Twenty-Five Poems. LC 75-127948. 190 p. 23cm. 1971. Coward, McCann & Geoghegan.
--Love Is Like the Lion's Tooth. LC 77-25659. 96p. (gr. 7 up). 1984. (ISBN 0-06-024138-1, HarpJ). (ISBN 0-06-024139-X). Har-Row.

McCullough, John G (1911-)
--At Our House. Duvoisin, Roger Antoine (1904-1980), illus. LC 43-15786. 41 p. illus. 25 x 21 cm. c.1943. W. R. Scott, Inc.
--Dark Is Dark. Shaw, Charles Green (1892-1974), illus. LC 47-30812. 34 p. col. illus. 25 cm. c.1947. W. R. Scott.
--Here Comes Daddy. Gropper, William (1897-1977), illus. LC 51-6804. unpaged. illus. 21 x 23 cm. 1951. W. R. Scott.

McCully, Emily Arnold, jt. auth. see Artis, Vicki Kimmel.

McCully, Emily Arnold, jt. auth. see Hapgood, Miranda.

McCully, Emily Arnold, jt. auth. see Hurd, Edith Thacher, Mrs.

McCully, Emily Arnold (1939-)
--First Snow. LC 84-43244. (Illus.). 32 p. 24cm. c.1985. (ISBN 0-06-024128-4). (ISBN 0-06-024129-2). Harper & Row.
--Picnic. 1st ed. LC 83-47913. (Illus.). (ps-2). c.1984. (ISBN 0-06-024099-7). (ISBN 0-06-024100-4). Harper & Row. **Award: (ALA).**

McCully, Helen & Crayder, Dorothy
--The Christmas Pony. Lee, Robert J. (1921-), illus. (Illus.). 101 p. 22cm. 1967. Bobbs-Merrill Co.

McCune, Evelyn
--Kim Rides the Tiger. McCune, Evelyn, illus. LC 51-12290. 150 p. illus. 20 cm. 1951. J. Day Co.

McCunn, Ruthanne L.
--Pie-Biter. Tang, You-Shah, illus. (Illus.). 32p. 1983. (ISBN 0-932538-09-6). (ISBN 0-932538-10-X). Design Ent SF.

McCurry, Bertha B Moore see Cannon, Brenda, pseud.

McCurry, Bertha B. Moore see Moore, Bertha B.

McCurry, Bertha B Moore (1890-)
--Autumn on Breezy Hill: A Story for Pre-Schoolchildren. LC 56-42781. 56p. 21cm. 1956. Zondervan Pub. House.
--Good Neighbors. Sorenson, Elizabeth Ann & DeWitt, Jayne Whistler, illus. LC 50-4467. 128 p. illus. 18 cm. (Colportage library, 198). 1950, c.1949. Moody Press.
--The Jolly J's Make Decisions. LC 51-11589. -125 p. 18 cm. 1951. Moody Press.
--Joy Shop. LC 51-11292. 59 p. 20 cm. 1951. Moody Press.

--Joy Shop Stories. LC 30-3873. 2 p. l., 7-71, l p. plates. 19 cm. 1929. Gospel Publishing House.
--On Silver Creek Knob. LC 51-46666. 123 p. illus. 18 cm. (Moody colportage library, 178.). 1939. Moody Press.
--On Silver Creek Knob. LC 40-1010. 123 p. inc. front., illus. 17 1/2 cm. (The Moody colportage library, no. 178). 1939. The Bible Institute Colportage Ass'n.
--A Picture for Joy Shop. LC 52-33572. 58 p. 20 cm. 1952. Moody Press.
--The Princess Beautiful: 108. Cannon, Brenda, pseud. LC 57-3486. 189p. illus. 20cm. 1957. Books, Inc.
--Spring on Breezy Hill. LC 52-14273. 56p. illus. 20cm. 1952. Zondervan Pub. House.
--The Three Bears. 88 p. 20cm. 1938. B. Eerdmans Publishing Co.
--The Triplets Become Good Neighbors. LC 45-8407. 87 p. 20 cm. 1945. Wm. B. Eerdmans Publishing Company.
--The Triplets Fly High. LC 50-7711. 87 p. 21 cm. 1950. Eerdmans.
--The Triplets Go Places. N.D. E. P. Dutton & Co.
--The Triplets Go Places. LC 42-23946. 72 p. 20 cm. 1942. Wm. B. Eerdmans Publishing Company.
--The Triplets Go South. LC 40-32985. 86 p. 20 cm. 1940. Wm. B. Eerdmans Publishing Co.
--The Triplets Go to Camp. LC 52-9302. 83 p. 20 cm. 1952. W. B. Eerdmans Pub. Co.
--The Triplets Have an Adventure. LC 47-24200. 89 p. 21 cm. 1947. W. B. Eerdmans Pub. Co.
--The Triplets in Business. LC 39-30182. 88 p. 20 cm. 1939. Wm. B. Eerdmans Publishing Company.
--The Triplets Make a Discovery. LC 48-6533. 89 p. 20 cm. 1948. Wm. B. Eerdmans Pub. Co.
--The Triplets Over J.O.Y. LC 41-17583. 79 p. 20 cm. N.D. Wm. B. Eerdmans Publishing Company,.
--The Triplets Receive a Reward. LC 47-15799. 88 p. 20 cm. 1946. Wm. B. Eerdmans Publishing Company.
--The Triplets Take Over. LC 53-1898. 89p. 21cm. (Her Triplets series). 1953. W. B.Eerdmans Pub. Co.
--The Triplets Try Television. LC 54-14736. 86p. 20cm. 1954. Eerdmans.

McCutchan, Philip Donald (1920-)
--On Course for Danger: A Story for Boys. LC 59-4833. 247p. illus. 21cm. 1959. St. Martin's Press.

McDaniel, Becky Bring
--Katie Couldn't. LC 85-11666. p. cm. (A Rookie Reader). 1985. (ISBN 0-516-02069-2). Childrens Press.
--Katie Did It. Axeman, Lois, illus. LC 83-7260. (Illus.). 30 p. 19cm. (A Rookie Reader). c.1983. (ISBN 0-516-02043-9). (ISBN 0-516-42043-7). Childrens Press.

McDaniel, Ruel (1896-)
--Deep Water Boy. Edwards, Parker F., illus. (Illus.). (gr. 7-11). 1964. (ISBN 0-87464-028-8). Golden Gate.

McDaniel, Suellen R
--Serpent Treasure. LC 78-24288. 129 p. 21cm. c.1978. (ISBN 0-89587-007-X). J. F. Blair.

McDaniels, M. Alberta
--Doris Marjorie and Her Tales of Fairy Land. LC 25-25026. 1 p. l., 76 p. 22 1/2 cm. c.1925. The Farmers Press.
--Doris Marjorie and Her Tales of Fairy Land. Putney, Effie Florence, illus. LC 30-131543. 119 p., 1 l. incl. front., illus. 20 cm. 1930. Educator Supply Company.

McDavid, Mittie Owen
--The Children of the Meadows. Heyer, Herman, illus. LC 13-321. 187 p. incl. plates. front. 19 1/2 cm. $1.0. 1912. The Cosmopolitan Press.

McDermoth, Cora A
--Almost Sleepy Time. LC 29-12469. 32 p. 23 cm. (Stratford poets). c.1929. The Stratford Company.

McDermott, Beverly Brodsky (1941-)
--The Crystal Apple: A Russian Tale. LC 74-3312. (Illus.). 32 p. 1974. (ISBN 0-670-25052-X). Viking Press.
--The Golem: A Jewish Folk Legend. 1975. Harper.
--The Golem: A Jewish Legend. McDermott, Beverly Brodsky (1941-), illus. LC 75-29136. (Illus.). 44 p. 32cm. c.1976. (ISBN 0-397-31674-7). Lippincott. **Awards: (ALA); (RCM).**

McDermott, Caroline & Aldrich, Andy
--Little Crow. 1974. (ISBN 0-307-60113-7, Golden Pr). Western Pub.

McDermott, Gerald (1941-), retold by.
--Anansi the Spider: A Tale from the Ashanti. 1st ed. McDermott, Gerald (1941-), illus. LC 76-150028. (Illus.). 41 p. 1972. (ISBN 0-03-080234-2). (ISBN 0-03-080236-9). Holt, Rinehart and Winston. **Awards: (ALA); (RCM).**
--Arrow to the Sun: A Pueblo Indian Tale. 1st ed. McDermott, Gerald (1941-), illus. LC 73-16172. (Illus.). 42 p. 1974. Viking Press. **Award: (RCM).**
--Daughter of Earth: A Roman Myth. McDermott, Gerald (1941-), illus. 1984. Delacorte.
--The Knight of the Lion. McDermott, Gerald (1941-), illus. LC 78-54680. p. cm. c.1978. (ISBN 0-590-07504-7). Four Winds Press.
--The Magic Tree. McDermott, Gerald (1941-), illus. LC 72-76567. 1973. H R & W. **Award: (BGH).**
--The Magic Tree: A Tale from the Congo. McDermott, Gerald (1941-), illus. (gr. k-3). 1977. Penguin.
--The Magic Tree: A Tale from the Congo. McDermott, Gerald (1941-), illus. LC 77-24035. (Illus.). 41 p. (Picture puffin). 1977, c.1973. (ISBN 0-14-050217-3). Puffin Books.
--Musicians of the Sun: An Aztec Myth. McDermott, Gerald (1941-), illus. LC 85-3805. p. cm. 1985. (ISBN 0-385-29405-0). Delacorte Press.
--Papagayo, the Mischief Maker. McDermott, Gerald (1941-), illus. LC 78-7911. p. cm. 1978. Windmill Books.
--The Stonecutter: A Japanese Folk Tale. McDermott, Gerald (1941-), illus. LC 77-25935. (Illus.). 32 p. 23cm. (Picture puffin.). 1978, c.1975. (ISBN 0-14-050289-0). Puffin Books.
--The Stonecutter: A Japanese Folk Tale. 1st ed. McDermott, Gerald (1941-), illus. LC 74-26823. (Illus.). 31 p. 28cm. 1975. (ISBN 0-670-67074-X). Viking Press.
--Sun Flight. McDermott, Gerald (1941-), illus. LC 79-5067. p. cm. 1980, c.1979. (ISBN 0-590-07632-9). Four Winds Press.
--The Voyage of Osiris: A Myth of Ancient Egypt. McDermott, Gerald (1941-), illus. LC 77-2861. (Illus.). 36 p. c.1977. (ISBN 0-525-61567-9). Windmill Books.

McDermott, Gerald (1941-), illus.
--The Adventures of Pinocchio. Mayer, Marianna (1945-), tr. from Ital. (Illus.). 128p. (gr. 3-6). 1981. (ISBN 0-590-07546-2, Four Winds). Scholastic Inc.

McDevitt, Jean
--Mister Apple's Family. (Illus.). (gr. 2-4). 1950. (ISBN 0-8382-0527-5). Hale.
--Mr. Apple's Family. 1st ed. MacKnight, Ninon (1908-), illus. Ninon, pseud. LC 50-7146. (Illus.). 118 p. 21cm. 1950. Doubleday.
--No, No, Taffy!. Gag, Flavia (1907-1979), illus. LC 52-9276. 1952. Doubleday & Co.
--The Twins and Trusty. Holmgren, John, illus. 96p. illus. 23cm. 1958. Row, Peterson.

McDole, Carol see Farley, Carol J.

MacDonald
--Light Princess. (The "Bimbi" Series of Children's Booklets). N.D. Thomas Y. Crowell.

Macdonald, Alexander (1878-)
--The Hidden Nugget: A Story of the Australian Gold Fields. (Illus.). N.D. Caldwell.
--The Invisible Island: A Tale of the Gulf of Carpentaria. Sheldon, Charles M., illus. (Illus.). 1910. Caldwell.
--The Island Traders: A Tale of the South Seas. Rainey, William R. I. (1852-1936), illus. LC 9-19036. 4 p. l., 283 p. front., 5 pl. 19 1/2 cm. c.1908. H. M. Caldwell Co.
--The Lost Explorers: A Story of the Trackless Desert. (Illus.). N.D. Caldwell.
--The Lost Explorers: A Story of the Trackless Desert. Buckland, Arthur H., illus. 5 p., 1 l., 11-378 p. 3 pl. 19 1/2 cm. 1906. Blackie & Son, Limited.
--The Pearl Seekers: A Story of Adventure in the Southern Seas. (Illus.). N.D. Caldwell.
--The Pearl Seekers: A Tale of the Southern Seas. Hodgson, Edward S., illus. LC 7-30434. 4 p. l., v-vi, 359 p. front., 6 pl., 2 maps. 20 cm. c.1907. Blackie and Son, Limited.
--Sung by the Sea. (Poetry, Music & Art). (MacMillan Bks. for Boys & Girls). (gr. 4-6). N.D. MacMillan Bks.
--Through the Heart of Tibet: A Tale of a Secret Mission to Lhasa. (Illus.). N.D. Caldwell.
--The White Trail: A Story of the Early Days of Klondike. (Illus.). N.D. Caldwell.

McDonald, Angus Henry (1903-)
--Old MacDonald had a Farm. Bartlett, Richard, illus. 1942. Houghton Mifflin Co.

MacDonald, Betty Bard
--Hello, Mrs. Piggle-Wiggle. Knight, Hilary (1926-), illus. LC 57-5613. (Illus.). (gr. k-3). 1957. (ISBN 0-397-30364-5, JBL-J). (ISBN 0-397-31708-5). Har-Row.
--Hello, Mrs. Piggle-Wiggle. Knight, Hilary (1926-), illus. LC 57-5613. (Illus.). 125 p. 21cm. 1957. Lippincott.
--Mrs. Piggle-Wiggle. Bennett, Richard Michael (1899-), illus. LC 47-1875. 118p. 1 p. incl. illus., col. plates. 21cm. 1947. J. B. Lippincott Company.
--Mrs. Piggle-Wiggle. Knight, Hilary (1926-), illus. LC 57-1911. (Illus.). 118 p. 21cm. 1957. Lippincott.
--Mrs. Piggle-Wiggle's Farm. 1st ed. Sendak, Maurice Bernard (1928-), illus. LC 54-72994. (Illus.). 127 p. 21cm. 1954. Lippincott.
--Mrs. Piggle-Wiggle's Magic. Knight, Hilary (1926-), illus. LC 57-248456. (Illus.). 126 p. 21cm. 1957. Lippincott.
--Mrs Piggle-Wiggle's Magic. 1st ed. Wiese, Kurt (1887-1974), illus. 126 p. illus. 26cm. 1949. Lippincott.
--Nancy and Plum. 1st ed. Hopkins, Hildegarde L., illus. LC 52-7456. (Illus.). 190 p. 21cm. 1952. Lippincott.
--Onions In The Stew. 256p. 1955. J. B. Lippincott.

MacDonald, Blackie, pseud., see Emrich, Duncan Black MacDonald.

MacDonald, Dora Mary
--Clever Plays. 95p. 1932. Northwestern Press.
--Clever Plays. 95p. N.D. T. S. Denison & Co.

Macdonald, Dwight (1906-1982), ed. see Poe, Edgar Allan.

MacDonald, Elizabeth Roberts
--Our Little Canadian Cousin. Bridgman, Lewis Jesse (1857-1931), illus. LC 4-18901. v p., 1 l., 129 p. front., 5 pl. 20 cm. (On verso of half-title: The little cousin series). 1904. L. C. Page & Company.

MacDonald, Elizabeth & Owen, Annie
--My Aunt and the Animals. LC 85-1287. p. cm. 1985. (ISBN 0-8120-5641-8). Barron's.

McDonald, Etta Austin Blaisdell see Murray, Clara, pseud.

McDonald, Etta Austin Blaisdell, Mrs., jt. auth. see Blaisdell, Mary Frances.

McDonald, Etta Austin Blaisdell, Mrs. (1872-) & Dalrymple, Julia
--Betty in Canada. LC 10-19959. 4 p.l., lll p. col. front., plates. 191/2cm. 1910. Little Brown.
--Betty in Canada. LC 10-19959. 4 p. l., 111 p. col. front., plates. 19 1/2 cm. (Little people everywhere). 1919. Little, Brown, & Company.
--Boris in Russia. LC 10-19960. vi p., 2 l., 129 p. incl. col. front. plates. 19 1/2 cm. (Little people everywhere). 1910. Little, Brown, and Company.
--Boy Blue and His Friends. school ed. LC 6-34637. 5 p. l., 3-165 p. incl. illus., plates. front. 19 x 15 1/2 cm. 1906. Little, Brown and Company.
--Bunny Rabbit's Diary. 193p. (The Boy Blue Ser.). N.D. Little, Brown.
--Bunny Rabbit's Playmates. N.D. Vantage Press.
--Chandra in India. LC 16-17496. vi p., 2 l., 111 p. col. front., plates. 19 1/2 cm. (Little people everywhere) $0.50). 1916. Little, Brown, and Company.
--Cherry-Tree Blossom. 126p. (The Boy Blue Ser.). N.D. Little, Brown.
--Cherry-Tree Children. N.D. Little Brown & Co.
--The Child at play: Little Stories for Little Children. Murray, Clara, pseud. LC 4-30591. 19 x 16cm. 11p. 1905. Little Brown & Co.
--Colette in France: A Geographical Reader. school ed. LC 13-18071. vi p., 2 l., 120 p. incl. col. front. plates. 19 1/2 cm. (Little people everywhere). 1914. Little, Brown, and Company.
--Donald in Scotland. LC 12-21321. 1 p. l., v-vi p., 2 l., 117 p. col. front., 8 pl. 19 1/2 cm. $0.6. (Little people everywhere). 1912. Little, Brown, and Company.
--Fritz in Germany. vi p., 2 l., 120 p. incl. col. front. plates. 19 1/2 cm. $0.6. (Little people everywhere). 1910. Little, Brown, and Company.
--Gerda in Sweden. vi p., 2 l., 120 p. incl. col. front. plates. 19 1/2 cm. $0.6. (Little people everywhere). 1910. Little, Brown, and Company.
--Hassan in Egypt. LC 11-245561. vi p., 2 l., 114 p. incl. col. front. plates. 19 1/2 cm. $0.6. (Little people everywhere). 1911. Little, Brown, and Company.
--Josefa in Spain. LC 12-213204. 1 p. l., v-vi p., 2 l., 117 p. col. front., 8 pl. 19 1/2 cm. (Little people everywhere). c.1912. Little, Brown, and Company.
--Kathleen in Ireland. vi p., 2 l., 118 p. incl. col. front. 8 pl. 19 1/2 cm. $0.6. (Little people everywhere). 1909. Little, Brown, and Company.
--The Kelpies. school ed. Fitts, Clara E. Atwood, illus. LC 25-3108. 147 p. col. front., col. illus. 19 cm. 1924. Little, Brown, and Company.
--The Kelpies Run Away. school ed. Fitts, Clara E. Atwood, illus. LC 30-167021. 156 p. incl. col. front., col. illus. 19 cm. 1930. Little, Brown, and Company.
--Manuel in Mexico. LC 9-24952. vi p., 2 l., 118 p. col. front., 8 pl. 19 1/2 cm. (Little people everywhere). 1909. Little, Brown & Company.
--Marta in Holland. LC 11-23499. vi p., 2 l., 116 p. incl. col. front. plates. 19 1/2 cm. (Little people everywhere). 1911. Little, Brown, and Company.
--My Garden of Stories. N.D. Little Brown & Co.
--Polly and Dolly. 173p. (The Boy Blue Ser.). N.D. Little, Brown.
--Pretty Polly Flinders. 188p. (The Boy Blue Ser.). N.D. Little, Brown.
--Rafael in Italy. LC 9-24951. vii p., 1 l., 119 p. incl. col. front. 8 pl. 19 1/2 cm. (Little people everywhere). 1909. Little, Brown, and Company.
--Rhymes and Tales for Children. Fitts, Clara E. Atwood, illus. 19cm. 125p. 1918. Little Brown & Co.
--Story Book Friends. Murray, Clara, pseud. LC 8-32391. 191 p. col. front., illus., col. plates. 19 x 16 cm. (On verso of half-title: The Playtime Ser.). c.1908. Little, Brown, and Company.
--Story Book Treasures. Murray, Clara, pseud. New Ed. ed. 1929. Little Brown & Co.
--Tommy Tinker's Book. 177p. (The Boy Blue Ser.). N.D. Little, Brown.
--Toy Town. N.D. Little Brown & Co.
--Twilight Town. 188p. (The Boy Blue Ser.). N.D. Little, Brown.
--Twilight Town. N.D. Little Brown & Co.
--Ume San in Japan. 4 p. l., 111 p. col. front., 8 pl. 18 1/2 cm. (Little people everywhere). 1909. Little, Brown, and Company.

MacDonald, Francis
--Star of the Mohawk: Kateri Tekakwitha. Dougherty, Charles L., illus. LC 58-13117. 183p. illus. 22cm. (Banner books). 1958. Benziger Bros.

Macdonald, George, jt. auth. see Davis, Caroline E. Kelly, Mrs.

MacDonald, Georg; see Watson, Jean.

MacDonald, George (1824-1905)
--At the Back of the North Wind. (Famous Bks. for Young Americans). N.D. A. L. Burt Co.
--At the Back of the North Wind. (Fireside Ser. for Girls). N.D. A. L. Burt's Publications.
--At the Back of the North Wind. (Illus.). (The Meade Series for Girls). N.D. A. L. Burt.
--At the Back of the North Wind. LC 75-32174. p. cm. (Classics of Children's Literature ; 1621-1932). 1976. (ISBN 0-8240-2286-6). Garland Pub.
--At the Back of the North Wind. (Illus.). 378p. N.D. George Routledge & Sons.
--At The Back of the North Wind. (Lippincott Juniors). N.D. J. B. Lippincott.
--At the Back of the North Wind. LC 50-10037. (Illus.). 21cm. 402p. (New children's classics). N.D. Macmillan.
--At the Back of the North Wind. Browning, Colleen (1929-), illus. LC 56-58963. 319p. illus. 22cm. 1956. Junior Deluxe Editions.
--At the Back of the North Wind. Brundage, Frances, illus. LC 27-18008. 406 p. incl. front., illus. 19 cm. (Half-title: Every child's library). c.1927. The Saalfield Publishing Company.
--At the Back of the North Wind. Dinnerstein, Harvey (1928-), illus. (Illus.). 310 p. 24cm. (Macmillan classics, 29). 1964. Macmillan.
--At the Back of the North Wind. Hauman, George (1890-1961) & Hauman, Doris, Mrs. (1897-), illus. LC 24-21078. 5 p. l., 376 p. col. front., illus. 19 1/2 cm. (The Macmillan children's classics). c.1924. The Macmillan Company.
--At the Back of the North Wind. Hughes, Arthur (1832-1915), illus. LC 4-18330. viii, 378 p. illus. 18 1/2 cm. 1882. G. Routledge & Sons.
--At the Back of the North Wind. Hughes, Arthur (1832-1915), illus. 1871. George Routledge & Sons.
--At the Back of the North Wind. Hughes, Arthur (1832-1915), illus. LC 66-8973. (Illus.). vi, 378 p. 24cm. (Legacy library facsimile). 1966. University Microfilms.
--At the Back of the North Wind. Kay, Gertrude Alice (1884-1939), illus. LC 34-28312. 3 p. l., 9-326 p. col. front., col. plates. 19 cm. (golden books). 1934. D. McKay.
--At the Back of the North Wind. Kay, Gertrude Alice (1884-1939), illus. LC 26-274472. 3 p. l., 9-326 p. col. front., col. plates. 19 1/2 cm. (Newberry classics). 1926. David McKay Company.
--At the Back of the North Wind. Lewis, Elizabeth, adapted by. Kirk, Maria Louise (1860-), illus. LC 9-24948. v, 1 p., 1 l., 303 p. 12 col. pl. (incl. front.) 21 cm. 1909. J. B. Lippincott Company.
--At the Back of the North Wind. Lewis, Elizabeth, adapted by. Kirk, Maria Louise (1860-), illus. LC 16-131189. v, 1 p., 1 l., 352 p. col. front., illus., col. plates. 21 cm. c.1909. J. B. Lippincott Company.
--At the Back of the North Wind. Lewis, Elizabeth, adapted by. (The Children's Classics). N.D. J. B. Lippincott.
--At the Back of the North Wind. Mozley, Charles (1915-), illus. (Illus.). vi, 276 p. 25cm. (Nonesuch cygnet). 1964. F. Watts.
--At the Back of the North Wind. Mozley, Charles (1915-), illus. LC 77-17650. (Illus.). vi, 276 p. 21cm. 1978. (ISBN 0-8052-0595-0). Schocken Books.
--At the Back of the North Wind. Shepard, Ernest Howard (1879-1976), illus. LC 57-610. 325p. illus. 22cm. (Children's illustrated classics). 1957. Dent.

--Mystery of the Long House. LC 56-6466. 191p. illus. 22cm. c.1956. Nelson.
--Mystery of the Long House. (Hi-Lo Reading Ser). (gr. 5-10,RL 5-6). 1968. Pyramid Pubns.
--Mystery of the Long House. (gr. 7-12). N.D. Pyramid Pubns.
--Pigtail Pioneer. 1st ed. Neville, Vera (1900-1978), illus. LC 56-5840. 152p. illus. 21cm. 1956. Winston.
--Stolen Letters. Orig. Title: Assignment in Ankara. (gr. 7-12). N.D. Pyramid Pubns.
--Stormy Year. LC 52-3631. 21cm. 1952. T. Nelson.
--Wing Harbor. LC 57-7463. 184p. illus. 21cm. 1957. Nelson.
--Winter's Answer. LC 61-13833. 190 p. 22cm. 1961. T. Nelson.

MacDonald, Lucy see Lucy, pseud.

MacDonald, Lucy
--Dumpy. Taylor, Cathryn, illus. LC 48-16128. (Illus.). 32p. 24cm. 1948. J. Martin's House.
--The Little Boy Who Ran Away ... Emmons, Marion, illus. LC 47-17004. 32 p. col. illus. 21 1/2 x 17 cm. 1946. John Martin's House, Inc.
--The Story of Toby. Lucy, pseud. Emmons, Marion, illus. Emmo, pseud. LC 51-27551. (Illus.). 24p. 20cm. (A Bonnie Bk.). 1950. S. Lowe Co.

MacDonald, Margaret
--WE Go By Boat. N.D. Carlton Press.

Macdonald, Marianne
--Black Bass Rock. N.D. Macmillan.

McDonald, Mary Reynolds (1888-)
--Little Stories About God. (Illus.). (gr. k-1). 1964. Dghtrs St Paul.

MacDonald, Reby Edmond
--The Ghosts of Austwick Manor. LC 81-10779. 144 p. 22cm. 1982. (ISBN 0-689-50212-5). Atheneum.

Macdonald, Robert Maclauchlan (1874-)
--The Great White Chief: A Story of Adventure in New Guinea. (Illus.). N.D. Caldwell.
--The Great White Chief: A Story of Adventure in Unknown New Guinea. Rainey, William R. I. (1852-1936), illus. LC 7-321540. 5 p. l., vii-viii, 374 p. front., 7 pl., map. 19 1/2 cm. c.1907. Blackie and Son, Limited.
--The Rival Treasure Hunters. (Illus.). N.D. Caldwell.

McDonald, Ruth, jt. auth. see White, Mary Sue.

Macdonald, Shelagh (1937-)
--No End to Yesterday. LC 78-74755. (Illus.). (gr. 7 up). 1979. (ISBN 0-233-96865-2). Andre Deutsch.

McDonald, Sue
--A New Song for Heng Wah. LC 77-113209. (Illus.). 31 p. 24cm. 1970. Convention Press.

Macdonald, Una
--Alys-All-Alone. Lyon, Helen F., illus. LC 11-20881. viii p., 1 l., 301 p. incl. front. plates. 20 cm. $1.5. 1911. L. C. Page & Company.
--Alys in Happyland. Marlowe, Diantha W. Horne, illus. LC 13-22287. viii p., 1 l., 334 p. front., plates. 20 cm. (Her The Alys series) $1.50). 1913. L. C. Page & Company.

McDonald, W. H.
--Creation Tales from the Salish. (Indian Culture Ser.). (gr. 3-9). 1973. (ISBN 0-89992-061-6). MT Coun Indian.

MacDonald, William Coll
--Sleepy Horse Range. N.D. World Publishing.

Macdonald, Zillah Katherine (1885-)
--The Bluenose Express. Rev ed. Fawcett, Robert, illus. LC 28-21490. 5 p. l., 134, 1 p. front., illus. 19 1/2 cm. 1928. D. Appleton & Company.
--A Cap for Corrine. N.D. Jullian Messner, Inc.
--Cobblecorners. Rev ed. LC 26-9575. 4 p. l., 245, 1 p. front., illus. (map) 19 1/2 cm. 1926. D. Appleton and Company.
--Courage to Command: A Story of the Capture of Louisbourg. 1st ed. Stein, Harve (1904-), illus. 177p. illus. 22cm. (Winston adventure books). 1953. Winston.
--Eileen's Adventures in Wordland: The Life Story of Our Word Friends. Rev ed. Hay, Stuart, illus. LC 20-17532. x p., 3 l., 3-241 p. incl. plates. col. front. 21 cm. 1920. Frederick A. Stokes Company.
--Fireman for a Day. Gotlieb, Jules, illus. LC 52-13596. 62 p. illus. 22 cm. (Everyday adventure story). 1952. J. Messner.
--Flower of the Fortress. LC 44-7470. 5 p. l., 3-231 p. 21 cm. 1944. The Westminster Press.
--Haunthouse. Rev ed. Merwin, Decie (1894-1961), illus. LC 31-8829. 5 p. l., 282, 1 p. front., illus. 19 1/2 cm. 1931. D. Appleton and Company.
--Little Travelers. Newton, Ruth E. & Carter, Betty, illus. LC 44-14013. 28 p. illus. (part col.) 23 1/2 x 30 cm. c.1937. Whitman Publishing Company.
--Marcia, Private Secretary. N.D. Julian Messner, Inc.
--Marcia: Private Secretary. (Career Romance Ser.). (gr. 7 up). 1949. (ISBN 0-671-76982-0). Messner.
--Mic Mac on the Track. Rev ed. Stoner, E. C., illus. LC 30-21416. 5 p. l., 156, 1 p. front., illus. 20 cm. 1930. D. Appleton and Company.
--Mystery of the Piper's Ghost. Beck, Charles, illus. (Illus., Pub. by Winston). (gr. 4-6). 1972 (Starline). Schol Bk Serv.
--Mystery of the Piper's Ghost. 1st ed. Troth, Eleanor, illus. LC 54-5070. 178p. illus. 22cm. 1954. Winston.
--Rosemary Wins Her Cap. LC 55-6925. 192 p. 22cm. (Romance for young moderns). 1955. J. Messner.
--Spindlespooks. Rev ed. LC 28-4241. vii, 255 p. front. 19 1/2 cm. 1928. D. Appleton and Company.
--The Tin Tin Car. 1st ed. Porter, Jean MacDonald (1906-), illus. LC 37-38597. 5 p. l., 5-138 p. incl. front., illus., plates. 21 1/2 cm. 1937. The Penn Publishing Company.
--A Tugboat Toots for Terry. Barnum, Jay Hyde (1888-1962), illus. LC 53-9064. 68p. illus. 23cm. (Everyday adventure story). 1953. Messner.
--Two on a Tow. Rev ed. Kidder, Harvey, illus. LC 42-5830. 3 p. l., 230, 1 p. front., illus. 21 1/2 cm. 1942. Houghton Mifflin Company.
--Windywhistle. Rev ed. LC 29-17219. 4 p. l., 226 p. front. 19 1/2 cm. 1929. D. Appleton and Company.

Macdonald, Zillah Katherine (1885-) & Ahl, Vivian J.
--Nurse Todd's Strange Summer. LC 60-124484. 192p. 22cm. (Career-romance for young moderns). 1960. Messner.

Macdonell, Anne
--The Italian Fairy Book. N.D. Frederick A. Stokes Co.

McDonnell, Christine (1949-)
--Don't Be Mad, Ivy. De Groat, Diane (1947-), illus. LC 81-65850. p. cm. 1981. (ISBN 0-8037-2127-7). (ISBN 0-8037-2128-5). Dial Press.
--Lucky Charms and Birthday Wishes. De Groat, Diane (1947-), illus. LC 83-19861. p. cm. 1984. (ISBN 0-670-44430-8). Viking Press.
--Toad Food and Measle Soup. De Groat, Diane (1947-), illus. LC 82-70204. p. cm. c.1982. (ISBN 0-8037-8476-7). Dial Press.
--Toad Food and Measle Soup. De Groat, Diane (1947-), illus. LC 83-19209. 1984. (ISBN 0-14-031724-4). Puffin Books.

McDonnell, Jack
--Ski Patrol. McClure, Herbert, illus. LC 65-197321. 144p. illus. 22cm. (Signal bk.). c.1965. (ISBN 0-385-05858-6). Doubleday.

McDonnell, Lois Eddy (1914-)
--Hana's New Home. Papy, Dorothy, illus. LC 57-6169. 127p. illus. 21cm. 1957. Friendship Press.
--Stevie's Other Eyes. Turkle, Brinton Cassaday (1915-), illus. LC 62-7856. 127p. illus. 21cm. 1962. (ISBN 0-377-22701-3). Friendship Press.
--Susan Comes Through the Fire. Walker, Jim, illus. LC 68-56619. (Illus.). 95 p. 21cm. 1969. Friendship Press.

McDonnell, Margot B.
--My Own Worst Enemy. LC 84-7722. 192p. (Pacer Bks.). (gr. 7 up). 1984. (ISBN 0-399-21102-0, Putnam). Putnam Pub Group.

McDonnell, Regina, tr. see Vildrac, Charles.

McDonnell, Virginia Bleecher see Kirby, Jean, pseud.

McDonnell, Virginia Bleecker (1917-)
--Aerospace Nurse. LC 66-8177. 192p. 21cm. (Career romance for young moderns). 1966. Messner.
--County Agent. 192 p. 21cm. (career romance for young moderns). 1968. J. Messner.
--Dee O'Hara, Astronauts' Nurse. 1965. Thomas Nelson & Sons.
--The Ski Trail Mystery. Wurzer, Karl, illus. LC 66-165205. 182p. illus. 22cm. c.1966. Macrae.
--Trouble at Mercy Hospital. 1st ed. Wolf, Jack, illus. 142 p. 22cm. (Doubleday signal books). 1968. Doubleday.

McDonough, Edmund F.
--Manty. (Illus.). 1974. (ISBN 0-682-47760-5). Exposition Press.

MacDonough, Glen (0000-1924) & Chapin, Anna Alice (1880-1930)
--Babes in Toyland. Betts, Ethel Franklin, illus. LC 4-23721. 1 p. l., vi, 180 p. col. front., illus., col. plates 24 x 18 1/2 cm. 1904. Fox, Duffield and Company.

McDonough, Jerome
--Limbo. 28p. (Orig.). 1984. (ISBN 0-88680-219-9). I E Clark.

McDonough, Marian McIntyre
--Caravans to Santa Fe. Lee, Manning De Villeneuve (1894-1980), illus. LC 40-7292. 287 p. front., illus., plates. 22 cm. c.1940. The Penn Publishing Company.
--Little Soldier of the Plains. Lee, Manning De Villeneuve (1894-1980), illus. LC 34-399410. 312 p. front., plates. 22 cm. c.1934. The Penn Publishing Company.
--The Rails Push West. LC 40-29880. 304 p. col. front., illus., 22 cm. c.1940. The Penn Publishing Company.
--Sun in the West. Lee, Manning De Villeneuve (1894-1980), illus. LC 37-386067. 307 p. front., illus., plates. 22 cm. c.1937. The Penn Publishing Company.
--Tenderfoot Gold: A Story of Cripple Creek. Hampson, Albert W., illus. LC 38-365079. 297 p. front., illus., plates. 22 cm. c.1938. The Penn Publishing Company.
--Wagon Wheels to Denver. 310p. 1960. Golden Bell Press.
--Westward to the Stars. Lee, Manning De Villeneuve (1894-1980), illus. LC 36-30322. 317 p. front., illus., plates. 22 cm. c.1936. The Penn Publishing Company.

McDonough, Mary E
--Professor Lou: A Story for Young People. LC 25-5388. 2 p l., 128 p. 19 cm. c.1924. Hamilton Bros., Scripture Truth Depot.

Macdougall, Allan Ross, tr. see Dussauze, Alice.

MacDougall, Mary Katherine
--Black Jupiter. Moyers, William (1916-), illus. LC 59-5867. 181p. illus. 22cm. 1960. Broadman Press.

McDougall, Walter Hugh (1858-1938)
--Fun and Fancy: Wonder Tales for the Children from 7 to 70. LC 27-119923. 26 p. front., illus. 23 1/2 cm. (On cover: Comic animal series). N.D. C. E. Graham & Co.
--The Rambillicus Book: Wonder Tales for Children from 7 to 70. McDougall, Walter Hugh (1858-1938), illus. LC 3-18180. 25cm. 239p. 1903. G. W. Jacobs & Co.

Macdowall, M. W., ed. see Wagner, Johann Wilhelm Ernst.

McDowell, Clemens Margaret
--Second Son. N.D. E . M. Hale and co.

McDowell, Elizabeth Tibbals (1912-)
--Nady Goes to Market. (Illus.). (Little Playmate series, set 3). (ps). 1960. (ISBN 0-377-68932-7). Friend Pr.
--Nady Goes to Market: A Story About Brazil. Turkle, Brinton Cassaday (1915-), illus. LC 61-8004. 32p. illus. 21cm. (Little playmate series, set 3). 1961. Friendship Press.
--Now I am Three. Wilde, Carol (1938-), illus. LC 69-18150. (Illus.). 24 p. 21cm. 1969. (ISBN 0-8170-0424-6). Judson Press.

McDowell, John Holmes (1946-)
--Children's Riddling. LC 78-19551. xii, 272 p. 22cm. c.1979. (ISBN 0-253-15020-5). Indiana University Press.

McDowell, Katherine Sherwood Bonner, Mrs. (1849-1883)
--Suwanee River Tales. Kirk, Sophia, ed. Merrill, Frank Thayer (1848-), illus. LC 73-38641. (Illus.). ix, 303 p. 23cm. (The Black Heritage Library Collection). 1972, c.1884. (ISBN 0-8369-8999-6). Books for Libraries Press.
--Suwanee River Tales. Kirk, Sophia, ed. Merrill, Frank Thayer (1848-), illus. LC 19-2909. xii, 303 p. front., plates, 17 1/2 cm. 1884. Roberts Brothers.

McDowell, Lillie Gilliland
--Elsie: A Mostly True Story. LC 46-271115. 95 p. 20 cm. 1945. Wm. B. Eerdmans Publishing Company.

McDowell, Margaret Clemens (1895-1955)
--New Friends for Nena. Pointer, Priscilla, illus. LC 53-9164. 127p. illus. 22cm. 1953. Friendship Press.
--Second Son. Wong, Jeanyee (1920-), illus. LC 55-11943. 127p. illus. 22cm. 1956. Friendship Press.

McDowell, Mildred
--The Little People. Whitaker, Arleen, illus. LC 72-133255. (Illus.). 39 p. 24cm. (Story and its verse books). 1971. (ISBN 0-87884-002-8). Unicorn Enterprises.
--The Squirrel and the Frog. Brennan, Nancy, illus. LC 76-133256. (Illus.). 39 p. 24cm. (Story and its verse books). 1971. (ISBN 0-87884-007-9). Unicorn Enterprises.

McDowell, Robert Eugene, jt. ed. see Lavitt, Edward.

McDowell, Robert Eugene (1928-) & Lavitt, Edward, eds.
--Third World Voices for Children. Isaac, Barbara K., illus. LC 71-169091. (Illus.). 156p. (Odarkai Bk). (gr. 5-9). 1971. (ISBN 0-89388-020-5, Odarkai). Okpaku Communications.

Macduff, John Ross (1818-1895)
--Bow in the Cloud. N.D. Robert Carter & Brothers.
--Fergus Morton: A Story of a Scottish Boy. (Illus.). 110p. N.D. Merrill.
--Tales of the Warrior King. N.D. American Tract Society.

Mace, Elisabeth (1933-)
--Brother Enemy. LC 80-29258. 175 p. 22cm. c.1979. (ISBN 0-8253-0031-2). Beaufort Books.
--The Ghost Diviners. LC 77-22444. p. cm. 22cm. 343p. c.1977. (ISBN 0-8407-6555-X). T. Nelson.
--Out There. 1st. ed. LC 77-26697. 181 p. 22cm. c.1975. (ISBN 0-688-80142-0). (ISBN 0-688-84142-2). Greenwillow Books.
--The Rushton Inheritance. LC 78-318421. 160 p. 21cm. 1978. (ISBN 0-233-96969-1). A. Deutsch.
--The Rushton Inheritance. LC 78-13559. 173 p. 21cm. c.1978. T. Nelson.
--The Travelling Men. LC 76-376162. 128 p. 21cm. 1976. (ISBN 0-233-96789-3). Deutsch.

Mace, Harry F., jt. auth. see Mace, Katherine Keeler.

Mace, Jean (1815-1894)
--Fairy Book. Booth, Mary L., tr. N.D. Harper & Bros.
--Home Fairy Tales. (Twilight Ser.). N.D. Harper & Bros.
--Home Fairy Tales. Booth, Mary L., tr. from Fr. LC 78-74517. (Illus.). 304p. Repr. of 1867 ed. (Children's Literature Reprint Ser.). (gr. 4-5). 1979. (ISBN 0-8486-0220-X). Core Collection.
--A Mouthful of Bread. N.D. Harper & Brothers.

Mace, Katherine Keeler (1921-)
--Let's Dance a Story. Hayes, William Dimitt (1913-), illus. LC 55-517027. unpaged. illus. 27cm. 1955. Abelard-Schuman.
--A Tail is a Tail. N.D. E. M. Hale & Co.
--A Tail Is a Tail. Graboff, Abner (1919-), illus. LC 57-5184. unpaged. illus. 27cm. 1957. Abelard-Schuman.
--When I Grow Up. Malvern, Corinne (1905-1956), illus. (A Little Golden Book, 96). 1950. Simon & Schuster.
--The Wonderful Dog Show. Berthold, illus. LC 50-12350. (Illus.). 29p. 29cm. (Treasure Bks.). 1950. Grosset & Dunlap.

Mace, Katherine Keeler (1921-) & Mace, Harry F. (1922-)
--Chief Dooley's Busy Day. LC 54-5239. unpaged. illus. 27cm. 1954. Abelard Press.
--Mr. Wiggington Joins the Circus. LC 52-2419. unpaged. illus. 28 cm. 1952. Abelard Press.

Mace, Varian
--Fairy Tales Coloring & Story Book. (Illus.). 48p. (Orig.). (gr. k-6). 1979. (ISBN 0-89844-006-8). Troubador Pr.

Mace, Varian, jt. auth. see Moen, Ann.

Mace, William H
--Stories of Heroism. N.D. Rand McNally.

MacEachen, Dougald B.
--Seven Boys and a Bandit. 192p. 1965. Astor Books.

McEleroy, Margaret Julia (1889-)
--The Adventures of Johnny T. Bear. N.D. E. P. Dutton & Co.

McElevey, Eva L.
--Dad and I. LC 30-18205. 4 p. 1. 11-110 p incl front illus 20". 1930. E. P. Dutton & Co.

McElfresh, Adeline see Wesley, Elizabeth, pseud.

McElfresh, Adeline (1918-)
--Career for Jenny. LC 58-9130. 222p. 21cm. 1958. Avalon Books.
--Polly's Summer Stock. Wesley, Elizabeth, pseud. LC 57-874221. 219p. 21cm. 1957. Avalon Books.
--Summer Change. 1st ed. Geer, Charles Hand (1922-), illus. LC 60-6940. 192p. illus. 22cm. 1960. Bobbs-Merrill.
--To Each Her Dream. LC 61-13144. (gr. 8 up). 1961. (ISBN 0-672-50541-X). Bobbs.

McElhone, James F
--Tim. LC 34-40513. 188 p. front. 19 cm. 1934. Benziger Brothers.

McElhone, Nell K.
--The Surprise Book. Wheelan, Albertine Randall (1863-), illus. 1901. Frederick A. Stokes Co.

McElrath, William N (1932-)
--I Sailed with Saul of Tarsus. LC 80-65215. (Illus.). 96 p. 21cm. c.1980. (ISBN 0-8054-7313-0). Broadman Press.
--Indian Treasure on Rockhouse Creek. LC 84-9527. (gr. 5-8). 1984. (ISBN 0-8054-4517-X). Broadman.
--Judges and Kings: God's Chosen Leaders. Johnston, Clifford, illus. LC 79-111945. (Illus.). 48 p. 24cm. (Biblearn series). c.1979. (ISBN 0-8054-4249-9). Broadman Press.

McElravy, May F
--Tortilla Girl. Bannon, Laura May (0000-1963), illus. LC 46-251816. 26 p. illus. (part col.) 26 cm. 1946. A. Whitman.

McElroy
--Jesus Forgives Peter. 24p. (Orig.). (Arch Bks.). (gr. k-4). 1985. (ISBN 0-570-06192-X). Concordia.

McElroy, Clifford D., ed.
--My Orange School. Unsworth, Bonnie D., illus. LC 79-39018. (Illus.). 48 p. 22cm. 1972. (ISBN 0-07-044943-0). McGraw-Hill.

McElroy, Frances Casseday
--The Fall of the Fairy Prince. Pallesen, Robert & Pallesen, Katharine, illus. LC 30-17104. 126 p. col. front., col. illus. 19 1/2 cm. c.1929. Johnson Publishing Company.

McElroy, Margaret Julia (1889-) & Younge, Jessica O.
--The Squirrel Tree. LC 27-18995. 94 p. illus. 19 1/2 cm. c.1927. American Book Company.
--Toby Chipmunk. LC 31-15940. 74 p. col. illus. 19 1/2 cm. c.1931. American Book Company.

McEntee, Dorothy, jt. auth. see Martin, Frances Gardiner McEntee.

McEvoy, Bernard L., ed.
--Stories from Across Canada. LC 67-17493. 109 p. 23cm. 1967, c.1966. Lippincott.

--The Most Wonderful Doll in the World. Stone, Helen (1904-), illus. LC 50-12175. (Illus.). 61 p. 21cm. 1950. Lippincott. **Award: (RCM).**
--A Name for Kitty. Rojankovsky, Feodor Stepanovich (1891-1970), illus. LC 49-713810. 28 p. col. illus. 21 cm. (Little golden library, 55.). 1948. Simon and Schuster.
--The Plain Princess. Harris, Aurand (1915-), adapted by. 1955. Children's Theatre Press.
--The Plain Princess. Stone, Helen (1904-), illus. LC 45-9782. 62, 2 p. illus. (part col.) 20 1/2 cm. 1945. J. B. Lippincott Company.
--Sugar and Spice: The ABC of Being a Girl. LC 60-11203. unpaged. illus. 26cm. 1960. F. Watts.
--Wonderful Time. Alcorn, John (1935-), illus. LC 66-835721. 47p. illus. 29cm. 1966. (ISBN 0-397-30926-0). Lippincott. **Award: (NYT).**
--Wonders & Surprises. LC 67-19271. 1968p. (gr. 6 up). 1960. (ISBN 0-397-31053-6). Har-Row.
--A Wreath of Christmas Legends. Weisgard, Leonard Joseph (1916-), illus. (Illus.). 32 p. 19cm. 1974, c.1967 (Collier Bks.). Macmillan.
--Year Without a Santa Claus. Werth, Kurt (1896-), illus. (Illus.). (gr. k-3). 1957. (ISBN 0-397-30399-8, JBL-J). (ISBN 0-397-31969-X). Har-Row.
--The Year Without a Santa Claus. Werth, Kurt (1896-), illus. LC 57-10332. unpaged. illus. 26cm. 32p. c.1957. Lippincott.

McGinley, Phyllis (1905-1978), ed.
--Wonders and Surprises: A Collection of Poems. LC 67-19271. 188 p. 22cm. 1968. Lippincott.

McGinn, Maureen, pseud., see Sautel, Maureen Ann.

McGinn, Maureen, pseud. (1951-)
--I Used to Be an Artichoke. Sautel, Maureen Ann. Norman, Anita, illus. LC 74-151235. (Illus.). 48 p. 27cm. 1973. (ISBN 0-570-03421-3). Concordia Pub. House.

McGinnis, Lila Sprague (1924-)
--Auras and Other Rainbow Questions. LC 84-4486. 1984. (ISBN 0-8038-0551-9). Hastings House.
--Auras & Other Rainbow Secrets. LC 84-4486. (gr. 3-7). 1984. (ISBN 0-8038-0551-9). Hastings.
--The Ghost Upstairs. Rowen, Amy, illus. LC 81-20337. (Illus.). 119 p. 22cm. c.1982. (ISBN 0-8038-2716-4). Hastings House.
--Secret of the Porcelain Cats. Frederick, Larry, illus. LC 78-15225. p. cm. (Pilot books). 1978. (ISBN 0-8075-7288-8). A. Whitman.

McGivern, Maureen Daly see Daly, Maureen.

McGivern, Maureen Daly (1921-)
--Ginger Horse. Dennis, Wesley (1903-1966), illus. (Illus.). (gr. 7 up). 1964. (ISBN 0-396-05043-3). Dodd.
--Patrick Takes a Trip. Simmons, Ellie, illus. LC 60-8741. unpaged. illus. 24cm. c.1960. Dodd, Mead.
--Patrick Visits the Farm. Simmons, Ellie, illus. LC 58-9725. unpaged. illus. 24cm. 1959. Dodd, Mead.
--Patrick Visits the Library. Lantz, Paul (1908-), illus. LC 61-14754. unpaged. illus. 24cm. 1961. (ISBN 0-396-06465-5). Dodd, Mead.
--Patrick Visits the Zoo. Savitt, Sam (1917-), illus. LC 63-8282. 47p. illus. (pt.col. c.1963. Dodd.
--Rosie, the Dancing Elephant. Bjorklund, Lorence F. (1913-1978), illus. LC 67-26152. (Illus.). 40 p. 24cm. 1967. (ISBN 0-396-05639-3). Dodd, Mead.
--Seventeenth Summer. Robinson, Jay, illus. (Illus.). (gr. 9 up). 1942. (ISBN 0-396-02322-3). Dodd.
--Seventeenth Summer. Robinson, Jay, illus. LC 48-10238. (Illus.). 255 p. 21cm. 1948. Dodd, Mead.
--Seventeenth Summer. Robinson, Jay, illus. 288p. Repr. 1981. (ISBN 0-89967-029-6). Harmony & Co.
--Sixteen, and Other Stories. Rossi, Kendall, illus. LC 61-10359. (Illus.). 157 p. 21cm. 1961. (ISBN 0-396-04501-4). Dodd, Mead.
--The Small War of Sergeant Donkey. Dennis, Wesley (1903-1966), illus. LC 66-20450. 85p. illus. 24cm. 1966. (ISBN 0-396-05409-9). Dodd.
--Small War of Sergeant Donkey. Wesley, Dennis, ed. (Illus.). (gr. 5-9). 1966. (ISBN 0-8382-1034-1). Hale.

McGivern, Maureen Daly (1921-), ed.
--My Favorite Mystery Stories. LC 66-9786. viii, 310 p. 21cm. 1966. (ISBN 0-396-05445-5). Dodd, Mead.
--My Favorite Stories. (gr. 9 up) 1948. (ISBN 0-396-03002-5). Dodd.
--My Favorite Suspense Stories. 192p. (gr. 8 up). 1968. (ISBN 0-396-05829-9). Dodd.

McGivern, Patrick
--The Ultimate Auto. Perl, Susan (1922-1983), illus. LC 74-75588. (Illus.). 48 p. 24cm. 1969. Putnam.

McGlennon, Pat
--The Musical Pussy Cat. N.D. Comet Press Books.

McGoldrick, Rita C., Mrs.
--The Corduroy Trail. Brown, Paul (1893-1958), illus. LC 35-1174. 5 p. l., 251 p. col. front. 20 1/2 cm. 1934. Doubleday, Doran & Company, Inc.

McGough, Edward Marcus see Marcus, Edward, pseud.

McGough, Edward Marcus
--Young Rider of the High Country. Marcus, Edward, pseud. 1st ed. Echohawk, Brummett, illus. LC 59-122344. 181p. illus. 21cm. 1959. Duell. Sloan and Pearce.

McGovern, Ann
--Annie Oakley and the Rustlers. Pictures by Mel Crawford. Crawford, Mel (1925-), illus. LC 55-161355. unpaged. illus. 21cm. (little Golden book, 221). 1955. Simon and Schuster.
--Arrow Book of Poetry. Dotzenko, Grisha, illus. LC 68-3527. 96 p. illus. 20 cm. (TX651). 1965. Scholastic Book Services.
--Black Is Beautiful. Wurmfeld, Hope, illus. LC 69-17247. (Illus.). 40 p. 1969. Four Winds Press.
--Feeling Mad-Feeling Sad-Feeling Bad-Feeling Glad. Wurmfeld, Hope, illus. LC 76-53374. (Illus.). (gr. k-5). 1978. (ISBN 0-8027-6295-6, Dist. by Walker & Co). Magic Circle Pr.
--Ghostly Fun. Glass, Marvin, illus. (gr. 4-6). 1971. (ISBN 0-590-04448-6, Schol Pap). Scholastic Inc.
--Ghostly Giggles. Gerberg, Mort, illus. (gr. 4-6). 1972. (ISBN 0-590-01616-4). Schol Bk Serv.
--Half a Kingdom. Langner, Nola (1930-), illus. (gr. 4-6). 1978. (ISBN 0-590-05373-6). (ISBN 0-590-20606-0). Scholastic Inc.
--Half a Kingdom: An Icelandic Folktale. Langner, Nola (1930-), illus. LC 76-45305. (Illus.). 41 p. c.1977. (ISBN 0-7232-6137-7). F. Warne.
--Hee Haw. Von Schmidt, Eric (1931-), illus. LC 75-86294. (Illus.). 31 p. 1969. Houghton Mifflin.
--If You Lived in Colonial Times. (Illus.). 80p. 1966. Four Winds Press.
--If You Sailed on the Mayflower. 80p. 1970. Four Winds Press.
--Little Wolf. Langner, Nola (1930-), illus. (Illus.). (Picture Book). (gr. k-3). 1965. (ISBN 0-200-71388-4). (ISBN 0-200-00020-9). Abelard.
--Mr. Skinner's Skinny House. Gerberg, Mort, illus. LC 79-18360. (Illus.). 48 p. 25cm. c.1980. (ISBN 0-590-07620-5). Four Winds Press.
--Nicholas Bentley Stoningpot III. De Paola, Tomie, pseud. (1934-), illus. De Paola, Thomas Anthony. LC 81-13226. p. cm. c.1982. (ISBN 0-8234-0443-9). Holiday House.
--Night Dive. Scheiner, Martin & Scheiner, James B., photos by LC 84-7163. (Illus.). 64p. (gr. 2-5). 1984. (ISBN 0-02-765710-8). Macmillan.
--Party in Shariland. Henderson, Doris & Henderson, Marion, illus. (Little Golden Book). 1959. Golden Press.
--Robin Hood of Sherwood Forest. Spilka, Arnold (1917-), illus. LC 68-1166. (Illus.). 164 p. 21cm. 1968. Crowell.
--Roy Rogers and the Mountain Lion. Crawford, Mel (1925-), illus. LC 55-3190. unpaged. illus. 21cm. (Little golden library, 231). 1955. Simon and Schuster.
--Ruff and Reddy. Eisenberg, Harvey & White, Al, illus. (Little Golden Book). 1959. Golden Press.
--Runaway Slave: The Story of Harriet Tubman. 64p. 1965. Four Winds Press.
--Scram, Kid!. 1st ed. Langner, Nola (1930-), illus. LC 73-20017. (Illus.). 40 p. 1974. (ISBN 0-670-62370-9). Viking Press. **Award: (BGH).**
--Shark Lady. (gr. 4-6). 1978. (ISBN 0-590-11896-X, Schol Pap). Schol Bk Serv.
--Squeals & Squiggles & Ghostly Giggles. Higginbottom, Jeffrey Winslow (1945-), illus. LC 72-87083. (Illus.). 76 p. 21cm. 1973. Four Winds Press.
--Stone Soup. Langner, Nola (1930-), illus. (gr. 2-3). 1971. (ISBN 0-590-01629-6). (ISBN 0-590-04393-5). Scholastic Inc.
--Too Much Noise. Taback, Simms, illus. (Illus.). 44 p. 1967. Houghton Mifflin.
--Treasure Book of Fairy Tales. (Illus.). N.D. Fawcett Pub Inc.
--Who Has a Secret. Langner, Nola (1930-), illus. (Illus.). (gr. k-3). 1964. (ISBN 0-395-06907-6). (ISBN 0-395-06908-4). HM.
--Why It's a Holiday. Wilson, Dagmar (1916-), illus. LC 60-124356. 64p. illus. 24cm. 1960. Random House.
--Winky Dink. Scarry, Richard McClure (1919-), illus. (Little Golden Bk.). 1956. Golden Press.
--Woody Woodpecker Takes a Trip. White, Al & DeNunez, Ben, illus. (Illus.). (gr. k-3). 1976. (ISBN 0-307-60445-4, Golden Pr). Western Pub.
--Zoo, Where Are You. (Illus.). (gr. k-2). 1964. (ISBN 0-8382-1005-8). Hale.
--Zoo, Where Are You. Keats, Ezra Jack (1916-1983), illus. (Illus.). (gr. k-3). 1964. (ISBN 0-06-024161-6, HarpJ). Har-Row.

McGovern, Ann, ed.
--Shakespearean Sallies, Sullies & Slanders: Insults for All Occasions. McCrea, James Craig, Jr. (1920-) & McCrea, Ruth Pirman (1921-), illus. LC 69-11826. (Illus.). index. 115p. (gr. 7 up). 1969. (ISBN 0-690-73092-6). T Y Crowell.
--Treasury of Christmas Stories. (Illus.). 160p. 1965. Four Winds Press.
--Treasury of Christmas Stories. Lockhart, David, illus. LC 73-88552. (Illus.). viii, 151 p. 22cm. 1974, c.1960. (ISBN 0-88365-043-6). Galahad Books.

McGovern, Ann, et al., eds.
--Hanna-Barbera Huckleberry Hound Treasury. N.D. Golden Press.

McGovern, Ann, adapted by see Damjan, Mischa.

McGovern, Ann & Hyatt, S. Quentin
--Huckleberry Hound & His Friends. White, Al, illus. 1962. Golden Press.

McGovern, James
--Martin Bormann. N.D (Tempo Books). Grosset & Dunlap.

McGovern, Mary Harriet (1881-)
--Fifty Famous Fairy Tales. Lee, Ella Dolbear, illus. LC 17-258866. vi p., 1 l., 9-254 p. col. front., illus., col. plates. 23 cm. c.1917. Whitman Publishing Co.

MacGowan, Alice (1858-)
--A Girl of the Plains Country. LC 24-20566. iv, 347 p. 19 1/2 cm. 1924. Frederick A. Stokes Company.
--Poole-Doodle of Doodle Farm. Wiese, Kurt (1887-1974), illus. N.D. J. B. Lippincott.
--The Trail of the Little Wagon. N.D. J. B. Lippincott.
--The Trail of the Little Wagon: A Novel for Boys and Girls. LC 28-6080. viii p., 1 l., 341 p. 19 1/2 cm. 1928. Frederick A. Stokes Company.

McGowan, Patricia
--House of Friends. LC 58-12231. 236p. 22cm. 1958. Bruce Pub. Co.

McGowan, Prudence R.
--Twinkie Flickertail. (Illus.). 1977. Dorrance.

McGowan, Susie W
--Teeny Tales for Tiny Tots. N.D. Lothrop,Lee & Shepard.

McGowen, Thomas see McGowen, Tom, pseud.

McGowen, Tom, pseud., see McGowen, Thomas.

McGowen, Tom, pseud. (1927-)
--The Apple Strudel Soldier. McGowen, Thomas. Johnson, John Emil (1929-), illus. LC 67-21154. (Illus.). 48 p. 27cm. 1968. Follett Pub. Co.
--The Biggest Toot in Toozelburg. McGowen, Thomas. Appleyard, Dev, illus. LC 70-125379. (Illus.). 30 p. 24cm. 1970. Reilly & Lee Books.
--Dragon Stew. McGowen, Thomas. Hyman, Trina Schart (1939-), illus. LC 68-14584. (Illus.). 31 p. 23cm. 1969. Follett Pub. Co.
--The Fearless Fossil Hunters. McGowen, Thomas. Scott, Frances Gruse, illus. LC 72-150804. (Illus.). 32 p. 24cm. 1971. (ISBN 0-8075-2306-2). A. Whitman.
--Hammet and the Highlanders. McGowen, Thomas. Stone, David Karl (1922-), illus. LC 73-93800. (Illus.). 47 p. 22cm. 1970. Follett Pub. Co.
--King's Quest. McGowen, Thomas. LC 83-91426. 160p. (Endless Quest Bks.). (gr. 5up). 1984. (ISBN 0-394-72460-7). Random.
--The Last Voyage of the Unlucky Katie Marie. McGowen, Thomas. Appleyard, Dev, illus. LC 72-91740. (Illus.). 32 p. 24cm. 1969. A. Whitman.
--Odyssey from River Bend. McGowen, Thomas. LC 74-34216. ix, 166 p. 21cm. 1975. (ISBN 0-316-55931-8). Little, Brown.
--The Only Glupmaker in the U.S. Navy. McGowen, Thomas. McGowen, Tom, pseud. (1927-), illus. McGowen, Thomas. LC 66-945945. 1v. (unpaged) illus. (pt. col.) 24cm. 1966. A. Whitman.
--Sir Machinery. McGowen, Thomas. Hyman, Trina Schart (1939-), illus. LC 78-118965. (Illus.). 160p. (gr. 4 up). 1971. (ISBN 0-695-80167-8). (ISBN 0-695-40167-X). Follett.
--Spirit of the Wild. McGowen, Thomas. (gr. 5-7). 1976. (ISBN 0-316-55933-4). Little.

McGrady, Mike, jt. auth. see Floherty, John Joseph, Jr.

McGrady, Mike (1933-)
--Crime Scientists. 160p. 1961. J B Lippincott Company.
--Jungle Doctors. 128p. 1962. J.

McGrath, Ann Sperry (1933-)
--Tony's Tunnel. Demi, pseud. (1942-), illus. Hitz, Demi. LC 81-2009. p. cm. c.1981. (ISBN 0-13-925099-9). Prentice-Hall.

McGrath, Fergal
--Adventure Island. LC 32-216654. 178 p. front., illus. (map) 19 cm. 1932. Benziger Brothers.
--The Last Lap. LC 25-102192. 249 p. front., plates. 19 cm. 1925. Benziger Brothers.

McGrath, Gayle, jt. auth. see Hithersay, Helen.

MacGrath, Harold
--The Adventures of Kathlyn: The/Motion-Picture Story. N.D. Bobbs-Merrill Co.
--The Best Man. Grefe, Will, illus. N.D. Bobbs-Merrill Co.
--The Carpet from Bagdad. Castaigne, Andre, illus. N.D. Bobbs-Merrill Co.
--Deuces Wild. Crosby, R. M., illus. N.D. Bobbs-Merrill Co.
--The Enchanted Hat. Grefe, Will, illus. N.D. Bobbs-Merrill Co.
--The Goose Girl. Casatigne, Andre, illus. N.D. Bobbs-Merrill Co.
--The Grey Cloak. Pierce, Thomas Mitchell, illus. N.D. Bobbs-Merrill Co.
--Half a Rogue. Fisher, Harrison, illus. N.D. Bobbs-Merrill Co.
--Hearts and Masks. Fisher, Harrison, illus. N.D. Bobb-Merrill Co.
--The Lure of the Mask. Fisher, Harrison & Anderson, Karl, illus. N.D. Bobbs-Merrill Co.
--The Man on the Box. Fisher, Harrison, illus. N.D. Bobbs-Merrill Co.
--Parrott & Co. Castaigne, Andre & Brown, Arthur William, illus. N.D. Bobbs-Merrill Co.
--Pidgin Island. Brown, Arthur William, illus. N.D. Bobbs-Merrill Co.
--The Place of Honeymoons. Keller, Arthur I., illus. N.D. Bobbs-Merrill Co.
--The Puppet Crown. Reay, Martine, illus. N.D. Bobbs-Merrill Co.
--A Splendid Hazard. Christy, Howard Chandler (1873-1952), illus. N.D. Bobbs-Merrill Co.
--The Voice in the Fog. Wenzell, A. B., illus. N.D. Bobbs-Merrill Co.

McGrath, Thomas M. (1916-) & Jenkyns, Chris (1924-)
--Beautiful Things. LC 60-15076. (Illus.). (gr. k-3). 1960. (ISBN 0-8149-0364-9). Vanguard.

McGraw, Al
--Timmie & His Little Brother. Cogancherry, Helen, illus. (Illus.). 1977. (ISBN 0-533-02872-8). Vantage.

McGraw, Eloise Jarvis (1915-)
--Crown Fire. LC 51-10751. 254 p. 21cm. 1951. Coward-McCann.
--Crown Fire. School ed. Schostak, Jerome, ed. LC 57-413212. 306p. illus. 22cm. (Teen-age bookshelf). 1957. Oxford Book Co.
--The Golden Goblet. LC 61-8256. 248 p. 21cm. 1961. Coward-McCann. **Awards: (ALA); (JNM).**
--Golden Goblet. 1961. (ISBN 0-8382-0295-0, Cadmus Books). E. M. Hale and Company.
--Greensleeves. LC 68-25191. 311 p. 22cm. 1968. Harcourt, Brace & World.
--Hideaway. 1st ed. LC 83-2786. 217 p. 22cm. 1983. (ISBN 0-689-50284-2). Atheneum.
--Joel and the Great Merlini. Arnosky, James E. (1946-), illus. LC 79-4580. p. cm. c.1979. (ISBN 0-394-94193-4). Pantheon Books.
--Mara. N.D E . M. Hale and Co.
--Mara, Daughter of the Nile. LC 53-9564. 279 p. 22cm. 1953. Coward-McCann.
--Mara, Daughter of the Nile. LC 85-567. (Illus.). viii, 279 p. 18cm. c.1985. (ISBN 0-14-031929-8). Puffin Books.
--Mara: Daughter of the Nile. Myers, Jack, illus. (Illus.). (gr. 5-8). 1953. (ISBN 0-698-20087-X, Coward). Putnam Pub Group.
--Master Cornhill. LC 72-85920. (Illus.). 206 p. 24cm. 1973. (ISBN 0-689-30320-3). Atheneum.
--Moccasin Trail. LC 52-12371. 247 p. 21cm. 1952. Coward-McCann. **Award: (JNM).**
--The Money Room. LC 81-3477. p. cm. 1981. (ISBN 0-689-50208-7). Atheneum.
--A Really Weird Summer. LC 76-28718. (Illus.). 216 p. 24cm. 1977. (ISBN 0-689-50077-7). Atheneum.
--Sawdust in His Shoes. LC 50-6964. 246 p. illus. 21 cm. 1950. Coward-McCann.
--Steady, Stephanie. 1962. Dramatic Publishing Company.

McGraw, Eloise Jarvis (1915-) & Wagner, Laurie McGraw
--Merry-Go-Round in Oz. Martin, Dick (1927-), illus. LC 63-19037. (Illus.). 303p. (gr. 4-6). 1963. (ISBN 0-8092-8557-6). Reilly & Lee.

McGraw, Tug (1944-)
--Lumpy: A Baseball Fable. LC 81-10658. p. cm. c.1981. (ISBN 0-89471-150-4). (ISBN 0-89471-151-2). Running Press.

McGraw, William Corbin see Corbin, William, pseud.

McGraw, William Corbin (1916-)
--The Day Willie Wasn't. Corbin, William, pseud. Fiammenghi, Gioia (1929-), illus. LC 76-126446. (Illus.). 48 p. 1971. Coward McCann & Geoghegan.
--Deadline. Corbin, William, pseud. LC 52-12095. 244 p. 22cm. 1952. Coward-McCann.
--The Everywhere Cat. Corbin, William, pseud. Joerns, Consuelo, illus. LC 76-90866. (Illus.). 47 p. 22cm. (ps-1). 1970. (ISBN 0-698-30072-6). Coward-McCann.
--Golden Mare. Corbin, William, pseud. Crowell, Pers (1910-), illus. LC 55-6891. (Illus.). 122 p. 22cm. 1955. Coward-McCann.
--High Road Home. Corbin, William, pseud. LC 53-9565. 250 p. 21cm. 1954. Coward-McCann.

--Horse in the House. Corbin, William, pseud. Savitt, Sam (1917-), illus. LC 64-17995. (Illus.). 288 p. 22cm. (gr. 3-6). 1964. Coward-McCann.
--Pony for Keeps. Corbin, William, pseud. Burchard, Peter Duncan (1921-), illus. LC 57-13160. (Illus.). 214 p. 22cm. 1958. Coward-McCann.
--The Prettiest Gargoyle. Corbin, William, pseud. LC 70-159757. 242 p. 22cm. 1971. Coward, McCann & Geoghegan.
--The Pup with the up-and-Down Tail. Corbin, William, pseud. Robinson, Charles (1931-), illus. LC 72-186651. (Illus.). 62 p. 24cm. 1972. Coward, McCann & Geoghegan.
--Smoke. Corbin, William, pseud. LC 67-24218. 253 p. 23cm. 1967. Coward-McCann.

McCray, Norm, ed. see Disney, Walter Elias (1901-1966) & Bedford, Annie North.

McGreal, William
--Andy, the Musical Ant. 1st ed. Unwin, Nora Spicer (1907-), illus. LC 49-11862. 46 p. illus. (part col.) 23 cm. 1949. Aladdin Books.
--Andy, the Musical Ant. Unwin, Nora Spicer (1907-), illus. N.D. E. P. Dutton & Co.
--Dennis the Donkey. Hall, Cyrus, illus. LC 40-10161. 2 p. l., 9-63, 1 p. col. front., illus. (part col.) 21 1/2 cm. c.1939. F. Warne & Co. Ltd.
--The Frog: The Penny and the Big Black Tree. Hall, Cyrus, illus. LC 40-10162. 3-68, 1 p. incl. col. front., illus. (part col.) 21 1/2 cm. c.1939. F. Warne & Co., Ltd.

MacGregor, Ellen (1906-1954)
--Miss Pickerell and the Geiger Counter. Galdone, Paul (1914-), illus. 1953. (ISBN 0-07-044561-3). McGraw Hill Book Company.
--Miss Pickerell & the Geiger Counter. Galdone, Paul (1914-), illus. 1961. McGraw.
--Miss Pickerell and the Geiger Counter. Galdone, Paul (1914-), illus. LC 53-5758. (Illus.). 123 p. 21cm. 1953. Whittlesey House.
--Miss Pickerell Goes to Mars. Galdone, Paul (1914-), illus. 1951. (ISBN 0-07-044560-5). McGraw Hill Book Company.
--Miss Pickerell Goes to Mars. Galdone, Paul (1914-), illus. LC 51-13241. (Illus.). 128 p. 21cm. 1951. Whittlesey House.
--Miss Pickerell Goes to the Arctic. Galdone, Paul (1914-), illus. 1961. McGraw.
--Miss Pickerell Goes to the Arctic. Galdone, Paul (1914-), illus. (Illus.). 126 p. 20cm. (Young pioneer book). 1967, c.1954. McGraw-Hill.
--Miss Pickerell Goes to the Arctic. Galdone, Paul (1914-), illus. LC 54-8816. (Illus.). 126 p. 21cm. 1954. Whittlesey House.
--Miss Pickerell goes to The Artic. Galdone, Paul (1914-), illus. (Illus.). 134 p. 18cm. 1981, c.1954. (ISBN 0-671-56021-2). Pocket Books.
--Miss Pickerell Goes Under Sea. Galdone, Paul (1914-), illus. 1953. (ISBN 0-07-044562-1). McGraw Hill Book Company.
--Miss Pickerell Goes Undersea. Galdone, Paul (1914-), illus. 1961. McGraw.
--Miss Pickerell Goes Undersea. Galdone, Paul (1914-), illus. LC 53-9890. (Illus.). 128 p. 21cm. 1953. Whittlesey House.
--Mister Ferguson of the Fire Department. Galdone, Paul (1914-), illus. (Illus.). (gr. k-2). 1956. (ISBN 0-07-044566-4). McGraw.
--Mr. Ferguson of the Fire Department. Galdone, Paul (1914-), illus. 1964. McGraw.
--Mr. Pringle and Mr. Buttonhouse. Galdone, Paul (1914-), illus. 1957. McGrawhill.
--Theodore Turtle. Galdone, Paul (1914-), illus. (gr. k-3). 1955. (ISBN 0-07-044567-2, GB). McGraw.
--Theodore Turtle. Galdone, Paul (1914-), illus. LC 55-8289. 32p. 1955. Whittlesey House.
--Tommy and the Telephone. Selover, Zabeth, illus. LC 47-12438. 32 p. illus. (part col.) 24 cm. 1947. A. Whitman.

MacGregor, Ellen (1906-1954) & Pantell, Dora F
--Miss Pickerell and the Blue Whale. Geer, Charles Hand (1922-), illus. LC 82-4624. (Illus.). 159 p. 21cm. c.1983. (ISBN 0-07-044592-3). McGraw-Hill.
--Miss Pickerell and the Earthquakes. Geer, Charles Hand (1922-), illus. 1977. McGraw Hill.
--Miss Pickerell and the Supertanker. Geer, Charles Hand (1922-), illus. LC 78-8241. p. cm. 1978. (ISBN 0-07-044588-5). McGraw-Hill.
--Miss Pickerell and the Weather Satellite. Geer, Charles Hand (1922-), illus. 1971. (ISBN 0-07-044569-9). McGraw Hill Book Company.
--Miss Pickerell Goes on a Dig. Geer, Charles Hand (1922-), illus. LC 62-200060. 128p. illus. 21cm. c.1966. (ISBN 0-07-044574-5). McGraw.
--Miss Pickerell Harvests the Sea. Geer, Charles Hand (1922-), illus. LC 68-28416. (Illus.). 144 p. 21cm. 1968. McGraw-Hill.
--Miss Pickerell Meets Mr. H.U.M. Geer, Charles Hand (1922-), illus. LC 74-2126. (Illus.). 160 p. 21cm. 1974. (ISBN 0-07-044577-X). (ISBN 0-07-044577-X). McGraw-Hill.
--Miss Pickerell on the Moon. Geer, Charles Hand (1922-), illus. LC 64-66411. 142p. illus. 21cm. c.1965. (ISBN 0-07-044551-6). Whittlesey-McGraw.
--Miss Pickerell on the Trail. Geer, Charles Hand (1922-), illus. LC 81-12316. p. cm. c.1981. (ISBN 0-07-044591-5). McGraw-Hill.
--Miss Pickerell Tackles the Energy Crisis. Geer, Charles Hand (1922-), illus. LC 79-24149. (Illus.). 173 p. 21cm. c.1980. (ISBN 0-07-044589-3). McGraw-Hill.
--Miss Pickerell Takes the Bull by the Horns. LC 75-41454. (Illus.). 160 p. 21cm. c.1976. (ISBN 0-07-044582-6). (ISBN 0-07-044583-4). McGraw-Hill.
--Miss Pickerell Takes the Bull by the Horns. Geer, Charles Hand (1922-), illus. (Illus.). 148 p. 18cm. (Archway Paperback)). 1980, c.1976. (ISBN 0-671-56029-8). Pocket Books.
--Miss Pickerell to the Earthquake Rescue. LC 76-52447. (Illus.). 158 p. 21cm. c.1977. (ISBN 0-07-044586-9). (ISBN 0-07-044587-7). McGraw-Hill.

MacGregor, Iona
--An Edinburgh Reel. (gr. 5 up). 1968. (ISBN 0-571-08362-5). Faber & Faber.
The Snake & the Olive. 166p. 1974. (ISBN 0-571-10582-3). Faber & Faber.
--The Tree of Liberty. N.D. (ISBN 0-571-10121-6, Pub. by Faber & Faber). Merrimack Pub Cir.

MacGregor, Marilyn
--Baby Takes a Trip. LC 85-4340. (Illus.). 32 p. c.1985. (ISBN 0-02-761940-0). Four Winds Press.

Macgregor, Mary
--Stories of Siegfried. Chisholm, Louey, ed. Fell, Herbert Granville, illus. (Illus.). 15cm. 118p. (Told to the Children Ser.). 1909. E. P. Dutton & Co.

MacGregor, Mary, retold by.
--Siegfried. (Illus.). N.D. Dutton & Co.

Macgregor, Mary, jt. ed. see Kingsley, Charles.

Macgregor, Mary Esther Miller see Keith, Marian, pseud.

MacGregor, Mary Esther Miller, Mrs. (1876-)
--Boy of Nazareth. Keith, Marian, pseud. Harper, Arthur, illus. LC 50-8724. 158 p. illus. 22 cm. 1950. Abingdon-Cokesbury Press.
--Glad Days in Galilee: A Story of the Boyhood of Jesus. Keith, Marian, pseud. 141 p. 21 cm. c.1935. The Abingdon Press.
--Little Miss Melody. Keith, Marian, pseud. LC 21-15433. vi p., 1 l., 9-302 p. 20 cm. c.1921. George H. Doran Company.
--Stories from the Ballads. Chisholn, Louey, ed. LC 234. xi, 115 p. 8 col. pl. (incl. front.) 15 cm. (Half-title: Told to the children series, No. 32). 1908. E. P. Dutton.
--Stories of Three Saints. Chisholn, Louey, ed. Traquair, P A, illus. LC 8-172. xi, 116 p. 8 col. pl. (incl. front.) 15 cm. (Half-title: Told to the children series; No. 28). 1908. E. P. Dutton & co.

MacGregor, Mary Esther Miller, Mrs. (1876-), retold by.
--Ballads and Stories Told to Children. (Illus.). N.D. Dutton & Co.
--Three Saints. (Illus.). N.D. Dutton & Co.
--Vikings: Told to Children. (Illus.). N.D. Dutton & Co.

Macgregor, Mary Esther Miller, Mrs. (1876-) & Malory, Thomas, Sir (0000-1471)
--Stories of King Arthur's Knights: Told to the Children. Cameron, Katharine, illus. LC 7-37553. viii p., 1 l., 115, 1 p. 8 col. pl. (incl. front.) 15 x 12 cm. (Half-title: Told to the children series). N.D. E. P. Dutton & Co.

Macgregor, Mary, Mrs., ed. see Andersen, Hans Christian.

McGregor, Reginald James
--Secret of Smugglers Wood. N.D. Penguin Bks.
--The Young Detectives. Grimmond, William (1907-), illus. LC 67-3916. (Illus.). 191 p. 18cm. (Puffin Books). 1967. Penguin Books.

McGuckin, Mildred Criss see Criss, Mildred.

McGuffey, William Holmes (1800-1873) & Dickson, Edith (1855-), eds.
--Meddlesome Mattie and Other Selections from McGuffey's Readers. LC 31-26714. 57 p. illus. 17 cm. 1931. Harper & Brothers.

McGuiness, Doreen, illus.
--Dinosaurs. (Illus.). 16p. (Animal Press-Out Bks.). (ps-2). 1984. (ISBN 0-911745-66-1, Bedrick Blackie). P Bedrick Bks.

McGuire, Alice Brooks, ed.
--Just Around the Corner. LC 61-17992. 373p. illus. 25cm. (Collier's junior classics series). 1962. Crowell-Collier Pub. Co.

McGuire, Catherine
--Captive Planet. LC 83-91425. 160p. (Endless Quest Bks.). (gr. 5up). N.D. (ISBN 0-394-72483-6). Random.
--Raid on Nightmare Castle. Holloway, Jim, illus. LC 83-51041. (Illus.). (An Endless Quest Bk.: No. 14). c.1983. (ISBN 0-88038-101-9). TSR, Inc.
--Trouble on Artule. LC 83-91425. 160p. (A Star Frontiers Endless Quest Bk.). (gr. 5 up). N.D. (ISBN 0-394-72805-X, Pub. by BYR). Random.

McGuire, Frances Lynch (1869-1947)
--Arizona Hide-Out. Murch, Frank J., illus. LC 53-6072. 128p. illus. 21cm. 1953. Dutton.
--The Case of the Smuggled Ruby. 1st ed. Abel, Raymond (1911-), illus. LC 56-63021. 128p. illus. 22cm. 1956. Dutton.
--Indian Drums Beat Again. 1st ed. Polgreen, John, illus. LC 52-129596. 123p. illus. 21cm. 1953. Dutton.
--Keys to Fortune. 1st ed. Orbaan, Albert F. (1913-), illus. LC 54-9307. 124p. illus. 21cm. 1954. Dutton.
--Red Fury. 1st ed. Wood, J. G., illus. LC [illegible] p. illus. 21 cm. 1954. Dutton.
--The Secret of Barnegat Light. Orbaan, Albert F. (1913-), illus. LC 52-5294. (Illus.). 21cm. 128p. N.D. Dutton.
--Wagon to a Star. Williamson, Gertrude M., illus. LC 51-11373. 200 p. illus. 24 cm. 1951. Caxton Printers.

McGuire, Leslie Sarah see Britton, Louisa, pseud.

McGuire, Leslie Sarah see Burton, Leslie, pseud.

McGuire, Leslie Sarah see Eyre, Dorothy, pseud.

McGuire, Leslie Sarah see Keyser, Sarah, pseud.

McGuire, Leslie Sarah see Leslie, Sarah, pseud.

McGuire, Leslie Sarah see Max, Leslie, pseud.

McGuire, Leslie Sarah (1945-)
--Bialosky's Christmas. Joyner, Jerry (1938-), illus. LC 84-80551. (Illus.). 24 p. 21cm. (A Golden Look-Look Book). c.1984. (ISBN 0-307-11891-6). (ISBN 0-307-61891-9). Golden Book.
--Miss Mopp's Lucky Day. Silver, Jody (1942-), illus. LC 81-4879. (Illus.). 38 p. 23cm. 1982, c.1981. (ISBN 0-8193-1061-1). (ISBN 0-8193-1062-X). Parents Magazine Press.
--Rainbow Brite and the Big Color Mix-up. LC 84-81583. (Illus.). 42 p. 29cm. c.1984. (ISBN 0-307-16001-7). (ISBN 0-307-66001-X). Western Pub. Co.
--Scooter Computer & Mr. Chips in the Computer in the Candy Store. Costanza, John, illus. LC 83-83175. (Illus.). (Golden Look-Look Bks). (ps-3). 1984. (ISBN 0-307-11819-3, Golden Bks). Western Pub.
--This Farm is a Mess. Mcguire, Leslie Sarah (1945-), illus. LC 80-25811. (Illus.). 42 p. 24cm. c.1981. (ISBN 0-8193-1045 X). (ISBN 0-8193-1046-8). Parents Magazine.

McGuire, Paula, tr. see Inkiow, Janakier Dimiter.

McHale, Ethel Kharasch, retold by.
--Son-of-Thunder: An Old Tale. Bornstein-Lercher, Ruth (1927-), illus. LC 74-4048. (Illus.). 32 p. 1974. (ISBN 0-516-08856-4). Childrens Press.

Machard, Alfred
--When Tytie Came: Paul et Virginie. Eskridge, Robert Lee, illus. O'Brien, Howard Vincent (1888-), tr. from Fr. LC 20-17171. 4 p. l., 13-316 p. illus. 20 cm. c.1920. The Reilly & Lee Co.

MacHarg, William
--Peewee. 1921. Reilly & Lee.

McHarge, Georges see Usher, Margo Scegge, pseud.

McHargne, Georgess, tr. see Heller, Friedrich C.

McHargue, Georgess (1941-)
--The Baker and the Basilisk. 1st ed. Quackenbush, Robert Mead (1929-), illus. LC 71-98276. (Illus.). 31 p. 1970. Bobbs-Merrill.
--Beasts of Never. Bozzo, Frank, illus. LC 67-18651. (Illus.). 9 duotones, 50 drawings. index. 112p. (gr. 8 up). 1968. (ISBN 0-672-50217-8). Bobbs.
--Elidor and the Golden Ball. 1st ed. Schongut, Emanuel, illus. LC 73-6029. (Illus.). 61 p. 24cm. 1973. (ISBN 0-396-06832-4). Dodd, Mead.
--Funny Bananas: The Mystery in the Museum. 1st ed. Palmer, Heidi (1948-), illus. LC 74-17259. (Illus.). 79 p. 22cm. 1975. (ISBN 0-03-013761-6). Holt, Rinehart and Winston.
--The Horseman's Word. LC 80-68736. viii, 259 p. 22cm. c.1981. (ISBN 0-440-04167-8). Delacorte Press.
--Meet the Werewolf. LC 75-34046. (gr. 2-5). 1976. (ISBN 0-397-31662-3, JBL-J). (ISBN 0-397-31663-1). Har-Row.
--Meet the Witches. LC 83-48446. (Illus.). 128p. (The Eerie Ser.). (gr. 4-7). 1984. (ISBN 0-397-32071-X, JBL-J). (ISBN 0-397-32072-8). Har-Row.
--The Mermaid and the Whale. 1st ed. Parker, Robert Andrew (1927-), illus. LC 73-7169. (Illus.). 40 p. 26cm. 1973. (ISBN 0-03-011166-8). Holt Rinehart & Winston.
--Stoneflight. 1st ed. Stewart, Arvis L., illus. LC 74-11146. 223 p. 22cm. 1975. (ISBN 0-670-67107-X). Viking Press. **Award: (ALA).**
--The Talking Table Mystery. 1st ed. Schongut, Emanuel, illus. LC 76-23794. (Illus.). 140 p. 22cm. c.1977. (ISBN 0-385-11353-6). (ISBN 0-385-11354-4). Doubleday.
--The Turquoise Toad Mystery. LC 81-69664. 137 p. 24cm. c.1982. (ISBN 0-440-08911-5). Delacorte Press.
--What's in Mommy's Pocketbook. Simpson, Jean, illus. (Illus.). 10p. (Golden Touch & Feel Bk). (ps). 1971. (ISBN 0-307-12150-X, Golden Pr). Western Pub.
--The Wonderful Wings of Harold Harrabescu. Hendrick, Joseph (1934-), illus. LC 78-108664. (Illus.). 25 p. 1971. Delacorte Press.

McHargue, Georgess (1941-), ed.
--Best of Both Worlds: An Anthology of Short Stories for All Ages. Bacon, Paul (1913-), illus. LC 68-22466. (Illus.). 60 linecuts. 600p. (gr. 7 up). 1968. (ISBN 0-385-03042-8). Doubleday.
--Hot & Cold Running Cities: An Anthology of Science Fiction. LC 74-8513. viii, 245 p. 22cm. 1974. (ISBN [illegible]). Holt, Rinehart and Winston.
--Little Victories, Big Defeats: War As the Ultimate Pollution. LC 74-5749. vi, 186 p. 22cm. 1974. (ISBN 0-440-04899-0). Delacorte Press.

McHargue, Georgess (1941-) & Foreman, Michael (1938-)
--Private Zoo. LC 74-17496. (Illus.). 32 p. 1975. (ISBN 0-670-57859-2). Viking Press.

McHargue, Georgress, tr. see Schouten, Alet.

Machetanz, Frederick, jt. auth. see Machetanz, Sara Burleson.

Machetanz, Frederick (1908-)
--On Arctic Ice. Machetanz, Frederick (1908-), illus. LC 40-30569. 8 p. l., 105 p. illus. (part col.) 21 cm. c.1940. C. Scribner's Sons.
--Panuck, Eskimo Sled Dog. Machetanz, Frederick (1908-), illus. LC 39-6119. 94, 1 p. illus. (part. col.) 21 cm. c.1939. (ISBN 0-684-12916-7). C. Scribner's Sons.

Machetanz, Sara Burleson (1918-)
--Puppy Named Gih. N.D. E. M Hale & Co.
--Rick of High Ridge. Machetanz, Frederick (1908-), illus. LC 52-12924. (Illus.). 177 p. 21cm. 1952. Scribner.
--Robbie and the Sled Dog Race. Machetanz, Frederick (1908-), illus. LC 64-22752. (Illus.). 48 p. 24cm. 1964. Scribner.

Machetanz, Sara Burleson (1918-) & Machetanz, Frederick (1908-)
--Barney Hits the Trail. Machetanz, Frederick (1908-), illus. LC 50-9824. (Illus.). 195 p. 22cm. 1950. Scribner.
--Puppy Named Gih. Machetanz, Frederick (1908-), illus. LC 57-6849. (Illus.). (gr. k-3). 1957. (ISBN 0-684-13038-6, ScribJ). Scribner.

Machin, Godall Daphne Edith see Stephan, Hanna.

McHugh, Arona (1924-)
--A Banner With A Strange Device. N.D. Doubleday & Co.
--The Sea Coast of Bohemia. N.D. Doubleday & Co.

McHugh, Elisabet
--Karen & Vicki. LC 83-14156. 160p. (gr. 5-9). 1984. (ISBN 0-688-02543-9). Greenwillow.
--Karen's Sister. LC 83-1741. p. cm. 1983. (ISBN 0-688-02472-6). Greenwillow Books.
--Raising a Mother Isn't Easy. 1st ed. LC 82-11714. 156 p. 22cm. c.1983. (ISBN 0-688-01827-0). Greenwillow Books.

McHugh, Florence, tr. see Baumann, Hans.

McHugh, Florence, tr. see Litgen, Kurt.

McHugh, Florence, tr. see Muhlenweg, Fritz.

McHugh, Gelolo
--Baby's House. Blair, Mary Robinson (1911-), illus. (Little Golden Book). 1950. Golden Press.
--Baby's House. Blair, Mary Robinson (1911-), illus. (Illus.). 24p. (gr. k-1). 1976. (ISBN 0-307-69051-2, Golden Pr). Western Pub.

McHugh, Isabel, tr. see Baumann, Hans.

McHugh, Isabel, tr. see Litgen, Kurt.

McHugh, Isabel, tr. see Muhlenweg, Fritz.

McHugh, Michael
--Giant of the Western Trail: Father Peter De Smet. Dougherty, Charles L., illus. LC 58-131194. 181p. illus. 22cm. (Banner books). 1958. Benziger Bros.

Maciel, Judith
--Martin's Important Day. Hampshire, Michael Allen, illus. LC 71-185059. (Illus.). 37 p. 24cm. 1972. (ISBN 0-8178-4701-4). Harvey House.

McIntyre, Jane, tr. see Lorenzini, Carlo.

McIlvaine, Jane (1919-)
--Cammie's Challenge. Dennis, Wesley (1903-1966), illus. LC 62-12877. 244p. illus. 22cm. 1962. Bobbs-Merrill.
--Cammie's Choice. 1961. (ISBN 0-672-50237-2). Bobbs-Merrill.
--Cammie's Cousin. (Illus.). N.D. Bobbs-Merrill Co, Inc.
--Cintra's Challenge. LC 55-6448. 219 p. 21cm. 1955. Macrae Smith.
--Cintra's Challenge. (gr. 7 up). 1971. Pyramid Pubns.
--Copper's Chance. Brown, Paul (1893-1958), illus. LC 51-14006. 232 p. illus. 22 cm. 1951. Macrae Smith.

--Front Page for Jennifer. Krush, Beth (1918-) & Krush, Joe (1918-), illus. LC 50-10059. 222 p. illus. 22 cm. 1950. Macrae Smith.
--The Sea Sprite. LC 52-10364. 204 p. 22 cm. 1952. Macrae Smith Co.
--Stardust for Jennifer. LC 56-618122. 221p. 21cm. 1956. Macrae Smith.

McIlwraith, Maureen Mollie Hunter McVeigh see Hunter, Mollie.

McIlwraith, Maureen Mollie Hunter McVeigh (1922-)
--The Ferlie. Cellini, Joseph (1924-), illus. LC 68-27998. (Illus.). 128 p. 21cm. 1968. Funk & Wagnalls.
--A Furl of Fairy Wind: Four Stories. LC 76-58732. p. cm. c.1977. (ISBN 0-06-022674-9). (ISBN 0-06-022675-7). Harper & Row.
--The Ghosts of Glencoe. LC 69-12155. (Illus.). 191 p. 22cm. 1969, c.1966. Funk & Wagnalls.
--The Haunted Mountain. Kubinyi, Laszlo (1937-), illus. LC 77-183164. (Illus.). 125 p. 21cm. 1972. (ISBN 0-06-022666-8). Harper & Row. **Award: (ALA).**
--The Kelpie's Pearls. Cellini, Joseph (1924-), illus. LC 66-835575. 112p. illus. 22cm. 1966, c.1964. Funk & Wagnalls. **Award: (ALA).**
--The Kelpie's Pearls. new ed. Gammell, Stephen, illus. LC 75-25404. (Illus.). 25cm. 134p. (gr. 3-7). 1976, c.1964. (ISBN 0-06-022656-0, HarpJ). (ISBN 0-06-022659-5). Har-Row.
--The Lothian Run. LC 70-100653. 212 p. 22cm. 1970. Funk & Wagnalls.
--A Sound of Chariots. LC 73-12635. 347 p. 25cm. 1973, c.1972. (ISBN 0-8161-6148-8). G. K. Hall.
--A Sound of Chariots. LC 72-76523. 242 p. 22cm. 1972. (ISBN 0-06-022668-4). (ISBN 0-06-022669-2). Harper & Row.
--A Stranger Came Ashore. (Story of Suspense Ser.). (gr. 5 up). 1977. (ISBN 0-06-440082-4, Trophy). Har-Row.
--The Stronghold. LC 73-14340. x, 259 p. 22cm. 1974. (ISBN 0-06-022653-6). (ISBN 0-06-022653-6). Harper & Row. **Award: (CMA).**
--The Third Eye. LC 78-22159. 276 p. 21cm. c.1979. (ISBN 0-06-022676-5). (ISBN 0-06-022677-3). Harper & Row.
--The Thirteenth Member: A Story of Suspense. LC 76-148423. 214 p. 21cm. 1971. (ISBN 0-06-022661-7). Harper & Row.
--Thomas and the Warlock. LC 67-22922. (Illus.). 128 p. 21cm. 1967. Funk & Wagnalls.
--The Walking Stones: A Story of Suspense. Hyman, Trina Schart (1939-), illus. LC 79-121807. (Illus.). 143 p. 19cm. (Trophy Book). 1973, c.1970. (ISBN 0-06-440034-4). Harper.
--The Wicked One: A Story of Suspense. LC 76-41515. 136 p. 21cm. c.1977. (ISBN 0-06-022647-1). (ISBN 0-06-022648-X). Harper & Row.

McInerney, Judith Whitelock
--Judge Benjamin, Superdog. Morrill, Leslie H., illus. LC 81-85092. (Illus.). 142 p. 22cm. c.1982. (ISBN 0-8234-0448-X). Holiday House.
--Judge Benjamin: The Superdog Rescue. Morrill, Leslie H., illus. (Illus.). 128p. (ps-7). 1984. (ISBN 0-8234-0515-X). Holiday.
--Judge Benjamin, the Superdog Secret. Morrill, Leslie H., illus. LC 82-48752. p. cm. c.1983. (ISBN 0-8234-0484-6). Holiday House.
--Judge Benjamin: The Superdog Surprise. Morrill, Leslie H., illus. LC 84-48745. (Illus.). 144p. (gr. 3-7). 1985. (ISBN 0-8234-0561-3). Holiday.

McInerny, Ralph M
--Quick As a Dodo. Butterworth, Pam, illus. LC 77-93301. (Illus.). 116 p. 22cm. c.1978. (ISBN 0-8149-0794-6). Vanguard Press.

MacInnes, Colin (1914-1976)
--Three Years to Play. LC 71-125157. 354p. 1970. (ISBN 0-374-27681-1). FS&G.

McInnes, Estelle
--Bobby Bear's Busy Day. McInnes, Estelle, illus. LC 52-2157. unpaged. illus. 21 cm. (Easy-to-read book, 4212). 1952. Saalfield Pub. Co.

MacInnes, Helen (1907-)
--Decision at Delphi. LC 60-15705. 1960. (ISBN 0-15-124221-6). HarBraceJ.
--Decision at Delphi. (Keith Jennison Large Type Bks). (gr. 7 up). N.D. (ISBN 0-531-00180-6). Watts.
--The Venetian Affair. LC 63-17774. (gr. 10 up). 1963. (ISBN 0-15-193501-7). HarBraceJ.

McInnes, John, jt. auth. see Ryckman, John.

McInnes, John (1927-)
--The Chocolate Chip Mystery. Frame, Paul (1913-), illus. LC 72-1773. (Illus.). 64 p. 23cm. 1972. (ISBN 0-8116-6964-5). Garrard Pub. Co.
--Drat the Dragon. Davidson, Rosalie (1921-), illus. LC 72-5285. (Illus.). 40 p. 23cm. 1973. (ISBN 0-8116-6720-0). Garrard Pub. Co.
--The Ghost Said Boo. Cunette, Lou, illus. LC 73-20392. (Illus.). 32 p. 23cm. 1974. (ISBN 0-8116-6055-9). Garrard Pub. Co.
--Goodnight Painted Pony. Stone, David Karl (1922-), illus. LC 76-155572. (Illus.). 40 p. 24cm. 1971. (ISBN 0-8116-6707-3). Garrard Pub. Co.
--Have You Ever Seen a Monster?. Eaton, Tom (1940-), illus. LC 73-20394. (Illus.). 32 p. 23cm. 1974. (ISBN 0-8116-6054-0). Garrard Pub. Co.
--How Pedro Got His Name. Malsberg, Edward, illus. LC 73-22082. (Illus.). 32 p. 23cm. 1974. (ISBN 0-8116-6064-8). Garrard Pub. Co.
--Leo Lion Paints It Red. Eaton, Tom (1940-), illus. LC 73-21586. (Illus.). 32 p. 23cm. 1974. (ISBN 0-8116-6060-5). Garrard Publishing Co.
--On with the Circus!. Hutchinson, William Miller (1916-), illus. LC 72-5283. (Illus.). 37 p. 23cm. 1973. (ISBN 0-8116-6722-7). Garrard Pub. Co.
--Who Ever Heard of a Tiger in a Tree. Davidson, Rosalie (1921-), illus. LC 72-155571. (Illus.). 40 p. 23cm. 1971. (ISBN 0-8116-6706-5). Garrard Pub. Co.

McIntire, Alta, jt. auth. see Harter, Helen.

McIntosh, Maria Jane see Cousin Kate, pseud.

McIntosh, Maria Jane (1803-1878)
--Aunt Kitty's Tales. N.D. D. Appleton.
--Blind Alice. (New Juvenile Library). 1876. D. Appleton.
--Blind Alice, 1 of 6 vols. (Home Library for Little Readers). N.D. Set. Thos Nelson & Sons.
--The Children's Mirror: A Treasury of Stories. Cousin Kate, pseud. N.D. Thos Nelson & Sons.
--The Cousins. N.D. Harper & Brother's Trade-List.
--Ellen Leslie, 1 of 7 vols. (New Juvenile Library: No.6). 1876. D. Appleton.
--Ellen Leslie. (Tales and Stories). N.D. D. Appleton & Co.
--Emily Herbert, 1 of 7 Vols. (New Juvenile Library: Vol. 4). N.D. Set. D. Appleton and Co.
--Emily Herbert: Or, The Happy Home. LC 44-39845. 2 p. l., 2, 5-165 p. front. 15 cm. (On cover: Appleton's library for young people). 1855. D. Appleton and Company.
--Evenings at Donaldson Manor. (Tales and Stories). N.D. D. Appleton & Co.
--An Eventful Night. Cousin Kate, pseud, 1 of 24 bks. (Illus.). (No. 3). N.D. Set. Thos Nelson & Sons.
--Florence Arnot. (New Juvenile Library). 1876. D. Appleton.
--Florence Arnot, 1 of 6 vols. (Home Library for Little Readers). N.D. Set. Thos Nelson & Sons.
--Florence Arnot: Is she Generous, 2 of 7 Vols. (New Juvenile Library). N.D. Set. D. Appleton and Co.
--Florence Arnot: Is she generous. (Home Library for Little Readers). N.D. Set. Thomas Nelson & Sons.
--Grace and Clara. (New Juvenile Library). 1876. D. Appleton.
--Grace & Clara, 1 of 6 vols. (Home Library for Little Readers). N.D. Set. Thos Nelson & Sons.
--Hope Campbell. N.D. A. D. F. Randolph.
--Horace and May. N.D. A. D. F. Randolph.
--I Want to Get on. Cousin Kate, pseud, 1 of 24 bks. (Illus.). (No. 1). N.D. Set. Thos Nelson & Sons.
--Is This Right?. Cousin Kate, pseud, 1 of 24 bks. (Illus.). (No. 2). N.D. Set. Thos Nelson & Sons.
--Jessie Graham. (New Juvenile Library). 1876. D. Appleton.
--Jessie Graham, 1 of 6 vols. (Home Library for Little Readers Ser.). N.D. Set. Thos Nelson & Sons.
--Kenneth and Hugh. N.D. A. D. F. Randolph.
--Lily Gordon. N.D. A. D. F. Randolph.
--Lofty and Lowly, 1 of 6 Vols. (Tales and Stories). N.D. Set. D. Appleton and Co.
--Meta Gray: Or, What Makes Home Happy. N.D. D. Appleton.
--New Juvenile Library: Containing: Grace and Clara, Florence Arnot, Blind Alice, Emily Herbert, Ellen Leslie, Rose and Lillie Stanhope, Jessie Graham, 7 Vols. (Illus.). N.D. Set. D. Appleton & Co.
--Rest and Unrest. N.D. A. D. F. Randolph.
--Rose and Lillie Stanhope. (New Juvenile Library). 1876. D. Appleton.
--Sydney Stuart. N.D. A. D. F. Randolph.
--Tales and Stories, 6 Vols. (Illus.). N.D. D. Appleton and Co.
--Tommy's Resolution. Cousin Kate, pseud, 1 of 24 bks. (Illus.). (Stories by Cousin Kate Packet "A": No. 1). N.D. Set. Thos Nelson & Sons.
--Two Lives. (Tales and Stories). N.D. D. Appleton & Co.
--Two Pictures. (Tales and Stories). N.D. D. Appleton & Co.

MacIntyre, A
--Skippy and Others. N.D. St Martin's Press.

McIntyre, Anna Theresa
--Blue Bells and Silver Chimes: Childhood Verse and Happy Rhymes for Boys and Girls. LC 35-29213. 2 p. l., 61 p. illus. 23 1/2 cm. c.1935. National Publishing Company.

MacIntyre, Carlyle Ferren (1890-)
--The Pig That Ate Truffles. Obligado, Lilian Isabel (1931-), illus. LC 63-9387. (Illus.). 19 x 26cm. 1963. Golden Press.

MacIntyre, Elisabeth (1916-)
--The Affable, Amiable Bulldozer Man. MacIntyre, Elisabeth (1916-), illus. LC 65-119661. 1v. (unpaged) col. illus. 27cm. (gr. k-3). 1965. (ISBN 0-394-90891-0). Knopf.
--Ambrose Kangaroo: A Story that Never Ends. MacIntyre, Elisabeth (1916-), illus. 1942. Charles Scribner's Sons.
--Hugh's Zoo. MacIntyre, Elisabeth (1916-), illus. (Illus.). (gr. k-2). 1964. Knopf.
--Jane Likes Pictures. MacIntyre, Elisabeth (1916-), illus. LC 59-6619. unpaged. illus. 26cm. 1959. Scribner.
--Mr. Koala Bear. MacIntyre, Elisabeth (1916-), illus. N.D. E. M. Hale & Co.
--Mr. Koala Bear. MacIntyre, Elisabeth (1916-), illus. LC 54-8608. unpaged. illus. 27cm. 1954. Scribner.
--Ninji's Magic. Funai, Mamoru R. (1932-), illus. (Illus.). 114 p. 22cm. 1966. Knopf.
--The Purple Mouse. MacIntyre, Elisabeth (1916-), illus. LC 75-1318. 108 p. 21cm. 1975. (ISBN 0-8407-6424-3). T. Nelson.
--Susan Who Lives in Australia. MacIntyre, Elisabeth (1916-), illus. LC 44-2099. 32 p. col. illus. 22 cm. 1944. C. Scribner's Sons.

McIntyre, Flora
--Children of the Golden Queen. LC 38-185291. 80 p. incl. front., illus. 23 1/2 cm. 1938. E. P. Dutton & Co., Inc.

McIntyre, Ida Mae
--Unicorn Magic. Hedin, Don, illus. LC 72-1922. (Illus.). 64 p. 23cm. c.1972. (ISBN 0-8116-6965-3). Garrard Pub. Co.

McIntyre, John Thomas (1871-)
--Blowing Weather. Mabie, George H., illus. N.D. Frederick A. Stokes.
--The Boy Tars of 1812. Deland, Clyde O., illus. LC 7-205141. 319 p. incl. front. 6 pl. 19 1/2 cm. 1907. The Penn Publishing Company.
--Fighting King George. LC 33-19402. 4, 7-372 p. front. 19 1/2 cm. (Historical Stories Ser.for Boys and Girls). 1933. The Penn Publishing Company.
--On the Borders with Andrew Jackson. Anderson, Frederic A., illus. LC 15-18914. 200 p. front., illus. 19 /2 cm. (His The buckskin books). 1915. The Penn Publishing Company.
--The Street Singer. Claghorn, Joseph C., illus. LC 8-15296. 356 p. front., illus., 6 pl. 19 1/2 cm. (Vacation Ser.). 1908. The Penn Publishing Company.
--With Fighting Jack Barry. Grant, Gordon H. (1875-1962), illus. LC 7-28972. 1 p. l., iii p., 1 l., 7-309, 1 p. col. front., 3 col. pl. 20 cm. 1907. J. B. Lippincott Company.
--With John Paul Jones. Deland, Clyde O., illus. LC 6-19773. 358 p. front., 6 pl. 19 1/2 cm. 1906. The Penn Publishing Company.
--The Young Continentals at Bunker Hill. Boyer, Ralph L., illus. (The Young Continentals Ser.). N.D. Penn.
--The Young Continentals at Lexington. Boyer, Ralph L., illus. (The Young Continental Ser.). N.D. Penn.
--The Young Continentals at Monmouth. Boyer, Ralph L., illus. LC 12-12485. 344 p. front., plates. 19 cm. 1912. The Penn Publishing Company.
--The Young Continentals at Trenton. Boyer, Ralph L., illus. (The Young Continentals Ser.). N.D. Penn.
--Young Patriots at Lexington. LC 49-5472. viii. 247 p. illus. 23 cm. 1949. Hearthstone Pub. Co.

McIntyre, LeGrand
--Flying Cloud, and Other Animal Stories. Bell, William P., illus. LC 49-50352. 167 p. illus 20 cm. 1949. Mathis, Van Nort.

McIntyre, Margaret A
--The Cave Boy of the Age of Stone. LC 7-15587. x, 131 p. incl. front., illus. 19 1/2 cm. (On verso of half-title: Stories of primitive life for primary grades)). 1907. D. Appleton and Company.

MacIntyre, Robert, ed. see Hawthorne, Nathaniel.

McIntyre, Vonda Neel, et al. (1948-)
--The Crystal Ship: Three Original Novellas of Science Fiction. Silverberg, Robert (1935-), ed. LC 76-26902. 1st U.S. edition. (Nelson's Science Fiction Ser.). (gr. 8 up). 1976. (ISBN 0-525-66527-7). Elsevier-Nelson.

MacIsaac, Janet (1926-) & Sennott, Robert Francis (1925-)
--The Donkey. Fitch, Robert, pseud. LC 52-14976. unpaged. illus. 17x23cm. 1952. Ravengate.
--For a Penny. Fitch, Robert, pseud. LC 52-14977. unpaged. illus. 17x23cm. 1952. Ravengate Press.
--Grandma. Fitch, Robert, pseud. LC 52-148987. unpaged. illus. 17x23cm. 1952. Ravengate Press.
--Jungle Jingle. Fitch, Robert, pseud. LC 52-14899. unpaged. illus. 17x23cm. 1952. Ravengate Press.

McIvers, Patricia T.
--Good Night, Mr. Christopher. 127p. 1975. Sheed Andrews & McMeel.

Mack, Brice, ed. see Disney, Walt, Productions.

Mack, Bruce
--Jesses Dream Skirt. Buchanan, Marian, illus. LC 79-89892. (Illus.). 34 p., 1 leaf of plates. 26cm. c.1979. (ISBN 0-914996-20-7). Lollipop Power.

Mack, Elsie Frances Wilson see Moore, Frances Sarah, pseud.

Mack, Elsie Frances Wilson (1909-)
--The Right Girl. Moore, Frances Sarah, pseud. LC 56-13508. 224p. 21cm. 1956. Avalon Books.

Mack, Gail
--Snowman. Blegvad, Erik (1923-), illus. LC 78-6090. p. cm. 1978. Pantheon.

Mack, Galen S., jt. auth. see Senogles, Galen D.

Mack, Glenn
--The Heart. LC 70-375961. (Illus.). 31 p. 22cm. (His Springboard topics, B5). 1968. Nelson (Australia.

Mack, Gwynne Dresser
--The Broolin. Mack, Gwynne Dresser, illus. LC 43-11961. ix, 107, 1 p. front., illus. 22 1/2 cm. 1943. W. Hebberd.
--Swish: The Sorrowful Sea Serpent. Mack, Gwynne Dresser, illus. LC 45-9094. vi, 1, 20, 1 p. illus. 21 1/2 cm. 1945. W. Hebberd.

Mack, Jacque (1948-) & Cassell, Robert H.
--Stanley Meets DoGood and BeBad. LC 77-29051. (Illus.). 32p. (Apple bks.). c.1978. (ISBN 0-570-07900-4). Concordia.

Mack, Lilian
--Two Little Girls. LC 4-4983. 18cm. 145p. 1904. Benziger Brothers.

Mack, Maynard, jt. auth. see Boynton, Robert W.

Mack, Mr. & Mack, Mrs.
--Old Father Santa Claus. (Illus.). 40p. N.D. Publications of E. P. Dutton & Co.

Mack, Nancy
--Why Me?. LC 76-13175. (Illus.). 32p. (Moods & Emotions Ser.). (gr. k-3). 1976. (ISBN 0-8172-0012-6). Raintree Pubs.

Mack, Nila Arah
--Animal Allies. Lazarus, Sidney, illus. LC 42-23955. (Based on an Idea by Ann Edison). (Illus.). 17. 22cm. 1942. J. Messner Inc.
--Let's Pretend: Stories Adapted from the Famous Radio Program "Let's Pretend" Heard Over the Columbia Broadcasting System. Barnes, Catherine J. (1918-), illus. LC 49-13598. 68 p. col. illus. 29 cm. (Cello-brite story books, 5066). 1948. Whitman Pub. Co.

Mack, Orin
--Indian Gold. Von Schmidt, Harold (1896-1982), illus. LC 33-25679. 6 p. l., 3-243, 1 p., 1 l. incl. front., illus. 19 1/2 cm. 1933. A. A. Knopf.

Mack, Robert Ellis
--Jack in The Box. Bennett, Harriet M., illus. N.D. Publications of E. P. Dutton & Co.

Mack, Robert Ellis, jt. auth. see Bennett, Harriet M.

Mack, Robert Ellis, jt. auth. see Lawson, Lizzie.

Mack, Stanley, jt. auth. see Kredenser, Gail.

Mack, Stanley (1935-)
--Belmont the Bat Catcher & Other Nutty Number Tales. Mack, Stanley (1935-), illus. (Illus.). 32p. (Orig.). (ps-3). 1983. (ISBN 0-590-31874-8). Scholastic Inc.
--The King's Cat Is Coming. Mack, Stanley (1935-), illus. LC 76-11033. p. cm. 1976. (ISBN 0-394-83302-3). (ISBN 0-394-93302-8). Pantheon Books.
--The Runaway Road. Mack, Stanley (1935-), illus. LC 79-5265. (Illus.). 40 p. 24cm. c.1980. (ISBN 0-8193-1017-4). (ISBN 0-8193-1018-2). Parents Magazine Press.
--Ten Bears in My Bed: A Goodnight Countdown. Mack, Stanley (1935-), illus. LC 74-151. (Illus.). 28 p. 1974. (ISBN 0-394-82902-6). (ISBN 0-394-82902-6). Pantheon Books.
--Where's My Cheese?. Mack, Stanley (1935-), illus. LC 77-3443. (Illus.). 32 p. c.1977. (ISBN 0-394-83452-6). (ISBN 0-394-93452-0). Pantheon Books.

MacKail, Denis
--Another Paul of the Wood. N.D. Houghton Mifflin Co.
--David's Day. N.D. Houghton Mifflin Co.
--Summertime. N.D. Houghton Mifflin Co.

AUTHOR INDEX MCKEEVER, HARRIET

Mackail, J. W.
--The Little Bible. New ed. 5x7 1/2cm. 350p. 1900. Doubleday, Page & Co.
Mackain, F. C.
--Buzzy. N.D. George W Jacobs.
Mackall, Lawton (1888-) & Mackall, Ruth
--Poodle-Oodle of Doodle Farm. Wiese, Kurt (1887-1974), illus. LC 29-23736. 3 p. l., 137 p. incl. col. front., illus. (part col.) 14 x 18 1/2 cm. 1929. Frederick A. Stokes Company.
Mackall, Ruth, jt. auth. see Mackall, Lawton.
Mackarness, Matilda Anne Planche (1826-1881)
--Amy's Kitchen. (The Star of Hope Ser.). N.D. Frederick Warne & Co.
--Broom. N.D. George Routledge & Sons.
--The Children's Sunday Album. (Album Library). N.D. Colby and Rich.
--The Children's Sunday Album, 1 of 4. (Illus.). 320p. (The Album Library Ser.). N.D. Lee & Shepard.
--The Cloud with the Silver Lining. (The Sunbeam Stories Library). 1875. George Routledge & Sons.
--The Dream Chintz. (The Sunbeam Stories Library). 1875. George Routledge & Sons.
--The Forget-me-not, 1 of 3 Vols. (Illus.). (The Wild Rose Library). N.D. Set. George Routledge & Sons.
--Minnie's Love. (The Sunbeam Stories Library). 1875. George Routledge & Sons.
--Old Saws New Set: By Author of "Trap to Catch a Sunbeam". Jones, W. L., illus. (Illus.). N.D. George Routledge & Sons.
--Snowdrop, and Other Tales: By Author of "Trap to Catch a Sunbeam". (Illus.). N.D. George Routledge & Sons.
--Sunbeam Library: Containing: "Cloud with a Silver Lining", "Dream Chintz", "Old Joliffe", & "Trap to Catch a Sunbeam", 4 Vols. (Illus.). N.D. James Miller.
--Sweet Flowers: By Author of "Trap to Catch a Sunbeam". (Illus.). N.D. George Routledge & Sons.
--Sweet Violets: By Author of "Trap to Catch a Sunbeam". (Illus.). N.D. George Routledge & Sons.
--Tell Mamma: By Author of "Trap to Catch a Sunbeam". (Illus.). N.D. George Routledge & Sons.
--A Trap to Catch a Sunbeam. (The Sunbeam Stories Library). 1875. George Routledge & Sons.
--A Trap to Catch a Sunbeam. LC 35-33777. 16cm. 60p. 1850. J. Munroe & Co.
--The Village Idol: By Author of "Trap to Catch a Sunbeam". (Illus.). N.D. George Routledge & Sons.
Mackay
--Family at Heatherdale. (Carters' Fireside Library). N.D. Robert Carter & Brothers.
MacKay, A Donald
--If you were a clown. (Illus.). 1965. James H. Heineman, Inc.
McKay, Alice
--Careyville Adventure. 135p. (gr. 4-9). 1981. (ISBN 0-941474-04-6). A McKay.
Mackay, Claire (1930-)
--Mini-Bike Hero. Smith, Merle, illus. (Illus.). (gr. 4-6). 1975. (ISBN 0-590-09874-8, Schol Pap). Schol Bk Serv.
--Mini-Bike Racer. (gr. 4-6). 1977. (ISBN 0-590-10346-6, Schol Pap). Schol Bk Serv.
Mackay, Constance D'Arcy (0000-1966)
--The Beau of Bath and Other One-Act Plays of Eighteenth-Century Life. 1915. Holt.
--Children's Theatres and Plays. LC 27-24136. xiii, 265 p. front., plates. 21 cm. (Half-title: The Drama league library of the theatre arts). 1927. D. Appleton and Company.
--Dick Whittington. N.D. Henry Holt.
--The Forest Princess and Other Masques. 1916. Holt.
--The House of the Heart: And Other Plays for Children. LC 9-32665. 6 p. l., 3-226 p. 17 1/2 cm. 1909. H. Holt and Company.
--Ladies of the White House. 1948. Baker.
--Midsummer Eve: An Outdoor Fantasy. 1929. French.
--Patriotic Plays & Pageants for Young People. 1912. Henry Holt.
--Plays of the Pioneers. 1915. Harper.
--The Silver Thread and Other Folk Plays for Young People: Containing: The Forest Spring, The Foam Maiden, Troll Magic, The Three Wishes, A Brewing of Brains, Siegfried, the Snow Witch. 1910. Henry Holt & Co.
--Youth's Highway and Other Folk Plays for Young People. N.D. Henry Holt & Co.
McKay, Herbert
--Noah and Rabbit: A Nursery Thriller. Lodge, Grace, illus. LC 32-17789. 3 p. l., 3-87 p. front., illus. 17 1/2 cm. c.1932. E. P. Dutton & Co., Inc.
Mackay, Isabel Ecclestone Macpherson, Mrs. (1875-)
--The Shining Ship: And Other Verse for Children. Grosvenor, Thelma Cudlipp, illus. LC 18-20173. 4 p. l., vii-ix p., 1 l., 11-82 p. col. front., illus., col. plates. 23 1/2 cm. c.1918. George H. Doran Company.
MacKay, J. S, jt. auth. see Keech, Roy A.
Mackay, Margaret Mackprang (1907-)
--Dolphin Boy. Fortnum, Peggy, pseud. (1919-), illus. Nuttall-Smith, Margaret Emily Noel. LC 65-20704. 92p. illus. 23cm. 1st U.S. edition. 1965, c.1963. (ISBN 0-399-20041-X). Putnam.
--The Flowered Donkey. Wiese, Kurt (1887-1974), illus. LC 50-10144. 91 p. illus. 21 cm. 1950. J. Day Co.
--Poetic Parrot. N.D. E. M. Hale and Co.
--The Poetic Parrot. Wiese, Kurt (1887-1974), illus. LC 51-597. 96 p. illus. 21 cm. 1951. J. Day Co.
Mackay, Mary L., jt. ed. see Roberts, Virginia Keller.
McKay, Robert (1921-)
--Bordy. LC 77-23305. 141 p. 21cm. c.1977. (ISBN [illegible]). T. Nelson.
--Canary Red. LC 68-26336. 186 p. 21cm. 1968. Meredith Press.
--Dave's Song. LC 74-91013. 181 p. 22cm. 1969. Meredith Press.
--The Girl Who Wanted to Run the Boston Marathon. LC 79-20928. 1980. (ISBN 0-525-66663-X). Lodestar Bks.
--The Running Back. LC 79-87523. p. cm. c.1979. (ISBN 0-15-269782-9). Harcourt Brace Jovanovich.
--The Troublemaker. LC 70-169037. 1st U.S. edition. (gr. 6 up). 1971. (ISBN 0-525-66168-9). Lodestar Bks.
MacKay, Ruth Clarage (1896-)
--Just Like Me. Doane, Pelagie (1906-1966), illus. LC 48-35008. 24 p. illus. (part col.) 18 x 20 cm. 1946. Abingdon-Cokesbury Press.
--They Sang a New Song. Laite, Gordon (1925-), illus. N.D. Abingdon Press.
McKay, Winsor
--Little Nemo in Slumberland. N.D. Duffield & Co.
Mackaye, Arthur Loring (1890-)
--The Slave Prince: A Tale of Ancient Greece and of the Siege of Troy. Merrill, Frank Thayer (1848-), illus. LC 26-15373. xii p., 1 l., 316 p. front., plates. 20 cm. c.1926. L. C. Page & Company.
--The Viking Prince: Or, The Adventure of Harald Trygvesen. (The Days of Chivalry Ser.). N.D. Page Co.
MacKaye, David Loring see David, Julian, pseud.
MacKaye, David Loring (1890-)
--The Far Distant Bugle. LC 48-4002. vi. 264 p. 22 cm. 1948. Longmans, Green.
--The Great Scoop. LC 56-6465. 192p. 21cm. c.1956. Nelson.
--Pat's New Worlds. Bennett, Richard Michael (1899-), illus. LC 54-9207. 242p. illus. 21cm. 1954. Longmans, Green.
--The Silver Disk. 1st ed. Johnson, Avery Fischer (1906-), illus. LC 55-8312. 195p. illus. 22cm. 1955. Longmans, Green.
--Trail from Taos. LC 55-100085. 191p. illus. 21cm. 1955. T. Nelson.
--We of Frabo Stand. Jemne, Elsa Laubach (1888-), illus. LC 44-8545. vi p., 2 l., 242 p. illus. 21 cm. 1944. Longmans, Green and Co.
MacKaye, David Loring (1890-), ed.
--Flock of Words: An Anthology of Poetry for Children & Others. Gill, Margery Jean (1925-), illus. De Mott, B., pref. by. LC 77-91070. index. notes. (gr. 10 up). 1970. (ISBN 0-15-228599-7, HJ). HarBraceJ.
MacKaye, Milton
--The Box Parade. N.D. Robert M. McBride & Co.
MacKaye, Percy Wallace (1875-1956), ed. see Chaucer, Geoffrey.
Mackaye, Percy Wallace (1875-1956)
--Poog & the Caboose Man. 1976. (ISBN 0-87027-175-X). Cumberland Pr.
--Poog's Pasture. 1976. (ISBN 0-87027-174-1). Cumberland Pr.
MacKaye, Percy Wallace (1875-1956), adapted by.
--Rip Van Winkle. N.D. Alfred A. Knopf.
McKean, Else
--David's Bad Day. McKean, Else, photos by. LC 49-10453. 46 p. illus. 25 cm. 1949. Shady Hill Press.
--David's Bad Day. McKean, Else, photos by. N.D. Vanguard Press.
--It's Mine!. LC 59-54. unpaged. illus. 23 cm. N.D. Vanguard Press.
McKean, Emma C., illus.
--Goldilocks and the Three Bears. LC 44-21221. (Illus.). 30cm. 14p. (Magic Fairy Tales). 1943. McLoughlin Bros., Inc.
--Little Red Riding Hood. LC 44-21952. (Illus.). 14p. 22 x 29cm. (Magic Fairy Tales). 1943. McLoughlin Bros. Inc.
McKean, May Field
--Florence Walton: Or, A Question of Duty. (Illus.). 235p. N.D. Sunday-School Publications.
--Flossie Thornton's Investment: Or, Bread Upon the Waters. 250p. N.D. Sunday-School Publications.
--Kezzie's Corner. 287p. N.D. Sunday-School Publications.
--Mrs. Goldworth's Charity. LC 12-36478. 2 p. l., 3-247 p. front., plates. 18 1/2 cm. c.1887. American Baptist Publication Society.
--Pearl Hanford's Summer. LC 12-364756. 2 p. l., 3-253 p. front., plates. 18 1/2 cm. c.1888. American Baptist Publication Society.
McKechnie, N. K.
--Heir of all the Ages. N.D. Bobbs-Merrill Co.
McKee, Craig & Holland, Margaret (1939-)
--Time to Swim. Robison, Don, illus. LC 84-52560. (Illus.). 24 p. 22cm. (Predictable Reading Books). c.1985. (ISBN 0-87406-003-6). Willowisp Press.
McKee, David (1935-), retold by see Asbjornsen, Peter Christen.
McKee, David (1935-)
--The Day the Tide Went Out ... and Out ... and Out ... and Out ... and Out ... and Out. McKee, David (1935-), illus. LC 75-18940. (Illus.). 28 p. 24cm. 1976, c.1975. (ISBN 0-200-00160-4). Abelard-Schuman.
--The Day the Tide Went Out- and Out-. McKee, David (1935-), illus. LC 85-30714. p. cm. c.1985. (ISBN 0-87226-064-X). P. Bedrick Books.
--Elmer: The Story of a Patchwork Elephant. McKee, David (1935-), illus. LC 68-29914. (Illus.). 45 p. 24cm. 1968. McGraw Hill.
--The Hill and the Rock. LC 84-14208. (Illus.). 24 p. 24cm. 1985, c.1984. (ISBN 0-89919-341-2). Clarion Books.
--I Hate My Teddy Bear. McKee, David (1935-), illus. LC 83-7605. (Illus.). 32p. (ps-3). 1984. (ISBN 0-89919-214-9, Clarion). HM.
--King Rollo & King Frank. (Illus.). 32p. (King Rollo Ser.). (gr. 1-3). 1982. (ISBN 0-87191-834-X). Creative Ed.
--King Rollo & the Balloons. (Illus.). 32p. (King Rollo Ser.). (gr. 1-3). 1982. (ISBN 0-87191-830-7). Creative Ed.
--King Rollo & the Bath. (Illus.). 32p. (King Rollo Ser.). (gr. 1-3). 1982. (ISBN 0-87191-833-1). Creative Ed.
--King Rollo and the Birthday. LC 79-53117. (Illus.). 27 p. 14cm. c.1979. (ISBN 0-316-56044-8). Little, Brown.
--King Rollo and the Bread. LC 79-53118. (Illus.). 27 p. 14cm. c.1979. (ISBN 0-316-56044-8). Little, Brown.
--King Rollo & the Breakfast. 32p. (King Rollo Ser.). (gr. k-2). 1982. (ISBN 0-87191-902-8). Creative Ed.
--King Rollo & the Dishes. (Illus.). 32p. (King Rollo Ser.). (gr. 1-3). 1982. (ISBN 0-87191-832-3). Creative Ed.
--King Rollo & the Dog. 32p. (King Rollo Ser.). (gr. k-2). 1982. (ISBN 0-87191-901-X). Creative Ed.
--King Rollo & the Mask. 32p. (King Rollo Ser.). (gr. k-2). 1982. (ISBN 0-87191-900-1). Creative Ed.
--King Rollo and the New Shoes. LC 79-53116. (Illus.). 28 p. 14cm. c.1979. (ISBN 0-316-56044-8). Little, Brown.
--King Rollo & the Playroom. 32p. (King Rollo Ser.). (gr. k-2). 1982. (ISBN 0-87191-899-4). Creative Ed.
--King Rollo & the Search. (Illus.). 32p. (King Rollo Ser.). (gr. 1-3). 1982. (ISBN 0-87191-835-8). Creative Ed.
--King Rollo & the Tree. (Illus.). 32p. (King Rollo Ser.). (gr. 1-3). 1982. (ISBN 0-87191-831-5). Creative Ed.
--King Rollo: Including "King Rollo & the New Shoes"; "King Rollo & the Birthday"; "King Rollo & the Bread. (gr. 1-3). 1980. (ISBN 0-316-56044-8, Pub. by Atlantic Monthly Pr). Little.
--Lord Rex, the Lion Who Wished. McKee, David (1935-), illus. LC 73-2156. (Illus.). 26 p. 26cm. 1973. (ISBN 0-200-72030-9). (ISBN 0-200-00109-4). Abelard-Schuman.
--The Magician and the Petnapping. McKee, David (1935-), illus. LC 77-367537. (Illus.). 28 p. 28cm. 1976. (ISBN 0-200-72451-7). Abelard-Schuman.
--The Magician and the Petnapping. McKee, David (1935-), illus. LC 76-20282. (Illus.). 28 p. 28cm. 1976. (ISBN 0-395-24916-3). Houghton Mifflin.
--The Magician and the Sorcerer. McKee, David (1935-), illus. LC 73-22280. (Illus.). 26 p. 27cm. 1974. (ISBN 0-8193-0772-6). (ISBN 0-8193-0772-6). Parents' Magazine Press.
--The Magician Who Lost His Magic. McKee, David (1935-), illus. LC 76-114289. (Illus.). 38 p. 28cm. 1970. Abelard-Schuman.
--Mark and the Monocycle. McKee, David (1935-), illus. LC 68-20809. (Illus.). 42 p. 27cm. 1968. (ISBN 0-200-71526-7). Abelard-Schuman.
--Mr. Benn: Red Knight. McKee, David (1935-), illus. LC 68-26313. (Illus.). 46 p. 1968. McGraw-Hill.
--Not Now, Bernard. McKee, David (1935-), illus. LC 80-21436. (Illus.). 26 p. 24cm. c.1980. (ISBN 0-416-30781-7). Metnuen.
--One, Two, Three, Four, Five, Six, Seven, Eight, Nine Benn. McKee, David (1935-), illus. LC 77-112839. (Illus.). 40 p. 25cm. 1970. McGraw-Hill.
--Tusk Tusk. McKee, David (1935-), illus. (Illus.). 1979. (ISBN 0-8120-5321-4). Barron.
--Two Admirals. McKee, David (1935-), illus. LC 77-5492. (Illus.). 32 p. 29cm. c.1977. (ISBN 0-395-25808-1). Houghton Mifflin.
--Two Can Toucan. McKee, David (1935-), illus. LC 65-10177. 1v. (unpaged) col. illus. 23cm. 1965, c.1964. Abelard.
--Two Can Toucan. McKee, David (1935-), illus. (Illus.). (gr. k-2). 1964. (ISBN 0-8382-0909-2). Hale.
--Two Monsters. McKee, David (1935-), illus. LC 85-22344. p. cm. 1986, c.1985. Bradbury Press.
McKee, David (1935-), retold by.
--Hans in Luck. McKee, David (1935-), illus. LC 67-181176. (Original Authors: The Brothers Grimm). (Illus.). (gr. k-3). 1967. Abelard.
McKee, Donald P.
--Travels of Tim the Telepathic Trunk. 1983. (ISBN 0-911197-02-8). Miracle Pub Co.
McKee, Douglas, tr. see Trez, Denise (1930-) & Trez, Alain.
McKee, Frances
--Rockabye to Monster Land. De Larrea, Victoria illus. LC 72-110317. (Illus.). 32 p. 1970. Putnam.
McKee, Gwendolyn
--Anchored to the Marsh. Morgan, Carrie Elizabeth, illus. LC 81-65367. (Illus.). 37 p. 1981. (ISBN 0-935304-20-7). August House.
McKee, Jessie Fulton, jt. auth. see Aldredge, Edna.
McKee, Louise & Summers, Richard
--Dusty Desert Tales. 191p. N.D. Caxton Printers.
--Dusty Desert Tales. 191p. N.D. Reilly & Lee Co.
McKee, Vallie
--Poems for Children. Liermann, Rosemary, illus. LC 46-2070. 21cm. 21p. 1945. Hobson Book Press.
McKeekin, Isabel McLennan
--Kentucky Derby Winner. N.D. Grosset & Dunlap.
McKeen, Frances (1871-)
--Stories in Prose and Rhyme and Nature Lessons for Little Children. LC 12-18010. 150 p. illus. 21 cm. c.1912. The American School for the Deaf.
McKeen, Phebe Fuller
--The Little Mother and her Christmas and Other Stories. White, E. E., illus. (Illus.). N.D. Lothrop Pub. Co.
--Thornton Hall: Or, Old Questions in Young Lives. LC 7-16302. 325 p. 19 cm. c.1872. A. D. F. Randolph & Company.
McKeever, B.
--Frederick Latimer: Or, What is the Standard. (Illus.). 320p. N.D. Sunday-School Publications.
McKeever, Harriet Burn, et al. (1807-1886)
--Little People's Home Library: Containing "Watercress Girl," "Christmas Tales," "Young Fisherman", 12 vols. N.D. Set. D. Lothrop & Co.
--Woodcliff Library: Containing "Woodcliff", "Legend and Record", "Edith's Ministry" and "Mark Wilton", 4 vols. (Illus.). N.D. Set. James A. Moore.
McKeever, Harriet Burn (1807-1886)
--Aunt Harriet's Tales About Little Words. LC 7-16291. 288 p. front., plates. 15 1/2 cm. c.1863. Presbyterian Board of Publication.
--Aunt Lou's Scrap-Book. 59 p. front., pl. 15 1/2 cm. c.1878. American Tract Society.
--Bertha's Coronet: Or, The House on the Heights. LC 7-19971. vi, 7-438 p. incl. front. 17 1/2 cm. 1881. Lutheran Publication Society.
--The Birthday Library Ser, 3 Vols. N.D. N. Tibbals & Sons.
--Breakers Ahead: Larry Dalton. N.D. Alfred Martien.
--Breakers Ahead: Or, Larry Dalton. LC 7-16292. 283 p. front., plates. 17 cm. 1869. J. P. Skelly & Co.
--Breakers Ahead: Or, Larry Dalton. (Illus.). N.D. James A. Moore.
--Children with the Poets. LC 12-5641. 360 p. 19 1/2 cm. 1868. Claxton, Remsen & Haffelfinger.
--Crown Jewels, 1 of 25 vols. (Selected Bks for Sunday School: The/Auburn Library). N.D. Set. Methodist Bk Concern.
--Crown Jewels. LC 7-19972. 243 p. front. 18 cm. 1883. Walden and Stowe.
--Edith's Ministry, 1 of 103 vols. (The Pearl Library: No. 20). 1900. Set. Hurst & Co.
--Edith's Ministry. (Illus.). N.D. James A. Moore.
--Eleanor's Three Birthdays, 1 of 3 Vols. (Birthday Library Ser.). N.D. Set. John C. Winston Co.
--Eleanor's Three Birthdays. Schell, Frederic B., illus. 295 p. front., plates. 16 1/2 cm. (Birthday series no. 1). N.D. Porter & Coates.

--Eleanor's Three Birthdays: or, "Charity Seeketh not her Own". (Illus.). 1888. Porter & Coates.
--The Flounced Robe. N.D. Bradley & Woodruff.
--The Flounced Robe. LC 7-16294. viii, 9-184 p. front. 17 1/2 cm. 1859. Lindsay & Blakiston.
--The Flounced Robe and What It Cost. 184p. N.D. Henry Hoyt.
--The Foot on the Sill: A Story of Home Influence. LC 7-19973. 189 p. front., plates. 17 1/2 cm. (A Bright Half Dozen Ser.). c.1879. American Tract Society.
--Golden Lines. LC 7-19974. 2 p. l., 3-399 p. front., plates. 18 cm. (Added t.-p.: The thousand dollar prize series). c.1873. D. Lothrop & Co.
--Good-Bye Stories for Little Children. LC 7-16295. 216 p. front. 15 1/2 cm. c.1866. Presbyterian Board of Publication.
--Heavenward Earthward. LC 7-16296. 369 p. front., plates. 17 cm. 1867. J. C. Garrigues & Co.
--Helen Graham: A Story for Young Girls. 279 p. front., pl. 17 1/2 cm. 1882. Garrigues Brothers.
--Jack and Florie: Or, The Pigeons' Wedding. 35, 1 p. incl. plates. 20 x 16 cm. 1870. Claxton, Remsen & Haffelfinger.
--Jack and Florie: Or, The Pigeon's Wedding. (Illus.). N.D. Thomas W. Hartley & Co.
--Jessie Morrison: Or, The Mission Flowers. 156 p. front., pl. 15 1/2 cm. c.1859. Presbyterian Board of Publication.
--Little Mary. LC 7-16298. 131 p. front. 15 1/2 cm. c.1867. Presbyterian Board of Publication.
--Little Mary and the Fairy. N.D. Claxton,Remsen & Haffelfinger.
--Little Mary and the Fairy. (Illus.). N.D. Thomas W. Hartley & Co.
--Little Red Cloak. LC 7-16230. 64 p. incl. col. plates. 20 x 15 1/2 cm. c.1866. Presbyterian Publication Committee.
--Lucy Forrester's Triumphs, 1 of 3 Vols. (Birhtday Library Ser.). N.D. Set. John C. Winston Co.
--Lucy Forrester's Triumphs. (Illus.). 1882. Porter & Coates.
--Lucy Forrester's Triumphs. (Illus.). 1888. Porter & Coates.
--Lucy Forrester's Triumphs, 1 of 3 vols. (Birthday Library: No. 3). 1891. Set. Porter & Coates.
--Lucy Forrester's Triumphs. Schell, Frederic B., illus. LC 7-16300. 298 p. front., plates. 16 1/2 cm. (Birthday series no. 3). c.1867. Porter & Coates.
--Lucy's Two Lives. N.D. Alfred Martien.
--Mary Leslie's Trials, 1 of 3 Vols. (Birthday Library Ser.). N.D. Set. John C. Winston Co.
--Mary Leslie's Trials, 1 of 3 vols. (Birthday Library Ser.: No. 2). 1891. Set. Porter & Coates.
--Mary Leslie's Trials: Or, Not Easily Provoked. (Illus.). 1882. Porter & Coates.
--Mary Leslie's Trials: Or, Not Easily Provoked. (Illus.). 1888. Porter & Coates.
--Mary Leslie's Trials: Or, Not Easily Provoked. Schell, Frederic B., illus. 301 p. front., plates. 16 1/2 cm. (Birthday series no. 2). c.1867. Porter & Coates.
--Maude and Miriam. N.D. Claxton, Remsen, & Haffelfinger.
--Maude & Miriam, 1 of 103 vols. (The Pearl Library: No. 61). 1900. Set. Hurst & Co.
--May Castleton's Mission. LC 7-16290. 228 p. front., plates. 15 1/2 cm. c.1866. Presbyterian Publication Committee.
--Merry Times: A Story and Picture Book for Boys and Girls. (Illus.). 1882. Porter & Coates.
--Milly's Taper: Or, What Can I Do?. N.D. Henry Hoyt.
--Nothing but Leaves. iv, 5-288 p. front., plates. 17 1/2 cm. (On cover: Woodcliff children series). 1882. E. Claxton & Company.
--Nothing but Leaves. LC 7-16289. iv, 5-288 p. front., plates. 17 cm. 1868. J. P. Skelly & Co.
--Nothing But Leaves. (Illus.). N.D. James A. Moore.
--Nothing But Leaves. (Illus.). (Woodcliff Children Ser.). 1891. Ward & Drummond.
--The Nursery Treasury. LC 7-19969. vii, 8-47 p. incl. col. front., col. plates. 19 cm. 1873. Claxton, Remsen & Haffelfinger.
--The Nursery Treasury. (Illus.). N.D. Thomas W. Hartley & Co.
--On the Border-Land. LC 7-19422. 2 p. l., 3-288 p. front., plates. 17 1/2 cm. c.1881. American Baptist Publication Society.
--Petite's Wand of Lilies. iv, 5-384 p. front., pl. 17 1/2 cm. (On cover: Woodcliff children series). 1882. E. Claxton & Company.
--Petite's Wand of Lilies. LC 7-19423. iv, 5-384 p. front., pl. 17 1/2 cm. 1877. J. A. Moore.
--Petite's Wand of Lilies, 1 of 10 Vols. (Illus.). (Woodcliff Children Ser.). 1891. Ward & Drummond.
--Rose Delaney's Secret. LC 7-16286. 216 p. front., plates. 15 1/2 cm. 1866. Presbyterian Publication Committee.
--Rupert Lawrence, 1 of 10 Vols. (Woodcliff Children Ser.). N.D. Ward & Drummond.
--Rupert Lawrence: Boy in Earnest. N.D. Alfred Martien.
--Rupert Lawrence: Or, A Boy in Earnest. LC 7-19421. 336 p. front., plates. 17 1/2 cm. (On cover: Woodcliff children series). 1882. E. Claxton & Company.
--Rupert Lawrence: Or, A Boy in Earnest. LC 7-16287. 336 p. front., plates. 16 1/2 cm. 1869. J. P. Skelly & Co.
--Rupert Lawrence: Or, A Boy in Earnest. (Illus.). N.D. James A. Moore.
--Silver Threads. LC 7-16288. 2 p. l., 3-376 p. front. 18 1/2 cm. 1868. Claxton, Remsen & Haffelfinger.
--Silver Threads, 1 of 103 vols. (The Pearl Library: No. 94). 1900. Set. Hurst & Co.
--Sunshine: Kate Vinton. N.D. Alfred Martien.
--Sunshine Library: Containing "Sunshine, or Kate Vinton", "Breakers Ahead", "Nothing but Leaves" and "Rupert Lawrence", 4 vols. (Illus.). N.D. James A. Moore.
--Sunshine: Or, Kate Vinton. LC 7-19420. 1 p. l., ix-xi, 13-372 p. front., plates. 17 1/2 cm. (On cover: Woodcliff children series). 1882. E. Claxton & Company.
--Sunshine: Or, Kate Vinton. (Illus.). N.D. James A. Moore.
--Sunshine: Or, Kate Vinton. (Illus.). (Woodcliff Children Ser.). 1891. Ward & Drummond.
--Tender and True. LC 7-19418. iv, 5-344 p. front., pl. 17 1/2 cm. 1877. J. A. Moore.
--The Three Rules, 1 of 10 Vols. (Illus.). (Woodcliff Children Ser.). 1891. Set. Ward & Drummond.
--Twice Crowned. N.D. Claxton, Remsen, & Haffelfinger.
--Twice Crowned, 1 of 103 vols. (The Pearl Library: No. 98). 1900. Set. Hurst & Co.
--Westbrook Parsonage. N.D. Claxton, Remsen, & Haffelfinger.
--Westbrook Parsonage, 1 of 103 vols. (The Pearl Library: No. 100). 1900. Set. Hurst & Co.
--Will Collins. N.D. Henry Hoyt.
--Woodcliff. N.D. Alfred Martien.
--Woodcliff, 1 of 103 vols. (The Pearl Library: No. 102). 1900. Set. Hurst & Co.
--Woodcliff. (Illus.). N.D. James A. Moore.
--Woodcliff Children. N.D. Alfred Martien.
--Woodcliff Children. LC 7-19417. ix-xvi, 17-248 p. front., plates. 17 cm. (On cover: Woodcliff children series). 1882. E. Claxton & Company.
--The Woodcliff Children. LC 7-19419. ix-xvi, 17-248 p. front., plates. 17 cm. 1872. J. P. Skelly & Co.
--Woodcliff Children. (Illus.). N.D. James A. Moore.
--Woodcliff Children, 1 of 10 Vols. (Illus.). (Woodcliff Children Ser.). 1891. Ward & Drummond.

McKellar, Shona
--The Beginning of the Rainbow. Kasuya, Masahiro (1937-), illus. LC 81-7954. p. cm. 1982, c.1977. (ISBN 0-687-02770-5). Abingdon.

MacKellar, William (1914-)
--Alfie and Me and the Ghost of Peter Stuyvesant. Stone, David Karl (1922-), illus. LC 74-3784. (Illus.). 150 p. 21cm. 1974. (ISBN 0-396-06976-2). Dodd, Mead.
--The Cat That Never Died. Stone, David Karl (1922-), illus. LC 75-38358. (Illus.). 183 p. 21cm. c.1976. (ISBN 0-396-07303-4). Dodd, Mead.
--Danger in the Mist. LC 55-12108. 159p. 21cm. 1956. Whittlesey House.
--A Dog Called Porridge. LC 85-4445. (Illus.). 153 p. 22cm. c.1985. (ISBN 0-396-08626-8). Dodd, Mead.
--Dog Like No Other. (Illus.). (gr. 4-6). 1965. (ISBN 0-8382-0215-2). Hale.
--A Dog Like No Other. Unwin, Nora Spicer (1907-), illus. LC 65-10193. 151p. illus. 21cm. c.1965. McKay.
--A Ghost Around the House. Miller, Marilyn Jean (1925-), illus. LC 79-125656. (Illus.). 117 p. 21cm. 1970. McKay.
--Ghost in the Castle. (Illus.). (gr. 4-6). 1960. (ISBN 0-8382-0282-9). Hale.
--Ghost in the Castle. Bennett, Richard Michael (1899-), illus. LC 60-11849. 86p. illus. 21cm. 1960. (ISBN 0-679-25052-2). D. McKay Co.
--The Ghost of Grannoch Moor. Lewin, Ted (1935-), illus. LC 73-6028. (Illus.). 115 p. 21cm. 1973. (ISBN 0-396-06834-0). Dodd, Mead.
--A Goal for Greg. LC 58-8465. 151p. 21cm. c.1958. D. McKay Co.
--A Goal For Greg. 1958. (ISBN 0-8382-0293-4, Cadmus Books). E. M. Hale and Company.
--Kenny and the Highland Ghost. Mars, Witold Tadeusz J. (1912-), illus. LC 79-6630. (Illus.). 185 p. 22cm. 1980. (ISBN 0-396-07811-7). Dodd, Mead.
--Kickoff. LC 55-5691. 184 p. 21cm. 1955. Whittlesey House.
--The Kid Who Owned Manhattan Island. Stone, David Karl (1922-), illus. LC 76-12504. (Illus.). 182 p. 21cm. c.1976. (ISBN 0-396-07363-8). Dodd, Meade.
--Mound Menace. Mocniak, George, illus. LC 69-10251. (Illus.). 187 p. 23cm. 1969. Follett.
--Mystery of Mordach Castle. Lazare, Gerald John (1927-), illus. LC 72-89578. (Illus.). 157 p. 22cm. 1970. Follett Pub. Co.
--The Mystery of the Ruined Abbey. LC 54-9713. (Illus.). 192 p. 21cm. 1954. Whittlesey House.
--A Place by the Fire. Koering, Ursula (1921-), illus. LC 66-13112. (Illus.). 85p. (gr. 4-6). 1966. (ISBN 0-679-25110-3). McKay.
--Score! A Baker's Dozen Sports Stories. viii, 148 p. 21cm. 1967. (ISBN 0-679-25127-8). D. McKay Co.
--The Secret of the Dark Tower. LC 67-21631. 150 p. 21cm. 1967. D. McKay Co.
--The Secret of the Sacred Stone. LC 79-101962. 132 p. 21cm. 1970. McKay.
--The Silent Bells. Lewin, Ted (1935-), illus. LC 78-7744. p. cm. 1978. (ISBN 0-396-07618-1). Dodd, Mead.
--The Smallest Monster in the World. Koering, Ursula (1921-), illus. LC 71-81901. (Illus.). 113 p. 21cm. 1969. D. McKay.
--The Soccer Orphans. LC 78-22435. 157 p. c.1979. (ISBN 0-396-07667-X). Dodd, Mead.
--The Team that Wouldn't Quit. 1956. McGraw.
--The Team That Wouldn't Quit. LC 56-10322. 160 p. 21cm. 1956. Whittlesey House.
--Terror Run. LC 82-45382. p. cm. 1982. (ISBN 0-396-08091-X). (ISBN 0-396-08091-X). Dodd, Mead.
--Two for the Fair. Unwin, Nora Spicer (1907-), illus. 1958. E M Hale.
--Two for the Fair. Unwin, Nora Spicer (1907-), illus. LC 58-111869. 61p. illus. 22cm. 1958. Whittlesey House.
--A Very Small Miracle. Mars, Witold Tadeusz J. (1912-), illus. LC 72-75069. (Illus.). 120 p. 22cm. 1969. Crown Publishers.
--Wee Joseph. 1957. E M Hale.
--Wee Joseph. Keats, Ezra Jack (1916-1983), illus. LC 57-9429. (Illus.). 76 p. 22cm. 1957. Whittlesey House.
--The Witch of Glen Gowrie. Lewin, Ted (1935-), illus. LC 77-16864. (Illus.). 144 p. 21cm. c.1978. (ISBN 0-396-07531-2). Dodd, Mead.

Mckelvey, David
--Bobby the Mostly Silky. (Illus.). 32p. 1984. (ISBN 0-931722-28-4). (ISBN 0-931722-27-6). Corona Pub.
--Commander the Gander. Asklin, William O., illus. LC 84-72455. (Illus.). 48p. 1984. (ISBN 0-931722-31-4). (ISBN 0-931722-30-6). Corona Pub.

McKelvey, Gertrude Della
--Gertrude D. McKelvey's Stories to Grow On: Five Everyday Parables for Boys and Girls. Busby, Jean, illus. LC 47-222327. 63 p. illus. 18 cm. 1947. The John C. Winston Company.
--Stories to Live By. Doane, Pelagie (1906-1966), illus. 1943. John C. Winston.

McKemy, Kay (1924-)
--Samuel Pepys of the Navy. LC 77-85217. (Illus.). (gr. 7-12). 1970. (ISBN 0-7232-6071-0). Warne.

Macken, Walter (1915-1967)
--The Flight of the Doves. LC 68-12083. 200 p. 22cm. 1967, c.1968. Macmillan.
--Island of the Great Yellow Ox. Keeping, Charles William James (1924-), illus. LC 66-11107. 206p. 21cm. c.1966. Macmillan.

McKenna, Dolores
--The Arrival of Mr. Widdle Waddle. (The Widdle Waddle Bks.). N.D. Penn.
--Mr. Widdle Waddle Brings the Family. (The Widdle Waddle Bks.). N.D. Penn.
--Tom Mitten's Cousins. LC 53-37576. (Illus.). 24cm. 1923. S. Gabriel Sons.
--Yellow Bill's Adventures. LC 53-56567. (Illus.). 24cm. 1923. S. Gabriel Sons.

McKenna, Helen, ed. see Carver, Marjorie Reineman.

MacKenna, Stephen Joseph (1837-1883)
--At School with an Old Dragoon. N.D. George Routledge & Sons.

McKenna, Terry (1949-)
--The Fox & the Circus Bear. McKenna, Terry (1949-), illus. (Illus.). 32p. 1st U.S. edition. (ps-3). 1982. (Pub. by Gollancz England). David & Charles.

McKenna, Tom, jt. auth. see Parker, Faye.

McKenney, Kenneth (1929-)
--The Plants. LC 75-34725. 1976. (ISBN 0-399-11627-3). Putnam Pub Group.

McKenney, Ruth (1911-1972)
--My Sister Eileen. large type ed. (Keith Jennison Bks). (gr. 7 up). N.D. (ISBN 0-531-00310-8). Watts.

McKenny, Margaret
--Abe and His Girl Friend, Amble. LC 45-10296. 1 p. l., 24, 1 p. illus. 28 1/2 cm. c.1945. Binfords & Mort.
--How the Hurricane Helped. Bromhall, Winifred, illus. LC 40-31803. 47 p. illus. (part col.) 17 1/2 x 14 cm. 1940. A. A. Knopf.

McKenzie, Cary Blair
--Classic Myth-Lore in Rhyme. Scott, J. Gardner, illus. LC 5-39031. (Founded on Bullfinch's Age of Fable). (Illus.). 22 1/2cm. 104p. c.1905. E. K. McKenzie.

Mackenzie, Charles Fraser (1880-), tr. see Bidpai.

McKenzie, Christine, jt. ed. see Holbrook, David Kenneth.

MacKenzie, Christine Beckwith Butchart (1917-)
--Out at Home. 176 p. 21cm. 1967. Bethany Press.
--A Year Is Forever. (gr. 7-10). 1964. (ISBN 0-8272-4400-2). Bethany Pr.

Mackenzie, Compton Edward Montague, Sir (1883-1972)
--Little Cat Lost. Boswell, James, illus. LC 66-156596. 134p. illus. 23cm. c.1965. (ISBN 0-02-761990-7). Macmillan.
--Santa Claus in Summer. LC 25-19315. 4 p. l., 3-298 p. illus. 21 cm. 1925. Frederick A. Stokes Company.
--The Stairs That Kept Going Down. Longtemps, Kenneth (1933-), illus. LC 72-96292. (Illus.). 57 p. 22cm. 1973. (ISBN 0-385-05376-2). (ISBN 0-385-05376-2). Doubleday.
--Told. LC 31-5764. vii, 1, 175 p. illus., col. mounted plates. 25 cm. 1930. D. Appleton and Company.

Mackenzie, Compton Edward Montague, Sir (1883-1972), retold by.
--Achilles. Stobbs, William (1914-), illus. 64p. (Golden Tales of Greece Ser.). 1973. (ISBN 0-529-04730-6). (ISBN 0-529-04734-9). Collins & World.
--The Book of Nursery Tales. Brock, Henry Matthew (1875-1960), illus. LC 35-6924. xx, 268 p. col. front., illus., col. plates. 20 1/2 cm. 1934. F. Warne & Co., Ltd.
--Jason. Stobbs, William (1914-), illus. (Illus.). 32p. (Golden Tales of Greece Ser.). (gr. 4-6). 1973. (ISBN 0-529-04732-2). (ISBN 0-529-04736-5). Collins-World.
--Perseus. Stobbs, William (1914-), illus. LC 72-87703. (Illus.). 64p. (Golden Tales of Greece Ser.). (gr. 4-6). 1973. (ISBN 0-529-04729-2). (ISBN 0-529-04733-0). Collins-World.
--Theseus. Stobbs, William (1914-), illus. LC 72-87704. (Illus.). 64p. (Golden Tales of Greece Ser.). (gr. 4-6). 1973. (ISBN 0-529-04731-4). (ISBN 0-529-04735-7). Collins-World.

McKenzie, Donald Alexander (1873-)
--Finn and His Warrior. Millar, Harold Robert (1869-1939), illus. N.D. Dodge Publishing Co.
--Indian Fairy Stories. LC 18-19581. (Legend and History Library). N.D. Dodge.
--Tales from the Northern Sagas. (Legend and History Library). N.D. Dodge.
--Wonder Tales of the East. (Legend and History Library). N.D. Dodge.

McKenzie, Ellen Kindt
--Drujienna's Harp. LC 70-135854. 1971. Dutton.
--Taash and the Jesters. LC 68-24763. 233 p. 22cm. 1968. Holt, Rinehart and Winston. **Award: (ALA).**

McKenzie, Isabel
--Through the Nursery Door. Freixas, James, illus. LC 17-16552. 95 p. incl. front., plates. 22 cm. 1914. The Neale Publishing Company.

MacKenzie, Jeanette Brown
--The Hawkness House Mystery. Norton, Jan, illus. LC 66-22209. 117 p. illus. 21 cm. 1966. I. Washburn.
--Mystery at the Pilgrim Dig. Norton, Jan, illus. LC 79-82647. (Illus.). 116 p. 21cm. 1969. I. Washburn.
--The Mystery of the Watching Eyes. Norton, Jan, illus. LC 65-12068. 119p. illus. 21cm. c.1965. Washburn Dist. McKay.
--Puss in the Corner Mystery. Norton, Jan, illus. (gr. 4-6). 1964. Washburn.

MacKenzie, Joy
--That's Him. Jones, Aletha & Lerner, Sheralyn, illus. (Illus.). (Especially for Children Ser.: Vol. 11). 1977. (ISBN 0-914850-13-X). Impact Tenn.

MacKenzie, Joy, jt. auth. see Forte, Imogene.

Mackenzie, Kathleen Guy (1907-)
--Starke Sisters. Abrahams, Hilary Ruth (1938-), illus. (Illus.). (gr. 5 up). 1963. (ISBN 0-685-21563-6). Verry.

MacKenzie, Lillian, jt. auth. see Sargant, Alice.

McKenzie, Roger
--Gremlins. Gonzales, Adrian, illus. LC 83-83380. (Illus.). 64p. (gr. 2 up). 1984. (ISBN 0-307-11365-5, Golden Bks). Western Pub.
--The Sun Bird Legacy. Gonzales, Adrian, illus. (Illus.). 24p. (gr. 3up). 1983. (ISBN 0-307-16010-6, Golden Bks). Western Pub.
--The Sword of Skeletor. Carrillo, Fred, illus. (Illus.). 24p. (Masters of the Universe Storybooks). (gr. k-3). 1983. (ISBN 0-307-11792-8, Golden Pr). Western Pub.
--The Thief of Castle Grayskull. Carrillo, Fred, illus. (Illus.). 24p. (Masters of the Universe Storybooks). (gr. k-3). 1983. (ISBN 0-307-11793-6, Golden Pr). Western Pub.
--Time Trouble. Barreto, Ed, illus. LC 83-83364. (Illus.). (Golden Super Adventure Bks.). (gr. k-5). 1984. (ISBN 0-307-11371-X, Golden Bks). Western Pub.

Maclean, Caroline (1909-1979)
--The Adventures of Maidilie. King, Joe (1909-1979), illus. LC 26-21778. 110 p. incl. col. front., illus. col. plates. 25 1/2 cm. 1926. E. Maclean.
McLean, Charles E. (1893-)
--Reversing History: An Adventure Story for Teen-Agers. MacLean, Charles E. (1893-), illus. LC 53-105471. 109p. illus. 21cm. 1953. Exposition Press.
McLean, George
--The Boys' Life Book of Wild Animal Stories. McLean, George, illus. LC 65-22174. (Illus.). 185 p. 22cm. (Boys' life library, 9). 1965. Random House.
MacLean, Janet (1946-) & MacLean, Andrew (1946-)
--The Steam Train Crew. (Illus.). 32p. (ps). 1983. (ISBN 0-19-554320-3, Pub by Oxford U Pr Childrens). Merrimack Pub Cir.
MacLean, Joan, tr. see Matute, Ana Maria.
MacLean, Katherine (1925-)
--Missing Man. 1975. (ISBN 0-399-11474-2). G. P. Putnam's Sons.
MacLean, Katherine (1925-) & West, Carl
--Dark Wing. McCrea, James Craig, Jr. (1920-) & McCrea, Ruth Pirman (1921-), illus. LC 78-10837. 35cm. 242p. 1979. (ISBN 0-689-30688-1, Argo). Atheneum.
McLean, Kathryn Anderson see Forbes, Kathryn, pseud.
McLean, Mina Gow, jt. auth. see Pieper, Elizabeth.
McLean, Mina Gow, jt. auth. see Wannamaker, Bruce.
McLean, Mollie & Wiseman, Anne
--The Adventures of Greek Heroes. Mars, Witold Tadeusz J. (1912-), illus. LC 61-10628. (Illus.). 184p. (gr. 4-6). 1972. (ISBN 0-395-13714-4, Sandpiper). HM.
--Adventures of the Greek Heroes. Mars, Witold Tadeusz J. (1912-), illus. LC 61-10628. 174p. col. illus. c.1961. (ISBN 0-395-06913-0). Houghton.
Maclean, Muriel
--Mags. Black, Ben, illus. LC 77-123881. (Illus.). 29 p. 23cm. (Magic circle book. Reading 360). 1971. Ginn.
MacLean, Ray Butts, jt. ed. see Flynn, Harry Eugene.
McLean, Robert Norris (1882-)
--The Flying Boat. Southard, Frank R. (1882-), illus. LC 35-5259. vi p., 1 l., 184 p. illus. 19 1/2 cm. c.1935. Friendship Press.
--Tommy Two-Wheels. Fax, Elton Clay (1909-), illus. LC 43-645110. 127 p. incl. front., illus. 19 1/2 cm. 1943. Friendship Press.
--The Traded Twins. LC 42-14592. 5 p. l., 150 p. illus. 19 1/2 cm. 1942. Friendship Press.
--The Traded Twins. rev. ed. Palacios, Rafael, illus. LC 51-3766. 136 p. illus. 21 cm. 1951. Friendship Press.
McLean, Sally Pratt
--Peter Patrick. N.D. D. Lothrop Co.
--Some Other Folks. N.D. De Wolfe, Fiske & Co.
--Towhead. N.D. De Wolfe, Fiske & Co.
McLean, Susan (1937-)
--Pennies for the Piper. LC 81-4073. 149 p. 22cm. c.1981. (ISBN 0-374-35791-9). Farrar, Straus, Giroux.
MacLear, G. F., ed. see Gaskoin, H., Mrs.
McLeary, Errol, jt. auth. see Minturn, Peter.
Maclehose, Sophia H., ed. see Spenser, Edmund.
McLeish, Kenneth (1940-)
--Chicken Licken. Ash, Julia, illus. LC 73-81975. (Illus.). 32 p. 1st U.S. edition. 1974, c.1973. (ISBN 0-87888-065-8). Bradbury Press.
McLeish, Kenneth (1940-) & Vautier, Ghislaine
--The Shining Stars: Greek Legends of the Zodiac. Con, Jacqueline Bezen, illus. LC 81-10161. (Illus.). 32 p. 1981. (ISBN 0-521-23886-2). Cambridge University Press.
MacLellan, Esther & Schroll, Catherine
--Mr. O'Riley and Brownie. N.D. Houghton Mifflin Co.
--Suzy & the Dog School. N.D. E. M. Hale & Co.
--Suzy and the Dog School. Bradfield, Margaret, illus. LC 53-7096. 46p. illus. 21cm. 1953. Ariel Books.
McLellan, Mary C
--Dr. Moore's Family. LC 44-1739. 4 p. l., 7-72 p. 20 cm. 1943. Wm. B. Eerdmans Publishing Co.
McLelland, Ernestine B.
--Angie: The Story of a Mischievous Little Scottie. (Illus.). 64p. (gr. 1). 1985. (ISBN 0-682-40198-6). Exposition Pr FL.
McLelland, Isabel Couper
--Hi! Teacher. 1st ed. Stevens, Mary E. (1920-1966), illus. LC 52-9041. (Illus.). 212 p. 21cm. 1952. Holt.
--Shadows on the Moor. Landau, Jacob (1917-), illus. LC 55-10570. (Illus.). 222 p. 21cm. 1955. Holt.
--Ski Cabin. LC 58-13064. 191 p. 21cm. 1958. Holt.
--Ten Beaver Road. Stevens, Mary E. (1920-1966), illus. LC 48-5585. 152 p. illus. 21 cm. 1948. H. Holt.
McLendon, Gloria Houston (1940-)
--My Brother Joey Died. Kelman, Harvey, photos by. LC 82-3537. (Illus.). 64p. (gr. 4-6). 1982. (ISBN 0-671-42401-7). Messner.
McLenighan, Valjean (1947-)
--Diana: Alone Against the Sea. Bennett, Russell, ed. Blair, Jay, illus. LC 79-21518. (Illus.). 46p. (Quest, Adventure, Survival). (gr. 4-9). 1982. (ISBN 0-8172-2055-0). Raintree Pubs.
--Ernie's Work of Art. Mathieu, Joseph (1945-), illus. (Illus.). (A Young Reader Ser.). (gr. k-3). 1979. (ISBN 0-307-60109-9, Golden Pr). Western Pub.
--I Know You Cheated. Jones, Brent, illus. LC 77-8623. p. cm. c.1977. (ISBN 0-8172-0962-X). Raintree Editions.
--Know When to Stop. Haesly, Jack, illus. LC 79-24520. (Illus.). 31 p. 21cm. (Follett beginning-to-read book). c.1981. (ISBN 0-695-41371-6). (ISBN 0-695-31371-1). Follett Pub. Co.
--New Wheels. Gubin, Mark, illus. LC 77-27052. (Illus.). 32 p. 25cm. c.1978. (ISBN 0-8172-1152-7). Childrens Press.
--Special Delivery: Featuring Jim Henson's Sesame Street Muppets. Brown, Richard Eric (1946-), illus. LC 79-57105. (Illus.). 26 p. 27cm. c.1980. (ISBN 0-307-23108-9). Western Pub. Co.
--Three Strikes and You're Out. Hamilton, Laurie, illus. LC 80-14020. p. cm. (Follett beginning-to-read book). 1980, c.1981. (ISBN 0-695-41462-3). (ISBN 0-695-31462-9). Follett.
--Turtle & Rabbit. McKissack, Vernon, illus. LC 80-13792. 32p. (Beginning-to-Read Ser.). 1980. (ISBN 0-695-41461-5, Dist. by Caroline Hse). (ISBN 0-695-31461-0). Modern Curr.
--What You See Is What You Get. Appleyard, Dev, illus. LC 79-24195. (Illus.). 31 p. 21cm. (Follett beginning-to-read book). c.1981. (ISBN 0-695-31370-3). (ISBN 0-695-41370-8). Follett Pub. Co.
--You Are What You Are. Reilly, Jack, illus. LC 77-156052. (Illus.). 31 p. 20cm. (Follet beginning-to-read book : Level 1). c.1977. (ISBN 0-695-30748-7). Follet Pub. Co.
--You Can Go Jump. Lee, Jared D, illus. LC 77-156064. (Illus.). 31 p. 20cm. (Follett beginning-to-read book). c.1977. (ISBN 0-695-40744-9). (ISBN 0-695-30744-4). Follett.
MacLennan, Phyllis
--Turned Loose on Irdra. LC 73-89128. 216p. (gr. 10 up). 1970. (ISBN 0-385-01547-X). Doubleday.
Macleod, Alexander
--The Wonderful Lamp. N.D. Robert Carter & Brothers.
--The Wonderful Lamp: And, Other Talks to Children. 262p. N.D. Merrill.
MacLeod, Ann
--English Fairy Tales. MacLeod, Ann, illus. (Illus.). (Illustrated Juvenile Classics). (gr. 1-4). N.D. (ISBN 0-601-07207-3, Pub. by Hamlyn). Tudor.
MacLeod, Barbara
--Children's Twilight Tales. Morgan, John, illus. LC 42-17152. 94 p., 1 l. incl. illus., plates. 21 cm. 1942. H. Harrison.
MacLeod, Beatrice Beach (1910-)
--On Small Wings. Simmons, Ellie, illus. LC 61-8765. 138p. illus. 23cm. 1961. Westminster Press.
MacLeod, Charlotte Matilda Hughes (1922-)
--Ask Me No Questions. LC 72-163291. 157 p. 21cm. 1971. (ISBN 0-8255-5508-6). Macrae Smith.
--Brass Pounder. LC 75-154966. 212 p. 22cm. 1971. Little, Brown.
--Cirak's Daughter. LC 82-1727. 22cm. 186p. N.D. (ISBN 0-689-30930-9). Atheneum.
--Fat Lady's Ghost. (gr. 7-11). N.D. Weybright.
--King Devil. LC 78-5981. 212 p. 25cm. 1978. (ISBN 0-689-30659-8). Atheneum.
--Maid of Honor. LC 83-15653. 168p. (gr. 7 up). 1984. (ISBN 0-689-31019-6). Atheneum.
--Mouse's Vineyard. Burke, Roseanne, illus. (Illus.). 152 p. 21cm. 1968. Weybright and Talley.
--We Dare Not Go A'Hunting. LC 79-22113. (gr. 6 up). 1980. (ISBN 0-689-30751-9). Atheneum.
MacLeod, Doug
--In the Garden of Badthings. Thomson, Peter, illus. LC 82-220744. (An Australian Picture Puffin). 1982. (ISBN 0-14-050412-5). Penguin Books.
MaCleod, Ellen Jane Anderson (1916-)
--Adventures on the Lazy N. 1957. Christian Literature Crusade.
--Alaska Star. 1960. Christian Literature Crusade.
--The Fourth Window. A Mystery-Adventure Story for Most Boys from Ages Ten Through Fifteen. LC 62-585. 127p. 21cm. 1961. Cowman Pub. Co.
--Headhunter's Moon. 1958. Christian Lit.
--Island in the Mist. LC 65-122939. 190p. 21cm. c.1965. Bethany.
--Mystery George. 1959. Christian Literature Crusade.
--Mystery of the tolling bell. 1960. Christian Literature Crusade.
--Seven Wise Owls. 1956. Christian Lit.
--Seven Wise Owls. 1958. Christin Literature Crusade.
McLeod, Emilie Warren (1926-1982), ed. see Corbett, Scott.
McLeod, Emilie Warren (1926-1982), ed. see Dabcovich, Lydia.
McLeod, Emilie Warren, ed. see John, Naomi.
McLeod, Emilie Warren, ed. see Weil, Lisl.
McLeod, Emilie Warren (1926-1982)
--The Bear's Bicycle. McPhail, Michael David (1940-), illus. LC 74-28282. (Illus.). 31 p. 1975. (ISBN 0-316-56203-3). Little, Brown. **Awards: (ALA); (BGH).**
--The Bear's Bicycle. McPhail, Michael David (1940-), illus. LC 77-21947. p. cm. 1977, c.1975. Puffin Books.
--Clancy's Witch. Weil, Lisl (1910-), illus. (Illus.). (A story about a most unusual witch). (gr. 2-6). 1959. (ISBN 0-316-56201-7, Pub. by Atlantic Monthly Pr). Little.
--One Snail & Me. 1st ed. Lorraine, Walter Henry (1929-), illus. LC 61-5333. (Illus.). (gr. k up). 1961. (ISBN 0-316-56197-5, Pub. by Atlantic Monthly Pr). Little.
--One Snail & Me. Lorraine, Walter Henry (1929-), illus. LC 61-5333. (ps-1). 1981. (ISBN 0-316-56198-3). (ISBN 0-316-56199-1). Little.
--The Seven Remarkable Bears. N.D. E. M. Hale & Co.
--Seven Remarkable Bears. Kepes, Juliet Appleby (1919-), illus. LC 53-6211. (Illus.). (gr. k-3). 1954. (ISBN 0-395-06915-7). HM.
McLeod, Grover Stephen (1923-)
--Sub Sailor. LC 64-55541. (Illus.). 315p. 22cm. 1964. Manchester Press.
MacLeod, Joseph Todd Gordon (1903-)
--Beauty and the Beast. N.D. Viking Press.
MacLeod, Mary, ed. see Malory, Thomas, Sir.
MacLeod, Mary (0000-1914)
--A Book of Ballad Stories. Walker, A. G., illus. Dowen, Edward (1843-1913), intro. by. LC 7-35074. xxiv, 402, 3 p. incl. front., plates. 21 cm. 1906. F.A.Stokes company.
--The Book of King Arthur. (Illus.). (Fine Art Juveniles Ser.). N.D. Frederick A. Stokes Ser.
--King Arthur & His Knights. Dobkin, Alexander (1908-1975), illus. (Illus.). (Rainbow Classics). (gr. 4-6). 1950. (ISBN 0-529-02829-8). (ISBN 0-529-02830-1). World Pub.
--King Arthur and His Noble Knights. (Famous Bks. for Young Americans). N.D. A. L. Burt Co.
--The Robins. (Illus.). (Children's Library). N.D. Frederick A. Stokes Co.
--Stories from the Faerie Queene (Pub. by Society for Promoting Christian Knowledge). N.D. E. & J. B Young & Co.
--Stories from The Faerie Queene. (Illus.). (Fine Arts Juvneiles Ser.). N.D. Frederick A. Stokes Co.
--Tiny True Tales. (Illus.). N.D. Frederick A. Stokes Co.
MacLeod, Mary (0000-1914), adapted by.
--The Red-Cross Knight and Sir Guyon. (Illus.). (The Children's Bookshelf). N.D. Dodge Publishing Company.
--Robin Hood. (Illus.). (The Children's Bookshelf). N.D. Dodge Publishing Company.
--The Shakespeare Story Book. N.D. A. S. Barnes & Co.
--The Story of King Arthur. (Illus.). (The Children's Bookshelf). N.D. Dodge Publishing Company.
McLeod, Norman (1812-1872)
--Aunt Mary, 2 Sets in 1. (Illus.). (Old Guard Ser.). N.D. Set. Dodd, Mead & Co.
--Billy Buttons, 2 Sets in 1. (Illus.). (Old Guard Ser.). N.D. Set. Dodd, Mead & Co.
--Gold Thread. (Illus.). N.D. George Routledge & Sons.
--The Gold Thread. 114p. N.D. Presbyterian Commitee of Publication.
--The Gold Thread. (Illus.). (Sunshine Library for Young People). 1900. T. Y. Crowell & Co.
--The Gold Thread: A Story for the Young. LC 7-20120. ix, 70 p. incl. front. 19 1/2 cm. c.1897. T. Y. Crowell & Company.
--A Highland Parish. vi, 7-318 p. front., plates. 17 1/2 cm. 1866. R. Carter & Brohters.
--The Highland Witch, 2 Sets In 1. (Illus.). (Old Guard Ser.). N.D. Set. Dodd, Mead & Co.
--The Old Guard, 2 Sets In 1. (Illus.). (Old Guard Ser.). N.D. Set. Dodd, Mead & Co.
--The Old Lieutenant and his Son. N.D. George Routledge & Sons.
--Our Bob, 2 Sets in 1. (Illus.). (Old Guard Ser.). N.D. Set. Dodd, Mead & Co.
--The Starling: A Scotch Story. N.D. George Routledge & Sons.
--T. T. Fitzroy, Esq, 2 Sets in 1. (Illus.). (Old Guard Ser.). N.D. Set. Dodd, Mead & Co.
--Wee Davie, 1 of 50 vols. (Heart Life Classics). N.D. American Tract Society.
--Wee Davie. N.D. George Routledge & Sons.
--Wee Davie. from the 27th London ed. LC 7-16070. 52 p. 18 1/2 cm. 1864. Presbyterian Committee of Publication.
--Wee Davie. (Fourth Ser.). (Carters' Fireside Library). N.D. Robert Carter & Bros.
MacLeod, Robert Parker
--The Medicine Bull. LC 63-10236. 222p. 21cm. c.1963. John Day.
--Tosco, the Stubborn One. Morse, Dorothy Bayley (1906-1979), illus. LC 59-12374. 180p. illus. 21cm. 1959. (ISBN 0-690-83245-1). Crowell.
MacLeod, Ruth (1903-)
--Arlene Perry: Orthopedics Nurse. LC 66-14013. 192p. 21cm. (Career romance for young moderns). c.1966. Messner.
--Buenos Dias, Teacher. LC 70-100574. 191 p. 21cm. (Career romance for young moderns). 1970. J. Messner.
--Cheryl Downing, School Nurse. LC 64-11364. 188 p. 21cm. (Career romance for young moderns). 1964. J. Messner.
McLerran, Alice (1933-)
--The Mountain That Loved a Bird. Carle, Eric (1929-), illus. LC 85-9391. (Illus.). 24 p. 29cm. c.1985. (ISBN 0-88708-000-6). Picture Book Studio USA : Distributed by Alphabet Press.
McLin, Ruth Arlene (1924-)
--The Family That Had Everything, but Money. Arrabito, James, illus. LC 76-16922. (Illus.). 128 p. 21cm. c.1976. Review and Herald Pub. Association.
MacIntyre, C. F.
--The Pig that Ate Truffles. Obligado, Lilian Isabel (1931-), illus. 1963. Golden Press.
McLoughlin Bros. Inc
--Youngsters at Play. McLoughlin Bros., illus. LC 79-121428. (Illus.). 18 p. 20cm. N.D. McLoughlin Bros.
McLoughlin, John C. (1949-)
--The Tree of Animal Life: A Tale of Changing Forms & Fortunes. McLoughlin, John C. (1949-), illus. (Illus.). (gr. 10 up). 1981. Dodd.
Maclure, David P., Jr.
--Land of the Milky Way. N.D. Vantage Press.
McMahan, Ian
--The Fox's Lair. Salzman, Yuri, illus. LC 83-61238. (Illus.). 98 p. 22cm. c.1983. (ISBN 0-02-765490-7). Macmillan.
McMahan, Valrie
--Bumps: The Golf Ball Kid and Little Caddie. McMahan, Valrie, illus. LC 30-5276. 2 p. l., 7-88, 1 p. illus. (part col.) 23 1/2 cm. c.1929. The Roycrofters.
--Fan and Fannie: The Baseball Twins. McMahan, Valrie, illus. LC 28-18558. 1 p. l., 62 p. col. illus. 21 cm. c.1928. Barse & Co.
MacMahon, Bryan Michael (1909-)
--Jack O'Moora and the King of Ireland's Son. 1st ed. Bennett, Richard Michael (1899-), illus. LC 50-9961. 86 p. illus. 21 cm. 1950. Dutton.
--Patsy-O and His Wonderful Pets. 1st ed. Gobbato, Imero (1923-), illus. LC 75-102741. (Illus.). 84 p. 22cm. 1970. E. P. Dutton.
McMahon, Jo (1883-)
--The Deenie Men. McMahon, Jo (1883-), illus. LC 30-683030. xi p., 1 l., 15-185 p. incl. front., illus. 19 cm. c.1930. E. P. Dutton & Co., Inc.
--Good Faery Tales: Irish Ones. McMahon, Jo (1883-), illus. LC 29-17317. 175 p. incl. front., illus. 19 cm. c.1929. E. P. Dutton & Company, Inc.
MacMahon, Percy, jt. auth. see Maze, Edward.
McMahon, William R.
--A Doodletown Dodger. Wegener, Kenneth, illus. LC 73-86944. (Illus.). 52p. (gr. 1-4). 1973. (ISBN 0-8059-1932-5). Dorrance.
--Pine Barrens Legends, Lore & Lies. LC 80-23518. (Illus.). 1980. (ISBN 0-912608-12-9). Mid Atlantic.
Macmann, Elaine (1926-)
--Ozzie and the 19th of April. Shortall, Leonard W., illus. LC 57-10263. (Illus.). 126 p. 21cm. 1957. Putnam.
--Risky Business. Shortall, Leonard W., illus. N.D. E. M. Hale & Co.
McManus, Blanche
--Our Little Belgian Cousin. McManus, Blanche, illus. (The Little Cousin Ser.). N.D. L. C. Page & Co.
McManus, Blanche, ed.
--Mother Goose: Songs for the Nursery, or Mother Goose's Melodies for Children. McManus, Blanche, illus. N.D. Wessels & Bissell Co.
--Told in the Twilight. McManus, Blanche, illus. LC 98-2209. 93p. 1898. E. R. Herrick & Co.
--Told in the Twilight: Stories to Tell to Children. McManus, Blanche, illus. N.D. A. Wessels Co.
Mac Manus, Seumas (1869-1960)
--The Bewitched Fiddle and Other Stories. 4 1/2x7cm. 240p. N.D. Doubleday, Page & Co.
--Bold Blades of Donegal. N.D. J. B. Lippincott.
--Bold Heroes of Hungry Hill. Chollick, Jay, illus. (Illus.). (ps-2). 1951. (ISBN 0-374-30858-6). FS&G.

AUTHOR INDEX MCNAUGHTON, COLIN

--The Bold Heroes of Hungry Hill: And Other Irish Folk Tales. Chollick, Jay, illus. LC 51-12254. 207 p. illus. 21 cm. 1951. Pellegrini & Cudahy.
--The Donegal Fairy Stories. N.D. Doubleday Page & Co.
--Donegal Fairy Stories. LC 1-29082. xii, 1, 255, 1 p. incl. plates. front. 19 1/2 cm. 1900. McClure, Phillips & Co.
--Donegal Fairy Stories. (Illus.). N.D. (ISBN 0-8446-2507-8). Peter Smith Publisher, Inc.
--Donegal Fairy Stories. Ver Beck, Frank (1858-1933), illus. LC 68-28406. (Illus.). xii, 256 p. 21cm. 1968. Dover Publications.
--The Donegal Wonder Book. LC 26-15585. 5 p. l., 283, 1 p. front., illus. 21 cm. 1926. Frederick A. Stokes Company.
--The Donegal Wonder Book. N.D. J. B. Lippincott.
--Hibernian Nights. Kennedy, Paul Edward (1929-), illus. LC 62-163160. (Illus.). 263 p. 25cm. 1963. Macmillan. **Award: (ALA).**
--In Chimney Corners. Merry Tales of Irish Folk-Lore. Smith, Pamela Colman, illus. LC 99-5104. xii p., 3 l., 281 p. incl. col. front., illus., col. plates. 20 1/2 cm. 1899. Doubleday & McClure Co.
--In Chimney Corners: Merry Tales of Irish Folk Lore. Smith, Pamela Colman, illus. LC 35-17774. 3 p. l., ix-xii p., 2 l., 281 p. illus. 19 1/2 cm. 1935. Doubleday, Doran & Company, Inc.
--The Well O' the World's End. Bennett, Richard Michael (1899-), illus. LC 39-19701. viii p., 3 l., 188, 1 p. incl. front., illus. 21 1/2 cm. 1939. The Macmillan Co.
--The Well O' the World's End, and Other Folk Tales. Bennett, Richard Michael (1899-), illus. LC 49-893845. viii, 188 p. illus. 21 cm. 1949, c.1939. Devin-Adair Co.
MacMartin, Louise, jt. auth. see Boyles, Trudy.
Macmaster, Eve Ruth Bowers (1942-)
--God Gives the Land. Converse, James, illus. LC 83-182. (Illus.). 168p. (Orig.). (Story Bible Ser.: Vol. 3). 1983. (ISBN 0-8361-3332-3). Herald Pr.
--God Rescues His People: Stories of God & his People: Exodus, Leviticus, Numbers & Deuteronomy. Converse, James, illus. LC 82-2849. (Illus.). 176p. (Orig.). (Story Bible Ser.: No. 2). 1982. (ISBN 0-8361-1994-0). Herald Pr.
--God's Chosen King. Converse, James, illus. LC 83-12736. (Illus.). 176p. (Orig.). (Story Bible Ser.: Vol. 4). (gr. 5-6). 1983. (ISBN 0-686-46597-0). Herald Pr.
--God's Family: Stories of God and His People : Genesis. Converse, James, illus. LC 81-6551. (Illus.). 166 p. 20cm. (Story Bible Series: Bk.1). 1981. (ISBN 0-8361-1964-9). Herald Press.
--God's Wisdom & Power. Converse, James, illus. LC 84-8974. (Illus.). 168p. (Orig.). (Story Bible Ser.: No. 5). (gr. 3-8). 1984. (ISBN 0-8361-3362-5). Herald Pr.
MacMaster, James Eric
--The Mutt: The Story of A Polo Pony. Ward, Richard F., illus. LC 55-6759. 104p. illus. 22cm. 1955. Caxton Printers.
McMeekin, Isabel McLennan (1895-)
--Ban-Joe and Grey Eagle. Dillon, Corinne Boyd, illus. LC 51-8553. 229p. illus. 21cm. 1951. Watts.
--Ban-Joe and Grey Eagle. Scott, Marguerite K., illus. 229p. (gr. 4-7). 1951. Franklin Watts, Inc.
--The Golden Glory. 1st ed. Orbaan, Albert F. (1913-), illus. LC 63-10358. (Illus.). 21cm. 1963. Duell, Sloan and Pearce.
--Journey Cake. Panesis, Nicholas (1913-), illus. LC 42-23634. 231 p. incl. illus., plates (1 double) 21 cm. 1942. J. Messner, Inc.
--Juba's New Moon. Panesis, Nicholas (1913-), illus. LC 44-8166. 224 p. illus. 21 cm. 1944. J. Messner, Inc.
--Kentucky Derby Winner. Dillon, Corinne Boyd, illus. LC 49-8758. 272 p. illus. 21 cm. 1949. D. McKay Co.
--The Postman's Pony. Kalm, Chet, illus. LC 60-12527. 96p. illus. 23cm. 1960. Putnam.
McMichael, Charles C
--Sonny. LC 17-3031. 280 p. front., plates. 20 cm. $1.00. 1916. W. B. Conkey Company.
MacMichael, Jane
--The Cat Who Wanted to Make Friends. Kincaid, Eric, illus. Repr. (gr. 1-3). 1972. (ISBN 0-88308-003-6). Lamplight Pub.
--The Ghost of Crumbling Castle. Embleton, Ronald, illus. (Illus.). Repr. (gr. 1-3). 1972. (ISBN 0-88308-002-8). Lamplight Pub.
--Kim & His Dog's Dreams. Hook, Richard, illus. Repr. (gr. 1-3). 1972. (ISBN 0-88308-001-X). Lamplight Pub.
--Tales of the Circus. Biro, Val, pseud. (1921-), illus. Biro, Balint Stephen. Repr. (gr. 1-3). 1972. (ISBN 0-685-84088-3). Lamplight Pub.
MacMillan, Annabelle, pseud. (1922-), tr. see Anckarsvard, Karin Inez Maria.
Macmillan, Annabelle, pseud. (1922-), tr. see Burman, Edor.
MacMillan, Annabelle, pseud. (1922-), tr. see Falk, Ann Mari.
MacMillan, Annabelle, pseud. (1922-), tr. see Hamori, Laszlo Deszo.
MacMillan, Annabelle, pseud. (1922-), tr. see Herrmanns, Ralph.
MacMillan, Annabelle, pseud. (1922-), tr. see Inger, Nan.
MacMillan, Annabelle, pseud. (1922-), tr. see Lindgren, Barbro.
MacMillan, Annabelle, pseud. (1922-), tr. see Ostman, Nan Inger.
MacMillan, Annabelle, pseud. (1922-), tr. see Oterdahl, Jeanna.
MacMillan, Annabelle, pseud. (1922-), tr. see Soderhjelm, Kai.
MacMillan, Annabelle, pseud. (1922-), tr. see Sundin-Wickman, Ulla.
MacMillan, Annabelle, pseud. (1922-), tr. see Thorvall, Kerstin.
MacMillan, Annabelle, pseud. (1922-), tr. see Wahlenberg, Anna.
MacMillan, Annabelle, pseud. (1922-), tr. see Warnlof, Anna Lisa.
McMillan, Brett, jt. auth. see McMillan, Bruce.
McMillan, Bruce
--Finest Kind O'Day. Lobstering in Maine. (Illus.). 1977. Harper.
McMillan, Bruce (1947-)
--The Alphabet Symphony: An Alphabet Book. McMillan, Bruce (1947-), photos by. LC 77-5491. (Illus.). 32 p. 26cm. c.1977. (ISBN 0-688-80112-9). (ISBN 0-688-84112-0). Greenwillow Books.
--Finest Kind o' Day. (Illus.). 48p (Pub. by Lippincott) (gr. 3-6). 1984. (ISBN 0-89272-185-5). Down East.
--Ghost Doll. LC 83-8386. p. cm. 1983. (ISBN 0-395-33073-4). Houghton Mifflin.
--Kitten Can... McMillan, Bruce (1947-), illus. (Illus.). 26p. (ps-1). 1984. (ISBN 0-688-02668-0). (ISBN 0-688-02669-9). Lothrop.
--The Remarkable Riderless Runaway Tricycle. LC 77-19027. (Illus.). 47 p. 1978. (ISBN 0-395-26496-0). Houghton Mifflin.
McMillan, Bruce (1947-) & McMillan, Brett
--Puniddles. McMillan, Bruce (1947-), illus. 1982. (ISBN 0-395-32082-8). (ISBN 0-395-32076-3). HM.
McMillan, Charles Stewart (1908-)
--Adjidaumo, the Squirrel. LC 73-83380. (Illus.). 10 p. 20cm. 1973. Franklin Pub. Co.
MacMillan, Cyrus
--Canadian Fairy Tales. N.D. Dodd Mead & Co.
--Glooskap's Country and other Indian Tales. Hall, John A., illus. 280p. 1956. Walck. **Award: (CLA).**
MacMillan, D. B.
--Kah-Da. N.D. Doubleday Doran & Co.
Macmillan, M., ed. see Goldsmith, Oliver.
MacMillan, Miriam Look
--Etuk, the Eskimo Hunter. Wiese, Kurt (1887-1974), illus. LC 50-9593. xiii, 177 p. illus., music. 21 cm. 1950. Dodd, Mead.
--Kudla and His Polar Bear. Woodward, Cleveland J. (1900-), illus. LC 53-9602. (Illus.). 96 p. 24cm. 1953. Dodd, Mead.
MacMillan, Polly Miller
--Little Lamb's Curls. Stubis, Talivaldis (1926-), illus. LC 61-17691. unpaged. illus. 23cm. c.1962. Lothrop, Lee & Shepard.
MacMillan, William (1890-)
--Arctic Adventure. LC 45-5186. 192 p. incl. front., illus. 21 cm. 1945. M. S. Mill Co., Inc.
--Arctic Adventure. 192p. 1945. William Morrow & Co.
--Dark Treasure. Poucher, Edward A., illus. LC 43-16891. 254 p. incl. front., plates. 21 cm. 1943. M. S. Mill Co., Inc.
--Mystery Ship. LC 44-47773. 185 p. incl. front. 20 1/2 cm. 1944. M. S. Mill Co., Inc.
McMillen, Ruth
--On Oleander Street. Moyler, Alan, illus. 1962. Exposition Press.
McMillion, Bonner (1921-)
--The Long Ride Home. LC 55-9153. 222 p. 22cm. 1955. Lippincott.
MacMinn, Edwin (1851-)
--Amal, a Prince of the Amalekites: A Prince of Sinai During the Exodus. 2 p. l., 3-315 p. front., plates. 18 1/2 cm. 1888. American Baptist Publication Society.
--Ben-Ammi, the Armorer's Son: A Story of the Days of Ahaz and Hezekiah. LC 7-20118. 2 p. l., 3-315 p. front., plates. 18 1/2 cm. 1885. American Baptist Publication Society.
--Brave Hearts Win. LC 7-20117. 2 p. l., 3-256 p. front., plates. 17 1/2 cm. 1883. American Baptist Publication Society.
--The Breaker-Boy Lansford. (Illus.). 288p. N.D. Sunday-School Publications.
--The Bushkill Social. LC 12-36472. 2 p. l., 3-320 p. front., plates. 19 cm. c.1886. American Baptist Publication Society.
--The Crystal Club: Or, A Summer's Outing. LC 7-20116. 2 p. l., 3-300 p. front., plates. 18 1/2 cm. 1890. American Baptist Publication Society.
--Eaglesmere Trio. 255p. N.D. Sunday-School Publications.
--From Cave to Palace: Or, The Anointed Shepherd. LC 7-20114. 352 p. 18 cm. c.1888. Presbyterian Board of Publication and Sabbath-School Work.
--Judith and Glaucia: A Story of the First Century. LC 7-20113. 2 p. l., 3-407 p. front., plates. 17 1/2 cm. 1884. American Baptist Publication Society.
McMinn, Janie L.
--Come & See. (ps-3). 1946. (ISBN 0-87213-630-2). Loizeaux.
--Come Before Winter. Murphy, E., illus. (ps-3). 1941. (ISBN 0-87213-631-0). Loizeaux.
--The Great Surprise: Children's Stories of the Resurrection and the Holy Spirit. N.D. Loizeaux Brothers Publications.
--Great Surprise: Children's Stories of the Resurrection & the Holy Spirit. Lofland, S., illus. (Illus.). (gr. 1-7). 1960. (ISBN 0-87213-632-9). Loizeaux.
McMorris, Helen, jt. auth. see Durfee, Burr.
McMullan, Kate
--The Mystery of the Missing Mummy. Prebenna, David, illus. (Illus.). 64p. (Orig.). (Pick-a-Path Bks.). (gr. 3-6). 1984. (ISBN 0-590-33143-4). Scholastic Inc.
McMullan, Kate, adapted by.
--Dr. Jekyll and Mr. Hyde. Van Munching, Paul, illus. LC 83-15972. (Original Author: Robert Louis Stevenson, 1850-1894). (Step-up Adventures). c.1984. (ISBN 0-394-96365-2). Random House.
McMullan, Kate & Eisenberg, Lisa
--Buggy Riddles. Taback, Simms, illus. LC 85-1450. p. cm. 1985. Dial Books for Young Readers.
McMullen, David W. (1939-)
--Mystery in Peru: The Lines of Nazca. McMullen, David W. (1939-), illus. LC 77-10456. (Illus.). 48 p. 24cm. c.1977. (ISBN 0-8172-1058-X). Contemporary Perspectives.
MacMullen, Grace Rice (1922-)
--A Reward for Jerry. 1st ed. Rice, Jessie Ruth, illus. LC 53-20023. (Illus.). 96p. 21cm. 1952. Sword of the Lord Publishers.
McMullen, Mary
--Rhymes. 46p. 18cm. 1975. Adams Press.
McMullen, Nigel
--Lucky: The Story of a Puppy. (Illus.). 32p. 1st U.S. edition. (ps-1). 1984. (ISBN 0-434-95136-6, Pub. by W Heinemann Ltd). David & Charles.
McMurry, Charles Alexander (1857-1929), ed. see Carroll, Lewis.
McMurry, Charles Alexander (1857-1929), ed. see Dodgson, Charles Lutwidge.
McMurry, James (1941-)
--The Catskill Witch and Other Tales of the Hudson Valley. 1st ed. Jones, Jeff, illus. LC 74-17067. (Illus.). viii, 156 p. 20cm. (York State book). 1974. (ISBN 0-8156-0105-0). Syracuse University Press.
McMurry, Lida Brown, Mrs. (1853-), adapted by.
--Classic Stories for the Little Ones. teachers' and mothers' ed. McMurray, Lida Brown, Mrs. (1853-), illus. LC 4-5481. 110, 33 p. illus. 17 cm. 1894. Public-School Publishing Company.
--Fifty Famous Fables. LC 11-338. (Illus.). 19 x 14cm. 126p. (Graded Classics Ser.). c.1910. B. F. Johnson Pub. Co.
McMurry, Lida Brown, Mrs. (1853-) & Gale, Agnes Spofford Cook, Mrs., eds.
--Songs of the Tree-Top and Meadow. McMurray, Lida Brown, Mrs. (1853-), illus. LC 99-3977. ix, 2, 11-192 p. incl. illus., pl., plates. 14 1/2 x 11 cm. 1899. Public-School Publishing Company.
McMurtrey, Martin Aloysias (1921-)
--Loose to the Wilds. LC 76-7101. 162 p. 22cm. c.1976. (ISBN 0-06-024158-6). (ISBN 0-06-024159-4). Harper & Row.
McMurtry, Judy
--Johnny & the Snow Owl. 1978. (ISBN 0-533-03846-4). Vantage.
McMurty
--The Bunjee Venture. (gr. 3-5). 1980. (ISBN 0-590-30162-4). Scholastic Inc.
Macnab, Iain (1890-1967)
--Nicht at Eenie: The Bairns' Parnassus. Macnab, Iain (1890-1967), illus. LC 77-28385. p. cm. 1977. (ISBN 0-8414-6236-4). Folcroft Library Editions.
--Nicht at Eenie: The Bairns' Parnassus. MacNab, Iain (1890-1967), illus. LC 73-22432. (Illus.). 37 p. 24cm. 1974. (ISBN 0-88305-422-1). Norwood Editions.
McNagny, Bob
--Noah's Nightmare. McNagny, Bob, illus. LC 26-19750. 67 p. col. front. illus., 30 col. pl. 16 1/2 cm. c.1926. The Bobbs-Merrill Company.
Macnair, Ian see Macnair, J. H., pseud.
MacNair, Ian see McNair, J. H., pseud.
MacNair, Ian & MacNair, Ruth
--The Adventures of Wong Wing Wu. authorized. MacNair, Ian & MacNair, Ruth, illus. LC 36-19828. 20 p. col. illus. 24 1/2 cm. c.1935. Artists and Writers Guild, Inc.
--Ginger. McNair, J. H., pseud. authorized. McNair, E. R., pseud. LC 36-19829. 20 p. illus, (part col.) 24 1/2 cm. c.1935. Artists and Writers Guild, Inc.
McNair, J. H., pseud., see MacNair, Ian.
Macnair, J. H., pseud.
--Animal Tales from Africa. Macnair, Ian. (Illus.). (Children's Library). N.D. Frederick A. Stokes Co.
McNair, John
--A Place Called Marathon. (Illus.). 1976. (ISBN 0-685-86598-3). State Mutual Bk.
--Wagonload. (Illus.). 1971. (ISBN 0-685-86603-3). State Mutual Bk.
MacNair, Julia, Mrs. (1840-1903)
--Graham's Laddie: A Story of God's Providence. 1886. Presbyterian Board of Pubn.
McNair, Kate
--A Book of Directions. LC 78-127595. 214 p. 21cm. 1970. Chilton Book Co.
--Sense of Magic. LC 65-23992. (gr. 7 up). 1965. (ISBN 0-8019-5059-7). Chilton.
MacNair, Ruth, jt. auth. see MacNair, Ian.
McNair Wright, J.
--The Cabin in the Brush. N.D. Alfred Martien.
McNally, Bruce, jt. auth. see Stevenson, Jocelyn.
McNally, E. Evalyn Grumbine see Child Life.
McNally, E. Evalyn Grumbine (1900-)
--Patsy Breaks into Advertising. Taylor, Douglas, frwd. by. LC 39-31418. x p., 1 l., 324 p. incl. plates. 21 cm. 1939. Dodd, Mead & Company.
--Patsy Succeeds in Advertising. LC 44-47310. x, 264 p. 19 1/2 cm. (Career books). 1944. Dodd, Mead & Company.
--Patsy's Mexican Adventure. McNally, Andrew, Jr., photos by. LC 53-9604. 245p. 21cm. (Dodd, Mead career books). 1953. Dodd, Mead.
McNamara, Ann Louise Greep
--Andy and Benny Catch a Thief. Dunnington, Tom, illus. LC 72-11926. (Illus.). 31 p. 25cm. 1973. Childrens Press.
--Henry's Pennies. McCully, Emily Arnold (1939-), illus. LC 74-161836. (Illus.). 40 p. 25cm. 1972. (ISBN 0-531-02019-3). Watts.
McNamara, John
--Extra!. N.D. Houghton Mifflin Co.
McNamara, John Regis
--Model Behavior. LC 85-4345. 174 p. 22cm. c.1985. (ISBN 0-385-29419-0). Delacorte Press.
--Revenge of the Nerd. LC 84-4328. 128p. (gr. 4-6). 1984. (ISBN 0-385-29348-8). Delacorte.
McNamee, James (1904-)
--My Uncle Joe. Parker, Lewis, illus. LC 63-12642. (Illus.). 63 p. 22cm. 1963, c.1962. Viking Press.
McNaught, Harry
--Muppets in My Neighborhood. McNaught, Harry, illus. LC 77-74472. (Illus.). (ps-k). 1977. (ISBN 0-394-83593-X, BYR). Random.
MacNaughtan, Donald
--The Moon Children. McNaughton, Colin, illus. LC 53-10300. 83p. illus. 23cm. 1954. Vantage Press.
McNaughton, Colin
--Anton B. Stanton and the Pirates. LC 79-7905. (Illus.). 38 p. c.1979. (ISBN 0-385-15759-2). (ISBN 0-385-15760-6). Doubleday.
--At Home. 16p. 1982. (ISBN 0-399-20878-X, Philomel). Putnam Pub Group.
--At Playschool. McNaughton, Colin, illus. 16p. 1982. (ISBN 0-399-20875-5, Philomel). Putnam Pub Group.
--At the Park. McNaughton, Colin, illus. 16p. 1982. (ISBN 0-399-20879-8, Philomel). Putnam Pub Group.
--At the Party. McNaughton, Colin, illus. 16p. 1982. (ISBN 0-399-20877-1, Philomel). Putnam Pub Group.
--At the Stores. McNaughton, Colin, illus. 16p. 1982. (ISBN 0-399-20876-3, Philomel). Putnam Pub Group.
--Autumn. McNaughton, Colin, illus. LC 83-45235. (Illus.). 11. (A Dial Very First Book). 1984, c.1983. (ISBN 0-8037-0043-1). Dial Books.
--Crazy Bear: Four Crazy Stories in One Big Book. McNaughton, Colin, illus. LC 82-23372. (Illus.). 47 p. 29cm. 1st U.S. edition. c.1983. (ISBN 0-03-063043-6). Holt, Rinehart, and Winston.
--The Great Zoo Escape. McNaughton, Colin, illus. LC 78-5138. (Illus.). 32 p. 21cm. 1979, c.1978. (ISBN 0-670-35145-8). Viking Press.
--The Rat Race: The Amazing Adventures of Anton B. Stanton. McNaughton, Colin, illus. LC 77-82648. (Illus.). 36 p. c.1978. (ISBN 0-385-13619-6). Doubleday.
--Soccer Crazy. McNaughton, Colin, illus. LC 80-67834. (Illus.). 32 p. 29cm. 1981. (ISBN 0-689-50189-7). Atheneum.
--Spring. McNaughton, Colin, illus. LC 83-45234. (A Dial Very First Book). 1984, c.1983. (ISBN 0-8037-0042-3). Dial Books for Young Readers.
--Winter. McNaughton, Colin, illus. LC 83-45236. (Illus.). 8 p. 19cm. (A Dial Very First Book). 1984. (ISBN 0-8037-0040-7). Dial Books for Young Readers.

McNaughton, Colin & Attenborough, Elizabeth
--Walk Rabbit Walk. McNaughton, Colin, illus. LC 76-58504. (Illus.). 32 p. 21cm. 1977. (ISBN 0-670-74918-4). Viking Press.
Mc Naughton, Colin & Low, Alice (1926-)
--If Dinosaurs Were Cats and Dogs. McNaughton, Colin, illus. LC 81-4874. (Illus.). 32 p. 27cm. 1981. (ISBN 0-590-07826-7). Four Winds Press.
McNeal, James (1925-)
--The Double Knights: More Tales from Round the World. Dimson, Theo Aeneas (1930-), illus. LC 64-22551. 128p. illus. 22cm. c.1964. Walck. **Award: (CLA).**
McNeal, Thomas Allen (1853-)
--Tom McNeal's Fables. Reid, Albert T., illus. 228p. illus. 191/2cm. 228p. 1905. Crane & Co.
McNear, Robert (1930-)
--The Marathon Race Mystery. Rogers, Jackie, illus. LC 84-16395. (Illus.). 128p. (Solve-It-Yourself Ser.). (gr. 3-7). 1985. (ISBN 0-8167-0444-9). (ISBN 0-8167-0445-7). Troll Assocs.
McNeely, Jeannette (1918-)
--Where's Izzy?. Morrison, Bill (1935-), illus. LC 78-184460. (Illus.). 32 p. 23cm. 1972. (ISBN 0-695-80318-2). (ISBN 0-695-40318-4). Follett.
McNeely, Marian Hurd, Mrs. (1877-1930)
--The Jumping-off Place. Siegel, William (1905-), illus. LC 29-16243. xi, 308 p. incl. front., illus. plates. 19 1/2 cm. 1929. Longmans, Green and Co. **Award: (JNM).**
--Rusty Ruston: A Story for Brothers and Sisters. Burns, Eloise (1904-), illus. LC 28-21226. 20cm. 293p. 1928. Longman's, Green & Co.
--The Way to Glory, and Other Stories. Esley, Joan, illus. Fisher, Dorothea Frances Canfield, Mrs. (1879-1958), pref. by. LC 32-235651. xv, 240 p. incl. front., illus., plates. 19 1/2 cm. 1932. Longmans, Green and Co.
--Winning Out. Price, Harriet Longstreet (1891-), illus. LC 31-28127. ix p., 1 l., 308 p. incl. front., illus., plates. 19 1/2 cm. 1931. Longmans, Green and Co.
McNeer, May Yonge, ed. see Marryat, Frederick.
McNeer, May Yonge (1902-)
--The American Indian Story. Ward, Lynd Kendall (1905-1985), illus. 96p. (Ariel Bks.). 1963. Farrar, Straus & Giroux.
--Armed With Courage. 1957. (ISBN 0-8382-0056-7, Cadmus Books). E. M. Hale and Company.
--Bloomsday for Maggie. Ward, Lynd Kendall (1905-1985), illus. LC 75-44359. (Illus.). 246 p. 22cm. 1976. (ISBN 0-395-24388-2). Houghton Mifflin.
--The California Gold Rush. Ward, Lynd Kendall (1905-1985), illus. LC 50-10705. (Illus.). 184 p. 22cm. (Landmark book 6). 1950. Random House.
--The Covered Wagon. Florian, illus. N.D. Grosset & Dunlap.
--Give Me Freedom. 1964. (ISBN 0-8382-0288-8, Cadmus Books). E. M. Hale and Company.
--The Gold Rush. Ward, Lynd Kendall (1905-1985), illus. N.D. Grosset & Dunlap.
--The Golden Flash. Ward, Lynd Kendall (1905-1985), illus. 227 p. illus. (part col.) 22 cm. 1947. Viking Press.
--Little Baptiste. Ward, Lynd Kendall (1905-1985), illus. LC 54-904253. unpaged. illus. 25cm. 1954. (ISBN 0-395-06922-X). Houghton Mifflin.
--My Friend Mac. (Illus.). (gr. 2-4). 1960. (ISBN 0-8382-0563-1). Hale.
--My Friend Mac. Ward, Lynd Kendall (1905-1985), illus. LC 60-11809. (Illus.). (gr. k-3). 1960. (ISBN 0-395-06923-8). (ISBN 0-395-06924-6). (ISBN 0-395-13715-2). HM.
--Prince Bantam: Being the Adventures of Yoshitsune the Brave and His Faithful Henchman, Great Benkei of the Western Pagoda. Ward, Lynd Kendall (1905-1985), illus. LC 29-9666. 7 p. l., 229 p., 1 l. col. front., illus. 23 1/2 cm. 1929. The Macmillan Company.
--Stop Tim!. The Tale of a Car. Ward, Lynd Kendall (1905-1985), illus. LC 30-27812. 39 p. col. illus. 18 1/2 cm. 1930. Farrar and Rinehart.
--Stranger in the Pines. Ward, Lynd Kendall (1905-1985), illus. LC 74-142826. (Illus.). 248 p. 22cm. 1971. (ISBN 0-395-12367-4). Houghton Mifflin.
--Tales from the Crescent Moon. Lederer, Charlotte Bacskay, Mrs. (1872-), illus. LC 30-32330. v, 1, 306 p. illus., col. plates. 24 1/2 cm. c.1930. Farrar & Rinehart Incorporated.
--Tinka, Minka and Linka. Lederer, Charlotte Bacskay, Mrs. (1872-), illus. LC 31-8216. 1 p. l., 30, 1 p. col. front., col. illus. 22 1/2 cm. 1931. A. A. Knopf.
--Up a Crooked River. Ward, Lynd Kendall (1905-1985), illus. LC 52-13713. 222 p. illus. 21 cm. 1952. Viking Press.
--Waif Maid. Ward, Lynd Kendall (1905-1985), illus. LC 30-28638. xi, 212 p. incl. col. front., illus. (incl. music) plates. 21 cm. 1930. The Macmillan Company.
--War Chief of the Seminoles. Ward, Lynd Kendall (1905-1985), illus. LC 54-6271. 180p. illus. 22cm. (Landmark books, 50). 1954. Random House.
--The Wolf of Lambs Lane. Ward, Lynd Kendall (1905-1985), illus. (Illus.). 64 p. 25cm. 1967. Houghton Mifflin.
MacNeice, Frederick Louis (1907-1963)
--The Penny that Rolled Away. Bileck, Marvin (1920-), illus. 39p. 1954. G. P. Putnam's Sons.
McNeil, Henry Everett (1862-1929)
--The Boy Forty-Niners. N.D. Doubleday Page & Co.
--The Boy Forty-Niners: Or, Across the Plains and Mountains to the Gold-Mines of California in a Prairie-Schooner. Heath, Howard & Treidler, Adolph, illus. LC 8-27102. xii p., 2 l., 3-433 p. front., 7 pl. 20 cm. 1908. The McClure Company.
--Buried Treasure: A Tale of an Old House. LC 19-15668. 4 p. l., 3-243 p. front., plates. 19 1/2 cm. $1.5. 1919. Duffield and Company.
--The Cave of Gold: A Tale of California in '49. LC 11-24407. vii p., 2 l., 376 p. front., plates. 21 1/2 cm. $1.5. c.1911. E. P. Dutton & Company.
--Dickon Bend the Bow. Wagner, Rob, illus. LC 3-24830. 1 p. l., cixxv, 1 p. col. illus. 25 x 20 1/2 cm. 1903. The Saalfield Publishing Company.
--For the Glory of France. LC 27-15600. ix p., 1 l., 483 p. front., plates. 20 cm. c.1927. E. P. Dutton & Company.
--In Texas with Davy Crockett: A Story of the Texas War of Indendence. LC 8-21926. xii, 398 p. front., 4 pl. 21 cm. c.1908. E. P. Dutton & Company.
--The Lost Nation. N.D. E P Dutton.
--The Lost Treasure Cave. N.D. E P Dutton.
--The Shadow of the Iroquois. N.D. E. P. Dutton & Co.
--The Shores of Adventure: Or, Exploring in the New World with Jacques Cartier, Wherein I Tell How I Came to Sail with Captain Cartier on the Voyage to America, in Which He Discovered That Great and Unknown River, Which Savages Called Hochelaga, (S. Lawrence); Together with an Account of the Marvelous Manner in Which the Casket of Quetzalbcoatl Came into My Possession... LC 29-162464. x, 371 p. col. front. 20 cm. c.1929. E. P. Dutton & Co., Inc.
--Tonty of the Iron Hand: Being an Account of My Great Adventure and the Remarkable Happenings That Brought About My Going with M. De La Salle and M. Henri De Tonty When They Explored the Mississippi River from the Mouth of the Illinois River to the Gulf of Mexico, Together with All That Befell Us During That Long and Hazardous Journey; from an Old French Manuscript Recently Discovered. LC 25-13301. ix p., 1 l., 357 p. front. plates. 19 1/2 cm. c.1925. E. P. Dutton & Company.
--With Kit Carson in the Rockies: A Tale of the Beaver Country. LC 9-22186. 5 p. l., 333 p. front., 4 pl. 21 cm. c.1909. E. P. Dutton & Company.
MacNeil, Marion Gill
--Monty Marine. Dobias, Frank (1902-), illus. 48p. 1943. Oxford University Press.
--Pinky and His Pals. 1942. Oxford University Press.
--Sailor Jack. MacNeil, Robert P., illus. LC 42-17475. 48 p. col. illus. 18 1/2 x 18 cm. 1942. Oxford University Press.
--Soldier Sammy. Doane, Pelagie (1906-1966), illus. LC 42-7640. 48 p. illus.(part col.) 18 1/2 x 18 cm. c.1942. Oxford University Press.
McNeil, Marion L.
--The Blue Elephant and the Pink Pig. Seignobosc, Francoise (1897-1961), illus. Francoise, pseud. LC 31-679. 38 p. col. front., illus. (part col.) 28 cm. c.1931. The Saalfield Publishing Company.
--I Want to Be a Circus Man. Bailey, Corinne Ringel, illus. cover-title, 12 p. illus. (part col.) 33 cm. c.1934. The Saalfield Pub Co.
--I Want to Be an Engineer. Bailey, Corinne Ringel, illus. cover-title, 12 p. illus. (part col.) 33 cm. c.1934. The Saalfield Pub. Co.
--Jingleman Jack, Aviator. Bailey, Corinne Ringel, illus. LC 29-20004. 42 p. illus. (part col.) 20 1/2 cm. c.1929. The Saalfield Publishing Company.
--Jingleman Jack, Circusman. Bailey, Corinne Ringel, illus. 42 p. illus. (part col.) 20 1/2 cm. c.1930. The Saalfield Publishing Company.
--Jingleman Jack, Cowboy. Bailey, Corinne Ringel, illus. LC 29-20002. 41 p. illus. (part col.) 20 1/2 cm. c.1929. The Saalfield Publishing Company.
--Jingleman Jack, Engineer. Bailey, Corinne Ringel, illus. 42 p. illus. (part col.) 21 cm. c.1930. The Saalfield Publishing Company.
--Jingleman Jack, Fireman. Bailey, Corinne Ringel, illus. LC 29-20003. 42 p. illus. (part col.) 20 1/2cm. c.1929. The Saalfield Publishing Company.
--Jingleman Jack, Policeman. Bailey, Corinne Ringel, illus. LC 29-20004. 42 p. illus. (part col.) 20 1/2 cm. c.1929. The Saalfield Publishing Company.
--The Little Green Cart. Seignobosc, Francoise (1897-1961), illus. Francoise, pseud. 38 p. col. front., illus. (part col.) 28 cm. c.1931. The Saalfield Publishing Company.
--Round the Mulberry Bush. Peat, Fern Bisel, Mrs. (1893-), illus. LC 33-223023. 34 p. col. illus. 30 1/2 cm. c.1933. The Saalfield Publishing Company.
McNeil, Robert
--Daniel Du Luth: Adventuring on the Great Lakes. N.D. E. P. Dutton & Co.
McNeile, Cyril
--Bulldog Drummond. (Detective Stories for Boys). N.D. Grosset & Dunlap.
McNeill, James (1925-)
--The Double Knights. Dimson, Theo Aeneas (1930-), illus. 128p. N.D. Henry Z. Walck Inc.
--Double Knights: More Tales from Round the World. Dimson, Theo Aeneas (1930-), illus. LC 64-22551. (Illus.). (gr. 4-6). 1964. (ISBN 0-8098-2372-1). Walck.
McNeill, James (1925-), ed.
--The Sunken City. (gr. 4-6). 1972 (Starline). Schol Bk Serv.
--The Sunken City, and Other Tales from Round the World. Dimson, Theo Aeneas (1930-), illus. LC 59-16365. 160p. illus. 22cm. 1959. H. Z. Walck.
McNeill, Janet (1907-)
--The Battle of St. George Without. Russon, Mary Georgina (1937-), illus. LC 68-11113. 188 p. illus. 21 cm. 1st U.S. edition. c.1966. Little, Brown.
--Best Specs. 1970. Faber.
--Billy Brewer Goes on Tour. 1976. Macmillan.
--Day Mom Came Home. 1976. MacMillan.
--The Day they Lost Grandad. Lawrence, John (1933-), illus. 1969. Macmillan.
--Dragons, Come Home, and Other Stories. 1969. Hamish Hamilton.
--Ever After. 160p. (gr. 7 up). 1975. (ISBN 0-316-56302-1). Little.
--Giant's Birthday. Erhard, Walter (1920-), illus. LC 64-21120. (Illus.). (gr. k-3). 1964. (ISBN 0-8098-1101-4). Walck.
--Goodbye, Dove Square. 1st ed. Russon, Mary Georgina (1937-), illus. LC 69-11785. (Illus.). 196 p. 21cm. 1969. Little, Brown. **Award: (ALA).**
--A Helping Hand. 1971. Hamish Hamilton.
--The Hermit's Purple Shirts. 1976. Macmillan.
--I Didn't Invite You to My Party. Paton, Jane Elizabeth (1934-), illus. 1967. Hamish Hamilton.
--It's Snowing Outside. 1969. Macmillan.
--A Light Dozen. 1957. Faber.
--Look Who's Here. 1976. Macmillan.
--The Magic Lollipop. American ed. Birch, Linda, illus. LC 75-40346. (Illus.). 24 p. 21cm. (Stepping stones). 1976, c.1974. (ISBN 0-516-03586-X). Childrens Press.
--A Monster Too Many. 1st ed. Fetz, Ingrid (1915-), illus. LC 77-113442. (Illus.). 60 p. 24cm. 1972. Little, Brown.
--The Mouse and the Mirage. 1964. Henry Z. Walck Inc.
--The Mouse and the Mirage. Erhard, Walter (1920-), illus. LC 66-729497. 1v. (unpaged) col. illus. 18x24cm. 1966. (ISBN 0-8098-1121-9). Walck.
--Much Too Much Magic. 1971. Hamish Hamilton.
--My Auntie. 1975. Mcmillan.
--My Friend Specs McCann. N.D. Transatlantic Arts.
--My Friend Specs McCann. Friers, Rowel Boyd (1920-), illus. 1955. Faber.
--The Other People. 1st ed. LC 73-97144. 185 p. 21cm. 1970. Little, Brown.
--A Pinch of Salt. Friers, Rowel Boyd (1920-), illus. 1956. Faber.
--The Prisoner in the Park. 1971. Faber.
--The Prisoner in the Park. 208p. (gr. 5-9). 1972. (ISBN 0-316-56300-5). Little.
--The Run-Around Robins. Braser-Creagh, Monica, illus. 1967. Hamish Hamilton.
--Special Occasions. Friers, Rowel Boyd (1920-), illus. 1960. Faber.
--Specs Fortissimo. 1958. Faber.
--This Happy Morning. Friers, Rowel Boyd (1920-), illus. 1959. Faber.
--The Three Crowns of King Hullabaloo. Cole, Michael, illus. LC 75-42151. (Illus.). 24 p. 21cm. (Stepping stones). 1976, c.1975. (ISBN 0-516-03593-2). Childrens Press.
--Tom's Tower. Russon, Mary Georgina (1937-), illus. 1965. Faber.
--Tom's Tower. Russon, Mary Georgina (1937-), illus. LC 67-3861. (Illus.). 182 p. 21cm. 1st U.S. edition. 1967, c.1965. Little, Brown.
--Umbrella Thursday. 1969. Hamish Hamilton.
--Various Specs. 1961. Faber.
--Various Specs. Friers, Rowel Boyd (1920-), illus. LC 75-145926. (Illus.). 127 p. 22cm. 1st U.S. edition. 1971. (ISBN 0-8407-6120-1). T. Nelson.
--Wait for it, and Other Stories. 1972. Faber.
--Wait for It & Other Stories. 190p. (Faber Fanfares Ser.). (gr. 4-7). 1979. (ISBN 0-571-11329-X). Faber & Faber.
--We Three Kings. 1974. Faber.
--We Three Kings. 1st ed. LC 74-7484. 181 p. 21cm. 1974. (ISBN 0-316-56301-3). Little, Brown.
--The Youngest Kite. Haines, Elizabeth, illus. 1970. Hamish Hamilton.
MacNess, Jay Jackson
--The American Witch. Bolognese, Donald Alan (1934-), illus. LC 66-16335. (Illus.). 144 p. 21cm. 1966. McGraw-Hill Book Co.

McNichols, Charles Longstreth (1895-)
--Crazy Weather. LC 77-20507. 195 p. 22cm. 1978, c.1944. (ISBN 0-670-24558-5). Viking Press.

McNickle, William D'Arcy (1904-1977)
--Runner in the Sun. Houser, Allan C. (1914-), illus. LC 54-7729. (Illus.). 234p. (Land of the Free Ser). (gr. 7-9). 1954. (ISBN 0-03-035060-3). HR&W.

McNicol, Jacqueline Morrell (1924-)
--Elizabeth for Lincoln. 1st ed. O'Sullivan, Tom, illus. LC 60-6705. 119p. illus. 20cm. 1960. Longmans, Green.
--Ride for Old Glory. Walker, Charles W., illus. (Illus.). (gr. 3-7). 1964. McKay.

McNulty, Faith (1918-)
--Arturito El Astuto, Arty the Smarty. Moore, Lilian, ed. Aquino, Albert, illus. (Easy Readers Ser). (gr. 1-3). N.D. (ISBN 0-448-04261-4). Wonder.
--The Elephant Who Couldn't Forget. Simont, Marc (1915-), illus. LC 79-2741. (Illus.). 62 p. 22cm. (I can read book). c.1980. (gr. k-3). (ISBN 0-06-024145-4). (ISBN 0-06-024146-2). Harper & Row.
--Hurricane. Owens, Gail, illus. 1983. Harper.
--Mouse and Tim. Simont, Marc (1915-), illus. LC 77-11845. (Illus.). 46 p. 27cm. c.1978. (ISBN 0-06-024156-X). (ISBN 0-06-024157-8). Harper & Row.
--Prairie Dog Summer. Johnson, Bonnie Helene, illus. LC 72-76689. (Illus.). 62 p. 24cm. 1972. (ISBN 0-698-20194-9). (ISBN 0-698-20194-9). Coward, McCann & Geoghegan.
--When a Boy Goes to Bed at Night. Weisgard, Leonard Joseph (1916-), illus. (Illus.). (gr. k-3). 1963. (ISBN 0-394-91811-8). Knopf.
--When a Boy Wakes up in the Morning. Weisgard, Leonard Joseph (1916-), illus. LC 62-14769. (Illus.). 27cm. (ps-2). 1962. (ISBN 0-394-91812-6). Knopf.
--Woodchuck. Sandin, Joan, illus. LC 74-3585. (Illus.). 5 7/8 x 8 1/2. 64p. (18 pt.). (Nature I Can Read Bks.). (gr. k-3). 1974. (ISBN 0-06-024167-5) Har-Row.
McNulty, Sally (1943-)
--Oceans. Higgs, Mike (1945-), illus. LC 84-2030. (Illus.). 32 p. 21cm. (Learn with Moonbird Ser.). c.1984. (ISBN 0-86592-744-8). Rourke Enterprises.
McNutt, Dave
--There Was an Old Man Who Lived in a One. (ps-3). 1979. (ISBN 0-88488-132-6). Creative Pubns.
Macon, J. A.
--Uncle Gabe Tucker. N.D. J. B. Lippincott Co.
MacOrlan, Pierre, pseud., see Dumarchais, Pierre.
MacOrlan, Pierre, pseud. (1882-1979)
--The Anchor of Mercy. Dumarchais, Pierre. Stone, David Karl (1922-), illus. Frenaye, Francis, tr. from Fr. LC 67-20211. 217 p. illus. 22 cm. 1st U.S. edition. 1967. Pantheon Books.
Macourek, Milos
--Curious Tales. 1st English ed. Born, Adolf (1930-), illus. Burg, Marie, tr. from Czech. LC 78-41180. (Illus.). 76 p. 25cm. 1980. (ISBN 0-19-271427-9). Oxford University Press.
McPhail, David see McPhail, Michael David.
McPhail, Laura
--A Child's Treasure of Poems. LC 51-12343. 112 p. 23 cm. 1951. Exposition Press.
McPhail, Michael David, jt. auth. see Iverson, Genie.
McPhail, Michael David (1940-)
--Alligators Are Awful: And They Have Terrible Manners, Too. McPhail, Michael David (1940-), illus. LC 79-7607. (Illus.). (gr. 1-3). 1980. Doubleday.
--Andrew's Bath. McPhail, Michael David (1940-), illus. LC 84-4368. (Illus.). 32 p. 20cm. c.1984. (ISBN 0-316-56319-6). Little, Brown.
--Annie & Company. McPhail, Michael David (1940-), illus. LC 84-9084. c.1984. (ISBN 0-03-071933-X). Holt, Rhinehart, and Winston.

--The Bear's Toothache. 1st ed. McPhail, Michael David (1940-), illus. LC 79-140482. (Illus.). 31 p. 22cm. 1972. Little, Brown.
--The Bear's Toothache. McPhail, Michael David (1940-), illus. LC 77-12312. (Illus.). 32 p. 23cm. 1978, c.1972. (ISBN 0-14-050263-7). Puffin Books.
--Bumper Tubbs. McPhail, Michael David (1940-), illus. LC 79-26360. (Illus.). 46 p. 1980. (ISBN 0-395-28477-5). Houghton Mifflin.
--Captain Toad and the Motorbike. 1st ed. McPhail, Michael David (1940-), illus. LC 78-59155. (Illus.). 32 p. 26cm. (Margaret K. McElderry book). 1978. (ISBN 0-689-50118-8). Atheneum.
--The Cereal Box. 1st ed. McPhail, Michael David (1940-), illus. LC 73-80036. (Illus.). 32 p. 19cm. 1974. (ISBN 0-316-56313-7). Little, Brown.
--The Dream Child. McPhail, Michael David (1940-), illus. LC 84-18755. (Illus.). 30 p. c.1985. (ISBN 0-525-44109-3). Dutton.
--Emma's Pet. McPhail, Michael David (1940-), illus. LC 85-4414. (Illus.). 22 p. 18cm. c.1985. (ISBN 0-525-44210-3). Dutton.
--Fix-it. McPhail, Michael David (1940-), illus. LC 83-16450. (Illus.). unpaged. c.1984. (ISBN 0-525-44093-3). (ISBN 0-525-44093-3). E. P. Dutton.
--The Glerp. McPhail, Michael David (1940-), illus. LC 72-162050. (Illus.). 23 p. (Magic Circle Book). 1972. (ISBN 0-663-22970-7). Ginn.
--Grandfather's Cake. McPhail, Michael David (1940-), illus. LC 79-15810. p. cm. 1979. (ISBN 0-684-16113-3). Scribner.
--Great Cat. McPhail, Michael David (1940-), illus. LC 81-12654. (Illus.). 32 p. 26cm. c.1982. (ISBN 0-525-45102-1). Dutton.
--Henry Bear's Park. McPhail, Michael David (1940-), illus. LC 75-25918. p. cm. 1975. (ISBN 0-316-56315-3). Little, Brown.
--Henry Bear's Park. McPhail, Michael David (1940-), illus. LC 78-59683. p. cm. 1978, c.1976. (ISBN 0-14-050291-2). Puffin Books.
--In the Summer I Go Fishing. McPhail, Michael David (1940-), illus. LC 76-146122. (Illus.). 32 p. 26cm. 1971. (ISBN 0-201-04612-1). Addison-Wesley.
--Lorenzo. McPhail, Michael David (1940-), illus. LC 79-7871. (Illus.). 64p. (gr. 1-3). 1984. (ISBN 0-385-15590-5). (ISBN 0-385-15591-3). Doubleday.
--The Magical Drawings of Moony B. Finch. McPhail, Michael David (1940-), illus. LC 76-23778. p. cm. c.1977. (ISBN 0-385-12103-2). Doubleday.
--Mistletoe. McPhail, Michael David (1940-), illus. LC 78-8372. p. cm. (Unicorn book). c.1978. (ISBN 0-525-35040-3). Dutton.
--Oh No Go. McPhail, Michael David (1940-), illus. (Illus.). (gr. k-3). 1973. (ISBN 0-316-56313-7, Pub. by Atlantic Monthly Pr). Little.
--Oh, No, Go: A Play. McPhail, Michael David (1940-), illus. LC 73-8144. (Illus.). 48 p. 27cm. 1973. Little, Brown.
--Pig Pig Goes to Camp. 1st ed. McPhail, Michael David (1940-), illus. LC 83-1412. (Illus.). 24 p. 26cm. c.1983. (ISBN 0-525-44064-X). Dutton.
--Pig Pig Grows up. McPhail, Michael David (1940-), illus. LC 80-350. (Illus.). 24 p. 26cm. (Unicorn book). c.1980. Dutton.
--Pig Pig Rides. McPhail, Michael David (1940-), illus. LC 82-9777. (Illus.). 24 p. 28cm. c.1982. (ISBN 0-525-44024-0). Dutton.
--Sisters. McPhail, Michael David (1940-), illus. LC 84-3775. (Illus.). 32p. (ps-3). 1984. (ISBN 0-15-275319-2, HJ). (ISBN 0-15-275319-2). HarBraceJ.
--Snow Lion. McPhail, Michael David (1940-), illus. (Illus.). 1983. Dutton.
--Snow Lion. McPhail, Michael David (1940-), illus. LC 82-8119. (Illus.). 41 p. 23cm. c.1982. (ISBN 0-8193-1097-2). (ISBN 0-8193-1098-0). Parents Magazine Press.
--Stanley, Henry Bear's Friend. McPhail, Michael David (1940-), illus. LC 78-11467. (Illus.). 47 p. 20cm. c.1979. (ISBN 0-316-56318-8). Little, Brown.
--That Grand Master Jumping Teacher, Bernard, Meets Jerome, the Great Jumping Glump. McPhail, Michael David (1940-), illus. LC 81-16507. (Illus.). 48 p. 23cm. c.1982. (ISBN 0-7232-6209-8). F. Warne.
--Those Terrible Toy-Breakers. McPhail, Michael David (1940-), illus. LC 80-10450. (Illus.). 41 p. 24cm. c.1980. (ISBN 0-8193-1019-0). (ISBN 0-8193-1020-4). Parents Magazine Press.
--The Train. McPhail, Michael David (1940-), illus. LC 76-45791. (Illus.). 32 p. 22cm. c.1977. (ISBN 0-316-56316-1). Little, Brown.
--The Train. McPhail, Michael David (1940-), illus. LC 78-17987. (Illus.). 32 p. 23cm. 1979, c.1977. (ISBN 0-14-050302-1). Puffin Books.
--Where Can an Elephant Hide?. McPhail, Michael David (1940-), illus. LC 78-31131. (Illus.). 32 p. c.1979. (ISBN 0-385-12940-8). (ISBN 0-385-12941-6). Doubleday.
--A Wolf Story. McPhail, Michael David (1940-), illus. LC 80-20277. p. cm. 1980. (ISBN 0-684-16713-1). Scribner.

McPharlin, Paul (1903-1948), tr. see Feuillet, Octave.

McPhedran, Marie
--David and the White Cat. 1st ed. Dowling, Victor J. (1906-), illus. LC 50-9652. (Illus.). 47 p. 21cm. 1950. Aladdin Books.
--Golden North. N.D. Macmillan.

MacPhee, Barbara
--Missin' the Left Behind Donkey. 1980. (ISBN 0-533-04067-1). Vantage.

McPhee, Colin
--A Club of Small Men. 62p. 1948. John Day Bks.

McPherrin, Ethel Warden
Peggy Goes West. LC 54-8332. 37p. 23cm. 1954. Vantage Press.

McPherson, Betty (1934-)
--A Mayflower Adventure. Di Stefano, Nancy (1943-), illus. (Illus.). 32p. (Pocket Tales Ser.: Bk. 1). 1984. (ISBN 0-918823-00-5). Boyce-Pubns.

MacPherson, Elizabeth H.
--A Tale of Tails. Williams, Garth Montgomery (1912-), illus. LC 62-52020. unpaged. illus. 33cm. (Big Golden Book). 1962. Golden Press.
--Tale of Tails. Williams, Garth Montgomery (1912-), illus. (Illus.). (ps). 1971. (ISBN 0-307-10351-X, Golden Pr). Western Pub.
--The Wonderful Whistle. Perl, Susan (1922-1983), illus. LC 65-133046. 48p. (chiefly illus. pt. col.) 22x26cm. c.1965. Putnam.

MacPherson, Georgia H, jt. auth. see Gianakoulis, Theodore P.

MacPherson, Georgia Harter
--Little Poems for Little People. LC 48-32864. 64 p. 23 cm. 1948. Exposition Press.

MacPherson, Imogene McCrary (1892-)
--And So the Wall Was Built. Wonsetler, John Charles (1900-), illus. LC 49-10827. 50 p. illus. (part col.) 17 x 23 cm. (Children's hour library). 1949. Westminster Press.
--The Little White Church. Kihl, Harold, illus. LC 49-8157. 47 p. illus. (part col.) 21 cm. 1949. Westminister Press.

Macpherson, Jean Jay (1931-)
--Four Ages of Man: The Classical Myths. MacPherson, Jean Jay (1931-), illus. LC 62-51813. 205p. illus., maps. 23cm. c.1962. St. Martin's.

Macpherson, Kathy
--The Adventures of Peter Pumpkin & Gregory Ghost. 1982. (ISBN 0-533-05076-6). Vantage.

McPherson, M. E. see Hartshorn, Nancy, pseud.

McPherson, M. E., Mrs.
--Nancy Hartshorn at Chautauqua. Hartshorn, Nancy, pseud. McPherson, M. E., Mrs., illus. Hartshorn, Nancy, pseud. LC 12-32950. 212 p. incl. front. (port.) illus. 18 cm. c.1882. J. S. Ogilvie & Company.

Macpherson, Margaret L.
--Australia Calling. Wiese, Kurt (1887-1974), illus. LC 47-365. viii p., 1 l., 199 p. illus., double map. 21 cm. 1946. Dodd, Mead & Company.
--New Zealand Beckons. Paterson, A. S., illus. LC 52-7339. 248 p. illus. 21 cm. 1952. Dodd, Mead.

MacPherson, Margaret McLean (1908-)
--The New Tenants. Hughes, Shirley (1929-), illus. LC 68-25190. (Illus.). 254 p. 21cm. 1968. Harcourt, Brace & World.
--Ponies for Hire. 1st ed. Parker, Robert Andrew (1927-), illus. LC 67-2902. (Illus.). 191 p. 21cm. 1967. Harcourt, Brace & World.
--The Rough Road. Hall, Douglas (1931-), illus. LC 65-21701. (Illus.). (gr. 7-9). 1966. (ISBN 0-15-269147-2, HJ). HarBraceJ. **Award: (ALA).**
--The Shinty Boys. 224p. 1963. Hartcourt Brace & World Inc.

McQuaid, Ina Debord
--Miss Hannah Ball: Lady of High Wycombe. McQuaid, Ina Debord, illus. N.D. Vantage Press.

McQueen, Anne, jt. auth. see Cooke, Grace MacGowan, Mrs.

McQueen, Lucinda, illus.
--Cabbage Patch Kids Pop-Up. (Illus.). 12p. (Cabbage Patch Kids Ser.). (gr. 1-5). 1984. (ISBN 0-910313-35-0). Parker Bro.

McQueen, Lucinda & Guitar, Jeremy, illus.
--Otis Lee. (Illus.). 12p. (Cabbage Patch Kids Ser.). (gr. 1-5). 1984. (ISBN 0-910313-33-4). Parker Bro.

McQueen, Mary Harris
--Baby Barefoot. (Illus.). N.D. D. Lothrop & Co.

McQueen, Mildred Hark see Hark, Mildred (1908-) & McQueen, Noel.

McQueen, Mildred Hark (1908-) & McQueen, Noel
--Junior Plays for All Occasions. N.D. Plays Inc Pub.
--Modern Comedies for Young Players. N.D. Plays Inc Pub.
--Special Plays for Special Days. N.D. Plays Inc Pub.
--Teen-Age Plays for All Occasions. N.D. Plays Inc Pub.
--Twenty-Five Plays for Holidays. N.D. Plays Inc Pub.

McQueen, Noel, jt. auth. see Hark, Mildred.

McQueen, Noel, jt. auth. see McQueen, Mildred Hark.

Macqueen-Pope, W. A.
--The Curtain Rises. 1961. Thomas Nelson & Sons.

McQueen, Priscilla L.
--We Can Read: Story Pack-54 Little Stories. 1973. (ISBN 0-685-47089-X). McQueen.

McQuilkin, Frank, jt. auth. see Malinowski, Paul.

Macquoid, Katherine Sarah Gadsen, Mrs. (1824-1917)
--At the Peacock. (Illus.). N.D. Society for Promoting Christian Knowledge.
--Little Vagabond, and Other Stories. N.D. E. & J. B. Young & Co.
--Patty. (Series of Works of Fiction). N.D. Macmillan & Co.
--The Story of Ives: A Brenton Legend. (Illus.). N.D. Society for Promoting Christian Knowledge.

Macquoid, Thomas Robert (1820-1912), illus.
--Little Bird Red and Little Bird Blue. Evens, Edmund, photos by. N.D. George Routledge & Sons.

McRae, ed. see Dickens, Charles John Huffam.

Macrae, Opal Wheeler see Deucher, Sybil & Wheeler, Opal.

Macrae, Opal Wheeler see Wheeler, Opal.

Macrae, Opal Wheeler see Wheeler, Opal (1898-) & Deucher, Sybil.

Macrae, Opal Wheeler see Wheeler, Opal (1898-) & Mother Goose.

McReavy, John Morgan
--Makah: Indian Whale hunters. Holmes, Robin (1940-), illus. LC 73-17011. (Illus.). 95 p. 22cm. 1973. (ISBN 0-87961-021-2). (ISBN 0-87961-020-4). Naturegraph Publishers.

McReynolds, Bob (1936-)
--Sleepy to the Rescue. Davenport, Roy (1936-), photos by. LC 49-10693. 62 p. illus. 21 x 23 cm. 1949. Viking Press.

McReynolds, Ginny
--Alone on a Desert Island. Bennett, Russell, ed. Shaw, Charles (1941-), illus. LC 79-22144. (Illus.). 46p. (Quest, Adventure, Survival Ser.). (gr. 4-9). 1982. (ISBN 0-8172-2050-X). Raintree Pubs.
--Woman Overboard. Gray, Mark, illus. LC 79-21834. (Illus.). 46p. (Quest, Adventure, Survival Ser.). (gr. 4-9). 1982. (ISBN 0-8172-2074-7). Raintree Pubs.

Macri, Angelika, tr. see Hartmann, Sven & Hartner, Thomas.

Macrow, Brenda Grace Joan Barton (1916-)
--The Amazing Mr. Whipper. Rose, Sheila, illus. 175p. 1963. Dodd, Mcad & Co.

McSavage, Frank, ed. see Lantz, Walter.

McShean, Gordon (1936-)
--Mr. Chillhead. McShean, Gordon (1936-), illus. LC 76-13743. (Illus.). 84 p. 28cm. c.1976. (ISBN 0-917112-03-2). Multinational Media.

McSherry, Frank David, Jr. (1927-) & Waugh, Charles
--Baseball Three Thousand. LC 81-3165. vi, 210 p. 21cm. c.1981. (ISBN 0-525-66732-6). Elsevier/Nelson Books.

MacSorley, Catherine Mary
--Aunt Dorothy's Tea Table (Pub. by Society for Promoting Christian Knowledge). N.D. E. & J. B Young & Co.
--The Children's Plan (Pub. by Society for Promoting Christian Knowledge). N.D. E. & J. B. Young & Co.
--The Dog at Number Twelve (Pub. by Society for Promoting Christian Knowledge). N.D. E. & J. B. Young & Co.
--Rosie's Friend (Pub. by Society for Promoting Christian Knowledge). N.D. E. & J. B. Young & Co.
--A Seaside Story (Pub. by Society for Promoting Christian Knowledge). N.D. E. & J. B Young & Co.
--The Vicarage Child (Pub. by Society for Promoting Christian Knowledge). N.D. E. J. B. Young & Co.

McSpadden, Joseph Walker, jt. auth. see Chaucer, Geoffrey.

McSpadden, Joseph Walker (1874-), ed. see Aesopus.

McSpadden, Joseph Walker (1874-), ed. see Dickens, Charles John Huffam.

McSpadden, Joseph Walker (1874-), ed. see Wagner, Richard.

McSpadden, Joseph Walker (1874-), tr. see Lorenzini, Carlo.

McSpadden, Joseph Walker (1874-)
--California: A Romantic Story for Young People. Hastings, Howard Livingston (1887-), illus. LC 26-24566. 127p. 1926. J. H. Sears & Co.
--How They Followed the Golden Trail: Stories of Man's Adventures in Quest of Gold. LC 41-27891. xii p., 2 l., 3-258 p. front., plates. 22 cm. 1941. Dodd, Mead & Company.
--The Land of Nod. Chase, Edward L., illus. N.D. Barse & Hopkins.
--The Land of Nod and what Tinkie and Tess Found There. Chase, Edward L., illus. LC 9-30120. 24cm. 137p. 1909. T. Y. Crowell & Co.
--Robin Hood. (Illus.). (Sunshine Library). 1915. Thomas Y Crowell.
--Robin Hood and His Merry Outlaws. Slobodkin, Louis (1903-1975), illus. Becker, May Lamberton (1873-1958), intro. by. LC 46-25026. 285, 3 p. col. front., illus., col. plates. 22 cm. (Half-title: Rainbow classics). (Rainbow Classics). 1946. The World Publishing Company.
--Robin Hood and His Merry Outlaws. Stewart, Allan (1865-), illus. LC 23-11063. xvi, 320 p. col. front., col. plates. 21 cm. c.1923. Thomas Y. Crowell Company.
--Stories from Dickens. (Children's Favorite Classics). N.D. Thomas Y.Crowell Company.
--Stories of Robin Hood & His Merry Outlaws. LC 4-27119. xvii, 313 p. front., plates. 17 1/2 cm. 1904. T. Y. Crowell & Co.

McSpadden, Joseph Walker (1874-), ed.
--Aesop's Fables. (Children's Favorite Classics). N.D. Thomas Y. Crowell Company.
--Famous Detective Stories. N.D. Thomas Y. Crowell Co.
--Famous Dogs in Fiction. rev. ed. LC 72-4373. xvii, 342 p. 22cm. (Short story index reprint series). 1972. (ISBN 0-8369-4184-5). Books for Libraries Press.
--Famous Dogs in Fiction. LC 21-18533. xvi, 265 p. front., plates. 20 cm. c.1921. Thomas Y. Crowell Company.
--Famous Dogs in Fiction. rev. ed. LC 30-8294 xix, 342 p. col. front., plates. 20 1/2 cm. c.1930. Thomas Y. Crowell Company.
--Famous Ghost Stories. N.D. Thomas Y. Crowell Co.
--Famous Mystery Stories. N.D. Thomas Y. Crowell Co.
--Robin Hood. (Illus.). (Children's Favorite Classics). N.D. Thomas Y. Crowell.
--Stories from Chaucer. (Illus.). (Children's Favorite Classics). N.D. Thomas Y. Crowell.
--Stories from Wagner. (Illus.). (Children's Favorite Classics). N.D. Thomas Y. Crowell.

McSweeney, Frank
--Cindy & Ricky Run a Pet Shop. McSweeney, Frank, photos by. (Illus.). 16 photos. (gr. 6 up). 1970. (ISBN 0-682-47207-7). Exposition.

McSweeny, Maxine (1905-)
--Christmas Plays for Young Players. LC 76-18480. 149 p. 22cm. c.1977. (ISBN 0-498-01959-4). A. S. Barnes.

McSwigan, Marie (1907-1962)
--All Aboard for Freedom!. 1st ed. Johnson, Eugene Harper, illus. Papanek, Jan, intro. by. LC 54-885523. 249p. illus. 22cm. 1954. Dutton.
--Binnie Latches On. 1st ed. Robinson, Jessie Berkowitz, illus. LC 50-9422. 214 p. illus. 21 cm. 1950. Dutton.
--Five on a Merry-Go-Round. Reardon, Mary A., illus. LC 43-7894. 4 p. l., 183 p. illus. 21 cm. 1943. E. P. Dutton and Company, Inc.
--Hi, Barney!. Dillon, Corinne Boyd, illus. LC 46-321194. 174, 1 p. incl. front., illus. 21 cm. 1946. E. P. Dutton and Company, Inc.
--Juan of Manila. 1st ed. Ayer, Margaret (0000-1981), illus. LC 47-4723. 132 p. illus. 22 cm. 1947. E. P. Dutton.
--The News Is Good. 1st ed. Elgin, Jill, illus. LC 52-7801. 223 p. illus. 21 cm. 1952. Dutton.
--Our Town Has a Circus. 1st ed. Burchard, Peter Duncan (1921-), illus. LC 49-616406. 176 p. illus. 21 cm. 1949. E. P. Dutton.
--Small Miracle at Lourdes. 1st ed. Lambo, Donald W. (1903-1966), illus. LC 58-11910. 122p. illus. 21cm. 1958. Dutton.
--Snow Treasure. Reardon, Mary A., illus. LC 42-28961. 178, 1 p. illus. 21 cm. 1942. E. P. Dutton and Company, Inc.
--Three's a Crowd. LC 53-8245. 192p. illus. 21cm. 1953. Dutton.
--Three's a Crowd (Pub. by Dutton). (gr. 7-12). 1972 (Starline). Schol Bk Serv.
--The Weather House People. Morse, Dorothy Bayley (1906-1979), illus. LC 40-30964. 155 p. incl. col. front., illus., col. plates. 21 x 16 cm. c.1940. J. B. Lippincott Company.

McTighe, Mary Adelaide
--The Fairies in the Old Clock & Other Fairies. H. M. Eaton, illus. LC 52-56515. 34 p. illus. 18 cm. 1906. H. M. Eaton.

McVay, Tracy & McVay, Myron, illus.
--Mother Goose Rhymes and Riddles. LC 73-90487. (Illus.). 42 p. 27cm. 42p. (Hallmark children's editions). c.1974. (ISBN 0-87529-380-8). Hallmark Cards.

McVey, R. Parker
--The Missing Rock Star Caper. Rogers, Jackie, illus. LC 84-8721. (Illus.). 128p. (Solve-It-Yourself Ser.). (gr. 3-7). 1985. (ISBN 0-8167-0398-1). (ISBN 0-8167-0399-X). Troll Assocs.

--Mystery at the Ball Game. Rogers, Jackie, illus. LC 84-8486. (Illus.). 120 p. 20cm. (Solve-It-Yourself). c.1985. (ISBN 0-8167-0336-1). (ISBN 0-8167-0337-X). Troll Associates.

MacVicar, Angus (1908-)

--Space Agent and the Isles of Fire. 1963. Roy.

McVicker, Charles, illus.

--Buck Rogers: A Pop-up Book. LC 79-56151. (Illus.). 16p. (Pop-up Ser.: No. 40). (ps-3). 1980. (ISBN 0-394-84437-8). Random.

--Buck Rogers in the 25th Century. Penick, Ib, designed by. LC 79-56151. (Illus.). 14 p. 24cm. (Pop-up book ; 40). c.1980. (ISBN 0-394-84437-8). Random House.

McWebb, Elizabeth U.

--Little Brown Bear. 2nd ed. Hartwell, Marjorie, illus. (Illus.). 55p. Repr. of 1962 ed (Pub. by Platt & Munk Pubs). 1978. (ISBN 0-940696-07-X). Monroe County Lib.

McWhirter, Millie, jt. auth. see Lewis, Al.

McWhirter, Millie & Lewis, Al (1901-)

--A Magic Morning with Uncle Al. Maestro, Giulio (1942-), illus. LC 71-88594. (Illus.). 64 p. 24cm. 1969. World Pub. Co.

Macy, William Hussey (1826-1891)

--There She Blows!. Or, The Log of the Arethusa. LC 16-7010. vii, 320 p. front., plates. 18 cm. 1877. Lee & Shepard.

Madda

--Rainy Day at School. (Illus.). (Play and Study Ser.). N.D. D. Lothrop Co.

Madden, Betsy

--The All-America Coeds. LC 75-134565. 143 p. 22cm. 1971. (ISBN 0-200-71785-5). Criterion Books.

Madden, Donald B.

--Lemonade Serenade: Or, The Thing in the Garden. Madden, Donald B. (1927-), illus. LC 66-8493. 1v. (unpaged) illus. (pt. col.) 24cm. 1966. A. Whitman.

Madden, Donald B., jt. auth. see Miklowitz, Gloria D.

Madden, Eva Annie (1863-)

--The I Can School. LC 2-20650. 118 p. front. 19 1/2 cm. (The golden hour series). 1902. Thomas Y. Crowell & Co.

--The Little Queen. Merrill, Frank Thayer (1848-), illus. (Illus.). 240p. 1910. W. A. Wilde Co.

--The Soldiers of the Duke. Merrill, Frank Thayer (1848-), illus. LC 4-25097. 279 p. front., plates. 19 1/2 cm. c.1904. W. A. Wilde Company.

--Stephen: A Story of the Little Crusaders. LC 1-185277. 3 p. l., 162 p. front. 19 1/2 cm. (Sunshine library). 1901. T. Y. Crowell & Co.

Madden, John J. (1856-)

--The Children of the Rocks: A Story of Tours. LC 44-6924. 192 p. incl. front. (map) 20 1/2 cm. 1944. Burton Publishing Company.

Madden, Walter

--Jason's Orchid. 1982. (ISBN 0-570-08401-6). Concordia.

Madden, William A. (1923-)

--Let's Read a Story About Princess Carolyn. Meyd, Orella S., illus. (gr. 1-3). 1970. (ISBN 0-682-46918-1). Exposition.

Maddigan, Barbara J.

--Shamrock, the Story of a Dog. Maddigan, Barbara J., illus. (gr. 2-7). 1975. (ISBN 0-88017-113-8). Ford Assocs.

Maddison, Angela Mary see Banner, Angela, pseud.

Maddock, Reginald Bertram (1912-)

--Danny Rowley. LC 77-108172. (gr. 3-7). 1970. (ISBN 0-316-54318-7). Little.

--The Dragon in the Garden. LC 70-77451. 168 p. 21cm. 1969, c.1968. Little, Brown.

--The Great Bow. Ambrus, Victor G., pseud. (1935-), illus. Ambrus, Gyozo Laszlo. LC 68-19436. (Illus.). 159 p. 22cm. 1968. Rand McNally.

--The Pit. Hall, Douglas (1931-), illus. LC 68-12350. 191p. illus. 21cm. 1st U.S. edition. c.1966. (ISBN 0-316-54316-0). Little, Brown.

--Thin Ice. LC 70-154954. 180 p. 21cm. 1971. Little, Brown.

Maddox, Bill (1938-) & Beeson, Harold (1939-)

--Rags and Patches. LC 78-3218. 192 p. 23cm. c.1978. (ISBN 0-695-80966-0). (ISBN 0-695-40966-2). Follett Pub. Co.

Maddox, Edith E.

--When I Grow Up. Maddox, Edith E., illus. LC 43-14576. 23, 1 p. col. illus. 20 1/2 cm. 1943. National College of Education.

Maddox, Hugh

--Billy Boll Weevil: A Pest Becomes a Hero. Maddox, Hugh, illus. LC 76-5188. (Illus.). 44 p. 28cm. c.1976. (ISBN 0-87397-097-7). Strode Publishers.

Mademoiselle Editors

--Mademoiselle Prize Stories: 1951-1975. Stoianoff, Ellen, frwd. by. LC 75-40393. 336p. (gr. 7 up). 1976. (ISBN 0-87131-202-6). M Evans.

Mader, Friedrich Wilhelm (1866-)

--Distant Worlds: The Story of a Voyage to the Planets. Graef, Robert A., illus. Schachtman, Max (1903-1972), tr. from Ger. LC 32-31035. vi p., 1 l., 343 p. front., plates. 21 1/2 cm. 1932. C. Scribner's Sons.

Madian, Jon (1941-)

--Beautiful Junk: A Story of the Watts Towers. 1st ed. Jacobs, Barbara & Jacobs, Louis, Jr. (1921-), photos by LC 68-21170. (Illus.). 44 p. 26cm. 1968. Little, Brown.

--Lines Make Me Lonely. Stelmach, Joe, illus. LC 73-166454. (Illus.). 23 p. 21cm. (Magic circle book). 1972. (ISBN 0-663-22968-5). Ginn.

--Two Is a Line. Jacobs, Louis, Jr. (1921-), illus. LC 76-142079. (Illus.). 31 p. 29cm. 1971. Platt & Munk.

Madigan, Margaret

--Good Night, Aunt Lilly. Dawson, Diane, illus. LC 82-84022. (Illus.). 24p. (Little Golden Bk.). (ps-2). 1983. (ISBN 0-307-02084-3, Golden Pr). (ISBN 0-307-02084-3). Western Pub.

Madison, Arnold (1937-)

--But This Girl is Different. 176p. (Orig.). (gr. 7 up). 1982. (ISBN 0-590-31998-1, Wishing Star). Scholastic Inc.

--Danger Beats the Drum. LC 66-7143. 191 p. 22cm. 1966. Holt, Rinehart and Winston.

--Fast Break to Danger. (Orig.). (gr. 4-6). 1973. (ISBN 0-515-00711-0). Pyramid Pubns.

--It Can't Happen to Me. 176p. (Orig.). (gr. 7-12). 1981. (ISBN 0-590-31254-5). Scholastic Inc.

--The Secret of the Carved Whale Bone. LC 70-86921. viii, 118 p. 21cm. 1969. D. McKay Co.

--Think Wild. LC 68-11828. 198 p. 22cm. 1968. Holt, Rinehart and Winston.

Madison, Lucy Foster, Mrs. (1865-)

--Captain Kitty, Colonial. Davis, Marguerite (1889-), illus. LC 23-10551. 4 p. l., 7-309 p. col. front., illus., plates. 23 cm. 1923. The Penn Publishing Company.

--A Colonial Maid of Old Virginia. (Historical Stories for Girls). N.D. Penn.

--A Daughter of the Union. (Historical Stories for Girls). N.D. Penn.

--In Doublet and Hose. Deland, Clyde O., illus. (Vacation Ser.). N.D. Penn Publishing Co.

--In Doublet and Hose: A Story for Girls. Deland, Clyde O., illus. LC 4-21666. 330 p. front., 6 pl. 19 cm. (Keystone Ser.). 1904. The Penn Publishing Company.

--A Maid at King Alfred's Court: A Story for Girls. Waugh, Ida, illus. LC 4746. vi, 7-362 p. front., plates. 19 cm. (Keystone Ser.). 1900. The Penn Publishing Company.

--A Maid of Salem Towne. N.D. Grosset & Dunlap.

--A Maid of Salem Towne. Merrill, Frank Thayer (1848-), illus. LC 34-5827. 315 p. incl. front. 19 1/2 cm. 1934. The Penn Publishing Company.

--A Maid of the First Century. (Illus.). (Vacation Ser.). N.D. Penn Publishing Co.

--A Maid of the First Century: A Story for Girls. Waugh, Ida, illus. LC 3906. 323 p. incl. front., plates. 19 cm. (Keystone Ser.). 1900. The Penn Publishing Company.

--Peggy Owen: A Story for Girls. Deland, Clyde O., illus. LC 8-22347. 456 p. front., 6 pl. 19 1/2 cm. 1908. The Penn Publishing Company.

--Peggy Owen: A Story for Girls. Peck, Henry J., illus. LC 36-10833. 2 p. l., 3-456 p. front., plates. 19 cm. 1936. The Penn Publishing Company.

--Peggy Owen and Liberty. Peck, Henry J., illus. LC 12-26369. 456 p. front., plates 19 cm. $1.2. 1912. The Penn Publishing Company.

--Peggy Owen at Yorktown. Peck, Henry J., illus. LC 11-28433. 405 p. front., plates, 19 1/2 cm. $1.2. 1911. The Penn Publishing Company.

--Peggy Owen, Patriot: A Story for Girls. Peck, Henry J., illus. LC 38-69815. 4 p. l., 11-437 p. front. 19 1/2 cm. c.1938. The Penn Publishing Company.

Madison, Winifred

--Becky's Horse. LC 74-26717. 152 p. 22cm. 1975. (ISBN 0-590-07361-3). Four Winds Press.

--Bird on the Wing. LC 73-17009. 249 p. 22cm. 1974. (ISBN 0-316-54361-6). Little, Brown.

--Call Me Danica. LC 76-48243. 202 p. 22cm. c.1977. (ISBN 0-590-07463-6). Four Winds Press.

--Dance with Me. 208p. (Orig.). 1981. (ISBN 0-590-31769-5, Wildfire). Scholastic Inc.

--The Genessee Queen: A Novel. LC 77-72634. 226 p. 21cm. c.1977. (ISBN 0-440-02809-4). Delacorte Press.

--Getting Out. LC 76-373303. 288 p. 23cm. c.1976. (ISBN 0-695-80634-3). (ISBN 0-695-40634-5). Follett Pub. Co.

--Growing up in A Hurry. 1973. Little Brown and Company.

--Growing up in a Hurry. LC 72-11957. 200 p. 18cm. (Archway book). 1975, c.1973. (ISBN 0-671-29704-X). Pocket Books.

--Homecoming Queen. 222p. (Orig.). (gr. 7 up). 1983. (ISBN 0-590-32369-5, Wildfire). Scholastic Inc.

--Maria Luisa. LC 79-159825. 187 p. 21cm. 1971. Lippincott.

--Marinka, Katinka, and Me (Susie). Pope, Miller, illus. LC 74-22853. (Illus.). 72 p. 24cm. c.1975. (ISBN 0-87888-080-1). Bradbury Press.

--Max's Wonderful Delicatessen. 1st ed. Armstrong, James (1934-), illus. LC 75-170852. (Illus.). 179 p. 22cm. 1972. Little, Brown.

--The Mysterious Caitlin McIver. LC 75-2966. 240 p. 23cm. c.1975. (ISBN 0-695-80591-6). (ISBN 0-695-40591-8). Follett Pub. Co.

--The Party That Lasted All Summer. Meiling, illus. LC 75-25812. p. cm. 1975. (ISBN 0-316-54362-4). Little, Brown.

--A Portrait of Myself: A Novel. LC 78-13897. 239 p. 22cm. c.1979. (ISBN 0-394-84021-6). (ISBN 0-394-94021-0). Random House.

--The Sketchbook of Catherine D'Amato. LC 78-10627. p. cm. 1979. (ISBN 0-394-84021-6). (ISBN 0-394-94021-0). Random House.

--Suzy Who?. 172p. (Orig.). 1981. (ISBN 0-590-31822-5, Wildfire). Scholastic Inc.

Madlee, Dorothy Haynes, jt. auth. see Norton, Andre.

Madlee, Dorothy Haynes (1917-1980)

--Miss Lindlow's Leopard. LC 65-11010. 222 p. 21 cm. 1965. Norton.

Madlee, Dorothy Haynes (1917-1980) & Norton, Andre, pseud. (1912-)

--Star Ka'at & the Plant People. Norton, Alice Mary. (Illus.). (gr. 3-6). 1979. (ISBN 0-8027-6342-1). (ISBN 0-8027-6343-X). Walker & Co.

Madler, Trudy

--Why Did Grandma Die?. Connelly, Gwen, illus. Lewis, Gloria, intro. by. LC 79-23892. p. cm. c.1980. (ISBN 0-8172-1354-6). Raintree Childrens Books.

Madsen, Jane M. & Bockoras, Diane

--Please Don't Tease Me. Brinko, Kathleen T., illus. LC 80-130599. (Illus.). 32 p. 24cm. c.1980. (ISBN 0-8170-0876-4). Judson Press.

Madsen, Lenora Kimball

--Green-Eye Phantoms: A Sicily Slatts Charm Story. 1st ed. Collett, Farrell R., illus. LC 53-11266. 197p. illus. 21cm. 1954. Exposition Press.

Maeda, Mieko (1930-)

--How Rabbit Tricked His Friends. Segawa, Yasuo (1932-), illus. Tresselt, Alvin R. (1916-), tr. LC 69-12615. (Illus.). 32 p. 27cm. c.1969. Parents' Magazine Press.

MaeLean, Katherine (1925-)

--The Diploids. 1981. (ISBN 0-8398-2510-2, Gregg). G K Hall.

Maestro, Betsy, jt. auth. see Maestro, Giulio.

Maestro, Betsy (1944-)

--Busy Day: A Book of Action Words. Maestro, Giulio (1942-), illus. LC 77-15635. (Illus.). (ps-1). 1978. Crown.

--Fat Polka-Dot Cat and Other Haiku. Maestro, Giulio (1942-), illus. LC 75-33641. (Illus.). 32 p. 20cm. c.1976. (ISBN 0-525-29625-5). Dutton.

--In My Boat. Maestro, Giulio (1942-), illus. LC 76-6095. p. cm. 1976. (ISBN 0-690-01251-9). Crowell.

Maestro, Betsy (1944-) & Maestro, Giulio (1942-)

--Around the Clock with Harriet. Maestro, Giulio (1942-), illus. LC 83-7664. (Illus.). 32p. (ps-1). 1984. (ISBN 0-517-55118-7). Crown.

--Harriet at Home. Maestro, Giulio (1942-), illus. LC 83-26365. (Illus.). 13 p. 16cm. (Little Harriet board books). c.1984. (ISBN 0-517-55417-8). Crown.

--Harriet at Play. Maestro, Giulio (1942-), illus. LC 83-27226. (Illus.). 11 p. 15cm. (Little Harriet board books). c.1984. (ISBN 0-517-55420-8). Crown.

--Harriet at School. Maestro, Giulio (1942-), illus. LC 83-27225. (Illus.). 10. (Little Harriet Board Books). c.1984. (ISBN 0-517-55419-4). Crown.

--Harriet at Work. Maestro, Giulio (1942-), illus. LC 83-26364. (Illus.). 10. (Little Harriet Board Books). c.1984. (ISBN 0-517-55418-6). Crown.

--Harriet Goes to the Circus. Maestro, Giulio (1942-), illus. LC 76-40204. (Illus.). 32 p. 29cm. (number concept book). c.1977. (ISBN 0-517-52844-4). Crown Publishers.

--Harriet Reads Signs. Maestro, Giulio (1942-), illus. LC 80-10438. p. cm. (Word concept book). c.1980. (ISBN 0-517-54167-X). Crown Publishers.

--The Key to the Kingdom. Maestro, Giulio (1942-), illus. LC 80-28071. (Illus.). 32 p. 26cm. c.1982. Harcourt Brace Jovanovich.

--Lambs for Dinner. Maestro, Giulio (1942-), illus. LC 78-6820. p. cm. c.1978. (ISBN 0-517-53380-4). Crown Publishers.

--Through the Year with Harriet: A Time Concept Book. Maestro, Giulio (1942-), illus. LC 84-29339. (Illus.). 32 p. 29cm. c.1985. (ISBN 0-517-55613-8). Crown Publishers.

--Where Is My Friend?. Maestro, Giulio (1942-), illus. LC 75-15902. p. cm. (Word concept book). 1976. (ISBN 0-517-52436-8). Crown Publishers.

--A Wise Monkey Tale. Maestro, Giulio (1942-), illus. LC 75-9749. (Illus.). 32 p. 29cm. 1975. (ISBN 0-517-52328-0). Crown Publishers.

Maestro, Giulio, jt. auth. see Maestro, Betsy.

Maestro, Giulio (1942-)

--Halloween Howls: Riddles That Are a Scream. 1st ed. Maestro, Giulio (1942-), illus. LC 83-1419. (Illus.). 64 p. 19cm. c.1983. (ISBN 0-525-44059-3). Dutton.

--Just Enough Rosie. Maestro, Giulio (1942-), illus. LC 82-83741. (Illus.). 32p. (Ready Readers Ser.). (gr. 1-3). 1983. (ISBN 0-448-21702-3, G&D). Putnam Pub Group.

--Leopard and the Noisy Monkeys. Maestro, Giulio (1942-), illus. LC 78-31701. (Illus.). 39 p. 22cm. (Greenwillow read-alone). c.1979. (ISBN 0-688-80221-4). (ISBN 0-688-84221-6). Greenwillow Books.

--Leopard Is Sick. Maestro, Giulio (1942-), illus. LC 78-1709. (Illus.). 48 p. 22cm. (Greenwillow read-alone). c.1978. (ISBN 0-688-80162-5). (ISBN 0-688-84162-7). Greenwillow Books.

--A Raft of Riddles. Maestro, Giulio (1942-), illus. LC 82-2402. (Illus.). 64p. (gr. 3-7). 1982. (ISBN 0-525-44017-8). Dutton.

--Razzle-Dazzle Riddles. Maestro, Giulio (1942-), illus. LC 85-3785. (Illus.). 64 p. 24cm. c.1985. (ISBN 0-89919-382-X). (ISBN 0-89919-405-2). Clarion Books.

--Remarkable Plant in Apartment Four. Maestro, Giulio (1942-), illus. LC 74-189021. (Illus.). 32p. (gr. k-3). 1973. (ISBN 0-87888-045-3). Bradbury Pr.

--The Remarkable Plant in Apartment Four. Maestro, Giulio (1942-), illus. (Illus.). 1973. E.P. Dutton & Co.

--Riddle Romp. Maestro, Giulio (1942-), illus. LC 83-2067. (Illus.). 64p. (gr. k-3). 1983. (ISBN 0-89919-180-0, Clarion). (ISBN 0-89919-207-6). HM.

--What's a Frank Frank?. Tasty Homograph Riddles. Maestro, Giulio (1942-), illus. 1984. Houghton.

--What's a Frank Frank?. Tasy Homograph Riddles. Maestro, Giulio (1942-), illus. LC 84-5021. (Illus.). c.1984. (ISBN 0-89919-297-1). Clarion Books.

Maestro, Giulio (1942-), retold by.

--The Tortoise's Tug of War. Maestro, Giulio (1942-), illus. LC 76-152223. (Illus.). 32 p. 27cm. 1971. (ISBN 0-87888-030-5). Bradbury Press.

Maestro, Giulio (1942-) & Maestro, Betsy (1944-)

--The Guessing Game. Maestro, Giulio (1942-), illus. (Illus.). 32p. (Ready Readers). (gr. 1-3). 1983. (ISBN 0-448-21701-5, G&D). Putnam Pub Group.

Maeterlinck, Maurice (1862-1949)

--Blue Bird. Leblanc, Georgette, Mrs., ed. (gr. 9 up). 1909. (ISBN 0-396-00944-1). Dodd.

--The Blue Bird for Children: The Wonderful Adventures of Tyltyl and Mytyl in Search of Happiness. Leblanc, Georgette, Mrs. & Perkins, Frederick Orville, eds. Teixeira De Mattos, Alexander Louis (1865-1921), tr. LC 14-4533. viii p., 1 l., 182 (i.e. 164) p. incl. col. front. plates. 20 cm. c.1914. Silver, Burdett & Company.

--The Bluebird Chooses: Being the Story of Maurice Maeterlinck's Play, "The Betrothal," Told for Children. Paus, Herbert, illus. Teixeira De Mattos, Alexander Louis (1865-1921), tr. LC 29-11504. 5 p. l., 3-159 p. col. mounted front., col. mounted plates. 24 1/2 cm. 1926. Dodd, Mead and Company.

--The Children's Blue Bird. Leblanc, Georgette, Mrs., ed. Paus, Herbert, illus. Teixeira De Mattos, Alexander Louis (1865-1921), tr. LC 13-22821. 5 p. l., 3-182 p. mounted col. front., plates. 23 cm. 1913. (ISBN 0-396-01979-X). Dodd, Mead and Company.

--Maeterlinck's The Children's Blue Bird. Leblanc, Georgette, Mrs., abridged by. Henderson, Doris & Henderson, Marion, illus. LC 40-3254. (Based on the Complete). 55 p. incl. col. front., illus. (part col.) 18 x 23 1/2 cm. c.1939. Grosset & Dunlap.

--Our Friend, the Dog. Shepard, Morgan (1865-), ed. Aspell, Seddie, illus. LC 24-22143. 36 p., 1 l. incl. front., illus. 23 1/2 cm. c.1924. Dodd, Mead and Company.

--Tyltyl: Being the Story of Maurice Maeterlinck's Play, "The Bethrothal". Paus, Herbert, illus. Teixeira De Mattos, Alexander Louis (1865-1921), tr. LC 20-18246. 5 p. l., 3-159 p. col., front., col. plates. 26 1/2 cm. $5.0. 1920. Dodd, Mead and Company.

Magaret, Helene (1906-)

--The Head on London Bridge: Life of St. Thomas More. Di Valentin, Louis, illus. LC 56-13234. 144p. illus. 22cm. 1956. Bruce Pub. Co.

Magdela, Sr.

--Little Joseph, Son of David. N.D. Bruce Pub Co.

Maiorano, Robert & Isadora, Rachel
--Backstage. Isadora, Rachel, illus. LC 77-21822. (Illus.). 32 p. c.1978. (ISBN 0-688-80130-7). (ISBN 0-688-84130-9). Greenwillow Books.
Mair, Henriette Willebeek see Le Mair, Henriette Willebeek.
Maison, Della
--The Care Bears' Garden. Bracken, Carolyn, illus. LC 82-61566. (Illus.). 32p. (Care Bear Mini-Storybooks). (gr. 1-6). 1983. (ISBN 0-394-85827-1). Random.
Maitland, Agnes C.
--Nellie O'Neil: Or, Our Summer Time. N.D. Thos Nelson & Sons.
Maitland, Antony Jasper (1935-)
--Ben Goes to the City. Maitland, Antony Jasper (1935-), illus. LC 67-3386. (Illus.). 1 v. (unpaged. 24cm. 1st U.S. edition. 1967, c.1964. Delacorte Press.
--Idle Jack. Maitland, Antony Jasper (1935-), illus. LC 77-10707. p. cm. 1979. (ISBN 0-374-33628-8). Farrar, Straus and Giroux.
--James & the Roman Silver. Maitland, Antony Jasper (1935-), illus. (Illus.). (gr. 1-4). 1965. (ISBN 0-685-21261-0). Verry.
--The Secret of the Shed. Maitland, Antony Jasper (1935-), illus. (Illus.). 1963. Duell Sloan & Pearce.
Maitland, Elizabeth
--Little Red Rickshaw. (Illus.). (gr. 1-3). 1954. Warne.
--Runaway Rickshaw. (Illus.). (gr. 1-3). 1958. Warne.
--Story of Porky Peek. Vise, Jennetta, illus. (Illus.). (gr. k-3). 1962. Warne.
Maitland, Ida, ed.
--The Humming Bird: A Christmas and New-Year's Gift. LC 15-17157. 1 p. l., 254 p. incl. pl. front., plates. 16 1/2 cm. N.D. Leavitt and Allen.
Maitland, Louise
--Heroes of Chivalry. LC 3-13631. xvii, 238 p. incl. front., 11 pl. 19 cm. (Stories of heroes). 1903. Silver, Burdett and Company.
Maitland-Nimmo, Frances
--Bed That Knew How to Fly. Brett, Molly, pseud., illus. Brett, Mary Elizabeth. LC 64-10118. (Illus.). 45p. (gr. k-3). 1964. Warne.
Maiyagawa, Yasue
--The Hare and the Bear, and Other Stories. Tresselt, Alvin R. (1916-) & Suzuki, Yushoharu (1916-), trs. LC 74-158840. (Illus.). 32 p. 27cm. 1971. (ISBN 0-8193-0517-0). Parents' Magazine Press.
Maizel, Clarice Matthews (1919-)
--Son of Condor. Howard, Simon (1903-1979), illus. (Illus.). 1964. Criterion Books.
Majewska, Maria
--Oscar Mouse Finds a Home. Miller, Moira (1939-), illus. LC 85-1665. p. cm. 1985. (ISBN 0-8037-0229-9). Dial Books for Young Readers.
Majima, Setsuko
--Song of the Sour Plum. Majima, Setsuko, illus. LC 68-26628. (Illus.). watercolors. 36p. 1st U.S. edition. (gr. k-3). 1968. (ISBN 0-8027-6068-6). Walker & Co.
Major, Beverly
--The Magic Pizza. Shortall, Leonard W., illus. LC 77-26993. p. cm. c.1978. (ISBN 0-13-545202-3). Prentice-Hall.
--Porcupine Stew. Ingraham, Erick, illus. LC 82-2268. p. cm. 1982. (ISBN 0-688-01272-8). W. Morrow.
Major, Charles (1856-1913)
--The Bears of Blue River. Frost, Arthur Burdett, et al. (1851-1928), illus. LC 67-31833. viii, 277p. illus. 22cm. 1967. Bobbs.
--The Bears of Blue River. Frost, Arthur Burdett, et al. (1851-1928), illus. LC 27-299486. vi, 277 p. incl. plates. front., illus. 19 1/2 cm. 1926. The Macmillan Company.
--The Little King. 249p. 1910. Macmillan.
--Uncle Tom Andy Bill. Ivory, P. Van E., illus. 344p. 1908. MacMillan.
Major, Clare Tree
--Playing Theatre: Six Plays for Children. Major, Clare Tree, illus. LC 30-305375. 6 p. l., 269 p. illus. 21 1/2 cm. c.1930. Oxford University Press.
Major, Kevin (1949-)
--Far from Shore. LC 81-65495. p. cm. 1981. (ISBN 0-440-02455-2). Delacorte Press.
--Hold Fast. LC 79-17544. (Illus.). 170 p. 21cm. 1980, c.1978. (ISBN 0-440-03506-6). Delacorte Press. **Awards: (CCCL); (CLA).**
--Thirty-Six Exposures. LC 84-4995. (gr. 7 up). 1984. (ISBN 0-385-29347-X). Delacorte.
Major, Ted, jt. ed. see Williams, Terry Tempest.
Major, W. Montgomery, ed.
--Flag of Our Hearts. Fisher, Elizabeth M., illus. LC 27-16939. 128 p. incl. col. front., illus. (part col.) 19 1/2 cm. c.1927. A. Whitman & Company.
--Merry Christmas Stories. Winter, Milo Kendall (1888-1956), illus. 128p. (The Holiday Library). N.D. A. Whitman & Co.
--Patriotic Stories. Fisher, Elizabeth M., illus. LC 36-17482. 128 p. incl. col. front., illus. (part col.; incl. port.) 18 1/2 cm. (On cover: The easy library). 1933. A. Whitman & Company.
Majors, G
--Who Would Want to Kill Hallie Pankey's Cat. LC 81-4270. 126 p. 22cm. c.1981. (ISBN 0-8038-8094-4). Hastings House.
Majors, Monroe Alphus (1864-)
--First Steps and Nursery Rhymes. LC 20-11593. (Illus.). 27cm. 48p. (The Colored Child Ser.: Bk. 1). 1920. McElray & Clark.
Makavova, T.
--The Brave Ant. 20p. 1976. (ISBN 0-8285-1117-9, Pub. by Progress Pubs USSR). Imported Pubns.
Makepeace, Emily, tr. see Musset, Paul Edme De.
Makerney, Edna Smith (1921-)
--Cissy's Texas Pride. Leibold, Margaret, illus. LC 75-2376. (Illus.). 80 p. 23cm. 1975. (ISBN 0-687-08564-0). Abingdon Press.
Makhanlall, David P.
--The Best of Brer Anansi. (gr. 1-6). 1978. (ISBN 0-8277-5442-6). British Bk Ctr.
Makin, Irene
--Wildcat. LC 70-81930. 160 p. 22cm. 1969. Lothrop, Lee & Shepard Co.
Makower, Sylvia
--Samson's Breakfast. Makower, Sylvia, illus. 1967. (ISBN 0-88302-364-4, Peter Possum). Mulberry Pr.
Maksimovic, Desanka (1898-)
--The Shaggy Little Dog. Wilkon, Jozef (1930-), illus. LC 82-24180. p. cm. 1983. (ISBN 0-571-12521-2). Faber and Faber.
Malan, A. N.
--Earnest Fairfield. (Illus.). (The Home and Enterprise Library Ser.). N.D. Frederick Warne & Co.
--Lost on Brown Willy. (Illus.). (The Home and Enterprise Library Ser.). N.D. Frederick Warne & co.
Malan, C.
--Idle Dick and the Poor Watchmaker. 82p. N.D. Presbyterian Committee of Publication.
Malan, D. D. Caesar
--Fox Hunter, 1 of 36 vols. (Illus.). (Primary Lib.: No. 8). N.D. Set. A. I. Bradley & Co.'s Pubs.
Malcolm, Arthur, pseud., see Williams, Henry Meade.
Malcolm, Claire
--Old Faithful. Galdone, Paul (1914-), illus. LC 41-16065. 27p. illus. (part. col) 21 1/2 x 17 1/2cm. c.1941. Grosset & Dunlap.
Malcolm, Mary
--Chaucer the Flying Saucer. Palmer, Edward F., illus. 1954. Exposition Press.
Malcolm-Smith, George
--Professor Peckam's Adventures in a Drop of Water. Ward, Keith, illus. LC 31-23676. 144 p. col. illus. 20 1/2 cm. c.1931. Rand, McNally & Company.
Malcolmson, Anne Burnett, Mrs. (1910-)
--Captain Ichabod Paddock: Whaler of Nantucket. Unada, pseud. (1927-), illus. Gliewe, Unada Grace. LC 78-96037. (Illus.). 40 p. 1970. (ISBN 0-8027-6015-5). Walker.
--Yankee Doodle's Cousins. McCloskey, John Robert (1914-1969), illus. LC 41-24262. xiii, 1, 267, 1 p. illus. 25 cm. 1941. (ISBN 0-395-06896-7). Houghton Mifflin Company.
Malcolmson, Anne Burnett, Mrs. (1910-), ed.
--Miracle Plays: Seven Medieval Plays for Modern Players. Baynes, Pauline Diana (1922-), illus. (gr. 10 up). 1959. (ISBN 0-395-06893-2). HM.
--Song of Robin Hood. Burton, Virginia Lee (1909-1968), illus. (Illus.). (gr. 7-9). 1947. (ISBN 0-395-06895-9). HM. **Award: (RCM).**
--A Taste of Chaucer: Selections from The Canterbury Tales. Arno, Enrico (1913-1981), illus. (Original Author: Geoffrey Chaucer, 1340-1400). 1964. Harcourt.
Malcolmson, Anne Burnett, Mrs. (1910-) & McCormick, Dell J. (1909-)
--Mister Stormalong. Tolford, Joshua (1909-), illus. LC 52-7196. 136 p. illus. 24 cm. 1952. Houghton Mifflin.
Malcolmson, David (1899-)
--Yipe: The Story of a Farm Dog. 1st ed. Dennis, Morgan (1891-1960), illus. LC 55-5188. 112p. illus. 22cm. c.1955. Little, Brown.
Malden, Richard Henry (1879-)
--The Personal History of David Copperfield. (Illus.). 1947. Oxford University Press.
Malet, H.
--Jacky Nory: Or, Do Your Best. N.D. Scribner, Welford & Armstrong.
Malet, Lucas, pseud., see Harrison, Mary ST. Leger Kingsley.
Malet, Lucas, pseud. (1852-)
--Little Peter. Harrison, Mary ST. Leger Kingsley. (Illus.). (Sunshine Library for Young People). 1900. T. Y. Crowell & Co.
--Little Peter. Harrison, Mary ST. Leger Kingsley. Brock, Charles Edmond (1870-1938), illus. (Illus.). N.D. George H. Doran.
--Little Peter: A Christmas Morality for Children of any Age. Harrison, Mary ST. Leger Kingsley. N.D. D. Appleton & Co.'s Pub.
Malet, Oriel, pseud., see Vaughan, Auriel Rosemary Malet.
Maley, Anneaka
--Have You Seen My Mother?. Sugita, Yutaka (1930-), illus. LC 76-82448. (Illus.). 31 p. 25cm. 1969. (ISBN 0-87614-001-0). Carolrhoda Books.
Mali, Jane Lawrence, jt. auth. see Herzig, Alison Cragin.
Malinowski, Paul (1936-) & McQuilkin, Frank
--The Town That Arrested Santa Claus. Rocco, Frank & Stang, Clayton, illus. LC 81-52991. (Illus.). 47 p. 29cm. (gr. k-7). c.1981. (ISBN 0-941316-00-9). (ISBN 0-941316-00-9). (ISBN 0-941316-01-7). TSM Productions.
Malinowski, Stanley B. & Melodia, Thomas V.
--The Easter Bunny Comes to Forgottenville. 48p. (ps-3). N.D. (ISBN 0-941316-02-5). TSM Prods.
Malka, Sora & Silverstein, Solomon
--Everyday Poems for the Jewish Child. (Illus.). 44p. (Orig.). 1st U.S. edition. (ps-6). 1980. (ISBN 0-89655-050-8). BRuach HaTorah.
Malkan, Pauline Darling see Malkan, Peedie, pseud.
Malkan, Pauline Darling (1889-) & De Vora, Anna
--The Scrambled Circus. Malkan, Peedie, pseud. Pearlman, Mal, illus. LC 39-22037. 26 p. col. front., col. illus. 23 1/2 cm. c.1939. Dorrance and Company.
Malkan, Peedie, pseud., see Malkan, Pauline Darling.
Malkus, Alida Wright Sims, Mrs., jt. auth. see Desmond, Alice Curtis, Mrs.
Malkus, Alida Wright Sims, Mrs. (1899-)
--Along the Inca Highway. Malkus, Alida Wright Sims, Mrs. (1899-), illus. LC 41-75120. 56 p. incl. col. front., illus. (part col.) 21 1/2 cm. (On cover: New world neighbors). c.1941. D. C. Health and Company.
--Beloved Island: A Cuban Family's Fight for Freedom. (gr. 8-10). 1967. (ISBN 0-8019-5193-3). Chilton.
--Caravans to Santa Fe. Lawson, Marie Abrams (1894-1956), illus. 1928. Harper & Bros.
--Chula of the Magic Islands. Malkus, Alida Wright Sims, Mrs. (1899-), illus. LC 48-22347. 90 p. illus. (part col.) 22 cm. (Saalfield treasure book). 1948. Saalfield Co.
--The Citadel of a Hundred Stairways. Pitz, Henry Clarence (1895-1976), illus. LC 41-24406. iii, 1 p., 1 l., 234 p. col. front., illus. 23 cm. c.1941. The John C. Winston Company.
--Colt of Destiny: A Story of the California Missions. Lee, Manning de Villeneuve (1894-1980), illus. LC 50-12675. (Illus.). xi, 244 p. 22cm. (Land of the Free series). 1950. Winston.
--Constancia Lona. 1st ed. Malkus, Alida Wright Sims, Mrs. (1899-), illus. LC 47-11497. 311 p. illus. 21 cm. 1947. Doubleday.
--The Dark Star of Itza: The Story of a Pagan Princess. Houser, Lowell, illus. LC 30-25187. xv p., 2 l., 3-217 p. incl, front., illus., plates. 22 1/2 cm. c.1930. Harcourt, Brace and Company. **Award: (JNM).**
--The Dragon Fly of Zuni. Best, Allena Champlin, Mrs. (1892-1974), illus. Berry, Erick, pseud. LC 28-20604. 5 p., l., 3-213 p. incl. front., illus., plates. 22 1/2 cm. c.1928. Harcourt, Brace and Company.
--Eastward Sweeps the Current. Sweeney, Dan, illus. N.D. John C. Winston.
--A Fifth for the King: A Story of the Conquest of Yucatan and of the Discovery of the Amazon. Best, Allena Champlin, Mrs. (1892-1974), illus. Berry, Erick, pseud. LC 31-507087. 6 p. l., 250 p. col. front., illus., plates, 2 double maps. 19 1/2 cm. 1931. Harper & Brothers.
--Little Giant of the North: The Boy Who Won a Fur Empire. 1st ed. Barnum, Jay Hyde (1888-1962), illus. LC 52-58. 178 p. illus. 22 cm. (Winston adventure books). 1952. Winston.
--Outpost of Peril. LC 61-17506. 189p. 24cm. (Daughters of valor series). 1961. J. Day Co.
--Pirates' Port: A Tale of Old New York. Justis, Lyle, illus. LC 29-23878. x p., 1 l., 251, 1 p. incl. 1 illus., plates. col. front.19 cm. c.1929. Harper & Brothers.
--Raquel of the Ranch Country. Avison, George F. (1885-), illus. LC 27-18965. 4 p. l., 3-314 p. front., plates. 19 1/2 cm. c.1927. Harcourt, Brace and Company.
--Sidi, Boy of the Desert. 1st ed. Lee, Manning de Villeneuve (1894-1980), illus. LC 56-5095. 210p. illus. 22cm. 1956. Winston.
--The Silver Llama. Malkus, Alida Wright Sims, Mrs. (1899-), illus. LC 39-31683. 107, 1 p. illus. (part col.) 28 1/2 cm. c.1939. The John C. Winston Company.
--The Spindle Imp and Other Tales of Maya Mith and Folk Lore. Best, Allena Champlin, Mrs. (1892-1974), illus. Berry, Erick, pseud. LC 31-22896. 5 p. l., 3-176 p. incl. illus., plates. front. 20 1/2 cm. c.1931. Harcourt, Brace and Company.
--Stone Knife Boy. Stoops, Herbert Morton, illus. LC 33-27399. viii, 270 p. incl. front., plates. 22 1/2 cm. c.1933. Harcourt, Brace and Company.
--The Story of Good Queen Bess. Meadowcroft, Enid La Monte, Mrs. (1898-1966), ed. Gorsline, Douglas Warner (1913-1985), illus. LC 52-137474. 177p. illus. 22cm. (Signature books, 18). 1953. Grosset & Dunlap.
--The Story of Louis Pasteur. Spier, Jo, illus. LC 52-11075. 178 p. illus. 22 cm. (Signature books). 1952. Grosset & Dunlap.
--There Really Was A Hiawatha. N.D. Grosset & Dunlap.
--Through the Wall: A Boy's Struggle for Freedom. Malkus, Alida Wright Sims, Mrs. (1899-), illus. LC 62-52304. 178p. illus. 22cm. 1962. Grosset & Dunlap.
--Timber Line. King, Ruth, illus. LC 29-21149. 5 p. l., 3-247 p. illus. 21 cm. c.1929. Harcourt, Brace and Company.
--We Were There at the Battle of Gettysburg. Miers, Earl S., ed. Vosburgh, Leonard W. (1912-), illus. LC 56-5041. 176p. illus. 24cm. (We were there books, 2). 1955. (ISBN 0-448-05002-1). Grosset & Dunlap.
--Young Inca Prince. 1st ed. Moyers, William (1916-), illus. LC 57-5263. 246p. illus. 22cm. 1957. (ISBN 0-394-91845-2). Knopf.
Mallan, Lloyd (1914-)
--Men, Rockets and Space Rats. N.D. Julian Messner, Inc.
Mallandaine, Catherine E.
--Flower and Thorn (Pub. by Society for Promoting Christian Knowledge). N.D. E. & J. B. Young & Co.
--The Girl Next Door (Pub. by Society for Promoting Christian Knowledge). N.D. E. & J. B. Young & Co.
--Grandfather's Secret (Pub. by Society for Promoting Christian Knowledge). N.D. E. & J. B. Young & Co.
--A Harbour Light (Pub. by Society for Promoting Christian Knowledge). N.D. E. & J. B. Young & Co.
--Jasper's Sweet Briar (Pub. by Society for Promoting Christian Knowledge). N.D. E. & J. B. Young & Co.
--Shadow of the Cliff (Pub. by Society for Promoting Christian Knoweledge). N.D. E. & J. B. Young & Co.
Mallari, Ismael V.
--When I Was a Little Boy. Alano, Ben, illus. LC 51-3765. (Stories for Children Based on Filipino Customs and Superstitions). 153 p. illus. 21 cm. 1951. Harper.
Mallary, M. Jeanie, Mrs.
--Aunt Clara's School. LC 12-36491. 2 p. l., 3-250 p. front., plates. 18 1/2 cm. c.1887. American Baptist Publication Society.
--Horace Wilde. LC 12-36504. iv, 5-295 p. 19 cm. 1868. J. B. Lippincott & Co.
--Jack: Or, "One Little Feather More.". LC 12-36493. 2 p. l., 3-192 p. front., plates.18 1/2 cm. c.1891. American Baptist Publication Society.
--Rosalie Wynnton: Or, Link to Link. LC 12-36492. 2 p. l., 3-312 p. front., plates. 18 1/2 cm. c.1889. American Baptist Publication Society.
--A Seeming Trifle. LC 12-36494. 250 p. front., 3 pl. 19 cm. c.1892. American Tract Society.
Maller, Allen S. (1938-)
--Jewish Children's Stories. Brandeis, Brigitta & Tov, Lika, illus. 1983. (ISBN 0-86628-053-7). Ridgefield Pub.
--Jewish Time Machine. Brandeis, Brigitta, illus. LC 82-10207. 40p. 1982. (ISBN 0-86628-030-8). Ridgefield Pub.
--The Rubic's Cube That Wanted to Be a Dreydel and Other Stories. LC 83-24735. p. cm. c.1984. (ISBN 0-86628-045-6). Ridgefield Pub. Co.
Malleson, Lucy Beatrice see Gilbert, Anthony, pseud.
Malleson, Lucy Beatrice (1899-1973)
--The Case Against Andrew Fane. Gilbert, Anthony, pseud. LC 31-19566. 3 p. l., 289, 1 p. 19 1/2 cm. 1931. Dodd, Mead & Company.
Mallet, Dennis, jt. auth. see McGill-Franzen, Anne.
Mallett, Anne (1913-)
--Here Comes Tagalong. Kellogg, Steven (1941-), illus. LC 78-153790. (Illus.). 32 p. 24cm. 1971. (ISBN 0-8193-0496-4). Parents' Magazine Press.
--The Secret Kitten. Mallett, Anne (1913-), illus. LC 70-174603. (Illus.). 40 p. 22cm. 1972. (ISBN 0-8193-0546-4). (ISBN 0-8193-0547-2). Parents' Magazine Press.
--Who'll Mind Henry?. Greenwald, Sheila, pseud. (1934-), illus. Green, Sheila Ellen. LC 65-17776. 59p. col. illus. 20cm. c.1965. Doubleday.

Mallette, Gertrude Ethel see Gregg, Alan, pseud.

Mallette, Gertrude Ethel (1887-)

--Bright Side up. LC 54-6785. 218 p. 22cm. 1954. Doubleday.

--Calling Doctor Marcia. LC 52-12670. 296p. 21cm. (Young moderns). 1954, c.1940. Doubleday.

--Chee-Cha-Ko. Stoops, Herbert Morton, illus. LC 38-33566. 3 p. l., 299 p. col. front. 20 1/2 cm. 1938. Doubleday, Doran & Co., Inc.

--Clear to Land. 1950. Doubleday & Co.

--Flying Wing Mystery. Gregg, Alan, pseud. 1st ed. Condon, Grattan, illus. LC 48-8638. 213 p. illus. 20 cm. 1948. Doubleday.

--For Keeps. Dean, Mallette, illus. LC 36-27268. 5 p. l., 309 p. incl. front., illus. 21 1/2 cm. 1936. Doubleday, Doran & Company, Inc.

--Hidden Wings Mystery. Gregg, Alan, pseud. LC 41-14050. 271 p. front 20 cm. 1941. Doubleday, Doran.

--Inside Out. (gr. 7-11). N.D. Doubleday Bks.

--Into the Wind. Reeves, Norman, illus. LC 41-181247. 3 p. l., 295 p. col. front. 20 1/2 cm. 1941. Doubleday, Doran & Co., Inc.

--Mystery in Blue. LC 45-9326. 3 p. l., 217 p. 20 1/2 cm. 1945. Doubleday, Doran & Company, Inc.

--The Mystery of Batty Ridge. Gregg, Alan, pseud. LC 46-20367. 213 p. 20 cm. 1946. Doubleday.

--No Vacancies. LC 46-7650. 3 p. l., 311 p. 20 1/2 cm. (Young moderns). 1946. Doubleday & Co., Inc.

--No Vacancies. 1st ed. Stoops, Herbert Morton, illus. LC 39-30325. 3 p. l., 311 p. front. 21 1/2 cm. 1939. Doubleday, Doran & Company, Inc.

--Once Is Forever. LC 46-11956. 3 p. l., 250 p. 20 1/2 cm. 1946. Doubleday & Company, Inc.

--Priceless Moment. LC 47-31100. 214 p. 21 cm. 1947. Doubleday.

--Private Props. (gr. 7-11). N.D. Doubleday Bks.

--Single Stones. Reeves, Norman, illus. LC 40-309670. 3 p. l., 296 p. col. front. 20 1/2 cm. 1940. Doubleday, Doran & Co., Inc.

--Unexpected Summer. LC 49-10409. 212 p. 21 cm. 1949. Doubleday.

--Wenderley. LC 43-15466. 3 p. l., 250 p. 20 1/2 cm. 1943. Doubleday, Doran & Co., Inc.

--Winged Mystery. Gregg, Alan, pseud. LC 40-30562. 302 p. front. 20 cm. 1940. Doubleday, Doran.

Mallison, Clare

--The Wooster-Poosters. Mallison, Clare, illus. LC 31-234596. 4 p. l., 87, 1 p. incl. col. illus., col. plates. 21 1/2 x 28 1/2 cm. c.1931. Frederick A. Stokes Co.

Mallon, Caroline H.

--Happy Gingerbread Boy: A Modern Version. Gehr, Mary, illus. LC 46-7499. 32 p. incl. col. front., col. illus. 26 cm. 1946. The Children's Company.

--The Story of the Man in the Moon. Gehr, Mary, illus. LC 46-21784. 32 p. col. illus. 25 1/2 cm. 1946. The Children's Company.

Mallory, Drew

--Target Manhattan. 1975. (ISBN 0-399-11496-3). G. P. Putnam's Sons.

Malloy, Judy

--Bad Thad. 1st ed. Durell, Ann, ed. Alexander, Martha G. (1920-), illus. LC 80-11349. (Illus.). 32 p. c.1980. (ISBN 0-525-26148-6). Dutton.

Malloy, Loncie L.

--The Wedding of Butternut Kisses & Fresco the Great. 1982. (ISBN 0-533-05138-X). Vantage.

Mally, Emma Louise (1908-), ed.

--Treasury of Animal Stories. N.D. Grosset & Dunlap.

Malmberg, Sybil

--Amos. Koski, Barbara, illus. LC 57-8113. 26p. col. illus. 21cm. (Bookland juvenile). 1957. Comet Press Books.

Malmgren, Ulf (1937-)

--When the Leaves Begin to Fall. Watkins, Jill, illus. Tate, Joan (1922-), tr. LC 78-24819. p. cm. 1979, c.1978. (ISBN 0-06-024046-6). (ISBN 0-06-024047-4). Harper & Row.

--When the Leaves Begin to Fall. Watkins, Jill, illus. Tate, Joan (1922-), tr. LC 79-40007. p. cm. 1979. (ISBN 0-19-271440-6). Oxford University Press.

Malmin, Gunnar J.

--Songs and Hymns for Children's Voices. N.D. Augsburg Publishing Hoose.

Malnate, Edmond V.

--Tuffy. Malnate, Edmond V., illus. LC 46-622632. 2 p. l., 47 p. col. illus. 27 1/2 x 21 cm. 1946. R. Speller.

Malocsay, Zoltan

--Galloping Wind. LC 77-9997. p. cm. c.1977. (ISBN 0-399-20619-1). Putnam.

Malois, Claude

--Giuliano, Boy of Sicily. LC 67-13530. (Illus.). photos. 48p. 1st U.S. edition. (gr. 3-5). 1969. (ISBN 0-695-43612-0). Follett.

Malone, Kemp (1889-1071)

--The Dodo and the Camel, A Fable in Verse for Children. 78p. 1938. John Hopkins Press.

Malone, Margaret Gay (1939-)

--Dolly the Dolphin. LC 78-3797. (Illus.). 96 p. 22cm. c.1978. (ISBN 0-671-32903-0). Messner.

Malone, Mary

--Dennie's Coat. Doane, Pelagie (1906-1966), illus. 159p. 1963. Dodd, Mead Co.

--Dennie's Way. Rossi, Kendall, illus. 185p. 1964. Dodd, Mead & Co.

--Here's Howie. 1962. (ISBN 0-8382-0329-9, Cadmus Books). E. M. Hale and Company.

--Here's Howie. Wiese, Kurt (1887-1974), illus. LC 62-7582. (Illus.). 173 p. 21cm. 1962. Dodd, Mead.

--This Was Bridget. Handville, Robert, illus. LC 60-6311. 247p. illus. 21cm. 1960. Dodd, Mead.

--Three Wishes for Sarah. Handville, Robert, illus. LC 61-5878. 159p. illus. 21cm. 1961. Dodd, Mead.

--Young Miss Josie Delaney, Detective. Horne, Rachel S., illus. LC 66-5596. (Illus.). 127 p. 21cm. 1966. Dodd, Mead.

Malone, P. Mae

--Reluctant Little Astronaut. (Illus.). (gr. 1-4). 1967. (ISBN 0-682-45743-4). Exposition.

Malone, Paul Bernard (1872-)

--A Plebe at West Point. Carter, F. A., illus. LC 5-29987. 430 p. front., 6 pl. 19 cm. (Adventure Stories Ser.). 1905. The Penn Publishing Company.

--A Plebe at West Point. Carter, F. A., illus. LC 10-3726. 4 p. l., 7-430 p. front., 6 pl. 19 1/2 cm. (West Point Ser.). 1909. The Penn Publishing Company.

--A West Point Cadet. 6 p., 1 l., 7-419 p. incl. front. 6 pl. 19 1/2 cm. (West Point Ser.). 1908. The Penn Publishing Company.

--A West Point Cadet. Carter, F. A., illus. LC 36-9865. 419 p. front. 19 cm. 1936. The Penn Publishing Company.

--A West Point Lieutenant. Carter, F. A., illus. LC 11-293523. 378 p. front., plates. 19 1/2 cm. $1.2. 1911. The Penn Publishing Company.

--A West Point Yearling. Carter, F. A., illus. LC 7-15319. 383 p. front., 6 pl. 19 1/2 cm. (West Point Ser.). 1907. The Penn Publishing Company.

--A West Point Yearling. Carter, F. A., illus. LC 35-8375. 4 p., 1 l., 9-383 p. front. 19 cm. c.1935. The Penn Publishing Company.

--Winning His Way to West Point. Carter, F. A., illus. 420 p. front., 6 pl. 19 cm. (Historical Stories Ser. for Boys and Girls). 1904. The Penn Publishing Company.

--Winning His Way to West Point. Carter, F. A., illus. LC 32-161173. 3 p. l., 5-420 p. front., plates. 19 cm. 1932. The Penn Publishing Company.

Malone, Ruth (1918-)

--Here No Evil. LC 72-8001. 139 p. 22cm. 1973. (ISBN 0-664-32522-X). Westminster Press.

--Mystery of the Golden Ram. LC 75-34158. 128 p. 21cm. c.1976. (ISBN 0-664-32585-8). Westminster Press.

Maloney, Shirley A

--Albi Angel, the Little Star of Bethlehem. Cassell, Robert H., illus. LC 77-23458. (Illus.). 40 p. 23cm. c.1977. (ISBN 0-570-03466-3). Concordia Pub. House.

Maloney, Thomas James (1904-)

--Isabelle Elizabeth, the Duck That Lived Alone. Mariinsky, Vaslov, illus. LC 45-2279. 65 p. col. illus. 26 cm. c.1944. U.S. Camera Publishers.

Malory, Thomas, Sir, jt. auth. see Creswick, Paul.

Malory, Thomas, Sir, jt. auth. see Macgregor, Mary Esther Miller, Mrs.

Malory, Thomas Sir, jt. auth. see Spenser, Edmund.

Malory, Thomas, Sir, jt. auth. see Sutcliff, Rosemary.

Malory, Thomas, Sir, jt. auth. see Tennyson, Alfred Lord.

Malory, Thomas, Sir (1410-1471)

--The Book of King Arthur and His Noble Knights. Macleod, Mary (0000-1914), ed. Pitz, Henry Clarence (1895-1976), illus. Patri, Angelo, intro. by. LC 49-9837. (Stories from Sir Thomas Malory's Morte D'Arthur). xvi, 824 p. illus. (part col.) 23 cm. (Lippincott classics). 1949. J. B. Lippincott Co.

--Book of King Arthur and of his Noble Knights of the Round Table. (Globe Ser.). N.D. Macmillan & Co.

--The Boy's King Arthur. Kappes, Alfred, illus. LC 4-11296. (Illus.). xvii, 403p. 20cm. (The Boy's Library of Legend and Chivalry). 1903. C. Scribner.

--The Boy's King Arthur. Lanier, Sidney (1842-1881), ed. Kappes, Alfred, illus. (Being Sir Thomas Malory's History of King Arthur and His Knights of the Round Table). xlvii, 408 p. front., 11 pl. 20 1/2 cm. (On cover: The boy's library of legend and chivalry). 1903. C. Scribner's Sons.

--The Boy's King Arthur. Lanier, Sidney (1842-1881), ed. Kappes, Alfred, illus. LC 8-30029. (Being Sir Thomas Malory's History of King Arthur and His Knights of the Round Table). xlvii, 403 p. front., 11 pl. 20 1/2 cm. (On back of cover: The boy's library of legend and chivalry). 1908. C. Scribner's Sons.

--The Boy's King Arthur. Lanier, Sidney (1842-1881), ed. Wyeth, Newell Convers (1882-1945), illus. LC 17-28104. (Sir Thomas Malory's History of King Arthur and His Knights of the Round Table). 7 p. l., 3-321 p. col. plates. 24 1/2 cm. 1917. C. Scribner's Sons.

--The Boy's King Arthur. Lanier, Sidney (1842-1881), ed. LC 24-24368. (Being Sir Thomas Malory's History of King Arthur and His Knights of the Round Table). xlvii, 403 p. incl. front. 19 1/2 cm. c.1924. C. Scribner's Sons.

--The Boy's King Arthur. Lanier, Sidney (1842-1881), ed. Wyeth, Newell Convers (1882-1945), illus. LC 73-173451. (Sir Thomas Mallory's History of King Arthur and His Knights of the Round Table). (Illus.). 321 p. 23cm. (Scribner library). (The Scribner Illustrated Classics). N.D. (ISBN 0-684-20871-7). (ISBN 0-684-13417-9). Scribner.

--King Arthur. MacLeod, Mary (0000-1914), retold by. Davenport, Basil, intro. by. LC 53-13343. (Stories from Sir Thomas Malory's Morte D'Arthur). 246p. illus. 22cm. (Great illustrated classics). 1953. Dodd, Mead.

--King Arthur. Macleod, Mary (0000-1914), retold by. Levit, Herschel (1912-), illus. Fadiman, Clifton, afterword by. LC 63-148306. (Stories from Thomas Malory's Morte D'Arthur). x, 316p. illus. (pt. col.) 24cm. (Macmillan classics). c.1963. Macmillan.

--King Arthur and His Knights. (Illus.). (Stories Old and New Ser.). N.D. Caldwell.

--King Arthur and His Knights. Kottmeyer, William (1910-), ed. LC 52-32077. 122 p. illus. 21 cm. (Junior everyreaders). 1952. Webster Pub. Co.

--King Arthur and His Knights. Kottmeyer, William (1910-), ed. (Illus.). 21cm. 122p. (Junior everyreaders). 1962, c.1952. Webster.

--King Arthur and His Knights. MacLeod, Mary (0000 1914), retold by. Pyle, Howard (1853-1911), illus. LC 64-15717. (Illus.). 324 p. 21cm. (Classics to grow on). 1966, c.1964. Parents' Magazine's Cultural Institute.

--King Arthur and His Knights: A Noble and Joyous History. Allen, Philip Schuyler (1871-), ed. Schaeffer, Mead (1898-1980) & Neill, John Rea (1878-1943), illus. LC 25-3028. xiii, 455 p. col. front., illus., col. plates. 23 1/2 cm. (Windermere series). c.1924. Rand, McNally & Company.

--King Arthur and His Knights of the Round Table. De luxe ed. Lanier, Sidney (1842-1881), ed. Florian, illus. LC 20-12314. (From Sir Thomas Malory's Le Morte D'Arthur). 282 p. illus. (part. col.) 24 cm. (Illustrated junior library). 1950. Grosset & Dunlap.

--King Arthur and His Knights of the Round Table. Popular ed. Lanier, Sidney (1842-1881), ed. Florian, illus. LC 20-12312. (From Sir Thomas Malory's Le Morte D'Arthur). 280 p. illus. (part. col.) 21 cm. (Illustrated junior library). 1950. Grosset & Dunlap.

--King Arthur and His Knights of the Round Table. Special ed. Lanier, Sidney (1842-1881), ed. Florian, illus. LC 50-12313. (From Sir Thomas Malory's Le Morte D'Arthur). 282 p. illus. (part col.) 24 cm. (illustrated junior library. 1950. Grosset & Dunlap.

--King Arthur & His Knights of the Round Table. Lanier, Sidney (1842-1881) & Pyle, Howard (1853-1911), eds. Florian, illus. (Illus.). (gr. 4-6). N.D. (ISBN 0-448-05816-2, G&D). (ISBN 0-448-06016-7). Putnam Pub Group.

--King Arthur and His Noble Knights. Macleod, Mary (0000-1914), ed. LC 4-11297. (Stories from Sir Thomas Malory's Morte D'Arthur). xxi, 383 p. front., illus. 19 cm. (On cover: The Home library). 1902. A. L. Burt Co.

--King Arthur and the Knights of the Round Table. Johnson, Clifton (1865-), ed. Thomson, Rodney, illus. LC 16-21578. xii, 335 p. col. front., illus., col. plates, map. 19 1/2 cm. 1916. The Macmillan Company.

--King Arthur and the Knights of the Round Table. Morris, Charles (1833-1922), ed. LC 12-37034. (A Modernized Version of the "Morte Darthur."). 3 v. 17 1/2 cm. 1891. J. B. Lippincott Company.

--King Arthur and the Knights of the Round Table. Stead, William Thomas (1849-), ed. Le Fanu, Brinsley, illus. LC 8-23089. 19cm. 64p. 1908. Penn Publishing Co.

--King Arthur and the Knights of the Round Table. Wright, T., illus. N.D. Distributed by Charles Scribner's Sons.

--King Arthur Stories from Malory. Stevens, Lillian O. & Allen, Edward Frank (1865-), eds. LC 8-37172. (Done from the Text of Sir Thomas Malory's Morte D'Athur). xiv, 188, 2 p. front., illus., 6 pl. (2 double) 18 cm. (Riverside literature series). c.1908. Houghton Mifflin Company.

--King Arthur: Stories from Sir Thomas Malory's Morte D'Arthur. MacLeod, Mary, ed. Levit, Herschel (1912-), illus. (gr. 6 up). 1963. Macmillan.

--Malory's King Arthur and His Knights. Lathrop, H. B., ed. (Illus.). N.D. Baker & Taylor Co.

--Merlin and Sir Balin. (Riverside Literature Ser.). N.D. Houghton Mifflin Co.

--Morte D'Arthur. N.D. (ISBN 0-671-00961-3). Monarch Pr.

--Stories from King Arthur. 96 p. illus., 6 col. pl. (incl. front.) 20 1/2 cm. (Great writers for young readers). 1935. Oxford University Press, H. Milford.

--Stories of King Arthur. (Illus.). 96p. (Fairy Tale Ser.). N.D. Cassell & Co.

--Stories of King Arthur. Cutler, Uriel Waldo (1854-), ed. Blaisdell, Elinore (1904-), illus. LC 41-16602. 4 p. l., 308 p. col. front., col. plates (part double) 21 1/2 cm. c.1941. Thomas Y. Crowell Company.

--Stories of King Arthur & His Knights. Cutler, Uriel Waldo (1854-), ed. LC 4-27124. xviii, 318 p. front., plates. 17 1/2 cm. 1904. T. Y. Crowell & Co.

--Stories of King Arthur and His Knights. Cutler, Uriel Waldo (1854-), ed. LC 24-14786. xix, 308 p. col. front., col. plates. 21 cm. c.1924. Thomas Y. Crowell Company.

--The Story of Sir Galahad. Sterling, Mary Blackwell, ed. Chapman, William Ernest, illus. LC 8-323748. (Retold from Le Morte D'Arthur of Sir Thomas Malory and the Original Stories). xii p., 1 l., 223 p. col. front., illus. (6 col. pl.) 21 1/2 cm. c.1908. E. P. Dutton & Co.

--The Wandering Knight. Schiller, Barbara, adapted by. Levit, Herschel (1912-), illus. LC 74-157949. (Illus.). 54 p. 22cm. 1971. (ISBN 0-525-42200-5). Dutton.

Malot, Hector Henri (1830-1907)

--The Adventures of Perrine: En Famille. Heal, Edith (1903-), ed. Winter, Milo Kendall (1888-1956), illus. Meynier, Gil (1902-), tr. LC 32-21196. 284 p. col. front., col. plates. 23 1/2 cm. (Windermere classics). c.1932. Rand, McNally & Company.

--Adventures of Remi. Schaeffer, Mead (1898-1980), illus. Allen, Philip Schuyler (1871-), tr. (Windermere Ser.). N.D. Rand McNally.

--The Little Sister: La Petite Soeur. Gooch, Thelma, illus. Crewe-Jones, Florence, tr. LC 28-16163. x p., 1 l., 303 p. front., plates. 20 cm. 1928. Cupples & Leon Company.

--Nobody's Boy. Crewe-Jones, Florence, tr. LC 62-131811. 307p. 23cm. 1962. Platt & Munk.

--Nobody's Boy. Gooch, Thelma, illus. Crewe-Jones, Florence, tr. LC 30-17177. 6 p. l., 307, 1 p. col. front. col. plates. 24 1/2 cm. c.1930. Cupples and Leon Company.

--Nobody's Boy. Gruelle, John Barton (1880-1938), illus. 384p. N.D. Cupples & leon Company.

--Nobody's Boy. Jones, Florence Crewe, illus. (Children's Classics). N.D. Platt & Munk.

--Nobody's Girl. Crewe-Jones, Florence, tr. LC 62-131821. 301p. 23cm. 1962. Platt & Munk.

--Nobody's Girl. Gooch, Thelma, illus. Crewe-Jones, Florence, tr. LC 29-24373. 6 p. l., 301 p. col. front., col. plates. 24 1/2 cm. c.1929. Cupples and Leon Company.

--Nobody's Girl: En Famille. Gooch, Thelma, illus. Crewe-Jones, Florence, tr. LC 22-176169. vi p., 2 l., 316 p. front., plates. 20 1/2 cm. 1922. Cupples & Leon Company.

--Remi. Herd, Constance, illus. (Illus.). drawings. (gr. 3-6). 1970. Hawthorn.

--Romain Kalbris, 1 of 3 Vols. (Illus.). (Holiday Library). N.D. Set. Porter & Coates.

--Romain Kalbris. Bayard, Emile, illus. Wright, Julia McNair, tr. (Illus.). (Roundabout Lib.). N.D. Henry T. Coates & Co.

--Romain Kalbris, His Adventures by Sea and Land. Bayard, Emile, illus. Wright, Julia McNair, tr. N.D. Porter & Coates.

--Ronnie: Romain Kalbris. Gooch, Thelma, illus. Crewe-Jones, Florence, tr. LC 37-9478. x, 310 p. front., plates. 20 cm. 1937. Cupples & Leon Company.

--Sea Shore: or, The Adventures of Romain Kalbris. Bayard, Emile, illus. Wright, Julia McNair, tr. from French. 1882. Porter & Coates.

Maloy, Lois (1902-)

--Arabella of the Merry-Go-Round. LC 35-27381. 64 p. illus. (part col.) 21 x 24 1/2 cm. c.1935. London, C. Scribner's Sons.

--Polly, Prue & Penny. LC 37-147397. 47 p. col. illus. 18 1/2 x 22 1/2 cm. 1937. Lothrop, Lee and Shepard Company.

--St. George and the Dragon. N.D. Charles Scribner's Sons.

--The Star Wish. LC 40-30570. 4 p. l., 109 p. illus., col. plates. 21 cm. 1940. C. Scribner's Sons.
--Swift Thunder of the Prairie: An American Adventure. LC 42-18440. 4 p. l., 73, 1 p. illus. (part col.) 24 cm. 1942. C. Scribner's Sons.
--Tea Party in Plumpudding Street. LC 46-8240. 52 p. illus. 23 1/2 cm. 1946. Grosset & Dunlap.
--Toby Can Fly. Maloy, Lois (1902-), illus. LC 48-3304. 32 p. col. illus. 19 cm. 1945. Grosset & Dunlap.
--Toby's House. LC 48-33054. 32 p. col. illus. 19 cm. c.1946. Grosset & Dunlap.
--Yankee Sails to China: An American Adventure. Maloy, Lois (1902-), illus. LC 43-17345. 3 p. l., 210 p. illus. 21 cm. 1943. C. Scribner's Sons.

Malpas, Philip Alfred
--The Little Builders and Their Voyage to Rangi. A Story for Children. Tingley, Katherine A. Westcott (1852-), ed. Machell, R. W., illus. LC 1-29772. 42 p. incl. illus., pl. 14 1/2 x 14 cm. 1900. The Theosophical Publishing Co.; Etc., Etc.

Malroy, Geneva de
--Hilla of Finland. Anderson, Frederic A., illus. 287p. N.D. Thomas Nelson & Sons.

Malter, Morton S
--Our Largest Animals. LC 58-12317. (Illus.). 32 p. 25cm. 1958. A. Whitman.

Malvern, Corinne (1905-1956)
--How Big?. Malvern, Corinne (1905-1956), illus. LC 49-48152. 28 p. col. illus. 21 cm. (Little golden library, no. 83). 1949. Simon and Schuster.

Malvern, Corinne (1905-1956), illus.
--Counting Rhymes. LC 47-1531. 42 p. illus. (part col.) 20 x 17 cm. (On cover: The Little golden library. 12). 1946. Simon and Schuster.
--Heidi. Reissue of 1956 ed. (Little Golden Book). N.D. Golden Press.
--The Little Golden Book of Poetry. LC 47-5528. 42 p. illus. (part col.) 20 cm. (The Little Golden Library). 1947. Simon and Schuster.
--Nursery Songs. Gale, Leah, contrib. by. (Little Golden Book). 1942. Golden Press.
--Storytime Tales. (Big Golden Book). 1950. Golden Press.
--Storytime Tales: A Treasury of 67 Favorite Stories, Poems, and Songs, Old and New. LC 50-9569. 208 p. col. illus. 28 cm. (Big golden book, 471). 1950. Simon and Schuster.

Malvern, Gladys (0000-1962)
--Ann Lawrence of Old New York. Malvern, Corinne (1905-1956), illus. LC 47-2263. 6 p. l., 203 p. illus. 19 1/2 cm. 1947. J. Messner, Inc.
--Behold Your Queen. Malvern, Corinne (1905-1956), illus. (gr. 6-9). 1951. (ISBN 0-679-20021-5). McKay.
--Brownie, the Little Bear Who Liked People. Malvern, Corinne (1905-1956), illus. LC 41-723. 59 p. incl. col. front., col. illus. 17 cm. (On cover: The little color classics). c.1939. McLoughlin Brothers, Inc.
--Curtain's at Eight: A Gladys Malvern Presentation. LC 57-6645. 207 p. 22cm. 1957. Macrae Smith.
--Dear Wife. Malvern, Corinne (1905-1956), illus. LC 53-7240. (Illus.). 245 p. 22cm. 1953. Longmans, Green.
--Eric's Girls. Malvern, Corinne (1905-1956), illus. LC 49-80881. 244 p. illus. 20 cm. 1949. J. Messner.
--Foreigner. Malvern, Corinne (1905-1956), illus. (Illus.). (gr. 9 up). 1954. (ISBN 0-679-20058-4). McKay.
--The Foreigner: The Story of a Girl Named Ruth. 1st ed. Malvern, Corinne (1905-1956), illus. LC 54-5952. 214p. illus. 27cm. 1954. Longmans, Green.
--Gloria, Ballet Dancer. LC 46-6362. 4 p. l., 184 p. 19 1/2 cm. 1946. J. Messner, Inc.
--Heart's Conquest. LC 62-18432. 185p. 22cm. 1962. Macrae Smith Co.
--Hollywood Star. LC 53-7454. 182p. 21cm. (Romance for young moderns). 1953. J. Messner.
--Jonica's Island. Malvern, Corinne (1905-1956), illus. LC 45-492460. 255 p. illus. 19 cm. 1945. J. Messner, Inc.
--Mamzelle: A Romance for Teen-Age Girls Set in the Days of Dolly Madison. LC 55-10733. 208 p. 21cm. 1955. Macrae Smith.
--Meg's Fortune. Malvern, Corinne (1905-1956), illus. LC 50-6059. viii, 182 p. 21cm. 1950. Messner.
--My Lady, My Love. LC 57-14840. (An Historical Junior Novel About Isabella of Valois). 206p. 22cm. 1957. Macrae Smith.
--Patriots Daughter: The Story of Anastasia Lafayette for Teen-Age Girls. LC 60-9184. 222p. 21cm. 1960. Macrae Smith.
--Prima Ballerina. LC 51-13113. 179 p. 21cm. (Romance for young moderns). 1951. Messner.
--The Queen's Lady. LC 63-12440. 191p. 22cm. c.1963. Macrae.
--Rhoda of Cyprus. LC 58-12066. 190 p. 22cm. 1958. Macrae Smith Co.
--Rogues and Vagabonds: A Novel About the First Acting Troupe to Play in America. LC 59-8242. 188p. 22cm. 1959. Macrae Smith Co.
--Saul's Daughter. 1st ed. Bock, Vera, illus. LC 56-5647. 241p. 21cm. 1956. Longmans, Green.
--So Great a Love. LC 62-10289. 190 p. 22cm. 1962. Macrae Smith Co.
--Stephanie. 221p. 21cm. 1956. Macrae Smith Co.
--The Story Book of Brownie and Rusty. Malvern, Corinne (1905-1956), illus. LC 40-8663. 34 p. incl. col. front., col. illus. 28 x 22 cm. c.1940. McLoughlin Bros., Inc.
--Tamar. LC 52-5737. 211 p. 21 cm. 1952. Longmans, Green.
--There's Always Forever. 1st ed. Thomas, Allan (1901-), illus. LC 57-10522. 182p. illus. 21cm. 1957. Longmans, Green.
--Valiant Minstrel. N.D. Julian Messner.
--Wilderness Island. LC 61-830163. 190p. c.1961. Macrae Smith.
--The World of Lady Jane Grey. LC 64-23320. (Illus.). 192 p. 22cm. 1964. Vanguard Press.
--Your Kind Indulgence: A Romance of the Theatre in Old New York. Malvern, Corinne (1905-1956), illus. LC 48-6281. vii, 213 p. illus. 21 cm. 1948. J. Messner.

Maly, Milos, retold by.
--Scandinavian Fairy Tales. Liesler, Josef, illus. LC 75-315633. (Illus.). 3, 195 p. 29cm. 1973. (ISBN 0-600-38077-7). Hamlyn.

Malzberg, Barry N., jt. auth. see Pronzini, Bill.
Malzberg, Barry N., jt. auth. see Zebrowski, George.
Malzberg, Barry N., jt. ed. see Ferman, Edward Lewis.
Malzberg, Barry N., jt. auth. see Holly, J. Hunter.

Malzberg, Barry N (1939-)
--Conversations. LC 74-17686. 87 p. 22cm. 1975. (ISBN 0-672-52043-5). Bobbs-Merrill.

Mamin, Dmitril Narkisovich (1852-1912)
--Verotchka's Tales. Artzybasheff, Boris Mikhailovich (1899-1965), illus. Davidson, Ray, tr. LC 22-209543. v. p., 1 l., 190 p. incl. illus., plates. 21 cm. c.1922. E. P. Dutton & Company.

Mamlock, Gwyneth
--Betsy's Adventure. Mamlock, Gwyneth, illus. LC 64-57445. (Illus.). 33cm. 1964. Golden Press.
--Magic Carpet to Animal Rhyme Land. (Illus.). (gr. k-3). 1962. (ISBN 0-8178-3341-2). Harvey.
--Magic Carpet to Nursery Rhyme Land. (Illus.). (gr. k-3). 1962. (ISBN 0-8178-3331-5). Harvey.

Mamlok, Gwyneth
--Sun Shone on the Elephant. Mamlok, Gwyneth, illus. (Illus.). 32p. (gr. 1-4). 1968 (Golden Pr). Western Pub.

Mammen, Edward William (1907-)
--The Buttons Go Walking. 1st ed. Robinson, Jessie Berkowitz, illus. LC 40-27702. 40 p. illus. 28 x 22 cm. c.1940. (ISBN 0-06-024051-2). Harper & Brothers.
--Jim's the Boy!. Robinson, Jessie Berkowitz, illus. LC 42-19687. 40 p. illus. 28 x 21 1/2 cm. 1942. Harper & Brothers.
--Tom, Dick and Jerry. Robinson, Jessie Berkowitz, illus. LC 41-20168. 32 p. illus. 19 1/2 x 24 1/2 cm. c.1941. Harper & Brothers.
--Turnipseed Jones. 1st ed. Robinson, Jessie Berkowitz, illus. LC 50-6441. (Illus.). 127 p. 21cm. 1950. Harper.

Mamoulian, Rouben (1897-)
--Abigayil: The Story of the Cat at the Manger. Goodman, Marshall, illus. 48p. 1964. New York Graphic Society.

Man, Mrs. D. H. see Gray, Rosalie.

Manchel, Frank (1935-)
--An Album of Great Science Fiction Films. (Illus.). 96p. (Picture Albums Ser.). (gr. 5 up). 1982. (ISBN 0-531-04504-8). Watts.
--An Album of Modern Horror Films. (Illus.). 96p. (Picture Album Ser.). (gr. 7 up). N.D. (ISBN 0-531-04661-3). Watts.

Manchester, Charles
--Papa Rooster & Baby Chick. LC 79-63000. 27p. 1980. (ISBN 0-533-04207-0). Vantage.

Manchester, Raymond Earl (1884-)
--A Child's Book of Verses. LC 17-18039. 15 l. 19 1/2 cm. $0.2. c.1917. George Banta Publishing Company.
--In and Out the Garden Gate. LC 29-6707. 47 p. 19 1/2 cm. 1929. Collegiate Press.

Mand, Ewald (1906-)
--The World is My Home. 176p. 1952. Friendship Press.

Mandal, Sant Ram (1891-1980)
--The Happy Flute. Lathrop, Dorothy Pulis (1891-1980), ed. Lathrop, Dorothy Pulis (1891-1980), illus. LC 39-28996. 3 p. l., 53, 1 p. front., illus. 23 1/2 cm. 1939. Frederick A. Stokes Company.
--The Happy Flute. Lathrop, Dorothy Pulis, illus. N.D. J. B. Lippincott.
--Hide and Go Seek. Lathrop, Dorothy Pulis (1891-1980), illus. LC 38-34328. 40 p. illus. 26 x 23 cm. 1938. The Macmillan Company.
--Let Them Live. Lathrop, Dorothy Pulis (1891-1980), illus. N.D. Macmillan.

Mandel, Corey
--Frankenstein Locks Himself Out. Huxtable, Jimmy & Woodruff, Daniel, illus. (Illus.). (Little Book Ser). (gr. k-6). 1975. (ISBN 0-89409-004-6). Childrens Art.

Mandel, J.
--Pari & the Prince. (Little Theater Ser). (gr. 4-6). 1967. (ISBN 0-07-039855-0). McGraw.

Mandel, Oscar (1926-)
--Chi Po and the Sorcerer: A Chinese Tale for Children and Philosophers. Koon-Chiu, Lo, illus. LC 63-11826. 85p. illus. 27cm. 1963. (ISBN 0-8048-0090-1). Tuttle.

Mandelkorn, Eugenia Miller see Miller, Eugenia.

Mandell, Judith J.
--Buffalo Blinkie & the Crazy Circus Caper. Reusable ed. Lessa, William, illus. (Illus.). (gr. 3-5). 1977. (ISBN 0-89039-196-3). (ISBN 0-89039-198-X). Ann Arbor FL.

Mandell, Muriel Hortence Levin (1921-)
--Jonathan's Sparrow. Helfgott, Gloria, illus. (Illus.). (gr. 2-4). 1963. (ISBN 0-8382-0392-2). Hale.

Manderson, M. A., Mrs., tr. see Hoffmann, Franz.

Mandeville
--Lost Sheep. (Ladybird Ser.). 1979. (ISBN 0-87508-849-X). Chr Lit.

Mandeville, Sylvia, jt. auth. see Pierson, Lance.

Mandigo, Pauline E
--Jean Reade in Public Relations. LC 54-6678. 248p. 21cm. (Dodd, Mead career books). 1954. Dodd, Mead.

Mandlelkorn, Eugenia Miller see Miller, Eugenia

Mandlin, Harvey, photos by.
--Early Childhood Series, 18 Bks. large type ed. Incl. Apple Is Red. Curry, Nancy LC 67-31186. (ISBN 0-8372-0252-3); Beautiful Day for a Picnic. Curry, Nancy LC 67-31187. (ISBN 0-8372-0255-8); Benny's Four Hats. Jaynes, Ruth M. (1899-) Curry, Nancy, ed. LC 67-26370. (ISBN 0-8372-0243-4); The Biggest House. Jaynes, Ruth M. (1899-) Curry, Nancy, ed. LC 67-31188. (ISBN 0-8372-0254-X); Box Tied with a Red Ribbon. Jaynes, Ruth M. (1899-) Curry, Nancy, ed. LC 68-17034. (ISBN 0-8372-0261-2); Colors. Radlauer, Ruth Shaw (1926-) & Radlauer, Edward (1921-) Curry, Nancy, ed. LC 68-17026. (ISBN 0-8372-0259-0); Do You Know What. Jaynes, Ruth M. (1899-) Curry, Nancy, ed. LC 67-31189. (ISBN 0-8372-0253-1); Do You Suppose Miss Riley Knows. Curry, Nancy LC 67-31327. (ISBN 0-8372-0263-9); Evening. Radlauer, Ruth Shaw (1926-) & Radlauer, Edward (1921-) Curry, Nancy, ed. LC 68-17033. (ISBN 0-8372-0269-8); Father Is Big. Radlauer, Ruth Shaw (1926-) & Radlauer, Edward (1921-) (ISBN 0-8372-0240-X); Follow the Leader. Crume, Marion W. (ISBN 0-8372-0242-6); Friends, Friends, Friends. Jaynes, Ruth M. Curry, Nancy, ed. LC 67-26371. (ISBN 0-8372-0245-0); Funny Mr. Clown. Crume, Marion W. Curry, Nancy, ed. LC 67-27124. (ISBN 0-8372-0248-5); Furry Boy. Crume, Marion W. Curry, Nancy, ed. LC 67-31474. (ISBN 0-8372-0264-7); I Like Cats. Crume, Marion W. Curry, Nancy, ed. LC 67-31475. (ISBN 0-8372-0260-4); Let Me See You Try. Crume, Marion W. Curry, Nancy, ed. LC 67-31185. (ISBN 0-8372-0256-6); Listen. Crume, Marion W. LC 68-54580. (ISBN 0-8372-0251-5); The Littlest House. Curry, Nancy LC 68-17032. (ISBN 0-8372-0258-2); Melinda's Christmas Stocking. Jaynes, Ruth M. (1899-) Curry, Nancy, ed. LC 68-17031. (ISBN 0-8372-0265-5); Morning. Crume, Marion W. Curry, Nancy, ed. LC 68-17030. (ISBN 0-8372-0268-X); My Friend Is Mrs. Jones. Curry, Nancy LC 67-26369. (ISBN 0-8372-0244-2); My Tricycle & I. Jaynes, Ruth M. (1899-) (ISBN 0-8372-0266-3); Tell Me, Please, What's That. Jaynes, Ruth M. (1899-) Curry, Nancy, ed. LC 68-17028. (ISBN 0-8372-0267-1); That's What It Is. Jaynes, Ruth M. (1899-) Curry, Nancy, ed. LC 67-31543. (ISBN 0-8372-0250-7); Three Baby Chicks. (ISBN 0-8372-0257-4); What Do You Say?. (ISBN 0-8372-0262-0); What Is a Birthday Child?. (ISBN 0-8372-0247-7); Where Is Whiffen?. (ISBN 0-8372-0246-9). (ps-3). 1967. (ISBN 0-8372-3543-X). Bowmar-Noble.
--Early Childhood Series. large-type ed. Incl. Three Baby Chicks. Jaynes, Ruth M. (1899-) Curry, Nancy, ed. LC 72-165174. (ISBN 0-8372-0257-4); Watch Me Indoors. Jaynes, Ruth M. (1899-) Curry, Nancy, ed. LC 67-31476. (ISBN 0-8372-0249-3); Watch Me Outdoors. Jaynes, Ruth M. (1899-) LC 67-25574. (ISBN 0-8372-0241-8); What Do You Say. Crume, Marion W. Curry, Nancy, ed. LC 67-31328. (ISBN 0-8372-0262-0); What Is a Birthday Child. Jaynes, Ruth M. (1899-) Curry, Nancy, ed. LC 67-27125. (ISBN 0-8372-0247-7); Where Is Whiffen. Jaynes, Ruth M. (1899-) Curry, Nancy, ed. LC 67-27126. (ISBN 0-8372-0246-9). (ps-3). 1967. Bowmar-Noble.

Mandry, Kathy
--The Cat and the Mouse and the Mouse and the Cat. Toto, Joe, illus. LC 72-175948. (Illus.). 32 p. 24cm. 1972. (ISBN 0-394-82401-6). (ISBN 0-394-92401-0). Pantheon Books.
--How to Make Elephant Bread. Toto, Joe, illus. (Illus.). (ps-4). 1971. (ISBN 0-394-92141-0). Pantheon.
--The World on My Windowsill. Toto, Joe, illus. LC 75-179937. (Illus.). 32 p. 32cm. 1971. Learning Child, Inc.

Manes, Esther & Manes, Stephen (1949-)
--The Bananas Move to the Ceiling. Samuels, Barbara, illus. LC 82-17519. p. cm. (An Easy-Read Story Book). 1983. (ISBN 0-531-03575-1). (ISBN 0-531-04517-X). F. Watts.

Manes, Stephen, jt. auth. see Manes, Esther.

Manes, Stephen (1949-)
--Be a Perfect Person in Just Three Days. Huffman, Tom, illus. LC 81-10275. (Illus.). 76 p. 21cm. c.1982. (ISBN 0-89919-064-2). Clarion Books.
--Be a Perfect Person in Just Three Days!. Huffman, Tom, illus. 1982. Houghton.
--The Boy Who Turned into a TV Set. Bass, Michael (1947-), illus. LC 78-31436. (Illus.). 32 p. c.1979. (ISBN 0-698-20491-3). Coward, McCann & Geoghegan.
--The Hoople's Haunted House. Weston, Martha, illus. LC 81-2216. (Illus.). 107 p. 24cm. c.1981. (ISBN 0-440-03733-6). (ISBN 0-440-03736-0). Delacorte Press.
--Hooples on the Highway. Peek, Merle (1938-), illus. LC 78-1710. (Illus.). 127 p. 23cm. c.1978. Coward, McCann & Geoghegan.
--I'll Live. LC 82-11538. p. cm. (Avon/Flare book). 1982. (ISBN 0-380-81737-3). Avon Books.
--Life Is No Fair!. Miller, Warren (1936-), illus. LC 84-21095. (Illus.). 32 p. 24cm. c.1985. (ISBN 0-525-44192-1). Dutton.
--Mule in the Mail. Chalmers, Mary Eileen (1927-), illus. LC 77-26193. p. cm. 1978. (ISBN 0-698-20453-0). Coward, McCann & Geoghegan.
--The Oscar J. Noodleman Television Network: The Second Strange Thing That Happened to Oscar Noodleman. Schlemme, Roy, illus. LC 83-8970. p. cm. c.1983. (ISBN 0-525-44075-5). E.P. Dutton.
--Slim Down Camp. LC 80-22725. 183 p. 22cm. c.1981. (ISBN 0-395-30170-X). Houghton Mifflin/Clarion Books.
--Socko: Every Riddle Your Feet Will Ever Need. Karlin, Nurit, illus. (Illus.). 32p. 1982. (ISBN 0-698-20538-3, Coward). Putnam Pub Group.
--That Game from Outer Space: The First Strange Thing That Happened to Oscar Noodleman. 1st ed. Auth, Tony, Jr., pseud. (1942-), illus. Auth, William Anthony. LC 82-21144. p. cm. c.1983. (ISBN 0-525-44056-9). Dutton.
--Video War. LC 82-22764. 249 p. 18cm. (Avon/Flare book). c.1983. (ISBN 0-380-83303-4). Avon Books.

Manfrini, Joseph
--Under the Buttonwood Tree. N.D. Vantage Press.

Mangelsdorf, Edward R., ed.
--A Christmas Gift. 14p. 1981. CSS Pub.

Manger, Maryland & Stevens, Robley D.
--Gobble Up Stories. N.D. (ISBN 0-8283-1400-4). Branden Press.

Mangin, Marie F.
--Suzette & Nicholas & the Seasons Clock. Ichikawa, Satomi (1939-), illus. (Illus.). 32p. (ps-k). 1982. (ISBN 0-399-20832-1, Philomel). Putnam Pub Group.

Mangin, Marie-France, jt. auth. see Lochak, Michele.

Mangione, Jerre Gerlando (1909-)
--Mount Allegro. LC 72-79794. viii, 290 p. 22cm. 1972. (ISBN 0-517-50071-X). Crown Publishers.

Mango, Karin N
--A Various Journey. LC 82-20968. 196 p. 22cm. c.1983. (ISBN 0-590-07856-9). Four Winds Press.

Mangurian, David
--Children of the Incas. (Illus.). (gr. 3-6). 1979. Four Winds.
--Lito The Shoe Shine Boy. 48p. 1975. (ISBN 0-590-07382-6). Four Wind Press.

--A Book of Devils and Demons. Jacques, Robin (1920-), illus. LC 79-116884. (Illus.). 124 p. 25cm. 1970. (ISBN 0-525-26794-8). Dutton.
--A Book of Dragons. LC 65-19578. (Illus.). 128 p. 24cm. 1965, c.1964. E. P. Dutton.
--A Book of Dwarfs. LC 64-17339. (Illus.). 127 p. 25cm. 1964, c.1963. Dutton.
--A Book of Enchantments and Curses. LC 76-58423. (Illus.). 128 p. 24cm. 1977, c.1976. Dutton.
--A Book of Ghosts and Goblins. Jacques, Robin (1920-), illus. LC 71-81719. (Illus.). 126 p. 21cm. (Dutton anytime books). 1974, c.1973. (ISBN 0-525-45014-9). E. P. Dutton.
--A Book of Giants. LC 63-157538. (Illus.). 124 p. 25cm. 1963, c.1962. Dutton.
--A Book of Kings and Queens. 1st ed. Jacques, Robin (1920-), illus. LC 77-16462. (Illus.). 125 p. 25cm. 1978, c.1977. (ISBN 0-525-26925-8). Dutton.
--A Book of Magic Animals. 1st ed. Jacques, Robin (1920-), illus. LC 74-28306. (Illus.). 127 p. 25cm. 1975, c.1974. (ISBN 0-525-26935-5). Dutton.
--Book of Witches. Jacques, Robin (1920-), illus. (gr. 2-6). 1966. Dutton.
--A Book of Witches. Jacques, Robin (1920-), illus. LC 66-14685. 126p. illus. 25cm. 1966, c.1965. Dutton.
--Damian & the Dragon: Modern Greek Folk & Fairy Tales. Papas, William (1927-), illus. (Illus.). (gr. 4-7). N.D. Roy.
--Elephant. N.D. J. B. Lippincott.
--Elephant. 1938. Stokes.
--Festivals. Briggs, Raymond Redvers (1934-), illus. (Illus.). 192p. (gr. 2-6). 1973. Dutton.
--Gianni & the Ogre. Stobbs, William (1914-), illus. LC 78-133113. (Illus.). 25 cm. 191p. 1971. (ISBN 0-525-30540-8). Dutton.
--Mystery at Penmarth. Suba, Susanne (1913-), illus. LC 41-16008. 246 p. incl. front., plates. 19 1/2 cm. c.1941. R. M. McBride & Company.
--Red Indian Folk and Fairy Tales. Hodges, Cyril Walter (1909-), illus. 1962. Roy.
--The Red King and the Witch. 1965. Roy Publishers, Inc.
--The Spaniards Are Coming!. Rizvi, Jacqueline, illus. LC 75-76151. (Illus.). 48 p. 23cm. (Long-ago children series). 1970, c.1969. F. Watts.
--Stories from the English and Scottish Ballads. Ridley, Trevor, illus. (Illus.). 148 p. 22cm. 1968. Dutton.

Manning-Sanders, Ruth (1895-), ed.
--A Book of Magical Beasts. Briggs, Raymond Redvers (1934-), illus. LC 79-123111. (Illus.). viii, 244 p. 26cm. 1st U.S. edition. 1970. T. Nelson.
--A Book of Mermaids. Jacques, Robin (1920-), illus. LC 68-13414. (Illus.). 127 p. 24cm. 1968, c.1967. Dutton. **Award: (ALA).**
--A Book of Monsters. 1st ed. Jacques, Robin (1920-), illus. LC 75-33252. (Illus.). 128 p. 25cm. c.1975. (ISBN 0-525-26951-7). Dutton.
--A Book of Ogres and Trolls. 1st ed. Jacques, Robin (1920-), illus. LC 73-77454. (Illus.). 127 p. 25cm. 1973, c.1972. Dutton.
--A Book of Princes and Princesses. 1st ed. Jacques, Robin (1920-), illus. LC 77-102739. (Illus.). 127 p. 24cm. 1970, c.1969. E. P. Dutton.
--A Book of Sorcerers and Spells. Jacques, Robin (1920-), illus. LC 73-16272. (Illus.). 125 p. 25cm. 1974, c.1973. (ISBN 0-525-27040-X). Dutton.
--A Book of Spooks and Spectres. 1st ed. Jacques, Robin (1920-), illus. LC 79-17673. (Illus.). 127 p. 25cm. 1979. (ISBN 0-525-27045-0). Dutton.
--A Book of Wizards. 1st ed. Jacques, Robin (1920-), illus. LC 67-2307. (Illus.). 126 p. 25cm. 1967, c.1966. Dutton.
--Bundle of Ballads. Stobbs, William (1914-), illus. (Illus.). (gr. 6-10). 1961. (ISBN 0-397-30541-9). Lippincott. **Award: (KGM).**
--A Choice of Magic. 1st ed. Jacques, Robin (1920-), illus. LC 70-157945. (Illus.). 318 p. 25cm. 1971. (ISBN 0-525-27810-9). Dutton.
--Damian and the Dragon: Modern Greek Folk-Tales. Papas, William (1927-), illus. LC 65-246413. 190 p. illus. (pt.col.) 22 cm. 1966, c.1965. Roy.
--The Glass Man and the Golden Bird: Hungarian Folk and Fairy Tales. Ambrus, Victor G., pseud. (1935-), illus. Ambrus, Gyozo Laszlo. (Illus.). 194 p. 23cm. 1968. Roy Publishers.
--Jonnikin and the Flying Basket: French Folk and Fairy Tales. 1st ed. Ambrus, Victor G., pseud. (1935-), illus. Ambrus, Gyozo Laszlo. LC 76-81720. (Illus.). 152 p. 23cm. 1969. Dutton.
--Jonnikin and the Flying Basket: French Folk and Fairy Tales. Ambrus, Victor G., pseud. (1935-), illus. Ambrus, Gyozo Laszlo. LC 73-403821. (Illus.). 23cm. vi, 152p. 1969. Oxford Univ. Press.
--Peter and the Piskies: Cornish Folk and Fairy Tales. Briggs, Raymond Redvers (1934-), illus. LC 66-115122. 215p. illus. 22cm. 1966, c.1958. Roy.
--The Red King and the Witch: Gypsy Folk and Fairy Tales. Ambrus, Victor G., pseud. (1935-), illus. Ambrus, Gyozo Laszlo. LC 65-10801. 175p. illus. (pt. col.) 23cm. 1965, c.1964. Roy.
--Stories from the English and Scottish Ballads. Ridley, Trevor, illus. LC 68-30827. 148p. illus. 22cm. 1st U.S. edition. 1968. Dutton.
--Tortoise Tales. Chaffin, Donald, illus. LC 73-18109. (Illus.). 95 p. 22cm. 1st U.S. edition. 1974. (ISBN 0-8407-6389-1). T. Nelson.

Mannix, Daniel Pratt (1911-)
--The Back-Yard Zoo. 256p. 1934. Coward-McCann.
--Drifter. 1974. (ISBN 0-88349-018-8). Readers Digest Pr.
--The Fox and the Hound. 1st ed. Schoenherr, John Carl (1935-), illus. LC 67-20531. (Illus.). 255 p. 22cm. 1967. Dutton.
--More Back-Yard Zoo. 252p. 1936. Coward-McCann.
--The Outcasts. Shortall, Leonard W., illus. LC 65-12182. (Illus.). 93p. illus. 21cm. c.1965. (ISBN 0-525-36496-X). Dutton.
--The Secret of the Elms. 213p. 18cm. (Berkley Medallion Book). 1977, c.1975. (ISBN 0-425-03359-7). Berkley Pub. Corp.
--The Secret of the Elms. LC 75-12935. 264 p. 21cm. 1975. (ISBN 0-88349-072-2). Reader's Digest Press : Distributed by Crowell.
--Walt Disney Productions Presents Tod and Vixey from the Fox and the Hound. Disney, Walt, Productions, illus. LC 81-5209. p. cm. (Disney's Wonderful World of Reading ; 50: No. 50). 1981. (ISBN 0-394-84904-3). (ISBN 0-394-94904-8). Random House.

Mannix, Jule
--Adventure Happy. 1954. Simon and Schuster.

Mannix, Mary
--Lee Devins, Copywriter. LC 57-65902. 187p. 21cm. (Romance for young moderns). 1957. J. Messner.

Mannix, Mary Ellen (1846-), tr. see Carnot, Maurus.

Mannix, Mary Ellen, Mrs. (1846-)
--As True As Gold. LC 7-40794. 162 p. front. 17 1/2 cm. (On verso of t.-p.: Benziger's juvenile series). c.1900. Benziger Brothers.
--The Children of Cupa. LC 5-35505. 169 p. front. 17 1/2 cm. 1905. Benziger Brothers.
--Cupa Revisited. vi, 7-136 p. front. 17 1/2 cm. $0.45. 1909. Benziger Brothers.
--The Fortunes of a Little Emigrant. LC 1308. 267 p. 18 cm. 1900. The Ave Maria.
--The Haldeman Children. LC 4-5915. 154 p. front. 17 1/2 cm. 1894. Benziger Brothers.
--In Quest of Adventure. N.D. Benziger Brothers.
--On the Old Camping Ground. LC 16-6315. 162 p. front. 19 cm. $0.85. 1916. Benziger Brothers.
--Pancho and Panchita. A Tale of the Southwest. 146 p. incl. front. 17 cm. 1900. Benziger Brothers.
--The Tales Tim Told Us. LC 99-1156. 158 p. 19 cm. c.1898. The Ave Maria.

Mannouth, E. H. see Homespun, Sophia, pseud.

Manoni, Mary H.
--Cynthia's Great Paint Adventure. Mahoney, Susan, ed. McKissack, Vernon, illus. (Illus.). 16p. (Raggedy Ann's & Raggedy Andy's Friends Ser.). (gr. k-3). N.D. (ISBN 0-89290-067-9). Soc for Visual.
--Raggedy Ann & the Mouse. Mahoney, Susan, ed. McKissack, Vernon, illus. (Illus.). 16p. (Raggedy Ann's & Raggedy Andy's Friends Book Cassettes). (gr. k-3). 1979. (ISBN 0-89290-064-4). Soc for Visual.
--Raggedy Arthur & Raggedy Andy. Mahoney, Susan, ed. McKissack, Vernon, illus. (Illus.). 16p. (Raggedy Ann's & Raggedy Andy's Friends Book Cassettes). (gr. k-3). 1979. (ISBN 0-89290-065-2). Soc for Visual.
--Scotty & the Kittens. Mahoney, Susan, ed. McKissack, Vernon, illus. (Illus.). 16p. (Raggedy Ann's & Raggedy Andy's Friends Ser.). (gr. k-3). 1979. (ISBN 0-89290-066-0). Soc for Visual.

Manoni, Mary Hallahan, jt. auth. see Himmel, Roger J.

Manoni, Mary Hallahan (1924-), ed. see Himmel, Roger J.

Mansbridge, Arthur
--Millicent Mouse and Her Funny Wee House. Ellerby, Jessie May, illus. N.D. Frederick Warne & Co.

Mansefield, John
--Bird of Dawning. 304p. (Century Seafarers Ser.). (gr. 6 up). 1984. (ISBN 0-7126-0334-4). Hippocrene Bks.

Mansell, C. R.
--Ragtail Patrol. Bertram, Prance, illus. N.D. Macmillan.

Mansergh, Jessie, pseud., see Vaizey, Jessie Bell.

Mansergh, Jessie, pseud. (1857-)
--The Daughters of a Genius. Vaizey, Jessie Bell. (The Girls' Own Library). N.D. David McKay.
--Sisters Three. Vaizey, Jessie Bell. (The Girls Own Library). N.D. David McKay.
--Tom and Some Other Girls. Vaizey, Jessie Bell. (The Girls' Own Library). N.D. David McKay.

Mansfield, Blanche McManus see McManus, Blanche.

Mansfield, Blanche McManus, Mrs. (1869-)
--Gerard: Our Little Belgian Cousin. Mansfield, Blanche McManus (1869-), illus. LC 11-4099. vi p., 2 l., 106 p. front., illus. (map) 5 pl. 19 1/2 cm. (The Little cousin series). 1911. L. C. Page & Company.
--Our Little Arabian Cousin. Mansfield, Blanche McManus (1869-), illus. LC 7-20709. vi p., 2 l., 93 p. front., illus. (map) 5 pl. 20 cm. (On verso of half-title: The little cousin series). 1907. L. C. Page & Company.
--Our Little Dutch Cousin. Mansfield, Blanche McManus (1869-), illus. LC 6-18353. vi p., 1 l., 2, 99 p. front., illus. (map) 5 pl. 19 1/2 cm. (On verso of half-title: The little cousin series). 1906. L. C. Page & Company.
--Our Little Egyptian Cousin. Mansfield, Blanche McManus (1869-), illus. LC 8-23100. vii p., 1 l., 2, 131 p. front., illus. (map) 5 pl. 20 cm. (On verso of half-title: The Little cousin series). N.D. L. C. Page & Company.
--Our Little English Cousin. Mansfield, Blanche McManus (1869-), illus. LC 5-24184. viii p., 2 l. 108 p. front., 1 illus. (map) 5 pl. 20 cm. (On verso of half-title: The little cousin series). 1905. L. C. Page & Company.
--Our Little French Cousin. Mansfield, Blanche McManus (1869-), illus. viii p., 1 l., 2, 116 p. front., illus. (map) 5 pl. 20 cm. (On verso of half-title: The little cousin series). 1905. L. C. Page & Company.
--Our Little Hindu Cousin. Mansfield, Blanche McManus (1869-), illus. LC 7-20708. vi p., 1 l., 2-103 p. front., illus. (map) 5 pl. 20 cm. (On verso of half-title: The Little cousin series). 1907. L. C. Page & Company.
--Our Little Scotch Cousin. Mansfield, Blanche McManus (1869-), illus. LC 6-15109. vi p., 1 l., 2, 95 p. front., illus. (map) 5 pl. 19 1/2 cm. (On verso of half-title: The little cousin series). 1906. L. C. Page & Company.

Mansfield, Blanche McManus, Mrs. (1869-), ed.
--Told in the Twilight: Stories to Tell to Children. Mansfield, Blanche McManus, Mrs. (1869-), illus. LC 98-2209. 23cm. 96p. 1898. E. R. Herrick & Co.

Mansfield, John
--Juma, the Little African. Escourido, Joseph, illus. LC 65-103917. 1v. (unpaged) col. illus. 23cm. c.1965. Nelson.

Mansfield, John, jt. auth. see Downing, Brownie.

Mansfield, Katherine, et al.
--Teen-Age Treasury for Girls. Manley, Seon, ed. LC 58-11366. 332p. 24cm. (Selections: Extracts, etc.). 1958. Funk & Wagnalls.

Mansfield, Norma Bicknell, Mrs.
--Keeper of the Wolves. N.D. Rinehart & Co.
--McAllister Patrol. King, Ruth, illus. LC 36-18965. vi, 201 p. front., illus. 19 1/2 cm. c.1936. Farrar & Rinehart, Incorporated.

Mansfield, Richard
--The Adventures of Beatrice and Jessie. (Cosy Corner Ser.). N.D. L. C. Page & Co.

Mansford, Charles J.
--Bully, Fag, and Hero. Vedder, S. H., illus. (Books for Young People). N.D. L. C. Page & Co.

Mansion, Horace, ed.
--Old English Nursery Songs. Anderson, Anne, illus. LC 23-26028. 87, 1 p. col. front., illus., col. plates. 28 x 21 1/2 cm. N.D. Brentano's.

Manso, Peter, jt. auth. see Hawkes, Ellen.

Manson, Beverlie
--The Fairies' Alphabet Book. LC 81-43401. (Illus.). 28 p. 29cm. c.1982. (ISBN 0-385-17544-2). Doubleday.
--The Fairies' Nighttime Book. 1st ed. LC 82-45531. (Illus.). 28 p. 29cm. (Doubleday balloon books). c.1983. (ISBN 0-385-18267-8). Doubleday.

Manson, Beverlie, illus.
--Fairy Poems for the Very Young. 1st ed. LC 80-2758. (Illus.). 30 p. 29cm. c.1982. (ISBN 0-385-17542-6). Doubleday.

Manson, Cecil & Manson, Celia
--The Adventures of Johnny Van Bart. Armour-Chelu, Ian, illus. LC 66-15490. (Illus.). vi, 202 p. 21cm. 1966, c.1965. Roy Publishers.
--Lonely One. Armour-Chelu, Ian, illus. (Illus.). (gr. 4-6). 1964. Roy.

Manson, Celia, jt. auth. see Manson, Cecil.

Mantel, S. G
--Tallmadge's Terry: Action and Espionage in the American Revolution. Ferguson, William, illus. LC 65-134954. vi.183, 1p. 21cm. bibl. c.1965. (ISBN 0-679-25147-2). McKay.
--The Youngest Conquistador. Ferguson, William, illus. LC 63-18874. (Illus.). vi, 182 p. 21cm. 1963. D. McKay Co.

Mantellini, Guetano Ettore Raffaele (1856-), tr. see Amicis, Edmondo De.

Mantinband, Gerda
--Bing Bong Bang and Fiddle Dee Dee. 1st ed. Rockwell, Anne F. (1934-), illus. LC 78-18562. (Illus.). 57 p. 25cm. (Reading-on-my-own book). c.1979. (ISBN 0-385-14211-0). (ISBN 0-385-14212-9). Doubleday.
--Papa and Mama Biederbeck. Weinhaus, Karen Ann, illus. LC 82-15619. p. cm. 1983. (ISBN 0-395-33228-1). Houghton Mifflin.

Mantle, Winifred Langford
--Chateau Holiday. Werth, Kurt (1896-), illus. LC 65-16485. (Illus.). 21cm. 207p. (gr. 5-7). 1965. (ISBN 0-03-051640-4). (ISBN 0-03-051645-5). HR&W.
--Hiding Place. Werth, Kurt (1896-), illus. LC 63-12747. (Illus.). 218p. (gr. 4-6). 1963. (ISBN 0-03-035900-7). (ISBN 0-03-035905-8). HR&W.
--Penderel Puzzle. LC 66-823751. 21cm. 224p. (gr. 4-6). 1966. (ISBN 0-03-059815-X). (ISBN 0-03-059820-6). HR&W.
--The Question of the Painted Cave. LC 66-12032. 207p. 21cm. 1966, c.1965. Holt.
--Tinker's Castle. Werth, Kurt (1896-), illus. LC 64-18254. (Illus.). 222p. (gr. 4-6). 1964. (ISBN 0-03-059820-6). HR&W.

Manton, Jo, pseud., see Gittings, Joan Grenville Manton.

Manton, Jo, pseud. (1919-) & Gittings, Robert William Victor (1911-)
--The Flying Horses: Tales from China. Gittings, Joan Grenville Manton. Collard, Derek, illus. LC 77-6344. p. cm. c.1977. (ISBN 0-03-022701-1). Holt, Rinehart and Winston.

Manuel, David, jt. auth. see Wilkerson, Don.

Manuel, Dino
--Paragraph of Life: Killer-Your Friend?. 64p. 1981. (ISBN 0-682-49724-X). Exposition.

Manuel, Don Juan (1282-1347)
--Tales from Count Lucanor. Negri, Rocco (1932-), illus. Talbot, Toby (1928-), tr. from Span. LC 73-120294. (Illus.). 64p. (gr. 4-6). 1970. Dial.

Manus, Willard (1930-)
--The Mystery of the Flooded Mine. 1st ed. Dwyer, James, illus. LC 64-13844. (Illus.). 144 p. 22cm. (Signal book). 1964. Doubleday.
--Sea Treasure. Ames, Lee Judah (1921-), illus. LC 61-12555. (Illus.). 139 p. 22cm. (Signal book). 1961. Doubleday.

Manushkin, Frances (1942-)
--The Adventures of Cap'n O. G. Readmore: To the Tune of "The Cat Came Back". Campana, Manny, illus. (Illus.). 32p. (Orig.). (ps-3). 1984. (ISBN 0-590-33246-5). Scholastic Inc.
--Annie & the Desert Treasure. Wildman, George, illus. LC 81-52853. (Illus.). 32p. (Annie Mini-Storybooks Ser.). (gr. 1-5). 1982. (ISBN 0-394-85207-9). Random.
--Annie & the Party Thieves. Wildman, George, illus. LC 81-52854. (Illus.). 32p. (Annie Mini-Storybooks Ser.). (gr. 1-5). 1981. (ISBN 0-394-85206-0). Random.
--Annie Finds Sandy. Wildman, George, illus. LC 81-52851. (Illus.). 32p. (Annie Mini-Storybooks Ser.). (gr. 1-5). 1981. (ISBN 0-394-85208-7). Random.
--Baby. Himler, Ronald Norbert (1937-), illus. LC 78-183159. (Illus.). 31 p. 1972. (ISBN 0-06-024061-X). (ISBN 0-06-024062-8). Harper & Row.
--Bubblebath!. 1st ed. Himler, Ronald Norbert (1937-), illus. LC 73-14329. (Illus.). 32 p. 1974. (ISBN 0-06-024058-X). (ISBN 0-06-024058-X). Harper & Row.
--Buster Loves Buttons!. Zimmer, Dirk, illus. LC 84-48332. (Illus.). 64p. (I Can Read Bk.). (gr. k-3). c.1985. (ISBN 0-06-024107-1). (ISBN 0-06-024108-X). HarpJ.
--Hocus & Pocus at the Circus. Hayes, Geoffrey (1947-), illus. LC 82-47704. (Illus.). 5 7/8 x 8 1/2. 64p. (18 pt.). (I Can Read Ser.). (gr. k-3). 1983. (ISBN 0-06-024091-1). (ISBN 0-06-024092-X). Har-Row.
--Hocus and Pocus at the Circus. Hayes, Geoffrey LC 82-47704. p. cm. (An I Can Read Book). c.1983. (ISBN 0-06-024091-1). (ISBN 0-06-024092-X). Harper & Row.
--Moon Dragon. Hayes, Geoffrey (1947-), illus. LC 81-20771. (Illus.). 32 p. 17cm. c.1982. (ISBN 0-02-762210-X). Macmillan.
--The Perfect Christmas Picture. Weinhaus, Karen Ann, illus. LC 79-2678. (Illus.). 5 7/8 x 8 1/2. 64p. (18 pt.). (I Can Read Bks.). (gr. k-3). 1980. (ISBN 0-06-024068-7). (ISBN 0-06-024069-5). Har-Row.
--The Perfect Christmas Picture. Weinhaus, Karen Ann, illus. LC 79-2678. p. cm. (I can read book). c.1980. (ISBN 0-06-024068-7). (ISBN 0-06-024069-5). Harper & Row.
--The Roller Coaster Ghost. Ross, David (1949-), illus. (Illus.). 64p. (Orig.). (Pick-a-Path Bks.: No. 2). (gr. 3-6). 1983. (ISBN 0-686-89402-2). Scholastic Inc.
--Shirleybird. Stuart, Carl, illus. LC 73-5489. (Illus.). 31 p. 21cm. 1975. (ISBN 0-06-024063-6). (ISBN 0-06-024064-4). Harper & Row.

AUTHOR INDEX MARICHALAR, ANTONIO

--Swinging and Swinging. Di Grazia, Thomas (0000-1983), illus. LC 74-2621. (Illus.). 23 p. 26cm. c.1976. (ISBN 0-06-024066-0). (ISBN 0-06-024067-9). Harper & Row.
--The Tickle Tree. Salzman, Yuri, illus. LC 81-12315. (Illus.). 30 p. 27cm. c.1982. (ISBN 0-89919-077-4). Clarion Books.
Manwaring, Randle (1912-)
--Crossroads of the Year: Songs of the Four Seasons). LC 75-328613. (Illus.). 10, 46 p. 21cm. 1975. (ISBN 0-85686-196-0). White Lion Publishers.
Manwell, B. M.
--Little House on the Cliff. (Illus.). 128p. (The Steadfast Ser.). N.D. Fleming H. Revell Co.
Manwell, Elizabeth Skelding Moore (1897-)
--Always Growing. (gr. 1-2). 1957. (ISBN 0-8070-1924-0). (ISBN 0-8070-1923-9). Beacon Pr.
--Always Growing. Ware, Charlotte, illus. LC 56-10077. 143p. illus. 25cm. 1957. Starr King Press.
--Growing Bigger. Fahs, Sophia Blanche Lyon (1876-1978) & Ware, Charlotte, illus. LC 42-256818. 130 p. illus. 24 1/2 x 21 cm. 1942. The Beacon Press.
Manwell, M. B.
The Boys of Monk's Harold. (The Treasure Library). N.D. Frederick Warne & Co.
Manz, Hans
--Wheeler!. Cavin, Ruth (1918-), retold by. Hofmann, Werner (1935-), illus. LC 77-125504. (Illus.). 40 p. 29cm. (Here-and-there book from Harlin Quist). c.1971. (ISBN 0-8252-0098-9). H. Quist.
--Wheeler. Hafmann, Werner (1935-), illus. (Illus.). (gr. k-3). 1970. (ISBN 0-531-01005-4) (ISBN 0-531-05005-X). Quist.
Manzi, Alberto
--White Boy. 1st ed. Molina, Charles, illus. Hughes, Serge, tr. from Ital. LC 63-14446. (Illus.). 202 p. 21cm. 1963. Macmillan.
Map, Walter
--King Herla's Quest: And Other Medieval Stories. Leekley, Thomas B., retold by. Troyer, Johannes (1902-), illus. LC 56-12037. 127p. illus. 22cm. 1956. Vanguard Press.
Mapes, Mary A., pseud., see Ellison, Virginia Howel.
Mapes, Mary A., pseud. (1910-)
--Surprise!. Ellison, Virginia Howel. N.D. Houghton Mifflin Co.
Maples, Evelyn Palmer (1919-)
--The Brass Plate Adventure. (Illus.). 16p. (Trumpet Bks.). (gr. 1-3). 1972. (ISBN 0-8309-0062-4). Herald Hse.
--Jomo, the Missionary Monkey: Trumpet Book. Farley, J. Robert, illus. LC 66-31223. (Illus.). 1966cm. 18p. 1966. Herald Pub. House.
--Lehi, Man of God. (Illus.). 20p. (Trumpet Bks.). (gr. 1-3). 1972. (ISBN 0-8309-0061-6). Herald Hse.
--The Many Selves of Ann-Elizabeth. Loeding, Charlene (1945-1970), illus. LC 72-95452. (Illus.). 34 p. 1973. (ISBN 0-8309-0093-4). Independence Press.
--Norman Learns About the Sacraments. Logan, Beverly, illus. (Illus.). 40p. Repr. of 1961 ed. (gr. 1-3). 1972. (ISBN 0-8309-0064-0). Herald Hse.
Mar, Graham
--The Little Tin Soldier. (Illus.). N.D. J B Lippincott.
Mar, Helena Harriet De see De Mar, Helena Harriet.
Mar, S. Y. Lu
--Chinese tales of folklore. Simon, Howard (1903-1979), illus. (Illus.). 1964. Criterion Books.
Marais, Eugene
--The Soul of the Cape. (Illus.). 1969. (ISBN 0-689-10175-9). Atheneum Publishers.
Marais, Josef (1905-1978)
--Koos, the Hottentot: Tales of the Veld. Stahlhut, Henry, illus. LC 45-35236. 2 p. l., 188, 8 p. illus. (part col.) col. plates. 21 x 16 cm. 1945. A. A. Knopf.
Maraja, pseud., see Maraja, Libico.
Maraja, Libico see Maraja, pseud.
Maraja, pseud. & Ripamonti, Aldo, illus.
--The Frog Prince. Maraja, Libico. LC 84-18765. p. cm. (Upside down books). c.1985. Educational Development Corp.
Maran, Rene (1887-1960)
--Batouala. Seltzer, Adele Szold, Mrs. (1876-), tr. from Fr. LC 22-19479. 4 p. l., 7-207 p. 20 cm. 1922. T. Seltzer.
Marangell, Virginia Johnson (1924-)
--Gianna Mia. LC 79-52047. (Illus.). 224 p., 1 leaf of leaves. 22cm. c.1979. Dodd, Mead.
Marath, Sparrow, pseud., see Roberts, Suzanne Fleisher.
Marbach, Ethel
--The Cabbage Moth & the Shamrock. Hague, Michael R., illus. (Illus.). 1978. (ISBN 0-914676-15-6, Star & Eleph Bks). Green Tiger Pr.
--The Cabbage Moth and the Shamrock. Hague, Michael R., illus. LC 79-105790. (Illus.). 32 p. 19cm. c.1978. Star and Elephant Books.
--A Christmas Tree For All Seasons. Day, Alexandra, illus. (Illus.). 12p. (Orig.). 1982. (ISBN 0-914676-60-1, Pub. by Envelope Bks). Green Tiger Pr.
--Dandelions, Fireflies, & Rhubarb Pie: The Adventures of Grandma Bagley & Her Friends. Myers, J. William, illus. Walker, Mary Lu, read by. LC 83-51403. (Illus.). 64p. (gr. 1-7). 1984. (ISBN 0-8358-0481-X). Upper Room.
--Emily's Rainbow. Demopoulos, Maria, illus. LC 80-105683. (Illus.). 29 p., 1 leaf of plates. 23cm. c.1978 (Star & Eleph. Bks.). (ISBN 0-914676-13-X). (ISBN 0-914676-20-2). Green Tiger Press.
--Once-Upon-a-Time Saints: Faith-Tales for Children. Brzustowica, Victoria, illus. (Illus.). (gr. k-6). N.D. (ISBN 0-912228-07-7). St Anthony Mess Pr.
Marber, Scott (1956-)
--A Lot of Lumps. Olson, Jamie, illus. LC 79-62879. p. cm. 1979. (ISBN 0-933556-00-4). Scoal Press.
Marble, Annie Russell, Mrs. (1864-1936)
--From Boston to Boston: A Story of Hannah and Richard Garrett in Old England and New England in 1630. Merrill, Frank Thayer (1848-), illus. LC 30-11714. 278 p. front., plates. 23 cm. c.1930. Lothrop, Lee & Shepard Co.
--The Story of Leatherstocking. N.D. Appleton Century Co.
Marburg, Theodore (1862-)
--Bobbylinkapoo. Ver Beck, Frank (1858-1933), illus. LC 37-17659. 78 p. incl. col. front., col. illus. 24 cm. c.1937. Dorrance and Company.
Marby, Thomas, jt. auth. see Dorrance, Ward.
Marceau, Marcel (1923-)
--The Story of Bip. 1st ed. Marceau, Marcel (1923-), illus. LC 75-598. (Illus.). 30 p. 31cm. c.1976. (ISBN 0-06-024052-0). (ISBN 0-06-024053-9). Harper & Row.
Marcelin, Pierre, jt. auth. see Thoby-Marcelin, Philippe.
March, Ann, et al.
--The One Thousand Dollar Prize Series, Part Two: Containing "The Old Stone House," "Into the Light," "Margaret Worthington,"Golden Lines," "Grace Avery's Influence," etc, 8 vols. N.D. D. Lothrop & Co.
March, George Otis see Humboldt, Archibald, pseud.
March, Lez
--Easter Monkeys? You're Kidding: The Story of the Fabulous E.E.E. Adventure. LC 76-58187. (Illus.). x, 119 p. 22cm. c.1977. Coast Book Publishers.
March, William, pseud., see Campbell, William Edward March.
March, William, pseud. (1893-1954)
--Ninety Nine Fables. Campbell, William Edward March. Going, T William, ed. Brough, Richard, illus. 202p. 1960. University of Alabama Press.
Marchant, Bessie (1862-1941)
--The Bonded Three. (Illus.). (Scribner-Blackie Series of Book for Young People). N.D. Charles Scribner's Sons.
--Captives of the Kaid. (The Forward Ser.). N.D. William Collins Co.
--Diana Carries On. N.D. Nelson.
--The Ghost of Rock Grange. N.D. E. & J. B. Young & Co.
--The Girl Captives. (Illus.). (Scribner-Blackie Series of Books for Young People). N.D. Charles Scribner's Sons.
--Millicent Gwent, Schoolgirl. (The Crown Library for Boys & Girls). N.D. Frederick Warne & Co.
--The Mistress of Purity Gap. 272p. N.D. Funk & Wagnalls Co.
--The Two New Girls. (The Magnet Library). N.D. Frederick Warne & Co.
--Waifs of Woollamoo. (Three Star Bks.). N.D. Frederick Warne & Co.
Marchant, Jill, jt. auth. see Marchant, Ralph.
Marchant, Ralph & Marchant, Jill
--The Little Painter. Peppe, Rodney Darrell (1934-), illus. LC 72-170148. (Illus.). 28 p. 27cm. 1971. (ISBN 0-87614-029-0). Carolrhoda Books.
Marcher, Marion Walden (1890-)
--Bob's Summer Sleighride. Medvey, Steven, illus. LC 51-12371. (Illus.). unpaged. 22cm. 1951. Aladdin Books.
--Monarch Butterfly. N.D. E. M. Hale & Co.
Marchesi, Steve
--Alfred Hitchcock's Witch's Brew. Hitchcock, Alfred Joseph (1899-1980), ed. Marchesi, Stephen, illus. LC 77-74457. (Illus.). 171 p. 26cm. c.1977. (ISBN 0-394-93592-6). Random House.
Marci, Alfeo, tr. see Bufalari, Giuseppe.
Marcin, Chester
--Rooster Scratch and Spade Fox. 1st ed. Kilgore, Al, illus. LC 53-12695. unpaged. illus. 21cm. 1953. Pageant Press.
Marcin, Marietta
--A Zoo in Her Bed. LC 63-15546. (Illus.). 1 v. (unpaged. 1963. Coward-McCann.
Marcomb, Margaret E.
--Red Feather Stories. (Illus.). 20cm. 128p. (Long Ago Ser.). c.1916. Lyons & Carnahan.
Marcus, Edward, pseud., see McGough, Edward Marcus.
Marcus, G. J.
--The Rebels. N.D. Frederick Warne & Co.
Marcus, Leonard S.
--Petrouchka: A Ballet Cutout Book. Kendall, Jane F., illus. (Illus.). (gr. 2). 1983. (ISBN 0-87923-469-5). Godine.
Marcuse, Katherine
--Never Ask for a Goochoo Bird: A Good Manners Story. Metzl, Ervine (1899-), illus. LC 62-13579. unpaged. illus. 30cm. 1962. Parents' Magazine Press.
Marcuse, Katherine & Zepelinski, Paul
--The Devil's Workshop. LC 78-24121. (Illus.). 157 p. 23cm. c.1979. Abingdon.
Marcy, Mary Edna Tobias, Mrs. (1877-)
--Rhymes of Early Jungle Folk. LC 22-23932. 3 p. l., 11-124 p. front., illus. 25 cm. c.1922. C. H. Kerr & Co.
Marder, Eva
--The Hedgehog-Mirror. Degler-Rummel, Gisela, illus. (gr. k-2). 1975. (ISBN 0-8277-4480-3). British Bk Ctr.
Mardesic, Salvador
--The Outdoor School Tales. (Illus.). 80p. 1975. Dorrance.
Mare, Colin De La see De La Mare, Colin.
Mare, Walter John De La see De La Mare, Walter John.
Mare, Walter John de La see Child Study Association of America.
Mare, Walter John de La see De La Mare, Walter John.
Marechal, Marie
--Nannette's Marriage. Mazergue, Aimee, tr. LC 12-36613. 170 p. front. 18 cm. 1888. P. J. Kenedy.
Marek, Margot
--Different, Not Dumb. Kirk, Barbara, illus. LC 84-21900. p. cm. c.1985. F. Watts.
Marenof, Martha, ed.
--Stories Round the Year: From Rosh Hashanah to Shavuot. 160p. music. 23cm. 1960. Dot Publications.
--Stories Round the Year: From Rosh Hashanah to Shavuot. 2d rev. ed. Quint, Frances H., illus. LC 70-12656. (Illus.). 159 p. 24cm. 1969. Dot Publications.
Margaret, Karla, pseud., see Andersdatter, Karla Margaret.
Margaret, Missy
--The Little C. Lions. Waddington, Margaret, illus. (Illus.). 65p. 1980. (ISBN 0-914960-29-6, Pub. by Academy Bks). C E Tuttle.
Margaret Patrice, Sr. (1900-)
--A Lovely Gate Set Wide: A Book of Catholic Verse for Young Readers. Gillespie, Jessie, illus. LC 47-364. 160 p. illus. (part. col.) 22 cm. 1946. The Bruce Publishing Company.
--Up the Shining Path. 1946. Bruce Publishing Co.
Marge, pseud., see Buell, Marjorie Henderson.
Marge, pseud. (1904-)
--Fun with Little Lulu. Buell, Marjorie Henderson. LC 44-41830. 1944. David McKay Co.
--Laughs with Little Lulu. Buell, Marjorie Henderson. N.D. David McKay Co.
--Little Lulu. Buell, Marjorie Henderson. N.D. Rand McNally & Co.
--Little Lulu and Her Pads. Buell, Marjorie Henderson. N.D. David McKay Co.
--Little Lulu on Parade. Buell, Marjorie Henderson. N.D. David McKay Co.
--Oh, Little Lulu. Buell, Marjorie Henderson. LC 43-16465. 1943. David McKay Co.
Marger, Mary Ann (1934-)
--Justice at Peachtree. LC 80-18639. p. cm. c.1980. (ISBN 0-525-66690-7). Elsevier/Nelson Books.
--Winner at the Dub-Dub Club. LC 79-1178. 72 p. 22cm. c.1979. (ISBN 0-525-66634-6). Elsevier/Nelson Books.
Margie, pseud., see Cooper, Marjorie.
Margo, Jan
--The Make-Believe Parade. Wilkin, Eloise Burns (1904-), illus. LC 51-38461. unpaged. illus. 21 cm. (Wonder books, 520). 1949. Wonder Books.
Margolis, Ellen (1934-)
--Idy the Fox-Chasing Cow, and Other Stories. 1st ed. Werth, Kurt (1896-), illus. LC 62-9062. 64p. illus. 22cm. 1962. World Pub. Co.
Margolis, Michael Stephen (1940-)
--King Grisly-Beard. Sendak, Maurice Bernard (1928-), illus. (Illus., Pub. by Farrar, Straus & Giroux). (Picture Puffins Ser.). (gr. 1-3). 1978. (ISBN 0-14-050231-9, Puffin). Penguin.
--Some Swell Pup. Sendak, Maurice Bernard (1928-), illus. (Illus., Pub. by Farrar, Straus & Giroux). (Picture Puffins Ser.). (gr. 1-3). 1978. (ISBN 0-14-050305-6, Puffin). Penguin.
Margolis, Richard Jules (1929-)
--Big Bear, Spare That Tree. Kent, Jack, pseud. (1920-), illus. Kent, John Wellington. LC 79-16303. (Illus.). 55 p. 22cm. (Greenwillow read-alone books). c.1980. (ISBN 0-688-80248-6). (ISBN 0-688-84248-8). Greenwillow Books.
--Big Bear to the Rescue. Lopshire, Robert Martin (1927-), illus. LC 75-8583. (Illus.). 40 p. 22cm. (Greenwillow read-alone). 1975. (ISBN 0-688-80005-X). (ISBN 0-688-84005-1). Greenwillow Books.
--Big Bear to the Rescue. Lopshire, Robert Martin (1927-), illus. LC 74-19042. p. cm. (Ready-to-read). 1975. (ISBN 0-02-762450-1). Macmillan.
--Homer and the Ghost. Kessler, Leonard P. (1921-), illus. LC 74-20751. p. cm. 1973, c.1972. (ISBN 0-02-044470-2). Collier Books.
--Homer & the Ghost. Kessler, Leonard P. (1921-), illus. LC 74-20751. (Illus.). 40p. (Ready to Read Ser.). Orig. Title: Homer, the Hunter. (gr. k-3). 1976. (ISBN 0-02-044470-2, Collier). Macmillan.
--Homer the Hunter. Kessler, Leonard P. (1921-), illus. LC 73-185220. (Illus.). 37 p. 22cm. 1972. Macmillan.
--Looking for a Place. 1st ed. Koehn, Ilse (1929-), illus. LC 70-82406. (Illus.). 70 p. 24cm. 1969. Lippincott.
--Only the Moon & Me. Keegan, Marcia K. (1943-), illus. (Illus.). halftones. 64p. (gr. 7 up). 1969. (ISBN 0-397-31094-3). Lippincott.
--Secrets of a Small Brother. Carrick, Donald (1929-), illus. LC 84-3878. (Illus.). 40p. (gr. 1-4). 1984. (ISBN 0-02-762280-0). Macmillan.
--The Upside-Down King. Lorenz, Lee, illus. LC 76-159153. (Illus.). 32 p. 29cm. 1971. (ISBN 0-87807-030-3). (ISBN 0-87807-031-1). Windmill Books.
--Wish Again, Big Bear. Lopshire, Robert Martin (1927-), illus. LC 75-160070. (Illus.). 34 p. 20cm. (Ready to read). 1974, c.1972. Collier Books.
Marguerite, Mary, Sr.
--Sally and the Angels. 1958. St. Anthony Guild Press.
Margueritte, Paul (1860-1918) & Margueritte, Victor (1866-)
--Poum: The Adventures of a Little Boy. Drillien, Berengere, tr. from Fr. LC 24-4589. 2 p. l., 7-170 p. col. front., col. plates. 22 x 17 cm. 1924. A. A. Knopf.
Margueritte, Victor, jt. auth. see Margueritte, Paul.
Margulies, Leo (1900-1975), ed.
--All American Football Stories: An Anthology ... LC 49-50116. ix, 239 p. front. 20 cm. 1949. Cupples and Leon.
--Wings Over the World. LC 44-7920. 4 p. l., 433 p. front. 22 cm. c.1942. The Hampton Publishing Company.
Mari, Enzo, jt. auth. see Mari, Iela.
Mari, Iela
--Eat and Be Eaten. LC 80-65392. (Illus.). 28 p. 22cm. 1980. Barron's.
--The Little Red Balloon. LC 78-66275. (Illus.). (gr. k-3). 1979. (ISBN 0-8120-5336-2). Barron.
--The Magic Balloon. LC 69-11041. (Illus.). 32 p. 22cm. 1969, c.1967. S. G. Phillips.
Mari, Iela & Mari, Enzo (1932-)
--The Apple and the Moth. LC 70-101180. 38 p. of col. illus. 22cm. 1970, c.1969. (ISBN 0-394-90857-0). Pantheon Books.
--The Chicken and the Egg. LC 74-101181. 30 p. of col. illus. 22cm. 1970, c.1969. (ISBN 0-394-90858-9). Pantheon Books.
Maria, Hannah
--Dolly's Resolutions: Or, Letters from Abroad. N.D. Claxton,Remsen & Haffelfinger.
Mariana, pseud., see Foster, Marian Curtis.
Maria Queen Consort of Ferdinand King of Rumania (1875-1938)
--The Magic Doll of Roumania: A Wonder Story in Which East and West Do Meet, Written for American Children. Petersham, Maud Sylvia Fuller, Mrs. (1890-1971) & Petersham, Miska, pseud. (1889-1960), illus. Petersham, Mihaly Petrezselyen. LC 29-25351. xi p., 2 l., 319 p. incl. col. front., illus., col. plates. 22 cm. 1929. Frederick A. Stokes Company.
--The Queen of Roumania's Fairy Book. Groseman-Bulyghin, N., illus. LC 27-910. 223 p. col. front., plates (part col.) 22 cm. 1926. Frederick A. Stokes Company.
--The Story of Naughty Kildeen. Onfroy De Breville, Jacques Marie Gaston (1858-), illus. LC 25-767. 2 p. l., 95, 1 p. illus. (part col.) 33 cm. 1922. H. Milford, Oxford University Press.
--The Story of Naughty Kildeen. Onfroy De Breville, Jacques Marie Gaston (1858-), illus. LC 27-27810. 148 p. col. front., illus., col. plates. 21 cm. 1927. Harcourt, Brace and Company.
Marichalar, Antonio
--The Perils and Fortune of the Duke of Osuna. De Onis, Harriet, tr. N.D. J. B. Lippincott.

Marie, Geraldine & Chessare, Michele
--The Magic Box. LC 80-26096. (Illus.). 32 p. 24cm. c.1981. (ISBN 0-525-66721-0). Elsevier/Nelson Books.
Marie, Jeanne
--Opera Ballerina. (Dodd, Mead Carrer Bks.). N.D. Dodd, Mead & Co.
--Yankee Ballerina. (Dodd, Mead Career Bks.). N.D. Dodd, Mead & Co.
Marie, Rhonda
--Sally's Secret. 1982. (ISBN 0-570-08409-1). Concordia.
Marie De France
--The Shadow of the Hawk, and Other Stories. Reeves, James (1909-), ed. Dalton, Anne, illus. LC 76-28949. 154 p. 24cm. 1977. (ISBN 0-8164-3188-4). Seabury Press.
Maril, Herman, jt. auth. see Maril, Nadja.
Maril, Lee
--Mr. Bunny Paints the Eggs. Lorentowicz, Irena (1910-), illus. LC 45-5127. 28 p. incl. col. front., col. illus. 21 x 25 1/2 cm. 1945. Roy Publishers.
Maril, Nadja (1954-) & Maril, Herman
--Me, Molly Midnight, the Artist's Cat. LC 77-22708. p. cm. 1977. (ISBN 0-916144-15-1). (ISBN 0-916144-16-X). Stemmer House Publishers.
--Runaway Molly Midnight, the Artist's Cat. LC 80-17097. p. cm. 1980. (ISBN 0-916144-62-3). (ISBN 0-916144-63-1). Stemmer House Publishers.
Marilue, pseud., see Johnson, Marilue Carolyn.
Marilue, pseud., see Johnson, Marilyn Carolyn.
Marilue, pseud.
--Bobby Bear Meets Cousin Boo. Johnson, Marilue Carolyn. LC 80-82952. (Illus.). (Bobby Bear Ser.). (ps-1). 1981. (ISBN 0-87783-155-6). Oddo.
--Bobby Bear's New Home. Johnson, Marilue Carolyn. LC 78-190265. (Illus.). 32 p. 25cm. 1972. (ISBN 0-87783-054-1). Oddo Pub.
--Bobby Bear's Red Raft. Johnson, Marilyn Carolyn. LC 71-190266. (Illus.). 32 p. 25cm. 1972. (ISBN 0-87783-055-X). Oddo Pub.
--Bobby Bear's Thanksgiving. Johnson, Marilue Carolyn. LC 77-83623. (Illus.). (Bobby Bear Ser.). (ps-1). 1978. (ISBN 0-87783-143-2). (ISBN 0-87783-147-5). (ISBN 0-87783-187-4). Oddo.
--Bobby Bear's Thanksgiving. Johnson, Marilue Carolyn. Marilue, pseud., illus. Johnson, Marilue Carolyn. LC 77-83623. (Illus.). 32 p. 24cm. c.1978. (ISBN 0-87783-142-4). Oddo Pub.
Marineau, Harriet
--Feats in the Fiords. (Illus.). (Sixty-Cents Juvenile Library). N.D. George Routledge & Sons.
Marineau des Chesnez, Baroness Elizabeth Lair
--Lady Green Satin and Her Maid Rosette: The History of Jean Paul and His Little White Mice. Bromhall, Winifred, illus. 1950. Macmillan.
Marino, Barbara Pavis (1948-)
--Eric Needs Stitches. Marino, Barbara Pavis (1948-), illus. 1979. Children's Press.
--Eric Needs Stitches. Rudinski, Richard, photos by. LC 78-31694. (Illus.). 28 p. c.1979. (ISBN 0-201-04401-3). Addison-Wesley.
--Eric Needs Stitches. Rudinski, Richard, photos by. LC 84-40753. p. cm. 1985, c.1979. (ISBN 0-201-04401-3). Lippincott.
Marino, Dorothy Bronson (1912-)
--Buzzy Bear and the Rainbow. LC 62-7750. unpaged. illus. 26cm. 1962. F. Watts.
--Buzzy Bear Goes Camping. LC 64-17395. (Illus.). 26 cm. 53p. (gr. k-3). 1964. (ISBN 0-531-01629-3). Watts.
--Buzzy Bear Goes South. LC 60-949677. unpaged. illus. 26cm. c.1961. F. Watts.
--Buzzy Bear in the Garden. (Illus.). (gr. k-3). 1963. (ISBN 0-531-01631-5). Watts.
--Buzzy Bear's Busy Day. LC 65-19463. (Illus.). 33 p. 26cm. 1965. F. Watts.
--Buzzy Bear's First Day at School. LC 76-117745. (Illus.). 38 p. 27cm. 1970. F. Watts.
--Buzzy Bear's Winter Party. LC 67-3775. (Illus.). 33 p. 27cm. 33p. 1967. Watts.
--Edward & the Boxes. Marino, Dorothy Bronson (1912-), illus. LC 57-108633. (Illus.). 19x22cm. (gr. k-3). 1957. (ISBN 0-397-30361-0). Lippincott.
--Fuzzy and Alfred. LC 61-11277. unpaged. illus. 19cm. 1961. F. Watts.
--Good-Bye Thunderstorm. LC 58-10143. unpaged. illus. 19x22cm. c.1958. Lippincott.
--Good Night Georgie. Marino, Dorothy Bronson (1912-), illus. LC 61-6488. unpaged. illus. 22cm. 1961. Dial Press.
--Grococo: A French Crow. Marokvia, Artur F. (1909-), illus. 48p. 1961. J B Lippincott Company.
--Little Angela and Her Puppy. Marino, Dorothy Bronson (1912-), illus. LC 54-5587. unpaged. illus. 19x23cm. 1954. Lippincott.
--Moving Day. Marino, Dorothy Bronson (1912-), illus. (Illus.). (gr. k-3). 1963. Dial.
--The Song of the Pine Tree Forest. LC 55-7989. unpaged. illus. 19x23cm. 1955. Lippincott.
--That's My Favorite. LC 56-9902. unpaged. illus. 19x23cm. 1956. Lippincott.
--Where Are the Mothers?. LC 59-12894. unpaged. illus. 19x23cm. c.1959. Lippincott.
Marino, Josef
--Hi! Ho! Pinocchio!. Donahey, William (1883-1970), illus. LC 40-32784. 127 p. col. front., illus. 29 cm. c.1940. Reilly & Lee.
Marins, Francisco
--The Mystery of the Gold Mines. Storni, Oswaldo, illus. (Illus.). (gr. 4-6). 1974. (ISBN 0-590-03057-4, Schol Trade Pap). Schol Bk Serv.
Marion, Francis (1886-1973)
--The Truant Tricycle. Crandall, C. Leslie, illus. LC 48-21642. 25 p. col. illus. 27 cm. c.1948. Hollow Tree House.
Mariotti, Jean
--Tales of Poindi. Rojankovsky, Feodor Stepanovich (1891-1970), illus. Averill, Esther, tr. from Fr. LC 38-38711. xi p., 1 l., 64, 2 p. illus. 28 cm. c.1938. Dominio Press.
Mariotti, Raffaello Marcello (1938-)
--The Three Kings. Mariotti, Raffaello Marcello (1938-), illus. LC 69-11537. (Illus.). 40 p. 1970. Knopf.
Mariotti, Raffaello Marcello (1938-) & Marchiori, Roberto, illus.
--Hanimals. (Illus.). 40p. (Orig.). 1st U.S. edition. Orig. Title: Animani. (gr. 4 up). 1982. (ISBN 0-914676-90-3, Star & Eleph Bks). Green Tiger Pr.
Maris, Roger (1934-) & Ogle, Jim, pseud. (1911-)
--Slugger in Right. Ogle, James Lawrence. LC 63-13383. 190p. 21cm. (The Argonaut All-Star Baseball Ser.). 1963. Argonaut Books.
Maris, Ron
--Are You There, Bear?. LC 84-4180. (Illus.). 32 p. 26cm. 1985, c.1984. (ISBN 0-688-03997-9). (ISBN 0-688-03998-7). Greenwillow Books.
--Better Move on Frog. Maris, Ron, illus. LC 82-81791. (Illus.). 32p. (Julia MacRae Bks.). (gr. k-1). 1982. (ISBN 0-531-04158-1, MacRae). (ISBN 0-531-04575-7). Watts.
--Is Anyone Home?. LC 85-5436. 7 7/8 x 9 7/8cm. 24p. c.1985. (ISBN 0-688-05899-X). (ISBN 0-688-05900-7). Greenwillow Books.
Marisa, pseud., see Nucera, Marisa Lonette.
Marisa, pseud. (1959-)
--One Day Means a Lot. Nucera, Marisa Lonette. 1st ed. Marisa, pseud. (1959-), illus. Nucera, Marisa Lonette. LC 65-18160. 1 v. (unpaged) col. illus. 18 cm. 1965. (ISBN 0-672-50414-6). Bobbs-Merrill.
Maritano, Adela Kay
--Playmate for Peter. Myers, Louise, illus. LC 51-8908. unpaged. illus. 17 cm. (tell-a-tale books). c.1951. Whitman Pub. Co.
Mark, Charles Christopher
--Run Away Home. 1960. Duell, Sloan and Pearce Pub.
Mark, David (1922-)
--The Sheep of the Lal Bagh. Kalish, Lionel, illus. LC 67-18472. (Illus.). 40 p. 26cm. 1967. Parents' Magazine.
Mark, Jan (1943-)
--Aquarius. LC 84-6176. 228p. (gr. 7 up). 1984. (ISBN 0-689-31051-X, Argo). Atheneum.
--Handles. LC 84-20467. 162 p. 24cm. 1985. (ISBN 0-689-31140-0). Atheneum. **Award: (ALA).**
--Handles. 1982. Viking. **Award: (CMA).**
--Nothing to Be Afraid Of. 5 3/8 x 8 13/16. (16-18 pt.). N.D (Pub. by Lythway Lg Print Bks). G K Hall.
--Nothing to Be Afraid of. LC 81-48064. 115 p. 21cm. c.1981. (ISBN 0-06-024087-3). (ISBN 0-06-024088-1). Harper & Row.
--Nothing to Be Afraid Of. Parkins, David, illus. (Illus.). 1980. Kestrel. **Award: (CMA).**
--Thunder and Lightnings. 1st ed. Russell, Jim (1933-), illus. LC 78-4778. (Illus.). 181 p. 21cm. 1979, c.1976. (ISBN 0-690-03901-8). (ISBN 0-690-03902-6). Crowell. **Award: (ALA).**
--Thunder and Lightnings. Russell, Jim (1933-), illus. 1976. Harper. **Award: (CMA).**
--Under the Autumn Garden. Brown, Judith Gwyn (1933-), illus. LC 78-4779. (Illus.). 211 p. 21cm. 1st U.S. edition. 1979, c.1977. (ISBN 0-690-03903-4). (ISBN 0-690-03904-2). Crowell.
Mark, Michael (1957-)
--Toba. Waldman, Neil, illus. LC 83-15679. (Illus.). 96p. (gr. 4-6). 1984. (ISBN 0-02-762300-9). Bradbury Pr.
--Toba at the Hands of a Thief. LC 84-20456. 136 p. 22cm. c.1985. (ISBN 0-02-762310-6). Bradbury Press.
Mark, Pauline Dahlin see Mark, Polly, pseud.
Mark, Polly, pseud., see Mark, Pauline Dahlin.
Mark, Polly, pseud. (1913-)
--Tani. Mark, Pauline Dahlin. Koering, Ursula (1921-), illus. (Illus.). (gr. 3-7). 1964. (ISBN 0-679-25148-0). McKay.
--The Way of the Wind. Mark, Pauline Dahlin. LC 65-23543. 186p. 21cm. c.1965. McKay.
Markandaya, Kamala, pseud., see Taylor, Kamala Purnaiya.
Markandaya, Kamala, pseud. (1924-)
--A Handful of Rice. Taylor, Kamala Purnaiya. LC 66-18782. 297p. 22cm. 1966. John Day Co.
--Nectar in a Sieve. Taylor, Kamala Purnaiya. (gr. 8 up). 1955. (ISBN 0-381-98153-3). John Day.
Markham, James L.
--King Tut & the Flying Carpet. (Illus., Orig.). 1979. (ISBN 0-89260-166-3). Hwong Pub.
Markham, Marion M.
--The Christmas Present Mystery. McCully, Emily Arnold (1939-), illus. LC 84-4557. (Illus.). 48p. (gr. 2-5). N.D. (ISBN 0-395-36383-7). HM.
--Escape from Velos. Carter, Derek, illus. LC 80-28114. p. cm. (Prime time adventures). 1981. (ISBN 0-516-02169-9). Childrens Press.
--The Halloween Candy Mystery. McCully, Emily Arnold (1939-), illus. LC 82-6054. (Illus.). 40 p. 24cm. 1982. (ISBN 0-395-32437-8). Houghton Mifflin.
Markham, Richard
--Colonial Days. (Illus.). N.D. Dodd, Mead & Company.
Markham, Virgil (1899-)
--Rogue's Road. N.D. MacMillan.
--The Scamp. (MacMillan Bks. for Boys & Girls). (gr. 7-9). N.D. MacMillan Bks.
Markham, Wyn
--The Gold Mine: An Adventure of Icky, Dicky and Licky. McKay, Dick, illus. LC 47-5612. 26 p. illus. 27 cm. 1946. Corwin Pub. Co.
Markley, Mary G
--Iowa Farm Stories. LC 77-112741. (Illus.). 31 p. 22cm. 1970. Dorrance.
Marko, Katherine Dolores (1913-)
--Away to Fundy Bay. LC 84-25680. p. cm. (Walker's American History Series for Young People). c.1985. (ISBN 0-8027-6576-9). Walker.
--God, When Will I Ever Belong?. Hackett, Michael, illus. LC 79-12244. (Illus.). 78 p. 21cm. c.1979. (ISBN 0-570-03624-0). Concordia Pub. House.
--God, Why Did Dad Lose His Job?". Counts, Kathy, illus. LC 82-7358. (Illus.). 83, 7 p. 21cm. c.1982. (ISBN 0-570-03629-1). Concordia Pub. House.
--The Sod Turners. Kane, Harry, illus. LC 77-112437. (Illus.). 207 p. 22cm. 1970. Criterion Books.
Markoe, Karen (1942-) & Phillips, Louis (1942-)
--Nuttier Nock Nocks. Gantz, David, illus. LC 80-24328. p. cm. (Funnybones). 1981. (ISBN 0-671-42249-9). Simon & Schuster.
--Nuttier Nock Nocks. Gantz, David, illus. LC 80-25822. p. cm. (Funnybones). 1981. (ISBN 0-671-42248-0). Wanderer Books.
--Nutty Nock Nocks. Kresse, Bill, illus. (Illus.). 64p. (Funnybones Ser.). (gr. 3-7). 1981. (ISBN 0-671-42249-9). Wanderer Bks.
--Sneakers. LC 80-24247. p. cm. (Funnybones). 1981. (ISBN 0-671-42117-4). Wanderer Books.
Markowa, Eugenia
--The Glowing Lily. LC 44-8304. 113 p. 19 cm. 1944. The Bruce Publishing Co.
Markowska, Wanda. & Milska, Anna
--The Coconut Thieves. Fournier, Catharine, ed. Domanska, Janina, illus. LC 64-16183. unpaged. col. illus. 26 cm. 1964. (ISBN 0-684-13454-3). Scribner. **Award: (ALA).**
Marks, Burton (1930-) & Marks, Rita (1938-)
--The Spook Book. Ernst, Lisa Campbell, illus. LC 81-5004. (Illus.). 56p. (gr. 1-4). 1981. (ISBN 0-688-00425-3). (ISBN 0-688-00426-1). Lothrop.
Marks, E. M.
--Events in the Life of Miss Dollikins. N.D. Thomas Nelson & Sons.
Marks, Holly L.
--Mrs. McDillydally's Candy Store. Fleischman, Joani, illus. (Illus.). (ps-3). 1979. (ISBN 0-682-49342-2). Exposition.
Marks, James Macdonald (1921-)
--Ayo Gurkha!. Douglas, Goray, illus. LC 73-7827. (Illus.). 253 p. 21cm. 1st U.S. edition. 1973. (ISBN 0-8407-6310-7). T. Nelson.
--Border Kidnap. LC 77-12725. p. cm. 1977, c.1974. (ISBN 0-8407-6551-7). T. Nelson.
--Hijacked!. LC 75-20482. 167 p. 21cm. 1975, c.1973. (ISBN 0-8407-6466-9). T. Nelson.
--The Triangle. Gibson, Robert, illus. LC 75-323911. (Illus.). 5, 136 p. 23cm. 1974. (ISBN 0-19-271370-1). Oxford University Press.
Marks, Jeannette Augustus (1875-)
--The Cheerful Cricket and Others. Brown, Edith, illus. 124 p. col. illus. 28 cm. 1907. Small, Maynard & Company.
--The Children in the Wood Stories. Burd, Clara Miller, illus. LC 19-10976. 3 p. l., 5-141 p. col. front., col. plates. 20 cm. 1919. Milton Bradley Company.
--Early English Hero Tales. 1915. Harper & Bros.
--Geoffery's Window: More Children in the Wood Stories. Burd, Clara Miller, illus. LC 21-11636. 3 p. l., 5-236 p. col. front., col. plates. 20 cm. 1921. Milton Bradley Company.
Marks, John Hugo Edgar Puempin (1908-), retold by.
--Spanish Fairy Tales. Moynihan, Roberta, illus. LC 58-5353. (Illus.). 22 cm. 181p. (gr. 3-7). 1958. (ISBN 0-394-91656-5). Knopf.
Marks, Marcia Bliss
--Swing Me, Swing Tree: Verse. 1st ed. Berger, David, illus. LC 59-5274. (Illus.). 26cm. 29p. c.1959. Little Brown.
Marks, Mickey Klar (1914-)
--Fine Eggs and Fancy Chickens. 1st ed. Polseno, Jo, illus. LC 56-10031. 96p. illus. 21cm. 1956. Holt.
--First You Like Me. Loewenstein, Bernice, illus. LC 69-13125. (Illus.). 160 p. 22cm. 1969. Parents' Magazine Press.
--Fish on the Tide. Wilde, Irma, illus. LC 56-4244. unpaged. illus. 25cm. 1956. Childrens Press.
--The Holiday Shop. 1st ed. Morse, Dorothy Bayley (1906-1979), illus. LC 57-116861. 125p. illus. 21cm. 1957. Holt.
--Let's Go to the Fair. Wilde, Irma, illus. 32p. col. illus. 21cm. (A Cozy Corner Book). 1951. Whitman.
--Little Peter: What's-My-Name?. Bracker, Charles Eugene (1895-), illus. LC 54-166645. unpaged. illus. 21cm. (Jolly books, 224). c.1953. Jolly Books.
--Straw Hat Theater. 1st ed. Tomes, Jacqueline, illus. LC 59-640768. 147p. illus. 21cm. 1959. Knopf.
--Straw Hat Theater. Tomes, Jacqueline, illus. (Illus.). (gr. 4-7). 1966. (ISBN 0-394-91698-0). Knopf.
--What Can I Buy?. Aliki, pseud. (1929-), illus. Brandenburg, Aliki Liacouras. LC 62-10129. unpaged. illus. 22cm. c.1962. Dial Press.
Marks, Rita, jt. auth. see Marks, Burton.
Marks, W. Parker & Moose, Don
--The Golden Doorstop. LC 77-151066. (Illus.). vii, 51 p. 23cm. c.1977. Meadowcreek Publications.
Markun, Patricia Maloney (1924-)
--The Secret of El Baru. Martin, Barry, illus. LC 58-978568. 213p. illus. 21cm. 1958. F. Watts.
Marlin, Jeffrey V. (1940-)
--Getting Out the Ghost. LC 84-7669. 176p. (Pacer Bks.). (gr. 7 up). 1984. (ISBN 0-399-21130-6, Putnam). (ISBN 0-399-21130-6). Putnam Pub Group.
Marline, Mark
--Lost on Volcano Island: Or, the Wreck of the Columbia. (Wide Awake Boys Ser.). N.D. A. L. Burt.
--Lost on Volcano Island: Or, The Wreck of the Columbia. LC 6669. iv, 218 p. front., plates. 19 cm. 1900. The Mershon Company.
--The Luck of a Castaway: Or, Fighting the Savages. 218p. 1900. Mershon Co.
--The Luck of the Castaway: Or, Fighting the Savages. (Wide Awake Boys Ser.). N.D. A. L. Burt.
Marlitt, E., pseud., see John, Eugenie.
Marlitt, E., pseud. (1825-1887)
--Gold Elsie. John, Eugenie. (Illus.). (The Wellesley Series for Girls). N.D. A. L. Burt's Pubs.
--Gold Elsie. John, Eugenie, 1 of 32 vols, Vol. 6. (Illus.). (Famous Books for Girls). N.D. H. M. Caldwell Co.
--Old Man'selle's Secret. John, Eugenie, 1 of 32 vols, Vol. 16. (Illus.). (Famous Books for Girls). N.D. H. M. Caldwell Co.
Marlow, Joyce, pseud., see Connor, Joyce Mary.
Marlow, Joyce, pseud. (1929-)
--The Man with the Glove. Connor, Joyce Mary. Webster, T. J., illus. LC 65-125660. 189p. illus. 20cm. 1966, c.1964. Roy.
Marlow, Ralph
--The Big Five Motorcycle Boys at the Front: Or, Carrying Dispatcher Through Belgium. (The Big Five Motorcycle Boys Ser.). N.D. A. L. Burt Company.
--The Big Five Motorcycle Boys in Tennessee Wilds: Or, The Secret of Walnut Ridge. (The Big Five Motorcycle Boys Ser.). N.D. A. L. Burt Company.
--The Big Five Motorcycle Boys on Florida Trails: Or, Adventures Among the Saw Plametto Crackers. (The Big Five Motorcycle Boys Ser.). N.D. A. L. Burt Company.
--The Big Five Motorcycle Boys on the Battle Line: Or, With the Allies in France. (The Big Five Motorcycle Boys Ser.). N.D. A. L. Burt Company.
--The Big Five Motorcycle Boys' Swift Road Chase: Or, Surprising the Bank Robbers. (The Big Five Motorcycle Boys Ser.). N.D. A. L. Burt Company.
--The Big Five Motorcycle Boys Through by Wireless: Or, A Strange Message From the Air. (The Big Five Motorcycle Boys Ser.). N.D. A. L. Burt.
--The Big Five Motorcycle Boys Under Fire: Or, With the Allies in the War Zone. (The Big Five Motorcycle Boys Ser.). N.D. A. L. Burt Company.
Marlow, Sidney, pseud., see Coggins, Paschal Heston.

Marlow, Sidney, pseud. (1852-1917)
--Harry Ambler. Coggins, Paschal Heston. (The Vacation Ser.). N.D. Penn.
--Harry Ambler. Coggins, Paschal Heston. (The Outdoor Bks.). N.D. Penn Publishing Co.
--Harry Ambler. Coggins, Paschal Heston. (Illus.). (The Little People's Ser.). N.D. Penn Publishing Co.
--Harry Ambler: Or, The Stolen Deed. Coggins, Paschal Heston. (Illus.). (Adventure Stories Ser.). N.D. Penn Publishing.
--The Moncasket Mystery. Coggins, Paschal Heston. (The Vacation Ser.). N.D. Penn.
--The Moncasket Mystery. Coggins, Paschal Heston. (The Outdoor Bks.). N.D. Penn Publishing Co.
--The Moncasket Mystery. Coggins, Paschal Heston. (Illus.). (Adventure Stories Ser.). N.D. Penn Publishing Co.
--The Moncasket Mystery. Coggins, Paschal Heston. (Illus.). (The Little People's Ser.). N.D. Penn Publishing Co.

Marlowe, Amy Bell, pseud., see Stratemeyer Syndicate.

Marlowe, Amy Bell, pseud.
--Frances of the Ranges: Or, The Old Ranchman's Treasure. Stratemeyer Syndicate. vi, 305 p. front., plates. 20 cm. (Amy Bell Marlowe's Books for Girls: No. 6). 1915. Grosset & Dunlap.
--The Girl from Sunset Ranch: Or, Alone in a Great City. Stratemeyer Syndicate. LC 14-145701. vi, 324 p. front., plates. 20 cm. (Amy Bell Marlowe's Books for Girls: No. 4). 1914. Grosset & Dunlap.
--The Girls of Hillcrest Farm: Or, The Secret of the Rocks. Stratemeyer Syndicate. Rogers, Walter S., illus. (Amy Bell Marlowe's Books for Girls: No. 2). 1914. Grosset & Dunlap.
--The Girls of Rivercliff School: Or, Beth Baldwin's Resolve. Stratemeyer Syndicate. Rogers, Walter S., illus. LC 16-19454. vi, 306 p. front., plates. 20 cm. (Amy Bell Marlowe's Books for Girls: No. 7). 1916. Grosset & Dunlap.
--A Little Miss Nobody: Or, With the Girls of Pinewood Hall. Stratemeyer Syndicate. Rogers, Walter S., illus. LC 14-145715. vi, 322 p. front., plates. 20 cm. (Amy Bell Marlowe's Books for Girls: No. 3). 1914. Grosset & Dunlap.
--The Oldest of Four: Or, Natalie's Way Out. Stratemeyer Syndicate. Rogers, Walter S., illus. LC 14-126354. vi, 304 p. front., plates. 20 cm. (Amy Bell Marlowe's Books for Girls: No. 1). 1914. Grosset & Dunlap.
--Oriole's Adventures. Stratemeyer Syndicate. Rogers, Walter S., illus. (A Four-in-one reprint. Includes: "When Oriole Came to Harbor Light"; "When Oriole Traveled Westward"; "When Oriole Went to Boarding School"; and, "The Girls of Rivercliff School"). 1933. Grosset & Dunlap.
--Sunset Ranch. Stratemeyer Syndicate. (A Four-in-one reprint. Titles from the series, "Amy Bell Marlowe's Books for Girls"). 1933. Grosset & Dunlap.
--When Oriole Came to Harbor Light. Stratemeyer Syndicate. Rogers, Walter S., illus. (Oriole Ser.: No. 1). 1920. Grosset & Dunlap.
--When Oriole Traveled Westward. Stratemeyer Syndicate. Rogers, Walter S., illus. (Oriole Ser.: No. 2). 1921. Grosset & Dunlap.
--When Oriole Went to Boarding School. Stratemeyer Syndicate. Rogers, Walter S., illus. (Oriole Ser.: No. 3). 1927. Grosset & Dunlap.
--Wyn's Camping Days: Or, the Outing of the Go-Ahead Club. Stratemeyer Syndicate. (Amy Bell Marlowe's Books for Girls: No. 5). 1914. Grosset & Dunlap.

Marlowe, Helena
--Clarabelle Hatches Ten: An Educational and Entertaining True Story. Vollmar, Clyde R., illus. LC 62-19338. 30p. col. illus. 29cm. c.1962. Bobbs.

Marlowe, Mabel
--Lazy Lob and other Stories. (Roundabout Ser.). N.D. D. Appleton & Co.
--The Wiggly Weasel. (Roundabout Ser.). N.D. D. Dppleton & Co.

Marlowe, Stephen see Lesser, Milton, pseud.

Marmer, Archie
--Makers of America: Hudson--Clark--Revere--Jackson--Fulton. LC 19-15600. 63 p. 20 cm. (Little folks' plays of American heroes). c.1919. R. G. Badger.

Marmorstein, Malcolm, jt. auth. see Key, Alexander Hill.

Marney, Dean (1952-)
--Just Good Friends. LC 81-19069. p. cm. c.1982. (ISBN 0-201-15877-9). Addison-Wesley.
--Just Good Friends. LC 84-40765. p. cm. 1985, c.1982. (ISBN 0-201-15877-9). Lippincott.

Marohn, Nancy (1927-)
--Tuttle. Landell, Harper (1918-), illus. LC 49-10601. (Illus.). 17p. 22cm. 1949. Winston Co.

Marokvia, Artur, jt. auth. see Marokvia, Mireille Journet.

Marokvia, Artur F., jt. auth. see Marokvia, Mireille Journet.

Marokvia, Mireille Journet (1918-)
--French School for Paul. Marokvia, Artur F. (1909-), illus. (Illus.). (gr. k-3). 1963. (ISBN 0-397-30657-1). (ISBN 0-397-30658-X). Lippincott.
--Grococo, A French Crow. Marokvia, Artur F. (1909-), illus. LC 69-13148. (Illus.). 45p. 26cm. 1969. Lippincott.
--Jannot, a French Rabbit. Marokvia, Artur (1909-), illus. LC 58-59934. (Illus.). (gr. 2-4). 1959. (ISBN 0-8382-0377-9). Hale.

Marokvia, Mireille Journet (1918-) & Marokvia, Artur (1909-)
--Belle Arabelle. LC 62-13148. (Illus.). 45 p. 26cm. c.1962. Lippincott.
--Nanette: A French Goat. Marokvia, Mireille (1918-), illus. LC 60-7620. 48p. 1960. J. B. Lippincott.

Marol, Jean-Claude
--Vagabul & His Shadow. (Illus.). 32p. (Vagabul Ser.). (gr. k-6). 1982. (ISBN 0-87191-889-7). Creative Ed.
--Vagabul Escapes. (Illus.). 32p. (Vagabul Ser.). (gr. k-6). 1982. (ISBN 0-87191-888-9). Creative Ed.
--Vagabul Goes Skiing. (Illus.). 32p. (Vagabul Ser.). (gr. k-6). 1982. (ISBN 0-87191-886-2). Creative Ed.
--Vagabul in the Clouds. (Illus.). 32p. (Vagabul Ser.). (gr. k-6). 1982. (ISBN 0-87191-887-0). Creative Ed.

Marquand, John Phillips (1893-)
--The Late George Apley: A Novel in the Form of a Memoir. (Pulitzer Prize Novel for 1938). 1937. (ISBN 0-316-54652-6). Little.

Marquand, Josephine, pseud., see Gladstone, Josephine.

Marquand, Josephine, pseud. (1938-)
--Chi Ming and the Tiger Kitten. Gladstone, Josephine. Binder, Pearl, pseud. (1904-), illus. Elwyn-Jones, Pearl Binder. LC 65-100893. 1v. (unpaged) illus. (pt. col.) 28cm. 1965, c.1964. Watts.
--Chi Ming and the Writing Lesson. Gladstone, Josephine. Binder, Pearl, pseud. (1904-), illus. Elwyn-Jones, Pearl Binder. LC 72-11858. (Illus.). 34 p. 29cm. 1970, c.1969. F. Watts.

Marquardt, Mervin
--Good Little King Josiah. (Illus.). (Arch Bk Ser.: No. 15). (gr. k-3). 1978. (ISBN 0-570-06118-0). Concordia.
--Grandfather's Story. LC 59-1239. (Illus.). (Arch Bk Ser.: No. 15). (gr. k-3). 1978. (ISBN 0-570-06121-0). Concordia.
--The Prisoner Who Freed Others. (Illus.). 32p. (Arch Book Ser.: No. 11). (gr. 1-4). 1974. (ISBN 0-570-06081-8). Concordia.
--Song for Joseph. (Arch Bks.: No. 18). (gr. k-4). 1981. (ISBN 0-570-06146-6). Concordia.

Marques, Rene
--The Oxcart. Pilditch, Charles, tr. (Illus.). 155p. (Scribner Student Paperback Ser.). 1969. (ISBN 0-684-51534-2). Charles Scribner's Sons.

Marquis, Helen
--The Longest Day of the Year. 1st ed. Vosburgh, Leonard W. (1912-), illus. LC 72-93840. (Illus.). 116 p. 21cm. 1969. (ISBN 0-696-69090-X). Meredith Press.

Marr-Johnson, Diana Maugham (1908-)
--Goodnight Pelican. 1958. St Martin's Press.

Marrandaine, E. E.
--The Shadow of the Cliff (Pub. by Society for Promoting Christian Knowledge). N.D. E. & J. B. Young & Co.

Marrero, Ramon A. (1925-)
--The Prophet's Disciple. LC 73-163077. 28 p. 22cm. 1971. (ISBN 0-8059-1586-9). Dorrance.

Marriott, Alice Lee (1910-)
--The Black Stone Knife. N.D. E. M. Hale and Co.
--The Black Stone Knife. Weiss, Harvey (1922-), illus. LC 57-6571. (Illus.). 180 p. 23cm. 1957. Crowell.
--Indian Annie: Kiowa Captive. 1965. (ISBN 0-8382-0365-5, Cadmus Books). E. M. Hale and Company.
--Indian Annie: Kiowa Captive. LC 65-141344. 179p. 21cm. c.1965. McKay.
--Saynday's People: The Kiowa Indians and the Stories They Told. N.D. University Of Nebraska Press.
--Sequoyah: Leader of the Cherokees. Riger, Bob, illus. LC 55-5823. 180p. illus. 22cm. (Landmark books). 1956. Random House.
--Winter-Telling Stories. Whitehorse, Roland, illus. 128p. (gr. 3-7). N.D. William Sloane Associates.

Marriott, Alice Lee (1910-), ed.
--Winter-Telling Stories. Cuffari, Richard (1925-1978), illus. LC 73-78264. (Illus.). 82 p. 24cm. 1969. Crowell.

Marriott, Alice Lee (1910-) & Rachlin, Carol
--Spider in the Sky. 1st ed. Rose, Anne K, adapted by. Owens, Gail, illus. LC 76-58722. (Illus.). 24 p. 24cm. c.1978. (ISBN 0-06-025073-9). (ISBN 0-06-025074-7). Harper & Row.

Marriott, H. B.
--The Adventures. (Illus.). N.D. Harper & Brothers.

Marrison, Lucile Curt
--The Mystery of Shadow Walk. 160p. 1963. Dodd, Mead & Co.

Marron, Carol A.
--Last Look from the Mountain. Ray, Deborah (1940-), illus. LC 83-6450. (Illus.). 32p. (Adventure Diaries). (gr. 3-6). 1983. (ISBN 0-940742-17-9, Pub. by Carnival Press). (ISBN 0-940742-17-9). Raintree Pubs.
--Mother Told Me So. Karn, George, illus. (Illus.). 32p. (Orig.). (ps-3). 1982. (ISBN 0-940742-00-4). Carnival Pr.
--Mother Told Me So. Karn, George, illus. LC 83-7271. (Illus.). 32p. (Family Bks.). (gr. k-3). 1983. (ISBN 0-940742-26-8, Pub. by Carnival Press). (ISBN 0-940742-26-8). Raintree Pubs.
--No Trouble for Grandpa. Burstein, Chaya M., illus. LC 83-7977. (Illus.). 32p. (Family Ser.). (gr. k-3). 1983. (ISBN 0-940742-27-6, Pub. by Carnival Press). (ISBN 0-940742-27-6). Raintree Pubs.
--Someone Just Like Me. Wheeler, Cindy (1955-), illus. LC 83-8898. (Illus.). 32p. (Imagination Bks.). (gr. k-3). 1983. (ISBN 0-940742-32-2, Pub. by Carnival Press). (ISBN 0-940742-32-2). Raintree Pubs.

Marron, Carol A., jt. auth. see Root, Phyllis.

Marryat, Augusta
--Left to Themselves, 15 of 15 Vols. (Illus.). (Warne's Hopeful Enterprise Library). N.D. Scribner & Welford.
--Lost in the Jungle. N.D. E. P. Dutton & Co.

Marryat, Emelia
--Amongst the Maories: A Book of Adventures, 1 of 15 Vols. (Illus.). (Warne's Hopeful Enterprise Library: Vol. 6). N.D. Scribner & Welford.
--Jack Stanley. (Warne's Golden Link Ser.). N.D. Frederick Warne & Co.

Marryat, Emma
--Long Evenings: Or, Stories for My Little Friends. N.D. E P Dutton.

Marryat, Florence
--The Little Marine and the Japanese Lily: Or, The Land of the Rising Sun. N.D. Thomas Whittaker.
--Open! Seasame!, No.21. (Lakeside Library Ser.). N.D. Donnelley, Loyd & Co.
--Petronel, No.119. (Seaside Library Ser.). N.D. George Munro: Dist. by American News Co.
--Sybil's Friend. (Illus.). N.D. George Routledge.
--Sybil's Friend, and How She Found Him. N.D. George Routledge & Sons.

Marryat, Frederick (1792-1848)
--The Children of the New Forest. LC 41-421452. 2 p. l., 428 p. front., plates. 20 cm. N.D. G. Routledge and Sons, Limited.
--The Children of the New Forest. (Illustrated Cabinet Editions). (The Works of Captain Marryat: Vol. 23). N.D. L. C. Page & Co.
--The Children of the New Forest. Courtney, W. L., intro. by. LC 24-16736. 23cm. 292p. 1898. D. Estes & Co.
--The Children of the New Forest. Edwards, Lionel Dalhousie Robertson (1878-), illus. (Children's Illustrated Classics). 1955. E. P. Dutton & Co.
--The Children of the New Forest. Good, Stafford C. (1890-), illus. LC 27-26378. 3 p. l., 372 p. col. plates, 25 cm. N.D. London.
--The Children of the New Forest. Good, Stafford C. (1890-), illus. LC 59-11854. 372p. illus. 24cm. 1959, c.1955. Scribner.
--The Children of the New Forest. McNeer, May Yonge, ed. LC 30-11283. x p., l., 322 p. incl. front., illus., plates. 20 cm. (The Macmillan children's classics). 1930. The Macmillan Company.
--The Children of the New Forest. Rhys, Ernest, ed. (Illus.). 18cm. 327p. (Everyman's Library for Young People). 1908. E. P. Dutton & Co.
--The Children of the New Forest. Smith, Elmer Boyd (1860-1943), illus. LC 11-28813. 2 p. l., 397 p. col. front., illus., col. plates. 21 cm. c.1911. H. Holt and Company.
--The Children of the New Forest. Thomas, Maurice Walton & Thomas, Gladys (1896-), eds. Branfield, Peter, illus. LC 66-6330. vii, 152p. illus. 19cm. (Shorter classics). 1966, c.1961. Ginn.
--The Henneker Diamonds: Based Upon an Episode in Captain Marryat's Famous Story--The Little Savage. Bernard, Joseph, ed. Holmes, Lenard, illus. LC 30-24519. 64 p. incl. front., illus., 21 cm. 1930. Thomas S. Rockwell Company.
--Jacob Faithful, 106 of 163 Vols. (Illus.). (The Cottage Library Ser.). N.D. R. Worthington.
--The Little Savage, No.184. (Seaside Library Ser.). N.D. George Munro: Dist. by American News Co.
--Little Savage. 1882. Harper's Trade-List.
--The Little Savage. viii, 269, 1 p. 18 cm. (Half-title: Everyman's library, ed. by Ernest Rhys For young people). 1907. J. M. Dent & Co.
--The Little Savage. Courtney, W. L., intro. by. LC 24-16737. 23cm. 241p. 1898. D. Estes & Co.
--The Little Savage. Gilbert, John Clitherae, illus. N.D. George Routledge & Sons.
--Masterman Ready. (Famous Bks. for Young People). N.D. A. L. Burt Co.
--Masterman Ready. (Marryat's Juvenile Stories). N.D. D. Appleton & Co.
--Masterman Ready. (Warne's Golden Link Series). N.D. Frederick Warne & Co.
--Masterman Ready. LC 75-32160. (Illus.). 3 v. 19cm. (Classics of Children's Literature, 1621-1932). 1976. (ISBN 0-8240-2274-2). Garland Pub.
--Masterman Ready. N.D. Grosset & Dunlap.
--Masterman Ready. (Harper Junior Classics Ser.). N.D. Harper & Bros.
--Masterman Ready. N.D. Longmans Green & Co.
--Masterman Ready. (The Forward Ser.). N.D. William Collins Co.
Masterman Ready: Or, the Wreck of the Pacific. (Illus.). (The Rugby Series for Boys). N.D. A. L. Burt's Pubs.
--Masterman Ready: Or, The wreck of the pacific. (Illus.). (Boys Presentation Library). N.D. Frederick Warne & Co.
--Masterman Ready: Or, The Wreck of the "Pacific". (Illustrated Cabinet Editions). (The Works of Captain Marryat: Vol.20). N.D. L. C. Page & Co.
--Mr. Midshipman Easy. (Famous Bks. for Young Americans). N.D. A. L. Burt Co.
--Mr. Midshipman Easy. N.D. G. P. Putnam Sons.
--Mr. Midshipman Easy. N.D. Grosset & Dunlap.
--Mr. Midshipman Easy. (Illustrated Cabinet Editions). (The Works of Captain Marryat: Vol. 8). N.D. L. C. Page & Co.
--Mr. Midshipman Easy. N.D. T. B. Peterson & Bros.
--Mr. Midshipman Easy. New ed. Burne, Harry H. A., illus. (The Father & Son Library). N.D. Sears Publishing Co.
--Mr. Midshipman Easy. Newbolt, Henry, illus. (Nelson Classics). N.D. Thomas Nelson & Sons.
--Mr. Midshipman Easy. Adapted for Young Readers. Polseno, Jo, illus. LC 67-5163. (Illus.). 314 p. 25cm. (Platt & Munk cricket book). 1967. Platt & Munk.
--Poor Jack. Stanfield, Clarkson, illus. (Boys Presentation Library). 1910. Frederick Warne & Co.
--Scenes in Africa. (Marryat's Juvenile Stories). N.D. D. Appleton & Co.
--Settlers in Canada. (Juvenile Stories). N.D. D. Appleton.
--The Story of Little Peter. Davidson, Bertha G. & Wheeler, L. J., illus. LC 4-22665. 19cm. 157p. (Famous Children of Literature Ser.). 1904. D. Estes & Co.
--Valerie. N.D. George Routledge & Sons.

Marryatt, Mollie
--Fairy Hours. LC 29-25968. 176 p. illus. 23 cm. c.1929. Arm Publishing Company.

Mars, Alastair (1915-)
--Fire in Anger: A Novel. LC 58-7581. 222p. 21cm. 1958. M. S. Mill Co.

Mars, Witold Tadeusz J. (1912-)
--The Baby Dragon. LC 59-5193. (Illus.). 26 cm. 27p. 1959. Houghton Mifflin.

Marsden, Catharine
--The Secret Elephants. Obligado, Lilian Isabel (1931-), illus. LC 65-212856. 76p. illus. 24cm. c.1966. Dutton.

Marsh, Brown Jesse
--Chip, the Chipmunk. 1962. Bethany Press.

Marsh, Carole
--The Haunt of Hope Plantation. Marsh, Carole, illus. (Illus.). 160p. (Orig.). (History Mystery Ser.). 1982. (ISBN 0-935326-03-0). Gallopade Pub Group.
--Mystery of the Lost Colony. (Illus.). 160p. (History Mystery Ser.). 1983. (ISBN 0-935326-05-7). Gallopade Pub Group.

Marsh, Charles, jt. auth. see Marsh, William John.

Marsh, Chester Gippert, Mrs.
--Singing Games and Drills. N.D. A. S. Barnes & Co.

Marsh, Corinna
--Flippy's Flashlight. Teichman, Dorothy, illus. LC 58-10817. unpaged. illus. 23cm. 1959. Dutton.

Marsh, D. E. (1900-)
--The Rajah of Gungra. Somerfield, Thomas (1870-), illus. LC 38-11647. 253 p. incl. illus., plates. col. front. 21 cm. 1937. David McKay Company.
--The Secret Aeroplane. Somerfield, Thomas (1870-) & Mills, Reginald, illus. LC 38-18912. vii, 9-256 p. incl. illus., plates, col. front. 21 cm. 1937. David McKay Company.

Marsh, Edith L.
--Trillium Hill. Duvoisin, Roger Antoine (1904-1980), illus. LC 53-6743. 159p. 22cm. 1955. Lothrop, Lee Shepard Co.
Marsh, Florence Anne, ed.
--Plays for Young People. LC 31-11523. x, 351 p. front., illus., plates, 18 cm. (Academy classics for junior high schools). c.1931. Allyn and Bacon.
Marsh, George Tracy (1876-)
--Flash, the Lead Dog. N.D. Grosset & Dunlap.
--Flash, the Lead Dog. Bull, Charles Livingston (1874-1932), illus. LC 27-21328. vi p., 1 l., 305 p. col. front., illus., plates. 20 cm. c.1927. The Penn Publishing Company.
--The Heart of the King-Dog. Bull, Charles Livingston (1874-1932), illus. LC 29-243626. 306 p. incl. front., illus. plates. 20 cm. c.1929. The Penn Publishing Company.
--Sled Trails and White Waters. Schoonover, Frank Earle (1877-1972), illus. N.D. Penn Publishing Co.
--Three Little Ojibwas: Amik (the Beaver) Nika (the Goose) Wabos (the Rabbit. LC 30-25625. 2 p. l., 3-215 p. incl. illus., plates. col. front. 19 cm. c.1930. The Penn Publishing Company.
Marsh, Gwen, tr. see Guillot, Rene.
Marsh, Irving T. (1907-1982) & Ehre, Edward (1905-), eds.
--Best Sports Stories - 1967: A Panorama of the 1966 Sports World. (Illus.). (gr. 7 up). N.D. (ISBN 0-525-06565-2). Dutton.
Marsh, Janet, Mrs.
--Don't Tread on Me. Torrey, Helen (1901-), illus. LC 41-21288. vii, 1 p., 1 l., 268, 1 p. illus. 22 cm. 1941. Houghton Mifflin Company.
--A 'prentice in Old London. Torrey, Helen (1901-), illus. LC 41-10780. 5 p. l., 242, 1 p. front., illus. 22 cm. 1941. Houghton Mifflin Company.
Marsh, Jeri (1940-) & Hanson, Joan (1938-)
--Hurrah for Alexander. LC 77-74013. (Illus.). 32 p. c.1977. (ISBN 0-87614-092-4). Carolrhoda Books.
Marsh, Jessie Brown
--Chip, the Chipmunk. Tudor, Bethany, illus. LC 61-16511. 95p. illus. 16 x 21cm. 1962. (ISBN 0-8272-0403-5). Bethany Press.
--Indian Folk Tales from Coast to Coast. Cunningham, Tanya, illus. (Illus.). (Indian Culture Ser.). (gr. 3-6). 1978. (ISBN 0-89992-068-3). Mt Coun Indian.
--The New Little Fuzzy Green Worm. LC 60-7181. 21 cm. 1960. (ISBN 0-8272-2502-4). Bethany Press.
Marsh, John B. (1835-)
--Life and Adventures of Robin Hood. N.D. E P Dutton.
--The Life and Adventures of Robin Hood. LC 12-36513. ix, 508 p. front., plates. 18 cm. N.D. G. Routledge and Sons.
Marsh, Lillian H.
--The Magic Shoes of Tiddlebinks. (Illus.). 72p. 1975. Dorrance.
Marsh, Mae (1897-)
--When They Ask Me My Name: A Book of Verse of Children. LC 33-7713. 1 p. l., 7-78 p. front., illus. 24 cm. c.1932. Castle Press.
Marsh, Olive Vincent
--The Galloping Horses. LC 42-221743. 95 p. incl. front. 18 cm. 1942. The Wartburg Press.
--Southern Highland Summer. LC 45-10056. 95 p. 18 cm. 1945. The Wartburg Press.
Marsh, Rebecca, pseud., see Neubauer, William Arthur.
Marsh, Reginald (1898-1954) & Gury, Jeremy
--The 'Round and 'Round Horse. N.D. Henry Holt & Co.
Marsh, Roy Simpson
--Kang. Baumann, Otto, illus. LC 62-11720. (Illus.). 188 p. 22cm. 1962. Macrae Smith.
--Moog. LC 58-12063. (Illus.). 188 p. 22cm. 1958. Macrae Smith.
--Rusty. Schule, Clifford H., illus. LC 61-8304. (Illus.). 169 p. 21cm. 1961. Macrae Smith.
--Tundra, Arctic Sled Dog. Geer, Charles Hand (1922-), illus. LC 68-18805. (Illus.). 158 p. 21cm. 1968. Macrae Smith Co.
--Wings and Runners: Tom's Alaskan Adventure. Abbott, Marsha, illus. LC 32-242795. 6 p. l., 258 p. incl. illus., plates, diagr. front. 20 cm. 1932. Frederick A. Stokes Company.
Marsh, William John (1918-) & Marsh, Charles
--Jimmy Huckleberry of Horse-Fly-Alley. 1st ed. LC 31-29417. 1 p. l., 2-3, 5-63 p. illus., plates, ports. 23 cm. 1931. Marsh Brothers.
Marshak, Ilia Iakovlevich see Ilin, M., pseud.
Marshak, Ilia Iakovlevich (1895-)
--Black on White. Ilin, M., pseud. Lapshin, N., illus. Kinkead, Beatrice, tr. N.D. J. B. Lippincott.
--Giant at the Crossroads. Ilin, M., pseud. Segal, E., illus. N.D. International Publishers.
--The Giant Widens His World. Ilin, M., pseud. Segal, E., illus. N.D. International Publishers.
Marshak, Ilia Iakovlevich (1895-) & Segal, E. A.
--A Ring and a Riddle. Ilin, M., pseud. Bock, Vera, illus. Kincead, Beatrice, tr. LC 44-5211. 65 p., 5 l. incl. front., illus. (part col.) 26 by 20 cm. 1944. J. B. Lippincott Company.
Marshak, Samuil Iakovlevich (1887-1964)
--House in the Meadow. Meyer-Rey, Ingeborg, illus. LC 77-80951. 48p. (gr. 2-5). 1971. (ISBN 0-8178-4552-6). Harvey.
--The Month Brothers. 1st ed. Nathan, Dorothy, adapted by. Shulevitz, Uri (1935-), illus. LC 67-20133. 95p. illus. 24cm. 1967. (ISBN 0-525-35161-2). Dutton.
--The Month Brothers: A Slavic Tale. Stanley, Diane (1943-), illus. Whitney, Thomas P., tr. from Rus. LC 82-7927. (Illus.). 32p. (gr. k up). 1983. (ISBN 0-688-01509-3). (ISBN 0-688-01510-7). Morrow.
--The Postman. McKean, Lloyd, illus. LC 48-9352. 23 p. col. illus. 17 x 21 cm. 1948. Shady Hill Press.
Marshak, Samuil Iakovlevich (1887-1964) & Harms, David
--The Merry Starlings. Zeldich, Arieh (1949-), illus. LC 82-47725. p. cm. 1983. (ISBN 0-06-024089-X). (ISBN 0-06-024090-3). Harper & Row.
Marshal, Emma & Besnon, Mary
--By the Light of the Nursery Lamp. 78p. (No. 410). N.D. Raphael Tuck & Sons.
Marshall, Alan (1902-)
--Four Sunday Suits & Other Stories. LC 75-9680. 1st U.S. edition. (gr. 7 up). 1975. (ISBN 0-8407-6467-7). Elsevier-Nelson.
--I Can Jump Puddles. 256p. 1957. The World Publishing Co.
--Whispering in the Wind. Newham, Jack, illus. (gr. 3-7). 1971. Tri-Ocean.
--The Wish Cat. (Illus.). 66p. 1966. Tri-Ocean Books.
Marshall, Archibald (1866-1934)
--Audacious Ann. Zian, Rita, illus. LC 23-268573. 3 p. l., 182 p. front., illus. 22 cm. 1924. Dodd, Mead and Company.
--The Dragon. 1st ed. Ardizzone, Edward Jeffrey Irving (1900-1979), illus. LC 67-2793. (Illus.). 32 p. 1967, c.1966. Dutton.
--Jimmy, the New Boy. LC 23-17724. 3 p. l., 255 p. col. front. 20 cm. 1923. Frederick A. Stokes Company.
--Joan and Nancy. Stephenson, Eunice Holmes, illus. LC 25-22636. 5 p. l., 207 p. incl. front. illus. 22 cm. 1925. Dodd, Mead and Company.
--John. Lehman, Agnes C., illus. LC 26-19023. 2 p. l., 168 p. front., illus. 22 cm. 1926. Dodd, Mead and Company.
--Peggy in Toyland. Barton, Helen M., illus. LC 20-18754. 5 p. l., 277 p. illus. 21 cm. 1920. Dodd, Mead and Company.
--Pippin. 1922. Dodd Mead & Co.
--Simple Stories. Morrow, George (1869-), illus. LC 68-12657. (Illus.). 86 p. 22cm. 1968. Pantheon Books.
--A Spring Walk in Provence. N.D. Dodd Mead & Co.
Marshall, Beatrice
--Nancy's Nephew: Or, Mike's First Campaign. N.D. Frederick Warne.
Marshall, Bernard G (1875-)
--Cedric the Forester. LC 21-12883. viii p., 1 l., 278, 1 p. incl. plates. front. 23 cm. 1921. D. Appleton and Company. **Award: (JNM).**
--Old Hickory's Prisoner: A Tale of the Second War for Independence. LC 25-17066. 5 p. l., 254, 1 p. incl. front., plates 23 cm. 1925. D. Appleton and Company.
--The Torch Bearers. LC 23-12963. (Illus.). 22 1/2 cm. v, 317p. 1923. D. Appleton-Century Co.
Marshall, Betty White
--Never Let Me Go. LC 56-133166. 223p. 21cm. c.1956. Avalon Books.
Marshall, Caroline Louise see Marshall, Carrie L., pseud.
Marshall, Caroline Louise, Mrs. (1849-)
--The Girl Ranchers. Marshall, Carrie L., pseud. Waugh, Ida, illus. (Keystone Ser.). N.D. Penn Publishing Co.
--The Girl Ranchers of the San Coulee: A Story for Girls. Marshall, Carrie L., pseud. Waugh, Ida, illus. LC 7-24678. 322 p. incl. front. plates. 19 cm. 1897. The Penn Publishing Company.
--Two Wyoming Girls and Their Homestead Claim: A Story for Girls. Marshall, Carrie L., pseud. Waugh, Ida, illus. 329 p. incl. front. plates. 19 cm. 1899. The Penn Publishing Company.
Marshall, Carolyn Louise see Marshall, Carrie L., pseud.
Marshall, Carolyn Louise, Mrs. (1849-)
--Story Bible. (Illus.). 220p. 1982. (ISBN 0-310-60270-X). Chosen Bks Pub.
--Two Wyoming Girls. Marshall, Carrie L., pseud. (The Vacation Ser.). N.D. Penn.
Marshall, Carrie L., pseud., see Marshall, Caroline Louise.
Marshall, Carrie L., pseud., see Marshall, Carolyn Louise.
Marshall, Catherine (1907-), retold by see Decoin, Didier.
Marshall, Catherine (1907-)
--Julie's Heritage. LC 57-7092. (Illus.). 231 p. 22cm. 1957. Longmans, Green.
--The Unwilling Heart. LC 55-6731. 246 p. 22cm. 1955. Longmans, Green.
Marshall, Clara
--Evenings at School. LC 7-24677. 270 p. 19 cm. 1891. Hunt & Eaton.
--Evenings at School. N.D. Methodist Bk Concern.
Marshall, Dean (1900-)
--Dig for a Treasure. 1st ed. Price, Christine Hilda (1928-1980), illus. LC 49-11007. 188 p. illus. 21 cm. 1949. E. P. Dutton.
--A House for Elizabeth. Kalab, Theresa, illus. LC 41-104659. 219 p. illus. 21 cm. 1941. E. P. Dutton and Company, Inc.
--The Invisible Island. 1st ed. Price, Christine Hilda (1928-1980), illus. LC 48-4788. 191 p. illus. 21 cm. 1948. E. P. Dutton.
--The Long White Month. Kalab, Theresa, illus. LC 42-161865. 5 p. l., 7-251, 1 p. illus. 21 cm. 1942. E. P. Dutton and Company, Inc.
--The Silver Robin. Dobias, Frank (1902-) & McGuckin, Malcolm, Jr., illus. LC 47-18370. 6 p. l., 15-246 p. illus. 21 cm. 1947. E. P. Dutton & Company, Inc.
--Wish on the Moon. Morse, Dorothy Bayley (1906-1979), illus. LC 51-11440. (Illus.). 21cm. 192p. N.D. E. P. Dutton.
Marshall, Donovan (1908-)
--God, Why Am I So Afraid?". Counts, Kathy, illus. LC 82-7360. (Illus.). 81, 11 p. 21cm. c.1982. (ISBN 0-570-03630-5). Concordia Pub. House.
Marshall, Edison (1894-1967)
--Campfire Courage: The Woodsmoke Boys in the Canadian Rockies. LC 26-16151. 3 p. l., 393 p. front., plates. 20 cm. c.1926. Harper & Brothers.
--Ocean Gold: A Novel for Young People. LC 25-17281. 5 p. l., 383 p. front., plates. 20 cm. c.1925. Harper & Brothers.
Marshall, Edward (1932-)
--Four on the Shore. Marshall, James (1942-), illus. LC 84-15610. (Illus.). 48 p. 23cm. c.1985. (ISBN 0-8037-0155-1). (ISBN 0-8037-0142-X). Dial Books for Young Readers. **Award: (ALA).**
--Fox All Week. Marshall, James (1942-), illus. LC 84-1708. (Illus.). (Easy-to-Read Bks.). (ps-3). 1984. (ISBN 0-8037-0062-8). (ISBN 0-8037-0062-8). Dial Bks for Young Readers.
--Fox and His Friends. Marshall, James (1942-), illus. LC 81-68769. (Illus.). 56 p. 23cm. (Dial Easy-to-Read). c.1982. (ISBN 0-8037-2668-6). (ISBN 0-8037-2669-4). Dial Press.
--Fox at School. Marshall, James (1942-), illus. LC 82-45506. (Dial Easy-to-Read). c.1983. (ISBN 0-8037-2674-0). Dial Press.
--Fox in Love. Marshall, James (1942-), illus. LC 82-70190. (Illus.). 48 p. 23cm. (Dial Easy-to-Read). c.1982. (ISBN 0-8037-2491-8). (ISBN 0-8037-2433-0). Dial Press.
--Fox on Wheels. Marshall, James (1942-), illus. 1983. Dial.
--Space Case. Marshall, James (1942-), illus. LC 80-13369. (Illus.). 40 p. c.1980. (ISBN 0-440-78005-5). (ISBN 0-440-78007-1). Dial Press.
--Three by the Sea. Marshall, James (1942-), illus. LC 80-26097. (Illus.). 48 p. 22cm. (Dial easy-to-read). c.1981. (ISBN 0-8037-8671-9). (ISBN 0-8037-8687-5). Dial Press.
--Troll Country. Marshall, James (1942-), illus. LC 79-19324. (Illus.). 56 p. 23cm. (Dial easy-to-read). c.1980. (ISBN 0-8037-6211-9). (ISBN 0-8037-6210-0). Dial Press.
Marshall, Emma Martin, Mrs. (1830-1899)
--Abigail Templeton. N.D. Thomas Whittaker.
--Alma: Or, The Story of a Little Music Mistress. N.D. Brentano's Publications.
--Alma: Or, The Story of a Little Music Mistress. 352p. N.D. Ward & Drummond.
--Between the Cliffs. N.D. Robert Carter & Brothers.
--Between the Cliffs: Or, Hal. Forrester's Anchor, 1 of 12 vols. (Illus.). 258p. (The Marshall Library). N.D. Set. Merrill.
--Bishop's Cranworth. N.D. E. P. Dutton & Co.
--Blue Bells. 289p. N.D. A. I. Bradley & Co.'s Pub.
--Born in the Purple. N.D. E. P. Dutton & Co.
--By the North Sea: Or, The Protector's Granddaughter. N.D. Thomas Whittaker.
--Cassandra's Casket. N.D. Robert Carter & Brothers.
--A Chip of the Old Block. N.D. Robert Carter.
--Christabel Kingscote. N.D. E. P. Dutton & Co.
--Consideration for Others. (Third Ser.). (Fireside Library). N.D. Robert Carter & Bros.
--Consideration for Others: Or, How Can We Help One Another, 1 of 12 vols. (Illus.). 180p. (The Marshall Library). N.D. Set. Merrill.
--The Court and the Cottage. (Illus.). (The Girl's Own Favorite Ser.). N.D. E. P. Dutton & Co.
--Crofton Cousins, 1 of 25 Vols. (Illus.). (Warne's Crofton Cousins Ser.: Vol. 2). N.D. Scribner & Welford.
--Dewdrops and Diamonds. (Violet and Lily Ser.). N.D. Robert Carter & Brothers.
--Dewdrops and Diamonds, 1 of 5 Vols. N.D. Thomas Whittaker.
--Eaglehurst Towers: A new Series for boys and girls, 1 of 4 Vols. (The Eaglehurst Ser.). N.D. White & Allen.
--Eastward Ho. N.D. E. P. Dutton & Co.
--Fanny & Her Friends. LC 1-29083. 19cm. 131p. (Lad and Lassie Ser.). 1915. George W Jacobs.
--Fine Gold: Or, Ravenswood Courtney. N.D. Thomas Whittaker.
--A Flight of Swallow: Or, Little Dorothy's Dream. 1891. Thomas Whittaker.
--Framilode Hall. (Primrose Ser.). N.D. Robert Carter & Brothers.
--Golden Silence. N.D. Thomas Whittaker.
--A Good Hearted Girl. (The Girls' Own Library). N.D. David McKay.
--A Good-Hearted Girl: Or, Present Day Heroine. (Illus.). N.D. E. P. Dutton & Co.
--Grandma's Wardrobe. N.D. Alfred Martien.
--The Happy Days at Fern Bank. N.D. Alfred Martien.
--Heather and Harebell, 1 of 5 Vols.. (Chimes Ser.). N.D. Set 6.25. Thomas Whittaker's.
--Hurly Burly. N.D. Thomas Whittaker's.
--In Colston's Days. N.D. E. P. Dutton & Co.
--In the East Country with Sir Thomas Browne. N.D. E. P. Dutton & Co.
--Katie's Work, 1 of 12 vols. (Illus.). 168p. (The Marshall Library). N.D. Set. Merrill.
--Katie's Work. (Third Ser.). (Fireside Library). N.D. Robert Carter & Bros.
--Lady Rosamond. N.D. E. P. Dutton & Co.
--Lessons of Love: Aunt Bertha's Visit to the Elms. N.D. Alfred Martien.
--Lily Among Thorns. N.D. E. P. Dutton & Co.
--Little Brothers, and Sisters. N.D. Robert Carter & Brothers.
--Little Brothers & Sisters: Three Little Brothers & Three Little Sisters in one vol. (Illus.). 376p. N.D. Merrill.
--Little May's Legacy, 1 of 7 Vols. (Always Do Right Library Ser). N.D. Set. T. Whittaker.
--Little May's Legacy: The Gipsy Boy. N.D. Alfred Martien.
--Little Miss Joy. (Illus.). (The Wellesley Series for Girls). 1915. A L Burt & Co.
--Little Miss Joy. (The Rugby Series for Boys and Girls). N.D. A. L. Burt Company.
--Little Miss Joy. (Illus.). (The Little Women Ser.). N.D. A. L. Burt's Pubs.
--Little Miss Joy. N.D. Thomas Whittaker.
--The Little Peat Cutters: Or, Songs of Love, 1 of 12 vols. (Illus.). 161p. (The Marshall Library). N.D. Merrill.
--The Little Peat Cutters: Or, The Song of Love. N.D. Robert Carter & Brothers.
--The Little Peat-Cutters: The Song Of Love. N.D. Bradley & Woodruff.
--Little Primrose. (Third Ser.). (Fireside Library). N.D. Robert Carter & Bros.
--Little Primrose: Or, The Bells of Old Effingham, 1 of 12 vols. 146p. (The Marshall Library). N.D. Set. Merrill.
--Little Queenie. (Illus.). 256p. N.D. A. I. Bradley & Co.'s Pubs.
--Lizette. N.D. E. P. Dutton & Co.
--The Lost Lilies. N.D. Alfred Martien.
--Master Martin. LC 99-467456. 3 p. l., 143 p. front., plates. 20 cm. c.1899. G. W. Jacobs & Co.
--Master Martin. (Lad and Lassie Ser.). 1915. George W Jacobs.
--Matthew Frost. N.D. Robert Carter & Brothers.
--Matthew Frost: Or, Little Snowdrop's Mission, 1 of 12 vols. 214p. (The Marshall Library). N.D. Set. Merrill.
--Michael's Treasure. N.D. Thomas Whittaker.
--Micheal's Treasures. N.D. Robert Carter & Brothers.
--Mistress of Tayne Court. N.D. E. P. Dutton & Co.
--The Mother's Chain. N.D. Thomas Whittaker.
--Mrs. Willoughby's Octave. 343p. 1884. E. P. Dutton & Co.
--My Grandmother's Pictures. 154p. 1884. Rob Carter & Brothers.
--My Lady Bountiful. N.D. Thomas Whittaker.
--Nature's Gentleman. N.D. Thomas Whittaker.
--Number Thirteen: Or, The Story of the Lost Vestal. (Illus.). 256p. (The Cross and Crown Ser.). N.D. Cassell & Co.'s Pubs.
--Only Susan. (Illus.). N.D. E. P. Dutton & Co.
--Pat's Inheritance. N.D. Thomas Whittaker.
--Peat Cutters. (Third Ser.). (Fireside Library). N.D. Robert.
--Poppies and Pansies. (Violet and Lily Ser.). N.D. Robert Carter & Brothers.
--Poppies and Pansies. (Chimes Ser.). N.D. Thomas Whittaker.
--Rex and Regina. (Viloet and Lily Ser.). N.D. Robert Carter & Brothers.
--Rex and Regina: Or, The Song of the River. (Chimes Ser.). N.D. Thomas Whittaker.

AUTHOR INDEX MARTIN, ANN

--Rhoda's Reward: Or, If Wishes Were Horses. Juv. ed. Garland, C. T., illus. N.D. Cassell & Co.
--The Rochemonts: A Story of Three Homes. (Illus.). N.D. E. P. Dutton & Co.
--Roger's Apprenticeship. (Third Ser.). (Fireside Library). N.D. Robert Carter & Bros.
--Roger's Apprenticeship: Or, Five Years of a Boy's Life, 1 of 12 vols. (Illus.). 180p. (The Marshall Library). N.D. Set. Merrill.
--Roman Maiden. N.D. George W Jacobs.
--Ruby and Pearl. (Primrose Ser.). N.D. Robert Carter.
--Salome: Or, "Let Patience Have Her Perfect Work". N.D. Thos Nelson & Sons.
--Silver Chimes: Or, Olive: A Story for Children. 372p. 1884. Rob Carter & Brothers.
--Sir Benjamin's Bounty. (Illus.). 160p. N.D. A. I. Bradley & Co.'s Pubs.
--Stellafont Abbey. N.D. Robert Carter & Brothers.
--Stellafont Abbey: Or, Nothing New, 1 of 12 vols. 247p. (The Marshall Library). N.D. Set. Merrill.
--Stories of the Cathedral Cities. (Primrose Ser.). N.D. Robert Carter & Brothers.
--Stories of the Cathedral Cities, 1 of 5 Vols. (Chimes Ser.). N.D. Set. Thomas Whittaker's
--Story of a Basket. N.D. Alfred Martien.
--Theodora's Childhood. N.D. Scribner, Welford & Armstrong.
--Three Little Brothers. (Illus.). (Golden Lily Ser.). N.D. D. Lothrop Co.
--Three Little Brothers, 1 of 15 vols. (Illus.). (Morning Glory Ser). N.D. Lothrop Pub. Co.
--Three Little Brothers, 1 of 12 vols. (Illus.). 196p. (The Marshall Library). N.D. Set. Merrill.
--Three Little Brothers. 1875. Robert Carter & Brothers.
--Three Little Sisters. N.D. Dodd & Mead.
--Three Little Sisters, 1 of 12 vols. (Illus.). 180p. (The Marshall Library). N.D. Set. Robert Carter & Brothers.
--Three Little Sisters. (Third Ser.). (Fireside Library). N.D. Robert Carter & Bros.
--Two Holidays: Or, To-day & Yesterday, 1 of 12 vols. 159p. (The Marshall Library). N.D. Set. Robert Carter & Brothers.
--The Two Margarets, 1 of 12 vols. (Illus.). 192p. (The Marshall Library). N.D. Set. Robert Carter & Brothers.
--Violet Douglas. N.D. D. Lothrop Co.
--Winifrede's Journal. N.D. Macmillan.

Marshall, Francesca, pseud., see Chadwick, Mara Louse Pratt.

Marshall, Francesca, pseud.
--The Cat School. Chadwick, Mara Louise Pratt. N.D. David McKay Co.
--The Nixie Well--The Goat and the Troll. Chadwick, Mara Louse Pratt. N.D. David McKay Co.

Marshall, George
--This Bus Is Stuffed to the Brim!. Huston, Ed, illus. (Illus., Orig.). 1976. (ISBN 0-918072-00-X). Mediaworks.

Marshall, Helen Laughlin
--A New Mexican Boy. Rush, Olive, illus. LC 40-12421. 85 p. col. illus. 22 cm. c.1940. Holiday House.

Marshall, Henrietta Elizabeth (1876-)
--Stories of Beowulf: Told to the Children. Chiholm, Louey, ed. Skelton, J. R., illus. xi, 114 p. 8 col. pl. (incl. front.) 15 cm. (Half-title: Told to the children series; ed. by Louey Chisholm. no. 32). 1908. T. C. & E. C. Jack.
--Stories of Guy of Warwick: Told to the Children. Chisholm, Louey, ed. LC 8-58765. xi, 109 p. 8 col. pl. (incl. front.) 15 x 12 cm. (Half-title: Told to the children series). N.D. T. C. & E. C. Jack.
--Stories of Robin Hood. Forrest, A. S., illus. 15cm. 122p. (Told to the Children Ser.). 1905. E. P. Dutton & Co.
--Stories of Roland. Luard, L. D., illus. 15cm. 116p. (Told to the Children Ser.). 1907. E. P. Dutton & Co.
--Stories of William Tell and His Friends: Told to the Children. Chisholm, Louey, ed. Gloag, I. L., illus. LC 7-25666. xi, 112 p. 8 col. pl. (incl. front.) 15 x 12 cm. (Half-title: Told to the children series.). N.D. T. C. & E. C. Jack.

Marshall, Henrietta Elizabeth (1876-), retold by.
--Uncle Tom's Cabin told to the Children. Forrest, A. S., illus. LC 8-13727. (Original Author: Mrs. Harriet Elizabeth Beecher Stowe, 1811-1896). 15cm. 115p. (Told to the Children Ser.). 1908. E. P. Dutton & Co.

Marshall, James, jt. auth. see Jameson, Cynthia.

Marshall, James, jt. auth. see Wolkstein, Diane.

Marshall, James Vance
--My Boy John That Went to Sea. Rosier, Lydia, illus. (Illus.). 144 p. 22cm. 1967, c.1966. Morrow.
--River Ran Out of Eden. Wilson, Maurice Charles John (1914-), illus. (Illus.). (gr. 9 up). 1963. Morrow.

Marshall, James (1942-)
--The Cut-Ups. Marshall, James (1942-), illus. (Illus.). 32p. (gr. 3-8). 1984. (ISBN 0-670-25195-X, Viking Kestrel). Viking.
--George and Martha. Marshall, James (1942-), illus. LC 74-184250. (Illus.). 46 p. 22cm. 1972. (ISBN 0-395-13731-4). (ISBN 0-395-13732-2). Houghton Mifflin. **Awards: (NYT); (ALA).**
--George & Martha Back in Town. Marshall, James (1942-), illus. LC 83-22842. (Illus.). 32p. (gr. k-3). 1984. (ISBN 0-395-35386-6). HM.
--George and Martha Encore. Marshall, James (1942-), illus. LC 73-5845. (Illus.). 46 p. 21cm. 1973. (ISBN 0-395-17512-7). Houghton Mifflin.
--George and Martha, One Fine Day. Marshall, James (1942-), illus. LC 78-60494. (Illus.). 46 p. 22cm. 1978. (ISBN 0-395-27154-1). Houghton Mifflin. **Award: (ALA).**
--George and Martha Rise and Shine. Marshall, James (1942-), illus. LC 76-14350. (Illus.). 46 p. 1976. (ISBN 0-395-24738-1). Houghton Mifflin.
--George and Martha, Tons of Fun. Marshall, James (1942-), illus. LC 80-13592. (Illus.). 46 p. 1980. (ISBN 0-395-29524-6). Houghton Mifflin Co.
--The Guest. Marshall, James (1942-), illus. LC 74-32043. (Illus.). 38 p. 22cm. 1975. (ISBN 0-395-20277-9). Houghton Mifflin.
--James Marshall's Mother Goose. Marshall, James (1942-), illus. LC 79-2574. (Illus.). 39 p. 27cm. 1979. (ISBN 0-374-33653-9). Farrar, Straus & Giroux.
--Merry Christmas, Space Case. Marshall, James (1942-), illus. LC 85-1664. p. cm. 1985. (ISBN 0-8037-0215-9). (ISBN 0-8037-0216-7). Dial Books for Young Readers.
--Miss Dog's Christmas Treat. Marshall, James (1942-), illus. LC 73-9824. (Illus.). 18 p. 1973. (ISBN 0-395-18154-2). Houghton Mifflin.
--Portly McSwine. Marshall, James (1942-), illus. LC 78-24814. (Illus.). 38 p. 21cm. 1979. (ISBN 0-395-28003-6). Houghton Mifflin.
--Rapscallion Jones. Marshall, James (1942-), illus. LC 83-48017. p. cm. 1983. (ISBN 0-670-58965-9). Viking.
--Speedboat. Marshall, James (1942-), illus. LC 75-40349. (Illus.). 47 p. 23cm. 1976. (ISBN 0-395-24384-X). Houghton Mifflin.
--A Summer in the South. Marshall, James (1942-), illus. LC 77-14018. p. cm. 1977. (ISBN 0-395-25840-5). Houghton Mifflin.
--Taking Care of Carruthers. Marshall, James (1942-), illus. LC 81-6619. p. cm. 1981. (ISBN 0-395-28593-3). Houghton Mifflin.
--What's the Matter with Carruthers?. Marshall, James (1942-), illus. LC 72-75607. (Illus.). 32 p. 28cm. 1972. (ISBN 0-395-13895-7). Houghton Mifflin.
--Willis. Marshall, James (1942-), illus. LC 74-5259. (Illus.). 46 p. 22cm. 1974. (ISBN 0-395-19494-6). Houghton Mifflin.
--Yummers!. Marshall, James (1942-), illus. LC 72-5400. (Illus.). 31 p. 1972. (ISBN 0-395-14757-3). Houghton Mifflin.

Marshall, James (1942-) & Murdock, Laurette
--Four Little Troubles. Marshall, James (1942-), illus. LC 75-12858. (Illus.). 4 v. in case. 13cm. c.1975. (ISBN 0-395-19880-1). Houghton Mifflin.

Marshall, Jean
--Little Story Books. Incl. Ducks Go to the Orchard; Ducks in the Village; Ducks on the Train; Hide & Seek; Jane; Little White Duck; Little Yellow Dog; A Pond for Ducks. (Illus.). (gr. k-2). 1965. Warne.

Marshall, John, tr. see Guillot, Rene.

Marshall, Logan
--Boys' and Girls' Book of Fairy Tales. (Illus.). (Standard Ser.). N.D. John C. Winston Co.
--Fairy Tales of All Nations. (The Challenge Ser.). N.D. John C. Winston.
--Famous Tales of Fact and Fancy. 320p. (The Famous "Retold" Series for Boys and Girls). N.D. John C. Winston.
--Happy Times at Home for Our Boys and Girls. LC 14-221344. (Amusing and Instructive Ways of Entertaining the Children of Our Own Land and Stories about Children of Other Lands). 252 p. col. front., illus., plates. 24 cm. c.1914. G. S. Ferguson, Printer.

Marshall, Logan, ed.
--Fairy Tales of All Nations. LC 11-10. (Famous Stories from the English, German French, Italian, Arabic, Russiea, Swedish, Danish, Norwegian, Bohemian, Japanese and Other Sources). 1 p. l., viii, 9-314 p. col. front., col. plates. 25 cm. c.1910. John C. Winston Company.
--Fairy Tales of Many Lands. LC 29-10212. (Famous Stories from the English, German, French, Italian, Arabic, Russian, Swedish, Danish, Norwegian, Bohemian, Japanese, and Other Sources). viii, 9-314 p. front., plates. 22 cm. 1928. The John C. Winston Company.
--Favorite Fairy Tales. (The Children's Book-Shelf). N.D. J. C. Winston Co.
--Myths and Legends of All Nations. LC 14-205448. (Famous Stories from the Greek, German, English, Spanish, Scandinavian, danish, French, Russian, Bohemian, Italian and Other Sources). 1 p. l., vi, 7-272 p. col. front., col. plates. 24 cm. c.1914. The John C. Winston Company.
--The Wonder Book of Bible Stories. (The Children's Bookshelf). 1921. John C. Winston.

Marshall, Logan, ed. see Mother Goose.

Marshall, Lydia & Oxendorf, Eric
--Nobody Likes to Lose. LC 79-22359. p. cm. 1980. (ISBN 0-516-01478-1). Childrens Press.

Marshall, Martha
--What Child Is This?. Conaway, James, illus. LC 82-7239. (Illus.). (gr. 1-2). 1982. (ISBN 0-89693-204-4). Dandelion Hse.

Marshall, Mary
--Teresa and the Scaredy-Cat. Marshall, Mary, illus. LC 72-181307. (Illus.). 27 p. 21cm. 1971. Bede Interprises.

Marshall, Miss
--Nancy's Nephew. (Illus.). (The Home and Enterprise Library Ser.). N.D. Frederick Warne & Co.

Marshall, Mollie
--Ready for Romance. 192p. (Orig.). (First Romance Ser.: No. 2). (gr. 6-12). 1982. (ISBN 0-8439-1129-8, Leisure Bks). Nordon Pubns.

Marshall, Mrs.
--Matthew Frost, Carrier, 1 of 4 Vols. (Treasure Library). N.D. Set. Pott, Young & Co.

Marshall, R. A.
--A Ride On A Rocking Horse. N.D. E. P. Dutton & Co.

Marshall, Ray
--Cats up: Purring Pop-Ups. Paul, Korky, illus. LC 83-112729. (Illus.). 10 p. 24cm. c.1982. (ISBN 0-671-45268-1). Little Simon.
--The Crocodile and the Dumper Truck: A Reptilian Guide to London. Paul, Korky, illus. LC 82-124652. (Illus.). 10 p. 26cm. 1982. (ISBN 0-689-20703-4). Atheneum Publishers.
--Hey Diddle Diddle. Kilmo, Kate, ed. Paul, Korky & Marshall, Ray, illus. (Illus.). 10p. (Chubby Pop-Ups Ser.). 1983. (ISBN 0-671-46239-3, Little Simon). S&S.
--Jack & Jill. Kilmo, Kate, ed. Paul, Korky & Marshall, Ray, illus. (Illus.). 10p. 1983. (ISBN 0-671-46238-5, Little Simon). S&S.
--Sing a Song of Sixpence. Kilmo, Kate, ed. Paul, Korky & Marshall, Ray, illus. (Illus.). 10p. (Chubby Pop-Ups Ser.). (ps-k). 1983. (ISBN 0-671-46237-7, Little Simon). S&S.

Marshall, Ray & Paul, Korky
--Humpty Dumpty. Klimo, Kate, ed. Marshall, Ray & Paul, Korky, illus. (Illus.). 10p. (Chubby Pop-Ups Ser.). 1983. (ISBN 0-671-46236-9, Little Simon). S&S.

Marshall, Rosamond Van Der Zee
--Kitty. N.D. World Publishing.
--None but the Brave: A Story of Holland. Duncan, Gregor, illus. LC 42-7641. 4 p. l., 184 p. incl. illus., plates. col. front. 22 cm. 1942. Houghton Mifflin Company.
--The Treasure of Shafto. Wonsetler, John Charles (1900-), illus. LC 46-4958. 3 p. l., 217 p. illus. 19 1/2 cm. 1946. J. Messner, Inc.

Marshall, Sarah Catherine Wood (1914-1983)
--Christy. (A Spire Book). N.D. (ISBN 0-8007-8008-6). Fleming H. Revell Co.
--God Loves You: Our Family's Favorite Stories & Prayers. Spanfeller, James John (1930-), illus. (gr. 1-5). 1967. (ISBN 0-07-040606-5). McGraw.

Marshall, Shirley E., ed.
--Young American's Treasury of English Poetry. (gr. 7 up). N.D. S&S.

Marshall, Sybil Mary Edwards (1913-)
--Polly at the Window. Anderson, Scoular, illus. (Illus.). 30 p. 20cm. (young puffin). 1975. (ISBN 0-14-030786-9). Penguin Books.

Marshell, Emma Martin, Mrs. (1830-1899)
--The Two Holidays. (Third Ser.). (Fireside Library). N.D. Robert Carter & Bros.
--The Two Margarets. (Third Ser.). (Fireside Library). N.D. Robert Carter & Bros.

Marsland, Alicia (1952-)
--The Wizard's Daughter. LC 77-10082. p. cm. 1977. (ISBN 0-87695-207-4). Aurora Publishers.

Marsland, May
--The Dolls of Castledale. Turner, William, illus. LC 41-1480. 4 p. l., 11-68, 1 p. incl. front., illus. 22 cm. 1940. W. Kibbee & Son.

Marsoli, Lisa A.
--Things to Know Before You Move. LC 84-50441. (Look Before You Leap Ser.). 1985. (ISBN 0-382-06783-5). (ISBN 0-382-06963-3). Silver.

Marsten, Richard
--Danger: Dinosaurs!. (Winston Science Fiction Ser.). N.D. John C. Winston Co.
--Rocket to Luna. (Winston Science Fiction Ser.). 1953. John C. Winston Co.

Marston, Elsa
--The Cliffs of Cairo. LC 80-26785. 160p. (gr. 7 up). 1981. (ISBN 0-8253-0032-0). Beaufort Bks NY.

Marston, Louise
--Bennie, The King's Little Servant. N.D. Robert Carter & Brothers.
--Blind Nettie. N.D. Robert Carter & Brothers.
--Cripple Jess. N.D. Robert Carter & Brothers.
--Rob and Mag. N.D. Robert Carter & Brothers.

Martel, Cruz & Pinkney, Jerry
--Yagua Days. LC 75-27601. (Illus.). 40 p. 27cm. c.1976. (ISBN 0-8037-9765-6). (ISBN 0-8037-9766-4). Dial Press.

Martel, Suzanne Chouinard
--The City Under Ground. Sibley, Ben, illus. LC 64-22968. (Illus.). 157 p. 21cm. 1964. Viking Press.

Martelli, Thomas R.
--What Would You Like to Be. Harlan, Warren, illus. (Illus.). 1981. (ISBN 0-533-04765-X). Vantage.

Marten, Elizabeth, jt. auth. see Crosby, Nina.

Martens, Anne Coulter (1906-)
--Be Nice to the Easter Bunny: An Easter Play for the Grades. 8p. 19cm. c.1956. Baker's Plays.
--Jimmy and the Same Old Stuff: A Thanksgiving Play for the Grades. 8p. 19cm. c.1958. Baker's Plays.
--Pictures in the Fire: A Lincoln's Birthday Play for the Grades. 7p. 19cm. c.1956. Baker's Plays.
--Popular Plays for Teen-Agers. 1968. (ISBN 0-8238-0063-6). Plays, Inc.
--The Tiniest Christmas Tree: A Christmas Play for the Grades. 10p. 19cm. c.1956. Baker's Plays.
--A Visit from Washington: A Washington's Birthday Play for the Grades. 6p. 19cm. c.1956. Baker's Plays.
--Weather or Not: An April Fool's Day Play for the Grades. 8p. 19cm. c.1956. Baker's Plays.
--Who Sent the Comic Valentine?. A Valentine Play for the Grades. 8p. 19cm. c.1956. Baker's Plays.
--You Are Watching!. A Columbus Day Play for the Grades. 8p. 19cm. c.1956. Baker's Plays.

Martens, Frederick Herman (1874-1932), tr. see Stroebe, Klara.

Martens, Frederick Herman (1874-1932), tr. see Wilhelm, Richard.

Martens, Frederick Herman (1874-1932)
--The Chinese Fairy Book. N.D. J. B. Lippincott.
--Fairy Tales from Far Away. Norman, Da Loria, illus. LC 23-180145. 5 p. l., 347 p. col. front., plates (part col.) 22 cm. 1923. R. M. McBride & Company.
--Fairy Tales from the Orient. Hood, George W., illus. LC 23-180134. 5 p. l., 293 p. col. front., illus., plates (part col.) 22 cm. 1923. R. M. McBride & Company.
--The Norwegian Fairy bk. N.D. J. B. Lippincott.
--The Swedish Fairy bk. N.D. J. B. Lippincott.
--Wonder Tales from Far Away. Norman, Da Loria, illus. LC 24-287130. vi p., 1 l., 343 p. col. front., plates (part col.) 22 cm. 1924. R. M. McBride & Company.

Martignoni, Margaret E., ed.
--Every Child's Story Book: A Horn of Plenty of Good Reading for Boys and Girls. Fiammenghi, Gioia (1929-), illus. LC 58-9787. 273p. illus. 26cm. 1959. (ISBN 0-531-01664-1). Watts.
--Illustrated Treasury of Children's Literature. Martignoni, Margaret E., intro. by. (Illus.). 152p. 512p. (gr. 5-8). 1955. (ISBN 0-448-04101-4, G&D). Putnam Pub Group.

Martignoni, Margaret E & Ernest, P. Edward, eds.
--The Illustrated Treasury of Children's Literature. LC 55-13739. 512p. illus. 27cm. 1955. Grosset and Dunlap.

Martignoni, Margaret E. & Larrick, Nancy G. (1910-), eds.
--The Illustrated Treasury of Children's Literature: Including Poems for Young Children. Smith, Kay Lovelace, illus. LC 65-5578. (Illus.). 2 vols. 27cm. xv, 512p. (Compton's beginner's bookshelf). 1965. Compton.

Martin
--The Dollar Hunt. N.D. Benziger Brothers.

Martin, A. H., Mrs.
--The Cuckoo in the Robin's Nest. (Illus.). N.D. Cassell & Co.
--For a Dream's Sake. (Illus.). (The Girl's Own Favorite Ser.). N.D. E. P. Dutton & Co.

Martin, Albert Y. & Lee, Warren
--Secret Spy. Lee, Warren, illus. LC 78-72332. (Illus.). (Pacesetters Ser.). (gr. 4 up). 1979. (ISBN 0-516-02188-5). Childrens.
--Secret Spy. Lee, Warren, illus. LC 78-72332. (Illus.). 56 p. 18cm. (Pacemaker bestellers book). c.1979. (ISBN 0-8224-5368-1). Fearon Pitman Publishers.

Martin, Ann Matthews (1955-)
--Bummer Summer. LC 82-48755. p. cm. c.1983. (ISBN 0-8234-0483-8). Holiday House.
--Inside Out. LC 83-18631. 160p. (ps-7). 1984. (ISBN 0-8234-0512-5). (ISBN 0-8234-0512-5). Holiday.

--Just You & Me. 192p. (Orig.). (gr. 7 up). 1983. (ISBN 0-590-32429-2, Wildfire). Scholastic Inc.
--Me and Katie (the Pest). Sims, Blanche, illus. LC 85-5558. (Illus.). 152 p. 22cm. c.1985. (ISBN 0-8234-0580-X). Holiday House.
--Stage Fright. Sims, Blanche, illus. LC 84-47834. (Illus.). 144p. (gr. 3-7). 1984. (ISBN 0-8234-0541-9). Holiday.

Martin, Anna
--Star Magicians. Rossit, Harry, illus. LC 78-105807. (Illus.). 79 p. 19cm. (Star Knights). c.1978. Leswing Press.
--Star Peril. Rossit, Harry, illus. LC 78-105806. (Illus.). 96 p. 19cm. (Star Knights). c.1978. Leswing Press.

Martin, Anne Crittendon (1922-)
--Kenji and the Lost Kite. Wright, Morris, illus. LC 62-115406. unpaged. illus. 25cm. c.1962. Convention Press.

Martin, B.
--Sandusky Sam: Wise Owl Books. 1971. Holt Reinhart and Winston.

Martin, Ben
--Alfred. Martin, Ben, illus. LC 40-31353. 47 p. of illus. 23 cm. c.1940. Simon and Schuster.
--Mr. Smith and Mr. Schmidt. N.D. Vanguard Press.

Martin, Bernard Davis (1897-)
--Red Treasure. LC 47-30912. 21cm. 188p. N.D. Viking Press.

Martin, Bernard Herman, jt. auth. see Martin, William Ivan, Jr.

Martin, Bernard Herman, jt. ed. see Martin, William Ivan, Jr.

Martin, Bertha D & Mead, Genevieve
--Finger Plays and Songs for Church, Home, and Day Schools. LC 37-4991. 63 p. illus. 22 cm. c.1936. Southern Publishing Association.

Martin, Bill, Jr.
--Old Man on Our Block. (Young Owl Bks.). 1971. (ISBN 0-03-085825-9). HR&W.
--Three Billy Goats Gruff. (Little Owl Books). 1971. (ISBN 0-03-085736-8). Holt Rinehart and Winston.

Martin, Bill see Martin, William Ivan, Jr.

Martin, Bill see Martin, William Ivan, Jr. (1916-) & Archambault, John.

Martin, Bill see Martin, William Ivan, Jr. (1916-) & Baten, Helen.

Martin, Bill see Martin, William Ivan, Jr. (1916-) & Martin, Bernard Herman.

Martin, Blanche Ralston
--Children of Lei Land: An Ancient Fable and a Modern Tale. 1st ed. Nagel, Stina (1918-), illus. LC 60-4869. 173p. illus. 22cm. 1960. Exposition Press.

Martin, Charles E. (1910-)
--Dunkel Takes a Walk. 1st ed. Martin, Charles E. (1910-), illus. LC 82-11833. (Illus.). 9 7/8 x 8. 24p. (14 pt.). (gr. k-3). 1983. (ISBN 0-688-01815-7). (ISBN 0-688-01816-5). Greenwillow.
--For Rent. LC 85-864. p. cm. c.1985. (ISBN 0-688-05716-0). (ISBN 0-688-05717-9). Greenwillow Books.
--Island Rescue. Martin, Charles E. (1910-), illus. LC 84-13672. (Illus.). 32 p. c.1985. (ISBN 0-688-04257-0). (ISBN 0-688-04258-9). Greenwillow Books.
--Island Winter. Marten, C'.arles E. (1910-), illus. LC 83-14098. (Illus.). 32p. (gr. k-3). 1984. (ISBN 0-688-02590-0). (ISBN 0-688-02592-7). Greenwillow.
--The Story of Jonah. Martin, Charles E. (1910-), illus. (Illus.). 24p. (Look-Look Bks.). (ps). 1981. (ISBN 0-307-11863-0, Golden Pr). (ISBN 0-307-61863-3). Western Pub.
--Summer Business. Martin, Charles E. (1910-), illus. LC 83-25422. (Illus.). 9 7/8 x 8. 32p. (14 pt.). (gr. k-3). 1984. (ISBN 0-688-03863-8). (ISBN 0-688-03863-8). Greenwillow.

Martin, Charles Morris (1891-)
--Cowboy Charley, 4-H Champ. Oughton, Taylor (1925-), illus. LC 53-8177. 220p. illus. 21cm. 1953. Viking Press.
--Monsters of Old Los Angeles: The Prehistoric Animals of the La Brea Tar Pits. Rayburn, Herb, illus. LC 50-9529. 127 p. illus. 26 cm. 1950. Viking Press.
--Once a Cowboy. Dennis, Wesley (1903-1966), illus. LC 48-8352. 191 p. illus. 21 cm. 1948. Viking Press.
--Orphans of the Range. Barnum, Jay Hyde (1888-1962), illus. LC 50-9493. 192 p. illus. 21 cm. 1950. Viking Press.

Martin, Clara Barnes
--The Little Nortons. N.D. Loring, Short & Harmon.

Martin, Clarence S
--Jo Jo: The Boogie-Man. Martin, Charles S., illus. LC 60-299217. unpaged. illus. 21cm. (Bookland juvenile). 1960. Comet Press Books.
--The Mouse and the Moon. Martin, Charles S., illus. N.D. Carlton Press Inc.

Martin, Clyde Inez, jt. auth. see Blanchette, Zelda Beth.

Martin, Clyde Inez, jt. auth. see Espy, Rosalie.

Martin, Clyde Inez, jt. auth. see Rickard, John Allison.

Martin, Dahris Butterworth
--Adventure in Ireland. De Muth, Flora Nash (1888-), illus. LC 49-8103. 178 p. illus., map. 22 cm. 1949. J. Messner.
--Adventure in Tunisia, the Fair at Kairwan. De Muth, Flora Nash (1888-), illus. LC 46-8272. 5 p. l., 162 p. front. (map) illus. 22 cm. 1916. J. Messner, Inc.
--Awisha's Carpet: The Story of a Little Girl. Cuming, B. L., illus. LC 30-24346. (Illus.). 21cm. xiii, 190p. N.D. Doubleday, Doran.
--Fatma Was a Goose: Tunis Tales. Cuming, B. L., illus. LC 29-26790. x, 195 p. incl. illus., plates. col. front. 21 cm. 1929. Doubleday, Doran & Company, Inc.
--Little Lamb. Somppi, Lilly, illus. LC 38-870035. 32 p. incl. col. front., col. illus. 20 x 26 cm. 1938. (ISBN 0-06-024065-2). Harper & Brothers.
--The Wonder Cat. Watson, Aldren Auld (1917-), illus. LC 42-19434. 2 p. l., 59, 1 p. col. illus. 21 cm. 1942. Thomas Y. Crowell Company.

Martin, David (1915-)
--Hughie. Brookes, Ron, illus. LC 72-180488. (Illus.). vii, 165 p. 23cm. 1971. (ISBN 0-17-002912-3). Thomas Nelson (Australia).

Martin, David (1946-)
--K9 and the Beasts of Vega. Martin, David (1946-), illus. LC 81-23424. (Illus.). 31 p. 19cm. c.1982. (ISBN 0-86625-115-4). Rourke Publications.

Martin, David (1946-) & Getz, Arthur
--Gator and Mary's Traveling Band. LC 80-20956. p. cm. c.1981. (ISBN 0-8037-4556-7). (ISBN 0-8037-4557-5). Dial Press.

Martin, Don (1931-)
--The Mad Adventures of Captain Klutz. Martin, Don (1931-), illus. N.D. New American Library.

Martin, Dorothy Louisa
--Munya the Lion. Kiddell-Monroe, Joan (1908-), illus. LC 47-292642. 48 p. illus. (part col.) 25 cm. 1946. Oxford Univ. Press.

Martin, Dorothy McKay (1921-)
--A Chapter Closed for Peggy. (Peggy Ser.). N.D. (ISBN 0-686-13838-4). Believers Bkshelf.
--Chapter Closed for Peggy. (Peggy Ser.). (gr. 8 up). 1966. (ISBN 0-8024-7608-2). Moody.
--Edge of Belonging for Peggy. N.D. (ISBN 0-686-13805-8). Believers Bkshelf.
--Faith at Work. (Peggy Ser.: No. 9). 1985. (ISBN 0-8024-8309-7). Moody.
--Heart's Surrender for Peggy. (Peggy Ser.). N.D. (ISBN 0-686-13836-8). Believers Bkshelf.
--Heart's Surrender for Peggy. (Peggy Ser.). (gr. 8 up). 1963. (ISBN 0-8024-7606-6). Moody.
--Hopes Fulfilled for Peggy. (Peggy Ser.). N.D. (ISBN 0-686-13835-X). Believers Bkshelf.
--Hopes Fulfilled for Peggy. (Peggy Ser.). (gr. 8 up). 1963. (ISBN 0-8024-7605-8). Moody.
--More Answers for Peggy. (Peggy Ser.). N.D. (ISBN 0-686-13833-3). Believers Bkshelf.
--More Answers for Peggy. (Peggy Ser.). (gr. 8 up). 1959. (ISBN 0-8024-7603-1). Moody.
--The Mystery of the Empty House. LC 80-25606. 143 p. 17cm. c.1981. Moody Press.
--The Mystery of the Fourteenth Floor. LC 79-24718. 144 p. 17cm. c.1980. (ISBN 0-8024-5700-2). Moody Press.
--The Mystery of the Jade Earring. LC 80-10195. 128 p. 17cm. (Her Vickie series ; 3). c.1980. (ISBN 0-8024-5702-9). Moody Press.
--The Mystery of the Missing Bracelets. LC 79-25799. 123 p. 18cm. c.1980. (ISBN 0-8024-5701-0). Moody Press.
--The Mystery of the Missing Dog. LC 82-6276. 144 p. 18cm. (Pioneer Family Adventures: 5). c.1982. (ISBN 0-8024-5704-5). Moody Press.
--Mystery of the Stolen Flight Bag. LC 83-728. p. cm. c.1983. (ISBN 0-8024-0273-9). Moody Press.
--Mystery Solved for Peggy. (Peggy Ser.). N.D. (ISBN 0-686-13834-1). Believers Bkshelf.
--Mystery Solved for Peggy. (Peggy Ser.). (gr. 8 up). 1962. (ISBN 0-8024-7604-X). Moody.
--A New Life for Peggy. (Peggy Ser.). N.D. (ISBN 0-686-13831-7). Believers Bkshelf.
--New Life for Peggy. (Peggy Ser.). (gr. 8 up). 1957. (ISBN 0-8024-7601-5). Moody.
--Open Doors for Peggy. (Peggy Ser.). N.D. (ISBN 0-686-13832-5). Believers Bkshelf.
--Open Doors for Peggy. (Peggy Ser.). (gr. 8 up). 1958. (ISBN 0-8024-7602-3). Moody.
--Prayer Answered for Peggy. LC 75-45474. 128 p. 17cm. c.1976. (ISBN 0-8024-7610-4). Moody Press.
--Wider Horizons for Peggy. (Peggy Ser.). N.D. (ISBN 0-686-13837-6). Believers Bkshelf.
--Wider Horizons for Peggy. (Peggy Ser.). (gr. 8 up). 1964. (ISBN 0-8024-7607-4). Moody.

Martin, E. LeBreton (1874-1944)
--Boys of the Otter Patrol. Baden-Powell, Robert, frwd. by. N.D. J.B. Lippincott.

Martin, Edgar Everett (1898-)
--Boots and the Mystery of the Unlucky Vase: A Story Based on the Famous Newspaper Strip "Boots and Her Buddies,". authorized. Martin, Edgar Everette (1898-), illus. LC 44-1335. 3 p. l., 11-248 p. illus. 20 1/2 cm. 1943. Whitman Publishing Company.

Martin, Edward Sandford (1856-1939)
--A Little Brother of the Rich and other Verses. N.D. Charles Scribner.

Martin, Ethel Bowyer
--Judy-Come-Lately. 1st ed. Fleur, Anne Elizabeth (1901-), illus. Sari, pseud. LC 49-5591. 218 p. illus. 21 cm. 1949. Harcourt, Brace.

Martin, Eugene, pseud., see Stratemeyer Syndicate.

Martin, Eugene, pseud.
--Randy Starr Above Stormy Seas: Or, The Sky Flyers on a Perilous Journey. Stratemeyer Syndicate. Repr. of 1931 ed (Pub. by Henry Altemus Co). (Sky Flyers Ser.: No. 2). N.D. Saalfield Publishing Co.
--Randy Starr Above Stormy Seas: Or, The Sky Flyers on a Perilous Journey. Stratemeyer Syndicate. Hastings, Howard Livingston (1887-), illus. LC 31-15549. iv, 5-216 p. front., plates. 20 cm. (Sky Flyers Ser.: No. 2). 1931. Henry Altemus Co.
--Randy Starr After an Air Prize: Or, The Sky Flyers in a Dash Down the States. Stratemeyer Syndicate. Repr. of 1931 ed (Pub. by Henry Altemus Co). (Sky Flyers Ser.: No. 1). N.D. Saalfield Publishing Co.
--Randy Starr After an Air Prize: Or, The Sky Flyers in a Dash Down the States. Stratemeyer Syndicate. Hastings, Howard Livingston (1887-), illus. LC 31-10517. iv, 5-212 p. front., plates. 20 cm. (Sky Flyers Ser.: No. 1). 1931. Henry Altemus Co.
--Randy Starr Leading the Air Circus: Or, The Sky Flyers in a Daring Stunt. Stratemeyer Syndicate. Repr. of 1932 ed (Pub. by Henry Altemus Co). (Sky Flyers Ser.: No. 3). N.D. Saalfield Publishing Co.
--Randy Starr Leading the Air Circus: Or, The Sky Flyers in a Daring Stunt. Stratemeyer Syndicate. Hastings, Howard Livingston (1887-), illus. LC 32-198270. iv, 5-216 p. front., plates. 20 cm. (Sky Flyers Ser.: No. 3). 1932. Henry Altemus Co.
--Randy Starr Tracing the Air Spy: Or, The Sky Flyers Seeking the Stolen Plane. Stratemeyer Syndicate. (Sky Flyers Ser.: No. 4). 1933. Henry Altemus Co.

Martin, Florence Marie (1913-) & Burnett, Elizabeth
--Rime, Rhythm and Song for the Child of Today. Wilhoite, Mariel, illus. LC 43-11127. 80 p. illus. 28 x 21 1/2 cm. 1942. Hall & McCreary Company.

Martin, Florence Marie (1913-) & White, Margaret Rose, eds.
--Songs Children Sing: Singing Games, Nursery Songs, Lullabies, Folk Songs, Patriotic Songs, Christmas Carols, Children's Hymns. LC 44-36607. 1 p. l., 126 p. 21 1/2 cm. 1943. Hall & McCreary Company.

Martin, Fran see Martin, Frances Gardiner McEntee.

Martin, Fran see Martin, Frances Gardiner McEntee (1906-) & McEntee, Dorothy.

Martin, Frances Gardiner McEntee (1906-)
--Knuckles Down!. McEntee, Dorothy (1902-), illus. LC 42-36295. vii, 230 p. front., illus. 21 cm. 1942. Harper & Brothers.
--Nine Tales of Coyote. McEntee, Dorothy (1902-), illus. 60p. (gr. 3-7). 1950. Harper & Bros.
--Nine Tales of Raven. McEntee, Dorothy (1902-), illus. (Illus.). 60p. (gr. 3-7). 1951. (ISBN 0-06-024075-X). Har-Row.
--No School Friday. McEntee, Dorothy (1902-), illus. LC 45-9574. 4 p. l., 135 p. incl. front., illus. 21 cm. 1945. Harper & Brothers.
--Pirate Island. McEntee, Dorothy (1902-), illus. (Illus.). (gr. 6-9). 1955. (ISBN 0-8382-0666-2). Hale.
--Pirate Island. 1st ed. McEntee, Dorothy (1902-), illus. LC 55-90207. 215p. illus. 23cm. 1955. (ISBN 0-06-024080-6). Harper.
--The Poet's Hour. N.D. Macmillan & Co.
--Sea Room. McEntee, Dorothy (1902-), illus. LC 47-110143. 229 p. illus. 21 cm. 1947. Harper.
--Spring Time with the Poets. N.D. Macmillan & Co.

Martin, Frances Gardiner McEntee (1906-) & McEntee, Dorothy (1902-)
--Raven-Who-Sets-Things-Right: Indian Tales of the Northwest Coast. rev. ed., with all new art, of nine tales of raven. LC 74-2631. (Illus.). 90 p. 23cm. 1975. (ISBN 0-06-024071-7). (ISBN 0-06-024072-5). Harper & Row.

Martin, Frank E. & Davis, George M.
--Firebrands. 219p. N.D. Little, Brown.

Martin, Fredric, pseud., see Christopher, Matthew F..

Martin, Fredric, pseud. (1917-)
--The Mystery at Monkey Run. Christopher, Matthew F.. 1st ed. Butterfield, Ned (1917-), illus. LC 66-7291. (Illus.). (Two boys set out to solve the mystery of a prowler along the shores of Monkey Run Cove). (gr. 3-7). 1966. (ISBN 0-316-54766-2). (ISBN 0-316-54768-9). Little.
--The Mystery on Crabapple Hill. Christopher, Matthew F.. 1st ed. Goldstein, Nathan (1927-), illus. LC 65-17853. (Illus.). 136 p. 20cm. 1965. Little, Brown.
--The Mystery Under Fugitive House. 1st ed. Teason, James G., illus. LC 67-19796. (Illus.). 146 p. 20cm. 1967. Little, Brown.

Martin, George, tr. see Calvino, Italo.

Martin, George Edward (1851-1920)
--Sunday Songs for Little Children. LC 99-1323. (Illus.). 105p. 1899. Westminster Press.

Martin, George Madden, Mrs. (1866-1946)
--Abbie Ann. Relyea, Charles M., illus. LC 7-29096. 4 p. l., 3-252 p. incl. 24 pl. col. front. 20 cm. 1907. The Century Co.
--The Angel of the Tenement. LC 18-20847. 2 p. l., 134 p. front. 20 cm. 1897. Bonnell, Silver & Co.
--Children in the Mist. N.D. D. Appleton and Company.
--Emmy Lou, Her Book & Heart. Galdone, Paul (1914-), illus. LC 36-10763. 4 p. l., 3-277, 2 p. front., illus. 21 cm. 1936. Doubleday, Doran & Company, Inc.
--Emmy Lou: Her Book & Heart. Galdone, Paul (1914-), illus. LC 31-244432. 4 p. l., 3-277, 2 p. front., illus. 20 cm. c.1931. Grosset & Dunlap.
--Emmy Lou: Her Book & Heart. Hinton, Charles Louis (1869-), illus. LC 2-27731. 3 p. l., 279 p. front., illus. 20 cm. 1902. McClure, Phillips & Co.
--Emmy Lou's Road to Grace. (Growing Literature Ser.). N.D. Grosset & Dunlap.
--Emmy Lou's Road to Grace: Being a Little Pilgrim's Progress. LC 16-20436. ix p., 3 l., 3-305, 1 p., 1 l. front., plates. 19 cm. 1916. D. Appleton and Company.
--March On. N.D. D. Appleton & Co.
--A Warwickshire Lad: The Story of the Boyhood of William Shakespeare. LC 16-6289. v, 1 p., 1 l., 9-111, 1 p. incl. plates. front., plates. 20 cm. 1916. D. Appleton and Company.

Martin, George Whitney (1926-)
--The Battle of the Frogs and the Mice: An Homeric Fable. Gwynne, Frederick Hubbard (1926-), illus. LC 62-7755. 55p. illus. 22cm. 1962. Dodd, Mead.

Martin, Graham Dunstan (1932-)
--Catchfire. LC 81-13195. (Illus.). 183 p. 22cm. 1982, c.1981. (ISBN 0-395-31861-0). Houghton Mifflin.
--Giftwish. LC 79-42716. 200 p. 23cm. 1982. (ISBN 0-04-823175-4). G. Allen & Unwin.
--Giftwish. LC 80-22592. 202 p. 22cm. 1981, c.1978. (ISBN 0-395-30348-6). Houghton Mifflin.

Martin, Gretchen Galloway (1903-)
--The Begging Student. LC 48-538. 173 p. 20 cm. 1947. Wartburg Press.
--Jamaica "Ginger,". A Boy of the Days of Clipper Ships. Dugger, L. E., illus. LC 28-22357. 250 p. front., plates. 19 1/2 cm. c.1928. Lothrop, Lee & Shepard Co.
--The Messenger of Faith. Cue, Harold, illus. LC 30-9969. 2 p. l., 7-100 p. incl. plates. 19 1/2 cm. c.1929. David C. Cook Publishing Co.
--Under the Roman Eagle. Dugger, L. E., illus. LC 29-13627. 119 p. incl. plates. 19 1/2 cm. c.1928. David C. Cook Publishing Co.

Martin, Guenn (1942-)
--Remember the Eagle Day. LC 83-26376. (gr. 6-8). 1984. (ISBN 0-8361-3351-X). Herald Pr.

Martin, Herbert, Mrs.
--Cast Adrift: The Story of a Waif. (Illus.). N.D. E P Dutton.
--Elsa's Little Boys. (Illus.). 1910. Frederick Warne & Co.
--A Musical Genius. (Illus.). (Scribner-Blackie series of books for young people). N.D. Charles Scribner's Sons.

Martin, Ivan William, Jr. (1916-)
--Little Red Cap. (Wise Owl Books). 1971. (ISBN 0-03-085817-8). Holt Rinehart and Winston.

Martin, Jacqueline Briggs
--Bizzy Bones and Uncle Ezra. Ormai, Stella, illus. LC 83-25618. (Illus.). 32p. (ps-2). 1984. (ISBN 0-688-03781-X). (ISBN 0-688-03782-8). Lothrop.

Martin, Janet, pseud., see Garfinkel, Bernard.

Martin, Janet, pseud. (1929-)
--Fast and Slow. Garfinkel, Bernard. Thomas, Philippe, illus. LC 67-20638. 1v. (unpaged) col. illus. 19x21cm. (Platt & Munk fun-to-read bk.). 1967, c.1965. Platt & Munk.

Martin, William Ivan, Jr., jt. auth. see Shepherd, Gene D.
Martin, William Ivan, Jr. (1916-), adapted by see Galea'i Fa'apouli, Sano M.
Martin, William Ivan, Jr. (1916-)
--Adam's Balm. Foreman, Michael (1938-), illus. LC 76-129125. (Illus.). 32 p. 21cm. (Bill Martin freedom book). 1970. Bowmar.
--America, I Know You: A Freedom Book. Rand, Ted, illus. LC 72-109212. (Illus.). 32 p. 21cm. (Bill Martin freedom book). 1970. Published by the Bill Martin Corp. for Bowmar.
--At Home on the Ice. (Wise Owl Books). 1971. Holt Rinehart and Winston.
--Baby Elephant. (Little Owl Books). 1971. Holt, Rinehart and Winston.
--Big Frogs Little Frogs. (Wise Owl Books). 1971. Holt, Rinehart and Winston.
--Brown Bear, Brown Bear, What Do You See?. Carle, Eric (1929-), illus. LC 67-9474. (Illus.). l v. (unpaged. 29cm. (Kin-Der owl book, KR1). 1967. Holt, Rinehart and Winston.
--Brown Bear, Brown Bear: What Do You See?. Carle, Eric (1929-), illus. LC 83-12779. (Illus.). 32p. (gr. k-2). 1983. (ISBN 0-03-064164-0). (ISBN 0-03-064164-0). HR&W.
--Brown Bear, Brown Bear, What Do You See?. Shimin, Symeon (1902-), illus. LC 67-9475. 1 v. (unpaged) col. illus. 29 cm. (Kin/Der owlbook, KC4). 1967. Holt, Rinehart and Winston.
--Captain Murphy's Tugboat. (Little Owl Books). 1971. (ISBN 0-03-085740-6). Holt, Rinehart and Winston.
--A Cat Story. (Little Owl Books). 1971. (ISBN 0-03-085707-4). Holt, Rinehart and Winston.
--The Caterpiller Man. (Wise Owl Books). 1971. (ISBN 0-03-085834-8). Holt Rinehart and winston.
--Daddy is Home. (Little Owl Books). 1971. (ISBN 0-03-085711-2). Holt Rinehart and Winston.
--David Was Mad. Shimin, Symeon (1902-), illus. LC 67-9475. (Illus.). l v. (unpaged. (Kin/Der owl book, KC4). 1967. Holt, Rinehart and Winston.
--David Was Mad. Shimin, Symeon (1902-), illus. (Kinder-Owl Books). (ps-1). 1971. (ISBN 0-03-085774-0, Holte). Holt, Rhinehart, Winston.
--The Emperor's Nightingale. (Wise Owl Books). 1971. (ISBN 0-03-085791-0). Holt Rinehart and Winston.
--Five is Five. (Little Owl Books). 1971. (ISBN 0-03-085741-4). Holt, Rinehart and Winston.
--A Fox Story. (Wise Owl Books). 1971. (ISBN 0-03-085812-7). Holt Rinehart and Winston.
--Freedom's Apple Tree. Rombola, John, illus. LC 79-109203. (Illus.). 30 p. 21cm. (Bill Martin freedom book). 1970. Bowmar.
--The Frightened Hare: Wise Owl Books. 1971. Holt Reinhart and Winston.
--The Funny Old Man and The Funny Old Women. (Wise Owl Books). 1971. (ISBN 0-03-085813-5). Holt Rinehart and Winston.
--A Ghost Story. Carle, Eric (1929-) & Barber, Ray, illus. LC 70-107089. (Illus.). 31 p. 17cm. (Bill Martin instant reader). 1970. (ISBN 0-03-084588-2). Holt, Rinehart and Winston.
--Going up Going Down. (Little Owl Books). 1971. (ISBN 0-03-085708-2). Holt, Rinehart and Winston.
--The Golden Crane: Wise Owl Books. (Wise Owl Books). 1971. (ISBN 0-03-085790-2). Holt Rinehart and Winston.
--Goodmorning Mr. Sun. (Little Owl Books). 1971. Holt Rinehart and Winston.
--Goodnight Mr. Beetle. (Little Owl Books). 1971. (ISBN 0-03-085710-4). Holt, Rinehart Winston.
--The Great Circus Parade. (Little Owl Books). 1971. (ISBN 0-03-085712-0). Holt, Rinehart and Winston.
--The Happy Hippopotami. Velde, Robert, illus. LC 78-106418. (Illus.). 32 p. 17cm. (Bill Martin instant reader). 1970. (ISBN 0-03-084596-3). Holt, Rinehart and Winston.
--The Haunted House. Lippman, Peter J. (1936-) & Barber, Ray, illus. LC 76-109193. (Illus.). 31 p. 17cm. (Bill Martin instant reader). 1970. (ISBN 0-03-084575-0). Holt, Rinehart and Winston.
--Here Comes Jimmy! Here Comes Jimmy's Dog. (Little Owl Bks.). 1971. (ISBN 0-03-085714-7). HR&W.
--The House Biter. (Little Owl Books). 1971. (ISBN 0-03-085728-7). Holt Rinehart and Winston.
--The House that Jack Built. (Little Owl Books). 1971. (ISBN 0-03-085715-5). Holt, Rinehart and Winston.
--I Paint the Joy of a Flower. Jablonsky, Carolyn, et al., illus. LC 74-111206. (Illus.). 32 p. 17cm. (Bill Martin instant reader). c.1970. (ISBN 0-03-084576-9). Holt, Rinehart and Winston.
--I Reach Out to the Morning. Markowitz, Henry, illus. LC 75-129130. (Illus.). 32 p. 21cm. (Bill Martin freedom book). 1970. Bowman.
--It's America for Me: A Freedom Book. Glanzman, Louis S. (1922-), illus. LC 79-129131. (Illus.). 30 p. 21cm. (Bill Martin freedom book). 1970. Bowmar.
--Joey Kangaroo: Little Owl Books. (Little Owl Books). 1971. Holt Rinehart and Winston.
--Kin-der Owl Books. Incl. David Was Mad. (ISBN 0-03-085774-0). (Social Studies Ser.). (ps-1). 1971 (HoltE). HR&W.
--Kin-der Owl Books. (Arithmetic Ser.). (ps-1). 1971 (HoltE). HR&W.
--King of the Mountain. Parry, Ivor, illus. LC 74-106417. (Illus.). 31 p. 17cm. (Bill Martin instant reader). 1970. (ISBN 0-03-084597-1). Holt, Rinehart and Winston.
--Knots on a Counting Rope. Smith, Joe (1936-), illus. LC 66-17925. (Illus.). 25 p. (Young Owl Book). c.1966. Holt, Rinehart and Winston.
--Little Princess Goodnight. Domjan, Joseph Spiri (1907-), illus. LC 67-9581. 1 v. (unpaged) col. illus. 29 cm. (Kin/Der owl book, KL2). 1967. ,Holt, Rinehart and Winston.
--The Maestro Plays. Murdocca, Salvatore & Barber, Ray, illus. LC 78-111207. (Illus.). 32 p. 17cm. (Bill Martin instant reader). 1970. Holt, Rinehart and Winston.
--Monday, Monday, I Like Monday. Leder, Dora, illus. LC 72-109192. (Illus.). 32 p. 17cm. (Bill Martin instant reader). c.1970. (ISBN 0-03-084579-3). Holt, Rinehart and Winston.
--Mr. Jolly's Sidewalk Market. (Little Owl Books). 1971. (ISBN 0-03-085719-8). Holt Rinehart And Winston.
--My Little Brother. (Little Owl Books). 1971. (ISBN 0-03-085723-6). Holt Rinehart and Winston.
--My Turtle Died Today. (Young Owl Bks.). 1971. (ISBN 0-03-085833-X). HR&W.
--Old Devil Wind. Lee, Robert J. (1921-) & Barber, Ray, illus. LC 70-109206. (Illus.). 31 p. 17cm. (Bill Martin instant reader). 1970. (ISBN 0-03-084590-4). Holt, Rinehart and Winston.
--Old Lucy Lindy. (Young Owl Bks.). 1971. (ISBN 0-03-085839-9). HR&W.
--Old Mother Goose. (Little Owl Books). 1971. (ISBN 0-03-085721-X). Holt, Rinehart and Winston.
--Old Mother Middle Muddle. Madden, Donald B. (1927-), illus. LC 72-109204. (Illus.). 30 p. 17cm. (Bill Martin instant reader). 1970. (ISBN 0-03-084589-0). Holt, Rinehart and Winston.
--The Old Women and Her Pig. (Little Owl Books). 1971. (ISBN 0-03-085722-8). Holt, Rinehart and Winston.
--Once There Were Bluebirds. Martin, Bernard Herman (1912-), illus. LC 77-129128. (Illus.). 32 p. 21cm. (Bill Martin freedom book). 1970. Bowmar.
--One Two Three Four. (Illus.). (Little Owl Books). 1971. (ISBN 0-03-085724-4). Holt Rinehart and Winston.
--Our New Home in the City. (Young Owl Bks.). 1971. (ISBN 0-03-085824-0). HR&W.
--Paulossie. (Young Owl Bks.). 1971. (ISBN 0-03-085827-5). HR&W.
--Poems for Counting. (Little Owl Books). 1971. (ISBN 0-03-085724-4). Holt Rinehart and Winston.
--Poems for Galloping. (Little Owl Books). 1971. (ISBN 0-03-085726-0). Holtl, Rinehart and Winston.
--Poor Old Uncle Sam: A Freedom Book. Murdocca, Salvatore, illus. LC 70-129126. (Illus.). 30 p. 21cm. (Bill Martin freedom book). 1970. Bowmar.
--The Proud Peacock. (Little Owl Books). 1971. (ISBN 0-03-085792-9). Holt Rinehart and Winston.
--Round as a Pancake. (Little Owl Books). 1971. (ISBN 0-03-085730-9). Holt, Rinehart and Winston.
--Smokey Poky. (Little Owl Books). 1971. (ISBN 0-03-085718-X). Holt Rinehart and Winston.
--Smoky Poky. Martin, Bernard Herman (1912-) & Martin, Bernard Herman (1912-), illus. (Winston Tell-Well Story Bks.). 1954. John C. Winston Co.
--Spoiled Tomatoes. Ells, Jay, illus. LC 73-129127. (Illus.). 32 p. 21cm. (Bill Martin freedom book). 1970. Bowman.
--A Spooky Story. Pucci, Albert John (1920-) & Barber, Ray, illus. LC 79-109211. (Illus.). 32 p. 17cm. (Bill Martin instant reader). c.1970. (ISBN 0-03-084600-5). Holt, Rinehart and Winston.
--The Steadfast Tin Soldier. (Young Owl Bks.). 1971. (ISBN 0-03-085829-1). HR&W.
--The Sun is a Star. (Little Owl Books). 1971. (ISBN 0-03-085718-X). Holt Rinehart and Winston.
--Tatty Mae & Catty Mae. Watson, Aldren Auld (1917-), illus. LC 70-109197. (Illus.). 32 p. 17cm. 1970. (ISBN 0-03-084578-5). Holt, Rinehart and Winston.
--Ten Little Caterpillars. Riswold, Gilbert, illus. LC 67-9476. 1 v. (unpaged) col. illus. 17 x 24 cm. (Kin/Der owl book, KA7). 1967. Holt, Rinehart and Winston.
--Ten Little Squirrels: An Old Rhyme. Martin, Bernard Herman (1912-), illus. LC 73-109207. (Illus.). 32 p. 17cm. (Bill Martin instant reader). 1970. (ISBN 0-03-084601-3). Holt, Rinehart and Winston.
--Ten Pennies for Candy. (Little Owl Books). 1971. (ISBN 0-03-085734-1). Holt, Rinehart and Winston.
--Three Little Dachshunds. (Little Owl Books). 1971. (ISBN 0-03-085737-6). Holt, Rinehart and Winston.
--The Tiger, the Brahman and the Jackal: An East Indian Legend. (Young Owl Bks.). 1971. (ISBN 0-03-085838-0). HR&W.
--Town Mouse, Country Mouse. (Young Owl Bks.). 1971. (ISBN 0-03-085811-9). HR&W.
--Up and Down the Escalator. Oechsli, Kelly (1918-), illus. LC 70-109194. (Illus.). 32 p. 17cm. (Bill Martin instant reader). 1970. (ISBN 0-03-084581-5). Holt, Rinehart and Winston.
--Welcome Home, Henry. Batherman, Muriel (1926-), illus. LC 75-109210. (Illus.). 32 p. 17cm. (Monkeying-around-with-print book.). (A Bill Martin Instant Reader). c.1970. (ISBN 0-03-084603-X). Holt, Rinehart and Winston.
--What is Big. (Little Owl Books). 1971. Holt Rinehart Winston.
--What is Pink. (Little Owl Books). 1971. Holt Rinehart and Winston.
--What to Say and When to Say It. Shein, Bob, illus. LC 77-115045. (Illus.). 32 p. 17cm. (Bill Martin instant reader). 1970. (ISBN 0-03-084856-3). Holt, Rinehart and Winston.
--When Great Greatmother was a Little Girl. (Little Owl Books). 1971. (ISBN 0-03-085807-0). Holt Rinehart and Winston.
--When It Rains ... It Rains. Luzzati, Emanuele (1921-), illus. LC 79-109191. (Illus.). 32 p. 17cm. (Bill Martin instant reader). c.1970. (ISBN 0-03-084582-3). Holt, Rinehart and Winston.
--Where is My Shoes?. (Little Owl Bks.). 1971. (ISBN 0-03-085716-3). HR&W.
--Whistle, Mary, Whistle. Luzzati, Emanuele (1921-), illus. LC 78-109199. (Illus.). 31 p. 17cm. (Bill Martin instant reader). 1970. (ISBN 0-03-084593-9). Holt, Rinehart and Winston.
--The Wizard. Murdocca, Salvatore & Martin, Bernard Herman (1912-), illus. LC 77-107088. (Illus.). 32 p. 17cm. (Bill Martin instant reader). 1970. (ISBN 0-03-084583-1). Holt, Rinehart and Winston.
--Young Owl Books. (Literature Ser.). (gr. 2-4). 1971 (HoltE). HR&W.

Martin, William Ivan, Jr. (1916-), adapted by.
--Fire! Fire! Said Mrs. McGuire. Schroeder, Ted (1931-1973), illus. LC 71-109201. (Illus.). 31 p. 17cm. (Bill Martin instant reader). 1970. (ISBN 0-03-084586-6). Holt, Rinehart and Winston.
--Sounds of the Storyteller. Brogan, Peggy (1916-), illus. LC 76-154051. (Illus.). 288 p. 24cm. (His Sounds of language readers). 1972. (ISBN 0-03-083355-8). Holt, Rinehart and Winston.

Martin, William Ivan, Jr. (1916-) & Archambault, John
--The Ghost-Eye Tree. Rand, Ted, illus. LC 85-8422. (Illus.). 32 p. 27cm. c.1985. Holt, Rinehart and Winston.

Martin, William Ivan, Jr. (1916-) & Baten, Helen
--I'm Going to Build a Supermarket One of These Days. Papas, William (1927-), illus. LC 70-109209. (Illus.). 32 p. 17cm. (Bill Martin instant reader). 1970. (ISBN 0-03-084595-5). Holt, Rinehart and Winston.

Martin, William Ivan, Jr. (1916-) & McKibben, Bill
--Which Do You Choose?. LC 67-9417. 1 v. (unpaged) col. illus. 29 cm. (Kin-Der Owl Book, KR10). 1967. Holt, Rinehart and Winston.

Martin, William Ivan, Jr. (1916-) & Martin, Bernard Herman (1912-)
--Bunny's Easter Gift. Martin, Bernard Herman (1912-), illus. LC 49-8862. 26 p. col. illus. 28 cm. c.1948. Tell-Well Press.
--Chicken Chuck. Martin, Bernard Herman (1912-), illus. LC 46-21744. 36 p. col. illus. 27 1/2 cm. c.1946. The Tell-Well Press, Inc.
--Christmas Puppy. Martin, Bernard Herman (1912-), illus. LC 49-49410. 26 p. col. illus. 28 cm. c.1949. Tell-Well Press.
--Golden Arrow. Martin, Bernard Herman (1912-), illus. LC 50-6658. (Illus.). 33 p. 28cm. 1950. Tell-Well Press.
--The Green-Eyed Stallion. Martin, Bernard Herman (1912-), illus. LC 53-12325. 128p. illus. 25cm. 1953. Tell-Well Press.
--Hook and Ladder, No. 3. Martin, Bernard Herman (1912-), illus. LC 49-16332. 26 p. col. illus. 28 cm. c.1948. Tell-Well Press.
--Hook and Ladder Number Three. Martin, Bernard Herman (1912-), illus. (Winston Tell-Well Story Bks.). 1954. John C. Winston Co.
--Lightning, A Cowboy's Colt. Martin, Bernard Herman (1912-), illus. (Winston Tell-Well Story Book). 1954. John C. Winston Co.
--Lightning: A Cowboy's Colt. Martin, Bernard Herman (1912-), illus. LC 48-2613. 28 p. col. illus. 28 cm. c.1948. Tell-Well Press.
--The Little Squeegy Bug. Martin, Bernard Herman (1912-), illus. LC 67-16453. (Illus.). 26 p. (Kin-Der Owl Book). c.1967. Holt, Rinehart and Winston.
--Little Squeegy Bug. Martin, Bernard Herman (1912-), illus. (Winsotn Tell-Well Story Bks.). 1954. John C. Winston Co.
--Little Squeegy Bug. Martin, Bernard Herman (1912-), illus. LC 45-8766. 32 p. col. illus. 21 1/2 cm. 1945. Tell-Well Press, Inc.
--Little Squeegy Bug. Martin, Bernard Herman (1912-), illus. LC 46-22070. 33 p. col. illus. 27 1/2 cm. 1946. Tell-Well Press.
--Palomino Pony. Martin, Bernard Herman (1912-), illus. LC 52-7592. unpaged. illus. 27 cm. (Quality juvenile books). 1952. Tell Well Press.
--Silver Stallion. Martin, Bernard Herman (1912-), illus. (Winston Tell-Well Story Bks.). 1954. John C. Winston Co.
--Silver Stallion. Martin, Bernard Herman (1912-), illus. LC 49-494118. 26 p. illus. (part col.) 28 cm. 1949. Tell-Well Press.
--Smoky Poky. Martin, Bernard Herman (1912-), illus. LC 47-6631. 32 p. col. illus. 28 cm. 1947. Tell-Well Press.
--Wild Horse Roundup. Martin, Bernard Herman (1912-), illus. 1952. The Tell-Well Press.

Martin, William Ivan, Jr. (1916-) & Martin, Bernard Herman (1912-), eds.
--The Brave Little Indian. LC 67-9418. 1 v.(unpaged) col. illus. 29 cm. (Kin-Der Owl Book, KL1). 1967. Holt, Rinehart and Winston.
--The Brave Little Indian. Bisch, Charlene, illus. LC 51-12848. (Illus.). unpaged. 28cm. 1951. Tell-Well Press.

Martin, William Ivan, Jr. (1916-) & Reed, Dorothy Tyler (1912-)
--Rosy Nose. Martin, Bernard Herman (1912-), illus. LC 46-86710. 33 p. col. illus. 27 x 21 cm. 1946. Tell-Well Press.

Martin, Winona Caroline (1882-1918)
--The Story of King Arthur. Martin, Winona Caroline (1882-1918), illus. 1928. Coward-McCann, Inc.
--The Story of King Arthur: In Twelve Tales. Martin, Winona Caroline (1882-1918), illus. LC 15-152896. xl, 1, 154 p. incl. front., illus. 22 1/2 cm. 1915. The Storytellers Company.

Martindale, Chris
--Duel of the Masters. LC 84-51002. 160p. (A Dungeons & Dragons Endless Quest Bk.). (gr. 5 up). 1984. (ISBN 0-394-72784-3, Pub. by BYR). Random.

Martineau, Harriet (1802-1876)
--Billow and Rock. New ed. Wheeler, E. J., illus. (Illus.). N.D. George Routledge & Sons.
--Feats on the Fiord: A Tale of Norwegian Life. (Illus.). N.D. L. C. Page & Co.
--The Peasant and the Prince. LC 25-18815. 16cm. 191p. (The Martineau Library). N.D. George Routledge & Sons.
--The Peasant and the Prince. Boynton, Henry Walcott, ed. LC 2-29919. viii, 204 p. 18 1/2 cm. (Riverside literature series. no. 152). 1902. Houghton, Mifflin and Company.
--The Peasant and the Prince. A Story of the French Revolution. LC 4-9594. viii, 212 p. 18 cm. 1886. Ginn & Company.
--The Peasant and the Prince: A Story of the French Revolution. Bryant, Sara Cone (1873-), ed. LC 17-5819. x, 298 p. illus. 18 cm. c.1917. Ginn and Company.
--The Peasant and the Prince: A Story of the French Revolution. Shaw, Edward R., ed. LC 99-5688. 183 p. 18 cm. (On cover: Standard literature series, no. 41). c.1899. University Publishing Company.
--The Playfellow: Comprising Miss Martineau's Juvenile Stories. (Illus.). N.D. George Routledge.

Martineau des Chesnez, Elizabeth Lair (1829-)
--Lady Green Satin and Her Maid Rosette: Or, The History of Jean Paul and his Little White Mouse. (Illus.). N.D. Porter and Coates.
--Lady Green Satin and Her Maid Rosette: The History of Jean Paul and His Little White Mice. Bromhall, Winifred, illus. Hunt, Clara Whitehill (1871-), tr. LC 23-12964. x, 275 p. incl. illus., plates. col. front. 20 cm. 1923. The Macmillan Company.

Martinek, Frank Victor (1895-)
--Don Winslow and the Scorpion's Stronghold. authorized. Bromhall, Winifred, illus. LC 46-7938. 2 p. l., 9-248 p. illus. 20 1/2 cm. 1946. Whitman Publishing Company.
--Don Winslow Breaks the Spy Net. LC 41-8990. 4 p. l., 211 p. incl. front. 19 1/2 cm. c.1941. Grosset & Dunlap.
--Don Winslow Face to Face with the Scorpion. Warren, Ferdinand E., illus. LC 40-33793. 4 p. l., 215 p. front. 19 1/2 cm. c.1940. Grosset & Dunlap.

--Don Winslow of the Navy. Warren, Ferdinand E., illus. LC 40-7528. vi p., 1 l., 214 p. incl. front. 19 1/2 cm. c.1940. Grosset & Dunlap.
--Don Winslow Saves the Secret Formula. Warren, Ferdinand E., illus. LC 41-194213. v, 218 p. incl. front. 19 1/2 cm. c.1941. Grosset & Dunlap.
--Don Winslow: U.S.N., in Ceylon with Kwang, Celebrated Chinese. LC 35-2967. 258 p. incl. plates. 19 1/2 cm. c.1934. Rosenow Co.

Martinez, Carmel
--Susan Peck: Late of Boston. LC 62-144009. 187p. 21cm. 1962. Putnam.

Martinez, Donna
--My Horse Knows Where Acoma Is. Sarracino, William L., illus. (Illus.). 10p. (Orig.). 1st U.S. edition. (ps-7). 1982. (ISBN 0-915347-00-8). Pueblo Acoma Pr.

Martinez, Mina, illus.
--O Jemima!. (Illus.). 48p. (Play School Books Ser.). (gr. k). N.D. (ISBN 0-563-09269-6). BBC.

Martinez, Raizizun May
--Your Own Little Elf. Rowland, Lucille, illus. LC 77-78912. (Illus.). 52 p. 21cm. (Quest book for children). 1969. Theosophical Pub. House.

Martinez del Rio, Ahelia
--The Sun, the Moon and a Rabbit. Charlot, Jean (1898-1979), illus. LC 35-145657. 191, 1 p. illus. (part col.) 18 1/2 x 26 cm. 1935. Sheed & Ward.

Martingale, H.
--Mark Rowland: A Sea Story for Boys. 1884. H. A. Sumner & Co.

Martingale, Hawser
--Jack in the Forecastle. N.D. Nichols & Hall.

Martini, Teri (1930-)
--All Because of Jill. LC 75-44167. 155 p. 21cm. c.1976. (ISBN 0-664-32589-0). Westminster Press.
--Fisherman's Ring. 1954. St. Anthony Guild Press.
--The Lucky Ghost Shirt. Gretzer, John, illus. LC 70-128642. (Illus.). 104 p. 24cm. 1971. (ISBN 0-664-32484-3). Westminster Press.
--Mystery of the Hard Luck House. Davis, Omar, illus. LC 65-15261. 153p. illus. 22cm. c.1965. Criterion.
--The Mystery of the Woman in the Mirror. Boehm, Linda, illus. LC 73-7901. (Illus.). 123 p. 21cm. 1973. (ISBN 0-664-32534-3). Westminster Press.
--The Mystery Waters of Tonbridge Wells. Boehm, Linda, illus. LC 74-28313. (Illus.). 139 p. 21cm. 1975. (ISBN 0-664-32565-3). Westminster Press.
--Patrick Henry Patriot. Jacobson, Robert, illus. 1972. (ISBN 0-664-32507-6). Westminster Press.
--Treasure of the Mohawks: The Story of the Indian Maiden Kateri Tekakwitha. Bradbury, Robert, illus. LC 56-427871. 113p. illus. 24cm. 1956. St. Anthony Guild Press.
--What a Frog Can Do. Polseno, Jo, illus. LC 62-7498. unpaged. illus. 26cm. 1962. Reilly & Lee.

Martinsen, Paul T., tr. see Wiemer, Rudolf Otto.

Martinson, Helen & Martinson, Melvin (1889-)
--Grandpa's Farm. Maltman, Chauncey, illus. LC 49-6163. 41 p. illus. 25 cm. c.1949. Childrens Press.

Martinson, Melvin, jt. auth. see Hoogstraal, Harry.

Martinson, Melvin, jt. auth. see Martinson, Helen.

Martorana, Carol A.
--The Drayco Dragon. (gr. 2-4). N.D. Carlton.

Marty, pseud., see Hancock, Myrtle J. Marti.

Marty, pseud.
--Mitzi. Hancock, Myrtle J. Marti. Thorne, Diana (1894-), illus. N.D. Grosset & Dunlap.

Martyn, Sarah Towne Smith, Mrs. (1805-1879)
--Dora's Mistake. N.D. American Tract Society.
--Will Thornton, the Crow Boy. 144p. (Alice and Willie Stories). N.D. Lockwood, Brooks, & Co. for American Tract Society.
--Winnie and her Grandfather. 144p. N.D. Hurd & Houghton for American Tract Society.
--Winnie and Her Grandfather. 144p. (Cozy House Stories). N.D. Lockwood, Brooks, & Co. for American Tract Society.

Martz, John, ed. see Bowling, David Louis & Bowling, Patricia Hendy.

Martz, Louis L., ed. see Bunyan, John.

Maruki, Toshi
--Hiroshima No Pika. 1982. Lothrop. **Award: (MLB).**

Marvel, Elinore, jt. ed. see Radin, Paul.

Marvin, Eleanor
--Mary Allen. Beard, Alice, illus. LC 16-6761. vii p., 2 l., 3-238, 2 p. front., plates. 19 1/2 cm. $1.2. 1916. Doubleday, Page & Company.

Marvin, Francis Sydney (1863-) & Mayor, Robert John Grote (1869-)
--The Adventures of Odysseus. Quiller-Couch, Arthur Thomas, Sir (1863-1944), ed. LC 26-12571. 221, 1 p. incl. front. (port.) illus. 15 1/2 cm. (Half-title: The Kings treasuries of literature; general editor, Sir A. T. Quiller Couch. 10). 1924. J. M. Dent & Sons, Ltd.

Marvin, H. N., Mrs.
--Rabbit Snares, and other stories. 128p. N.D. Hurd & Houghton for American Tract Society.
--Rabbit Snares, and Other Stories. 128p. (Gay Cottage Stories). N.D. Lockwood, Brooks, & Co. for American Tract Society.

Marvin, Mayor & Marvin, Stawell
--The Adventures of Odysseus. N.D. E. P. DUtton & Co.

Marvin, Stawell, jt. auth. see Marvin, Mayor.

Marwick, Ernest W.
--The Folklore of Orkney and Shetland: Ledgends, Folk-Tales and Customs. 1975. (ISBN 0-87471-681-0). Rowman and Littlefield.

Marwood, Desmond
--The Enchanted Island. LC 77-184851. (Illus.). 30p. (Scratch & Sniff Books). (gr. k-3). 1972. (ISBN 0-529-04493-5). World Pub.
--Granny Bear's Birthday. Manchipp, Ben, illus. LC 70-184852. (Illus.). 30p. (Scratch & Sniff Books). (gr. k-3). 1972. World Pub.

Marx, W. J
--For the Admiral. LC 7-28959. viii p., 1 l., 333 p. front., 5 pl. 20 1/2 cm. 1907. G. W. Jacobs & Company.

Marxhausen, Ben, jt. auth. see Marxhausen, Joanne G

Marxhausen, Evelyn
--The Man Who Slept Through a Sermon. (Illus.). (Arch Bk.: No. 16). 1979. (ISBN 0-570-06128-8). Concordia.

Marxhausen, Joanne G. (1935-)
--I Am a Cloud. Marxhausen, Benjamin W., illus. LC 78-12751. p. cm. c.1979. (ISBN 0-570-07951-9). Concordia Pub. House.
--I Am a Tree. Marxhausen, Benjamin W., illus. (Illus.). 1979. (ISBN 0-570-07952-7). Concordia.
--I Am the Sun. Marxhausen, Benjamin W., illus. (Illus.). 1979. (ISBN 0-570-07950-0). Concordia.
--The Mysterious Star. Morris, Susan Stoehr, illus. LC 75-310771. (Illus.). 48 p. 26cm. 1974. (ISBN 0-570-03433-7). Concordia Pub. House.
--Thank God for Circles: Story. Johnson, Daniel E., illus. LC 75-159012. (Illus.). 32 p. 27cm. 1971. (ISBN 0-8066-1135-9). Augsburg Pub. House.

Marxhausen, Joanne G. (1935-) & Marxhausen, Ben
--I Am People. (Illus.). 1979. (ISBN 0-570-07953-5). Concordia.

Mary, Agnes
--Albert in Wonderland. Ryan, Connelly, illus. N.D. Vantage Press.

Mary Adrian, pseud., see Venn, Mary Eleanor.

Mary Charitina, ed. see Spenser, Edmund.

Mary Immaculate, Sr. (1908-), ed.
--The Cry of Rachel: An Anthology of Elegies on Children. LC 66-21477. xxiv, 196 p. 25cm. 1966. Random House.

Maryland Webb, David
--The Little Seed... Harris, Janet Barnes, illus. LC 79-67086. (Illus.). 39p. (Orig.). (gr. 3-8). 1979. (ISBN 0-935054-00-6). Webb-Newcomb.

Marylla
--Stella Matutina; A Star Story. Marylla, illus. LC 37-729. (Illus.). 31p. 23cm. 1936. The Franciscan Missionaries of Mary.

Mary Marguerite, Sr. (1895-)
--Martin's Mice. Busoni, Rafaello (1900-1962), illus. LC 54-10096. 32cm. 32p. N.D. Wilcox & Follett Co.

Mary Thomas, Sr.
--Not Words but Deeds: The Story of Nano Nagle. Jagodits, Carolyn Lee, illus. LC 68-23382. (Illus.). 92 p. 22cm. 1968. Dujarie Press.

Marzetti, Salli L.
--Santa Spreads Love Through God. 1979. (ISBN 0-685-62887-6). Vantage.
--Santa Spreads Love Through God. (Illus.). 1980. (ISBN 0-533-03800-6). Vantage.

Marzollo, Claudio, jt. auth. see Marzollo, Jean.

Marzollo, Jean (1942-)
--Amy Goes Fishing. Schweninger, Ann (1951-), illus. LC 80-11598. (Illus.). 56 p. 24cm. (Dial easy-to-read). c.1980. (ISBN 0-8037-0109-8). (ISBN 0-8037-0111-X). Dial Press.
--Baxter's Bad Day: A Read & Play Storybook. Thornton, Shelley, illus. (Illus.). 32p. (Orig.). (ps-3). 1983. (ISBN 0-590-32652-X). Scholastic Inc.
--Close Your Eyes. Jeffers, Susan, illus. LC 76-42935. (Illus.). 32 p. 26cm. c.1978. (ISBN 0-8037-1609-5). (ISBN 0-8037-1610-9). Dial Press.
--Do You Love Me, Harvey Burns?. LC 82-73218. p. cm. c.1983. (ISBN 0-8037-1668-0). Dial Press.
--Doll House Adventure. Thornton, Shelley, illus. (Illus.). 32p. (Orig.). (A Punch & Play Storybook Ser.). (ps-3). 1984. (ISBN 0-590-33094-2). Scholastic Inc.
--Halfway Down Paddy Lane. LC 80-25854. 178 p. 22cm. c.1981. (ISBN 0-8037-3329-1). Dial Press.
--Out of Time, Into Love. 176p. (gr. 7 up). 1982. (ISBN 0-590-32502-7). Scholastic Inc.
--Superkids. LC 80-8691. (Illus.). 1982. (ISBN 0-06-090939-0, CN). Har-Row.
--Uproar on Hollercat Hill. Kellogg, Steven (1941-), illus. LC 79-22201. (Illus.). 32 p. 28cm. c.1980. (ISBN 0-8037-9027-9). (ISBN 0-8037-9028-7). Dial Press.

Marzollo, Jean (1942-) & Marzollo, Claudio
--Blue Sun Ben. Meddaugh, Susan (1944-), illus. LC 83-18808. (Illus.). 48p. (Easy to Read Book Ser.). (ps-3). 1984. (ISBN 0-8037-0063-6). (ISBN 0-8037-0056-3). (ISBN 0-8037-0063-6). Dial Bks Young.
--Jed and the Space Bandits. Sis, Peter, illus. LC 84-15616. p. cm. (Science and fiction easy-to-read). 1985. (ISBN 0-8037-0135-7). (ISBN 0-8037-0136-5). Dial Books for Young Readers
--Jed's Junior Space Patrol: A Science Fiction Easy-to-Read. Rose, David S. (1947-), illus. LC 81-12483. (Illus.). 56 p. 22cm. (Dial Easy-to-Read). c.1982. (ISBN 0-8037-4288-6). (ISBN 0-8037-4287-8). Dial Press.
--Red Sun Girl. Meddaugh, Susan (1944-), illus. 1983. Dial.
--Robin of Bray. Stanley, Diane (1943-), illus. LC 82-1573. (Illus.). 56 p. 23cm. (Dial Easy-to-Read). c.1982. (ISBN 0-8037-7332-3). (ISBN 0-8037-7329-3). Dial Press.
--Ruthie's Rude Friends. Meddaugh, Susan (1944-), illus. LC 84-1707. (Easy-to-Read Bks.). (ps-3). 1984. (ISBN 0-8037-0115-2). (ISBN 0-8037-0116-0). Dial Bks for Young Readers.

Masani, Shakuntala
--Nehru's Story. N.D. Oxford University Press.

Maschke, Ruby
--Bible People Story-N-Puzzle Book. Sparks, Judith Ann, ed. 48p. (Orig.). (gr. 7 up). 1983. (ISBN 0-87239-673-8). Standard Pub.
--Blinkety Blanks, 1 & 2. Zapel, Arthur L., ed. Zapel, Michelle, illus. (Illus., Orig.). (gr. 6-12). 1981. (ISBN 0-916260-10-0). Meriwether Pub.
--Disciples of Christ Story-N-Puzzle Book. 48p. (Orig.). (gr. 7 up). 1983. (ISBN 0-87239-675-4). Standard Pub.

Maschler, Fay, jt. auth. see Lord, John Vernon.

Maschler, Fay & Selig, Sylvie
--T. G. and Moonie Go Shopping. Maschler, Fay & Selig, Sylvie (1942-), illus. LC 77-18451. (Illus.). 32 p. 22cm. c.1978. (ISBN 0-385-14147-5). (ISBN 0-385-14148-3). Doubleday.
--T. G. and Moonie Have a Baby. Maschler, Fay & Selig, Sylvie (1942-), illus. LC 79-3951. (Illus.). 32 p. 22cm. 1979. (ISBN 0-385-15332-5). Doubleday.
--T. G. and Moonie Move Out of Town. Maschler, Fay & Selig, Sylvie (1942-), illus. LC 77-15344. (Illus.). 32 p. 22cm. 1978, c.1977. (ISBN 0-385-14145-9). (ISBN 0-385-14146-7). Doubleday.

Mascott, R. D
--Double O Three and One Half: The Adventures of James Bond Junior. Jackson, Michael, illus. LC 68-23666. (Illus.). 236 p. 24cm. 1968. Random House.

Masefield, John Edward (1878-1967)
--The Bird of Dawning: Or, The Fortune of the Sea. 1958. Macmillan.
--A Book of Discoveries. Browne, Gordon Frederick (1858-1932), illus. xii, 353 p. front., illus., plates. 21 cm. 1910. F. A. Stokes.
--The Box of Delights: Or, When the Wolves Were Running. LC 35-23309. viii p., 1 l., 311 p. illus. 20 cm. 1935. The Macmillan Company.
--The Box of Delights: Or, When the Wolves Were Running. Crampton, Patricia, abridged by. Jaques, Faith (1923-), illus. LC 84-14404. p. cm. 1984. (ISBN 0-02-762740-3). Macmillan.
--The Box of Delights: When the Wolves Were Running. Crampton, Patricia, ed. Jaques, Faith (1923-), illus. LC 85-104257. (Illus.). viii, 168 p. 19cm. c.1984. (ISBN 0-440-40853-9). Dell.
--Jim Davis. LC 14-17989. vii, 244 p. front., plates. 20 cm. (Everyboy's library--Boy scout edition). 1913. Grosset & Dunlap.
--Jim Davis. (Thrushwood Bks.). N.D. Grosset & Dunlap.
--Jim Davis. Brundage, Frances, illus. LC 27-328. 246 p. front., illus. 19 cm. (Half-title: Every child's library). c.1926. The Saalfield Publishing Company.
--Jim Davis. Dean, Bob, illus. LC 51-13058. (Illus.). 20cm. 242p. N.D. Macmillan.
--Jim Davis. Reid, Stephen (1873-1934), illus. 2 p. l., 244 p. col. front., col. pl. 20 cm. (Golden books). 1924. D. McKay.
--Jim Davis. Reid, Stephen (1873-1934), illus. 1 p. l., 244 p. col. front. 21 cm. (Newbery classics). 1942. D. McKay Company.
--Jim Davis. Schaeffer, Mead (1898-1980), illus. LC 24-26801. 6 p. l., 226 p. col. front., col. plates. 21 cm. 1924. Frederick A. Stokes Company.
--Jim Davis: Or, The Captive of the Smugglers. (The American Boy's Library). N.D. L. C. Page & Co.
--Jim Davis: Or, The Captive of the Smugglers. Dean, Bob, illus. LC 33-27042. 5 p. l., 3-242, 1 p. incl. front., illus. col. plates. 21 cm. 1932. T. Nelson & Sons.
--Martin Hyde, the Duke's Messenger. Dugdale, T. C., illus. 289p. (The Beacon Hill Bookshelf). 1910. Little,Brown & Co.
--Midnight Folk. 1927. MacMillan.
--Salt-Water Poems & Ballads. Pears, Charles (1873-1958), illus. (gr. 7 up). 1953. (ISBN 0-02-581000-6). (ISBN 0-02-069930-1). Macmillan.
--Salt-Water Poems and Ballads. Pears, Charles (1873-1958), illus. 1960. Macmillan.

Masefield, Judith
--Shepherdess of France: Remembrances of Jeanne D'Arc. Weisgard, Leonard Joseph (1916-), illus. LC 76-83488. (Illus.). 192 p. 24cm. 1969. Coward-McCann.

Masey, Mary Louise (1932-)
--Branislav the Dragon: A New Tale of Old Russia. Basilevsky, Helen (1939-), illus. LC 67-18264. (Illus.). 1 v. (unpaged. 22cm. 1967. D. McKay Co.
--Stories of the Steppes: Kazakh Folk-Tales. LC 68-20183. (Illus.). xvii, 142 p. 21cm. 1968. D. McKay Co.

Masey, Mary Louise (1932-) & Forman, Frieda
--Teddy and the Moon. Basilevsky, Helen (1939-), illus. LC 72-76400. (Illus.). 45 p. 21cm. 1972. (ISBN 0-8178-4901-7). (ISBN 0-8178-4901-7). Harvey House.

Masha, pseud., see Stern, Marie Simchow.

Masha, pseud. (1909-)
--Masha's Cats and Kittens. Stern, Marie Simchow. LC 77-95735. (Illus.). 39 p. 29cm. 1970. American Heritage Press.
--Toys. Stern, Marie Simchow. Osswald, Edith, illus. LC 48-4728. (Illus.). 21cm. 42p. (The Little Golden Library). N.D. Simon & Schuster.

Masha, pseud. (1909-), ed.
--Masha's Stuffed Mother Goose. Stern, Marie Simchow. 1st ed. Masha, pseud. (1909-), illus. Stern, Marie Simchow. LC 46-3219. 64, 1 p. col. illus. 28 cm. c.1946. Garden City Publishing Co., Inc.

Masha, pseud. (1909-), illus.
--Bedtime Stories. Stern, Marie Simchow. N.D (Wonder Books). Grosset & Dunlap.
--Nursery Tales. Stern, Marie Simchow. (Little Golden Book). 1943. Golden Press.
--Nursery Tales. Stern, Marie Simchow. LC 43-13842. 42 p. illus. (part col.) 20 x 17 cm. (On cover: The Little golden library. 14). 1943. Simon and Schuster.
--Three Little Kittens. Stern, Marie Simchow. Reissue of 1957 ed. (Little Golden Book). 1959. Golden Press.
--Three Little Kittens. Stern, Marie Simchow. LC 42-24236. 42 p. illus. (part col.) 20 1/2 x 17 1/2 cm. (On cover: The Little golden library. 1). 1942. Simon and Schuster, Inc.
--Three Little Kittens. Stern, Marie Simchow. (Illus.). (ps-1). 1942 (Golden Pr). Western Pub.
--The Three Little Kittens. Stern, Marie Simchow. (Illus.). 24p. (First Little Golden Bks.). (ps). 1982. (ISBN 0-307-11154-7, Golden Pr). Western Pub.
--Three Little Kittens. Stern, Marie Simchow. (Illus.). (ps-3). 1982. (ISBN 0-307-68127-0). Western Pub.

Maskell, A. E. Anderson-, Mrs.
--Nell and Nan: Or, Trying to Be Good. LC 12-36626. 3 p. l., 5-192 p. front., plates. 18 1/2 cm. c.1888. American Baptist Publication Society.

Maskelyne, A. S.
--True and False Riches: or, the Ore Seekers. 1875. Scribner, Welford, & Armstrong.

Masland, Anne C.
--The Witch Who Became Someone Else. Servello, Joe (1932-), illus. (Illus.). 32p. 1983. (ISBN 0-682-40133-1). Exposition.

Masolle, Aina, illus.
--Cinderella. N.D. Grosset & Dunlap.

Mason, Alfred Bishop (1851-1933)
--Tom Strong, Boy-Captain: A Story of America. Mason, Alfred Bishop (1851-1933), illus. LC 13-17998. 5 p. l., 3-318 p. front., illus. (incl. maps) plates, ports. 19 1/2 cm. $1.2. 1913. H. Holt and Company.
--Tom Strong, Junior: A Story of the Young United States. Mason, Alfred Bishop (1851-1933), illus. LC 15-188193. xiii, 344 p. front., illus., plates, ports. 19 1/2 cm. 1915. H. Holt and Company.
--Tom Strong, Lincoln's Scout: A Story of the United States in the Times That Tried Men's Souls. Mason, Alfred Bishop (1851-1933), illus. LC 19-155754. xiii, 324 p. incl. front., illus., ports., map. plates, port. 19 1/2 cm. 1919. H. Holt and Company.
--Tom Strong, Third: A Story of the United States When Railroads and the West Were New. Mason, Alfred Bishop (1851-1933), illus. LC 16-23207. x p., 1 l., 333 p. front., illus. (incl. ports.) plates. 19 1/2 cm. $1.3. 1916. H. Holt and Company.

--Tom Strong, Washington's Scout: A Story of Patriotism. Mason, Alfred Bishop (1851-1933), illus. LC 11-262520. vi p., 1 l., 313 p. front., illus. (incl. maps) plates, ports. 19 1/2 cm. 1911. H. Holt and Company.

Mason, Alfred Edward Woodley

--Clementina. Partridge, B., illus. LC 1-18551. 364p. 1901. F. A. Stokes Co.

Mason, Alice L. & Iverson, Barbara A. Leedy

--Larry the Lion. Audeck, Kurt, illus. (Illus.). 16p. (gr. k-6). 1984. (ISBN 0-8249-8068-9). Ideals.

Mason, Alice Leedy

--Katie the Camel. Flint, Russ, illus. (Illus.). 16p. (gr. k-6). 1984. (ISBN 0-8249-8066-2). Ideals.

--Katie the Camel. Hockerman, Dennis, illus. LC 84-23089. p. cm. (Teaching Tales). c.1984. (ISBN 0-516-09121-2). Childrens Press.

--Oscar the Otter. Flint, Russ, illus. LC 84-23088. p. cm. (Teaching Tales). c.1984. (ISBN 0-516-09124-7). Childrens Press.

--Oscar the Otter. Flint, Russ, illus. (Illus.). 16p. (gr. k-6). 1984. (ISBN 0-8249-8065-4). Ideals.

--Simon the Snake. Hockerman, Dennis, illus. (Illus.). 16p. (gr. k-6). 1984. (ISBN 0-8249-8069-7). Ideals.

Mason, Alice Leedy, retold by.

--Sammy the Sloth. Hockerman, Dennis, illus. LC 84-23139. p. cm. (Teaching Tales). 1984. (ISBN 0-516-09125-5). Childrens Press.

--Sammy the Sloth. Hockerman, Dennis, illus. (Illus.). 16p. (gr. k-6). 1984. (ISBN 0-8249-8064-6). Ideals.

Mason, Alice Leedy, jt. ed. see Goldsmith, Howard.

Mason, Alice Leedy, retold by see Hilliard, Susan E.

Mason, Alice Leedy & Iverson, Barbara A

--Larry the Lion. Avdek, Kurt, illus. LC 84-23145. p. cm. (Teaching Tales). c.1984. (ISBN 0-516-09122-0). Childrens Press.

Mason, Arthur (1876-)

--From the Horn of the Moon. Lawson, Robert (1892-1957), illus. LC 31-28915. 6 p. l., 3-259 p. incl. illus., plates. front. 23 1/2 cm. 1931. Doubleday, Doran & Company, Inc.

--From the Horn of the Moon. Lawson, Robert (1892-1957), illus. LC 37-30937. 7 p. l., 3-259 p. incl. front., illus., plates. 22 1/2 cm. 1937. Garden City Publishing Co., Inc.

--An Ocean Boyhood. Burne, Harry H. A., illus. LC 27-21132. vi p., 1 l., 297 p. incl. plates. front. 20 cm. c.1927. J. H. Sears & Company, Inc.

--The Roving Lobster. Lawson, Robert (1892-1957), illus. LC 31-14057. x p., 1 l., 131, 1 p. incl. front., illus., plates. 21 cm. 1931. Doubleday, Doran & Company, Inc.

--Salt Horse: From Fo'c'sle to Bridge. Burne, Harry H. A., illus. 306p. N.D. Sears Publishing Co.

--The Wee Men of Ballywooden. Lawson, Robert (1892-1957), illus. 7 p. l., 3-266 p., 1 l. incl. front., illus., plates. 23 1/2 cm. 1930. Doubleday, Doran & Company, Inc.

--The Wee Men of Ballywooden. Lawson, Robert (1892-1957), illus. LC 37-309388. 7 p. l., 3-266 p., 1 l. incl. front., illus. plates. 22 1/2 cm. 1937. Garden City Publishing Co., Inc.

--The Wee Men of Ballywooden. Lawson, Robert (1892-1957), illus. LC 52-115581. 214p. illus. 22cm. 1952, c.1930. Viking Press.

Mason, Arthur (1876-) & Frank, Mary

--The Fossil Fountain. Van Everen, Jay, illus. LC 28-27778. viii p., 1 l., 198 p. incl. illus., plates. col. front. 21 cm. 1928. Doubleday, Doran & Company, Inc.

Mason, Betty Oxford (1930-)

--I Go to School. Myers, Bill (1940-), illus. LC 73-157406. (Illus.). 31 p. 1971. (ISBN 0-8054-4221-9). Broadman Press.

Mason, Beverly, jt. auth. see Finley, Virginia.

Mason, Bobbie Ann (1940-)

--The Girl Sleuth. LC 74-22313. p. cm. 1974. (ISBN 0-912670-17-7). Feminist Press.

Mason, Caroline Atwater, Mrs. (1853-)

--A Loyal Heart, 1 of 60 vols. LC 12-36618. 316 p. front., plates. 18 1/2 cm. (Crescent Lib.). c.1892. Set. American Baptist Publication Society.

Mason, Edna Warren

--The Treasure Hunt: Cruising Through the West Indies. LC 27-4067. 4 p. l., 332 p. front., plates. 19 1/2 cm. c.1927. T. Nelson & Sons.

Mason, Evelyn

--The Baby Hugs Bear and Baby Tugs Bear Look and Find Book. Cooke, Tom, illus. LC 84-14905. (Illus.). 44 p. 29cm. (A Parker Brothers Good Start Book). c.1984. (ISBN 0-910313-73-3). Parker Bros.

--A Sister for Sam. Cooke, Tom, illus. LC 83-2236. p. cm. c.1982. (ISBN 0-910313-03-2). Parker Bros.

Mason, Francis Van Wyck see Mason, Frank W., pseud.

Mason, Francis Van Wyck (1901-1978)

--Flight into Danger. Mason, Frank W., pseud. Beaudouin, Frank, illus. LC 46-119664. 173, 1 p. incl. illus., plates. 20 1/2 cm. 1946. J. B. Lippincott Company.

--Pilots, Man Your Planes!. Mason, Frank W., pseud. Beaudouin, Frank, illus. LC 44-37527. 213 p. incl. illus., plates. col. front. 21 cm. 1944. J. B. Lippincott Company.

--Q-Boat. Mason, Frank W., pseud. Rev ed. Beaudouin, Frank, illus. LC 43-51191. 243, 1 p. col. front., illus. 21 cm. 1943. J. B. Lippincott Company.

--The Winter at Valley Forge. Johnson, Eugene Harper, illus. LC 53-6258. 180p. illus. 22cm. (Landmark books, 33). 1953. Random House.

Mason, Frank W., pseud., see Mason, Francis Van Wyck.

Mason, George Evan (1932-) & Sheldon, William Denley (1915-)

--Full Count. LC 73-87092. (Illus.). 60 p. 21cm. (Breakthrough). 1974. Allyn and Bacon.

--On the Level. LC 73-87091. (Illus.). 63 p. 21cm. (Breakthrough). 1974. Allyn and Bacon.

Mason, George Frederick (1904-)

--The Bear Family. Mason, George Frederick (1904-), illus. LC 60-5081. 96p. illus, 22cm. 1960. Morrow.

--The Deer Family. Mason, George Frederick (1904-), illus. LC 62-11351. (Illus.). 96p. 22cm. 1962. Morrow.

Mason, Grace Sartwell, Mrs. (1877-)

--The Godparents. N.D. Houghton Mifflin.

--Licky and His Gang. Deremeaux, Irma, illus. LC 12-23507. 5 p. l., 260, 2 p. col. front., col. plates. 18 cm. $1.0. 1912. Houghton Mifflin Company.

Mason, Gregory (1889-)

--Lemon Pie, and Other Stories. LC 61-7180. 177p. 22cm. 1961. Twayne Publishers.

Mason, Haven A.

--Rainbow Gold. Wilson, Helen Hughes, illus. LC 51-9995. 299 p. illus. 24 cm. 1951. Caxton Printers.

Mason, Henry Burrall (1848-1932)

--Letters from Uncle Henry: Being His Adventures with Children, Dogs, Fairies, Ambitious Pigs and Others. Mason, Henry Burrall (1848-1932), illus. LC 26-16339. 7 p. l., 109 p. col. front., illus. 26 cm. 1926. Frederick A. Stokes Company.

Mason, James, ed.

--The Old Fairy Tales. 29th thousand. ed. Smith, John Moyr, illus. LC 43-373780. viii, 9-160 p. incl. front., illus. 17 1/2 cm. N.D. Cassell & Company, Limited.

Mason, Laura Anne

--The Dancing Meteorite. LC 83-47705. 217 p. 21cm. c.1984. (ISBN 0-06-024098-9). (ISBN 0-06-024097-0). Harper & Row.

Mason, Leckie & Ohanian, Phyllis B.

--God's Wonderful World. Dillon, Corinne Boyd, illus. (Illus.). (gr. 1-3). 1954. (ISBN 0-394-80719-7). (ISBN 0-394-90719-1). Random.

Mason, Michael, jt. auth. see Heyman, Ken.

Mason, Michael (1939-)

--The Book That Jason Wrote. Bolognese, Donald Alan (1934-), illus. LC 68-13071. (Illus.). 29 p. 26cm. (Fun & frolic book). 1968. Funk & Wagnalls.

--Casey's Cove: A Village on the New England Seacoast. Hanna, John (1942-), illus. LC 75-77096. (Illus.). 32 p. (Our living neighborhoods). 1969. McGraw-Hill.

Mason, Miriam Evangeline (1899-1973)

--Becky and Her Brave Cat, Bluegrass. Maclean, Robert (1926-), illus. LC 60-12288. 135p. illus. 21cm. c.1960. (ISBN 0-02-762950-3). Macmillan.

--Benjamin Lucky. Guthrie, Vee, illus. LC 56-9935. 138p. illus. 22cm. 1956. Macmillan.

--Broomtail, Brother of Lightning. Moyers, William (1916-), illus. LC 52-12587. (Illus.). 135 p. 21cm. 1952. Macmillan.

--Caroline and Her Kettle Named Maud. Voute, Kathleen (1892-), illus. LC 51-13835. (Illus.). 134 p. 21cm. 1951. Macmillan.

--Caroline and Her Kettle Named Maud. Voute, Kathleen (1892-), illus. 1967. MacMillan Publishing Company.

--Caroline & the Seven Little Words. Frame, Paul (1913-), illus. LC 66-31758. (gr. 2-4). 1967. (ISBN 0-02-763330-6). Macmillan.

--Dan Beard: Boy Scout. Fiorentino, Al, illus. LC 62-12694. 200p. illus. 20cm. (Childhood of famous Americans). 1962. Bobbs-Merrill.

--Freddy. Guthrie, Vee, illus. LC 57-6717. 85p. illus. 21 cm. 1957. Macmillan.

--The Gray-Nosed Kitten. Nichols, Marie C. (1905-), illus. LC 50-8856. 118 p. illus. 22 cm. 1950. Houghton Mifflin.

--Happy Jack. Hauman, George (1890-1961) & Hauman, Doris, Mrs. (1897-), illus. LC 45-10359. 136 p. incl. front., illus. 21 cm. 1945. The Macmillan Company.

--Herman, the Brave Pig. Hauman, George (1890-1961) & Hauman, Doris, Mrs. (1897-), illus. 120 p. illus. 21 cm. 1949. Macmillan Co.

--Hominy and His Blunt-nosed Arrow. Hauman, George (1890-1961) & Hauman, Doris, Mrs. (1897-), illus. 145p. 1950. Macmillan.

--Hominy & His Blunt-Nosed Arrow. Hauman, George (1890-1961) & Hauman, Doris, Mrs. (1897-), illus. (gr. 2-4). 1967. (ISBN 0-02-763720-4). Macmillan.

--Hoppity. Wiese, Kurt (1887-1974), illus. LC 47-11164. 76 p. illus. 21 cm. 1947. Macmillan Co.

--A House for Ten. Seredy, Kate (1899-1975), illus. LC 49-8206. v. 186 p. col. illus. 24 cm. 1949. Ginn.

--John Audubon: Boy Naturalist. Patterson, Robert (1899-), illus. LC 62-12692. 200p. illus. 20cm. (Childhood of famous Americans). 1962. Bobbs-Merrill.

--John Smith: Man of Adventure. Freeman, Charles, illus. LC 58-13690. 192p. illus. 22cm. (Piper books). 1958. Houghton Mifflin.

--Kate Douglas Wiggin, the Little Schoolteacher. Locke, Vance, illus. LC 62-925141. 200p. illus. 20cm. (Childhood of famous Americans). 1962. Bobbs-Merrill.

--Kate Douglas Wiggin: The Little Schoolteacher. 1st ed. Morse, Dorothy Bayley (1906-1979), illus. LC 57-12854. 191p. illus. 20cm. (Childhood of famous Americans series 103). 1958. Bobbs-Merrill.

--Katie Kittenheart. (gr. 4-6). 1973 (Starline). Schol Bk Serv.

--Katie Kittenheart. Geer, Charles Hand (1922-), illus. LC 57-10477. 131p. illus. 21cm. 1957. Macmillan.

--A Lion for Patsy. Neville, Vera (1900-1978), illus. LC 47-5502. 32 p. illus. (part col.) 24 cm. 1947. D. McKay Co.

--Little Bunny Little: Magic Bridge Reader Two. 1963. (ISBN 0-13-537837-0). P-H.

--Little Jonathan. Hauman, George (1890-1961) & Hauman, Doris, Mrs. (1897-), illus. LC 44-7721. 127, 1 p. incl. front., illus. 21 cm. 1944. The Macmillan Company.

--The Major and His Camels. Gay, Zhenya (1906-1978), illus. LC 53-128151. 130p. illus. 21cm. 1953. Macmillan.

--Mark Twain: Boy of Old Missouri. Gillette, Henry Sampson (1915-), illus. LC 62-12706. 200p. illus. 20cm. (Childhood of famous Americans). 1962. Bobbs.

--Mark Twain: Boy of Old Missouri. Laune, Paul Sidney (1899-), illus. LC 42-216432. vii p., 1 l., 11-164 p. illus. 20 cm. (Boyhood of famous Americans series). 1942. The Bobbs-Merrill Company.

--Mary Mapes Dodge: Jolly Girl. 1st ed. Dowd, Victor, illus. LC 49-8117. 199 p. illus. 20 cm. (The Childhood of Famous Americans Series). 1949. Bobbs-Merrill Co.

--Matilda and Her Family. Wohlberg, Meg (1905-), illus. LC 42-25369. 144 p. incl. front., illus. 21 x 16 cm. 1942. The Macmillan Company.

--The Middle Sister. Paull, Grace A. (1898-), illus. LC 47-30194. 160 p. illus. 21 cm. 1947. The Macmillan Company.

--Miney and the Blessing. Morse, Dorothy Bayley (1906-1979), illus. LC 61-15160. (Illus.). 157 p. 21cm. 1961. Macmillan.

--Miss Posy Longlegs. Petersham, Maud Sylvia Fuller, Mrs. (1890-1971) & Petersham, Miska (1889-1960), illus. LC 55-14473. 54p. illus. 21cm. 1955. Macmillan.

--Mr. Meadowlark. Nichols, Marie C. (1905-), illus. LC 58-12898. 110p. illus. 22cm. 1959. Hastings House.

--O Happy Day!. Woodbury, Mabel Jones, illus. LC 39-22581. 6 p. l., 216 p. front., illus. 21 cm. 1939. Frederick A. Stokes Company.

--O Happy Day!. Woodbury, Mabel Jones, illus. N.D. J. B. Lippincott.

--A Pony Called Lightning. Anderson, Clarence William (1891-1971), illus. LC 48-9570. 142 p. illus. 21 cm. 1948. Macmillan Co.

--Sara and the Winter Gift. Frame, Paul (1913-), illus. LC 68-12091. (Illus.). 152 p. 22cm. 1968. Macmillan.

--A Small Farm for Andy. Guthrie, Vee, illus. LC 58-11301. (Illus.). 137 p. 21cm. 1958. Macmillan.

--Smiling Hill Farm. Seredy, Kate (1899-1975), illus. LC 38-27137. vii, 311, 1 p. illus. 23 cm. c.1937. The Junior Literary Guild and Ginn and Company.

--Stevie, and His Seven Orphans. Gretzer, John, illus. LC 64-15916. 22cm. 1964. Houghton Mifflin.

--The Sugarbush Family. Gay, Zhenya (1906-1980), illus. LC 54-12842. (Illus.). 137 p. 21cm. 1954. Macmillan.

--Susannah: The Pioneer Cow. Petersham, Maud Sylvia Fuller, Mrs. (1890-1971) & Petersham, Miska (1889-1960), illus. LC 41-258298. 151, 1 p. illus. (part col.) 21 cm. 1941. (ISBN 0-02-765150-9). The Macmillan Co.

--Three Ships Came Sailing in: A Story of John Smith's Jamestown. 1st ed. John, Charles V., illus. LC 50-7477. (Illus.). 246 p. 21cm. 1950. Bobbs-Merrill.

--William Penn: Friendly Boy. Dresser, Lawrence T., illus. LC 53-699. 210p. illus. (Childhood of famous Americans series). 1953. Bobbs-Merrill.

--William Penn: Friendly Boy. Dresser, Lawrence T., illus. LC 44-8405. 210 p. illus. 19 1/2 cm. (The Childhood of famous Americans series). 1944. The Bobb-Merrill Company.

--William Penn: Friendly Boy. Pearson, Justin, illus. LC 60-7722. 200p. illus. 20cm. (Childhood of famous Americans). 1962. Bobbs-Merrill.

--Young Mr. Meeker and His Exciting Journey to Oregon. James, Sandra, illus. LC 52-5822. (Illus.). 168 p. 21cm. 1952. (ISBN 0-672-50599-1). Bobbs-Merrill.

--Yours with Love Kate. (Illus.). 1952. Houghton Mifflin Company.

Mason, Miriam Evangeline (1900-1973)

--Frances Willard: Girl Crusader. Goldstein, Leslie, illus. LC 61-15556. 200p. col. illus. (Childhood of famous Americans). c.1961. Bobbs.

Mason, Patrice G., jt. auth. see Rosenberg, Amye.

Mason, Rowena

--Salty, the Sea Horse. Evans, Cynthia, illus. LC 66-14246. 1v. (unpaged) illus. 29cm. 1965, c.1966. (ISBN 0-8119-0149-1). Fell.

Mason, S. M.

--Panacea. N.D. E. & J. B .Young & Co.

Mason, T. Edward, ed.

--Songs of Fairy Land. Humphrey, Maud (1868-), illus. N.D. Putman & Sons.

Mason, Theodore K.

--Two Against the Ice: Amundsen & Ellsworth. LC 82-45383. (Illus.). 224p. (gr. 7 up). 1982. (ISBN 0-396-08092-8). Dodd.

Mason, Van Wyck see Mason, Francis Van Wyck.

Mason, Victor

--The Haughty Toad, and Other Tales from Bali. Mason, Victor, illus. LC 77-369269. (Illus.). 56 p. 31cm. 1975. PT Bali Art Print.

Mason, Walt

--Rippling Rhymes. N.D. A. C. McClurg.

Mason, Walter M

--We Like to Do Things. Lerch, Steffie E. (1908-), illus. LC 50-5802. 42 p. col. illus. 20 cm. (Little golden library, 62). c.1949. Simon and Schuster.

Massa, Gilda, tr. see Vigil, Constancio C.

Massaquoi, Princess Fatima

--The Leopards Daughter. N.D. (ISBN 0-8283-1402-0). Branden Press.

--The Leopard's Daughter: A Folk Tale from Liberia. Humphrey, Martha Burnham, illus. LC 61-11713. 14p. illus. 28cm. 1961. Bruce Humphries.

Massaro, Cora D.

--The Circus Is Here. Garr, Anton, ed. Yolanda, illus. LC 83-72068. (Illus.). 16p. (Koala Collection Ser.). (gr. 1-3). N.D. (ISBN 0-914855-04-2). Alta Pub Co.

--My Happy Days. Garr, Anton, ed. Mary-Ann, illus. LC 83-72067. (Illus.). 16p. (Koala Collection Ser.). (gr. 2-4). N.D. (ISBN 0-914855-03-4). Alta Pub Co.

--The Way We Travel. Garr, Anton, ed. Yolanda, illus. LC 83-72066. (Illus.). 16p. (Koala Collection Ser.). (gr. 1-3). N.D. (ISBN 0-914855-02-6). Alta Pub Co.

Massee, May, tr. see Kastner, Erich.

Masselink, Ben (1919-)

--The Danger Islands. LC 64-12361. 21cm. 177p. (A Tale of the South Seas filled with the ingenuity & skill that man can call upon to survive). (gr. 7 up). 1964. (ISBN 0-316-54974-6). Little.

--Deadliest Weapon. (gr. 7 up). 1965. Little.

--Green: The Story of a Caribbean Turtle's Struggle for Survival. 1st ed. Wilson, Maurice Charles John (1914-), illus. LC 69-10661. (Illus.). 111 p. 22cm. 1969. Little, Brown.

Massey, Craig

--Brown Shadow. 41p. N.D. Zondervan Publishing House.

--Captain Daley's Crew and the Jungle Ship. 128p. 1964. Moody Press.

--Captain Daley's Crew and the Jungle Ship. LC 58-153702. 58p. 21cm. c.1957. Zondervan Pub. House.

--Captain Daley's Crew & the Missing Houseboat. 128p. (gr. 5-8). 1962. Moody.

--Captain Daley's Crew & the Peg-Legged Tramp. (gr. 5-9). 1963. (ISBN 0-8024-4103-3). Moody.

--Captain Daley's Crew and the Peg-Legged Tramp. A Mystery Story for Boys and Girls. LC 55-186. 91p. 20cm. 1954. Zondervan Pub. House.

--Captain Daley's Crew at Thunderhead Lake. 128p. 1963. Moody Press.

--Captain Daley's Crew at Thunderhead Lake. LC 52-4185. 90 p. 20 cm. 1952. Zondervan Pub. House.

--Captain Daley's Crew in Danger. LC 54-284. 86p. 20cm. c.1953. Zondervan Pub. House.

--Captain Daley's Missing Houseboat: A Mystery Story for Boys and Girls. LC 51-4040. 72 p. 20 cm. 1951. Zondervan Pub. House.

--Chip, Roger and the Barefoot Hermit. 63p. 1964. Moody Press.

--Bessie at School, 1 0f 6 vols. LC 12-36665. viii, 9-357 p. front., plates. 17 1/2 cm. (On back of cover: The Bessie books. 5). 1869. R. Carter and Brothers.
--Bessie at School, 1 of 6 vols. Kennedy, J. W. Ferguson, illus. (Illus.). (Bessie Books Ser.). N.D. Per vol. Set. H. M. Caldwell.
--Bessie at the Sea-Side, 1 of 6 vols. LC 12-36661. 357 p. front., plates. 17 1/2 cm. (On back of cover: The Bessie books. 1). 1868. R. Carter & Brothers.
--Bessie at the Seaside, 1 of 6 vols. Kennedy, J. W. Ferguson, illus. (Illus.). (Bessie Books Ser.). N.D. Set. Per vol. H. M. Caldwell Co.
--The Bessie Books. (Illus.). N.D. De Wolfe, Fiske & Co.
--Bessie Bradford's Prize: The Third of a Series of Sequels to "The Bessie Books,". Harper, W. St. John, illus. LC 12-36840. 4 p. l., 7-266 p. front., plates. 17 cm. 1890. Frederick A. Stokes Company.
--Bessie Bradford's Secret. (Author of the "Bessie Books."). (Illus.). 256p. N.D.-Cassell, Petter, Galpin.
--Bessie in the City, 2 0f 6 vols. LC 12-36662. 395 p. front., plates. 17 1/2 cm. (On back of cover: The Bessie books. 2). 1868. R. Carter & Brothers.
--Bessie in the City, 1 of 6 vols. Kennedy, J. W. Ferguson, illus. (Illus.). (Bessie Books Ser.). N.D. Per Vol. Set. H. M. Caldwell Co.
--Bessie on Her Travels, 6 0f 6 vols. LC 12-36666. 376 p. front., plates. 17 1/2 cm. (On back of cover: The Bessie books. 6). 1870. R. Carter and Brothers.
--Bessie on Her Travels, 1 of 6 vols. Kennedy, J. W. Ferguson, illus. (Illus.). (Bessie Books Ser.). N.D. Set. Per vol. H. M. Caldwell Co.
--Blackberry Jam, 1 of 6 vols. (Haps and Mishpas). N.D. Per Vol. Set. H. M. Caldwell Co.
--Blackberry Jam. LC 12-36624. 305 p. front., 2 pl. 17 1/2 cm. (Half-title: Haps and mishaps. III). 1878. R. Carter and Brothers.
--The "Bradford" Library: Containing: Follow My Leader, Bound By A Spell, For Fortune And Glory, Champion Of Odin. Juv. ed. N.D. Cassell & Co.
--Breakfast for Two. LC 12-36625. v, 7-296 p. front., pl. 18 1/2 cm. c.1879. D. Lothrop and Co.
--Breakfast for Two. (The Girls' Own Library). N.D. David McKay.
--Breakfast for Two. (Illus.). (Library for Boys and Girls Ser.). N.D. Frederick A. Stokes Co.
--The Broken Mallet, 1 of 6 vols. (Haps and Mishaps). N.D. Per Vol. Set. H. M. Caldwell Co.
--The Broken Mallet. 1877. Robert Carter & Bros.
--The Broken Mallet and the Pigeon's Eggs, 1 of 6 vols. LC 12-366236. 325 p. front., 2 pl. 17 1/2 cm. (Half-title: Haps and mishaps. II). 1877. R. Carter and Brothers.
--Daisybank. 190p. N.D. American Tract Society.
--Daisy's Work. (The Flowerets). N.D. Robert Carter & Brothers.
--Dora's Motto, 1 of 6 Vols. (Little Sunbeams Series.). N.D. Set. Frederick Stokes.
--Dora's Motto.., 1 0f 6 vols. LC 12-36731. 237 p. front., 2 pl. 17 1/2 cm. (Half-title: Little sunbeams. II). 1871. R. Carter and Brothers.
--Eleanor's Visit, 1 of 6 vols. (Miss Ashton's Girls). N.D. Per Vol. Set. H. M. Caldwell Co.
--Eleanor's Visit, 1 of 6 vols. LC 12-36658. 352 p. front., 2 pl. 17 1/2 cm. (Half-title: Miss Ashton's girls. IV). 1875. R. Carter and Brothers.
--Elsie's Santa Claus, 1 of 6 vols. (Miss Ashton's Girls). N.D. Per Vol. Set. H. M. Caldwell Co.
--Elsie's Santa Claus, 1 of 6 vols. LC 12-366606. 4 p. l., 7-346 p. front., 2 pl. 17 1/2 cm. (Half-title: Miss Ashton's girls. VI). 1876. R. Carter and Brothers.
--Fanny's Birthday gift, 1 of 6 vols. (Miss Ashton's Girls). N.D. Per Vol. Set. H. M. Caldwell.
--Fanny's Birthday Gift, 1 of 6 vols. LC 12-36655. 368 p. front., 2 pl. 17 1/2 cm. (Half-title: Miss Ashton's girls. I). 1874. R. Carter and Brothers.
--Frankie Bradford's Bear. (Illus.). (Library for Boys and Girls Ser.). N.D. Frederick A. Stokes Co.
--Frankie Bradford's Bear. The Fifth of a Series of Sequels to "The Bessie Books,". Harper, W. St. John, illus. LC 12-366094. 4 p. l., 7-253 p. front., plates. 17 cm. c.1893. Frederick A. Stokes Company.
--Fred Bradford's Debt. (Author of "Bessie Bradford's Secret."). (Illus.). 256p. N.D. Cassell, Petter, Galpin.
--Haps and Mishaps. (6 vols.). N.D. De Wolfe, Fiske & Co.
--Hyacinthe and her Brothers. (The Flowerets). N.D. Robert Carter & Brothers.
--Jessie's Parrot, 1 of 6 Vols. (Illus.). (Little Sunbeams Series.). N.D. Set. Frederick Stokes.
--Jessie's Parrot... LC 12-367334. 3 p. l., 9-245 p. front., 2 pl. 17 1/2 cm. (Half-title: Little sunbeams. IV). 1872. R. Carter and Brothers.
--Kitty and Lulu Books: Containing: Toutou and Pussy, Kitty's Scrap Book, The White Rabbit, Kitty's Robins, Rudie's Goat, Kitty's Visit. N.D. Frederick A. Stokes.
--Kitty's Robins, 1 of 6 Vols. (Illus.). (Kitty and Lulu Books). N.D. Set. Frederick Stokes.
--Kitty's Robins. LC 12-36726. 230 p. incl. front. 2 pl. 18 cm. (Half-title: Kitty and Lulu books. ii). 1872. R. Carter and Brothers.
--Kitty's Scrap Book, 1 of 6 Vols. (Kitty and Lulu Books.). N.D. Set. Frederick Stokes.
--Kitty's Scrap-Book. LC 12-367292. 214 p. front. 2 pl. 18 cm. (Half-title: Kitty and Lulu books. vi). 1873. R. Carter and Brothers.
--Kitty's Visit, 1 of 6 Vols. (Illus.). (Kitty and Lulu Books). N.D. Set. Frederick Stokes.
--Kitty's Visit to Grandmamma. LC 12-36728. 229 p. front., 2 pl. 18 cm. (Half-title: Kitty and Lulu books. v). 1873. R. Carter and Brothers.
--Lily Norris' Enemy, 1 of 6 Vols. (Illus.). (Little Sunbeams Series). N.D. Set 3.60. Frederick Stokes.
--Lily Norris' Enemy.., 1 of 6 vols. LC 12-367323. 240 p. front., 2 pl. 17 1/2 cm. (Half-title: Little sunbeams. III). 1872. R. Carter and Brothers.
--Lily's Lesson. (The Flowerets). N.D. Robert Carter & Brothers.
--Little Friends at Glenwood. LC 12-366676. 318 p. front., 2 pl. 17 1/2 cm. (Half-title: Haps and mishaps. I). 1876. R. Carter and Brothers.
--Little Friends of Glenwood, 1 of 6 vols. (Haps and Mishaps). N.D. Per Vol. Set. H. M. Caldwell Co.
--Little Sunbeam Series: Containing: "Lilly Norris'Enemy," "Jessie's Parrot" "Dora's Motto, Belle Powers' Locket" Nellie's Housekeeping," "Mamie's Watchword.". N.D. Set. Frederick A. Stokes.
--Mabel Walton's Experiment, 1 of 6 vols. (Miss Ashton's Girls). N.D. Per Vol. Set. H. M. Caldwell Co.
--Mabel Walton's Experiment. LC 12-366593. 347 p. front., 2 pl. 17 1/2 cm. (Half-title: Miss Ashton's girls. V). 1875. R. Carter and Brothers.
--Maggie Bradford's Club. The First of a Series of Sequels to "The Bessie Books,". Harper, W. St. John, illus. LC 12-366610. vi, 7-250 p. front., plates. 17 cm. 1889. F. A. Stokes & Brother.
--Maggie Bradford's Fair. The Fourth of a Series of Sequels to "The Bessie Books,". Harper, W. St. John, illus. LC 12-366085. 271 p. front., plates. 17 cm. 1892. Frederick A. Stokes Company.
--Maggie Bradford's School-Mates. The Second of a Series of Sequels to "The Bessie Books.". Harper, W. St. John, illus. LC 12-366071. vi, 7-256 p. front., plates. 17 cm. (No. 6). 1890. Frederick A. Stokes Company.
--Maggie Bradford's Schoolmates. (Library for Boys and Girls Ser.: No. 6). N.D. Set. Frederick Stokes.
--Mamie's Watchword, 1 of 6 Vols. (Little Sunbeams Series). N.D. Set. Frederick Stokes.
--Mamie's Watchword.., 1 of 6 vols. LC 12-36735. 3 p. l., 9-233 p. front., 2 pl. 17 1/2 cm. (Half-title: Little sunbeams. V). 1872. R. Carter and Brothers.
--Milly's Whims, 1 of 6 vols. (Haps and Mishaps Ser.). N.D. Per Vol. Set. H. M. Caldwell Co.
--Milly's Whims. LC 12-366684. 292 p. front., 2 pl. 17 1/2 cm. (Half-title: Haps and mishaps. IV). 1878. R. Carter and Brothers.
--Miss Ashton's Girls. (6 vols.). N.D. De Wolfe, Fiske & Co.
--Nellie's Housekeeping, 1 of 6 Vols. (Illus.). (Little Sunbeams Series). N.D. Set. Frederick Stokes.
--Nellie's Housekeeping.., 1 of 6 vols. LC 12-36734. 267 p. front., 2 pl. 17 1/2 cm. (Half-title: Little sunbeams. VI). 1872. R. Carter and Brothers.
--The New Scholars, 1 of 6 vols. (Miss Ashton's Girls). N.D. Per Vol. Set. H. M. Caldwell Co.
--The New Scholars. LC 12-366567. 376 p. front. 2 pl. 17 1/2 cm. (Half-title: Miss Ashton's girls. II). 1874. R. Carter and Brothers.
--Pinkie and the Rabbits. (The Flowerets). N.D. Robert Carter & Brothers.
--Rosalie's Pet, 1 of 6 vols. (Miss Ashton's Girls). N.D. Per Vol. Set. H. M. Caldwell Co.
--Rosalie's Pet, 1 of 6 vols. LC 12-366573. 373 p. front., 2 pl. 17 1/2 cm. (Half-title: Miss Ashton's girls. III). 1875. R. Carter and Brothers.
--Rose's Temptation. (The Flowerets). N.D. Robert Carter & Brothers.
--Rudie's Goat, 1 of 6 Vols. (Illus.). (Kitty and Lulu Books). N.D. Set. Frederick Stokes.
--Rudie's Goat. LC 12-36727. 237 p. front., 2 pl. 17 1/2 cm. (Kitty and Lulu books. IV). 1873. R. Carter and Brothers.
--Toutou and Pussy, 1 of 6 Vols. (Kitty and Lulu Books). N.D. Set 3.60. Frderick Stokes.
--Toutou and Pussy. LC 12-367253. 243 p. front., 2 pl. 17 1/2 cm. (Half-title: Kitty and Lulu Books. I). 1872. R. Carter and Brothers.
--Uncle Joe's Thanksgiving, 1 of 6 vols. (Haps and Mishaps Ser.). N.D. Per Vol. Set. H. M. Caldwell Co.
--Uncle Joe's Thanksgiving. 1877. Robert Carter & Bros.
--Uncle Rutherford's Attic. (The Girls' Own Library). N.D. David McKay.
--Uncle Rutherford's Attic: A Story for Girls. LC 12-36606. 282 p. front., plates. 19 cm. (No. 1). 1887. F. A. Stokes.
--Uncle Rutherford's Nieces. (The Girls' Own Library). N.D. David McKay.
--Uncle Rutherford's Nieces. Harper, W. St. John, illus. N.D. Frederick A. Stokes.
--Violet's Idol. (The Flowerets). N.D. Robert Carter & Brothers.
--The White Rabbit, 1 of 6 Vols. (Illus.). (Kitty and Lulu Books). N.D. Set. Frederick Stokes.
--The White Rabbit. (Kitty and Lulu Bks.). N.D. Robert Carter & Brothers.

Mathews, Julia A.
--Allan Haywood. (Drayton Hall Ser.). N.D. Robert Carter & Brothers.
--Christy's Grandson. (Drayton Hall Ser.). N.D. Robert Carter & Brothers.
--Crossing-Sweeper, 1 of 103 vols. (The Pearl Library: No. 16). 1900. Set. Hurst & Co.
--Eagle Crag. (Drayton Hall Ser.). N.D. Robert Carter & Brothers.
--Frank Austin's Diamond. LC 61-55549. (Illus.). 18cm. 196p. (Drayton Hall Ser.). 1871. Robert Carter & Brothers.
--Giuseppe's Home. (Illus.). 343p. N.D. Merrill.
--Giuseppe's Home, 1 of 5 Vols. LC 58-52813. (Illus.). 18cm. 343p. (Dare to Do Right). 1874. Robert Carter & Brothers.
--Grandfather's Faith, 1 of 5 Vols. (Dare to Do Right). N.D. Robert Carter & Brothers.
--How Jennie Found Her Lord. (Golden Ladder Ser.). N.D. Robert Carter & Brothers.
--Jolly and Katy in the Country. (Golden Ladder Ser.). N.D. Robert Carter & Brothers.
--Katy and Jim. New ed. 1877. Robert Carter & Bros.
--Lawrence Bronson's Victory. (Illus.). 191p. N.D. Merrill.
--Lawrence Bronson's Victory, 1 of 6 vols. (Illus.). 191p. (Drayton Hall Ser.). N.D. Set. Robert Carter & Brothers.
--Lilies and Thistledown. N.D. Robert Carter & Brothers.
--Little Katy and Jolly Jim. (Golden Ladder Ser.). N.D. Robert Carter & Brothers.
--Little Margery, 1 of 103 vols. (The Pearl Library: No. 54). 1900. Set. Hurst & Co.
--Margery's City Home, 1 of 103 vols. (The Pearl Library: No. 60). 1900. Set. Hurst & Co.
--Margery's Home, & Crossing Sweeper. N.D. Merrill.
--Ned Dolan's Garret, 1 of 103 vols. (The Pearl Library: No. 66). 1900. Set. Hurst & Co.
--Nellie's Stumbling Block. (Illus.). 246p. N.D. Merrill.
--Nellie's Stumbling-Block, 1 of 5 Vols. (Dare to Do Right). N.D. Robert Carter & Brothers.
--Nettie's Mission, 1 of 103 vols. (The Pearl Library: No. 67). 1900. Set. Hurst & Co.
--Our Four Boys. (Illus.). 324p. N.D. Merrill.
--Our Four Boys, 1 of 5 Vols. (Dare to Do Right). N.D. Robert Carter & Brothers.
--Rosy Conroy's Lessons, 1 of 103 vols. (The Pearl Library: No. 91). 1900. Set. Hurst & Co.
--Susy's Sacrifice. (Illus.). 306p. N.D. Merrill.
--Susy's Sacrifice, 1 of 5 Vols. (Dare to Do Right). N.D. Robert Carter & Brothers.
--True to His Flag. (Drayton Hall Ser.). N.D. Robert Carter & Brothers.

Mathews, Louise (1950-)
--Bunches & Bunches of Bunnies. Bassett, Jeni Crisler, illus. LC 78-7625. (Illus.). (ps-3). 1978. Dodd.
--Cluck One. Bassett, Jeni Crisler, illus. LC 81-12532. (Illus.). 32 p. 1982. (ISBN 0-396-08029-4). Dodd, Mead.

Mathews, Louise (1950-) & Bassett, Jeni
--Gator Pie. LC 79-1512. (Illus.). 32 p. c.1979. (ISBN 0-396-07694-7). Dodd, Mead.
--The Great Take-Away. LC 80-12961. (Illus.). 46 p. c.1980. (ISBN 0-396-07846-X). Dodd, Mead.

Mathews, Marcia Mayfield
--The Freedom Star. Johnson, Bonnie Helene, illus. LC 70-165483. (Illus.). 94 p. 23cm. 1971. Coward, McCann & Geoghegan.

Mathews, Margaret Harriet
--Dame Prism. (Illus.). (Library for Boys and Girls Ser.). N.D. Frederick A. Stokes Co.
--Dell Daffodils. (Illus.). N.D. White & Stokes.
--Dr. Gilbert's Daughter. N.D. John C. Winston.
--Dr. Gilbert's Daughters. (Illus.). (Roundabout Lib.). N.D. Henry T. Coates & Co.
--Mr. Gilbert's Daughters: A Story for Girls. (Illus.). 1888. Porter & Coates.

Mathews, Shirley
--The Big Round Moon Book. Spicer, Jesse, illus. LC 49-6580. 20 p. col. illus. 22 cm. N.D. Distributed by W. Roberts.

Mathews, Vere Laughton, Mrs.
--Fanta-Sea Children, Designs and Story. LC 39-115071. 8 p. l., 21-127 p. incl. plates. 27 1/2 cm. c.1938. Guilders Publishing Center.

Mathewson, Christopher see Mathewson, Christy, pseud.

Mathewson, Christopher (1880-1925)
--Catcher Craig. Mathewson, Christy, pseud. (The Christy Mathewson Books for Boys). N.D. Grosset & Dunlap.
--Catcher Craig. Relyea, Charles M., illus. LC 15-8155. 5 p. l., 3-347 p. front., plates. 20 1/2 cm. c.1915. Dodd, Mead and Company.
--First Base Faulkner. Mathewson, Christy, pseud. (The Christy Mathewson Books for Boys). N.D. Grosset & Dunlap.
--First Base Faulkner. Relyea, Charles M., illus. LC 16-9067. 5 p. l., 3-328 p. front., plates. 20 cm. c.1916. Dodd, Mead and Company.
--Pitcher Pollock. Mathewson, Christy, pseud. (The Christy Mathewson Books for Boys). N.D. Grosset & Dunlap.
--Pitcher Pollock. Relyea, Charles M., illus. LC 14-6794. 5 p. l., 3-335 p. front., plates. 20 1/2 cm. c.1914. Dodd, Mead and Company.
--Pitching in a Pinch. Mathewson, Christy, pseud. (The Christy Mathewson Books for Boys). N.D. Grosset & Dunlap.
--Second Base Sloan. Mathewson, Christy, pseud. (The Christy Mathewson Books for Boys). N.D. Grosset & Dunlap.
--Second Base Sloan. Caswell, Edward C., illus. LC 17-130762. 5 p. l., 3-302 p. front., plates. 20 cm. c.1917. Dodd, Mead and Company.
--Won in the Ninth. Mathewson, Christy, pseud. Aulick, Will Wroth (1873-), ed. Mahony, Felix, illus. 2 p. l., 298 p. front., illus., plates. 19 1/2 cm. (Matty books). 1910. R. J. Bodmer Company.
--Won in the Ninth. Aulick, Will Wroth (1873-), ed. Mahony, Felix, illus. 2 p. l., 298 p. fornt., illus., plates. 19 1/2 cm. (Matty books. 1). c.1916. The New York Book Company.

Mathewson, Christy, pseud., see Mathewson, Christopher.

Mathias, Robert, retold by.
--The Stories of Hans Andersen. Lawrie, Robin, illus. LC 85-61399. (Original Author: Hans Christian Andersen, 1805-1875). (Illus.). 76 p. 28cm. 1985. (ISBN 0-382-09153-1). Silver Burdett.

Mathiesen, Egon (1907-1976)
--The Blue-Eyed Pussy. Mathiesen, Egon (1907-1976), illus. Rye, Karen, tr. LC 51-12291. 111 p. illus. 21 cm. (junior books. 1951. Doubleday.
--Jungle in the Wheat Field. (gr. k-3). N.D. G&D.
--Jungle in the Wheat Field. Mathiesen, Egon (1907-1976), illus. Birch, Robert, tr. LC 60-9047. (Illus.). (gr. k-3). 1960. (ISBN 0-8392-3014-1). Astor-Honor.
--Oswald the Monkey. (gr. k-3). N.D. G&D.
--Oswald the Monkey. Mathiesen, Egon (1907-1976), illus. (Illus.). (gr. k-3). 1959. (ISBN 0-8392-3025-7). Astor-Honor.
--Oswald the Monkey. 1st ed. Mathiesen, Egon (1907-1976), illus. LC 60-113492. unpaged. illus. 23 x 26cm. (Astor book). N.D. McDowell-Obolensky.

Mathiesen, Eric
--The True Story of Jumbo the Elephant. Jaques, Faith (1923-), illus. (Illus.). (gr. 4-6). 1964. (ISBN 0-698-30377-6, Coward). Putnam Pub Group.

Mathieson, Theodore (1913-)
--The Door to Nowhere. LC 64-10412. 192p. 1964. G P Putnam's Sons.
--Island in the Sand. Mathieson, David, illus. LC 64-15673. (Illus.). 22cm. 184p. (gr. 7-9). 1964. (ISBN 0-672-50329-8). Bobbs.

Mathieu, Joseph, jt. auth. see Lerner, Sharon Ruth.

Mathieu, Joseph (1945-)
--The Amazing Adventures of Silent E Man. Mathieu, Joseph (1945-), illus. LC 73-276. (Illus.). 24cm. 18p. (Electric Company Pop-up Ser.: No. 2). (gr. 2-5). 1973. (ISBN 0-394-82640-X, BYR). Random.
--Big Joe's Trailer Truck. (Illus.). (A Pictureback Book). 1974. (ISBN 0-394-82925-5). Random House.
--I Am a Monster. Mathieu, Joseph (1945-), illus. LC 77-360600. (Illus.). 22 p. 25cm. (Golden/Sesame street sturdy book). c.1976. (ISBN 0-307-12139-9). Golden Press.
--The Magic Word Book, Starring Marko the Magician!. Mathieu, Joseph (1945-), illus. LC 73-277. 18 p. (chiefly col. illus. 24cm. 1973. (ISBN 0-394-82641-8). Random House.
--The Sesame Street Mix or Match Storybook: Over Two Hundred Thousand Funny Combinations : Featuring Jim Henson's Muppets. LC 77-70853. (Illus.). 9 leaves (incl. cover). c.1977. (ISBN 0-394-83547-6). Random House.

Mathieu, Joseph (1945-), illus.
--Bathtime on Sesame Street. LC 82-80571. (Illus.). 12 p. 15cm. (Little pops). c.1983. (ISBN 0-394-85449-7). Random House/Children's Television Workshop.

AUTHOR INDEX MAUERMANN, MARY

Mathiews, F. K., ed. see Porter, William Sydney.
Mathiews, Franklin K., ed.
--The Boy Scout Year Bks. (Stories of Brave Boys and Fearless Men). N.D. D. Appleton-Century Co.
--The Boy Scouts Book of Campfire Stories. LC 21-146981. vi p., 1 l., 294, 1 p. front., illus. 22 1/2 cm. 1921. D. Appleton and Company.
--The Boy Scouts' Book of Good Turn Stories. LC 31-13592. x p., 2 l., 3-353 p; front., illus., plates. 22 cm. 1931. C. Scribner's Sons.
--Boy Scouts Book of Stories. N.D. D. Appleton and Company.
--The Boy Scouts Books of Adventurous Youth. N.D. Appleton-Century-Crofts.
--The Boy Scouts Year Books. (Stories of Boy Scout Courageous). N.D. D. Appleton-Century Co.
--The Boy Scouts Year Books. (Stories of Patriots and Pioneers). N.D. D. Appleton-Century Co.
--The Boy Scouts Year Books. (Wild Animal Stories). N.D. D. Appleton-Century Co.
--The Boy Scouts Year Books: Fun in Fiction. (Boy Scout Books). N.D. D. Appleton-Century Co.
--The Boy Scouts Year Books: Stories Boys Like Best. N.D. Appleton Century Crofts.
--The Boy Scouts Year Books: Stories of Adventurous Fliers. (Boy Scout Bks.). N.D. D. Appleton-Century Co.
--The Boy Scouts Year Books: Stories of Boy Heroes. (Boy Scouts Bks.). N.D. D. Appleton-Century Co.
--Chuckles and Grins. Schuyler, Remington (1884-1955) & Lauderback, Walt, illus. LC 28-15626. v, 3 9-224 p. front., illus. 26 cm. c.1928. Grosset & Dunlap.
--Laugh, Boy, Laugh!. A Book of Humorous Stories for Boys. Comstock, Enos Benjamin (1879-1945) & Pitz, Henry Clarence (1895-1976), illus. LC 32-9888. 192 p. front., illus. 26 cm. c.1932. Grosset & Dunlap.
--Skyward Ho!. LC 30-14003. 239, 1 p. incl. front., illus. 26 cm. c.1930. Grosset & Dunlap.
--Stories of Adventurous Fliers. N.D. Appleton-Century-Crofts.
--Wild Animal Trails. LC 28-15620. 192 p. incl. front., illus. 26 cm. c.1928. Grosset & Dunlap.
Mathiews, Franklin K., ed. see London, Jack.
Mathiews, Franklin K., ed. see Porter, William Sydney.
Mathis, Sharon Bell (1937-)
--Brooklyn Story. 1st ed. Bible, Charles (1937-), illus. LC 70-126794. (Illus.). 56 p. 20cm. (Challenger book. Black series). 1970. (ISBN 0-394-02013-8). Hill and Wang; Distributed by Random House.
--The Hundred Penny Box. 1st ed. Dillon, Leo (1933-) & Dillon, Diane (1933-), illus. LC 74-23744. (Illus.). 47 p. 24cm. 1975. (ISBN 0-670-38787-8). Viking Press. **Awards: (ALA); (BGH); (JNM).**
--Listen for the Fig Tree. LC 73-19797. 175 p. 22cm. 1974. (ISBN 0-670-43016-1). Viking Press.
--Sidewalk Story. 1st ed. Carty, Leo (1931-), illus. LC 71-136830. (Illus.). 71 p. 23cm. 1971. (ISBN 0-670-64377-7). Viking Press.
--Teacup Full of Roses. LC 73-8831. 159 p. 25cm. 1973, c.1972. (ISBN 0-8161-6121-6). G. K. Hall.
--Teacup Full of Roses. LC 74-162675. 125 p. 22cm. 1972. (ISBN 0-670-69434-7). Viking Press.
Mathison, Lorraine C.
--Blackie & the Proud Kitten. (gr. 3-6). N.D. Vantage.
Mathison, Melissa, jt. auth. see Kotzwinkle, William.
Mathleson, Theodore
--The Sign of the Flame. LC 64-18043. 21cm. 192p. (A Sleuth Club Mystery). 1964. Putnam.
Mathurin, Dondo
--The Pie and the Tart. N.D. D. Appleton & Co.
--Two Blind Men and a Donkey. N.D. D. Appleton & Co.
Matias, pseud., see Henrioud, Charles.
Matias, pseud.
--Little Donkey: Un Petit Ane. Henrioud, Charles. (Illus.). (gr. k-3). 1959. Walck.
Matias, see Henrioud, Charles.
Matimore, Patrick Henry (1891-)
--A Child's Garden of Religion Stories. Boog, Carle Michel, illus. LC 29-19206. x, 280 p. incl. col. front., col. illus. 19 cm. (Half-title: The Madonna series). 1929. The Macmillan Company.
Matlack, Margaret Moore
--Sergeant Jane. Bickford, Nana French, illus. LC 20-16159. 5 p. l., 278 p. front., plates. 19 1/2 cm. 1920. Little, Brown, and Company.
Matranga, Frances C.
--Secret Behind the Blue Door. 96p. (Orig.). (Voyager Ser.). 1981. (ISBN 0-8010-6121-0). Baker Bk.
Matrinez, Larry, jt. auth. see Caggiano, Rosemary.
Matschat, Cecile Hulse
--Ladd of the Big Swamp: A Story of the Okefenokee Settlement. 1st ed. Key, Alexander Hill (1904-1979), illus. LC 54-7732. 179p. illus. 22cm. (Winston adventure books). 1954. Winston.
Matschat, Cecile Hulse, jt. ed. see Del Rey, Lester.
Matschat, Cecile Hulse & Carmer, Carl Lamson (1893-1976), eds.
--American Boy Adventure Stories. Rudolph, Norman Guthrie (1896-1983), illus. LC 52-5490. 24cm. 367p. 1952. John C. Winston Co.
Matson, Emerson Nelson (1926-), ed.
--Legends of the Great Chiefs. LC 72-5870. (Illus.). 125 p. 22cm. 1972. (ISBN 0-8407-6214-9). T. Nelson.
--Longhouse Legends. Bjorklund, Lorence F. (1913-1978), illus. LC 68-22747. (Illus.). 128 p. 22cm. 1968. T. Nelson.
Matson, Henrietta
--The Mississippi Schoolmaster. 219p. N.D. Pilgrim Press.
Matsui, Tadashi (1926-)
--Oniroku and the Carpenter. Akaba, Suekichi, illus. Matsuno, Masako (1935-), tr. LC 63-18116. (Illus.). 28 p. 1963. Prentice-Hall.
--Peeka, the Traffic Light: A Story from Japan. 1st ed. Cho, Shinta (1927-), illus. LC 79-96056. (Illus.). 28 p. 27cm. 1970. (ISBN 0-8348-2001-3). (ISBN 0-8348-2008-0). Walker/Weatherhill.
Matsumura, Masako, illus.
--The Bird's Wedding. Meredith, Lucy, tr. (Illus.). 26p. (gr. k-3). 1982. (ISBN 0-571-11896-8) Faber & Faber.
Matsuno, Masako (1935-), tr. see Kishida, Eriko.
Matsuno, Masako (1935-), tr. see Matsui, Tadashi.
Matsuno, Masako (1935-), tr. see Matsutani, Miyoko.
Matsuno, Masako (1935-)
--Chie and the Sports Day. Mizumura, Kazue, illus. LC 65-13416. 1v. (unpaged) col. illus. 21x24cm. c.1965. World.
--Chie & the Sports Day. Mizumura, Kazue, illus. (Illus.). (gr. k-3). 1965. World Pub.
--A Pair of Red Clogs. 1st ed. Mizumura, Kazue, illus. LC 60-12901. (Illus.). unpaged. 1960. World Pub. Co.
--Taro & the Bamboo Shoot. LC 64-18322. (Illus.). 32p. (Pinwheel Bks). (gr. k-3). 1974. (ISBN 0-394-82802-X). Pantheon.
--Taro and the Bamboo Shoot: A Japanese Tale. Segawa, Yasuo (1932-), illus. LC 64-18322. (Illus.). 32 p. 1964. (ISBN 0-394-91727-8). (ISBN 0-394-91727-8). Pantheon.
--Taro and the Tofu. Mizumura, Kazue, illus. LC 62-9058. unpaged. illus. 26cm. 1962. World Pub. Co.
Matsuno, Masako (1935-) & Mizumura, Kazue
--A Pair of Red Clogs. 1st U.S. pbk. Ed. ed. Mizumura, Kazue, illus. LC 81-941. p. cm. 1981. (ISBN 0-399-20796-1). Philomel Books.
Matsutani, Miyoko (1925-)
--The Crane Maiden. Iwasaki, Chihiro (1918-1974), illus. LC 68-13357. (Illus.). 32 p. 27cm. 1968. Parents' Magazine Press.
--The Fisherman Under the Sea. Iwasaki, Chihiro (1918-1974), illus. LC 69-13126. (Illus.). 32 p. 27cm. 1969. Parents' Magazine Press.
--The Fox Wedding. Segawa, Yasuo (1932-), illus. Matsuno, Masako (1935-), tr. LC 63-18350. (Illus.). 27cm. 32p. 1963. Encyclopedia Britannica Press.
--Gengoroh and the Thunder God. Segawa, Yasuo (1932-), illus. LC 70-99582. (Illus.). 32 p. 27cm. 1970. Parents' Magazine Press.
--How the Withered Trees Blossomed: How the Wintered Trees Blossomed. Segawa, Yasuo (1932-), illus. LC 75-141769. (Illus.). 40 p. 29cm. 1971, c.1969. Lippincott.
--Taro, the Dragon-Boy. 1st ed. Kuwata, Masakazu, illus. Boone, Donald C., tr. LC 67-167723. 127p. illus. (pt. col.) 22cm. 1967. Kodansha.
--The Witch's Magic Cloth. American ed. Segawa, Yasuo (1932-), illus. LC 79-77787. (Illus.). 32 p. 27cm. 1969. Parents' Magazine Press.
Matsuura, Richard & Matsuura, Ruth
--Kalani and Primo. Olcott, Candice, ed. Chao, Linus, illus. LC 80-113230. (Illus.). 32 p. 23cm. c.1979. Orchid Isle Pub. Co.
Matsuura, Ruth, jt. auth. see Matsuura, Richard.
Matt, Christopher
--Wing-T Fullback. (Illus.). 160p. 1960. Franklin Watts, Inc.
Mattam, Donald (1909-), ed.
--English Poems for All Peoples. Samuel, D. T., illus. LC 66-211433. (An Anthology for Children Studying English As a Second Language). v. illus. 20cm. (Commonwealth & intl. lib.). 1966. Pergamon.
Mattenklodt, Wilhelm
--Fugitive in the Jungle. N.D. Little, Brown & Co.
Matter, John & Matter, Robert
--The Amateur Vagabond. LC 18-20942. 340 p. 21 1/2 cm. $1.5. c.1918. George H. Doran Company.
Matter, Robert, jt. auth. see Matter, John.
Mattern, Marjorie, adapted by.
--The Three Musketeers. Greene, Hamilton, illus. (An abridgement of the novel by Alexandre Dumas). (A Golden Picture Classic). 1957. Golden Press.
Mattews, Mollie, jt. auth. see Mattews, Patrick.
Mattews, Patrick & Mattews, Mollie
--Teddy Edward's Magic Music Box. 32p. 1976. (ISBN 0-7207-0812-5, Pub. by Michael Joseph). Merrimack Pub Cir.
Matthew, Jean Marian, ed. see Bunyan, John.
Matthew, Margolis, jt. auth. see Sendak, Maurice Bernard.
Matthew, Ray, jt. auth. see Abdullah, Mena.
Matthews, Agnes Rounds, Mrs. (1860-)
--The Seven Champions of Christendom: A Legendary Romance of Chivalry. LC 11-24418. x, 161 p. incl. front., illus. 19 cm. $0.4. c.1911. Ginn and Company.
Matthews, Ann, adapted by.
--The Journey of Natty Gann Storybook. Rosenberg, Jeanne & Walt Disney Pictures LC 85-18220. (Based on the Motion Picture from Walt Disney Pictures.). p. cm. c.1985. (ISBN 0-671-60502-X). Little Simon.
Matthews, Asimov
--Lucky Star and Big Sun of Mercury. N.D. New American Company.
--Lucky Star and The Moons of Jupiter. N.D. New American Company.
--Lucky Star and the Ocean of Venus. N.D. New American Company.
--Lucky Star and the Pirates of the Asteroids. N.D. New American Company.
--Lucky Starr and the Rings of Saturn. N.D. New American Company.
Matthews, Brander (1852-1929)
--Tom Paulding: The Story of a Search for Buried Treasure in the Streets of New York. LC 7-32308. 6 p. l., 254 p. incl. front., illus., plates. 19 1/2 cm. 1892. The Century Co.
Matthews, Clayton Harley see Brisco, Patty, pseud.
Matthews, Cornelius, compiled by.
--The Enchanted Moccasins and Other Legends. N.D. G P Putnam's Sons.
Matthews, Ellen (1950-)
--Debugging ROVER. Thompson, Arthur (1951-), illus. LC 85-12951. (Illus.). 127 p. 21cm. c.1985. (ISBN 0-396-08729-9). Dodd, Mead.
--Getting Rid of Roger. 1st ed. Duffy, Pat (1952-), illus. LC 77-12311. (Illus.). 96 p. 21cm. c.1978. (ISBN 0-664-32622-6). Westminster Press.
--Putting up with Sherwood. 1st ed. Unada, pseud. (1927-), illus. Gliewe, Unada Grace. LC 80-17574. (Illus.). 137 p. 21cm. c.1980. (ISBN 0-664-32672-2). Westminster Press.
--The Trouble with Leslie. 1st ed. Unada, pseud. (1927-), illus. Gliewe, Unada Grace. LC 79-12348. (Illus.). 109 p. 21cm. c.1979. (ISBN 0-664-32653-6). Westminster Press.
Matthews, Irma Blanchard (1872-)
--Under a Circus Tent. (Illus.). (Lad and Lassie Series.). 1915. George W Jacobs.
--Under a Circus Tent. LC 7-29099. 136 p. front., 4 pl. 19 1/2 cm. 1907. G.W. Jacobs & Company.
Matthews, Jacklyn Meek, pseud., see Meek, Jacklyn O'Hanlon.
Matthews, Jacklyn Meek, pseud. (1933-)
--Edward and the Night Horses. Meek, Jacklyn O'Hanlon. Freeman, Don (1908-1978), illus. LC 78-141156. (Illus.). 48 p. 26cm. 1971. (ISBN 0-87464-165-9). Golden Gate Junior Books.
Matthews, Margaret Harriet
--Dame Prism: A Story for Girls. Tucker, Elizabeth S., illus. LC 20-16481. vi, 429 p. front., plates. 19 1/2 cm. c.1895. Frederick A. Stokes Company.
Matthews, Maria
--My Little Pony, Baby Firefly's Adventure and Other My Little Pony Stories. Beylon, Catherine M., illus. LC 85-42537. p. cm. 1985. (ISBN 0-394-87386-6). Random House.
--The Snorks & the Bubble Gum Mystery. Wildman, George, illus. LC 84-17752. (Illus.). 32p. (ps-3). 1985. (ISBN 0-394-87108-1, BYR). (ISBN 0-394-87109-X). Random.
--The Snorks & the Magic Pearl. Wildman, George, illus. LC 84-17728. (Illus.). 32p. (ps-3). 1985. (ISBN 0-394-87109-X, BYR). (ISBN 0-394-87108-1). Random.
Matthews, Mollie, jt. auth. see Matthews, Patrick.
Matthews, Patricia Anne (1927-)
--Too Much in Love. (Written under the Pseudonym Patty Brisco). (gr. 7 up). 1980. (ISBN 0-590-32199-4, Wishing Star Bks). Scholastic Inc.
Matthews, Patrick & Matthews, Mollie
--Snowy Toes & the Magic Music Box. 32p. 1976. (ISBN 0-7207-0813-3, Pub. by Michael Joseph). Merrimack Pub Cir.
--Teddy Edward's Magic Journey. 32p. 1976. (ISBN 0-7207-0814-1, Pub. by Michael Joseph). Merrimack Pub Cir.
Matthews, Rodney, illus.
--Back to Earth. (Illus.). (Blue Planet Ser.). 1975. (ISBN 0-85953-058-2, Pub. by Childs's Play England). Playspaces.
Matthias, Catherine (1945-)
--I Love Cats. Dunnington, Tom, illus. LC 83-7215. (Illus.). 29 p. 19cm. (A Rookie Reader). c.1983. (ISBN 0-516-02041-2). Childrens Press.
--Out the Door. Neill, Eileen Mueller, illus. LC 81-17060. p. cm. (A Rookie Reader). 1982. (ISBN 0-516-03560-6). Childrens Press.
--Over-Under. Sharp, Gene (1923-), illus. LC 83-21005. (Prepared under the Direction of Robert L. Hillerich, 1929-). (Illus.). 32p (Rookie Readers). (ps-2). 1984. (ISBN 0-516-02048-X). (ISBN 0-516-42048-8). Childrens.
--Too Many Balloons. Sharp, Gene (1923-), illus. LC 81-15520. (Illus.). 29 p. 19cm. (A Rookie Reader). c.1982. (ISBN 0-516-03633-5). (ISBN 0-516-43633-3). Childrens Press.
Matthias, Virginia Park
The Big Bending Tree. Stone, David Karl (1922-), illus. LC 60-5583. 120p. illus. 21cm. 1960. F. Watts.
Matthiesen, Thomas
--ABC: An Alphabet Book. Matthiesen, Thomas, photos by. LC 66-13382. 1 v. unpaged. col. illus. 21cm. 1966. Platt & Munk.
Matthiessen, Peter (1927-)
--Seal Pool. 1st ed. Du Bois, William Sherman Pene (1916-), illus. LC 73-101981. (Illus.). 78 p. 22cm. 1972. Doubleday.
Matthiessen, Wilhelm (1891-1966)
--Folk Tales. Bartlett, Ruth, illus. LC 68-23586. (Illus.). 206 p. 24cm. 1968. Grove Press.
Mattingley, Christobel Rosemary (1931-)
--The Angel with a Mouth-Organ. Lacis, Astra, illus. LC 84-168606. (Illus.). 32 p. 1984. (ISBN 0-340-33333-2). Hodder and Stoughton.
--The Angel with a Mouth-Organ. Lacis, Astra, illus. LC 85-16424. p. cm. 1986, c.1984. (ISBN 0-8234-0593-1). Holiday House.
--The Long Walk. Sallis, Helen, illus. LC 77-360920. (Illus.). 47 p. 22cm. 1976. (ISBN 0-17-005047-5). Thomas Nelson (Australia).
Mattmuller-Frick, Felix
--We Want a Little Sister. Schneider, Marcus, illus. LC 65-25946. (Illus.). 1 v. (unpaged). (Foreign Land Bks). 1965. Lerner Publications Co.
Mattos, Alexander Louis Teixeira De see Maeterlinck, Maurice.
Mattson, Olle (1922-)
--Mickel and the Lost Ship. Gross, Sarah Chokla, ed. Sax, Robert M., illus. Spurge, Anna & Sprigge, Elizabeth, trs. LC 60-11176. 214p. illus. 21cm. 1960. F. Watts.
--Mickel, Seafarer. Gross, Sarah Chokla (1906-1976), ed. Sturge, Anna & Sprigge, Elizabeth, trs. from Swedish LC 61-6304. 21cm. 179p. 1962, c.1961. F. Watts.
Matulay, Laszlo (1912-), illus.
--Fairy Tales. N.D (Wonder Books). Grosset & Dunlap.
--Read Aloud Fairy Tales. LC 57-4199. (Illus.). 160p. 1957. Wonder Books Inc.
Matus, Greta (1936-)
--Where Are You, Jason?. LC 74-4118. (Illus.). 32 p. 21cm. 1974. (ISBN 0-688-41584-9). (ISBN 0-688-41584-9). Lothrop, Lee & Shepard Co.
Matute, Ana Maria (1926-)
--The Lost Children. MacLean, Joan, tr. from Spanish. LC 65-11570. 22cm. 538p. 1965. Macmillan.
Matz, Dale, jt. auth. see Edgar, Pamela.
Matzdorff, Hyde
--Limpy, Tale of a Monkey Hero. (Illus.). (gr. 3-5). 1957. (ISBN 0-8382-0439-2). Hale.
--Limpy: Tale of a Monkey Hero. Wiese, Kurt (1887-1974), illus. LC 57-8239. 87p. illus. 21cm. 1957. J. Day Co.
Maud, Constance Elizabeth
--Heroines of Poetry. Ospovat, Henry, illus. LC 2-27240. 4 p. l., 299 p. front., pl. 20 cm. 1903. J. Lane.
Maude, Alymer, tr. see Tolstoy, Leo Nikolaevich.
Maude, Louise Shanks, tr. see Tolstoy, Leo Nikolaevich.
Mauermann, Mary Anne (1927-)
--The Magic Tower. 1965. David McKay Company Inc.
--The Magic Tower. LC 65-20770. 150p. 21cm. N.D. Washburn.
--Spotlight Summer. 1964. David McKay Company Inc.
--Spotlight Summer. LC 64-12014. 154 p. 21cm. 1964. I. Washburn.
--Strangers Into Friends. 1965. David McKay Company.
--Strangers into Friends. LC 76-86238. 153 p. 21cm. 1969. I. Washburn.

Mauersberger, Helga, adapted by.
--The Sun: Cockadoodledo Tells the Story of the Sun and the Seasons of the Year. Winter, Klaus (1928-) & Bischoff, Helmut, illus. LC 61-1867. (Illus.). 33cm. 1961. F. Watts.
Mauge
--Prairie Boys. N.D. Hurst & Company.
Mauge, Roger
--The Story of a Goldfish. LC 62-15023. unpaged. illus. 31cm. 1962, c.1960. Orion Press.
Maugham, William Somerset (1874-1965)
--Princess September. 1st ed. Ayer, Jacqueline (1930-), illus. LC 69-13776. (Illus.). 38 p. 22cm. 1969. Harcourt, Brace & World.
--Princess September and the Nightingale. Jones, Richard C. (1910-), illus. LC 39-27811. 31 p. illus. (part col.) 25 1/2 cm. c.1939. Oxford University Press.
Maughan, Joyce Bowen, ed.
--Stories You'll Want to Remember. LC 75-82122. 84 p. 16cm. 1969. Deseret Book Co.
Mauldin, Bill, pseud., see Mauldin, William Henry.
Mauldin, Bill, pseud. (1921-)
--A Sort of Saga. Mauldin, William Henry. Mauldin, Bill, pseud. (1921-), illus. Mauldin, William Henry. 301p. N.D. William Sloane Associates.
Mauldin, William Henry see Mauldin, Bill, pseud.
Maule, Hamilton Bee see Maule, Tex, pseud.
Maule, Hamilton Bee (1915-)
--Beatty of the Yankees. Maule, Tex, pseud. 1963. David McKay Company Inc.
--Last Out. Maule, Tex, pseud. (gr. 7 up). 1964. (ISBN 0-679-25076-X). McKay.
Maule, Mary Katherine Finigan, Mrs. (1861-)
--The Bryne Girls, How They Worked and Won. Goss, John, illus. LC 21-14797. 394 p. front., plates. 19 1/2 cm. 1921. Lothrop, Lee & Shepard Co.
--For Mamsie's Sake: The Story of a Boy's Ambition. LC 7-25584. 88 p. plates. 21 cm. 1893. J. North & Company.
--The Little Knight of the X-Bar-B. LC 10-4044. viii.p. 1 1, 461 p front. plates 20. 1910. Grosset & Dunlap.
--The Little Knight of the X Bar B. N.D. Lothrop Lee & Shepard Co.
--A Prairie-Schooner Princess. N.D. Lothrop,Lee & Shepard.
Maule, Tex, pseud., see Maule, Hamilton Bee.
Maum, Emmett
--Over the Hurdles. LC 40-12853. 2 p. l., 248 p. 20 1/2 cm. c.1940. The World Publishing Company.
--Over the Hurdles. LC 48-11674. 216 p. front. 20 cm. (Falcon books, A-18). 1948. World Pub. Co.
Maupassant, Guy De see De Maupassant, Guy.
Maupassant, Guy De (1850-1893)
--The Diamond Necklace, and Four Other Stories. Quackenbush, Robert Mead (1929-), illus. (Illus.). 82 p. 23cm. 1967. F. Watts.
Maurel, Micheline
--Jade Tales. Delhumeau, Annick, illus. LC 64-15586. (Illus.). 62p. (gr. 3-7). 1964. (ISBN 0-87663-052-2). Universe.
Mauriac, Francois (1885-1970)
--The Holy Terror. Fetz, Ingrid (1915-), illus. LC 67-26039. (Illus.). 63 p. 22cm. 1967. Funk & Wagnalls.
Maurice, Dominique
--The Tale About the Owl. (Illus.). 8p. (Orig.). 1982. (ISBN 0-914676-59-8, Pub. by Envelope Bks). Green Tiger Pr.
Maurier, Daphne Du see Du Maurier, Daphne.
Maurois, Andre (1885-1967)
--Fatapoufs & Thinifers. Bruller, Jean Marcel (1902-), illus. Benet, Rosemary Carr, Mrs., tr. LC 40-34734. 2 p. l., 9-92 p., 1 l. illus. (part col.) 29 cm. 1940. H. Holt and Company.
--Fattypuffs & Thinifers. Wegner, Fritz (1924-), illus. LC 69-17508. (Illus.). 87 p. 27cm. 1st U.S. edition. 1969, c.1968. Knopf.
Maurois, Andre (1885-1967) & Maurois, Gerald
--The French Boy. LC 57-59556. unpaged. illus. 31cm. 1957. Sterling Pub. Co.
Maurois, Gerald, jt. auth. see Maurois, Andre.
Maury, Inez (1909-)
--My Mother the Mail Carrier - Mi Mama la Cartera. McCrady, Lady (1951-), illus. Alemany, Norah, tr. LC 96-14295. (Illus.). 32p. (Orig.). (gr. 1-2). 1976. (ISBN 0-912670-23-1). (ISBN 0-912670-23-1). Feminist Pr.
Maury, Jean West, Mrs.
--A First Bible. (980). 1934. (ISBN 0-8098-2302-0). David McKay Company.
--Old Raven's World. Kutcher, Ben (1895-), illus. LC 31-29632. xiv p., 2 l., 3-284 p., 1 l. incl. plates. col. front. 20 1/2 cm. 1931. Little, Brown, and Company.
Mauser, Patricia Rhoads (1943-)
--A Bundle of Sticks. 1st ed. Owens, Gail, illus. LC 81-8098. (Illus.). 169 p. 22cm. 1982. (ISBN 0-689-30899-X). Atheneum.
--How I Found Myself at the Fair. 1st ed. McCully, Emily Arnold (1939-), illus. LC 80-12058. (Illus.). 58 p. 22cm. 1980. (ISBN 0-689-30780-2). Atheneum.
--Rip-off. LC 85-7958. p. cm. 1985. (ISBN 0-689-31134-6). Atheneum.
Mauthner, Maria, jt. auth. see De Jaeger, Charles.
Mauzey, Merritt (1897-1975)
--Cotton-Farm Boy. Mauzey, Merritt (1897-1975), tr. Putcamp, Luise, Jr. (1924-), intro. by. LC 53-10940. 79p. illus. 26cm. 1953. H. Schuman.
--Oilfield Boy. LC 56-10386. 80p. illus. 27cm. 1957. Abelard-Schuman.
--Rice Boy. LC 57-952638. 67p. illus. 27cm. 1958. Abelard-Schuman.
--Rubber Boy. Mauzey, Merritt (1897-1975), illus. LC 62-13629. 60p. illus. 26cm. 1962. Abelard-Schuman.
--Texas Ranch Boy. LC 55-85390. 77p. illus. 27cm. 1955. Abelard-Schuman.
Mavor, William Fordyce (1758-1837)
--A Father's Gift to His Children: Consisting of Original Essays, Tales, Fables, Reflections, &C. LC 45-46886. v. 15 cm. N.D. Published by M. Carey.
Maw, Margaret Peterson (1874-)
--Nikoline's Academy. LC 51-2268. 249 p. illus. 21 cm. 1951. Oxford University Press.
--Nikoline's Career. LC 56-6749. 188p. 21cm. 1956. Oxford University Press.
--Nikoline's Choice. Woodbury, Mabel Jones, illus. LC 47-3370. 289 p. incl. front., illus. 21 cm. (Oxford books for boys and girls). 1947. Oxford University Press.
Mawhinney, Thomas A. H
--English Oak and Spanish Gold. Lee, Manning De Villeneuve (1894-1980), illus. 4 p. l., 7-315 p. front., illus., plates. 21 cm. 1943. David McKay Company.
--English Oak and Spanish Gold. Lee, Manning De Villeneuve (1894-1980), illus. LC 26-14835. 315 p. front., illus., plates. 19 1/2 cm. 1926. The Penn Publishing Company.
--The Messenger of the Black Prince. (Dollar Mystery and Adventure Ser.). N.D. David McKay Co.
--The Messenger of the Black Prince. Lee, Manning De Villeneuve (1894-1980), illus. LC 28-23543. 299 p. front., illus., plates. 20 cm. 1928. The Penn Publishing Company.
--The Sword of the House of De Marillac. Lee, Manning De Villeneuve (1894-1980), illus. LC 25-16205. 293 p. front., illus., plates. 19 1/2 cm. 1925. The Penn Publishing Company.
Mawicke, Tran, jt. auth. see Hall, Lynn.
Max, Leslie, pseud., see McGuire, Leslie Sarah.
Max, Leslie, pseud. (1945-)
--Barney's Picnic. McGuire, Leslie Sarah. 14p. (Play & Learn Shape Board Bks). (gr. k-3). 1981. (ISBN 0-89828-101-6, Ottenheimer Pubs Inc). Tuffy Bks.
--Dino's Happy & Sad Book. McGuire, Leslie Sarah. 14p. (Play & Learn Shape Board Bks). (gr. k-3). 1981. (ISBN 0-89828-103-2, Ottenheimer Pubs Inc). Tuffy Bks.
--Huckleberry Hound Takes a Trip. McGuire, Leslie Sarah. 14p. (Play & Learn Shape Board Bks). (gr. k-3). 1981. (ISBN 0-89828-105-9, Ottenheimer Pubs Inc). Tuffy Bks.
--Pebbles & Bamm-Bamm. McGuire, Leslie Sarah. 14p. (Play & Learn Shape Board Bks). (gr. k-3). 1981. (ISBN 0-89828-102-4, Ottenheimer Pubs Inc). Tuffy Bks.
Max, Peter (1937-)
--The Peter Max Land of Blue. LC 72-125535. (Illus.). 31 p. 29cm. 1970. (ISBN 0-531-01958-6). F. Watts.
--The Peter Max Land of Blue and How the Cousins Got There. Max, Peter (1937-), illus. 30p. (gr. k-3). 1970. (ISBN 0-531-01958-6). Watts.
--The Peter Max Land of Red. LC 76-125536. (Illus.). 31 p. 29cm. 1970. (ISBN 0-531-01960-8). F. Watts.
--Peter Max Land of Red and BoyGreen's Surprise in the Cosmic Color Tunnel. 32p. (gr. k-3). 1970. (ISBN 0-531-01960-8). Watts.
--The Peter Max Land of Yellow. LC 70-125537. (Illus.). 31 p. 29cm. 1970. (ISBN 0-531-01959-4). F. Watts.
--Peter Max Land of Yellow and How the Purple King Nearly Lost Himself There. Max, Peter (1937-), illus. (gr. k-3). 1970. (ISBN 0-531-01958-6). Watts.
Maxey, Dale (1927-)
--Fidgit. LC 65-28060. 1v. (unpaged) col. illus. 33cm. c.1965. Dodd.
--The Trouble with Timothy. LC 79-102639. (Illus.). 40 p. 29cm. 1970. (ISBN 0-695-80126-0). Follett.
Maxfield, Mina Rosenthal
--The Perilous Adventures of the Golden Princes. Buckman, Betty Brunner, illus. LC 53-11166. 201p. illus. 21cm. 1953. Christopher Pub. House.
Maxon, Anne (1892-1974)
--The House that Jill Built. Best, Allena Champlin, Mrs. (1892-1974), illus. Berry, Erick, pseud. LC 34-28615. 1934. Dodd Mead & Co.
Maxon, Olivia J.
--The Story of the Two Grunches. (gr. 4-6). 1979. (ISBN 0-533-03268-7). Vantage.
Maxwell, Allen, jt. auth. see Hudson, Wilson Mathis.
Maxwell, Arthur Stanley (1896-1970)
--The Children's Hour with Uncle Arthur ... LC 46-1715. v. col. front., illus., plates (part col) 23 1/2 cm. c.1945. Review and Herald Publishing Association.
--The Secret of the Cave: A Thrilling, Inspiring Mystery Story for Boys and Girls. Atterbury, John W., illus. LC 51-11441. 96 p. col. illus. 23 cm. 1951. Pacific Press Pub. Association.
--Uncle Arthur's Bedtime Stories. LC 50-3160. v. col. illus. 21 cm. N.D. Review and Herald.
--Uncle Arthur's Bedtime Stories ... LC 28-11922. v. fronts., illus. 19 1/2 cm. N.D. Review and Herald Publishing Company.
--Uncle Arthur's Storytime. LC 77-113040. (Illus.). v. 22cm. (Penguin series). N.D. Review and Herald Pub. Association.
--Uncle Jim's Visitors. LC 27-3036. 152 p. illus. 19 1/2 cm. c.1927. Pacific Press Publishing Association.
Maxwell, Edith (1923-)
--Game of Truth. LC 75-38354. 185 p. 21cm. c.1976. (ISBN 0-396-07305-0). Dodd, Mead.
--Just Dial a Number. LC 70-140059. 178 p. 21cm. 1971. (ISBN 0-396-06291-1). Dodd, Mead.
Maxwell, Gavin (1914-1969)
--The Otters' Tale. LC 62-7807. 124p. illus. 25cm. 1st U.S. edition. 1962. Dutton.
Maxwell, Ian
--MacGee and MacGill and Me. LC 69-19891. (Illus.). 98 p. 22cm. 1969. Dorrance.
Maxwell, Kathleen
--The Crater and the Krater. (Illus.). N.D. (ISBN 0-8111-0406-0). The Naylor Company.
Maxwell, L. E.
--Boy Wanted and Other Stories. 1956. Eerdmans.
Maxwell, Marjorie, pseud., see Aspinwall, Marguerite.
Maxwell, Mary Elizabeth Braddon see M. E. B. , pseud.
Maxwell, Mary Elizabeth Braddon
--Brave Nelly: Or, Weak Hands and a Willing Heart. M. E. B. , pseud. (Illus.). N.D. E P Dutton.
--Clement's Trial and Victory. M. E. B. , pseud. (Illus.). N.D. E P Dutton.
--Gem of an Aunt, and the Treat She Gave. (Illus.). N.D. Publications of E. P. Dutton & Co.
--The New Girl: Or, The Rivals. M. E. B. , , pseud. (Illus.). N.D. E P Dutton.
--The Three Wishes. M. E. B. , pseud. (Illus.). N.D. E P Dutton.
Maxwell, Mary H, Mrs.
--The Juvenile Annual: Or, Holiday Melodies. 2nd ed. LC 15-16822. iv, 5-101 p. front., plates. 12 cm. 1852. Stone & Pratt.
--Willie Drew and His School-Mates. Kidder, Daniel Parish (1815-1891), ed. LC 15-234406. 1 p. l. 5-36 p. front. 11 cm. 1849. Lane & Scott.
Maxwell, R. H
--Cowboy on Ice. Williams, Lee, illus. LC 74-23771. (Illus.). 64 p. 25cm. 1975. (ISBN 0-516-07631-0). Childrens Press.
Maxwell, Robert
--Close-up. (gr. 7 up). N.D. Pyramid Pubns.
Maxwell, Ruth (1925-)
--Look with May Ling. Dewey, Kenneth Francis, illus. LC 73-81590. (Illus.). 16 p. (Magic circle book). 1974. (ISBN 0-663-25452-3). Ginn.
Maxwell, Violet, jt. auth. see Hill, Helen.
Maxwell, Violet & Hill, Helen
--The Adventures of Galley Jack: Ship's Cat to the Susan P. Meservey. Hill, Helen & Maxwell, Violet, illus. LC 29-16076. 6 p. l. 112 p. incl. illus., plates. col. front. 17 1/2 cm. 1929. Harper & Brothers.
--Charlie and His Kitten Topsy. Maxwell, Violet & Hill, Helen, illus. LC 22-17222. 6 p. l. 90 p. col. front., illus., col. plates. 18 cm. (Half-title: The Charlie stories). 1922. The Macmillan Company.
--Galley Jack Crosses the Line. Hill, Helen & Maxwell, Violet, illus. LC 30-21941. 6 p. l. 105 p. incl. illus., plates. col. front. 17 1/2 cm. 1930. Harper & Brothers.
Maxwell, William (1908-)
--The Heavenly Tenants. Karasz, Ilonka (1896-1981), illus. LC 46-11959. 3 p. l., 9-56, 2 p. incl. illus., double plates. 25 x 20 cm. 1946. Harper & Brothers. **Award: (JNM).**
May, Ann
--Phoebe, the Swishy Witch. 1st ed. Marash, Megan, illus. LC 67-20457. (Illus.). 91 p. 24cm. 1967. Bobbs-Merrill.
May, Anna Mackall
--Grandma's Spinning Wheel. LC 12-26912. (Illus.). 18cm. 51p. c.1912. Lord Baltimore Press.
May, Barbara
--Buckle Horse. 1st ed. Brown, Paul (1893-1958), illus. LC 56-10036. 128p. illus. 25cm. 1956. Holt.
May, Carrie L., Mrs.
--Bertie's Telegraph. (Little Pitcher Stories). N.D. Henry A. Young.
--Brownie Sandford. (Sweet Clover Stories). N.D. Henry A. Young.
--Brownie Sandford: Or, The Recovered Pearl. LC 12-36639. 2 p. l., 3-301 p. plates. 17 cm. (Sweet clover stories. 2). 1866. W. H. Hill, Jr. & Co.
--Charley's Calico Rooster. LC 12-36640. 1 p. l., 7-174 p. front., plates. 15 1/2 cm. (Little pitcher stories). 1869. W. H. Hill, Jr., & Co.
--Charlie's Calico Rooster. (Little Pitcher Stories). N.D. Henry A. Young.
--Four Little Pitchers. (Little Pitcher Stories). N.D. Henry A. Young.
--Grandma's Strong Box. (Little Pitcher Stories). N.D. Henry A. Young.
--Nellie Milton's Housekeeping. (Sweet Clover Stories). N.D. Henry A. Young.
--Nellie Milton's Housekeeping: Or, Sweet Clover. LC 12-866414. 2 p. l. iii-v, 7-280 p. 17 cm. (Half-title: Sweet clover stories. v. 1). 1867. W. H. Hill, Jr., & Co.
--Ruth Lovell. (Sweet Clover Stories). N.D. Henry A. Young.
--Ruth Lovell: Or, Holidays at Home. LC 12-36643. 2 p. l. 3-304 p. plates. 17 cm. (Sweet clover stories 4). 1868. W. H. Hill, Jr & Co.
--Sweet Clover Stories For Girls, 4 Vols. 1884. A Sumner & Co.
--Sylvia's Burden. (Sweet Colver Stories). N.D. Henry A. Young.
--Sylvia's Burden. LC 12-36644. vi, 9-290 p. plates 17 cm. (Half-title: Sweet clover stories. v. 3). c.1867. W. H. Hill, Jr., & Co.
--Trials of the Baby Pitcher. (Little Pitcher Stories). N.D. Henry A. Young.
--Uncle Barney's Fortune. (Little Pitcher Stories). N.D. Henry A. Young.
May, Catharine E.
--Life at Hartwell: Or, Frank and His Friends, 1 of 4 Vols. (Hartwell Library Ser.). N.D. Set. T. Whittaker.
May, Charles Paul (1920-)
--Box Turtle Lives in Armor. N.D. E . M . Hale and Co.
--High-Noon Rocket. Turkle, Brinton Cassaday (1915-), illus. LC 66-77612. 1v. (unpaged) col. illus. 20x23cm. 1966. Holiday House.
--Left by Themselves. Ambrus, Victor G., pseud. (1935-), illus. Ambrus, Gyozo Laszlo. (gr. k-3). 1973. (ISBN 0-590-06228-X). Schol Bk Serv.
--Little Mouse. Loeffler, Gisella (1900-), illus. LC 62-15074. unpaged, illus. 22cm. (Reading-made-easy book). 1962. Barnes.
--Pink Pig and the Nut Tree. Daniel, Frank, illus. LC 62-150757. unpaged. illus. 22cm. (Wonderful world book). 1962. A. S. Barnes.
--Stranger in the Storm. Ambrus, Victor G., pseud. (1935-), illus. Ambrus, Gyozo Laszlo. LC 75-156849. (Illus.). 92 p. 22cm. 1972. (ISBN 0-200-71821-5). (ISBN 0-200-71822-3). Abelard-Schuman.
--When Animals Change Clothes. Ferguson, Walter (1930-), illus. LC 65-815608. 55p. illus. 24cm. c.1965. Holiday House.
May, Charles R. (1920-)
--Stranger in the Storm. Ambrus, Victor G., pseud. (1935-), illus. Ambrus, Gyozo Laszlo. LC 75-156849. (Illus.). drawings. 96p. (gr. 3 up). 1972. (ISBN 0-200-71822-3). Abelard.
May, Earl Chapin (1873-)
--The Circus, From Rome to Ringling. N.D. Dodd, Mead & Co.
--The Prairie Pirates. Dean, Bob, illus. N.D. Dodd, Mead & Co.
--The Prairie Pirates. Dean, Bob, illus. LC 32-28973. 5 p. l. 3-360 p. plates. 21 cm. c.1932. Duffield & Green.
May, Edith J.
--Dashwood Priory: Or, Mortimer's College Days, 1 of 3 Vols. Gilbert, John Clitherae, illus. (Illus.). (School and College Library). N.D. Set. George Routledge & Sons.
--Louis' School-Days, 1 of 4 Vols. (Library of the School-Boy Philosopher). N.D. Set. A D F Randolph & Co.
--Louis' School Days: A Story for Boys. LC 45-291626. viii, 9-325 p. front., plates. 17 1/2 cm. 1852. D. Appleton & Company.
--Louis's School-Days: A/Story for Boys, 1 of 3 Vols. (School and College Library). N.D. Set. George Routledge & Sons.
--Saxelford. N.D. George Routledge & Sons.
--Saxelford, 1 of 3 Vols. (Illus.). (School and College Library). N.D. Set. George Routledge & Sons.
May, Edith Rogers (1876-)
--The True Fairy Tales. LC 24-16901. c.1923. The Four Seas Company.

--Terrible Troll. Mayer, Mercer (1943-), illus. (Illus.). 32 p. 25cm. 1968. Dial Press.
--There's a Nightmare in My Closet. Mayer, Mercer (1943-), illus. (Illus.). unpaged. 26cm. (Pied piper book). 1976, c.1968. (ISBN 0-8037-8574-7). Dial Press.
--Too's Bracelet. Mayer, Mercer (1943-), illus. (Illus.). (Little Critter Books). 1983. (ISBN 0-590-32810-7). Scholastic Inc.
--Two Moral Tales. Mayer, Mercer (1943-), illus. LC 74-7487. 48 p. of illus. 16cm. 1974. (ISBN 0-590-07366-4). (ISBN 0-590-07367-2). Four Winds Press.
--Two Moral Tales: Bird's New Hat & Bear's New Clothes. (Illus.). 48p. (ps-3). 1974. (ISBN 0-590-07366-4, Four Winds). Scholastic Inc.
--Two More Tales: Sly Fox's Folly & Just A Pig at Heart. (Illus.). 48p. (ps-3). 1974. (ISBN 0-590-07367-2, Four Winds). Scholastic Inc.
--Walk, Robot, Walk. Mayer, Mercer (1943-), illus. LC 72-97336. 32 p. of illus. 20cm. (Magic circle book). 1974. (ISBN 0-663-25443-4). Ginn.
--What Do You Do with a Kangaroo?. Mayer, Mercer (1943-), illus. LC 72-87073. (Illus.). 44 p. 24cm. 1974, c.1973. Four Winds Press.
--When I Get Bigger. Mayer, Mercer (1943-), illus. LC 82-84110. (Illus.). 32p. (Little Critter Library). (ps-1). 1983. (ISBN 0-307-10602-0, Golden Pr). Western Pub.
--You're the Scaredy-Cat. Mayer, Mercer (1943-), illus. LC 80-16859. p. cm. 1980, c.1974. (ISBN 0-590-07783-X). Four Winds Press.
--You're the Scaredy-Cat. Mayer, Mercer (1943-), illus. LC 73-22185. (Illus.). 40 p. 24cm. 1974. (ISBN 0-8193-0762-9). (ISBN 0-8193-0762-9). Parents' Magazine Press.

Mayer, Mercer (1943-), ed.
--A Poison Tree and Other Poems. Mayer, Mercer (1943-), illus. LC 76-57732. (Illus.). 46 p. 24cm. c.1977. (ISBN 0-684-14904-4). Scribner.
--The Sleeping Beauty. Mayer, Mercer (1943-), illus. LC 84-7195. (Illus.). 48p. 1984. (ISBN 0-02-765340-4). (ISBN 0-02-765340-4). Macmillan.

Mayer, Mercer (1943-) & Mayer, Marianna (1945-)
--Mine. LC 76-123243. 38 p. (chiefly illus. 17cm. 1970. Simon and Schuster.
--One Frog Too Many. Mayer, Mercer (1943-), illus. LC 75-6325. (Illus.). 32 p. 15cm. 1975. (ISBN 0-8037-4858-2). Dial Press.
--A Special Trick. Mayer, Mercer (1943-), illus. LC 69-18220. (Illus.). 30 p. 23cm. 1970. (ISBN 0-8037-8189-X). Dial Press.

Mayer, Mercer (1943-) & Mayer, Marianna (1945-), illus.
--Frog & a Friend. (Illus.). 1971. Dial.

Mayer, Peter (1936-)
--An Idea Is Like a Bird: The Story of Herbert-Up-High-in-the-Sky. Francois, Andre (1915-), illus. LC 62-15024. unpaged. illus. 32cm. 1962. Orion Press.

Mayer, Robert (1939-)
--The Grace of Shortstops. LC 83-40146. 264p. 1984. (ISBN 0-385-19049-2). (ISBN 0-385-19049-2). Doubleday.

Mayers, Patrick
--Just One More Block. Hawkinson, Lucy Ozone (1924-1971), illus. LC 72-115896. 32 p. (chiefly illus., part col. 19cm. 1970. (ISBN 0-8075-4081-1). A. Whitman.
--Lost Bear, Found Bear. Darwin, Beatrice, illus. LC 72-13353. (Illus.). 32 p. 18cm. 1973. (ISBN 0-8075-4760-3). A. Whitman.

Mayerson, Evelyn Wilde (1935-)
--Coydog: A Novel. LC 81-13624. p. cm. 1981. (ISBN 0-684-17159-7). (ISBN 0-684-17159-7). Scribner.

Mayfield, Albert U
--Wally Wish and Maggie Magpie. Rev ed. Brinley, Neil, illus. LC 8-3413. 57 p. illus. 26 1/2 cm. c.1907. The Democrat Publishing Co.

Mayfield, James L
--The Vvirbrr and the King: A Story of Potential. Townsley, Patti Hughes, illus. LC 79-65809. (Illus.). ix, 77 p. 21cm. 1980, c.1979. (ISBN 0-934524-00-9). Eclectic Pub. Co.

Mayhar, Ardath, jt. auth. see Dunn, Mary Lois.

Mayhar, Ardath (1930-)
--Lords of the Triple Moons. LC 82-16241. p. cm. 1983. (ISBN 0-689-30978-3). Atheneum.
--Medicine Walk. LC 85-7469. 83 p. 22cm. 1985. (ISBN 0-689-31135-4). Atheneum.
--The Runes of the Lyre. LC 82-1730. x, 214 p. 22cm. 1982. (ISBN 0-689-30932-5). Atheneum.
--The Saga of Grittel Sundotha. LC 84-21523. viii, 196 p. 22cm. 1985. (ISBN 0-689-31097-8). Atheneum.
--Soul Singer of Tyrnos. LC 81-5023. p. cm. 1981. (ISBN 0-689-30852-3). Atheneum.

Mayhew, Ann
--The Rose: Folklore Myths & Legends. Pollard, Michael, illus. (Illus.). 1979. (ISBN 0-8027-0642-8). Walker & Co.

Mayhew, Augustus Septimus, jt. auth. see Mayhew, Henry.

Mayhew, Henry (1812-1887)
--The Peasant Boy Philosopher. N.D. George Routledge & Sons.
--The Wonders of Science: Or, Young Humphrey Davy. Gilbert, John Clitherae, illus. N.D. George Routledge & Sons.

Mayhew, Henry (1812-1887) & Mayhew, Augustus Septimus (1826-1875)
--Good Genius that Turned Everything into Gold. N.D. JUV. George Routledge.
--Good Genius that turned Everything into Gold. (Illus.). (Harper's Fireside Library). 1882. Harper & Bros.
--The Magic of Kindness: Or, The Wondrous Story of the Good Huan. Crane, Walter (1845-1915), illus. LC 16-720127. iv, 220 p. front., plates. 17 x 13 1/2 cm. 1869. Cassell, Petter, and Galpin.
--Magic of Kindness: Or, The Wondrous Story of the Good Huan. Crane, Walter (1845-1915), illus. 1882. Harper's.
--The Magic of Kindness: Or,The Wondrous Story of the Good Huan. (Illus.). (Harper's Fireside Library). N.D. Harper & Bros.

Mayhew, Ralph & Johnson, Burges (1877-1963)
--Animal Bubble Book, No. 4. Chase, Rhoda Campbell, illus. 1917. Harper & Brothers.
--The Bubble Book, No. 1. Chase, Rhoda Campbell, illus. 1917. Harper & Brothers.
--Child's Garden of Verses Bubble Book, No.13. Chase, Rhoda Campbell, illus. (No. 13). N.D. Harper & Brothers.
--The Chimney Corner Bubble Book, No.14. Chase, Rhoda Campbell, illus. 1922. Harper & Brothers.
--The Funny Froggy Bubble Book, No.7. Chase, Rhoda Campbell, illus. 1919. Harper & Brothers.
--Gay Games Bubble Book, No.12. Chase, Rhoda Campbell, illus. 1920. Harper & Brothers.
--The Happy Go Lucky Bubble Book, No.8. 1919. Harper & Brothers.
--Little Mischief Bubble Book, No.10. Chase, Rhoda Campbell, illus. 1920. Harper & Brothers.
--The Merry Midget Bubble Book, No. 9. Chase, Rhoda Campbell, illus. 1920. Harper & Brothers.
--The Pet Bubble Book, No. 6. Chase, Rhoda Campbell, illus. 1919. Harper & Brothers.
--Pie Party Bubble Book, No. 5. Chase, Rhoda Campbell, illus. 1919. Harper & Brothers.
--The Second Bubble Book, No. 11. Chase, Rhoda Campbell, illus. 1918. Harper & Brothers.
--The Third Bubble Book. Chase, Rhoda Campbell, illus. 1918. Harper & Brothers.
--Tippy-Toe Bubble Book, No. 11. Chase, Rhoda Campbell, illus. 1920. Harper & Brothers.

Mayle, Peter
--Chilly Billy. Robbins, Arthur (1928-), illus. LC 82-21211. p. cm. c.1983. (ISBN 0-517-54959-X). Harmony Books.

Maynard, Christopher & Berry, Roland
--All About Ghosts. Berry, Roland, illus. LC 77-17613. (Illus.). 32 p. 29cm. (World of the unknown). c.1978. (ISBN 0-88436-469-0). EMC Corp.

Maynard, Colton
--Elliott Gray, Jr. A Chronicle of School Life. LC 12-5554. 2 p. l., 7-226 p. 19 1/2 cm. c.1911. Fleming H. Revell Company.

Maynard, Joyce (1953-)
--Camp-Out. Bethel, Steve, illus. LC 85-5504. (Illus.). 32 p. c.1985. (ISBN 0-15-214077-8). Harcourt Brace Jovanovich.

Maynard, Lorraine
--Dilly Was Different: The Story of a Little Pilgraim. Hill, Mabel Betsy (1877-), illus. LC 32-13679. 1 p. l., 7-105 p. incl. illus., col. plates. col. front. 23 1/2 cm. c.1932. S. Gabriel Son & Company.
--Twinkle, Little Movie Star. Maturo, Joseph A., illus. LC 27-20755. 6 p. l., 3-284 p. front., plates. 19 1/2 cm. c.1927. The Century Co.

Maynard, Mary Harris Ewer, Mrs. (1857-)
--Our Little Pitchers: A Budget of True Tales Concerning the Funny Adventures of Four Children. Paley, Joan, illus. LC 13-22205. 196 p. incl. plates, front. 19 cm. 1913. The Nyvall Print.

Maynard, Priscilla
--A Summer to Remember. 160p. (Orig.). (gr. 7 up). 1982. (ISBN 0-590-32166-8, Wishing Star Bks). Scholastic Inc.

Maynard, Priscilla M
--Stop! Look!. Paley, Joan, illus. LC 73-82000. (Illus.). 16 p. 20cm. (Magic circle book). 1974. (ISBN 0-663-25456-6). Ginn.

Maynard, Sara Katherine Casey
--Here Come the Penguins. LC 43-51028. 84, 1 p. illus. (part col.) 20 cm. 1942. St. Anthony Guild Press.

Mayne, Maude Rittenhouse
--A Candid Critic, and Other Storis for Girls. Chapin, illus. LC 12-36605. 245 p. front., illus., plates. 20 1/2 cm. c.1897. American Baptist Publication Society.

Mayne, William James Carter, jt. ed. see Farjeon, Eleanor.

Mayne, William James Carter (1928-)
--The Battlefield. 1st ed. Russon, Mary Georgina (1937-), illus. (Illus.). 158 p. 22cm. 1967. Dutton.
--The Blue Boat. Spence, Geraldine (1931-), illus. (Illus.). (gr. 3-6). 1960, c.1957. (ISBN 0-525-26737-9). Dutton. **Award: (ALA).**
--The Blue Boat. 1st ed. Spence, Geraldine (1931-), illus. LC 57-42293. 173p. illus. 23cm. 1957. Oxford University Press. **Award: (CMA).**
--The Blue Book of Hob Stories. Benson, Patrick, illus. LC 84-4231. p. cm. 1984. (ISBN 0-399-21037-7). (ISBN 0-399-21037-7). Philomel Books.
--Book of Heroes. Turska, Krystyna Zofia (1933-), illus. (gr. 2-6). 1966. Dutton.
--Changeling. Ambrus, Victor G., pseud. (1935-), illus. Ambrus, Gyozo Laszlo. (Illus.). (gr. 4-7). 1963. Dutton.
--Choristers' Cake. Hodges, Cyril Walter (1909-), illus. LC 58-126072. 160p. illus. 23cm. 1958, c.1956. Bobbs-Merrill.
--The Dark Crystal. Knowlden, Martin, illus. LC 81-48468. (Illus.). 48p. (Muppet Press Bks.). (gr. 2-5). 1982. (ISBN 0-394-85304-0). (ISBN 0-394-95304-5). Random.
--A Day Without Wind. Gill, Margery Jean (1925-), illus. 1964. Dutton.
--Earthfasts. LC 67-16464. 154 p. 22cm. 1967, c.1966. Dutton.
--A Game of Dark. 1st ed. LC 70-154012. 143 p. 22cm. 1971. (ISBN 0-525-30346-4). Dutton.
--Glass Ball. Duchesne, Janet (1930-), illus. (gr. 3-7). 1962. Dutton.
--A Grass Rope. Lamb, Lynton Harold (1907-1977), illus. LC 62-7492. (Illus.). 21cm. 166p. (gr. 5-7). 1962. Dutton. **Award: (ALA).**
--A Grass Rope. 1st ed. Lamb, Lynton Harold (1907-1977), illus. LC 59-182616. 166p. illus. 23cm. 1957. Oxford University Press. **Award: (CMA).**
--The Green Book of Hob Stories. Benson, Patrick, illus. LC 83-17317. (Illus.). 32p. (gr. k-4). 1984. (ISBN 0-399-21039-3, Philomel). Putnam Pub Group.
--The Hill Road. 1st ed. LC 69-18906. 143 p. 22cm. 1969, c.1968. Dutton.
--The House on Fairmount. 1st ed. Wegner, Fritz (1924-), illus. (Illus.). 32 p. 27cm. 1968. Dutton.
--The Incline. Stubley, Trevor Hugh (1932-), illus. LC 72-75506. 192 p. 22cm. 1972. (ISBN 0-525-32550-6). Dutton.
--It. 1st ed. LC 78-1902. 189 p. 22cm. c.1977. (ISBN 0-688-80173-0). (ISBN 0-688-84173-2). Greenwillow Books.
--The Jersey Shore. 1st ed. LC 72-89843. 159 p. 22cm. 1973. (ISBN 0-525-32765-7). Dutton.
--Max's Dream. Acs, Laszlo Bela (1931-), illus. LC 77-12728. (Illus.). 88 p. 24cm. 1977. (ISBN 0-688-80131-5). (ISBN 0-688-84131-7). Greenwillow Books.
--The Mouldy. Bayley, Nicola (1935-), illus. LC 83-6163. (Illus.). 32p. (ps-3). 1983. (ISBN 0-394-96211-7). (ISBN 0-394-86211-2). Knopf.
--The Mouse and the Egg. Turska, Krystyna Zofia (1933-), illus. LC 80-15084. (Illus.). 32 p. 26cm. 1st U.S. edition. 1981, c.1980. (ISBN 0-688-80301-6). (ISBN 0-688-84301-8). Greenwillow Books.
--The Old Zion. 1st ed. Gill, Margery Jean (1925-), illus. LC 67-1294. (Illus.). 64 p. 26cm. 1967, c.1966. Dutton.
--Over the Horizon: Or, Around the World in Fifteen Stories. Kennedy, Richard (1910-), illus. LC 60-11677. 192p. illus. 20cm. N.D. Duell, Sloan, and Pearce.
--Parcel of Trees. Gill, Margery Jean (1925-), illus. N.D. Penguin Books.
--The Patchwork Cat. Bayley, Nicola (1935-), illus. p. cm. c.1981. (ISBN 0-394-95021-6). Knopf : Distributed by Random House.
--Pig in the Middle. Russon, Mary Georgina (1937-), illus. LC 66-5271. 160p. illus. 22cm. 1966, c.1965. Dutton.
--Pig in the Middle. Russon, Mary Georgina (1937-), illus. (Illus.). (gr. 4-7). 1966. (ISBN 0-525-37007-2). Dutton.
--Plot Night. 1st ed. Duchesne, Janet (1930-), illus. LC 68-24725. (Illus.). 126 p. 22cm. 1968. Dutton.
--Ravensgill. LC 70-81721. 174 p. 22cm. 1970. Dutton.
--The Red Book of Hob Stories. Benson, Patrick, illus. LC 83-15125. (Illus.). 32p. (gr. k-4). 1984. (ISBN 0-399-21047-4, Philomel). Putnam Pub Group.
--Royal Harry. LC 74-154013. 158 p. 22cm. 1972. (ISBN 0-525-38690-4). E. P. Dutton.
--Salt River Times. LC 80-20806. 182 p. 22cm. 1st U.S. edition. 1981. (ISBN 0-688-80311-3). (ISBN 0-688-84311-5). Greenwillow Books.
--Sand. Gill, Margery Jean (1925-), illus. LC 65-21277. 206p. illus. 22cm. 1965, c.1964. Dutton.
--A Swarm in May. Hodges, Cyril Walter (1909-), illus. LC 57-138877. 199p. illus. 23cm. 1957, c.1955. Bobbs-Merrill.
--Underground Alley. Foster, Marcia Lane (1897-), illus. (Illus.). (gr. 3-7). N.D. (ISBN 0-525-41840-7). Dutton.
--Underground Alley. 1st ed. Foster, Marcia Lane (1897-), illus. LC 61-330786. 168p. illus. 22cm. 1958. Oxford University Press.
--Whistling Rufus. Briggs, Raymond Redvers (1934-), illus. LC 65-121834. 120p. illus. 22cm. 1965, c.1964. Dutton.
--A Year and a Day. 1st ed. Turska, Krystyna Zofia (1933-), illus. LC 75-34160. 86 p. 22cm. c.1976. (ISBN 0-525-43450-X). Dutton.
--The Yellow Airplane. Stubley, Trevor Hugh (1932-), illus. LC 74-3057. (Illus.). 128 p. 21cm. 1st U.S. edition. 1974. (ISBN 0-8407-6395-6). T. Nelson.
--The Yellow Book of Hob Stories. Benson, Patrick, illus. LC 84-4230. (Illus.). 26 p. 18cm. 1984. (ISBN 0-399-21050-4). Philomel Books.
--The Yellow Book of Hob Stories. Benson, Patrick, illus. (The Hob Stories Ser.). (ps-4). 1984. (ISBN 0-399-21050-4). Putnam Pub Group.

Mayne, William James Carter (1928-), compiled by.
--William Mayne's Book Of Giants. Briggs, Raymond Redvers (1934-), illus. N.D. Doubleday.
--William Mayne's Book of Giants: Stories. 1st ed. Briggs, Raymond Redvers (1934-), illus. LC 69-13368. (Illus.). viii, 215 p. 24cm. 1969. Dutton.
--William Mayne's Book of Heroes: Stories and Poems. Turska, Krystyna Zofia (1933-), illus. (Illus.). x, 230 p. 25cm. 1968, c.1967. Dutton.

Mayo, Allen
--The Fortress of Miguel. LC 57-12987. (Illus.). 21cm. 160p. 1974. Tex-Mex Books.

Mayo, Gretchen, jt. auth. see Grant, Eva H.

Mayo, Isabella Fyvie see Garrett, Edward, pseud.

Mayo, Isabella Fyvie, Mrs. (1843-)
--Mayo's Stories and Thoughts for Girls. (Illus.). N.D. George Routledge & Sons.

Mayo, Lucy Graves (1909-)
--Wendy Scott, Secretary. Gibbs, Blanche L., illus. LC 61-12919. 331p. 21cm. (Dodd, Mead career books). 1961. Dodd, Mead.

Mayo, Margaret
--Polly of the Circus. (Playbooks). N.D. (ISBN 0-679-39057-X). McKay.

Mayo, Margaret, compiled by.
--The Book of Magical Horses. Ambrus, Victor G, pseud. (1935-), illus. Ambrus, Gyozo Laszlo. LC 79-58963. (Illus.). 119 p. 23cm. 1977, c.1976. (ISBN 0-8038-0778-3). Hastings House.

Mayo, William Starbuck (1812-1895)
--The Adventures of Jonathan Romer. The Framazugda ed. (Illus.). 24cm. 389p. 1900. G. P. Putnam & Co.
--Kaloolah, Adventures of Jonathan Romer of Nantucket. (Illus.). 19cm. 1872. G. P. Putnam & Sons.

Mayol, Lurline Bowles, Mrs.
--The Big Canoe. Kihn, W. Langdon, illus. LC 33-22930. vi p., 4 l., 3-257 p. incl. front., illus. 21 cm. c.1933. D. Appleton-Century Company Incorporated.
--Billy Whiskers, Stowaway: Continuing the Famous Billy Whiskers Series. Jadwyn, David, illus. LC 30-25852. 3 p. l., 11-146 p., 1 l. col. front., illus., col. plates. 23 1/2 cm. (The Billy Whiskers Series, V. 32: Vol. 32). c.1930. The Saalfield Publishing Company.
--Billy Whiskers, Tourist: Continuing the Famous Billy Whiskers Series. Jadwyn, David, illus. LC 30-1313. 3 p. l., 11-161 p. col. front., illus., col. plates. 23 1/2 cm. (The Billy Whiskers series, v. 31). c.1929. The Saalfield Publishing Company.
--Jiji Lou. Peat, Fern Bisel, Mrs. (1893-), illus. LC 23-30111. 5 p. 1., 13-142 p. col. front., illus., col. plates. 26 cm. c.1928. The Saalfield Publishing Company.
--Talking Totem Pole. Morgan, Edward, illus. (Illus.). (gr. 4-9). 1943. (ISBN 0-8323-0158-2). Binford.
--The Talking Totem Pole: The Tales it Told to the Indian Children of the Northwest. Morgan, Edward, illus. LC 43-159633. 2 p. l., 13-142 p. col. front., illus. 24 cm. 1943. Binfords & Mort.
--The Talking Totem Pole: The Tales It Told to the Indian Children of the Northwest. Morgan, Edward, illus. LC 30-18292. 142 p. incl. col., front., illus. col. plates. 23 1/2 cm. c.1930. The Saalfield Publishing Company.

Mayor, Robert John Grote, jt. auth. see Marvin, Francis Sydney.

Mayorga, Margaret Gardner (1894-), ed.
--The World's a Stage: Short Plays for Juniors. LC 44-2132. 6 p. l., 3-272 p. 21 cm. N.D. Los Angeles Etc.

Mayr-Pletschen, Heide, illus.
--A Christmas Carol Book. (Illus.). (gr. 3 up). N.D. (ISBN 0-685-24603-5). Merry Thoughts.

Mayrocker, Friederike, jt. auth. see Kaufmann, Angelika.

--The Girls of Castle Rocco. Smith, Elizabeth Thomasina Meade. (Illus.). (The Meade Series.). 1915. A L Burt & Co.
--The Girls of King's Roval. Smith, Elizabeth Thomasina Meade. New Copyrighted. N.D. Hurst & Co.
--The Girls of Mrs. Pritchard's School. Smith, Elizabeth Thomasina Meade. (Illus.). (Fascinating Stories for Girls). N.D. A. L. Chatterton Co.
--The Girls of St. Wode's. Smith, Elizabeth Thomasina Meade. (Illus.). (The Meade Series.). 1915. A L Burt & Co.
--The Girls of St. Wode's. Smith, Elizabeth Thomasina Meade. (Illus.). (The Wellesley Series for Girls). N.D. A. L. Burt.
--The Girls of St. Wode's. Smith, Elizabeth Thomasina Meade. (Illus.). N.D. Caldwell.
--The Girls of St Wode's. Smith, Elizabeth Thomasina Meade. (Illus.). (Famous Books for Girls). N.D. Dodge Publishing Co.
--The Girls of St. Wode's. Smith, Elizabeth Thomasina Meade, 1 of 20 vols. (Illus.). (Mrs. L. T. Meade Ser.). N.D. Set. George M Hill Co.
--The Girls of St. Wode's. Smith, Elizabeth Thomasina Meade. (L. T. Meade Ser.). N.D. Hurst & Co.
--Girls of the Forest. Smith, Elizabeth Thomasina Meade. (Illus.). (The Meade Series.). 1915. A L Burt & Co.
--Girls of the Forest. Smith, Elizabeth Thomasina Meade. (Illus.). (The Wellesley Series for Girls). N.D. A. L. Burt.
--Girls of the True Blue. Smith, Elizabeth Thomasina Meade. (Illus.). (The Wellesley Series for Girls). N.D. A. L. Burt.
--Girls of the True Blue. Smith, Elizabeth Thomasina Meade. (The Girls' Own Library). N.D. David McKay.
--Girls of the True Blue. Smith, Elizabeth Thomasina Meade. (L. T. Meade Ser.). N.D. Hurst & Co.
--Girls of True Blue. Smith, Elizabeth Thomasina Meade, 31 vols. (Illus.). (Famous Books for Girls Ser.: No. 10). 1905. Set. H M Caldwell Co.
--The Golden Lady. Smith, Elizabeth Thomasina Meade, 1 of 12 Vols. (Dickory Dock Series.). N.D. Thomas Whittaker.
--Good Luck. Smith, Elizabeth Thomasina Meade. (The Meade Series for Girls). N.D. A. L. Burt Co.
--Good Luck. Smith, Elizabeth Thomasina Meade. (Illus.). (The Wellesley Series for Girls). N.D. A. L. Burt.
--Good Luck. Smith, Elizabeth Thomasina Meade. Empire ed. 1905. American News Co.
--Good Luck. Smith, Elizabeth Thomasina Meade, 1 of 20 vols. (Illus.). (Mrs. L. T. Meade Ser.). N.D. Set. George M Hill Co.
--Good Luck. Smith, Elizabeth Thomasina Meade. (L. T. Meade Ser.). N.D. Hurst & Co.
--A Handful of Silver. Smith, Elizabeth Thomasina Meade. (Illus.). N.D. E. P. Dutton & Co.
--The Harman Girls. Smith, Elizabeth Thomasina Meade. (The Meade Series for Girls). N.D. A. L. Burt Co.
--The Heart of Gold. Smith, Elizabeth Thomasina Meade. N.D. Frederick Warne & Co.
--The Heart of Gold. Smith, Elizabeth Thomasina Meade. (L. T. Meade Ser.). N.D. Hurst & Co.
--Hermie's Rosebuds and Other Stories. Smith, Elizabeth Thomasina Meade. (Illus.). 1888. Thomas Whittaker.
--The Hill-Top Girl. Smith, Elizabeth Thomasina Meade. (The Meade Series for Girls). N.D. A. L. Burt Co.
--The Hill-Top Girl. Smith, Elizabeth Thomasina Meade. (The Girls' Own Library). N.D. David McKay.
--Hill-top Girl. Smith, Elizabeth Thomasina Meade. (Illus.). N.D. J. B. Lippincott.
--The Honorable Miss. Smith, Elizabeth Thomasina Meade. (Illus.). N.D. Caldwell.
--The Honorable Miss. Smith, Elizabeth Thomasina Meade. (L. T. Meade Ser.). N.D. Hurst & Co.
--The House of Surprises. Smith, Elizabeth Thomasina Meade. (The Meade Series for Girls). N.D. A. L. Burt Co.
--The House of Surprises. Smith, Elizabeth Thomasina Meade. (Illus.). (The Wellesley Series for Girls). N.D. A. L. Burt.
--The House of Surprises. Smith, Elizabeth Thomasina Meade. N.D. Longmans Green & Co.
--The House of Surprises. Smith, Elizabeth Thomasina Meade. 1891. Thomas Whittaker.
--How it All Came Round. Smith, Elizabeth Thomasina Meade. (L. T. Meade Ser.). N.D. Hurst & Co.
--Jill, the Irresistible. Smith, Elizabeth Thomasina Meade. New Copyrighted. N.D. Hurst & Co.
--Kingfisher's Egg. Smith, Elizabeth Thomasina Meade. N.D. E. P. Dutton & Co.
--The Kingfisher's Egg. Smith, Elizabeth Thomasina Meade, 1 of 15 vols. (Illus.). (Dainty Ser. of Choice Gift Bks: No. 7). 1905. Set. Henry Altemus Co.
--A Knight of To-Day. Smith, Elizabeth Thomasina Meade. N.D. Robert Carter.
--Lady of the Forest. Smith, Elizabeth Thomasina Meade. (Illus.). (Fireside Series for Girls). N.D. A. L. Burt's Pubs.
--Lady of the Forest. Smith, Elizabeth Thomasina Meade. (Illus.). (The Wellesley Series for Girls). N.D. A. L. Burt's Pubs.
--Lady of the Forest. Smith, Elizabeth Thomasina Meade. (Illus.). (The Meade Series for Girls). N.D. A. L. Burt.
--Lady of the Forest. Smith, Elizabeth Thomasina Meade. (L. T. Meade Series.). N.D. Hurst & Co.
--The Least of These. Smith, Elizabeth Thomasina Meade. (Illus.). N.D. Publications of the Methodist Book Concern.
--The Least of These, & Other Stories. Smith, Elizabeth Thomasina Meade. (Illus.). N.D. Methodist Bk Concern.
--Light O' the Morning. Smith, Elizabeth Thomasina Meade. (The Meade Series for Girls). N.D. A. L. Burt Co.
--Light o' the Morning. Smith, Elizabeth Thomasina Meade. (Illus.). (The Wellesley Series for Girls). N.D. A. L. Burt.
--Light o' the Morning. Smith, Elizabeth Thomasina Meade, 1 of 20 vols. (Illus.). (Mrs. L. T. Meade Ser.). N.D. Set. George M Hill Co.
--Light of the Morning. Smith, Elizabeth Thomasina Meade. (Illus.). N.D. E. P. Dutton & Co.
--Lil Carrington. Smith, Elizabeth Thomasina Meade. (Illus.). (Fascinating Stories for Girls). N.D. A. L. Chatterton Co.
--Little Mary. Smith, Elizabeth Thomasina Meade. 1891. Thomas Whittaker.
--A Little Mother to the Others. Smith, Elizabeth Thomasina Meade. (The Albion Library). N.D. Frederick Warne & Co.
--A Little Mother to the Others. Smith, Elizabeth Thomasina Meade. (Illus.). (Warne's Golden Link Ser.). N.D. Frederick Warne & co.
--Little Princess of Tower Hill. Smith, Elizabeth Thomasina Meade. (Illus.). (The Meade Series). 1915. A L Burt & Co.
--Little Princess of Tower Hill. Smith, Elizabeth Thomasina Meade. (Illus.). (The Little Women Ser.). N.D. A. L. Burt's Pubs.
--Little Princess of Tower Hill. Smith, Elizabeth Thomasina Meade. (Illus.). (The Wellesley Series for Girls). N.D. A. L. Burt.
--Little Princess of Tower Hill. Smith, Elizabeth Thomasina Meade. (L. T. Meade Ser.). N.D. Hurst & Co.
--The Little Princess of Tower Hill. Smith, Elizabeth Thomasina Meade. 1891. Thomas Whittaker.
--Little School Mothers. Smith, Elizabeth Thomasina Meade. (The Girls' Own Library). N.D. David McKay.
--A Little Silver Trumpet. Smith, Elizabeth Thomasina Meade. Pym, T. O., illus. N.D. Methodist Book Concern.
--A Madcap. Smith, Elizabeth Thomasina Meade. (Illus.). (Fascinating Stories for Girls). N.D. A. L. Chatterton Co.
--The Manor School. Smith, Elizabeth Thomasina Meade. (Illus.). (Fascinating Stories for Girls). N.D. A. L. Chatterton Co.
--Me and My Dolls. Smith, Elizabeth Thomasina Meade. (Little Wanderer Ser.). N.D. D. Lothrop Co.
--Me and My Dolls. Smith, Elizabeth Thomasina Meade. (Illus.). (Lady Gay Ser.). N.D. Lothrop Lee & Shepard Co.
--Merry Girls of England. Smith, Elizabeth Thomasina Meade. (Illus.). 288p. N.D. A. I Bradley & Co.'s Pubs.
--The Merry Girls of England. Smith, Elizabeth Thomasina Meade. (Illus.). (The Meade Series.). 1915. A L Burt & Co.
--Merry Girls of England. Smith, Elizabeth Thomasina Meade. (Illus.). (The Wellesley Series for Girls). N.D. A. L. Burt.
--Merry Girls of England. Smith, Elizabeth Thomasina Meade. Empire ed. 1905. American News Co.
--Merry Girls of England. Smith, Elizabeth Thomasina Meade. (Illus.). N.D. Cassell & Co.
--Merry Girls of England. Smith, Elizabeth Thomasina Meade. (L. T. Meade Series.). N.D. Hurst & Co.
--Miss Nonentity. Smith, Elizabeth Thomasina Meade. (Illus.). (The Meade Series for Girls). 1915. A. L. Burt Co.
--Miss Nonentity. Smith, Elizabeth Thomasina Meade. (Illus.). N.D. Caldwell.
--Miss Nonentity. Smith, Elizabeth Thomasina Meade. (L. T. Meade Series.). N.D. Hurst & Co.
--Miss Nonentity. Smith, Elizabeth Thomasina Meade. (Illus.). 1900. J B Lippincott.
--A Modern Tomboy. Smith, Elizabeth Thomasina Meade. (The Meade Series for Girls). N.D. A. L. Burt Co.
--A Modern Tomboy. Smith, Elizabeth Thomasina Meade. (Illus.). (The Wellesley Series for Girls). N.D. A. L. Burt.
--Mother Herring's Chicken. Smith, Elizabeth Thomasina Meade. N.D. Robert Carter.
--Mother Mary. Smith, Elizabeth Thomasina Meade. N.D. J.B. Lippincott.
--Nobody's Neighbors. Smith, Elizabeth Thomasina Meade. N.D. Thomas Whittaker.
--Nora Crena. Smith, Elizabeth Thomasina Meade. N.D. Robert Carter.
--Oceana's Girlhood. Smith, Elizabeth Thomasina Meade. N.D. Hurst & Co.
--The Odds and Evens. Smith, Elizabeth Thomasina Meade. (The Meade Series for Girls). N.D. A. L. Burt Co.
--The Odds and Evens. Smith, Elizabeth Thomasina Meade. (The Girls' Own Library). N.D. David McKay.
--The Odds and the Evens. Smith, Elizabeth Thomasina Meade. (Illus.). (The Wellesley Series for Girls). N.D. A. L. Burt.
--The Odds and the Evens. Smith, Elizabeth Thomasina Meade. (Illus.). N.D. E. P. Dutton & co.
--Out of Fashion. Smith, Elizabeth Thomasina Meade. (Illus.). (Fascinating Stories for Girls). N.D. A. L. Chatterton Co.
--Out of the Fashion. Smith, Elizabeth Thomasina Meade. Empire ed. 1905. American News Co.
--Out of the Fashion. Smith, Elizabeth Thomasina Meade, 1 of 20 vols. (Illus.). (Mrs. L. T. Meade Ser.). N.D. Set. George M Hill Co.
--The Palace Beautiful. Smith, Elizabeth Thomasina Meade. (Illus.). (The Meade Series.). 1915. A L Burt & Co.
--The Palace Beautiful. Smith, Elizabeth Thomasina Meade. (Illus.). (Fireside Series for Girls). N.D. A. L. Burt's Pubs.
--The Palace Beautiful. Smith, Elizabeth Thomasina Meade. (Illus.). (The Wellesley Series for Girls). N.D. A. L. Burt's Pubs.
--Palace Beautiful. Smith, Elizabeth Thomasina Meade. Empire ed. 1905. American News Co.
--Palace Beautiful. Smith, Elizabeth Thomasina Meade. (Illus.). N.D. Caldwell.
--The Palace Beautiful. Smith, Elizabeth Thomasina Meade. 384p. N.D. Cassell & Co.
--Palace Beautiful. Smith, Elizabeth Thomasina Meade. (The Girls' Own Library). N.D. David McKay.
--The Palace Beautiful. Smith, Elizabeth Thomasina Meade, 1 of 20 vols. (Illus.). (Mrs. L. T. Meade Ser.). N.D. Set. George M Hill Co.
--Palace Beautiful. Smith, Elizabeth Thomasina Meade. (L. T. Meade Ser.). N.D. Hurst & Co.
--Peter the Pilgrim. Smith, Elizabeth Thomasina Meade. (Illus.). (The Little Men Ser.). N.D. A. L. Burt's Pubs.
--Peter the Pilgrim: The Story of a Boy and His Pet Rabbit. Smith, Elizabeth Thomasina Meade. (Illus.). (The Rugby Ser.). N.D. A. L. Burt.
--Petronella. Smith, Elizabeth Thomasina Meade. (The Meade Series for Girls). N.D. A. L. Burt Co.
--Petronella. Smith, Elizabeth Thomasina Meade. (Illus.). (The Wellesley Series for Girls). N.D. A. L. Burt.
--Petronella. Smith, Elizabeth Thomasina Meade. N.D. J.B. Lippincott.
--Playmates. Smith, Elizabeth Thomasina Meade, 36 vols. (Illus.). (St. Nicholas Ser.). 1905. Set. A L Burt Co.
--Playmates. Smith, Elizabeth Thomasina Meade. (The Meade Series for Girls). N.D. A. L. Burt Co.
--Playmates. Smith, Elizabeth Thomasina Meade. (Illus.). (The Wellesley Series for Girls). N.D. A. L. Burt.
--Playmates. Smith, Elizabeth Thomasina Meade. N.D. Thomas Whittaker.
--A Plucky Girl. Smith, Elizabeth Thomasina Meade. N.D. Hurst & Co.
--A Plucky Girl. Smith, Elizabeth Thomasina Meade. Waugh, Ida, illus. LC 1-120. (Illus.). viii, 330. 12cm. 1900. G. W. Jacobs.
--Polly. Smith, Elizabeth Thomasina Meade. (Illus.). (The Wellesley Series for Girls). N.D. A. L. Burt's Pubs.
--Polly. Smith, Elizabeth Thomasina Meade, 1 of 31 vols. (Illus.). (Famous Books for Girls Ser.: No. 19). 1905. Set. H M Caldwell Co.
--Polly: A New-Fashioned Girl. Smith, Elizabeth Thomasina Meade. (The Meade Series for Girls). N.D. A. L. Burt Co.
--Polly, A New Fashioned Girl. Smith, Elizabeth Thomasina Meade. (Illus.). (Fireside Ser. for Girls). N.D. A. L. Burt's Publications.
--Polly, a New Fashioned Girl. Smith, Elizabeth Thomasina Meade. Empire ed. 1905. American News Co.
--Polly: A New-fashioned Girl. Smith, Elizabeth Thomasina Meade. (Illus.). (Story Books for Girls). N.D. Cassell & Co.'s Pubs.
--Polly, a New Fashioned Girl. Smith, Elizabeth Thomasina Meade. (The Girls' Own Library). N.D. David McKay.
--Polly, a New-Fashioned Girl. Smith, Elizabeth Thomasina Meade, 1 of 20 vols. (Illus.). (Mrs. L. T. Meade Ser.). N.D. Set. George M Hill Co.
--Polly, A New-Fashioned Girl. Smith, Elizabeth Thomasina Meade. (L. T. Meade Ser.). N.D. Hurst & Co.
--Polly: A New-Fashioned Girl. Smith, Elizabeth Thomasina Meade. N.D. New York Book Co.
--Poor Miss Carolina. Smith, Elizabeth Thomasina Meade, 1 of 12 Vols. (Dickory Dock Series.). 1891. Thomas Whittaker.
--The Princess of the Revels. Smith, Elizabeth Thomasina Meade. (The Meade Series for Girls). N.D. A. L. Burt Co.
--Princess Who Gave Away All. Smith, Elizabeth Thomasina Meade. N.D. E. P. Dutton & Co.
--Queen of the Day. Smith, Elizabeth Thomasina Meade. (Illus.). (Dainty Ser.). N.D. Henry Altemus Co.
--Queen Rose. Smith, Elizabeth Thomasina Meade. (The Meade Series for Girls). N.D. A. L. Burt Co.
--Queen Rose. Smith, Elizabeth Thomasina Meade. (The Girls' Own Library). N.D. David McKay.
--The Rebel of the School. Smith, Elizabeth Thomasina Meade. (Illus.). (The Meade Series.). 1915. A L Burt & Co.
--The Rebel of the School. Smith, Elizabeth Thomasina Meade. (Illus.). (The Wellesley Series for Girls). N.D. A. L. Burt.
--The Rebel of the School. Smith, Elizabeth Thomasina Meade. (Illus.). N.D. Caldwell.
--The Rebel of the School. Smith, Elizabeth Thomasina Meade. (The Girls' Own Library). N.D. David McKay.
--The Rebel of the School. Smith, Elizabeth Thomasina Meade. (L. T. Meade Ser.). N.D. Hurst & Co.
--The Rebel of the School. Smith, Elizabeth Thomasina Meade. N.D. J.B. Lippincott.
--Red Rose and Tiger Lily. Smith, Elizabeth Thomasina Meade. (Illus.). (Fascinating Stories for Girls). N.D. A. L. Chatterton Co.
--Red Rose and Tiger Lily. Smith, Elizabeth Thomasina Meade. (Illus.). (Story Books for Girls). N.D. Cassell & Co.'s Pubs.
--Red Rose & Tiger Lily. Smith, Elizabeth Thomasina Meade, 1 of 20 vols. (Illus.). (Mrs. L. T. Meade Ser.). N.D. Set. George M Hill Co.
--A Ring of Rubies. Smith, Elizabeth Thomasina Meade. (Illus.). (Fascinating Stories for Girls). N.D. A. L. Chatterton Co.
--A Ring of Rubies. Smith, Elizabeth Thomasina Meade. Empire ed. 1905. American News Co.
--A Ring of Rubies. Smith, Elizabeth Thomasina Meade, 1 of 20 vols. (Illus.). (Mrs. L. T. Meade Ser.). N.D. Set. George M Hill Co.
--Rosa Regina. Smith, Elizabeth Thomasina Meade. N.D. J.B. Lippincott.
--Scamp and I. Smith, Elizabeth Thomasina Meade. 1877. Robert Carter & Bros.
--The Scamp Family. Smith, Elizabeth Thomasina Meade. (The Meade Series for Girls). N.D. A. L. Burt Co.
--The School Favorite. Smith, Elizabeth Thomasina Meade. (The Meade Series for Girls). N.D. A. L. Burt Co.
--The School Favorite. Smith, Elizabeth Thomasina Meade. (The Girls' Own Library). N.D. David McKay.
--The School Favorite. Smith, Elizabeth Thomasina Meade. N.D. J. B. Lippincott Co.
--The School Queens. Smith, Elizabeth Thomasina Meade. (The Meade Series for Girls). N.D. A. L. Burt Co.
--Seven Maids. Smith, Elizabeth Thomasina Meade. (The Meade Series for Girls). N.D. A. L. Burt Co.
--Seven Maids. Smith, Elizabeth Thomasina Meade. (Illus.). (The Wellesley Series for Girls). N.D. A. L. Burt.
--Seven Maids. Smith, Elizabeth Thomasina Meade. (The Girls' Own Library). N.D. David McKay.
--A Soldier of Fortune. Smith, Elizabeth Thomasina Meade, 1 of 32 vols, Vol. 1. (Illus.). (Famous Books for Girls). N.D. Per vol. H. M. Caldwell Co.
--A Soldiers Fortune. Smith, Elizabeth Thomasina Meade. (Illus.). (Caldwell's ILlustrated Library of Famous Books by Famous Authors). N.D. H. M. Caldwell Co.
--The Strange Adventures of Mopsy and Hans. Smith, Elizabeth Thomasina Meade, 1 of 6 vols. (Sunny Land Ser.). N.D. D. Lothrop Co.
--Sweet Girl Graduate. Smith, Elizabeth Thomasina Meade. (The Meade Series for Girls). N.D. A. L. Burt Co.
--Sweet Girl Graduate. Smith, Elizabeth Thomasina Meade. (Illus.). (Fireside Ser. for Girls). N.D. A. L. Burt's Publications.
--Sweet Girl Graduate. Smith, Elizabeth Thomasina Meade. (Illus.). (The Wellesley Series for Girls). N.D. A. L. Burt's Pubs.

--A Sweet Girl Graduate. Smith, Elizabeth Thomasina Meade. Empire ed. 1905. American News Co.
--A Sweet Girl Graduate. Smith, Elizabeth Thomasina Meade. (Illus.). (The Young Folks Library). N.D. Caldwell.
--A Sweet Girl Graduate. Smith, Elizabeth Thomasina Meade. (Illus.). (Story Books for Girls). N.D. Cassell & Co.'s Pubs.
--Sweet Girl Graduate. Smith, Elizabeth, Thomasina Meade. (The Girls' Own Library). N.D. David McKay.
--A Sweet Girl Graduate. Smith, Elizabeth Thomasina Meade, 1 of 20 vols. (Illus.). (Mrs. L. T. Meade Ser.). N.D. Set. George M Hill Co.
--The Sweet Girl Graduate. Smith, Elizabeth Thomasina Meade. (The Good Value Books). N.D. Grosset & Dunlap.
--Sweet Girl Graduate. Smith, Elizabeth Thomasina Meade. N.D. Grosset & Dunlap.
--A Sweet Girl Graduate. Smith, Elizabeth Thomasina Meade, 31 vols. (Illus.). (Famous Books for Girls Ser.: No. 3). 1905. Set. H M Caldwell Co.
--A Sweet Girl Graduate. Smith, Elizabeth Thomasina Meade. (L. T. Meade Series.). N.D. Hurst & Co.
--Sweet Girl Graduate. Smith, Elizabeth Thomasina Meade. (Home Series for Girls). N.D. Hurst & Co.
--Sweet Nancy. Smith, Elizabeth Thomasina Meade. 1891. Thomas Whittaker.
--Temptation of Olive Latimer. Smith, Elizabeth Thomasina Meade. (Illus.). (Fascinating Stories for Girls). N.D. A. L. Chatterton Co.
--The Temptation of Oliver Latimer. Smith, Elizabeth Thomasina Meade, 1 of 20 vols. (Illus.). (Mrs. L. T. Meade Ser.). N.D. Set. George M Hill Co.
--The Palace Beautiful. Smith, Elizabeth Thomasina Meade. (Illus.). (Story Books for Girls). N.D. Cassell & Co's Pubs.
--Their Little Mother. Smith, Elizabeth Thomasina Meade. (Illus.). (The Meade Series.). 1915. A L Burt & Co.
--Their Little Mother. Smith, Elizabeth Thomasina Meade. (Illus.). (The Wellesley Series for Girls). N.D. A. L. Burt.
--Their Little Mother. Smith, Elizabeth Thomasina Meade. (L. T. Meade Ser.). N.D. Hurst & Co.
--Three Girls from School. Smith, Elizabeth Thomasina Meade. (The Meade Series for Girls). N.D. A. L. Burt Co.
--Three Girls from School. Smith, Elizabeth Thomasina Meade. (Illus.). (The Wellesley Series for Girls). N.D. A. L. Burt.
--Three Girls From School. Smith, Elizabeth Thomasina Meade. N.D. J. B. Lippincott Co.
--The Time of Roses. Smith, Elizabeth Thomasina Meade. (Illus.). (The Wellesley Series for Girls). N.D. A. L. Burt.
--The Time of Roses. Smith, Elizabeth Thomasina Meade. (L. T. Meade Ser.). N.D. Hurst & Co.
--The Time of the Roses. Smith, Elizabeth Thomasina Meade. (Illus.). (The Meade Series for Girls). N.D. A. L. Burt.
--A Very Naughty Girl. Smith, Elizabeth Thomasina Meade. (The Meade Series for Girls). N.D. A. L. Burt Co.
--A Very Naughty Girl. Smith, Elizabeth Thomasina Meade. (Illus.). (The Wellesley Series for Girls). N.D. A. L. Burt.
--A Very Naughty Girl. Smith, Elizabeth Thomasina Meade, 31 vols. (Illus.). (Famous books for Girls Ser.: No. 6). 1905. Set. H M Caldwell Co.
--A Very Naughty Girl. Smith, Elizabeth Thomasina Meade. (L. T. Meade Ser.). N.D. Hurst & Co.
--Water Gipsies. Smith, Elizabeth Thomasina Meade. N.D. Robert Carter.
--A Wild Irish Girl. Smith, Elizabeth Thomasina Meade. N.D. Hurst & Co.
--Wild Kitty. Smith, Elizabeth Thomasina Meade. (Illus.). (Fireside Series for Girls). N.D. A. L. Burt's Pubs.
--Wild Kitty. Smith, Elizabeth Thomasina Meade. (Illus.). (The Wellesley Series for Girls). N.D. A. L. Burt's Pubs.
--Wild Kitty. Smith, Elizabeth Thomasina Meade. Empire ed. 1905. American News Co.
--Wild Kitty. Smith, Elizabeth Thomasina Meade. (Illus.). N.D. Caldwell.
--Wild Kitty. Smith, Elizabeth Thomasina Meade. (The Girls' Own Library). N.D. David McKay.
--Wild Kitty. Smith, Elizabeth Thomasina Meade. (Famous Books for Girls). N.D. Dodge Publishing Co.
--Wild Kitty. Smith, Elizabeth Thomasina Meade. (Illus.). N.D. E. P. Dutton & Co.
--Wild Kitty. Smith, Elizabeth Thomasina Meade, 1 of 20 vols. (Illus.). (Mrs. L. T. Meade Ser.). N.D. Set. George M Hill Co.
--Wild Kitty. Smith, Elizabeth Thomasina Meade. (L. T. Meade Ser.). N.D. Hurst & Co.
--Wild Kitty. Smith, Elizabeth Thomasina Meade. N.D. New York Book Co.
--Wild Kitty: A Story of Middleton School. Smith, Elizabeth Thomasina Meade. (Illus.). (The Meade Series.). 1915. A L Burt & Co.
--Wilful Cousin Kate. Smith, Elizabeth Thomasina Meade. (The Meade Series for Girls). N.D. A. L. Burt Co.
--A World of Girls. Smith, Elizabeth Thomasina Meade. (Illus.). (Fireside Ser. for Girls). N.D. A. L. Burt's Publications.
--A World of Girls. Smith, Elizabeth Thomasina Meade. (Illus.). (The Wellesley Series for Girls). N.D. A. L. Burt's Pubs.
--A World of Girls. Smith, Elizabeth Thomasina Meade. Empire ed. 1905. American News Co.
--A World of Girls. Smith, Elizabeth Thomasina Meade. (Illus.). (Story Books for Girls). N.D. Cassell & Co.'s Pubs.
--A World of Girls. Smith, Elizabeth Thomasina Meade, 1 of 20 vols. (Illus.). (Mrs. L. T. Meade Ser.). N.D. Set. George M Hill Co.
--World of Girls. Smith, Elizabeth Thomasina Meade, 31 vols. (Illus.). (Famous Books for Girls Ser.: No. 26). 1905. Set. H M Caldwell Co.
--World of Girls. Smith, Elizabeth Thomasina Meade. (L. T. Meade Ser.). N.D. Hurst & Co.
--A World of Girls. Smith, Elizabeth Thomasina Meade. N.D. New York Book Co.
--A World of Girls. A Story of a School. Smith, Elizabeth Thomasina Meade. (The Meade Series for Girls). N.D. A. L. Burt Co.
--A Young Heroine. Smith, Elizabeth Thomasina Meade. (The Meade Series for Girls). N.D. A. L. Burt Co.
--A Young Mutineer. Smith, Elizabeth Thomasina Meade. (Illus.). (Fireside Series for Girls). N.D. A. L. Burt's Pubs.
--A Young Mutineer. Smith, Elizabeth Thomasina Meade. (Illus.). (The Wellesley Series for Girls). N.D. A. L. Burt's Pubs.
--A Young Mutineer. Smith, Elizabeth Thomasina Meade, 1 of 20 vols. (Illus.). (Mrs. L. T. Meade Ser.). N.D. Set. George M Hill Co.
--A Young Mutineer. Smith, Elizabeth Thomasina Meade. (L. T. Meade Ser.). N.D. Hurst & Co.
--A Young Mutineer. Smith, Elizabeth Thomasina Meade. Browne, Gordon Frederick (1858-1932), illus. N.D. E. & J. B. Young & Co.
--A Young Mutineer: A Story for Girls. Smith, Elizabeth Thomasina Meade. (Illus.). (The Meade Series.). 1915. A L Burt & Co.
--Your Brother and Mine. Smith, Elizabeth Thomasina Meade. N.D. Robert Carter.

Meade, L. T., pseud. (1854-1914) & Fenn, George Manville (1831-1909)
--Sunny Days. Smith, Elizabeth Thomasina Meade. N.D. E. P. Dutton and Co.

Meade, Marion (1934-)
--The Little Book of Big Bad Jokes. Cummings, Chris, illus. LC 77-78092. (Illus.). 32. 16cm. c.1977. Harvey House.
--Little Book of Big Riddles. Ross, David (1949-), illus. LC 76-15135. (Illus.). 1st U.S. edition. (Little Bks Ser.). (gr. 2-4). 1976. (ISBN 0-8178-5512-2). Harvey.

Meade, T. M
--Dorothy: A Tale. 1888. Thomas Whittaker.

Meader, Emma Blakely Grant, Mrs., jt. auth. see Olmstead, Emma Gertrude.

Meader, Stephen Warren (1892-)
--Away to Sea. Balmer, Clinton, illus. LC 31-25233. 5 p. l., 3-233 p. incl. illus., plates. front. 22 cm. c.1931. Harcourt, Brace and Company.
--Bat: The Story of a Bull-Terrier. N.D. Grosset & Dunlap.
--Bat: The Story of a Bull Terrier. Shenton, Edward (1895-), illus. LC 39-6267. 5 p. l., 3-273 p. incl. front., illus., plates (part double) 22 1/2 cm. c.1939. Harcourt, Brace and Company.
--Behind the Ranges. Shenton, Edward (1895-), illus. LC 47-11000. 6 l., 3-222 p. illus. 21 cm. 1947. Harcourt, Brace.
--The Black Buccaneer. Rev ed. Meader, Stephen Warren (1892-), illus. LC 20-16856. 2 p. l., 281 p. incl. illus., plates. front. 19 1/2 cm. 1920. Harcourt, Brace and Howe.
--The Black Buccaneer. Rev ed. Schaeffer, Mead (1898-1980), illus. LC 29-21547. 4 p. l., 3-269 p. col. front., illus., col. plates 23 1/2 cm. c.1929. Harcourt, Brace and Company.
--The Black Buccaneer. Rev ed. Shenton, Edward (1895-) & Meader, Stephen Warren, illus. LC 42-50074. x p., 1 l., 287 p. incl. illus., plates. 19 1/2 cm. (On cover: The Discovery series). 1942. Harcourt, Brace and Company.
--Blow for Liberty. X ed. Mays, Lewis Victor, Jr. (1927-), illus. LC 65-17991. (Illus.). 21cm. 187p. (gr. 7 up). 1965. (ISBN 0-15-208823-7). HarBraceJ.
--Blueberry Mountain. Shenton, Edward (1895-), illus. LC 41-51869. 4 p. l., 8-309 p. incl. illus., plates (part double) front. 22 cm. c.1941. Harcourt, Brace and Company.
--Boy with a Pack. Shenton, Edward (1895-), illus. LC 39-27870. 2 p. l., 297 p. front., illus. 22 cm. c.1939. Harcourt, Brace and Company. **Award: (JNM).**
--The Buckboard Stranger. Calle, Paul, illus. LC 54-8574. (Illus.). 213 p. 21cm. 1954. Harcourt, Brace.
--Buffalo and Beaver. 1st ed. Beck, Charles, illus. LC 60-10246. 189p. illus. 22cm. 1960. Harcourt, Brace.
--Bulldozer. School ed. Murphy, Geraldine, ed. Schmidt, Edwin, illus. LC 55-408. 261p. illus. 21cm. 1955. Harcourt, Brace.
--Bulldozer. 1st ed. Schmidt, Edwin, illus. LC 51-12740. (Illus.). 239 p. 21cm. 1951. Harcourt, Brace.
--The Cape May Packet. 1st ed. Frankenberg, Robert Clinton (1911-), illus. LC 78-82636. (Illus.). 218 p. 21cm. 1969. (ISBN 0-15-214094-8). Harcourt, Brace & World.
--Cedar's Boy. 1st ed. Townsend, Lee (1895-), illus. LC 49-10523. 234 p. illus. 21 cm. 1949. Harcourt, Brace.
--Clear for Action!. Beaudouin, Frank, illus. LC 40-27736. 4 p. l., 3-323 p. incl. illus., plates. front. 22 cm. c.1940. Harcourt, Brace and Company.
--The Commodore's Cup. 1st ed. Sibley, Don (1922-), illus. LC 58-8733. (Illus.). 192 p. 21cm. 1958. Harcourt, Brace.
--Down the Big River. Rev ed. Meader, Stephen Warren (1892-), illus. LC 24-8257. 2 p. l., 270 p. front., plates. 19 1/2 cm. c.1924. Harcourt, Brace and Company.
--Everglades Adventure. 1st ed. Beck, Charles, illus. LC 57-10350. (Illus.). 192 p. 22cm. 1957. Harcourt, Brace.
--The Fish Hawk's Nest. 1st ed. Shenton, Edward (1895-), illus. LC 52-10065. 236 p. illus. 21 cm. 1952. Harcourt, Brace.
--Guns for the Saratoga. 1st ed. O'Hara, John, illus. LC 55-8680. (Illus.). 207 p. 21cm. 1955. Harcourt, Brace.
--Jonathan Goes West. Shenton, Edward (1895-), illus. LC 46-6955. 4 p. l., 3-241 p. front., illus. 21 cm. 1946. Harcourt, Brace and Company.
--Keep 'em Rolling. Savitt, Al, illus. LC 67-17155. (Illus.). 21cm. 192p. (gr. 7 up). 1967. (ISBN 0-15-242195-5, HJ). HarBraceJ.
--King of the Hills. Rev ed. Townsend, Lee (1895-), illus. LC 33-27403. 3 p. l., 3-250 p. incl. illus., plates. front. (map) 22 cm. c.1933. Harcourt, Brace and Company.
--Lonesome End. 1st ed. Butterfield, Ned (1917-), illus. LC 68-25192. (Illus.). 190 p. 21cm. 1968. Harcourt, Brace & World.
--The Long Trains Roll. Shenton, Edward (1895-), illus. LC 44-40175. 3 p. l., 3-259 p. incl. front., illus. 21 cm. 1944. (ISBN 0-15-248651-8). Harcourt, Brace and Company.
--Longshanks. Caswell, Edward C., illus. LC 28-20763. 4 p. l., 243 p. front., plates, 19 1/2 cm. c.1928. Harcourt, Brace and Company.
Longshanks. Shenton, Edward (1895-), illus. 243p. N.D. Harcourt, Brace and Co., Inc.
--Lumberjack. Rev ed. Pitz, Henry Clarence (1895-1976), illus. LC 34-31292. viii p., 2 l., 3-277 p. incl. front., illus., plates (part double) 22 cm. c.1934. Harcourt, Brace and Company.
--Muddy Road to Glory. X ed. Hughes, George, illus. LC 63-17005. (Illus.). 22cm. 190p. (gr. 7-9). 1963. (ISBN 0-15-256260-5, HJ). HarBraceJ.
--The Open Road. Compton, Ray & Brown, Marjorie Dowling, eds. 366p. 1938. Harcourt, Brace.
--Phantom of the Blockade. Mays, Lewis Victor, Jr. (1927-), illus. LC 62-13333. (Illus.). 21cm. 190p. (gr. 7-9). 1962. (ISBN 0-15-261340-4). HarBraceJ.
--Red Horse Hill. Rev ed. Townsend, Lee (1895-), illus. LC 30-23594. 6 p. l., 3-244 p. incl. front., illus., plates. 22 cm. c.1930. Harcourt, Brace and Company.
--River of the Wolves. Shenton, Edward (1895-), illus. LC 48-867205. ix, 248 p. illus. 21 cm. 1948. Harcourt, Brace.
--Sabre Pilot. 1st ed. Polgreen, John, illus. LC 56-9551. 173p. illus. 21cm. 1956. Harcourt, Brace.
--The Sea Snake. Shenton, Edward (1895-), illus. LC 43-51265. 3 p. l., 3-255 p. incl. illus., plates. front. 21 cm. 1943. Harcourt, Brace and Company.
--Shadow in the Pines. Rev ed. Shenton, Edward (1895-), illus. LC 42-36279. 4 p. l., 3-281 p. illus. 22 cm. 1942. Harcourt, Brace and Company.
--Skippy's Family. Korn, Elizabeth P., illus. LC 45-84112. 4 p. l., 3-158 p. illus. 21 cm. 1945. Harcourt, Brace and Company.
--Snow on Blueberry Mountain. 1st ed. Sibley, Don (1922-), illus. LC 61-10112. (Illus.). 189 p. 21cm. 1961. Harcourt, Brace & World.
--Sparkplug of the Hornets. 1st ed. Sibley, Don (1922-), illus. LC 53-7868. (Illus.). 245 p. 21cm. 1953. Harcourt, Brace.
--Stranger on Big Hickory. 1st ed. Lambo, Donald W. (1903-1966), illus. LC 64-20975. (Illus.). 186 p. 21cm. 1964. Harcourt, Brace & World.
--T-Model Tommy. Rev ed. Shenton, Edward (1895-), illus. LC 38-23547. 5 p. l., 3-305 p. incl. fr228., illus., plates (part double) 22 1/2 cm. c.1938. Harcourt, Brace and Company.
--T-Model Tommy. Shenton, Edward (1895-), illus. LC 40-432526. x, 3-312 p. incl. front., illus., plates (part double) 19 1/2 cm. (On cover: The discovery series). c.1940. Harcourt, Brace and Company.
--Topsail Island Treasure. Brown, Marbury, illus. LC 66-10078. (Illus.). (gr. 6-7). 1966. (ISBN 0-15-289465-9). HarBraceJ.
--Topsail Island Treasure. 1st ed. Brown, Marbury, illus. LC 66-5274. 189p. illus. 21cm. c.1966. Harcourt.
--Trap-Lines North. Comstock, Enos Benjamin (1879-1945), illus. N.D. Dodd, Mead & Co.
--The Voyage of the Javelin. 1st ed. Cosgrave, John O'Hara, II (1908-1968), illus. LC 59-6564. (Illus.). 189 p. 21cm. 1959. Harcourt, Brace.
--Whaler Round the Horn. 1st ed. Shenton, Edward (1895-), illus. LC 50-9530. viii, 244 p. illus. 21 cm. 1950. Harcourt, Brace.
--Who Rides in the Dark?. MacDonald, James, illus. LC 37-27469. 4 p. l., 3-281 p. incl. front., illus., plates 22 cm. c.1937. Harcourt, Brace and Company.
--Who Rides in the Dark. Rev ed. MacDonald, James, illus. LC 37-274692. (Illus.). 20cm. 281p. (Voyager bk.: AVB44). 1966, c.1937. Harcourt.
--Wild Pony Island. Beck, Charles, illus. (Illus.). 21cm. 192p. (gr. 6-10). 1959. (ISBN 0-15-297139-4). HarBraceJ.
--The Will to Win and Other Stories. Gincano, John, illus. LC 36-19165. 7 p. l., 3-300 p. incl. front., plates. 22 cm. c.1936. Harcourt, Brace and Company.

Meadowcroft, Enid La Monte (1898-1966), ed. see Collier, Edmund.

Meadowcroft, Enid La Monte (1898-1966), ed. see Du Bois, Shirley Graham.

Meadowcroft, Enid La Monte (1898-1966), ed. see Wilson, Hazel Hutchins, Mrs.

Meadowcroft, Enid La Monte, Mrs. (1898-1966), ed. see Gordon, Patricia.

Meadowcroft, Enid La Monte, Mrs. (1898-1966), ed. see Graham, Shirley.

Meadowcroft, Enid La Monte, Mrs. (1898-1966), ed. see Hickok, Lorena A.

Meadowcroft, Enid La Monte, Mrs. (1898-1966), ed. see Malkus, Alida Wright Sims, Mrs.

Meadowcroft, Enid La Monte, Mrs. (1898-1966)
--The Adventures of Peter Whiffen. Bennetts, Beatrice H., illus. 148p. N.D. Thomas Y. Crowell Co.
--Along the Erie Towpath. MacKnight, Ninon (1908-), illus. Ninon, pseud. LC 40-324382. 2 p. l., 227 p. incl. col. front., illus. col. plates. 22 1/2 x 17 cm. c.1940. Thomas Y. Crowell Co.
--Aren't We Lucky!. LC 39-10238. 63 p. illus. (incl. maps) 21 x 26 cm. 1939. Thomas Y. Crowell Company.
--By Secret Railway. Pitz, Henry Clarence (1895-1976), illus. LC 48-8747. (Illus.). 21cm. 275p. (gr. 4-7). 1948. (ISBN 0-690-16431-9, TYC-J). T Y Crowell.
--By Wagon and Flatboat. MacKnight, Ninon (1908-), illus. Ninon, pseud. LC 38-32408. (Illus.). (gr. 5 up). 1938. (ISBN 0-690-16502-1, TYC-J). Har-Row.
--The First Year. Paull, Grace A. (1898-), illus. LC 46-22591. 6 p. l., 11-153 p. illus. (incl. map) 21 cm. 1946. Thomas Y. Crowell Company.
--The First Year: A Story of the Pilgrims in America. Phares, Frank E., illus. LC 37-3589. 152 p. incl. front., illus. 21 cm. c.1937. Thomas Y. Crowell Company.
--Holding the Fort with Daniel Boone. Coe, Lloyd (1899-1976), illus. LC 58-6563. 147p. illus. 21cm. 1958. Crowell.
--On Indian Trails with Daniel Boone. Coe, Lloyd (1899-1976), illus. LC 47-3536. 4 p. l., 136 p. incl. col. front., illus. 20 1/2 cm. 1947. Thomas Y. Crowell Company.
--Scarab for Luck. Weisgard, Leonard Joseph (1916-), illus. LC 63-18417. (Illus.). 21cm. 229p. (gr. 3-7). 1964. (ISBN 0-690-72027-0, TYC-J). Crowell.
--Ship Boy with Columbus. Robinson, Jessie Berkowitz, illus. LC 42-14387. 5 p. l., 120 p. plates, map. 21 cm. 1942. Thomas Y. Crowell Company.
--Silver for General Washington (Pub. by Crowell). (gr. 4-6). N.D (Starline). Schol Bk Serv.
--Silver for General Washington: A Story of Valley Forge. Ames, Lee Judah (1921-), illus. LC 57-10281. 247p. illus. 21cm. 1957. Crowell.
--Silver for General Washington: A Story of Valley Forge. James, Sandra, illus. LC 44-44997. 3 p. l., 138 p. illus. 23 1/2 cm. 1944. Thomas Y. Crowell Company.
--The Story of Andrew Jackson. Hendrickson, David (1896-), illus. LC 52-13742. (Illus.). 182 p. 22cm. (Signature books). 1953. Grosset & Dunlap.

--The Story of Benjamin Franklin. Wilson, Edward Arthur (1886-), illus. LC 52-11069. 182 p. illus. 22 cm. (Signature books). 1952. Grosset & Dunlap.
--The Story of Crazy Horse. Reusswig, William, illus. LC 54-5860. (Illus.). 181 p. 22cm. (Signature books, 28). 1954. Grosset & Dunlap.
--The Story of Davy Crockett. Falls, Charles Buckles (1874-1960), illus. LC 52-11067. (Illus.). 178 p. 22cm. (Signature books). 1952. Grosset & Dunlap.
--The Story of George Washington. Wilson, Edward Arthur (1886-), illus. LC 52-11076. 180 p. illus. 22 cm. (Signature books). 1952. Grosset & Dunlap.
--The Story of Thomas Alva Edison. Stein, Harve (1904-), illus. LC 52-11068. 181 p. illus. 22 cm. (Signature books). 1952. Grosset & Dunlap.
--Texas Star. Coe, Lloyd (1899-1976), illus. LC 50-13236. 148 p. illus. 21 cm. 1950. Crowell.
--We Were There at the Opening of the Erie Canal. McCann, Gerald (1916-), illus. LC 58-9838. (Historical consultant:Sylvester Vigilante). (Illus.). 182 p. 22cm. (We were there books, 19). 1958. Grosset & Dunlap.

Meager, Marijane see Kerr, M. E, pseud.

Meagher, James L. (1888-)
--The Knight of the Bow. LC 49-490957. vii, 214 p. front. 23 cm. 1949. Bruce.

Meaker, Mabel Sears
--The Prospector's Promise. Segal, Louis, illus. LC 59-15449. 183p. illus. 22cm. 1960. Lothrop, Lee & Shepard.
--The Secret of Hollow Hill. Geer, Charles Hand (1922-), illus. LC 61-5275. 154p. illus. 21cm. 1961. Watts.

Meaker, Marijane see Kerr, M. E, pseud.

Meakin, Naomi B
--The Seasons, for Young Folks. LC 31-2660. 56 p. 19 1/2 cm. c.1930. Done by the Bookfellows at the Torch Press.

Meaney, Mary L.
--Grace Harlowe with the Marines at Chateau Thierry. (The Grace Harlowe Overseas Ser.). N.D. Henry Altemus Co.

Means, Carl, jt. auth. see Means, Florence Crannell, Mrs.

Means, Florence Crannell, Mrs. (1891-1980)
--Assorted Sisters. Blair, Helen (1910-), illus. LC 47-11468. 250 p. col. illus. 21 cm. 1947. Houghton Mifflin Co.
--Our Cup Is Broken. LC 69-19935. 229 p. 22cm. 1969. Houghton Mifflin.
--Pepita's Adventure in Friendship. 1929. Friendship Press.
--Smith Valley. LC 73-8842. 297 p. 22cm. 1973. (ISBN 0-395-17710-3). Houghton Mifflin.

Means, Florence Crannell, Mrs. (1891-1980) & Fullen, Harriet Louise
--A Candle in the Mist. De Angeli, Marguerite Lofft, Mrs. (1889-), illus. Brandinger, Alice, contrib. by. LC 73-4929. vii, 196 p. 22cm. (Riverside reading series). 1968. Houghton Mifflin.
--A Candle in the Mist: A Story for Girls. De Angeli, Marguerite Lofft, Mrs. (1889-), illus. LC 31-25049. 5 p. l., 252, 1 p. front., illus., plates. 21 cm. 1931. Houghton Mifflin Company.
--Rafael and Consuelo. 1929. Friendship Press.

Means, Florence Crannell, Mrs. (1891-1980) & Means, Carl
--Alicia. Barss, William (1916-), illus. LC 53-6205. 266p. illus. 22cm. 1953. Houghton Mifflin Co.
--Borrowed Brother. Morse, Dorothy Bayley (1906-1979), illus. LC 58-8167. 239p. illus. 22cm. 1958. Houghton Mifflin.
--But I Am Sara. LC 61-513639. 231p. 21cm. 1961. Houghton Mifflin.
--Carver's George. N.D. E. M. Hale and Co.
--Carver's George. (Illus.). 1952. Houghton Mifflin.
--Emmy and the Blue Door. Nicholas, Frank, illus. LC 59-9722. 217p. illus. 22cm. 1959. Houghton Mifflin.
--Hetty of the Grande Deluxe. Blair, Helen (1910-), illus. LC 51-283. 188 p. col. illus. 29 cm. 1951. Houghton Mifflin.
--It Takes All Kinds. 1964. (ISBN 0-8382-0374-4, Cadmus Books). E. M. Hale and Company.
--It Takes All Kinds. LC 64-21743. 22cm. 234p. (gr. 7-9). 1964. (ISBN 0-395-06931-9). HM.
--Knock at the Door, Emmy. Lantz, Paul (1908-), illus. LC 56-5547. (Illus.). 240 p. 22cm. 1956. Houghton Mifflin.
--The Rains Will Come. Kabotie, Fred (1900-), illus. LC 54-9043. 241p. illus. 22cm. 1954. Houghton Mifflin.
--Reach for a Star. LC 57-7201. 247p. 22cm. 1957. Houghton Mifflin.
--The Silver Fleece. Schmidt, Edwin, illus. (Land of the Free Ser.). 1950. Holt, Rinehart and Winston.
--That Girl Andy. LC 62-16793. 227 p. 22cm. 1962. Houghton Mifflin.
--Tolliver. LC 63-15289. (Illus.). 22cm. 234p. (gr. 7-9). 1963. (ISBN 0-395-06940-8). HM.
--Us Maltbys. LC 66-12099. (Illus.). 250 p. 1966. Houghton Mifflin.

Means, Florence Crannell, Mrs. (1891-1980) & Riggs, Frances
--Across the Fruited Plain. Smalley, Janet (1893-), illus. LC 40-11704. xii p., 1 l., 112, 1 p. illus. 19 1/2 cm. c.1940. Friendship Press.
--Adella Mary in Old New Mexico. Stoops, Herbert Morton, illus. LC 39-21783. (Illus.). 6 p. l., 3-226, 1 p. incl. front., illu. 1939. Houghton Mifflin Company.
--At the End of Nowhere. Hendrickson, David (1896-), illus. LC 40-32069. 5 p. l., 232 p. plates. 21 1/2 cm. 1940. Houghton Mifflin Company.
--A Bowlful of Stars: A Story of the Pioneer West. Pitz, Henry Clarence (1895-1976), illus. LC 34-246285. vi p., 1 l., 247 p. incl. front., illus. 21 cm. 1934. Houghton Mifflin Company.
--Children of the Promise. Smalley, Janet (1893-), illus. LC 41-7697. 4 p. l., 119, 1 p. incl. front., illus. 19 1/2 cm. c.1941. Friendship Press.
--Dusky Day: A College Story. Lee, Manning De Villeneuve (1894-1980), illus. LC 33-240909. 5 p. l., 271 p. front., plates. 21 cm. 1933. Houghton Mifflin Company.
--Great Day in the Morning. Blair, Helen (1910-), illus. LC 46-252952. 5 p. l., 3-182, 1 p. col. plates. 21 cm. 1946. Houghton Mifflin Company.
--The House Under the Hill. Blair, Helen (1910-), illus. LC 49-11585. 184 p. col. illus. 22 cm. 1949. Houghton Mifflin Co.
--The Moved-Outers. (gr. 7-9). 1945. (ISBN 0-395-06933-5). HM. **Award: (JNM).**
--Penny for Luck: A Story of the Rockies. Revised. Quinn, Paul, illus. LC 35-15043. 4 p. l., 232 p. illus., paltes. 21 1/2 cm. 1935. Houghton Mifflin Company.
--Peter of the Mesa. Smalley, Janet (1893-), illus. LC 44-5275. 19 1/2cm. 120p. 1944. Friendship Press.
--Rainbow Bridge. Lattimore, Eleanor Frances (1904-), illus. LC 34-110871. 3 p. l., 152 p. incl. front., illus. pl. 19 1/2 cm. c.1934. Friendship Press.
--Ranch and Ring: A Story of the Pioneer West. Peck, Henry J., illus. LC 32-22538. 5 p. l., 260 p. front., illus. 21 cm. 1932. Houghton Mifflin Company.
--Shadow Over Wide Ruin. Bjorklund, Lorence F. (1913-1978), illus. LC 42-22718. 5 p. l., 227 p. illus., col. plates 22 cm. 1942. Houghton Mifflin Company.
--Shuttered Windows. Sperry, Armstrong W. (1897-1976), illus. LC 38-19939. 5 p. l., 205, 1 p. front., plates. 21 1/2 cm. 1938. Houghton Mifflin Company.
--The Singing Wood: A College Story. Lee, Manning De Villeneuve (1894-1980), illus. LC 37-17505. vi p., 1 l., 241 p. front., plates. 21 cm. 1937. Houghton Mifflin Company.
--Tangled Waters: A Navajo Story. Stoops, Herbert Morton, illus. LC 36-18757. 5 p. l., 212 p. col. front., illus. 21 1/2 cm. 1936. Houghton Mifflin Company.
--Teresita of the Valley. Panesis, Nicholas (1913-), illus. LC 43-15999. 5 p. l., 166 p. plates. 21 cm. 1943. Houghton Mifflin Company.
--Whispering Girl: A Hopi Indian Story of Today. Howard, Oscar, illus. LC 41-140540. 4 p. l., 225 p., 1 l. col. front., illus. 21 1/2 cm. 1941. Houghton Mifflin Company.

Means, Nathalie T.
--Aminah. 97p. (gr. 6-8). 1979. Dorrance.

Means, Philip Ainsworth (1892-)
--Tupak of the Incas. Dalgliesh, Alice (1893-), ed. Herget, H. M., illus. LC 42-4726. 4 p. l., 136 p. illus. 24 cm. 1942. C. Scribner's Sons.

Meany, Tom
--The Yankee Story. (Illus.). N.D. E. P. Dutton & Co.

Mearian, Judy Frank (1936-)
--Someone Slightly Different. LC 79-22514. 197 p. 22cm. c.1980. (ISBN 0-8037-8370-1). (ISBN 0-8037-8371-X). Dial Press.
--Two Ways About It. LC 79-10029. 166 p. 22cm. c.1979. (ISBN 0-8037-8797-9). (ISBN 0-8037-8796-0). Dial Press.

Mearns, Hughes, frwd. by see Baruch, Dorothy Walter, Mrs.

Mearns, Martha
--H M S Pinafore. Johnstone, Anne Grahame & Johnstone, Janet Grahame, illus. (gr. 4-6). N.D. (ISBN 0-531-01765-6). Watts.
--The Mikado. LC 66-31703. (Illus.). 1 v. (unpaged. (Curtain raiser book). 1966, c.1965. F. Watts.

Mearns, Martha, ed. see Gilbert, William Schwenck, Sir (1836-1911) & Sullivan, Arthur Seymour, Sir.

Mearns, Martha, tr. see Haar, Jaap Ter.

Mears, Henrietta Cornelia (1890-), ed. see Walton, Thelma.

Mears, James R
--The Iron Boys As Foremen: Or, Heading the Diamond Drill Shift. LC 12-23930. 251 p. incl. front., plates. 19 1/2 cm. (His The boys of steel series). c.1912. Henry Altemus Company.
--The Iron Boys in the Mines: Or, Starting at the Bottom of the Shaft. LC 12-239299. 256 p. incl. front., plates. 19 1/2 cm. (His The boys of steel series). c.1912. Henry Altemus Company.

M. E. B. , pseud., see Maxwell, Mary Elizabeth Braddon.

Mechelen, B. Van see Van Mechelen, B.

Medary, Marjorie (1890-)
--Buckeye Boy. MacDonald, James, illus. LC 44-7722. 3 p. l., 265 p. illus. 21 cm. 1944. Longmans. Green and Co.
--College in Crinoline. Berger, William Merritt (1872-), illus. LC 37-274703. viii p., 1 l., 403, 2 p. incl. front., illus. 21 cm. 1937. Longmans, Green and Co.
--Edra of the Islands. Morse, Dorothy Bayley (1906-1979), illus. LC 40-13170. 4 p. l., 280 p. illus. 22 cm. 1940. Toronto, Longmans, Green and Co.
--Hetty's Orange Winter. N.D. Grosset & Dunlap.
--Joan and the Three Deer. Wiese, Kurt (1887-1974), illus. LC 39-27556. 5 p. l., 3-160 p. incl. illus., plates. 23 cm. c.1939. Random House.
--Prairie Anchorage. Gincano, John, illus. LC 33-274042. viii p., 1 l., 278 p. incl. front., illus. 20 cm. 1933. Longmans, Green and Co.
--Prairie Printer. Lee, Manning De Villeneuve (1894-1980), illus. LC 49-9720. ix, 288 p. 22 cm. 1949. Longmans, Green.
--The Store at Crisscross Corners. Smalley, Janet (1893-), illus. LC 46-7180. 47, 1 p. illus. (part col.) 21 by 16 1/2 cm. 1946. Abingdon-Cokesbury Press.
--Topgallant: A Herring Gull. Ward, Lynd Kendall (1905-1985), illus. LC 35-22401. 159 p. illus. 23 cm. c.1935. H. Smith and R. Haas.
--Topgallant: The Story of a Herring Gull. Ward, Lynd Kendall (1905-1985), illus. N.D. Random House.

Meddaugh, Susan (1944-)
--Beast. Meddaugh, Susan (1944-), illus. LC 80-24851. (Illus.). 32 p. 1981. (ISBN 0-395-30349-4). Houghton Mifflin.
--Maude and Claude Go Abroad. LC 79-26460. (Illus.). 32 p. 1980. (ISBN 0-395-29162-3). Houghton Mifflin.
--Too Many Monsters. LC 81-7068. (Illus.). 31 p. 24cm. 1982. (ISBN 0-395-31862-9). Houghton Mifflin.
--Too Short Fred. Meddaugh, Susan (1944-), illus. LC 78-60942. (Illus.). 39 p. 23cm. 1978. (ISBN 0-395-27155-X). Houghton Mifflin.

Medearis, Mary (1915-)
--Big Doc's Girl. new ed. (gr. 7-9). 1950. (ISBN 0-397-30164-2). Har-Row.
--Big Doc's Girl. N.D. J. B. Lippincott.
--Big Doc's Girl. (gr. 7-10). N.D. Pyramid Pubns.

Medica, Jack, jt. auth. see Fishel, Richard Mark.

Medina, Frank
--Once Upon a Cotton Picking Time. N.D. Vantage Press Inc.

Medoff, Francine
--The Mouse in the Matzah Factory. Goldstein, David (1948-), illus. LC 82-23349. (Illus.). 40 p. 27cm. c.1983. (ISBN 0-930494-18-0). (ISBN 0-930494-19-9). Kar-Ben Copies.

Medon, Florence, Mrs. (1916-)
--Mother's Helpers. Grider, Dorothy (1915-), illus. LC 47-11269. 49 p. illus. 29 cm. 1947. Garden City Pub. Co.

Medora, Marie
--Patty McGill: Investigator. LC 36-32331. 206 p. front. 20 cm. c.1936. The Penn Publishing Company.

Medvedev, Roy A. & Medvedev, Zhores
--A Question of Madness. (gr. 9 up). 1971. (ISBN 0-394-47900-9). Knopf.

Medvedev, Zhores, jt. auth. see Medvedev, Roy A.

Mee, Arthur (1875-) & Thompson, Holland (1873-), eds.
--The Everyday Library for Young People. LC 16-11711. (Illus.). 25cm. 1916. The Grolier Society.

Mee, Charles L, Jr., jt. auth. see Munowitz, Ken.

Mee, Charles L., Jr. (1938-)
--Moses, Moses. Munowitz, Ken (1935-1977), illus. LC 76-41516. (Illus.). (gr. k-3). 1977. (ISBN 0-06-024178-0, HarpJ). (ISBN 0-06-024179-9). Har-Row.
--Noah. Munowitz, Ken (1935-1977), illus. LC 77-11839. (Illus.). 1978. (ISBN 0-06-024183-7, HarpJ). (ISBN 0-06-024184-5). Har-Row.

Mee, Josiah
--Sunday Talks to the Young. (Illus.). (The Staincliffe Ser.: Vol. 6). N.D. Fleming H. Revell Co.

Meecham, J.
--South American Fairy Tales. (gr. 1-4). 1971. (ISBN 0-584-62392-5). Transatlantic.

Meek, Jacklyn O'Hanlon see Matthews, Jacklyn Meek, pseud.

Meek, Jacklyn O'Hanlon see O'Hanlon, Jacklyn.

Meek, Mary Elizabeth, jt. auth. see David, Alfred.

Meek, Pauline Palmer (1917-)
--All Day Long. (Illus.). (ps-k). 1965. (ISBN 0-8042-2711-X). John Knox.
--The Broken Vase. Forberg, Ati, pseud. (1925-), illus. Forberg, Beate Gropius. (Illus.). (ps). 1965. (ISBN 0-8042-2733-0). John Knox.
--God Speaks to Me. Forberg, Ati, pseud. (1925-) & Zander, Hans (1937-), illus. Forberg, Beate Gropius. LC 73-160570. (Illus.). 95 p. 21cm. (Covenant life curriculum). 1973, c.1972. John Knox Press.
--Just-Alike Princes. Poehlmann, Joanna, illus. LC 67-2241. (Illus.). 25 p. 30cm. (Whitman small world library book). c.1966. Whitman Pub. Co.
--Knock! Knock!. (Illus.). (ps). 1965. (ISBN 0-8042-2873-6). John Knox.
--Noah & the Ark. Byrd, Pam, illus. (Illus.). 8p. of color ils. 20p. (gr. k-3). 1970. (ISBN 0-87529-038-8). Hallmark.
--When Joy Came: The Story of the First Christmas. Stirnweis, Shannon (1931-), illus. LC 77-27407. (Illus.). 25 p. 32cm. (Big golden book). 1971. Golden Press.
--Who Is Debbie?. (Illus.). (ps). 1965. (ISBN 0-8042-2986-4). John Knox.

Meek, Sterner St. Paul (1894-1972)
--Bellfarm Star: The Story of a Pacer. McCann, Gerald (1916-), illus. LC 55-9248. 213p. illus. 21cm. 1955. Dodd, Mead.
--Boots: The Story of a Working Sheep Dog. LC 48-8238. xiii, 234 p. 20 cm. 1948. A. A. Knopf.
--Boy: An Ozark Coon Hound. LC 51-13015. 238 29. (gr. 7-11). 1952. Knopf.
--Dignity,. A Springer Spaniel. N.D. Alfred A. Knopf.
--Dignity: A Springer Spaniel. Abbott, Jacob Bates (1803-1879), illus. LC 37-34171. 304 p. front., illus., plates. 23 cm. c.1937. The Penn Publishing Company.
--Franz: A Dog of the Police. (gr. 7-11). 1944. Knopf.
--Franz: A Dog of the Police. Abbott, Jacob Bates (1803-1879), illus. LC 35-223991. 319 p. front., illus., plates. 22 cm. c.1935. The Penn Publishing Company.
--Frog, The Horse that Knew no Master. N.D. Alfred A. Knopf.
--Frog: The Horse That Knew No Master. N.D. Grosset & Dunlap.
--Frog, The Horse That Knew No Master. Hargens, Charles, Jr. (1893-), illus. N.D. Penn Publishing Co.
--Frog: The Horse That Knew No Master. Hargens, Charles, Jr. (1893-), illus. LC 33-360745. 302 p. front., illus., plates. 22 cm. c.1933. The Penn Publishing Company.
--Gustav,. A Son of Franz. N.D. Alfred A. Knopf.
--Gustav: A Son of Franz. Abbott, Jacob Bates (1803-1879), illus. LC 40-347403. 296 p. front., illus., plates. 22 cm. c.1940. The Penn Publishing Company.
--Gypsy Lad: The Story of a Champion Setter. Dennis, Morgan (1891-1960), illus. LC 34-32936. xii , 1 l. 314 col. front., illus. 21. 1934. William Morrow & Co.
--Hans: A Dog of the Border Patrol. X ed. LC 50-5748. (Illus.). 20cm. xiv, 253p. (gr. 7-11). 1950. Knopf.
--Jerry: The Adventures of an Army Dog. Balmer, Clinton, illus. LC 32-9671. xi, 235 p. incl. illus., plates. 20 cm. c.1932. The Century Co.
--Jerry: The Story of an Army Dog. N.D. Appleton Century Co.
--Midnight: A Cow Pony. LC 49-75963. xiii, 217 p. 20 cm. 1949. A. A. Knopf.
--Omar: A State Police Dog. LC 53-7636. 240p. 20cm. (Barzol books for young people). 1953. Knopf.
--Omar: A State Police Dog. (gr. 7 up). 1963. (ISBN 0-394-81460-6). (ISBN 0-394-91460-0). Knopf.
--Pagan: A Bomber Patrol Horse. LC 51-9814. 238 p. 20 cm. 1951. Knopf.
--Pat: The Story of a Seeing Eye Dog. LC 47-1965. xv, 190 p., 1 l. 22 cm. 1947. A. A. Knopf.
--Pierre of the Big Top: The Story of a Circus Poodle. Wiese, Kurt (1887-1974), illus. LC 56-9315. 203p. illus. 21cm. 1956. Dodd, Mead.
--Ranger: A Dog of the Forest Service. LC 49-10348. xvii, 232 p. 20 cm. 1949. A. A. Knopf.
--Red: A Trailing Bloodhound. LC 51-11074. 225 p. 20 cm. 1951. Knopf.
--Rip: A Game Protector. LC 52-6399. 266 p. 20cm. 1952. (ISBN 0-394-81547-5). Knopf.
--Rusty,. A Cocker Spaniel. N.D. A. A. Knopf.
--Rusty: A Cocker Spaniel. Abbott, Jacob Bates (1803-1879), illus. LC 54-8559. 296p. illus. 22cm. (Famous dog stories). 1954, c.1938. Grosset & Dunlap.

Melcher, Marguerite Fellows (1879-1969)
--Catch of the Season. 1st ed. Cook, Stephen, illus. LC 60-5875. 195p. illus. 21cm. 1960. Little, Brown.
--Lost Pond. Lantz, Paul (1908-), illus. LC 56-14187. 190p. illus. 21cm. 1956. Viking Press.
--Why Don't You Draw a Dog. 1st ed. Zemach, Margot (1931-), illus. LC 62-8311. 28p. illus. 24cm. 1962. Little Brown.
Melcon, H. A., tr. see Spyri, Johanna Heusser.
Meldrum, Roy
--Col and Joy. (Roundabout Ser.). N.D. D. Appleton & Co.
Melin, Grace Hathaway (1892-1973)
--Dorothea Dix. Dowd, Victor, illus. LC 63-17663. 200 p. col. illus. 20 cm. (Childhood of famous Americans). 1963. Bobbs-Merrill.
--Henry Wadsworth Longfellow, Gifted Young Poet. Plummer, William Kirtman, illus. LC 68-55146. (Illus.). 200 p. 20cm. (Childhood of famous Americans). 1968. Bobbs-Merril Co.
--Maria Mitchell, Girl Astronomer. 1st ed. Davis, Bette J. (1923-), illus. LC 54-10847. 192p. illus. 20cm. (Childhood of famous Americans series). 1954. Bobbs-Merrill.
--Maria Mitchell, Girl Astronomer. Giacoia, Frank, illus. LC 59-13998. 192p. illus. 20cm. (Childhood of famous Americans). 1960. Bobbs-Merrill.
Melinda, Luke
--Junior's Day in Space: An Astronik Adventure. Jacquet, Jean-Pierre, illus. LC 83-62910. (Illus.). 32p. (Astroniks Mini-storybooks). (ps-3). 1984. (ISBN 0-394-86393-3, BYR). Random.
Meling, O. R.
--The Druid's Tune. 240p. (gr. 7 up). 1985. (ISBN 0-14-031778-3, Puffin). Penguin.
Mellanby, Kenneth (1908-)
--Talpa,. The Story of a Mole. Kitchen, Bert, illus. LC 76-54964. (Illus.). (gr. 4-6). 1977. (ISBN 0-529-05338-1). Collins Pubs.
Mellandaine, C. E.
--The Carrier's Cart (Pub. by Society for Promoting Christian Knowledge). N.D. E. & J. B. Young & Co.
Melle, Gerta & Redies, Reiner
--The Cats' Party: A Picture Book. Kimber, Rita, tr. LC 85-15676. p. cm. 1985. (ISBN 0-8120-3643-3). Barron's Educational Series.
Mellen, Ida May (1877-)
--Twenty Little Fishes. N.D. Julian Messner.
Meller, Celine
--The April Time. LC 54-7892. 199 p. 21cm. 1954. Bruce Pub. Co.
Meller, Sidney
--Home Is Here. LC 41-9783. 5 p. l., 405 p. 21 cm. 1941. The Macmillan Company.
Mellett, James S.
--Willy and Sand Grain. N.D. Carlton Press.
Mellett, John Calvin see Brooks, Jonathan, pseud.
Mellett, John Calvin (1888-)
--Jimmy Makes the Varsity. Brooks, Jonathan, pseud. Avison, George F. (1885-), illus. LC 28-21063. 6 p. l., 11-283 p. front., plates. 21 cm. c.1928. The Bobbs-Merrill Company.
--Pigskin Soldier. Brooks, Jonathan, pseud. Condon, Grattan, illus. LC 31-23362. 5 p. l., 3-215 p. front. 20 cm. 1931. Doubleday, Doran & Company, Inc.
--Varsity Jim. Brooks, Jonathan, pseud. Laune, Paul Sidney (1899-), illus. LC 39-21295. 320 p. col. front. 21 cm. c.1939. The Bobbs-Merrill Company.
Mellick, Jim
--Sunny Gems: As Told to Sonny Jim, Sonny Jim, Sonny Lou, and Their Boy and Girl Friends. LC 67-6832. (Illus.). 109 p. 21cm. 1966. Vantage Press.
Mellin, Jeanne (1929-)
--Pidgy's Surprise. 1st ed. Mellin, Jeanne (1929-), illus. LC 55-8880. 124p. illus. 21cm. 1955. Dutton.
Mellon, Joseph, adapted by.
--Aladdin,. Or, the Wonderful Lamp. Laufer, Susan, illus. LC 78-72133. (Illus.). 32p. (gr. 3-5). 1979. Dandelion Pr.
Mellon, Joseph, adapted by see Frame, Paul (1913-) & Grimm, Jakob Ludwig Karl.
Mellon, Joseph, adapted by see Grimm, Jakob Ludwig Karl.
Mellon, Joseph (1785-1863), adapted by see Grimm, Jakob Ludwig Karl (1785-1863) & Grimm, Wilhelm Karl.
Mellon, Robert C, ed.
--A Treasury of Laughs. Berenzy, Roberta, illus. LC 60-13197. 127p. illus. 27cm. 1960. Hart Pub. Co.
Mellor, Kathleen C., jt. ed. see Schaefer, Charles E.
Melloy, Camille, tr. see Windham, Joan.
Melnikoff, Pamela
--The Star and the sword. Schwarz, Hans, illus. LC 68-26551. 157p. illus. 22cm. 1968, c.1965. Crown.
Melnyk, Bohdan (1914-), tr. see Franko, Ivan.
Melodia, Thomas V., jt. auth. see Malinowski, Stanley B.
Melton, David (1934-)
--A Boy Called Hopeless. LC 75-37943. (Illus.). 231 p. 21cm. c.1976. (ISBN 0-8309-0148-5). Independence Press.
--The One & Only Autobiography of Ralph Miller: The Dog Who Knew He Was a Boy. Melton, David (1934-), illus. (Illus.). (gr. 3-6). 1979. (ISBN 0-8309-0233-3). Ind Pr MO.
--The One and Only Second Autobiography of Ralph Miller: The Dog Who Knew He Was a Boy. Melton, David (1934-), illus. LC 83-18408. (Illus.). 116, 2 p. 22cm. c.1983. (ISBN 0-8309-0380-1). Independence Press.
Meltzer, Milton (1915-)
--The Terrorists. LC 82-48858. (Illus.). 192p. (gr. 7 up). 1983. (ISBN 0-06-024193-4, HarpJ). (ISBN 0-06-024194-2). Har-Row.
--Underground Man: A Novel. LC 72-80317. (Illus.). 220 p. 24cm. 1972. (ISBN 0-87888-051-8). Bradbury Press.
Meltzoff, Nancy (1952-)
--A Sense of Balance. x ed. LC 77-18508. 159 p. 21cm. c.1978. (ISBN 0-664-32629-3). Westminster Press.
Melvill, Heather
--Four Pigs & a Bee. Galvani, Maureen, illus. (Dinosaur Ser.). (ps-1). 1978. (ISBN 0-85122-080-0, Pub. by Dino Pub). Merrimack Pub Cir.
Melville, Herman, jt. auth. see Cooper, James Fenimore.
Melville, Herman (1819-1891)
--Billy Budd. N.D. Parents' Magazine Press.
--Billy Budd. (Illus.). 64p. (Now Age Illustrated V Ser.). (gr. 4-12). 1979. (ISBN 0-88301-397-5). (ISBN 0-88301-385-1). (ISBN 0-88301-409-2). Pendulum Pr.
--Billy Budd. (gr. 8 up). 1972. (ISBN 0-590-02520-1, Schol Trade Pap). Schol Bk Serv.
--Billy Budd & Other Tales. (gr. 9 up). N.D. Lancer.
--Billy Budd, Foretopman. large type complete and unabridged. vi, 132 p. 29cm. N.D. F. Watts.
--Billy Budd, Foretopman. Quackenbush, Robert Mead (1929-), illus. LC 68-10284. (Illus.). 126 p. 23cm. 1968. F. Watts.
--Billy Budd, Sailor, and Other Stories. Beaver, Harold Lothar (1929-), ed. N.D. (ISBN 0-8446-0799-1). Peter Smith Publishing, Inc.
--The Confidence Man. (gr. 9 up). N.D. Lancer.
--Five Tales. (Illus.). (Great Il. Classics). (gr. 9 up). 1967. (ISBN 0-396-05500-1). Dodd.
--Melville. Incl. Best of Moby Dick; Typee; Billy Budd Complete. (Great Writers Collection Ser). (gr. 7 up). 1964. Platt.
--Moby Dick. N.D. Albert & Charles Boni.
--Moby Dick. Abridged. 1926. Alfred A. Knopf.
--Moby Dick. (Everyman's Library). N.D. E. P. Dutton & Co.
--Moby Dick. N.D. Grosset & Dunlap.
--Moby Dick. N.D. Harper & Bros.
--Moby Dick. (The Winston Clear-Type Popular Classics). N.D. John C. Winston.
--Moby Dick. (The Fairmount Classics). N.D. Macrae Smith.
--Moby Dick. (World Classics). N.D. Oxford University Press-American Branch.
--Moby Dick. (Classics, Giant Eds.). (gr. 7 up). N.D. (ISBN 0-531-00421-X). Watts.
--Moby Dick. (Keith Jennison Large Types Bks). (gr. 7 up). N.D. (ISBN 0-531-00238-1). Watts.
--Moby Dick. N.D. William Collins Sons & Co.
--Moby Dick. Arvin, Newton, ed. 566p. 1948. Rinehart & Co.
--Moby Dick. Beals, Frank Lee (1881-1972), adapted by. Beals, Frank Lee (1881-1972), retold by. (Illus.). (Famous Story Ser.). N.D. Naylor.
--Moby Dick. Daniels, Patricia, adapted by. Kelley, Gary, illus. LC 81-15386. (Illus.). 48p. (Raintree Short Classics). (gr. 4-12). 1983. (ISBN 0-8172-2016-X). Raintree Pubs.
--Moby Dick. Fadiman, Clifton Paul (1904-), intro. by. (Harper's Modern Classics). N.D. Harper & Brothers.
--Moby Dick. Fink, Joanne, adapted by. LC 84-50431. (Illus.). 26 p., 1 leaf of plates. 26cm. (Classics for Kids). 1984. (ISBN 0-382-06807-6). Silver Burdett Co.
--Moby Dick. Fischer, Anton Otto (1882-), illus. (The Children's Bookshelf). N.D. John C. Winston.
--Moby Dick. Hayford, Harrison & Parker, Hershel (1935-), eds. 1967. (ISBN 0-393-04284-7). (ISBN 0-393-09670-X). Norton & Co.
--Moby Dick. new ed. Shapiro, Irwin (1911-), ed. Nino, Alex, illus. LC 73-75458. (Illus.). footnotes. 64p. (Orig.). (Now Age Illustrated Ser.). (gr. 5-10). 1973. (ISBN 0-88301-212-X). (ISBN 0-88301-099-2). Pendulum Pr.
--Moby Dick. Shore, Robert (1924-), illus. (Illus.). (gr. 7 up). 1962. (ISBN 0-02-766830-4). Macmillan.
--Moby Dick. New ed. Whiting, John Downes (1884-), illus. (The Father and Son Library). N.D. Sears Publishing Co.
--Moby Dick. Adapted for Young Readers. Sutton, Felix (1910-), adapted by. Vestal, Herman B., illus. LC 56-58632. 69p. illus. 29cm. 1956. Grosset& Dunlap.
--Moby Dick: Or, the Whale. Robinson, Boardman, illus. 638p. N.D. Heritage Press.
--Moby Dick: Or, the White Whale. Fischer, Anton Otto (1882-), illus. McFee, William, intro. by. N.D. John C. Winston Co.
--Moby Dick: Or, The White Whale. Schaeffer, Mead (1898-1980), illus. 1942. Dodd.
--Moby Dick: Or, The White Whale. Schaeffer, Mead (1898-1980), illus. (Illus.). (Great Illustrated Classics). 1979. Dodd.
--Moby Dick: Or, The White Whale. Shute, A. Burnham, illus. N.D. Dana Estes & Co.
--Moby Dick: Or, The White Whale. Shute, A. Burnham & Merrill, Frank Thayer (1848-), illus. N.D. Page Co.
--Moby Dick: The Whale. N.D. Ginn & Co.
--Moby Dick: The White Whale. N.D. Dodd Mead & Co.
--Omoo. 1958. Grove Press.
--Omoo. N.D. Page Co.
--Omoo. Schaeffer, Mead (1898-1980), illus. N.D. Dodd Mead & Co.
--Typee. (Astor Library). N.D. Dodd Mead & Co.
--Typee. (Magnum Easy Eye Classic Ser). (gr. 7-12). N.D. Lancer.
--Typee. N.D. Page Co.
Melville, Velma Caldwell
--White Dandy: Or, Master and I. N.D. J. S. Ogilvie Publishing Co.
Melvin, Arthur Gordon (1894-)
--Adventures on Midsummer Evenings. Melvin, Lorna Strong, illus. LC 51-11616. 61 p. front. 22 cm. 1951. Exposition Press.
Melwood, Mary, pseud., see Lewis, E. M..
Melwood, Mary, pseud.
--Five Minutes to Morning. Lewis, E. M.. 1966. New Plays.
--Nettlewood. Lewis, E. M.. LC 74-19426. 352p. (gr. 6 up). 1975. (ISBN 0-395-28919-X, Clarion). HM.
--Nettlewood: A Novel. Lewis, E. M.. LC 74-19426. 351 p. 22cm. 1975, c.1974. (ISBN 0-8164-3142-6). Seabury Press.
--The Tingalary Bird. Lewis, E. M.. 1964. New Plays.
--The Watcher Bee. Lewis, E. M.. (Illus.). 272p. (gr. 9 up). 1983. (ISBN 0-233-97432-6). Andre Deutsch.
Melzack, Ronald (1929-)
--The Day Tuk Became a Hunter & Other Eskimo Stories. Jones, Carol, illus. LC 67-26842. (Illus.). 92 p. 25cm. 1967. Dodd, Mead.
--Raven, Creator of the World. Gal, Laszlo (1933-), illus. LC 70-122535. (Illus.). 91 p. 25cm. 1st U.S. edition. 1970. (ISBN 0-316-56650-0). Little, Brown.
Memling, Carl, jt. auth. see Disney, Walt, Productions.
Memling, Carl, jt. auth. see Hanna-Barbera Productions.
Memling, Carl (1918-1969), adapted by see Disney, Walter Elias.
Memling, Carl (1918-1969), retold by see Disney, Walt, Productions.
Memling, Carl (1918-1969), adapted by see UPA Pictures, Inc.
Memling, Carl (1918-1969), adapted by see Wyss, Johann David Von.
Memling, Carl (1918-1969)
--A B C Rhymes. Rodegast, Roland, illus. (Illus.). (ps-3). 1970. (ISBN 0-307-60543-4, Golden Pr). Western Pub.
--The Amazing Adventures of Dennis the Menace. Memling, Carl (1918-1969), adapted by. Holley, Lee, illus. LC 61-117332. unpaged. illus. 29cm. 1961. Random House.
--Barbie's Adventures at Camp. Burris, Burmah, illus. LC 64-12426. 1 v. (unpaged) col. illus. 29 cm. 1964. Random House.
--Captain Kangaroo and His Animal Friends. Nonnast, Marie (1924-), illus. LC 59-3151. unpaged illus. 29. (Big Golden Book, 399). 1959. Golden Press.
--Dennis the Menace. Pratt, Hawley & Holley, Lee, illus. (Little Golden Book). 1959. Golden Press.
--Dennis the Menace Storybook. Holley, Lee, illus. LC 60-14458. (Illus.). unpaged illus. 29. (gr. 1-5). 1960. (ISBN 0-394-80711-1). Random.
--A Gift-Bear for the King. Hoban, Lillian (1925-), illus. LC 66-11385. 47p. col. illus. 26cm. c.1966. Dutton.
--Happy-Go-Lucky Skipper. Porter, Raymond, illus. LC 65-120373. 56p. illus. (pt. col.) 24cm. c.1965. (ISBN 0-394-81222-0). Random.
--Hey There -- It's Yogi Bear. Pratt, Hawley, illus. LC 64-2228. 1 v. (unpaged) col. illus. 33 cm. (big Golden book). 1964. Golden Press.
--Hi, All You Rabbits. McGee, Myra, illus. LC 78-117558. (Illus.). 40 p. 24cm. 1970. (ISBN 0-8193-0430-1). Parents' Magazine Press.
--Huckleberry Hound. McGrary, Norman & Pratt, Hawley, illus. LC 61-224. unpaged. illus. 29cm. (Big golden book, 384). 1960. Golden Press.
--I Can Count. LC 63-22978. 1 v. (unpaged) col. illus. 33 cm. (Big golden book). c.1963. Golden Press.
--Life with Mindy. 1st ed. Johnson, John Emil (1929-), illus. LC 66-8330. (Illus.). 48 p. 27cm. 1966. Dutton.
--The Little Bear's Mother. Fern, Eugene A. (1919-), illus. LC 59-511852. unpaged. illus. 29cm. 1959. Ariel Books.
--Maverick. Leone, John, illus. (Little Golden Book). 1959. Golden Press.
--Old Man Riddle. Faulkner, John Frink (1922-), illus. LC 77-188432. (Illus.). 32p. (gr. k-3). 1972. (ISBN 0-8075-5964-4). A Whitman.
--Quick Draw McGraw. White, Al & Pratt, Hawley, illus. (Little Golden Book). 1960. Golden Press.
--Riddles, Riddles from A to Z. Hyman, Trina Schart (1939-), illus. (ps-3). 1962. (ISBN 0-307-60940-5, Golden Pr). Western Pub.
--Ride, Willy, Ride!. Mardon, John, illus. LC 78-85950. (Illus.). 31 p. 21cm. (Follett beginning-to-read books). 1970. Follett Pub. Co.
--Seals for Sale. Edwards, Peter William (1934-), illus. LC 63-16216. 1 v. (unpaged) col. illus. 27 cm. c.1963. Abelard-Schuman.
--Ten Big Passengers. Cooke, Tom, illus. LC 68-58456. (Illus.). 24 p. 29cm. (Carousel book). 1969. L. W. Singer Co.
--Ten Little Animals. Rojankovsky, Feodor Stepanovich (1891-1971), illus. LC 68-7887. (Illus.). 24 p. 23cm. 1961. Golden Press.
--We Went to the Doctor. Carten, Virginia, illus. LC 55-9318. 22cm. 1955. Abelard-Schuman, Inc.
--What's in the Dark?. Carten, Virginia, illus. LC 54-10211. (Illus.). unpaged. 27cm. 1954. Abelard-Schuman.
--What's in the Dark?. Johnson, John Emil (1929-), illus. LC 74-136993. (Illus.). 41 p. 1971. (ISBN 0-8193-0445-X). Parents' Magazine Press.
Memling, Carl (1918-1969), adapted by.
--Tom Thumb. Dugan, William J., illus. (Little Golden Book). 1959. Golden Press.
Memling, Carl (1918-1969) & Ketcham, Hank, pseud. (1920-), eds.
--The Dennis the Menace Storybook. Ketcham, Henry King. Denice the Menace, Television Program Holley, Lee, illus. LC 60-14458. unpaged. illus. 29cm. 1960. Random House.
Menard, Belle, jt. auth. see Gertude, J.
Menconi, Lee
--Pony That Lost Her Neigh. Colton, Jan, illus. N.D. Vantage Press.
Mendel, Florence Emma Voigt, Mrs. (1874-)
--Our Little Austrian Cousin. Marlowe, Diantha W. Horne, illus. LC 13-151680. 3 p. l., v-vi p., 2 l., 157 p. front., plates. 20 cm. (The little cousin series). 1913. L. C. Page & Company.
--Our Little Polish Cousin. O'Brien, Harriet, illus. LC 12-11855. ix p., 2 l., 147 p. front., plates. 20 cm. (The Little cousin series). 1912. L. C. Page & Company.
Mendel, Jo, pseud., see Bond, Gladys Baker.
Mendel, Jo, pseud. (1912-)
--The Tuckers: The Cottage Holiday. Bond, Gladys Baker. Tomes, Jacqueline, illus. LC 64-4813. 282 p. illus. 20 cm. c.1962. Whitman Publ. Co.
Mendel, Marcella
--A Story Book for Very Young Children. Shriber, Anne, photos by. LC 35-172. 1 p. l., 7-58, 1 p. illus. 16 cm. c.1935. Whitman Publishing Company.
Mendel, Rosalie G.
--Spark, the Story of a Bull-Terrier and His Dog Friends. LC 13-119. (Illus.). 19cm. 4p. c.1913. A. Flannagan Co.
Mendelsohn, Zora see Benson, Nora, pseud.
Mendelsohn, Zora
--Joan Takes a Bow. Benson, Nora, pseud. LC 50-9681. 183 p. 22 cm. 1950. Lothrop, Lee & Shepard.
Mendelssohn-Bartholdy, Felix, jt. auth. see Shakespeare, William.
Mendenhall, Susan
--Livingstone Hero Stories. N.D. Friendship Press.
Mendes, Catulle (1841-1909)
--The Fairy Spinning Wheel and the Tales it Spun. Peabody, Marion L., illus. Vivian, Thomas Jondrie (1855-), tr. from Fr. LC 98-1858. (Illus.). 8cm. 146p. 1898. G. Badger & Co.
--The Family Spinning Wheel and the Tales it Spun. Peabody, Marion L., illus. Vivian, Thomas Jondrie (1855-), tr. from French. LC 98-1858. (Illus.). 146p. 1898. R. G. Badger & Co.
Mendes, Henry Pereira (1852-)
--In Old Egypt. Humphrey, Mabel L. (1859-), illus. (Illus.). (Popular Ser. for Young People). N.D. Frederick A. Stokes Co.

--Don't Think About a White Bear. Tinkelman, Murray (1933-), illus. LC 65-13302. 47p. col. illus. 20x24cm. c.1965. Putnam.
--Finding a Poem. 1st ed. Chwast, Seymour (1931-), illus. LC 76-115077. (Illus.). 68 p. 22cm. 1970. Atheneum. **Awards: (NYT).**
--Funny Town. Ness, Evaline Michelow, Mrs. (1911-), illus. LC 63-8301. 63 p. illus. 30 cm. (Modern masters book for children). 1963. Crowell Collier Press.
--A Gaggle of Geese. Galdone, Paul (1914-), illus. LC 60-8603. unpaged. illus. 26cm. 1960. Knopf.
--Good Night to Annie. Wallner, John C (1945-), illus. LC 79-5068. p. cm. c.1979. (ISBN 0-590-07485-7). Four Winds Press.
--I Am a Man: Ode to Martin Luther King, Jr. Verrier, Suzanne, illus. (Illus.). 22 halftones. 48p. (gr. 1-5). 1971. (ISBN 0-385-07006-3). (ISBN 0-385-08701-2). Doubleday.
--Independent Voices. Stewart, Arvis L., illus. LC 68-18453. (Illus.). xi, 79 p. 22cm. 1968. Atheneum.
--It Doesn't Always Have to Rhyme. Spooner, Malcolm, illus. LC 64-11893. (Illus.). 83 p. 22cm. 1964. Atheneum.
--Love Poems. Diamond, Donna (1950-), illus. LC 83-4377. p. cm. 1983. (ISBN 0-394-86043-8). (ISBN 0-394-96043-2). A.A. Knopf.
--Miss Tibbett's Typewriter. 1st ed. Schreiter, Rick (1936-), illus. LC 66-137797. 26p. illus. 23cm. (Read alone bks.). c.1966. (ISBN 0-394-91413-9). Knopf.
--Mommies at Work. Montresor, Beni (1926-), illus. LC 61-8126. (Illus.). (ps-2). 1961. (ISBN 0-394-90737-X). (ISBN 0-394-80737-5). Knopf.
--Mommies at Work. Montresor, Beni (1926-), illus. 1973. Scholastic.
--Out Loud. Sherman, Harriet, illus. LC 72-86942. (Illus.). 50 p. 22cm. 1973. Atheneum.
--Project One-Two-Three. Sherman, Harriet, illus. LC 77-163295. (Illus.). 40 p. 27cm. 1971. (ISBN 0-07-041516-1). McGraw-Hill.
--Rainbow Writing. LC 76-4468. p. cm. 1976. (ISBN 0-689-30527-3). Atheneum.
--Small Fry. MacKenzie, Garry. (1921-), illus. LC 65-119631. 40p. illus. (pt. col.) 26cm. 1965. Knopf.
--There is No Rhyme for Silver. 1st ed. Schindelman, Joseph (1923-), illus. LC 62-10254. (Illus.). 70p. 22cm. 1962. Atheneum.
--Unhurry Harry. Owens, Gail, illus. LC 78-1302. (Illus.). 32 p. 21cm. c.1978. (ISBN 0-590-07480-6). Four Winds Press.
--What Can You Do with a Pocket?. Sherman, Harriet, illus. LC 63-9112. 1 v. (unpaged) col. illus. 29 cm. c.1964. Knopf; Distributed by Random House.
--A Word or Two with You: New Rhymes for Young Readers. Nez, John A, illus. LC 81-1282. p. cm. 1981. (ISBN 0-689-30862-0). Atheneum.

Merriam, Lillie Fuller
--Jenny and Tito. Troth, Emma, illus. (The Cosy Corner Ser.). N.D. L C Page & Co.
--Jenny's Bird-house. Butler, C. L., illus. LC 10-28334. (Illus.). 20cm. 91p. 1910. C. M. Clark Publishing Co.
--Jenny's Bird House. Butter, C. L., illus. (The Cosy Corner Ser.). N.D. L C Page & Co.

Merriam, Robert L.
--Abigail Challenges the Telephone Company. Merriam, Robert L., illus. (Illus.). 8p. (Orig.). 1972. (ISBN 0-686-32483-8). R L Merriam.
--Santa Claus' Snack. Roberts, William, illus. (Illus.). 14p. N.D. (ISBN 0-686-32491-9). R L Merriam.

Merrick, Donna & Clark, Ginnie (1910-)
--Christopher A. Moose III: Christopher Discovers a Secret. Tauer, Roi (1941-), created by. Clark, Robert (1911-), illus. LC 77-76781. (Illus.). 48p. (gr. k-3). 1977. (ISBN 0-516-03439-1). Childrens.

Merrick, James Kirk (1905-)
--Brian. Merrick, James Kirk (1905-), illus. LC 48-520994. 62 p. illus. 22 x 26 cm. 1948. Rockport Press.

Merrill, Anna Darby
--College Days: Mary Lee and Her College Chums Grow up. LC 27-22473. 1 p. l., 7-187 p. illus. 20 cm. c.1927. Whitman Publishing Co.
--The Story of Cinderella. Bennett, Juanita C., illus. LC 35-327671. 1 p. l., 7-44 p. col. illus., col. plates. 33 cm. c.1935. Whitman Publishing Company.

Merrill, Anna Darby, adapted by see Spyri, Johanna Heusser.

Merrill, B. J., jt. auth. see Crafts, F. W.

Merrill, Flora
--Flush of Wimpole Street and Broadway. N.D. Robert M. McBride & Co.
--Kippy of the Cavendish. N.D. Robert M. McBride & Co.

Merrill, Frank Thayer (1848-), illus.
--Grandmother. N.D. Dana Estes & Co.
--Prisoners of the Pirates. N.D. The Page Co.

Merrill, George Edmands (1846-1908)
--Battle Lost and Won, 1 of 50 vols. (Illus.). 350p. (Sunday-School Lib: No. 14). N.D. Set. Lothrop Pub Co.
--Master Hathorne's Family: A Story of the Early Boston Baptists. LC 12-366128. 2 p. l., 3-384 p. front., plates. 17 cm. c.1870. American Baptist Publication Society.

Merrill, Harrison R (1884-)
--Ko-I Chito: The Indian Boy. Collett, Farrell R. & Smith, Cecil, illus. LC 37-7077. 127, 1 p. col. front., illus., col. plates. 17 cm. c.1937. Bridgham Young University Press.

Merrill, J. M.
--His Mother's Letter: Or, The Boy Wails Search. Fry, W. H., illus. 20cm. 303p. 1902. The Saalfield Pub. Co.

Merrill, Jean
--The Pushcart War. Solbert, Ronni, pseud. (1925-), illus. Solbert, Romaine G.. LC 84-43131. p. cm. 1985, c.1964. Harper & Row.

Merrill, Jean, ed. see Issa.

Merrill, Jean Fairbanks (1923-)
--The Black Sheep. Solbert, Ronni, pseud. (1925-), illus. Solbert, Romaine G.. LC 76-77431. (Illus.). 80p. (gr. 3-5). 1969. (ISBN 0-394-90887-2). Pantheon.
--Blue's Broken Heart. (Illus.). (gr. k-2). 1960. (ISBN 0-8382-0103-2). Hale.
--Blue's Broken Heart. Solbert, Ronni, pseud. (1925-), illus. Solbert, Romaine G.. LC 60-773110. unpaged. illus. 23cm. c.1960. Whittlesey House.
--Boxes. Solbert, Ronni, pseud. (1925-), illus. Solbert, Romaine G.. LC 53-9563. 26cm. 1953. Coward-McCann, Inc.
--The Elephant Who Liked to Smash Small Cars. Solbert, Ronni, pseud. (1925-), illus. Solbert, Romaine G.. LC 67-20215. (Illus.). 32 p. 26cm. 1967. Pantheon Books.
--Emily Emerson's Moon. Solbert, Ronni, pseud. (1925-), illus. Solbert, Romaine G.. LC 60-9345. (Illus.). 22 cm. 32p. (ps up). 1960. (ISBN 0-316-56746-9). Little.
--Henry, the Hand Painted Mouse. LC 51-12295. unpaged. illus. 26 cm. 1951. Coward-McCann.
--High, Wide & Handsome. 48p. (gr. k-3). 1964. (ISBN 0-201-09225-5, A-W Childrens). A-W.
--High, Wide & Handsome. Solbert, Ronni, pseud. (1925-), illus. Solbert, Romaine G.. (Illus.). (Cadmus Bks). (gr. k-2). 1964. (ISBN 0-8382-0332-9). Hale.
--High, Wide, and Handsome and Their Three Tall Tales. Solbert, Ronni, pseud. (1925-), illus. Solbert, Romaine G.. LC 64-13584. (Illus.). 25cm. 48p. 1964. Young Scott Books.
--High,Wide and Handsome. 48p. 1964. Young Scott Books.
--Maria's House. 1st ed. Scott, Frances Gruse, illus. LC 74-75565. (Illus.). 55 p. 21cm. 1974. (ISBN 0-689-30412-9). Atheneum.
--Mary, Come Running. Solbert, Ronni, pseud. (1925-), illus. Solbert, Romaine G.. (Illus.). 1970. E.P. Dutton & Co.
--Mary, Come Running. Solbert, Ronni, pseud. (1925-), illus. Solbert, Romaine G.. LC 74-122153. (Illus.). 32 p. 29cm. 1970. (ISBN 0-8415-2021-6). McCall Pub. Co.
--Please, Don't Eat My Cabin. Scott, Frances Gruse, illus. LC 70-165818. (Illus.). 64 p. 24cm. 1971. (ISBN 0-8075-6551-2). A. Whitman.
--The Pushcart War. Solbert, Ronni, pseud. (1925-), illus. Solbert, Romaine G.. 1964. Children's Press.
--Pushcart War. Solbert, Ronni, pseud. (1925-), illus. Solbert, Romaine G.. 1964. E M Hale.
--The Pushcart War. Solbert, Ronni, pseud. (1925-), illus. Solbert, Romaine G.. N.D. (ISBN 0-448-04804-3, Universal Library). Grosset & Dunlap.
--The Pushcart War. Solbert, Ronni, pseud. (1925-), illus. Solbert, Romaine G.. LC 64-13581. (Illus.). 222 p. 23cm. 1964. W. R. Scott. **Award: (ALA).**
--Red Riding. Solbert, Ronni, pseud. (1925-), illus. Solbert, Romaine G.. LC 68-12656. (Illus.). 4-color ils. 32p. (gr. 1-3). 1968. (ISBN 0-394-91534-8). Pantheon.
--Red Riding: A Story of How Katy Tells Tony a Story Because It Is Raining. Solbert, Ronni, pseud. (1925-), illus. Solbert, Romaine G.. (Illus.). 32 p. 29cm. 1968. (ISBN 0-394-82736-8). Pantheon Books.
--Shan's Lucky Knife. 48p. (gr. 3-7). 1960. (ISBN 0-201-09341-3, Young Scott Bks). A-W.
--Shan's Lucky Knife. (Illus.). (gr. 3-5). 1960. (ISBN 0-8382-0745-6). Hale.
--Shan's Lucky Knife. Solbert, Ronni, pseud. (1925-), illus. Solbert, Romaine G.. LC 60-1743. (Illus.). 48 p. 26cm. (Young Scott books). 1960. W. R. Scott.
--A Song for Gar. Solbert, Ronni, pseud. (1925-), illus. Solbert, Romaine G.. LC 56-11721. (Illus.). 31 p. 26cm. (Whittlesey House books for young people). 1957. Whittlesey House.
--The Superlative Horse. Solbert, Ronni, pseud. (1925-), illus. Solbert, Romaine G.. LC 61-16201. (Illus.). 79 p. 24cm. 1961. W. R. Scott. **Award: (ALA).**
--Tell About the Cowbarn, Daddy. Wronker, Lili Cassell (1925-), illus. LC 63-19196. 1 v. (unpaged) col. illus. 25 cm. 1963. Young Scott Books.
--The Toothpaste Millionaire. (Illus.). 1974. Houghton.
--The Toothpaste Millionaire. Palmer, Janice, illus. LC 73-22055. (Illus.). 90 p. 24cm. c.1972. (ISBN 0-395-18511-4). (ISBN 0-395-18511-4). Houghton Mifflin.
--The Travels of Marco. Solbert, Ronni, pseud. (1925-), illus. Solbert, Romaine G.. LC 56-5079. 28cm. 42p. 1956. Knopf.
--Travels of Marco. Solbert, Ronni, pseud. (1925-), illus. Solbert, Romaine G.. LC 56-5079. (Illus.). (gr. k-3). 1965. (ISBN 0-394-91765-0). Knopf.
--The Tree House of Jimmy Domino. Solbert, Ronni, pseud. (1925-), illus. Solbert, Romaine G.. 1954. Coward-McCann, Inc.
--The Tree House of Jimmy Domino. Solbert, Ronni, pseud. (1925-), illus. Solbert, Romaine G.. LC 55-869587. unpaged. illus. 20 x 27cm. 1955. Oxford University Press.
--The Tree House of Jimmy Domino. Solbert, Ronni, pseud. (1925-), illus. Solbert, Romaine G.. 29p. 1955. Walck.
--The Very Nice Things. Solbert, Ronni, pseud. (1925-), illus. Solbert, Romaine G.. LC 59-8976. unpaged. illus. 19x22cm. 1959. Harper.
--The Woover. Solbert, Ronni, pseud. (1925-), illus. Solbert, Romaine G.. LC 52-13099. (Illus.). 31 p. 23cm. 1952. Coward-McCann.

Merrill, Jean Fairbanks (1923-) & Scott, Frances Gruse
--The Bumper Sticker Book. LC 73-7319. (Illus.). 32p. (gr. 1-4). 1973. (ISBN 0-8075-0930-2). A Whitman.
--Here I Come, Ready or Not. LC 76-115897. (Illus.). 24cm. 32p. (gr. 1-3). 1970. (ISBN 0-8075-3244-4). A Whitman.
--How Many Kids Are Hiding on My Block?. LC 70-126431. (Illus.). 32 p. 24cm. 1970. (ISBN 0-8075-3418-8). A. Whitman.

Merrill, Jenny Biggs
--Bible Pictures and Stories for Little Folks. Juv ed. (Illus.). N.D. Cassell & Co.
--Little Folks' Bible Gallery. (Illus.). N.D. Cassell, Petter, Galpin.

Merrill, Lewis C
--Fuzzy Britches. 1st ed. Kilgore, Al, illus. LC 53-119537. 55p. illus. 21cm. 1953. Pageant Press.

Merrill, Marion
--My Cut and Paste Story Book. LC 39-8127. (Illus.). 26 1/2 x 30cm. 47p. c.1938. McLoughlin Bros.
--Syd of Tar-Paper Shack. Merrill, Marion, illus. LC 47-17964. 4 p. l., 259, 1 p. front., illus. 20 cm. 1947. Wilcox & Follett Co.
--Treasure Cave Trail: An Adventure of the Young Billings. James, Sandra, illus. LC 43-10068. 158, 2 p. col. front., illus. 21 cm. 1943. W. Morrow and Company.
--The Young Billings of Buckhorn. James, Sandra, illus. LC 42-17986. 71, 1 p. col. front., illus., col. plates. 22 x 17 cm. 1942. W. Morrow and Company.

Merrill, Marion, ed. see Three Little Kittens.

Merrill, Marion, ed. see Three Little Pigs.

Merrill, Susan
--Washday. LC 77-12621. (Illus.). 32 p. c.1978. (ISBN 0-8164-3206-6). Seabury Press.

Merriman, Effie Woodward, Mrs. (1857-)
--The Conways. LC 12-36611. 303 p. front., plates. 18 cm. 1893. Lee and Shepard.
--The Conways. (Illus.). (Stories for our Daughters). N.D. Lee & Shepards.
--The Little Millers. LC 12-366164. 245 p. front., plates. 17 cm. 1891. Lee and Shepard.
--The Little Millers, 1 of 3 vols. (Illus.). (Street Arab Ser.). 1900. Set. Lee & Shepard.
--Mollie Miller. LC 12-366151. 285 p. front., plates. 18 cm. (Stories for our daughters, v. 1). 1895. Lee and Shepard.
--Mollie Miller. (Illus.). (Stories for Our Daughters Ser). N.D. Lee & Shepard.
--Pards, 1 of 3 vols. (Illus.). (Street Arab Ser.). 1900. Set. Lee & Shepard.
--Pards: A Story of Two Homeless Boys. LC 12-366141. 202 p. plates. 17 cm. 1891. Lee and Shepard.
--A Queer Family. LC 12-366176. 2 p. l., 7-215 p. front., plates. 17 cm. 1891. Lee and Shepard.
--A Queer Family, 1 of 3 vols. (Illus.). (Street Arab Ser.). 1900. Set. Lee & Shepard.
--Sir Jefferson Nobody. (Illus.). 286p. 1900. A C McClurg Co.

Merriman, Elsie A, jt. auth. see Mills, Harriette Melissa.

Merriman, Henry Seton
--Barlasch of the Guard. (Illus.). (Childrens Illustrated Classics Ser). 1971. (ISBN 0-460-05089-3, Pub. by J. M. Dent England). Biblio Dist.
--Barlasch of the Guard. Gough, Philip (1908-), illus. N.D. (ISBN 0-525-26197-4). Dutton.
--The Phantom Future. (Phenix Ser.). N.D. Dodd, Mead & Co.
--Young Mistley. (Phenix Ser.). N.D. Dodd, Mead & Co.

Merrit, Dora W.
--The Story of Four Little Sabots. Merrit, Dora W., illus. (The Cosy Corner Ser.). N.D. Frederick Warne & Co.

Merritt, Lizzie K
--Forever and Ever Stories. LC 56-12715. 80p. illus. 24cm. 1957, c.1956. Pageant Press.

Merritt, Mabel C.
--Dance of the Mayflies & Other Nature Stories. Graham, Robert, illus. (Illus.). 63p. (gr. 4-6). 1973. (ISBN 0-682-47645-5). Exposition.

Merritt, Muriel (1905-)
--Give Them Wings: Poems for Children. 1st ed. Merritt, Muriel (1905-), illus. LC 73-87289. 44 p. Illus. 24 cm. c.1973. H Stewart.

Merrivale, J.
--The Fallen Flyer: Or, Camping in Canada. N.D. Macmillan.

Merriweather, Magnus, pseud., see Talbot, Charles Remmington.

Merriweather, Magnus, pseud. (1851-1891)
--Honor Bright. Talbot, Charles Remmington, 1 of 3 vols. (Honor Bright Series). 1882. D Lothrop.
--Honor Bright Series. Talbot, Charles Remmington, 3 vols. 1882. Set. D Lothrop.
--Royal Lowrie. Talbot, Charles Remmington, 1 of 3 vols. (Honor Bright Ser.). 1882. D Lothrop.
--Royal Lowrie's Last Year at St. Olaves. Talbot, Charles Remmington, 1 of 3 vols. (Honor Bright Ser.). 1882. D Lothrop.

Merry, Robert, pseud., see Stearns, John Newton.

Merry Thoughts Staff
--Fairy Tales Pop up Book. (Illus.). (ps-3). N.D. (ISBN 0-685-24616-7). Merry Thoughts.
--Rhyme Time Pop up Book. Merry Thoughts Staff, tr. (Illus.). (ps-3). N.D. (ISBN 0-685-24615-9). Merry Thoughts.

Merryman, Mildred Plew (1892-)
--Bonbon and Bonbonette. LC 25-1292. 96 p. incl. col. front., col. illus. col. plates. 24 cm. 1924. Rand, McNally & Company.
--Quack! Said Jerusha. Phipps, Mary, illus. LC 30-28919. 56 p. incl. col. front., col. illus. 24 cm. c.1930. Sears Publishing Company.
--The Road to Raffydiddle. Aloise, Frank E., illus. LC 66-10572. 1v. (unpaged) col. illus. 21cm. N.D. (ISBN 0-687-36526-0). Abingdon.

Mers, Joe De see De Mers, Joseph.

Mers, Joseph De see De Mers, Joseph.

Merschel, Sylvia E., jt. auth. see Perry, Donald R.

Mersereau, Ann
--The Story of Li-Lo. LC 37-35179. 32 p. incl. col. front., illus. (part col.) 19 x 19 cm. 1937. Harper & Brothers.

Merten, George
--Plays for Puppet Performance. (gr. 3-10). 1979. (ISBN 0-8238-0234-5). Plays.

Mertens, Robert, jt. auth. see Pinkwater, Daniel Manus.

Merton, Ambrose, pseud., see Thoms, William John.

Mertz, Barbara Gross see Michaels, Barbara, pseud.

Mertz, Barbara Gross see Peters, Elizabeth, pseud.

Mervyn, Louise
--Daddy Dinks. Lawrence, T. Cromwell, illus. LC 3-22890. (Illus.). 19cm. 94p. 1903. The Saalfield Pub. Co.

Merwin, Decie, jt. auth. see Bechdolt, John Ernest.

Merwin, Decie (1894-1961)
--Mostly the Meldons. 1st ed. Merwin, Decie (1894-1961), illus. LC 56-11887. 147p. illus. 21cm. 1957. Lippincott.
--Parachute Pup. Merwin, Decie (1894-1961), illus. LC 41-13400. 63 p. incl. col. front., illus. (part col.) 24 cm. c.1941. J. B. Lippincott Company.
--Pink-Tails. LC 50-10577. 102 p. illus. 21 cm. (Oxford books for boys and girls). 1950. Oxford University Press.
--Rafferty Red. Merwin, Decie (1894-1961), illus. LC 52-14894. 128p. illus. 21cm. 1952. Abelard Press.
--Robin and Mr. Jones. LC 53-5546. (Illus.). 111 p. 22cm. (Oxford books for boys and girls). 1953. Oxford University Press.
--Scottish Treasure Mystery. 1 st. ed. LC 60-13867. 159p. illus. 21cm. 1960. Lippincott.
--Somerhaze Farm. 1st ed. Merwin, Decie (1894-1961), illus. LC 58-7534. 188p. illus. 21cm. 1958. Lippincott.
--Time for Tammie. Merwin, Decie (1894-1961), illus. LC 46-15977. 39p. incl. col. front., col. ill. 19 x 15 1/2cm. 1946. Oxford University Press.
--Where's Teresa?. LC 56-5709. unpaged. illus. 19x23cm. c.1956. Lippincott.

Merwin, Frances Maude Spaits (1872-)
--The Eye Single. LC 28-27808. (Illus.). 19 1/2cm. 191p. N.D. Parker Pub. Co.

Merwin, Samuel
--Bad Penny. N.D. Robert M. McBride & Co.

--The Merry Anne. (Every Boy's and Every Girl's Ser.). N.D. The Macmillan Co.

Merwine, Effie Kline
--Starlight Sterling and Other Stories and Poems for Boys and Girls. LC 98-2289. 56 p. front. 27 cm. 1898. Chaplin Printing Co.

Merz, Robert Griffith (1934-)
--The Mockingbird Book. Tinkelman, Murray (1933-), illus. LC 62-17965. unpaged (chiefly illus.) 24 cm. 1962. Harper & Row.

Meseraull, Elaine & Van Dolson, Bobbie Jane, eds.
--Your Story Hour, with Uncle Dan and Aunt Sue: Stories. Woody, Ann Munro, illus. LC 77-86277. (Illus.). v. 26cm. c.1979. Review and Herald Pub. Association.

Mesfin Habte-Mariam
--The Rich Man and the Singer: Folktales from Ethiopia. Price, Christine Hilda (1928-1980), ed. Price, Christine Hilda (1928-1980), illus. LC 73-102738. (Illus.). viii, 84 p. 25cm. 1971. Dutton. 0-525-38224-0.

Meshover, Leonard & Feistel, Sally
--The Guinea Pigs That Went to School. Hoffmann, Eve, illus. LC 68-10488. (Illus.). 63 p. 26cm. 1968. Follett Pub. Co.
--The Monkey That Went to School. Hoffmann, Eve, illus. LC 77-88636. (Illus.). 64 p. c.1978. (ISBN 0-695-10878-X). (IEDN 0-695-30878-5). Follett Pub. Co.

Mesick, Helen Winne
--Thelma's Story of a Happy Family. Mesick, Helen Winne, illus. LC 40-6335. 21 p. illus. 20 cm. c.1940. F. H. Evory & Co., Inc.

Messager, Charles see Vildrac, Charles, pseud.

Messe, Mildred Foulke, Mrs.
--The Wagon to the Star: A Novel for Girls. Costello, Louise, illus. LC 39-21781. 318 p. illus. 21 cm. c.1939. The New York, Bobbs-Merrill Company.

Messer, Clarence Johnson
--Mr. Responsibility, Partner: How Bobby and Joe Achieved Success in Business. Hubbard, Charles D., illus. LC 12-175481. 379 p. incl. front. plates. 20 cm. 1912. Lothrop, Lee & Shepard Co.
--Next-Night Stories. Bridgman, Lewis Jesse (1857-1931), illus. LC 12-17515. 6 p. l., 3-261 p. front., illus., plates. 20 cm. 1912. Lothrop, Lee & Shepard Co.
--Next-Night Stories. Maurer, Adam C., illus. LC 11-147175. 5 p. l., 7-142 p. front., plates. 21 cm. 1911. Broadway Publishing Co.

Messer, Ronald Keith (1942-)
--Shumway. LC 74-34488. 190 p. 21cm. 1975. (ISBN 0-8407-6419-7). T. Nelson.

Messick, Dale
--Brenda Starr, Girl Reporter. authorized. Messick, Dale, illus. LC 44-835. (An original story based on the famous newspaper strip "Brenda Starr".) 20 1/2cm. 248p. 1943. Whitman Pub.

Messieres, Nicole de see De Messieres, Nicole.

Messmann, John
--Willie Whistle. Brady, William, illus. LC 42-17635. 24 p. illus. 26 cm. 1942. Harbinger House.

Messmer, Otto
--Felix the Cat. (gr. k-3). N.D. Wonder.

Meta
--Foolish Chrissy. (The Young Folks Ser.: No. 4). N.D. Fleming H. Revell Co.

Metcalf, Charles
--Honors Divided: Or, The Pirate's Lair. N.D. E. P. Dutton & Co.

Metcalf, John, compiled by.
--The Speaking Earth: Canadian Poetry. 1973. Von Nostrand.

Metcalf, Suzanne, pseud., see Baum, Lyman Frank.

Metcalf, Suzanne, pseud. (1856-1919)
--Annabel: A Novel for Young Folk. Baum, Lyman Frank. Nuyttens, Joseph Pierre, illus. LC 6-32106. 19cm. 231p. N.D. The Reilly & Britton Co.
--Annnabel: A Novel for Young Folk. Baum, Lyman Frank. Nuyttens, Joseph Pierre, illus. LC 12-13905. 213p. front., plates. 20cm. N.D. Reilly & Britton Co.

Metcalf, Vicky (1901-)
--Unwanted Legacy. Haas, Dorothy F. (1926-), illus. LC 54-41711. 195p. illus. 20cm. c.1953. Gospel Pub. House.
--Unwanted Legacy. Haas, Dorothy F. (1926-), illus. 164 p. 18cm. (Radiant books). 1976, c.1953. (ISBN 0-88243-623-6). Gospel Pub. House.

Metcalfe, Barry
--The Square Gang. 160p. (gr. 5 up). 1981. (ISBN 0-571-11681-7). Faber & Faber.

Metcalfe, J Powell & Stainer, J, eds.
--The School Round-Book: A Collection of One Hundred Rounds, Catches, and Canons. new and rev. ed. vi, 73 p. 20 cm. N.D. Novello, Ewer and Co.

Metcalfe, James J. (1906-)
--Poems for Children. McLean, Mina Gow, illus. LC 50-8351. (Illus.). 23cm. 48p. 1950. Garden City Pub. Co.

Metcalfe, William C.
--Aboveboard. N.D. Thomas Whittaker.
--Billows and Bergs. (The Treasure Library). N.D. Frederick Warne & Co.
--Steady Your Helm: Or, Stowed Away. N.D. Thomas Whittaker.

Meteyard, Eliza see Silverpen, pseud.

Meteyard, Eliza (1816-1879)
--The Delf Jug. Silverpen, pseud. (Illus.). N.D. Cassell & Co.
--The Doctor's Little Daughter. (Illus.). (Routledge's Welcome Series of Girls' Books). N.D. George Routledge & Sons.
--Dora and Her Papa. (Illus.). (Routledge's Welcome Series of Girls' Books). N.D. George Routledge & Sons.
--Lillian's Golden Hours. Absolon, illus. N.D. (Illus.). Routledge & Son.
--The Meteyard's Doctor's Little Daughter: A Book for Girls. (Illus.). N.D. George Routledge & Sons.

Meteyard, Peter
--Stanley, the Tale of the Lizard. Firmin, Peter (1928-), illus. LC 78-74466. (Illus.). 32 p. 26cm. 1979. (ISBN 0-233-97071-1). Deutsch.

Metheny, Mary E, Mrs.
--Philip St. John. LC 12-366280. 300 p. front., plates, 18 cm. c.1884. Presbyterian Board of Publication and Sabbath School Work.

Methley, Alice A, ed. see Cervantes Saavedra, Miguel de.

Methley, Violet M
--Derry Down-Under: A Story of Adventure in Australia. Lupton, L. F., illus. LC 45-22123. 236 p. front. 18 1/2 cm. c.1943. F. Warne & Co., Ltd.

Metro-Goldwyn-Mayer, Inc., illus.
--M-G-M's Tom and Jerry. LC 51-39074. unpaged. illus. 21 cm. (Little golden library, 117). 1951. Simon and Schuster.
--M-G-M's Tom and Jerry and the Toy Circus. authorized. LC 54-21759. unpaged. illus. 17 cm. (Tell-a-tale books, 933). 1954, c.1953. Whitman Pub. Co.
--M-G-M's Tom and Jerry and Their Friends. LC 50-7522. 125 p. col. illus. 18 cm. (Golden story book, 11). 1950. Simon and Schuster.
--M-G-M's Tom and Jerry in Model Mice. authorized. LC 52-16444. unpaged. illus. 17 cm. (Tell-a-tale books). c.1951. Whitman Pub. Co.
--M-G-M's Tom and Jerry in Tom's Happy Birthday. authorized. LC 55-40528. unpaged illus. 17 cm. (Tell-a-tale books, 2562). c.1955. Whitman Pub. Co.
--M-G-M's Tom and Jerry Meet Little Quack. LC 53-3482. unpaged. illus. 21 cm. (Little golden library, 181). 1953. Simon and Schuster.

Metropolitan Museum of Art (New York, N.Y.) see Koch, Kenneth (1925-) & Farrell, Kate.

Metropolitan Opera Guild see Johnston, Johanna.

Metropolitan Opera Guild see Verdi, Giuseppe.

Metz, Lois Lunt (1906-)
--Action Songs and Rhythms for Children. LC 62-18843. 110p. 29cm. c.1962. Denison.
--Hop, Skip, and Sing: A Collection of Twenty-Five Songs and Rhythms Based on the Interests and Activities of Children. LC 59-1033. 87 p. 29 cm. c.1959. T. S. Denison.

Metzdorf, Robert Frederic (1912-)
--Short Rhymes for a Little Girl. LC 41-4810. 211p. 11 x 14cm. 1940. Strever Hobby Press.

Metzger, Berta
--Picture Tales from India. Buchanan, Mina, illus. LC 42-22997. 87 p. illus. 14 x 18 1/2 cm. 1942. Frederick A. Stokes Company.
--Picture Tales from the Chinese. Lattimore, Eleanor Frances (1904-), illus. LC 34-30045. xii p., 1 l., 106, 3 p. incl. illus., plates. 14 x 19 cm. 1934. Fredrick A. Stokes Company.
--Tales Told in Hawaii. Tallman, Verna, illus. LC 29-17319. xii, 116 p. incl. front., illus. 22 cm. 1929. Frederick A. Stokes Company.
--Tales Told in Hawaii. Tallman, Verna, illus. N.D. J. B. Lippincott.
--Tales Told in India. Buchanan, Mina, illus. LC 36-3544. viii, 160 p. illus. 22 cm. 1935. H. Milford, Oxford University Press.
--Tales Told in Korea. Park, Arthur Y., illus. LC 32-23577. xvi p., 1 l., 247 p. incl. plates. col. front. 20 cm. 1932. Frederick A. Stokes Company.
--Tales told in Korea. Park, Arthur Y., illus. N.D. J. B. Lippincott.

Mewees, Tim
--Treehouse Gang to the Rescue. 32p. (Better Living Ser.). (ps). 1981. (ISBN 0-8127-0311-1). Review & Herald.

Meyer, Alice
--Through the Moon Gate. LC 55-24403. 23cm. 36p. 1954. Comet Press Books.

Meyer, Alma E
--Wassara and His Tale of the Far North. Bigham, John C., illus. LC 62-21412. (Illus.). 32 p. (Reading-go-round books). c.1962. E.C. Seale.

Meyer, Ann
--Nibby. Wiese, Kurt (1887-1974), illus. LC 52-10454. 26cm. 31p. 1952. Coward-McCann, Inc.

Meyer, Carolyn (1935-)
--C. C. Poindexter. LC 78-6102. 207 p. 22cm. 1978. (ISBN 0-689-50119-6). Atheneum.
--The Center: From a Troubled Past to a New Life. LC 79-12509. 216p. (gr. 9 up). 1979. (ISBN 0-689-50143-9, McElderry Bk). Atheneum.
--The Luck of Texas McCoy. LC 84-3061. 204p. (gr. 7 up). 1984. (ISBN 0-689-50312-1, McElderry Bk). Atheneum.
--The Needlework Book of Bible Stories. McCaffery, Janet, illus. LC 75-10135. (Illus.). 96p. (gr. 5 up). 1975. (ISBN 0-15-256793-3, HB). Harcourt.
--Rock Band: Big Men in a Great Big Town. LC 80-13349. 168p. (gr. 9 up). 1980. (ISBN 0-689-50181-1, McElderry Bk). Atheneum.
--The Summer I Learned About Life. LC 83-6390. p. cm. 1983. (ISBN 0-689-50285-0). Atheneum.

Meyer, Edith Paterson, jt. auth. see Loveland, Seymour.

Meyer, Edith Paterson (1895-)
--Bible Stories for Young Readers. Simon, Howard (1903-1979), illus. N.D. Abingdon Press.
--Three Guardsmen & Other Stories from the Apocrypha. Simon, Howard (1903-1979), illus. (Illus.). (gr. 5-10). 1960. (ISBN 0-687-41904-2). Abingdon.
--Tim Chick. Ward, Keith, illus. LC 32-16247. 42 p. col. illus. 23 cm. c.1932. Rand, McNally & Company.

Meyer, Edith Paterson (1895-), retold by.
--Stories From the Bible-New Testament. Linge, Lis, illus. N.D. Grosset & Dunlap.

Meyer, Elizabeth Cooper (1958-)
--The Blue China Pitcher. Meyer, Elizabeth Cooper (1958-), illus. LC 73-15935. (Illus.). 25 p. 21cm. 1974. (ISBN 0-687-03625-9). Abingdon Press.

Meyer, Franklyn Edward (1932-)
--Me & Caleb. Smith, Lawrence Beall (1909-), illus. LC 62-156698. (Illus.). (gr. 4-6). 1962. (ISBN 0-695-45640-7). Follett.
--Me and Caleb Again. Liese, Charles, illus. LC 69-19423. (Illus.). 185 p. 23cm. 1969. Follett Pub. Co.

Meyer, Josephine Amelia (1884-)
--The Green E: A High School Story. Meyer, Josephine Amelia (1884-), illus. LC 12-24820. 5 p. l., 315, 1 p. front., plates. 19 cm. 1912. Harper & Brothers.

Meyer, Kathleen Allan
--God Sends the Seasons. McIlrath, James, illus. LC 81-80712. (Illus.). 32 p. 27cm. c.1981. (ISBN 0-87973-668-2). Our Sunday Visitor.
--The Time to Sleep Book. Ruth, Rod (1912-), illus. (Illus.). (gr. k-2). 1978. (ISBN 0-307-68889-5, Golden Pr). Western Pub.

Meyer, Lewis
--The Tipsy Witch & Other Fairy Tales. LC 74-11183. (Illus.). 160p. (gr. 1 up). 1974. (ISBN 0-07-041743-1, GB). McGraw.

Meyer, Lois
--The Store-Bought Doll. Sanderson, Ruth, illus. LC 82-83070. (Illus.). 24p. (Little Golden Bk.). (ps-2). 1983. (ISBN 0-307-02044-4, Golden Pr). (ISBN 0-307-60193-5). Western Pub.

Meyer, Louis Albert Jr. (1942-)
--The Clean Air and Peaceful Contentment Dirigible Airline. 1st ed. Meyer, Louis Albert, Jr. (1942-), illus. LC 73-169011. (Illus.). 47 p. 1972. Little, Brown.
--The Gypsy Bears. Meyer, Louis Albert, Jr. (1942-), illus. LC 73-129904. (Illus.). 51 p. 27cm. 1971. Little, Brown.

Meyer, Lucy Jane Rider, Mrs. (1849-1922)
--The Fairy Land of Chemistry: Or, Real Fairy Folks. N.D. Lothrop Publishing Co.
--Real Fairy Folks: Explorations in the World of Atoms. LC 12-36587. 3 p. l., xi-xiv, 15-389 p. front., illus. 19 cm. c.1887. D. Lothrop and Company.

Meyer, Lynn
--Paperback Thriller. 1975. (ISBN 0-394-49767-8). Random.

Meyer, Margaret
--Mei Ling's Mountain. LC 68-31698. vii, 116 p. 21cm. 1968. Chilton Book Co.

Meyer, Mildred Elizabeth
--Four on an Island. Norris, Homer, illus. LC 66-5279. 125p. illus. 21cm. c.1966. Southern Pub.

Meyer, Renate (1930-)
--Hide-and-Seek: A Picture Book. LC 70-174350. 25 p. (p. 2-25 col. illus. 1972, c.1969. (ISBN 0-87888-039-9). Bradbury Press.
--Vicki. Meyer, Renate (1930-), illus. LC 69-11859. (Illus.). 26cm. 28p. (ps-3). 1969. (ISBN 0-689-20276-8). (ISBN 0-689-20277-6). Atheneum.

Meyer-Rey, Ingeborg
--The Silly Goose. Meyer-Rey, Ingeborg, illus. LC 73-103605. (Illus.). 24 p 24cm. 1971. (ISBN 0-87614-011-8). Carolrhoda Books.

Meyer, Rosemary
--Wendy's World. 1982. (ISBN 0-533-05146-0). Vantage.

Meyer, Zoe
--Flowers of the Trail. N.D. Little Brown & Co.
--Followers of the Trail. Stecher, William Frederick (1864-), illus. LC 26-12230. viii p., 1 l., 217 p. incl. illus., plates. front. 20 cm. 1926. Little, Brown, and Company.
--The Garden of Happiness. Atwood, Clara E., illus. (Illus.). 19cm. 172p. 1923. Little Brown & Co.
--The Little Green Door. Atwood, Clara E., illus. LC 21-269863. 3 p. l., 3-157 p. col. front., illus. 19 cm. 1921. Little, Brown, and Company.
--Orchard and Meadow. 143p. N.D. Little Brown.
--Stories from The Dawn-Breakers. (Illus.). (gr. 3-5). 1955. (ISBN 0-87743-035-7). Baha'i.
--Sunshine Farm. Young, Florence Liley, illus. LC 27-26864. vi, 159 p. col. front., illus. 19 cm. 1927. Little, Brown, and Company.
--Under the Blue Sky. Atwood, Clara E., illus. (Illus.). 19cm. 123p. 1917. Little Brown & Co.
--Under the Maple Tree. Young, Florence Liley, illus. LC 27-100723. vi, 159 p. col. front. illus. 19 cm. 1927. Little, Brown, and Company.

The, Meyers, illus.
--Mother Goose in Five Languages. Harold, Margaret, ed. 1964. Allied Publications, Inc.

Meyers, Bernice
--Charlie's Birthday Present. Meyers, Bernice, illus. (Illus., Orig.). (gr. k-3). 1981. (ISBN 0-590-31992-2). Scholastic Inc.
--Not This Bear. Meyers, Bernice, illus (Illus.). (gr. k-3). 1971. (ISBN 0-590-01556-7). (ISBN 0-590-20741-5). Scholastic Inc.

Meyers, Bernice & Meyers, Lou, illus.
--Puss-In-Boots. (Illus.). (ps-k). 1969. (ISBN 0-528-88886-2). Rand.

Meyers, Gertrude Barlow (1902-)
--The Blue Runner. LC 60-70366. 205p. 21cm. 1960. Westminster Press.
--Fireball. LC 56-8521. 208 p. 21cm. 1956. Westminster Press.
--Last of the Wild Stallions. N.D. The Westminster Press.
--Struggle at Saddle Bow. LC 54-6430. 236p. 21cm. 1954. Westminster Press.
--Tumbleweed. LC 52-7256. 192 p. illus. 22 cm. 1952. Westminster Press.

Meyers, Lou
--Tutti-Frutti. Myers, Lou, illus. (Illus.). (gr. 1-3). 1967. (ISBN 0-394-81773-7). Pantheon.

Meyers, Ruth S. & Banfield, Beryle, eds.
--Embers: Stories for a Changing World. LC 82-73499. (Illus.). 168p. 1st U.S. edition. (gr. 3-7). 1983. (ISBN 0-935312-16-1). (ISBN 0-935312-17-X). Feminist Press.

Meyers, Susan (1942-)
--The Cabin on the Fjord. 1st ed. Hyman, Trina Schart (1939-), illus. LC 68-22467. (Illus.). 128 p. 25cm. 1968. Doubleday.
--Melissa Finds a Mystery. LC 66-9225. 143 p. 21cm. 1966. Dodd, Mead.
--The Mysterious Bender Bones. 1st ed. Ohlsson, Ib (1935-), illus. LC 79-87974. (Illus.). 119 p. 22cm. 1970. Doubleday.
--Pearson, a Harbor Seal Pup. Hartmann, Ilka, illus. LC 80-13041. (Illus.). 64p. (gr. 3-7). 1980. Dutton.
--P.J. Clover, Private Eye: The Case of the Stolen Laundry. LC 81-14183. 127 p. 20cm. c.1981. (ISBN 0-671-44325-9). Messner.
--P.J. Clover, Private Eye: The Case of the Stolen Laundry. LC 81-7611. p. cm. 1981. (ISBN 0-671-43360-1). Wanderer Books.

Meyler, Eileen
--The Gloriet Tower. Walker, Monica, illus. LC 57-10698. 131p. illus. 21cm. N.D. Roy Publishers.
--The Story of Elswyth. Walker, Monica, illus. LC 59-13393. 136p. illus. 20cm. 1959. Roy Publishers.

Meynell, Alice Christina Gertrude Thompson, Mrs. (1847-1922), ed.
--The School of Poetry: An Anthology Chosen for Young Readers. 241, 1 p. front. (port.) 21 cm. 1924. Charles Scribner's Sons.

Meynell, Francis, ed.
--Memorable Poetry. (gr. 7 up). 1966. (ISBN 0-531-01725-7). Watts.

Meynell, Laurence Walter see Tring, Stephen, pseud.

Meynell, Laurence Walter (1899-)
--Bridge Under the Water: A Story of the Age of Steam. Goodall, S., illus. 158p. illus. 21cm. (Pageant books). 1957. Roy Publishers.
--Young Master: A Boy in the Reign of Edward III. Tring, Stephen, pseud. Jessell, Alan, illus. LC 57-9674. arver. (Pageant books). N.D. Roy Publishers.

Meynier, Gil (1902-), tr. see Malot, Hector Henri.

Meyst, Lucille
--Legend of the Silver Hoofs. 128p. (gr. 4-6). 1973. (ISBN 0-8024-3470-3). Moody.

--Tyler Lane and the Gold Nugget Mystery. LC 76-4808. 126 p. 18cm. c.1976. (ISBN 0-8024-3849-0). Moody Press.
--Tyler Lane & the Wolf Dog Mystery. 87p. (gr. 9 up). 1971. Beacon Hill.
--The Watch Goat Mystery. 128p. (Preteen Ser.). (gr. 4-8). 1974. (ISBN 0-8024-4914-X). Moody.

Mezger, Max (1876-)
--Monica Goes to Madagascar. Wilkins, Hugo, illus. Darnton, Maida Castelhun, Mrs., tr. LC 36-19436. 252 p. incl. front., illus. 22 cm. c.1936. Coward, McCann, Inc.

Mezieres, Jean-Claude, jt. auth. see Christin, Pierre.

M. H. S.
--Mollie's Christmas Stocking and Other Stories. N.D. E P Dutton & Co.

Mian, Mary Lawrence Shipman
--The Net to Catch War. LC 74-29444. vii, 241 p. 22cm. 1975. (ISBN 0-395-20491-7). Houghton Mifflin.
--Nip and Tuck War. 1964. E M Hale.
--The Nip and Tuck War. Krush, Beth (1918-) & Krush, Joe (1918-), illus. LC 64-14520. 156 p. illus. 22 cm. 1964. Houghton-Mifflin.
--Take Three Witches. Von Schmidt, Eric (1931-), illus. LC 70-142825. (Illus.). 279 p. 22cm. 1971. (ISBN 0-395-12368-2). Houghton Mifflin.

Michael, Maurice Albert
--Fairy Tales from Germany. (Illus.). 1957. Dufour.

Michael, Maurice Albert & Michael, Pamela
--Fairy Tales from Bohemia. Lathey, John, illus. LC 68-13804. (Illus.). 182 p. 23cm. (World fairy tale collections). 1968, c.1966. Follett Pub. Co.
--German Folk and Fairy Tales. Jauss, Anne Marie (1907-), illus. 189 p. illus. 22 cm. (folk and fairy tales from many lands. 1st U.S. edition. 1963, c.1958. Putnam.
--Portuguese Fairy Tales. Toothill, Ilse & Toothill, Harry, illus. LC 67-5920. (Illus.). 185 p. 23cm. (World fairy tale collections). 1967, c.1965. Follett Pub. Co.

Michael, Pamela, jt. auth. see Michael, Maurice Albert.

Michael Cervantes, Esther De & Cervantes, Alex
--Senora Pepino and Her Bad Luck Cats: Senora Pepino y Sus Gatos De Mala Suerte. Cervantes, Alex, illus. Cervantes, Alex, tr. LC 76-4818. (Illus.). 39 p. 24cm. 1976. (ISBN 0-87917-052-2). B. Ethridge-Books.

Michaelis-Jena, Ruth
--Scottish Folk Tales. Breheny, Thomas R., illus. LC 77-359302. (Illus.). 144 p. 23cm. 1977. (ISBN 0-584-62393-3). Muller.

Michaelis, Karin, pseud., see Stangeland, Katharina Maria Bech Brondum Michaelis.

Michaelis, Karin, pseud. (1872-)
--Bibi: A Little Danish Girl. Stangeland, Katharina Maria Bech Brondum Michaelis. Bibi & Collin, Hedvig, illus. Hanson, Lida Siboni, tr. LC 27-24343. viii p., 1 l., 357, 1 p. incl. illus., plates col. front., col. plates 22 cm. 1927. Doubleday, Page & Company.
--Bibi: A Little Danish Girl. Stangeland, Katharina Maria Bech Brondum Michaelis. Bibi & Collin, Hedvig, illus. Hanson, Lida Siboni, tr. LC 39-181643. viii p., 1 l., 355, 1 p. incl. illus., plates. front. 21 cm. (Young moderns books). 1936. Doubleday, Doran & Company, Inc.

Michaelis-Jena, Ruth, ed. see Grimm, Jakob Ludwig Karl (1785-1863) & Grimm, Wilhelm Karl.

Michaelis-Jena, Ruth, tr. see Ditzen, Rudolf.

Michaelis-Jena, Ruth, tr. see Voegeli, Max.

Michaels, Barbara, pseud., see Mertz, Barbara Gross.

Michaels, Barbara, pseud. (1927-)
--Master of Blacktower. Mertz, Barbara Gross. (gr. 7-9). 1966. Hawthorn.
--Prince of Darkness. Mertz, Barbara Gross. (gr. 7-9). 1969. (ISBN 0-696-75821-0). Hawthorn.
--Sons of the Wolf. Mertz, Barbara Gross. (gr. 7-9). 1967. Hawthorn.

Michaels, Mike
--What's the Matter with That Dog. LC 69-20498. (Illus.). 64p. (Easy Readers Ser). (gr. 1-3). 1969. Wonder.
--What's the Matter with That Dog?. Wood, Ruth, illus. LC 69-20498. (Illus.). 61 p. 22cm. (Easy reader). 1969. Grosset & Dunlap.

Michaels, Philip Verrill (1869-1911)
--The Crystal Sceptre: A Story of Adventure. LC 1-15262. 389p. 1901. R. F. Fenno & Co.

Michajluk, Elizabeth Jane see Brinhart, Betty, pseud.

Michajluk, Elizabeth Jane (1922-)
--Golden Men of Mitas Town. Brinhart, Betty, pseud. LC 53-20940. 160p. 21cm. 1952. Pageant Press.

Michalkow, Sergej
--Naughty Little Kid. Nast, Bernhard, illus. LC 70-86133. (Illus.). 32p. 1st U.S. edition. (Easy-Reading Picture Story Book). (gr. k-3). 1969. (ISBN 0-516-03552-5). Childrens.

Michel, Bernard E.
--The Belfry That Moved and Other Stories Based on American Moravian History. Wolff, Ted, illus. LC 60-23471. 64p. illus. 20cm. 1959. Comenius Press.

Michel, Dana
--Cat in the Box. Rev ed. Welcher, Rosalind (1922-), illus. LC 63-18951. 61 p. col. illus. 22 cm. 1963. Grosset & Dunlap.

Michel, Emilie Louise (1909-)
--Tales from the Elves Forest. Heaton-Sessions, Charlotte, illus. LC 50-8069. 138p. illus. 34cm. 1950. Caxton Printers.

Michel, Sandra Seaton (1935-), ed. see Smith, Viola B.

Michell, Gladys Turley
--Through My Window. LC 54-36458. unpaged. illus. 21cm. (Cosy-corner-book). c.1954. Whitman Pub. Co.
--When We Grow Up. Michell, Gladys Turley, illus. LC 44-5933. 24 x 19 cm. 32p. 1943. A. Whitman & Co.

Michell, Mrs.
--The Diamond Ring. (Illus.). N.D. E & J B Young.

Michels, Barbara & White, Bettye
--Apples on Stick: The Folklore of Black Children. Pinkney, Jerry (1939-), illus. LC 82-14385. p. cm. 1983. (ISBN 0-698-20567-7). Coward, McCann & Geoghegan.

Michels, Tilde
--No Zoo Without Mumba. (gr. 4-6). N.D. (ISBN 0-448-02100-5). (ISBN 0-448-25997-4). G&D.
--Sophie the Rag Picker. (gr. k-1). N.D. G&D.
--Sophie the Rag Picker. Scholss, Lisolette L. (1928-) & Fromm, Lilo, illus. 24p. (gr. k-1). 1962. (ISBN 0-8392-3036-2). Astor Company.

Michels, Tilde & Fromm, Lilo
--No Zoo Without Mumba. LC 62-16991. unpaged. illus. 29 cm. 1962. Norton.

Michelson, Florence B
--The Defiant Heart. LC 64-12912. 288 p. 20 cm. (Whitman teen novels). 1964. Whitman Pub. Co.

Michener, James Albert (1907-)
--The Bridges at Toko-Ri. (gr. 10 up). 1953. (ISBN 0-394-41780-1). Random.

Michl, Reinhard
--A Day on the River. LC 85-18551. p. cm. 1986, c.1985. (ISBN 0-8120-3644-1). Barron's.

Micklish, Rita (1931-)
--Sugar Bee. Lewin, Ted (1935-), illus. LC 78-176034. (Illus.). 195 p. 24cm. 1972. Delacorte Press.

Micocci, Harriet Palmer
--Captain Orkle's Treasure. (gr. 4-6). N.D. G&D.
--Captain Orkle's Treasure. Dora, illus. (Illus.). (gr. 3-7). 1961. (ISBN 0-8392-3003-6). Astor-Honor.
--Captain Orkle's Treasure. Dora, illus. LC 61-9933. 153p. illus. 26cm. (Astor book). 1961. I. Obolensky.

Middleton, Charles
--Two Little Patriots and the Declaration of Independence. Vitelli, Ferdinand, illus. LC 39-22341. (Illus.). 30cm. 36p. 1939. Bystander Press.

Middleton, Don
--Roy Rogers and the Gopher Creek Gunman: An Original Story Featuring Roy Rogers, Famous Motion Picture Star, As the Hero. authorized. Hess, Erwin L., illus. LC 45-105935. 3 p. l., 11-248 p. illus. 20 cm. 1945. Whitman Publishing Company.

Middleton, Leella
--Chick-Chick. N.D. Carlton Press.

Middleton, Lilian
--Christmas Comes to Michael. N.D. Bruce Humpries.

Middleton, Martha
--Sainthood for Rex. (Illus.). (gr. 3-8). 1980. (ISBN 0-89554-025-8). Brasch & Brasch.

Mido, pseud., see Reznikoff, Dominique.

Miers, Earl S., ed. see Malkus, Alida Wright Sims, Mrs.

Miers, Earl Schenck, ed. see Sutton, Felix.

Miers, Earl Schenck (1910-1972)
--The Backfield Feud. Beebe, Robb (1891-), illus. LC 36-18565. xi p., 1 l., 302 p. incl. front., illus., plates. 19 1/2 cm. 1936. D. Appleton-Century Company, Incorporated.
--Ball of Fire. 1st ed. Galdone, Paul (1914-), illus. LC 56-5316. 220p. illus. 21cm. 1956. World Pub. Co.
--Big Ben. N.D. The Westminster Press.
--Billy Yank and Johnny Reb. 1959. (ISBN 0-8382-0083-4, Cadmus Books). E. M. Hale and Company.
--Career Coach. LC 41-928119. 258 p. illus. 19 1/2 cm. 1941. The Westminster Press.
--The Guns of Vicksburg. LC 57-12215. (Illus.). 187 p. 21cm. 1958, c.1957. Putnam.
--The Ivy Years. LC 45-35116. xiv, 229 p. 21 cm. 1945. Rutgers University Press.
--The Kid Who Beat the Dodgers, and Other Sports Stories. 1st ed. Galdone, Paul (1914-), illus. LC 54-8171. 190p. illus. 21cm. 1954. World Pub. Co.
--The Magnificent Mutineers. Mars, Witold Tadeusz J. (1912-), illus. LC 68-15067. (Illus.). 124 p. 21cm. 1968. Putnam.
--Mark Twain on the Mississippi. 1st ed. Frankenberg, Robert Clinton (1911-), illus. LC 57-5892. (Illus.). 246 p. 22cm. 1957. World Pub. Co.
--Monkey Shines, a Baseball Story. 1st ed. Galdone, Paul (1914-), illus. LC 52-8423. 207 p. illus. 21 cm. 1952. World Pub. Co.
--The Night We Stopped the Trolley. 128p. 1969. Four Winds Press.
--Pirate Chase. Burchard, Peter Duncan (1921-), illus. LC 65-12791. (Illus., Orig.). (Younger Readers Ser). (gr. 4-7). 1965. (ISBN 0-910412-69-3). Colonial Williamsburg.
--Pirate Chase. Colonial Williamsburg. Burchard, Peter Duncan (1921-), illus. LC 65-12791. 129p. illus. 24cm. c.1965. (ISBN 0-03-051035-X). Holt.
--The Story of Thomas Jefferson. Pollak, Reynold C., illus. LC 55-10740. (Illus.). 179 p. 22cm. (Signature books, 36). 1955. Grosset & Dunlap.
--Touchdown Trouble. 1st ed. Galdone, Paul (1914-), illus. LC 53-6642. 221p. illus. 21cm. 1953. World Pub. Co.
--We Were There When Grant Met Lee at Appomattox. Catton, Bruce (1899-1978), ed. Vosburgh, Leonard W. (1912-), illus. LC 60-52136. 176p. illus. 22cm. (We were there books, 23). 1960. (ISBN 0-448-05023-4). Grosset & Dunlap.
--We Were There When Washington Won at Yorktown. Rankin, Hugh Franklin (1913-), ed. Vestal, Herman B., illus. LC 58-5701. 176p. illus. 22cm. (We were there books, 17). 1958. (ISBN 0-448-05017-X). Grosset & Dunlap.
--We Were There with Lincoln in the White House. Castellon, Federico (1914-), illus. (Illus.). (gr. 4-8). 1963. (ISBN 0-448-05036-6). G&D.
--We Were There with Lincoln in the White House. Geer, Charles Hand (1922-), illus. LC 63-3697. (Historical Consultant: Joseph Allan Nevins). 179 p. illus. 22 cm. (We were there books, 36). 1963. Grosset & Dunlap.
--Yankee Doodle Dandy. 1963. Rand McNally Publication.

Mies Bouhys
--Broken Jug. Lichtveld, Noni, illus. (Illus.). (Bibletimes Ser.: Vol. 4). (gr. 9-12). 1969. (ISBN 0-8091-6501-5). Paulist Pr.
--Wise Men of the East. Lichtveld, Noni, illus. (Illus.). (Bibletimes Ser.: No. 1). (gr. 9-12). 1969. (ISBN 0-8091-6524-4). Paulist Pr.

Miescke, Lori
--Shaggy Dog Riddles. Karas, G. Brian, illus. LC 83-16743. p. cm. 1983. (ISBN 0-8075-7329-9). A. Whitman.

Miessner, William Otto
--Play for Me: Original Melodies. LC 45-14250. cover-title, 63, 1 p. illus. 23 x 31 cm. 1944. McKinley Publishers, Inc.
--Sing to Me. La Mont, Violet, illus. LC 45-14266. 63, 1 p. illus. 23 x 31 cm. c.1944. McKinley Publishers Inc.

Mighels, Ella Sterling Clark, Mrs. (1853-)
--Fairy Tale of the White Man: Told from the Gates of Sunset. Briggs, W. Kimball, illus. LC 16-2212. 5 p. l., 13-72 p. illus. 24 cm. $1.00. 1915. Pacific Publication Company.

Mighels, Philip Verrill (1869-1911)
--Adventures with Indians. LC 8-3518. xp., 2 l., 233, 1 pl. 18 1/2 cm. (On verse of l.-p.: Harper's adventure series). 1908. Harper & Brothers.
--When a Witch is Young: A Historical Novel. LC 1-15263. 442p. 1901. R. F. Fenno & Co.

Mighels, Philip Verrill (1869-1911) & Stoddard, W O
--Boy's Book of Indians. LC 24-26908. x p., 1 l., 243 p. front., plates. 20 cm. 1924. Harper & Brothers.

Mikhalkov, Sergei Vladimirovich (1913-)
--Jolly Hares. 118p. 1969. (ISBN 0-8285-1170-5, Pub. by Progress Pubs USSR). Imported Pubns.
--Let's Fight and Other Russian Fables. Foreman, Michael (1938-), illus. Daniels, Guy, tr. LC 68-24561. 54p. col. illus. 23cm. 1968. (ISBN 0-394-81304-9). Pantheon Books.
--The Naughty Little Kid. american ed. Koenig, Marion, adapted by. Nast, Bernhard, illus. LC 70-86133. (Illus.). 30 p. 27cm. 1969, c.1967. Childrens Press.

Miklowitz, Gloria D., jt. auth. see Young, Wesley A.

Miklowitz, Gloria D (1927-)
--Barefoot Boy. Collins, Jim (1934-), illus. LC 64-21040. (Illus.). 29 p. 21cm. (Follett beginning-to-read books). 1964. Follett Pub. Co.
--Close to the Edge. LC 82-72817. p. cm. c.1983. (ISBN 0-440-00990-1). Delacorte Press.
--The Day the Senior Class Got Married: A Novel. LC 83-5343. 157 p. 22cm. c.1983. (ISBN 0-385-29304-6). Delacorte Press.
--Did You Hear What Happened to Andrea?. LC 78-72972. 168 p. 22cm. c.1979. (ISBN 0-440-01923-0). Delacorte Press.
--The Love Bombers. LC 80-65836. 199 p. 21cm. c.1980. (ISBN 0-440-04640-8). Delacorte Press.
--The Marshmallow Caper. Pelavin, Cheryl (1946-), illus. LC 72-156319. (Illus.). 48 p. 23cm. (See and read beginning to read storybook). 1971. (ISBN 0-399-60449-9). Putnam.
--Sad Song, Happy Song. Thollander, Earl Gustave (1922-), illus. LC 70-187137. (Illus.). 32 p. 23cm. (See and read beginning to read book). 1973. (ISBN 0-399-20304-4). (ISBN 0-399-20304-4). Putnam.
--Save That Raccoon!. St. Tamara, pseud., illus. Kolba, St. Tamara. LC 77-12031. (Illus.). 48 p. 22cm. (Let me read book). c.1978. (ISBN 0-15-270241-5). (ISBN 0-15-679476-4). Harcourt Brace Jovanovich.
--A Time to Hurt, a Time to Heal. (Orig.). (gr. 6 up). 1974. (ISBN 0-448-05771-9, Tempo). G&D.
--Turning off. LC 72-76739. 128 p. 22cm. 1972, c.1973. (ISBN 0-399-20260-9). (ISBN 0-399-20260-9). Putnam.
--The War Between the Classes. LC 84-19883. 158 p. 22cm. c.1985. (ISBN 0-385-29375-5). Delacorte Press.
--The Zoo That Moved. Madden, Donald B. (1927-), illus. LC 68-13791. (Illus.). 32 p. 22cm. 1968. Follett Pub. Co.

Miklowitz, Gloria D. (1927-) & Desbery, Peter
--Ghastly Ghostly Riddles. Ross, David (1949-), illus. (gr. 5-8). 1978. (ISBN 0-590-11849-8, Schol Pap). Scholastic Inc.

Miklowitz, Gloria D (1927-) & Madden, Donald B. (1927-)
--The Parade Starts at Noon. LC 68-22263. (Illus.). 43 p. 23cm. (See and read beginning to read book). 1970, c.1969. Putnam.

Mikolaycak, Charles, ed. see Asbjornsen, Peter Christen (1812-1885) & Moe, Jorgen Engebretsen.

Mikolaycak, Charles (1937-), retold by.
--Baboushak: An Old Russian Tale. Mikolaycak, Charles (1937-), illus. LC 84-500. (Illus.). 32p. 1984. (ISBN 0-8234-0520-6). (ISBN 0-8234-0520-6). Holiday House. **Award: (NYT).**

Mikolaycak, Charles (1937-), illus.
--Little Red Riding-Hood. (Illus.). 24 p. 19cm. (Stardust books). 1968. C. R. Gibson Co.

Miksch, M. K.
--Curtain Raisers. 124p. N.D. Northwestern Press.

Mikulova, Milada, illus.
--Coppelia. (Illus.). color ils. 64p. (Curtain-Raiser Bks). (gr. 4-6). 1971. (ISBN 0-531-01926-8). Watts.

Mikura, Vera Ferra (1923-)
--Twelve People Are Not a Dozen. Kennedy, Paul Edward (1929-), illus. Hutter, Catherine, tr. from Ger. LC 65-21398. 121p. illus. 22cm. 1965. Bobbs.

Milan, Helen
--The Little Ladies. Harding, Emily J., illus. (Illus.). N.D. J. B. Lippincott Co.

Milcsik, Margie (1950-)
--Cupid Computer. LC 81-2045. p. cm. 1981. (ISBN 0-689-30855-8). Atheneum.

Miler, Warren
--Pablo Paints a Picture. 1st ed. Sorel, Edward (1929-), illus. LC 59-5284. unpaged. illus. 20x26cm. 1959. Little, Brown. **Award: (NYT).**

Miles, Alfred H.
--Fifty-two More Stories for Boys. N.D. D. Appleton & Co.
--Fifty-two More Stories for girls. N.D. D. Appleton & Co.
--Fifty-two Stories for Boys. N.D. D. Appleton & Co.
--Fifty-two Stories for Girls. N.D. D. Appleton & Co.
--The Sweep of the Sword. N.D. D. Appleton & Co.

Miles, Bernard (1907-)
--Favorite Tales from Shakespeare. 1984 school and library ed. Ambrus, Victor G., pseud. (1935-), illus. Ambrus, Gyozo Laszlo. LC 84-21344. (Illus.). 125 p. 29cm. 1984, c.1976. (ISBN 0-516-09840-3). Childrens Press Choice.
--Favorite Tales from Shakespeare. Ambrus, Victor G., pseud. (1935-), illus. Ambrus, Gyozo Laszlo. LC 76-58597. (Illus.). (gr. 5-9). 1977. (ISBN 0-528-82100-8). Rand.
--Robin Hood, His Life and Legend. school and library ed. Ambrus, Victor G., pseud. (1935-), illus. Ambrus, Gyozo Laszlo. LC 84-20063. (Illus.). 125 p. 29cm. 1984, c.1979. (ISBN 0-516-09841-1). Childrens Press Choice.
--Robin Hood, His Life and Legend. Ambrus, Victor G, pseud. (1935-), illus. Ambrus, Gyozo Laszlo. LC 79-64615. (Illus.). 125 p. 29cm. 1979. (ISBN 0-528-82340-X). Rand McNally.

--Robin Hood: His Life & Legend. Ambrus, Victor G., pseud. (1935-), illus. Ambrus, Gyozo Laszlo. LC 79-64615. (Illus.). (gr. 4 up). N.D. (ISBN 0-528-82340-X). Rand.

Miles, Betty (1928-)

--All It Takes Is Practice. LC 76-13057. 101 p. 22cm. c.1976. (ISBN 0-394-83325-2). Knopf.

--A Day of Autumn. Auerbach, Marjorie Hoffberg (1932-), illus. LC 67-15800. (Illus.). 22 cm. 1967. Borzoi Books.

--A Day of Spring. Auerbach, Marjorie Hoffberg (1932-), illus. LC 78-94008. (Illus.). 32p. 22cm. 1970. Knopf.

--A Day of Summer. Remy, Charlip, illus. LC 60-5506. 23cm. 1960. Borzoi Books.

--A Day of Winter. Remy, Charlip, illus. LC 61-12307. 23cm. 1961. Borzoi Books.

--The Feast on Sullivan Street. Werth, Kurt (1896-), illus. LC 63-9102. (Illus.). 22 cm. 48p. 1963. Borzoi Books.

--Having a Friend. Blegvad, Erik (1923-), illus. LC 59-10024. unpaged. illus. 19cm. 1959. Knopf.

--A House for Everyone. Lowry, Jo, illus. LC 58-5349. unpaged. illus. 28cm. 1958. Knopf.

--A House for Everyone. Lowry, Jo, illus. LC 72-9558. (Illus.). 32 p. 23cm. 1973. c.1958. (ISBN 0-394-82618-3). Random House.

--I Would If I Could. LC 81-8458. 128p. (gr. 3-6). 1982. (ISBN 0-394-93929-8). (ISBN 0-394-83929-3). Knopf.

--Just the Beginning. LC 75-28454. 143 p. 22cm. c.1976. (ISBN 0-394-83226-4). (ISBN 0-394-93226-9). Knopf.

--Looking on: A Novel. LC 77-15946. 187 p. 22cm. c.1978. (ISBN 0-394-83582-4). (ISBN 0-394-93582-9). Knopf : Distributed by Random House.

--Maudie and Me and the Dirty Book. LC 79-19783. 144 p. 22cm. c.1980. (ISBN 0-394-84343-6). (ISBN 0-394-94343-0). Knopf : Distributed by Random House.

--Mister Turtle's Mystery. Tomes, Jacqueline, illus. LC 60-13025. (Illus.). (Read Alone Bk). (gr. k-3). 1961. (ISBN 0-394-91426-0). Knopf.

--The Real Me. LC 74-160. 122 p. 22cm. 1974. (ISBN 0-394-82838-0). (ISBN 0-394-82838-0). Knopf; Distributed by Random House.

--The Secret Life of the Underwear Champ. Jones, Dan (1948-), illus. LC 80-15651. (Illus.). 117 p. 20cm. (Capers). c.1981. (ISBN 0-394-84563-3). (ISBN 0-394-94563-8). Knopf.

--The Trouble with Thirteen. LC 78-31678. 108 p. 22cm. c.1979. (ISBN 0-394-83930-7). (ISBN 0-394-93930-1). Knopf ; Distributed by Random House.

Miles, Betty (1928-) & Blos, Joan Winsor (1928-)

--Just Think. 1st ed. Porter, Patricia Grant, illus. LC 77-151848. (Illus.). 40 p. 27cm. 1971. (ISBN 0-394-92290-5). Knopf.

Miles, H. A.

--A Boy Hero: A Story Founded on Fact. 22p. 1884. J. B. Young & Co.

Miles, H. I. A.

--The Old, Old Story. 40p. 1885. A. D. F. Randolph & Co.

Miles, Mary Patricia

--Mind Pirates. 160p. (gr. 5-9). 1984. (ISBN 0-241-10989-2, Pub. by Hamish Hamilton England). David & Charles.

Miles, Mary Patricia (1930-)

--A Disturbing Influence. LC 79-14234. 160 p. 22cm. c.1979. (ISBN 0-688-41911-9). (ISBN 0-688-51911-3). Lothrop, Lee & Shepard Co.

--The Gods in Winter. LC 77-16704. 140 p. 22cm. 1978. (ISBN 0-525-30748-6). E. P. Dutton.

--Nobody's Child. LC 75-13688. 149 p. 22cm. 1975. (ISBN 0-525-36020-4). Dutton.

Miles, Miska, pseud., see Martin, Patricia Miles.

Miles, Miska, jt. auth. see Clymer, Theodore.

Miles, Miska, pseud. (1899-)

--Aaron's Door. Martin, Patricia Miles. 1st ed. Cober, Alan Edwin (1935-), illus. LC 76-41159. (Illus.). 46 p. 25cm. c.1977. (ISBN 0-316-57017-6). Little, Brown.

--Annie and the Old One. Martin, Patricia Miles. 1st ed. Parnall, Peter (1936-), illus. LC 79-129900. (Illus.). 44 p. 24cm. 1971. Little, Brown. **Awards: (ALA); (JNM).**

--Apricot ABC. Martin, Patricia Miles. 1st ed. Parnall, Peter (1936-), illus. LC 68-22072. (Illus.). 32 p. 1969. Little, Brown.

--Beaver Moon. Martin, Patricia Miles. 1st ed. Schoenherr, John Carl (1935-), illus. LC 77-20921. (Illus.). 31 p. 27cm. c.1978. (ISBN 0-316-57018-4). Little, Brown.

--Chicken Forgets. Martin, Patricia Miles. 1st ed. Arnosky, Jim (1946-), illus. LC 76-12458. (Illus.). 31 p. 23cm. c.1976. (ISBN 0-316-56972-0). Little, Brown.

--Dusty & the Fiddlers. Martin, Patricia Miles. 1st ed. Blegvad, Erik (1923-), illus. LC 62-12382. (Illus.). 52 p. 22cm. 1962. Little, Brown.

--Eddie's Bear. Martin, Patricia Miles. 1st ed. Schoenherr, John Carl (1935-), illus. LC 74-97147. (Illus.). 43 p. 1970. Little, Brown.

--The Fox and the Fire. Martin, Patricia Miles. 1st ed. Schoenherr, John Carl (1935-), illus. LC 66-10820. (Illus.). 40 p. 1966. Little, Brown. **Award: (ALA).**

--Gertrude's Pocket. Martin, Patricia Miles. 1st ed. McCully, Emily Arnold (1939-), illus. LC 70-97146. (Illus.). 55 p. 22cm. 1970. Little, Brown.

--Hoagie's Rifle-Gun. Martin, Patricia Miles. 1st ed. Schoenherr, John Carl (1935-), illus. LC 69-16096. (Illus.). 40 p. 24cm. 1970. Little, Brown.

--Hoagie's Rifle Gun. Martin, Patricia Miles. Schoenherr, John Carl (1935-), illus. 1970. Little, Brown.

--Jenny's Cat. Martin, Patricia Miles. 1st ed. Watson, Wendy McLeod (1942-), illus. LC 79-11501. (Illus.). 39 p. 23cm. (Unicorn book). c.1979. (ISBN 0-525-32746-0). Dutton.

--Kickapoo. Martin, Patricia Miles. 1st ed. Dennis, Wesley (1903-1966), illus. LC 61-9286. 54p. illus. 22cm. 1961. Little, Brown.

--Mississippi Possum. Martin, Patricia Miles. Schoenherr, John Carl (1935-), illus. LC 64-13984. (Illus.). (A picture storybook concerned with the nature of possums). (gr. 2-6). 1965. (ISBN 0-316-57116-1, Pub. by Atlantic Monthly Pr). Little.

--Mouse Six and the Happy Birthday. Martin, Patricia Miles. 1st ed. Morrill, Leslie H, illus. LC 78-7517. (Illus.). 32 p. 23cm. (Unicorn book). c.1978. (ISBN 0-525-35230-9). Dutton.

--Nobody's Cat. Martin, Patricia Miles. 1st ed. Schoenherr, John Carl (1935-), illus. LC 68-12351. (Illus.). 43 p. 1969. Little, Brown. **Award: (ALA).**

--Noisy Gander. Martin, Patricia Miles. 1st ed. Morrill, Leslie H, illus. LC 77-25938. (Illus.). 32 p. 23cm. (Unicorn book). c.1978. (ISBN 0-525-36026-3). Dutton.

--Otter in the Cove. Martin, Patricia Miles. 1st ed. Schoenherr, John Carl (1935-), illus. LC 73-18398. (Illus.). 47 p. 1974. (ISBN 0-316-56970-4). Little, Brown.

--The Pieces of Home. Martin, Patricia Miles. 1st ed. Ambrus, Victor G., pseud. (1935-), illus. Ambrus, Gyozo Laszlo. LC 67-17549. (Illus.). 60 p. 22cm. 1967. Little, Brown.

--Pony in the Schoolhouse. Martin, Patricia Miles. 1st ed. Blegvad, Erik (1923-), illus. LC 64-10179. 60 p. illus. 22 cm. 1964. Little, Brown.

--See a White Horse. Martin, Patricia Miles. Dennis, Wesley (1903-1966), illus. (Illus.). (gr. 3-5). 1963. (ISBN 0-316-57008-7, Pub. by Atlantic Monthly Pr). Little.

--Small Rabbit. Martin, Patricia Miles. 1st ed. Arnosky, Jim (1946-), illus. LC 77-3436. (Illus.). 31 p. c.1977. (ISBN 0-316-56973-9). Little, Brown.

--Swim, Little Duck. Martin, Patricia Miles. 1st ed. Arnosky, James E. (1946-), illus. LC 75-30700. (Illus.). 30 p. c.1976. (ISBN 0-316-57033-8). Little, Brown.

--Teacher's Pet. Martin, Patricia Miles. 1st ed. Lasell, Elinor Hegemann (1929-), illus. LC 66-17684. (Illus.). 54 p. 25cm. 1966. Little, Brown.

--Tree House Town. Martin, Patricia Miles. 1st ed. McCully, Emily Arnold (1939-), illus. LC 74-3358. (Illus.). 30 p. 22cm. 1974. (ISBN 0-316-56971-2). Little, Brown.

--Uncle Fonzo's Ford. Martin, Patricia Miles. Watson, Wendy McLeod (1942-), illus. LC 67-19798. (Illus.). 54p. 24cm. 1968. Little, Brown.

--Wharf Rat. Martin, Patricia Miles. Schoenherr, John Carl (1938-), illus. LC 70-176300. (Illus.). 47p. 20 x 26cm. 1972. Little, Brown.

Miles, Miska, pseud. (1899-) & Morrill, Leslie H

--This Little Pig. Martin, Patricia Miles. 1st ed. p. cm. (Unicorn book). c.1980. Dutton.

Miles, Patricia see Miles, Mary Patricia.

Miles, Sande, pseud., see Adams, Lawrence Stowell.

Milgram, Mary

--Brothers Are All the Same. Hausherr, Rosemarie, illus. LC 77-25940. (Illus.). 32 p. c.1978. (ISBN 0-525-27243-7). Dutton.

Milgrom, Harry (1912-)

--Adventures with a Ball. Strimban, Robert & Strimban, Jack, illus. (Illus.). 1965. Dutton.

--Adventures with a String. Funk, Thompson (1911-), illus. 32p. col. illus. 22cm. (First sci. experiments). c.1965. Dutton.

Milhous, Katherine (1894-1977)

--Appolonia's Valentine. Milhous, Katherine (1894-1977), illus. LC 54-7248. illus. 26cm. 32p. 1954. Scribner.

--Corporal Keeperupper. Milhous, Katherine (1894-1977), illus. LC 43-15468. 2 p. l. 7-62, 1 p. col. illus. 19 1/2 cm. 1943. C. Scribner's Sons.

--The Egg Tree. Milhous, Katherine (1894-1977), illus. LC 50-6017. (Illus.). 32 p. 26cm. 1950. (ISBN 0-684-12716-4, Aladdin). (ISBN 0-689-70492-5). Scribner. **Award: (RCM).**

--The First Christmas Crib. Milhous, Katherine (1894-1977), illus. LC 44-8906. 3 p. l. 47 p. illus. (part col.) 19 1/2 cm. 1944. C. Scribner's Sons.

--Herodia, the Lovely Puppet. Milhous, Katherine (1894-1977), illus. LC 42-24592. 4 p. l. 3-193 p. illus., col. plates. 23 cm. 1942. C. Scribner's Sons.

--Lovina: A story of the Pennsylvania Country. N.D. Charles Scribner's Sons.

--Patrick and the Golden Slippers. Milhous, Katherine (1894-1977), illus. LC 51-12317. (Illus.). unpaged. 26cm. c.1951. Scribner.

--Peter Piper's Pickled Peppers. Milhous, Katherine (1894-1977), illus. N.D. J. B. LIppincott.

--Snow over Bethlehem. Milhous, Katherine (1894-1977), illus. LC 45-37876. (Illus.). 21cm. vi, 98p. 1945. Charles Scribner's Sons.

--With Bells on. Milhous, Katherine (1894-1977), illus. LC 55-14936. 32p. 1955. Scribner.

Milius, Winifred

--Here Comes Daddy. Milius, Winifred, illus. LC 44-8303. (Illus.). 21 x 23 1/2 cm. 22p. (Young Scott Bks.). 1944. William R. Scott Inc.

Millais, J. E., illus.

Little Songs for Me to Sing. Leslie, Henry, contrib. by. N.D. Cassell, Petter & Galpin.

Millar, Barbara Finn, jt. auth. see Luis, Earlene W.

Millar, Harold Robert (1869-1939)

--The Dreamland Express. Millar, Harold Robert (1869-1939), illus. LC 27-19087. 5 p. l., 56 p. col. front., illus., plates (part col., 1 double) 22 1/2 cm. 1927. Dodd, Mead & Company.

Millar, Susie McKinnon

--George of the Parsonage. N.D. Wm. B. Eerdmans Publishing Co.

Millard

--Flaming Star. (gr. 3-5). N.D. (ISBN 0-590-11923-0, Schol Pap). Scholastic Inc.

Millard, Adele

--Dogs in Fact & Legend. Minn, illus. LC 76-51176. (Illus.). 96 p. 21cm. c.1977. (ISBN 0-8069-3736-X). (ISBN 0-8069-3737-8). Sterling Pub. Co.

Millard, Edith E.

--Mr. Skiddleywinks. N.D. Frederick A. Stokes Co.

Millard, Florence Grace

--Verses Small for One and All. LC 32-16550. 59, 1 p. incl. col. front., illus. (part col.) 22 cm. c.1932. New Publishing Company.

Millay, Cora Buzzelle, Mrs.

--Little Otis. Hall, Helen Jameson, illus. LC 28-22729. 4 p. l., 3-103 p. illus. 19 1/2 cm. c.1928. W. W. Norton & Company, Inc.

Millay, Edna St. Vincent (1892-1950)

--Edna St. Vincent Millay's Poems Selected for Young People. New Ed. ed. Keller, Ronald, illus. LC 77-25671. (Illus.). 115 p. 24cm. 1979, c.1951. (ISBN 0-06-024218-3). (ISBN 0-06-024219-1). Harper & Row.

--Edna St.Vincent Millay's Poems Selected for Young People. Paget-Fredericks, Joseph E. P. Rous-Marten (1903-1963), illus. (Illus.). (gr. 3-7). 1929. (ISBN 0-06-024205-1, HarpJ). (ISBN 0-06-024206-X). Har-Row.

--Edna St.Vincent Millay's Poems Selected for Young People. Paget-Fredericks, Joseph E. P. Rous-Marten (1903-1963), illus. 1962. Harper & Bros.

Millay, Kathleen

--The Beggar at the Gate. N.D. Liveright Publishing.

--The Evergreen Tree. N.D. Liveright Publishing.

--The Hermit Thrush. N.D. Liveright Publishing.

Mille, Agnes De see De Mille, Agnes.

Mille, Alban Bertram De see Hughes, Thomas.

Mille, James De see DeMille, James.

Mille, Pierre

--Barnavaux. Drillien, Berengere, tr. N.D. John Lane.

--Joffre Chaps. Drillien, Berengere, tr. N.D. John Lane.

--Louise & Barnavaux. Drillien, Berengere, tr. N.D. John Lane.

--Two Little Parisians. Drillien, Berengere, tr. N.D. John Lane.

--Under the Tricolour. Drillien, Berengere, tr. N.D. John Lane.

Mille, William Churchill De see De Mille, William Churchill (1878-) & Barnard, Charles.

Millen, Muriel

--Wild West Bill Rides Home. LC 46-18721. (Illus.). 24 cm. 32p. 1946. Albert Whitman & Co.

Millen, Nina

--The Friendly Missionary. N.D. Friendship Press.

--Off to Brazil. Smalley, Janet (1893-), illus. LC 51-10945. 126 p. illus. 20 cm. 1951. Friendship Press.

--A Sari for Sita. (India and the Moslem World). N.D. Friendship Press.

--Surprise for Min Deh. LC 48-8069. 55 p. illus. 23 cm. 1948. Friendship Press.

--Tiger Tail Village. Herric, Pru, illus. LC 62-785710. 127p. illus. 19cm. 1962. Friendship Press.

Millender, Dharathula Hood (1920-)

--Crispus Attucks: Boy of Valor. Morrow, Gray, illus. LC 65-14977. 200 p. col. illus. 20 cm. (Childhood of famous Americans). 1965. Bobbs-Merrill.

Miller, jt. auth. see Hinds.

Miller, Aaron B.

--Backwards Tree. (gr. 2-6). N.D. Carlton.

Miller, Ada L., ed. see Isaac, Ella M.

Miller, Agnes

--The Chimes of Daskam High. Warren, Elizabeth B., illus. LC 25-17704. 311 p. front., plates. 19 cm. c.1925. Lothrop, Lee & Shepard Co.

--The Linger Nots and the Mystery House: Or, The Story of Nine Adventurous Girls. 3 p. l., 204 p. front. 19 1/2 cm. (Her Linger-nots series). c.1923. Cupples & Leon Company.

--The Linger-Nots and the Secret Maze: Or, Treasure-Trove on Battlefield Hill. LC 31-14181. 3 p. l., 206 p. front., 1 illus. 19 1/2 cm. (Her Linger-nots series). c.1931. Cupples & Leon Company.

--The Linger-Nots and the Valley Feud: Or, The Great West Point Chain. 3 p. l., 210 p. front. 19 1/2 cm. (Her Linger-nots series). c.1923. Cupples & Leon Company.

--The Linger-Nots and the Whispering Charm: Or, The Secret from Old Alaska. LC 25-11592. 3 p. l., 210 p. front. 19 1/2 cm. (Her Linger-nots series). c.1925. Cupples & Leon Company.

--The Linger-Nots and Their Golden Quest: Or, The Log of the Ocean Monarch. 3 p. l., 210 p. front. 19 1/2 cm. (Her Linger-nots series). c.1923. Cupples & Leon Company.

--Mystery Stories for Girls. LC 34-6273. 3 p. l., 204 p., 2 l., 210 p., 2 l., 210 p., 2 l., 210 p. front. 21 1/2 cm. c.1934. Cupples & Leon Co.

--Two Girls and Two Treasures. Hoopes, Florence J., illus. LC 27-19181. 317 p. front., plates. 19 1/2 cm. c.1927. Lothrop, Lee & Shepard Co.

Miller, Albert see Mills, Alan, pseud.

Miller, Albert G., adapted by see Carroll, Lewis.

Miller, Albert G., ed. see Lorenzini, Carlo.

Miller, Albert Griffith, jt. auth. see Baum, Lyman Frank.

Miller, Albert Griffith (1905-1982)

--The ABC Dog Show. Silverstein, Donald (1932-), illus. LC 72-89032. (Illus.). 57 p. (ABC serendipity). 1974. (ISBN 0-8372-1814-4). Bowmar.

--Backward Beasts. Taylor, Paul L., illus. (ABC Serendipity Ser). (gr. 2-6). 1973. (ISBN 0-8372-0819-X). Bowmar-Noble.

--Backward Beasts from A to Z. Taylor, Paul L., illus. LC 72-89034. (Illus.). 58 p. (ABC serendipity). 1974. Bowmar.

--Captain Whopper. 64p. 1965. Astor Books.

--Captain Whopper. Komisarow, Don, illus. LC 67-30942. (Illus.). 45 p. 23cm. 1967. Astor-Honor.

--Dog That Said Wow-Bow. Taylor, Paul L., illus. (Illus.). color ils. 28p. (Play-Along Books No. 4). 1968. (ISBN 0-394-81408-8). Random.

--A Friend for Shadow. Obligado, Lilian Isabel (1931-), illus. LC 70-79220. (Illus.). 48 p. 24cm. (Carousel book). 1969. L. W. Singer Co.

--Fury. Thorne, Alice, adapted by. Kinstler, Everett Raymond (1926-), illus. LC 64-24426. 59 p. illus. (part col.) 29 cm. (Silver dollar). 1964. Grosset & Dunlap.

--Fury & the Mustangs. 224p. (gr. 3-7). 1981. (ISBN 0-590-31294-4). Scholastic Inc.

--Fury and the Mustangs. 1st ed. Savitt, Sam (1917-), illus. LC 60-10769. 186p. illus. 22cm. 1960. Holt, Rinehart and Winston.

--Fury & the Mustangs. Schucker, James, illus. (gr. 4-10). 1963. (ISBN 0-448-07072-3). G&D.

--Fury and the White Mare. 1st ed. LC 62-921086. 189p. 22cm. 1962. Holt, Rinehart and Winston.

--Fury & the White Mare. Schucker, James, illus. (gr. 4-10). 1963. (ISBN 0-448-07073-1). G&D.

--Fury, Stallion of Broken Wheel Ranch. (gr. 3-5). 1980. (ISBN 0-590-31260-X, Schol Pap). Scholastic Inc.

--Fury, Stallion of Broken Wheel Ranch. Schucker, James, illus. (gr. 4-10). 1963. (ISBN 0-448-07071-5). G&D.

--Fury, Stallion of Broken Wheel Ranch. 1st ed. Schucker, James, illus. LC 59-5086. 177p. illus. 22cm. 1959. Winston.

--How Many Tadpoles?, Bk.1. (Illus.). (Play-Along Ser.). 1968. (ISBN 0-394-81412-6). Random House.

--Mark Twain in Love. LC 73-5243. 190 p. 22cm. 1973. (ISBN 0-15-230295-6). Harcourt Brace Jovanovich.

--More Captain Whopper Tales. Komisarow, Don, illus. (Illus.). (gr. 3-7). 1968. (ISBN 0-8392-3060-5). Astor-Honor.

--Our Friends the ABC's. Wysocki, Harry, illus. LC 72-89033. (Illus.). 59 p. (ABC serendipity). 1974. (ISBN 0-8372-1812-8). (ISBN 0-8372-1812-8). (ISBN 0-8372-0820-3). Bowmar.

--Pop-up Noah & the Ark. Taylor, Paul L., illus. (Illus.). pop-ups. (Pop-up Books Ser). (gr. k-3). 1969. (ISBN 0-394-80788-X). Random.
--Silver Chief's Big Game Trail. (Illus.). (gr. 6-10). N.D. (ISBN 0-448-00945-5). G&D.
--Silver Chief's Big Game Trail. Wiese, Kurt (1887-1974), illus. LC 62-522236. 191p. illus. 22cm. (Famous dog stories). 1962, c.1961. Grosset & Dunlap.
--Silver Chief's Big Game Trail. 1st ed. Wiese, Kurt (1887-1974), illus. LC 61-904850. 191p. illus. 22cm. 1961. Holt, Rinehart and Winston.
--Talking Letters. Wysocki, Harry, illus. LC 72-89035. (Illus.). 55 p. (ABC serendipity). 1974. (ISBN 0-8372-1816-0). Bowmar.
--Twenty-Six Riddles from A to Z. Luap, Rolyat L., pseud., illus. Taylor, Paul L.. LC 72-89036. (Illus.). 58 p. (ABC serendipity). 1974. (ISBN 0-8372-1813-6). (ISBN 0-8372-1813-6). (ISBN 0-8372-0821-1). Bowmar.
--Who Popped Out. (Illus.). color pop ups. 26p. (Play-Along Books: No. 2). (ps-4). 1968. (ISBN 0-394-81416-9). Random.
--The Wonderful Magic-Motion Machine. Taylor, Paul L., designed by. N.D. Random House.

Miller, Albert Griffith (1905-1982), ed.
--Adventures of Chitty Chitty Bang Bang. LC 68-28467. (Illus.). 72p. (gr. k-4). 1968. (ISBN 0-394-81955-1). (ISBN 0-394-91955-6). Random.
--Aladdin & the Wonderful Lamp. (Illus.). (Pop-Up Classics: No. 7). (ps up). 1970. (ISBN 0-394-81105-4). Random.
--Knock, Knock. (Illus.). (Pop-Up Bks.). (ps up). 1969. (ISBN 0-394-80696-4). Random.
--Pop-up Aladdin & the Wonderful Lamp. Taylor, Paul L., illus. (Illus.). color ils. 24p. (Pop-up Classics Ser.: No. 7). 1970. (ISBN 0-394-81105-4, BYR). Random.
--The Pop-up Book of Jokes: Pop Corn. Walton, Tony, illus. LC 72-386. (Illus.). 20 p. 24cm. 1972. (ISBN 0-394-82447-4). Random House.
--Pop-up David & Goliath. Svensson, Borje, illus. (Illus.). color ils. 24p. 1970. (ISBN 0-394-82021-5). Random.
--Pop-up Little Red Riding Hood. Gordon, Gwen, illus. (Illus.). color ils. 24p. (gr. k-3). 1970. (ISBN 0-394-80437-6). Random.
--Pop-up Mother Goose. (Illus.). (Pop-up Books Ser). (ps). 1966. (ISBN 0-394-81588-2, BYR). Random.
--Pop-Up Sound-Alikes. (Illus.). (Pop-Up Bks.). (ps up). 1967. (ISBN 0-394-81868-7). Random.
--Pop-up Three Little Pigs. Taylor, Paul L., illus. (Illus.). color ils. 24p. (Pop-up Fairy Tales: No. 3). (gr. k-3). 1970. (ISBN 0-394-80436-8). Random.
--Ring of Bright Water. (A Golden Paperback Special). N.D. Golden Press.
--Robin Hood. Taylor, Paul L., illus. (Illus.). pop-ups. 24p. (Pop-up Classic Ser). (gr. k-4). 1969. (ISBN 0-394-80790-1). Random.
--Snow White. (Illus.). (Pop-up Classics,). (ps-3). 1970. (ISBN 0-394-82000-2). Random.
--Walt Disney's Bambi Gets Lost. LC 72-4859. (Illus.). 42 p. 25cm. (Disney's wonderful world of reading, 2). 1972. (ISBN 0-394-82520-9). (ISBN 0-394-82520-9). Random House.

Miller, Albert (1914-)
--The Hungry Goat. Mills, Alan, pseud. Graboff, Abner (1919-), illus. LC 64-14398. 48p. col. illus. 24cm. c.1964. Rand.

Miller, Alexander McVeigh
--Bonnie Dora and Little Golden Daughters. LC 3-26214. 19cm. 140p. (Clover Ser.: No. 118). c.1896. Street & Smith.
--Bonnie Dora: Or, Winning the Heir. LC 3-26212. 19cm. 126p. c.1883. International Book Co.
--Bonnie Dora: Or, Winning the Heir. LC 3-26215. 18cm. 126p. (Lovell's Library Ser.: No. 1253). c.1883. J. W. Lovell Co.
--Bonnie Dora: Or, Winning the Heir. LC 3-26213. 19cm. 127p. (Munro's Library: Vol. 1 No. 1). c.1883. N. L. Munro Co.
--Brunette and Blonde: Or, The Struggle for a Birthright. 246p. (Street & Smith's Select Ser.: No. 5). 1887. Street & Smith.
--Little Golden's Daughter: Or, The Dream of Her Lifetime. 1905. American News Co.

Miller, Alice Duer (1874-1942)
--Cinderella. Alajalov, Constantin (1900-), illus. LC 43-16088. 64 p. illus. 23 1/2 cm. 1943. Coward-McCann, Inc.
--The White Cliffs. 1940. Coward-McCann Inc.

Miller, Alice Patricia McCarthy
--The Heart of Camp Whippoorwhill. Shortall, Leonard W., illus. (gr. 4-6). 1976. (ISBN 0-590-10132-3, Schol Trade Pap). Schol Bk Serv.
--The Heart of Camp Whippoorwill. Ilsley, Velma Elizabeth (1918-), illus. LC 60-5714. (Illus.). (gr. 3-5). 1960. (ISBN 0-397-30497-8). Lippincott.
--The Little Store on the Corner. Lawrence, John (1933-), illus. LC 61-7134. unpaged. illus. 21cm. c.1961. Abelard-Schuman.
--The Little Store on the Corner. Weil, Lisl (1910-), illus. (Illus.). (gr. k-3). 1974. (ISBN 0-590-04839-2). (ISBN 0-590-20740-7). Scholastic Inc.
--Make Way for Peggy O'Brien!. 1st ed. Geer, Charles Hand (1922-), illus. LC 61-14639. 120p. illus. 21cm. 1961. Lippincott.
--Melissa the Mouse. Flint, Russ, illus. (Illus.). N.D. (ISBN 0-516-09116-6). Childrens.
--Melissa the Mouse. Flint, Russ, illus. 16p. (Orig.). (gr. k-6). 1982. (ISBN 0-8249-8982-1). Ideals.
--The Mouse Family's Blueberry Pie. 1st ed. Bloch, Carol, illus. LC 81-2204. p. cm. c.1981. (ISBN 0-525-66745-8). Elsevier/Dutton Books.

Miller, Allan, jt. ed. see Winn, Marie.

Miller, Anne Archbold
--Huldy's Whistle. Donahey, William (1883-1970), illus. LC 19-127182. 286, 1 p. incl. front., illus., plates. 19 1/2 cm. c.1919. The Reilly & Lee Co.
--Little Bigs. Westmacott, Bernard (1887-), illus. LC 25-180551. 64 p. incl. col. front., illus. (part col.) 23 1/2 cm. c.1925. Greenberg, Inc.

Miller, Arthur (1915-)
--Jane's Blanket. McCully, Emily Arnold (1939-), illus. LC 76-183764. (Illus.). 47 p. 24cm. 1972. (ISBN 0-670-40568-X). Viking Press.
--Jane's Blanket. Parker, Al, illus. LC 63-8300. 64 p. illus. 30 cm. (Modern masters books for children). 1963. Crowell-Collier Press.

Miller, Ashley, adapted by.
--Mr. Scrooge: A Dramatization of Dickens' A Christmas Carol. N.D. Dodd Mead & Co.

Miller, Barbara, jt. auth. see Hewson, Isabel Manning.

Miller, Barbara Brakeley, ed. see Lessing, Erich.

Miller, Barry (1946-)
--Alphabet World. LC 77-127470. 29 l. (chiefly illus., part col. 24cm. 1971. Macmillan Co.

Miller, Basil William (1897-)
--Kay and Kim in Wild Horse Canyon. LC 46-22072. 80 p. 20 cm. 1946. Zondervan Publishing House.
--Ken and the Cattle Thieves. LC 53-13077. 88p. 20cm. 1953. Zondervan Pub. House.
--Ken and the Lost Indian Treasure. LC 58-15374. 57p. 20cm. 1957. Zondervan Pub. House.
--Ken and the Navajo Treasure Map. LC 56-18683. 56p. 20cm. 1955. Zondervan Pub. House.
--Ken Bails Out: A High Sierra Adventure Story for Boys. LC 42-23231. 4 p. l. 7-76 p. 19 1/2 cm. 1942. Zondervan Publishing House.
--Ken Captures a Foreign Agent: A Christian Adventure Story for Boys. LC 43-10171. 3 p. l. 9-82 p. 20 cm. 1943. Zondervan Publishing House.
--Ken Follows the Chuck Wagon. LC 50-11792. 58 p. 20 cm. 1950. Zondervan Pub. House.
--Ken Hits the Cowboy Trail. LC 51-2300. 58 p. 20 cm. 1951. Zondervan.
--Ken in Alaska. LC 45-1082. 71 p. 19 1/2 cm. 1944. Zondervan Publishing House.
--Ken on the Anchor D Ranch. LC 56-42789. 57p. 20cm. 1956. Zondervan Pub. House.
--Ken on the Argentine Pampas. LC 47-25852. 57 p. 20 cm. 1947. Zondervan Pub. House.
--Ken on the Navajo Trail. LC 48-8076. 56 p. 20 cm. 1948. Zondervan Pub. House.
--Ken, Range Detective. LC 51-14994. 58 p. 20 cm. 1952. Zondervan Pub. House.
--Ken, Range Hero. LC 55-156. 88p. 20cm. 1954. Zondervan Pub. House.
--Ken Rides the Range: A Boy's Story of the Painted Desert. LC 42-141610. 4 p. l., 7-76 p. 19 1/2 cm. c.1941. Zondervan Publishing House.
--Ken Saddles up. LC 46-448108. 68 p. 20 cm. 1945. Zondervan Publishing House.
--Ken South of the Border. LC 47-313091. 57 p. 20 cm. 1947. Zondervan Pub. House.
--Ken's Mercy Flight to Australia. LC 44-74683. 64 p.20 cm. 1944. Zondervan Publishing House.
--Koko and the Eskimo Doctor. LC 50-5087. 88 p. 20 cm. 1949. Zondervan.
--Koko and the Fur Thieves. LC 53-744489. 57p. 20cm. 1953. Zondervan Pub. House.
--Koko and the Mounties. LC 56-427864. 57p. 20cm. 1956. Zondervan Pub. House.
--Koko and the Timber Thieves. LC 51-14504. 71 p. 20 cm. 1951. Zondervan Pub. House.
--Koko, King of the Arctic Trail. LC 47-23972. 87 p. incl. front. 20 cm. 1947. Zondervan Publishing House.
--Koko of the Airways. LC 48-7263. (Illus.). 20 cm. 88p. (The Koko Dog Ser.). 1948. Zondervan Publishing House.
--Koko on the Yukon. LC 55-205. 88p. 20cm. 1954. Zondervan Pub. House.
--Patty Lou and the Seminole Indians. LC 56-18684. 58p. 20cm. 1955. Zondervan Pub. House.
--Patty Lou and the White Gold Ranch. LC 43-151753. 74 p. 19 1/2 cm. 1943. Zondervan Publishing House.
--Patty Lou at Sunset Pass. LC 52-14265. 57p. 21cm. 1952. Zondervan Pub. House.
--Patty Lou, Flying Missionary. LC 48-724948. 57 p. illus. 20 cm. 1948. Zondervan Pub. House.
--Patty Lou Home on the Range. LC 51-6038. 57 p. 20 cm. 1951. Zondervan.
--Patty Lou in the Coast Guard. LC 45-1209. 1944. Zondervan Publishing House.
--Patty Lou in the Wilds of Central America. LC 49-8605. 56 p. illus. 20 cm. 1949. Zondervan Pub. House.
--Patty Lou Lost in the Jungle. LC 53-130781. 89p. 20cm. 1953. Zondervan Pub. House.
--Patty Lou of the Golden West: A Girl's Adventure Story. LC 42-232307. 67 p. 20 cm. 1942. Zondervan Publishing House.
--Patty Lou, Range Nurse. LC 55-204. 89p. 20cm. 1954. Zondervan Pub. House.
--Patty Lou, the Girl Forester. LC 47-23056. 64 p. 19 1/2 cm. 1947. Zondervan Publishing House.
--Patty Lou Under Western Skies. LC 50-4411. 57 p. 20 cm. 1950. Zondervan Pub. House.
--Patty Lou, Western Nurse. LC 58-163438. 58p. 20cm. c.1957. Zondervan Pub. House.
--Patty Lou's Pot of Gold. LC 43-10172. 67 p. 20 cm. 1943. Zondervan Publishing House.
--Patty Lou,the Flying Nurse. LC 45-10688. 62 p. 20 cm. 1945. Zondervan Publishing House.
--Silver Star and the Black Raider. LC 51-15788. 88 p. 29 cm. 1950. Zondervan.
--Silver Star and the Mustang Roundup. LC 51-14995. 73 p. 20 cm. 1951. Zondervan Pub. House.
--Silver Star and the Navajos. LC 54-808407. 89p. 20cm. 1953. Zondervan Pub. House.
--Silver Star in Rainbow Valley. LC 54-8084. 20 cm. 80p. (The Silver Star Horse Ser.). 1953. Zondervan Publishing House.
--Silver Star on the Painted Desert. LC 57-153448. 57p. 20cm. 1956. Zondervan Pub. House.

Miller, Bob
--Rumples and the Bugs. Miller, Bob, illus. LC 82-14577. (Illus.). 30 p. 24cm. c.1982. (ISBN 0-516-03636-X). Childrens Press.
--Rumples' Supper-Time Problem. Miller, Bob, illus. LC 82-9522. (Illus.). 31 p. 24cm. (Rumples Books). c.1982. (ISBN 0-516-03637-8). (ISBN 0-516-43637-6). Childrens Press.

Miller, Bob & Paul, Sherry (1934-)
--Blossom Bird Falls in Love: A Bob Miller Picture Story. Miller, Bob, illus. LC 81-7995. p. cm. (A See How I Read Classroom Edition). 1981. (ISBN 0-87895-152-0, Modern Curriculum). Contemporary Perspectives, Inc.
--Blossom Bird Falls in Love: A Bob Miller Picture Story. Miller, Bob, illus. LC 81-9578. (Illus.). 32 p. 23cm. (Orange blossom see how I read book). 1981. (ISBN 0-675-01081-0, C. E. Merrill). (ISBN 0-675-01081-0). Contemporary Perspectives, Inc.
--Blossom Bird Finds a Family: A Bob Miller Picture Story. Miller, Bob, illus. LC 81-7992. p. cm. (A See How I Read Classroom Edition). 1981 (Modern Curriculum). Contemporary Perspectives, Inc.
--Blossom Bird Finds a Family: A Bob Miller Picture Story. Miller, Bob, illus. LC 81-9580. (Illus.). 32 p. 23cm. (An Orange Blossom See How I Read Book). c.1981. (ISBN 0-675-01079-9, C. E. Merrill). Contemporary Perspectives, Inc.
--Blossom Bird Finds a Family: A Bob Miller Picture Story. Miller, Bob, illus. LC 81-9980. p. cm. (A See How I Read Book). 1981. (ISBN 0-516-02352-7, Children's Press). Contemporary Perspectives, Inc.,.
--Blossom Bird Goes South: A Bob Miller Picture Story. Miller, Bob, illus. LC 81-8623. (Illus.). 32 p. 23cm. (An Orange Blossom See How I Read Book). c.1981. (ISBN 0-675-01080-2, C. E. Merrill). C.E. Merrill.
--Blossom Bird Goes South: A Bob Miller Picture Story. Miller, Bob, illus. LC 81-7991. p. cm. (A See How I Read Classroom Edition). 1981. (ISBN 0-87895-151-2, Contemporary Perspectives). Contemporary Perspectives, Inc.
--Finn, the Foolish Fish: Trouble with Bubbles : a Bob Miller Picture Story. Miller, Bob, illus. LC 81-9978. p. cm. (A See How I Read Book). 1981. (ISBN 0-516-02354-3, Children's Press). Contemporary Perspectives, Inc.
--Finn, the Foolish Fish: Trouble with Bubbles. Miller, Bob, illus. LC 81-7990. (A Bob Miller Picture Story). p. cm. (A See How I Read Classroom Edition). 1981. (ISBN 0-87895-155-5, Modern Curriculum). Contemporary Perspectives, Inc.
--Finn the Foolish Fish: Trouble with Bubbles. Miller, Bob, illus. (Illus.). 32p. (Orig.). (See How I Read). (ps-2). N.D. (ISBN 0-675-01084-5). Contemp Perspectives.
--Two-B and the Rock n Roll Band: A Bob Miller Picture Story. Miller, bob, illus. LC 81-9579. (Illus.). 32 p. 23cm. (An Orange Blossom See How I Read Book). 1981. (ISBN 0-675-01082-9). Contemporary Perspectives, Inc.
--Two-B and the Space Visitor: A Bob Miller Picture Story. Miller, Bob, illus. LC 81-9577. (Illus.). 32 p. (An Orange Blossom See How I Read Book). c.1981. (ISBN 0-675-01083-7). Contemporary Perspectives, Inc.

Miller, C. S., Mrs.
--Ralph Weston's Secret: Or, Unto the Fourth Generation. LC 12-36414. 247 p. front., plates. 18 cm. c.1886. Presbyterian Board of Publication.

Miller, Calvin (1936-)
--When the Aardvark Parked on the Ark, and Other Poems. Harrison, Marc, illus. LC 84-47894. (Illus.). 185 p. 24cm. c.1984. (ISBN 0-317-13380-2). (ISBN 0-06-065748-0). Harper & Row.

Miller, Carey
--All About Monsters. LC 77-17933. (Illus.). 32 p. 29cm. (World of the unknown). c.1978. (ISBN 0-88436-467-4). EMC Corp.

Miller, Carl, compiled by.
--Rockabye Baby: Lullabies from Many Nations & Peoples. (gr. k-8). 1975. (ISBN 0-935738-04-5). US Comm Unicef.
--Sing Children Sing. (gr. k up). 1972. (ISBN 0-935738-05-3). US Comm Unicef.

Miller, Christopher R.
--Stroke of Luck. LC 80-82989. (Illus.). 64p. (SporTellers Ser.). (gr. 4 up). 1981. (ISBN 0-516-02268-7). Childrens.

Miller, David Lee
--Baby the Lost Legend. (gr. 3 up). 1985. (ISBN 0-671-54091-2, Little Simon). S&S.
--Baby: The Storybook. LC 84-14352. (Illus.). 58 p., 1 leaf of plates. 29cm. c.1985. (ISBN 0-671-54091-2). Simon & Schuster.

Miller, David Reed
--The Red Swan's Neck. N.D. Sherman,French & Co.

Miller, Deborah Uchill
--Only Nine Chairs: A Tall Tale for Passover. LC 82-80035. (Illus.). 40p. (ps-4). 1982. (ISBN 0-930494-12-1). (ISBN 0-930494-13-X). Kar Ben.
--Poppy Seeds, Too: A Twisted Tale for Shabbat. Ostrove, Karen, illus. LC 82-84021. (Illus.). 48 p. 26cm. c.1982. (ISBN 0-930494-16-4). (ISBN 0-930494-17-2). Kar-Ben Copies, Inc.

Miller, Don (1923-), illus.
--The Boys' Life Book of Sports Stories. LC 65-18980. (Illus.). 185 p. 22cm. (Boys' life library, 8). 1965. Random House.

Miller, Doris R., pseud., see Mosesson, Gloria Rubin.

Miller, Doris R., pseud., retold by
--The Little Red Hen. Mosesson, Gloria Rubin. Ramirez, Pablo, illus. Little Red Hen LC 66-14053. 32p. col. illus. 24cm. (Holly story bk. lib. Q1046). N.D. World.

Miller, Doris R, jt. auth. see Aladdin.

Miller, Doris R., pseud., ed. see Grimm, Jakob Ludwig Karl (1785-1863) & Grimm, Wilhelm Karl.

Miller, Doris R., pseud. (1924-), ed. see Mother Goose.

Miller, Doris R, retold by see Perrault, Charles.

Miller, Doris R, pseud., retold by see Puss in Boots.

Miller, Dorothy Shirley
--Showboat Round the Bend. Stevens, Mary E. (1920-1966), illus. LC 57-6518. 243p. illus. 21cm. 1957. Dodd, Mead.

Miller, Dupont, Mrs., jt. auth. see Miller, Harold Blaine.

Miller, E. Lorraine
--Rooney Crooney's Second Chance. Stuker, Chris, illus. LC 77-88334. (Illus.). (Self Help Ser.). (ps-4). 1978. (ISBN 0-89566-351-1). Miller Ent.

Miller, Edgar H., Jr., tr. see De Vasconcelos, Jose M.

Miller, Edna Anita (1920-)
--Duck,Duck. Miller, Edna Anita (1920-), illus. LC 78-151761. (Illus.). 32 p. 1971. (ISBN 0-8234-0195-2). Holiday House.
--Duck,Duck. Miller, Edna Anita (1920-), illus. LC 80-28344. p. cm. 1981, c.1971. (ISBN 0-13-220962-4). (ISBN 0-13-220962-4). Prentice-Hall.
--The Jumping Bean Book. Miller, Edna Anita (1920-), illus. LC 79-15434. p. cm. c.1979. (ISBN 0-13-512384-4). Prentice-Hall.
--Mousekin Finds a Friend. Miller, Edna Anita (1920-), illus. LC 67-18924. (Illus.). 32 p. 24cm. 1967. Prentice-Hall.
--Mousekin Takes a Trip. Miller, Edna Anita (1920-), illus. LC 75-35922. (Illus.). 32 p. 24cm. c.1976. (ISBN 0-13-604363-1). Prentice-Hall.
--Mousekin's ABC. Miller, Edna Anita (1920-), illus. LC 79-176159. (Illus.). 32 p. 24cm. 1972. (ISBN 0-13-604389-5). Prentice-Hall.
--Mousekin's Birth. Miller, Edna Anita (1920-), illus. (Illus.). 32p. (gr. k-3). 1982. (ISBN 0-13-604132-9, Pub. by Treehouse). P-H.
--Mousekin's Christmas Eve. Miller, Edna Anita (1920-), illus. LC 65-25244. (Illus.). 32 p. 24cm. 1965. Prentice-Hall.
--Mousekin's Close Call. 1980. Prentice Hall.

--Little Rabbit's Big Surprise. Miller, John Parr (1913-), illus. LC 81-52360. (Illus.). 24p. (Shape Bks.). (ps-1). 1982. (ISBN 0-394-85137-4). Random.
--Little Rabbit's Merry Christmas. LC 82-80385. (Illus.). 24 p. 17cm. (A Sniffy Book). c.1982. (ISBN 0-394-85427-6). Random House.
--The Little Red Hen: A Favorite Folk Tale. Miller, John Parr (1913-), illus. LC 54-14959. unpaged. illus. 21cm. (Little golden book, 209). 1954. Simon and Schuster.
--Sniffy the Mouse: Eight Fragrances to Scratch and Sniff. LC 79-66558. (Illus.). 22 p. 17cm. (Sniffy book). c.1980. (ISBN 0-394-84397-5). Random House.
--Tiny Tiger Learns a Lot: About the Alphabet, About Numbers, About Ways to Go, About Colors. Miller, John Parr (1913-), illus. LC 76-1305. (Illus.). 37 p. 29cm. c.1976. (ISBN 0-307-13770-8). Golden Press.
--Tiny Tiger Tales: Nine Stories in Full Color. LC 77-103097. (Illus.). 93 p. 14cm. 1970. Golden Press.
--What Did Santa Bring?. LC 80-54290. (Illus.). 10 p. 16cm. (Happy house). c.1981. (ISBN 0-394-84839-X). Random House.
--What Time Is It, Little Rabbit?. LC 85-2225. (Illus.). 20 p. 31cm. (Knee-high book). c.1985. (ISBN 0-394-87533-8). (ISBN 0-394-97533-2). Random House.

Miller, John Parr (1913-), ed.
--Brave Little Tailor & Puss in Boots: Two Folk Tales. Miller, John Parr (1913-), illus. 36p. (Golden Favorites). (gr. 3-6). 1971. (ISBN 0-307-12036-8, Golden Pr). Western Pub.
--Favorite Tales for the Very Young. Miller, John Parr (1913-), illus. 1966. (ISBN 0-394-80652-2). Random House.
--The House That Jack Built. Miller, John Parr (1913-), illus. LC 73-77487. foldout. (ps-2). 1973. (ISBN 0-307-15002-X, Golden Pr). Western Pub.
--The House That Jack Built: A Mother Goose Rhyme. Miller, John Parr (1913-), illus. LC 55-106692. unpaged. illus. 21cm. (Little golden book, 218). 1955, c.1954. Simon and Schuster.

Miller, John Parr (1913-) & Grimm, Jakob Ludwig Karl (1785-1863)
--Two Folk Tales: The Brave Little Tailor and Puss in Boots. Miller, John Parr (1913-), illus. LC 77-143403. (Illus.). 34 p. (incl. cover. 32cm. (Golden book favorite). 1971, c.1953. Golden Press.

Miller, Joseph, tr. see Kraft, Ruth.

Miller, Joseph Shields
--Johnny Freedom Grows up: The Story of a True-Blue American Boy. LC 56-863259. 161p. illus. 20cm. c.1956. Dorrance.
--Johnny Freedom's High School Battles. LC 60-2158. 362p. 21cm. 1960. Pageant Press.

Miller, Joseph (1922-)
--Parables. (gr. 8-12). N.D. Miller Bks.
--Parables. (Illus.). (gr. 4-10). 1966. (ISBN 0-8111-0149-5). Naylor.
--Tales from the Wandering Gypsies. Culver, Larry, illus. LC 72-87908. (Illus.). 72 p. 23cm. 1969. Miller Books.

Miller, Judith Ransom
--Nabob and the Geranium. Neuhart, Marilyn, illus. LC 67-5309. (Illus.). 44 p. 25cm. 1967. Golden Gate Junior Books.

Miller, Kate B., jt. auth. see Borski, Lucia Merecka, Mrs.

Miller, Kate B., jt. tr. see Borski, Lucia Merecka, Mrs.

Miller, Katherine, ed.
--Five Plays from Shakespeare. Ward, Lynd Kendall (1905-1985), illus. (gr. 9 up). 1964. (ISBN 0-395-06943-2). HM.

Miller, Katherine E. James
--Apollo. Berger, Vivian, illus. LC 72-105248. (Illus.). 78 p. 25cm. 1970. Houghton Mifflin.
--Saint George: A Christmas Mummer's Play. Tripp, Wallace Whitney (1940-), illus. (gr. 5 up). 1967. (ISBN 0-395-06944-0). HM.

Miller, Kathryn
--Good Thought Stories for the Children. LC 24-24955. v. front. 17 1/2 cm. c.1922. Kathryn Miller.

Miller, Lena
--The Doll Wedding: Being the Tale of the Wedding of the Dolls of Ada and Vada at the Old Farm House. LC 16-24231. 18cm. 22p. 1916. H. S. Crocker Company.

Miller, Leo Edward (1887-)
--Adrift on the Amazon. LC 23-720215. 7 p. l., 263 p. front., plates. 21 cm. 1923. C. Scribner's Sons.
--The Black Phantom. LC 22-18797. 6 p. l., 225 p. front., plates. 19 1/2 cm. 1922. C. Scribner's Sons.
--The Hidden People: The Story of a Search for Incan Treasure. Bransom, Paul (1885-), illus. LC 20-16498. 6 p. l., 321 p. front., plates. 21 cm. 1920. C. Scribner's Sons.
--In the Tiger's Lair. Bransom, Paul (1885-), illus. LC 21-16799. x p., 1 l., 252 p. front., plates. 21 cm. 1921. C. Scribner's Sons.
--The Jungle Pirates. LC 25-21421. 5 p. l., 235 p. front., plates. 21 cm. 1925. C. Scribner's Sons.

Miller, Lewis Bennett (1861-)
--The Crooked Trail. Kennedy, J. W. Ferguson, illus. N.D. Dana Estes & Co.
--Fort Blocker Boys. LC 17-291811. 380 p. plates. 22 cm. c.1917. The Standard Publishing Company.
--Saddles and Lariats. Kennedy, J. W. Ferguson, illus. N.D. L. C. Page & Co.
--The White River Raft. Kennedy, J. W. Ferguson, illus. (Pioneer Stories). N.D. Dana Estes & Co.

Miller, Lida Brooks, ed.
--Rip Van Winkle, and Other Wonderful Tales: Retold for our Little Boys and Girls of to-Day. LC 49-30241. 286 p. illus. (part col.) 25 cm. 1897. Monarch Book Co.

Miller, Llwellyn
--What is This Thing Called Love: The Difference Between Love, in Love, Like and Ugh. Dauber, Elizabeth, illus. LC 73-13252. (Illus.). 16cm. 50p. 1970. (ISBN 0-671-10465-9). Essandess Special Editions.

Miller, Lorraine E.
--Free with Biz Bee. LC 77-82754. (Illus.). (Self-Help Book). 1977. (ISBN 0-89566-350-3). Miller Ent.

Miller, Luree, jt. auth. see Silverstone, Marilyn.

Miller, Luree (1926-)
--Gurkhas and Ghosts. The Story of a Boy in Nepal. Silverstone, Marilyn, illus. LC 68-31712. (Illus.). 144 p. 24cm. 1970. Criterion Books.

Miller, Lyle (1950-), illus.
--Mysteries of Sherlock Holmes. Conaway, Judith, adapted by. LC 81-15751. (Illus.). 96p. (Step-up Adventures Ser.: No. 3). (gr. 2-5). 1982. (ISBN 0-394-95086-0). (ISBN 0-394-85086-6). Random.

Miller, M. E., Mrs.
--Bessie Kirkland. 87p. N.D. American Tract Society.
--Little Margery. 102p. N.D. American Tract Society.
--More Happy Days, 1 of 4 vols. (Books For Bright Eyes). N.D. Set. American Tract Society.
--Mountain Tops. (Books For Bright Eyes). N.D. American Tract Society.
--On the Farm, 1 of 4 vols. (Book For Bright Eyes). N.D. Set. American Tract Society.
--One Day In Our Vacation, 1 of 4 vols. (Books For Bright Eyes). N.D. Set. American Tract Society.
--Riverside Farmhouse. 48p. N.D. American Tract Society.

Miller, M. Hughes, ed. see Blyton, Enid Mary.

Miller, M. L
--Dizzy from Fools. Tharlet, Eve, illus. LC 85-9390. p. cm. c.1985. (ISBN 0-88708-004-9). Picture Book Studio USA.

Miller, Madge (1918-), adapted by see Andersen, Hans Christian.

Miller, Madge (1918-), adapted by see Carroll, Lewis.

Miller, Madge (1918-), adapted by see Defoe, Daniel.

Miller, Madge (1918-)
--The Emperor's Nightingale. 1961. Children's Theatre Press.
--The Land of the Dragon. 1946. Children's Theatre Press.
--The Pied Piper of Hamelin. 1951. Children's Theatre Press.
--Pinocchio. 1954. Children's Theatre Press.
--Puss in Boots. 1954. Children's Theatre Press.
--Snow White and Rose Red. 1954. Children's Theatre Press.
--The Unwicked Witch: An Unlikely Tale. 1964. Children's Theatre Press.

Miller, Madge (1918-), ed.
--Hansel and Gretel. (Original Authors: The Brothers Grimm). 1951. Children's Theatre Press.

Miller, Margaret J., pseud., see Dale, Margaret Jessy Miller.

Miller, Margaret J., pseud. (1911-)
--Doctor Boomer. Dale, Margaret Jessy Miller. Jacques, Robin (1920-), illus. (Illus.). (gr. 3-6). 1964. (ISBN 0-685-21058-8). Verry.
--Knights, Beasts, and Wonders: Tales and Legends from Mediaeval Britain. Dale, Margaret Jessy Miller. Keeping, Charles William James (1924-), illus. LC 69-13470. (Illus.). 127 p. 23cm. 1969. D. White.
--Queen's Music. Dale, Margaret Jessy Miller. Jacques, Robin (1920-), illus. (Illus.). (gr. 5-9). 1961. (ISBN 0-685-21455-9). Verry.

Miller, Margaret Y.
--Precious Memories. 1978. (ISBN 0-533-03631-3). Vantage.

Miller, Marge, compiled by.
--Adventures from God's Word. rev. ed. (Illus.). 128p. (Basic Bible Readers Ser.). (gr. 3). 1983. (ISBN 0-87239-663-0). Standard Pub.
--Growing with Bible Heroes: Grade 4. rev. ed. (Illus.). 128p. (Basic Bible Readers Ser.). (gr. 4). 1983. (ISBN 0-87239-664-9). Standard Pub.

Miller, Marguerite
--The Flying Twins. N.D. Vantage Press.

Miller, Marie Clark
--Holidays in Verse: Poems for Children. LC 48-154528. 38 p. illus. 24 cm. 1948. Christopher Pub. House.

Miller, Marjorie, ed. see Stortz, Diane.

Miller, Mark
--Fight for Your Life. 1st ed. Camana, Joseph C., illus. LC 55-5017. 209p. illus. 22cm. 1955. Winston.
--The Singing Wire. Savage, Steele (1900-), illus. (Winston Adventure Bks.). 1955. Holt, Rinehart and Winston.
--The Singing Wire: A Story of the Telegraph;. 1st ed. Savage, Steele (1900-), illus. LC 53-62334. 172p. illus. 22cm. (Winston adventure books). 1953. Winston.
--White Captive of the Sioux. Avison, George F. (1885-), illus. LC 52-12897. (Illus.). 211p. (gr. 6-9). 1952. (ISBN 0-03-034185-X). HR&W.
--White Captive of the Sioux. Avison, George F. (1885-), illus. LC 52-128977. 211p. illus. 22cm. 1953. Winston.

Miller, Martha, pseud., see Ivan, Martha Miller Pfaff.

Miller, Marvin & Robinson, Nancy K.
--TACK Against Time. Tiegreen, Alan, illus. (Illus.). 128p. (Orig.). (TACK Books Ser.). (gr. 3-6). 1983. (ISBN 0-590-32406-3). Scholastic Inc.
--TACK into Danger. Tiegreen, Alan, illus. (Illus.). 128p. (Orig.). (TACK Books Ser.). (gr. 3-6). 1983. (ISBN 0-590-32405-5). Scholastic Inc.
--TACK Secret Service. Tiegreen, Alan, illus. (Illus., Orig.). (TACK Books Ser.). (gr. 3-6). 1983. (ISBN 0-590-32404-7). Scholastic Inc.
--TACK to the Rescue. Tiegreen, Alan, illus. (Illus.). 128p. (Orig.). (TACK Books Ser.). (gr. 3-6). 1982. (ISBN 0-590-32403-9). Scholastic Inc.

Miller, Mary Britton (1883-1975)
--All Aboard: Poems. Sokol, Bill, pseud. (1925-), illus. Sokol, William. Sokol, Bill, pseud. (1925-), designed by Sokol, William. LC 58-6094. 47p. illus. 21cm. 1958. Pantheon. **Award: (NYT).**
--Give a Guess: Poems. Kepes, Juliet Appleby (1919-), illus. LC 57-561860. unpaged. illus. 23cm. c.1957. Pantheon.
--A Handful of Flowers: Poems. Vaughan-Jackson, Genevieve (1913-), illus. LC 59-671487. 46p. illus. 21cm. 1959. Pantheon.
--Jungle Journey. Schneebaum, Tobias (1921-), illus. LC 59-11966. (Illus.). unpaged. 23cm. c.1959. Pantheon.
--Listen-- the Birds: Poems. Ness, Evaline Michelow, Mrs. (1911-), illus. LC 61-14777. 46p. illus. 23cm. 1961. Pantheon. **Award: (NYT).**
--Menagerie. LC 28-231504. xi, 124 p. incl. col. front., illus., plates. 19 1/2 cm. 1928. The Macmillan Company.

Miller, Mary Christina
--The Arnold Family. LC 13-33852. 352 p. front., plates. 18 cm. (Arnold-family series, no. 1). 1881. Presbyterian Board of Publication.
--Ned and Sydney. LC 12-367703. iv, 5-341 p. 15 1/2 cm. 1874. Cumberland Presbyterian Board of Publication.

Miller, Mary Esther
--Brother Ben. 260p. N.D. Congregational Sunday-School and Publishing Society.
--Old Mr. Pro. 117p. N.D. Congregational Sunday-School and Publishing Society.

Miller, May
--Dust of Uncertain Journey. 1st ed. LC 75-40977. 67p. 1975. (ISBN 0-916418-05-7). Lotus.
--Halfway to the Sun. Pauker, John, intro. by. LC 81-50427. (Illus.). 50p. (Orig.). (VI Ser.). (gr. 6). 1981. (ISBN 0-931846-17-X). Wash Writers Pub.

Miller, May Halsey (1865-)
--Raoul and Iron Hand: Or, Winning the Golden Spurs. De Luce, Percival, illus. 330p. N.D. E. P. Dutton & Co.

Miller, Minnie Tarr
--Grandma's Tiny Kitten. (Illus.). 85p. 1974. (ISBN 0-87881-014-5). Mojave Books.
--Grandma's Tiny Kitty. 130p. (gr. k-3). 1975. (ISBN 0-87881-014-5). Mojave Bks.
--Why the March Hare Went Mad & Other Stories. 55p. (gr. k-4). 1972. (ISBN 0-87881-002-1). Mojave Bks.

Miller, Minnie Willis Baines see Baines, Minnie Willis.

Miller, Mitchell (1947-), ed.
--The Glass Slipper: Charles Perrault's Tales of Times Past. Miller, Mitchell (1947-), illus. Bierhorst, John (1936-), tr. from Fr. LC 80-66243. (Illus.). 120p. 1981. (ISBN 0-590-07603-5, Four Winds). Scholastic Inc.
--One Misty Moisty Morning: Rhymes from Mother Goose. Miller, Mitchell (1947-), illus. LC 70-149215. (Illus.). 47 p. 20cm. 1971. (ISBN 0-374-35647-5). Farrar, Straus and Giroux.

Miller, Muriel
--Otter's Gala Event. Pickett, Barbara, illus. (Illus.). 32p. (Woodlander-Gorilla Bks.: No. 2). (gr. 1-4). 1985. (ISBN 0-915677-15-6). Roundtable Pub.
--Rufus Fox Goes Hunting. Pickett, Barbara, illus. (Illus.). 32p. (Woodlander-Gorilla Bks.: No. 4). (gr. 1-4). 1985. (ISBN 0-915677-17-2). Roundtable Pub.
--Samantha the Hungry Squirrel. Pickett, Barbara, illus. (Illus.). 32p. (Woodlander & Gorilla Bks.: No. 1). (gr. 1-4). 1985. (ISBN 0-915677-14-8). Roundtable Pub.
--The Well Traveled Rabbits. Pickett, Barbara, illus. (Illus.). 32p. (Woodlander & Gorilla Bks.: No. 3). (gr. 1-4). 1985. (ISBN 0-915677-16-4). Roundtable Pub.

Miller, Muriel, jt. auth. see Dumpledon, Bernard.

Miller, Nancy Minerva Haynes (1831-)
--Mother Truth's Melodies. Common Sense for Children. A Kindergarten. new and enl. ed. LC 6-39128. 352 p. incl. front., illus. 19 1/2 cm. 1887. Fairbanks & Palmer Publishing Co.
--Mother Truth's Melodies. Common Sense for Children. A Kindergarten. LC 6-30760. 215 p. incl. front., illus. 19 cm. 1879. G. W. Carleton & Co.
--Mother Truth's Melodies. Common Sense for Children. A Kindergarten. new and enl. 45th thousand. ed. LC 6-462417. 352 p. incl. front., illus. 19 1/2 cm. c.1906. G. W. Dillingham Co.

Miller, Nell
--Strawberry Shortcake & the Crazy Pie Baking Contest. Sustendal, Pat, illus. (Illus.). 40p. (Strawberry Shortcake Ser.). (ps-3). 1983. (ISBN 0-910313-09-1). Parker Bro.

Miller, Olive Kennon Beaupre, Mrs.
--Engines and Brass Bands. LC 33-334566. 3 p. l., 376 p. front., illus. 23 1/2 cm. 1933. The Book House for Children.
--Heroes, Outlaws and Funny Fellows. Bennett, Richard Michael (1899-), illus. 1939. Doubleday Doran & Co.
--Whisk Away on a Sunbeam. Enright, Maginel Wright, illus. LC 19-16209. c.1919. P. F. Volland Company.

Miller, Olive Kennon Beaupre, Mrs., ed.
--Flying Sails of My Book House. LC 37-1367. 250 p. illus. (part col.) 24 cm. c.1936. The Bookhouse for Children.
--Flying Sails of My Book House. LC 38-548. 2 p. l., 7-224 p. illus. (part col.) 24 cm. c.1937. The Book House for Children.
--From the Tower Window of My Book House. LC 21-15435. 4 p. l., 11-448 p. illus. (part col.) 24 cm. c.1921. The Bookhouse for Children.
--From the Tower Window of My Book House. LC 33-3083. 4 p. l., 11-448 p. illus. (part col.) 24 cm. c.1932. The Bookhouse for Children.
--From the Tower Window of My Book House. LC 37-1364. 240 p. illus. (part col.) 24 cm. c.1936. The Bookhouse for Children.
--From the Tower Window of My Book House. LC 38-550. 2 p. l., 7-240 p. illus. (part col.) 24 cm. c.1937. The Book House for Children.
--Halls of Fame of My Book House. LC 38-780. 3 p. l., 11-280 p. illus. (part col.) 24 cm. c.1937. The Book House for Children.
--In Shining Armor of My Book House. LC 37-1365. 216 p. illus. (part col.) 24 cm. c.1936. The Bookhouse for Children.
--In Shining Armor of My Book House. LC 38-779. 216 p. illus. (part col.) 24 cm. c.1937. The Book House for Children.
--In the Nursery of My Book House. LC 20-4479. 7 p. l., 432 p. illus. (part col.) 24 cm. c.1920. The Bookhouse for Children.
--In the Nursery of My Book House. LC 25-21163. 448 p. illus. (part col.) 24 cm. c.1925. The Bookhouse for Children.
--In the Nursery of My Book House. LC 38-541. 6 p. l., 17-224 p. illus. (part col.) 24 cm. c.1937. The Book House for Children.
--The Latch Key of My Book House. LC 22-11853. 320 p. illus. (part col.) 24 cm. c.1922. The Bookhouse for Children.
--The Latch Key of My Book House. LC 25-21161. 448 p. illus. (part col.) 24 cm. c.1925. The Bookhouse for Children.
--The Magic Garden of My Book House. LC 38-547. 2 p. l., 11-224 p. illus. (part col.) 24 cm. c.1937. The Book House for Children.
--My Book House. LC 50-14984. 12 v. illus. (part col.) 24 cm. 1950. Book House for Children.
--My Book House. 12v. illus. (part col.) 24cm. 1956. Book House for Children.
--My Book House. LC 60-6365. 12 v. illus. (part col.) 24 cm. c.1960. Book House for Children.
--My Book House. LC 65-23921. 12 v. illus. (part col.) 24 cm. 1965. Book House for Children.
--My Book House. LC 74-155096. (Illus.). 12 v. 25cm. 1971. Book House for Children.
--Nursery Friends from France. Petersham, Maud Sylvia Fuller, Mrs. (1890-) & Petersham, Miska (1889-1960), illus. LC 50-4604. 191 p. col. illus. 29 cm. 1950. Book House for Children.

--The Doll Dramas: Contains; The Doll's Drama, A Midsummer Day Queen, Mistress Mary Quite Contrary, The Princess and the Swineherd, The Lucky Sixpence and The Revolution in Sugar-Canida. (Half Hour Play Series.: Vol. 2). N.D. Frederick Stokes.

Milman, Emily

--The Little Sunbeam of the Farm House. (Illus.). N.D. Methodist Bk Concern.

Milman, Helen, pseud., see Crofton, Helen Rose Ann Milman.

Milman, Helen, pseud. (1857-)

--Little Ivan's Hero. Crofton, Helen Rose Ann Milman. (Illus.). (The Rugby Series.). 1915. A L Burt & Co.

--Little Ivan's Hero. Crofton, Helen Rose Ann Milman. (Illus.). (The Little Men Ser.). N.D. A. L. Burt's Pubs.

--Little Ivan's Hero. Crofton, Helen Rose Ann Milman. (Illus.). N.D. E. P. Dutton & Co.

--Little Ivan's Hero: A Story of Child Life. Crofton, Helen Rose Ann Milman. (The Rugby Series for Boys and Girls). N.D. A. L. Burt Company.

--The Little Ladies. Crofton, Helen Rose Ann Milman. N.D. J. B. Lippincott.

--Of High and Low Degree. Crofton, Helen Rose Ann Milman. N.D. E. & J. B. Young & Co.

--Those Children. Crofton, Helen Rose Ann Milman. (Illus.). N.D. E P Dutton.

--Uncle Bill's Children. Crofton, Helen Rose Ann Milman. N.D. J. B. Lippincott.

Milman, Robert (1816-1876)

--The Way Through the Desert: Or, The Caravan. LC 50-40330. 110 p. illus. 16 cm. 1863. General Protestant Episcopal S. School Union.

Miln, Louise Jordan

--Rice. N.D. Frederick A. Stokes Co.

Milne, A. A. see Milne, Alan Alexander (1882-1956) & Disney, Walt, Productions.

Milne, Alan Alexander, ed. see Grahame, Kenneth.

Milne, Alan Alexander (1882-1956), adapted by see Mother Goose.

Milne, Alan Alexander (1882-1956)

--The Christopher Robin Birthday Book. N.D. E. P. Dutton & Co.

--The Christopher Robin Book of Verse. 1st. ed. Shepard, Ernest Howard (1879-1976), illus. (Illus.). 62 p. 27cm. 1967. Dutton.

--The Christopher Robin Reader: From When We Were Very Young, Now We Are Six, Winni-the-Pooh, The House at Pooh Corner. LC 29-17532. 2 p. l., vii-xiii p. 1 l., 171 p. illus. 19 1/2 cm. c.1929. E. P. Dutton & Co., Inc.

--The Christopher Robin Story Book. LC 66-12251. (Illus.). xi, 171 p. 21cm. 1966, c.1929. Dutton.

--The Christopher Robin Story Book: From When We Were Very Young. Now We Are Six, Winnie-the-Pooh, The House at Pooh Corner. LC 29-209749. xiii p., 1 l., 171 p. illus. 19 1/2 cm. c.1929. E. P. Dutton & Co., Inc.

--The Christopher Robin Verse: Being 'When We Were Very Young; and 'Now We Are Six'. (With a Preface for Parents). xi, 210 p., 1 l. col. front., illus., col. plates. 21 cm. c.1932. E. P. Dutton & Co., Inc.

--The Christopher Robin Verses. Shepard, Ernest Howard (1879-1976), illus. LC 32-31502. (Illus.). xi,210p. 21cm. 1932. E. P. Dutton & Co.

--Fourteen Songs from "When We Were Very Young". N.D. E. P. Dutton & Co.

--A Gallery of Children. Le Mair, Henriette Willebeek (1889-1966), illus. Saida, pseud. LC 25-20978. 105 p. col. plates. 30 1/2 cm. c.1925. David McKay Company.

--A Gallery of Children. Watson, A. H, illus. LC 76-41919. (Illus.). 125 p. 18cm. 1976, c.1925. D. McKay Co.

--A Gallery of Children. Watson, A. H., illus. LC 46-31652. 125 p. incl. front., illus. 19 1/2 cm. N.D. David McKay Company.

--The House at Pooh Corner. Shepard, Ernest Howard (1879-1976), illus. LC 61-16260. (Illus.). 180 p. 20cm. 1961, c.1928. Dutton.

--The House at Pooh Corner. Shepard, Ernest Howard (1879-1976), illus. LC 28-24272. xi, 178 p., 1 l. incl. front., illus. 20 cm. c.1928. E. P. Dutton & Co., Inc.

--The Hums of Pooh. N.D. E P Dutton & Co.

--Introducing Winnie-the-Pooh, and Other Selections. Shepard, Ernest Howard (1879-1976), illus. LC 47-6000. 23 p. illus. 25 cm. 1947. E. P. Dutton.

--The King's Breakfast, and Other Selections. Shepard, Ernest Howard (1879-1976), illus. LC 47-600160. 23 p. illus. 25 cm. c.1947. E. P. Dutton.

--The Magic Hill, and Other Stories. Sewell, Helen Moore (1896-1957), illus. LC 39-23413. 40 p. incl. col. front., illus. (part col) 27 1/2 cm. c.1937. Grosset & Dunlap.

--More "Very Young" Songs. N.D. E. P. Dutton & Co.

--Now We Are Six. Shepard, Ernest Howard (1879-1976), illus. 104p. illus. 20cm. 1961, c.1927. Dutton.

--The Old Sailor, and Other Selections. Shepard, Ernest Howard (1879-1976), illus. LC 47-6002. 23 p. illus. 23 cm. 1947. E. P. Dutton.

--Once on a Time. N.D. Grosset & Dunlap.

--Once on a Time. Brock, Henry Matthew (1875-1960), illus. 358p. 1922. G P Putnam's Sons.

--Once on a Time. Perl, Susan (1922-1983), illus. (Illus.). (gr. 5 up). 1962. (ISBN 0-8212-0267-7). NYGS.

--Pooh Song Book. Shepard, Ernest Howard (1879-1976), illus. (gr. 1-4). 1961. Dutton.

--The Pooh Story Book. Shepard, Ernest Howard (1879-1976), illus. LC 65-19580. 77 p. illus. (part col.) 26 cm. 1965. Dutton.

--Pooh's Alphabet Book. Shepard, Ernest Howard (1879-1976), illus. LC 75-12507. (Illus.). 60 p. 15cm. 1975. (ISBN 0-525-37370-5). Dutton.

--Pooh's Bedtime Book. 1st ed. Shepard, Ernest Howard (1879-1976), illus. LC 80-65523. (Illus.). 40 p. 28cm. c.1980. (ISBN 0-525-37373-X). Dutton.

--Pooh's Birthday Book. 1st ed. Shepard, Ernest Howard (1879-1976), illus. LC 63-15754. (Illus.). 16cm. 1963. Dutton.

--Pooh's Counting Book. Shepard, Ernest Howard (1879-1976), illus. LC 82-5170. p. cm. c.1982. (ISBN 0-525-44016-X). Dutton.

--Pooh's Library, 4 bks. Shepard, Ernest Howard (1879-1976), illus. Incl. Winnie the Pooh; When We Were Very Young; Now We Are Six; House at Pooh Corner. (Illus.). (gr. k-4). 1961. Set. (02718-820). Dutton.

--Pooh's Pot O'honey. Shepard, Ernest Howard (1879-1976), illus. LC 68-24726. (Illus.). 4 v. (in case. 1968. Dutton.

--Pooh's Quiz Book. 1st ed. Shepard, Ernest Howard (1879-1976), illus. LC 77-6204. (Illus.). 58 p. 15cm. c.1977. (ISBN 0-525-37485-X). Dutton.

--Prince Rabbit. Shepard, Mary (1900-), illus. Bd. with Princess Who Could Not Laugh. (gr. 1-5). N.D. (ISBN 0-525-37687-9). Dutton.

--Prince Rabbit, and the Princess Who Could Not Laugh. 1st ed. Shepard, Mary Eleanor (1909-), illus. LC 66-7120. 72p. illus. (pt. col.) 26cm. 1966. (ISBN 0-525-37687-9). Dutton.

--The Princess and the Apple Tree, and Other Stories. Sewell, Helen Moore (1896-1957), illus. LC 37-32161. 40 p. col. front., col. illus. 27 1/2 cm. c.1937. Grosset & Dunlap.

--Sneezles, and Other Selections. Shepard, Ernest Howard (1879-1976), illus. LC 47-6003. 23 p. illus. 25 cm. 1947. E. P. Dutton.

--Songs from "Now We Are Six". N.D. E. P. Dutton & Co.

--Teddy Bear. N.D. E. P. Dutton & Co.

--Toad of Toad Hall: A Play. (Adapted from the book by Kenneth Grahame, 1859-1932). (gr. 4 up). 1965. (ISBN 0-684-82169-9). Scribner.

--Toad of Toad Hall: A Play from Kenneth Grahame's Book. 1957. Scribner.

--The Very Young Calendar, 1930. Shepard, Ernest Howard (1879-1976), illus. LC 30-279139. cover-title, 13 l. col. illus. 25 1/2 cm. 1929. E. P. Dutton & Co., Inc.

--Walt Disney's Pooh's Adventures with Words. LC 84-8065. 1984. (ISBN 0-525-67158-7). Dutton.

--Walt Disney's Winnie-the-Pooh: A Tight Squeeze. Disney Walt,Studio, illus. (Illus.). (ps-3). 1962. (ISBN 0-307-10859-7, Golden Pr). (ISBN 0-307-60859-X). Western Pub.

--Walt Disney's Winnie-the-Pooh and the Pebble Hunt. LC 81-83002. (Illus.). 24 p. 16cm. (First little golden book). c.1982. (ISBN 0-307-10121-5). (ISBN 0-307-68121-1). Golden Press.

--Walt Disney's Winnie-the-Pooh and the Windy Day. LC 84-194252. (Illus.). 22 p. 23cm. (Disney's Wonderful World of Reading). c.1984. (ISBN 0-394-86179-5). Random House.

--Walt Disney's Winnie the Pooh and Tigger Too. LC 75-20349. (Illus.). 42 p. 25cm. (Disney's wonderful world of reading ; 35). 1976, c.1975. (ISBN 0-394-82569-1). Random House.

--Walt Disney's Winnie-the-Pooh Scratch & Sniff Book. Disney, Walt, Studio, illus. (Illus.). 32p. (Golden Scratch & Sniff Bk.). (ps-6). 1974. (ISBN 0-307-13528-4, Golden Pr). (ISBN 0-307-63528-7). Western Pub.

--When We Were Very Young. Shepard, Ernest Howard (1879-1976), illus. LC 61-162592. 102p. illus. 20cm. 1961, c.1924. Dutton.

--When We Were Very Young. Shepard, Ernest Howard (1879-1976), illus. LC 24-29102. xii, p., 1 l., 100 p. incl. front., illus. 19 1/2 cm. 1924. E. P. Dutton & Co.

--When We Were Very Young. Shepard, Ernest Howard (1879-1976), illus. 1966. E.P. Dutton & Co.

--Winnie-Ille-Pu: A Latin Version of A. A. Milne's Winnie-the-Pooh. Shepard, Ernest Howard (1879-1976), illus. Lenard, Alexander, tr. 120p. 1984. (ISBN 0-525-24267-8). Dutton.

--Winnie-the Pooh. (A Reproduction of the Original Manuscript). (gr. k up). 1971. Dutton.

--Winnie the Pooh. LC 71-81727. 221p. 26cm. 1971. Dutton.

--Winnie the Pooh. colored. (gr. 1-5). 1974. Dutton.

--Winnie-the-Pooh. xi, 1 l., 158 p. illus., plates. 20 cm. c.1926. E. P. Dutton & Company.

--Winnie-the-Pooh. (Illus.). 8p. (Baby's First Golden Bks.). (ps). 1982. (ISBN 0-307-02217-X, Golden Pr). Western Pub.

--Winnie-the-Pooh. Page, Helen, illus. LC 46-22514. 32 p. col. illus. 26 1/2 x 23 1/2 cm. 1946. John Martin's House, Inc.

--Winnie-the-Pooh. Shepard, Ernest Howard (1879-1976), illus. LC 55-2595. viii, 159p. illus. 20cm. 1954, c.1926. Dutton.

--Winnie-the-Pooh. Shepard, Ernest Howard (1879-1976), illus. x, 161 p. illus. 19 cm. 1961, c.1954. Dutton.

--Winnie-the-Pooh. Shepard, Ernest Howard (1879-1976), illus. LC 63-22987. (Illus.). x, 161p. 19cm. 1961, c.1926. Dutton.

--Winnie-the-Pooh. Shepard, Ernest Howard (1879-1976), illus. LC 74-7215. (Illus.). xi, 161 p. 22cm. 1974, c.1926. (ISBN 0-525-43034-2). Dutton.

--Winnie-the-Pooh. 1st ed. Shepard, Ernest Howard (1879-1976) & Scott, Hilda, illus. LC 74-7215. (Illus.). xi,161p. 22cm. 1974, c.1926. (ISBN 0-525-43034-2). Dutton.

--Winnie-the-Pooh. Shepard, Ernest Howard (1879-1976), illus. LC 26-18391. (Illus.). 20cm. 158p. 1926. E. P. Dutton & Co.

--Winnie-the-Pooh: A Pop-Up Book. (Illus.). 12p. 1984. (ISBN 0-525-44119-0). Dutton.

--Winnie-the-Pooh & Eeyore's House. Disney, Walt, Studio, illus. (Illus.). (Tell-a-Tale Reader). (gr. k-3). 1976. (ISBN 0-307-68620-5, Whitman). Western Pub.

--Winnie-the-Pooh and Eeyore's Tail. Shepard, Ernest Howard (1879-1976), illus. LC 52-8249. unpaged. illus. 25 cm. (A Pop-up Picture Book). 1952. Dutton.

--Winnie-the-Pooh and the Bees. Shepard, Ernest Howard (1879-1976), illus. LC 52-8248. unpaged. illus. 25 cm. (Pop-up picture book). 1952. Dutton.

--Winnie-the-Pooh & the Blustery Day. (Illus.). (Tell-a-Tale Readers). (gr. k-3). 1979. (ISBN 0-307-68577-2, Whitman). Western Pub.

--Winnie-the-Pooh & the Pebble Hunt. (Illus.). 24p. (First Little Golden Bks.). (ps). 1982. (ISBN 0-307-10121-5, Golden Pr). (ISBN 0-307-68121-1). Western Pub.

--Winnie-the-Pooh & Tigger. Disney, Walt, Studio, illus. (Illus.). (gr. k-3). 1976. (ISBN 0-307-60121-8, Golden Pr). Western Pub.

--Winnie-the-Pooh & Tigger. Disney, Walt, Studio, illus. (Illus.). (Walt Disney Square Bks.). (gr. k-3). 1978. (ISBN 0-307-66097-4, Golden Pr). Western Pub.

--Winnie-the-Pooh Meets Gopher. Disney, Walt, Studio, illus. (Illus.). 24p. (gr. k-3). 1976. (ISBN 0-307-60017-3, Golden Pr). Western Pub.

--The Winnie-the-Pooh Scratch and Sniff Book: In Which Tigger Is Unbounced and Pooh and Piglet Find Their Way Home by a Nose. LC 74-14158. (Illus.). 28 p. 25cm. (Golden fragrance book). 1974. (ISBN 0-307-13528-4). Golden Press.

--Winnie-the-Pooh: The Unbouncing of Tigger : a Story. LC 76-54827. (Illus.). 24 p. 32cm. 1977, c.1974. (ISBN 0-307-10504-0). Golden Press.

--Winnie-the-Pooh: The Unbouncing of Trigger. Disney, Walt, Studio, illus. (Illus.). (Tell-a-Tale Readers). (gr. k-3). 1978. (ISBN 0-307-60504-3, Whitman). (ISBN 0-686-77046-3). Western Pub.

--Winnie-the-Pooh's Rhymes. (Baby's First Golden Bks.). 1977. (ISBN 0-307-10749-3, Golden Pr). Western Pub.

--The World of Christopher Robin: The Complete When We Were Very Young and Now We Are Six. Shepard, Ernest Howard (1879-1976), illus. LC 58-9571. 234p. illus. 24cm. 1958. Dutton.

--The World of Pooh: The Complete Winnie-the-Pooh and The House at Pooh Corner. Shepard, Ernest Howard (1879-1976), illus. LC 57-8986. (Illus.). 314 p. 24cm. 1957. Dutton.

Milne, Lorus J. & Milne, Margery

--The Crab that Crawled Out of the Past. Gosner, Kenneth, illus. (Illus.). (gr. 4-8). N.D. (ISBN 0-689-20278-4). (ISBN 0-689-20279-2). Atheneum.

--The Mystery of the Bog Forest. (Illus.). 128p. (gr. 5up). 1984. (ISBN 0-396-08318-8). Dodd.

Milne, Margery, jt. auth. see Milne, Lorus J.

Milne, Ruth

--TV Girl Friday. King, Ruth, illus. LC 57-5517. 248p. illus. 20cm. 1957. Little, Brown.

Milner, A.

--Louisa Broadhurst. (Illus.). (Happy Home Library). N.D. E. P. Dutton & Co.

Milner, Edith

--The Lily of Lumley. N.D. Macmillan & Co.

Milner, Thomas

--Half-Hour Readings for Sunday Afternoons. N.D. Thomas Nelson & Sons.

Milner-White, Eric (1884-) & Duckett, Eleanor Shipley (1880-1976)

--The Book of Hugh and Nancy. Lufkin, Raymond H. (1897-), illus. LC 38-11473. 278p. 21cm. 1938. Macmillan Co.

Miloche, Hilda & Kane, Wilma

--At Teddy Bear's House. Miloche, Hilda & Kane, Wilma, illus. LC 52-1966. unpaged. illus. 21 cm. (Easy-to-read book, 4203). 1952. Saalfield Pub. Co.

--Judy and Jim. Miloche, Hilda & Kane, Wilma, illus. (Big Golden Book). 1947. Golden Press.

--Judy and Jim. Miloche, Hilda & Kane, Wilma, illus. (Big Golden Book: 430). 1947. Simon and Schuster.

--The Little Golden Paper Dolls. LC 52-368. unpaged illus. 21 cm. (Little golden library, 113). 1951. Simon and Schuster.

--Mother Goose Land with Judy and Jim. Miloche, Hilda & Kane, Wilma, illus. (Big Golden Book: 431). 1949. Simon and Schuster.

--One More Story Please!. Miloche, Hilda & Kane, Wilma, illus. LC 48-15383. (Illus.). 22cm. 40p. (A Cozy Corner Bk.). 1947. Whitman Pub. Co.

--The Paper Doll Wedding. Miloche, Hilda & Kane, Wilma, illus. Reissue of 1954 ed. (Little Golden Book). 1958. Golden Press.

Milone, Karen

--Beauty and the Beast. Milone, Karen, illus. LC 81-612. p. cm. c.1981. (ISBN 0-89375-464-1). (ISBN 0-89375-465-X). Troll Associates.

Milord, Jerry, jt. auth. see Milord, Sue.

Milord, Sue & Milord, Jerry

--Maggie and the Goodbye Gift. 1st ed. Milord, Sue & Milord, Jerry, illus. LC 79-12424. (Illus.). 33 p. 26cm. c.1979. (ISBN 0-688-41912-7). (ISBN 0-688-51912-1). Lothrop, Lee & Shepard.

Milostan, Harry

--Folksy Fables. Sarnacki, John & Milostan, Harry, illus. LC 84-61017. (Illus.). 80p. (Orig.). 1984. (ISBN 0-918020-07-7). Masspac Pub.

Milska, Anna, jt. auth. see Markowska, Wanda.

Milton, Constance Cozzens

--The Giraffe's Necktie. Priest, Joyce, illus. LC 69-16195. (Illus.). 32 p. 1969. Nelson.

Milton, Hilary Herbert (1920-)

--Blind Flight. LC 79-23279. 138 p. 22cm. 1980. (ISBN 0-531-04108-5). Watts.

--The Brats and Mr. Jack. LC 80-23114. 220 p. 21cm. c.1980. (ISBN 0-8253-0004-5). Beaufort Books.

--Craven House Horrors. LC 82-7020. p. cm. (Plot Your Own Horror Stories: No. 1). c.1982. (ISBN 0-671-45631-8). Wanderer Books.

--Dognappers!. LC 81-16016. p. cm. c.1982. (ISBN 0-671-44475-1). Wanderer Books.

--Emergency Ten-Thirty-Three Eleven. LC 76-30292. p. cm. 1977. (ISBN 0-531-02905-0). (ISBN 0-531-02905-0). F. Watts.

--Escape from High Doom. Frame, Paul (1913-), illus. (Illus.). 128p. (Plot-it-yourself Horror Stories). (gr. 3-7). 1984. (ISBN 0-671-53039-9). Messner.

--Escape from High Doom. Schwartz, Betty, ed. Frame, Paul (1913-), illus. LC 84-7372. (Illus.). 128p. (Orig.). (Plot It Yourself Horror Stories Ser.: No. 5). (gr. 3-7). 1984. (ISBN 0-671-52405-4). Wanderer Bks.

--Fun House Terrors!. Frame, Paul (1913-), illus. (Illus.). 128p. (Plot-it-yourself Horror Stories). (gr. 3-7). 1984. (ISBN 0-671-53041-0). Messner.

--Fun House Terrors. Schwartz, Betty, ed. Frame, Paul (1913-), illus. LC 84-7374. (Illus.). 128p. (Orig.). (Plot It Yourself Horror Stories Ser.: No. 6). (gr. 3-7). 1984. (ISBN 0-671-52406-2). Wanderer Bks.

--The Gitaway Box. (gr. 4-9). 1980. (ISBN 0-89191-243-6). Cook.

--The Gitaway Box. LC 68-21534. 1968. (ISBN 0-88331-025-2). Luce.

--Horror Hotel. Frame, Paul (1913-), illus. LC 83-12453. (Illus.). (Plot-Your-Own Horror Stories: No. 4). c.1983. (ISBN 0-671-49249-7). Wanderer Books.

--The Longest Highway. LC 78-74526. 1979. (ISBN 0-89191-138-3). Cook.

--Mayday! Mayday!. LC 78-24007. 152 p. 22cm. 1979. (ISBN 0-531-02890-9). F. Watts.

--Museum of the Living Dead. Frame, Paul (1913-), illus. LC 84-23709. (Illus.). 120 p. 19cm. (Plot-it-Yourself Horror Stories: No. 7). c.1985. (ISBN 0-671-54447-0). Wanderer Books.

--Nightmare Store. LC 82-7027. (Illus.). 121 p. 19cm. (Plot Your Own Horror Stories: No. 2). c.1982. (ISBN 0-671-45630-X). Wanderer Books.

--November's Wheel. LC 75-23040. 186 p. 21cm. 1976. (ISBN 0-200-00159-0). Abelard-Schuman.

--Nowhere to Run. LC 78-2798. 153 p. 22cm. 1978. (ISBN 0-531-02247-1). F. Watts.

Mitchell, Adrian (1932-), adapted by.
--The Baron on the Island of Cheese: More Adventures of Baron Munchausen. Benson, Patrick, illus. LC 85-28423. (Original Author: Rudolf Erich Raspe, 1737-1794). p. cm. N.D. (ISBN 0-399-21309-0). Philomel Books.
--The Baron Rides Out. Benson, Patrick, illus. LC 85-3715. (Original Author: Rudolf Erich Raspe, 1737-1794). p. cm. 1985. (ISBN 0-399-21280-9). Philomel Books.

Mitchell, Anne Templeton, Mrs. (1859-)
--The Indians and the Oki: A Story of Old France in the New World. LC 25-228983. vi, 282 p. incl. front, illus. 19 cm. c.1925. Row, Peterson and Company.

Mitchell, Barbara (1941-)
--Cornstalks & Cannonballs. Ritz, Karen, illus. LC 79-91304. (Illus.). (Carolrhoda on My Own Books). (gr. 1-2). 1980. (ISBN 0-87614-121-1). Carolrhoda Bks.
--Hush, Puppies. Wyman, Cherie R., illus. LC 82-4465. p. cm. (A Carolrhoda On My Own Book). c.1983. (ISBN 0-87614-201-3). Carolrhoda Books.
--The Old Fasnacht. Kiedrowski, Priscilla, illus. LC 82-23619. p. cm. (A Carolrhoda On My Own Book). c.1983. (ISBN 0-87614-221-8). Carolrhoda Books.

Mitchell, Cynthia, jt. auth. see Ichikawa, Satomi.

Mitchell, Cynthia (1922-)
--Halloweena Hecatee, and Other Rhymes to Skip to. Browne, Eileen, illus. LC 78-60175. (Illus.). 32 p. 20cm. 1979, c.1978. (ISBN 0-690-03925-5). (ISBN 0-690-03926-3). Crowell.
--Playtime. Ichikawa, Satomi (1939-), illus. LC 78-13326. (Illus.). 32 p. 1979, c.1978. (ISBN 0-529-05514-7). (ISBN 0-529-05515-5). Collins.
--Under the Cherry Tree. Ichikawa, Satomi (1939-), illus. LC 79-11579. (Illus.). 1979. (ISBN 0-529-05543-0, Philomel). (ISBN 0-529-05544-9). Putnam Pub Group.

Mitchell, Don, jt. auth. see Grimm, Gary.

Mitchell, Don, jt. auth. see Wayman, Joe.

Mitchell, Don & Grimm, Gary
--Cemetery Box. (gr. 3-8). 1976. (ISBN 0-916456-01-3). Good Apple.

Mitchell, Don & Wayman, Joe
--Ballad of Lucy Lum. (gr. k-8). 1977. (ISBN 0-916456-10-2). Good Apple.

Mitchell, Donald Charles Peter (1925-), ed. see Biss, Roderick.

Mitchell, Donald Charles Peter (1925-), ed.
--Every Child's Book of Nursery Songs. Howard, Alan (1922-), illus. Blyton, Carey (1932-), contrib. by. LC 69-11683. (Music Arranged by Carey Blyton). (Illus.). 175 p. 29cm. 1969, c.1968. Crown Publishers.

Mitchell, Edith
--The Otherside Book. (Illus.). N.D. The Reilly & Britton Co.

Mitchell, Elizabeth Harcourt
--The Beautiful Face: A Tale. (Illus.). N.D. E & J B Young.
--Beautiful Face: A Tale. (Illus.). N.D. E. P. Dutton & Cp.
--The Beautiful Face: A Tale. 1891. Thomas Whittaker.
--Diamond Ring. (Illus.). N.D. E. P. Dutton & Co.
--The Diamond Ring. N.D. Thomas Whittaker.
--Engel the Fearless (Pub. by Society for Promoting Christian Knowledge). N.D. E. & J. B. Young & Co.
--Golden Horseshoes. (Illus.). N.D. E. P. Dutton & Co.
--Golden Horseshoes: A Tale of Chivalry for Young and Old. 1891. Thomas Whittaker.
--Her Majesty's Bear. 1891. Thomas Whittaker.
--Her Majesty's Bear: A Tale. (Illus.). N.D. E. P. Dutton & Co.
--Little Blue Lady, and Other Tales. (Illus.). N.D. E P Dutton.
--The Little Blue Lady and Other Tales. 1891. Thomas Whittaker.
--Norton Hall. (Author of "The Beautiful Face."). (Illus.). N.D. E P Dutton.
--Norton Hall. 1891. Thomas Whittaker.

Mitchell, Eloise A.
--Songs & Games for Pre-School Children. (gr. k-1). N.D. Carlton.

Mitchell, Elyne see Mitchell, Sibyl Elyne Keith.

Mitchell, Fay Langellier (1884-1964)
--Every Road Has Two Directions. 1st ed. LC 60-13546. 212p. 22cm. 1960. Doubleday.
--Pitch in His Hair. 1st ed. Crowell, Pers (1910-), illus. LC 54-5901. 224p. illus. 22cm. 1954. Doubleday.
--The Tide Always Turns. Bennett, Richard Michael (1899-), illus. LC 57-11434. (Illus.). 215 p. 22cm. 1957. Doubleday.

Mitchell, George William (1873-)
--King Kuriosity. LC 26-17111. (Illus.). 23cm. 95p. 1926. Small, Maynard & Company.
--Sergeant Giggles. Mitchell, George William (1873-), illus. LC 29-25036. 118 p. incl. illus., plates. (part col.) col. front. 21 1/2 cm. 1929. J. B. Lippincott Company.

Mitchell, Harley W., tr. see Baumbach, Rudolf.

Mitchell, Isla
--The Beginning Was a Dutchman. Kennedy, Richard (1910-), illus. LC 46-4397. vi p., 1 l., 196 p., 1 l. illus. 21 cm. 1946. Dodd, Mead & Company.

Mitchell, Joan
--Our God Gives Life. (gr. 1-3). 1984. (ISBN 0-89837-098-1, Pub. by Pflaum Press). Peter Li.

Mitchell, John Ames (1845-1918)
--Life's Fairy Tales. Gibson, Charles Dana, et al. (1867-1944), illus. N.D. Frederick A. Stokes.

Mitchell, Kitty
--Maynard, the Nehalem River White Duck & Other Stories. Anderson, Rus, illus. (Illus.). 31p. 1974. (ISBN 0-682-47771-0). Exposition.

Mitchell, Kurt
--Jonah. (Illus.). 27p. 1981. (ISBN 0-89107-224-1, Crossway Bks). Good News.
--Poor Ralph. Mitchell, Kurt, illus. LC 83-120988. (Illus.). 32 p. 27cm. 1982. (ISBN 0-89107-273-X). Crossway Books.

Mitchell, Laisdell
--Tony: The Story of a Waif. 58p. N.D. American Baptist Publication Society.

Mitchell, Lebbeus (1879-)
--Bobby in Search of a Birthday. Nuyttens, Joseph Pierre, illus. LC 17-2477. 64 p. illus. 19 cm. 1916. P. F. Volland & Co.
--The Circus Comes to Town. (Junior Bks. for Boys and Girls). N.D. Cupples & Leon Co.
--The Circus Comes to Town. Chase, Rhoda Campbell, illus. LC 21-181683. 4 p. l., 204 p., 1 l., col. front., illus., col. plates. 20 1/2 cm. $1.7. 1921. Little, Brown, and Company.
--Here, Tricks, Here!. (Junior Bks. for Boys and Girls). N.D. Cupples & Leon Co.
--Here, Tricks, Here!. Maturo, Joseph A., illus. LC 23-132603. 5 p. l., 3-232 p. front., plates, 19 1/2 cm. $1.5. 1923. The Century Co.
--Kippy, the Dog of Carlow: A Story for Children of Ten to Fourteen Years. LC 51-1077. 209 p. front. 21 cm. 1950. Cupples and Leon.
--One Boy Too Many. (Junior Bks. for Boys and Girls). N.D. Cupples & Leon Co.
--One Boy Too Many. Berger, William Merritt (1872-), illus. LC 26-15712. vii, 191 p. front., plates, 19 1/2 cm. $1.7. c.1926. The Century Co.

Mitchell, Louvina, jt. auth. see Lyman.

Mitchell, Lucy Sprague, Mrs. (1878-)
--Another Here and Now Story Book. Slocum, Rosalie (1906-), illus. N.D. E. P. Dutton & Co.
--Fix It, Please!. Wilkin, Eloise Burns (1904-), illus. LC 48-1846. 42 p. illus. (part col.) 21 cm. (The Little Golden Library: No. 32). 1947. Simon and Schuster.
--Guess What's in the Grass. Glannon, Edward John (1911-), illus. LC 45-35206. 30 p. col. illus. 21 x 25 1/2 cm. (Young Scott books). c.1945. W. R. Scott, Inc.
--The Here & Now Story Book. rev. & enl. ed. Van Loon, Henrik Willem (1882-1944) & Price, Christine Hilda (1928-1980), illus. (Illus.). (ps-2). 1948. (ISBN 0-525-31651-5). Dutton.
--The New House in the Forest. Reed, Mary, ed. Wilkin, Eloise Burns (1904-), illus. (Little Golden Library). 1945. Simon & Schuster.
--The New House in the Forest. Wilkin, Eloise Burns (1904-), illus. LC 46-32237. 42 p. illus. (part col.) 20 x 17 cm. (The Little golden library. 24). 1946. Simon and Schuster.
--The Red, White & Blue Auto. Gergely, Tibor (1900-1978), illus. LC 43-15138. 33 p. col. illus. 13 x 21 cm. c.1943. W. R. Scott.
--A Year in the City. Gergely, Tibor (1900-1978), illus. LC 48-8178. 42 p. illus. (part col) 21 cm. (Little golden library 48). 1948. Simon and Schuster.
--A Year on the Farm. Floethe, Richard (1901-), illus. LC 48-62164. 42 p. illus. (part col.) 21 cm. (The Little Golden Library: No. 37). c.1948. Simon and Schuster.

Mitchell, Lucy Sprague, Mrs. (1878-), ed.
--Boats and Bridges: Stories for Children Under Seven. LC 33-11065. 20cm. 32p. 1933. John Day Co.
--Streets: Stories for Children Under Seven. LC 33-11064. 20cm. 32p. (Cooperating School Pamphlets: No. 2). 1933. John Day Co.
--Trains: Stories for Children Under Seven. LC 33-11066. 32 p. 19 1/2 cm. (co-operating school pamphlets. no. 4). c.1933. The John Day Company.

Mitchell, Lucy Sprague, Mrs. (1878-) & Black, Irma Simonton (1906-1972)
--The Taxi That Hurried. Gergely, Tibor (1900-1978), illus. LC 46-3222. 42 p. illus. (part col.) 20 x 17 cm. (The Little golden library. 25). 1946. Simon and Schuster.

Mitchell, Lucy Sprague, Mrs. (1878-) & Black, Irma Simonton (1906-1972), eds.
--Believe and Make Believe. 1st ed. Gordon, Ayala, illus. LC 56-8316. 190p. illus. 21cm. 1956. Dutton.

Mitchell, M. A.
--Two Doll's House. N.D. E & J B Young & Co.

Mitchell, Marie, Mrs.
--The Night the Coyotes Sang. LC 66-12125. 151p. 21cm. c.1966. McKay.

Mitchell, Minnie Belle Alexander, Mrs. (1860-)
--Gray Moon Tales. Vawter, Will, illus. LC 26-10512. 7 p. l., 169 p. illus. 20 cm. c.1926. The Bobbs-Merrill Company.
--Hoosier Boy: James Whitcomb Riley. Browne, Syd, illus. LC 42-21963. 179 p. illus. 20 cm. (The Childhood of famous Americans series). 1942. The Bobbs-Merrill Company.
--James Whitcomb Riley: Hoosier Boy. Elgin, Kathleen (1923-), illus. LC 62-12696. 200p. illus. 20cm. (Childhood of famous Americans). 1962. Bobbs-Merrill.

Mitchell, Mrs.
--King's Stirrup (Pub. by Society for Promoting Christian Knowledge). N.D. E. & J. B. Young & Co.

Mitchell, Muriel Moscrip
--The Adventures of Nip and Tuck. Ellsworth, Mary, illus. LC 27-23293. 40 p. col. illus. 19 cm. (Lettered on cover: Volland Sunny book series). c.1927. The P. F. Volland Company.

Mitchell, Pryce
--Deep Water. N.D. Little Brown & Co.

Mitchell, Ruth
--Aunt Lucia's Locket, and Other Stories, 1 of 6 vols. (Illus.). (The Little Pitcher Library). N.D. Cassell, Petter, Galpin.
--Marion's Two Homes, 1 of 6 vols. (Illus.). 230p. (The Evening Hour Library). N.D. Cassell, Petter, Galpin.

Mitchell, Sibyl Elyne Keith (1913-)
--The Silver Brumby. Thompson, Ralph & Savitt, Sam (1917-), illus. LC 59-11498. 191p. illus. 21cm. 1959, c.1958. Dutton.
--The Snow Filly. Huxtable, Grace, illus. LC 61-5872. 21cm. 192p. 1961, c.1960. Dutton.

Mitchell, Silas Weir, jt. auth. see Stevenson, Elizabeth Wister.

Mitchell, Silas Weir (1829-1914)
--Mr. Kris Kringle: A Christmas Tale. LC 75-317269. 20cm. 48p. 1893. G. W. Jacobs.
--Mr. Kris Kringle: A Christmas Tale. De Land, Clyde O., illus. LC 4-22669. 105p. 1 p. 5 col. pl. (incl. front.) 19 1/2cm. 1904. G. W. Jacobs & Co.
--Prince Little Boy, and Other Tales Out of Fairy Land. New ed. (Illus.). 160p. N.D. The Century Co.
--Prince Little Boy and Other Tales Out of Fairy-Land. Church, Frederick S. & Mowbray, Siddons, illus. LC 12-36844. ix, 7-157 p. front., illus., plates. 20 1/2 cm. 1888. J. B. Lippincott Company.
--A Venture in Seventeen Seventy-Seven. 120 p. incl. col. front. 3 col. pl. 20 x 15 1/2 cm. 1908. G. W. Jacobs & Company.

Mitchell, William (1892-)
--Tom in the Wind. 1st ed. Mitchell, William (1892-), illus. LC 66-13487. 1 v. (unpaged) illus. 24 cm. 1966. Duell, Sloan and Pearce.

Mitchella
--Some Snow-Hill Girls. (Illus.). (Child Life Ser.). N.D. D. Lothrop Co.

Mitchison, Naomi Margaret Haldane, Mrs. (1897-)
--The Family at Ditlabeng. Stubbs, Joanna, illus. LC 71-125149. (Illus.). xii, 143 p. 21cm. 1st U.S. edition. (Ariel book). 1970, c.1969. (ISBN 0-374-32265-1). Farrar, Straus & Giroux.
--Friends and Enemies. Sassoon, Caroline, illus. LC 68-11185. (Illus.). 192 p. 21cm. 1st U.S. edition. 1968. John Day Co.
--The Hostages and Other Stories for Boys and Girls. Southby, Logi, illus. LC 31-506793. viii p., 2 l., 3-332 p. incl. front., illus., plates. 21 cm. c.1931. Harcourt, Brace and Company.
--Ketse and the Chief. Bloomer, Christine, illus. LC 67-13921. 59p. illus., (pt. col.) 18cm. (Salamander bks.). 1967, c.1965. Nelson.
--Nix-Nought-Nothing: Four Plays for Children. Bromhall, Winifred, illus. 1929. Harcourt Brace & Co.
--Sun and Moon. Wilkinson, Barry, illus. LC 72-13012. (Illus.). 93 p. 22cm. 1st U.S. edition. 1973. (ISBN 0-8407-6290-9). (ISBN 0-8407-6291-7). T. Nelson.
--Sunrise Tomorrow: A Story of Botswana. LC 72-97004. 120 p. 21cm. 1973. (ISBN 0-374-37298-5). Farrar, Straus and Giroux.

Mitchnik, Helen
--Egyptian and Sudanese Folk-Tales. Fraser, Eric, illus. LC 78-40202. p. cm. (Oxford myths and legends). 1978. (ISBN 0-19-274122-5). Oxford University Press.

Mitford, Mary Russell (1787-)
--Children of the Village. New ed. Murray, C. O., illus. N.D. George Routledge.

Mitford, Miss
--Tales and Stories. N.D. Scribner, Welford & Armstrong.

Mitgutsch, Ali
--The Busy Book. LC 75-34689. (Illus.). 1976. (ISBN 0-307-13768-6, Golden Pr). (ISBN 0-307-63768-9). Western Pub.
--Pedro's Sombrero. LC 60-16916. (Illus.). 27 x 28 cm. 1960. Bobbs-Merrill Co.

Mittelmann, Gertrude, ed.
--The Bird of the Golden Feather, and Other Arabic Folktales. LC 69-14546. (Illus.). 125 p. 21cm. 1969. Roy Publishers.

Mitten, Homer H
--The Enchanted Canyon: A Fairy Story. Eulalie, pseud. (1896-), illus. Banks, Eulalie M.. LC 33-19401. 3 p. l., v-ix, 1, 111 p. incl. illus. (part col. mounted) col. mounted plates. 24 1/2 cm. c.1932. Suttonhouse.
--The Enchanted Canyon: A Fairy Story. Eulalie, pseud. (1896-), illus. Banks, Eulalie M.. LC 33-24538. 3 p. l., v-ix, 1, 111 p. incl. illus. (part col. mounted) col. mounted plates. 24 1/2 cm. c.1933. Williams Publishing Company.

Mitton, G E, jt. ed. see Wyss, Johann Rudolf.

Mitton, Geraldine Edith, Miss, ed.
--Swiss Family Robinson. Rountree, Harry (1878-1950), illus. N.D. Macmillan.

Mityayev, A.
--The Ant & the Astronaut. 16p. 1973. (ISBN 0-8285-1099-7, Pub. by Progress Pubs USSR). Imported Pubns.

Miyazawa, Kenji (1896-1933)
--Winds and Wildcat Places. 1st ed. Taniuchi, Rokur O., illus. LC 67-26309. (Illus.). 95 p. 22cm. 1967. Kodansha International.
--Winds from Afar. Leach, Bernard, illus. Bester, John, tr. LC 75-174216. (Illus.). 164 p. 27cm. 1972. (ISBN 0-87011-171-X). Kodansha International Ltd.

Miyoshi, Sekiya (1924-)
--The Christmas Lamb. LC 80-112762. (Illus.). 32 p. c.1978. (ISBN 0-89742-010-1). Dawne-Leigh Publications.
--Jonah and the Big Fish. LC 81-3635. p. cm. 1981. (ISBN 0-687-20541-7). Abingdon Press.
--The Oldest Story in the World. Jensh, Barbara L, adapted by. Miyoshi, Sekiya (1924-), illus. LC 69-18145. (Illus.). 24 p. 25cm. 1969. (ISBN 0-8170-0436-X). Judson Press.
--Pooke and Kark in the Ark. Miyoshi, Sekiya (1924-), illus. LC 67-1272. 25cm. 25p. 1966, c.1964. Hawthorn Books.
--Singing David. LC 74-110722. (Illus.). 25 p. 25cm. (Watts international picture book). 1970, c.1969. (ISBN 0-531-01936-5). F. Watts.
--Singing David. 1971. (ISBN 0-531-01936-5). Franklin Watts.

Mizner, Elizabeth Howard see Howard, Elizabeth, pseud.

Mizumura, Kazue
--Flower, Moon, Snow: A Book of Haiku. Mizumura, Kazue, illus. LC 76-41180. (Illus.). 48 p. c.1977. (ISBN 0-690-01291-8). Crowell.
--Flower Moon Snow: A Book of Haiku. Mizumura, Kazue, illus. 1977. Harper.
--The Greedy One. (Illus.). 1964. Rand McNally Pub.
--I See the Winds. Mizumura, Kazue, illus. LC 66-12670. (Illus.). 1 v. (unpaged). 1966. Crowell. **Award: (ALA).**
--If I Built a Village. Mizumura, Kazue, illus. LC 77-140645. (Illus.). 32 p. 26cm. 1971. (ISBN 0-690-42903-7). Crowell. **Award: (BGH).**
--If I Were a Cricket ... Mizumura, Kazue, illus. LC 73-3495. (Illus.). 32 p. 26cm. 1973. (ISBN 0-690-00075-8). (ISBN 0-690-00075-8). Crowell.
--If I Were a Mother. Mizumura, Kazue, illus. LC 68-23668. 1v. (unpaged) illus. (pt. col.) 26cm. 1968. T. Y. Crowell. **Award: (ALA).**
--The Way of an Ant. Mizumura, Kazue, illus. LC 72-87155. (Illus.). 34 p. 27cm. 1970. T. Y. Crowell Co.

Mizumura, Kazue, jt. auth. see Matsuno, Masako.

Mizuta, Yone, tr. see Ishii, Momoko.

Mlagala, Martha V
--Yasin's Nightmare. LC 76-980209. (Illus.). 34 p. 19cm. 1976. East African Pub. House.

M. M. S, tr. see Kokhanovsky.

Moberg, Verne, tr. see Widerberg, Siv.

Mobley, Jane
--The Star Husband. 1st ed. Vojtech, Anna, illus. LC 78-1213. (Illus.). 32 p. 22cm. c.1979. (ISBN 0-385-14282-X). (ISBN 0-385-14283-8). Doubleday.

Moche, Dinah Rachel Levine (1936-)
--We're Taking an Airplane Trip. Bracken, Carolyn, illus. (Illus.). 24p. (Golden Look-Look Bks.). (ps-2). 1982. (ISBN 0-307-11869-X, Golden Pr). Western Pub.

Mockler, Geraldine
--A Dreadful Mistake. (Illus.). (Scribner-Blackie Series of Books for Young People). N.D. Charles Scribner's Sons.
--The Girls of St. Bede's: A Story of School Life. LC 29-20981. 248 p. front. 19 1/2 cm. c.1929. The World Syndicate Publishing Company.
--Proud Miss Sidney, 36 vols. (Illus.). (St. Nicholas Ser.). 1905. Set. A L Burt Co.
--Proud Miss Sydney. (Illus.). (The Wellesley Series for Girls). N.D. A. L. Burt.
--The Rambles of Three Children. (Illus.). (Stories Old and New Ser.). N.D. Caldwell.
--School Days at St. Bede's. (The Girl's World Ser.). N.D. World Publishing Co.
--The Summer Holidays. (Illus.). 1900. Thomas Nelson & Sons.

Mockrin, Ida
--The Big Parade. Brodsky, Harry, illus. (Illus.). 16p. (ps-1). 1983. (ISBN 0-9612244-0-1). Honeycomb Pr.
Modell, Frank
--Goodbye Old Year, Hello New Year. Modell, Frank, illus. LC 84-4020. (Illus.). 32p. (gr. k-3). 1984. (ISBN 0-688-03938-3). (ISBN 0-688-03939-1). Greenwillow.
--Look Out, It's April Fools' Day. LC 84-4138. (Illus.). 24 p. 26cm. c.1985. (ISBN 0-688-04016-0). (ISBN 0-688-04017-9). Greenwillow Books.
--One Zillion Valentines. Modell, Frank, illus. LC 81-2215. (Illus.). 32 p. 26cm. c.1981. (ISBN 0-688-00565-9). (ISBN 0-688-00569-1). Greenwillow Books.
--[illegible] (ISBN 0-688-03703-8). (ISBN 0-688-03706-2). Greenwillow Books.
--Seen Any Cats?. Modell, Frank, illus. LC 79-11607. (Illus.). 32 p. 26cm. c.1979. (ISBN 0-688-80229-X). (ISBN 0-688-84229-1). Greenwillow Books.
--Tooley! Tooley!. Modell, Frank, illus. LC 76-49645. (Illus.). 28 p. 26cm. c.1979. (ISBN 0-688-80092-0). (ISBN 0-688-84092-2). Greenwillow Books.
Moderow, Gertrude, et al., eds.
--Six Great Stories. Key, ALexander Hill (1904-1979), illus. LC 37-2245. 3 p. l., 531 p. incl. front., illus. 21 1/2 cm. c.1937. Scott, Foresman and Company.
Moderow, Gertrude, ed. see Sandrus, Mary Yost.
Moderow, Gertrude, adapted by see Stratton, Clarence.
Moe, Barbara A. (1937-)
--The Ghost Wore Knickers. LC 74-26980. 127 p. 21cm. 1975. (ISBN 0-8407-6427-8). T. Nelson.
--Pickles and Prunes. LC 75-41347. 122 p. 21cm. c.1976. (ISBN 0-07-042643-0). McGraw-Hill.
Moe, Christian Hollis (1929-) & Payne, Darwin Reid, eds.
--Six New Plays for Children. Triplett, Jane Dinsmoor, pref. by. LC 70-112391. xviii, 284 p. 24cm. 1971. (ISBN 0-8093-0453-8). Southern Illinois University Press.
Moe, Jorgen Engebretsen, jt. auth. see Asbjornsen, Peter Christen.
Moe, Jorgen Engebretsen (1812-1885) & Jorgen, Moe (1813-1882)
--Norwegian Folk Tales. Werenskiold, Erik & Kittelsen, Theodor, illus. 1978. Vanous.
Moe, Louis Maria Niels Peder Halling (1859-)
--The Adventures of Three Little Pigs. N.D. Longmans Green & Co.
--The Forest Party. N.D. Coward McCann.
--Little Bear-Cub and the Dressed up Pig: Picture Tales for Children. LC 30-7747. 21 p. illus. 17 x 25 cm. c.1930. Coward-McCann, Inc.
--Peter Kroak: The Largest Green Frog in the Pond. LC 33-986. 17 p. illus. (part col.) 21 1/2 x 28 1/2 cm. 1932. A. Whitman & Company.
--Tommy-Tatters and the Four Bears. N.D. Longs Green & Co.
--The Vain Pussy Cat and Other Picture-Tales for Children. LC 29-19910. 32 p. illus. 17 x 25 1/2 cm. c.1929. Coward-McCann, Inc.
--The Vain Pussy Cat, and Other Picture-Tales for Children Including Little Bear Cub. LC 38-29063. 53 p. illus. 17 x 25 cm. 1938. Coward-McCann, Inc.
Moe, Phyllis, jt. ed. see Benardete, Jane Johnson.
Moed-Kass, Pnina
--Stevie's Tricycle. Tomei, Lorna, illus. LC 81-83006. (Illus.). 24 p. 16cm. (First little golden book). c.1982. (ISBN 0-307-10119-3). (ISBN 0-307-68119-X). Golden Press.
Moen, Ann & Mace, Varian
--Fairy Tales. (Illus.). 48p. 1979. (ISBN 0-89844-006-8). Troubador Pr.
Moeri, Louise (1924-)
--Downwind. LC 83-20802. 144p. (gr. 4-7). 1984. (ISBN 0-525-44096-8). (ISBN 0-525-44096-8). Dutton.
--First the Egg. LC 82-5145. p. cm. c.1982. (ISBN 0-525-44006-2). Dutton.
--The Girl Who Lived on the Ferris Wheel. LC 79-11359. 117 p. 22cm. c.1979. (ISBN 0-525-30659-5). Dutton.
--How the Rabbit Stole the Moon. Brown, Marc Tolon (1946-), illus. LC 77-3158. p. cm. 1977. (ISBN 0-395-25765-4). Houghton Mifflin.
--Save Queen of Sheba. LC 80-23019. 116 p. 22cm. c.1981. (ISBN 0-525-33202-2). E. P. Dutton. **Award: (ALA).**
--Star Mother's Youngest Child. Hyman, Trina Schart (1939-), illus. LC 75-9743. (Illus.). 48 p. 16cm. 1975. (ISBN 0-395-21406-8). Houghton Mifflin.
--The Unicorn and the Plow. 1st ed. Goode, Diane (1949-), illus. LC 81-15287. (Illus.). 31 p. 23cm. c.1982. (ISBN 0-525-45116-1). E.P. Dutton.

Moeri, Louise (1924-) & Owens, Gail
--A Horse for X.Y.Z. 1st ed. Owens, Gail, illus. LC 76-55739. (Illus.). 98 p. 23cm. c.1977. (ISBN 0-525-32220-5). Dutton.
Moery, Robert
--Kevin. Keith, Eros, illus. LC 71-113497. (Illus.). 32 p. 28cm. 1970. Bradbury Press.
Moeschlin, Elsa
--The Little Boy with the Big Apples. LC 33-27030. 23 p. col. illus. 28 cm. 1932. Coward-McCann, Inc.
--The Red Horse. LC 29-26171. 19, 1 p. col. illus. 20 cm. 1929. Coward McCann Inc.
--The Red Horse. LC 44-20102. 19, 1 p. col. illus. 28 cm. 1944. Coward-McCann Inc.
Moffat, A. S., Mrs.
--One-Armed Hugh. N.D. D. Lothrop Co.
--One-Armed Hugh. 1 of 10 Vols. (Woodcliff Children Ser.). N.D. Ward & Drummond.
--One-Armed Hugh: The Little Corn Merchant. N.D. Andrew F. Graves.
Moffat, Alfred Edward (1866-)
--Little Songs of Long Ago: More old Nursery Rhymes. Le Mair, Henriette Willebeek (1889-1966), illus. 22 x 30cm. 64p. 1913. David McKay.
--Our Old Nursery Rhymes. Le Mair, Henriette Willebeek (1889-1966), illus. N.D. David McKay Co.
Moffat, Derry, ed.
--The Lady & the Tramp. (Illus.). (Disney Classics Ser.). (gr. k-4). 1980. (ISBN 0-448-16109-5, G&D). Putnam Pub Group.
Moffat, William David (1866-)
--The Crimson Banner: A Story of College Baseball. 2 p. l., 9-287 p. front., plates. 19 cm. c.1907. Chatterton-Peck Company.
--The Crimson Banner: A Story of College Baseball. (The Enterprise Bks.). N.D. Grosset & Dunlap.
--Not Without Honor. N.D. Arnold and Company.
Moffatt, Sara Bullard (1867-) & Hidden, Julia
--The Children's Sunday hour of Story and Song. LC 12-966. 135p. 1911. T. W. Ripley Co.
Moffett, Martha Leatherwood (1934-)
--A Flower Pot Is Not a Hat. Perl, Susan (1922-1983), illus. LC 72-179048. lv. (chiefly illus. 21cm. (Dutton anytime books). 1974, c.1972. (ISBN 0-525-45025-4). Dutton.
Moffitt, Frederick James (1896-)
--The Best Burro. Bolognese, Donald Alan (1934-), illus. LC 67-16755. 32p. col. illus. 27cm. (Our world of people ser., Mexico). 1967. Silver Burdett.
--A Busy Day for Okoth. Gerhard, Mae, illus. LC 67-167565. 32p. col. illus. 27cm. (Our world of people ser., Kenya). 1967. Silver Burdett.
--Diary of a Warrior King: Adventures from the Odyssey. Shields, Bill, illus. LC 67-18717. (Original Author: Homerus). (Illus.). 90 p. 25cm. (Folk literature around the world). 1967. Silver Burdett Co.
--Karl and the Clockmaker. Kredel, Fritz (1900-1973), illus. (Illus.). 32 p. 27cm. (Our world of people series, Germany). 1968. Silver Burdett Co.
--Tales from Ancient Greece. Shields, Bill, illus. LC 78-56059. (Illus.). 90 p., 2 leaves of plates. 25cm. (The World Folktale Library). c.1979. (ISBN 0-382-50008-3). Silver Burdett Co.
Moffitt, Virginia May (1909-)
--Great Horse: A Forest Pony of Long Ago. LC 38-31622. xi, 179 p. incl. front., illus. 23 cm. c.1938. The John C. Winston Company.
--The Jayhawker and the Adventures of Brett Pruitt, with the Outlaws and the Indians of the Texas Plains. Candy, Robert (1920-), illus. LC 49-830027. xiii, 275 p. illus. 22 cm. 1949. L. C. Page.
--Pollyanna at Six Star Ranch. (The Pollyanna Bks.). N.D. Grosset & Dunlap.
--Pollyanna at Six Star Ranch. 4 p. l., 295 p. col. front. 20 cm. (Pollyanna glad books). 1947. L. C. Page & Company.
--Pollyanna of Magic Valley. LC 47-4480. (Illus.). 20 cm. iv, 295p. (The Pollyanna Glad Bks.). 1947. L. C. Page & Co.
Mogensen, Jan
--Teddy and the Chinese Dragon. North American ed. LC 85-26091. p. cm. (Quality time books). (Teddy Tales). 1985. (ISBN 1-555-32003-1). (ISBN 1-555-32002-3). G. Stevens Pub.
--Teddy in the Undersea Kingdom. North American ed. LC 85-26093. p. cm. (Quality time books). (Teddy Tales). 1985. (ISBN 1-555-32001-5). (ISBN 1-555-32000-7). G. Stevens Pub.
--Teddy's Christmas Gift. North American ed. LC 85-26095. p. cm. (Quality time books). (Teddy Tales). 1985. (ISBN 1-555-32005-8). (ISBN 1-555-32004-X). G. Stevens Pub.
--When Teddy Work Early. North American ed. LC 85-26096. p. cm. (Quality time books). (Teddy Tales). 1985. (ISBN 1-555-32007-4). (ISBN 1-555-32006-6). G. Stevens Pub.
Mogridge, George (1787-1854)
--Half-Hours with Old Humphrey. (Illus.). N.D. Methodist Book Concern.

Mogus, Bette
--I'm a Goo. Mogus, Bette & Martin, Teresa, illus. 1959. Exposition Press.
Mohammed, Rasheed
--Animals I Love & Other Stories. Sherman, Larry, illus. (gr. k-4). 1978. (ISBN 0-682-48948-4). Exposition.
Mohammed, Rasheed & Mohammed, Tinamarie
--My First Trip to the Library. 66p. 1980. (ISBN 0-533-04357-3). Vantage.
Mohammed, Tinamarie, jt. auth. see Mohammed, Rasheed.
Mohan, Beverly Moffett (1918-), retold by.
--Punia and the King of the Sharks: A Hawaiian Tale. Bolognese, Donald Alan (1934-), illus. LC 64-15634. (Illus.). 32 p. 26cm. 1964. Follett Pub. Co.
Mohne, Wilhelmina, jt. ed. see Ross, Frances.
Mohne, Wilhelmina & Rudy, Stella M., eds.
--Tales of Long Ago. LC 39-32047. (Illus.). 21cm. 32p. (Unity Study Book: No.331). 1939. American Education Press.
Mohr, Joseph
--Silent Night. Jeffers, Susan, illus. LC 84-8113. (Illus.). 32p. (gr. k up). 1984. (ISBN 0-525-44144-1). Dutton.
Mohr, Nicholasa (1935-)
--El Bronx Remembered: A Novella & Stories. LC 75-6303. 256p. (gr. 7 up). 1975. (ISBN 0-06-024313-9, HarpJ). (ISBN 0-06-024314-7). Har-Row.
--Felita. Cruz, Raymond (1933-), illus. LC 79-50151. (Illus.). 112 p. 22cm. c.1979. (ISBN 0-8037-3143-4). (ISBN 0-8037-3144-2). Dial Press.
--In Nueva York. LC 76-42931. (gr. 7 up). 1977. Dial Bks Young.
--Nilda. Mohr, Nicholasa (1935-), illus. LC 73-8046. (Illus.). 272p. (gr. 5 up). 1973. (ISBN 0-06-024331-7, HarpJ). (ISBN 0-06-024332-5). Har-Row.
Mohringer, J.
--Life at the Creekbank. N.D. Carlton Press.
Moir, Kathleen
--The Mystery of the Dolls House. Whittam, Geoffrey William (1916-), illus. LC 62-12503. 128p. illus. 21cm. 1962. F. Warne.
Mokreja, Lillian F., tr. see Wenig, Adolf.
Mokrohisky, Patricia Ann (1934-)
--Chris Cuspid. Taylor, Bernard (1937-), illus. LC 55-43671. (Illus.). 26cm. 34p. 1955. Chris Enterprises.
Molarsky, Osmond (1909-)
--The Bigger They Come. Hyman, Trina Schart (1939-), illus. LC 79-133297. (Illus.). 47 p. 24cm. 1971. (ISBN 0-8098-1166-9). H. Z. Walck.
--A Different Ball Game. Zingarelli, James, illus. LC 78-23793. (Illus.). 48 p. 23cm. c.1979. (ISBN 0-698-20462-X). Coward, McCann & Geoghegan.
--The Fearless Leroy. Bartram, Robert, illus. LC 76-51344. (Illus.). 57 p. 24cm. c.1977. (ISBN 0-8098-0008-X). H. Z. Walck.
--The Good Guys and the Bad Guys. Berson, Harold (1926-), illus. LC 73-4588. (Illus.). 60 p. 24cm. 1973. (ISBN 0-8098-1213-4). H. Z. Walck.
--Montalvo Bay. LC 75-37482. p. cm. c.1976. (ISBN 0-8098-5000-1). H. Z. Walck.
--The Peasant and the Fly. Coville, Katherine (1939-), illus. LC 80-11609. p. cm. c.1980. (ISBN 0-15-260153-8). Harcourt Brace Jovanovich.
--Piper: The Sailboat That Came Back. (Illus.). (gr. 3-5). 1965. (ISBN 0-8382-0665-4). Hale.
--Piper: The Sailboat That Came Back. Shortall, Leonard W., illus. LC 65-10069. (Illus.). (gr. 1-4). 1965. (ISBN 0-8212-0268-5). NYGS.
--Right Thumb, Left Thumb. Johnson, John Emil (1929-), illus. LC 69-15797. (Illus.). 32 p. 27cm. (Addisonian Press book). 1969. Addison-Wesley.
--Robbery in Right Field. Sauber, Rob, illus. LC 78-5204. (Illus.). 52 p. 24cm. c.1978. (ISBN 0-8098-6425-8). H. Z. Walck.
--Scrappy. LC 82-45991. 127 p. 21cm. c.1983. (ISBN 0-396-08120-7). Dodd, Mead.
--Song of the Empty Bottles. Feelings, Thomas (1933-), illus. LC 68-23889. (Illus.). 1 v. unpaged. 24cm. 55p. 1968. H. Z. Walck.
--Song of the Smoggy Stars. Ford, George Cephas, Jr., illus. LC 77-182534. (Illus.). 55 p. 24cm. c.1972. (ISBN 0-8098-1199-5). H. Z. Walck.
--Take It or Leave It. Hyman, Trina Schart (1939-), illus. LC 76-158870. (Illus.). 62 p. 24cm. 1971. (ISBN 0-8098-1187-1). H. Z. Walck.
--Where the Good Luck Was. Fetz, Ingrid (1915-), illus. LC 74-82678. (Illus.). 63 p. 24cm. 1970. H. Z. Walck.
Molbech, Christian (1783-1857)
--The Fox, the Dog, and the Griffin. Anderson, Poul William (1926-), ed. Kubinyi, Laszlo (1937-), illus. LC 66-10862. (A Folk Tale Adapted from the Danish). 20cm. 62p. c.1966. Doubleday.

Mole, John (1941-) & Norman, Mary
--Once There Were Dragons: A Book of Riddles in Words and Pictures. LC 79-64262. (Illus.). 64 p. 21cm. 1979. (ISBN 0-233-97112-2). A. Deutsch.
Molesworth, Mary Louisa Stewart see Graham, Ennis, pseud.
Molesworth, Mary Louisa Stewart, Mrs. (1842-1921)
--The Abbey of the Sea, and Another Story. N.D. Society for Promoting Christian Knowledge.
--The Adventures of Herr Baby. Crane, Walter (1845-1915), illus. 1886. Macmillan & Co.
--The Bewitched Lamp. N.D. Thomas Whittaker.
--Blanche. Barnes, Robert, illus. 1894. Thomas Whittaker.
--The Blue Baby and Other Stories. Foster, Maud C., illus. 1904. Dutton.
--The Boys and I. (Illus.). N.D. E. P. Dutton & Co.
--The Boys and I: A Child's Story for Children. New ed. Edwards, Ellen M., illus. N.D. George Routledge & Sons.
--Carrots. LC 12-36899. 231 p. col. front., plates. 17 cm. c.1895. T. Y. Crowell & Company.
--Carrots. (Children's Favorite Classics). 1900. Thomas Y. Crowell & Co.
--Carrots and A Christmas Child, 1 of 10 Vols. Cranc, Walter (1845-1915) & Brooke, Leonard Leslie (1862-1940), illus. N.D. Set. Macmillian & Co.
--Carrots: Just a Little Boy. (Illus.). (The Little Men Ser.). N.D. A. L. Burt's Pubs.
--Carrots: Just a Little Boy. (Illus.). (The Rugby Ser.). N.D. A. L. Burt.
--Carrots: Just a Little Boy. Crane, Walter (1845-1915), illus. LC 4-17546. 4 p. l., 253 p. illus., 8 pl. (incl. front.) 18 1/2 cm. N.D. A. L. Burt Company.
--Carrots: Just a Little Boy. Crane, Walter (1845-1915), illus. 20cm. 166p. 1921. Macmillan Co.
--Carrots: Just a Little Boy. Crane, Walter (1845-1915), illus. (Juvenile Ladder Library for Children). N.D. Macmillan.
--Carrots: Just a Little Boy. Crane, Walter (1845-1915), illus. (Series of Books for the Young). N.D. Macmillan & Co.
--Carrots: Just a Little Boy. Crane, Walter (1845-1915), illus. 1957. St Martin's Press.
--Carrots: Just a Little Boy. Oldham, Marion Mildred, illus. LC 26-27702. 171 p. col. front., col. plates. 20 1/2 cm. (Stories All Children Love Ser.). 1926. J. B. Lippincott Company.
--Carrots: Just a Little Boy. Wheelhouse, M. V., illus. 18cm. 1500p. (Queen's Treasures Ser.). 1920. Harcourt, Brace & Howe.
--Carrots: Just a Little Boy and A Christmas Child. Crane, Walter (1845-1915), illus. LC 4-23578. 2 v. in 1. fronts., plates. 19 cm. 1893. Macmillan and Co.
--The Carved Lions. Brooke, Leonard Leslie (1862-1940), illus. 1898. Macmillan.
--The Carved Lions. Hart, Lewis, illus. LC 64-56555. x, 144 p. illus. 22 cm. (Children's illustrated classics no. 65). 1964. New York, Dutton.
--A Charge Fulfilled. Woodville, Richard Caton (1856-), illus. 1886. Young.
--The Children of the Castle, 36 vols. (Illus.). (St. Nicholas Ser.). 1905. Set. A L Burt Co.
--The Children of the Castle. (The Rugby Series for Boys and Girls). N.D. A. L. Burt Company.
--The Children of the Castle. (Illus.). (The Wellesley Series for Girls). N.D. A. L. Burt.
--The Children of the Castle. Crane, Walter (1845-1915), illus. 1890. Macmillan.
--The Children of the Castle, and Four Winds Farm, 1 of 10 Vols. Crane, Walter (1845-1915) & Brooke, Leonard Leslie (1862-1940), illus. N.D. Set. Macmillan & Co.
--The Children's Hour, 36 vols. (Illus.). (St. Nicholas Ser.). 1905. Set. A L Burt Co.
--The Children's Hour. (Illus.). (The Wellesley Series for Girls). N.D. A. L. Burt.
--The Children's Hour. (Illus.). 1900. Thomas Nelson & Sons.
--A Child's Book of Country Stories. Smith, Jessie Willcox (1863-1935), illus. (Dial Library of Illustrated Bks. for Children). N.D. Dial Press.
--A Child's Book of Modern Stories. Smith, Jessie Willcox (1863-1935), illus. (Dial Library of Illustrated Bks. for Children). N.D. Dial Press.
--A Child's Book of Old Verse. Cooke, Edna W., illus. (Dial Library of Illustrated Bks. for Children). N.D. Dial Press.
--A Christmas Child. (Illus.). (The Little Men Ser.). N.D. A. L. Burt's Pubs.
--A Christmas Child. (Illus.). (The Rugby Ser.). N.D. A. L. Burt.
--A Christmas Child: A Sketch of a Boy-life. Crane, Walter (1845-1915), illus. LC 16-19171. (Illus.). 17 1/2 cm. viii, 223p. 1896. Macmillan & Co.
--A Christmas Posy. Crane, Walter (1845-1915), illus. 1888. Macmillan.
--Christmas-Tree Land and A Christmas Posy. LC 12-36900. 2 v. in 1. fronts., plates. 19 cm. 1893. Macmillan and Co.

--Christmas-Tree Land, and A Christmas Posy, 1 of 10 Vols. Crane, Walter (1845-1915) & Brooke, Leonard Leslie (1862-1940), illus. 1884. Set. Macmillan & Co.
--The Cuckoo Clock. (Illus.). (The Little Women Ser.). N.D. A. L. Burt's Pubs.
--The Cuckoo Clock. (Illus.). (The Wellesley Series for Girls). N.D. A. L. Burt's Pubs.
--The Cuckoo Clock. (Illus.). (Burt's Young Folks' Library). N.D. A. L. Burt's Pubs.
--The Cuckoo Clock. N.D. Grosset & Dunlap.
--The Cuckoo Clock, 25 vols. (Illus.). (The Editha Ser.: No. 16). 1905. Set. H M Caldwell Co.
--The Cuckoo Clock. N.D. St. Martin's Press.
--The Cuckoo Clock. LC 12-368983. 4 p. l., 224 p. col. front., plates. 17 cm. c.1895. T. Y. Crowell & Company.
--Cuckoo Clock. (Children's Favorite Classics). 1900. Thomas Y. Crowell & Co.
--The Cuckoo Clock. (Illus.). (Children's Classics). N.D. Thomas Y. Crowell & Co.
--The Cuckoo Clock. Brock, Charles Edmond (1870-1938), illus. LC 79-21253. p. cm. (Facsimile Classic Series). 1980. Mayflower Books.
--The Cuckoo Clock. Cooke, Sherman, illus. LC 30-29260. 282, 1 p. col. front., illus., col. plates. 21 cm. (The stories all children love series). c.1930. J. B. Lippincott Company.
--The Cuckoo Clock. Crane, Walter (1845-1915), illus. LC 4-21563. 4 p. l., 253 p. 7 pl. (incl. front.) 18 cm. N.D. A. L. Burt.
--The Cuckoo Clock. Crane, Walter (1845-1915), illus. 1 p. l., vi p., 1 l., 162 p. front., pl. 20 cm. 1921. Macmillan Company; Etc., Etc.
--The Cuckoo Clock. Crane, Walter (1845-1915), illus. (Series of Books For the Young). N.D. MacMillan & Co.
--The Cuckoo Clock. Kirk, Maria Louise (1860-), illus. LC 14-17992. 282, 1 p. col. front., col. plates. 21 cm. (On verso of half-title: "Stories all children love"). 1914. J. B. Lippincott Company.
--The Cuckoo Clock. Shepard, Ernest Howard (1879-1976), illus. (Children's Illustrated Classics). N.D. E. P. Dutton & Co.
--The Cuckoo Clock. Williams, Florence White, illus. LC 27-18006. 246, 1 p. incl. front., illus. 19 cm. (Half-title: Every child's library). c.1927. The Saalfield Publishing Company.
--The Cuckoo Clock and Other Stories. N.D. Grosset & Dunlap.
--Cuckoo Clock and The Tapestry Room. (Children's Classics Ser.). N.D. Macmillan.
--The Cuckoo Clock and The Tapestry Room. Crane, Walter (1845-1915), illus. Bull, Angela, pref. by. LC 75-32182. (Illus.). 502 p. in various pagings, 14 leaves of plates. 19cm. (Classics of Children's Literature, 1621-1932). 1976. (ISBN 0-8240-2294-7). Garland Pub.
--The Cuckoo Clock and The Tapestry Room. Crane, Walter (1845-1915), illus. LC 4-16842. viii p., 3 l., 162 p., 2 l., 207 p. fronts., plates. 19 cm. 1893. Macmillan and Co.
--The Cuckoo Clock and the Tapestry Room. Crane, Walter (1845-1915), illus. LC 4-17547. 2 v. in 1. fronts., plates. 19 1/2 cm. (On cover: Mrs. Molesworth's stories for children ...). 1904. The Macmillan Company.
--Earthlings: The Story of a Stray and a Waif. Broadley, G. M., illus. 1892. Young.
--Edmee: A Story of the French Revolution. (True Might-Be-True Stories). N.D. MacMillan Bks.
--An Enchanted Garden: Fairy Stories. Hennessy, W. J., illus. 1892. Cassell.
--Fairy Stories. Green, Roger Gilbert Lancelyn (1918-), selected by. LC 58-9343. 159p. illus. 19cm. 1958. Roy Publishers.
--Family Troubles. Morgan, Walter J., illus. 1890. Young.
--The February Boys. Attwell, Mabel Lucie (1879-1964), illus. 1909. Dutton.
--Five Minute Stories. Browne, Gordon Frederick, et al. (1858-1932), illus (Pub. by Society for Promoting Christian Knowledge). 1888. E. & J. B. Young & Co.
--Five Minute Stories. Morgan, Walter J., illus. N.D. E. J. B. Young & Co.
--Four Winds Farm. Crane, Walter (1845-1915), illus. 1886. Macmillan.
--Four Winds Farm and The Children of the Castle. Green, Roger Gilbert Lancelyn (1918-), pref. by. LC 75-32192. (Illus.). 398 p. in various pagings. 19cm. (Classics of Children's Literature, 1621-1932: No.54). 1977. (ISBN 0-8240-2303-X). Garland Pub.
--Friendly Joey. Morgan, Walter J., illus (Pub. by Society for Promoting Christian Knowledge). N.D. E. & J. B. Young & Co.
--The Girls and I, 36 vols. (Illus.). (St. Nicholas Ser.). 1905. Set. A L Burt Co.
--The Girls and I. (The Rugby Series for Boys and Girls). N.D. A. L. Burt Company.
--The Girls and I. (Illus.). (The Wellesley Series for Girls). N.D. A. L. Burt.
--The Girls and I. Brooke, Leonard Leslie (1862-1940), illus. 1892. Macmillan.
--Grandmother Dear, 36 vols. (Illus.). (St. Nicholas Ser.). 1905. Set. A L Burt Co.
--Grandmother Dear. (Illus.). (The Wellesley Series for Girls). N.D. A. L. Burt.
--Grandmother Dear. (Home Series for Girls). N.D. Hurst & Co.
--Grandmother Dear. Crane, Walter (1845-1915), illus. (True Might-Be-True Stories). 1878. MacMillan Bks.
--Grandmother Dear. Crane, Walter (1845-1915), illus. (Series of Books for the Young). N.D. MacMillan & Co.
--Grandmother Dear and Two Little Waifs. Crane, Walter (1845-1915), illus. LC 12-36912. 2 v. in 1. fronts., plates. 19 cm. 1893. Macmillan and Co.
--Grandmother Dear, and Two Little Waifs, 1 of 10 Vols. Crane, Walter (1845-1915) & Brooke, Leonard Leslie (1892-1940), illus. N.D. Set. Macmillian.
--Great Uncle Hoot-Toot. Browne, Gordon Frederick (1858-1932) & Morgan, Walter J., illus. (Pictorial Ser.). N.D. E. & J. B. Young & Co.
--Greyling Towers. (Illus.). N.D. E. P. Dutton & Co.
--The Grim House. N.D. Thomas Whittaker.
--Hermy. (Illus.). N.D. E. P. Dutton & Co.
--Hermy: The Story of a Little Girl. New ed. Edwards, Mary Ellen, illus. 1880. George Routledge & Sons.
--Hoodie and I. (Illus.). N.D. E. P. Dutton & Co.
--Hoodie and I. New ed. Edwards, Ellen M., illus. N.D. George Routledge & Sons.
--The House that Grew. (Illus.). (The Wellesley Series for Girls). N.D. A. L. Burt.
--The House That Grew, 31 vols. (Illus.). (Famous Books for Girls Ser.: No. 11). 1905. Set. H M Caldwell Co.
--The House that Grew. (Home Series for Girls). N.D. Hurst & Co.
--The House that Grew. Woodward, Alice Bolingbroke (1862-), illus. 1900. Macmillan.
--The House that Grew: A Girl's Story. (The Rugby Series for Boys and Girls). N.D. A. L. Burt Company.
--A House to Let. Morgan, Walter J., illus (Pub. by Society for Promoting Christian Knowledge). N.D. E. & J. B. Young & Co.
--Imogen: Or, Only Eighteen. Bone, Herbert A., illus. 1892. Thomas Whittaker.
--Jasper: A Story for Children. Hammond, Gertrude Demain, illus. LC 7-15926. vii, 235 p. 8 pl. (incl. front.) 19 cm. 1906. Macmillan and Co., Limited.
--The Laurel Walk. (Illus.). 12cm. 454p. 1899. Drexel Biddle's Pub.
--Lettice. Dadd, Frank, illus. 1884. Young.
--A Little Child's Book of Stories. Smith, Jessie Willcox (1863-1935), illus. (Dial Library of Illustrated Bks. for Children). N.D. Dial Press.
--The Little Guest. Hammond, Gertrude Demain, illus. (Illus.). 1907. Macmillan Co.
--Little Miss Peggy. (Illus.). (The Little Women Ser.). N.D. A. L. Burt's Pubs.
--Little Miss Peggy. (Illus.). (The Wellesley Series for Girls). N.D. A. L. Burt.
--Little Miss Peggy: A Nursery Story. (Illus.). 1915. A L Burt & Co.
--Little Miss Peggy, and Nurse Heather-Dale's Story, 1 of 10 Vols. Crane, Walter (1845-1915) & Brooke, Leonard Leslie (1862-1940), illus. N.D. Set. Macmillian & Co.
--Little Miss Peggy: Only a Nursery Story. LC 4-17548. 5 p. l., 260 p. front., plates. 18 1/2 cm. N.D. A. L. Burt.
--Little Miss Peggy: Only a Nursery Story. Crane, Walter (1845-1915), illus. 1887. Macmillan.
--Little Mother Bunch. (Illus.). N.D. Cassell & Co.'s Pubs.
--Little Mother Bunch. Edwards, Mary Ellen, illus. (Illus.). (The Wellesley Series for Girls). 1903. A. L. Burt.
--Little Mother Bunch: A Story for Girls. (The Rugby Series for Boys and Girls). N.D. A. L. Burt Company.
--The Little Old Portrait, 36 vols. (Illus.). (St. Nicholas Ser.). 1905. Set. A L Burt Co.
--Little Old Portrait. (Illus.). (The Wellesley Series for Girls). 1915. A L Burt & Co.
--The Little Old Portrait. (The Rugby Series for Boys and Girls). N.D. A. L. Burt Company.
--The Little Old Portrait. Gunston, William Tudor (1927-), illus. (Illus.). (A New Series of Books). 1884. E. & J. B. Young & Co.
--The Lucky Duck. Morgan, Walter J., illus (Pub. by Society for Promoting Christian Knowledge). N.D. E. &. J. B. Young & Co.
--The Lucky Ducks and Other Tales. Morgan, Walter J., illus. (Pictorial Ser.). N.D. E.& J. B. Young & Co.
--Magic Nuts. 1905. Henry Altemus Co.
--Magic Nuts. (Illus.). (Boys' and Girls' Classics). N.D. Henry Altemus Co.
--The Magic Nuts. (Illus.). (Petit-Trainon Ser.). N.D. Henry Altemus Co.
--Magic Nuts. Rosie, M. M., illus. (Illus.). 1898. Macmillan Co.
--The Man With the Pan Pipes (Pub. by Society for Promoting Christian Knowledge). N.D. E. & J. B. Young & Co.
--The Man with the Pan-Pipes, and Other Stories. Morgan, Walter J., illus. (Pictorial Ser.). 1892. E.& J. B. Young & Co.
--Mary: A Nursery Story for Very Little Children. Brooke, Leonard Leslie (1862-1940), illus. LC 12-369023. vi p., 1 l., 204 p. plates. 19 cm. 1893. Macmillan and Co.
--Meg Langholme. (Illus.). 1900. J B Lippincott.
--Meg Langholme: Or, The Day After Tomorrow. Rainey, William R. I. (1852-1936), illus. LC 12-36910. 1 p. l., v-ix, 7-299 p. front., plates. 19 1/2 cm. 1897. J. B. Lippincott Company.
--Miss Mouse and Her Boys. (Illus.). (The Little Women Ser.). N.D. A. L. Burt's Pubs.
--Miss Mouse and Her Boys. Brooke, Leonard Leslie (1862-1940), illus. 1897. Macmillan.
--Miss Mouse and Her Boys: A Story for Girls. (Illus.). (The Wellesley Series for Girls). 1915. A L Burt & Co.
--Miss Mouse and Her Boys: A Story for Girls. (The Rugby Series for Boys and Girls). N.D. A. L. Burt Company.
--My New Home. Brooke, Leonard Leslie (1862-1940), illus. 1898. Macmillan.
--My Pretty and Her Little Brother Too , and Other Stories. Baumer, Lewis (1870-), illus. 1901. Whitaker.
--Mystery of the Pine Wood. (The Rosebud Ser.). N.D. E. P. Dutton & Co.
--Neighbours. Edwards, Mary Ellen, illus. 1891. Thomas Whittaker.
--Nesta, 1 of 12 Vols. (Dickory Dock Series). N.D. Thomas Whittaker.
--Next Door House, 31 vols. (Illus.). (Famous Books for Girls Ser.: No. 15). 1905. Set. H M Caldwell Co.
--Next Door House. (Home Series for Girls). N.D. Hurst & Co.
--The Next-Door House. LC 1-30612. 3 p. l., 271 p. front., plates. 19 cm. 1901. The Mershon Company.
--The Next-Door House. Hatherell, William, illus. LC 44-28981. 3 p. l., 271 p. front., plates. 19 cm. 1892. Cassell Publishing Company.
--Nurse Heatherdale's Story, 36 vols. (Illus.). (St. Nicholas Ser.). 1905. Set. A L Burt Co.
--Nurse Heatherdale's Story. (A Story for Girls). N.D. A. L. Burt Company.
--Nurse Heatherdale's Story. Brooke, Leonard Leslie (1862-1940), illus. (Illus.). (The Wellesley Series for Girls). 1891. A. L. Burt.
--Nurse Heatherdale's Story and Little Miss Peggy. Brooke, Leonard Leslie (1862-1940) & Crane, Walter (1845-1915), illus. LC 12-36901. 2 v. in 1. fronts., plates. 19 cm. 1893. Macmillan and Co.
--The Old Pincushion and Other Fairy Tales. (Illus.). N.D. E. P. Dutton & Co.
--The Old Pincushion: Or, Aunt Clotilda's Guests. Hope, Adrian, Mrs., illus. (Illus.). 1890. E. P. Dutton & Company.
--Olivia. (Illus.). 1900. J B Lippincott.
--Olivia: A Story for Girls. Barnes, Robert, illus. LC 12-36909. 311 p. incl. plates. front. 19 1/2 cm. 1895. J. B. Lippincott Company.
--Opposite Neighbours and Other Stories. Morgan, Walter J., illus. (Pictorial Ser.). 1895. E. & J. B. Young & Co.
--The Oriel Window. Brooke, Leonard Leslie (1862-1940), illus. 1896. The Macmillan Co.
--The Palace in the Garden. 1891. Thomas Whittaker.
--The Palace in the Garden. Bennett, Harriet M., illus. 1887. Thomas Whittaker.
--Peterkin. (Illus.). (The Rugby Ser.). N.D. A. L. Burt.
--Peterkin. Limited. Millar, Harold Robert (1869-1939), illus. LC 4-18274000002. 19cm. 196p. 1902. Macmillan And Co.
--Philippa. (Illus.). 1900. J B Lippincott.
--Philippa. Finnemore, J., illus. LC 12-36908. 328 p. front., plates. 19 1/2 cm. 1896. J. B. Lippincott Company.
--Puff: An Autobiography of a Dog. Morgan, Walter J., illus (Pub. by Society for Promoting Christian Knowledge). N.D. E. & J. B. Young & Co.
--The Rectory Children. Crane, Walter (1845-1915), illus. LC 16-19170. (Illus.). 19 cm. viii, 212p. (True Or Might-Be-True Stories). 1889. MacMillan Bks.
--The Red Grange. Browne, Gordon Frederick (1858-1932), illus. 1891. Thomas Whittaker.
--Robin Redbreast. Barnes, Robert, illus. 1892. Thomas Whittaker.
--Robin Redbreast: A Story for Girls. (Illus.). (The Wellesley Girls). 1915. A L Burt & Co.
--Rosy. (The Rugby Series for Boys and Girls). N.D. A. L. Burt Company.
--Rosy. (Illus.). (The Little Women Ser.). N.D. A. L. Burt's Pubs.
--Rosy. (Illus.). (The Wellesley Series for Girls). N.D. A. L. Burt.
--Rosy. Crane, Walter (1845-1915), illus. (True Or Might-Be-True Stories). 1882. MacMillan Bks.
--Rosy, and The Girls and I, 1 of 10 Vols. Crane, Walter (1845-1915) & Brooke, Leonard Leslie (1862-1940), illus. N.D. Set. Macmillian & Co.
--The Ruby Ring. Pitman, Rosie M. M., illus. 1904. Macmillan.
--Sheila's Mystery. Brooke, Leonard Leslie (1862-1940), illus. 1895. Macmillan.
--Silverthorns. (Illus.). N.D. Publications of E. P. Dutton & Co.
--Stories. Cooke, Edna W., illus. N.D. Duffield.
--Stories by Mrs. Molesworth. Baldwin, Sidney, compiled by. LC 22-19474. 4 p. l., 353 p. col. front., col. plates. 24 cm. 1922. Duffield and Company.
--Stories of the Saints for Children. N.D. Longmans, Green, & Co.
--The Story of a Little Girl. (Illus.). N.D. George Routledge & Sons.
--Story of a Spring Morning and Other Tales. Edwards, Mary Ellen, illus. 1890. Longmans Green & Co.
--Story of a Year. (Illus.). N.D. Macmillan Co.
--Summer Stories for Boys and Girls. 1882. Macmillan & Co.
--Sweet Content. (The Rugby Series for Boys and Girls). N.D. A. L. Burt Company.
--Sweet Content. (Illus.). (The Little Women Ser.). N.D. A. L. Burt's Pubs.
--Sweet Content. (Illus.). (The Wellesley Series for Girls). N.D. A. L. Burt.
--Sweet Content. Rainey, William R. I. (1852-1936), illus. (Illus.). 148p. 1891. E. P. Dutton & Co.
--The Tapestry Room. (The Rugby Series for Boys and Girls). N.D. A. L. Burt Company.
--The Tapestry Room. (Illus.). (The Little Women). N.D. A. L. Burt's Pubs.
--The Tapestry Room. (Illus.). (The Wellesley Series for Girls). N.D. A. L. Burt.
--Tapestry Room. LC 62-894. (Illus.). 217p. illus. 20cm. (Looking Glass Library). (gr. 4 up). 1961. (ISBN 0-394-80477-5). (ISBN 0-394-90477-X). Random.
--The Tapestry Room: A Child's Romance. LC 15-20300. (Illus.). 17 1/2 cm. iv, 237p. 1879. Macmillan & Co.
--Tell Me a Story. Crane, Walter (1845-1915), illus. (Series of Books for the Young). N.D. MacMillan & Co.
--Tell Me a Story and the Adventures of Herr Baby. Crane, Walter (1845-1915), illus. LC 12-36907. 2 v. in 1. fronts., plates. 19 cm. 1893. Macmillan and Co.
--Tell Me a Story, and The Adventures of Herr Baby, 1 of 10 Vols. Crane, Walter (1845-1915) & Brooke, Leonard Leslie (1862-1940), illus. N.D. Set. Macmillian & Co.
--The Third Miss St. Quenin. 1888. Thomas Whittaker.
--The Thirteen Little Black Pigs. Morgan, Walter J., illus. (Pictorial Ser.). N.D. E.& J. B. Young & Co.
--The Thirteen Little Black Pigs, and Other Stories. (Illus.). (The Wellesley Series for Girls). N.D. A. L. Burt.
--The Thirteen Little Black Pigs and Other Stories. Morgan, Walter J., illus (Pub. by Society for Promoting Christian Knowledge). 1901. E. & J. B. Young & Co.
--This and That: A Tale of Two Tinies. Thomson, Hugh (1860-1920), illus. 1899. Macmillan.
--The Three Witches. Baumer, Lewis (1870-), illus. 1900. Lippincott.
--Twelve Tiny Tales. Morgan, Walter J., illus (Pub. by Society for Promoting Christian Knowledge). 1890. E. & J. B. Young & Co.
--Twelve Tiny Tales. Morgan, Walter J., illus. (Pictorial Ser.). N.D. E.& J. B. Young & Co.
--Two Little Waifs. (Illus.). (The Little Women Ser.). 1915. A. L. Burt's Pubs.
--Two Little Waifs. (The Rugby Series for Boys and Girls). N.D. A. L. Burt Company.
--Two Little Waifs. (Illus.). (The Wellesley Series for Girls). N.D. A. L. Burt.
--Two Little Waifs. Crane, Walter (1845-1915), illus. LC 15-20299. (Illus.). 18 1/2 cm. vi, 216p. (True Or Might-Be-True Stories). 1883. MacMillan Bks.
--Uncanny Tales. N.D. Longmans Green & Co.
--Us,. LC 12-369061. 2 v. in 1. fronts., plates. 19 cm. 1893. Macmillan and Co.
--Us. (Every Boy's and Every Girl's Ser.). N.D. The Macmillan Co.
--Us: An Old-Fashioned Story, 1 of 32 vols, Vol. 23. (Illus.). (Famous Books for Girls). N.D. H. M. Caldwell.
--Us: An Old-Fashioned Story. (Home Series for Girls). N.D. Hurst & Co.
--Us: An Old Fashioned Story. LC 51-52461. 19cm. 129p. (The Seaside Library: No. 654). 1885. Munro Co.
--Us: An Old Fashioned Story. N.D. Thomas Whittaker.
--Us,. An Old-Fashioned Story. Crane, Walter (1845-1921), illus. LC 12-25425. cover-title, 209 p. incl. front., plates. 17 1/2 cm. (Harper's handy series, no. 39). 1885. Harper & Brothers.

--Us, and the Rectory Children, 1 of 10 Vols. Crane, Walter (1845-1915) & Brooke, Leonard Leslie (1862-1940), illus. N.D. Set. MacMillan & Co.
--A Very Little Child's Book of Stories. Smith, Jessie Willcox (1863-1935), illus. (Dial Library of Illustrated Bks. for Children). N.D. Dial Press.
--White Turrets. Rainey, William R. I. (1852-1936), illus. 1895. Thomas Whittaker.
--The Wooden-Pigeon and Mary. Millar, Harold Robert (1869-1939), illus. LC 2-16206. 19cm. 192p. 1901. Macmillan & Co. Limited.

Molesworth, Mary Louisa Stewart, Mrs. (1842-1921), ed.
Through the Looking Glass and What Alice Found There. (Illus.). (The Little Women Ser.). N.D. A. L. Burt's Pubs.

Molesworth, Olive
--The Trio in the Square (Pub. by Society for Promoting Christian Knowledge). N.D. E. & J. B Young & Co.

Molesworth, Olive & Bingham, Clifton
--Sunny Land Stories. Bennett, Harriet M., illus. N.D. Dutton.

Molière, Jean Baptiste
--A Doctor in Spite of Himself. Harris, Aurand, adapted by. 1968. Anchorage Press.

Molin, Charles, ed.
--Ghosts, Spooks, and Spectres. 236 p. 23cm. (David White collection). 1967. D. White Co.

Moline, Earl W., jt. auth. see Howard, Matthew V.

Molles, Emmy, jt. ed. see Sawyer, Ruth Estelle.

Molley, Anne Stearns Baker (1907-)
--Uncle Andy's Island. Tolford, Joshua (1909-), illus. LC 50-217. 243 p. illus. 21 cm. 1950. Houghton Mifflin.

Mollikin, Virginia Greene
--The Friendly Light. N.D. Abingdon Press.

Molloy, Anne G., ed. see Barnum, Frances Courtenay Baylor, Mrs.

Molloy, Anne Stearns Baker (1907-)
--A Bird in Hand. Reardon, Mary A., illus. LC 45-8771. 5 p. l., 181 p. col. illus. 20 1/2 cm. 1945. Houghton Mifflin Company.
--Blanche of the Blueberry Barrens. Thomson, Arline K. (1912-), illus. LC 59-7465. 168p. illus. 22cm. 1959. (ISBN 0-8038-0688-4). Hastings House.
--Captain Waymouth's Indians. Gorsline, Douglas Warner (1913-1985), illus. LC 56-11304. 189p. illus. 22cm. 1956. (ISBN 0-8038-1079-2). Hastings House.
--Celia's Lighthouse. Koering, Ursula (1921-), illus. LC 49-7323. 248 p. illus. 22 cm. 1949. Houghton Mifflin Co.
--The Christmas Rocket. N.D. E. M. Hale & Co.
--The Christmas Rocket. (Illus.). 48p. (Blackbird Bks). (gr. 5-8). 1984. (ISBN 0-531-03754-1, Macrae). Watts.
--Christmas Rocket. Marokvia, Artur F. (1909-), illus. (Illus.). (gr. 2-4). 1958. (ISBN 0-8038-1098-9). Hastings.
--Coast Guard to Greenland. Delano, John L., illus. LC 42-6007. 4 p. l., 122, 1 p. front., plates. 25 1/2 cm. 1942. Houghton Mifflin Company.
--Decky's Secret. Hauman, George (1890-1961) & Hauman, Doris, Mrs. (1897-), illus. LC 44-8681. 4 p. l., 120 p. col. plates. 21 cm. 1944. Houghton Mifflin Company.
--The Girl from Two Miles High. Jackson, Pauline (1918-), illus. LC 67-18383. (Illus.). 184 p. 22cm. 1967. Hastings House.
--Lucy's Christmas. LC 50-14376. (Illus.). 25cm. 46p. 1950. Houghton Mifflin.
--The Monkey's Fist. Tolford, Joshua (1909-), illus. LC 53-6209. (Illus.). 227 p. 22cm. 1953. Houghton Mifflin.
--The Mystery of the Pilgrim Trading Post. Torbert, Floyd James (1922-), illus. LC 64-13478. (Illus.). 160 p. 22cm. 1964. Hastings House.
--The Pigeoneers. Converse, Elizabeth, illus. LC 47-30395. 179 p. illus. 25 cm. 1947. Houghton Mifflin Co.
--A Proper Place for Chip. Maitland, Antony Jasper (1935-), illus. LC 62-22119. (Illus.). 26cm. 47p. (gr. 1-4). 1963. (ISBN 0-8038-5734-9). Hastings.
--The Secret of the Old Salem Desk. (Illus.). (gr. 2-5). 1955. FS&G.
--The Secret of the Old Salem Desk. Thomson, Arline K. (1912-), illus. LC 55-9595. 243p. illus. 22cm. 1955. Ariel Books.
--Shaun and the Boat: An Irish Story. Cooney, Barbara (1917-), illus. LC 64-19082. (Illus.). 43 p. 25cm. 1965. (ISBN 0-8038-6655-0). Hastings House.
--Shooting Star Farm. Cooney, Barbara (1917-), illus. LC 46-7310. 4 p. l., 231 p. incl. front., illus. 23 cm. 1946. Houghton Mifflin Company.
--Three-Part Island: A Maine Mystery. Thomson, Arline K. (1912-), illus. LC 60-10584. (Illus.). 178 p. 22cm. 1960. Hastings House.
--The Tower Treasure. Marokvia, Artur F. (1909-), illus. LC 58-6291. 165p. illus. 22cm. 1958. Hastings House.
--Where Away?. Tolford, Joshua (1909-), illus. LC 52-5913. 241 p. illus. 24 cm. 1952. Houghton Mifflin.

Molloy, Maurice Kent
--Jeremiah and the Gorgecus Gopher. Wilson, Joyce Lancaster, illus. LC 53-9918. unpaged. illus. 28cm. 1953. Borden Pub. Co.

Molloy, Paul, ed.
--One Hundred Plus American Poems. (Illus., Pub. by Schol B Serv). (gr. 7-12). 1972. (ISBN 0-590-04486-9, Schol Trade Pap). Schol Bk Serv.
--Poetry, U.S.A. (gr. 7-12). N.D. (ISBN 0-590-03371-9, Schol Trade Pap). Schol Bk Serv.

Molloy, William Fillmore & Butler, Arthur
--Silver King: His Own Story ... LC 33-1841. viii, 379 p. plates, ports. 24 cm. c.1932. Silver King Associates.

Molnar, Agnes
--Jack and the Beanstalk. Molnar, Agnes, illus. LC 78-12222. p. cm. (Goodnight Book). 1979. (ISBN 0-394-84101-8). Knopf.

Molnar, Ferenc (1878-1952)
--The Blue-Eyed Lady. Sewell, Helen Moore (1896-1957), illus. LC 42-50585. 46 p. col. illus. 26 cm. 1942. The Viking Press.

Molnar, Joe
--Graciela: A Mexican-American Child Tells Her Story. Molnar, Joe, illus. LC 77-182297. (Illus.). 48p. (gr. 4-7). 1972. (ISBN 0-531-02023-1). Watts.
--Sherman. 1973. (ISBN 0-531-02613-2). Franklin Watts.

Moloney, Louis, jt. auth. see Wilson, Alice.

Molony, A.
--Lion's Crouch. N.D. Transatlantic Arts.

Molter, Bennet A.
--Knights of the Air. N.D. D. Appleton and Company.

Momaday, Natachee Scott
--Owl in the Cedar Tree. Perceval, Don Louis (1908-), illus. LC 65-25051. (Illus.). iii, 114 p. 22cm. (Ginn book-length stories). 1965. Ginn.

Momary, Douglas, jt. auth. see Atlas, Barbara.

Momens, Norman (1922-)
--Fifofus and the Red Indians. LC 60-7646. (Illus.). unpaged. 26 cm. (A Wonderful World Book). 1960. A. S. Barnes & Co.

Mommens, Norman (1922-)
--Dib Dib and the Red Indians. N.D. Transatlantic Arts, Inc.

Monahan, Douglas
--The Tales of Running Deer. Ecuyer, Andre, illus. LC 76-111382. (Illus.). 48 p. 22cm. 1970. (ISBN 0-8096-1774-9). Association Press.

Monahan, Helen Thurston
--The Adventures of Gally, Golly: And Kaptain Kid at the Zoo; Puss in the Zoo. LC 40-35427. 3 p. l., 143 p. incl. front., illus. pl. 26 cm. c.1940. The Greystone Press.
--Gally and Golly and Kaptain Kid: The Adventures of Three Little Cats at the Fair. LC 34-372432. x, 125, 1 p. incl. front., illus. pl. 27 cm. 1934. A. Kroch.

Monath, Elizabeth (1907-)
--The Other End of the String. Monath, Elizabeth (1907-), illus. LC 64-12635. 64p. 1964. Viking Press.
--Topper and the Giants. Monath, Elizabeth (1907-), illus. LC 60-1893. 59p. illus. 24cm. 1960. Viking Press.

Monckton, Ella (1899-)
--The Boy and the Mountain. Webb, Clifford Cyril (1895-1972), illus. LC 61-154299. unpaged. illus. 22cm. 1961. F. Warne.
--The Gates Family. Webb, Clifford Cyril (1895-1972), illus. N.D. Frederick Warne & Co.
--The Go-to-Bed Book. Webb, Clifford Cyril (1895-1972), illus. LC 36-10724. 75, 1 p. col. front., illus., col. plates. 22 cm. 1935. F. Warne & Co., Inc.
--The Key and the Chest. Kennedy, Richard (1910-), illus. 155p. illus. 19cm. 1957. Warne.
--Tim Minds the Baby. Turner, Patricia W., illus. LC 60-14708. (Illus.). 17cm. 43p. (gr. 1-3). 1960. (ISBN 0-7232-0439-X). Warne.
--Tim Minds the Shop. (Illus.). (gr. k-2). 1954. (ISBN 0-7232-0972-3). Warne.
--Tim Thinks of Something. Turner, Patricia W., illus. LC 64-13625. 43p. illus. (col.) 17cm. ('Prettimouse' ser.). c.1964. (ISBN 0-7232-0440-3). Warne.

Moncrieff, Ascott Robert Hope see Hope, Ascott R., pseud.

Moncrieff, Ascott Robert Hope (1846-)
--Arthur Fortescue: Or, The Schoolboy Hero. 1873. Leavitt & Allen Bros.
--The Lyceum Boys: A Sketch of Schoolboy Life in France, 1 of 25 vols. (Illus.). 175p. (Selected Bks for Sunday School: No. 18). N.D. Set. Methodist Bk Concern.

Moncure, Jane Belk see Wannamaker, Bruce, pseud.

Moncure, Jane Belk, jt. auth. see Nielsen-Barsuhn, Rochelle.

Moncure, Jane Belk (1926-), retold by see Grimm, Jakob Ludwig Karl (1785-1863) & Grimm, Wilhelm Karl.

Moncure, Jane Belk (1926-)
--About Me. Hohag, Linda Sommers, illus. LC 76-16556. (Illus.). 32 p. 25cm. c.1976. (ISBN 0-913778-52-4). Child's World.
--All by Myself. Hook, Frances Arnold (1912-), illus. LC 76-5487. 29cm. 32p. 1976, c.1975. Children's Press.
--Barbara's Pony, Buttercup. Altschuler, Franz (1923-), illus. LC 76-52921. (Illus.). 32 p. 25cm. c.1977. (ISBN 0-913778-74-5). Child's World.
--A Beach in My Bedroom. Endres, Helen Elise, illus. LC 77-12960. (Illus.). 30 p. 23cm. (Her Creative dramatics). c.1978. (ISBN 0-89565-003-3). Child's World.
--Birds, Baboons, and Barefoot Bears. Endres, Helen Elise, illus. LC 77-13025. (Illus.). 30 p. 23cm. (Creative Dramatics). N.D. (ISBN 0-89565-006-1). Child's World.
--Bunny Finds a Home. Jaffe, Morris H., photos by. LC 62-150258. unpaged. illus. 26cm. 1962. Orion Press.
--The Bunny Who Knew All About Plants. Endres, Helen Elise, illus. LC 75-12958. (Illus.). 23 p. 29cm. 1975. (ISBN 0-913778-08-7). Child's World.
--But I'm Thankful, I Really Am. Hook, Frances Arnold (1912-), illus. LC 79-1062. p. cm. c.1979. (ISBN 0-89565-069-X). Child's World.
--Fall Is Here!. Hook, Frances Arnold (1912-), illus. LC 75-14019. p. cm. 1975. (ISBN 0-913778-13-3). Child's World.
--Fixing Fences. Wannamaker, Bruce, pseud. Williams, Jenny (1939-), illus. LC 84-7037. (Illus.). 32 p. 25cm. c.1984. (ISBN 0-89693-223-0). (ISBN 0-89693-226-5). Dandelion House.
--Flip, the True Story of a Dairy Farm Goat. Jaffe, Morris H., photos by. LC 64-12770. 48 p. illus. 26 cm. 1964. Ariel Books.
--Happy Birthday, Word Bird. Hohag, Linda Sommers, illus. LC 83-15256. (Illus.). 32p. (Word Birds for Early Birds Ser.). (gr. k-2). 1983. (ISBN 0-89565-256-0). Childs World.
--Hi, Word Bird!. Hohag, Linda Sommers, illus. LC 80-15919. p. cm. (An Early Bird Reader). c.1980. (ISBN 0-89565-159-9). Child's World.
--Hide-and-Seek Word Bird. Hohag, Linda Sommers, illus. LC 81-18068. (Illus.). 32 p. 25cm. (Word Birds for Early Birds). c.1982. (ISBN 0-89565-218-8). Child's World.
--How Beautiful God's Gifts. Hook, Frances Arnold (1912-), illus. LC 80-15434. p. cm. 1980. (ISBN 0-89565-172-6). Child's World.
--I Never Say I'm Thankful, but I Am. Hook, Frances Arnold (1912-), illus. LC 78-21577. (Illus.). 30 p. 27cm. c.1979. (ISBN 0-89565-023-1). Child's World.
--If a Dinosaur Came to Dinner. Endres, Helen Elise, illus. LC 77-12957. (Illus.). 30 p. 23cm. (Creative Dramatics). c.1978. (ISBN 0-89565-008-8). Child's World.
--In God's Great Way. Karch, Pat, illus. LC 82-7446. (Illus.). 30 p. 25cm. c.1982. (ISBN 0-89693-201-X). Dandelion House.
--It Happened at Mackey's Point. 32p. 1984. (ISBN 0-89693-220-6). Victor Bks.
--It Happened at Mackey's Point: A Story About God's Power ... and About Trusts. Halverson, Lydia, illus. LC 84-7039. (Illus.). 32 p. 25cm. (A Book for Competent Readers). c.1984. (ISBN 0-89693-220-6). Dandelion House.
--Jennie & the Black Stockings. 32p. 1984. (ISBN 0-89693-225-7). Victor Bks.
--Jennie and the Black Stockings. Halverson, Lydia, illus. LC 84-7036. (Illus.). 32 p. 25cm. (A Book for Early Readers). c.1984. (ISBN 0-89693-225-7). Dandelion House.
--John's Choice. Halverson, Lydia, illus. LC 82-7461. (Illus.). 30 p. 25cm. c.1982. (ISBN 0-89693-207-9). Dandelion House.
--John's Choice. Halverson, Lydia, illus. LC 82-19897. p. cm. (Making Choices). 1983. (ISBN 0-89565-252-8). Dandelion House.
--John's Choice: A Story about Honesty. Halverson, Lydia, illus. LC 82-19897. (Illus.). 30p. (Making Choices Ser.). (gr. k-3). 1983. (ISBN 0-516-06381-2). Childrens.
--Julie' New Home. Karch, Pat, illus. LC 82-19900. (Illus.). 32p. (Making Choices). (gr. 3-4). 1983. (ISBN 0-89565-254-4). Dandelion Hse.
--Just the Right Place. Endres, Helen, illus. LC 75-34176. (Illus.). 25cm. 32p. c.1976. (ISBN 0-913778-36-2). Children's Press.
--The Kindness Weapon. Wannamaker, Bruce, pseud. Lexa, Susan, illus. LC 84-7038. (Illus.). 32 p. 25cm. c.1984. (ISBN 0-89693-219-2). Dandelion House.
--The Lad Who Made the Princess Laugh. (Illus.). 32p. (Folk Tales Ser.). (gr. k-4). 1980. (ISBN 0-516-06481-9). Childrens.
--The Lad Who Made the Princess Laugh: A Folk Tale from Germany. Axeman, Lois, illus. LC 79-25835. p. cm. c.1980. (ISBN 0-89565-109-2). Child's World.
--The Little Boy Samuel. Karch, Paul, illus. LC 79-12174. (Illus.). 31 p. 25cm. c.1979. (ISBN 0-89565-084-3). Child's World.
--Magic Monsters Act Out the Alphabet. Endres, Helen Elise, illus. LC 79-23841. p. cm. (Magic Monster Series). c.1980. (ISBN 0-89565-116-5). Child's World.
--Magic Monsters Count to Ten. Fudala, Rose Mary, illus. LC 78-23634. (Illus.). 30 p. 25cm. (Magic Monster Series). c.1979. (ISBN 0-89565-058-4). (ISBN 0-516-06185-2). Distributed by Childrens Press.
--Magic Monsters Learn About Health. Endres, Helen Elise, illus. LC 79-24240. (Illus.). (Magic Monster Ser.). (ps-3). 1980. (ISBN 0-89565-117-3). Childs World.
--Magic Monsters Learn About Space. (Illus.). 32p. (Magic Monsters Ser.). (ps-3). 1980. (ISBN 0-516-06463-0). Childrens.
--Magic Monsters Learn About Space. Hohag, Linda Sommers, illus. LC 79-25765. (Illus.). (Magic Monster Ser.). (ps-3). 1980. (ISBN 0-89565-119-X). Childs World.
--Magic Monsters Look for Colors. Magnuson, Diana, illus. LC 78-23792. (Illus.). 31 p. 25cm. (Magic Monster Series). c.1979. (ISBN 0-89565-056-8). Child's World.
--Magic Monsters Look for Shapes. Magnuson, Diana, illus. LC 78-21529. (Illus.). 32 p. 25cm. (Magic Monster Series). c.1979. (ISBN 0-89565-057-6). Child's World.
--My "A" Book. special rev. ed. Peltier, Pam, illus. LC 84-17535. p. cm. (My First Steps to Reading). (My First Steps to Reading). c.1984. (ISBN 0-89565-272-2). Child's World.
--My "A" Sound Box. Peltier, Pam, illus. LC 84-17024. (Illus.). 31 p. (Sound Box Books). c.1984. (ISBN 0-89565-296-X). Child's World.
--My "B" Book. special rev. ed. Hohag, Linda Sommers, illus. LC 84-17536. p. cm. (My first steps to reading). c.1984. (ISBN 0-89565-277-3). Child's World.
--My B Sound Box. Hohag, Linda Sommers, illus. LC 77-23588. (Illus.). 29 p. (Sound Box Books). c.1977. Child's World.
--My Baby Brother Needs a Friend. Hook, Frances Arnold (1912-), illus. LC 78-21935. (Illus.). 30 p. 27cm. c.1979. (ISBN 0-89565-019-3). Child's World.
--My Baby Brother Needs Me. Hook, Frances Arnold (1912-), illus. LC 79-1074. p. cm. c.1979. (ISBN 0-89565-070-3). Child's World.
--My "C" Book. special rev. ed. Hohag, Linda Sommers, illus. LC 84-17534. p. cm. (My first steps to reading). c.1984. (ISBN 0-89565-278-1). Child's World.
--My C Sound Box. Hohag, Linda Sommers, illus. LC 78-23638. (Illus.). 30 p. (Sound Box Bks.). c.1979. (ISBN 0-89565-053-3). Child's World.
--My "D" Book. special rev. ed. Hohag, Linda Sommers, illus. LC 84-17544. p. cm. (My first steps to reading). c.1984. (ISBN 0-89565-279-X). Child's World.
--My D Sound Box. Hohag, Linda Sommers, illus. LC 78-8450. (Illus.). 29 p. (Sound Box Books). c.1978. (ISBN 0-89565-044-4). Child's World.
--My "E" Book. special rev. ed. Gohman, Vera Kennedy (1922-), illus. LC 84-17545. p. cm. (My first steps to reading). c.1984. (ISBN 0-89565-273-0). Child's World.
--My "E" Sound Box. Gohman, Vera Kennedy (1922-), illus. LC 84-17021. (Illus.). 29 p. (Sound Box Books). c.1984. (ISBN 0-89565-297-8). Child's World.
--My "F" Book. special rev. ed. Hohag, Linda Sommers, illus. LC 84-17546. p. cm. (My first steps to reading). c.1984. (ISBN 0-89565-280-3). Child's World.
--My F Sound Box Book. Hohag, Linda Sommers, illus. LC 77-9377. p. cm. (Sound Box Books). c.1977. (ISBN 0-913778-93-1). Child's World.
--My First Thanksgiving Book. Connelly, Gwen, illus. LC 84-9433. (Illus.). 30 p. 25cm. c.1984. (ISBN 0-516-02903-7). Childrens Press.
--My "G" Book. special rev. ed. Hohag, Linda Sommers, illus. LC 84-17547. p. cm. (My first steps to reading). c.1984. (ISBN 0-89565-281-1). Child's World.
--My G Sound Box. Hohag, Linda Sommers, illus. LC 78-22037. (Illus.). 31 p. (Sound Box Books). c.1979. (ISBN 0-89565-053-3). Child's World.
--My "H" Book. special rev. ed. Hohag, Linda Sommers, illus. LC 84-17541. p. cm. (My first steps to reading). 1984. (ISBN 0-89565-282-X). Child's World.
--My H Sound Box Book. Hohag, Linda Sommers, illus. LC 77-8977. p. cm. (Sound Box Books). c.1977. (ISBN 0-913778-94-X). Child's World.
--My "I" Book. special rev. ed. Gohman, Vera Kennedy (1922-), illus. LC 84-17542. p. cm. (My first steps to reading). c.1984. (ISBN 0-89565-274-9). Child's World, Inc.
--My "J" Book. special rev. ed. Hohag, Linda Sommers, illus. LC 84-17543. p. cm. (My First steps to reading). c.1984. (ISBN 0-89565-283-8). Child's World.

--My J Sound Box. Hohag, Linda Sommers, illus. LC 78-23178. (Illus.). 29 p. (Sound Box Books). c.1979. (ISBN 0-89565-049-5). Child's World.
--My "K" Book. special rev. ed. Hohag, Linda Sommers, illus. LC 84-17539. p. cm. (My first steps to reading). c.1984. (ISBN 0-89565-284-6). Child's World.
--My K Sound Box. Hohag, Linda Sommers, illus. LC 78-22034. (Illus.). 29 p. (Sound Box Books). c.1979. Child's World.
--My "L" Book. special rev. ed. Hohag, Linda Sommers, illus. LC 84-17540. p. cm. (My first steps to reading). c.1984. (ISBN 0-89565-285-4). Child's World.
--My L Sound Box. Hohag, Linda Sommers, illus. LC 78-8373. (Illus.). 29 p. (Sound Box Books). c.1978. (ISBN 0-89565-044-4). Child's World.
--My "M" Book. special rev. ed. Hohag, Linda Sommers, illus. LC 84-17556. p. cm. (My first steps to reading). c.1984. (ISBN 0-89565-286-2). Child's World.
--My M Sound Box. Hohag, Linda Sommers, illus. LC 78-24458. (Illus.). 29 p. (Sound Box Books). c.1979. (ISBN 0-89565-051-7). Child's World.
--My "N" Book. special rev. ed. Hohag, Linda Sommers, illus. LC 84-17537. p. cm. (My first steps to reading). c.1984. (ISBN 0-89565-287-0). Child's World.
--My N Sound Box. Hohag, Linda Sommers, illus. LC 78-22053. (Illus.). 29 p. (Sound Box Books). c.1979. (ISBN 0-89565-054-1). Child's World.
--My "O" Book. special rev. ed. Gohman, Vera Kennedy (1922-), illus. LC 84-17538. p. cm. (My first steps to reading). c.1984. (ISBN 0-89565-275-7). Child's World.
--My "O" Sound Box. Gohman, Vera Kennedy (1922-), illus. LC 84-17023. (Illus.). 29 p. (Sound Box Books). c.1984. (ISBN 0-89565-299-4). Child's World.
--My "P" Book. special rev. ed. Hohag, Linda Sommers, illus. LC 84-17553. p. cm. (My first steps to reading). c.1984. (ISBN 0-89565-288-9). Child's World.
--My P Sound Box. Hohag, Linda Sommers, illus. LC 78-7841. (Illus.). 29 p. (Sound Box Books). c.1978. (ISBN 0-89565-047-9). Child's World.
--My Parade of Sounds. Hohag, Linda Sommers, illus. LC 79-15930. p. cm. (Sound Box Books). c.1979. (ISBN 0-89565-103-3). Child's World.
--My "Q" Book. special rev. ed. Hohag, Linda Sommers, illus. LC 84-17554. p. cm. (My first steps to reading). c.1984. (ISBN 0-89565-289-7). Child's World.
--My Q Sound Box. Hohag, Linda Sommers, illus. LC 79-13085. (Illus.). 29 p. (Sound Box Books). c.1979. (ISBN 0-89565-100-9). Child's World.
--My "R" Book. special rev. ed. Hohag, Linda Sommers, illus. LC 84-17555. p. cm. (My first steps to reading). c.1984. (ISBN 0-89565-290-0). Child's World.
--My R Sound Box. Hohag, Linda Sommers, illus. LC 78-7842. (Illus.). 29 p. (Sound Box Books). c.1978. (ISBN 0-89565-048-7). Child's World.
--My "S" Book. special rev. ed. Hohag, Linda Sommers, illus. LC 84-17551. p. cm. (My first steps to reading). c.1984. (ISBN 0-89565-291-9). Child's World.
--My S Sound Box Book. Hohag, Linda Sommers, illus. LC 77-8970. p. cm. (Sound Box Books). c.1977. (ISBN 0-913778-95-8). Child's World.
--My Sound Box. Gohman, Vera Kennedy (1922-), illus. LC 84-17022. (Illus.). 31 p. 20cm. (Sound Box Books). c.1984. (ISBN 0-89565-298-6). Child's World.
--My "T" Book. special rev. ed. Hohag, Linda Sommers, illus. LC 84-17552. p. cm. (My first steps to reading). c.1984. (ISBN 0-89565-292-7). Child's World.
--My-T-Sound Box Book. Hohag, Linda Sommers, illus. LC 77-23587. p. cm. (Sound Box Books). c.1977. (ISBN 0-913778-96-6). Child's World.
--My "U" Book. special rev. ed. Peltier, Pam, illus. LC 84-17548. p. cm. (My first steps to reading). c.1984. (ISBN 0-89565-276-5). Child's World.
--My "U" Sound Box. Peltier, Pam, illus. LC 84-17012. (Illus.). 31 p. (Sound Box Books). c.1984. (ISBN 0-89565-300-1). Child's World.
--My "V" Book. special rev. ed. Hohag, Linda Sommers, illus. LC 84-17549. p. cm. (My first steps to reading). c.1984. (ISBN 0-89565-293-5). Child's World.
--My "V" Sound Box. Hohag, Linda Sommers, illus. LC 79-13084. (Illus.). 29 p. (Sound Box Books). N.D. (ISBN 0-89565-101-7). Child's World.
--My "W" Book. special rev. ed. Hohag, Linda Sommers, illus. LC 84-17550. p. cm. (My first steps to reading). c.1984. (ISBN 0-89565-294-3). Child's World.
--My W Sound Box. Hohag, Linda Sommers, illus. LC 78-8614. (Illus.). 29 p. (Sound Box Books). c.1978. (ISBN 0-89565-046-0). Child's World.
--My "Xyz" Book. special rev. ed. Hohag, Linda Sommers, illus. LC 84-17561. p. cm. (My first steps to reading). c.1984. (ISBN 0-89565-295-1). Child's World.
--A New Boy in Kindergarten. Siculan, Daniel (1922-), illus. LC 76-15634. (Illus.). 32 p. 25cm. (Learning About Living). c.1976. Child's World.
--No! No! Word Bird. Hohag, Linda Sommers, illus. LC 80-29491. p. cm. (Word Birds for Early Birds). 1981, c.1980. (ISBN 0-89565-161-0). Child's World.
--Now I Am Five. Endres, Helen Elise, illus. LC 83-25264. (Illus.). 32p. (Now I Am Ser.). (ps). 1984. (ISBN 0-516-01879-5). (ISBN 0-516-41879-3). Childrens.
--Now I Am Four. Hutton, Kathryn, illus. LC 83-25270. (Illus.). 32p. (Now I Am Ser.). (ps). 1984. (ISBN 0-516-01878-7). (ISBN 0-516-41878-5). Childrens.
--Now I Am Three. Hohag, Linda Sommers, illus. LC 83-20892. (Illus.). 32p. (Now I Am Ser.). (ps). 1984. (ISBN 0-516-01877-9). (ISBN 0-516-41877-7). Childrens.
--Now I Am Two. Hutton, Kathryn, illus. LC 83-20891. (Illus.). 32p. (Now I Am Ser.). (ps). 1984. (ISBN 0-516-01876-0). (ISBN 0-516-41876-9). Childrens.
--Now I Am Two!. Hutton, Kathryn, illus. LC 83-20891. (Created by Child's World (Firm)). (Illus.). 31 p. 25cm. c.1984. (ISBN 0-516-01876-0). (ISBN 0-516-41876-9). Childrens Press.
--One Little World. Lafferty, Ed, illus. LC 75-35975. (Illus.). 32 p. 25cm. 1976, c.1975. (ISBN 0-913778-31-1). Child's World.
--Our Easter Book. LC 75-37698. (Illus.). 32p. (Special-Day Bks.). (ps-3). 1976. (ISBN 0-516-05890-8). Childrens.
--Pinny's Day at Play School. Jaffe, Morris H, photos by. LC 55-7028. unpaged. illus. 29cm. 1955. Lothrop, Lee and Shepard.
--Play with "A" and "T". Endres, Helen Elise, illus. LC 73-4740. (Illus.). 25 p. 1973. Child's World.
--Play with "E" and "D". Endres, Helen Elise, illus. LC 73-4743. (Illus.). 25 p. 1973. Child's World.
--Play with "I" and "G". Endres, Helen Elise, illus. LC 73-4739. (Illus.). 25 p. 1973. Child's World.
--Play with "O" and "G". Endres, Helen Elise, illus. LC 73-4742. (Illus.). 25 p. 1973. Child's World.
--Play with "U" and "G". Endres, Helen Elise, illus. LC 73-4741. (Illus.). 25 p. 1973. Child's World.
--A Rabbit Has a Habit. Endres, Helen Elise, illus. LC 75-35608. (Illus.). (ps-3). 1976. (ISBN 0-913778-35-4). Childs World.
--Rhyme Me a Rhyme. Belenchia, Marc, illus. LC 76-16538. (Illus.). 32 p. c.1976. (ISBN 0-913778-42-7). Child's World.
--Riddle Me a Riddle. Belenchia, Marc, illus. LC 76-30822. (Illus.). 32 p. c.1977. (ISBN 0-913778-80-X). Child's World ; Chicago : Distributed by Childrens Press.
--The Shoemaker & the Christmas Elves. (Illus.). 32p. (Folk Tales Ser.). (ps-3). 1980. (ISBN 0-516-06482-7). Childrens.
--Skip Aboard a Space Ship. Endres, Helen Elise, illus. LC 77-12958. p. cm. (Creative Dramatics). 1978. (ISBN 0-89565-009-6). Child's World.
--Spring. Monchaux, Marie-Claude, illus. LC 85-11672. p. cm. c.1985. (ISBN 0-89565-327-3). Child's World.
--Spring Is Here!. Hook, Frances Arnold (1912-), illus. LC 75-14202. p. cm. 1975. (ISBN 0-913778-11-7). Child's World.
--Stop! Go! Word Bird. Hohag, Linda Sommers, illus. LC 80-16273. p. cm. (An Early Bird Reader). c.1980. (ISBN 0-89565-160-2). Child's World.
--Summer. Monchaux, Marie-Claude, illus. LC 85-12823. p. cm. c.1985. (ISBN 0-89565-328-1). Child's World.
--Summer Is Here!. Hook, Frances Arnold (1912-), illus. LC 75-12945. p. cm. 1975. (ISBN 0-913778-12-5). Child's World.
--Talking Tabby Cat. (Illus.). 32p. (Folk Tales Ser.: No. 34). (gr. k-4). 1980. (ISBN 0-516-06483-5). Childrens.
--The Talking Tabby Cat: A Folk Tale from France. Endres, Helen Elise, illus. LC 79-26193. p. cm. c.1980. (ISBN 0-89565-107-6). Child's World.
--Terry's Turn-Around. Wannamaker, Bruce, pseud. Endres, Helen Elise, illus. LC 82-7467. (Illus.). 30 p. 25cm. c.1982. (ISBN 0-89693-200-1). (ISBN 0-89693-200-1). Dandelion House: Distributed by Scripture Press Publications.
--Thank You, Animal Friends. Gohman, Vera Kennedy (1922-), illus. LC 75-29241. (Illus.). (ps-3). 1975. (ISBN 0-913778-15-X). Childs World.
--Thank You, God, for Fall. rev. ed. Hook, Frances Arnold (1912-), illus. LC 79-10030. (Illus.). 24 p. (Four Seasons.). (The Four Seasons). c.1979. (ISBN 0-89565-081-9). Child's World.
--Thank You, God, for Spring. rev. ed. Hook, Frances Arnold (1912-), illus. LC 79-10031. (Illus.). 24 p. (Four seasons.). (The Four Seasons). c.1979. (ISBN 0-89565-079-7). Child's World.
--Thank You, God, for Summer. rev. ed. Hook, Frances Arnold (1912-), illus. LC 79-10032. (Illus.). 24 p. (The Four Seasons). c.1979. Child's World.
--Thank You, God, for Winter. Hook, Frances Arnold (1912-), illus. LC 79-11398. (Illus.). 24 p. (The Four Seasons). c.1979. (ISBN 0-89565-082-7). Child's World.
--Thank You, Lord, for Me. rev. ed. Hohag, Linda Sommers, illus. LC 79-10033. (Illus.). 32 p. 25cm. (A Values Series). c.1979. (ISBN 0-89565-077-0). Child's World.
--Tick, Tock, the Popcorn Clock. Endres, Helen Elise, illus. LC 77-13120. (Illus.). (Creative Dramatics Ser.). (ps-3). 1978. (ISBN 0-89565-010-X). (ISBN 0-89565-043-6). Childs World.
--Try on a Shoe. Weisgard, Leonard Joseph (1916-), illus. LC 73-4738. (Illus.). 32 p. 32cm. 1973. (ISBN 0-913778-00-1). Child's World.
--Wait," ... Says His Father. Endres, Helen Elise, illus. LC 75-12956. (Illus.). 20 p. 29cm. 1975. (ISBN 0-913778-07-9). Child's World.
--Watch Out! Word Bird. Hohag, Linda Sommers, illus. LC 81-21570. p. cm. (Word Birds for Early Birds). c.1982. (ISBN 0-89565-219-6). Child's World.
--We Visit the Farm. McLean, Mina Gow, illus. LC 76-15975. (Illus.). 32 p. (Going places Ser.). c.1976. (ISBN 0-913778-43-5). Child's World.
--We Visit the Zoo. Magnuson, Diana, illus. LC 76-15639. (Illus.). 31 p. (Going Places Ser.). c.1976. (ISBN 0-913778-61-3). Child's World.
--What Do the Animals Do in the Zoo?. Magnuson, Diana, illus. LC 75-33954. (Illus.). 32 p. 25cm. c.1976. (ISBN 0-913778-31-1). Child's World.
--What Does a Koala Bear Need?. Endres, Helen Elise, illus. LC 75-33956. (Illus.). 31 p. 25cm. c.1976. (ISBN 0-913778-34-6). Distributed by Childrens Press.
--What Does Word Bird See?. Gohman, Vera Kennedy (1922-), illus. LC 81-21594. (Illus.). 32 p. 25cm. (Word Birds for Early Birds). c.1982. (ISBN 0-89565-220-X). Child's World.
--What Will It Rain?. A Book About Fall. Endres, Helen Elise, illus. LC 76-46295. (Illus.). (ps-3). 1977. (ISBN 0-913778-69-9). Childs World.
--When I'm Afraid. special rev. ed. Hook, Frances Arnold (1912-), illus. LC 79-1504. (Based on Sometimes in I'm Afraid, by Sylvia Root Teser, 1939). (Illus.). 30 p. 26cm. c.1979. (ISBN 0-89565-071-1). Child's World.
--Where Things Belong. Siculan, Daniel (1922-), illus. LC 76-13865. (Illus.). 32 p. 25cm. c.1976. (ISBN 0-913778-44-3). Child's World.
--Winter. Monchaux, Marie-Claude, illus. LC 85-11663. p. cm. c.1985. (ISBN 0-89565-330-3). Child's World.
--Winter Is Here!. Hook, Frances Arnold (1912-), illus. LC 75-14201. p. cm. 1975. (ISBN 0-913778-10-9). Child's World.
--Wise Owl's Book of Sounds. Endres, Helen Elise, illus. LC 81-18094. p. cm. (Wise Owl plus). c.1982. (ISBN 0-516-06564-5). Child's World.
--Wise Owl's Days of the Week. Endres, Helen Elise, illus. LC 81-9971. (Created by Child's World (Firm)). (Illus.). 31 p. 25cm. (Wise Owl books). c.1981. (ISBN 0-516-06563-7). Childrens Press.
--Wise Owl's Time Book. Endres, Helen Elise, illus. LC 81-38546. p. cm. (Wise Owl plus). c.1981. (ISBN 0-516-06566-1). (ISBN 0-516-46566-X). Childrens Press.
--Wishes, Whispers, and Secrets. Hook, Frances Arnold (1912-), illus. LC 78-31295. p. cm. c.1979. (ISBN 0-89565-024-X). Child's World.
--Word Bird Asks: What? What? What?. Gohman, Vera Kennedy (1922-), illus. LC 83-15258. (Illus.). 32 p. 25cm. (Word Birds for Early Birds). c.1983. (ISBN 0-89565-258-7). Child's World.
--Word Bird Builds a City. Gohman, Vera Kennedy (1922-), illus. LC 83-15257. (Illus.). 32p. (Word Birds for Early Birds Ser.). 1983. (ISBN 0-89565-257-9). Childs World.
--Word Bird Makes Words with Cat. Hohag, Linda Sommers, illus. LC 83-23948. c.1984. (ISBN 0-89565-259-5). Child's World.
--Word Bird Makes Words with Dog. Gohman, Vera Kennedy (1922-), illus. LC 83-23946. c.1984. (ISBN 0-89565-263-3). Child's World.
--Word Bird Makes Words with Duck. Hohag, Linda Sommers, illus. LC 83-23943. c.1984. (ISBN 0-89565-261-7). Child's World.
--Word Bird Makes Words with Hen. Hohag, Linda Sommers, illus. LC 83-23944. c.1984. (ISBN 0-89565-260-9). Child's World.
--Word Bird Makes Words with Pig. Gohman, Vera Kennedy (1922-), illus. LC 83-23945. c.1984. (ISBN 0-89565-262-5). Child's World.
--Word Bird's Circus Surprise. Hohag, Linda Sommers, illus. LC 80-29528. p. cm. (Word Birds for Early Birds). 1981, c.1980. (ISBN 0-89565-162-9). Child's World.
--Word Bird's Hats. Gohman, Vera Kennedy (1922-), illus. LC 81-18065. (Illus.). 32 p. 25cm. (Word Birds for Early Birds). c.1982. (ISBN 0-89565-221-8). Child's World.
--Word Bird's Shapes. Hohag, Linda Sommers, illus. LC 83-15255. (Illus.). 32p. (Word Birds for Early Birds Ser.). (gr. k-2). 1983. (ISBN 0-89565-255-2). Childs World.

Mond, Frank L. Du see Du Mond, Frank L.

Mondello, Anita, tr. see De Brisville, Jean-Claude.

Mongiardini-Rembodi, G.

--Pinocchio under the Sea. LC 13-19424. (Illus.). 20cm. 201p. 1913. MacMillan.

Mongo, C.

--Uncle Happy's Cat. (Illus., Orig.). N.D. Dghtrs St Paul.

Monheit, Alfred

--Picnic in the Park. Lewis, Anne, illus. LC 60-943629. (Illus.). (gr. k-3). 1960. (ISBN 0-8178-3241-6). (ISBN 0-8178-3242-4). Harvey.

Monheit, Helen

--Suzy. LC 72-81257. (Illus.). 20cm. 39p. 1969. Franklin Pub. Co.

Monigold, Glenn W

--Folk Tales from Vietnam. Wong, Jeanyee (1920-), illus. LC 64-3909. 61 p. col. illus. 19 cm. 1964. Peter Pauper Press.

Monjo, F. N., tr. see Zimnik, Reiner.

Monjo, Ferdinand Nicolas, III (1924-1978)

--Clarence and the Burglar. Galdone, Paul (1914-), illus. LC 72-85622. (Illus.). 47 p. 23cm. (Break-of-day book). 1973. (ISBN 0-698-20237-6). (ISBN 0-698-20237-6). Coward, McCann & Geoghegan.
--The Drinking Gourd. Brenner, Fred (1920-), illus. LC 68-10782. (Illus.). 5 7/8 x 8 1/2. 64p. (16 pt.). (I Can Read History Bks.). (gr. k-3). 1970. (ISBN 0-06-024330-9) (ISBN 0-06-444042-7) Har-Row.
--Gettysburg: Tad Lincoln's Story. Gorsline, Douglas Warner (1913-1985), illus. LC 75-6695. (Illus.). 48 p. 26cm. c.1976. (ISBN 0-525-61534-2). Windmill Books.
--Grand Papa and Ellen Aroon. Cuffari, Richard (1925-1978), illus. LC 73-17435. (Being an Account of Some of the Happy Times Spent Together by Thomas Jefferson and His Favorite Grand-daughter). (Illus.). 58 p. 24cm. 1974. (ISBN 0-03-012091-8). Holt, Rinehart and Winston.
--The House on Stink Alley: A Story About the Pilgrims in Holland. Quackenbush, Robert Mead (1929-), illus. LC 77-3469. (Illus.). 64 p. 24cm. c.1977. (ISBN 0-03-016651-9). Holt, Rinehart and Winston.
--Indian Summer. Lobel, Anita Kempler (1934-), illus. LC 68-10206. (Illus.). 5 7/8 x 8 1/2. 64p. (18 pt.). (I Can Read History Bks.). (gr. k-3). 1968. (ISBN 0-06-024328-7) Har-Row.
--The Jezebel Wolf. Schoenherr, John Carl (1935-), illus. LC 73-144225. (Illus.). 47 p. 22cm. 1971. (ISBN 0-671-65191-9). Simon and Schuster.
--King George's Head Was Made of Lead. Tomes, Margot Ladd (1917-), illus. LC 74-79705. (Illus.). 47 p. 24cm. 1974. (ISBN 0-698-20298-8). Coward, McCann & Geoghegan.
--Letters to Horseface. Bolognese, Donald Alan (1934-) & Raphael, Elaine, pseud. (1933-), illus. Bolognese, Elaine Raphael Chionchio. LC 74-23766. (Being the Story of Wolfgang Amadeus Mozart's Journey to Italy, 1769-1770, When He Was a Boy of Fourteen). p. cm. 1975. (ISBN 0-670-42738-1). Viking Press.
--Me and Willie and Pa: The Story of Abraham Lincoln and His Son Tad. Gorsline, Douglas Warner (1913-1985), illus. 1973. (ISBN 0-671-65191-9). Simon & Schuster.
--A Namesake for Nathan: Being an Account of Captain Nathan Hale by His Twelve-Year-Old Sister, Joanna. Keith, Eros, illus. LC 76-58325. (Illus.). 127 p. 24cm. c.1977. (ISBN 0-698-20411-5). Coward, McCann & Geoghegan.
--The One Bad Thing About Father. Negri, Rocco (1932-), illus. LC 71-85036. (Illus.). 62 p. 22cm. (I can read history book). 1970. Harper & Row.
--Pirates in Panama. Tripp, Wallace Whitney (1940-), illus. LC 79-101891. (Illus.). 59 p. 24cm. 1970. Simon and Schuster.
--Poor Richard in France. Turkle, Brinton Cassaday (1915-), illus. LC 72-76582. (Illus.). 58 p. 24cm. 1973. (ISBN 0-03-088597-3). Holt, Rinehart and Winston. **Award: (ALA).**
--The Porcelain Pagoda. Egielski, Richard (1952-), illus. LC 75-38574. (Illus.). 11, 243 p. 25cm. c.1976. (ISBN 0-670-56565-2). Viking Press.

--Prisoners of the Scrambling Dragon. Geisert, Arthur, illus. LC 79-4449. (Illus.). 95 p. 24cm. c.1980. (ISBN 0-03-016656-X). Holt, Rinehart and Winston.
--Rudi and the Distelfink. Kraus, George (1909-), illus. LC 72-86275. (Illus.). 32 p. 1972. (ISBN 0-525-61002-2). Windmill Books.
--The Sea Beggar's Son. Hodges, Cyril Walter (1909-), illus. LC 73-78320. (Illus.). 32 p. 26cm. 1975, c.1974. (ISBN 0-698-20277-5). Coward, McCann & Geoghegan.
--The Secret of the Sachem's Tree. Tomes, Margot Ladd (1917-), illus. LC 72-76699. (Illus.). 60 p. 23cm. (Break-of-day book). 1972. (ISBN 0-698-20199-X). (ISBN 0-698-20199-X). Coward, McCann & Geoghegan.
--Slater's Mill. Kubinyi, Laszlo (1937-), illus. LC 73-179990. (Illus.). 78 p. 24cm. 1972. (ISBN 0-671-65178-1). Simon and Schuster.
--The Vicksburg Veteran. Gorsline, Douglas Warner (1913-1985), illus. LC 77-144226. (Illus.). 62 p. 27cm. 1971. (ISBN 0-671-65156-0). Simon and Schuster. **Award: (ALA).**
--Willie Jasper's Golden Eagle. Gorsline, Douglas Warner (1913-1985), illus. LC 75-36603. 96p (gr. 1-5). 1976. Doubleday.
--Willie Jasper's Golden Eagle: Being an Eyewitness Account of the Great Steamboat Race Between the Natchez and the Robert E. Lee. 1st ed. Gorsline, Douglas Warner (1913-1985), illus. LC 75-28455. (Illus.). 95 p. 29cm. c.1976. (ISBN 0-385-07268-6). Doubleday.
--Zenas and the Shaving Mill. Cuffari, Richard (1925-1978), illus. LC 75-32531. (Illus.). 44 p. 27cm. c.1976. (ISBN 0-698-20326-7). Coward, McCann & Geoghegan.

Monjo, J. N., tr. see Janzarik, Hilde.

Monmouth, Harper, Mrs.
--Blue-Eyed Jimmie. (Illus.). (Child Life Ser.). N.D. D. Lothrop Co.
--Johnny Jones. (Illus.). (Child Life Ser.). N.D. D. Lothrop Co.
--Much Fruit. (Illus.). (Child Life Ser.). N.D. D. Lothrop Co.
--Nettie Nesmith. (Illus.). (Child Life Ser.). N.D. D. Lothrop Co.
--Ruthie Shaw. (Illus.). (Child Life Ser.). N.D. D. Lothrop Co.

Monninger, Werner H
--Salute to Teen-Age. Glore, Charles F., illus. 61p. illus. 21cm. 1957. Exposition Press.

Monniot, Victorine (1824-)
--Marguerite's Journal: A Story for Girls. Harris, Miriam Coles (1834-1925), ed. Baxter, Lucy W. (1834-1925), tr. (With an Editorial Introduction by the Author of Rutledge, Louie's, Last Term at St. Mary's). 328 p. 19 cm. 1875. G. W. Carleton & Co.; Etc., Etc.

Monrad, Jean (1917-)
--How Many Kisses Good Night?. Bloch, Lucienne (1909-), illus. LC 49-8112. (Illus.). 20p. 21 x 24cm. (Young Scott Bks.). 1949. Scott.

Monreal, Guy
--Alala. Claveloux, Nicole, illus. (Illus.). (gr. 3 up). 1970. (ISBN 0-531-04016-X). (ISBN 0-531-05016-5). Quist. **Award: (NYT).**
--The Teletrips of Alala. Claveloux, Nicole, illus. LC 73-125503. (Illus.). 36 p. 28cm. 1970. (ISBN 0-8252-0040-7). Harlin Quist.

Monro, C. Bedell
--The Quest of the Moon Fish. Harrison, William Don, illus. LC 27-21015. 5 p. l., 205 p. incl. plates. col. front. 20 cm. 1927. W. Morrow & Company.

Monro, Edward (1815-1866)
--Basil the Schoolboy: Or, The Heir of Arundel. (Illus.). N.D. E J B Young.
--Basil the Schoolboy: Or, the Heir of Arundel. 1891. Thomas Whittaker.
--The Dark Mountains. 1891. Thomas Whittaker.
--Dark Mountains: Being a Sequel to The Journey Home. New ed. N.D. E. P. Dutton.
--Dark River. N.D. E. P. Dutton.
--Journey Home. N.D. E. P. Dutton.
--The Journey Home. 1891. Thomas Whittaker.
--The Vast Army. 1891. Thomas Whittaker.
--Walter the Schoolmaster. (Illus.). N.D. E & J B Young.
--Walter the Schoolmaster. 1891. Thomas Whittaker.

Monroe, Alex
--Barnacle & His Friends. (Illus.). 42p. (Orig.). (gr. 1-6). 1980. (ISBN 0-933614-07-1). Peregrine Pr.

Monroe, Doris
--When Marcia Goes to Church. Dugan, Maggie, illus. (gr. 1-3). 1966. (ISBN 0-8054-4216-2). Broadman.

Monroe, Irene R.
--Heavenly A B C's. (Illus.). (ps-3). N.D. Dghtrs St Paul.

Monroe, Jane B.
--The Four Magic Boxes. Endres, Helen Elise, illus. LC 77-12959. (Illus.). (Creative Dramatics Ser.). (ps-3). 1978. (ISBN 0-89565-007-X). (ISBN 0-89565-040-1). Childs World.

Monroe, Keith see Keith, Donald, pseud.

Monroe, Marion (1898-) & Artley, Stern
--The New Tall Tales. Robinson, Helen M., ed. Moran, Constance Oehler (1898-), illus. LC 67-21911. (Illus.). 1964. Scott Foresman.

Monsell, Helen Albee (1895-1971)
--Boy of Old Virginia, Robert E. Lee. Funk, Clotilde Embree, illus. LC 53-701. 165p. illus. 20cm. (Childhood of famous Americans series). 1953. Bobbs-Merrill.
--Boy of Old Virginia, Robert E. Lee. Funk, Clotilde Embree, illus. LC 38-1037. 165 p illus. 20 cm. c.1937. The Bobbs-Merrill Company.
--Dolly Madison, Quaker Girl. 1st ed. James, Sandra, illus. LC 44-3726. (Illus.). 162p. 19 x 15cm. (Childhood of Famous Americans Ser.). 1944. Bobbs-Merrill.
--Dolly Madison, Quaker Girl. James, Sandra, illus. LC 53-700. (Illus.). 20cm. 182p. (Childhood of Famous Americans Series). 1953. Bobbs-Merrill.
--Dolly Madison, Quaker Girl. Morrow, Gray, illus. LC 60-7715. 200p. illus. 20cm. (Childhood of famous Americans). 1961. Bobbs-Merrill.
--Dolly Madison, Quaker Girl. Sandra, James, illus. LC 44-3793. 182 p. illus. 19 1/2 x 15 cm. (Childhood of famous Americans Ser.). 1944. The Bobbs-Merrill Company.
--Henry Clay, Mill Boy of the Slashes. John, Charles V., illus. 183 p. illus. 20 cm. (The Childhood of famous Americans ser.). 1947. The Bobbs-Merrill Company.
--Henry Clay, Young Kentucky Orator. Morrow, Gray, illus. LC 62-16625. (Illus.). 200 p. 20cm. (Childhood of famous Americans). 1963. Bobbs-Merrill.
--Her Own Way: The Story of Lottie Moon. Pitz, Henry Clarence (1895-1976), illus. LC 58-9919. 188p. illus. 21cm. 1958. Broadman Press.
--John Marshall, Boy of Young America. 1st ed. Browne, Syd, illus. LC 49-8116. 206 p. illus. 20 cm. (The Childhood of Famous Americans Ser.). 1949. Bobbs-Merrill Co.
--John Marshall, Boy of Young America. Pellicer, Joseph Luis, illus. LC 62-16621. (Illus.). 20cm. 200p. (Childhood of Famous Americans). 1962. Bobbs-Merrill.
--Lucy Lou Fights for Her Rights. Laune, Paul Sidney (1899-), illus. LC 40-80191. (Illus.). 20cm. 280p. 1940. Bobbs-Merrill.
The Mystery of Grandfather's Coat. 1st ed. Page, Joseph, illus. LC 48-6637. 234 p. illus. 21 cm. 1948. Bobbs-Merrill Co.
--Paddy's Christmas. Wiese, Kurt (1887-1974), illus. LC 42-18463. 48 p. incl. front., illus. (part col.) 17 x 23 cm. 1942. A. A. Knopf.
--Robert E. Lee, Boy of Old Virginia. Arthur, James & Morrow, Gray, illus. LC 59-140001. 192p. illus. 20cm. (Childhood of famous Americans). 1960. Bobbs-Merrill.
--The Secret of the Chestnut Tree: A Mystery Story of a Girls' School in Old Virginia. Laune, Paul Sidney (1899-), illus. LC 36-19099. 308 p. illus. 19 1/2 cm. c.1936. The Bobbs-Merrill Company.
--The Secret of the Gold Earring: A Mystery Story of Two Southern Girls in Little Old New York. Laune, Paul Sidney (1899-), illus. LC 38-24563. 298 p. incl. front., illus. 20 cm. c.1938. The Bobbs-Merrill Company.
--Susan Anthony, Girl Who Dared. Fiorentino, Al, illus. LC 60-7704. 192p. illus. 20cm. (Childhood of Famous Americans). 1960. Bobbs-Merrill.
--Susan Anthony, Girl Who Dared. 1st ed. Laune, Paul Sidney (1899-), illus. LC 54-6062. 192p. illus. 20cm. (The Childhood of Famous Americans Ser.: No. 81). 1954. Bobbs-Merrill.
--Tom Jackson, Young Stonewall. Rawson, Maurice, illus. LC 60-7720. 200p. illus. 20cm. Reissue of 1942 ed. (Childhood of famous Americans). 1961. Bobbs-Merrill Co.
--Tom Jefferson, a Boy in Colonial Days. Funk, Clotilde Embree, illus. LC 53-703. 168p. illus. 20cm. (Childhood of Famous Americans ser.). 1953. Bobbs-Merrill.
--Tom Jefferson: A Boy in Colonial Days. Funk, Clotilde Embree, illus. LC 39-21294. 168, 1 p. illus. 20 cm. c.1939. The Bobbs-Merrill Company.
--Tom Jefferson, Boy of Colonial Days. Wagner, Kenneth (1911-), illus. LC 62-12688. 200p. illus. 20cm. (Childhood of famous Americans). 1962. Bobbs-Merrill.
--With Patrick Henry's Help. Hutchinson, William William (1916-), illus. LC 66-10385. 192 p. illus. 21 cm. c.1966. Broadman Press.
--Woodrow Wilson, Boy President. Bolden, Melvin Reed (1919-), illus. LC 50-9475. (Illus.). 186 p. 20cm. (Childhood of famous Americans ser.). 1950. Bobbs-Merrill.
--Woodrow Wilson Boy President. 1st ed. Bolden, Melvin Reed (1919-), illus. LC 59-14004. 192p. illus. 20cm. (Childhood of famous Americans). 1959. Bobbs-Merrill.
--Young Stonewall, Tom Jackson. John, Charles V., illus. LC 53-702762. 177p. illus. 20cm. (Childhood of famous Americans series). 1953. Bobbs-Merrill.
--Young Stonewall, Tom Jackson. John, Charles V., illus. LC 42-217587. vii p., 1 l., 9-177 p. illus. 20 cm. (The Boyhood of famous Americans series). 1942. The Bobbs-Merrill Company.

Monsell, John Robert (1877-), ed. see Grimm, Jakob Ludwig Karl (1785-1863) & Grimm, Wilhelm Karl.

Monsell, John Robert (1877-)
--The Hooded Crow: This Is the Tale of the Hooded Crow, a Story Which Every Child Should Know. Monsell, John Robert (1877-), illus. LC 34-20677. 58 p. illus. 29 cm. 1931. Oxford University Press.
--Jingle Book. Monsell, John Robert (1877-), illus. (Illus.). N.D. E. P. Dutton & Co.
--The Pink Knight. Monsell, John Robert (1877-), illus. N.D. Dodd, Mead & Co.
--The Pink Knight. Monsell, John Robert (1877-), illus. (Illus.). (Dumpy Books for Children Ser.). N.D. Frederick A. Stokes Co.
--Polichinelle: Old Nursery Songs of France. Monsell, John Robert (1877-), illus. LC 30-2905. 2 p. l., 7-55, 1 p. col. illus. 19 x 20 cm. 1928. H. Milford, Oxford University Press.

Monsell, John Samuel Bowley (1811-1875)
--Nursery Carols. Pletsch, Oscar, et al. (1830-1888), illus. N.D. Pott, Young & Co.

Monsma, Hester, adapted by see Schmidt, William.

Monson, Dianne L, jt. ed. see Ruddell, Robert Byron.

Monsour, Sally (1929-), ed.
--Folk Songs of the Arab World. (gr. 4 up). N.D. Bowmar.

Montagu, Elizabeth (1917-)
--This Side of the Truth. LC 58-6937. 193 p. 21cm. 1958, c.1957. Coward-McCann.

Montague, Clinton
--Old Tiger Eye, the Death Shot: Or, the White Squaw of the Dacotahs. (Champion Stories). 1877. C. T. DeWitt.

Montague, Louise see Athearn, Louise Montague.

Montaufier, Poupa
--One Summer at Grandmother's House. Montaufier, Poupa, illus. (Illus.). 32p. 1985. (ISBN 0-87614-238-2). Carolrhoda Bks.

Monteiro, George (1932-), intro. by.
--The Man Who Never Was. Levine, David (1926-) & Negreiros, Almada, illus. LC 81-83226 (Illus.) 195p (Orig.) 1982 (ISBN 0-943722-07-1). (ISBN 0-943722-08-X). Gavea-Brown.

Monteiro, Irene-Anne & Watson, Jenny, eds.
--Favourite Stories from Singapore. (Favourite Stories Ser.). 1977. (ISBN 0-686-60427-X). Heinemann Ed.
--Favourite Stories from Singapore. bilingual ed. (Orig.). (The Favourite Stories Ser.). 1981. (ISBN 0-686-73753-9). Heinemann Ed.

Monteith, Augusta
--The Pink Book of Verse for Very Little Children. Robin, illus. LC 35-27057. vi p., 1 l., 255, 1 p. illus. 25 cm. 1934. Sheed & Ward.

Montero, Anibal Diaz
--Young Peter and His Friends. N.D. Carlton Press.

Montero, Jaime A.
--Gatan & Talaw. (Illus., Orig.). (Sagada Folk Tales Ser.: No. 1). 1984. (ISBN 971-10-0164-0, Pub. by New Day Philippines). Cellar.

Montgolfier, Adelaide De (1789-1880)
--Piccolissima. Follen, Eliza Lee Cabot, Mrs. (1787-1860), tr. LC 30-14036. 96 p. incl. front., illus. 16 cm. (Half-title: Mrs. Follen's twilight stories no. 11). 1858. Whittemore, Niles, and Hall.

Montgomerie, Norah Mary (1913-)
--One, Two, Three: A Little Book of Counting Rhymes. Montgomerie, Norah Mary (1913-), illus. LC 68-10102. (Illus.). 23 p. 21cm. 1968. (ISBN 0-200-71488-0). Abelard-Schuman.
--This Little Pig Went to Market. Gill, Margery Jean (1925-), illus. (Illus.). 112p. 1983. (ISBN 0-370-30938-3, Pub by The Bodley Head). Merrimack Pub Cir.
--This Little Pig Went to Market: Play Rhymes. Gill, Margery Jean (1925-), illus. LC 67-20349. (Illus.). 111 p. 26cm. 1967, c.1966. (ISBN 0-531-01814-8). F. Watts.
--Twenty-Five Fables. Montgomerie, Norah Mary (1913-), illus. LC 61-14843. 60p. illus. 21cm. 1961. Abelard-Schuman.

Montgomerie, Norah Mary (1913-), retold by.
--The Merry Little Fox. Montgomerie, Norah Mary (1913-), illus. LC 64-12740. 61 p. col. illus. 21 cm. 1964. Abelard-Schuman.
--To Read & to Tell. Gill, Margery Jean (1925-), illus. LC 64-11464. 272p. illus. 23cm. 1964, c.1962. Arco.

Montgomerie, Norah Mary (1913-) & Montgomerie, William, eds.
--A Book of Scottish Nursery Rhymes. Ritchie, T. & Montgomerie, Norah Mary (1913-), illus. LC 65-14598. 157p. illus. 21cm. 1965, c.1964. (ISBN 0-19-500403-5). Oxford.
--Scottish Nursery Rhymes. 158p. 1978. (ISBN 0-7012-0003-0, Pub. by Chatto Bodley Jonathan). Merrimack Pub Cir.
--The Well at the World's End: Folk Tales of Scotland. new ed. Gill, Margery Jean (1925-), illus. LC 78-311097. (Illus.). 272 p. 23cm. 1980. (ISBN 0-370-01280-1). Bodley Head.

Montgomerie, William, jt. ed. see Montgomerie, Norah Mary.

Montgomery
--Montgomery's Heroic Ballads. (Classics for Children). N.D. Ginn and Company.

Montgomery, ed. see Bunyan, John.

Montgomery, Bobbie Carmichael (1918-)
--Artie Lizard's Long Tail and Other Stories. LC 53-3686. 58p. illus. 23cm. 1953. Vantage Press.
--The Cat's Got Her Tongue. LC 85-12155. p. cm. c.1985. (ISBN 0-8163-0615-X). Pacific Press Pub. Association.
--The Donkey-Car Kids. LC 80-15656. 128p. (Orion Ser.). (gr. 1-6). 1980. (ISBN 0-8127-0286-7). Review & Herald.

Montgomery-Campbell, M
--Uncle Ben's Whims: Or, Friends All Round Wrekin. N.D. E J B Young & Co.

Montgomery, Elizabeth Rider
--Half-Pint Fisherman. McCann, Gerald (1916-), illus. LC 56-8608. 202p. illus. 21cm. 1956. Dodd, Mead.
--The Mystery of Edison Brown. Beeby, Betty (1923-), illus. LC 60-104731. 218p. illus. 22cm. 1960. Scott, Foresman.
--The Mystery of the Boy Next Door. Gold, Ethel, illus. LC 77-14019. (Illus.). 44 p. 23cm. (For real book). c.1978. (ISBN 0-8116-4309-3). Garrard Pub. Co.
--Second-Fiddle Sandra. Norling, Ernest Ralph (1892-), illus. LC 58-9728. (Illus.). 205 p. 21cm. 1958. Dodd, Mead.
--Seeing in the Dark. Howell, Troy, illus. LC 79-11736. (Illus.). 44 p. 23cm. (For real book). 1979. (ISBN 0-8116-4312-3). Garrard Pub. Co.
--Susan and the Storm. LC 60-7289. 191 p. 22cm. 1960. T. Nelson.
--Three Miles an Hour. LC 52-10604. 245 p. 21 cm. 1952. Dodd, Mead.
--Tide Treasure Camper. LC 63-16688. (Illus.). 21cm. 122p. 1963. David McKay Company Inc.
--Tide Treasure Camper. Dawson, Isabel, illus. LC 63-16688. (Illus.). 122 p. 21cm. 1963. I. Washburn
--Trouble is His Name. Vestal, Herman B, illus. LC 76-18136. (Illus.). 39 p. 23cm. c.1976. (ISBN 0-8116-4303-4). Garrard Pub. Co.
--Two Kinds of Courage. LC 66-14584. vii, 150p. 21cm. c.1966. Washburn.

Montgomery, Elizabeth Rider, Mrs., jt. auth. see Baruch, Dorothy Walter, Mrs.

Montgomery, Florence
--Peggy and Other Tales. N.D. Cassell, Petter, Galpin.

Montgomery, Frances Trego see Wheeler, F. G., pseud.

Montgomery, Frances Trego
--Billy Whiskers Adventures. rev. ed. Hawthorne, Paul, illus. LC 53-56571. 162p. illus. 23cm. (The Billy Whiskers Ser.: Vol. 22). 1920. Saalfield Pub. CO.
--Billy Whiskers Adventures. Hawthorne, Paul, illus. LC 53-56572. 186p. illus. 23cm. (The Billy Whiskers Ser.: Vol. 24). 1922. Saalfield.
--Billy Whiskers at Home. Frank, C. D. & Brundage, Frances, illus. LC 24-32084. 169 p. col. front., illus., col. plates. 23 cm. c.1924. The Saalfield Publishing Company.
--Billy Whiskers at the Fair. DeBebian, Arthur, illus. LC 78-101854. (Illus.). 163 p. 24cm. c.1909. Saalfield Pub. Co.
--Billy Whiskers Friends. Hofsten, Hugo Von, illus. LC 6-25694. 139 p. col. front., illus., 5 col. pl. 24 x 21 cm. 1906. Brewer, Barse & Company.
--Billy Whiskers Frolics. Hawthorne, Paul, illus. LC 53-56573. 157p. illus. 23cm. (The Billy Whiskers Ser.: Vol. 25). 1923. Saalfield.
--Billy Whiskers' Grandchildren. Hofsten, Hugo Von, illus. LC 43-20443. 152 p. col. front., illus., col. plates. 22 1/2 x 18 cm. (The Billy Whiskers Ser. 9). 1909. The Saalfield Publishing Company.
--Billy Whiskers' Grandchildren of the Ojibways. Von Hofsten, Hugo, illus. 24 x 20cm. 152p. c.1909. Brewer, Barse & Co.
--Billy Whiskers in an Aeroplane. White, Constance, illus. LC 12-111642. 2 p. l., 9-219 p. col. front., illus., col. plates. 24 x 21 cm. c.1912. The Saalfield Publishing Company.
--Billy Whiskers in Camp. Fitzgerald, William, illus. LC 18-15720. 153 p. col. front., illus., col. plates. 23 x 19 cm. c.1918. The Saalfield Publishing Company.

AUTHOR INDEX MOORE, BERTHA

--Rough Riders Ho!. Wittmack, Edgar Franklin, illus. LC 46-5052. 228 p. illus. 21 cm. 1946. David McKay Company.
--Rufus. Nenninger, Jerome D., illus. LC 78-150819. (Illus.). 137 p. 22cm. 1973. (ISBN 0-87004-227-0). Caxton Printers.
--Sea Raiders Ho!. Wittmack, Edgar Franklin, illus. LC 45-10298. 224 p. col. front., illus. 21 cm. 1945. David McKay Company.
--Seecatch: A Story of a Fur Seal. (Ginn Book-Length Stories). 1955. Ginn & Co.
--The Silver Hills. Frankenberg, Robert Clinton (1911-), illus. LC 58-5776. 213p. illus. 21cm. 1958. World Pub. Co.
--Snowman. (Illus.). (gr. 5-8). 1962. (ISBN 0-8015-6900-1). Hawthorn.
--Stan Ball of the Rangers. Abbott, Jacob Bates ([illegible]), illus. (Dollar Mystery and Adventure Ser.). (gr. 5-11). N.D. David McKay Co.
--The Stubborn One. Miller, Donald George (1909-), illus. LC 65-14404. vii, 118p. 21cm. c.1965. Duell Dist. Meredith.
--Tenderfoot at Bar X. 202p. N.D. Reilly & Lee Co.
--Thornbush Jungle. Bjorklund, Lorence F. (1913-1978), illus. LC 66-13900. 159 p. illus. 21 cm. 1966. World Pub. Co.
--Thumbs Up!. Wittmack, Edgar Franklin, illus. LC 42-25519. 256 p. col. front., illus. 21 cm. 1942. David McKay Company.
--Timberline Tales. Abbott, John Bates, illus. LC 39-258754. 264 p. col. front., illus., col. plates. 22 cm. c.1939. David McKay Company.
--Tim's Mountain. DeMiskey, Julian (1908-1976), illus. LC 59-6657. (Illus.). 218 p. 21cm. 1959. World Pub. Co.
--Tom Pittman, U. S. A. F. Kueskin, Sam, illus. 1957. Duell, Sloan, Pearce.
--The Trail of the Buffalo. Wiese, Kurt (1887-1974), illus. LC 39-30070. 5 p. l., 217, 1 p. incl. col. front., illus. 22 cm. 1939. Houghton Mifflin Company.
--Trappers' Trail. Cressingham, Harold, illus. LC 43-16890. 5 p. l., 226 p. illus. 21 cm. 1943. H. Holt and Company.
--Troopers Three. Gay, Zhenya (1906-1978), illus. 1932. Caxton Publishers.
--Troopers Three. Gay, Zhenya (1906-1978), illus. LC 32-22710. x p., 1 l., 233 p. incl. illus., plates. col. front. 21 cm. 1932. Doubleday, Doran & Company, Inc.
--Wapiti the Elk. 1st ed. Christensen, Gardell Dano (1907-), illus. LC 52-8339. (Illus.). 186 p. 21cm. 1952. Little, Brown.
--War Wings. Knight, Clayton (1891-1969), illus. LC 43-7554. 224 p. col. front., illus. 21 cm. 1943. David McKay Company.
--Warhawk Patrol. Knight, Clayton (1891-1969), illus. (Dollar Mystery and Adventure Ser.). (gr. 5-11). 1944. David McKay Co.
--White Mountaineer. 1st ed. Christensen, Gardell Dano (1907-), illus. LC 53-7326. 177p. illus. 21cm. 1953. Little, Brown.
--Whitetail: The Story of a Prairie Dog. Nonnast, Marie (1924-), illus. LC 58-11155. (Illus.). 64 p. 22cm. 1958. World Pub. Co.
--A Yankee Flier in Italy. Avery, Al, pseud. Laune, Paul Sidney (1899-), illus. 5 p. l., 212 p. incl. front. 19 1/2 cm. 1944. Grosset & Dunlap.
--A Yankee Flier in North Africa. Avery, Al, pseud. Laune, Paul Sidney (1899-), illus. LC 43-103285. v p., 1 l., 214 p. incl. front. 19 1/2 cm. 1943. Grosset & Dunlap.
--A Yankee Flier in the Far East. Avery, Al, pseud. Laune, Paul Sidney (1899-), illus. LC 42-13421. v, 216 p. incl. front. 20 cm. 1942. Grosset & Dunlap.
--A Yankee Flier in the South Pacific. Laune, Paul Sidney (1899-), illus. LC 43-2345. vii p., 1 l., 208 p. incl. front. 19 1/2 cm. 1943. Grosset & Dunlap.
--A Yankee Flier on a Rescue Mission. Avery, Al, pseud. Knight, Clayton (1891-1969), illus. LC 46-12927. vii p., 1 l., 210p. incl. front. 19cm. 1945. Grosset & Dunlap.
--A Yankee Flier over Berlin. Avery, Al, pseud. Laune, Paul Sidney (1899-), illus. LC 44-5245. 212p. 1944. Grosset & Dunlap.
--A Yankee Flier Under Secret Orders. Avery, Al, pseud. Knight, Clayton (1891-1969), illus. LC 46-5258. 5 p. l., 204 p. incl. front. 19 1/2 cm. 1946. Grosset & Dunlap.
--Yellow Eyes. (gr. 6-9). N.D. (ISBN 0-590-02429-9, Schol Trade Pap). Schol Bk Serv.
--Yellow Eyes. Cram, L. D. (1898-), illus. 243p. 1932. Caxton Printers.
--Yellow Eyes. Cram, L. D. (1898-), illus. 243p. 1936. Reilly & Lee Co.
Montgomery, Rutherford George (1894-) & Heiman, Grover George, Jr. (1920-)
--Jet Navigator: Strategic Air Command. LC 59-6001. 216 p. 21cm. 1959. Dodd, Mead.
Montgomery, Virginia Louise (1896-)
--The Pest and Decoy, Sandy Cove Dog Stories. LC 37-17508. 23cm. 25p. 1937. Whig Pub. Co.
Montgomery, Vivian
--Mr. Jellybean. Waide, Jan (1952-), illus. LC 79-24867. p. cm. c.1979. (ISBN 0-88319-045-1). Shoal Creek Publishers.
Montgomery, Walter, ed.
--The Boys of the Sierras: Or, The Young Gold Hunters. (Illus.). N.D. Estes & Lauriat's.
--Tales of Ancient Troy, and the Adventure of Ulysses. (Illus.). N.D. Estes & Lauriat's.
Montgomery, Walter, ed. see Homer.
Montolieu, ed. see Wyss, Johann David Von.
Montreal, Mary
--Wings or Weights. N.D. AMerican Sunday-School Union.
Montresor, Beni (1926-), adapted by see Rossini, Gioacchino Antonio.
Montresor, Beni (1926-)
--A for Angel: Beni Montresor's A B C Picture-Stories. LC 68-15320. 39 p. (chiefly col. illus. 1969. Knopf.
--Bedtime!. LC 78-108581. (Illus.). 32 p. c.1978. (ISBN 0-06-024354-6). Harper & Row.
--Cinderella. Montresor, Beni (1926-), illus. (Illus.). (gr. k-3). 1965. (ISBN 0-394-91055-9). Knopf.
--House of Flowers, House of Stars. LC 62-9473. (Illus.). unpaged. 29cm. 1962. Knopf.
--I Saw a Ship a-Sailing: Or, The Wonderful Games That Only Little Flower-Plant Children Can Play. LC 67-19486. (Illus.). 1 v. (unpaged). 29cm. 1967. (ISBN 0-394-91870-3). Knopf.
--The Witches of Venice. Montresor, Beni (1926-), illus. LC 63-9114. 1 v. (unpaged) illus. 29 cm. 1963. Knopf.
Montreuil, Anna B, Mrs.
--Dumb-Bell. LC 29-23887. 264 p. 21 cm. c.1929. The Christopher Publishing House.
Montrose, Anne
--The Winter Flower, and Other Fairy Stories. LC 64-21476. 143 p. illus. 25 cm. 1964. Viking Press.
Moodey, Marion McCook
--Here Comes the Peddler!. Markham, Kyra, illus. LC 47-31149. 32 p. illus. 24 cm. 1947. Holiday House.
Moody, Ann
--Judy & Her Ballerina Doll. (gr. k-2). N.D. Carlton.
Moody, Anne (1940-)
--Mr. Death: Four Stories. LC 75-9391. 96p. (gr. 5 up). 1975. (ISBN 0-06-024312-0, HarpJ). Har-Row.
Moody, J. B., jt. auth. see Idriess, Ion L.
Moody, Ralph Owen (1898-)
--Little Britches. 1950. Norton Company.
--Riders of the Pony Express. 1958. Houghton Mifflin Company.
Moody, Randolh
--The Home Ranch. 1956. Norton Company.
Moody, S.
--The Fairy Tree: Or, Stories from Far and Near. N.D. Thomas Nelson & Sons.
Moody, Winfield Scott (1856-)
--The Pickwick Ladle. (Illus.). N.D. Charles Scribner's Sons.
Mook, Charles Craig, jt. auth. see Walker, Edith B.
Mook, Jane Day
--The Secret of the Drumstick Tree. Nagy, Al, illus. (gr. 1-3). 1972. (ISBN 0-377-12701-9). Friend Pr.
Moon, Carl, jt. auth. see Moon, Grace Purdie, Mrs.
Moon, Carl (1879-1948)
--The Flaming Arrow. N.D. Frederick A. Stokes Co.
--The Flaming Arrow. N.D. J. B. Lippincott.
--Painted Moccasin. LC 31-217588. 5 p. l., 318 p. col. front. 21 cm. 1931. Frederick A. Stokes Company.
--Tah-Kee: The Boy from Nowhere. Moon, Carl (1879-1948), illus. LC 32-24137. 6 p. l., 282, 1 p. col. front., plates. 19 cm. 1932. Frederick A. Stokes Company.
Moon, Grace Purdie, Mrs. (1877-1947)
--The Arrow of Tee-May. Moon, Carl (1879-1948), illus. (The Grace Moon Bks.). N.D. A. L. Burt Co.
--The Arrow of Tee-May. Moon, Carl (1879-1948), illus. LC 31-318481. 6 p. l., 284 p. incl. illus., plates. col. front. 21 cm. 1931. Doubleday, Doran & Company, Inc.
--The Book of Nah-Wee. Moon, Carl (1879-1948), illus. LC 32-17515. 2 p. l., 59 p. illus. (part col.) 26 cm. c.1932. Doubleday, Doran & Company.
--Chi-Wee and Loki of the Desert. Moon, Carl (1879-1948), illus. LC 26-27596. x p., 1 l., 208 p. col. front., illus., plates. 21 cm. 1926. Doubleday, Page & Co.
--Chi-Wee: The Adventures of a Little Indian Girl. Moon, Carl (1879-1948), illus. LC 25-26908. xi p., 1 l., 289 p. col. front., illus., plates. 21 cm. 1925. Doubleday, Page & Co.
--Daughter of Thunder. Moon, Carl (1879-1948), illus. LC 42-21562. 184 p. col. front. 21 cm. 1942. The Macmillan Company.
--Far-Away Desert. Moon, Carl (1879-1948), illus. LC 32-246707. 6 p. l., 261 p. incl. illus., plates. col. front. 20 cm. 1932. Doubleday, Doran & Company, Inc.
--Indian Legends in Rhyme. Moon, Carl (1879-1948), illus. N.D. Frederick A Stokes Co.
--Lost Indian Magic. Moon, Carl (1879-1948), illus. N.D. J. B. Lippincott.
--Lost Indian Magic: A Mystery Story of the Red Man As He Lived Before the White Men Came. Moon, Carl (1879-1948), illus. LC 18-17664. xi p., 2 l., 301 p. col. front., col. plates. 21 cm. c.1918. Frederick A. Stokes Company.
--The Magic Trail. Moon, Carl (1879-1948), illus. (The Grace Moon Bks.). N.D. A. L. Burt Co.
--The Magic Trail. Moon, Carl (1879-1948), illus. LC 29-18411. 6 p. l., 234 p. incl. illus., plates. col. front. 21 cm. 1929. Doubleday, Doran and Company.
--The Magic Trail. Moon, Carl (1879-1948), illus. LC 38-23550. 6 p. l., 234 p. incl. illus., plates. col. front., double map. 21 cm. (Young moderns bookshelf). 1938. The Sun Dial Press, Inc.
--The Missing Katchina. Moon, Carl (1879-1948), illus. (The Grace Moon Bks.). N.D. A. L. Burt Co.
--The Missing Katchina. Moon, Carl (1879-1948), illus. LC 30-24140. xii p., 1 l., 286 p. incl. plates. col. front 21 cm. 1930. Doubleday, Doran & Company, Inc.
--The Missing Katchina. Moon, Carl (1879-1948), illus. LC 39-24303. xii p., 1 l., 286 p. incl. illus., plates, col. front. 21 cm. (Young Moderns Bookshelf). 1939. The Sun Dial Press, Inc.
--Nadita. Moon, Carl (1879-1948), illus. LC 46-7668. 7 p. l., 274 p. incl. front., illus., plates. 20 1/2 cm. (Young Moderns). 1946. Doubleday & Co., Inc.
--Nadita: Little Nothing. Moon, Carl (1879-1948), illus. LC 27-19154. 7 p. l., 274 p. incl. plates. col. front. 21 cm. 1927. Doubleday, Page & Co.
--Nadita: Little Nothing. Moon, Carl (1879-1948), illus. LC 36-106092. 6 p. l., 274 p. incl. illus., plates. front. 21 cm. (Young Moderns Books). 1936. Doubleday, Doran & Company, Inc.
--Nadita: Little Nothing. Moon, Carl (1879-1948), illus. LC 37-229789. 6 p. l., 274 p. incl. illus., plates. col. front. 21 cm. (Young Moderns Bookshelf). 1937. The Sun Dial Press, Inc.
--One Little Indian. rev. ed. Moon, Carl (1879-1948), illus. (Illus.). (ps-2). 1967. (ISBN 0-8075-6092-8). A Whitman.
--One Little Indian. Moon, Carl (1879-1948), illus. LC 50-6281. (Illus.). 25cm. 32p. 1950. Whitman.
--The Runaway Papoose. Moon, Carl (1879-1948), illus. LC 28-217329. 6 p. l., 264 p. incl. illus., plates. col. front. 21 cm. 1928. Doubleday, Doran & Company, Inc. **Award: (JNM).**
--Shanty Ann. Moon, Carl (1879-1948), illus. LC 35-157421. 6 p. l., 200 p. col. front., plates. 21cm. 1935. Frederick A. Stokes Company.
--Shanty Ann. Moon, Carl (1879-1948), illus. N.D. J. B. Lippincott.
--Singing Sands. Moon, Carl (1879-1948), illus. LC 36-274382. 6 p. l., 3-245 p. col. front., illus., plates. 21 cm. 1936. Doubleday, Doran & Company, Inc.
--Singing Sands. Moon, Carl (1879-1948), illus. LC 46-7651. 5 p. l., 3-245 p. 20 1/2 cm. (Young Moderns). 1946. Doubleday & Co., Inc.
--Solita. Moon, Carl (1879-1948), illus. LC 38-341807. 6 p. l., 241 p. incl. plates. col. front. 21 cm. 1938. Doubleday, Doran & Company, Inc.
--Tita of Mexico. Moon, Carl (1879-1948), illus. LC 31-31073. 5 p. l., 213 p. incl. plates. col. front. 21 cm. 1934. Frederick A. Stokes Company.
--Tito of Mexico. Moon, Carl (1879-1948), illus. N.D. J. B. Lippincott.
--White Indian. Moon, Carl (1879-1948), illus. LC 37-208868. 5 p. l., 221 p. incl. illus., plates. col. front. 21 cm. 1937. Doubleday, Doran & Company, Inc.
Moon, Grace Purdie, Mrs. (1877-1947) & Moon, Carl (1879-1948)
--Wongo and the Wise Old Crow. Moon, Carl (1879-1948), illus. LC 23-5851. 4 p. l., 13-188 p. col. front., illus., plates. 21 cm. c.1923. The Reilly & Lee Co.
Moon, Henrietta Jones
--Angelina Amelia, a Doll. Moon, Henrietta Jones, illus. LC 50-13237. 89 p. illus. (part col.) 18 cm. 1950. Crowell.
Moon, Sheila Elizabeth (1910-)
--Hunt Down the Prize. Schindelman, Laurel, illus. LC 75-154757. (Illus.). 244 p. 24cm. 1971. Atheneum.
--Knee-Deep in Thunder. 1st ed. Parnall, Peter (1936-), illus. LC 67-18996. (Illus.). 307 p. 25cm. 1967. (ISBN 0-689-20287-3). Atheneum. **Awards: (NYT).**
Mooney, Bel
--Liza's Yellow Boat. (Illus.). 1981. (ISBN 0-7043-2268-4, Pub. by Quartet England). Charles River Bks.
Mooney, Elizabeth Comstock (1918-)
--The Mystery of the Narrow Land. Fitch, Winnie, illus. LC 69-15977. (Illus.). 128 p. 23cm. (Merit mystery). 1969. Follett Pub. Co.
--The Sandy Shoes Mystery. Nebel, Gustave E., illus. LC 75-101902. (Illus.). 128 p. 21cm. 1970. Lippincott.
Mooney, James (1861-1921)
--Cherokee Animal Tales. Scheer, George Fabian (1917-), ed. Frankenberg, Robert Clinton (1911-), illus. (Illus.). 79 p. 23cm. 1968. Holiday House.
Mooney, Mark
--Zoo School. Smith, Jane C., illus. LC 51-21607. 64 p. illus. 23 cm. c.1950. The Camera.
Mooney, Thomas J., ed. see Carlson, Gordon.
Mooney, Thomas J., ed. see Doyle, Tim.
Mooney, Thomas J., ed. see Otfinoski, Steven.
Mooney, Thomas J., ed. see Schleifer, Jay.
Mooney, Thomas J., ed. see Verdick, Mary Peyton.
Mooney, Thomas J. (1927-), ed.
--The Big Freeze. Rich, Harry & Smolinski, Dick, illus. (Illus., Orig.). (Pal Paperbacks Ser., Kit A-Plus). (gr. 7-12). 1976. (ISBN 0-8374-3489-0). Xerox Ed Pubns.
--Old Yellow Eyes. Sovek, Charles, illus. (Illus., Orig.). (Pal Paperbacks Ser., Kit A Plus). (gr. 7-12). 1976. (ISBN 0-8374-3491-2). Xerox Ed Pubns.
--One Cool Sister. Noyes, David, illus. (Illus., Orig.). (Pal Paperbacks Ser., Kit A-Plus). (gr. 7-12). 1976. (ISBN 0-8374-3496-3). Xerox Ed Pubns.
--Race for Glory. Wenzel, David & Carreiro, Ron, illus. (Illus., Orig.). (Pal Paperbacks Kit B Ser.). (gr. 7-12). 1973. (ISBN 0-8374-3519-6). Xerox Ed Pubns.
--Varoom. Sovek, Charles, illus. (Illus., Orig.). (Pal Paperbacks Kit A Ser.). (gr. 7-12). 1973. (ISBN 0-8374-3469-6). Xerox Ed Pubns.
--Varoom!. Eight Short Stories of Wheels and Speed. Sovek, Charles, illus. LC 72-83370. (Illus.). 96 p. 18cm. (Pal paperback, R3). 1972. Xerox Education Publications.
Mooney, Tom, ed. see Oldham, Neild.
Moorat, Joseph, ed.
--Humpty Dumpty and Other Songs. Woodroffe, Paul Vincent (1875-1945), illus. N.D. Dodge Publishing Co.
--Thirty Old-Time Nursery Songs. Woodroffe, Paul Vincent (1875-1945), illus. LC 80-16025. (Illus.). 33p. (ps). 1980. (ISBN 0-87099-242-2). Metro Mus Art.
--Thirty Old-Time Nursery Songs. Woodroffe, Paul Vincent (1875-1945), illus. Reissue of 1980 ed. (ps-3). N.D. Norton.
Moore, Alice G.
--A Triangle of Stories For Younger Girls: The Palace Beautiful, The Patch of Blue, and The Orchard. N.D. Womans Press.
Moore, Anne Carroll, jt. auth. see Greenaway, Kate.
Moore, Annie Carroll (1871-1961), ed. see Diaz, Abby Morton, Mrs.
Moore, Annie Carroll (1871-1961), ed. see Irving, Washington.
Moore, Annie Carroll (1871-1961)
--My Roads. 1939. Doubleday Doran & Co.
--Nicholas: A Manhattan Christmas Story. Everen, Jay Van, illus. LC 24-24347. ix, 331, 1 p. col. front., illus. 19 cm. 1924. G. P. Putnam's Sons. **Award: (JNM).**
--Nicholas and the Golden Goose. Everen, Jay Van, illus. LC 32-23280. x, 259, 3 p. col. front., illus., pl. 19 cm. 1932. G. P. Putnam's Sons.
Moore, Barbara (1934-)
--Hard on the Road. LC 73-13091. 312p. 1974. Doubleday.
Moore, Beatrix T.
--Kerry. Johnson, Eugene Harper, illus. LC 59-792957. 80p. illus. 22cm. 1959. Morrow.
--Swim for It, Bridget!. Johnson, Eugene Harper, illus. LC 58-5024. 80p. illus. 22cm. (Morrow junior books). 1958. Morrow.
Moore, Bertha B. (1890-)
--The Baer's Christmas. N.D. E. P. Dutton & Co.
--The Three Baers. LC 38-21321. 88 p. 20 cm. 1938. Wm. B. Eerdmans Publishing Co.
--Triplets Become Good Neighbors. N.D. E. P. Dutton & Co.
--Triplets Over J.O.Y. N.D. E. P. Dutton & Co.
--Triplets Receive a Reward. N.D. Wm. B. Eerdmans Publishing Co.
--Triplets Sign Up. (Triplets Ser). (gr. 2-4). N.D. Eerdmans.

--Thrilling Stories for Boys. Stratemeyer Syndicate. (A Four-in-one reprint. Includes: "Wrecked on Cannibal Island"; "Lost in the Caves of Gold"; "Cast Away in the Land of Snow"; and, "Prisoners on the Pirate Ship" from the series, "Jerry Ford Wonder Stories"). 1937. Cupples & Leon Co.
--Wrecked on Cannibal Island: Or, Jerry Ford's Adventures Among Savages. Stratemeyer Syndicate. Tandy, Russell H., illus. LC 31-143404. 2 p. l., 210 p. front. 20 cm. (Jerry Ford Wonder Stories: No. 1). 1931. Cupples & Leon Co.

Moore, Frances C.
--Prince Uno: Uncle Frank's Visit to Fairy-Land. Stevens, W. D., illus. LC 44-33928. xi, 1 p., 1 l., 241, 3 p. incl. front., illus. 19 cm. 1897. Doubleday & McClure Co.

Moore, Frances Sarah, pseud., see Mack, Elsie Frances Wilson.

Moore, H. Keatley, ed.
--Nursery Song Book. Sandheim, May, illus. N.D. Dutton.

Moore, Hannah Woodbridge Hudson, Mrs. (1857-1927)
--Deeds of Daring Done by Girls. Gunn, Archie, illus. LC 6-40212. 6 p. l., 300 p. col. front., 5 col. pl. 20 cm. 1906. Frederick A. Stokes Company.

Moore, Harry
--The Sad Dad. Tootill, Ginger, illus. LC 69-18157. (Illus.). 26 p. (incl. cover. 21cm. 1969. (ISBN 0-8170-0432-7). Judson Press.

Moore, Henry Charles
--Afloat on the Dogger Bank: A Story of Adventure in the North Sea and in China. Prater, J., illus. LC 6-23699. 6 p.. l.., 11-321 p.. front., 7 pl. 20 cm. c.1906. D. Estes & Company.

Moore, Ida Cecil
--Lucky Orphan. Robertson, Primrose McPherson, illus. LC 47-2535. 3 p. l., 121, 1 p. illus. 21 x 16 cm. 1947. C. Scribner's Sons.

Moore, Inga
--Aktil's Bicycle Ride. Moore, Inga, illus. (Illus.). 32p. (ps). 1983. (ISBN 0-19-554319-X, Pub by Oxford U Pr Childrens). Merrimack Pub Cir.
--Aktil's Big Swim. Moore, Inga, illus. (Illus.). 32p. (ps). 1983. (ISBN 0-19-554250-9, Pub by Oxford U Pr Childrens). Merrimack Pub Cir.
--Aktil's Big Swim. Moore, Inga, illus. (Illus.). 32p. (gr. k-3). 1981. (ISBN 0-19-554250-9). Oxford U Pr.
--Aktil's Rescue. Moore, Inga, illus. (Illus.). 32p. 1st U.S. edition. (ps-2). 1984. (ISBN 0-318-00785-1, Pub. by Oxford U Pr Childrens). Merrimack Pub Cir.
--The Vegetable Thieves. Moore, Inga, illus. LC 83-14487. (Illus.). 32p. 1st U.S. edition. (gr. k-3). 1984. (ISBN 0-670-74380-1, Viking Kestrel). Viking.

Moore, Isabel Kellogg, Mrs. (1872-)
--The Bardolph Turvey Stories. The Land of Dimm. LC 17-31036. 1 p. l., 5-45 p. 24 cm. 1917. R. C. Penfield.

Moore, J. F., Mrs. (1875-)
--The Clifford Household, 1 of 5. (The Clifford Library). N.D. Dodd, Mead.
--The Clifford Household, 1 of 10 vols. (Popular Ser.). N.D. Dodd, Mead & Company.
--Linside Farm. N.D. Bradley & Woodruff.
--Linside Farm. N.D. Henry Hoyt.
--Linside Farm. (Illus.). 346p. N.D. Ira Bradley & Co's.
--Miriam Brandon: Or, Trials and Triumphs. (Illus.). 318p. N.D. A. I. Bradley & Co.'s Pubs.
--Miriam Brandon: Or, Trials and Triumphs. 1875. Henry Hoyt.
--Rescued. N.D. Henry Hoyt.

Moore, Jane Shearer
--The Story of Toby. Grider, Dorothy (1915-), illus. LC 50-14875. 17cm. 32p. (A Rand McNally Book-Elf Junior). c.1950. Rand McNally.
--The Story of Toby. Grider, Dorothy (1915-), illus. LC 57-10612. unpaged. illus. 26cm. (Rand McNally storytime book). 1957, c.1950. Rand McNally.

Moore, Jessie Eleanor (1886-)
--A Bell for Baby Brother. Wallower, Lucille (1910-), illus. LC 44-6543. 126, 1 p. illus. 21 cm. 1944. Friendship Press.
--The Little Child and His Crayon. N.D. Abingdon Press.
--Welcome House. Hill, Mabel Betsy (1877-), illus. LC 39-106357. 95, 1 p. incl. front., illus. 24 cm. c.1939. Friendship Press.

Moore, Jessie Eleanor (1886-), ed.
--Eyes for Eric, and Other Stories: For Children from Four to Eight Years of Age. Johnston, Clifford, illus. LC 63-4645. 127 p. illus. 21 cm. 1963. Published for the Cooperative Publication Association by Abingdon Press.
--Songs in Our Bible. (Illus.). (gr. 3-7). 1966. (ISBN 0-8170-0346-0). Judson.
--Valuable Kindling. McKeehan, Murray, illus. LC 63-4639. 190p. illus. 21cm. c.1963. Pub. for the Cooperative Pubn. Assn. by Abingdon.

Moore, John Travers, et al. (1908-)
--Christmas Classics for Children. 1981. (ISBN 0-570-04058-2). Concordia.

Moore, John Travers, jt. auth. see Moore, Margaret Rumberger.

Moore, John Travers (1908-)
--All Along the Way. Inderieden, Nancy, illus. LC 72-11084. (Illus.). 27cm. 32p. (gr. k-4). 1973. (ISBN 0-87614-034-7). Carolrhoda Bks
--Cinnamon Seed. Hyman, Trina Schart (1939-), illus. LC 67-23310. (Illus.). 47 p. 24cm. 1967. Houghton Mifflin.
--God's Wonderful World. Mickelson, Melva, illus. LC 64-21503. 32p. 28cm. (gr. k-3). 1964. (ISBN 0-8066-0418-2). Augsburg.
--Story of Silent Night. LC 65-19252. (gr. 2-3). 1965. (ISBN 0-570-03430-2). Concordia.
--There's Motion Everywhere. Taback, Simms, illus. LC 70-98518. (Illus.). 40 p. 24cm. 1970. Houghton Mifflin Co.
--Town and Countryside Poems. Allen, Lois, illus. LC 68-22194. (Illus.). 39 p. 19cm. 1968. A. Whitman.

Moore, John & Wright, Martin
--Granny Stickleback. (Illus.). 32p. 1st U.S. edition. (ps-3). 1982. (Pub. by Hamish Hamilton England). David & Charles.

Moore, Joseph A
--Hot Shot at Third. 1st. LC 58-6763. 184p. 21cm. 1958. Duell, Sloan and Pearce.
--Two Strikes on Lefty. Cue, Harold, illus. LC 54-10626. 224p. illus. 22cm. 1954. W. A. Wilde Co.

Moore, Katharine Yeo (1898-)
--The Little Stolen Sweep. (Illus.). 128p. (gr. 5-8). 1982. (ISBN 0-8052-0107-X, Pub. by Allison & Busby England). Schocken.
--Moog. Moore, Jane, illus. (Illus.). 96p. 1st U.S. edition. 1983. (ISBN 0-8052-8140-1, Pub. by Allison & Busby England). Schocken.

Moore, Leo T.
--Leo Moore's Little Scroll. N.D. Vantage Press.

Moore, Lilian
--Bear Trouble. Werth, Kurt (1896-), illus. LC 60-10609. (gr. k-4). 1960. (ISBN 0-07-042895-6). (ISBN 0-07-042896-4). McGraw.
--Everything Happens to Stuey. Stevens, Mary, illus. LC 60-10028. 82p. illus. 24cm. 1960. (ISBN 0-394-90117-7). Random House.
--Go with the Poem. (gr. 4 up). 1979. (ISBN 0-07-042880-8, GB). McGraw.
--The Golden Picture Book of Stories. Malvern, Corinne (1905-1956), illus. 1955. Golden Press.
--The Golden Picture Book of Stories. Malvern, Corinne (1905-1956), illus. LC 55-14840. 29cm. 48p. (Fun to Learn Book: 5). 1955. Simon and Schuster.
--I Feel the Same Way. Quackenbush, Robert Mead (1929-), illus. LC 67-18989. (Illus.). 1 v. (unpaged). 19cm. 1967. Atheneum.
--I Feel the Same Way. Quackenbush, Robert Mead (1929-), illus. LC 76-371679. (Illus.). 32 p. 18cm. (Aladdin book). c.1967. (ISBN 0-689-70424-0). Atheneum.
--I Thought I Heard the City. Dunton, Mary Jane, illus. LC 69-18964. (Illus.). 39 p. 22cm. 1969. Atheneum.
--The Important Pockets Of Paul. N.D. E. M. Hale & Co.
--The Important Pockets of Paul. Hayes, William Dimitt (1913-), illus. LC 54-9094. 73p. illus. 24cm. 1954. D. McKay Co.
--Junk Day on Juniper Street & Other Easy to Read Stories. Lobel, Arnold Stark (1933-), illus. LC 69-12611. (Illus.). 72p. 24cm. (gr. k-5). 1968. (ISBN 0-8193-0241-4). (ISBN 0-8193-0242-2). Parents.
--Just Right. Watson, Aldren Auld (1917-), illus. LC 68-11658. (Illus.). 1 v. (unpaged. 1968. Parents' Magazine Press.
--Little Raccoon and No Trouble at All. Fiammenghi, Gioia (1929-), illus. LC 70-39002. (Illus.). 48 p. 22cm. 1972. (ISBN 0-07-042909-X). McGraw-Hill.
--Little Raccoon and Poems from the Woods. Fiammenghi, Gioia (1929-), illus. LC 75-14303. (Illus.). 40 p. 22cm. 1975. (ISBN 0-07-042914-6). McGraw-Hill.
--Little Raccoon and the Outside World. Fiammenghi, Gioia (1929-), illus. LC 64-66412. (Illus.). 44 p. 22cm. 1965. Whittlesey House.
--Little Raccoon & the Thing in the Pool. Fiammenghi, Gioia (1929-), illus. (Illus.). (gr. k-4). 1963. (ISBN 0-07-042892-1, GB). McGraw.
--The Magic Spectacles. Lobel, Arnold Stark (1933-), illus. LC 66-13333. 70 p.illus. (part col.) 24 cm. 1966, c.1965. Parents' Magazine Press.
--Mr Twitmeyer & The Poodle. (Illus.). 1963. Random House Inc.
--My Big Golden Counting Book. Williams, Garth Montgomery (1912-), illus. LC 57-4317. unpaged. illus. 33cm. (Big Golden Book 458). c.1957. Simon and Schuster.
--My First Counting Book. Williams, Garth Montgomery (1912-), illus. LC 56-13805. unpaged. illus. 21cm. (Golden Book, 445). 1956. Simon and Schuster.
--Once Upon a Holiday. Fiammenghi, Gioia (1929-), illus. LC 59-1070. 95p. illus. 22cm. 1959. Abingdon Press.
--Once Upon a Season. Fiammenghi, Gioia (1929-), illus. LC 62-7865. 95p. illus. 22cm. 1962. Abingdon Press.
--Papa Albert. Fiammenghi, Gioia (1929-), illus. LC 64-11889. 1 v. (unpaged) col. illus.22 x 26 cm. 1964. Atheneum.
--A Pickle for a Nickel. Perl, Susan (1922-1983), illus. LC 61-12364. (Illus.). 22cm. 30p. 1961. Golden Press.
--The Riddle Walk. Pucci, Albert John (1920-), illus. LC 76-157819. (Illus.). 40 p. 24cm. 1971. (ISBN 0-8116-6715-4). Garrard Pub. Co.
--Sam's Place: Poems from the Country. Stubis, Talivaldis (1926-), illus. LC 73-76325. (Illus.). 32 p. 27cm. 1973. (ISBN 0-689-30116-2). Atheneum.
--See My Lovely Poison Ivy and Other Verses about Witches, Ghosts, and Things. Dawson, Diane, illus. LC 75-8581. (Illus.). 40 p. 21cm. 1975. (ISBN 0-689-30468-4). Atheneum.
--Shadows. Robison, Deborah, illus. LC 80-13496. 1980. (ISBN 0-689-30782-9). Atheneum.
--The Snake That Went to School. Stevens, Mary, illus. LC 57-10204. (Illus.). 114 p. 22cm. 1957. Random House.
--Something New Begins: New and Selected Poems. Dunton, Mary Jane, illus. LC 82-1723. p. cm. 1982. (ISBN 0-689-30818-3). Atheneum. **Award: (ALA).**
--Think of Shadows. Robison, Deborah, illus. LC 80-13496. (Illus.). 40p. (gr. 2 up). 1980. (ISBN 0-689-30782-9). Atheneum. **Award: (ALA).**
--Tony the Pony. Dennis, Wesley (1903-1966), illus. LC 58-59667. (Illus.). 21cm. 48p. (gr. k-4). 1959. (ISBN 0-07-042898-0). (ISBN 0-07-042899-9). (ISBN 0-07-042892-1). McGraw.
--Too Many Bozos. Perl, Susan (1922-1983), illus. LC 60-4083. 22cm. 30p. (Golden Beginning Reader: 4009). 1960. Golden Press.
--Too Many Bozos. Perl, Susan (1922-1983), illus. (Illus.). 32p. (Golden Beginning Readers Ser.). (gr. k-2). 1969. (ISBN 0-307-61157-4, Golden Pr). Western Pub.
--Wobbly Wheels. Krush, Beth (1918-), illus. LC 56-14076. (Illus.). 21cm. 47p. (gr. k-3). 1956. (ISBN 0-687-45949-4). Abingdon.

Moore, Lilian, et al., eds.
--Duck on the Truck. (Illus.). (Easy Readers). (gr. k-4). N.D. Wonder.

Moore, Lilian, ed. see Andersen, Hans Christian.

Moore, Lilian, ed. see Bonsall, Crosby Barbara Newell.

Moore, Lilian, ed. see McNulty, Faith.

Moore, Lilian, ed. see Newman, Paul.

Moore, Lilian, jt. ed. see Peter, Jonathan.

Moore, Lilian, ed. see Tarcov, Edith.

Moore, Lilian, compiled by see Thurman, Judith.

Moore, Lilian & Adelson, Leone (1908-)
--Old Rosie, the Horse Nobody Understood. Shortall, Leonard W., illus. LC 60-7198. 64p. illus. 24cm. 1960. Random House.
--Old Rosie: The Horse That Nobody Understood. Shortall, Leonard W., illus. LC 52-5855. (Illus.). 33 p. 29cm. 1952. Random House.

Moore, Lilian & Webster, Lawrence (1947-), eds.
--Catch Your Breath: A Book of Shivery Poems. Wilson, Gahan (1930-), illus. LC 72-11759. (Illus.). 64 p. 24cm. (Reading Shelf Ser.). 1973. (ISBN 0-8116-4113-9). Garrard Pub. Co.

Moore, Lillian
--Wobbly Wheels. N.D. E. M. Hale & Co.

Moore, Lillian, jt. auth. see Adelson, Leone.

Moore, Louis, jt. auth. see Harris, Delmer William.

Moore, Mamie Wiser, jt. auth. see Black, Elizabeth Griswold.

Moore, Margaret Eileen (1911-)
--Willie Without. Unwin, Nora Spicer (1907-), illus. LC 52-7126. 85p. illus. 21cm. 1952, c.1951. Coward-McCann.

Moore, Margaret Rumberger (1903-) & Moore, John Travers (1908-)
--Certainly, Carrie, Cut the Cake: Poems A to Z. Anderson, Laurie, illus. LC 70-137713. (Illus.). 32 p. 19cm. 1971. (ISBN 0-672-51395-1). Bobbs-Merrill.
--The Little Band and the Inaugural Parade. Faulkner, John Frink (1922-), illus. LC 68-9121. (Illus.). 40 p. 24cm. 1968. A. Whitman.
-On Cherry Tree Hill. 1st ed. Geer, Charles Hand (1922-), illus. LC 60-13601. 160p. illus. 22cm. 1960. Bobbs-Merrill.
--Pepito's Speech at the United Nations. Overlie, George, illus. LC 78-128821. (Illus.). 47 p. 23cm. 1971. (ISBN 0-87614-024-X). Carolrhoda Books.
--Sing-Along Sary. 1st ed. Moment, John, illus. LC 51-9996. (Illus.). 150 p. 21cm. 1951. Harcourt, Brace.
--The Three Tripps. Funk, Clotilde Embree, illus. LC 59-10203. 159p. illus. 21cm. 1959. (ISBN 0-672-50535-5). Bobbs-Merrill.

Moore, Marianne (1887-), retold by see Perrault, Charles.

Moore, Marianne Craig, tr. see Stifter, Adelbert.

Moore, Marie Drury (1926-)
--Two Princes, a Witch and Miss Katie O'Flynn. Morrison, Sean, illus. LC 68-19145. (Illus.). 40 p. 26cm. 1970. Prentice-Hall.

Moore, Marie Eslanda
--Little White Shoes. 1975. (ISBN 0-682-48217-X). Exposition Press.

Moore, Marvin (1937-)
--Witnesses Through Trial. LC 78-24294. 128 p. 17cm. (Orion). c.1979. (ISBN 0-8127-0216-6). Southern Pub. Association.

Moore, Mary F.
--The Lion Who Ate Tomatoes. N.D. British Book Centre.

Moore, Mary Furlong (1910-) & Fuller, Muriel (1901-), eds.
--The Baby-Sitter's Storybook. LC 60-15279. 180p. (bibls.) illus. 21cm. c.1960. Longmans, Green.

Moore, Marylu
--A Present for Dino. LC 61-75580. unpaged. illus. 25cm. c.1961. Convention Press.

Moore, Mavis Garey
--Pony for a Prize. Moyers, William (1916-), illus. LC 51-12892. 210 p. illus. 21 cm. 1951. Macmillan.
--Whale Mountain. Moore, John, illus. LC 53-7573. (Illus.). 234 p. 21cm. 1953. Macmillan.

Moore, Nancy (1908-)
--The Sandman Who Lost His Sand. Leight, Edward, illus. LC 59-7769. unpaged. illus. 27cm. 1959. (ISBN 0-8149-0371-1). Vanguard Press.

Moore, Nancy (1908-) & Leight, Edward
--Ermintrude. Leight, Edward, illus. LC 60-9730. (Illus.). (ps). 1960. (ISBN 0-8149-0370-3). Vanguard.
--Miss Harriet Hippopotamus and the Most Wonderful. Leight, Edward, illus. LC 63-11499. unpaged. illus. 29 cm. 1963. Vanguard Press.
--The Unhappy Hippopotamus. Leight, Edward, illus. LC 57-76849. unpaged. illus. 29cm. c.1957. (ISBN 0-8149-0368-1). Vanguard Press. **Award: (NYT).**

Moore, Patrick Alfred (1923-)
--Crater of Fear. (gr. 7 up). 1962. (ISBN 0-8178-3351-X). Harvey.
--Peril on Mars. Lambo, Donald W. (1903-1966), illus. LC 65-13305. (Illus.). 158 p. 22cm. 1st U.S. edition. 1965, c.1958. Putnam.

Moore, Peggy S.
--My Very First Book of Poetry & Other Things. Moore, Peggy S., illus. 16p. (Poetry & Essays Ser.: No. 1). (gr. 3-5). 1982. (ISBN 0-9613078-0-3). Detroit Black.

Moore, Ray see Robertson, Dale.

Moore, Raymond S. (1915-) & Moore, Dorothy Nelson (1915-)
--Guess Who Took the Battered-up Bike: A Story of Kindness. Downing, Julie, illus. LC 85-13602. (Illus.). 32 p. 29cm. (The Schoolhouse Gang). c.1985. Thomas Nelson.
--Oh, No! Miss Dent's Coming to Dinner. Downing, Julie, illus. LC 85-13604. (Illus.). 32 p. 29cm. c.1985. (ISBN 0-8407-6654-8). T. Nelson.
--Quit? Not Me!. A Story of Dependability. Downing, Julie, illus. LC 85-13603. (Illus.). 32 p. 29cm. c.1985. (ISBN 0-8407-6652-1). T. Nelson.

Moore, Renate, tr. see Mayrocker, Friederike.

Moore, Robert J. (1907-)
--The Magical Mr. Tiz and the Grumpops. Moore, Robert J., illus. LC 53-11179. 24cm. 30p. 1953. Pageant Press, Inc.

Moore, Robin & Dempsey, Al
--Phase of Darkness. LC 73-92799. 1974. (ISBN 0-89388-136-8). Okpaku Communications.

Moore, Roger E.
--Jason's First Quest. LC 84-51004. 80p. (Fantasy Forest Adventures Ser.). (gr. 2-5). N.D. (ISBN 0-394-72788-6, Pub. by BYR). Random.

Moore, Ruth
--Jeb Ellis of Candlemas Bay. Wilson, William N., illus. LC 52-5069. (Illus.). 21cm. 238p. 1952. Morrow.

Moore, Ruth Kolster
--Snooty. LC 42-201786. 89 p. col. illus. 22 x 18 cm. c.1941. Institute Press.

Moore, Ruth Nulton (1923-)
--Danger in the Pines. Converse, James, illus. LC 82-15770. (Illus.). 164 p. 20cm. 1983. (ISBN 0-8361-3313-7). (ISBN 0-8361-3314-5). Herald Press.
--Frisky: The Playful Pony. Brudi, Theresa, illus. LC 66-15169. 96 p. illus. 22 cm. 1966. Criterion Books.

--The Ghost Bird Mystery. Moon, Ivan, illus. LC 77-10438. (Illus.). 143 p. 22cm. 1977. (ISBN 0-8361-1829-4). (ISBN 0-8361-1830-8). Herald Press.
--Hiding the Bell. Snyder, Andrew A., illus. LC 68-10398. (Illus.). 126 p. 22cm. 1968. Westminster Press.
--In Search of Liberty. Converse, James, illus. LC 83-10827. p. cm. 1983. (ISBN 0-8361-3340-4). Herald Press.
--Mystery at Indian Rocks. Bond, Magi, illus. LC 80-25803. (Illus.). 183 p. 20cm. 1981. (ISBN 0-8361-1944-4). Herald Press.
--Mystery of the Lost Heirloom. Converse, James, illus. LC 85-27334. p. cm. (Sara and Sam series ; bk. 3). ((Series: Moore, Ruth Nulton.). (Sara and Sam series ; bk. 3.). 1985. (ISBN 0-8361-3408-7). Herald Press.
--Mystery of the Lost Treasure. Converse, James, illus. LC 78-11748. 32 311cm. 177p. 1978. (ISBN 0-8361-1868-5). (ISBN 0-8361-1869-3). Herald Press.
--Mystery of the Missing Stallions. Converse, James, illus. LC 84-19764. (Illus.). 133 p. 20cm. (Orig.). (Sara and Sam series ; bk. 1). (gr. 3-8). 1984. (ISBN 0-8361-3376-5). Herald Press.
--Mystery of the Secret Code. Converse, James, illus. LC 85-5441. (Illus.). 123 p. 20cm. (Sara and Sam series ; bk. 2). 1985. (ISBN 0-8361-3394-3). Herald Press.
--Peace Treaty. Espe, Marvin, illus. LC 76-48922. (Illus.). 153 p. 22cm. 1977. (ISBN 0-8361-1804-9). (ISBN 0-8361-1805-7). Herald Press.
--The Sorrel Horse. Converse, James, illus. LC 82-3136. (Illus.). 154 p. 20cm. 1982. (ISBN 0-8361-3303-X). Herald Press.
--Tomas and the Talking Birds. Graber, Esther Rose, illus. LC 78-23509. (Illus.). 115 p. 22cm. 1979. (ISBN 0-8361-1873-1). (ISBN 0-8361-1874-X). Herald Press.
--Wilderness Journey. Eitzen, Allan (1928-), illus. LC 79-20489. p. cm. 1979. (ISBN 0-8361-1906-1). (ISBN 0-8361-1907-X). Herald Press.

Moore, Samuel C.
--Historical Poem's. N.D. Dresser, McLellan & Co.

Moore, Samuel Taylor (1893-1974)
--Aces All. Lufkin, Raymond H. (1897-), illus. LC 32-20529. 3 p. l., 237 p. front., illus. 20 cm. c.1932. McLoughlin Brothers, Incorporated.
--Fighting Aces. Lufkin, Raymond H. (1897-), illus. LC 32-205289. 3 p. l., 235 p. front., illus. 20 cm. c.1932. McLoughlin Brothers, Incorporated.
--Under Sea Heroes. Lufkin, Raymond H. (1897-), illus. LC 32-20527. 3 p. l., 234 p. front., illus. 26 cm. c.1932. McLoughlin Brothers, Incorporated.

Moore, Sarah E.
--Diego. Flynn, Barbara (1928-), illus. LC 72-76368. (Illus.). 48 p. 22cm. 1972. (ISBN 0-15-223470-5). Harcourt Brace Jovanovich.
--Secret Island. Brown, Judith Gwyn (1933-), illus. LC 77-7331. (Illus.). 213 p. 22cm. c.1977. (ISBN 0-590-07479-2). Four Winds Press.

Moore, Sarah L.
--Merry Jingles: A Book for the Little Ones. Webster, H., illus. Nichols, Helen, photos by. LC 1-23063. 59p. 1901. Zimmerman's.

Moore, Sheila
--Samson Svenson's Baby. 1st ed. Weinhaus, Karen Ann, illus. LC 82-48262. p. cm. c.1983. (ISBN 0-06-022612-9). (ISBN 0-06-022613-7). Harper & Row.

Moore, Silas
--Scarlet Arena 30303. Oddo, Genevieve, ed. Luering, Jacqueline M., illus. LC 74-190272. 196p. 1st U.S. edition. (gr. 8-12). 1972. (ISBN 0-87783-063-0). Oddo.

Moore, Smith
--Tall Tales. N.D. Vantage Press Inc.

Moore-Smith, G. C., tr. from Danish.
--Queen Bee. (Illus.). N.D. Thomas Nelson & Sons.

Moore, Sparky, ed. see Disney, Walt, Productions.

Moore, Thomas Sturge (1870-1944)
--The Little School, a Posy of Rhymes. LC 47-392813. 45, 2 p. illus. 18 1/2 cm. 1905. Eragny Press.

Moore, Tom (1950-)
--Good-Bye Momma. LC 77-356825. 70 p. 21cm. c.1976. (ISBN 0-919948-19-7). (ISBN 0-919948-18-9). Breakwater Books.

Moore, Vardine Russell (1906-)
--Mice Are Rather Nice: Poems About Mice. Jamison, Doug, illus. LC 80-23121. (Illus.). xiv, 76 p. 22cm. 1981. (ISBN 0-689-30819-1). Atheneum.
--Mystery of the Bells. Kendrick, Alcy, illus. LC 55-7794. 156p. illus. 21cm. 1955. Westminster Press.
--Picnic Pony. Werth, Kurt (1896-), illus. LC 56-9149. unpaged. illus. 23cm. c.1956. Lothrop, Lee & Shepard Co.
--The Pleasure of Poetry with and by Children: A Handbook. LC 80-29015. ix, 133 p. 23cm. 1981. (ISBN 0-8108-1399-8). Scarecrow Press.

Moore, Vardine Russell (1906-) & Conkling, Fleur
--Billy Between. Crumling, Roger, illus. LC 51-10032. 175 p. illus. 22 cm. 1951. Westminster Press.
--House Next Door. Smalley, Janet (1893-), illus. LC 54-5216. 220p. illus. 21cm. 1954. Westminster Press.

Moore, W. Mark
--Together with Daddy. Karch, Paul, illus. LC 77-364701. (Illus.). 32 p. 24cm. 1977, c.1976. (ISBN 0-8054-4153-0). Broadman Press.

Moore-Betty, Maurice, jt. auth. see Travers, Pamela Lyndon.

Moorehead, Caroline (1944-), adapted by see Clot, S. & Quinel, Charles.

Moores, Dick, ed. see Disney, Walt, Productions.

Moores, Richard, ed. see Disney, Walt, Productions.

Moores, Richard see Disney, Walt, Productions.

Moorhead, Kent, jt. auth. see Moorhead, Rod.

Moorhead, Rod & Moorhead, Kent
--Aunt Tillie's Adventure: A Nutritious Story. LC 82-147084. (Illus.). 32 p. c.1981. University of Mississippi in Cooperation with the Mississippi State Dept. of Education.

Moorhouse, Reed
--With Pipe and Tabor: Junior Class-Room Plays. LC 34-20556. 191, 1 p. incl. front., illus. 16 cm. (Half-title: The Kings Treasuries of Literature, General Editor: Sir A. T. Quiller Couch). 1928. J. M. Dent & Sons, Ltd.

Moorsom, Sasha, tr. see Perrault, Charles.

Moos, Michael, jt. ed. see Bradford, Gigi.

Moose, Don, jt. auth. see Marks, W. Parker.

Moose, George L., ed. see Mother Goose.

Mooser, Stephen (1941-)
--Funnyman and the Penny Dodo. De Paola, Tomie, pseud. (1934-), illus. De Paola, Thomas Anthony. LC 84-2185. (Illus.). 30 p. 22cm. (An Easy-Read Story Book). 1984. (ISBN 0-531-03576-X). (ISBN 0-531-04393-2). F. Watts.
--Funnyman's First Case. De Paola, Tomie, pseud. (1934-), illus. De Paola, Thomas Anthony. LC 80-29637. (Illus.). 32 p. 22cm. (An Easy-Read Story Book). 1981. (ISBN 0-531-03538-7). (ISBN 0-531-04300-2). Watts.
--The Ghost with the Halloween Hiccups. De Paola, Tomie, pseud. (1934-), illus. De Paola, Thomas Anthony. LC 77-6271. (Illus.). 32 p. 22cm. (Easy-Read Story Book). 1977. (ISBN 0-531-01316-2). (ISBN 0-531-02483-0). (ISBN 0-531-02483-0). F. Watts.
--Into the Unknown: Nine Astounding Stories. Stevenson, Dinah, ed. LC 79-3336. (Illus.). (gr. 5 up). N.D. (ISBN 0-397-31855-3, JBL-J). (ISBN 0-397-31904-5). Har-Row.
--Orphan Jeb at the Massacree. Dos Santos, Joyce Audy, illus. LC 83-99. (Illus.). 96p. (Borzoi Bks.). (gr. 3-8). 1984. (ISBN 0-394-85731-3). (ISBN 0-394-95731-8). Knopf.

Moot, Barbara
--Henry the Bug. Moot, Barbara, illus. LC 66-9618. (Illus.). 33 p. 26cm. 1966. Story House Corp.

Mora, J. J., ed. see Aesopus.

Mora, Joseph Jacinto (1876-), illus.
--Reynard the Fox. (Illus.). N.D. Dana Estes and Company.

Moran, Connie see Bradbury, Bianca.

Moran, Connie, jt. auth. see Thorne, Diana.

Moran, Connie & Thorne, Diana
--Chips, The Story of a Cocker Spaniel. N.D. John C. Winston.

Moran, Edward Percy (1862-)
--Rhymes and Stories of Olden Times. N.D. Frederick A. Stokes.

Moran, James Sterling (1909-)
--Miserable: A Story about a Dinosaur. Howard, Ric, illus. LC 60-7167. 1960. Bobbs-Merrill Co.
--Sophocles the Hyena. N.D. E. M. Hale and Co.
--Sophocles the Hyena: A Fable. Duvoisin, Roger Antoine (1904-1980), illus. LC 54-10641. (Illus.). 26cm. 48p. (gr. 1-5). 1954. Whittlesey House.

Moran, Mabel O'Connell see O'Moran, M., pseud.

Moran, Mabel O'Connell (1899-1952)
--Red Eagle: Buffalo Bill's Adopted Son. Hargens, Charles, Jr. (1893-), illus. LC 48-8128. x, 212 p. illus. 21 cm. 1948. J. B. Lippincott Co.
--State Boy. O'Moran, M., pseud. LC 54-8106. 182p. 21cm. (gr. 7-9). 1954. (ISBN 0-397-30282-7). Lippincott.
--Trail of the Little Paiute. Davison, Claire, illus. LC 52-5105. 189 p. illus. 21 cm. 1952. Lippincott.

Moran, Martha Manker
--Sugar and Mr. Duck. (Illus.). 1 v. (unpaged. 1973. (ISBN 0-682-47763-X). Exposition Pr.
--Sugar Gets the Skunk. Wilkey, Elmira, illus. (Illus.). (gr. k-4). 1977. (ISBN 0-682-48778-3). Exposition.

Moran, Nancy, photos by.
--Bialosky Goes Out. LC 84-80116. (Illus.). (Golden Photo Board Bks.). (ps). 1984. (ISBN 0-307-06090-X, Golden Bks). Western Pub.

Moran, Tom
--Bicycle Motocross Racing. (Illus.). 48p. (Superwheels & Thrill Sports Ser.). (gr. 4 up). 1985. (ISBN 0-8225-0510-X). Lerner Pubns.

Moraski, Al, illus.
--Q'bert's Quazy Questions: A Riddle Book to Make You Laugh. (Illus.). 32p. (gr. 2-6). 1983. (ISBN 0-910313-13-X). Parker Bro.

Moray-Williams, Ursula see Williams, Ursula Moray.

Moray Williams, Ursula (1911-)
--Adventures of the Little Wooden Horse. Brisley, Joyce Lankester (1896-), illus. 204p. N.D. J. B. Lippincott.
--Adventures of the Little Wooden Horse. Fortnum, Peggy, pseud. (1919-), illus. Nuttall-Smith, Margaret Emily Noel. LC 59-4909. 170p. illus. 18cm. (Puffin Books, PS125). 1959. (ISBN 0-14-030125-9). Baltimore Penguin Books.
--Adventures of the Little Wooden Horse. Pitz, Henry Clarence (1895-1976), illus. LC 39-21774. 203, 1 p. col. front., illus. 22 cm. c.1939. J. B. Lippincott Company.
--Beware of This Animal. Paton, Jane Elizabeth (1934-), illus. LC 64-22792. (Illus.). 114 p. 21cm. 1965. Dial Press.
--Bogwoppit. LC 78-57534. 174 p. 21cm. 1st U.S. edition. c.1978. (ISBN 0-8407-6597-5). T. Nelson.
--Boy in a Barn. Dalley, Terence, illus. LC 79-102411. (Illus.). 128 p. 22cm. 1st U.S. edition. 1970. T. Nelson.
--Castle Merlin. LC 72-4074. 142 p. 22cm. 1972. (ISBN 0-8407-6246-1). T. Nelson.
--Crown for a Queen. Hughes, Shirley (1929-), illus. (Illus.). (gr. 3-6). 1969. (ISBN 0-696-56932-9). Hawthorn.
--Cruise of the Happy-Go-Gay. Edwards, Gunvor, illus. LC 68-15002. (Illus.). 38 line drawings. 160p. (gr. 3-6). 1968. (ISBN 0-696-56940-X). Hawthorn.
--The Cruise of the Happy-Go-Gay. 1st U.S. ed. Edwards, Gunvor, illus. LC 68-15002. (Illus.). vii,151p. 21cm. 1967. Meredith Press.
--Earl's Falconer. Geer, Charles Hand (1922-), illus. (Illus.). (gr. 7-9). 1961. Morrow.
--Gobbolino, the Witch's Cat. (gr. k-3). 1973. (ISBN 0-14-030239-5, Puffin). Penguin.
--Gobbolino the Witch's Cat. (gr. 1-5). 1974. (ISBN 0-14-030239-5, Puffin). Penguin.
--Island MacKenzie. Ardizzone, Edward Jeffrey Irving (1900-1979), illus. (Illus.). (gr. 3-6). 1960. Morrow.
--Jockin the Jester. LC 72-14324. 224 p. 22cm. 1st U.S. edition. 1973. (ISBN 0-8407-6276-3). T. Nelson.
--Johnnie Golightly and His Crocodile. Jaques, Faith (1923-), illus. LC 70-113715. (Illus.). 32 p. 26cm. 1st U.S. edition. 1971, c.1970. (ISBN 0-8178-4761-8). Harvey House.
--Johnnie Tigerskin. John, Diana, illus. LC 66-13489. 117p. illus. 21cm. 1st U.S. edition. 1966, c.1964. Duell Dist. Meredith.
--Kelpie, the Gipsies' Pony. Williams, Barbara Moray (1911-), illus. LC 35-6460. 255, 1 p. col. front., illus. 20 cm. c.1935. J. B. Lippincott Company.
--Malkin's Mountain. Hughes, Shirley (1929-), illus. LC 70-164972. (Illus.). 159 p. 21cm. 1st U.S. edition. 1972, c.1971. (ISBN 0-8407-6178-3). (ISBN 0-8407-6179-1). T. Nelson.
--Moonball. Paton, Jane Elizabeth (1934-), illus. (Illus.). (gr. 3-5). 1967. (ISBN 0-696-71859-6). Hawthorn.
--The Moonball. Paton, Jane Elizabeth (1934-), illus. LC 67-14749. 138p. illus. 21cm. 1st U.S. edition. 1967, c.1965. Meredith.
--The Moonball. Paton, Jane Elizabeth (1934-), illus. (Illus., Pub. by Meredith). (gr. 4-6). 1972 (Starline). Schol Bk Serv.
--The Nine Lives of Island Mackenzie. Ardizzone, Edward Jeffrey Irving (1900-1979), illus. LC 80-670265. (Illus.). 128 p. 22cm. 1979. (ISBN 0-7011-0227-6). Chatto and Windus.
--No Ponies for Miss Pobjoy. LC 76-8404. 159 p. 21cm. 1st U.S. edition. 1976, c.1975. (ISBN 0-8407-6477-4). Nelson.
--Peter and the Wanderlust. Pitz, Henry Clarence (1895-1976), illus. LC 40-33285. 5 p. l., 295 p. col. front., illus. 21 cm. c.1940. J. B. Lippincott Company.
--Pretenders' Island. Brisley, Joyce Lankester (1896-), illus. LC 43-2004. 5 p. l., 3-209 p., 1 l. incl. front., illus., plates. 19 cm. 1942. A. A. Knopf.
--The Three Toymakers. Hughes, Shirley (1929-), illus. LC 79-152875. (Illus.). 156 p. 22cm. 1st U.S. edition. 1971. (ISBN 0-8407-6114-7). T. Nelson.
--Tiger Nanny. Edwards, Gunvor, illus. LC 74-14518. p. cm. 1st U.S. edition. 1974. (ISBN 0-8407-6405-7). Nelson.
--The Toymaker's Daughter. Hughes, Shirley (1929-), illus. LC 73-80287. (Illus.). 134 p. 21cm. 1st U.S. edition. 1969, c.1968. Meredith Press.

Mord, E Ed.
--Arabian Tales. (Illus.). N.D. Frederick A. Stokes.
--Nursery Favorites. (Illus.). N.D. Frederick A. Stokes.
--Persian Tales. (Illus.). N.D. Frederick A. Stokes.

Mordaunt, Elinor, pseud., see Mordaunt, Evelyn May.

Mordaunt, Elinor, pseud.
--Blitz Kids. Mordaunt, Evelyn May. Trier, Walter (1890-1951), illus. LC 42-242806. 100 p. incl. front., illus. 19 cm. 1941. Oxford University Press.
--Shoe and Stocking Stories. Mordaunt, Evelyn May. Sichel, Harold M. (1881-), illus. LC 15-21392. 221 p. col. front., illus. (part col.) 22 cm. 1915. John Lane Company.

Mordaunt, Evelyn May see Mordaunt, Elinor, pseud.

Mordillo, Guillermo
--Crazy Cowboy. LC 72-78356. (Illus.). 36 p. 27cm. 1976, c.1972. (ISBN 0-8252-1843-8). (ISBN 0-8252-0087-3). Quist.
--Crazy Cowboy. Mordillo, Guillermo, illus. (Illus.). 36p. (Harlin Quist Bks). (ps-5). 1973. (ISBN 0-8252-0087-3). (ISBN 0-8252-0088-1). Dial.
--The Damp and Daffy Doings of a Daring Pirate Ship. Mordillo, Guillermo, illus. LC 72-146838. 28 p. (chiefly col. illus.). 24cm. 1971. (ISBN 0-8252-0071-7). (ISBN 0-8252-0072-5). H. Quist.

Mordvinoff, Nicolas see Nicolas, pseud.

Mordvinoff, Nicolas, jt. auth. see Lipkind, William.

Mordvinoff, Nicolas (1911-1973)
--Bear's Land. Nicolas, pseud. Mordvinoff, Nicolas (1911-1973), illus. Nicolas, pseud. LC 55-10772. unpaged. illus. 23cm. 1955. Coward-McCann.
--Coral Island. Nicolas, pseud. Mordvinoff, Nicolas (1911-1973), illus. Nicolas, pseud. LC 56-8231. unpaged. illus. 29cm. 1957. Doubleday.

More, B., ed. see Ballantyne, Robert Michael.

More, Blanche Rebecca
--Kit Cottage. Price, Harriet Longstreet (1891-), illus. LC 37-34667. 320 p. incl. front., illus., plates. 22 1/2 cm. c.1937. The Penn Publishing Company.
--Two in Patches. LC 34-393603. 304 p. incl. front., illus., plates. 22 cm. c.1934. The Penn Publishing Company.

More, Caroline, pseud., see Cone, Molly Lamken.

More, Caroline, pseud. (1918-)
--A Batch of Trouble. Cone, Molly Lamken. Smith, Lee (1925-), illus. LC 63-9778. 85 p. illus.22 cm. 1963. Dial Press.

More, Florence E
--Sportsmen, Beware!. Thirty Minutes of Fun for Actors and Audience. LC 38-3498. 21, 1 p. diagr. 18 1/2 cm. c.1937. S. French.

More, Grace Van Dyke
--John and Betty Stories: Tales of John More and Betty Taylor More, Pioneers in Delaware County, New York. Roediger, Virginia More, illus. LC 32-12718. 93, 3 p. illus. (incl. maps) 21 cm. 1930. Rogers, Kellogg, Stillson Company.

More, Hannah, jt. auth. see A Friend of Youth.

More, Hannah, jt. auth. see Barbauld, Anna Letitia Aikin, Mrs.

More, Hannah (1745-1833)
--The Shepherd of Salisbury. N.D. American Sunday-School Union.
--Stories for the Young. 1440p. N.D. American Tract Society.

Morecamp, Arthur, pseud., see Pilgrim, Thomas.

Morehead, Albert Hodges see Hodges, Turner, pseud.

Morehouse, Carrie Warner, Mrs.
--Legend of Psyche and Other Verses. LC 24-7036. 18 x 12cm. 98p. 1889. C. T. Walter.

Morel, Eve
--Noses Are for Smelling Roses. Sears, Nancy, illus. LC 74-163159. (Illus.). 28 p. 27cm. 1971. (ISBN 0-448-02808-5). Grosset & Dunlap.

Morel, Eve, compiled by.
--Fairy Tales and Fables. Fujikawa, Gyo, illus. LC 70-122562. (Illus.). 32cm. 124p. 1970. (ISBN 0-448-02824-7). Grosset & Dunlap.
--Hans Christian Andersen's Fairy Tales. Morel, Eve, illus. (Original Author: Hans Christian Andersen, 1805-1875). N.D. (ISBN 0-448-00323-6, Silver Dallor Library). Grosset & Dunlap.

Morel, Eve, ed. see Grimm, Jakob Ludwig Karl (1785-1863) & Grimm, Wilhelm Karl.

Moreland, Mary Leona
--The School on the Hill. (Illus.). 374p. N.D. Ira Bradley & Co's.

AUTHOR INDEX MORIER, JAMES

--Which: Right or Wrong?. LC 12-36897. iv, 5-312 p. front., plates. 18 1/2 cm. 1883. Lee and Shepard.
--Which: Right or Wrong?. A Story of Life at Lakeview, 1 of 30 vols. (American Girls' Ser.: No. 24). 1900. Set. Lee & Shepard.
Moremen, Grace
--No, No, Natalie. Fulton, Geoffrey P., photos by. LC 72-10213. (Illus.). 46 p. 1973. (ISBN 0-516-07624-8). Childrens Press.
Morenus, Constance Gay, jt. auth. see Suddeth, Ruth Elgin.
Morenus, Richard
--Frozen Trails. Kramer, Frank, illus. LC 56-8709. 235p. illus. 21cm. 1956. Dodd, Mead.
--Northland Adventure. LC 51-6655. 250 p. 21cm. 1951. Dodd, Mead.
Moreton, Ada Margarette Smith, Lady, ed. see Coloma, Luis P.
Moreton, John, pseud., see Cohen, Morton N..
Moreton, John, pseud. (1921-)
--The Love for Three Oranges. Cohen, Morton N.. Tinkelman, Murray (1933-), illus. Prokofief, Mrs., intro. by. LC 66-14335. (Illus.). 61 p. 28cm. (Opera stories for young people). 1966. G. P. Putnam's Sons.
--Punky, Mouse for a Day. Cohen, Morton N.. Tinkelman, Murray (1933-), illus. LC 64-25763. 60 p. illus. 24 cm. 1st U.S. edition. c.1965. Putman.
--Punky: Mouse for a Day. Cohen, Morton N.. Tinkelman, Murray (1933-), illus. (Illus.). (gr. 2-5). 1964. (ISBN 0-399-60525-8). Putnam.
Morey, Francina
--The Bears of Log Cabin Village. Nagel, Stina (1918-), illus. 1960. Exposition Press.
Morey, Kathleen
--Otto Shares a Fright. Morey, Kathleen, illus. (Illus.). 32p. (Otto Shares Ser.). 1984. (ISBN 0-912249-03-X). Kid-Love Unltd.
--Otto Shares a Giggle. Morey, Kathleen, illus. (Illus.). 32p. (Otto Shares Ser.). (gr. k-3). 1984. (ISBN 0-912249-01-3). Kid-Love Unltd.
--Otto Shares a Hug & a Kiss. Morey, Kathleen, illus. LC 83-80189. (Illus., Orig.). (Otto Shares Ser.). (gr. k-3). 1983. (ISBN 0-912249-00-5). Kid-Love Unltd.
--Otto Shares a Tear. Morey, Kathleen, illus. (Illus.). 32p. (Otto Shares Ser.). 1984. (ISBN 0-912249-02-1). Kid-Love Unltd.
Morey, R.
--Kevin. 1970. (ISBN 0-13-514828-6). P-H.
Morey, Sheena (1905-)
--Old MacDonald's Farm. Scrydloff, Mary (1926-), illus. LC 66-15969. 29p. col. illus. 30x14cm. (Read-aloud bk.). 1966. Follett.
--Old MacDonald's Farm. Scrydloff, Mary (1926-), illus. LC 50-23976. 27 p. col. illus. 22 cm. (Bonnie Book). 1949. John Martin's House.
--Pat 'n' Penny. Scott, Martha, illus. LC 47-1781. 32 p. col. illus. 21 x 28 1/2 cm. 1946. Wilcox & Follett Co.
Morey, Sheena (1905-), retold by.
--The Old Man and the Turnip. Mathieu, Dorothea, illus. LC 65-16159. 1v. (unpaged) col. illus. 30x14cm. (Readaloud Bk.). c.1965. Follett.
--The Old Man and the Turnip: An Old Folk Tale. Mathieu, Dorothea, illus. LC 49-16459. 28 p. col. illus. 21 cm. (Bonnie Book). 1948. John Martin's House.
Morey, Sheenathea (1786-1859), ed. see Grimm, Jakob Ludwig Karl (1785-1863) & Grimm, Wilhelm Karl.
Morey, Walter Nelson (1907-)
--Angry Waters. 1st ed. Cuffari, Richard (1925-1978), illus. LC 73-81722. (Illus.). 224 p. 22cm. 1969. Dutton.
--Canyon Winter. LC 72-79126. 202 p. 22cm. 1972. (ISBN 0-525-27410-3). E. P. Dutton.
--Deep Trouble. LC 72-133117. 214 p. 22cm. 1971. (ISBN 0-525-28620-9). E. P. Dutton.
--Gentle Ben. 1st ed. Schoenherr, John Carl (1935-), illus. LC 65-21290. (Illus.). 191 p. 22cm. 1965. Dutton. **Award: (ALA).**
--Gloomy Gus. LC 76-121588. 245 p. 22cm. 1970. Dutton.
--Home Is the North. 1st ed. Shore, Robert (1924-), illus. LC 67-20132. (Illus.). 223 p. 22cm. 1967. Dutton.
--Kavik the Wolf Dog. 1st ed. Parnall, Peter (1936-), illus. LC 68-24727. 192p. illus. 22cm. 1968. Dutton.
--Kavik the Wolf Dog. Parnall, Peter (1936-), illus. LC 68-24727. (Illus.). 192 p. 20cm. (Dutton anytime book, AB10). 1973, c.1968. (ISBN 0-525-45018-1). E. P. Dutton & Co.
--The Lemon Meringue Dog. LC 80-171. 165 p. 22cm. c.1980. (ISBN 0-525-33455-6). Dutton.
--Run Far, Run Fast. LC 74-4228. 173 p. 22cm. 1974. (ISBN 0-525-38728-5). Dutton.
--Runaway Stallion. LC 73-77450. 217 p. 22cm. 1973. (ISBN 0-525-38738-2). Dutton.
--Sandy & the Rock Star. LC 78-12375. (gr. 4-7). 1979. Dutton.
--Scrub Dog of Alaska. LC 73-157954. 212 p. 22cm. 1971. (ISBN 0-525-38908-3). Dutton.
--Year of the Black Pony. LC 75-33805. 152 p. 22cm. c.1976. (ISBN 0-525-43455-0). Dutton.
Morford, Cyretta
--That Rascal Buddy. 1970. Carlton.
Morgan
--Baron Bruno. (Series of Books for the Young). N.D. MacMillan & Co.
Morgan, Alfred
--Aquarium Book for Boys & Girls. Morgan, Alfred, illus. (Illus.). (gr. 3-9). N.D. (ISBN 0-684-12668-0, ScribJ). Scribner.
Morgan, Alice
--The Boy Who Brought Christmas. Jackson, John Edwin, illus. LC 11-27807. 6 p. l., 3-139 p. col. front., col. plates. 18 1/2 cm. $0.5. 1911. Doubleday, Page & Company.
Morgan, Alison Mary (1930-)
--All Kinds of Prickles. LC [illegible]. p. cm. c.1979. (ISBN 0-525-66664-8). Elsevier/Nelson Books.
--At Willie Tucker's Place. Stubley, Trevor Hugh (1932-), illus. LC 76-41183. (Illus.). 95p. 1st U.S. edition. (gr. 4-12). 1976, c.1975. (ISBN 0-525-66515-3). (ISBN 0-8407-6515-0). Elsevier-Nelson.
--A Boy Called Fish. Sandin, Joan (1942-), illus. LC 72-9859. (Illus.). 201 p. 21cm. 1973. (ISBN 0-06-024351-1). (ISBN 0-06-024351-1). Harper & Row.
--Paul's Kite. LC 82-3957. 120p. (gr. 5-9). 1982. (ISBN 0-689-50245-1, McElderry Bk). Atheneum.
--Pete. LC 73-5490. 241 p. 21cm. 1973. (ISBN 0-06-024349-X). (ISBN 0-06-024349-X). Harper & Row.
--River Song. Schoenherr, John Carl (1935-), illus. LC 74-2619. (Illus.). 135 p. 22cm. c.1975. (ISBN 0-06-024343-0). (ISBN 0-06-024344-9). Harper & Row.
--Ruth Crane. LC 74-9075. 244 p. 21cm. 1974. (ISBN 0-06-024347-3). Harper and Row.
Morgan, Anna Blunt
--Little Folks Tramping and Camping: A Nature-Study Story of Real Children and a Real Camp. Cue, Harold James, illus. LC 20-17826. 356p. 20cm. 1920. Lothrop, Lee and Shepard Co.
Morgan, Appleton, jt. auth. see Carnes, William F.
Morgan, Barbara Ellen
--Hand of the King. Simon, Howard (1903-1979), illus. LC 63-11949. 176 p. illus.,map. 22 cm. 1963. Random House.
--Journey for Tobiyah. Mars, Witold Tadeusz J. (1912-), illus. LC 66-15410. (Illus.). 22cm. 152p. (gr. 4-7). 1966. (ISBN 0-394-81327-8). Random.
Morgan, Bryan Stanford & Morgan, Joan
--Pepe's Island. Payne, Roger, illus. LC 66-15168. 94p. illus. 21cm. (Criterion bk. for young people). c.1966. Criterion.
Morgan, Carol McAfee
--Hunt for the Yule Log. Wildsmith, Brian Lawrence (1930-), illus. LC 57-9471. 159p. illus. 21cm. 1957. Abelard-Schuman.
--A New Home for Pablo. Weiss, Harvey (1922-), illus. LC 55-8537. 144p. illus. 22cm. 1955. Abelard-Schuman.
Morgan, Caroline Starr, Mrs.
--Charlotte's Revenge. LC 12-36896. 423 p. front., plates. 18 1/2 cm. (On cover: The Crown series). c.1895. American Baptist Publication Society.
--Esther Lawrence: Or, She Hath Done What She Could, 1 of 60 vols. LC 12-36895. 2 p. l., 3-224 p. front., plates. 18 1/2 cm. (Crescent Lib.). c.1890. Set. American Baptist Publication Society.
--Jingles and Rhymes for Nursery and Playroom. Hudson, illus. 20cm. 57p. c.1907. Broadway Publishing Co.
--Marmaduke Multiply Stories... LC 12-36988. 2 v. col. fronts., illus. 19 cm. c.1897. American Baptist Publication Society.
--A Sheaf of Happy Holidays. LC 7-39191. 213 p. 9 pl. 20 cm. 1907. The Griffith & Rowland Press.
--Ways That Win: A/Tale of a Year. (Illus.). 352p. N.D. Sunday-School Publications.
Morgan, David Page (1927-)
--True Adventures of Railroaders. 1st ed. Akin, W. A., Jr., illus. LC 54-5119. 209p. illus. 20cm. (True adventure library). 1954. Little, Brown.
Morgan, De Wolfe, pseud., see Williamson, Thames Ross.
Morgan, De Wolfe pseud.
--Great Pyramid Mystery. (gr. 7-9). 1973 (Starline). Schol Bk Serv.
Morgan, Earlaine, pseud., see Earle, Teda Morgan.
Morgan, Elizabeth
--In the Deep Blue Sea. Plasencia, Peter P., illus. LC 62-14740. 72p. illus. 22cm. 1962. Prentice-Hall.
Morgan, Flora
--The Adventures of Willie the Kid. (gr. 4-7). N.D. Carlton.
Morgan, Fred Troy (1926-)
--Ghost Tales of the Uwharries. Ingram, Virginia, illus. LC 68-58501. (Illus.). 10 woodcuts. vii & 152p. 1980. (ISBN 0-910244-52-9). Blair.
--Uwharrie Magic. 1975. (ISBN 0-87716-050-3). Moore Publishing Company: Distributed by Acropolis LTD.
Morgan, Geoffrey (1916-)
--Lame Duck. Stubbs, Joanna, illus. (gr. 1-4). 1977. (ISBN 0-8277-5392-6). (ISBN 0-8277-5391-8). British Bk Ctr.
--A Small Piece of Paradise. Knight, David (1923-), illus. LC 68-22245. (Illus.). 110 p. 22cm. 1968, c.1967. Knopf.
Morgan, Gwladys M
--Our Little Welsh Cousin. Gooch, Thelma, illus. LC [illegible]. 4 p. l., 107 p. front., illus. (incl. map) plates. 19 1/2 cm. (The little cousin series). 1924. L. C. Page & Company (Incorporated.
Morgan, Harriet
--The Island Impossible. Pyle, Katharine D. (0000-1938), illus. LC 99-5299. 5 p. l., 206 p., 1 l. front., plates. 19 cm. 1899. Little, Brown & Co.
Morgan, Helen Gertrude Louise Axford (1921-)
--Little Old Lady. (Illus.). (gr. k-2). N.D. Transatlantic.
--Mary Kate. Hughes, Shirley (1929-), illus. LC 70-181676. (Illus.). 89 p. 21cm. 1st U.S. edition. 1972. (ISBN 0-8407-6215-1). T. Nelson.
--Mrs. Pinny & the Salty Sea Day. Hughes, Shirley (1929-), illus. (Illus.). (ps-5). N.D. (ISBN 0-571-09863-0). Faber & Faber.
--Satchkin Patchkin. Hughes, Shirley (1929-), illus. LC 75-113384. (Illus.). 64 p. 22cm. 1970, c.1966. M. Smith Co.
--Tales Of Tigg's Farm. N.D. Transatlantic Arts.
Morgan, Helen L.
--Mistress of the White House: The Story of Dolly Madison. Cote, Phyllis N. (1921-), illus. LC 46-3479. 4 p. l., 11-248 p. plates. 21 cm. 1946. The Westminister Press.
Morgan, Henry, pseud., see Von Ost, Henry Lerner.
Morgan, Henry, pseud. (1915-)
--O-Sono and the Magician's Nephew, and the Elephant. Von Ost, Henry Lerner. Spanfeller, James John (1930-), illus. LC 64-56972. 1 v. (unpagсd) illus. (port col.) 26 cm. (Edward Ernest book). 1964. Vanguard Press.
Morgan, Ike, jt. auth. see Boylan, Grace Duffie, Mrs.
Morgan, Jim
--Circus Comes to Town. Falck, Cheryl, illus. (Illus.). 20p. (gr. k-3). 1971. Hallmark.
Morgan, Joan, jt. auth. see Morgan, Bryan Stanford.
Morgan, John De see De Morgan, John.
Morgan, Len (1894-)
--Abilene Trail. Hamaker, William B., illus. LC 41-101529. 1 p. l., vii-ix, 205 p. incl. illus., plates. front. (fold. map) 22 cm. 1941. T. Nelson & Sons.
--Klondike Adventure. Hamaker, William B., illus. LC 40-32441. 199 p. front., illus. 20 1/2 cm. 1940. T. Nelson and Sons.
Morgan, Lenore H. (1908-1976)
--Dragons & Stuff. Hastings, Ian (1912-), illus. LC 70-108725. (Illus.). 32p. (gr. 2-4). 1970. (ISBN 0-87783-012-6). (ISBN 0-87783-091-6). Oddo.
--Peter's Pockets. LC 65-27622. (Illus.). (gr. k-2). 1968. (ISBN 0-87783-029-0). Oddo.
--Peter's Pockets. Lysaker, Gene, illus. LC 65-27622. 32p. illus. (pt. col.) 26cm. c.1965. Oddo Pub.
--Peter's Pockets. Lysaker, Gene, illus. (Illus.). (gr. k-2). 1978. (ISBN 0-89508-063-X). Rainbow Bks.
Morgan, Margaret, tr. see Day, Veronique.
Morgan, Mary, pseud., see Powell, Miriam.
Morgan, Mary see De Morgan, Mary.
Morgan, Mary De see DeMorgan, Mary.
Morgan, Mary De see DeMorgan, Mary & DeMorgan, William Frend.
Morgan, Myra Boyd
--The Little Girl and the Gobolin. The Birds and Other Poems. Berryman, Clifford, illus. LC 12-15152. 29 p. illus. 18 cm. 1912. B. S. Adams.
Morgan, Nellie
--Mrs. Squirrel's Problem & Other Tales. (gr. k-5). N.D. Carlton.
Morgan, Nina Hermanna
--Prairie Star. Henneberger, Robert G. (1921-), illus. LC 55-1412. (Illus.). 189 p. 22cm. 1955. Viking Press.
Morgan, Nina Lillian
--How Edith Found Fairy-land. 16cm. 1899. F. M. Harley Pub. Co.
Morgan, S. E. De see DeMorgan, S. E.
Morgan, Sharon Antonia see Fufuka, Karama, pseud.
Morgan, Shirley
--Rain, Rain, Don't Go Away. 1st ed. Ardizzone, Edward Jeffrey Irving (1900-1979), illus. LC 76-179049. (Illus.). 32 p. 23cm. 1972. (ISBN 0-525-38030-2). Dutton.
Morgan, Sidney T.
--Elmer the Elf. (gr. 1-3). N.D. Carlton.
Morgan, Stephanie
--The Witch Down the Street. Cooke, Tom, illus. LC 82-22329. p. cm. c.1982. (ISBN 0-910313-02-4). Parker Brothers.
Morgan, Violet
--Sebastian and the Dragon. LC 70-105400. (Illus.). 77 p. 27cm. 1970, c.1968. Scroll Press.
Morgan, Walter Amos (1882-)
--The Dreams of Youth. LC 28-6304. xiv, 246 p. 19 1/2 cm. $2.0. c.1928. The Century Co.
Morgan, Walter J., compiled by.
--Nursery Rhymes and Fables. Morgan, Walter J., illus (Pub. by Society for Promoting Christian Knowledge). N.D. E. & J. B. Young & Co.
Morgan, William Frend De see DeMorgan, Mary & DeMorgan, William Frend.
Morganson, Margaret Caroline
--The Faith of an Indian. LC 38-367458. 130 p. 19 1/2 cm. c.1938. Dorrance and Company.
Morgenthaler, Verena
--The Legend of St. Nicholas. 1970. Henry Z. Walck Inc.
Morgenroth, Barbara
--Demons at My Door. LC 80-12053. p. cm. 1980. Atheneum.
--In Real Life I'm Just Kate. LC 81-1421. p. cm. 1981. (ISBN 0-689-30851-5). Atheneum.
--Last Junior Year. LC 78-2750. 179 p. 22cm. 1978. (ISBN 0-689-30663-6). Atheneum.
--Nicki & Wynne. LC 81-10965. (Illus.). 139 p. 22cm. 1982. (ISBN 0-689-30886-8). Atheneum.
--Ride a Proud Horse. LC 77-21111. 181 p. 22cm. 1978. (ISBN 0-689-30624-5). Atheneum.
--Tramps Like Us. LC 78-13739. 145 p. 22cm. 1979. (ISBN 0-689-30690-3). Atheneum.
--Will the Real Renie Lake Please Stand up?. 1st ed. LC 80-21904. 164 p. 22cm. 1981. (ISBN 0-689-30820-5). Atheneum.
Morgenroth, Barbara & Ilsley, Velma Elizabeth (1918-)
--Impossible Charlie. LC 79-10447. (Illus.). 153 p. 22cm. 1979. (ISBN 0-689-30718-7). Atheneum.
Morgenstern, Christian, jt. auth. see Freyhold, K. F. E. Von.
Morgenstern, Christian (1871-1914)
--The Great Lalula and Other Nonsense Rhymes. Svatos, Ladislav, illus. Knight, Max (1909-), tr. LC 68-24527. (Illus.). 61 p. 22cm. 1969. (ISBN 0-399-60212-7). Putnam.
--Three Nursery Poems. Bohdal, Susi (1951-), illus. Cutler, May Ebbitt (1923-), tr. from Ger. LC 77-89348. (Illus.). (Children's Books As Works of Art Ser.). (ps-1). 1977. (ISBN 0-912766-85-9). Tundra Bks.
--The Three Sparrows, and Other Nursery Poems. Hogrogian, Nonny (1932-), illus. Knight, Max (1909-), tr. LC 68-29366. (Illus.). 1 v. (unpaged. 1968. Scribner.
Morgenstern, Susie Hoch
--It's Not Fair. Abrams, Kathie, illus. LC 83-81535. (Illus.). 101p. N.D. (ISBN 0-374-33649-0). FS&G.
Morgenthaler, Verena
--The Legend of St. Nicholas. LC 70-93676. (Illus.). 30 p. 1970. H. Z. Walck.
Moriarty, Henry C. & Cerf, Bennet Alfred (1898-1971)
--Young Northeast. N.D. Random House.
Moriarty, M. L., ed. see La Fontaine, Jean de.
Moric, Rudo
--Tale of a Wild Duck. Cerna, Dagmar, illus. LC 66-16420. (Illus.). (Foreign Lands Bks). (gr. k-5). 1966. (ISBN 0-8225-0357-3). Lerner Pubns.
Morice, Dave (1946-)
--Dot Town. Morice, Dave (1946-), illus. (Illus.). 36p. (Orig.). (gr. 2-4). 1981. (ISBN 0-915124-38-6, Bookslinger). Toothpaste.
--The Happy Birthday Handbook. Morice, Dave (1946-), illus. LC 82-19429. p. cm. 1982. (ISBN 0-915124-67-X). Toothpaste Press.
--A Visit from St. Alphabet: Poem & Drawings. Morice, Dave (1946-), illus. LC 80-24865. (Illus.). 19 p. 1980. (ISBN 0-915124-47-5). Toothpaste Press.
Morice, Stella Margery
--The Book of Wiremu. Parker, Nancy Winslow (1930-), illus. LC 66-69695. 2, 51p. front., illus. 25cm. 1966. Blackwood & J. Paul.
Morier, James Justinian (1780-1849)
--The Adventures of Hajji Baba of Ispahan. 20cm. 1895. Stone and Kimballs.
--The Adventures of Hajji Baba of Ispahan, 2 Vols, Vol. 1 & 2. Browne, S. E., intro. by. 1985. Set. Vol. 1, 242pp. Stone & Kimball's.
--The Adventures of Hajji Baba of Ispahan. Millar, Harold Robert (1869-1939), illus. LC 75-36062. (Illus.). xxxvi, 455 p. 22cm. c.1976. (ISBN 0-8055-1173-3). (ISBN 0-8055-0249-1). Hart Pub. Co.

--The Adventures of Hajji Baba of Ispahan. Millar, Harold Robert (1869-1939), illus. N.D. Macmillian & Co.
Morland, Nigel (1905-)
--The Goofus Man. LC 37-337782. 51 p. 18 1/2 cm. (On cover: French's plays for juvenile performers. no. 40). c.1937. S. French, Ltd.
Morley, Christopher Darlington (1890-1957)
--The Goldfish Under the Ice. N.D. J. B. Lippincott.
--The Goldfish Under the Ice. Wiese, Kurt (1887-1974), illus. LC 32-317246. 5 p. l., 3-69 p. incl. illus., plates. front. 19 1/2 cm. 1932. Doubleday, Doran & Company, Inc.
--I Know a Secret. N.D. J. B. Lippincott.
--I Know a Secret. Warmuth, Jeanette, illus. LC 27-24950. viii p., 3 l., 235 p., 1 l. incl. illus., plates. col. front. 20 1/2 cm. 1927. Doubleday, Page & Company.
--Max and Moritz. Morley, Christopher Darlington (1890-1957), tr. (Orig.). 1934. William Morrow & Co.
Morley, Henry, jt. auth. see Hakluyt.
Morley, Henry (1822-1894), ed. see Ramasvami Raju, P. V.
Morley, Henry (1822-1894)
--The Chicken Market, and Other Fairy Tales. Bennett, Charles Henry (1829-1867), illus. 368p. N.D. Cassell, Petter, & Galpin.
--Fairy Tales. 5th ed. Bennett, Charles Henry (1829-1867), illus. LC 27-201716. 2 p. l., ix-xvi, 362 p. front., illus., pl. 20 cm. (Half-title: Books and papers by Henry Morley, 1851-1866. vol. iv). 1893. G. Routledge and Sons, Limited.
Morley, Margaret Warner (1858-1923)
--The Apple Tree Sprite. LC 15-21390. 6, 207 p. illus. 19 1/2 cm. 1915. A. C. McClurg & Co.
--The Bee People. N.D. A. C. McClurg.
--Donkey John of the Toy Valley. LC 9-25981. xi, 13-297, 1 p. illus. 19 1/2 cm. 1909. A. C. McClurg & Co.
--Donkey John of the Toy Valley. LC 39-610. viii p., 1 l., 13-297, 1 p. 19 1/2 cm. 1938. A. C. McClurg & Co.
--The Honey-Makers. N.D. A. C. McClurg.
--Life and Love. N.D. A. C. McClurg.
--Little Mitchell: The Story of a Mountain Squirrel. Horsfall, Robert Bruce (1869-1948), illus. N.D. A. C. McClurg.
--A Song of Life. N.D. A. C. McClurg.
Morningstar, Mildred Whaley
--Christian Nursery Rhymes. N.D. Zondervan Publihing House.
--Danger at the Sheep Ranch. LC 83-1032. p. cm. c.1983. (ISBN 0-8024-0267-4). Moody Press.
Moroso, John Antonio (1874-)
--Cap Fallon, Fire Fighter. LC 23-5519. 4 p. l., 236, 1 p. front. 19 1/2 cm. 1923. D. Appleton and Company.
Morpurgo, Michael
--War Horse. LC 83-1747. 148 p. 22cm. 1st U.S. edition. 1983, c.1982. (ISBN 0-688-02296-0). Greenwillow Books.
Morra, Madeleine
--Snoozy, the Tortoise, and Other Stories. 1st ed. Lyons, Dave, illus. LC 55-12520. (Illus.). 42p. 21cm. 1955. Pageant Press.
Morreale, Vin, Jr.
--The Day the Woods Were One. (Orig.). (gr. 3 up). 1985. (ISBN 0-88734-507-7). Players Pr.
Morrell, Edith Whitcomb, tr. see Purdy, Nina Sutherland.
Morrell, Henry
--Magic Jelly Bean. 1980. (ISBN 0-8062-1565-8). Carlton.
Morressy, John (1930-)
--The Drought on Ziax II. Skardinski, Stanley, illus. LC 77-14651. (Illus.). 77 p. 22cm. 1978. (ISBN 0-8027-6315-4). (ISBN 0-8027-6316-2). Walker.
--The Humans of Ziax II. Skardinski, Stanley, illus. LC 73-92455. (Illus.). 62 p. 24cm. 1974. (ISBN 0-8027-6187-9). Walker.
--The Humans of Ziax II: The Drought on Ziax II. (gr. 3-5). 1980. (ISBN 0-590-30382-1). Scholastic Inc.
--The Windows of Forever. Atkinson, Allen, illus. LC 74-31904. (Illus.). 86 p. 22cm. 1975. (ISBN 0-8027-6219-0). Walker.
Morrill, Belle Chapman
--Simon Called Peter. Larkin, E. Louise, illus. LC 49-71271. 95 p. illus. 21 cm. 1948. Judson Press.
Morrill, Leslie H, jt. auth. see Miles, Miska.
Morrill, Lily Logan, Mrs. (1877-)
--Virginia's War. LC 35-20295. 185 p. 19 1/2 cm. c.1935. Dorrance & Company.
Morrill, Madge Haines
--Happy Children. LC 48-21610. 125 p. illus. (part col.) 24 cm. 1948. Southern Pub. Assn.
Morris, Alfred E.
--The Last Viking: A Fable. 1977. (ISBN 0-682-48738-4). Exposition.
Morris, Alice Talwyn
--The Trouble of Tatters, and Other Stories. (Illus.). (The Wellesley Series for Girls). N.D. A. L. Burt.
--The Troubles of Tatters, and Other Stories, 36 vols. (Illus.). (St. Nicholas Ser.). 1905. Set. A L Burt Co.
--Troubles of Tatters and Other Stories. (Illus.). (Scribner-Blackie Series of Books for Young People). N.D. Charles Scribner's Sons.
Morris, Alton Chester (1903-), compiled by.
--Folksongs of Florida. N.D. University of Florida Press.
Morris, Celia F.
--New Friends, New Places. 97p. 1982. (ISBN 0-533-03390-X). Vantage.
Morris, Charles (1833-1922), ed. see Malory, Thomas, Sir.
Morris, Charles Dexter (1883-)
--Land of the Whatsit ... Adventures of Billy and Betty. Banks, Joe, illus. LC 35-32774. 333 p. illus. 20 cm. c.1935. The Macaulay Company.
Morris, Charles (1833-1922), adapted by.
--King Arthur and the Knights of the Round Table. (Illus.). N.D. J. B. Lippincott Co.
Morris, Clara (0000-1925)
--Little "Jim Crow" and Other Stories of Children. LC 143. vii p., 1 l., 226 p. front. 18 cm. 1899. The Century Co.
Morris, Cora
--Four Gypsy Children. Fouse, Dorothea, illus. LC 31-962382. 5 p. l., 80 p., 1 l. incl. illus., plates. front. 22 cm. 1931. The Macmillan Company.
--Stories Always New: As Told for Children. Inglis, Antoinette, illus. LC 21-680431. 197 p. col. front., col. plates. 20 1/2 cm. c.1921. Lothrop, Lee & Shepard Co.
Morris, Cora, ed.
--The Gypsy Story Teller. Dobias, Frank (1902-), illus. LC 31-201961. xvi, 206 p. col. front., illus. 23 1/2 cm. 1931. The Macmillan Company.
Morris, Dorothy B
--Morning Glory Cottage. LC 48-6532. 72 p. illus. 21 cm. 1948. W. B. Eerdmans Pub. Co.
Morris, Dudley Henry (1912-)
--Mike, the Monk. LC 42-23635. 56 p. col. illus. 25 cm. 1942. G. P. Putnam's Sons.
--Peter and Patrick. 29 p. illus. (part. col.) 21 x 28 cm. 1947. G. P. Putnam's Sons.
--The Truck that Flew. Morris, Dudley Henry (1912-), illus. LC 42-2897. 32 p.col.illus. 21x28 cm. c.1942. G. P. Putnam's Sons.
Morris, Earl J
--The Cop. LC 51-2763. 126 p. 22 cm. 1951. Exposition Press.
Morris, Gilbert
--Barney Buck and the Flying Solar-Cycle. LC 85-50031. 151 p. 18cm. c.1985. (ISBN 0-8423-0131-3). WindRider Books.
Morris, Harrison Smith (1856-), ed.
--In the Yule-Log Glow. Special ed. (Illus.). N.D. J. B. Lippincott Co.
Morris, Helen
--Grandma's Girls. Hoyt, P. L., illus. LC 2-22671. 19cm. 3p. 1902. Little Brown and Co.
Morris, Ida Dorman
--Golden Fluff. LC 1-26948. 152 p. front. 20 cm. 1901. The Abbey Press.
Morris, James Humphrey (1926-)
--The Upstairs Donkey & Other Stolen Stories. Baynes, Pauline Diana (1922-), illus. LC 61-146641. 126p. illus. 21cm. 1961. (ISBN 0-394-81788-5). Pantheon Books.
Morris, Jay
--Mystery at Stony Cove. Stevens, Mary, illus. LC 55-3581. 64p. illus. 26cm. (Trumpet book, BT60). c.1955. S. Gabriel Sons.
Morris, Jean (1924-)
--Twist of Eight. Knox, Jolyne, illus. LC 82-670080. (Illus.). 128 p. 21cm. 1981. (ISBN 0-7011-2557-8). Chatto & Windus.
Morris, Jennie Guthrie (1888-)
--The Three Purse. Morris, Jennie Guthrie (1888-), illus. LC 55-16985. 74p. illus. 29cm. c.1954. W. C. Morris.
Morris, Jill
--The Boy Who Painted the Sun. Hocking, Geoff, illus. (Illus.). 32p. (ps-3). 1984. (ISBN 0-7226-6052-9, Viking Kestrel). Viking.
Morris, Jill & Wu, Cheng-En (1500-1582)
--Monkey and the White Bone Demon. Sheng, Lin & Chang Fu, Fei, illus. LC 83-17670. p. cm. 1984. (ISBN 0-670-48574-8). (ISBN 0-670-48574-8). Viking Press.
Morris, Johnny
--Delilah. Wood, Leslie, illus. LC 65-10039. 24p. illus. 26cm. 1964. F. Watts.
Morris, Johnny, ed.
--The Faber Book of Animal Stories. 1978. (ISBN 0-571-11221-8). Faber & Faber.
--The Faber Book of Animal Stories. LC 84-13537. 1984. (ISBN 0-571-13281-2). Faber and Faber.
Morris, Joseph (1889-) & Adams, St. Clair (1883-), eds.
--Mother's Baby Book. LC 25-24373. 21 p. l., 214 p. 18 cm. c.1925. G. Sully & Company.
Morris, Judy K
--The Crazies & Sam. LC 84-17941. 136 p. 20cm. 1985, c.1983. (ISBN 0-14-031833-X). Puffin Books.
--The Crazies and Sam. LC 82-8380. p. cm. 1983. (ISBN 0-670-24545-3). Viking Press.
Morris, Kenneth see Morus, Cenydid, pseud.
Morris, Kenneth (1879-1937)
--Book of the Three Dragons. LC 77-84257. (Illus.). xii, 206 p., 7 leaves of plates. 24cm. (Lost Race and Adult Fantasy Fiction). 1978, c.1930. (ISBN 0-405-11001-4). Arno Press.
--Book of the Three Dragons. Horvath, Ferdinand Huszti (1891-), illus. LC 30-23656. xii, 206 p. front., illus., plates. 26 cm. c.1930. Longmans, Green and Co.
--The Fates of the Princes of Dyfed. Morus, Cenydid, pseud. Machell, R. W., illus. LC 14-17491. 4 p. l., v-xiv, 4, 3-365 p. incl. front., illus. 25 cm. c.1914. Aryan Theosophical Press.
--The Fates of the Princes of Dyfed. Morus, Cenydid, pseud. Machell, R. W., illus. LC 78-106149. (Illus.). xix, 355 p. 21cm. (Newcastle Forgotten Fantasy library ; v. 15). 1978. (ISBN 0-87877-114-X). Newcastle Pub. Co.
Morris, L., retold by.
--Pilgrim's Progress: Retold for Children. (Original Author: John Bunyan, 1628-1688). 1954. Christian Lit.
Morris, Louis, ed.
--Great Humorous Stories. Greene, Hamilton, illus. LC 64-24883. 191p. illus. 23cm. (Sunrise lib.). 1965. Hart.
Morris, M. C. O., jt. auth. see DeBosschere, Jean.
Morris, M. C. O., tr. see Bosschere, Jean De.
Morris, M. C. O., tr. see Ridder, Andre De.
Morris, Marilyn Ritner
--Mother Married a Diplomat. LC 65-2619. 123p. illus. 32cm. c.1965. Pageant.
Morris, Mary
--Vanishing Animals & Other Stories. (Illus.). 192p. 1980. (ISBN 0-87923-388-5). Godine.
Morris, Mike
--Mouse in My Garden. 12p. (Orig.). (Mouse Board Bks.). 1984. (ISBN 0-8431-1195-X). Price Stern.
--Mouse in My Room. 12p. (Orig.). (Mouse Board Bks.). 1985. (ISBN 0-8431-1194-1). Price Stern.
--Mouse in My Toybox. 12p. (Orig.). (Mouse Board Bks.). 1984. (ISBN 0-8431-1196-8). Price Stern.
Morris, Neil see Lorenzini, Carlo.
Morris, Neil & Morris, Ting
--The Black Knight's Plot. Clarke, Anna (1919-), illus. LC 85-40304. p. cm. 1985, c.1983. (ISBN 0-382-09110-8). (ISBN 0-382-09105-1). Silver Burdett Co.
--Fire in the Town. Clarke, Anna (1919-), illus. LC 85-40303. p. cm. 1985, c.1983. (ISBN 0-382-09111-6). (ISBN 0-382-09107-8). Silver Burdett Co.
--Queen of the Tournament. Clarke, Anna (1919-), illus. LC 85-40299. p. cm. 1985, c.1983. (ISBN 0-382-09113-2). (ISBN 0-382-09109-4). Silver Burdett Co.
--Secret of the Forest. Clarke, Anna (1919-), illus. LC 85-40300. p. cm. 1985. (ISBN 0-382-09112-4). (ISBN 0-382-09108-6). Silver Burdett Co.
Morris, Patricia, tr. see Gant, Roland.
Morris, Phyllis
--Peter Pencil. N.D. (ISBN 0-8283-1154-4). Branden Press.
Morris, Rhoda, pseud., see Morris-Stephenson, Delia.
Morris, Rhoda, pseud. & Nelson, Rhoda
--Bad Penny. Morris-Stephenson, Delia. Nelson, Arthur R., illus. LC 37-23778. (Rhoda Morris is a Joint Pseud. for Delia Morris-Stephenson & Rhoda Nelson.). (Illus.). 20 1/2cm. v, 254p. 1937. Little, Brown.
--Peter's Pencil. Morris-Stephenson, Delia. LC 21-275936. (Rhoda Morris is a Joint Pseud. for Delia Morris-Stephenson & Rhoda Nelson.). 123 p. incl. front., plates. 26 cm. 1920. John Lane.
--Sun Bird. Morris-Stephenson, Delia. Nelson, Arthur R., illus. LC 36-20255. (Rhoda Morris is a Joint Pseud. for Delia Morris-Stephenson & Rhoda Nelson.). 4 p. l., 3-255 p. incl. illus., plates. front. 20 1/2 cm. 1936. Little, Brown, and Company.
--Susan and Arabella: Pioneers. Morris-Stephenson, Delia. Hauman, George & Hauman, Doris, Mrs. (1897-), illus. LC 35-18080. (Rhoda Morris is the Joint Pseud. for Delia Morris-Stepnenson and Rhoda Nelson). 5 p. l., 3-247 p. incl. plates. front. 20 1/2 cm. 1935. Little, Brown, and Company.
--Susan and Little Bird Lost. Morris-Stephenson, Delia. Hauman, George (1890-1961) & Hauman, Doris, Mrs. (1897-), illus. LC 41-17582. (Rhoda Morris is the joint Pseud. of Delia Morris-Stephenson and Rhoda Nelson). 4 p. l., 3-239 p. incl. illus., plates. col. front. 20 1/2 cm. 1941. Little, Brown and Company.
Morris, Robert A.
--Dolphin. Funai, Mamoru R. (1932-), illus. LC 75-6292. (Illus.). 5 7/8 x 8 1/2. 64p. (18 pt.). (Nature I Can Read Bks.). (gr. k-3). 1975. (ISBN 0-06-024342-2) (ISBN 0-06-444043-5) Har-Row.
--Seahorse. LC 70-146004. (Illus.). 5 7/8 x 8 1/2. 64p. (18 pt.). (Nature I Can Read Bks.). (gr. k-3). 1972. (ISBN 0-06-024342-2) Har-Row.
Morris, Robert Hugh (1876-)
--The Prince and the Pig's Gate and Other Sermons in Story. Martin, Paul, illus. LC 28-13490. viii p., 2 l., 203, 1 p. front., plates. 20 cm. 1928. Harper & Brothers.
Morris, Rosamund, ed.
--Great Detective Stories. Kramer, Frank, illus. LC 64-24881. 191 p. illus. 23 cm. (Sunrise library). 1965. Hart Pub. Co.
--Great Horror Stories. Greene, Hamilton, illus. LC 64-24882. 191p. illus. 23cm. (Sunrise lib.). c.1965. Hart.
--Great Suspense Stories. 192p. 1962. Hart Publishing Co., Inc.
Morris, Ruth Ellen Allen
--The White Dog. 109 p. 21cm. 1974. (ISBN 0-533-00999-5). Vantage Press.
Morris, Ruth (1926-)
--Runaway Girl. Krush, Beth (1918-), illus. LC 62-17239. 216p. illus. 21cm. 1962. Random House.
--Runaway Girl. Krush, Beth (1918-), illus. (Illus.). (gr. 5-10). 1966. (ISBN 0-394-91568-2). Random.
Morris-Stephenson, Delia see Morris, Rhoda, pseud.
Morris-Suzuki, Tessa
--Odo, the Snail. (Illus.). N.D. (ISBN 0-85122-161-0, Pub. by Dinosaur Pubns). Merrimack Pub Cir.
Morris, Terry Nell
--Goodnight, Dear Monster!. Morris, Terry Nell, illus. LC 79-26904. (Illus.). 28 p. 15cm. (ps-2). c.1980. (ISBN 0-394-84221-9). (ISBN 0-394-94221-3). Knopf : Distributed by Random House.
--Just Sixteen. 176p. (Orig.). (gr. 7 up). 1980. (ISBN 0-590-31341-X, Wildfire). Scholastic Inc.
--Lucky Puppy! Lucky Boy!. Morris, Terry Nell, illus. LC 79-27024. (Illus.). 28 p. 15cm. c.1980. (ISBN 0-394-84220-0). (ISBN 0-394-94220-5). Knoph : Distributed by Random House.
--On Your Toes. 176p. (Orig.). (gr. 7 up). 1984. (ISBN 0-590-33692-4, Wildfire). Scholastic Inc.
Morris, Ting, jt. auth. see Morris, Neil.
Morris, Toni
--Oldie, the Engine that Won. LC 53-13119. 35p. 1953. Pageant Press, Inc.
Morris-Vann, Artie M.
--My Dad Is Unemployed... but. Orlowski, Dennis, illus. (Illus.). 40p. (Orig.). (It's Not the End of the World Ser.). (ps-5). 1981. (ISBN 0-940370-01-8). (ISBN 0-940370-05-0). Aid-U Pub.
Morris, Victoria S.
--The Hand Puppet Show: Methods & Plays. rev ed. (gr. 1-8). 1976. (ISBN 0-914318-01-2). V S Morris.
Morris, Walter
--Bob Porter at Lakeview Academy. (The Boys Own Library). N.D. David McKay.
--Bob Porter at Lakeview Academy. LC 3-17002. 294p. 19cm. (Boys' Own Library). 1903. Street & Smith.
Morris, William Barrett
--The Longest Journey in the World. Fraser, Betty M., pseud. (1928-) & Barber, Ray, illus. Fraser, Elizabeth Marr. LC 73-107087. (Illus.). 31 p. 17cm. (Bill Martin Instant Reader). 1970. (ISBN 0-03-084577-7). Holt, Rinehart and Winston.
--The Oyster's Secret. Morris, William Barrett, illus. LC 78-188861. (Illus.). 32 p. 1972. Hubbard Press.
Morris, William (1834-1896)
--Stories from The Earthly Paradise. Evans, Charles Seddon (1883-), retold by. vii, 247 p. col. front., plates. 19 cm. 1915. Longmans, Green & Co.
--Story of Sigurd. N.D. Longmans, Green.
--Story of the Glittering Plain. N.D. Longmans, Green.
--Tale of Beowulf. N.D. Longmans, Green.
--Water of the Wondrous Isles. N.D. Longmans, Green.
--The Wolf's-Head and the Queen. Shepard, Morgan (1865-), ed. Grofe, Nelson, illus. LC 31-25769. (Retold from "Child Christopher."). xiv p., 2 l., 243, 1 p.incl. illus., plates. col. front. 23 cm. 1931. C. Scribner's Sons.
Morris, William (1834-1896) & Hosford, Dorothy Grant (1900-1952), eds.
--Sons of the Volsungs. Dobias, Frank (1902-), illus. LC 49-8722. x, 168 p. illus. 22 cm. 1949. Holt.

AUTHOR INDEX MORROW, ELIZABETH

--Sons of the Volsungs. Dobias, Frank (1902-), illus. LC 32-30926. x p., 2 l., 168 p., 1 l. incl. front., illus. plates. 22 1/2 cm. 1932. The Macmillan Company.

Morris, Willie

--Good Old Boy. LC 75-157897. 196p. (gr. 5 up). 1971. (ISBN 0-06-024336-8, HarpJ). Har-Row.

Morris, Winifred

--With Magical Horses to Ride. LC 84-21633. (Illus.). 152 p., 1 leaf of plates. 22cm. 1985. (ISBN 0-689-31108-7). Atheneum.

Morrison, Bill (1935-)

--Louis James Hates School. Morrison, Bill (1935-), illus. LC 78-60496. (Illus.). 32 p. 1978. (ISBN 0-395-27156-8). Houghton Mifflin.

--[illegible] Says. Morrison, Bill (1935-), illus. LC 83-9431. (Illus.). 32 p. 20cm. c.1983. (ISBN 0-316-58475-4). Little, Brown.

--Squeeze a Sneeze. Morrison, Bill (1935-), illus. LC 76-62503. 32p. (gr. k-3). 1977. (ISBN 0-395-25151-6). HM.

Morrison, Carrie E.

--The Adventures of the Pixies and Elaines. Birch, Reginald Bathurst, et al. (1856-1943), illus. LC 4218. 20 x 16cm. 125p. 1900. D. Estes & Co.

The Pixie & Elaine Stories. Birch, Reginald Bathurst (1856-1943), illus. N.D. Dana Estes & Co.

Morrison, Dorothy Nafus

--Mystery of the Last Concert. LC 72-130525. 143p. 1971. (ISBN 0-664-32486-X). Westminster Press.

--Whisper Goodbye. LC 84-21626. 183 p. 22cm. 1985. (ISBN 0-689-31109-5). Atheneum.

Morrison, Frank M. (1914-)

--Adventure Stories for Boys. LC 75-99266. (Illus.). 98 p. 25cm. 1969. T. S. Denison.

Morrison, Gertrude W., pseud., see Stratemeyer Syndicate.

Morrison, Gertrude W., pseud.

--The Girls of Central High Aiding the Red Cross: Or, Amateur Theatricals for a Worthy Cause. Stratemeyer Syndicate. Owen, Robert Emmett (1878-), illus. (The Girls of Central High Ser.: Vol. 7). 1919. Grosset & Dunlap.

--The Girls of Central High Aiding the Red Cross: Or, Amateur Theatricals for a Worthy Cause. Stratemeyer Syndicate. Owen, Robert Emmett (1878-), illus. Repr. of 1919 ed (Pub. by Grosset & Dunlap). (The Girls of Central High Ser.: Vol. 7). N.D. Saalfield Publishing Co.

--The Girls of Central High Aiding the Red Cross: Or, Amateur Theatricals for a Worthy Cause. Stratemeyer Syndicate. Owen, Robert Emmett (1878-), illus. Repr. of 1919 ed (Pub. by Grosset & Dunlap). (The Girls of Central High Ser.: Vol. 7). N.D. World Syndicate Publishing Co.

--The Girls of Central High at Basketball: Or, The Great Gymnasium Mystery. Stratemeyer Syndicate. Repr. of 1914 ed (Pub. by Grosset & Dunlap). (The Girls of Central High Ser.: Vol. 3). N.D. Goldsmith Publishing Co.

--The Girls of Central High at Basketball: Or, The Great Gymnasium Mystery. Stratemeyer Syndicate. (Illus.). (The Girls of Central High Ser.: Vol. 3). 1914. Grosset & Dunlap.

--The Girls of Central High at Basketball: Or, The Great Gymnasium Mystery. Stratemeyer Syndicate. Repr. of 1914 ed (Pub. by Grosset & Dunlap). (The Girls of Central High Ser.: Vol. 3). N.D. Saalfield Publishing Co.

--The Girls of Central High at Basketball: Or, The Great Gymnasium Mystery. Stratemeyer Syndicate. Repr. of 1914 ed (Pub. by Grosset & Dunlap). (The Girls of Central High Ser.: Vol. 3). N.D. World Syndicate Publishing Co.

--The Girls of Central High in Camp: Or, The Old Professor's Secret. Stratemeyer Syndicate. Rogers, Walter S., illus. (The Girls of Central High Ser.: Vol. 6). 1915. Grosset & Dunlap.

--The Girls of Central High in Camp: Or, The Old Professor's Secret. Stratemeyer Syndicate. Rogers, Walter S., illus. Repr. of 1915 ed (Pub. by Grosset & Dunlap). (The Girls of Central High Ser.: Vol. 6). N.D. Saalfield Publishing Co.

--The Girls of Central High in Camp: Or, The Old Professor's Secret. Stratemeyer Syndicate. Rogers, Walter S., illus. Repr. of 1915 ed (Pub. by Grosset & Dunlap). (The Girls of Central High Ser.: Vol. 6). N.D. World Syndicate Publishing Co.

--The Girls of Central High on Lake Luna: Or, The Crew that Won. Stratemeyer Syndicate. Richards, Jim H., illus. Repr. of 1914 ed (Pub. by Grosset & Dunlap). (The Girls of Central High Ser.: Vol. 2). N.D. Goldsmith Publishing Co.

--The Girls of Central High on Lake Luna: Or, The Crew that Won. Stratemeyer Syndicate. Richards, Jim H., illus. (The Girls of Central High Ser.: Vol. 2). 1914. Grosset & Dunlap.

--The Girls of Central High on Lake Luna: Or, The Crew that Won. Stratemeyer Syndicate. Richards, Jim H., illus. Repr. of 1914 ed (Pub. by Grosset & Dunlap). (The Girls of Central High Ser.: Vol. 2). N.D. Saalfield Publishing Co.

--The Girls of Central High on Lake Luna: Or, The Crew that Won. Stratemeyer Syndicate. Richards, Jim H., illus. Repr. of 1914 ed (Pub. by Grosset & Dunlap). (The Girls of Central High Ser.: Vol. 2). N.D. World Syndicate Publishing Co.

--The Girls of Central High on the Stage: Or, The Play that Took the Prize. Stratemeyer Syndicate. Richards, Dick, illus. Repr. of 1914 ed (Pub. by Grosset & Dunlap). (The Girls of Central High Ser.: Vol. 4). N.D. Goldsmith Publishing Co.

--The Girls of Central High on the Stage: Or, The Play that Took the Prize. Stratemeyer Syndicate. Richards, Dick, illus. (The Girls of Central High Ser.: Vol. 4). 1914. Grosset & Dunlap.

--The Girls of Central High on the Stage: Or, The Play that Took the Prize. Stratemeyer Syndicate. Richards, Dick, illus. Repr. of 1914 ed (Pub. by Grosset & Dunlap). (The Girls of Central High Ser.: Vol. 4). N.D. Saalfield Publishing Co.

--The Girls of Central High on the Stage: Or, The Play that Took the Prize. Stratemeyer Syndicate. Richards, Dick, illus. Repr. of 1914 ed (Pub. by Grosset & Dunlap). (The Girls of Central High Ser.: Vol. 4). N.D. World Syndicate Publishing Co.

--The Girls of Central High on Track and Field: Or, The Girl Champions of the School League. Stratemeyer Syndicate. Repr. of 1914 ed (Pub. by Grosset & Dunlap). (The Girls of Central High Ser.: Vol. 5). N.D. Goldsmith Publishing Co.

--The Girls of Central High on Track and Field: Or, The Girl Champions of the School League. Stratemeyer Syndicate. (Illus.). (The Girls of Central High Ser.: Vol. 5). 1914. Grosset & Dunlap.

--The Girls of Central High on Track and Field: Or, The Girl Champions of the School League. Stratemeyer Syndicate. Repr. of 1914 ed (Pub. by Grosset & Dunlap). (The Girls of Central High Ser.: Vol. 5). N.D. Saalfield Publishing Co.

--The Girls of Central High on Track and Field: Or, The Girl Champions of the School League. Stratemeyer Syndicate. Repr. of 1914 ed (Pub. by Grosset & Dunlap). (The Girls of Central High Ser.: Vol. 5). N.D. World Syndicate Publishing Co.

--The Girls of Central High: Or, Rivals for all Honors. Stratemeyer Syndicate. Richards, Dick, illus. Repr. of 1914 ed (Pub. by Grosset & Dunlap). (The Girls of Central High Ser.: Vol. 1). N.D. Goldsmith Publishing Co.

--The Girls of Central High: Or, Rivals for all Honors. Stratemeyer Syndicate. Richards, Dick, illus. (The Girls of Central High Ser.: Vol. 1). 1914. Grosset & Dunlap.

--The Girls of Central High: Or, Rivals for all Honors. Stratemeyer Syndicate. Richards, Dick, illus. Repr. of 1914 ed (Pub. by Grosset & Dunlap). (The Girls of Central High Ser.: Vol. 1). N.D. Saalfield Publishing Co.

--The Girls of Central High: Or, Rivals for all Honors. Stratemeyer Syndicate. Richards, Dick, illus. Repr. of 1914 ed (Pub. by Grosset & Dunlap). (The Girls of Central High Ser.: Vol. 1). N.D. World Syndicate Publishing Co.

Morrison, Harry Steele (1880-)

--The Adventures of a Boy Reporter, 39 vols. (Illus.). (Famous Books for Boys Ser.: No. 16). 1905. Set. H M Caldwell Co.

--The Adventures of a Boy Reporter. Bridgman, Lewis Jesse (1857-1931), illus. 20cm. 153p. 1900. L. C. Page & Co.

--The Adventures of a Boy Reporter in the Phillipines. (Illus.). (The Boy's Own Authors Ser.). N.D. Dana Estes & Co.

--A Yankee Boy's Success. (Illus.). (Library for Boys and Girls Ser.). N.D. Frederick A. Stokes Co.

--A Yankee Boy's Success. Tobin, George T., illus. Depew, C. M., intro. by. LC 98-1414. 278p. 1898. F. A. Stokes Co.

Morrison, Helena V.

--Class of Seventy, 1 of 20 vols. New ed. (Illus.). 350p. (Sunday-School Lib: No. 13). 1895. Set. Lothrop Pub. Co.

Morrison, J. Strang, pseud., see Thom, William Albert Strang.

Morrison, Lenora Marianne

--The Little Engine Who Could Blow Smoke Rings. Morrison, William James (1909-), illus. LC 47-254646. 19 p. illus. 22 cm. 1947. Press of the Crippled Turtle.

Morrison, Lillian (1917-)

--The Break Dance Kids: Poems of Sport, Motion, and Locomotion. LC 84-23396. (Illus.). 63 p. 22cm. c.1985. (ISBN 0-688-04553-7). (ISBN 0-688-04554-5). Lothrop, Lee & Shepard Books.

Morrison, Lillian (1917-), compiled by.

--A Diller, A Dollar: Rhymes and Sayings for the Ten O'Clock Scholar. Bauernschmidt, Marjorie (1926-), illus. 160p. 1955. Thomas Y. Crowell.

--Best Wishes, Amen: A New Collection of Autograph Verses. Lustig, Loretta, illus. LC 74-2456. (Illus.). xii, 195 p. 1974. (ISBN 0-690-00579-2). Crowell.

--Black Within & Red Without: A Book of Riddles. Spier, Jo, illus. LC 53-8420. (Illus.). 120p. (gr. 4 up). 1953. (ISBN 0-690-14656-6, TYC-J). Har-Row.

--A Diller, a-Dollar: Rhymes and Sayings for the Ten O'Clock Scholar. 1955. Harper.

--Overheard in a Bubble Chamber & Other Sciencepoems. De Lanux, Eyre, illus. LC 80-26522. (Illus.). 64p. (gr. 7 up). 1981. (ISBN 0-688-00490-3). (ISBN 0-688-00493-8). Lothrop.

--Remember Me When This You See: A New Collection of Autograph Verses. Bauernschmidt, Marjorie (1926-), illus. LC 60-11536. (Illus.). 182 p. 8p. 1961. Crowell.

--Remember Me When This You See: A New Collection of Autograph Verses. Authorized abridged. Bauernschmidt, Marjorie (1926-), illus. (Illus.). 11 x 16cm. 96p. 1964, c.1961. Scholastic.

--The Sidewalk Racer, and Other Poems of Sports and Motion. LC 77-907. (Illus.). 62 p. 22cm. c.1977. (ISBN 0-688-41805-8). (ISBN 0-688-51805-2). Lothrop, Lee & Shepard Co.

--Sprints & Distances: Sports in Poetry & the Poetry in Sport. Ross, Clare Romano (1922-) & Ross, John (1921-), illus. LC 65-14906. (Illus.). (gr. 5 up). 1965. (ISBN 0-690-76571-1, TYC-J). Har-Row. **Award: (ALA).**

--Touch Blue. Lee, Doris Emrick (1905-1983), illus. 1958. T. Crowell.

--Who Would Marry a Mineral?. Riddles, Runes, and Love Tunes. Leydon, Rita Floden (1949-), illus. LC 78-2494. (Illus.). 61 p. 22cm. c.1978. (ISBN 0-688-41846-5). (ISBN 0-688-51846-X). Lothrop, Lee & Shepard Co.

--Yours Till Niagara Falls. Bauernschmidt, Marjorie (1926-), illus. LC 50-6508. 182 p. illus. 14 x 19 cm. 1950. Crowell.

Morrison, Lucile Phillips (1896-)

--The Attic-Child. Pyne, Mable Mandeville (1903-1969), illus. LC 29-167739. 6 p. l., 299 p. col. front., illus. 19 1/2cm. 1929. Frederick A. Stokes Company.

--The Blue Bandits. Pyne, Mable Mandeville (1903-1969), illus. LC 30-20593. 5 p. l., 818 p. col. front., illus. 19 1/2cm. 1930. Frederick A. Stokes Company.

--The Blue Bandits. Pyne, Mable Mandeville (1903-1969), photos by. N.D. J. B. Lippincott.

--The Lost Queen of Egypt. Geritz, Franz & Brunton, Winifred, illus. LC 37-28730. xii p., 1 l., 867, 1 p. col. front., illus. 21 1/2cm. c.1937. Frederick A. Stokes Company.

--The Lost Queen of Egypt. Geritz, Franz, illus. 1937. J. B. Lippincott Co.

--Mystery Gate. Bromhall, Winifred, illus. LC 28-21489. 6 p. l., 257 p. incl. plates. col. front. 19 1/2cm. 1928. Frederick A. Stokes Company.

--Mystery Gate. Bromhall, Winifred, illus. N.D. J. B. Lippincott.

--The Mystery of Shadow Walk. LC 63-18784. 183 p. 21 cm. 1964. Dodd, Mead.

Morrison, Margaret Mackie see Morrison, Peggy, pseud.

Morrison, Mary

--Every-Day Margaret. 349p. N.D. Congregational Sunday-School and Publishing Society.

--Over the Threshold to Manhood. LC 12-150. 1 p. l., 5-64 p. illus. 17 1/2cm. $0.12. c.1911. David C. Cook Publishing Co.

Morrison, Mary Jane Whitney, Mrs. (1832-1904), compiled by.

--Songs and Rhymes for the Little Ones. LC 13-17859. xi, 234 p. 20 1/2cm. 1884. G. P. Putnam's Sons.

--Songs and Rhymes for the Little Ones. (Gift Book Ser.). N.D. L. C. Page & Co.

--Songs and Rhymes for the Little Ones. New ed. Whitney, Adeline Dutton Train, Mrs. (1824-1906) LC 4-13834. xi, 244 p. front., plates. 20cm. 1896. J. Knight Company.

--Songs and Rhymes for the Little Ones. New ed. Whitney, Adeline Dutton Train, Mrs. (1824-1906), intro. by. (Illus.). 12mocm. N.D. L. C. Page & Co.

--Stories True and Fancies New. Bridgman, Lewis Jesse (1857-1931), illus. (Little People's Ser.). N.D. Dana Estes and Company.

--Stories True and Fancies New. Bridgman, Lewis Jesse (1857-1931), illus. Sacker, Amy, designed by. (The Story Book House). N.D. Dana Estes and Company.

Morrison, Peggy, pseud., see Morrison, Margaret Mackie.

Morrison, Peggy, pseud. (0000-1973)

--The Bitter Green of the Willow: Four Fairy Tales. Morrison, Margaret Mackie. Anderson, Anne, illus. LC 67-23818. (Illus.). 76 p. 26cm. 1967. Chilton Book Co.

Morrison, Sarah Elizabeth

--Chilhowee Boys. (Illus.). (Crowell's Young People Ser.). N.D. Thomas Y. Crowell.

--Chilhowee Boys. LC 12-37080. v. 434 p. front., 2 pl. 19cm. c.1893. T.Y. Crowell & Co.

--Chilhowee Boys at College. (Illus.). (The Chilhowee Ser.). 1905. Thomas Y. Crowell & Co.

--Chilhowee Boys at College. (Illus.). (Crowell's Young People Ser.). N.D. Thomas Y. Crowell.

--Chilhowee Boys in Harness. vi, 384 p. front., plates. 18 1/2cm. (The Chilhowee series). 1898. T. Y. Crowell & Company.

--Chilhowee Boys in Harness. (Illus.). (The Chilhowee Ser.). 1905. Thomas Y. Crowell & Co.

--Chilhowee Boys in War Time. LC 12-37079. vi, 382 p. front., plates. 18 1/2cm. (The Chillhowee series). c.1895. T. Y. Crowell & Company.

--Chilhowee Boys in War Time. (Illus.). (The Chilhowee Ser.). 1905. Thomas Y. Crowell & Co.

--Chilhowee Boys in War Time. (Illus.). (Crowell's Young People Ser.). N.D. Thomas Y. Crowell.

Morrison, Sean

--Is That a Happy Hippopotamus?. Aliki, pseud. (1929-), illus. Brandenberg, Aliki Liacouras. LC 66-7771. (Illus.). 1 v. (unpaged). 22cm. 1966. Crowell.

Morrison, Velma Ford see Ford, Hildegarde, pseud.

Morrison, William, pseud., see Samachson, Joseph.

Morrison, William, jt. auth. see Wood, Audrey.

Morrison, William James

--Charley Circus Among the Indians of Brazil. (Charley Circus Stories). N.D. Cokesbury Press.

--Charley Circus Among the Indians of Brazil. LC 14-214291. 135 p. col. front., illus. (part col.) 19 1/2cm. (Morrison's System of Natural History Stories). c.1913. Publishing House M. E. Church, South, Smith & Lamar; Agents.

--Charley Circus Hunting and Trapping in Brazil. (Charley Circus Stories). N.D. Cokesbury Press.

--Charley Circus Hunting and Trapping in Brazil. LC 14-21430. 135 p. col. front., illus. (part col.) 19 1/2cm. (Morrison's System of Natural History Stories). c.1914. Publishing House M. E. Church, South, Smith & Lamar, Agents.

--Charley Circus in the Wilds of Brazil. (Charley Circus Stories). N.D. Cokesbury Press.

--Charley Circus in the Wilds of Brazil. LC 14-214314. 139 p. col. front. col. illus. 19 1/2cm. (Morrison's System of Natural History Stories). c.1914. Publishing House M. E. Church, South, Smith & Lamar, Agents.

--Willie Wyld. LC 14-17623. 131 p. front., illus. 19 1/2 cm. (Morrison's System of Natural History Stories)). c.1912. Publishing House M. E. Church, South, Smith & Lamar, Agents.

--Willie Wyld: His Wonderful Voyage to the Island of Zanzibar. (Willie Wyld Stories). N.D. Cokesbury Press.

--Willie Wyld Hunting Big Game in Africa. (Willie Wyld Stories). N.D. Cokesbury Press.

--Willie Wyld lost in the Jungles of Africa. (Willie Wyld Stories). N.D. Cokesbury Press.

Morriss, Frank (1923-)

--Alfred of Wessex, the King Who Saved His Country. Boucher, Joseph, illus. LC 59-13271. 148p. illus. 22cm. (Catholic treasury books). 1959. Bruce Pub. Co.

--Boy of Philadelphia: A Story About the Continental Congress. LC 55-848416. 133p. illus. 22cm. (Catholic Treasury Books). 1955. Bruce Pub. Co.

Morrow, Barbara, ed.

--Well Done. 1st ed. Morrow, Barbara, illus. LC 73-20074. (Illus.). 32 p. 1974. (ISBN 0-03-012391-7). Holt, Rinehart and Winston.

Morrow, Betty, pseud., see Bacon, Elizabeth.

Morrow, Elizabeth Reeve Cutter, Mrs. (1873-1955)

--My Favorite Age. Suba, Susanne (1913-), illus. LC 43-160433. 220 p. incl. front., illus. 21 cm. 1943. The Macmillan Company.

--The Painted Pig. D'Harnoncourt, Rene (1901-1968), illus. 1942. Borzoi Books.

--The Painted Pig: A Mexican Picture Book. D'Harnoncourt, Rene (1901-1968), illus. LC 30-269763. 3 p. l., 3-32, 2 p. col. front., illus. (part col. 28cm. 1930. A. A. Knopf.

--A Pint of Judgment. LC 39-32007. 3p. 1939. Alfred A. Knopf.

--A Pint of Judgment: A Christmas Story. Berson, Harold (1926-), illus. LC 60-50261. unpaged. illus. 19cm. 1960. Knopf.

--The Rabbit's Nest. LC 40-35456. (Illus.). 43p. 13 x 10cm. 1940. The Macmillan Co.

--Shannon. 1st ed. Torrey, Helen (1901-), illus. LC 41-21554. 3 p. l., 63, 1 p. incl. front., illus. 13 1/2cm. 1941. The Macmillan Company.

Morrow, Honore McCue Willsie, Mrs. (1880-1940)

--On to Oregon!. The Story of a Pioneer Boy. LC 26-16049. 247p. 19cm. 1926. W. Morrow.

--On to Oregon. The Story of a Pioneer Boy. Shenton, Edward (1895-), illus. LC 46-252327. 239 p. incl. front., illus. (part col.) 20 1/2 cm. (Morrow Junior Books). 1946. W. Morrow and Company.

--Seven Alone. (gr. 7-12). 1977. (ISBN 0-590-10291-5). Scholastic Inc.

Morrow, Honore McCue Willsie, Mrs. (1880-1940) & Swartman, William John

--Ship's Monkey. Grant, Gordon H. (1875-1962), illus. LC 33-25682. 6 p. l., 8-188 p. incl. illus., plates (part col.) col. front. 21cm. 1933. W. Morrow & Company.

--Ship's Parrot. Grant, Gordon H. (1875-1962), illus. LC 36-28561. 4 p. l., 3-180 p. col. front., illus. 21cm. 1936. W. Morrow & Company.

Morrow, Suzanne Stark

--Inatuk's Friend. 1st ed. Raskin, Ellen (1928-1984), illus. LC 68-11114. (Illus.). 48 p. 27cm. 1968. Little, Brown.

--There Was a Time: The Story of Evolution. Arno, Enrico (1913-1981), illus. LC 65-21291. 40p. col. illus. 27cm. 1965. Dutton.

Morse, Anita

--Cissie-Sweet Child of Grace. N.D. Vantage Press Inc.

Morse, Ann, jt. auth. see Morse, Charles.

Morse, Ann & Morse, Charles

--Forward Roll. Bay, Stuart, photos by. LC 73-14698. (Illus.). 31 p. (Their Just like you, just like me). 1973. (ISBN 0-88436-033-4). (ISBN 0-88436-033-4). EMC Corp.

--Lost and Found. Brooks, Nan, illus. LC 73-14687. (Illus.). 32 p. (Their Just Like You, Just Like Me). 1973. (ISBN 0-88436-035-0). (ISBN 0-88436-035-0). EMC Corp.

--Max-I-Fish. Brooks, Nan, illus. LC 73-14783. (Illus.). 32 p. (Their Just Like You, Just Like Me). 1973. (ISBN 0-88436-029-6). (ISBN 0-88436-029-6). EMC Corp.

--On a Tight Rope. Bay, Stuart, photos by. LC 73-14685. (Illus.). 31 p. (Their Just Like You, Just Like Me). 1973. (ISBN 0-88436-031-8). (ISBN 0-88436-031-8). EMC Corp.

Morse, Carol, pseud., see Yeakley, Marjory Hall.

Morse, Charles, jt. auth. see Morse, Ann.

Morse, Charles & Morse, Ann

--Whobody There?. (Illus.). 63p. (Orig.). 1st U.S. edition. (gr. k-6). 1971. (ISBN 0-88489-001-5). St Marys.

Morse, David (1940-)

--Grandfather Rock: The New Poetry & the Old. LC 76-156048. 224p. (gr. 7 up). 1972. Delacorte.

Morse, Douglas

--Long Tom. Cooke, Tom, illus. LC 75-313672. (Illus.). 16 p. 29cm. (His A Storyfold treasure chest book). 1974. (ISBN 0-89008-000-3). Storyfold.

Morse, Elizabeth, Mrs.

--Chang of the Siamese Jungle. Best, Allena Champlin, Mrs. (1892-1974), illus. Berry, Erick, pseud. LC 30-21774. xi, 195 p. incl. front., illus., plates. 20cm. c.1930. E. P. Dutton & Co., Inc.

--The Coconut Monkey. Ayer, Margaret (0000-1981), illus. LC 38-12961. 223, 1 p. illus. 19 1/2cm. 1938. E. P. Dutton & Co., Inc.

--The Siamese Cat. Seymour, Ruth, illus. LC 30-4743. 62p. c.1929. E. P. Dutton & Co.

--The Whistling Snake. Ayer, Margaret (0000-1981), illus. LC 35-15478. 246 p. incl. front., plates. 19 1/2 cm. c.1935. E. P. Dutton & Co., Inc.

Morse, Emily Hewitt

--Happy Days at Hillside. Davidson, Clara D., illus. LC 11-12035. 20cm. 222p. c.1911. E. P. Dutton Co.

Morse, Evangeline

--Brown Rabbit: Her Story. Martin, David Stone (1913-), illus. LC 67-4993. (Illus.). 191 p. 23cm. 1967. (ISBN 0-695-40864-X). Follett Pub. Co.

Morse, Flo (1921-)

--How Does It Feel to Be a Tree?. Watson, Clyde (1947-), illus. LC 75-19177. (Illus.). 30 p. 23cm. c.1976. (ISBN 0-8193-0829-3). (ISBN 0-8193-0830-7). Parents' Magazine Press.

Morse, George

--Extra!. LC 32-11123. 3 p. l., 18-247 p. 19 1/2cm. c.1932. The Goldsmith Publishing Company.

--Vanishing Liner. LC 39-10513. 3 p. l., 11-252 p. 19 1/2cm. c.1934. The Goldsmith Publishing Company.

Morse, Joyce

--Peter Sinks in the Water. 32p. (Orig.). (Books I Can Read). (gr. 2). 1980. (ISBN 0-8127-0281-6). Review & Herald.

Morse, Katharine Duncan (1888-)

--Goldtree and Silvertree: Fairy Plays to Read and Act. Bromhall, Winifred, illus. Le Bron, Marion E., contrib. by. LC 25-24495. vii, 159 p. illus. 19 1/2cm. 1925. The Macmillan Company.

--Peter Was a Pirate. Downer, Marion (1892-1971), illus. LC 39-21145. 65 p. incl. col. front., col. illus. 18 1/2 x 23cm. 1939. E. P. Dutton and Company, Inc.

--The Pig That Danced a Jig. Bromhall, Winifred, illus. LC 38-29525. 33 p. incl. col. front., col. illus. 20 x 24 1/2cm. 1938. E. P. Dutton & Co., Inc.

Morse, Kenneth (1913-)

--A is for Angels: An Alphabet Book for Christmas. Miller, Joyce (1932-), illus. LC 78-5806. p. cm. 1978. (ISBN 0-87178-017-8). Brethen Press.

Morse, Livingston Burrill

--The Road to Nowhere. A Story for Children. Morse, Edna, illus. LC 6279. 3 p. l., 236 p. col. front., col. illus. 19cm. 1900. Harper & Bros.

Morse, Lucy Gibbons, Mrs. (1839-)

--Breezes. LC 21-18888. (Illus.). viii, 46p. 22cm. 1921. Houghton Mifflin Company.

--Rachel Stanwood: A Story of the Middle of the Nineteenth Century. LC 19-6562. 3 p. l., 441 p. 18 1/2cm. 1893. Houghton, Mifflin and Company.

Morse, Mary Lincoln & Baruch, Dorothy Walter, Mrs., eds.

--Stories & Verse. Torrey, Helen (1901-), illus. LC 37-5362. xi, 5, 272 p. illus. (part col.) 23 1/2cm. (Half-title: Childhood, the Beginning Years and Beyond ... vol. IV; edited by the Association for childhood education)). 1937. Houghton Mifflin Company.

Morse, Murray see Morse, Ray, pseud.

Morse, Murray (1921-)

--Cadets at Kings Point. Morse, Ray, pseud. LC 49-11183. 249 p. 21 cm. 1949. Aladdin Books.

Morse, Ray, pseud., see Morse, Murray.

Morse, Samuel French (1916-)

--All in a Suitcase. Cooney, Barbara (1917-), illus. (Illus.). (Original verse in an alphabet-game book that collects rare animals for a favorite trip). (gr. 1-3). 1966. (ISBN 0-316-58513-0). Little.

--Sea Sums. Akino, Fuku (1908-), illus. LC 70-91229. (Illus.). 32 p. 1970. Little, Brown.

Morss, Lee (1903-), ed.

--The "Claytoon" Book of Fairy Tales ... Sass-Dorne Studios, Los Angeles, illus. LC 47-19783. 32 p. col. illus. 27 1/2 cm. 1946. J. L. Schilling Co.

Morss, Willard N. & Herren, Janet M., eds.

--Stolen Princess: A Northwest Indian Legend. Millard, Carolyn, illus. LC 83-82920. (Illus.). 44p. (Orig.). (gr. 4-8). 1983. (ISBN 0-9613025-0-X). J M Herren.

Mortenson, Dagny, tr. see Aanrud, Hans.

Mortimer, Favell Lee Bevan, Mrs. (1802-1878)

--Bible Stories. (By the author of "Peep of Day." Eight books with bright colors in a box.). 1879. American Tract Society.

--Peep of Day. (Illus.). N.D. George Routledge & Sons.

--The Peep of Day: Or, A Series of the Earliest Religious Instruction the Infant Mind Is Capable of Receiving. LC 27-3646. xiv, 15-238 p. 15 cm. 1849. Baker and Scribner.

--The Peep of Day: Or, A Series of the Earliest Religious Instruction the Infant Mind Is Capable of Receiving. 5th American, from the 7th London ed. LC 21-30496. xiv, 15-228 p. 15 cm. 1848. American Tract Society.

Mortimer, M. L.

--The Shepherd Boy & the Dancing Dog. (Illus.). (ps-3). N.D. Dghtrs St Paul.

Morton, Elizabeth

--The Illuminated Bible Story Book. N.D. John C. Winston Co.

--Rags, the Firehouse Dog. Morgan, Dennis, illus. LC 52-8979. (Illus.). 42p. (gr. k-4). 1952. (ISBN 0-03-035130-8). HR&W.

Morton, Elizabeth, intro. by see Lorenzini, Carlo.

Morton, G. E.

--From Egypt to Canaan. (Sequel to "From the Beginning). N.D. Thos Nelson & Sons.

--From the Beginning: Or, Stories from Genesis. N.D. Thos Nelson & Sons.

Morton, Jane (1931-)

--I Am Rubber, You Are Glue. LC 81-2751. p. cm. 1981. (ISBN 0-8253-0055-X). Beaufort Books.

--Running Scared. LC 79-1495. 118 p. 21cm. c.1979. (ISBN 0-525-66631-1). Elsevier/Nelson Books.

Morton, Lois

--Let's Find Charlie. (Illus.). (Animated Bks). (ps-2). 1969. (ISBN 0-394-80699-9, BYR). Random.

--Pickles Don't Grow on Trees. Schwarz, Walter, illus. (Illus.). pop-ups. (gr. k-2). 1969. (ISBN 0-394-80789-8). Random.

Morton, Miriam, ed. see Rozenfeld, Semen Efimovich.

Morton, Miriam, ed. see Vivier, Colette.

Morton, Miriam (1918-), tr. see Sholokhov, Mikhail Aleksandrovich.

Morton, Miriam (1918-), tr. see Tolstoy, Leo Nikolaevich.

Morton, Miriam (1918-), tr. see Vangeli, Spiridon.

Morton, Miriam, tr. see Vivier, Colette.

Morton, Miriam (1918-), ed.

--A Harvest of Russian Children's Literature. Viguers, Ruth Hill, frwd. by. LC 67-21384. (Illus.). xiv, 474 p. 28cm. 1967. University of California Press.

--The Moon Is Like a Silver Sickle: A Celebration of Poetry by Russian Children. Keith, Eros, illus. LC 72-77768. (Illus.). 93 p. 21cm. 1972. (ISBN 0-671-65198-6). Simon and Schuster.

--Russian Plays for Young Audiences: Five Contemporary Selections. Morton, Miriam (1918-), tr. LC 77-82856. (Illus.). vi, 401 p. 22cm. c.1977. New Plays Books.

--Said the Little Raccoon to the Moon. Provest, Jon, illus. LC 73-75068. (Illus.). 24 p. (Magic circle book). 1974. (ISBN 0-663-25472-8). Ginn.

Morton, Miriam (1918-), tr.

--Voices from France: Ten Stories by French Nobel Prize Winners. LC 78-79971. 240p. (gr. 9 up). 1969. (ISBN 0-385-02451-7). Doubleday.

Morus, Cenydid, pseud., see Morris, Kenneth.

Mosca, Frank

--All American Boys. 09/1983 ed. 100p. (Orig.). (gr. 7-12). N.D. (ISBN 0-932870-44-9). Alyson Pubns.

Mosel, Arlene Jirchy (1921-), retold by.

--The Funny Little Woman. 1st ed. Hearn, Lafcadio (1850-1904) & Lent, Blair (1930-), illus. LC 75-179046. (Illus.). 40 p. 1972. (ISBN 0-525-30265-4). Dutton. **Awards: (RCM); (IBBY); (ALA).**

--Tikki Tikki Tembo. 1st ed. Lent, Blair (1930-), illus. (Illus.). 45 p. 26cm. 1968. Holt, Rinehart and Winston. **Awards: (BGH); (ALA).**

Moseley, L H, jt. auth. see Craine, Edith Janice.

Moser, Barry, jt. auth. see Carroll, Lewis.

Moser, Don see Moser, Donald Bruce.

Moser, Donald Bruce (1932-)

--A Heart to the Hawks. LC 74-18190. 208 p. 22cm. 1975. (ISBN 0-689-50024-6). Atheneum.

Moses, Anna Mary Robertson see Grandma Moses, pseud.

Moses, Belle

--Helen Ormesby. LC 12-22811. 4 p. l., 309, 1 p. col. front., col. plates. 20 cm. $1.50. 1912. D. Appleton and Company.

Moses, Horace S.

--Here Comes the Circus. N.D. Houghton Mifflin & Co.

Moses, Joseph

--The Great Rain Robbery. Levine, David (1926-), illus. LC 74-20814. (Illus.). 28 p. 1975. (ISBN 0-395-20275-2). Houghton Mifflin.

Moses, Montrose Jonas (1878-1934), ed.

--Another Treasury of Plays for Children. Sarg, Tony, pseud. (1882-1942), illus. Sarg, Anthony Frederick. LC 26-18753. ix p., 2 l., 3-614 p. col. front., plates. 21 cm. 1926. Little, Brown, and Company.

--Ring up the Curtain!. A Collection of Plays for Children. Scott, Janet Laura, illus. 7 p. l., 3-398 p., 1 l. incl. plates. col. front. 23 cm. 1932. Little, Brown, and Company.

--A Treasury of Plays for Children. Sarg, Tony, pseud. (1882-1942), illus. Sarg, Anthony Frederick. LC 21-26987. xiii, 550 p. col. front., plates. 20 1/2 cm. 1921. Little, Brown, and Company.

Mosesson, Gloria Rubin see Miller, Doris R., pseud.

Mosheim, Lilly

--Elizabeth and Her Doll, Susan. Walker, Audrey, illus. LC 61-6083. (Illus.). 19cm. 1961, c.1959. F. Watts.

--Elizabeth's Cat Tiny. (Illus.). (ps-1). 1961. Verry.

--A Garden Picnic for Elizabeth and Peter. Walker, Audrey, illus. LC 61-6085. (Illus.). 19cm. 1961, c.1960. F. Watts.

--Peter and His Tricycle, Flash. Walker, Audrey, illus. LC 61-6084. (Illus.). 19cm. 1961, c.1959. F. Watts.

--A Secret Birthday Present for Elizabeth. Walker, Audrey, illus. LC 61-6086. (Illus.). 19cm. 1961, c.1960. F. Watts.

--Where is John?. Ford, Sally, illus. 1963. (ISBN 0-685-47582-4). (ISBN 0-685-47583-2). Verry.

Mosher, Bruce & Mosher, Dottie

--How Do You Spell TV. Gretzer, John, illus. (Illus.). 64p. (Orig.). (gr. 1-3). 1970. (ISBN 0-377-00751-X). Friend Pr.

Mosher, Dottie, jt. auth. see Mosher, Bruce.

Moshkovskaya, E.

--Little Chick Goes to Clucky-Cluck. 12p. 1976. (ISBN 0-8285-1185-3, Pub. by Progress Pubs USSR). Imported Pubns.

Moskin, Marietta Dunston (1928-), tr. see Tisna, Udayana Pandji & Last, Jef, pseud. (1898-1972)

Moskin, Marietta Dunston (1928-)

--Adam and the Wishing Charm. Scrofani, Joseph, illus. LC 76-43093. (Illus.). 59 p. 24cm. c.1977. (ISBN 0-698-20404-2). Coward, McCann & Geoghegan.

--The Best Birthday Party. LC 64-20703. 189 p. illus. 21 cm. 1964. John Day Co.

--Day of the Blizzard. Gammell, Stephen, illus. LC 78-6461. p. cm. 1978. (ISBN 0-698-20468-9). Coward, McCann & Geoghegan.

--Dream Lake. LC 80-18999. (Illus.). 138 p. 22cm. 1981. (ISBN 0-689-30821-3). Atheneum.

--I Am Rosemarie. LC 72-2413. 190 p. 22cm. 1972. John Day Co.

--Lysbet and the Fire Kittens. Tomes, Margot (1917-), illus. LC 72-67615. (Illus.). 46p. 23cm. (A Break-of-Day Book). c.1973. (ISBN 0-686-20270-8). Coward, McCann & Geoghgan.

--Lysbet and the Fire Kittens. Tomes, Margot Ladd (1917-), illus. LC 73-97315. (Illus.). 48p. (Break-of-Day Bk). (gr. 1-3). 1974. (ISBN 0-698-30522-1, Coward). Putnam Pub Group.

--A Paper Dragon. LC 68-11310. 221 p. 21cm. 1968. John Day Co.

--Rosie's Birthday Present. Rose, David S. (1947-), illus. LC 81-2220. p. cm. 1981. (ISBN 0-689-30854-X). Atheneum.

--A Royal Gift. Stock, Catherine, illus. LC 81-7800. (Illus.). 56 p. 23cm. (Break-of-day book). c.1982. (ISBN 0-698-30734-8). Coward, McCann & Geoghegan.

--A Royal Gift. Stock, Catherine, illus. (gr. 3-4). 1982. Putnam.

--Sky Dragons & Flaming Swords: The Story of Eclipses, Comets, & Other Strange Happenings in the Sky. 96p. (gr. 3-6). 1985. (ISBN 0-8027-6575-0). Walker & Co.

--Toto. Negri, Rocco (1932-), illus. LC 70-153989. (Illus.). 48 p. 1971. Coward, McCann & Geoghegan.

--Waiting for Mama. Lebenson, Richard, illus. LC 74-21068. 91 p. 20cm. 1975. (ISBN 0-698-20319-4). Coward, McCann & Geoghegan.

--With an Open Hand. Grifalconi, Ann (1929-), illus. LC 66-9818. (Illus.). 190 p. 22cm. 1967. J. Day Co.

Moskof, Martin Stephen, jt. auth. see Chwast, Seymour.

Moskof, Martin Stephen, jt. auth. see Hefter, Richard.

Moskof, Martin Stephen see Rogers, Fred McFeely.

Moskowitz, Stewart

--Fred's Pyramid. LC 82-7910. p. cm. c.1982. (ISBN 0-671-45889-2). J. Messner : Little Simon.

--The Legend of the American Rabbit. LC 82-7930. p. cm. c.1982. (ISBN 0-671-45885-X). J. Messner.

--A Patchwork Fish Tale. LC 82-7959. p. cm. c.1982. (ISBN 0-671-45890-6). J. Messner.

--Tooloose, the Chocolate Moose. LC 82-7918. p. cm. c.1982. (ISBN 0-671-45886-8). (ISBN 0-671-45329-7). J. Messner : Little Simon.

Mosley, Elizabeth Robards, jt. auth. see Wilkie, Katharine Elliott.

Mosley, Zack

--Smilin' Jack and the Daredevil Girl Pilot: A New Story Based on the Famous Comic Strip. authorized. LC 42-22611. 3 p. l., 11-248 p. illus. 20 1/2 cm. 1942. Whitman Publishing Company.

Moss, Charles Norman

--The Wreck of the Pied Piper. LC 78-23264. 136 p. 21cm. (Pathfinder: Series. 4). 1979, c.1973. (ISBN 0-310-37831-1). Zondervan Pub. House.

Moss, Elaine, ed. see Swift, Jonathan.

Moss, Elaine Dora (1924-), selected by see Ichikawa, Satomi.

Moss, Elaine Dora (1924-)

--Polar. Baker, Jeannie (1950-), illus. (Illus.). (ps-1). 1979. (ISBN 0-233-96695-1). Andre Deutsch.

--Twirly. Ellentuck, Shan, illus. LC 65-108786. 1V. (unpaged) col. illus.21cm. 1965, c.1963. Coward.

Moss, Elaine Dora (1924-) & Roberts, Doreen (1922-)

--Story of Saul the King. Roberts, Doreen (1922-), illus. (gr. 4 up). 1966. D White.

Moss, Geoffrey

--Arthur's Artichoke. LC 73-102833. (Illus.). 32 p. 24cm. 1970. Dial Press.

Moss, Hilda

--Wild Rose of the King's Chase. Vise, Jennetta, illus. LC 60-7745. (Illus.). 21cm. 256p. 1960. F. Warne.

Moss, Howard (1922-) & Belli, Frederick Henry

--Tigers & Other Lilies. LC 77-1998. (Illus.). 40 p. 24cm. 1977. (ISBN 0-689-30592-3). Atheneum.

Moss, Jeffrey

--People in My Family. (Illus.). 24p. (gr. k-2). 1976. (ISBN 0-307-68968-9, Golden Pr). Western Pub.

--People in Your Neighborhood. Brown, Richard Eric (1946-), illus. (Illus.). 32p. (Golden Melody Bks.). (ps-2). 1984. (ISBN 0-307-12247-6, Golden Pr). Western Pub.

--The Songs of Sesame Street in Poems and Pictures: Featuring Jim Henson's Sesame Street Muppets. Chartier, Normand (1945-), illus. LC 83-3329. 1983. (ISBN 0-394-85245-1). Random House.

Moss, Jeffrey & Hart, Bruce

--Songs of Sesame Street in Poems & Pictures. Axelrod, David, illus. LC 83-3329. (Illus.). 48p. (ps-3). 1983. (ISBN 0-394-85245-1). (ISBN 0-394-95245-6). Random.

Moss, Jeffrey & Raposo, Joe

--Sesame Street Songbook. LC 74-161217. (Illus.). 1971. (ISBN 0-671-21036-X, Fireside). S&S.

--The Sesame Street Songbook. 1978. (ISBN 0-671-24208-3, Fireside). S&S.

Moss, Jeffrey & Stiles, Norman

--The Sesame Street ABC Storybook: Featuring Jim Henson's Muppets. Cross, Peter, et al., illus. LC 74-5522. (Illus.). 65 p. 29cm. 1974. (ISBN 0-394-82921-2). (ISBN 0-394-82921-2). Random House.

Moss, Marion

--Doll House. Weil, Lisl (1910-), illus. N.D. World Publishing Co.

Moss, Mildred E. W.

--The Little Dog's Search. N.D. Pageant Press, Inc.

Mossiker, Frances Sanger (1906-)

--More than a Queen: The Story of Josephine. Eagle, Michael (1942-), illus. 1971. Borzoi Books.

Mossman, T. A.

--A Mother's Favorite Lullaby Book. Greinke, Geri & Barbour, Judith K. M., illus. LC 84-2060. c.1984. (ISBN 0-89471-261-6). Running Press.

Most, Bernard (1937-)

--Boo!. Most, Bernard (1937-), illus. (Illus.). 31p. 1980. (ISBN 0-13-079780-4). P-H.

--If the Dinosaurs Came Back. Most, Bernard (1937-), illus. LC 77-23911. (Illus.). 32 p. c.1978. Harcourt Brace Jovanovich.

--My Very Own Octopus. Most, Bernard (1937-), illus. LC 80-12786. p. cm. c.1980. (ISBN 0-15-256641-4). Harcourt Brace Jovanovich.

--There's an Ant in Anthony. Most, Bernard (1937-), illus. LC 79-23089. (Illus.). 32 p. 26cm. 1980. (ISBN 0-688-22226-9). (ISBN 0-688-32226-3). Morrow.

--There's an Ape Behind the Drape. Most, Bernard (1937-), illus. LC 80-24280. (Illus.). 32 p. 26cm. 1981. (ISBN 0-688-00380-X). (ISBN 0-688-00381-8). W. Morrow.

--Whatever Happened to the Dinosaurs?. Most, Bernard (1937-), illus. LC 84-3779. (Illus.). 40p. (ps-1). 1984. (ISBN 0-15-295295-0, HJ). (ISBN 0-15-295295-0). HarBraceJ.

Moston, Meredith, jt. auth. see Bjerke, Odd.

Mother Goose

--The Animated Mother Goose. Frees, Harry Whittier, photos by. LC 21-19154. 168 p. incl. front., illus. 21 1/2 cm. 1921. Lothrop, Lee & Shepard Co.

--Animated Mother Goose. Wehr, Julian, illus. LC 62-52303. unpaged. illus. 27cm. 1962. McLoughlin Bros.

--Animated Story Rhymes: A New Book of Old Favorites. Wehr, Julian, illus. LC 44-47300. 24 p. col. illus. 20 1/2 x 26 1/2 cm. c.1944. Garden City Publishing Co., Inc.

--The Annotated Mother Goose. Baring-Gould, William Stuarty (1913-1967) & Baring-Gould, Ceil, annotations by. Crane, Walter (1845-1915), illus. 350p. 1962 (Potter). Crown.

--The Annotated Mother Goose, Nursery Rhymes Old and New. Baring-Gould, William Stuart (1913-1967) & Baring-Gould, Ceil, eds. Crane, Walter (1845-1915) & Simon, E. M., illus. LC 62-21606. 350 p. illus. 28cm. c.1962. C. N. Potter.

--Baby's Mother Goose. (Illus.). (ps). N.D. (ISBN 0-448-46804-2, Peggy Cloth Bks.). Platt.

--Baby's Mother Goose. Stearns, Sharon (1912-), illus. LC 38-19922. 16 p. illus. (part col.) 16 1/2 x 14 1/2 cm. c.1938. Grosset & Dunlap.

--Baby's Mother Goose. Wilkin, Eloise Burns (1904-), illus. 24p. (ps). 1975. (ISBN 0-307-10411-7, Golden Pr). Western Pub.

--Berta and Elmer Hader's Picture Book of Mother Goose. Hader, Berta Hoerner (1890-1976) & Hader, Elmer Stanley (1889-1976), illus. LC 30-29908. 152 p. incl. col. front., illus. (part col.) 23 1/2 x 22 cm. c.1930. Coward-McCann, Inc.

--Berta and Elmer Hader's Picture Book of Mother Goose. Hader, Berta Hoerner (1890-1976) & Hader, Elmer Stanley (1889-1973), illus. LC 44-799619. 4 p. l., 144 p. incl. col. front., illus. (part col.) 21 x 19 1/2 cm. 1944. Coward-McCann, Inc.

--Blessed Mother Goose: Favorite Nursery Rhymes. Scully, Frank (1892-1964), retold by. Luke, Keye, illus. LC 54-7116. 95p. illus. 26cm. 1954, c.1951. Greenberg.

--Blessed Mother Goose: Nursery Rhymes for Today's Children. Scully, Frank (1892-1964), retold by. Luke, Keye, illus. LC 51-8659. 104 p. illus. 28 cm. 1951. House-Warven.

--Bo-Peep. Mother Goose Melodies ... cover-title, 14 p. illus. (part col.) 27 cm. c.1887. McLoughlin Bros.

--A Book of Nursery Rhymes. Welsh, Charles (1850-1914), ed. Atwood, Clara E., illus. LC 3-12252. 2 pt. fronts., illus. 19 cm. (On cover: Heath's Home and School Classics. no. 25-26). 1901. D. C. Heath & Co.

--The Boyd Smith Mother Goose: With Numerous Illustrations in Color and in Black and White. Elmendorf, Lawrence, ed. Smith, Elmer Boyd (1860-1943), illus. LC 19-160313. 1 p. l., v-xx, 223 p. col. front., illus., col. plates, facsims. 27 1/2 cm. c.1919. G. P. Putnam's Sons.

--Boys and Girls from Mother Goose. Scott, Marguerite K., illus. LC 55-36716. unpaged. illus. 21cm. (Cosy-Corner Book, 2451). c.1955. Whitman Pub. Co.

--Brian Wildsmith's Mother Goose: A Collection of Nursery Rhymes. Wildsmith, Brian Lawrence (1930-), illus. LC 65-10040. 80p. col. illus. 28cm. 1964. Watts.

--Carolyn Wells Edition of Mother Goose. Wells, Carolyn (1869-1942), ed. Cooper, Marjorie (1910-) & Robson, Janet, illus. LC 47-2032. 5-125 p. col. illus. 33 x 26 1/2 cm. c.1946. Garden City Publishing Co., Inc.

--Chimes, Rhymes, and Jingles: Or, Mother Goose's Songs, Being the Remainder of Her Melodies. Billings, Hammatt (1818-1874) & Hartwell, illus. LC 16-3093. 3-160 p. front., illus. 15 1/2 x 13 cm. c.1845. Munroe and Francis.

--The Comic Adventures of Old Mother Hubbard & Her Dog. Martin, Sarah Catherine (1768-1826), ed. Lobel, Arnold Stark (1933-), illus. LC 68-9052. (Illus.). 32p. (ps-1). 1968. (ISBN 0-87888-003-8). Bradbury Pr.

--The Complete Mother Goose. Betts, Ethel Franklin, illus. LC 9-281297. 3 p. l., v-xviii p., 2 l., 227 p. col. front., illus., col. plates. 21 1/2 cm. 1909. Frederick A. Stokes Company.

--Corinne Malvern's Mother Goose. Malvern, Corinne (1905-1956), illus. LC 53-3884. 64p. illus. 28cm. (Big Golden Book, 480). 1953. Simon and Schuster.

--The Crooked Man. Barto, Emily Newton (1886-), illus. LC 40-13275. 56 p. illus. 17 x 14 cm. c.1940. Longmans Green & Co.

--Curly Locks. Mother Goose Melodies. LC 15-23986. 34 p. illus. (part col.) 20 cm. c.1887. McLoughlin Bros.

--The Dandelion Mother Goose. Goldsborough, June (1923-), illus. LC 78-72131. (Illus.). 32 p. 23cm. 1979. (ISBN 0-89799-052-8). (ISBN 0-89799-097-8). Dandelion Press.

--Denslow's Mother Goose. Denslow, William Wallace (1856-1915), ed. Denslow, William Wallace (1856-1915), illus. LC 1-25765. (Being the Old Familiar Rhymes and Jingles of Mother Goose). 94 p. col. illus 28 1/2 cm. 1901. McClure, Phillips & Company.

--The Ella Dolbear Lee Mother Goose. Lee, Ella Dolbear, illus. LC 18-10008. 10 p. l., 17-280, 2 p. incl. col. front., illus. (part col.) col. plates. 26 cm. c.1918. M. A. Donohue & Company.

--Everychild's Mother Goose. Wilson, Edith R. (1864-), illus. Wells, Carolyn (1869-1942), intro. by. LC 18-21114. xiii, 308 p. incl. col. front., col. illus. 19 cm. $2.0. 1918. The Macmillan Company.

--Everychild's Mother Goose. Wilson, Edith R. (1864-), illus. Wells, Carolyn (1869-1942), intro. by. LC 20-83. xv, 83, 308 p. incl. front., col. illus. 19 1/2 cm. 1919. The Macmillan Company.

--The Family Mother Goose. Weisgard, Leonard Joseph (1916-), illus. LC 51-11661. 3 v. illus. 18 cm. 1951. Harper.

--Famous Rhymes, Mother Goose. Piper, Watty, pseud. (1896-), ed. Braggs, Mabel Caroline. LC 28-21940. 86 p. col. front., illus. (part col.) col. plates. 27 1/2 cm. c.1928. The Platt & Munk Co., Inc.

--Famous Rhymes, Mother Goose. Piper, Watty, pseud. (1870-1945), ed. Bragg, Mabel Caroline. LC 33-5086. 120 p. incl. col. front., illus. (part col.) 28 1/2 cm. c.1933. The Platt & Munk Co., Inc.

--The Fanny Cory Mother Goose: Mother Goose Rhymes and Jingles. Cory, Fanny Young, illus. 29cm. 72p. c.1913. The Bobbs-Merrill Co.

--Favorite Nursery Rhymes. Betts, Ethel Franklin, illus. LC 6-33533. 47 p. col. front., illus., 5 col. pl. 26 cm. 1906. F. A. Stokes Company.

--Favorite Rhymes from Mother Goose. Humphrey, Maud (1868-), illus. LC 16-309285. 12 l. col. illus. 28 1/2 x 23 1/2 cm. 1891. Frederick A. Stokes Company.

--Fifty Favorite Rhymes of Mother Goose. Winship, Florence Sarah, illus. LC 63-6018. 28p. illus. 32cm. (Giant tell-a-tale bk.). 1963. Whitman Pub.

--Fuzzy Friends in Mother Goose. Cunningham, Dellwyn, illus. LC 53-16721. 16p. illus. 17cm. c.1952. Whitman Pub. Co.

--The Gay Mother Goose. Dalgliesh, Alice (1893-1979), ed. Seignobosc, Francoise (1897-1961), illus. Francoise, pseud. LC 38-21324. 63 p. incl. col. illus., col. plates. 26 cm. c.1938. C. Scribner's Sons.

--Happi-Time Mother Goose. Dawson, Muriel & Henderson, Doris, illus. LC 42-14591. viii, 2, ix-xv, 17-317, 2 p. col. front., illus. (part col.) col. plates. 28 1/2 cm. c.1941. Sears, Roebuck & Co.

--Hilary Knight's Mother Goose. Knight, Hilary (1926-), illus. LC 62-21635. 61p. illus. 33cm. (Big Golden Book). c.1962. Golden Press.

--Hilary Knight's Mother Goose. Knight, Hilary (1926-), illus. LC 62-21635. (Illus.). 63 p. 25cm. (Golden Book). 1973, c.1962. Golden Pr.

--How Eight Men Became One: Magical Changes with Mother Goose Melodies. cover-title, 16 p. col. illus. 19 cm. (Star Ser. No. 5). c.1879. G. W. Carleton & Co.

--Humpty Dumpty, and Other Mother Goose Rhymes. Chase, Mary Jane, illus. LC 52-34937. unpaged. illus. 17 cm. (Rand McNally book-elf junior, 674). c.1952. Rand McNally.

--The Humpty Dumpty Book. Simpson, Jean, illus. LC 64-57440. 1 v. (unpaged) col. illus. 22 cm. (Golden Book for Kindergarten). 1964. Golden Press.

--Humpty Dumpty: Magical Changes with Mother Goose Melodies. LC 17-1855. (Illus.). 19cm. 16p. (Star Ser.: No. 6). c.1879. G. W. Carleton & Co.

--Jack Horner and Song of Sixpence. Barto, Emily Newton (1886-), ed. Barto, Emily Newton (1886-), illus. LC 43-15297. 48 p. illus. 16 1/2 x 13 1/2 cm. 1943. Longmans, Green & Co.

--The Jessie Willcox Smith Mother Goose. Smith, Jessie Willcox (1863-1935), illus. LC 14-20546. (A Careful and Full Selection of the Rhymes, with Numerous Illustrations in Full Color and Black and White). 173 p. col. front., illus., plates (part col.) 22 1/2 x 30 1/2 cm. c.1914. Dodd, Mead & Company.

--The Jolly Jump-Ups Mother Goose Book. Clyne, Geraldine, ed. LC 44-9739. 13 p. col. illus. 27 cm. c.1944. McLoughlin Bros., Inc.

--Jolly Rhymes of Mother Goose. Piper, Watty, pseud. (1870-1945), ed. Bragg, Mabel Caroline. Lenski, Lois (1893-1974), illus. LC 32-15183. 118 p., col. front., illus. (part col.) 10 cm. c.1932. The Platt & Munk Co., Inc.

--The Julian Wehr Mother Goose. Wehr, Julian, illus. LC 45-7056. 1 p. l., 7-104 p. col. illus. 28 cm. 1945. Grosset and Dunlap.

--A Little Golden Mother Goose. Rojankovsky, Feodor Stepanovich (1891-1970), illus. LC 57-1223. unpaged. illus. 21cm. (Little golden book, 283). 1957. Simon and Schuster.

--The Little Kittens' Mother Goose Rhymes. Frees, Harry Whittier, photos by. LC 41-16605. 61 p. illus. 17 x 14 cm. c.1941. Rand McNally & Company.

--The Little Mother Goose. Smith, Jessie Willcox (1863-1935), illus. LC 18-18792. xv, 176 p. col. front., illus., col. plates. 14 1/2 x 18 1/2 cm. c.1918. Dodd, Mead & Company.

--Littlefolks' Mother Goose. Rule, Christopher, illus. LC 26-19295. 158 p., 1 l. incl. front., illus. 29 1/2 cm. c.1926. J. H. Sears & Company, Inc.

--The Littlest Mother Goose. Steiner, Charlotte, ed. Steiner, Charlotte, illus. LC 64-223954. 1 v. (unpaged) col. illus. 13 cm. (Mail-me books). 1964. Random House.

--Lois Lenski's Mother Goose. Lenski, Lois (1893-1974), illus. LC 37-7818. ix p., 1 l., 83, 1 p. illus. (part col.) 20 1/2 cm. 1936. Harper & Brothers.

--Magic Mother Goose. Falk, Nat, illus. LC 33-327709. 31 p. illus. 26 cm. c.1933. The Vanguard Press.

--The Merry Mother Goose. Ruhman, Ruth M., illus. LC 68-11121. 223p. col. illus. 27cm. (Whitman lib. of giant bks.). 1968. Whitman Pub.

--More Mother Goose Rhymes. Rojankovsky, Feodor Stepanovich (1891-1970), illus. (Little Golden Book). 1958. Golden Press.

--Mother Goose, 12 vols. (Illus.). 400p. (Juvenile Classics Ser.). 1905. Set. H M Caldwell Co.

--Mother Goose, 1 of 10 vols. (Aunt Virginia Ser.). 1900. Set. Hurst & Co.

--Mother Goose. LC 35-20669. 1 p. l., 7-284 p. col. front., illus. 20 cm. c.1934. Whitman Publishing Company.

--Mother Goose. Benet, William Rose (1886-), ed. Duvoisin, Roger Antoine (1904-1980), illus. LC 36-32644. 144 p. illus. (part col.) 34 cm. c.1936. The Heritage Press.

--Mother Goose. Chadburn, Mabel, illus. LC 27-26606. 125p., 1 p. col. front., illus., col. plates. 18 1/2 cm. (Half-title: Tales for children from many lands). 1927. J. M. Dent & Sons, Limited.

--Mother Goose. Daniel, Frank, ed. (Illus.). (ps). 1979. (Gingerbread). Dutton.

--Mother Goose. Doane, Pelagie (1906-1966), illus. LC 40-335284. 52 p. incl. col. front, illus. (part col.) 24 1/2 x 21 cm. c.1940. Random House.

--Mother Goose. Dorne, Maxwell, illus. LC 49-11043. 69 p. illus. (part col.) 29 cm. 1949. Random House.

--Mother Goose. Duenewald, Doris, ed. (Illus.). color ils. (ps-1). 1971. (ISBN 0-448-00394-5). G&D.

--Mother Goose. Falls, Charles Buckles (1874-1960), illus. LC 24-31195. 96 p. col. illus. 31 cm. 1924. Doubleday, Page & Company.

--Mother Goose. Fraser, Phyllis Maurine (1915-), ed. Elliott, Miss, illus. LC 42-50764. 41p., 1 p. illus. (part col.) 20 1/2 x 17 1/2 cm. (On cover: The Little golden library, 4). 1942. Simon and Schuster, Inc.

--Mother Goose. Friend, Esther, illus. LC 47-3423. 3 p. l., 3-46p., 2 p. col. illus. 21 x 17 1/2 cm. (On cover: A Rand McNally book-elf book). c.1947. Rand McNally & Company.

--Mother Goose. Fujikawa, Gyo, illus. LC 68-29949. (Illus.). 125 p. 32cm. 1968. Grosset & Dunlap.

--Mother Goose. the original volland ed. Grover, Eulalie Osgood (1873-1958), ed. Richardson, Frederick (1862-1937), illus. LC 83-23939. (Illus.). 123 p. 29cm. 1985. (ISBN 0-517-43619-1). Derrydale Books : Distributed by Crown Publishers.

--Mother Goose. Grover, Eulalie Osgood (1873-1958), ed. Richardson, Frederick (1862-1937), illus. 1947. M. A. Donohue & Co.

--Mother Goose. Grover, Eulalie Osgood, ed. Richardson, Frederick (1862-1937), illus. LC 15-201563. 119 p. col. illus. 31 1/2 cm. c.1915. P. F. Volland & Co.

--Mother Goose. the classic volland ed. Grover, Eulalie Osgood (1873-1958), ed. Richardson, Frederick (1862-1937), illus. LC 76-16156. (Illus.). 159 p. 31cm. 1976, c.1971. (ISBN 0-528-88559-6). Rand McNally.

--Mother Goose. Hirsch, Joseph (1910-), illus. LC 46-21747. 40 p. illus. (part col.) 25 x 19 1/2 cm. 1946. Wonder Books.

--Mother Goose. Ives, Ruth, illus. LC 39-277718. 41 p. illus. (part col.) 12 1/2 cm. c.1939. Holiday House, Inc.

--Mother Goose. Joyce, William, illus. LC 84-1955. (Illus.). (Knee-High Bks.). (ps-1). 1984. (ISBN 0-394-86534-0, Pub. by BYR). (ISBN 0-394-96534-5). Random.

--Mother Goose. Leaf, Anne Sellers, illus. LC 58-8219. unpaged. illus. 21cm. (Tip-top elf book, 1028). c.1958. Rand McNally.

--Mother Goose. Leaf, Anne Sellers, illus. LC 65-182885. 1v. (unpaged) col. illus. 32cm. 1965, c.1958. (ISBN 0-528-88806-4). Rand McNally.

--Mother Goose. MacKenzie, Garry (1921-), illus. LC 49-112958. 177 p. illus. 24 cm. 1949. Crowell Co.

--Mother Goose. Miller, Doris R., pseud. (1924-), ed. Mosesson, Gloria Rubin. Ramirez, Pablo, illus. LC 66-14056. 1 v. (unpaged) col. illus. 24 cm. (Holly Story Book Library). 1966. World Pub. Co.

--Mother Goose. Milne, Alan Alexander (1882-1956), adapted by. Shepard, Ernest Howard (1879-1976), illus. N.D. E. P. Dutton & Co.

--Mother Goose. Moose, George L., ed. N.D. (ISBN 0-448-07352-8). (ISBN 0-448-00757-6). Grosset & Dunlap.

--Mother Goose. Newton, Ruth E. & Horn, Mable G., illus. LC 34-405162. 28 p. illus. (part col.) 30 1/2 cm. c.1934. Whitman Publishing Co.

--Mother Goose. Opper, Frederick Burr (1857-1937), ed. N.D. J.B. Lippincott.

--Mother Goose. Orr, Munro Scott (1874-), illus. LC 22-12848. 255, 1 p. col. front., illus., col. plates. 23 1/2 cm. c.1915. D. McKay.

--Mother Goose. Paschal, Rose, illus. LC 51-28019. 32p. col. ill. 21cm. (A Cozy Corner Book). c.1951. Whitman Pub.

--Mother Goose. Peat, Fern Bisel, Mrs. (1893-) & Peat, Frank, illus. LC 29-10197. 60 p. col. illus. 31 cm. c.1929. The Saalfield Publishing Company.

--Mother Goose. Peat, Fern Bisel, Mrs. (1893-), illus. LC 34-4682. 18 p. illus. (part col.) 32 cm. c.1934. The Saalfield Publishing Co.

--Mother Goose. Provensen, Alice (1918-) & Provensen, Martin (1916-), eds. Provensen, Alice (1918-) & Provensen, Martin (1916-), illus. LC 76-8548. p. cm. 1976. (ISBN 0-394-82122-X). (ISBN 0-394-92122-4). Random House. **Award: (NYT).**

--Mother Goose. Rackham, Arthur (1867-1939), illus. 262p. N.D. Century Co.

--Mother Goose. Classic Volland ed. Richardson, Frederick (1862-1937), illus. Grover, Eulalie Osgood (1873-1958), intro. by. LC 72-161577. 160p. (ps-4). 1915. (ISBN 0-528-82800-2). Rand.

--Mother Goose. Russell, Mary La Fetra, illus. LC 38-31288. 24 p. col. illus. 30 1/2 x 26 cm. 1938. S. Gabriel Son & Company.

--Mother Goose. Saviozzi, Adriana (1928-), illus. LC 63-445539. 95 p. illus. 27 cm. (Golden Storytime Book). 1963, c.1957. Golden Press.

--Mother Goose. Smith, Elmer Boyd (1860-1843), ed. Smith, Elmer Boyd (1860-1943), illus. N.D. G.P. Putnam's Sons.

--Mother Goose. Smith, Harry, ed. (Illus.). N.D. Duffield & Co.

--Mother Goose. Sweeney, illus. N.D. D. Lothrop Co.

--Mother Goose. Tate, Sally, retold by. Tate, Sally, illus. LC 48-15378. 40 p. illus. 22 cm. (Cozy-corner book). 1947. Whitman Pub. Co.

--Mother Goose. Tenggren, Gustaf (1896-1970), illus. LC 40-34871. 133, 3 p. incl. col. front., col. illus. 28 1/2 cm. 1940. Little, Brown and Company.

--Mother Goose. Tudor, Tasha (1915-), illus. 1944. Walck. **Award: (RCM).**

--Mother Goose. Vaughan, Eileen Fox, illus. LC 50-4105. 52 p. illus. (part col.) 17 cm. (Story Hour Ser.). c.1950. Whitman Pub. Co.

--Mother Goose. Vaughan, Eileen Fox, illus. LC 53-31783. unpaged. 17cm. (Tell-a-Tale Books). c.1953. Whitman Pub. Co.

--Mother Goose. Wehr, Julian, illus. LC 42-25480. (A Unique Version with Animated Illustrations). 24 p. col. illus. 20 1/2 x 27 cm. 1942. Grosset & Dunlap, Inc.

--Mother Goose. Weihs, Erika (1917-), illus. LC 45-826. 53 p. illus. (part col.) 17 cm. (Story Hour Ser.). c.1944. Whitman Publishing Company.

--Mother Goose. Wells, Carolyn (1869-1942), ed. (Illus.). (gr. k-3). 1953. (ISBN 0-385-02128-3). Doubleday.

--Mother Goose. Wildsmith, Brain Lawrence (1930-), retold by. Wildsmith, Brain Lawrence (1930-), illus. (Illus.). 80p. 1982. (ISBN 0-19-279611-9, Pub. by Oxford U Pr Childrens). Merrimack Pub Cir.

--Mother Goose. Workman, Arthur, ed. Paris, Pat, illus. (Illus.). 8p. of color ils. 20p. (gr. k-3). 1970. (ISBN 0-87529-036-1). Hallmark.

--Mother Goose A, B, C,. (Illus.). (Kindergarden A, B, C, Bks.). N.D. DeWolfe, Fiske & Co.

--Mother Goose: A Complete Compilation of Mother Goose Melodies. Lohman, Fred D., illus. LC 38-8834. 1 p. l., 9-113p. , 3 p. col. front., illus. (part col.) 31 cm. c.1938. The Saalfield Publishing Company.

--Mother Goose: A Complete Compilation of Mother Goose Melodies. Lohman, Fred D. & Hays, Ethel, illus. LC 41-12319. 93p., 3 p. col. front., illus., col. plates. 31 x 24 1/2cm. c.1941. The Saalfield Publishing Company.

--Mother Goose: A Comprehensive Collection of the Rhymes. Benet, William Rose (1886-), ed. Duvoisin, Roger Antoine (1904-1980), illus. LC 44-162. 112 p. col. illus. 27 1/2 x 21 cm. 1943. The Heritage Press.

--Mother Goose: An Anthology. Wood, Clement (1888-), ed. 64 p. 13 cm. (Little Blue Book No. 716, ed. by E. Haldeman-Julius). c.1924. Haldeman-Julius Company.

--Mother Goose and Fairyland. (Illus.). (The Progressive Ser.). N.D. John C. Winston & Co.

--Mother Goose and Fairyland. (The Superb Ser.). N.D. John C. Winston Co.

--Mother Goose, and Favorite Fairy Tales. Marshall, Logan, ed. LC 17-24171. 256, 256 p. col. front., illus., col. plates 24 1/2 cm. $1.2. c.1917. The John C. Winston Company.

--Mother Goose and Her Goslings. Allyn, Rose, ed. Burd, Clara Miller & Higgins, Violet Moore, illus. LC 18-22195. 5 p. l., 9-125 p. col. front., illus. pl. plates. 23 1/2 cm. c.1918. Stanton and Van Vliet Co.

--Mother Goose and Nursery Rhymes. LC 30-19658. 343 p. illus. 25 cm. c.1929. The World Syndicate Publishing Company.

--Mother Goose and Nursery Rhymes. 1st ed. Reed, Philip G. (1908-), illus. LC 63-72784. 57 p. col. illus. 28 cm. 1963. Atheneum. **Awards: (ALA); (RCM).**

--Mother Goose, and Other Poems. Evans, Katherine Floyd (1901-1964) & Bauer, Margaret, illus. LC 51-12239. unpaged. illus. 34 cm. (Big Silver Star Book). 1951. Children's Press.

--Mother Goose and Other Stories. Stretton, Hesba (1832-1911), illus. (Illus.). (The Happy Hour Ser.). N.D. John C. Winston & Co.

--Mother Goose Book. Bolenius, Emma Miller & Kellogg, Marion George, eds. Tenggren, Gustaf (1896-1970), illus. LC 29-434524. 128 p. col. illus. 21 cm. c.1929. Houghton Mifflin Company.

--The Mother Goose Book: Gathered from Many Sources. Roetter, Sonia, illus. LC 47-3982. 78 p. col. front., col. illus. 16 x 21 1/2 cm. 1946. The Peter Pauper Press.

--Mother Goose: Books for the Little Folk. (Illus.). (Novelty Ser.). N.D. Dewolfe, Fiske & Co.

--Mother Goose Complete. (Illus.). (Hurst's Fairy Tale Ser.). N.D. Hurst and Company.

--Mother Goose Complete. (Illus.). (Hurst's Presentation Ser.). N.D. Hurst and Company.

--The Mother Goose: Containing All the Melodies the Old Lady Ever Wrote. LC 16-3091. 64 p. front. (port.) illus. 15 x 12 cm. 1851. G. S. Appleton.

--Mother Goose Fairy Tales. (Illus.). (Ever New Books for Young People). N.D. Henry Altemus Company Publications.

--Mother Goose Favorites. (Illus.). 32p. N.D. Rand McNally & Co.

--Mother Goose Festival. (School Entertainment Ser.). 1901. E L Kellogg.

--Mother Goose Finger Plays. Cullison, Irene Margaret, adapted by. LC 19-15140. 32 p. incl. mounted col. front., illus. 26 1/2 x 23 1/2 cm. c.1915. G. W. Jacobs & Co.

--Mother Goose from Germany. Richter, Ludwig, et al. (1803-1884), illus. LC 16-10101. 72 p. illus. 22 cm. 1864. F. Leypoldt.

--Mother Goose: Her Best-Known Rhymes. Peat, Fern Bisel, Mrs. (1893-), illus. LC 33-22599. 34 p. illus. (part col.) 30 1/2 cm. c.1933. The Saalfield Publishing Company.

--Mother Goose: Her Book. Smith, Harry L., illus. LC 7-10592. 25 x 21cm. 48p. 1906. Duffield & Co.

--Mother Goose: Her Own Book. Royt, Mary, illus. LC 32-23576. 55 p. illus. (part col.) 33 cm. c.1932. The Reilly & Lee Co.

--Mother Goose: Her Rhymes and Riddles for Little Folks. Peat, Fern Bisel, Mrs. (1893-), illus. LC 42-313934. 16 p. illus. (part col.) 26 1/2 x 24 cm. c.1939. The Saalfield Publishing Company.

--Mother Goose in Holland. Post, May Audubon, illus. LC 12-21149. 90, 4 p. col. front., plates (part col.) 28 x 22 cm. $1.2. 1912. G. W. Jacobs & Company.

--Mother Goose in Silhouettes. Buffum, Katharine Gough (1884-), illus. LC 7-30443. 3 p. l., 78, 2 p., 1 l. illus. 15 1/2 x 16 cm. 1907. Houghton, Mifflin & Company.

--Mother Goose in Song and Rhyme. Burd, Clara Miller & Irwin, Grace (1891-), illus. Knecht, Joseph, contrib. by. LC 30-189675. 87, 1 p. incl. col. front., illus. (part col.) 27 1/2 cm. c.1930. C. E. Graham & Co.

--Mother Goose in White. Goodridge, J. F., illus. (Illus.). 1900. Lee & Shepard.

--Mother Goose in White. Mother Goose Rhymes. Goodridge, J. F., illus. LC 16-3090. 102, 1 p. illus. 15 1/2 x 19 cm. 1879. Lee and Shepard.

--Mother Goose Jingles. Sweeney, illus. (Illus.). N.D. D. Lothrop & Co.

--Mother Goose Jingles. Jolly Rhymes and Jingles for the Little Folks. 64 p. col. front., illus., col. plates. 25 1/2 cm. c.1895. Lothrop Publishing Company.

--Mother Goose Jungle Book. Von Hofsten, Hugo, illus. LC 3-17561. 27cm. 63p. 1903. The Madison Book Co.

--Mother Goose Library: Containing: "Mother Goose's Jingles", "Mother Goose's Melodies", "Mother Goose at Home", "Mother Goose Telling Stories, 4 Vols. (Illus.). N.D. George Routledge & Sons.

--Mother Goose Melodies. 64p. (Mother Goose Ser.). N.D. Donohue, Henneberry & Co.

--Mother Goose Melodies and Nursery Rhymes ... Willard, James Hartwell (1847-), ed. LC 16-10102. 96 p. front., illus., plates. 25 cm. 1897. Publishers Union.

--Mother Goose Melodies and Nursery Ryhmes. (Illus.). N.D. Monarch Book Company.

--Mother Goose Melodies with Magical Changes. 3 v. col. illus. 19 cm. (Star Ser. No. 1-3). c.1879. G. W. Carleton & Co.

--Mother Goose Moving Pictures & Five Cut-Out Puzzle Pictures with Famous Old Nursery Rhymes. Wood, Stacy H. 37 l. col. illus. 26 cm. $2.5. c.1928. G. P. Putnam's Sons.

--The Mother Goose Nursery Almanac. 1st ed. Palazzo, Tony (1905-1970), ed. Palazzo, Tony (1905-1970), illus. LC 60-5673. 88p. illus. 33cm. c.1960. Garden City Books.

--Mother Goose Nursery Rhymes. LC 46-440. 1 p. l., 213 p. illus. 21 1/2 cm. 1946. Books, Inc.

--Mother Goose Nursery Rhymes. (Illus.). (Beautiful Mother Goose and Fairy Books for the Little Folks). N.D. DeWolfe, Fiske & Co.

--Mother Goose Nursery Rhymes. (Illus.). (The Little Red Hen Ser.). N.D. George H. Doran.

--Mother Goose Nursery Rhymes. (Nursery Series of Linen Bks.). N.D. John C. Winston.

--Mother Goose Nursery Rhymes. LC 36-8199. 192 p. illus. 28 1/2 cm. c.1936. Whitman Publishing Company.

--Mother Goose Nursery Rhymes. Eulalie, pseud. (1896-), illus. Banks, Eulalie M.. LC 53-12973. unpaged. illus. 22x26cm. c.1953. Platt and Munk.

--Mother Goose Nursery Rhymes. Eve, Esme, illus. LC 59-3591. 200p. illus. 27cm. c.1958. Grosset & Dunlap.

--Mother Goose Nursery Rhymes. Marshall, Logan, ed. Green, Julia, illus. LC 29-255853. 256 p. col. front., illus., col. plates. 20 1/2 cm. (The Winston Clear-Type Popular Classics). 1928. The John C. Winston Company.

--Mother Goose Nursery Rhymes. Rackham, Arthur (1867-1939), illus. LC 69-11186. (Illus.). 153 p. 21cm. 1969. F. Watts.

--Mother Goose Nursery Rhymes. Reprint ed. Rackham, Arthur (1867-1939), selected by. Rackham, Arthur (1867-1939), illus. LC 75-16242. (Illus.). 153 p., 6 leaves of plates. 25cm. (Studio book). 1975. (ISBN 0-670-49003-2). Viking Press.

--Mother Goose Nursery Rhymes and Melodies. (Mother Goose Ser.). N.D. Hurst & Company.

--Mother Goose Nursery Rhymes: Children's Favorite Rhymes and Jingles. Mansfield, Blanche McManus (1869-), illus. LC 44-30633. viii, 136 p. illus. 20 1/2 cm. c.1912. The Platt & Peck Co.

--Mother Goose Nursery Tales. (Illus.). (Wee Books for Wee Folks). N.D. Henry Altemus Company Publicatons.

--Mother Goose: Or, The Old Nursery Rhymes, After Kate Greenaway. Greenaway, Kate (1846-1901), illus. LC 12-32710. 48 p. incl. col. front., col. illus. 25 cm. 1882. McLaughlin Bro's.

--Mother Goose: Or, The Old Nursery Rhymes. Greenaway, Kate (1846-1901), illus. LC 16-216438. 48 p. incl. col. front., col. illus. 17 1/2 cm. 1881. G. Routledge and Sons.

--Mother Goose: Or, The Old Nursery Rhymes. Greenaway, Kate (1846-1901), illus. LC 12-327095. 48 p. incl. col. front., col. illus. 17 1/2 cm. 1881. G. Routledge and Sons.

--Mother Goose Picture Book with Rhymes. Deane, Elsie, illus. LC 39-30533. p. l., 7-119 p., 1 l. illus. (part col.) 19 1/2 cm. c.1939. S. Gabriel Sons & Company.

--Mother Goose Playpictures: Tom, Tom, the Piper's Son. Pritchard, Clarence F., ed. LC 27-24449. 57 p. col. illus. 25 1/2 cm. c.1927. G. P. Putnam's Sons.

--Mother Goose Puzzle Pictures. (Illus.). (Young Folks' Puzzle Pictures Ser.). N.D. Henry Altemus Company Publications.

--Mother Goose Rhymes. (Illus.). (The Mother Goose Ser.). N.D. A. L. Burt's Pubs.

--Mother Goose Rhymes. (ps-3). N.D. (ISBN 0-685-27828-X). Borden.

--Mother Goose Rhymes. (Illus.). (The Favorite Lib.). N.D. DeWolfe, Fiske & Co.

--Mother Goose Rhymes. (Illus.). (ps). N.D. (ISBN 0-448-40114-2). Platt.

--Mother Goose Rhymes. (Illus.). (Young People's Classics). N.D. R. F. Fenno & Co.

--Mother Goose Rhymes. (Illus.). (ps). N.D. (ISBN 0-528-88007-1). Rand.

--Mother Goose Rhymes. LC 42-46326. 16 p. illus. (part col.) 30 x 28 1/2 cm. c.1934. The Platt & Munk Co., Inc.

--Mother Goose Rhymes ... LC 43-15331. 40 p. col. illus. 21 1/2 x 18 1/2 cm. c.1943. The Saalfield Pub. Co.

--Mother Goose Rhymes. Austin, Margot, Mrs., illus. LC 44-534531. 40 p. incl. col. front., illus. (part col.) 23 x 19 1/2 cm. 1944. The Platt & Munk Co., Inc.

--Mother Goose Rhymes. Fleur, Anne Elizabeth (1901-), illus. Sari, pseud. LC 46-224439. 32 p. illus. (part col.) 22 1/2 x 19 cm. c.1946. John Martin's House, Inc.

--Mother Goose Rhymes. De luxe ed. Piper, Watty, pseud. (1870-1945), ed. Bragg, Mabel Caroline. Eulalie, pseud. (1896-) & Lenski, Lois (1893-1974), illus. Banks, Eulalie M.. LC 56-592291. 107p. illus. 31cm. (Star Books for Children). 1956. Platt and Munk Co.

--Mother Goose Rhymes. Piper, Watty, pseud. (1870-1945), ed. Bragg, Mabel Caroline. Eulalie, pseud. (1896-) & Lenski, Lois (1893-1974), illus. Banks, Eulalie M.. LC 31-11919. 120 p. col. front., illus. 25 1/2 cm. c.1931. The Platt & Munk Co. Inc.

--Mother Goose Rhymes. New rev. ed. Piper, Watty, pseud. (1870-1945), ed. Bragg, Mabel Caroline. Eulalie, pseud. (1896-) & Lenski, Lois (1893-1974), illus. Banks, Eulalie M.. LC 32-2238. 106 p. col. front., illus. (part col.) 31 cm. c.1932. The Platt & Munk Co., Inc.

--Mother Goose Rhymes. Piper, Watty, pseud. (1870-1945), ed. Bragg, Mabel Caroline. LC 39-15597. 24 p. incl. col. front., illus. (part col.) 26 cm. c.1938. The Platt & Munk Co., Inc.

--Mother Goose Rhymes. Piper, Watty, pseud. (1870-1945), ed. Bragg, Mabel Caroline. Austin, Margot, Mrs., illus. LC 40-32642. 83 p. col. front., col. illus 28 1/2 x 23 cm. c.1940. The Platt & Munk Co., Inc.

--Mother Goose Rhymes. Robson, Janet (1902-) & Kippy, illus. LC 50-32366. (Illus.). 20cm. (A Friendly Bk). 1950. John Martin's House.

--Mother Goose Rhymes. Rojankovsky, Feodor Stepanovich (1891-1970), illus. (Giant Little Golden Book). 1958. Golden Press.

--Mother Goose Rhymes. Wedde, Janice, illus. LC 42-14737. 62 p. illus. (part col.) 17 x 13 cm. 1942. Rand McNally & Company.

--Mother Goose Rhymes and A B C's. (Choice Bits of Verse and Entertaining Stories for Little Folks of All Ages and with Special Illuminated Alphabet). 130 p. illus. (part col.) 24 1/2 x 18 1/2 cm. N.D. C.

--Mother Goose Rhymes and Fairy Tales. (Illus.). (Pleasant Hour Ser.). N.D. Barse and Hopkins.

--Mother Goose Rhymes and Nursery Tales. Piper, Watty, pseud. (1870-1945), ed. Bragg, Mabel Caroline. LC 27-24305. (Illus.). 103p. c.1927. Platt & Munk.

--Mother Goose Rhymes, Chimes, and Jingles. (Illus.). (Beautiful Mother Goose and Fairy Books for the Little Folks). N.D. DeWolfe, Fiske & Co.

--Mother Goose Rhymes, Jingles, and Fairy Tales. LC 44-30630. 254 p. incl. front., illus. 16 cm. (Altemus' Young People's Library). 1896. H. Altemus.

--Mother Goose Rhymes, Jingles and Fairy Tales. (Illus.). (Children's Gift Ser.). N.D. Henry Altemus Company Publications.

--Mother Goose Rhymes My Children Love Best of All. Johnson, Clifton (1865-1940), ed. Knowles, Machan, illus. LC 18-22196. ix, 206 p. incl. front., illus. col. plates. 21 cm. 1917. A. L. Noble.

--Mother Goose Rhymes Set to Music. Sheldon, Louise Patterson, ed. Eulalie, pseud. (1896-), illus. Banks, Eulalie M.. LC 30-34400. 31 p. 20 x 27 1/2 cm. 1930. The Sierra Press.

--Mother Goose Rhymes Tales, and Jingles. (Illus.). 1888. R Worthington.

--Mother Goose: Seventy-Seven Rhymes. Tudor, Tasha (1915-), illus. LC 58-58523. (Illus.). (gr. k-3). 1944. (ISBN 0-8098-1901-5). McKay.

--Mother Goose: Seventy-Seven Verses. Tudor, Tasha (1915-), illus. LC 44-8553. (Starling Burgess Legally Changed name to Tasha Tudor). 87 p. illus. (part col.) 19 x 17 cm. 1944. Oxford University Press.

--Mother Goose Tells Time. Schneider, Alice, ed. Paflin, Roberta, pseud. (1903-), illus. Petty, Roberta Harris Pfafflin. LC 45-3542. 28 p. col. illus. 26 x 22 1/2 cm. 1945. The Citadel Press.

--Mother Goose: The Complete Book of Nursery Rhymes. Miloche, Hilda & Kane, Wilma, illus. LC 53-29502. 380p. illus. 27cm. 1953. Whitman Pub. Co.

--Mother Goose: The Complete Book of Nursery Rhymes. Snow, Dorothea Johnston (1909-), illus. LC 41-22516. 2 p. l., 9-380 p. illus. (part col.) 26 1/2 cm. c.1941. Whitman Publishing Company.

--Mother Goose: The Most Popular Nursery Jingles. LC 3-14818. (Illus.). 23cm. 107p. 1902. Homewood Pub. Co.

--Mother Goose: The Old Nursery Rhymes. Rackham, Arthur (1867-1939), illus. LC 13-234258. xxiii, 262 p. incl. col. front., illus., col. plates. 24 1/2 cm. 1913. The Century Co.

--The Mother Goose Treasury. Briggs, Raymond Redvers (1934-), ed. Briggs, Raymond Redvers (1934-), illus. LC 66-12045. 217p. illus. (pt. col.) 30cm. 1st U.S. edition. 1966. Coward. **Awards: (ALA); (KGM).**

--The Mother Goose Treasury. Briggs, Raymond Redvers (1934-), ed. Briggs, Rayond Redvers (1934-), illus. (Illus.). 224p. 1980. (ISBN 0-698-20094-2, Coward). Putnam Pub Group.

--Mother Goose Wonder Book. 44p. (Little Red Riding Hood Ser.). N.D. Hurst & Co.

--Mother Goose's A. B. C. Book. 48p. (Playtime Picture Ser.). N.D. Donohue, Henneberry & Co.

--Mother Goose's Complete Nursery Rhymes, Tales, and Jingles for Children. (Illus.). 576p. N.D. Frederick Warne & Co.

--Mother Goose's Complete Rhymes and Melodies. (Illus.). 196p. (St. Nicholas Ser.). N.D. Hurst & Co.

--Mother Goose's Jingles. (Illus.). N.D. George Routlegde & Sons.

--Mother Goose's Jingles, 1 of 10 vols. (Cinderella Ser.). 1900. Set. Hurst & Co.

--Mother Goose's Jingles. 68p. (Christmas Tree Ser.). N.D. Hurst & Co.

--Mother Goose's Melodies. (Illus.). N.D. George Routledge & Sons.

--Mother Goose's Melodies. N.D. J. B. Lippincott & Co.

--Mother Goose's Melodies ... 79 p. col. front., illus. 25 1/2 cm. c.1904. Lothrop Publishing Company.

--Mother Goose's Melodies. LC 41-421478. 18 l. col. illus. 27 x 24 cm. N.D. Porter & Coates.

--Mother Goose's Melodies, 1 of 12 Vols. (Illus.). (Kriss Kringle Library). N.D. Set. Pousford & Co.
--Mother Goose's Melodies. Bennett, Charles Henry (1829-1967), illus. (Illus.). N.D. Porter & Coates.
--Mother Goose's Melodies. Uncle Solomon, selected by. 96p. N.D. Happy Hours Company.
--Mother Goose's Melodies: Or, Songs for the Nursery. Kappes, Alfred, illus. LC 14-22478. xix, 1 p., 1 l., 186 p. illus., 8 col. pl. (incl. front.) 25 1/2 x 20 cm. 1879. Osgood and Company.
--Mother Goose's Melodies: Or, Songs for the Nursery. Wheeler, William Adolphus (1833-1874), ed. LC 4-10452. xix, 1, 186 p. front., illus., plates. 24 cm. N.D. Houghton, Mifflin and Company.
--Mother Goose's Melody: Or, Sonnets for the Cradle. Thomas, Isaiah (1749-1831) & Shakespeare, William (1564-1616), eds. x, 11-94 p., 1 l. incl. front., illus. 9 1/2 cm. N.D. Printed by Isaiah Thomas, and Sold at His Book-Store.
--Mother Goose's Nursery Rhymes. 48p. (Pleasant Picture Ser.). N.D. Donohue, Henneberry & Co.
--Mother Goose's Nursery Rhymes. (Illus.). (Mother Goose Ser.). N.D. Hurst and Company.
--Mother Goose's Nursery Rhymes. LC 99-4827. 3 p. l., 128 p. illus. (part col.) 28 x 21 1/2 cm. 1899. McLoughlin Bros.
--Mother Goose's Nursery Rhymes. Atkinson, Allen, illus. LC 83-48846. (Illus.). (gr. k up). 1984. (ISBN 0-394-53699-1). Knopf.
--Mother Goose's Nursery Rhymes. Cooke, Edna W., illus. LC 30-173080. 384 p. col. front., illus., col. plates. 21 1/2 cm. c.1930. Cupples & Leon Company.
--Mother Goose's Nursery Rhymes. Gilbert, John Clitherae & Tenniel, John, Sir (1820-1914), illus. N.D. George Routledge & Sons.
--Mother Goose's Nursery Rhymes. Gilbert, John Clitherae & Tenniel, John, Sir (1820-1914), illus. (Illus.). N.D. George Routledge & sons.
--Mother Goose's Nursery Rhymes. Jerold, Walter Copeland, ed. Hassall, John (1868-1948), illus. (Illus.). N.D. Dodge Publishing Company.
--Mother Goose's Nursery Rhymes. Opper, Frederick Burr (1857-1937), illus. LC 15-23982. 320 p. col. front., illus. 21 cm. 1900. J. B. Lippincott Company.
--Mother Goose's Nursery Rhymes. Opper, Frederick Burr (1857-1937), illus. LC 16-23240. 320 p. col. front., illus. (part col.) 21 1/2 cm. $1.5. c.1916. J. B. Lippincott Company.
--Mother Goose's Nursery Rhymes. Walter, Lavinia Edna, ed. Folkard, Charles James (1878-1963), illus. LC 24-26903. vii, 1 216 p. col. front., illus., col. plates. 19 1/2 cm. (Macmillan children's classics). 1924. The Macmillan Company.
--Mother Goose's Nursery Rhymes. A Collection of Alphabets, Rhymes, Tales, and Jingles. Gilbert, John Clitherae & Tenniel, John, Sir (1820-1914), illus. LC 16-3087. 2 p. l., iii-vi, 7-271 p. incl. front., illus. 21 1/2 cm. c.1886. J. D. Williams.
--Mother Goose's Nursery Rhymes and Fairy Tales. (Illus.). 400p. (Colored Classics). N.D. David Mckay.
--Mother Goose's Nursery Rhymes and Fairy Tales. (Illus.). 447p. N.D. George Routledge & Sons; Dist. by E. P. Dutton.
--Mother Goose's Nursery Rhymes and Melodies. (Pictorial Ser). N.D. Hurst & Company.
--Mother Goose's Nursery Rhymes & Melodies, 1 of 10 vols. 1900 ed. (Mother Goose Ser.). N.D. Set. Hurst & Co.
--Mother Goose's Nursery Rhymes, Tales, and Jingles. 576p. 1891. Frederick Warne.
--Mother Goose's Nursery Rhymes, Tales and Jingles. Gannon, W., ed. xiii, 15-416 p. col. front., illus., col. pl. 21 cm. 1902. Hurst & Company.
--Mother Goose's Rhymes. (Illus.). (The Mother Goose Ser.). N.D. A. L. Burt.
--Mother Goose's Rhymes. (Illus.). N.D. George Routledge & Sons.
--Mother Goose's Rhymes. LC 16-3076. 67-132 p. illus. 19 cm. 1886. McLoughlin Bros.
--Mother Goose's Rhymes, Chimes and Jingles. LC 16-3074. iv, 5-132 p. illus. 20 cm. 1886. McLoughlin Bro's.
--Mother Goose's Rhymes, Chimes and Melodies. (Illus.). 1888. Porter & Coates.
--Mother Goose's Rhymes, Jingles and Fairy Tales. (Illus.). (Young Poeple's Lib.). N.D. Henry Altemus.
--Mother Goose's Rhymes, Jingles and Fairy Tales. (Illus.). (Boys and Girls' Classics). N.D. Henry Altemus.
--Mother Goose's Story Book. LC 16-10100. 66 p. col. illus. 28 cm. c.1899. McLoughlin Bros.
--Mother Goose's Teddy Bears. Cavally, Frederick L., Jr., adapted by. Cavally, Frederick L., Jr., illus. LC 7-31379. 64p. illus. 23 x 26 cm. 29 x 26cm. 64p. 1907. Bobbs-Merrill.
--My First Mother Goose. Watkins, Sylvestre C. (1911-), ed. Gehr, Mary, illus. LC 46-22442. 32 p. illus. (part col.) 23 1/2 x 18 cm. 1946. Wilcox & Follett Co.
--Nursery Rhymes ... LC 42-1759. 16 p. col. illus. 32 cm. c.1941. Whitman Publishing Company.
--Nursery Rhymes and Songs. Malvern, Corinne (1905-1956), illus. Dallam, Helen, contrib. by. LC 45-11390. 63 p. col. illus. 28 1/2 cm. c.1944. Whitman Publishing Company.
--The Old Fashioned Mother Goose' Melodies, Complete, with Magic Colored Pictures. Donaldson Brothers, Designers & Printers. 96 p. col. illus. 19 cm. 1879. G. W. Carleton & Co.
--Old Mother Goose. cover-title, 3-15 p. col. illus. 19 cm. c.1852. J. B. Keller.
--Old Mother Goose. Haines, Frank (0000-1963), adapted by. Richardson, Frederick, illus. LC 63-12406. (Illus.). 26 p. 24cm. (Little owl book). 1963. Holt, Rinehart & Winston.
--Old Mother Goose in a New Dress. Whitcomb, Adah Frances, ed. Hall, Douglas (1931-), illus. LC 32-26677. 45 p. col. illus. 22 x 28 1/2 cm. 1932. Laidlaw Brothers.
--The Old Mother Goose Nursery Rhyme Book. LC 25-27468. 143, 1 p. incl. col. front., illus. (part col.) 29 1/2 cm. N.D. T. Nelson and Sons.
--The Old Mother Goose Nursery Rhyme Book. LC 44-1740. 127, 1 p. incl. col. front., illus. (part col.) 29 1/2 x 24 cm. N.D. T. Nelson and Sons.
--Old Mother Hubbard & Her Dog. Ness, Evaline Michelow, Mrs. (1911-), illus. LC 74-182788. (Illus.). 32p. (ps-1). 1972. (ISBN 0-03-088369-5). (ISBN 0-03-005721-3). HR&W. **Award: (ALA).**
--Old Nurse's Mother Goose. LC 16-3075. 66 p. illus. 19 cm. 1886. McLoughlin Bros.
--The Only True Mother Goose Melodies. Hale, Edward Everett (1822-1909), intro. by. LC 5-27154. (An Exact Reproduction of the Text and Illustrations of the Original Edition). xii, 103 p. illus. 14 1/2 x 12 1/2 cm. 1905. Lee and Shepard.
--Original Melodies from Mother Goose. Hillegas, Rose T., selected by. Deming, Kathryn O., illus. LC 38-20651. 96 p. illus. (part col.) 24 cm. c.1938. F. A. Davis Company.
--The Original Mother Goose Melodies. Goodridge, J. F., illus. LC 16-30838. 103 p. illus. 15 1/2 x 19 cm. 1878. Lee and Shepard.
--The Original Mother Goose's Melody. Newbery, John (1713-1767) & Thomas, Isaiah (1749-1831), eds. Samber, Robert, tr. LC 16-5939. 1 p. l., 117 p. front. (port.) illus. 23 1/2 cm. 1892. Damrell & Upham.
--Our Own Mother Goose. Reid, Carol McMillan, ed. The, Koehne Studios, Inc. LC 35-23323. cover-title, 34 p. illus. 33 1/2 cm. c.1934. Whitman Publishing Co.
--The Piper's Son. Barto, Emily Newton (1886-), illus. Barto, Emily Newton (1886-), intro. by. LC 42-218951. 56 p. illus. 16 1/2 x 14 cm. 1942. Longmans Green & Co.
--The "Pop-up" Mother Goose. Lentz, Harold B., illus. LC 34-15308. 96 p. incl. front., illus. (part col.) 22 1/2 cm. c.1933. Blue Ribbon Books, Inc.
--The "Pop-up" Mother Goose. Lentz, Harold B., illus. 18 p. front., illus. (part col.) 23 1/2 cm. c.1934. Blue Ribbon Press.
--The Rainbow Mother Goose. Becker, May Lamberton (1873-1958), ed. Cassel, Lili, pseud. (1924-), illus. Wronker, Lili Cassel. LC 47-310905. 160 p. illus. (part col.) 22 cm. (Rainbow Classics). 1947. World Pub. Co.
--The Read Aloud Mother Goose. Stang, Judy (1921-1977), illus. LC 57-4178. 160p. illus. 21cm. (Wonder Read Aloud Books, 2006). 1957. Wonder Books.
--The Real Mother Goose. LC 32-28025. 61 p. col. illus. 23 cm. 1932. Rand, McNally & Company.
--The Real Mother Goose. LC 43-43402. 134, 1 p. incl. col. front., illus. (part col.) 31 1/2 x 25 cm. 1940. Rand McNally & Co.
--The Real Mother Goose. Wright, Blanche Fisher (1878-), illus. LC 41-51995. 31 x 25cm. 134p. N.D. Rand McNally Publication.
--Rhymes and Melodies. Webb, J. L., illus. Lane, E. I., contrib. by. 52 p. col. illus. 26 1/2 cm. c.1888. Cassell & Company, Limited.
--Richard Scarry's Animal Mother Goose: One Hundred Favorite Old Rymes. Scarry, Richard McClure (1919-), illus. LC 64-25953. (Illus.). 1 v. (unpaged). 33cm. 1964. Golden Press.
--Rojankovsky's Mother Goose. Rojankovsky, Feodor Stepanovich (1891-1970), illus. LC 42-36352. 120p. incl. col., illus. (part col.) 31 1/2 x 13cm. Reissue of 1957 ed. (Little Golden Book). 1959. Golden Press.
--The Romney Gay Mother Goose ... Gay, Romney, ed. LC 36-17312. 4 p. l., 7-56 p. illus. (part col.) 26 1/2 x 24 1/2 cm. c.1936. Grosset & Dunlap, Inc.
--The Shoe Mother Goose. Gringhuis, Richard H. (1918-1974), illus. Gringhuis, Dirk, pseud. LC 47-2030. 32 p. illus. (part col.) 21 1/2 x 29 cm. (Story Hour Book). 1946. The Fideler Company.
--The Singing Mother Goose Book. Fujikawa, Gyo, illus. LC 55-1059. (Illus.). unpaged. 21cm. (Magic talking books, T 1). 1955. J. C. Winston Co.
--The So Big Book of Mother Goose. LC 50-7941. 24p. col. illus. 32 x 15cm. (So Big Ser.). 1950. Garden City Pub. Co.
--Songs and Pictures from Mother Goose Land. LC 42-40670. (Twenty-two Rhymes with Music and Pictures for Coloring). cover-title, 47 p. illus. 30 1/2 cm. c.1941. Remick Music Corporation.
--Stardust Mother Goose. Rutherford, Bonnie & Rutherford, Bill, eds. Rutherford, Bonnie & Rutherford, Bill, illus. LC 68-21792. 1. v. (unpaged) illus. by col.) 19cm. (Stardust Bks.). 1968. C. R. Gibson.
--Stokes' Wonder Book of Mother Goose. Choate, Florence & Curtis, Elizabeth, illus. LC 19-19073. xiv p., 1 l., 240 p. col. front., illus., col. plates. 28 cm. c.1919. Frederick A. Stokes Company.
--Tall Book of Mother Goose. Rojankovsky, Feodor Stepanovich (1891-1970), illus. (Illus.). (Tall Book Ser.). (ps-1). 1942. (ISBN 0-06-025055-0, HarpJ). (ISBN 0-06-025056-9). Har-Row.
--The Teenie Weenie Man's Mother Goose. Donahey, William (1883-1970), illus. LC 21-14441. (The Most Complete Mother Goose Published in America--700 Rhymes). 126 p. col. front., illus., col. plates. 28 1/2 cm. c.1921. The Reilly & Lee Co.
--A Tiny Book of Nursery Rhymes from Mother Goose. Van Nortwick, Chester K., illus. LC 34-37990. 2 p. l., 7-61 p. illus. (part col.) 17 1/2 cm. c.1934. The Harter Publishing Company.
--Tom Tom The Piper's Son. Galdone, Paul (1914-), illus. LC 63-21537. 19 x 26cm. 32p. 1964. (ISBN 0-07-022711-X). Whittlesey House.
--Tommy Tittlemouse: Nursery Rhymes. Evans, Katherine Floyd (1901-1964), illus. LC 47-202254. 37 p. illus. (part col.) 19 1/2 x 17 cm. (Star-Bright Book, S-302). 1947. Childrens Press, Inc.
--Tommy Tucker. Mother Goose Melodies ... cover-title, 14 p. illus. (part col.) 27 cm. c.1887. McLoughlin Bros.
--The Toyland Mother Goose. Beard, Patten, ed. Beard, Patten, illus. LC 17-298789. xi, 147 p. incl. front., illus. 28 cm. c.1917. Frederick A. Stokes Company.
--The True Mother Goose. Or, Mother Goose's Melodies for Children. Mansfield, Blanche McManus (1869-), illus. LC 15-239834. x, 138 p. illus. 25 cm. 1896. Lamson, Wolffe and Company.
--The True Mother Goose: Songs for the Nursery, Or Mother Goose's Melodies for Children. McManus, Blanche, illus. 136p. 1901. A. Wessels Co.
--Twenty Four Pictures from Mother Goose. G. B. J., illus. 1 p. l., 23 numb. l., 9 p. illus. 23 cm. c.1881. S. W. Tilton & Co.
--Walt Disney's Mother Goose. Disney, Walt, Studio, illus. LC 52-3177. unpaged illus. 21 cm. (See-saw books, S-4). 1952. Simon and Schuster.
--Willy Pogany's Mother Goose. Pogany, Willy (1882-1955), illus. LC 28-25391. 152 p. incl. col. front., illus. (part col.) 23 1/2 cm. c.1928. T. Nelson & Sons.

Mother Goose & Anglund, Joan Walsh (1926-)
--In a Pumpkin Shell, a Mother Goose ABC. 1st ed. LC 60-10243. unpaged. illus: 25cm. 1960. Harcourt, Brace.
--In a Pumpkin Shell: A Mother Goose ABC. LC 76-41001. 23cm. 32p. (A Voyager book; A V B 109). 1977, c.1960. (ISBN 0-15-644425-9). Hardcourt Brace Jovanovich.

Mother Goose & Disney, Walt, Productions
--Mickey Mouse and Mother Goose. LC 52-317. 2 p. l., 9-136, 4 p. illus. (part col.) 20 cm. c.1937. Whitman Publishing Company.

Mother Goose & Fisher & Brother,Philadelphia, Pub
--Delightful Ditties. LC 32-305686. cover-title, p. 12-19, col. illus. 14 cm. (Fisher and brother's funny toys). 1860. Fisher & Brother.
--Nursery Rhymes. LC 32-30569. cover-title, 20-26, 1 p. col. illus. 14 cm. (Fisher and brother's funny toys). N.D. Fisher & Brother.

Mother Goose & Francis, Jane Shaw
--The Christmas Mother Goose. Hannan, Tom, illus. LC 54-44836. unpaged. illus. 21 x 24cm. c.1954. American Press.

Mother Goose & Low, Joseph (1911-)
--Mother Goose Riddle Rhymes. 1st ed. Low, Joseph (1911-), illus. LC 53-902685. unpaged. illus. 28cm. 1953. Harcourt, Brace. **Award: (NYT).**

Mother Goose, jt. auth. see Broadhurst, Jean.
Mother Goose, jt. auth. see Cornish, Mary Taylor.
Mother Goose, jt. auth. see Downer, Marion.
Mother Goose see Doyle, Emma Lyons.
Mother Goose, jt. auth. see Haubiel, Charles.
Mother Goose, jt. auth. see Martin, Sarah Catherine.
Mother Goose see Scott, William Rufus.
Mother Goose, jt. auth. see Smith, Laura Rountree.
Mother Goose, jt. auth. see Wheeler, Opal.

Mother Goose & Rion, Hanna
--Ver Beck's Bears in Mother Goose Land. VerBeck, Frank (1858-1933), illus. N.D. George H Doran & Co.

Motley, Ann, jt. auth. see Schiever, Shirley.

Motor, R. R.
--The Upward Path: A Reader for Colored Children. Pritchard, Myron T. & Ovington, Mary W., eds. N.D. Harcourt Brace.

Mott, Michael Charles Alston (1930-)
--The Blind Cross: A Novel of the Children's Crusade. LC 68-27739. 208 p. 21cm. 1970, c.1969. Delacorte Press.
--Master Entrick. (gr. 3-7). 1965. (ISBN 0-440-05489-3). Delacorte.
--Master Entrick. LC 66-77271. (An Adventure). 190p. 21cm. 1st U.S. edition. 1966, c.1965. (ISBN 0-440-05489-3). Delacorte.

Mott, Sarah Minnie & Lynch, Maude Darrows Dutton, Mrs. (1880-)
--Fishing and Hunting. LC 5-416333. 127 p. illus. 19 cm. (World at Work Series ...I). c.1905. American Book Company.

Motte-Fouque, Friedrich Heinrich Karl La see La Motte-Fouque, Friedrich Heinrich Karl.

Motter, Charlott L
--Poca. Kelley, Onetia, illus. LC 81-68859. (Illus.). 20 p., 1 leaf of plates. c.1981. (ISBN 0-937268-12-7). C.L. Motter.

Motteux, Peter Anthony (1663-1718), tr. see Cervantes Saavedra, Miguel de.

Motz, Lloyd
--The Mouse. N.D. (ISBN 0-448-03049-7). Grosset & Dunlap.

Moule, Arthue Evans (1836-1918), ed.
--Chinese Stories for Boys and Girls. Moule, Arthur Evans, tr. N.D. Charles Scribner.

Moule, Arthur Evans, tr. see Moule, Arthue Evans.

Moulton, Charles
--Mother Goose's Melodies For Children: Or, Songs For The Nursery. N.D. Houghton, Mifflin And Co.

Moulton, Louise Chandler, Mrs. (1835-1908)
--Against Wind and Tide. LC 99-496093. 1 p. l., 90 p. front., plates. 20 cm. c.1899. Little, Brown and Company.
--Bed-Time Stories, 1 of 5 Vols. (Illus.). (Bed-Time Series). 1910. Little Brown & Co.
--Bed-Time Stories. LC 7-333205. 239 p. front., plates. 18 cm. 1874. Roberts Brothers.
--Bed-Time Stories. Ledyard, Addie, illus. LC 1-21995. (Illus.). 18cm. 239p. (The Boys' and Girls' Books). 1899. Little, Brown and Company.
--Firelight Stories, 1 of 5 Vols. (Illus.). (Bed-Time Stories). 1910. Little Brown & Co.
--Firelight Stories. LC 7-33319. 232 p. front., plates. 18 cm. 1883. Roberts Brothers.
--Four of Them. LC 99-106. (Illus.). 12cm. 78p. 1899. Little Brown & Co.
--Her Baby Brother. LC 1-20923. (Illus.). 62p. (The Children's Friend Ser.). 1901. Little, Brown and Company.
--In Childhood's Country. Reed, Ethel, illus. LC 99-2816. ix, 13-69 p. incl. plates, 1 l. pl. 23 x 18 cm. (yellow hair library v. 2). 1896. Copeland & Day.
--In Childhood's Country. Reed, Ethel, illus. N.D. Small, Maynard & Co.
--Jessie's Neighbor, 1 of 4 vols. (Illus.). 190p. (Out of School Ser.). N.D. D Lothrop.
--Jessie's Neighbor. LC 6024. 1 p. l., 64 p. front., plates. 19 1/2 cm. (The Children's Friend Ser.). c.1900. Little, Brown and Company.
--Jessie's Neighbor & Other Stories. LC 1-5520. 50 p. front., illus., plates. 18 cm. c.1877. D. Lothrop and Company.
--Miss Eyre from Boston and others. LC 7-33318. 339 p. 19 cm. 1889. Roberts Brothers.
--More Bed-Time Stories, 1 of 5 Vols. (Illus.). (Bed-Time Series.). 1910. Little Brown & Co.
--More Bed-Time Stories. (Illus.). (The Boys' and Girls' Books). N.D. Little, Brown and Company.
--More Bed-Time Stories. Ledyard, Addie, illus. 238 p. front., pl. 18 cm. 1901. Little, Brown, and Company.

--More Bed-Time Stories. Ledyard, Addie, illus. LC 7-33317. 238 p. front., plates. 18 cm. 1875. Roberts Brothers.

--New Bed-Time Stories. LC 8-20576. 230 p., 1 l. front., plates. 18 cm. 1907. Little, Brown, and Company.

--New Bed-Time Stories, 1 of 5 Vols. (Illus.). (Bed-Time Series). 1910. Little Brown & Co.

--New Bed-Time Stories. Ledyard, Addie, illus. LC 7-33316. 230 p. front., plates. 18 cm. 1880. Roberts Brothers.

--Some Women's Hearts. N.D. Messrs. Roberts Brothers.

--Stories Told at Twilight, 1 of 5 Vols. (Illus.). (Bed-Time Series.). 1910. Little Brown & Co.

--Stories Told at Twilight. LC 7-33315. 3 p. l., 5-229 p. front., plates. 18 cm. 1890. Roberts Brothers.

Moulton, Nathalie Forbes

--Buddie and Blossom. N.D. Little Brown & Co.

--The Health Guard Brownies. N.D. Little Brown & Co.

Moulton, R. Dwayne

--The Mystery of the Pink Waterfall. Headley, Adriane Moulton, illus. LC 80-84116. (Illus.). 177 p. 28cm. 1980. (ISBN 0-9605236-0-X). Pandora's Treasures.

Mounce, Mildred Howard

--Carolee in Candyland. Mounce, Mildred Howard, illus. LC 46-19684. 4 p. l., 50 p. incl. illus., col. plates. 20 1/2 x 17 cm. c.1946. Milmo Publishing Company.

Mount, Adela Frances

--Margery's Quest. N.D. Thomas Nelson & Sons.

Mountain, Lee Harrison

--Space Carnival: The Story Behind Our Space Trips. Love, Dane, illus. LC 76-114439. (Illus.). 41 p. 29cm. (Spin-a-tale book). 1970. Pictorial Publishers.

--Uncle Sam & the Flag. LC 77-83633. (Illus.). (gr. 2-3). 1978. (ISBN 0-87783-145-9). (ISBN 0-87783-148-3). (ISBN 0-87783-232-3). Oddo.

Mountain, Robert, pseud., see Montgomery, Raymond A..

Mountevans, Edward Ratcliffe Garth Russell Evans (1880-1957)

--Ghosts of the Scarlet Fleet. Lee, Manning de Villeneuve (1894-1980), illus. LC 32-32260. 4 p. l., 3-310 p. front. 21 cm. 1932. Farrar & Rinehart, Incorporated.

--The Mystery Chest. Caswell, Edward C., illus. LC 32-2879. vi, 279 p. incl. front. 21 1/2 cm. 1931. Farrar & Rinehart, Incorporated.

--Noel Howard Midshipman. LC 35-10479. x, 246 p. col. front., plates. 21 cm. 1935. F. Warne & Co., Ltd.

--Pirate's Doom. LC 30-33970. viii, 272 p. front. 21 1/2 cm. 1930. Farrar & Rinehart Incorporated.

Mountsier, Mabel, ed.

--Singing Youth. 216p. 1927. Harper & Bros.

Mourning Dove (1888-)

--Coyote Stories. Guie, Heister Dean, ed. Guie, Heister Dean, illus. McWhorter, L. V., notes by. LC 33-32589. 228 p. incl. illus., plates. front. (port.) pl. 20 cm. 1933. The Caxton Printers, Ltd.

Moussard, Jacqueline see Cervon, Jacqueline, pseud.

Moustache, Vieux

--Boarding-School Days. Nast, Thomas (1840-1902) & Darley, Felix Octavius Carr (1822-1888), illus. (An Old Boy's Stories). N.D. Hurd & HOughton.

--Our Fresh and Salt Tutors. Nast, Thomas (1840-1902) & Darley, Felix Octavius Carr (1822-1888), illus. (An Old Boy's Stories). N.D. Hurd & Houghton.

--Two Lives in One. Nast, Thomas (1840-1902) & Darley, Felix Octavius Carr (1822-1888), illus. (An Old Boy's Stories). N.D. Hurd & Houghton.

Mowat, Farley McGill (1921-)

--The Black Joke. Mays, Lewis Victor, Jr. (1927-), illus. LC 63-13462. (Illus.). 218 p. 21cm. 1st U.S. edition. 1963, c.1962. Little, Brown.

--The Curse of the Viking Grave. Geer, Charles Hand (1922-), illus. LC 66-14904. (Illus.). x, 243 p. 21cm. 1966. Little, Brown.

--Lost in the Barrens. Geer, Charles Hand (1922-), illus. LC 56-5628. (Illus.). 244 p. 22cm. (Atlantic Monthly Press book). 1956. Little, Brown. **Award: (CLA).**

--Owls in the Family. Frankenberg, Robert Clinton (1911-), illus. 1962. Little.

--The Snow Walker. 1976. (ISBN 0-316-58693-5, Pub. by Atlantic Monthly Pr). Little.

Mowell, Harriet P. H. see Mannering, May, pseud.

Mowell, Harriet P. H., Mrs.

--The Little Spaniard. Mannering, May, pseud. (Helping Hand Ser.). N.D. Colby and Rich.

Mower, Nancy Alpert

--I Visit My Tutu and Grandma. Wozniak, Patricia A., illus. LC 84-3280. (Illus.). 24 p. 26cm. (Treasury of Children's Hawaiian Stories). c.1984. (ISBN 0-916630-41-2). Press Pacifica.

Mower, Nancy Alpert & Akina, Allen

--The Voyage to Tahiti. Akina, Allen, illus. LC 76-1782. (Illus.). 47 p. 28cm. (Na puke huakai kamalii = Books for children on Sea Voyaging ; Book 3). (Na Puke Huakai Kamalii Ser.: 3). Orig. Title: Ka Huakai I Kahiki. c.1976. Polynesian Voyaging Society.

Mower, Nancy Alpert & Kumm, Sharon

--The Vision of Moikeha. LC 76-1780. (Illus.). 47 p. 28cm. (Na Puke Huakai Kamalii = Books for Children on Sea Voyaging ; Book 1). Orig. Title: Ka Moeuhane O Moikeha. 1976. Polynesian Voyaging Society.

Mowery, Gilbert

--Animaland Homily. 1983. (ISBN 0-8062-1999-8). Carlton.

Moxon, Keith

--Charlie Cockatoo and the Mysterious Signals, and Other Astonishing Adventures in the Insect World. LC 60-10071. 88 p. illus. 20 cm. 1960. Beacon Hill Press.

--Charlie Cockatoo Visits the Insect World: The Astonishing Adventures of a Very Talkative Bird. LC 59-8630. 95p. illus. 20cm. 1959. Beacon Hill Press.

Moyes, Patricia (1923-)

--Helter-Skelter. LC 68-11840. (Illus.). 243 p. 22cm. 1968. Holt, Rinehart and Winston.

Moynihan, Roberta

--Futility, the Tapir. LC 59-1692. 52p. illus. 21x27cm. 1959. Viking Press.

Mozley, Charles (1915-), ed.

--Arabian Nights. The First Book of Tales of Ancient Araby. LC 60-120157. 66p. illus. 23cm. 1960. F. Watts.

--The First Book of Tales of Ancient Egypt. LC 60-12016. 67p. illus. 23cm. (First books, 121). 1960. F. Watts.

Mozley, Charles (1915-), illus.

--Oscar Wilde Fairy Tales. (Illus.). 190p. (gr. 4-8). 1980. (ISBN 0-370-01042-6, Pub. by Chatto Bodley Jonathan). Merrimack Pub Cir.

Mozley, Juliet, illus.

--Wooden Horse of Troy. (Illus.). 7 color ils. 48p. (gr. k-3). 1971. (ISBN 0-531-01975-6). Watts.

Mrs. Dr. T

--Helper for Santa. (gr. 2-4). 1970. Vantage.

Mrs E. , pseud., see Elliott, Glynn S..

Mrs E. , pseud. & Charlie D. , pseud.

--Thumpalong. Elliott, Glynn S.. new ed. Dikkens, Charlie. Fredrick C. , pseud., illus. Miller, Fredrick C.. (Illus.). 30p. 1st U.S. edition. (Teaching Human Values Ser.: Vol. 2). (gr. 3-8). 1975. (ISBN 0-914242-06-7). (ISBN 0-914242-05-9). Bookworld Comm.

Mrstikova, Marie

--Tales the Wind Told. Wilson, Paul & Manasek, Ludek, illus. LC 76-356709. (Illus.). 202 p. 29cm. 1974. (ISBN 0-600-38704-6). Hamlyn.

Ms. Foundation see Thomas, Marlo.

Muchnik, Michoel (1952-)

--The Cuckoo Clock Castle of Shir. Muchnik, Michoel (1952-), illus. LC 79-55560. (Illus.). 32 p. 20cm. c.1980. (ISBN 0-8197-0476-8). Bloch Pub. Co.

Muddock, Joyce Emerson Preston (1843-1934)

--Maid Marian & Robin Hood. Wood, Stanley L. (1866-1928), illus. (Illus.). 1900. J B Lippincott.

--Maid Marian and Robin Hood. A Romance of Old Sherwood Forest. Wood, Stanley L. (1866-1928), illus. iv p., 1 l., 326 p. front., 11 pl. 20 cm. 1892. J. B. Lippincott Company.

Mudge

--Grace Goodwin, a Story for Girls. N.D. Hurst & Company.

Mudge, Zachariah Atwell, jt. auth. see Kingston, William Henry Giles.

Mudra, Marie

--David Farragut, Sea Fighter. LC 53-10510. 177p. illus. 22cm. 1953. J. Messner.

--A Feather for His Cap. 1st ed. MacLean, Robert (1926-), illus. LC 58-9573. 160p. illus. 22cm. 1959. Dutton.

--Look Beyond Tomorrow. 1st ed. LC 57-8963. 192p. 21cm. 1957. Dutton.

Muehl, Lois Baker (1920-)

--The Hidden Year of Devlin Bates. Martinez, John, illus. LC 67-3652. (Illus.). 138 p. 22cm. 1967. Holiday House.

--My Name Is-. A Game of Letters and Their Sounds. LC 59-16189. (Illus.). unpaged. 20cm. 1959. Holiday House.

--Worst Room in the School. Freeman, Don (1908-1978), illus. LC 61-2309. (Illus.). 159 p. 22cm. 1961. Holiday House.

Mueller, Amelia (1911-)

--Sissy Kid Brother. Van Demark, Paul, illus. LC 74-17385. (Illus.). 236 p. 23cm. 1975. (ISBN 0-8361-1753-0). (ISBN 0-8361-1753-0). Herald Press.

Mueller, Arnold Carl (1891-)

--Bible Heroes. Hook, Richard, illus. LC 56-1128. (Illus.). color ils. 16p. (Bible Story Booklet Ser). (gr. 3-5). 1981. (ISBN 0-570-06700-6). Concordia.

--Jesus & His Friends. Hook, Richard, illus. (Illus.). color ils. 16p. (Bible Story Booklets Ser.). (gr. 3-5). 1971. (ISBN 0-570-06703-0). Concordia.

--Jesus Helps People. Hook, Richard, illus. (Illus.). color ils. 16p. (Bible Story Booklets Ser). (gr. 3-5). 1971. (ISBN 0-570-06704-9). Concordia.

--Jesus with Us. Hook, Richard, illus. (Illus.). color ils. 16p. (Orig.). (Bible Story Booklets Ser). (gr. 3-5). 1971. (ISBN 0-570-06702-2). Concordia.

--My Good Shepherd: Bible Story Book. Brune, Lillian, ed. Hook, Richard, illus. LC 70-89876. (Illus.). 175 p. 29cm. 1969. (ISBN 0-570-03400-0). Concordia Pub. House.

--Our Savior Lives. Hook, Richard, illus. (Illus.). color ils. 16p. (Bible Story Booklets Ser). (gr. 3-5). 1971. (ISBN 0-570-06705-7). Concordia.

--People God Chose. Hook, Richard, illus. LC 56-1129. (Illus.). color ils. 16p. (Bible Story Booklets Ser). (gr. 3-5). 1971. (ISBN 0-570-06701-4). Concordia.

Mueller, Elmer

--Charley the Ant and His Magic Cane. (Illus.). N.D. (ISBN 0-8181-0098-2). Pageant Press International Corp.

--Charlie the Ant & His Magic Cane. (gr. 1 up). N.D. (ISBN 0-8181-0098-2). Pageant-Poseidon.

Mueller-Guggenbuehl, Fritz (1922-), retold by.

--Swiss-Alpine Folk-Tales. Kiddell-Monroe, Joan (1908-), illus. Potts, Katherine, tr. LC 58-199882. 225p. illus. 23cm. (Oxford myths and legends). 1958. Oxford University Press.

--Swiss-Alpine Folk-Tales. Potts, Katherine & Kiddell-Monroe, Joan (1908-), trs. LC 64-8652. (Illus.). (Myths & Legends Ser). (gr. 4-7). 1958. (ISBN 0-8098-2332-2). Walck.

Mueller, Madeline, tr. see De Jong, Dola.

Mueller, Madeline, tr. see Diekmann, Miep.

Mueller, Margarethe (1862-)

--Elsbeth: A Story of German Home Life. LC 14-188086. 5 p. l., vii-xxi p., 1 l., 296 p. col. front., plates. 20 cm. (On verso of half-title: Little Schoolmate Ser. ed by F. Converse). c.1914. E. P. Dutton & Company.

Mueller, Marie Hinrichs

--Little Betta in the Red Heather Country. LC 56-10549. 118p. 21cm. 1957. Vantage Press.

Mueller, Theodore J., adapted by see Wulff, Trolli Neutzsky.

Mueller, Virginia (1924-)

--Clem, the Clumsy Camel. (Illus.). 32p. (Arch Book: No. 11). (gr. 1-4). 1974. (ISBN 0-570-06085-0). Concordia.

--The King's Invitation: Matthew 22: 1-14 for Children. Roberts, Jim, illus. (Illus.). 32 p. 21cm. (Arch books). 1968. (ISBN 0-570-06033-8). Concordia Pub. House.

--Monster and the Baby. Munsinger, Lynn (1951-), illus. LC 85-3127. (Illus.). 22 p. 1985. (ISBN 0-8075-5253-4). A. Whitman.

--A Playhouse for Monster. Munsinger, Lynn (1951-), illus. LC 85-3144. (Illus.). 24 p. 1985. (ISBN 0-8075-6541-5). A. Whitman.

--The Secret Journey: Matthew 2: 13-23 for Children. Wind, Betty, illus. (Illus.). 32 p. 21cm. (Arch books). 1968. Concordia Pub. House.

--Silly Skyscraper. (Illus.). 32 full color. 32p. (Orig.). (Arch Bks: Set 7). (ps-4). 1970. (ISBN 0-570-06050-8). Concordia.

Mueser, Annie

--Face at the Window. (Illus.). (Pal Paperbacks). (Pal Skills II Ser.). (gr. 5-12). 1980. (ISBN 0-8374-3562-5). Xerox Ed Pubns.

Mugilevskaya, S.

--Maxim. 18p. 1978. (ISBN 0-8285-1205-1, Pub. by Progress Pubs USSR). Imported Pubns.

Muhlenweg, Fritz (1898-)

--Big Tiger & Christian: Their Adventures in Mongolia. Busoni, Rafaello (1900-1962), illus. McHugh, Isabel & McHugh, Florence, trs. LC 52-9672. (Illus.). 22cm. 592p. (gr. 7-9). 1952. (ISBN 0-394-80946-7). (ISBN 0-394-90946-1). Pantheon.

Mui, Shan

--The Seven Magic Orders. Tabrah, Ruth, ed. Mui, Y. T., illus. LC 72-86743. (Illus.). 27cm. 80p. (An island heritage book). (gr. 1-7). 1972. (ISBN 0-8348-3013-2). Weatherhill.

Muir, Frank (1920-)

--What-a-Mess. Wright, Joseph, illus. LC 77-82646. (Illus.). 30 p. 28cm. 1st U.S. edition. c.1977. (ISBN 0-385-13621-8). Doubleday.

--What-a-Mess, the Good. Wright, Joseph, illus. LC 78-8807. (Illus.). 32 p. 28cm. 1st U.S. edition. c.1978. (ISBN 0-385-14699-X). (ISBN 0-385-14700-7). Doubleday.

Muir, John

--Stickeen: The Story of a Dog. N.D. Houghton Mifflin Co.

Muir, Kirby, ed.

--Fairy Tale Sampler: A Collection of World Famous Tales. La Mont, Violet, illus. LC 47-121199. 46 p. illus. (part col.) 29 cm. 1947. Ziff-Davis Pub. Co.

Muir, Lydia

--Santa Comes to Creepy Corners. Borozinski, Len, photos by. LC 82-50476. (Illus.). 20p. (Orig.). (gr. k-3). 1982. (ISBN 0-943332-00-1). Sonoran.

Muir, Lynette

--The Unicorn Window. Baynes, Pauline Diana (1922-), illus. LC 60-13695. 168p. illus. 21cm. 1961. Abelard-Schuman.

Muir, Marie (1904-)

--The Torridons' Surprise. Acheson, Joseph, illus. LC 62-7425. (Illus.). 21cm. 192p. 1962, c.1961. F. Watts.

--The Torridons' Triumphant Summer. LC 61-6074. 186p. 21cm. 1st U.S. edition. 1961, c.1960. F. Watts.

Muir, Percival Horace (1894-1979), tr. see Le Prince De Beaumont, Marie.

Muir, Percival Horace (1894-1979), tr. see Sleeping Beauty & Perrault, Charles.

Mukerji, Dhan Gopal (1890-1936), tr. see Valmiki.

Mukerji, Dhan Gopal (1890-1936)

--Bunny, Hound and Clown. Wiese, Kurt (1887-1974), illus. LC 31-22899. 4 p. l., 11-124 p. illus. 22 cm. c.1931. E. P. Dutton & Company, Inc.

--Chief of the Herd. Blaine, Mahlon, illus. 168p. c.1929. E. P. Dutton & Co.

--Fierce-Face: The Story of a Tiger. Lathrop, Dorothy Pulis (1891-1980), illus. LC 36-18969. 75, 2 p. incl. front., illus., plates. 22 cm. 1936. E. P. Dutton & Company, Incorporated.

--Gay-Neck; the Story of a Pigeon. Artzybasheff, Boris Mikhailovich (1899-1965), illus. LC 68-13419. (Illus.). 191 p. 21cm. 1968, c.1927. (ISBN 0-525-30400-2). Dutton.

--Gayneck: The Story of a Pigeon. 1927. Dutton. **Award: (JNM).**

--Ghond the Hunter. Artzybasheff, Boris Mikhailovich (1899-1965), illus. 1928. Dutton.

--Hari: The Jungle Lad. Stinemetz, Morgan, illus. LC 24-25647. ix, 220 p. front., plates. 22 cm. c.1924. (ISBN 0-525-31481-4). E. P. Dutton & Company.

--Hindu Fables: For Little Children. Wiese, Kurt (1887-1974), illus. LC 29-10057. xi, 1 p., 2 l., 3-113 p. incl. front., illus., plates. 22 cm. 1929. E. P. Dutton & Co., Inc.

--Jungle Beasts and Men. Allen, James E., illus. LC 23-13123. ix, 160 p. col. front., plates. 22 cm. 1923. E. P. Dutton & Company.

--Kari, the Elephant. Allen, James E., illus. (Illus.). (gr. 5-7). 1922. Dutton.

--Kari, the Elephant. Allen, James E., illus. 1949. Dutton.

--The Master Monkey. Weber, Florence, illus. LC 32-21554. xvi p., 2 l., 3-261 p. incl. front., plates. (1 double) 22 cm. c.1932. E. P. Dutton & Co., Inc.

Muko, Hatoju, pseud., see Kubota, Hikoho.

Muko, Hatoju, pseud. (1905-)

--The Golden Footprints. Kubota, Hikoho. 1st ed. Yashima, Taro, pseud. (1908-), illus. Iwamatsu, Jun Atsushi. Yashima, Taro, pseud. (1908-), tr. Iwamatsu, Jun Atsushi. LC 59-11543. (Illus.). 50 p. 22cm. 1960. World Pub. Co. **Award: (ALA).**

Muku, Hotoju, jt. auth. see Yashima, Taro.

Mulcahy, Lucille Burnett

--The Blue Marshmallow Mountains. Lambo, Donald W. (1903-1966), illus. LC 59-6488. 128p. illus. 23cm. 1959. Nelson.

--Dark Arrow. Danska, Herbert (1928-), illus. LC 53-8939. 209p. illus. 22cm. 1953. Coward-McCann.

--Fire on Big Lonesome. LC 67-30296. (Illus.). 97 p. 25cm. 1967. Elk Grove Press.

--Magic Fingers. Lambo, Donald W. (1903-1966), illus. LC 58-6118. 124p. illus. 23cm. 1958. Nelson.

--Natoto. LC 60-11473. 192p. 21cm. 1960. T. Nelson.

--Pita. LC 54-11355. 218 p. 22cm. 1954. Coward-McCann.

Mulets, Lenore Elizabeth see Muller, Mary, pseud.

Mulets, Lenore Elizabeth (1876-)

--Bird Stories. Schneider, Sophie, illus. LC 3-30473. viii p., 1 l., 240 p. front., 5 pl. 21 cm. (Her Phyllis' Field Friends). 1904. L. C. Page and Company.

--Flower Stories (Pub. by Society for Promoting Christian Knowledge). 1900. E. & J. B. Young & Co.

--Flower Stories. Schneider, Sophie, illus. LC 3-30472. ix p., 1 l., 241 p. front., 5 pl. 21 cm. (Her Phyllis' Field Friends). 1903. L. C. Page and Company,.

--Insect Stories. Schneider, Sophie, illus. LC 3-30474. viii p., 1 l., 294 p. front., 5 pl. 21 cm. (Her Phyllis' Field Friends). 1904. L. C. Page and Company.

--Little People of Japan: A Story of Japanese Child-Life. Starr, Laura B., photos by. LC 3-710. 195 p. front., illus. 18 cm. c.1902. A. Flanagan Company.

--Little People of Japan: A Story of Japanese Child-Life. Starr, Laura B., photos by. LC 25-3027. 190 p. front., illus. 19 cm. (Little People of Other Lands Ser.). 1925. A. Flanagan Company.
--Little People of the Snow. Muller, Mary, pseud. Gilbert, John Clitherae, illus. LC 25-310789. 2 p. l., 135, 4 p. illus. 19 cm. (Little People of Other Lands Ser.). 1925. A. Flanagan Company.
--Little People of the Snow. A Tale of the Frozen North. Muller, Mary, pseud. Gilbert, John Clitherae, illus. LC 1-29543. 108 p. incl. illus., pl. front. 20 cm. 1900. A. Flanagan Co.
--Phyllis' Bird Stories. N.D. L. C. Page & Co.
--Phyllis' Flower Stories. N.D. L. C. Page & Co.
--Phyllis' Insect Stories. N.D. L. C. Page & Co.
--Phyllis' Stories of Big Animals. (Illus.). (The Phyllis Ser.). N.D. The Page Company.
--Phyllis' Stories of Little Animals. (Illus.). (The Phyllis Ser.). N.D. The Page Company.
--Phyllis' Stories of Little Fishes. (Illus.). (The Phyllis Ser.). N.D. The Page Company.
--Phyllis' Tree Stories. (Illus.). (The Phyllis Ser.). N.D. The Page Company.
--Stories of Big Animals. Bull, Charles Livingston (1874-1932) & Smith, Frank Vining, illus. LC 13-166553. viii p., 2 l., 3-298 p. incl. front. plates. 21 cm. (Her Phyllis' field friends). 1913. L. C. Page & Company.
--Stories of Little Animals. Schneider, Sophie, illus. LC 4-17925. ix p., 2 l., 3, 279 p. front., 5 pl. 21 cm. (Her Phyllis' Field Friends). 1905. L. C. Page and Company.
--Stories of Little Fishes. Schneider, Sophie, illus. LC 5-8297. ix p., 2 l., 3-288 p. front., 5 pl. 21 cm. (Her Phyllis' Field Friends). 1905. L. C. Page and Company.
--The Story of Akimakoo: An African Boy. Muller, Mary, pseud. LC 4-12773. 171 p. front., illus. 18 cm. 1904. A. Flanagan Company.
--The Story of Akimakoo: An African Boy. Muller, Mary, pseud. LC 24-3775. 160 p. illus. 18 cm. 1924. A. Flanagan Company.
--Sunshine Lands of Europe. Goldberg, Elias, illus. LC 18-14100. 159 p. illus. (incl. maps) 19 cm. (Children of the world). 1918. World Book Company.
--Tree Stories. Schneider, Sophie, illus. LC 4-26112. xi, 292 p. front., plates. 21 cm. (Her Phyllis' Field Friends). 1905. L. C. Page and Company.
--Wretched Flea: Or, The Story of a Chinese Boy. Muller, Mary, pseud. LC 2-242460. 2 p. l., 3-157, 1 p. front., illus. 18 cm. 1901. A. Flanagan Company.

Mulford, Clarence Edward (1883-1956), created by.
Hopalong Cassidy and Lucky at Copper Gulch. Crowe, Jack, illus. LC 50-8546. (Illus.). 28cm. 24p. 1950. Garden City Pub. Co.
--Hopalong Cassidy and Lucky at the Double X Ranch. Crowe, Jack, illus. LC 50-8547. (Illus.). 28cm. 21p. 1950. Garden City Pub. Co.

Mulford, Philippa Greene
--If It's Not Funny, Why Am I Laughing?. LC 82-70321. 166 p. 22cm. c.1982. (ISBN 0-440-03961-4). Delacorte Press.

Mulgrave, Dorothy Irene, jt. auth. see Kono, Keora.

Mulherin, Jennifer, ed.
--Favorite Fairy Tales. (Illus.). 1983. (ISBN 0-448-01339-8, G&D). Putnam Pub Group.
--Popular Nursery Rhymes. (Illus.). 1983. (ISBN 0-448-01346-0, G&D). Putnam Pub Group.

Mulholland, Clara
--Bunt and Bill. LC 8-2606. 158 p. front. 18 cm. (On verso of t.-p.: Benziger's Juvenile Ser.). c.1902. Benziger Brothers.
--Dimpling's Success. LC 1-30787. 150 p. incl. front., 16 degrees. 1901. Benziger Bros.
--Kathleen Mavourneen. LC 12-369687. 143 p. 19 cm. 1890. J. Murphy & Co.
--Naughty Miss Bunny, 36 vols. (Illus.). (St. Nicholas Ser.). 1905. Set. A L Burt.
--Naughty Miss Bunny. (Illus.). (The Wellesley Series). 1915. A L Burt & Co.
--Naughty Miss Bunny. (The Rugby Series for Boys and Girls). N.D. A. L. Burt Company.

Mulholland, Rosa, pseud., see Gilbert, Rosa Mulholland.

Mulholland, Rosa, pseud. (1841-1921)
--Banshee Castle. Gilbert, Rosa Mulholland. (Illus.). (Scribner-Blackie Series of Books for Young People). N.D. Charles Scribner's Sons.
--Cynthia's Bonnet Shop. Gilbert, Rosa Mulholland. (Illus.). N.D. Charles Scribner's Sons.
--Eldergowan, and Other Tales. Gilbert, Rosa Mulholland. N.D. Pott, Young & Co.
--Four Little Mischiefs. Gilbert, Rosa Mulholland, 36 vols. (Illus.). (St. Nicholas Ser.). 1905. Set. A L Burt Co.
--Four Little Mischiefs. (The Rugby Series for Boys and Girls). N.D. A. L. Burt Company.
--Four Little Mischiefs. Gilbert, Rosa Mulholland. (Illus.). (The Wellesley Series for Girls). N.D. A. L. Burt.
--Four Little Mischiefs. Gilbert, Rosa Mulholland. (Illus.). (Scribner-Blackie Series of books for young people). N.D. Charles Scribner's Sons.
--Gianetta. Gilbert, Rosa Mulholland. (Illus.). (Fireside Series for Girls). N.D. A. L. Burt's Pubs.
--Gianetta. Gilbert, Rosa Mulholland. (Illus.). (The Wellesley Series for Girls). N.D. A. L. Burt's Pubs.
--Gianetta. Gilbert, Rosa Mulholland. (Illus.). (Scribner-Blackie Series of books for young people). N.D. Charles Scribner's Sons.
--Hetty Gray. Gilbert, Rosa Mulholland. (Scribner-Blackie Series of books for young people). N.D. Charles Scribner's Sons.
--The Late Miss Hollingford. Gilbert, Rosa Mulholland. (Scribner-Blackie Series of books for young people). N.D. Charles Scribner's Sons.
--The Little Flower-Seekers: The Adventures of Trot and Daisy in a Wonderful Garden by Moonlight. Gilbert, Rosa Mulholland. N.D. Scribner, Welford & Armstrong.
--Puck and Blossom: A Fairy Tale. Gilbert, Rosa Mulholland. N.D. Pott, Young & Co.
--The Squire's Granddaughter. Gilbert, Rosa Mulholland, 1 of 7 vols. (Catholic Library). 1891. Set. McCauley & Kllner.

Mullan, Carol
--Bible Picture Stories from the Old and New Testaments. Laite, Gordon (1925-), illus. LC 74-187764. (Illus.). 20 p. 32cm. (Golden Books). 1974. (ISBN 0-307-10496-6). Golden Press.
--New Testament Bible Stories. Waring, Dan, illus. LC 75-312224. (Illus.). 20 p. 32cm. 1975. (ISBN 0-307-10502-4). Golden Press.

Mullen, Mary Joanna Funk, Mrs. (1914-) & Mullen, William Boone (1911-)
--The Little Monkey with Wings on His Tail. LC 39-7259. 32 p. incl. front., illus. 25 cm. 1939. Harper & Brothers.

Mullen, Michael
--Sea Wolves from the North. Dunne, Jeanette, illus. (Illus.). 108p. (gr. 3-9). 1984. (ISBN 0-905473-94-9, Pub. by Wolfhound Pr Ireland). (ISBN 0-86327-023-9, Pub. by Wolfhound Pr Ireland). Irish Bks Media.

Mullen, William Boone, jt. auth. see Mullen, Mary Joanna Funk, Mrs.

Mullens, Hannah Catherine, Mrs.
--Life by the Ganges: Or, Faith and Victory. Dulles, John Welsh (1823-1887), ed. LC 12-37035. 288 p. front., plates. 18 cm. c.1867. Presbyterian Publication Committee.

Muller, Adelaide
--Me, Billy!. (Illus.). 64p. (ps-2). 1973. (ISBN 0-682-47744-3). Exposition.

Muller, Carolyn Edna
--God Planned It That Way. LC 52-11653. (Illus.). unpaged. c.1952. Abingdon-Cokesbury Press.

Muller, Charles George Geoffrey (1897-)
--The Baseball Detective. LC 28-19389. 6 p. l., 333, 1 p. front., plates. 20 cm. 1928. Harper & Brothers.
--The Commodore. LC 29-16075. viii p., 1 l., 264 p. front., illus. 20 cm. 1929. Harper & Brothers.
--Curry Was Right. Rigney, Francis Joseph (1882-), illus. LC 31-16336. xii p., 2 l., 3-210 p. incl. front., illus., plates. 21 cm. c.1931. Harcourt, Brace and Company.
--Hero of Champlain. LC 61-12721. 192p. illus. 21cm. 1961. John Day Co.
--Hero of Two Seas. 1968. David McKay Company.
--Laziest Man on the Campus. Starrett, Henrietta McCaig, illus. LC 46-887. 3 p. l., 5-253 p. front., illus. 20 1/2 cm. 1945. W. A. Wilde Company.
--Puck Chasers, Incorporated. LC 27-19314. 5 p. l., 246 p. front., plates. 20 cm. c.1927. Harper & Brothers.
--Ship a-Hoyden?. Picken, Henry Moore, illus. LC 46-8461. 6 p. l., 11-292 p. front., illus. 21 cm. 1946. W. A. Wilde Company.
--Shipwrecked on Mystery Island. Martin, P. L., illus. LC 43-17451. 247 p. front., plates. 21 cm. 1943. W. A. Wilde Company.
--Unburied Treasure. Starrett, Henrietta McCaig, illus. LC 45-5781. 294 p. front., plates. 21 cm. 1944. W. A. Wilde Company.

Muller, Charles George Geoffrey (1897-) & Mazet, Horace Sawyer (1903-)
--Tigers of the Sea. LC 46-2255. 20 1/2cm. 223p. 1946. The Westminster press.

Muller, Christine
--The Burgomaster's Family. (Library of Choice Fiction). N.D. Charles Scribner's Sons.

Muller, Daniel Cody (1889-)
--Chico of the Up Ranch. Muller, Daniel Cody (1889-), illus. LC 38-29550. 5 p. l., 15-249 p. front., illus. 24 cm. c.1938. Reilly & Lee.

Muller, Gerda Maria
--The Dressed-up Rabbit. LC 72-75160. (Illus.). 29 p. 33cm. (Golden book). 1972. Golden Press.

Muller, Jorg
--The Changing Countryside. LC 76-46647. (Illus.). 1977. (ISBN 0-689-50085-8, McElderry Bk). Atheneum.

Muller, Loraine (1933-)
--The Brownie & The Green Elf. LC 63-20436. 96p. (Children's Picture Bks.). 1963. T. S. Denison & Co.

Muller, Loraine (1933-) & Kidder, Barbara Ann
--Little Sardine. Kidder, Barbara Ann (1933-), illus. LC 61-15235. unpaged. illus. 29cm. 1961. T. S. Denison.

Muller, Mary, pseud., see Mulets, Lenore Elizabeth.

Muller, Olga Helen Clara Erbsloh (1894-)
--The Silvery Flute: Verses for Children. Very, Marjorie, illus. LC 45-7902. 44 p., 1 l. col. frontis. illus., col. pl. 21 1/2 cm. 1943. B. Humphries, Inc.

Mullett, George Merrick
--Betsy Lane, Patriot. Fink, Denman, illus. LC 19-14007. 6 p. l., 3-208 p. front., plates. 19 cm. 1919. The Century Co.

Mulley, Jane, tr. see Grundtvig, Svend Hersleb.

Mulligan, Kevin
--Kid Brother. LC 81-20725. 157 p. 22cm. c.1982. (ISBN 0-688-00896-8). Lothrop, Lee & Shepard Books.

Mulliken, Barbara, jt. auth. see Berry, Ruth Eugenie.

Mulliken, E. G., Mrs.
--The Giant of the Treasure Caves. (Illus.). N.D. Dana Estes & Co.

Mulliken, Sarah Elizabeth
--Boys and Girls of Colonial Times. Sichel, Harold M. (1881-), illus. LC 28-11165. ix, 232 p. incl. front., illus. 19 cm. c.1928. Ginn and Company.
--The Voyage of the Anna Smith. LC 40-142001. 292 p. illus. 23 x 17 cm. c.1940. The Bobbs-Merrill Company.

Mullin, Penn
--Search and Rescue. LC 81-22894. (Illus.). 44 p. 18cm. (Perspectives). c.1982. (ISBN 0-87879-292-9). Academic Therapy Publications.

Mullins, Edward Swift (1922-)
--Animal Limericks. Mullins, Edward Swift (1922-), illus. LC 65-20063. (Illus.). 27cm. 32p. (ps-3). 1965. (ISBN 0-695-80427-8). Follett.
--The Big Book of Limericks. Mullins, Edward Swift (1922-), illus. LC 77-75890. (Illus.). 96 ils. 96p. (gr. 1-6). 1969. Platt.

Mullins, Isla May Hawley, Mrs. (1859-1936)
--Captain Pluck. N.D. Baptist Sunday School Beard.
--Captain Pluck. LC 23-12713. 235 p. 20 cm. c.1923. George H. Doran Company.

Mullins, Patricia Ann (1952-)
--Fabulous Beasts. LC 77-352653. (Illus.). 30 p. 30cm. 1976. (ISBN 0-00-185019-9). Collins.

Mullins, Richard
--Most Valuable Player. LC 62-16174. 179p. 22cm. 1962. Funk & Wagnalls.
--Swimmer. LC 57-10580. 243 p. 22cm. 1957. Funk & Wagnalls.

Mullins, Vera Annie Cooper (1903-)
--Kala and the Sea Bird. Thollander, Earl Gustave (1922-), illus. LC 65-10260. 130p. illus. 25cm. c.1966. (ISBN 0-87464-048-2). (ISBN 0-87464-049-0). Golden Gate.
--Ronnie and the Texas Camel. LC 75-38756. p. cm. c.1976. (ISBN 0-8024-3740-0). Moody Press.

Mulock, Dinah Maria see Craik, Dinah Maria Mulock, Mrs.

Mulock, Dinah Maria see Witt, Henriette Elizabeth Guizot.

Mulock, Dinah Maria, pseud. (1826-1887)
--The Little Lame Prince. Craik, Dinah Maria Mulock. Nielsen, Jon (1912-), illus. 1948. World Pub.

Multon, Charles
--Mother Goose's Melodies for Children: Or, Songs for the Nursery. Stephens, Henry Louis (1824-1882) & Kappes, Charles, illus. N.D. Houghton Mifflin.

Mulvany, May Melanie Dauteur (1904-)
--Joan and Pierre. Mulvaney, May Melanie Dauteur (1904-), illus. LC 31-25568. 64 p. col. illus. 26 cm. c.1931. Doubleday, Doran & Company, Inc.

Mumford, Edwin
--The Five Flights of the Starfire. 1974. (ISBN 0-682-47882-2). Exposition Press.
--Flight of the Starfire. 48p. 1972. (ISBN 0-682-47432-0). Exposition.
--The Fourth Flight of the Starfire. 64p. (gr. 10 up). 1972. (ISBN 0-682-47574-2). Exposition.
--The Second Flight of the Starfire: A Fantasy. 64p. (gr. 4-8). 1972. (ISBN 0-682-47462-2). Exposition.
--The Third Flight of the Starfire. 166p. (gr. 5-6). 1972. (ISBN 0-682-47503-3). Exposition.

Mumford, Lawrence Quincy (1903-), ed. see Goldsmith, Oliver (1728-1774) & Jones, Giles.

Mumford, Mary Eno Bassett, Mrs. (1842-)
--A Regular Tomboy. Andrade, Mary F., illus. LC 13-20397. 235 p. incl. front., illus. 20 cm. 1913. The Penn Publishing Company.

Munari, Bruno (1907-)
--ABC. Munari, Bruno (1907-), illus. LC 60-11461. (Illus.). unpaged. 30cm. (Munari Picture Books). 1960. World Pub. Co. **Award: (NYT).**
--Animals For Sale. 1957. World Pub.
--Animals for Sale. Munari, Bruno (1907-), illus. LC 79-19097. (Illus.). 15 p. 32cm. 1980, c.1959. (ISBN 0-529-05567-8). W. Collins.
--The Birthday Present. Munari, Bruno (1907-), illus. LC 79-19082. (Illus.). Orig. Title: L'uomo del camion. (ps-2). 1980. (ISBN 0-529-05565-1, Philomel). Putnam Pub Group.
--The Birthday Present. Munari, Bruno (1907-), illus. (Illus.). (gr. k-2). 1959. (ISBN 0-529-03593-6). World Pub.
--Bruno Munari's Zoo. Munari, Bruno (1907-), illus. 1963. Putnam.
--Bruno Munari's Zoo. Munari, Bruno (1907-), illus. LC 63-14773. 1 v. (unpaged, chiefly col. illus.) 30 cm. (Munari Picture Books). 1963. World Pub. Co. **Award: (ALA).**
--The Circus in the Mist. Munari, Bruno (1907-), illus. LC 78-82766. (Illus.). 57 p. 22cm. 1969, c.1968. World Pub. Co. **Awards: (NYT); (ALA).**
--Elephant's Wish. Munari, Bruno (1907-), illus. (Illus.). (gr. k-2). 1959. (ISBN 0-529-03595-2). World Pub.
--From Afar It Is an Island. Munari, Bruno (1907-), illus. LC 71-155071. (Illus.). photos. 40p. (gr. k-3). 1972. (ISBN 0-529-01284-7). (ISBN 0-529-01285-5). Collins-World.
--Jimmy Has Lost His Cap. Munari, Bruno (1907-), illus. LC 79-18841. (Illus.). Orig. Title: Gigi cera il suo berretto. (ps-2). 1980. (ISBN 0-529-05563-5, Philomel). Putnam Pub Group.
--Jimmy Has Lost His Cap. Munari, Bruno (1907-), illus. (Illus.). (gr. k-2). 1959. (ISBN 0-529-03597-9). World Pub.
--Jimmy Has Lost His Cap: Where Can It Be?. Munari, Bruno (1907-), illus. LC 79-18841. (Illus.). 11 p. 32cm. 1980, c.1959. (ISBN 0-529-05563-5). W. Collins.
--Tic, Tac, and Toc. 1957. World Pub.
--Tic, Tac, and Toc. Munari, Bruno (1907-), illus. LC 79-18852. (Illus.). 21 p. 32cm. 1980, c.1959. (ISBN 0-529-05564-3). W. Collins.
--Who's There? Open the Door!. Munari, Bruno (1907-), illus. LC 79-19012. (Illus.). Repr. of 1957 ed. (ps-2). 1980. (ISBN 0-529-05568-6, Philomel). Putnam Pub Group.
--Who's There?, Open the Door. Munari, Bruno (1907-), illus. LC 79-19012. (Illus.). 12 p. 32cm. 1980. (ISBN 0-529-05568-6). W. Collins.
--Who's There, Open the Door. Munari, Bruno (1907-), illus. (Illus.). (gr. k-2). 1957. (ISBN 0-529-03520-0). World Pub.

Munce, Ruth Hill see Hill, Ruth Livingston.

Munch, Theodore William (1919-) & De Vault, M. Vere
--Road Runner. Rogers, Carol, illus. (gr. 2-4). 1958. (ISBN 0-8114-7587-5). Steck-V.

Munch, Theodore William (1919-) & Winthrop, Robert D. (1932-)
--Thunder on Forbidden Mountain. LC 75-35852. 155 p. 21cm. c.1976. (ISBN 0-664-32588-2). Westminster Press.

Munch, W. Theodore, jt. auth. see DeVault, Marion Vere.

Munchausen
--The Adventures of Baron Munchausen. Dore, Louis Christophe Paul Gustave (1832-1883), illus. LC 44-10705. (With, as issued: Arabian Nights. The Adventures of Sinbad the Sailor). 206 p. incl. front., illus., plates. 22 cm. c.1936. Three Sirens Press.
--Baron Munchhausen: His Wonderful Travels and Adventures. Kastner, Erich (1899-1974), retold by. Trier, Walter (1890-1951), illus. Winston, Richard & Winston, Clara, trs. LC 57-11502. 68p. illus. 27cm. (Harlequin books). 1957. Messner.

Munchhausen, Angelita Von see Von Munchhausen, Angelita.

Muncy, Leroy Lee (1899-)
--The Boy from McGregor: A Story of Enterprise and Integrity for Young and Old Americans of Today. LC 59-943795. 186p. 21cm. 1959. Greenwich Book Publishers.

Mundy, V M
--Brave Journey. LC 58-12696. 181p. 22cm. 1958. Prentice-Hall.
--Mission to Bayou Pierre. LC 61-13541. 180p. 21cm. 1961. Prentice-Hall.

Munger, J. S.
--Suzie Belle. N.D. Carlton.

Munkittrick, Richard Kendall (1853-1911)
--The Moon Prince. LC 12-36987. xi, 340 p. incl. front., illus., plates. 19 cm. 1893. Harper & Brothers.

--Moon Prince. (Harper's Selected Juveniles). 1910. Harper & Brothers.
--More Mother Goose: Little Bo-peep Continued. Loomis, Chester, illus. (Illus.). 12p. 1898. R. H. Russell.

Munkres, Alberta (1888-)

--I Wonder: Stories for Little Children. Howe, Gertrude Herrick (1902-), illus. LC 30-33609. 54 p. col. illus. 21 cm. c.1930. The Abingdon Press.

Munn, Charles Clark (1848-1917)

--Boyhood Days on the Farm. Merrill, Frank Thayer (1848-), illus. (Illus.). 403p. 1907. Lothrop.
--Camp Castaway. Shettsline, William J., Jr., illus. LC 16-7916. 4 p. l., 325, 1 p. col. front., col. plates. 20 cm. 1916. D. Appleton and Company.

Munn, Ian

--Five Beds for Bitsy: A Puppy Grows up. Webbe, Elizabeth, illus. (Illus.). 17cm. 33p. c.1950. Rand McNally.
--Five Beds for Bitsy: A Puppy Grows Up. Webbe, Elizabeth, illus. LC 57-10610. unpaged. illus. 27cm. (Rand McNally Storytime Book). 1957, c.1950. Rand McNally.
--Johnny & the Birds. LC 50-4867. (Illus.). 21cm. 33p. (A Rand McNally book-elf book). (gr. k-2). 1950. (ISBN 0-8382-0386-8). Hale.
--Little Mailman of Bayberry Lane. 1952. (ISBN 0-8382-0460-0, Hale Giant Books). E. M. Hale and Co.
--The Little Mailman of Bayberry Lane. Webbe, Elizabeth, illus. LC 52-33574. unpaged. illus. 21 cm. (Rand McNally Book-Elf Book, 458). c.1952. Rand McNally.

Munn, W.

--Three Men on a Chinese Houseboat. (Illus.). N.D. Fleming H. Revell Co.

Munowitz, Ken (1935-1977) & Mee, Charles L, Jr. (1938-)

--Noah. LC 77-11839. p. cm. c.1978. (ISBN 0-06-024183-7). (ISBN 0-06-024184-5). Harper & Row.

Munro, pseud., see Munro, John Kirkby.

Munro, Douglas, tr. see Dumas, Alexandre.

Munro, Eleanor

--Through Vermilion Gates. 1971. (ISBN 0-394-82034-7). Pantheon Books.

Munro, Elsie Smeaton

--Topsy Turvy Tales. N.D. Frederick A. Stokes.

Munro, Frances

--Johnnie Snoozle Mouse in the Big House. (Stories for Little Children). N.D. Penn.

Munro, Hector Hugh see Saki, pseud.

Munro, John Kirkby see Munro, pseud.

Munro, John Kirkby (1908-)

--Busy Bee. Munro, pseud. Hick, Grace Floyd, illus. LC 36-18910. 63 p. illus. 17 cm. c.1936. Farrar & Rinehart, Inc.
--Catherine Caterpillar. Munro, pseud. Hick, Grace Floyd, illus. LC 37-200599. 63 p. illus. 2 cm. c.1937. Farrar & Rinehart, Incorporated.

Munro, Leaf

--Walt Disney's Ferdinand the Bull. Disney, Walt, Productions, adapted by. Lawson, Robert (1892-1957), illus. LC 39-16745. (Based on the Story "The Story of Ferdinand"). (Illus.). 30cm. 1938. Whitman Publishing Company.

Munro, Roxie

--The Inside-Outside Book of New York City. 1985. Dodd Mead.

Munroe, Kirk (1850-1930)

--At War with Pontiac: Or, The Totem of the Bear; a Tale of Redcoat and Redskin. Finnemore, J., illus. LC 7-172559. 1 p. l., v-vii, 320 p. front., 7 pl. 19 cm. 1895. C. Scribner's Sons.
--The Belt of Seven Totems: A Story of Massasolt. McConnell, Emlen, illus. LC 1-25044. 326 p. front., plates. 20 cm. 1902. J. B. Lippincott Company.
--Big Cypress. 164p. 1910. W. A. Wilde.
--Big Cypress. The Story of an Everglade Homestead. Burgess, H., illus. LC 7-32284. 164 p. front., plates. 19 cm. c.1894. W. A. Wilde & Company.
--The Blue Dragon: A Tale of Recent Adventure in China. LC 4-27984. viii, 268 p. front., 6 pl., map. 19 cm. 1904. Harper & Brothers.
--Brethren of the Coast: A Tale of the West Indies. Zogbaum, Rufus F., illus. LC 5107. vi p., 1 l., 303 p. front., 7 pl. 19 cm. 1900. C. Scribner's Sons.
--Cab and Caboose: The Story of a Railroad Boy. LC 13-2066. v, 264 p. front., 11 pl. 20 cm. (Rail and water series). 1892. G. P. Putnam's Sons.
--Campmates: A Story of the Plains. LC 4-23601. vi, 333 p. 21 pl. (incl. front.) 19 cm. 1891. Harper & Brothers.
--Campmates: A Story of the Plains. LC 4-189317. vi, 333 p. 16 pl. (incl. front.) 19 cm. 1903. Harper & Brothers.
--Canoemates: A Story of the Florida Reef and Everglades. LC 4-23602. vi, 324 p. 25 pl. (incl. front.) 19 cm. 1893. Harper & Brothers.
--Canoemates: A Story of the Florida Reef and Everglades. LC 4-18932. vi, 324 p. 16 pl. (incl. front.) 19 cm. 1903. Harper & Brothers.
--Chrystal, Jack, & Co. and Delta Bixby. LC 11-8225. 221 p. incl. front., plates. 17 cm. 1889. Harper & Brothers.
--The Copper Princess: A Story of Lake Superior Mines. Rogers, W. A., illus. LC 98-1605. iv p., 1 l., 237 p. front., 11 pl. 19 cm. 1898. Harper & Brothers.
--The Coral Ship. (Illus.). (Putnam's Knickerbocker Ser.). N.D. G. P. Putman's Sons.
--The Coral Ship: A Story of the Florida Reef. LC 7-322836. iv p., 1 l., 261 p. front., 13 pl. 20 cm. (On cover: Rail and water Ser. No. 4). 1893. G. P. Putnam's Sons.
--Crab and Caboose. (Illus.). (Putnam's Knickerbocker Ser.). N.D. G. P. Putman's Sons.
--Derrick Sterling: A Story of the Mines. LC 7-32282. vi, 256 p. front., 19 pl. 17 x 12 cm. (Harper's young people series). 1888. Harper & Brothers.
--Dory Mates: A Tale of the Fishing Banks. LC 13-7649. 357 p. incl. front 23 pl. 17 x 12 cm. (Harper's young people series). 1890. Harper & Brothers.
--Dorymates: A Tale of the Fishing Banks. LC 4-17528. 357 p. incl. front 23 pl. 19 cm. 1903. Harper & Brothers.
--The Flamingo Feather. N.D. Grosset & Dunlap.
--The Flamingo Feather. LC 4-16145. vi, 255 p. incl. plates. front. 17 x 12 cm. (Harper's Young People Ser.). 1887. Harper & Brothers.
--The Flamingo Feather. Kottmeyer, William (1910-), adapted by. Hines, Lee, illus. LC 49-486583. 138 p. illus. 21 cm. (The Everyreader Ser.). 1949. Webster Pub. Co.
--The Flamingo Feather. Schoonover, Frank Earle (1877-1972), illus. LC 23-174710. vii p., 1 l., 222 p. col. front., illus., col. plates. 25 cm. c.1923. Harper & Brothers.
--For the Mikado: Or, A Japanese Middy in Action. LC 5-33974. iv p., 2 l., 270 p. front., 6 pl., map. 19 cm. 1905. Harper & Brothers.
--Forward March: A Tale of the Spanish-American War. LC 99-427697. vi p., 1 l., 254 p. front., 19 pl. 19 cm. 1899. Harper & Brothers.
--The Fur-Seal's Tooth: A Story of Alaskan Adventure. LC 4-23584. viii, 267 p. front., plates, map. 19 cm. (Pacific Coast Ser.). 1894. Harper & Brothers.
--The Golden Days of '49: A Tale of the California Diggings. LC 14-1066. ix, 351 p. front. (double) plates (double) 19 cm. c.1889. Dodd, Mead and Company.
--The Golden Days of '49: A Tale of the California Diggings. Crump, Leslie (1894-), illus. LC 41-38145. ix, 351 p. col. front., plates. 21 cm. 1924. Dodd, Mead & Company.
--In Pirate Waters: A Tale of the American Navy. LC 98-926. vi p., 1 l., 345 p. front., plates. 19 cm. 1898. C. Scribner's Sons.
--In the Heart of the Everglades. Burgess, H. & Martin, P. L., illus. LC 26-21117. 3 p. l., 5-164 p. col. front., plates. 19 cm. c.1926. W. A. Wilde Company.
--The Mates, 4 vols. (Illus.). (The Mates Ser). N.D. Harper & Brothers.
--Midshipman Stuart: Or, The Last Cruise of the "Essex"; a Tale of 1812. LC 99-4277. vi p., 1 l., 339 p. front., plates. 19 cm. 1899. C. Scribner's Sons.
--The Outcast Warrior: A Tale of the Red Frontier. LC 5-32852. vi p., 1 l., 279 p. col. front., 3 col. pl. 21 cm. 1905. D. Appleton and Company.
--The Painted Desert. (Pacific Coast Ser.). N.D. Harper & Brothers.
--Prince Dusty. (Illus.). (Putnam's Knickerbocker Ser.). N.D. G. P. Putman's Sons.
--Prince Dusty: A Story of the Oil Regions. LC 7-32281. iv p., 1 l., 300 p. front., 7 pl. 20 cm. (On cover: Rail and water series. no. 2). 1891. G. P. Putnam's Sons.
--Raftmates: A Story of the Great River. LC 4-31657. viii, 341 p. incl. front 19 pl. 19 cm. 1893. Harper & Brothers.
--Raftmates: A Story of the Great River. LC 4-18933. viii, 341 p. incl. front 15 pl. 19 cm. 1903. Harper & Brothers.
--The Ready Rangers: A Story of Boys, Boats, and Bicycles, Fire-Buckets and Fun. Rogers, W. A., illus. LC 7-32279. 334 p. front. 5 pl. 20 cm. c.1897. Lothrop Publishing Company.
--Rick Dale. N.D. Grosset & Dunlap.
--Rick Dale: A Story of the Northwest Coast. Rogers, W. A., illus. LC 7-32280. vi, 282 p. front., 19 pl. 19 cm. 1896. Harper & Brothers.
--Shine Terrill: A Sea Island Ranger. 317 p. incl. front. 4 pl. 20 cm. c.1899. Lothrop Publishing Company.
--Silent Pete. (Harper's Young People Ser.). N.D. Harper & Brothers.
--Snow-Shoes and Sledges. N.D. Grosset & Dunlap.
--Snow-Shoes and Sledges. LC 7-32278. (A Sequel to "The Fur-Seal's Tooth"). viii, 271 p. 26 pl. (incl. front.) 19 cm. 1895. Harper & Brothers.
--A Son of Satsuma: Or, With Perry in Japan. LC 1-24531. vi p., 1 l., 306 p. front., 7 pl. 19 cm. 1901. C. Scribner's Sons.
--Through Swamp and Glade: A Tale of the Seminole War. Perard, Victor Semon (1870-1957), illus. LC 7-17256. ix p., 1 l., 353 p. front., 7 pl. 19 cm. 1896. C. Scribner's Sons.
--Under Orders. (Illus.). (Putnam's Knickerbocker Ser.). N.D. G. P. Putman's Sons.
--Under Orders: The Story of a Young Reporter. LC 12-36986. vii, 348 p. front., plates. 20 cm. 1890. G. P. Putnam's Sons.
--Under the Great Bear, 8 vols. (Illus.). 384p. (Books for Boys). 1905. Set. Cassell & Co.
--Under the Great Bear. (Illus.). N.D. Harper & Bros.
--Under the Great Bear. Giles, Howard, illus. LC 5785. 6 p. l., 3-313 p. incl. front., 11 pl. 20 cm. 1900. Doubleday, Page & Co.
--Wakulla. N.D. Grosset & Dunlap.
--Wakulla: A Story of Adventure in Florida. LC 13-7650. 255 p. incl. 22 pl. 20 x 12 cm. (Harper's young people series). 1886. Harper & Brothers.
--Wakulla: A Story of Adventure in Florida. 255 p. incl. front., illus., plates. 18 cm. 1903. Harper & Brothers.
--The White Conquerors: A Tale of Toltec and Aztec. Stacey, W. S., illus. LC 7-17257. vi p., 1 l., 326 p. front., 7 pl. 19 cm. 1893. C. Scribner's Sons.
--With Crockett and Bowie: Or, Fighting for the Lone-Star Flag; a Tale of Texas. Perard, Victor Semon (1870-1957), illus. LC 7-17265. 3 p. l., v-vi p., 1 l., 347 p. front. 7 pl. 19 cm. 1897. C. Scribner's Sons.

Munson, Amelia H., selected by see Blake, William.

Munson-Benson, Tunie (1946-)

--A Fistful of Sun. Cuffari, Richard (1925-1978), illus. LC 74-6420. (Illus.). 127 p. 22cm. 1974. (ISBN 0-688-41647-0). (ISBN 0-688-51647-5). Lothrop, Lee & Shepard Co.

Munson, C. A., Mrs.

--Oline: Or, One Year at the Nest. (The River Home Library). N.D. N. Tibbals & Sons.

Munson, Howard A.

--The Adventures of Smudgie: The Story of a Beautiful and Very Clever Cat. Baerg, Harry John (1909-), illus. LC 58-154077. 64p. illus. 26cm. c.1957. Review and Herald Pub. Association.
--Perky, the Partridge. LC 56-15376. 63p. illus. 26cm. c.1955. Review and Herald Pub. Association.

Munson, Joan Foster

--The Giant Book of Giants. Gray, Leslie, illus. LC 68-3066. (Illus.). 1 v. (unpaged. 32cm. (Whitman juveniles). c.1967. Whitman Pub. Co.

Munson, Nelson Henry see Nels, pseud.

Munson, Nelson Henry (1904-)

--Animal Friends of Pleasant Valley. Dummer, H. Boylston (1878-), illus. LC 42-35205. 34 p. col. front., illus. (part col.) 28 x 21 1/2 cm. 1938. McLoughlin Bros.
--Who's Who in Tony Sarg's Zoo. Nels, pseud. Sarg, Anthony Frederick. LC 38-37579. (Illus.). 25cm. 34p. 1937. McLoughlin Bros. Inc.

Munsterhjelm, Erik (1905-)

--A Dog Named Wolf. 172 p. 18cm. (Laurel-leaf library). 1973, c.1972. Dell Pub. Co.

Muntean, Michaela

--All About Me. Appleby, Ellen, illus. (Illus.). 48p. (ps-3). 1984. (ISBN 0-8193-1123-5). Parents.
--Alligator's Garden. Rubel, Nicole (1953-), illus. LC 83-7703. (Illus.). 22p. (Playbooks). (ps-3). 1984. (ISBN 0-8037-0025-3). Dial Bks Young.
--Bicycle Bear. Cushman, Doug, illus. LC 83-3980. p. cm. 1983. (ISBN 0-8193-1103-0). (ISBN 0-8193-1104-9). Parents Magazine Press.
--Big & Little Stories. Swanson, Maggie, illus. (Illus.). 24p. (Golden Storytime Bks.). (ps-1). 1982. (ISBN 0-307-11963-7, Golden Pr). Western Pub.
--The Doozer Disaster. Hearn, Diane Dawson, illus. LC 84-6527. (Illus.). (Fraggle Rock Bks.). (gr. 1-4). 1984. (ISBN 0-03-000707-0). HR&W.
--Fraggle Countdown. Hearn, Diane Dawson, illus. LC 84-19107. (Illus.). 32 p. 21cm. c.1985. (ISBN 0-03-003264-4). Holt, Rinehart, and Winston.
--A Garden for Miss Mouse. Santoro, Christopher, illus. LC 82-2135. (Illus.). 48p. (ps-3). 1982. (ISBN 0-8193-1083-2). (ISBN 0-8193-1084-0). Parents.
--Get Ready: Seasons. Cooke, Tom, illus. (Illus.). 64p. (Sesame Street Get Ready Books). (ps). N.D. (ISBN 0-307-35403-2, Golden Bks). Western Pub.
--The House That Bear Built. Rubel, Nicole (1953-), illus. LC 83-7703. (Illus.). 22p. (Playbooks). (gr. k-3). 1984. (ISBN 0-8037-0026-1). (ISBN 0-8037-0026-1). Dial Bks for Young Readers.
--I Have a Friend: Featuring Jim Henson's Sesame Street Muppets. Winborn, Marsha, illus. Children's Television Workshop Henson, James Maury (1936-), created by. LC 80-84523. (Illus.). 26 p. 26cm. c.1981. (ISBN 0-307-23133-X). Western Pub. Co.
--I Like School: Featuring Jim Henson's Sesame Street Muppets. Herbert, Tom, illus. Children's Television Workshop Henson, James Maury (1936-), created by. LC 80-50236. (Illus.). 26 p. 27cm. c.1980. (ISBN 0-307-23111-9). Western Pub. Co.
--If I Lived Alone: Featuring Jim Henson's Sesame Street Muppets. Nicklaus, Carol, illus. Children's Television Workshop Henson, James Maury (1936-), created by. LC 80-51205. (Illus.). 25 p. 26cm. c.1980. (ISBN 0-307-23118-6). Western Pub. Co.
--Little Lamb Bakes a Cake. Rubel, Nicole (1953-), illus. LC 83-14266. (Illus.). 20 p. c.1984. (ISBN 0-8037-0048-2). Dial Books for Young Readers.
--Look What I Found!. Featuring Jim Henson's Sesame Street Muppets. Costanza, John, illus. Children's Television Workshop Henson, James Maury (1936-), created by. LC 80-84522. (Illus.). 28 p. 26cm. c.1981. (ISBN 0-307-23134-8). Western Pub. Co. in Conjunction with Children's Television Workshop.
--Meet the Fraggles. Lanza, Barbara, illus. LC 84-19182. (Illus.). 40 p. 27cm. c.1985. (ISBN 0-03-003263-6). Holt, Rinehart, and Winston.
--Monkey's Marching Band. Rubel, Nicole (1953-), illus. LC 83-14267. (Illus.). 20 p. (Playbook Ser.). c.1984. (ISBN 0-8037-0047-4). Dial Books for Young Readers.
--Muppet Babies Through the Year. McNally, Bruce, illus. LC 83-16041. c.1984. (ISBN 0-394-86544-8). Muppet Press,Random House.
--The Old Man and the Afternoon Cat. Weissman, Bari, illus. Morrison, Duncan, contrib. by. LC 81-11047. (Illus.). 46 p. 23cm. 1982, c.1981. (ISBN 0-8193-1071-9). (ISBN 0-8193-1072-7). Parents Magazine Press.
--Panda Bear's Paintbox. Santoro, Christopher, illus. (First Little Golden Bks.). (ps). 1981. (ISBN 0-307-10105-3, Golden Pr). (ISBN 0-307-68105-X). Western Pub.
--Panda Bear's Secret. Santoro, Christopher, illus. (Illus.). 24p. (First Little Golden Bk.). (ps). 1983. (ISBN 0-307-10136-3, Golden Pr). (ISBN 0-307-68136-X). Western Pub.
--The Tale of Traveling Matt. McCue, Lisa, illus. LC 83-23711. (Illus.). 1984. (ISBN 0-03-071092-8). HR&W.
--Theodore Mouse Goes to Sea. McQueen, Lucinda, illus. LC 82-82290. (Illus.). 24 p. 20cm. (Little Golden Book). c.1983. (ISBN 0-307-02015-0). (ISBN 0-307-60198-6). Golden Press.
--The Very Bumpy Bus Ride. Wiseman, Bernard (1922-), illus. LC 81-16905. (Illus.). 46 p. 23cm. c.1981. (ISBN 0-8193-1079-4). (ISBN 0-8193-1080-8). Parents Magazine Press.
--What Do Doozers Do?. Venning, Sue, illus. LC 83-22709. 1984. (ISBN 0-03-071091-X). (ISBN 0-03-071888-0). HR&W.

Munthe, Adam John (1946-)

--Anna and the Echo-Catcher. Falconer, Elizabeth, illus. (Illus.). 32p. 1st U.S. edition. (gr. k-3). 1981. (ISBN 0-7011-2498-9, Pub. by Chatto-Bodley-Jonathan). Merrimack Pub Cir.
--I Believe in Unicorns. Falconer, Elizabeth, illus. (Illus.). 32p. (gr. 1-4). 1980. (ISBN 0-7011-2437-7, Pub. by Chatto, Bodley Head & Jonathan). Merrimack Pub Cir.

Munves, James Albert (1922-)

--The Treasure of Diogenes Sampuez. LC 78-21768. 186 p. 22cm. c.1979. (ISBN 0-590-07384-2). Four Winds Press.
--We Were There at the Opening of the Atomic Era. Brey, Charles, illus. LC 60-51562. (Historical Consultant: John R Dunning). (Illus.). 22cm. 175p. (We were there books, 82.). (gr. 4-9). 1960. (ISBN 0-448-05032-3). Grosset & Dunlap.
--We Were There with Lewis and Clark. Glaubke, Robert, illus. LC 59-5671. 180p. illus. 22cm. (We Were There Books, 22). 1959. Grosset & Dunlap.

Muppet Press

--Robin Hood, a High Spirited Tale of Adventure: The Muppet Press. LC 80-5083. p. cm. 1980. (ISBN 0-394-84568-4). (ISBN 0-394-94568-9). Random House.

Murad, Maria B.

--The Magic Words. Morgado, Dick, illus. LC 83-23706. (Illus.). 40p. (Care Bears Ser.). (ps-3). 1984. (ISBN 0-910313-17-2). (ISBN 0-910313-17-2). Parker Bro.

AUTHOR INDEX MURRAY, WILLIAM

Murch, Elizabeth
--Ettie May: A Story of Civil War Days for the Children. LC 33-11063. 45 p. 20 cm. 1933. Meador Publishing Co.
Murdocca, Salvatore
--The Boy Who Was a Raccoon. Murdocca, Salvatore, illus. LC 73-21728. (Illus.). 32 p. 26cm. 1974. (ISBN 0-688-41583-0). (ISBN 0-688-41583-0). Lothrop, Lee & Shepard.
--The Boy Who Was a Raccoon. Murdocca, Salvatore, illus. 1974. (ISBN 0-688-41583-0). William Morrow and Company.
--The Hero of Hamblett. Murdocca, Salvatore, illus. LC 80-11346. p. cm. 1980. (ISBN 0-440-04457-X). (ISBN 0-440-04458-8). Delacorte Press.
--The Nothing. LC 84-11428. (Illus.). 32 p. 24cm. c.1986. (ISBN 0-517-55505-2). Crown.
--Sir Hamm and the Golden Sundial. LC 81-65489. p. cm. c.1981. (ISBN 0-440-08302-8). (ISBN 0-440-08316-8). Delacorte Press.
--Take Me to the Moon. Murdocca, Salvatore, illus. LC 76-6113. 61 ill. 22. (Fun-to-read book). 1976. (ISBN 0-688-41766-3). (ISBN 0-688-51766-8). Lothrop, Lee & Shepard Co.
--Tuttle's Shell. Murdocca, Salvatore, illus. LC 75-17516. (Illus.). 64 p. 22cm. c.1976. (ISBN 0-688-41724-8). (ISBN 0-688-51724-2). Lothrop, Lee & Shepard.
--Video Cat. (Illus.). 96p. (Write Your Own Story Bks.). (gr. 2-8). 1983. (ISBN 0-394-86196-5). Random.
--The Visitor. (Illus.). 96p. (Write Your Own Story Bks.). (gr. 2-7). 1983. (ISBN 0-394-86195-7). Random.
Murdoch, Royal (1898-)
--New Friends of Mother Goose. LC 58-2506. 78p. 21cm. 1958. Fine Editions Press.
Murdock, Laurette, jt. auth. see Marshall, James.
Murdock, Marie, jt. auth. see Treuhardt, Beverly Huie.
Mure, Eleanor (1798-1885)
--The Story of the Three Bears. LC 67-199328. (Illus.). 32 p. 1967. H. F. Walck.

Murfree, Mary Noacilles see Craddock, Charles Egbert, pseud.

Murgo, Jane, tr. see Sperandio, Guido.

Murphey, Eleanor Albertson
--Nihal. Keats, Ezra Jack (1916-1983), illus. LC 59-11396. 25cm. 39p. 1960. Thomas Y. Crowell.
Murphey, Sara
--The Animal Hat Shop. Pekarsky, Mel, illus. LC 64-10268. (Illus.). 30 p. 21cm. (Follett Beginning-To-Read Series). 1964. Follett Pub. Co.
--Bing-Bang Pig. Perl, Susan (1922-1983), illus. LC 64-10271. (Illus.). 30 p. 21cm. (Follett beginning-to-read series). 1964. Follett Pub. Co.
Murphy, Arthur George (1906-)
--ABC Animal Book. LC 43-15958. 47 p. illus. 16 x 24 1/2 cm. 1943. Coward-McCann.
Murphy, Barbara Beasley (1933-)
--Home Free. Murphy, Bill (1931-), illus. LC 72-87171. (Illus.). 83 p. 21cm. 1970. (ISBN 0-440-03675-5). Delacorte Press.
--No Place to Run. LC 76-57911. 176 p. 22cm. c.1977. (ISBN 0-87888-116-6). Bradbury Press.
--One Another. LC 81-18074. 192p. (gr. 7 up). 1982. (ISBN 0-02-767710-9). (ISBN 0-87888-196-4). Bradbury Pr.
Murphy, Barbara Beasley (1933-) & Wolkoff, Judie
--Ace Hits Rock Bottom. LC 85-3776. 202 p. 22cm. c.1985. (ISBN 0-385-29412-3). Delacorte Press.
--Ace Hits the Big Time. LC 81-65496. p. cm. c.1981. (ISBN 0-440-00299-0). Delacorte Press.
Murphy, Bernadette
--The House in the Country. LC 28-3686. 170 p., 1 l. front. 20 cm. 1927. G. P. Putnam's Sons, Ltd.
Murphy, C. L., pseud., see Murphy, Charlotte Alice.
Murphy, C. L., pseud. (1924-) & Murphy, Lawrence Augustus, pseud. (1924-)
--Buffalo Grass. Murphy, Charlotte Alice. Murphy, Lawrence Augustus. Kidwell, Carl (1910-), illus. LC 66-12836. (C.L. Murphy joint Pseud. for Charlotte Alice Murphy & Lawrence Augustus). 174 p. illus. 22 cm. 1966. Dial Press.
Murphy, Carol, ed. see George, David L.
Murphy, Carol, jt. ed. see Wright, Glen.
Murphy, Charlotte Alice see Murphy, C. L., pseud.
Murphy, Chuck, jt. auth. see Lokvig, Tor.
Murphy, Edward Francis (1892-)
--The Tale of Two Brothers: "God Is Love", A Brave Coward, Two Mothers. Burroughs, John F., illus. LC 23-739483. 210 p. incl. front., plates. 20 cm. c.1921. O'Donovan Brothers.
Murphy, Elspeth Campbell
--Danny Petrowski. Kenyon, Tony LC 85-16568. (Illus.). 105 p. 19cm. (The Kids from Apple Street Church: No. 2). 1985. (ISBN 0-89191-730-6). Chariot Books.
--God Cares When I Do Something Stupid. Nelson, Jane E., illus. LC 83-72504. (Illus.). 23 p. (God's word in my heart ; 7). c.1984. (ISBN 0-89191-792-6). Chariot Books.
--God Cares When I Don't Know What to Do. Nelson, Jane E., illus. LC 84-15595. (Illus.). 23 p. (God's word in my heart ; #11). c.1984. (ISBN 0-89191-948-1). Chariot Books.
--God Cares When I Don't Know What to Do. Nelson, Jane E., illus. 24p. (God's Word in My Heart Ser.). (gr. 1-3). 1985, c.1984. (ISBN 0-89191-948-1, Chariot Bks). Cook.
--God Cares When I Need to Talk to Somebody. Nelson, Jane E., illus. LC 84-1914. c.1984. (ISBN 0-89191-887-6). Chariot Books.
--God Cares When I'm All Tired Out. Nelson, Jane E., illus. LC 83-71233. (Illus.). 23 p. (God's Word in My Heart). c.1983. (ISBN 0-89191-757-8). Chariot Books.
--God Cares When I'm Disappointed. Nelson, Jane E., illus. LC 82-73574. (Illus.). 23 p. c.1983. (ISBN 0-89191-725-X). Chariot Books.
--God Cares When I'm Feeling Mean. Nelson, Jane E., illus. LC 83-72501. 24p. (God's Word in My Heart Ser.). (gr. 1-3). 1985. (ISBN 0-89191-789-6, Chariot Bks). Cook.
--God Cares When I'm Sorry. Nelson, Jane E., illus. LC 82-73573. (Illus.). 23 p. (God's Word in My Heart). c.1983. (ISBN 0-89191-724-1). Chariot Books.
--God Cares When I'm Wondering. Nelson, Jane E., illus. LC 84-15594. p. cm. c.1984. (ISBN 0-89191-791-8). Chariot Books.
--God Cares When I'm Wondering. Nelson, Jane E., illus. (Illus.). 24p. (God's Word in My Heart Ser.). (gr. 1-3). 1985. (ISBN 0-89191-791-8, Chariot Bks). Cook.
--God Cares When Somebody Hurts Me. Nelson, Jane E., illus. LC 83-72502. 1984. (ISBN 0-89191-790-X). Chariot Books.
Murphy, Emily Ferguson, Mrs.
--Our Little Canadian Cousin of the Great Northwest. Gooch, Thelma, illus. LC 23-11216. viii p., 2 l., 86 p. front., plates. 20 cm. (The Little Cousin Ser.). 1923. L. C. Page & Company, Inc.
Murphy, Emmy Lou Osborne (1910-)
--Paco and Paquita of Mexico. LC 62-53433. unpaged. illus. 29 cm. 1962. Zondervan Pub. House.
Murphy, Frances Salomon
--A Nickel for Alice. Woodbury, Mabel Jones, illus. LC 51-9836. (Illus.). 184 p. 21cm. 1951. Crowell.
--Ready-Made Family. Woodbury, Mabel Jones, illus. LC 53-8421. (Illus.). 184 p. 21cm. 1953. Crowell.
--Runaway Alice. Orig. Title: A Nickel for Alice. (gr. 4-6). 1972 (Starline). Schol Bk Serv.
Murphy, Freda Lindsley
--In a Children's World. LC 48-116734. 11 p. 22 cm. (William-Frederick Poets, No. 47). 1948. William-Frederick Press.
Murphy, Geraldine, ed. see Meader, Stephen Warren.
Murphy, Gerard, retold by.
--Tales from Ireland. MacNeill, Seamus, illus. LC 48-1254. 192 p. illus. 22 cm. 1947. Desmond & Stapleton.
Murphy, Helen, ed. see Kozisek, Josef.
Murphy, Jill (1949-)
--Peace at Last. Murphy, Jill (1949-), illus. LC 80-15659. p. cm. 1980. (ISBN 0-8037-6757-9). (ISBN 0-8037-6758-7). Dial Press.
--What Next, Baby Bear!. Murphy, Jill (1949-), illus. LC 83-7316. (Illus.). 32p. (ps-2). 1984. (ISBN 0-8037-0027-X). (ISBN 0-8037-0027-X). Dial Bks for Young Readers.
--The Worst Witch. Murphy, Jill (1949-), illus. 72p. (gr. 3-6). 1980. (ISBN 0-8052-8019-7, Pub. by Allison & Busby England). Schocken.
--The Worst Witch Strikes Again. Murphy, Jill (1949-), illus. (Illus.). 72p. (gr. 3-6). 1980. (ISBN 0-8052-8020-0, Pub. by Allison & Busby England). Schocken.
Murphy, Jim (1947-)
--Death Run. LC 81-10265. 174 p. 24cm. c.1982. (ISBN 0-89919-065-0). Clarion Books.
--Harold Thinks Big. Natti, Susanna (1948-), illus. LC 79-24199. (Illus.). 48 p. 22cm. c.1980. (ISBN 0-517-53912-8). Crown Publishers.
--Rat's Christmas Party. Gackenbach, Dick, illus. LC 79-13094. p. cm. c.1979. (ISBN 0-13-753111-7). Prentice-Hall.
Murphy, Lawrence Augustus, jt. auth. see Murphy, C. L.
Murphy, M. E.
--Damascus Steel: Adventure in Arabia. Schmidt, O. F., illus. LC 28-10295. 5 p., l., 287 p. col. front. 20 cm. 1928. Doubleday, Doran & Company, Inc.
Murphy, Mabel Ansley (1870-)
--When America Was Young. Smith, Cecil Alden, illus. LC 72-38326. (Illus.). 319 p. 23cm. (Biography index reprint series). 1972, c.1948. (ISBN 0-8369-8126-X). Books for Libraries Press.
--When America Was Young. Smith, Cecil Alden, illus. LC 48-1962. 319 p. illus. 24 cm. 1948. Caxton Printers.
--When Jefferson Was Young. LC 42-51971. (Illus.). 262p. 23cm. 1942. A. Whitman & Co.
Murphy, Marguerite
--The Necklace of Jewels. LC 18-16984. 6 p. l., 3-123 p. col. front., illus. col. plates. 20 cm. 1918. The Page Company.
--Patricia and the Other Girls. Withington, Elizabeth R., illus. LC 26-16270. 320 p. front., plates. 20 cm. c.1926. Lothrop, Lee & Shepard Co.
--Patricia from New York. Withington, Elizabeth R., illus. LC 25-177061. 316 p. front., plates. 20 cm. c.1925. Lothrop, Lee & Shepard Co.
--Patricia's Problem. Withington, Elizabeth R., illus. LC 27-191850. 293 p. front., plates. 20 cm. c.1927. Lothrop, Lee & Shepard Co.
--Peter's Wonderful Adventure. Wylie, Samuel B., illus. LC 27-153926. v, 274 p. illus. 19 cm. 1927. Ginn and Company.
Murphy, Martha, tr. see Korschunow, Irina.
Murphy, Patrick John, jt. auth. see Murphy, Shirley Rousseau.
Murphy, Patrick John (1926-) & Murphy, Shirley Rousseau (1928-)
--Carlos Charles. LC 78-162676. 154 p. 23cm. 1971. (ISBN 0-670-20494-3). (ISBN 0-670-20495-1). Viking Press.
Murphy, Richard
--Sailing to an Island. (gr. 1-4). 1963. Chilmark.
Murphy, Robert William (1902-1971)
--The Haunted Journey. 192p. 1969. (ISBN 0-374-32904-4). Farrar, Straus and Giroux.
--The Stream. Hines, Robert W., illus. (Illus.). 205p. 1971. (ISBN 0-374-27092-9). Farrar, Straus and Giroux.
--The Warm Hearted Polar Bear. 1st ed. Kaufmann, John (1931-), illus. LC 57-8044. (Illus.). 47 p. 27cm. 1957. Little, Brown.
--Wild Geese Calling. Kaufmann, John (1931-), illus. LC 66-5569. 96 p. illus. 22 cm. 1966. Dutton.
Murphy, Ruby Bradford
--American Riddles in Rhyme. McKee, John Dukes, illus. LC 55-14817. (Illus.). 21cm. 48p. (gr. 3-5). 1955. (ISBN 0-687-01265-1). Abingdon.
--Who's Who in Mother Goose Land. Combet, Fernande, illus. LC 37-15346. 32 p. col. illus. 17 cm. c.1937. Rand, MacNally & Company.
Murphy, Ruth
--Wonderful Wee Folk in Florida. (Illus.). 64p. (gr. 1-4). 1974. (ISBN 0-682-47919-5). Exposition.
Murphy, Shirley Rousseau, jt. auth. see Murphy, Patrick John.
Murphy, Shirley Rousseau (1928-)
--The Castle of Hope. LC 79-22764. (Illus.). viii, 172 p. 25cm. (Argo Book). 1980. (ISBN 0-689-30753-5). Atheneum.
--Caves of Fire and Ice. LC 80-12887. p. cm. (Argo book). 1980. (ISBN 0-689-30784-5). Atheneum.
--Elmo Doolan and the Search for the Golden Mouse. Kredel, Fritz (1900-1973), illus. LC 79-123024. (Illus.). 125 p. 22cm. 1970. (ISBN 0-670-29237-0). Viking Press.
--The Flight of the Fox. Sibley, Don (1922-), illus. Cuffari, Richard (1925-1978), designed by. LC 78-5436. (Illus.). 164 p. 22cm. 1978. (ISBN 0-689-30620-2). Atheneum.
--The Grass Tower. Robinson, Charles (1931-), illus. LC 75-23151. (Illus.). 244 p. 22cm. 1976. (ISBN 0-689-30512-5). Atheneum.
--The Joining of the Stone. LC 81-2351. p. cm. 1981. (ISBN 0-689-30822-1). Atheneum.
--Nightpool. LC 85-42626. 250 p. 22cm. c.1985. (ISBN 0-06-024360-0). (ISBN 0-06-024361-9). Harper & Row.
--The Pig Who Could Conjure the Wind. Lefkowitz, Mark, illus. LC 77-20512. (Illus.). 58 p. 1978. (ISBN 0-689-30639-3). Atheneum.
--Poor Jenny, Bright As a Penny. LC 72-9911. 174 p. 24cm. 1974. Viking Press.
--The Ring of Fire. LC 77-1576. (Illus.). 232 p. 25cm. 1977. (ISBN 0-689-30594-X). Atheneum.
--The Sand Ponies. Weihs, Erika (1917-), illus. LC 67-20960. (Illus.). 175 p. 22cm. 1967. Viking Press.
--Silver Woven in My Hair. Tiegreen, Alan, illus. LC 76-25578. (Illus.). 121 p. 22cm. 1977. (ISBN 0-689-30558-3). Atheneum.
--Soonie and the Dragon. Vaeth, Susan, illus. LC 79-11728. (Illus.). 84 p. 21cm. 1979. (ISBN 0-689-30720-9). Atheneum.
--Tattie's River Journey. De Paola, Tomie, pseud. (1934-), illus. De Paola, Thomas Anthony. LC 82-45508. p. cm. c.1983. (ISBN 0-8037-8767-7). Dial Press.
--Valentine for a Dragon. Chorao, Ann McKay Sproat (1936-), illus. LC 83-17911. (Illus.). 48p. (gr. k-3). 1985. (ISBN 0-689-31016-1). (ISBN 0-689-71049-6, Aladdin). Atheneum.
--White Ghost Summer. McGee, Barbara J. (1943-), illus. LC 67-3590. (Illus.). 191 p. 22cm. 1967. Viking Press.
--The Wolf Bell. LC 78-10415. (Illus.). 182 p. 24cm. 1979. (ISBN 0-689-30692-X). Atheneum.
Murphy, Shirley Rousseau (1928-) & Murphy, Patrick John (1926-)
--Mrs. Tortino's Return to the Sun. Russo, Susan (1947-), illus. LC 79-20694. (Illus.). 30 p. 26cm. c.1980. (ISBN 0-688-41921-6). (ISBN 0-688-51921-0). Lothrop, Lee & Shepard Books.
Murray, A. A.
--Anybody's Spring. N.D. The Vanguard Press.
--The Blanket. N.D. (ISBN 0-8149-0164-6). The Vanguard Press.
Murray-Aaron, Eugene (1852-1941)
--The Butterfly Hunters in the Caribbees. LC 19-10807. xv. 1, 269 p. front., plates. 21 cm. 1894. C. Scribner's Sons.
Murray, Andrew
--Alone in London, 1 of 50 vols. (Heart Life Classics). N.D. American Tract Society.
Murray, C. O.
--Mustard and Cress-Their Suprising Adventures: And The Downfall of Burdock. (Illus.). N.D. Thomas Nelson & Sons.
Murray, Clara, pseud., see McDonald, Etta Austin Blaisdell.
Murray, Clara Elizabeth (1894-), compiled by.
--Story-land. LC 9-35908. (Illus.). 224p. 19 x 15cm. (The Playtime Ser.). 1908. Little, Brown.
Murray, Gilbert (1865-)
--The Airplane Spider. Cady, Walter Harrison (1877-1970), illus. LC 21-966. xi, 86 p. col. front., col. plates. 18 cm. 1920. Little, Brown, and Company.
Murray, Gladys Hall
--Mystery of the Talking Totem Pole. LC 65-23291. viii, 208 p. 21cm. 1965. Dodd, Mead.
Murray, Gretchen Ostrander
--Shoes for Sandy. LC 36-17306. (Illus.). 25cm. 39p. c.1936. Grosset & Dunlap.
Murray, Gretchen Ostrander, Mrs., jt. ed. see Hill, Patty Smith.
Murray, Jane W. (1915-)
--Walk the High Horizon. LC 74-6309. 144 p. 22cm. 1974. (ISBN 0-664-32551-3). Westminster Press.
Murray, John (1923-)
--Comedies and Farces for Teen-Agers. N.D. (ISBN 0-8238-0050-4). Plays, Inc.
--Comedies and Mysteries for Young Actors: A Collection of One-Act, Royalty-Free Plays for Teen-Agers. LC 76-190199. vi, 339 p. 22cm. 1972. (ISBN 0-8238-0133-0). Plays.
--Comedy Roundup for Teen-Age Actors. N.D. (ISBN 0-8238-0051-2). Plays, Inc.
--Fifteen Plays for Teen-Agers: A Collection of One-Act Royalty-Free Comedies and Mysteries. LC 78-16588. p. cm. c.1978. (ISBN 0-8238-0227-2). Plays, Inc.
--Fifteen Plays for Today's Teen-Agers. 1982 ed. (gr. 7-12). 1979. (ISBN 0-8238-0258-2). Plays.
--Mystery Plays for Young Actors. LC 84-11329. 188 p. 23cm. c.1984. (ISBN 0-8238-0265-5). Plays, Inc.
--Mystery Plays for Young People. N.D. Plays Inc Pub.
Murray, Judith Michele Freedman (1933-1974)
--The Crystal Nights. LC 72-93807. 320p. (gr. 6 up). 1973. (ISBN 0-395-28920-3, Clarion). Seabury.
--Nellie Cameron. Prince, Leonora E., illus. LC 75-133060. (Illus.). 185 p. 22cm. 1971. Seabury Press.
Murray, Kathryn Kohnfelder (1906-)
--The Best Day for Every Little Girl. Rosse, Allianora, illus. LC 60-12585. unpaged. illus. 29cm. 1960. Simon and Schuster.
Murray, M. A., tr. see Lorenzini, Carlo.
Murray, Marguerite
--The Sea Bears. LC 84-2945. 168p. (gr. 4-9). 1984. (ISBN 0-689-31050-1). Atheneum.
Murray, Marina
--Here Comes the Circus. Vranian, F. Richard, illus. 1954. The Dietz Press.
Murray, Mary, illus.
--Pat-A-Cake. (Illus.). (A Peggy Cloth Book). (ps). 1978. (ISBN 0-448-46833-6). Platt.
Murray, Mary Alice, tr. see Lorenzini, Carlo.
Murray, Michele see Murray, Judith Michele Freedman.
Murray, Patricia Hagen, jt. auth. see Steveson, Florence.
Murray, Ruth Adams, ed. see Together Magazine.
Murray, William D.
--Bible Stories to Tell Children. LC 10-22076. 1858-cm. 211p. c.1910. Fleming H. Revell Co.

Murray, William Henry Harrison (1840-1904)
--The Mystery of the Woodsand,the Man Who Missed it. (Illus.). (Adirondack Tales. Volume Two). N.D. DeWolfe, Fiske & Co.
--The Story that the Keg Told Me, and The Story of the Man Who Didn't Know Much. (Adirondack Tales. Volume one). N.D. DeWolfe, Fiske & Co.
Murrell, Elsie Kathleen Seth-Smith see Seth-Smith, Elsie K.
Murrie, Merle, pseud., see Newman, Fannie J..
Murrie, Merle, pseud.
--The Story of Lillian. Newman, Fannie J.. 20cm. 247p. (Neely's Imperial Library: No. 40). 1899. F. T. Neely.
Murrill, William Alphonso (1869-)
--Three Young Crusoes: Their Life and Adventures on an Island in the West Indies. LC 19-172. xiv, 218 p. incl. illus., pl. 2 col. pl. 20 cm. 1918. W. A. Murrill.
Murschetz, Luis
--A Hamster's Journey. LC 76-9788. p. cm. c.1976. (ISBN 0-13-372383-6). Prentice-Hall.
--Mister Mole. LC 75-34162. (Illus.). 33 p. 24cm. 1976. (ISBN 0-13-604728-9). Prentice-Hall.
Murstad, Tomm
--Skiing With Per and Kari. N.D. Grosset & Dunlap.
Murtaugh, Janet
--Wonder Tales of Giants and Dwarfs. Florian, illus. LC 45-37875. 33cm. 65p. 1945. Random House.
Murton, Jessie Wilmore
--A Child's Book of Verses. LC 52-68721. 62p. illus. 22cm. 1952. Review and Herald Pub. Association.
--Christopher Cricket. (ps-k). N.D. Review & Herald.
--Grandfather's Farm, and Other Poems for Boys and Girls. Cole, Dick, illus. LC 60-10099. unpaged. illus. 24cm. 1960. Pacific Press Pub. Association.
--Make-Believe Journeys. (gr. 1-5). N.D. Review & Herald.
Musaus, Johann Karl, jt. auth. see Eichenberg, Fritz.
Musgrave, Florence (1902-)
--A Boy for You, a Horse for Me. Stevens, Mary, illus. LC 59-10850. 157p. illus. 22cm. 1959. Hastings House.
--Catherine's Bells. Gay, Zhenya (1906-1978), illus. 248p. illus. 22cm. 1954. Ariel Books.
--Dogs in the Family. Henneberger, Robert G. (1921-), illus. LC 52-6897. (Illus.). 245 p. 22cm. 1952. Houghton Mifflin.
--Like a Red, Red Rose. Stevens, Mary, illus. LC 58-8273. (Illus.). (gr. 6-9). 1958. (ISBN 0-8038-4236-8). Hastings.
--Marged: The Story of a Welsh Girl in America. Thomson, Arline K. (1912-), illus. LC 56-6166. 250p. illus. 22cm. 1956. Ariel Books.
--Mary Lizzie. Candy, Robert (1920-), illus. LC 50-9375. (Illus.). 187 p. 22cm. 1950. Houghton Mifflin.
--Merrie's Miracle. N.D. Hastings House, Publishers, Inc.
--Oh Sarah. Candy, Robert (1920-), illus. LC 52-12379. (Illus.). 247 p. 21cm. 1953. Ariel Books.
--Robert E. Stevens, Mary, illus. LC 57-7450. 191p. illus. 22cm. 1957. Hastings House.
--Sarah Hastings. Stevens, Mary, illus. LC 60-105817. 160p. illus. 22cm. 1960. Hastings House.
--Stars Over the Tent. Candy, Robert (1920-), illus. LC 53-620696. 214p. illus. 22cm. 1953. Houghton Mifflin Co.
--Trailer Tribe. Vaughan-Jackson, Genevieve (1913-), illus. LC 55-556496. 244p. illus. 22cm. 1955. Ariel Books.
--Two Dates for Mike. 1964. E M Hale.
--Two Dates for Mike. Neale, Sidnee, illus. LC 73-4248. (Illus.). 208 p. 25cm. 1973, c.1964. (ISBN 0-8161-6100-3). G. K. Hall.
--Two Dates for Mike. Neale, Sidnee, illus. LC 64-13480. (Illus.). 150 p. 22cm. 1964. Hastings House.
Musgrave, Susan (1951-)
--Gullband Thought Measles Was a Happy Ending. Rikki, illus. LC 75-305961. (Illus.). 26cm. 49p. 1974. (ISBN 0-88894-058-0). J. J. Douglas.
Musial, Joseph W (1905-1977)
--Matey Visits New York. LC 42-7642. 15 p. illus. (part. col.) 27 x 26 1/2 cm. c.1941. David McKay Company.
Music, Peter
--Meemyself the Wicked Elf & Zem the Little Queen. Pierre, Jake, illus. LC 78-62832. (Illus.). 29p. Repr. of 1972 ed. (gr. 3-6). 1978. (ISBN 0-915238-01-2). Peace Pr.
Musicant, Elke Alice (1919-) & Musicant, Tobias Ted (1921-)
--The Night Vegetable Eater. Bassett, Jeni Crisler, illus. LC 80-22389. (Illus.). 48 p. 24cm. c.1981. (ISBN 0-396-07923-7). Dodd, Mead.
Musicant, Ted see Musicant, Elke Alice (1919-) & Musicant, Tobias Ted.
Musicant, Tobias Ted, jt. auth. see Musicant, Elke Alice.
Musick, A L
--Jigger Flies First. LC 58-338322. unpaged. illus. 29cm. c.1957. Sage Books.
Musick, J. R.
--Banker of Bedford, 1 of 18 vols. (Library of Romance Ser). N.D. Lothrop Pub. Co.
Musick, Ruth Ann
--Green Hills of Magic: West Virginia Folktales from Europe. (Illus.). 336p. 1970. (ISBN 0-8131-1191-9). University Press Of Kentucky.
--The Telltale Lilac Bush and Other West Virginia Ghost Tales. (Illus.). 189p. 1965. (ISBN 0-8131-1094-7). University Press Of Kentucky.
Musil, Rosemary Gabbert
--The Ghost of Mr. Penny. (Illus.). 48p. (Thespian Ser.: Bk. 2). c.1939. Children's Theatre Press.
--Seven Little Rebels. (Illus.). 68p. c.1938. Children's Theatre Press.
Musser, Joseph L. (1936-)
--Behold a Pale Horse. N.D. Zondervan Publishing House.
Musset, Paul Edme De (1804-1880)
--Mr. Wind and Madam Rain. Bennett, Charles Henry (1829-1867), illus. Makepeace, Emily, tr. LC 5-323845. xiv p., 1 l., 151 p. incl. front., illus., plates. 22 cm. 1905. G. P. Putnam's Sons.
--Mr. Wind and Madam Rain. Bennett, Charles Henry (1829-1867), illus. Makepeace, Emily, tr. LC 9-351806. 126 p. incl. illus., plates. front. 19 cm. 1908. Harper & Brothers.
--Mr. Wind and Madame Rain. (Illus.). 1882. Harper & Brothers.
--Mr. Wind and Madame Rain. Bennett, Charles Henry (1829-1867), illus. Makepeace, Emily, tr. 126p. 1864. Harper & Bros.
--Mr. Wind & Madame Rain. Bennett, Charles Henry (1829-1867), illus. Makepeace, Emily, tr. (Wonderland Ser.). 1908. Harper & Bros.
Mussey, Barrows, tr. see Haar, Jaap Ter.
Mussey, Barrows, tr. see Hauser, Henrich.
Mussey, June Barrows (1910-), tr. see Franke, Simon.
Mussey, June Barrows, tr. see Salten, Felix.
Mussey, Virginia Howell (1910-)
--Fala: A President's Dog. Vandoren, Margaret (1917-), illus. LC 41-18906. 30, 2 p. illus. 26 cm. c.1941. Howell, Soskin.
Mussi, Mary see Howard, Mary, pseud.
Musso, Laurie D., jt. auth. see Duston, Nettie M.
Musson, Bennet
--Maisie and Her Dog Snip in Fairyland. LC 3-25726. 22 x 18cm. 165p. 1903. Harper & Brothers.
Mussorgsky, Modest P.
--Night on Bald Mountain. Semba, Taro, illus. (Pictorial Fantasia Ser). (gr. 3-6). 1969. Silver.
Mutch, Margaret, tr. see Grund, Josef Carl.
Mutch, William James
--Graded Bible Stories. LC 14-1692. 20cm. 582p. c.1914. Christian Nurture.
Mutt, Eugenie, adapted by.
--Fairy Tales from Baltic Shores: Folk-Lore Stories from Estonia. Berkowitz, Jeannette, illus. LC 30-30343. 382 p. col. front., illus., col. plates. 25 cm. N.D. The Penn Publishing Company.
Muzick, Terra
--Teddy Bear Paper Dolls. 32p. 1984. (ISBN 0-8431-1724-9). Price Stern.
Muzzy, Alice M.
--Bennie Winklefield. N.D. Methodist Bk Concern.
Mwenye Hadithi
--Greedy Zebra. Kennaway, Adrienne (1945-), illus. LC 83-83381. (Illus.). 32 p. c.1984. (ISBN 0-316-33721-8). (ISBN 0-316-33721-8). Little, Brown.
Myers, Agnes, retold by.
--A King is Born. Myers, Irwin, illus. N.D. Grosset & Dunlap.
Myers, Alexander John William (1877-)
--Children's Adventures with Nature and People. 1st ed. LC 59-3770. (A Collection of Stories for Children about Animals, Plants, Biblical and Other Events to be Narrated by Ministers, Teachers, and Parents.). 108p. 21cm. 1959. Exposition Press.
Myers, Amy
--I Know a Monster. Myers, Amy, illus. LC 78-11692. (Illus.). 31 p. c.1979. (ISBN 0-201-04990-2). Addison-Wesley.
Myers, Bernice
--The Apple War. Myers, Bernice, illus. LC 72-8191. (Illus.). 40 p. 27cm. 1973. (ISBN 0-8193-0650-9). (ISBN 0-8193-0650-9). Parents' Magazine Press.
--Come Out Shadow, Wherever You Are. Myers, Bernice, illus. (Illus.). (gr. k-3). 1971. (ISBN 0-590-04441-9, Schol Pap). Scholastic Inc.
--The Extraordinary Invention. Myers, Bernice, illus. LC 84-3884. (Illus.). 48p. (gr. k-3). 1984. (ISBN 0-02-767780-X). Macmillan.
--Herman and the Bears Again. Myers, Bernice, illus. LC 76-45635. (Illus.). 47 p. 22cm. c.1976. (ISBN 0-590-07494-6). Four Winds Press.
--Herman & the Bears & the Giant. (gr. k-3). 1978. (ISBN 0-590-05375-2). Scholastic Inc.
--Herman & the Bears Behind Bars. Myers, Bernice, illus. (Illus.). (gr. k-3). 1979. (ISBN 0-590-05745-6). Scholastic Inc.
--Little John Bear in the Big City. LC 78-15595. (Illus.). 32 p. 22cm. c.1978. (ISBN 0-590-07601-9). Four Winds Press.
--A Lost Horse. LC 74-23888. (Illus.). 32 p. 22cm. 1975. (ISBN 0-385-08361-0). (ISBN 0-385-08406-4). Doubleday.
--My Mother Is Lost. Myers, Bernice, illus. (gr. k-3). 1971. (ISBN 0-590-04478-8). (ISBN 0-590-20694-X). Scholastic Inc.
--Not at Home. LC 80-16288. (Illus.). 47 p. 22cm. c.1981. (ISBN 0-688-51974-1). (ISBN 0-688-41974-7). Lothrop, Lee & Shepard Books.
--Not This Bear!. LC 68-12387. (Illus.). 1 v. (unpaged. 24cm. 1968, c.1967. Four Winds Press.
--Sally's Secret. (gr. k-3). 1977. (ISBN 0-590-10418-7). Scholastic Inc.
--Sidney Rella and the Glass Sneaker. LC 85-3044. (Illus.). 32 p. 24cm. 1985. (ISBN 0-02-767790-7). Macmillan.
Myers, Beth McHenry (1910-)
--The Doctor Is a Lady. LC 54-7967. 255p. 21cm. 1954. Avalon Books.
Myers, Byrona
--Turn Here Strawberry Roan. LC 50-6921. 134 p. illus. 23 cm. 1950. Bobbs-Merrill.
--Yo Ho for Strawberry Roan. LC 51-9934. 155 p. illus. 23 cm. 1951. Bobbs-Merrill.
Myers, Caroline Elizabeth Clark (1887-1980), ed.
--Children's Own Stories. Rao, Anthony, illus. (Illus.). line ils. 32p. (Orig.). (Highlights Handbooks Ser.). (gr. 2-6). 1970. (ISBN 0-87534-142-X). Highlights.
Myers, Cora Estelle
--Scot. LC 23-180152. vii, 198 p. incl. front. 19 cm. 1923. The Author.
Myers, E. L. (1940-)
--The Blatherskite's: A Fable. Blue, Sharon, illus. (Illus.). 32 p. 22cm. 1974. (ISBN 0-682-47997-7). Exposition Press.
--The Blatherskite's Reward. Blue, Sharon, illus. (Illus.). (gr. 5 up). 1974. (ISBN 0-682-47997-7). Exposition.
Myers, Elisabeth Perkins (1918-)
--Edward Bok: Young Editor. Sternweiss, Shannon, illus. LC 67-26336. (Illus.). 200 p. 20cm. (Childhood of Famous Americans). 1967. Bobbs-Merrill.
--F. W. Woolworth: Five and Ten Boy. Morrow, Gray, illus. LC 62-16590. 200p. col. illus. 20cm. (Childhood of Famous Americans). c.1962. Bobbs.
--Katharine Lee Bates: Girl Poet. Rawson, Maurice, illus. LC 61-12320. 200p. col. illus. (Childhood of Famous Americans). c.1961. Bobbs.
Myers, Garry Cleveland (1884-1971)
--Christmas Wishes. Rao, Anthony, illus. LC 73-184396. (Illus.). 32 p. 19cm. c.1972. (ISBN 0-87534-602-2). Highlights for Children.
--For Beginning the School Day. LC 66-27820. (Illus.). 96 p. 29cm. (Highlights Jumbo handbook). 1966. Highlights for Children.
--Wishes. Allen, Lois, illus. LC 70-101373. (Illus.). 32 p. 19cm. 1969. Hewitt House.
Myers, Grayce Silverton
--The Fishing Cat. N.D. E. M. Hale & Co.
--The Fishing Cat. Galdone, Paul (1914-), illus. LC 53-11614. unpaged. 19 x 23cm. c.1953. Abingdon-Cokesbury.
Myers, Helen Elizabeth (1910-), retold by.
--Noah's Ark. Steiner, Charlotte, illus. LC 41-22953. (Illus.). 26 x 26cm. 17p. 1941. Garden City Publishing Co.
Myers, Hortense Powner (1913-) & Burnett, Ruth
--Carl Ben Eielson,. Young Alaskan Pilot. Morrow, Gray, illus. LC 60-148340. 192p. illus. 20cm. (Childhood of famous Americans). c.1960. Bobbs-Merrill.
--Cecil B. DeMille: Young Dramatist. Goldstein, Nathan (1927-), illus. LC 63-10311. 200p. col. illus. 20cm. (Childhood of Famous Americans). c.1963. Bobbs.
Myers, Jack & Myers, Louise
--Little Star. LC 52-24660. (Illus.). 21cm. 16p. (A Cozy-Corner Bk.). 1952. Whitman.
Myers, Jane Pentzer
--Stories of Enchantment: Or, The Ghost Flower. Roosevelt, Harriet, illus. 19cm. 215p. 1901. A. C. McClurg & Co.
Myers, Lou
--Ha, Ha, Ha, Hyenas. LC 74-153990. (Illus.). 48 p. 23cm. (Break-of-Day Bk.). 1971. Coward, McCann & Geoghegan.
--In Plenty of Time. LC 71-183551. (Illus.). 48 p. 23cm. (Break-of-Day Bk.). 1972. Coward, McCann & Geoghegan.
--Tutti-Frutti. LC 67-14231. (Illus.). 32 p. 1967. Pantheon Books.
Myers, Lou, illus.
--The Wonder Book of Christmas. Including The Night Before Christmas, and Ten Other Stories. LC 51-7286. unpaged. illus. 21 cm. (Wonder Bks. 575). 1951. Wonder Books.
Myers, Louise, jt. auth. see Myers, Jack.
Myers, Madeleine Neuberger (1896-)
--The Courting-Lamp Mystery. 1st ed. Vasiliu, Mircea (1920-), illus. LC 58-6517. 190p. illus. 21cm. 1958. Holt.
--Pocketful of Feathers. LC 50-2846. 159p. 21cm. 1950. Westminster Press.
--Pulling Strings. Adams, Adrienne (1906-), illus. LC 54-5739. (Illus.). 228 p. 21cm. 1954. Holt.
--Touch the Harvest Moon. 1st ed. Mitchell, Michael, illus. LC 55-10571. 258p. illus. 21cm. (Holt books for young people). 1955. Holt.
Myers, Sarah Ann Irwin, Mrs. (1800-1876)
--Faithful Nicolette: Or, The French Nurse, 1 of 25 vols. (Illus.). (Selected Bks for Sunday School: No. 21). N.D. Set. Methodist Bk Concern.
--Little Shoemaker: Or, The Orphans' Victory, 1 of 25 vols. (Illus.). (Selected Bks for Sunday School: No. 21). N.D. Set. Methodist Bk Concern.
--The Little Shoemaker: Or, the Orphan's Victory. 232p. N.D. Presbyterian Committee of Publication.
Myers, Sarah Ann Irwin, Mrs. (1800-1876) & Cottage, Rose
--Our Katie, 1 of 25 vols. (Illus.). (Selected Bks for Sunday School: No. 21). N.D. Set. Methodist Bk Concern.
Myers, Sarah Ann Irwin (1800-1876), compiled by.
--The Balloon. Myers, Sarah Ann Irwin (1800-1876), tr. LC 66-57586. 123 p. col. plates. 16 cm. (Child's Library). 1855. C. G. Henderson.
Myers, Steven
--The Enchanted Sticks. Diamond, Donna (1950-), illus. LC 78-27725. p. cm. 1979. (ISBN 0-698-20483-2). Coward, McCann & Geoghegan.
Myers, Walter Dean (1937-)
--Adventure in Granada. LC 85-43041. p. cm. (Arrow Adventure Ser.). 1985. (ISBN 0-14-032011-3). Puffin Books.
--The Black Pearl and The Ghost: Or, One Mystery After Another. 1st ed. Quackenbush, Robert Mead (1929-), illus. LC 79-20268. (Illus.). 36 p. 24cm. 1980. (ISBN 0-670-17284-7). Viking Press.
--Brainstorm. Freedman, Chuck, photos by. LC 77-6462. (Illus.). 90 p. 22cm. (Triumph book). 1977. (ISBN 0-531-01325-1). Watts.
--The Dancers. Rockwell, Anne F. (1934-), illus. LC 79-174600. (Illus.). 40 p. 22cm. 1972. (ISBN 0-8193-0567-7). (ISBN 0-8193-0568-5). Parents' Magazine Press.
--The Dragon Takes a Wife. Grifalconi, Ann (1929-), illus. LC 71-172340. (Illus.). 32 p. 24cm. 1972. Bobbs-Merrill.
--Fast Sam, Cool Clyde, and Stuff. LC 74-32383. 190 p. 22cm. 1975. (ISBN 0-670-30874-9). Viking Press. **Award: (ALA).**
--Fly, Jimmy, Fly!. Barnett, Moneta (1922-1976), illus. LC 73-88813. (Illus.). 32 p. 25cm. 1974. (ISBN 0-399-20394-X). (ISBN 0-399-60884-2). Putnam.
--The Golden Serpent. Provensen, Alice (1918-) & Provensen, Martin (1916-), illus. LC 80-12731. p. cm. 1980. (ISBN 0-670-34445-1). Viking Press.
--The Hidden Shrine. LC 85-43042. p. cm. (Arrow Adventure Ser.). 1985. (ISBN 0-14-032010-5). Puffin Books.
--Hoops: A Novel. LC 81-65497. p. cm. 1981. (ISBN 0-440-03707-7). (ISBN 0-440-03707-7). Delacorte Press.
--It Ain't All for Nothin'. 1st ed. LC 78-57516. 217 p. 22cm. 1978. (ISBN 0-670-40301-6). Viking Press. **Award: (ALA).**
--The Legend of Tarik. Howell, Troy, illus. LC 80-27655. p. cm. 1981. (ISBN 0-670-42312-2). Viking Press.
--Mojo and the Russians. LC 77-23454. p. cm. 1977. (ISBN 0-670-48437-7). Viking Press.
--Motown & Didi: A Love Story. LC 84-3632. 192p. (gr. 7 up). 1984. (ISBN 0-670-49062-8, Viking Kestrel). Viking. **Award: (CSKA).**
--Mr. Monkey & the Gotcha Bird. Morrill, Leslie H., illus. LC 82-18241. (Illus.). 32p. (ps-3). 1984. (ISBN 0-385-29292-9). (ISBN 0-385-29293-7). Delacorte.
--The Nicholas Factor. LC 82-60083. p. cm. 1983. (ISBN 0-670-51055-6). Viking Press.
--The Outside Shot. LC 84-4271. 192p. (gr. 7 up). 1984. (ISBN 0-385-29353-4). Delacorte.
--Tales of a Dead King. LC 83-5373. (gr. 5-9). 1983. (ISBN 0-688-02413-0). Morrow.
--Where Does the Day Go?. Carty, Leo (1931-), illus. LC 69-12616. (Illus.). 41 p. 1969. (ISBN 0-8193-0317-8). Parents' Magazine Press.
--Won't Know Till I Get There. 11 x 12 1/2. 188p. Repr. of 1982 ed (Pub. by Viking Press). (15 pt.). (gr. 6-9). N.D. Am Printing Hse.
--Won't Know till I Get There. 1st ed. LC 81-71128. 176 p. 22cm. 1982. (ISBN 0-670-77862-1). Viking Press.
--The Young Landlords. LC 79-13264. p. cm. 1979. (ISBN 0-670-79454-6). Viking Press. **Awards: (CSKA); (ALA).**

Nash, Frederic Ogden (1902-1971), ed.
--Everybody Ought to Know. LC 61-9102. (Illus.). (gr. 7-11). 1961. (ISBN 0-397-30545-1). Har-Row.
--I Couldn't Help Laughing: Stories. 1st ed. LC 57-10337. 231p. 22cm. 1957. Lippincott.
--The Moon Is Shining Bright As Day: An Anthology of Good-Humored Verse. LC 53-7143. (Illus.). 177 p. 22cm. 1953. (ISBN 0-397-30244-4). Lippincott.
Nash, Harriet A.
--Polly's Secret. Price, Harriet Longstreet (1891-), illus. LC 26-15065. 4 p. l., 292 p. col. front., col. plates. 23 cm. (Beacon Hill book-shelf). 1926. Little, Brown and Company.
--Polly's Secret: A Story of the Kennebec. Edwards, Harry C., illus. LC 2-23901. 4 p. l., 291 p. front., plates. 19 x 15 cm. 1902. Little, Brown, and Company.
Nash, Mary Hughes (1925-)
--Mrs. Coverlet's Detectives. Price, Garrett W. (1896-1979), illus. LC 65-16846. (Illus.). 153 p. 22cm. 1965. Little, Brown.
--Mrs Coverlet's Magicians. Price, Garrett W. (1896-1979), illus. LC 61-5326. (Illus.). 189 p. 22cm. 1961. Little, Brown.
--While Mrs. Coverlet Was Away. Price, Garrett W. (1896-1979), illus. LC 58-8489. (Illus.). 133 p. 22cm. 1958. Little, Brown.
Nash, N. Richard (1913-)
--East Wind, Rain. 1st ed. LC 76-40433. 317. 25cm. 1976. Atheneum.
Nash, Nancy (1943-)
--A Pet for Kei-Chan. Nash, Nancy (1943-), illus. LC 66-25301. 1 v. (unpaged) col. illus. 19 cm. 1966. C. E. Tuttle Co.
--Wumpy's Christmas Gift. Floethe, Richard (1901-), illus. LC 56-9150. (Illus.). 29. 25cm. 1956. Lothrop, Lee and Shepard.
Nash, Nellie Clayton
--Cape Split Ducklings. Leland, Stanley F., illus. LC 19-15083. 4 p. l., 3-86 p. front., illus. 21 cm. c.1918. The Cornhill Company.
Nash, Ogden, jt. auth. see Alger, Joseph.
Nash, Ogden see Lear, Edward (1812-1888) & Vash, Fredric Ogden.
Nash, Ogden see Nash, Frederic Ogden.
Nash, Roy (1929-)
--I'll Bow Sadly: A Story of Giuseppe Verdi. Ruplinger, Harold, Bro., illus. LC 56-15677. 96p. illus. 24cm. 1955. Dujarie Press.
Nason, Janet
--Little Women Paper Dolls. 8p. (gr. 8-12). 1982. (ISBN 0-914510-13-4). Evergreen.
Nason, Thelma Campbell
--Under the Wide Sky: Tales of New Mexico and the Spanish Southwest. Kane, Herbert Kawainui, illus. LC 65-23421. 191p. illus. 23cm. c.1965. Follett.
Nasreddin, Hoca (1924-), compiled by see Shah, Idries Sayed.
Nassau, Robert H.
--Where Animals Talk. N.D. Bruce Humphries.
Nast, Elsa Ruth, pseud., see Watson, Jane Werner.
Nast, Elsa Ruth, pseud. (1915-)
--Chatterly Squirrel and Other Animal Stories. Watson, Jane Werner. Miller, John Parr (1913-), illus. (Golden Bks.). 1949. Simon & Schuster.
--Christopher Bunny and Other Animal Stories. Watson, Jane Werner. Scarry, Richard McClure (1919-), illus. (Golden Story Book). 1949. Golden Press.
--Happy Birthday. Watson, Jane Werner. Worcester, Retta, illus. Reissue of 1960 ed. (Little Golden Book). 1951. Golden Press.
--Our Puppy. Watson, Jane Werner. Rojankovsky, Feodor Stepanovich (1891-), illus. Reissue of 1949 ed. (Little Golden Book). 1957. Golden Press.
--Tex and His Toys. Watson, Jane Werner. Malvern, Corinne (1905-1956), illus. LC 52-8416. unpaged. illus. 21cm. (Little golden library, 129). 1952. Simon and Schuster.
--A Wood's Story. Watson, Jane Werner. N.D. Harper & Bros.

Nast, Thomas (1840-1902), illus.
--Yankee Doodle. LC 72-285992. (Illus.). 16p. 27cm. 1872. McLoughlin Bros.
--Yankee Doodle. LC 79-285921. (Illus.). 16p. 27cm. (Aunt Louisa's Big Picture Ser.). 1879. McLoughin Bros.
Nastick, Sharon
--Mr. Radagast Makes an Unexpected Journey. 1st ed. Glasser, Judith, illus. LC 80-8017. (Illus.). 85 p. 21cm. c.1981. (ISBN 0-690-04051-2). (ISBN 0-690-04050-4). Crowell.
Nathan, A. G., jt. auth. see Ernst, Margaret Samuels.
Nathan, Adele Gutman, jt. auth. see Loeb, Elinor G.
Nathan, Adele Newburger Gutman
--Seven Brave Companions. 1st ed. Kredel, Fritz (1900-1973), illus. LC 53-12190. 164p. illus. 20cm. 1953. Aladdin Books.
--Seven Brave Companions. Kredel, Fritz (1900-1973), illus. N.D. E. P. Dutton & Co.
--Wheat Won't Wait. McGee, Millard, illus. LC 52-11820. 192 p. illus. 21 cm. (American Heritage Ser.). 1952. Aladdin Books.
--When Lincoln Went to Gettysburg. 1st ed. Weiss, Emil (1896-1965), illus. LC 55-6509. 221p. illus. 20cm. 1955. Aladdin Books.
Nathan, Dorothy, adapted by see Marshak, Samuil Iakovlevich.
Nathan, Dorothy Goldeen (0000-1966)
--The Shy One. Cather, Carolyn, illus. LC 66-9788. (Illus.). 178 p. 22cm. 1966. Random House.
Nathan, Emily
--I Know a Farmer. Abel, Raymond (1911-), illus. LC 75-92817. (Illus.). 24 cm. 43p. (Community Helper Bks.). (gr. 1-3). 1970. (ISBN 0-399-60279-8). Putnam Pub Group.
Nathan, Robert Gruntal (1894-1985)
--Sir Henry. 1st ed. LC 54-12039. 187p. 21cm. 1955, c.1954. Knopf.
--The Snowflake and the Starfish. Weisgard, Leonard Joseph (1916-), illus. LC 59-12571. (Illus.). 68 p. 23cm. 1959. Knopf.
--Tappy. Burn, Doris (1923-), illus. LC 68-11172. (Illus.). 60 p. 22cm. 1968. Knopf.
Nathan, Stella
--Porky Pig & Bugs Bunny - Just Like Magic. Totten, Bob & McKimson, Tom, illus. (Illus.). (ps-3). N.D. (ISBN 0-307-60146-3, Golden Pr). Western Pub.
--Rumpelstiltskin. Tiffany, Virginia, illus. LC 68-7728. (Illus.). 26 p. 32cm. (Whitman Giant Tell-a-Tale Bk.). 1968. Whitman Pub. Division.
Nathanson, Laura
--Abigail and the Thing with Feathers. LC 85-12166. p. cm. c.1985. (ISBN 0-399-21269-8). Putnam.
Nation, Terry
--Rebecca's World. Learmonth, Larry, tr. LC 76-39725. (Illus.). 114p. (gr. 3-5). 1977. (ISBN 0-8149-0779-2). Vanguard.
National Association of Junior Chautauqua Directors
--Fun Folk and Fairy Tales. LC 23-10977. 160 p. 1 illus. 20 cm. c.1923. Fleming H. Revell Company.
--Through Story-land with the Children. Faulkner, Georgene, intro. by. LC 24-22123. (Illus.). 20cm. 153p. (Junior Chautauqua Series). 1924. Revell Co.
National Child Labor Committee, New York
--Poems of Child Labor. 53 p. 20 cm. (Its Publication, No. 316). 1924. National Child Labor Committee.
National Wildlife Federation
--Ranger Rick's Storybook: A Keepsake Collection of Animal Tales from Ranger Rick Magazine. LC 83-8060. p. cm. c.1983. (ISBN 0-912186-47-X). National Wildlife Federation.
Natti, Marylee Kingman see Kingman, Lee, pseud.
Nauman, Mary D.
--The Enchanted Princess. N.D. Claxton, Remsen & Haffelfinger.
--Eva's Adventures In Shadowland. N.D. J. B. Lippincott.
--Twisted Threads. N.D. Claxton, Remsen, and Haffelfinger.
Naumburg, Elsa H., tr. see Froschel, George.
Navaho Curriculum Center see Callaway, Sydney M. & Witherspoon, Gary.
Navaho Curriculum Center see Roessel, Robert A., Jr. & Platero, Dillon.
Navajo Childern, jt. auth. see Brandt, Rose Katherine.
Navarra, John Gabriel (1927-)
--Earthquake. LC 79-8938. (Illus.). 96p. (gr. 6-7). 1980. (ISBN 0-385-15081-4). Doubleday.
--A Turtle in the House. 1st ed. Komoda, Kiyoaki (1937-), illus. (Illus.). 58 p. 24cm. 1968. Doubleday.
Nay, Carol
--Timmy Rides the China Clipper. Nay, Carol, photos by. LC 39-30372. 94, 2 p. incl. col. front., illus. (part col., incl. maps) 24 cm. (Junior Press Bks.). 1939. A. Whitman & Co.
Naylor, James Ball (1860-1945)
--The Cabin in the Big Woods. Elliott, Fred A., illus. LC 4-28419. 20cm. 239p. 1904. The Saalfield Pub. Co.
--The Little Green Goblin. Miller, Harry Lambright, illus. LC 7-24772. 187 p. incl. col. front., illus. 5 col. pl. 24 x 21 cm. c.1907. The Saalfield Publishing Company.
--Witch Crow and Barney Bylow. Williams, Carll B., illus. LC 6-45177. 2 p. l., 118 p. col. front., illus., 5 col. pl. 24 x 21 cm. c.1906. The Saalfield Publishing Company.
Naylor, Phyllis Reynolds (1933-)
--The Agony of Alice. LC 85-7957. 131 p. 22cm. 1985. (ISBN 0-689-31143-5). Atheneum. **Award: (ALA).**
--All Because I'm Older. LC 80-18586. (Illus.). 32p. (ps-4). 1981. (ISBN 0-689-30824-8). Atheneum.
--An Amish Family. 1975. (ISBN 0-87955-209-3). J. Philip O'Hara Inc.
--The Bodies in the Bessledorf Hotel. LC 83-17920. 128p. (Escapade Ser.). (gr. 4-6). 1985. (ISBN 0-689-31379-9). Atheneum.
--The Boy with the Helium Head. Chorao, Ann Mckay Sproat (1936-), illus. LC 82-1807. (Illus.). 32p. (ps-3). 1982. (ISBN 0-689-30934-1). Atheneum.
--The Dark of the Tunnel. LC 84-20441. p. cm. 1985. (ISBN 0-689-31098-6). Atheneum.
--Eddie, Incorporated. Sims, Blanche, illus. LC 79-22589. (Illus.). 101 p. 22cm. 1980. (ISBN 0-689-30754-3). Atheneum.
--Faces in the Water. LC 80-24057. (Illus.). 167 p. 22cm. (The York Trilogy: Bk. 2). 1981. (ISBN 0-689-30823-X). Atheneum.
--Footprints at the Window. LC 81-1944. p. cm. 1981. (ISBN 0-689-30856-6). Atheneum.
--Galloping Goat & Other Stories. Jefferson, Robert Louis (1929-), illus. LC 65-14092. (Illus.). col. illus. 21 cm. 112p. (gr. 3-7). 1965. (ISBN 0-687-13914-7). Abingdon.
--Grasshoppers in the Soup: Short Stories for Teenagers. Bailey, Elsa, illus. LC 65-21819. 131p. illus. 19cm. c.1965. Fortress.
--Jennifer Jean: The Cross-Eyed Queen. Lamson, Harold K., illus. LC 67-15701. (Illus.). 32 p. 24cm. 1967. (ISBN 0-8225-0263-1). Lerner Publications Co.
--Just Because I'm Older. Kramer, Tony, illus. LC 80-18586. p. cm. 1981. (ISBN 0-689-30824-8). Atheneum.
--Knee Deep in Ice Cream and Other Stories. 144p. 1967. Lutheran Publications.
--The Mad Gasser of Besseldorf Street. LC 83-6430. p. cm. (Escapade). 1983. (ISBN 0-689-31375-6). Atheneum.
--Making It Happen. LC 73-118929. 128 p. 23cm. 1970. (ISBN 0-695-80144-9). Follett.
--Meet Murdock. Fiammenghi, Gioia (1929-), illus. LC 69-10247. (Illus.). 32 p. 27cm. 1969. Follett Pub. Co.
--The New Schoolmaster. Funai, Mamoru R. (1932-), illus. LC 67-16757. (Illus.). 32 p. 27cm. (Our World of Peoples Ser. India). 1967. Silver Burdett Co.
--A New Year's Surprise. Endewelt, Jack, illus. LC 67-167587. (Illus.). 32 p. 27cm. (Our World of Peoples Ser.). 1967. Silver Burdett Co.
--Night Cry. LC 83-15569. 168p. 1984. (ISBN 0-689-31017-X). Atheneum.
--No Easy Circle. LC 74-161556. 152 p. 23cm. 1972. (ISBN 0-695-80242-9). (ISBN 0-695-40242-0). Follett Pub. Co.
--Old Sadie & the Christmas Bear. Newton, Patricia Montgomery, illus. LC 84-2995. (Illus.). 32p. (ps-2). 1984. (ISBN 0-689-31052-8). Atheneum.
--Private I, & Other Stories. (gr. 8 up). 1969. (ISBN 0-8006-1125-X). Fortress.
--Shadows on the Wall. LC 80-12967. p. cm. 1980. (ISBN 0-689-30785-3). Atheneum.
--Ships in the Night. LC 79-133037. (Illus.). vi, 121 p. 20cm. 1971, c.1970. Fortress Press.
--The Solomon System. LC 83-2661. p. cm. 1983. (ISBN 0-689-30991-0). Atheneum.
--A String of Chances. 1st ed. LC 82-1790. 244 p. 22cm. 1982. (ISBN 0-689-30935-X). Atheneum. **Award: (ALA).**
--To Make a Wee Moon. Krush, Beth (1918-) & Krush, Joe (1918-), illus. LC 79-83313. (Illus.). 190 p. 23cm. 1969. Follett Pub. Co.
--To Shake a Shadow. LC 67-7049. 144 p. 22cm. 1967. Abingdon Press.
--To Walk the Sky Path. LC 72-85583. 144 p. 23cm. 1973. (ISBN 0-695-80368-9). (ISBN 0-695-80368-9). Follett Pub. Co.
--A Triangle Has Four Sides. LC 83-72123. (True-to-Life Stories Show How Teens Deal with Feelings & Problems). 1984. (ISBN 0-8066-2067-6). Augsburg Pub. House.
--Walking Through the Dark. 1st. ed. LC 75-23039. 212 p. 22cm. 1976. (ISBN 0-689-30509-5). Atheneum.
--What the Gulls Were Singing. Smith, Jack, illus. LC 67-211165. (Illus.). 191 p. 23cm. 1967. Follett Pub. Co.
--When Rivers Meet. Eitzen, Allan (1928-), illus. LC 67-27802. 160p. illus. 20cm. 1968. Friendship.
--The Witch Herself. 1st ed. Owens, Gail, illus. LC 78-5437. (Illus.). 164 p. 22cm. 1978. (ISBN 0-689-30625-3). Atheneum.
--Witch Water. 1st ed. Owens, Gail, illus. LC 77-1057. (Illus.). 179 p. 22cm. 1977. (ISBN 0-689-30595-8). Atheneum.
--Witch's Sister. 1st ed. Owens, Gail, illus. LC 74-19268. (Illus.). 150 p. 22cm. 1975. (ISBN 0-689-30453-6). Atheneum.
--Wrestle the Mountain. LC 79-121413. 249p. 23cm. c.1971. (ISBN 0-695-80181-3). Follett.
Naylor, Phyllis Reynolds (1933-) & Daniel, Alan (1939-)
--How Lazy Can You Get?. LC 79-10444. p. cm. 1979. (ISBN 0-689-30721-7). Atheneum.
Ndirangu, Eutychus
--Island of Yo. Moore, Adrienne (1945-), illus. Kennaway, Adrienne, photos by. LC 76-980746. (Illus.). 24 p. (Lioncub Bk. 8). 1976. East African Pub. House.
Neago, Fanny Louise, tr. see Baudouy, Michel Aime.
Neal, Barbara
--Melody's Christmas. 32p. (gr. k-3). 1975. (ISBN 0-682-48296-X). Exposition.
Neal, Berniece Roer
--Chicken. Lindberg, Jeffrey K., illus. LC 78-72119. (Illus.). 32 p. 23cm. 1979. (ISBN 0-89799-092-7). (ISBN 0-89799-018-8). Dandelion Press.
Neal, Harry Edward (1906-)
--The Story of the Kite. Moment, John, illus. LC 52-11121. 61p. illus. 25cm. 1954. Vanguard Press.
Neal, Hazel G
--Mary's Reward: Or, The First Commandment with Promise. LC 24-2324. 96 p. incl. front., illus. 19 cm. c.1923. Gospel Trumpet Company.
Neal, John (1793-1876)
--Goody Gracious! And the Forget-Me-Not. (Little Classics). N.D. James R Osgood & Co.
--Great Mysteries and Little Plagues. LC 12-28069. iv p., 1 l., 7-271 p. front. 18 cm. 1870. Roberts Brothers.
Neal, Michael
--Gremlins: A New Friend. Dominguez, Luis, illus. LC 83-83378. (Illus.). 24p. (ps). 1984. (ISBN 0-307-11372-8, Golden Bks). Western Pub.
Neale, Gay Weeks
--Banners Over Terre D'Or. LC 82-20592. (Illus.). 246 p. 22cm. c.1982. (ISBN 0-89587-024-X). J.F. Blair.
Neall, Beatrice M.
--Outside the Gate. (gr. 8 up). 1976. (ISBN 0-8127-0126-7). Review & Herald.
--Outside the Gate. (gr. 8 up). 1976. (ISBN 0-8127-0126-7). Southern Pub.
Neally, Amy, ed.
--Favorite Poems from the Best Authors. LC 11-30742. vii, 234 p. front., plates. 14 cm. 1894. E. P. Dutton & Co.
--Poetry for Children. LC 11-33532. 280, v p. front., illus. 18 cm. 1880. E. P. Dutton and Company.
Nealy, Sid H.
--In the Trail of the Pack-Mule. Nealy, Sid H., illus. LC 22-160251. ix p., 1 l., 261 p. front., plates. 21 cm. c.1902. F. T. Neely.
Nearing, Penny (1916-) & Roscoe, Esther B.
--Big Enough. (Indian Culture Ser.). (gr. 2-5). 1974. (ISBN 0-89992-070-5). MT Coun Indian.
Neasi, Barbara J
--Just Like Me. Axeman, Lois, illus. LC 83-23154. (Illus.). 30 p. 19cm. (A Rookie Reader). 1984. (ISBN 0-516-02047-1). (ISBN 0-516-02047-1). (ISBN 0-516-42047-X). Childrens Press.
Neavles, Janet Talmadge (1919-)
--Beyond the Mist Lies Thule. Zaidenberg, Arthur, illus. LC 61-7093. 216p. illus. 21cm. (Wonderful World Bk.). 1961. A. S. Barnes.
--For Life and Liberty. Marcel, Delia, illus. LC 60-10203. 200p. illus. 21cm. (Wonderful World Bk.). 1960. Barnes.
--The Mystery of the Pharaoh's Treasure. Roselli, Luciana, photos by. LC 63-9862. (Illus.). 192 p. 21cm. 1963. Lippincott.
Nedobeck, Don
--Nedobeck's Twelve Days of Christmas. (Illus.). 32p. (gr. k-6). 1982. (ISBN 0-8249-8043-3). Ideals.

Neebe, William
--The Three Billy Goats Gruff. (Illus.). 24p. (gr. k-3). N.D. (ISBN 0-528-88869-2). Rand.
Needle, Jan (1943-)
--Another Fine Mess. Bentley, Roy, illus. (Illus.). 192p. (gr. 5-7). N.D. (ISBN 0-233-97370-2). Andre Deutsch.
--Rottenteeth. Bentley, Roy, illus. LC 79-8650. (Illus.). 32 p. 26cm. 1980. (ISBN 0-233-97205-6). A. Deutsch.
--The Size Spies. Bentley, Roy, illus. (Illus.). 156p. (gr. 3-6). 1983. (ISBN 0-233-97003-7). Andre Deutsch.
Needles, Cora Blanche (1876-)
--The Stories My School Children Loved: A Manual of Ethical Training for Children. LC 41-6969. 5 p. l., 13-304 p. incl. front. (port.) 23 cm. c.1941. The Pyramid Press.
Neeland, Barbara S.
--Coming of the Reindeer. Stevens, Gloria, illus. LC 66-7538. (Illus.). 1 v. (unpaged) col. 24 cm. (gr. 1-4). 1966. (ISBN 0-8313-0080-9). Lantern.
Neely, Henry Milton (1876-1963)
--Fred Spencer, Reporter. Blum, A. A., illus. LC 12-24482. viii p., 1 l., 357, 1 p. front., plates. 20 cm. c.1912. Small, Maynard and Company.
Neely, Kate Hill
--Florry Forrester: Or, Three Dreadful Days. (Illus.). 320p. N.D. Sunday-School Publications.

Neely, Kate J.
--Actions Speak Louder Than Words. LC 41-421463. 238 p. front., plates. 18 cm. (Added t.-p.: The Proverb Ser. by Mrs. M. E. Bradley and Kate J. Neely no. 5). 1871. Lee and Shepard.
--Fine Feathers Do Not Make Fine Birds, 1 of 25 vols. (Illus.). (Mayflower Ser. for Girls: No. 8). 1900. Lee & Shepard.
--One Good Turn Deserves Another, 1 of 25 vols. (Illus.). (Mayflower Ser. for Girls: No. 19). 1900. Lee & Shepard.
Neely, Kate J., jt. auth. see Bradley, Mary Emily Neely, Mrs.
Neese, Marcia A.
--Everyone Is Special. Oelerich, Marjorie L. & Cranfill, John, eds. Neese, Marcia A., illus. LC 83-22404. (Illus.). 32p. (The Boulder Gang Ser.). (gr. k-4). 1984. (ISBN 0-914867-02-4). Baker St Prod.
--Have You Ever Tried. Oelerich, Marjorie L. & Cranfill, John, eds. Neese, Marcia A., illus. LC 83-22399. (Illus.). 32p. (The Boulder Gang Ser.). (gr. k-4). 1984. (ISBN 0-914867-00-8). Baker St Prod.
--Homesick. Oelerich, Marjorie L. & Cranfill, John, eds. Neese, Marcia A., illus. LC 83-21488. (Illus.). 32p. (The Boulder Gang Ser.). (gr. k-4). 1984. (ISBN 0-914867-06-7). Baker St Prod.
--I'm Afraid of the Dark. Oelerich, Marjorie, ed. Neese, Marcia A., illus. LC 83-22392. (Illus.). 32p. (The Boulder Gang Ser.). (gr. k-4). 1984. Baker St Prod.
--It's Great to Be Me. Oelerich, Marjorie L. & Cranfill, John, eds. LC 83-25876. 1984. (ISBN 0-914867-07-5). Baker Street Productions.
--Not a Thing to Wear. Oelerich, Marjorie L. & Cranfill, John, eds. Neese, Marcia A., illus. LC 83-22373. (Illus.). 32p. (The Boulder Gang Ser.). (gr. k-4). 1984. (ISBN 0-914867-05-9). Baker St Prod.
--To Be a Friend. Oelerich, Marjorie L. & Cranfill, John, eds. Neese, Marcia A., illus. LC 83-22342. (Illus.). 32p. (The Boulder Gang Ser.). (gr. k-4). 1984. (ISBN 0-914867-01-6). Baker St Prod.
--When You've Done Your Best. Oelerich, Marjorie L. & Cranfill, John, eds. LC 83-22424. 1984. (ISBN 0-914867-03-2). Baker Street Productions.
Neff, Carolyn & Verett, Dotty
--Blue Jean Days. Bachelis, Faren, ed. Franklin, Jean, illus. 32p. (gr. 4-8). 1982. (ISBN 0-931724-20-1). Dandy Lion.
Neff, Ethel Maxine
--Packy: The Runaway Elephant. Munson, Harold W. (1920-), illus. LC 57-14976. unpaged. illus. 24cm. 1957. Pacific Press Pub. Association.
--Pokey the Runaway Bear. Munson, Harold W. (1920-), illus. LC 50-14873. illus. 24 cm. 42p. (gr. k-3). N.D. Pacific Pr Pub Assn.
--Sally the Runaway Monkey. Munson, Harold W. (1920-), illus. LC 55-8491. (Illus.). 24 cm. (ps-3). N.D. Pacific Pr Pub Assn.
Neff, Lavonne
--God's Gift Baby. (Arch Book Series Fourteen). 1977. (ISBN 0-570-06113-X). Concordia.
--Simon was Safe. (Illus.). 32p. (Arch Bks: No. 13). (ps-4). 1976. (ISBN 0-570-06104-0). Concordia.
Neff, Priscilla Holton
--Little Miss Callie. 1955. (ISBN 0-8382-0461-9, Cadmus Books). E. M. Hale And Company.
--Little Miss Callie. 1st ed. Geer, Charles Hand (1922-), illus. LC 55-6732. 116p. illus. 21cm. 1955. Longmans, Green.
--Tressa's Dream. 1965. E M Hale.
--Tressa's Dream. Howe, Marcia, illus. LC 65-20934. 86 p. illus. 21 cm. 1965. D. McKay Co.
Neher, Bertha Miller
--Among the Giants: A Story Introducing Six Common Giants. LC 12-37092. 122 p. incl. illus., pl. 20 cm. 1895. A. Flanagan.
Neibuhr, Barthold George (1776-1831)
--The Greek Heroes. 96p. 1910. Cassell & Co.
Neidlinger, William Harold (1863-1924)
--Earth, Sky and Air in Song. Bobbett, Walter, illus. LC 2-719. 2 v. illus. (part col.) 24 x 20 cm. 1900. American Book Company.
--The Owl and the Woodchuck. Bobbett, Walter, illus. N.D. Rand, McNally & Co.
--The Squirrel and the Crow. Bobbett, Walter, illus. N.D. Rand, McNally & Co.
Neigoff, Anne
--A Cap for Jack, a Coat for Jill. Axeman, Lois, illus. LC 72-83685. (Illus.). 32p. (Career Awareness-Community Helpers Ser.). (gr. k-2). 1972. (ISBN 0-8075-1062-9). A Whitman.
--New House, New Town. Axeman, Lois, illus. LC 72-13352. (Illus.). 32p. (Career Awareness-Community Helpers Ser.). (gr. k-2). 1973. (ISBN 0-8075-5570-3). A Whitman.
--Parade of Stories. LC 73-3180. (Illus.). 190 p. 26cm. (Child horizons). 1974, c.1973. Standard Educational Corporation.
Neigoff, Mike (1920-)
--Beat the Gang. Tiedemann, Berthold, illus. LC 73-87293. (Illus.). 95 p. 23cm. (Inner-city series). 1974. Benefic Press.
--Best in Camp. Irvin, Fred M. (1914-), illus. LC 78-79545. (Illus.). 127 p. 22cm. (Albert Whitman Pilot Bks.). 1969. (ISBN 0-8075-0660-5). A. Whitman.
--Dive In. Irvin, Fred M. (1914-), illus. LC 65-23885. (Illus.). 22 cm. 128p. (Pilot Book Ser). (gr. 3-5). 1965. (ISBN 0-8075-1644-9). A Whitman.
--Free Throw. Irvin, Fred M. (1914-), illus. LC 68-9122. (Illus.). 128 p. 22cm. 1968. A. Whitman.
--Goal to Go. Irvin, Fred M. (1914-), illus. LC 70-115808. (Illus.). 127 p. 22cm. (Pilot Bks.). 1970. (ISBN 0-8075-2974-5). A. Whitman.
--Hal, Tennis Champ. Irvin, Fred M. (1914-), illus. LC 70-150806. (Illus.). 126p. 22cm. 1971. A. Whitman.
--It Will Never Be the Same Again. LC 79-1018. p. cm. 1979. Holt, Rinehart, and Winston.
--New Boy in School. Tiedemann, Berthold, illus. LC 73-87294. (Illus.). 95 p. 23cm. (Inner-city series). 1974. (ISBN 0-8175-2804-0). Benefic Press.
--Nine Make a Team. Neebe, William, illus. LC 63-13331. 128 p. illus. 21 cm. 1963. A. Whitman.
--Playmaker. Irvin, Fred M. (1914-), illus. LC 73-7314. (Illus.). 127 p. 21cm. (Pilot books). 1973. (ISBN 0-8075-6543-1). A. Whitman.
--Runaway. Magnani, Rudolph, illus. LC 74-112727. (Illus.). 95 p. 23cm. (Inner-City Ser.). 1974. Benefic Press.
--Runner-up. Irvin, Fred (1914-), illus. LC 75-1089. (Illus.). 128 p. 22cm. (Pilot Bks.). 1975. (ISBN 0-8075-7181-4). A. Whitman.
--Ski Run. Irvin, Fred M. (1914-), illus. LC 70-188433. (Illus.). 126 p. 21cm. (Pilot Bks. Ser.). 1972. (ISBN 0-8075-7396-5). A. Whitman.
--Smiley Sherman, Substitute. LC 64-7721. 127 p. illus. 22 cm. 1964. A. Whitman.
--Soccer Hero. Armstrong, George Douglas (1927-), illus. LC 76-18750. (Illus.). 128 p. 22cm. (Pilot books). c.1976. (ISBN 0-8075-7529-1). A. Whitman.
--Terror on the Ice. Irvin, Fred M. (1914-), illus. LC 74-3405. (Illus.). 128 p. 22cm. (Pilot books series). 1974. (ISBN 0-8075-7808-8). A. Whitman.
--Two on First. Irvin, Fred M. (1914-), illus. LC 67-17419. (Illus.). 21 cm. 127p. (Pilot Book Ser). (gr. 3-5). 1967. (ISBN 0-8075-8161-5). A Whitman.
--Up Sails. Irvin, Fred M. (1914-), illus. LC 66-16080. (Illus.). 128 p. Illus. 22 cm. (Pilot Book Ser). (gr. 3-5). 1966. (ISBN 0-8075-8331-6). A Whitman.
Neikirk, Mabel E
--All About Oscar, the Trained Seal. O'Brian, William, illus. LC 43-12649. ix, 131 p. incl. col. front., illus. (part col.) 23 1/2 cm. 1943. The John C. Winston Company.
--Oscar on the Radio. Hanson, Marguerite, illus. LC 49-16731. 64 p. col. illus. 29 cm. (Cello-brite story books). c.1948. Whitman Pub. Co.
--Oscar the Trained Seal. Dobias, Frank (1902-), illus. LC 40-27463. 24 p. incl. col. front., illus. (part col.) 22 x 26 cm. (story parade picture book). c.1940. Grosset & Dunlap.
Neill, Alexander Sutherland
--Last Man Alive. Araquistain, Sonia, illus. LC 70-94832. (Illus.). 12 linecuts. 272p. 21 cm. 255p. (Orig.). Repr. of 1938 ed. (gr. 5 up). 1969. Hart.
Neill, John Rea (1878-1943)
--Lucky Bucky in Oz. Neill, John Rea (1878-1943), illus. Baum, Lyman Frank (1856-1919), created by. LC 42-25231. 6 p. l., 17-280, 1 p. illus. 23 1/2 cm. 1942. Reilly & Lee.
--The Scalawagons of Oz. Neill, John Rea (1878-1943), illus. Baum, Lyman Frank (1856-1919), created by. LC 41-23278. 6 p. l., 17-309 p. illus. 23 1/2 x 18 cm. c.1941. Reilly & Lee.
--The Wonder City of Oz. Neill, John Rea (1878-1943), illus. LC 49-34282. (Based on Stories created by Frank Lyman Baum, 1856-1919). 5 p. l., 17-318 p. illus. 24 x 18 cm. c.1940. Reilly & Lee.
Neill, John Rea (1878-1943), illus.
--The Adventures of a Brownie, 2 in 1. 64p. (Children's Red Book: Vol. 6). N.D. Reilly & Britton Co.
--Alice's Adventures in Wonderland and Through The Looking Glass, 2 Vols. in 1. (Vol. 10). N.D. Reilly & Britton Co.
--Andersen's Fairy Tales, 2 Vols. in 1. (Children's Red Book: Vol. 11). N.D. Reilly & Britton Co.
--Baum's Own Book. (Illus.). (Baum Populars). N.D. The Reilly & Britton Co.
--Black Beauty and The Little Lame Prince, 2 Vols. in 1. (Children's Red Book: Vol. 4). N.D. Reilly & Britton Co.
--Cinderella and The Three Bears, 2 Vols in 1. (Children's Red Book: Vol.8). N.D. Reilly & Britton Co.
--The Foolish Fox. LC 43-35774. 4 p. l., xi-xii p., 1 l., 15-92 p., 1 l. incl. col. front., illus. (part col.) 14 1/2 cm. (Altemus' Wee books for wee folks). 1904. Henry Altemus Company.
--The Foolish Fox, 1 of 6 vols. New ed. (Illus.). (Wee Books for Wee Folks: No. 4). 1905. Set. Henry Altemus Co.
--Grimm's Fairy Tales and Snow White and Rose Red, 2 Vols. in 1. (Children's Red Book: Vol. 12). N.D. Reilly & Britton Co.
--Jack and the Bean Stalk and Robinson Crusoe, 2 Vols. in 1. (Children's Red Book: Vol. 9). N.D. Reilly & Britton Co.
--Little Black Sambo and Uncle Tom's Cabin, 2 Vols. in 1. (Children's Red Book: Vol. 2). N.D. Reilly & Britton Co.
--Little Red Riding Hood and Sleeping Beauty, 2 Vols. in 1. (Children's Red Book: Vol. 7). N.D. Reilly & Britton Co.
--The Little Small Red Hen. N.D. David McKay Co.
--The Night Before Christmas and Mother Goose Rhymes and Jingles, 2 Vols. in 1. (Children's Red Book: Vol. 3). N.D. Reilly & Britton Co.
--Peter Rabbit and Dick Whittington, 2 Vols. in 1. 64p. (Children's Red Books: Vol. 1). N.D. Reilly & Britton Co.
--Rab and His Friends and J. Cole, 2 Vols. in 1. 64p. (Children's Red Book: Vol. 5). N.D. Reilly & Britton Co.
--Three Little Pigs. N.D. David McKay Co.
Neill, John Rea (1878-1943) & Enright, Walter J. Pat (1879-), illus.
--Children's Stories That Never Grow Old. 320p. N.D. Reilly & Britton & Co.
Neilson, Frances Fullerton Jones, Mrs. (1910-) & Neilson, Winthrop
--Bruce Benson on Trails of Thunder. LC 50-14558. 190 p. illus. 21 cm. 1950. Dutton.
--Bruce Benson: Son of Fame. Ayer, Margaret (0000-1981), illus. LC 48-452610. 173 p. illus. 21 cm. 1948. E. P. Dutton.
--Bruce Benson: Thirty Fathoms Deep. 1st ed. Wonsetler, John Charles (1900-), illus. LC 49-11008. 179 p. illus., map (on lining-papers) 21 cm. 1949. E. P. Dutton.
--The Donkey from Dorking. 1st ed. Vitale, Lydia & Hopkins, Janet, illus. LC 42-6282. 4 p. l., 11-84, 2 p. illus. 22 c. 1942. E. P. Dutton & Co., Inc.
--Dusty for Speed!. 1st ed. Kreis, Hans, illus. LC 47-5701. 219 p. illus. 21 cm. 1947. E. P. Dutton.
--Giant Mountain. Reardon, Mary A., illus. LC 46-18021. 120 p. illus. 20 cm. 1946. E. P. Dutton & Company, Inc.
--Mocha the Djuka. Johnson, Avery Fischer (1906-), illus. LC 43-12122. 142, 1 p. illus. 21 cm. 1943. E. P. Dutton & Company, Inc.
--Storm on Giant Mountain. (Illus.). (gr. 4-6). 1975. (ISBN 0-590-09989-2, Schol Trade Pap). Schol Bk Serv.
Neilson, Harry B.
--Jolly Jumbo. (Illus.). N.D. Frederick A. Stokes Co.
Neilson, Harry B., jt. auth. see Harner, S. H.
Neilson, Kenneth P
--The Littlest Giant. LC 79-54240. (Illus.). 35 p. c.1979. All Seasons Art.
Neilson, Linda Apolzon
--Max Helps Out. Stott, Dorothy M., illus. LC 83-83292. (Illus.). 24 p. 15cm. (First little golden book). c.1984. (ISBN 0-307-10130-4). (ISBN 0-307-68154-8). Golden Book.
Neilson, William Allan (1869-)
--The Junior Classics. LC 12-28704. 10 v. col. fronts., illus., plates. 21 cm. c.1912. P. F. Collier & Son.
--The Junior Classics. Eliot, Charles W., intro. by. LC 18-8318. 10 v. col. front., illus., plates. 20 cm. c.1918. P. F. Collier & Son.
Neilson, Winthrop, jt. auth. see Neilson, Frances Fullerton Jones, Mrs.
Nekrasov, A.
--Visiting Captain Fibbur. (Illus.). 21p. 1976. (ISBN 0-8285-1579-4, Pub. by Progress Pubs USSR). Imported Pubns.
Nelles, Gay
--All the Nuts Aren't in the Fruitcake. 75 p. 21cm. 1974. (ISBN 0-533-00952-9). Vantage Press.
Nelms, Rosalie C., jt. auth. see Stowe, Julia M.
Nels, pseud., see Munson, Nelson Henry.
Nelsen, Donald
--Sam and Emma. Gorey, Edward St. John (1925-), illus. LC 72-136998. (Illus.). 40 p. 1971. (ISBN 0-8193-0467-0). Parents' Magazine Press.
--The Spotted Cow. Peek, Merle (1938-), illus. LC 73-5738. (Illus.). 41 p. 27cm. 1973. (ISBN 0-8193-0694-0). (ISBN 0-8193-0694-0). Parents' Magazine Press.
Nelson, A W
--Yankee Swanson: Chapters from a Life at Sea. N.D. Macmillan.
Nelson, Betty
--What Do You Do When You Go to the Zoo. Standish, Jan, illus. LC 75-32303. (Illus.). 26 p. 29cm. c.1975. Alura Press.
Nelson, Brenda
--Mud For Sale. Brown, Richard Eric (1946-), illus. LC 84-4515. (Illus.). 32 p. 22cm. 1984. (ISBN 0-395-36175-3). Houghton Mifflin.
Nelson, Carl A., ed. see United Danish Evangelical Lutheran Church in America. Central Committee of Young People's Leagues.
Nelson, Carol
--Dear Angie: Your Family Is Getting a Divorce. LC 79-57210. (gr. 5-8). 1980. (ISBN 0-89191-246-0). Cook.
Nelson, Cholmondeley M. (1903-)
--With Bolivar Over the Andes. Relf, Douglas, illus. LC 63-19042. 197 p. illus., port., maps. 21 cm. 1963. Reilly & Lee.
--With Nelson at Trafalgar. Relf, Douglas, illus. LC 61-118339. 206p. illus. 21cm. 1961, c.1960. Reilly &Lee.
--With Wellington at Waterloo. Relf, Douglas, illus. LC 62-14445. 208p. illus. 22cm. 1962. Reilly & Lee.
Nelson, Cordner Bruce (1918-)
--The Miler. LC 79-85003. 158 p. 22cm. 1969. S. G. Phillips.
Nelson, Darrel
--Little Millard Mustardseed. LC 78-72834. (Illus.). 48 p. (Chariot Bks.). c.1979. (ISBN 0-89191-063-8). D. C. Cook Pub. Co.
Nelson-Erichsen, Jean
--Copito: The Christmas Chihuahua. Atcheson, Marguerite, illus. Davenport, May, intro. by. LC 82-72080. (Illus.). 80p. (The Copito Stories). (gr. k-5). 1982. (ISBN 0-943864-08-9). (ISBN 0-943864-07-0). Davenport.
Nelson, Esther L. (1928-)
--Dancing Games for Children of All Ages. Matsuda, Shizu, illus. LC 83-18147. p. cm. 1984, c.1973. (ISBN 0-8069-7818-X). Sterling Pub. Co.
--The Funny Songbook. Behr, Joyce (1929-), illus. LC 84-89. (Illus.). 96p. (gr. k-5). 1984. (ISBN 0-8069-4682-2). (ISBN 0-8069-7832-5). (ISBN 0-8069-4683-0). Sterling.
--Holiday Singing & Dancing Games. LC 80-52331. (Illus.). 72p. (gr. k-3). 1980. (ISBN 0-8069-4630-X). (ISBN 0-8069-4631-8). Sterling.
--Musical Games for Children of All Ages. Matsuda, Shizu, illus. LC 76-19804. (Illus.). (gr. 3 up). 1976. (ISBN 0-8069-4540-0). (ISBN 0-8069-4541-9). (ISBN 0-686-77162-1). Sterling.
--The Silly Songbook. Behr, Joyce (1929-), illus. LC 81-50989. (Illus.). 128p. (gr. k-7). 1981. (ISBN 0-8069-4650-4). (ISBN 0-8069-4651-2). (ISBN 0-8069-7552-0). Sterling.
--Singing & Dancing Games for the Very Young. LC 77-79513. (Illus.). 1982. (ISBN 0-8069-4568-0). (ISBN 0-8069-4569-9). (ISBN 0-8069-7572-5). Sterling.
Nelson, Ethel see Nina, pseud.
Nelson, Faith
--Randolph: The Bear Who Said No. 1st ed. Nelson, Faith, illus. LC 40-6906. 59 p. col. illus. 21 cm. c.1940. Random House.
--Randolph: The Bear Who Said No. Walker, Nedda, illus. LC 46-81979. 31 p. illus. (part col.) 25 x 19 1/2 cm. 1946. Wonder Books, Inc.
Nelson, Felice
--Zoo's Who. Hord, Bob, illus. LC 72-191960. (Illus.). 21 p. 23cm. 1972. Potamus Books.
--Zoo's Who Two. Hord, Bob, illus. LC 72-191225. (Illus.). 21 p. 23cm. 1972. Potamus Books.
Nelson, Florence
--Adventuring: Poems. LC 41-31412. 62 p. illus. 23 x 24 cm. 1939. The Patrician Press.
--O Come to the Fair: A Child's Day at the Fair, Poems. Lipton, Monroe H., illus. LC 41-31413. 53 p. illus. 23 x 24 cm. 1939. The Patrician Press.
Nelson, Gladys Tirrell
--War Drums at Eden Prairie. Nelson, Gladys Tirrell, illus. LC 78-104895. (Illus.). 115 p. 23cm. c.1976. (ISBN 0-87839-023-5). North Star Press.
Nelson, Jewell Wells
--Mommy Comes for Me. McCracken, Helen Dolman, illus. LC 69-17899. (Illus.). 31 p. 21cm. (CE: Children's easy books). 1969. Broadman Press.
Nelson, Kathleen Gray
--The Fox That Wanted Nine Golden Tails. LC 15-20148. 91 p. front. 22 cm. c.1915. The Devin-Adair Company.
Nelson, Marg Raibley (1899-)
--The Crew of the Mermaid. Porter, Jean Macdonald (1906-), illus. LC 57-11047. 181p. illus. 21cm. c.1957. I. Washburn.
--A Girl Called Chris. LC 62-7707. 184 p. 22cm. 1962. Ariel Books.
--Mystery at Land's End. LC 61-8935. 192 p. 22cm. 1961. Ariel Books.

--Mystery at Little Squaw River. LC 62-14498. 185 p. 22cm. 1963. Ariel Books.

--Mystery in Hawaii. LC 69-14970. 151 p. 22cm. 1969. Farrar, Straus & Giroux.

--Mystery of the Missing Cannon. LC 66-5507. 149p. 22cm. (Ariel bk.). c.1966. Farrar.

--Mystery of the Missing Dowry. LC 65-170253. 183p. 22cm. (Ariel bks.). c.1965. Farrar.

--Mystery of the Starboard List. LC 68-23750. 134 p. 22cm. (An Ariel Bk.). 1968. Farrar, Straus and Giroux.

--Mystery on a Full Moon. LC 77-109555. 166 p. 22cm. (Ariel book). 1970. Farrar, Straus & Giroux.

--Mystery on a Minus Tide. LC 64-17813. 182 p. 22 cm. 1964. Ariel Books.

--Mystery Rides the Charter Boat. LC 67-19882. 152 p. 22cm. (An Ariel Bk.). 1967. Farrar, Straus and Giroux.

--One Summer in Alaska. LC 77-149214. 185 p. 21cm. 1971. (ISBN 0-374-35650-5). Farrar, Straus & Giroux.

--Storm at Anderson Point. LC 57-6606. 186p. 21cm. 1957. I. Washburn.

--Valiant Venture. LC 58-11496. 186p. illus. 21cm. c.1958. I. Washburn.

Nelson, Margaret Worthing

--Pinky Finds a Home. Heyneman, Anne (1910-), illus. LC 40-110246. 118, 1 p. col. front., illus. (part col.) 17 cm. c.1940. Holiday House.

Nelson, Marguerite, pseud., see Florence, Lee.

Nelson, Marguerite, pseud.

--Forever This Love. Florence, Lee. LC 57-135589. 221p. 21cm. 1957. Avalon Books.

Nelson, Mary Ann, ed.

--A Comparative Anthology of Children's Literature. LC 74-177980. (Illus.). xxvi, 1060 p. 27cm. 1972. (ISBN 0-03-083379-5). Holt, Rinehart and Winston.

Nelson, May

--The Redbirds Are Flying. Kidwell, Carl (1910-), illus. LC 63-19078. 189p. illus., map. 22cm. c.1963. Criterion.

Nelson, O. T

--The Girl Who Owned a City. LC 75-319646. 179 p. 23cm. 1975. (ISBN 0-8225-0956-3). Lerner Publications Co.

Nelson, Ralph, tr.

--Popol Vuh: The Great Mythological Book of the Ancient Maya. 1976. (ISBN 0-395-24302-5). (ISBN 0-395-25168-0). HM.

Nelson, Rhoda, jt. auth. see Morris, Rhoda.

Nelson, Rhoda Louise Smith, Mrs. (1891-)

--High Timber. Boyle, Mildred, illus. LC 41-22954. 4 p. l., 3-280 p. incl. illus., plates. 20 cm. 1941. Thomas Y. Crowell Company.

--This Is Freedom. Nelson, Mary Elizabeth & Nelson, Rhoda Louise Smith, Mrs. (1891-), illus. LC 40-318044. ix, 302 p. incl. illus., plates. 21 cm. 1940. Dodd, Mead & Company.

--Wagon Train West. Blaisdell, Elinore (1904-), illus. LC 39-32046. 2 p. l., 224 p. incl. col. front., illus. plates (part col.) 22 cm. 1939. Thomas Y. Crowell Company.

Nelson, Steve (1907-) & Rollins, Jack (1906-)

--Here Comes Peter Cottontail. LC 61-158218. unpaged. illus. 33cm. 1961. (ISBN 0-394-80660-3). Random House.

Nelson, Zaida, jt. auth. see Mills, G. R.

Nemcova, Bozena (1820-1862), ed.

--The Shepherd and the Dragon: Fairy Tales from the Czech of Bozena Nemcova. Siegel, William (1905-), illus. Ledbetter, Eleanor Edwards, Mrs., tr. LC 30-30199. 5 p. l., 3-206 p. incl. illus., plates. col. front. 24 cm. 1930. R. M. McBride & Company.

Nemcova, Jeanne, tr. see Prague, Statni Zidovske Museum.

Nemeth, A. P.

--Father Baker's Children. N.D. Vantage Press Inc.

Nemeth, Doris I., et al., eds.

--Poet, Autumn, Nineteen Seventy-Nine. Bearden, Wanda, illus. LC 79-84762. (Illus.). 1979. (ISBN 0-932192-01-7). Fine Arts Soc.

Nemeth, Doris I. & Kenzie, Peggy, eds.

--The Poet. Bearden, Wanda, illus. (Illus.). 400p. (gr. 5 up). 1982. (ISBN 0-932192-04-1). Fine Arts Soc.

Nemo, Dina Di see Di Nemo, Dina.

Nephew, William & Chester, Michael

--Beyond Mars. Buehr, Walter Franklin (1897-1971), illus. LC 60-12530. (Illus.). 72 p. 23cm. 1960. Putnam.

--Planet Trip. Buehr, Walter Franklin (1897-1971), illus. LC 60-6896. 72p. illus. 23cm. 1960. Putnam.

Nerlove, Evelyn

--Who Is David?. A Story of an Adopted Adolescent and His Friends. Nerlove, Evelyn, illus. LC 85-3837. (Illus.). 113 p. 23cm. c.1985. (ISBN 0-87868-233-3). Child Welfare League of America.

Nerlove, Miriam

--I Made a Mistake. LC 85-6018. (Based on a Jump Rope Rhyme with New Verses and Illustrations). p. cm. 1985. (ISBN 0-689-50327-X). Atheneum.

Nerman, Einar (1888-)

--A Trip to Gingerbread Land. LC 42-31394. 19 p. col. illus. 19 x 26 cm. c.1939. Whitman Publishing Company.

Nerman, Einar (1888-), retold by.

--Fairy Tales from the North. Nerman, Einar (1888-), illus. LC 46-7904. 5 p. l., 3-128 p. illus., col. plates. 26 x 20 1/2 cm. (Borzoi books for young people). 1946. A. A. Knopf.

Nervaud, Marie De see De Nervaud, Marie.

Nesbit, E., pseud., see Bland, Edith Nesbit.

Nesbit, E., ed. see Browne, Frances.

Nesbit, E., ed. see Herbertson, Agnes Grozier.

Nesbit, E., ed. see Kingsley, Charles.

Nesbit, E., ed. see Yonge, Charlotte Mary.

Nesbitt, E. (1858-1924), pseud.

--Conscience Pudding. Blegvad, Erik (1923-), illus. LC 70-120095. (Illus.). line drawings. 48p. 1st U.S. edition. (gr. 3-6). 1970. (ISBN 0-698-30054-8). Coward.

--Five of Us - and Madeline. Sharp, Clifford, Mrs., ed. Unwin, Nora Spicer (1907-), illus. 1926. Adelphi.

--House of Arden. Millar, Harold Robert (1869-1939), illus. (Illus.). (gr. 3-4). 1958. (ISBN 0-486-21495-8). Dover.

--Oswald Bastable and Others. Brock, Charles Edmond (1870-1938) & Millar, Harold Robert (1869-1939), illus. 1960. Coward.

Nesbitt, Troy, pseud., see Folsom, Franklin Brewster.

Nesbitt, Troy, pseud. (1907-)

--The Indian Mummy Mystery. Folsom, Franklin Brewster. Busch, Paul, illus. LC 54-3653. 282p. illus. 20cm. 1954. Whitman Pub. Co.

--The Jinx of Payrock Canyon. Folsom, Franklin Brewster. Koering, Ursula (1921-), illus. 282p. illus. 21cm. c.1954. Whitman Pub. Co.

--Sand Dune Pony. Folsom, Franklin Brewster. Gotlieb, Jules, illus. LC 52-4446. 250 p. illus. 21 cm. 1952. Whitman Pub. Co.

Nesbitt, Wilbur Dick (1871-1927)

--As Children Do: Poems of Childhood. Friend, Ellery, illus. LC 29-13451. 96 p. illus. 19 cm. 12p. c.1929. The P. F. Volland Company.

--The Jolly Kid Book. Meyers, Marie Honre, illus. LC 26-13508. 12 p. col. illus. 20 x 28 cm. (Volland Jolly kid book series). c.1926. P. F. Volland Co.

--Little Henry's Slate. LC 3-30986. 128p. 1903. W. S. Lord.

Nesbit, Z. A. R.

--Bushy Tales. (Fireside Library). N.D. Thomas Nelson & Sons.

--Firelight Tales. LC 42-43990. 96 p. col. front., illus., col. plates. 19 1/2 x 15 cm. (Nelson's fireside library). 1930. T. Nelson and Sons.

Nesbitt, Alexander, tr. see Grimm, Jakob Ludwig Karl (1785-1863) & Grimm, Wilhelm Karl.

Nesbitt, F.

--The Magic Whistle and Other Fairy Tale Plays. N.D. Longmans Green & Co.

Nesbitt, Nell Smidell (1906-)

--Bumpy Bison. Dowling, Colista, illus. LC 47-2603. 3 p. l., 92 p. plates. 24 1/2 cm. 1947. Binfords & Mort.

--Cobi Camel. LC 44-7838. 159 p. illus. 23 1/2 cm. 1944. The Caxton Printers, Ltd.

Nesbitt, Philip

--Nicholas Needlefoot. LC 44-558544. 32 p. col. illus. 20 1/2 x 18 1/2 cm. c.1944. Wilcox & Follett Co.

--Trum Peter's Tea Party. Nesbitt, Philip, illus. LC 31-29310. 31 p. col. illus. 25 cm. 1931. Coward-McCann, Inc.

Nesbitt, Rosemary Sinnett (1924-)

--Colonel Meacham's Giant Cheese. Burns, Raymond Howard (1924-), illus. LC 77-173789. (Illus.). 63 p. 24cm. 1972. (ISBN 0-8116-4255-0). Garrard Pub. Co.

--The Great Rope. Gorsline, Douglas Warner (1913-1985), illus. LC 67-18035. 127p. illus. 22cm. 1968. (ISBN 0-688-51018-3). Lothrop.

Neshamit, Sarah, pseud., see Dushnitzky-Shiner, Sara.

Neshamit, Sarah, pseud. (1913-)

--The Children of Mapu Street: A Novel. Dushnitzky-Shiner, Sara. Dudden, Adrianne, illus. Segal, David, tr. LC 73-105066. 324 p. 22cm. 1970. Jewish Publication Society of America.

Nesmith, Robert I, ed. see Cochran, Hamilton.

Ness, Evaline Michelow, Mrs., jt. auth. see Zimelman, Nathan.

Ness, Evaline Michelow, Mrs. (1911-)

--Do You Have the Time, Lydia?. 1st ed. Ness, Evaline Michelow, Mrs. (1911-), illus. LC 79-157950. (Illus.). 32 p. 24cm. 1971. (ISBN 0-525-28790-6). E. P. Dutton.

--A Double Discovery. LC 65-22404. 1 v. (unpaged) col. illus. 26cm. c.1965. Scribners. **Award: (NYT).**

--Exactly Alike. Ness, Evaline Michelow, Mrs. (1911-), illus. LC 64-12036. (Illus.). col. illus. 21x36 cm. 32p. (gr. k-3). 1964. (ISBN 0-684-12403-3). Scribner. **Award: (NYT).**

--Fierce the Lion. Ness, Evaline Michelow, Mrs. (1911-), illus. LC 80-10172. (Illus.). 32 p. 26cm. c.1980. (ISBN 0-8234-0412-9). Holiday House.

--A Gift for Sula Sula. Ness, Evaline Michelow, Mrs. (1911-), illus. LC 63-14659. (Illus.). 1 v. (unpaged. 27cm. 1963. Scribner.

--The Girl and the Goatherd: Or, This and That and Thus and So. 1st ed. Ness, Evaline Michelow, Mrs. (1911-), illus. LC 72-116885. (Illus.). 32 p. 26cm. 1970. E. P. Dutton.

--Josefina February. Ness, Evaline Michelow, Mrs. (1911-), illus. LC 63-10390. (Illus.). 1 v. (unpaged. 26cm. 1963. Scribner. **Award: (ALA).**

--Marcella's Guardian Angel. Ness, Evaline Michelow, Mrs. (1911-), illus. LC 78-10414. (Illus.). 40 p. 21cm. c.1979. (ISBN 0-8234-0343-2). Holiday House.

--Mr. Miacca: An English Folk Tale. 1st ed. Ness, Evaline Michelow, Mrs. (1911-), illus. LC 67-5425. (Illus.). 32 p. col. illus. 17 x 26cm. 1967. Holt, Rinehart and Winston.

--Pavo & the Princess. Ness, Evaline Michelow, Mrs. (1911-), illus. LC 64-18806. (Illus.). (gr. k-3). 1964. (ISBN 0-684-20898-9). Scribner.

--Sam, Bangs & Moonshine. Ness, Evaline Michelow, Mrs. (1911-), illus. LC 66-10113. (Illus.). 48p. (ps-2). 1966. (ISBN 0-03-012716-5). (ISBN 0-03-080111-7). HR&W. **Awards: (RCM); (ALA).**

--A Shaker Paper House. Ness, Evaline Michelow, Mrs. (1911-), illus. (Illus.). (Encore Edition). 1979. (ISBN 0-684-17386-7, ScribJ). Scribner.

--The Warmint. Ness, Evaline Michelow, Mrs. (1911-), illus. LC 76-454. (Illus.). 32p. (Encore Edition Ser.). (gr. k-2). 1976. (ISBN 0-684-17387-5, ScribJ). Scribner.

--Yeck Eck. 1st ed. Ness, Evaline Michelow, Mrs. (1911-), illus. LC 74-3406. (Illus.). 40 p. 19x23 cm. 1974. (ISBN 0-525-43470-4). Dutton.

Ness, Evaline Michelow, Mrs. (1911-), selected by.

--Amelia Mixed the Mustard and Other Poems. Ness, Evaline Michelow, Mrs. (1911-), illus. LC 74-14077. (Illus.). 47 p. 27cm. 1975. (ISBN 0-684-14271-6). Scribner. **Award: (ALA).**

--Long, Broad & Quickeye. Ness, Evaline Michelow, Mrs. (1911-), illus. LC 69-17060. (Illus.). 39 p. 27cm. 1969. Scribner.

Nestlerode, Mildred R

--The Avengers. LC 53-11177. 104p. 21cm. 1953. Pageant Press.

Nestrick, Nova

--Little Red Hen & the Grain of Wheat. Rutherford, Bonnie & Rutherford, Bill, illus. LC 61-13224. (Illus.). 23cm. 28p. (ps-3). N.D. Platt.

Nestrick, Nova, ed.

--Billy Goats Gruff. Remington, Barbara, illus. LC 42-22617. 28 p. illus. 23 cm. (An Early-Fun-to Read Classic Ser.). (ps-3). N.D. Platt.

--Gingerbread Boy. (Illus.). (ps-3). 1961. Platt.

--Old Man Rabbit's Dinner Party. Robinson & Rutherford, Bonnie, illus. LC 61-13225. (Based on the original story by Carolyn Sherwin Bailey.). (Illus.). 25cm. 28p. (An Early fun-to-read classic). (ps-3). 1961. Platt.

--The Rooster, Mouse, Red Hen. Rutherford, Bonnie & Rutherford, Bonnie, illus. LC 61-13226. (Illus.). (ps-3). 1961. Platt.

--The Tale of Peter Rabbit. (Illus.). (gr. 3-7). 1961. Platt.

--The Three Bears and Goldilocks. LC 62-12641. (Illus.). 28 p. 24cm. (Early Fun-to-Read Classic). 1962. Platt & Munk.

--The Three Little Pigs. (Illus.). (ps-3). 1961. Platt.

Nestrick, Nova, ed. see Beskow, Elsa Maartman.

Nethaway, Iva, ed.

--Poems for Us. Street, Neva, illus. LC 81-51090. (Illus.). 115p. 1981. (ISBN 0-533-05028-6). Vantage.

Netherclift, Beryl Constance (1911-)

--Mystery at Castle Steep. Eagle, Michael (1942-), illus. LC 70-121348. (Illus.). 141 p. 22cm. 1970. Knopf.

--The Snowstorm. LC 68-15326. 180 p. 22cm. 1967. Knopf.

--The Snowstorm. Schindelman, Joseph (1923-), illus. 1968. Borzoi Books.

Nett, Roger

--Thorntree Meadows. LC 57-5879. 180p. illus. 21cm. 1957. Houghton Mifflin.

Neubauer, William Arthur see Hatheway, Jan, pseud.

Neubauer, William Arthur see Marsh, Rebecca, pseud.

Neubauer, William Arthur (1916-)

--But Love Remains. Marsh, Rebecca, pseud. LC 56-8986. 224p. 20cm. 1956. Arcadia House.

--Dream's End. LC 54-7484. 221p. 20cm. 1954. Arcadia House.

--The Key of Gold. Hatheway, Jan, pseud. 223 p. 20 cm. (Arcadia teen-age romance, 2). 1963. Arcadia House.

--Robynn's Way. Hatheway, Jan, pseud. LC 64-9171. 223 p. 20 cm. (Arcadia teen-age romance, 5). 1963. Arcadia House.

--Treasure of the Redwoods. Hatheway, Jan, pseud. 224 p. 20 cm. (Arcadia teenage romance). c.1961. Arcadia.

Neuberger, Phyllis J.

--Suppose You Were a Kitten. LC 82-91105. (Illus.). (gr. 1-3). 1982. (ISBN 0-9610050-0-9). P J Neuberger.

Neudeck-Jobin, Marilyn

--A New Home for Bili. 40p. (gr. 2-4). N.D. Dorrance.

Neuendorffer, Mary Jane

--Journey to Nine Villages. Carlson, Albert W. D., illus. LC 62-136021. (Illus.). 139 p. 25cm. 1962. F. Ungar Pub. Co.

Neufeld, Elizabeth E

--Meet the Winners, Jimmy and Joe. Wheeler, Herschel D., photos by. LC 52-11422. 136 p. illus. 23 cm. 1952. Pacific Press Pub. Association.

Neufeld, John Arthur (1938-)

--Edgar Allan. Dunlap, Loren, illus. LC 68-31175. (Illus.). 96p. (gr. 5-8). 1968. (ISBN 0-87599-149-1). S G Phillips. **Award: (ALA).**

--Freddy's Book. LC 72-11056. 132 p. 22cm. 1973. (ISBN 0-394-82135-1). (ISBN 0-394-82135-1). Random House.

--Lisa, Bright & Dark. 128p. (gr. 7 up). 1969. (ISBN 0-87599-153-X). S G Phillips.

--Sleep Two Three Four. 1971. Harper & Row Pub.

--Touching. 1970. Phillips Inc.

Neufeld, Rose (1924-), retold by.

--Beware the Man Without a Beard & Other Greek Folk Tales. Auerbach, Marjorie Hoffberg (1932-), illus. LC 68-15323. (Illus.). 74p. (gr. 3-7). 1969. (ISBN 0-394-90945-3). Knopf.

Neugroschel, Joachim, jt. auth. see Driz, Ovsei Ovseevich.

Neuhaus, David

--His Finest Hour. Neuhaus, David, illus. LC 83-23547. (Illus.). 32p. (gr. 2-3). 1984. (ISBN 0-670-37260-9, Viking Kestrel). Viking.

Neumann, Daisy

--Timothy Travels. Neuman, Daisy, illus. 320p. N.D. Coward McCann.

Neumann, Dorothy

--Come Meet the Clowns!. Furbush, Lydia, illus. LC 41-73164. 35 p. col. illus. 24 x 19 cm. 1941. The Macmillan Company.

Neumann, Gustav Julius (1888-)

--The Door That Walked Away, and Other Stories. Schminke, Arthur F., illus. LC 57-4342. 96p. illus. 20cm. 1957. Wartburg Press.

Neumann, Rudolf (1926-1971)

--The Bad Bear. Rubin, Eva Johanna (1926-), illus. Prelutsky, Jack, tr. LC 67-17211. 1v. (unpaged) col. illus. 29cm. 1st U.S. edition. 1967. Macmillan.

--The Hat in the Apple Tree. Bluhm, Helen, illus. Bluhm, Ina R., tr. LC 63-9329. iv, 104 p. illus. 22 cm. 1963. D. McKay.

--The Very Special Animal. Heuck, Sigrid, illus. McClintock, Theodore (1902-1971), tr. from Ger. LC 65-10757. 31p. col. illus. 25cm. c.1965. Rand McNally.

Neumeier, Marty & Glaser, Byron

--Action Alphabet. Neumeier, Marty & Glaser, Byron, illus. LC 84-25322. 56p. (ps-1). 1985. (ISBN 0-688-05703-9). (ISBN 0-688-05704-7). Greenwillow.

Neumeyer, Helen, tr. see Careme, Maurice.

Neumeyer, Peter, tr. see Baumann, Hans.

Neumeyer, Peter Florian, jt. auth. see Gorey, Edward St. John.

Neumeyer, Peter Florian (1929-)

--Donald and the ... Gorey, Edward St. John (1925-), illus. LC 69-15800. (Illus.). 40 p. (Addisonian press book). 1969. Addison-Wesley.

--Dream Cat. (Orig.). 1982. (ISBN 0-914676-84-9, Pub. by Envelope Bks). Green Tiger Pr.

--The Faithful Fish. Stewart, Arvis L., illus. LC 70-135849. (Illus.). 48 p. 26cm. 1971. (ISBN 0-8240-0000-5). Young Scott Books.

--Fenstermachers's Boulder. Carnehl, Jeff, illus. (Illus.). 12p. (Orig.). N.D. (ISBN 0-914676-61-X, Pub. by Envelope Bks). Green Tiger Pr.

--Why We Have Day and Night. Gorey, Edward St. John (1925-), illus. LC 77-120942. (Illus.). 38 p. 1970. Young Scott Books.

Neve, Margaret

--More and Better. LC 77-2006. p. cm. c.1977. (ISBN 0-13-600981-6). Prentice-Hall.

Nevil, Susan R.

--The Biblical Zoo. Nevil, Susan R., illus. N.D. David McKay Co.

Nevill, E. Mildred (1899-)

--Ah Fu, a Chinese River Boy. Wood, Elsie Anna, illus. LC 35-9699. 60, 1 p. col. illus. 14 cm. (Nursery Series). c.1932. Friendship Press.

--Ah Fu: A Chinese River Boy. 1951. Friendship Press.

--Esa: A Little Boy of Nazareth. 64p. 1951. Friendship Press.

--Esa, a Little Boy of Nazareth. Wood, Elsie Anna, illus. LC 35-9700. 60, 1 p. col. illus. 14 cm. (Nursery series). c.1930. Friendship Press.

Neville, C. J.
--Little Long-Nose and His Animal Friends. N.D. St. Martin's Press.
Neville, Emily Cheney (1919-)
--Berries Goodman. 1965. (ISBN 0-8382-0069-9, Cadmus Books). E. M. Hale and Company.
--Berries Goodman. LC 65-14485. 178p. 22cm. c.1965. Harper. **Award: (ALA).**
--Fogarty. LC 73-85023. 182 p. 22cm. 1969. Harper & Row.
--Garden of Broken Glass. LC 74-22630. 215 p. 21cm. 1975. (ISBN 0-440-04839-7). Delacorte Press.
--It's Like This, Cat. 1st ed. Weiss, Emil (1896-1965), illus. LC 62-21292. (Illus.). 180 p. 22cm. 1963. Harper & Row. **Awards: (JNM); (ALA).**
--Seventeenth-Street Gang. McCully, Emily Arnold (1939-), illus. LC 66-7116. (Illus.). 148p. (gr. 5-7). 1966. (ISBN 0-06-024395-3, HarpJ). Har-Row.
--The Seventeenth-Street Gang. McCully, Emily Arnold (1939-), illus. LC 66-7116. 148p. illus. 22cm. 1966. Harper.
--Traveler from a Small City. Mocniak, George, illus. 1969. Harper & Row Pub.
--Traveler From a Small Kingdom. Mocniak, George, illus. 1968. (ISBN 0-06-024388-0). Harper and Row.
Neville, Mary (1915-)
--The First and Last Annual Pet Parade. Chwast, Jacqueline (1932-), illus. LC 68-12651. (Illus.). 48 p. 1968. Pantheon Books.
--Woody and Me. Solbert, Ronni, pseud. (1925-), illus. Solbert, Romaine G.. LC 66-12461. (Illus.). 1 v. (unpaged. 25cm. 1966. Pantheon Books.
Neville, Mary (1915-), ed.
--If a Poem Bothers You. (Illus.). 64p. (Orig.). 1980. (ISBN 0-913678-14-7). New Day Pr.
Neville, Ralph
--Lloyd Pennant: A Tale of The West. N.D. Kelly, Piet & Co.
Neville, Vera (1900-1978)
--Little Bo. Neville, Vera (1900-1978), illus. LC 40-10194. 64 p. illus. 23 x 20 cm. 1940. T. Nelson and Sons.
--The Meddlesome Mouse. LC 31-20195. 36 p. col. illus. 23 cm. 1931. The Macmillan Company.
--Safety for Sandy. Neville, Vera (1900-1978), illus. LC 40-31805. 47 p. illus. (part col.) 22 x 17 cm. 1940. T. Nelson and Sons.
Nevin, Evelyn Cook (1910-)
--Captive of the Delawares. Sanchez, Fred, illus. LC 52-8367. (Illus.). 127 p. 22cm. 1952. Abingdon-Cokesbury Press.
--The Extraordinary Adventures of Chee Chee McNerney. LC 73-142535. (Illus.). 224 p. 22cm. 1971. Four Winds Press.
--The Lost Children of the Shoshones. Lee, Manning de Villeneuve (1894-1980), illus. LC 46-37500. 3 p. l., 11-123, 2 p. incl. col. front., col. illus., col. plates. 22 cm. 1946. The Westminster Press.
--The River Spirit and the Mountain Demons. Benarde, Anita, illus. LC 65-25534. xi, 145p. illus. 21cm. 1965. Van Nostrand.
--The Sign of the Anchor. LC 47-5405. 157 p. illus. 22 cm. 1947. Westminster Press.
--Underground Escape. LC 49-10637. 191 p. illus. 22 cm. 1949. Westminster Press.
Nevins, Albert J. (1915-), tr. see Rey, Alfonso.
Nevins, Albert J. (1915-)
--The Adventures of Duc of Indochina. Wiese, Kurt (1887-1974), illus. LC 55-7210. 276p. illus. 21cm. 1955. Dodd, Mead.
--The Adventures of Kenji of Japan. Wiese, Kurt (1887-1974), illus. LC 52-9407. (Illus.). 275 p. 21cm. 1952. Dodd, Mead.
--The Adventures of Pancho of Peru. Wiese, Kurt (1887-1974), illus. LC 53-532145. 246p. illus. 21cm. 1953. Dodd, Mead.
--The Adventures of Ramon of Bolivia. Wiese, Kurt (1887-1974), illus. LC 54-5795. (Illus.). 272 p. 21cm. 1954. Dodd, Mead.
--The Adventures of Wu Han of Korea. Wiese, Kurt (1887-1974), illus. LC 51-9642. (Illus.). 244 p. 21cm. 1951. Dodd, Mead.
--St. Francis of The Seven Seas. Manso, Leo, illus. 192p. (Vision Bk.: No. 4). 1955. Farrar, Straus & Giroux.
--St. Francis of the Seven Seas. Manso, Leo, illus. LC 55-9794. 184p. illus. 22cm. (Vision books, 4). 1955. Vision Books.
--The Young Conquistador. LC 60-13400. viii, 270p. map 21cm. c.1960. Dodd, Mead.
Nevins, Ann
--From the Horse's Mouth. Nevins, Daniel, illus. (Illus.). (gr. 3-8). 1981. (ISBN 0-13-331462-6). P-H.
New Mexico People & Energy Collective, et al.
--Red Ribbons for Emma. LC 80-83883. (Illus.). 48p. (Orig.). (gr. 3 up). 1981. (ISBN 0-938678-07-8). New Seed.
New, Michael
--The Year of the Apple. Arnosky, Jim (1946-), illus. LC 80-15933. (Illus.). 128p. (gr. 3-7). 1980. (ISBN 0-201-05220-2, A-W Childrens). A-W.
New York Principals' Association & New York World's Fair, Inc.
--Trix, the Runaway Monkey: A Social Studies Story Book about Shelter. Johnson, Carl E., illus. LC 39-19350. 21cm. 32p. (The World of Tomorrow series). 1939. Grosset & Dunlap.
New Zoo Revue Joint Venture
--Mostly Happy Henrietta. (Illus.). 32p. (Orig.). (gr. 2-6). 1973. Hawthorn.
Newall, George
--Scooter Computer & Mr. Chips. Yohe, Tom, illus. (Illus.). 49p. (Texas Instruments Magic Wand Speaking Library). (ps-3). 1983. (ISBN 0-89512-088-7). Tex Instr Inc.
Newbauer, William Arthur see Bennett, Christine, pseud.
Newberg, Beth
--Three Strikes & You're Out. 1982. (ISBN 0-570-08404-0). Concordia.
Newberg, John see Aesop, Abraham, pseud.
Newberger, Eli, ed. see Tutela, Dawn.
Newbern, Kenneth, jt. auth. see Kuhmerker, Lisa.
Newberry, Clare Turlay, Mrs. (1903-1970)
--April's Kittens. Newberry, Clare Turlay, Mrs. (1903-1970), illus. LC 40-32442. 30, 2 p., 1 l. illus., pl. 27 1/2 x 23 cm. 1940. Harper & Brothers. **Award: (RCM).**
--Babette. Newberry, Clare Turlay, Mrs. (1903-1970), illus. LC 37-25347. 30, 2 p. incl col. front., illus. (part col.) 24 cm. 1937. Harper & Brothers.
--Barkis. Newberry, Clare Turlay, Mrs. (1903-1970), illus. Newberry, Clare Turlay, photos by. LC 38-27880. 30, 2 p., incl. front., illus. 1938. Harper & Brothers. **Award: (RCM).**
--Cat Velours. (Illus.). (gr. k-6). 1970. Comox.
--Cousin Toby. Newberry, Clare Turlay, Mrs. (1903-1970), illus. LC 39-24445. 32 p. incl. front., illus. 24 cm. 1939. Harper & Brothers.
--Frosty. Newberry, Clare Turlay, Mrs. (1903-1970), illus. LC 61-577246. (Illus.). 24 cm. 92p. (gr. 1-5). 1961. (ISBN 0-06-024431-3, HarpJ). Har-Row.
--Herbert the Lion. 41p. (gr. k-3). N.D. Harcourt, Brace & Co.
--Herbert the Lion. LC 39-612138. 64 p. col. illus. 22 x 27 cm. 1939. Harper & Brothers.
--Herbert the Lion. Newberry, Clare Turlay, Mrs. (1903-1970), illus. LC 31-32954. 41 p. col. illus. 24 1/2 x 28 cm. 1931. Brewer, Warren & Putnam Inc.
--Herbert, the Lion. Newberry, Clare Turlay, Mrs. (1903-1970), illus. LC 56-531800. unpaged. illus. 21 x 24cm. 1956. Harper.
--Ice Cream for Two. (Illus.). (gr. 1-4). 1971. Comox.
--Ice Cream for Two. Newberry, Clare Turlay, Mrs. (1903-1970), illus. LC 53-7116. 58p. illus. 24cm. 1953. Harper.
--The Kittens' ABC. LC 46-8583. 36 p. col. illus. 33 x 25 1/2 cm. 1946. Harper & Brothers.
--The Kittens' ABC. Verse. New rev. ed. Newberry, Clare Turlay, Mrs. (1903-1970), illus. LC 64-19712. 1v. (unpaged) illus. (pt. col.) 33cm. 1965. Harper.
--Lambert's Bargain. N.D. E. M. Hale & Co.
--Lambert's Bargain. LC 41-896178. 30, 2 p. illus. 24 x 19 cm. c.1941. Harper & Brothers.
--Marshmallow. Newberry, Clare Turlay, Mrs. (1903-1970), illus. LC 42-22858. (Illus.). 1978. (ISBN 0-06-024460-7, HarpJ). (ISBN 0-06-024461-5). Har-Row.
--Marshmallow. Newberry, Clare Turlay, Mrs. (1903-1970), illus. LC 42-22858. (Illus.). 31 p. 1942. Harper & Brothers. **Award: (RCM).**
--Mittens. N.D. E. M. Hale & Co.
--Mittens. Newberry, Clare Turlay, Mrs. (1903-1970), illus. LC 36-23259. 28 p., 2 l., incl. col. front. col. illus. 24cm. 1936. Harper & Brothers.
--Pandora. rev. ed. Newberry, Clare Turlay, illus. (Illus.). (gr. k-3). 1970. Comox.
--Pandora. Newberry, Clare Turlay, Mrs. (1903-1970), illus. LC 44-97508. 35 p. incl. fronts., illus. 33 x 25 cm. 1944. Harper & Brothers.
--Percy, Polly, and Pete. Newberry, Clare Turlay, Mrs. (1903-1970), illus. LC 52-7848. (Illus.). 1 v. (unpaged. 27cm. 1952. Harper.
--Smudge. Newberry, Clare Turlay, Mrs. (1903-1970), illus. LC 48-8624. (Illus.). (ps-1). 1948. (ISBN 0-06-024496-8, HarpJ). Har-Row.
--T-Bone, the Baby-Sitter. Newberry, Clare Turlay, Mrs. (1903-1970), illus. LC 50-9922. (Illus.). 32p. (gr. k-3). 1950. (ISBN 0-06-024506-9, HarpJ). Har-Row. **Award: (RCM).**
--Widget. Newberry, Clare Turlay, Mrs. (1903-1970), illus. LC 58-7759. (Illus.). unpaged. 1958. Harper.
Newberry, Fannie Ellsworth Stone, Mrs. (1848-1942)
--All Aboard. (Illus.). (The Wellesley Series for Girls). N.D. A. L. Burt.
--All Aboard. Barry, Etheldred Breeze (1870-), illus. LC 98-391. 324 p. incl. front. plates. 19 1/2 cm. 1898. A. I. Bradley & Co.
--All Aboard: A Story for Girls. (The Girl Comrades Ser.). N.D. A. L. Burt Company.
--Brian's Home. 342p. N.D. Pilgrim Press.
--Brian's Home. 342p. N.D. SUnday-School Library.
--Bubbles: A Girl's Story. (The Girl Comrades Ser.). N.D. A. L. Burt Company.
--Comrades. (Illus.). (St. Nicholas Ser.). 1905. Set. A L Burt Co.
--Comrades. (The Girl Comrades Ser.). N.D. A. L. Burt Company.
--Comrades. (Illus.). (The Rugby Ser.). N.D. A. L. Burt.
--Comrades. 308p. N.D. Pilgrims Press.
--Everyday Honor: Or, A Story for Young People. pl. 12cm. 429p. 1898. W. J. Jacobs & Co.
--Joyce's Investments: A Story for Girls. (The Girl Comrades Ser.). N.D. A. L. Burt Company.
--Millicent Raymond: A Story for Girls. (The Girl Comrades Ser.). N.D. A. L. Burt Company.
--Not for Profit. (Illus.). (The Wellesley Series for Girls). N.D. A. L. Burt.
--Not for Profit: A Story for Girls. (The Girl Comrades Ser.). N.D. A. L. Burt Company.
--The Odd One: A Story for Girls. (The Girl Comrdes Ser.). N.D. A. L. Burt Company.
--Sara, a Princess: A Story for Girls. (The Girl Comrades Ser.). N.D. A. L. Burt Company.
--Transplanted. LC 12-37258. 391 p. front., plates. 19 1/2 cm. c.1889. Congregational Sunday-School and Publishing Society.
--Transplanted. 391p. N.D. Pilgrim Press.
Newberry, Perry (1870-)
--Black Boulder Claim. N.D. Alfred A. Knopf.
--Black Boulder Claim. Pitz, Henry Clarence (1895-1976), illus. LC 21-15887. 303 p. col. front., illus., plates. 22 cm. 1921. The Penn Publishing Company.
--Castaway Island. N.D. Alfred A. Knopf.
--Castaway Island. Anderson, Frederic A., illus. LC 17-23974. 320 p. col. front., illus. (incl. maps) plates. 22 cm. 1917. The Penn Publishing Company.
--Forward Ho!. Newberry, Perry, illus. N.D. Frederick A. Stokes Co.
--The House-Boat Mystery. Beebe, Robb (1891-), illus. LC 35-15741. 5 p. l., 240 p. incl. plates. front. 19 1/2 cm. 1935. Frederick A. Stokes Company.
Newbery, F.
--Cries of London. Lurie, Alison & Schiller, Justin G., eds. Incl. Cries of New York. Wood, Samue. LC 75-32142. (Classics of Children's Literature 1621-1932 Ser.). N.D. (ISBN 0-8240-2258-0). Garland Pub.
Newbery, John
--The History of Little Goody Two-Shoes. Platt, Michael, pref. by. Bd. with The Fairing or a Golden Toy for Children. Repr. of 1768 ed. LC 75-32141. Repr. of 1765 ed. (Classics of Children's Literature, 1621-1932 Ser.: Vol. 8). 1976. (ISBN 0-8240-2257-2). Garland Pub.
Newbery, John, jt. auth. see Goody Two Shoes.
Newbery, John, jt. auth. see Thwaite, M. F.
Newbery, John, ed. see Mother Goose.
Newbolt, Henry, ed. see Hughes, Thomas.
Newbolt, Henry (1911-), ed. see Stevenson, Robert Louis.
Newbolt, Henry John, Sir (1862-1938)
--The Book of the Grenvilles. Ford, Henry Justice (1860-1941), illus. LC 21-17580. 4 p. l., 263 p. col. front., 4 port. 20 cm. $2.5. 1921. Longmans, Green and Co.
--The Book of the Happy Warrior. new ed. Ford, Henry Justice (1860-1941), illus. LC 29-165593. xiv, 284 p. front., illus., col. plates. 20 cm. 1928. Longmans, Green and Co., Ltd.
--Rilloby-Rill. Gretz, Susanna (1937-), illus. LC 73-8809. (Illus.). 1 vol. unpaged. 18cm. 1974, c.1973. (ISBN 0-87955-107-0). J. Philip O'Hara.
Newbolt, Henry, Sir, ed. see Austen, Jane.
Newbolt, Henry, Sir, jt. ed. see Cox, George Williams.
Newbolt, Henry, Sir, ed. see Dana, Richard Henry, Jr.
Newbolt, Henry, Sir, ed. see Dickens, Charles John Huffam.
Newbolt, Henry, Sir, ed. see Dumas, Alexandre.
Newbolt, Henry, Sir, ed. see Eliot, George.
Newbury, Norman Frederick & Armstrong, H. A
--The Young Experimenter. LC 61-10412. (Illus.). 96 p. 23cm. (Science in Action, Book 1). 1961, c.1960. Sterling Pub. Co.
Newby, Dorothy D., jt. auth. see Clinard, Dorothy Long.
Newby, Percy Howard (1918-)
--The Spirit of Jem: A Novel. 1st ed. (gr. 7 up). Wojciechowake, Maia, frwd. by. LC 67-6424. 185 p. 22cm. 1967. Delacorte Press.
Newcom, Grethel C., jt. auth. see Hadsell, Virginia T.
Newcomb, Ambrose
--Eagles of the Sky: Or, With Jack Ralston Along the Air Lanes. LC 31-15295. 3 p. l., 13-245 p. 19 1/2 cm. c.1930. The Goldsmith Publishing Co.
--Flying the Coast Skyways: Or, Jack Ralston's Swift Patrol. LC 31-15410. 2 p. l., 13-251 p. 19 1/2 cm. c.1931. The Goldsmith Publishing Co.
--The Sky Detectives: Or, How Jack Ralston Got His Man. LC 31-154113. 3 p. l., 13-254 p. 19 1/2 cm. c.1930. The Goldsmith Publishing Co.
--The Sky Pilot's Great Chase: Or, Jack Ralston's Dead Stick Landing. LC 31-15412. 3 p. l., 13-254 p. 19 1/2 cm. c.1930. The Goldsmith Publishing Co.
--Trackers of the Fog Pack: Or, Jack Ralston Flying Blind. LC 31-154137. 2 p. l., 7-242 p. 19 1/2 cm. c.1931. The Goldsmith Publishing Co.
--Wings Over the Rockies: Or, Jack Ralston's New Cloud Chaser. LC 31-154143. 3 p. l., 13-249 p. 19 1/2 cm. c.1930. The Goldsmith Publishing Co.
NewComb, C. G.
--The Smoke Hole. N.D. (ISBN 0-8111-0178-9). The Naylor and Company.
Newcomb, Covelle, jt. auth. see Burbank, Addison Bushnell.
Newcomb, Covelle (1908-)
--Silver Saddles. 1st. ed. Burbank, Addison Bushnell (1895-), illus. LC 43-51266. ix, 261, 1 p. illus. 21 cm. 1943. Longmans, Green & Co.
--Vagabond in Velvet: The Story of Miguel De Cervantes. 1st ed. Burbank, Addison Bushnell (1895-), illus. LC 42-21762. ix, 262 p. incl. front., illus. 22 cm. 1942. Longmans, Green and Co.
Newcomb, Ellsworth, pseud., see Kenny, Ellsworth Newcomb.
Newcomb, Ellsworth, pseud. (1909-)
--Anchor for Her Heart. Kenny, Ellsworth Newcomb. 1st. ed. LC 47-30630. 187 p. 20 cm. 1947. E. P. Dutton.
--Mystery Beyond the Wall. Kenny, Ellsworth Newcomb. 1st. ed. LC 50-9153. 192 p. front. 20 cm. 1950. Dutton.
--Stars Above. Kenny, Ellsworth Newcomb. 1st ed. LC 49-11009. 191 p. 20 cm. 1949. E. P. Dutton.
--Three Came Riding. Kenny, Ellsworth Newcomb. Christensen, Christina F., illus. LC 64-17535. (Illus.). 82 p. 24cm. 1964. Norton.
--Window on the Sea. Kenny, Ellsworth Newcomb. LC 48-4729. 192 p. 20 cm. 1948. E. P. Dutton.
--With This Ring. Kenny, Ellsworth Newcomb. LC 51-12692. 183 p. illus. 20 cm. 1951. Dutton.
Newcomb, Frances Lynette Johnson (1889-) & Harvey, Lillian, eds.
--Navajo Bird Tales Told by Hosteen Clah Chee. Na-Ton-Sa-Ka (1943-), illus. LC 71-108760. (Illus.). xiii, 125 p. 22cm. (Quest book for children). 1970. Theosophical Pub. House.
Newcombe, J. S.
--The Adventures of Mr. Bumble the Policeman. 24p. N.D. British Book Centre.
Newcombe, Jack
--The Fireball: Baseball's Fastest Pitcher. N.D. G P Putnum's Sons.
--Six Days to Saturday: Joe Paterno and Penn State. Swanson, Dick, photos by. 128p. 1974. (ISBN 0-374-36975-5). Farrar, Straus and Giroux.
Newell, Averil
--Fly-by-Nights. N.D. Macmillan.
Newell, Charles Martin see Captain Barnacle, pseud.
Newell, Cicero
--Indian Stories. LC 12-52031. vii, 191 p. front., illus. (incl. ports.) 19 1/2 cm. c.1912. Silver, Burdett and Company.
Newell, Crosby, pseud., see Bonsall, Crosby Barbara Newell.
Newell, David McCheyne (1898-)
--Cougars & Cowboys. LC 27-22946. xi, 222 p. illus. 20 cm. 1927. Century Co.
Newell, Eadie
--Trouble Brewing. LC 68-11222. 254 p. 22cm. 1968. Steck-Vaughn Co.
Newell, Edythe Weatherford (1910-)
--The Rescue of the Sun. Altschuler, Franz (1923-), illus. LC 76-91741. (Illus.). 142 p. 23cm. 1970. (ISBN 0-8075-6948-8). A. Whitman.
Newell, Harriet P. H. see Mannering, May, pseud.
Newell, Harriet P. H., Mrs.
--Climbing the Rope. Mannering, May, pseud, 1 of 25 vols. (Illus.). (Pilgrim Ser. for Boys: No. 7). 1900. Lee & Shepard.
--Cruise of the Dashaway: Or, Katie Putnam's Voyage. Mannering, May, pseud, 1 of 25 vols. (Illus.). (Mayflower Ser. for Girls: No. 6). 1900. Lee & Shepard.
--Little Maid of Oxbow. Mannering, May, pseud, 1 of 25 vols. (Illus.). (Mayflower Ser. for Girls: No. 13). 1900. Lee & Shepard.
Newell, Hope Hockenberry, Mrs. (1896-1965)
--A Cap for Mary Ellis. N.D. (ISBN 0-425-01234-4). Berkley Publishing Company.

--A Cap for Mary Ellis. LC 53-8547. 200 p. 22cm. 1953. Harper.
--Cinder Ike. Peck, Anne Merriman (1884-), illus. LC 42-22617. 121, 1 p. incl. front., illus. 22 1/2 cm. 1942. T. Nelson and Sons.
--Little Old Woman Carries On. N.D. Thomas Nelson & Co.
--The Little Old Woman Carries On. Peck, Anne Merriman (1884-), illus. LC 47-19863. 64 p. incl. front., illus. 22 cm. 1947. T. Nelson & Sons.
--The Little Old Woman Who Used Her Head. Ruse, Margaret, photos by. LC 35-14391. (Illus.). 63 p. incl. front., illus., plates. 22 cm. 1935. T. Nelson and Sons.
--The Little Old Woman Who Used Her Head and Other Stories. Ruse, Margaret & Peck, Anne Merriman (1884-), illus. LC 73-17036. (Illus.). 127 p. 20cm. 1973. (ISBN 0-8407-6328-X). T. Nelson.
--Mary Ellis, Student Nurse. LC 58-6621. (Illus.). 196 p. 22cm. 1958. Harper.
--More About the Little Old Woman Who Used Her Head. Ruse, Margaret, photos by. LC 38-172773. (Illus.). 62 p. incl. front., illus. 22 cm. 1938. T. Nelson and Sons.
--Penny's Best Summer. Mars, Witold Tadeusz J. (1912-), illus. LC 54-8975. (Illus.). 244 p. 22cm. 1954. Harper.
--Selections from the Little Old Woman Who Used Her Head. Ruse, Margaret, illus. (Illus., Pub. by Nelson). (gr. k-3). 1972 (Starline). Schol Bk Serv.
--Steppin and Family. Peck, Anne Merriman (1884-), illus. 190p. 1924. Oxford University Press.
--Steppin and Family. Peck, Anne Merriman (1884-), illus. LC 42-36134. 6 p. l., 11-198 p. col. front., illus., col. plates (1 double) 22 cm. 1942. Oxford University Press.
--The Story of Christina. Peck, Anne Merriman (1884-), illus. LC 47-30885. viii, 207 p. illus. 22 cm. 1947. Harper.

Newell, Peter (1832-1924), ed.
--Alice Through the Looking-Glass. (Harper's Selected Juveniles). 1910. Harper & Brothers.

Newell, Peter (1862-1924)
--The Hole Book. LC 8-34150. 51 p. col. illus. 22 1/2 cm. 1908. Harper & Brothers.
--Hunting the Snark. (Harper's Selected Juveniles). 1910. Harper & Brother.
--Jungle-Jangle. (Illus.). N.D. Harper & Brothers.
--Pictures and Rhymes. LC 99-5698. 4p. N.D. Harper & Brothers.
--The Rocket Book. LC 69-12080. (Illus.). 51 p. 23cm. 1969. C. E. Tuttle Co.
--The Rocket Book. LC 68-9155. (Illus.). 44 p. 21cm. 1974, c.1912. (ISBN 0-486-22044-3). Dover Publications.
--The Rocket Book. LC 12-23935. (Illus.). 47x. 22cm. 1912. Harper & Brothers.
--The Slant Book. LC 67-12304. (Illus.). 52 p. 22cm. 1967. C. E. Tuttle Co.
--The Slant Book. LC 10-25818. 47p. 1910. Harper & Brothers.
--Topsys & Turvys. LC 64-18861. 72p. (chiefly illus., pt. col.) 16x23cm. 1964. Dover.
--Topsys and Turvys, 2 Vols, No. 1. LC 16-5309. (Illus.). 24cm. 31p. 1893. The Century Co.
--Topsys and Turvys, 2 Vols, No. 2. LC 2-22691. (Illus.). 24cm. 36p. 1902. The Century Co.

Newell, Peter (1862-1924) & Bennett, Francis I., illus.
--Favorite Fairy Tales: The Childhood Choice of Representative Men and Women. LC 7-34176. xviii p., 2 l., 354 p., 1 l. front., 15 pl. 23 cm. 1907. Harper & Brothers.

Newell, Robert R.
--Blowy the Whale. Newell, Robert R., illus. LC 48-3302. 32 p. col. illus. 17 x 26 cm. c.1945. T. Y. Crowell Co.

Newell, William Wells (1839-1907)
--Games and Songs of American Children. LC 5-29289. xii, 242 p. incl. front. 23 cm. 1883. Harper & Brothers.
--Games and Songs of American Children. Withers, Carl (1900-1970), intro. by. LC 63-3347. 289p. illus. 22cm. (Dover bk. T534 rebound). c.1963. P. Smith.
--Games and Songs of American Children: Collected and Compared. LC 40-37826. xii, 242 p. incl. front., diagr. 23 cm. 1884. Harper & Brothers.
--Games and Songs of American Children: Collected and Compared. new and enl. ed. LC 3-29283. xv, 282 p. incl. front. 23 1/2 cm. 1903. Harper & Brothers.
--Lady Featherflight. An English Folk-Tale. LC 44-12295. 1 p. l., 10 p. 19 cm. 1892. The Salem Press Publishing and Printing Co.

Newell, William Wells (1839-1907), ed.
--Journal of American Folk-Lore. N.D. Houghton, Miffin & Company.

Newfeld, Frank, jt. auth. see Lee, Dennis Benyon.

Newfeld, Frank (1928-) & Toye, William Eldred (1926-)
--Simon and the Golden Sword. LC 76-384030. (Illus.). 24 p. 25cm. 1976. (ISBN 0-19-540270-7). Oxford University Press.

Newfield, Marcia
--A Book for Jodan. 1st ed. De Groat, Diane (1947-), illus. LC 74-18192. (Illus.). 48 p. 22cm. (A Margaret K. McElderry Bk.). 1975. (ISBN 0-689-50010-6). Atheneum Publishers.
--Iggy. Chwast, Jacqueline (1932-), illus. LC 72-75609. (Illus.). 46 p. 20x24 cm. 1972. (ISBN 0-395-13898-1). Houghton Mifflin.
--Six Rags Apiece: Five Stories About Fuzzy Bear and Velvet Belly. Langner, Nola (1930-), illus. LC 76-6776. (Illus.). 48 p. 22 x 28cm. c.1976. (ISBN 0-7232-6132-6). Frederick Warne.
--Where Did You Put Your Sleep?. DaRif, Andrea, illus. LC 83-2785. p. cm. 1983. (ISBN 0-689-50286-9). Atheneum.

Newhall, Charles Stedman (1842-1935)
--Ruthie's Story. LC 12-37257. (Illus.). 187p. 18cm. 1888. Presbyterian Board of Publication.

Newhouse, Edward (1911-)
--Anything Can Happen. LC 41-21721. 6 p. l., 286 p. 21 cm. c.1941. Harcourt, Brace and Company.

Newhouse, Wilfred John (1894-)
--Sandman Tales. Sardella, Lou, illus. LC 54-23525. v. illus. 28cm. c.1954. Sandman Press.
--Six Stories about Mollie the Bell Cow. Sardella, Lou, illus. LC 57-42297. (Illus.). 26p. 28cm. (Sandman Tales). 1957. Sandman Press.
--Six Stories about Prim the Kitten and Curly the Collie. Sardella, Lou, illus. LC 57-42296. (Illus.). 26p. 28cm. (Sandman Tales). 1957. Sandman Press.

Newkirk, Clyde see Newkirk, Newton, pseud.

Newkirk, Clyde
--The Stork Book. Newkirk, Newton, pseud. Goldsmith, Wallace, illus. LC 7-28481. 18cm. 123p. c.1907. H. M. Caldwell Co.

Newkirk, Garrett (1847-1921)
--Rhymes of the States. Fenn, Harry (1838-1911), illus. LC 16-3079. 4 p. l., 96 p. illus. 24 1/2 cm. 1896. The Century Co.

Newkirk, Newton, pseud., see Newkirk, Clyde.

Newman, Alyse (1953-)
--It's Me, Claudia!. LC 80-29525. (Illus.). 32 p. 22cm. (Easy-Read Story Book). 1981. (ISBN 0-531-03539-5). F. Watts.

Newman, Bernard Charles (1897-1968)
--The Cavalry Goes Through!. LC 30-19633. 276 p. illus. (maps) 19 1/2 cm. c.1930. H. Holt and Company.

Newman, Carol
--Strella's Children. Krahn, Fernando (1935-), illus. LC 66-5949. 40p. illus. 25cm. N.D. Atheneum.

Newman, Daisy (1904-)
--Mount Joy. LC 68-12232. (Illus.). 279 p. 24cm. 1968. Atheneum.
--Sperli the Clockmaker. Thompson, Edward Thorne, photos by. LC 32-6895. 7 p. l., 117 p. incl. illus., plates. col. front. 23 cm. 1932. The Macmillan Company.

Newman, Deborah
--Holiday Plays for Little Players: A Collection of Royalty-Free Plays for Children. LC 57-9953. 286 p. 21cm. 1957. Plays, Inc.

Newman, Fannie J. see Murrie, Merle, pseud.

Newman, Gertrude
--Delicia and Adolphus, Happy Plays Days of Two Rag Dolls. Benson, Russell R., photos by. LC 38-10619. 33 illus. 21x19. 1938. Rand McNally & Co.
--Polly Poppingay: Milliner. Meyer, Edith Paterson (1895-) & Paull, Grace A. (1898-), illus. LC 43-13935. 226 p. incl. col. front., illus. col. plates. 21 cm. 1943. J. B. Lippincott Company.
--The Story of Delicia: A Rag Doll. LC 35-16897. 61 p. illus. 23 1/2 cm. c.1935. Rand, McNally & Company.

Newman, Isidora
--Fairy Flowers: Nature Legends of Facts & Fantasy. Pogany, Willy (1882-1955), illus. LC 26-224212. ix p., 1 l., 196 p. incl. col. mounted front., illus. col. mounted plates. 26 cm. c.1926. H. Holt and Company.
--Fairy Flowers: Nature Legends of Facts & Fantasy. Pogany, Willy (1882-1955), illus. LC 27-12936. viii p., 2 l., 160 p. col. mounted front., illus., col. mounted plates. 28 cm. 1926. H. Milford, Oxford University Press.

Newman, J. P., Mrs., ed.
--Dew-Drops and Sunshine. N.D. Methodist Book Concern.
--Dew-Drops and Sunshine. N.D. Nelson & Phillips.

Newman, Joseph Simon (1891-)
--One Summer Day. Greenwald, Sheila, pseud. (1934-), illus. Green, Sheila Ellen. LC 62-9059. unpaged. illus. 20cm. 1962. World Pub. Co.

Newman, Louis, ed. see Newman, Shirley.

Newman, Louis, ed. see Newman, Shirley & Jewish, Theological Seminary of America. Melton Research Cernter.

Newman, Lucy Wheeler, Mrs.
--Friends. LC 36-22174. (Being a Story of Two Little American Girls Who Lived in China When the Yellow Flag with a Black Dragon Still Waved, and Airplanes Were Unknown). 3 p. l., 9-89 p. illus. 21 cm. c.1936. Sheffield Press.

Newman, Marjorie
--Knocked Out!. 48p. (gr. 6-9). 1984. (ISBN 0-241-11072-6, Pub. by Hamish Hamilton England). David & Charles.

Newman, Matt H., ed.
--Goldilocks & the Three Bears. Laite, Gordon (1925-), illus. LC 66-3459. (Illus.). 18p. (Children's Bk.). (ps). 1980. (ISBN 0-89290-085-7). Soc for Visual.
--Little Red Riding Hood. Kane, Sharon Koester, illus. LC 66-3456. (Illus.). 18p. (Children's Stories Bk). (ps). 1980. (ISBN 0-89290-084-9). Soc for Visual.
--Rumpelstiltskin. Laite, Gordon (1925-), illus. LC 66-3460. (Illus.). 18p. (Children's Stories Bk). (ps). 1980. (ISBN 0-89290-086-5). Soc for Visual.
--Thanksgiving for King. Bendel, Ruth, illus. LC 66-3416. (Illus.). 18p. (Children's Stories Bk). (ps). 1980. (ISBN 0-89290-087-3). Soc for Visual.

Newman, Maxine M.
--The Robins Raise a Family. N.D. Carlton Press.

Newman, Miriam
--Phoebe and the Duck. Grace, Marjorie, illus. LC 41-14056. 19 p. illus. 24 cm. c.1941. House of Field, Inc.

Newman, Nanette
--That Dog!. Hafner, Marylin (1925-), illus. LC 81-43892. (Illus.). 48p. (gr. 1-4). 1983. (ISBN 0-690-04229-9, TYC-J). (ISBN 0-690-04230-2). Har-Row.

Newman, Paul
--The Birthday Party. Zamaky, Jessica & Moore, Lilian, illus. LC 64-9920. 61 p. col. illus. 22 cm. "3463. 1964. Grosset & Dunlap.
--No Place to Play. Moore, Lilian, ed. Lockhart, David, illus. LC 69-18262. (Illus.). 58 p. 22cm. (Easy Reader). 1969. Grosset & Dunlap.
--Noah & the Ark. LC 72-79767. (Illus.). 14p. (Pop-up Panorama Bks.). (gr. k-2). 1972. (ISBN 0-529-04865-5). World Pub.

Newman, Robert Howard (1909-)
--The Boy Who Could Fly. Sagsoorian, Paul (1923-), illus. LC 67-2716. (Illus.). 121 p. 22cm. 1967. Atheneum.
--The Case of the Baker Street Irregular: A Sherlock Holmes Story. LC 77-15463. vii, 216 p. 22cm. 1978. (ISBN 0-689-30641-5). Atheneum. **Award: (ALA).**
--The Case of the Etruscan Treasure. LC 83-2632. p. cm. 1983. (ISBN 0-689-30992-9). Atheneum.
--The Case of the Frightened Friend. LC 83-15887. 180p. (gr. 4-8). 1984. (ISBN 0-689-31018-8). Atheneum.
--The Case of the Murdered Players. LC 85-7956. 174 p. 21cm. 1985. (ISBN 0-689-31155-9). Atheneum.
--The Case of the Somerville Secret. LC 80-18584. vii, 184 p. 22cm. 1981. (ISBN 0-689-30825-6). Atheneum.
--The Case of the Threatened King. LC 81-10802. 212 p. 22cm. 1982. (ISBN 0-689-30887-6). Atheneum.
--The Case of the Vanishing Corpse. LC 79-22078. x, 221 p. 22cm. 1980. (ISBN 0-689-30755-1). Atheneum.
--Grettir the Strong. Gretzer, John, illus. LC 68-21608. (Illus.). 21cm. 190p. 1968. Crowell.
--Identity Unknown. LC 45-4852. 3 p. l., 3-92 p. 21 cm. 1945. Ziff-Davis Publishing Company.
--Merlin's Mistake. Lebenson, Richard, illus. LC 68-18454. (Illus.). 237 p. 22cm. 1970. Atheneum.
--Night Spell. Burchard, Peter Duncan (1921-), illus. LC 76-25207. (Illus.). 189 p. 22cm. 1977. (ISBN 0-689-30559-1). Atheneum.
--The Shattered Stone. 1st ed. Gretzer, John, illus. LC 75-6834. (Illus.). 231 p. 22cm. 1975. (ISBN 0-689-30481-1). Atheneum.
--The Testing of Tertius. Cuffari, Richard (1925-1978), illus. LC 72-86944. (Illus.). 186 p. 22cm. 1973. Atheneum.
--The Twelve Labors of Hercules. Keeping, Charles William James (1924-), illus. LC 75-132300. (Illus.). 150 p. 21cm. (Crowell hero tales). 1972. (ISBN 0-690-83920-0). Crowell.

Newman, Shirlee Petkin (1924-)
--Tell Me, Grandma, Tell Me, Grandpa. Drescher, Joan ELizabeth (1939-), illus. LC 78-23711. (Illus.). 30 p. 1979. Houghton Mifflin.
--Yellow Silk for May Lee. Goldstein, Leslie, illus. LC 61-15548. (gr. 2-6). 1961. Bobbs.

Newman, Shirlee Petkin (1924-), adapted by.
--Folk Tales of Japan. LC 63-14586. 24cm. 111p. (Folk Tales Around the World Series). (gr. 4-7). N.D. (ISBN 0-672-50276-3). Bobbs.

Newman, Shirlee Petkin (1924-) & Chall, Jeanne, eds.
--Folk Tales of Latin America. 1st ed. LC 62-22152. (Illus.). 123p. 24cm. (Folk Tales Around the World Ser.). 1962. Bobbs-Merrill.

Newman, Shirlee Petkin (1924-) & Gotlieb, Jules, illus.
--The Shipwrecked Dog. 1st ed. LC 63-19018. 127 p. illus. 22 cm. 1963. Bobbs-Merrill.

Newman, Shirley
--A Child's Introduction to the Early Prophets. Newman, Louis, ed. Wallace, Lucille, illus. LC 75-14052. (Illus.). 128 p. 26cm. c.1975. (ISBN 0-87441-244-7). Behrman House.
--A Child's Introduction to Torah. Newman, Louis, ed. Zemsky, Jessica, illus. LC 72-2056. (Illus.). 128 p. 26cm. 1972. (ISBN 0-87441-067-3). Published by Behrman House for the Melton Research Center of the Jewish Theological Seminary of America.

Newman, Winifred Barnum
--The Secret in the Garden. Newman, Winifred Barnum, illus. LC 81-123472. (Illus.). 32 p. 22cm. c.1980. (ISBN 0-87743-151-5). Baha'i Pub. Trust.
--The Spotlessly Leopard. Newman, Winifred Barnum, illus. LC 82-24423. p. cm. c.1983. (ISBN 0-87743-700-9). Bellwood Press.

Newman & Boulanger
--Sunflakes & Snowshine. (ps-3). N.D. (ISBN 0-590-05412-0, Schol Pap). Scholastic Inc.

Newmark, John
--To the Zoo in a Plastic Box. (Illus.). 1965. Random House Inc.

Newport, W.
--Two Boys: A Boy's Romance. N.D. Fords, Howard & Hulbert.

Newsham, Wendy
--The Monster Hunt. Newsham, Ian, illus. (Illus.). 32p. (gr. 3-6). 1983. (ISBN 0-241-10859-4, Pub by Hamish Hamilton). David & Charles.

Newsome, Effie Lee, Mrs.
--Gladiola Garden: Poems of Outdoors and Indoors for Second Grade Readers. Jones, Lois Mailou, illus. LC 41-3681. xv, 1, 167 p. incl. front., illus. 23 1/2 cm. 1940. The Associated Publishers.

Newth, Mette
--The Little Viking. Holl, Adelaide Hinkle (1910-), retold by. Schmitt-Menzel, Isolde, illus. LC 73-84542. (Original Author: Mette Newth). (Illus.). 32 p. 28cm. 1975. (ISBN 0-307-15691-5). Golden Press.

Newth, Philip.
--Roly Goes Exploring. LC 81-5899. (A Book for Blind and Sighted Children, in Braille and Standard Type, with Pictures to Feel As Well As See). p. cm. 1981, c.1977. (ISBN 0-399-20815-1). Philomel Books.

Newton, Elizabeth
--Stay Near Me. (gr. 2-5). N.D. Carlton.

Newton, Lucilda A.
--Big Peanuts in Trouble. 1976. (ISBN 0-915374-18-8). Rapids Christian.

Newton, Patricia Montgomery
--The Five Sparrows: A Japanese Folktale. LC 82-3881. (Illus.). 32p. (ps-3). 1982. (ISBN 0-689-30936-8). Atheneum.
--The Frog Who Drank the Waters of the World. Newton, Patricia Montgomery, illus. LC 83-2594. p. cm. 1983. (ISBN 0-689-30993-7). Atheneum.

Newton, Richard (1813-1887)
--Bible Animals and the Lessons Taught by Them. LC 6-32902. 450 p. front., plates. 19 1/2 cm. c.1888. R. Carter and Brothers.
--The King in His Beauty. (Illus.). 348p. 1905. American Tract Society.
--The King in His Beauty. LC 12-37239. 347 p. front., plates. 17 1/2 cm. 1878. R. Carter and Brothers.
--Nature's Wonders. LC 12-37279. 335 p. front., plates. 17 1/2 cm. 1872. R. Carter and Brothers.
--Pearls From the East. (Illus.). 176p. N.D. American Sunday-School Union's.
--Pebbles from the Brook. (Illus.). 312p. 1905. American Tract Society.

Newton, Rosamond
--Londonderry Heir. Goss, John, illus. LC 34-345947. 3 p. l., 5-306 p. front., illus. 20 1/2 cm. 1934. Lothrop, Lee and Shepard Company.

Newton, Ruth E.
--Soap and Bubbles: A Picture Story Book. Kovar, Edith May (1905-), illus. Windsor, Mary, pseud. LC 35-147. 16 p. col. illus. 32 1/2 cm. c.1935. Whitman Publishing Co.

Newton, Sandra S.
--Enjoying the Arts: Poetry. 1977. (ISBN 0-8239-0398-2). Rosen Group.

Newton, Stan
--Paul Bunyan of the Great Lakes. N.D. Hendricks House-Farrar, Straus.

Newton, Suzanne (1936-)
--C O Arnold's Corners. LC 73-18063. 176 p. 21cm. 1974. (ISBN 0-664-32545-9). Westminster Press.

--The Laird of Cockpen. Alger, Leclaire Gowans. LC 68-19993. (Illus.). 32p. Repr. of 1969 ed. (Owlet Bks.). 1973. (ISBN 0-03-071745-0). HR&W.
--The Laird of Cockpen. Alger, Leclaire Gowans. Adams, Adrienne (1906-), illus. LC 68-19993. (Illus.). 32 p. 23cm. (Holt Owlet). 1973, c.1969. (ISBN 0-03-005726-4). Holt.
--Laird of Cockpen. Alger, Leclaire Gowans. Adams, Adrienne (1906-), illus. LC 68-19993. (Illus.). color ils. 32p. Repr. of 1969 ed. (gr. k-3). 1969. (ISBN 0-03-071745-0). (ISBN 0-03-071750-7). HR&W.
--Scottish Songbook. Alger, Leclaire Gowans. Ness, Evaline Michelow, Mrs. (1911-), illus. LC 69-12805. (Illus.). 32 3-color ils. footnotes. 64p. (gr. 3-8). 1969. (ISBN 0-03-079915-5). (ISBN 0-03-080265-2). HR&W.
--Sea-Spell & Moor-Magic: Tales of the Western Isles. Alger, Leclaire Gowans. Bock, Vera, illus. LC 68-12271. (Illus.). 11 drawings. glossary. 224p. (gr. 4-7). 1968. (ISBN 0-03-068865-5). (ISBN 0-03-068870-1). HR&W. **Award: (ALA).**
--Twelve Great Black Cats, and Other Eerie Scottish Tales. Alger, Leclaire Gowans. Bock, Vera, illus. LC 73-135855. (Illus.). xiii, 173 p. 24cm. 1971. Dutton. **Award: (ALA).**

Nic Leodhas, Sorche, pseud. (1898-1969), retold by
--By Loch & by Lin: Tales from Scottish Ballads. Alger, Leclaire Gowans. Bock, Vera, illus. LC 69-11812. (Illus.). 130p. (gr. 4-7). 1969. (ISBN 0-03-076450-5). (ISBN 0-03-076455-6). HR&W.
--Claymore and Kilt: Tales of Scottish Kings and Castles. Alger, Leclaire Gowans. 1st ed. Dillon, Leo (1933-) & Dillon, Diane (1933-), illus. LC 67-6499. (Illus.). 157 p. 25cm. 1967. (ISBN 0-03-063985-9). Holt, Rinehart and Winston.
--Thistle and Thyme: Tales and Legends from Scotland. Alger, Leclaire Gowans. 1st ed. Ness, Evaline Michelow, Mrs. (1911-), illus. LC 62-11043. 143p. illus. 24cm. 1962. (ISBN 0-03-035210-X). Holt, Rinehart and Winston. **Awards: (ALA); (JNM).**

Nicol, Nina, Mrs., jt. auth. see Fogler, Doris.

Nicolai, D. Miles
--The Summer the Flowers Had No Scent. 3rd ed. Poyser, Victoria, illus. (Illus.). 28p. (Color-a-Story Ser.). (gr. 3-5). 1977. (ISBN 0-933992-19-X). Coffee Break.

Nicolas, pseud., see Mordvinoff, Nicolas.

Nicolas, jt. auth. see Will.

Nicolas, pseud. (1911-1973) & Will, pseud. (1904-1974)
--Russet & the Two Reds. Mordvinoff, Nicolas. Lipkind, William. Nicolas, pseud. (1911-1973), illus. Mordvinoff, Nicolas. (gr. k-2). 1962. (ISBN 0-8382-0716-2). Hale.

Nicole, pseud., see Duplaix, Georges.

Nicole, Christopher Robin (1930-)
--Operation Destruct. 1st ed. 230p. 22cm. 1969. Holt, Rinehart, and Winston.
--Operation Manhunt. LC 76-98919. 22cm. 225p. (gr. 7 up). 1970. (ISBN 0-03-084260-3). (ISBN 0-03-084261-1). HR&W.
--Operation Neptune. LC 76-182783. 222 p. 22cm. 1972. (ISBN 0-03-091309-8). Holt, Rinehart & Winston.
--Where the Cavern Ends. LC 74-119097. 171 p. 22cm. 1970. (ISBN 0-03-085115-7). Holt, Rinehart and Winston.

Nicole (1895-)
--The Happy Family. Elliott, Gertrude, illus. (Little Golden Book). 1947. Golden Press.
--The Happy Family. Elliott, Gertrude, illus. LC 47-3634. 42 p. illus. (part col.) 20 x 17 1/2 cm. (On cover: The Little golden library, no. 35). 1947. Simon and Schuster.
--The Happy Family. Malvern, Corinne (1905-1956), illus. (Little Golden Book). 1955. Golden Press.

Nicolet, Vera Ogden, Mrs.
--Tiny Poems for Tiny Tots. LC 37-22680. 69 p. illus. 20 1/2 cm. c.1937. Huxley.

Nicoll, Helen & Pienkowski, Jan (1936-)
--Meg and Mog. LC 72-86945. (Illus.). 30 p. 22cm. 1973, c.1972. Atheneum.
--Meg and Mog. LC 77-360921. (Illus.). 31 p. 21cm. (Picture Puffins). 1975. (ISBN 0-14-050117-7). Puffin Books.
--Meg & Mog Birthday Book. (Illus.). 32p. 1st U.S. edition. (Meg & Mog Ser.). (ps-1). 1983. (ISBN 0-434-95428-4, Pub. by W. Heinemann England). David & Charles.
--Meg at Sea. LC 74-83409. (Illus.). 30p. 21cm. 1976, c.1974. (ISBN 0-8178-5281-6). (ISBN 0-8178-5282-4). Harvey House.
--Meg on the Moon. LC 74-83410. (Illus.). 30p. 21cm. 1976, c.1974. (ISBN 0-8178-5271-9). (ISBN 0-8178-5272-7). Harvey House.
--Meg's Car. (Illus.). 32p. 1st U.S. edition. (Meg & Mog Ser.). (ps-1). 1983. (ISBN 0-434-95426-8, Pub. by W. Heinemann). David & Charles.
--Meg's Castle. (Illus.). 32p. 1st U.S. edition. (Meg & Mog Ser.). (ps-1). 1983. (ISBN 0-434-95427-6, Pub. by W. Heinemann). David & Charles.
--Meg's Eggs. LC 73-163935. (Illus.). 30 p. 22cm. 1973, c.1972. Atheneum.
--Meg's Eggs. LC 77-359000. (Illus.). 32 p. 21cm. (Picture puffins). 1975. (ISBN 0-14-050118-5). Puffin Books.
--Meg's Veg. (Illus.). 32p. 1st U.S. edition. (Meg & Mog Ser.). (ps-1). 1983. (ISBN 0-434-95639-2, Pub. by W. Heinemann). David & Charles.
--Mog at the Zoo. (Illus.). 32p. 1st U.S. edition. (Meg & Mog Ser.). (ps-1). 1983. (ISBN 0-434-95429-2, Pub. by W. Heinemann). David & Charles.
--Mog in the Fog. (Illus.). 32p. 1st U.S. edition. (ps). 1984. (ISBN 0-434-95430-6, Pub. by W Heinemann Ltd). David & Charles.
--Mog's Mumps. (Illus.). 32p. 1st U.S. edition. (Meg & Mog Ser.). (ps-1). 1983. (ISBN 0-434-95640-6, Pub. by W. Heinemann). David & Charles.
--Mog's Mumps. LC 84-234639. (Illus.). 32 p. 21cm. (Picture puffins). 1982, c.1976. (ISBN 0-14-050357-9). Puffin Books.
--Owl at School. (Illus.). 32p. 1st U.S. edition. (ps). 1984. (ISBN 0-434-95431-4, Pub. by W Heinemann Ltd). David & Charles.
--Quest for the Gloop. (Illus.). 32p. 1st U.S. edition. (gr. 1-3). 1983. (ISBN 0-434-95641-4, Pub. by W. Heinemann England). David & Charles.

Nida, Stella Humphrey, ed. see Defoe, Daniel.

Nida, Stella Humphrey, adapted by see Scott, Walter, Sir.

Nida, Stella Humphrey, Mrs.
--Monkey Monk. Zetterstrom, Martin, illus. LC 40-12859. 55 p. illus. 22 x 18 cm. c.1940. Cupples and Leon Company.

Nida, Stella Humphrey, Mrs., jt. auth. see Nida, William Lewis.

Nida, William Lewis, ed. see Defoe, Daniel.

Nida, William Lewis (1874-)
--Ab, the Cave Man. Waterloo, Stanley (1846-), adapted by. Stearns, Fred, illus. LC 23-562826. (A Story of the Time of the Stone Age, Adapted for Young Readers from The Story of Ab). 3 p. l., 5-166 p. front., plates. 19 cm. c.1918. A. Flanagan Company.
--Ab, The Caveman. (The Children's Hour Bks). N.D. Grosset & Dunlap.
--Fleetfoot, The Cave Boy. N.D. Laidlaw Bros.
--The Story of Man. N.D. Laidlaw Bros.
--Taming the Animals. N.D. Laidlaw Bros.
--The Tree Boys. N.D. Laidlaw Bros.

Nida, William Lewis (1874-) & Nida, Stella Humphrey, Mrs.
--Little White Chief. Dulin, Dorothy, illus. LC 23-16089. 128 p. col. illus. 18 1/2 cm. 1923. A. Flanagan Company.

Niebling, Richard F., ed.
--Journey of Poems. (gr. 9 up). 1967. Delacorte.

Niebuhr, Barthold George (1776-1831)
--Greek Hero Stories. Hoppin, Augustus (1828-1896), illus. N.D. Dodd, Mead & Company.
--Greek Heroes by Lechner. Rackham, Arthur (1867-1939), illus. N.D. Longmans,Green & Co.

Niebuhr, Hulda
--Greatness Passing By. N.D. Charles Scribner's Sons.
--One Story. Lear, John, illus. (Illus.). (gr. 7-9). 1949. (ISBN 0-664-46430-0). Westminster.
--Ventures in Dramatics with Boys and Girls of the Church School. LC 35-38149. xix p., 1 l., 224 p. 20 cm. 1935. C. Scribner's Sons.

Niedermeyer, Mabel A. (1899-)
--My Indian Picture Story Book. Jefferson, Louise E., contrib. by. LC 44-6288. 55 p. illus. 22 1/2 x 19 cm. 1944. Friendship Press.
--My Story Book about the Bible. N.D. Friendship Press.

Niedermeyer, Maud Wilcox
--Billy Boy's Sea Adventures. Tilgner, Helen, illus. N.D. A. L. Burt Co.
--Billy Boy's Sea Adventures. Tilgner, Helen, illus. LC 30-14695. 6 p. l., 145 p. col. front., illus. 21 cm. c.1930. G. Sully and Company, Inc.
--The Wonderful World of Make-Believe. Tilgner, Helen, illus. LC 29-7733. xii p., 1 l., 240 p. incl. illus., plates. col. front. 19 cm. c.1929. G. Sully & Company.

Niehardt, John G.
--The Splendid Wayfaring. N.D. Macmillan.

Niehuis, Charles Carroll (1907-)
--Beegee. LC 63-20496. 187 p. 21cm. 1963. Macrae Smith.
--Steel Dust. Toschik, Larry (1922-), illus. LC 59-6600. 267 p. illus. 21 cm. 1959. Dodd, Mead.
--Trapping the Silver Beaver. Kenyon, Chris A., illus. LC 56-5230. 208 p. illus. 22 cm. 1956. Dodd, Mead.

Nielsen-Barsuhn, Rochelle (1958-)
--Sometimes I Feel ... Connelly, Gwen, illus. LC 85-10351. p. cm. (A Book for Early Readers). c.1985. (ISBN 0-89693-228-1). Dandelion House.

Nielsen-Barsuhn, Rochelle & Moncure, Jane Belk (1926-)
--Fall. Monchaux, Marie-Claude, illus. LC 85-12817. p. cm. c.1985. (ISBN 0-89565-329-X). Child's World.

Nielsen, Billie, illus.
--Big Meeting Day and Other Festival Tales. 240p. (gr. 3-7). N.D. Aladdin Bks.

Nielsen, Harry A.
--Olaf and the Frump. Stuecklin, Karl W., illus. LC 74-78713. (Illus.). 63 p. 20cm. 1969. Doubleday.

Nielsen, Jean Sarver see Sarver, Hannah, pseud.

Nielsen, Jean Sarver (1922-)
--Because of Sheila. Sarver, Hannah, pseud. Chan, Eddie, illus. LC 64-17432. 151 p. illus. 21 cm. 1964. Funk & Wagnalls Co.
--Choose This Day. Sarver, Hannah, pseud. LC 59-8810. 245 p. 22cm. 1959. (ISBN 0-308-80086-9). Funk & Wagnalls.
--Fair Exchange. Sarver, Hannah, pseud. LC 57-10579. (Illus.). 278 p. 22cm. 1957. Funk & Wagnalls.
--The Golden Dream. Sarver, Hannah, pseud. LC 59-10895. 248 p. 22cm. 1959. Funk & Wagnalls.
--Green Eyes. Sarver, Hannah, pseud. Korach, Mimi (1922-), illus. LC 55-11100. (Illus.). 250 p. 22cm. 1955. Funk & Wagnalls.
--Halfpenny Linda. LC 63-15392. 185p. 21cm. 1963. Funk & Wagnalls.
--Island Exile. Sarver, Hannah, pseud. LC 56-10703. 250 p. 22cm. 1956. Funk & Wagnalls.
--Libby-Come-Lately. Sarver, Hannah, pseud. LC 60-127537. 246p. 22cm. 1960. Funk & Wagnalls.
--The Phantom Palomino. Sarver, Hannah, pseud. Donahue, Vic, illus. LC 66-12584. 126p. illus. 21cm. c.1966. Funk & Wagnalls.
--Redhead. Sarver, Hannah, pseud. LC 61-12966. 245 p. 22cm. 1961. Funk & Wagnalls Co.
--The Square Peg. Sarver, Hannah, pseud. LC 62-16175. 243p. 22cm. 1962. Funk & Wagnalls.
--Walk Under the Trees. Sarver, Hannah, pseud. LC 58-11502. 280 p. 22cm. 1958. Funk & Wagnalls.
--Where My Heart Is. Sarver, Hannah, pseud. LC 60-6428. 251 p. 22cm. 1960. Funk & Wagnalls.
--Where My Heart Is. Nielsen, Jean Sarver. Sarver, Hannah, pseud. (gr. 7-11). N.D. (ISBN 0-308-80195-4). Funk & W.

Nielsen, Jon, jt. auth. see Nielsen, Kay.

Nielsen, Kay Rasmus, jt. auth. see Andersen, Hans Christian.

Nielsen, Kay Rasmus (1886-1957), illus.
--Three Princesses in the Blue Mountains. 64p. 1975. (ISBN 0-915112-03-5). Seattle Bk.
--Three Princesses of Whiteland. 64p. 1975. (ISBN 0-915112-02-7). Seattle Bk.

Nielsen, Kay (1923-) & Nielsen, Jon (1912-), eds.
--The Wishing Pearl, and Other Tales of Vietnam. Nielsen, Jon (1912-), illus. Lam Chan Quan, tr. LC 69-17737. (Illus.). 47 p. 21x26 cm. 1969. Harvey House.

Nielsen, Martin
--Brownie Numbers Combine Work and Fun. Sauve, Philip & Wehn, James A., illus. LC 35-7443. 27 p., 1 l. illus. 35 cm. 1935. Farwest Lithograph & Printing Co.

Nielsen, Virginia, pseud., see McCall, Virginia Nielsen.

Nielsen, Virginia, pseud. (1909-)
--Adassa & Her Hen. McCall, Virginia Nielsen. Koering, Ursula (1921-), illus. (Illus.). (gr. 2-5). 1971. (ISBN 0-679-20000-2). (ISBN 0-679-25001-8). McKay.
--The House of Three Sisters. McCall, Virginia Nielsen. 176p. (Orig.). (gr. 7 up). 1982. (ISBN 0-590-32283-4, Windswept). Scholastic Inc.
--Keoni, My Brother. McCall, Virginia Nielsen. (gr. 9 up). 1965. (ISBN 0-679-20090-8). McKay.
--Kimo and Madame Pele: The Story of a Volcanic Eruption. McCall, Virginia Nielsen. Koering, Ursula (1921-), illus. LC 66-8458. 117p. illus. 22cm. 1966. (ISBN 0-679-20091-6). McKay.
--Mirror, Mirror. McCall, Virginia Nielsen. 160p. (Orig.). (gr. 7 up). 1983. (ISBN 0-590-32546-9, Windswept). Scholastic Inc.
--Mystery of Secret Town. McCall, Virginia Nielsen. LC 69-13783. (gr. 4-6). 1969. (ISBN 0-679-20125-4). (ISBN 0-679-25097-2). McKay.
--Road to the Valley. McCall, Virginia Nielsen. Earle, Vana (1917-), illus. (Illus.). (gr. 9-11). 1961. McKay.
--Weekend of Fear. McCall, Virginia Nielsen. 176p. (Orig.). (gr. 7 up). 1984. (ISBN 0-590-33253-8, Windswept Bks). Scholastic Inc.
--The Whistling Winds: A Novel for Young Adults. McCall, Virginia Nielsen. LC 63-16696. 152 p. 21 cm. 1965. D. McKay Co.

Nielson, Edith M., tr. see Hartmann, John.

Nielson, Jean Sarver see Sarver, Hannah, pseud.

Niemeier, Minnie A
--New Plays for Every Day the Schools Celebrate. LC 28-6115. vi, 243 p. illus. 21 cm. c.1928. Noble and Noble.
--New Plays for Every Day the Schools Celebrate. LC 29-9209. vii, 268 p. illus. 21 cm. c.1929. Noble and Noble.
--New Plays for Every Day the Schools Celebrate. enl. ed. LC 36-13053. viii, 382 p. illus. 21 cm. c.1936. Noble and Noble, Publishers, Inc.

Niemeyer, Marie
--The Moon Guitar. Nebel, Gustave E., illus. LC 69-11521. (Illus.). 151 p. 21cm. 1969. F. Watts.

Niemi, Matt, jt. auth. see Sharp, Mary.

Nieritz, Karl Gustav (1795-1876)
--Betty's Decision. Ireland, Mary Eliza Haines, Mrs. (1834-1927), tr. from Ger. LC 18-12002. iv, 5-145 p. 17 cm. (On cover: The Fatherland series). c.1886. Lutheran Publication Society.
--Christian Beck's Grandson. Ireland, Mary Eliza Haines, Mrs. (1834-1927), tr. from Ger. LC 12-34606. 232 p. 20 cm. 1894. Presbyterian Committee of Publication.
--Driven Out. Ireland, Mary Eliza Haines, Mrs. (1834-1927), tr. from Ger. LC 12-346077. 156 p. 19 cm. 1893. Presbyterian Committee of Publication.
--Erna, the Forest Princess: Or, Pilgrimage of the Three Wise Men to Bethlehem. Conant, H. C., tr. from Ger. N.D. Erastus Darrow.
--Her First and Only School Friend. Ireland, Mary Eliza Haines, Mrs. (1834-1927), tr. from Ger. LC 21-12958. 165 p. 17 cm. N.D. United Brethren Publishing Company.
--In Fair Silesia. Ireland, Mary Eliza Haines, Mrs. (1834-1927), tr. from Ger. LC 12-346046. 156 p. 20 cm. 1894. Presbyterian Committee of Publication.
--In the Days of Peter the Great: A True Story. Ireland, Mary Eliza Haines, Mrs. (1834-1927), tr. from Ger. LC 20-231651. iv, 5-135 p. 17 cm. 1902. United Brethren Publishing House.
--Lenchen's Brother and The Platzbacker of Plauen. Ireland, Mary Eliza Haines, Mrs. (1834-1927), tr. from Ger. LC 12-37240. 313 p. front., plates. 18 cm. c.1887. Presbyterian Board of Publication.
--The School on Luneburg Heath. Ireland, Mary Eliza Haines, Mrs. (1834-1927), tr. from Ger. LC 12-34605. 148 p. 20 cm. 1895. The Presbyterian Committee of Publication.
--The Shepherd's Family. Ireland, Mary Eliza Haines, Mrs. (1834-1927), tr. from Ger. LC 12-34603. 111 p. 19 cm. 1894. Presbyterian Committee of Publication.
--The Siberian Exile. Ireland, Mary Eliza Haines, Mrs. (1834-1927), tr. from Ger. LC 12-346021. 122 p. 19 cm. 1894. Presbyterian Committee of Publication.
--Stolen for Ransom. Ireland, Mary Eliza Haines, Mrs. (1834-1927), tr. from Ger. LC 21-414457. 138 p. 16 cm. 1901. United Brethren Publishing House.
--The Tall Man, No.76. (Illus.). (Lakeside Library Ser.). N.D. Donnelley, Loyd & Co.
--The Three Kings. Schively, Rebecca H., tr. from Ger. LC 12-37242. viii, 9-223 p. front., 2 pl. 17 cm. (Added t.-p.: The fatherland series). 1871. Lutheran Board of Publication.

Nieritz, Karl Gustav (1795-1876) & Franz, Agnes (1794-1843)
--The Bears of Augustusburg: An Episode in Saxon History. Trauermantel, tr. from Ger. LC 42-436118. 3 p. l., 3-251 p. col. front., col. plates. 17 1/2 cm. 1859. Crosby, Nichols, & Co.

Niggli, Josephina
--A Miracle for Mexico. Hidalgo, Alejandro Rangel, illus. LC 64-14893. (Illus.). 179 p. 25cm. 1964. New York Graphic Society Publishers.

Nightingale, Agnes
--Nursery Rhymes. N.D. Macmillan.

Nightingale, Charles Thrupp (1878-) & Nightingale, Madeline (1879-)
--Roundabout Tabitha. (Roundabout Ser.). N.D. D. Appleton & Co.

Nightingale, Madeline, jt. auth. see Nightingale, Charles Thrupp.

Niizaka, Kazuo (1943-)
--Clouds. Niizaka, Kazuo (1943-), illus. LC 74-19155. (Illus.). 24p. 1st U.S. edition. (gr. k-3). 1975. (ISBN 0-201-00574-3, A-W Childrens). A-W.

Nikanov, Fedor, tr. see Tolstoy, Aleksei Nikolaevich.

Niklaus, Thelma, tr. see Cervon, Jacqueline.

Niklaus, Thelma, tr. see Peyrouton De Ladebat, Monique.

Niklaus, Thelma Jones (1912-), tr. see Bonzon, Paul-Jacques.

Niklaus, Thomas, tr. see Baudouy, Michel Aime.

Niklewiczowa, Maria
--Sparrow's Magic. Yamanaka, Fuyuji, illus. Tresselt, Alvin R. (1916-), tr. LC 73-99583. (Japanese). (Illus.). 4 color ils. Orig. Title: Suzume No Mahou. (gr. k-3). 1970. (ISBN 0-8193-0412-3, Four Winds). (ISBN 0-8193-0413-1). Scholastic Inc.
Nikly, Michelle
--The Emperor's Plum Tree. LC 82-902. (Illus.). 24 p. 30cm. 1982. (ISBN 0-688-01243-4). (ISBN 0-688-01244-2). Greenwillow Books.
--The Princess on the Nut: Or, the Curious Courtship of the Son of the Princess of the Pea. Claverie, Jean (1946-), illus. Meredith, Lucy, tr. from Ger. LC 82-70025. (Illus.). 24 p. 29cm. 1981. (ISBN 0-571-11846-1). Faber and Faber.
Niland, Deborah (1951-)
--ABC of Monsters. LC 78-7939. p. cm. 1978. (ISBN 0-07-046560-6). McGraw-Hill.
Niles, John Jacob, jt. auth. see Niles, Rena.
Niles, John Jacob (1892-1980)
--Rhymes for A. Wince. Bruer, John Michael, illus. Kentucky University Libraries. Dept. of Special Collections. LC 78-29865. (Illus.). 20 p. 16cm. 1971. Margaret I. King Library, Dept. of Special Collections.
Niles, Katherine (1899-)
--The Angel in the Hayloft. Merwin, Decie (1894-1961), illus. Littell, Robert, frwd. by. LC 54-8868. 60p. illus. 18cm. 1954. Dutton.
Niles, M. E., tr. see Bjoernson, Bjoernstjerne Martinius.
Niles, Rena & Niles, John Jacob (1892-)
--Mr. Poof's Discovery. McDonald, Harriet, illus LC 47-12477. (Illus.). 17p. 21cm. 1947. Bur Press.
Nilsson, Betty
--Elsa's Mission Contribution, and Three Other Missionary Stories. LC 23-13109. 128 p. incl. front., plates. 18cm. c.1923. Augustana Book Concern.
Nims, Bonnie
--Always at Home: The Story of Seashells. 1790. (ISBN 0-8382-1050-3, Hale House Bks.). E. M. Hale and Company.
--I Wished I Lived at the Playground: Yo Quisiera Vivir En un Parque De Juegos. Orellana, Ramon F., illus. Orellana, Ramon S., tr. LC 79-186886. (Illus.). 64p. 1st U.S. edition. (ps-3). 1972. (ISBN 0-87955-200-X). (ISBN 0-87955-800-8). O'Hara.
Nims, Clara Felt
--Cowboys and Roundups. Gauss, Charlotte Wilhelmina (1891-), illus. LC 36-10945. (Illus.). 144p. 22cm. (Junior Press Bks.). 1936. A.Whitman & Co.
Nina, pseud., see Nelson, Ethel.
Nina, pseud.
--The Kitten's Surprise. Nelson, Ethel. Rojankovsky, Feodor Stepanovich (1891-1970), illus. LC 51-40028. unpaged. illus. 21 cm. (Little Golden-Library, 107). 1951. Simon and Schuster.
Nindorf, Quentin C.
--The Williwaw Cubs. Jordan, John, illus. LC 56-5171. 179p. illus. 21cm. 1956. Dodd, Mead.
Ninon, pseud., see MacKnight, Ninon.
Nipote, Collodi, pseud., see Lorenzini, Paolo.
Nipp, Susan, jt. auth. see Beall, Pamela.
Nirdlinger, Daisy Ella
--Althea: Or, The Children of Rosemont Plantation. LC 8-11706. 205 p. front. 19 cm. 1908. Benziger Brothers.
--Dear Friends. N.D. Benziger Bros.
Nirodi, Hira (1930-)
--Chikka. McMillan, Constance (1949-), illus. LC 62-16307. (Illus.). 154p. 21cm. 1962. Reilly & Lee.
Nishimaki, Kayako & Nakamura, Shigeo
--The Land of Lost Buttons. Nishimaki, Kayako, illus. Tresselt, Alvin R. (1916-), tr. LC 71-99135. (Illus.). 40 p. 1970. (ISBN 0-8193-0410-7). Parents' Magazine Press.
Nishizaki, Ichiro, ed. see Hearn, Lafcadio.
Nissen, Betty B
--Sam on the Jolly Blue. Oechsli, Kelly (1918-), illus. LC 68-23672. (Illus.). 48 p. 27cm. 1968. Random House.
Nist, Al, jt. auth. see Jameson, Mack.
Nister, Ernest
--Animal Tales. Nister, Ernest, illus. (Illus.). N.D. (ISBN 0-399-20801-1, Philomel). Putnam Pub Group.
--Animal Tales: A Reproduction from an Antique Book. LC 80-10199. (Illus.). 10 p. 1980. (ISBN 0-529-05612-7). Collins.
--The Children's Picture Book: A Reproduction from an Antique Book. LC 80-7613. (Illus.). 16 p. 26cm. c.1980. (ISBN 0-440-01540-5). Delacorte Press.
--Land of Sweet Surprises: A Revolving Picture Book. LC 83-4082. (A Reproduction from and Antique Book). c.1983. (ISBN 0-399-20993-X). Philomel Books.
--Little Tales from Long Ago. Nister, Ernest, illus. LC 79-87798. (Illus.). 1979. Boxed Set. Delacorte.
--Magic Windows: A Revolving Picture Book. LC 80-20821. p. cm. 1981. (ISBN 0-399-20773-2). Philomel Books.
--Merry Magic-Go-Round: A Reproduction of an Antique Book of Changing Pictures. LC 82-13243. (Illus.). 12 p. 24cm. 1983, c.1982. (ISBN 0-399-20946-8). Philomel Books.
--Playtime Surprises with Reproductions of Antique Changing Pictures. LC 84-16579. (Illus.). 12 p. 25cm. c.1985. (ISBN 0-399-21214-0). Philomel Books.
--Revolving Pictures: A Reproduction from an Antique Book. LC 79-12438. p. cm. 1979. (ISBN 0-529-05551-1). Collins.
Nister, Ernest & Bingham, Clifton
--Revolving Pictures. LC 79-12438. (Illus.). (ps-4). 1979. (ISBN 0-399-20802-X, Philomel). Putnam Pub Group.
Nitzsche, Elsa Koenig, Mrs. (1880-)
--Dickel and the Penguin. LC 24-25554. 32 p. col. illus. 32 cm. 1924. The Stratford Company.
Nivedita, Sr., jt. auth. see Coomaraswamy, Ananda Kentish.
Niven, Larry & Pournelle, Jerry
--The Mote in God's Eye. 576p. 1974. (ISBN 0-671-21833-6). S&S.
Niven, Laurence Van Cott, jt. auth. see Gerrold, David.
Nivola, Ruth
--The Messy Rabbit. Nivola, Claire, illus. LC 78-6018. p. cm. 1978. (ISBN 0-394-83764-9). (ISBN 0-394-93764-3). Pantheon Books.
Niwa, Tamako, tr. see Tsugawa, Shuichi.
Nix, Marguerite Obets
--What the Little Fairy Saw. 1st ed. Kilgore, Al, illus. LC 53-111817. unpaged. illus. 16x24cm. 1953. Pageant Press.
Nixon, Joan Lowery (1927-)
--The Adventures of the Red Tape Gang. 144p (Pub. by Putnam). (gr. 3-6). 1983. (ISBN 0-590-31761-X). Scholastic Inc.
--The Alligator Under the Bed. Hughes, Jan, illus. LC 72-94263. (Illus.). 32 p. 1974. (ISBN 0-399-60914-8). (ISBN 0-399-20423-7). (ISBN 0-399-60914-8). Putnam.
--The April Fool Mystery. Cummins, James (1914-), illus. LC 80-18809. p. cm. (First read-alone mystery). 1980. (ISBN 0-8075-0406-8). A. Whitman.
--Bigfoot Makes a Movie. Hoff, Sydney (1912-), illus. LC 78-31106. (Illus.). 48 p. 24cm. 1979. (ISBN 0-399-20684-1). Putnam.
--The Boy Who Could Find Anything. Hoff, Sydney (1912-), illus. LC 77-15061. (Illus.). 64 p. 22cm. (Let me read book). c.1978. (ISBN 0-15-210697-9). (ISBN 0-15-613748-8). Harcourt Brace Jovanovich.
--The Butterfly Tree. McIlrath, James, illus. LC 78-71264. (Illus.). 30 p. 29cm. (OSV Read-along Bk.). c.1979. (ISBN 0-87973-355-1). Our Sunday Visitor.
--Casey and the Great Idea. Rowen, Amy, illus. LC 80-13617. (Illus.). 136 p. 22cm. c.1980. Dutton.
--Casey and the Great Idea. Rowen, Amy, illus. (gr. 5-7). 1980. Scholastic.
--The Christmas Eve Mystery. Cummins, James (1914-), illus. LC 81-345. (Illus.). 32 p. 21cm. (First read-alone mysteries). c.1981. (ISBN 0-8075-1150-1). A. Whitman.
--Danger in Dinosaur Valley. Simont, Marc (1915-), illus. LC 77-6397. p. 23 cm. 47p. c.1978. (ISBN 0-399-61109-6). Putnam.
--Days of Fear. Wallner, John C. (1945-), illus. Menschenfreund, Joan, photos by. LC 81-12655. p. cm. (Skinny Bk.). c.1983. (ISBN 0-525-45106-4). Dutton.
--A Deadly Game of Magic. 1st ed. LC 83-8379. 148 p. 22cm. c.1983. (ISBN 0-15-222954-X). Harcourt Brace Jovanovich.
--Delbert, the Plainclothes Detective. Smith, Philip (1936-), illus. LC 71-134564. (Illus.). 89 p. 24cm. 1971. (ISBN 0-200-71787-1). Criterion Books.
--The Easter Mystery. Cummins, James (1914-), illus. LC 81-13011. p. cm. (First Read-Alone Mysteries). 1981. (ISBN 0-8075-1874-3). Whitman.
--Five Loaves & Two Fishes. Van Woerkom, Dorothy O'Brien (1924-), ed. Cunningham, Aline, illus. LC 76-15288. (Illus.). 48p. (I Can Read a Bible Story Ser.). (gr. 1-3). 1976. (ISBN 0-570-07311-1). Concordia.
--The Ghosts of Now: A Novel of Psychological Suspense. LC 84-4007. (gr. 7 up). 1984. (ISBN 0-385-29349-6). Delacorte.
--The Gift. Glass, Andrew, illus. LC 82-17994. p. cm. 1983, c.1982. (ISBN 0-02-768160-2). Macmillan.
--Gloria Chipmunk, Star!. Dawson, Diane, illus. LC 79-23431. (Illus.). 48 p. 21cm. c.1980. (ISBN 0-395-29103-8). Houghton Mifflin/Clarion Books.
--The Halloween Mystery. Cummins, James (1914-), illus. LC 79-166. (Illus.). 32 p. 21cm. (First Read-alone Mysteries). 1979. (ISBN 0-8075-3136-7). A. Whitman.
--The Halloween Mystery. Cummins, James (1914-), illus. LC 81-8768. p. cm. 1981, c.1979. (ISBN 0-671-42543-9). Simon & Schuster.
--The Happy Birthday Mystery. Cummins, James (1914-), illus. LC 79-18362. p. cm. (First Read-alone Mysteries). 1979. (ISBN 0-8075-3150-2). A. Whitman.
--The Happy Birthday Mystery. Cummins, James (1914-), illus. LC 81-8168. p. cm. (First Read-Alone Mysteries). 1981, c.1979. (ISBN 0-671-42546-3). Little Simon.
--If You Say So, Claude. Cauley, Lorinda Bryan (1951-), illus. LC 80-12254. p. cm. 1980. (ISBN 0-7232-6163-0). F. Warne.
--Kidnapped on Astarr. Frame, Paul (1913-), illus. LC 80-11740. p. cm. 1980. (ISBN 0-8116-7450-9). Garrard Pub. Co.
--The Kidnapping of Christina Lattimore. LC 78-20570. 179 p. 21cm. c.1979. (ISBN 0-15-242657-4). Harcourt Brace Jovanovich.
--Maggie, Too. LC 84-19766. 101 p. 24cm. c.1985. (ISBN 0-15-250350-1). Harcourt Brace Jovanovich.
--Magnolia's Mixed-up Magic. Bucholtz-Ross, Linda (1946-), illus. LC 82-16684. p. cm. 1983. (ISBN 0-399-20956-5). Putnam.
Muffie & the Birthday Party. (ps-3). 1980. (ISBN 0-590-30064-4). Scholastic Inc.
--Muffie Mouse and the Busy Birthday. Hayes, Geoffrey (1947-), illus. LC 77-28866. p. cm. c.1978. (ISBN 0-8164-3213-9). Seabury Press.
--The Mysterious Prowler. 1st ed. Amoss, Berthe (1925-), illus. LC 75-29314. (Illus.). 61 p. 22cm. (Let me read book). c.1976. (ISBN 0-15-256355-5). (ISBN 0-15-256356-3). Harcourt Brace Jovanovich.
--The Mysterious Queen of Magic. Frame, Paul (1913-), illus. LC 80-21845. p. cm. (Her Kleep, Space Detective). 1981. Garrard Pub. Co.
--The Mysterious Red Tape Gang. Sandin, Joan (1942-), illus. LC 73-87218. (Illus.). 159 p. 21cm. 1974. Putnam.
--Mystery Dolls from Planet Urd. Frame, Paul (1913-), illus. LC 81-5098. (Illus.). 64 p. 23cm. (Kleep, Space Detective). c.1981. (ISBN 0-8116-7452-5). Gerrard Pub. Co.
--Mystery of Hurricane Castle. Ilsley, Velma Elizabeth (1918-), illus. LC 64-13731. 144 p. illus. 22 cm. 1964. Criterion Books.
--The Mystery of the Grinning Idol. Smith, Alvin (1933-), illus. LC 65-15260. 127p. illus. 21cm. c.1965. Criterion.
--Mystery of the Haunted Woods. Brudi, Theresa, illus. LC 67-23453. (Illus.). 144 p. 21cm. 1967. Criterion Books.
--Mystery of the Hidden Cockatoo. Lewis, Richard William (1933-1966), illus. LC 66-23738. (Illus.). 144 p. 22cm. (Criterion Book for Young People). 1966. Criterion Books.
--Mystery of the Secret Stowaway. Drescher, Joan Elizabeth (1939-), illus. LC 68-15236. (Illus.). 128 p. 22cm. 1968. Criterion Books.
--The New Year's Mystery. Cummins, James (1914-), illus. LC 79-172. (Illus.). 31 p. 21cm. (First Read-alone Mysteries). 1979. (ISBN 0-8075-5592-4). A. Whitman.
--The Seance. LC 79-90031. 142 p. 21cm. c.1980. (ISBN 0-15-271158-9). Harcourt Brace Jovanovich.
--The Secret Box Mystery. Grant, Alice Leigh (1947-), illus. LC 73-84469. (Illus.). 45 p. 23cm. 1974. (ISBN 0-399-20380-X). (ISBN 0-399-20380-X). Putnam.
--The Son Who Came Home Again. (Illus.). 48p. (I Can Read a Bible Story Ser.: No. 2). (gr. 2-4). 1977. (ISBN 0-570-07323-5). (ISBN 0-570-07317-0). Concordia.
--The Specter. LC 82-70322. 184 p. 22cm. c.1982. (ISBN 0-440-08063-0). Delacorte Press.
--The Stalker. LC 84-16962. 180 p. 22cm. c.1985. (ISBN 0-385-29376-3). Delacorte.
--The Thanksgiving Mystery. Cummins, James (1914-), illus. LC 79-27346. (Illus.). 32 p. 21cm. (First Read-alone Mysteries). c.1980. (ISBN 0-8075-7820-7). A. Whitman.
--The Thanksgiving Mystery. Cummins, James (1914-), illus. LC 81-8192. p. cm. (First read-alone mysteries). 1981. (ISBN 0-671-42544-7). Little Simon.
--The Valentine Mystery. Cummins, James (1914-), illus. LC 79-17055. p. cm. (First Read-alone Mysteries). 1979. (ISBN 0-8075-8450-9). A. Whitman.
--The Valentine Mystery. Cummins, James (1914-), illus. LC 81-8226. p. cm. (First Read-Alone Mysteries). 1981. (ISBN 0-671-44422-0). Little Simon.

Nixon, Kathleen Irene Blundell see Nixon, K., pseud.

Nixon, K., pseud., see Nixon, Kathleen Irene Blundell.

Nixon, Kathleen Irene Blundell
--Bushy Tail Family. Nixon, K., pseud. LC 64-10130. (Illus.). (gr. 1-3). 1964. (ISBN 0-7232-0405-5). Warne.
--Pindi Poo. Nixon, K., pseud. Nixon, Kathleen Irene Blundell, illus. LC 57-12978. (Illus.). unpaged. illus. 22cm. 1957. F. Warne.
--Pindi Poo. Nixon, K., pseud. Nixon, Kathleen Irene Blundell, illus. Nixon, K., pseud. (Illus.). (gr. 1-3). 1959. (ISBN 0-7232-0402-0). Warne.
--Poo & Pushti. (Illus.). (gr. 1-3). 1959. (ISBN 0-7232-0404-7). Warne.
--Poo Pushti. Nixon, K., pseud. Nixon, Kathleen Irene Blundell, illus. LC 59-11982. unpaged. illus. 22cm. c.1959. F. Warne.
--Pushti. Nixon, Kathleen Irene Blundell, illus. LC 57-422. unpaged. illus. 22cm. 1956. F. Warne.
Strange Animal Friendships. Nixon, K., pseud. Nixon, Kathleen Irene Blundell, illus. Nixon, K., pseud. LC 68-10152. 40p. illus. (pt. col.) 23x26cm. c.1967. Warne.
Nixon, Kathleen Irene Blundell, retold by.
--Animal Legends. Nixon, Kathleen Irene Blundell, illus. LC 66-10486. 56p. illus. (pt. col.) 24x26cm. 1966. (ISBN 0-7232-0407-1). Warne.
Animals and Birds in Folklore. Nixon, K., pscud. Nixon, Kathlcen Irene Blundell, illus. Nixon, K., pseud. LC 77-91866. (Illus.). 41p. 23 x 26cm. 1969. (ISBN 0-7232-1099-3), F. Warne.
Nixon, Lucille M. (1908-1963)
--Young Ranchers at Oak Valley. 1st ed. Litton, Martin & Coleberd, Frances, illus. LC 60-8354. 63p. illus. 24cm. (Sunset junior book). 1960. Lane Book Co.
Nixon-Roulet, Mary F.
--The Little Marshalls at the Lake. N.D. Benziger Bros.
--Seven Little Marshalls. N.D. Benziger Bros.
Nixon-Roulet, Mary F. & Taggart, Marion Ames
--The Trail of the Dragon, and Other Stories. LC 6-35448. 256p. 1906. Benziger Bros.
Nixon, Vesta Tharp
--The White Cat. Shonkweiler, J. H., illus. LC 23-17556. 119 p. incl. front., illus., 21 cm. 1923. The Standard Publishing Company.

Njala see Treece, Henry.

Njala (1870-)
--Heroes of Iceland. French, Allen (1870-), intro. by. French, Allen, pref. by. (Adapted from Dasent's Translation of "The Story of Burnt Njal", the Great Icelandic Saga.). 297p. front., 3 pl. 19 1/2cm. 1905. Little Brown.
Noa, Henrietta
--Plays for the Kindergarten. Richter, Charles John, contrib. by. N.D. E Steiger, New York.
Noa, Henrietta, jt. auth. see Richter, Charles John.
Noad, Frederick
--The Guitar Songbook. (Illus.). (gr. 7 up). 1969. (ISBN 0-02-080980-8, Collier). Macmillan.
Nobens, C. A
--The Happy Baker. LC 79-88198. (Illus.). 47 p. 23cm. (On My Own Books). c.1979. (ISBN 0-87614-109-2). Carolrhoda Books.
Noble, Annette Lucile, jt. auth. see Keeney, Ella Beckwith, Mrs.
Noble, Annette Lucile (1844-1932)
--After the Failure;. Or, A Loss and A Gain. LC 7-33159. 336P. 18cm. 1887. Presbyterian Board of Publication and Sabbath-School Work.
--Dave Marquand. LC 7-33158. 357p. 19cm. 1886. The National Temperance Society and Publication House.
--Eleanor Willoughby's Self. (Illus.). 300p. N.D. A. I. Bradley & Co.'s Pub.
--Elsie's Miracle, 1 of 4 Vols. Penney, L., ed. 72p. (The Never-Begin Series). N.D. Per set in box 3.00. National Temperance Society.
--Eugene's Quest. LC 6-32859. 308 p. front., plates. 19 cm. c.1906. American Tract Society.
--How Billy Went up in the World. A Story for Boys. LC 7-333434. 396 p. front. 18 cm. 1883. National Temperance Society and Publication House.
--Jacob's Heiress. LC 7-33342. 310 p. 18 cm. c.1894. Presbyterian Board of Publication and Sabbath-School Work.
--Little Pilgrims' Pets. LC 7-33340. 64 p. illus. 18 cm. (On cover: Little pilgrim library). c.1896. American Tract Society.
--Little Pilgrims' Pets, 1 of 6 vols. (Illus.). (The Little Pilgrim Library). 1905. Set. American Tract Society.
--Miss Janet's Old House. LC 7-33339. 428 p. front. 18 cm. 1884. National Temperance Society and Publication House.
--Miss Roberts' Lodgers: A Little Welsh Town. LC 7-33338. 315 p. front. 20 cm. 1892. The National Temperance Society and Publication House.
--The Professor's Girls. LC 7-33337. 384 p. front., plates. 18 cm. c.1885. Presbyterian Board of Publication.

--The Queer Home in Rugby Court. LC 7-33336. 450 p. 18 cm. 1878. National Temperance Society and Publication House.
--Rachel's Farm. LC 7-33334. 223 p. front., plates. 19 cm. c.1894. American Tract Society.
--The Sailor Boy. LC 7-33335. 64 p. illus. 18 cm. (On cover: Little pilgrim library). c.1896. American Tract Society.
--The Sailor Boy, 1 of 6 vols. (Illus.). (Little Pilgrim Library). 1905. Set. American Tract Society.
--Silas Gower's Daughters. LC 7-33157. 320 p. front., plates. 18 cm. 1878. Presbyterian Board of Publication.
--The Silent Man's Legacy. LC 7-33156. 379 p. front., plates. 18 cm. c.1888. Presbyterian Board of Publication and Sabbath-School Work.
--St. Augustine's Ladder. LC 7-33341. 441 p. front. 18 cm. 1873. D. Lothrop & Co.
--St. Augustine's Ladder, 1 of 4 Vols. (Annie Maylie Ser.). N.D. Set. D Lothrop & Co.
--Tarryport School-Girls. LC 7-33344. 272 p. front., plates. 18 cm. c.1882. American Tract Society.
--Tarryport School-Girls. (Illus.). (Sunday-Hour Lib.). 1882. American Tract Society.
--Under Shelter. LC 7-33345. 208 p. front., plates. 18 cm. c.1876. American Tract Society.
--Under Shelter, 1 of 50 vols. (Library of Best Authors). 1905. Set. American Tract Society.

Noble, Annette Lucile (1844-1932) & Hunter, E. A.
--Between-Times Stories, 1 of 4 vols. (Illus.). (Cosey Corner Stories). 1905. Set. American Tract Society.
--Cosey Corner Stories, 4 Vols. (Illus.). 1905. American Tract Society.
--Fido and His Friends, 1 of 4 Vols. (Illus.). (Cosey Corner Stories). 1905. American Tract Society.
--Fireside Stories, 1 of 4 vols. (Illus.). (Cosey Corner Stories). 1905. Set. American Tract Society.
--Home Favorites, 1 of 4 vols. (Illus.). (Cosey Corner Stories). 1905. Set. American Tract Society.

Noble , Emily, pseud.
--Sue Andrews, Career Girl. Gifford, James Noble. Noble, Emmily, pseud. LC 57-9400. 220p. 20cm. 1957. Arcadia House.

Noble, Gurre Ploner (1902-)
--Gwendolyn, the Hawaiian Water Buffalo. Schubert, Mel, illus. LC 48-15207. (Illus.). 29p. 29cm. 1947. K. Stone.

Noble, Iris Davis (1922-)
--Courage in Her Hands. LC 67-21625. 190 p. 22cm. 1967. J. Messner.
--Megan. LC 65-12961. 192 p. 21cm. 1965. J. Messner.
--One Golden Summer. LC 59-12766. 191 p. 22cm. 1959. Messner.
--Stranger No More. LC 61-13825. 190 p. 22cm. 1961. J. Messner.
--The Tender Promise. LC 62-16678. 192 p. 22cm. 1962. Messner.

Noble, June (1979-)
--Two Homes for Lynn. Salzman, Yuri, illus. LC 78-14090. (Illus.). 32 p. 24cm. c.1979. (ISBN 0-03-046186-3). Holt, Rinehart and Winston.
--Where Do I Fit in?. Salzman, Yuri, illus. LC 79-1073. (Illus.). 32 p. 24cm. c.1981. (ISBN 0-03-046181-2). Holt, Rinehart and Winston.

Noble, Margaret Elizabeth see Sister Nivedita, pseud.

Noble, Margaret Elizabeth (1867-1911), ed.
--Cradle Tales of Hinduism. Sister Nivedita, pseud. LC 8-13677. xv, 343 p. front. 20 cm. 1907. Longmans, Green, and Co.
--Cradle Tales of Hinduism. Sister Nivedita, pseud. (Illus.). 329p. (gr. 3-12). 1972. (ISBN 0-87481-170-8). (ISBN 0-87481-131-7). Vedanta Pr.
--A Selection from Cradle Tales of Hinduism. Sister Nivedita, pseud. LC 53-25467. vi, 112p. 19cm. 1945. Longmans, Green.

Noble, Olivette
--The Mouse Cradle. 1981. (ISBN 0-8062-1818-5). Carlton.

Noble, T. Tertius, jt. ed. see Sewell, Helen Moore.

Noble, Thomas Tertius (1867-), compiled by.
--A Round of Carols. Sewell, Helen Moore (1896-1957), illus. N.D. Henry Z. Walck Inc.

Noble, Trinka Hakes
--Apple Tree Christmas. Noble, Trinka Hakes, illus. LC 84-1901. (Illus.). 32p. (ps-2). 1984. (ISBN 0-8037-0102-0). Dial Bks Young.
--The Day Jimmy's Boa Ate the Wash. Kellogg, Steven (1941-), illus. LC 80-15098. p. cm. c.1980. (ISBN 0-8037-1723-7). (ISBN 0-8037-1724-5). Dial Press. Award: (ALA).
--Hansy's Mermaid. Noble, Trinka Hakes, illus. LC 82-45509. (Illus.). 31 p. 28cm. c.1983. (ISBN 0-8037-3605-3). (ISBN 0-8037-3606-1). Dial Press.
--Jimmy's Boa Bounces Back. Kellogg, Steven (1941-), illus. LC 83-14289. 1984. (ISBN 0-8037-0049-0). (ISBN 0-8037-0050-4). Dial.
--The King's Tea. Noble, Trinka Hakes, illus. LC 79-50749. (Illus.). 32 p. c.1979. (ISBN 0-8037-4529-X). (ISBN 0-8037-4530-3). Dial Press.

Nobokov, Vladimir
--The Gift. 384p. 1963. G P Putnam's Sons.

Noboru, Baba
--Eleven Hungry Cats. Noboru, Baba, illus. 48p. 1970. (ISBN 0-8193-0375-5). Parents' Magazine Press.

Noda, Phyllis, jt. auth. see Ganz, Barbara.

Nodier, Charles (1780-1844)
--Trilby: The Fairy of Argyle. Smith, Minna Caroline (1860-1929), tr. from Fr. N.D. Frederick Stokes Co.
--Trilby: The Fairy of Argyle. Smith, Minna Caroline (1860-1929), tr. from Fr. LC 44-306355. 4 p. l., 111, 1 p. 17 cm. 1895. Lamson, Wolffe and Company.

Nodset, Joan L., pseud., see Lexau, Joan M..

Nodset, Joan L., pseud.
--Come Here, Cat. Lexau, Joan M.. Kellogg, Steven (1941-), illus. LC 72-9858. (Illus.). 32p. (ps-3). 1973. (ISBN 0-06-024558-1, HarpJ). (ISBN 0-06-024558-1). Har-Row.
--Come Here, Cat. Lexau, Joan M.. Kellogg, Steven (1941-), illus. LC 73-162019. (Illus.). 32 p. 16cm. 1973. (ISBN 0-06-023869-0). Harper & Row.
--Go Away, Dog. Lexau, Joan M.. (Illus.). (gr. k-2). 1963. (ISBN 0-8382-0292-6). Hale.
--Go Away Dog. Lexau, Joan M.. Bonsall, Crosby Barbara Newell (1921-), illus. LC 63-11162. 1 v. (unpaged) illus. 16 cm. (gr. k-3). 1963. Harper & Row.
--Go Away, Dog. Lexau, Joan M.. Bonsall, Crosby Barbara Newell (1921-), illus. (Illus., Pub. by Har-Row). (gr. k-3). 1972. (ISBN 0-590-09301-0, Schol Pap). Scholastic Inc.
--Where Do You Go When You Run Away. Lexau, Joan M.. (gr. k-3). 1964. (ISBN 0-672-50574-6). Bobbs.
--Who Took the Farmer's Hat. Lexau, Joan M.. (gr. k-2). 1963. (ISBN 0-8382-0949-1). Hale.
--Who Took the Farmer's Hat. Lexau, Joan M.. Siebel, Fritz (1913-), illus. LC 62-17964. (Illus.). 18cm. 31p. (gr. k-3). 1963. (ISBN 0-06-024566-2, HarpJ). Har-Row.
--Who Took the Farmer's Hat?. Lexau, Joan M.. Siebel, Fritz (1913-), illus. 32p. (gr. k-3). 1970. (ISBN 0-590-02950-9). Scholastic Inc.

Noe, Tom
--The Sixth Day. McKissack, Vernon, illus. LC 79-55296. (Illus.). 77 p. c.1979. (ISBN 0-87793-190-9). Ave Maria Press.

Noel, Bernard (1930-), adapted by.
--Sindbad the Sailor. Le Foll, Alain, illus. Smith, C. Ross, tr. LC 79-185306. (Illus.). 31 p. 27cm. 1972. Good Book, Inc.; Distributed by Doubleday, Garden City, N.Y.

Noel, Sybille Graham, Mrs., ed.
--The Magic Bird of Chomo-Lung-Ma: Tales of Mount Everest, the Turquoise Peak. Avinoff, Andry (1884-), illus. LC 31-336821. 5 p. l., 310 p. front., illus., plates. 24 cm. 1931. Doubleday, Doran & Company, Inc.

Noella, Lucia
--Grandpa & the Ghost Dog. (Illus.). 48p. 1984. (ISBN 0-89962-345-X). Todd & Honeywell.

Nofziger, Edward C. (1913-)
--Krazy Kangaroo Kartoons. (gr. 7 up). 1977. (ISBN 0-590-11867-6, Schol Pap). Scholastic Inc.
--Shorty. LC 41-120283. 35 p. col. illus. 26 x 25 cm. 1941. Simon and Schuster.

Noguere, Suzanne (1947-)
--Little Raccoon. Chen, Tony (1929-), illus. LC 80-26171. (Illus.). 32p. (gr. k-3). 1981. (ISBN 0-03-054826-8). HR&W.

Nohelty, Sally, ed.
--Eleven and Three Are Poetry. Oechsli, Kelly (1918-), illus. LC 64-12023. 1 v. (unpaged) col. illus. 17x24cm. (Young Owl Bk.). 1964. Holt.

Nohelty, Sally, jt. ed. see Jacobs, Leland Blair.

Nolan, Aretas Wilbur (1874-), ed.
--Short Stories for Future Farmers. LC 37-7085. 307 p. illus. 19 1/2 cm. 1936. The Interstate Printers and Publishers.

Nolan, Dennis
--Alphabrutes. LC 76-45439. (Illus.). 32 p. 24cm. c.1977. (ISBN 0-13-022822-2). Prentice-Hall.
--Big Pig. LC 75-35694. p. cm. c.1976. (ISBN 0-13-076158-3). Prentice-Hall.
--Monster Bubbles: A Counting Book. LC 76-10167. (Illus.). 32 p. 24cm. c.1976. (ISBN 0-13-600635-3). Prentice-Hall.
--Witch Bazooza. LC 79-12715. p. cm. c.1979. (ISBN 0-13-961573-3). Prentice-Hall.
--Wizard McBean and His Flying Machine. LC 77-3472. p. cm. 32p. c.1977. (ISBN 0-13-961607-1). Prentice-Hall.

Nolan, Frederick W., tr. see Goscinny, Rene.

Nolan, Jeannette Covert, Mrs. (1896-1974)
--Abraham Lincoln. Ames, Lee Judah (1921-), illus. LC 53-807586. 182p. illus. 22cm. 1953. J. Messner.
--Andrew Jackson. Ames, Lee Judah (1921-), illus. LC 49-8105. (Illus.). 178p. 22cm. 1949. J. Messner.
--Barry Barton's Mystery. Gardner, Mary Ponton, illus. LC 32-21668. 211 p. front., plates. 20 cm. 1932. R. M. McBride & Company.
--Belle Boyd, Secret Agent. LC 67-21613. 191 p. 22cm. 1967. Messner.
--Benedict Arnold, Traitor to His Country. LC 56-104525. 190p. 22cm. 1956. J. Messner.
--Dolley Madison. LC 58-11079. 192p. 22cm. 1958. Messner.
--The Gay Poet: The Story of Eugene Field. Robison, Robert S., illus. LC 40-27767. 7 p. l., 3-230 p. incl. front., illus., plates. 24 cm. c.1940. J. Messner, Inc.
--George Rogers Clark, Soldier and Hero, November 19, 1752--February 13, 1818. Ames, Lee Judah (1921-), illus. LC 54-10592. 190p. illus. 22cm. 1954. J. Messner.
--Hobnailed Boots. Hargens, Charles, Jr. (1893-), illus. LC 39-21780. xi, 187 p. col. front., illus. 23 cm. c.1939. The John C. Winston Company.
--James Whitcomb Riley: Hoosier Poet. Robison, Robert S., illus. LC 41-19422. xvi p., 2 l., 3-265 p. incl. illus., plates. front. 24 cm. c.1941. J. Messner, Inc.
--LaSalle and the Grand Enterprise. LC 51-12789. 178 p. illus. 22 cm. 1951. Messner.
--O. Henry: The Story of William Sydney Porter. Greene, Hamilton, illus. LC 43-17447. vii, 263 p. illus. 22 cm. 1943. J. Messner, Inc.
--Patriot in the Saddle. Annand, George, illus. LC 45-6200. 239 p. illus. 21 cm. 1945. J. Messner, Inc.
--Red Hugh of Ireland. Bennett, Richard Michael (1899-), illus. LC 38-32009. 4 p. l., 3-250 p. illus. 21 cm. 1938. Harper & Brothers.
--The Story of Joan of Arc. Meadowcroft, Enid La Monte, Mrs. (1898-1966) & Lape, Pranas (1921-), illus. LC 52-13744. 178p. illus. 22cm. (Signature books, 19). 1953. (ISBN 0-448-05619-4). Grosset & Dunlap.
--The Story of Martha Washington. Dillon, Corinne Boyd, illus. LC 54-5864. 174p. illus. 22cm. (Signature books, 32). 1954. Grosset & Dunlap.
--The Story of Ulysses S. Grant. Ward, Lynd Kendall (1905-1985), illus. LC 52-11070. 180 p. illus. 22 cm. (Signature Bks.). 1952. Grosset & Dunlap.
--Treason at the Point. Pitz, Henry Clarence (1895-1976), illus. LC 44-8164. 224 p. illus. 21 cm. 1944. J. Messner, Inc.
--The Victory Drum. Bjorklund, Lorence F. (1913-1978), illus. LC 53-8451. 152p. illus. 22cm. 1953. Messner.
--The Young Douglas. Key, Alexander Hill (1904-1979), illus. LC 34-360351. xiv, 285 p. incl. front., illus., plates. 22 cm. 1934. R. M. McBride & Company.

Nolan, Lucy
--Secret at Summerhaven. LC 83-15568. p. cm. (Escapade). 1985. (ISBN 0-689-31383-7). Atheneum/Escapade.

Nolan, Madeena Spray (1943-)
--My Daddy Don't Go to Work. LaMarche, Jim, illus. LC 78-53640. (Illus.). 32 p. 20cm. c.1978. (ISBN 0-87614-093-2). Carolrhoda Books.

Nolan, Paul Thomas (1919-), ed.
--Folk Tale Plays Round the World: A Collection of Royalty-Free, One-Act Plays for Young People About Lands Far and Near. LC 82-14188. vi, 248 p. 21cm. c.1982. (ISBN 0-8238-0253-1). Plays, Inc.
--Round-the-World Plays for Young People: A Collection of Royalty-Free, One-Act Plays About Lands Far and Near. LC 71-17098. vi, 285 p. 21cm. 1970. Plays, Inc.

Nolan, Walter K., ed. see Spenser, Edmund.

Nolan, Winefride Bell (1913-)
--Exiles Come Home. Tresilian, Cecil Stuart (1891-), illus. LC 55-4833. 292p. illus. 21cm. 1955. Macmillan.

Nolen, Barbara (1902-), adapted by see Sewell, Anna.

Nolen, Barbara (1902-), ed.
--Children of American. LC 39-27394. x, 194 p., 1 l. illus. (incl. music) 24 cm. c.1939. The John C. Winston Company.

Nolen, Barbara (1902-) & Johnson, Eleanor Murdoch (1892-), eds.
--What Next?. Adventure and Surprise. LC 57-3392. 125p. illus. 26cm. 1957. American Education Publications.

Nolen, Eleanor Weakley, Mrs.
--The Cherry Street House. Neville, Vera (1900-1978), illus. LC 39-341573. 3 p. l., 11-193 p. front., illus. (incl. music) 22 cm. 1939. T. Nelson and Sons.
--The Cowhide Trunk. Merwin, Decie (1894-1961), illus. LC 41-5302. 85 p, 11 incl. front illus. 312. 21 cm. 85p. 1941. Oxford University Press.
--A Job for Jeremiah. Johnson, Iris Beatty, illus. LC 40-27280. 80 p. incl. front., illus., plates. 21 cm. c.1940. Oxford University Press.
--Plantation on the Potomac. Deane, Elsie & Finnan, Margaret Nowell, illus. LC 41-14439. 103 p. incl. front., illus., plates. 20 cm. (Half-title: Yesterday and Today Ser.). 1941. T. Nelson and Sons.
--Secret on the Potomac. Cote, Phyllis N. (1921-), illus. LC 45-102622. 3 p. l., 215 p. incl. front., illus., plates. 21 cm. 1945. David McKay Company.
--A Shipment for Susannah. Best, Allena Champlin, Mrs. (1892-1974), illus. Berry, Erick, pseud. LC 38-17090. 3 p. l., 11-82 p. front., illus. 22 cm. 1938. T. Nelson and Sons.

Noll, Arthur Howard, ed. see English, Thomas Dunn.

Noll, Florence English, ed. see English, Thomas Dunn.

Noll, Frances
--Let's Get Together. 24p. 1946. Friendship Press.

Noll, Sally
--Off and Counting. LC 84-17943. (Illus.). 24 p. (Picture Puffins). 1985. (ISBN 0-14-050502-4). Puffin Books.
--Off & Counting. Noll, Sally, illus. LC 83-16366. (Illus.). 9 7/8 x 8. 24p. (40 pt.). (ps-1). 1984. (ISBN 0-688-02795-4). (ISBN 0-688-02796-2). Greenwillow.

Nolte, Nancy, adapted by.
--Gingerbread Man. Scarry, Richard McClure (1919-), illus. (Little Golden Book: 165). 1953. Simon and Schuster.

Nonidez, Jose Fernandez (1892-1947)
--Fuzzy and His Neighbors: A True Story. Nonidez, Jose Fernandez (1892-1947), illus. LC 32-78116. viii, 139 p. illus. 21 cm. c.1932. The Century Co.

Nonnen, Emily (1812-1905)
--Fortunes of Life: Or, Struggles of the Ornshield Family. N.D. Augustana Book Concern.
--The Fortunes of Life: Or, Struggles of the Ornshield Family. Nystrom, Jenny, illus. Olson, Ernst Wilhelm (1870-), tr. LC 9-11255. 170 p. front., plates. 18 cm. 1909. The Engberg-Holmberg Pub. Co.
--The Fugitives: Or, The Motto Above the Door. Nystrom, Jenny, illus. Olson, Ernst Wilhelm (1870-), tr. LC 10-1355. 160 p. front., 5 pl. 18 cm. 1909. The Engberg-Holmberg Pub. Co.
--The Fugitives: Or, The Motto Over the Door. N.D. Augustana Book Concern.
--Lost and Found. LC 26-459. 125 p. col. front., col. pl. 18 cm. c.1925. Augustana Book Concern.
--The Stork's Necklace: A Story. LC 23-15586. 128 p. incl. front. 18 cm. c.1923. Augustana Book Concern.

Noodles, pseud., see Hahn, Frank G..

Noodles, pseud.
--The False-Face Detective. Hahn, Frank G.. Murdocca, Salvatore, illus. LC 79-117432. (Illus.). 32 p. 17cm. c.1979. (ISBN 0-03-047356-X). Holt, Rinehart, and Winston.
--How to Catch a Ghost. Hahn, Frank G.. Foreman, Michael (1938-), illus. LC 79-117444. (Illus.). 32 p. 16cm. c.1979. (ISBN 0-03-047631-3). Holt, Rinehart, and Winston.
--The Night of the Ooley Bugs: A Story. Hahn, Frank G.. Endicott, James R, illus. LC 79-117448. (Illus.). 32 p. 16cm. c.1979. (ISBN 0-03-047371-3). Holt, Rinehart, and Winston.
--The Phantom Athlete: A Diary of Great Events in My Life. Hahn, Frank G.. Rand, Ted, illus. LC 79-117430. (Illus.). 32 p. 17cm. c.1979. (ISBN 0-03-047346-2). Holt, Rinehart, and Winston.
--Spooky Sounds. Hahn, Frank G.. Maitin, Samuel, illus. LC 79-117450. (Illus.). 32 p. 16cm. c.1979. (ISBN 0-03-047351-9). Holt, Rinehart, and Winston.
--This Little Thing. Hahn, Frank, G.. Lippman, Peter J. (1936-), illus. LC 79-117445. (Illus.). 32 p. 16cm. c.1979. (ISBN 0-03-047361-6). Holt, Rhinehart, and Winston.
--Where Do Ghosts Live?. Hahn, Frank G.. Lee, Robert J. (1921-), illus. LC 79-117435. (Illus.). 32 p. 17cm. c.1979. (ISBN 0-03-047336-5). Holt, Rinehart, and Winston.

Noodles, ed. see Elliot, David.

Noon, Elizabeth F (1914-), ed.
--Poems Children Enjoy. Karb, Ruth B. & Palmer, James E., illus. LC 53-13476. 116p. illus. 33cm. (Instructor Activity Guide Series). 1953. F. A. Owen Pub. Co.

Noonan, Daniel
--The Piedmont Flyer. (Illus.). 40p. (gr. 3-8). N.D. (ISBN 0-686-97486-7). Oak Tree Pubns.

Noonan, Julia (1946-)
--The Best Thing to Be. 1st ed. Noonan, Julia (1946-), illus. LC 78-120472. (Illus.). 32 p. 20x24 cm. 1971. Doubleday.

Noonan, Michael John (1921-)
--Air Taxi. Rowe, Barry, illus. LC 68-9527. (Illus.). 148 p. 21cm. 1st U.S. edition. 1968, c.1967. Meredith Press.
--Flying Doctor. LC 61-828368. 191p. 21cm. 1961. John Day Co.
--Flying Doctor & the Secret of the Pearls. (Illus.). (gr. 5 up). 1962. (ISBN 0-685-21130-4). Verry.

--Sargasso of Space. Norton, Alice Mary. 1955. Gnome Press.

North, Carol, retold by.

--Jack and the Beanstalk. Dabaghian, Brenda, illus. LC 81-83347. (Illus.). 20 p. 24cm. (Golden storytime book). c.1982. (ISBN 0-307-11951-3). Golden Press.

--The Three Bears. McCue, Lisa, illus. LC 82-82650. (Illus.). 24p. (First Little Golden Bk.). (ps). 1983. (ISBN 0-307-10147-9, Golden Pr). (ISBN 0-307-10147-9). Western Pub.

North, Emily

--Old Friends, New Friends. Sims, Lynda, illus. LC 79-22046. p. cm. 1980. (ISBN 0-516-01479-X). Childrens Press.

North, Eric, pseud., see Cronin, Bernard.

North, Eric, pseud.

--The Ant Men. Young, Florence Liley, illus. LC 55-6522. 216p. (Winston Science Fiction Ser). (gr. 7-9). 1955. (ISBN 0-03-033545-0). HR&W.

North, Grace May see Norton, Carol, pseud.

North, Grace May (1876-)

--Adele Doring at Boarding-School. Young, Florence Liley, illus. LC 21-21145. 251 p. col. front., col. plates. 20 cm. 1921. Lothrop, Lee & Shepard Co.

--Adele Doring at Vineyard Valley. Young, Florence Liley, illus. LC 23-12522. 3 p. l., v-vii, 9-334 p. col. front., col. plates. 20 cm. c.1923. Lothrop, Lee & Shepard Co.

--Adele Doring in Camp. Young, Florence Liley, illus. LC 22-18550. ix, 11-238 p. col. front., col. plates. 20 cm. c.1922. Lothrop, Lee & Shepard Co.

--Adele Doring of the Sunnyside Club. Young, Florence Liley, illus. LC 20-2648. 374 p. col. front., col. plates. 20 cm. c.1919. Lothrop, Lee & Shepard Co.

--Adele Doring on a Ranch. Young, Florence Liley, illus. LC 21-2068. 278 p. col. front., col. plates. 19 cm. c.1920. Lothrop, Lee & Shepard Co.

--Bobs, a Girl Detective. Norton, Carol, pseud. LC 28-13224. 245 p. front. 20 cm. (Mystery and adventure series for girls). c.1928. A. L. Burt Company.

--Dixie Martin: The Girl of Woodford's Canon. Warren, Elizabeth B., illus. LC 25-384868. 363 p. front., plates. 20 cm. c.1924. Lothrop, Lee & Shepard Co.

--Meg of Mystery Mountain. LC 26-9749. 311 p. front. 20 cm. c.1926. A. L. Burt Company.

--Nan of the Gypsies. LC 26-121409. 235 p. front. 20 cm. c.1926. A. L. Burt Company.

--The Phantom Town. Norton, Carol, pseud. LC 33-121106. 272 p. incl. front. 20 cm. (Mystery and adventure series for girls). c.1933. A. L. Burt Company.

--The Phantom Town Mystery. Norton, Carol, pseud. LC 33-12109. 256 p. front. 20 cm. (Mystery and adventure series for girls). c.1933. A. L. Burt Company.

--The Phantom Yacht. Norton, Carol, pseud. LC 28-132218. 249 p. front. 20 cm. (Mystery and adventure series for girls). c.1928. A. L. Burt Company.

--Rilla of the Lighthouse. (Grace May North Books for Girls). N.D. A L Burt Co.

--The Seven Sleuths' Club. Norton, Carol, pseud. LC 28-13222. 236 p. front. 20 cm. (Mystery and adventure series for girls). c.1928. A. L. Burt Company.

--Sisters. LC 28-11927. 320 p. front. 20 cm. c.1928. A. L. Burt Company.

--Virginia at Vine Haven. LC 24-17246. 242 p. front., plates. 20 cm. (Her Virginia Davis series). c.1924. A. L. Burt Company.

--Virginia of V. M. Ranch. LC 24-13017. 288 p. front., plates. 20 cm. (Her The Virginia Davis series). c.1924. A. L. Burt Company.

--Virginia's Adventure Club. LC 24-180921. 274 p. front., plates. 20 cm. (Her Virginia Davis series). c.1924. A. L. Burt Company.

--Virginia's Ranch Neighbors. LC 24-19023. 287 p. front., plates. 20 cm. (Her Virginia Davis series). c.1924. A. L. Burt Company.

--Virginia's Romance. LC 24-190224. 279 p. front., plates. 20 cm. (Her Virginia Davis series). c.1924. A. L. Burt Company.

North, Jessica

--River Rising. 1975. (ISBN 0-394-49001-0). Random.

North, Joan (1920-)

--The Cloud Forest. LC 66-53618. 180p. 20cm. 1st U.S. edition. (Ariel bk.). 1966, c.1965. Farrar.

--The Cloud Forest. LC 66-10653. (gr. 7 up). 1966. (ISBN 0-374-31386-5). FS&G.

--The Light Maze. LC 70-161370. 185 p. 22cm. (Ariel book). 1971. (ISBN 0-374-34450-7). Farrar, Straus & Giroux.

--Whirling Shapes. (gr. 6-10). 1967. (ISBN 0-374-38349-9). FS&G.

North, Rose Dennis

--Dell and Dot in Fairyland. LC 25-1690. 64 p. 21 cm. c.1924. R. G. Badger.

North, Sterling, jt. auth. see Disney, Walt, Productions.

North, Sterling (1906-1974)

--The Five Little Bears. Biers, Clarence & Frazee, Hazel, illus. LC 35-22662. 32 p. illus. (part col.) 21 x 19 cm. c.1935. Rand, McNally & Company.

--The Five Little Bears. Tamburine, Jean (1930-), illus. LC 55-81853. unpaged. illus. 21cm. (Rand McNally elf book, 498). c.1955. Rand McNally.

--Greased Lightning. Wiese, Kurt (1887-1974), illus. LC 40-34539. 93 p. incl. col. front., illus. (part col.) 26 cm. c.1940. The John C. Winston Company.

--Little Rascal. 1st ed. Burger, Carl Victor (1888-1967), illus. LC 65-19579. 78 p. illus. 24 cm. 1965. Dutton.

--Midnight and Jeremiah. Wiese, Kurt (1887-1974), illus. LC 43-17083. 125 p. incl. col. front., illus. (part. col.) 23 cm. (gr. 3-5). 1943. John C. Winston Co.

--Rascal: A Memoir of a Better Era. Schoenherr, John Carl (1935-), illus. (Illus.). (gr. 5 up). 1963. Dutton. **Awards: (ALA); (JNM).**

--So Dear to My Heart. Holland, Bradford, illus. (Illus.). 240 p. 22cm. 1968. Doubleday.

--Son of the Lamp Maker: The Story of a Boy Who Knew Jesus. Lee, Manning De Villeneuve (1894-1980), illus. LC 56-9427. 60p. illus. 23cm. 1956. Rand McNally.

--The Wolfling. 256p (Pub. by Dutton). (gr. 3-7). 1980. (ISBN 0-590-30254-X). Scholastic Inc.

--The Zipper ABC Book. Ward, Keith, illus. LC 37-36659. 59 p. col. illus. 20 cm. c.1937. Rand, McNally & Company.

Northall, G. F., compiled by.

--English Folk-Rhymes. N.D. Gale Reprint.

Northcote, Stafford M.

--Little Verses for Little People. (Illus.). 45p. 32cm. 1898. S. M. Northcote.

Northcott, William Cecil (1902-)

--People of the Bible. Wrigley, Denis, illus. LC 67-12336. (Illus.). 157 p. 26cm. 1967. Westminster Press.

Northey, Neil Wayne

--Bluebirds & Their Neighbors. (gr. k-3). N.D. Pacific Pr Pub Assn.

--Mallards & Their Neighbors. (gr. 4-6). N.D. Pacific Pr Pub Assn.

--Old Homestead Tales. LC 30-13909. v. illus., pl. 20 cm. c.1930. Pacific Press Publishing Association.

--Paddletail the Beaver. (gr. 4-6). N.D. Pacific Pr Pub Assn.

--Wild Animal Stories, 2 Vols. De Bolt, Byron, illus. v. illus. 20.5 cm. 1934. Pacific Press Publishing Association.

--Wild Animals of Africa. Wilke, William, illus. LC 49-439. (Illus.). 205p. 23cm. 1948. Pacific Press Pub.

Northmore, Elizabeth Florence see Stucley, Elizabeth Florence.

Northrop, Grace Emmert

--Fantasy in Verse. 1977. (ISBN 0-682-48718-X). Exposition.

Northrop, Hazel

--Stories from 'round the World. LC 23-14271. 4 p. l., 7-152 p. front. 20 cm. c.1923. F. H. Revell Company.

Northrop, Hazel, jt. auth. see Pierce, Cora Banks.

Northrup, Marguerite, ed.

--Christmas Story: From the Gospels of Matthew & Luke. LC 65-23504. (Illus.). (gr. 3 up). 1966. (ISBN 0-87099-047-0, Pub. by Metro Mus Art). NYGS.

--Easter Story: From the Gospels. (Illus.). (gr. 3 up). 1967. (ISBN 0-87099-058-6, Dist. by NYGS). Metro Mus Art.

Northrup, Melvin

--Toby's Gift. 32p. (Orig.). (Books I Can Read). (gr. 2). 1980. (ISBN 0-8127-0291-3). Review & Herald.

Northrup, Mili

--The Watch Cat. 1st ed. Salisbury, Kent, designed by. LC 67-18655. (Illus.). 32 p. 23x29cm. 1968. Bobbs-Merrill Co.

Northstein, Ira O.

--Our Father's Care. N.D. Augustana Book Concern.

Northup, Truman

--Arctic Raider. LC 37-281539. (Being the story of the trials and tribulations of a young superintendant of a Government Reindeer Station on the North Coast of Alaska). 320 p. front., plates. 21 cm. c.1936. W. A. Wilde Company.

--The Phantom Code. LC 37-24839. 4 p. l., 7-294 p. front., plates. 21 cm. c.1937. W. A. Wilde Company.

Norton, Alice Mary see North, Andrew, pseud.

Norton, Alice Mary see Norton, Andre, pseud.

Norton, Alice Mary, jt. auth. see Reynard the Fox. English.

Norton, Alice Mary (1912-)

--Android at Arms. Norton, Andre, pseud. LC 77-152695. 253 p. 22cm. 1971. (ISBN 0-15-203497-8). Harcourt Brace Jovanovich.

--The Defiant Agents. Norton, Andre, pseud. 1st ed. LC 62-90630. 224p. 21cm. 1962. World Pub. Co.

--Dragon Magic. Norton, Andre, pseud. Jacques, Robin (1920-), illus. LC 70-158697. (Illus.). 213 p. 21cm. 1972. (ISBN 0-690-24489-4). Crowell.

--Dread Companion. Norton, Andre, pseud. 1st ed. LC 72-115758. 234p. 20cm. 1970. (ISBN 0-15-224201-5). Harcourt, Brace, Jovanovich.

--Exiles of the Stars. Norton, Andre, pseud. LC 72-136817. 255 p. 22cm. 1971. (ISBN 0-670-30112-4). Viking Press.

--Forerunner Foray. Norton, Andre, pseud. LC 72-91403. 286 p. 22cm. 1973. (ISBN 0-670-32357-8). Viking Press.

--Fur Magic. Norton, Andre, pseud. Kaufmann, John (1931-), illus. LC 68-26970. (Illus.). 174 p. 21cm. 1968. World Pub. Co.

--Galactic Derelict. Norton, Andre, pseud. 1st ed. LC 59-11542. 224p. 21cm. 1959. World Pub. Co.

--Here Abide Monsters. Norton, Andre, pseud. LC 73-75438. 215 p. 22cm. (A Margaret K. McElderry Bk.). 1973. (ISBN 0-689-30422-6). Atheneum.

--Huon of the Horn: Being a Tale of That Duke of Bordeaux Who Came to Sorrow at the Hands of Charlemagne and Yet Won the Favor of Oberon, the Elf King, to His Lasting Fame and Great Glory. Norton, Andre, pseud. 1st ed. Krush, Joe (1918-), illus. LC 51-13839. (Illus.). 208 p. 21cm. 1951. Harcourt, Brace.

--Ice Crown. Norton, Andre, pseud. LC 72-102928. 256 p. 22cm. 1970. (ISBN 0-670-39139-5). Viking Press.

--Key Out of Time. Norton, Andre, pseud. LC 63-10861. 224 p. 21 cm. 1963. World Pub. Co.

--Octagon Magic. Norton, Andre, pseud. Conner, Mac, illus. LC 67-13822. (Illus.). 189 p. 21cm. 1967. World Pub. Co.

--Ordeal in Otherwhere. Norton, Andre, pseud. LC 79-25691. 191 p. 22cm. (Gregg Press science fiction series). 1980, c.1964. (ISBN 0-8398-2634-6). Gregg Press.

--Ordeal in Otherwhere. Norton, Andre, pseud. LC 64-12354. 224 p. 21 cm. 1964. World Pub. Co.

--Postmarked the Stars. Norton, Andre, pseud. LC 69-18626. 223 p. 21cm. 1969. Harcourt, Brace & World.

--The Prince Commands: Being Sundry Adventures of Michael Karl, Sometime Crown Prince & Pretender to the Throne of Morvania. Norton, Andre, pseud. 1st ed. Seredy, Kate (1899-1975), illus. LC 34-3730. viii p., 1 l., 268, 1 p. front., illus. 20 cm. 1934. D. Appleton-Century Company, Incorporated.

--Quest Crosstime. Norton, Andre, pseud. LC 65-18159. 253 p. 21cm. 1965. Viking Press.

--Rebel Spurs. Norton, Andre, pseud. LC 62-139445. 224p. 22cm. 1962. World Pub. Co.

--Ride Proud, Rebel!. Norton, Andre, pseud. 1st ed. LC 61-665742. 255p. 21cm. 1961. World Pub. Co.

--Star Man's Son: Twenty-Two Fifty A.D. Norton, Andre, pseud. LC 79-26128. (Illus.). 253 p. 22cm. (Gregg Press science fiction series). 1980, c.1952. (ISBN 0-8398-2636-2). Gregg Press.

--Star Man's Son: Twenty-Two Fifty A.D. Norton, Andre, pseud. 1st ed. Mordvinoff, Nicolas (1911-1973), illus. Nicolas, pseud. LC 52-6906. (Illus.). 248 p. 21cm. 1952. Harcourt, Brace.

--Steel Magic. Norton, Andre, pseud. Jacques, Robin (1920-), illus. LC 65-19714. 155p. illus. 21cm. (gr. 5-9). c.1965. World.

--Storm over Warlock. Norton, Alice Mary. Norton, Andre, pseud. LC 60-7204. 251 p. 21 cm. 1960. The World Publishing Co.

--The Time Traders. Norton, Andre, pseud. 1st ed. LC 58-11154. 219p. 21cm. 1958. World Pub. Co.

--Uncharted Stars. Norton, Andre, pseud. LC 69-13080. 253 p. 22cm. 1969. Viking Press.

--Yankee Privateer. Norton, Andre, pseud. 1st ed. Vosburgh, Leonard W. (1912-), illus. LC 55-5281. (Illus.). 300 p. 21cm. 1955. World Pub. Co.

--The Zero Stone. Norton, Andre, pseud. LC 68-16065. 286 p. 21cm. 1968. Viking Press.

Norton, Alice Mary (1912-) & Donaldy, Ernestine, eds.

--Gates to Tomorrow: An Introduction to Science Fiction. Norton, Andre, pseud. LC 72-85921. 264 p. 22cm. 1973. (ISBN 0-689-30321-1). Atheneum.

Norton, Alice Whitson (1897-)

--Cheery Mary. LC 45-12220. 94 p. 18 cm. 1944. The Wartburg Press.

--The Other Side of Baldy. LC 45-10057. 96 p. 18 cm. 1945. The Wartburg Press.

Norton, Andre, pseud., see Norton, Alice Mary.

Norton, Andre, jt. auth. see Madlee, Dorothy Haynes.

Norton, Andre, pseud. (1912-)

--At Swords' Points. Norton, Alice Mary. LC 54-8575. 279 p. 21cm. 1954. (ISBN 0-15-283893-7). Harcourt, Brace.

--The Beast Master. Norton, Alice Mary. LC 59-8955. 192 p. 21cm. 1959. (ISBN 0-15-206049-9). Harcourt, Brace.

--Catseye. Norton, Alice Mary. LC 61-11750. (gr. 9 up). 1961. (ISBN 0-15-215536-8). HarBraceJ.

--The Crystal Gryphon. Norton, Alice Mary. LC 70-190559. (gr. 7 up). 1972. (ISBN 0-689-50014-9, McElderry Bk). Atheneum.

--Dark Piper. Norton, Alice Mary. LC 68-25193. 256p. (gr. 7 up). 1968. (ISBN 0-15-222127-1). HarBraceJ.

--The Defiant Agents. Norton, Alice Mary. LC 78-20923. 190 p. 21cm. (The Time Traders Ser.). 1978. Gregg Press.

--The Factor. Norton, Alice Mary. LC 65-17992. 191 p. 21cm. 1965. Harcourt, Brace & World.

--Follow the Drum. Norton, Alice Mary. N.D. Alfred A. Knopf.

--Follow the Drum. Norton, Alice Mary. LC 42-23640. (Being the ventures and misadventures of one Johanna Lovell, sometime Lady of Catkept Manor in Kent County of Lord Baltimore's Proprietary of Maryland, in the gracious reign of King Charles the Second). (Illus.). vi, 312 p. 21cm. 1942. Wm. Penn Publishing Corp.

--Galactic Derelict. Norton, Alice Mary. LC 78-26944. 192 p. 21cm. (The Time Traders Ser.). 1978. (ISBN 0-8398-2422-X). Gregg Press.

--Gryphon in Glory. Norton, Alice Mary. LC 80-24835. 242 p. 22cm. (Argo book). 1981. (ISBN 0-689-50195-1). Atheneum.

--Iron Cage. Norton, Alice Mary. 1st ed. LC 74-6310. 288 p. 22cm. 1974. (ISBN 0-670-40151-X). Viking Press.

--Judgment on Janus. Norton, Alice Mary. LC 63-16035. (gr. 9 up). 1963. (ISBN 0-15-240950-5). HarBraceJ.

--Key Out of Time. Norton, Alice Mary. LC 78-27244. 188 p. 21cm. (The Time Traders Ser.). 1978. (ISBN 0-8398-2424-6). Gregg Press.

--Knave of Dreams. Norton, Alice Mary. LC 75-14444. 252 p. 25cm. 1975. (ISBN 0-670-41467-0). Viking Press.

--Lavender-Green Magic. Norton, Alice Mary. Brown, Judith Gwyn (1933-), illus. LC 73-21941. (Illus.). 241 p. 21cm. 1974. (ISBN 0-690-00429-X). Crowell.

--Lord of Thunder. Norton, Alice Mary. LC 62-14247. 192 p. 21cm. 1962. (ISBN 0-15-249357-3). Harcourt, Brace & World.

--Moon Called. Norton, Alice Mary. LC 82-236312. (Illus.). 301 p. 21cm. c.1982. (ISBN 0-671-45716-0). Simon & Schuster : Distributed by Pocket Books.

--Moon of Three Rings. Norton, Alice Mary. (gr. 7 up). 1966. (ISBN 0-670-48815-1). (ISBN 0-670-48816-X). Viking Pr.

--Night of Masks. Norton, Alice Mary. LC 64-16266. (gr. 9 up). 1964. (ISBN 0-15-257435-2). HarBraceJ.

--No Night Without Stars. Norton, Alice Mary. LC 75-6948. 246 p. 22cm. 1975. (ISBN 0-689-50033-5). Atheneum.

--Operation Time Search. Norton, Alice Mary. LC 67-17156. (gr. 8 up). 1967. (ISBN 0-15-258700-4, HJ). HarBraceJ.

--Outside. Norton, Alice Mary. Colonna, Bernard, illus. LC 73-92454. (Illus.). 126 p. 22cm. 1974. (ISBN 0-8027-6185-2). Walker.

--Quag Keep. Norton, Alice Mary. LC 77-17771. 224 p. 22cm. 1978. (ISBN 0-689-50107-2). Atheneum.

--Ralestone Luck. Norton, Alice Mary. Reid, James (1907-), illus. LC 38-21549. (Illus.). xii p., 1 l. 20cm. 1938. D. Appleton-Century Company, Incorporated.

--Red Hart Magic. Norton, Alice Mary. Diamond, Donna (1950-), illus. LC 76-3539. (Illus.). 179 p. 21cm. c.1976. (ISBN 0-690-01147-4). Crowell.

--Scarface. Norton, Alice Mary. Bjorklund, Lorence F. (1913-1978), illus. LC 48-8179. (Illus.). 21cm. 263p. (gr. 7-9). 1948. (ISBN 0-15-270485-X). HarBraceJ.

--Sea Siege. Norton, Alice Mary. LC 57-8586. (gr. 5-8). 1957. (ISBN 0-15-271738-2, HJ). HarBraceJ.

--Shadow Hawk. Norton, Alice Mary. 1st ed. LC 60-10247. (Illus.). 237 p. 21cm. 1960. (ISBN 0-15-273170-9). Harcourt, Brace.

--Space Service. Norton, Alice Mary. N.D. World Publishing Co.

--Stand to Horse. Norton, Alice Mary. Norton, Andre, pseud. LC 56-8354. 242 p. 21cm. (Voyager book, AVB 55). 1956. (ISBN 0-15-684890-2). Harcourt, Brace.

--Star Born. Norton, Alice Mary. Norton, Andre, pseud. LC 57-5898. 212 p. 21cm. 1957. World Pub. Co.

--Star Gate. Norton, Alice Mary. LC 58-8626. (gr. 10-12). 1958. (ISBN 0-15-278710-0). HarBraceJ.

--Star Guard. Norton, Alice Mary. LC 55-7612. (Illus.). 247 p. 21cm. 1955. (ISBN 0-15-279068-3). Harcourt, Brace.
--Star Rangers. Norton, Alice Mary. LC 53-7869. 280p. (gr. 7 up). 1953. (ISBN 0-15-279426-3, HJ). HarBraceJ.
--The Stars Are Ours!. Norton, Alice Mary. LC 54-8169. 237 p. 21cm. 1954. World Pub. Co.
--Storm Over Warlock. Norton, Alice Mary. LC 79-24953. 251 p. 22cm. (Gregg Press science fiction series). 1980, c.1960. (ISBN 0-8398-2512-9). Gregg Press.
--Sword in Sheath. Norton, Alice Mary. 1st ed. Bjorklund, Lorence F (1913-1978), illus. LC 49-10979. (Illus.). 246 p. 21cm. 1949. Harcourt, Brace.
--The Sword Is Drawn. Norton, Alice Mary. Norton, Andre, pseud. Coburn, Duncan, illus. LC 44-40054. (Illus.). viii, 2, 178, 2 p. 21cm. 1944. Houghton Mifflin Company.
--The Time Traders. Norton, Alice Mary. LC 78-26925. xiv, 220 p. 21cm. (The Time Traders Ser.). 1978. (ISBN 0-8398-2421-1). Gregg Press.
--The Time Traders. Norton, Alice Mary. 1958. Harcourt Brace.
--Troy of Swords. Norton, Alice Mary. LC 77-72636. 180 p. 22cm. 1977. (ISBN 0-448-14348-8). Grosset & Dunlap.
--Victory on Janus. Norton, Alice Mary. LC 66-10079. (gr. 7 up). 1966. (ISBN 0-15-293760-9). HarBraceJ.
--Ware Hawk. Norton, Alice Mary. LC 83-2835. p. cm. 1983. (ISBN 0-689-50287-7). Atheneum.
--Wraiths of Time. Norton, Alice Mary. LC 75-43607. 210 p. 22cm. (A Margaret K. Elderry Bk.). 1976. (ISBN 0-689-50057-2). Atheneum.

Norton, Andre, pseud. (1912-), ed.
--Baleful Beasts and Eerie Creatures. Norton, Alice Mary. Ruth, Rod (1912-), illus. LC 76-20529. 124 p. c.1976. (ISBN 0-528-82171-7). (ISBN 0-528-80211-9). Rand McNally.
--Small Shadows Creep. Norton, Alice Mary. LC 74-5408. ix, 195 p. 24cm. 1974. (ISBN 0-525-39505-9). Dutton
--Space Pioneers. Norton, Alice Mary. (gr. 5-9). N.D. (ISBN 0-529-03465-4). World Pub.

Norton, Andre, pseud. (1912-) & Gilbert, Michael Francis (1912-)
--The Day of the Ness. Norton, Alice Mary. Gilbert, Michael Francis, illus. LC 74-78111. (Illus.). 119 p. 22cm. 1975. (ISBN 0-8027-6195-X). Walker.

Norton, Andre, pseud. (1912-) & Madlee, Dorothy Haynes (1917-1980)
--Star Ka'at. Norton, Alice Mary. Colonna, Bernard, illus. LC 75-36018. (Illus.). 122 p. 22cm. 1976. (ISBN 0-8027-6249-2). (ISBN 0-8027-6250-6). Walker.
--Star Ka'at World. Norton, Alice Mary. Jenkins, Jean, illus. LC 77-79268. (Illus.). 130 p. 22cm. c.1978. (ISBN 0-8027-6300-6). (ISBN 0-8027-6301-4). Walker.
--Star Ka'ats and the Plant People. Norton, Alice Mary. Jenkins, Jean, illus. LC 78-67177. (Illus.). 122 p. 22cm. 1979. (ISBN 0-8027-6342-1). (ISBN 0-8027-6343-X). Walker.
--Star Ka'ats and the Winged Warriors. Norton, Alice Mary. Jenkins, Jean, illus. LC 81-11692. p. cm. 1981. (ISBN 0-8027-6416-9). (ISBN 0-8027-6417-7). Walker.

Norton, Andre, pseud. (1912-) & Miller, Phyllis
--House of Shadows. Norton, Alice Mary. LC 83-16197. 216p. (gr. 5-9). 1984. (ISBN 0-689-50298-2, McElderly Bk). Atheneum.
--Ride the Green Dragon. Norton, Alice Mary. LC 85-7329. p. cm. 1985. (ISBN 0-689-50331-8). Atheneum.
--Seven Spells to Sunday. Norton, Alice Mary. Colonna, Bernard, illus. LC 78-24362. 136 p. 22cm. 1979. (ISBN 0-689-50134-X). Atheneum.

Norton, Browning (1909-)
--Johnny Bingo. LC 77-158368. 185 p. 22cm. 1971. Coward, McCann & Geoghegan.
--Help Me, Charley Buoy. LC 74-79698. 158 p. 22cm. 1974. (ISBN 0-698-20297-X). (ISBN 0-698-30549-3). Coward, McCann & Geoghegan.
--Wreck of the Blue Plane. LC 77-18507. 168 p. 22cm. c.1978. (ISBN 0-698-20448-4). Coward, McCann & Geoghegan.

Norton, Carol, pseud., see North, Grace May.

Norton, Charles Eliot (1827-1908), ed.
--The Story Teller. LC 55-21376. 316p. illus. (part col.) 21cm. (Young Folks Library: No. 1). c.1955. Auxiliary Educational League.

Norton, Charles G
--Bobby Travels up a Tree. LC 52-6963. 78 p. 23 cm. 1952. Vantage Press.

Norton, Charles Ledyard (1837-1909)
--Jack Benson's Log: Or, Afloat with the Flag in '61. Gibbs, George, illus. front, 4 pl. 19 cm. 281p. (Fighting for the Flag Ser.). N.D. W. A. Wilde Co.
--A Medal of Honor Man: Or, Cruising Among Blockade Runners. Gibbs, George, illus. LC 4-16462. 281 p. front., 4 pl. 19 cm. (On cover: Fighting for the flag series). 1896. W. A. Wilde & Company.
--Midshipman Jack. Gibbs, George, illus. LC 4-16147. 290 p. front., 4 pl. 19 cm. (On cover: Fighting for the flag series). 1897. W. A. Wilde & Company.
--The Queen's Rangers: A Story of Revolutionary Times. Stecher, William Frederick (1864-), illus. LC 99-4680. 351 p. front., plates. 20 cm. c.1899. W. A. Wilde Company.
--A Soldier of the Legion: A Story of the Great Northwest. Small, Frank O., illus. 2 p. l., 7-291 p. front., plates. 20 cm. c.1898. W. A. Wilde & Company.

Norton, Edith Constance Egbert, Mrs.
--Little Black Eyes: The Story of a Little Girl in Japan. Snell, Carroll C., illus. LC 27-23025. xvii p. 1 l., 134 p. incl. illus., plates. col. front., col. plates. 20 cm. 1927. The Macmillan Company.

Norton, Frank Henry (1836-1921)
--The Days of Daniel Boone. (The Excelsior Edition). N.D. The American News Co.

Norton, Frank R. Browning see Norton, Browning.

Norton, Grace K
--Cappy Can. Wolcott, Elizabeth Tyler (1892-), illus. LC 48-3301. 31 p. illus. (part col.) 14 x 21 cm. N.D. D. Appleton-Century.

Norton, June Mary
--The June Norton Sing-It-Again Book for Small Children. Kindergarten children, illus. LC 38-32163. 48 p. col. illus. 31 cm. 1935. The June Norton Publications.
--Sing and Be Happy. Byj, Charlot, illus. 48p. 1951. John Day Books.
--The Sunflower Song Book. Byj, Charlot, illus. 48p. 1956. John Day Books.

Norton, Lottie Tresner
--The Big Insect Mystery. Pomerantz, Norman, illus. LC 58-13705. (Illus.). 44p. 21cm. 1959, c.1958. Greenwich Book Publishers.

Norton, Mary, Mrs. (1903-)
--Adventures of the Borrowers, 4 vols. Krush, Beth (1918-) & Krush, Joe (1918-), illus. (Illus.). 784p. (gr. 4 up). 1975. Set. (ISBN 0-15-613605-8, VoyB). HarBraceJ.
--Are All the Giants Dead?. Froud, Brian, illus. LC 75-10133. (Illus.). 123 p. 24cm. 1st U.S. edition. 1975. (ISBN 0-15-203810 8). Harcourt Brace Jovanovich.
--Are All the Giants Dead?. Froud, Brian, illus. LC 78-6622. p. cm. (Voyager/HBJ book). 1978, c.1975. (ISBN 0-15-607888-0). Harcourt Brace Jovanovich.
--Bed-Knob and Broomstick. Blegvad, Erik (1923-), illus. LC 57-11341. (Illus.). 189 p. 21cm. 1957. Harcourt, Brace.
--Bed-Knob and Broomstick. 1st ed. Blegvad, Erik (1923-), illus. LC 74-17497. p. cm. (Voyager book, AVB 91). 1975, c.1957. Harcourt Brace Jovanovich.
--The Borrowers. Krush, Beth (1918-) & Krush, Joe (1918-), illus. LC 53-7870. (Illus.). (gr. 3 up). 1965. (ISBN 0-15-613600-7, VoyB). HarBraceJ.
--The Borrowers. Krush, Beth (1918-) & Krush, Joe (1918-), illus. LC 53-78700. 180p. illus. 22cm. 1st U.S. edition. 1953. (ISBN 0-15-209987-5). Harcourt, Brace. **Awards: (ALA); (CMA).**
--The Borrowers Afield. x ed. Krush, Beth (1918-) & Krush, Joe (1918-), illus. LC 55-11011. 215p. illus. 22cm. (gr. 3up). 1955. (ISBN 0-15-613601-5). Harcourt, Brace. **Award: (ALA).**
--The Borrowers Afloat. 1st ed. Krush, Beth (1918-) & Krush, Joe (1918-), illus. LC 59-5630. 191p. illus. 22cm. 1959. Harcourt, Brace. **Award: (CMA).**
--The Borrowers Afloat. Krush, Beth (1918-) & Krush, Joe (1918-), illus. (Illus.). 191 p. (Voyager Book). 1973, c.1959. (ISBN 0-15-613603-1). Harcourt.
--The Borrowers Aloft. Krush, Beth (1918-) & Krush, Joe (1918-), illus. LC 61-11751. 193p. illus. 21cm. 1st U.S. edition. 1961. Harcourt, Brace & World. **Award: (ALA).**
--The Borrowers Aloft. Krush, Beth (1918-) & Krush, Joe (1918-), illus. LC 73-12865. (Illus.). 192 p. 20cm. (Voyager book, AVB 83). 1974, c.1961. (ISBN 0-15-613604-X). Harcourt Brace Jovanovich.
--The Borrowers Avenged. Krush, Beth (1918-) & Krush, Joe (1918-), illus. LC 82-47937. p. cm. c.1982. (ISBN 0-15-210530-1). Harcourt Brace Jovanovich. **Award: (ALA).**
--The Complete Adventures of the Borrowers. Krush, Beth (1918-) & Krush, Joe (1918-), illus. LC 67-25003. (Illus.). 180, 215, 191, 192 p. 22cm. 1st U.S. edition. 1967. Harcourt, Brace & World.
--The Magic Bed-Knob: How to Become a Witch in Ten Easy Lessons. Peirce, Waldo (1884-1970), illus. LC 44-381. 50 p. illus. (part. col.) 28 cm. c.1943. The Hyperion Press, Distributed by G. O. Putnam's Sons.
--Poor Stainless: A New Story About the Borrowers. Krush, Beth (1918-) & Krush, Joe (1918-), illus. LC 70-140781. (Illus.). 31 p. 21cm. 1971, c.1966. (ISBN 0-15-263221-2). Harcourt Brace Jovanovich.
--Poor Stainless: A New Story About the Borrowers. Krush, Beth (1918-) & Krush, Joe (1918-), illus. LC 85-5443. p. cm. 1985, c.1966. (ISBN 0-15-263221-2). Harcourt Brace Jovanovich.

Norton, Miriam
--The Kitten Who Thought He Was a Mouse. Williams, Garth Montgomery (1912-), illus. LC 55-1001. unpaged. illus. 21cm. (Little golden book, 210). 1955, c.1954. Simon and Schuster.

Norton, Nancy R.
--Rainbowland. 1979. (ISBN 0-533-03638-0). Vantage.

Norton, Natalie
--A Little Old Man. N.D. E. M. Hale & Co.
--A Little Old Man. Huntington, Will, illus. LC 59-6968. (Illus.). unpaged. 26cm. 1959. Rand McNally.

Norton, Roy
--Drowned Gold: Being a Story of a Sailor's Life. N.D. Houghton Mifflin.

Norway, G.
--Hussein the Hostage. (Scribner-Blackie Series of Books for Young People). N.D. Charles Scribner's Sons.
--The Loss of John Humble. (Illus.). (Scribner-Blackie Series of Books for Young People). N.D. Charles Scribner's Sons.
--A Prisoner of War. (Illus.). (Scribner-Blackie Series of Books for Young People). N.D. Charles Scribner's Sons.
--A True Cornish Maid. (Illus.). (Scribner-Blackie Series of Books for Young People). N.D. Charles Scribner's Sons.

Norwood, Edwin P (1881-)
--The Adventures of Diggeldy Dan. Peyton, A. Conway, illus. LC 22-19211. xi, 240 p. col. front., col. plates. 21 cm. 1922. Little, Brown, and Company.
--Davy Winkle in Circusland. Peyton, A. Conway, illus. LC 26-105133. 4 p. l., 202 p. col. front., plates. 20 1/2 cm. 1926. Little, Brown and Company.
--The Friends of Diggeldy Dan. Peyton, A. Conway, illus. LC 24-22941. xii p., 1 l., 215 p. col. front., col. plates. 20 1/2 cm. (His Diggeldy Dan Series). 1924. Little, Brown, and Company.
--In the Land of Diggeldy Dan. Peyton, A. Conway, illus. LC 23-13488. ix, 226 p. col. front., col. plates. 21 cm. (His Diggeldy Dan series). 1923. Little, Brown, and Company.
--The Other Side of the Circus. N.D. Doubleday Doran & Co.

Nosov, Nikolai Nikolaevich (1908-)
--The Adventures of Tolya Klyukvin & Other Stories. Solasko, Fianna, tr. from Rus. LC 74-164817. 174p. (Stormy Petrel Ser.). 1973. (ISBN 0-8285-1098-9, Pub. by Progress Pubs USSR). Imported Pubns.
--Dunno Takes Music Lessons. Wettlin, Margaret, tr. 24p. 1983. (ISBN 0-8285-2621-4, Pub. by Raduga Pubs USSR). Imported Pubns.
--Eleven Stories for Boys and Girls. Yudin, Georgi, illus. Riordan, Jim, et al., trs. from Russian LC 82-114899. (Illus.). 184 p. 26cm. c.1981. Progress.
--How Dunno Became an Artist. Wettlin, Margaret, tr. 17p. (ps-3). 1983. (ISBN 0-8285-2581-1, Pub. by Raduga Pubs USSR). Imported Pubns.
--Mites of Flower Town. Wettlin, Margaret, tr. 16p. 1983. (ISBN 0-8285-2582-X, Pub. by Raduga Pubs USSR). Imported Pubns.

Nostlinger, Christine
--The Cucumber King. Bell, Anthea, tr. LC 84-18497. 126p. (gr. 3-7). 1984, c.1983. (ISBN 0-930267-01-X). Bergh Pub.
--Fly Away Home. Bell, Anthea, tr. LC 75-16255. 135 p. 21cm. 1975. (ISBN 0-531-01096-1). F. Watts.
--Girl Missing: A Novel. LC 76-13893. 139 p. 22cm. 1976. (ISBN 0-531-00346-9). F. Watts.
--Konrad. Nicklaus, Carol, illus. Bell, Anthea, tr. from Ger. LC 77-7489. (Illus.). 135 p. 22cm. 1977. F. Watts. **Award: (MLB).**
--Luke and Angela. Bell, Anthea, tr. from Ger. LC 81-1422. p. cm. 1981. (ISBN 0-15-249902-4). Harcourt Brace Jovanovich. **Award: (ALA).**
--Marrying off Mother. Bell, Anthea, tr. from Ger. LC 82-47938. 140 p. 21cm. 1st U.S. edition. 1982, c.1978. (ISBN 0-15-252138-0). Harcourt Brace Jovanovich.

Nothdurft, Lillian
--Folklore and Early Customs of Southeast Missouri. 1972. (ISBN 0-682-47495-9). Exposition Press.

Noto, Andrea Di see DiNoto, Andrea.

Nottingham, Ronald M., Sr.
--The Fairy Tales of Ronald M. Nottingham Sr. 1979. (ISBN 0-533-03888-X). Vantage.

Notzh, Helen, tr. see Cerny, Vaclav, et al.

Nourse, Alan Edward (1928-)
--The Bladerunner. LC 74-6534. 245 p. 21cm. 1974. (ISBN 0-679-20289-7). D. McKay Co.
--The Counterfeit Man. LC 63-15883. 185 p. 21cm. (More science fiction stories). 1963. (ISBN 0-679-20040-1). D. McKay Co.
--The Counterfeit Man & Other Science Fiction Stories. (gr. 7-12). 1975. (ISBN 0-590-09804-7, Schol Trade Pap). Schol Bk Serv.
--Junior Intern. LC 55-5525. 210 p. 22cm. 1955. Harper.
--Mercy Men. (gr. 7 up). 1968. (ISBN 0-679-20110-6). McKay.
--PSI High & Others. (gr. 10 up). 1967. (ISBN 0-679-20270-6). McKay.
--Raiders from the Rings. x ed. LC 61-8729. 211p. 21cm. 1962. D. Mc Kay Co.
--Rocket to Limbo. LC 57-12177. 184p. illus. 21cm. c.1957. (ISBN 0-679-20162-9). D. McKay Co.
--Rx for Tomorrow. Anderson, Rus, illus. (gr. 6 up). N.D. McKay.
--Scavengers in Space. LC 59-5114. 180p. illus. 21cm. 1959. D. McKay Co.
--Star Surgeon: Science Fiction. LC 60-7199. 22 cm. 182p. (gr. 7-11). 1960. (ISBN 0-679-20193-9). McKay.
--Tiger by the Tail and other Science Fiction Stories. LC 61-6108. 184 p. 21cm. 1961. D. McKay Co.
--Trouble on Titan. Schomburg, Alex, illus. LC 54-5067. (Illus.). 208 p. 22cm. (Science fiction novel). 1954. Winston.
--Universe Between. (gr. 7 up). 1965. (ISBN 0-679-20226-9). (ISBN 0-685-14519-0). McKay.

Novas, Higby
--Rocking in London. 144p. (Mirrors Ser.). (gr. 7 up). 1984. (ISBN 0-317-13556-2). Putnam Pub Group.

Novick, Sandra, jt. auth. see Boiko, Claire.

Novikoff, Alex
--Climbing Our Family Tree. English, John, illus. N.D. International Publishers.
--From Head to Foot. Nydorf, Seymour, illus. N.D. International Publishers.

Novinger, Virginia B
--Round Trip for Johnny. Gringhuis, Richard H. (1918-1974), illus. Gringhuis, Dirk, pseud. LC 51-14691. unpaged. illus. 24 cm. 1951. Whitman.
--Skip Sees the Signs. Wilson, Beth, illus. LC 54-8775. (Illus.). 25cm. 1953. A. Whitman.
--Tommy on Time. Evans, Katherine Floyd (1901-1964), illus. LC 52-14406. unpaged. illus. 24 cm. 1952. A. Whitman.

Novotny, Louise Miller (1889-)
--Primary Playlets and Dramatizations. LC 36-7854. 3 p. l., 9-141 p. 20 cm. c.1936. The Standard Publishing Company.

Novros, Lester (1909-)
--Who Was Aesop?. "Aesop's Fables," a "Who Story" for Children Who Ask Questions... LC 47-166173. cover-title, 16 p. col. illus. 26 x 27 1/2 cm. (Graphic educational phono-book. A-103). 1946. Graphic Educational Productions Inc.

Novy, Karel
--The Kingfishers. Hanak, Mirko, illus. Avis, Peter & Tvarochova, Jirina, trs. LC 68-11963. (Illus.). 100 p. 25cm. 1968, c.1967. Funk & Wagnalls.

Nowell, Elizabeth Cameron see Clemons, Elizabeth, pseud.

Nowell, Elizabeth Cameron
--We Live on a Farm. Wilde, Irma & Elgin, Kathleen, illus. 1956. Grosset & Dunlap.
--A Wish for Billy. Elgin, Angela (1923-) & Elgin, Kathleen, illus. 1956. Grosset & Dunlap.

Nowell, Harriet P. H. see Mannering, May, pseud.

Nowell, Harriet P. H., Mrs.
--Billy Grimes' Favorite. Mannering, May, pseud, 1 of 25 vols. (Illus.). (Pilgrim Ser. for Boys: No. 4). 1900. Lee & Shepard.
--Billy Grimes' Favorite: Or, Johnny Greenleaf's Talent. Mannering, May, pseud. LC 12-36525. 3 p. l., 5-191 p. front., 2 pl. 16 1/2 cm. (Added t.-p.: The helping hand series by May Mannering. 2). 1868. Lee and Shepard.
--Billy Grimes's Favorite. Mannering, May, pseud. (Helping Hand Ser.). N.D. Colby and Rich.
--Billy Grimes's Favorite. Mannering, May, pseud, 1 of 6 vols. (Illus.). 191p. (Helping Hand Ser.). 1882. Lee & Shepard.
--Billy Grimes's Favorite. Mannering, May, pseud. (Salt-Water Dick Stories). N.D. Lee and Shepard.
--Climbing the Rope. Mannering, May, pseud. (Helping Hand Ser.). N.D. Colby and Rich.
--Climbing the Rope. Mannering, May, pseud. (Salt-Water Dick Stories). N.D. Lee and Shepard.
--Climbing the Rope: Or, "God helps those who try to help themselves. Mannering, May, pseud, 1 of 6 vols. LC 12-36526. (Illus.). 4 p 1, 7-224 p 2 pl. 224p. (Helping Hand Ser.). 1868. Lee & Shepard.

--The Cruise of the Dashaway. Mannering, May, pseud. (Helping Hand Ser.). N.D. Colby and Rich.
--The Cruise of the Dashaway. Mannering, May, pseud, 1 of 6 vols. (Illus.). 221p. (Helping Hand Ser.). 1882. Lee & Shepard.
--The Cruise of the Dashaway: Or, Katie Putnam's Voyage. Mannering, May, pseud. LC 12-36527. 3 p. l., 5-221 p. front., 2 pl. 16 1/2 cm. (Added t.-p.: The helping hand series by May Mannering. 3). 1868. Lee and Shepard.
--Helping Hand Series. Mannering, May, pseud, 6 vols. (Illus.). 1882. Set. Lee & Shepard.
--The Little Maid of Owbow. Mannering, May, pseud. LC 12-365243. 207 p. incl. front., 2 pl. 16 1/2 cm. (Added t.-p.: The helping hand series by May Mannering. 6). 1871. Lee and Shepard.
--Little Maid of Oxbow. Mannering, May, pseud. (Helping Hand Ser.). N.D. Colby and Rich.
--Little Maid of Oxbow. Mannering, May, pseud, 1 of 6 vols. (Illus.). 207p. (Helping Hand Ser.). 1882. Lee & Shepard.
--Little Maid of Oxbow. Mannering, May, pseud. (Salt-Water Cick Stories). N.D. Lee and Shepard.
--The Little Spaniard. Mannering, May, pseud, 1 of 6 vols. (Illus.). 221p. (Helping Hand Ser.). 1882. Lee & Shepard.
--Little Spaniard. Mannering, May, pseud, 1 of 25 vols. (Illus.). (Pilgrim Ser. for Boys: No. 18). 1900. Lee & Shepard.
--The Little Spaniard. Mannering, May, pseud. (Salt-Water Dick Stories). N.D. Lee and Shepard.
--The Little Spaniard: Or, Old Jose's Grandson. Mannering, May, pseud. LC 12-36522. 3 p. l., 5-221 p. front., pl. 16 1/2 cm. (Added t.-p.: The helping hand series by May Mannering. 4). 1869. Lee and Shepard.
--Salt Water Dick. Mannering, May, pseud. (Helping Hand Ser.). N.D. Colby and Rich.
--Salt-Water Dick. Mannering, May, pseud. LC 12-36523. 4 p. l., 7-230 p. front., 2 pl. 16 1/2 cm. (Added t.-p.: The helping hand series by May Mannering. 5). 1869. Lee and Shepard.
--Salt-Water Dick. Mannering, May, pseud, 1 of 25 vols. (Illus.). (Pilgrim Ser. for Boys: No. 16). 1900. Lee & Shepard.

Nowels, Conrad
--The Burned Letter. 192p. (Orig.). (gr. 7 up). 1984. (ISBN 0-590-32516-7, Windswept Bks). Scholastic Inc.
--The Disappearing Teacher. 190p. (Orig.). (gr. 7-12). 1981. (ISBN 0-590-31464-5). Scholastic Inc.

Nowlan, Nora
--The Shannon: River of Loughs & Legends. LC 66-12285. (Illus.). (Rivers of the World Ser.). (gr. 4-7). 1965. (ISBN 0-8116-6363-9). Garrard.

Nowlan, Philip Frances, jt. auth. see Calkins, Dick.

Nowlin, Clifford Hiram (1863-)
--The Story Teller and His Pack. LC 29-22390. xvii, 408 p. 20 cm. c.1929. Milton Bradley Co.

Noy, Dov, ed.
--Folktales of Israel. Baharav, Gena, tr. 220p. 1963. The University Of Chicago.

Noyes, Alfred (1880-1958)
--Daddy Fell into the Pond. Kredel, Fritz (1900-1973), illus. LC 52-10618. 46p. N.D. Shedd & Ward, Inc.
--The Highwayman. Mikolaycak, Charles (1937-), illus. LC 83-725. (Illus.). 40p. (gr. 5 up). 1983. (ISBN 0-688-02117-4). (ISBN 0-688-02118-2). Lothrop.
--The Highwayman. Mikolaycak, Charles, illus. (Illus.). 32p. 1982. (ISBN 0-19-279748-4, Pub. by Oxford U Pr Childrens). Merrimack Pub Cir.
--The Secret of Pooduck Island. (Illus.). 176p. 1959. (ISBN 0-910334-22-6). Catholic Authors Press.
--The Secret of Pooduck Island. De Muth, Flora Nash (1888-), illus. LC 43-13640. 4 p. l., 183 p. incl. front.,114lus. 21 cm. 1943. Frederic A. Stokes Company.
--The Secret of Pooduck Island. DeMuth, Flora Nash (1888-), illus. 1943. J. B. Lippincott Co.
--Sherwood: Robin Hood & the Three Kings. Nichols, Spencer Baird (1875-), illus. N.D. Frederick A Stokes Co.

Noyes, Alfred (1880-1958), ed.
--The Magic Casement: An Anthology of Fairy Poetry. Reid, Stephen (1873-1934), illus. 20cm. 390p. 1909. E. P. Dutton & Co.

Noyes, Beppie & United States. John F. Kennedy Center for the Performing Arts
--Mosby, the Kennedy Center Cat. Noyes, Beppie, illus. LC 78-12640. (Illus.). x, 127 p. 24cm. c.1978. (ISBN 0-87491-263-6). Acropolis Books.

Noyes, Ernest, ed. see Sandrus, Mary Yost.

Noyes, Marion Ingalls Osgood, Mrs. (1859-) & Ray, Blanche H.
--Little Plays for Little People. LC 10-24046. (Illus.). 19cm. 122p. 1910. Ginn & Co.

Noyes, Minna Bertha, adapted by.
--Twilight Stories. Noyes, Minna Bertha, tr. LC 17-12874. 2 p. l., 154 p. illus. 19 cm. c.1917. Parker P. Simmons Co., Inc.

Noyes, Minna Bertha, tr.
--Twilight Stories. LC 20-20032. 2 p. l., 211 p. front., illus., pl. 19 1/2 cm. c.1920. Parker P. Simmons Co., Incorporated.

Nucera, Marisa Lonette see Marisa, pseud.

Nucera, Vincent
--Pigeon on My Head. 1st ed. Nucera, Marisa Lonette (1959-), illus. Marisa, pseud. LC 65-28412. 1 v. (unpaged) col. illus. 17 cm. 1965. Bobbs-Merrill.

Nugent, Alys, illus.
--My ABC Book. (Illus.). 32p. (Golden Melody Book). (gr. k-2). 1983. (ISBN 0-307-12245-X, Golden Bks). Western Pub.

Nuhn, Elizabeth, jt. auth. see Christensen, Vera.

Numeroff, Laura Joffe, jt. auth. see Richter, Alice Numeroff.

Numeroff, Laura Joffe (1953-)
--Amy for Short. Numeroff, Laura Joffe (1953-), illus. LC 76-8842. (Illus.). p. cm. 23 cm. 48p. (Ready-to-read). c.1976. (ISBN 0-02-768180-7). Macmillan.
--Beatrice Doesn't Want to. Numeroff, Laura Joffe (1953-), illus. LC 81-447. (Illus.). 32 p. 22cm. (Easy-read story book). 1981. (ISBN 0-531-03537-9). F. Watts.
--Digger. 1st ed. Numeroff, Laura Joffe (1953-), illus. LC 82-18242. p. cm. c.1983. Dutton.
--Does Grandma Have an Elmo Elephant Jungle Kit?. Numeroff, Laura Joffe (1953-), illus. LC 79-16301. (Illus.). 55 p. 22cm. (Greenwillow read-alone books). c.1980. (ISBN 0-688-80249-4). (ISBN 0-688-84249-6). Greenwillow Books.
--If You Give a Mouse a Cookie. Numeroff, Laura Joffe (1953-) & Bond, Felicia, illus. LC 84-48343. (Illus.). 32p. (ps-2). 1985. (ISBN 0-06-024586-7). (ISBN 0-06-024587-5). HarpJ.
--Phoebe Dexter Has Harriet Peterson's Sniffles. Numeroff, Laura Joffe (1953-), illus. LC 76-54661. (Illus.). 32 p. 21cm. c.1977. (ISBN 0-688-80091-2). (ISBN 0-688-84091-4). Greenwillow Books.
--The Ugliest Sweater. Numeroff, Laura Joffe (1953-), illus. LC 79-18618. (Illus.). 32 p. 22cm. (Easy-read story book). 1980. (ISBN 0-531-02393-1). (ISBN 0-531-04097-6). F. Watts.
--Walter. Numeroff, Laura Joffe (1953-), illus. LC 77-10343. (Illus.). 32 p. 26cm. c.1978. (ISBN 0-02-768190-4). Macmillan.

Numeroff, Laura Joffe (1953-) & Richter, Alice Numeroff (1941-)
--Emily's Bunch. Numeroff, Laura Joffe (1953-), illus. LC 78-2637. (Illus.). 32 p. 26cm. c.1978. (ISBN 0-02-768430-X). Macmillan.

Nunn, Jessie Alford, ed.
--African Folk Tales. Crichlow, Ernest T. (1914-), illus. LC 72-80706. (Illus.). 141 p. 21cm. 1969. Funk & Wagnalls.

Nura, pseud., see Ulreich, Nura Woodson.

Nurenberg, Thelma (1903-)
--My Cousin, the Arab. LC 65-12125. 224p. 21cm. c.1965. Abelard.
--The Time of Anger. LC 75-2396. 207 p. 21cm. 1975. (ISBN 0-200-00153-1). Abelard-Schuman.

Nusbaum, Aileen Baehrens, Mrs.
--The Seven Cities of Cibola. Finnan, Margaret, illus. LC 26-186415. xi, 167 p. illus., 6 double col. pl. 21 cm. 1926. G. P. Putnam's Sons.
--Zuni Indian Tales. xi, 167 p. incl. illus., 6 double col. pl. 21 cm. c.1926. G. P. Putnam's Sons.

Nussbaum, Albert F. see Frederick, Lee, pseud.

Nuss baum, Albert F. see Hiller, Doris, pseud.

Nussbaum, Albert F. see Oreshnik, A. F., pseud.

Nussbaum, Albert F. (1934-)
--Gypsy. LC 77-76671. (Illus.). 64p. (Pacesetters Ser.). (gr. 4 up). 1978. (ISBN 0-516-02170-2). Childrens.

Nussbaumer, Mares & Nussbaumer, Paul Edmund (1934-)
--Away in a Manger: A Story of the Nativity. Nussbaumer, Paul Edmund (1934-), illus. LC 65-670632. 1v. (unpaged) col. illus. 22x23cm. 1st U.S. edition. 1965. Harcourt.

Nussbaumer, Paul Edmund, jt. auth. see Nussbaumer, Mares.

Nutt, Grady (1934-)
--Being Me. LC 71-145984. 96p. (gr. 7 up). 1971. (ISBN 0-8054-6909-5). Broadman.

Nutt, Laetitia L. A.
--Courageous Journey. 88p. N.D. (ISBN 0-912458-53-4). E. A. Seemann Publishing Inc.

Nuwer, Patricia
--The Birthday Party. (gr. k-2). 1978. Dorrance.

Nyabongo, Akiki K. (1905-)
--Winds and Lights: African Fairy Tales. Hewit, B., illus. LC 39-17420. (Illus.). 45p. 24p. 1939. The Voice of Ethiopia.

Nyblom, Helena Augusta Roed (1843-1926)
--The Little Maid Who Danced to Every Mood, and the Knight Who Wanted the Best of Everything. Stringer, Agnes & Andrewes, D., illus. James, A. W., tr. from Swedish. (Illus.). N.D. Dana Estes & Co.
--The Witch of the Woods: Fairy Tales from Sweden. Hald, Nils Christian, illus. Lundbergh, Holger, tr. LC 68-11175. 209p. illus. 24cm. 1st U.S. edition. 1968. Knopf.

Nyce, Vera (1862-1925)
--The Adventures of the Greyfur Family. Nyce, Helen Von Strecker (1885-1969), illus. 16cm. 76p. 1917. J. B. Lippincott Co.
--The Greyfur's Neighbors: The Twinkletails and the Twitchets. Nyce, Helen Von Strecker (1885-1969), illus. 16cm. 76p. 1917. J. B. Lippincott Co.
--A Jolly Christmas at the Patterprints. Nyce, Helen Von Strecker (1885-1969), illus. LC 76-153795. (Illus.). 27 p. 1971. (ISBN 0-8193-0522-7). Parents' Magazine Press.

Nye, A. A.
--The Adventures of Prince Curly. N.D. St. Martin's Press.
--The Witch's Cat. Reeves, William, illus. N.D. St. Martin's Press.

Nye, Harriet Kamm
--Destination Danger. LC 61-10954. 189p. 21cm. 1961. Westminster Press.
--Uncertain April. LC 58-6451. 277 p. 21cm. 1958. Dodd, Mead.
--Wishing on a Star. LC 56-6832. 247p. 21cm. 1956. Dodd, Mead.

Nye, Nelson Coral (1907-)
--Caliban's Colt. LC 50-10888. 278 p. 21 cm. 1950. Dodd, Mead.

Nye, Peter, pseud., see White, Wallace.

Nye, Peter
--The Storm. LC 82-4852. (Illus.). 96p. (Triumph Bks.). (gr. 7 up). 1982. (ISBN 0-531-04425-4). Watts.

Nye, Robert (1939-)
--Poor Pumkin. Collard, Derek, illus. 1971. Hill and Wang.
--Taliesin. Maas, Dorothy, illus. LC 67-23518. (Illus.). 121 p. 21cm. 1st U.S. edition. 1967, c.1966. Hill and Wang.
--Wishing Gold. Craig, Helen, illus. LC 79-116876. (Illus.). 107 p. 22cm. 1971, c.1970. (ISBN 0-8090-9774-5). Hill & Wang.

Nye, Robert (1939-), ed.
--Beowulf: A New Telling. Cober, Alan Edwin (1935-), illus. LC 68-14792. (Illus.). 116 p. 24cm. 1st U.S. edition. 1968. Hill and Wang.
--Cricket: Three Tales. Cole, Joanne, illus. LC 73-13233. (Illus.). 96p. (ps-2). 1975. (ISBN 0-672-51582-2). Bobbs.
--March Has Horse's Ears and Other Stories. Maas, Dorothy, illus. LC 67-146523. 88p. illus. 23cm. 1st U.S. edition. 1967, c.1966. Hill & Wang.
--The Mathematical Princess, and Other Stories. Bruner, Paul, illus. LC 79-185428. (Illus.). 125 p. 22cm. 1972, c.1971. (ISBN 0-8090-6806-0). Hill & Wang.

Nye, Robert (1939-) & Freshman, Shelley
--Cricket: Three Stories. LC 77-362778. (Illus.). 86 p. 24cm. c.1975. Bobbs-Merrill Co.

Nye, Russel Blaine, ed. see Baum, Lyman Frank.

Nygaard, Jakob Johannes Bech (1911-)
--Tobias, the Magic Mouse. Olsen, Ib Spang (1921-), illus. McCormick, Edith Joan (1934-), tr. from Danish. LC 68-26427. 1 v. (unpaged) col. illus. 25cm. 1st U.S. edition. 1968. (ISBN 0-15-289058-0). Harcourt.

Nyhart, Nina, jt. auth. see Gensler, Kinereth D.

Nystrom, Carolyn
--Growing Jesus' Way. (Children's Bible Basics Ser.). 1982. (ISBN 0-8024-5999-4). Moody.

O, A V
--Jack. 2 p. l., 51 p., 2 l. 35 1/2 x 25 cm. 1905. Althea Press.
--Jack. LC 6-25692. vii, 122 p. front. 18 cm. 1906. Benziger Brothers.

Oakes, Chandler Alban (1854-1915)
--Tobytown. Carlson, George L., illus. LC 17-30362. 4 p. l., 138 p. col. front., col. illus., col. plates. 19 1/2 cm. 1917. Sully and Kleinteich.

Oakes, Donald Thomas see Thomas, Paul, pseud.

Oakes, Donald Thomas (1923-)
--The Promise. Thomas, Paul, pseud. Simon, Howard (1903-1979), illus. LC 58-2308. (Illus.). 211p. 21cm. (The Seabury Ser.). 1959. Seabury Press.

Oakes, Vanya, pseud., see Oakes, Virginia Armstrong.

Oakes, Virginia Armstrong see Oakes, Vanya, pseud.

Oakes, Virginia Armstrong (1909-1963)
--The Bamboo Gate: Stories of Children of Modern China. Oakes, Vanya, pseud. Kingman, Dong Moy Shu (1911-), illus. LC 46-37770. ix, 157 p. incl. front., illus. 22 1/2 cm. 1946. The Macmillan Company.
--By Sun and Star. Oakes, Vanya, pseud. LC 48-11367. ix, 166p. 22cm. 1948. Macmillan Co.
--Desert Harvest. Oakes, Vanya, pseud. Kashiwagi, Isami (1925-), illus. (Land of the Free Ser.). 1953. Holt, Rinehart and Winston.
--Desert Harvest: A Story of the Japanese in California. Oakes, Vanya, pseud. Kashiwagi, Isami (1925-), illus. LC 52-14256. (Illus.). 236 p. 22cm. (Land of the Free). N.D. Winston.
--Footprints of the Dragon. Oakes, Vanya, pseud. Wong, Tyrus, illus. N.D. John C. Winston Co.
--Hawaiian Treasure. Oakes, Vanya, pseud. Kashiwagi, Isami (1925-), illus. LC 57-11509. 153p. illus. 22cm. 1957. Messner.
--Island of Flame: A Novel. Oakes, Vanya, pseud. LC 60-10950. (Illus.). 191 p. 21cm. (Your fair land series). 1960. John Day Co.
--Roy Sato: New Neighbor. Oakes, Vanya, pseud. Kashiwagi, Isami (1925-), illus. LC 55-6928. 157p. illus. 21cm. 1955. J. Messner.
--Willy Wong, American. Oakes, Vanya, pseud. Yap, Weda (1894-), illus. LC 51-9838. (Illus.). 174 p. 21cm. 1951. Messner.

Oakeshott, R. Ewart
--Knight & His Castle. (Illus.). (gr. 5-9). 1964. Dufour.

Oakley, Donald G. (1927-)
--Two Muskets for Washington. LC 72-103862. (Illus.). 166 p. 22cm. 1970. Bobbs-Merrill.

Oakley, G R
--The Children's Year. N.D. Macmillan.

Oakley, Graham (1929-)
--The Church Cat Abroad. 1980. (ISBN 0-689-70472-0, Aladdin). Atheneum.
--The Church Cat Abroad. Oakley, Graham (1929-), illus. LC 73-76327. (Illus.). 40p. (gr. k-3). 1973. (ISBN 0-689-30124-3). Atheneum.
--The Church Mice Adrift. Oakley, Graham (1929-), illus. LC 76-25705. 27cm. 36p. 1977, c.1976. (ISBN 0-689-30562-1). Atheneum. **Awards: (NYT); (KGM).**
--The Church Mice and the Moon. 1st American ed. Oakley, Graham (1929-), illus. LC 74-75569. (Illus.). 36p. 22 x 27cm. 1974. (ISBN 0-689-30437-4). Atheneum.
--The Church Mice at Bay. Oakley, Graham (1929-), illus. LC 78-62260. 36p. 1979, c.1978. (ISBN 0-689-30629-6). Atheneum.
--The Church Mice at Christmas. Oakley, Graham (1929-), illus. LC 80-14518. p. cm. 1980. (ISBN 0-689-30797-7). Atheneum.
--The Church Mice in Action. Oakley, Graham (1929-), illus. LC 82-11394. p. cm. 1983. (ISBN 0-689-30949-X). Atheneum.
--The Church Mice Spread Their Wings. 1st American ed. Oakley, Graham (1929-), illus. LC 75-15102. (Illus.). 39. 21 x 26cm. 39p. 1976, c.1975. (ISBN 0-689-30496-X). Atheneum.
--The Church Mouse. Oakley, Graham (1929-), illus. LC 72-75276. (Illus.). 36 p. 26cm. 1972. Atheneum.
--Graham Oakley's Magical Changes. Oakley, Graham (1929-), illus. LC 79-2784. (Illus.). 34 p. 1980. (ISBN 0-689-30732-2). Atheneum. **Awards: (ALA); (BGH).**
--Hetty and Harriet. Oakley, Graham (1929-), illus. LC 81-8024. (Illus.). 32 p. 1982, c.1981. (ISBN 0-689-30888-4). Atheneum.

Oakley, Helen McKelvey (1906-)
--The Enchanter's Wheel. Geer, Charles Hand (1922-), illus. LC 62-16390. 183 p. illus. 22 cm. 1962. W. W. Norton.
--Freedom's Daughter. LC 68-11382. (Illus.). 179 p. 21cm. 1968. W. W. Norton.
--The Horse on the Hill. 1st ed. Koering, Ursula (1921-), illus. LC 57-9200. 247p. illus. 22cm. 1957. Knopf.
--The Ranch by the Sea. 1st ed. Geer, Charles Hand (1922-), illus. LC 59-640900. 209p. illus. 22cm. 1959. Knopf.

Oaks, Gladys
--Nursery Rhymes for Children of Darkness. N.D. Robert M. McBride & Co.

Oana, Katherine (1929-)
--Bertrand the Bull. 1982. Ideals Publishing.
--Bobby Bear & the Blizzard. LC 80-82950. (Illus.). (Bobby Bear Ser.). (ps-1). 1981. (ISBN 0-87783-151-3). Oddo.
--Bobby Bear Goes to the Beach. LC 80-82951. (Illus.). (Bobby Bear Ser.). (ps-1). 1981. (ISBN 0-87783-153-X). Oddo.
--Gertrude the Goat. 1982. Ideals Publishing.
--Harry the Horse. 1982. Ideals Publishing.
--Leonard the Leopard. 1982. Ideals Publishing.
--The Little Dog Who Wouldn't Be. Russo, Robert, illus. LC 77-18351. (Illus.). 32 p. 25cm. c.1978. (ISBN 0-87783-150-5). Oddo Pub.
--Potter the Otter. 1982. Ideals Publishing.
--Timmy Tiger & the Butterfly Net. LC 80-82954. (Illus.). (Timmy Tiger Ser.). (ps-4). 1981. (ISBN 0-87783-160-2). Oddo.
--Timmy Tiger & the Masked Bandit. LC 80-82955. (Illus.). (Timmy Tiger Ser.). (ps-4). 1981. (ISBN 0-87783-161-0). Oddo.

Oana, Katherine (1929-) & Stephens, Jackie
--Robbie and the Raggedy Scarecrow. LC 77-18349. (Illus.). 32 p. 25cm. c.1978. (ISBN 0-87783-154-8). Oddo Publ.

O'Connell, Loretta
--The Letters of Mark O. LC 39-34156. viii, 20 p. illus. 23 cm. 1939. K. Gordon.
O'Conner, Jane & Milton, Joyce
--The Amazing Bubble Gum Caper. Zimmerman, Jerry, illus. (Illus.). 64p. (Orig.). (Pick-a-path Bks.: No. 4). (gr. 3-6). 1983. (ISBN 0-590-32893-X). Scholastic Inc.
O'Connor, Barry
--Turf Fire Stories and Fairy Tales of Ireland. (Illus.). 405p. N.D. P. J. Kenedy.
O'Connor, Betty, compiled by.
--Better Homes and Gardens Story Book: Favorite Stories and Poems from Children's Literature. LC 50-9504. viii, 151 p. illus. (part col.) 27 cm. 1950. Meridith Pub. Co.
O'Connor, Daniel Stephen (1880-), ed. see Barrie, James Matthew, Sir.
O'Connor, Dick (1930-)
--Foul Play. LC 80-82985. (Illus.). 64p. (SporTellers Ser.). (gr. 4 up). 1981. (ISBN 0-516-02263-6). Childrens.
O'Connor, Edward Dennis (1922-)
--The G-Man's Son. LC 36-417. 4 p. l., 13-249 p. 19 1/2 cm. c.1936. The Goldsmith Publishing Company.
O'Connor, Edwin Greene (1918-1968)
--Benjy: A Ferocious Fairy Tale. 1st ed. Forberg, Ati, pseud. (1925-), illus. Forberg, Beate Gropius. LC 57-119946. 143p. illus. 22cm. 1957. Little, Brown.
O'Connor, Jane
--Just Good Friends. 1st ed. LC 82-48851. 216 p. 22cm. c.1983. (ISBN 0-06-024588-3). (ISBN 0-06-024591-3). Harper & Row.
--Yours Til Niagara Falls, Abby. Apple, Margaret, illus. LC 79-19782. xiv, 141 p. 24cm. 1979. (ISBN 0-8038-8601-2). Hastings House.
--Yours Till Niagara Falls, Abby. Apple, Margaret, illus. (Illus.). 128p. (gr. 3-6). 1982. (ISBN 0-590-31957-4, Apple Paperbacks). Scholastic Inc.
O'Connor, Jane, ed.
--Dr. Jerkyl & Mr. Hyde. Van Munching, Paul, illus. McMullan, Kate LC 83-15972. (Illus.). 96p. (Step-Up Adventures Ser.: 9). (gr. 2-5). 1984. (ISBN 0-394-86365-8, BYR). (ISBN 0-394-96365-2). Random.
O'Connor, Jane, ed. see Miller, John Parr.
O'Connor, Jane & Milton, Joyce
--The Dandee Diamond Mystery. Cagle, Daryl, illus. (Illus.). 64p. (Orig.). (Pick-a-Path Bks.: No. 1). (gr. 3-6). 1983. (ISBN 0-590-32742-9). Scholastic Inc.
O'Connor, Jane & O'Connor, Jim
--The Magic Top Mystery. Callahan, Kevin, illus. (Illus.). 64p. (Orig.). (Pick-a-Path Bks.). (gr. 3-6). 1984. (ISBN 0-590-33142-6). Scholastic Inc.
O'Connor, Jane & Risom, Ole, eds.
--Noah's Ark. McKie, Roy, illus. LC 83-19189. (Illus.). 24p. (Knee-High Bks.). (gr. 1-2). 1984. (ISBN 0-394-86584-7, BYR). (ISBN 0-394-96584-1). Random.
O'Connor, Jim, jt. auth. see O'Connor, Jane.
O'Connor, Mary Ignatia, jt. auth. see Mahoney, Florence Jerome.
O'Connor, Patrick, pseud., see Wibberley, Leonard Patrick O'Connor.
O'Connor, Patrick, pseud., see Wibberly, Leonard Patrick O'Connor.
O'Connor, Patrick, pseud. (1915-)
--Beyond Hawaii. Wibberly, Leonard Patrick O'Connor. LC 69-14865. 160p. (gr. 7-9). 1969. Washburn.
--The Black Tiger. Wibberly, Leonard Patrick O'Connor. N.D. E . M. Hale and Co.
--The Black Tiger. Wibberly, Leonard Patrick O'Connor. (Illus.). (gr. 7-9). 1956. (ISBN 0-679-27005-1). Washburn.
--The Black Tiger at Bonneville. Wibberly, Leonard Patrick O'Connor. (Illus.). (gr. 6 up). 1960. (ISBN 0-8382-0093-1). Hale.
--The Black Tiger at Bonneville. Wibberly, Leonard Patrick O'Connor. (gr. 7-9). 1961. Washburn.
--The Black Tiger at Indianapolis. Wibberly, Leonard Patrick O'Connor. (gr. 7-9). 1962. Washburn.
--The Black Tiger at Le Mans. Wibberly, Leonard Patrick O'Connor. (gr. 7-9). 1958. (ISBN 0-679-24005-5, Pub. by Washburn). McKay.
--A Car Called Camellia. Wibberly, Leonard Patrick O'Connor. (gr. 6-9). 1970. Washburn.
--The Lost Harpooner. Wibberly, Leonard Patrick O'Connor. 1957. Ives Washburn Inc.
--The Lost Harpooner. Wibberly, Leonard Patrick O'Connor. 1947. Washburn.
--Raising of the Dubhe. Wibberly, Leonard Patrick O'Connor. (gr. 6-8). 1964. Washburn.
--South Swell. Wibberly, Leonard Patrick O'Connor. (gr. 6-8). 1967. Washburn.
--Treasure at Twenty Fathoms. Wibberly, Leonard Patrick O'Connor. (Illus.). (gr. 6-10). 1961. (ISBN 0-8382-0892-4). Hale.
--Treasure at Twenty Fathoms. Wibberly, Leonard Patrick O'Connor. (gr. 7-9). 1961. (ISBN 0-679-27070-1). Washburn.
O'Connor, William (1941-)
--Legend of Horn Mountain. Schlegel, Ralph A., illus. LC 70-117990. (Illus.). 160 p. 20cm. 1970. Criterion Books.
O'Conor, Norreys Jephson (1885-)
--There Was Magic in Those Days. Parks, J. Gower, illus. LC 30-27100. 3 p. l., 5-62 p., 1 l. col. plates. 22 cm. 1930. Frederick A. Stokes Co.
Odaga, Asenath
--Jande's Ambition. (gr. 7 up). 1966 (Pub. by East African Publ Hse). Northwestern U Pr.
O'Daniel, Janet (1921-)
--Garrett's Crossing. LC 69-11997. 185 p. 22cm. 1969. Lippincott.
--A Part for Addie. LC 74-7479. 230 p. 22cm. 1974. (ISBN 0-395-19495-4). Houghton Mifflin.
O'Day, Dean, ed.
--Shirley Temple Story Book. Authorized. Bailey, Corinne Ringel & Bailey, Bill, illus. LC 35-20301. 2 p. l., 9-106 p. col. front., illus. 23 1/2 cm. c.1935. The Saalfield Publishing Company.
Oddie, Alan, jt. auth. see Dickmeyer, Lowell A.
Oddo, Genevieve, ed. see Moore, Silas.
Odell, Carol
--Jimmy hurley to the rescue. 184p. 1964. Tri-Ocean Books.
--Mark and His Pictures. Rose, Gerald Hembdon Seymour (1935-), illus. LC 68-28151. (Illus.). 32 p. 25cm. 1968, c.1962. Walker.
--Wake up! It's Night. Janjic, Penelope, illus. LC 66-28942. 1v. (unpaged) col. illus. 26cm. 1967, c.1966. Angus & Robertson.
Odell, Frank Iglehart (1886-)
--Larry Burke, Freshman. Edwards, Harry C., illus. LC 10-118717. 310 p. front., plates. 20 cm. 1910. Lothrop, Lee & Shepard Co.
--Larry Burke, Sophomore. Edwards, Harry C., illus. LC 11-16264. 379 p. incl. front. plates. 20 cm. (His The Larry Burke books). 1911. Lothrop, Lee & Shepard Co.
Odell, Margaretta C. (0000-1908)
--The Story Shop. Cunnings, Edith May, illus. Clemens, Margaret M., intro. by. LC 38-216971. 9 p. l., 3-288 p. front., illus. 21 cm. c.1938. The Judson Press.
O'Dell, Marie W.
--Charles & Mary Stories. 1981. (ISBN 0-8062-1582-8). Carlton.
Odell, Mary Clemens (1904-)
--Another Story Shop. Cunnings, Edith May, illus. LC 47-4064. 7 p. l., 189 p. front., illus. 21 cm. 1947. The Judson Press.
Odell, Samuel W.
--Atlanteans. Adam Lore's Choice: A Story for Young Men. N.D. Methodist Bk Concern.
--Atlanteans. Adam Lore's Choice. Stories for Young Men. LC 7-32517. 310 p. 19 cm. 1889. Hunt & Eaton.
--The Unequal Four. A Story for Young Ladies. LC 7-32516. 442 p. 19 1/2 cm. 1893. Cranston & Hunt.
--Unequal Four: A Story for Young Ladies, 1 of 25 vols. (Selected Bks for Sunday School: The/Clifton Library). N.D. Set. Methodist Bk Concern.
O'Dell, Scott (1903-)
--Alexandra. 1984. Houghton.
--The Amethyst Ring. LC 82-23388. 212 p. 22cm. 1983. (ISBN 0-395-33886-7). Houghton Mifflin.
--The Black Pearl. Johnson, Milton (1932-), illus. LC 67-23311. 140 p. 22cm. 1967. Houghton Mifflin. **Award: (JNM).**
--The Captive. LC 79-15809. p. cm. 1979. (ISBN 0-395-27811-2). Houghton Mifflin.
--Carlota. LC 77-9468. vi, 153 p. 22cm. 1977. (ISBN 0-395-25487-6). Houghton Mifflin.
--The Castle in the Sea. 192p. (gr. 7up). 1983. (ISBN 0-395-34831-5). HM.
--Child of Fire. LC 76-3540. 261 p. 24cm. 1976, c.1974. (ISBN 0-8161-6359-6). G. K. Hall.
--Child of Fire. LC 74-8718. 213 p. 22cm. 1974. (ISBN 0-395-19496-2). Houghton Mifflin.
--The Cruise of the Arctic Star. Repr (Pub. by HM). (Young Adult Ser.). (gr. 7 up). 1973. (ISBN 0-8161-6146-1, Large Print Bks). G K Hall.
--The Cruise of the Arctic Star. Bryant, Samuel Hanks, illus. (Illus.). 224p. (gr. 7-12). 1973. (ISBN 0-395-16034-0). HM.
--The Dark Canoe. Johnson, Milton (1932-), illus. LC 68-29354. (Illus.). 165 p. 22cm. 1968. Houghton Mifflin.
--The Feathered Serpent. LC 81-7888. p. cm. 1981. (ISBN 0-395-30851-8). Houghton Mifflin.
--The Hawk That Dare Not Hunt by Day. LC 75-17029. xi, 222 p. 22cm. 1975. (ISBN 0-395-21892-6). Houghton Mifflin.
--Island of the Blue Dolphins. LC 73-20214. 231 p. 24cm. 1974, c.1960. (ISBN 0-8161-6170-4). G. K. Hall.
--Island of the Blue Dolphins. LC 60-5213. 184 p. 22cm. 1960. Houghton Mifflin. **Awards: (JNM); (IBBY); (ALA).**
--Journey to Jericho. 1st ed. Weisgard, Leonard Joseph (1916-), illus. LC 71-82479. (Illus.). 39 p. 25cm. 1969. Houghton Mifflin.
--Kathleen, Please Come Home. LC 78-3567. 196 p. 22cm. 1978. (ISBN 0-395-26453-7). Houghton Mifflin.
--The King's Fifth. Bryant, Samuel Hanks, illus. LC 66-7763. 264p. illus., maps. 22cm. 1966. Houghton. **Awards: (ALA); (JNM).**
--The Road to Damietta. LC 85-11720. 230 p. 22cm. 1985. (ISBN 0-395-38923-2). Houghton Mifflin.
--Sarah Bishop. LC 79-28394. vii, 184 p. 22cm. 1980. (ISBN 0-395-29185-2). Houghton Mifflin.
--Sing Down the Moon. LC 71-98513. 137 p. 22cm. 1970. Houghton Mifflin. **Award: (JNM).**
--The Spanish Smile. LC 82-9276. 182 p. 22cm. 1982. (ISBN 0-395-32867-5). Houghton Mifflin.
--The Treasure of Topo-el-Bampo. Ward, Lynd Kendall (1905-1985), illus. LC 72-135138. (Illus.). 47 p. 25cm. 1972. (ISBN 0-395-12576-6). (ISBN 0-395-12577-4). Houghton Mifflin.
--The Two Hundred Ninety. LC 76-42097. vi, 118 p. 22cm. 1976. (ISBN 0-395-24737-3). Houghton Mifflin.
--Zia. Lewin, Ted (1935-), illus. LC 75-44156. 179 p. 22cm. 1976. (ISBN 0-395-24393-9). Houghton Mifflin. **Award: (ALA).**
Odenwald, Tomi
--Cornelius. Morales, Ricardo A., illus. (Illus.). (gr. 3-6). 1971. Vantage.
Odescalchi, Esther Kando (1938-)
--The Little Shoe That Ran Away. LC 75-32079. (Illus.). 27 p. 29cm. c.1976. (ISBN 0-914226-04-5). Cyclopedia Pub. Co.
Odhams
--Stirring Stories For Boys. N.D. Transatlantic Arts.
--Stirring Stories For Girls. N.D. Transatlantic Arts.
Odlum, Jerome
--Nine Lives Are Not Enough. LC 40-35816. 253 p. 20 cm. c.1940. Sheridan House.
O'Donnell, Elliott (1872-1965)
--The Boys' Book of Sea Mysteries. Schaeffer, Mead (1898-1980), illus. 1930. Dodd Mead & Co.
O'Donnell, James E (1924-)
--Japanese Folk Tales. Nagao, Kasumi, illus. LC 57-5250. 92p. illus. 28cm. 1958. Caxton Printers.
O'Donnell, Jan
--A Funny Girl Like Me. 160p. (Orig.). (gr. 7 up). 1981. (ISBN 0-590-31358-4, Wildfire). Scholastic Inc.
O'Donnell, K. M., jt. auth. see Binder, Eando.
O'Donnell, William F.
--Mother Santa Claus Stories. (Illus.). (Illustrated Mother Stories Ser.). N.D. Henry Altemus Company Publications.
--Mother Santa Claus Stories: A Book of the Best Santa Claus Stories That Mothers Can Tell Their Children. LC 9-25389. 94 p. front., illus. 22 cm. c.1909. H. Altemus Company.
O'Donoghue, Michael
--The Incredible Thrilling Adventures of the Rock. Wende, Philip (1939-), illus. LC 68-28533. (Illus.). 47 p. 20cm. 1968. Random House.
Odor, Ruth Shannon (1926-)
--Baby in a Basket. Endres, Helen Elise, illus. LC 79-12092. (Illus.). 31 p. 25cm. c.1979. (ISBN 0-89565-086-X, Standard Pub). (ISBN 0-89565-086-X). Childs World.
--Bible Adventures. Mahany, Patricia, ed. Wahl, Richard (1939-), illus. (Illus.). 16p. (Orig.). (Flip-a-Bible-Story Bks.). (ps-4). 1982. (ISBN 0-87239-561-8). Standard Pub.
--Bible Heroes. Mahany, Patricia, ed. Wahl, Richard (1939-), illus. (Illus.). 16p. (Orig.). (Flip-a-Bible-Story Bks.). (ps-4). 1982. (ISBN 0-87239-562-6). Standard Pub.
--Bible Heroes. Seward, James E., illus. (Illus.). 128p. (Basic Bible Readers Ser.). (gr. 4). 1963. (ISBN 0-87239-261-9). Standard Pub.
--Brian's Trip to the Hospital. 1977. (ISBN 0-87239-265-1). Standard Pub.
--Cissy, the Pup. Altschuler, Franz (1923-), illus. LC 76-15633. (Illus.). 32 p. 25cm. (Learning about living). c.1976. (ISBN 0-913778-50-8). Child's World.
--Do You Know?. Gehring, Jack, illus. (Illus.). 24p. (gr. k-2). 1977. (ISBN 0-87239-267-8). Standard Pub.
--A Friend Is One Who Helps. rev. ed. Endres, Helen Elise, illus. LC 79-10996. (Illus.). 32 p. 25cm. (Values Ser.). c.1979. (ISBN 0-89565-074-6). Child's World.
--Growing up. rev. ed. Simon, Helen, illus. LC 79-11393. (Illus.). 31 p. 25cm. (A Values Series). c.1979. (ISBN 0-89565-075-4). Child's World.
--Learning About Giants. Axeman, Lois, illus. LC 81-10101. p. cm. c.1981. (ISBN 0-516-06534-3). Children's Press.
--The Little Lost Lamb. Sommers, Linda, illus. LC 79-13155. (Illus.). (Bible Story Books). (ps-3). 1979. (ISBN 0-89565-088-6). Childs World.
--Lori's Day. Simon, Helen, illus. LC 76-16082. (Illus.). 32 p. 25cm. (Learning about living). c.1976. (ISBN 0-913778-48-6). Child's World.
--My Quiet Book. Hook, Frances Arnold (1912-), illus. LC 76-44814. (Illus.). 32 p. 17x23cm. c.1977. (ISBN 0-913778-65-6). Children's World.
--My Wonder Book. Hook, Frances Arnold (1912-), illus. LC 76-44309. (Illus.). 32 p. c.1977. (ISBN 0-913778-64-8). Children's World.
--Parables of Jesus. (Illus., Orig.). (Programs for Children Ser.). (gr. 1-2). 1975. (ISBN 0-87239-316-X). Standard Pub.
--Please. Inderieden, Nancy, illus. LC 79-25319. (Illus.). (What Does It Mean? Ser.). (ps-2). 1980. (ISBN 0-89565-115-7). Childs World.
--The Pup Who Did As She Pleased. rev. ed. Altschuler, Franz (1923-), illus. LC 79-10774. (Illus.). 32 p. 25cm. (Values Series). c.1979. (ISBN 0-89565-078-9). Child's World.
--Sarah Lou's Untied Shoe. Endres, Helen Elise, illus. LC 76-13892. (Illus.). 32 p. 25cm. (Learning about living). c.1976. (ISBN 0-913778-46-X). Child's World.
--Thank You, God, for Quiet Things. Hook, Frances Arnold (1912-), illus. LC 80-15099. p. cm. c.1980. (ISBN 0-89565-169-6). Child's World.
--Thank You, God, for Wonderful Things. Hook, Frances Arnold (1912-), illus. LC 80-16106. p. cm. c.1980. (ISBN 0-89565-170-X). Child's World.
Oechsle, Robert
--Ducky, Ucky, and Mucky. (Illus.). 40 p. 21cm. 1975. Flourtown Pub. Co.
Oechsli, Helen, retold by.
--Peter Bull: An Old Danish Tale. 1st ed. Oechsli, Kelly (1918-), illus. LC 79-136824. (Illus.). 32 p. 24cm. 1971. (ISBN 0-670-54925-8). Viking Press.
Oechsli, Kelly, jt. auth. see Kroll, Steven.
Oechsli, Kelly, jt. ed. see Hautzig, Deborah.
Oechsli, Kelly (1918-)
--Home Sweet Home. LC 83-8607. c.1983. (ISBN 0-940742-30-6). Raintree Publishers.
--It's Schooltime. Oechsli, Kelly (1918-), illus. LC 67-9477. (Illus.). 1 v. of col. (Kin/Der owl book, KA15). 1967. Holt, Rinehart and Winston.
--Surprise! Surprise! Guess What's Inside. Oechsli, Kelly (1918-), illus. LC 67-9416. 25 p. (chiefly illus. 29cm. (Kin/Der owl book, KA14). 1967. Holt, Rinehart and Winston.
--Too Many Monkeys!. A Counting Rhyme. LC 80-50287. (Illus.). 20 p. 24cm. (Golden storytime book). c.1980. (ISBN 0-307-11984-X). Golden Press.
Oechsli, Kelly (1918-), illus.
--Humpty Dumpty's Bedtime Stories. LC 79-136997. (Illus.). 71 p. 24cm. 1971. (ISBN 0-8193-0503-0). Parents' Magazine Press.
--Humpty Dumpty's Holiday Stories. LC 72-8116. (Illus.). 70 p. 24cm. 1973. (ISBN 0-8193-0644-4). (ISBN 0-8193-0644-4). Parents' Magazine Press.
Oelerich, Marjorie L., ed. see Neese, Marcia A.
Oelerich, Marjorie L, ed. see Sanders, Sheila.
Oemler, Marie Conway, Mrs. (1879-)
--Slippy McGee. N.D. Grosset & Dunlap.
--Where the Young Child Was: And Also The Spirit of the House, The Youngest Officer, Linden Goes Home, The Little Brown House, That Makes the World Go Round. LC 21-16533. 6 p. l., 3-242 p. front., plates. 19 1/2 cm. 1921. The Century Co.
Oertel, Theodore Eugene (1864-)
--Blackbeard's Treasure: A Tale of the Famous Pirate, Captain Teach. Pugh, Mabel (1891-), illus. LC 27-16096. xv, 368 p. front., plates. 21 cm. c.1927. Thomas Y. Crowell Company.
--Jack Sutherland: A Tale of Bloody Marsh. Hastings, Howard Livingston (1887-), illus. LC 74-2401. (Illus.). ix, 325 p. 22cm. 1974, c.1926. (ISBN 0-87152-183-0). Reprint Co.
--Jack Sutherland: A Tale of Bloody Marsh. Hastings, Howard Livingston (1887-), illus. LC 26-7019. ix, 325 p. col. front., col. plates, map. 20 1/2 cm. c.1926. Thomas Y. Crowell Company.
Oetting, Rae
--The Chieftain of Chaucer. Raymond, Don, illus. LC 73-87806. (Illus.). 31 p. 25cm. c.1974. (ISBN 0-87783-137-8). (ISBN 0-87783-138-6). Oddo Pub.
--Father Nature Takes a Tour. Spiegel, Lawrence M., illus. LC 61-18090. (Illus.). (Nature & Science Bk. Ser.). (gr. k-6). 1962. (ISBN 0-513-00326-6). Denison.

AUTHOR INDEX O'HARE, KATHERINE

--The Gray Ghosts of Gotham. Raymond, Don, illus. LC 73-87804. (Illus.). 31 p. 25cm. 1974. (ISBN 0-87783-136-X). Oddo Publishing.
--The Gray Ghosts of Gotham. Raymond, Don, illus. (Illus.). (gr. 2-5). 1978. (ISBN 0-89508-059-1). Rainbow Bks.
--Keiki of the Islands. Pearson, Jeanne & Pearson, Charles, illus. LC 71-108728. (Illus.). 96 p. 25cm. 1970. Oddo Pub.
--Marilee and the Calico Cat. Spiegel, Lawrence M., illus. LC 60-10299. unpaged. illus. 29cm. 1960. T. S. Denison.
--Orderly Cricket. Marilue, pseud. (1931-), illus. Johnson, Marilue Carol. LC 68-16395. (Illus.). (gr. 2-3). 1967. (ISBN 0-87783-028-2). Oddo.
--Prairie Dog Town. LC 68-56829. (Illus.). (gr. 2-5). 1968. (ISBN 0-87783-030-4). (ISBN 0-87783-157-2). Oddo.
--Prairie Dog Town. Johnson, Marilue Carolyn (1931-), illus. LC 65-22297. 48p. col. illus. 26cm. 1965. Oddo.
--Timmy Tiger and the Elephant. Cantone, Vic, illus. LC 73-108731. (Illus.). 32 p. 25cm. 1970. Oddo Pub.
--Timmy Tiger to the Rescue. Cantone, Vic, illus. LC 70-108733. (Illus.). 32 p. 25cm. 1970. Oddo Pub.
Timmy Tiger's New Coat. Cantone, Vic, illus. LC 74-108734. (Illus.). (Timmy Tiger Ser). (ps-2). 1970. (ISBN 0-87783-044-4). (ISBN 0-87783-113-0). (ISBN 0-87783-230-7). Oddo.
--Timmy Tiger's New Friend. Cantone, Vic, illus. LC 77-108732. (Illus.). (Timmy Tiger Ser). (ps-2). 1970. (ISBN 0-87783-042-8). (ISBN 0-87783-114-9). (ISBN 0-87783-231-5). Oddo.
--When Jesus Was a Lad. Johnson, Marilue Carolyn (1931-), illus. LC 64-25749. 32 p. col. illus., ports. 27 cm. (Wonderful world of children's readers). 1964. Oddo Pub.

Oetting, Rae, jt. auth. see Oetting, Robert B.

Oetting, Robert B. & Oetting, Rae
--Quetico Wolf. Carlson, Kenneth L., illus. LC 66-11439. 112p. col. illus. 27cm. (Wonderful World of Children's Bks.). 1966. Oddo.
--Quetico Wolf. Carlson, Kenneth L., illus. LC 71-190274. (Illus.). 48 p. 25cm. 1972. (ISBN 0-87783-059-2). Oddo Pub.

O'Faolain, Eileen, Mrs.
--High Sang the Sword. 1st ed. Wildsmith, Brian Lawrence (1930-), illus. LC 64-56838. viii, 247 p. illus. 23 cm. 1959. Oxford University Press.
--The King of the Cats. Bock, Vera, illus. LC 42-166152. 158, 1 p. illus. 23 1/2 cm. 1942. W. Morrow & Co.
--The Little Black Hen: An Irish Fairy Story. LC 40-27615. 135 p. illus. 23 cm. 1940. Random House.
--The Little Black Hen: An Irish Fairy Story. Jones, Trefor, illus. LC 40-31951. 128 p. illus. (part col.) 21 x 16 cm. 1940. Oxford University Press.
--Miss Pennyfeather and the Pooka. Watson, Aldren Auld (1917-), illus. LC 46-25216. 4 p. l., 3-154 p. incl. col. illus., col. plates. 24 cm. 1946. Random House.

O'Faolain, Eileen, Mrs., ed.
--Children of the Salmon and other Irish Folktales. Hyman, Trina Schart (1939-), illus. LC 65-108942. xvii, 349p. illus. 22cm. bibl. c.1965. Atlantic-Little.
--Irish Sagas and Folk-Tales. Kiddell-Monroe, Joan (1908-), illus. LC 54-13304. 245p. illus. 22cm. (Oxford books for boys and girls). (Oxford Myths and Legends). (gr. 4-7). 1954. (ISBN 0-8098-2317-9). Oxford University Press.

Ofek, Uriel, pseud., see Popik, Uriel.

Ofek, Uriel, jt. ed. see Zim, Jacob.

Ofek, Uriel, pseud. (1926-)
--Smoke Over Golan: A Novel of the 1973 Yom Kippur War in Israel. Popik, Uriel. Bloom, Lloyd, illus. Taslitt, Israel Isaac, tr. from Hebrew. LC 78-22488. (Illus.). 192p. (gr. 4-7). 1979. (ISBN 0-06-024613-8, HarpJ). (ISBN 0-06-024614-6). Har-Row.

Ofek, Uriel, pseud. (1926-), ed.
--The Dog That Flew and other Favorite Stories from Isreal. Popik, Uriel. LC 72-82700. 154 p. 22cm. (Sabra books). 1969. Funk and Wagnalls.

Offer, Charles K
--Salt Above Gold, and Other Bohemian Folk Stories. Lewis, Wendy D., illus. LC 68-16602. (Illus.). 64 p. 23cm. 1968. F. Watts.

Offerman, Lynn, jt. auth. see Brown, Mik.

Offerman, Lynn, ed. see Daly, Kathleen N.

Offit, Sidney (1928-)
--The Adventures of Homer Fink. Galdone, Paul (1914-), illus. LC 66-14635. (Illus.). 181 p. 22cm. 1966. St. Martin's Press.
--The Boy Who Made a Million. Mayer, Mercer (1943-), illus. LC 68-16719. (Illus.). 148 p. 22cm. 1968. St. Martin's Press.
--The Boy Who Won the World Series. LC 59-15451. 160p. 21cm. 1960. Lothrop. Lee & Shepard.
--Cadet Attack. Burchard, Peter Duncan (1921-), illus. LC 64-10918. 173 p. illus. 21 cm. 1964. St Martin's Press.
--Cadet Command. Heyer, William, illus. LC 62-17667. (Illus.). 192 p. 21cm. 1962. St. Martin's Press.
--Cadet Quarterback. Fisher, Leonard Everett (1924-), illus. LC 61-13382. (Illus.). 183 p. 21cm. 1961. St. Martin's Press.
--Not All Girls Have Million Dollar Smiles and other Tales from Sam Orlinski's Scene. LC 73-158367. 158 p. 22cm. 1971. Coward, McCann & Geoghegan.
--Only a Girl Like You. LC 72-76696. 126 p. 21cm. 1972. (ISBN 0-698-20176-0). (ISBN 0-698-20176-0). Coward, McCann & Geoghegan.
--Soupbone. Galdone, Paul (1914-), illus. LC 63-12639. 127 p. illus. 22 cm. 1963. St Martin's Press.
--Topsy Turvy. LC 65-15745. 169p. 24cm. c.1965. St Martin's.
--What Kind of Guy Do You Think I Am?. LC 77-9378. p. cm. c.1977. (ISBN 0-397-47372-9). Lippincott.

Offord, Lenore Glen (1905-)
--Enchanted August. 1st ed. LC 56-968432. 245p. 22cm. 1956. Bobbs-Merrill.

Offutt, Andrew Jefferson (1934-)
--The Galactic Rejects. Cuffari, Richard (1925-1978), illus. LC 73-4948. (Illus.). 191 p. 22cm. 1973. (ISBN 0-688-41552-0). (ISBN 0-688-41552-0). Lothrop, Lee & Shepard Co.

O'Flaherty, Joseph S.
--Those Powerful Years. The South Coast & Los Angeles 1887-1917. 1978. (ISBN 0-682-49103-9, Lochinvar). Exposition Pr FL.

O'Flaherty, Liam (1896-)
--The Test of Courage & All Things Come of Age. O'Connell, Terence, illus. (Illus.). 48p. (ps-5). 1984. (ISBN 0-86327-048-4, Pub. by Wolfhound Pr Ireland). (ISBN 0-86327-044-1). Irish Bks Media.

Ogan, George F., jt. auth. see Ogan, Margaret E. Nettles.

Ogan, Margaret E. Nettles (1923-1979) & Ogan, George F. (1912-)
--Acuna Brutes. LC 73-3161. 94 p. 22cm. 1973. (ISBN 0-664-32529-7). Westminster Press.
--Backyard Winner. LC 63-15393. 180 p. 21 cm. 1963. Funk & Wagnalls Co.
--Big Iron. LC 78-181722. 122 p. 21cm. 1972. (ISBN 0-664-32492-4). Westminster Press.
--Choicy. Donahue, Vic, illus. LC 68-27143. (Illus.). 126 p. 22cm. 1968. Funk & Wagnalls.
--Desert Road Racer. LC 75-110725. 125 p. 21cm. 1970. Westminster Press.
--Devil Drivers. LC 61-12967. 183p. 22cm. 1961. Funk and Wagnalls Co.
--Donavan's Dusters. LC 75-17760. 156 p. 21cm. 1975. (ISBN 0-664-32576-9). Westminster Press.
--Goofy Foot. Dohanue, Vic, illus. LC 67-22924. (Illus.). 123 p. 21cm. 1967. Funk & Wagnalls.
--Grand National Racer. LC 76-54662. 114 p. 21cm. c.1977. (ISBN 0-664-32608-0). Westminster Press.
--The Green Galloper. Donahue, Vic, illus. LC 66-8240. 123p. 21cm. 1966. Funk & Wagnalls.
--Green Thirteen. LC 77-15935. 126 p. 21cm. c.1978. (ISBN 0-664-32624-2). Westminster Press.
--Number One Son. Donahue, Vic, illus. LC 76-80707. (Illus.). 127 p. 22cm. 1969. Funk & Wagnalls.
--Pancake Special. LC 65-19345. 190p. 22cm. c.1965. (ISBN 0-308-80146-6). Funk & Wagnalls.
--Place for Ingrid. LC 62-16176. 22cm. 182p. (gr. 7-11). 1962. (ISBN 0-308-80153-9). Funk & W.
--Raceway Charger. LC 74-2280. 141 p. 21cm. 1974. (ISBN 0-664-32550-5). Westminster Press.
--Tennis Bum. LC 76-8008. 122 p. 21cm. c.1976. (ISBN 0-664-32593-9). Westminster Press.
--Water Rat. Donahue, Vic, illus. LC 77-119785. (Illus.). 118 p. 22cm. 1970. Funk & Wagnalls.

Ogburn, Charlton, Jr. (1911-)
--Big Caesar. Krush, Joe (1918-), illus. LC 58-8169. (Illus.). 118 p. 22cm. 1958. Houghton Mifflin.
--The Bridge. Ness, Evaline Michelow, Mrs. (1911-), illus. LC 57-5886. 68p. illus. 24cm. 1957. Houghton Mifflin.
--The White Falcon. Bryson, Bernarda (1905-1977), illus. LC 55-5220. 51p. illus. 22cm. 1955. (ISBN 0-395-06965-3). Houghton Mifflin.

Ogden, Harriet V. C.
--Then Came Molly. (The Outdoor Bks.). N.D. Penn.

Ogden, Peggy, ed. see Vrooman, Christine W.

Ogden, Rollo (1856-), tr. see Isaacs, Jorge.

Ogden, Ruth, pseud., see Ide, Frances Otis Ogden.

Ogden, Ruth, pseud. (1853-1927)
--Courage. Ide, Frances Otis Ogden. Gordon, Frederick C., illus. (Children's Library). N.D. Frederick A. Stokes.
--His Little Royal Highness. Ide, Frances Otis Ogden. Rainey, William R. I. (1852-1936), illus. N.D. E. P. Dutton & Co.
--A Little Queen of Hearts. Ide, Frances Otis Ogden. (Illus.). (Popular Ser. for Young People). N.D. Frederick A. Stokes Co.
--Loyal Hearts and True. Ide, Frances Otis Ogden. (Illus.). (Library For Boys and Girls Ser.). N.D. Frederick A. Stokes Co.
--A Loyal Little Red Coat. Ide, Frances Otis Ogden. (Illus.). (Popular Ser. for Young People). N.D. Frederick A. Stokes Co.
--Tattine. Ide, Frances Otis Ogden, 1 of 15 vols. (Illus.). (Dainty Ser. of Choice Gift Bks: No. 8). 1905. Set. Henry Altemus Co.

Ogier le Danois & De Paris, Raimbert
--The Misfortunes of Ogier the Dane. Bois, Marie, ed. Linker, Robert, tr. Shewmake, Mitzi, illus. LC 64-8377. 107 p. illus. 23 cm. 1964. J. F. Blair.

Ogilby, John (1600-1676)
--The Fables of Aesop: Paraphras'd in Verse (1668). Miner, Earl Roy (1927-), compiled by. William Andrews Clark Memorial Library, Univ. of California at Los Angeles LC 65-9240. (Illus.). 25cm. xv, 211p. 1965. William Andrews Clark Memorial Lib., Univ. of Calif.

Ogilvie, Elisabeth May (1917-)
--Becky's Island. LC 61-16967. (gr. 6 up). 1961. (ISBN 0-07-047624-1). (ISBN 0-07-047620-9). McGraw.
--Blueberry Summer. LC 56-7565. 186p. 21cm. 1956. Whittlesey House.
--Ceiling of Amber. LC 64-25373. 175 p. 21cm. 1964. McGraw-Hill.
--Come Aboard and Bring Your Dory. LC 69-16258. 176 p. 22cm. 1969. McGraw-Hill.
--The Fabulous Year. LC 58-7423. 223p. 21cm. 1958. Whittlesey House.
--A Forgotten Girl. 176p. (Orig.). (gr. 7 up). 1982. (ISBN 0-590-32544-2, Windswept). Scholastic Inc.
--How Wide the Heart. 1 st. ed. LC 59-8556. 186p. 21cm. (gr. 7-10). 1959. (ISBN 0-07-047615-2). Whittlesey House.
--Masquerade at Sea House. LC 65-25549. 173p. 21cm. c.1965. McGraw.
--The Pigeon Pair. LC 67-2714. 182 p. 21cm. 1967. McGraw-Hill.
--A Steady Kind of Love. (gr. 7-10). 1979. (ISBN 0-590-04599-7, Schol Pap). Scholastic Inc.
--Too Young to Know. 192p. (Orig.). (gr. 7 up). 1982. (ISBN 0-590-31710-5, Wildfire). Scholastic Inc.
--Turn Around Twice. LC 62-18859. 160 p. 21 cm. 1962. Whittlesey House.
--Until the End of Summer. 192p. (Orig.). 1981. (ISBN 0-590-31327-4). Scholastic Inc.
--Whistle for a Wind: Maine 1820. Geer, Charles Hand (1922-), illus. LC 54-8789. 241p. illus. 21cm. (Strength of the Union). 1954. Scribner.
--The Young Islanders. Henneberger, Robert G. (1921-), illus. LC 60-14802. 160p. illus. 21cm. 1960. (ISBN 0-07-047623-3). Whittlesey House.

Ogilvie, Marta
--George and Robert. Ogilvie, Marta, illus. LC 78-103627. (Illus.). 21, 21 p., 1 leaf of plates. c.1978. Flyingfish Press.
--Sailing on Firefly. Ogilvie, Marta, illus. LC 78-103629. (Illus.). 27 i.e. 54 p. 20x22cm. c.1978. Flyingfish Press.

Ogle, Jim, jt. auth. see Maris, Roger.

Ogle, Lucille & Thoburn, Tina
--I Hear: Sounds in a Child's World. Wilkins, Eloise Burns (1904-), illus. LC 75-134277. 98p. col. illus. 21cm. 1971. (ISBN 0-07-047543-1). American Heritage Press.
--I Spy: A Picture Book of Objects in a Child's Home Enviornment. Kaufman, Joe (1911-), illus. LC 77-117362. 189p. col. illus. 21cm. 1970. (ISBN 0-07-047548-2). American Heritage Press.

Oglebay, Kate, ed. see Drama League of America.

Oglevee, Louise McAroy, Mrs. (1872-)
--Bible Text Stories for Boys and Girls. LC 35-58017. 262 p. 20 cm. c.1935. The Standard Publishing Company.
--Child's First Songs in Religious Education. app. index. viii & 71. (gr. 2-5). 1927. (ISBN 0-8192-1060-9). Morehouse.
--Seventy-Eight Year-Round Stories for Beginners and Primary Children. LC 32-808413. 205 p. illus. 20 cm. c.1932. The Standard Publishing Company.
--Story Poems for Children. LC 33-7836. 111 p. illus. 20 cm. c.1933. The Standard Publishing Company.

Ogliby, John (1600-1676), ed. see Aesopus.

Ognall, Leopold Horace see Carmichael, Harry, pseud.

O'Gorman, Edward Charles see O'Gorman, Ned, pseud.

O'Gorman, Ned, pseud., see O'Gorman, Edward Charles.

O'Gorman, Ned, pseud. (1929-)
--The Blue Butterfly. O'Gorman, Edward Charles. 1st ed. Di Grazia, Thomas (0000-1983), illus. LC 70-105491. (Illus.). 57 p. 23cm. 1971. (ISBN 0-06-024604-9). Harper & Row.

O'Grady, Alice
--The Story Tellers Book. Throop, Frances (1838-), illus. N.D. Rand McNally.

O'Grady, Alice, ed. see Asbjornsen, Peter Christen.

O'Grady, Alice, tr. see Asbjornsen, Peter Christen.

O'Grady, Caroline Geraldine
--The Dog That Went to the Doctor and other true stories of Real Animals. Berger, William Merritt (1872-), illus. LC 29-19720. 183 p. incl. illus., plates. col. front. 20 cm. c.1929. Lothrop, Lee & Shepard Co.

O'Grady, Philippe
--Escape from the Island of Ice. Zoellick, Scott, illus. LC 79-22723. (Illus.). 46p. (Quest, Adventure, Survival). (gr. 4-9). 1982. (ISBN 0-8172-2057-7). Raintree Pubs.

O'Grady, Standish see Page, Eileen.

O'Grady, Standish James (1846-1928)
--The Chain of Gold: Or, In Crannied Rocks; a Boys' Tale of Adventure on the Wild West Coast of Ireland. LC 12-37270. 1 p. l., vii-viii, 304 p. plates. 20 cm. 1895. Dodd, Mead and Company.
--Fionn and His Companions. Ni Rinn, Brid, illus. LC 77-287553. (Illus.). 21cm. 124p. 1970. Talbot Press.

Ogston, Helen
--Piney Bear. Davis, James H., illus. LC 48-1894. 53 p. illus. (part col.) 24 cm. 1948. R. M. McBride.

Ohanian, Phyllis B., jt. auth. see Mason, Leckie.

Ohanian, Phyllis Brown
--Favorite Nursery Songs. 1956. Random House.
--Songs to Sing to the Very Young. (Illus.). (ps). 1956. (ISBN 0-394-80675-1). Random.

Ohanian, Phyllis Brown, ed.
--Songs to Sing with the Very Young. Chanslor, Marjorie Torrey Hood (1899-), illus. Torrey, Marjorie, pseud. LC 66-9481. (Illus.). 24 p. 33cm. 1966. Random House.

O'Hanlon, Jacklyn (1933-)
--The Door. LC 77-86269. 84 p. 22cm. c.1978. (ISBN 0-8037-8983-1). (ISBN 0-8037-8979-3). Dial Press.
--Fair Game. LC 76-42929. p. cm. 1977. (ISBN 0-8037-2660-0). Dial Press.
--The Other Michael. LC 76-42930. p. cm. 22cm. 109p. c.1977. (ISBN 0-8037-6744-7). (ISBN 0-8037-6745-5). Dial Press.

O'Hanlon, M. A.
--Chris of Coorabeen. 1954. Bruce Publishing Co.

O'Hanlon, Virginia, jt. auth. see Church, Francis Pharcellus.

O'Hara, David, pseud., see Snell, Roy Judson.

O'Hara, David
--Candid Camera Detective. (Jimmie Drury Ser.). N.D. Grosset & Dunlap.
--Caught by the Camera. (Jimmie Drury Ser.). 1939. Grosset & Dunlap.
--What the Dark Room Revealed. (Jimmie Drury Ser.). N.D. Grosset & Dunlap.

O'Hara, Mary (1885-1980)
--The Catch Colt. 126p. 1st U.S. edition. 1981. (ISBN 0-7710-6843-3, HarpT). Har-Row.
--Green Grass of Wyoming. (gr. 7-9). 1946. (ISBN 0-397-00011-1). Har-Row.
--My Friend Flicka. (gr. 7-9). 1941. (ISBN 0-397-00008-1). Lippincott.
--My Friend Flicka. (Keith Jennison Large Type Bks). (gr. 6 up). N.D. (ISBN 0-531-00244-6). Watts.
--My Friend Flicka. new ed. Blossom, David, illus. LC 73-6611. (Illus.). 272p. (gr. 7-9). 1973. (ISBN 0-397-00981-X). (ISBN 0-397-00008-1). Har-Row.
--Sometimes Sad, Sometimes Glad. Tureck, Karen, designed by. LC 73-2737. (Illus.). 30 p. 27cm. 1973. Friendship Press.
--Thunderhead. (gr. 7-9). 1943. (ISBN 0-397-00007-3). Har-Row.

O'Hara, Vera (1902-), adapted by see Pyle, Howard.

O'Hara, Veronica
--Learn-to-Live Plays: Eight Character Plays in Verse for Intermediate Grades and Junior High Schools. LC 40-4005. 235 p. incl. front., illus. 20 cm. (Educational play-book series). c.1939. Beckley-Cardy Company.

O'Hare, Colette, ed.
--What Do You Feed Your Donkey On?. Rodwell, Jenny, illus. LC 77-17155. (Illus.). (ps-8). 1978. (ISBN 0-00-183703-6, Philomel). (ISBN 0-00-183734-6). Putnam Pub Group.
--What Do You Feed Your Donkey on?. Rhymes from a Belfast Childhood. Rodwell, Jenny, illus. LC 77-17155. (Illus.). 32 p. 21cm. 1978. Collins. **Award: (BGH).**

O'Hare, Katherine & Toomey, Elizabeth, eds.
--Old Testament Stories. (The Junior Everyreaders). N.D. Webster Publishing Co.

O'Hearn, Nila
--Fun in the Firehouse. Fleur, Anne Elizabeth (1901-), illus. Sari, pseud. LC 53-39528. unpaged. illus. 21cm. (Jolly books, 221). c.1953. Avon Publications.
O'Higgins, Harvey J.
--The Adventures of Detective Barney. 305p. N.D. Century Co.
--The Smoke-Eaters. N.D. Appleton Century Co.
Ohio. State University Columbus. Ohio State Center for Textual Studies see Hawthorne, Nathaniel.
Ohlsson, Ib, jt. auth. see Dauer, Rosamond.
Okamura, Koson, jt. ed. see Cassedy, Sylvia.
O'Kane, Walter C
--Jim & Peggy at Apple-Top Farm. N.D. Macmillan.
--Jim & Peggy at Meadowbrook Farm. N.D. Macmillan.
Oke, Janette (1935-)
--New Kid in Town. Mann, Brenda, illus. (Illus.). 125p. (Orig.). (gr. 3 up). 1983. (ISBN 0-934998-16-7). Bethel Pub.
Okeke, Uchefuna (1933-), retold by.
--Tales of Land of Death: Igbo Folktales. Okeke, Uchefuna (1933-), illus. LC 70-144286. (Illus.). xiii, 114 p. 22cm. 1st U.S. edition. 1971. Zenith Books.
Okimoto, Jean Davies (1942-)
--It's Just Too Much. LC 80-15411. 126 p. 22cm. c.1980. (ISBN 0-399-20737-6). Putnam
--My Mother Is Not Married to My Father. LC 78-26924. 109 p. 21cm. 1979. (ISBN 0-399-20664-7). Putnam.
--Norman Schnurman, Average Person. LC 82-9045. p. cm. c.1982. (ISBN 0-399-20913-1). Putnam.
--Who Did It, Jenny Lake?. LC 83-15971. p. cm. c.1983. (ISBN 0-399-21014-8) Putnam.
Oklahoma State Dept. of Education, jt. auth. see Wise, Lu Celia.
Oksner, Robert M.
--The Incompetent Wizard. McCaffery, Janet, illus. LC 65-20951. 1v. (unpaged) col. illus. 27cm. c.1965. Morrow.
O'Kun, Lan, jt. auth. see Lewis, Shari.
Okun, Lillian
--Let's Listen to a Story: Radio Scripts for Children. Straus, Helen Sachs, frwd. by. LC 59-14512. 273p. 20cm. 1959. Wilson.
Okun, Milt (1923-)
--Something to Sing About. (Illus.). 60 ils. 256p. (gr. 7 up). 1968. (ISBN 0-02-592820-1). Macmillan.
Olander, Joseph D, jt. ed. see Greenberg, Martin Harry.
O'Lantern, Jack
--A Book for Little Children. (Illus.). N.D. Robert Carter.
Olbracht, Ivan, as told by see Zeman, Kamil.
Olcott, Candice, ed. see Matsuura, Richard & Matsuura, Ruth.
Olcott, Frances Jenkins, jt. auth. see Williamson, John Ernst.
Olcott, Frances Jenkins, ed. see Grimm, Jakob Ludwig Karl (1785-1863) & Grimm, Wilhelm Karl.
Olcott, Frances Jenkins (1872-1963), ed. see Topelius, Zakarias.
Olcott, Frances Jenkins (1872-1963), tr. see Siebe, Josephine.
Olcott, Frances Jenkins (1872-1963), tr. see Veltman, Jan.
Olcott, Frances Jenkins (1872-1963)
--Bible Stories for Anniversaries. N.D. Houghton Mifflin Co.
--Bible Stories to Read and Tell. N.D. Blue Ribbon Books Inc.
--Bible Stories to Read and Tell. N.D. Houghton Mifflin Co.
--The Book of Elves and Fairies for Story-Telling and Reading Aloud and for the Children's Own Reading. Winter, Milo Kendall (1888-1956), illus. LC 18-217104. xix p., 1 l., 430 p., 1 l., col. front., col. plates. 21 cm. 1918. Houghton Mifflin Company.
--The Children's Reading. N.D. Houghton Mifflin Co.
--Good Stories for Anniversaries. Price, Harriet Longstreet (1891-), illus. LC 37-21242. 237p. N.D. Houghton Mifflin Company.
--Good Stories for Great Birthdays. (Illus.). (gr. 4-6). N.D. (ISBN 0-395-06966-1). HM.
--The Red Indian Fairy Book for the Children's Own Reading and for Story-Tellers. Richardson, Frederick (1862-1937), illus. (Riverside Literature Ser.). 1917. Houghton Mifflin Co.
--Story-Telling Poems. (Selected and Arranged for Story-Telling and Reading Aloud and for the Children's Own Reading). 1913. Houghton Mifflin Co.
--Wonder Tales from Baltic Wizards. Candell, Victor G. (1903-), illus. LC 28-24516. 234p. 1928. Longmans, Green and Co.
Olcott, Frances Jenkins (1872-1963), ed.
--The Adventures of Haroun Er Raschid: And Other Tales from the Arabian Nights. Pogany, Willy (1882-1955), illus. LC 23-17856. x p., 1 l., 363 p. col. front., illus. 21 1/2 cm. 1923. H. Holt & Company.
--The Arabian Nights. N.D. Henry Holt & Co.
--Good Stories for Great Holidays: Arranged for Story-Telling and Reading Aloud and for the Children's Own Reading. Sacker, A., illus. LC 14-19135. xxi p., 2 l., 3-461, 1 p. col. front., col. plates. 21 cm. 1914. (ISBN 0-395-06967-X). Houghton Mifflin Company.
--The Isles of Colored Shells: Tales and Poems of Fact and Beauty for Reading Aloud and for the Children's Own Reading. Fay, Herman B., Jr., illus. LC 34-39939. xv p., 2 l., 3-169 p. front., plates. 22 cm. 1934. Houghton Mifflin Company.
--More Tales from the Arabian Nights. Pogany, Willy (1882-1955), illus. Lane, Edward William (1801-1876), tr. LC 16-722. ix, 274 p. col. front., col. plates. 22 cm. $1.5. 1915. H. Holt and Company.
--Story-Telling Ballads. LC 81-84881. (Selected and Arranged for Story-Telling and Reading Aloud, and for the Boys' and Girls' Own Reading). xx, 394 p. 22cm. (Granger Poetry Library). 1982. (ISBN 0-89609-234-8). Granger Book Co.
--Story-Telling Ballads. (Selected and Arranged for Story-Telling and Reading Aloud and for the Boys' and Girls' Own Reading). (Riverside Literature Ser.). 1920. Houghton Mifflin Co.
--Story-Telling Poems: Selected and Arranged for Story-Telling and Reading Aloud and for the Children's Own Reading. LC 77-128155. xvi, 384 p. 21cm. (Granger index reprint series). 1970, c.1913. (ISBN 0-8369-6182-X). Books for Libraries Press.
--Tales of the Persian Genii. Pogany, Willy (1882-1955), illus. LC 17-298000. x p., 1 l., 225, 1 p. col. front., col. plates. 21 cm. 1917. Houghton Mifflin Company.
--Tales of the Persian Genii. New and enlarged. Pogany, Willy (1882-1955), illus. LC 31-18737. ix p., 1 l., 276 p. col. front., col. plates. 21 cm. c.1931. Houghton Mifflin Company.
--The Wonder Garden: Nature Myths and Tales from All the World Over for Story-Telling and Reading Aloud and for the Children's Own Reading. Winter, Milo Kendall (1888-1956), illus. LC 19-19157. xxiii p., 2 l., 3-468, 1 p. col. front., col. plates. 21 cm. 1919. Houghton Mifflin Company.
--Wonder Tales from China Seas. Walker, Dugald Stewart (1888-1937), illus. LC 25-24607. xviii, 233 p. col. front., illus. 20 cm. 1925. Longmans, Green and Co.
--Wonder Tales from Fairy Isles: England, Cornwall, Wales, Scotland, Man, and Ireland. Whittemore, Constance, illus. LC 29-19562. xx, 235 p. incl. illus., plates. col. front. 20 cm. 1929. Longmans, Green and Co.
--Wonder Tales from Goblin Hills: From the German and English. Sichel, Harold M. (1881-), illus. LC 30-24472. xix, 268 p. col. front., illus., 20 cm. 1930. Longmans, Green and Co.
--Wonder Tales from Pirate Isles: Chiefly Translated from the Dutch. Rosse, Herman, illus. LC 27-19511. 256 p. col. front., illus. 20 cm. 1927. Longmans, Green and Co.
--Wonder Tales from Windmill Lands: From the Dutch and Other Sources. Rosse, Herman, illus. LC 26-19755. xvii, 1, 238 p. col. front., illus. 19 cm. 1926. Longmans, Green and Co.
Olcott, Frances Jenkins (1872-1963) & Pendleton, Amena, eds.
--The Jolly Book for Boys and Girls. LC 15-27925. xiv, 409, 1 p. front., plates. 21 cm. 1915. Houghton Mifflin Company.
Olcott, Harriet Mead
--The Children's Fairyland. N.D. Henry Holt.
--The Whirling King and other French Fairy Tales. LC 20-16112. 5 p. l., 3-177 p. illus. 21 cm. 1920. H. Holt and Company.
Olcott, Julia, as told by see Segur, Sophie Rostopchine, Mrs.
Olcott, Julia, tr. see Foa, Eugenie Rodrigues-Gradis.
Olcott, Susan
--Rusty and Al. Fodor, Laszlo (1898-), illus. LC 45-9580. 27 x 21 1/2cm. 32p. 1945. Diamond Pub.
Olcott, Virginia
--Adventures in France: The Story of Jean and Fanchon. Whittemore, Constance, illus. LC 53-510392. 168p. illus. 22cm. (Her The world's children series). 1953. Grosset & Dunlap.
--Adventures in Holland: The Story of Klass and Jansje. Whittemore, Constance, illus. LC 53-5108. 152p. illus. 22cm. (Her The world's children series). 1953. Grosset & Dunlap.
--Adventures in Italy: The Story of Beppo and Lucia. Whittemore, Constance, illus. LC 53-5105. 162p. illus. 22cm. (Her The world's children series). 1953. Grosset & Dunlap.
--Adventures in Norway: The Story of Olaf and Ane. Whittemore, Constance, illus. 168p. illus. 22cm. (Her The world's children series). 1953. Grosset &Dunlap.
--Adventures in Sweden: The Story of Erik and Britta. Whittemore, Constance, illus. LC 53-5107. 168p. illus. 22cm. (Her The world's children series). 1953. Grosset & Dunlap.
--Adventures in Switzerland: The Story of Anton and Trini. Whittemore, Constance, illus. LC 53-510408. 152p. illus. 22cm. (Her The world's children series). 1953. Grosset & Dunlap.
--Anton and Trini, Children of the Alpland. Whittemore, Constance, illus. LC 30-1705. vii, 1, 152 p. illus. (part col.) 20 cm. c.1930. Silver, Burdett and Company.
--Beppo and Lucia, Children of Sunny Italy. Whittemore, Constance, illus. LC 34-33273. vii, 1, 168 p. illus. (part col.) 20 cm. (On cover: The world's children). c.1934. Silver, Burdett and Company.
--Concetta, the Coral Girl. Smith, Catherine, illus. LC 28-21421. xiv, 77, 5 p. col. front., col. illus. 22 cm. 1928. Frederick A. Stokes Company.
--Dino of the Golden Boxes. Smith, Catherine, illus. N.D. J. B. Lippincott.
--Dino of the Golden Boxes: A Story of Florence. Smith, Catherine, illus. LC 30-25161. xi, 89 p., 1 l. col. front., col. illus. 22 cm. 1930. Frederick A. Stokes Company.
--Erik and Britta, Children of Flowery Sweden. Whittemore, Constance, illus. LC 37-359473. vii, 1, 168 p. illus. (part col.) 20 cm. (On cover: The world's children). c.1937. Silver Burdett Company.
--Everyday Plays for Home, School and Settlement: Flowers in the Palace Garden, and Other Plays. LC 25-22898. 8 p. l., 5-167 p. col. front., illus., col. plates. 20 cm. 1925. Dodd, Mead and Company.
--Holiday Plays for Home, School and Settlement. Olcott, Harriet, illus. N.D. Dodd Mead & Co.
--Holiday Plays for Home, School and Settlement. Olcott, Harriet Mead, illus. LC 17-25837. 7 p. l., 5-197 p. col. front., illus., col. plates. 20 cm. 1917. Moffat, Yard & Company.
--Household Plays for Young People. Egan, Florence, illus. LC 28-8648. ix, 275 p. incl. plates. col. front., col. plates. 20 cm. 1928. Dodd, Mead & Company.
--Industrial Plays for Young People. Egan, Florence, illus. LC 27-5961. xi, 257 p. col. front., plates (port col.) 20 cm. 1927. Dodd, Mead and Company.
--International Plays for Young People. Egan, Florence, illus. LC 25-21518. vii, 245 p. col. front., illus., col. plates. 20 cm. 1925. Dodd, Mead and Company.
--Jean and Fanchon, Children of Fair France. Whittemore, Constance, illus. LC 31-28698. vii, 1, 168 p. illus. (part col.) 20 cm. c.1931. Silver, Burdett and Company.
--Karl and Gretel, Children of the Fatherland. Whittemore, Constance, illus. LC 32-28984. vii, 1, 168 p. illus. (part col.) 20 cm. c.1932. Silver, Burdett and Company.
--Klaas and Jansje, Children of the Dikes. Whittemore, Constance, illus. LC 33-38001. vii, 1, 152 p. illus. (part col.) 20 cm. (On cover: The world's children). c.1933. Silver, Burdett and Company.
--Market Day and Holiday: Stories of the World's Children. Whittemore, Constance, illus. LC 41-18904. 192 p. illus. (part col.) 21 x 16 cm. (Her The world's children). c.1941. Silver Burdett Company.
--Olof and Ane, Children of the Northland. Whittemore, Constance, illus. LC 38-35989. vii, 1, 168 p. illus. (part col.) 19 cm. (On cover: The world's children). c.1938. Silver Burdett Company.
--Patriotic Plays for Young People. Olcott, Harriet Mead, illus. LC 18-11134. xi, 1, 174 p. col. front., illus., col. plates. 20 cm. 1918. Dodd, Mead and Company.
--Plays for Home, School and Settlement: Flowers in the Palace Garden, and Other Plays. LC 16-18615. 7 p. l., 5-133 p. col. front., illus., col. plates. 20 cm. 1916. Moffat, Yard & Company.
Olcott, Virginia, tr. see Rosmer, Jean.
Olcott, Virginia, tr. see Segur, Sophie Rostopchine, Mrs.
Old Woman and Her Pig
--The Old Woman and Her Pig. Harwood, John, illus. LC 46-15978. 32 p. illus. (part col.) 18 cm. (Baby Puffin book). 1944. Penguin Books, Limited.
--The Old Woman and Her Pig. Wadsworth, Wallace Carter (1894-1933), retold by. Brice, Tony, illus. LC 44-6707. 62 p. illus. (part col.) 17 cm. 1944. Rand McNally & Company.
--The Old Woman and Her Pig. Wadsworth, Wallace Carter (1894-1933), retold by. Friend, Esther, illus. LC 52-64156. unpaged. illus. 21cm. (Rand McNally book-elf book, 464). c.1952. Rand McNally.
Old Coyote, Sally & Toineeta, Joy Yellow Tail
--Indian Tales of the Northern Plains. (Indian Culture Ser.). (gr. 2-5). 1972. (ISBN 0-89992-018-7). MT Coun Indian.
Oldden, Richard, jt. auth. see Kraus, Robert.
Oldenburg, Egbert William (1936-1974)
--Potawatomi Indian Summer. Beeby, Betty (1923-), illus. LC 75-12857. (Illus.). 134 p. 24cm. 1975. (ISBN 0-8028-1614-2). Eerdmans.
Oldenburg, Richard, tr. see Geijerstam, Brita Af.
Oldenburg, Richard E., tr. see Lagerlof, Selma Ottiliana Lovisa.
Oldfellow, Alfred, pseud., see Beach, Alfred.
Oldfellow, Alfred, pseud.
--Uncle Nat Library: Containing: "Joe Nichols, of Difficulties overcome", "Tom Randall, or the Way to Success", & "Uncle Nat". Beach, Alfred, 3 Vols. N.D. James Miller.
Oldfield, Jenny (1949-)
--Secret of the Seasons. LC 76-371439. 7, 143 p. 22cm. 1976. (ISBN 0-434-95562-0). Heinemann.
Oldfield, Margaret J.
--Fat Cat and Ebenezer Geezer the Teeny Tiny Mouse. 2nd ed. Oldfield, Margaret J., illus. (Illus.). (gr. k-2). 1980. (ISBN 0-934876-13-4). Creative Storytime.
--Finger Puppets & Finger Plays. (Illus.). (ps-3). 1982. (ISBN 0-934876-18-5). Creative Storytime.
--Lots More Tell & Draw Stories. (Illus.). (ps-3). 1973. (ISBN 0-934876-07-X). (ISBN 0-934876-03-7). Creative Storytime.
--More Tell & Draw Stories. (Illus.). (ps-3). 1969. (ISBN 0-934876-06-1). (ISBN 0-934876-02-9). Creative Storytime.
--Tell & Draw Paper Bag Puppet Book. 2nd ed. Oldfield, Margaret J., illus. (Illus.). (gr. k-2). 1981. (ISBN 0-934876-16-9). Creative Storytime.
Oldfield, Pamela
--The Halloween Pumpkin. american ed. Eccles-Williams, Ferelith, illus. LC 75-41346. (Illus.). 24 p. 21cm. (Stepping stones). 1976, c.1974. (ISBN 0-516-03582-7). Childrens Press.
--Melanie Brown & the Jar of Sweets. Dinan, Carolyn, illus. (Illus.). 64p. (ps-5). 1974. (ISBN 0-571-10619-6). Faber & Faber.
--Melanie Brown Goes to School. Dinan, Carolyn, illus. (Illus.). (ps-5). 1970. (ISBN 0-571-09421-X). Faber & Faber.
--Melanie Brown Goes to School. Dinan, Carolyn, illus. (Illus.). 64p. 1st U.S. edition. (Faber Fanfare Ser.). (ps-4). 1979. (ISBN 0-571-11334-6). Faber & Faber.
--Simon's Extra Gran. Lucas, Derek, illus. LC 75-42148. (Illus.). 24 p. 21cm. (Stepping stones). 1976, c.1974. (ISBN 0-516-03592-4). Childrens Press.
Oldfield, Reuben Bertram see Field, Ben, pseud.
Oldfield, Reuben Bertram (1878-)
--Exciting Adventures of Mister Bob White. Field, Ben, pseud. LC 28-130252. 4 p. l., 119 p. col. front., col. plates. 20 cm. (His Wildwood series). c.1928. A. L. Burt Company.
--Exciting Adventures of Mister Gerald Fox. Field, Ben, pseud. LC 28-142780. 4 p. l., 115 p. col. front., col. plates. 20 cm. (His Wildwood series). c.1928. A. L. Burt Company.
--Exciting Adventures of Mister Jim Crow. Field, Ben, pseud. LC 28-10520. 4 p. l., 114 p. col. front., col. plates. 20 cm. (His Wildwood series). c.1928. A. L. Burt Company.
--Exciting Adventures of Mister Melancthon Coon. Field, Ben, pseud. LC 28-12121. 4 p. l., 119 p. col. front., col. plates. 20 cm. (His Wildwood series). c.1928. A. L. Burt Company.
--Exciting Adventures of Mister Robert Robin. Field, Ben, pseud. LC 28-14493. 3 p. l., 119 p. col. front., col. plates. 20 cm. (His Wildwood series). c.1928. A. L. Burt Company.
--Exciting Adventures of Mister Tom Squirrel. Field, Ben, pseud. LC 28-121222. 4 p. l., 113 p. col. front., col. plates. 20 cm. (His Wildwood series). c.1928. A. L. Burt Company.
Oldham, Etta Baldwin, Mrs.
--Pedro's Pirate. Cannon, Martin, illus. LC 41-7321. 4 p. l., 215 p. illus. 21 cm. c.1941. Lothrop, Lee & Shepard Co.
Oldham, Mary (1944-)
--A Horse for Her. Hodgson, Robert, illus. LC 69-16556. (Illus.). 157 p. 22cm. 1st U.S. edition. 1969, c.1968. Hastings House.
--The White Pony. LC 81-4135. 119 p. 22cm. c.1981. (ISBN 0-8038-0800-3). Hastings House.

--Masie & the Persian Pink Petunias. Obligado, Lilian Isabel (1931-), illus. LC 79-105255. (Illus.). color ils. 48p. (gr. k-3). 1970. (ISBN 0-200-72024-4). Abelard.

Olsen, Alfa-Betty, jt. auth. see Efron, Marshall.

Olsen, Eilene

--Just Imagine. Langelier, Joyce, illus. LC 63-5639. (Illus.). 21cm. 135p. 1963. Rolton House.

Olsen, Einar A

--Adrift on a Raft. Le Blanc, Lee, illus. LC 68-16397. (Illus.). 48 p. 27cm. (Wonderful World of Children's Books). 1968. Oddo Publishing.

--Killer in the Trap. Le Blanc, Lee, illus. LC 68-16399. (Illus.). 48 p. 24cm. (Wonderful World of Children's Books). 1968. Oddo Publishing.

--The Lobster King. Le Blanc, Lee, illus. LC 68-16400. (Illus.). 48 p. 25cm. (Wonderful World of Children's Books). 1968. Oddo Publishing.

--Mystery at Salvage Rock. Le Blanc, Lee, illus. LC 68-16401. (Illus.). 48 p 25cm. (Wonderful World of Children's Books). 1968. Oddo Publishing.

Olsen, Gunder E.

--The Volcano House. 92p. 1974. (ISBN 0-912180-22-6). The PetroGlyph Press.

Olsen, Ib Spang (1921-)

--The Boy in the Moon. Jensen, Virginia Allen, tr. LC 74-1418. p. 1977. (ISBN 0-8193-0733-5). (ISBN 0-8193-0734-3). Parents' Magazine Press.

--The Boy in the Moon. Olsen, Ib Spang (1921-), illus. Jensen, Virginia Allen (1927-), tr. from Danish. LC 62-11150. unpaged. illus. 13 x 18 cm. c.1963. Abingdon Press.

--Cat Alley. Olsen, Ib Spang (1921-), illus. Jensen, Virginia Allen (1927-), tr. LC 73-161608. (Illus.). 32 p. 26cm. 1st U.S. edition. 1971. Coward, McCann & Geoghegan.

--Little Locomotive. Jensen, Virginia Allen, tr. LC 75-35513. (Illus.). 32 p. 25cm. 1976. (ISBN 0-698-20364-X). Coward, McCann & Geoghegan.

--The Little Shunting Engine. Jensen, Virginia Allen, tr. LC 77-351984. (Illus.). 32 p. 25cm. 1976. (ISBN 0-437-64571-1). World's Work.

--The Marsh Crone's Brew. Olsen, Ib Spang (1921-), illus. Jensen, Virginia Allen (1927-), tr. LC 60-6812. unpaged. illus. 18cm. c.1960. Abingdon Press.

--Smoke. Jensen, Virginia Allen, tr. LC 78-171614. (Illus.). 34 p. 1972. Coward, McCann & Geoghegan.

Olsen, Jack

--The Night of the Grizzlies. (Illus.). 1969. G P Putnum's Sons.

Olsen, James P

--Powdersmoke Paddy. LC 40-13802. 283 p. 20 cm. 1940. E. P. Dutton & Company, Inc.

Olsen, Johanna Bugge

--Stray Dog. Edwards, Gunvor, illus. LC 68-15242. (Illus.). 160 p 22cm. 1st U.S. edition. 1968, c.1966. Criterion Books.

Olsen, Judy C.

--Dive into Danger. Olsen, Judy C., illus. 147p. Repr. of 1979 ed (Pub. by Ensign Pubs). (gr. 9-12). 1980. (ISBN 0-934126-04-6). Raymont Pubs.

Olsen, Theodore Victor (1932-)

--Summer of the Drums. 1st ed. LC 72-79413. 22cm. 152p. 1972. (ISBN 0-385-05694-X). Doubleday.

Olsen, Violet

--The Growing Season. 1st ed. LC 82-1763. 220 p. 22cm. 1982. (ISBN 0-689-30938-4). Atheneum.

--Never Brought to Mind. LC 84-21664. 176 p. 22cm. 1985. (ISBN 0-689-31110-9). Atheneum.

Olsen, Zora L.

--Herman the Great. Cooney, Barbara (1917-), illus. (illus.). (gr. 2-3). 1976. (ISBN 0-590-09807-1, Schol Trade Pap). Schol Bk Serv.

Olson, Arielle North

--Hurry Home, Grandma!. Dabcovich, Lydia, illus. LC 84-1529. (Illus.). 32p. (ps-1). 1984. (ISBN 0-525-44113-1). (ISBN 0-525-44113-1). Dutton.

Olson, Enid Martell, ed.

--Bushes & Bears: Adventures in Imagination and Reality. LC 79-134357. (Illus.). vii, 184 p. 21cm. (Reader's digest story world). 1971, c.1969. Reader's Digest Services.

--Corner of the Moon: Folk Tales for Reading Pleasure. LC 78-134354. (Illus.). vii, 151 p. 21cm. (Reader's digest story world). 1971, c.1969. Reader's Digest Services.

--Moons, Suns, and Rush-Candles: Stories of Fantasy. LC 75-134356. (Illus.). vii, 132 p. 21cm. (Reader's digest story world). 1971, c.1969. Reader's Digest Services.

Olson, Enid Martell & Sideman, Belle Becker, eds.

--Lamps of Joy: Stories of Humor from Western Europe. LC 70-134352. (Illus.). vii, 150 p. 21cm. (Reader's digest story world). 1971, c.1967. Reader's Digest Services.

--Lions & Lizards: Stories from Asia, Africa, and Eastern Europe. LC 74-134353. (Illus.). vii, 182 p. 21cm. (Reader's digest story world). 1971, c.1967. Reader's Digest Services.

Olson, Ernst Wilhelm (1870-), tr. see Nonnen, Emily.

Olson, Ernst Wilhelm (1870-)

--Bobby Beggum's Birthday. 48p. N.D. Augustana Book Concern.

Olson, Evelyn F.

--The Months of the Year in Verse. (Illus.). 64p. 1984. (ISBN 0-682-40152-8). Exposition.

Olson, Gene (1922-)

--Bailey and the Bearcat. LC 64-10665. 191 p. 21 cm. 1964. Westminster Press.

--The Ballhawks. LC 60-7811. 186p. 21cm. 1960. Westminster Press.

--Between Me and the Marshal. LC 64-10677. 209 p. 21cm. 1964. Dodd, Mead.

--Bonus Boy: The Story of a Southpaw Pitcher. LC 63-11544. 184 p. 21cm. 1963. Dodd, Mead.

--The Bucket of Thunderbolts: A Sports Car Racing Adventure. LC 59-11692. 176 p. 21cm. 1959. Dodd, Mead.

--Cross-Country Chaos. LC 66-10225. 168p. 22cm. c.1966. Westminster.

--Drop into Hell. LC 69-12128. 156 p. 21cm. 1969. Westminster Press.

--Fullback Fury. LC 64-23288. (gr. 7-9). 1964. (ISBN 0-396-05073-5). Dodd.

--Iron Foxhole. (gr. 7-10). 1968. (ISBN 0-664-32409-6). Westminster.

--The Most Beautiful Girl in the World. LC 68-16857. 168 p. 22cm. 1968. Westminster Press.

--Pistons and Powderpuffs. LC 67-10613. 188 p. 21cm. 1967. Westminster Press.

--The Red, Red Roadster. LC 62-18431. 192p. 22cm. 1962. Macrae Smith.

--The Red, Red Roadster (Pub. by Masrae). (gr. 7-12). 1972 (Starline). Schol Bk Serv.

--Roaring Road. LC 62-12205. (gr. 7-9). 1962. Dodd.

--Sacramento Gold. LC 61-14957. 180 p. 22cm. 1961. Macrae Smith Co.

--The Tall One: A Basketball Story. LC 56-8710. 21cm. 211p. (gr. 7-9). 1956. (ISBN 0-396-03885-9). Dodd.

--Three Men on Third. LC 65-11209. 174p. 21cm. c.1965. Westminster.

--The Tin Goose. LC 61-9792. 189p. 21cm. c.1962. Westminster Press.

Olson, Helen Kronberg

--The Secret of Spirit Mountain. Benjamin, Hameed, illus. LC 80-1014. (Illus.). 157 p. 21cm. c.1980. (ISBN 0-396-07856-7). Dodd, Mead.

--The Strange Thing That Happened to Oliver Wendell Iscovitch. Lewin, Betsy (1937-), illus. LC 82-45990. p. cm. 1983. (ISBN 0-396-08147-9). Dodd, Mead.

--Stupid Peter and Other Tales: New Stories to Read Together. Delano, Irene (1919-) & Delano, Jack, illus. LC 79-107599. (Illus.). 96p. (gr. 2-5). 1970. (ISBN 0-394-80798-7). (ISBN 0-394-90798-1). Random.

Olson, Jim

--The Reindeer & the Easter Bunny. Van Vleck, Jane & Olson, Sally, eds. (Illus.). 18p. (Orig.). 1st U.S. edition. (gr. 1-4). 1981. (ISBN 0-943806-00-3). Greenprint Pr.

Olson, John Helmer

--The Bluebells of Nola. Bystrom, Gerald, illus. LC 28-29230. 94 p. incl. front., illus. 20 cm. c.1928. Augustana Book Concern.

--Fearless Freddie. (Illus.). (gr. 1-3). 1967. (ISBN 0-8382-0247-0). Hale.

Olson, Lyla Mae, jt. auth. see Seybert, Mildred.

Olson, Margaret J.

--Aloysious Alligator. 2nd ed. Olson, Margaret J., illus. (Illus.). (gr. k-2). 1980. (ISBN 0-934876-14-2). Creative Storytime.

--Tell & Draw Animal Cut-Outs. 3rd ed. (gr. k-2). 1963. (ISBN 0-934876-15-0). Creative Storytime.

--Tell & Draw Stories. (Illus.). (ps-3). 1963. (ISBN 0-934876-05-3). (ISBN 0-934876-01-0). Creative Storytime.

Olson, Marjorie E.

--Benji the Bug: Directionality Concepts for Children. (Illus.). 21p. (gr. k-1). 1973. (ISBN 0-89039-099-1). Ann Arbor FL.

--Finton the Fish: Visual Discriminations for Children. (Illus.). 29p. (gr. k-1). 1974. (ISBN 0-89039-100-9). Ann Arbor FL.

--The Sly Spy & Other Stories. Reusable ed. (Illus.). (Educational Ser.). (gr. 2-3). 1979. (ISBN 0-89039-242-0). Ann Arbor FL.

Olson, Sally, ed. see Olson, Jim.

Olujic, Grozdana

--Rose of Mother-of-Pearl: A Fairy Tale. Jacobi, Kathy, illus. Olujic, Grozdana & Kessler, Jascha, trs. from Serbo-Croatian LC 83-18254. (Illus.). 23 p. 16cm. (Hot Chocolate Fairy Tale Series ; 1). c.1983. (ISBN 0-915124-90-4). Hot Chocolate Books.

O'Malley, Mary Dolling Sanders see Bridge, Ann, pseud.

O'malley, Patricia see Strickland, Catherine Patricia O'Malley.

O'Malley, Patricia (1900-)

--Airline Girl. LC 44-47955. 209p. 19cm. 1944. Dodd, Mead.

O'Malley, Raymond Morgan & Thompson, Denys (1907-), eds.

--The Bough on the Tree. (Illus.). 122 p 22cm. (Their the Tree in the Wood, 4). 1968, c.1966. F. Watts.

--The Egg in the Nest. LC 68-19241. (Illus.). 85 p 22cm. (Their the Tree in the Wood, 1). 1968, c.1966. F. Watts.

--The Nest on the Twig. LC 68-19242. (Illus.). 93 p. 22cm. (Their the Tree in the Wood, 2). 1968, c.1966. F. Watts.

--The Twig on the Bough. (Illus.). 103 p. 22cm. (Their the Tree in the Wood, 3). 1968, c.1966. F. Watts.

O'Malley, Sallie Margaret

--An Heir of Dreams. LC 12-37289. 168 p. 17 cm. 1897. Etc. Benziger Brothers.

Oman, Carola Mary Anima (1897-1978)

--Alfred, King of the English. Uden, E. Boye, illus. N.D. E. P. Dutton & Co.

--Robin Hood. (Illus.). 254p. Repr. of 1949 ed. (Childrens Illustrated Classics). 1974. (ISBN 0-460-05007-9, Pub. by J. M. Dent England). Biblio Dist.

--Robin Hood. Van Abbe, Salaman (1883-1955), illus. (Children's Illustrated Classics). 1949. E. P. Dutton & Co.

O'Meara, Frances Jacobi

--Young MacDonald had a Farm. N.D. Carlton Press Inc.

O'Meara, Kathleen

--Mabel Stanhope, 1 of 7 vols. (Premium Library: No. 1). 1891. Set. McCauley & Kilner.

O'Meara, Walter Andrew (1897-)

--The Devil's Cross. 1st ed. LC 57-10309. 291p. 22cm. 1957. Knopf.

--The Sioux Are Coming. Bjorklund, Lorence F. (1913-1978), illus. LC 79-161647. (Illus.). 105 p. 22cm. 1971. (ISBN 0-395-12759-9). Houghton Mifflin.

O'Mellish, Phineas, jt. auth. see Berman, Sam.

Omer, Devorah (1932-)

--Gideonites: The Story of the Nili Spies in the Middle East. Reznik, Ruth, ed. Reznik, Ruth, tr. from Hewbrew. LC 68-55545. (Illus.). 256p. 23cm. (gr. 3-6). 1968 (Sabra). Funk & W.

--Path Beneath the Sea: A Novel. Taslitt, Israel Isaac, tr. from Hebrew. LC 69-13469. (Illus.). 191 p. 23cm. (Sabra book). 1969. Funk and Wagnalls.

O'Moran, M., pseud., see Moran, Mabel O'Connell.

O'More, Peggy see Blocklinger, Betty, pseud.

O'More, Peggy (1897-)

--Girl at Sea. LC 64-9170. 223 p. 20 cm. (Arcadia teen-age romance, 12). c.1962. Arcadia House.

--House by the Orchard. LC 52-11402. 220 p. 21 cm. 1952. Arcadia House.

--Lesson in Love. LC 62-569496. 220p. 20cm. 1962. Arcadia House.

--Pretty Polly. Blocklinger, Betty, pseud. LC 54-7489. 224p. 20cm. 1954. Arcadia House.

Onassis, Jacqueline Kennedy (1929-), ed.

--The Firebird and Other Russian Fairy Tales. Zvorykin, Boris Vasilevich (1872-), illus. LC 78-5235. 78 29. (Studio book). 1978. (ISBN 0-670-31544-3). Viking Press.

Oncken, Clara

--Hickory Sam. Wood, Stanley L. (1866-1928), illus. LC 39-24444. 6 p. l., 276 p. incl. illus., plates. 21 cm. c.1939. H. Holt and Company.

Onclincx, Georges

--Einar, the Viking. Dolan, Ellen M., adapted by. Wabbes, Marie, illus. LC 75-2536. (Illus.). 26 p. (Children of other times). c.1968. (ISBN 0-07-017369-9). Webster Division, McGraw-Hill.

O'Neal, Charles E. (1904-)

--The Three Wishes of Jamie McRuin. N.D. Julian Messner, Inc.

Oneal, Elizabeth see Oneal, Zibby, pseud.

Oneal, Zibby, pseud., see Oneal, Elizabeth.

Oneal, Zibby, pseud. (1934-)

--A Formal Feeling: A Novel. Oneal, Elizabeth. LC 82-2018. (Illus.). 168p. 1st U.S. edition. (gr. 7 up). 1982. (ISBN 0-670-32488-4). Viking Pr. **Award: (ALA).**

--The Improbable Adventures of Marvelous O'Hara Soapstone. Oneal, Elizabeth. 1st ed. Galdone, Paul (1914-), illus. LC 72-80516. (Illus.). 128 p. 22cm. 1972. (ISBN 0-670-39424-6). Viking Press.

--In Summer Light. Oneal, Elizabeth. LC 85-50806. 149 p. 22cm. 1985. (ISBN 0-670-80784-2). Viking Kestrel. **Award: (ALA).**

--The Language of Goldfish: A Novel. Oneal, Elizabeth. LC 79-19167. 179 p. 22cm. 1980. (ISBN 0-670-41785-8). Viking Press. **Award: (ALA).**

--Maude and Walter. Oneal, Elizabeth. Chambliss, Maxie, illus. LC 84-48357. (Illus.). 28 p. 20cm. c.1985. (ISBN 0-397-32150-3). (ISBN 0-397-32151-1). Lippincott.

--Turtle and Snail. Oneal, Elizabeth. Tomes, Margot Ladd (1917-), illus. LC 78-14826. (Illus.). 47 p. 24cm. (Lippincott I-like-to-read book). c.1979. (ISBN 0-397-31829-4). Lippincott.

--War Work. Oneal, Elizabeth. 1st ed. Porter, George, illus. LC 77-162673. (Illus.). 251 p. 22cm. 1971. (ISBN 0-670-75000-X). (ISBN 0-670-75001-8). Viking Press.

O'Neil, Beverly J.

--Tales for Tots. (ps up) 1984. (ISBN 0-8062-2330-8). Carlton.

O'Neil, George

--Tomorrow's House: The Tiny Angel. O'Neill, Rose Cecil (1874-), illus. LC 30-20206. 21cm. 159p. 1930. E. P. Dutton & Co.

O'Neill, David Patrick (1918-)

--The Book of Rewi: A Utopian Tale. LC 75-14445. p. cm. (Continuum Book). 1975. (ISBN 0-8164-9267-0). Seabury Press.

O'Neill, Eugene Gladstone (1888-1953)

--The Emperor Jones. Herzberg, Max J., ed. N.D. Appleton-Century-Crofts.

O'Neill, G

--Song Garden for Children. N.D. Longmans,Green & Co.

O'Neill, Jean

--Cotton Top. LC 53-6729. (Illus.). unpaged. 26cm. 1953. Lothrop, Lee and Shepard.

O'Neill, Mary Le Duc (1908-)

--Ali. 1st ed. Barberis, Juan Carlos, illus. LC 68-25411. (Illus.). 122 p. 25cm. 1968. Atheneum.

--Anna Amelia's Apteryx. 1st ed. Groedel, Burton, illus. LC 65-20464. 1 v. (unpaged) illus. (part col.) 20 cm. 1966. Doubleday.

--Big Red Hen. 1st ed. Piussi-Campbell, Judy, illus. LC 73-139452. (Illus.). 48 p. 20cm. 1971. Doubleday.

--The Boy. 1st ed. LC 70-116241. 156 p. 22cm. 1970. Doubleday.

--Fingers Are Always Bringing Me News. 1st ed. Bolognese, Donald Alan (1934-), illus. LC 69-12200. (Illus.). 40 p. 24cm. 1969. Doubleday.

--Hailstones and Halibut Bones: Adventures in Color. LC 60-7138. (Illus.). 1 v. (unpaged. 24cm. (Zephyr Book). 1973, c.1961. Doubleday.

--Hailstones and Halibut Bones: Adventures in Colour. Weisgard, Leonard Joseph (1916-), illus. LC 60-7138. 59 p. illus. 24 cm. (gr. k-12). 1961. (ISBN 0-385-07912-5). (ISBN 0-385-07911-7). Doubleday.

--Hailstones and Halibut Bones: Adventures in Colour. Weisgard, Leonard Joseph (1916-), illus. LC 65-22854. 59 p. col. illus. 24 cm. 1962. Surrey, The World's Work () Ltd.

--People I'd Like to Keep. Galdone, Paul (1914-), illus. LC 63-12991. 64 p. illus. (part col.) 25 cm. 1964. Doubleday.

--Poor Merlo. 1st ed. Piussi-Campbell, Judy, illus. LC 67-18995. (Illus.). 48 p. 1967. Atheneum.

--Take a Number. Nagy, Al, illus. LC 68-12378. (Illus.). 63 p. 25cm. 1968. Doubleday.

--What Is That Sound. Ehlert, Lois Jane (1934-), illus. LC 66-5958. (Illus.). 26cm. 54p. (gr. 2-6). 1966. (ISBN 0-689-20320-9). (ISBN 0-689-20321-7). Atheneum.

--The White Palace. Hogrogian, Nonny (1932-), illus. LC 65-161810. 1v. (unpaged) illus. (pt. col.) 26cm. 48p. c.1966. Crowell.

--Winds. Barkley, James Edward (1941-), illus. LC 73-116242. (Illus.). 64 p. 1970. Doubleday.

--Words, Words, Words. 1st ed. Piussi-Campbell, Judy, illus. LC 66-10110. 61 p. illus. (part col). 25cm. 1966. Doubleday.

O'Neill, Moira

--The Elf-Errant. Britten, W. E. F., illus. LC 7-4462. (Illus.). 20 x 15cm. vi, 109p. 1895. Dodd, Mead and Co.

O'Neill, Paul (1928-)

--Barnstormers & Speed Kings. (Epic of Flight Ser.). N.D. (ISBN 0-8094-3276-5). Silver.

--Legends of a Lost Tribe: Folk Tales of the Beothuck Indians of Newfoundland. LC 77-355751. (Illus.). 94 p. 23cm. c.1976. (ISBN 0-7710-6878-6). McClelland and Stewart.

O'Neill, Rose Cecil (1874-)

--The Kewpies and Dotty Darling: Verse. O'Neill, Rose Cecil (1874-), illus. LC 14-13378. 79 p. incl. col. front., illus. (part col.) col. plates. 28 cm. 1912. Frederick A. Stokes Company.

--The Kewpies and Dotty Darling: Verse and Pictures. O'Neill, Rose Cecil (1874-), illus. LC 12-25990. 88 p. incl. col. front., col. illus. 28 cm. c.1912. George H. Doran Company.

--This Wonderful Day: Poems of Prayer and Thanksgiving. Doane, Pelagie (1906-1966), illus. LC 58-14444. 52p. illus. 25cm. 1958. Union of American Hebrew Congregations.
--Within Thy Hand: My Poem Book of Prayers. Forst, Sigmund, illus. (Illus.). (gr. 6 up). 1961. UAHC.
--The Wonder Book of Fun: Poems. Cunningham, Dellwyn, illus. LC 51-14570. unpaged. illus. 21 cm. (Wonder books, 576). 1951. Wonder Books.
--The Zoo that Grew. Berson, Harold (1926-), illus. LC 60-15920. 23cm. 47p. 1960. Henry Z. Walck, Inc.
Orlev, Uri (1931-)
--The Island on Bird Street. Halkin, Hillel, tr. from Hebrew. LC 83-26524. 22 cm. xi, 162p. 1984, c.1983. (ISBN 0-395-33887-5). Houghton Mifflin. **Awards: (ALA); (MLB).**
Orlob, Helen (1908-)
--The Commodore's Boys: Naval Campaigns of the War of 1812. 1967. (ISBN 0-664-32374-X). Westminster Press.
--Darling Young Men in the Flying Machines. 1960. Thomas Nelson & Sons.
--Navy Style. Vosburgh, Leonard W. (1912-), illus. LC 62-10561. 191p. illus. c.1962. Nelson.
Orloff, Nicholas W. (1895-), tr. see Khachatriants, Iakov Samsonovich.
Orlowsky, Wallace (1939-) & Perera, Thomas Biddle (1938-)
--Who Will Wash the River?. Cuffari, Richard (1925-1978), illus. LC 78-121382. (Illus.). 47 p. 22cm. (Science is what and why books). 1970. Coward-McCann.
Ormerod, Jan
--Dad's Back. Ormerod, Jan, illus. LC 84-12614. p. cm. 24p. (Jan Ormerod's Baby Books). (ps). 1985. (ISBN 0-688-04126-4). Lothrop, Lee & Shepard Books. **Award: (ALA).**
--Messy Baby. LC 84-12610. p. cm. (Jan Ormerod's Baby books). (ps). 1985. (ISBN 0-688-04128-0). Lothrop, Lee & Shepard Books. **Award: (ALA).**
--Moonlight. Ormerod, Jan, illus. LC 81-8290. (Illus.). 28 p. (ps-2). c.1982. (ISBN 0-688-00846-1). (ISBN 0-688-00847-X). Lothrop, Lee & Shepard Books. **Award: (ALA).**
--One-Hundred-One Things to Do With a Baby. Ormerod, Jan, illus. LC 84-4401. 1984. (ISBN 0-688-03801-8). (ISBN 0-688-03802-6). Lothrop.
--Reading. LC 84-12628. p. cm. (Jan Ormerod's Baby books). ((Series: Ormerod, Jan.). (Baby books.). (ps). 1985. (ISBN 0-688-04127-2). Lothrop, Lee & Shepard Books.
--Rhymes Around the Day. Thompson, Pat, selected by. LC 82-24001. (Illus.). 32 p. 24cm. 1st U.S. edition. c.1983. (ISBN 0-688-02073-9). (ISBN 0-688-02074-7). Lothrop, Lee & Shepard Books.
--Sleeping. LC 84-12627. (Illus.). 20 p. 18cm. (Jan Ormerod's Baby books). ((Series: Ormerod, Jan.). (Baby books.). (ps). c.1985. (ISBN 0-688-04129-9). Lothrop, Lee & Shepard Books.
--Sunshine. LC 80-84971. (Illus.). 32p. (ps-1). 1981. (ISBN 0-688-00552-7). (ISBN 0-688-00553-5). Lothrop. **Award: (ALA).**
--Sunshine. (Illus.). 32p. (Picture Puffin Ser.). (ps-k). 1984. (ISBN 0-14-050362-5, Puffin). Penguin.
Ormondroyd, Edward (1925-)
--All in Good Time. Robbins, Ruth (1917-), illus. LC 75-1688. (Illus.). 206 p. 22cm. c.1975. (ISBN 0-87466-072-6). (ISBN 0-87466-073-4). Parnassus Press.
--Broderick. Larrecq, John Maurice (1926-1980), illus. LC 77-83752. (Illus.). 33 p. 1969. Parnassus Press. **Award: (ALA).**
--Castaways on Long Ago. Robbins, Ruth (1917-), illus. LC 73-77122. 21cm. 182p. 1973. Parnassus Press.
--David & the Phoenix. 152p. (Orig.). (gr. 4-6). 1957. (ISBN 0-590-31276-6). Scholastic Inc.
--David and the Phoenix. Raysor, Joan, illus. LC 57-8280. (Illus.). (gr. 4-6). 1957. (ISBN 0-695-41875-0). Follett.
--Imagination Greene. Lewis, John Denzil, illus. LC 73-77123. (Illus.). 33 p. 20cm. 1973. (ISBN 0-87466-064-5). (ISBN 0-87466-064-5). Parnassus Press.
--Johnny Castleseed. Thewlis, Diana, illus. LC 85-8189. (Illus.). 32 p. 24cm. 1985. (ISBN 0-395-38355-2). Houghton Mifflin.
--Jonathan Frederick Aloysius Brown. Spector, Suzi, illus. LC 64-10545. 1 v. (unpaged) col. illus. 24 x 26 cm. 1964. Golden Gate Junior Books.
--Michael, the Upstairs Dog. Szekeres, Cyndy (1933-), illus. LC 67-16209. (Illus.). 40 p. 1967. Dial Press.
--Tale of Alain. Frankenberg, Robert Clinton (1911-), illus. LC 60-9370. (Illus.). (gr. 4-6). 1960. (ISBN 0-695-48450-8). Follett.
--Theodore. Larrecq, John Maurice (1926-1980), illus. LC 66-9502. (Illus.). 1 v. (unpaged. 1966. Parnassus Press. **Award: (ALA).**
--Theodore's Rival. Larrecq, John Maurice (1926-1980), illus. LC 76-156876. (Illus.). 33 p. 1971. (ISBN 0-87466-001-7). Parnassus Press.
--Time at the Top. Bach, Peggie, illus. LC 63-10140. (Illus.). (gr. 4-7). 1963. (ISBN 0-395-27698-5). Parnassus. **Award: (ALA).**
Ormsby, Virginia Haire
--The Big Banyan Tree. Ormsby, Virginia Haire, illus. LC 64-11445. 1 v. (unpaged) col. illus. 24 cm. 1964. Lippincott.
--Cunning Is Better Than Strong. 1st ed. Ormsby, Virginia Haire, illus. LC 60-7616. (Illus.). (gr. 4-6). 1960. (ISBN 0-397-30484-6). Lippincott.
--Here We Go. Ormsby, Virginia Haire, illus. LC 55-7991. unpaged. illus. 24cm. 1955. Lippincott.
--It's Saturday. Ormsby, Virginia Haire, illus. LC 56-5710. unpaged. illus. 24cm. 1956. Lippincott.
--The Little Country Schoolhouse. Ormsby, Virginia Haire, illus. LC 58-10144. unpaged. illus. 24cm. 1958. Lippincott.
--Long, Lonesome Train Whistle. 1st ed. Ormsby, Virginia Haire, illus. LC 61-11735. 106p. illus. 22cm. (gr. 4-6). 1961. Lippincott.
--Mountain Magic for Rosy. Kennedy, Paul Edward (1929-), illus. LC 78-75073. (Illus.). 137 p. 22cm. 1969. Crown Publishers.
--Right-Handed Horse. Ormsby, Virginia Haire, illus. LC 63-9866. (Illus.). 23cm. 110p. (gr. 4-6). 1963. Lippincott.
--Twenty-One Children. Ormsby, Virginia Haire, illus. LC 57-10336. unpaged. illus. 24cm. 1957. Lippincott.
--Twenty-One Children Plus Ten. Ormsby, Virginia Haire, illus. LC 78-141460. (Illus.). 32 p. 24cm. 1971. Lippincott.
--What's Wrong with Julio?. Ormsby, Virginia Haire, illus. LC 65-21671. 1 v. col. illus. 24 cm. 26p. 1965. Lippincott.
Ornitz, Samuel Badisch (1890-1957)
--Round the World with Jocko the Great. Shell, Carol C., illus. LC 25-20743. 232 p. col. front., illus., col. plates. 24 cm. c.1925. The Macaulay Company.
Orosz-O'Gara, M, jt. auth. see Cassie, Dyan.
O'Rourke, Frank (1916-)
--Bonus Rookie. LC 50-14743. 179p. 21cm. (A Barnes Sports Novel). 1950. A. S. Barnes.
O'Rourke, Robert
--What God Did for ZEKE the Fuzzy Caterpillar. Sparks, Judith, ed. (Illus.). 24p. (Orig.). (A Happy Day Bks.). (gr. 1-3). 1980. (ISBN 0-87239-406-9). Standard Pub.
Orr, A. S., Mrs.
--Mountain Patriots, 1 of 7. (The Mossdale Ser.). N.D. Cassell, Petter, & Galpin.
Orr, Ethel McCrossin & Reed, Edna M., eds.
--Stories from Near and Far. Dowling, Victor J. (1906-), illus. LC 51-3932. (Illus.). 21cm. viii, 440p. (Reading Today Ser.). 1951. Scribner.
Orr, Gulielma Day & Schiele, Henriette
--Sally in South Africa. Ayer, Margaret (0000-1981), illus. LC 29-18335. ix, 242 p. front., plates. 20 cm. c.1929. The Century Co.
Orr, Jack, illus.
--Nursery Rhymes. N.D. Thomas Nelson & Sons.
Orr, James Lee
--Ned Dawson in Wilful Land. LC 13-25441. 3 p. l., 118 p. plates. 19 cm. c.1913. M. A. Donohue & Co.
Orr, Munro Scott (1874-), illus.
--Mother Goose. N.D. David McKay.
Orr, Rebecca
--Gunner's Run. LC 79-9613. p. cm. c.1980. (ISBN 0-06-024617-0). (ISBN 0-06-024618-9). Harper & Row.
Orr, Stewart
--Two Jolly Mariners. Orr, Stuart, illus. N.D. Dodge Publishing Co.
Orrell, Robert
--Over the Fells. (Illus.). 114p. (gr. 3-7). 1984. (ISBN 0-19-273152-1, Pub. by Oxford U Pr Childrens). Merrimack Pub Cir.
Orska, Krystyna, illus.
--Illustrated Poems for Children. Peterson, Miriam, intro. by. LC 73-78379. (Illus.). 160p. (ps-3). 1973. (ISBN 0-528-82803-7). Rand.
Ort, Jane
--Mr. Mogo Mouse. LC 30-141101. 39 p. incl. col. front., col. illus. 19 cm. (On cover: Volland sunny book series). c.1930. The P. F. Volland Company.
Ortiz, Elisabeth Lambert see Lambert, Elisabeth, pseud.
Ortiz, Simon J. & Graves, Sharol
--The People Shall Continue. LC 77-83856. (Illus.). (Fifth World Tales Ser.). (gr. k-6). N.D. (ISBN 0-89239-015-8, Imprenta de Libros Infantiles). Childrens Book Pr.
Ortman, Blache Sellers, Mrs.
--The Old House, and Other Stories. LC 11-592. 17cm. 54p. 1910. Ortman.
Ortman-Holtz
--Candy. 1979. (ISBN 0-533-04006-X). Vantage.
Orton, George W (1873-)
--Bob Hunt at Camp Pontiac. LC 14-225591. 4 p. l., 7-322 p. col. front., col. plates. 20 cm. 1914. G. W. Jacobs & Company.
--Bob Hunt in Canada. LC 17-3887. 294 p. col. front., col. plates. 20 cm. 1916. George W. Jacobs & Company.
--Bob Hunt, Senior Camper. 20cm. 340p. 1915. G. W. Jacobs & Co.
Orton, Helen Fuller, Mrs. (1872-1955)
--Bobby of Cloverfield Farm. N.D. J. B. Lippincott.
--Bobby of Cloverfield Farm. Owen, Robert Emmett (1878-), illus. LC 22-224397. 2 p. l., 122 p. col. front., col. illus. 20 cm. c.1922. Frederick A. Stokes Company.
--The Brave Frontier. Mansfield, Louise, illus. N.D. J. B. Lippincott.
--The Brave Frontier: A Story of Old Schoharie. Mansfield, Louise, illus. LC 40-31725. xvi, 259 p. incl. front., illus. 21 cm. 1940. Frederick A. Stokes Company.
--The City Mrs. Winkle Built. Price, Luxor, illus. LC 31-5064. 3 p. l., 87, 1 p. col. front., col. illus. 16 cm. 1931. Frederick A. Stokes Company.
--The City Mrs. Winkle Built. Price, Luxor, illus. N.D. J. B. Lippincott.
--Cloverfield Farm Stories. Owen, Robert Emmett (1878-), illus. LC 47-30860. 108, 122, 122, 122 p. illus. 20 cm. 1947. J. B. Lippincott Co.
--Daddy's Adventure with the Animals. LC 33-27406. 3 p. l., 81, 1 p. incl. illus., plates. 20 cm. 1933. Frederick A. Stokes Company.
--Daddy's Adventure with the Animals. Price, Luxor, illus. N.D. J. B. Lippincott.
--Danny's Country Store. Hill, Mabel Betsy (1877-), illus. LC 35-15740. 4 p. l., 108 p. col. front., illus. 20 cm. 1935. Frederick A. Stokes Company.
--Danny's Country Store. Hill, Mabel Betsy (1877-), illus. 1935. J. B. Lippincott Co.
--The Gold-Laced Coat: A Story of Old Niagara. Ball, Robert (1890-), illus. LC 34-30242. x, 226 p. illus., maps. 21 cm. 1934. Frederick A. Stokes Co.
--The Gold-Laced Coat: A Story of Old Niagra. Ball, Robert (1890-), illus. 1934. J. B. Lippincott Co.
--Grandmother's Cooky Jar. Frantz, Marie Louise, illus. LC 30-22897. 128, 1 p. incl. col. front., illus. 22 cm. 1930. Frederick A. Stokes Company.
--Grandmother's Cooky Jar. Frantz, Marie Louise, illus. 1930. J. B. Lippincott Co.
--Hoof-Beats of Freedom. De Feo, Charles, illus. LC 36-20367. x, 235 p. illus. (incl. map) 21 cm. 1936. Frederick A. Stokes Company.
--Hoof-Beats of Freedom. De Feo, Charles, illus. N.D. J. B. Lippincott.
--Knights of the Snowstorm. Ayer, Margaret (0000-1981), illus. LC 39-22580. 5 p. l., 116 p. illus. 22 cm. 1939. Frederick A. Stokes Company.
--A Lad of Old Williamsburg. N.D. J. B. Lippincott.
--A Lad of Old Williamsburg. Blaisdell, Elinore (1904-), illus. LC 38-29529. ix, 218 p. incl. plates. col. front. 21 cm. 1938. Frederick A. Stokes Company.
--The Little Lost Pigs. Price, Luxor, illus. LC 25-19644. 96 p. incl. col. front., illus., plates (part col.) 14 x 19 cm. 1925. Frederick A. Stokes Company.
--The Little Lost Pigs in Town. Comstock, Enos Benjamin (1879-1945), illus. LC 42-21436. 95, 1 p. incl. col. front., illus., plates (part col.) 13 1/2 x 18 1/2 cm. 1942. Frederick A. Stokes Co.
--The Little Lost Pigs in Town. Comstock, Enos Benjamin (1879-1945), illus. N.D. J. P. Lippincott.
--Mystery at the Little Red School-House. Owen, Robert Emmett (1878-), illus. LC 41-15013. (Illus.). 4 p., l., 126 p. 22cm. c.1941. Frederick A. Stokes Company.
--Mystery at the Little Red School House. Owen, Robert Emmett (1878-), illus. N.D. J. B. Lippincott.
--Mystery at the Old Place. James, Sandra, illus. LC 43-14780. (Illus.). 3 p. 21cm. 113p. 1943. Frederick A. Stokes Company.
--Mystery in the Apple Orchard. 1st ed. Doremus, Robert (1913-), illus. LC 54-8108. (Illus.). 115 p. 21cm. 1954. Lippincott.
--Mystery in the Old Cave. 1st ed. Doremus, Robert (1913-), illus. (Illus.). (gr. 4-6). 1950. (ISBN 0-397-30173-1, JBL-J). Har-Row.
--Mystery in the Old Cave. 1st ed. Doremus, Robert (1913-), illus. LC 50-14371. (Illus.). 121 p. 21cm. 1950. Lippincott.
--Mystery in the Old Red Barn. 1st ed. Doremus, Robert (1913-), illus. LC 52-7461. (Illus.). 115 p. 21cm. 1952. Lippincott.
--Mystery in the Pirate Oak. 1st ed. Doremus, Robert (1913-), illus. LC 49-9989. (Illus.). 120 p. 21cm. 1949. Lippincott Co.
--Mystery of the Hidden Book. Doremus, Robert (1913-), illus. LC 53-7142. (Illus.). 119 p. 21cm. 1953. Lippincott.
--Mystery of the Lost Letter. Doremus, Robert (1913-), illus. LC 46-7568. (Illus.). v, 112 p. 21cm. 1946. Lippincott.
--Mystery of the Secret Drawer. James, Sandra, illus. LC 45-6319. (Illus.). 3 p. 21cm. 105p. 1945. J. B. Lippincott Company.
--Mystery Over the Brick Wall. Doremus, Robert (1913-), illus. LC 51-11175. (Illus.). vii, 114 p. 21cm. 1951. Lippincott.
--Mystery up the Chimney. Doremus, Robert (1913-), illus. LC 47-4012. 4 p. l., 3-109 p. incl. illus., plates. 21 cm. 1947. J. B. Lippincott Company.
--Mystery up the Winding Stair. Doremus, Robert (1913-), illus. LC 48-8113. 120 p. illus. 21 cm. 1948. J. B. Lippincott Co.
--Prancing Pat. Day, Maurice (1892-), illus. N.D. Frederick A. Stokes Co.
--Prancing Pat. Day, Maurice (1892-), illus. N.D. J. B. Lippincott.
--Prince and Rover of Cloverfield Farm. N.D. J. B. Lippincott.
--Prince and Rover of Cloverfield Farm. Spencer, Hugh, illus. LC 21-26988. viii, 103 p. incl. col. front., col. illus. 20 cm. c.1921. Frederick A. Stokes Company.
--Queenie: The Story of a Cow. Day, Maurice (1892-), illus. LC 29-155671. 119 p. incl. col. front., illus., plates (part col.) 14 cm. 1929. Frederick A. Stokes Company.
--Queenie: The Story of a Cow. Day, Maurice (1892-), illus. 1929. J. B. Lippincott Co.
--The Secret of the Rosewood Box. Ball, Robert (1890-), illus. LC 37-28568. 7 p. l., 112 p. incl. col. front., illus. 22 cm. 1937. Frederick A. Stokes Company.
--The Secret of the Rosewood Box. Ball, Robert (1890-), illus. N.D. J. B. Lippincott.
--Snappy, the Puppy-Dog. Frantz, Marie Louise, illus. LC 31-220705. 52 p. col. illus. 23 cm. 1931. R. M. McBride & Company.
--Summer at Cloverfield Farm. N.D. J. B. Lippincott.
--Summer at Cloverfield Farm. Owen, Robert Emmett (1878-), illus. LC 24-26937. 3 p. l., 122 p. incl. col. front., col. illus. 20 cm. 1924. Frederick A. Stokes Company.
--The Treasure in the Little Trunk. Ball, Robert (1890-), illus. LC 32-22715. vi p., 1 l., 198 p. illus. 21 cm. 1932. Frederick A. Stokes Company.
--The Treasure in the Little Trunk. Ball, Robert (1890-), illus. 1932. J. B. Lippincott Co.
--The Twin Lambs. Flack, Marjorie (1897-1958), illus. LC 31-280507. 3 p. l., 106 p. incl. col. front., illus., plates (part col.) 14 x 19 cm. 1931. Frederick A. Stokes Company.
--The Winding River: A Story of French Emigres on the Susquahanna. LC 44-686763. xi, 239 p. illus. 21 cm. 1944. J. B. Lippincott Company.
--Winter at Cloverfield Farm. N.D. J. B. Lippincott.
--Winter at Cloverfield Farm. Blossom, Ethel & Babbitt, Helen, illus. LC 26-27597. 3 p. l., 122 p. incl. col. front., col. illus. 20 cm. 1926. Frederick A. Stokes Company.
Orton, James K.
--Beach Boy Joe: Or, Among the Life Savers. LC 2-19167. 19cm. 258p. 1902. Street & Smith.
--Last Chance Mine: Or, Dale Wrightman's Pluck. LC 2-19020. (Lieutenant James K. Orton). 19cm. 256p. 1902. Street & Smith.
--The Secret Chart: Or, Treasure Hunting in Hayti. LC 2-19168. 19cm. 257p. 1902. Street & Smith.
--Tom Haven with the White Squadron: The Adventures of a Young Inventor of a Submarine Boat. (Famous Adventure Ser.). N.D. David McKay.
--Tom Havens with the White Squadron. LC 3-17006. 19cm. 293p. (Boy's Own Library). 1903. Street & Smith.
Orton, John Overton Cone, jt. auth. see Attiwill, Kenneth.
Orton, Ruth
--Pepito, the Colt: The Childhood of a Polo Pony. Thorne, Diana (1894-), illus. LC 33-29343. 1 p. l., 36, 1 p. front., illus. 21 x 28 cm. 1933. Houghton Mifflin Co.
Ortzen, Len, tr. see Gainier-Raymond, Philippe.
Orvieto, Laura Cantoni
--The Birth of Rome. Pitz, Henry Clarence (1895-1976), illus. Oberholtzer, Beatrice Cerboni, tr. LC 35-291. 301, 1 p. incl. col. front., illus. 21 cm. c.1935. J. B. Lippincott Company.
Orville, Florence, ed.
--Pollyanna Annual: The Yearly Glad Book. LC 17-28852. v. col. front., illus., col. plates. 26 cm. N.D. The Page Company.
Orwell, George, pseud., see Blair, Eric Hugh.
Orwell, George, pseud. (1903-1950)
--Animal Farm. Blair, Eric Hugh. Batchelor, Joy (1914-) & Halas, John (1912-), illus. LC 54-11330. (Illus.). (gr. 10 up). 1954. (ISBN 0-15-107252-3). HarBraceJ.
--Nineteen Eighty-Four. Blair, Eric Hugh. LC 66-91393. (gr. 10 up). N.D. (ISBN 0-15-166038-7). HarBraceJ.
O'Ryan, Anna Wynne, jt. auth. see O'Ryan, Francis.

--Boy Alone. Pearson, Clyde, illus. LC 66-11204. 191 p. illus. 21 cm. 1st U.S. edition. 1966, c.1965. Harcourt. **Award: (ALA).**
--Brumbie Dust: A Selection of Stories. LC 69-11598. 143 p. 21cm. 1969. Harcourt, Brace & World.
--Giselle. LC 68-25194. 159 p. 21cm. 1968. Harcourt, Brace & World.
--Jim Grey of Moonbah. LC 77-106596. 159 p. 21cm. 1970. Harcourt, Brace & World.
--No More Tomorrow. LC 78-137758. 107 p. 21cm. 1971. (ISBN 0-15-257495-6). Harcourt Brace Jovanovich.
--Rain Comes to Yamboorah. Hales, Robert, illus. LC 68-115031. 159p. illus. 21cm. 1st U.S. edition. 1968, c.1967. Harcourt.
--The Roan Colt. Parry, David, illus. LC 67-348. (Illus.). 159 p. 21cm. 1st U.S. edition. Orig. Title: The Roan Colt of Yamboorah. 1967. Harcourt, Brace & World.
--The War on William Street. LC 72-13252. 160 p. 22cm. 1973. (ISBN 0-8407-6298-4). T. Nelson.

Otto, Margaret Glover (1909-1976)
--Cocoa. 1st ed. Spier, Peter Edward (1927-), illus. LC 53-8971. (Illus.). 90 p. 21cm. 1953. Holt.
--Great Aunt Victoria's House. N.D. E. M. Hale & Co.
--Great-Aunt Victoria's House. Adams, Adrienne (1906-), illus. LC 56-10032. (Illus.). 122p. (gr. 4-6). 1956. (ISBN 0-03-032400-9). HR&W.
--The Little Brown Horse. Cooney, Barbara (1917-), illus. LC 59-6405. (Illus.). unpaged. 23cm. 1959. Knopf.
--The Little Lost Puppy. Spicer, Jesse, illus. LC 50-6648. 41p. (A Wonder Book for Children, 528.). 1950 (Wonder books). Grosset & Dunlap.
--The Little Old Train. Blegvad, Erik (1923-), illus. LC 60-8605. (Illus.). unpaged. 22cm. 1960. Knopf.
--The Man in the Moon. Galdone, Paul (1914-), illus. LC 57-11687. (Illus.). 1957. Holt, Rinehart and Winston, Inc.
--Mr. Kipling's Elephant. Berson, Harold (1926-), illus. LC 61-15569. 106p. illus. c.1961. Knopf.
--Mr. Magic. 1st ed. Knight, Susan, illus. LC 55-589455. 201p. illus. 21cm. 1955. Holt.
--Pumpkin, Ginger, and Spice. N.D. E. M. Hale & Co.
--Pumpkin, Ginger, and Spice. Cooney, Barbara (1917-), illus. LC 54-5741. (Illus.). 116p. (gr. 4-6). 1954. (ISBN 0-03-036095-1). HR&W.
--Roly-Poly Snowman. 1st ed. Suba, Susanne (1913-), illus. LC 54-10388. 83p. illus. 21cm. 1954. Holt.
--Stephen's Train. 1953. E M Hale.
--Stephen's Train. 1st ed. Stevens, Mary E. (1920-1966), illus. LC 52-130691. unpaged. illus. 20x26cm. c.1953. Holt.
--Syrup. 1st ed. Jackson, Polly, pseud. (1918-), illus. Jackson, Pauline. LC 56-6231. 159p. illus. 21cm. 1956. Holt.
--Three Little Dachshunds. Haines, Frank, adapted by. Cooney, Barbara (1917-), illus. LC 63-12408. 25 p. col. illus. 17 x 24 cm. (Little Owl Book). 1963. Holt, Rinehart and Winston.
--The Tiny Man. (gr. 3-5). 1955. (ISBN 0-8382-0878-9). Hale.
--The Tiny Man. 1st ed. Burchard, Peter Duncan (1921-), illus. LC 55-105739. 122p. illus. 21cm. 1955. Holt.

Otto, Svend (1916-)
--Taxi Dog. Otto, Svend (1916-), illus. LC 77-24127. (Illus.). 32 p. 26cm. c.1978. (ISBN 0-8193-0915-X). (ISBN 0-8193-0916-8). Parents' Magazine Press.

Otto, Svend (1916-), retold by.
--The Wonderful Pumpkin. Otto, Svend (1916-), illus. Hellsing, Lennart (1919-), tr. from Swedish. LC 75-24223. p. cm. 1976. (ISBN 0-689-10717-X). Atheneum.

Otto, William N, ed. see Parker, Gilbert.

Ottum, Bob
--Busy Days with Raggedy Ann & Andy. Cummins, James (1914-), illus. (Illus.). (Golden Touch & Feel Bk.). (ps-k). 1976. (ISBN 0-307-12143-7, Golden Pr). Western Pub.

Ottum, Bob, ed.
--The Three Bears. LaSalle, Janet (1926-), illus. (Illus.). (ps-1). 1973. (ISBN 0-307-68971-9, Golden Pr). Western Pub.

Ottum, Bob & Wood, JoAnne
--Santa's Beard Is Soft & Warm. Ruth, Rod (1912-), illus. (Golden Touch & Feel Bk). 1974. (ISBN 0-307-12148-8, Golden Pr). Western Pub.

Ouida, pseud., see De La Ramee, Marie Louise.

Ouida, Sebestyen
--I. O. U. 192p. (gr. 7 up). 1982. (ISBN 0-686-79042-1, Pub. by Atlantic Monthly Pr). Little.

Our Young Folks
--Yesterday's Children: An Anthology, Compiled from the Pages of Our Young Folks, 1865-1873. Blum, John Morton (1921-), selected by. LC 58-9054. 276p. illus. 22cm. 1959. Houghton Mifflin.

Oursler, Charles-Fulton see Oursler, Fulton.

Oursler, Fulton (1893-1952)
--A Child's Life of Jesus. 1951. Franklin Watts, Inc.
--A Child's Life of Jesus. Blaisdell, Elinore (1904-), illus. N.D. Doubleday & Co.

Ourth, John & Sawitz, Mike
--Hooray, It's Raining. (gr. k-6). 1979. (ISBN 0-916456-50-1). Good Apple.

Ousley, Odille (1897-)
--Cowboy Bill and the Big Umbrella. Irvin, Fred M. (1914-), illus. LC 65-25818. 28p. col. illus. 23cm. 1966. Ginn.
--Mr. Bear's Bow Ties. LC 65-209. 44 p. col. illus. 24 cm. (Ginn Story-Time Ser.). 1964. Ginn.

Ousley, Odille (1897-), ed.
--V Is for Verses. LC 65-464. (Illus.). vii, 135 p. 27cm. 1964. Ginn.

Ousley, Odille (1897-) & Duffield, Lois
--The Little Pig Who Listened. Battaglia, Aurelius (1910-), illus. LC 65-25817. 21p. col. illus. 23cm. 1966. Ginn.

Outcault, Richard Felton (1863-1928)
--Buster and Tige Here Again. N.D. Frederick A. Stokes Co.
--Buster Brown Abroad. Outcault, Richard Felton (1863-1928), illus. LC 4-33214. (Illus.). N.D. Frederick A. Stokes Co.
--Buster Brown and His Chum Tige. N.D. Frederick A. Stokes Co.
--Buster Brown and His Pets. (Illus.). (Buster Brown Books.). 1915. Cupples & Leon.
--Buster Brown and His Resolution. N.D. Frederick A. Stokes.
--Buster Brown at Home. N.D. Frederick A. Stokes Co.
--Buster Brown at Play. (Illus.). (Buster Brown Bks.: No. 1). 1915. Cupples & Leon.
--Buster Brown, His Dog Tige and Their Jolly Times. (Illus.). (Buster Brown Series.: No. 8). 1915. Cupples & Leon.
--Buster Brown, His Dog Tige and Their Troubles. N.D. Frederick A. Stokes.
--Buster Brown's Amusing Capers. (Illus.). (Buster Brown Books: No. 5). 1915. Cupples & Leon.
--Buster Brown's Antics. N.D. Frederick A. Stokes.
--Buster Brown's Autobiography. LC 7-33214. 4 p. l., 70 p., 1 l. col. front., illus., col. plates. 26 x 22 cm. 1907. F. A. Stokes Company.
--Buster Brown's Funny Tricks. (Illus.). (Buster Brown Books.: No. 2). 1915. Cupples & Leon.
--Buster Brown's Happy Days. (Illus.). (Buster Brown Books.: No. 4). 1915. Cupples & Leon.
--Buster Brown's Latest Frolics. (Illus.). (Buster Brown Books: No. 6). 1915. Cupples & Leon.
--Buster Brown's Pranks. N.D. Frederick A. Stokes.
--Outcault's Buster Brown and Company. N.D. Frederick A. Stokes.
--Outcault's Buster, Mary Jane and Tige. N.D. Frederick A. Stokes.
--Outcault's The Real Buster and the Only Mary Jane. N.D. Frederick A. Stokes.
--Tige: His Story. Outcault, Richard Felton (1863-1928), illus. LC 5-33027. (Illus.). 26cm. 61p. 1905. Frederick A. Stokes Co.

Outhwaite, Ida Rentoul
--The Little Fairy Sister. N.D. E P Dutton.

Outhwaite, Ida Rentoul, jt. auth. see Rentoul, Annie R.

Outhwaite, Ida Rentoul & Rentoul, Annie R
--Fairyland of Ida Rentoul Outhwaite. LC 29-21811. 164, 2 p. incl. col. front., illus., col. plates. 34 cm. 1929. Frederick A. Stokes Company.
--The Little Green Road to Fairy Land. N.D. E P Dutton.

Overbeck, Alicia O'Reardon
--Sven the Wise and Svea the Kind, and Other Stories of Lappland. Tenggren, Gustaf (1896-1970), illus. LC 32-25177. 6 p. l., 3-171 p. incl. illus., plates. col. front., col. pl. 23 cm. 1932. Harper & Brothers.

Overbeck, Cynthia
--Figaro the Horse. Hammarberg, Dyan, tr. from Fr. LC 76-29453. (Illus.). (Animal Friends Books). (gr. k-4). 1977. (ISBN 0-87614-079-7). Carolrhoda Bks.
--Rusty the Irish Setter. Hammarberg, Dyan, tr. from Fr. LC 76-29463. (Illus.). (Animal Friends Books). (gr. k-4). 1977. (ISBN 0-87614-080-0). Carolrhoda Bks.
--Splash the Dolphin. Hammarberg, Dyan, tr. from Fr. LC 76-1218. (Illus.). 24p. (The Animal Friends Bks). (gr. k-4). 1976. (ISBN 0-87614-061-4). Carolrhoda Bks.
--Tanya the Turtle Dove. Hammarberg, Dyan, tr. from Fr. LC 76-29464. (Illus.). (Animal Friends Books). (gr. k-4). 1977. (ISBN 0-87614-084-3). Carolrhoda Bks.
--Tippy the Fox Terrier. Hammarberg, Dyan, tr. from Fr. LC 76-1230. (Illus.). 24p. (The Animal Friends Bks). (gr. k-4). 1976. (ISBN 0-87614-071-1). Carolrhoda Bks.

Overbeck, Cynthia, rev. by see Pajot, Anne Marie.

Overend, Campbell
--A Noble Printer. N.D. D. Lothrop Co.

Overend, W. H.
--The North Pole and How Charlie Wilson Discovered It. Overend, W. H., illus. N.D. E. P. Dutton & Co.

Overholser, Wayne D., jt. auth. see Patten, Lewis Byford.

Overholser, Wayne D. (1906-) & Patten, Lewis Byford (1915-1981)
--The Meeker Massacre. LC 70-87086. (Illus.). 136 p. 22cm. 1969. Cowles.

Overlie, George
--The Tallest Tree. Overlie, George, illus. LC 65-201158. 1v. (unpaged) col. illus. 27cm. c.1965. Lerner.

Overlie, George, jt. auth. see Prince, Gary Michael.

Overton, Gwendolen (1876-)
--The Captain's Daughter. Jones, Frances D, illus. 20cm. 270p. 1903. Macmillan.

Overton, Jenny Margaret Mary (1942-)
--Creed Country. geneal. 224p. 1st U.S. edition. (gr. 7 up). 1970. (ISBN 0-02-769000-8). Macmillan.
--The Thirteen Days of Christmas. Hughes, Shirley (1929-), illus. LC 74-10277. (Illus.). 154 p. 21cm. 1st U.S. edition. 1974. (ISBN 0-8407-6406-5). T. Nelson.

Overton, Mark
--Jack Winters' Baseball Team: Or, The Rivals of the Diamond. LC 30-1377. 2 p. l., 11-183 p. front. 19 cm. (His The American boys' sport series). c.1919. The New York Book Company.

Overton, Robert
--After School: Books of Adventure For Boys. Thiele, Reinhold, illus. N.D. Frederick A Stokes Co.
--A Chase Round the World. (Illus.). (Warne's Adventure Library). N.D. Frederick Warne & Co.
--Decoyed Across the Sea. (The Albion Library). N.D. Frederick Warne & Co.
--Friend or Fortune. Yohn, F. C., illus. (Illus.). N.D. Duffield & Co.
--Friend or Fortune?. A Story for Boys. Yohn, Frederic, illus. LC 7-22771. 243 p., 1 l. 19 cm. 1896. Stone & Kimball.
--The King's Pardon. (Illus.). (The Round Table Ser.). N.D. A. L. Burt's Pubs.
--The King's Pardon. (Illus.). (Famous Books for Boys). N.D. H. M. Caldwell Co.
--The King's Pardon. Margetson, W. H., illus. N.D. Dana Estes & Co.
--The King's Pardon: A Story of Land and Sea. (The Rugby Series for Boys and Girls). N.D. A. L. Burt Company.
--The King's Pardon: Or, The Boy Who Saved His Father. Margetson, W. H., illus. N.D. Frederick A Stokes Co.
--Light Out. Thiele, Reinhold, illus. N.D. Dana Estes & Co.
--Lights Out. (Illus.). (Famous Books for Boys). N.D. H. M. Caldwell Co.
--Lights Out: Book Of Adventure For Boys. Thiele, Reinhold, illus. N.D. Frederick A. Stokes Co.

Ovington, Mary W., ed. see Motor, R. R.

Ovington, Mary White (1865-1951)
--Hazel. Roseland, Harry, illus. LC 72-4639. (Illus.). vii, 162 p. 22cm. (The Black Heritage Library Collection). 1972. (ISBN 0-8369-9117-6). Books for Libraries Press.
--Hazel. Roseland, Harry, illus. LC 14-9527. vii, 7-162 p. front., plates. 20 cm. c.1913. Crisis Publishing Company.
--Zeke. Davis, Natalie H., illus. LC 31-22145. 3 p. l., 3-205 p. incl. illus., pl. front. 21 cm. c.1931. Harcourt, Brace and Company.

Owen
--Star Streak: Stories of Space. (gr. 7-9). N.D. (ISBN 0-590-31264-2, Schol Pap). Scholastic Inc.

Owen, A. J.
--The Great Cranberry Quarrel. N.D. E. & J. B. Young & Co.

Owen, Annie, jt. auth. see MacDonald, Elizabeth.

Owen, Benjamin Evan see Owen, Evan.

Owen, Bessie
--The Carrot Club. N.D. Chapman & Grimes.

Owen, Betty, ed. see London, Jack.

Owen, Betty Meek (1913-), ed.
--Eleven Great Horror Stories. 239p. (gr. 7-12). 1970. (ISBN 0-590-08723-1, Schol Pap). Scholastic Inc.
--Eleven Great Horror Stories. Repr. (Starbright Editions). (gr. 7-12). 1973. Schol Bk Serv.
--The Ghostmasters: Weird Stories by Famous Writers. (gr. 7 up). 1977. (ISBN 0-590-02623-2). Scholastic Inc.
--Nine Strange Stories. (gr. 7-12). 1975. (ISBN 0-590-09933-7, Schol Pap). Scholastic Inc.

Owen, Betty Meek (1913-) & Macewen, Mary E., eds.
--A Wreath of Carols. HYman, Trina Schart (1939-), illus. 88p. 1967. Four Winds Press.
--Wreath of Carols. Hyman, Trina Schart (1939-), illus. LC 67-23552. 88p. (gr. 1 up). 1968 (Four Winds). Schol Bk Serv.

Owen, D F
--Book of Fairy Poetry. N.D. Longmans,Green & Co.

Owen, Dilys, pseud., see Grater, Dilys.

Owen, Dilys, pseud. (1944-)
--Leo Possessed. Grater, Dilys. Gammell, Stephen, illus. LC 78-20572. p. cm. 1st U.S. edition. 1979, c.1975. (ISBN 0-15-244897-7). Harcourt Brace Jovanovich.

Owen, Ethel
--Hallowe'en Tales and Games. Hubbard, Eleanore Mineah, illus. 128p. (The Holiday Library). N.D. A. Whitman & Co.
--The Pumpkin People. Enslow, Constance, illus. LC 27-234479. 128 p. incl. col. front., illus. (part col.) 21 cm. (A Just right book). c.1927. A. Whitman & Company.

Owen, Ethel & Owen, Frank (1893-)
--The Blue Highway. Tobin, George T., illus. LC 32-781023. 5 p. l., 15-140 p. front., illus. 20 cm. c.1932. The Abingdon Press.
--Coat Tales from the Pockets of the Happy Giant. LC 27-18927. 106 p. incl. col. front., illus., col. plates. 24 cm. c.1927. The Abingdon Press.
--The Dream Hills of Happy Country. LC 28-18828. 159, 1 p. col. front., illus., col. plates. 24 cm. c.1928. The Abingdon Press.
--Wind Blown Stories. Tobin, George T., illus. LC 30-20818. 191 p. incl. col. front., col. plates. 24 cm. c.1930. The Abingdon Press.

Owen, Evan (1918-)
--On Your Own. LC 78-56517. (Illus.). (Breakthrough Ser.). (gr. 5 up). 1978. (ISBN 0-8178-5979-9). Harvey.

Owen, Frank, jt. auth. see Owen, Ethel.

Owen, Frank (1893-)
--Harty, The Wanderer. (Illus.). (The Boy's Own Favorite Ser.). N.D. E. P. Dutton & Co.
--Morris the Midget Moose. LC 45-7647. 47 p. col. illus. 25 cm. 1945. G. P. Putnam's Sons.
--Pictureland. Fifty-Two Children, illus. LC 29-8292. xiii, 117, 1 p. incl. front., illus. 23 cm. 1929. The Lantern Press.
--Teen-Age Victory Parade. Ricketts, William B., illus. LC 50-7056. 255 p. illus. 22 cm. 1950. Lantern Press.

Owen, Frank (1893-), ed.
--Teen-age Baseball Stories. N.D. Grosset & Dunlap.
--Teen-Age Baseball Stories. Haff, Drayton S., illus. LC 48-7426. 255 p. illus. 21 cm. (Teen-age library). 1948. Lantern Press.
--Teen-age Companion. (The Teen-age Library). N.D. Grosset & Dunlap.
--Teen-Age Companion. LC 46-25279. vi p., 1 l., 280 p. illus. 21 cm. 1946. Lantern Press, Inc.
--Teen-age Football Stories. (The Teen-age Library). N.D. Grosset & Dunlap.
--Teen-Age Football Stories. LC 48-8815. 252 p. illus. 21 cm. (Teen-age library). 1948. Lantern Press.
--Teen-age Mystery Stories. (The Teen-age Library). N.D. Grosset & Dunlap.
--Teen-Age Mystery Stories. LC 49-787. 247 p. illus. 21 cm. (Teen-age library). 1948. Lantern Press.
--Teen-age Outdoor Stories. (The Teen-age Library). N.D. Grosset & Dunlap.
--Teen-Age Outdoor Stories. LC 47-30665. viii, 242 p. illus. 21 cm. (Teen-age library). 1947. Lantern Press.
--Teen-age Sports Stories. (The Teen-age Library). N.D. Grosset & Dunlap.
--Teen-Age Sports Stories. LC 47-30471. viii, 239 p. illus. 21 cm. (Teen-age library). 1947. Lantern Press.
--Teen-age Stories of Action. (The Teen-age Library). N.D. Grosset & Dunlap.
--Teen-Age Stories of Action. LC 48-8283. 255 p. illus. 21 cm. (Teen-age library). 1948. Lantern Press.
--Teen-Age Victory Parade. N.D. Grosset & Dunlap.
--Teen-age Winter Sports Stories. (The Teen-age Library). N.D. GRosset & Dunlap.
--Teen-Age Winter Sports Stories. Osborne, Richard N., illus. LC 49-8941. 256 p. illus. 22 cm. 1949. Lantern Press.

Owen, H J
--The Robber Bridegroom: A Fairy Tale from Grimm. N.D. Macmillan.

Owen, Helen Hammett, tr. see Avelot, Henri.

Owen, Hetty
--Christmas Wreath. new ed. (gr. 7-12). 1977. (ISBN 0-590-08038-5, Schol Pap). Schol Bk Serv.

Owen, John S.
--The Giant of Oldborne. N.D. Houghton Mifflin Co.
--Granmua, the Autobiography of a Cat. rev. ed. Owen, John S., illus. LC 2557. 18cm. 86p. c.1899. American Pub, Co.

Owen, Letitia White, Mrs. (1853-)
--The Life and History of Mary and Her Little Lamb. LC 13-8910. (Illus.). 31p. 20cm. 1913. The Davis Press.

--Jimmie Dale and the Phantom Clue. N.D. A L Burt Co.
--Pawned. N.D. A L Burt Co.
--The Red Ledger. N.D. A L Burt Co.
--The White Moll. N.D. A L Burt Co.
--The Wire Devils. N.D. A L Burt Co.

Packard, Hazel, ed.
--Bedtime Tales: A Treasury of Thirty-Six Stories, Old and New. Malvern, Corinne (1905-1956), illus. LC 51-8265. 192 p. illus. 28 cm. (Big golden book, 558). 1951. Simon and Schuster.

Packard, Mary
--Fun Factory. Barish, Wendy, ed. 64p. (Orig.). (Mickey's Magic Answer Ser.). (gr. 3-8). 1983. (ISBN 0-671-47729-3). Wanderer Bks.
--Riddles, Codes, & Games. Barish, Wendy, ed. 64p. (Magic Answer Ser.). (gr. 7 up). 1983. (ISBN 0-671-47731-5). Wanderer Bks.
--A Visit to the Dentist. Leder, Dora, illus. (Illus.). 64p. (New Feelings Activity Bks.). (ps-3). 1981. (ISBN 0-671-43099-8, Little Simon). S&S.

Packard, Mary, adapted by.
--The Adventures of the Gummi Bears Storybook. LC 85-18133. p. cm. c.1985. (ISBN 0-671-60510-0). Little Simon.

Packard, Virginia
--Jerry the Giraffe. LC 45-4467. 23 p. illus. (part col.) 23 1/2 x 11 1/2 cm. 1945. Thomas Y. Crowell Company.

Packard, Winthrop, jt. auth. see Pyle, Howard.

Packard, Winthrop (1862-)
--The Young Ice Whalers. LC 3-22109. 4 p. l., 397, 1 p. front., 15 pl. 20cm. 1903. Houghton, Mifflin and Company.

Packer, Eleanor Lewis
--Jane Withers and the Hidden Room: An Original Story Featuring Jane Withers, Famous Motion-Picture Star, As the Heroine. authorized. Vallely, Henry E., illus. LC 42-22297. 4 p. l., 13-246 p. incl. 1 illus., plates. 20 1/2 cm. 1942. Whitman Publishing Company.

Packie, Robert M.
--Storm Treasure. Streeter, Sherry, illus. LC 81-66266. (Illus.). 160p. (Orig.). (gr. 6). 1981. Down East.

Paczynells, Maria, tr. see Werner, Jadwiga.

Pad, Peter, pseud., see Stratemeyer, Edward L..

Pad, Peter, pseud. (1862-1930)
--Mayor Liederkranz of Hoboken: Or, The Jolly Captain of the Pretzel Schuten Corps. Stratemeyer, Edward L.. (New York Five Cent Library: No. 40). 1893. Street & Smith.

Paddock, Anna Georgia
--Prairie Dogs' Pranks. Crank, Bess Bethell & Wuenscher, N. G., illus. LC 31-16673. 128 p. illus. 19 1/2 cm. c.1931. The Bethany Press.

Paddock, Charles Lee, jt. auth. see Reynolds, Louis Bernard.

Paddock, Charles Lee (1891-)
--Don't Rope Those Calves and Other Stories. LC 39-15279. 127 p. illus. 20 1/2 cm. c.1939. Pacific Press Publishing Association.
--The Eagle that Went to War and Other Stories. Padgett, Jim, illus. LC 62-41430. (Illus.). 20cm. 107p. 1962. Southern Pub, Association.
--Going up. Thollander, Earl Gustave (1922-), illus. LC 53-10773. 128p. illus. 23cm. 1953. Pacific Press Pub. Association.
--Little Builders. LC 24-8796. 124 p. incl. front., illus., plates. 20 cm. c.1924. Southern Publishing Association.
--Little Builders. 96p. illus. 21cm. 1967. Southern Pub.
--Only a Dog and Other Stories. LC 39-13751. 126 p. incl. front., illus. 20 1/2 cm. c.1939. Pacific Press Publishing.

Padelford, F. M., ed. see Browning, Robert.

Padgett, James
--Jesus: God's Son, Savior, Lord. Chamberlain, Eugene, illus. LC 76-382763. (Illus.). 47 p. 24cm. (Biblearn series). c.1976. (ISBN 0-8054-4226-X). Broadman Press.

Paehr, Gunhild
--The Lonely Witch. Bartsch, Jochen (1906-), illus. Koenig, Marion, tr. LC 65-15103. 61 p. illus. 22 cm. 1965. (ISBN 0-8075-4752-2). A. Whitman.

Paek, Min
--Aekyung's Dream. Paek, Min, illus. LC 78-59168. (Illus.). (Fifth World Tales Ser.). (gr. k-6). 1979. (ISBN 0-89239-018-2, Imprenta de Libros Infantiles). Childrens Book Pr.

Pagano, John
--Johnny and the Winged Horse. LC 70-130890. (Illus.). 52 p. 22cm. 1970. (ISBN 0-8059-1479-X). Dorrance.

Page, Carole Gift
--Heather's Choice. LC 82-3417. 128p. N.D. (ISBN 0-8024-3490-8). Moody.
--Maria: A Story of Loneliness. LC 85-18852. 136 p. 18cm. c.1985. (ISBN 0-8024-5179-9). Moody Press.
--Neeley Never Said Good-Bye. LC 84-6627. c.1984. (ISBN 0-8024-0342-5). Moody Press.
--The Two Worlds of Tracy Corbett. LC 79-54117. (Illus.). 128 p. 20cm. c.1980. (ISBN 0-8066-1767-5). Augsburg Pub. House.

Page, Curtis Hidden, tr. see France, Anatole.

Page, David
--Ferocious, the Puppy Dragon. (Picture Ser). (gr. 3-6). 1974. (ISBN 0-14-050049-9, Puffin). Penguin.

Page, Eileen, pseud., see Heal, Edith.

Page, Eileen, pseud. (1903-), retold by
--The Hound of Culain: Or,The Child of Promise. Heal, Edith. Cuchulain & O'Grady, Standish (1846-1928) LC 31-3840. 62 p. incl. front., illus. 20 1/2 cm. 1930. Thomas S. Rockwell Company.

Page, Grover, Jr. (1918-)
--The Brave Bookmobile. Reisner, Joe, illus. LC 65-15361. (Illus.). 47 p. 24cm. 1966. E. C. Seale.
--The Haunted Bookmobile. Reisner, Joe, illus. LC 74-151515. (Illus.). 32 p. c.1971. Three Pages.

Page, H. A.
--Out and All About. N.D. George Routledge & Sons.

Page, Irene F, ed.
--Big Book for Special Days: A Collection of Original Plays and Poems. LC 47-3397. vii, 1, 248 p. illus. 21 1/2 cm. 1947. Beckley-Cardy Company.

Page, Isaac Marshall, Dr. (1885-) & China Inland Mission
--When the Donkey Jumped and Other Stories. LC 45-916412. 94 p. illus., plates, 2 port. (incl. front.) 21 cm. 1945. China Inland Mission.

Page, Jessie
--A Boy's Friendship, 1 of 6 Vols. (Illus.). 96p. (The Young Folk Series.). N.D. Set. F H Revell.

Page, Margaret
--In Childhood Land. Greenland, Katherine Hawyard, illus. LC 3-25528. (Illus.). 58p. 29cm. 1903. Saalfield Pub. Co.

Page, Marguerita
--Why Roosty Sang Cock-a-Doodle-Doo. Winship, Florence Sarah, illus. LC 49-4087. (Illus.). 17cm. 32p. (Tell-a-tale Books). c.1948. Whitman Pub, Co.

Page, Michael F. (1922-)
--The Runaway Punt. Ingpen, Robert R, illus. LC 76-379338. (Illus.). 30 p. 26cm. (Rigby opal books). 1976. (ISBN 0-7270-0119-1). Rigby.

Page, Thomas Nelson (1853-1922)
--Among the Camps: Or, Young People's Stories of the War. LC 4-17530. 6 p. l., 163 p. incl. plates. front. 21 1/2 cm. 1902. C. Scribner's Sons.
--Among the Camps: Or, Young Poeple's Stories of the War. LC 11-105013. 7 p. l., 163 p. incl. front., plates. 21 1/2 cm. 1891. C. Scribner's Sons.
--A Captured Santa Claus. Jacobs, W. L., illus. LC 2-25758. 4 p. l., 81 p. col. front., col. pl. 20 cm. 1902. C. Scribner's Sons.
--The Page Story Book. Spaulding, Frank Ellsworth (1866-) & Bryce, Catherine Turner (1871-), eds. LC 6-16650. xii p., 1 l., 125 p. front. (port.) 5 pl. 19 cm. 1906. C. Scribner's Sons.
--Pastime Stories. Frost, Arthur Burdett (1851-1928), illus. 1898. Charles Scribner's Sons'.
--Polly. Castaigne, Andre, illus. N.D. Charles Scribner's Sons.
--Santa Claus's Partner. Glackens, W., illus. LC 99-531119. 4 p. l., 176, 1 p., 1 l. col. plates. 19 cm. 1899. C. Scribner's Sons.
--Tommy Trot's Visit to Santa Claus. Anderson, Victor C., illus. LC 8-35741. 21cm. 94p. 1908. C. Scribner's Sons.
--Tommy Trot's Visit to Santa Claus and A Captured Santa Claus. (Scribner's Series for Young People). N.D. Charles Scribner's Sons.
--Two Little Confederates. LC 4-16463. 4 p. l., 156 p. incl. plates. front. 21 1/2 x 17 cm. 1888. C. Scribner's Sons.
--Two Little Confederates. LC 21-4142. 5 p. l., 156 p. incl. front., plates. 22 cm. 1889. C. Scribner's Sons.
--Two Little Confederates. LC 24-222361. 5 p. l., 169 p. incl. front., plates. 21 cm. 1923. C. Scribner's Sons.
--Two Little Confederates. LC 76-29926. (Illus.). xiv, 156, 102 p. 23cm. 1976. (ISBN 0-8240-2305-6). Garland.
--Two Little Confederates. Thomason, John W., Jr., illus. LC 32-253275. viii, 189, 2 p. incl. illus., tables. col. front. 23 cm. 1932. C. Scribner's Sons.
--Two Little Confederates. Thomason, John W., Jr., illus. 1953. Charles Scribner's Sons.
--Two Prisoners. New ed. (Illus.). N.D. Harper & Brothers Trade-List.
--Two Prisoners. LC 7-34707. 82 p. incl. front 191 cm. 1898. R. H. Russell.
--Two Prisoners. Keep, Virginia, illus. LC 3-25407. 82 p. col. front., 4 col. front., 4 col. pl. 20 1/2 cm. 1903. R. H. Russell.

Page, Thomas (1942-)
--The Hephaestus Plague. 1973. (ISBN 0-399-20125-4). G. P. Putnam's Sons.

Page, Valerie King
--Pi Gal. Callaert, Jacques, illus. LC 78-105287. (Illus.). 127 p. 24cm. 1970. Dodd, Mead.

Paget, A. M. F.
--Three More Tales. Redden, H. P., illus. N.D. Publications of E. P. Dutton & Co.

Paget, Francis Edward see Churne, William, pseud.

Paget, Francis Edward (1806-1882)
--The Hope of the Katzekopfs: A Fairy Tale. Churne, William, pseud. LC 68-18214. (With a New Preface). xv, 211p. illus. 16cm. Repr. of 1844 ed. (Early Children's Bks.). 1968. Johnson Reprint, Print.
--Luke Sharp: Or, Knowledge Without Religion. A Tale of Modern Education. LC 24-24999. 238 p. front. 15 1/2 cm. 1846. General Protestant Episcopal S.S. Union.

Paget-Fredericks, Joseph E. P. Rous-Marten (1903-1963)
--Green Pipes: Poems and Pictures. Paget-Fredericks, Joseph E. P. Rous-Marten (1903-1963), illus. LC 29-28659. vi p., 2 l., 42 p., 3 l. col. front., illus., col. plates (1 double) 31 cm. 1929. Macmillan.
--Miss Pert's Christmas Tree. Paget-Fredericks, Joseph E. P. Rous-Marten (1903-1963), illus. LC 29-286354. 5 p. l., 24, 3 p. col. front., illus., col. plates (1 double) 31 cm. 1929. Macmillan.

Paget, Walter, illus.
--Treasure Island. N.D. Charles Scribner's Sons.

Pagliaro, Penny, ed.
--I Like Poems and Poems Like Me. Chee, Wendy Kim, illus. LC 76-50343. (Illus.). xi, 98 p. 19cm. 1977. (ISBN 0-916630-03-X). Press Pacifica.

Pahz, Anne Cheryl see Goldfeder, Cheryl, pseud.

Pahz, Anne Cheryl Suzanne, jt. auth. see Pahz, James Alon.

Pahz, Cheryl see Pahz, James Alon (1943-) & Pahz, Anne Cheryl Suzanne.

Pahz, James Alon (1943-) & Pahz, Anne Cheryl Suzanne (1949-)
--Robin Sees a Song. Pahz, Anne Cheryl Suzanne (1949-), illus. LC 76-17710. (Illus.). 51 p. 29cm. (People potential series ; 2). c.1977. National Association of the Deaf.

Paige, Douglass, tr. see Bufalari, Giuseppe.

Paige, Harry W. (1922-)
--Johnny Stands. LC 82-4912. 138 p. 22cm. c.1982. (ISBN 0-7232-6213-6). F. Warne.
--Shadow on the Sun. LC 83-21567. 192p. (gr. 5-9). 1984. (ISBN 0-7232-6258-6). Warne.
--The Summer War. LC 82-24822. 176p. (gr. 6-10). 1983. (ISBN 0-7232-6223-3). Warne.

Pain, Barry Eric Odell (1864-1928)
--Two: A Story of English Schoolboy Life. Roush, L. L., illus. 1 p. l., 328 p. front., plates. 19 cm. c.1901. The Mershon Company.

Paine, Albert Bigelow (1861-1937)
--The Arkansaw Bear. VerBeck, Frank (1858-1933), illus. 1925. Harper.
--The Arkansaw Bear: A Tale of Fanciful Adventure told in Song and Story. New ed. VerBeck, Frank (1858-1933), illus. LC 3-1968. 17cm. 255p. 1902. Henry Altemus Co.
--The Arkansaw Bear: A Tale of Fanciful Adventure; Told in Song and Story. VerBeck, Frank (1858-1933), illus. LC 98-1871. 118, 2 p. incl. front., illus. 22 1/2 x 17 1/2 cm. 1898. R. H. Russell; Etc., Etc.
--The Arkansaw Bear: Complete, Being "The Arkansaw Bear" and "The Arkansaw Bear and Elsie"...Told in Song and Story. VerBeck, Frank (1858-1933), illus. LC 29-10439. 297 p. incl. col. front., illus. (incl. music) col. plates. 24 cm. c.1929. H. Altemus Company.
--The Beacon Prize Medals, and other stories. Wright, G. E. & Heustis, Louise, illus. 12cm. 325p. 1899. Baker & Taylor Co.
--Elsie and the Arkansaw Bear: Told in Song and Story. Beck, Frank Ver, illus. LC 9-28044. 3 p. l., xi-xiv p., 1 l., 17-253 p. incl. col. front., col. illus., col. plates. 19 cm. c.1909. H. Altemus Company.
--Gobolinks, for Young and Old. Stuart, Ruth McEnery, illus. N.D. The Century Co.
--Golden Cat. Doane, Pelagie (1906-1966), illus. LC 34-35887. 208 p. incl. illus., plates. col. front. 22 1/2 cm. c.1934. The Penn Publishing Company.
--The Hollow Tree. Rev ed. Conde, J. M., illus. LC 98-929. 128 p. incl. front., illus. 23 1/2 cm. 1898. R. H. Russell.
--The Hollow-Tree and Deep-Woods Book. (Twilight Ser.). N.D. Harper & Bros.
--The Hollow Tree and Deep Woods Book. Conde, J. M., illus. LC 1-27055. 135, 137, 1 p. front., illus. 20 1/2 cm. 1901. R. H. Russell.
--Hollow-Tree Nights and Days. (Twilight Ser.). N.D. Harper & Bros.
--Hollow Tree Nights and Days: Being a Continuation of the Stories About the Hollow Tree and Deep Woods People. Conde, J. M., illus. LC 16-183136. 290 p. incl. front., illus. 20 1/2 cm. 1916. Harper & Brothers.
--The Hollow Tree Snowed-in Book: Being a Continuation of the Stories About the Hollow Tree and Deep Woods People. Conde, J. M., illus. LC 10-23133. 285 p. front., illus. 20 1/2 cm. 1910. Harper & Brothers.
--Hollow-Tree Stories. (Illus.). N.D. Harper & Brothers Trade-List.
--How Mr. Dog Got Even. (Hollow-Tree Stories Ser.). 1915. Harper & Bros.
--How Mr. Rabbit Lost His Tail. (Hollow-Tree Stories Ser.). 1915. Harper & Bros.
--In the Deep Woods. Conde, J. M., illus. LC 1638. 3 p. l., 134 p. front., illus. 24 1/2 cm. 1899. R. H. Russell.
--A Little Garden Calendar. New ed. (Illus.). N.D. Henry Altemus Co.
--The Little Lady, Her Book. New ed. Heustis, Louise M. & Humphrey, Mabel L. (1859-), illus. 1905. Henry Altemus Co.
--The Little Lady, Her Book. Humphrey, Mabel L., et al. (1859-), illus. 19cm. 315p. 1901. Henry Altemus Company.
--Making Up with Mr. Dog. (Hollow-Tree Stories Ser.). 1915. Harper & Bros.
--Mr. Crow and the Whitewash: Hollow Tree Stories. Conde, J. M., illus. LC 17-29235. 119, 1 p. incl. front., illus. 18 1/2 cm. 1917. Harper & Brothers.
--Mr. Possum's Great Balloon Trip. (Hollow-Tree Stories Ser.). 1915. Harper & Bros.
--Mr. Rabbit's Big Dinner. 115p. (Hollow-Tree Stories Ser.). 1915. Harper & Bro.
--Mr. Rabbit's Wedding: Hollow Tree Stories. LC 17-29236. 123, 1 p. incl. front., illus. 18 1/2 cm. 1917. Harper & Brothers.
--Mr. Turtle's Flying Adventure: Hollow Tree Stories. LC 17-29237. 119, 1 p. incl. front., illus. 18 1/2 cm. 1917. Harper & Brothers.
--The Wanderings of Joe and Little Em. Conacher, J., illus. LC 3-20577. ix p., 1 l., 13-146 p. incl. illus., pl. front. 18 cm. 1903. H. Altemus Company.
--The Wanderings of Joe and Little Em, 1 of 21 vols. Conacher, J., illus. (Boys & Girls Booklovers Ser.: No. 5). 1905. Set. Henry Altemus Co.
--When Jack Rabbit Was a Little Boy. (Hollow-Tree Stories Ser.). N.D. Harper & Bros.

Paine, Dorothy Charlotte
--Hilda of the Hippodrome. Stanlaws, Penrhyn, illus. LC 10-16981. 282 p. incl. col. front., illus. 19 cm. 1910. The Reilly & Britton Co.
--A Little Florida Lady. LC 3-31030. 277 p. front., plates. 19 1/2 cm. 1903. George W. Jacobs & Company.
--A Little Florida Lady. (Little Maid Ser.). N.D. George W. Jacobs.
--A Little Florida Lady. (Illus.). (Little Maid Ser.). N.D. Hurst and Company.
--A Little Florida Lady. (The Vacation Bks.). (gr. 2-7). N.D. Penn Publishing Co.
--A Maid of the Mountains. LC 6-383940. 348 p. front., 7 pl. 19 1/2 cm. 1906. G. W. Jacobs & Company.
--A Maid of the Mountains. (Little Maid Ser.). N.D. George W. Jacobs.
--A Maid of the Mountains. (The Vacation Bks.). (gr. 2-7). N.D. Penn Publishing Co.

Paine, Lauran Bosworth see Carrell, Mark, pseud.

Paine, Merrill P., ed. see Dickens, Charles John Huffam.

Paine, Ralph Delahaye (1871-1925)
--Blackbeard: Buccaneer. Schoonover, Frank Earle (1877-1972), illus. LC 22-19214. 309 p. col. front., plates. 22 cm. 1922. The Penn Publishing Company.
--A Cadet of the Black Star Line. Varian, George, illus. LC 10-19384. 5 p. l., 3-198 p. front., plates. 19 1/2 cm. 1910. C. Scribner's Sons.
--Campus Days. Bohnert, Herbert F., illus. LC 12-193300. 5 p. l., 3-356 p. front., plates. 20 1/2 cm. 1912. C. Scribner's Sons.
--Comrades of the Rolling Ocean. LC 23-899016. 3 p. l., 322, 1 p. front. 19 1/2 cm. 1923. Houghton Mifflin Company.
--The Dragon and the Cross. Varian, George, illus. LC 12-19324. 5 p. l., 3-241 p. front.,/ plates. 19 1/2 cm. 1912. C. Scribner's Sons.
--First Down, Kentucky!. LC 21-19389. 3 p. l., 347, 1 p., 1 l. 19 1/2 cm. 1921. Houghton Mifflin Company.
--The Fugitive Freshman. Stevens, E. Dalton, illus. LC 10-216414. 5 p. l., 3-304 p. front., 5 pl. 20 1/2 cm. 1910. C. Scribner's Sons.
--The Golden Table. Cavaliere, R. J., illus. LC 25-19833. 329 p. front., illus., plates. 20 cm. 1925. The Penn Publishing Company.
--Midshipman Wickham. LC 26-15278. 2 p. l., 220 p. front. 19 1/2 cm. 1926. Houghton Mifflin Company.

AUTHOR INDEX PALMER, BERNARD

--Privateers of Seventy-Six. Schoonover, Frank Earle (1877-1972), illus. LC 23-141171. 316 p. col. front., illus., plates. 22 1/2 cm. 1923. The Penn Publishing Company.
--Sandy Sawyer: Sophomore. Johnson, C. Everett, illus. LC 11-22330. 5 p. l., 3-285 p. front., plates. 20 1/2 cm. 1911. C. Scribner's Sons.
--The Wrecking Master. Varian, George, illus. LC 11-221314. v p., 2 l., 3-185 p. front., plates. 19 1/2 cm. 1911. C. Scribner's Sons.
Paine, Stuart D. L., jt. auth. see Walden, Jane Brevoort.
Painter, Barbara
--Smarty Pants. Nena, illus. LC 51-15960. (Illus.). 65p. 24cm. (Gusto Issues). 1950. House-Warven.
Painton, Edith F. A. U. Palmer, Mrs. (1878-)
--Dialogues and Plays for Entertainment Days. LC 18-1365. 115 p. 19 cm. c.1917. Beckley-Cardy Company.
--King Desire and His Knights: A Fairy-Tale for Children and Some Parents. LC 13-18068. 218 p. incl. front. 19 1/2 cm. c.1913. R. F. Fenno & Company.
Pairpoint, Nellie M
--Jacinth and Her Fairy Friends. Pairpoint, Nellie M., illus. LC 23-226. 93 p. incl. front., illus. 20 cm. c.1922. W. A. Wilde Company.
--Noel and the Little People of the Woods. Pairpoint, Nellie M., illus. LC 22-6651. 83 p. incl. front., illus. 19 1/2 cm. c.1921. W. A. Wilde Company.
Pai She Chuan
--The Legend fof the White Serpent. Kwan Sang-mei, illus. Prior, A. Fullarton, tr. from Chinese. N.D. Charles E. Tuttle Co.
Paisley, A. Gardner (1904-), ed. see Ford, Robert.
Paisley, Tom see Bethancourt, T. Ernesto, pseud.
Pajot, Anne Marie
--Boots the Kitten. Pursell, Margaret Sanford, adapted by. Matte, L'Enc, illus. Bouet, Sophie, photos by. Hammarberg, Dyan, tr. from Fr. LC 76-1277. (Illus.). 24 p. 22cm. (Animal friends books). 1976. (ISBN 0-87614-066-5). Carolrhoda Books.
--Curly, the Piglet. Overbeck, Cynthia, rev. by. Matte, L'Enc, illus. Dhuit, Guy, photos by. Hammarberg, Dyan, tr. LC 76-3431. p. cm. (Animal friends books). 1976. (ISBN 0-87614-069-X). Carolrhoda Books.
--Jessie the Chicken. Pursell, Margaret Sanford, adapted by. Matte, L'Enc, illus. Fayn, Claudie, photos by. Hammarberg, Dyan, tr. from Fr. LC 76-29458. (Illus.). (Animal Friends Books). (gr. k-4). 1977. (ISBN 0-87614-074-6). Carolrhoda Bks.
--Mandy the Monkey. Pursell, Margaret Sanford, adapted by. Matte, L'Enc, illus. Vial, Yves, photos by. Hammarberg, Dyan, tr. from Fr. LC 76-41410. p. cm. (Animal friends books). 1976. (ISBN 0-87614-082-7). Carolrhoda Books.
--Polly the Guinea Pig. Pursell, Margaret Sanford, adapted by. Matte, L'Enc, illus. Barrere, Antoinette, photos by. Hammarberg, Dyan, tr. from Fr. LC 76-29449. (Illus.). 24 p. 23cm. (Animal friends books). 1977. (ISBN 0-87614-077-0). Carolrhoda Books.
--Shelley the Seagull. Pursell, Margaret Sanford, adapted by. Matte, L'Enc, illus. David, Jean-Christian & Dhuit, Guy, photos by LC 76-29454. (Illus.). (Animal Friends Books). (gr. k-4). 1977. (ISBN 0-87614-083-5). Carolrhoda Bks.
--Sprig the Tree Frog. Pursell, Margaret Sanford, adapted by. Matte, L'Enc, illus. Vial, Yves, photos by. Hammarberg, Dyan, tr. from Fr. LC 76-1224. (Illus.). 24p. (The Animal Friends Bks). (gr. k-4). 1976. (ISBN 0-87614-064-9). Carolrhoda Bks.
Pajot, Anne Marie, jt. auth. see Anders, Rebecca.
Pak, Chong-Yong & Carroll, Jock
--Korean Boy. LC 55-7030. 184 p. 22cm. 1955. Lothrop, Lee and Shepard Co.
Pal, George
--George Pal Presents Jasper and the Watermelons. Pal, George, illus. LC 45-173. (Illus.). 32p. 27 x 21cm. 1945. Diamond Publishing Co.
Palacios, Argentina, jt. auth. see Rothman, Joel.
Palacios, Argentina, ed. see Cruz, Raymond.
Palacios, Argentina, tr. see Bridwell, Norman.
Palatini, Margie
--Capricorn & Co. 160p. (The Zodiac Club Ser.: No. 5). (gr. 7 up). 1984. (ISBN 0-399-21186-1). Putnam Pub Group.
Palau, Douglas & Palau, Margaret
--Our Teddies, Ourselves: A Guide to the Well Bear. 1st ed. Cassidy, Dianne, illus. LC 83-11347. p. cm. c.1983. (ISBN 0-316-68920-3). Little, Brown.
Palau, Margaret, jt. auth. see Palau, Douglas.
Palazzo, Anthony D. see Palazzo, Tony.
Palazzo-Craig, Janet
--Case of the Missing Cat. Shire, Ellen, illus. LC 81-7635. p. cm. (A Troll Easy-to Read Mystery). c.1982. (ISBN 0-89375-594-X). (ISBN 0-89375-595-8). Troll Associates.
--Mystery of the Missing Wigs. Harvey, Paul (1926-), illus. LC 81-7615. p. cm. (A Troll Easy-to-Read Mystery). c.1982. (ISBN 0-89375-592-3). (ISBN 0-89375-593-1). Troll Associates.
Palazzo-Craig, Janet, adapted by.
--Adventures in the Wild Wood. Baer, Mary Alice, illus. LC 81-16417. (Original Author: Kenneth Grahame, 1859-1932). (Illus.). 32p. (The Wind in the Willows Ser.: No.2). (gr. 2-5). 1982. (ISBN 0-89375-638-5). (ISBN 0-89375-639-3). Troll Assocs.
Palazzo, Tony (1905-1970), selected by see Lear, Edward.
Palazzo, Tony (1905-1970), ed. see Mother Goose.
Palazzo, Tony (1905-1970), retold by see The, Three Bears
Palazzo, Tony (1905-1970)
--Amerigo, the Wandering Tortoise. Palazzo, Tony (1905-1970), illus. LC 65-16276. 1 v. (unpaged) col. illus. 28 cm. 1965. Duell, Sloan and Pearce.
--Bianco and the New World. Palazzo, Tony (1905-1970), illus. N.D. E. M. Hale & Co.
--Bianco and the New World. Palazzo, Tony (1905-1970), illus. LC 57-13709. 64p. illus. 28cm. 1957. Viking Press.
--A Bird Alphabet. Palazzo, Tony (1905-1970), illus. LC 64-12450. 58 p. illus. (part col.) 29 cm. (Tony Palazzo ABC book). 1964. Duell, Sloan and Pearce.
--Charley the Horse. Palazzo, Tony (1905-1970), illus. LC 67-433. (Illus.). 1 v. (unpaged. 26cm. 1966. Abelard-Schuman.
--Charley the Horse. Palazzo, Tony (1905-1970), illus. LC 50-7278. (Illus.). 56 p. 28cm. 1950. Viking Press.
--A Dinosaur Alphabet. Palazzo, Tony (1905-1970), illus. LC 63-16844. 1 v. (unpaged) illus. (part col.) 29 cm. (Tony Palazzo ABC book). c.1963. Duell, Sloan and Pearce.
--An Elephant Alphabet. LC 61-11959. (Illus.). 29cm. (ABC Bk.). 1961. Duell, Sloan and Pearce.
--Federico, the Flying Squirrel. Palazzo, Tony (1905-1970), illus. LC 51-10301. (Illus.). 54 p. 28cm. 1951. Viking Press.
--Fireman, Save My Cat!. Palazzo, Tony (1905-1970), illus. LC 64-12743. 42 p. col. illus. 25 cm. 1964. Abelard-Schuman.
--Golden Girl. Palazzo, Tony (1905-1970), illus. LC 63-9221. 43 p. illus. 25 cm. 1963. Garrard Pub. Co.
--The Great Othello: The Story of a Seal. Palazzo, Tony (1905-1970), illus. LC 52-12508. (Illus.). 48 p. 1952. Viking Press.
--A Horse Alphabet. Palazzo, Tony (1905-1970), illus. LC 62-15472. unpaged. illus. 29cm. (Tony Palazzo ABC book). 1962. Duell, Sloan and Pearce.
--Jan and the Reindeer. Palazzo, Tony (1905-1970), illus. LC 63-7849. 42 p. illus. 25 cm. 1963. Garrard Pub. Co.
--Magic Crayon. Palazzo, Tony (1905-1970), illus. LC 67-18481. (Illus.). 22cm. 42p. (gr. k-2). 1967. (ISBN 0-87460-003-0). (ISBN 0-87460-089-8). Lion Press.
--Mister Whistle's Secret. Palazzo, Tony (1905-1970), illus. LC 53-12308. 52p. illus. 26cm. 1953. Viking Press.
--A Monkey Alphabet. Palazzo, Tony (1905-1970), illus. LC 62-15473. unpaged. illus. 29cm. (Tony Palazzo ABC book). c.1962. Duell, Sloan and Pearce.
--A Pig for Tom. LC 63-19128. 42 p. illus. 25 cm. (Palazzo books). 1963. Garrard Pub. Co.
--Ramona Knew What She Wanted!. Palazzo, Tony (1905-1970), illus. LC 64-22345. 1 v. (unpaged) col. illus. 26 cm. 1964. Abelard-Schuman.
--The Secret of Alexander's Horse. 1st ed. Palazzo, Tony (1905-1970), illus. LC 65-16277. (Illus.). 1 v. (unpaged. 29cm. 1965. Duell, Sloan and Pearce.
--Simple Simon. 1st ed. Palazzo, Tony (1905-1970), illus. LC 59-8891. unpaged. illus. 27cm. (Tony Palazzo nursery classic). c.1959. Garden City Books.
--The Story of Snowman, the Cinderella Horse. 1st ed. Palazzo, Tony (1905-1970), illus. LC 62-8534. unpaged. illus. 28cm. c.1962. Duell, Sloan and Pearce.
--Susie, the Cat. Palazzo, Tony (1905-1970), illus. LC 63-10364. unpaged. illus. 28 cm. 1963. Duell, Sloan and Pearce.
--Susie, the Cat. Palazzo, Tony (1905-1970), illus. LC 49-8393. 50 p. col. illus. 28 cm. 1949. Viking Press.
--Thai, Kao, and Tone: An Elephant Story. Palazzo, Tony (1905-1970), illus. LC 66-14118. 1v. (unpaged) col. illus. 27cm. 1966. Abelard.
--A Time for All things. Palazzo, Tony (1905-1970), illus. 1966. (ISBN 0-8098-1122-7). David McKay Company.
--Waldo the Woodchuck. 1st Ed. ed. Palazzo, Tony (1905-1970), illus. LC 64-12449. (Illus.). 29cm. 42p. 1964. Duell Sloan & Pearce.
Palazzo, Tony (1905-1970), retold by.
--Animal Folk Tales of America. 1 st. ed. Palazzo, Tony (1905-1970), illus. LC 61-7822. 88p. col. illus. 32cm. c.1961. Doubleday.
--Animals 'round the Mulberry Bush. 1st ed. Palazzo, Tony (1905-1970), illus. LC 58-8794. unpaged. illus. 27cm. (Tony Palazzo Nursery Classic). c.1958. Garden City Books.
--Anna Sewell's Black Beauty. 1st ed. Palazzo, Tony (1905-1970), illus. LC 59-11303. (Original Author: Anna Sewell, 1820-1878). 92p. illus. 32cm. c.1959. Garden City Books.
--Edward Lear's Nonsense Book. Palazzo, Tony (1905-1970), illus. N.D. Doubleday.
--The Giant Nursery Book. Palazzo, Tony (1905-1970), illus. LC 57-11318. 188p. illus. 32cm. c.1957. Garden City Books.
--The Giant Playtime Nursery Book. 1st ed. Palazzo, Tony (1905-1970), illus. LC 59-105152. 187p. illus. 32cm. c.1959. Garden City Books.
--Henny-Penny and Chicken-Little. 1st ed. Palazzo, Tony (1905-1970), illus. LC 59-8892. unpaged. illus. 27cm. (Tony Palazzo nursery classic). c.1960. Garden City Books.
--Let's Go to the Jungle. Palazzo, Tony (1905-1970), illus. (Illus.). (gr. k-3). 1962. Doubleday.
--The Little Red Hen. 1st ed. Palazzo, Tony (1905-1970), illus. LC 58-8793. unpaged. ii. 27cm. (Tony Palazzo sursery classic). c.1958. Garden City Books.
--Peter and the Wolf. Palazzo, Tony (1905-1970), illus. (gr. 1-3). N.D. (ISBN 0-385-07932-X). (ISBN 0-385-07933-8). Doubleday.
--Story of Noah's Ark. Palazzo, Tony (1905-1970), illus. (gr. k-3). N.D. (ISBN 0-385-02143-7). Doubleday.
--The Story of Noah's Ark. Palazzo, Tony (1905-1970), illus. LC 55-9717. unpaged. illus. 32cm. 1955. Garden City Books.
--Tales of Don Quixote. Palazzo, Tony (1905-1970), illus. (gr. 1-3). N.D. (ISBN 0-385-02237-9). Doubleday.
--Tales of Don Quixote and His Friends. Palazzo, Tony (1905-1970), illus. LC 58-69213. (Original Author: Miguel de Saavedra Cervantes, 1547-1616). 84p. illus. 32cm. c.1958. Garden City Books.
--Three Little Kittens. 1st ed. Palazzo, Tony (1905-1970), illus. LC 61-5119. (Illus.). 27cm. (A Tony Palazzo Nursery Classic). 1961. Doubleday.
--Three Little Pigs. 1st ed. Palazzo, Tony (1905-1970), illus. LC 60-12697. unpaged. illus. 27 cm. (Tony Palazzo nursery classic). 1961. Doubleday.
Palazzo, Tony (1905-1970) & Fox, Robin
--A Passel of 'possums and Other Animal Families. Palazzo, Tony, illus. LC 68-19692. (Illus.). 45 p. 26cm. c.1968. Lion Press.
Palazzo-Craig, Janet, adapted by see Grahame, Kenneth.
Palecek, Josef
--The Surprise Kitten. Parents Magazine Press, ed. Palecek, Josef, illus. LC 76-4806. p. cm. (ps-2). 1976. (ISBN 0-8193-0877-3, Four Winds). Parents' Magazine Press.
Palecek, Libuse
--The Magic Grove: A Persian Folktale. Palecek, Josef, illus. LC 84-26533. p. cm. 1985, c.1984. (ISBN 0-907234-72-0). Picture Book Studio USA : Distributed by Alphabet Press.
Palencia, Isabel De
--Juan: Son of the Fisherman. Palencia y Alvares Tabau, Ceferino (1882-), illus. LC 41-19427. v p., 1 l., 207 p. incl. illus., plates. 21 x 16 cm. 1941. Longmans, Green and Co.
--Saint Anthony's Pig. Palencia y Alvares Tabau, Ceferino (1882-), illus. LC 40-13979. 3 p. l., 11-60 p. illus. 17 x 14 cm. c.1940. Longmans, Green and Co.
Paley, Claudia
--Benjamin the True. 1st ed. Hyman, Trina Schart (1939-), illus. LC 69-10663. (Illus.). 88 p. 24cm. 1969. Little, Brown.
Palgrave, Francis Turner (1824-1897), selected by.
--The Children's Treasury of English Song. LC 43-41833. viii, 302 p. 16 cm. (Golden Treasury Ser.). 1875. Macmillan and Co.
--The Children's Treasury of English Song. viii, 302 p. 19 1/2 cm. (Macmillan's juvenile library). 1916. The Macmillan Company.
--The Children's Treasury of Lyrical Poetry. LC 4-13924. x p., 1 l., 332 p. 16 1/2 cm. (Half-title: Golden treasury series). 1898. Macmillan and Co., Limited.
--Children's Treasury of Songs and Lyrics. (Poetry, Music & Art). (MacMillan Bks. for Boys & Girls). (gr. 4-6). N.D. MacMillan Bks.
--The Five Days of Entertainment at Wentworth Grange. LC 7-35781. xi, 1, 328 p. illus., plates. 21 cm. 1868. Roberts Brothers; Etc., Etc.
--The Five Days of Entertainments at Wentworth Grange. Hughes, Arthur (1832-1915), illus. N.D. Macmillan & Co.
--The Golden Treasury. N.D. A L Burt Co.
--The Golden Treasury. (Golden Treasury Series). N.D. Macmillan & Co.
--The Golden Treasury. N.D. William Collins Sons & Company Ltd.
--The Golden Treasury. Parrish, Frederick Maxfield (1870-1966), illus. N.D. Duffield.
--The Golden Treasury of Songs. (The Golden Treasury Ser.). N.D. Johm Allyn.
--The Golden Treasury of Songs and Lyrics. (The Golden Treasury Ser.). N.D. John Allyn.
--Golden Treasury of Songs and Lyrics. (Golden Treasury Ser.). N.D. Macmillan & Co.
--Golden Treasury of Songs and Lyrics. Bell, Robert Anning, illus. N.D. Dutton & Co.
--The Golden Treasury of Songs and Lyrics. Parrish, Frederick Maxfield (1870-1966), illus. (The Treasure House Bks.). N.D. Dodd, Mead & Co.
--Scott's Lady of the Last Minstrel. N.D. MacMillian.
Palgrave, Mary E
--Blind Jem and His Fiddle: A New Series. (Illus., Pub. by Society for Promoting Christian Knowledge). N.D. E & J B Young.
--In Charge. N.D. Thomas Whittaker.
--A Promise Kept. N.D. Thomas Whittaker.
Palladino, Tony (1930-)
--Once There Was a General. Palladino, Tony (1930-), illus. LC 58-5815. (Illus.). 12 x 17cm. 1958. F. Watts.
Pallas, Norvin (1918-)
--The Abandoned Mine Mystery. LC 65-12067. 143p. 21cm. (A Ted Wilford Mystery). c.1965. Washburn Dist. McKay.
--The Baseball Mystery. LC 63-12150. 147 p. 21 cm. 1963. I. Washburn.
--The Big Cat Mystery. LC 61-6978. 147p. 21cm. 1961. Washburn.
--The Counterfeit Mystery. LC 58-8450. 184 p. 21cm. 1958. Washburn.
--The Empty House Mystery. LC 57-11048. 176p. illus. 21cm. c.1957. Washburn.
--Greenhouse Mystery. LC 67-12965. (A Ted Wilford Mystery). (gr. 6-8). 1967. Washburn.
--The Locked Safe Mystery. LC 54-12220. 184p. 21cm. 1954. Washburn.
--The Missing Witness Mystery. LC 62-107568. 172p. 21cm. 1962. I. Washburn.
--The Mystery of Rainbow Gulch. LC 64-12764. 163 p. 21 cm. (A Ted Wilford Mystery). 1964. I. Washburn.
--The S. S. Shamrock Mystery. LC 66-14237. 149 p. 21cm. 1966. I. Washburn.
--The Scarecrow Mystery. LC 60-710875. 179p. illus. 21cm. 1960. Washburn.
--The Secret of Thunder Mountain. Kinnear, Paul, illus. LC 51-12241. (Illus.). 192 p. 21cm. 1951. Washburn.
--The Singing Trees Mystery. LC 56-590260. 183p. 21cm. 1956. Washburn.
--The Star Reporter Mystery. LC 55-14945. 177p. 21cm. 1955. I. Washburn.
--Stolen Plans Mystery. 1959. E M Hale.
--The Stolen Plans Mystery. LC 59-9052. 169 p. 21cm. 1959. Washburn.
Palm, Amy
--Wanda and Greta at Broby Farm. McIntosh, Frank (1901-), illus. Andrews, Siri, tr. from Swedish. LC 30-20455. vii p., 1 l., 198 p. col. front., illus. col. plates. 20 1/2 cm. 1930. Longmans, Green and Co.
Palm, Edith Cling
--Little Folks' Hour: Stories and Poems for Children. LC 31-30612. 40 p. front., illus. 21 1/2 cm. c.1931. Augustana Book Concern.
Palmer, Adelaide
--Blacky Daw: The Story of a Pet Crow. Saunders, Dorothy, illus. LC 31-1283. 128 p. incl. col. front., col. illus. 20 cm. c.1930. Beckley-Cardy Company.
Palmer, Adell Reese
--Butterfly Childern. 48p. 1974. (ISBN 0-89036-036-7). Hawkes Publishing Inc.
Palmer, Anna Campbell see Archibald, George, pseud.
Palmer, Anna Campbell, Mrs. (1854-)
--A Dozen Good Times That Georgiana and Dolly Had. Archibald, George, pseud. LC 12-37417. 5 p. l., 7-136 p. incl. front., illus., 12 pl. 17 cm. c.1898. Lothrop Publishing Company.
--Lady Gay: The Story of a Little Girl and Her Friends. Archibald, George, pseud. LC 12-37416. 4 p. l., 7-118 p. incl. front., illus., plates. 17 cm. 1898. Lothrop Publishing Company.
--A Little Brown Seed: Or, An Improved Opportunity. Archibald, George, pseud. LC 12-374184. 197 p. front., 2 pl. 19 cm. 1891. Hunt & Eaton.
Palmer, Bell Elliott
--Peggy, Betsy, and Mary Ann. LC 7-29727. 4 p. l., 161 p. col. front., 3 col. pl. 19 1/2 cm. 1907. D. Appleton and Company.
Palmer, Bernard Alvin see Runyan, John, pseud.
Palmer, Bernard Alvin (1914-)
--Angry Water. LC 74-224. (Illus.). 128 p. 20cm. 1968. Moody Press.
--Barbara Nichols, Fifth Grade Teacher. 1960. Moody.
--The Brigade Boys and the Basketball Mystery. (Illus.). (gr. 4-6). 1963 (MYL). Moody.

--The Brigade Boys and the Burning Barn. (gr. 2-5). N.D (MYL). Moody.
--The Brigade Boys and the Disappearing Stranger. (Illus.). (gr. 4-6). 1961 (MYL). Moody.
--The Brigade Boys and the Flight to Danger. (Illus.). (gr. 4-6). 1960 (MYL). Moody.
--The Brigade Boys in the Arctic Wilderness. (Illus.). (gr. 4-6). 1961 (MYL). Moody.
--The Case of the Missing Dinosaur. LC 80-65059. 160p. (Orig.). (Powell Family Ser.). (gr. 7-10). 1981. (ISBN 0-89636-050-4). Accent Bks.
--The Clue of the Old Sea Chest. LC 80-65060. 160p. (Orig.). (Powell Family Ser.). (gr. 7-10). 1981. (ISBN 0-89636-051-2). Accent Bks.
--Danny and Ron Orlis and the Mexican Jungle Mystery. 1965. Moody.
--Danny and Ron Orlis in the Canadian Wilderness. 1960. Moody.
--Danny and Ron Orlis in the Sacred Cave. 1956. Moody.
--Danny Orlis & Excitement at Circle-R Ranch. (gr. 5-10). N.D. (ISBN 0-8024-7233-8). Moody.
--Danny Orlis and Fritz McCloud, High School Star. (Danny Orlis Ser.). N.D. (ISBN 0-686-13785-X). Believers Bkshelf.
--Danny Orlis & Fritz McCloud, High School Star. 128p. (Orig.). (gr. 5-10). 1968. (ISBN 0-8024-7224-9). Moody.
--Danny Orlis and Hal's Great Victory. 1958. Moody.
--Danny Orlis & His Big Chance. (gr. 5-10). 1958. (ISBN 0-8024-7216-8). Moody.
--Danny Orlis and Jim's Northern Adventures. (Danny Orlis Ser.). N.D. (ISBN 0-686-13794-9). Believers Bkshelf.
--Danny Orlis and Johnny's New Life. (Danny Orlis Ser.). N.D. (ISBN 0-686-13789-2). Believers Bkshelf.
--Danny Orlis and Linda's New Mother. 1964. Moody.
--Danny Orlis and Linda's Struggle. 1964. Moody.
--Danny Orlis and Marilyn's Great Trial. 1959. Moody.
--Danny Orlis and Ron's Call to Service. 1963. Moody.
--Danny Orlis and the Accident that Shook Fairview. (Danny Orlis Ser.). N.D. (ISBN 0-686-13790-6). Believers Bkshelf.
--Danny Orlis & the Accident That Shook Fairview. (gr. 5-10). N.D. (ISBN 0-8024-7225-7). Moody.
--Danny Orlis & the Alaskan Highway Adventure. 128p. (Danny Orlis Ser.). (gr. 5-10). 1972. (ISBN 0-8024-7238-9). Moody.
--Danny Orlis and the Angle Inlet Mystery. (Danny Orlis Ser.). N.D. (ISBN 0-686-13781-7). Believers Bkshelf.
--Danny Orlis & the Angle Inlet Mystery. (gr. 5-10). 1954. (ISBN 0-8024-7201-X). Moody.
--Danny Orlis and the Bewildered Runaway. (Danny Orlis Ser.). N.D. (ISBN 0-686-13799-X). Believers Bkshelf.
--Danny Orlis and the Bewildered Runaway. (gr. 5-10). N.D. (ISBN 0-8024-7235-4). Moody.
--Danny Orlis and the Big Indian. 1956. Moody.
--Danny Orlis & the Boy Who Would Not Listen. (gr. 5-10). 1957. (ISBN 0-8024-7214-1). Moody.
--Danny Orlis and the Canadian Caper. (Danny Orlis Ser.). N.D. (ISBN 0-686-13800-7). Believers Bkshelf.
--Danny Orlis & the Colorado Challenge. 128p. (gr. 5-10). 1972. (ISBN 0-8024-7239-7). Moody.
--Danny Orlis and the Contrary Mrs. Forester. 1956. Moody.
--Danny Orlis and the Crisis at Cedarton. (Danny Orlis Ser.). N.D. (ISBN 0-686-13795-7). Believers Bkshelf.
--Danny Orlis and the Drugstore Mystery. 1962. Moody.
--Danny Orlis and the Dry Gulch Mystery. (Danny Orlis Ser.). N.D. (ISBN 0-686-13787-6). Believers Bkshelf.
--Danny Orlis & the Dry Gulch Mystery. 128p. (gr. 5-10). 1969. (ISBN 0-8024-7227-3). Moody.
--Danny Orlis and the Girl Who Dared. (Danny Orlis Ser.). N.D. (ISBN 0-686-13804-X). Believers Bkshelf.
--Danny Orlis & the Girl Who Dared. (Teen Ser.). (gr. 5-10). 1974. (ISBN 0-8024-7243-5). Moody.
--Danny Orlis & the Guatemala Adventure. (Orig.). (gr. 5-10). 1963. (ISBN 0-8024-7221-4). Moody.
--Danny Orlis and the Headstrong Linda Penner. 1963. Moody.
--Danny Orlis and the Hunters. (Danny Orlis Ser.). N.D. (ISBN 0-686-13793-0). Believers Bkshelf.
--Danny Orlis and the Hunters. 1955. Moody.
--Danny Orlis and the Ice Fishing Escapade. 1964. Moody.
--Danny Orlis and the Live-in Tragedy. (Danny Orlis Ser.). N.D. (ISBN 0-686-13802-3). Believers Bkshelf.
--Danny Orlis & the Live-in Tragedy. (Danny Orlis Ser). (gr. 5-10). 1972. (ISBN 0-8024-7236-2). Moody.
--Danny Orlis and the Man from the past. 1959. Moody.
--Danny Orlis and the Mexican Kidnapping. (Danny Orlis Ser.). N.D. (ISBN 0-686-13798-1). Believers Bkshelf.
--Danny Orlis & the Mexican Kidnapping. (gr. 5-10). N.D. (ISBN 0-8024-7234-6). Moody.
--Danny Orlis & the Model Plane Mystery. (gr. 4-8). 1975. (ISBN 0-8024-7246-X). Moody.
--Danny Orlis & the Mysterious Intruder. 128p. (Orig.). (Moody Teen Bks.). (gr. 5-10). 1974. (ISBN 0-8024-7244-3). Moody.
--Danny Orlis and the Mysterious Visitor. (Danny Orlis Ser.). N.D. (ISBN 0-686-13784-1). Believers Bkshelf.
--Danny Orlis & the Mysterious Visitor. (gr. 7 up). N.D. (ISBN 0-8024-7231-1). Moody.
--Danny Orlis & the Mystery at Northwest High. 128p. (gr. 5-10). 1973. (ISBN 0-8024-7240-0). Moody.
--Danny Orlis and the Mystery of the Sunken Ship. 1960. Moody.
--Danny Orlis and the Ordeal at Camp. 1963. Moody.
--Danny Orlis and the Point Barrow Mystery. (Danny Orlis Ser.). N.D. (ISBN 0-686-13788-4). Believers Bkshelf.
--Danny Orlis and the Point Barrow Mystery. N.D. Moody.
--Danny Orlis & the Rock Point Rebel. (gr. 6-10). 1974. (ISBN 0-8024-7245-1). Moody.
--Danny Orlis & the Rocks That Talk. (gr. 5-10). 1955. (ISBN 0-8024-7211-7). Moody.
--Danny Orlis & the Sacred Cave. 128p. (gr. 5-10). N.D. (ISBN 0-8024-7210-9). Moody.
--Danny Orlis & the Ski Slope Emergency. 128p. (gr. 5-10). 1973. (ISBN 0-8024-7242-7). Moody.
--Danny Orlis and the Strange Forest Fires. 1955. Moody.
--Danny Orlis and the Time of Testing. 1961. Moody.
--Danny Orlis and the Wrecked Plane. (Danny Orlis Ser.). N.D. (ISBN 0-686-13778-7). Believers Bkshelf.
--Danny Orlis & the Wrecked Plane. (gr. 5-10). 1956. (ISBN 0-685-16812-3). Moody.
--Danny Orlis and Trouble on the Circle R Ranch. (Danny Orlis Ser.). N.D. (ISBN 0-686-13803-1). Believers Bkshelf.
--Danny Orlis, Big Brother. 1959. Moody.
--Danny Orlis, Bush Pilot. 1961. Moody.
--Danny Orlis Changes School. (Danny Orlis Ser.). N.D. (ISBN 0-686-13786-8). Believers Bkshelf.
--Danny Orlis Changes Schools. 1956. Moody.
--Danny Orlis Goes to School. (Danny Orlis Ser.). N.D. (ISBN 0-686-13779-5). Believers Bkshelf.
--Danny Orlis Goes to School. 1955. Moody.
--Danny Orlis in the Canadian Wilderness. (Danny Orlis Ser.). 1960. Moody.
--Danny Orlis in The Mysterious Zandeland. 1960. Moody.
--Danny Orlis in the Sacred Cave. (gr. 5-10). 1956. (ISBN 0-8024-7210-9). Moody.
--Danny Orlis Makes the Team. 1956. Moody.
--Danny Orlis on Superstition Mountain. (Danny Orlis Ser.). N.D. (ISBN 0-686-13780-9). Believers Bkshelf.
--Danny Orlis on Superstition Mountain. N.D. Moody.
--Danny Orlis on the Valiant. 1959. Moody.
--Danny Orlis Plays Hockey. 1957. Moody.
--Danny Orlis, Star Back. (Danny Orlis Ser.). N.D. (ISBN 0-686-13777-9). Believers Bkshelf.
--Danny Orlis, Star Back. 1957. Moody.
--Dell Norton and the Hidden Caves. (Dell Norton Ser.). 1959. Moody.
--Dell Norton in the Ozarks. (Dell Norton Ser.). 1958. Moody.
--The Echo Mountain Hermit. (Dell Norton Ser.). 1958. Moody.
--Eyes in the Jungle. LC 74-80945. (Illus.). 128 p. 20cm. 1969. Moody Press.
--Felicia Cartwright & the Black Phantom. 728p. (Orig.). (gr. 8 up). 1968. (ISBN 0-8024-7415-2). Moody.
--Felicia Cartwright and the Case of the Antique Bookmark. (Felicia Cartwright Ser.). N.D. (ISBN 0-686-13816-3). Believers Bkshelf.
--Felicia Cartwright and the case of the Antique Bookmark. 1963. Moody.
--Felicia Cartwright and the Case of the Black Phantom. (Felicia Cartwright Ser.). N.D. (ISBN 0-686-13819-8). Believers Bkshelf.
--Felicia Cartwright and the Case of the Dancing Fire. (Felicia Cartwright Ser.). N.D. (ISBN 0-686-13811-2). Believers Bkshelf.
--Felicia Cartwright and the Case of the Dancing Fire. 1960. Moody.
--Felicia Cartwright and the Case of the Frightened Student. (Felicia Cartwright Ser.). N.D. (ISBN 0-686-13809-0). Believers Bkshelf.
--Felicia Cartwright & the Case of the Frightened Student. (gr. 8 up). 1959. (ISBN 0-8024-7404-7). Moody.
--Felicia Cartwright and the Case of the Green Medallion. 1958. Moody.
--Felicia Cartwright and the Case of the Lost Puppy. (Felicia Cartwright Ser.). N.D. (ISBN 0-686-13817-1). Believers Bkshelf.
--Felicia Cartwright & the Case of the Lost Puppy. (gr. 8 up). 1965. (ISBN 0-8024-7412-8). Moody.
--Felicia Cartwright & the Case of the Hungry Fiddler. (gr. 8 up). 1962. (ISBN 0-8024-7410-1). Moody.
--Felicia Cartwright & the Case of the Lonely Skiboot. (gr. 8 up). 1969. (ISBN 0-8024-7416-0). Moody.
--Felicia Cartwright and the Case of the Lonely Teacher. (Felicia Cartwright Ser.). N.D. (ISBN 0-686-13812-0). Believers Bkshelf.
--Felicia Cartwright & the Case of the Lonely Teacher. (gr. 8 up). 1960. (ISBN 0-8024-7407-1). Moody.
--Felicia Cartwright & the Case of the Missing Sideboard. 1958. Moody.
--Felicia Cartwright and the Case of the Pink Poodle. (Felicia Cartwright Ser.). N.D. (ISBN 0-686-13822-8). Believers Bkshelf.
--Felicia Cartwright & the Case of the pink Poodle. (gr. 8 up). N.D. (ISBN 0-8024-7418-7). Moody.
--Felicia Cartwright and the Case of the Sad-Eyed Girl. (Felicia Cartwright Ser.). N.D. (ISBN 0-686-13821-X). Believers Bkshelf.
--Felicia Cartwright and the Case of the Storm Scarred Mountain. (Felicia Cartwright Ser.). N.D. (ISBN 0-686-13813-9). Believers Bkshelf.
--Felicia Cartwright & the Case of the Storm Scarred Mountain. (gr. 8 up). 1961. (ISBN 0-8024-7408-X). Moody.
--Felicia Cartwright and the Case of the Twisted Key. (Felicia Cartwright Ser.). N.D. (ISBN 0-686-13810-4). Believers Bkshelf.
--Felicia Cartwright & the Case of the Twisted Key. (gr. 8 up). 1959. (ISBN 0-8024-7405-5). Moody.
--Felicia Cartwright and the Case of the Troubled Rancher. (Felicia Cartwright Ser.). N.D. (ISBN 0-686-13814-7). Believers Bkshelf.
--Felicia Cartwright & the Case of the Troubled Ranch. (gr. 8 up). 1961. (ISBN 0-8024-7409-8). Moody.
--Felicia Cartwright and the Case of the Uncut Diamond. (Felicia Cartwright Ser.). N.D. (ISBN 0-686-13808-2). Believers Bkshelf.
--Felicia Cartwright and the Case of the Uncut Diamond. 1958. Moody.
--Felicia Cartwright and the Frantic Search. (Felicia Cartwright Ser.). N.D. (ISBN 0-686-13806-6). Believers Bkshelf.
--Felicia Cartwright & the Frantic Search. (gr. 8 up). N.D. (ISBN 0-8024-7401-2). Moody.
--Felicia Cartwright and the Green Medallion. (Felicia Cartwright Ser.). N.D. (ISBN 0-686-13807-4). Believers Bkshelf.
--Felicia Cartwright & the Green Medallion. (gr. 8 up). 1958. (ISBN 0-8024-7402-0). Moody.
--Felicia Cartwright and the Honorable Traitor. 128p. 1967. Moody Press.
--Felicia Cartwright & the Knotted Wire. (Orig.). (gr. 8 up). 1966. (ISBN 0-8024-7413-6). Moody.
--Felicia Cartwright and the Lone Ski Boot. 122p. 1969. Moody Press.
--Felicia Cartwright and the Sad-Eyed Girl. 122p. 1969. Moody Press.
--The Fire Detectives. (Mickey Turner Ser.). 1955. Moody.
--The First Bull Run. Repr. 1965. MacMillan Co.
--Frosty Roberts and the Golden Jade Mystery. LC 75-330360. (Illus.). 124 p. 20cm. 1975. (ISBN 0-8024-2883-5). Moody Press.
--Golden Boy. LC 51-8262. 96 p. 20 cm. 1951. Van Kampen Press.
--Goon Walford Fights Back. LC 47-18104. (Illus.). 96p. 20cm. 1946. Van Kampen Press.
--The Halliway Boys and the Case of the Missing Film Mystery. 1960. Moody.
--The Halliway Boys and the Disappearing Staircase. 1958. Moody.
--The Halliway Boys and the Mysterious Treasure Map. 1960. Moody.
--The Halliway Boys on a Dangerous Voyage. 1958. Moody.
--The Halliway Boys on Crusade Island. 1957. Moody.
--The Halliway Boys on Forbidden Mountain. 1962. Moody.
--The Halliway Boys on Secret African Safari. 1962. Moody.
--The Halliway Boys on the Secret Expedition. 156p. 1958. Moody.
--Hitched to a Star. LC 81-9636. p. cm. c.1981. (ISBN 0-8024-3584-X). Moody Press.
--Jim Dunlap & the Mysterious Orbiting Rocket. 128p. (Pre-Teen Bks). Orig. Title: Pat Collins and the Mysterious Orbiting Rocket. (gr. 5-7). 1968. (ISBN 0-8024-4303-6). Moody.
--Jim Dunlap & the Secret Rocket Formula. 128p. (Pre-Teen Bks). (gr. 3-6). 1967. (ISBN 0-8024-4301-X). Moody.
--Jim Dunlap & the Wingless Plane. 128p. (Pre-Teen Bks). Orig. Title: Pat Collins and the Wingless Plane. (gr. 3-6). 1968. (ISBN 0-8024-4302-8). Moody.
--Jim Shelton, Radio Engineer. 128p. 1964. Moody.
--Jungle Jim. 159p. 1956. Moody.
--Little Feather and the Mystery Mine. LC 48-9597. 20cm. 57p. (The Little Feather Ser.). 1948. Zondervan Publishing House.
--Little Feather and the River of Grass. LC 54-8087. 55p. 20cm. 1953. Zondervan Pub. House.
--Little Feather and the Secret Package. LC 51-4041. 59 p. 20 cm. 1951. Zondervan.
--Little Feather at Big Bear Lake. LC 45-108018. 73 p. 19 1/2 cm. 1944. Zondervan Publishing House.
--Little Feather at Tonka Bay. LC 50-11745. 56 p. 20 cm. 1950. Zondervan Pub. House.
--Little Feather Goes Hunting. Matthews, Evan, illus. LC 46-19191. 80 p. illus. 20 cm. 1946. Zondervan Publishing House.
--Little Feather Rides Herd. LC 47-25853. 60 p. front. 20 cm. 1947. Zondervan Pub. House.
--Lori Adams & the Adopted Rebel. (Illus.). 128p. (Pre-Teen Bks). (gr. 3-7). 1971. (ISBN 0-8024-4502-0). Moody.
--Lori Adams & the Jungle Search. 128p. (gr. 6-10). 1974. (ISBN 0-8024-4504-7). Moody.
--Lori Adams & the Old Carter House Mystery. 128p. (Orig.). (gr. 6-10). 1969. (ISBN 0-8024-4501-2). Moody.
--Lori Adams and the River Boat Mystery. (Lori Adams Ser.). N.D. (ISBN 0-686-13828-7). Believers Bkshelf.
--Lori Adams & the Riverboat Mystery. (Illus.). 128p. (Pre-Teen Bks). (gr. 3-7). 1971. (ISBN 0-8024-4503-9). Moody.
--Mel Webb and the Border Collie. (Mel Webb Ser.). 1964. Moody.
--Mel Webb & the Stolen Dog Mystery. N.D. (ISBN 0-8024-3522-X). Moody.
--Mel Webb on the Danger Trail (Pub. by Moody). (Pre-Teens Ser). (gr. 6-8). 1972. (ISBN 0-8024-3522-X). Moody.
--Mickey Turner and the Phantom Dog. (Mickey Turner Ser.). 1955. Moody.
--Mickey Turner, Ranger's Son. (Mickey Turner Ser.). 1955. Moody.
--The Mystery at Poor Boy's Folly. LC 80-65058. 160 p. 18cm. (The Powell Family Series for Young Readers). c.1981. (ISBN 0-89636-049-0). Accent Books.
--Mystery of Dungu-re. 124p. 1961. Moody.
--Mystery of the Musty Ledger. 123p. 1960. Moody.
--The Orlis Twins and Jim Morgan's Ordeal. 159p. 1962. Moody.
--The Orlis Twins and Mike's Last Chance. 153p. 1960. Moody.
--The Orlis Twins and Ron's Big Problem. 158p. 1962. Moody.
--The Orlis Twins and Roxie's Triumph. 158p. 1963. Moody.
--The Orlis Twins and the High School Gang. 159p. 1959. Moody.
--The Orlis Twins and the New Coach. 160p. 1960. Moody.
--The Orlis Twins and the Secret of the Mountain. 159p. 1959. Moody.
--The Orlis Twins Live for Christ. 159p. 1959. Moody.
--Outlaw: Another Golden Boy Story. LC 55-18717. 75p. 20cm. c.1954. Van Kampen Press.
--Pat Collins and the Hidden Treasure. LC 57-2558. 63p. 21cm. 1957. Moody Press.
--Pat Collins and the Peculiar Dr. Brockton. LC 57-2559. 61p. 21cm. 1957. Moody Press.
--Pat Collins and the Secret Engine. LC 57-2560. 63p. 21cm. 1957. Moody Press.
--Pat Collins and the Wingless Plane. LC 57-264657. 60p. 21cm. 1957. Moody Press.
--Peggy Archer, Missionary Candidate. 126p. 1961. Moody.
--Silent Thunder: Based on the New Ken Anderson Motion Picture. LC 74-21363. 90 p. 18cm. 1975. (ISBN 0-87123-531-5). Dimension Books.
--Student Nurse. 1960. Moody Press.
--Sue Riley and the Mysterious Cargo. 64p. 1968. Moody Press.
--The Tattered Lion Cloth Mystery. 189p. 1962. Moody.
--Ted & Terri & the Broken Arrow. (gr. 3-7). N.D. (ISBN 0-8024-4902-6). Moody.
--Ted & Terri & the Crooked Trapper. (gr. 3-7). N.D (MYL). Moody.
--Ted & Terri & the Secret Captive. (gr. 3-7). N.D. (ISBN 0-8024-4901-8). Moody.
--Ted & Terri & the Stubborn Bully. (gr. 3-7). N.D (MYL). Moody.
--Ted & Terri & the Troubled Trumpeter. (gr. 3-7). N.D (MYL). Moody.

AUTHOR INDEX PALMER, SUE

--Ted and the Secret Club. Van Severen, Joe, illus. LC 79-67407. (Illus.). 118 p. 20cm. (Winner book). c.1980. (ISBN 0-88207-487-3). Victor Books.
--Trapped on Sugar Loaf Mountain. (Mickey Turner Ser.). 1955. Moody.
--The Vanishing Mountain Lion. (Dell Norton Ser.). 1958. Moody.
--The Wild Float Trip. (Dell Norton Ser.). 1958. Moody.

Palmer, Bernard Alvin (1914-) & Palmer, Marjorie Matthews (1919-)
--Fifth Grade Teacher. (Career Books Ser). (gr. 8 up). N.D (MYL). Moody.
--The Flood. Webb, Gary A., illus. (Illus.). 32p. (Orig.). 1982. (ISBN 0-934998-10-8). Bethel Pub.
The Pioneer Girls and the Dutch Mill Mystery (Orig.). (gr. 5-9). 1968 (MYL). Moody.
--The Pioneer Girls and the Mysterious Bedouin Cave. (Orig.). (gr. 5-9). 1963 (MYL). Moody.
--The Pioneer Girls and the Mystery of Oak Ridge Manor. (Orig.). (gr. 5-9). 1959 (MYL). Moody.
--Pioneer Girls and the Mystery of the Missing Cocker. 64p. 1959. Moody.
--The Pioneer Girls and the Secrets of the Jungle. (Orig.). (gr. 5-9). 1962 (MYL). Moody.
--The Pioneer Girls and the Strange Adventures on Tomahawk Hill. (Orig.). (gr. 5-9). 1959 (MYL). Moody.
--Pioneer Girls at Caribou Flats. 64p. 1959. Moody.
--Who Helps. Webb, Gary A., illus. (Illus.). 32p. (Orig.). 1982. (ISBN 0-934998-08-6). Bethel Pub.

Palmer, Cox
--Another Brownie Book: Containing: The Brownies' Snow Man, The Brownies at Niagara Falls, The Brownies' Fancy Ball, The Brownies Birthday Dinner and Twenty other Brownie Adventures. 144p. N.D. The Century Co.
--Brownies Abroad. 144p. N.D. The Century Co.
--The Brownies Around the World. 144p. N.D. The Century Co.
--The Brownies at Home. 150p. N.D. The Century Co.
--The Brownies. Their Book. (Illus.). N.D. The Century Co.
--The Brownies Through the Union. 144p. N.D. The Century Co.

Palmer, Cyril Everard (1930-)
--Baba and Mr. Big. Lynch, Lorenzo (1932-), illus. LC 72-75891. (Illus.). 110 p. 20cm. 1972. Bobbs-Merrill.
--Big Doc Bitteroot. LC 71-136420. 157 p. 21cm. 1971, c.1968. Bobbs-Merrill.
--The Cloud with the Silver Lining. Acs, Laszlo Bela (1931-), illus. LC 67-20213. (Illus.). 164 p. 24cm. 1st U.S. edition. 1967, c.1966. Pantheon Books.
--A Cow Called Boy. Gaines, Charles E., illus. LC 76-172344. (Illus.). 112 p. 20cm. 1972. Bobbs-Merrill.
--A Dog Called Houdini. Wilson, Maurice Charles John (1914-), illus. LC 78-321833. (Illus.). 100 p. 21cm. 1979. (ISBN 0-233-96985-3). Deutsch.
--Houdini, Come Home. Rowe, Gavin, illus. LC 81-67109. 96 p. 20cm. 1981. (ISBN 0-233-97359-1). Deutsch.
--The Sun Salutes You. LC 73-156110. 144 p. 21cm. 1971, c.1970. Bobbs-Merrill.

Palmer, Donald Ellsworth (1922-)
--Boy Scout Explorers at Emerald Valley. LC 56-263. 224p. illus. 20cm. 1955. Cupples and Leon Co.
--Boy Scout Explorers at Headless Hollow. LC 57-4962. 217p. illus. 20cm. 1957. Cupples and Leon Co.
--The Boy Scout Explorers at Treasure Mountain. LC 56-264. 220p. illus. 20cm. 1955. Cupples and Leon Co.

Palmer, Edith
--Tea Meeting Winner. Payne, Joan Balfour (1923-1973), illus. LC 64-19081. (Illus.). 25cm. 46p. (gr. 2-4). 1964. (ISBN 0-8038-7017-5). Hastings.

Palmer, Elizabeth, Mrs.
--Give Me a River. Holberg, Richard A. (1889-1942), illus. LC 39-27820. 152 p. incl. illus., col. double plates. 21 cm. 1939. C. Scribner's Sons.
--Good Old Clipsy. Brown, Paul (1893-1958), illus. LC 41-14774. 4 p. l., 194 p. incl. front., col. illus. 21 x 16 cm. 1941. C. Scribner's Sons.
--The Nightingale House. Peters, Marjorie, illus. LC 37-27471. 4 p. l., 3-122 p. incl. illus., plates. col. front., col. plates. 21 cm. 1937. C. Scribner's Sons.
--Up the River to Danger. Holberg, Richard A. (1889-1942), illus. LC 40-30968. 183, 1 p. incl. illus., col. double plates. 21 x 16 cm. 1940. C. Scribner's Sons.

Palmer, Ellen
--Nonna, 1 of 6. (Home and School Reward Ser.: No. 1). N.D. Cassell, Petter, & Galpin.
--The Standard-Bearer, 1 of 7. (The Mossdale Ser.). N.D. Cassell, Petter, & Galpin.

Palmer, Frances
--Dogged Jack. (Illus.). N.D. E. P. Dutton & Co.
--Dogged Jack. N.D. Wells, Gardner, Darton & Co.'s.
--True Under Trial: A Tale for Boys. (Illus.). N.D. E. P. Dutton & Co.
--True Under Trial: A Tale For Boys. N.D. Wells, Gardner, Darton & Co.'s.

Palmer, Francis Paul
--Old Tales for the Young. N.D. George Routledge & Sons.

Palmer, Francis Sterne
--Strange Stories of Colonial Days. LC 7-17360. 1907. Harper & Brothers.

Palmer, Geoffrey & Lloyd, Noel
--A [illegible] of Witchcraft. Friers, Rowel Boyd (1920-), illus. LC 65-10803. 160 p. illus. 22 cm. 1965. Roy Publishers.
--Ghost Stories Round the World. Friers, Rowel Boyd (1920-), illus. (Illus.). (gr. 5 up). 1968. Roy.
--Journey by Broomstick. Friers, Rowel Boyd (1920-), illus. LC 67-10271. (Illus.). 160 p. 22cm. 1966. Roy Publishers.
--Moonshine and Magic. Friers, Rowel Boyd (1920-), illus. LC 67-27959. (Illus.). 158 p. 22cm. 1966. Roy Publishers.
--Starlight and Spells. Friers, Rowel Boyd (1920-), illus. LC 74-90931. (Illus.). 144 p. 22cm. 1969. Roy Publishers.

Palmer, Geoffrey & Lloyd, Noel, eds.
--Round About Eight: Poems for Today. Wrigley, Denis, illus. LC 72-81148. (Illus.). 128 p. 25cm. 1973, c.1972. (ISBN 0-7232-1470-0). (ISBN 0-7232-1470-0). F. Warne.

Palmer, Helen Marion, pseud., see Geisel, Helen.

Palmer, Helen Marion, adapted by see Disney, Walter Elias.

Palmer, Helen Marion (1898-1967), adapted by see Disney, Walt, Productions.

Palmer, Helen Marion, pseud. (1898-1967), adapted by see Disney, Walt, Productions & North, Sterling.

Palmer, Helen Marion, pseud. (1898-1967)
--Bobby and His Airplanes. Geisel, Helen. Gergely, Tibor (1900-1978), illus. LC 49-48154. 20cm. 42p. (Little Golden Book: 69). 1949. Simon and Schuster.
--Do You Know What I'm Going to Do Next Saturday?. Geisel, Helen. Fayman, Lynn, photos by. LC 63-17572. 62 p. illus. 24 cm. 1963. Beginner Books.
--Do You Know What I'm Gonna Do Next Saturday. Geisel, Helen. Fayman, Lynn, photos by. (Illus.). 1963. Random House Inc.
--Donald Duck Sees South America. Geisel, Helen. LC 45-5599. 3 p. l., 137 1 p. illus. (part col., incl. maps) 21 1/2 cm. (Walt Disney story books). 1945. D. C. Heath and Company.
--A Fish Out of Water. Geisel, Helen. Eastman, Philip Dey (1909-), illus. LC 61-9579. 64p. illus. 24cm. (Beginner books, B-23). 1961. Beginner Books.
--A Fish Out of Water. Geisel, Helen. Eastman, Philip Dey (1909-), illus. (Illus.). 1961. Random House Inc.
--A Fish Out of Water. Geisel, Helen. Rivera, Carlos, tr. (Illus.). (Spanish Beginner Bks.). (gr. k-3). 1967. (ISBN 0-394-91598-4). Random.
--A Fish Out of Water. Geisel, Helen. Vallier, Jean, tr. (Illus.). (French Beginner Bks). 1967. (ISBN 0-394-90172-X). Beginner.
--I Was Kissed by a Seal at the Zoo. Geisel, Helen. Fayman, Lynn, photos by. LC 62-151139. 62p. illus. 24cm. (Beginner books, B-26). c.1962. (ISBN 0-394-90026-X). Beginner Books.
--Johnny's Machines. Geisel, Helen. DeWitt, Cornelius Hugh (1905-), illus. LC 50-5804. 42p. (Little Golden Library). 1949. Simon and Shuster.
--The Smile on the Face of the Lion. Geisel, Helen. (Illus.). 1965. Random HOuse INc.
--Three Caballeros. Geisel, Helen. LC 44-47730. 1 p. l., 7-56 p. illus. (part col.) 28 1/2 x 23 cm. 1944. Random House.
--Tommy's Wonderful Rides. Geisel, Helen. Miller, John Parr (1913-), illus. LC 49-7107. 42p. (Little Golden Library). 1948. Simon and Shuster.
--Why I Built the Booglehouse. Geisel, Helen, Bk.35. Fayman, Lynn, photos by. LC 64-11459. (Illus.). 23cm. 63p. (Beginner Book Ser.). 1964. (ISBN 0-394-80035-4). (ISBN 0-394-90035-9). Random House INc.

Palmer, Jan, illus.
--Who Lives in the Zoo?. (Illus.). 24p. (Golden Storytime Bks.). (ps). 1981. (ISBN 0-307-11958-0, Golden Pr). (ISBN 0-307-61958-3). Western Pub.

Palmer, Joan E
--The Red Petticoat. Mars, Witold Tadeusz J. (1912-), illus. LC 71-81928. (Illus.). 128 p. 22cm. 1969. Lothrop, Lee & Shepard.

Palmer, Julius A., Jr.
--One Voyage. N.D. Lothrop Pub. Co.

Palmer, Katherine Stedman
--The Fat Frog of Pau. LC 20-930. 26 p. 10 1/2 cm. 1919. The Neale Publishing Comapny.

Palmer, Lynde, pseud., see Peebles, Mary Louise Parmelee.

Palmer, Lynde, pseud. (1833-1915)
--A Question of Honour. Peebles, Mary Louise Parmelee. (Roundabout Lib.). N.D. Henry T. Coates & Co.
--Archie's Shadow. Peebles, Mary Louise Parmelee. (The Magnet Stories). N.D. H. B. Nims & Co.
--Archie's Shadow. Peebles, Mary Louise Parmelee. New ed. (The Magnet Stories) N.D. Joseph Knight Co.
--Archie's Shadow. Peebles, Mary Louise Parmelee. (The Magnet Stories). N.D. L. C. Page & Co.
--Drifting and Steering. Peebles, Mary Louise Parmelee. (The Magnet Stories). N.D. H. B. Nims & Co.
--Drifting and Steering. Peebles, Mary Louise Parmelee. New ed. (The Magnet Stories). N.D. Joseph Knight Co.
--Drifting and Steering. Peebles, Mary Louise Parmelee. (The Magnet Stories). N.D. L. C. Page & Co.
--Drifting and Steering. Peebles, Mary Louise Parmelee. 304p. (The Magnet Stories). 1888. Nims & Knight.
--The Good Fight. Peebles, Mary Louise Parmelee. 208p. (Pleasant-grove Ser.). N.D. Lockwood, Brooks, & Co. for American Tract Society.
--Half Hours in Story Land. Peebles, Mary Louise Parmelee. (Illus.). 1891. Nims & Knight.
--Helps for Boys: First Series. Peebles, Mary Louise Parmelee. N.D. H. B. Nims & Co.
--Helps for Boys: Second Series. Peebles, Mary Louise Parmelee. (Illus.). N.D. H. B. Nims & Co.
--Helps for Girls: First Series. Peebles, Mary Louise Parmelee. N.D. H. B. Nims & Co.
--Helps Over Hard Places: Stories for Boys. Peebles, Mary Louise Parmelee, 1 of 50 vols. 224p. (Heart Life Classics). 1905. American Tract Society.
--Helps Over Hard Places: Stories for Girls. Peebles, Mary Louise Parmelee. (Illus.). 224p. 1905. American Tract Society.
--The Honorable Club and Other Stories. Peebles, Mary Louise Parmelee. 270p. (Honor-bright Library). N.D. Lockwood, Brooks, & Co. for American Tract Society.
--John-Jack. Peebles, Mary Louise Parmelee. New ed. (The Magnet Stories). N.D. Joseph Knight Co.
--John-Jack. Peebles, Mary Louise Parmelee. (The Magnet Stories). N.D. L. C. Page & Co.
--John Jack. Peebles, Mary Louise Parmelee. 320p. (The Magnet Stories). 1888. Nims & Knight.
--The Little Captain. Peebles, Mary Louise Parmelee. 131p. N.D. Hurd & Houghton for American Tract Society.
--The Little Captain. Peebles, Mary Louise Parmelee. 131p. N.D. Lockwood, Brooks, & Co. for American Tract Society.
--One Day's Weaving. Peebles, Mary Louise Parmelee. New ed. (The Magnet Stories). N.D. Joseph Knight Co.
--One Day's Weaving. Peebles, Mary Louise Parmelee. (The Magnet Stories). N.D. L. C. Page & Co.
--One Day's Weaving. Peebles, Mary Louise Parmelee. 320p. (The Magnet Stories). 1888. Nims & Knight.
--Twinkle and Wrinkle. Peebles, Mary Louise Parmelee, 2 bks. 220p. N.D. American Tract Society.
--Twinkle and Wrinkle. Peebles, Mary Louise Parmelee. (Illus.). N.D. Joseph Knight Co.
--Twinkle and Wrinkle and Other Stories. Peebles, Mary Louise Parmelee. (Illus.). N.D. Nims & Knight.
--Two Blizzards and Other Stories. Peebles, Mary Louise Parmelee. 220p. (The Golden Rod Lib.). N.D. American Tract Society.
--The Two Blizzards and Other Stories. Peebles, Mary Louise Parmelee. (Illus.). N.D. Nims & Knight Troy.
--The Two Blizzards and Other Stories: Stories for Boys and Girls. Peebles, Mary Louise Parmelee. (Illus.). N.D. Joseph Knight Co.

Palmer, Marion, adapted by see Disney, Walter Elias.

Palmer, Marion (1898-), retold by see Harris, Joel Chandler.

Palmer, Marjorie Mathews, jt. auth. see Palmer, Bernard Alvin.

Palmer, Marjorie Matthews, jt. auth. see Palmer, Bernard Alvin.

Palmer, Marjorie Matthews (1919-)
--God Helps David. (Illus.). (My Bible Story Reader Ser.: Vol. 1). (gr. 2 up). 1983. (ISBN 0-8024-0191-0). Moody.
--God Saves Noah. (Illus., Orig.). (My Bible Story Reader Ser.: Vol. 2). (gr. 2). 1983. (ISBN 0-8024-0192-9). Moody.

Palmer, Mary Babcock (1916-)
--The Dolmop of Dorkling. Lasell, Elinor Hegemann (1929-), illus. LC 67-14702. (Illus.). 155 p. 22cm. 1967. Houghton Mifflin.
--The Magic Knight. Sokol, Bill, pseud. (1925-), illus. Sokol, William. 1964. E M Hale.
--The Magic Knight. Sokol, Bill, pseud. (1925-), illus. Sokol, William. LC 64-205350. (Illus.). 93 p. 22cm. 1964. Houghton Mifflin.
--The No-Sort-of-Animal. LC 64-10726. 48 p. col. illus. 24 x 25 cm. 1964. Houghton Mifflin.
--The Teaspoon Tree. Dodge, Carlota, illus. LC 63-7327. 114 p. illus. 22 cm. 1963. Houghton Mifflin Co.

Palmer, Michele
--Zoup Soup. Gugler, Janine, illus. LC 78-66342. (Illus.). 24 p. c.1978. (ISBN 0-932306-00-4). Rocking Horse Press.

Palmer, Michele, ed.
--A Mother Goose Feast: Rhymes & Recipes. LC 79-65819. (Illus.). (ps-12). 1979. (ISBN 0-932306-01-2). Rocking Horse.
--Rainy Day Rhymes: A Collection of Chants, Forecasts & Tales. Guerin, Penny, illus. LC 84-60412. (Illus.). 24p. (Orig.). 1984. (ISBN 0-932306-02-0). Rocking Horse.

Palmer, Myron Tim
--At the Lion Gate. Palmer, Myron Tim, illus. LC 61-5140. 155p. illus. 22cm. 1962. (ISBN 0-395-06982-3). Houghton Mifflin.
--The Egyptian Necklace. Palmer, Myron Tim, illus. LC 61-5141. 135p. illus. 22cm. 1961. (ISBN 0-395-06984-X). Houghton Mifflin.
--Treachery in Crete. LC 61-982451. 167p. illus. 22cm. 1961. Houghton Mifflin.

Palmer, Nena
--That Stewart Girl. LC 53-5251. 246p. 21cm. 1953. Morrow.

Palmer, Robin (1911-)
--The Barkingtons. Gag, Flavia (1907-1979), illus. LC 48-7153. 21cm. 111p. (gr. 3-7). 1948. Harper & Bros.
--Centaurs, Sirens, and Other Classical Creatures: A Dictionary, Tales & Verse from Greek & Roman Mythology. Bolognese, Donald Alan (1934-), illus. LC 78-82679. (Illus.). 92 p. 24cm. 1969. H. Z. Walck.
--Demons, Monsters & Abodes of the Dead. (gr. 7-12). 1978. (ISBN 0-590-11839-0). Scholastic Inc.
--Dragons, Unicorns, and Other Magical Beasts: A Dictionary of Fabulous Creatures with Old Tales and Verses About Them. Bolognese, Donald Alan (1934-), illus. LC 66-6506. (Illus.). 95 p. 24cm. 1966. H. Z. Walck.
--Furry Ones: An/Animal Picture Book. LC 42-31600. (Illus.). 47p. 24 x 19cm. 1938. Whitman Publishing Company.
--Mickey Never Fails. Disney, Walt, Studio, illus. LC 39-190084. 3 p. l., 102 p. illus. (part col.) 22 cm. c.1939. D. C. Heath and Company.
--Ship's Dog. Busoni, Rafaello (1900-1962), illus. LC 46-6227. 28 p. incl. col. front., illus. (part col.) 23 x 21 cm. (Story parade picture book). c.1945. Grosset and Dunlap.
--Wise House. Merwin, Decie (1894-1961), illus. LC 51-13614. 138 p. illus. 22 cm. 1951. Harper.

Palmer, Robin (1911-) & Doane, Pelagie (1906-1966)
--Fairy Elves: A Dictionary of the Little People with Some Old Tales and Verses About Them. Doane, Pelagie (1906-1966), illus. LC 64-21123. 92 p. illus. (part col.) 24 cm. 1964. (ISBN 0-8098-2373-X). H. Z. Walck.

Palmer, Ruth Candida (1926-)
--Kim Ann and the Yellow Machine. Mayer, Mercer (1943-), illus. LC 70-166456. (Illus.). 16 p. 24cm. (Magic circle book). 1972. (ISBN 0-663-22972-3). Ginn.
--A Ride on High. Hall, H. Tom, illus. LC 66-109043. (Illus.). (gr. k-3). 1966. (ISBN 0-397-30914-7). (ISBN 0-397-30915-5). Lippincott.
--Snow Storm Before Christmas. Hall, H. Tom, illus. LC 65-21672. 32p. illus. 23cm. c.1965. (ISBN 0-397-31623-2). (ISBN 0-397-30834-5). Lippincott.
--The Soapsuds Fairy. Stirnweis, Shannon (1931-), illus. LC 78-157442. (Illus.). 32 p. 23cm. (Magic circle book: reading 360). 1971, c.1972. (ISBN 0-663-22984-7). Ginn.

Palmer, S. Lady
--Mrs Penicott's Lodger and Other Stories. N.D. MacMillian.

Palmer, Sarah Elizabeth, jt. auth. see Hall, Mary Leora.

Palmer, Sue
--Tales in Rhyme. Jones, Joan, illus. (Illus.). 1978. (ISBN 0-682-48904-2). Exposition.

Palmer, Winthrop Bushnell, Mrs., ed. see McCleary, Fione.

Palmer, Winthrop Bushnell, Mrs. (1899-)

--Abdul: The Story of an Egyptian Boy. Linson, Corwin Knapp, illus. LC 28-22883. ix p., 1 l., 90 p. incl. illus., plates (3 double) col. front. 21 cm. 1928. The Macmillan Company.

Palmerston, Nicholas

--At Mr. Crump's. (Roundabout Ser.). N.D. D. Appleton & Co.

Paltenghi, Madeleine (1899-)

--Honey on a Raft. Anderson, Clarence William (1891-1971), illus. LC 41-51039. 31 p. illus. 26 x 21 cm. c.1941. Garden City Publishing Co., Inc.

--Honey, the City Bear. Anderson, Clarence William (1891-1971), illus. LC 37-8153. 31, 1 p. illus. 20 cm. c.1937. Grosset & Dunlap.

--Remus Goes to Town. Anderson, Clarence William (1891-1971), illus. LC 38-18606. 1 p. l., 29 p. illus. 26 x 21 cm. c.1938. Grosset & Dunlap.

--Rumpus Rabbit. 1st Ed. ed. Anderson, Clarence William (1891-1971), illus. LC 39-24224. 1 p. l., 25, 3 p. front., illus. 29 x 22 cm. 1939. London, Harper & Brothers.

Paltrowitz, Donna, jt. auth. see Paltrowitz, Stuart.

Paltrowitz, Stuart & Paltrowitz, Donna

--More Mystery & Adventure Computer Stories. (Illus.). 128p. (Orig.). 1984. (ISBN 0-943392-42-X). Tribeca Comm.

--More Mystery and Adventure Computer Stories. LC 84-8537. p. cm. 1985. (ISBN 0-943392-42-X). Tribeca Communications.

--More Science Fiction Computer Stories. LC 84-8600. p. cm. 1985. (ISBN 0-943392-43-8). Tribeca Communications.

--The Mystery and Adventure Computer Storybook. 1st ed. LC 83-9302. (Illus.). 116 p. 26cm. 1983. (ISBN 0-943392-23-3). Tribeca Communications.

--The Science Fiction Computer Storybook. 1st ed. LC 83-9303. (Illus.). 116 p. 26cm. 1983. (ISBN 0-943392-22-5). Tribeca Communications.

Paludan, Lis

--Playing with Puppets. Crowley, Christine (Illus.). 144 p. 22cm. 1975, c.1974. (ISBN 0-263-05465-9). Plays, Inc.

Pameroy, Pete

--Wipeout. 160p. 1968. Four Winds Press.

Pan American Union

--Children of Other Americas: A Collection of Short Stories. LC 45-42399. 26p. 28 x 21cm. N.D. Pan American Union.

Pancoast, Morris H

--The Rejuvenation of Mama and Papa Goose. LC 17-11924. 85 p. incl. front., illus. (part col.) 30 cm. $1.3. c.1916. Britton Publishing Company.

Panek, Dennis

--Catastrophe Cat. Panek, Dennis, illus. LC 77-90951. (Illus.). 34 p. 29cm. c.1978. (ISBN 0-87888-130-1). Bradbury Press.

--Catastrophe Cat at the Zoo. Panek, Dennis, illus. LC 78-26369. (Illus.). 32 p. 29cm. c.1979. (ISBN 0-87888-147-6). Bradbury Press.

--Detective Whoo. Panek, Dennis, illus. LC 81-7703. (Illus.). 32 p. c.1981. (ISBN 0-87888-183-2). Bradbury Press.

--Matilda Hippo Has a Big Mouth. Panek, Dennis, illus. LC 80-13260. (Illus.). 32 p. c.1980. (ISBN 0-87888-161-1). Bradbury Press.

Panetta, George (1915-1969)

--A Kitchen Is Not a Tree. 1st ed. Servello, Joe (1932-), illus. LC 79-88127. (Illus.). 77 p. 24cm. 1970. Norton.

--Sea Beach Express. McCully, Emily Arnold (1939-), illus. LC 66-7402. (Illus.). 24cm. 64p. (gr. 3-6). 1966. (ISBN 0-06-024620-0, HarpJ). Har-Row.

--The Shoeshine Boys. Servello, Joe (1932-), illus. LC 79-130855. (Illus.). 99 p. 24cm. 1971. (ISBN 0-448-21404-0). Grosset & Dunlap.

Panetta, Perla

--The Legend of the Easter Basket. Panetta, Perla, illus. (ps-3). N.D. Dghtrs St Paul.

Panlsen, Martha, pseud., see Swindler, Leona Martha Olsen.

Pannell, L., jt. auth. see Henry, R.

Pannell, Lucile, jt. ed. see Cavanah, Frances.

Pannell, Lucile & Cavanah, Frances (1899-1982), eds.

--Holiday Round Up. Lee, Manning de Villeneuve (1894-1980), illus. LC 50-10063. 335 illus. 24. (gr. 3-8). 1950. Macrae Smith Co.

Pannullo, Aldo Joseph see Arlen, Al, pseud.

Pannullo, Aldo Joseph (1933-)

--The Story of Shivers. Arlen, Al, pseud. Parnell, Louise, ed. LC 59-11172. 26p. 18cm. 1959. Notch Pub. House.

Panova, Vera Fedorovna (1905-)

--On Faraway Street. White, Anne Terry (1896-), ed. Gabel, Rya, tr. from Rus. LC 68-12891. (Illus.). 132 p. 22cm. (Venture book). 1968. G. Braziller.

Panowski, Eileen Thompson see Thompson, Eileen.

Panshin, Alexei

--Farewell to Yesterday's Tomorrow. 1975. (ISBN 0-399-11505-6). G. P. Putnam's Sons.

Pansy, pseud., see Alden, Isabella Macdonald.

Pansy, jt. auth. see Huntington, Faye.

Pansy, pseud. (1841-1930)

--Bernie's White Chicken. Alden, Isabella Macdonald. 1874. D. Lothrop & Co.

--Bernie's White Chicken. Alden, Isabella Macdonald, 1 of 4 vols. (Illus.). (Pansy Ser.). N.D. D. Lothrop & Co.

--The Chautauqua girls Library: Containing "Randolphs", "Four Girls at Chautauqua", "Chautauqua Girls at Home", and "Echoing and Re-Echoing". Alden, Isabella Macdonald, 4 vols. N.D. Set. D. Lothrop & Co.

--Chrissy's Endeavor. Alden, Isabella Macdonald. (Mrs. Isabella Alden also Known as " Mrs. G. R. Alden"). (The Pansy Books). N.D. Lothrop Pub.

--Christmas Time. Alden, Isabella Macdonald. (Illus.). N.D. D. Lothrop & Co.

--Daisy and Grandpa. Alden, Isabella Macdonald. (Illus.). N.D. D. Lothrop & Co.

--David Ransom's Watch. Alden, Isabella MacDonald. LC 5-16123. 20cm. 354p. 1905. Lothrop Publishing Company.

--Dorris Farrand's Vocation. Alden, Isabella MacDonald. LC 4-13288. 20cm. 335p. 1904. Lothrop Publishing Company.

--The Easter Reid Library: Containing "Three People," "Ester Reid," "Julia Reid," etc. Alden, Isabella Macdonald, 5 vols. N.D. Set. D. Lothrop & Co.

--Ester Reid. Alden, Isabella Macdonald. (Illus.). N.D. D. Lothrop & Co.

--Four Mothers at Chautauqua. Alden, Isabella Macdonald. (Illus.). 20cm. 408p. 1913. Lothrop, Lee & Shepard Co.

--Grandpa's Darlings. Alden, Isabella Macdonald. (Illus.). N.D. D. Lothrop & Co.

--Helen Lester. Alden, Isabella MacDonald. 1874. D. Lothrop & Co.

--Household Puzzles. Alden, Isabella MacDonald. 20cm. 370p. 1903. D. Lothrop Publishing Company.

--Julia Ried. Alden, Isabella Macdonald. (Illus.). N.D. D. Lothrop & Co.

--Little Minnie. Alden, Isabella Macdonald. (Illus.). N.D. D. Lothrop & Co.

--Our Darlings: What They Think, Say and Do. Alden, Isabella Macdonald. (Illus.). N.D. D. Lothrop & Co.

--A Package for Rose, and Other Stories, from The Pansy. Alden, Isabella Macdonald. LC 20-16492. 95 p. incl. front., plates. 17 cm. c.1887. D. Lothrop and Company.

--Pansies: A New Book of Stories. Alden, Isabella Macdonald. (Illus.). N.D. D. Lothrop & Co.

--The Pansy Library: Containing "Three People", "Ester Reid", "Julia Reid", "King's Daughter," etc. Alden, Isabella Macdonald, 16 vols. N.D. Set. D. Lothrop & Co.

--The Pansy Ser. Containing "Jessie Wells," "Bernie's White Chicken," "Docia's Journal," etc. Alden, Isabella Macdonald, 4 vols. N.D. Set. D. Lothrop & Co.

--Pansy's New Library for Boys and Girls: Containing "Pansies", "Getting Ahead", and "Two Boys". Alden, Isabella Macdonald. N.D. Set. D. Lothrop & Co.

--Pansy's Picture Library: Containing "Daisy and Grandpa," "Little Minnie," "Robbie and the Stars," and "Pictures from Bobby's Life". Alden, Isabella Macdonald. N.D. D. Lothrop & Co.

--The Randolphs. Alden, Isabella MacDonald, 1 of 5 vols. (Illus.). (Household Library). N.D. D. Lothrop & Co.

--Robbie and the Stars. Alden, Isabella Macdonald. (Illus.). N.D. D. Lothrop & Co.

--Side by Side. Alden, Isabella Macdonald. (Pansy-Also known as Alden/Mrs. G. R.). (Illus.). N.D. D. Lothrop Co.

--The Teacher's Helper. Alden, Isabella MacDonald. 19cm. 243p. 1880. D. Lothrop & Co.

--Those Boys. Alden, Isabella Macdonald. (Illus.). N.D. D. Lothrop & Co.

Pantale, Richard

--The Pink Poodle. Schaffer, Virginia, illus. LC 68-59010. (Illus.). 25cm. 36p. (Early Childhood Bk.). (ps-2). 1968. Denison.

Pantaleoni, Hewitt (1933-), ed. see Serwadda, William Moses.

Pantell, Dora F

--Miss Pickerell and the War of the Computers. Geer, Charles Hand (1922-), illus. LC 84-7581. (Illus.). 136 p. 22cm. 1984. (ISBN 0-531-04841-1). F. Watts.

Pantell, Dora F., jt. auth. see MacGregor, Ellen.

Panter, Carol (1936-)

--Beany and His New Recorder. Gobbato, Imero (1923-), illus. LC 72-77802. (Illus.). 42 p. 26cm. 1972. Four Winds Press.

Panting, James Harwood

--Clive of Clair College. (The Albion Library). N.D. Frederick Warne & Co.

--The Hero of Garside School. (The Albion Library). N.D. Frederick Warne & Co.

--The Hero of Garside School. (Illus.). (Warne's Adventure Library). N.D. Frederick Warne & Co.

--The Two Runaways. (The Albion Library). N.D. Frederick Warne & Co.

--The Two Runaways. (Illus.). (Warner's Adventure Library). N.D. Frederick Warne & Co.

Panzer, Martin see Paul, Marcia, pseud.

Panzer, Martin (1905-)

--Mary Allen, Publicity Girl. Paul, Marcia, pseud. LC 47-2491. 4 p. l., 3-215 p. 19 1/2 cm. 1947. J. Messner, Inc.

Panzer, Pauline (1911-1972)

--Magic in Her Voice. LC 53-105127. 184p. 21cm. (Romance for young moderns). 1953. J. Messner.

Paola, Tomie de see Calhoun, Mary.

Paola, Tomie de see Dasent, George Webbe, Sir.

Paola, Tomie de see De Paola, Tomie.

Paola, Tomie de see Epstein, Samuel (1909-) & Epstein, Beryl Williams.

Paola, Tomie de see Farber, Norma.

Paola, Tomie de see Fritz, Jean Guttery.

Paola, Tomie de see Gauch, Patricia Lee.

Paola, Tomie de see Hancock, Sibyl.

Paola, Tomie de see Johnston, Susan T.

Paola, Tomie de see Kroll, Steven.

Paola, Tomie de see Moore, Clement Clarke.

Paola, Tomie de see Mooser, Stephen.

Paola, Tomie de see Rose, Anne K.

Paola, Tomie de see Schneider, Nina.

Paola, Tomie de see De Paola, Tomie.

Paola, Tomie de see Jacobs, Leland Blair.

Paola, Tomie de see Winston Press Editorial Staff.

Papa, Ethyl R.

--A Very Special Family: A Story Book to Color & Teach Your Child to Read. (Illus.). 32p. (ps-2). 1983. Innovative Pub.

Papantoniou, D.

--Greek Stories. (gr. 3-4). N.D. Divry.

Papas, Theodore

--The Story of Mr. Nero. Papas, William (1927-), illus. LC 66-10337. 1v. (unpaged) col. illus. 26cm. 1966, c.1965. (ISBN 0-698-30337-7). Coward.

--The Story of Mr. Nero. Papas, William (1927-), illus. LC 66-31250. 1 v. (unpaged) col. illus. 26 cm. 1965. Oxford University Press.

Papas, William

--No Mules. Papas, William, illus. LC 67-26121. (Illus.). 32 p. 1968, c.1967. Coward-McCann.

--Tarash the Tea Planter. Papas, William, illus. LC 77-365915. (Illus.). 29cm. 32p. 1968. Oxford Univ. Press.

--Taresh the Tea Planter. Papas, William, illus. LC 69-15245. (Illus.). 32 p. 29cm. 1st U.S. edition. 1969, c.1968. World Pub. Co.

--Tasso. LC 67-485. 1v. (unpaged) col. illus. 29cm. 1967, c.1966. Coward.

--Tasso. Papas, William, illus. LC 67-72032. 32 p. col. illus. 29 cm. (24034). 1966. Oxford U.P.

--Theodore: Or, The Mouse Who Wanted to Fly. Papas, William, illus. LC 75-99160. (Illus.). 24 p. 26cm. 1970, c.1969. World Pub. Co.

--The Zoo. Papas, William, illus. LC 75-312323. (Illus.). 32 p. 28cm. 1974. (ISBN 0-19-279701-8). Oxford University Press.

Papas, William, ed.

--Armenian Folk-Tales & Legends. Papas, William & Downing, Charles, illus. (Illus.). (Oxford Myths & Legends Ser.). (gr. 6 up). 1979. (ISBN 0-19-274117-9). Oxford U Pr.

Papashvily, George (1898-1978) & Papashvily, Helen Waite (1906-)

--Yes and No Stories: A Book of Georgian Folk Tales. Lissim, Simon (1900-1981), illus. LC 46-781580. 4 p. l., 3-227, 1 p. incl. col. front., col. illus. 19 1/2 cm. 1946. Harper & Brothers.

Papashvily, Helen Waite, jt. auth. see Papashvily, George.

Pape, Agnes M

--Fair Folk of Many Lands. N.D. Macmillan.

Pape, Donna Lugg, et al. (1930-)

--Puzzles & Silly Riddles. (gr. 4-6). 1974. (ISBN 0-590-06120-8). Scholastic Inc.

Pape, Donna Lugg (1930-)

--The Big White Thing. Morrison, Bill (1935-), illus. LC 75-6747. (Illus.). 32 p. 23cm. 1975. (ISBN 0-8116-6066-4). Garrard Pub. Co.

--A Bone for Breakfast. Morrison, Bill (1935-), illus. LC 73-22079. p. cm. (Easy venture). 1974. (ISBN 0-8116-6059-1). Garrard Pub. Co.

--Come Out, Come Out, Wherever You Are. Reiss, Susan, illus. LC 78-73528. (Illus.). (First Reader Ser.). (gr. k-3). N.D. Dandelion Pr.

--Count on Leo Lion. Eaton, Tom (1940-), illus. LC 72-9093. (Illus.). 23cm. 40p. (Venture Ser). (gr. 1). 1973. (ISBN 0-8116-6724-3). Garrard.

--Doghouse for Sale. Eaton, Tom (1940-), illus. LC 78-11685. (Illus.). 40 p. 23cm. (Imagination books). 1979. (ISBN 0-8116-4415-4). Garrard Pub. Co.

--Jack Jump Under the Candlestick. Trivas, Irene, illus. LC 82-1918. (Illus.). 32 p. 19cm. (Self-Starter Books). c.1982. (ISBN 0-8075-3753-5). A. Whitman.

--King Robert, the Resting Ruler. Frank, Lola Sharle, illus. LC 68-56823. (Illus.). 48 p. 26cm. (Wonderful world of children's books). 1968. Oddo Publishing.

--Leo Lion Looks for Books. Eaton, Tom (1940-), illus. LC 72-1078. (Illus.). 64 p. 23cm. 1972. (ISBN 0-8116-6956-4). Garrard Pub. Co.

--The Little Bird. Bloch, Carol, illus. LC 78-73535. (Illus.). (First Reader Ser.). (gr. k-3). N.D. Dandelion Pr.

--Liz Dearly's Silly Glasses. Frank, Lola Sharle, illus. LC 68-56824. (Illus.). (Oddo Sound Ser.). (gr. 2-5). 1968. (ISBN 0-87783-023-1). Oddo.

--Mary Lou, the Kangaroo. (Illus.). (gr. 1-3). 1967. (ISBN 0-8382-0507-0). Hale.

--The Mouse at the Show. 1st ed. Gibbons, Gail (1944-), illus. LC 80-26690. (Illus.). 32 p. 24cm. c.1981. (ISBN 0-525-66722-9). Elsevier/Nelson Books.

--Mr. Mogg in the Log. Korach, Mimi (1922-), illus. LC 72-1472. (Illus.). 60 p. 23cm. 1972. (ISBN 0-8116-6961-0). Garrard Pub. Co.

--Mrs. Twitter the Animal Sitter. Leder, Dora, illus. LC 72-1470. (Illus.). 62 p. 23cm. 1972. (ISBN 0-8116-6960-2). Garrard Pub. Co.

--My Fish Got Away!. Silverstein, Donald (1932-), illus. LC 68-58307. (Illus.). 32 p. 29cm. (Carousel book). 1969. L. W. Singer.

--Professor Fred & the Fid Fuddlephone. Frank, Lola sharle, illus. LC 68-56825. (Illus.). (Oddo Sound Ser.). (gr. 2-5). 1968. (ISBN 0-87783-032-0). Oddo.

--Scientist Sam. Frank, Lola Sharle, illus. LC 68-56826. (Illus.). (Oddo Sound Ser.). (gr. 2-5). 1968. (ISBN 0-87783-034-7). Oddo.

--The Seal Who Wanted to Ski. (Illus.). (gr. 2-4). 1967. (ISBN 0-8382-0731-6). Hale.

--Shoemaker Fooze. Frank, Lola Sharle, illus. LC 68-56827. (Illus.). 48 p. 26cm. (Wonderful world of children's books). 1968. Oddo Pub.

--The Sleep-Leaping Kangaroo. Eaton, Tom (1940-), illus. LC 72-7810. (Illus.). 40 p. 24cm. 1973. (ISBN 0-8116-6723-5). Garrard Pub. Co.

--The Snoino Mystery. Hutchinson, William Miller (1916-), illus. LC 79-17908. (Illus.). 40 p. 23cm. (Garrard mystery book). c.1980. (ISBN 0-8116-6410-4). Garrard Pub. Co.

--Snowman for Sale. Burns, Raymond Howard (1924-), illus. LC 76-23308. (Illus.). 39 p. 23cm. (For real book). c.1977. (ISBN 0-8116-4304-2). Garrard Pub. Co.

--Taffy Finds a Halloween Witch. Nicklaus, Carol, illus. LC 75-11590. (Illus.). 32 p. 23cm. 1975. (ISBN 0-8116-6067-2). Garrard Pub. Co.

--Three Thinkers of Thay-Lee. Frank, Lola Sharle, illus. LC 68-56828. (Illus.). (Oddo Sound Ser.). (gr. 2-5). 1968. (ISBN 0-87783-040-1). Oddo.

--A Very Special Birthday. Leavitt, Beth, illus. (Illus.). 32p. (gr. 1-3). 1975. (ISBN 0-8024-9156-1). Moody.

--Where Is My Little Joey?. Eaton, Tom (1940-), illus. LC 78-1022. (Illus.). 44 p. 23cm. (Imagination book). c.1978. (ISBN 0-8116-4411-1). Garrard Pub. Co.

Pape, Donna Lugg (1930-) & Kessler, Leonard P. (1920-)

--Play Ball, Joey Kangaroo!. Eaton, Tom (1940-), illus. LC 79-19343. (Illus.). 47 p. 23cm. (Imagination book). c.1980. (ISBN 0-8116-4420-0). Garrard Pub. Co.

Pape, Frank Cheyne (1878-) & Coffman, Ramon, eds.

--The Picture Story of Robinson Crusoe. Pape, Frank Cheyne (1878-), illus. LC 32-28983. (Original Author: Daniel DeFoe, 1661-1731). 6 p., 1 l., 7-213 p. col. front., illus. 24 1/2 cm. c.1932. The Reilly & Lee Co.

Pape, Lee

--The First Doll in the World. Weisgard, Leonard Joseph (1916-), illus. LC 61-120291. unpaged. illus. 26cm. c.1961. Lothrop, Lec & Shepard.

Paperny, Myra (1932-)

--The Wooden People. 1st ed. Stampnick, Ken, illus. LC 76-24816. (Illus.). 168 p. 21cm. c.1976. (ISBN 0-316-69040-6). Little, Brown. **Award: (CCCL).**

Pappas, Michael G.

--Sweet Dreams for Little Ones. Wenz-Victor, Else, illus. LC 81-69553. (Illus.). 64 p. 20cm. c.1982. (ISBN 0-86683-641-1). Winston Press.

Paquin, Samuel Savil

--The Garden Fairies. Chamberlin, Emily Hall, illus. LC 8-31834. (Illus.). 23cm. 179p. 1908. Moffat, Yard & Co.

Paradis, Adrian Alexis (1912-)

--Gail Borden: Resourceful Boy. Goldstein, Nathan (1927-), illus. LC 64-24809. 200p. col. illus. 20cm. (Childhood of famous Americans) Bibl.). c.1964. Bobbs.

Paradis, Marjorie Bartholomew, jt. auth. see De Leeuw, Adele Louise.

Paradis, Marjorie Bartholomew (1886-1970)

--Flash Flood at Hollow Creek. Michini, Albert, illus. LC 63-7180. 159 p. illus. 21 cm. 1963. Westminster Press.

--Jeanie. Stein, Alex, illus. LC 63-11550. 159 p. illus. 23 cm. 1963. Westminster Press.

Parker, Anne, tr. see Beckman, Gunnel.
Parker, Anne, tr. see Hallqvist, Britt G.
Parker, Anne, tr. see Linde, Gunnel.
Parker, Anne, tr. see Thorvall, Kerstin.
Parker, Arthur Caswell (1881-1955), ed. see Dam, Cornelia H, Mrs.
Parker, Arthur Caswell (1881-1955)
--Gustango Gold. Dobias, Frank (1902-) & Goldfield, Robert, illus. LC 30-21943. viii p., 1 l., 258 p. col. front. 21 cm. 1930. Doubleday, Doran & Company, Inc.
--Red Streak of the Iroquois. Heldbron, I, illus. LC 50-7769. (Illus.). 191 p. 22cm. 1950. Childrens Press.
--Rumbling Wings and Other Indian Tales. Crawford, Will, illus. LC 28-24256. 1928. Doubleday Doran & Co.
--Skunny Wundy. (Junior Library). N.D. Doubleday Doran & Co.
--Skunny Wundy: Seneca Indian Tales. Armstrong, George Douglas (1927-), illus. LC 73-115899. (Illus.). 224 p. 22cm. 1970, c.1926. (ISBN 0-8075-7405-8). A. Whitman.
Parker, B.
--The A's and the K's. Parker, Nancy Winslow (1930-), illus. (Illus.). N.D. Frederick A. Stokes Co.
--The Browns: A Book of Bears. Parker, Nancy Winslow (1930-), illus. (Illus.). 1906. Frederick A. Stokes Co.
--Frolic Farm. Parker, Nancy Winslow (1930-), illus. (Illus.). N.D. Frederick A. Stokes Co.
--Funny Bunnies. Parker, Nancy Winslow (1930-), illus. N.D. Frederick A. Stokes.
--The Lays of The Grays. Parker, Nancy Winslow (1930-), illus. (Illus.). N.D. Frederick A. Stokes.
Parker, Barbara, jt. ed. see Reynolds, Charlotte.
Parker, Barbara S
--My Street. Schreiter, Rick (1936-), illus. LC 67-5986. (Illus.). 1 v. 32p. (Carousel book). 1967. S. W. Singer Co.
Parker, Benson
--The Adventures of Little Fuzzy. Whelan, Michael & Wenzel, David, illus. (gr. k-5). 1983. (ISBN 0-448-47496-4, G&D). Putnam Pub Group.

Parker, Bertha Morris (1890-1980)
--The Wonders of the Seasons. Wilkin, Eloise Burns (1904-), illus. LC 67-3650. (Illus.). 28p. 33cm. (A Big Golden Bk.). 1967, c.1966. Golden Press.

Parker Brothers Inc.
--Bert's Quazy Questions: A Riddle Book to Make You Laugh. Maraski, Al, illus. LC 83-12113. c.1983. (ISBN 0-910313-13-X). Parker Bros.

Parker, Caroline E. R., Mrs.
--Grandmamma's Trunkful of Stories. 166p. N.D. The American News Co.
--Wilson's Kindling Depot. (Illus.). 144p. 1905. American Tract Society.
--Wilson's Kindling-Depot. A Story for Boys. LC 12-37463. 144 p. front., pl. 16 cm. c.1873. American Tract Society.

Parker, Charles E.
--The Whipper-Snapper. Hastings, Howard Livingston (1887-), illus. LC 26-10200. v p., 1 l., 245 p. col. front. 20 cm. 1926. Frederick A. Stokes Company.

Parker, Donald Dean
--Gabriel Renville, Young Sioux Warrior: The Adventures of an Indian Boy in Early Minnesota. 1st ed. LC 73-86547. (Illus.). 1973. (ISBN 0-682-47719-2). Exposition Press.

Parker, Dorothy D
--Liam's Catch. Parker, Robert Andrew (1927-), illus. LC 77-184354. (Illus.). 35 p. 1972. (ISBN 0-670-42744-6). Viking Press.

Parker, Edgar (1925-)
--The Dream of the Dormouse. Parker, Edgar (1925-), illus. LC 62-7536. (Illus.). 47 p. 26cm. 1963. Houghton Mifflin.
--Duke of Sycamore. Parker, Edgar (1925-), illus. (Illus.). (gr. 3-5). 1959. (ISBN 0-8382-0216-0). Hale.
--Duke of Sycamore. Parker, Edgar (1925-), illus. LC 57-12081. (Illus.). 26cm. 38p. (gr. k-3). 1959. (ISBN 0-395-06992-0). (ISBN 0-395-06993-9). HM.
--Enchantress. Parker, Edgar (1925-), illus. LC 60-11490. (Illus.). 25cm. 36p. (gr. 2-5). 1960. (ISBN 0-394-91123-7). Pantheon.
--Flower of the Realm. Parker, Edgar (1925-), illus. LC 65-19299. (Illus.). 59p. (gr. 3-5). 1966. (ISBN 0-395-06989-0). HM.
--Question of a Dragon. Parker, Edgar (1925-), illus. (Illus.). (gr. 2-5). 1964. (ISBN 0-394-81528-9). Pantheon.
--Rogue's Gallery. Parker, Edgar (1925-), illus. LC 70-77432. (Illus.). 62 p. 27cm. 1969. Pantheon Books.
--Stuff and Nonsense. Parker, Edgar (1925-), illus. LC 61-14775. (Illus.). 32 p. 27cm. 1961. Pantheon.

Parker, Edward
--Jack and the Beanstalk. Parker, Edward, illus. LC 78-18072. (Illus.). 32 p. 24cm. c.1979. (ISBN 0-89375-125-1). Troll Associates.
Parker, Elinor Milnor (1906-), compiled by.
--A Birthday Garland. Primrose, Jean Logan (1917-), illus. LC 49-11878. 281p. 1949. Thomas Y. Crowell.
--Echoes of the Sea: Poems. Vallario, Jean, illus. LC 76-54719. (Illus.). x, 134 p. 22cm. c.1977. (ISBN 0-684-14852-8). Scribner.
--Four Seasons, Five Senses. De Groat, Diane (1947-), illus. LC 73-14402. (Illus.). 144p. (gr. 5 up). 1974. (ISBN 0-684-13661-9). Scribner.
--Here & There: One Hundred Poems About Places. Spier, Peter Edward (1927-), illus. (gr. 4 up). 1967. (ISBN 0-690-37875-0). T Y Crowell.
--I Was Just Thinking, A Book of Essays. Leighton, Clare Veronica Hope (1899-), illus. 192p. 1959. Thomas Y. Crowell Co.
--One Hundred More Story Poems. Spier, Peter Edward (1927-), illus. LC 60-11543. (Illus.). 374 p. 21cm. 1960. Crowell.
--One Hundred Poems About People. David, Ismar, illus. (Illus.). 234p. (gr. 7 up). 1955. (ISBN 0-690-59744-4). T Y Crowell.
--One Hundred Story Poems. Pitz, Henry Clarence (1895-1976), illus. LC 51-6759. (Illus.). 499 p. 21cm. 1951. Crowell.
--Singing & the Gold: Poems Translated from World Literature. Leighton, Clare Veronica Hope (1899-), illus. (Illus.). (gr. 7 up). 1962. (ISBN 0-690-73802-1). T Y Crowell.
Parker, Everett & Oledoska
--The Secret of No Face: An Ireokwa Epic. (gr. 7 up). N.D. Naturegraph.
Parker, Faye
--The Mystery Rocket. (Children's Theatre Playscript Ser.). 1961. (ISBN 0-88020-042-1). Coach Hse.
--Tom Edison & the Wonderful "Why". (Children's Theatre Playscript Ser.). 1961. (ISBN 0-88020-061-8). Coach Hse.
--Young Ben: Franklin's Fight for Freedom. (Children's Theatre Playscript Ser.). 1958. (ISBN 0-88020-065-0). Coach Hse.
--Young Stephen Foster. (Children's Theatre Playscript Ser.). 1968. (ISBN 0-88020-067-7). Coach Hse.
Parker, Faye & McKenna, Tom
--Maggie's Magic Teapot. (Children's Theatre Musical Playscript Ser.). 1963. (ISBN 0-88020-038-3). (ISBN 0-88020-031-6). Coach Hse.
Parker, Frances
--Marjie of the Lower Ranch. LC 4-525245. 4 p. l., 393 p. col. front., 7 col. pl. 20 cm. 1903. C. M. Clark Publishing Co.
Parker, Gilbert
--The Seats of the Mighty. Otto, William N, ed. (Appleton Modern Literature Ser.). N.D. Appleton-Century-Crofts.
Parker, Gordon W.
--The Deer Lodge Series, 3 Vols. (Illus.). 1905. Lee and Shepard Company.
Parker, Helen F., Mrs.
--Blind Florette. 318p. N.D. Congregational Sunday-School and Publilshing Society.
--Frank's Search after Sea-Shells. 349p. N.D. Hurd & Houghton for American Tract Society.
Parker, Hershel, jt. ed. see Harrison, Hayford.
Parker, Hershel, ed. see Melville, Herman.
Parker, Irene Ruth (1920-)
--Sam Gaw. Granstaff, William (1925-), illus. LC 66-27467. 189 p. illus. 24 cm. 1966. Southern Pub. Association.
Parker, Jenny Marsh see Parker, Permelia Jane Marsh, Mrs.
Parker, K. Langloh
--Australian Legendary Tales. Drake-Brochman, H., ed. Durack, Elizabeth (1916-), illus. (Illus.). (gr. 7 up). 1966. (ISBN 0-670-14193-3). (ISBN 0-670-14194-1). Viking Pr.

Parker, Lockie, ed. see Story Parade Magazine.
Parker, Lois Mary (1912-)
--Brothers of the Longhouse. Davis, Thomas A, ed. Crews, Terry (1950-), illus. LC 79-13190. (Illus.). 124 p. 21cm. 1979. Review and Herald Pub. Association.
--Duncan, Son of Malcolm. LC 77-12724. p. cm. 96p. 1977. (ISBN 0-8127-0156-9). Southern Publishing Association.
--A New Friend for Kelly. LC 66-19422. (Illus.). 32 p. 23cm. 1966. Review and Herald Pub. Association.
--Once Upon a Summer. Padgett, Jim, illus. LC 77-110396. (Illus.). 93 p. 22cm. 1970. Southern Pub. Association.
--Princess of the Two Lands. Myers, Bill (1940-), illus. LC 74-26245. (Illus.). 125 p. 21cm. (Crown book). 1975. (ISBN 0-8127-0088-0). Southern Pub. Association.
--Quack-quack and Duck-duck. Baerg, Harry John (1909-), illus. LC 61-11975. (Illus.). 25p. 23cm. 1961. Review and Herald Pub. Association.
--Thee, Patience. LC 74-78021. (Illus.). 124 p. 21cm. (Penguin series). 1974. Review and Herald Pub. Association.
--They of Rome: A Story of Early Christianity. LC 81-110496. 128 p. 21cm. (Crown book). c.1980. (ISBN 0-8127-0308-1). Southern Pub. Association.
--The Yellow Cat of Cottonwood Creek. Baerg, Harry John (1909-), illus. LC 59-16700. 124p. illus. 26cm. N.D. Review and Herald Pub. Association.
Parker, M.
--For the Sake of a Friend. (Illus.). (Scribner-Blackie Series of books for Young People). N.D. Charles Scribner's Sons.
Parker, Mark (1954-)
--Horses, Airplanes, and Frogs. Childrens, Press (1922-) LC 76-54805. (Illus.). 30 p. 25cm. 1977. (ISBN 0-913778-71-0). Child's World.
Parker, Mary Moncure Paynter, Mrs.
--The Birds and the Bird Man. LC 19-6344. 24p. 18cm. 1919. Laura W. Greene.
--Happy Plays for Happy Days: Twelve New One-Act Plays. 154 p. 19 cm. 1934. Play Fair Publishing Company.
Parker, Mrs.
--Grandmamma's Recollections. (Illus.). 261p. N.D. Merrill.
Parker, Nancy Winslow (1930-)
--The Christmas Camel. Parker, Nancy Winslow (1930-), illus. LC 83-9045. (Illus.). 32 p. (Uncle Clyde Ser.: Bk. 3). c.1983. (ISBN 0-396-08220-3). Dodd, Mead.
--Cooper, the McNallys' Big Black Dog. Parker, Nancy Winslow (1930-), illus. LC 80-21905. (Illus.). 32 p. c.1981. (ISBN 0-396-07914-8). Dodd, Mead.
--The Crocodile Under Louis Finneberg's Bed. Parker, Nancy Winslow (1930-), illus. LC 77-16875. (Illus.). 44 p. c.1978. (ISBN 0-396-07542-8). Dodd, Mead.
--Love from Aunt Betty. Parker, Nancy Winslow (1930-), illus. LC 82-45988. p. cm. 1983. (ISBN 0-396-08135-5). Dodd, Mead.
--Love from Uncle Clyde. Parker, Nancy Winslow (1930-), illus. LC 76-54957. (Illus.). 32. c.1977. (ISBN 0-396-07426-X). Dodd, Mead.
--The Man with the Take-Apart Head. Parker, Nancy Winslow (1930-), illus. LC 74-2595. (Illus.). 46 p. 1974. Dodd, Mead.
--Mrs. Wilson Wanders off. Parker, Nancy Winslow (1930-), illus. LC 76-6112. (Illus.). 44 p. 24cm. c.1976. (ISBN 0-396-07333-6). Dodd, Mead.
--Mystery Aboard the Murrabit. Parker, Nancy Winslow (1930-), illus. 132p. 1964. Tri-Ocean Books.
--The Ordeal of Byron B. Blackbear. Parker, Nancy Winslow (1930-), illus. LC 78-12140. (Illus.). 70 p. 24cm. 197p. c.1979. (ISBN 0-396-07642-4). Dodd, Mead.
--The Party at the Old Farm: A Halloween Story. 1st ed. Parker, Nancy Winslow (1930-), illus. LC 75-6754. (Illus.). 35 p. 23cm. 1975. (ISBN 0-689-50034-3). Atheneum.
--Poofy Loves Company. Parker, Nancy Winslow (1930-), illus. LC 79-20095. (Illus.). 32 p. 1980. Dodd, Mead. **Award: (ALA).**
--Puddums, the Cathcarts' Orange Cat. 1st ed. Parker, Nancy Winslow (1930-), illus. LC 79-23088. (Illus.). 32 p. 25cm. 1980. (ISBN 0-689-50159-5). Atheneum.
--The Spotted Dog: The Strange Tale of a Witch's Revenge. 1st ed. Parker, Nancy Winslow (1930-), illus. LC 80-13363. (Illus.). 46 p. 22cm. c.1980. (ISBN 0-396-07845-1). Dodd, Mead.
Parker, Permelia Jane Marsh, Mrs. (1836-1913)
--The Boy Missionary. LC 7-34979. 162 p. front., pl. 16 cm. 1858. General Protestant Episcopal S. School Union, and Church Book Society.
--Dick Wortley: Or, Choosing a Profession. LC 7-34978. 149 p. front., plates. 16 cm. 1863. Gen. Prot. Episcopal Sunday School Union, and Church Book Society.
--Frank Earnest: Or, Going into the Master's Vineyard ... LC 7-39647. 64 p. 15 cm. (On cover: The little church library). 1858. Stanford & Delisser.
--Losing the Way. 2d ed. LC 7-34976. 232 p. front., plates. 15 cm. 1859. General Protestant Episcopal Sunday School Union, and Church Book Society.
--Taking Sides: A Story for School Boys. LC 7-34977. 32 p. 16 cm. 1876. E. P. Dutton & Company.
Parker, Richard (1915-)
--Almost Lost. Shortall, Leonard W., illus. LC 62-10580. 107p. illus. 23cm. 1962. T. Nelson.
--The Boy Who Wasn't Lonely. Spanfeller, James John (1930-), illus. LC 64-25317. x, 141p. illus. 22cm. c.1965. Bobbs.
--Four Desperate Days. Repr. of 1975 ed (Pub. by Thomas Nelson). (gr. 4-6). 1976. (ISBN 0-590-01499-4, Schol Trade Pap). Schol Bk Serv.
--Gilda. Orig. Title: The House That Gilda Drew. (gr. 4-6). 1972 (Starline). Schol Bk Serv.
--He Is Your Brother. LC 76-6116. 98 p. 21cm. c.1974. (ISBN 0-8407-6495-2). T. Nelson.
--The Hendon Fungus. LC 68-26333. 185 p. 21cm. 1968, c.1967. Meredith Press.
--He's Your Brother. new ed. (gr. 4-6). 1977. (ISBN 0-590-10401-2). Scholastic Inc.
--The House that Guilda Drew. Funai, Mamoru R. (1932-), illus. LC 64-17115. 117 p. illus. 22 cm. 1964. Bobbs-Merrill.
--The Impossible Pet. Sibley, Don (1922-), illus. (Illus.). Orig. Title: No House for a Mouse. (gr. 4-6). 1972. (ISBN 0-590-08739-8, Schol Trade Pap). Schol Bk Serv.
--Lion at Large. Werth, Kurt (1896-), illus. LC 61-6808. 126p. illus. 22cm. 1961. T. Nelson.
--M for Mischief. Geer, Charles Hand (1922-), illus. LC 66-12605. 90 p. illus. 21 cm. 1st U.S. edition. 1966. Duell, Sloan and Pearce.
--The Midnight Beast (Pub. by Thomas Nelson & Son). Orig. Title: Lion at Large. (gr. 4-6). 1972 (Starline). Schol Bk Serv.
--New in the Neighborhood. LC 66-8497. v, 185p. 22cm. 1st U.S. edition. 1966. Duell.
--No House for a Mouse. Mars, Witold Tadeusz J. (1912-), illus. LC 68-13808. (Illus.). 96 p. 22cm. 1st U.S. edition. 1968. Follett Pub. Co.
--The Old Powder Line. LC 72-152876. 143 p. 21cm. 1971. (ISBN 0-8407-6170-8). T. Nelson.
--Paul and Etta. Rowe, Gavin, illus. LC 72-13011. (Illus.). 128 p. 22cm. 1973. (ISBN 0-8407-6282-8). T. Nelson.
--Perversity of Pipers. Kennedy, Richard (1910-), illus. LC 64-7489. 159 p. illus. 21 cm. 1964. Van Nostrand.
--Private Beach. Ambrus, Victor G., pseud. (1935-), illus. Ambrus, Gyozo Laszlo. LC 65-23020. 184p. illus. 21cm. 1st U.S. edition. 1965, c.1964. Duell Dist. Meredith.
--Private Beach. Ambrus, Victor G., pseud. (1935-), illus. Ambrus, Gyozo Laszlo. (Illus.). (gr. 5-8). 1965. (ISBN 0-696-75832-6). Hawthorn.
--Quarter Boy. LC 77-355740. 4, 82 p. 21cm. 1976. (ISBN 0-434-95810-7). Heinemann.
--Quarter Boy. LC 76-22665. 92 p. 21cm. c.1976. (ISBN 0-8407-6522-3). T. Nelson.
--The Runaway. LC 77-24291. p. cm. c.1977. (ISBN 0-8407-6568-1). T. Nelson.
--Second-Hand Family. Floyd, Gareth (1940-), illus. LC 66-25287. (Illus.). 114 p. 22cm. 1966, c.1965. Bobbs-Merrill.
--A Sheltering Tree. LC 76-93841. (Illus.). 223 p. 21cm. 1969. Meredith Press.
--Spell Seven. Ridley, Trevor, illus. LC 76-140082. (Illus.). 127 p. 22cm. 1st U.S. edition. 1971. (ISBN 0-8407-6116-3). T. Nelson.
--The Sword of Ganelon. Ferguson, William, illus. LC 58-846626. 213p. illus. 21cm. c.1958. D. McKay Co.
--Three by Mistake. LC 74-13214. 128 p. 21cm. 1974. (ISBN 0-8407-6417-0). T. Nelson.
--The Three Pebbles. Ferguson, William, illus. LC 56-795958. 218p. illus. 21cm. 1956. D. McKay Co.
--A Time to Choose: A Story of Suspense. LC 73-18708. 151 p. 22cm. (gr. 7up). 1974. (ISBN 0-06-024678-2). Harper & Row.
--Valley Full of Pipers. Kennedy, Richard (1910-), illus. LC 63-19020. (Illus.). 22cm. 156p. (gr. 2-6). 1962. (ISBN 0-672-50556-8). Bobbs.
--Voyage to Tasmania. Seward, Prudence, illus. LC 63-11660. (Illus.). 22cm. 127p. (gr. 2-6). N.D. (ISBN 0-672-50560-6). Bobbs.
Parker, Robert Andrew (1927-), ed. see Shelley, Mary Wollstonecraft Godwin.
Parker, Robert Andrew (1927-)
--Mortal Stakes. LC 75-20273. 192p. 1975. (ISBN 0-395-21969-8). HM.
--Sweet Betsy from Pike: A Song from the Gold Rush Days. 1st ed. Parker, Robert Andrew (1927-), illus. LC 77-13924. (Illus.). 32 p. 1978. (ISBN 0-670-68632-8). Viking Press.
Parker, Robert Ross
--Myrtle the Turtle. Evans, Alice Lois, illus. N.D. E. P. Dutton & Co.
--The Strange Adventures of Myrtle the Turtle. 1st ed. Evans, Alice Lois, illus. LC 37-21371. (Illus.). 44p. 22cm. 1937. E. P. Dutton & Co.
Parker, Rosa Abbott, Mrs.
--Alexis the Runaway. N.D. Colby and Rich.
--Alexis the Runaway: Or, Afloat in the World. LC 12-374641. 4 p. l., 7-216 p. front., 2 pl. 17 cm. (Added t.-p.: Rosa Abbott stories. v. 2). 1868. Lee and Shepard.
--Jack of All Trades. N.D. Colby and Rich.
--Jack of All Trades. LC 12-37465. 4 p. l., 7-229 p. front., 2 pl. 17 cm. (Added t-p.: Rosa Abbott storie v. 1). 1868. Lee and Shepard.
--The Pinks and Blues. N.D. Colby and Rich.
--The Pinks and Blues: Or, The Orphan Asylum. LC 12-374690. 214 p. front., plates. 18 cm. (Added t-p.: Rosa Abbott stories. v. 6). 1871. Lee and Shepard.
--Tommy Hickup. N.D. Colby and Rich.
--Tommy Hickup: Or, A Pair of Black Eyes. LC 12-37466. 4 p. l., 7-254 p. front., 2 pl. 17 cm. (Added t-.p.: Rosa Abbott stories v. 3). 1868. Lee and Shepard.
--Upside Down. N.D. Colby and Rich.

AUTHOR INDEX PARRY, MICHEL

--Upside Down: Or, Will and Work. LC 12-374671. 4 p. l., 7-252 p. front., 2 pl. 17 cm. (Added t.-p.: Rosa Abbott stories. v. 4). 1868. Lee and Shepard.
--The Young Detective. N.D. Colby and Rich.
--The Young Detective: or, Which Won?. LC 12-37468. 4 p. l., 7-256 p. front., plates. 18 cm. (Added t.-p.: Rosa Abbott stories. v. 5). 1870. Lee and Shepard.
Parker, Rosina Ruth see Park, Rosina Ruth Lucia.
Parker, Sale, Mrs.
--Uncle John's Adventures in Prairie-Land. 311p. 1884. Routledge & Sons.
Parker, Sue Amsden
--Little Black Kitten. LC 40-13276. 19 p. illus. 20 cm. c.1940. Weaver Publishing Co.
Parker, Thomas Drayton (1871-)
--The Air Raider: Or, Winning the Gold and Silver Chevron. Merrill, Frank Thayer (1848-), illus. LC 21-4508. 291 p. front. 20 cm. c.1920. W. A. Wilde Company.
--The Cruise of the Deep Sea Scouts: Boy Scouts Afloat. Copeland, Charles, illus. LC 18-138635. 287 p. col. front. 20 cm. c.1917. W. A. Wilde Company.
--Sailing Under Sealed Orders: A Story of the Navigator of the "Greenville". Merrill, Frank Thayer (1848-), illus. LC 22-6524. 3 p. l., 5-286 p. front. 20 cm. c.1921. W. A. Wilde Company.
--The Spy on the Submarine: Or, Over and Under the Sea. LC 19-6659. 298 p. front. 20 cm. c.1918. W. A. Wilde Company.
Parker, W. Karl, ed. see Ramos, Francie.
Parker, Warren W.
--Elfie Jingle: Santa's Right Hand Man. (Illus.). 64p. 1980. (ISBN 0-682-49628-6). Exposition.
Parker, Wendy
--The Christmas Doll. Parker, Wendy, illus. LC 79-4067. p. cm. 1979. (ISBN 0-03-047111-7). Holt, Rinehart and Winston.
Parker, William Gordon (1875-)
--Grant Burton the Runaway: or, The Mishaps of a Schoolboy. 1899. Lothrop, Lee & Shepard.
--Rival Boy Sportsmen: Or, The Mink Lake Regatta. Parker, William Gordon (1875-), illus. (Illus.). ix, 363p. (Deer Lodge Ser.). 1900. Lee & Shepard.
--Six Young Hunters: Or, The Adventures of the Greyhound Club. Parker, William Gordon (1875-), illus. vi, 335 p. front., illus., plates. 19 cm. 1898. Lee and Shepard.
--Two Boys in the Blue Ridge. Parker, William Gordon (1975-), illus. LC 1-13994. (Illus.). 289p. (The Boys Own Authors Ser.). 1901. Dana Estes & Co.
Parker, Willie L., ed. see Aesopus.
Parker, Willis A.
--Our Friendly Neighbors. 1st ed. Hoffman, George Daniel, illus. LC 46-1032. (Illus.). 31p. 24cm. 1945. The Stephens Press.
Parker & Lambert
--Black Hills Ghost Towns. N.D. The Swallow Press.
Parker Chiropractic Research Foundation see Ramos, Francie.
Parkes, Anna L, Mrs.
--The Unconscious Influence. LC 24-19024. 4 p. l., 224 p. 19 cm. 1924. The Stratford Company.
Parkes, Haddon
--Nowell. N.D. E. & J. B. Young & Co.
Parkhurst, Lucia A.
--Good-Night Stories. N.D. Abingdon Press.
--Good-Night Stories. (Illus.). N.D. Methodist Book Concern.
--Sona Mona Singh. N.D. Abingdon Press.
Parkhurst, Ted, ed.
--Fruitbowl of Rhinos: Little Poems by Little People. Strauss, Stan & Purvis, Susan, photos by LC 80-65461. (Illus.). 56p. (gr. 1-6). 1980. (ISBN 0-935304-13-4). (ISBN 0-935304-12-6). August Hse.
Parkin, Rex
--The Red Carpet. Parkin, Rex, illus. LC 48-6703. 27cm. 48p. 1948. Macmillan.
--The Red Carpet. Parkin, Rex, illus. (Illus.). (gr. k-3). 1967. (ISBN 0-02-770020-8). Macmillan.
--The Red Carpet. Parkin, Rex, illus. LC 48-6703. (ps-1). 1972 (Collier). Macmillan.
--The Shadow Train. Parkin, Rex, illus. LC 62-8912. unpaged (chiefly illus.) 23 x 26cm. 1962. Macmillan.
Parkinson, Cyril Northcote (1909-)
--Ponies' Plot. Morgan, Violet (1898-), illus. LC 65-193008. 184p. illus. 22cm. c.1965. (ISBN 0-395-06994-7). Houghton.
Parkinson, Ethel
--Dutchie Doings. Parkinson, Ethel, illus. N.D. Dodge Publishing Co.
--Sambo and Susanna. Parkinson, Ethel, illus. Byron, May N.D. Dodge Publishing Co.
Parkinson, Ethelyn Minerva (1906-)
--Double Trouble for Rupert. (gr. 4-6). 1972. (ISBN 0-590-08720-7, Schol Pap). Schol Bk Serv.
--Elf King Joe. Brown, Cornelia, illus. LC 68-15401. (Illus.). 40 p. 27cm. 1968. Abingdon Press.
--Good Old Archibald. N.D. E . M. Hale and Co.
--Good Old Archibald. Stevens, Mary E. (1920-1966), illus. LC 60-6816. (Illus.). 22cm. 100p. (gr. 4-6). 1960. (ISBN 0-687-15567-3). Abingdon.
--Higgins of the Railroad Museum. McPheeters, William N., illus. LC 75-95196. (Illus.). 176 p. 24cm. 1970. Abingdon Press.
--Merry Mad Bachelors. Kredel, Fritz (1900-1973), illus. LC 62-11151. (Illus.). 21cm. 176p. (gr. 3-7). 1962. (ISBN 0-687-24881-7). Abingdon.
--Never Go Anywhere with Digby. Vosburgh, Leonard W. (1912-), illus. LC 70-135042. (Illus.). 160 p. 24cm. 1971. (ISBN 0-687-27714-0). Abingdon Press.
--The Operation That Happened to Rupert Piper. Kamen, Gloria (1923-), illus. LC 66-10139. 176p. illus. 22cm. (gr. 3-7). c.1966. (ISBN 0-687-29315-4). Abingdon.
--Rupert Piper and Megan, the Valuable Girl. Kamen, Gloria (1923-), illus. LC 71-186230. (Illus.). 160 p. 24cm. 1972. (ISBN 0-687-36657-7). Abingdon Press.
--Rupert Piper & the Boy Who Could Knit. Padgett, Jim, illus. LC 78-24001. (Illus.). 159 p. 23cm. c.1979. Abingdon.
--Rupert Piper and the Dear, Dear Birds. Kamen, Gloria (1923-), illus. LC 76-11645. 23cm. 175p. 1976. (ISBN 0-687-36655-0). Abingdon.
--The Terrible Troubles of Rupert Piper. Stevens, Mary, illus. LC 63-10809. 111 p. illus. 22 cm. 1963. Abington Press.
--Today I Am a Ham. N.D. (ISBN 0-671-29567-5). Simon & Schuster (Archway).
--Today I Am a Ham. McDonald, Ralph J., illus. LC 68-10705. (Illus.). 192 p. 22cm. 1968. Abingdon Press.
--Triple Trouble for Rupert. (Orig.). (gr. 4-6). N.D. (ISBN 0-590-08109-8, Schol Trade Pap). Schol Bk Serv.
Parkinson, Kathy
--The Enormous Turnip. LC 85-14432. p. cm. 1986. (ISBN 0-8075-2062-4). A. Whitman.
Parkinson, Virginia
--Cleanliness, Starring Johnny Toothbrush. Sass-Dorne Studio & Wales, Marjorie, illus. Fahs, Philip, photos by. LC 44-24889. (Illus.). 30p. 28cm. (Pointers for Little Persons). 1943. J. L. Schilling Co.
--Manners. (Illus.). (Pointers for Little Persons Ser). (gr. k-3). 1961. (ISBN 0-8178-5042-2). Harvey.
--Manners: Starring Mr. Do and Mr. Don't. Phillips, Isabel & Fahs, Philip, illus. LC 93-16083. 28 p. col. illus. 28 cm. (Pointers for little persons. Book 1). 1943. J. L. Schilling Co.
--Obedience. (Pointers for Little Persons Ser). (gr. k-3). 1961. (ISBN 0-8178-5052-X). Harvey.
--Safety. (Illus.). (Pointers for Little Persons Ser). (gr. k-3). 1961. (ISBN 0-8178-5062-7). Harvey.
--Safety: Starring Roy Raccoon and Rob Rabbit. Wales, Marjorie & Fahs, Philip, illus. LC 44-24888. 29 p. col. illus. 28 cm. (Pointers for little persons. Book 2). c.1943. J. L. Schilling Co.
Parkman, Alice
--Slices of Mother Goose. Champ, pseud. (1843-1903), illus. Champney, James Wells. LC 17-856. 16 l. illus. 27 cm. c.1877. Lockwood, Brooks & Co.
Parks, Aileen Wells (1901-)
--Bedford Forrest: Boy on Horseback. 1st ed. Laune, Paul Sidney (1899-), illus. LC 52-5818. 192 p. illus. 20 cm. (Childhood of Famous Americans Ser.). 1952. Bobbs-Merrill.
--Bedford Forrest: Horseback Boy. Morrow, Gray, illus. LC 62-16611. 200p. col. illus. 20cm. (The Childhood of Famous Americans Ser.). 1963. Bobbs.
--Davy Crockett, Young Rifleman. 1st ed. John, Charles V., illus. LC 49-8115. 194 p. illus. 20 cm. (The Childhood of Famous Americans Ser.). 1949. Bobbs-Merrill Co.
--Davy Crockett, Young Rifleman. Pearson, Justin, illus. LC 62-9248. 200p. col. illus. 20cm. (The Childhood of Famous Americans Ser.). 1962. Bobbs.
--James Oglethorpe, Young Defender. Lees, Harry Hanson, illus. LC 57-9340. 20 cm. 191p. (The Childhood of Famous American Ser.). 1958. Bobbs-Merrill.
--James Oglethorpe, Young Defender. Rawson, Maurice, illus. LC 60-7711. 20 cm. 192p. (Childhood of Famous American Ser.). 1960. Bobbs-Merrill.
Parks, Carrie Belle, ed. see Wescott, Edward N.
Parks, Edd Winfield (1906-1968)
--Little Long Rifle. 1st ed. Meyers, Robert William (1919-), illus. LC 49-7862. 139 p. illus. 22 cm. 1949. Bobbs-Merrill Co.
--Pioneer Pilot: A Boys' Story of the First Steamboat Voyage from Pittsburgh to New Orleans. LC 47-30932. 298 p. illus. 21 cm. 1947. Bobbs-Merrill Co.
--Safe on Second: The Story of a Little Leaguer. 1st ed. Wenzel, Al, illus. LC 52-14025. 199p. illus. 22cm. 1953. Bobbs-Merrill.
--Teddy Roosevelt: All Around Boy. Morrow, Gray, illus. LC 60-77193. 200p. illus. 20cm. (Childhood of Famous American Ser.). 1961. Bobbs-Merrill.
--Teddy Roosevelt, All-Round Boy. 1st ed. James, Sandra, illus. LC 53-9869. 192p. illus. 20cm. (Childhood of famous Americans Ser.). 1953. Bobbs-Merrill.
Parks, Mahalinda
--Little Castles in the Air. 1st ed. LC 63-15450. (Illus.). 24 x 31cm. 1963. Eastern Shore News.
Parks, Michael
--The Prince of the Golden Apple. 112p. 1975. (ISBN 0-571-10702-8). Faber & Faber.
Parks, Patricia
--Treasure. N.D. Carlton.

Parley, Peter, pseud., see Goodrich, Samuel Griswold.

Parley, Peter, pseud. (1793-1860)
--Bible Stories. Goodrich, Samuel Griswold. New & Revised. (Parley's Juvenile Ser.). N.D. Charles Desilver & Sons.
--The Every Day Book for Youth. Goodrich, Samuel Griswold. LC 14-22483. (Illus.). 16cm. 415p. 1831. Carter, Hendee & Co.
--Fagots for The Fireside: Or, Fact and Fancy. Goodrich, Samuel Griswold. N.D. D. Appleton & Co.
--Juvenile Tales. Goodrich, Samuel Griswold. New & Revised. (Parley's Juvenile Ser.). N.D. Charles Desilver & Sons.
--Merry Stories: Fact, Fancy, and Fiction. Goodrich, Samuel Griswold. N.D. James Miller.
--One Thousand and One Lives. Goodrich, Samual Griswold. N.D. D. Lothrop Co.
--Parley's Merry Stories. Goodrich, Samuel Grisowld. (Parley's Fireside Library). N.D. James Miller.
--Parley's New York. Goodrich, Samuel Griswold. (Aunt Mary's Story Bks.). 1873. Leavitt & Allen Bros.
--Parley's Thousand and One Stories. Goodrich, Samuel Grisowld. (Parley's Fireside Library). N.D. James Miller.
--The Tales of Peter Parley About America. Goodrich, Samuel Griswold. 192p. Repr. of 1827 ed. (Pub. by Carter, Hendee & Co.). 1974. Dover.
--The Tales of Peter Parley About America. Goodrich, Samuel Griswold. enl. ed. Mussey, Barrows, intro. by. (Illus.). (gr. 1 up). 1975. Dover.
--Tales of the Sea. Goodrich, Samuel Griswold. New & Revised. (Parley's Juvenile Ser.). N.D. Charles Desilver & Sons.
--Thousand and One Stories of Fact and Fancy, Wit and Humor, Rhyme, Reason, and Romance. Goodrich, Samuel Griswold. N.D. James Miller.
--Wanderers By Sea and Land. Goodrich, Samuel Griswold. N.D. D. Appleton & co.
--Winter Evening Tales. Goodrich, Samuel Griswold. New & Revised. (Parley's Juvenile Ser.). N.D. Charles Desilver & Sons.
Parlin, John, pseud., see Graves, Charles Parlin.
Parlin, John, pseud. (1911-1972)
--Skeleton Creek. Graves, Charles Parlin. Russell, James, illus. LC 63-16220. 159 p. illus. 21 cm. 1963. Abelard-Schuman.
Parma, Clemens, pseud., see Menzel, Roderich.
Parma, Clemens, pseud. (1907-)
--Wandering Shoe. Menzel, Roderich. Sengler, Johanna (1924-), illus. Jopp, Regina, tr. from Ger. LC 66-14897. (Illus.). (Foreign Lands Bks). (gr. k-5). 1966. (ISBN 0-8225-0358-1). Lerner Pubns.
Parmalee, Ted, adapted by see Disney, Walt, Productions.
Parmenter, Christine Whiting, Mrs. (1877-)
--David's Star of Bethlehem. Anderson, Victor C., illus. 32p. N.D. Thomas Y Crowell Co.
--I Was Christabel. LC 38-33008. 207 p. 21 cm. c.1938. J. Messner, Inc.
--Jean's Winter with the Warners. Federer, Charles A., illus. LC 24-24138. 230 p. illus., col. pl. 20 cm. c.1924. Rand, McNally & Company.
--The Real Reward. Price, Harriet Longstreet (1891-), illus. LC 27-20081. 6 p. l., 3-259 p. incl. plates. col. front. 21 cm. 1927. Little, Brown, and Company.
--The Treasure at Shady Vale. LC 25-879127. viii p. 1 l., 281 p. col. front. 20 cm. 1925. Doubleday, Page & Company.
--The Unknown Port. LC 27-20465. 276, 1 p. 19 cm. c.1927. Thomas Y. Crowell Company.
Parnall, Peter (1936-)
--Alfalfa Hill. 1st ed. Parnall, Peter (1936-), illus. LC 74-186. (Illus.). 32 p. 20 x 24 cm. 1975. (ISBN 0-385-02448-7). (ISBN 0-385-02200-X). Doubleday.
--The Great Fish. 1st ed. Parnall, Peter (1936-), illus. LC 73-183908. (Illus.). 48 p. 20 x 24 cm. 1973. (ISBN 0-385-04589-1). (ISBN 0-385-04589-1). Doubleday.
--The Mountain. 1st ed. Parnall, Peter (1936-), illus. LC 72-145751. (Illus.). 32 p. 1971. Doubleday.
Parnell, Louise, ed. see Pannullo, Aldo Joseph.
Parnell, Thomas (1679-1718)
--The Hermit. (Clarendon Press Ser.). N.D. MacMillian.
--The Hermit. LC 78-315551. (Illus.). 48 p. 14cm. 1813. S. Woods.
Parr, Adolph Henry (1900-)
--Because of a Promise. LC 61-18404. 199p. 21cm. c.1961. Franciscan Herald Press.
Parr, Harriet see Lee, Holme, pseud.
Parr, Letitia Evelyn (1906-)
--Green is for Growing. (Illus.). 32p. 1968. Tri-Ocean Books.
--When Sun and Sky Are Blue. Watts, John Francis (1926-), illus. LC 78-151272. (Illus.). 32 p. 25cm. 1971, c.1970. (ISBN 0-207-95351-1). Scroll Press.
Parr, Lucy (1924-)
--Family Christmas Stories. LC 73-86052. 74 p. 23cm. 1973. Bookcraft.
--Pioneer and Indian Stories. LC 70-79421. (Illus.). vii, 136 p. 24cm. 1969. Bookcraft.
Parrish, Anne (1888-1957)
--Clouded Star. 1948. (ISBN 0-06-013285-X, HarpT). Har-Row.
--The Dream Coach ... Parrish, Dillwyn, illus. LC 24-22958. 5 p. l., 3-143 p. incl. illus., plates, double pl. 22 cm. 1924. The Macmillan Company. **Award: (JNM).**
--Floating Island. Doll, Mr. & Parrish, Anne (1888-1957), illus. LC 30-28183. vii p., 1 l., 265 p. front., illus., plates (1 double col.) 24 cm. c.1930. Harper & Brothers. **Award: (JNM).**
--The Story of Appleby Capple. Parrish, Anne (1888-1957), illus. LC 50-10673. (Illus.). 184 p. 31cm. 1950. Harper. **Award: (JNM).**
Parrish, Anne (1888-1957) & Parrish, Dillwyn
--Knee-High to a Grasshopper. Parrish, Anne (1888-1957) & Parrish, Dillwyn, illus. LC 23-126098. 5 p. l., 209 p. incl. illus., plates. 21 cm. 1923. The Macmillan Company.
Parrish, Dillwyn, jt. auth. see Parrish, Anne.
Parrish, Jean J., pseud., see Church, Elsie.
Parrish, Mable Corinne
--Dot & Peppy on a Florida Farm. (gr. 2-4). 1970. Vantage.
--Dot and Peppy, Playmates and Friends. Norwood, Jean, illus. LC 60-10101. unpaged. illus. 24cm. 1960. Pacific Press Pub. Association.
Parrott, Alonzo Leslie (1922-)
--Toby and His Beach House. LC 56-23071. unpaged. illus. 21cm. (Zondervan stori-picture book). 1955. Zondervan Pub. House.
Parrott, Cecil, tr. see Hasek, Jaroslav.
Parrott, Irene Juanita, jt. auth. see Carr, Deirdre.
Parrott, Leslie see Parrott, Alonzo Leslie.
Parrott, Mary A.
--Aunt Milly's Childhood. (Illus.). 200p. N.D. A. I. Bradley & Co.'s Pub.
--Aunt Milly's Childhood, 1 of 25 vols. (Illus.). (Intermediate Primary and Infant Libs.). N.D. A. I. Bradley & Co.'s Pubs.
Parry, David Harold (1868-1950)
--For Glory and Renown, 8 vols. (Illus.). 384p. (Story Books for Boys). 1905. Set. Cassell & Co.
--The Sunken Million. (The Treasure Library). N.D. Frederick Warne & Co.
--With Haig on the Somme. LC 17-27904. vi p., 1 l, 301, 1 p. front., col. plates. 21 cm. 1917. Cassell and Company, Ltd.
Parry, Emma Louise, tr. see Hoffmann, Franz.
Parry, Judge, ed. see Cervantes Saavedra, Miguel de.
Parry, Marian (1924-), adapted by.
--The Birds of Basel. Parry, Marian (1924-), illus. LC 69-17503. (Illus.). 56 p. 21cm. 1969. Knopf.
--City Mouse, Country Mouse & Two More Mouse Tales from Aesop. Parry, Marian (1924-), illus. (Illus.). (gr. 2-3). 1971. (ISBN 0-590-04438-9). (ISBN 0-590-04353-6). Scholastic Inc.
--City Mouse, Country Mouse & Two More Mouse Tales from Aesop. Parry, Marian (1924-), illus. Repr. (Starbright Editions). (gr. k-3). 1973. Schol Bk Serv.
--I Am a Big Help. Parry, Marian (1924-), illus. LC 79-16638. (Illus.). 32 p. c.1980. (ISBN 0-688-80250-8). (ISBN 0-688-84250-X). Greenwillow Books.
--King of the Fish. Parry, Marian (1924-), illus. LC 76-46922. (Adapted from a Korean Folk Tale). (Illus.). 26cm. 32p. (gr. k-3). 1977. (ISBN 0-02-770200-6). Macmillan.
--Roger and the Devil. Parry, Marian (1924-), illus. LC 73-106142. (Illus.). 64 p. 22cm. 1972. (ISBN 0-394-82293-5). (ISBN 0-394-92293-X). Knopf.
Parry, Michel
--Hounds of Hell: Stories of Canine Horror & Fantasy. LC 73-16635. 192p. 1974. (ISBN 0-8008-3945-5). Taplinger.

Parry, Thomas Wood
--When Daddy Was a Boy. 280p. N.D. Little, Brown.
--When Daddy Was a Boy. Wood, H., illus. LC 7-39999. 280 p. incl. front., illus., plates. 21 cm. 1907. Press of F. Hudson Publishing Company.

Parsley, Mary, compiled by.
--I Can Choose My Bedtime Story. Kailer, Claude & Lowndes, Rosemary, illus. LC 77-152557. (Illus.). 116 p. 29cm. 1971. (ISBN 0-448-02820-4). Grosset & Dunlap.
--My All Day Read and Play Book. LC 71-39154. (Illus.). 156 p. 29cm. 1972, c.1971. (ISBN 0-07-038831-8). (ISBN 0-07-038833-4). American Heritage Press.
--My Book of Stories for All Seasons: Spring, Summer, Fall, Winter. Kailer, Claude & Lowndes, Rosemary, illus. LC 74-78600. (Illus.). 116 p. 28cm. 1974, c.1972. (ISBN 0-88332-063-0). Larousse.
--Two-Minute Stories. Escott, Tony, illus. LC 84-7675. p. cm. c.1984. (ISBN 0-517-43926-3). Derrydale Books.

Parson, George Burton
--Time to Stop Running. LC 77-10478. 127 p. 18cm. (Spire books). c.1977. (ISBN 0-8007-8293-3). F. H. Revell Co.

Parsons, Arthur Hudson, Jr. (1910-)
--The Horn that Stopped the Band. N.D. E . M. Hale and Co.
--The Horn That Stopped the Band. Ward, Lynd Kendall (1905-1985), illus. LC 54-5950. (Illus.). unpaged. 28cm. 1954. F. Watts.

Parsons, Arthur M
--Eyes of the Wilderness. LC 30-205980. 296 p. 20 cm. c.1930. The Reilly & Lee Co.

Parsons, Charles R.
--Amos Truelove: A Story of the Last Generation, 1 of 25 vols. (Illus.). 240p. (Selected Bks for Sunday School: No. 18). N.D. Set. Methodist Bk Concern.

Parsons, Elizabeth (1937-)
--The Upside-Down Cat. Himler, Ronald Norbert (1937-), illus. LC 80-13507. p. cm. 1981. (ISBN 0-689-50187-0). Atheneum.

Parsons, Ellen, pseud., see Dragonwagon, Crescent.

Parsons, Ellen, pseud. (1952-)
--Rainy Day Together. Dragonwagon, Crescent. 1st ed. Hoban, Lillian (1925-), illus. LC 72-135781. (Illus.). 32 p. 1971. (ISBN 0-06-024688-X). Harper & Row.

Parsons, George A
--Cut Bait, Johnny. 1st ed. Liebman, Oscar (1919-), illus. LC 58-6516. 189p. illus. 21cm. 1958. Holt.
--Put Her to Port, Johnny. 1st ed. Liebman, Oscar (1919-), illus. LC 57-5747. 223p. illus. 21cm. 1957. Holt.

Parsons, Henrietta Grace (1875-)
--The Jimpy Stories. LC 8-25124. 4 p. l., 7-257 p. front., 6 pl. 20 cm. c.1908. E. P. Dutton & Company.

Parsons, Julia Warth see Warth, Julian, pseud.

Parsons, Kitty
--Up & Down & Roundabout. Coe, Lloyd (1899-1976), illus. LC 67-29564. (Illus.). 64p. (gr. 2-4). 1967. (ISBN 0-8233-0080-3). Golden Quill.

Parsons, Margaret Colby Getchell, Mrs. (1891-)
--The Cloud Bird. Price, Edith Ballinger (1897-), illus. LC 16-24230. 5 p. l., 9-78 p. col. front., illus. 21 cm. c.1916. The Davis Pres, Inc.
--One Night Stand. (Five One-Act Plays for Young People). 116p. 1942. Woman's Press.
--Red Letter Day Plays. LC 22-711. x, 224 p. 19 cm. 1921. The Womans Press.

Parsons, Virginia
--Animal Parade. 1st ed. Parsons, Virginia, selected by. Parsons, Virginia, illus. LC 68-13726. (Illus.). 27 color ils. 64p. 20cm. 54p. (gr. 1-3). 1970. (ISBN 0-385-09084-6). Doubleday.
--A Christmas Panorama. Parsons, Virginia, illus. (gr. 1-3). 1977. Doubleday.
--Christmas Panorama. Parsons, Virginia, illus. (Illus.). (gr. k-3). N.D. (ISBN 0-385-04269-8). Doubleday.
--The Giant Happy Nursery Book. Parsons, Virginia, illus. LC 75-121096. (Illus.). 168 p. 29cm. 1970. Doubleday.
--Homes. Parsons, Virginia, illus. N.D. Doubleday.
--Homes. 1st ed. Parsons, Virginia, illus. LC 58-10034. (Illus.). unpaged. 27cm. (A Happy Nursery Bk.). 1958. Garden City Books.
--Lots and Lots of Bedtime Stories. Parsons, Virginia, illus. LC 73-140959. (Illus.). 91 p. 27cm. 1971. (ISBN 0-07-048519-4). (ISBN 0-07-048520-8). American Heritage Press.
--Loud. 1st ed. Parsons, Virginia, illus. LC 67-15221. (Illus.). 24 p. 17 x 19 cm. (A Holly Bk.). 1967. World Pub. Co.
--Night. 1st ed. Parsons, Virginia, illus. LC 58-10035. (Illus.). unpaged. 27cm. (Happy Nursery Bk.). 1958. Garden City Books.
--Play. 1st ed. Parsons, Virginia, illus. LC 63-11387. (Illus.). unpaged. 27cm. (Happy Nursery Bk.). 1963. Doubleday.
--Quiet. 1st ed. Parsons, Virginia, illus. LC 66-14035. (Illus.). 24 p. 17 x 19 cm. 1967. World Pub. Co.
--Rain. 1st ed. Parsons, Virginia, illus. LC 61-10941. unpaged. illus. 27cm. (Happy Nursery Bk.). (ps-3). 1961. Doubleday.
--Rainbow Rhymes. LC 73-79295. (Illus.). 26 p. 33cm. 1974. Golden Press.
--Rides. 1st ed. Parsons, Virginia, illus. LC 64-10272. (Illus.). 1 v. (unpaged. 27cm. (Happy Nursery Bk.). 1964. Doubleday.
--Ring for Liberty. Parsons, Virginia, illus. LC 74-33242. (Illus.). 32 p. 29cm. 1975. (ISBN 0-307-15694-X). Golden Press.
--Snow. Parsons, Virginia, illus. LC 62-7329. (Illus.). (ps-3). 1962. Doubleday.

Parsons, Virginia, ed.
--Pinocchio and Geppetto. Parsons, Virginia, illus. LC 78-11844. (Based on the Story by Carlo Collodi,1826-1890). (Illus.). 32 p. 22cm. 1979. (ISBN 0-07-048531-3). McGraw-Hill.
--Pinocchio and the Money Tree. Parsons, Virgina, illus. LC 78-12183. (Based on a Story by Carlo Collodi,1826-1890). (Illus.). 32 p. 22cm. 1979. (ISBN 0-07-048533-X). McGraw-Hill.
--Pinocchio Goes on the Stage. Parsons, Virginia, illus. LC 78-12323. (Based on a Story by Carlo Collodi, 1826-1890). (Illus.). 32 p. 22cm. 1979. (ISBN 0-07-048532-1). McGraw-Hill.
--Pinocchio Plays Truant. Parsons, Virginia, illus. LC 78-11843. (Based on a Story by Carlo Collodi, 1826-1890). (Illus.). 32 p. 22cm. 1979. (ISBN 0-07-048530-5). McGraw-Hill.

Parsons, Virginia, illus.
--First Things. 20p. (Block Bk.). (ps). 1982. (ISBN 0-307-10629-2, Golden Pr). Western Pub.

Parsons, Virginia & Waters, Sheila, illus.
--The Friendly Beasts & A Partridge in a Pear Tree: A Christmas Panorama. LC 66-4870. 1v. col. illus. 12x186cm. fold. to 12cm. 1966. Doubleday.

Partch, Virgil Franklin see Vip, pseud.

Partch, Virgil Franklin, II (1916-)
--VIP Quips. Vip, pseud. (ps-3). 1975. (ISBN 0-525-61527-X, Windmill Bks). Dutton.

Partch, Virgil Franklin, II (1916-) & Kraus, Robert (1925-)
--The Christmas Cookie Sprinkle Snitcher. LC 80-13641. (Illus.). 32 p. 31cm. 1980, c.1969. (ISBN 0-671-41199-3). Windmill Books/Simon and Schuster.
--Christmas Cookie Sprinkle Snitcher. Vip, pseud. Partch, Virgil Franklin, II (1916-), illus. Vip, pseud. LC 76-84138. (Illus.). color ils. 32p. (ps-3). 1969. (ISBN 0-671-66513-8, Windmill Bks.). (ISBN 0-671-66514-6). S&S.
--Ludwig: the Dog Who Snored Symphonies. Vip, pseud. Partch, Virgil Franklin, II (1916-), illus. Vip, pseud. LC 70-159149. (Illus.). 32 p. 29cm. 1971. (ISBN 0-87807-028-1). (ISBN 0-87807-029-X). Windmill Books.
--Shaggy Fur Face. Vip, pseud. Partch, Virgil Franklin, II (1916-), illus. Vip, pseud. LC 80-13485. 32p. (Windmill paperbacks). (ps). 1980, c.1971. (ISBN 0-671-41358-9). Windmill Books.

Partelow, Jennie R.
--Lively Nancy of Old South County. LC 28-18507. 2 p.l.,49 p. 20cm. 1928. The Branwell Co.

Partington, pseud., see Shillaber, Benjamin Penhallow.

Partington, Mrs., pseud. (1814-1890)
--Mrs. Partington's Mother Goose: The Original Mother Goose Melodies. Shillaber, Benjamin Penhallow. Shillaber, B. P., intro. by. 1882. Lee & Shepard.

Partington, Wilfred, jt. ed. see Walpole, Hugh Seymour, Sir.

Parton, Ethel (1862-1944)
--The House Between. Platt, Margaret, illus. LC 43-5777. 21cm. 343p. 1943. Viking Press.
--The Lost Locket: The Newburyport of 1830. Platt, Margaret, illus. LC 40-321452. 317 p. illus. 21 cm. 1940. The Viking Press.
--Melissa Ann: A Little Girl of the Eighteen Twenties. Lawson, Marie Abrams (1894-1956), illus. LC 31-26735. 6 p. l., 280 p. incl. illus., plates. col. front. 21 cm. 1931. Doubleday, Doran & Company, Inc.
--The Mule of the Parthenon and Other New Stories of Ancient Greece. Gay, Zhenya (1906-1978), illus. LC 32-26907. 5 p. l., 3-243 p. col. front., illus. 21 cm. 1932. Doubleday, Doran & Company, Inc.
--Penelope Ellen and Her Friends: Three Little Girls of 1840. LC 36-6475. 6 p. l., 3-300 p. front., illus. 21 cm. 1936. The Viking Press.
--Runaway Prentice: By the Story of Jeffrey, Susan, Tris, and Tibby in the Year 1800. LC 39-29716. 5 p. l., 3-280 p. illus. 21 cm. 1939. The Viking Press.
--Tabitha Mary: A Little Girl of 1810. Platt, Margaret, illus. LC 33-23355. 6 p. l., 3-244, 2 p. incl. double paltes. front., facsim. (music) 21 cm. 1933. The Viking Press.
--Vinny Applegay: Her First Year in New York. LC 37-28700. 6 p. l., 3-293 p. incl. front., illus. 21 cm. 1937. The Viking Press.
--The Year Without a Summer: A Story of 1816. Platt, Margaret, illus. LC 45-8599. 288 p. illus. 21 1/2 cm. 1945. The Viking Press.

Partridge, Bellamy
--Cousins. LC 25-18276. viii p., 1 l., 306 p. front., pl. 20 cm. c.1925. Brentano's.

Partridge, Benjamin Waring, jt. auth. see Cheney, Cora.

Partridge, Chuck
--Mile High Surprise. Partridge, Chuck, illus. (Illus.). (Pal Paperbacks). (Pal Skil ls II Ser.). (gr. 5-12). 1980. (ISBN 0-8374-3558-7). Xerox Ed Pubns.

Partridge, E. N.
--Glooscap the Great Chief: Legends of the Micmac Indians. N.D. Macmillan.
--Joyful Star: Indian Stories for Camp Fire Girls. N.D. Macmillan.

Partridge, Edward Bellamy
--Sube Cane. LC 17-13316. 8 p. l., 356 col. front., illus., col. plates. 20 cm. 1917. The Penn Publishing Company.

Partridge, Jenny Lilian (1947-)
--Colonel Grunt. Partridge, Jenny Lilian (1947-), illus. LC 81-7067. (Illus.). 28 p. 17cm. 1982, c.1980. Holt, Rinehart and Winston.
--Dominic Sly. Partridge, Jenny Lilian (1947-), illus. LC 82-21331. (Illus.). 26 p. 16cm. 1st U.S. edition. 1983, c.1981. (ISBN 0-03-062972-1). Holt, Rinehart, and Winston.
--Grandma Snuffles. 1st ed. Partridge, Jenny Lilian (1947-), illus. LC 82-21257. (Illus.). 28 p. 17cm. 1983, c.1981. (ISBN 0-03-062974-8). Holt, Rinehart, and Winston.
--Harriet Plume. Partridge, Jenny Lilian (1947-), illus. LC 82-21256. (Illus.). 24p. (Oakapple Wood Stories Ser.). (gr. k-3). 1983. (ISBN 0-03-062971-3). HR&W.
--Hopfellow. Partridge, Jenny Lilian (1947-), illus. LC 81-7070. (Illus.). 28 p. 17cm. 1982, c.1980. Holt, Rinehart and Winston.
--Lop-Ear. Partridge, Jenny Lilian (1947-), illus. LC 82-23204. p. cm. 1st U.S. edition. (An Oakapple Wood Story). 1983, c.1981. (ISBN 0-03-062973-X). Holt, Rinehart, and Winston.
--Mr. Squint. Partridge, Jenny Lilian (1947-), illus. LC 81-7065. (Illus.). 28 p. 17cm. 1982, c.1980. Holt, Rinehart and Winston.
--Peterkin Pollensnuff. Partridge, Jenny Lilian (1947-), illus. LC 81-7069. (Illus.). 28 p. 17cm. 1982, c.1980. Holt, Rinehart, and Winston.

Parvis, Gladys
--The Street of the Seven Little Sisters: A/Tale of Old Cairo and the Great Desert. LC 25-15987. (Illus.). 104p. 23cm. 1925. R. F. Seymour.

Pascal, David (1918-)
--The Silly Knight. Pascal, David (1918-), illus. LC 67-26041. (Illus.). 36 p. 28cm. 1967. Funk & Wagnalls.

Pascal, Francine
--The Hand-Me-Down Kid. LC 79-5462. 172 p. 22cm. 1980. (ISBN 0-670-35969-6). Viking Press.
--Hangin' Out with Cici. LC 76-57700. 152 p. 24cm. 1977. (ISBN 0-670-36045-7). Viking Press.
--Love and Betrayal & Hold the Mayo!. LC 84-20905. 210 p. 22cm. 1985. (ISBN 0-670-80547-5). Viking Kestrel.
--My First Love and Other Disasters. LC 78-25720. p. cm. 1979. (ISBN 0-670-49952-8). Viking Press.

Pascal, Jamie, jt. auth. see Pascal, Laurie.

Pascal, Jamie & Pascal, Laurie
--The Ballerina Mystery. Jenkins, Jean, illus. 64p. (Orig.). (Pick-a-Path Bks.: No. 12). (gr. 3-5). 1984. (ISBN 0-590-33048-9). Scholastic Inc.

Pascal, Laurie, jt. auth. see Pascal, Jamie.

Pascal, Laurie & Pascal, Jamie
--Mystery at Mockingbird Manor. Prebenna, David, illus. (Illus.). 64p. (Orig.). (Pick-a-Path Bks.: No. 6). (gr. 3-6). 1983. (ISBN 0-590-32812-3). Scholastic Inc.

Paschal, Nancy, pseud., see Trotter, Grace Violet.

Paschal, Nancy, pseud. (1900-)
--Magnolia Heights. Trotter, Grace Violet. King, Ruth, illus. LC 47-30412. 272 p. illus. 21 cm. 1947. T. Nelson.

Paschall, Alma, jt. auth. see Pearson, Francis Bail.

Paschang, Adolph
--Dragon Treasure. 1st ed. Wiese, Kurt (1887-1974), illus. LC 32-23566. (Illus.). v, 265p. 20cm. 1932. Longmans, Green and Co.

Pascheles, Wolf (1814-1857)
--Jewish Legends of the Middle Ages. Field, Claud Herbert Alwyn (1863-), ed. Mulliner, Mary, illus. LC 15-14527. viii, 152 p. illus., 20 cm. N.D. Bloch Publishing Company.

Paschos, Jacqueline & Destang, Francoise
--Mom's Birthday. (Rejoice Ser.). (ps). N.D. (ISBN 0-8091-6512-0). Paulist Pr.

Pashin, Gertrude, tr. see Einhorn, David.

Pashko, Stanley (1913-)
--Black Sheep Patrol. Rigney, Francis Joseph (1882-), illus. LC 46-8528. 180, 1 p. incl. col. front., illus. (part col.) plates (part col.) 21 cm. 1946. Roy Publishers.
--Ross Duncan at Bataan. LC 50-9598. 161 p. 21 cm. 1950. Messner.

Pasley, Louisa Maria Sabine & Pasley, M. S. (1848-1939)
--The Adventures of Madalene and Louisa. LC 79-5541. (Illus.). 43 p. 28cm. 1980. (ISBN 0-394-50946-3). Random House.

Pasley, M. S., jt. auth. see Pasley, Louisa Maria Sabine.

Pasma, Henry Kay (1881-)
--The Enchanted Sword. Westmacott, Bernard (1887-), illus. LC 32-253190. xi, 275 p. incl. front., illus., plates. 20 cm. 1932. Longmans, Green and Co.

Pastore, Edward W
--African Safari. Dowling, Victor J. (1906-), illus. LC 56-8708. 231p. illus. 21cm. 1956. Dodd, Mead.

Patapoff, Elizabeth, jt. auth. see Adair, Margaret Weeks.

Patch, Claye
--The Burro in Bethlehem. Nagel, Stina (1918-), illus. 1959. Exposition Press.

Patch, Dan E. L (1886-)
--Linda Lu Comes Through. LC 45-10698. 80 p. 20 cm. 1945. Zondervan Publishing House.
--Linda Lu-Girl Detective. LC 48-18885. 82p. 20cm. 1948. Zondervan Pub. House.
--Tug Turns Detective. LC 45-120606. 95 p. 20 cm. 1944. Zondervan Publishing House.
--Tug's Secret Mission. LC 47-15514. 2 p. l., 9-102 p. 19 1/2 cm. 1946. Zondervan Publishing House.

Patch, Kate Whiting, Mrs. (1870-)
--Old Lady and Young Laddie: Two Christmas Stories. Davidson, Bertha G., illus. LC 1-29096. 32 p. front., pl. 20 cm. c.1900. J. H. West Company.
--Prince Yellowtop. Barry, Etheldred Breeze (1874-), illus. LC 3-15229. 95 p. incl. front., illus., plates. 19 cm. (Cosy corner series). 1904. L. C. Page & Company.
--Prince Yellowtop. Barry, Etheldred Breeze (1874-), illus. (Illus.). (Goldenrod Library Ser.). 1905. L. C. Page & Co.
--Rainy Days and Sunny Days. LC 99-5313. 69 p. 1 illus. 20 cm. 1899. M. Bradley Company.

Patch, Olive, pseud., see Hamer, Mrs. Sarah Sharp Heaton.

Patch, Olive, pseud. (1839-1927)
--Happy Little People. Hamer, Mrs. Sarah Sharp Heaton. (Illus.). N.D. Cassell, Petter, Galpin.
--A Parcel of Children. Hamer, Mrs. Sarah Sharp Heaton. (Illus.). N.D. Cassell, Petter, Galpin.

Patchen, Joan
--Two Beastly Tales. LC 75-21155. (Illus.). 51, 44 p. c.1975. Lamplighters Roadway Press.

Patchett, Mary Osborne Elwyn (1897-)
--Ajax and the Haunted Mountain. LC 66-18284. 135p. 22cm. 1966, c.1963. Bobbs.
--Ajax, Golden Dog of the Australian Bush. Tansley, Eric, illus. LC 54-9495. (Illus.). 172 p. 21cm. 1st U.S. edition. 1954, c.1953. Bobbs-Merrill.
--Brumby, Come Home. Tresilian, Cecil Stuart (1891-), illus. LC 62-10026. 191p. illus. 22cm. 1962. Bobbs-Merrill.
--Brumby, Come Home. (Illus.). (gr. 6-10). 1962. (ISBN 0-8382-0123-7). Hale.
--Brumby, the Wild White Stallion. McCann, Gerald (1916-), illus. LC 59-9607. 224p. illus. 21cm. 1959, c.1958. Bobbs-Merrill.
--The Chance of Treasure. Hickey, Tom, illus. LC 57-9338. 220p. illus. 21cm. 1957. (ISBN 0-672-50247-X). Bobbs- Merrill.
--Cry of the Heart. LC 57-10357. 255p. 21cm. 1957. Abelard-Schuman.
--Dangerous Assignment. LC 64-15671. 22cm. 181p. (gr. 6-10). 1964. Bobbs.
--Dingo. LC 63-12944. 155 p. 22cm. 1963, c.1962. Doubleday.
--End of the Outlaws. Payne, Roger, illus. LC 63-19004. (Illus.). 22cm. 157p. (gr. 5-9). 1961. (ISBN 0-672-50263-1). Bobbs.
--The Golden Wolf. Payne, Roger, illus. LC 64-25318. 174p. 22cm. 1965, c.1962. Bobbs.
--The Great Barrier Reef. Kiddell-Monroe, Joan (1908-), illus. LC 58-12918. (Illus.). 21cm. 211p. 1958. Bobbs-Merril.
--The Quest of Ati Manu. 1st ed. Tresilian, Cecil Stuart (1891-), illus. LC 62-19326. 188p. illus. 22cm. 1962. Bobbs-Merrill.
--Send for Johnny Danger: The Amazing Adventures of Captain Danger and His Crew on the Moon. LC 58-9258. 174p. 19cm. 1958. Whittlesey House.
--Space Captives of the Golden Men. LC 55-7537. 222p. 21cm. 1st U.S. edition. c.1953. Bobbs-Merrill Co.
--Stranger in the Herd. Tresilian, Cecil Stuart (1891-), illus. LC 66-8712. 132p. illus. 21cm. 1966, c.1964. Duell.
--Stranger in the Herd. Tresilian, Cecil Stuart (1891-), illus. (Illus.). (gr. 5-8). 1966. (ISBN 0-696-81719-5). Hawthorn.

--Summer on Wild Horse Island. Payne, Roger, illus. LC 67-147512. (Illus.). 116 p. 21cm. 1967, c.1965. Meredith Press.
--Summer on Wild Horse Island. Tresilian, Cecil Stuart (1891-), illus. (Illus.). (gr. 5-8). 1967. (ISBN 0-696-82038-2). Hawthorn.
--Tam the Untamed. McCann, Gerald (1916-), illus. LC 55-10891. 186p. illus. 21cm. 1st U.S. edition. 1955. (ISBN 0-672-50528-2). Bobbs-Merrill.
--Tiger in the Dark. Payne, Roger, illus. LC 66-8989. 166p. illus. 21cm. 1st U.S. edition. 1966, c.1964. Duell.
--Tiger in the Dark. Payne, Roger, illus. (Illus.). (gr. 5-8). 1966. (ISBN 0-696-83575-4). Hawthorn.
--Warrimoo. 1st ed. Payne, Roger, illus. LC 63-11664. 189 p. illus. 22 cm. 1963. Bobbs-Merrill.

Patchin, Frank Gee (1861-1925)
--The Battleship Boys at Sea: Or, Two Apprentices in Uncle Sam's Navy. (The Battleship Boys Ser.). N.D. Henry Altemus Company.
--The Battleship Boys First Step Upward: Or, Winning Their Grades as Petty Officers. (The Battleship Boys Ser.). N.D. Henry Altemus Company.
--The Battleship Boys in Foreign Service: Or, Earning New Ratings in European Seas. (The Battleship Boys Ser.). N.D. Henry Altemus Company.
--The Battleship Boys in the Tropics: Or, Upholding the American Flag in Hondurus Revolution. LC 12-18550. 252 p. incl. front., plates. 20 cm. c.1912. Henry Altemus Company.
--The Battleship Boys in the Wardroom: Or, Winning Their Commissions As Line Officers on the Eve of the Great War. LC 18-20100. 255 p. incl. front., illus. 20 cm. (His The battleship boys series). c.1918. Henry Altemus Company.
--The Battleship Boys On Sky Patrol: Or, Fighting the Hun from Above the Clouds. (The Battleship Boys Ser.). N.D. Henry Altemus Company.
--The Battleship Boys Under Fire: Or, The Dash for the Besieged Kam Shav Mission. (The Battleship Boys Ser.). N.D. Henry Altemus Company.
--The Battleship Boys with the Adriatic Chasers: Or, Blocking the Path of the Undersea Raiders. (The Battleship Boys Ser.). N.D. Henry Altemus Company.
--The Pony Rider Boys in Alaska: Or, The Gold Diggers of Taku Pass. LC 55-47051. 20cm. 252p. (The Pony Rider Boys Series). 1955. Henry Altemus Co.
--The Pony Rider Boys in Louisiana: Or,Following the Game Trails in the Canebrake. (The Pony Rider Boys Series). N.D. Henry Altemus Co.
--The Pony Rider Boys in Montana: Or, The Mystery of the Old Custer Trail. (The Pony Rider Boys Ser.). N.D. Henry Altemus Company.
--The Pony Rider Boys in New England: Or, An Exciting Quest in the Maine Wilderness. LC 74-194167. (Illus.). 255 p. 20cm. c.1924. H. Altemus.
--The Pony Rider Boys in New Mexico: Or, The End of the Silver Trail. (The Pony Rider Boys Ser.). N.D. Henry Altemus Company.
--The Pony Rider Boys in Texas: Or, The Veiled Riddle of the Plains. (The Pony Rider Boys Ser.). N.D. Henry Altemus Company.
--The Pony Rider Boys in the Alkali: Or, Finding a Key to the Desert Maze. LC 14-9887. 252 p. incl. front., plates. 20 cm. (His Pony Rider Boys Series). c.1910. Henry Altemus Company.
--The Pony Rider Boys in the Grand Canyon: Or, The Mystery of Bright Angel Gulch. (The Pony Rider Boys Series). N.D. Henry Altemus Company.
--The Pony Rider Boys in the Ozarks: Or, The Secret of Ruby Mountain. (The Pony Rider Boys Ser.). N.D. Henry Altemus Company.
--The Pony Rider Boys in the Rockies: Or, The Secret of the Lost Claim. (The Pony Rider Boys Ser.). N.D. Henry Altemus Company.
--The Pony Rider Boys on the Blue Ridge: Or, A Lucky Find in the Carolina Mountains. (Pony Rider Boys Series). N.D. Henry Altemus Co.
--The Pony Rider Boys with the Texas Rangers: Or, On the Trail of the Border Bandits. (The Pony Rider Boys Ser.). N.D. Henry Altemus Company.
--The Range and Grange Hustlers on the Ranch: Or, The Boy Sheperds of the Great Divide. LC 12-207881. 250 p. incl. front., plates. 20 cm. (His The Range and Grange Hustlers Series). c.1912. Henry Altumus Company.
--Ted Jones at Desperation Island: Or, The Affair with the Yellow Coral Prince. LC 28-22315. 258 p. incl. front., plates. 20 cm. (His Fortune Hunters Ser.). c.1928. Henry Altemus Company.
--Ted Jones, Fortune Hunter: Or, The Adventures of the Luckless Three in Pearl Fishing. LC 28-22779. 256 p. incl. front., illus. 20 cm. c.1928. Henry Altemus Company.
--Ted Jones Under Sealed Orders: Or, The Mysterious Treasure Trail to the Red Lagoon. LC 28-22773. ix, 11-254 p. incl. front., illus. 20 cm. (His Fortune Hunters Ser.). c.1928. Henry Altemus Company.
--Ted Jones' Weeks of Terror: Or, The Luckless Three's Revolt Against the Sandalwood Sharpers. LC 28-22576. 256 p. incl. front., illus. 20 cm. c.1928. Henry Altemus Company.

Patchin, Frank Glines see Patchin, Frank Gee.

Pateman, May
--Babo: A South Seas Boy. Pateman, May, illus. 56. 3 p. col. illus. 14 cm. (Nursery series). c.1931. Friendship Press.

Patent, Dorothy H.
--The Sheep Book. Munoz, William, photos by. (Illus.). 80p. (gr. 2-5). 1985. (ISBN 0-396-08607-1). Dodd.

Paterson, Andrew Barton (1864-1941)
--The Animals Noah Forgot. Lindsay, Norman Alfred William (1879-1969), illus. LC 76-31405. (Illus.). 71 p. 25cm. 1970. Lansdowne.
--A Bush Christening. Poem. Hole, Quentin, illus. LC 77-356096. (Illus.). 16 leaves. 1976. (ISBN 0-00-185023-7). Collins.
--The Man from Ironbark. Hole, Quentin, illus. LC 74-24653. (Illus.). 32 p. 1975. (ISBN 0-529-05260-1). (ISBN 0-529-05262-8). Collins-World.
--Mulga Bill's Bicycle. Niland, Kilmeny & Niland, Deborah (1951-), illus. LC 74-12286. (Illus.). 40p. 1st U.S. edition. (ps-3). 1975. (ISBN 0-8193-0777-7, Four Winds). (ISBN 0-8193-0778-5). Scholastic Inc.
--Mulga Bill's Bicycle: Poem. Niland, Kilmeny & Niland, Deborah (1951-), illus. LC 74-12286. (Illus.). 30 p. 27cm. 1975, c.1973. (ISBN 0-8193-0777-7). (ISBN 0-8193-0778-5). Parents' Magazine Press.
--Waltzing Matilda. Digby, Desmond, illus. LC 79-155869. (Illus.). 36 p. 1972, c.1970. (ISBN 0-03-086748-7). (ISBN 0-03-086749-5). Holt, Rinehart and Winston.

Paterson, Brian, jt. auth. see Paterson, Cynthia.

Paterson, Cynthia & Paterson, Brian
--The Foxwood Treasure. Paterson, Cynthia & Paterson, Brian, illus. LC 85-1407. (Illus.). 32 p. 21cm. (Foxwood Tales). 1985. (ISBN 0-8120-5664-7). Barron's.
--Robbery at Foxwood. Paterson, Cynthia & Paterson, Brian, illus. LC 85-3854. (Illus.). 33 p. 20cm. (Foxwood Tales). 1985. (ISBN 0-8120-5665-5). Barron's.

Paterson, Diane, jt. auth. see Harris, Robie H.

Paterson, Diane R. Cole (1946-)
--The Bathtub Ocean. Paterson, Diane R. Cole (1946-), illus. LC 78-72517. (Illus.). 32 p. c.1979. (ISBN 0-8037-0460-7). (ISBN 0-8037-0462-3). Dial Press.
--The Biggest Snowstorm Ever. Paterson, Diane R. Cole (1946-), illus. LC 74-2884. (Illus.). 31 p. 24cm. 1974. Dial Press.
--Eat!. Paterson, Diane R. Cole (1946-), illus. LC 74-23491. (Illus.). 32 p. 1975. (ISBN 0-8037-4830-2). (ISBN 0-8037-4831-0). Dial Press.
--Eat!. Paterson, Diane R. Cole (1946-), illus. LC 74-18596. (Illus.). 32 p. (Pied Piper Book). 1977, c.1975. (ISBN 0-8037-2205-2). Dial Press.
--Hey, Cowboy!. Patterson, Diane R. Cole (1946-), illus. LC 81-20851. (Illus.). 48 p. 19cm. c.1983. (ISBN 0-394-85341-5). (ISBN 0-394-95341-X). Knopf.
--If I Were a Toad. Paterson, Diane R. Cole (1946-), illus. LC 76-42925. (Illus.). 32 p. 16cm. c.1977. (ISBN 0-8037-4803-5). (ISBN 0-8037-4804-3). Dial Press.
--Smile for Auntie. Paterson, Diane R. Cole (1946-), illus. LC 76-2285. p. cm. c.1976. (ISBN 0-8037-8066-4). (ISBN 0-8037-8067-2). (ISBN 0-8037-7981-X). Dial Press.
--Soap and Suds. Paterson, Diane R. Cole (1946-), illus. 1984. Knopf.
--Stone Soup. Paterson, Diane R. Cole (1946-), illus. LC 80-27947. (Illus.). 32 p. 24cm. c.1981. (ISBN 0-89375-478-1). (ISBN 0-89375-479-X). Troll Associates.
--Wretched Rachel. Paterson, Diane R. Cole (1946-), illus. LC 77-71515. (Illus.). 32 p. 16cm. c.1978. (ISBN 0-8037-9715-X). (ISBN 0-8037-9695-1). Dial Press.

Paterson, Huntley, tr. see Salten, Felix.

Paterson, Katherine, tr. see Yagawa, Sumiko.

Paterson, Katherine Womeldorf (1932-)
--Angels and Other Strangers: Family Christmas Stories. LC 79-63797. p. cm. c.1979. (ISBN 0-690-03992-1). Crowell.
--Angels and Other Strangers: Family Christmas Stories. 1979. Harper.
--Bridge to Terabithia. Diamond, Donna (1950-), illus. LC 77-2221. 24cm. 128p. 1977. (ISBN 0-690-01359-0). Crowell. **Awards: (JNM).**
--Bridge to Terabithia. Diamond, Donna (1950-), illus. 1977. Harper.
--Come Sing, Jimmy Jo. LC 84-21123. 197 p. 22cm. c.1985. (ISBN 0-525-67167-6). Dutton. **Award: (ALA).**
--The Great Gilly Hopkins. LC 77-27075. 148 p. 24cm. (gr. 4-6). c.1978. (ISBN 0-690-03837-2). (ISBN 0-690-03838-0). Crowell. **Awards: (NBA); (ALA); (JNM).**
--Jacob Have I Loved. LC 80-668. p. cm. c.1980. (ISBN 0-690-04079-2). (ISBN 0-690-04078-4). Crowell. **Awards: (JNM); (ALA).**
--Jacob Have I Loved. 1980. Harper.
--The Master Puppeteer. Wells, Haru, illus. LC 75-8614. (Illus.). 179 p. 24cm. c.1975. (ISBN 0-690-00913-5). Crowell. **Awards: (NBA); (ALA).**
--The Master Puppeteer. Wells, Haru, illus. (gr. 6-9). 1976. Harper & Row.
--Of Nightingales that Weep. Wells, Haru, illus. LC 74-8294. (Illus.). xiii, 170 p. 24cm. 1974. (ISBN 0-690-00485-0). Crowell.
--Rebels of the Heavenly Kingdom. 1st ed. LC 83-1529. x, 229 p. 22cm. c.1983. (ISBN 0-525-66911-6). E.P. Dutton.
--The Sign of the Chrysanthemum. Landa, Peter, illus. LC 72-7553. (Illus.). x, 132 p. 24cm. 1973. (ISBN 0-690-73625-8). Crowell.

Putino, Ernesto (1911-)
--A Boy Named Paco. Un Nino Llamado Paco. Perez Torres, Arturo, illus. Olivas, Herlinda P., tr. LC 74-13661. (Illus.). v, 43 p. 21cm. Orig. Title: Un Nino Llamado Paco. 1974. (ISBN 0-8111-0528-8). Naylor.

Patmore, Coventry Kersey Dighton (1823-1896), selected by.
--The Children's Garland. New & Cheaper Ed. ed. (Golden Treasury Ser.). N.D. MacMillan.
--The Children's Garland from the Best Poets. LC 73-167478. xi, 354 p. 21cm. (Granger Index reprint Ser.). 1971. (ISBN 0-8369-6283-4). Books for Libraries Press.
--The Children's Garland from the Best Poets. (The Golden Treasury Ser.). N.D. John Allyn.
--The Children's Garland from the Best Poets. LC 7-41816. xvi, 344 p. 17 cm. (Half-title: Golden Treasury Series). 1906. Macmillan and Co., Limited.
--The Children's Garland from the Best Poets. 17cm. xvi, 344p. Repr. of 1861 ed. (Golden Treasury Ser.). 1906. Macmillan & Co.
--The Children's Garland from the Best Poets. (Illus.). (Series of Books for the Young). N.D. MacMillan & Co.

Paton, M. Joe & Glass, Malcolm Sanford (1936-), eds.
--Grab Me a Bus and other Award Winning Poems from Scholastic Writing Awards. Scholastic-Kodak Photography Awards, photos by. (Illus.). (gr. 7-12). 1975. (ISBN 0-590-05217-9, Schol Trade Pap). Schol Bk Serv.

Paton, Noel, Sir
--The Fairy Book: The Best Popular Fairy Stories. Craik, Dinah Maria Mulock, Mrs. (1826-1887), selected by. (Golden Treasury Series). N.D. MacMillan & Co.

Paton Walsh, Gillian see Paton Walsh, Jill, pseud.

Paton Walsh, Jill, pseud., see Paton Walsh, Gillian.

Paton Walsh, Jill, pseud., see Walsh, Gillian Paton.

Paton Walsh, Jill, pseud. (1937-)
--Babylon. Paton Walsh, Gillian. (Illus.). 32p. (gr. k-3). 1982. (ISBN 0-233-97362-1). Andre Deutsch.
--Babylon. Walsh, Gillian Paton. Northway, Jennifer, illus. 1982. Dutton.
--A Chance Child. Paton Walsh, Gillian. LC 78-21521. p. cm. 1978. (ISBN 0-374-31236-2). Farrar, Straus and Giroux. **Award: (ALA).**
--Children of the Fox. Paton Walsh, Gillian. Easton, Robin, illus. LC 78-8138. (Illus.). 115 p. 22cm. 1978. (ISBN 0-374-31242-7). Farrar, Straus and Giroux.
--The Dolphin Crossing. Paton Walsh, Gillian. LC 67-17767. 134p. (gr. 7-9). 1967. St Martin.
--The Emperor's Winding Sheet. Paton Walsh, Gillian. LC 73-90970. 273 p. 21cm. 1974. (ISBN 0-374-32160-4). Farrar, Straus and Giroux.
--Fireweed. Paton Walsh, Gillian. LC 73-109554. 133 p. 21cm. (Ariel book). 1970, c.1969. Farrar, Straus & Giroux.
--Fireweed. Paton Walsh, Gillian. LC 73-330950. 127 p. 18cm. (Puffin books). 1972. (ISBN 0-14-030560-2). Penguin.
--Gaffer Samson's Luck. Paton Walsh, Gillian. Cole, Brock, illus. LC 84-10180. (Illus.). 118 p. 25cm. 1984. (ISBN 0-374-32498-0). Farrar/Straus/Giroux. **Award: (ALA).**
--Goldengrove. Paton Walsh, Gillian. LC 72-81484. 130 p. 21cm. 1972. (ISBN 0-374-32696-7). Farrar, Straus and Giroux.
--Goldengrove. Paton Walsh, Gillian. LC 73-4809. 189 p. 24cm. 1973. (ISBN 0-8161-6104-6). G. K. Hall.
--The Green Book. Paton Walsh, Gillian. Bloom, Lloyd, illus. LC 81-12620. p. cm. 1st U.S. edition. 1981. (ISBN 0-374-32778-5). Farrar, Straus, Giroux.
--Hengest's Tale. Paton Walsh, Gillian. Margrie, Janet, illus. LC 66-66607. 6, 151p. 21cm. 1966. Macmillan.
--Hengest's Tale. Paton Walsh, Gillian. Margrie, Janet, illus. LC 66-66607. (Illus.). 21cm. 151p. (gr. 5-9). 1966. St Martin.
--The Huffler. Paton Walsh, Gillian. Palmer, Juliette (1930-), illus. LC 75-25917..22cm. 83p. 1st U.S. edition. 1975. (ISBN 0-374-33505-2). Farrar, Straus, and Giroux.
--A Parcel of Patterns. Paton Walsh, Gillian. LC 83-48143. 139p. (gr. 7 up). N.D. (ISBN 0-374-35750-1). (ISBN 0-374-35750-1). FS&G.
--Toolmaker. Paton Walsh, Gillian. Roy, Jeroo, illus. LC 73-7126. (Illus.). 45 p. 23cm. 1974, c.1973. (ISBN 0-8164-3109-4). Seabury Press.
--Unleaving. Paton Walsh, Gillian. LC 76-8857. 145 p. 21cm. 1976. (ISBN 0-374-38042-2). Farrar, Straus, and Giroux. **Award: (BGH).**

Paton Walsh, Jill, pseud. (1939-) & Crossley-Holland, Kevin (1941-)
--Wordhoard. Paton Walsh, Gillian. 136p. 1969. (ISBN 0-374-38514-9). Farrar, Straus and Giroux.
--Wordhoard: Anglo-Saxon Stories. Paton Walsh, Gillian. LC 70-85364. 21cm. 122p. (gr. 7 up). 1969. (ISBN 0-374-38042-2). FS&G.
--Wordhoard:. Anglo-Saxon Stories. Paton Walsh, Gillian. LC 74-183335. 139 p. 19cm. (Puffin books). 1972. (ISBN 0-14-030511-4). Penguin.

Patri, Angelo (1876-), tr. see Cherubini, Eugenio.

Patri, Angelo (1896-), tr. see Lorenzini, Carlo.

Patri, Angelo (1876-)
--Pinocchio in America. Liddell, Mary, illus. LC 28-21821. xiv, 255 p. col. front., illus., plates. 21 cm. 1928. Doubleday, Doran & Company, Inc.
--Pinocchio's Visit to America. Gallagher, Sears (1869-1955), illus. LC 29-13623. vi, 250 p. illus. 18 cm. (On cover: Once-upon-a-time series). c.1929. Ginn and Company.

Patrick, Gloria
--A Bug in a Jug & Other Funny Poems. Hanson, Joan (1938-), illus. (Illus.). (gr. k-3). 1973. (ISBN 0-590-09387-8, Schol Pap). Schol Bk Serv.
--This Is ... Hanson, Joan (1938-), illus. LC 70-84092. (Illus.). 104 p. 24cm. 1970. Carolrhoda Books.

Patrick, Mae C.
--My Red-Letter Christmas. LC 26-9915. 28 p. 19 1/2cm. c.1926. R. G. Badger.

Patrick, Pearl Haley (1883-)
--O'po of the Omaha. Jacobson, Dan, illus. LC 57-5244. 229p. illus. 22cm. 1957. Caxton Printers.

Patrick, Stanley L.
--Laughing, Singing, Jumping for Joy. 1981. (ISBN 0-8062-1855-X). Carlton.

Patten, Brian (1946-)
--Mr. Moon's Last Case. Moore, Mary (1946-), illus. LC 76-10070. (Illus.). 158 p. 22cm. c.1975. (ISBN 0-684-14674-6). Scribner.

Patten, Clara Irene (1877-)
--The Log House in the Woods. LC 48-15209. 88 p. 18 cm. 1947. Wartburg Press.
--Miss Hadley's Finishing School. LC 31-977. 143 p. 20 cm. c.1930. Meador Publishing Company.

Patten, Gilbert see Standish, Burt L., pseud.

Patten, Gilbert (1866-1945)
--Ben Oakman, Stroke. Standish, Burt L., pseud. Hastings, Howard Livngston (1887-), illus. LC 25-10693. 3 p. l., 11-249 p. front. 20 cm. c.1925. Barse & Hopkins.
--Bill Bruce of Harvard. Standish, Burt L., pseud. Poucher, Edward A., illus. LC 10-20847. viii, p., 1 l., 371 p. front., plates. 20 cm. 1910. Dodd, Mead and Company.
--Boltwood of Yale. Standish, Burt L., pseud. LC 14-28985. 300 p. incl. col. front. col. plates 21 cm. c.1914. Barse & Hopkins.
--Boy Boomers. Standish, Burt L., pseud. (The Boys' Own Library). N.D. David McKay.
--Boy Cattle King. Standish, Burt L., pseud. (The Boys' Own Library). N.D. David McKay.
--Boy From the West. Standish, Burt L., pseud. (The Boys' Own Library). N.D David McKay.
--The Boy from the West. Standish, Burt L., pseud. 218p. (Medal Library: No. 24). 1899. Street & Smith.
--Brick King, Backstop. Standish, Burt L., pseud. LC 14-6232. 317 p. incl. front. plates. 21 cm. (His The Big League Ser.). c.1914. Barse & Hopkins.
--The Call of the Varsity. Standish, Burt L., pseud. (The College Life Ser.). N.D. Barse & Hopkins.
--Clif Stirling Behind the Line. Standish, Burt L., pseud. LC 11-28365. 19cm. 336p. (Clif Stirling Ser.). 1911. D. McKay.

--Clif Stirling, Captain of the Nine. Standish, Burt L., pseud. LC 10-18955. 4 p., 1 l., 9-322 p. col. front., plates. 20 cm. (On cover: Clif Stirling Ser.). c.1910. D. McKay.
--Clif Stirling, Freshman at Stormbridge. Standish, Burt L., pseud. LC 13-21743. 329 p. col. front., plates. 20 cm. (On cover: Clif Stirling Ser.). c.1913. D. McKay.
--Clif Stirling, Sophomore at Stormbridge. Standish, Burt L., pseud. LC 24-222182. 4, 7-333 p. col. front. 19 cm. (His Clif Stirling Ser.). c.1916. D. McKay.
--Clif Stirling, Stroke of the Crew. Standish, Burt L., pseud. LC 12-5550. 19cm. 331p. (Clif Sterling Ser.). 1912. D. McKay.
--The College Rebel. Standish, Burt L., pseud. LC 14-7562. 313 p. incl. col. front. col. plates. 21 cm. c.1914. Barse & Hopkins.
--The College Rebel. Standish, Burt L., pseud. LC 30-12309. 3 p. l., 11-313 p. front. 20 cm. (His The College Life Ser.). N.D. Barse & Hopkins.
--Courtney of the Center Garden. Standish, Burt L., pseud. Angell, Clare, illus. LC 15-7818. 320 p. incl. front. plates. 21 cm. (His The Big League Ser.). c.1915. Barse & Hopkins.
--Covering the Look-in Corner. Standish, Burt L., pseud. Wrenn, Charles L., illus. LC 15-781974. 316 p. incl. front. plates. 21 cm. (His The Big League Ser.). c.1915. Barse & Hopkins.
--Crossed Signals. Standish, Burt L., pseud. LC 28-10869. 2 p. l., 9-220 p. front. 20 cm. (His The Big League Ser.). c.1928. Barse & Co.
--The Deadwood Trail. Standish, Burt L., pseud. LC 4-17926. 20cm. 261p. (The Boys' Own Library). 1904. David McKay.
--Don Kirk, the Boy Cattle King. Standish, Burt L., pseud. 220p. (Medal Library: No. 10). 1899. Street & Smith.
--Don Kirke's Mine. Standish, Burt L., pseud. (The Boys' Own Library). N.D. David McKay.
--Don Kirk's Mine: Or, The Fight for a Lost Fortune. Standish, Burt L., pseud. (A companion story to The Boy Cattle King). 210p. (Medal Library: No. 12). 1899. Street & Smith.
--Frank Merriwell's Champions. Standish, Burt L., pseud. LC 12-37534. 1 p. l., 7-318 p. 18 cm. (On cover: Medal Library, No. 240). c.1904. Street & Smith.
--Frank Merriwell's Chums. Standish, Burt L., pseud. LC 2-16919. 1 p. l., ii, 9-282 p. front., pl. 19 cm. 1902. Street & Smith.
--Frank Merriwell's Chums: Or, Tried and True. Standish, Burt L., pseud. Rudman, Jack, ed. LC 73-151839. 252 p. 18cm. (His Merriwell Ser. No. 2). c.1972. (ISBN 0-8373-9302-7). (ISBN 0-8373-9002-8). Smith Street Publications.
--Frank Merriwell's Foes. Standish, Burt L., pseud. LC 2-16920. 19cm. 271p. 1902. Street & Smith.
--Frank Merriwell's Foes. Standish, Burt L., pseud. Rudman, Jack, ed. N.D. (ISBN 0-8373-9303-5). (ISBN 0-8373-9003-6). F Merriwell.
--Frank Merriwell's Foes: Or, An Uphill Fight. Standish, Burt L., pseud. Rudman, Jack, ed. LC 70-151838. 252 p. 18cm. (Merriwell Ser. No. 3). c.1972. (ISBN 0-8373-9303-5). (ISBN 0-8373-9003-6). Smith Street Publications.
--Frank Merriwell's Own Company: Or, Fun Behind the Footlights. Standish, Burt L., pseud. LC 58-528069. 213p. 18cm. (His The Merriwell Ser. No. 35). 1922, c.1898. Street & Smith Corp.
--Frank Merriwell's Return to Yale. Standish, Burt L., pseud. LC 12-375358. 1 p. l., 5-247 p. 18 cm. (On cover: Medal Library, No. 244). c.1904. Street & Smith.
--Frank Merriwell's School Days. Standish, Burt L., pseud. LC 1-26272. 19cm. 302p. 1901. Street & Smith.
--Frank Merriwell's Schooldays: Or, A Tale of School Life at Fardale Academy. Standish, Burt L., pseud. Rudman, Jack, ed. LC 76-151837. (Merriwell Ser.: No. 1). 1971. Smith Street Pub.
--Frank Merriwell's Sports Afield. Standish, Burt L., pseud. (The Frank Merriwell Stories). N.D. David McKay.
--Frank Merriwell's Sports Afield. Standish, Burt L., pseud. LC 12-375365. 1 p. l., 7-384 p. 18 cm. (On cover: Medal Library, No. 209). c.1903. Street & Smith.
--The Grip of the Game. Standish, Burt L., pseud. Wrenn, Charles L., illus. LC 24-12763. 2 p. 9-245 p. front. 20 cm. (His Big League Ser.). c.1924. Barse & Hopkins.
--Jud and Joe. Standish, Burt L., pseud. (The Boys' Own Library). N.D. David McKay.
--Jud and Joe, Printers and Publishers. Standish, Burt L., pseud. 202p. (Medal Library: No. 33). 1899. Street & Smith.
--Lefty Locke: Owner. Standish, Burt L., pseud. LC 25-10975. 1 p. l., vii-viii, 9-242 p. front. 20 cm. (Lettered on cover: The Big League Ser.). c.1925. Barse & Hopkins.
--Lefty O' the Big League. Standish, Burt L., pseud. LC 14-6157. 311 p. incl. front. plates. 21 cm. (His The Big League Ser.). c.1914. Barse & Hopkins.
--Lefty O' the Blue Stockings. Standish, Burt L., pseud. LC 14-6231. 299 p. incl. front. plates. 21 cm. (His The big league series). c.1914. Barse & Hopkins.
--Lefty O' the Bush. Standish, Burt L., pseud. LC 29-25273. 3 p. l., 11-305 p. front. 20 cm. (His Big League Ser.). 1914. Barse & Hopkins.
--Lefty O' the Training Camp. Standish, Burt L., pseud. LC 14-6156. 295 p. incl. front. plates. 21 cm. (His The Big League Ser.). c.1914. Barse & Hopkins.
--Lego Lamb, Southpaw. Standish, Burt L., pseud. Hastings, Howard Livingston (1887-), illus. LC 23-582521. 2 p. l., 9-250 p. front. 20 cm. (His The Big League Ser.). c.1923. Barse & Hopkins.
--The Making of a Big Leaguer. Standish, Burt L., pseud. Owen, Robert Emmett (1878-), illus. LC 15-7589. 3 p. l., 11-307 p. front., plates. 21 cm. (His The Big League Ser.). c.1916. Barse & Hopkins.
--On College Battlefields. Standish, Burt L., pseud. (The College Life Ser.). N.D. Barse & Hopkins.
--The Rockspur Eleven. Standish, Burt L., pseud. (The Boys' Own Library). N.D. David McKay.
--The Rockspur Eleven: A Story of Football. Standish, Burt L., pseud. 300p. 1900. Street & Smith.
--The Rockspur Nine. Standish, Burt L., pseud. (The Boys' Own Library). N.D. David McKay.
--The Rockspur Nine: A Story of Baseball. Standish, Burt L., pseud. LC 6682. 287p. 1900. Street & Smith.
--The Rockspur Rivals. Standish, Burt L., pseud. (The Boys' Own Library). N.D. David McKay.
--The Rockspur Rivals: A Story of Winter Sports. Standish, Burt L., pseud. LC 2-22673. 20cm. 2p. 1901. Street & Smith.
--Sons of Old Eli. Standish, Burt L., pseud. Hastings, Howard Livingston (1887-), illus. LC 23-7641. 248 p. incl. front., plates. 20 cm. c.1923. Barse & Hopkins.

Patten, Lewis Byford, jt. auth. see Overholser, Wayne D.

Patten, Lewis Byford (1915-) & Overholser, Wayne D. (1906-)
--Meeker Massacre. LC 70-87086. (Illus.). 160p. (gr. 5-9). 1969. (ISBN 0-8092-8502-9). Contemp Bks.

Patterson, Anne Virginia Sharpe, Mrs. (1841-)
--Dickey Downy: The Autobiography of a bird. 192p. N.D. American Baptist Publication Society.
--Dickey Downy: The Autobiography of a Bird. (The Phoenix Ser.). N.D. George W. Jacobs & Co.
--Dickey Downy: The Autobiography of a Bird. phoenix ed. Hallowell, Elizabeth M., illus. Lacey, J. F., intro. by. LC 2-11138. 192 p. col. pl. 16 cm. 1899. A. F. Rowland.

Patterson, Antoinette De Coursey, Mrs., tr. see Wahlenberg, Anna (1858-1933) & Thomsen, Frede.

Patterson, Antoinette De Coursey, Mrs.
--The Enchanted Bird, and Other Fairy Stories. Pilsbry, ELizabeth, illus. LC 18-19165. 63 p. incl. col. front., illus. col. plates. 21 cm. 1917. The Penn Publishing Company.

Patterson, Arthur Willis (1888-)
--Redcoats at Castine. Quinn, Paul, illus. LC 38-33568. 4 p. l., 203 p. incl. front. (map) illus. 21 cm. 1938. Stephen Daye Press.

Patterson, Carolyn
--Mr. Gomp and the Opti-Goblins: Optical Illusions and Other Eye-Fooling Fun. Wagner, John, illus. LC 78-104746. (Illus.). 24 p. 24cm. (Children's Corner). c.1977. Hallmark.

Patterson, Elizabeth
--Judy, Heroine: A Tale of the Days of Roger Williams. Ives, Sarah Noble, illus. LC 6-6052. 92 p. col. front., illus. 20 cm. c.1906. McLoughlin Brothers.

Patterson, Emma Lillie (1904-)
--Midnight Patriot. McGee, Millard, illus. (Illus.). (gr. 10 up). N.D. (ISBN 0-679-20112-2). McKay.
--The World Turned Upside Down. LC 52-12699. 281 p. 22cm. 1953. Longsmans, Green.
--The World Turned Upside Down. 1953. McKay.

Patterson, Frances Taylor
--Catherine Tekakwitha. LC 58-58795. 159p. 21cm. 1958. Sheed & Ward.

Patterson, Gardner (1914-)
--Docker. LC 80-13514. 145 p. 22cm. 1980. (ISBN 0-689-50182-X). Atheneum.

Patterson, Geoffrey (1943-)
--Chestnut Farm. Patterson, Geoffrey (1943-), illus. 1980. Deutsch.
--A Pig's Tale. Patterson, Geoffrey (1943-), illus. LC 82-72113. (Illus.). 32p. (gr. k-3). 1984. (ISBN 0-233-97477-6, Andre Deutsch). Dutton.

Patterson, Grace
--The Secret Visitor. (Illus.). 96p. 1982. (ISBN 0-682-49860-2). Exposition.

Patterson, Henry W
--Frenchman's Island. LC 29-6344. 4 p. l., 3-238 p. front., plates. 20 cm. c.1929. The Century Co.
--Meetinghouse Bay. Whiting, John Downes (1884-), illus. LC 41-8633. 4 p. l., 3-250 p. illus. 20 cm. c.1941. Coward-McCann, Inc.
--The Secret Empire: a Boy with La Salle. Cheney, Philip, illus. LC 31-25416. 4 p. l., 3-269 p. illus. 20 cm. c.1931. Coward-McCann, Inc.

Patterson, Lillie G.
--Christmas Trick or Treat. Oechsli, Kelly (1918-), illus. LC 78-11308. p. cm. (Happy Holiday Books). 1979. Garrard Pub. Co.
--The Grouchy Santa. Cunette, Lou, illus. LC 78-21936. (Illus.). 39 p. 23cm. (First Holiday Books). c.1979. (ISBN 0-8116-7254-9). (ISBN 0-8116-7254-9). Garrard Pub. Co.
--Haunted Houses on Halloween. Cushman, Doug, illus. LC 78-11382. (Illus.). 47 p. 23cm. c.1979. (ISBN 0-8116-7253-0). Garrard Pub. Co.
--The Jack-O'lantern Trick. Hutchinson, William Miller (1916-), illus. LC 78-11307. (Illus.). 38 p. 23cm. (First Holiday Books). 1979. (ISBN 0-8116-7250-6). Garrard Pub. Co.
--Janey, the Halloween Spy. Dawson, Diane, illus. LC 78-11538. (Illus.). 37 p. 23cm. c.1979. (ISBN 0-8116-7251-4). Garrard Pub. Co.
--Poetry for Spring. Oechsli, Kelly (1918-), illus. LC 73-3186. (Illus.). 64 p. 24cm. 1973. (ISBN 0-8116-4114-7). Garrard Pub. Co.

Patterson, Nancy-Lou & Long, James
--Cartoon Catechism. Patterson, Nancy-Lou & Long, James, illus. N.D. Morehouse-Barlow.

Patterson, Samuel White
--When St. Nicholas got Back: A Tale of Christmas Morning, 1822. LC 59-510. 21cm. 37p. (Bookland Juvenile). 1959. Carlton Press Inc.

Patterson, Valeria, illus.
--Favorite Nursery Rhymes. LC 50-2912. 24p. illus. (part col.) 21cm. 1950, c.1942. Martin's House.

Patterson, William H.
--I Wish I Were: Little Verses for Little Children. Freeman, Elinor, illus. 1977. (ISBN 0-682-48696-5). Exposition.

Patterson, Yvonne
--Happy Hannah. Hutton, Kathryn, illus. (Illus.). 24p. (Happy Day Bible Stories Bks.). (ps-2). 1984. (ISBN 0-87239-764-5). Standard Pub.
--My Happy Week. Sparks, Judith, ed. Arthur, Lorraine, illus. LC 81-86705. (Illus.). 24p. (Orig.). (Happy Day Bks.). (ps-3). 1982. (ISBN 0-87239-542-1). Standard Pub.
--The Wise King & the Baby. LC 59-1258. (Illus.). (Arch Bk.: No. 18). (gr. k-4). 1981. Concordia.

Patteson, Madge Lisbeth
--Marco: The Gypsy Elf. LC 18-22194. 96 p. incl. front., 1 illus., plates. 20 cm. 1918. Hine Brothers.

Patteson, Susanna Louise, Mrs. (1853-1922)
--Kitty Kat Kimmie. Patteson, Susanna Louise, Mrs. (1853-1922), illus. (Illus.). N.D. George W. Jacobs & Co.
--Letters from Pussycatville. Patteson, Susanna Louise, Mrs. (1853-1922), illus. Butterworth, Hezekiah, intro. by. LC 3-25886. 19cm. 281p. 1903. G. W. Jacobs & Co.
--Pussy Meow. (The Phoenix Ser.). N.D. George W. Jacobs & Co.
--Pussy Meow. (The Phoenix Ser.). N.D. Macrae Smith.
--Pussy Meow: The Autobiography of a Cat. Bolton, Sarah K., intro. by. LC 1-23690. 237 p. front., plates. 19 cm. c.1901. G. W. Jacobs & Co.

Patton, Carl Safford (1866-)
--More Two-Minute Stories. LC 38-9499. 6 p. l., 130 p. 19 cm. 1937. Willett, Clark & Company.

Patton, Dee, jt. auth. see Patton, Jim.

Patton, Don (1892-)
--The Bunch Quitter. Clowes, Paul, illus. LC 35-22400. 256 p. illus. 23 cm. 1935. Macrae Smith Company.

Patton, Frances Gray (1906-)
--Good Morning, Miss Dove. Price, Garrett W. (1896-1979), illus. (Illus.). (gr. 7 up). 1954. Dodd.

Patton, Harris
--Young Eagles. LC 35-32200. 3 p. l., 11-123 p. 20 cm. (His Young Eagles Ser.). c.1932. The Goldsmith Publishing Company.

Patton, Jim (1950-) & Patton, Dee (1953-)
--Grandmother's Heart. LC 80-15968. p. cm. c.1980. (ISBN 0-87123-190-5). Bethany Fellowship.

Patton, Kay
--Jenny Wren's New House. Wilde, Irma, illus. LC 55-20868. unpaged. illus. 21cm. (Coxy-corner book, 2442). c.1954. Whitman Pub. Co.

Patton, Lucia
--Little Echo in the Hills. Patton, Lucia, illus. (Illus.). 25cm. 32p. 1950. Albert Whitman & Co.
--The Little House on Stilts. Patton, Lucia, illus. LC 48-8961. 31 p. illus. (part col.) 25 cm. 1948. A. Whitman.
--The Little River of Gold. Patton, Lucia, illus. N.D. Albert Whitman & Co.

Patton, Lucia, jt. auth. see Friskey, Margaret Richards.

Patton, Willoughby
--The Florentine Giraffe: A Tale of the Italian Renaissance. Hutchinson, William Miller (1916-), illus. (Illus.). 151 p. 21cm. 1967. D. McKay Co.
--Manuel's Discovery: A Story of Bermuda. Hutchinson, William Miller (1916-), illus. LC 70-111213. (Illus.). viii, 118 p. 21cm. 1970. D. McKay Co.
--Sea Venture. 1st ed. Hutchinson, William Miller (1916-), illus. LC 59-112657. 146p. illus. 21cm. 1959. Longmans, Green.

Patz, Nancy
--Moses Supposes His Toeses Are Roses: And Seven Other Silly Old Rhymes. 1st ed. Patz, Nancy, illus. LC 82-3099. p. cm. (gr. k-3). c.1983. (ISBN 0-15-255690-7). Harcourt Brace Jovanovich.
--Nobody Knows I Have Delicate Toes. Patz, Nancy, illus. LC 79-16304. (Illus.). 32 p. 29cm. 1980. (ISBN 0-531-02392-3). F. Watts.
--Pumpernickel Tickle and Mean Green Cheese. Patz, Nancy, illus. LC 78-2915. (Illus.). 32 p. 29cm. 1978. (ISBN 0-531-02221-8). Watts.

Paul, Anthony (1941-)
--The Tiger Who Lost His Stripes. Foreman, Michael (1938-), illus. LC 81-83987. (Illus.). 32 p. 1st U.S. edition. 1982, c.1980. (ISBN 0-15-287681-2). Harcourt Brace Jovanovich.

Paul, Frances L.
--Kahtahah. Munoz, Rie (1921-), illus. LC 76-17804. (Illus., Orig.). (ps-8). 1976. (ISBN 0-88240-058-4). Alaska Northwest.

Paul, Frank A., illus.
--Blue Bug & the Bullies in Sign Language. (Illus.). 1977. (ISBN 0-917002-21-0). Joyce Media.

Paul, Jan S.
--Hortense. Linden, Madelaine Gill, illus. LC 83-45055. (Illus.). 40p. (gr. k-2). 1984. (ISBN 0-690-04370-8, TYC-J). (ISBN 0-690-04371-6). Har-Row.

Paul, Julian, jt. auth. see Yeakley, Marjory Hall.

Paul, Korky, jt. auth. see Marshall, Ray.

Paul, Leslie Allen (1905-)
--The Waters and the Wild. LC 75-9493. 181 p. 21cm. c.1975. St. Martin's Press.

Paul, Louis (1901-)
--Papa Luigi's Marionettes. Weiss, Emil (1896-1965), illus. LC 62-18468. 117p. illus. 22cm. 1st U.S. edition. 1962. I. Washburn.

Paul, Marcia, pseud., see Panzer, Martin.

Paul, Mrs.
--Children of Elf-Land. 1875. Scribner, Welford, & Armstrong.
--Hans Andersen's Fairy Tales. (Warne's Lansdowne Fairy Library). N.D. Scribner, Welford, & Armstrong.

Paul, Nance, jt. auth. see Helme, Eleanor Edith.

Paul, Paula G
--Dance with Me, Gods. LC 82-2509. p. cm. c.1982. (ISBN 0-525-66760-1). Lodester Books.
--Sarah, Sissy Weed, and the Ship of the Desert. LC 85-3818. v, 128 p. 23cm. 1985. (ISBN 0-89015-504-6). Eakin Press.
--You Can Hear a Magpie Smile. LC 80-20783. 96 p. 21cm. c.1980. (ISBN 0-525-66709-1). Elsevier/Nelson.

Paul, Sherry, jt. auth. see Miller, Bob.

Paul, Sherry (1934-)
--Blossom Bird Falls in Love. Miller, Bob, illus. (Illus.). 32p. (Orig.). (See How I Read Ser.). (ps-2). 1981. (ISBN 0-675-01081-0). Contemp Perspectives.
--Blossom Bird Falls in Love. Miller, Bob, illus. 32p. (See How I Read Ser.). (gr. 1). 1981. (ISBN 0-87895-152-0). Modern Curr.
--Blossom Bird Finds a Family. Miller, Bob, illus. (Illus.). 32p. (Orig.). (See How I Read Ser.). (ps-2). 1981. (ISBN 0-686-31343-7). Contemp Perspectives.
--Blossom Bird Finds a Family. Miller, Bob, illus. 32p. (See How I Read Ser.). (gr. 1). 1981. (ISBN 0-87895-150-4). Modern Curr.
--Blossom Bird Goes South. Miller, Bob, illus. (Illus.). 32p. (Orig.). (See How I Read Ser.). (ps-2). 1981. (ISBN 0-675-01080-2). Contemp Perspectives.
--Blossom Bird Goes South. Miller, Bob, illus. 32p. (See How I Read Ser.). (gr. 1). 1981. (ISBN 0-87895-151-2). Modern Curr.
--Two-B & the Rock & Roll Band. Miller, Bob, illus. 32p. (See How I Read Ser.). (gr. 1). 1981. (ISBN 0-87895-153-9). Modern Curr.

Pavel, Frances K. (1907-), retold by.
--The Elves and the Shoemaker. Hewitt, Joyce, illus. LC 61-5351. 26 p. illus. 24cm. (Read it Myself Book). 1961. Holt, Rinehart & Winston.
--The Frog Prince. Helms, Georgeanne, illus. LC 61-12325. 42 p. ill. 24cm. (Read it myself book). 1962. Holt, Rinehart & Winston.
--Hansel and Gretel. Kendrick, Alcy, illus. LC 60-14376. 58 p. illus. 24 cm. (Read it myself book). 1961. Holt, Rinehart and Winston.
--Peter and the Wolf. Eitzen, Allan (1928-), illus. LC 61-12324. (Illus.). 42p. 24cm. (A Read it Myself Bk.). 1962. Holt, Rinehart and Winston.
--Snow White and The Seven Dwarfs. Smith, Edward John, illus. LC 61-12326. (Illus.). 58p. 24cm. (A Read it Myself Bk.). 1962. Holt, Rinehart and Winston.
--The Ugly Duckling. Kitzmiller, Carol, illus. LC 61-5350. 58p. illus. 24cm. (Read it myself book). 1961. Holt, Rinehart and Winston.
Pavey, Anne, Mrs., ed.
--Our Little Tot's Speaker. Windes, Susan A., illus. LC 99-5711. (Containing a Choice of Poems and Jingles Dear to the Hearts of the Little Ones; Suitable for All Classes of Entertainments). 222 p. front. (port.) illus., plates. 25 cm. 1899. Imperial Publishing Company.
--Our Little Tot's Speaker. (Illus.). 224p. N.D. Monarch Book Company.
Pavey, Peter
--I'm Taggarty Toad. Pavey, Peter, illus. LC 80-16696. p. cm. 32p. 1980. (ISBN 0-87888-172-7). (ISBN 0-02-770240-5). Bradbury Press.
--One Dragon's Dream. Pavey, Peter, illus. LC 79-12008. (Illus.). 32 p. 1979, c.1978. (ISBN 0-87888-148-4). Bradbury Press.
Pavlova, N.
--Fijate y Veras. 96p. 1983. (ISBN 0-8285-2647-8, Pub. by Raduga Pubs USSR). Imported Pubns.
Pawlowska, Harriet
--Merrily We Sing. 283p. 1961. (ISBN 0-8143-1143-1). Wayne State UNiversity Press.
Paxman, Monroe, jt. auth. see Paxman, Shirley.
Paxman, Shirley & Paxman, Monroe
--To Bed to Bed the Doctor Said. Zurcher, Cheryl, illus. (Illus.). 40p. (gr. 3-10). 1975. (ISBN 0-914510-05-3). Evergreen.
Paxson, Mary Scarborough (1872-)
--Mary Paxson: Her Book. Doane, Pelagie (1906-1966), illus. LC 31-22439. 4 p. l., 3-98 p. incl. illus., plates. facsim. 20 cm. 1931. Doubleday, Doran & Company Inc.
--Mary Paxson: Her Book 1880-1884. Doane, Pelagie (1906-1966), illus. LC 36-21187. 4 p. l., 3-98 p. incl. illus., plates. facsim. 20 cm. 1936. Doubleday, Doran & Co., Inc.
Paxton, Lois
--Quiet Sound of Fear. (gr. 7-9). 1971. Hawthorn.
Paxton, Mary
--River Gold. N.D. Grosset & Dunlap.
--River Gold. Whiting, John Downes (1884-), illus. LC 28-5167. 5 p. l., 13-250, 1 p. front., plates. 21 cm. c.1928. The Bobbs-Merrill Company.
Paxton, S. H., pseud., see Smith, Ralph.
Paxton, Thomas R. see Paxton, Tom.
Paxton, Tom (1937-)
--Jennifer's Rabbit. Tripp, Wallace Whitney (1940-), illus. LC 78-110313. (Illus.). 31 p. 22cm. 1970. Putnam.
Paxton, William A
--Rhymes for Children Young and Old. LC 54-11675. 62p. illus. 22cm. 1954. Vantage Press.
Payes, Cosgrove see Cosgrove, Rachel R, pseud.
Payler, Esther Miller (1896-)
--Arrows Over Jamestown. 1 st. ed. LC 56-129183. 83p. 21cm. 1957. Vantage Press.
Payn, James
--Travels and Adventures, No.33. (Lakeside Library Ser.). N.D. Donnelley, Loyd & Co.
Payne
--Across the Water. N.D. Bradley & Woodruff.
--Where the Rockies Ride Herd. N.D. The Swallow Press.
Payne, A. M. M.
--One Winter's Work: A Temperance Tale, 1 of 25 vols. (Illus.). (Selected Bks for Sunday School: The/Avondale Library). N.D. Set. Methodist Bk Concern.
Payne, Annie Mitchell
--The Cash Boy's Trust. N.D. Robert Carter & Brothers.
--The Odd One. N.D. Robert Carter & Brothers.
--Outside the Walls. N.D. Robert Carter.
--Rhoda's Corner. 1873. Robert Carter & Brothers.
Payne, Bernal C., Jr.
--It's About Time. LC 83-24910. 170 p. 22cm. c.1984. (ISBN 0-02-770230-8). Macmillan.
Payne, Bruce R., jt. ed. see Mims, Edwin.
Payne, Darwin R., retold by see Wilde, Oscar Fingal O'Flahertie Wills.
Payne, Darwin Reid, jt. ed. see Moe, Christian Hollis.
Payne, Donald Gordon see Gordon, Donald, pseud.
Payne, Emmy, pseud., see West, Emily Govan.
Payne, Emmy, pseud. (1919-)
--Johnny Groundhog's Shadow. West, Emily Govan. Pascal, Theo, illus. LC 48-6107. (Illus.). 29cm. 32p. 1948. Houghton Mifflin Co.
--Katy No-Pocket. West, Emily Govan. 1944. (ISBN 0-8382-0400-7, Cadmus Books). E. M. Hale And Company.
--Katy No-Pocket. West, Emily Govan. Rey, Hans Augusto (1898-1977), illus. LC 44-8099. 32 p. col. illus. 28 1/2 x 23 1/2 cm. 1944. Houghton Mifflin Company.
Payne, Fanny Ursula (1875-)
--Plays for Anychild. LC 18-14353. 8 p. l., 5-144, 1 p. front. 20 cm. c.1918. Harper & Brothers.
Payne, Grace Visher
--The Khanum and Her Treasures. 1958. Friendship Press.
Payne, Joan Balfour, jt. auth. see Justus, May.
Payne, Joan Balfour (1923-1973)
--Ambrose. Payne, Joan Balfour (1923-1973), illus. LC 56-8122. (Illus.). 48 p. 28cm. 1956. Hastings House.
--Charlie from Yonder. Payne, Joan Balfour (1923-1973), illus. LC 62-16191. (Illus.). 46 p. 25cm. 1962. Hastings House.
--General Billycock's Pigs. Payne, Joan Balfour (1923-1973), illus. LC 60-16951. (Illus.). 62 p. 25cm. 1961. Hastings House.
--The Leprechaun of Bayou Luce. Payne, Joan Balfour (1923-1973), illus. LC 57-107331. 60p. illus. 25cm. 1957. Hastings House.
--Leprechaun of Bayou Luce. Payne, Joan Balfour (1923-1973), illus. LC 57-10733. (Illus.). 40 drawings. 64p. (gr. 2-4). 1969. (ISBN 0-8038-4227-9). Hastings.
--Magnificent Milo. Payne, Joan Balfour (1923-1973), illus. LC 58-8278. (Illus.). 64 p. 27cm. 1958. Hastings House.
--Pangur Ban. Payne, Joan Balfour (1923-1973), illus. LC 66-11900. (Illus.). 46p. (gr. 2-4). 1966. (ISBN 0-8038-5693-8). Hastings.
--The Piebald Princess. Payne, Joan Balfour (1923-1973), illus. LC 54-5892. (Illus.). 79 p. 24cm. 1954. Ariel Books.
--The Piebald Princess. Payne, Joan Balfour (1923-1973), illus. N.D. E. M. Hale and Co.
Payne, Joan Balfour (1923-1973), retold by.
--The Raven, and Other Fairy Tales. Payne, Joan Balfour (1923-1973), illus. LC 72-81379. (Illus.). 51 p. 27cm. 1969. Hastings House.
Payne, John
--Arabian Nights: The Book of Thousand Night and Night, 9 Vols. (Illus.). N.D. Worthington Company.
Payne, Josephine Balfour
--The Journey of Josiah talltatters. Payne, Joan Balfour (1923-1973), illus. N.D. E . M. Hale and Co.
--The Journey of Josiah Taltatters. Payne, Joan Balfour (1923-1973), illus. LC 52-123786. 51p. illus. 22x26cm. c.1953. Ariel Books.
--The Last Giant. Payne, Joan Balfour (1923-1973), illus. LC 47-4822. 54 p. illus. 23 cm. 1947. G. P. Putnam's Sons.
--The Little Green Island. Payne, Joan Balfour (1923-1973), illus. LC 42-22140. 32 p. illus. 22 1/2 cm. 1942. G. P. Putnam's Sons.
--Once There was Olga. Payne, Joan Balfour (1923-1973), illus. LC 44-6670. 44, 1 p. illus. 20 1/2 cm. 1944. G. P. Putnam's Sons.
--The Sable that Stayed. Payne, Joan Balfour (1923-1973), illus. N.D. E. M. Hale & Co.
--The Stable that Stayed. Payne, Joan Balfour (1923-1973), illus. LC 52-5922. (Illus.). 47 p. 24cm. 1952. Ariel Books.
Payne, Lucile Vaughan
--The Boy Upstairs and other Stories. LC 65-238028. 183p. 22cm. c.1965. (ISBN 0-695-40813-5). Follett.
Payne, Marvin & Randle, Guy (1951-)
--The Planemaker. LC 83-14197. p. cm. c.1983. (ISBN 0-912085-03-7). Ensign Productions.
Payne, Nina
--All the Day Long. 1st ed. Schindelman, Laurel, illus. LC 73-76328. (Illus.). 34 p. 23cm. 1973. (ISBN 0-689-30117-0). Atheneum.
Payne, Sherry Neuwirth
--A Contest. Kyle, Jeff, illus. LC 81-15440. (Illus.). 40 p. 19cm. c.1982. (ISBN 0-87614-176-9). Carolrhoda Books.
Payne, Stephen
--Teen-age Cowboy Stories. (The Teen-age Library). N.D. Grosset & Dunlap.
--Teen-Age Cowboy Stories. Haff, Drayton S., illus. LC 49-10656. 256 p. illus. 21 cm. (teen-age library. 1949. Lantern Press.
--Teen-age Stories of the West. (The Teen-age Library). N.D. Grosset & Dunlap.
--Teen-Age Stories of the West. Margulies, Leo (1900-1975), intro. by. LC 49-1065. 253 p. illus. 21 cm. (Teen-age library). 1947. Lantern Press.
--Young Hero of the Range. Geer, Charles Hand (1922-), illus. LC 54-7282. 191p. illus. 21cm. (Young heroes library). 1954. Lantern Press.
--Young Readers Stories of the West. Geer, Charles Hand (1922-), illus. LC 52-6044. 192 p. illus. 21 cm. (Young readers bookshelf). 1951. Lantern Press.
Payson, Dale (1943-)
--Almost Twins. Payson, Dale (1943-), illus. LC 74-5044. (Illus.). 32 p. 23cm. 1974. (ISBN 0-13-022780-3). Prentice-Hall.
Payson, Dale (1943-) & Wyatt, Karen, eds.
--The Sleepy Time Treasury. Payson, Dale (1943-), illus. LC 75-11624. 64 16 x 24. 1975. (ISBN 0-13-812891-X). Prentice-Hall.
Payson, Edward
--Doctor Tom. N.D. Dresser, McLellan & Co.
Payson, Elizabeth Payson (1818-1878)
--Little Susie's Little Servants. N.D. A. D. F. Randolph.
Payson, Frances & Kendrick, Vane
--Down Among the Fairies. N.D. T. S. Denison.
Payson, Lieut. Howard, pseud., see Goldfrap, John Henry.
Payson, Lieut. Howard, pseud. (1879-1917)
--The Boy Scouts and the Army Airship. Goldfrap, John Henry. (Payson's Boy Scout Ser.). N.D. A L Burt Co.
--The Boy Scouts at the Canadian Border. Goldfrap, John Henry. (Payson's Boy Scout Ser.). N.D. A L Burt Co.
--The Boy Scouts at the Panama Canal. Goldfrap, John Henry. (Payson's Boy Scout Ser.). N.D. A L Burt Co.
--The Boy Scouts at the Panama Canal. Goldfrap, John Henry. (The Boy Scout Ser.). N.D. Hurst & Co.
--The Boy Scouts at the Panama-Pacific Exposition. Goldfrap, John Henry. (The Boy Scout Ser.). N.D. Hurst & Co.
--The Boy Scouts at the Panama-Pacific Exposition. Goldfrap, John Henry. Wrenn, Charles L., illus. (Payson's Boy Scout Ser.). N.D. A L Burt Co.
--The Boy Scouts' Badge of Courage. Goldfrap, John Henry. (Payson's Boy Scout Ser.). N.D. A L Burt Co.
--The Boy Scouts' Campaign for Preparedness. Goldfrap, John Henry. (Payson's Boy Scout Ser.). N.D. A L Burt Co.
--The Boy Scouts for Uncle Sam. Goldfrap, John Henry. Wrenn, Charles L., illus. (Payson's Boy Scout Ser.). N.D. A L Burt Co.
--The Boy Scouts' Mountain Camp. Goldfrap, John Henry. (Payson's Boy Scout Ser.). N.D. A L Burt Co.
--The Boy Scouts' Mountain Camp. Goldfrap, John Henry. (The Boy Scout Ser.). N.D. Hurst & Co.
--The Boy Scouts on Belgian Battlefields. Goldfrap, John Henry. (The Boy Scout Ser.). N.D. Hurst & Co.
--The Boy Scouts on Belgian Battlefields. Goldfrap, John Henry. Wrenn, Charles L., illus. (Payson's Boy Scout Ser.). N.D. A L Burt Co.
--The Boy Scouts on the Eagle Patrol. Goldfrap, John Henry. (Payson's Boy Scout Ser.). N.D. A L Burt Co.
--The Boy Scouts Under Fire in Mexico. Goldfrap, John Henry. (The Boy Scout Ser.). N.D. Hurst & Co.
--The Boy Scouts Under Sealed Orders. Goldfrap, John Henry. (Payson's Boy Scout Ser.). N.D. A L Burt Co.
--The Boy Scouts with the Allies in France. Goldfrap, John Henry. (Payson's Boy Scout Ser.). N.D. A L Burt Co.
--The Boy Scouts With the Allies in France. Goldfrap, John Henry. (The Boy Scout Ser.). N.D. Hurst & Co.
--The Motor Cycle Chums Around the World. Goldfrap, John Henry. Wrenn, Charles L., illus. LC 12-14114. 288 p. front., plates. 20 cm. (The Motor Cycle Ser.). c.1912. Hurst & Company.
--The Motor Cycle Chums in the Gold Fields. Goldfrap, John Henry. Wrenn, Charles L., illus. LC 12-24625. 288 p. front., plates. 20 cm. (The Motor Cycle Ser.). c.1912. Hurst & Company.
--The Motor Cycle Chums of the Northwest Patrol. Goldfrap, John Henry. Wrenn, Charles L., illus. LC 12-17207. 301 p. front., plates. 20 cm. (The Motor Cycle Ser.). c.1912. Hurst & Company.
--The Motor Cycle Chums South of the Equator. Goldfrap, John Henry. (The Motor Cycle Ser.). N.D. Hurst & Co.
--The Motor Cycle Chums through Historic America. Goldfrap, John Henry. (Illus.). (The Motor Cycle Ser.). N.D. Hurst & Co.
--The Motor Cycle Chums Whirlwind Tour. Goldfrap, John Henry. (Illus.). (The Motor Cycle Ser.). N.D. Hurst & Co.
Payton, Colleen M.
--The Adventures of Wilbur H. Worm & His Friends. 1983. (ISBN 0-8062-2254-9). Carlton.
Payzant, Charles
--Moko, the Circus Monkey. Parmelee, Ted, illus. LC 52-675332. unpaged. illus. 21cm. (Jolly books, 202). 1952. Avon Pub. Co.
--The Sea Searchers. 1968. (ISBN 0-516-08853-X). Childrens Press.
--Windows in the Sea. 1973. (ISBN 0-516-08876-9). Childrens Press.
Payzant, Charles, jt. auth. see Shannon, Terry.
Peabody, Elizabeth P, ed. see Froebel, Friedrich Wilhelm August.
Peabody, Josephine Preston (1874-1922)
--Old Greek Folk-Stories Told Anew. LC 12-37444. 3 p. l., 123 p. 18 cm. (Riverside Literature Series. No. 114). c.1897. Houghton, Mifflin and Company.
Peabody, Leila Rose (1867-)
--A Little book of Verse. 1912. Sherman French & Co.
Peachey, Caroline, tr. see Andersen, Hans Christian.
Peachy, Caroline, tr. see Andersen, Hans Christian.
Peacock, Margaret
--Use-Over Nursery Rhymes. Langworthy, Emma, ed. Strimple, Helen, illus. LC 40-34373. (Music, Piano-Xylophone; Pictures. Color the same picture as often as you like, mistakes rub off with ease. A fascinating educational book in four colors; Pictures, Stories, Poems, Music). cover-title, 40 p. illus. (part col.) 27 1/2 x 22 cm. c.1940. Hand-Craft Industries.
Peake, Elmore Elliott (1871-)
--The Little King of Angel's Landing. LC 6-34050. 4 p. l., 228 p. front., 3 pl. 20 cm. 1906. D. Appleton and Company.
Peake, Helena
--The Boy's Books of Heroes, 1 of 15 vols. (Illus.). (Warne's Daring Deeds Library: No. 6). N.D. Scribner & Welford.
Peake, Katy
--The Indian Heart of Carrie Hodges. 1st Ed. ed. Allen, Thomas Burt (1928-), illus. LC 72-80518. (Illus.). 125 p. 22cm. 1972. (ISBN 0-670-39788-1). Viking Press.
Peake, Mervyn Laurence, jt. auth. see Dodgson, Charles Lutwidge.
Peake, Mervyn Laurence, jt. auth. see Stevenson, Robert Louis.
Peake, Mervyn Lawrence (1911-1968)
--Captain Slaughterboard Drops Anchor. Peake, Mervyn Lawrence (1911-1968), illus. LC 67-15095. (Illus.). 48 p. 27cm. 1967, c.1939. Macmillan.
--Captain Slaughterboard Drops Anchor. Peake, Mervyn Lawrence (1911-1968), illus. N.D. Transatlantic Arts, Inc.
Peake, Mervyn Lawrence (1911-1968), illus.
--Ride a Cock-Horse and other Nursey Rhymes. LC 75-509235. (Illus.). 32p. 1st U.S. edition. (ps-2). 1979. (ISBN 0-7011-5015-7, Pub. by Chatto Bodley Jonathan). (ISBN 0-7011-1945-4, Pub. by Chatto Bodley Jonathan). Merrimack Pub Cir.
Peale, Norman Vincent (1898-)
--Bible Stories. Grabianski, Janusz (1928-1976), illus. LC 73-4481. (gr. 1 up). 1973. (ISBN 0-531-02634-5). Watts.
--He Was a Child. Busoni, Rafaello (1900-1962), illus. LC 57-12422. unpaged. illus. 25cm. 1957. Prentice Hall.
Pearce, Ann Philippa, jt. auth. see Fairfax-Lucy, Brian.
Pearce, Ann Philippa (1920-)
--The Battle of Bubble & Squeak. 5 3/8 x 8 13/16. (16-18 pt.). N.D (Pub. by Lythway Lg Print Bks). G K Hall.
--Battle of Bubble & Squeak. Baker, Alan (1951-), illus. (Illus.). 21cm. 82p. (gr. 2-7). 1978. (ISBN 0-233-96986-1). Andre Deutsch.
--A Dog So Small. LC 63-9869. (Illus.). 142 p. 23cm. 1963, c.1962. Lippincott. **Award: (ALA).**
--Lion at School and Other Stories. Sharpe, Caroline (1947-), illus. LC 85-17588. p. cm. c.1985. (ISBN 0-688-05996-1). Greenwillow Books.
--The Minnow Leads to Treasure. Ardizzone, Edward Jeffrey Irving (1900-1979), illus. LC 79-18256. p. cm. (Gregg Press Children's Literature Series). 1979, c.1958. (ISBN 0-8398-2609-5). Gregg Press.
--The Minnow Leads to Treasure. Ardizzone, Edward Jeffrey Irving (1900-1979), illus. LC 58-5773. (Illus.). 253 p. 22cm. 1958. World Pub. Co. **Award: (ALA).**
--Mrs. Cockle's Cat. Maitland, Antony Jasper (1935-), illus. LC 61-14298. (Illus.). 26cm. (gr. k-3). 1962. (ISBN 0-397-30622-9). Lippincott. **Award: (KGM).**
--The Shadow-Cage, and Other Tales of the Supernatural. Lewin, Ted (1935-), illus. LC 77-3174. 21cm. 152p. 1977. (ISBN 0-690-01396-5). Crowell.
--The Squirrel Wife. Collard, Derek, illus. LC 70-168556. (Illus.). 61 p. 22cm. 1972, c.1971. (ISBN 0-690-76678-5). (ISBN 0-690-76679-3). Crowell. **Award: (ALA).**
--Tom's Midnight Garden. Einzig, Susan (1922-), illus. 240p. 1959. J B Lippincott Company. **Award: (CMA).**
--Tom's Midnight Garden. Einzig, Susan (1922-), illus. LC 59-16380. 229p. illus. 23cm. 1959, c.1958. Oxford University Press.

AUTHOR INDEX PEASE, CLARENCE

--The Way to Sattin Shore. Voake, Charlotte, illus. LC 83-14152. (Illus.). 192p. c.1983. (ISBN 0-688-02319-3). (ISBN 0-688-02320-7). (ISBN 0-688-02320-7). Greenwillow Books. **Award: (ALA).**
--The Way to Sattin Shore. Voake, Charlotte, illus. LC 84-23729. (Illus.). 190 p. 18cm. 1985, c.1983. (ISBN 0-14-031644-2). Puffin Books.
--What the Neighbors Did, and Other Stories. Jaques, Faith (1923-), illus. LC 73-3170. (Illus.). 130 p. 21cm. 1st U.S. edition. 1973, c.1972. (ISBN 0-690-87932-6). (ISBN 0-690-87933-4). Crowell. **Award: (ALA).**

Pearce, Ann Philippa (1920-), retold by.
--Beauty and the Beast. Barrett, Alan, illus. LC 71-188314. (Illus.). 41 p. 22cm. 1972. (ISBN 0-690-12561-5). (ISBN 0-690-12562-3). Crowell.

Pearce, C. E.
--The Golden Island. 168p. N.D. American News Co.

Pearce, Jessie H., illus.
--Aunt Reesie and the Triplets. 1st ed. LC 54-9056. (Illus.). 21cm. 30p. 1954. Exposition Press.

Pearce, Samuel W.
--The Boy Yacthsman: Or, The Cruise of the "Storm King". 1 p. l., 5-128 p. 19 cm. (On cover: The Boy's Dashaway Ser., No. 12). c.1893. G. Munro's Sons.

Pearce, William Houghton Sprague (1864-)
--Toot! Toot! Puff! Puff! Ding! Dong!. Pearce, William Houghton Sprague (1864-), illus. LC 34-503. (Illus.). 31cm. 32p. 1934. Stoll & Einson Games Inc.

Peard, Frances Mary (1835-1923)
--The Abbot's Bridge. N.D. Thomas Whittaker.
--The Blue Dragon. N.D. Thomas Whittaker.
--Jacob and the Raven. N.D. E. P. Dutton & Co.
--The Locked Desk. N.D. Thomas Whittaker.
--Mademoiselle. 260p. N.D. E. P. Dutton & Co.
--Mother Molly. (Queen's Treasures Ser.). N.D. Harcourt Brace & Co.
--Prentice Hugh. N.D. Thomas Whittaker.
--Scapegrace Dick. N.D. Thomas Whittaker.
--To Horse and Away. N.D. Thomas Whittaker.

Peare, Catherine Owens (1911-)
--The Lost Lakes. Bjorklund, Lorence F. (1913-1978), illus. (Illus.). 20cm. 122p. 1967, c.1963. Scholastic.
--The Lost Lakes: A Story of the Texas Rangers. 1st ed. Bjorklund, Lorence F. (1913-1978), illus. LC 53-960958. 176p. illus. 22cm. (Winston Adventure Bks). 1953. Winston.
--Melor, King Arthur's Page. Frame, Paul (1913-), illus. LC 63-9685. 157p. illus. 21cm. c.1963. Putnam.

Pearl, Christie
--Little Sheaves for Little Gleaners. 234p. (Golden Sheaves Library). N.D. Lockwood, Brooks, & Co. for American Tract Society.

Pearl, Elaine W.
--Mouse That Smiled. N.D. (ISBN 0-685-46202-1). Vantage.

Pearl, Jack, pseud., see Pearl, Jacques Bain.

Pearl, Jack, pseud. (1923-)
--Bruce Larkin: Air Force Cadet. Pearl, Jacques Bain. LC 62-10581. 205p. illus. 22cm. (Young Falcons Ser.). 1962. C. S. Hammond.
--The Young Falcons. Pearl, Jacques Bain. LC 62-15658. 219p. 22cm. (His Young Falcons Ser.). 1962. C. S. Hammond.

Pearl, Jacques Bain see Pearl, Jack, pseud.

Pearl, Minnie & Cannon, Sarah O.
--Christmas at Grinders Switch. (gr. 7 up). N.D. (ISBN 0-687-07754-0). Abingdon.

Pearlberg, Deborah
--Wembley Fraggle Gets the Story. Schindler, Steven D., illus. LC 84-6586. (Illus.). (Fraggle Rock Ser.). (gr. 1-4). 1984. (ISBN 0-03-000718-6). HR&W.

Pearn, Violet A
--The Invisible Playmate: A Play in Three Acts. Cyphus, Henry, contrib. by. LC 30-12636. (Music by Henry Cyphus and Barbara Thornley). 65, 1 p. diagr. 22 cm. (On cover: French's Acting edition, No. 1736). c.1930. S. French, Ltd.

Pearsall, William
--Junior Skipper. (gr. 5 up). N.D. (ISBN 0-448-25930-3). G&D.

Pearse, Mark Guy
--Mister Horn and His Friends: Or, Givers and Giving. (Illus.). 180p. 1876. Nelson & Phillips.

Pearse, S B
--Mother Goose Fun. (The Pearse Mother Goose). N.D. Frederick A Stokes Co.
--Mother Goose Jingles. (The Pearse Mother Goose). N.D. Frederick A Stokes Co.
--Mother Goose Rhymes. (The Pearse Mother Goose). N.D. Frederick A Stokes.
--Mother Goose Verses. (The Pearse Mother Goose). N.D. Frederick A Stokes Co.
--Tinker, Tailor. N.D. George Sully & Co.

Pearson, Adelaide
--The Laughing Lion and other Stories. Bromhall, Winifred, illus. LC 21-199560. xiii, 196 p. incl. illus., plates. col. front. 20 cm. c.1921. E. P. Dutton & Company.

Pearson, Bill (1922-)
--Olive & Swee' Pea Wash Up!. Mann, Philip Alan (1934-), ed. Wildman, George, illus. (Illus.). 14p. (Shape Board Play Book). (gr. k-3). 1980. (ISBN 0-89828-126-1). Tuffy Bks.
--Popeye & His Pals Stay in Shape. Mann, Philip Alan (1934-), ed. Wildman, George, illus. (Illus.). 14p. (Shape Board Play Book). (gr. k-3). 1980. (ISBN 0-89828-125-3). Tuffy Bks.

Pearson, Carol Lynn (1944-)
--I Believe in Make Believe. (Orig.). 1984. (ISBN 0-87602-255-7). Anchorage.
--Today, Tomorrow, & Four Weeks from Tuesday. LC 83-71869. c.1983. (ISBN 0-88494-496-4). Bookcraft.

Pearson, Charles Henry (1830-1894)
--The Cabin on the Prairie. (Illus.). (Famous Books for Boys). N.D. H. M. Caldwell Co.
--The Cabin on the Prairie, 1 of 50 vols. (Illus.). (The Norwood Ser.: No. 34). 1900. Lee & Shepard.
--The Cabin on the Prairie, 1 of 5. (Illus.). 299p. (The Frontier Ser.). N.D. Lee & Shepard.
--The Young Pioneers. (Illus.). (Famous Books for Boys). N.D. H. C. Caldwell Co.
--The Young Pioneers of the North-West. LC 7-35804. 1 p. l., 7-331 p. plates. 18 cm. (Frontier Ser.). 1871. Lee and Shepard.
--The Young Pioneers of the Northwest. (Frontier Ser.). N.D. Colby and Rich.
--The Young Pioneers of the Northwest, 1 of 50 vols. (Illus.). (The Norwood Ser.: No. 35). 1900. Lee & Shepard.

Pearson, Edmund Lester (1880-1937)
--The Believing Years. LC 11-24405. ix, 303 p. 18 cm. 1911. The Macmillan Company.
--The Voyage of the Hoppergrass. 5 p. l., 348 p. front., illus. 20 cm. 1924. The Macmillan Company.
--The Voyage of the Hoppergrass. Fogarty, Thomas (1873-), illus. LC 13-22818. 5 p. l., 348 p. illus. 20 cm. 1913. The Macmillan Company.

Pearson, Elizabeth J., jt. ed. see Brodkin, Sylvia Z.

Pearson, Francis Bail (1853-) & Paschall, Alma
--The Thrift Twins. Warren, Elizabeth B., illus. LC 22-117. 4 p. l., 147 p. front., plates. 20 cm. c.1921. The Bobbs-Merrill Company.

Pearson, Gilbert T.
--Stories of Bird Life. (Illus.). N.D. B. F. Johnson Publishing Co.

Pearson, Helen C.
--Roy's Search: Or, Lost in the Cars. 364p. N.D. National Temperance Society Pub.

Pearson, John (1934-), illus.
--Begin Sweet World. LC 75-9228. (Illus.). 112 p. 28cm. 1976. (ISBN 0-385-11065-0). Doubleday.

Pearson, M. Jeanne
--A Pony in the Yard. Pearson, Charles E. & Pearson, Jeanne, illus. LC 78-154345. (Illus.). 32 p. 29cm. 1971. (ISBN 0-513-01152-8). T. S. Denison.
--Pony of the Sioux. 1st ed. Pfeufer, Carl, illus. LC 61-9756. (Illus.). 143 p. 22cm. (Signal book). 1961. Doubleday.
--Ride the Red-Eyed Wind. Pearson, Charles E., illus. LC 78-2206. (Illus.). 175 p. 22cm. c.1978. (ISBN 0-87518-157-0). Dillon Press.

Pearson, Michael, jt. ed. see Williams-Ellis, Amabel, Mrs.

Pearson, Molly Winston, Mrs. (1876-) & Bullis, Franklin Howard (1860-)
--Injuns Comin'!. Hurd, Peter (1904-1984), illus. LC 35-206732. x p., 1 l., 300 p. incl. illus., plates. 21 cm. 1935. C. Scribner's Sons.

Pearson, Mrs., jt. auth. see Ruskin, John.

Pearson, Mrs., jt. auth. see Sharpe, Richard Scrafton.

Pearson, Mrs. & Sharpe, Richard Scrafton (0000-1852)
--Dame Wiggins of Lee and Her Seven Wonderful Cats: A Famous Ballad, Told and Sung in England. Meldrum, Roy, illus. LC 25-26906. 2 p. l., 9-76 p. col. illus. 17 cm. (Little library). 1925. The Macmillan Company.
--Dame Wiggins of Lee and Her Seven Wonderful Cats: A Humorous Tale Written Principally by a Lady of Ninety. Marshall, Francesca, adapted by. LC 10-25831. 90 p. illus. 20 cm. c.1908. Educational Publishing Co.

Pearson, Pauline Stewart
--Ski Town: A Children's Story of Life in the Black Hills. LC 52-12345. 94 p. 21 cm. 1952. Exposition Press.

Pearson, Ronald Hooke (1915-)
--A Seal Flies by. rev. ed. (Illus.). (gr. 6-9). 1967. (ISBN 0-8027-6064-3). Walker & Co.

Pearson, Susan (1946-)
--Everybody Knows That!. Paterson, Diane R. Cole (1946-), illus. LC 78-51311. (Illus.). 32 p. 24cm. c.1978. (ISBN 0-8037-2417-9). (ISBN 0-8037-2418-7). Dial Press.
--Happy Birthday, Grampie, I Love You. Dillon, Leo (1933-) & Dillon, Diane (1933-), illus. LC 78-51327. p. cm. c.1978. (ISBN 0-8037-3457-3). Dial Press.
--Izzie. Parker, Robert Andrew (1927-), illus. LC 74-18597. (Illus.). 40 p. 1975. (ISBN 0-8037-4904-X). (ISBN 0-8037-4905-8). Dial Press.
--Karin's Christmas Walk. Noble, Trinka Hakes, illus. LC 80-11739. p. cm. c.1980. (ISBN 0-440-74431-8). (ISBN 0-440-74432-6). Dial Press.
--Molly Moves Out. Kellogg, Steven (1941-), illus. LC 78-31840. (Illus.). 64 p. 23cm. c.1979. (ISBN 0-8037-5802-2). (ISBN 0-8037-5803-0). Dial Press.
--Monday I Was an Alligator. Murdocca, Salvatore, illus. LC 78-23618. (Illus.). 40 p. 24cm. (Lippincott I-like-to-read book). c.1979. (ISBN 0-397-31830-8). Lippincott.
--Monnie Hates Lydia. Paterson, Diane R. Cole (1946-), illus. LC 75-9198. (Illus.). 32 p. 1975. (ISBN 0-8037-5443-4). (ISBN 0-8037-5445-0). Dial Press.
--Saturday, I Ran Away. Jeschke, Susan (1942-), illus. 1981. (ISBN 0-397-31958-4). Har-Row.
--That's Enough for One Day, J. P.!. Chorao, Ann Mckay Sproat (1936-), illus. LC 76-42923. (Illus.). 32 p. 21cm. c.1977. (ISBN 0-8037-8566-6). (ISBN 0-8037-8567-4). Dial Press.

Pearson, Tracey Campbell
--Old MacDonald Had a Farm. Pearson, Tracey Campbell, illus. LC 83-18815. (Illus.). 32p. (ps-2). 1984. (ISBN 0-8037-0068-7). (ISBN 0-8037-0070-9). (ISBN 0-8037-0070-9). Dial Bks for Young Readers.
--Sing a Song of Sixpence. Pearson, Tracey Campbell, illus. LC 84-14206. (Illus.). 26 p. c.1985. (ISBN 0-8037-0151-9). (ISBN 0-8037-0152-7). Dial Books for Young Readers.
--We Wish You a Merry Christmas. Pearson, Tracey Campbell, illus. LC 82-22224. (Illus.). 32p. (Dial Book for Young Readers Ser.). 1983. (ISBN 0-8037-9368-5). (ISBN 0-8037-9400-2). Dutton.

Pearson, Violet T., jt. auth. see Walter, Frances.

Pearson, Wanda Lynn
--Buttons and His Sunday Coat. Cobb, Betty, illus. LC 59-5606. (Illus.). 32 p. 24cm. 1959. (ISBN 0-8114-7507-7). Steck Co.

Pearson, William Harris see Pearson, Bill.

Peart, Hendry
--The Loyal Grenvilles. 1st ed. Powers, Richard M. Gorman (1921-), illus. LC 58-994031. 207p. illus. 22cm. 1958. (ISBN 0-394-81365-0). Knopf.
--Red Falcons of Tremoine. Brevannes, Maurice (1904-), illus. LC 56-8895. (Illus.). 22cm. 244p. (gr. 5-9). 1956. (ISBN 0-394-91537-2). Knopf.

Peary, Marie Ahnighito, jt. auth. see Peary, Robert Edwin.

Peary, Marie Ahnighito (1893-1978)
--Little Tooktoo: The Story of Santa Claus' Youngest Reindeer. Wiese, Kurt (1887-1974), illus. LC 30-25121. 5 p. l., 9-62 p. col. front., illus., col. plates. 23 cm. c.1930. W. Morrow & Co.
--Ootah and His Puppy. Wiese, Kurt (1887-1974), illus. LC 42-9590. 64 p. incl. col. front., illus. (part col.) 21-1/2 cm. (Half-title: New World Neighbors). c.1942. D.C. Heath and Company.
--Over the Moon. (Folk Lore & Fairy Tales). (MacMillan Bks. for Boys & Girls). (gr. 4-6). N.D. MacMillan Bks..
--The Red Caboose with Peary in the Arctic. Rev ed. Horvath, Ferdinand Huszti (1891-), illus. LC 32-28090. 128 p. incl. col. front., illus., col. plates. 19 cm. 1932. W. Morrow & Company.

Peary, Robert Edwin (1856-1920)
--Adventures of Uncle Sam's Sailors. LC 7-34286. x. 1 p. front., 7 pl. 18 1/2 cm. (On verse of l.-p.: Harper's Adventure Series). 1907. Harper & Brothers.

Peary, Robert Edwin (1856-1920) & Peary, Marie Ahnighito (1893-1978)
--Snowland Folk: The Eskimos, the Bears, the Dogs, the Musk Oxen, and Other Dwellers in the Frozen North. Peary, Robert Edwin (1856-1920) & Operti, Albert, illus. 1 p. l., 7-97 p. front., illus. 27 x 20 cm. 1904. F. A. Stokes Company.

Pease, Clarence Howard see Pease, Howard,

Pease, Clarence Howard (1894-1974)
--The Black Tanker: The Adventures of a Landlubber on the Illfated Last Voyage of the Oil Tank Steamer "Zambora". Fischer, Anton Otto (1882-), illus. LC 41-51814. 5 p. l., 3-312 p. col. front. 21 cm. 1941. (ISBN 0-385-07228-7). Doubleday, Doran & Company, Inc.
--Bound for "Singapore". Being a True & Faithful Account of the Making of an Adventurer. Fischer, Anton Otto (1882-), illus. LC 48-8749. 21cm. 243p. (gr. 7-11). 1948. Doubleday Bks.
--Captain of the Araby: The Story of a Voyage. Fischer, Anton Otto (1882-), illus. LC 53-5296. 247 p. 21cm. 1953. Doubleday.
--Captain Pinnacle. Pont, Charles Ernest (1898-), illus. LC 38-20647. vi, 160 p. incl. illus., plates. 22 cm. 1938. Dodd, Mead & Company.
--Dark Adventure. Fischer, Anton Otto (1882-), illus. (gr. 7-11). 1950. (ISBN 0-385-07275-9). Doubleday.
--Foghorns. Fischer, Anton Otto (1882-), illus. LC 37-29658. (A Story of the San Francisco Water Front). 3 p. l., v-vi, 295 p. col. front. 21 cm. 1937. Doubleday, Doran & Company, Inc.
--The Gypsy Caravan. Wood, Harrie (1902-), illus. LC 30-21863. (Being the Merry Tale of the Travels of Betty and Joe With the Gypsies--Their Amazing Adventures with Robin Hood--with Richard the Lion-Hearted--with Roland--and Sundry Other Great and Famous Persons.). ix p., 2 l., 3-254 p. incl. illus., plates. col. front. 21 cm. 1930. Doubleday, Doran & Company, Inc.
--The Gypsy Caravan. Wood, Harrie (1902-), illus. LC 46-8612. (Being the Merry Tale of the Travels of Betty and Joe, with the Gypsies--Their Amazing Adventures with Robin Hood--with Richard the Lion-Hearted--with Roland--and Sundry Other Great and Famous Persons.). ix p., 2 l. 3-254 p. incl. illus., plates. front.20 1/2 cm. (Young Moderns). 1946. Doubleday & Company, Inc.
--Heart of Danger. Fischer, Anton Otto (1882-), illus. LC 46-73902. (A Tale of Adventure on Land and Sea with Tod Moran, Third Mate of the Tramp Steamer "Araby."). 6 p. l., 3-336 p. 20 1/2 cm. 1946. (ISBN 0-385-07315-1). Doubleday & Company, Inc.
Highroad to Adventure. Dobias, Frank (1902-), illus. LC 39-337443. (What Happened to Tod Moran When He Traveled South into Old Mexico). vi p., 1 l., 297 p. 21 cm. 1939. Doubleday, Doran & Co., Incorporated.
--Hurricane Weather. Fischer, Anton Otto (1882-), illus. LC 36-27441. (How Stan Ridley Met Adventure on the Trading Schooner "Wind-Rider."). 3 p. l., v-vi, 296 p. col. front. 21 cm. 1936. Doubleday, Doran & Co., Inc.
--The Jinx Ship. LC 46-7652. (The Dark Adventure that Befell Tod Morgan When He Shipped As Fireman Aboard the Tramp Steamer "Congo," Bound Out of New York for Caribbean Ports). viii p., 1 l., 324 p. 1 illus. 20 1/2 cm. (Young moderns). 1946. (ISBN 0-385-07320-8). Doubleday & Co., Inc.
--The Jinx Ship. Blaine, Mahlon, illus. LC 27-25541. (The Dark Adventure that Belfell Tod Moran When He Shipped as Fireman Aboard the Tramp Steamer "Congo," Bound Out of New York for Caribbean Ports). viii p., 1 l., 324 p. col. front. 21 cm. 1927. Doubleday, Page & Company.
--The Jinx Ship. Fischer, Anton Otto (1882-), illus. LC 37-210382. (The Dark Adventure that Belfell Tod Morgan When He Shipped as Fireman Aboard the Tramp Steamer "Congo," Bound Out of New York for Caribbean Ports). viii p., 1 l., 324 p. col. front., 1 illus. 21 cm. (Young Moderns Bookshelf). 1937. The Sun Dial Press, Inc.
--Jungle River. Sperry, Armstrong W. (1897-1976), illus. LC 38-28913. 5 p. l., 295 p. col. front. 21 cm. 1938. Doubleday, Doran & Company, Inc.
--Long Wharf: A Story of Young San Francisco. Lee, Manning de Villeneuve (1894-1980), illus. LC 39-993424. 6 p. l., 219 p. illus. 23 cm. 1939. Dodd, Mead & Company.
--Long Wharf: A Story of Young San Francisco. Lee, Manning de Villeneuve (1894-1980), illus. LC 47-20167. 6 p. l. 219 p. illus. 20 1/2 cm. 1947. Doubleday & Company, Inc.
--Mystery at Thunderbolt House (Pub. by Doubleday). (gr. 7-12). 1972. (ISBN 0-590-02902-9, Schol Pap). Schol Bk Serv.
--Mystery on Telegraph Hill: Tod Moran Mystery. 1st ed. LC 61-954132. 216p. 22cm. 1961. Doubleday.
--Night Boat, and Other Tod Moran Mysteries. LC 42-25520. xvii, 267 p. 20 1/2 cm. 1942. Doubleday, Doran & Company, Inc.
--Secret Cargo. 1943. Doran.
--Secret Cargo. Forster, Paul Q., illus. LC 31-11920. (The Story of Larry Mathews and His Dog Sambo, Forecastle Mates on the Tramp Steamer "Creole Trader", New Orleans to the South Seas). vi, 272 p. front., illus. 12 cm. 1931. Doubleday, Doran & Company, Inc.
--Secret Cargo. Forster, Paul Q., illus. LC 46-7669. (The Story of Larry Mathews and His Dog Sambo, Forecastle Mates on the Tramp Steamer "Creole Trader," New Orleans to the South Seas). vi, 272 p. front., illus.20 1/2 cm. (Young Moderns). 1946. Doubleday & Co.,Inc.
--Secret Cargo. Forster, Paul Q., illus. LC 39-24304. (The Story of Larry Mathews and His Dog Sambo, Forecastle Mates on the Tramp Steamer "Creole Trader," New Orleans to the South Seas). vi, 272 p. front., illus. 21 cm. (Young Moderns Bookshelf). 1939. The Sun Dial Press, Inc.
--Shanghai Passage. 1943. Doubleday Doran & Co.

--Shanghai Passage. Forster, Paul Q., illus. LC 29-187021. (Being a Tale of Mystery and Adventure on the High Seas in Which Stuart Ormsby is Shanghaied Aboard the Tramp Steamer "Nanking", Bound for Ports on the China Coast). viii, 301 p. front., illus. 21 cm. 1929. Doubleday, Doran & Company, Inc.
--Shanghai Passage. 1st ed. Forster, Paul Q., illus. LC 46-7670. (Being a Tale of Mystery and Adventure on the High Sease in Which Stuart Ormsby is Shanghaied Aboard the Tramp Steamer "Hanking", Bound for Ports on the China Coast). viii, 301 p. front., illus. 20 1/2 cm. Repr. of 1929 ed. (Young Moderns). 1946. Doubleday & Co., Inc.
--Shanghai Passage: Mystery and Adventure on the Pacific. LC 35-7679. viii, 301 p. front., illus. 21 cm. (Young Moderns Bks). 1935. Doubleday, Doran & Company, Inc.
--Shanghai Passage: Mystery and Adventure on the Pacific. LC 39-181659. viii, 301 p. front., illus. 21 cm. (Young Moderns Books). 1936. Doubleday, Doran & Company, Inc.
--The Ship Without a Crew. Fischer, Anton Otto (1882-), illus. LC 34-19670. (The Strange Adventures of Tod Morgan, Third Mate of the Tramp Steamer "Araby."). x, 304 p. front. 21 cm. 1934. (ISBN 0-385-07489-1). Doubleday, Doran & Company, Inc.
--Shipwreck. LC 57-11435. (The Strange Adventures of Renny Mitchum, Mess Boy of the Trading Schooner "Samarang."). 237p. 22cm. 1957. Doubleday.
--Tattooed Man. 1944. Doubleday Doran & Co.
--Tattooed Man. LC 37-24123. (A Tale of Strange Adventures Belfalling Tod Moran, Mess Boy of the Tramp Steamer "Araby," Upon His First Voyage from San Francisco to Genoa, Via the Panama Canal). 2 p. l., vii-viii p., 2 l., 332 p. col. front., illus., plates. 21 cm. (Young Moderns Bookshelf). 1937. The Sun Dial Press, Inc.
--The Tattooed Man. Blaine, Mahlon, illus. LC 26-18320. (A Tale of Strange Adventures, Befalling Tod Moran, Mess Boy of the Tramp Steamer "Araby," Upon His First Voyage from San Francisco to Genoa, Via the Panama Canal). viii p., 2 l., 332 p. col. front., illus., plates 20 cm. 1926. Doubleday, Page & Company.
--The Tattooed Man. Pease, Clarence Howard. Blaine, Mahlon, illus. LC 46-7671. (A Tale of Strange Adventures Belfalling Tod Moran, Mess Boy of the Tramp Steamer "Araby," Upon His First Voyage from San Francisco to Genoa, Via the Panama Canal). viii p., 2 l., 332 p. illus., plates. 20 1/2 cm. (Young Moderns). 1946. (ISBN 0-385-07519-7). Doubleday & Co., Inc.
--Thunderbolt House. Sperry, Armstrong W. (1897-1976), illus. LC 44-4098. viii, 287 p. 21 cm. 1944. Doubleday, Doran and Company, Inc.
--Wind in the Rigging. LC 35-12673. (An Adventurous Voyage of Tod Moran on the Tramp Steamer "Sumatra," New York to North Africa). 4 p. l., vii-xii p., 333 p. col. front. 21 cm. 1935. Doubleday, Doran & Company, Inc.

Pease, Cyril Arthington (1868-), tr. see Homerus.

Pease, Eleanor Fairchild, Mrs.
--Book of Horses and Their Pictures. Cannon, James L., illus. LC 49-50337. (Illus.). 34p. 26cm. 1949. A. Whitman.
--Brave Tales of Real Dogs. Rice, R. J., illus. LC 31-30255. 160 p. incl. front., illus. 23 cm. c.1931. A. Whitman & Co.
--Heroes All: Tales of Real Dogs. Orloff, Gregory, illus. LC 40-32221. (Illus.). 223p. 22cm. 1940. A. Whitman.
--The Jolly Little Clown and Other Stories. Hetherington, Mildred Lyon, illus. LC 27-21136. 126 p. incl. col. front., illus. (part col.) 24 cm. (just right book). c.1927. Albert Whitman Company.

Pease, Eleanor Fairchild, Mrs. & De Melik, Beatrice, Mrs.
--Gay Pippo. Wiese, Kurt (1887-1974), illus. LC 36-33400. 79, 1 p. col. illus. 26 cm. 1936. A. Whitman & Co.

Pease, F. W., Miss
--Winnie's Temptation. 96p. (Popular Ser). N.D. American Tract Society.

Pease, Howard see Pease, Clarence Howard.

Pease, Josephine Van Dolzen
--The Children That Lived in a Shoe. Friend, Esther, illus. LC 42-16616. 62 p. illus. (part col.) 17 x 18 cm. 1942. Rand McNally & Company.
--The Children That Lived in a Shoe. Webbe, Elizabeth, illus. LC 51-6018. unpaged. illus. 21 cm. (Rand McNally Book-Elf Bk 453). c.1951. Rand McNally.
--The Children That Lived in a Shoe. Webbe, Elizabeth, illus. LC 55-9032. unpaged. illus. 33cm. (Rand McNally Giant Bk). 1955, c.1951. Rand McNally.
--Fun with Letters from A to Z. Pointer, Priscilla, illus. LC 44-6666. 61 p. illus. (part col.) 17 cm. 1944. Rand McNally & Company.
--Nimbo: The Story of an African Boy. Young, Eleanor Mussey, illus. LC 34-34580. 64 p. incl. col. front., col. illus. 22 cm. c.1934. A. Whitman & Co.
--One, Two, Cock-A-Doodle-Do. (Illus.). (gr. k-2). 1950. (ISBN 0-8382-0619-0). Hale.
--One, Two, Cock-a-Doodle-Doo. Friend, Esther, illus. LC 43-16220. 2 p. l., 7-62, 2 p. illus. (part col.) 17 x 13 cm. 1943. Rand McNally & Company.
--One, Two, Cock-a-Doodle-Doo: Counting Rhymes and Number Fun. Wosmek, Frances, illus. LC 50-4806. (Illus.). 36p. 21cm. (A Rand McNally Book-Elf Bk.). 1950. Rand McNally.
--One, Two, Cock-a-Doodle-Doo: Counting Rhymes and Number Fun. Wosmek, Frances (1917-), illus. LC 68-13404. (Illus.). 22 p. (incl. lining papers. 33cm. (Rand McNally Giant Bk.). 1968, c.1950. (ISBN 0-528-88827-7). Rand McNally.
--Safe All Day with the Happies: Simple Stories of Safety at Home and Outdoors. Friend, Esther, illus. LC 42-10027. 48 p. illus. (part col.) 17 cm. c.1939. Rand McNally & Company.
--This Is the World. Friend, Esther, illus. LC 44-9356. 71, 1 p. illus. (part col.) 26 1/2 x 21 cm. 1944. Rand McNally & Company.
--We Love America: Simple Stories of American Living. Friend, Esther, illus. LC 41-7322. 48 p. illus. (part col.) 17 x 14 cm. (On cover: American Patriot's Series). c.1941. Rand McNally & Company.

Pease, Leonora
--The Child You Used to Be. Perkins, Lucy Fitch (1865-1937), illus. LC 9-25394. (Illus.). 198p. 23cm. 1909. A. C. McClurg & Co.

Pease, R.
--When Grandfather Was A Boy. Kerwood, L. O., illus. 1973. (ISBN 0-07-049131-3). McGraw Hill Book Company.

Peat, Emily May Caskill
--The Boat with a Red Sail. Oehler, Bernice Olivia (1881-), illus. LC 48-4315. 32p. illus. part. col. 22cm. c.1948. Saalfield Pub. Co.

Peat, Fern Bisel, Mrs. (1893-), illus.
--Four Stories That Never Grow Old: Little Black Sambo, The Tale of Peter Rabbit, Hansel and Gretel and Cinderella. LC 44-35022. 60 p. illus. (part col.) 23 1/2 x 25 1/2 cm. 1943. Distributed Exclusively by the American Crayon Co.
--Little Red Hen. The Cock, the Mouse and the Little Red Hen. Unrevised. 20 p. illus. (part col.) 23 cm. (Lettered on cover: Calico classics). c.1932. The Saalfield Publishing Company.
--Stories Children Like. LC 33-22301. 34 p. illus. (part col.) 30 1/2 cm. c.1933. The Saalfield Publishing Company.
--The Three Little Pigs. LC 32-910. 20 p. illus. (part col.) 22 1/2 cm. (Lettered on cover: Calico Classics). c.1932. The Saalfield Publishing Company.

Peat, Fern Bisel, Mrs. (1893-) & Brueggeman, Binnie, illus.
--Three Little Kittens. LC 40-31954. 16 p. illus. (part col.) 27 x 24 cm. c.1940. The Saalfield Publishing Company.

Peattie, Elia Wilkinson, Mrs. (1862-)
--Azalea at Sunset Gap. Nuyttens, Joseph Pierre, illus. LC 14-11803. 286 p. front., plates. 20 cm. (Her The Blue Ridge series). c.1914. The Reilly & Britton Co.
--Azalea: The Story of a Girl in the Blue Ridge Mountains. Roberts, Hazel, illus. LC 12-17545. 272 p. front., plates. 20 cm. c.1912. The Reilly & Britton Co.
--Edda and the Oak. Merrill, Katherine, illus. LC 12-193335. vi, 134 p. col. illus., col. pl. 23 cm. c.1911. Rand, McNally and Co.
--Ickery Ann and Other Girls and Boys. LC 99-1347. 5 p. l., 286 p. 20 cm. 1899. H. S. Stone & Company.
--Sarah Brewster's Relatives. Stevens, W. D., illus. LC 16-194564. 4 p. l., 198, 2 p. front., plates. 19 cm. 1916. Houghton Mifflin Company.
--With Scrip and Staff: A Tale of the Children's Crusade. Mitchell, Edith & Randolph, Grace F., illus. LC 7-33488. 182 p. incl. front., illus. 19 cm. c.1891. A. D. F. Randolph and Co.

Peavy, Linda (1943-)
--Allison's Grandfather. 11 x 12 1/2. 40p. Repr. of 1981 ed (Pub. by Scribners). (18 pt.). (gr. 3-4). N.D. Am Printing Hse.
--Allison's Grandfather. Himler, Ronald Norbert (1937-), illus. LC 81-2297. p. cm. 1981. Scribner.

Peck, Anne Merriman (1884-)
--Jo Ann of the Border Country. Peck, Anne Merriman (1884-), illus. LC 52-9254. 21cm. 216p. 1952. Dodd Mead & Co.
--Manoel and the Morning Star. Peck, Anne Merriman (1884-), illus. LC 43-6568. 4 p.l. 31 p. col. front., illus., col. plates. 26 x 21 1/2 cm. 1943. Harper & Brothers.
--Rene and Paton. Peck, Anne Merriman (1884-), illus. LC 38-328572. 59, 5 p. incl. col. front., illus. (part col.) 24 cm. 1938. A. Whitman & Co.

Peck, Anne Merriman (1884-) & Johnson, Enid (1892-)
--Wings Over Holland. Peck, Anne Merriman (1884-), illus. LC 32-6100. 6 p. l., 145 p. incl. illus., plates. col. front 23 cm. 1932. The Macmillan Company.
--Young Americans from Many Lands. Peck, Anne Merriman (1884-), illus. LC 35-24889. 7 p. l., 21-273 p. incl. illus., col. plates (part double) col. front. 23 cm. 1935. A. Whitman & Co.

Peck, George Wilbur (1840-1916)
--The Grocery Man and Peck's Bad Boy. LC 79-104538. (Illus.). xiv, 240 p. 23cm. 1970. Literature House.
--Peck's Bad Boy. Harris, Aurand (1915-), adapted by. 1974. Anchorage Press.
--Peck's Bad Boy Abroad. Groesbeck, E. S. & Taylor, R. W., illus. LC 5-16891. 1905. Thompson & Thomas.
--Peck's Bad Boy and His Pa. Smith, Gean, illus. LC 12-37641. 1 p. l., vii-xiv p., 1 l., 9-196 p. front., plates. 19 cm. 1883. Belford, Clarke & Co.
--Peck's Bad Boy and His Pa. Complete Ed. ed. Williams, True, illus. Bleiler, E. F., intro. by. LC 58-143767. 347p. illus. 21cm. 1958. Dover Publications.
--Pecks Bad Boy and His Pa. Williams, True, illus. 1900. George M Hill Co.
--Peck's Bad Boy and His Pa. Williams, True, illus. N.D. Thompson & Thomas.
--Peck's Bad Boy and His Pa. Williams, True, illus. LC 12-37642. (Complete Ed). 2 v. in 1. front. (port.) illus. 21 cm. c.1893. W. B. Conkey Company.
--Peck's Bad Boy and the Grocery Man. LC 13-12931. (Illus.). vii- xiv,240p. 19cm. 1883. Belford, Clarke & Co.
--Peck's Bad Boy and the Groceryman. LC 2-9796. (Illus.). ix-xiv,240p. 19cm. (Franklin Ser.). 1901. Homewood Pub. Co.
--Peck's Bad Boy and the Groceryman. LC 2-9798. 20cm. 240p. (Franklin Ser.: No. 10). 1901. W. B. Conkey Co.
--Peck's Bad Boy Number Two: Being a Continuation of Peck's Bad Boy and His Pa. LC 5-25859. 20cm. 240p. (White City Ser: Vol. 1 No. 3). 1894. W. B. Conkey Co.
--Peck's Bad Boy with the Circus. Frink, C., illus. LC 6-28761. 1 p. l., 5-319 p. front., illus., plates. 22 cm. 1906. Thompson & Thomas.
--Peck's Bad Boy with the Cowboys. LC 7-28449. 303 p. front., illus. 22 cm. 1907. Thompson & Thomas.
--Peck's Boss Book. (Illus.). N.D. Belford, Clarke & Co.
--Peck's Fun. 1883. Belford, Clarke & Co.
--Peck's Fun. (Illus.). (The Household Library). N.D. Belford, Clarke & Co's.
--Peck's Sunshine. Hopkins, illus. LC 41-31335. (Being a Collection of Articles Written for Peck's Sun, Milwaukee, Wis., Generally Calculated to Throw Sunshine Instesd of Clouds on the Faces of Those Who Read Them.). vi, 9-154 p. illus. 23 1/2 cm. (With, as issued, His Peck's Bad Boy and His Pa. Chicago, c1893). c.1893. W. B. Conkey Company.
--Peck's Uncle Ike and the Red Headed Boy. LC 99-5714. (Illus.). 217p. 20cm. 1899. A. Belford.

Peck, Harry Thurston see Pyke, Rafford, pseud.

Peck, Harry Thurston (1856-1914)
--The Adventures of Mabel. Pyke, Rafford, pseud. Norton, Melanie Elizabeth, illus. LC 44-31336. 5 p. l. 245 p. incl. plates. front. 22 cm. 1897. Dodd, Mead and Company.
--The Adventures of Mabel. Norton, Melanie Elizabeth, illus. 20cm. 245p. 1909. Dodd, Mead & Co.
--The Adventures of Mabel. Rountree, Harry (1878-1950), illus. LC 16-19460. 6 p. l., 223 p. col. front., illus., col. plates. 25 cm. c.1916. Dodd, Mead and Company.
--The Adventures of Mabel. Wohlberg, Meg (1905-), illus. LC 63-8627. 173 p. illus. 21 cm. 1963. New York Graphic Society.
--Hilda and the Wishes. Norton, Melanie Elizabeth, illus. LC 7-36100. 20cm. 240p. 1907. Dodd, Mead & Co.

Peck, Helen Estelle (1910-) & Dearmin, Jennie Tarascou (1924-)
--The Smiling Dragon. Sevillia, Leon, illus. (Illus.). (Second Grade Bk.). (gr. 2-3). 1963. Denison.

Peck, Kathryn Blackburn (1904-1975)
--Everyday and Sunday. Costanza, Peter, illus. LC 59-3180. unpaged. illus. 23cm. 1959. Warner Press.

Peck, Leigh
--Don Coyote. Burton, Virginia Lee (1909-1968), illus. LC 42-8283. 1 p. l., 78 p. col. illus. 26 cm. 1942. Houghton Mifflin Company.
--Pecos Bill and Lightning. N.D. E . M. Hale and Co.
--Pecos Bill and Lightning. Wiese, Kurt (1887-1974), illus. LC 40-335293. 1 p. l., 68 p. col. illus. 25 x 19 cm. 1940. Houghton Mifflin Company.
--They Were Made of Rawhide. Watson, Aldren Auld (1917-), illus. LC 52-11453. 181p. illus. 22cm. 1954. Houghton Mifflin.

Peck, Lora B
--Stories East and West. Chase, Rhoda Campbell, illus. LC 27-4667. (A Supplementary Reader). xii, 218 p. incl. illus., plates. col. front. 19 cm. 1927. Little, Brown, and Company.
--Stories for Good Children. Chase, Rhoda Campbell, illus. LC 20-18926. xvi p., 1 l., 174 p. incl. illus., plates. col. front. 19 cm. 1920. Little, Brown, and Company.

Peck, M. E.
--The Boy Peddler: A Christmas Story. N.D. James Pott.

Peck, Minnie Seamans
--Doings of the Pansy Family. Peck, Mimi Seamans, illus. LC 7-2059. 73 p. incl. illus., plates. 20 cm. c.1905. C. W. Bardeen.

Peck, Richard (1934-)
--Are You in the House Alone?. 1st ed. LC 76-28810. 22cm. 156p. 1976. (ISBN 0-670-13241-1). Viking Press.
--Close Enough to Touch. LC 81-65498. p. cm. 1981. (ISBN 0-440-01362-3). Delacorte Press.
--Don't Look and It Won't Hurt. 1st ed. LC 70-185053. 173 p. 22cm. 1972. (ISBN 0-03-091466-3). (ISBN 0-03-091467-1). Holt, Rinehart and Winston.
--The Dreadful Future of Blossom Culp. LC 83-5165. 183 p. 22cm. c.1983. (ISBN 0-385-29300-3). Delacorte Press.
--Dreamland Lake. 1st ed. LC 72-11066. 22 cm. 147p. 1973. (ISBN 0-03-007886-5). Holt, Rinehart and Winston.
--Father Figure. LC 78-7909. 22cm. 192p. 1978. (ISBN 0-670-30930-3). Viking Press.
--The Ghost Belonged to Me. LC 74-34218. 183 p. 22cm. 1975. (ISBN 0-670-33767-6). Viking Press. **Award: (ALA).**
--Ghosts I Have Been. 1st Ed. ed. LC 77-9469. p. cm. 22cm. 214p. 1977. (ISBN 0-670-33813-3). Viking Press.
--Monster Night at Grandma's House. 1st ed. Freeman, Don (1908-1978), illus. LC 76-42463. (Illus.). 32 p. 24cm. 1977. (ISBN 0-670-48680-9). Viking Press.
--Remembering the Good Times. LC 84-19962. 181 p. 22cm. c.1985. (ISBN 0-385-29396-8). Delacorte Press. **Award: (ALA).**
--Representing Super Doll. LC 74-8690. 188 p. 22cm. 1974. (ISBN 0-670-59492-X). Viking Press.
--Secrets of the Shopping Mall. LC 79-50675. 185 p. 22cm. c.1979. (ISBN 0-440-07664-1). Delacorte Press.
--Through a Brief Darkness. LC 73-5151. 142 p. 22cm. 1973. (ISBN 0-670-71094-6). Viking Press.

Peck, Richard (1934-), ed.
--Mindscapes: Poems for the Real World. LC 70-146821. 160p. (gr. 7 up). 1971. Delacorte.
--Sounds & Silences: Poetry for Now. (gr. 7 up). 1970. (ISBN 0-440-08165-3). Delacorte.
--Transitions: A Literary Paper Casebook. LC 74-10794. (Illus.). 141 p. 22cm. (Random House English Ser.). 1974. (ISBN 0-394-02740-X). Random House.

Peck, Robert Newton (1928-)
--Banjo. Glass, Andrew, illus. LC 82-15347. (Illus.). 96p. (gr. 3-6). 1982. (ISBN 0-394-85394-6). (ISBN 0-394-95394-0). Knopf.
--Basket Case. LC 78-60298. 94 p. 22cm. c.1979. (ISBN 0-385-14361-3). (ISBN 0-385-14362-1). Doubleday.
--Bee Tree & Other Stuff. Lydecker, Laura, illus. LC 75-10054. (Illus.). 128p. (gr. 3 up). 1975. (ISBN 0-8027-6227-1). (ISBN 0-8027-6232-8). Walker & Co.
--Clunie. LC 78-24335. 124 p. 22cm. c.1979. Knopf : Distributed by Random House.
--A Day No Pigs Would Die. LC 73-3147. 175p. 24cm. N.D. G. K . Hall.
--A Day No Pigs Would Die. LC 72-259. 22cm. 150p. (gr. 7 up). 1972. (ISBN 0-394-48235-2). Knopf.
--Dukes. LC 84-4272. 200p. (gr. 5-9). 1984. (ISBN 0-910923-06-X). (ISBN 0-910923-06-X). Pineapple Pr.
--Fawn. LC 74-19078. 1975. (ISBN 0-316-69652-8). Little.
--Hamilton. 1st ed. Lydecker, Laura, illus. LC 75-12515. 27cm. 32p. 1975. (ISBN 0-316-69653-6). Little, Brown.
--Hang for Treason. 1st Ed. ed. LC 75-14836. 24cm. 232p. 1976. Doubleday.
--Hub. Lewin, Ted (1935-), illus. LC 78-11763. (Illus.). 104 p. 22cm. c.1979. (ISBN 0-394-83968-4). (ISBN 0-394-93968-9). Knopf : Distributed by Random House.
--Jo Silver. LC 85-3720. 132 p. 23cm. c.1985. (ISBN 0-910923-20-5). Pineapple Press.
--Justice Lion. LC 80-24283. 243 p. 22cm. c.1981. (ISBN 0-316-69658-7). Little, Brown.

--King of Kazoo. Park, William Bryan (1936-), illus. LC 76-5783. (Illus.). 81p. (gr. 4-7). 1976. (ISBN 0-394-83295-7, Dist by Random Hse). (ISBN 0-394-93295-1). Knopf.
--Kirk's Law. LC 80-2058. 204 p. 22cm. c.1981. (ISBN 0-385-17242-7). Doubleday.
--Last Sunday. 1st ed. Stahl, Ben F., illus. LC 76-42381. (Illus.). 142 p. 22cm. c.1977. (ISBN 0-385-12531-3). (ISBN 0-385-12532-1). Doubleday.
--Millie's Boy. LC 73-5739. 22cm. 195p. 1973. (ISBN 0-394-82699-X). (ISBN 0-394-92699-4). Knopf.
--Mr. Little. 1st ed. Stahl, Ben F., illus. LC 78-22347. (Illus.). 87 p. 22cm. c.1979. (ISBN 0-385-13657-9). (ISBN 0-385-13658-7). Doubleday.
--Patooie. Lewin, Ted (1935-), illus. LC 77-3548. (Illus.). 138 p. 22cm. c.1977. (ISBN 0-394-83580-8). (ISBN 0-394-93580-2). Knof ; Distributed by Random House.
--Rabbits and Redcoats. Lydecker, Laura, illus. LC 75-43449. p. cm. 1976. (ISBN 0-915892-06-5). Regional Center for Educational Training.
--Rabbits and Redcoats. Lydecker, Laura, illus. LC 75-43449. (Illus.). 56p. 22cm. c.1976. (ISBN 0-8027-6241-7). (ISBN 0-8027-6242-5). Walker.
--Soup. Gehm, Charles C., illus. LC 73-15117. (Illus.). 96 p. 22cm. 1974. (ISBN 0-394-82700-7). (ISBN 0-394-92700-1). Knopf.
--Soup & Me. Lilly, Charles, illus. LC 75-9514. (Illus.). 115 p. 22cm. 1975. (ISBN 0-394-83157-8). (ISBN 0-394-93157-2). Knopf.
--Soup for Christmas. Robinson, Charles (1931-), illus. LC 85-218. p. cm. 1985. (ISBN 0-394-87613-X). (ISBN 0-394-97613-4). Knopf.
--Soup for President. Lewin, Ted (1935-), illus. LC 77-13522. (Illus.). 107 p. 22cm. c.1978. (ISBN 0-394-83675-8). (ISBN 0-394-93675-2). Knopf : Distributed by Random House.
--Soup in the Saddle. Robinson, Charles (1931-), illus. LC 82-14010. p. cm. 1983. (ISBN 0-394-85294-X). Knopf.
--Soup on Wheels. Robinson, Charles (1931-), illus. LC 80-17661. (Illus.). 103 p. 22cm. c.1981. (ISBN 0-394-84581-1). (ISBN 0-394-94581-6). Knopf.
--Soup's Drum. Gehm, Charles C., illus. 1980. Knopf.
--Soup's Drum. Robinson, Charles (1931-), illus. LC 79-17982. p. cm. c.1979. (ISBN 0-394-84251-0). (ISBN 0-394-94251-5). Knopf : Distributed by Random House.
--Soup's Goat. Robinson, Charles (1931-), illus. LC 83-16245. (Illus.). 112p. (gr. 4-6). 1984. (ISBN 0-394-96322-9). (ISBN 0-394-86322-4). Knopf.
--Spanish Hoof. LC 84-21776. 181 p. 22cm. c.1985. (ISBN 0-394-87261-4). (ISBN 0-394-97261-9). Knopf.
--Trig. 1st ed. Johnson, Pamela, illus. LC 76-26497. (Illus.). 58 p. 21cm. c.1977. (ISBN 0-316-79131-8). Little, Brown.
--Trig Goes Ape. 1st ed. Johnson, Pamela, illus. LC 80-17066. p. cm. c.1980. Little, Brown.
--Trig or Treat. 1st ed. Johnson, Pamela, illus. LC 81-20700. (Illus.). 89 p. 21cm. c.1982. (ISBN 0-316-69659-5). Little, Brown.
--Trig Sees Red. 1st ed. Johnson, Pamela, illus. LC 78-18348. (Illus.). 59 p. 21cm. c.1978. (ISBN 0-316-69656-0). Little, Brown.
--Two Buck. 200p. (gr. 5-9). 1984. (ISBN 0-910923-07-8). Pineapple Pr.
--Wild Cat. Frenck, Hal, illus. LC 74-21792. (Illus.). 64 p. 23cm. 1975. (ISBN 0-8234-0257-6). Holiday House.

Peck, S. M.
--The Golf Girl. Humphrey, Maud (1868-), illus. LC 99-5259. (Illus.). 15p. 1899. Stokes Co.

Peck, Winifred
--The King of Melido. Anderson, Florence Mary, illus. 191p. (Round Table Ser.). 1928. Harper & Bros.

Pecker The Cat
--A Rug Before My Time: Memoirs of Pecker the Cat. (Illus.). 32p. 1982. (ISBN 0-9604894-1-X). Borf Bks.

Peckham, Betty Clock (1906-)
--Other People's Children. Imhoff, Howard, illus. LC 43-5112. 4 p. l., 196 p. front., illus. 22 1/2 cm. 198p. 1943. T. Nelson and Sons.
--Tangle-Britches. Pitz, Henry Clarence (1895-1976), illus. N.D. E. P. Dutton & Co.
--Tangle-Britches, a Pennsylvania Dutch Story. 1st ed. Pitz, Henry Clarence (1895-1976), illus. LC 54-9273. 166p. illus. 22cm. 1954. Aladdin Books.

Peckham, Howard Henry (1910-)
--Nathanael Greene: Independent Boy. Goldstein, Nathan (1927-), illus. LC 62-16620. 200 p. illus. 20 cm. (Childhood of Famous Americans). 1963. Bobbs-Merrill.
--Nathanael Greene, Independent Boy. Laune, Paul Sidney (1899-), illus. LC 56-9686. 192p. illus. 20cm. (Childhood of Famous Americans Ser. No. 95). 1956. Bobbs-Merrill.
--Pontiac, Young Ottawa Leader. Doremus, Robert (1913-), illus. LC 62-12708. 200p. col. illus. 20cm. (Childhood of Famous Americans). 1963. Bobbs.
--William Henry Harrison, Young Tippecanoe. Fiorentino, Al, illus. LC 62-16598. 200 p. illus. 20 cm. (Childhood of Famous Americans). 1962. Bobbs-Merrill.

Peckham, Mary C., Mrs.
--Father Gabrielle's Fairy. (Illus.). 193p. (Prize Story Bks.). N.D. American Unitarian Association.

Peckinpah, Betty
--Coco Is Coming. Foster, Marian Curtis (1909-1978), illus. Mariana, pseud. LC 56-6698. unpaged. illus. 26cm. c.1956. Lothrop, Lee & Shepard Co.
--Patrick Michael Kevin. (Illus.). (gr. k-2). 1961. (ISBN 0-8382-0633-6). Hale.
--Patrick Michael Kevin. Stubis, Talivaldis (1926-), illus. LC 61-11919. unpaged. illus. 23cm. c.1961. (ISBN 0-688-51219-4). Lothrop, Lee & Shepard Co.

Peddicord, Florence E.
--Sam and Betty on the Farm. Peddicord, Florence E., illus. LC 56-10539. 63p. illus. 21cm. 1957, c.1956. Vantage Press.

Peden, Pearle
--Bilibili & the Kangaroos. Maniscalco, Joseph (1926-), illus. LC 68-59221. (Illus.). 32p. (gr. 3-7). 1969. (ISBN 0-8127-0016-3). Southern Pub.
--Pony Boy. Padgett, Jim, illus. LC 63-12809. 48 p. col. illus. 28 cm. 1963. Southern Pub. Association.

Peden, William Harwood (1913-)
--Golden Shore: Great Short Stories Selected for Young Readers. Stuecklin, Karl W., illus. (Illus.). (gr. 6 up). 1967. Platt.

Pedersen, Edith Snyder (1904-)
--After Their Own Pleasure. LC 39-25038. 186 p. 20 cm. c.1939. Fleming H. Revell Company.
--Teddy and the "Witch's" Lamp. LC 51-13354. 20cm. 75p. 1951. Moody Press.
--The Witchs Lamp. (Illus.). 128p. (Childrens Bk.). Orig. Title: Teddy & the Witchs Lamp. (gr. 1-5). 1970. (ISBN 0-8024-1960-7). Moody.

Pedersen, Elsa Kienitz (1915-)
--Alaska Harvest. (Illus.). (gr. 5-8). 1960. (ISBN 0-8382-0018-4). Hale.
--Alaska Harvest. Werth, Kurt (1896-), illus. LC 61-7042. (Illus.). 192p. 22cm. 1960. Abingdon Press.
--Cook Inlet Decision. Ferro, Walter, illus. LC 63-7279. (Illus.). 203 p. 22cm. 1963. Atheneum.
--Dangerous Flight. D'Adamo, Anthony, illus. LC 60-6810. 224p. illus. 22cm. 1960. Abingdon Press.
--Fisherman's Choice. 1964. (ISBN 0-8382-0253-5, Cadmus Books). E. M. Hale and Company.
--Fisherman's Choice. Smith, Alvin (1933-), illus. LC 64-19568. 182 p. illus. 22 cm. 1964. Atheneum.
--House Upon a Rock. Shaw, Charles Green (1892-1974), illus. LC 68-12231. (Illus.). 218 p. 22cm. 1968. Atheneum.
--The Mountain of Gold Mystery. Case, Bernard, illus. LC 64-18908. 122 p. illus. 21 cm. 1964. I. Washburn.
--Mountain of the Sun. D'Adamo, Anthony, illus. LC 62-11152. (Illus.). 224 p. 22cm. 1962. Abingdon Press.
--The Mystery of Kama Lu. Lewis, Richard William (1933-1966), illus. LC 66-23252. 134p. illus. 21cm. 1966. Washburn.
--The Mystery of the Alaska Queen. Koering, Ursula (1921-), illus. LC 70-82642. (Illus.). 145 p. 21cm. 1969. I. Washburn.
--Mystery on Malina Straits. LC 63-17264. (Illus.). 116 p. 21cm. 1963. I. Washburn.
--Petticoat Fisherman. 1st ed. Shaw, Charles Green (1892-1974), illus. LC 69-13526. (Illus.). 231 p. 22cm. 1969. Atheneum.
--Victory at Bear Cove: A Story of Alaska. Shenton, Edward (1895-), illus. LC 59-7497. (Illus.). 207 p. 22cm. 1959. Abingdon Press.

Peebles, J. Winston
--My Funny Cloud. 1st ed. Beach, Bettye Rene, illus. LC 81-50915. (Illus.). 32 p. 29cm. 1981. (ISBN 0-938232-00-2). Winston-Derek Publishers.

Pedley, Ethel
--Dot and the kangaroo. 128p. 1965. Tri-ocean Books.

Peebles, Mary Louise Parmelee see Palmer, Lynde, pseud.
Peebles, Mary Louise Parmelee, Mrs. (1833-1915)
--The Honorable Club. Palmer, Lynde, pseud. N.D. American Tract Society.
--Little Captain. Palmer, Lynde, pseud. (Illus.). 131p. (Popular Ser.). N.D. American Tract Society.
--One Day's Weaving. Palmer, Lynde, pseud. LC 54-46567. (Illus.). 308p. 18cm. (The Magnet Stories). 1868. Moore & Nims.

Peedie, Jean Murdoch
--Donald in Numberland. Hader, Elmer Stanley (1889-1973) & Hader, Berta Hoerner (1890-1976), illus. LC 27-16680. 64 p. col. illus. 22 cm. c.1927. Rae D. Henkle Co., Inc.

Peek, Merle (1938-)
--Roll Over. Peek, Merle (1938-), illus. LC 80-16675. p. cm. 1980. (ISBN 0-395-29438-X). Houghton Mifflin/Clarion Books.

Peek, Merle (1938-), adapted by.
--Mary Wore Her Red Dress, and Henry Wore His Green Sneakers. Peek, Merle (1938-), illus. LC 84-12733. (Illus.). 25 p. c.1985. (ISBN 0-89919-305-6). Clarion Books.

Peekner, Ray, jt. auth. see Paulsen, Gary.
Peel, Arthur J. & Robinson, Evangeline
--Pon My Sole!. Wilson, Paul R., illus. 100p. N.D. House of Field.

Peel, Hazel Mary (1930-)
--Fury, Son of the Wilds. Kiddell-Monroe, Joan (1908-), illus. LC 59-13680. (Illus.). 152 p. 21cm. 1959. F. Watts.
--Pilot, the Chaser. Money, Keith (1935-), illus. LC 64-12630. 151 p. illus. 21 cm. 1964. F. Watts.
--Pilot, the Hunter. Money, Keith (1935-), illus. LC 61-10074. 172p. illus. 21cm. 1962. F. Watts.
--Show Jumper. Lyne, Michael, illus. LC 65-101590. 180p. illus. 21cm. 1965. Watts.

Peel, Neville, Mrs.
--Autobiography of a Bull Dog. N.D. Thomas Whittaker.

Peeling, Kitty
--The Unwanted. N.D. Vantage Press.

Peeples, Edwin Augustus, Jr. (1915-)
--Blue Boy. Shenton, Edward (1895-), illus. LC 64-21742. (Illus.). 176 p. 22cm. 1964. Houghton Mifflin.
--A Hole in the Hill. Wiggins, George, illus. 189p. 1969. (ISBN 0-9600080-2-0). Edwin A. Peeples.
--A Hole in the Hill. Wiggins, George, illus. LC 77-82913. (Illus.). 189 p. 21cm. 1969. T. Nelson.

Peery, Wilson Kimsey
--Silver Streams. 96p. N.D. Binfords & Mort.
--Silver Streams. Ackerman, Marion, illus. LC 38-7731. 2 p. l., 7-95 p. illus. 20 cm. c.1936. Metropolitan Press.

Peet, Bill, pseud., see Peet, William Bartlett.
Peet, Bill, jt. auth. see Disney, Walter Elias.
Peet, Bill, pseud. (1915-)
The Ant and the Elephant. Peet, William Bartlett. Peet, Bill, pseud. (1915-), illus. Peet, William Bartlett. LC 74-179918. (Illus.). 46 p. 26cm. 1972. (ISBN 0-395-13733-0). (ISBN 0-395-13734-9). Houghton Mifflin.
--Big Bad Bruce. Peet, William Bartlett. Peet, Bill, pseud. (1915-), illus. Peet, William Bartlett. LC 76-62502. (Illus.). 38 p. 26cm. 1977. (ISBN 0-395-25150-8). Houghton Mifflin.
--Buford, the Little Big Horn. Peet, William Bartlett. Peet, Bill, pseud. (1915-), illus. Peet, William Bartlett. LC 67-3499. (Illus.). 46 p. 26cm. 1967. Houghton Mifflin.
--The Caboose Who Got Loose. Peet, William Bartlett. Peet, Bill, pseud. (1915-), illus. Peet, William Bartlett. LC 79-155554. (Illus.). 48 p. 26cm. 1971. (ISBN 0-395-12578-2). Houghton Mifflin Co.
--Capyboppy. Peet, William Bartlett. Peet, Bill, pseud. (1915-), illus. Peet, William Bartlett. LC 66-8337. (Illus.). 62 p. 24cm. 1966. Houghton, Mifflin.
--Chester, the Wordly Pig. Peet, William Bartlett. Peet, Bill, pseud. (1915-), illus. Peet, William Bartlett. LC 65-11023. 48p. col. illus. 26cm. c.1965. Houghton.
--Countdown to Christmas. Peet, William Bartlett. Peet, Bill, pseud. (1915-), illus. Peet, William Bartlett. LC 72-78394. (Illus.). 48 p. 26cm. 1972. (ISBN 0-87464-198-5). (ISBN 0-87464-199-3). Golden Gate Junior Books.
--Cowardly Clyde. Peet, William Bartlett. Peet, Bill, pseud. (1915-), illus. Peet, William Bartlett. LC 78-24343. (Illus.). 38 p. 26cm. 1979. (ISBN 0-395-27802-3). Houghton Mifflin.
--Cyrus the Unsinkable Sea Serpent. Peet, William Bartlett. Peet, Bill, pseud. (1915-), illus. Peet, William Bartlett. LC 74-20646. (Illus.). 46 p. 26cm. 1975. (ISBN 0-395-20272-8). Houghton Mifflin.
--Eli. Peet, William Bartlett. Peet, Bill, pseud. (1915-), illus. Peet, William Bartlett. LC 77-17500. (Illus.). 38 p. 26cm. 1978. (ISBN 0-395-26454-5). Houghton Mifflin.
--Ella. Peet, William Bartlett. Peet, Bill, pseud. (1915-), illus. Peet, William Bartlett. LC 63-20703. (Illus.). 48 p. 26cm. 1964. Houghton Mifflin.
--Encore for Eleanor. Peet, William Bartlett. Peet, Bill, pseud. (1915-), illus. Peet, William Bartlett. LC 80-15918. (Illus.). 38 p. 26cm. 1981. (ISBN 0-395-29860-1). Houghton Mifflin.
--Farewell to Shady Glade. Peet, William Bartlett. Peet, Bill, pseud. (1915-), illus. Peet, William Bartlett. LC 66-12100. (Illus.). 38 p. 26cm. 1966. Houghton Mifflin.
--Fly, Homer, Fly. Peet, William Bartlett. Peet, Bill, pseud. (1915-), illus. Peet, William Bartlett. LC 76-82480. (Illus.). 60 p. 25cm. 1969. Houghton Mifflin.
--The Gnats of Knotty Pine. Peet, William Bartlett. Peet, Bill, pseud. (1915-), illus. Peet, William Bartlett. LC 75-17024. (Illus.). 46 p. 26cm. 1975. (ISBN 0-395-21405-X). Houghton Mifflin.
--How Droofus the Dragon Lost His Head. Peet, William Bartlett. Peet, Bill, pseud. (1915-), illus. Peet, William Bartlett. LC 75-135136. (Illus.). 46 p. 26cm. 1971. Houghton Mifflin Co.
--Hubert's Hair-Raising Adventure. Peet, William Bartlett. Peet, Bill, pseud. (1915-), illus. Peet, William Bartlett. (Illus.). (gr. k-3). 1979. (ISBN 0-395-28267-5). HM.
--Hubert's Hair-Raising Adventure. Peet, William Bartlett. Peet, Bill, pseud. (1915-), illus. Peet, William Bartlett. LC 59-7478. (Illus.). 38 p. 26cm. 1959. (ISBN 0-395-15083-3). Houghton Mifflin.
--Huge Harold. Peet, William Bartlett. Peet, Bill, pseud. (1915-), illus. Peet, William Bartlett. LC 61-5131. (Illus.). 26cm. 45p. (gr. k-2). 1961. (ISBN 0-395-18449-5). HM.
--Huge Harold. Peet, William Bartlett. Peet, Bill, pseud. (1915-), illus. Peet, William Bartlett. (gr. k-3). 1982. (ISBN 0-395-32923-X). HM.
--Jennifer and Josephine. Peet, William Bartlett. Peet, Bill, pseud. (1915-), illus. Peet, William Bartlett. LC 67-20373. (Illus.). 46 p. 26cm. 1967. Houghton Mifflin.
--Kermit The Hermit. Peet, Bill, pseud. (1915-), illus. Peet, William Bartlett. 1958. (ISBN 0-8382-0405-8, Cadmus Books). E. M. Hale And Company.
--Kermit the Hermit. Peet, William Bartlett. Peet, Bill, pseud. (1915-), illus. Peet, William Bartlett. LC 65-20482. (Illus.). 48 p. 26cm. 1965. Houghton Mifflin.
--The Kweeks of Kookatumdee. Peet, William Bartlett. Peet, bill, pseud. (1915-), illus. Peet, William Bartlett. LC 84-22379. (Illus.). 32 p. 26cm. 1985. (ISBN 0-395-37902-4). Houghton Mifflin.
--The Luckiest One of All. Peet, William Bartlett. Peet, Bill, pseud. (1915-), illus. Peet, William Bartlett. LC 81-7094. (Illus.). 30 p. 25cm. 1982. (ISBN 0-395-31863-7). Houghton Mifflin.
--Merle the High Flying Squirrel. Peet, William Bartlett. Peet, Bill, pseud. (1915-), illus. Peet, William Bartlett. LC 73-18371. (Illus.). 30 p. 25cm. 1974. (ISBN 0-395-18452-5). Houghton Mifflin.
--No Such Things. Peet, William Bartlett. Peet, Bill, pseud. (1915-), illus. Peet, William Bartlett. LC 82-23234. p. cm. 1983. (ISBN 0-395-33888-3). Houghton Mifflin.
--Pamela Camel. Peet, William Bartlett. LC 83-18594. (Illus.). 30 p. 26cm. 1984. (ISBN 0-395-35975-9). Houghton Mifflin.
--The Pinkish, Purplish, Bluish Egg. Peet, William Bartlett. Peet, Bill, pseud. (1915-), illus. Peet, William Bartlett. LC 63-7328. (Illus.). 46 p. 26cm. 1963. Houghton Mifflin.
--Randy's Dandy Lions. Peet, William Bartlett. Peet, Bill, pseud. (1915-), illus. Peet, William Bartlett. LC 64-19983. (Illus.). 48 p. 26cm. 1964. Houghton Mifflin.
--Smokey. Peet, William Bartlett. Peet, Bill, pseud. (1915-), illus. Peet, William Bartlett. LC 61-10626. (Illus.). 38 p. 26cm. 1962. Houghton Mifflin.
--The Spooky Tail of Prewitt Peacock. Peet, William Bartlett. Peet, Bill, pseud. (1915-), illus. Peet, William Bartlett. LC 72-7930. (Illus.). 30 p. 25cm. 1972, c.1973. (ISBN 0-395-15494-4). Houghton Mifflin.
--The Whingdingdilly. Peet, William Bartlett. Peet, Bill, pseud. (1915-), illus. Peet, William Bartlett. LC 71-98521. (Illus.). 60 p. 26cm. 1970. Houghton Mifflin.
--The Wump World. Peet, William Bartlett. Peet, Bill, pseud. (1915-), illus. Peet, William Bartlett. LC 72-124999. (Illus.). 44 p. 25cm. 1970. Houghton-Mifflin.

Peet, Creighton Byrd (1899-1977)
--Captain Teddy and Sailor Chips. Peet, Creighton Byrd (1899-1977), photos by. LC 35-17489. 96 p. incl. front., illus. 24 cm. c.1935. Loring & Mussey.
--Dude Ranch: The Story of a Modern Cowboy. Peet, Creighton Byrd (1899-1977), photos by. LC 39-178011. 96 p. incl. front., illus. 24 cm. 1939. A. Whitman & Co.

--Mike the Cat. Peet, Creighton Byrd (1899-1977), photos by. LC 40-9821. 63 p. illus. 21 x 26 cm. c.1939. H. Holt. and Company.
--Mike the Cat. Peet, Creighton Byrd (1899-1977), photos by. LC 34-19678. 64 p. illus. 21 x 26 cm. 1934. Loring & Mussey.
--The Runaway Train. Peet, Creighton Byrd (1899-1977), photos by. LC 43-48584. 71 p. illus. 21 x 26 cm. 1943. H. Holt and Company.

Peet, William Bartlett see Peet, Bill, pseud.

Peg, Gianni & Ferraro, Renato
--Alex, the Amazing Juggler. Peg, Gianni, illus. LC 81-80742. (Illus.). 32 p. 32cm. 1981. (ISBN 0-03-059891-5). Holt, Rinehart and Winston.

Peggy
--A Tail of Hair. Linnell, Harry, illus. (Illus.). N.D. Dodge Publishing Company.

Pegis, Jessie Corrigan (1907-)
--Best Friends: A Canadian Story. Unwin, Nora Spicer (1907-), illus. LC 64-19079. (Illus.). 22 cm. 128p. (gr. 4-6). 1964. (ISBN 0-8038-0676-0). Hastings.

Pei, Mario Andrew (1901-1978)
--Tales of the Natural & Supernatural. LC 72-149813. 310p. (gr. 7 up). 1971. (ISBN 0-8159-6901-5). (ISBN 0-685-24483-0). (ISBN 0-685-24484-9). Devin.

Peil, William
--The Big Story. (Illus.). 62p. (gr. 2-4). 1973. (ISBN 0-87793-124-0). Ave Maria.

Peirce, Gerry see Stutters, Percival, pseud.

Peirce, Gerry
--How Percival Caught the Python. Stutters, Percival, pseud. Peirce, Gerry, illus. Stutters, Percival, pseud. LC 37-17503. 89 p. col. illus. 11 x 12 cm. c.1937. Holiday House.
--How Percival Caught the Tiger. Stutters, Percival, pseud. Peirce, Gerry, illus. Stutters, Percival, pseud. LC 36-20842. 113 p. illus. (part col.) 11 cm. c.1936. Holiday House.

Peirce, S H, ed.
--Little Gems for Little People. LC 11-30318. xii, 13-239 p. front., illus., plates. 17 cm. 1871. Claxton, Remsen & Haffelfinger.

Peirce, Waldo (1884-1970), illus.
--The Children's Hour. LC 44-9741. 71, 1 p. incl. col. front., illus. (part col.) 28 cm. 1944. The Hyperion Press, Distributed by Duell, Sloan and Pearce.

Pelaez, Jill (1924-)
--Donkey Tales. Padgett, Jim, illus. LC 70-127376. (Illus.). 79 p. 25cm. 1971. (ISBN 0-687-11151-X). Abingdon Press.

Pelavin, Cheryl (1946-)
--The Little Brown Bear. Pelavin, Cheryl (1946-), illus. LC 73-166986. (Illus.). 30 p. 25cm. 1972. Putnam.
--Ruby's Revenge. Pelavin, Cheryl (1946-), illus. LC 76-185403. (Illus.). 32 p. 25cm. 1972. (ISBN 0-399-60776-5). Putnam.
--There Once Was a Cat. Pelavin, Cheryl (1946-), illus. LC 76-85545. (Illus.). 32 p. 25cm. 1969. Dial Press.

Pelgrave, E. J. (1805-1875), adapted by see Andersen, Hans Christian.

Pelgrom, Els
--The Winter When Time Was Frozen. Rudnik, Raphael & Rudnik, Maryka, trs. from Dutch LC 80-21224. (Illus.). 253 p. 22cm. 1980. (ISBN 0-688-22247-1). (ISBN 0-688-32247-6). Morrow. **Awards: (MLB); (ALA).**

Pell, Olive Bigelow (1886-1980)
--Belinda. N.D. Vantage Press.

Peller, Jackie & Tamburine, Jean (1930-), illus.
--Little Red Riding Hood and The Three Little Pigs. N.D. Grosset & Dunlap.
--Little Red Riding Hood and The Three Little Pigs. N.D. Wonder Books.

Pelletier, Ingrid (1912-)
--Daughter of Lapland. Tierney, Carolyn Cather, illus. LC 72-92819. (Illus.). 157 p. 22cm. 1970. Putnam.

Pelletreau, Ella Marie
--The Magic Scissors and Other Fairy Stories. Rubins, Winfield, illus. LC 3-2038. 20 x 20cm. 84p. 1902. Abbey Press.

Pellowski, Anne (1933-)
--Betsy's Up-and-Down Year. Watson, Wendy McLeod (1942-), illus. LC 82-22344. p. cm. 1983. (ISBN 0-399-20970-0). Philomel Books.
--First Farm in the Valley: Anna's Story. Watson, Wendy McLeod (1942-), illus. LC 82-5323. (Illus.). 189 p. 24cm. 1982. (ISBN 0-399-20887-9). Philomel Books.
--Nine Crying Dolls: A Story from Poland. Mikolaycak, Charles (1937-), illus. LC 79-25975. (Illus.). 31 p. 22cm. c.1980. (ISBN 0-529-05582-1). Philomel Books in Cooperation with the U.S. Committee for UNICEF.
--Stairstep Farm: Anna Rose's Story. Watson, Wendy McLeod (1942-), illus. LC 81-8476. p. cm. 1981. (ISBN 0-399-20814-3). Philomel Books.
--Willow Wind Farm: Betsy's Story. Watson, Wendy McLeod (1942-), illus. (Illus.). 176p. (gr. 9-12). 1981. (ISBN 0-399-20781-3, Philomel). Putnam Pub Group.
--Winding Valley Farm: Annie's Story. Watson, Wendy McLeod (1942-), illus. LC 81-15908. p. cm. 1982. (ISBN 0-399-20863-1). Philomel Books.

Pellowski, Michael Joseph (1949-)
--Clara Cow Joins the Circus. Kelley, True Adelaide (1946-), illus. LC 80-25602. p. cm. 1981. (ISBN 0-8193-1057-3). (ISBN 0-8193-1058-1). Parents Magazine Press.

Pelous, Donald
--Angel of Peace: A Story of St. Elizabeth of Portugal. Jagodits, Carolyn Lee, illus. 95p. illus. 24cm. 1960. Dujarie Press.

Pelsner, Stella
--Footsteps on the Stairs. 160p. (gr. 3-6). 1984. (ISBN 0-671-52411-9). Archway.

Peltier, Florence (1862-)
--A Japanese Garland. Yeto, Genjiro, illus. N.D. Lothrop Lee & Shepard Co.
--Through the Rainbow. Morrison, Jewel Lendrum, illus. LC 17-314533. 117 p. col. front., illus., col. plates. 22 cm. c.1917. Fleming H. Revell Company.

Peltzman, Ronne
--Mr. Bell's Fixit Shop. Battaglia, Aurelius (1910-), illus. LC 80-85031. (Illus.). 24 p. 21cm. (Little golden book). c.1981. (ISBN 0-307-02104-1). (ISBN 0-307-60214-1). Golden Press.

Pelzel, Helene
--Nanka of Old Bohemia. Wallower, Lucille (1910-), illus. LC 37-23785. 6 p. l., 17-254 p. incl. illus., plates. col. front., col. plates. 23 cm. 1937. A. Whitman & Co.

Pember, Edna Dole
--Rag Carpet Verses. 1st ed. Jeannine, illus. LC 53-20515. (Illus.). 39p. 24cm. 1952. Pageant Press.

Pemberton, Lois, ed.
--The Stork Didn't Bring You. 1966. Nelson Junior Books.

Pemberton, P. D.
--Richard's M-Class Cows. (Puffin Story Books). (gr. 4-6). 1976. (ISBN 0-14-030790-7, Puffin). Penguin.

Pemsteen, Hans & Cross, Beverly, pseud. (1931-)
--Clash of the Titans. Cross, Alan Beverly. Eagle, Michael (1942-), illus. LC 80-84679. (Illus.). 35 p. 29cm. c.1981. (ISBN 0-307-16801-8). Golden Press.

Pena, Sylvia Cavazos, ed.
--Kikiriki: Stories & Poems in English & Spanish for Children. Pena, Narciso, illus. LC 81-68072. 116p. (Orig.). (gr. k-6). 1981. (ISBN 0-934770-15-8). Arte Publico.
--Tun-Ta-Ca-Tun: More Stories & Poems in English & Spanish for Children. LC 84-72297. 80p. (Orig.). 1985. (ISBN 0-934770-43-3). Arte Publico.

Pender, Lydia Podger, jt. auth. see Gilmore, Mary Cameron.

Pender, Lydia Podger (1907-)
--Barnaby: And The Horses. 1961. (ISBN 0-8382-0059-1, Cadmus Books). E. M. Hale and Company.
--Barnaby and the Horses. Evers, Alie, illus. LC 61-6683. (Illus.). unpaged. 26cm. c.1961. Abelard-Schuman.
--Barnaby and the Horses. Moore, Inga, illus. LC 80-497354. (Illus.). 32 p. 1980. Oxford University Press.
--Dan McDougall & the Bulldozer. Rose, Gerald Hembdon Seymour (1935-), illus. LC 63-8107. (Illus.). 26 cm. (Picture Book). (gr. k-3). 1963. Abelard.
--Sharpur, the Carpet Snake. Smith, Virginia, illus. LC 67-136008. 1v. (unpaged), col. illus. 27cm. 26 cm. 1967. Abelard.
--The Useless Donkeys. Cowell, Judith, illus. LC 79-25304. p. cm. 1980. (ISBN 0-454-00025-1). F. Warne.

Pendergraft, Exer Vinson (1892-)
--Little Man in the Woods. Stephens, Marty, illus. LC 75-24121. (Illus.). 62 p. 22cm. c.1975. Creative Press.

Pendergrass, Mark D., jt. auth. see Wright, Samuel.

Pendery, Rosemary Schmitz
--A Home for Hopper. Quackenbush, Robert Mead (1929-), illus. LC 70-120612. (Illus.). 40 p. 26cm. 1971. Morrow.

Pendexter, Hugh (1875-1940)
--A Virginia Scout. LC 22-7880. 5 p. l., 353 p. front. 20 cm. c.1922. The Bobbs-Merrill Company.
--The Young Fishermen: Or, The King of Smugglers' Island. Copeland, Charles, illus. LC 12-25075. vii p., 1 l., 421 p. front., plates. 20 cm. (His Along the Coast Ser. Vol. 1). c.1912. Small, Maynard & Company.
--Young Gem Hunters: Or, The Mystery of the Haunted Comp. Copeland, Charles, illus. LC 11-28356. 4 p. l., 408 p. front., plates. 20 cm. (Camp and Trail Ser., Vol. 2). c.1911. Small, Maynard & Company.
--The Young Loggers: Or, The Gray Axeman of Mt. Crow. Copeland, Charles, illus. 6 p. l., 436 p. front., plates. 20 cm. (His The camp and trail series, v. 5). c.1917. Small, Maynard & Company.
--The Young Sea-Merchants: Or, After Hidden Treasure. Copeland, Charles, illus. LC 14-944875. 6 p. l., 443 p. front., plates. 20 cm. (His Along the coast series v. 2). c.1913. Small, Maynard & Company.
--The Young Timber-Cruisers: Or, Fighting the Spruce Pirates. Copeland, Charles, illus. LC 11-256808. 6 p. l., 408 p. front., plates. 20 cm. (The Camp and Trail Ser., Vol. 1). c.1911. Small, Maynard & Company.
--The Young Trappers: Or, The Quest of the Giant Moose. Copeland, Charles, illus. LC 13-214788. 5 p. l., 423 p. front., plates. 20 cm. (The Camp and Trail Ser., Vol. 4). c.1913. Small, Maynard & Company.
--The Young Woodsmen: Or, Running Down the Squawtooth Gang. Copeland, Charles, illus. LC 12-2926. ix, 413 p. front., plates. 20 cm. (The Camp and Trail Ser., Vol. 3). c.1912. Small, Maynard & Company.

Pendleton, Amena
--The Golden Heart and Other Stories. Sellner, Eudora, illus. LC 22-23720. ix p., 1 l., 79 p. illus. 21 cm. 1922. The Academy of the New Church.

Pendleton, Amena, ed. see Masson, Elsie.

Pendleton, Amena, jt. ed. see Olcott, Frances Jenkins.

Pendleton, Amena, retold by see Segur, Sophie Rostopchine, Mrs.

Pendleton, Amena, tr. see Foa, Eugenie Rodrigues-Gradis.

Pendleton, Cora Landrum
--Children of the King. Pendleton, Cora Landrum, illus. LC 55-12612. (Illus.). 96p. 23cm. 1955. Review and Herald Association.
--Richard and Judy. Pendleton, Cora Landrum, illus. LC 54-44831. 96p. illus. 23cm. 1954. Printed by the Review and Herald Pub. Association.

Pendleton, Frank
--Tim and Roy in Camp. Kennedy, J. W. Ferguson, illus. LC 10-15599. 4 p. l., 368 p. front., plates. 21 cm. 1910. Lothrop, Lee & Shepard Co.

Pendleton, Leo
--Divine Lines in Rhyme for Children. 1981. (ISBN 0-533-04923-7). Vantage.

Pendleton, Louis Beauregard (1861-1939)
--Captain Ted: A Boy's Adventures Among Hiding Slackers in the Great Georgia Swamp. LC 18-188916. 4 p. l., 315, 1 p. col. front., col. plates. 20 cm. 1918. D. Appleton and Company.
--In Assyrian Tents: The Story of the Strange Adventures of Uriel. LC 4-13657. 248 p. front., plates. 19 cm. 1904. The Jewish Publication Society of America.
--In the Camp of the Creeks. Carter, F. A., illus. LC 3-26867. 1 p. l., 328 p. front., 6 pl. 19 cm. (Adventure Stories Ser.). 1903. The Penn Publishing Company.
--In the Okefenokee: A Story of War Time and Great Georgia Swamp. LC 21-8702. vi, 182 p. front., plates. 20 cm. 1895. Roberts Brothers.
--In the Okefenokee: A Story of War Time and the Great Georgia Swamp. LC 72-1558. vi, 182 p. 22cm. (The Black Heritage Library Collection). 1972, c.1895. (ISBN 0-8369-9045-5). Books for Libraries Press.
--Kidnapping Clarence: A Boy's Adventures by Canoe and Portage Trail. LC 22-6522. iv p., 2 l., 3-322 p. front., plates. 20 cm. 1922. H. Holt and Company.
--King Tom and the Runaways: The Story of What Befell Two Boys in a Georgia Swamp. LC 12-37575. 4 p. l., 273 p. front., plates. 20 cm. 1890. D. Appleton and Company.
--Lost Prince Almon. LC 98-2008. 3 p. l., 218 p. front., plates. 19 cm. 1898. The Jewish Publication Society of America.

Pendleton, Margaret & Wilkins, David Schermerhorn, eds.
--Recent Short Stories. LC 28-24696. xvi p., 1 l., 418 p. 20 cm. c.1928. D. Appleton and Company.

Penick, Ib
--The Lone Ranger. Barr, Ken, illus. (Illus.). (Pop-Up Bks.). (ps-3). N.D. (ISBN 0-394-84691-5). Random.

Penman, Stella Jaques, Mrs.
--Child-Rhymes and Other Recitations. Gill, Mildred & Bailey, Donna, illus. LC 18-18879. 183, 1 p. incl. front., illus. (part col.) ports. 21 cm. c.1918. The Arts & Crafts Press.

Penn, Audrey (1950-)
--Blue Out of Season. Ewing, C. S., illus. LC 84-13584. 1984. (ISBN 0-915556-14-6). Great Ocean Publishers.

Penn, Bridget
--A Story of Seven. (Illus.). N.D. Thomas Nelson & Sons.

Penn, Margaret (0000-1981)
--Manchester, Fourteen Miles. LC 48-6449. v. 240 p. 19 cm. 1947. Univ. Press.

Penn, Rachel
--Cherriwink. (Illus.). 1900. J B Lippincott.

Penn, Ruth Bonn, pseud., see Rosenberg, Ethel Clifford.

Pennell, Mary Elizabeth, jt. auth. see Wilson, Clara Owsley.

Penney, Grace Jackson (1904-)
--Moki. Miret, Gil, illus. LC 60-5214. 146p. illus. 22cm. 1960. Houghton Mifflin.
--Spiky, the Mini-Monster. Gard, Judy Richardson, illus. LC 74-82660. (Illus.). 60 p. 21cm. 1974. Word Books.
--Tales of the Cheyennes. (Illus.). 1953. Houghton Mifflin.

Penney, L., ed. see Chellis, Mary Dwinell.

Penney, L., ed. see Farley, Helen Hall Moyer, Mrs.

Penney, L., ed. see Hartough, M. S.

Penney, L., ed. see Noble, Annette Lucile.

Penney, Lizzie, Miss
--Buttercups and Daisies. Penney, Lizzie, Miss, illus. (Illus.). (Pet and Pussy Ser.). N.D. DeWolfe, Fiske & Co.
--Buttercups and Daisies. Penney, Lizzie, Miss, illus. (Illus.). (Quarto Picture Books). N.D. Dodd, Mead & Co.
--Buttercups and Daisies. Penney, Lizzie, Miss, illus. (Illus.). 56p. (Buttercups and Daisies Ser.). N.D. George H. Doran.
--Home Stories for Little Folks. Penney, Lizzie, Miss, illus. LC 99-302. 72 p. illus. 17 cm. 1898. J. B. Dunn.
--Stories of Little Heroes. Penney, Lizzie, Miss, illus. LC 99-303. 72 p. incl. illus., pl. 19 cm. 1898. J. B. Dunn.
--Wee Girls and Boys. Penney, Lizzie, Miss, illus. LC 99-304. 72 p. illus. 17 cm. 1898. J. B. Dunn.

Penney, Lizzie, Miss, ed.
--Brave Boys and Girls, 1 of 6 Vols. Penney, Lizzie, Miss, illus. (Illus.). 72p. (The Water-Lily Ser.). N.D. Set. 1.50. National Temperance Society.
--Bright Stories for Young Readers, 1 of 6 Vols. Penney, Lizzie, Miss, illus. (Illus.). 72p. (The Water-Lily Ser.). N.D. Set. 1.50. National Temperance Society.
--Dainty Bits, 1 of 6 Vols. Penney, Lizzie, Miss, illus. (Illus.). 72p. (The Water-Lily Ser.). N.D. Set. 1.50. National Temperance Society.
--Fire-Side Stories. Penney, Lizzie, Miss, illus. (Illus.). (The Brooklet Ser.). N.D. National Temperance Society's Publications.
--Gems for Bands of Hope. Penney, Lizzie, Miss, illus. (Illus.). (The Brooklet Ser.). N.D. National Temperance Society's Publications.
--Little Dew-Drops, 1 of 6 Vols. Penney, Lizzie, Miss, illus. (Illus.). 72p. (The Water-Lily Ser.). N.D. Set.1.50. National Temperance Society.
--Little Drops of Water. (Illus.). (The Brooklet Ser.). N.D. NAtional Temperance Society's Publications.
--Little People's Favorite, 1 of 6 Vols. Penney, Lizzie, Miss, illus. (Illus.). 72p. (The Water-Lily Ser.). N.D. Set. 1.50. National Temperance Society.
--Little Stories for Little People. Penney, Lizzie, Miss, illus. (Illus.). (The Brooklet Ser.). N.D. National Temperance Society's Publications.
--Our Pets. Penney, Lizzie, Miss, illus. (Illus.). (The Brooklet Ser.). N.D. National Temperance Society's Publications.
--Pebbles and Pearls, 1 of 6 Vols. Penney, Lizzie, Miss, illus. (Illus.). 72p. (The Water-Lily Ser.). N.D. Set. 1.50. National Temperance Society.
--Pebbles from the Brook. Penney, Lizzie, Miss, illus. (Illus.). (The Brooklet Ser.). N.D. National Temperance Society's Publications.

Penney, R. L.
--The Penguins Are Coming!. Eaton, Tom (1940-), illus. LC 78-85027. (Illus.). 5 7/8 x 8 1/2. 64p. (18 pt.). (Nature I Can Read Bks.). (gr. k-3). 1969. (ISBN 0-06-024693-6) Har-Row.

Pennington, Eunice (1923-)
--Perry, the Pet Pig. Pennington, Eunice (1923-), illus. 80p. (gr. 4-7). 1966. (ISBN 0-685-19374-8). (ISBN 0-685-19375-6). Pennington.

Pennington, Lillian Boyer
--Choo-Choo Train. Kessler, Leonard P. (1921-), illus. (Illus.). (Nursery Treasury Ser). (ps). N.D. G&D.
--Little Train Said Choo Choo. N.D. Grosset & Dunlap.
--Snafu: The Littlest Clown. Gardner, Earle Stanley (1889-1970), illus. LC 73-90113. (Illus.). 29 cm. 28p. (gr. 1-6). 1972. (ISBN 0-685-59387-8). (ISBN 0-87783-225-0). High Country Press.

Pennoyer, Sara Waller (1900-)
--Maggie in Fashion:. Advertising, Display, Promotion. Spades, Jean, illus. LC 61-15586. (Illus.). 277p. 21cm. (Dodd Mead Career Bks.). 1961. Dodd, Mead.
--Polly Tucker: Merchant. (Dodd, Mead Career Bks.). N.D. Dodd, Mead & Co.

Penrose, Ethel
--The Fairy Cobbler's Gold. N.D. Thos Nelson & Sons.
Penrose, Margaret, pseud., see Stratemeyer Syndicate.
Penrose, Margaret, pseud.
--Burglar's Daughter. Stratemeyer Syndicate, 25 vols. (Illus.). (The Editha Ser.: No. 3). 1905. Set. H M Caldwell Co.
--The Burglar's Daughter. Stratemeyer Syndicate. (Illus.). (The Young Folks Lib.). N.D. H. M. Caldwell Co.
--The Burglar's Daughter. Stratemeyer Syndicate. Merrill, Frank Thayer (1848-), illus. N.D. Set. Dana Estes & Co.
--The Burglar's Daughter: Or, A True Heart Wins Friends. Stratemeyer Syndicate. Merrill, Frank Thayer (1848-), illus. LC 99-5454. 60p. 1900. Jordan, Marsh & Co.
--The Campfire Girls at Forest Lodge: Or, The Strange Hut in the Swamp. Stratemeyer Syndicate. 1930cm. Repr. of 1924 ed (Pub. by Cupples & Leon Co). (The Campfire Girls Ser.: No. 4). Orig. Title: The Radio Girls at Forest Lodge. N.D. Goldsmith.
--The Campfire Girls of Roselawn: Or, A Strange Message from the Air. Stratemeyer Syndicate. Repr. of 1922 ed (Pub. by Cupples & Leon Co). (The Campfire Girls Ser.: No. 1). Orig. Title: The Radio Girls of Roselawn. 1930. Goldsmith.
--The Campfire Girls on Station Island: Or, The Wireless from the Steam Yacht. Stratemeyer Syndicate. Repr. of 1922 ed (Pub. by Cupples & Leon Co). (The Campfire Girls Ser.: No. 3). Orig. Title: The Radio Girls on Station Island. 1930. Goldsmith.
--The Campfire Girls on the Program: Or, Singing and Reciting at the Sending Station. Stratemeyer Syndicate. Repr. of 1922 ed (Pub. by Cupples & Leon Co). (The Campfire Girls Ser.: No. 2). Orig. Title: The Radio Girls on the Program. 1930. Goldsmith.
--Dorothy Dale, A Girl of Today. Stratemeyer Syndicate. Nuttall, Charles, illus. LC 8-20575. 2 p. l., 242 p. front., plates. 20 cm. (The Dorothy Dale Ser.: Vol. 1). c.1908. Cupples & Leon Company.
--Dorothy Dale and Her Chums. Stratemeyer Syndicate. Nuttall, Charles, illus. LC 9-206676. 2 p. l., 252 p. front., plates. 20 cm. (The Dorothy Dale Ser.: Vol. 4). c.1909. Cupples & Leon Company.
--Dorothy Dale at Glenwood School. Stratemeyer Syndicate. Nuttall, Charles, illus. LC 8-197225. 2 p. l., 227 p. front., plates. 20 cm. (The Dorothy Dale Ser.: Vol. 2). c.1908. Cupples & Leon Company.
--Dorothy Dale in the City. Stratemeyer Syndicate. LC 13 751835. (Illus.). 2 p. l., 246 p. front., plates. 20 cm. (The Dorothy Dale Ser.: Vol. 8). c.1913. Cupples & Leon Company.
--Dorothy Dale in the West. Stratemeyer Syndicate. Rogers, Walter S., illus. LC 15-15303. 2 p. l., 250 p. front., plates. 20 cm. (The Dorothy Dale Ser.: Vol. 10). c.1915. Cupples & Leon Company.
--Dorothy Dale to the Rescue. Stratemeyer Syndicate. LC 24-14879. 2 p. l., 246 p. front., plates. 20 cm. (The Dorothy Dale Ser.: Vol. 13). c.1924. Cupples & Leon Company.
--Dorothy Dale's Camping Days. Stratemeyer Syndicate. Boehm, H. Richard, illus. 2p. 1., 237p. front., plates. 19.5cm. (The Dorothy Dale Ser.: Vol. 6). 1911. Cupples & Leon Company.
--Dorothy Dale's Engagement. Stratemeyer Syndicate. Owen, Robert Emmett (1878-), illus. LC 17-138206. 2 p. l., 248 p. front., 20 cm. (The Dorothy Dale Ser.: Vol. 12). c.1917. Cupples & Leon Company.
--Dorothy Dale's Great Secret. Stratemeyer Syndicate. Nuttall, Charles, illus. 2p. 1., 240p. front., plates. 19.5cm. (The Dorothy Dale Ser.: Vol. 3). 1909. Cupples & Leon Company.
--Dorothy Dale's Promise. Stratemeyer Syndicate. Rogers, Walter S., illus. LC 24-262714. 2 p. l., 252 p. front., plates. 20 cm. (The Dorothy Dale Ser.: Vol. 9). c.1914. Cupples & Leon Company.
--Dorothy Dale's Queer Holidays. Stratemeyer Syndicate. Nuttall, Charles, illus. LC 10-113625. 2 p. l., 250 p. front., plates. 20 cm. (The Dorothy Dale Ser.: Vol. 5). c.1910. Cupples & Leon Company.
--Dorothy Dale's School Rivals. Stratemeyer Syndicate. LC 12-179691. (Illus.). 2 p. l., 240 p. front., plates. 20 cm. (The Dorothy Dale Ser.: Vol. 7). c.1912. Cupples & Leon Company.
--Dorothy Dale's Strange Discovery. Stratemeyer Syndicate. Owen, Robert Emmett (1878-), illus. (The Dorothy Dale Ser.: Vol. 11). 1916. Cupples & Leon Company.
--The Motor Girls at Camp Surprise: Or, The Cave in the Mountains. Stratemeyer Syndicate. Repr. of 1916 ed (Pub. by Cupples & Leon Co). (The Motor Girls Ser.: Vol. 9). N.D. Goldsmith Publishing Co.
--The Motor Girls at Camp Surprise: Or, The Cave in the Mountains. Stratemeyer Syndicate. Rogers, Walter S., illus. (The Motor Girls Ser.: Vol. 9). 1916. Cupples & Leon Company.
--The Motor Girls at Lookout beach: Or, In Quest of the Runaways. Stratemeyer Syndicate. (Illus.). (The Motor Girls Ser.: Vol. 3). 1911. Cupples & Leon Company.
--The Motor Girls at Lookout Beach: Or, In Quest of the Runaways. Stratemeyer Syndicate. Repr. of 1911 ed (Pub. by Cupples & Leon Co). (The Motor Girls Ser.: Vol. 3). N.D. Goldsmith Publishing Co.
--The Motor Girls in the Mountains: Or, The Gypsy Girl's Secret. Stratemeyer Syndicate. Repr. of 1917 ed (Pub. by Cupples & Leon Co). (The Motor Girls Ser.: Vol. 10). N.D. Goldsmith Publishing Co.
--The Motor Girls in the Mountains: Or, The Gypsy Girl's Secret. Stratemeyer Syndicate. Owen, Robert Emmett (1878-), illus. (The Motor Girls Ser.: Vol. 10). 1917. Cupples & Leon Company.
--The Motor Girls on a Tour: Or, Keeping a Strange Promise. Stratemeyer Syndicate. Repr. of 1910 ed (Pub. by Cupples & Leon Co). (The Motor Girls Ser.: Vol. 2). N.D. Goldsmith Publishing Co.
--The Motor Girls on a Tour: Or, Keeping a Strange Promise. Stratemeyer Syndicate. Nuttall, Charles, illus. (The Motor Girls Ser.: Vol. 2). 1910. Cupples & Leon Company.
--The Motor Girls on Cedar Lake: Or, The Hermit of Fern Island. Stratemeyer Syndicate. (Illus.). 2p. 1., 246p. front., plates. 19.5cm. (The Motor Girls Ser.: Vol. 5). c.1912. Cupples & Leon Company.
--The Motor Girls on Cedar Lake: Or, The Hermit of Fern Island. Stratemeyer Syndicate. Repr. of 1912 ed (Pub. by Cupples & Leon Co). (The Motor Girls Ser.: Vol. 5). N.D. Goldsmith Publishing Co.
--The Motor Girls on Crystal Bay: Or, The Secret of the Red Oar. Stratemeyer Syndicate. Repr. of 1914 ed (Pub. by Cupples & Leon Co). (The Motor Girls Ser.: Vol. 7). N.D. Goldsmith Publishing co.
--The Motor Girls on Crystal Bay: Or, The Secret of the Red Oar. Stratemeyer Syndicate. Rogers, Walter S., illus. (The Motor Girls Ser.: Vol. 7). 1914. Cupples & Leon Company.
--The Motor Girls on the Coast: Or, The Waif From the Sea. Stratemeyer Syndicate. (Illus.). (The Motor Girls Ser.: Vol. 6). 1913. Cupples & Leon Company.
--The Motor Girls on the Coast: Or, The Waif from the Sea. Stratemeyer Syndicate. Repr. of 1913 ed (Pub. by Cupples & Leon Co). (The Motor Girls Ser.: Vol. 6). N.D. Goldsmith Publishing Co.
--The Motor Girls on Waters Blue: Or, The Strange Cruise of the Tartar. Stratemeyer Syndicate. Repr. of 1915 ed (Pub. by Cupples & Leon Co). (The Motor Girls Ser.: Vol. 8). N.D. Goldsmith Publishing Co.
--The Motor Girls on Waters Blue: Or, The Strange Cruise of the Tartar. Stratemeyer Syndicate. Rogers, Walter S., illus. (The Motor Girls Ser.: Vol. 8). 1915. Cupples & Leon Company.
--The Motor Girls: Or, A Mystery of the Road. Stratemeyer Syndicate. Repr. of 1910 ed (Pub. by Cupples & Leon Co). (The Motor Girls Ser.: Vol. 1). N.D. Goldsmith Publishing Co.
--The Motor Girls: Or, A Mystery of the Road. Stratemeyer Syndicate. Kaiser, G. M., illus. 2p. 1., 250p. front., plates. 19.5cm. (The Motor Girls Ser.: Vol. 1). c.1910. Cupples & Leon Company.
--The Motor Girls Through New England: Or, Held By the Gypsies. Stratemeyer Syndicate. (Illus.). 2p. 1., 247p. front., plates. 19.5cm. (The Motor Girls Ser.: Vol. 4). c.1911. Cupples & Leon Company.
--The Motor Girls through New England: Or, Held by the Gypsies. Stratemeyer Syndicate. Repr. of 1911 ed (Pub. by Cupples & Leon Co). (The Motor Girls Ser.: Vol. 4). N.D. Goldsmith Publishing Co.
--The Radio Girls at Forest Lodge: Or, the Strange Hut in the Swamp. Stratemeyer Syndicate. LC 24-14878. (Illus.). 2p. 1. 201p. 19cm. (The Radio Girls Ser.: Vol. 4). c.1924. Cupples & Leon Company.
--The Radio Girls of Roselawn: Or, A Strange Message from the Air. Stratemeyer Syndicate. Gooch, Thelma, illus. (The Radio Girls Ser.: Vol. 1). 1922. Cupples & Leon Co.
--The Radio Girls on Station Island: Or, The Wireless from the Steam Yacht. Stratemeyer Syndicate. Gooch, Thelma, illus. (The Radio Girls Ser.: Vol. 3). 1922. Cupples & Leon Co.
--The Radio Girls on the Program: Or, Singing and Reciting at the Sending Station. Stratemeyer Syndicate. Gooch, Thelma, illus. (The Radio Girls Ser.: Vol. 2). 1922. Cupples & Leon Co.

Penwell, Lora Hayward (1877-)
--The Enchanted Cottage. Rosemary, illus. LC 53-24259. unpaged. illus. 27cm. 1952. Bellevne Books.
Pepe
--No-Hitter. (gr. 7 up). 1977. (ISBN 0-590-02977-0). Scholastic Inc.
Peple, Edward Henry (1869-1924)
--The Littlest Rebel. LC 36-14628. (With Illus. from the Motion Picture Featuring Shirley Temple). 4 p. l., 258, 1 p. front., plates. 20 cm. 1935. Dodd, Mead & Company.
--The Littlest Rebel. LC 14-18340. (With Illus. from Motion Picture Featuring Shirley Temple). 3 p. l., 258, 1 p. front., plates, 20 cm. c.1914. Grosset & Dunlap.
--The Littlest Rebel. LC 11-23062. 5 p. l., 85 p. front. 8 pl. 20 cm. 1911. Moffat, Yard and Company.
--The Littlest Rebel. LC 59-12362. (With Illus. from the Motion Picture Featuring Shirley Temple. Shirley Temple Ed.). 214p. illus. 20cm. 1959, c.1939. Random House.
Peple, Florence Selden
--The Red and White Secret. Hill, Mabel Betsy (1877-), illus. LC 31-29633. ix p., 1 l., 129 p. incl. fron., illus. 21 cm. 1931. Garrett & Massie.
Peploe, Annie Molyneux (1805-1880)
--Alypius of Tagaste. LC 12-403664. 379 p. front., plates. 18 cm. 1865. Presbyterian Board of Publication.
Peppe, Rodney Darrell (1934-)
--The Alphabet Book. Peppe, Rodney Darrell (1934-), illus. LC 68-27275. (Illus.). 1 v (unpaged. 26cm. 1968. Four Winds Press.
--Cat & Mouse. Peppe, Rodney Darrell (1934-), illus. (Puffin Picture Bks.). 1980. (ISBN 0-14-050297-1). Penguin.
--Cat & Mouse: A Book of Rhymes. Peppe, Rodney Darrell (1934-), illus. LC 73-1569. (Illus.). 48p. (gr. k-3). N.D. (ISBN 0-03-010321-5). HR&W.
--Humpty Dumpty. Peppe, Rodney Darrell (1934-), illus. LC 75-38580. p. cm. 1976, c.1975. (ISBN 0-670-38673-1). Viking Press.
--The Kettleship Pirates. Peppe, Rodney Darrell (1934-), illus. LC 82-23993. (Illus.). 32p. (ps-1). 1983. (ISBN 0-688-02075-5). Lothrop.
--The Mice and the Flying Basket. Peppe, Rodney Darrell (1934-), illus. LC 84-14360. (Illus.). 32 p. 28cm. 1st U.S. edition. c.1985. (ISBN 0-688-04252-X). Lothrop, Lee & Shepard Books.
--The Mice Who Lived in a Shoe. Peppe, Rodney Darrell (1934-), illus. LC 81-82061. (Illus.). 32 p. 28cm. 1982, c.1981. (ISBN 0-688-00844-5). Lothrop, Lee & Shepard Books.
--Odd One Out. 1st American ed. Peppe, Rodney Darrell (1934-), illus. LC 73-17298. (Illus.). 26 p. 23 x 28 cm. 1974. (ISBN 0-670-52029-2). Viking Press.
--Run Rabbit, Run. Peppe, Rodney Darrell (1934-), illus. LC 82-70307. (Illus.). 12p. (ps-2). 1982. (ISBN 0-440-07397-9). Delacorte.
Peppe, Rodney Darrell (1934-), ed.
--Hey, Riddle Diddle. Peppe, Rodney Darrell (1934-), illus. (Picture Puffins Ser.). (ps-3). 1979. (ISBN 0-14-050295-5, Puffin). Penguin.
--Hey Riddle Diddle: A Book of Traditional Riddles. LC 74-141009. (Illus.). 41 p. 1971. (ISBN 0-03-086233-7). (ISBN 0-03-020911-0). Holt, Rinehart and Winston.
--The House That Jack Built. LC 78-112054. (Illus.). 32 p. 1st U.S. edition. 1970. Delacorte Press.
--Simple Simon. LC 76-185052. (Illus.). 30 p. 1st U.S. edition. 1973, c.1972. Holt, Rinehart and Winston.

Peppe, Rodney Darrell (1934-) & Jacobs, Joseph (1854-1916)
--Three Little Pigs. Peppe, Rodney Darrell (1934-), illus. LC 79-14974. (Illus.). 32 p. 28cm. 1st U.S. edition. c.1979. (ISBN 0-688-41923-2). (ISBN 0-688-51923-7). Lothrop, Lee & Shepard Books.
Pepper, Dennis
--The Elephant Book. Pepper, Dennis, illus. (Illus.). 96p. 1st U.S. edition. (gr. 1-5). 1984. (ISBN 0-19-278100-6, Pub. by Oxford U Pr Childrens). Merrimack Pub Cir.
Pepper, Nancy
--Teen-Age Blues. Verses. Damerow, Abbi, illus. LC 48-5477. 72 p. illus. 22 cm. 1948. J. Messner.
Pepper, Wilma D.
--Fairy Tales for Me. (gr. k-3). N.D. Ann Arbor Pubs.
--More Fairy Tales for Me. (gr. k-3). N.D. Ann Arbor Pubs.
--Read with Me. 165p. (gr. 1). 1967. (ISBN 0-89039-052-5). Ann Arbor Pubs.
Percival, Emily
--The Wreath of Gems. (Illus.). N.D. John E Potter & Co.
Percival, Frances E
--Sweet Home: or, Friendship's Golden Altar. (Illus.). N.D. John E Potter.

Percival, Leila
--Professor Archie. LC 26-23547. 104 p. incl. front. 19 cm. 1902. T. Nelson and Sons.
Percy
--Charlie Dikkens. (Learning Human Values Ser: Vol.3). 1976. (ISBN 0-685-69517-4). (ISBN 0-685-69518-2). Bookworld Comm.
Percy, Caroline B.
--Victoria Enters a Doll Museum: A Staffordshire Doll Tells Her Story. N.D. Pageant Press, Inc.
Percy, E. Arthur
--You Are the Captain. 1963. Steck-Vaughn Company.
Percy, Graham, illus.
--Sleeping Beauty. LC 79-18233. (Illus.). 24p. (Goodnight Bks). (gr. 1). 1980. (ISBN 0-394-84384-3). Knopf.
Percy, Stephen, pseud., see Cundall, Joseph.
Percy, Stephen, pseud.
--Robin Hood and His Merry Foresters. (Illus.). N.D. James Miller.
--Robin Hood and His Merry Forresters. (Illus.). N.D. Thomas R. Knox & Co.
Perdew, Myrtle Mosher
--Tenderfoot at Bar X. 202p. 1942. Caxton Printers.
Perdue, Hannah Avis (1858-)
--How Other Children Live. LC 27-4666. 216 p. front., illus. 20 cm. c.1927. Rand, McNally & Company.
Perera, Lydia
--Frisky. Liebman, Oscar (1919-), illus. LC 55-13595. (Illus.). unpaged. 21cm. c.1955. Holiday House.
Perera, Thomas Biddle, jt. auth. see Orlowsky, Wallace.
Peres, Antonio Martin
--Twisters and Other Poems. N.D. Vantage Press.
Peretz, Isaac Loeb (1851-1915)
--The Case Against the Wind, and Other Stories. Hautzig, Esther Rudomin (1930-), adapted by. Shtainmets, Leon, illus. Hautzig, Esther Rudomin (1930-), tr. LC 75-14193. (Illus.). xiv, 96p. 24cm. 1975. (ISBN 0-02-770990-6). Macmillan.
--The Magician. Shulevitz, Uri (1935-), adapted by. Shulevitz, Uri (1935-), illus. LC 72-85186. (An Adaptation from the Yiddish of I. L. Peretz). (Illus.). 32 p. 23cm. 1973. Macmillan.
--The Magician. Shulevitz, Uri (1935-), adapted by. Shulevitz, Uri (1935-), illus. LC 85-10666. (An Adaptation from the Yiddish of I. L. Peretz). 32p. 1985, c.1973. (ISBN 0-02-782770-4). Macmillan Pub. Co.
--The Sabbath Treasure & Other Stories. Hautzig, Esther Rudomin (1930-), retold by. Ray, Deborah (1940-), illus. N.D. Jewish Pubn.
--The Three Canopies. Horodisch, Alice, illus. Feinerman, Tehilla, tr. LC 48-28259. 128 p. col. illus. 22 cm. 1948. Shoulson Press.
Peretz, Josephine
--American History Plays & Playlets for Children. (gr. 1-7). N.D. Vantage.
Perez, Carla, jt. auth. see Robison, Deborah.
Perez-Guerra, Anne
--Poppy: Or, The Adventures of a Fairy. West, Benton, illus. LC 31-172853. 89 p. illus. 24 cm. c.1931. Rand, McNally & Company.
--Poppy: The Adventures of a Fairy. Barclay, Betty, illus. LC 42-16711. 63 p. illus. (part' col.) 17 x 13 cm. 1942. Rand McNally & Company.
Perez, Irene, jt. auth. see Rohmer, Harriet.
Perez, Norah A
--The Passage. LC 74-32278. 191 p. 21cm. 1975. (ISBN 0-397-31616-X). Lippincott.
--The Slopes of War. LC 83-26436. (Illus.). 192p. (gr. 7 up). 1984. (ISBN 0-395-35642-3). HM.
--Strange Summer in Stratford. 1st ed. Ihrig, Robert, illus. LC 68-21175. (Illus.). 176 p. 22cm. 1968. Little, Brown.
Perine, George Corbin (1874-)
--Poems for Children. LC 26-8442. 47 p. 21 cm. c.1926. The Christopher Publishing House.
Perkes, Alden
--The Santa Claus Book. LC 82-10241. p. cm. 1982. (ISBN 0-8184-0327-6). L. Stuart.

Perkins, Agnes Regan, jt. ed. see Hill, Helen Morey.

Perkins, Al see Perkins, Albert Rogers.

Perkins, Al (1904-1975)
--Meet Doctor Dolittle. Lofting, Hugh John (1886-1947), ed. Jason, Leon, illus. LC 67-25851. (Illus.). 22 p. 33cm. 1967. Random House.
Perkins, Albert Rogers (1904-1975), adapted by see Fleming, Ian Lancaster.
Perkins, Albert Rogers, jt. ed. see Lofting, Hugh John.
Perkins, Albert Rogers (1904-1975)
--The Digging-Est Dog. Gurney, J. Eric (1910-), illus. LC 67-21920. (Illus.). 63 p. 24cm. 1967. Beginner Books.
--Don and Donna Go to Bat. Tobey, Barney, illus. LC 66-8558. (Illus.). 63 p. 24cm. 1966. Beginner Books.

--The Ear Book. O'Brian, William, illus. LC 68-28464. (Illus.). 28 p. 24cm. (Bright and Early Books for Beginners BE3). 1968. Random House.
--Hand, Hand, Fingers, Thumb. Gurney, J. Eric (1910-), illus. LC 76-77841. (Illus.). 28p. 24cm. (A Bright & Early Bk.). 1969. Random House.
--King Midas & the Golden Touch. Berson, Harold (1926-), illus. LC 70-85290. (Illus.). 24cm. 62p. (ps-3). 1969. (ISBN 0-394-80054-0). (ISBN 0-394-90054-5). Beginner.
--The Nose Book. McKie, Roy, illus. LC 71-117540. (Illus.). 28 p. 24cm. (Bright & early book, BE 8). 1970. (ISBN 0-394-80623-9). Random House.
--Tubby and the Lantern. Wilson, Rowland B., illus. LC 70-158390. (Illus.). 64 p. 24cm. 1971. (ISBN 0-394-92297-2). Beginner Books, Random House.
--Tubby and the Poo-Bah. Wilson, Rowland B., illus. LC 72-42. (Illus.). 64 p. 24cm. 1972. (ISBN 0-394-82469-5). (ISBN 0-394-92469-X). Beginner Books.

Perkins, Albert Rogers (1904-1975), adapted by.
--Hugh Lofting's Travels of Doctor Dolittle in English & Spanish. Rivera, Carlos, tr. (Illus.). (Spanish Beginner Bks.). (gr. k-3). 1968. (ISBN 0-394-91579-8). Random.
--Ian Fleming's Story of Chitty Chitty Bang Bang!. The Magical Car. Tobey, Barney, illus. LC 68-28461. (Original Author: Ian Fleming, 1908-1964). (Illus.). 63 p. 24cm. 1968. Beginner Books.
--Meet Chitty Chitty Bang Bang. Hanna, John (1942-), illus. LC 68-28466. (Original Author: Ian Fleming, 1908-1964). (Illus.). 4-color ils. 32p. 33 cm. 29p. (gr. k-2). 1968. (ISBN 0-394-90653-5). Random.

Perkins, Barbara C.
--Come, Walk with Me. Padgett, Jim, illus. LC 68-12563. (Illus.). (ps). 1968. (ISBN 0-8054-4142-5). Broadman.

Perkins, Carol Morse
--Little Pierre: The True Story of a Baby Chimpanzee at the Saint Louis Zoological Gardens. 1 st ed. LC 66-8348. 1v. (unpaged) illus. 23cm. 1966. (ISBN 0-910600-04-X). Folkstone Pr.

Perkins, Charles
--The Pinto Horse. Wister, Owen, frwd. by. (Illus.). 82p. (gr. 7 up). 1960. (ISBN 0-8159-6504-4). Devin.
--Wilderness Friend. LC 69-12157. 142 p. 21cm. 1969, c.1966. Funk & Wagnalls.

Perkins, Clella Lester & Trimingham, Ann
--The Silver Book of Songs: Song Material for All Grades. LC 38-2901. 132 p. 22 cm. c.1935. Hall & McCreary Company.

Perkins, Eleanor Ellis, jt. auth. see Perkins, Lucy Fitch, Mrs.

Perkins, Eleanor Ellis (1893-) & Perkins, Lucy Fitch, Mrs. (1865-1937)
--The Scotch Twins: A Play for Children,. (A Play based on the book of that title by Lucy Fitch Perkins). 2p.l. 76p. 19cm. c.1930. S. French.

Perkins, Frederick Orville, ed. see Barrie, James Matthew, Sir.

Perkins, Frederick Orville, ed. see Maeterlinck, Maurice.

Perkins, Jeanette Eloise
--The Adventures of Savoy Rabbit. Spencer, Hugh, illus. N.D. Cupples & Leon Co.
--The Knights of Anytown. Young, Florence Liley, illus. LC 24-3460. 5 p. l., 159 p. plates. 21 cm. c.1923. The Pilgrim Press.
--The Rest of the Family. Young, Florence Liley, illus. LC 24-3403. 5 p. l., 139 p. plates. 21 cm. c.1923. The Pilgrim Press.

Perkins, Jeannette Gamble
--Bobby Bruin of the Big Horn Mountains. Perkins, Jeannette Gamble, illus. LC 18-13306. 115 p. incl. front. plates. 20 cm. c.1917. Burton Publishing Company.

Perkins, Lucy Fitch, ed. see Aesopus.

Perkins, Lucy Fitch, Mrs., jt. auth. see Perkins, Eleanor Ellis.

Perkins, Lucy Fitch, Mrs. (1865-1937)
--The American Twins of the Revolution. Perkins, Lucy Fitch, Mrs. (1865-1937), illus. LC 26-16267. 6 p. l., 3-207, 1 p. illus. (incl. map) 22 cm. 1926. Houghton Mifflin Company.
--The American Twins of 1812. Perkins, Lucy Fitch, Mrs. (1865-1937), illus. LC 25-21913. 6 p. l., 3-188, 1 p. incl. front., illus. 22 cm. c.1925. Houghton Mifflin Company.
--The American Twins of 1812. Perkins, Lucy Fitch, Mrs. (1865-1937), illus. LC 72-81230. (Illus.). 188 p. 22cm. 1969, c.1925. Walker.
--The Belgian Twins. Perkins, Lucy Fitch, Mrs. (1865-1937), illus. LC 17-29863. 7 p. l., 7-197, 1 p., 1 l. illus. (incl. map, music) 22 cm. 1917. Houghton Mifflin Company.
--The Cave Twins. Perkins, Lucy Fitch, Mrs. (1865-1937), illus. LC 16-21403. 5 p. l., 162, 4 p. front., illus. 22 cm. 1916. Houghton Mifflin Company.
--The Cave Twins. Perkins, Lucy Fitch, Mrs. (1865-1937), illus. LC 68-28148. (Illus.). 162 p. 21cm. (Twins Ser.). 1968, c.1916. Walker.
--The Chinese Twins. Perkins, Lucy Fitch, Mrs. (1865-1937), illus. LC 35-23921. xvii, 3, 165, 1 p. col. front., illus. 22 cm. 1935. Houghton Mifflin Company.
--The Colonial Twins of Virginia. Perkins, Lucy Fitch, Mrs. (1865-1937), illus. LC 24-28337. iii, 1 p., 2 l., 3-204, 1 p. front., illus. 22 cm. 1924. Houghton Mifflin Company.
--Cornelia: The Story of a Benevolent Despot. Perkins, Lucy Fitch, Mrs. (1865-1937), illus. LC 19-7717. 4 p. l., 202 p., 1 l. front., plates. 20 cm. 1919. Houghton Mifflin Company.
--The Dutch Twins. Perkins, Lucy Fitch, Mrs. (1865-1937), illus. LC 11-25745. 5 p. l., 3-189, 3 p. illus. 22 cm. 1911. Houghton, Mifflin Company.
--The Dutch Twins. Perkins, Lucy Fitch, Mrs. (1865-1937), illus. (Illus.). 189 p. 21cm. (Twins Ser.). 1968, c.1911. Walker.
--The Eskimo Twins. Perkins, Lucy Fitch, Mrs. (1865-1937), illus. 1914. Houghton Mifflin.
--The Eskimo Twins. Perkins, Lucy Fitch, Mrs. (1865-1937), illus. LC 69-11618. (Illus.). 191 p. 21cm. 1969, c.1942. Walker.
--The Farm Twins. Perkins, Lucy Fitch, Mrs. (1865-1937), illus. LC 28-25021. 4 p. l., 3-305, 1 p. illus. 22 cm. 1928. Houghton Mifflin Company.
--The Filipino Twins. Perkins, Lucy Fitch, Mrs. (1865-1937), illus. LC 23-13263. 4 p. l., 3-150, 2 p. illus. 22 cm. 1923. Houghton Mifflin Company.
--The French Twins. Perkins, Lucy Fitch, Mrs. (1865-1937), illus. LC 18-185675. 5 p. l., 3-201, 3 p. incl. front. (map) illus. 22 cm. 1918. Houghton Mifflin Company.
--The Goose Girl: A Mother's Lap Book of Rhymes and Pictures. Perkins, Lucy Fitch, Mrs. (1865-1937), illus. LC 6-38342. 88 p. illus. 31 cm. 1906. A. C. McClurg & Co.
--The Indian Twins. Perkins, Lucy Fitch, Mrs. (1865-1937), illus. LC 30-29559. ix, 1, 201, 1 p. incl. front., illus. 22 cm. 1930. Houghton Mifflin Company.
--The Indian Twins. Perkins, Lucy Fitch, Mrs. (1865-1937), illus. LC 78-81229. (Illus.). ix, 201 p. 21cm. 1969, c.1930. Walker.
--The Irish Twins. Perkins, Lucy Fitch, Mrs. (1865-1937), illus. LC 13-243170. 6 p. l., 3-205, 1 p., 1 l. illus. 22 cm. 1913. Houghton Mifflin Company.
--The Italian Twins. Perkins, Lucy Fitch, Mrs. (1865-1937), illus. LC 20-15958. 4 p. l., 3-148, 2 p. illus. 22 cm. 1920. Houghton Mifflin Company.
--The Japanese Twins. Perkins, Lucy Fitch, Mrs. (1865-1937), illus. LC 12-25844. 5 p. l., 3-177, 3 p. illus. 22 cm. 1912. Houghton Mifflin Company.
--The Japanese Twins. Perkins, Lucy Fitch, Mrs. (1865-1937), illus. LC 68-28149. (Illus.). 177 p. 21cm. (The Twins Ser.). 1968, c.1912. Walker.
--Kit and Kat: More Adventures of the Dutch Twins. Perkins, Lucy Fitch, Mrs. (1865-1937), illus. LC 29-23127. ix, 1 p., 1 l., 181, 2 p. incl. front., illus. 22 cm. 1929. Houghton Mifflin Company.
--The Mexican Twins. Perkins, Lucy Fitch, Mrs. (1865-1937), illus. LC 15-249142. 5 p. l., 183 (i. e. 195), 3 p. incl. front., illus. 22 cm. 1915. Houghton Mifflin Company.
--Mr. Chick: His Travels and Adventures. Perkins, Lucy Fitch, Mrs. (1865-1937), illus. LC 26-147959. 5 p. l., 116 p., 1 l. illus. 21 x 27 cm. 1926. Houghton Mifflin Company.
--The Norwegian Twins. Perkins, Lucy Fitch, Mrs. (1865-1937), illus. LC 33-30559. viii, 2, 149, 1 p. illus. 22 cm. 1933. Houghton Mifflin Company.
--The Norwegian Twins. Perkins, Lucy Fitch, Mrs. (1865-1937), illus. LC 76-81231. (Illus.). viii, 149 p. 21cm. 1969, c.1933. Walker.
--The Pickaninny Twins. Perkins, Lucy Fitch, Mrs. (1865-1937), illus. LC 31-31452. v, 1, 152, 1 p. illus. 22 cm. 1931. Houghton Mifflin Company.
--The Pioneer Twins. Perkins, Lucy Fitch, Mrs. (1865-1937), illus. LC 27-224812. 5 p. l., 3-221, 1 p. illus. 22 cm. 1927. Houghton Mifflin Company.
--The Pioneer Twins. Perkins, Lucy Fitch, Mrs. (1865-1937), illus. LC 68-28147. (Illus.). 221 p. 21cm. (Twins Ser.). 1968, c.1927. Walker.
--The Puritan Twins. Perkins, Lucy Fitch, Mrs. (1865-1937), illus. LC 21-187992. 4 p. l., 3-178, 2 p., 1 l. illus. 22 cm. 1921. Houghton Mifflin Company.
--The Scotch Twins. Perkins, Lucy Fitch, Mrs. (1865-1937), illus. LC 19-18221. 6 p. l., 3-225, 3 p. illus. 22 cm. c.1919. Houghton Mifflin Company.
--The Scotch Twins. Perkins, Lucy Fitch, Mrs. (1865-1937), illus. LC 69-11619. (Illus.). 225 p. 21cm. (The Twins Ser.). 1969, c.1919. Walker.
--The Spanish Twins. Perkins, Lucy Fitch, Mrs. (1865-1937), illus. LC 34-34598. xiii, 1, 171 p., 1 l. illus. 22 cm. 1934. Houghton Mifflin Company.
--The Spanish Twins. Perkins, Lucy Fitch, Mrs. (1865-1937), illus. LC 75-81070. (Illus.). xiii, 171 p. 21cm. 1969, c.1934. Walker.
--The Spartan Twins. Perkins, Lucy Fitch, Mrs. (1865-1937), illus. LC 18-21686. 6 p. l., 3-160, 3 p. front., illus. (incl. plan) 20 cm. c.1918. Houghton Mifflin Company.
--The Spartan-Twins. Perkins, Lucy Fitch, Mrs. (1865-1937), illus. LC 20-150692. 6 p. l., 3-160 p., 1 l. front., illus. (incl. plan) 22 cm. c.1920. Houghton Mifflin Company.
--The Spartan Twins. Perkins, Lucy Fitch, Mrs. (1865-1937), illus. LC 69-11617. (Illus.). 160 p. 21cm. (The Twins Ser.). 1969, c.1918. Walker.
--The Swiss Twins. Perkins, Lucy Fitch, Mrs. (1865-1937), illus. LC 22-21943. 4 p. l., 3-131, 1 p. illus. 22 cm. c.1922. Houghton Mifflin Company.
--The Swiss Twins. Perkins, Lucy Fitch, Mrs. (1865-1937), illus. LC 69-13167. (Illus.). 131 p. 21cm. 1969, c.1922. Walker.
--A Wonder Book. N.D. Frederick A. Stokes.

Perkins, Lucy Fitch, Mrs. (1865-1937), selected by.
--Robin Hood. Perkins, Lucy Fitch, Mrs. (1865-1937), illus. N.D. Frederick A. Stokes.
--Robin Hood. Perkins, Lucy Fitch, Mrs. (1865-1937), illus. N.D. Houghton Mifflin Co.
--The Twenty Best Fairy Tales Hans Andersen. Perkins, Lucy Fitch, Mrs. (1865-1937), illus. LC 7-28460. (Illus.). 164p. (The Dandelion Classics for Children). 1907. Frederick A. Stokes.

Perkins, Lucy Fitch, Mrs. (1865-1937) & Perkins, Eleanor Ellis (1893-)
--The Dutch Twins and Little Brother. Perkins, Lawrence Bradford, illus. LC 38-32622. 4 p. l., 78, 1 p. illus. 21 cm. 1938. Houghton Mifflin Company.

Perkins, Marlin, pseud., see Perkins, Richard Marlin.

Perkins, Marlin, pseud. (1905-)
--One Magic Night: A Story from the Zoo. Perkins, Richard Marlin. Timba, Peggy (1901-1965) & Evans, Katherine Floyd (1901-1964), illus. LC 52-13347. unpaged. illus. 26 cm. 1952. H. Regnery Co.
--Zooparade. Perkins, Richard Marlin. N.D. Rand McNally & Co.

Perkins, Mary (1928-) & Perkins School,Lancaster, Mass
--It Was Such a Blue Day: An International Story Book. LC 76-29893. (Illus.). 71 p., 27 leaves of plates. 35cm. Orig. Title: Byl Takovej Modrej Den. c.1977. Mijjilee Press.

Perkins, Raymond
--The Dansant for Little Folks. Woodroffe, Paul Vincent (1875-1945), illus. (The Playtime Book). 1930. Harper & Brothers Trade-List.
--Mother Goose Rhymes and Tunes. Woodroffe, Paul Vincent (1875-1945), illus. (The Playtime Book). N.D. Harper & Brothers Trade-List.
--The Playtime Book. Woodroffe, Paul Vincent (1875-1945), illus. N.D. Penn.
--The Playtime Books: Containing: "Mother Goose Rhymes and Tunes" "Playtime Songs, Old and New" "The Dansant for Little Folks", 3 books. Woodroffe, Paul Vincent (1875-1945), illus. (Illus.). N.D. Set. Harper & Brothers.
--Playtime Songs, Old and New. Woodroffe, Paul Vincent (1875-1945), illus. (The Playtime Books). N.D. Harper & Brothers.

Perkins, Richard Marlin see Perkins, Marlin, pseud.

Perkins School,Lancaster, Mass, jt. auth. see Perkins, Mary.

Perl, Lila
--Annabelle Starr, E.S.P. LC 83-2068. 160p. (gr. 4-7). 1983. (ISBN 0-89919-187-8, Clarion). HM.
--Candles, Cakes, & Donkey Tails: Birthday Symbols & Celebrations. De Larrea, Victoria, illus. LC 84-5803. (Illus.). 80p. (gr. 3-6). 1984. (ISBN 0-89919-250-5, Clarion). (ISBN 0-89919-315-3). HM.
--Don't Ask Miranda. (gr. 5-7). 1979. Houghton Mifflin.
--Don't Ask Miranda. LC 78-23835. 164 p. 21cm. c.1979. (ISBN 0-8164-3229-5). Seabury Press.
--Dumb Like Me, Olivia Potts. LC 76-7986. (Illus.). 181 p. 22cm. c.1976. (ISBN 0-8164-3178-7). Seabury Press.
--Hey, Remember Fat Glenda?. LC 80-28258. 168 p. 22cm. c.1981. (ISBN 0-395-31023-7). Ticknor & Fields.
--Marleen, the Horror Queen. LC 85-3740. 164 p. 22cm. c.1985. (ISBN 0-89919-368-4). Clarion Books.
--Me and Fat Glenda. LC 71-179439. 185p. 22cm. 1972. (ISBN 0-8164-3043-8). Seabury Press.
--No Tears for Rainey. LC 69-12008. 158 p. 22cm. 1969. Lippincott.
--Pieface and Daphne. LC 79-23815. 184 p. 22cm. c.1980. Houghton Mifflin/Clarion Books.
--Telltale Summer of Tina C. (Illus.). (gr. 4-6). 1977. (ISBN 0-590-10422-5). Scholastic Inc.
--The Telltale Summer of Tina C. LC 75-9518. 160 p. 22cm. 1975. (ISBN 0-8164-3156-6). Seabury Press.
--That Crazy April. 1974. Houghton.
--That Crazy April. LC 73-14812. (Illus.). 188 p. 22cm. 1974. (ISBN 0-8164-3117-5). Seabury Press.
--Tybee Trimble's Hard Times. LC 84-4310. 160p. (gr. 4-7). 1984. (ISBN 0-89919-288-2, Clarion). HM.

Perlberg, Deborah
--Wembley Fraggle Gets the Story. 1st ed. Schindler, Steven D., illus. LC 84-6586. (Illus.). 42 p. 22cm. c.1984. Muppet Press : Holt, Rinehart, and Winston.

Perle, Ruth L., ed. see Abisch, Roz.

Perle, Ruth Lerner, adapted by.
--Sleeping Beauty, with Benjy and Bubbles. Maestro, Giulio (1942-), illus. LC 78-55625. p. cm. (Read with Me Ser.). 1978. (ISBN 0-03-044966-9). Holt, Rinehart and Winston.
--Snow White and the Seven Dwarfs, with Benjy and Bubbles. Razzi, James (1931-), illus. LC 77-17680. (Illus.). 34 p. 25cm. (Read With Me Ser.). c.1978. (ISBN 0-03-040231-X). Holt, Rinehart, and Winston.
--Stories from Miss E. Abisch, Roz (1927-) & Kaplan, Boche (1926-), illus. (Illus.). (Alpha Vowel Books). (gr. k-1). 1977. (ISBN 0-89796-851-4). Arista Corp NDE.

Perle, Ruth Lerner, ed. see Abisch, Roz.

Perle, Ruth Lerner, ed. see Grimm, Jakob Ludwig Karl.

Perle, Ruth Lerner, ed. see Hefter, Richard.

Perle, Ruth Lerner, jt. ed. see Horowitz, Susan.

Perle, Ruth Lerner, ed. see Reinach, Jacquelyn Krasne.

Perle, Ruth Lerner, ed. see Ross, Jessica.

Perle, Ruth Lerner & Perrault, Charles (1628-1703)
--Cinderella with Benjy and Bubbles. Razzi, James (1931-), illus. LC 77-27870. (Illus.). 32 p. 25cm. (Series: Read with Me Series.). c.1978. (ISBN 0-03-040236-0). Holt, Rinehart and Winston.

Perlmutter, William, jt. auth. see Jackson, Jacqueline.

Peron, Rene, jt. auth. see Chandon, G.

Peroni, Carlo, jt. ed. see Gallagher, Elizabeth Lucy.

Perovskaya, Olga
--Wolf in Olga's Kitchen. Culfogienis, Angeline, illus. Glagoleva, Fainna, tr. LC 69-12440. (Illus.). 12 four-color halftone ils. 200p. 24 cm. 229p. Orig. Title: Kids & Cubs. (gr. 4-8). 1969. (ISBN 0-672-50590-8). Bobbs.

Perram, Frances Annie
--Go Work: A Book for Girls. N.D. Methodist Book Concern.

Perrault, Charles, et al. (1628-1703)
--Complete Fairy Tales. Robinson, William Heath (1872-1944), illus. Johnson, Alfred Edwin (1879-), tr. LC 61-6938. (Illus.). 183 p. 25cm. 1961. Dodd, Mead.
--Favorite Fairy Tales Told in France. 1st ed. Haviland, Virginia (1911-), retold by. Duvoisin, Roger Antoine (1904-1980), illus. LC 59-7346. 91p. illus. 25cm. 1959. Little, Brown.
--Perrault's Fairy Tales. (Illus.). N.D. George Routledge & Sons.

Perrault, Charles, jt. auth. see Little Red Riding Hood.

Perrault, Charles, jt. auth. see Perle, Ruth Lerner.

Perrault, Charles, jt. auth. see Puss in Boots.

Perrault, Charles, jt. auth. see Sleeping Beauty.

Perrault, Charles, jt. auth. see Wilkinson, Barry.

Perrault, Charles (1628-1703), retold by see Little Red Riding Hood.

Perrault, Charles (1628-1703)
--All the French Fairy Tales. Untermeyer, Louis (1885-1977), retold by. Dore, Louis Christophe Paul Gustave (1832-1883), illus. Untermeyer, Louis (1885-1977), frwd. by. LC 46-84593. 92, 2 p. incl. col. front., col. illus. 25 x 20 1/2 cm. 1946. Didier.
--The Awful History of Bluebeard. Thackeray, William Makepeace (1811-1863), illus. LC 75-308266. (Illus.). 32 p. 23cm. 1924. J. Kern.
--Bluebeard and Other Fairy Tales. Lambert, Saul (1928-), illus. Howard, Richard, tr. DeBeauvoir, Simone (1908-), intro. by. LC 64-9849. 38 p. col. illus. 34 cm. 1964. Macmillan.
--Bluebeard, Cinderella, and Other Tales. Smith, Lloyd E., retold by. LC 26-675. 64 p. 13 cm. (Little Blue Book, No. 836, ed. by E. Haldeman-Julius). c.1925. Haldeman-Julius Company.
--Cinderella. N.D. Golden Press.
--Cinderella. Dutfoy, Serge, illus. Coen, Fabio, tr. LC 79-18772. (Illus.). 21 p. 17cm. c.1980. (ISBN 0-394-84382-7). Knopf : Distributed by Random House.

--A Flock of Girls. N.D. Houghton & Mifflin.
--A Flock of Girls and Boys. Parker, Charlotte Tiffany, illus. 1895. Little, Brown, & Co.
--Hope Benham: A Story for Girls. Rev ed. Merrill, Frank Thayer (1848-), illus. LC 4-35674. 322 p. illus. 19 cm. 1894. Little, Brown.
--Hope Benham: A Story for Girls. Rev ed. Merrill, Frank Thayer (1848-), illus. LC 4-18935. 322 p. illus. 19 cm. 1903. Little, Brown.
--Ju Ju's Christmas Party. Perry, Nora (1831-1896), illus. LC 1-19478. 59 p. illus. 20 cm. 1901. Little, Brown.
--Lyrics and Legends. (Illus.). N.D. Little, Brown , and Co.
--May Bartlett's Stepmother. Perry, Nora (1831-1896), illus. LC 6048. 79 p. illus. 20 cm. 1900. Little, Brown.
--New Songs and Ballads. (Illus.). N.D. Houghton & Mifflin.
--A New Volume of Poems. N.D. Little, Brown, and Co.
--A New Year's Call. LC 3-17530. 1 p. l., 34 p., 1 l. front, plates. 19 1/2 cm. (The Children's Friend Series). 1903. Little, Brown, and Company.
--A Rosebud Garden of Girls. Gordon, Frederick C., illus. LC 12-37614. 287 p. illus. 20 cm. 1892. Little, Brown.
--That Little Smith Girl. Rev ed. Parker, Charlotte Tiffany, illus. LC 99-4974. 72 p. illus. 19 cm. 1899. Little, Brown.
--Three Little Daughters of the Revolution. Merrill, Frank Thayer (1848-), illus. N.D. Houghton & Mifflin.
--The Youngest Miss Lorton: And Other Stories. Perry, Nora (1831-1896), illus. N.D. Houghton & Mifflin.
--The Youngest Miss Lorton and Other Stories. Perry, Nora (1831-1896), illus. LC 12-37615. 290 p. illus. 19 cm. 1889. Ticknor.

Perry, Octavia Jordan (1893-)
--My Head's High From Proudness: The Adventures of a Ballad Singing Bear Hunter Named Burnie Waters. 1963. (ISBN 0-910244-34-0). John F. Blair Publisher.

Perry, Patricia, jt. auth. see Lynch, Marietta.

Perry, Patricia (1949-) & Lynch, Marietta (1947-)
--Mommy and Daddy Are Divorced. LC 77-86268. (Illus.). 32 p. 29cm. c.1978. (ISBN 0-8037-5770-0). (ISBN 0-8037-5771-9). Dial Press.

Perry, Phyllis Jean
--A Trip through the Zoo. Furan, Barbara J., illus. LC 68-24645. (Illus.). 31p. 29cm. 1968. T.S. Denison.

Perry, Shauneille & Jackson, Donald
--Mio & Other Plays for Young People. LC 73-92790. (gr. 4 up). 1976. (ISBN 0-89388-154-6). Okpaku Communications.

Perry, Stella George Stern, Mrs. (1877-)
--Barbara of Telegraph Hill. Gooch, Thelma, illus. LC 25-17278. 4 p. l., 296 p. col. front. 20 cm. 1925. Frederick A. Stokes Company.
--Girls'-Nest. Kirk, Maria Louise (1860-), illus. LC 18-16899. 4 p. l., 310 p. col. front. 20 cm. c.1918. Frederick A. Stokes Company.
--The Kind Adventure. Glidden, Carlton & Kirk, Maria Louise (1860-), illus. LC 14-15364. 5 p. l., 318 p. col. front., col. plates. 20 cm. c.1914. Frederick A. Stokes Company.
--Melindy. LC 12-29982. 4 p. l., 250 p. front. 19 cm. 1912. Moffat, Yard and Company.

Perry, Stella George Stern, Mrs. (1877-), ed.
--Go to Sleep: Bedtime Tales. Runyon, S. D., illus. LC 12-29. 24cm. 40p. 1911. Frederick A. Stokes Co.

Perry, Tuner, ed.
--The Unlikely Ghosts. N.D. (ISBN 0-8008-7940-6). Taplinger.

Perry, Verena M
--The Party That Went Wrong. 28p. 1962. Pitman Publishing Corporation.
--The Piped Piper. 32p. 1964. Pitman Publishing Corporation.
--Puss-in-Boots. 32p. 1964. Pitman Publishing Corporation.

Perry, Walter Copland (1814-1911) & Homerus
--The Boy's Iliad. Jacomb-Hood, George Percy (1857-), illus. LC 3-2126. xi, 1, 411 p. 8 pl. (incl. front.) 19 cm. 1902. Macmillan and Co., Limited.
--The Boy's Odyssey. Jacomb-Hood, George Percy (1857-), illus. LC 2-24495. 5 p. l., 204 p. 8 pl. (incl. front.) 19 cm. 1902. Macmillan and Co., Limited.

Perry, William B., pseud., see Brown, William Perry.

Perryman, Jennifer
--Where Are All the Kittens?. Brett, Jan (1949-), illus. LC 83-63492. (Illus.). 14p. (Cuddle Shape Bks.). (ps-1). 1984. (ISBN 0-394-86793-9, Pub. by BYR). Random.

Persaud, Pat
--Through a Child's Eye: A Book of Poetry for Children. 1st ed. Thompson, Norman, ed. Wong, Audrey, illus. LC 80-112474. (Illus.). 16 p. 23cm. N.D. S.N.

Perske, Robert (1927-)
--Show Me No Mercy: A Compelling Story of Remarkable Courage. 144p. (Orig.). 1984. (ISBN 0-687-38435-4). Abingdon.

Persky, Louise J., ed.
--Adventures in Sport. LC 37-5116. (Illus.). viii, 327p. 20cm. 1937. Ginn and Company.

Person, Charles
--From the Jungle to the Zoo. Cross, Elizabeth & Congdon, Allen, illus. LC 33-21888. 95, 1 p. illus. 19 cm. c.1933. Stephen Daye Press.

Person, Tom, pseud., see Person, William Thomas.

Person, William Thomas see Person, Tom, pseud.

Person, William Thomas (1900-)
--Abner Jarvis. LC 43-6453. 254 p. 21 cm. 1943. The Westminster Press.
--Bar-Face. Person, Tom, pseud. 1st ed. Cram, L. D. (1898-), illus. LC 52-8449. (Illus.). 155 p. 22cm. 1953. Ariel Books.
--The Land and the Water. Duncan, Matt, illus. LC 52-12380. (Illus.). 181 p. 21cm. 1953. Ariel Books.
--New Dreams for Old. Person, Tom, pseud. 1st ed. McGee, Millard, illus. LC 57-6618. (Illus.). 184 p. 22cm. 1957. Longmans, Green.
--The Rebellion of Ran Chatham. 1st ed. Johnson, Avery Fischer (1906-), illus. LC 57-10520. (Illus.). 185 p. 22cm. 1957. Longmans, Green.
--Sedge-Hill Setter. Person, Tom, pseud. 1st ed. Johnson, Eugene Harper, illus. LC 60-10884. (Illus.). 154 p. 21cm. 1960. Longmans, Green.
--Trouble on the Trace: A Story of the Natchez Trace in the Year 1801. 1st ed. Tolford, Joshua (1909-), illus. LC 53-7095. (Illus.). 184 p. 24cm. 1954. Ariel Books.

Persons, Helen M
--Finding the Lost Treasure. LC 33-12106. 256 p. front. 20 cm. (Mystery and adventure series for girls). c.1933. A. L. Burt Company.
--The Mystery of Arnold Hall. LC 34-857495. 3 p. l., 5-253 p. front. 20 cm. (Mystery and Adventure Series for Girls). c.1934. A. L. Burt Company.

Pertwee, Roland (1885-1963)
--The Islanders. Shepard, Ernest Howard (1879-1976), illus. LC 56-13273. 267p. illus. 22cm. 1956. Bobbs- Merrill.
--Rough Water. Orbaan, Albert F. (1913-), illus. LC 57-128532. 224p. illus. 22cm. 1957. Bobbs-Merrill Co.

Perugini, Donna
--The Flight of Orville Wright Caterpillar. Perugini, Donna, illus. (Illus.). 32p. (Orig.). 1983. (ISBN 0-89274-297-6). Harrison Hse.

Peschel, Enid Rhodes, jt. auth. see Rhodes, Irma G.

Pesek, Ludek (1919-)
--The Earth Is Near. Bell, Anthea, tr. from Ger. LC 73-88617. 205 p. 22cm. 1974, c.1973. (ISBN 0-87888-066-6). Bradbury Press.
--Log of a Moon Expedition. Pesek, Ludek (1919-), illus. Schmidt, Helene (1919-), tr. Motz, Lloyd, intro. by. LC 72-84015. (Illus.). 111 p. 24cm. 1969. Knopf.
--Trap for Perseus. LC 79-24862. 168 p. 22cm. 1980. Bradbury Press.

Peshkov, Alexiri Maximovich see Gorky, Maxim, pseud.

Pessin, Deborah
--The Aleph-Bet Story Book. Simon, Howard (1903-1979), illus. LC 46-2506. 6 p. l., 176 p. illus. 27 x 20 1/2 cm. N.D. The Jewish Publication Society of America.

Pester, Sylvia Root (1939-)
--Parade!. Hauge, Carl & Hauge, Mary, illus. LC 80-12389. p. cm. (Easy-read book). c.1980. (ISBN 0-89565-155-6). Child's World.

Petach, Heidi
--Daniel & the Lions. Petach, Heidi, illus. (Illus.). 24p. (Happy Day Bible Stories Bks.). (ps-2). 1984. (ISBN 0-87239-762-9). Standard Pub.
--The Lost Sheep. Petach, Heidi, illus. (Illus.). 24p. (Happy Day Bible Stories Bks.). (ps-2). 1984. (ISBN 0-87239-765-3). Standard Pub.

Petaja, Emil Theodore (1915-)
--The Star Mill. 1966. Ace Books.

Peter, Diana
--Claire & Emma. Findlay, Jeremy, photos by. LC 77-629. (Illus.). (gr. k-4). 1977. (ISBN 0-381-90059-2, JD-J). Har-Row.

Peter, Edith Marshall, jt. auth. see Silvester, M. Genevieve.

Peter, John (1917-)
--My Own Book of Fun and Play. Riley, Bob, illus. LC 54-12612. unpaged. illus. 20cm. (Treasure books, 885). 1954. Treasure Books.
--What Time Is It?. Zabinski, Joseph, illus. (Illus.). 20 p. 30cm. (Nursery treasure books). 1968, c.1954. Grosset & Dunlap.
--What Time Is It?. Zabinski, Joseph, illus. LC 54-4948. unpaged. illus. 21cm. (Treasure books, 889). 1954. Treasure Books.

Peter, Jonathan, ed.
--Jokes & Riddles. Lockhart, David, illus. (Illus.). (gr. k-3). 1963. G&D.

Peter, Jonathan & Moore, Lilian, eds.
--More Jokes and Riddles. Aquino, Albert, illus. LC 63-18952. 61 p. col. illus. 22 cm. 1963. Grosset & Dunlap.

Peter Pauper Press
--Child's Own Book of Favorite Poems. Bock, Vera, illus. LC 52-44808. (Illus.). 18cm. 61p. N.D. Peter Pauper Press.
--Peter Pauper's Limerick Book. N.D. The Peter Pauper Press.

Peterkin, Julia Mood (1880-1961)
--A Plantation Christmas. N.D. Houghton Mifflin Co.
--A Plantation Christmas. Hendrickson, David (1896-), illus. LC 72-4563. Repr. of 1934 ed. (Black Heritage Library Collection Ser.). N.D. (ISBN 0-8369-9119-2). Ayer Co.

Peter Pauper Press, jt. auth. see Aesopus.

Peter Pauper Press, Mount Vernon, N. Y see Aesopus.

Peters, Caroline
--St. Michael: God's Warrior Angel. (gr. 1-3). 1963. St Anthony.

Peters, Donald L. (1925-)
--Stories for Thinking Teens. 1 st. ed. LC 68-101451. 159p. 22cm. (Personal Guidance Social Adjustment Ser.). c.1968. Rosen.

Peters, Elizabeth, pseud., see Mertz, Barbara Gross.

Peters, Elizabeth, pseud. (1927-)
--Camelot Caper. Mertz, Barbara Gross. (gr. 7-9). 1969. Hawthorn.
--The Murders of Richard Third. Mertz, Barbara Gross. LC 73-21160. 256p. 1974. (ISBN 0-396-06936-3). Dodd.

Peters, John Punnett (1852-1921)
--The Animals' Christmas Tree. LC 17-23337. 3 p. l., 32 p. 15 cm. c.1916. E. P. Dutton & Company.
--The Animals Christmas Tree. Erhard, Walter, illus. LC 62-17481. 48p. 1962. Henry Z. Walck, Inc., Publishers.

Peters, Lane, pseud., see Lapidus, Elaine.

Peters, Lane, pseud. (1939-)
--Here Comes Charlie. Lapidus, Elaine. (gr. 4-6). 1971 (StarLine). Schol Bk Serv.
--Mystery at the Moscow Fair. Lapidus, Elaine. Brudi, Theresa, illus. LC 66-23739. (Illus.). 160 p. 22cm. 1966. Criterion Books.

Peters, Lisa
--The Big Jump-Up Animal Book. Bartlett, William, illus. LC 50-12767. (Illus.). 24p. 29cm. (An Activity Bk.). 1950. Grosset & Dunlop.
--The Wonder Book of Cowboys. Vaughn, Frank E., illus. LC 56-19038. unpaged. illus. 21cm. (Wonder books, 640). 1955, c.1956. Wonder Books.
--The Wonder Book of Trucks. Schucker, James, illus. LC 54-242242. unpaged. illus. 21cm. (Wonder books, 616). c.1954. Wonder Books.

Peters, Madison Clinton (1859-1918), ed.
--Our Children in Heaven: A Collection of Consolatory Poems. LC 27-1086. 94 p. incl. front. 20 cm. 1897. Wilmore-Andrews Publishing Co.

Peters, Marjorie
--Nancy Goes Places. Peters, Marjorie, illus. LC 39-19700. (Being the Story of a Little Girl with a Gereat Big Imagination). 56 p. illus. 22 x 26 cm. 1939. The Macmillan Company.

Peters, Sharon
--Five Little Kittens. Rosenberg, Amye, illus. LC 81-2317. p. cm. 1981. (ISBN 0-89375-503-6). (ISBN 0-89375-504-4). Troll Associates.
--The Goofy Ghost. Garcia, Tom, illus. LC 81-2573. (Illus.). 31 p. 24cm. (A Giant First-Start Reader). c.1981. (ISBN 0-89375-533-8). (ISBN 0-89375-534-6). Troll Associates.
--Happy Birthday. Harvey, Paul (1926-), illus. (Illus.). 32p. (gr. k-2). 1980. (ISBN 0-89375-379-3). (ISBN 0-89375-279-7). Troll Assocs.
--Happy Jack. Harvey, Paul (1926-), illus. (Illus.). 32p. (gr. k-2). 1980. (ISBN 0-89375-380-7). (ISBN 0-89375-280-0). Troll Assocs.
--Here Comes Jack Frost. Connor, Eulala, illus. LC 81-4093. p. cm. c.1981. (ISBN 0-89375-513-3). (ISBN 0-89375-514-1). Troll Associates.
--The Marching Band Mystery. Trivas, Irene, illus. LC 84-8783. (Illus.). 48p. (gr. 2-4). 1985. (ISBN 0-8167-0406-6). (ISBN 0-8167-0407-4). Troll Assocs.
--Messy Mark. Trivas, Irene, illus. (Illus.). 32p. (gr. k-2). 1980. (ISBN 0-89375-381-5). (ISBN 0-89375-281-9). Troll Assocs.
--Puppet Show. Lee, Alan, illus. (Illus.). 32p. (gr. k-2). 1980. (ISBN 0-89375-385-8). (ISBN 0-89375-286-X). Troll Assocs.
--Ready, Get Set, Go!. Trivas, Irene, illus. (Illus.). 32p. (gr. k-2). 1980. (ISBN 0-89375-386-6). (ISBN 0-89375-285-1). Troll Assocs.
--Santa's New Sled. McCarthy, Kathy, illus. LC 81-5028. p. cm. c.1981. (ISBN 0-89375-523-0). (ISBN 0-89375-524-9). Troll Associates.
--Stop That Rabbit. Silverstein, Donald (1932-), illus. (Illus.). 32p. (gr. k-2). 1980. (ISBN 0-89375-388-2). (ISBN 0-89375-288-6). Troll Assocs.
--The Tooth Fairy. Sims, Deborah, illus. LC 81-5100. p. cm. c.1981. (ISBN 0-89375-519-2). (ISBN 0-89375-520-6). Troll Associates.
--Trick or Treat Halloween. Hall, Susan T. (1940-), illus. (Illus.). 32p. (gr. k-2). 1980. (ISBN 0-89375-392-0). (ISBN 0-89375-292-4). Troll Assocs.

Peters, W. T., jt. auth. see Ledyard, Laura.

Petersen, Emma Marr
--Choose Ye this Day. Kilbourn, Dale, illus. LC 58-47579. (Illus.). 146p. 24cm. 1956. Bookcraft.

Petersen, Grace A
--Sea Foam. Petersen, Grace A., illus. LC 36-10468. 61 p. incl. plates. 22 cm. c.1935. The Poets Press.

Petersen, John
--Silly Mysteries. Williams, Garth Montgomery (1912-), illus. (Illus.). (gr. k-3). 1976. (ISBN 0-590-10151-X, Schol Pap). Scholastic Inc.

Petersen, Melba Francis (1919-)
--Beya's Train Ride. Turkle, Brinton Cassaday (1915-), illus. LC 61-8005. 21cm. 32p. (Little Playmate Series: Set 8). 1961. (ISBN 0-685-11643-3). (ISBN 0-377-68901-7). Friendship Press.

Petersen, P. J
--The Boll Weevil Express. LC 82-72816. 211 p. 22cm. c.1983. (ISBN 0-440-00856-5). Delacorte Press.
--Corky and the Brothers Cool. LC 84-15579. 181 p. 22cm. c.1985. (ISBN 0-385-29377-1). Delacorte.
--Here's to the Sophomores. LC 83-14362. 192p. (gr. 7 up). 1984. (ISBN 0-385-29319-4). Delacorte.
--Nobody Else Can Walk It for You: A Novel. LC 81-69669. 215 p. 22cm. c.1982. (ISBN 0-440-06415-5). Delacorte Press.
--Would You Settle for Improbable?. LC 80-69465. 185 p. 22cm. c.1981. (ISBN 0-440-09601-4). (ISBN 0-440-09672-3). (ISBN 0-440-09672-3). Delacorte Press.

Petersen, Palle
--Sally Can't See. LC 77-628. (Illus.). (gr. k-4). 1977. (ISBN 0-381-90058-4, JD-J). John Day.

Petersham, Maud Sylvia Fuller see Hutchins, Pat, et al.

Petersham, Maud Sylvia Fuller, Mrs. (1890-1971) & Petersham, Miska (1888-1960)
--The Ark of Father Noah and Mother Noah. Petersham, Maud Sylvia Fuller, Mrs. (1890-1971) & Petersham, Miska (1888-1960), illus. LC 30-29907. 72 p. col. illus. 22 cm. 1930. Doubleday, Doran & Company, Inc.
--Auntie and Celia Jane and Miki. Petersham, Maud Sylvia Fuller, Mrs. (1890-1971) & Petersham, Miska (1888-1960), illus. LC 32-32568. 64 p. col. illus. 26 cm. 1932. Doubleday, Doran & Company, Inc.
--The Box with Red Wheels. Petersham, Maud Sylvia Fuller, Mrs. (1890-1971) & Petersham, Miska (1888-1960), illus. LC 49-11325. 32 p. col. illus. 26 cm. 1949. Macmillan Co.
--The Boy Who Had No Heart. Petersham, Maud Sylvia Fuller, Mrs. (1890-1971) & Petersham, Miska (1888-1960), illus. LC 55-14297. (Illus.). 32 p. 27 cm. 1955. Macmillan.
--Christ Child. Petersham, Maud Sylvia Fuller, Mrs. (1890-1971) & Petersham, Miska (1888-1960), illus. (gr. 4 up). 1931. Doubleday.
--Circus Baby. Petersham, Maud Sylvia Fuller, Mrs. (1890-1971) & Petersham, Miska (1888-1960), illus. (Illus.). (gr. k-2). 1950. (ISBN 0-8382-0172-5). Hale.
--The Circus Baby. Petersham, Maud Sylvia Fuller, Mrs. (1890-1971) & Petersham, Miska (1888-1960), illus. LC 50-9295. (Illus.). 20cm. 32p. 1950. Macmillan.
--Circus Baby. Petersham, Maud Sylvia Fuller, Mrs. (1890-1971) & Petersham, Miska (1888-1960), illus. (Illus.). (gr. k-3). 1968. (ISBN 0-02-771670-8). Macmillan.
--David. Petersham, Maud Sylvia Fuller, Mrs. (1890-1971) & Petersham, Miska (1888-1960), illus. (Illus.). (gr. 4-6). 1967. (ISBN 0-02-771900-6). Macmillan.
--David: From the Story Told in the First Book of Samuel and the First Book of Kings. Petersham, Maud Sylvia Fuller, Mrs. (1890-1971) & Petersham, Miska (1888-1960), illus. LC 58-8035. (Illus.). unpaged. 24cm. 1958. Macmillan.
--Get-a-Way and Hary Janos. Petersham, Maud Sylvia Fuller, Mrs. (1890-1971) & Petersham, Miska (1888-1960), illus. LC 33-29354. 64 p. incl. col. front., illus. (part col.) 29 cm. 1933. The Viking Press.
--Joseph and His Brothers, from the Story Told in the Book of Genesis. Petersham, Maud Sylvia fuller, Mrs. (1890-1971) & Petersham, Miska (1888-1960), illus. (Illus.). 32 p. 24cm. 1958. Macmillan.
--Miki. Petersham, Maud Sylvia Fuller, Mrs. (1890-1971) & Petersham, Miska (1888-1960), illus. LC 29-23125. 63 p. col. illus. 26 cm. 1929. Doubleday, Doran & Company Inc.

--Miki and Mary, Their Search for Treasures. Petersham, Maud Sylvia Fuller, Mrs. (1890-1971) & Petersham, Miska (1888-1960), illus. LC 34-37833. 64 p. illus. (part col.) 29 cm. 1934. The Viking Press.

--Moses, from the Story Told in the Old Testament. Petersham, Maud Sylvia Fuller, Mrs. (1890-1971) & Petersham, Miska (1888-1960), illus. (Illus.). 32 p. 24cm. 1958, c.1938. Macmillan.

--Nursery Friends from France. Miller, Olive Kennon Beaupre, Mrs., tr. LC 25-24499. 1 p. l., 5-190 p. col. illus. 28 1/2 cm. c.1925. The Book House for Children.

--Off to Bed. Petersham, Maud Sylvia fuller, Mrs. (1890-1971) & Petersham, Miska (1888-1960), illus. (gr. k-1). 1961. Macmillan.

--Off to Bed. Seven Stories for Wide-Awakes. Petersham, Maud Sylvia Fuller, Mrs. (1890-1971) & Petersham, Miska (1888-1960), illus. LC 54-13044. (Illus.). 30 p. 26cm. 1954. Macmillan.

--The Peppernuts. Petersham, Maud Sylvia Fuller, Mrs. (1890-1971) & Petersham, Miska (1888-1960), illus. LC 58-6963. (Illus.). 62 p. 21cm. 1958. Macmillan.

--Rooster Crows. Petersham, Maud Sylvia Fuller, Mrs. (1890-1971) & Petersham, Miska (1888-1960), illus. (Illus.). (gr. k-1). 1969. (ISBN 0-02-773100-6). Macmillan.

--The Rooster Crows: A Book of American Rhymes and Jingles. Petersham, Maud Sylvia Fuller, Mrs. (1890-1971) & Petersham, Miska (1888-1960), illus. 1955. Macmillan.

--Rooster Crows: A Book of American Rhymes and Jingles. abr. ed. Petersham, Maud Sylvia Fuller, Mrs. (1890-1971) & Petersham, Miska (1888-1960), illus. (Illus.). color ils. 48p. (ps-1). 1971. (ISBN 0-02-044840-6, Collier). Macmillan.

--The Rooster Crows: A Book of American Rhymes and Jingles. Petersham, Maud Sylvia Fuller (1890-1971) & Petersham, Miska (1888-1960), illus. LC 46-446. 61 p. col. illus. 26 1/2 x 21 cm. 1945. The Macmillan Company. **Award: (RCM).**

--Ruth: From the Story Told in the Book of Ruth. Petersham, Maud Sylvia Fuller, Mrs. (1890-1971) & Petersham, Miska (1888-1960), illus. (Illus.). 32 p. 24cm. 1958, c.1938. Macmillan.

--Shepherd Psalm. Petersham, Maud Sylvia Fuller, Mrs. (1890-1971) & Petersham, Miska (1888-1960), illus. (Illus.). (gr. 1-4). 1962. Macmillan.

--Silver Mace. Petersham, Maud Sylvia Fuller, Mrs. (1890-1971) & Petersham, Miska (1888-1960), illus. N.D. E. M. Hale and Co.

--The Silver Mace. Petersham, Maud Sylvia Fuller, Mrs. (1890-1971) & Petersham, Miska (1888-1960), illus. 1964. Macmillan Co.

--Story of Jesus. rev. ed. Petersham, Maud Sylvia Fuller, Mrs. (1890-1971) & Petersham, Miska (1888-1960), illus. (gr. 2-4). 1967. (ISBN 0-02-773850-7). Macmillan.

Petersham, Miska see Hutchins, Pat, et al.

Petersham, Miska, jt. auth. see Petersham, Maud Sylvia Fuller, Mrs.

Peterson, Alice Fessenden

--Jolita of the Jungle: A Story of the Bush People. Peterson, Alice Fessenden, illus. LC 30-19639. 194 p. incl. col. front., illus. 19 cm. 1929. Beckley-Cardy Company.

Peterson, Alvin Martin (1884-)

--Powderpuff: The Story of a Cottontail Rabbit. Peterson, Alvin Martin (1884-), illus. LC 31-1278. 104 p. illus. 30 cm. 1930. Bruce Pub. Co.

Peterson, Antoinette Rotan

--Rhymes of Cho Cho's Grandma. Gillespie, Jessie, illus. 19cm. 19p. 1922. Macmillan Co.

Peterson, Barbara Burns & Peterson, Russell Francis

--Whitefoot Mouse. Peterson, Russell Francis, illus. 1959. E M Hale.

--Whitefoot Mouse. Peterson, Russell Francis, illus. LC 59-16490. 52p. illus. 21cm. (Life-Cycle Stories). 1959. Holiday House.

Peterson, Barbara N. & Peterson, Edward C.

--To Find Jesus. Padgett, Jim, illus. (Illus.). (gr. 2-4). 1967. (ISBN 0-687-42204-3). Abingdon.

Peterson, Barby, jt. auth. see Peterson, Glen.

Peterson, Barby & Peterson, Glen

--Come Visit Me. Peterson, Barby & Peterson, Glen, photos by LC 73-84350. (Illus.). 23 p. 21cm. 1974. Golden Press.

Peterson, Beatrice E

--Charley, the Pet Crow. McCoy, Jeanie, illus. LC 63-17763. 128 p. col. illus. 26 cm. 1963. Review and Herald Pub. Association.

--Farm Life With Danny. Baerg, Harry John (1909-), illus. LC 62-14168. 150p. illus. 22cm. 1962. Review and Herald Pub.

Peterson, Bettina

--Christmas Is for Giving. Norton, Jan, illus. (Illus.). 62 p. 22cm. 1960. Washburn.

--The Cranberry Train. Norton, Jan, illus. LC 58-11494. unpaged. illus. 24cm. c.1958. I. Washburn.

--Thanksgiving Is for What We Have. Norton, Jan, illus. (Illus.). 55 p. 22cm. 1959. Washburn.

Peterson, Carolyn Sue (1938-)

--Christmas Story Programs. Sterchele, Christina L., illus. (Illus.). (ps-6). 1981. (ISBN 0-913545-01-5). Moonlight FL.

Peterson, Cheryl, illus.

--The Animals' Christmas: A Twelfth Century Christmas Carol. LC 83-42694. (Illus.). 12p. (Board Bks.). (ps). 1983. (ISBN 0-394-85305-9). Random.

Peterson, Christian

--The Treasure of Troon. 1950. Roy Publishers.

Peterson, Edward C., jt. auth. see Peterson, Barbara N.

Peterson, Esther Allen (1934-)

--Frederick's Alligator. Natti, Susanna (1948-), illus. LC 78-15597. (Illus.). 19 x 21 cm. 32p. (gr. k-3). 1979. Crown.

--Frederick's Alligator. Natti, Susanna (1948-), illus. (Illus.). 32p. (ps-3). 1981. (ISBN 0-590-30385-6). Scholastic Inc.

--Penelope Gets Wheels. Natti, Susanna (1948-), illus. LC 81-7856. p. cm. c.1982. (ISBN 0-517-54467-9). Crown.

Peterson, Florence K., selected by.

The Big Book of Favorite Dog Stories. Greene, Hamilton, illus. (Illus.). 336p. (gr. 3-9). N.D. (ISBN 0-448-42640-4). Platt.

--Dogs: Heroes, Adventurers, Friends: A Collection of 30 Outstanding Stories. Greene, Hamilton, illus. Mowat, Farley, frwd. by. LC 64-11546. (Illus.). 336 p. 23cm. 1964. Platt & Munk.

Peterson, Gail Mahan

--Adventures and Surprises with Raggedy Ann and Andy. Paris, Pat, illus. LC 75-310189. (Illus.). 16 p. 24cm. (Hallmark children's editions). (A Hallmark Play-Time Bk.). 1974. Hallmark Cards.

--All About You. Mihel, Merrily, illus. LC 67-21541. (Illus.). 16cm. 1967. Hallmark Editions.

--The Bible Storybook. Klemushin, Fred, illus. LC 73-90489. (Illus.). 44 p. 27cm. (Hallmark children's editions). 1974. (ISBN 0-87529-382-4). Hallmark Cards.

--The Gold of Friendship. Conklin, Marilyn, illus. LC 67-21540. (Illus.). 16cm. 1967. Hallmark Editions.

Peterson, Gayle & Kelley, Ying, eds.

--A Chance to Live: Children's Poems for Peace in a Nuclear Age. (Illus.). 102p. 1983. (ISBN 0-939508-03-6). Mindbody.

Peterson, Glen, jt. auth. see Peterson, Barby.

Peterson, Glen & Peterson, Barby

--Come Fly with Me. Peterson, Barby & Peterson, Glen, illus. 36p. (Getting Acquainted Bks). (ps). 1974. (ISBN 0-307-12102-X, Golden Pr). Western Pub.

Peterson, Hans (1922-)

--The Big Snowstorm. Wiberg, Harald Albin (1908-), illus. Bibb, Eric, tr. LC 75-7675. (Illus.). 25 p. 29cm. 1st U.S. edition. 1975. (ISBN 0-698-30599-X). Coward, McCann & Geoghegan.

--Brownie. Galdone, Paul (1914-), illus. LC 65-13822. (Illus.). 32 p. 16cm. 1965. Lothrop, Lee & Shepard.

--Erik and the Christmas Horse. Wikland, Ilon (1930-), illus. Hyatt, Christine, tr. LC 74-81926. (Illus.). 32 p. 27cm. 1st U.S. edition. 1970, c.1969. Lothrop, Lee & Shepard Co.

--Liselott and the Goloff. Galdone, Paul (1914-), illus. LC 64-13067. (Illus.). 157 p. 21cm. 1st U.S. edition. 1964. Coward-McCann.

--Magnus and the Ship's Mascot. Wikland, Ilon (1930-), illus. Turner, Marianne, tr. LC 67-20217. 119p. illus. 22cm. 1st U.S. edition. 1967, c.1964. (ISBN 0-394-91890-8). Pantheon.

--Magnus and the Squirrel. N.D. E. M. Hale and Co.

--Magnus and the Squirrel. Wikland, Ilon (1930-), illus. Hamilton, Madeleine, tr. LC 59-16434. (Illus.). 128 p. 22cm. 1959. Viking Press.

--Magnus and the Wagon Horse. Wikland, Ilon (1930-), illus. Turner, Marianne, tr. LC 66-9787. (Illus.). 138 p. 22cm. 1st U.S. edition. 1966, c.1961. Pantheon Books.

--Magnus in Danger. Wikland, Ilon (1930-), illus. Turner, Marianne, tr. LC 67-14224. (Illus.). 135 p. 22cm. 1st U.S. edition. 1967, c.1963. Pantheon Books.

--Magnus in the Harbor. Wikland, Ilon (1930-), illus. Turner, Marianne, tr. LC 66-31470. (Illus.). 117 p. 22cm. 1st U.S. edition. 1966, c.1962. Pantheon Books.

--Mickey and Molly. Montelius, Olle, illus. LC 64-14433. (Illus.). 32 p. 16cm. (Lothrop little book). 1964. Lothrop, Lee & Shepard Co.

--The New House. Ware, Kay (1916-) & Sutherland, Lucille, eds. Kallstrom, Ylva, illus. LC 64-6416. (Illus.). 23cm. (The Read for Fun Ser.). 1964. Webster Division, McGraw-Hill.

--The Old Man and the Bird. Ware, Kay (1916-) & Sutherland, Lucille, eds. Kallstrom, Ylva, illus. LC 64-7024. (Illus.). 23cm. (The Read for Fun Ser.). 1964. Webster Division, McGraw-Hill.

--Peter Johnson and His Guitar. Clante, Iben, illus. Ware, Kay (1916-), adapted by. LC 61-66405. unpaged. illus. 23cm. (Read for fun series). c.1961. Webster Pub. Co.

--Tom and Tabby. Montelius, Olle, illus. LC 65-133944. 1v. (unpaged) col. illus. 16cm. (Lothrop little bk.). 1965. Lothrop.

--When Peter Was Lost in the Forest. Wiberg, Harald Albin (1908-), illus. LC 74-120096. (Illus.). 32 p. 22 cm. 1970. Coward-McCann.

Peterson, Harry L

--Their Pot O' Gold: The Tale of a Prospector. LC 58-9677. 215p. 21cm. c.1958. Dorrance.

Peterson, Holly & Peterson, John Lawrence (1924-)

--Terry's Treasure Hunt. Peterson, Holly & Peterson, John Lawrence (1924-), illus. (gr. 5-8). 1977. (ISBN 0-590-10324-5, Schol Pap). Schol Bk Serv.

--Tony's Treasure Hunt. Peterson, Holly & Peterson, John Lawrence (1924-), illus. 48p. 1965. Pitman Publishing Corporation.

--Tony's Treasure Hunt. Peterson, Holly & Peterson, John Lawrence (1924-), illus. (Illus.). (gr. k-3). 1972. (ISBN 0-590-00120-5, Schol Trade Pap). Schol Bk Serv.

Peterson, Isabel J., selected by.

--The First Book of Poetry. Elgin, Kathleen (1923-), illus. (Illus.). 114 p. 23cm. (First books 37). 1954. F. Watts.

--Poetry. Elgin, Kathleen (1923-), illus. (Illus.). (gr. 7 up). 1954. (ISBN 0-531-01076-7). Watts.

Peterson, Jeanne Whitehouse, pseud., see Whitehouse, Jeanne.

Peterson, Jeanne Whitehouse, pseud. (1939-)

--I Have a Sister, My Sister Is Deaf. Whitehouse, Jeanne. Ray, Deborah (1940-), illus. LC 76-24306. (Illus.). (gr. k-3). 1977. (ISBN 0-06-024701-0, HarpJ). (ISBN 0-06-024702-9). Har-Row.

--That Is That. Whitehouse, Jeanne. Ray, Deborah (1940-), illus. LC 77-25676. (Illus.). 32 p. c.1979. (ISBN 0-06-024708-8). (ISBN 0-06-024709-6). Harper & Row.

--While the Moon Shines Bright. Whitehouse, Jeanne. Apple, Margot, illus. LC 79-2697. p. cm. c.1981. (ISBN 0-06-024710-X). (ISBN 0-06-024711-8). Harper & Row.

Peterson, Jim

--Broomhilda DewDrop. Peterson, Jim, illus. (Illus.). 32p. (gr. k-5). 1975. (ISBN 0-685-63894-4). (ISBN 0-685-63895-2). Amhara Corp.

Peterson, John Lawrence, jt. auth. see Peterson, Holly.

Peterson, John Lawrence (1924-)

--The Cowboy. Peterson, John Lawrence (1924-), illus. (Illus.). (gr. k-3). 1972. (ISBN 0-590-00512-X, Schol Pap). (ISBN 0-590-20796-2). Scholastic Inc.

--Enemies of the Secret Hide-Out. Peterson, John Lawrence (1924-), illus. LC 66-9442. (Illus.). 46 p. 22cm. 1966. Four Winds Press.

--The Littles. Clark, Roberta Carter, illus. (Illus.). 80p. (gr. 4-6). 1970. (ISBN 0-590-32006-8). Scholastic Inc.

--The Littles. Clark, Roberta Carter, illus. Repr. (Starbright Editions). (gr. k-3). 1973. Schol Bk Serv.

--The Littles & the Big Storm. Clark, Roberta Carter, illus. (Littles Ser.). (gr. 4-6). 1979. (ISBN 0-590-05752-9). Scholastic Inc.

--The Littles & the Trash Tinies. Clark, Roberta Carter, illus. (gr. 4-6). 1977. (ISBN 0-590-10404-7). Scholastic Inc.

--The Littles & Their Friends. Peterson, John Lawrence (1924-), illus. (Illus.). 24p. (Orig.). (ps-3). 1981. (ISBN 0-590-31394-0). Scholastic.

--The Littles' Give a Party. Clark, Roberta Carter, illus. (Illus.). (gr. 4-6). 1974. (ISBN 0-590-32004-1). Scholastic Inc.

--The Littles Have a Wedding. Clark, Roberta Carter, illus. (Illus.). (gr. 4-6). 1972. (ISBN 0-590-32009-2). Scholastic Inc.

--The Littles Take a Trip. Clark, Roberta Carter, illus. (Illus.). (gr. 4-6). 1972. (ISBN 0-590-02563-5). Scholastic Inc.

--The Littles to the Rescue. Clark, Roberta Carter, illus. (Illus.). (gr. 4-6). 1971. (ISBN 0-590-32007-6). Scholastic Inc.

--The Littles to the Rescue. Peterson, John Lawrence (1924-), illus. (Illus.). 48p. (ps-3). 1981. (ISBN 0-448-47491-3, G&D). Putnam Pub Group.

--Mean Max. (gr. k-3). N.D (Schol Trade Pap). Schol Bk Serv.

--Mystery in the Night Woods. Szekeres, Cyndy (1933-), illus. (Illus.). (gr. k-3). N.D. (ISBN 0-590-08748-7). Scholastic Inc.

--The Secret Hide-Out. Peterson, John Lawrence (1924-), illus. LC 66-33865. 47p. col. illus. 22cm. 1966, c.1965. Four Winds Dist. Scholastic.

--Tom Little's Great Halloween Scare. Peterson, John Lawrence (1924-), illus. (gr. 5-8). 1976. (ISBN 0-590-04702-7). Scholastic Inc.

Peterson, John V.

--Rock the Big Rock. ca. 200p. 1970. Curtis.

Peterson, Livia Y. (1886-) & Plummer, Myrtes Marie (1886-)

--Fair Wind. Nelson, Don, illus. LC 47-2602. 234 p. incl. front., illus., plates. 21 cm. 1947. Wilcox & Follett Co.

Peterson, Lorraine

--Falling Off Cloud Nine & Other High Places. Dugan, LeRoy, illus. LC 81-38465. (Illus.). 159p. (Orig.). (gr. 8-12). 1981. (ISBN 0-87123-167-0). Bethany Hse.

Peterson, Mike

--The Biggest Giraffe. Gadbois, Robert, illus. LC 77-1981. (Illus.). 31 p. 25cm. c.1977. (ISBN 0-87191-609-6). Creative Education.

Peterson, Phyllis Lee

--The Log Cabin in the Forest. Forberg, Ati, pseud. (1925-), illus. Forberg, Beate Gropius. LC 54-9050. (Illus.). 24. 24cm. 1954. Houghton Mifflin.

Peterson, Russell Francis, jt. auth. see Peterson, Barbara Burns.

Peterson, Stella Parker

--From Honeymoon to Massacre: The Story of Marcus and Narcissa Whitman. Peterson, Stella Parker, illus. LC 41-21728. 192 p. incl. front. (ports.) illus. 20 cm. c.1941. Review and Herald Publishing Association.

Peterson, William (1938-) & Hallmark Cards, Inc.

--Hallmark Presents the Patch Family. Peterson, William (1938-), illus. LC 75-18546. (Illus.). 28 p. 22 x 26 cm. c.1976. (ISBN 0-87529-471-5). Hallmark.

Peterson, Willis & Clifford, Eth, pseud.

--Wapiti, King of the Woodland. Rosenberg, Ethel Clifford. Peterson, Willis, photos by. (Illus.). 32 p. 29cm. c.1961. Follett Pub. Co.

Petersson, Jon, jt. auth. see Wade, Anne.

Petie, Haris, pseud., see Petty, Roberta Harris Pfafflin.

Petie, Haris, pseud. (1915-)

--The Seed the Squirrel Dropped. Petty, Roberta Harris Pfafflin. Petie, Haris, pseud. (1915-), illus. Petty, Roberta Harris Pfafflin. LC 75-35848. (Illus.). 32 p. 24cm. c.1976. (ISBN 0-13-799627-6). Prentice-Hall.

--That's Our Cleo!. And Other Stories About Cats. Petty, Roberta Harris Pfafflin. Petie, Haris, pseud. (1915-), illus. Petty, Roberta Harris Pfafflin. LC 66-9205. (Illus.). 156 p. 22cm. (Whitman Teen age Book). 1967, c.1966. Whitman Pub. Co.

Petie, Haris, pseud. (1915-) & McKenna, John F., illus.

--Lullaby Lyrics. Petty, Roberta Harris Pfafflin. LC 44-4183. 32 p. col. illus. 24 1/2 cm. 1944. E. P. Dutton.

Petis De la Croix, Francois, jt. auth. see Fehse, Willi Richard.

Petisvka, E., ed. see Hoffmann, Ernst Theodor Amadeus.

Petitclerc, Grace Myers (1896-)

--The Mystery of the Missing Goat. Weaver, Jack (1925-), illus. LC 55-6894. 187p. illus. 20cm. 1955. Coward-McCann.

Peto, Gladys Emma, ed.

--The China Cow: Tales and Jingles for Children. Peto, Gladys Emma, illus. LC 27-3824. viii, 120 p. col. front., illus., col. plates. 26 cm. 1926. Houghton Mifflin Company.

Petrakis, Harry Mark (1923-)

--Pericles on Thirty-First Street. viii, 213p. (gr. 7 up). 1965. (ISBN 0-8129-0021-9). Quadrangle.

Petrezselyem, Mihaly see Spyri, Johanna Heusser.

Petrides, Heidrun (1944-)

--Hans and Peter. Petrides, Heidrun (1944-), illus. LC 63-1031. (Illus.). 1 v. (unpaged. 1963, c.1962. Harcourt, World.

Petrie, Catherine (1947-)

--Hot Rod Harry. Sharp, Paul (1927-), illus. LC 81-15549. (Illus.). 30 p. 19cm. (A Rookie Reader). c.1982. (ISBN 0-516-03493-6). (ISBN 0-516-43493-4). Childrens Press.

--Joshua James Likes Trucks. Warshaw, Jerry (1929-), illus. LC 81-17076. (Illus.). 29 p. 19cm. (A Rookie Reader). c.1982. (ISBN 0-516-03525-8). (ISBN 0-516-03525-8). (ISBN 0-516-43525-6). Childrens Press.

--Sandbox Betty. Elzaurdia, Sharon, illus. LC 81-15547. (Illus.). 30 p. 19cm. (A Rookie Reader). c.1982. (ISBN 0-516-03578-9). (ISBN 0-516-43578-7). Childrens Press.

Petrie, Helen

--The Little Pilgrim. Petrie, Helen, illus. LC 16-10112. 61 p. incl. front., illus. plates. 23 cm. 1880. E. P. Dutton & co.

Petrie, Stuart

--The Voyage of Barracks. 1st U.S. ed. Petrie, Stuart, illus. LC 68-26498. (Illus.). 120 p. 21cm. 1968, c.1967. Meredith Press.

Petroff, Boris George (1895-)

--Son of the Danube. Mueller, Hans Alexander (1888-), illus. LC 40-27408. 4 p. l., 3-277 p. illus. 22 cm. 1940. The Viking Press.

Petroski, Catherine Ann Groom (1939-)

--Beautiful My Mane in the Wind. Parker, Robert Andrew (1927-), illus. LC 82-12120. p. cm. 1983. (ISBN 0-395-33074-2). Houghton Mifflin.

--The Summer That Lasted Forever. LC 84-12930. (gr. 6-8). 1984. (ISBN 0-395-35388-2). Houghton Mifflin.

Petroulas, Elias N

--The Prodigal Angel. LC 41-1357. 96 p. 22 cm. c.1940. Pegasus Publishing Co.

Petrovich, Michael B., tr. see Kusan, Ivan.

Petrovskaya, Kyra (1918-)

--Quest for the Golden Fleece. Mars, Witold Tadeusz J. (1912-), illus. LC 61-17695. (Illus.). 128p. (gr. 4-6). 1961. (ISBN 0-688-41248-3). Lothrop.

Petry, Ann Lane (1911-)

--The Drugstore Cat. Suba, Susanne (1913-), illus. LC 49-6316. 87 p. illus. 24 cm. 1949. T. Y. Crowell Co.

--Harriet Tubman, Conductor on the Underground Railroad. LC 55-9215. 247 p. 21cm. 1955. Crowell.

--Legends of the Saints. Rockwell, Anne F. (1934-), illus. LC 72-106576. (Illus.). 47 p. 24cm. 1970. Crowell.

--Tituba of Salem Village. LC 64-20691. 254 p. 21cm. 1964. Crowell. **Award: (ALA).**

Petry, Mercedes Mills

--Ruth Ann and Polly; a Story for Children. 1st ed. Rausch, Jane, illus. LC 56-12377. (Illus.). 36p. 14 x 22cm. 1956. Exposition Press.

Pettee, Florence Mae (1888-)

--Blunder's Mystery Companions. Key, Alexander Hill (1904-1979), illus. Harper, Wilhelmina, intro. by. LC 29-234952. 272 p. incl. front., illus. 20 cm. (Boys' and girls' adventure library). c.1929. A. Whitman & Co.

Pettee, Frank H

--The Orange Cat. Chapling, Ralph, illus. LC 32-288352. 120 p. incl. front., illus. 21 x 21 cm. c.1932. The Reilly & Lee Co.

Petter, Helen Mary

--The Number Book. Adams, George A., illus. LC 48-3498. 31 p. illus. (part col.) 21 cm. (Lothrop color book). 1946. Lothrop, Lee & Shepard Co.

Pettersson, Allan Rune (1936-)

--Frankenstein's Aunt. LC 81-2617. 125 p. 22cm. c.1980. (ISBN 0-316-70320-6). Little, Brown.

Pettigrew, Shirley

--There Was an Old Lady. Henry, Steve, illus. LC 73-88538. (Illus.). 46 p. 23cm. (Break-of-day book). c.1974. (ISBN 0-698-20289-9). (ISBN 0-698-30541-8). Coward, McCann & Geoghegan.

Pettit, Terry, et al.

--Watermarks. Hollis, James, ed. Miller, Kevin, illus. (Illus.). 4p. of drawings. 79p. (Orig.). 1971. (ISBN 0-87178-924-8). Brethren.

Petty, Emma

--Boy of the Wilderness. Doremus, Robert (1913-), illus. LC 48-7645. 171 p. illus., map (on lining-papers) 21 cm. 1948. Broadman Press.

--Brave Men of the Bible. Richards, H. O., illus. (Little Treasure Series). (gr. 1-4). 1956. (ISBN 0-8054-4209-X). Broadman.

Petty, Roberta Harris Pfafflin see Petie, Haris, pseud.

Peuleve, Marie-Louise, tr. see Andersen, Hans Christian.

Pevsner, Stella

--And You Give Me a Pain, Elaine. LC 78-5857. p. cm. c.1978. (ISBN 0-8164-3219-8). Seabury Press.

--Break a Leg!. Seuling, Barbara (1937-), illus. LC 73-90998. (Illus.). 160 p. 22cm. 1969. Crown Publishers.

--Call Me Heller, That's My Name. Cuffari, Richard (1925-1978), illus. 1973. Houghton.

--Call Me Heller, That's My Name. Cuffari, Richard (1925-1978), illus. LC 72-90084. (Illus.). 183 p. 22cm. 1973. (ISBN 0-8164-3095-0). Seabury Press.

--Cute Is a Four Letter Word. 190p. (gr. 3-6). 1980. (ISBN 0-395-29106-2, Clarion). HM.

--Footsteps on the Stairs. Seuling, Barbara (1937-), illus. LC 77-127517. (Illus.). 128 p. 22cm. 1970. Crown Publishers.

--I'll Always Remember You . . . Maybe. 192p. (gr. 6 up). 1981. (ISBN 0-395-31024-5, Clarion). HM.

--Keep Stompin Till the Music Stops. (gr. 5-7). 1977. Houghton Mifflin.

--Keep Stompin' Till the Music Stops. LC 76-27845. 136 p. 22cm. c.1977. (ISBN 0-8164-3187-6). Seabury Press.

--Lindsay, Lindsay, Fly Away Home. LC 83-2115. 184 p. 22cm. c.1983. (ISBN 0-89919-187-8). Clarion Books.

--New Girl. Seuling, Barbara (1937-), illus. (Illus.). 192p. (gr. 3-6). 1983. (ISBN 0-590-04483-4, Apple Paperbacks). Scholastic Inc.

--A Smart Kid Like You. 1975. Houghton.

--A Smart Kid Like You. LC 74-19320. (Illus.). 216 p. 22cm. 1975. (ISBN 0-8164-3138-8). Seabury Press.

Pevsner, Stella, adapted by.

--Me, My Goat, & My Sister's Wedding. Peek, Merle (1938-), illus. LC 84-12734. 192p. (gr. 4-7). 1985. (ISBN 0-89919-305-6, Clarion). HM.

Peyo, pseud., see Culliford, Pierre.

Peyo, pseud.

--Baker Smurf's Sniffy Book. Culliford, Pierre. Peyo, pseud., illus. Culliford, Pierre. LC 81-52359. (Illus.). 24p. (Sniffy Bks.). (ps-2). 1982. (ISBN 0-394-85138-2). Random.

--The Fake Smurf. Culliford, Pierre. Peyo, pseud., illus. Culliford, Pierre. LC 81-50256. (Illus.). 32p. (Smurf Mini-Storybooks). (ps-5). 1981. (ISBN 0-394-84932-9). Random.

--The Hundredth Smurf. Culliford, Pierre. Peyo, pseud., illus. Culliford, Pierre. LC 81-85941. (Illus.). 32p. (Smurf Mini-Storybooks). (ps-5). 1982. (ISBN 0-394-85374-1). Random.

--King Smurf. Culliford, Pierre. Peyo, pseud., illus. Culliford, Pierre. LC 81-52356. (Illus.). 48p. (Smurf Bks.). (gr. 4-8). 1982. (ISBN 0-394-85141-2). Random.

--A Little Smurf Bedtime Story. Culliford, Pierre. Peyo, pseud., illus. Culliford, Pierre. LC 81-52474. (Illus.). 12 p. 15cm. (Little pops). c.1982. (ISBN 0-394-85170-6). Random House.

--Rainy Day: A Smurf Book of Feelings. Culliford, Pierre. Peyo, pseud., illus. Culliford, Pierre. LC 81-52358. (Illus.). 24 p. 17cm. c.1982. (ISBN 0-394-85139-0). Random House.

--Smurf Cake. Culliford, Pierre. Peyo, pseud., illus. Culliford, Pierre. LC 81-50254. (Illus.). 32p. (Smurf Mini-Storybooks). (ps-5). 1981. (ISBN 0-394-84930-2). Random.

--The Smurf-Catching Trap. Culliford, Pierre. Peyo, pseud., illus. Culliford, Pierre. LC 81-52473. (Illus.). 12p. (Smurf Little Pops Ser.). (ps-3). 1982. (ISBN 0-394-85169-2). Random.

--Smurf on the Grow. Culliford, Pierre. Peyo, pseud., illus. Culliford, Pierre. LC 81-52475. (Illus.). 12 p. 16cm. (Little pops). c.1982. (ISBN 0-394-85171-4). Random House.

--A Smurf Picnic. Culliford, Pierre. Peyo, pseud., illus. Culliford, Pierre. LC 81-52476. (Illus.). 12 p. 15cm. (Little pops). c.1982. (ISBN 0-394-85172-2). Random House.

--Smurf Water Fun. Culliford, Pierre. Peyo, pseud., illus. Culliford, Pierre. (Illus.). 10p. (A Bathtime Book Ser.). (gr. k-1). 1983. (ISBN 0-394-86072-1). Random.

--The Smurfic Games & Smurf of One & Smurf a Dozen of the Other. Cuilliford, Pierre. Bell, Anthea & Hockridge, Derek, trs. from French LC 82-60259. (Illus.). 1984. (ISBN 0-394-85619-8). Random.

--The Smurfs & the Howlibird. Culliford, Pierre. Peyo, pseud., illus. Culliford, Pierre. (Illus.). 48p. (Smurf Adventures Ser.). (gr. 9-12). 1983. (ISBN 0-394-86075-6). Random.

--The Smurfs & the Magic Flute. Culliford, Pierre. Peyo, pseud., illus. Culliford, Pierre. LC 82-63150. (Illus.). 64p. (Smurf Adventures Ser.). 1983. (ISBN 0-394-86074-8). Random.

--The Smurfs & Their Woodland Friends. Culliford, Pierre. Peyo, pseud., illus. Culliford, Pierre. LC 81-85940. (Illus.). 28p. (Chunky Bks.). (ps). 1983. (ISBN 0-394-85370-9). Random.

--The Smurf's Apprentice. Culliford, Pierre. Peyo, pseud., illus. Culliford, Pierre. LC 81-85942. (Illus.). 32p. (Smurf Mini-Storybooks). (ps-5). 1982. (ISBN 0-394-85373-3). Random.

--Smurphony in C. Culliford, Pierre. Peyo, pseud., illus. Culliford, Pierre. LC 81-85943. (Illus.). 32p. (Smurf Mini-Storybooks). (ps-5). 1982. (ISBN 0-394-85372-5). Random.

--Through the Seasons with Smurfette. Culliford, Pierre. Peyo, pseud., illus. Culliford, Pierre. LC 82-60093. (Illus.). 16p. (Smurf Hummingbird Bks.). (ps-3). 1983. (ISBN 0-394-85620-1). Random.

--The Wandering Smurf. Culliford, Pierre. Peyo, pseud., illus. Culliford, Pierre. LC 81-50253. (Illus.). 32p. (Smurf Mini-Storybooks). (ps-5). 1981. (ISBN 0-394-84931-0). Random.

--What Do Smurfs Do All Day?. Culliford, Pierre. Peyo, pseud., illus. Culliford, Pierre. LC 83-6070. (Illus.). 48p. (Beginner Bks.: No. 70). (ps-3). 1983. (ISBN 0-394-86078-0). (ISBN 0-394-96078-5). Random.

--The Wonderful World of Smurfs. Culliford, Pierre. Peyo, pseud., illus. Culliford, Pierre. LC 81-85493. (Illus.). 1982. (ISBN 0-394-85189-7). Random.

Peyo, pseud. & Delporte, pseud.

--The Astrosmurf. Culliford, Pierre. Delporte, Yvan. Peyo, pseud., illus. Cuillford, Pierre. Bell, Anthea & Hockridge, Derek, trs. LC 81-52357. (Illus.). 40 p. 28cm. 1st U.S. edition. (A Smurf Adventure). 1983, c.1979. (ISBN 0-394-85140-4). Random House.

Peyo, pseud. & Matagne, Michel

--The Smurfs and the Miller. Culliford, Pierre. Peyo, pseud., illus. Culliford, Pierre. LC 83-3302. 1st U.S. edition. 1984. (ISBN 0-394-86076-4). Random House.

--The Smurfs and the Toyshop. Culliford, Pierre. Peyo, pseud., illus. Culliford, Pierre. LC 83-3301. 1st U.S. edition. 1984. (ISBN 0-394-86077-2). Random House.

Peyrouton De Ladebat, Monique (1909-)

--The Village That Slept. Gill, Margery Jean (1925-), illus. Niklaus, Thelma, tr. from Fr. LC 65-10881. (Illus.). 188 p. 21cm. 1st U.S. edition. 1965, c.1963. Coward-McCann.

--The Village That Slept. Gill, Margery Jean (1925-), illus. LC 79-18363. p. cm. (Gregg Press Children's Literature Series). 1979, c.1963. (ISBN 0-8398-2610-9). Gregg Press.

Peyser, Ethel

--The House That Music Built. N.D. Robert M. McBride & Co.

Peyton, K. M., pseud., see Peyton, Kathleen Wendy.

Peyton, K. M., pseud. (1929-)

--The Beethoven Medal. Peyton, Kathleen Wendy. Peyton, K. M., pseud. (1929-), illus. Peyton, Kathleen Wendy. LC 71-175109. 185 p. 21cm. 1972, c.1971. (ISBN 0-690-12846-0). Crowell.

--The Beethoven Medal. Peyton, Kathleen Wendy. Peyton, K. M., pseud. (1929-), illus. Peyton, Kathleen Wendy. LC 71-888177. (Illus.). 4 152 p. 23cm. 1971. (ISBN 0-19-271328-0). Oxford University Press.

--The Edge of the Cloud. Peyton, Kathleen Wendy. Ambrus, Victor G., pseud. (1935-), illus. Ambrus, Gyozo Laszlo. LC 79-82785. (Illus.). 207 p. 21cm. 1st U.S. edition. 1970, c.1969. World Pub. Co.

--Flambards. Peyton, Kathleen Wendy. Ambrus, Victor G., pseud. (1935-), illus. Ambrus, Gyozo Laszlo. LC 82-22391. p. cm. 1982, c.1967. (ISBN 0-399-20925-5). Philomel Books.

--Flambards. Peyton, Kathleen Wendy. Ambrus, Victor G., pseud. (1935-), illus. Ambrus, Gyozo Laszlo. LC 68-26977. (Illus.). 206 p. 21cm. 1st U.S. edition. 1968, c.1967. World Pub. Co. **Awards: (ALA); (BGH); (CMA).**

--Flambards Divided. Peyton, Kathleen Wendy. LC 81-15720. 272 p. 22cm. 1982, c.1981. (ISBN 0-399-20864-X). Philomel Books.

--Flambards in Summer. Peyton, Kathleen Wendy. LC 71-23034. (Illus.). 23cm. v, 165p. 1969. (ISBN 0-19-271312-4). Oxford University Press.

--Flambards in Summer. Peyton, Kathleen Wendy. Ambrus, Victor G., pseud. (1935-), illus. Ambrus, Gyozo Laszlo. LC 76-101850. (Illus.). 191 p. 21cm. 1st U.S. edition. 1970, c.1969. World Pub. Co.

--Fly-by-Night. Peyton, Kathleen Wendy. Peyton, K. M., pseud. (1929-), illus. Peyton, Kathleen Wendy. LC 74-404821. (Illus.). 23cm. vii, 163p. 1968. Oxford Univ. Press.

--Fly-by-Night. Peyton, Kathleen Wendy. Peyton, K. M., pseud. (1929-), illus. Peyton, Kathleen Wendy. LC 69-13057. (Illus.). 189 p. 21cm. 1969, c.1968. World Pub. Co.

--Free Rein. Peyton, Kathleen Wendy. LC 83-8151. p. cm. 1983. (ISBN 0-399-20995-6). Philomel Books.

--Going Home. Peyton, Kathleen Wendy. LC 81-22703. p. cm. 1982. (ISBN 0-399-20889-5). Philomel Books.

--If I Ever Marry. Peyton, Kathleen Wendy. (gr. 7-12). 1976. (ISBN 0-590-05195-4, Schol Pap). Scholastic Inc.

--The Maplin Bird. Peyton, Kathleen Wendy. Ambrus, Victor G., pseud. (1935-), illus. Ambrus, Gyozo Laszlo. LC 79-18257. p. cm. (Gregg Press Children's Literature Series). 1979, c.1965. (ISBN 0-8398-2611-7). Gregg Press.

--The Maplin Bird. Peyton, Kathleen Wendy. Ambrus, Victor G., pseud. (1935-), illus. Ambrus, Gyozo Laszlo. LC 65-13077. (Illus.). 237 p. 21cm. 1st U.S. edition. 1965. World Pub. Co. **Awards: (ALA); (CMA).**

--Marion's Angels. Peyton, Kathleen Wendy. LC 79-40676. p. cm. 1979. (ISBN 0-19-271432-5). Oxford University Press.

--A Midsummer Night's Death. Peyton, Kathleen Wendy. LC 78-9822. p. cm. c.1978. (ISBN 0-529-05453-1). CollinsWorld. **Award: (ALA).**

--North to Adventure. Peyton, Kathleen Wendy. LC 65-15197. 206p. 20cm. c.1965. Platt & Munk.

--A Pattern of Roses. Peyton, Kathleen Wendy. Peyton, K. M., pseud. (1929-), illus. Peyton, Kathleen Wendy. LC 73-3387. (Illus.). 186 p. 21cm. 1973, c.1972. (ISBN 0-690-61199-4). Crowell. **Award: (ALA).**

--A Pattern of Roses. Peyton, Kathleen Wendy. Peyton, K. M., pseud. (1929-), illus. Peyton, Kathleen Wendy. LC 72-172220. (Illus.). 5, 132 p. 23cm. 1972. (ISBN 0-19-271347-7). Oxford University Press.

--Pennington's Heir. Peyton, Kathleen Wendy. Peyton, K. M., pseud. (1929-), illus. Peyton, Kathleen Wendy. LC 74-8692. (Illus.). 229 p. 21cm. 1974, c.1973. (ISBN 0-690-00615-2). Crowell.

--Pennington's Last Term. Peyton, Kathleen Wendy. Peyton, K. M., pseud. (1929-), illus. Peyton, Kathleen Wendy. LC 75-139099. (Illus.). 216 p. 21cm. 1971, c.1970. (ISBN 0-690-61271-0). Crowell.

--Pennington's Seventeenth Summer. Peyton, Kathleen Wendy. Peyton, K. M., pseud. (1929-), illus. Peyton, Kathleen Wendy. LC 71-23322. (Illus.). 23cm. v, 183p. 1970. (ISBN 0-19-271318-3). Oxford Univ. Press.

--The Plan for Birdsmarsh. Peyton, Kathleen Wendy. Ambrus, Victor G., pseud. (1935-), illus. Ambrus, Gyozo Laszlo. LC 66-97792. 172 p. illus. 23 cm. 1965. Oxford University Press.

--The Plan for Birdsmarsh. Peyton, Kathleen Wendy. Ambrus, Victor G., pseud. (1935-), illus. Ambrus, Gyozo Laszlo. LC 66-13901. 239 p. illus. 21 cm. 1st U.S. edition. 1966. World Pub. Co.

--Prove Yourself a Hero. Peyton, Kathleen Wendy. LC 78-18802. p. cm. 22 cm. 182p. 1978, c.1977. (ISBN 0-529-05452-3). Collins.

--Sea Fever. Peyton, Kathleen Wendy. Ambrus, Victor G., pseud. (1935-), illus. Ambrus, Gyozo Laszlo. LC 63-18464. (Illus.). 21 cm. 240p. (gr. 6 up). 1963. (ISBN 0-529-03801-3). Collins Pubs. **Award: (ALA).**

--Sea Fever. Peyton, Kathleen Wendy. Ambrus, Victor G., pseud. (1935-), illus. Ambrus, Gyozo Laszlo. 240p. 1963. World Publishing Company.

--Sing a Song of Ambush. Peyton, Kathleen Wendy. LC 64-18262. 20cm. 208p. (A Junior adventure). 1964. Platt and Munk.

--So Once Was I. Peyton, Kathleen Wendy (Pub. by T. Y. Crowell). (gr. 7-12). 1976. (ISBN 0-590-03890-7, Schol Pap). Schol Bk Serv.

--The Team. Peyton, Kathleen Wendy. Peyton, K. M., pseud. (1929-), illus. Peyton, Kathleen Wendy. LC 75-34092. 21 cm. 213p. 1976. (ISBN 0-690-01083-4). Crowell.

--Thunder in the Sky. Peyton, Kathleen Wendy. Ambrus, Victor G., pseud. (1935-), illus. Ambrus, Gyozo Laszlo. LC 67-13831. (Illus.). 158 p. 21cm. 1st U.S. edition. 1967, c.1966. World Pub. Co.

--Who, Sir? Me, Sir?". Peyton, Kathleen Wendy. LC 83-670261. 171 p. 23cm. 171p. 1983. (ISBN 0-19-271470-8). Oxford University Press.

Peyton, Kathleen Wendy see Herald, Kathleen, pseud.

Peyton, Kathleen Wendy see Peyton, K. M, pseud.

Pezzi, Maria Pia

--Curly the Pig. Daly, Kathleen N., adapted by. Lavraghi, Virginio, illus. LC 64-5440. (Illus.). 23cm. (A Big Golden Bk.). 1964. Golden Press.

Pfaender, Ann McLelland

--Miss Library Lady.'. LC 54-6772. 184p. 22cm. (Romance for young moderns). 1954. J. Messner.

Pfaffle, Hope, compiled by.

--Mother Goose Song Book. Smith, Marion Frederick, illus. LC 48-11342. 100 p. col. illus. 21 x 29 cm. 1948. Garden City Pub. Co.

Pfeffer, Susan Beth (1948-)

--About David. LC 80-10581. 167 p. 22cm. c.1980. (ISBN 0-440-00093-9). Delacorte Press.

--Awful Evelina. Pacini, Kathy, ed. Dawson, Diane, illus. LC 79-108. (Illus.). (Concept Bk.: Level I). (gr. k-3). 1979. (ISBN 0-8075-0494-7). A Whitman.

--The Beauty Queen. 1st ed. LC 73-11634. 134 p. 22cm. 1974. (ISBN 0-385-02256-5). Doubleday.

--Better Than All Right. LC 72-76197. 111 p. 22cm. 1972. Doubleday.

--Courage, Dana. Rutherford, Jenny, illus. LC 82-72821. (Illus.). 134 p. 22cm. c.1983. (ISBN 0-440-00922-7). Delacorte Press.

--Fantasy Summer. 192p. (Perfect Image Ser.). (gr. 7 up). 1984. (ISBN 0-399-21086-5, Putnam). Putnam Pub Group.

--Just Between Us. Tomei, Lorna, illus. LC 79-53606. (Illus.). 116 p. 21cm. c.1980. (ISBN 0-440-05045-6). (ISBN 0-440-05046-4). Delacorte Press.

--Just Morgan. LC 73-100709. 199 p. 21cm. 1970. (ISBN 0-8098-3088-4). H. Z. Walck.

--Kid Power. Grant, Alice Leigh (1947-), illus. LC 77-1975. (Illus.). 121 p. 22cm. 1977. (ISBN 0-531-00123-7). F. Watts.

--Kid Power Strikes Back. Grant, Alice Leigh (1947-), illus. (Illus.). 128p. (Single Title Ser.). 1984. (ISBN 0-531-04839-X). Watts.

--Marly the Kid. LC 74-33658. 137 p. 22cm. (Doubleday signal books). 1975. (ISBN 0-385-03693-0). (ISBN 0-385-03983-2). Doubleday.
--A Matter of Principle: A Novel. LC 81-15288. 181 p. 22cm. c.1982. (ISBN 0-440-05612-8). Delacorte Press.
--Rainbows & Fireworks. LC 72-10709. 131 p. 21cm. 1973. (ISBN 0-8098-3114-7). H. Z. Walck.
--Starring Peter and Leigh: A Novel. LC 78-72855. 200 p. 22cm. c.1979. (ISBN 0-440-08226-9). Delacorte Press.
--Starting with Melodie. LC 82-70412. 122 p. 22cm. c.1982. (ISBN 0-590-07859-3). Four Winds Press.
--Truth or Dare. LC 83-20635. 128p. 1984. (ISBN 0-590-07853-4). Four Winds Press.
--What Do You Do When Your Mouth Won't Open?. A Novel. Tomei, Lorna, illus. LC 80-68731. (Illus.). 128p. (gr. 4-7). 1981. Delacorte.
--Whatever Words You Want to Hear. LC 74-5478. 152 p. 21cm. 1974. (ISBN 0-8098-3120-1). H. Z. Walck.

Pfloog, Jan
--The Bear Book. Pfloog, Jan, illus. LC 66-9493. 1 v. (unpaged) col. illus. 22 cm. (Golden book for kindergarten). 1965. Golden Press.
--The Bear Book. Pfloog, Jan, illus. LC 66-78546. 24 p. col. illus. 20 1/2 cm. 2/. 1966. Golden Pleasure Books.
--The Puppy Book. Pfloog, Jan, illus. (Illus.). (ps-1). 1968. (ISBN 0-307-68946-8, Golden Pr). Western Pub.

Pflug, Betsy
--Egg-Speriment. Pflug, Betsy, illus. (Illus.). 40p. 1973. J. B. Lippincott Company.
--Funny Bags. Pflug, Betsy, illus. 48p. Repr. 1970. J B Lippincott Company.
--Funny Bags. Pflug, Betsy, illus. (Illus.). 40 p. 27cm. 1968. Van Nostrand.
--Pint-Size Fun. Pflug, Betsy, illus. LC 73-172153. (Illus.). 40 p. 26cm. 1972. (ISBN 0-397-31216-4). (ISBN 0-397-31290-3). Lippincott.

Pfrimmer, Mildred
--Books to Learn & Live by, 5 bks. Incl. Bk. 1. The ABC's of Creation; Bk. 2. The ABC's of the Flood; Bk. 3. The Aardvark in the Ark; Bk. 4. Elephant in Eden; Bk. 5. The Tale of the Whale. (The Little Talkers Ser.). (gr. 3-9). 1977. Set. (ISBN 0-685-80546-8). Triumph Pub.

Phaedrus
--Select Fables. Walpole, A. S., adapted by. (Elementary Classics). N.D. MacMillan.

Phang, Ruth & Roth, Susan L.
--Patchwork Tales. Roth, Susan L., illus. LC 84-2987. (Illus.). 32p. (gr. k-3). 1984. (ISBN 0-689-31053-6). Atheneum.

Phegley, Mallie
--Children of Hawaii. LC 39-33010. x p., 1 l., 208 p. illus. 23 cm. c.1939. Manfred, Van Nort & Co.

Phelan, Margaret S G, Mrs.
--Candlelight Tales. Woodward, Hildegard (1898-), illus. LC 34-33678. x, 9-68 p. incl. front., illus. 20 cm. (Our changing world). 1934. T. Nelson and Sons.

Phelan, Mary Kay (1914-)
--Midnight Alarm;. The/Story of Paul Revere's Ride. Weisgard, Leonard Joseph (1916-), illus. LC 68-17080. (Illus.). 131p. 21cm. 1968. Crowell.

Phelan, Terry Wolfe (1941-)
--Best Friends-Hands Down. LC 82-16038. p. cm. c.1983. (ISBN 0-590-07629-9). Four Winds Press.
--The S. S. Valentine. (gr. 4-6). 1979. Scholastic.
--The S. S. Valentine. Glasser, Judith, illus. LC 79-10037. (Illus.). 40 p. 22cm. c.1979. (ISBN 0-590-07578-0). Four Winds Press.
--The Week Mom Unplugged the TVs. Schick, Joel (1945-), illus. LC 78-12180. (Illus.). 36 p. 22cm. c.1979. (ISBN 0-590-07561-6). Four Winds Press.

Phelps, Agnes
--One Year at Our Boarding School. N.D. Loring.

Phelps, Almira Hart Lincoln, Mrs.
--The Blue Ribbon Society: Or, The School Girls Rebellion. N.D. Claxton, Remsen & Haffelfinger.
--Caroline Westerley. 1882. Harper's Trade-List.
--Caroline Westerley. (Illus.). (Harper's Boys' and Girls' Library). N.D. Harper & Brothers'.
--Fireside Friend. 1882. Harper's Trade-List.

Phelps, Edith May (1881-), ed.
--Book and Library Plays for Elementary and High School Use. LC 38-289140. v. diagrs. 20 cm. N.D. The H. W. Wilson Company.

Phelps, Edith P.
--Mrs. Tippoo Tib (Pub. by Society for Promoting Christian Knowledge). N.D. E. & J. B. Young & Co.

Phelps, Elizabeth Stuart see Trusta, H., pseud.

Phelps, Elizabeth Stuart see Ward, Elizabeth Stuart Phelps, Mrs.

Phelps, Elizabeth Stuart, Mrs. (1815-1852)
--Gypsy Breynton. N.D. Dodd Mead & Co.
--Little Mary: Or, Talks and Tales for Children. Trusta, H., pseud. LC 31-35235. vii, 1 l., 11-186 p. front., plates. 17 cm. 1854. Phillips, Sampson and Company.
--Tiny's Sunday Nights, 1 of 4 Vols. (Tiny Ser.). N.D. Set. Congregational Publishing Society.

Phelps, Ethel Johnston (1914-), compiled by.
--The Maid of the North: Feminist Folk Tales from Around the World. Bloom, Lloyd, illus. LC 80-21500. (Illus.). 192p. (gr. 2-6). 1981. (ISBN 0-03-056893-5). (ISBN 0-03-062374-X). HR&W.
--Tatterhood and Other Tales: Stories of Magic and Adventure. Baldwin-Ford, Pamela, illus. LC 78-9352. p. cm. 1978. (ISBN 0-912670-49-5). Feminist Press.

Phelps, Frances Brown
--Nikita, a Story of Russia. De Gogorza, Maitland, illus. LC 32-23277. 5 p. l., 3-263 p. incl. front., plates. 22 cm. c.1932. Harcourt, Brace and Company.

Phelps, Guy Fitch
--Mountains of the Morning. N.D. Abingdon Press.

Phelps, L. L., Miss
--The Veil on the Heart, 1 of 5 vols. (Illus.). (Edith Prescot Library). N.D. D. Lothrop Co.

Phelps, Lavinia H.
--Dramatic Stories for Home and School Entertainment. N.D. S. C. Griggs.

Phelps, Margaret
--Antelope Boy and Other Stories. Eshner, Ann, illus. LC 46-8271. 152 p. illus. (part col.) 22 cm. 1946. Macrea-Smith-Company.
--Chia and the Lambs. Eshner, Ann, illus. LC 44-3691. 5 p. l., 9-158 p. illus. 22 1/2 cm. 1941. Macrae Smith Co.
--Gard and Golden Boy. Copelman, Evelyn, illus. LC 50-7379. 204 p. illus. 23 cm. 1950. Macrae-Smith.
--Jaro and the Golden Colt. Copelman, Evelyn, illus. LC 54-7151. (Illus.). 168 p. 23cm. 1954. Macrae Smith Co.
--Ketch Dog. Copelman, Evelyn, illus. LC 51-13083. 223 p. illus. 23 cm. 1951. Macrae Smith.
--Pico and the Silver Mountain. Eshner, Ann, illus. LC 42-25239. 5 p. l., 13-126 p., 1 l. illus., col. plates. 22 1/2 cm. 1942. Macrae-Smith-Company.
--Regular Cowboys. Copelman, Evelyn, illus. LC 48-8611. 224 p. illus. 23 cm. 1948. Macrae Smith Co.
--Territory Boy. Copelman, Evelyn, illus. LC 52-140027. 224p. illus. 23cm. 1953. Macrae Smith.
--Toby on the Sheep Drive. Copelman, Evelyn, illus. LC 49-650544. 197 p. illus. 23 cm. 1949. Macrae Smith Co.

Phelps, Netta Sheldon, Mrs. (1861-)
--The Valiant Seven. Wilson, Helen Hughes, illus. LC 41-4139. 221 p. col. front., illus., plates. 24 cm. 1941. The Caxton Printers, Ltd.

Phelps, Norris McDonald
--Baby Blue Eyes, and Other Stories. Mier, Richard John, illus. LC 49-6366. (Illus.). 1941. W. G. Clark.

Phelps, Phebe H.
--Henry Day Learning to Obey Bible Commands. (Mary and Henry Day Ser.). N.D. Thompson, Brown & Co.
--Henry Day's Story Book. (Mary and Henry Day Ser.). N.D. Thompson, Brown & Co.
--Mary Day Forming Good Habits. (Mary and Henry Day Ser.). N.D. Thompson, Brown & Co.
--Mary Day's Story Book. (Mary and Henry Day Ser.). N.D. Thompson, Brown & Co.

Phelps, R. P
--Tom Martin the Breaker Boy. Hastings, Howard Livingston (1887-), illus. LC 26-18319. 4 p. l., 374 p front plates. 20 cm. c.1926. Cupples & Leon Company.

Phelps, S. B., Mrs.
--Sister Eleanor's Brood, 1 of 4 vols. (Sister Eleanor Ser.). N.D. D. Lothrop & Co.
--Sister Eleanor's Brood, 1 of 5 vols. (Illus.). (Favorite Books for Girls). N.D. D. Lothrop Co.
--Sister Eleanor's Brood, 1 of 50 vols. (Illus.). 350p. (Sunday-School Lib: No. 14). N.D. Set. Lothrop Pub. Co.

Pheobe, pseud., see Hoss, Phoebe Wilson.

Philadelphia Yearly Meeting of the Society of Friends
--The Children's Story Garden. Broomell, Anna Pettit, ed. Wireman, Katharine Richardson & Wireman, Eugenie M., illus. LC 20-7726. 246, 1 p. col. front., plates. 20 cm. 1920. J. B. Lippincott Company.
--The Children's Story Garden. Broomell, Anna Pettit, ed. Wireman, Katharine Richardson & Wireman, Eugenie M., illus. LC 38-12762. 216, 1 p. col. front., plates. 20 cm. N.D. J. B. Lippincott Company.

Philbrick, Charles Horace, II (1922-1971)
--Westaway. 1st ed. Hollerbach, Serge, illus. LC 68-15425. (Illus.). 119 p. 21cm. 1968. Harcourt, Brace & World.

Philbrook, Clement E. (1917-)
--Captured by the Abnakis. Tolford, Joshua (1909-), illus. LC 66-13281. 125 p. illus. 22 cm. 1966. Hastings House.
--Hickory Wings. LC 51-13735. 177 p. 21cm. 1951. Macmillan.
--Key Log. LC 53-81803. 188p. 21cm. 1953. Macmillan.
--Live Wire. Tolford, Joshua (1909-), illus. LC 66-20537. (Illus.). 22cm. 126p. (gr. 6-9). 1966. (ISBN 0-8038-4248-1). Hastings.
--The Magic Bat. Geary, Clifford N. (1916-), illus. LC 54-8603. 167p. 21cm. 1954. Macmillan.
--Ollie, the Backward Forward. Chauncy, Francis, illus. LC 73-126421. (Illus.). 96 p. 22cm. 1970, c.1971. (ISBN 0-8038-5361-0). Hastings House.
--Ollie, the Foul Shooter. Chauncy, Francis, illus. 128p. (gr. 3-7). 1984. (ISBN 0-8038-5400-5). Hastings.
--Ollie's Team and the Alley Cats. Chauncy, Francis, illus. LC 77-170630. (Illus.). 126 p. 22cm. 1971. (ISBN 0-8038-5366-1). Hastings House.
--Ollie's Team and the Baseball Computer. Chauncy, Francis, illus. LC 67-15343. 122p. illus. 22cm. 1967. Hastings.
--Ollie's Team and the Basketball Computer. Chauncy, Francis, illus. LC 73-85232. (Illus.). 125 p. 22cm. 1969. Hastings House.
--Ollie's Team and the Football Computer. Chauncy, Francis, illus. LC 68-21354. (Illus.). 128 p. 22cm. 1968. Hastings House.
--Ollie's Team and the Million Dollar Mistake. Chauncy, Francis, illus. LC 73-1644. (Illus.) 125 p. 22cm. 1973. (ISBN 0-8038-5373-4). Hastings House.
--Ollie's Team and the Two Hundred Pound Problem. Chauncy, Francis, illus. LC 72-360. (Illus.). 125 p. 22cm. 1972. (ISBN 0-8038-5371-8). Hastings House.
--Ollie's Team Plays Biddy Baseball. Chauncy, Francis, illus. LC 72-104748. (Illus.). 123 p. 22cm. 1970. Hastings House.
--Skimeister. LC 55-14824. 164p. 21cm. 1955. Macmillan.
--Slope Dope. Kramer, Frank, illus. LC 66-8495. (Illus.). (gr. 6-9). 1966. (ISBN 0-8038-6658-5). (ISBN 0-8038-6659-3). Hastings.

Philbrook, Elizabeth
--Far from Marlborough Street. Chanslor, Marjorie Torrey Hood (1899-), illus. Torrey, Marjorie, pseud. LC 44-3679. viii p., 1 l., 302 p. incl. illus., plates. 21 cm. 1944. The Viking Press.
--Hobo Hill. Freeman, Don (1908-1978), illus. LC 54-9317. 96p. illus. 25cm. 1954. Viking Press.

Philbrook, Rose (1911-)
--The Wings of Dr. Smidge. Bolin, Jim, illus. LC 52-11880. (Illus.). 138p. 24cm. 1954. Caxton Printers.

Philipe, Anne
--Atom, the Little Moon Monkey. (gr. k up). N.D. (ISBN 0-531-04004-6). (ISBN 0-531-05004-1). Quist.

Philipps, Myra
--Smooth As Silk. 2nd ed. Ramon, Estelle, illus. (Illus.). 1979. (ISBN 0-686-10960-0). Basin Pub.

Philips, John
--The Bomb that Wouldn't Go Off. N.D. Bruce Humphries.

Philips, Mary Alice
--The Beast in the Cave. Gide, Torson, illus. LC 59-5260. 182p. illus. 21cm. 1959. F. Watts.

Philipson, Morris H. (1926-)
--Everything Changes. Oechsli, Kelly (1918-), illus. LC 76-175949. (Illus.). 32 p. 27cm. 1972. (ISBN 0-394-82396-6). (ISBN 0-394-92396-0). Pantheon Books.

Philipson, Susan S.
--Lion for Niccolby Sacher. Guarcello, Giovanni, illus. LC 63-15483. (Illus.). 29cm. (gr. k-3). 1963. (ISBN 0-394-91344-2). Pantheon.

Phillimore, Catherine Mary
--Princess Opportunity and the Lady Remorse. (Illus.). N.D. E & J B Young.

Phillips, Agnes Lucas
--One Clear Call: A Novel About Nursing. 1 st. ed. LC 55-11129. 120p. 21cm. 1955. Exposition Press.

Phillips, Ann
--The Multiplying Glass. (Illus.). 157p. 1982. (ISBN 0-19-271455-4, Pub. by Oxford U Pr Childrens). Merrimack Pub Cir.
--The Oak King and the Ash Queen. 1985. Oxford Univ Press.

Phillips, Barbara
--Don't Call Me Fatso. Cogancherry, Helen, illus. LC 79-23888. p. cm. c.1980. (ISBN 0-8172-1350-3). Raintree Childrens Books.
--Nok Noy and the Charcoal Man. Selig, Sylvie (1942-), illus. LC 70-110346. (Illus.). 32 p. 24cm. 1970. (ISBN 0-201-05825-1). Addison-Wesley.

Phillips, Betty L.
--Go! Fight! Win!. Herkimer, Lawrence Russell (1925-), illus. Shepherd, Francis, photos by. LC 79-53607. (Illus.). 160p. (gr. 6 up). 1981. Delacorte.

Phillips, C. A., jt. auth. see Briggs, E. B.

Phillips, Carolyn E.
--Our Family Got a Divorce. Taylor, Paul L., illus. LC 78-74006. 112p. (gr. k-6). 1979. (ISBN 0-8307-0677-1). Regal.
--When Someone Really Loves You. LC 83-17837. p. cm. 1983. (ISBN 0-8307-0914-2). Regal Books.

Phillips, Charles Fox
--The Hoity-Toity Mouse, and Other Bayou Tales. LC 78-22643. (Illus.). 48 p. 27cm. c.1979. (ISBN 0-385-14546-2). Doubleday.

Phillips, Cheryl M., ed. see Stirrup Associates, Inc.

Phillips, Cheryl M. & Harvey, Bonnie C., eds.
--My Jesus Pocketbook of God's Fruit. Fulton, Ginger A., illus. LC 83-50194. (Illus.). 32p. (My Jesus Pocketbook Ser.). (ps). 1983. (ISBN 0-937420-08-5). Stirrup Assoc.
--My Jesus Pocketbook of the Lord's Prayer. Fulton, Ginger A., illus. LC 83-50193. (Illus.). 32p. (My Jesus Pocketbook Ser.). (ps). 1983. (ISBN 0-937420-07-7). Stirrup Assoc.

Phillips, David L.
--It's a Small World. N.D. (ISBN 0-8283-1111-0). Branden Press.

Phillips, Dorothy Evans (1909-)
--Big-Enough Boat. Frankenberg, Robert Clinton (1911-), illus. LC 56-9866. 96p. illus. 23cm. 1956. (ISBN 0-695-40770-8). Follett Pub. Co.

Phillips, Dorothy Waldo, as told to.
--Dear Mrs. Bender,. Dictated by Children in a Summer Resort; Illustrated by an Adult in a City. Calder, Mildred Bussing, illus. xiii, 126 p. incl. col. front., illus. (part col.) port. group. 23 cm. c.1937. The John C. Winston Company.

Phillips, Ethel Calvert (0000-1947)
--Belinda and the Singing Clock. Burton, Virginia Lee (1909-1968), illus. LC 38-27883. 5 p. l., 112 p. front., plates. 22 cm. 1938. Houghton Mifflin Company.
--Black-Eyed Susan. Cue, Harold, illus. LC 21-18797. 3 p. l., 170 p. col. front. 20 cm. c.1921. Houghton Mifflin Co.
--Brian's Victory. Merwin, Decie (1894-1961), illus. LC 42-228611. 4 p. l., 86, 1 p. illus. 25 1/2 cm. 1942. Houghton Mifflin Company.
--Bunchy: Or, The Children of Scarsbrook Farm. (Illus.). N.D. Publications of E. P. Dutton & Co.
--Calico. LC 37-35185. 4 p. l., 139 p. incl. col. front., illus. 21 cm. 1937. Houghton Mifflin Company.
--Christmas Light. LC 22-19686. 5 p. l., 128 p. col. front. 20 cm. 1922. Houghton Mifflin Company.
--Gay Madelon. LC 31-172806. 4 p. l., 142, 1 p. col. front., illus., col. plates. 21 cm. 1931. Houghton Mifflin Company.
--Grandfather. N.D. Publications of E. P. Dutton & Co.
--Hilda and Her Doll. (Illus.). N.D. E. P. Dutton & Co.
--Humpty Dumpty House. Preston, Alice Bolam (1889-), illus. LC 24-24814. 3 p. l., 140 p. col. front. 20 cm. c.1924. Houghton Mifflin Co.
--Jeanne-Marie and Her Golden Bird. Blair, Helen (1910-), illus. LC 34-259312. 4 p. l., 112, 1 p. front., plates. 21 cm. 1934. Houghton Mifflin Company.
--Little Friend Lydia. Butler, Edith F., illus. LC 21-280. 4 p. l., 181, 1 p. col. front., illus., col. plates. 20 cm. 1920. Houghton Mifflin Company.
--Little Rag Doll. Lenski, Lois (1893-1974), illus. LC 30-299902. 5 p. l., 173, 1 p. col. front., illus., col. plates. 21 cm. 1930. Houghton Mifflin Company.
--Little Sally Waters. Butler, Edith F., illus. LC 26-146803. 4 p. l., 143 p. col. front., col. plates. 21 cm. 1926. Houghton Mifflin Company.
--The Lively Adventures of Johnny Ping Wing. Perkins, Jack, illus. LC 29-188809. 5 p. l., 153 p. col. front., illus. 21 cm. 1929. Houghton Mifflin Company.
--Marty Comes to Town. Schreiber, Georges (1904-1977), illus. LC 35-19146. 3 p. l., 95, 1 p. col. front., illus. 21 cm. 1935. Houghton Mifflin Company.
--A Name for Obed. Lenski, Lois (1893-1974), illus. LC 41-5681. 4 p. l., 116, 1 p., 1 l. illus. (part col.) 26 x 20 cm. 1941. Houghton Mifflin Company.
--Our Aubrey. N.D. E. P. Dutton & Co.
--Peter Peppercorn. Bischoff, Ilse Marthe (1903-), illus. LC 30-30181. viii p., 1 l., 148, 1 p. incl. front., illus. 24 cm. 1939. Houghton Mifflin Company.
--The Popover Family. LC 27-19508. 4 p. l., 132 p. col. front., col. plates. 20 cm. 1927. Houghton Mifflin Company.
--Pretty Polly Perkins. Butler, Edith F., illus. LC 25-191225. 3 p. l., 122 p. col. front., col. plates. 21 cm. 1925. Houghton Mifflin Company.
--Punch. (Illus.). N.D. E. P. Dutton & Co.

--Pyxie, a Little Boy of the Pines. Barney, Maginel Wright, Mrs. (1881-1966), illus. LC 32-25175. 4 p. l., 164 p. col. front., illus., plates. 21 cm. 1932. Houghton Mifflin Company.
--Ride-the-Wind. Stoops, Herbert Morton, illus. LC 33-29647. 4 p. l., 192 p. incl. front., illus. 21 cm. 1933. Houghton Mifflin Company.
--The Santa Claus Brownies. LC 28-25092. 3 p. l., 3-139 p. col. front., illus. 21 cm. 1928. Houghton Mifflin Company.
--The Saucy Betsy. De Gogorza, Maitland, illus. LC 36-21348. 4 p. l., 122 p. front., illus., plates. 21 cm. 1936. Houghton Mifflin Company.
--A Story of Nancy Hanks. Hall, Kleber, illus. LC 23-13193. 5 p. l., 125 p. front., plates. 20 cm. 1923. Houghton Mifflin Company.
--Wee Ann; a Story for Little Girls: A Story for Little Girls. LC 19-14474. 4 p. l., 134 p., 1 l. col. front., col. plates. 21 cm. 1919. Houghton Mifflin Company.

Phillips, Ethel M. (1916-)
--Bible Boys and Girls. LC 47-4174. 64 p. col. illus. 22 1/2 cm. 1947. The Warner Press.

Phillips, Eula Mark (1905-)
--Chucho, the Boy with the Good Name. Simon, Howard (1903-1979), illus. LC 57-11027. 141p. illus. 25cm. 1957. (ISBN 0-695-41240-X). Follett Pub. Co.

Phillips, Irving W. (1908-)
--The Twin Witches of Fingle Fu. Pinkney, Jerry (1939-), illus. LC 72-79226. (Illus.). 48 p. (Carousel book). 1969. L. W. Singer.

Phillips, Isabel
--Punkey, the Angel Monkey. LC 41-10469. (Illus.). 20p. 15 x 23cm. 1941. Weaver Publishing Co.

Phillips, James D.
--The Misadventures of Norse. 1985. (ISBN 0-8062-2463-0). Carlton.

Phillips, Joan
--Gretchen and the Lost Carousel. Sargent, Barbi, illus. LC 82-80871. (Illus.). 44 p. 26cm. (A Gretchen Book). c.1982. (ISBN 0-448-16576-7). Grosset & Dunlap.

Phillips, Kathleen C
--Katie McCrary and the Wiggins Crusade. LC 80-21467. p. cm. c.1980. (ISBN 0-525-66717-2). Elsevier/Nelson Books.
--Sly As a Fox and Cross As a Bear. Funai, Mamoru R. (1932-), illus. LC 68-10506. (Illus.). 48 p. 23cm. 1967, c.1968. Watts.

Phillips, Loretta (1893-) & Phillips, Prentice (1894-)
--Two Silly Kings. Hunter, Warren, illus. LC 64-17590. (Illus.). 22cm. 31p. (gr. k-3). 1964. (ISBN 0-8114-7566-2). Steck-V.

Phillips, Louis, jt. auth. see Markoe, Karen.

Phillips, Louis (1942-)
--The Brothers Wrong & Wrong Again. Higginbottom, Jeffrey Winslow (1945-), illus. LC 79-11737. p. cm. 1979. (ISBN 0-07-049805-9). McGraw-Hill.
--How Do You Get a Horse Out of the Bathtub?. Profound Answers to Preposterous Questions. Stevenson, James Walker (1929-), illus. 1983. Viking.
--The Man Who Stole the Atlantic Ocean. Phillips, Louis (1942-), illus. LC 77-167909. (Illus.). 48 p. 22cm. 1971, c.1969. (ISBN 0-13-548289-5). Prentice-Hall.
--Theodore Jonathan Wainwright Is Going to Bomb the Pentagon: A Comic Novella. LC 72-10212. 115 p. 22cm. 1973. (ISBN 0-13-913004-7). Prentice-Hall.
--The Upside Down Riddle Book. Gardner, Beau, illus. LC 82-73. (Illus.). 32p. (gr. k up). 1982. (ISBN 0-688-00931-X). (ISBN 0-688-00932-8). Lothrop.

Phillips, Louis (1942-) & Braswell, Lynn
--The Animated Thumbtack Railroad Dollhouse & All-Around Surprise Book, Evening Edition. LC 75-12637. (Illus.). 95 p. 27cm. 1975. (ISBN 0-397-31646-1). (ISBN 0-397-31647-X). Lippincott.

Phillips, Louis (1942-) & Koziakin, Vladimir
--Riddlemazes. 64p. (Orig.). (Puzzlebacks Ser.). (gr. 3-7). 1981. (ISBN 0-671-43366-0). Wanderer Bks.

Phillips, Louise
--The Bald Eagle's Flying Shadow: A Fourth of July Celebration. (Illus.). 64p. 1984. (ISBN 0-682-40193-5). Exposition Pr FL.

Phillips, Lynn
--Exactly Like Me. (ps-3). 1972. Lollipop Power.

Phillips, Marjorie Fell (1910-)
--The Midshipman and the Rajah. 1st ed. Walker, Gil, illus. LC 63-11658. (Illus.). 190p. 22cm. 1963. Bobbs-Merrill.
--Two of Red and Two of Blue: The Story of a Page and a Prince. Walsh, David, illus. LC 56-580908. 221p. illus. 21cm. N.D. Bobbs-Merrill.

Phillips, Mary
--The Bushman Speaks. Johnson, Townley, illus. LC 78-207028. 59 p. illus. 25cm. 1961. H. Timmins.

Phillips, Mary Elizabeth (1857-)
--Laurel Leaves for Little Folk. Phillips, Mary Elizabeth (1857-), illus. LC 3-26883. xviii, 148, 4 p. incl. front., illus., ports. 23 cm. 1903. Lee & Shepard.

Phillips, Mary Hibbs Geisler, Mrs. (1881-1964)
--Ant Hills and Soap Bubbles. Norcross, Grace & Force, Albert W., illus. N.D. Macrae Smith Co.
--Dragonflies and Damselflies. Jauss, Anne Marie (1907-), illus. 1960. (ISBN 0-690-24454-1). Thomas Y. Crowell.
--Honey Bees and Fairy Dust. Edmonston, Ellen, illus. LC 26-16525. 213 p. col. front., illus. 21 cm. 1926. Macrae Smith Company.
--Little Lamb's Hat. Corwin, Eleanor, illus. LC 53-314031. unpaged. illus. 17cm. (Rand McNally book-elf junior, 675). c.1952. Rand McNally.
--Spider Webs and Sunflowers. Greer, Blanche (1884-) & Force, Albert W., illus. LC 28-24754. 257 p. incl. illus., plates. col. front. 21 cm. c.1928. Macrae Smith Company.
--Things That Go: Stories for the Smallest Ones. Chisholm, Christine, illus. LC 37-16648. 47 p. ill. 22 x 20 1/2cm. c.1937. Rand McNally & Co.
--What's Behind the Door?. Canizares, Stephanie, illus. LC 63-12330. (Illus.). 27p. 27cm. 1963. Rand McNally.

Phillips, Mary J.
--Young Gold Seeker, 1 of 25 vols. (Illus.). (Selected Bks for Sunday School: No. 21). N.D. Set. Methodist Bk Concern.

Phillips, Maurice Jack (1914-1976)
--Lightning on Ice. 1st ed. Quigley, Ray, illus. LC 63-8733. (Illus.). 143 p. 22cm. (Signal book). 1963. Doubleday.

Phillips, Michael James (1876-)
--Bunty Prescott at Englishman's Camp. Nelson, Emile A., illus. LC 12-18011. 279 p. front., plates. 20 cm. c.1912. The Reilly & Britton Co.

Phillips, Mildred
--The Sign in Mendel's Window. Zemach, Margot (1931-), illus. LC 85-5049. (Illus.). 30 p. 26cm. c.1985. (ISBN 0-02-774600-3). Macmillan Pub. Co. **Award: (ALA).**

Phillips, Myra Porter
--Bubble Eyes, The Friendly Crab. Rosemary, illus. LC 53-24260. (Illus.). 27cm. 1953. Bellevue Bks.
--Sniffer and Peanuts, a Story of Two Dogs. Phillips, Myra Porter, illus. LC 54-9374. (Illus.). 27p.cm. 1955. Bellevue Books.

Phillips, Prentice, jt. auth. see Phillips, Loretta.

Phillips, Rose
--Sketches for the Fireside. N.D. Claxton, Remsen & Haffelfinger.

Phillips, Scott G.
--Tonto Trails. N.D. Bruce Humphries, Inc.

Phillips, Walter Shelley see El Comancho, pseud.

Phillips, Walter Shelley (1867-)
--Indian Campfire Tales. El Comancho, pseud. (Illus.). (gr. 3-7). 1963. Platt.
--Indian Tales for Little Folks. El Comancho, pseud. 80p. N.D. Nourse.
--Indian Tales for Little Folks. El Comancho, pseud. 80p. N.D. Platt & Munk Co.
--Indian Tales for Little Folks. El Comancho, pseud. Phillips, Walter Shelley (1867-), illus. El Comancho, pseud. 22 x 30cm. 80p. 1914. Platt & Peck Co.
--Just About a Boy. El Comancho, pseud. N.D. Duffield.
--Just About a Boy. El Comancho, pseud. LC 99-5717. 5 p. l., 233 p. 18 cm. 18cm. 233p. 1899. H. S. Stone & Company.
--Teepee Tales. El Comancho, pseud. Bull, Charles Livingston (1874-1932) & Phillips, Walter Shelley (1867-), illus. El Comancho, pseud. LC 27-8760. 4 p. l., viii, 208 p. illus. 23 cm. c.1927. The Reilly & Lee Co.
--The Sandman: His Indian Stories. El Comancho, pseud. Phillips, Walter Shelley (1867-), illus. El Comancho, pseud. (The Sandman Ser.). N.D. L. C. Page & Co.
--Three Boys in the Indian Hills. El Comancho, pseud. Elwell, R. Farrington, illus. LC 18-168947. 3 p. l., v-vii, 3, 326 p. col. front., illus., plates. 20 cm. (The American Boy's Library). 1918. The Page Company.
--Two Young Crusoes. El Comancho, pseud. Phillips, Walter Shelley (1867-), illus. El Comancho, pseud. LC 6-3123. 217 p. front., illus. 21 cm. c.1906. Star Publishing Company.

Phillips, Walter Shelley (1867-), compiled by.
--Indian Fairy Tales. El Comancho, pseud. (Illus.). N.D. Reilly & Britton Co.

Phillips, William P.
--Playmates in Japan. N.D. Broadman Press.

Phillips-Wooley, C
--Gold, Gold in Cariboo. (Illus.). (Scribner-Blackie Series of Books for Young People). N.D. Charles Scribner's Sons.

Phillpotts, Eden (1862-1960)
--The Flint Heart: A Fairy Story. Folkard, Charles James (1878-1963), illus. LC 10-20974. 334 p. front., plates. 20 cm. c.1910. E. P. Dutton & Company.
--Golden Island. Morrow, George (1869-), illus. LC 38-37583. (Illus.). 186p. 1938. M. Joseph Ltd.
--The White Camel. Ahmed, Sheikh, illus. LC 38-144471. 3 p. l., 165, 1 p. incl. front., illus. plates. 22 cm. 1938. E. P. Dutton & Co., Inc.

Philpott, Alexis Robert
--Let's Look at Puppets. Burgin, Norma, illus. LC 67-265176. 63 p. illus. (part col.) 21 cm. (Let's look at series). 1967, c.1966. A. Whitman.

Philpott, Alexis Robert, ed.
--Eight Plays for Hand Puppets. (gr. 5-12). 1968. (ISBN 0-8238-0103-9). Plays.

Philrook, Rose (1911-)
--The Wings of Dr. Smidge. Bolin, Jim, illus. LC 52-11880. 158p. illus. 24cm. 1954. Caxton Printers.

Phipps, Mary
--All About Patsy. Phipps, Mary, illus. LC 30-219552. 4 p. l., 136 p. incl. illus., plates. col. front., col. plates. 20 cm. 1930. Doubleday, Doran & Co. Inc.
--Liza Jane and the Kinkies. Phipps, Mary, illus. LC 29-13586. 91 p. col. front., col. illus. 28 cm. c.1929. J. H. Sears and Company, Inc.

Phipson, Joan, pseud., see Fitzhardinge, Joan Margaret.

Phipson, Joan, pseud. (1912-)
--Birkin. Fitzhardinge, Joan Margaret. Horder, Margaret L'Anson (1911-), illus. LC 66-11205. (Illus.). 224p. (gr. 4-7). 1966, c.1965. (ISBN 0-15-207929-7). HarBraceJ. **Award: (ALA).**
--The Boundary Riders. Fitzhardinge, Joan Margaret. Duchesne, Janet (1930-), illus. LC 63-7900. (Illus.). 189 p. 21cm. 1st U.S. edition. 1963, c.1962. Harcourt, Brace & World.
--The Cats. Fitzhardinge, Joan Margaret. LC 75-43608. 168 p. 22cm. 1976. (ISBN 0-689-50061-0). Atheneum.
--Cross Currents. Fitzhardinge, Joan Margaret. Duchesne, Janet (1930-), illus. LC 67-1340. (Illus.). 192 p. 21cm. 1st U.S. edition. Orig. Title: The Crew of the Merlin. 1967, c.1966. Harcourt, Brace & World.
--The Family Conspiracy. Fitzhardinge, Joan Margaret. Horder, Margaret L'Anson (1911-), illus. LC 64-11494. (Illus.). 224 x. 21cm. 1st U.S. edition. 1964, c.1962. Harcourt, Brace & World. **Award: (ALA).**
--Fly Free. Fitzhardinge, Joan Margaret. LC 79-14661. 134 p. 22cm. 1979. (ISBN 0-689-50149-8). Atheneum.
--Fly into Danger. Fitzhardinge, Joan Margaret. LC 76-28717. vi, 152 p. 22cm. 1977. Atheneum.
--Good Luck to the Rider. Fitzhardinge, Joan Margaret. Horder, Margaret L'Anson (1911-), illus. LC 68-11504. (Illus.). 186 p. 21cm. 1st U.S. edition. 1968. Harcourt Brace & World.
--The Haunted Night. Fitzhardinge, Joan Margaret. LC 70-96320. 187 p. 21cm. 1970. Harcourt, Brace & World.
--Hit and Run. Fitzhardinge, Joan Margaret. 1985. McElderry Atheneum. **Award: (ALA).**
--Horse with Eight Hands. Fitzhardinge, Joan Margaret. LC 74-76280. 199 p. 22cm. 1974. (ISBN 0-689-50013-0). Atheneum.
--Peter and Butch. Fitzhardinge, Joan Margaret. LC 69-11599. 222 p. 21cm. 1969. Harcourt, Brace & World.
--Polly's Tiger. Fitzhardinge, Joan Margaret. 1st ed. Blegvad, Erik (1923-), illus. LC 73-77465. (Illus.). 43 p. 24cm. 1974. (ISBN 0-525-37325-X). Dutton.
--Six and Silver. Fitzhardinge, Joan Margaret. Horder, Margaret L'Anson (1911-), illus. LC 70-152696. (Illus.). 190 p. 21cm. 1971. (ISBN 0-15-275330-3). Harcourt Brace Jovanovich.
--Threat to the Barkers. Fitzhardinge, Joan Margaret. 1st US Ed. ed. Horder, Margaret L'Anson (1911-), illus. LC 65-10962. (Illus.). 21cm. 219p. (gr. 4-6). 1965. (ISBN 0-15-286310-9, HJ). HarBraceJ.
--A Tide Flowing. Fitzhardinge, Joan Margaret. LC 80-24375. 156 p. 22cm. 1981. (ISBN 0-689-50196-X). Atheneum.
--The Watcher in the Garden. Fitzhardinge, Joan Margaret. LC 82-3960. 288p. 1982. (ISBN 0-689-50246-X, Argo). Atheneum.
--The Way Home. Fitzhardinge, Joan Margaret. LC 73-75440. 184 p. 22cm. 1973. Atheneum.
--When the City Stopped. Fitzhardinge, Joan Margaret. LC 78-6930. 181 p. 22cm. 1978. (ISBN 0-689-50121-8). Atheneum.

Phleger, Fred B. (1909-)
--Ann Can Fly. LC 59-13406. (Illus.). (gr. 1-2). 1959. (ISBN 0-394-90012-X). Beginner.
--Red Tag Comes Back. Lobel, Arnold Stark (1933-), illus. LC 61-11452. (Illus.). 5 7/8 x 8 1/2. 64p. (18 pt.). (Nature I Can Read Bks.). (gr. k-3). 1961. (ISBN 0-06-024706-1) Har-Row.
--The Whales Go by. Galdone, Paul (1914-), illus. LC 59-9740. (Illus.). 62 p. 24cm. 1959. Beginner Books; Distributed by Random House.

Phleger, Fred B (1909-) & Phleger, Marjorie Temple
--Off to the Races. Summers, Leo, illus. LC 68-28458. (Illus.). 63 p. 23cm. 1968. Beginner Books.
--You Will Live Under the Sea. Brackett, Ward, illus. LC 66-9297. (Illus.). 61 p. 24cm. 1966. Beginner Books.

Phleger, Marjorie Temple
--Pilot Down, Presumed Dead. LC 63-16244. (Illus.). 206 p. 22cm. 1963. Harper & Row.
--Pilot Down, Presumed Dead. (Illus.). 206 p. 22cm. (Harper Trophy book). 1975. Harper & Row.

Phleger, Marjorie Temple, jt. auth. see Phleger, Fred B.

Phumla
--Nomi & the Magic Fish: A Story from Africa. Byard, Carole M., illus. LC 73-187292. (Illus.). 27cm. 30p. (gr. 1-2). 1972. (ISBN 0-385-04414-3). Doubleday.

Piatt, John James (1835-1917) & Piatt, Sarah Morgan Bryan, Mrs. (1836-)
--The Children Out-of-Doors: A Book of Verses by Two in One House. LC 24-18689. vi, 7-83 p. 19 cm. 1885. R. Clarke & Co.

Piatt, Sarah Morgan Bryan, Mrs., jt. auth. see Piatt, John James.

Piatt, Sarah Morgan Bryan, Mrs. (1836-)
--A Book About Baby. N.D. D. Lothrop Co.
--A Book About Baby and Other Poems in Company with Children. LC 24-18697. viii, 9-162 p. incl. front. (port.) illus. 18 cm. c.1882. D. Lothrop and Company.
--Poems in Company with Children. Humphrey, Lizzie B. & Curtis, Jesse, illus. LC 24-18703. viii, 9-162 p. incl. front., (port.) illus. 17 x 15 cm. 1877. D. Lothrop and Company.

Piatti, Celestino
--Animal ABC. Piatti, Celestino (1922-), illus. Reid, John, tr. LC 66-12851. (Illus.). 1 v. (unpaged). 1966. Atheneum. **Awards: (NYT); (ALA).**
--The Happy Owls. 1st US Ed. ed. Piatti, Celestino (1922-), illus. LC 64-3620. (Illus.). 31 p. 31cm. 1964, c.1963. Atheneum. **Awards: (NYT); (ALA).**

Piatti, Celestino & Piatti, Ursula
--Barbara and the Dormouse. LC 77-351306. (Illus.). 28 p. 31cm. 1976. (ISBN 0-237-44860-2). Evans.

Piatti, Ursula, jt. auth. see Piatti, Celestino.

Picard, Barbara Leonie (1917-), ed. see Firdawsi.

Picard, Barbara Leonie (1917-), ed. see Homerus.

Picard, Barbara Leonie (1917-)
--The Faun & the Woodcutter's Daughter. (Illus.). (gr. 5-8). 1964. (ISBN 0-8382-0246-2). Hale.
--The Faun & the Woodcutter's Daughter. Stewart, Charles William (1915-), illus. LC 63-19081. (Illus.). 255p. (gr. 3-7). 1964. (ISBN 0-200-71999-8, Criterion Bks). Abelard. **Award: (ALA).**
--The Goldfinch Garden: Seven Tales. Linton, Anne, illus. LC 65-240153. 121p. illus. 21cm. 1st U.S. edition. (Criterion bk. for young people). 1965, c.1963. Criterion.
--The Lady of the Linden Tree. Stewart, Charles William (1915-), illus. LC 62-8943. (Illus.). 214 p. 22cm. 1st U.S. edition. 1962. Criterion Books.
--Lady of the Linden Tree. Stewart, Charles William (1915-), illus. 1954. Oxford Univ. Pr. **Award: (CMA).**
--Lost John: A Young Outlaw in the Forest of Arden. Keeping, Charles William James (1924-), illus. LC 63-12458. (Illus.). 224 p. 22cm. 1st U.S. edition. 1963, c.1962. Criterion Books.
--The Mermaid and the Simpleton. Gough, Philip (1908-), illus. LC 68-31716. (Illus.). 254 p. 22cm. 1970. Criterion Books.
--One Is One. LC 66-83408. 287 p. 22cm. 1966, c.1965. Holt, Rinehart and Winston.
--Ransom for a Knight. Hodges, Cyril Walter (1909-), illus. 1956. (ISBN 0-8098-3011-6). David McKay Company.
--Ransom for a Knight. Hodges, Cyril Walter (1909-), illus. LC 67-6443. (Illus.). vi, 314 p. 23cm. 1967. H. Z. Walck.
--Ransom for a Knight. Hodges, Cyril Walter (1909-), illus. LC 56-3686. 314p. illus. 23cm. 1956. Oxford University Press. **Award: (CMA).**
--Ransom for a Knight. Hodges, Cyril Walter (1909-), illus. 314p. 1956. Walck.
--Three Ancient Kings: Gilgamensh,Hrolf Kraki,Conary. Gough, Philip (1908-), illus. LC 72-187502. (Illus.). 160p. (gr. 3-7). 1972. (ISBN 0-7232-6091-5). Warne.
--The Young Pretenders. Ambrus, Victor G., pseud. (1935-), illus. Ambrus, Gyozo Laszlo. LC 66-17589. 231 p. illus. 23 cm. 1966. Criterion Books.
--The Young Pretenders. Ambrus, Victor G., pseud. (1935-), illus. Ambrus, Gyozo Laszlo. LC 66-73395. 231p. front., 5 illus. 23cm. 1st U.S. edition. c.1966. E. Ward.

--Among the Meadow People. N.D. E. P. Dutton & Co.
--Dooryard Stories. N.D. E P Dutton.
--The Millers and Their New Home. LC 8-21922. vii, 333 p. front., 5 pl. 18 1/2 cm. c.1908. E. P. Dutton and Company.
--The Millers and Their Playmates. LC 7-289752. vii, 334 p. front., 5 pl. 18 1/2 cm. 1907. E. P. Dutton & Company.
--The Millers at Pencroft. LC 6-35325. v, 274 p. front., 5 pl. 18 1/2 cm. 1906. E. P. Dutton & Company.
--Plow Stories. Cartwright, Charles E., illus. LC 23-13728. xiv p., 1 l., 179 p. incl. front., illus., plates. 20 cm. c.1923. E. P. Dutton & Company.
--The Plucky Allens. LC 25-15851. xi p., 1 l., 327 p. front., illus. 19 1/2 cm. c.1925. E. P. Dutton & Company.
--Tales of a Poultry Farm. LC 4-21729. xi, 195 p. front., 7 pl. 20 cm. 1904. E. P. Dutton and Company.
--Three Little Millers: A Story of the Boys and Girls of Pencroft. LC 5-32846. v, 308 p. front., 7 pl. 18 1/2 cm. 1905. E. P. Dutton and Company.

Pierson, Clara Dillingham, jt. auth. see Harrington, Helen.

Pierson, Cornelia Tuthill, Mrs. (1820-1870), ed.
--The Girls and Boys' Miscellany ... LC 15-12443. 2 p. l., iii-vii, 19-200 p. front., illus., plates. 21 cm. 1848. Lindsay and Blakiston.

Pierson, Helen Wall, Mrs.
--Bible Stories in Easy Words. LC 34-4485. 1 p. l., 134 p. col. front., illus., col. plates. 25 x 20 1/2 cm. 1904. McLoughlin Brothers.
--Edith Vaughan's Victory: Or, How to Conquer. LC 43-40889. 289 p. incl. front. 17 cm. 1860. D. Appleton and Company.

Pierson, Inez Skrede
--Tilda from Tustin: A Schoolgirl's Journal, 1892. Pierson, Inez Skrede, illus. LC 67-1897. (Illus.). 36 p. 24cm. 1966. Pioneer Press.

Pierson, Jan (1937-)
--The Carson Kids & the Mystery of the Cove Point Stallion. 128p. (Orig.). (Carson Kids Ser.). (gr. 5-10). 1984. (ISBN 0-8423-4661-9). Tyndale.
--The Mystery of Five Finger Island. Furmanski, Ralph, illus. LC 78-63616. (Illus.). 123 p. 18cm. c.1979. (ISBN 0-8423-4663-5). Tyndale House Publishers.
--The Mystery of Skull Rocks Mansion, No. 3. (gr. 5-10). 1983. (ISBN 0-8423-4665-1). Tyndale.

Pierson, Jessie Alma
--Babyhood Days. N.D. Barse and Hopkins.

Pierson, Lance & Mandeville, Sylvia
--God's Friends. Deverell, Richard, illus. (gr. 1-3). 1978. (ISBN 0-8307-0595-3). Regal.

Pietroforte, Alfred
--Songs of the Yokuts & Paiutes, of California & Nevada. (Illus.). 11 photos. 6 ils. 72p. (Indian Bks). (gr. 4 up). 1965. (ISBN 0-911010-21-1). (ISBN 0-911010-20-3). Naturegraph.

Piggin, Julia
--Mini Mysteries. 160p. Repr. (gr. 5 up). 1974 (Schol Trade Pap). Schol Bk Serv.

Piggott, Juliet
--Fairy Tales of Japan. Harris, Jennifer Drury, illus. LC 61-65154. unpaged. illus. 21cm. c.1961. Cassell.
--Great Day in Japan: The Bigger Fish. Thompson, Peter, illus. LC 60-13088. (Illus.). 32 p. 22cm. c.1962. Abelard-Schuman.
--Japanese Fairy Tales. Toothill, Harry, illus. LC 67-21173. (Illus.). 198 p. 23cm. (World fairy tale collections). 1967. Follett Pub. Co.

Pihl, Herman Gottfrid (1894-) & Beckman, Karin (1904-)
--Follow Me: Stories from the Bible for Children. Carney, Edward, tr. LC 67-1574. (Illus.). 95 p. 20cm. c.1966. Association Press.

Pike, Christopher
--Slumber Party. LC 84-20238. 170 p. 18cm. (Point paperback). (gr. 7up). c.1985. (ISBN 0-590-33409-3). Scholastic.

Pike, Frances West Atherton see Athern, Anna, pseud.

Pike, Frances West Atherton, Mrs.
--Every Day. LC 21-4124. v, 282 p. 19 1/2 cm. 1871. Noyes, Holmes, and Company.
--Here and Hereafter: Or, The Two Altars. Athern, Anna, pseud. LC 21-4123. iv, 376 p. 19 1/2 cm. 1858. Crosby, Nichols, and Company; Etc., Etc.
--Katherine Morris: An Autobiography. LC 21-4125. 1 p. l., 353 p. 19 1/2 cm. 1860. Walker, Wise and Company.

Pike, Harper
--Here's Extra Help!. (gr. 4-8). 1980. (ISBN 0-916456-96-X). Good Apple.

Pike, Henry Lee Mitchell (1865-)
--Our Little Korean Cousin. Bridgman, Lewis Jesse (1857-1931), illus. LC 5-20922. vi p., 2 l., 96 p. front., 5 pl. 20 cm. (On verso of half-title: The little cousin series). 1905. L. C. Page & Company.
--Our Little Panama Cousin. Bridgman, Lewis Jesse (1857-1931), illus. LC 6-27350. 3 p. l., v-vi p., 2 l., 118 p. front., 5 pl. 20 cm. (On verso of half-title: The little cousin series). (The Little Cousin Ser.). 1906. L. C. Page & Company.

Pike, Henry Lee Mitchell (1865-) & Etzkorn, Leo Rudolph
--Our Little Panama Cousin. new rev. ed. Bridgman, Lewis Jesse (1857-1931), illus. LC 32-24680. vii p., 2 l., 135 p. col. front., plates. 19 1/2 cm. 1932. L. C. Page & Company.

Pike, Judith, jt. auth. see Hollister, C. Warren.

Pike, Norman
--The Peach Tree. 1st ed. LC 83-4393. p. cm. c.1983. (ISBN 0-88045-014-2). Stemmer House Publishers.

Pike, Robert Everding (1905-)
--Fighting Yankee. Lee, Manning De Villeneuve (1894-1980), illus. LC 55-7038. 231p. illus. 22cm. 1955. Abelard-Schuman.

Pilant, Elizabeth (1905-)
--Sky Bears: Verse for Childern. LC 52-11673. 64p. 21cm. 1953, c.1952. Exposition Press.

Pilditch, Charles, tr. see Marques, Rene.

Pilgrim, Anne, pseud., see Allan, Mabel Esther.

Pilgrim, Anne, pseud. (1915-)
--Clare Goes to Holland. Allan, Mabel Esther. LC 62-13625. 191p. 21cm. 1962. Abelard-Schuman.
--The First Time I Saw Paris. Allan, Mabel Esther. LC 61-7146. 191 p. 21cm. 1961. Abelard-Schuman.
--Selina's New Family. Allan, Mabel Esther. Byfield, Graham, illus. LC 67-136106. 191p. illus., map. 22cm. 1967. Abelard.
--Strangers in New York. Allan, Mabel Esther. LC 64-22348. 192 p. map. 21 cm. 1964. New York, Abelard-Schuman.
--A Summer in Provence. Allan, Mabel Esther. LC 63-16223. 190 p. 21 cm. 1963. New York, Abelard-Schuman.

Pilgrim, Jane
--The Adventures of Walter. May, Frederick Stocks (1891-), illus. (Blackberry Farm Bks.). 1954. David McKay Co.
--The Birthday Picnic. May, Frederick Stocks (1891-), illus. (Blackberry Farm Bks.). 1955. David McKay Co.
--A Bunny in Trouble. May, Frederick Stocks (1891-), illus. LC 74-166484. (Illus.). 1st U.S. edition. (Blackberry Farm Books). (ps-1). 1973. (ISBN 0-87955-010-4, Potato Pr). O'Hara.
--Christmas at Blackberry Farm. May, Frederick Stocks (1891-), illus. (Blackberry Farm Bks.). 1954. David McKay Co.
--Ernest Owl Starts a School. May, Frederick Stocks (1891-), illus. (Blackberry Farm Bks.). 1954. David McKay Co.
--Ernest Owl Starts a School. May, Frederick Stocks (1891-), illus. LC 74-168172. (Illus.). 29cm. 16p. 1st U.S. edition. (Blackberry Farm Books). (ps-1). 1973. (ISBN 0-87955-009-0, Potato Pr). O'Hara.
--Henry Goes Visiting. May, Frederick Stocks (1891-), illus. (Blackberry Farm Bks.). 1955. David McKay Co.
--Henry Goes Visiting. May, Frederick Stocks (1891-), illus. LC 73-153550. (Illus.). 15p. 1st U.S. edition. (Blackberry Farm Ser.). (ps-2). 1972. (ISBN 0-87955-007-4). O'Hara.
--Little Martha. May, Frederick Stocks (1891-), illus. (Blackberry Farm Bks.). 1955. David McKay Co.
--Lucy Mouse Keeps a Secret. May, Frederick Stocks (1891-), illus. (Blackberry Farm Bks.). 1954. David McKay Company Inc.
--Lucy Mouse Keeps a Secret. May, Frederick Stocks (1891-), illus. (Illus.). 20p. 1st U.S. edition. (Blackberry Farm Ser.). (ps-2). 1972. (ISBN 0-87955-006-6). O'Hara.
--Mother Hen and Mary. May, Frederick Stocks (1891-), illus. LC 74-166424. 16 p. (chiefly col. illus. 29cm. (Her A Blackberry Farm book). 1973. Brockhampton Press.
--Mother Hen and Mary. May, Frederick Stocks (1891-), illus. (Blackberry Farm Bks.). 1954. David McKay Co.
--Mother Hen & Mary. May, Frederick Stocks (1891-), illus. (Illus.). 1st U.S. edition. (Blackberry Farm Books). (ps-1). 1973. (ISBN 0-87955-008-2, Potato Pr). O'Hara.
--Mr. Nibble Calls a Doctor. May, Frederick Stocks (1891-), illus. LC 73-153239. (Illus.). 16p. 1st U.S. edition. (Blackberry Farm Ser.). (ps-2). 1972. (ISBN 0-87955-004-X). O'Hara.
--Mrs. Nibble. May, Frederick Stocks (1891-), illus. LC 73-152875. (Illus.). 16p. 1st U.S. edition. (Blackberry Farm Ser.). (ps-2). 1972. (ISBN 0-87955-005-8). O'Hara.
--Mrs. Squirrel and Hazel. May, Frederick Stocks (1891-), illus. (Blackberry Farm Bks.). 1955. David McKay Co.
--Naughty George. May, Frederick Stocks (1891-), illus. (Blackberry Farm Bks.). 1955. David McKay Co.
--Postman Joe. May, Frederick Stocks (1891-), illus. LC 74-166423. 16 p. (chiefly col. illus. 29cm. (Her A Blackberry Farm book). 1973. Brockhampton Press.
--Postman Joe. May, Frederick Stocks (1891-), illus. (Blackberry Farm Bks.). 1954. David McKay Co.
--Postman Joe. May, Frederick Stocks (1891-), illus. (Illus.). 1st U.S. edition. (Blackberry Farm Books). (ps-1). N.D. (ISBN 0-87955-011-2, Potato Pr). O'Hara.
--Rusty the Sheep Dog. May, Frederick Stocks (1891-), illus. (Blackberry Farm Bks.). 1955. David McKay Co.

Pilgrim, Mariette Shaw
--Oogaruk: The Aleut. Wilson, Helen Hughes, illus. LC 47-12106. 223 p. illus. 24 cm. 1947. Caxton Printers.

Pilgrim, Thomas see Morecamp, Arthur, pseud.

Pilgrim, Thomas (0000-1882)
--Live Boys in the Black Hills: Or,the Young Texas Gold Hunters. Morecamp, Arthur, pseud, 1 of 50 vols. (Illus.). (The Norwood Ser.: No. 33). 1900. Lee & Shepard.
--Live Boys: Or, Charlie and Nasho in Texas. Morecamp, Arthur, pseud. (Illus.). 1882. Lee & Shepard.
--Live Boys: Or,Charlie and Nasho in Texas. Morecamp, Arthur, pseud, 1 of 50 vols. (Illus.). (The Norwood Ser.: No. 32). 1900. Lee & Shepard.

Pilkington, Francis Meredith (1907-), ed.
--The Three Sorrowful Tales of Erin. Ambrus, Victor G., pseud. (1935-), illus. Ambrus, Gyozo Laszlo. LC 66-13952. (Illus.). 232 p. 23cm. 1966, c.1965. H. Z. Walck. **Award: (ALA).**

Pilkington, R. M.
--Shamrock & Spear: Tales & Legends from Ireland. Dillon, Leo (1933-) & Dillon, Diane (1933-), illus. (gr. 4-7). 1968. (ISBN 0-03-067955-9). HR&W.

Pilkington, Roger Windle (1915-)
--Chesterfield Gold. (Orig.). 1st U.S. edition. (gr. 4-6). 1969. (ISBN 0-14-030375-8, Puffin). Penguin.
--The Chesterfield Gold. Klaasse, Piet, illus. LC 57-13741. 252p. illus. 21cm. 1957. Macmillan.
--The Dalia's Cargo. Edwards, Peter William (1934-), illus. LC 59-4719. 233p. illus. 21cm. 1959. Macmillan.
--Don John's Ducats. Edwards, Peter William (1934-), illus. LC 60-52353. 205p. illus. 21cm. 1960. Macmillan.
--The Eisenbart Mystery. Edwards, Peter William (1934-), illus. LC 63-5133. 192 p. illus. 21 cm. 1963. St. Martin's Press.
--The Face in the River. LC 76-371746. 124 p. 21cm. 1976. (ISBN 0-233-96787-7). Deutsch.
--I Sailed on the Mayflower. A Boy's Discovery of the New World. Bisset, Douglas, illus. LC 66-16607. v. 216 p. illus. 22 cm. 1966. St. Martin's Press.
--Jan's Treasure. Klaasse, Piet, illus. LC 55-12610. 258p. illus. 21cm. 1955. St. Martins Press.
--The Missing Panel. Klaasse, Piet, illus. LC 58-810. 235p. illus. 20cm. 1958. St. Martins Press.
--Nepomuk of the River. Edwards, Peter William (1934-), illus. LC 62-4317. 224p. illus. 21cm. 1962. St. Martins Press.

Pillet, Roger
--Andre Francois Villeneuve. Pillett, Roger & Campbell, Nancy, illus. Hudspeth, De Layne, photos by. LC 65-28895. (Illus.). 28cm. 31p. (ps-3). 1965. (ISBN 0-695-40410-5). Follett.

Pilpay
--The Fables of Pilpay. Anderson, Alexander (1775-1870), illus. N.D. Hurd & Houghton.
--Pilpay's Fables. Anderson, Alexander (1775-1870), illus. N.D. Houghton Mifflin.

Pim, Paul
--Telling Tommy About Mother Nature's Curious Children. LC 39-11081. 2 p. l., 7-93 p. illus. 22 cm. c.1939. Cupples and Leon Company.

Pimberton, May
--Christmas Plays for Children. Godfrey, Rupert, illus. 1915. T Y Crowell.

Pimplehuber, pseud., see Trobisch, David.

Pimsleur, Paul, jt. auth. see Rimanelli, Giose.

Pinchot, Ann
--Rival to My Heart. LC 54-7187. 256p. 20cm. 1954. Avalon Books.

Pinchot, Ann, ed. see Beatty, Jane.

Pinchot, Gifford, Jr.
--Giff and Stiff in the South Seas. N.D. John C. Winston Co.

Pinckney, Harriet see Huse, Harriet Pinckney, Mrs.

Pincus, Harriet (1938-)
--Little Red Riding Hood: A Story. Pincus, Harriet (1938-), illus. LC 68-11505. (Illus.). 1 v. (unpaged). 22cm. (Voyager Book). 1973, c.1968. (ISBN 0-15-652850-9). Harcourt.
--Minna and Pippin. Pincus, Harriet (1938-), illus. LC 79-188253. (Illus.). 32 p. 1972. (ISBN 0-374-34991-6). Farrar, Straus and Giroux.

Pindar, Susan Cooper
--Story Book, Comprising Fireside Fairies: Or, Christmas at Aunt Elsie's. LC 49-44452. 18cm. 205p. 1853. D. Appleton.
--The Wentworths. (Fern Glen Ser.). N.D. D. Lothrop Co.

Pinelli, Babe
--Mr. Ump. 1953. Westminster Press.

Pineo, Craig, illus.
--Happy Puppy. rev. ed. (Illus.). (Play & Learn Bk). (gr. k-2). 1967. (ISBN 0-307-10737-X, Golden Pr). Western Pub.
--My Animal Babies. (Illus.). 8p. (Golden Cloth Bk). (ps). 1972. (ISBN 0-307-10746-9, Golden Pr). Western Pub.

Pini, Richard, jt. auth. see Pini, Wendy.

Pini, Wendy & Pini, Richard
--ElfQuest, Book 4. Reynolds, Kay, ed. LC 81-5401. 172p. (ElfQuest Ser.). 1984. (ISBN 0-89865-377-0). (ISBN 0-89865-378-9). Donning Co.

Pinkerton, Allan (1819-1884)
--Bank-Robbers and the Detectives. LC 12-376333. 1 p. l., v-x, 11-339 p. front., plates. 19 cm. 1883. G. W. Carleton & Co.; Etc., Etc.

Pinkerton, Colin McKenzie
--Buckeye-Hawkeye, School-Master: Or, The Life of Carl MacKenzie : Dedicated to the School-Teachers of America. LC 75-302976. (Illus.). 176 p., 1 leaf of plates. 20cm. 1895. W. B. Conkey Co.

Pinkerton, E. Percy, tr. see Hauff, Wilhelm.

Pinkerton, Kathrene Sutherland Gedney, Mrs. (1887-1967)
--Adventure North. Voorhies, Stephen J., illus. LC 40-31726. 268 p. illus., pl. 21 cm. c.1940. Carrick & Evans, Inc.
--Adventure North. Voorhies, Stephen J., illus. 1940. Harcourt.
--Farther North. Stein, Harve (1904-), illus. LC 44-295385. 4 p. l., 3-181 p. incl. illus., plates. front. 20 1/2 cm. 1944. Harcourt, Brace and Company.
--Fox Island. Hazelton, Isaac Brewster, illus. LC 42-21973. 3 p. l., 3-195 p. illus. 21 cm. 1942. Harcourt, Brace and Company.
--A Good Partner. LC 48-81814. 269 p. 21 cm. 1948. Harcourt, Brace.
--Hidden Harbor. LC 51-13356. 20cm. 278p. (A Voyager Bk.: AVB46). 1951. Harcourt.
--Peddler's Crew. LC 54-515563. 243p. 21cm. 1954. Harcourt, Brace.
--Second Meeting. LC 56-6919. 204p. 21cm. 1956. Harcourt, Brace.
--The Silver Strain. LC 46-6383. 3 p. l., 3-263 p. 21 cm. 1946. Harcourt, Brace and Company.
--Steer North!. LC 62-83467. 219p. 21cm. 1962. (ISBN 0-15-280210-X). Harcourt, Brace & World.
--Tomorrow Island. LC 60-137033. 217p. 22cm. 1960. Harcourt, Brace.
--Windigo. LC 45-35156. 3 p. l., 3-223 p. 21 cm. 1945. Harcourt, Brace and Company.
--Year of Enchantment. LC 57-11342. 224 p. 21cm. 1957. Harcourt, Brace.

Pinkney, Jerry, jt. auth. see Martel, Cruz.

Pinkwater, Daniel Manus, jt. auth. see Keele, Luqman.

Pinkwater, Daniel Manus (1941-)
--Alan Mendelsohn, the Boy from Mars. LC 78-12052. 248 p. 22cm. c.1979. (ISBN 0-525-25360-2). Dutton.
--Around Fred's Bed. Mertens, Robert, illus. LC 76-8834. 23cm. 32p. c.1976. (ISBN 0-13-046581-X). Prentice-Hall.
--Attila the Pun: A Magic Moscow Book. LC 80-28504. p. cm. 1981. Four Winds Press.
--Bear's Picture. Pinkwater, Daniel Manus (1941-), illus. LC 83-25369. 1984. (ISBN 0-525-44102-6). Dutton.
--Bear's Picture. Pinkwater, Daniel Manus (1941-), illus. LC 72-76577. (Illus.). 40 p. 24cm. 1972. (ISBN 0-03-091980-0). Holt, Rinehart and Winston.
--The Big Orange Splot. Pinkwater, Daniel Manus (1941-), illus. LC 76-49825. (Illus.). 30 p. c.1977. (ISBN 0-8038-0777-5). Hastings House.
--Blue Moose. Pinkwater, Daniel Manus (1941-), illus. LC 75-12575. (Illus.). 47 p. 24cm. 1975. (ISBN 0-396-07151-1). Dodd, Mead.
--The Blue Thing. LC 77-3470. (Illus.). 32 p. 24cm. c.1977. (ISBN 0-13-077818-4). Prentice-Hall.
--Devil in the Drain. Pinkwater, Daniel Manus (1941-), illus. LC 83-16468. (Illus.). 32p. (gr. k-2). 1984. (ISBN 0-525-44092-5). Dutton.
--Ducks. Pinkwater, Daniel Manus (1941-), illus. LC 83-22210. (Illus.). (gr. 1-3). 1984. (ISBN 0-316-70810-0). Little.
--Fat Elliot and the Gorilla. Pinkwater, Daniel Manus (1941-), illus. LC 73-88074. (Illus.). 47 p. 26cm. 1974. Four Winds Press.
--Fat Men from Space. Pinkwater, Daniel Manus (1941-), illus. LC 77-6091. (Illus.). 57 p. 24cm. c.1977. (ISBN 0-396-07461-8). Dodd, Mead.
--I Was a Second Grade Werewolf. 1st ed. Pinkwater, Daniel Manus (1941-), illus. LC 82-17715. p. cm. 1983. (ISBN 0-525-44038-0). E.P. Dutton.

Pitts, Lilla Belle
--Singing and Rhyming. Wilkin, Eloise Burns (1904-) & Cummings, Alison, illus. LC 50-7166. 191 p. illus. 24 cm. (Our Singing World). 1950. Ginn.
--Singing Every Day. LC 51-7993. 203 p. col. illus. 24 cm. (Our Singing World). 1950. Ginn.
--Singing in Harmony. Wood, Ruth, illus. LC 51-8988. 239 p. illus. 24 cm. (Our Singing World). 1951. Ginn.
Pitts, Lilla Belle & Glenn, Mabelle
--Singing As We Play. Fox, Dorothea Warren (1914-), illus. LC 49-27209. 48 p. col. illus. 21 x 25 cm. (Our Singing World). c.1949. Ginn.
Pittsburgh. Carnegie Library
--Stories from the Ballads of Robin Hood. LC 15-25841. (With Lists of Other Ballads to Tell and to Read Aloud. Outlines for Story-Telling to Children Over Nine Years of Age). 37 p. 23 cm. 1914. Carnegie Library.
--Stories from the Norse: Historical Tales, Myths, and Sagas. LC 14-12935. (Outlines for Story-Telling to Children Over Nine Years of Age.). 22 p. 23 cm. 1914. Carnegie Library.
Pitz, Henry Clarence (1895-1976)
--One Thousand Poems for Children. Sechrist, Elizabeth Hough, Mrs. (1903-), ed. Ingpen, Roger (1868-1936), selected by. LC 46-4924. xiii p., 1 l., 601 p. illus. 24 1/2 cm. 1946. (ISBN 0-8255-8146-X). Macrae-Smith Company.
--You Fight for Treasure. 320p. 1932. William Morrow & Co.
Pitzele, Patricia, tr. see Van Iterson, Siny Rose.
Pizzo, Joan E.
--Amy Avocet. Geronimi, Clyde, illus. (Illus.). (Tales of the Back Bay). (gr. k-8). 1983. (ISBN 0-939126-06-0). Back Bay.
--Little Crumb. Geronimi, Clyde, illus. (Illus.). 29p. (Orig.). (gr. k-6). 1980. (ISBN 0-939126-00-1). (ISBN 0-939126-01-X). (ISBN 0-939126-03-6). Back Bay.

Place, Marian Templeton see White, Dale, pseud.

Place, Marian Templeton (1910-)
--The Boy Who Came Back. Gaughan, Jack, illus. LC 66-23740. (Illus.). 190 p. 22cm. 1967, c.1966. Criterion Books.
--The Boy Who Saw Bigfoot. LC 78-23199. 96 p. 21cm. c.1979. (ISBN 0-396-07644-0). Dodd, Mead.
--Brad's Flying Saucer. (Illus.). 1969. David McKay Company.
--Brad's Flying Saucer. Lambo, Donald W. (1903-1966), illus. LC 69-12913. (Illus.). 148 p. 21cm. 1969. I. Washburn.
--The First Astrowitches. O'Sullivan, Tom, illus. LC 84-10266. (Illus.). 128p. (gr. 2-5). 1984. (ISBN 0-396-08456-7). (ISBN 0-396-08456-7). Dodd.
--The Frontiersman: The True Story of Billy Dixon. 1st ed. LC 67-1963. (Illus.). 128 p. 22cm. 1967. Holt, Rinehart and Winston.
--Hold Back the Hunter: A Novel. White, Dale, pseud. LC 59-6722. 189p. illus. 21cm. (Your Fair Land Series). 1959. J. Day Co.
--The Johnny Cake Mine. White, Dale, pseud. Bennett, Richard Michael (1899-), illus. LC 54-8234. (Illus.). 222 p. 21cm. 1954. Viking Press.
--Lets go the Fish Hatchery: Lets go Series. (Illus.). 1966. G P Putman's sons.
--Lotta Crabtree, Girl of the Gold Rush. 1st ed. Burns, Raymond Howard (1924-), illus. LC 58-12910. 192p. illus. 20cm. (Childhood of Famous American Series: 106). 1958. Bobbs-Merrill.
--Lotta Crabtree, Gold Rush Girl. Morrow, Gray, illus. LC 62-16612. 200p. col. illus. 20cm. (Childhood of Famous Americans). 1963, c.1958. Bobbs.
--Mystery of Wild Horse Trap. LC 70-137772. (Illus.). 212 p. 24cm. 1971. (ISBN 0-87004-206-8). Caxton Printers.
--Nobody Meets Bigfoot. LC 75-40030. 192 p. 21cm. c.1976. (ISBN 0-396-07290-9). Dodd, Mead.
--The Resident Witch. Miller, Marilyn Jean (1925-), illus. LC 72-102664. (Illus.). 119 p. 21cm. 1970. Washburn.
--Retreat to the Bear Paw: The Story of the Nez Perce. 192p. 1969. Four Winds Press.
--The Singing Boones. White, Dale, pseud. Morse, Dorothy Bayley (1906-1979), illus. LC 57-13721. 285p. illus. 21cm. 1957. Viking Press.
--Steamboat up the Missouri. Geer, Charles Hand (1922-), illus. LC 58-59956. 185p. illus. 21cm. 1958. Viking Press.
--Thunder in His Moccasins. White, Dale, pseud. Geer, Charles Hand (1922-), illus. LC 62-154529. 222p. illus. 21cm. 1962. Viking Press.
--Vigilantes, Ride!. White, Dale, pseud. Sentz, James, illus. LC 56-1626. 285p. illus. 21cm. 1956. Viking Press.
--The Wild-Horse Trap. White, Dale, pseud. Bennett, Richard Michael (1899-), illus. LC 55-675. 192p. illus. 21cm. 1955. Viking Press.
--The Witch Who Saved Halloween. Miller, Marilyn Jean (1925-), illus. LC 70-165011. (Illus.). 150 p. 21cm. 1971. Washburn.
--Young Deputy Smith. Hite, Dale, pseud. Geer, Charles Hand (1922-), illus. LC 61-116792. 191p. illus. 21cm. 1961. Viking Press.
--The Yukon. 1967. David McKay Company.
Place, Marian Templeton (1910-) & Preston, Charles G
--Juan's Eighteen-Wheeler Summer. LC 82-7251. 158 p. 21cm. c.1982. (ISBN 0-396-08078-2). Dodd, Mead.
Place, Tom
--The Trail Sweepers. Nair, Christina, illus. (Illus.). 1977. (ISBN 0-533-02830-2). Vantage.
Plaisted, Ralph & Plaisted, Riki
--Wildness Adventure. 192p. 1975. (ISBN 0-87518-097-3). Dillon Press inc.
Plaisted, Riki, jt. auth. see Plaisted, Ralph.
Planche, James Robison (1796-1880), tr. see Aulnoy, Marie Catherine Jumelle de Berneville.
Planche, James Robison (1796-1880)
--Four-and-Twenty Fairy Tales. Godwin, James & Corbould, illus. N.D. George Routledge & Sons.
--An Old Fairy Tale,. The Sleeping Beauty in the Wood. Doyle, Richard (1824-1883) & Daziell, George (1815-1902), illus. N.D. George Routledge & Sons.
Planche, Matilda Anne see MacKarness, Matilda Anne Planche.
Plant, Richard & Seidlin, Oskar
--S.O.S. Geneva. Du Bois, William Sherman Pene (1916-), illus. LC 39-30323. 246 p. incl. illus., plates. 21 cm. 1939. The Viking Press.
Plante, Patricia, ed. see La Fontaine, Jean De.
Plasmati, Valdine
--Algernon and the Pigeons. Mizumura, Kazue, illus. LC 63-8528. 37 p. illus. 26 cm. 1963. Viking Press.
--Magnificent Pumpkin. 1959. E M Hale.
--The Magnificent Pumpkin. Ogawa, Heidi, illus. LC 59-16367. (Illus.). 40 p. 1959. Viking Press.
Platero, Dillon, jt. ed. see Roessel, Robert A., Jr.
Plath, Sylvia (1932-1963)
--The Bed Book. Blake, Quentin (1932-), illus. LC 76-360384. (Illus.). 32 p. 21cm. 1976. (ISBN 0-571-10929-2). Faber.
--The Bed Book. McCully, Emily Arnold (1939-), illus. LC 76-3825. (Illus.). 40 p. 29cm. c.1976. (ISBN 0-06-024746-0). (ISBN 0-06-024747-9). Harper & Row.
Platonov, Andrei Platonovich (1899-1951)
--Finist, the Falcon Prince: A Russian Folk Tale. Chagnon, Mary, illus. Regehr, Lydia, tr. LC 72-186860. (Illus.). 32p. 27cm. c.1973. (ISBN 0-87614-032-0). Carolrhoda Books.
Platt, Edith Guldi, jt. auth. see Bradley, Margaret Hope.
Platt, Harrison Gray (1902-), ed.
--One Hundred and Ten Favorite Children's Poems. LC 43-983945. 152 p. illus. 21 1/2 x 12 cm. 1943. Reilly and Lee.
Platt, Kin (1911-), ed. see Stevenson, Robert Louis.
Platt, Kin (1911-)
--The Ape Inside Me. LC 79-2402. p. cm. c.1979. (ISBN 0-397-31826-X). (ISBN 0-397-31863-4). Lippincott.
--Big Max. Lopshire, Robert Martin (1927-), illus. LC 65-14488. (Illus.). 5 7/8 x 8 1/2. 64p. (18 pt.). (I Can Read Mysteries Ser.). (gr. k-3). 1965. (ISBN 0-06-024751-7) (ISBN 0-06-444006-0) Har-Row.
--Big Max in the Mystery of the Missing Moose. Lopshire, Robert Martin (1927-), illus. LC 76-58727. (Illus.). 5 7/8 x 8 1/2. 64p. (18 pt.). (I Can Read Mysteries Ser.). (gr. k-3). 1977. (ISBN 0-06-024756-8) (ISBN 0-06-024757-6) (ISBN 0-06-444044-3) Har-Row.
--The Blue Man. LC 61-12088. 185p. 22cm. 1961. Harper.
--The Boy Who Could Make Himself Disappear. LC 68-24842. 216 p. 21cm. 1968. Chilton.
--Brogg's Brain. LC 79-9622. 128p. (gr. 6 up). 1981. (ISBN 0-397-31945-2, JBL-J). (ISBN 0-397-31946-0). Har-Row.
--Brogg's Brain. 112p. (gr. 7 up). 1982. (ISBN 0-590-32828-X). Scholastic Inc.
--Chloris and the Creeps. LC 72-13920. 146 p. 21cm. 1973. (ISBN 0-8019-5825-3). Chilton Book Co.
--Chloris and the Freaks: A Novel. LC 75-11113. 217 p. 22cm. c.1975. (ISBN 0-87888-089-5). Bradbury Press.
--Chloris and the Weirdos. LC 78-55214. 231 p. 22cm. c.1978. (ISBN 0-87888-137-9). Bradbury Press.
--Crocker. LC 82-48456. p. cm. (A Lippincott Page Turner). c.1983. (ISBN 0-397-32025-6). (ISBN 0-397-32026-4). Lippincott.
--The Doomsday Gang. LC 77-18864. 185 p. 22cm. c.1978. (ISBN 0-688-80155-2). (ISBN 0-688-84155-4). Greenwillow Books.
--Dracula, Go Home!. Mayo, Frank, illus. LC 78-11335. (Illus.). 87 p. 22cm. (Triumph book). 1979. (ISBN 0-531-01464-9). F. Watts.
--Flames Going Out. LC 79-23625. p. cm. c.1980. (ISBN 0-416-30621-7). Methuen.
--Frank and Stein and Me. LC 81-16322. 124 p. 22cm. (Triumph book). 1982. (ISBN 0-531-04169-7). F. Watts.
--The Ghost of Hellsfire Street. LC 80-10446. ix, 246 p. 22cm. c.1980. (ISBN 0-440-02795-0). (ISBN 0-440-02796-9). Delacorte Press.
--Headman. LC 75-11808. 186 p. 22cm. 1975. (ISBN 0-688-80011-4). (ISBN 0-688-84011-6). Greenwillow Books.
--Hey, Dummy. LC 71-180202. 169 p. 21cm. 1971. (ISBN 0-8019-5644-7). Chilton Book Co.
--Mystery of the Witch, Who Wouldn't. LC 70-91658. 265 p. 20cm. 1969. Chilton Book Co.
--Sinbad and Me. LC 66-5259. viii, 296p. 21cm. c.1966. Chilton.
Platt, Kin (1911-) & Freedman, Chuck
--Run for Your Life. LC 77-3172. (Illus.). 95 p. 22cm. (Triumph book). 1977. (ISBN 0-531-01327-8). Watts.
Platt, Penny
--Hi-Ho Hortense. 176p. (Orig.). (Platt Early Reading Program Ser.). (gr. 1-3). 1973. (ISBN 0-201-05841-3, Sch Div). A-W.
Platt, S, retold by.
--Stories from the Old Testament. N.D. Dodge Publishing Co.
Platt, Samuel C. see See, Sam, pseud.
Platt, Samuel C. (1888-)
--Where Are You?. See, Sam, pseud. Lieberman, Frank Joseph (1910-), illus. LC 41-25880. (Illus.). 29. 21 x 19cm. 1941. Simon and Schuster.
Plaut, Abraham Lincoln
--Stan Begins to Fight: A Story About a Boy for Youthful People of All Ages. LC 45-5919. 181 p. 21 cm. 1944. House of Field Inc.
Playfair, Robert Smith
--Colonel of the Crimson. LC 40-30969. 3 p. l., 233 p. illus. 21 1/2 cm. 1940. Houghton Mifflin Company.
--The Crimson Road. Lee, Manning De Villeneuve (1894-1980), illus. LC 38-22276. 6 p. l., 3-234 p. front., plates. 21 1/2 cm. 1938. Houghton Mifflin Company.
--Fuller at Harvard. Adams, Bruce, illus. LC 40-12422. 4 p. l., 231 p. illus., diagrs. 21 cm. 1939. Houghton Mifflin Company.
--Fuller at Harvard. Lee, Manning De Villeneuve (1894-1980), illus. LC 39-217791. 4 p. l., 231 p. illus. 21 cm. 1939. Houghton Mifflin Company.
Playne, Alfred C., ed. see Bland, Edith Nesbit, Mrs. (1858-1924) & Weedon, L. L.
Playne, C. F.
--An Old Maid's Child. (Illus.). N.D. Society for Promoting Christian Knowledge.
Plays: The Drama Magazine for Young People (1916-)
--Little Plays for Little Players: Fifty Non-Royalty Plays for Children. Kamerman, Sylvia E., ed. LC 52-6320. 335 p. 21 cm. 1952. Plays, Inc.
--One Hundred Plays for Children: An Anthology of Nonroyalty One-Act Plays. Burack, Abraham Saul (1908-1978), ed. LC 49-6791. ix, 886 p. 22 cm. 1949. Plays, Inc.
Pleadwell, Theodora Hunt
--Sylvester, the Christmas Mouse. LC 79-49758. (Illus.). 26 p. 23cm. c.1979. (ISBN 0-932384-11-0). Tashmoo Press.
Pleasanton, Louise M
--The Fairyland of Opera. Price, Harriet Longstreet (1891-), illus. N.D. Penn Publishing Co.
--A Nursery Story of the Bible. N.D. Frederick A. Stokes.
Plenn, Doris Troutman
--Green Song. Galdone, Paul (1914-), illus. LC 54-9468. (Illus.). 22cm. 126p. (gr. 3-7). 1954. (ISBN 0-679-20068-1). McKay.
--The Violet Tree. Troyer, Johannes (1902-), illus. LC 62-7204. 128p. illus. 22cm. 1962. Ariel Books.
Pletsch, Oscar (1830-1888), illus.
--Buttercups and Daisies. 1875. George Routledge & Sons.
--Chimes and Rhymes for Youthful Times. N.D. George Routledge & Sons.
Pliant, Elizabeth
--Sky Bears. 1953. Exposition Press.
Plimpton, George Ames (1927-)
--The Rabbit's Umbrella. N.D. E. M. Hale and Co.
--The Rabbit's Umbrella. Du Bois, William Sherman Pene (1916-), illus. LC 55-14925. (Illus.). 159 p. 22cm. 158p. 1955. (ISBN 0-670-58704-4). Viking Press.
Pliss, Louise
--Little Sam & the Tigers. (Illus.). (gr. 4-6). 1963. (ISBN 0-8382-0470-8). Hale.
--Little Sam and The Tigers. D'Adamo, Anthony, illus. LC 63-19041. 21cm. 160p. 1963. Reilly & Lee Company.
--The Strange Journey of Kippy Brooks. Aloise, Frank E., illus. LC 65-26900. 121p. illus. 21cm. c.1965. Reilly & Lee.
--That Summer on Catalpa Street. D'Adamo, Anthony, illus. LC 61-12111. 157p. illus. 21cm. 1961. Reilly & Lee.
--The Trip Down Catfish Creek. D'Adamo, Anthony, illus. LC 62-16395. 21cm. 160p. 1962. Reilly & Lee Company.
Plomer, William Charles Franklin, jt. auth. see Aldridge, Alan.
Ploss, Douglas A.
--The Tweens at Deep Lake: An Original American Fantasy. Ploss, Douglas A., illus. LC 79-90996. (Illus.). 88p. (gr. 3 up). 1979. D A Ploss.
Plotz, Helen, ed. see Stevenson, Robert Louis.
Plotz, Helen Ratnoff (1913-), ed. see Dickinson, Emily.
Plotz, Helen Ratnoff (1913-), ed. see Hardy, Thomas.
Plotz, Helen Ratnoff (1913-), selected by.
--As I Walked Out One Evening: A Book of Ballads. LC 76-10306. p. cm. c.1976. (ISBN 0-688-80054-8). (ISBN 0-688-84054-X). Greenwillow Books.
--The Earth Is the Lord's: Poem's of the Spirit. Leighton, Clare Veronica Hope (1899-), illus. (Illus.). (gr. 4 up). 1965. (ISBN 0-690-25093-2). T Y Crowell. **Award: (ALA).**
--Eye's Delight: Poems of Art and Architecture. 1983. Greenwillow.
--The Gift Outright: America to Her Poets. LC 77-8555. xv, 204 p. 24cm. c.1977. (ISBN 0-688-80109-9). (ISBN 0-688-84109-0). Greenwillow Books.
--Gladly Learn and Gladly Teach: Poems of the School Experience. LC 81-2344. 160p. (gr. 5-9). 1981. (ISBN 0-688-00594-2). Greenwillow.
--Imagination's Other Place: Poems of Science & Mathematics. Leighton, Clare Veronica Hope (1899-), illus. LC 55-9216. (Illus.). 200p. (gr. 7-11). 1955. (ISBN 0-690-43413-8, TYC-J). Har-Row.
--Life Hungers to Abound: Poems of the Family. LC 78-5829. 192p. (gr. 5-9). 1978. (ISBN 0-688-80176-5). (ISBN 0-688-84176-7). Greenwillow.
--Marvelous Light: Poets and Poetry. index. 192p. (gr. 7 up). 1970. (ISBN 0-690-52183-9). T Y Crowell.
--Poems from the German. David, Ismar, illus. (Poems of the World Ser). (gr. 4 up). 1967. (ISBN 0-690-63578-8). (ISBN 0-690-63579-6). T Y Crowell.
--Saturday's Children: Poems of Work. LC 82-3087. xv, 174 p. 24cm. c.1982. (ISBN 0-688-01406-2). Greenwillow Books.
--This Powerful Rhyme: A Book of Sonnets. LC 79-14037. 160p. (gr. 6 up). 1979. (ISBN 0-688-80226-5). (ISBN 0-688-84226-7). Greenwillow.
--Untune the Sky: Poems of Music and the Dance. Leighton, Clare Veronica Hope (1899-), illus. LC 57-10285. (Illus.). (gr. 7 up). 1957. (ISBN 0-690-85020-4). T Y Crowell.
Plourde, Francois
--The Legend of the Seventh Son. N.D. Vantage Press.
Plowhead, Ruth Gipson, Mrs. (1877-)
--Holidays With Betty Sue and Sally Lou. Moore, Agnes Kay Randall, illus. 234p. 1946. Caxton Printers.
--Holidays with Betty Sue and Sally Lou. Moore, Agnes Kay Randall, illus. LC 39-244426. 234 p. incl. col. front., illus. col. pl. 21 1/2 cm. 1939. The Caxton Printers, Ltd.
--Josie and Joe. De Angeli, Marguerite Lofft, Mrs. (1889-), illus. LC 38-80807. 23cm. 262p. 1938. Caxton Publications.
--Josie and Joe Carry on. Lund, Johanna E., illus. LC 42-24770. 291 p. incl. col. front., illus. 22 1/2 cm. 1942. The Caxton Printers, Ltd.
--Lucretia Ann in the Golden West. Moore, Agnes kay Randall, illus. LC 35-1480. 294, 1 p. col. front., illus., col. pl. 19 1/2cm. 1935. Caxton Printers, Ltd.
--Lucretia Ann on the Oregon Trail. Moore, Agnes Kay Randall, illus. LC 31-25267. 244 p. col. front., illus., col. plates. 19 1/2cm. 1931. The Caxton Printers, Ltd.
--Lucretia Ann on the Sagebrush Plains. Moore, Agnes Kay Randall, illus. LC 36-35048. 357, 1 p. col. front., illus., col. plates. 21 1/2cm. 1936. Caxton Printers, Ltd.
--Mile High Cabin. Lund, Johanna E., illus. LC 46-815983. 4 p. l., v-vii p., 1 l., 229 p. incl. illus., plates. col. front 22 cm. 1945. The Caxton Printers, Ltd.
--The Silver Nightingale and Other Stories. Moore, Agnes Kay Randall, illus. LC 55-6754. 22cm. 252p. 1955. Caxton Printers.
Plowman, Stephanie (1922-)
--My Kingdom for a Grave. LC 71-147903. (Illus.). 239 p. 22cm. 1971, c.1970. (ISBN 0-395-12429-8). Houghton Mifflin.
--The Road to Sardis. LC 66-17173. (Illus.). 380 p. 22cm. 1966, c.1965. Houghton Mifflin.
--Three Lives for the Czar. LC 76-105249. (Illus.). 269 p. 22cm. 1970, c.1969. Houghton Mifflin Co.

Pluff, Barbara Littlefield see Clayton, Barbara, pseud.

Plum, jt. auth. see Wayman.

Plume, Ilse

--The Bremen Town Musicians. 1st ed. Plume, Ilse, illus. LC 79-6622. (Illus.). 32 p. c.1980. (ISBN 0-385-15161-6). (ISBN 0-385-15162-4). Doubleday. **Awards: (ALA); (RCM).**

--The Story of Befana: An Italian Christmas Tale. LC 81-6896. p. cm. 1981. (ISBN 0-87923-420-2). D.R. Godine.

Plumer, William Swan, jt. auth. see Sherwood, Mary Martha Butt, Mrs.

Plummer, Cameron, ed. see Staples, Alfred.

Plummer, Dorothy

--Joan's Freshman Year at Stanford. LC 39-33083. xv, 1, 11-369 p. incl. front., illus. 20 1/2 cm. c.1939. Lothrop, Lee & Shepard Company.

Plummer, Geraldine Mary Simpson, Mrs.

--The Old Mrs. Plummer Stories for Little Ones. LC 31-30701. (Illus.). 27p. 31cm. 1931. Clipe Printing Co.

Plummer, Gladys

--The Baby and the Princess. Foster, Marcia Lane (1897-), illus. (Little Folks Bible Story Books). (gr. k-6). 1969. (ISBN 0-87162-076-6). Warner Press.

--Benjamin's Brother. Foster, Marcia Lane (1897-), illus. (Illus.). (gr. k-6). 1969. (ISBN 0-87162-073-1). Warner Pr.

--The Boy Who Gave His Dinner Away. Foster, Marcia Lane (1897-), illus. (Illus.). (gr. k-6). 1969. (ISBN 0-87162-077-4). Warner Pr.

--The General and the Slave Girl. Foster, Marcia Lane (1897-), illus. (Illus.). (Little Folks Bible Story Books). (gr. k-6). 1969. (ISBN 0-87162-080-4). Warner Pr.

--In the Den of Lions. Foster, Marcia Lane (1897-), illus. (Illus.). (gr. k-6). 1969. (ISBN 0-87162-078-2). Warner Pr.

--Noah's Ark. Foster, Marcia Lane (1897-), illus. (Illus.). (gr. k-6). 1969. (ISBN 0-87162-081-2). Warner Pr.

--The Son Who Came Home: Little Folks Bible Stories. Foster, Marcia Lane (1897-), illus. (Illus.). (Little Folks Bible Story Bks). (gr. k-6). 1969. (ISBN 0-87162-074-X). Warner Pr.

--The Story of Anna. Foster, Marcia Lane (1897-), illus. (Illus.). (gr. k-6). 1969. (ISBN 0-87162-082-0). Warner Pr.

--Who Is My Neighbor. Foster, Marcia Lane (1897-), illus. (Illus.). (Little Folks Bible Story Bks.). (gr. k-6). 1969. (ISBN 0-87162-075-8). Warner Pr.

Plummer, Louise

--A Walk to Grow on: Story. LC 85-505. p. cm. (A Tale from the Care Bear Cousins). c.1985. (ISBN 0-910313-85-7). Parker Bros.

Plummer, Mary Wright (1856-1916)

--Roy & Ray in Canada. N.D. Henry Holt.

--Roy & Ray in Mexico. N.D. Henry Holt.

--Stories from the Chronicle of the Cid. LC 10-28009. vi p., 2 l., 155, 1 p. incl. illus., plates. front. 19 1/2cm. 1910. H. Holt and Company.

Plummer, Myrtes Marie, jt. auth. see Hollmann, Clide Anne.

Plummer, Myrtes Marie, jt. auth. see Peterson, Livia Y.

Plumptre, Annabella (1795-1812)

--Stories for Children. LC 78-219410. (Illus.). ix, 111p. 12cm. 1824. S. King.

Plunket, Zoe

--The Girl With Golden Locks, 1 of 6 vols. (The Golden Library). N.D. Cassell, Petter, Galpin.

Plunkett, Barbara

--Sam Diego, a Coloring Adventure in San Diego, California. Plunkett, Barbara, illus. (Illus.). (ps). 1977. (ISBN 0-914488-14-7). Rand-Tofua.

Plunkett, Isabel

--The Children's Band. (Incident and Adventure Library). N.D. Scribner, Welford & Armstrong.

--Children's Band: Or, The Trial of Paul's Faith. N.D. E. P. Dutton.

--Hester's Fortune: Or, Pride and Humility. (Illus.). N.D. Scribner, Welford & Armstrong.

Plutarch

--Plutarch's Lives. Handy Volume, Large Type ed. (Illus.). (Beauxarts Ser.). N.D. Henry Altemus.

Plutarchus

--Tales from Plutarch. Rowbotham, Frances Jameson, ed. LC 5-26114. iii, 346 p. col. front., plates. 18 cm. c.1905. T. Y. Crowell & Co.

Plutarchus & Gould, Frederick James (1855-)

--The Children's Plutarch: Tales of the Greeks. Crane, Walter (1845-1915), illus. LC 10-15773. xiii, 1 p., 1 l., 166 p., 1 l. front., plates. 19 cm. 1910. Harper & Brothers.

Plyer, Arthur Mabb

--Dawn in the Shadow: A Novel. LC 41-1832. 2 p. l., 3-284 p. 23 cm. c.1940. The Welrad Corporation.

Plympton, Almira George (1852-1939)

--Betty, a Butterfly. Plympton, Almira George (1852-1939), illus. LC 7-37408. 198 p. incl. front., illus. pl. 19 cm. 1891. Roberts Brothers.

--The Black Dog and Other Stories. Plympton, Almira George (1852-1939), illus. LC 7-37407. 230 p. front., illus., plates. 18 cm. 1896. Roberts Brothers.

--A Brave Coward: Also,the Girl Without a Conscience. LC 1-20282. 1 p. l., 70 p. c.1901. Little, Brown, and Company.

--A Child of Glee. (Illus.). (The Boys' and Girls' Books). N.D. Little, Brown and Company.

--A Child of Gleee and How She Saved the Queen. Edwards, Harry C., illus. LC 5117. 3 p. l., 300 p. front., 5 pl. 19 cm. 1900. Little, Brown and Company.

Dear Daughter Dorothy. Plympton, Almira George (1852-1939), illus. 321p. N.D. Little, Brown.

--Dear Daughter Dorothy. Plympton, Almira George (1852-1939), illus. LC 7-37406. 190 p. front., plates. 20 cm. 1890. Roberts Brothers.

--Dorcaster Days. Kennedy, J. W. Ferguson, illus. LC 7-31228. 3 p. l., 242 p. front., 3 pl. 19 cm. 1907. Little, Brown, and Company.

--Dorothy and Anton. LC 7-374059. (Sequel to "Dear Daughter Dorothy"). 131 p. front., illus., plates. 19 cm. 1895. Roberts Brothers.

--A Flower of the Wilderness. (Illus.). (The Boys' and Girls' Books). N.D. Little, Brown and Company.

--A Flower of the Wilderness. Rev ed. Plympton, Almira George (1852-1939), illus. LC 99-5119. 3 p. l., 260 p. front., 9 pl. 19 cm. 1899. Little, Brown, and Company.

--Gerald and Geraldine and Other Stories. 4 p. l., 15-128 p. incl. 11 pl. (5 col.) col. front. 24 cm. c.1898. De Wolfe, Fiske & Co.

--Little Folks' Ladder. (Author of "The Glad Year Round."). 1882. Dodd, Mead & Co.

--Little Olive the Heiress. (Illus.). (The Children's Friend Ser.). N.D. Little, Brown and Company.

--Little Olive the Heiress. Plympton, Almira George (1852-1939), illus. 1.p l., bop. front, illus. 19 c. c.1899. Little, Brown, and Company.

--The Little Sister of Wilifred. Plympton, Almira George (1852-1939), illus. LC 7-37404. 211 p. incl. front., illus., pl. 19 cm. 1892. Roberts Brothers.

--The Mary Jane Papers, 36 vols. (Illus.). (St. Nicholas Ser.). 1905. Set. A L Burt Co.

--The Mary Jane Papers. (Illus.). (The Wellesley Series for Girls). N.D. A. L. Burt.

--The Mary Jane Papers. New ed. (Illus.). N.D. Frederick A. Stokes Co.

--The Mary Jane Papers. Plympton, Almira George (1852-1939), illus. LC 6-40213. viii p., 3 l., 113 p. incl. front. 7 pl. 18 cm. 1906. F. A. Stokes Company.

--The Mary Jane Papers: A Book for Girls. Plympton, Almira George (1852-1939), illus. LC 7-37403. vi p., 1 l., 9-127 p. incl. front., illus., plates. 18 cm. 1884. White, Stokes, & Allen.

--The Mary Jane Papers: A Story for Girls. (Illus.). N.D. White, Stokes & Allen.

--Old-Home Day at Hazeltown. Atwood, Clara E., illus. LC 6-29780. 3 p. l., 159, 1 p., 1 l. front., 5 pl. 19 cm. 1906. Little, Brown, and Company.

--Penelope Prig and Other Stories. Plympton, Almira George (1852-1939), illus. LC 7-37402. 4 p. l., 13-194 p. front., illus., plates. 19 cm. 1894. Roberts Brothers.

--Rags and Velvet Gowns. (Illus.). (The Children's Friend Ser.). N.D. Little Brown and Company.

--Rags and Velvet Gowns. Plympton, Almira George (1852-1939), illus. LC 7-37401. 91 p. illus. 19 cm. 1894. Roberts Brothers.

--Robin Recruit. PLympton, Almira George (1852-1939), illus. LC 12-37851. 5 p. l., 9-179 p. front., illus. 19 cm. 1893. Roberts Brothers.

--The Schoolhouse in the Woods. Atwood, Clara E., illus. LC 5-28004. 4 p. l., 272 p., 1 l. front., 5 pl. 19 cm. 1905. Little, Brown, and Company.

--Two Dogs and a Donkey. Plympton, Almira George (1852-1939), illus. (Illus.). 12cm. 82p. (The Children's Friend Ser.). 1900. Little, Brown and Company.

--Wanolasset, The-Little-One-Who-Laughs. Plympton, Almira George (1852-1939), illus. LC 7-37400. vi, 203 p. front., illus., plates. 19 cm. 1897. Roberts Brothers.

Po, Lee, retold by.

--The Sycamore Tree & Other African Tales. 1st ed. Byard, Carole M., illus. LC 74-755. (gr. 2-4). 1974. (ISBN 0-385-00561-X). (ISBN 0-385-02840-7). Doubleday.

Poala, Tomie de see De Paola, Tomie.

Pocci, Franz

--Chimpanzee, the Darwin Ape. Zahl, Jagna, tr. from It. LC 72-84057. 30p. (gr. 1 up). 1973. (ISBN 0-8283-1503-5). Branden.

--Kasper: The Portrait Painter. N.D. (ISBN 0-8283-1249-4). Branden Press.

--The Wishing Fairy. N.D. (ISBN 0-8283-1251-6). Branden Press.

Pocock, Doris Alice

--A Flag Kept Flying. LC 27-4064. vi p., 1 l., 280 1 p. front. 19 cm. 1927. D. Appleton and Company.

--The Mystery of the Marsh. LC 29-6455. 3 p. l., 234, 1 p. front. 19 1/2 cm. 1929. D. Appleton & Company.

--A Runaway Rebel. LC 29-19256. v, 241, 1 p. front. 19 1/2 cm. 1929. D. Appleton and Company.

--The Secret of Hallowdene Farm. LC 24-7320. 4 p. l., 243, 1 p. front. 19 1/2 cm. 1924. D. Appleton and Company.

--Summer at Hallowdene Farm. LC 26-5890. 3 p. l., 274, 1 p. front. 19 1/2 cm. 1926. D. Appleton and Company.

Pocock, Guy Noel (1880-), selected by.

--A Poetry Book for Boys and Girls. LC 37-118. xvi, 366 p., 1 l. 18 cm. (Half-title: Everyman's library, ed. by Ernest Rhys. For young people. no. 894). 1933. E. P. Dutton & Co.

Poddany, Eugene & Geisel, Theodor Seuss (1904-)

--The Cat in the Hat Song Book. Dr. Seuss, pseud. LC 67-21921. 1 v. (unpaged) col. illus. 29cm. 1967. Random.

Podendorf, Illa E. (1903-1983), ed. see Friskey, Margaret Richards.

Podendorf, Illa E. (1903-1983)

--The True Book of Animal Babies. Adams, Pauline Batchelder (1897-), illus. LC 55-701. (Illus.). 44p. 22cm. (The True Book Ser.). 1955. Childrens Press.

Podendorf, Illa (1903-1983)

--Toby on the Move. Herrington, Roger, illus. LC 72-123802. (Illus.). 48 p. 23cm. (Stepping into science). 1970. (ISBN 0-516-01554-0). Childrens Press.

--Touching for Telling. Frederick, Florence, illus. LC 73-160600. (Illus.). 47 p. 22cm. (Her Stepping into science). 1971. (ISBN 0-516-01576-1). Childrens Press.

--The True Book of Sounds We Hear. Maltman, Chauncey, illus. LC 55-14801. (Illus.). 46 p. 22cm. ("True book" series). 1955. Childrens Press.

Podmore, William

--Fee, Fi, Fo and Fum, and Other Famous Fairy Stories in Rhyme. Morris, Howard, illus. LC 51-11861. 96 p. illus. 22 cm. 1951. Exposition Press.

Podolin, Si

--The Man-Eater of Shark Island. 1st ed. Mays, Lewis Victor, Jr. (1927-), illus. LC 61-6120. 159p. illus. 21cm. 1961. Harcourt, Brace and World.

Podulka, Fran

The Wonder Jungle. 1974. (ISBN 0-399-11198-0). G. P. Putnam's Sons.

Poduschka, Christl, jt. auth. see Poduschka, Walter.

Poduschka, Walter & Poduschka, Christl

--Dearest Prickles: The Story of a Hedgehog Family. N.D. (ISBN 0-8008-2124-6). Taplinger.

Poe, Edgar Allan (1809-1849) see Cutts, David E.

Poe, Edgar Allan (1809-1849)

--The Best of Poe. new & abr. ed. Farr, Naunerle, ed. Taloac, Gerry & Redondo, N., illus. (Illus.). (Now Age Illustrated III Ser.). (gr. 4-12). 1977. (ISBN 0-88301-281-2). (ISBN 0-88301-269-3). Pendulum Pr.

--The Cask of Amontillado. (Illus.). 32p. (Creative's Classics Ser.). (gr. 5-9). 1980. (ISBN 0-87191-773-4). Creative Ed.

--The Cask of Amontillado. Toulmin-Rothe, Ann, illus. Cutts, David E., adapted by. LC 81-15997. (Illus.). 32p. (gr. 6-11). 1982. (ISBN 0-89375-622-9). (ISBN 0-89375-623-7). Troll Assocs.

--The Devil in the Belfry. Overlie, George, illus. LC 72-13328. (Illus.). 32 p. 20cm. (Seedling book). 1974. (ISBN 0-8225-0281-X). Lerner Publications.

--Edgar Allan Poe Stories. (Great Writers Collection). (gr. 7 up). 1961. (ISBN 0-448-41104-0). Platt.

--Edgar Allan Poe's The Masque of the Red Death. Cutts, David E., adapted by. Lawn, John, illus. LC 81-15959. (Illus.). 32 p. 24cm. c.1982. (ISBN 0-89375-620-2). (ISBN 0-89375-621-0). Troll Associates.

--Edgar Allan Poe's The Pit and the Pendulum. Cutts, David, adapted by. Eisenberg, Monroe, illus. LC 81-16432. (Illus.). 32 p. 24cm. c.1982. (ISBN 0-89375-626-1). (ISBN 0-89375-627-X). Troll Associates.

--Eight Tales of Terror. Repr. (Starbright Editions). (gr. 7-12). 1973. Schol Bk Serv.

--The Fall of the House of Usher. Crowell, James (1936-), illus. Cutts, David E., adapted by. LC 81-15958. (Illus.). 32p. (gr. 6-11). 1982. (ISBN 0-89375-624-5). (ISBN 0-89375-625-3). Troll Assocs.

--The Fall of the House of Usher, and Four Other Tales: The Black Cat, Ms. Found in a Bottle, Three Sundays in a Week, The Oval Portrait. Schreiter, Rick (1936-), illus. (Illus.). 82 p. 23cm. 1967. (ISBN 0-531-01066-X). F. Watts.

--The Gold Bug. (Illus.). (Every Boy's Library). N.D. Caldwell.

--The Gold Bug. (Illus.). (The Young Folks Library). N.D. Caldwell.

--The Gold Bug. (Classic Ser.). N.D. World Publishing Co.

--The Gold Bug. Kennedy, J. W. Ferguson, illus. N.D. Set. Dana Estes & Co.

--Gold Bug and Other Stories. 91p. 1965. Publications of Bruce Humphries.

--The Gold Bug and Other Stories. Kottmeyer, William, ed. (The Everyreader Library). N.D. Webster Publishing Co.

--The Gold Bug, and Other Tales. N.D. A. L. Burt Co.

--The Gold Bug and Other Tales. N.D. International Pocket Library.

--The Gold Bug and Other Tales and Poems. LC 53-848822. (Illus.). 225 p. 22cm. (New children's classics). (The New Children's Classics). 1953. Macmillan.

--The Gold Bug and Other Tales of Mystery. Landau, Jacob (1917-), illus. LC 70-79988. (Illus.). 224p. (Fun-To-Read Classics). (gr. 6 up). 1969. (ISBN 0-516-04244-0). Childrens.

--The Gold-Bug, the Purloined Letter, and Other Tales. (Riverside Literature Ser.). N.D. Houghton Mifflin Co.

--The Masque of the Red Death. Lawn, John, illus. Cutts, David E., adapted by. LC 81-15959. (Illus.). 32p. (gr. 6-11). 1982. (ISBN 0-89375-620-2). (ISBN 0-89375-621-0). Troll Assocs.

--The Pit and the Pendulum. LC 80-21646. p. cm. 1980. (ISBN 0-87191-771-8). Creative Education.

--The Pit and the Pendulum and Five Other Tales. Schreiter, Rick (1936-), illus. (Illus.). (gr. 7 up). 1967. (ISBN 0-531-01075-9). Watts.

--Poems of Edgar Allan Poe. Macdonald, Dwight (1906-1982), ed. Raskin, Ellen (1928-1984), illus. LC 65-21417. (Illus.). (Poets Ser). (gr. 7 up). 1965. (ISBN 0-690-64217-2, TYC-J). Har-Row.

--Poe's Tales, 8. Rackham, Arthur (1867-1939), illus. N.D. J. P. Lippincott.

--Poe's Tales of Mystery & Terror. (Magnum Easy Eye Classic Ser). (gr. 9-12). N.D. Lancer.

--The Purloined Letter. Schreiter, Rick (1936-), illus. Bd. with The Murders in the Rue Morgue. (Illus.). 96p. (gr. 7up). 1966. (ISBN 0-531-01078-3). Watts.

--Selected Stories and Poems. (Franklin Watts Classics). (gr. 7 up). 1969. (ISBN 0-531-00409-0). Watts.

--Selected Stories and Poems. large type ed. Zulli, Floyd, Jr. (1922-1980), ed. (Keith Jennison Bks). (gr. 6 up). N.D. (ISBN 0-531-00263-2). Watts.

--Stories. (gr. 7 up). N.D. Pyramid Pubns.

--Stories by Edgar Allan Poe. Harris, David P., ed. 128p. 1973. (ISBN 0-87789-080-3). English Language Service.

--Tales. (Illus.). (Great Illus. Classics). 1952. Dodd.

--Tales. (Great Ill, Classic Ser.). (gr. 9 up). 1979. Dodd.

--Tales. (New Pocket Classics). N.D. Macmillan.

--Tales. Benet, Laura (1884-1979), intro. by. (Great Illustrated Classics). N.D. Dodd Mead & Co.

--Tales. Benet, Laura (1884-1979), intro. by. (Illus.). N.D. Dodd, Mead & Co.

--Tales and Poems of Edgar Allan Poe. 1963. MacMillan Co.

--Tales and Poems of Edgar Allan Poe. Hoban, Russell Conwell (1925-), illus. (gr. 7 up). 1967. (ISBN 0-02-774620-8). Macmillan.

--Tales of Edgar Allan Poe. 420 p. 21cm. (Classics to grow on). 1966, c.1964. Parent's Magazine's Cultural Institute.

--Tales of Edgar Allan Poe. Forberg, Ati, pseud. (1925-), illus. Forberg, Beate Gropius. LC 79-105826. (Illus.). 252 p. 22cm. (Golden Press classics library). c.1979. (ISBN 0-307-12227-1). Golden Press.

--Tales of Edgar Allan Poe. Forberg, Ati, pseud. (1925-), illus. Forberg, Beate Gropius. 420 p. 21cm. (Classics to grow on). 1966, c.1964. Parent's Magazine's Cultural Institute.

--Tales of Edgar Allan Poe. Stewart, Diana, adapted by. Shaw, Charles (1941-), illus. LC 80-14064. p. cm. (Raintree Short Classics). c.1980. (ISBN 0-8172-1662-6). Raintree Publishers.

--Tales of Mystery and Imagination. (The Nelson Classics). N.D. Nelson Bks.

--Tales of Mystery and Imagination. (World's Classics Ser). (gr. 7 up). N.D. (ISBN 0-19-250021-X). Oxford U Pr.

--Tales of Mystery & Imagination. Henniker-Major, retold by. Owen, C., illus. (Illus.). (Oxford Progressive English Readers Ser.). (gr. 3 up). 1975. (ISBN 0-19-580511-9). Oxford U Pr.
--Tales of Poe. (Classic Ser.). N.D. World Pub.
--Tales of Terror and Fantasy. Green, Roger Gilbert Lancelyn (1918-), ed. (Illus.). 1st U.S. edition. (Childrens Illustrated Classics Ser). 1971. (ISBN 0-460-05091-5, Pub. by J. M. Dent England). Biblio Dist.
--Tales of Terror and Fantasy. Rackham, Arthur (1867-1939), illus. Green, Roger Gilbert Lancelyn (1918-), intro. by. (Illus.). (Children's Illustrated Classics). (gr. 5 up). 1972. (ISBN 0-525-40750-2). Dutton.
--Tales of the Raven and Other Poems. N.D. Brown Book Company.
--The Tell-Tale Heart. LC 80-21462. p. cm. 1980. Creative Education.
--The Tell-Tale Heart and Other Stories. (O.s.i.). (gr. 7-12). 1972 (Starline). Schol Bk Serv.
--Ten Great Mysteries. Conklin, Groff (1904-1968), ed. (gr. 7 up). 1968. (ISBN 0-590-08595-6, Schol Pap). Scholastic Inc.
--Three Poems. (gr. 7 up). 1966. (ISBN 0-07-050358-3). (ISBN 0-07-050359-1). McGraw.

Poehlmann, JoAnna, illus.
--The Poky Little Puppy. (Color & Wipe-off Ser.). (ps). 1981. (ISBN 0-307-01857-1, Golden Pr). Western Pub.

Pogany, Elaine Cox, Mrs.
--The Golden Cockerel. Pogany, Willy (1882-1955), illus. N.D. Thomas Nelson & Co.

Pogany, Elaine Cox, Mrs., ed. see Pushkin, Alexander Sergeyevich.

Pogany, Elaine Cox, Mrs. & Pogany, Willy (1882-1955)
--Peterkin. Pogany, Elaine Cox, Mrs. & Pogany, Willy (1882-1955), illus. LC 40-31952. 40 p. incl. front., illus. (part col.) 26 x 22 cm. c.1940. David McKay Company.

Pogany, Nandor, ed.
--The Hungarian Fairy Book. Pogany, Willy, illus. 1913. Frederick A. Stokes.
--The Hungarian Fairy Book. Pogany, Willy (1882-1955), illus. N.D. J. B. Lippincott.
--Magyar Fairy Tales from Old Hungarian Legends. Pogany, Willy (1882-1955), illus. LC 30-202044. 5 p. l., 268 p. incl. front., illus. 22 cm. c.1930. E. P. Dutton & Co.

Pogany, Willy, jt. auth. see Pogany, Elaine Cox, Mrs.

Pogany, Willy (1882-1955)
--The Hungarian Fairy Book. Pogany, Willy (1882-1955), illus. (The Fairy Stories). N.D. Frederick A. Stokes Co.

Pogrebin, Letty Cottin (1939-), ed.
--Stories for Free Children. LC 82-9981. p. cm. c.1982. (ISBN 0-07-050389-3). McGraw-Hill.

Pogue, Kate
--Fritzie Goes Home. Augustiny, Sally, illus. (Illus.). (A Young Reader Ser.). (gr. k-3). 1979. (ISBN 0-307-60301-6, Golden Pr). Western Pub.

Pohl, Frederik (1919-) & Williamson, Jack (1908-)
--Undersea City. LC 57-14673. 188 p. 21cm. 1958. Gnome Press.
--Undersea Fleet. 1st ed. LC 55-12189. 187p. 22cm. 1956. Gnome Press.
--Undersea Quest. 1st ed. LC 54-7256. 189 p. 21 cm. (A Jim Eden adventure). 1954. Gnome Pr.

Pohl, Louis
--It's Really Nice. Pohl, Louis, illus. LC 60-9340. 18cm. 31p. 1960. Little, Brown.

Pohl, Victor
--Farewell the Little People. Heath, Jane, illus. LC 71-433688. (Illus.). viii, 146 p. 22cm. 1968. Oxford University Press.

Pohlmann, Lillian Grenfell (1902-)
--Calypso Holiday. 1959. (ISBN 0-8382-0142-3, Cadmus Books). E. M. Hale and Company.
--Calypso Holiday. Petie, Haris, pseud. (1915-), illus. Petty, Roberta. LC 59-11446. 187p. illus. 21cm. 1959. Coward-McCann.
--Love Can Say No. LC 66-10140. 170 p. 21cm. 1966. Westminster Press.
--Myrtle Albertina's Secret. Blegvad, Erik (1923-), illus. LC 56-7098. 128p. illus. 22cm. 1956. Coward-McCann.
--Myrtle Albertina's Secret. Blegvad, Erik (1923-), illus. (Illus.). (gr. 4-6). 1975. (ISBN 0-590-09321-5, Schol Trade Pap). Schol Bk Serv.
--Myrtle Albertina's Song. Blegvad, Erik (1923-), illus. LC 58-7008. (Illus.). 218 p. 22cm. 1958. Coward-McCann.
--Owls and Answers. Fiorentino, Al, illus. LC 63-13354. 176 p. illus. 23 cm. 1964. Westminster Press.
--Sing Loose. LC 68-19639. 160 p. 22cm. 1968. Westminster Press.
--Summer of the White Reindeer. (Illus.). (gr. 4-6). 1965. (ISBN 0-8382-0821-5). Hale.
--Summer of the White Reindeer. large type ed. Krush, Beth (1918-) & Krush, Joe (1918-), illus. LC 65-10042. (Illus.). 23cm. 154p. (gr. 3-6). 1965. (ISBN 0-664-32340-5). Westminster.
--Tall, Skinny, Towheaded, and Miserable. LC 74-22398. 22cm. 124p. 1975. (ISBN 0-664-32564-5). Westminster Press.
--The Unsuitable Behavior of America Martin. LC 76-40408. 21cm. 157p. c.1976. (ISBN 0-664-32603-X). Westminster Press.
--Wolfskin. (gr. 4-6). N.D. (ISBN 0-448-02131-5). (ISBN 0-448-26089-1). G&D.
--Wolfskin. 1st ed. LC 68-16570. 143 p. 24cm. 1968. Norton.

Point, Charles H. (1918-), illus.
--Senor El Dik Dak in the Land of the Gauchos. LC 57-5242. (Illus.). 22cm. 221p. 1957. Caxton Printers.

Pointer, Priscilla
--Ten Little Fingers: A Book of Finger Plays. LC 54-198411. unpaged. illus. 21cm. (Treasure books, 875). 1954. Treasure Books.

Pointer, Priscilla, illus.
--Little Boy Blue and Other Poems for Children. LC 41-221490. 59 p. incl. col. front., illus. (part col.) 17 x 14 cm. (The Little Color Classics). c.1941. McLoughlin Bros., Inc.

Points, Maureen
--The Adventures of Pepe the Poodle & Other Stories. Points, Maureen, illus. (Illus.). 1978. (ISBN 0-9601594-1-X). Maureen Points.

Poix, Carol de see De Poix, Carol.

Pokorska, Christina
--Make Me a Farm. Makowski, Julius, illus. (Illus.). (gr. k-3). N.D. Roy.

Pokrovskaia, Magdalina, tr. see Karazin, Nikolai Nikolnevich.

Polacheck, Janet G
--Mystery on Wheels. LC 60-5207. 174p. 21cm. 1960. Westminster Press.

Polakoff, P. Byron
--Arnold Palmer & the Golfin' Dolphin. Mackall, Debbie, illus. (Illus.). 48p. 1984. (ISBN 0-943084-14-8). Turnbull & Willoughby.

Pole, James T.
--Midshipman Plowright. (Illus.). maps. (gr. 8 up). 1969. (ISBN 0-396-05886-8). Dodd.

Polese, Carolyn
--Promise Not to Tell. Barrett, Jennifer, illus. LC 84-19767. (Illus.). 65 p. 24cm. c.1985. (ISBN 0-89885-239-0). Human Sciences Press.
--Something About a Mermaid. 1st ed. Owens, Gail, illus. LC 77-15585. p. cm. 22cm. 27p. c.1978. (ISBN 0-525-39590-3). Dutton.

Polese, Marcia Ann (1949-) & Wender, Dorothea
--Frankie and the Fawn. Stone, David Karl (1922-), illus. LC 74-4236. (Illus.). 126 p. 23cm. 1974. (ISBN 0-687-13454-4). Abingdon Press.

Polette, Nancy Jane (1930-)
--Katie Penn. Molina, Charles, illus. LC 77-20495. (Illus.). 111 p. 24cm. (Midwestern Memories). c.1978. (ISBN 0-570-07807-5). (ISBN 0-570-07802-4). Concordia Pub. House.

Polgreen, Cathleen, jt. auth. see Polgreen, John.

Polgreen, John
--The Stars Tonight. Polgreen, Cathleen, illus. 1967. Harper & Row Pub.

Polgreen, John & Polgreen, Cathleen
--Good Morning, Mr. Sun. LC 63-9570. (Illus.). 26p. 24cm. (A Little Owl Bk.). 1963. Holt, Rinehart, and Winston.

Polhamus, Jean Burt
--Dinosaur Funny Bones: Poems. Funai, Mamoru R. (1932-), illus. LC 74-8331. (Illus.). 41 p. 22cm. 1974. (ISBN 0-13-214536-7). Prentice-Hall.
--Doctor Dinosaur. O'Neill, Steve, illus. 29p. 1975. (ISBN 0-13-217083-3). P-H.

Poling, James
--The Man Who Saved Robinson Crusoe. N.D (W. W. Norton). Grosset & Dunlap Pub.

Politi, Leo (1908-)
--A Boat for Peppe. Politi, Leo (1908-), illus. LC 50-9534. (Illus.). 32 p. 27cm. 1950. Scribner.
--The Butterflies Come. Politi, Leo (1908-), illus. LC 57-6848. (Illus.). unpaged. 26cm. 1957. Scribner.
--Emmet. Politi, Leo (1908-), illus. LC 74-142388. (Illus.). 30 p. 27cm. 1971. (ISBN 0-684-12320-7). Scribner's.
--Juanita. Politi, Leo (1908-), illus. LC 48-1509. 31 p. illus. (part col.) 27 cm. 1948. C. Scribner's Sons. **Award: (RCM).**
--Lito and the Clown. Politi, Leo (1908-), illus. LC 64-21295. 31 p. col. illus. 26 cm. 1964. Scribner.
--Little Leo. Politi, Leo (1908-), illus. LC 51-12320. (Illus.). 26cm. 28p. 1951. Scribner.
--Little Pancho. Politi, Leo (1908-), illus. LC 38-303814. 41 p. illus. 16 cm. 1938. The Viking Press.
--Mieko. Politi, Leo (1908-), illus. LC 69-15402. (Illus.). 31 p. 30cm. 1969. Golden Gate Junior Books.
--The Mission Bell. Politi, Leo (1908-), illus. LC 53-12756. (Illus.). unpaged. c.1953. Scribner.
--Moy Moy. Politi, Leo (1908-), illus. LC 60-6413. unpaged. illus. 26cm. 1961. Scribner.
--Mr. Fong's Toy Shop. LC 78-1547. (Illus.). 32 p. 26cm. c.1978. (ISBN 0-684-15583-4). Scribner.
--The Nicest Gift. Politi, Leo (1908-), illus. LC 73-1377. (Illus.). 32 p. 27cm. 1973. (ISBN 0-684-13383-0). Scribner.
--Pedro, the Angel of Olvera Street. Politi, Leo (1908-), illus. (Illus.). (ps-2). 1946. (ISBN 0-684-12628-1, ScribJ). Encore ed. (ISBN 0-684-17411-1, ScribJ). Scribner. **Award: (RCM).**
--Piccolo's Prank. Politi, Leo (1908-), illus. LC 65-21365. (Illus.). 32 p. 26cm. 1965. Scribner.
--Rosa. Politi, Leo (1908-), illus. LC 63-17237. 1 v. (unpaged) col. illus. 26 cm. 1963. Scribner.
--Saint Francis and the Animals. 1959. Charles Scribner's Sons.
--Song of the Swallows. Politi, Leo (1908-), illus. LC 49-821515. 32 p. col. illus., music. 26 cm. c.1949. C. Scribner's Sons. **Award: (RCM).**
--Three Stalks of Corn. Politi, Leo (1908-), illus. LC 75-35009. (Illus.). 32 p. 27cm. c.1976. (ISBN 0-684-14572-3). Scribner.

Politzer, Anie & Defoe, Daniel (1660-1731)
--My Journals and Sketchbooks: By Robinson Crusoe. Politzer, Michel, illus. LC 74-2240. (Illus.). 78 p. 32cm. 1st U.S. edition. 1974. (ISBN 0-15-267836-0). Harcourt Brace Jovanovich.

Politzer, Anie & Politzer, Michel
--Reader's Digest Treasury for Young Readers. Politzer, Anie & Politzer, Michel, illus. LC 78-78139. (Illus.). 255 p. 29cm. c.1979. (ISBN 0-89577-064-4). Reader's Digest Association.

Politzer, Michel, jt. auth. see Politzer, Anie.

Polk, William T.
--The Fallen Angel and Other Stories. 188p. 1956. University Of North Carolina.

Poll, Ruth
--The American Holiday Parade. Gilbert, Gar, illus. LC 40-367070. 40 p. col. illus. 26 cm. c.1939. Elektra Press.

Pollack, Merrill S. (1924-)
--Phaethon. Hofmann, William, illus. LC 66-10899. (Illus.). 24cm. 54p. (gr. 4-6). 1966. (ISBN 0-397-30905-8). Lippincott.
--Shem & Doon: A Fairy Tale. 1st ed. Fraser, Betty M., pseud. (1928-), illus. Fraser, Elizabeth Marr. LC 62-19329. (Illus.). 24 312cm. 64p. (gr. 3-7). 1962. Bobbs.

Pollack, Pam, compiled by.
--Moonbeam Fairy Tales. LC 77-154249. (Illus.). 47 p. 28cm. c.1977. (ISBN 0-8055-0355-2). Hart Pub. Co.

Pollack, Reginald (1924-)
--The Magician and the Child. LC 77-154760. (Illus.). 40 p. 1971. Atheneum.

Polland, Madeleine Angela Cahill (1918-)
--Alhambra. Gaaze, Mary Frances, illus. LC 76-121955. (Illus.). 178 p. 22cm. 1970. Doubleday.
--Beorn the Proud. Stobbs, William (1914-), illus. LC 62-9805. (Illus.). 175 p. 21cm. 1962, c.1961. Holt, Rinehart and Winston. **Award: (ALA).**
--Children of the Red King. 1st ed. Macarthur-Onslow, Annette Rosemary (1933-), illus. LC 61-7625. 159p. illus. 21cm. 1961, c.1959. Holt, Rinehart and Winston.
--Chuiraquimba and the Black Robes. 1st ed. Barberis, Juan Carlos, illus. LC 62-8858. (Illus.). 189 p. 22cm. (Clarion book). 1962. Doubleday.
--City of the Golden House. 1st ed. Summers, Leo, illus. LC 63-8751. 190p. 22cm. (Clarion bk.). c.1963. Doubleday.
--Daughter of the Sea. LC 72-90367. 176p. (gr. 7-9). 1972. (ISBN 0-385-01143-1). (ISBN 0-385-07046-2). Doubleday.
--Deirdre. Morrison, Sean, illus. LC 67-2903. (Illus.). 166 p. 22cm. 1967. Doubleday.
--Fingal's Quest. Mars, Witold Tadeusz J. (1912-), illus. LC 61-543. 191p. (Clarion books). c.1961. Doubleday.
--Flame Over Tara. 1st ed. Davis, Omar, illus. LC 64-11285. 192p. illus. 22cm. 1964. Doubleday.
--Mission to Cathay. 1st ed. Landa, Peter, illus. LC 65-14019. 229 p. illus., map (on lining papers) 22 cm. 1965. Doubleday.
--Queen Without Crown. Danska, Herbert (1928-), illus. LC 66-7762. (Illus.). 190p. (gr. 7-9). 1966. (ISBN 0-03-060750-7). HR&W.
--The Queen's Blessing. 1st ed. Fraser, Betty M., pseud. (1928-), illus. Fraser, Elizabeth Marr. LC 64-14577. 176p. illus. 22cm. c.1964. Holt.
--Shattered Summer. LC 71-103772. 212 p. 22cm. 1970, c.1969. Doubleday.
--Stranger in the Hills. Ambrus, Victor G., pseud. (1935-), illus. Ambrus, Gyozo Laszlo. LC 68-11760. (Illus.). 190 p. 22cm. 1st U.S. edition. 1968. Doubleday.
--To Kill a King. 1st ed. Holder, John, illus. LC 79-98917. 187 p. 22cm. 1971. (ISBN 0-03-084264-6). Holt, Rinehart and Winston.
--To Tell My People. 1st ed. Powers, Richard M. Gorman (1921-), illus. LC 68-11832. (Illus.). 209 p. 22cm. 1968. Holt, Rinehart and Winston.
--Town Across the Water. Nesbitt, Esta (1918-), illus. LC 63-10512. (Illus.). 174p. (gr. 4-6). 1963. (ISBN 0-03-035850-7). (ISBN 0-03-035855-8). HR&W.
--The White Twilight. 1st ed. Cober, Alan Edwin (1935-), illus. LC 65-12424. 152 p. illus. 21 cm. 1965, c.1962. Holt, Rinehart and Winston.

Polland, Madeleine Angela Cahill (1918-) & Coatsworth, Elizabeth (1892-)
--Children of the Red King. Deny, Maurice (1892-), illus. LC 66-1018. 78p. (gr. 4-6). 1961. (ISBN 0-03-059745-5). HR&W.

Pollard, A. W., ed. see Chaucer, Geoffrey.

Pollard, Arthur
--The Romance of King Arthur. Rackham, Arthur (1867-1939), illus. (Illus.). (Facsimile Classics Ser.). 1979. (ISBN 0-8317-7460-6, Mayflower Bks). Smith Pubs.

Pollard, Edwina Obenauer (1902-)
--Come With Me: Especially for Children. LC 52-23442. 47p. 24cm. 1952. Cullen Print Co.

Pollard, Eliza Frances
--The Green Mountain Boys. N.D. Dodd, Mead & Co.
--The King's Signet. (Scribner-Blackie Series of books for young people). N.D. Charles Scribner's Sons.
--The Lady Isobel. (Scribner-Blackie Series of books for young people). N.D. Charles Scribner's Sons.
--Roger the Ranger. N.D. Dodd, Mead & Co.
--A Saxon Maid. (Illus.). (Stories Old and New Ser.). N.D. Caldwell.

Pollard, Josephine (1834-1892), ed. see Grimm, Jakob Ludwig Karl (1785-1863) & Grimm, Wilhelm Karl.

Pollard, Josephine, Miss, jt. ed. see Vincent, John Heyl.

Pollard, Josephine, Miss (1834-1892)
--Elfin Land. Poems. Saterlee, Walter, designed by. LC 16-3875. 2 p. l., 7-40 p. col. front., col. illus. 25 x 33 cm. c.1882. G. W. Harlan & Co.
--Gellivor. A Christmas Legend of the North Land. Satterlee, Walter, illus. LC 16-3097. 10 l. plates. 17 x 14 cm. c.1882. A. D. F. Randolph & Co.
--Gipsy in New York, 1 of 6 Vols. (Illus.). (Gipsy Books Ser.). N.D. Methodist Book Concern.
--Gipsy in New York. (Illus.). (Gipsy Bks.). N.D. Nelson & Phillips.
--Gipsy's Adventures, 1 of 6 vols. (Illus.). (Gipsy Bks). N.D. Set. Methodist Bk Concern.
--Gipsy's Adventures. (Illus.). (Gipsy Bks.). N.D. Nelson & Phillips.
--Gipsy's Early Days, 1 of 6 Vols. (Illus.). (Gipsy Books Ser.). N.D. Methodist Book Concern.
--Gipsy's Early Days. (Illus.). (Gipsy Bks.). N.D. Nelson & Phillips.
--Gipsy's Quest, 1 of 6 Vols. (Illus.). (Gipsy Books Ser.). N.D. Methodist Book Concern.
--Gipsy's Quest. (Illus.). (Gipsy Bks.). N.D. Nelson & Phillips.
--Gipsy's Travels, 1 of 6 vols. (Illus.). (Gipsy Books Ser.). N.D. Methodist Book Concern.
--Gipsy's Travels. (Illus.). (Gipsy Bks.). N.D. Nelson & Phillips.
--Lydia's Duty. N.D. A. D. F. Randolph.
--The Other Gipsy, 1 of 6 vols. (Illus.). (Gipsy Bks). N.D. Set. Methodist Bk Concern.
--Plays and Games for Little Folks: Sports of All Sorts, Fireside Fun, and Singing Games. Mathews, Ferdinand Schuyler (1854-), illus. LC 5-29307. 2 p. l., 4, 128 p. col. illus. 27 cm. 1889. McLoughlin Bros.
--Singing Games. Mathews, Ferdinand Schuyler (1854-), illus. LC 5-29306. 2 p. l., 97-128 p. col. illus. 27 cm. 1890. McLoughliu Bros.
--The Story of Bonnybelle. LC 16-3098. cover-title, 11, 1 p. col. plates. 28 x 21 cm. (On cover: Grimm's series). c.1883. McLoughlin Bro's.
--Two Little Tots on Their Way Through the Year. Sunter, Pauline J., Mrs., illus. LC 16-3876. 13 l. col. front., illus., col. plates. 22 cm. 1890. Frederick A. Stokes Company.

Pollard, Josephine, Miss (1834-1892) & Grimm, Jakob Ludwig Karl (1785-1863)
--Hours in Fairy Land. Enchanted Princess, White Rose and Red Rose, Six Swans. LC 16-3867. 1 p. l., 1, 14, 1, 14 p., 1 l., 12 p. col. plates. 28 x 22 cm. c.1883. McLoughlin Bro's.
--Tales of the Fairy World. Bonny Belle, Brave Little Tailor, Snow White. LC 16-3868. 2 p. l., 11, 1 p., 1 l., 12 p., 1 l., 12 p. col. plates. 28 x 22 cm. c.1883. McLoughlin Bro's.

Pollard, M. M.
--Aunt Hetty's Will. (Illus.). (The Girl's Own Favorite Ser.). N.D. E. P. Dutton & Co.
--Beneath a Sultry Sky. (Illus.). 128p. (The Steadfast Ser.). N.D. Fleming H. Revell Co.
--The Brother's Legacy: Or, Better than Gold. N.D. Nelson & Phillips.
--Brother's Legacy: Or,Better Than Gold. (Illus.). N.D. Methodist Book Concern.
--An Earl's Daughter, 1 of 6. (Home and School Reward Ser.: No. 2). N.D. Cassell, Petter, & Galpin.
--Miner's Son and Margaret Vernon. (Illus.). N.D. Methodist Book Concern.

--The Miner's Son, and Margaret Vernon. N.D. Nelson & Phillips.
--Nellie's Secret. N.D. Robert Carter.
--The Old Farmhouse: Or, Alice Morton's Home, and Other Stories. (Illustrated Juvenile Ser.). N.D. The American News Co.
--The Two Sisters, 1 of 6. (Home and School Reward Ser.: No. 1). N.D. Cassell, Petter, & Galpin.

Pollard, Nancy D. (1925-), illus.
--The Bunny Book. LC 50-23544. 18 p. col. illus. 22 cm. (A Bonnie Bk.). 1949. John Martin's House.

Pollock, Bruce (1945-)
--It's Only Rock and Roll. LC 80-355. 232 p. 22cm. 1980. (ISBN 0-395-29182-8). Houghton Mifflin.
--Mr. Minsky & Max. LC 78-15599. 242 p. 22cm 1978. (ISBN 0-395-26455-3). Houghton Mifflin.
--Playing for Change. LC 76-62498. 204 p. 22cm. 1977. Houghton Mifflin.

Pollock, Dean
--Joseph, Chief of the Nez Perce. Pollock, Dean, illus. N.D. Binfords & Mort.

Pollock, Frank Lillie
--Northern Diamonds. LC 17-24854. 4 p. l., 259, 1 p. front., plates. 20 cm. 1917. Houghton Mifflin Company.
--The Timber Treasure. LC 23-11926. 6 p. l., 3-269 p. front., plates. 20 cm. 1923. The Century Co.
--Wilderness Honey. Edwards, Harry C., illus. LC 17-243984. 8 p. l., 3-325 p. incl. front., plates. 20 cm. 1917. The Century Co.
--The Woods-Rider. Jackson, John Edwin & Edwards, Harry C., illus. LC 22-17972. 5 p. l., 3-384 p. front., plates. 20 cm. 1922. The Century Co.

Pollock, Katherine G. see Ward, Kate, pseud.

Pollock, Katherine G (1904-)
--The Gaucho's Daughter. Bart, Barry, illus. LC 41-7318. 56 p. incl. col. front., illus. (part col.) 22 cm. (New world neighbors). c.1941. D. C. Heath and Company.
--Sandalio Goes to Town. Busoni, Rafaello (1900-1962), illus. LC 42-4728. 5 p. l., 144 p. col. front., illus. 21 cm. 1942. C. Scribner's Sons.
--Sir Toby and the Murrays. Fleur, Anne Elizabeth (1901-), illus. Sari, pseud. LC 45-9824. 3 p. l., 201 p. illus. 21 cm. 1945. C. Scribner's Sons.
--Sky Ride. Wood, Ruth, illus. LC 44-654272. 3 p. l., 131 p. front., illus. 21 cm. 1944. C. Scribner's Sons.
--Sly Mongoose. Wiese, Kurt (1887-1974), illus. LC 43-12454. 5 p. l., 78 p. col. illus. 23 cm. 1943. C. Scribner's Sons.
--A Story That Has No End. Ward, Kate, pseud. Dirks, John, illus. LC 49-8168. 50 p. illus. (part col.) 17 x 23 cm. (Children's hour library). 1949. Westminster Press.

Pollock, Louise, Mrs. (0000-1901)
--Cheerful Echoes. From the National Kindergarten, for Children from 3 to 10 Years of Age. LC 41-23490. vi, 3-72 p. 20 cm. c.1888. De Wolfe, Fiske & Co.
--National Kindergarten Songs and Plays. LC 40-25914. 77 p. 20 cm. c.1880. De Wolfe, Fiske & Co.

Pollock, Louise, Mrs. (0000-1901), tr. from Ger.
--The Life and Adventures of Chanticleer the Intelligent Rooster: An Interesting Story in Verse for Children. LC 44-14176. 96 p. front., plates. 20 1/2 cm. 1862. A. Williams & Co.

Pollock, Marylee, illus.
--Come Out and Play. Poems. LC 47-270947. 60 p. illus. (part col.) 26 cm. (Saalfield treasure books). c.1947. Saalfield Pub. Co.

Pollock, Miriam S., jt. auth. see Pollock, Morris P.

Pollock, Morris P. & Pollock, Miriam S.
--The Clown Family Speech Book: We Want Toto!. (Illus.). 168p. (gr. 3-6). 1960. (ISBN 0-398-01505-8). C C Thomas.

Pollock, Penny (1935-)
--Ants Don't Get Sunday Off. Cauley, Lorinda Bryan (1951-), illus. LC 78-8283. (Illus.). 45 p. 23cm. (See and Read Storybook). 1979. (ISBN 0-399-61129-0). Putnam.
--Garlanda: The Ups and Downs of an Uppity Teapot. Tomes, Margot Ladd (1917-), illus. LC 80-12966. p. cm. c.1980. (ISBN 0-399-20713-9). Putnam.
--Keeping it Secret. Diamond, Donna (1950-), illus. LC 82-3831. p. cm. 1982. (ISBN 0-399-20934-4). Putnam.
--The Slug Who Thought He Was a Snail. Cauley, Lorinda Bryan (1951-), illus. LC 79-17719. (Illus.). 46 p. 23cm. (See and Read Book). c.1980. (ISBN 0-399-61147-9). Putnam.
--The Spitbug Who Couldn't Spit. Cauley, Lorinda Bryan (1951-), illus. LC 80-17063. p. cm. (See and read book). 1980. (ISBN 0-399-61152-5). Putnam.
--Stall Buddies. Owens, Gail, illus. LC 84-9947. (Illus.). 63 p. 23cm. c.1984. (ISBN 0-399-21118-7). (ISBN 0-399-21118-7). Putnam.

Pollok, Robert (1798-1827)
--Course of Time. N.D. Robert Carter.
--Helen of Glen. N.D. Robert Carter.
--Helen of the Glen: A Tale of the Scotch Covenanters. (Illus.). 113p. N.D. Merrill.
--Helen of the Glen: A Tale of the Scotch Covenanters. LC 1736. 2 p. l., 3-113 p. plates. 20 cm. c.1900. Presbyterian Committee of Publication.
--The Persecuted Family, 1 of 3 vols. (Illus.). 115p. (Tales of the Covenanters Ser.). N.D. Set. Robert Carter & Brothers.
--Ralph Gemmell. N.D. Robert Carter.
--Ralph Gemmell: Or, The Banks of the Irvine. (Illus.). 103p. N.D. Merrill.
--Tales of the Covenanters, 3 vols. (Illus.). N.D. Set. Merrill.
--Tales of the Scottish Covenanters. LC 42-32085. 1 p. l., 113 p., 1 l., v-viii, 9-115, 108 p. 16 cm. 1844. R. Carter.

Pollowitz, Melinda Kilborn (1944-)
--Cinnamon Cane. LC 76-58690. 154 p. 21cm. c.1977. (ISBN 0-06-024762-2). (ISBN 0-06-024763-0). Harper & Row.

Polowe, David (1893-)
--The Adventures of Jimmy Martin, Stowaway. LC 47-267. 160 p. 21 1/2 cm. 1946. The Colt Press.

Polseno, Jo
--This Hawk Belongs to Me. Polseno, Jo, illus. LC 76-12745. p. cm. c.1976. (ISBN 0-679-20324-9). D. McKay Co.

Polsky, Milton, et al.
--The King of Escapes. (Orig.). (gr. 3-12). 1985. (ISBN 0-88734-510-7). Players Pr.

Poltarnees, Welleran, jt. ed. see Edens, Cooper.

Polter, David
--Say Hello to the Care Bear Cousin. Neher, Julie & Redding, Jane, illus. (Illus.). 64p. (ps-3). 1985. (ISBN 0-394-87114-6, BYR). Random.

Polushkin, Maria
--Bubba and Babba. De Groat, Diane (1947-), illus. LC 75-15914. (Based on a Russian Folktale). (Illus.). 32 p. 29cm. c.1976. (ISBN 0-517-52435-X). Crown.
--The Little Hen & the Giant. Salzman, Yuri, illus. LC 76-58712. (Illus.). 31p. (gr. k-3). 1977. (ISBN 0-06-024783-5, HarpJ). (ISBN 0-06-024783-5). Har-Row.
--The Little Hen & the Giant. Salzman, Yuri, illus. (Illus.). (gr. k-3). 1979. (ISBN 0-590-12102-2, Schol Pap). Scholastic Inc.
--Mama's Secret. Bond, Felicia, illus. LC 83-14144. (Illus.). 32p. 1984. (ISBN 0-590-07892-5). Four Winds Press.
--Morning. Morrison, William (1935-), illus. LC 82-21076. p. cm. c.1983. (ISBN 0-590-07871-2). Four Winds Press.
--Mother, Mother, I Want Another. Dawson, Diane, illus. LC 78-5443. p. cm. 32p. 1978. (ISBN 0-517-53401-0). Crown Publishers.

Polushkin, Maria, tr. see Aleksin, Anatolii Georgievich.

Polushkin, Maria, tr. see Linevski, A.

Polushkin, Maria & Suteyev, Vladimir Grigorevich
--Who Said Meow?. 1st ed. Maestro, Giulio (1942-), illus. LC 74-19500. (Illus.). 36 p. 29cm. 1975. (ISBN 0-517-51846-5). Crown Publishers.

Polyzoides, G.
--Stories from the Old Testament. (Illus.). 71p. N.D. Divry.

Pomerans, A. J., tr. see Dickmann, Miep.

Pomerantz, Charlotte, jt. auth. see Barton, Byron.

Pomerantz, Charlotte (1930-)
--All Asleep. Tafuri, Nancy, illus. LC 83-25337. (Illus.). 7 1/2 x 9. 32p. (14 pt.). (ps-1). 1984. (ISBN 0-688-03762-3). (ISBN 0-688-03763-1). (ISBN 0-688-03763-1). Greenwillow.
--Ask the Windy Sea. Grossman, Nancy S. (1940-) & Siegel, Anita, illus. LC 68-27029. (Illus.). 32 p. 27cm. 1968. Young Scott Books.
--The Ballad of the Long-Tailed Rat. Parry, Marian (1924-), illus. LC 74-13611. (Illus.). 32 p. 1975. (ISBN 0-02-774890-1). Macmillan.
--The Bear Who Couldn't Sleep. Wohlberg, Meg (1905-), illus. LC 65-10138. 1 v. (unpaged) col. illus. 26 cm. 1965. Morrow.
--Buffy and Albert. 1st ed. Abolafia, Yossi, illus. LC 81-20144. (Illus.). 47 p. 22cm. (Greenwillow Read-Alone Books). c.1982. (ISBN 0-688-00920-4). (ISBN 0-688-00921-2). Greenwillow Books.
--The Day They Parachuted Cats on Borneo: A Drama of Ecology. Aruego, Jose (1932-), illus. LC 75-141664. (Illus.). (gr. 3-7). 1971 (A-W Childrens). A-W.
--Detective Poufy's First Case: Or, the Missing Battery-Operated Pepper Grinder. Mathieu, Joseph (1945-) & Norman, Marty, illus. LC 75-2283. p. cm. 64p. 1976. (ISBN 0-201-05853-7). Addison-Wesley.
--The Downtown Fairy Godmother. Natti, Susanna (1948-), illus. LC 78-1014. (Illus.). 42 p. 23cm. c.1978. (ISBN 0-201-05858-8). Addison-Wesley.
--The Half-Birthday Party. DeSalvo-Ryan, DyAnne, illus. LC 84-4963. (Illus.). 48p. (gr. 1-4). 1984. (ISBN 0-89919-273-4, Clarion). HM.
--If I Had a Paka: Poems in Eleven Languages. Tafuri, Nancy, illus. LC 81-6624. (Illus.). 32 p. c.1982. (ISBN 0-688-00836-4). (ISBN 0-688-00837-2). Greenwillow Books.
--The Mango Tooth. Hafner, Marylin (1925-), illus. LC 76-22664. (Illus.). 32 p. 26cm. c.1977. (ISBN 0-688-80070-X). (ISBN 0-688-84070-1). Greenwillow Books.
--The Moon Pony. Trezzo, Loretta, illus. LC 67-9540. 1 v. (unpaged) col. illus. 27 cm. 1967. Young Scott Books.
--Noah's and Namah's Ark. Carson, Kelly K. M, illus. LC 80-14595. (Illus.). 38 p. 24cm. c.1981. (ISBN 0-03-057629-6). Holt, Rinehart, and Winston.
--One Duck, Another Duck. Aruego, Jose (1932-) & Dewey, Ariane (1937-), illus. LC 83-20767. (Illus.). 9 7/8 x 8. 24p. (22 pt.). (ps-1). 1984. (ISBN 0-688-03744-5). (ISBN 0-688-03745-3). Greenwillow.
--The Piggy in the Puddle. Marshall, James (1942-), illus. LC 73-6047. (Illus.). 30 p. 19cm. 1974. (ISBN 0-02-774900-2). Macmillan.
--Posy. Stock, Catherine, illus. LC 83-1452. p. cm. 1983. (ISBN 0-688-02298-7). (ISBN 0-688-02299-5). Greenwillow Books.
--The Princess and the Admiral. Chen, Tony (1929-), illus. LC 73-15525. (Illus.). 48 p. 23cm. 1974. (ISBN 0-201-05852-9). Addison-Wesley.
--The Tamarindo Puppy & Other Poems. Barton, Byron (1930-), illus. LC 79-16584. (Byron Barton is the legal name change of Byron Vartanian.). (Illus.). 32p. (gr. k-3). 1980. (ISBN 0-688-80251-6). (ISBN 0-688-84251-8). Greenwillow. **Award: (ALA).**
--Where's the Bear?. Barton, Byron (1930-), illus. LC 83-1697. (Byron Barton is the legal name change of Byron Vartanian.). (Illus.). 9 7/8 x 8. 32p. (40 pt.). (ps-1). 1984. (ISBN 0-688-01752-5). (ISBN 0-688-01753-3). Greenwillow.
--Whiff, Sniff, Nibble, & Chew: The Gingerbread Boy Retold. Incisa, Monica, illus. LC 83-14179. (Illus.). 7 x 9. 24p. (14 pt.). (gr. k-3). 1984. (ISBN 0-688-02551-X). (ISBN 0-688-02552-8). Greenwillow.

Pomeroy, Pete, pseud., see Roth, Arthur Joseph.

Pomeroy, Pete, pseud. (1925-)
--Wipeout!. Roth, Arthur Joseph. LC 68-12391. (gr. 7-12). 1968. (ISBN 0-590-07083-5, Four Winds). Schol Bk Serv.
--Wipeout!. Roth, Arthur Joseph. (gr. 7-12). 1972. (ISBN 0-590-08769-X, Schol Pap). Scholastic Inc.

Pomeroy, Sarah Gertrude (1882-)
--Christmas in Spain: Or, Mariquita's Day of Rejoicing. Hoxie, Bertha Davidson, illus. LC 10-25794. (Illus.). 29p. (Christmas in Many Lands Ser.). 1910. Dana Estes & Co.
--Christmas in Sweden: Or, A Festival of Light. Hoxie, Bertha Davidson, illus. LC 11-21582. 32 p. incl. col. front., col. illus. 20 cm. c.1911. D. Estes & Company.
--A Loyal Little Subject: A Christmas in Holland. Hoxie, Bertha Davidson, illus. LC 8-22609. 31 p. incl. front., illus. 20 cm. c.1908. D. Estes & Company.
--Saburo's Reward: A Christmas in Japan. Horne, Diantha W., illus. LC 9-30323. (Illus.). (Christmas in Many Lands Ser.). 1909. Dana Estes & Co.

Pomeroy, Vivian Towse (1883-)
--Another Story, Please!. LC 47-12051. 101 p. illus. 27 cm. 1947. Beacon Press.
--The Enchanted Children. Rev ed. Backharsch, H. I., illus. LC 25-20306. 3 p. l., 137, 1 p. incl. illus., plates. col. front. 21 cm. 1925. Houghton Mifflin Company.
--Kings, Donkeys and Dreams. LC 37-21962. 3 p. l., 94 p. 19 1/2 cm. 1937. The Beacon Press, Inc.

Ponder, Hazel K
--Deep in the Hills. LC 78-108569. 94 p. 22cm. 1970. Dorrance.

Pong, Ted
--Quilt. Fraser, Diane, illus. LC 81-90056. (Illus.). 87p. (Orig.). 1981. (ISBN 0-939966-00-X). Pong.

Ponicsan, Darryl (1938-)
--The Accomplice. LC 74-5802. 1975. Harper & Row.

Pons, Helene
--Story of Vania. Pons, Helene, illus. LC 63-18359. (Illus.). 24p. (gr. 1-3). 1963. (ISBN 0-670-67560-1). Viking Pr.

Ponsot, Marie, adapted by.
--Once Upon a Time Stories. Huens, Jean Leon & Ivanovsky, Elizabeth, illus. 1v. (unpaged) col. illus. 29cm. 1965, c.1945. Grosset.

Ponsot, Marie, tr. see Baudouy, Michel Aime.

Ponsot, Marie (1922-), tr. see Bay, Andre.

Ponsot, Marie, tr. see Clair, Andree.

Ponsot, Marie, tr. see La Fontaine, Jean de.

Ponsot, Marie, tr. see Perrault, Charles.

Ponsot, Marie Birmingham, ed.
--My Big Book of Cat Stories. Segur, Adrienne, illus. (Illus.). (gr. 3-6). 1967 (Golden Pr). Western Pub.

Ponsot, Marie Birmingham, tr. see Grimm, Jakob Ludwig Karl (1785-1863) & Grimm, Wilhelm Karl.

Ponsot, Marie Birmingham (1922-), adapted by.
--Once upon a Time Stories. Ivanovsky, Elizabeth & Huens, Jean Leon, illus. Ponsot, Marie Birmingham (1922-), tr. LC 59-4382. (Illus.). 31cm. 1959. Grosset & Dunlop.

Pont, Clarice Holt (1907-)
--The Immediate Gift. LC 61-6397. 216 p. 21cm. 1961. D. McKay Co.
--No School on Friday: A Story of Saudi Arabia. Stevens, Mary, illus. LC 53-11360. 213p. illus. 21cm. 1953. D. McKay Co.
--Sally on the Fence. Genia, pseud. (1930-), illus. Wennerstrom, Genia Katherine. LC 55-6318. 192p. 21cm. 1955. Nelson.
--Ten Minus Nine Equals Joanie. Maloy, Lois (1902-), illus. LC 65-10565. 180p. illus. 22cm. c.1965. Golden Gate.
--Three Times Easier. Gag, Flavia (1907-1979), illus. LC 51-10220. (Illus.). 111 p. 21cm. 1951. McKay.

Ponter, James J., illus.
--Henny-Penny. LC 54-22404. unpaged. illus. 20cm. (Treasure books, 882). c.1954. Treasure Books.

Pontiflet, Ted (1932-)
--Poochie. Fufuka, Mahiri, illus. LC 78-51321. 25cm. 40p. c.1978. (ISBN 0-8037-7029-4). Dial Press.

Pontigny De Chatelain, Clara De see Chatelain, Clara De Pontigny De.

Poochoo, pseud., see Wisler, Israel Menahem.

Pool, Eugene Hillhouse (1943-)
--The Captain of Battery Park. Morrill, Leslie H, illus. LC 77-12711. (Illus.). 124 p. 22cm. c.1978. (ISBN 0-201-05857-X). Addison-Wesley.

Pool, Maria Louise (1841-1898)
--Boss and Other Dogs. (Illus.). (Editha Ser.). N.D. Caldwell.
--Boss and Other Dogs. (Illus.). (The Young Folks Library). N.D. Caldwell.
--Chums. (Illus.). (The Girls' Own Authors Ser.). N.D. Dana Estes & Co.
--Chums, 31 vols. (Illus.). (Famous Books for Girls Ser.: No. 28). 1905. Set. H M Caldwell Co.
--Chums. Bridgman, Lewis Jesse (1857-1931), illus. LC 19-173. 8cm. 241p. (Gift Book Series for Boys and Girls). 1900. L. C. Page & Co.
--Little Bermuda. Bridgman, Lewis Jesse (1856-1931), illus. (Illus.). 8cm. 163p. (Gift Book Series for Boys and Girls). 1899. L. C. Page & Co.

Poole, Evered Travers
--Flower Stories for our Little Folks. (Illus.). 128p. (The Steadfast Ser.). N.D. Fleming H. Revell co.

Poole, Gray Johnson (1933-)
--Mistletoe: Fact & Folklore. 1976. Dodd.

Poole, Josephine (1933-)
--Catch As Catch Can: A Story of Suspense. Komoda, Kiyoaki (1937-), illus. LC 78-105461. (Illus.). 21cm. 163p. (gr. 5-7). 1970. (ISBN 0-06-024766-5, HarpJ). (ISBN 0-06-440014-X). Har-Row.
--Moon Eyes. Hyman, Trina Schart (1939-), illus. LC 67-1936. (Illus.). 151 p. 21cm. 1st U.S. edition. 1967. Little, Brown.
--Touch & Go. LC 76-3829. 21cm. 169p. (Story of Suspense Ser.). (gr. 7 up). 1976. (ISBN 0-06-024758-4, HarpJ). (ISBN 0-06-024759-2). Har-Row.
--Touch & Go. (gr. 9 up). 1977. (ISBN 0-06-440089-1, Trophy). Har-Row.
--The Visitor. LC 72-80367. 21cm. 148p. (Story of Suspense Ser.). (gr. 7 up). 1972. (ISBN 0-06-024769-X, HarpJ). (ISBN 0-06-024769-X). Har-Row.

Poole, L. E., Mrs.
--Johnnie, The Railroad Boy. (Crowell's Library For Young People). N.D. Thomas Y. Crowell & Co.'s Catalogue.

Poole-Lane, Stanley, ed.
--Stories from The Arabian Nights. (3 Vols.). N.D. Putman's & Sons.

Poolman, Kenneth
--The Kelly. 1956. Norton Company.

Poor, Lucy Tappan (1855-)
--A Summer Siege: A Story for Girls. LC 14-20366. 2 p. l., 318 p. 21 cm. 1914. Sherman, French & Company.
Poortvliet, Rien
--The Pop-up Book of Gnomes. Huygen, Willibrord Joseph (1922-), adapted by. LC 80-108229. (Illus.). 12 p. 28cm. c.1979. (ISBN 0-8109-0966-9). H. N. Abrams.
Poortvliet, Rien, illus.
--Teeny Tiny Gnome Tomes, 3 vols. (Illus.). 48p. (gr. 1-5). 1981. (ISBN 0-8109-1681-9). Abrams.
Pope, Billy N & Emmons, Ramona Ware
--Your World; Let's Go to School. (Illus.). 32 p. 28cm. 1967. Taylor Pub. Co.
--Your World; Let's Visit a Paper Mill. LC 68-59071. (Illus.). 32 p. 28cm. 1969. Taylor Pub. Co.
--Your World: Let's Visit a Silver Company. LC 77-28289. (Illus.). 32 p. 28cm. 1971. (ISBN 0-87833-031-3). Taylor Pub. Co.
Pope, Edith
--The Biggety Chameleon. Grider, Dorothy (1915-), illus. LC 46-25222. 32 p. col. illus. 18 x 21 cm. 1946. C. Scribner's Sons.
Pope, Elizabeth Marie (1917-)
--The Perilous Gard. Cuffari, Richard (1925-1978), illus. LC 76-115. 447 p. 24cm. 1976, c.1974. (ISBN 0-8161-6353-7). G. K. Hall.
--The Perilous Gard. Cuffari, Richard (1925-1978), illus. LC 73-21648. (Illus.). 280 p. 22cm. 1974. (ISBN 0-395-18512-2). Houghton Mifflin. **Award: (JNM).**
--The Sherwood Ring. Ness, Evaline Michelow, Mrs. (1911-), illus. LC 57-12085. (Illus.). 266 p. 22cm. 1958. Houghton Mifflin. **Award: (ALA).**
Pope, Jessie
--Adventures of Silversuit. (Illus.). (The Happy Child's Library). N.D. Dodge Publishing Co.
Pope, Ray (1924-)
--Desperate Breakaway. Floyd, Gareth (1940-), illus. LC 79-102359. (Illus.). 128 p. 22cm. 1970, c.1969. Childrens Press.
--Salvage from Strosa. Floyd, Gareth (1940-), illus. LC 75-102358. (Illus.). 144 p. 22cm. 1970, c.1967. Childrens Press.
--Strosa Light. Floyd, Gareth (1940-), illus. LC 71-102357. (Illus.). 183 p. 21cm. 1970, c.1965. Childrens Press.
Pope, William (1922-)
--Penniless Dreamer. 1st ed. LC 52-2508. 21cm. 186p. 1952. Pageant Press.
Popescu, Christine see Pullein-Thompson, Christine.
Popham, Hugh (1920-)
--The Fabulous Voyage of the Pegasus. Oakley, Graham (1929-), illus. LC 59-659168. 149p. illus. 22cm. (Criterion book for young people). 1959, c.1958. Criterion Books.
--The Fabulous Voyage of the Pegasus. Oakley, Graham (1929-), illus. LC 59-6591. (Illus.). (gr. 4-8). 1959. (ISBN 0-87599-092-4). S G Phillips.
Popik, Uriel see Ofek, Uriel, pseud.
Popper, E. M., tr. see Spyri, Johanna Heusser.
Porazinska, Janina
--In Voytus' Little House. Bobinski, Stanislaw (1897-), illus. Borski, Lucia Merecka, pseud., tr. from Polish. Szczepanowixz, Luica Merecka. LC 44-8334. (Illus.). 1944. Roy Publishers.
--Nine Cry-Baby Dolls: A Folk-Tale. Lorentowicz, Irena (1910-), illus. Bernhard, Josephine Butkowska, Mrs., tr. from Pol. LC 45-35088. 28 p. incl. col. front., col. illus. 21 x 25 1/2 cm. 1945. Roy Publishers.
Porazinski, Janinna
--My Village. Bobinski, Stanislaw (1897-), illus. Borski, Lucia Merecka, tr. from Polish. LC 44-8335. 24cm. 46p. 1944. Roy Publishers.
Porcari, Constance Kwolek see Kwolek, Constance.
Porcher, Mary F. Wickham, pseud., see Bond, Mary Fanning Wickham.
Porcher, Mary F. Wickham, pseud. (1898-)
--Cherique. Bond, Mary Fanning Wickham. LC 28-23049. 3 p. l., 203, 1 p. front., map. 20 cm. 1928. D. Appleton and Company.
--Gloom Creek. Bond, Mary Fanning Wickham. LC 29-17285. v. 221, 1 p. front. 20 cm. 1929. D. Appleton & Company.
Porcher, Peggie
--The Magic City of Children. LC 37-137828. 16 p. col. illus. 33 cm. c.1936. Lynn Publishing Company.
--The Magic Garden of Flowers. LC 37-13795. 16 p. col. illus. 33 cm. c.1936. Lynn Publishing Company.
Porcsa, Micheal
--Under the Brightness of Alien Stars. N.D. Vantage Press.
Pordes, Ilse, retold by.
--Favourite Stories from Japan. (Favourite Stories Ser.). 1975. (ISBN 0-686-60424-5). Heinemann Ed.
Portch, Elizabeth, tr. see Jansson, Tove.
Portch, Elizabeth, tr. see Otava, Merja.
Porte, Barbara Ann
--Harry's Dog. Abolafia, Yossi, illus. LC 83-14129. (Illus.). 47 p. 22cm. (Greenwillow read-alone). (gr. 1-3). c.1984. (ISBN 0-688-02555-2). (ISBN 0-688-02555-2). (ISBN 0-688-02556-0). Greenwillow Books.
--Harry's Mom. Abolafia, Yossi, illus. LC 84-25955. (Illus.). 55 p. 22cm. (Greenwillow read-alone). c.1985. (ISBN 0-688-04817-X). (ISBN 0-688-04818-8). Greenwillow Books.
--Harry's Visit. Abolafia, Yossi, illus. LC 81-20188. (Illus.). 6 1/4 x 8 3/8. 48p. (16 pt.). (gr. 1-3). 1983. (ISBN 0-688-01207-8). (ISBN 0-688-01208-6). Greenwillow. **Award: (ALA).**
--Jesse's Ghost and Other Stories. 1st ed. LC 83-1451. 105 p. 22cm. c.1983. (ISBN 0-688-02301-0). Greenwillow.
--The Kidnapping of Aunt Elizabeth. LC 84-18757. (Illus.). 145 p. 22cm. c.1985. (ISBN 0-688-04302-X). (ISBN 0-688-04305-4). Greenwillow Books.
Porteous, S. R.
--The Tambai Treasure. Stackpool, Will, illus. 168p. 1958. Tri-Ocean Books.
Porter, Alma Florence
--Nigger Baby and Nine Beasts. Verbeek, Gustave, illus. LC 1-29370. 196, 1 p. front., plates. 21 cm. 1901. Ess Ess Publishing Company.
Porter, Ann E.
--Captain John. N.D. Henry Hoyt.
Porter, Barton
--Listen to the Millrace. Casad, Mike, illus. LC 78-66449. (Illus.). (gr. 6 up). 1978. (ISBN 0-9601888-0-0). M J Stone.
Porter, Bertha Currier
--Trudy and Timothy. Aiken, May, illus. LC 17-29734. 217 p. front., plates. 20 cm. 1917. The Penn Publishing Company.
--Trudy and Timothy and the Trees. Aiken, May, illus. LC 21-1356. 224 p. front., plates. 20 cm. 1920. The Penn Publishing Company.
--Trudy and Timothy, Foresters. Aiken, May, illus. LC 22-190486. 213 p. front., plates. 20 cm. 1922. The Penn Publishing Company.
--Trudy and Timothy Out-of-Doors. Aiken, May, illus. LC 19-138439. 224 p. front., plates. 20 cm. 1919. The Penn Publishing Company.
--Wonder-Oak. Aiken, May, illus. LC 13-26100. vi, 163 p. col. front., illus. plates. 21 cm. c.1913. Eaton & Mains.
Porter, C. Fayne (1920-)
--The Battle of the Thousand Slain & Other Stories Selected from Our Indian Heritage. (gr. 7-12). 1972 (Starline). Schol Bk Serv.
Porter, Cyrus
--If I Had a Dog. LC 73-19197. (Illus.). 17p. (Stretch Bks). (gr. k-3). 1974. (ISBN 0-448-11739-8, G&D). Putnam Pub Group.
--If I Had a House. LC 73-19196. (Illus.). 17p. (Stretch Bks). (gr. k-3). 1974. (ISBN 0-448-11738-X, G&D). Putnam Pub Group.
--If I Met Mother Goose. (Illus.). 17p. (Stretch Bks.). (ps-2). 1975. (ISBN 0-448-12085-2, G&D). Putnam Pub Group.
--If I Say A B C. (Illus.). 17p. (Stretch Bks.). (ps-2). 1975. (ISBN 0-448-12084-4, G&D). Putnam Pub Group.
Porter, David Lord (1944-)
--Help! Let Me Out!. Macaulay, David Alexander (1946-), illus. LC 82-1110. (Illus.). 36 p. 27cm. 1982. (ISBN 0-395-32438-6). Houghton Mifflin.
--Mine!. LC 81-6310. p. cm. 1981. (ISBN 0-395-31607-3). Houghton Mifflin.
Porter, David R., ed.
--Poems of Action. N.D. Association Press.
Porter, Eleanor Hodgman see Stuart, Eleanor, pseud.
Porter, Eleanor Hodgman, jt. auth. see Disney, Walter Elias.
Porter, Eleanor Hodgman, Mrs. (1868-1920)
--Cross Currents: The Story of Margaret. Stecher, William Frederick (1864-), illus. LC 7-276181. 207 p. front., 3 pl. 19 cm. c.1907. W. A. Wilde Company.
--Little Pardner and Other Stories. LC 70-142273. 302 p. 20cm. (Short story index reprint series). 1970. (ISBN 0-8369-3757-0). Books for Libraries Press.
--Mary Marie. Grose, Helen Mason (1880-), illus. N.D. Houghton Mifflin.
--Pollyanna. (The Pollyanna Bks.). N.D. Grosset & Dunlap.
--Pollyanna. Harrington, Molly, ed. (gr. 4-6). 1976. (ISBN 0-590-10146-3, Schol Trade Pap). Schol Bk Serv.
--Pollyanna. Abridged. Vinton, Iris, adapted by. Dawson, Isabel, illus. LC 60-16262. 60p. illus. 29cm. 1960. Grosset & Dunlap.
--Pollyanna Grows Up. (The Pollyanna Bks.). N.D. Grosset & Dunlap.
--Pollyanna Grows Up: The Second Glad Book. Taylor, H. Weston, illus. (The Pollyanna Bks.). 1919. Page Co.
--Pollyanna Jewels. (The Pollyanna Bks.). N.D. Grosset & Dunlap.
--Pollyanna: The First Glad Book. Mulford, Stockton, illus. (The Pollyanna Bks.). 1915. L. C. Page.
--Pollyanna: The Glad Girl. (The Glad Book). N.D. Grosset & Dunlap.
--Six Star Ranch. Murch, Frank J. & Elwell, R. Farrington, illus. LC 16-2367. 4 p. l., 353 p. col. front., plates. 20 cm. c.1916. The Page Company.
--The Sunbridge Girls at Six Star Ranch. Stuart, Eleanor, pseud. Rev ed. Murch, Frank J., illus. LC 13-9247. 4 p. l., 353 p. front., plates. 21 cm. 1913. L. C. Page & Company.
Porter, Ella Williams
--Footprints on the Sand. LC 49-8056. 163 p. 22 cm. 1949. Macmillan Co.
--Prairie Shadows. King, Ruth, illus. LC 52-12598. 22cm. 154p. 1952. Macmillan.
--Sandra Kendall of the Four-H: The Career Story of a Young Home Demonstration Agent. LC 42-19646. ix p., 1 l., 271 p. diagrs. 21 cm. (Dodd, Mead career books). 1942. Dodd, Mead & Company.
--A Song for Julie. LC 51-13028. 160 p. 22cm. 1951. Macmillan.
--The Wind's in the West. LC 50-6589. 163 p. 21cm. 1950. Macmillan.
Porter, Gene Stratton see Porter, Geneva Grace Stratton, Mrs.
Porter, Geneva Grace Stratton, Mrs. (1863-1924)
--Freckles. Crawford, Earl Stetson, illus. 1904. Doubleday.
--A Girl of the Limberlost. 1909. Doubleday.
--The Harvester. 560p. 1977. (ISBN 0-89966-225-0). Buccaneer Bks.
--The Magic Garden. LC 76-41378. 23cm. 41p. 1976, c.1927. (ISBN 0-89190-942-7). American Reprint Co.
--The Magic Garden. Thayer, Emma Redington Lee (1874-1973), illus. LC 27-5604. 5 p. l., 271, 1 p. 20 cm. 1927. Doubleday, Page & Company.
--Morning Face. Porter, Geneva Grace Stratton, Mrs. (1863-1924), illus. LC 16-22428. (Illus.). 26cm. 127p. 1916. Doubleday.
Porter, Horace, pseud., see De Hart, Horace Porter Biddle.
Porter, Horace, pseud. (1863-)
--Our Young Aeroplane Scouts at the Marne: Or, Hurrying the Huns From Allied Battleplanes. De Hart, Horace Porter Biddle. (Our Young Aeroplane Scouts). N.D. A. L. Burt Company.
--Our Young Aeroplane Scouts at Verdun: Or, Driving Armored Motors Over Flaming Battle Fronts. De Hart, Horace Porter Biddle. (Our Young Aeroplane Scouts). N.D. A. L. Burt Company.
--Our Young Aeroplane Scouts in at the Victory: Or, Speedy High Flyers Smashing the Hindenburg Line. De Hart, Horace Peter Biddle. LC 19-13154. 228p. 19cm. (Our Young Aeroplane Scout Ser.). 1919. A. L. Burt Company.
--Our Young Aeroplane Scouts in England: Or, Twin Stars in the London Sky Patrol. De Hart, Horace Porter Biddle. (Our Young Aeroplane Scouts). N.D. A. L. Burt Company.
--Our Young Aeroplane Scouts in Russia: Or, Lost on the Frozen Steppes. De Hart, Horace Porter Biddle. (Our Young Aeroplane Scouts). N.D. A. L. Burt Company.
--Our Young Aeroplane Scouts in the Balkans: Or, Wearing the Red Badge of Courage Among Warring Legions. De Hart, Horace Porter Biddle. (Our Young Aeroplane Scouts). N.D. A. L. Burt Company.
--Our Young Aeroplane Scouts in the War Zone: Or, Serving Uncle Sam in the Great Cause of the Allies. De Hart, Horace Porter Biddle. (Our Young Aeroplane Scouts). N.D. A. L. Burt Company.
--Our Young Aeroplane Scouts in Turkey: Or, Bringing the Light to Yusef. De Hart, Horace Porter Biddle. (Our Young Aeroplane Scouts). N.D. Al.L. Burt Company.
--Our Young Airplane scouts in Germany: Or, Winning the Iron Cross. De Hart, Horace Porter Biddle. (Our Young Airplane Scouts Ser.). N.D. A. L. Burt.
Porter, Jane (1776-1850)
--Biffy Buffalo. Smalley, Janet (1893-), illus. LC 42-17150. 63, 1 p. incl. front., illus. (part col.) 23 x 19 cm. 1942. W. Morrow and Company.
--Scottish Chiefs. (Illus.). (Famous Books for Boys). N.D. H. M. Caldwell Co.
--Scottish Chiefs. (The Young People's Library). N.D. John C. Winston.
--Scottish Chiefs. (Illus.). (The Junior Library: Vol. 12). 1910. Rand McNally & Co.
--Scottish Chiefs. (Illus.). (The Young People's Library). N.D. William Collins Co.
--Scottish Chiefs, 1 of 3 Vols. Darley, Felix Octavius Carr (1822-1888), illus. (Illus.). (Library of Classic Fiction, No. 1). N.D. Set. Porter & Coates.
--The Scottish Chiefs. Wyeth, Newell Convers (1882-1945), illus. (Illustrated Classics). 1956. Scribner.
--Thaddeus of Warsaw, 98 vols. (The Rugby Ser.). 1905. Set. A L Burt Co.
--Thaddeus of Warsaw. Darley, Felix Octavius Carr (1822-1888), illus. (World-Famous Fiction). N.D. Porter & Coates.
--The Scottish Chiefs. Wiggin, Kate Douglas Smith (1856-1923) & Smith, Nora Archibald, eds. Wyeth, Newell Convers (1882-1945), illus. (Scribner Illustrated Classics). 1921. (ISBN 0-684-20914-4). Charles Scribner's Sons.
Porter, John Shepard (1900-)
--Mutiny in the Christmas Tree. Underwood, Bettie Porter, illus. LC 54-7407. 64p. illus. 22cm. 1954. Vantage Press.
Porter, Katherine Anne (1890-1980)
--Collected Stories of Katherine Anne Porter. LC 65-19706. (gr. 9 up). 1965. (ISBN 0-15-118992-7). HarBraceJ.
Porter, Lydia Ann Emerson, Mrs. (1816-1898)
--Millie Lee, 1 of 4 Vols. (Annie Maylie Ser.). N.D. Set. D Lothrop & Co.
--Millie Lee, 1 of 50 vols. (Young People's Library: No. 22). N.D. Set. Lothrop Publishing Co.
Porter, Mark, pseud., see Leckie, Robert Hugh.
Porter, Mark, pseud. (1920-)
--Duel on the Cinders. Leckie, Robert Hugh. LC 60-8129. 218p. 20cm. (His A Win Hadley sport story, 6). 1960. Simon and Schuster.
--Keeper' Play. Leckie, Robert Hugh. LC 60-8130. 192p. 20cm. (His A Win Hadley sport story, 2). 1960. Simon and Schuster.
--Overtime Upset. Leckie, Robert Hugh. LC 60-8131. 192p. 20cm. (His A Win Hadley sport story, 3). 1960. Simon and Schuster.
--Set Point. Leckie, Robert Hugh. LC 60-8133. 224p. 20cm. (His A Win Hadley sport story, 4). 1960. Simon and Schuster.
--Slashing Blades. Leckie, Robert Hugh. N.D. (ISBN 0-448-04837-X, Pitman Art Instruction Guides). Grosset & Dunlap.
--Slashing Blades. Leckie, Robert Hugh. LC 60-813281. 218p. 20cm. (His A Win Hadley Sport Story, 5). 1960. Simon and Schuster.
--Winning Pitcher. Leckie, Robert Hugh. LC 60-812881. 190p. 20cm. (His A Win Hadley Sport Story, 1). 1960. Simon and Schuster.
Porter, Mary H., compiled by see Russell, Nellie Naomi.
Porter, Mary W.
--Five Little Southerners, 1 of 4 vols. (Bark Cabin Library). 1882. Lothrop Pub. Co.
--Jack and Bessie in Rome: Or, Poor Papa. N.D. Lothrop Pub. Co.
--Poor Papa. LC 21-15396. 218 p. incl. front. plates. 18 cm. c.1879. D. Lothrop and Company.
--Poor Papa, 1 of 7 vols. (Illus.). (Idle Hour Ser.). N.D. D Lothrop.
Porter, Myrtle Crist (1902-)
--Little Red Hummy. Dailey, Paul, illus. LC 49-4962. 76 p. illus., music. 23 cm. 1949. House of the Church of Brethren.
Porter, Penny
--Howard's Monster. (gr. k-3). 1978. (ISBN 0-682-49144-6). Exposition.
Porter Productions
--Elbert Goes House Hunting. LC 76-267. (Illus.). 16p. (Play with Me Bks.). (ps-2). 1976. (ISBN 0-448-12472-6). G&D.
--If I Met Raggedy Andy. LC 78-71510. (Stretch Bk.). (ps-k). 1979. (ISBN 0-448-16364-0, G&D). Putnam Pub Group.
--If I Met Raggedy Ann. LC 78-71509. (Illus.). (Stretch Bk.). (ps-k). 1979. (ISBN 0-448-16365-9, G&D). Putnam Pub Group.
--The Little Engine That Could. (Illus.). 16p. (Stretch Bks.). (ps). 1981. (ISBN 0-448-16266-0, G&D). Putnam Pub Group.
--Mom & Me. (Illus.). 16p. (Walking Books Ser.). (ps-3). 1975. (ISBN 0-448-11986-2, Pretzel Pr). G&D.
--Santa's Workshop. (Illus.). 16p. (Fold-A-Bks.). (ps). 1981. (ISBN 0-448-11772-X, G&D). Putnam Pub Group.
--Touch & Read Books. Incl. The Bear Who Found a Hat; The Cow Who Liked What She Saw. (ISBN 0-448-12880-2). (ISBN 0-448-13431-4); The Elephant Who Wanted to Be a Leopard. (ISBN 0-448-12881-0). (ISBN 0-448-13432-2); The Chicken Who Went to a Party. (ISBN 0-448-12882-9). (ISBN 0-448-13433-0); The Pig Who Needed a Bath. (ISBN 0-448-12883-7). (ISBN 0-448-13434-9); The Rabbit Who Slept & Slept. (ISBN 0-448-12884-5). (ISBN 0-448-13435-7). (Illus.). (ps-3). 1977. (ISBN 0-685-80827-0, Pretzel Pr). (ISBN 0-685-80828-9). G&D.
--Whose House Is This. LC 76-320. (Illus.). 16p. (Play with Me Bks.). (ps-2). 1976. G&D.
Porter, R. G. see Gilderoy, pseud.
Porter, R. G.
--Odd Hours for Young People. Gilderoy, pseud. LC 21-8700. 222 p. 18 cm. 1891. Publishing House of the Methodist Episcopal Church, South.
Porter, Rose
--Summer Driftwood for the Winter Fire. N.D. A. D. F. Randolph.
Porter, Ruth Stephens
--The Toy Circus. Macrae, Ruth K., illus. LC 63-19847. 1 v. (unpaged) col. illus. 29 cm. 1963. Dorrance.
Porter, S. K., Mrs., tr. see Hoffmann, Franz.

AUTHOR INDEX POTTER, HELEN

Porter, Sheena (1935-)
--The Bronze Chrysanthemum. Hughes, Shirley (1929-), illus. LC 65-17041. 152 p. illus. 28 cm. 1965. Van Nostrand.
--Bronze Chrysanthemum Mystery. (Illus.). (gr. 5-8). 1965. (ISBN 0-8382-0118-0). Hale.
--Deerfold. Ambrus, Victor G., pseud. (1935-), illus. Ambrus, Gyozo Laszlo. LC 67-71841. xii, 144 p. illus. 22 1/2 cm. 15/. (B 66-24036). 1966. Oxford U. P.
--The Hospital. Jacques, Robin (1920-), illus. LC 74-163288. (Illus.). 7, 112 p. 23cm. 1973. (ISBN 0-19-271355-8). Oxford University P.
--Nordy Bank. Macarthur-Onslow, Annette Rosemary (1933-), illus. 1964. Roy Publishers. **Award: (CMA).**
--Nordy Bank. Macarthur-Onslow, Annette Rosemary (1933-), illus. LC 67-1261. (Illus.). 144 p. 23cm. 1967, c.1964. Roy Publishers.

Porter, Sue, et al., illus.
--Baa Baa Black Sheep. LC 83-22505. (Illus.). 8p. 1st U.S. edition. (Nursery Rhyme Press-Out Bks.). (gr. k-2). 1984. (ISBN 0-911745-26-2). Bedrick-Blackie: Dist. by Harper & Row.
--Hey Diddle Diddle. (Illus.). 8p. 1st U.S. edition. (Nursery Rhyme Press-Out Bks.). (gr. k-2). 1984. (ISBN 0-911745-27-0). P Bedrick Bks.
--Little Boy Blue. LC 83-22503. (Illus.). 8p. 1st U.S. edition. (Nursery Rhyme Press-Out Bks). (gr. k-2). 1984. (ISBN 0-911745-28-9). Bedrick-Blackie: Dist. By Harper & Row.
--Sing a Song of Sixpence. LC 83-22510. (Illus.). 8p. (Nursery Rhyme Press-Out Books). (gr. k-2). 1984. (ISBN 0-911745-29-7). Bedrick-Blackie Dist. by Harper & Row.

Porter, Wesley
--About Monkeys in Trees: An African Folk Legend. Churchill, Dominique, illus. LC 79-10834. (Illus.). 31 p. 20cm. 1979. (ISBN 0-531-02506-3). Watts.
--Dragons of Peking: A Chinese Folk Legend. Sweat, Lynn, illus. LC 79-10278. (Illus.). 32 p. 20cm. 1979. (ISBN 0-531-02500-4). (ISBN 0-531-04079-8). F. Watts.
--The First Tom-Tom: An American Indian Folk Legend. Matera, Fran (1891-), illus. LC 79-10199. (Illus.). 30 p. 20cm. 1979. (ISBN 0-531-04080-1). F. Watts.
--First Winter, First Summer: An American Indian Folk Legend. Sweat, Lynn, illus. LC 79-10339. (Illus.). 32 p. 20cm. 1979. (ISBN 0-531-04081-X). (ISBN 0-531-02502-0). F. Watts.
--The Hare, the Elephant, and the Hippo: An African Folk Legend. Behr, Joyce (1929-), illus. LC 79-10832. (Illus.). 32 p. 20cm. 1979. (ISBN 0-531-02503-9). (ISBN 0-531-04082-8). F. Watts.
--Kate Shelley and the Midnight Express. An American Folk Legend. Lasker, Joseph Leon (1919-), illus. LC 79-10385. (Illus.). 32 p. 20cm. 1979. (ISBN 0-531-02504-7). F. Watts.
--The Magic Kettle: A Japanese Folk Legend. Sweat, Lynn, illus. LC 79-10807. (Illus.). 32 p. 20cm. 1979. (ISBN 0-531-02505-5). (ISBN 0-531-04084-4). Watts.
--Old Tortoise and the Baboon: An African Folk Legend. Stone, E. Robert, illus. p. cm. 1979. (ISBN 0-531-02508-X). (ISBN 0-531-04087-9). F. Watts.
--Why the Sea Is Salty: Scandinavian Folk Legend. Einsel, Naiad & Einsel, Walter (1926-), illus. LC 79-10806. (Illus.). 32 p. 20cm. 1979. (ISBN 0-531-04088-7). (ISBN 0-531-02509-8). F. Watts.

Porter, Wesley & Grimm, Jakob Ludwig Karl (1785-1863)
--The Musicians of Bremen: German Folk Legend. Mitchell, Kenneth W., illus. LC 79-11301. (Illus.). 32 p. 20cm. 1979. (ISBN 0-531-04086-0). (ISBN 0-531-02507-1). F. Watts.

Porter, William Sydney see Henry, O., pseud.

Porter, William Sydney (1862-1910)
--The Best of O. Henry. new & abr. ed. Fago, John N., ed. Caravana, Anton, illus. (Illus.). (Now Age Illustrated III Ser.). (gr. 4-12). 1977. (ISBN 0-88301-280-4). (ISBN 0-88301-268-5). Pendulum Pr.
--The Ransom of Red Chief. 1st ed. Frame, Paul (1913-), illus. LC 79-92641. (Illus.). 48 p. 21cm. 1970, c.1907. Hawthorn Books.
--The Ransom of Red Chief. Mathiews, F. K., ed. N.D. Grosset & Dunlap.
--The Ransom of Red Chief: And Other O. Henry Stories for Boys. Mathiews, Franklin K., ed. Grant, Gordon H. (1875-1962), illus. LC 18-4550. xiii, 329, 1 p. front., plates. 20 cm. 1918. Doubleday, Page & Company.

Portor, Laura Spencer
--Genevieve: A Story of French School Days. Converse, F., ed. LC 14-18803. 5 p. l., vii-xxv, 327 p. col. front., plates. 20 cm. (On Verso of Half-Title: Little Schoolmate Ser). c.1914. E. P. Dutton & Company.

Portor, Laura Spencer, jt. auth. see Pyle, Katharine D.

Portugal, Jan
--ABC Sillies. Portugal, Jan, illus. (Illus.). 56p. (Orig.). (Living on This Planet Ser.). (ps-1). 1983. (ISBN 0-937148-13-X). Wild Horses.

Posesi Fanual, Tupou
--Po Fananga: Folk Tales of Tonga. Rott, Nick, illus. LC 74-34532. (Illus.). 96p. (Orig.). 1975. (ISBN 0-914488-04-X). Rand-Tofua.

Posey, Anita E
--Rings and Things and Other Poems. Maas, Julie, illus. LC 67-13589. 32p. col. illus. 22cm. 1967. Crowell-Collier.

Poskanzer, Susan Cornel
--A Surprise for Baby Blueberry Muffin. Sustendal, Pat, illus. LC 83-22103. (Baby Strawberry Shortcake). c.1984. (ISBN 0-910313-23-7). Parker Bros.

Poskanzer, Susan Cornell, ed. see Stevenson, Robert Louis.

Posner, Grace
--In My Sister's Eyes. LC 80-20781. p. cm. c.1980. (ISBN 0-8253-0013-4). Beaufort Books.

Post, Walter
--The Fulgora and Other Children's Poems. LC 64-6604. 50 p. illus. 29 cm. 1964. Buddha Press.

Poston, Margaret Lois (1915-)
--Maggie and Friend. Furan, Barbara J., illus. LC 73-81600. (Illus.). 31 p. 29cm. 1969. T. S. Denison.

Postgate, Oliver
--Ivor the Engine. Firmin, Peter (1928-), illus. LC 62-8073. 26cm. 48p. 1962. Abelard-Schumann.

Postgate, Oliver & Firmin, Peter (1928-)
--The Ice Dragon. LC 77-222. (Illus.). 48 p. 16cm. (Their the Saga of Noggin the Nog). (No.2). 1968. Holiday House.
--King of the Nogs. LC 70-223. (Illus.). 48 p. 16cm. (Their the Saga of Noggin the Nog_1). (No.1). 1968. Holiday House.
--Nogbad and the Elephants. LC 67-23583. (Illus.). 47 p. 21cm. 1967. D. White.
--Noggin and the Moon Mouse. LC 67-23584. (Illus.). 47 p. 21cm. 1967. D. White.
--Noggin and the Whale. LC 67-5966. (Illus.). 47 p. 21cm. (Starting to Read Books). (No.2). 1967, c.1965. D. White.
--Noggin, the King. LC 67-1057. 47 p. col. illus. 21 cm. (Starting to Read Books). (No.11). 1966, c.1965. D. White.
--Silly Old Uncle Feedle. 32p. 1975. (ISBN 0-7207-0783-8, Pub. by Michael Joseph). Merrimack Pub Cir.
--The Song of the Pongo. 32p. 1975. (ISBN 0-7207-0782-X, Pub. by Michael Joseph). Merrimack Pub Cir.

Posthuma, Mary Louise
--A Boy Named Jeff. Thompson, R., illus. LC 73-90728. (Illus.). 87 p. 23cm. 1973. Center of Team Learning.

Posthumus, C., jt. auth. see Clutton, C.

Postma, Lidia (1952-), ed. see Perrault, Charles.

Postma, Lidia (1952-)
--The Stolen Mirror. LC 75-43888. (Illus.). 26 p. 28cm. 1976. (ISBN 0-07-050533-0). (ISBN 0-07-050534-9). McGraw-Hill.
--The Witch's Garden. Postma, Lidia (1952-), illus. LC 78-11414. (Illus.). 25 p. 29cm. 1979, c.1978. (ISBN 0-07-050535-7). McGraw-Hill.

Postnikov, Fedor Alexis (1872-)
--Our Little Cossack Cousin in Siberia. Rogers, Walter S., illus. LC 16-25217. vi p., 2 l., 136 p. front., plates, port. 20 cm. (On verso of half-title: The little cousin series). 1916. The Page Company.

Poston, Elizabeth (1905-), ed.
--The Baby's Song Book. Stobbs, William (1914-), illus. LC 74-186815. (Illus.). 190 p. 27cm. 1972, c.1971. T. Y. Crowell Co.
--Children's Song Book. Einzig, Susan (1922-), illus. (gr. 3 up). 1963. Dufour.
--The Children's Song Book. Einzig, Susan (1922-), illus. LC 79-670259. 160p. 1979. (ISBN 0-370-01044-2, Pub. by Chatto Bodley Jonathan). Merrimack Pub Cir.

Poston, Martha Lee
--Ching-Li. Yap, Weda, illus. LC 41-13240. 23cm. 40p. 1941. Thomas Nelson & Sons.
--The Girl Without a Country. Ayer, Margaret (0000-1981), illus. LC 44-8546. 226 p. illus. (incl. map) 21 cm. 1944. T. Nelson and Sons.
--The Mystery of the Eighth Horse. Yap, Weda (1894-), illus. LC 49-9657. 192 p. illus. 22 cm. 1949. T. Nelson.

Posy, Arnold (1894-)
--Holiday Night Dreams. N.D. Bloch Publishing Co.
--Israeli Tales and Legends. N.D. Bloch Publishing Co.

Pothast-Gimberg, C. E.
--Corso the Donkey. Van Beek, Elly, illus. Van Stockum, Hilda Gerarda, tr. LC 63-8588. (Illus.). 128p. (gr. 3-6). 1963. (ISBN 0-525-28245-9). Dutton.

Pott, Prunella C., illus.
--Hedgehog's Jacket. 48p. (gr. k-3). N.D. (ISBN 0-87460-157-6). Lion.

Pott, William Hawks
--Stories from Dreamland. LC 6060. (Illus.). 206p. 17cm. 1900. J. Pott & Co.
--Strange Adventures in Dreamland. (Illus.). N.D. James Pott & Co.

Pottebaum, Gerald A. (1934-)
--The Christmas Story. (Little People's Paperbacks Ser.). 1979. (ISBN 0-8164-2241-9). Seabury.
--The Easter Lamb. (Little People's Paperbacks Ser.). 1979. (ISBN 0-8164-2247-8). Seabury.
--The Festival of Art. Roberts, Ken, illus. LC 79-135224. (Illus.). 32 p. 27cm. 1971. (ISBN 0-8066-1107-3). Augsburg Pub. House.
--The Generous Vine Grower. (Little People's Paperbacks Ser.). 1979. (ISBN 0-8164-2252-4). Seabury.
--Generous Vinegrower. Strobridge, Robert, illus. (Illus., Orig.). (gr. k-2). 1965. Pflaum Standard.
--The Good Samaritan. (Little People's Paperbacks Ser.). 1979. (ISBN 0-8164-2249-4). Seabury.
--The Great Harvest. (Little People's Paperbacks Ser.). 1979. (ISBN 0-8164-2253-2). Seabury.
--How the Animals Got Their Names. (Little People's Paperbacks Ser.). N.D. (ISBN 0-8164-2240-0). Seabury.
--The King & the Servant. (Little People's Paperbacks Ser.). N.D. (ISBN 0-8164-2251-6). Seabury.
--The Loving Father. (Little People's Paperbacks Ser.). 1979. (ISBN 0-8164-2250-8). Seabury.
--Ninety-Nine Plus One. Johnson, Daniel E., illus. LC 72-135225. (Illus.). 32 p. 27cm. (Tree House Production). 1971. (ISBN 0-8066-1108-1). Augsburg Pub. House.
--Psalm Eight from Voices of Children. (Little People's Paperbacks Ser.). 1979. (ISBN 0-8164-2254-0). Seabury.
--Psalm Eighty-Four: The Sparrow Finds a Home. (Little People's Paperbacks Ser.). 1979. (ISBN 0-8164-2256-7). Seabury.
--Psalm Ninety-Eight: Sing a New Song. (Little People's Paperbacks Ser.). 1979. (ISBN 0-8164-2257-5). Seabury.
--Psalm One Hundred Fifty: The Praise Parade. (Little People's Paperback Ser.). 1979. (ISBN 0-8164-2258-3). Seabury.
--Psalm Twenty-Three: My Shepard is the Lord. (Little People's Paperbacks Ser.). 1979. (ISBN 0-8164-2255-9). Seabury.
--The Story of Emmaus. (Little People's Paperbacks Ser.). 1979. (ISBN 0-8164-2248-6). Seabury.
--The Three Wise Men. (Little People's Paperbacks Ser.). 1979. (ISBN 0-8164-2242-7). Seabury.

Potter, Beatrix see Potter, Helen Beatrix.

Potter, Beatrix see Potter, Helen Beatrix (1866-1943) & Erickson, Phoebe.

Potter, Beatrix see Potter, Helen Beatrix (1866-1943) & Stewart, Pat.

Potter, Bronson
--Antonio. 1st ed. Grifalconi, Ann (1929-), illus. LC 68-18457. (Illus.). 41 p. 25cm. 1968. Atheneum. **Award: (ALA).**
--Chibia, the Dhow Boy. 1st ed. Robinson, Charles (1931-), illus. LC 70-154761. (Illus.). 239 p. 25cm. 1971. Atheneum.
--Isfendiar and the Bears of Mazandaran. 1st ed. White, David Omar (1927-), illus. LC 69-12778. (Illus.). 72 p. 25cm. 1969. Atheneum.
--Isfendiar and the Wild Donkeys. 1st ed. Barberis, Juan Carlos, illus. LC 67-2639. (Illus.). 41 p. 24cm. 1967. Atheneum.
--The Poet Who Couldn't Wait for Spring. Rosenkranz, Patricia, illus. LC 64-8451. (Illus.). 1 v. (unpaged. 24cm. 1965, c.1964. Reilly & Lee Co.

Potter, Bronson & Ashworth, Rala
--Shadow, the Cigar-Smoking Cat. 1st ed. Nicklaus, Carol, illus. LC 72-75279. (Illus.). 36 p. 23cm. 1972. (ISBN 0-689-30061-1). Atheneum.

Potter, Charles Francis (1885-1962), ed.
--More Tongue Tanglers and a Rigmarole. 1st ed. Weisner, William, illus. LC 64-12359. (Illus.). 42 p. 19cm. 1964. World Pub. Co.
--Tongue Tanglers. Wiesner, William (1899-), illus. LC 62-13945. (Illus.). 19cm. 42p. (gr. 3-6). 1962. (ISBN 0-529-03718-1). World Pub.

Potter, Dan
--Crazy Moon Zoo: A Novel. LC 85-6157. p. cm. 1985. (ISBN 0-531-10076-6). F. Watts.

Potter, Edna
--Land from the Sea. Potter, Edna, illus. LC 39-22034. 62 p. incl. front. map. 24 cm. c.1939. Longmans, Green and Co.
--Mamie, a Little Girl of 1875. N.D. Oxford Univerity Press.

Potter, Edna, ed.
--This Way and That: A Book of Singing Games. Potter, Edna, illus. LC 30-14504. 52 p. illus. (part col.) 28 x 31 cm. c.1930. Oxford University Press.

Potter, Frederick Scarlett (1834-)
--Amrose Oran: Or, With the Buccaneers. (Illus.). N.D. E & J B Young.
--Drowsey Dell. (Illus.). N.D. E & J B Young.
--Elfin Hollow. (Illus.). N.D. E & J B Young.
--Erling: Or, the Days of St. Olaf, 1 of 4 Vols. (Illus.). (Tales of Heroes). N.D. Set. Pott, Young & Co.
--Heroes of the North, 1 of 4 Vols. (Illus.). (Tales of Heroes). N.D. Set. Pott, Young & Co.
--Out of Doors Friends. (Illus.). N.D. E & J B Young.
--Paul and His Troubles. N.D. E. & J. B. Young & Co.
--Princess Myra, and Her Adventures Amongst the Fairy Folk. (Illus.). N.D. E. & J. B. Young & Co.
--The Raven's Nest. (Illus.). N.D. E & J B Young.
--Three Boys on the Tramp. N.D. E P Dutton.
--A Wonderful Goldsmith. (Illus.). N.D. E & J B Young.

Potter, Grace Elizabeth & Gilbert, Constance
--Giants and Fairies. LC 64-13113. 128p. col. illus. 24 cm. (Told-again tales from many lands). 1964. C. E. Merrill Books.

Potter, Grace Elizabeth & Harley, Ruth
--First Fairy Tales. De Luna, Tony, illus. LC 64-13114. 128 p. illus. (part col.) 24 cm. (Told-Again Tales from Many Lands). 1964. C. E. Merrill Books.

Potter, Helen Beatrix, jt. auth. see Carlson, David

Potter, Helen Beatrix, jt. auth. see Laurie, Rona.

Potter, Helen Beatrix (1866-1943)
--Appley Dappley's Nursery Rhymes. Potter, Helen Beatrix (1866-1943), illus. LC 65-29402. (Illus.). 34p. 15cm. (The Peter Rabbit Bks.). 1965. F. Warne.
--Appley Dapply's Nursery Rhymes. Potter, Helen Beatrix (1866-1943), illus. LC 65-29402. 34 p. col. illus. 15 cm. (Her The Peter Rabbit books,). 1965. F. Warne.
--Appley Dapply's Nursery Rhymes. Potter, Helen Beatrix (1866-1943), illus. LC 63-22863. 52 p. col. illus. 15 cm. N.D. F. Warne.
--Beatrix Potter Giant Treasury. LC 83-20890. (Illus.). x, 51 p. 29cm. 1985, c.1984. (ISBN 0-517-43121-1). Derrydale Books ; Distributed by Crown.
--Beatrix Potter's Birthday Book. Linder, Enid, ed. Potter, Helen Beatrix (1866-1943), illus. LC 73-89833. (Illus.). appendix. 156p. (gr. 1 up). 1974. (ISBN 0-7232-1758-0). (ISBN 0-7232-1815-3). Warne.
--Beatrix Potter's Nursery Rhyme Book. 56p. (ps-4). 1984. (ISBN 0-7232-3254-7). Warne.
--Cecil Parsley's Nursery Rhymes. Potter, Helen Beatrix (1866-1943), illus. 1922. Warne.
--Cecily Parsley's Nursery Rhymes. LC 66-4155. 52 p. col. illus. 15 cm. 34p. (Her The Peter Rabbit Books). 1964. F. Warne.
--The Complete Adventures of Peter Rabbit. LC 82-10861. p. cm. 1982. (ISBN 0-7232-6165-2). F. Warne.
--The Complete Adventures of Peter Rabbit. 80p. (Picture Puffins Ser.). 1984. (ISBN 0-14-050444-3, Puffin). Penguin.
--The Complete Adventures of Tom Kitten and His Friends. original and authorized. Potter, Helen Beatrix (1866-1943), illus. LC 85-135831. (Illus.). 79 p. 29cm. c.1984. (ISBN 0-7232-3288-1). F. Warne.
--The Fairy Caravan. new ed. LC 51-10124. 225 p. illus. 22 cm. 1951, c.1929. Warne.
--The Fairy Caravan. Potter, Helen Beatrix (1866-1943), illus. LC 29-22257. 225 p. col. front., illus., col. plates. 22 cm. c.1929. David McKay Company.
--Famille Flopsaut: The Flopsy Bunnies. (gr. 3-7). N.D. (ISBN 0-7232-0655-4). Warne.
--Ginger and Pickles. Potter, Helen Beatrix (1866-1943), illus. LC 85-13641. p. cm. 1985, c.1909. (ISBN 0-486-24969-7). Dover Publications.
--Ginger & Pickles. Potter, Helen Beatrix (1866-1943), illus. LC 9-30322. 52 p. incl. col. front., illus., col. plates. 19 cm. c.1909. F. Warne & Co.
--Jeannot Lapin: Benjamin Bunny. (gr. 3-7). N.D. (ISBN 0-7232-0651-1). Warne.
--The Jemima Puddle-Duck Pop-up Book. Twinn, Colin, ed. LC 85-122092. (From the Tale of Jemima Puddle-Duck, the original and authorized edition). (Illus.). 13 p. 28cm. 1985. (ISBN 0-7232-3304-7). F. Warne.
--Mrs. Tittlemouse and Other Mouse Tales. Potter, Helen Beatrix (1866-1943), illus. LC 85-40386. p. cm. 1985. (ISBN 0-7232-3324-1). Warne.
--Operetta of Peter Rabbit. (Illus.). (gr. 4-7). 1962. (ISBN 0-7232-0499-3). Warne.
--Peter Rabbit. Erickson, Phoebe (1907-), illus. LC 47-20368. 36 p. illus. (part col.) 19 1/2 x 17 1/2 cm. (Star-bright book. S-300). 1947. Childrens Press, Inc.
--Peter Rabbit. Frantz, Estelle V., illus. (The "Just Right" Edition). (Enlarged Picture Library). N.D. A. Whitman & Co.
--Peter Rabbit. Musial, Joseph W. (1905-1977), illus. LC 37-467. cover-title, 16 p. col. illus. 33 1/2 cm. c.1936. Whitman Publishing Company.

--Peter Rabbit. Nosworthy, Florence England, illus. LC 43-29576. 32 p. illus. 18 1/2 cm. (Instructor Library Books. 308). c.1918. Hall & McCreary Company.
--Peter Rabbit. Potter, Helen Beatrix (1866-1943), illus. LC 56-51688. (Illus.). 34p. 17cm. (The Little Color Classics). 1928. McLoughlin Bros.
--Peter Rabbit. Potter, Helen Beatrix (1866-1943), illus. LC 42-34435. (Illus.). 16p. 30 x 25cm. 1934. The Platt & Munk Co. Inc.
--Peter Rabbit. Saviozzi, Adriana (1928-), illus. (Little Golden Book). 1958. Golden Press.
--Peter Rabbit. Wadsworth, Wallace Carter (1894-1933), retold by. Leaf, Anne Sellers, illus. LC 54-16668. unpaged. illus. 17cm. (Rand McNally book-elf junior, 681). c.1953. Rand McNally.
--Peter Rabbit. Wadsworth, Wallace Carter (1894-1933), retold by. Leaf, Anne Sellers, illus. LC 56-6742. unpaged. illus. 33cm. (Rand McNally giant book). 1956, c.1953. Rand McNally.
--Peter Rabbit. Weisgard, Leonard Joseph (1916-), illus. LC 55-267875. unpaged. illus. 34cm. (Big treasure books). c.1955. Grosset Dunlap.
--Peter Rabbit. Wilson, Beth, illus. LC 54-21575. unpaged. illus. 17cm. (Tell-a-tale books, 929). 1954, c.1953. Whitman Pub. Co.
--Peter Rabbit. Winship, Florence Sarah, illus. LC 56-26797. unpaged. illus. 17cm. (Tell-a-tale books, 2515). c.1955. Whitman Pub. Co.
--Peter Rabbit: Also Henny Penny and Puss-in-Boots. 1 p. l., 5-64 p. col. illus. 17 cm. c.1934. Rand, McNally & Company.
--Peter Rabbit and Chicken Little. Kalab, Theresa, illus. LC 49-877. 40 p. col. illus. 22 cm. (Cozy corner book). c.1948. Whitman Pub. Co.
--Peter Rabbit & His Friends. (Beatrix Potter's Coloring Bks.). (ps-1). 1984. (ISBN 0-7232-3258-X). Warne.
--Peter Rabbit & His Friends. Carlson, David, illus. (Illus.). 14p. (Beatrix Potter Board Bks). (ps-k). 1982. (ISBN 0-671-44519-7, Little Simon). S&S.
--Peter Rabbit, and Other Stories. LC 77-84327. (Illus.). 94 p. 29cm. c.1977. (ISBN 0-89009-187-0). Castle Books.
--Peter Rabbit, and Other Stories. Berry, Anne Scheu, illus. LC 48-154501. 52 p. illus. (part col.) 17 cm. (Story Hour Series). c.1947. Whitman Pub. Co.
--Peter Rabbit Birthday Book. (Illus.). 256p. (ps up). 1983. (ISBN 0-517-40303-X, Greenwich Hse). Outlet Bk Co.
--Peter Rabbit Books, 23 Vols. (Illus.). (ps-2). N.D. Set. (ISBN 0-7232-1374-7). Warne.
--The Peter Rabbit Pop-Up Book. LC 84-109194. (From the "Tale of Peter Rabbit"). 12p. 1983. (ISBN 0-7232-2950-3). (ISBN 0-7232-2950-3). Warne.
--The Peter Rabbit Story Book. LC 62-13187. 62p. illus. 25cm. (Platt & Munk classic, 113). 1962. Platt & Munk.
--Peter Rabbit's Giant Treasury. derrydale ed. Potter, Helen Beatrix (1866-1943), illus. LC 80-13368. (Illus.). 92 p. 29cm. 1980. (ISBN 0-517-31687-0). Derrydale Books.
--The Pie and the Patty Pan. N.D. (ISBN 0-531-05115-3). Franklin Watts.
--The Pie and the Patty-Pan. Potter, Helen Beatrix (1866-1943), illus. LC 5-35793. 51, 1 p. incl. front., illus., col. plates. 19 cm. c.1905. F. Warne & Co.
--Roly Poly Pudding. (Illus.). (ps-2). 1908. (ISBN 0-7232-0607-4). Warne.
--Sister Anne. Sturges, Katharine, illus. LC 32-34678. 154 p. incl. plates. pl. 20 cm. c.1932. David McKay Company.
--The Sly Old Cat. Potter, Helen Beatrix (1866-1943), illus. LC 73-163984. 35 p. (chiefly col. illus.). 17cm. 1971. (ISBN 0-7232-1420-4). F. Warne.
--The Songs of Peter Rabbit. Glass, Dudley, contrib. by. N.D. Frederick Warne & Co.
--The Story of a Fierce Bad Rabbit. Potter, Helen Beatrix (1866-1943), illus. LC 66-4154. 15cm. 34p. (Peter Rabbit Books). (ps-2). 1964. (ISBN 0-7232-0611-2). Warne.
--The Story of Miss Moppet. Potter, Helen Beatrix (1866-1943), illus. LC 66-4153. (Illus.). 15cm. 34p. (Peter Rabbit Books). (ps-2). 1964. (ISBN 0-7232-0612-0). Warne.
--The Story of Miss Moppett. (Peter Possum Paperbacks Ser). 1967. (ISBN 0-531-05118-8). Watts.
--The Story of Peter Rabbit. Easthill, Ruth, illus. LC 37-21956. 34 p. illus. (part col.) 17 cm. c.1937. Whitman Publishing Company.
--The Story of Peter Rabbit. Ward, Keith, illus. LC 35-201087. 16 p. illus. 34 cm. c.1935. Whitman Publishing Co.
--Tailor of Gloucester. 1903. E M Hale.
--Tailor of Gloucester. N.D. (ISBN 0-531-05103-X). Franklin Watts.
--The Tailor of Gloucester. LC 73-84196. (Illus.). 57 p. 14cm. 1973. (ISBN 0-486-20176-7). Dover Publications.
--The Tailor of Gloucester. Potter, Helen Beatrix (1866-1943), illus. LC 3-26374. 59 p. col. illus. 15 cm. (Her The Peter Rabbit books). 1903. F. Warne.
--The Tailor of Gloucester. Potter, Helen Beatrix (1866-1943), illus. LC 66-4151. (Illus.). 59p. 15cm. (The Peter Rabbit Books). 1964. F. Warne.
--The Tailor of Gloucester. Potter, Helen Beatrix (1866-1943), illus. LC 68-27844. (Illus.). 64 p. 25cm. 1968. F. Warne.
--The Tailor of Gloucester. Potter, Helen Beatrix (1866-1943), illus. LC 68-59598. (Illus.). x, 126 p. 25cm. 126p. 1968. F. Warne.
--The Tale of Benjamin Bunny. LC 74-78812. (Illus.). 59p. 1974. (ISBN 0-486-21102-9). Dover Books.
--Tale of Benjamin Bunny. 1904. E M Hale.
--The Tale of Benjamin Bunny. LC 65-24140. 58 p. col. illus. 15 cm. (Her The Peter Rabbit books). 1965. F. Warne.
--Tale of Benjamin Bunny. N.D. (ISBN 0-531-05126-9). Franklin Watts.
--The Tale of Benjamin Bunny. Kirk, Tim, illus. LC 74-78812. (Illus.). 59 p. 14cm. 1974. (ISBN 0-486-21102-9). Dover Publications.
--The Tale of Benjamin Bunny. Kirk, Tim, illus. LC 80-27468. p. cm. c.1981. (ISBN 0-89375-484-6). (ISBN 0-89375-485-4). Troll Associates.
--The Tale of Benjamin Bunny. Potter, Helen Beatrix (1866-1943), illus. LC 4-26876. 85, 1 p. incl. col. front., col. plates. 15 cm. 1904. F. Warne & Co.
--Tale of Benjamin Bunny: With a Bunny. N.D. (ISBN 0-686-08950-2). Merrimack.
--The Tale of Ginger & Pickles. LC 66-4152. 75 p. illus (part col.) 15 cm. (Her The Peter Rabbit books,). 1964. F. Warne.
--The Tale of Jemima Puddle-Duck. LC 65-24145. 59 p. col. illus 15 cm. (Her The Peter Rabbit books). 1965. F. Warne.
--The Tale of Jemima Puddle-Duck. Potter, Helen Beatrix (1866-1943), illus. LC 8-23555. 85, 1 p. incl. col. front., col. plates. 15 cm. c.1908. F. Warne & Co.
--Tale of Jeremy Fisher. N.D. (ISBN 0-531-05128-5). Franklin Watts.
--The Tale of Jimina Puddle-Duck. LC 84-7977. 1984. (ISBN 0-486-24634-5). Dover Publications.
--The Tale of Johnny Town-Mouse. LC 66-4164. 58 p. col. illus. 15 cm. (Her The Peter Rabbit books,). 1964. F. Warne.
--The Tale of Johnny Town-Mouse. Potter, Helen Beatrix (1866-1943), illus. LC 18-23515. 84, 1 p. incl. col. front., col. plates. 24 cm. c.1918. F. Warne and Co.
--The Tale of Little Pig Robinson. LC 51-9162. 111 p. illus. 15 cm. 1950, c.1930. Warne.
--The Tale of Little Pig Robinson. Potter, Helen Beatrix (1866-1943), illus. LC 30-310401. 3 p. l., 141 p. col. front., illus., col. plates. 22 cm. c.1930. David McKay Company.
--The Tale of Mr. Jeremy Fisher. (Illus.). 59p. 1906. (ISBN 0-486-23066-X). Dover Books.
--The Tale of Mr. Jeremy Fisher. LC 74-75269. (Illus.). 59 p. 15cm. 1974. (ISBN 0-486-23066-X). Dover Publications.
--The Tale of Mr. Jeremy Fisher. LC 65-24143. 58 p. col. illus. 15 cm. (Her The Peter Rabbit books,). 1964. F. Warne.
--Tale of Mr. Jeremy Fisher. Potter, Helen Beatrix (1866-1943), illus. LC 6-27353. (Illus.). 15cm. 85p. (ps-2). 1906. (ISBN 0-7232-0598-1). Warne.
--The Tale of Mr. Tod. LC 12-26289. 93 p. illus. part col. 15 cm. (Her The Peter Rabbit books,). 1912. F. Warne.
--The Tale of Mr. Tod. Potter, Helen Beatrix (1866-1943), illus. LC 66-4159. (Illus.). 23p. 15cm. (The Peter Rabbit Bks.). 1964. F. Warne.
--Tale of Mr. Tod. Potter, Helen Beatrix (1866-1943), illus. LC 12-27197. (Illus.). (ps-2). 1912. (ISBN 0-7232-0605-8). Warne.
--The Tale of Mrs. Tiggy-Winkle. (Illus.). 58p. 1905. (ISBN 0-486-20546-0). Dover Books.
--The Tale of Mrs. Tiggy-Winkle. LC 73-84197. (Illus.). 54 p. 14cm. 1973. (ISBN 0-486-20546-0). Dover Publications.
--The Tale of Mrs. Tiggy-Winkle. LC 65-24141. 59 p. col. illus. 15 cm. (Her The Peter Rabbit books). 1963. F. Warne.
--Tale of Mrs. Tiggy Winkle. N.D. (ISBN 0-531-05122-6). Franklin Watts.
--The Tale of Mrs. Tiggy-Winkle. Potter, Helen Beatrix (1866-1943), illus. LC 5-32528. 84, 2 p. incl. front., col. plates. 15 x 11 cm. c.1905. F. Warne & Co.
--The Tale of Mrs. Tittlemouse. LC 65-24147. 58 p. col. illus. 15 cm. (Her The Peter Rabbit books). 1964. F. Warne.
--The Tale of Mrs. Tittlemouse. Potter, Helen Beatrix (1866-1943), illus. LC 11-196652. 84 p., 1 l. incl. col. front., col. plates. 15 cm. c.1910. F. Warne & Co.
--The Tale of Peter Rabbit. N.D. David McKay Co.
--The Tale of Peter Rabbit. Facsimile ed. LC 72-75248. (Illus.). 15cm. 55p. 1972. (ISBN 0-486-22827-4). Dover Books.
--The Tale of Peter Rabbit. LC 7-33592. 1 p. l., 7-70 p. col. front., illus. 21 cm. c.1907. H. Altemus Company.
--The Tale of Peter Rabbit. Apple, Margot, illus. LC 78-18071. (Illus.). 32 p. 24cm. c.1979. (ISBN 0-89375-124-3). Troll Associates.
--The Tale of Peter Rabbit. Cloud, Claude Carey (1899-), illus. (With Pop-Up Pictures). 1 p. l., 5-58 (i. e. 60) p. illus. (1 col.) 13 cm. (On cover: The midget pop-up books). c.1934. Blue Ribbon Press.
--The Tale of Peter Rabbit. Cloud, Claude Carey (1899-), illus. LC 51-14500. unpaged. illus. 15 cm. N.D. F. Warne.
--The Tale of Peter Rabbit. Cloud, Claude Carey (1899-), illus. LC 51-14500. (Illus.). 15cm. (The Peter Rabbit Ser.). 1951. Frederick Warne & Co.
--The Tale of Peter Rabbit. Gringhuis, Richard H. (1918-1974), illus. Dirk, pseud. LC 47-2029. 28 p. col. illus. 26 1/2 x 22 1/2 cm. (On cover: Story hour library). 1946. The Fideler Company.
--The Tale of Peter Rabbit. Lohse, William R., illus. LC 4-16170. 2 p. l., 9-127 p. incl. col. plates. col. front. 14 cm. (Altemus' Wee Books for Wee Folks). 1904. H. Altemus Company.
--The Tale of Peter Rabbit. Lohse, William R., illus. LC 55-2242. unpaged. illus. 21cm. (Magic talking books, T 10). 1955. Winston.
--The Tale of Peter Rabbit. Masha, pseud. (1909-), illus. Stern, Marie Simchow. LC 42-18286. 23 p. incl. col. front., illus. (part col.) 24 x 21 cm. 1942. Grosset & Dunlap.
--The Tale of Peter Rabbit. Potter, Helen Beatrix (1866-1943), illus. 1901. Warne.
--The Tale of Peter Rabbit. Rosenberg, Amye, illus. LC 81-83346. (Illus.). 20 p. 24cm. (Golden storytime book). c.1982. (ISBN 0-307-11950-5). Golden Press.
--The Tale of Peter Rabbit. Rutherford, Bonnie & Rutherford, Bill, illus. Banks, Eulalie M.. LC 61-13223. (Illus.). 27 p. 25cm. (Early fun-to-read classic). 1961. Platt & Munk.
--Tale of Peter Rabbit & Other Children's Favorites, 4 vols. Incl. The Tale of Peter Rabbit; The Tale of Benjamin Bunny; The Tale of Squirrel Nutkin; The Tale of Two Bad Mice. (Illus.). (gr. 3 up). 1975. Crown.
--The Tale of Peter Rabbit & Other Favorite Stories, 7 vols. 447p. N.D. Boxed Set. (ISBN 0-486-23903-9). Dover.
--The Tale of Peter Rabbit and Other Stories. Atkinson, Allen, illus. LC 82-47808. (Illus.). 141 p. 27cm. 1982. (ISBN 0-394-52845-X). A.A. Knopf.
--The Tale of Peter Rabbit and Other Stories. Delacre, Lulu, illus. LC 85-174133. (Illus.). 37 p. 29cm. c.1985. (ISBN 0-671-54562-0). J. Messner.
--The Tale of Peter Rabbit and Other Stories. Delacre, Lulu, illus. LC 85-123388. (Illus.). 39 p. 29cm. 1985. (ISBN 0-671-52403-8). Simon & Schuster.
--The Tale of Peter Rabbit Animated!. Wehr, Julian, illus. LC 44-1703. 24 p. col. illus. 21 1/2 x 23 cm. 1943. Grosset & Dunlap.
--The Tale of Peter Rabbitt. LC 65-24139. 59 p. col. illus. 15 cm. (Her The Peter Rabbit books). 1964. F. Warne.
--The Tale of Pigling Bland. LC 66-4163. 93 p. illus. part col. 15 cm. (Her The Peter Rabbit Books). 1964. F. Warne ?.
--The Tale of Pigling Bland. Potter, Helen Beatrix (1866-1943), illus. LC 14-233. 93, 1 p. incl. front., illus., col. plates. 15 cm. c.1913. F. Warne & Co.
--The Tale of Samuel Whiskers: Or, the Roly-Poly Pudding. Potter, Helen Beatrix (1866-1943), illus. LC 66-4162. (Illus.). 73p. 15cm. (The Peter Rabbit Bks.). 1965. F. Warne.
--The Tale of Squirrel Nutkin. Facsimile ed. (Illus.). 60p. 1903. (ISBN 0-486-22828-2). Dover Books.
--The Tale of Squirrel Nutkin. LC 72-75249. (Illus.). 55 p. 15cm. 1972. (ISBN 0-486-22828-2). Dover Publications.
--The Tale of Squirrel Nutkin. LC 42-463271. 84, 1 p. incl. col. front., col. plates 14 cm. (Her The Peter Rabbit Books). c.1905. F. Warne & Co.
--Tale of Squirrel Nutkin. N.D. (ISBN 0-531-05116-1). Franklin Watts.
--The Tale of Squirrel Nutkin. Potter, Helen Beatrix (1866-1943), illus. 84, 2 p. incl. col. front., col. plates. 15 cm. 1903. F. Warne & Co.
--The Tale of Squirrel Nutkin. Potter, Helen Beatrix (1866-1943), illus. LC 66-4161. (Illus.). 58p. 15cm. (The Peter Rabbit Bks.). 1964. F. Warne.
--The Tale of the Faithful Dove. Angel, Marie (1923-), illus. LC 56-42785. unpaged. illus. 16cm. 1st U.S. edition. 1956. F. Warne.
--The Tale of the Faithful Dove. 2d ed. Angel, Marie (1923-), illus. LC 75-109403. (Illus.). 47 p. 15cm. 1970. F. Warne.
--The Tale of the Faithful Dove. Angel, Marie (1923-), illus. LC 72-171850. (Illus.). 47 p. 17cm. 1971. (ISBN 0-7232-1336-4). F. Warne.
--The Tale of the Faithful Dove. Potter, Helen Beatrix (1866-1943), illus. LC 56-15684. (Illus.). 31p. 14cm. 1955. F. Warne.
--The Tale of the Flopsy Bunnies. LC 65-24146. 59 p. col. illus 15 cm. (Her The Peter Rabbit books). 1962. F. Warne.
--The Tale of the Flopsy Bunnies. Potter, Helen Beatrix (1866-1943), illus. LC 84-21041. (Illus.). 59 p. 14cm. 1985. (ISBN 0-486-24806-2). Dover.
--The Tale of the Flopsy Bunnies. Potter, Helen Beatrix (1866-1943), illus. LC 9-17660. 85, 1 p. incl. col. front., col. plates. 15 cm. c.1909. F. Warne & Co.
--The Tale of the Pie and the Patty-Pan. Potter, Helen Beatrix (1866-1943), illus. LC 66-4160. (Illus.). 75p. 15cm. (Peter Rabbit Bks.). Orig. Title: The Pie and the Patty Pan, 1905. 1964. F. Warne.
--The Tale of Timmy Tiptoes. LC 65-24148. 58 p. col. illus. 15 cm. (Her The Peter Rabbit books). 1964. F. Warne.
--The Tale of Timmy Tiptoes. Potter, Helen Beatrix (1866-1943), illus. LC 11-32424. 84 p., 1 l. incl. front., col. plates. 15 cm. c.1911. F. Warne & Co.
--The Tale of Tom Kitten. LC 7-28973. 84, 2 p. incl. col. front., col. plates. 15 x 11 cm. c.1907. F. Warne & Co.
--The Tale of Tom Kitten. Potter, Helen Beatrix (1866-1943), illus. LC 82-18272. p. cm. 1983. (ISBN 0-486-24502-0). Dover.
--The Tale of Tom Kitten. Potter, Helen Beatrix (1866-1943), illus. LC 65-24144. 59 p. col. illus. 15 c. (Her The Peter Rabbit books). 1965. F. Warne.
--The Tale of Tuppeny. Second Edition ed. Angel, Marie (1923-), illus. LC 72-89477. (Illus.). 39 p. 15cm. 1973, c.1971. (ISBN 0-7232-6097-4). F. Warne.
--The Tale of Two Bad Mice. LC 74-75268. (Illus.). 56 p. 15cm. 1974. (ISBN 0-486-23065-1). Dover Publications.
--The Tale of Two Bad Mice. LC 65-24142. (Illus.). 58 p. 15cm. (Her The Peter Rabbit books). 1964. F. Warne.
--Tale of Two Bad Mice. N.D. (ISBN 0-531-05117-X). Franklin Watts.
--The Tale of Two Bad Mice. Potter, Helen Beatrix (1866-1943), illus. LC 4-27991. 84, 2 p. incl. col. front., col. plates. 15 cm. 1904. F. Warne & Co.
--Tale of Two Bad Mice: With Fur Mouse. N.D. (ISBN 0-686-08951-0). Merrimack.
--Tales of Peter Rabbit. N.D. (ISBN 0-531-05107-2). Franklin Watts.
--The Tales of Peter Rabbit. Special ed. N.D. Frederick Warne & Co.
--Tales of Peter Rabbit and His Friends: 13 Tales. Potter, Helen Beatrix (1866-1943), illus. LC 84-11427. (Illus.). xi, 137 p. 25cm. c.1984. (ISBN 0-517-44901-3). Chatham River Press : Distributed by Crown Publishers.
--A Tiny Tale of Peter Rabbit. Carlson, David, illus. (Illus.). 14p. (Beatrix Potter Board Bks.). (ps-k). 1982. (ISBN 0-671-44518-9, Little Simon). S&S.
--A Treasury of Peter Rabbit and Other Stories: A Collection of Classics. LC 78-105544. (Illus.). ca. 300 p. 21cm. 1978. (ISBN 0-531-01353-7). Watts.
--Wag-by-Wall. Lankes, Julius J. (1884-1960), illus. LC 44-40204. 30 p. incl. mounted front. (port.) illus. 16 cm. 1944. The Horn Book Inc.
--Yours Affectionately, Peter Rabbit. Potter, Helen Beatrix (1866-1943), illus. (Illus.). 96p. 1984. (ISBN 0-317-01688-1). Warne.

Potter, Helen Beatrix (1866-1943) & Almond, Linda Stevens

--The Peter Rabbit Playtime Story Book. Willis, Bess Goe, illus. LC 31-5757. 62 p., 1 l. incl. col. front., col. illus. 25 cm. c.1931. Henry Altemus Company.

Potter, Helen Beatrix (1866-1943) & Chicken Little

--Peter Rabbit, Henny Penny. Erickson, Phoebe (1907-), illus. LC 47-11563. 41 p. illus. (part col.) 25 cm. (wonder book for children). 1947. Wonder Books; Distributed by Random House.

Potter, Helen Beatrix (1866-1943) & Erickson, Phoebe (1918-)

--Favorite Animal Stories. LC 53-11880. (Peter Rabbit by Beatrix Potter; The Story of a Little Fox by Phoebe Erickson). unpaged. illus. 32cm. (Big silver star book). 1953. Childrens Press.

Potter, Helen Beatrix (1866-1943) & Le Fleming, Christopher

--Squirrel Nutkin: A Children's Play. Potter, Helen Beatrix (1866-1943), illus. LC 68-10756. (Illus.). line sketches. 24p. (gr. 1-4). 1968. (ISBN 0-7232-0501-9). Warne.

Powell, Harriett
--Game Songs with Prof. Dogg's Troupe: Forty-four Songs and Games with Activities. McKee, David (1935-), illus. (Illus.). 64p. (Orig.). (ps-3). 1984. (ISBN 0-7136-2306-3, Pub. by A & C Black UK). Sterling.
--The World Was Gay. Rochester, Anne, illus. 144 p. incl. plates. col. front. 22 cm. N.D. Oxford University Press, H. Miford.
Powell, Ida Adaline Campbell, Mrs. (1877-)
--A Little Leaven. LC 42-265682. 4 p. l., 3-177 p. port. 19 cm. 1923. Britt Pub. Co.
--Zoe: An Allegory. N.D. A. D. F. Randolph.
Powell, Meredith (1886-1965) & Yokubinas, Gail
--What to Be?. Miodock, Richard, illus. LC 77-178497. (Illus.). 31p. 25cm. 1972. (ISBN 0-516-03662-9). Childrens Press.
Powell, Miriam see Morgan, Mary, pseud.
Powell, Miriam
--Jareb. Morgan, Mary, pseud. Simont, Marc (1915-), illus. LC 52-7040. (Illus.). 241 p. 21cm. 1952. Crowell.
--Rainbow for Susan. Morgan, Mary, pseud. Kennedy, Richard (1910-), illus. LC 62-9067. 159p. illus. 21cm. 1962. Abelard-Schuman.
Powell, Pamela, jt. auth. see Fairholme, Elizabeth.
Powell, Patience
--Dollie Doe. LC 51-14794. unpaged, illus. 13 cm. (Peekobook). 1949. Perry Colour Books.
--Hetty the Hen. LC 51-14795. unpaged. illus. 13 cm. (Peekobook). 1950. Perry Colour Books.
--Hubert the Hare. LC 51-14796. unpaged. illus. 13 cm. (Peekobook). 1951. Perry Colour Books.
--Katy the Kitten. LC 49-161881. unpaged, illus. 13 cm. (Peekobook). 1947. Perry Colour Books.
--Peggy the Penguin. LC 52-164510. unpaged. illus. 13 cm. (Peekobook). 1947. Perry Colour Books.
--Ruby the Robin. LC 52-164504. unpaged. illus. 13 cm. (Peekobook). 1947. Perry Colour Books.
Powell-Price, Evelyn
--Pumpkin Palace. Steed, Cicely, illus. LC 50-45028. 75 p. illus. (part col.) 26 cm. c.1949. F. Warne.
Powell, Van
--The Ghost of Mystery Airport. LC 32-12120. 288 p. front. 19 cm. (His The Sky scouts series). c.1932. A. L. Burt Company.
--The Haunted Hangar. LC 32-12122. 288 p. front. 19 cm. (His The Sky scouts series). c.1932. A. L. Burt Company.
--The Mystery Boys and Captain Kidd's Message. LC 31-13593. 281 p. front. 20 cm. (His The Mystery boys). c.1931. A. L. Burt Company.
--Mystery Boys and Captain Kidd's Message. (Mystery Boys Ser.). N.D. World Publishing Co.
--The Mystery Boys and the Chinese Jewels. LC 31-135963. 288 p. front. 20 cm. (His The Mystery boys). c.1931. A. L. Burt Company.
--Mystery Boys and the Chinese Jewels. (Mystery Boys Ser.). N.D. World Publishing Co.
--The Mystery Boys and the Hindu Treasure. LC 31-135953. 288 p. front. 20 cm. (His The Mystery boys). c.1931. A. L. Burt Company.
--Mystery Boys and the Hindu Treasure. (Mystery Boys Ser.). N.D. World Publishing Co.
--The Mystery Boys and the Inca Gold. LC 31-135971. 283 p. front. 20 cm. (His The Mystery boys). c.1931. A. L. Burt Company.
--The Mystery Boys and the Inca Gold. (Mystery Boys Ser.). N.D. World Publishing Co.
--The Mystery Boys and the Inca Gold, and The Mystery Boys and Captain Kidd's Message: Two Books in One. N.D. World Publishing Co.
--The Mystery Boys and the Secret of the Golden Sun. LC 31-13594. 285 p. front. 20 cm. (His The Mystery boys). c.1931. A. L. Burt Company.
--The Mystery Boys and the Secret of the Golden Sun. (Mystery Boys Ser.). N.D. World Publishing Co.
--The Mystery Crash. LC 32-12123. 285 p. front. 19 cm. (His The Sky scouts series). c.1932. A. L. Burt Company.
--The Mystery of the Fifteen Sounds. LC 38-3588. 2 p. l., 9-248 p. 20 cm. 1938. The Goldsmith Publishing Company.
--Racket Busters. N.D. World Publishing Co.
--The Vanishing Air Liner. LC 32-121218. 284 p. front. 19 cm. (His The Sky scouts series). c.1932. A. L. Burt Company.
Power, Barbara
--I Wish Laura's Mommy was My Mommy. Hafner, Marylin (1925-), illus. 1979. Harper.
--I Wish Laura's Mommy Was My Mommy. Hafner, Marylin (1925-), illus. LC 79-2406. p. cm. (Lippincott I-Like-to-Read Book). c.1979. (ISBN 0-397-31838-3). (ISBN 0-397-31859-6). Lippincott.
Power, Effie Louise, jt. auth. see Everson, Florence McClurg.
Power, Effie Louise (1873-), ed.
--Bag O' Tales. Bell, Corydon Whitten (1894-), illus. (Illus.). 10 line drawings. bibl. index. 340p. (Pub. by Dutton). (gr. k-6). 1970. Dover.
--Bag O' Tales. Bell, Corydon Whitten (1894-), illus. N.D. Gale Reprint.
--Bag O' Tales: A Source Book for Story-Tellers. Bell, Corydon Whitten (1894-), illus. LC 34-24147. 340 p. illus. 24 cm. 1934. E. P. Dutton and Co., Inc.
--Bag O' Tales: A Source Book for Story-Tellers. Bell, Corydon Whitten (1894-), illus. LC 68-26598. (Illus.). 340 p. 22cm. 1968. Singing Tree Press.
--Bag O' Tales: Sixty-Three Famous Stories for Storytellers. Bell, Corydon Whitten (1894-), illus. LC 78-96393. (Illus.). 22cm. 340p. 1934. (ISBN 0-486-22527-5). Dover Books.
--Bag O' Tales: Sixty-Three Famous Stories for Storytellers. Bell, Corydon Whitten (1894-), illus. N.D. (ISBN 0-8446-4796-9). Peter Smith Publisher, Inc.
--Bag O'Tales: Sixty-Three Famous Stories for Storytellers. Bell, Corydon Whitten (1894-), illus. LC 78-98693. (Illus.). 340 p. 22cm. 1969. Dover Publications.
--Blue Caravan Tales. Doane, Pelagie (1906-1966), illus. LC 35-27281. 128 p. illus. 20 cm. c.1935. E. P. Dutton & Co.
--From Umar's Pack. 1st ed. Bayley, Dorothy (1906-1979), illus. LC 37-16376. 123 p. illus. 20 cm. c.1937. E. P. Dutton & Co., Inc.
--Osceola Buddy: A Florida Farm Mule. Simon, Howard (1903-1979), illus. LC 41-8962. 56, 1 p. illus. (incl. music) 23 1/2 cm. 1941. E.P. Dutton & Co., Inc.
--Stories to Shorten the Road. LC 36-27393. 3 p. l., 5-126 p. illus. 20 cm. c.1936. E. P. Dutton & Co., Inc.
Power, Helena M., retold by.
--More Stories from Dickens. LC 61-59614. 21cm. 141p. 1961. Exposition Press.
--Stories from Dickens. 1959. Exposition Press.
Power, Leonore St. John, selected by see Van Loon, Hendrik Willem.
Power, Norman Sandiford (1916-)
--Fear in Finland. (Illus.). N.D. (ISBN 0-8202-0204-5). Sherbourne.
--Forgotten Kingdom. (Illus.). (gr. k-3). N.D. (ISBN 0-8202-0205-3). Sherbourne.
Power, P. B.
--Babe at the Wedding. (Carters' Fireside Library). N.D. Robert Carter & Brothers.
--Babe at the Wedding, and Other Narratives. N.D. Thomas Whittaker.
--Bag of Blessings. (Carters' Fireside Library). N.D. Robert Carter & Brothers.
--Bag of Blessings: Or, The Singing Tailor. N.D. Thomas Whittaker.
--Fagot of Stories. (Carters' Fireside Library). N.D. Robert Carter & Brothers.
--Fagot of Stories for Young Folks. N.D. Thomas Whittaker.
--Father's Joy and Other Stories. (Illus.). 80p. N.D. Fleming H. Revell Co.
--Last Shilling. (Carters' Fireside Library). N.D. Robert Carter & Brothers.
--Last Shilling: Or, The Selfish Child. N.D. Thomas Whittaker.
--Little Knitter. 63p. (Moss-rose Stories). N.D. Lockwood, Brooks, & Co. for American Tract Society.
--The Moss Rose. 62p. (Moss-Rose Stories). N.D. Lockwood, Brooks & Co. for American Tract Society.
--Sambo's Legacy. (Carters' Fireside Library). N.D. Robert Carter & Brothers.
--Sambo's Legacy and Other Narratives. N.D. Thomas Whittaker.
--Stamp on it, John. (Carters' Fireside Library). N.D. Robert Carter & Brothers.
--Stamp on It, John, and Other Narratives. N.D. Thomas Whittaker.
--Take Care of Number One. N.D. Robert Carter.
--Take Care of Number One and Other Narratives. N.D. Thomas Whittaker.
--Three Cripples. (Carters' Fireside Library). N.D. Robert Carter & Brothers.
--Three Cripples. N.D. Thomas Whittaker.
--Truffle Nephews. N.D. Robert Carter & Brothers.
--Truffle Nephews, and How They Commenced a New Charity. N.D. Thomas Whittaker.
--Two Brothers. (Carters' Fireside Library). N.D. Robert Carter & Brothers.
--Two Brothers and the Two Paths. N.D. Thomas Whittaker.
Power, Phyllis M.
--Sabotage in the Snowy Mountains. King, Gustav, illus. (Illus.). (gr. 7 up). 1961. (ISBN 0-685-21493-1). Verry.
Power, Rhoda Dolores (1890-1957)
--The Big Book of Stories from Many Lands. Watts, Anna Bernadette (1942-), illus. LC 68-30962. (Illus.). 238 p. 25cm. 340p. 1970, c.1969. Watts.
--From the Fury of the Norsemen and Other Stories from History. Baynes, Pauline Diana (1922-), illus. 1957. Houghton Mifflin.
--How It Happened: Myths & Folk-Tales. Parker, Agnes Miller, Mrs. (1895-), illus. LC 31-267384. viii p., 2 l., 188, 2 p. incl. illus., plates. 24 cm. 1930. The University Press.
--Redcap Runs Away. Hodges, Cyril Walter (1909-), illus. LC 54-8384. 303p. illus. 21cm. 1953. Houghton Mifflin.
--Stories from Everywhere. Brisley, Nina K., illus. 1931. Macmillan.
Power-Waters, Alma Shelley (1896-)
--The Giving Gift. Ilsley, Velma Elizabeth (1918-), illus. LC 62-16279. 157p. illus. 22cm. (Bell Books). 1962. Farrar, Straus & Cudahy.
--Moon in My Pocket. LC 56-8293. 224 p. 21cm. 1956. Dutton.
--St. Catherine Laboure & The Miraculous Medal. Fox, James J., illus. 192p. (Vision Bks.: No. 54). 1962. Farrar, Straus & Giroux.
--Virginia Giant: The Story of Peter Francisco. 1st ed. Bjorklund, Lorence F. (1913-1978), illus. LC 57-7599. 224p. illus. 21cm. 1957. Dutton.
Powers, Alfred
--Alexander's Horses. 1st ed. Mackey, John, illus. LC 59-9293. 213p. illus. 22cm. 1959. Longmans, Green.
--Alexander's Horses. Mackey, John, illus. (gr. 7-11). 1959. (ISBN 0-679-25006-9). McKay.
--Chains for Columbus. LC 48-4044. 219 p. map (on lining-papers) 22 cm. 1948. Westminster Press.
--Hannibal's Elephants. Reid, James (1907-), illus. LC 44-8547. 3 p. l., 272 p. front., illus. 21 cm. 1944. Longmans, Green & Co.
--Hannibal's Elephants. Reid, James (1907-), illus. 1944. McKay.
--A Long Way to Frisco. Daugherty, James Henry (1889-1974), illus. 1951. Little, Brown.
--Marooned in Crater Lake. (Illus.). (gr. 5-11). N.D. Binfords.
--Prisoners of the Redwoods: An Adventure Story of San Francisco and the Northern California Coast in the Fifties. LC 48-4959. 246 p. 22 cm. 1948. Coward-McCann.
Powers, Anne (1913-)
--Ride with Danger. LC 58-8391. 256p. 21cm. 1958. Bobbs-Merrill.
Powers, Bill (1931-)
--Break Him Down!. Powers, Bill (1931-), illus. LC 76-39894. (reading consultants, irene swinburne, laurence swinburne). (Illus.). 48 p. (Target book). 1977. (ISBN 0-531-01273-5). Watts.
--Flying High. Powers, Bill (1931-), illus. LC 77-14290. (Reading Consultants: Irene Swinburne and Laurence Swinburne). (Illus.). 48 p. 23cm. (Target book). 1978. (ISBN 0-531-01461-4). Watts.
--A Test of Love. Aron, Bill, illus. LC 78-12913. (Illus.). 90 p. 22cm. (Triumph book). 1979. (ISBN 0-531-02888-7). F. Watts.
--The Weekend. Joseph, Meryl, illus. LC 77-10710. (Illus.). 90 p. 22cm. (Triumph book). 1978. (ISBN 0-531-01467-3). F. Watts.
Powers, Ella Marie (1865-)
--Stories of Indian Days. LC 12-19154. 127 p. illus. 20 cm. c.1912. Educational Publishing Company.
Powers, Jessica, Sr.
--The Little Alphabet. Rose of God, Sr., illus. LC 55-4826. unpaged. illus. 21cm. (Christian Child's Stories, 5). 1955. Bruce Pub. Co.
Powers, Mabel
--Round An Iroquois Story Fire. N.D. Frederick A. Stokes Co.
Powers, Mala (1931-)
--Follow the Star. Tanner, Suzy-Jane, illus. LC 80-66664. (Illus.). 112 p. 29cm. c.1980. (ISBN 0-89742-046-2). Dawne-Leigh Publications.
Powers, Richard M. Gorman (1921-)
--Double Decker. Powers, Richard M. Gorman (1921-), illus. LC 52-13411. (Illus.). unpaged. 1952. Coward-McCann.
Powers, Steven
--Muskingum Legends. N.D. J. B. Lippincott Co.
Powers, Thetis
--Little Book of Daffinitions. Cummings, Chris, illus. LC 77-85135. (Illus.). (Little Bks. Ser.). (gr. 2-4). 1977. (ISBN 0-8178-5682-X). Harvey.
Powers, Tom (1890-)
--A Scotch Circus: The Story of Tammas Who Rode the Dragon. Lenski, Lois (1893-1974), illus. LC 34-32271. 4 p. l., 3-95, 1 p. illus. (part col.) 21 cm. 1934. Houghton Mifflin Company.
Powicke, Hilda B.
--Barrier. (gr. 9 up). 1964. Friend Pr.
--No Certain Harbor. (gr. 9 up). 1962. (ISBN 0-377-80231-X). Friend Pr.
Pownall, David (1938-)
--The Bunch from Bananas. Fitzgerald, Frank, illus. LC 80-27422. (Illus.). 72 p. 22cm. 1st U.S. edition. 1981, c.1980. (ISBN 0-02-775090-6). Macmillan.
Powys, Theodore Francis (1875-1953)
--Fables. N.D. Viking Press.
Poynter, E. F.
--My Little Lady. (The Leisure Hour Ser.). N.D. Henry Holt.
Poynter, Margaret & Sherrod, David
--Crazy Minnie. Sherrod, David, illus. LC 78-12887. (Illus.). 56 p. 24cm. c.1978. (ISBN 0-87191-680-0). Creative Education.
Poynter, May H.
--Scarlet Town (Pub. by Society for Promoting Christian Knowledge). N.D. E. & J. B Young & Co.
Poznak, Joan Gilbert Van see Agay, Denes & Gilbert Van Poznak, Joan.
Pradier, Mireille
--Aurora: Story of the Little Princess Who Won a Kingdom by Sharing a Secret. Sabran, Guy, illus. Dawes, C. Burr (1902-), tr. LC 47-24771. (Illus.). 31p. 31cm. 1947. Tell-Well Press.
Praeger, S. R.
--The Adventures of Three Bold Babes. N.D. Longmans Green & Co.
--Further Doings of the Three Bold Babes. N.D. Longmans Green & Co.
--How They Went to School. (Illus.). N.D. Frederick A. Stoke.
--How They Went to the Seaside. (Illus.). N.D. Frederick A. Stokes.
--Wee Tony: A Day in His Life. (Illus.). N.D. Dodge Publishing Co.
Prager, Annabelle
--The Four Getsys and What They Forgot. Darrow, Whitney, Jr. (1909-), illus. LC 81-5029. (Illus.). 43 p. 24cm. (An I Am Reading Book). c.1982. (ISBN 0-394-84833-0). (ISBN 0-394-94833-5). Pantheon Books.
--The Spooky Halloween Party. De Paola, Tomie, pseud. (1934-), illus. De Paola, Thomas Anthony. LC 81-1945. p. cm. (I Am Reading Book). c.1981. (ISBN 0-394-84370-3). Pantheon Books.
--The Surprise Party. De Paola, Tomie, pseud. (1934-), illus. De Paola, Thomas Anthony. LC 76-40309. (Illus.). 43 p. 24cm. (Read Alone Book). c.1977. (ISBN 0-394-83235-3). (ISBN 0-394-93235-8). Pantheon Books.
Prague, Statni Zidovske Museum
--Children's Drawings and Poems. Terezin, Nineteen-Forty-Two to Nineteen-Forty-Four. Volavkova, Hana, ed. Weil, Jiri, intro. by. Nemcova, Jeanne, tr. LC 62-51351. 80p. illus. (pt. col.) 29cm. 1962. Vanous.
Prague & Volavkova, Hana
--I Never Saw Another Butterfly: Children's Drawings and Poems from Terezin Concentration Camp, 1942-1944. 2d ed. LC 78-3542. p. cm. 1978. (ISBN 0-8052-0598-5). Schocken Books.
Prall, Dorothea, tr. see With, Karl Henrik.
Pratchett, Terry
--The Carpet People. (gr. 3-6). 1976. (ISBN 0-8277-4530-3). British Bk Ctr.
Prather, Ray
--Anthony and Sabrina. LC 73-3888. (Illus.). 32 p. 24cm. 1973. (ISBN 0-02-775030-2). Macmillan.
--Double Dog Dare. LC 74-13316. (Illus.). 40 p. 22cm. (Ready-to-read). 1975. (ISBN 0-02-775040-X). Macmillan.
--New Neighbors. LC 74-14703. (Illus.). 32 p. 26cm. 32p. 1975. (ISBN 0-07-050671-X). (ISBN 0-07-050670-1). (ISBN 0-07-050670-1). McGraw-Hill.
--No Trespassing. LC 73-19056. (Illus.). 32 p. 1974. (ISBN 0-02-775020-5). Macmillan.
--The Ostrich Girl. LC 78-9710. (Illus.). 32 p. 26cm. c.1978. (ISBN 0-684-15889-2). Scribner.
Pratt
--Little Cave Dwellers. (The "Bimbi" Series of Children's Booklets). N.D. Thomas Y. Crowell.
Pratt, ed.
--Grimm's Fairy Tales. (Original Authors: The Brothers Grimm). (Vol. 1). N.D. Educational Publishing Company.
Pratt, Alice Day
--Animal Babies. Rev. ed. Wiese, Kurt (1887-1974), illus. LC 59-7048. (Illus.). 125p. 25cm. 1959. Beacon Press.
--Animal Babies. Wiese, Kurt (1887-1974), illus. LC 41-9385. vii p., 2 l., 148 p. illus. (part col.) 24 x 21 cm. c.1941. The Beacon Press.
--Animals of a Sagebrush Ranch. Wiese, Kurt (1887-1974), illus. Seton, Ernest Evan Thompson (1860-1946), frwd. by. LC 31-32407. 208 p. illus., col. plates. 24 cm. c.1931. Rand, McNally & Company.
Pratt, Anna M.
--Flower Folk. Hills, Laura C., illus. LC 16-3880. (Illus.). 24cm. 1890. Frederick A. Stokes.
--Friends from My Garden. Hills, Laura C., illus. LC 16-3878. 128 p. incl. col. front., col. plates. 23 x 20 cm. 1890. Frederick A. Stokes Company.
--Little Rhymes for Little People. LC 15-18026. 60 p. 21 cm. 1896. P. Lemperly, F. A. Hilliard and F. E. Hopkins.
Pratt, Charles Stuart (1854-)
--Buz-Buz: His Twelve Adventures. Bridgman, Lewis Jesse (1857-1931), illus. xi p., 1 l., 15-102 p. incl. front., illus., plates. 20 cm. 1898. Lothrop Publishing Company.

--Bye O Baby Ballads. Hassam, F. Childe (1859-1935), illus. LC 16-3877. 61 p. col. front., col. illus. 25 cm. c.1887. D. Lothrop & Co.

--Little Peterkin Vandike. (Illus.). (Every Boy's Library). N.D. Caldwell.

--Little Peterkin Vandike. (Illus.). (Goldenrod Library Ser.). 1905. L. C. Page & Co.

--Little Peterkin Vandike. (Illus.). (Cosy Corner Ser.). N.D. L. C. Page & Co.

--Stick-and -Pea Plays. (Illus.). N.D. Lothrop, Lee & Shepard.

Pratt, Davis & Kula, Elsa

--Magic Animals of Japan. LC 67-17483. (Illus.). 1 v. (unpaged. 1967. Parnassus Press.

Pratt, Eliza Anna Farman see Pratt, Ella Farman, Mrs.

Pratt, Ella Farman, Mrs., et al. (1843-1907)

--The Play Lady: A Story for Other Girls. LC 4299. 2 p. l., 132 p. front. 20 cm. (Sunshine library). c.1900. T. Y. Crowell & Co.

Pratt, Ella Farman, Mrs. (1843-1907)

--Anna Maylie, 1 of 9 vols. (Illus.). (Ella Farman's Books). N.D. Lothrop Pub. Co.

--Anna Maylie, 1 of 50 vols. (Illus.). 350p. (Sunday-School Lib: No. 14). N.D. Set. Lothrop Pub. Co.

--Birdie's Twelfth Birthday. (Illus.). 80p. (The Rosebud Ser.). N.D. Fleming H. Revell.

--Bo-Peep's Stocking. REv ed. LC 21-8705. (Illus.). 60 p. front., illus. 17 cm. c.1883. D. Lothrop and Company.

--The Cooking Club of Tu-Whit Hollow. LC 21-13955. 223 p. incl. front. plates. 18 cm. 1876. D. Lothrop & Co.

The Cooking Club of Tu-Whit Hollow, 1 of 9 vols. (Illus.). (Ella Farman's Bks.). N.D. D. Lothrop & Co.

--A Dozen Darlings and Their Doings. 24 p. illus. pl. 4 degrees. 1898. Lothrop Pub. Co.

--A Girl's Money, 1 of 9 vols. (Illus.). (Ella Farman's Bks.). N.D. D. Lothrop & Co.

--A Girl's Money, 1 of 50 vols. (Illus.). 350p. (Sunday-School Lib: No. 14). N.D. Set. Lothrop Pub.

--Good-For-Nothing Polly, 1 of 9 vols. (Illus.). (Ella Farman's Bks.). N.D. D. Lothrop & Co.

--Good-for-Nothing Polly, 1 of 50 vols. (Illus.). 350p. (Sunday-School Lib: No. 14). N.D. Set. Lothrop Pub. Co.

--Grandma Crosby's Household, 1 of 9 vols. (Illus.). (Ella Farman's Bks.). N.D. D. Lothrop & Co.

--Happy Children: A Book of Bed Time Stories. LC 11-19663. vii, 157 p. incl. col. front. col. plates. 20 cm. c.1911. Thomas Y. Crowell Company.

--Home Primer. (Illus.). N.D. Lothrop Pub. Co.

--The Little Cave-Dwellers. LC 1-25757. (Illus.). 12cm. 96p. (The From Nine to Twelve Ser.). 1901. Thomas Y. Crowell & Co.

--The Little Owls at Red Gates. Foster, Edith Francis, illus. LC 3-14265. 79, 1 p. front., illus. 18 x 23 cm. 1903. D. Estes & Company.

--A Little Woman, 1 of 9 vols. (Illus.). (Ella Farman's Books). N.D. D. Lothrop & Co.

--A Little Woman, 1 of 3 Vols. (Illus.). (Allie Bird Ser.). N.D. Set. D Lothrop & Co.

--A Little Woman, 1 of 50 vols. (Illus.). 350p. (Sunday-School Lib: No. 14). N.D. Set. Lothrop Pub. Co.

--A Little Woman, 1 of 50 vols. (Boys' & Girls' Library: No. 26). N.D. Set. Lothrop Publishing Co.

--A Little Woman: A Story for Other Little Women. LC 20-19329. 195 p. incl. front., pl. 18 cm. (Added t.-p.: The Allie-Bird series). 1873. D. Lothrop & Co.

--Mrs. Hurd's Niece, 1 of 9 vols. (Illus.). (Ella Farman Bks.). N.D. D. Lothrop& Co.

--Mrs. Hurd's Niece, 1 of 50 vols. (Illus.). 350p. (Sunday-School Lib: No. 14). N.D. Set. Lothrop Pub. Co.

--Mrs. Hurd's Niece. (Illus.). (The Kitty Kent Library). N.D. Set. Ward & Drummond.

--Mrs. Hurd's Niece: Six Months of a Girl's Life. LC 20-19331. vii, 7-357 p. front., pl. 18 cm. (On cover: The young folks library. no. 4). 1884. D. Lothrop and Company.

--Mrs. White's Party and Other Stories. LC 20-19328. 105 p. front., illus. plates. 18 cm. 1879. D. Lothrop and Company.

--Sugar Plums. Northam, C. A., illus. LC 15-254. v, 7-100 p. front., illus. 17 cm. c.1877. D. Lothrop and Company.

--A White Hand, 1 of 9 vols. (Illus.). (Ella Farman's Bks.). N.D. D. Lothrop & Co.

--A White Hand, 1 of 50 vols. (Illus.). 350p. (Sunday-School Lib: No. 14). N.D. Set. Lothrop Pub. Co.

Pratt, Ella Farman, Mrs. (1843-1907), ed.

--Christmas Snowflakes. LC 17-16406. 158 p. front., illus. 26 cm. 1879. D. Lothrop & Co.

Pratt, Ellen F.

--Amy and the Cloud Basket. Russell, Lisa, illus. LC 75-25035. (Illus.). 38 p. 25cm. c.1975. Lollipop Power.

--Jerry. LC 21-16874. 1 p. l., 5-234 p. 19 cm. 1889. J. B. Alden Company.

Pratt, Fletcher, jt. auth. see Coggins, Jack.

Pratt, Frances Lee

--Agnes and Her Neighbors. In Three Parts. LC 21-13956. 360 p. front., plates. 17 cm. 1872. D. Lothrop & Co.

Pratt, Laura

--Tales of Doggie Dutch. N.D. Carlton.

Pratt, Mara Louise, Mrs., ed. see Grimm, Jakob Ludwig Karl (1785-1863) & Grimm, Wilhelm Karl.

Pratt, Margaret

--Flash of Washington Square. Duvoisin, Roger Antoine (1904-1980), illus. LC 54-101894. unpaged. illus. 26cm. c.1954. Lothrop, Lee & Shepard Co.

--The Talking Typewriter. 1st Ed. ed. Gergely, Tibor (1900-1978), illus. LC 40-82779. 26cm. 38p. 1940. Lothrop Lee & Shepard.

Pratt, Mary Elizabeth Smith

--Rhoda Thornton's Girlhood, 1 of 32 vols, Vol. 20. (Illus.). (Famous Books for Girls). N.D. H. M. Caldwell Co.

--Rhoda Thornton's Girlhood, 1 of 6 vols. (Illus.). (Girlhood Ser.). N.D. Set. Lee & Shepard.

--Rhoda Thornton's Girlhood. Rev ed. Bush, C. G., illus. LC 2-11143. 273 p. incl. front. pl. 19 cm. (American girl's series, v. 16). 1901. Lee & Shepard.

Pratt, Robert A., ed.

--The Tales of Canterbury and Shorter Poems. 1973. Houghton Mifflin Company.

Pratt, S. G.

--The Brownie Song Book. (Illus.). N.D. Laird & Lee's Publication.

Pratt, Sabina Carlin

--Range Land Animal Tales. 1959. Exposition Press.

--Skip & Skid. 1962. Exposition Press.

Pratt, Theodore (1901-1969)

--The Barefoot Mailman. N.D. Duell, Sloan & Pearce.

--Miss Dilly Says No. N.D. Duell, Sloan & Pearce.

--Mr. Thurtle's Trolley. N.D. Duell, Sloan & Pearce.

--Mr. Winkle Goes to War. N.D. Duell, Sloan & Pearce.

--Perils in Provence. N.D. Duell, Sloan & Pearce.

--Thunder Mountain. LC 44-4728. 3 p. l., 3-249 p. 21 1/2 cm. 1944. Duell, Sloan and Pearce.

--Thunder Mountain. N.D. World Publishing.

--Valley Boy. N.D. Duell, Sloan & Pearce.

Pratt, Waldo S., ed.

--Saint Nicholas Songs. (Illus.). 200p. N.D. The Century Co.

Pratt, Waldo S., ed. see St. Nicholas Magazine.

Pratten, Albra

--Winkie the Grey Squirrel. Thompson, Ralph, illus. 1950. Oxford University Press.

Preble, Donna Louise (1882-)

--Yamino-Kwiti. Preble, Donna Louise (1882-), illus. Margolin, Malcolm, intro. by. (Illus.). 256p (Pub. by Caxton Printers (Caldwell Idaho)). (gr. 4-10). 1983. (ISBN 0-930588-09-6). Heyday Bks.

--Yamino-Kwiti: Boy Runner of Siba. Preble, Donna Louise (1882-), illus. LC 40-33794. 236 p. col. front., illus., plates (part col.) 24 cm. 1940. The Caxton Printers, Ltd.

Preble, Laura E., ed. see Bennett, John.

Prechtl, Louise Boylston

--The Golden Swan. Prechtl, Louise Boylston, illus. LC 60-15146. unpaged. illus. 29cm. 1960. T.S.Denison.

Pree, Mildred De see DePree, Mildred.

Prehn, Monika

--A Christmas Crib. N.D. (ISBN 0-8008-1550-5). Taplinger.

Preiss, Byron Cary

--The Bat Family. Smith, Kenneth, illus. LC 83-23986. c.1985. (ISBN 0-89845-237-6). Caedmon.

--The Little Blue Brontosaurus. Stout, William (1949-) & Morgan, Don, illus. LC 83-7424. (Illus.). 48p. (ps-3). 1983. (ISBN 0-89845-165-5). (ISBN 0-89845-127-2). Caedmon.

Prelutsky, Jack

--The Baby Uggs Are Hatching. Stevenson, James Walker (1929-), illus. LC 81-7266. p. cm. 1982. (ISBN 0-688-00922-0). (ISBN 0-688-00923-9). Greenwillow Books.

--Circus. Lobel, Arnold Stark (1933-), illus. LC 77-16496. (Illus.). 32 p. 1978, c.1974. (ISBN 0-02-044760-4). Collier Books.

--Circus. Lobel, Arnold Stark (1933-), illus. LC 73-6055. (Illus.). 32 p. 1974. (ISBN 0-02-775060-4). Macmillan.

--A Gopher in the Garden, and Other Animal Poems. Leydenfrost, Robert J. (1925-), illus. LC 67-4720. (Illus.). 1 v. (unpaged. 26cm. 1967. Macmillan.

--A Gopher in the Garden: And Other Animal Poems. Leydenfrost, Robert J. (1925-), photos by. LC 67-4720. (Illus.). 1970. Macmillan Company.

--The Headless Horseman Rides Tonight: More Poems to Trouble Your Sleep. 1st ed. Lobel, Arnold Stark (1933-), illus. LC 80-10372. (Illus.). 40p. (gr. 1-4). 1980. (ISBN 0-688-80273-7). (ISBN 0-688-84273-9). Greenwillow. **Awards: (NYT).**

--It's Christmas. Hafner, Marylin (1925-), illus. LC 81-1100. p. cm. c.1981. (ISBN 0-688-00439-3). (ISBN 0-688-00440-7). Greenwillow Books.

--It's Halloween. Hafner, Marylin (1925-), illus. LC 77-2141. (Illus.). 56 p. 22cm. (Greenwillow Read-Alone). c.1977. (ISBN 0-688-80102-1). (ISBN 0-688-84102-3). Greenwillow Books.

--It's Snowing! It's Snowing!. Titherington, Jeanne, illus. LC 83-16583. (Illus.). 7 x 9. 48p. (20 pt.). (gr. 1-3). 1984. (ISBN 0-688-01512-3). (ISBN 0-688-01513-1). (ISBN 0-688-01513-1). Greenwillow.

--It's Thanksgiving. Hafner, Marylin (1925-), illus. LC 81-1929. p. cm. (Greenwillow Read-Alone Books). c.1981. (ISBN 0-688-00441-5). (ISBN 0-688-00442-3). Greenwillow Books.

--It's Valentine's Day. Abolafia, Yossi, illus. LC 83-1449. p. cm. 1983. (ISBN 0-688-02311-8). (ISBN 0-688-02312-6). Greenwillow Books.

--Kermit's Garden of Verses. McNally, Bruce, illus. LC 82-480. (Illus.). 54 p. 18cm. 1982. Muppet Press/Random House.

--Lazy Blackbird & Other Verses. Janosch, pseud. (1931-), illus. Eckert, Horst. LC 69-14273. (Illus.). color ils. 24p. 1st U.S. edition. (gr. k-2). 1969. (ISBN 0-02-775080-9). Macmillan.

--The Mean Old Mean Hyena. Lobel, Arnold Stark (1933-), illus. LC 78-2300. (Illus.). 32 p. 26cm. 1st U.S. edition. c.1978. (ISBN 0-688-80163-3). (ISBN 0-688-84163-5). Greenwillow Books.

--My Parents Think I'm Sleeping: Poems. Abolafia, Yossi, illus. LC 84-13640. (Illus.). 47 p. 24cm. (gr. 1-4). c.1985. (ISBN 0-688-04018-7). (ISBN 0-688-04019-5). Greenwillow Books.

--New Kid on the Block: Poems. 1st ed. Stevenson, James Walker (1929-), illus. LC 83-20621. (Illus.). 24 cm. 159p. 1984. (ISBN 0-688-02271-5). (ISBN 0-688-02272-3). (ISBN 0-688-02272-3). Greenwillow. **Award: (ALA).**

--Nightmares: Poems to Trouble Your Sleep. Lobel, Arnold Stark (1933-), illus. LC 76-4820. (Illus.). 38 p. 26cm. c.1976. (ISBN 0-688-80053-X). (ISBN 0-688-84053-1). Greenwillow Books. **Award: (ALA).**

--No End of Nonsense. Blecher, Wilfried, illus. LC 68-17512. (Illus.). 4 color ils. 24p. 1st U.S. edition. (gr. k-2). 1968. Macmillan.

--The Pack Rat's Day and Other Poems. Graham, Margaret Bloy (1920-), illus. LC 72-81061. p. 1974. (ISBN 0-02-775050-7). Macmillan.

--The Queen of Eene. Chess, Victoria (1939-), illus. LC 77-17311. (Illus.). 32 p. c.1978. (ISBN 0-688-80144-7). (ISBN 0-688-84144-9). Greenwillow Books. **Award: (ALA).**

--Rainy Rainy Saturday. Hafner, Marylin (1925-), illus. LC 79-22217. (Illus.). 47 p. 22cm. (Greenwillow Read-Alone). c.1980. (ISBN 0-688-80252-4). (ISBN 0-688-84252-6). Greenwillow Books.

--Ride a Purple Pelican. Williams, Garth Montgomery (1912-), illus. LC 84-6024. p. cm. c.1985. (ISBN 0-688-04031-4). (ISBN 0-688-04032-2). Greenwillow Books.

--Rolling Harvey Down the Hill. Chess, Victoria (1939-), illus. LC 79-18236. (Illus.). 30 p. c.1980. (ISBN 0-688-80258-3). (ISBN 0-688-84258-5). Greenwillow Books.

--The Sheriff of Rottenshot. Chess, Victoria (1939-), illus. LC 81-6420. (Illus.). 9 7/8 x 8. 32p. (14 pt.). (gr. k-3). 1982. (ISBN 0-688-00205-6) (ISBN 0-688-00198-X) Greenwillow.

--The Snopp on the Sidewalk, and Other Poems. Barton, Byron (1930-), illus. LC 76-46323. (Byron Barton is the lagal name change of Byron Vartanian.). (Illus.). 31 p. c.1977. (ISBN 0-688-80084-X). (ISBN 0-688-84084-1). Greenwillow Books.

--The Terrible Tiger. Lobel, Arnold Stark (1933-), illus. LC 75-89592. (Illus.). 1 v. (unpaged. 23cm. 38p. (Collier juvenile paperbacks). 1969, c.1970. Collier Books.

--Three Saxon Nobles & Other Verses. Rubin, Eva Johanna (1926-), illus. LC 69-14272. (Illus.). 4 color ils. 24p. 23p. 1st U.S. edition. (gr. k-2). 1969. Macmillan.

--Toucans Two, and Other Poems. Aruego, Jose (1932-), illus. LC 70-102970. (Illus.). 32 p. 23cm. 1970. Macmillan.

--What I Did Last Summer. Abolafia, Yossi, illus. LC 83-11561. (Illus.). 6 1/4 x 8 3/8. 48p. (16 pt.). (gr. 1-3). 1984. (ISBN 0-688-01754-1). (ISBN 0-688-01755-X). Greenwillow.

--Zoo Doings and Other Animal Poems. Zelinsky, Paul O., illus. LC 82-11996. p. cm. c.1983. (ISBN 0-688-01782-7). (ISBN 0-688-01784-3). Greenwillow Books.

Prelutsky, Jack, compiled by.

--The Random House Book of Poetry for Children. Lobel, Arnold Stark (1933-), illus. LC 83-2990. p. cm. 1983. (ISBN 0-394-85010-6). (ISBN 0-394-95010-0). Random House. **Award: (ALA).**

Prelutsky, Jack, adapted by see Lindgren, Barbro.

Prelutsky, Jack, tr. see Blecher, Wilfried.

Prelutsky, Jack, tr. see Hoffmann-Donner, Heinrich.

Prelutsky, Jack, tr. see Kruss, James.

Prelutsky, Jack, tr. see Lindgren, Barbro.

Prelutsky, Jack, tr. see Neumann, Rudolf.

Prempeh, Albert Kofi, jt. ed. see Courlander, Harold.

Prendergast, John

--Great Operas Told for Children. (Illus.). N.D. Frederick A. Stokes.

Prensky, Frieda, jt. ed. see Eisenstein, Judith K.

Prentice, Amy

--Billy Goat's Story. Davis, J. Watson, illus. LC 6-10310. 72 p. col. front., illus., plates. 19 cm. (Half-title: Aunt Amy's animal stories). c.1906. A. L. Burt Company.

--Brown Owl's Story. Davis, J. Watson, illus. LC 6-10309. 75 p. col. front., illus., plates. 19 cm. (Half-title: Aunt Amy's Animal Storics). c.1906. A. L. Burt Company.

--Bunny Rabbit's Story. Davis, J. Watson, illus. LC 6-10308. 2 p. l., 3-73 p. col. front., illus., plates. 19 cm. (Half-title: Aunt Amy's animal stories). c.1906. A. L. Burt Company.

--Croaky Frog's Story. Davis, J. Watson, illus. LC 6-42433. 72 p. col. front., illus., plates. 19 cm. (Half-title: Aunt Amy's Animal Stories). c.1906. A. L. Burt Company.

--Frisky Squirrel's Story. Davis, J. Watson, illus. LC 6-36426. 2 p. l., 3-69 p. col. front., illus., plates. 19 cm. (Half-title: Aunt Amy's animal stories). c.1906. A. L. Burt Company.

--Gray Goose's Story. Davis, J. Watson, illus. LC 6-36427. 74 p. col. front., illus., plates. 19 cm. (Half-title: Aunt Amy's animal stories). c.1906. A. L. Burt Company.

--Mickie Monkey's Story. Davis, J. Watson, illus. (Aunt Amy's Animal Stories). N.D. A. L. Burt.

--Mouser Cat's Story. Davis, J. Watson, illus. LC 6-10307. 75 p. col. front., illus., plates. 19 cm. (Half-title: Aunt Amy's animal stories). c.1906. A. L. Burt Company.

--Plodding Turtle's Story. Davis, J. Watson, illus. LC 6-103068. 2 p. l., 3-69 p. col. front., illus., plates. 19 cm. (Half-title: Aunt Amy's animal stories). c.1906. A. L. Burt Company.

--Quacky Duck's Story. Davis, J. Watson, illus. LC 6-10305. 70 p. col. front., illus., plates. 19 cm. (Half-title: Aunt Amy's animal stories). c.1906. A. L. Burt Company.

--Speckled Hen's Story. Davis, J. Watson, illus. (Aunt Amy's Animal Stories). N.D. A. L. Burt Co.

--Towser Dog's Story. Davis, J. Watson, illus. LC 6-10311. 74 p. col. front., illus., plates. 19 cm. (Half-title: Aunt Amy's animal stories). c.1906. A. L. Burt Company.

Prentice, Harry

--Ben Burton: The Slate-Picker. LC 12-37751. 275 p. incl. front., illus. 19 cm. (On cover: Boys' library. v. 1, no. 6). c.1888. A. L. Burt.

--The Boy Explorers. (The Alger Series for Boys). N.D. A. L. Burt's Pubs.

--The Boy Explorers: Or, The Adventures of Two Boys in Alaska. LC 12-37854. 1 p. l., 314 p. front., plates, map. 19 cm. c.1895. A. L. Burt.

--The Boy Explorers: The Adventures of Two Boys in Alaska. (Wide Awake Boys Ser.). N.D. A. L. Burt.

--Captured by Apes: Or, How Philip Garland Became King of Apeland. LC 12-377527. 286 p. incl. front., illus. 19 cm. c.1892. A. L. Burt.

--Captured by Apes: Or, How Philip Garland Became King of Apeland. (The Alger Series For Boys). N.D. A. L. Burt's Pubs.

--Captured by Apes: Or, How Philip Garland Became King of Apeland. (Wide Awake Boys Ser.). N.D. A. L. Burt.

--Captured by Zulus. A Story of Trapping in Africa. LC 12-37753. 282 p. incl. front., illus. 20 cm. (On cover: Boy's home library. no. 24). c.1890. A. L. Burt.

--Captured by Zulus: A Story of Trapping in Africa. (The Alger Series for Boys). N.D. A. L. Burt's Pubs.

--Captured by Zulus: A Story of Trapping in Africa. (Wide Awake Boys Ser.). N.D. A. L. Burt.

--The King of Apeland. The Wonderful Adventures of a Young Animal Trainer. LC 12-37755. 286 p. incl. front., illus. 19 cm. (On cover: Boys' library. v. 1, no. 18). c.1888. A. L. Burt.

--The Slate Picker. (Illus.). (The Alger Series for Boys). N.D. A. L. Burt's Pubs.

--The Slate-Picker. A Story of Boy's Life in the Coal Mines. LC 12-37754. 275 p. incl. front., illus. 19 cm. c.1892. A. L. Burt.

--The Slate Picker: Story of a Boy's Life in the Coal Mines. (Wide Awake Boys Ser.). N.D. A. L. Burt.

Prentice, William Kelly (1871-), tr. see Leander, Richard.

Prentice, William Kelly (1871-), tr. see Volkmann, Richard von.

Prentiss, Annie L.

--Mother Annie and her Little Maggie. N.D. G. P. Putman's Sons.

Prentiss, Elizabeth Payson, Mrs. (1818-1878)

--Aunt Jane's Hero. LC 7-30082. 92 p. 20 cm. 1871. A. D. F. Randolph & Co.

--Aunt Jane's Hero. 1898. A. Wessels Co.

--The Flower of the Family. 12cm. 1898. A. Wessels Co.

--The Flower of the Family: A Book for Girls. new stereotype ed. with an introductory note. LC 7-30081. vii p., 1 l., 9-370 p. 20 cm. 1883. A. D. F. Randolph & Company.

--The Flower of the Family: A Book for Girls. new ed. with an introductory note. vii, 9-370 p. 18 cm. (The Flower of the Family Ser.). c.1898. A. D. F. Randolph Company.

--Fred, and Maria, and Me. Rev ed. Magrath, W., illus. LC 7-30080. 3 p. l., 3-71 p. front., plates. 17 cm. 1868. C. Scribner & Company.

--Henry and Bessie: Or, What They Did in the Country. LC 7-30079. 198 p. front., illus. 18 cm. (On cover: Golden thread series). c.1883. A. D. F. Randolph & Co.

--The Home at Greylock. LC 7-30078. 1 p. l., 338 p. 20 cm. 1876. A. D. F. Randolph & Company.

--The Home at Greylock. LC 98-1632. 1 p. l., 338 p. 18 cm. c.1898. A. D. F. Randolph Company.

--The Home at Greylock. N.D. A. Wessels Co.

--Little Lou's Sayings and Doings. Rev ed. Stone, M. L., illus. LC 7-30077. 1 p. l., 287 p. front. 20 cm. 1868. Hurd and Houghton.

--The Little Preacher. N.D. A. D. F. Randolph.

--Little Susy Stories. (Illus.). (The Wellesley Series for Girls). N.D. A. L. Burt.

--Little Susy Stories. LC 1-31489. vi, 3-73, 105, 95 p. front., 2 pl. 19 cm. c.1901. The Mershon Company.

--Little Susy Stories. Davis, J. Watson, illus. LC 26-7500. 2 p. l., 88 p. front. 19 cm. 1912. A. L. Burt Company.

--Little Susy Story. (Home Series for Girls). N.D. Hurst & Co.

--Little Susy's Library: Containing: Little Susy's Six Birthdays, Little Susy's Six Teachers, LittleSusy's Little Servants, 3 Vols. 1882. A D F Randolph.

--Little Susy's Little Servants. LC 78-240581. 15cm. (The Little Susy Library). 1869. A. D. F. Randolph.

--Little Susy's Little Servants. 2 v. in 1. front., 2 pl. 18 cm. c.1883. A. D. F. Randolph & Company.

--Little Susy's Six Birthdays. 2 v. in l. fronts., 2 pl. 18 cm. c.1883. A. D. F. Randolph & Company.

--Little Susy's Six Birthdays. LC 98-1634. 2 v. fronts., plates. 18 cm. c.1898. A. D. F. Randolph Company.

--Little Susy's Six Birthdays, Six Teachers, Little Servants, 3 Vols in 1. (Illus.). 1910. Frederick Warne & Co.

--Little Susy's Six Birthdays, Six Teachers, Six Servants. LC 7-30969. iv p., 4 l., 3-258 p. front., plates. 22 cm. c.1895. A. D. F. Randolph and Company.

--Little Susy's Six Servants. (Illus.). N.D. A. Wessels Co.

--Little Susy's Six Teachers. 2 v. in 1. fronts., 2 pl. 18 cm. c.1883. A. D. F. Randolph & Company.

--Little Susy's Six Teachers. (Illus.). N.D. A. Wessels Co.

--Little Threads. (Illus.). N.D. Set. Cheap Sunday-School Library.

--Little Threads: Or, Tangle Thread, Silver Thread, and Golden Thread. LC 7-300752. 191 p. incl. front. pl. 18 cm. 1863. A. D. F. Randolph.

--Nidworth and His Three Magic Wands. LC 7-30074. iv, 279 p. front. 17 cm. 1870. Roberts Brothers.

--Only a Dandelion and Other Stories. LC 7-300728. vi, 9-308 p. front. 18 cm. 1884. A. D. F. Randolph & Company.

--Only a Dandelion, and Other Stories. By the Author of "Little Susy's Six Birthdays", and "The Flower of the Family" ... LC 7-30073. 3 p. l., v-vi, 9-308 p. front., plates. 18 cm. 1854. A. D. F. Randolph.

--Pemaquid: A Story of Old Times in New England. N.D. A. Wessels Co.

--The Percys. LC 7-30071. 341 p. front. 17 cm. (The Flower of the Family Ser.). 1870. A. D. F. Randolph & Co.

--Peterchen and Gretchen. (Illus.). (The Golden Thread Ser.). N.D. A D F Randolph & Co.

--Six Little Princesses. (Home Series for Girls). N.D. Hurst & Co.

--Six Little Princesses and What They Turned Into. LC 7-30070. 75 p. front., plates. 19 cm. 1871. A. D. F. Randolph & Company.

--Six Little Princesses and What They Turned Into, 36p(Illus.). (St. Nicholas Ser.). 1904. Set. A L Burt Co.

--Six Little Princesses and What they Turned Into. (Illus.). (The Wellesley Series for Girls). N.D. A. L. Burt.

--Six Little Princesses,and What They Turned Into. (Illus.). N.D. Caldwell.

--Stepping Heavenward. (Illus.). N.D. A. Wessels Co.

--The Story Lizzie Told. LC 7-30122. 48 p. front., pl. 19 cm. 1870. A. D. F. Randolph & Co.

--The Story Lizzie Told and Six Little Princesses. N.D. A D F Randolph & Co.

--Thirteen Little Black Pigs, and Other Stories, 36 vols. (Illus.). (St. Nicholas Ser.). 1905. Set. A L Burt Co.

--Urbane and His Friends. N.D. A. Wessels Co.

Presberg, Miriam Goldstein see Gilbert, Miriam, pseud.

Presbyterian Church in the U. S. A

--When the Little Child Wants to Sing: For Use with Four-and Five-Years-Olds in Home, School, and Church School. Laufer, Calvin Welss (1874-), ed. LC 35-9481. x, 104 p. 26 cm. 1935. The Westminster Press.

Prescott, D. M.

--Noah & His Ark. (Very First Bible Stories Ser.). (gr. k-4). 1984. (ISBN 0-87162-273-4). Warner Pr.

Prescott, Della R.

--A Day in a Colonial Home. Dana, John Cotton, ed. N.D. Marshall Jones Co.

Prescott, E. Livingston, pseud., see Jay, Edith Katharine Spicer.

Prescott, John Brewster (1919-)

--The Beautiful Ship: A Story of the Great Lakes. Thomas, Allan (1901-), illus. LC 52-5640. 182 p. illus. 21 cm. 1952. Longmans, Green.

--Meeting in the Mountains. Tomchik, Larry, illus. LC 53-6668. (Illus.). 181 p. 21cm. 1953. Longmans, Green.

--The Renegade. LC 54-5389. 232p. 20cm. 1954. Random House.

Prescott, Mary N.

--Matt's Follies. 1873. James R. Osgood.

--Matt's Follies. (Illus.). N.D. James Miller.

Prescott, Michael

--Duggie the Digger and His Friends. Downes, Gerry, illus. LC 72-192515. (Illus.). 120 p. 20cm. (Puffin books). (A Young Puffin Original). 1972. (ISBN 0-14-030532-7). Penguin Books.

Prescott, Orville (1908-), ed.

--A Father Reads to His Children: An Anthology of Prose and Poetry. 1st ed. LC 65-19455. 352 p. 24 cm. 1965. Dutton.

--Robin Hood: The Outlaw of Sherwood Forest. Beck, Charles, illus. LC 59-6144. 51p. illus. 22cm. (Legacy books, Y-8). 1959. Random House.

Presencer, Alain

--Roaring Lion Tales. Van der Meer, Ron, illus. (Illus.). (gr. 1-5). 1984. (ISBN 0-911745-65-3, Bedrick Blackie). P Bedrick Bks.

Pressense, Domitille De see De Pressense, Domitille.

Presto, Linda

--Pink Panther Book. Baker, Darrell, illus. (Illus.). (A Golden Book for Early Childhood Ser.). (gr. k-3). 1979. (ISBN 0-307-68944-1, Golden Pr). Western Pub.

Preston, Annie A, Mrs. & Thayer, E. S.

--Drop's Dog, and Other Stories. LC 44-14234. (Illus.). 18cm. 68p. 1878. D. Lothrop & Co.

Preston, Annie & Butterworth, Hezekiah (1839-1905)

--Robin Hood Series: Includes "Drop's Dog," Jack's First Contract," "Robin Hood's Miarcle," "Bunch and Joker," "Tyrant Tom," and "What Johnny Found.", 6 vols. (Illus.). N.D. Set. D Lothrop.

Preston, Carol

--A Trilogy of Christmas Plays for Children. LC 67-171573. (Illus.). 135 p. 21cm. 1967. Harcourt, Brace & World.

Preston, Charles

--Robby's Dream Rocket. (Illus.). 76p. (gr. k-2). 1975. (ISBN 0-8181-0343-4). Pageant-Poseidon.

Preston, Charles G, jt. auth. see Place, Marian Templeton.

Preston, Chloe

--Peek-A-Boos at Play. N.D. George H Doran.

Preston, David R. (1922-)

--Uncle Pockets. Doty, Roy, created by. Doty, Roy (1922-), illus. LC 51-14149. unpaged illus. 25 cm. N.D. Dodd, Mead.

Preston, Edna Mitchell

--The Boy Who Could Make Things. 1st ed. Kessler, Leonard P. (1921-), illus. LC 77-102921. (Illus.). 48 p. 24cm. 1970. Viking Press.

--Horrible Hepzibah. 1st ed. Cruz, Raymond (1933-), illus. LC 71-136822. (Illus.). 42 p. 21cm. 1971. (ISBN 0-670-37877-1). Viking Press.

--Ickle Bickle Robin. Sandin, Joan (1942-), illus. LC 72-3985. (Illus.). 32 p. 25cm. 1973. (ISBN 0-531-02591-8). F. Watts.

--Monkey in the Jungle. Hurd, Clement (1908-), illus. LC 68-27563. (Illus.). 1 v. (unpaged. 1968. Viking Press. **Award: (BGH).**

--One Dark Night. Werth, Kurt (1896-), illus. LC 76-85868. (Illus.). 28 p. 1969. Viking Press.

--Pop Corn & Ma Goodness. Parker, Robert Andrew (1927-), illus. LC 71-85864. (Illus.). 35 p. 1969. Viking Press. **Awards: (ALA); (RCM).**

--The Sad Story of the Little Bluebird and the Hungry Cat. Cooney, Barbara (1917-), illus. LC 75-12570. (Illus.). 32 p. 1975. (ISBN 0-590-07370-2). Four Winds Press.

--Squawk to the Moon, Little Goose. 1st ed. Cooney, Barbara (1917-), illus. LC 72-91394. (Illus.). 32 p. 24cm. 1974. Viking Press.

--Squawk to the Moon, Little Goose. Cooney, Barbara (1917-), illus. (Illus.). 32p. 23cm. (Viking seafarer books). 1976, c.1974. (ISBN 0-670-05103-9). Viking Press.

--The Temper Tantrum Book. Bennett, Rainey (1907-), illus. LC 76-29003. p. cm. (Puffin books). 1976. (ISBN 0-14-050181-9). Penguin Books.

--The Temper Tantrum Book. Bennett, Rainey (1907-), illus. LC 69-13075. (Illus.). 36 p. 26cm. 1969. Viking Press.

--Toolittle. Servello, Joe (1932-), illus. LC 69-13074. (Illus.). 47 p. 25cm. 1969. Viking Press.

--Where Did My Mother Go?. Conover, Chris (1950-), illus. LC 77-15064. (Illus.). 28 p. 21cm. c.1978. (ISBN 0-590-07347-8). Four Winds Press.

Preston, Effa Estelle (1884-)

--High School Assembly Plays. 192p. N.D. T. S. Denison & Co Inc.

--Homer on the Range. 68p. 1937. T. S. Denison & Co.

--Plays for Special Occasions. 249p. 1934. T. S. Denison & Co.

--Ten Clever Plays for Children. 78 p., 1 l. 19 cm. c.1926. Eldridge Entertainment House, Inc.

--The Upper Grades Closing Day Book. 227p. N.D. T.S. Denison & Co Inc.

Preston, Effa Estelle (1884-) & Casey, Beatrice Marie

--The Closing Day Program Book. 190p. N.D. T. S. Denison & Co Inc.

--Good Things for Closing Day. 163p. N.D. T. S. Denison & Co Inc.

Preston, Effa Estelle (1884-) & Winston, Carol

--The Cobbler of Fairyland. N.D. T. S. Denison.

Preston, Hall & Barr, Catherine

--The Bear Cubs Escape. LC 53-9193. unpaged. illus. 26cm. (Oxford books for boys and girls). 1953. Oxford University Press.

--Monkey's Big Discovery. LC 59-12016. unpaged. illus. 28cm. 1950. H. Z. Walck.

--Smokey's Big Discovery. LC 59-12016. (Illus.). 28cm. 1959, c.1950. H. Z. Walck.

--Smokey's Big Discovery. LC 50-6947. (Illus.). 32 p. 28cm. (Oxford books for boys and girls). 1950. Oxford University Press.

--Snoop Waits for Dinner. LC 52-7000. unpaged. illus. 28 cm. (Oxford books for boys and girls). 1952. Oxford University Press.

Preston, Helen Bradley

--Blue Nets and Red Sails. Braley, Margaret Temple, illus. LC 36-27394. 38, 2 p. incl. col. front., illus. (part col.) 24 cm. c.1936. Longmans, Green and Co.

--Cinnamon Spice. Braley, Margaret Temple, illus. LC 39-19608. 40 p. illus. (part col.) 21 x 24 cm. c.1939. Grosset & Dunlap.

Preston, I. S., Mrs.

--Gaboon Stories. 160p. N.D. American Tract Scoiety.

Preston, John, pseud., see Johnson, Preston P..

Preston, Judy J.

--The Outer Banks Story. Preston, Judy J., illus. (Illus.). 117p. (Orig.). (gr. 5 up). 1985. (ISBN 0-9613824-0-6). Seabright.

Preston, L. E.

--Ching's Magic Brush. Mitsch, Evelyn, illus. LC 72-7659. (Illus.). 27cm. 40p. (gr. 2-5). 1973. (ISBN 0-87614-037-1). Carolrhoda Bks.

Preston, Margaret Junkin, Mrs. (1820-1897)

--Aunt Dorothy: Old Virginia Plantation Story. N.D. Lentlehon & Co.

--Chimes for Church-Children. LC 12-37740. 111 p. 15 x 12 cm. c.1889. Presbyterian Board of Publication and Sabbath-School Work.

Preston, Margaret M.

--As a White Candle. N.D. Pageant Press, Inc.

Preston, Phyllis, ed. see Thackeray, William Makepeace.

Preston, Tom

--The Peek-A-Boo Japs. Preston, Chloe, illus. N.D. George H Doran.

--The Peek-A-Boo Twins. Preston, Chloe, illus. N.D. George H Doran.

--The Peek-A-Boos and Mr. Plopper. Preston, Chloe & Howard-Vyse, George, illus. N.D. George H Doran.

--The Peek-A-Boos Holiday. Preston, Chloe, illus. N.D. George H Doran.

Prestopino, Gregorio, illus.

--The Reluctant Dragon. N.D. (ISBN 0-448-01889-6, Picture Story Books). Grosset & Dunlap.

Preus, Johan Carl Keyser (1881-)

--The Friend of the Prince. LC 48-9596. (Illus.). 78p. 19cm. 1948. Augsburg Pub. House.

Preussler, Otfried (1923-)

--The Adventures of Strong Vanya. Bell, Anthea, tr. from Ger. LC 70-120916. (Illus.). 173 p. 22cm. 1970. Abelard-Schuman.

--The Further Adventures of the Robber Hotzenplotz: A Story About Kasperl. Tripp, Franz Josef, illus. Bell, Anthea, tr. LC 71-132192. (Illus.). 124 p. 23cm. 1971. (ISBN 0-200-71706-5). Abelard-Schuman.

--The Little Ghost. Tripp, Franz Josef, illus. Bell, Anthea, tr. LC 67-16786. (Illus.). 125 p. 22cm. 1967. Abelard-Schuman.

--The Little Water Sprite. Gayler, Winnie, illus. LC 61-5791. 21cm. 127p. 1961. Abelard-Schuman.

--The Little Water-Sprite. Gayler, Winnie, illus. Bell, Anthea, tr. LC 60-13154. (Illus.). 109p. 21cm. Orig. Title: Der Kleine Wassermann, 1957. 1961, c.1960. Abelard-Schuman.

--The Little Witch. Gayler, Winnie, illus. Bell, Anthea, tr. LC 61-5791. (Illus.). 127 p. 21cm. 1961. Abelard-Schuman.

--Robber Hotzenplotz. Tripp, Franz-Josef, illus. Bell, Anthea, tr. from Ger. LC 65-10234. (Illus.). (gr. 1-4). 1965. (ISBN 0-200-71272-1). (ISBN 0-200-00013-6). Abelard.

--The Satanic Mill. Bell, Anthea, tr. LC 74-20752. p. cm. 18cm. 128p. 1970. (ISBN 0-02-044770-1). Collier Books.

--The Satanic Mill. Bell, Anthea, tr. LC 72-90992. 250 p. 22cm. 1973. (ISBN 0-02-775170-8). Macmillan. **Award: (ALA).**

--Thomas Scarecrow. Gayler, Winnie, illus. Bell, Anthea, tr. LC 64-10281. (Illus.). 21cm. 91p. (gr. 1-4). 1963. Abelard.

--The Wise Men of Schilda. Tripp, Frannz Josef, illus. Bell, Anthea, tr. from Ger. LC 63-7058. (Illus.). 185p. 21cm. 1963. Abelard-Schuman.

Prevert, Jaques Henri Marie, jt. auth. see Lamorisse, Albert Emmanuel.

Prevert, Patricia D.

--Patrick, Yes You Can. (Illus.). 48p. (Everyday Heroes Ser). 1983. (ISBN 0-87191-891-9). Creative Ed.

Prevost, M. C.

--Terra Cotta Plays: Contains; "The Sleeping Beauty", "The White Cat", and "Snowdrop and the Seven Dwarf". (Half Hour Play Series: Vol. 3). N.D. Frederick Stokes.

Prewett, Gloria McRae

--Dandy Doodle Day. McMahon, Sara Morgan, illus. LC 68-13296. (Illus.). 28 p. 20cm. 1968. Naylor Co.

Price, jt. auth. see Watson.

Price, Al

--Haunted by a Paintbrush. 1968. (ISBN 0-516-04834-1). Childrens Press.

Price, Barbara Pradal

--The Miracle of the Golden Doors. Bernstein, Zena, illus. LC 75-124177. (Illus.). 64 p. 19cm. 1971. (ISBN 0-13-585281-1). Prentice-Hall.

Price, Beverley Joan see Randell, Beverly, pseud.

Price, C. Eleanor

--Two Half Sovereigns: A Christmas Story. N.D. E J B Young.

Price, Christine Hilda, jt. ed. see Keely, Harry Harris.

Price, Christine Hilda (1928-1980), ed. see Mesfin Habte-Mariam.

Price, Christine Hilda (1928-1980)

--David and the Mountain. 1st ed. Price, Christine Hilda (1928-1980), illus. LC 59-8305. 135p. illus. 22cm. 1959. Longmans, Green.

--The Dragon and the Book. 1st ed. Price, Christine Hilda (1928-1980), illus. LC 53-8760. (Illus.). 196 p. 22cm. 1953. Longmans, Green.

--Made in The Midldle Ages. Price, Christine Hilda (1928-1980), illus. N.D. E. P. Dutton & Co.

--One Is God: Two Old Counting Songs. Price, Christine Hilda (1928-1980), illus. LC 72-100339. (Illus.). 48 p. 1970. (ISBN 0-7232-6075-3). F. Warne.

--Sixty at a Blow: A Tall Tale from Turkey. 1st ed. Price, Christine Hilda (1928-1980), illus. LC 68-16253. (Illus.). 44 p. 26cm. 1968. Dutton.

--Song of the Wheels. 1st. ed. LC 56-9219. 214p. illus. 21cm. 1956. Longmans, Green.

--Three Golden Nobles. 1st ed. Price, Christine Hilda (1928-1980), illus. LC 51-12261. (Illus.). 239 p. 21cm. 1951. Longmans, Green.

--Widdecombe Fair. Price, Christine Hilda (1928-1980), illus. LC 68-10978. (Illus.). 2-color line cuts. 40p. (gr. k-4). 1968. Warne.

AUTHOR INDEX PRIESTLEY, LEE

Price, Christine Hilda (1928-1980), retold by.
--The Valiant Chattee-Maker: A Folktale of India. LC 65-10030. 1 v. (unpaged) illus. (pt. col.) 22x23cm. c.1965. (ISBN 0-7232-0348-2). Warne.
Price-Clarke, Robyn
--Stories for Children. 1979. (ISBN 0-533-03493-0). Vantage.
Price, Edith Ballinger (1897-)
--Blue Magic. Price, Edith Ballinger (1897-), illus. LC 19-14008. 6 p. l., 3-130 p. front., plates. 20 cm. 1919. The Century Co.
--A Citizen of Nowhere. Price, Edith Ballinger (1897-), illus. LC 27-229989. 4 p. l., 264 p. col. front., plates. 20 cm. c.1927. Greenberg.
--The Enchanted Admiral. Price, Edith Ballinger (1897-) & Dutch, C. I., illus. LC 31-22650. ix, 281 p. incl. front., illus., plates. 20 cm. c.1931. The Century Co.
--The Fork in the Road. Price, Edith Ballinger (1897-), illus. LC 30-23903. vii, 240 p. front., plates. 20 cm. c.1930. The Century Co.
--The Fortune of the Indies. Price, Edith Ballinger (1897-), illus. LC 22-17388. 6 p. l., 3-255 p. front., plates. 20 cm. 1922. The Century Co.
--The Four Winds. Price, Edith Ballinger (1897-), illus. N.D. Frederick A. Stokes Co.
Garth: Able Seaman. 200p. N.D. Century Co.
--Gervaise of the Garden. Price, Edith Ballinger (1897-), illus. LC 27-340888. v, 162 p. illus. 20 cm. c.1927. The Century Co.
--The Happy Venture. Price, Edith Ballinger (1897-), illus. LC 21-15253. 5 p. l., 3-204 p. front., plates. 20 cm. 1921. The Century Co.
--John and Susanne. Price, Edith Ballinger (1897-), illus. LC 26-15710. vii, 244 p. front., plates. 20 cm. c.1926. The Century Co.
--Lubber's Luck. Price, Edith Ballinger (1897-), illus. LC 35-17495. x p., 2 l., 3-275 p. incl. front., plates. 21 cm. 1935. Little, Brown, and Company.
--The Luck of Glenlorn. Todd, Robert, illus. LC 29-195142. vii p., 2 l., 3-224 p. front., plates. 20 cm. c.1929. The Century Co.
--Ship of Dreams. Price, Edith Ballinger (1897-), illus. LC 27-18850. ix, 267 p. front., plates. 20 cm. 1927. The Century Co.
--Silver Shoal Light. 351p. N.D. Century Co.
--Turn of Tide: The Mystery of Piper's Island. Price, Edith Ballinger (1897-), illus. LC 37-18439. 6 p. l., 276 p. incl. front., illus. 20 cm. 1937. D. Appleton-Century Company, Incorporated.
--Us and the Bottle Man. Price, Edith Ballinger (1897-), illus. LC 20-14292. 4 p. l., 3-154 p. front., plates. 20 cm. 1920. The Century Co.
Price, Edward
--Storm Nelson & the Sea Leopard. (gr. 7 up). N.D. Soccer.
Price, Elizabeth Robinson Walker, Mrs. (1863-)
--The Jolly Shipleys. LC 19-45140. 3 p. l., 244 p. front. 20 cm. c.1918. The Pilgrim Press.
Price, Emerson
--Cranberry Bear. (gr. 2-6). N.D. Carlton.
Price, Helen F
--On the Hilltop. LC 27-8147. 115, 1 p. 21 cm. c.1927. Dorrance and Company.
Price, Hilda Cumings
--No Way Back: A Story of the Civil War in England in the Reign of King Charles the First. 1st ed. Price, Christine Hilda (1928-1980), illus. LC 52-12958. (Illus.). 192 p. 21cm. 1953. Dutton.
--Song of Roland. Price, Christine Hilda (1928-1980), illus. (Illus.). (gr. 7-10). 1961. (ISBN 0-7232-0258-3). Warne.
--Two's Company: A Story for Children. Wynne, D. L., illus. LC 51-14509. 176p. illus. 19cm. c.1951. Warne.
Price, James T.
--The Big Red Choo Choo. N.D. (ISBN 0-685-33195-4). Vantage.
Price, Lee
--The Tree that Always Said No. LC 73-90617. (Illus.). 24cm. 35p. c.1973. St. Paul Editions.
Price, Lillian Louise (1865-)
--Lads and Lassies of Other Days. LC 6-138. 180 p. incl. front., illus., plates. 20 cm. (Stories of colony and nation). c.1905. Silver, Burdett and Company.
Price, Lillian Louise (1865-) & Gilbert, Charles Benajah (1855-1913)
--Heroes of Myth. LC 2-23757. xv, 176 p. incl. front., illus., plates. 19 cm. (Stories of heroes ed. by C. B. Gilbert). 1902. Silver,Burdett and Company.
Price, Lucien
--Winged Sandals. N.D. Little, Brown & Co.
Price, Luxor
--The Quoks. LC 24-20508. 62, 2 p. incl. col. front., illus. (part col.) 31 cm. 1924. Frederick A. Stokes Company.
Price, Margaret Evans, Mrs. (1888-1973)
--Animals Marooned. LC 43-16957. 5 p. l., 185 p. incl. front., illus. 21 1/2 cm. 1943. Harper & Brothers.
--A Child's Book of Myths. Price, Margaret Evans, Mrs. (1888-1973), illus. LC 24-30802. 2 p. l., 3-112 p. col. illus., col. pl. 27 cm. c.1924. Rand, McNally & Company.
--Down Comes the Wilderness. LC 37-4380. ix p., 1 l., 212 p. incl. front., illus., plates. 21 cm. 1937. Harper & Brothers.
--Enchantment Tales for Children. Price, Margaret Evans, Mrs. (1888-1973), illus. LC 26-15412. 118 p. col. illus. 27 cm. c.1926. Rand, McNally & Company.
--Monkey-Do. Price, Margaret Evans, Mrs. (1888-1973), illus. LC 34-6717. xi p., 1 l., 149 p. incl. front., illus. 22 cm. 1934. Harper & Brothers.
--Mota and the Monkey Tree. LC 35-18846. ix p., 1 l., 146 p. incl. front., illus. 22 cm. 1935. Harper & Brothers.
--The Windy Shore: A Tale of Old Marseilles. Price, Margaret Evans, Mrs. (1888-1973), illus. LC 30-25451. vii p., 1 l., 181 p. col. front., illus., plates (part double) 24 cm. 1930. Harper & Brothers.
Price, Margaret Evans, Mrs. (1888-1973), retold by.
--Legends of the Seven Seas. Price, Margaret Evans, Mrs. (1888-1973), illus. LC 29-15599. 23cm. 168p. 1929. Harper & Brothers.
--Myths and Enchantment Tales. Price, Margaret Evans, Mrs. (1888-1973), illus. LC 36-123192. 160 p. incl. col. front., illus. (part col.) col. pl. 24 cm. 1935. Rand, McNally & Company.
--Myths and Enchantment Tales. Urbanowich, Evelyn, illus. LC 60-8267. 192p. col. illus. 23cm. c.1960. Rand McNally.
--A Treasure Chest of Nursery Favorites. Winter, Milo Kendall, illus. LC 36-10236. 160 p. incl. col. front., illus. (part col.) 23 1/2 cm. c.1936. Rand, McNally & Company.
Price, Marjorie
--Alphadabbles: A Playful Alphabet. LC 79-18129. (Illus.). 128p. 1980. (ISBN 0-394-84303-7). Pantheon.
Price, Mathew
--I Want My Mommy. Claverie, Jean (1946-), illus. LC 85-23175. p. cm. 1986, c.1985. (ISBN 0-394-88180-X). Knopf : Distributed by Random House.
--Knock! Knock! Who's There?. Claverie, Jean (1946-), illus. LC 85-7677. p cm. 1st U.S. edition. c.1985. (ISBN 0-394-87536-2). Knopf.
--My Daddy. Claverie, Jean (1946-), illus. LC 85-7573. p. cm. 1st U.S. edition. c.1985. (ISBN 0-394-87537-0). Knopf.
--Peekaboo!. Claverie, Jean (1946-), illus. LC 84-40451. (Illus.). 20 p. 24cm. c.1985. (ISBN 0-394-87142-1). Knopf : Distributed by Random House.
Price, Michelle
--Mean Melissa. LC 77-75361. p. cm. 26cm. 32p. c.1977. (ISBN 0-87888-126-3). Bradbury Press.
Price, Norman Mills (1877-1951), tr. see Lang, Jeanie, Mrs.
Price, Olive, adapted by see London, Jack.
Price, Olive, adapted by see Lothrop, Harriet Mulford Stone, Mrs.
Price, Olive M. see Cherryholmes, Anne, pseud.
Price, Olive M. (1903-), ed. see Ollivant, Alfred.
Price, Olive M (1903-)
--The Blue Harbor. LC 56-1658. 176p. 21cm. 1956. Washburn.
--The Boy with One Shoe. Frame, Paul (1913-), illus. LC 63-10170. 95 p. illus. 21 cm. 1963. Coward-McCann.
--The Dog That Watched the Mountain. Miller, Marilyn Jean (1925-), illus. LC 67-152887. 123p. illus. 22cm. 1967. Coward.
--A Donkey for the King. Angelo, Valenti (1897-), illus. LC 45-3925. 6 p. l., 73 p. col. illus. 21 cm. 1945. Whittlesey House.
--The Donkey with Diamond Ears: A Salute to Little Donkeys at Work in the Jewel Mines of Brazil. Hunter, Mel (1927-), illus. LC 62-8007. 96p. illus: 22cm. 1962. Coward-McCann.
--From Picture Book Towne. LC 31-28770. 1 p. l., 10 p. 23 cm. 1931. United States George Washington Bicentennial Commission.
--The Glass Mountain. LC 54-123861. 178p. illus. 21cm. 1954. I. Washburn.
--The Golden Wheel. Eshner, Ann, illus. LC 58-8142. 175p. illus: 21cm. 1958. Westminster Press.
--The Island of the Silver Spoon. Cherryholmes, Anne, pseud. Jaeger, Elinor, illus. LC 63-8211. 93 p. illus. 21 cm. 1963. Coward-McCann.
--The Island of the Voyageurs. Cherryholmes, Anne, pseud. Jaeger, Elinor, illus. LC 64-17998. 125 p. illus. 21 cm. 1964. Coward-McCann.
--Kim Walk-in-My-Shoes. Funai, Mamoru R. (1932-), illus. LC 68-14318. (Illus.). 126 p. 22cm. 1968. Coward-McCann.
--Miracle by the Sea. Burbank, Addison Bushnell (1895-), illus. LC 47-11734. 136 p. illus. 21 cm. 1947. Whittlesey House.
--Mystery of the Sunken City. Hall, H. Tom, illus. LC 62-726762. 140p. illus: 21cm. 1962. Westminster Press.
--The Phantom Reindeer. Hunter, Mel (1927-), illus. LC 61-8259. 94p. illus: 22cm. 1961. Coward-McCann.
--The Redbud Tree. LC 31-287803. 1 p. l., 18 p. 23 cm. 1931. United States George Washington Bicentennial Commission.
--Reindeer Island. Hall, H. Tom, illus. LC 60-5359. (Illus.). 158 p. 21cm. 1960. Westminster Press.
--River Boy. Hamilton, Bill, illus. LC 59-5524. 176p. illus. 21cm. 1959. Wetminster Press.
--Snifty. Hamilton, Bill, illus. LC 57-8071. 157p. illus. 21cm. 1957. Westminster Press.
--Story of Clara Barton. Ives, Ruth, illus. (Illus.). (gr. 4-6). 1954. (ISBN 0-448-05625-9, Sign). G&D.
--The Story of Marco Polo. Castellon, Federico (1914-), illus. LC 53-8125. 179p. illus. 22cm. (Signature books, 22). 1953. (ISBN 0-448-05622-4). Grosset & Dunlap.
--Three Golden Rivers. LC 48-8227. 272 p. 21 cm. 1948. Bobbs-Merrill Co.
--The Valley of the Dragon: A Story of the Times of Kublai Khan. 1st ed. Moment, John, illus. LC 51-9968. 250 p. illus. 21 cm. (Stories of children in great times). 1951. Bobbs-Merrill.
Price, Pattie
--Bantu Tales. Smith, Desmond, illus. LC 38-148941. 64 p. col. illus. 23 cm. 1938. E. P. Dutton & Co., Inc.
Price, Ralston R.
--Duckie: Memoirs of a Cowboy. N.D. Pageant Press, Inc.
Price, Roger (1921-)
--Captain America Mad Libs. 48p. (Orig.). (Marvel Mad Libs Ser.). 1981. (ISBN 0-8431-0702-2). Price Stern.
--Casper, the Friendly Ghost Mad Libs. 48p. (Orig.). 1981. (ISBN 0-8431-0704-9). Price Stern.
--Incredible Hulk Mad Libs. 48p. (Orig.). (Marvel Comics Mad Libs Ser.). 1981. (ISBN 0-8431-0716-2). Price Stern.
--The Last Little Dragon. Funai, Mamoru R. (1932-), illus. LC 71-77943. (Illus.). 31 p. 1969. Harper & Row.
--Pebbles & Bamm-Bamm with Dino Mad Libs. 48p. 1981. (ISBN 0-8431-0705-7). Price Stern.
--Popeye Mad Libs. 48p. 1981. (ISBN 0-8431-0703-0). Price Stern.
--Scooby-Doo & Scrappy-Doo Mad Libs. 48p. 1981. (ISBN 0-8431-0706-5). Price Stern.
--Spiderman Mad Libs. 48p. (Marvel Mad Libs Ser.). 1981. (ISBN 0-8431-0701-4). Price Stern.
--Spiderwoman Mad Libs. 48p. (Marvel Mad Libs Ser.). 1981. (ISBN 0-8431-0715-4). Price Stern.
Price, Susan (1955-)
--The Carpenter and Other Stories. LC 82-670029. 126 p. 21cm. 1981. (ISBN 0-571-11731-7). Faber and Faber.
--Christopher Uptake. 208p. (gr. 5-12). 1981. (ISBN 0-571-11660-4). Faber & Faber.
--The Devil's Piper. LC 75-29467. 216 p. 22cm. 1976, c.1973. (ISBN 0-688-80030-0). (ISBN 0-688-84030-2). Greenwillow Books.
--From Where I Stand. LC 83-20827. 128p. (gr. 6 up). 1984. (ISBN 0-571-13247-2). (ISBN 0-571-13247-2). Faber & Faber.
--Ghosts at Large. Price, Alison, illus. LC 84-13510. (Illus.). 90p. (gr. 2-6). 1984. (ISBN 0-571-13282-0). (ISBN 0-571-13282-0). Faber & Faber.
--Home from Home. LC 77-360148. 123 p. 21cm. 1977. (ISBN 0-571-11022-3). Faber and Faber.
--In a Nutshell. LC 82-25152. p. cm. 1983. (ISBN 0-571-13075-5). Faber and Faber.
--Sticks & Stones. 136p. (gr. 6-8). N.D. (ISBN 0-571-10842-3). Faber & Faber.
Price, Willard DeMille (1887-)
--African Adventure. LC 62-20146. 189 p. 21 cm. 1963. John Day Co.
--Amazon Adventure. LC 49-109441. x, 242 p. 21 cm. 1949. J. Day Co.
--Cannibal Adventure. Marriott, Patricia (1920-), illus. LC 78-179785. (Illus.). 244 p. 21cm. 1973, c.1972. (ISBN 0-381-99640-9). John Day Co.
--Diving Adventure. LC 70-117170. 181 p. 21cm. 1970. John Day Co.
--Elephant Adventure. LC 64-10449. 20cm. 192p. 1964. John Day & Co.
--Gorilla Adventure. LC 69-11856. 189 p. 22cm. 1969. John Day Co.
--Lion Adventure. LC 67-13581. 189 p. 22cm. 1967. John Day Co.
--Safari Adventure. LC 66-15103. 187 p. 21cm. 1966. John Day Co.
--South Sea Adventure. Price, Willard DeMille, illus. LC 52-6179. (Illus.). 243 p. 21cm. 1952. J. Day Co.
--Tiger Adventure. Marriott, Patricia (1920-), illus. (Illus.). 240p. (gr. 3-6). 1980. (ISBN 0-224-01674-1, Pub. by Chatto Bodley Jonathan). Merrimack Pub Cir.
--Underwater Adventure. LC 54-11494. 191p. illus. 21cm. 1954. J. Day Co.
--Volcano Adventure. 192p. 1956. John Day & Co.
--Volcano Adventure. (Illus.). 192p. (gr. 3 up). 1983. (ISBN 0-224-60624-7, Pub by Jonathan Cape). Merrimack Pub Cir.
--Whale Adventure. LC 60-5649. 191p. 22cm. 1960. J. Day Co.
Price & Watson
--Animal Stories. (Animal Story Books). (gr. k-4). 1982. (ISBN 0-86020-666-1, Usborne-Hayes). EDC.
Prichard, Katharine Susannah (1884-)
--The Wild Oats of Han. Melrose, Genevieve, illus. LC 72-92446. (Illus.). 184 p. 22cm. 1973. (ISBN 0-02-775200-3). Macmillan.
Prichard, Lillian
--Stormy, The Brave Sponge Diver. Key, Alexander Hill (1904-1979), illus. 1955. The Dietz Press.
Prichard, Marianna Nugent
--Long Night to Tokyo. Hutchinson, William Miller (1916-), illus. LC 67-11856. 127p. illus. 19cm. 1967. Friendship.
Prichard, Sarah Johnson (1830-1909)
--Aunt Saidee's Cow. LC 7-300684. vii, 5-357 p. incl. front., plates. 18 cm. 1873. R. Carter and Brothers.
--Faye Mar of Storm-Cliff. LC 7-300678. 1 p. l., iv, 5-351 p. 18 cm. 1868. Wynkoop & Sherwood.
--Hugh's Fire on the Mountain. N.D. A D F Randolph & Co.
--Joe and Jim. N.D. A D F Randolph & Co.
--Marjie's Matches. LC 7-300657. iv, 5-174 p. 16 cm. 1866. A. D. F. Randolph.
--The Old Stone Chimney. N.D. A D F Randolph & Co.
--Rose Marbury. LC 7-30066. vi, 7-304 p. 18 cm. 1871. R. Carter and Brothers.
--Shawny and the Light House. N.D. Robert Carter & Brothers.
--What Shawny Did to the Light-House. LC 7-300644. 144 p. front., plates. 18 cm. 1871. R. Carter and Brothers.
--The Wonderful Christmas in Pumpkin Delight Lane. LC 8-33784. 2 p. l., 185 p. 21 cm. 1908. The Tuttle Morehouse & Taylor Company.
Priddy, Frances Rosaleen (1931-)
--Barbie. LC 60-5180. 173p. 21cm. c.1960. Westminster Press.
--Challenge for Angel. LC 63-8066. 206 p. 22 cm. 1963. Westminister Press.
--The Ghosts of Lee House. 1st ed. Abrams, Abby, illus. LC 68-27813. (Illus.). 144 p. 22cm. (Doubleday Signal Books). 1968. Doubleday.
--The Grand Rogue. LC 58-6496. 244 p. 21cm. 1958. Dodd, Mead.
--Let's Go Steady. LC 61-5180. 185p. 21cm. 1961. Westminster Press.
--Sam's Country: A Small Town in the Midwest. Oughton, Taylor (1925-), illus. LC 79-77097. (Illus.). 32 p. 1969. McGraw-Hill.
--Shell Beach Mystery. 21cm. 278p. 1963. Westminster Press.
--The Social Swim. LC 62-7263. 173p. 21cm. 1962. Westminster Press.
--TV Bandstand. LC 59-5902. 192p. 21cm. 1959. Westminster Press.
Pridham, Radost (1922-)
--A Gift from the Heart: Folk Tales from Bulgaria. Baynes, Pauline Diana (1922-), illus. LC 67-13819. (Illus.). 156 p. 21cm. 1st U.S. edition. 1967, c.1966. World Pub. Co.
Priest, Jane, jt. auth. see Gordon, Elizabeth.
Priest, S. M.
--Little Pieces for Little Speakers: A Collection of Poetry. N.D. Lee & Shepard.
Priester, Gertrude Ann
--People Who Knew God. Schmidt, Eric von, illus. LC 64-14501. (Illus.). 92p. 23cm. 1964. United Church Press.
Priestley, Harold Edford (1901-)
--John Stranger. LC 62-13287. (Illus.). 21cm. 178p. (gr. 7 up). 1962. Roy.
Priestley, John Boynton (1894-)
--Snoggle. Flynn, Barbara (1928-), illus. LC 74-188966. (Illus.). 158 p. 21cm. 1st U.S. edition. 1972, c.1971. (ISBN 0-15-276430-5). Harcourt Brace Jovanovich.
Priestley, Lee Shore, et al. (1904-)
--Teen-Age Outer Space Stories. Furman, Abraham Loew (1902-), ed. LC 62-9533. 190p. illus. c.1962. Lantern Pr.
Priestley, Lee Shore (1904-)
--Believe in Spring. LC 64-12841. 191 p. 21 cm. 1964. J. Messner.
--Everygirls Detective Stories. Furman, Abraham Loew (1902-), ed. McCann, Gerald (1916-), illus. LC 61-5218. 195p. front. (Everygirls library). c.1961. (ISBN 0-8313-0060-4). Lantern Press.
--Now for Nola. LC 70-123176. 191 p. 22cm. 1970. J. Messner.
--Rocket Mouse. Theobalds, Prue, illus. LC 61-7141. 93p. illus. 21cm. 1961. Abelard-Schuman.
--Rocket to the Stars. LC 59-7016. 192 p. 22cm. 1959. J. Messner.
--A Second Look for Avis. LC 61-13823. 190 p. 22cm. 1961. J. Messner.
--A Teacher for Tibby. Sherman, Theresa (1916-), illus. LC 60-7411. (Illus.). 96 p. 22cm. (Morrow Junior Books). 1960. Morrow.

Priestman, Barbara
--The Two Houses. N.D. Nelson Bks.
Prieto, Mariana Beeching (1912-), compiled by see Armando, Baez.
Prieto, Mariana Beeching (1912-)
--Ah Ucu and Itzo: A/Story of the Mayan People of the Yucatan. Smith, Lee (1925-), illus. LC 64-10244. (Illus.). 48p. 25cm. 1964. John Day Co.
--Johnny Lost: Juanito Perdido. Hanley, Catherine, illus. LC 69-10490. (Illus.). 48p. (gr. 2-4). 1969. (ISBN 0-381-99727-8, JD-J). John Day.
--Kite for Carlos. Smith, Lee (1925-), illus. (Illus.). (gr. 2-4). 1966. John Day.
--Pablo's Petunias. Furan, Barbara Howell, illus. LC 72-190269. (Illus.). 32 p. 25cm. 1972. (ISBN 0-87783-058-4). Oddo Pub.
--Play it in Spanish: Spanish Games and Folk Songs for Children. (Illus.). 1973. (ISBN 0-381-99726-X). John Day.
--Raimundo, the Unwilling Warrior. Darwin, Beatrice, illus. LC 77-148103. (Illus.). 45 p. 27cm. 1971. (ISBN 0-8178-4821-5). Harvey House.
--Tomato Boy. Smith, Lee (1925-), illus. LC 67-630. (Illus.). 23cm. 48p. (gr. 2-4). 1967. (ISBN 0-381-99725-1, JD-J). Har-Row.
--Tomato Boy. Smith, Lee (1925-), illus. LC 67-630. (Illus.). 48 p. 25cm. 1967. John Day Co.
--When the Monkeys Wore Sombreros. Quackenbush, Robert Mead (1929-), illus. LC 69-10586. (Illus.). 36 p. 1969. Harvey House.
--The Wise Rooster. El Gallo Sabio. Smith, Lee (1925-), illus. LC 62-14901. (Illus.). unpaged. 26cm. 1962. John Day Co.
Prieto, Mariana Beeching (1912-), ed.
--Play It in Spanish: Spanish Games & Folk Songs for Children. Shekerjian, Regina, illus. Nielson, Elizabeth C., compiled by. LC 79-140474. (Illus.). music examples. 48p. 1st U.S. edition. (gr. 1-4). 1973. (ISBN 0-381-99726-X, JD-J). Har-Row.
Priley, Margaret Hubbard see Hubbard, Margaret Ann.
Primachenko, Maria, illus.
--Hey Hey My Dapple Greys. (Illus.). 16p. 1976. (ISBN 0-8285-1159-4, Pub. by Progress Pubs USSR). Imported Pubns.
Primary Assn. General Board, jt. ed. see Deseret Sunday School Union Board.
Primavera, Elise
--Basil & Maggie. 1st ed. Primavera, Elise, illus. LC 82-48455. (Illus.). 31 p. c.1983. (ISBN 0-397-32027-2). (ISBN 0-397-32028-0). Lippincott.
Primavera, Elise, jt. auth. see Crayder, Dorothy.
Primavera, Elise, jt. auth. see St. Peter, Joyce.
Prime, Honor
--Matthew's Ear. Spence, Geraldine (1931-), illus. (Illus.). (ps-5). N.D. (ISBN 0-571-06063-3). Faber & Faber.
--Moonface. N.D. Transatlantic Arts.
Prime, Samuel Irenaeus (1812-1885)
--The Prodigal Reclaimed. Or, The Sinner's Ruin and Recovery. LC 7-30062. 220 p. front. 16 cm. 1843. Massachusetts Sabbath School Society.
Primmer, Phyllis Cora Griesbach (1926-)
--At the River's Turning. LC 60-51916. 120p. 20cm. 1960. Zondervan Pub. House.
Primrose, pseud., see Robertson, Primrose McPherson.
Prince Ahmed
--The Flying Carpet: Retold from Richard Burton's Translation of the Arabian Nights. Brown, Marcia (1918-), ed. Brown, Marcia (1918-), illus. LC 56-10258. unpaged. illus. 26cm. 1956. Scribner. **Award: (ALA).**
Prince, Alison (1931-)
--The Doubting Kind. LC 77-21945. 21cm. 287p. 1977, c.1975. (ISBN 0-688-32126-7). Morrow.
--House on the Common. Mars, Witold Tadeusz J. (1912-), illus. LC 73-109562. (Illus.). 144p. 1st U.S. edition. (gr. 4 up). 1970. (ISBN 0-374-33466-8). FS&G.
--Night Landings. Thompson, Ellen, illus. LC 83-19304. (gr. 5-8). 1984. (ISBN 0-688-02753-9). (ISBN 0-688-02753-9). Morrow.
--The Red Jaguar. 1st ed. Shortall, Leonard W., illus. LC 72-75280. (Illus.). 126 p. 22cm. 1972. Atheneum.
--The Sinister Airfield. Thompson, Ellen, illus. LC 82-18877. (Illus.). 128p. 1st U.S. edition. (gr. 4-6). 1983. (ISBN 0-688-01741-X). Morrow.
--The Turkey's Nest. LC 79-28126. 223 p. 21cm. 1980. (ISBN 0-688-22224-2). (ISBN 0-688-32224-7). Morrow.
Prince, Dorothy E.
--Speedy Gets Around. Warren, Betsy, pseud. (1916-), illus. Warren, Elizabeth Avery. LC 65-12089. (Illus.). (gr. k-3). 1965. (ISBN 0-8114-7562-X). Steck-V.
Prince, E. M., tr. see Voegeli, Max.
Prince, Florence Ellenore
--At Shadow Time: Stories in Verse for Children. LC 36-10758. 52 p., 1 l. illus. 20 cm. (Contemporary poets of Dorrance (145). c.1936. Dorrance & Company.
Prince, Gary Michael (1948-) & Overlie, George
--Vanya and the Clay Queen. Baranov, I. A., illus. LC 74-9035. (Illus.). 32 p. 19cm. 1975. (ISBN 0-87614-049-5). Carolrhoda Books.
Prince, Helen Albee, Mrs.
--Grandma's Album Quilt. Shaw, George Eleanor, illus. LC 36-7790. 5 p. l., 127, 1 p. front., illus. 23 cm. 1936. Falmouth Book House.
Prince, Marjorie M.
--The Cheese Stands Alone. Lewin, Ted (1935-), illus. LC 73-6737. (Illus.). 170 p. 22cm. 1973. (ISBN 0-395-17511-9). Houghton Mifflin.
Prince, Pamela
--The Secret World of Teddy Bears: A Rare and Privileged Glimpse into the Lives They Lead When You're Not There. Keenan, Elaine Faris, illus. LC 83-27. p. cm. 1983. (ISBN 0-517-55022-9). Harmony Books.
--Teddy Bears' Christmas. Keenan, Elaine Faris & Sansone, Ken, illus. 1985. Crown Publishers.
--Teddy Bears' Christmas: Holiday Greetings from the Secret World of Teddy Bears. Keenan, Elaine Faris & Sansone, Ken, illus. LC 85-5454. (Illus.). 47 p. 29cm. c.1985. (ISBN 0-517-55671-5). Harmony Books.
Prince, Victor
--The Other Kingdom. N.D. Doubleday & Co.
Prince of Wales (1948-)
--The Old Man of Lochnager. Casson, Hugh Maxwell, Sir (1910-), illus. (Illus.). (gr. k up). 1980. (ISBN 0-374-35613-0). FS&G.
Prince Uno
--Uncle Frank's Visit to Fairyland. (Illus.). 5x7 1/2cm. 241p. N.D. Doubleday, Page & Co.
Prindle, Elinor Pauline
--Polly Prindle's Jolly Jingles. Prindle, Elinor Pauline, illus. LC 32-325509. 59 p., 1 l. incl. plates. 19 cm. 1932. The Exccelsior Press.
Pringle, Mary Poague & Urann, Clara A.
--Yule-Tide in Many Lands. Bridgman, Lewis Jesse (1857-1931), illus. N.D. Lothrop,Lee & Shepard.
Pringle, Patrick
--Danger Mountain. 232p. illus. 19cm. 1954. Roy Publishers.
--Great Day in Spain: Jose's Own Fiesta. De Guarino, Margarita Maria, illus. LC 60-13690. (Illus.). 32 p. 22cm. 1962, c.1961. Abelard-Schuman.
Prinz, Renato
--Pallina and Her Wondrous Grandmothers. Albicocco, Paul & Forlani, George, illus. LC 64-18264. 1 v. (unpaged) illus. (part col.) 27 cm. 1964. Platt & Munk.
Priolo, Pauline Pizzo (1907-)
--Bravo Marco!. Peterson, Betty Ferguson (1917-), illus. (Illus.). Repr (Pub. by Parnassus). (gr. 4-6). 1963. (ISBN 0-395-27654-3). HM.
--Bravo Marco: A Picture Book in English and Italian. LC 63-10141. (Illus.). 48 p. 26cm. 1963. Parnassus Press.
--Piccolina & the Easter Bells. Fava, Rita (1932-), illus. LC 61-9289. (Illus.). 26cm. 47p. (gr. 1 up). 1962 (Pub. by Atlantic Monthly Pr). (ISBN 0-316-71939-0). Little.
Prior, A. Fullarton, tr. see Pai She Chuan.
Prior, Beatrix, Mrs.
--Lota of the Little Trees. Mallon, Grace, illus. LC 37-124327. 4 p. l., 138, 1 p. col. front., illus. 21 cm. 1936. Suttonhouse, Ltd.
--The Shadow Cat. Arrows, Russell, illus. LC 36-706. 103 p. incl. illus., plates. 24 cm. c.1935. Suttonhouse, Ltd.
Priscilla, Carden
--Young Brave Algonquin. N.D. E . M. Hale and Co.
Prishvin, Mikhail Mikhailovich (1873-)
--The Treasure Trove of the Sun. Rojankovsky, Feodor Stepanovich (1891-1970), illus. Balkoff-Drowne, Tatiana, tr. LC 52-12492. 79 p. col. illus. 28 cm. 1952. Viking Press.
Pritchard, Clarence F., ed. see Mother Goose.
Pritchard, Clarence F & White, W. C.
--Mother Goose Circus Parade. Wood, Stacy H., illus. LC 27-24490. 122 p. illus. 30 cm. c.1927. G. P. Putnam's Sons.
Pritchard, Hesketh
--November Joe. N.D. Grosset & Dunlap.
Pritchard, Myron T., ed. see Motor, R. R.
Pritchard, S. J., Miss
--Kenny Carle's Uniform. 119p. N.D. Hurd & Houghton for American Tract Society.
--Kenny Carle's Uniform. 119p. N.D. Lockwood, Brooks, & Co. for American Tract Society.
Pritchard, Thomas W.
--Happy Andy: The Willing Worker. (Illus.). (gr. 7 up). 1976. (ISBN 0-533-02087-5). Vantage.
Pritchard, Virginia Cole
--A Christmas Story. Hickey, Frances B., illus. LC 39-22035. 26, 1 p. incl. front., illus. 25 cm. 1939. E. P. Dutton and Company, Inc.
Pritchett, Lulita Crawford
--The Cabin at Medicine Springs. D'Adamo, Anthony, illus. LC 58-9973. 195p. illus. 21cm. 1958. F. Watts.
--The Shining Mountains. Tousey, Thomas Sanford, illus. LC 39-23295. 3 p. l., 15-296 p. incl. illus., plates. col. front., col. pl. 23 cm. 1939. A. Whitman & Co.
Pritt, Carmel Lee
--Walk the Path in the Hills. LC 74-20066. (Illus.). 232 p. 22cm. 1975. (ISBN 0-87012-201-0). McClain Printing Company.
Prittie, Edwin John, adapted by.
--Robin Hood. Prittie, Edwin John, illus. Harvey, George Cockburn, intro. by. LC 57-12795. 278p. illus. 22cm. (Children's classics). 1957. Winston.
Probst, Pierre (1913-)
--Caroline at the Ranch. Probst, Pierre (1913-), illus. Dabrowska, Beata, tr. 1961. Golden Press.
--Caroline in Europe. Probst, Pierre (1913-), illus. Witty, Susan (1913-), tr. LC 62-52841. unpaged. col. illus. 32cm. (Big golden bk., 12008). 1962, c.1960. Golden.
--The Golden Treasury of Caroline & Her Friends. Probst, Pierre (1913-), illus. LC 61-2910. 32cm. 1961. Golden Press.
--Kenny and His Raft. LC 68-29536. (Illus.). 27 p. 32cm. 1968, c.1966. Hart Pub. Co.
--Kenny and His Raft. Probst, Pierre (1913-), illus. 48p. N.D. (ISBN 0-87460-159-2). Lion Press.
Prochawska, Jan
--Long Live the Republic: All About Me, & Julie, & the End of the Great War. Kussi, Peter, tr. from Czech. LC 72-76183. 264p. (gr. 6-8). 1973. (ISBN 0-385-04753-3). (ISBN 0-385-05836-5). Doubleday.
Procopio, Andrew B.
--Mister Beumpy: An Animal Fantasy. (gr. 2-6). 1970. Carlton.
Procter, E. H
--Rabbits Day in Town. (Illus.). (Happy Child's Library). N.D. Dodge Publishing Co.
Procter, Gilbert
--Panchita. (Illus.). (gr. 10 up). 1960. (ISBN 0-8111-0146-0). Naylor.
Procter, Leslie Chambers (1886-)
--For Freedom's Sake. Jones, L. Raymond, illus. LC 44-956. 347 p. incl. front., illus. (incl. maps) 21 1/2 cm. 1944. Beckley-Cardy Company.
Procter, Marjorie
--The Little Grey Donkey. (Very First Bible Stories Ser.). (gr. k-4). 1984. (ISBN 0-87162-272-6). Warner Pr.
--The Little Lost Lamb. (Very First Bible Stories Ser.). (gr. k-4). 1984. (ISBN 0-87162-276-9). Warner Pr.
Proctor, Beth
--Little Sally Dutcher. Turpin, Fay, illus. LC 24-24954. (Illus.). 58p. 23cm. (Jordan Juvenile Ser.). 1924. Jordan Pub. Co.
--The Tale of a Lucky Dog: A Japanese Story. Turpin, Fay, illus. LC 24-25640. 59 p. col. illus. 24 cm. (Jordan juvenile series). c.1924. Jordan Publishing Company.
Proctor, Everitt, pseud., see Montgomery, Rutherford George.
Proctor, Everitt, pseud. (1894-)
--The Last Cruise of the Jeannette. Montgomery, Rutherford George. LC 44-6669. 4 p. l., 195 p. 21 cm. 1944. The Westminster Press.
--Men Against the Ice. Montgomery, Rutherford George. Barnett, Isa, illus. LC 46-6429. 148 p. illus. 21 cm. 1946. The Westminster Press.
--Thar She Blows. Montgomery, Rutherford George. LC 45-353824. 4 p. l., 143 p. incl. front., illus. 21 cm. 1945. The Westminster Press.
Proctor, Mary
--Giant Sun and His Family. N.D. Silver Burdett & Co.
--Stories from Starland. N.D. Silver, Burdett & Co.
Proctor, Warren, jt. auth. see Burnham, Clara Louise Root, Mrs.
Prodanovic, Nada Cureija
--Yugoslav Folk Tales. 1975. (ISBN 0-8098-2328-4). David McKay Company.
--Yugoslav Folk-Tales. Kiddell-Monroe, Joan (1908-), illus. (Myths and Legends Ser.). 1957. Henry Z. Walck Inc.
Proddow, Penelope
--Art Tells a Story: Greek & Roman Myths. LC 76-18364. (Illus.). 1979. Doubleday.
--The Spirit of Spring: A Tale of the Greek God Dionysos. Jeffers, Susan, illus. LC 76-104339. (Illus.). 133 p. 22cm. 1970. (ISBN 0-13-835397-2). Bradbury Press.
Proddow, Penelope, tr. see Homerus.
Prohl, Hedwig Taube (1823-1886)
--Where Is Heaven?. Butcher, M. P., tr. LC 45-47541. 230 p. front. 17 cm. (On cover: The Fatherland series). 1884. Lutheran Publication Society.
Prokofiev, Sergei Sergeevich, jt. auth. see Disney, Walt, Productions.
Prokofiev, Sergei Sergeevich (1891-1953)
--Peter and the Wolf. Chappell, Warren (1904-), illus. 1940. Alfred A. Knopf.
--Peter and the Wolf. Chappell, Warren (1904-), illus. LC 60-16759. (Illus.). 1 v. (unpaged). 1961. F. Watts.
--Peter and the Wolf. Chappell, Warren (1904-), illus. LC 72-9557. (Illus.). 32 p. 1973, c.1940. (ISBN 0-394-82613-2). Random House.
--Peter and the Wolf. Chappell, Warren (1904-), illus. LC 81-40404. p. cm. 1981, c.1940. (ISBN 0-8052-0684-1). Schocken Books.
--Peter and the Wolf. Haacken, Frans, illus. 64p. 1962. Franklin Watts.
--Peter and the Wolf. 1st ed. Mikolaycak, Charles (1937-), illus. Carlson, Maria, tr. LC 81-70402. (Illus.). 32 p. 27cm. 1982. (ISBN 0-670-54919-3). Viking Press.
--The Story of Peter and the Wolf. Howard, Alan (1922-), illus. LC 59-12811. (Illus.). 24cm. 31p. 1960. A. S. Barnes & Co.
--The Story of Peter and the Wolf. 1st ed. Palazzo, Tony (1905-1970), illus. LC 61-5517. (Illus.). 88p. 32cm. 1961. Doubleday.
Prokofieva, S.
--Raggity & the Cloud. 160p. 1982. (ISBN 0-8285-2530-7, Pub. by Progress Pubs USSR). Imported Pubns.
Prokop, Phyllis Stillwell (1922-)
--The Sword & the Sundial. (gr. 5 up). 1981. (ISBN 0-89191-376-9). Cook.
Pronzini, Bill (1943-)
--Snowbound. 1974. (ISBN 0-399-11264-2). G. P. Putnam's Sons.
Pronzini, Bill (1943-) & Malzberg, Barry N. (1939-)
--The Running of Beasts. LC 75-24874. 320p. 1976. (ISBN 0-399-11647-8). Putnam.
Propper, Robert A. (1934-)
--High Diddle Diddle: Rhymes from Mother Goose. LC 75-15062. (Illus.). 47 p. 24cm. c.1975. (ISBN 0-87070-377-3). Museum of Modern Art.
Prosser, Mrs.
--The Cheery Chime of Garth and Other Stories. N.D. Thomas Nelson & Sons.
--The Door without a Knocker and Other Tales. N.D. Thomas Nelson & Sons.
--Fables. (Gift Bks. for Children). N.D. Hurd & Houghton for American Tract Society.
--Fables. 160p. N.D. Lockwood, Brooks, & Co. for American Tract Society.
--Fables for the Young Folks. (Illus.). 160p. N.D. American Tract Society.
Protas, Julius, ed. see Three Little Kittens.
Protas, Julius, ed. see Three Little Pigs.
Protestant Episcopal Church in the U.S.A
--Short Stories and Lessons of the Festivals, Fasts, and Saints' Days of the Protestant Episcopal Church. 4th amer. ed. LC 65-81455. 334 p. 20 cm. N.D. T. Whittaker.
Protheroe, Ruth Hepburn
--Beyond the Mountains. Escourido, Joseph, illus. LC 57-562419. 240p. illus. 22cm. 1957. Abelard Schuman.
--Little Chief of the Gaspe. Hogner, Nils (1893-1970), illus. LC 55-6217. 115p. illus. 22cm. 1955. Abelard-Schuman.
Protter, Eric, ed.
--A Children's Treasury of Folk and Fairy Tales. LC 82-4387. p. cm. 1982. (ISBN 0-8253-0112-2). Beaufort Books.
--A Children's Treasury of Folk and Fairy Tales. Richter, Ludwig (1803-1884) & Hostnig, Hildegade, illus. Foley, Martha, intro. by. LC 61-172151. 211p. illus. 28cm. 1961. Channel Press.
--Folk & Fairy Tales of Far-off Lands. Rosenwasser, Dorothy Eckmann (1917-), illus. (Illus.). (gr. 4-8). 1966. Hawthorn.
--Monster Festival: Classic Tales of the Macabre. Gorey, Edward St. John (1925-), illus. LC 79-56028. (Illus.). (gr. 7 up). N.D. (ISBN 0-8149-0377-0). Vanguard.
--Story Time with the Great Painters. Protter, Nancy LC 67-27290. (Illus.). 93 p. 29cm. 1967. Lion Press.
Protter, Eric & Protter, Nancy, eds.
--Celtic Folk and Fairy Tales. 1st ed. Keeping, Charles William James (1924-), illus. Donohue, H. E. F., intro. by. LC 67-1943. (Illus.). x, 209 p. 25cm. 1966. Duell, Sloan and Pearce.
--Folk and Fairy Tales of Far-off Lands. 1st ed. Rosenwasser, Dorothy Eckmann (1917-), illus. Egan, Robert, tr. Cassill, Ronald Verlin (1919-), intro. by. LC 65-26811. xii, 196p. illus. 24cm. 1966, c.1965. Duell Dist. Meredith.
--Gypsy Tales. Cather, Carolyn, illus. LC 67-18484. (Illus.). 190 p. 24cm. 1968, c.1967. Lion Press.
Protter, Nancy, jt. ed. see Protter, Eric.
Proudfit, Isabel Katherine, Mrs.
--Come & See the Battle Family. Matson, Caroline Whitehead, illus. LC 38-22129. 38p. 1938. David McKay Co.
--Come and See the Broom Closet Family. Matson, Caroline Whitehead, illus. LC 38-21178. 19cm. 38p. (The Family Bks.). 1938. David McKay Co.

--Come and See the Icebox Family. Matson, Caroline Whitehead, illus. LC 45-5082. 18cm. 40p. (The Family Bks.). N.D. David McKay Co.
--Come and See the Pantry Family. Matson, Caroline Whitehead, illus. LC 42-9473. 18cm. 38p. N.D. David McKay Co.
--The Ugly Duckling. N.D. Robert M. McBride Co.
Proudfoot, Alice-Boyd, pseud., see Stockdale, Alice Boyd.
Proudfoot, Andrea Hofer, Mrs.
--Child's Christ Tales. (Illus.). N.D. George M Hill Co.
Prout, Vera Julia
--Prairie Windwagon. McCann, Gerald (1916-), illus. LC 58-9727. 173p. illus. 21cm. 1958. Dodd, Mead.
--The Race for Land. Wiese, Kurt (1887-1974), illus. LC 54-6050. 179p. illus. 21cm. 1954. Dodd, Mead.
Prouty, Olive Higgins (1882-1974)
--Bobbie, General Manager. N.D. Frederick A. Stokes.
--Bobbie, General Manager. N.D. Grosset & Dunlap.
Provan, Eldoris Angel
Drummer for the Americans. LC 65-11890. 21cm. 127p. 1965. Chilton Book Co.
Provence, Jean
--Easy Stunt Plays from Literature. 96p. N.D. Northwestern Press.
Provencher, Dennis
--Three Nice Smelling Skunks. N.D. Vantage Press INC.
Provensen, Alice, jt. auth. see Martin, Sarah Catherine.
Provensen, Alice, ed. see Lawrence, David Herbert.
Provensen, Alice, ed. see Mother Goose.
Provensen, Alice (1918-) & Provensen, Martin (1916-)
--The Animal Farm. Provensen, Alice (1918-) & Provensen, Martin (1916-), illus. LC 52-148373. 76p. illus. 33cm. (Giant Golden Book, 751). 1952. Simon and Schuster. **Award: (NYT).**
--A Horse and a Hound, a Goat and a Gander. Provensen, Alice (1918-) & Provensen, Martin (1916-), illus. LC 80-13259. p. cm. 1980. (ISBN 0-689-30793-4). (ISBN 0-689-20700-X). Atheneum.
--Karen's Curiosity. Provensen, Alice (1918-) & Provensen, Martin (1916-), illus. LC 63-8558. (Illus.). unpaged. 15 x 18cm. 1963. Golden Press. **Award: (NYT).**
--Karen's Opposites. Provensen, Alice (1918-) & Provensen, Martin (1916-), illus. LC 63-8559. unpaged. illus. 15 x 18 cm. 1963. Golden Press
--My Little Hen. Provensen, Alice (1918-) & Provensen, Martin (1916-), illus. LC 73-4444. (Illus.). 33 p. 21cm. 1973. (ISBN 0-394-82684-1). (ISBN 0-394-92684-6). Random House.
--Our Animal Friends at Maple Hill Farm. Provensen, Alice (1918-) & Provensen, Martin (1916-), illus. LC 74-828. (Illus.). 57 p. 33cm. 1974. (ISBN 0-394-82123-8). (ISBN 0-394-92123-2). Random House.
--An Owl and Three Pussycats. Provensen, Alice (1918-) & Provensen, Martin (1916-), illus. LC 81-2855. p. cm. 1981. (ISBN 0-689-30857-4). Atheneum.
--A Peaceable Kingdom: The Shaker Abecedarius. Provensen, Alice (1918-) & Provensen, Martin (1916-), illus. LC 80-24866. (Illus.). 42 p. (Picture puffin). 1981, c.1978. (ISBN 0-14-050370-6). Puffin Books.
--A Peaceable Kingdom: The Shaker Abecedarius. Provensen, Alice (1918-) & Provensen, Martin (1916-), illus. LC 78-125. p. cm. 1978. (ISBN 0-670-54500-7). Viking Press. **Awards: (NYT); (ALA).**
--Roses Are Red. Are Violets Blue? A First Book About Color. Provensen, Alice (1918-) & Provensen, Martin (1916-), illus. LC 73-4352. (Illus.). 32 p. 21cm. 1973. (ISBN 0-394-92680-3). (ISBN 0-394-82680-9). Random House.
--What Is a Color?. Provensen, Alice (1918-) & Provensen, Martin (1916-), illus. LC 67-7701. (Illus.). 1 v. (unpaged. 33cm. (Big Golden Book). 1967. Golden Press.
--Who's in the Egg. Provensen, Alice (1918-) & Provensen, Martin (1916-), illus. LC 73-103096. (Illus.). 32 p. 32cm. 1970. Golden Press.
--The Year at Maple Hill Farm. Provensen, Martin (1916-) & Provensen, Alice (1918-), illus. LC 77-18578. 23cm. 327p. 1978. (ISBN 0-689-30642-3). Atheneum.
Provensen, Alice (1918-) & Provensen, Martin (1916-), eds.
--The Provensen Book of Fairy Tales. Provenen, Alice (1918-) & Provensen, Martin (1916-), illus. LC 76-155600. (Illus.). 140 p. 29cm. 1971. (ISBN 0-394-82121-1). (ISBN 0-394-92121-6). Random House.
Provensen, Alice (1918-) & Provensen, Martin (1916-), illus.
--The First Noel. (Big Golden Book). 1959. Golden Press.
--Old Mother Hubbard. LC 76-24176. (Illus.). 32p. (Picturebacks Ser.). (ps-2). 1982. (ISBN 0-394-93460-1). (ISBN 0-394-83460-7). Random.
Provensen, Martin, jt. auth. see Provensen, Alice.
Provensen, Martin, ed. see Lawrence, David Herbert.
Provensen, Martin, ed. see Mother Goose.
Provensen, Martin, jt. ed. see Provensen, Alice.
Provenzano, Natalie
--First Things. (Illus.). (ps-1). 1980. (Gingerbread). Dutton
Provines, Mary Virginia
--Bright Heritage. Hoeflich, Sherman C., illus. LC 39-27686. viii p., 1 l., 261 p. illus. 22 cm. 1939. Longmans, Green and Co.
--A Home for Keeps. Aver, Margaret, illus. LC 37-27474. viii p., 1 l., 277 p. incl. front., illus. 21 cm. 1937. Longmans, Green and Co.
--Liz'beth Ann's Goat. Paull, Grace A. (1898-), illus. LC 47-31382. 26cm. 40p. N.D. Viking Press.
Provost, Gary (1944-)
--The Pork Chop War. LC 82-9589. p. cm. 1982. (ISBN 0-87888-205-7). Bradbury Press.
Provost, Gary (1944-) & Levine-Provost, Gail
--Good If It Goes. LC 83-15681. 192p. (gr. 6-8). 1984. (ISBN 0-02-774950-9). Bradbury Pr.
--Popcorn. LC 84-20444. p. cm. 1985. (ISBN 0-02-774960-6). Bradbury Press.
Provost, Katherine
--Margaret Worthington. N.D. D. Lothrop & co.
Provost, Marjorie
--Vagabond's Ward. Stein, Harve (1904-), illus. LC 31-21538. x p., 1 l., 236 p. col. front., illus., plates (1 double) 20 cm. 1931. Harper and Brothers.
Proysen, Alf
--Down the Mouse Hole. Ware, Kay (1916-) & Sutherland, Lucille, eds. Nordra, Willie, illus. LC 64-6956. 23cm. (Read for Fun Ser.). 1964. (ISBN 0-07-068251-8). McGraw Hill Book Company.
--A Friend Can Be. (Illus.). 32p. 1969. (ISBN 0-8392-3075-3). Astor Books.
--The Goat That Learned to Count. Ware, Kay & Sutherland, Lucille, eds. Berg, Bjorn (1923-), illus. LC 61-66406. unpaged. illus. 23cm. (Read for Fun Series). c.1961. Webster Pub. Co.
--Little Old Mrs. Pepperpot. Berg, Bjorn (1923-), illus. Helweg, Marianne, tr. (gr. 1-4). 1960. (ISBN 0-8392-3021-4). Astor-Honor.
--Little Old Mrs. Pepperpot, and Other Stories. Berg, Bjorn (1923-), illus. Helweg, Marianne, tr. LC 60-8978. 95p. illus. 24cm. (Astor book). 1960, c.1959. McDowell, Obolensky.
--Mrs. Pepperpot Again. (gr. 1-4). N.D. G&D.
--Mrs. Pepperpot Again. Berg, Bjorn (1923-), illus. Helweg, Marianne, tr. (Illus.). (gr. 1-4). 1961. (ISBN 0-8392-3023-0). Astor-Honor.
--Mrs. Pepperpot Again, and Other Stories. Rev ed. Berg, Bjorn (1923-), illus. Helweg, Marianne, tr. LC 61-8504. 98p. illus. 24cm. (Astor book). c.1960. I. Obolensky.
--Mrs. Pepperpot in the Magic Wood. Berg, Bjorn (1923-), illus. Helweg, Marianne, tr. LC 68-12654. (Illus.). 40 line drawings. 76p. 84p. (gr. 2-5). 1968. (ISBN 0-394-81434-7). (ISBN 0-394-91434-1). Pantheon.
--Mrs. Pepperpot to the Rescue. Berg, Bjorn (1923-), illus. Helweg, Marianne, tr. LC 64-11883. (Illus.). 24cm. 65p. (gr. 1-4). 1964. (ISBN 0-394-91429-5). Pantheon.
--Mrs. Pepperpot's Outing. Berg, Bjorn (1923-), illus. Helweg, Marianne, tr. LC 71-153976. (Illus.). 90 p. 24cm. 1971. (ISBN 0-394-82347-8). (ISBN 0-394-92347-2). Pantheon Books.
--Time is Day. (Illus.). 1968. (ISBN 0-8392-3065-6). Astor Books.
--The Town That Forgot It Was Christmas. Ware, Kay & Sutherland, Lucille, eds. Stodberg, Nils, illus. LC 61-59875. unpaged. illus. 23cm. (Read for fun series). c.1961. Webster Pub. Co.
Prudden, Theodore Mitchell
--The Frigate Philadelphia. Wonsetler, John Charles (1900-), illus. LC 66-16906. x, 144p. illus. 23cm. c.1966. Van Nostrand.
Prude, Agnes George see De Mille, Agnes, pseud.
Prud'Hommeaux, Rene
--The Extra Hand. Abel, Raymond (1911-), illus. LC 53-93086. 190p. illus. 22cm. 1953. Viking Press.
--Hidden Lights. Busoni, Rafaello (1900-1962), illus. LC 56-14289. (Illus.). 246 p. 21cm. 1956. Viking Press.
--The Mystery of Marr's Hill. LC 58-120655. 190p. 22cm. 1958. Macrae Smith.
--The Port of Missing Men. LC 52-8710. 192 p. illus. 22 cm. 1952. Viking Press.
--The Sunken Forest. Busoni, Rafaello (1900-1962), illus. LC 49-11408. 248 p. illus. 22 cm. 1949. Viking Press.
Pruitt, Anna Seward & Weeks, Nan F.
--The Chinese Boat Baby. N.D. Broadman Press.
--Whirligigs in China: Stories for Juniors. rev. ed. Keller, Mathilda, illus. LC 48-10429. 119 p. illus. 19 cm. 1948. Broadman Press.
Pruitt, Jo Ann
--All It Could Be. (Illus.). (gr. 4-10). 1978. (ISBN 0-8054-4512-9). Broadman.
Pruitt, Olga Reed (1896-)
--Trouble with Yukon. LC 64-8949. 135 p. 23 cm. N.D. American Southern,C.
Pruitt, Pamela see McCluskey, John.
Pruitt, Pamela & Johnston, Brenda
--Henry Box Brown: Struggle for Freedom. 22p. N.D. (ISBN 0-913678-08-2). New Day Press.
Prusina, Katica, jt. auth. see Mann, Peggy.
Pryor, Bonnie
--Grandpa Bear. Degen, Bruce, illus. LC 84-25545. (Illus.). 32 p. 26cm. c.1985. (ISBN 0-688-04551-0). (ISBN 0-688-04552-9). Morrow.
Pryor, Ethel V
--Thoughtful Cathy. (Illus.). 30 p. 22cm. 1974. (ISBN 0-533-01182-5). Vantage Press.
Pryor, Helen Sloman, jt. auth. see Pryor, William Clayton.
Pryor, William Clayton & Pryor, Helen Sloman
--The Glass Book: A Photographic Picture-Book with a Story. LC 35-272821. 4 p. l., 100 p. illus., pl. 23 cm. c.1935. Harcourt, Brace and Company.
--The Train Book. 107p. (gr. k-3). N.D. Harcourt, Brace & Co.
P. S, tr. see Segur, Sophie Rostopchine, Mrs.
Pucci, Mario, jt. auth. see Andrews, Martin.
Puccinelli, Marie
--Catch a Fish. Watson, Aldren Auld (1917-), illus. LC 65-26499. 45p. col. illus. 24cm. 1966, c.1965. Bobbs.
--The Time of the Puffins. Kaufmann, John (1931-), illus. LC 65-17706. 39 p. col. illus. 24cm. c.1965. Bobbs.
Puckett, G. A
--Ten Kittens. Walley, Helen, illus. LC 20-2503. 73 p. incl. illus., plates. 19 cm. c.1919. Burton Publishing Company.
Pucmer, Inka
--The Crystal Sphere: (From Grimm's Fairy Tales). (Illus.). 37p. (gr. k-5). 1983. (ISBN 0-88010-068-0). Anthroposophic.
Pudney, John
--Camel fighter. (Illus.). N.D. British Book Centre.
Puett, Judith Flippo
--Trigo-Kit. Puett, Judith Flippo, illus. LC 74-129651. (Illus.). ix, 98 p. 22cm. 1970. (ISBN 0-8111-0374-9). Naylor Co.
Puffer, Garry
--Billy Bumbry's Year. Servello, Joe (1932-), illus. LC 81-940. (Illus.). 192p. (gr. 7 up). 1981. (ISBN 0-688-00737-6). (ISBN 0-688-00738-4). Lothrop.
Puffer, Joseph Adams
--The Boy and His Gang. N.D. Houghton Mifflin.
Pugh, Ellen Tiffany (1920-)
--The Adventures of Yoo-Lah-Teen: A Legend of the Salish Coastal Indians. Kubinyi, Laszlo (1937-), illus. LC 75-9199. p. cm. 1975. (ISBN 0-8037-6318-2). (ISBN 0-8037-6319-0). Dial Press.
--Brave His Soul. LC 70-117619. (Illus.). bibl. index. photos. & maps. notes. 160p. (gr. 7 up). 1970. Dodd.
--More Tales from the Welsh Hills. (Illus.). 1971. (ISBN 0-396-06294-6). Dodd, Mead & Company.
--Tales from the Welsh Hills. Sandin, Joan (1942-), illus. LC 68-24025. (Illus.). 143 p. 24cm. 1968. Dodd, Mead.
Pugh, Mabel (1891-)
--Little Carolina Blue Bonnet. Pugh, Mabel (1891-), illus. LC 33-21386. 5 p. l., 3-171 p. col. front., illus. (part col.) 22 cm. c.1933. Thomas Y. Crowell Co.
Puglise, Francis
--Too Smart?. (Illus.). 23p. (Orig.). 1980. (ISBN 0-936920-01-7). Ridgeview Jr High Pr.
Pulis, Clifford A
--Ashanti. LC 83-19852. p. cm. c.1983. (ISBN 0-310-46951-1). Zondervan Pub. House.
Pullein-Thompson, Christine (1930-)
--I Rode a Winner. (gr. 7 up). 1978. (ISBN 0-685-47065-2, Schol Pap). Scholastic Inc.
Pullein-Thompson, Diana
--The Boy and the Donkey. Cassel, Lili, pseud. (1924-), illus. Wronker, Lili Cassel. LC 58-11463. 190p. illus. 22cm. (Criterion book for young people). 1958. Criterion Books.
--Boy & the Donkey. Cassel, Lili, pseud. (1924-), illus. Wronker, Lili Cassel. LC 58-11463. (Illus.). (gr. 2-6). 1958. (ISBN 0-87599-089-4). S G Phillips.
Pullein-Thompson, Joanna Maxwell see Cannan, Joanna, pseud.
Pullein-Thompson, Josephine Mary Wedderburn & Pullein-Thompson, Diana
--Black Beauty's Clan. Grant, Elisabeth, illus. LC 80-19168. (Illus.). 285 p. 22cm. 1980. (ISBN 0-07-050913-1). McGraw-Hill.
--Black Beauty's Family. Grant, Elisabeth, illus. LC 80-23731. (Illus.). 282 p. 22cm. 1980, c.1978. (ISBN 0-07-050914-X). McGraw-Hill.
Pullein-Thompson, Diana, jt. auth. see Pullein-Thompson, Josephine Mary Wedderburn.
Pullen, Alan & Rapstoff, Cyril
--The Black Pigeon. Kennedy, Richard (1910-), illus. (Illus.). N.D. (ISBN 0-685-24591-8). Merry Thoughts.
--Black Pigeon. Kennedy, Richard (1910-), illus. (Illus.). (gr. 7 up). 1965. (ISBN 0-685-20968-7). Verry.
--Devil's Dump. Kennedy, Richard (1910-), illus. (Illus.). N.D. (ISBN 0-685-24597-7). Merry Thoughts.
Last Straw. (Illus.). (gr. 7 up). 1966. Verry
--The Last Straw. Kennedy, Richard (1910-), illus. (Illus.). N.D. (ISBN 0-685-24594-2). Merry Thoughts.
--The Man in the Train. Kennedy, Richard (1910-), illus. (Illus.). N.D. (ISBN 0-685-24590-X). Merry Thoughts.
--Man in the Train. Kennedy, Richard (1910-), illus. (Illus.). (gr. 7 up). 1965. (ISBN 0-685-21325-0). Verry.
--A Night in Town. Kennedy, Richard (1910-), illus. (Illus.). N.D. (ISBN 0-685-24592-6). Merry Thoughts.
--Night in Town. Kennedy, Richard (1910-), illus. (Illus.). (gr. 7 up). 1966. (ISBN 0-685-21382-X). Verry.
--The Old House. Kennedy, Richard (1910-), illus. (Illus.). N.D. (ISBN 0-685-24598-5). Merry Thoughts.
--Old House. Kennedy, Richard (1910-), illus. (Illus.). (gr. 7 up). 1965. (ISBN 0-685-21391-9). Verry.
--On the Hook. Kennedy, Richard (1910-), illus. (Illus.). N.D. (ISBN 0-685-24599-3). Merry Thoughts.
--On the Hook. Kennedy, Richard (1910-), illus. (Illus.). (gr. 7 up). 1966. (ISBN 0-685-21393-5). Verry.
--Over the Wall. (Illus.). N.D. (ISBN 0-685-24595-0). Merry Thoughts.
--River Cats. Kennedy, Richard (1910-), illus. (Illus.). N.D. (ISBN 0-685-24601-9). Merry Thoughts.
--A Spoke in the Wheel. Kennedy, Richard (1910-), illus. (Illus.). N.D. (ISBN 0-685-24593-4). Merry Thoughts.
--Spoke in the Wheel. Kennedy, Richard (1910-), illus. (Illus.). (gr. 7 up). 1966. (ISBN 0-685-21559-8). Verry.
--The Thing on the Line. Kennedy, Richard (1910-), illus. (Illus.). N.D. (ISBN 0-685-24589-6). Merry Thoughts.
--Thing on the Line. Kennedy, Richard (1910-), illus. (Illus.). (gr. 7 up). 1965. (ISBN 0-685-21607-1). Verry.
Puller, Edwin Seward (1870-)
--Biff McCarty: The Eagle Scout. LC 15-7730. 297 p. front., plates. 20 cm. (Books for Boys Scouts). c.1915. The Abingdon Press.
Pulliam, Roy Avron, ed. see Irving, Washington.
Pulliam, Roy Avron, ed. see Stevenson, Robert Louis.
Pulliam, Roy Avron (1902-) & Darby, Oscar Nolan, eds.
--Stories I Like. Vail, Claudine Cook, illus. LC 49-49615. 224 p. illus. (part col.) 23 cm. (Treasure books). 1949. Steck Co.
Pulling, Norah
--Mary Belinda and the Ten Aunts. Einzig, Susan (1922-), illus. LC 46-3013. (Illus.). 27p. 16 x 13cm. 1946. Transatlantic Arts Ltd.
Pullman, Philip
--Count Karlstein. 166p. 1st U.S. edition. (gr. 5-12). 1983. (ISBN 0-7011-2649-3, Pub. by Chatto & Windus). Merrimack Pub Cir.
Pulsford, Henry A
--Old Brig's Cargo. Rines, Frank M., illus. LC 25-7275. 4 p. l., 3-278 p. front. 21 cm. c.1925. The Atlantic Monthly Press.
Pulver, Mary Brecht
--Tales That Nimko Told. Wright, Mabel Sherwood, illus. LC 25-17707. xv, 119 p. illus. 20 cm. c.1925. The Century Co.
Pulzker, Mrs.
--From Peasant to Prince. (Illus.). N.D. E. P. Dutton & Co.
Puma, Thomas
--The Adventures of Tom & Fiore. Guerriero, Salvatore, Jr., illus. 1983. (ISBN 0-533-05384-6). Vantage.
Pumphrey, Margaret Blanche
--Pilgrim Stories. Hall, Elvajean (1910-), ed. (Illus.). (gr. 4-6). 1962. (ISBN 0-528-80338-7). Rand.
--Stories of the Pilgrims. Perkins, Lucy Fitch, Mrs. (1865-1937), illus. N.D. Rand McNally.
--Yucca Ranch. Preibisus, Hilda, illus. LC 49-10391. 265 p. illus. 24 cm. 1949. Caxton Printers.
Punch
--Dog Stories from Punch. Morrow, George (1869-), illus. LC 28-26156. viii p., 1 l., 11-211 p. illus. 24 cm. 1927. George H. Doran Company.

Punch and Judy
--Punch and Judy: A Play for Puppets. 1st ed. Emberley, Edward Randolph (1931-), illus. LC 65-10793. (Illus.). 27 cm. 27p. 1965. Little, Brown. **Award: (NYT).**
Pundt, Helen Marie
--The Judge's Daughters. LC 66-6821. 219 p. 21cm. 1966. (ISBN 0-690-46821-0). Crowell.
--Mystery of the Castle Coins. LC 67-23671. 150 p. 21cm. 1967. Crowell.
--Spring Comes First to the Willows. LC 63-9212. 231 p. 21 cm. 1963. Crowell.
--Zenty. LC 64-20690. 239 p. 22cm. 1964. Crowell.
Puner, Helen Walker (1915-)
--Daddies-What They Do All Day. Duvoisin, Roger Antoine (1904-1980), illus. LC 46-17063. (Illus.). 34p. (gr. k-3). 1946. (ISBN 0-688-51234-8). Lothrop.
--I Am Big; You Are Little. Rice, Eve Hart (1951-), illus. LC 72-10218. (Illus.). 31 p. 1973. Young Scott Books.
--Sitter Who Didn't Sit. 1949. E M Hale.
--The Sitter Who Didn't Sit. LC 49-8457. 26 p. col. illus. 26 cm. c.1949. Lothrop,Lee & Shepard Co.
Pungo
--Scissors: A Story to Make Your Eyes Shine. LC 27-13383. 34, 1 p., 2 l. incl. front., illus. 26 cm. 1926. The Spiral Press.
Punnett, Richard Douglas (1924-)
--Double-Rhyme-Our Brat Cat. Rauh, Herb, illus. LC 84-23027. (Illus.). 30 p. 26cm. (Double-Rhyme Books). c.1985. (ISBN 0-89565-303-6). Child's World.
--Double-Rhyme-Peek-a-Boo Sue. Dunnington, Tom LC 84-23003. (Illus.). 30 p. 26cm. (Double-Rhyme Books). c.1985. (ISBN 0-89565-305-2). Child's World.
--Talk Along-Count the Possums. Dunnington, Tom, illus. LC 81-21773. p. cm. (Talk-Along Book). 1982. (ISBN 0-89565-215-3). Child's World.
--Talk Along-Help Jumbo Escape. Dunnington, Tom, illus. LC 81-21667. (Illus.). 30 p. 26cm. (A Talk-Along Book). c.1982. (ISBN 0-89565-214-5). Child's World.
--Talk Along-Name Lizzy's Colors. Dunnington, Tom, illus. LC 82-1172. (Illus.). 30 p. 26cm. (A Talk-Along Book). c.1982. (ISBN 0-89565-216-1). Child's World.
--Talk Along-Name Patty's Pets. Dunnington, Tom, illus. LC 81-18056. (Illus.). 30 p. 26cm. (A Talk-Along Book). c.1982. (ISBN 0-89565-213-7). Child's World.
Punot, S.
--Tim's Little Mother. N.D. Robert Carter & Brothers.
Pupils of Washington Seminary
--The Magic Ladder, and Other Stories. Brooks, Mary Wallace, ed. Scott, Harriet Clark, illus. LC 5-42527. (Illus.). 67p. 21cm. 1905. H. F. Ward.
Purdon, Eric Sinclaire (1913-)
--The Valley of the Larks: A Story of Inner Mongolia, by Eric Purdon. Peck, Graham, illus. LC 39-305386. 6 p. l., 3-134 p. illus. 22 cm. c.1939. Farrar & Rinehart, Inc.
Purdon, K. F.
--Kevin and the Cats. (True Or Might-Be-True Stories). N.D. MacMillan Bks.
Purdy, Carol
--Iva Dunnit and the Big Wind. Kellogg, Steven (1941-), illus. LC 84-17441. (Illus.). 30 p. 28cm. 1985. (ISBN 0-8037-0183-7). (ISBN 0-8037-0184-5). Dial Books for Young Readers.
Purdy, Nina Sutherland (1889-)
--Four-Leaf-Clover. Greer, M. L., illus. LC 18-15379. 5 p. l., 210 p. front., plates. 20 cm. c.1918. Small, Maynard and Company.
--Wide-Open-Eye. Morrell, Edith Whitcomb, tr. LC 25-8122. vii, 1 p., 1 l., 218 p. col. front. 20 cm. 1925. Doubleday, Page & Company.
Purdy, Susan Gold (1939-)
--Be My Valentine: Charms for Captivating and Capturing Your Love. LC 67-10300. (Illus.). 47 p. 19cm. 1967, c.1966. Lippincott.
--If You Have a Yellow Lion. LC 66-11014. (Illus.). 1 v. (unpaged. 23cm. 1966. Lippincott.
--My Little Cabbage: Mon Petit Chou. LC 65-13438. 1v. (unpaged) col. illus., 18x22cm. c.1965. Lippincott.
Puricelli, Luigi, jt. auth. see Cristini, Ermanno.
Purnell, Idella (1901-), as told by see Disney, Walt, Productions & Salten, Felix.
Purnell, Idella (1901-)
--Forbidden City. N.D. MacMillan.
--Little Yusf: The Story of a Syrian Boy. McCreery, James L., illus. LC 31-6490. 7 p. l., 121 p. incl. front., illus., plates. double col. pl. 23 cm. 1931. The Macmillan Company.
--The Merry Frogs. Wenden, Nadine, illus. LC 37-12221. 109, 1 p. illus. (part col.) 22 cm. c.1936. Suttonhouse, Ltd.
--The Wishing Owl: A Maya Storybook. LC 31-30264. xii p., 1 l., 95 p. incl. illus., plates. col. front. 23 cm. 1931. The Macmillan Company.
Purnell, Idella (1901-) & Weatherwax, John M.
--The Talking Bird: An Aztec Story Book: Tales Told to Little Paco by His Grandfather. Dehlsen, Frances Purnell, illus. LC 30-286377. ix p., 1 l., 95 p., 1 l. incl. plates. col. front., illus., plates. 23 cm. 1930. The Macmillan Company.
--Why the Bee Is Busy and Other Rumanian Fairy Tales Told to Little Marcu by Baba Maritza. Smith, Helen, illus. 7 p. l., 134 p. incl. illus., plates. col. front. 20 cm. 1930. The Macmillan Company.
Purscell, Phyllis (1934-)
--Old Boy's Tree House & Other Deep Forest Tales. Arndt, Ursula, illus. LC 68-12861. (Illus.). 64p. (gr. 1-5). 1968. Weybright.
Pursell, Margaret Sanford, adapted by see Pajot, Anne Marie.
Pursell, Thomas F
--The Burning Barn Mystery. Overlie, George, illus. LC 77-74011. (Illus.). 32 p. 16cm. (Carolrhoda mini-mystery). c.1977. (ISBN 0-87614-085-1). Carolrhoda Books.
--Mr. Kruger's Treasure. Overlie, George, illus. LC 77-74012. (Illus.). 32 p. 16cm. (Carolrhoda mini-mystery). c.1977. (ISBN 0-87614-087-8). Carolrhoda Books.
--The Mysterious Radio Code. Overlie, George, illus. LC 77-74009. (Illus.). 32 p. 16cm. (Carolrhoda mini-mystery). c.1977. (ISBN 0-87614-088-6). Carolrhoda Books.
--The Mystery of Lost Beach. Overlie, George, illus. LC 77-74007. (Illus.). 32 p. 16cm. (Carolrhoda mini-mysteries). c.1977. (ISBN 0-87614-086-X). Carolrhoda Books.
--The Mystery of the Zebra Butterfly. Overlie, George, illus. LC 77-74008. (Illus.). 16cm. 32p. (A Carolrhoda mini-mystery). c.1977. (ISBN 0-87614-090-8). Carolrhoda Books.
--The Prize Tomatoes Mystery. Overlie, George, illus. LC 77-74010. (Illus.). 32 p. 16cm. (Carolrhoda mini-mystery). c.1977. (ISBN 0-87614-089-4). Carolrhoda Books.
Purtill
--Lord of the Elves and Eldils. N.D. Zondervan Publishing House.
Purvis, Mary E.
--Animal Alphabet: Wild Animals. Purvis, Mary, illus. LC 83-73382. (Illus.). 32p. (Orig.). (ps-6). 1984. (ISBN 0-915861-02-X). (ISBN 0-915861-03-8). Childrens Ctr.
--Mrs. Purvis Visits the SEASHORE. Purvis, Kenny, illus. LC 83-73382. (Illus.). 32p. (Orig.). (ps-6). 1983. (ISBN 0-915861-00-3). (ISBN 0-915861-01-1). Childrens Ctr.
Pushkin, Alexander Sergeyevich (1799-1837)
--Golden Cockerel. Pogany, Elaine Cox, Mrs., ed. Pogany, Willy (1882-), illus. LC 38-18911. 31cm. 48p. (gr. 7-9). 1938. T. Nelson and sons.
--Golden Cockerel. Richards, Rosalie, illus. Hulick, Elizabeth C., tr. (Illus.). 1962. (ISBN 0-8392-1039-6). Astor-Honor.
--Golden Cockerel & Other Stories. Reeves, James (1909-), ed. Lebis, Jan, illus. (gr. 4-6). 1969. (ISBN 0-531-01895-4). Watts.
--On Seashore Far, a Green Oak Tower. 126p. 1983. (ISBN 0-8285-2718-0, Pub. by Raduga Pubs USSR). Imported Pubns.
--Pushkin's Fairy Tales. Boyd, Arthur, illus. Dalley, Janet, tr. from Rus. (Illus.). 1979. (ISBN 0-8317-7139-9, Mayflower Bks). Smith Pubs.
--Six Russian Tales. Wilde, Carol (1938-), illus. White, Anne Terry (1896-), tr. from Russian. LC 69-14832. (Illus.). 96 p. 24cm. (Reading Shelf Book). 1969. (ISBN 0-8116-4203-8). Garrard Pub. Co.
--The Snow Storm. 40p. (Classic Short Stories). 1983. (ISBN 0-87191-923-0). Childrens Bk Co.
--The Snow Storm. Redpath, Ann, ed. 32p. (Creative's Classic Short Stories Ser.). 1983. (ISBN 0-87191-923-0). Creative Ed.
--The Tale of the Golden Cockerel. Bilbin, Ivan Iakovlevich (1876-1942), illus. Lowe, Patrica (1876-1942), tr. LC 75-4623. (Illus.). (gr. 1-5). 1975. (ISBN 0-690-00790-6, TYC-J). Har-Row.
--Tale of the Tsar Saltan. Bilibin, Ivan Iakovlevich (1876-1942), illus. (Illus.). 18p. 1978. (ISBN 0-8285-1240-X, Pub. by Progress Pubs USSR). Imported Pubns.
--Tales by Alexander Pushkin. Bilibin, Ivan Iakovlevich (1876-1942), illus. (Illus.). 15p. (ps-3). 1982. (ISBN 0-8285-2365-7, Pub. by Malysh Pubs USSR). Imported Pubns.
Puss in Boots
--Puss in Boots. Cloud, Claude Carey (1899-) & Lentz, Harold B., illus. 18 p. incl. front., illus. (part col.) 24 cm. c.1934. Blue Ribbon Press.
--Puss in Boots. Dobias, Frank (1902-), illus. LC 37-24114. 41 p. col. illus. 15 x 15 cm. 1937. The Macmillan Company.
--Puss in Boots. Fleur, Anne Elizabeth (1901-), illus. Sari, pseud. LC 41-22146. 59 p. incl. col. front., illus. (part col.) 17 x 19 cm. (The little color classics). c.1941. McLoughlin Bros., Inc.
--Puss in Boots. Hale, Kathleen (1898-), illus. LC 51-6680. unpaged. illus. 18 cm. (Peepshow books). c.1951. Houghton Mifflin.
--Puss in Boots. Miller, Doris R, pseud., retold by Mosesson, Gloria Rubin. Ramirez, Pablo, illus. LC 66-14052. 1v. (unpaged) col. illus. 24cm. (Holly story bk. lib.). 1966. World.
--Puss in Boots and Other Famous Stories. Liebman, Oscar (1919-), illus. LC 62-17122. unpaged. col. illus. 30cm. (Commended classics). c.1962. Parents' Magazine Pr., Vanderbilt Ave.
Puss in Boots & Perrault, Charles (1628-1703)
--The Adventures of Puss in Boots ... Lentz, Harold B., illus. LC 25-878. 15 p. col. illus. 19 cm. c.1852. J. B. Keller.
--Puss in Boots. Brock, Henry Matthew (1875-1960), illus. LC 8-35520. 2 p. l., 15 numb. l., 1 l. 8 col. pl. (incl. front.) 32 cm. (Half-title: The fairy library). N.D. F. Warne & Co.
--Puss-in-Boots. Rev ed. Myers, Bernice (1875-1960) & Myers, Lou, illus. LC 55-8192. unpaged. 21cm. (Rand McNally alf book, 507). c.1955. Rand McNally.
Putcamp, Luise, Jr. (1924-)
--The Night of the Child: A Christmas Story. Teichman, Dorothy, illus. LC 76-160302. (Illus.). 39 p. 21cm. 1971. Word Books.
Putman, Peter
--The Triumph of the Seeing Eye. 1963. Harper & Row Publishers.
Putnam, Alice (1916-)
--The Spy Doll. LC 79-18364. p. cm. c.1979. (ISBN 0-525-66667-2). Elsevier/Nelson Books.
--The Whistling Swans. Hiestand, Scott, illus. (Illus.). 64p. (gr. 3-6). 1981. (ISBN 0-671-41688-X). Messner.

Putnam, Arthur Lee, pseud., see Alger, Horatio Jr..

Putnam, Arthur Lee, pseud. (1832-1899)
--Ben's Nuggett: Or, A Boy's Search for Fortune. Alger, Horatio Jr., 1 of 4 vols. (Illus.). (Roundabout Lib.). (Pacific Ser.). N.D. Henry T. Coates & Co.
--Ned Newton. Alger, Horatio. LC 62-57449. (Illus.). 348. 19cm. (The Berkeley Series of Books for Boys). 1890. American Publishers Corp.
--Number Ninety-One. Alger, Horatio Jr.. (Illus.). (St. Nicholas Seies for Boys). N.D. International Book Co.
--Tom Tracy. Alger, Horatio Jr.. (Illus.). (St. Nicholas Series for Boys). N.D. International Book Co.
--Young Acrobat. Alger, Horatio Jr.. (Illus.). (St. Nicholas Series for Boys). N.D. International Book Co.
--The Young Adventurer: Or, Tom's Trip Across the Plains. Alger, Horatio Jr., 1 of 4 vols. (Illus.). (Roundabout Lib.). (Pacific Ser.). N.D. Set. Henry T. Coates & Co.
--The Young Explorer: Or, Among the Sierras. Alger, Horatio Jr., 1 of 4 vols. (Illus.). (Roundabout Lib.). (Pacific Ser.). N.D. Set. Henry T. Coates & Co.
--The Young Miner: Or, Tom Nelson in California. Alger, Horatio Jr., 1 of 4 vols. (Illus.). (Roundabout Lib.). (Pacific Ser.). N.D. Set. Henry T. Coates & Co.
Putnam, Brenda, jt. auth. see Kovalsky, Olga.
Putnam, Claude George
--Dickey Wickey, the Flying Frog: Desert Fairy Tales. Putnam, Claude George, illus. LC 33-19486. 3 p. l., 210 p. illus. 19 cm. c.1933. Suttonhouse.
Putnam, David Binney (1913-)
--David Goes to Baffin Land. N.D. G. P. Putnam Sons.
--David Goes to Greenland. N.D. G. P. Putnam Sons.
--David Goes Voyaging. Cooper, Isabel & Dickerman, Don, illus. LC 25-19287. viii, 132 p. front., iillus., plates, ports. 21 cm. 1925. G. P. Putnam's Sons.
Putnam, Edward Hall
--Watty & Co. LC 19-14194. 4 p. l., 202 p. front., illus. 20 cm. 1919. The Macmillan Company.
Putnam, Eleanor, pseud., see Bates, Harriet Leonora Vose.
Putnam, Eleanor, pseud. (1856-1886)
--Bob's Breaking In. Bates, Harriet Leonora Vose, 1 of 4 vols. (Illus.). (Winter Sunshine Ser.). N.D. D Lothrop.
--Bob's Father. Bates, Harriet Leonora Vose, 1 of 6 vols. (Illus.). (Firelight Stories). 1882. D Lothrop.
Putnam, Eleanor, pseud. (1856-1886) & Bates, Arlo
--Prince Vance: The Story of a Prince with a Court in his Box. Bates, Harriet Leonora Vose. Myrick, Frank (1850-1918), illus. N.D. Robert Brothers.
Putnam, George Haven
--The Little Gingerbread Man. Herbert, Robert Gaston, illus. LC 10-29639. 22cm. 20p. 1910. G. P. Putnam's Sons.
Putnam, H. A., Mrs.
--Through Trials to Triumph: A Story of Boy's School-Life. (Illus.). N.D. Methodist Book concern.
--Through Trials to Triumph: A Story of Boys' School Life. LC 78-313276. (Illus.). 277 p. 18cm. 1873. Nelson & Phillips.
Putnam, Harriet (1862-)
--Father Gander: Tales of a Golden Rule King. Pyle, Katharine D. (0000-1938), illus. LC 34-74. 3 p. l., 5-62 p. front., illus. 14 x 21 cm. c.1933. The Christopher Publishing House.
Putnam, Nina Wilcox, Mrs. (1888-)
--Lynn, Cover Girl. LC 50-9600. 186 p. 21 cm. 1950. Messner.
Putnam, Polly
--The Mystery of Sara Beth. Friedman, Judith (1935-), illus. LC 81-3282. p. cm. c.1981. (ISBN 0-695-41628-6). (ISBN 0-695-31628-1). Follett Pub. Co.
Putnam, Say
--Freddie Fighting His Way, 1 of 103 vols. (The Pearl Library: No. 26). 1900. Set. Hurst & Co.
--Little Freddie Feeding his Soul. 125p. N.D. American Tract Society.
Puttcamp, Rita
--Borrowed Boots. Geary, Clifford N. (1916-), illus. LC 56-14290. 186p. illus. 21cm. 1956. Viking Press.
--Polly & Whispering Voice. 128p. 1952. Moody.
--The Singing Bridge. Escourido, Joseph, illus. LC 59-6046. 125p. illus. 20cm. 1959. Friendship Press.
--Texas Treasure. Werth, Kurt (1896-), illus. LC 58-118206. 155p. illus. 22cm. 1959. Lothrop, Lee and Shepard.
Puttcamp, Rita & Willman, Gordon
--Operation Bro-Kee. Puttcamp, Rita, illus. LC 77-13307. (Illus.). 115 p. 23cm. (Bro-kee series). c.1978. (ISBN 0-570-07761-3). Concordia Pub. House.
Puzo, Mario (1920-)
--The Runaway Summer of Davie Shaw. Sherwood, Stewart, illus. LC 66-5268. 186p. illus. 22cm. c.1966. Platt & Munk.
Pyk, Ann (1934-), tr. see Loefgren, Ulf.
Pyk, Ann Phillips (1937-), retold by.
--The Hammer of Thunder. Pyk, Jan (1934-), illus. Edda, Samundar LC 72-187135. (Illus.). 32 p. 27cm. 1972. (ISBN 0-399-20278-1). (ISBN 0-399-20278-1). Putnam.
Pyke, Gertrude V & Pyke, Helen Godfrey (1941-)
--Student Nurse. LC 77-70846. 126 p. 21cm. c.1977. (ISBN 0-8127-0134-8). Southern Pub. Association.
Pyke, Helen Godfrey, jt. auth. see Pyke, Gertrude V.
Pyke, Helen Godfrey (1941-)
--Sword Unsheathed. 128p. (gr. 5-8). 1970. (ISBN 0-8127-0037-6). Southern Pub.
--A Wind to the Flame. Myers, J. William, illus. LC 73-80237. (Illus.). 121, 5 p. 21cm. (Crown book). 1973. (ISBN 0-8127-0061-9). Southern Pub. Association.
--A Wind to the Flames. Meyers, J. William, Jr., illus. 128p. (Orig.). (gr. 7-9). 1973. (ISBN 0-8127-0061-9). Review & Herald.
Pyke, Rafford, pseud., see Peck, Harry Thurston.
Pyle, Howard, ed. see Malory, Thomas, Sir.
Pyle, Howard (1853-1911)
--The Book of King Authur. complete and unabridge ed. King, Ron, illus. LC 77-79987. (Illus.). 192 p. 29cm. 1969. (ISBN 0-516-04243-2). Childrens Press.
--Fairy Tales. Rev ed. Stevens, Beatrice (1876-), illus. LC 3-17907. 2 p. l., vii, 587 p. col. front., illus., col. pl. 21 cm. (Added t.-p.: Library for young people. vol. iv). 1903. P. F. Collier & Son.
--The Garden Behind the Moon: A Real Story of the Moon Angel. Pyle, Howard (1853-1911), illus. LC 4-16148. vii, 192 p. incl. illus., plates. front., 22 cm. 1895. C. Scribner's Sons.
--Howard Pyle's Book of Pirates: Fiction, Fact and Fancy Concerning the Buccaneers of the Spanish Main. Johnson, Merle De Vore (1874-1935), ed. Pyle, Howard (1853-1911), illus. (Illus.). (gr. 7-9). 1921. (ISBN 0-06-024791-6, HarpJ). Har-Row.
--Jack Ballister's Fortunes. N.D. Appleton Century Co.
--King Arthur and the Knights of the Round Table. Schneider, Estelle B, adapted by. Barnum, Jay Hyde (1888-1962), illus. LC 54-7018. unpaged. illus. 29cm. c.1954. (ISBN 0-394-90663-2). Random House.
--King Stork. 1st ed. Hyman, Trina Schart (1939-), illus. LC 78-182249. (Illus.). 48 p. 26cm. 1973. (ISBN 0-316-72440-8). Little, Brown. **Award: (BGH).**
--Men of Iron. vi, 328 p. 21 pl. (incl. front.) 22 cm. 1892. Harper & Brothers.
--Men of Iron. LC 4-18936. (Illus.). 22p.cm. 1904. Harper & Brothers.
--Men of Iron. (Harper's Selected Juveniles). 1910. Harper & Brothers.
--Men of Iron. 1919. Harper.

--Mother Goose: The Old Nursery Rhymes. (Illus.). Repr. of 1912 ed. 1978. (ISBN 0-932106-02-1, Pub by Marathon Pr). S J Durst.
--The Sleeping Beauty. Large Paper ed. N.D. J.B. Lippincott.
Rackman, Arthur, ed. see Grahame, Kenneth.
Rackow, Sonja R
--Elmer: The Little Red Schoolhouse. N.D. Carlton Press.
Rada, Warren
--Little Boat That Almost Sank. 32p. 1965. Lutheran Publications.
Radau, Hanns (1901-)
--Illampu. Rothfuchs, Heiner, illus. 160p. 1962. Abelard-Schuman.
--The Last Chief, Alaskan Trapper. Rothfuchs, Heiner, illus. Long, Dorothy, tr. from Ger. LC 65-18558. (Illus.). 156 p. 21cm. 1965. Abelard-Schuman.
--Little Fox, Alaskan Trapper. Rothfuchs, Heiner, illus. Long, Dorothy, tr. LC 63-10718. (Illus.). 157 p. 21cm. 1963. Abelard-Schuman.
Radcliffe, S. T. A.
--Diamonds in the Sand, and Other Stories, 1 of 6 vols. (Illus.). (The Little Pitcher Library). N.D. Cassell, Petter, Galpin.
--The Giant's Cradle and Other Stories, 1 of 6 vols. (Illus.). (The Little Pitcher Library). N.D. Cassell, Petter, Galpin.
Raddall, Thomas Head (1903-)
--Son of the Hawk. Turner, Stanley, illus. 247p. 1950. John C. Winston Co.
Radebaugh, Marie Herman (1906-)
--Woody, the Termite. Medoff, Eve Lowenthal (1904-), illus. LC 48-1106. 30 p. illus. (part col.) 29 cm. 1947. Seven Stars Press.
Radebaugh, Marie Herman (1906-) & Radebaugh, William Henry (1909-)
--A Fishy ABC: Or, An Alphabet of the Sea. LC 48-178764. 16 i. col. illus. 17 x 26 cm. c.1947. Seven Stars Press.
Radebaugh, William Henry, jt. auth. see Radebaugh, Marie Herman.
Radford, Alice E
--Little Brown Bruno. Rawson, Clayton (1906-1971), illus. LC 31-17564. 80 p. illus. 24 cm. c.1931. Rand, McNally & Company.
Radford, Beatrice
--The Bell in the Forest (Pub. by Society for Promoting Christian Knowledge). N.D. E. & J. B. Young & Co.
Radford, Dollie, Mrs.
--Songs and Other Verses. LC 28-2744. 18 cm. 18p. 1895. J. B. Lippincott Co.
Radford, Ruby Lorraine see Bailey, Matilda, pseud.
Radford, Ruby Lorraine see Ford, Marcia, pseud.
Radford, Ruby Lorraine (1891-1971)
--Anne Fuller, Librarian. Ford, Marcia, pseud. LC 57-87488. 220p. 21cm. 1957. Avalon Books.
--A Cruise for Judy. Ford, Marcia, pseud. LC 57-126868. 224p. 20cm. 1957. Avalon Books.
--Dixie Nurse. Ford, Marcia, pseud. LC 53-118893. 255p. 21cm. 1953. Avalon Books.
--Dorothy Lamour and the Haunted Lighthouse: An Original Story Featuring Dorothy Lamour As the Heroine. Bailey, Matilda, pseud. authorized. Vallely, Henry E., illus. LC 49-380985. 249 p. illus. 21 cm. 1947. Whitman Pub. Co.
--The Enchanted Cove. LC 57-12675. 223p. 21cm. 1957. Avalon Books.
--The Enchanted Hill. Evans, Jane A., illus. LC 68-4751. (Illus.). 127 p. 22cm. (Quest book for children). 1968. (ISBN 0-8356-0416-0). Theosophical Pub. House.
--Kathy Phillips, Scriptwriter. Ford, Marcia, pseud. LC 56-58091. 222p. 20cm. 1956. Avalon Books.
--Kitty Carter, Canteen Girl. Vallely, Henry E., illus. LC 45-102313. 3 p. l., 11-248 p. illus. 20 1/2 cm. (Fighters for freedom series). 1944. Whitman Publishing Company.
--Marie of Old New Orleans. Snyder, Harold E., illus. LC 44-6549. 271 p. front., illus., plates. 21 cm. 1943. David McKay Company.
--Marie of Old New Orleans. Snyder, Harold E., illus. LC 31-24664. 271 p. front., illus., plates. 20 cm. c.1931. The Penn Publishing Company.
--The Mystery of Adventure Island. (Dollar Mystery and Adventure Ser.). N.D. David McKay Co.
--The Mystery of Adventure Island. McCollum, Katharine, illus. LC 28-172732. 307 p. front., plates. 20 cm. 1928. The Penn Publishing Company.
--The Mystery of Magnolia Beach. Stein, Harve (1904-), illus. LC 42-25516. 254 p. col. front., illus. 21 cm. 1942. David McKay Company.
--The Mystery of Myrtle Grove. Snyder, Harold E., illus. LC 33-354787. 320 p. front., plates. 20 cm. c.1933. The Penn Publishing Company.
--The Mystery of Palmetto Lodge. Hargens, Charles, Jr. (1893-), illus. LC 29-186992. 306 p. front., plates. 20 cm. c.1929. The Penn Publishing Company.
--The Mystery of Pelican Cove. Homer, Caroline, illus. LC 34-390566. 304 p. front., plates. 20 cm. c.1934. The Penn Publishing Company.
--The Mystery of the Bradley Pearls. Sweeney, Nora, illus. LC 30-256239. 320 p. front., plates. 20 cm. c.1930. The Penn Publishing Company.
--Mystery of the Nancy Lee. N.D. David McKay Co.
--The Mystery of the Nancy Lee. Hargens, Charles, Jr. (1893-), illus. LC 32-324153. 320 p. front., plates. 20 cm. c.1932. The Penn Publishing Company.
--Mystery of the White Knight. N.D. David McKay Co.
--The Mystery of the White Knight. McCollum, KatHarine, illus. LC 27-148032. 314 p. front., plates. 20 cm. 1927. The Penn Publishing Company.
--Nancy Craig and the Fire Opal of Guatemala. Bailey, Matilda, pseud. authorized. Hedwig, Jo Meixner, illus. LC 49-3807. 248 p. illus. 21 cm. 1948. Whitman Pub. Co.
--Nancy Dale Army Nurse. Vallely, Henry E., illus. LC 45-958. 3 p. l., 11-248 p. illus. 20 1/2 cm. (Fighters for freedom series). 1944. Whitman Publishing Company.
--Nurse in the Pinelands. Ford, Marcia, pseud. LC 55-13904. 252p. 21cm. 1955. Avalon Books.
--Pamela Lee ,Home Economist. Ford, Marcia, pseud. LC 56-13315. 224p. 21cm. c.1956. Avalon Books.
--Patty O'Neal on the Airways. Vallely, Henry E., illus. LC 46-22725. 2 p. l., 9-248 p. illus. 20 1/2 cm. 1946. Whitman Publishing Company.
--Peacehaven. Ford, Marcia, pseud. LC 54-8726. 252p. 21cm. 1954. Avalon Books.
--Peggy Parker, Girl Inventor. Colburn, Dorothy, illus. LC 46-22726. 3 p. l., 11-248 p. illus. 20 1/2 cm. 1946. Whitman Publishing Co.
--Rose-Colored Glasses. 2d rev. ed. White, Iris Weddell, illus. LC 79-110698. (Illus.). 56 p. 22cm. (Quest book for children). 1970. Theosophical Pub. House.
--Sandra of the Girl Orchestra. Fomeko, Lise, illus. LC 46-22727. 3 p. l., 11-248 p. illus. 20 1/2 cm. 1946. Whitman Publishing Company.
--Scout Counselor. Ford, Marcia, pseud. LC 58-9136. 223p. 21cm. 1958. Avalon Books.
--Secret of Ocean House. Hart, Lewis, illus. LC 61-7143. 157p. illus. 21cm. 1961. Abelard-Schuman.
--The Secret of Peach Orchard Plantation. Kennedy, Richard (1910-), illus. LC 63-8105. 160 p. illus. 20 cm. 1963. Abelard-Schuman.
--Secret of the Bay. Hedwig, Jo Meixner, illus. LC 46-2669. 4 p. l., 11-197 p. 21 cm. (Junior mystery league book). 1946. Howell, Soskin.
--Sylvia Sanders and the Tangled Web: The Story of a Girl's Struggle for a Radio Career. LC 46-6143. 2 p. l., 9-248 p. illus. 20 1/2 cm. 1946. Whitman Publishing Company.
--Tomorrow's Promise. LC 56-13310. 224p. 21cm. c.1956. Avalon Books.
Radice, William, tr. see Raychaudhuri, Upendrakishore.
Radin, Paul & Marvel, Elinore, eds.
--African Folktales and Sculpture. 355p. (Bollinger Ser.: No. 32). 1952. Pantheon Books Inc.
Radin, Ruth Yaffe
--A Winter Place. O'Kelley, Mattie Lou, illus. LC 82-15349. (Illus.). 32p. (gr. 3 up). 1982. (ISBN 0-316-73218-4, Pub. by Atlantic Monthly Pr). Little. **Award: (ALA).**
Radius, Marianne
--New Testament Story Sermons for Children's Church. 120p. 1984. (ISBN 0-8010-7723-0). Baker Bk.
--Ninety Story Sermons for Children's Church. (Illus.). 286p. 1976, c.1966. (ISBN 0-8010-7641-2). Baker Book House.
--Tent of God. Overvoorde, Cris, illus. (Illus.). 320p. (gr. 5-10). 1968. (ISBN 0-8028-4057-4). Eerdmans.
Radke, Martha Elizabeth
--The Cat Who Conducted with His Tail. Tootill, Ginger, illus. LC 81-90803. (Illus.). 19 p. 19cm. c.1979. (ISBN 0-9607994-0-0). G.E. Radke.
--The Cat Who Conducted With His Tail. Tootill, Ginger, illus. LC 81-90803. (Illus.). 28p. (Orig.). (ps-3). 1982. (ISBN 0-9607994-0-0). GE Radke.
Radlauer, Edward, jt. auth. see Radlauer, Ruth Shaw.
Radlauer, Edward (1921-)
--Minibike Challenge. Radlauer, Dan, illus. LC 72-131218. (Illus.). 82 p. 25cm. (Rally series). 1970. Elk Grove Press.
--Monster Mania. LC 79-18666. p. cm. (Ready, get set, go). c.1979. (ISBN 0-516-07472-5). Childrens Press.
--Motorcycle Challenge. Radlauer, Dan, illus. LC 77-167767. (Illus.). 68p. (Rally Ser.). 1971. (ISBN 0-516-07405-9, Elk Grove Bks). Childrens.
Radlauer, Edward (1921-) & Radlauer, Ruth Shaw (1926-)
--BMX Winners. LC 84-7818. (Illus.). 47 p. 25cm. (Fact and fiction books). c.1984. (ISBN 0-516-07813-5). Childrens Press.
--Buggy-Go-Round. Radlauer, Edward (1921-) & Radlauer, Ruth Shaw (1926-), illus. LC 76-15188. (Illus.). photos. glossary. 48p. (Sports Action Bks). (gr. 3 up). 1971. (ISBN 0-531-01991-8). Watts.
--Chopper Cycle. Radlauer, Edward (1921-) & Radlauer, Ruth Shaw (1921-), illus. LC 79-180239. (Illus.). 47 p. 1972. (ISBN 0-531-02033-9). Watts.
--Drag Racing Pix Dix. Radlauer, Edward (1921-) & Radlauer, Ruth Shaw (1926-), illus. (Language Lab). (gr. 3 up). 1970. (ISBN 0-8372-0564-6). (ISBN 0-8372-0565-4). Bowmar-Noble.
--Dragstrip Challenge. Radlauer, Edward (1921-) & Radlauer, Ruth Shaw (1926-), illus. LC 78-84220. (Illus.). (Rally Ser.). 1969. (ISBN 0-516-07401-6, Elk Grove Bks). Childrens.
--Dragstrip Challenge. Radlauer, Edward (1921-) & Radlauer, Ruth Shaw (1926-), illus. LC 72-85201. (Illus.). 83 p. 25cm. c.1972. Childrens Press.
--Foolish Filly. LC 73-17048. (gr. 3 up). 1974. (ISBN 0-531-02680-9). Watts.
--Horse Show Challenge. Radlauer, Edward (1921-) & Radlauer, Ruth Shaw (1926-), illus. LC 72-10214. (Illus.). 79 p. 25cm. (Rally series). 1973. (ISBN 0-516-07406-7). Childrens Press.
--Karting Challenge. Radlauer, Edward (1921-) & Radlauer, Ruth Shaw (1926-), illus. LC 77-90755. (Illus.). 1969. (ISBN 0-516-07402-4, Elk Grove Bks). Childrens.
--Karting Winners. LC 82-1129. (Illus.). 47 p. 24cm. (Fact and fiction books). c.1982. (ISBN 0-516-07811-9). Childrens Press.
--Minibike Winners. LC 82-1150. (Illus.). 47 p. 25cm. (Fact & fiction books). c.1982. Childrens Press.
--Motorcycle Mania. Radlauer, Edward (1921-) & Radlauer, Ruth Shaw (1926-), illus. LC 73-6657. (Illus.). 32p. (Ready, Get Set, Go Ser.). (gr. 1-4). 1973. (ISBN 0-516-07421-0, Elk Grove Bks). (ISBN 0-516-47421-9). Childrens.
--Motorcycle Mutt. Radlauer, Edward (1921-) & Radlauer, Ruth Shaw (1926-), photos by LC 73-942. (Illus.). 48 p. 25cm. (Sports action book). 1973. (ISBN 0-531-02091-6). F. Watts.
--Motorcycle Winners. LC 82-1177. (Illus.). 47 p. 24cm. (Fact and fiction books). c.1982. (ISBN 0-516-07815-1). Childrens Press.
--On the Drag Strip. Radlauer, Edward (1921-) & Radlauer, Ruth Shaw (1926-), illus. LC 70-151889. (Illus.). photos. glossary. 48p. (Sports Action Ser). (gr. 3 up). 1971. (ISBN 0-531-01995-0). Watts.
--Parade Mania. LC 82-4133. (Illus.). (Mania Bks.). (gr. k-5). 1982. (ISBN 0-516-07793-7). (ISBN 0-516-47793-5). Childrens.
--Quarter Midget Challenge. LC 73-87568. (Illus.). 80p. (gr. 4-8). 1969. (ISBN 0-516-07404-0, Elk Grove Bks). Childrens.
--Soap Box Winners. LC 82-17867. p. cm. (Fact and fiction books). c.1983. (ISBN 0-516-07816-X). Childrens Press.
Radlauer, Ruth Shaw, jt. auth. see Radlauer, Edward.
Radlauer, Ruth Shaw (1926-)
--Get Ready for School. Krieger, Carol, illus. LC 67-22724. 36p. illus. col. 24cm.6. 1967. Elk Grove Press.
--Good Times Drawing Lines. Radlauer, Ruth Shaw (1926-), illus. LC 61-5054. unpaged. illus. 25cm. (Look, read, learn). 1961. Melmont Publishers.
--Of Course, You're a Horse. Graboff, Abner (1919-) & Greenwald, Sheila, pseud. (1934-), illus. Green, Sheila Ellen. Sheila, pseud. LC 59-5604. unpaged illus. 21cm. 1959. Abelard Schuman.
--Stein, the Great Retriever. Perl, Susan (1922-1983), illus. LC 64-25319. 32p. illus. (pt. col.) 16x22cm. (gr. k-3). 1965. (ISBN 0-672-50513-4). Bobbs.
--What Can You Do with a Box?. Rivkin, Jay, illus. LC 72-10216. (Illus.). 40 p. 24cm. 1973. (ISBN 0-516-07623-X). Childrens Press.
Radlauer, Ruth Shaw (1926-) & Radlauer, Edward (1921-)
--Colors. Curry, Nancy, ed. Mandlin, Harvey, photos by. LC 68-17026. (Early Childhood Ser.). (ps-3). 1967. (ISBN 0-8372-0259-0). Bowmar-Noble.
--Evening. Curry, Nancy, ed. Mandlin, Harvey, photos by. LC 68-17033. (Early Childhood Ser.). (ps-3). 1967. (ISBN 0-8372-0269-8). Bowmar-Noble.
--Evening. Radlauer, Edward (1921-) & Radlauer, Ruth Shaw (1926-), illus. LC 68-17033. (Illus.). 1 v. (unpaged. (Bowmar early childhood series). 1968. Bowmar Pub. Corp.
--Father Is Big. Mandlin, Harvey, photos by. LC 67-25575. (Illus.). 1 v. (unpaged. (Bowmar early childhood series). 1967. Bowmar Pub. Corp.
--Guide Dog Winners. LC 82-17825. p. cm. (Fact and fiction books). c.1983. (ISBN 0-516-07812-7). Childrens Press.
Radley, Gail (1951-)
--CF in His Corner. LC 83-20677. 128p. 1984. (ISBN 0-590-07901-8). (ISBN 0-590-07901-8). Four Winds Press.
--The Night Stella Hid the Stars. Wallner, John C (1945-), illus. LC 78-55545. p. cm. c.1978. Crown.
--Nothing Stays the Same Forever. LC 81-12515. p. cm. c.1981. (ISBN 0-517-54465-2). Crown.
--Special Strengths. Boddy, Joe, illus. LC 84-21658. (Illus.). 56 p. 21cm. c.1984. (ISBN 0-87743-702-5). (ISBN 0-87743-198-1). BellwoodPress.
--The World Turned Inside Out. LC 82-19796. p. cm. c.1982. (ISBN 0-517-54616-7). Crown Publishers.
--Zahra's Search. Newman, Winifred Barnum, illus. LC 82-11583. p. cm. 1982, c.1981. (ISBN 0-87743-161-2). Baha'i Pub. Trust.
Radlov, Nikolal Ernestovich (1889-)
--The Cautious Carp and Other Fables in Pictures. Black, Helen (1890-), tr. LC 38-27423. 48 p. col. illus. 20 x 28 cm. c.1938. Coward McCann, Inc.
Radnor, Marvin & Stevenson, Robert Louis (1850-1894)
--Songs for Little Children. LC 35-27161. (Music by Marvin Radnor). 2 p. l., 3-27 p. 24 cm. (Book 1). 1923. M. Radnor.
Rae, Gwynedd (1892-)
--Mary Plain & the Twins. 1952. (ISBN 0-7100-1995-5). Routledge & Kegan.
--Mary Plain Goes Bob-a-Jobbing. 1954. (ISBN 0-7100-1996-3). Routledge & Kegan.
--Mary Plain Goes to America. 1957. (ISBN 0-7100-1997-1). Routledge & Kegan.
--Mary Plain in Town. 1935. (ISBN 0-7100-1989-0). Routledge & Kegan.
--Mary Plain in Trouble. 1940. (ISBN 0-7100-1991-2). Routledge & Kegan.
--The Mary Plain Omnibus. Williamson, Irene, illus. LC 77-364253. (Illus.). 8, 458 p. 20cm. 1976. (ISBN 0-7100-8437-4). Routledge and Kegan Paul.
--Mary Plain's Big Adventure. 1944. (ISBN 0-7100-1992-0). Routledge & Kegan.
--Mary Plain's 'Whodunit'. 1965. (ISBN 0-7100-1999-8). Routledge & Kegan.
--Mostly Mary. Harris, Audrey, illus. LC 31-22143. 88 p. incl. front., illus. 20 cm. 1931. W. Morrow & Company.
Rae, Hugh Crauford see Crawford, Robert, pseud.
Rae, Jess Campbell
--Beach Magic. Newton, Margaret, illus. 48p. N.D. Binfords & Mort.
Rae, John Malcolm (1931-)
--The Third Twin: A Ghost Story. LC 80-16001. (Illus.). 111 p. 23cm. 1981, c.1980. (ISBN 0-7232-6192-X). F. Warne.
Rae, John (1882-1963)
--The Big Family and Their Good Times. Rae, John (1882-1963), illus. LC 17-10436. 5 p. l., 50 p. illus. (part col.) 20 x 28 cm. c.1916. Dodd, Mead and Company.
--Granny Goose!. Verses and Pictures for Your Children. Gordon Volland ed. Volland, Gordon, ed. Rae, John (1882-1963), illus. LC 26-219930. 48 p. col. illus. 30 cm. c.1926. The P. F. Volland Company.
--Grasshopper Green. Rae, John (1882-1963), illus. 40p. (Sunny Bks.). N.D. P. F. Volland Co.
Rae, Judy
--Boogie Man, O Please. Lalo, illus. (Illus.). 44p. (ps-5). 1982. (ISBN 0-939728-07-9). (ISBN 0-939728-08-7). Touchstone Ent ND.
--Bye, Bye Boogieman. Rev. ed. Lalo, illus. Timm, Stephen A., intro. by. LC 83-70412. (Illus.). 42p. (Orig.). (ps-3). 1984. (ISBN 0-939728-09-5). Touchstone Ent ND.
Raebeck, Lois (1921-)
--Who Am I?. Activity Songs for Young Children. Goldsborough, June (1923-), illus. LC 69-15985. (Illus.). 32 p. 1970. Follett Pub. Co.
Raedal, Margit
--Mischievious Kitten. Proft, Irmhild & Proft, Hilmar, illus. (Illus.). (gr. k-3). 1970. (ISBN 0-87614-010-X, Disb. by Silver). Carolrhoda Bks.
Raedel, Margit, jt. auth. see Schempf, Bonnie Winck.
Rael, Rick, jt. auth. see Rubin, Jeff.
Raffensperger, Anna Frances, Mrs.
--Fritz's Ranch. A Book for Boys. LC 12-37954. 195 p. front., plates. 19 cm. c.1887. American Tract Society.
--Happy Hours. (Illus.). 48p. 1905. American Tract Society.
--Little Folks' Stories. 48p. N.D. American Tract Society.
--Little Stories for Good Little People, 1 of 50 vols. (Illus.). 48p. (Model Library No. 4). 1905. Set. American Tract Society.
--Seventeen and Twice Seventeen. A Story of New England. LC 12-37955. 320 p. front., plates. 19 cm. 1884. American Tract Society.
Rafill, Stewart see Crume, Vic.

AUTHOR INDEX RAND, EDWARD

Rafilson, Sidney, illus.
--My Dog, My Friend. (Illus.). 32p. (ps-1). 1972. (ISBN 0-307-10461-3, Golden Pr). Western Pub.
--My Dog, My Friend: In Pictures and Rhyme. LC 67-2915. (Illus.). 32cm. 28p. 1966. Whitman.
Raftery, Gerald Bransfield (1905-)
--City Dog. Cram, L. D. (1898-), illus. LC 53-7108. 216p. illus. 21cm. 1953. Morrow.
--Copperhead Hollow. LC 52-5066. 185 p. 20 cm. (Morrow junior books). 1952. Morrow.
--Gray Lance. LC 50-6575. 223 p. 20 cm. (Morrow Junior books). 1950. Morrow.
--The Natives Are Always Restless. Geer, Charles Hand (1922-), illus. (Illus.). (gr. 7-12). N.D. (ISBN 0-8149-0380-0). Vanguard.
--Silver Cloud. LC 67-30666. 184 p. 22 cm. 1967. Vanguard Press.
--Snow Cloud. LC 51-187. 189 p. 20cm. (Morrow junior books). 1951. Morrow.
--Twenty-Dollar Horse. 1955. E M Hale.
--Twenty-Dollar Horse. Safran, Bernard, illus. LC 55-9862. (Illus.). 192 p. 22cm. 1955. Messner.
Ragozin, Zenaide Alexeievna, jt. ed. see Burt, Mary Elizabeth.
Ragozin, Zenaide Alexeievna, ed. see Homerus.
Ragozin, Zenaide Alexeievna (1835-1924)
--Salammbo. N.D. G. P. Putnam's Sons.
--Siefried, the Hero Of the North, and Beowulf, the Hero of the Anglo-Saxons. Tobin, George T., illus. LC 96-1153. xxv, 332 p. front., 7 pl. 20 cm. (Tales of the heroic ages.). 1898. G. P. Putnam's Sons.
--Siegried and Beowulf. N.D. G. P. Putnam's Sons.
Ragozin, Zenaide Alexeievna (1835-1924) & Tegner, Esais (1782-1846)
--Frithjof, the Viking of Norway, and Roland, the Paladin of France. LC 695. vii, 295 p. front., plates, facsim. 20 cm. (Tales of the heroic ages). 1899. G. P. Putnam's Sons.
Ragsdale, Karl S., jt. ed. see Fair, Martha Harris.
Rahmas, Sigrid
--A Day in Fairy Land. LC 67-2703. (Illus.). 28 p. 25cm. 1967. Story House Corp.
Rahmas, Sigrid, ed. see Johnson, Margie L.
Rahmas, Sigrid, ed. see Smith, Vivian Brian.
Rahmlow, Lavina
--Granny Glee & Whoppity Sock. (Illus.). (gr. 2-4). 1979. (ISBN 0-682-49457-7). Exposition.
Rahr, Ruth, Mrs. & Rahr, William
--The Journey of the Toys. Ertz, Bruno (1873-), illus. LC 34-35311. 88 p. col. illus. 26 cm. c.1934. Color Craft Printers, Inc.
Rahr, William, jt. auth. see Rahr, Ruth, Mrs.
Raihle, Paul Henry (1892-) & Raihle, Sylvia
--The Visit of Santa Claus: As Inspired by the Poem, "A Visit from St. Nicholas". LC 39-9823. 31 p. illus. 24 cm. 1939. Chippewa Valley Courier.
Raihle, Sylvia, jt. auth. see Raihle, Paul Henry.
Raile, Vilate & Russell, Frank Alden (1908-)
--So There!. Dickeman, Mildred R., illus. LC 43-771343. 53 p. incl. col. front., illus. (part col.) 23 cm. 1942. Bookmark Press.
Railton, Ione, illus.
--Robin Hood and His Merry Men. N.D. Dutton & Co.
Raimondi, Emily
--Secret of the Sea Legacy. Tamer, Salem, illus. LC 73-83033. (Illus.). 173 p., 5 leaves of plates. 21cm. 1974. (ISBN 0-8149-0725-3). Vanguard Press.
Rainbird, Alice, ed. see Dickens, Charles John Huffam.
Rainboldt, Jo, jt. auth. see Gingras, Louie.
Rainbow, Elizabeth
--Concha and the Silver Star. 1st ed. Wilson, George, illus. LC 65-25360. vii, 118 p. illus. 22 cm. 1965. Duell, Sloan and Pearce.
--Mystery at Witchwood. Loehle, Richard, illus. LC 68-12862. (Illus.). 122 p. 21cm. 1968. Weybright and Talley.
Raine, William MacLeod (1871-)
--A Daughter of the Dons: A Story of New Mexico to-Day. LC 14-17091. 320 p. front., pl. 20 cm. c.1914. G. W. Dillingham Company.
Rainey, William R. I. (1852-1936), illus.
--Orden Ruth: His Little Royal Highness. 260p. N.D. E. P. Dutton & Company.
Rains, Marie Curtis
--Lazy Liza Lizard. Neville, Vera (1900-1978), illus. LC 38-24145. 182, 2 p. incl. col. front., illus. (part col.) 21 cm. c.1938. The John C. Winston Company.
--Lazy Liza Lizard's Tricks. 1st ed. Neville, Vera (1900-1978), illus. LC 53-6138. (Illus.). 119 p. 21cm. 1953. Winston.
Rainwater, Janette
--A Dragon in a Wagon. Gilbert, John, illus. (Illus.). (ps-3). 1966. (ISBN 0-307-60555-8, Golden Pr). Western Pub.
Raisbeck, Ana M.
--A Gem for Princess Zuleira. (Illus.). 32p. 1984. (ISBN 0-89962-380-8). Todd & Honeywell.
Rajanen, Aini
--A Tale for Saint Urho's Tay. Kilbride, Robert, illus. LC 81-295. p. cm. c.1981. (ISBN 0-87518-215-1). Dillon Press.
Raleigh, Francis
--Ralph Somerby at Panama. N.D. The Page Co.
Raleigh-King, Robin Victor Lethbridge see King, Robin, pseud.
Ralphson, G. Harvey (1879-)
--Boy Scouts Beyond the Arctic Circle: Or, The Lost Expedition. LC 44-27712. 2 p. l., 255 p. front. 19 1/2 cm. c.1913. M. A. Donahue & Company.
--Boy Scouts in a Motor Boat: Or, Adventures on the Columbia River. LC 12-13466. 246 p. incl. front. 20 cm. c.1912. M. A. Donohue & Company.
--Boy Scouts in a Submarine: Or, Searching an Ocean Floor. LC 13-2326. 217 p. incl. front. 20 cm. c.1912. M. A. Donohue & Company.
--Boy Scouts in an Airship: Or, The Warning from the Sky. LC 13-23126. 232 p. incl. front. 20 cm. c.1912. M. A. Donohue & Company.
--Boy Scouts in Belgium: Or, Under Fire in Flanders. LC 16-2568. 308 p. incl. front. 20 cm. (His Boy scouts series). c.1915. M. A. Donohue & Company.
--Boy Scouts in Mexico: Or, On Guard with Uncle Sam. LC 12-13468. 283 p. front., plates. 20 cm. (His Boy scouts series). c.1911. M. A. Donohue & Company.
--Boy Scouts in Southern Waters: Or, Spaniard's Treasure Chest. LC 16-2569. 279 p. incl. front. 20 cm. (His Boy scouts series). c.1915. M. A. Donohue & Company.
--Boy Scouts in the Canal Zone: Or, The Plot Against Uncle Sam. LC 12-13470. 255 p. front., plates. 20 cm. (His Boy scouts series). c.1911. M. A. Donohue & Company.
--Boy Scouts in the North Sea: Or, "Mystery of U-13,". LC 16-2567. 252 p. incl. front. 20 cm. (His Boy scouts series). c.1915. M. A. Donohue & Company.
--Boy Scouts in the Northwest: Or, Fighting Forest Fires. LC 12-134670. 255 p. incl. front. plates. 20 cm. (His Boy scouts series). c.1911. M. A. Donohue & Company.
--Boy Scouts in the Philippines: Or, The Key to the Treaty Box. LC 12-134691. 254 p. incl. front. plates. 20 cm. (His Boy scouts series). c.1911. M. A. Donohue & Company.
--Boy Scouts on Motor Cycles: Or, With the Flying Squadron. LC 13-237. 221 p. incl. front. 20 cm. c.1912. M. A. Donohue & Company.
Ralston, Jan, pseud., see Dunlop, Agnes Mary Robertson.
Ralston, Jan, pseud. (0000-1982)
--Mystery of the Good Adventure. Dunlop, Agnes Mary Robertson. Trotter, A. Mason, illus. LC 50-13846. 245 p. illus. 21 cm. 1950. Dodd, Mead.
Ralston, W. R. S.
--Krilof and his Fables. (Illus.). N.D. George Routledge.
--Russian Fairy Tales, 1 of 264 vols. (The New Argyle Ser.: No.264). 1900. Hurst & Co.
Ramage, Corinne
--The Joneses. LC 75-2491. (Illus.). 39 p. 23cm. 1975. (ISBN 0-397-31644-5). Lippincott.
Ramage, Rosalyn Rikel
--A Book About People. Fields, Don, illus. LC 79-7737. (Illus.). 64 p. 21cm. c.1980. (ISBN 0-8054-4258-8). Broadman Press.
--A Book for All Seasons. Shelton, Dean, illus. LC 77-81370. (Illus.). (gr. k-3). 1977. (ISBN 0-8054-4245-6). Broadman.
Ramakrishna, Swami
--Tales from Ramakrishna. Chakravarty, Biswaranjan, illus. Ray, Irene R. & Gupta, Mallika C., retold by. (Illus.). 54p. (Orig.). (gr. 1-5). 1975. (ISBN 0-87481-152-X). Vedanta Pr.
Ramakrishnan, Prema
--King Kamel. Joshi, Jagadish, illus. (Illus.). 24p. (Orig.). (gr. k-3). 1980. (ISBN 0-89744-210-5, Pub. by Children's Bk Trust India). Auromere.
Ramasvami Raju, P. V
--The Tales of the Sixty Mandarins. 2nd ed. Morley, Henry (1822-1894), ed. Browne, Gordon Frederick (1858-1932), illus. LC 8-210. xv, 280 p. incl. front., illus. 20 cm. 1886. Cassell & Company, Limited.
--The Tales of the Sixty Mandarins. Morley, Henry (1822-1894), ed. Browne, Gordon Frederick (1858-1932), illus. LC 43-40131. xv, 280 p. incl. front., illus. plates. 19 cm. 1943, c.1886. Cassell & Company, Limited.
Rambo, Dottie
--Down by the Creek Bank. Beatty, Dill, illus. (Creek Bank Kids Ser.: Vol. 1). (ps-8). 1979. (ISBN 0-914850-50-4). Impact Tenn.
--Germs, Vol. 3. (Creek Bank Kids Ser.). (ps-8). 1979. (ISBN 0-914850-49-0). Impact Tenn.
Rambo, Dottie & Huntsinger, Dave
--He Plants Me Like a Seed. (Creek Bank Kids Ser.: Vol. 7). (ps-8). 1980. (ISBN 0-914850-90-3). Impact Tenn.
--Is There Anything I Can Do for You?. Beatty, Dill, illus. (Creek Bank Kids Ser.: Vol. 5). (ps-8). 1979. (ISBN 0-914850-74-1). Impact Tenn.
Ramdsen, Evelyn, tr. see Sommerfelt, Aimee.
Ramee, Marie Louise de La see De La Ramee, Marie Louise.
Ramella, Richard
--The Lightyear Excuse: A Computer Space Adventure. (Illus.). 144p. (gr. 4-9). 1984. (ISBN 0-89588-222-1). SYBEX.
--Rainbow Quest: Color Computer Version. Porter, Coni, illus. (Illus.). (gr. 3-6). 1984. (ISBN 0-88006-064-6). Green Pub Inc.
Rames, Helen, jt. auth. see Rames, Ruth.
Rames, Ruth & Rames, Helen
--The Quinducklets: The Adventures of Five Little Ducks Who Were Quinducklets. Lynch, Jack, illus. LC 48-3676. 32 p. illus. 21 x 28 cm. 1945. Murray & Gee.
Ramholt, Toni, tr. see Hopp, Zinken.
Ramirez, Carolyn Holmes (1933-)
--Foot and Feet. Gates, Frieda (1933-), illus. LC 73-79451. (Illus.). 47 p. 24cm. 1973. (ISBN 0-8178-5121-6). (ISBN 0-8178-5121-6). Harvey House.
--Small As a Raisin, Big As the World. Ramirez, Carl, illus. LC 61-13358. (Illus.). unpaged. 28cm. 1961. Harvey House.
Ramirez, Sharon (1936-)
--Brinktown. LC 81-7704. p. cm. 1981. (ISBN 0-932112-12-9). Carolina Wren Press.
Ramos, Francie
--The Land of Health. Parker, W. Karl, ed. Hall, Bill, illus. Parker Chiropractic Research Foundation LC 79-114692. (Illus.). 39 p. 29cm. c.1977. Parker Chiropractic Research Foundation.
Ramsay, DeVere Maxwell
--God's Church: A Book of Stories About the Church for Young Children. Endhoven, Rita, illus. LC 65-28567. 18 p. illus. 27 cm. 1966. W. B. Eerdmans Pub. Co.
--God's Promises. (Illus.). (gr. 3-7). 1964. (ISBN 0-8028-4019-1). Eerdmans.
Ramsay, Janet
--Singing Bird. King, Ruth, illus. LC 39-33743. 3 p. l., xi-xii, 13-267 p. illus. 21 cm. 1939. T. Nelson and Sons.
--Stars Rising. LC 38-16871. xi, 13-218 p. illus. 21 cm. 1938. T. Nelson and Sons.
Ramsay, Marjorie B.
--Nyra. Ramsay, Marjorie B., illus. (Illus.). (gr. 4-7). 1979. (ISBN 0-917182-10-3). Triumph Pub.
Ramsay, Tamara
--The Toy Workshop in the Land of Silvery-Blue. LC 33-5937. 31 p. illus. (part col.) 27 cm. 1932. A. Whitman & Company.
Ramsbotham, Helen, tr. see Recher, Robert.
Ramsden, Evelyn, tr. see Braenne, Berit.
Ramsden, Evelyn, tr. see Franzen, Nils Olof.
Ramsden, Evelyn, tr. see Hamre, Leif.
Ramsden, Evelyn, tr. see Holmvik, Oyvind (1914-) & Faye-Lund, Hans.
Ramsden, Evelyn, tr. see Kullman, Harry.
Ramsden, Evelyn, tr. see Lindgren, Astrid Ericsson.
Ramsden, Evelyn, tr. see Rasmussen, Sigurd.
Ramsden, Evelyn, tr. see Rongen, Bjorn.
Ramsden, Evelyn, tr. see Senje, Sigurd.
Ramsden, Lewis
--Quest of the Luck. (The Forward Ser.). N.D. William Collins Co.
Ramsey, Helen
--The Halloween Festival Book. 133p. N.D. T. S. Denison & Co Inc.
--The Primary Closing Day Book. 93p. N.D. T. S. Denison & Co Inc.
Ramsey, John O.
--Rocky, the Kitten Who Wins by a Squeak. McNeill, Cecily, illus. LC 84-158735. (Illus.). 32 p. 22cm. c.1984. (ISBN 0-533-05794-9). Vantage Press.
Ramstad, Josie Winship & Benson, Ethel Mitchell
--Ferocious Sarah. Ramstad, Josie Winship, illus. LC 79-118530. (Illus.). 44 p. c.1979. (ISBN 0-934926-00-X). Talespinner Publications.
Ramtha & Mahr, Douglas J.
--The Ominous Dragoon of Dothdura. Banghart, Jerry, illus. LC 84-62175. (Illus.). 48p. (gr. k-9). 1985. (ISBN 0-931317-13-4). Masterworks Inc.
Rand, Addison, pseud., see Regli, Adolph Casper.
Rand, Ann Binkley
--Did a Bear Just Walk There. (Illus.). (gr. k-2). N.D. (ISBN 0-8382-1011-2). Hale.
--Did a Bear Just Walk There?. Birnbaum, Abe (1899-), illus. LC 66-11206. (Illus.). 1v.(unpaged) illus.(pt. colored) 29cm. (ps-3). 1966. (ISBN 0-15-223457-8). HarBraceJ.
--Edward & The Horse. N.D. E. M. Hale & Co.
--Edward & the Horse. 1 st. ed. Eksell, Olle (1918-), illus. LC 61-6121. (Illus.). (gr. k-2). 1961. (ISBN 0-15-225202-9, HJ). HarBraceJ.
--I Know a Lot of Things. 1 st. ed. Rand, Paul (1914-), illus. LC 56-5576. unpaged. illus. 27cm. 1956. Harcourt, Brace. **Award: (NYT).**
--I Know a Lot of Things. Rand, Paul (1914-), illus. (Illus.). 1 v. (unpaged). 23cm. (Voyager Book). 1973, c.1956. (ISBN 0-15-644400-3). Harcourt.
--The Little River. 1 st. ed. Rojankovsky, Feodor Stepanovich (1891-1970), illus. LC 59-7520. unpaged. illus. 23x26cm. 1959. Harcourt, Brace.
--So Small. 1st ed. Rojankovsky, Feodor Stepanovich (1891-1970), illus. LC 62-17447. unpaged. illus. 19cm. (gr. k-3). 1962. (ISBN 0-15-277110-7). Harcourt, Brace & World.
--Umbrellas, Hats and Wheels. 1 st. ed. Snyder, Jerome (1916-1976), illus. LC 61-10113. unpaged. illus. 27cm. 1961. Harcourt, Brace & World. **Award: (NYT).**
Rand, Ann Binkley & Rand, Paul (1914-)
--Tiger! Tiger! LC 70-91011. (Illus.). 27cm. 31p. (ps-3). 1970. (ISBN 0-15-245580-9, HJ). HarBraceJ.
--Little One. LC 62-15628. (Illus.). (gr. k-3). 1962. (ISBN 0-15-246315-1). HarBraceJ.
--Sparkle and Spin: A Book About Words. 1 st. ed. LC 57-9445. unpaged. illus. 26cm. 1957. Harcourt, Brace. **Award: (NYT).**
--Voyager Book. 32p. N.D. Harcourt Brace Jovanovich.
Rand, C. H. see Hazelton, Mabel, pseud.
Rand, Edward Augustus (1837-1903)
--After the Freshet. N.D. Lothrop Pub. Co.
--The Atlantic Surfman. LC 4-27121. 20 cm. 1904. Eaton and Mains.
--The Bark-Cabin on Kearsarge. LC 28-179111. 209 p. incl. front. plates. 18 cm. (On cover: Out of school series). 1880. D. Lothrop and Company.
--Bark Cabin on Kearsarge, 1 of 1 vols. (Illus.). (Bark Cabin Library). 1882. Lothrop Pub. Co.
--The Bark Cabin on Kearsarge. N.D. Thomas Whittaker.
--The Camp at Surf Bluff. LC 8-599. 304 p. 19 cm. (Up-the-ladder club series, round 4. Vacation). 1886. Phillips & Hunt.
--A Candle in the Sea: Or, A Winter at Seal's Head. N.D. Thomas Whittaker.
--Christmas Jack. LC 8-600. 231 p. front., plates. 18 cm. (Sunday-Hour Lib.). c.1878. American Tract Society.
--Christmas Jack. (Illus.). 231p. 1905. American Tract Society.
--The Drummer-Boy of the Rappahannock: Or, Taking Sides. LC 8-601. 336 p. front. 19 cm. 1889. Hunt & Eaton.
--The Drummer-Boy of the Rappahannock: Or, Taking Sides. (Illus.). N.D. Methodist Bk Concern.
--Fifer Boy of the Boston Siege. LC 4776. 20 cm. 326p. 1900. A. I. Bradley & Co.
--Her Christmas and Her Easter, 1 of 50 vols. 187p. (Library of Best Authors). 1905. Set. American Tract Society.
--Hymns of Help and Hope. LC 5-36805. 20 cm. 53p. c.1905. The Grafton Press.
--Kindling-Wood Jimmy, 2 of 4 Vols. 252p. (The Schooner on the Beach Ser.). N.D. Set. American Sunday-School Union.
--Knight that Smote the Dragon. (Illus.). N.D. Methodist Book Concern.
--A Knight That Smote the Dragon: Or, The Young People's Gough. LC 12-37974. 19 cm. 1892p. N.D. Cranston & Stowe.
--Little Brown-Top, and the People Under It, 1 of 3 vols. (Illus.). (School and Camp Ser.). N.D. D Lothrop.
--Making the Best of It: Or, Tumble-up Tom. LC 8-60201. 3 p. l., 281 p. front., pl. 20 cm. (Look ahead series, no. 1). 1888. T. Whittaker.
--Manhood: Out of the Breakers, 1 of 5 vols. (Up-the-Ladder Club Ser.: No. 5). N.D. Set. Methodist Bk Concern.
--Margie at the Harbor-Light. A Story Succeeding "Her Christmas and Her Easter.". LC 8-60399. 264 p. front., plates. 19 cm. c.1888. American Tract Society.
--The Mill at Sandy Creek. LC 8-6049. 2 p. l., 360 p. front., 2 pl. 19 cm. (Fighting the sea series, no. 3). 1893. T. Whittaker.
--Nellie's New Year, 1 of 50 vols. LC 8-605. 351 p. front., plates. 18 cm. (Model Library: No. 3). c.1879. Set. American Tract Society.
--Our Clerk from Barkton: Or, Right Rather Than Rich. LC 8-606. 3 p. l., 342 p. front., 2 pl. 20 cm. (Added t.-p.: Look ahead series, no. 4). 1891. T. Whittaker.
--Out of the Breakers. LC 8-607. 336 p. 19 cm. (Up-the-ladder club series, round 5. Manhood). 1886. Phillips & Hunt.
--Play: Knights of the White Shield, 1 of 5 vols. (Up-the-Ladder Club Ser.: No. 1). N.D. Set. Methodist Bk Concern.
--Pushing Ahead: Or, Big Brother Dave, 1 of 3 vols. LC 8-608. viii, 9-314 p. front., plates. 19 cm. (School and camp series no. 1). c.1880. D. Lothrop and Company.
--Roy's Dory at the Sea-Shore. LC 8-609. 346 p. front., 2 pl. 19 cm. (School and camp series, no. 2). c.1880. D. Lothrop and Company.
--Sailor-Boy Bob. N.D. Methodist Bk Concern.
--Sailor-Boy Bob. LC 8-610. 367 p. 19 cm. 1887. Phillips & Hunt.

--A Salt Water Hero. LC 8-611. 2 p. l., 330 p. front., 2 pl. 20 cm. (Fighting the sea series, no. 4). c.1894. T. Whittaker.
--School and Camp Series, 3 vols. (Illus.). N.D. Set. D Lothrop.
--The School in the Light-House. LC 8-612. 324 p. 19 cm. (Up-the-ladder club series, round 2. School). 1885. Phillips & Hunt.
--School in the Lighthouse, 1 of 5 vols. (Up-the-Ladder Club Ser.: No. 2). N.D. Set. Methodist Bk Concern.
--The Schooner on the Beach. LC 8-613. 272 p. front., plates. 18 cm. 1879. American Sunday-School Union.
--The Schooner on the Beach Series, 4 Vols. N.D. American Sunday-School Union.
--Ship Ashore. LC 3-24532. 20 cm. 235p. 1903. Eaton and Mains.
--The Tent in the Notch. LC 72-2040. (Illus.). 183 p. 22cm. (The Black Heritage Library Collection). 1972, c.1881. (ISBN 0-8369-9054-4). Books for Libraries Press.
--The Tent in the Notch. LC 8-614. 178 p. front., 2 pl. 18 cm. c.1881. D. Lothrop & Company.
--The Tent in the Notch, 1 of 4 vols. (Bark Cabin Library). 1882. D Lothrop.
--The Tent in the Notch. N.D. Thomas Whittaker.
--Too Late for the Tidemill. LC 8-615. 2 p. l., 307 p. front., 2 pl. 20 cm. (Look ahead series no. 3). 1890. T. Whittaker.
--Two Boys and a Fire. 112 p. front., pl. 19 cm. 1900. T. Whittaker.
--Two College Boys: Or, The Old Man of the Mountain. LC 8-663. 166 p. front., pl. 19 cm. (White Mountain series, no. 3). c.1895. T. Whittaker.
--Under the Lantern at Black Rocks. LC 8-616. 347 p. 19 cm. 1890. Hunt & Eaton.
--Under the Lantern at Black Rocks. N.D. Methodist Bk Concern.
--Up North in a Whaler: Or, Would He Keep His Colors Flying?. LC 8-61706. 3 p. l., 350 p. front., plates. 20 cm. (Look ahead series. no. 2). 1889. T. Whittaker.
--Up-the-Ladder Club: Or, The Knights of the White Shield. LC 8-658. 330 p. 19 cm. (Up-the-ladder club series, round 1. Play). 1885. Phillips & Hunt.
--Vacation: Camp at Surf Bluff, 1 of 5 vols. (Up-the-Ladder Club Ser.: No. 4). N.D. Set. Methodist Bk Concern.
--When the War Broke Out: Or, Sailor-Boy Bob's Sister. N.D. Methodist Bk Concern.
--When the War Broke Out: Or, Sailor-Boy Bob's Sister. LC 8-662. 368 p. 19 cm. 1885. Phillips & Hunt.
--The Whistle in the Alley. 269 p. front., plates. 20 cm. 1899. A. I. Bradley & Co.
--The Whistle in the Alley. (Bks. for Boy Scouts). N.D. Abingdon Press.
--Work: Yardstick & Scissors, 1 of 5 vols. (Up-the-Ladder Club Ser.). N.D. Set. Methodist Bk Concern.
--Yard-Stick and Scissors. 306 p. 19 cm. (Up-the-ladder club series, round 3. Store). 1886. Phillips & Hunt.

Rand, George Hart
--Sherman Hale, the Harvard Half-Back. LC 10-21745. 1 p. l., vii-viii, 9-326 p. col. front., col. plates. 21 cm. 1910. R. F. Fenno & Company.

Rand, Kenneth
--The Dirge of the Sea-Children. N.D. Sherman, French & Co.
--The Rainbow Chaser. N.D. Sherman, French & Co.

Rand McNally and Company
--Galactic Adventures. LC 80-80321. (Illus.). 188 p., 2 leaves of plates. 27cm. 1980. (ISBN 0-528-82374-4). Rand McNally.
--A Treasury of Elf Storybooks: Twenty -Eight Best-Loved Stories. LC 79-65640. (Illus.). 92 p. 29cm. c.1979. (ISBN 0-528-82788-X). Rand McNally.

Rand, Mary Abbott
--Holly and Mistletoe. (Illus.). N.D. T. Y. Crowell.
--Homespun Yarns for Christmas Stockings. (Illus.). N.D. T. Y. Crowell.

Rand, Paul, jt. auth. see Rand, Ann Binkley.

Randal, Vera
--You Get Used to a Place. 1972. (ISBN 0-399-11019-4). G. P. Putnam's Sons.

Randall, Billie
--Golden Girl and the Guardians of the Gemstones. Ruiz, Aristides, illus. LC 85-2047. p. cm. 1985. (ISBN 0-394-87450-1). Random House.

Randall, Blossom E. (1902-)
--Fun for Chris. Smith, Eunice Young, illus. LC 56-7753. (Illus.). (gr. k-3). 1956. (ISBN 0-8075-2674-6). A Whitman.

Randall, Dudley
--A Litany of Friends: Poems Selected & New. LC 80-85234. 101p. 1981. (ISBN 0-916418-33-2). (ISBN 0-916418-29-4). Lotus.

Randall, E. T.
--Cosmic Kidnappers. Rogers, Jackie, illus. LC 84-8579. (Illus.). 128p. (Alien Adventures Ser.). (gr. 4-7). 1985. (ISBN 0-8167-0328-0). (ISBN 0-8167-0329-9). (ISBN 0-8167-0329-9). Troll Assocs.
--Target: Earth. Rogers, Jackie, illus. LC 84-2740. (Illus.). 128p. (Alien Adventures Ser.). (gr. 3-7). 1985. (ISBN 0-8167-0326-4). (ISBN 0-8167-0327-2). Troll Assocs.
--Thieves from Space. Rogers, Jackie, illus. LC 84-8538. (Illus.). 128p. (Alien Adventures Ser.). (gr. 3-7). 1985. (ISBN 0-8167-0330-2). (ISBN 0-8167-0331-0). Troll Assocs.
--Town in Terror. Rogers, Jackie, illus. LC 84-5617. (Illus.). 116 p. 20cm. (Alien Adventures). c.1985. (ISBN 0-8167-0332-9). (ISBN 0-8167-0333-7). Troll Associates.

Randall, Florence Engel (1917-)
--All the Sky Together. LC 83-2604. p. cm. 1983. (ISBN 0-689-30996-1). Atheneum.
--The Almost Year. LC 78-134819. 239 p. 25cm. 1971. Atheneum. **Award: (ALA).**
--A Watcher in the Woods. LC 75-23044. 229 p. 22cm. 1976. (ISBN 0-689-30511-7). Atheneum.

Randall, George Archibald (1887-)
--Saddle up. Randall, George Archibald (1887-), illus. LC 41-11238. 3 p. l., 9-223, 1 p. illus. 21 cm. 1941. E. P. Dutton & Company, Inc.

Randall, Homer
--Army Boys in France: Or, From Training Camp to Trenches. Herbert, Robert Gaston, illus. LC 18-10272. iv, 216 p. front. 19 cm. (His Army boys series). c.1918. G. Sully & Company.
--Army Boys in the Big Drive: Or, Smashing Forward to Victory. (Army Boys Ser.). N.D. George Sully & Co.
--Army Boys in the French Trenches: Or, Hand to Hand Fighting with the Enemy. Herbert, Robert Gaston, illus. LC 18-15089. iv, 214 p. front. 20 cm. (His Army boys series). c.1918. G. Sully & Company.
--Army Boys Marching into Germany: Or, Over the Rhine with the Stars and Stripes. LC 19-16661. iv, 214 p. front. 20 cm. (His Army boys series). c.1919. G. Sully & Company.
--Army Boys on German Soil: Or, Our Doughboys Quelling the Mobs. (Army Boys Ser.). N.D. George Sully & Co.
--Army Boys on the Firing Line: Or, Holding Back the German Drive. (Army Boys Ser.). N.D. George Sully & Co.

Randall, Jane
--When Toys Could Talk. Peat, Fern Bisel, Mrs. (1893-), illus. LC 39-16852. 16 p. illus. (part col.) 27 x 24 cm. c.1939. The Saalfield Publishing Company.

Randall, Janet, pseud., see Young, Janet Randall.
Randall, Janet, pseud., see Young, Randall.
Randall, Janet, pseud. (1919-) & Young, Robert William (1916-1969)
--Brave Young Warriors. Young, Janet Randall. LC 73-85137. (Janet Randall is the joint pseud. of Janet Randall Young and Robert William Young). 160p. (gr. 6-9). 1969. (ISBN 0-679-25029-8). McKay.
--The Buffalo Box. Young, Janet Randall. Koering, Ursula (1921-), illus. LC 69-12949. (Janet Randall is the Joint Pseud. of Janet Randall Young(1919-) and Robert William Young(1916-1969)). (Illus.). 120 p. 21cm. 1969. D. McKay Co.
--Burro Canyon. Young, Janet Randall. Lewis, Richard William (1933-1966), illus. LC 64-22403. (Janet Randall is the pseud. of Janet Randall Young & Robert William Young). 183 p. illus. 21 cm. 1964. D. McKay.
--Desert Venture. Young, Janet Randall. LC 63-12142. (Janet Randall is the joint pseud. of Jamet Randall Young & Robert William Young). 182 p. illus. 21 cm. 1963. D. McKay Co.
--The Girl from Boothill. Young, Janet Randall. Lantz, Paul (1908-), illus. LC 62-107588. (Janet Randall is the joint pseud. for Janet Randall & Robert William Young). 186p. illus. 21cm. 1962. D. McKay Co.
--Island Ghost. Young, Janet Randall. Kidwell, Carl (1910-), illus. (Janet Randall is the joint pseud. of Janet Randall Young & Robert William Young). (Illus.). (gr. 3-5). 1970. (ISBN 0-679-25068-9). McKay.
--Jellyfoot. Young, Janet Randall. LC 64-14845. (Janet Randall is the joint pseud. of Janet Randall Young & Robert William Young). 184 p. illus. 21 cm. 1964. D. McKay Co.
--Miracle of Sage Valley. Young, Janet Randall. LC 58-10762. (Janet Randall is the pseud. of Janet Randall Young & Robert William Young). (Illus.). 185 p. 21cm. 1958. Longmans, Green.
--Pony Girl. Young, Janet Randall. Morse, Dorothy Bayley (1906-1979), illus. LC 63-13175. (Janet Randall is the joint pseud. for Janet Randall Young & Robert William Young). (Illus.). 151 p. 21cm. 1963. McKay.
--Saddles for Breakfast. Young, Janet Randall. (Janet Randall is the joint pseud. of Janet Randall Young & Robert William Young). (Illus.). (gr. 6-9). 1961. (ISBN 0-679-20166-1). McKay.
--Saddles for Breakfast. Young, Janet Randall. 1 st. ed. Laune, Paul Sidney (1899-), illus. LC 61-11304. (Janet Randall is the joint pseud. of Janet Randall Young & Robert William Young). 186p. illus. 21cm. 1961. Longmans, Green.
--The Seeing Heart. Young, Randall. LC 65-21597. (Janet Randall is the joint pseud. of Janet Randall Young & Robert William Young). 187 p. illus. 21 cm. 1965. D. McKay Co.
--Topi Forever. Young, Janet Randall. (Janet Randall is the joint pseud. of Janet Randall Young & Robert William Young). (Illus.). 90 p. 21cm. 1968. D. McKay Co.
--Tumbleweed Heart. Young, Janet Randall. (Janet Randall is the joint pseud. of Janet Randall Young & Robert William Young). 1959. McKay.
--Tumbleweed Heart. Young, Janet Randall. 1 st. ed. O'Sullivan, Tom, illus. LC 59-11266. (Janet Randall is the joint pseud. of Janet Randall Young & Robert William Young). 183p. 21cm. 1959. Longmans, Green.

Randall, Julia
--Adam's Dreams. 1969. (ISBN 0-394-40310-X). Borzoi Books.

Randall, Kenneth Charles
--Wild Hunter. Lee, Manning De Villeneuve (1894-1980), illus. LC 51-9969. (Illus.). 236 p. 22cm. 1951. F. Watts.

Randall, Louise A.
--Scripture Stories for Tiny Tots. LC 83-83429. 38p. (Orig.). (gr. k-3). 1983. (ISBN 0-88290-209-1). Horizon Utah.

Randall, Rona
--Girls in White. LC 52-14857. 224p. 21cm. 1952. Arcadia House.

Rande, Mary Abbot
--Holly and Mistletoe. (Illus.). N.D. Belford, Clarke & Co.
--Home-Spun Yarns. (Illus.). N.D. Belford, Clarke & Co's.

Randell, Beverly, pseud., see Price, Beverley Joan.
Randell, Beverly, pseud. (1933-)
--John, the Mouse Who Learned to Read. Price, Beverley Joan. (Illus.). Repr. of 1969 ed. (gr. k-2). 1975. (ISBN 0-00-195367-2). Collins-World.

Randle, Guy, jt. auth. see Payne, Marvin.
Randolph, Boris, jt. ed. see Hoke, Helen L., Mrs.

Randolph, Clare
--The Adventures of Jack & Jill. Crandall, C. Leslie, illus. LC 48-4220. 26 p. col. illus. 27 cm. 1948. Hollow-Tree House.
--Nautical Ned. Crandall, C. Leslie, illus. LC 48-421986. 25 p. col. illus. 27 cm. 1948. Hollow Tree House.

Randolph, Helen
--Crossed Trails in Mexico. LC 36-9683. 255 p. front. 21 cm. (Her Mexican mystery stories for girls). c.1936. A. L. Burt Company.
--The Mystery of Carlitos. LC 36-924083. 247 p. front. 21 cm. (Her Mexican mystery stories for girls). c.1936. A. L. Burt Company.
--The Secret of Casa Grande. LC 36-9385. (Illus.). 21cm. 250p. (Mexican Mystery Stories for Girls). 1936. A. L. Burt Co.

Randolph, Henry Fitz (1856-1892)
--Christmas-Tide in Song. LC 11-26533. 18 cm. 80p. N.D. A. D. F. Randolph and Co.

Randolph, Jane
--The Circus in Peter's Closet. Freeman, Don (1908-1978), illus. LC 55-9217. 50p. 1956. Thomas Y. Crowell Co.

Randolph, Richard W, as told to.
--Sweet Medicine and Other Stories of the Cheyenne Indians. Hall, R. H., illus. LC 37-21028. 196 p. incl. col. front., illus. 22 cm. 1937. The Caxton Printers, Ltd.

Randolph, Vance (1892-)
--The Camp on Wildcat Creek. Simon, Howard (1903-1979), illus. LC 34-31447. vii, 1-210, 2 p. illus. 20 cm. 1934. A. A. Knopf.

Randolph, Vance (1892-), ed.
--Hot Springs and Hell. Cechak, William, illus. LC 65-26776. 297p. 1965 (Gale Reprints). Folklore Associates.

Random House, New York see Kingsley, Emily Perl.

Rands, Minnie Frost (1889-)
--Punki, Her Story of the Island of Java. Rands, Audrey, illus. LC 47-170016. x, 153 p. illus., plates, map. 22 cm. 1947. Island Press.

Rands, William Brighty, jt. auth. see Shulevitz, Uri.

Rands, William Brighty (1823-1882)
--Lilliput Lectures. (Illus.). N.D. George Routledge & Sons.
--Lilliput Legends. (Illus.). N.D. George Routldge & Sons.
--Lilliput Levee. N.D. A. D. F. Randolph.
--Lilliput Levee: Poems of Childhood, Child-Fancy, and Childlike Moods. LC 22-19861. (With the Addition of Several New Poems, Written Expressly for This Edition). viii, 213, 1 p. plates. 15 cm. 1868. G. Routledge & Sons.
--Lilliput Revels. (Illus.). N.D. George Routledge & Sons.
--Lilliput Revels. Innocents' Island. Johnson, Reginald Brimley (1867-), ed. Wedderburn, Griselda, illus. LC 22-239762. 10 p., 1 l., 17-224, 1 p. front., 31 pl. 19 cm. 1905. John Lane.

Rands, William Brighty (1823-1882) & Millais, J. E., illus.
--Lilliput Levee: A Book of Rhymes for Children. N.D. George Routledge & Sons.

Raney, Gail T.
--Another to Love. Miller, Cathy B., illus. (Illus.). 48p. 1983. (ISBN 0-938934-06-6). (ISBN 0-938934-05-8). C&M Pubns.

Ranft, Max
--The Witch Book. Ranft, Max, illus. LC 76-16572. (Illus.). 64 p. 29cm. c.1976. (ISBN 0-528-82007-9). (ISBN 0-528-80013-2). Rand McNally.

Ranger, Mary (1934-)
--Benjamin of Nazareth: A Boyhood Friend of Jesus Discovers the Answers at the Foot of the Cross. LC 77-1584. (Illus.). 53 p. 23cm. (gr. 5-8). c.1977. (ISBN 0-570-03615-1). Concordia Pub. House.
--Daniel's Star: A Weaver's Son Seeks the Meaning of the Star, the Cross and the Tomb. LC 77-2650. (Illus.). 56 p. 23cm. (Starlight books). c.1977. (ISBN 0-570-03614-3). Concordia Pub. House.
--Rebellious Rebecca: A Tax Collector's Daughter Finds Her Life Changing After Christ's Visit. LC 77-3550. (Illus.). 56 p. 23cm. (Starlight books). c.1977. (ISBN 0-570-03612-7). Concordia Pub. House.
--Simon the Small: A Young Galilean Wonders Why Peter Becomes a Fisher of Men. LC 77-3551. (Illus.). 55 p. 23cm. (Starlight books). c.1977. (ISBN 0-570-03613-5). Concordia Pub. House.

Ranger, Robin, pseud., see Freeman, James Midwinter.
Ranger, Robin, pseud. (1827-1900)
--Christmas Time in the Crocus Family. Freeman, James Midwinter. (Illus.). N.D. Methodist Book Concern.

Ranke, Kurt, ed.
--Folktales of Germany. Baumann, Lotte, tr. (Folktales of the World Ser.). 1966. Univ. of Chicago Press.

Rankin, Carroll Watson, Mrs. (1870-)
--The Adopting of Rosa Marie. Shinn, Florence Scovel, illus. LC 8-24300. (A Sequel to dandelion Cottage). vi p., 2 l., 300 p. front., 3 pl. 20 cm. (Her Dandelion series). 1908. H. Holt and Company.
--The Castaways of Pete's Patch. Williamson, Ada Clendenin, illus. LC 11-288143. (A Sequel to the Adopting of Rosa Marie). xiii, 290 p. front., plates. 20 cm. (Her Dandelion series). 1911. H. Holt and Company.
--The Cinder Pond. Williamson, Ada Clendenin, illus. LC 15-18624. 20cm. 316p. 1915. Henry Holt.
--Dandelion Cottage. Shinn, Florence Scovel & Finley, Elizabeth R., illus. LC 4-32150. xi, 312 p. front., 4 pl. 20 cm. 1904. H. Holt and Company.
--Dandelion Cottage. Stevens, Mary, illus. LC 46-417447. 5 p. l., 229 p. illus. 21 cm. 1946. H. Holt and Company.
--Finders Keepers. LC 30-277610. 261 p. incl. front. plates. 20 cm. c.1930. H. Holt and Company.
--Gipsy Nan. Selss, Mariam, illus. LC 26-14678. viii, 2 l., 3-246 p. col. front., plates. 20 cm. c.1926. H. Holt and Company.
--The Girls of Gardenville. LC 6-6746. 19cm. 317p. 1906. Henry Holt & Co.
--Girls of Highland Hall: Further Adventures of the Dandelion Cottagers. LC 21-16795. v, 1 p., 1 l., 268 p. front., plates. 20 cm. 1921. H. Holt and Company.
--Stump Village. LC 35-19004. 5 p. l., 248 p. col. front., 1 illus., plates. 19 cm. c.1935. H. Holt and Company.
--Wolf Rock. LC 33-32594. (Sequel to "The Cinder Pond"). viii, 286 p. 20 cm. c.1933. H. Holt and Company.

Rankin, Hugh Franklin (1913-), ed. see Miers, Earl Schenck.

Rankin, Jean, jt. auth. see Leach, John.

Rankin, Katherine
--A Summer on Beaverbrook. Howie, Bob, illus. LC 64-16890. viii, 168p. ill. 24cm. 1964. Itawamba Times.

Rankin, Katherine, jt. ed. see Langdon, Mary Ramon, Sr.

Rankin, Louise S. (1897-)
--Daughter of the Mountains. Wiese, Kurt (1887-1974), illus. LC 48-1649. 191 p. illus. 25 cm. 1948. Viking Press. **Award: (JNM).**

--The Gentling of Jonathan. Townsend, Lee (1895-), illus. LC 50-10412. (Illus.). 223 p. 22cm. 1950. Viking Press.

Rankin, Ruth I.

--Don't Walk on Your Feet. LC 74-20032. 60p. 1975. (ISBN 0-8283-1596-5). Branden.

Rankin, S. B.

--Climbing Poems. 1875. Turnbull Bros.

Rankin, Sloan

--Dink. LC 80-81545. (Illus.). 77 p. c.1980. (ISBN 0-396-07837-0). Dodd, Mead.

Ranlett, Susan Alice (1853-)

--Boiling Springs. LC 32-23575. 166 p. front. 21 cm. 1932. Meador Publishing Company.

Rannells, Will, jt. auth. see Youmans, Eleanor Williams, Mrs.

Ranney, Agnes V (1916-)

--Flash of Phantom Canyon. LC 63-12460. (Illus.). 160 p. 22cm. 1963. Criterion Books.

Ransom, Abbie Eliose Fosdick, Mrs. (1860-)

--Bigelow Boys: The Tale of a Street Car Strike. Miller, Harry Lambright, illus. LC 7-30452. 348 p. front., 3 pl. 21 cm. c.1907. The Saalfield Publishing Co.

Ransom, Candice F.

--Amanda. 368p. (gr. 7 up). 1984. (ISBN 0-590-32774-7, Sunfire). Scholastic Inc.

Ransom, Fletcher C.

Adventures of a Freshman. N.D. Charles Scribner's Sons.

Ransom, Marie D.

--Prose & Poetic Expressions of a Black Woman. White, Mosezelle N., ed. Morant, Mack B. LC 80-54319. 40p. 1st U.S. edition. 1982. (ISBN 0-936026-13-8). R&M Pub Co.

Ransome, Arthur Michell (1884-1967)

--Aladdin and His Wonderful Lamp. N.D. Brentano's.

--The Big Six. Ransome, Arthur Michell (1884-1967), illus. 1980. Merrimack.

--The Big Six. Ransome, Arthur Michell (1884-1967), illus. LC 41-5682. ix p., 2 l., 353 p. incl. front., illus. 21 cm. 1941. The Macmillan Company.

--Coot Club. Ransome, Arthur Michell (1884-1967) & Carter, Helene (1887-1960), illus. LC 35-7174. 342, 1 p. incl. front., illus. double maps. 21 cm. c.1935. J. B. Lippincott Company.

--Coot Club. Ransome, Arthur Michell (1884-1967), illus. 1980. Merrimack.

--The Fool of the World & the Flying Ship. Shulevitz, Uri (1935-), illus. LC 68-54105. (Illus.). color ils. ca. 48p. (ps-3). 1968. (ISBN 0-374-32442-5). FS&G. **Awards: (RCM); (ALA).**

--Great Northern. LC 48-7170. 350 p. illus., col. map (on lining-papers) 21 cm. 1948, c.1947. Macmillan Co.

--Great Northern. Ransome, Arthur Michell (1884-1967), illus. 1980. Merrimack.

--Missee Lee. LC 42-8280. 6 p. l., 321 p. front., illus. 21 cm. 1942. The Macmillan Company.

--Missee Lee. Ransome, Arthur Michell (1884-1967), illus. 1980. Merrimack.

--Old Peter's Russian Tales. (Illus.). N.D. (ISBN 0-8446-0867-X). Peter Smith Publisher, Inc.

--Old Peter's Russian Tales. Jaques, Faith (1923-), illus. (Illus.). 1976. (ISBN 0-525-66497-1). Elsevier-Nelson.

--Old Peter's Russian Tales. Jaques, Faith (1923-), illus. LC 84-249440. (Illus.). viii, 243 p. 23cm. 1984, c.1971. (ISBN 0-224-02959-2). J. Cape.

--Old Peter's Russian Tales. Jaques, Faith (1923-), illus. LC 75-311793. (Illus.). 254 p. 18cm. 1974. (ISBN 0-14-030696-X). Puffin Books.

--Old Peter's Russian Tales. Mitrokhin, Dmitri Isidorovich (1883-), illus. (Illus.). 334p. 1916. (ISBN 0-486-22406-6). Dover Books.

--Old Peter's Russian Tales. Mitrokhin, Dmitri Isidorovich (1883-), illus. LC 79-88072. (Illus.). 334 p. 21cm. 1969. Dover Publications.

--Old Peter's Russian Tales. Mitrokhin, Dmitri Isidorovich (1883-), illus. LC 17-26894. viii p., 1 l., 11-334 p. illus., 7 col. pl. (incl. front.) 23 cm. 1917. Frederick A. Stokes Company.

--Old Peter's Russian Tales. Mitrokhin, Dmitri Isidorovich (1883-), illus. LC 79-88072. (Illus.). 334p. 1969. Nelson Junior Books.

--Old Peter's Russian Tales. Mitrokhin, Dmitri Isidorovich (1883-), illus. LC 38-27663. viii p., 1 l., 11-334 p. col. front., illus., col. plates. 21 cm. 1938. T. Nelson and Sons.

--Peter Duck. Carter, Helene (1887-1960), illus. LC 33-12106. 427 p. incl. illus., pl. 21 cm. c.1933. J. B. Lippincott Company.

--Peter Duck. Ransome, Arthur Michell (1884-1967), illus. 1980. Merrimack.

--The Picts and the Martyrs: Or, Not Welcome at All. LC 43-16040. x p., 1 l., 308 p. incl. front., illus. 21 cm. 1943. The Macmillan Company.

--The Picts & the Martyrs: Or, Not Welcome at All. Ransome, Arthur Michell (1884-1967), illus. (Illus.). 304p. (gr. 4-8). 1980. (ISBN 0-224-60641-7, Pub. by Chatto Bodley Jonathan). Merrimack Pub Cir.

--Pigeon Post. Ransome, Arthur Michell (1884-1967), illus. 1980. Merrimack.

--Pigeon Post. Shepard, Mary Eleanor (1909-), illus. LC 37-2567. 349 p. illus. 21 cm. c.1937. J. B. Lippincott Company.

--Russian Fairy Tales. Gorecka-Egan, Erica, illus. LC 46-5863. 122 p., 1 l. col. illus. 16 x 21 1/2 cm. N.D. Peter Pauper Press.

--Secret Walter. Ransome, Arthur Michell (1884-1967), illus. 1980. Merrimack.

--Secret Water. LC 40-7529. xii p., 1 l., 363 p. incl. front., illus. (incl. maps) 21 cm. 1940. The Macmillan Company.

--The Soldier and Death: A Russian Folk Tale Told in English. 1922. Huebsch.

--Swallowdale. LC 73-367182. (Illus.). 19cm. 441p. (Puffin bks.: PS 339). 1968. Penguin.

--Swallowdale. Carter, Helene (1887-1960), illus. LC 32-4755. 393 p. illus., plates. 21 cm. 1932. J. B. Lippincott Company.

--Swallowdale. Ransome, Arthur Michell (1884-1967), illus. 1980. Merrimack.

--Swallows & Amazons. LC 30-248533. 349, 1 p. incl. front. (map) 21 cm. 1930. J. Cape.

--Swallows and Amazons. Carter, Helene (1887-1960), illus. LC 31-1519. 343 p. incl. illus., pl. 21 cm. 1931. J. B. Lippincott Company.

--Swallows and Amazons. Ransome, Arthur Michell (1884-1967), illus. 1980. Merrimack.

--We Didn't Mean to Go to Sea. LC 80-26323. p. cm. (Gregg Press Children's Literature Series). 1981, c.1938. (ISBN 0-8398-2698-2). Gregg Press.

--We Didn't Mean to Go to Sea. Ransome, Arthur Michell (1884-1967), illus. LC 38-9837. xii p., 1 l., 335 p. incl. front., illus. 21 cm. 1938. The Macmillan Company.

--Winter Holiday. Carter, Helene (1887-1960), illus. LC 34-6051. 350 p. incl. front., illus. 21 cm. c.1934. J. B. Lippincott Company.

--Winter Holiday. Ransome, Arthur Michell (1884-1967), illus. 1980. Merrimack.

Ransome, Arthur Michell (1884-1967), illus.

--My Big Book of Nursery Tales. LC 79-52804. (Illus.). 18 p. 34cm. 1979, c.1975. (ISBN 0-517-29265-3). Derrydale Books.

Ranson, Nancy Richey, Mrs.

--The Bucking Burro. McKinley, Frances, illus. LC 32-13192. x p., 1 l., 70, 2 p. illus. 20 cm. 1932. The Kaleidograph Press.

Ranucci, Renato

--Piccoletto: The Story of the Little Chimney Sweep. Di Majo, Ennio, illus. Gemming, Mary Elizabeth (1932-), tr. LC 61-660391. 62p. illus. 30cm. 1961. Pantheon Books.

Rao, Anthony, illus.

--The Highlights Book of Nursery Rhymes. Highlights for Children Inc LC 73-10279. (Illus.). 32 p. 1974. (ISBN 0-87534-771-1). (ISBN 0-87534-772-X). Highlights for Children, Inc.

Rao, Raja

--The Cow of the Barricades and Other Stories. N.D. Oxford University Press.

Rao, Shanta R.

--Seethu: A Novel. 160p. 1980. (ISBN 0-86131-178-7, Pub. by Orient Longman Ltd India). Apt Bks.

Raoul-Duval, Francois

--Hum-Hum and Gurigoo: Or, How the Rivers and the Oceans Were Created. Molnar, Agnes, illus. LC 77-359287. (Based on Legends of the South-American Indians). (Illus.). 34 p. 1976. (ISBN 0-903895-67-6). Robson Books.

--Petali & Gurigoo. (gr. k-3). N.D. (ISBN 0-685-28654-1). Merry Thoughts.

Rapaport, Stella Fread

--The Bear, Ship of Many Lives. Rapaport, Stella Fread, illus. LC 62-17930. (Illus.). 146 p. 24cm. 1962. Dodd, Mead.

--Binkley's Bottleneck. N.D. E. M. Hale & Co.

--Binkley's Bottleneck. Rapaport, Stella Fread, illus. LC 56-10270. (Illus.). 71 p. 23cm. 1956. Putnam.

--Horse Chestnut Hideaway. Rapaport, Stella Fread, illus. LC 56-10270. 71p. illus. 23cm. 1956. Putnam.

--Reindeer Rescue. Rapaport, Stella Fread, illus. LC 55-10108. (Illus.). 119 p. 21cm. 1955. Putnam.

--A Whittle Too Much. Rapaport, Stella Fread, illus. LC 55-5786. 23cm. 45p. 1955. G. P. Putnam's Sons.

Raphael, Arthur Michael

--The Great Jug. Benton, Clifford P., illus. LC 36-15972. 136 p. col. front., illus. 24 cm. c.1936. The Reilly & Lee Co.

Raphael, Elaine, pseud., see Bolognese, Elaine Raphael Chionchio.

Raphael, Elaine, pseud. (1933-) & Bolognese, Donald Alan (1934-)

--Donkey and Carlo. Bolognese, Elaine Raphael Chionchio. LC 77-25660. (Illus.). 31 p. 22cm. c.1978. (ISBN 0-06-024838-6). (ISBN 0-06-024839-4). Harper & Row.

--Donkey It's Snowing. Bolognese, Elaine Raphael Chionchio. LC 80-8449. p. cm. 1981. (ISBN 0-06-020554-7). (ISBN 0-06-020555-5). Harper & Row.

--Sam Baker, Gone West. Bolognese, Elaine Raphael Chionchio. LC 76-27314. p. cm. 1977. Viking Press.

--Turnabout. Bolognese, Elaine Raphael Chionchio. LC 80-11866. p. cm. 1980. (ISBN 0-670-73281-8). Viking Press.

Raphael, Morris

--How Do You Know When You're in Acadiana. Hebert, Carrie, illus. (Illus.). 32p. (Orig.). (gr. 5 up). 1984. (ISBN 0-9608866-3-X). M Raphael.

Raphael, Ralph B

--Water, Water Everywhere. Seiden, Art, illus. LC 53-29592. unpaged. illus. 21cm. (Wonder books, 607). 1953. Wonder Books.

Raphael, Sipora, tr. see Livne, Zvi.

Rapin, William (1949-)

--A Penguin in New York. Rapin, William (1949-), illus. LC 84-15609. c.1984. (ISBN 0-918273-04-8). Coffee House Press.

Rapoport, Eileen, tr. see Schnack, Friedrich.

Rapoport, Eileen, tr. see Spang, Gunter.

Raposo, Joe, jt. auth. see Moss, Jeffrey.

Raposo, Joseph G

--Being Green. Delessert, Etienne (1941-), illus. LC 73-82468. (Illus.). 20 p. 32cm. (Sesame Street Book). 1973. Western Pub. Co.

Rappaport, Doreen

But She's Still My Grandma. Simmons, Bernadette, illus. LC 81-20236. p. cm. 1982. (ISBN 0-89885-072-X). Human Sciences Press.

Rapport, Samuel, jt. ed. see Wright, Helen.

Rapson, Linda Buckmaster

--Kipper. LC 81-11175. p. cm. c.1981. (ISBN 0-8024-4558-6). Moody Press.

--Kipper Plays Cupid. LC 81-11294. p. cm. c.1981. (ISBN 0-8024-4559-4). Moody Press.

Rapstoff, Cyril, jt. auth. see Pullen, Alan.

Rardin, Susan Lowry

--Captives in a Foreign Land. LC 84-12858. 224p. (gr. 5 up). 1984. (ISBN 0-395-36216-4). HM.

Rarick, Carrie

--Jeanies Valentines. Magnuson, Diana, illus. 32p. (Beginning-to-Read Ser.). (gr. k-3). 1982. (ISBN 0-695-41674-X, Dist. by Caroline Hse). (ISBN 0-695-31674-5). Modern Curr.

--The Three Bears Visit Goldilocks. McKinley, Clare, illus. LC 51-9780. 33p. col. illus. 21cm. c.1951. Rand McNally.

--The Three Bears Visit Goldilocks. McKinley, Clare, illus. LC 56-8665. unpaged. illus. 33cm. (Rand McNally giant book). 1956, c.1950. Rand McNally.

Rarig, Frances H

--The Ant Queen's Home and Other Stories. LC 32-137332. v, 170 p. illus. 19 cm. (Heath supplementary readers). c.1932. D. C. Heath and Company.

Rasbach, Hubert H.

--The Dinkywinkies & Snickity Snackety Snort. Ingram, Fred & Jennings, Elkay, illus. LC 79-89378. (Illus.). (ps-4). 1982. (ISBN 0-934822-05-0). Plus One Pub.

Rasch, Sunna, jt. ed. see Hopkins, Lee Bennett.

Raskin, A.

--When Daddy Was a Little Boy. Glagoleva, Fainna, tr. from Russian. LC 68-51021. 124p. 1976. (ISBN 0-8285-1262-0, Pub. by Progress Pubs USSR). Imported Pubns.

Raskin, Edith L., jt. auth. see Greenberg, Sylvia S.

Raskin, Edith Lefkowitz, jt. auth. see Raskin, Joseph.

Raskin, Edith Lefkowitz, jt. ed. see Raskin, Joseph.

Raskin, Edith Lefkowitz (1908-)

--Indian Tales. Raskin, Joseph (1897-1982), retold by. Siegl, Helen (1924-), illus. LC 69-17444. (Illus.). 63 p. 24cm. 1969. Random House.

--Many Worlds: Seen and Unseen. Jauss, Anne Marie (1907-), illus. 1960. David McKay Co.

Raskin, Ellen (1928-1984)

--A & The: Or, Willian T. E. C.umgarten Comes to Town. Raskin, Ellen (1928-1984), illus. LC 75-115074. (Illus.). (gr. 1-4). 1970. (ISBN 0-689-20609-7). Atheneum.

--And It Rained. Raskin, Ellen (1928-1984), illus. LC 69-18967. (Illus.). 48 p. 22cm. 1969. Atheneum. **Award: (ALA).**

--Figgs & Phantoms. Raskin, Ellen (1928-1984), illus. LC 73-17309. (Illus.). vi, 152 p. 24cm. 1974. (ISBN 0-525-29680-8). E. P. Dutton. **Award: (JNM).**

--Franklin Stein. Raskin, Ellen (1928-1984), illus. LC 75-175560. (Illus.). 32 p. 24cm. 1972. Atheneum.

--Franklin Stein. Raskin, Ellen (1928-1984), illus. LC 75-321549. (Illus.). 32 p. 23cm. (Aladdin book). 1972. (ISBN 0-689-70417-8). Atheneum.

--Ghost in a Four-Room Apartment. Raskin, Ellen (1928-1984), illus. LC 69-13521. (Illus.). 48 p. 18cm. 1969. (ISBN 0-689-20354-3). Atheneum.

--Moe Q. McGlutch, He Smoked Too Much. Raskin, Ellen (1928-1984), illus. LC 73-4383. (Illus.). 40 p. 27cm. 1973. (ISBN 0-8193-0686-X). (ISBN 0-8193-0686-X). Parents' Magazine Press.

--Moose, Goose, and Little Nobody. Raskin, Ellen (1928-1984), illus. LC 80-15287. p. cm. 1980, c.1974. (ISBN 0-590-07775-9). Four Winds Press.

--Moose, Goose, and Little Nobody. Raskin, Ellen (1928-1984), illus. LC 73-23053. (Illus.). 31 p. 26cm. 1974. (ISBN 0-8193-0768-8). (ISBN 0-8193-0768-8). Parents' Magazine Press.

--The Mysterious Disappearance of Leon (I Mean Noel). 1st ed. Raskin, Ellen (1928-1984), illus. LC 70-157953. (Illus.). 24 cm. viii, 149p. (gr. 4-7). 1971. Dutton. **Award: (ALA).**

--The Mysterious Disappearance of Leon (I Mean Noel). Raskin, Ellen (1928-1984), illus. 1980. Dutton.

--The Mysterious Disappearance of Leon (I Mean Noel). Raskin, Ellen (1928-1984), illus. LC 70-157953. (Illus.). 149 p. 20cm. (Dutton anytime books, AB02). 1973, c.1971. (ISBN 0-525-45010-6). E. P. Dutton & Co.

--Nothing Ever Happens on My Block. Raskin, Ellen (1928-1984), illus. LC 66-12853. (Illus.). 1 v. 1966. Atheneum. **Awards: (NYT); (ALA).**

--Silly Songs and Sad. Raskin, Ellen (1928-1984), illus. LC 67-18522. (Illus.). 48 p. 21cm. 1967. Crowell.

--Songs of Innocence. 1st ed. Raskin, Ellen (1928-1984), illus. Weissman, Dick, contrib. by. LC 66-3935. 48p. col. illus. 21x27cm. 1966. Doubleday.

--Spectacles. Raskin, Ellen (1928-1984), illus. LC 68-12234. (Illus.). 48 p. 1968. Atheneum. **Awards: (NYT); (ALA).**

--The Tattooed Potato and Other Clues. Raskin, Ellen (1928-1984), illus. LC 74-23764. 170 p. 24cm. 1975. (ISBN 0-525-40805-3). Dutton. **Award: (ALA).**

--Twenty-Two, Twenty-Three. Raskin, Ellen (1928-1984), illus. LC 76-5475. 28cm. 24p. 1976. (ISBN 0-689-30529-X). Atheneum. **Award: (ALA).**

--The Westing Game. LC 77-18866. 185 p. 24cm. c.1978. (ISBN 0-525-42320-6). Dutton. **Awards: (JNM); (BGH); (ALA).**

--Who, Said Sue, Said Whoo?. Raskin, Ellen (1928-1984), illus. LC 72-86947. (Illus.). 32 p. 1973. Atheneum. **Awards: (ALA); (BGH).**

--The World's Greatest Freak Show. Raskin, Ellen (1928-1984), illus. LC 72-134820. (Illus.). 32 p. 1971. Atheneum.

Raskin, Joseph (1897-1982), retold by see Raskin, Edith Lefkowitz.

Raskin, Joseph (1897-1982) & Raskin, Edith Lefkowitz (1908-)

--Guilty or Not Guilty?. Tales of Justice in Early America. Bock, William Sauts Netamux'we (1939-), illus. LC 74-22008. p. cm. 1975. (ISBN 0-688-41684-5). (ISBN 0-688-51684-X). Lothrop, Lee & Shepard.

--The Newcomers: Ten Tales of American Immigrants. Werth, Kurt (1896-), illus. LC 74-6420. (Illus.). 128p. (gr. 3-7). 1974. (ISBN 0-688-41590-3). (ISBN 0-688-51590-8). Lothrop.

--Of Whales and Wolves and Other Adventures in Early America. Bock, William Sauts Netamux'we (1939-), illus. LC 77-15662. (Illus.). 126 p. 22cm. c.1978. (ISBN 0-688-41826-0). (ISBN 0-688-51826-5). Lothrop, Lee and Shepard Co.

--Strange Shadows: Spirit Tales of Early America. Bock, William Sauts Netamux'we (1939-), illus. LC 76-54515. (Illus.). (gr. 3-7). 1977. (ISBN 0-688-41795-7). (ISBN 0-688-51795-1). Lothrop.

--Tales of Indentured Servants. Bock, William Sauts Netamux'we (1939-), illus. (Illus.). (gr. 4-6). 1978. (ISBN 0-688-41871-6). (ISBN 0-688-51871-0). Lothrop.

--Tales Our Settlers Told. Bock, William Sauts Netamux'we (1939-), illus. LC 76-152842. (Illus.). 96 p. 22cm. 1971. Lothrop, Lee, and Shepard Co.

Raskin, Joseph (1897-1982) & Raskin, Edith Lefkowitz (1908-), eds.

--Ghosts and Witches Aplenty: More Tales Our Settlers Told. Bock, William Sauts Netamux'we (1939-), illus. LC 73-4949. (Illus.). 128 p. 22cm. 1973. (ISBN 0-688-41554-7). (ISBN 0-688-41554-7). Lothrop, Lee & Shepard Co.

Rasmussen, A. H.

--Sea Feaver. N.D. Hastings House.

Rasmussen, Carrie

--Let's Say Poetry Together and Have Fun: For Primary Grades. Lundin, Morris, illus. LC 62-13792. x, 114p. illus. 17x22cm. c.1962. Burgess Pub. Co.

--Let's Say Poetry Together and Have Fun. Lundin, Morris, illus. LC 63-17518. (For Intermediate Grades.). xii, 179p. illus. (pt. col.) 17x22cm. c.1963. Burgess.

--Poems for Playtime. Mathews, Eleanor J., illus. LC 42-18151. 93 p. illus. (part col.) 24 cm. 1942. Expression Company.

Rasmussen, Halfdan Wedel (1915-)

--Long Peter Madsen: How Shorty Madsen Became Long Peter Madsen and Back Again!. 1 st. Eng. ed. Clausen, Ernst, illus. LC 60-12369. unpaged. illus. 36x14cm. 1960. F. Watts.

Rasmussen, Hope

--Bronto's Christmas. 1983. (ISBN 0-8062-2175-5). Carlton.

Rasmussen, Inger Margrete, Mrs., retold by see Asbjornsen, Peter Christen (1812-1885) & Moe, Jorgen Engebretsen.

Rasmussen, Knud Johan Victor, jt. auth. see Field, Edward.

Rasmussen, Knud Johan Victor (1879-1933)

--The Eagle's Gift. Hansen, Ernst, illus. Hutchinson, Isobel, tr. N.D. Doubleday Doran.

Rasmussen, Knud Johan Victor (1879-1933), compiled by.

--Beyond the High Hills: A Book of Eskimo Poems. 1st ed. Mary-Rousseliere, Guy, photos by. Rasmussen, Knud Johan Victor (1879-1933), tr. LC 61-14072. (Illus.). 29 cm. 32p. 1961. World. **Award: (ALA).**

Rasmussen, Sigurd see Senje, Sigurd, pseud.

Rasmussen, Sigurd

--Escape!. Senje, Sigurd, pseud. Ramsden, Evelyn, tr. LC 64-12509. 156 p. 21cm. 1964. Harcourt, Brace & World.

--Escape!. Senje, Sigurd, pseud. Ramsden, Evelyn, tr. LC 66-6701. 156 p. 20cm. (Voyager book). 1964. Harcourt, Brace & World.

Rasp-Nuri, Grace (1897-)

--Yusuf, Boy of Cyprus. Brownjohn, Maxwell J., tr. from Ger. LC 58-5901. 22cm. 222p. 1958. Criterion Bks. Inc.

--Yusuf, Boy of Cyprus. Cassel, Lili, pseud. (1924-), illus. Wronker, Lili Cassel. LC 58-5901. (Illus.). (gr. 5-9). 1958. (ISBN 0-87599-095-9). S G Phillips.

Raspe, Rudolf Erich (1737-1794)

--The Adventures of Baron Munchausen, 1 of 12 vols. New ed. (Illus.). (Good Time Ser.: No. 12). 1905. Set. Henry Altemus Co.

--Baron Munchausen. (New Alpha Library). N.D. Rand, McNally & Co.'s.

--Baron Munchausen. (Illus.). (Children's Classics). N.D. Thomas Y. Crowell & Co.

--The Children's Munchausen. Shephard, Morgan (1865-), retold by. Martin, John, pseud. Ross, Gordon, illus. LC 21-19483. xv p., 2 l., 3-185, 1 p. col. front., illus., plates (part col.) 23 cm. 1921. Houghton Mifflin Company.

--Singular Travels, Campaigns & Adventures of Baron Munchausen. Carswell, John Patrick (1918-), ed. Dore, Louis Christophe Paul Gustave (1832-1883), illus. (Illus.). (gr. 4-8). N.D. (ISBN 0-486-20698-X). Dover.

Rassussen, Inger Margrete, Mrs., tr. see Asbjornsen, Peter Christen (1812-1885) & Moe, Jorgen Engebretsen.

Raswan, Carl

--Drinkers of the Wind. (Illus.). 1962. (ISBN 0-374-31881-6). FS&G.

Ratcliff, Arthur, ed. see Grimm, Jakob Ludwig Karl (1785-1863) & Grimm, Wilhelm Karl.

Ratcliff, Arthur, tr. see Ditzen, Rudolf.

Ratcliff, Arthur, tr. see Voegeli, Max.

Ratcliffe, Dorothy Una (1891-)

--Rosemary Isle, and Other Rhymes. Unwin, Nora Spicer (1907-), illus. LC 46-19670. (Illus.). vi, 95p. 22cm. 1945. T. Nelson and Sons Ltd.

Ratel, Simonne

--The Weathercock. N.D. D. Appleton-Century Co.

Ratera, Rosario K.

--A Gift. (Illus.). 1972. (ISBN 0-686-09524-3). Cellar.

Rath, Ida Ellen

--Francis and Her Little Brother: A Story for Young People. LC 55-11829. (Illus.). 22cm. 42p. 1955. Exposition.

--The Year of Charles. LC 56-13554. 218p. 22cm. c.1955. Naylor Co.

Rathborne, St. George see Adams, Harrison, pseud.

Rathborne, St. George see Clifton, Oliver Lee, pseud.

Rathborne, St. George (1854-1928)

--Adrift on a Junk: Or, Boy Sailors of the China Sea. Rockwell, Ida May, illus. LC 5-32854. 19 cm. 329p. 1905. The Saalfield Publishing Co.

--Baron Sam: A Novel. LC 12-37992. 241 p. 18 cm. (On cover: The favorite library. no. 98). c.1893. The American News Company.

--The Boy Cruisers: Or, Adventures in Florida. (The Rugby Series for Boys and Girls). N.D. A. L. Burt Company.

--The Boy Cruisers: Or, Adventures in Florida. (The Alger Series for Boys). N.D. A. L. Burt's Pubs.

--The Boy Cruisers: Or, Adventures in Florida. (Wide Awake Boys Ser.). N.D. A. L. Burt.

--The Camp Fire Boys at Log Cabin Bend: Or, Four Chums Afoot in the Tall Timber. Clifton, Oliver Lee, pseud. Wrenn, Charles L., illus. LC 23-7124. vii, 9-248 p. incl. front., plates. 20 cm. c.1923. Barse & Hopkins.

--The Camp Fire Boys' Canoe Cruise: Or, Stormbound on the Upper Rockaway. Clifton, Oliver Lee, pseud. Foster, John M., illus. LC 25-10469. 1 p. l., v-vii, 9-244 p. incl. plates. front., map. 20 cm. c.1925. Barse & Hopkins.

--The Camp Fire Boys in Muskrat Swamp: Or, A Hunt for the Missing Plane Pilot. Clifton, Oliver Lee, pseud. Wrenn, Charles L., illus. LC 23-7547. vi p., 1 l., 9-248 p. 20 cm. c.1923. Barse & Hopkins.

--Canoe and Camp Fire. (The Boys' Own Library). N.D. David McKay.

--Canoe and Campfire. 1 p. l., 5-187 p. 18 cm. (On cover: Medal library, no. 40). c.1900. Street & Smith.

--Canoe Mates in Canada: Or, Three Boys Afloat on the Saskatchewan. LC 13-236754. 238 p. incl. front. 20 cm. (Canoe and campfire series). c.1912. M. A. Donohue & Co.

--A Chase for a Bride: A Romance of the Philippines. 19 cm. 337p. 1899. Street & Smith.

--Chums in Dixie: Or, The Strange Cruise of a Motorboat. LC 13-235. 232 p. incl. front. 20 cm. c.1912. M. A. Donohue & Co.

--Chums of the Prairie. (Ranch and Ranch Ser.). N.D. David McKay.

--Chums of the Prairie. LC 2-19162. 19 cm. 1902. Street & Smith.

--Down the Amazon: Or, The Story of a Wonderful Cruise in a Canvas Canoe. Shute, A. Burnham, illus. LC 5-32921. 19 cm. 246p. 1905. The Saalfield Publishing Co.

--The Fair Maid of Fez: A Novel. 16 cm. 267p. c.1895. Home Book Company.

--A Goddess of Africa: A Story of the Golden Fleece. 267p. 1899. Street & Smith.

--The Gulf Cruisers. (The Boys Own Library). N.D. David McKay.

--The Gulf Cruisers: Or, The Voyage of the Lost Canoe. LC 2-18933. 19 cm. 209p. 1902. Street & Smith.

--The House Boat Boys: Or, Drifting Down to the Sunny South. LC 12-10651. 313 p. incl. front. 20 cm. (His Canoe and campfire series). c.1912. M. A. Donohue & Co.

--Lend-a-Hand Boys As Wild Game Protectors: Or, The Little Four-Footed Brother in the Fur Coat. LC 31-15548. 3 p. l., 13-254 p. 20 cm. (His Lend-a-hand boys series). c.1931. The Goldsmith Publishing Co.

--Lend-a-Hand Boys of Carthage: Or, Waking up the Home Town. LC 31-15553. 3 p. l., 13-248 p. 20 cm. (His Lend-a-hand boys series). c.1931. The Goldsmith Publishing Co.

--Lend-a-Hand Boy's Sanitary Squad: Or, When the Fever Came to Blairstown. LC 31-155529. 3 p. l., 13-247 p. 20 cm. (His Lend-a-hand boys series). c.1931. The Goldsmith Publishing Co.

--Lend-a-Hand Boys' Team-Work: Or, Putting Their Shoulders to the Wheel. LC 31-155475. 3 p. l., 13-242 p. 20 cm. (His Lend-a-hand boys series). c.1931. The Goldsmith Publishing Co.

--The Man from Wall Street: A Novel. LC 3-14823. 21 cm. 324p. c.1892. Morrill, Higgins & Co.

--The Man from Wall Street: A Novel. LC 3-14822. 21 cm. 324p. c.1894. W. B. Conkey Company.

--Paddling Under Palmettos. (The Boys Own Library). N.D. David McKay.

--Paddling Under Palmettos. LC 1-26275. 2 p. l. ii, 9-288 p. front., plates. 19 cm. c.1901. Street & Smith.

--Rival Canoe Boys. (The Boy's Own Library). N.D. David McKay.

--Rival Canoe Boys: Or, With Pack and Paddle on the Nipigon. LC 2-19163. 19 cm. 191p. 1902. Street & Smith.

--A Sailor's Sweetheart: Or, Fighting for Love and Country. 284p. 1900. Street & Smith.

--Shifting Winds. (The Boys Own Library). N.D. David McKay.

--Shifting Winds: Or, The Cruise of the Coast Canoes. LC 2-18932. 19 cm. 212p. 1902. Street & Smith.

--Sunset Ranch. (Ranch and Ranch Ser.). N.D. David McKay.

--Sunset Ranch: A Boy's Story of Adventure in the West. LC 2-13611. 19 cm. 272p. 1901. Street & Smith.

--Young Castaways: Or, Marooned on a Sand-Key in the Caribbean. Rockwell, Ida May, illus. LC 5-32922. 19 cm. 261p. 1905. The Saalfield Publishing Co.

--The Young Fur-Takers: Or, Traps and Trails in the Wilderness. LC 12-10650. 258 p. incl. front. 20 cm. (His Canoe and campfire series). c.1912. M. A. Donohue & Co.

--Young Range Riders. (Ranch and Range Ser.). N.D. David McKay.

--The Young Range Riders: Or, Two Yankee Cowboys on a Mexican Ranch. LC 2-19164. 19 cm. 253p. 1902. Street & Smith.

--Young Voyagers of the Nile: Or, The Chase for the Fugitive Dahabeah. Shute, A. Burnham, illus. LC 5-32697. 19 cm. 205p. 1905. The Saalfield Publishing Co.

Rathbun, Helen Kelleher (1918-)

--Easter Surprise. Neville, Vera (1900-1978), illus. LC 47-26016. 62 p. incl. col. front., col. illus. 20 1/2 cm. 1947. Thomas Y. Crowell Company.

Rathjen, Carl Henry (1909-)

--Cruise of the Catalyst. LC 62-16177. 209p. 22cm. 1962. Funk & Wagnalls.

--Haunted Highway. LC 60-127542. 218p. 22cm. 1960. Funk & Wagnalls.

--Ken Tompkins, Animal Doctor. LC 56-9007. 279 p. 21cm. 1956. Dodd, Mead.

--Shadow on the Ice. Otero, Ben, illus. LC 75-314679. (Illus.). 210 p. 20cm. (Whitman sports adventure ; 1501). 1975. (ISBN 0-307-01501-7). Western Pub. Co.

--Smoke River Mystery. LC 68-23986. 188 p. 21cm. 1968. Lantern Press.

--Teen-Age Great Rescue Stories. Furman, Abraham Loew (1902-), ed. LC 64-15172. 190p. 21cm. 1964. Lantern.

--Teen-Age Haunted Stories. Furman, Abraham Loew (1902-), ed. LC 65-126022. 190p. 21cm. c.1965. Lantern.

Ratigan, Eleanor Eldridge (1916-)

--Deep Water. Lonette, Reisie Dominee (1924-), illus. LC 60-53426. 158p. illus. 22cm. 1961. Lothrop, Lee & Shepard.

Ratigan, William (1910-)

--Adventures of Paul Bunyan and Babe: Michigan Folklore. 1958. Eerdmans.

--The Blue Snow: Michigan Folklore. 1958. Eerdmans.

--Tiny Tim Pine: Michigan Folklore. 1958. Eerdmans.

Rattiner, Dan

--Attack of the Space Creatures. Shepard, Richard, illus. LC 79-67492. (Illus.). 59 p. 26cm. N.D. (ISBN 0-932966-07-1). Permanent Press.

Ratzesberger, Anna

--Camel Bells: A Boy of Baghdad. Wiese, Kurt (1887-1974), illus. LC 35-24892. 80 p. col. illus. 29 cm. 1935. A. Whitman & Co.

--Donkey Beads: A Tale of a Persian Donkey. Wiese, Kurt (1887-1974), illus. LC 38-16533. 62, 1 p. incl. col. front., illus. (part col.) 24 cm. 1938. A. Whitman & Co.

--Farm Pets. Phillips, Katherine L., illus. LC 54-28806. unpaged. illus. 17cm. 1954. Rand McNally.

--Jasmine: A Story of Present Day Persia. Wiese, Kurt (1887-1974), illus. 5 p. l., 15-286 p. incl. illus., plates. col. front., col. plates. 23 cm. 1937. A. Whitman & Co.

--Pets. Webbe, Elizabeth, illus. LC 54-24186. unpaged. illus. 21cm. c.1954. Rand McNally.

--Pets. Webbe, Elizabeth, illus. LC 59-9036. unpaged. illus. 33cm. (Rand McNally giant book). 1960, c.1954. Rand McNally.

--Ponies. Webbe, Elizabeth, illus. LC 54-177415. unpaged. illus. 17cm. (Rand McNally book-elf junior, 683). c.1953. Rand McNally.

--Puppy and Me. Bannister, Constance, photos by. LC 55-898914. unpaged. illus. 21cm. (Rand McNally elf book, 504). c.1955. Rand McNally.

--Wild Animals. Vlasaty, J. L., illus. LC 52-18197. unpaged. illus. 21 cm. (Rand McNally book-elf book, 454). c.1951. Rand McNally.

Rau, Margaret, Mrs. (1913-)

--The Band of the Red Hand. Low, Joseph (1911-), illus. LC 38-32229. 5 p. l., 3-250 p. illus. 21 cm. 1938. A. A. Knopf.

--Jimmy of Cherry Valley. LC 73-5398. (Illus.). index. 64p. 1st U.S. edition. (gr. 3-6). 1973. (ISBN 0-671-32613-9). (ISBN 0-671-32614-7). Messner.

Rauch, Constance (1937-)

--The Landlady. 1975. (ISBN 0-399-11507-2). G. P. Putnam's Sons.

Rauch, Mabel Thompson (1888-1972)

--The Little Hellion: A Story of 'Egypt' Southern Illinois. LC 60-128488. 180p. illus. 21cm. 1960. Duell, Sloan and Pearce.

--Vinnie and the Flag Tree. 1959. Duell, Sloan and Pearce Pub.

Raucher, Herman (1928-)

--A Glimpse of Tiger. 1971. (ISBN 0-399-10340-6). G. P. Putnam's Sons.

Rausiri, Supa

--The Beautiful Chick. Rodriguez, Gloria F., ed. Chang, Phillip, illus. Pinta, Thanom, tr. (Illus.). (gr. k-2). 1979. (ISBN 0-686-26620-X, Pub. by New Day Publishers Philippines). Cellar.

Ravel, Maurice, jt. auth. see Colette, Sidonie Gabrielle.

Raverat, Gwendolen Mary Darwin, jt. auth. see Wedgwood, Henry Allen.

Rawlings, James R. see McCulloch, J. H., pseud.

Rawlings, Marjorie Kinnan (1896-1953)

--Golden Apples. N.D. World Publishing.

--The Secret River. Weisgard, Leonard Joseph (1916-), illus. LC 55-6916. (Illus.). (gr. 1-4). 1955. (ISBN 0-684-12636-2, ScribT). Scribner. **Award: (JNM).**

--The Yearling. (Illus.). 1962. (ISBN 0-684-20922-5, ScribJ). (ISBN 0-684-51547-4, ScribC). (ISBN 0-684-71878-2, ScribJ). pap. text ed. ibner. RCM). 4, ScribJ). Scribner.). ner. 356-5, ScribJ). Scribner. , ScribJ). Scribner. **Award: (ALA).** ic Inc. idge. pap. 3.95 rack size. (ISBN 0-684-51547-4). Scribner.

--The Yearling. (Keith Jennison Large Type Bks). (gr. 9 up). 1966. (ISBN 0-531-00307-8). Watts.

--The Yearling. Shenton, Edward (1895-), illus. (Illus.). (gr. 9 up). 1938. (ISBN 0-684-10490-3). Scribner.

--The Yearling. Wyeth, Newell Convers (1882-1945), illus. (The Scribner Illustrated Classics). N.D. Charles Scribner's Sons.

--The Yearling. Wyeth, Newell Convers (1882-1945), illus. LC 77-362867. (Illus.). 431 p., 16 leaves of plates. 23cm. 1977. Franklin Library.

--The Yearling. Wyeth, Newell Convers (1882-1945), illus. LC 85-40301. (Illus.). x, 400 p., 14 leaves of plates. 24cm. 1985. (ISBN 0-684-18461-3). Scribner.

Rawlins, Margaret G., compiled by.

--Round About Six. Wrigley, Denis, illus. LC 73-80254. (Illus.). 96 p. 25cm. 1973. (ISBN 0-7232-1728-9). F. Warne.

Rawlinson, Eleanor

--Introduction to Literature for Children. LC 31-9385. xvi, 493 p. 24 cm. c.1931. W. W. Norton & Company, Inc.

--Introduction to Literature for Children. rev. ed. LC 37-8814. xvii, 499 p. 24 cm. c.1937. W. W. Norton & Company, Inc.

Rawls, Dorothy Dickens

--Little China Pig. Blake, Vivienne, illus. N.D. Rand McNally & Co.

Rawls, Wilson

--Where the Red Fern Grows: The/Story of Two Dogs and a Boy. LC 61-9201. 1961. Doubleday.

Rawson

--Dragons. (Story Books). (gr. k-4). 1980. (ISBN 0-86020-337-9, Usborne-Hayes). (ISBN 0-88110-055-2). (ISBN 0-86020-336-0). EDC.

--Dragons, Giants & Witches. (Story Books). (gr. k-4). 1979. (ISBN 0-86020-342-5, Usborne-Hayes). EDC.

Rawson, jt. auth. see Cartwright.

Rawson, Elsie Lewis

--Adventures of Cuddles and Chuckles. Baerg, Harry John (1909-), illus. LC 76-102117. (Illus.). 96 p. 22cm. (Penguin series). 1970. Review and Herald Pub. Association.

--Nicku, Little Orphan Puppy. Baerg, Harry John (1909-), illus. LC 62-141661. 96p. illus. 24cm. 1962. Review and Herald Pub. Association.

--Rajah, the Story of a Bird. Quade, Lester, illus. LC 50-31780. (Illus.). 73. 21cm. 1949. Review and Herald Pub. Association.

--Up from the Sidewalk. Larkin, Howard C., illus. LC 66-19424. 96 p. illus. 22 cm. 1966. Review and Herald Pub. Association.

Rawson, Marianna S.

--A Life of Jesus for Boys and Girls. LC 11-26488. 21 cm. 115p. 1911. The Biddle Press.

Ray, Anna Chapin see Howard, Sidney, pseud.

Ray, Anna Chapin (1865-1945)

--Buddie: A Story of a Boy. Richards, Harriet Roosevelt, illus. LC 11-10758. 4 p. l., 286 p., 1 l. front., 3 pl. 20 cm. (Her The Buddie books). 1911. Little, Brown, and Company.

--Buddie at Gray Buttes Camp. Richards, Harriet Roosevelt, illus. LC 12-21734. vii, 261 p. front., plates. 20 cm. (Her The Buddie books). 1912. Little, Brown, and Company.

--Bumper & Baby John, 1 of 21 vols. Wager-Smith, Curtis, illus. LC 4-31607. 18cm. 146p. (Boys & Girls Booklovers Ser.: No. 1). 1904. Set. Henry Altemus Co.

--The Cadets of Flemming Hall. LC 7-36655. 300, 3 p. front., plates. 19 cm. c.1892. T. Y. Crowell & Co.

--Day: Her Year in New York. Richards, Harriet Roosevelt, illus. LC 7-30834. 3 p. l., 317 p. front., 3 pl. 19 cm. (Her The "Sidney" books vol. iii). 1907. Little, Brown, and Company.

--Dick: A Story for Boys and Girls. LC 7-36654. 280 p. incl. front. plates. 20 cm. c.1896. T. Y. Crowell & Company.

--Half a Dozen Boys: An Every-Day Story. LC 7-36653. 318 p. front., plates. 21 cm. 1890. T. Y. Crowell & Company.

--Half a Dozen Boys: An Every-Day Story. Merrill, Frank Thayer (1848-), illus. LC 7-36652. 318 p. front., plates. 19 cm. 1895. T. Y. Crowell & Co.

--Half a Dozen Girls. LC 7-36651. 2 p. l., 3-369 p. front., illus. 21 cm. 1891. T. Y. Crowell & Company.

--Half a Dozen Girls. Merrill, Frank Thayer (1848-), illus. LC 7-36650. 369 p. front., plates. 19 cm. 1896. T. Y. Crowell & Co.

Raymond, Nancy, pseud. & Fideler, Raymond Edwin
--Forgetful Bear. Fideler, Nancy B.. Harper, Frank Robert (1908-), illus. LC 43-16038. (Nancy Raymond is a Joint Pseud. of Nancy B. Fideler and Raymond Edwin Fideler.). (Illus.). 28p. 27cm. 1943. Fideler Co.
--Frisky at the Fair. Fideler, Nancy B.. Gringhuis, Richard H. (1918-1974), illus. Dirk, pseud. LC 48-4405. (Nancy Raymond is the Joint Pseud. of Nancy B. Fideler and Raymond Edwin Fideler.). (Illus.). 27p. 27cm. (Story Hour Library). 1947. Fideler Co.
--Grabby Pup. Fideler, Nancy B.. Gringhuis, Richard H., pseud. (1918-1974), illus. Gringhuis, Richard H.. Dirk, pseud. LC 45-8442. (Nancy Raymond is the Joint Pseud. of Nancy B. Fideler and Raymond Edwin Fideler). (Illus.). 28p. 27cm. (A Story Hour Bk.). 1945. Fideler Co.
--Smoky, the Little Kitten Who Didn't Want to. Fideler, Nancy B.. Gringhuis, Richard H., pseud. (1918-1974), illus. Gringhuis, Richard H.. Dirk, pseud. LC 45-8443. (Nancy Raymond is the Joint Pseud. of Nancy B. Fideler and Raymond Edwin Fideler.). (Illus.). 20p. 27cm. (A Story Hour Bk.). 1945. Fideler Co.
--Unhappy Rabbit. Fideler, Nancy B.. Harper, Frank Robert (1908-), illus. LC 44-2948. (Nancy Raymond is the Joint Pseud. of Nancy B. Fideler and Raymond Edwin Fideler.). (Illus.). 20p. 27cm. 1943. Fideler Co.

Raymond, Robert R.
--Shakespeare for the Young: Containing: "A Midsummer Night's Dream," "As You Like It" and "Julius Caesar.". N.D. Fords, Howard & Hulbert.

Raymond, Rossiter Worthington (1840-1918)
--Camp and Cabin: Life and Luck in the Sierras. (Little Classic). N.D. Fords, Howard & Hulbert.
--Hoyty-Toyty. N.D. J. B. Ford.
--The Man in the Moon, and Other People. 347p. 1876, c.1874. American News Co.
--The Man in the Moon, and Other People. LC 14-19348. 3 p. l., 9-347 p. 10 pl. 20 cm. 1875. J. B. Ford & Company.
--The Merry-Go-Round: Stories for Boys and Girls. (Author of "The Man in the Moon."). (Illus.). N.D. Fords, Howard & Hulbert.
--Two Ghosts and Other Christmas Tales. (Illus.). N.D. Lothrop Publishing Co.

Raymond, Rossiter Worthington (1840-1918) & Lippincott, Sara Jane Clarke, Mrs. (1823-1904)
--Treasures from Fairy Land. Greenwood, Grace, pseud. (Illus.). 534p. (The Excelsior Edition). 1879. American News Co.
--Treasures from Fairy Land. Greenwood, Grace, pseud. LC 44-31054. 2 p. l., 9-321, 185 p. front., illus., plates 19 cm. 1879. The American News Company.
--Treasures from Fairyland. Empire ed. Greenwood, Grace, pseud. 1905. American News Co.

Raymund, Carl
--Little Man Dressed in Red. Raymund, Carl, illus. LC 57-9208. (Illus.). (ps-1). 1957. (ISBN 0-06-024840-8). Har-Row.

Raynal, Francois, jt. auth. see Guyot, Jacqueline.

Rayner, Mary (1933-)
--Crocodarling. LC 85-11395. p. cm. 1986, c.1985. (ISBN 0-02-775770-6). Bradbury Press.
--Garth Pig and the Ice Cream Lady. Rayner, Mary (1933-), illus. LC 77-1647. p. cm. 1977. (ISBN 0-689-30598-2). Atheneum.
--Garth Pig and the Ice Cream Lady. Rayner, Mary (1933-), illus. (Illus.). 32 p. 21cm. 1st U.S. edition. 1981, c.1977. (ISBN 0-689-70495-X). Atheneum.
--Garth Pig and the Ice Cream Lady. Rayner, Mary (1933-), illus. 1977. Macmillan. **Award: (KGM).**
--Mr. and Mrs. Pig's Evening Out. Rayner, Mary (1933-), illus. LC 76-4476. (Illus.). 32 p. 27cm. c.1976. (ISBN 0-689-30530-3). Atheneum. **Award: (ALA).**
--Mrs. Pig's Bulk Buy. Rayner, Mary (1933-), illus. LC 80-19875. p. cm. 1981. (ISBN 0-689-30831-0). Atheneum.
--The Rain Cloud. Rayner, Mary (1933-), illus. LC 79-3069. (Illus.). 32 p. 18cm. 1980. (ISBN 0-689-30763-2). Atheneum.
--The Witchfinder. Rayner, Mary (1933-), illus. LC 76-22600. p. cm. 1976, c.1975. (ISBN 0-688-22082-7). (ISBN 0-688-32082-1). Morrow.

Rayner, William (1929-)
--Stag Boy. LC 72-91232. 160 p. 21cm. 1973. (ISBN 0-15-278400-4). Harcourt Brace Jovanovich.

Rayson, Steven (1932-)
--The Crows of War. A Novel of Maiden Castle. LC 74-19355. (Illus.). 269 p. 22cm. 1975, c.1974. (ISBN 0-689-30455-2). Atheneum.

Razumivevich, V.
--Order Number One. 111p. 1977. (ISBN 0-8285-1219-1, Pub. by Progress Pubs USSR). Imported Pubns.

Razzi, James (1931-)
--The Dennis Bones Mystery Book. (gr. k-3). 1979. (ISBN 0-590-12082-4, Schol Pap). Scholastic Inc.
--Don't Open This Box!. LC 72-10219. (Illus.). 39 p. 22cm. 1973. (ISBN 0-8193-0669-X). Parents' Magazine Press.
--The Empire Strikes Back Panorama Book. Daly, Gerry, illus. (Illus.). (ps up). 1981. (ISBN 0-394-84688-5). Random.
--Simply Fun. Razzi, James (1931-), illus. 64p. 1968. Parents' Magazine Press.

Razzi, Jim
--The Get Along Gang & the Missing Caboose. Williams, A. O., illus. (Illus.). 32p. (Orig.). (Get Along Gang Ser.). (ps-2). 1984. (ISBN 0-590-33187-6). Scholastic Inc.

Read, Albert, tr. see Lindgren, Astrid Ericsson.

Read, Beryl J
--Pip's Mountain. LC 79-26357. 94 p. 21cm. (Path Finder Ser.). 1980, c.1976. (ISBN 0-310-37901-6). Zondervan Pub. House.
--The Runaway Girl. LC 78-31367. 89 p. 21cm. (Pathfinder Ser.). 1979, c.1976. (ISBN 0-310-37851-6). Zondervan Pub. House.

Read, Edyth Ellerbeck, jt. auth. see Jacobs, Caroline Elliott Hoogs, Mrs.

Read, Elfreida (1920-)
--Brothers by Choice. LC 73-21858. 153 p. 21cm. 1974. (ISBN 0-374-30996-5). Farrar, Straus and Giroux.
--The Magical Egg. Green, Alison, illus. LC 65-13434. 95 p. illus. 22 cm. 1st U.S. edition. 1965, c.1963. Lippincott.
--No One Need Ever Know. Delfino, Matte, illus. LC 79-123879. (Illus.). 23 p. 24cm. (Magic circle book). 1971. Ginn.
--The Spell of Chuchuchan. Fraser, Betty M., pseud. (1928-), illus. Fraser, Elizabeth Marr. LC 67-23345. (Illus.). 110 p. 20cm. 1967, c.1966. World Pub. Co.

Read, Emily
--Jasper, the Carver and Aunt Gracie's Trust. LC 12-346208. v, 7-174 p. front., plates. 18 cm. c.1877. American Sunday-School Union.

Read, G. W., jt. auth. see Gaines, Ruth Louise.

Read, Helen S.
--Billy's Letter. N.D. Charles Scribner's Sons'.
--Jip and the Fireman. N.D. Charles Scribner's Sons'.
--Mary and the Policeman. N.D. Charles Scribner's Sons'.
--Mr. Brown's Grocery Store. N.D. Charles Scribner's Sons'.
--My Blue Book: Adventures for Young Children. Hill, Patty Smith & Reed, Mary Maud (1880-1960), eds. Lee, Eleanor, illus. N.D. Charles Scribner's Sons.

Read, Herbert Edward, Sir (1893-1968), ed.
--This Way, Delight: A Book of Poetry for the Young. Kepes, Juliet Appleby (1919-), illus. LC 56-6014. 155p. illus. 25cm. 1956. (ISBN 0-394-91741-3). Pantheon. **Award: (ALA).**

Read, Isobel
--Chitter Chatter. LC 49-21349. 32 p. col. illus. 17 cm. (Tell-a-tale books, 889). c.1948. Whitman Pub. Co.

Read, Maggie, illus.
--Going to School. LC 81-52654. (Illus.). 28 p. 20cm. (Starters Facts: No. 5). c.1981. (ISBN 0-382-06482-8). (ISBN 0-382-06551-4). Silver Burdett Co.

Read, Mary Lyle
--The Ghost of Emma Louise. Koepcke, Ingrid, illus. LC 79-3686. (Illus.). 128 p. 21cm. c.1980. (ISBN 0-687-14218-0). Abingdon.
--The Sack Man and the Grave. LC 80-26913. 160 p. 21cm. c.1981. (ISBN 0-687-36690-9). Abingdon.

Read, Nora, jt. auth. see Hemery, Paul Arnold Valentine.

Reade, Charles
--The Cloister and the Hearth. (Great Il. Classics - Titans). (gr. 9 up). 1944. (ISBN 0-396-05512-5). Dodd.

Reade, Compton
--The Father's Crown. (The Golden Crowns Ser.). N.D. Cassell Petter & Galpin.
--The Little Girl's Crown. (The Golden Crowns Ser.). N.D. Cassell Petter & Galpin.
--The Maiden's Crown. (The Golden Crowns Ser.). N.D. Cassell Petter & Galpin.
--The Orphan's Crown. (The Golden Crown Ser.). N.D. Cassel Petter & Galpin.
--The Poor Man's Crown. (The Golden Crowns Ser.). N.D. Cassell Petter & Galpin.
--The Wife's Crown. (The Golden Crown Ser.). N.D. Cassell Petter & Galpin.

Reade, F. E.
--After the Winter (Pub. by Society for Promoting Christian Knowledge). N.D. E. & J. B. Young & Co.
--Brave Tiny. N.D. E.& J. B. Young & Co.
--Edith's Charity (Pub. by Society for Promoting Christian Knowledge). N.D. E. & J. B. Young & Co.
--The False Character. (Illus.). N.D. E & J B Young.
--How Sandy Learned the Creed (Pub. by Society for Promoting Christian Knowledge). N.D. E. & J. B Young & Co.
--Janie Fletcher. N.D. E. & J. B. Young & Co.
--Mrs. Heritage. N.D. E & J B Young & Co.
--Nell's Bondage. N.D. E . J B Young & Co.
--The Parting Ways. N.D. E. & J. B. Young & Co.
--Patty Burton: Or, The Ninth Commandment. N.D. E. & J. B Young & Co.
--Seven Idols. N.D. E. & J. B. Young & Co.
--Wife from the Country. N.D. E J B Young & Co.

Reade, Louis (1857-1926), ed.
--Hans Andersen's Fairy Tales. (Illus.). N.D. Harper & Brothers Trade-List.

Reader, Dennis Joel (1939-)
--Coming Back Alive. LC 79-5147. 233 p. 21cm. c.1981. (ISBN 0-394-84359-2). (ISBN 0-394-94359-7). Random House.

Reader, Ethel
--The Little Merman. Pape, Frank Cheyne (1878-) & Johnson, Bob (1950-), illus. LC 79-12762. (Illus.). (gr. 4 up). 1979. (ISBN 0-89742-024-1, Dawne-Leigh). (ISBN 0-89742-018-7). Celestial Arts.
--The Story of the Little Merman. Pape, Frank Cheyne (1878-) & Johnson, Bob (1950-), illus. LC 79-12762. p. cm. c.1979. (ISBN 0-89742-024-1). Dawne-Leigh Publications.

The, Reader's Digest Editors
--Great Stories for Young Readers. (gr. 6 up). N.D. Funk & W.
--New Treasury for Young Readers. LC 63-159383. 200 p. illus. (part col.) 29 cm. 1963. Reader's Digest Association.
--Storytime. LC 82-80898. (Illus.). 448p. (gr. 1-8). 1982. (ISBN 0-89577-145-4). RD Assn.
--Teen-Age Treasury. LC 58-1546. (A Collection of Articles and Stories from the "Reader's Digest", Selected by Teen-Agers and Compiled by the Editors.). 4v. illus. 20cm. c.1957. Reader's Digest Association.
--Treasury for Young Readers. 1 st. ed. LC 61-11278. 202p. illus. 29cm. 1961. Reader's Digest Association.
--World's Best Fairy Tales. Kredel, Fritz (1900-1973), illus. (Illus.). (gr. k-6). 1967. Funk & W.

Reading, J. P
--Bouquets for Brimbal. LC 79-2002. p. cm. 1980. (ISBN 0-06-024843-2). (ISBN 0-06-024844-0). Harper & Row.

Ready, Dolores
--The Boy Who Made His Pennies Go a Long Way: A Story about Martin De Porres. (Stories about Christian Heroes Ser.). (gr. 1-5). 1977. (ISBN 0-03-022106-4). Winston Pr.

Reagan, Rocky (1883-)
--Rocky's Chuck Wagon Stories. LC 68-59005. (Illus.). vii, 160 p. 22cm. 1968. Naylor Co.
--Rocky's Chuck Wagon Stories. LC 79-4688. 22cm. 171p. 1969. Naylor Co.
--Rocky's Yarn. (Illus.). N.D. (ISBN 0-8111-0482-6). The Naylor and Company.

Ream, Gerald L.
--The Land of Charlie Cornsilk. Scaduto, Al, illus. (Illus.). 64p. (gr. 3-5). 1973. (ISBN 0-682-47581-5). Exposition.

Reams, Olive Mann, Mrs.
--Toys and Joys: Rhymes for Sleepy Times. Burdick, Doris, illus. LC 22-10491. 39 p. incl. front., illus. 26 cm. c.1921. The Four Seas Company.

Reaney, G. S. mrs. see Reaney, Isabel Edis.

Reaney, Isabel Edis (1847-)
--Clovie and Madge: A Book for Girls. (Illus.). (The Eaglehurst Ser.). N.D. White & Allen.
--Daisy Snowflake's Secret. (Illus.). (Sunday-Hour Lib.). N.D. American Tract Society.
--The Gypsy Queen: A New series for Boys and Girls, 1 of 4 Vols. (Illus.). (The Eaglehurst Ser.). N.D. White & Allen.
--Just in Time. 374p. N.D. American Tract Society.
--Little Glory Mission, 1 of 50 vols. (The Golden Rod Lib.). 1905. Set. American Tract Society.

Reardon, Mark S
--The Christmas Present, and Other Stories for Children. 1st ed. Lyons, Dave, illus. LC 55-12067. 85p. illus. 21cm. 1955. Pageant Press.

Reason, Joyce (1894-)
--Bran the Bronze-Smith: A Tale of the Bronze Age in the British Isles. Reason, Joyce (1894-), illus. LC 32-17788. xi, 285 p. incl. front., illus. plates. 20 cm. c.1932. E. P. Dutton & Co., Inc.
--To Capture the King!. The Story of a Jacobite Plot. Walsh, David, illus. LC 57-7083. (Illus.). 144 p. 21cm. (Pageant books). 1957. Roy Publishers.

Reavin, Sam
--Hurray for Captain Jane!. McCully, Emily Arnold (1939-), illus. LC 79-153793. (Illus.). 32 p. 27cm. 1971. (ISBN 0-8193-0511-1). Parents' Magazine Press.

Rebald, Aime
--Scalawag. Dennis, Morgan (1891-1960), illus. Hoppin, Frederick Street, tr. from Fr. N.D. J. B. Lippincott.
--Scalawag: The Story of a Little Dog. Dennis, Morgan (1891-1960), illus. Hoppin, Frederick Street, tr. LC 31-23354. 5 p. l., 115 p. incl. illus., plates. col. front. 22 cm. 1931. Frederick A. Stokes Company.

Rebin, Norman
--The Forgotten Christmas. N.D. Carlton Press.

Reboul, Antoine (1914-)
--Thou Shalt Not Kill. Craig, Stephanie, tr. LC 77-77312. 157 p. 22cm. 1969. S. G. Phillips.

Recheis, Kathe
--No Room for the Baker. Gergely, Tibor (1900-1978), illus. LC 74-81697. (Illus.). 47 p. 27cm. 1969. Four Winds Press.

Recher, Robert
--Rudi of the Mountains. Gray, Reginald S., illus. Ramsbotham, Helen, tr. from Fr. LC 65-23589. 158p. illus. 21cm. 1st U.S. edition. 1965, c.1964. Criterion.

Rechnitzer, Ferdinand Edsted (1894-)
--Bonny's Boy. Kirmse, Marguerite (1885-1954), illus. LC 47-30005. 3 p. l., 266 p. front., illus. 22 cm. 1946. The John C. Winston Company.
--Bonny's Boy Returns. Cortese, Edward F., illus. LC 52-14257. (Illus.). 213p. (gr. 5-9). 1952. (ISBN 0-03-034350-X). HR&W.
--Captain Jeep. 1st ed. Gretzer, John, illus. LC 51-13737. 209 p. illus. 22 cm. 1951. Winston.
--Jinks of Jayson Valley. 1st ed. Kirmse, Marguerite (1885-1954), illus. LC 50-10758. (Illus.). 216 p. 22cm. 1950. Winston.
--Midnight Alarm. LC 55-10575. (Illus.). 192 p. 21cm. 1955. Holt.
--Raff: The Story of an English Setter. Kirmse, Marguerite (1885-1954), illus. LC 48-10567. ix, 240 p. illus. 22 cm. 1948. J. C. Winston Co.

Reck, Alma Kehoe (1901-)
--All Aboard for Tin Cup. Frankenberg, Robert Clinton (1911-), illus. LC 62-9664. 160p. illus. 21cm. 1962. Scribner.
--The Lost Little Boy. Patton, Lucia, illus. LC 46-18713. 32 p. illus. (part col.) 24 x 19 1/2 cm. 1946. A. Whitman & Company.

Reck, Franklin Mering (1896-1965), ed. see The, American Boy.

Reck, Franklin Mering (1896-1965)
--Sergeant Pinky. LC 31-29629. 3 p. l., 257 p. 20 cm. 1931. Dodd, Mead & Company.
--Varsity Letter. 238p. (gr. 7-11). 1942. Thomas Y. Crowell Co.

Reck, Franklin Mering (1896-1965), ed.
--Stories Boys Like. LC 65-212095. 2)03p. 21cm. c.1965. Crowell.

Rector, Margaret Hayden
--Norton and Gus. James, Toni & James, Ron (1938-), photos by LC 76-46259. (Illus.). 238 p. 22cm. c.1976. (ISBN 0-913182-77-X). Grossmont Press.

Reddin, Gladys M.
--The Johnny Bruin Children Stories. (gr. 4-7). N.D. (ISBN 0-8181-0219-5). Pageant-Poseidon.

Redding, Robert Hull (1919-)
--Aluk: An Alaskan Caribou. 1st ed. Komoda, Kiyoaki (1937-), illus. (Illus.). 107 p. 22cm. 1967. Doubleday.
--Mara: An Alaskan Weasel. Komoda, Kiyoaki (1937-), illus. LC 68-19316. (Illus.). 10 linecuts. 144p. (gr. 7-9). 1968. (ISBN 0-385-02719-2). Doubleday.
--North to the Wilderness: The Story of an Alaskan Boy. LC 76-97682. 192p. (gr. 7 up). 1970. (ISBN 0-385-00141-X). (ISBN 0-385-04081-4). Doubleday.

Reddix, Valerie (1955-)
--The Claw & the Spiderweb. (Pennypincher Bks.). (gr. 3-6). 1982. (ISBN 0-89191-709-8). Cook.
--The Treasure of the Scroll. LC 84-12735. 128 p. 18cm. c.1984. (ISBN 0-89191-884-1). Chariot Books.
--The Treasure of the Scroll. 128p. (Pennypincher Ser.). (gr. 5-9). 1984. (ISBN 0-89191-884-1). Cook.

Reddy, Marie E
--Mr. Simmie: Or, The Square Dance in the Clearing. Quarterman, Leonora, illus. LC 40-7603. 1 p. l., 5-50 p. illus., 24 cm. c.1940. The Christopher Publishing House.

Redfield, Fern, pseud., see Koch, Frieda Redfield.

Redford, Christian
--Frank's Life Battle: Or, The Three Friends, 1 vol. Juv ed. Stacey, W. S., illus. N.D. Cassell & Co.

Redford, Polly (1925-1972)
--The Christmas Bower. 1st ed. Gorey, Edward St. John (1925-), illus. (Illus.). 192 p. 21cm. 1967. Dutton.

Redford, Ruby Lorraine
--The Mystery of the Bradley Pearls. (Dollar Mystery and Adventure Ser.). N.D. David McKay Co.

Redies, Reiner, jt. auth. see Melle, Gerta.

--The Story of Kurri Kurri the Kookaburra. (John Sands Nature Ser.). (gr. 2-5). N.D. Tri-Ocean Books.
--The Story of Russ the Australian Tree Kangaroo. (John Sands Nature Ser.). (gr. 2-5). N.D. Tri-Ocean Books.
--The Story of Sarli the Great Barrier Reef Turtle. (John Sands Nature Ser.). (gr. 2-5). N.D. Tri-Ocean Books.
--The Story of Shadow the Rock Wallaby. (John Sands Nature Ser.). (gr. 2-5). N.D. Tri-Ocean Books.
--Story of Shy the Platypus. (gr. 2-5). N.D (Pub. by Cowman). Tri-Ocean.
--The Story of Shy the Platypus. (John Sands Nature Ser.). (gr. 2-5). N.D. Tri-Ocean Books.
--The Story of Two Thumbs the Koala. (John Sands Nature Ser.). (gr. 2-5). N.D. Tri-Ocean Books.
--The Story of Wy-Lah the Cuckoo. (John Sands Nature Ser.). (gr. 2-5). N.D. Tri-Ocean Books.

Rees-Hansen, Gloria
--Desi & Gooie's Desert Tails. Rees-Hansen, Gloria, illus. (Illus.). (gr. 2 up). 1984. (ISBN 0-533-05602-0). Vantage.

Rees, Helen Christina Easson Evans see Oliver, Jane, pseud.

Rees, Jennifer Larcombe (1942-)
--The Fire Brand. LC 80-20276. p. cm. (Pathfinder Ser.). c.1980. (ISBN 0-310-37911-3). Zondervan Pub. House.

Rees, Leslie see Rees, George Leslie Clarence.

Rees, Lucy
--Wild Pony. 136p. (gr. 5-8). 1978. (ISBN 0-571-10685-4). Faber & Faber.

Reese, Albert
--Dark of the Moon. N.D. Carlton.

Reese, Bob
--Arbor Day. Jordan, Alton, ed. Reese, Bob, illus. (Illus.). (Holidays Ser.). (gr. k-3). 1977. (ISBN 0-89868-031-X, Read Res). (ISBN 0-89868-064-6). ARO Pub.
--Calico Jack and the Desert Critters. Reese, Bob, illus. LC 83-7550. (Illus.). 31 p. 22cm. (Critterland Adventures). c.1983. (ISBN 0-516-02321-7). Childrens Press.
--Coral Reef. Reese, Bob, illus. LC 82-23610. (Illus.). 24p. (Critterland Ocean Adventures Ser.). (ps-2). 1983. (ISBN 0-516-02312-8). (ISBN 0-516-42312-6). Childrens.
--Crab Apple. Wasserman, Dan, ed. Reese, Bob, illus. (Illus.). (Ten Word Bks.). (gr. k-1). 1979. (ISBN 0-89868-072-7). (ISBN 0-89868-083-2). ARO Pub.
--The Critter Race. Reese, Bob, illus. LC 81-3874. p. cm. (Critterland Adventures). 1981. (ISBN 0-516-02302-0). Childrens Press.
--Dale the Whale. Reese, Bob, illus. LC 82-23588. (Critterland Adventures). c.1983. (ISBN 0-516-02313-6). Children's Press.
--Huzzard Buzzard. Reese, Bob, illus. LC 81-6118. p. cm. (Critterland Adventures). 1981. (ISBN 0-516-02303-9). Childrens Press.
--Lactus Cactus. Reese, Bob, illus. LC 81-3866. p. cm. (Critterland Adventures). 1981. (ISBN 0-516-02304-7). Childrens Press.
--Little Dinosaur. Wasserman, Dan, ed. Reese, Bob, illus. (Illus.). (Ten Word Bks.). (gr. k-1). 1979. (ISBN 0-89868-070-0). (ISBN 0-89868-081-6). ARO Pub.
--Ocean Fish School. Reese, Bob, illus. LC 82-23572. (Illus.). 24p. (Critterland Ocean Adventures Ser.). (ps-2). 1983. (ISBN 0-516-02314-4). (ISBN 0-516-42314-2). Childrens.
--Oola Oyster. Reese, Bob, illus. LC 82-23609. (Illus.). 24p. (Critterland Ocean Adventures Ser.). (ps-2). 1983. (ISBN 0-516-02311-X). (ISBN 0-516-42311-8). Childrens.
--The Pamba and the Bink. Reese, Bob, illus. LC 84-21631. (Illus.). 31 p. 31cm. c.1984. (ISBN 0-89868-153-7). Aro Pub.
--Rapid Robert and Hiss the Snake. Reese, Bob, illus. LC 83-7622. (Illus.). 31 p. 22cm. (A Critterland Reader). c.1983. (ISBN 0-516-02322-5). Childrens Press.
--Rapid Robert Roadrunner. Reese, Bob, illus. LC 81-6090. p. cm. (Critter Land Adventures). 1981. (ISBN 0-516-02305-5). Childrens Press.
--Scary Larry Meets Big Willie. Reese, Bob, illus. LC 83-7553. p. cm. (Critterland Adventures). 1983. (ISBN 0-516-02323-3). Childrens Press.
--Scary Larry the Very Very Hairy Tarantula. Reese, Bob, illus. LC 81-3871. (Illus.). 24p. (Critterland Desert Adventures Ser.). (ps-2). 1981. (ISBN 0-516-02306-3). (ISBN 0-516-42306-1). Childrens.
--Spongee Sponge. Reese, Bob, illus. LC 82-23608. (Illus.). 24p. (Critterland Ocean Adventures Ser.). (ps-2). 1983. (ISBN 0-516-02315-2). (ISBN 0-516-42315-0). Childrens.
--Sunshine. Wasserman, Dan, ed. Reese, Bob, illus. (Illus.). (Ten Word Bks.). (gr. k-1). 1979. (ISBN 0-89868-073-5). (ISBN 0-89868-084-0). ARO Pub.
--Tweedle-De-Dee Tumbleweed. Reese, Bob, illus. LC 81-6155. p. cm. (Critterland Adventures). 1981. Childrens Press.
--Wellington Pelican. Reese, Bob, illus. LC 82-23587. (Illus.). 24p. (Critterland Ocean Adventures Ser.). (ps-2). 1983. (ISBN 0-516-02316-0). (ISBN 0-516-42316-9). Childrens.
--Who's a Silly Egg?. Jordan, Alton, ed. (Illus.). (Buppet Series). (gr. k-3). 1981. (ISBN 0-89868-092-1, Read Res). (ISBN 0-89868-103-0). ARO Pub.

Reese, Irene see Irene, pseud.

Reese, Irene
--Holidays in the Country: Or, Tessie, Beth, Rob, and Will. Irene, pseud. LC 12-34610. 73 p. incl. front., illus. 17 1/2 cm. 1889. Publishing House of the M. E. Church, South.

Reese, John Henry
--Big Mutt. Ruth, Rod (1912-), illus. LC 52-7057. (Illus.). 190 p. 21cm. 1952. Westminster Press.
--Dinky. LC 64-20953. 134 p. 21cm. 1964. D. McKay Co.
--The Shouting Duke: A Story Scientifically Calibrated to the Tastes, Needs & Educational Development of the Nine to Ninety Age Groups. Horwitz, Richard, illus. LC 51-8505. 133 p. illus. 22 cm. 1952. Westminster Press.
--Three Wild Ones. LC 63-9951. 188 p. 21 cm. 1963. Westminster Press.

Reese, Nancy
--I Can Eat an Elephant. Jordan, Alton, ed. Reese, Bob, illus. (Illus.). (Elephant Ser.). (gr. k-3). 1975. (ISBN 0-89868-012-3, Read Res). (ISBN 0-89868-045-X). ARO Pub.
--Purple Bear. Jordan, Alton, ed. Reese, Bob, illus. (Illus.). (Elephant Ser.). (gr. k-3). 1975. (ISBN 0-89868-013-1, Read Res). (ISBN 0-89868-046-8). ARO Pub.
--Smiley Snake. Jordan, Alton, ed. Reese, Bob, illus. (Illus.). (I Can Read Underwater Bks). (gr. k-3). 1974. (ISBN 0-89868-010-7, Read Res). (ISBN 0-89868-043-3). ARO Pub.

Reese, Ron
--Crazy Cat. Jordan, Alton, ed. Reese, Bob, illus. (Illus.). (I Can Read Underwater Bks). (gr. k-3). 1974. (ISBN 0-89868-002-6, Read Res). (ISBN 0-89868-035-2). ARO Pub.
--Crazy Cat's Bad Day. Jordan, Alton, ed. (Illus.). (Buppet Ser.). (gr. k-3). 1981. (ISBN 0-89868-090-5, Read Res). (ISBN 0-89868-101-4). ARO Pub.
--Halloween. Jordan, Alton, ed. Reese, Bob, illus. (Illus.). (Holidays Ser.). (gr. k-3). 1977. (ISBN 0-89868-023-9, Read Res Ser.). (ISBN 0-89868-056-5). ARO Pub.
--Mosquito. Jordan, Alton, ed. Reese, Bob, illus. (Illus.). (Elephant Ser.). (gr. k-3). 1975. (ISBN 0-89868-014-X, Read Res). (ISBN 0-89868-047-6). ARO Pub.
--Sammy Skunk. Jordan, Alton, ed. Reese, Bob, illus. (Illus.). (I Can Read Underwater Bks). (gr. k-3). 1974. (ISBN 0-89868-009-3, Read Res). (ISBN 0-89868-042-5). ARO Pub.

Reesink, Maryke (1919-)
--The Fisherman's Family. Apol, Georgette, illus. LC 68-5573. (Illus.). 32 p. 29cm. 1968. Harcourt, Brace & World.
--The Golden Treasure. Tol, Jaap, illus. LC 68-7103. (Illus.). 1 v. (unpaged. 29cm. 1st U.S. edition. 1968. Harcourt, Brace & World.
--The Magic Horse. Hospes, Adrie (1946-), illus. LC 74-8512. p. cm. 1974. (ISBN 0-07-030456-4). (ISBN 0-07-030456-4). McGraw-Hill.
--Peter and the Twelve-Headed Dragon. Hospes, Adrie (1946-), illus. LC 77-11137. (Illus.). 32 p. 29cm. 1st U.S. edition. 1970. Harcourt, Brace & World.
--The Princess Who Always Ran Away. Tresy, Francoise (1943-), illus. LC 80-16849. (Illus.). 26 p. 29cm. 1981. (ISBN 0-07-051714-2). McGraw-Hill.
--The Two Windmills. Apol, Georgette, illus. LC 67-6406. (Illus.). 1 v. (unpaged. 29cm. 1967. Harcourt, Brace & World.
--The Wishing Balloons. Hospes, Adrie (1946-), illus. LC 78-146712. (Illus.). 24 p. 29cm. 1971. (ISBN 0-03-086302-3). Holt, Rinehart and Winston.

Reev
--Susie in the Algrave: Or, Susie the Tail-Wagger. 1977. (ISBN 0-682-48842-9). Exposition.

Reeve, Arthur Benjamin (1880-)
--The Boy Scouts Craig Kennedy. LC 25-17415. xi p., 1 l., 237 p. front., plates. 19 cm. c.1925. Harper & Brothers.
--Craig Kennedy Listens In. (Detective Stories for Boys). N.D. Grosset & Dunlap.
--The Treasure Train. N.D. Grosset & Dunlap.

Reeve, Joan P.
--Jerry & the Missing Cuckoo. (gr. 2-5). N.D (MYL). Moody.
--Strange Boy of the Island. 128p. (Pre-Teen Ser). (gr. 4-6). 1972. (ISBN 0-8024-3835-0). Moody.

Reeve, Joel, pseud., see Cox, William Robert.

Reeves, Ada Morrow
--The Christmas Parade. Brevannes, Maurice (1904-), illus. LC 51-6292. 23 p. illus. 21 cm. 1951. Houghton Mifflin.

Reeves, Bruce Douglas (1940-)
--Street Smarts. LC 80-28256. 222 p. 22cm. c.1981. (ISBN 0-8253-0047-9). Beaufort Books.

Reeves, Catharine
--Lucky: The Palomino Colt. 1978. (ISBN 0-533-03542-2). Vantage.

Reeves, Helen Buckingham Mathers see Mathers, Helen Buckingham.

Reeves, James (1909-), ed. see Aesopus.

Reeves, James (1909-), retold by see Cervantes Saavedra, Miguel de.

Reeves, James (1909-), ed. see De France, Marie.

Reeves, James (1909-), retold by see Grimm, Jakob Ludwig Karl (1785-1863) & Grimm, Wilhelm Karl.

Reeves, James (1909-), retold by see Homerus.

Reeves, James (1909-), ed. see Marie De France.

Reeves, James (1909-), ed. see Pushkin, Alexander Sergeyevich.

Reeves, James (1909-)
--The Angel and the Donkey. Ardizzone, Edward Jeffrey Irving (1900-1979), illus. LC 75-102453. (Illus.). 32 p. 1970, c.1969. McGraw-Hill.
--The Blackbird in Lilac: Verses. Ardizzone, Edward Jeffrey Irving (1900-1979), illus. 1952. Dutton.
--The Blackbird in the Lilac: Verses for Children. 1st ed. Ardizzone, Edward Jeffrey Irving (1900-1979), illus. LC 59-5841. (Illus.). 21cm. 95p. (gr. k-3). 1959. (ISBN 0-525-26652-6). Dutton.
--Christmas Book. Briggs, Raymond Redvers (1934-), illus. LC 68-17168. (Illus.). (gr. 4-6). 1970. (ISBN 0-525-27821-4). Dutton.
--The Clever Mouse. Swiderska, Barbara, illus. LC 76-377754. (Illus.). 24 p. 1976. (ISBN 0-7011-5085-8). Chatto and Windus.
--Exploits of Don Quixote. Ardizzone, Edward Jeffrey Irving (1900-1979), illus. LC 85-11170. (Original Author: Miguel De Cervantes Saavedra). p. cm. 1985, c.1959. (ISBN 0-87226-025-9). (ISBN 0-87226-028-3). P. Bedrick Books.
--Fables from Aesop. Wilson, Maurice Charles John (1914-), illus. LC 85-11138. p. cm. 1985, c.1961. (ISBN 0-87226-027-5). (ISBN 0-87226-028-3). P. Bedrick Books.
--Mr. Horrox & the Gratch. Blake, Quentin (1932-), illus. (gr. 1-4). 1975. (ISBN 0-8277-4481-1). British Bk Ctr.
--Mulcaster Market. 1951. (ISBN 0-435-21003-3). Heinemann Ed.
--The Peddler's Dream, and Other Plays. LC 63-8592. 96 p. 20 cm. 1963. Dutton.
--Prefabulous Animiles: Verses. 1st ed. Ardizzone, Edward Jeffrey Irving (1900-1979), illus. LC 60-11859. (Illus.). 56 p. 21cm. 1960, c.1957. Dutton.
--Ragged Robin. Paton, Jane Elizabeth (1934-), illus. LC 61-65416. unpaged. illus. 30cm. 1961. Dutton. **Award: (CMA).**
--Rhyming Will. Ardizzone, Edward Jeffrey Irving (1900-1979), illus. LC 68-12425. (Illus.). 32 p. 1968, c.1967. McGraw-Hill.
--Sailor Rumbelow, and Other Stories. Ardizzone, Edward Jeffrey Irving (1900-1979), illus. LC 62-14699. (Illus.). 221 p. 21cm. 1st U.S. edition. 1962. Dutton.
--The Story of Jackie Thimble. 1st ed. Ardizzone, Edward Jeffrey Irving (1900-1979), illus. LC 64-10693. 31 p. illus. 17 cm. 1964. Dutton.
--The Strange Light. Kocsis, James C. (1936-), illus. Paul, James, pseud. LC 66-7397. 152p. illus. 22cm. 1966. Rand McNally.
--Titus in Trouble. Ardizzone, Edward Jeffrey Irving (1900-1979), illus. 1972. (ISBN 0-8098-2014-5). David McKay Company.
--Titus in Trouble. Ardizzone, Edward Jeffrey Irving (1900-1979), illus. LC 60-7633. (Illus.). unpaged. 29cm. 1960, c.1959. H. Z. Walck.
--The Wandering Moon. Ardizzone, Edward Jeffrey Irving (1900-1979), illus. LC 60-118608. 73p. illus. 22cm. 1st U.S. edition. 1960. Dutton.

Reeves, James (1909-), retold by.
--English Fables and Fairy Stories. Kiddell-Monroe, Joan (1908-), illus. (Myths and Legends Ser.). 1954. Henry Z. Walck Inc. **Award: (CMA).**
--English Fables & Fairy Stories. Kiddell-Monroe, Joan (1908-) & Curl, Beverly, illus. (Illus.). Repr. of 1954 ed. (Oxford Myths & Legends). (gr. 6-12). 1978. (ISBN 0-19-274101-2). Oxford U Pr.
--Golden Land. 496p. (gr. 4 up). 1963. Dufour.
--A Golden Land: Stories, Poems, Songs, New and Old. Conway, Gillian, et al., illus. LC 58-135632. (Illus.). 496 p. 25cm. 1958. Hastings House.
--Heroes & Monsters. Nechamkin, Sarah, illus. (Illus., Orig.). 1978. (ISBN 0-8467-0539-7, Pub. by Two Continents). Hippocrene Bks.
--Maildun the Voyager. Negri, Rocco (1932-), illus. LC 72-3211. (Illus.). 104 p. 21cm. 1972, c.1971. (ISBN 0-8098-2421-3). H. Z. Walck.
--The Merry-Go-Round: A Collection of Rhymes and Poems. Abridged. LC 68-97654. (Illus.). 301p. (Puffin bks.). 1967. Penguin.
--One's None: Old Rhymes for New Tongues. Watts, Anna Bernadette (1942-), illus. LC 68-16779. (Illus.). 125 p. 23cm. 1969. (ISBN 0-531-01756-7). F. Watts.
--Snow-White & Red-Rose. Rodwell, Jenny, illus. 32p. 1981. (ISBN 0-905478-47-9, Pub. by Andersen-Hutchinson England). State Mutual Bk.
--Three Tall Tales, Chosen from Traditional Sources. Ardizzone, Edward Jeffrey Irving (1900-1979), illus. LC 64-149048. 42 p. col. illus. 27 cm. 1964. Abelard-Schuman.

Reeves, Joyce see Gard, Joyce, pseud.

Reeves, Katherine
--The Cloud Eater. Golbin, Andree, illus. LC 63-12331. 48 p. illus. 23 cm. 1963. Rand McNally.
--Curious Doings at the Mouse-House. Nichols, Marie C. (1905-), illus. LC 57-876286. 93p. illus. 22cm. 1957. Sterling Pub. Co.
--The Farmer's Cat Nap. Nichols, Marie C. (1905-), illus. LC 56-11142. unpaged. illus. 22cm. 1956. Sterling Pub. Co.
--A Feather Bed for Toby Tod. N.D. E. M. Hale & Co.
--A Feather Bed for Toby Tod. Paull, Grace A. (1898-), illus. LC 59-113972. (Illus.). 21cm. 55p. (gr. 2-7). 1959. (ISBN 0-690-29426-3). T Y Crowell.

Reeves, Lawrence F. see Lyfick, Warren, pseud.

Reeves, Marjorie Ethel (1905-), ed. see Bolton, James.

Reeves, Ruth M
--Stories of Liberian Life. LC 77-367914. (Illus.). 96 p. 22cm. N.D. S.N.

Regan, Mary
--Paddy's Moon. Hansen, Evelyn, illus. LC 51-16438. unpaged. illus. 27 cm. 1951. Erle Press.

Regehr, Lydia, tr. see Platonov, Andrei Platonovich.

Regehr, Lydia (1903-)
--Bible Riddles of Birds & Beasts & Creeping Things. (Illus.). 36p. (Orig.). (gr. 7-12). 1982. (ISBN 0-89323-030-8). BMA Pr.

Reggiani, Renee (1925-)
--Five Children and a Dog. Tomes, Margot Ladd (1917-), illus. Lambert, Mary & Chisholm, Anne, trs. LC 65-132851. 249p. illus. 21cm. 1st U.S. edition. N.D. (ISBN 0-698-20043-8). Coward.
--The Sun Train. Creagh, Patrick (1930-), tr. from Ital. LC 66-13143. 251p. 21cm. 1st U.S. edition. c.1966. Coward.
--Tomorrow and the Next Day. Chisholm, Anne, tr. from Italian. LC 67-9580. 255 p. 21cm. 1967. Coward-McCann.

Regli, Adolph Casper see Rand, Addison, pseud.

Regli, Adolph Casper, jt. auth. see Anderson, Anita Melva.

Regli, Adolph Casper (1896-1952)
--Fiddling Cowboy. Edson, Nat, illus. 1949. David McKay Co.
--Fiddling Cowboy in Search of Gold. LC 51-8070. (Illus.). 243 p. 22cm. 1951. Watts.
--Partners in the Saddle. LC 50-6250. 248 p. 22cm. 1950. F. Watts.
--Southpaw Fly Hawk. Rand, Addison, pseud. 1st ed. Ricketts, William B., illus. LC 52-5641. 183p. illus. 21cm. 1952. Longmans Green.
--Young Readers Cowboy Stories. LC 51-7857. 188 p. illus. 21 cm. (Young Readers bookshelf). 1951. Lantern Press.
--Young Readers Cowboy Stories. Geer, Charles Hand (1922-), illus. LC 53-11999. 188p. illus. 22cm. (Young readers bookshelf 6). 1953, c.1951. Grossett & Dunlap.

Regniers, Beatrice Schenk Freedman de see De Regniers, Beatrice Schenk Freedman.

Reich, Ali
--The Care Bears and the Terrible Twos. Bracken, Carolyn, illus. LC 83-4494. 32p. (A Random House Pictureback). (gr. k-3). c.1983. (ISBN 0-394-85918-9). Random House.
--Meet the Care Bears. Gray, J. M. L., illus. LC 82-61672. (Illus.). 32p. (Care Bear Mini-Storybooks). (gr. 1-6). 1983. (ISBN 0-394-85844-1). Random.

Reich, Ali, selected by.
--Annie Jump-Rope Jingles. Wildman, George, illus. Starr, Leonard, created by. LC 82-13317. (Illus.). 16 p. 19cm. (Hummingbird book). c.1983. (ISBN 0-394-85674-0). Random House.

Reich, Hanns, ed. see Bucher, Otmar.

Reichert, Edwin C., jt. auth. see Bracken, Dorothy Kendall.

Reichert, Edwin Clark (1909-)
--Freight Train. Pollard, George, illus. LC 56-7104. unpaged. illus. 22cm. (Rand McNally elf book, 534). c.1956. Rand McNally.
--Happy Holidays, and Other Fun Days Around the Year. Bruce, Suzanne, illus. LC 54-15101. unpaged. illus. 21cm. (Rand McNally book-elf book, 482). c.1953. Rand McNally.

--My Truck Book. Grider, Dorothy (1915-), illus. LC 48-7988. 40 p. col. illus. 22 cm. (Rand McNally book-elf book). c.1948. Rand McNally.
--Space Ship to the Moon. Bilder, Arthur K., illus. LC 53-16715. unpaged. illus. 21cm. (Rand McNally book-elf book, 473). 1953, c.1952. Rand McNally.
--Tim and His Train. Mastri, Fiore & Mastri, Jackie, illus. N.D. Rand McNally & Co.
--To the Store We Go. Walker, Ora, illus. LC 52-33987. unpaged. illus. 21 cm. (Rand McNally book-elf book). c.1952. Rand McNally.

Reichman, Edith
--Bobby Bear. Champion, Hope Loring (1913-), illus. LC 50-13843. (Illus.). 21cm. 23p. (A Bonnie Blinky Bk.). 1950. John Martin's House.
--Danny Dog. Champion, Hope Loring (1913-), illus. LC 50-13847. (Illus.). 23p. 26cm. (A Bonnie Blinky Bk.). 1950. John Martin's House.
--Katy Cat. Martin, Winifred, illus. LC 50-13849. (Illus.). 24p. 20cm. (A Bonnie Blinky Bk.). 1950. John Martin's House.

Reichman, Edith, illus.
--The Busy Children. LC 50-23545. 18 p. col. illus. 22 cm. (Bonnie book). 1949. John Martin's House.

Reid, Ace
--Cowpokes Cookbook & Cartoons. 12th ed. Reid, Ace, illus. (Illus.). 64p. (gr. 5 up). N.D. (ISBN 0-917207-06-8). Reid Ent.
--Cowpokes Cow Country Cartoons. 14th ed. Reid, Ace, illus. Barker, S. Omar, intro. by. (Illus.). 38p. (gr. 5 up). N.D. (ISBN 0-917207-00-9). Reid Ent.
--Cowpokes Rarin' to Go. 2nd ed. Reid, Ace, illus. (Illus.). 74p. (gr. 5 up). N.D. (ISBN 0-917207-09-2). Reid Ent.
--Cowpokes Tales & Cartoons. 2nd ed. Reid, Ace, illus. Pickens, Slim, intro. by. (Illus.). 64p. (gr. 5 up). N.D. (ISBN 0-917207-10-6). Reid Ent.
--Cowpokes Wanted. 12th ed. Reid, Ace, illus. Gipson, Fred, intro. by. (Illus.). 62p. (gr. 5 up). N.D. (ISBN 0-917207-02-5). Reid Ent.
--Draggin' S Ranch Cowpokes. 14th ed. Reid, Ace, illus. (Illus.). 65p. (gr. 5 up). N.D. (ISBN 0-917207-04-1). Reid Ent.
--More Cowpokes. 14th ed. Reid, Ace, illus. Robertson, Frank C., intro. by. (Illus.). 60p. (gr. 5 up). N.D. (ISBN 0-917207-01-7). Reid Ent.

Reid, Alastair, jt. auth. see Gill, Bob.

Reid, Alastair (1926-)
--Allth. Lorraine, Walter Henry (1929-), illus. LC 57-12078. 51p. illus. 24cm. 1958. Houghton Mifflin. **Award: (ALA).**
--Fairwater. (Illus.). (gr. 3-5). 1957. (ISBN 0-8382-0240-3). Hale.
--I Will Tell You of a Town. Lorraine, Walter Henry (1929-), illus. LC 56-5550. (Illus.). 22cm. 36p. 1956. Houghton, Mifflin. **Award: (NYT).**
--Oddments, Inklings, Omens, Moments: Poems. 22cm. 52p. 1960. Dent.
--Oddments, Inklings, Omens, Moments: Poems. LC 59-5933. 22cm. 52p. 1959. Little, Brown.
--Ounce, Dice, Trice. 1st ed. Shahn, Benjamin (1898-1969), illus. LC 58-10685. (Illus.). 27cm. 57p. 1958. Little Brown.
--Supposing. 1st ed. Birnbaum, Abe (1899-), illus. LC 60-5879. (Illus.). 25cm. 48p. 1960. Little Brown.

Reid, Barbara (1922-)
--Carlo's Cricket. Grifalconi, Ann (1929-), illus. LC 67-24442. (Illus.). 48 p. 26cm. 1967. McGraw-Hill.
--Miguel and His Racehorse. Cellini, Joseph (1924-), illus. LC 72-13604. (Illus.). 32 p. 1973. (ISBN 0-688-20077-X). (ISBN 0-688-20077-X). Morrow.

Reid, Barbara (1922-) & Reid, Ewa Malewicz
--The Cobbler's Reward. Mikolaycak, Charles (1937-), illus. LC 78-4638. p. cm. c.1978. (ISBN 0-02-775800-1). Macmillan.

Reid, Carol McMillan, ed. see Mother Goose.

Reid, Christian, pseud., see Tiernan, Frances Christine Fisher.

Reid, Christian, pseud. (1846-1920)
--Carmela. Tiernan, Frances Christine Fisher, 1 of 9 vols. (Catholic Library). 1891. Set. McCauley & Kilner.
--Carmen's Inheritance. Tiernan, Frances Christine Fisher. (Illus.). N.D. Claxton, Remsen, and Haffelfinger.
--Child of Mary. Tiernan, Frances Christine Fisher, 1 of 7 vols. (Catholic Library). 1891. Set. McCauley & Kilner.
--Philip's Restitution. Tiernan, Frances Christine Fisher, 1 of 9 vols. (Catholic Library). 1891. Set. McCauley & Kilner.

Reid, Dorothy M.
--Tales of Nanabozho. Grant, Donald, illus. 1963. Henry Z. Walck Inc. **Award: (CLA).**
--Tales of Nanabozho. Grant, Donald, illus. LC 80-473787. (Illus.). 128 p. 21cm. 1979. (ISBN 0-19-540322-3). Oxford University Press.

Reid, Eugenie Chazal (1924-)
--Mystery of the Carrowell Necklace. Werner, Barbara, illus. LC 65-13389. 159p. illus. 22cm. c.1965. (ISBN 0-688-41394-3). Lothrop.
--The Mystery of the Second Treasure. Lonette, Reisie Dominee (1924-), illus. LC 67-3308. (Illus.). 192 p. 22cm. 1967. Lothrop, Lee & Shepard.

Reid, Ewa Malewicz, jt. auth. see Reid, Barbara.

Reid, Forrest
--Pender Among the Residents. N.D. Houghton Mifflin.
--Pirates of the Spring. N.D. Houghton Mifflin.
--The Spring Song. N.D. Houghton Mifflin.
--Tom Barber: Containing: "Young Tom", "The Retreat", and "Uncle Stephen". 512p. 1955. Pantheon Books Inc.

Reid, James (1907-)
--Peter, Peter, Pumpkin Eater. Reid, James (1907-), illus. LC 76-16532. (Illus.). 32 p. 33cm. 1970. Fortress Press.

Reid, James (1907-), illus.
--The Gypsy and the Bear and Other Fairy Tales. Borski, Lucia Merecka, Mrs. & Miller, Kate B., trs. from Pol. Kelly, Eric P., frwd. by. LC 33-272513. xxii p., 1 l., 129 p. incl. front., illus., plates. 21 cm. 1933. Longmans, Green and Co.

Reid, Jane Brewster
--Carcy of St. Ursula's. LC 11-208254. 267 p. front., plates. 19 cm. $1.25. 1911. The Baker & Taylor Company.

Reid, John, tr. see Piatti, Celestino.

Reid, John Calvin (1901-)
--Bird Life in Wington. (Illus.). (gr. 3-6). 1954. (ISBN 0-8028-4024-8). Eerdmans.
--Filsky Finds a Treasure. Schwarz, Macy, illus. LC 64-16594. 31 p. col. illus. 23 cm. 1964. Eerdmans.
--Parables from Nature: Earthly Stories with a Heavenly Meaning. The Parables of Jesus Retold and Interpreted for Young Minds. Weidenaar, Reynold H., illus. LC 54-10729. 89p. illus. 21cm. (ps-6). 1954. (ISBN 0-8028-4025-6). Eerdmans.
--Secrets from Field & Forest. Tuma, Rick, illus. LC 79-63458. (Illus.). 106 p. 19cm. 1980, c.1979. (ISBN 0-8423-5858-7). Tyndale House Publishers.
--Surprise for Dr. Retriever. Schwarz, Macy, illus. LC 61-10863. unpaged. illus. 23 cm. (gr. 3-6). c.1962. Eerdmans.
--Thirty Favorite Bible Stories for Boys and Girls. Seward, James E., illus. LC 81-21514. (Illus.). 192 p. 22cm. 1982. (ISBN 0-87239-498-0). (ISBN 0-87239-496-4). Standard Pub.
--War of the Birds. (gr. 3-6). 1963. Eerdmans.

Reid, Lionel Meredith (1900-)
--Bobo Dee. Denison, R. (1900-), illus. 48p. 1935. Oxford University Press.
--The Piper Had the Penny and Did You See What I Saw?. LC 50-7095. 40 p. illus. (part col.) 23 cm. (Double story book). 1949. Garden City Pub. Co.

Reid, Lionel Meredith (1900-) & Holt, Marion E.
--Oliver and Hugo Sand Willie Woodchuck Builds a Back Door. LC 49-10605. 40 p. illus. (part col.) 23 cm. N.D. Garden City Pub. Co.,.

Reid, Lizzie C.
--The Way of a Girl. N.D. Cassell & Co.

Reid, M. Francis
--Doodle: A California Boy. LC 26-712027. viii p., 1 l., 293 p. 19 cm. 1926. Dodd, Mead & Company.

Reid, Maynard
--Death Shot. N.D. E P Dutton.

Reid, Mayne see Reid, Thomas Mayne.

Reid, Meta Mayne
--All Because of Dawks. Whittam, Geoffrey William (1916-), illus. LC 55-1361. 237p. illus. 20cm. 1955. Macmillan.
--The Cuckoo at Coolnean. N.D. Transatlantic Arts, Inc.
--Dawks Does It Again. Whittam, Geoffrey William (1916-), illus. LC 56-23821. 199p. illus. 21cm. 1956. Macmillan.
--Dawks on Robbers' Mountain. Whittam, Geoffrey William (1916-), illus. LC 57-4426. 241p. illus. 21cm. 1957. St Martin's Press.
--Sandy & the Hollow Book. (Illus.). (gr. 2-4). N.D. Transatlantic.
--Storm on Kildoney. Whittam, Geoffrey William (1916-), illus. LC 61-1338. 189p. illus. 21cm. 1961. St Martin's Press.
--The Tobermillin Oracle. N.D. Transatlantic Arts.
--The Two Rebels. N.D. (ISBN 0-571-08967-4, Pub. by Faber & Faber). Merrimack Pub Cir.
--With Angus in the Forest. (Illus.). (gr. 2-4). N.D. Transatlantic.

Reid, Sydney
--Josey and the Chipmunk. Cory, Fanny Young, illus. 301p. (New Books for Boys and Girls). 1900. The Century Co.

Reid, Terry
--Nikos and the Ikon. Reid, Terry, illus. LC 69-10321. (Illus.). 61 p. 22cm. 1970, c.1969. Abelard-Schuman.

Reid, Terry, retold by.
--Brother Jerome & the Lion. Reid, Terry, illus. LC 66-100842. (Illus.). (Picture Book). (ps up). 1966. Abelard.

Reid, Thomas Mayne (1818-1883)
--Afloat in the Forest. (Captain Mayne Reid Ser.). 1910. Hurst & Co.
--Afloat in the Forest. (St. Nicholas Series for Boys). N.D. International Book Co.
--Afloat in the Forest, 1 of 19 vol. set. (Illus.). (Complete Works of Mayne Reid). N.D. International Book Co.
--Afloat in the Forest, 1 of 5 Vols. (Illus.). (Captain Mayne Reid's Travels by Sea and Land). N.D. Set. James Miller.
--Afloat in the Forest: Or, A Voyage Among the Tree-Tops. (Illus.). N.D. James Miller.
--Afloat in the Forest: Or, A Voyage Among the Tree Tops. LC 1-29559. (Medal Library: No. 8). 1900. Street & Smith.
--Afloat in the Forest: Or, A Voyage Among the Tree-Tops. New ed. LC 12-379351. 1 p. l., 4 iii-v, 292 p. front., plates. 19 cm. 1885. T. R. Knox & Co.
--Afloat in the Forest: Or, A Voyage Among the Tree-Tops. LC 49-40826. v. 292 p. illus. 19 cm. 1867. Ticknor and Fields.
--Boy Hunters. N.D. E P Dutton.
--Boy Hunters, 1 of 64 vols. (Young America Library: No. 9). 1900. Set. Hurst & Co.
--Boy Hunters. (Captain Mayne Reid Ser.). 1910. Hurst & Co.
--Boy Hunters. (Illus.). (The Cambridge Classics). N.D. Hurst and Company.
--Boy Hunters. (St. Nicholas Series for Boys). N.D. International Book Co.
--The Boy Hunters, 1 of 18 vol. set. (Illus.). (Complete Works of Mayne Reid). N.D. International Book Co.
--Boy Hunters, 1 of 6 Vols. (Illus.). (Captain Mayne Reid's Tales of American Adventure). N.D. Set. James Miller.
--The Boy Hunters of the Mississippi. Rhys, Ernest, ed. 18 cm. 250p. 1912. E. P. Dutton & Co.
--The Boy Hunters: Or, Adventures in Search of a White Buffalo. nimrod ed. LC 12-37938. xiii, 397 p. front., plates. 19 cm. 1896. G. P. Putnam's Sons.
--The Boy Hunters: Or, Adventures in Search of a White Buffalo. (Illus.). (Putnam's Knickerbocker Ser.). N.D. G. P. Putman's Sons.
--The Boy Hunters: Or, Adventures in Search of a White Buffalo. New ed. Harvey, William (1796-1866), illus. Stoddard, R. H., memoir by. LC 49-40697. 364 p. 20 cm. N.D. J. W. Lovell Co.
--The Boy Hunters: Or, Adventures in Search of a White Buffalo. New ed. Harvey, William (1796-1866), illus. Stoddard, R. H., memoir by. LC 13-12906. 2 p. l., 8 p., 1 l., 9-364 p. front. plates. 19 1/2 cm. 1885. T. R. Knox & Co.
--The Boy Hunters: Or, Adventures in Search of a White Buffalo. New ed. Stoddard, Richard Henry (1825-1903), memoir by. LC 68-23725. (Illus.). 364 p. 23cm. 1968. Gregg Press.
--Boy Slaves, 1 of 64 vols. (Young America Library: No. 10). 1900. Set. Hurst & Co.
--Boy Slaves. (Captain Mayne Reid Ser.). 1910. Hurst & Co.
--Boy Slaves. (Illus.). (The Cambridge Classics). N.D. Hurst and Company.
--Boy Slaves. (St. Nicholas Series for Boys). N.D. International Book Company.
--The Boy Slaves, 1 of 18 vol. set. (Illus.). (Complete Works of Mayne Reid). N.D. International Book Co.
--The Boy Slaves. LC 42-26113. 2 p. l., iii-v, 321 p. front., plates. 18 cm. 1876. J. Miller.
--Boy Slaves, 1 of 5 Vols. (Illus.). (Captain Mayne Reid's Travels by Sea and Land). N.D. Set. James Miller.
--The Boy Slaves. LC 22-16029. v, 321 p. plates. 18 1/2 cm. 1865. Ticknor and Fields.
--The Boy Slaves. Rhys, Ernest, ed. Pocock, Guy N., intro. by. 18 cm. 268p. 1927. E. P. Dutton.
--The Boy Slaves. New ed. Stoddard, Richard Henry (1825-1903), memoir by. LC 12-37937. 2 p. l., 4 iii-v, 321 p. front., plates. 19 cm. 1885. T. R. Knox & Co.
--Boy Tar, 1 of 64 vols. (Young America Library: No. 11). 1900. Set. Hurst & Co.
--Boy Tar. (Captain Mayne Reid Ser.). 1910. Hurst & Co.
--The Boy Tar. (Illus.). (The Cambridge Classics). N.D. Hurst and Company.
--Boy Tar. (St. Nicholas Series for Boys). N.D. International Book Company.
--The Boy Tar, 1 of 19 vol. set. (Illus.). (Complete Works of Mayne Reid). N.D. International Book Co.
--Boy Tar, 1 of 6 Vols. (Illus.). (Captain Mayne Reid's Tales of Foreign Adventure). N.D. Set. James Miller.
--The Boy Tar: Or, A Voyage in the Dark. new ed. Keene, Charles S., illus. Stoddard, Richard Henry (1825-1903), memoir by. LC 12-37932. 1 p. l., 4 iii-iv, 356 p. front., plates. 19 cm. 1885. T. R. Knox & Co.
--Bruin. (St. Nicholas Series for Boys). N.D. International Book Co.
--Bruin, 1 of 6 Vols. (Illus.). (Captain Mayne Reid's Tales of American Adventure). N.D. Set. James Miller.
--Bruin: Or, The Bear Hunt, 1 of 18 vol. set. (Illus.). (Complete Works of Mayne Reid). N.D. International Book Co.
--Bruin: The Grand Bear Hunt. LC 22-16028. v, 371 p. plates. 17 cm. 1864. Ticknor and Fields.
--Bruin: The Grand Bear Hunt. New ed. Stoddard, Richard Henry (1825-1903), memoir by. LC 12-379363. 1 p. l., 4, iii-v, l, 371 p. front., plates 19 cm. 1885. T. R. Knox & Co.
--Bush Boys. (St. Nicholas Series for Boys). N.D. International Book Co.
--The Bush Boys, 1 of 18 vol. set. (Illus.). (Complete Works of Mayne Reid). N.D. International Book Co.
--Bush Boys, 1 of 6 Vols. (Illus.). (Captain Mayne Reid's Tales of Foreign Adventure). N.D. Set. James Miller.
--The Bush Boys: Or, the History and Adventures of a Cape Farmer in the Wild Karoos of Southern Africa. nimrod ed. LC 7-1494. xi, 387, 1 p. front., pl. 20 cm. 1896. G. P. Putnam's Sons.
--The Bush-Boys: Or, The History and Adventures of a Cape Farmer and His Family in the Wild Karoos of Southern Africa. LC 7-1624, iv, 356 p. front., 11 pl. 17 1/2 cm. 1862. Ticknor and Fields.
--The Bush-Boys: Or, The History and Adventures of a Cape Farmer and His Family in the Wild Karoos of Southern Africa. Stoddard, Richard Henry (1825-1903), memoir by. LC 7-1493. 1 p. l., 4 iii-iv, 356 p. front., 11 pl. 19 1/2 cm. 1885. T. R. Knox & Co.
--The Castaways: A Story of Adventure in the Wilds of Borneo. LC 22-16027. 237 p. plates. 19 cm. 1870. Sheldon & Company.
--The Cliff-Climber: Or, The Lone Home in the Himalayas. New ed. Stoddard, Richard Henry (1825-1903), memoir by. LC 12-37940. (A/Sequel to "The Plant-HUnters"). 1 p. l., 4, v-vii, 304 p. front., plates. 19 cm. 1885. T. R. Knox & Co.
--Cliff Climbers. N.D. E P Dutton.
--Cliff Climbers. (St. Nicholas Series for Boys). N.D. International Book Co.
--The Cliff Climbers, 1 of 18 vol. set. (Illus.). (Complete Works of Mayne Reid). N.D. International Book Co.
--Cliff Climbers, 1 of 6 Vols. (Illus.). (Captain Mayne Reid's Tales of Foreign Travels). N.D. Set. James Miller.
--Cris Rock: A Novel. 376 p. front. 18 cm. (popular series. no. 32). 1893. R. Bonner's Sons.
--Cris Rock: Or, A Lover in Chains; A Novel. LC 12-37926. 376 p. front. 18 1/2 cm. c.1889. R. Bonner's Sons.
--Desert Home. N.D. E P Dutton.
--The Desert Home. (Illus.). (St. Nicholas Series for Boys). N.D. International Book Company.
--The Desert Home, 1 of 18 vol. set. (Illus.). (Complete Works of Mayne Reid). N.D. International Book Co.
--Desert Home, 1 of 6 Vols. (Illus.). (Captain Mayne Reid's Tales of American Adventure). N.D. Set. James Miller.
--The Desert Home: Or, the Adventures of a Lost Family in the Wilderness. New ed. Harvey, William (1796-1866), illus. Stoddard, Richard Henry (1825-1903), memoir by. LC 13-12905. 411 p. incl. front. plates. 19 1/2 cm. 1885. T. R. Knox & Co.
--The Desert Home: Or, the Adventures of a Lost Family in the Wilderness. Harvey, William (1796-1866), illus. LC 7-1630. 7 p., 1 l., 9-411 p. incl. front. plates. 17 1/2 cm. 1864. Ticknor and Fields.
--Flag of Distress. N.D. E P Dutton.
--Flag of Distress. (Illus.). (Famous Books for Boys). N.D. H. M. Caldell Co.
--Flag of Distress. (Illus.). (St. Nicholas Series for Boys). N.D. International Book Co.
--The Flag of Distress, 1 of 18 vol. set. (Illus.). (Complete Works of Mayne Reid). N.D. International Book Co.
--Flag of Distress, 1 of 5 Vols. (Illus.). (Captain Mayne Reid's Travels by Sea and Land). N.D. Set. James Miller.
--The Flag of Distress: A Tale of the South Sea. LC 13-12904. 1 p. l., 4, 3-409 p. front. 19 1/2 cm. 1884. T. R. Knox & Co.
--The Flag of Distress: A Tale of the South Sea. New ed. Stoddard, Richard Henry (1825-1903), memoir by. LC 12-37939. 1 p. l., 4, 3-409 p. front. 19 cm. 1885. T. R. Knox & Co.
--Forest Exiles. N.D. E P Dutton.
--Forest Exiles. (Illus.). (St. Nicholas Series for Boys). N.D. International Book Co.

--The Forest Exiles, 1 of 18 vol. set. (Illus.). (Complete Works of Mayne Reid). N.D. International Book Co.
--Forest Exiles, 1 of 6 Vols. (Illus.). (Captain Mayne Reid's Tales of American Adventure). N.D. Set. James Miller.
--The Forest Exiles: Or, The Perils of a Peruvian Family Amid the Wilds of the Amazon. New ed. Stoddard, Richard Henry (1825-1903), memoir by. LC 12-37930. 2 p. l., 360 p. front., plates. 19 cm. 1885. T. R. Knox & Co.
--Gaspar the Gaucho: A Tale of the Gran Cacho, A Story of Adventure for Boys. (Illus.). N.D. George Routledge.
--Gasper the Gaucho. N.D. E P Dutton.
--The Giraffe-Hunters. LC 15-12451. (A/Sequel to "The Bush Boys" and "The/Young Yagers"). 20 cm. 392p. 1913. E. P. Dutton and Co.
--Giraffe Hunters, 1 of 64 vols. (Young America Library: No. 21). 1900. Set. Hurst & Co.
--Giraffe Hunters. (Captain Mayne Reid Ser.). 1910. Hurst & Co.
--Giraffe Hunters. (Illus.). (St. Nicholas Series for Boys). N.D. International Book Co.
--The Giraffe Hunters, 1 of 18 Vol. set. (Illus.). (Complete Works of Mayne Reid). N.D. International Book Co.
--Giraffe Hunters, 1 of 5 Vols. (Illus.). (Captain Mayne Reid's Travels by Sea and Land). N.D. Set. James Miller.
--The Giraffe-Hunters. Stoddard, R. H., memoir by. LC 12-37931. 1 p. l., 4, (iii-v, 298 p. front., plates. 19 cm. 1885. T. R. Knox & Co.
--The Giraffe-Hunters: A Sequel to "The Bush Boys" and "The Young Yagers,". LC 15-12451. 2 p. l., ii, 3-392 p. front., plates 19 1/2 cm. N.D. G. Routledge and Sons, Limited.
--Guerilla Chief and Other Tales. N.D. E P Dutton.
--Gwen Wynn. N.D. E P Dutton.
--Headless Horseman. N.D. E P Dutton.
--The Headless Horseman. A Novel. LC 12-37949. 406 p. 18 cm. 1892. G. W. Dillingham.
--Hunter's Feast. N.D. E P Dutton.
--The Hunter's Feast. (Illus.). N.D. G W Carleton & Co.
--The Hunter's Feast: Or, Conversations Around the Camp Fire. LC 12-37962. vi, 9-364 p. 18 cm. 1891. G. W. Dillingham.
--The Hunters' Feast: Or, Conversations Around the Camp-Fire. Orr, N., designed by. LC 21-4155. vi, 7-364 p. front., plates. 18 1/2 cm. 1856. De Witt & Davenport.
--The Land of Fire. (Illus.). (Warne's Adventure Library). N.D. Frederick Warne & Co.
--Lone Ranch. N.D. E P Dutton.
--Lone Ranch. (Captain Mayne Reid Ser.). 1910. Hurst & Co.
--The Lone Ranch. LC 51-50183. 398 p. 19 cm. N.D. M. A. Donohue.
--The Lone Ranch. A Novel. LC 19-12053. 398 p. front., plates. 19 cm. 1884. G. W. Carleton & Co. Etc.
--The Lone Ranch. A Novel. LC 12-37961. 2 p. l., 9-398 20 cm. (primrose series no. 15). 1891. Street & Smith.
--Lost Leonore. N.D. G. W. Dillingham Co.
--Man Eaters, 1 of 6 Vols. (Illus.). (Captain Mayne Reid's Tales of American Adventure). N.D. Set. James Miller.
--Maroon. N.D. E P Dutton.
--The Maroon. N.D. G. W. Dillingham.
--The Maroon: Or, Planter Life in Jamaica. Orr, N., illus. LC 12-37943. vi, 7-383 p. front., plates. 18 1/2 cm. c.1864. R. M. De Witt.
--No Quarter!. 20 cm. 456p. 1905. E. P. Dutton & Co.
--No Quarter!. LC 44-49401. viii, 456 p. 18 1/2 cm. N.D. Hurst and Company.
--Ocean Waifs. N.D. E P Dutton.
--The Ocean Waifs. (Illus.). (St. Nicholas Series for Boys). N.D. International Book Co.
--The Ocean Waifs, 1 of 18 vol. set. (Illus.). (Complete Works of Mayne Reid). N.D. International Book Co.
--The Ocean Waifs, 1 of 5 Vols. (Illus.). (Captain Mayne Reid's Travels by Sea and Land). N.D. Set. James Miller.
--The Ocean Waifs: A Story of Adventure on Land and Sea. New ed. Stoddard, Richard Henry (1825-1903), memoir by. LC 12-37933. 1 p. l., 4, iii-v, 366 p. front., plates. 19 cm. 1885. T. R. Knox & Co.
--Odd People. (Illus.). (St. Nicholas Series for Boys). N.D. International Book Co.
--Odd People, 1 of 18 vol. set. (Illus.). (Complete Works of Mayne Reid). N.D. International book Co.
--Osceola, the Seminole. (Illus.). N.D. G W Carleton & Co.
--Osceola the Seminole: Or, The Red Fawn of the Flower Land. LC 12-37960. 1 p. l., 9-454 p. 18 cm. 1891. G. W. Dillingham.
--Plant Hunters. (Illus.). (St. Nicholas Series for Boys). N.D. International Book Co.
--The Plant Hunters, 1 of 18 vol. set. (Illus.). (Complete Works of Mayne Reid). N.D. International Book Co.
--Plant Hunters, 1 of 6 Vols. (Illus.). (Captain Mayne Reid's Tales of Foreign Adventure). N.D. Set. James Miller.
--The Plant Hunters: Or, Adventures Among the Himalaya Mountains. author's ed. LC 4-8703. vi, 353 p. front., 11 pl. 17 1/2 cm. 1864. Ticknor and Fields.
--The Plant Hunters: Or, Adventures Among the Himalaya Mountains. New ed. Stoddard, Richard Henry (1825-1903), memoir by. LC 13-12903. 1 p. l., 4 v-vi, 353 p. front., plates. 19 cm. 1885. T. R. Knox & Co.
--The Quadroon. N.D. G. W. Dillingham.
--The Quadroon: Or, A Lover's Adventures in Louisiana. LC 12-37928. 2 p. l., vi-xii, 13-384 p. front., plates. 19 1/2 cm. c.1856. R. M. De Witt.
--Ran Away to Sea. N.D. E P Dutton.
--Ran Away to Sea. (Illus.). (Famous Books for Boys). N.D. H. M. Caldwell Co.
--Ran Away to Sea. (Illus.). (St. Nicholas Series for Boys). N.D. International Book Co.
--Ran Away to Sea, 1 of 18 vol. set. (Illus.). (Complete Works of Mayne Reid). N.D. International Book Co.
--Ran Away to Sea, 1 of 6 Vols. (Illus.). (Captain Mayne Reid's Tales of Foreign Adventure). N.D. Set. James Miller.
--Ran Away to Sea: An Autobiography for Boys. New ed. Stoddard, Richard Henry (1825-1903), memoir by. LC 4-872. 359 p. front., plates. 19 cm. (On cover: St. Nicholas series for boys and girls. v. 71). 1889. American Publishers Corporation.
--Ran Away to Sea: An Autobiography for Boys. New ed. Stoddard, Richard Henry, memoir by. LC 12-37997. 1 p. l., 4, 3-359 p. front., pl. 19 cm. 1885. T. R. Knox & Co.
--Reid's Library of Travel and Adventure, 10 vols. (Contains "Afloat in the Forest," "Boy HUnters," "Bruin," "Forest Exiles," etc.). (Illus.). N.D. James Miller.
--Reid's Tales of American Adventure, 6 vols. (Containing "Boy Hunters," Bruin," "Desert Home," etc.). (Illus.). N.D. James Miller.
--Reid's Tales of Foreign Adventure: Containing "Boy Tar", "Bush Boys", "Cliff Climbers", etc, 6 vols. (Illus.). N.D. Set. James Miller.
--Reid's Travels by Sea and Land, 5 vols. (Containing "Afloat in the Forest," "Boy Slaves," "Flag od Distress," etc.). (Illus.). N.D. James Miller.
--The Rifle Ranger. N.D. G. W. Dillingham.
--The Rifle Rangers. (The Albion Library). N.D. Frederick Warne & Co.
--The Rifle Rangers. (Illus.). N.D. G W Carleton & Co.
--Rifle Rangers, 1 of 64 vols. (Young America Library: No. 36). 1900. Set. Hurst & Co.
--Rifle Rangers. (Captain Mayne Reid Ser.). 1910. Hurst & Co.
--The Rifle Rangers: A Thrilling Story of Daring Adventure and Hairbreadth Escapes During the Mexican War. LC 688. 432 p. illus., plates. 18 1/2 cm. 1899. Hurst & Co.
--The Scalp Hunters. (The Albion Library). N.D. Frederick Warne & Co.
--The Scalp Hunters. (Illus.). N.D. G W Carleton & Co.
--Scalp Hunters, 1 of 64 vols. (Young America Library: No. 38). 1900. Set. Hurst & Co.
--Scalp Hunters. (Captain Mayne Reid Ser.). 1910. Hurst & Co.
--The Scalp Hunters: A Thrilling Tale of Adventure and Romance in Northern Mexico. LC 6891. 468 p. illus. 18 1/2 cm. 1899. Hurst & Co.
--The Scalp Hunters: Or, Romantic Adventures in Northern Mexico. LC 21-4156. iv, 9-204 p. 23 1/2 cm. 1851. Lippincott, Grambo and Co.
--The Scalp Rangers. N.D. G. W. Dillingham Co.
--Stories about Animals. (Illus.). (St. Nicholas Series for Boys). N.D. International Book Co.
--Stories about Animals, 1 of 18 vol. set. (Illus.). (Complete Works of Mayne Reid). N.D. International Book Co.
--Stories About Animals. New ed. Stoddard, Richard Henry (1825-1903), memoir by. LC 12-37996. 1 p. l., 4 p., 1 l., 13-305 p. front., illus., plates. 19 cm. 1885. T. R. Knox & Co.
--The Tiger Hunter. (Illus.). N.D. G W Carleton & Co.
--The Tiger-Hunter: Or, A Hero in Spite of Himself. LC 12-37958. 1 p. l., 9-368 p. 18 cm. 1892. G. W. Dillingham.
--Vee-Boers. N.D. E P Dutton.
--The War-Trail: Or, The Hunt of the Wild Horse; a Romance of the Prairie. LC 12-37944. 1 p. l., v-vii, 9-489 p. 18 cm. 1892. G. W. Dillingham.
--The War-Trail: Or, The Hunt of the Wild Horse. LC 51-542210. 489 p. plates. 19 cm. 1870. Carleton.
--War Trails. N.D. E P Dutton.
--The White Chief. (Illus.). N.D. G W Carleton & Co.
--The White Chief. A Legend of North Mexico. LC 12-37945. 1 p. l., 9-401 p. 18 cm. 1891. G. W. Dillingham.
--The White Chief: A Legend of North Mexico. LC 68-23726. (Illus.). 4, 401 p. 22cm. 1968. Gregg Press.
--The White Gauntlet. A Novel. LC 12-37946. 2 p. l., 7-405 p. 18 cm. 1892. G. W. Dillingham.
--The Wild Huntress. (Illus.). N.D. G W Carleton & Co.
--The Wild Huntress: Or, Love in the Wilderness. LC 12-37947. 1 p. l., 9-466 p. 18 cm. 1892. G. W. Dillingham.
--The Wood Rangers. (Illus.). N.D. G W Carleton & Co.
--The Wood Rangers. N.D. G. W. Dillingham Co.
--Young Voyagers. (Captain Mayne Reid Ser.). 1910. Hurst & Co.
--Young Voyagers. (Illus.). (St. Nicholas Series for Boys). N.D. International Book Co.
--The Young Voyagers, 1 of 18 vol. set. (Illus.). (Complete Works of Mayne Reid). N.D. International Book Co.
--Young Voyagers, 1 of 6 Vols. (Illus.). (Captain Mayne Reid's Tales of American Adventure). N.D. Set. James Miller.
--The Young Voyagers: Or, The Boy Hunters in the North, 1 of 64 vols. (Young America Library: No. 64). 1900. Set. Hurst & Co.
--The Young Voyageurs: Or, The Boy Hunters in the North. nimrod ed. LC 12-37942. xiii, 392 p. front., plates. 19 cm. 1896. G. P. Putnam's Sons.
--The Young Voyageurs: Or, The Boy Hunters in the North. (Illus.). (Putnam's Knickerbocker Ser.). N.D. G. P. Putman's Sons.
--The Young Voyageurs: Or, The Boy Hunters in the North. New ed. Harvey, William (1796-1866), illus. Stoddard, Richard Henry (1825-1903), memoir by. LC 12-37941. 2 p. l., 360 p. front., plates. 19 cm. 1885. T. R. Knox & Co.
--The Young Voyageurs: Or, The Boy Hunters in the North. Harvey, William (1796-1866), illus. LC 22-160262. 356 p. plates. 16 1/2 cm. 1857. Ticknor and Fields.
--Young Yagers. (Illus.). (St. Nicholas Series for Boys). N.D. International Book Co.
--The Young Yagers, 1 of 18 vol. set. (Illus.). (Complete Works of Mayne Reid). N.D. International Book Co.
--Young Yagers, 1 of 6 Vols. (Illus.). (Captain Mayne Reid's Tales of Foreign Adventure). N.D. Set. James Miller.
--The Young Yagers: Or, A Narrative of Hunting Adventures in Southern Africa. New ed. Harvey, William (1796-1866), illus. Stoddard, Richard Henry (1825-1903), memoir by. LC 12-37934. 2 p. l., 4, v-vi, 328 p. front., plates. 19 cm. 1885. T. R. Knox & Co.

Reida, Bernice, jt. auth. see Irwin, Annabelle Bowen.

Reidel, Marlene
--Jacob and the Robbers. LC 67-19007. (Illus.). 31cm. 1967. Atheneum.

Reidman, Sarah
--Masters Of the Scalpel. 1962. E M Hale.

Reiff, Betty J.
--The Cow That Couldn't Moo. N.D. Carlton Press.

Reifsnyder, Marylou
--The Boy Who Got Caught. LC 77-39595. p. 1972. (ISBN 0-394-82369-9). (ISBN 0-394-92369-3). Knopf.
--The Golden Cup. Beif-Snyder, Marylou, illus. LC 71-106139. (Illus.). 32 p. 1970. Knopf.

Reig, June (1933-)
--The Diary of the Boy King, Tut Anhk Amen. Reig, June (1933-), illus. LC 78-26359. p. cm. 22cm. 147p. 1979. Scribner.

Reiget
--Wake up It's Night. (ps-3). N.D. (ISBN 0-590-05404-X, Schol Pap). Scholastic Inc.

Reighard, Catherine F
--Plays for People and Puppets. LC 28-17805. 7 p. l., 3-390 p. front., plates. 20 cm. c.1928. E. P. Dutton & Company.

Reilly, Bernard James see Yorke, Anthony, pseud.

Reilly, Bernard James (1865-)
--Billy Glenn, of the Broken Shutters. Yorke, Anthony, pseud. LC 6-18583. 3 p. l., 5-261 p. front., plates. 19 1/2 cm. c.1906. P. J. Kenedy & Sons.
--A College Boy. Yorke, Anthony, pseud. LC 99-1910. 224 p. 19 1/2 cm. 1899. Benziger Bros.

Reilly, Frank A.
--Freddie. Gunn, Donald, illus. N.D. Farrar & Rinehart.
--The Hideout Club. Geary, Clifford N. (1916-), illus. LC 48-5855. 147 p. 20 cm. 1948. Rinehart.

Reilly, Genevieve, jt. auth. see Semple, Daisy.

Reilly, Robert Thomas (1922-)
--Fighting Prince of Donegal (Pub. by FS&G). Orig. Title: Red Hugh Prince of Donegal. (gr. 7-12). 1972 (Starline). Schol Bk Serv.
--Massacre at Ash Hollow. Gringhuis, Richard H. (1918-1974), illus. Gringhuis, Dirk, pseud. LC 60-141237. 156p. illus. 22cm. (Catholic treasury books). 1960. Bruce Pub. Co.
--Rebels in the Shadows. LC 78-66069. (Illus.). x, 179 p. 21cm. 1979, c.1962. University of Pittsburgh Press.
--Red Hugh, Prince of Donegal. (gr. 2-6). 1957. (ISBN 0-374-36237-8). FS&G.
--Red Hugh, Prince of Donegal. Gringhuis, Richard H. (1918-1974), illus. Gringhuis, Dirk, pseud. LC 57-103826. 155p. illus. 22cm. (Catholic treasury books). 1957. Bruce Pub. Co.

Reimers, Henry L
--Spokane Country Homestead. LC 81-2624. (Illus.). 106, 1 p. 23cm. 1981. (ISBN 0-87770-244-6). Homestead House.

Reimuller, Vera
--Otto the Beaver. Reimuller, Vera, illus. N.D. Beechhurst Press.
--Otto The Beaver. Reimuller, Vera, illus. LC 45-4303. 24 p. col. illus. 21 1/2 x 28cm. 1945. Bernard Ackerman.
--Scampy and Pineky. Reimuller, Vera, illus. N.D. Beechhurst Press.
--Scampy and Piney. Reimuller, Vera, illus. LC 44-20104. 38 p. illus. 23 1/2cm. 1944. B. Ackerman, Inc.

Reinach, Jacquelyn, jt. auth. see Lewis, Shari.

Reinach, Jacquelyn Krasne (1930-)
--A Bad Break. Perle, Ruth Lerner, ed. Hefter, Richard (1942-), illus. LC 80-22264. p. cm. (Sweet Pickles Ser.). 1980. (ISBN 0-937524-04-2). Euphrosyne Incorporated.
--Elephant Eats the Profits. Perle, Ruth Lerner, ed. Hefter, Richard (1942-), illus. LC 77-7254. p. cm. 26cm. 32p. (Sweet Pickles Ser.). 1977. (ISBN 0-03-021426-2). Holt, Rinehart, and Winston.
--Fish and Flips. Perle, Ruth Lerner, ed. Hefter, Richard (1942-), illus. LC 77-14577. (Illus.). 36 p. 25cm. (Sweet Pickles Ser.). c.1977. (ISBN 0-03-042016-4). Holt, Rinehart and Winston.
--Fixed by Camel. Perle, Ruth Lerner, ed. Hefter, Richard (1942-), illus. LC 76-43091. p. cm. (Sweet Pickles Ser.). c.1977. Holt, Rinehart and Winston.
--Goose Goofs Off. Perle, Ruth Lerner, ed. Hefter, Richard (1942-), illus. LC 76-44313. (Illus.). 32 p. 26cm. (Sweet Pickles Ser.). c.1977. (ISBN 0-03-018086-4). Holt, Reinhart and Winston.
--Happy Birthday Unicorn. Perle, Ruth Lerner, ed. Hefter, Richard (1942-), illus. LC 78-9585. (Illus.). 36 p. 25cm. (Sweet Pickles Ser.). c.1978. (ISBN 0-03-042066-0). Holt, Rinehart, and Winston.
--Hippo Jogs for Health. Perle, Ruth Lerner, ed. Hefter, Richard (1942-), illus. LC 77-16320. (Illus.). (gr. k-2). 1978. (ISBN 0-03-042026-1). HR&W.
--Ice Cream Dreams. Perle, Ruth Lerner, ed. Hefter, Richard (1942-), illus. LC 80-24625. p. cm. (Sweet Pickles Ser.). 1980. (ISBN 0-937524-05-0). Euphrosyne Inc.
--Jackal Wants Everything. Perle, Ruth Lerner, ed. Hefter, Richard (1942-), illus. LC 77-16324. (Illus.). 36 p. 25cm. (Sweet Pickles Ser.). c.1978. Holt, Rinehart and Winston.
--Me Too, Iguana. Perle, Ruth Lerner, ed. Hefter, Richard (1942-), illus. LC 76-43090. (Illus.). 32 p. 26cm. (Sweet Pickles Ser.). c.1977. (ISBN 0-03-018071-6). Holt, Rinehart and Winston.
--Nuts to Nightingale. Perle, Ruth Lerner, ed. Hefter, Richard (1942-), illus. LC 77-16325. (Illus.). 33 p. 25cm. (Sweet Pickles Ser.). c.1978. (ISBN 0-03-042041-5). Holt, Rinehart and Winston.
--Octopus Protests. LC 78-54981. p. cm. 25cm. 363p. (Sweet Pickles Ser.). 1978. (ISBN 0-03-042046-6). Holt, Rinehart, and Winston.
--Quail Can't Decide. Perle, Ruth Lerner, ed. Hefler, Richard, illus. LC 77-7249. p. cm. (Sweet Pickles Ser.). 1977. (ISBN 0-03-021451-3). Holt, Rinehart, and Winston.
--Rainy Day Parade. Perle, Ruth Lerner, ed. Hefter, Richard (1942-), illus. LC 80-19071. (Illus.). 34 p. 21cm. (Sweet Pickles Ser.). c.1981. (ISBN 0-937524-01-8). Euphrosyne.
--Rest, Rabbit, Rest. Perle, Ruth Lerner, ed. Hefter, Richard (1942-), illus. LC 77-13311. (Illus.). 32 p. 25cm. (Sweet Pickles Ser.). c.1977. (ISBN 0-03-042056-3). Holt, Rinehart and Winston.
--Scaredy Bear. Perle, Ruth Lerner, ed. Hefter, Richard (1942-), illus. LC 78-16814. p. cm. (Sweet Pickles Ser.). 1979. (ISBN 0-03-042021-0). Holt, Rinehart and Winston.
--Wait! Wait! Wait!. weekly reader books' ed. Perle, Ruth Lerner, ed. Hefter, Richard (1942-), illus. LC 80-19072. (Illus.). 32 p. 21cm. (Sweet Pickles Ser.). c.1980. (ISBN 0-937524-00-X). Euphrosyne.
--What a Mess!. Perle, Ruth Lerner, ed. Hefter, Richard (1942-), illus. LC 80-22262. (Illus.). 32 p. 21cm. (Sweet Pickles Ser.). c.1981. (ISBN 0-937524-03-4). Euphrosyne.
--What's So Great About Nice?. Perle, Ruth Lerner, ed. Hefter, Richard (1942-), illus. LC 80-21438. p. cm. (Sweet Pickles Ser.). 1980. (ISBN 0-937524-02-6). Euphrosyne Press.

--Who Stole Alligator's Shoe?. Perle, Ruth Lerner, ed. Hefter, Richard (1942-), illus. LC 77-7251. p. cm. 26cm. 32p. (Sweet Pickles Ser.). 1977. (ISBN 0-03-021431-9). Holt, Rinehart, and Winston.
--Xerus Won't Allow It. Perle, Ruth Lerner, ed. Hefter, Richard (1942-), illus. LC 78-54979. (Illus.). (Sweet Pickles Ser.). (gr. k-2). 1978. (ISBN 0-03-042076-8). HR&W.

Reinecke, Alma G
--Your Own World. LC 74-77461. (Illus.). 124 p. 21cm. c.1974. Spoken Arts.

Reinecke, Carl, ed. see Hoffmann, Ernst Theodor Amadeus.

Reinecke, Esther E.
--Punkin's First Halloween. Nolan, Gary William, illus. LC 60-12263. (Illus.). 29cm. (Second Grade Bk.). (gr. 2-3). 1960. Denison.
--Tim and the Green-Eyed Monster. Skaff, Lamese M., illus. LC 59-14405. unpaged. illus. 29cm. 1959. (ISBN 0-513-00420-3). T. S. Denison.
--Tim & The Green-Eyed Monster. Skaff, Lamese M., illus. 32p. (Children's Picture Bks.). N.D. T. S. Denison & Co.
--Tim and the Lucky Straw. Schaphorst, Dorothy, illus. LC 63-16003. unpaged. illus. 29 cm. 1963. T. S. Denison.
--Tim Listens and Learns. Skaff, Lamese M., illus. LC 60-15143. unpaged. illus. 29cm. 1960. (ISBN 0-513-00423-8). Denison.

Reiner, D. E.
--Jesus Never Fails. (gr. 7 up). N.D. Southern Pub.

Reiner, William Buck (1910-1975)
--The Flying Rangers. Ramstad, Ralph, illus. LC 54-677321. 62p. illus. 22cm. (Everyday science stories). 1954. J. Messner.

Reinert, Rick
--The Tooth Chicken. (Illus.). 16p. (Good Friends Ser.). (gr. k-6). 1982. (ISBN 0-686-84018-6). Ideals.

Reinertsen, Emma May Alexander (1853-)
--Five Cousins in California: A Sunny Picture of a Sunny Land. LC 9-29501. 4 p. l., 287 p. front., plates, ports., 19 1/2 cm. $1.50. 1909. The C. M. Clark Publishing Company.

Reinfeld, Fred, jt. auth. see Boehm, David Alfred.

Reingold, Beverly, ed.
--The Animal Storybook. Frank, Robert, illus. LC 77-90512. (Illus.). 41 p. 31cm. c.1978. (ISBN 0-448-47613-4). (ISBN 0-448-13028-9). Platt & Munk.
--Classics: A Child's Introduction to Treasure Island by Robert Louis Stevenson; Black Beauty by Anna Sewell; The Adventures of Tom Sawyer by Mark Twain, and Robin Hood by Henry Gilbert. Craft, Kinuko Y., illus. LC 77-76562. (Illus.). 61 p. 31cm. c.1977. (ISBN 0-8228-7232-3). Platt & Munk.

Reinhard, Florence
--The Donkey, Daniel: A Christmas Story. Littman, Wally, illus. (Illus.). 1 vol. unpage. 22cm. 1974. (ISBN 0-533-01356-9). Vantage Press.

Reinhardt, Rosamond, tr. see Kyber, Manfred.

Reinherz, Nathan (1910-)
--Quest of the Sages' Stone. Pitz, Henry Clarence (1895-1976), illus. LC 51-937. ix, 262 p. illus. 21 cm. 1951. Crowell.
--Trumpets at the Crossroads. Ray, Ralph (1920-1952), illus. LC 48-8537. vii, 263 p. illus. 21 cm. 1948. T. Y. Crowell Co.

Reinick, Robert (1805-1852)
--The Root-Princess. A Christmas Story. Fuller, Fanny, tr. LC 44-31055. 72 p. col. front., col. plates. 22 cm. 1865. F. Leypoldt.

Reiniger, Lotte (1899-1981)
--Shadow Puppets, Shadow Theatres & Shadow Films. (Illus.). 128p. Repr. of 1970 ed (Pub. by Watson Guptill). 1975. (ISBN 0-8238-0198-5). Plays.

Reinius, Trish (1936-)
--The Planet of Tears. Johnson, Bob (1950-), illus. LC 79-15753. p. cm. c.1979. (ISBN 0-89742-025-X). (ISBN 0-89742-016-0). Dawne-Leigh Publications.

Reinke de Vos & Reynard the Fox. English
--King Lion and Reynard the Fox. Forrest, John L, retold by. Mora, Joseph Jacinto (1876-), illus. LC 22-1733. xi, 186 p. col. front., illus., plates. 23 1/2 cm. c.1920. A. Whitman & Company.

Reinl, Edda
--The Little Snake. LC 82-60894. (Illus.). 28p. 1982. (ISBN 0-907234-15-1, Pub. by Picture Bk Studio USA). Neugebauer Pr.

Reinl, Edda, illus.
--The Three Little Pigs. LC 83-8256. p. cm. (Picture Book Studio). c.1983. (ISBN 0-907234-32-1). Neugebauer Press USA.

Reinstedt, Randall A
--Dinosaur Dan. Hampshire, Michael Allen, illus. LC 70-123882. (Illus.). 22 p. 23cm. (Magic circle book). 1971. Ginn.

Reioux, Margaret L.
--Thomas Augustus Pedro William Roadrunner. 1978. (ISBN 0-533-03671-2). Vantage.

Reiser, Joanne
--Hannah's Alaska. Downing, Julie, illus. LC 83-8668. (Illus.). 32p. (Heritage Bks.). (gr. 3-6). 1983. (ISBN 0-940742-23-3, Pub. by Carnival Press). (ISBN 0-940742-23-3). Raintree Pubs.

Reisig, Phyllis C.
--Here Comes Hubert. (gr. 1-6). 1970. Vantage.

Reiss, Elayne & Friedman, Rita
--A-Choo. (Illus.). (gr. k-1). 1978. (ISBN 0-89796-864-6). Arista Corp NDE.
--A Buttonmat for Beautiful Buttons. (gr. k-1). 1978. (ISBN 0-89796-865-4). Arista Corp NDE.
--Hat Helpers Hullaballoo. (gr. k-1). N.D. (ISBN 0-89796-868-9). Arista Corp NDE.
--The Tale of Tall Toothbrush. (gr. k-1). 1978. (ISBN 0-89796-869-7). Arista Corp NDE.

Reiss, Johanna
--The Upstairs Room. 1972. Crowell. **Award: (JNM).**

Reiss, John J.
--Colors. Reiss, John J., illus. LC 69-13653. (Illus.). full-color pictures. 32p. 32p. (ps-2). 1969. (ISBN 0-02-776130-4). Bradbury Pr.

Reiss, Julian J.
--The Story of Santa Claus. 1959. Bruce Pub Co.

Reiss, Malcolm
--China Boat Boy. 1st ed. Wong, JeanYee (1920-), illus. LC 54-730234. 157p. illus. 21cm. 1954. Lippincott.

Reiss, Marilyn Leitner
--Thackeray Turtle. Rice, Elizabeth (1913-), illus. LC 70-76604. 32 full-color ils. 32p. (gr. 1-2). 1969. (ISBN 0-8114-7659-6). Steck-V

Reit, Ann
--Phone Calls. 192p. (Orig.). (gr. 7 up). 1983. (ISBN 0-590-32189-7, Wildfire). Scholastic Inc.
--Worried Ghost. (gr. 4-7). 1977. (ISBN 0-590-10259-1). Schol Bk Serv.
--Yours Truly, Love, Janie. 176p. (Orig.). (gr. 7-12). 1981. (ISBN 0-590-31849-7, Wildfire). Scholastic Inc.

Reit, Ann, compiled by.
--Alone Amid All This Noise: A Collection of Women's Poetry. LC 75-38705. index. 144p. (gr. 5 up). 1976. (ISBN 0-590-07359-1, Four Winds). Scholastic Inc.
--Wildfire: Every Young Girl's Dream. 64p. (Orig.). 1981. (ISBN 0-590-31872-1, Schol Pap). Scholastic Inc.
--The World Outside: Collected Short Fiction About Women at Work. Bitzer, Lucy Martin, illus. LC 77-7986. 21cm. 214p. (gr. 7 up). 1977. (ISBN 0-590-07484-9, Four Winds). (ISBN 0-685-79849-6). Scholastic Inc.

Reit, Seymour, jt. auth. see Dietrich, Fred.

Reit, Seymour (1918-)
--Animals Around My Block. Sobolewski, Alex V., illus. LC 70-100207. (Illus.). 29 p. 27cm. (My world series, for early childhood). 1970. McGraw-Hill.
--Aurora Presents Don Bluth Productions' "The Secret of NIMH Storybook". Don Bluth Productions, illus. LC 81-86147. (Illus.). 33 p. 29cm. c.1982. (ISBN 0-307-96821-9). (ISBN 0-307-66821-5). Golden Press.
--Benvenuto. Winslow, Will, illus. LC 73-15625. (Illus.). 126 p. 21cm. 1974. (ISBN 0-201-06297-6). Addison-Wesley.
--Benvenuto and the Carnival. Miller, Marilyn Jean (1925-), illus. LC 76-11265. (Illus.). 93 p. 21cm. (Weekly Reader Children's Book Club edition). c.1976. (ISBN 0-88375-212-3). Xerox Education Publications.
--Bugs Bunny Goes to the Dentist. Cunette, Lou, illus. LC 77-88808. (Illus.). 24 p. 21cm. (Golden look-look book). c.1978. (ISBN 0-307-11843-6). Golden Press.
--Bugs Bunny's Space Carrot. Heimdahl, Ralph (1909-) & Lorencz, William, illus. LC 76-53955. (Illus.). 24 p. 21cm. (Golden look-look book). c.1977. (ISBN 0-307-11831-2). Golden Press.
--Child of the Navajos. Conklin, Paul s., photos by. LC 74-162608. (Illus.). (gr. 2-5). 1971. Dodd.
--Dear Uncle Carlos. Brody, Sheldon, illus. LC 70-90020. (Illus.). 30 p. 26cm. (My world series, for early childhood). 1969. McGraw-Hill.
--The Fox & the Hound Storybook. 40p. (Specials Ser.). (ps-3). 1981. (ISBN 0-307-16802-6, Golden Pr). Golden Pr. (ISBN 0-307-66802-9). Western Pub.
--The Ginghams. (Illus.). (A Golden Book of Picture Postcards Ser.). (ps-4). 1977. (ISBN 0-307-11101-6, Golden Pr). Western Pub.
--Ironclad!. A True Story of the Civil War. Reit, Seymour, illus. LC 76-50649. (Illus.). 92 p. 21cm. 1977. (ISBN 0-396-07403-0). Dodd, Mead.
--Jamie Visits the Nurse. Brody, Sheldon, illus. LC 77-90022. (Illus.). 30 p. 26cm. (My world series, for early childhood). 1969. McGraw-Hill.
--The King Who Learned to Smile. Laite, Gordon (1925-), illus. LC 60-4082. (Golden Beginning Reader). 1960. Golden Press.
--Look! Look!. A/Clown Book. Nigro, Joanne, illus. LC 62-9857. (Illus.). 30p. 27cm. (A Golden Reader). 1962. Golden Press.
--Race Against Death: A True Story of the Far North. LC 75-38355. (Illus.). 94 p. 21cm. c.1976. (ISBN 0-396-07293-3). Dodd, Mead.
--Rice Cakes and Paper Dragons. 1973. (ISBN 0-396-06735-2). Dodd, Mead & Company.
--Round Things Everywhere. Basen, Carol, illus. LC 73-90021. (Illus.). 32 p. 27cm. (My world series. For early childhood). 1969. McGraw-Hill Co.
--Tiny & Tony. Kent, Jack, pseud. (1920-), illus. Kent, John Wellington. (Illus.). (Golden Book of Picture Postcards Ser.). (ps-4). 1977. (ISBN 0-307-11103-2, Golden Pr). Western Pub.
Tweety and Sylvester Birds of a Feather. Cunette, Lou, illus. LC 76-53956. (Illus.). 24 p. 22cm. (Golden look-look book). c.1977. (ISBN 0-307-11833-9). Golden Press.
--Where's Willie?. Blegvad, Erik (1923-), illus. LC 61-11966. (Illus.). 31 p. 22cm. (Golden beginning reader). 1961. Golden Press.

Reit, Seymour (1918-), ed.
--America Laughs: A Treasury of Great Humor. Huehnergarth, John, illus. LC 66-8145. (Illus.). viii, 152 p. 22cm. (America in the making). 1966. Crowell-Collier Press.

Reit, Seymour (1918-) & Hooks, William H
--When Small Is Tall and Other Read-Together Tales. Munsinger, Lynn (1951-), illus. LC 83-9811. (Illus.). 32 p. 21cm. (Please read to me). (Random House pictureback). c.1985. (ISBN 0-394-95836-5). (ISBN 0-394-85836-0). Random House.

Reitci, Rita Krohne see Ritchie, Rita, pseud.

Reiter, David
--The Way Back. LC 53-103041. 218p. 22cm. c.1953. Vantage Press.

Reiter, Herman William, ed. see Gilbert, William Schwenck, Sir (1836-1911) & Sullivan, Arthur Seymour, Sir.

Rekemchuk, A.
--Boys Who Did a Singing Go. 247p. 1972. (ISBN 0-8285-1116-0, Pub. by Progress Pubs USSR). Imported Pubns.

Relf, Patricia
--The Adventures of Superman. Schaffenberger, Kurt & Hunt, David, illus. LC 81-81955. (Illus.). 24 p. 22cm. (Golden look-look book). c.1982. (ISBN 0-307-61861-7). (ISBN 0-307-11861-4). Golden Press.
--The First Day of School. DiSalvo-Ryan, DyAnne, illus. LC 80-84776. (Illus.). 20 p. 24cm. (Golden storytime book). c.1981. (ISBN 0-307-11957-2). Golden Press.
--Show and Tell, Featuring Jim Henson's Sesame Street Muppets. Cooke, Tom, illus. Henson, Jim, pseud. (1936-), created by Henson, James Maury. Children's Television Workshop LC 80-50139. (Illus.). 28 p. 26cm. (Sesame Street Read-Aloud StoryBooks). c.1980. (ISBN 0-307-23112-7). Western Pub. Co. in Conjunction with Children's Television Workshop.
--That New Baby!. DiSalvo-Ryan, DyAnne, illus. LC 80-50286. (Illus.). 20 p. 24cm. (Golden storytime book). c.1980. (ISBN 0-307-11989-0). Golden Press.

Rembao, Alberto
--Lupita. 192p. 1935. Friendship Press.

Remi, Georges see Herge, pseud.

Remi, Georges (1907-1983)
--The Broken Ear. Herge, pseud. Lonsdale-Cooper, Leslie & Turner, Michael, trs. LC 77-90970. (Illus.). 62 p. 30cm. (His The adventures of Tintin). c.1978. Little, Brown.
--The Calculus Affair. Herge, pseud. Lonsdale-Cooper, Leslie & Turner, Michael, trs. LC 76-13280. (Illus.). 62 p. 30cm. (Adventures of Tintin). c.1976. (ISBN 0-316-35847-9). Little, Brown.
--The Crab with Golden Claws. Herge, pseud. Lonsdale-Cooper, Leslie & Turner, Michael, trs. LC 73-21249. (Illus.). 62 p. 30cm. (Atlantic Monthly Press book). (The Adventures of Tintin). 1974. (ISBN 0-316-35833-9). Little, Brown.
--Explorers on the Moon. Herge, pseud. Lonsdale-Cooper, Leslie & Turner, Michael, trs. LC 76-13297. (Illus.). 62 p. 30cm. (Adventures of Tintin). c.1976. (ISBN 0-316-35846-0). Little, Brown.
--King Ottokar's Sceptre. Herge, pseud. Lonsdale-Cooper, Leslie & Turner, Michael, trs. LC 73-21251. (Illus.). 62 p. 30cm. (Atlantic Monthly Press book). (The Adventures of Tintin Ser.). 1974. (ISBN 0-316-35831-2). Little Brown.
--Red Rackham's Treasure. Herge, pseud. Lonsdale-Cooper, Leslie & Turner, Michael, trs. LC 73-21253. (Illus.). 62 p. 30cm. (Atlantic Monthly Press book). (The Adventures of Tintin). 1974. (ISBN 0-316-35834-7). Little, Brown.
--The Secret of the Unicorn. Herge, pseud. Lonsdale-Cooper, Leslie & Turner, Michael, trs. LC 73-21250. (Illus.). 62 p. 30cm. (Atlantic Monthly Press book). (The Adventures of Tintin). 1974. (ISBN 0-316-35832-0). Little, Brown.
--Tintin in America. Herge, pseud. (Illus.). 62p. N.D. (ISBN 0-416-86120-2). French & Eur.
--Tintin in America. Herge, pseud. Lonsdale-Cooper, Leslie & Turner, Michael, trs. LC 79-64865. (Illus.). 62 p. 30cm. (His The adventures of Tintin). c.1979. (ISBN 0-316-35852-5). Little, Brown.

Remick, Grace May
--Glenloch Girls. Williamson, Ada Clendenin, illus. LC 9-25397. 337 p. front., 6 pl. 19 1/2 cm. $1.25. 1909. The Penn Publishing Company.
--Glenloch Girls. Williamson, Ada Clendenin, illus. LC 37-8409. 337 p. front. 19 cm. c.1937. The Penn Publishing Company.
--Glenloch Girls Abroad. Williamson, Ada Clendenin, illus. LC 10-14907. 354 p. front., plates. 19 1/2 cm. $1.25. 1910. The Penn Publishing Company.
--Glenloch Girls Abroad. Williamson, Ada Clendenin, illus. LC 38-6987. 3, 1, 1 l., 9-354 p. front. 19 cm. c.1938. The Penn Publishing Company.
--Glenloch Girls at Camp West. Williamson, Ada Clendenin, illus. LC 12-14711. 377 p. front., plates. 19 1/2 cm. $1.25. 1912. The Penn Publishing Company.
--Glenloch Girl's Club. Williamson, Ada Clendenin, illus. (The Glenloch Books). N.D. Penn Publishing Co.
Jane Stuart at Rivercroft. Williamson, Ada Clendenin, illus. LC 15-16341. (The Jane Stuart Books). 1915. Penn Publishing Co.
--Jane Stuart, Comrade. Williamson, Ada Clendenin, illus. LC 16-16523. 376 p. front., plates. 20 cm. $1.25. 1916. The Penn Publishing Company.
--Jane Stuart, Twin. Williamson, Ada Clendenin, illus. LC 13-167931. 354 p. front., plates. 20 cm. $1.25. 1913. The Penn Publishing Company.
--Jane Stuart's Chum. Williamson, Ada Clendenin, illus. LC 14-12632. 361p. (The Jane Stuart Books). 1914. Penn Publishing Co.
--The Sheldon Six: Anne. Caley, Isabel W., illus. LC 20-142967. 366 p. front., plates. 20 cm. 1920. The Penn Publishing Company.
--The Sheldon Six: Connie. Caley, Isabel W., illus. LC 23-110795. 369 p. front., plates. 19 1/2 cm. 1923. The Penn Publishing Company.
--The Sheldon Six: Rose. Caley, Isabel W., illus. LC 21-211439. 367 p. front., plates. 19 1/2 cm. 1921. The Penn Publishing Company.
--The Sheldon Six: Susan. Caley, Isabel W., illus. LC 24-304455. 351 p. front., plates. 19 1/2 cm. 1924. The Penn Publishing Company.

Remington, Barbara
--Boat. LC 70-180101. (Illus.). 48 p. 1975. (ISBN 0-385-02676-5). (ISBN 0-385-02676-5). Doubleday.

Remington, Ella-Carrie see Alden, Carella, pseud.

Remington, Roger W.
--Adventures of These Three. (Illus.). 112p. (gr. 1-4). 1976. (ISBN 0-682-48471-7). Exposition.

Rempel, Ruth W
--Deegie and the Fairy Princess. Rempel, Dietrich G., illus. LC 50-36060. 32 p. col. illus. 32 cm. c.1949. Rempel Manufacturing Incorporated.

Remy, Jean S., retold by see Grimm, Jakob Ludwig Karl (1785-1863) & Grimm, Wilhelm Karl.

Renault, Mary, pseud., see Challans, Mary.

Renault, Mary, pseud. (1905-1983)
--The Lion in the Gateway. Challans, Mary. 1964p. N.D. Harper & Row Pub.
--The Persian Boy. Challans, Mary. 1972. (ISBN 0-394-48191-7). Pantheon Books.

Renberg, Dalia Hardof
--Hello, Clouds. Frankel, Alona, illus. LC 83-49477. (Illus.). 32 p. 18cm. c.1985. (ISBN 0-06-024838-6). (ISBN 0-06-024839-4). Harper & Row.

Rendina, Laura Jones Cooper (1902-)
--Debbie Jones. LC 50-121187. (Illus.). 244 p. 20cm. 1950. Little, Brown.
--Destination Capri. LC 68-21176. 214 p. 22cm. 1968. Little, Brown.
--Lolly Touchberry. 1 st. ed. Rendina, Mario, illus. LC 57-5511. 213p. illus. 21cm. 1957. Little, Brown.
--My Love for One. King, Ruth, illus. LC 55-51894. (Illus.). 20cm. (A Debbie Jones story. Frontispiece by Ruth King). (gr. 7 up). 1955. (ISBN 0-316-74004-7). Little.
--Roommates. 1st ed. King, Ruth, illus. LC 48-5979. 214 p. illus. 20 cm. 1948. Little, Brown.
--Summer for Two. 1 st ed. King, Ruth, illus. LC 52-6794. 216 p. illus. 20 cm. 1952. Little, Brown.
--Trudi. 1 st ed. LC 59-910757. 230p. 22cm. 1959. Little, Brown.
--World of Their Own. LC 68-13464. (gr. 9 up). 1963. (ISBN 0-316-74009-8). Little.

Rene, Blanche, pseud., see Larsen, Blanche Ida.

Renfro, Nancy & Armstrong, Beverly

--Make Amazing Puppets. 32p. (Gifted & Talented Ser.). (gr. 1-6). 1979. (ISBN 0-88160-007-5). Learning Wks.

Renick, Dorothy

--Star Myths from Many Lands. N.D. Charles Scribner's Sons.

Renick, James L & Renick, Marion Lewis (1905-)

--David Cheers the Team. Machetanz, Frederick (1908-), illus. LC 41-14775. 4 p. l., 125 p. illus. 21 x 17 1/2 cm. c.1941. C. Scribner's Sons.

--Steady: A Baseball Story. Machetanz, Frederick (1908-), illus. LC 42-7376. 3 p. l., 137 p. incl. front., illus. 21 cm. c.1942. C. Scribner's Sons.

--Tommy Carries the Ball. Machetanz, Frederick (1908-), illus. LC 40-32633. 4 p. l., 78 p. illus., diagr. 21 x 17 cm. c.1940. C. Scribner's Sons.

Renick, Marion Lewis, jt. auth. see Renick, James L.

Renick, Marion Lewis (1905-)

--Bats & Gloves of Glory. Herric, Pru, illus. LC 56-5667. (Illus.). 215p. (gr. 3-7). 1956. (ISBN 0-684-13478-0). Scribner.

--The Big Basketball Prize. Galdone, Paul (1914-), illus. LC 63-19908. (Illus.). 32p. (gr. k-4). 1963. (ISBN 0-684-12706-7). Scribner.

--Boy at Bat. Galdone, Paul (1914-), illus. LC 61-7229. (Illus.). (gr. k-4). 1961. (ISBN 0-684-13166-8). Scribner.

--Champion Caddy. Fulton, John, illus. LC 43-3197. 4 p. l., 131 p. illus. 21 x 17 1/2 cm. 1943. C. Scribner's Sons.

--The Dooleys Play Ball. Logan, Dwight, illus. LC 49-8451. 165 p. illus. 20 cm. 1949. C. Scribner's Sons.

--The Famous Forward Pass Pair. Robinson, Charles (1931-), illus. LC 77-2943. (Illus.). 55 p. 21cm. c.1977. (ISBN 0-684-15037-9). Scribner.

--Five Points for Hockey. Robinson, Charles (1931-), illus. LC 72-7732. (Illus.). 132 p. 22cm. 1973. (ISBN 0-684-13211-7). Scribner.

--Football Boys. Lynch, Donald, illus. LC 67-24050. (Illus.). 144 p. 20cm. 1967. Scribner.

--The Heart for Baseball. Galdone, Paul (1914-), illus. LC 53-8959. i34p. illus. 20cm. 1953. Scribner.

--Jimmy's Own Basketball. Herric, Pru, illus. LC 52-13498. (Illus.). 1952. Charles Scribner's Sons.

--John's Back Yard Camp. Herric, Pru, illus. LC 54-6303. (Illus.). 124 p. 20cm. 1954. Scribner.

--Little Fish Hard-to-Catch. Schroeder, Ted (1931-1973), illus. LC 74-79221. (Illus.). 24 p. 24cm. (Carousel book). 1969. L. W. Singer.

--Nicky's Football Team. Honigman, Marian, illus. LC 51-12895. (Illus.). 115 p. 20cm. 1951. Scribner.

--Pete's Home Run. Herric, Pru, illus. LC 52-9349. 117 p. illus. 20 cm. 1952. Scribner.

--Ricky in the World of Sport. Grossman, Nancy S. (1940-), illus. LC 67-24460. (Illus.). 124 p. 21cm. 1967. Seabury Press.

--Sam Discovers Soccer. Blossom, David, illus. LC 74-27237. (Illus.). 102 p. 22cm. 1975. (ISBN 0-684-14215-5). Scribner.

--Seven Simpsons on Six Bikes. Howe, Gertrude Herrick (1902-), illus. LC 56-9282. 122p. illus. 20cm. 1956. Scribner.

--The Shining Shooter. Logan, Dwight, illus. LC 50-6844. (Illus.). 218 p. 20cm. 1950. Scribner.

--Skating Today. Vartanian, Raymond J., illus. LC 45-373931. 2 p. l., 171 p. illus., diagr. 20 cm. 1945. C. Scribner's Sons.

--Steve Marches with the General. Herric, Pru, illus. LC 62-964854. 175p. illus. 20cm. 1962. Scribner.

--Swimming Fever. Logan, Dwight, illus. LC 47-37472. 4 p. l., 181 p. illus. 19 1/2 cm. 1947. C. Scribner's Sons.

--The Tail of the Terrible Tiger: A/Football Story. Galdone, Paul (1914-), illus. LC 59-11855. (Illus.). 27cm. 1959. Scribner.

--Take a Long Jump. Robinson, Charles (1931-), illus. LC 71-158885. (Illus.). 154 p. 20cm. 1971. (ISBN 0-684-12496-3). Scribner.

--Todd's Snow Patrol. Herric, Pru, illus. LC 55-6917. 123p. illus. 20cm. 1955. Scribner.

--A Touchdown for Doc. Logan, Dwight, illus. LC 48-100641. 170 p. illus. 20 cm. 1948. C. Scribner's Sons.

--Watch Those Red Wheels Roll. Shortall, Leonard W., illus. LC 65-14766. (Illus.). 125 p. 20cm. 1965. Scribner.

--Young Mr. Football. Shortall, Leonard W., illus. LC 57-8490. (Illus.). 211 p. 20cm. 1957. Scribner.

Renick, Marion Lewis (1905-) & Tyler, Margaret Carey

--Buckskin Scout, and Other Ohio Stories. 1st ed. Galdone, Paul (1914-), illus. LC 53-9044. 192p. illus. 21cm. 1953. World Pub. Co.

Renier, Anne Cliff & Renier, Fernand Gabriel (1905-)

--Little Wide-Awake. De Vries, Leonard, ed. LC 67-23362. (An Anthology from Victorian Children's Books and Periodicals in the Collecton of Anne and Fernand G. Renier). (Illus.). 240 p. 27cm. 1967. World Pub. Co.

Renier, Fernand Gabriel, jt. auth. see Renier, Anne Cliff.

Renken, Aleda (1907-)

--Adventure on Padre Island. Norman, Michael, illus. LC 75-5945. (Illus.). iii p. 18cm. (Haley adventure book). 1975. (ISBN 0-570-07231-X). Concordia Pub. House.

--Donnie's Danger. Kirchhoff, Art, illus. LC 80-22721. (Illus.). 68 p. 18cm. (Her A Haley adventure book). c.1981. (ISBN 0-570-07235-2). Concordia Pub. House.

--Grandma Haley. Kirchhoff, Art, illus. LC 80-22143. (Illus.). 96 p. 18cm. (Her A Haley adventure book). c.1981. (ISBN 0-570-07234-4). Concordia Pub. House.

--Jeff and the Bad Guy. Norman, Michael, illus. LC 73-75863. (Illus.). 76 p. 18cm. (Haley adventure book). 1973. (ISBN 0-570-03602-X). Concordia Pub. House.

--Kathy. 150 p. 21cm. 1967. F. Watts.

--The Mystery of Cottage Cove. Norman, Michael, illus. LC 75-5578. (Illus.). 96 p. 18cm. (Haley adventure book). 1975. (ISBN 0-570-07232-8). Concordia Pub. House.

--Never the Same Again. LC 75-133253. 156 p. 21cm. 1971. (ISBN 0-664-32487-8). Westminster Press.

--Pat's Problems. LC 80-23228. (Haley Adventures Ser.). 1981. (ISBN 0-570-07236-0). Concordia.

--Picked-on Pat. Norman, Michael, illus. LC 73-75864. (Illus.). 96 p. 18cm. (Haley adventure book). 1973. (ISBN 0-570-03601-1). Concordia Pub. House.

--Rough Rapids Ahead. LC 74-38. (Illus.). 95 p. 18cm. (Haley adventure book). 1974. (ISBN 0-570-03605-4). Concordia.

--Trouble at Briden High. Molina, Charles, illus. LC 77-20060. (Illus.). 132 p. 24cm. (Midwestern Memories Series). c.1978. (ISBN 0-570-07808-3). (ISBN 0-570-07803-2). Concordia Pub. House.

--The Two Christmases. LC 74-37. (Illus.). 96 p. 18cm. (Haley adventure book). c.1974. (ISBN 0-570-03604-6). Concordia Pub. House.

Renner, Beverly Hollett (1929-)

--The Hideaway. 158p (Pub. by Harper & Row). (gr. 3-7). 1980. (ISBN 0-590-31308-8, Schol Pap). Scholastic Inc.

--The Hideaway Summer. 1st ed. Sanderson, Ruth, illus. LC 77-11848. 134 p. 21cm. c.1978. (ISBN 0-06-024862-9). (ISBN 0-06-024863-7). Harper & Row.

Renninger, Elizabeth D. & Firdausi

--The Story of Rustem, and Other Persian Hero Tales from Firdusi. Williams, J. L. S., illus. LC 9-26015. xix, 361 p. col. front., 11 col. pl. 20 1/2 cm. 1909. C. Scribner's Sons.

Reno, Esther Watson see Fleming, Lisa, pseud.

Reno, Esther Watson

--Patsy's Picture. Smith, Charlotte Helen (1905-), illus. Charims, pseud. LC 44-166286. 22 p. col. illus. 22 1/2 x 18 1/2 cm. 1943. R. M. McBride and Company.

--The Pup Called Cinderella. Weisgard, Leonard Joseph (1916-), illus. LC 39-21778. (Illus.). 32p. 1939. Bobbs-Merrill Co.

--Up and Down the Street. Fleming, Lisa, pseud. Miller, Jane Judith (1925-), illus. LC 53-11737. unpaged. illus. 21cm. 1953. Oxford University Press.

Renshaw, V. Corinne

--Thalassine. Gill, Margery Jean (1925-), illus. LC 72-168630. (Illus.). 110 p. 22cm. 1972, c.1971. (ISBN 0-7232-1306-2). F. Warne.

Renstrom, Moiselle

--Musical Adventures. (gr. 1-4). N.D. Deseret Bk.

Renton, Cam, pseud., see Armstrong, Richard.

Renton, Cam, pseud. (1903-)

--The Ship Stealers. Armstrong, Richard. Biro, Val, pseud. (1921-), illus. Biro, Balint Stephen. LC 63-4336. 120 p. illus. 19 cm. 1963. Friday Press.

Rentoul, Annie R, jt. auth. see Outhwaite, Ida Rentoul.

Rentoul, Annie R. & Outhwaite, Ida Rentoul

--Little Green Road to Fairyland. N.D. Macmillan.

Renvoize, Jean

--A Wild Thing. 256p. (gr. 7 up). 1971. (ISBN 0-316-74050-0, Pub. by Atlantic Monthly Pr). Little.

Reorganized Church of Jesus Christ and Latter-Day Saints. Children's Division, jt. auth. see Strand, Ruby.

Reppy, Nell

--The Little Builders ABC. LC 43-15784. 56p. col. illus. 22 1/2 x 17 1/2cm. 1943. Simon & Schuster.

Reque, Anna C., tr. see Kalkar, Georg & Hill, Frank Ernest.

Resnick, Seymour (1920-), ed.

--Spanish-American Poetry: A Bilingual Selection. Jauss, Anne Marie (1907-), illus. LC 64-14514. (Illus.). (gr. 5 up). 1964. (ISBN 0-8178-3492-3). Harvey.

Resnick, William S

--The Dragon Ship: A Story of the Vikings in America. Busoni, Rafaello (1900-1962), illus. LC 42-23867. ix, 214 p. incl. col. front., illus. (part col.) 23 1/2 cm. 1942. Coward-McCann Inc.

Respighi, Ottorino (1879-1936)

--The Fantastic Toy Shop: La Boutique Fantasque. Weil, Lisl (1910-), retold by. Weil, Lisl (1910-), illus. LC 67-107. (Illus.). 47 p. 29cm. c.1966. Abelard-Schuman.

Ressler, Theodore Whitson

--Treasury of American Indian Tales. LC 57-5046. 310p. 20cm. 1957. Association Press.

Ressner, Philip (1922-)

--August Explains. 1963. (ISBN 0-8382-0056-7, Cadmus Books). E. M. Hale and company.

--August Explains. Bonsall, Crosby Barbara Newell (1921-), illus. LC 62-13327. unpaged. illus. 30 cm. 1963. Harper & Row.

--Dudley Pippin. Lobel, Arnold Stark (1933-), illus. LC 65-20252. 46p. illus. 24cm. 1965. Harper.

--Dudley Pippin's Summer. Shecter, Ben (1935-), illus. LC 78-19831. (Illus.). 40 p. 24cm. c.1979. (ISBN 0-06-024887-4). (ISBN 0-06-024888-2). Harper & Row.

--Jerome. Snyder, Jerome (1916-1976), illus. LC 67-18469. (Illus.). 1 v. (unpaged). 26cm. 1967. Parents' Magazine Press.

--The Park in the City. 1st ed. Binzen, Bill, illus. LC 70-133111. (Illus.). 32 p. 27cm. 1971. (ISBN 0-525-36620-2). Dutton.

Rest, Karl Heinrich Albert (1908-)

--Story Talks for Children. 133p. 1942. The Wartburg Press.

Retan, Walter, et al. (1920-)

--Santa's Footprints and Other Christmas Stories. Price, Christine Hilda (1928-1980), illus. N.D. E. P. Dutton & Co.

Retan, Walter (1920-)

--Mystery of the Haunted Cliff. 1st ed. Chapman, Frederick Trench (1887-), illus. LC 49-8673. 131 p. illus. 21 cm. 1949. Aladdin Books.

--Mystery of the Haunted Cliff. Chapman, Frederick Trench (1887-), illus. N.D. E. P. Dutton & Co.

--The Steam Shovel That Wouldn't Eat Dirt. Duvoisin, Roger Antoine (1904-1980), illus. LC 48-10017. 3? p. illus. (part col.) 26 cm. 1948. Aladdin Books.

--Wanted Two Bikes. 1st ed. Chapman, Frederick Trench (1887-), illus. LC 48-10015. 174 p. illus. 21 cm. 1948. Aladdin Books.

Retner, Beth A., pseud., see Brown, Beth.

Retner, Beth A., pseud.

--That's That. Brown, Beth. 1925. Doubleday Page & Co.

Rettich, Margret

--The Silver Touch and Other Family Christmas Stories. Rettich, Rolf, illus. Crawford, Elizabeth D., tr. from Ger. LC 78-6817. (Illus.). 191 p. 21cm. 1978. (ISBN 0-688-22164-5). (ISBN 0-688-32164-X). W. Morrow.

--The Tightwad's Curse and Other Pleasantly Chilling Stories. Rettich, Rolf, illus. Crawford, Elizabeth D., tr. from Ger. LC 79-17832. (Illus.). 189 p. 21cm. 1979. (ISBN 0-688-22211-0). (ISBN 0-688-32211-5). Morrow.

--The Voyage of the Jolly Boat. Jones, Olive, tr. from Ger. LC 80-21408. (Illus.). 32 p. 27cm. c.1981. (ISBN 0-416-30791-4). Methuen.

Reuben, Paula, jt. auth. see Dodson, Fitzhugh James.

Reufenacht, Peter, jt. auth. see Bauer, Fred.

Reuter, Carol, jt. auth. see Fiedler, Jeanette Feldman.

Reuter, Carol Joan, jt. auth. see Fiedler, Jeanette Feldman.

Reuter, Carol Joan (1931-)

--The Secret of the Sea Rocks. LC 67-21182. 217 p. 21cm. 1967. D. McKay Co.

Reuter, Margaret

--My Mother Is Blind. Lanier, Philip, illus. LC 78-12645. p. cm. 1979. Childrens Press.

--You Can Depend on Me. Swenson, Seri, illus. LC 79-22285. p. cm. 1980. (ISBN 0-516-01481-1). Childrens Press.

Reuther, Ruth E (1917-)

--Gray C, Circus Horse. Rosier, Lydia, illus. LC 74-107946. (Illus.). 84 p. 25cm. (Merit books). 1970. Houghton Mifflin.

Reveaux, Darryl

--The Great Wild Egg Hunt. (Illus.). (Little Book Ser). (gr. k-3). 1975. (ISBN 0-89409-002-X). Childrens Art.

Revius, Jacobus (1586-1658)

--Noah's Ark. Spier, Peter Edward (1927-), illus. Spier, Peter Edward (1927-), tr. from Dutch. LC 76-43630. (Illus.). 46p. 21 x 27cm. c.1977. (ISBN 0-385-09473-6). (ISBN 0-385-12730-8). Doubleday.

Revoil, M.

--In the Bush & on the Trail. (Illus.). N.D. Thos Nelson & Sons.

Rew, Lois Johnson

--God's Green Liniment. Thomas, Avis Johnson, illus. LC 81-84183. (Illus.). 204 p. 22cm. c.1981. (ISBN 0-938462-02-4). Green Leaf Press.

Rexford, Eben E.

--Grandmother's Garden. Spaulding, Mary Cecilia, illus. 1891. McClurg.

Rexroth, Kenneth (1905-1982)

--Collected Shorter Poems. LC 66-17818. 1967. (ISBN 0-8112-0367-0). (ISBN 0-8112-0178-3). New Directions.

Rey, Alfonso

--The Lost Sheep & Other Parables. Beaumont, illus. Nevins, Albert J. (1915-), tr. from Sp. LC 78-71329. (Illus.). (gr. 4-6). 1979. (ISBN 0-87973-712-3). Our Sunday Visitor.

--Poor Lazarus and Other Parables: The Parable of the Sower, the Good Shepherd. Beaumont, illus. Nevins, Albert J. (1915-), tr. from Sp. LC 78-71328. (Illus.). 60 p. 31cm. c.1979. (ISBN 0-87973-711-5). Our Sunday Visitor.

Rey, Barbara

--Tales of the Primitive Area. LC 76-12897. (Illus.). v. 23cm. N.D. B. Dolls.

Rey, Hans Augusto, jt. auth. see Rey, Margret Elisabeth Waldstein.

Rey, Hans Augusto (1898-1977)

--Anybody at Home!. LC 42-50767. cover-title, 24 p. col. illus. 21 x 24 cm. c.1942. Houghton Mifflin Company.

--Au Clair De la Lune and Other French Nursery Songs. LC 42-12506. 31 p. incl. col. plates. 21 1/2 x 28 cm. c.1941. Greystone Press.

--Cecily G. & the Nine Monkeys. LC 42-20276. (Illus.). 30cm. 31p. (gr. 1-3). 1942. (ISBN 0-395-18430-4). HM.

--Cecily G. & the Nine Monkeys. Rey, Hans Augusto (1898-1977), illus. (gr. k-3). 1977. (ISBN 0-395-25380-2). HM.

--A Christmas Manger. N.D. Houghton Mifflin Co.

--Curious George Rides a Bike. LC 52-8728. (Illus.). 45 p. 27cm. 1952. Houghton Mifflin.

--Elizabite: The Adventures of a Carnivorous Plant. Rey, Hans Augusto (1898-1977), illus. (Illus.). (gr. k-3). 1962. (ISBN 0-06-024896-3, HarpJ). Har-Row.

--Humpty Dumpty and Other Mother Goose Songs. Rey, Hans Augusto (1898-1977), illus. LC 43-51362. 23 p. col. illus. 21 1/2 x 27 1/2 cm. 1943. Harper & Brothers.

--Uncle Gus's Circus. N.D. Houghton Mifflin Co.

--Uncle Gus's Farm. N.D. Houghton Mifflin Co.

--We Three Kings. N.D. Harper & Bros.

Rey, Hans Augusto (1898-1977) & Rey, Margret Elisabeth Waldstein (1906-)

--Billy's Picture. Rey, Hans Augusto (1898-1977), illus. LC 48-7929. (Illus.). 22 p. 26cm. 1948. (ISBN 0-06-024906-4). Harper.

--Cecily G. and the Nine Monkeys. Rey, Hans Augusto (1898-1977), illus. LC 42-20276. 31, 1 p. col. illus. 30 cm. 1942. Houghton Mifflin Company.

--Curious George. Rey, Hans Augusto (1898-1977), illus. LC 41-160545. 55 p. col. illus. 26 1/2 x 22 cm. 1941. Houghton Mifflin Company.

--Curious George. Rey, Hans Augusto (1898-1977), illus. LC 73-162780. (Illus.). 46 p. 23cm. (Sandpiper books). 1973, c.1941. (ISBN 0-395-15024-8). Houghton Mifflin.

--Curious George Flies a Kite. LC 58-8163. (Illus.). 80 p. 24cm. 1958. (ISBN 0-395-16965-8). Houghton Mifflin.

--Curious George Gets a Medal. Rey, Hans Augusto (1898-1977), illus. LC 57-7206. (Illus.). 47 p. 27cm. 1957. Houghton Mifflin. **Award: (NYT).**

--Curious George Goes to the Hospital. Rey, Hans Augusto (1898-1977), illus. LC 65-19301. (Illus.). (gr. 1-5). 1966. (ISBN 0-395-18158-5). (ISBN 0-395-07062-7). HM.

--Curious George Goes to the Hospital. Rey, Hans Augusto (1898-1977), illus. 48p. (gr. k-3). 1970 (Starline). Schol Bk Serv.

--Curious George Learns the Alphabet. Rey, Hans Augusto (1898-1977), illus. LC 62-12261. (Illus.). 72p. (gr. k-3). 1973. (ISBN 0-395-13718-7, Sandpiper). (ISBN 0-395-16031-6). HM.

--Curious George Rides a Bike. Rey, Hans Augusto (1898-1977), illus. LC 73-180856. (Illus.). 45 p. 23cm. (Sandpiper books). 1973, c.1952. (ISBN 0-395-17444-9). Houghton Mifflin.

--Curious George Takes a Job. Rey, Hans Augusto (1898-1977), illus. LC 47-5527. 47 p. col. illus. 27 cm. 1947. Houghton Mifflin Co.

--Curious George Takes a Job. Rey, Hans Augusto (1898-1977), illus. (Illus.). 47 p. 23cm. (Sandpiper book). 1974, c.1947. (ISBN 0-395-18649-8). Houghton, Mifflin.

--Elizabite: The Adventures of a Carnivorous Plant. Rey, Hans Augusto (1898-1977), illus. LC 42-11251. (Illus.). 32 p. 1942. Harper & Brothers.

--Feed the Animals. Rey, Hans Augusto (1898-1977), illus. LC 44-40376. 24 p. col. illus. 20 1/2 x 24 cm. c.1944. Houghton Mifflin Company.

--How Do You Get There?. Rey, Hans Augusto (1898-1977), illus. LC 43-12354. cover-title, 22 p. col. illus. 21 x 24 1/2 cm. c.1941. Houghton Mifflin Company.

--See the Circus. Rey, Hans Augusto (1898-1977), illus. LC 56-14089. unpaged. illus. 14 x 16cm. 1956. Houghton Mifflin.

--Spotty. LC 45-9836. (Illus.). 25cm. 30p. (ps-1). 1945. (ISBN 0-06-024921-8, HarpJ). Har-Row.

--Tit for Tat. Rey, Hans Augusto (1898-1977), illus. LC 42-24738. 30 p. col. illus. 26 1/2 x 24 cm. 1942. Harper & Brothers.

--Where's My Baby!. Rey, Hans Augusto (1898-1977), illus. LC 43-17320. 24 p. col. illus. 20 1/2 x 24 cm. c.1943. Houghton Mifflin Company.

Rey, Lester del

--Space Flight. Polgreen, John, illus. 1959. Golden Press.

Rey, Lester Del see Del Rey, Lester.

Rey, Lillian Elizabeth Becker (1868-)

--The Woodcraft Girls in the City. LC 18-11834. 1918. George H. Doran Co.

Rey, Margret Elisabeth Waldstein, jt. auth. see Rey, Hans Augusto.

Rey, Margret Elisabeth Waldstein (1906-)

--Arabian Nights Entertainment. N.D. Harper & Bros.

--Curious George and the Dump Truck. Shalleck, Alan J., ed. LC 84-16824. (Illus.). 32p. (ps-2). 1984. (ISBN 0-395-36635-6). (ISBN 0-395-36629-1). (ISBN 0-395-36629-1). HM.

--Pretzel. 1st ed. Rey, Hans Augusto (1898-1977), illus. LC 44-9584. (Illus.). 32 p. 1944. Harper & Brothers.

--Pretzel and the Puppies. Rey, Hans Augusto (1898-1977), illus. LC 46-7187. 30 p. col. illus. 26 x 21 cm. 1946. Harper & Brothers.

Rey, Margret Elisabeth Waldstein (1906-) & Rey, Hans Augusto (1898-1977)

--Curious George Flies a Kite. Rey, Hans Augusto (1898-1977), illus. (Illus.). (gr. k-3). 1977. (ISBN 0-395-25937-1). HM.

Rey, Margret Elisabeth Waldstein (1906-) & Shalleck, Alan J., eds.

--Curious George and the Pizza. LC 85-2434. (Illus.). 32 p. 21cm. 1985. (ISBN 0-395-39039-7). Houghton Mifflin.

--Curious George at the Fire Station. LC 85-2471. (Illus.). 32 p. 21cm. 1985. (ISBN 0-395-39037-0). (ISBN 0-395-39031-1). Houghton Mifflin.

--Curious George Goes Hiking. LC 85-2433. p. cm. 1985. (ISBN 0-395-39038-9). (ISBN 0-395-39032-X). Houghton Mifflin.

--Curious George Goes Sledding. LC 84-16827. p. cm. 1984. (ISBN 0-395-36637-2). (ISBN 0-395-36631-3). Houghton Mifflin.

--Curious George Goes to the Aquarium. LC 84-16828. p. cm. 1984. (ISBN 0-395-36634-8). (ISBN 0-395-36634-8). (ISBN 0-395-36628-3). Houghton Mifflin.

--Curious George Goes to the Circus. LC 84-16826. p. cm. 32p. 1984. (ISBN 0-395-36636-4). (ISBN 0-395-36630-5). Houghton Mifflin.

--Curious George Visits the Zoo. LC 85-2415. (Illus.). 30 p. 22cm. 1985. (ISBN 0-395-39036-2). (ISBN 0-395-39030-3). Houghton Mifflin.

Rey, Pierre

--The Greek. 1974. (ISBN 0-399-11347-9). G. P. Putnam's Sons.

Reyher, Ferdinand

--David Farragut, Sailor. 1st ed. LC 53-10218. 238p. illus. 22cm. 1953. Lippincott.

Reyher, Rebecca Hourwich (1897-)

--My Mother is the Most Beautiful Woman in the World. Gannett, Ruth Chrisman Arens (1896-1979), illus. 1945. (ISBN 0-688-51251-8). William Morrow and Company.

--My Mother Is the Most Beautiful Woman in the World: A Russian Folktale. Gannett, Ruth Chrisman Arens (1896-1979), illus. LC 45-832684. 39 p. illus. (part col.) 21 1/2 x 17 1/2 cm. 1945. Howell, Soskin.

Reyher, Rebecca Hourwich (1897-), adapted by.

--My Mother is the Most Beautiful Woman in the World: A Russian Folktale. Gannett, Ruth Chrisman Arens (1896-1979), illus. (Illus.). (gr. 1-4). 1945. (ISBN 0-688-51251-8). Lothrop. **Award: (RCM).**

Reyman, N

--The Little Lady of the Hall. N.D. Benziger Brothers.

Reynard the Fox. English

--Reynard the Fox. Evans, Charles Seddon (1883-), as told by. Brightwell, Leonard Robert (1889-), illus. LC 23-26860. 127, 1 p. incl. col. front., illus., col. plates. 27 1/2 cm. 1923. Dodd, Mead & Company.

--Reynard the Fox. Firman, Sidney Grant, retold by. Richardson, Frederick, illus. LC 30-5279. ix, 86 p. col. front., illus., col. pl. 21 cm. (The child's garden of charming books). c.1929. The John C. Winston Company.

--Reynard the Fox: The/Little Red Hen and the Sly Old Fox. Best, Susie M., retold by. LC 43-29582. 32 p. illus. 18 1/2 cm. (Instructor library books) No. 50). c.1913. Hall & McCreary Company.

--The Story of Reynard the Fox. Larrieu, Odette, tr. from Fr. Lorioux, F., illus. LC 28-14546. 5 p. l., 254 p. incl. illus., plates. col. front., col. plates. 19 1/2 cm. (The Macmillan children's classics). 1928. The Macmillan Company.

Reynard the Fox. English & Day, Samuel Phillips

--The Rare Romance of Reynard the Fox, the Crafty Courtier, in Words of One Syllable. LC 44-35366. 95 p. incl. front., illus. 21 1/2 x 17 1/2 cm. (One syllable series). 1888. Cassell Publishing Company.

Reynard the Fox. English & Norton, Alice Mary (1912-)

--Rogue Reynard: Being A tale of the Fortunes and Misfortunes and Divers Misdeeds of That Great Villain, Baron Reynard, the Fox, and How Was Served with King Lion's Justice, Based Upon the Beast Saga. Norton, Andre, pseud. Bannon, Laura May (0000-1963), illus. LC 47-3707. vii, 96 p. illus. 24 1/2 cm. 1947. Houghton, Mifflin Company.

Reynard the Fox. English & Owens, Harry James (1894-)

--The Scandalous Adventures of Reynard the Fox: A Modern American Version. Ward, Keith, illus. LC 45-5277. xvii 1 p., 1 l., 115, 3 p. incl. front. illus. plates. 22 cm. 1945. A. A. Knopf.

Reynard the Fox. English & Von Goethe, Johann Wolfgang (1749-1832)

--Reynard the Fox. Johnson, Clifton (1865-), adapted by. LC 24-15090. x, 155 p. front., illus., plates. 19 cm. c.1924. Milton Bradley Company.

Reynard the Fox. English, jt. auth. see Reinke de Vos.

Reynolds, Alfred Christopher (1911-)

--The Adventures of Rattlesnake Ralph. McKenna, Paul, illus. LC 73-5193. (Illus.). 152 p. 22cm. 1973. (ISBN 0-684-13434-9). Scribner.

--Kiteman of Karanga. LC 84-14351. 217 p. 22cm. c.1985. (ISBN 0-394-86347-X). (ISBN 0-394-96347-4). Knopf.

--The Pond on My Windowsill. Reynolds, Alfred Christopher (1911-), illus. 1970. Pantheon Books.

Reynolds, Barbara Leonard

--Cabin Boy and Extra Ballast. Geer, Charles Hand (1922-), illus. LC 58-6742. (Illus.). 250 p. 21cm. 1958. Scribner.

--Emily San. Shigaki, Tack, illus. LC 55-6918. 180p. illus. 21cm. 1955. Scribner.

--Hamlet and Brownswiggle. Henneberger, Robert G. (1921-), illus. LC 54-5925. (Illus.). 203 p. 22cm. 1954. Scribner.

--Pepper. N.D. E . M. Hale and Co.

--Pepper. Cooney, Barbara (1917-), illus. LC 52-9132. (Illus.). 169 p. 22cm. 1952. Scribner.

Reynolds, Barbara Leonard, jt. auth. see Doi, Hiroyuki.

Reynolds, Betty J

--A Skunk Named Zorri. LC 72-83040. (gr. 4 up). 1972. (ISBN 0-679-20182-3). McKay.

Reynolds, Charlotte & Parker, Barbara, eds.

--Poetry Please. Hafner, Marylin (1925-), illus. LC 68-55408. (Illus.). 46p. 29cm. (Carousel Book). 1968. L. W. Singer.

Reynolds, Cuyler (1866-)

--The Rosamond Tales: Sixteen Short Stories Intended for Children. Reynolds, Cuyler (1866-), illus. LC 1-24850. xv p., 2 l., 19-284 p. incl. front. pl. 20 front., pl. 20 1/2 cm. (Princess series). 1901. L. C. Page & Co.

Reynolds, Dickson, pseud., see Reynolds, Helen Mary Greenwood Campbell Dickson.

Reynolds, Dorothy

--The Sons of the Smiling Tiger. Davis, M. J., illus. LC 55-9889. 202p. illus. 21cm. 1955. (ISBN 0-8114-7642-1). Steck Co.

Reynolds, Feza M

--Shug the Pup: The Story of a Real Dog. LC 28-352. 127 p. incl. col. front., col. illus. 19 1/2 cm. c.1927. Beckley-Cardy Company.

Reynolds, Florence Krag, jt. auth. see Krag, Martha Ann.

Reynolds, G. W. M. (1814-1879)

--Wagner, the Wher Wolf. N.D. De Witt.

Reynolds, Helen Mary Greenwood Campbell Dickson see Reynolds, Dickson, pseud.

Reynolds, Helen Mary Greenwood Campbell Dickson (1884-1969)

--Angry River. Reynolds, Dickson, pseud. Geary, Clifford N. (1916-), illus. LC 51-7314. 181p. 21cm. 1951. Nelson.

--Brother Scouts. LC 52-10879. 158 p. 21 cm. 1952. T. Nelson.

--Captain Peggy of the Mamie L. Merrill, Marion, illus. LC 43-13834. 176 p. incl. front., illus. 22 cm. 1943. T. Nelson and Sons.

--Carol of Long Chance Mine. LC 59-8040. 216 p. 22cm. 1959. Funk & Wagnalls.

--Cherries Are Ripe. Morse, Dorothy Bayley (1906-1979), illus. LC 50-9008. 191 p. illus. 21 cm. 1950. Nelson.

--The Fire Patrol. Reynolds, Dickson, pseud. LC 49-965833. 192 p. 21 cm. 1949. T. Nelson.

--Fortune Trail. Reynolds, Dickson, pseud. Fitzgerald, Edmond J., illus. LC 54-6363. 213p. illus. 22cm. 1954. Funk & Wagnalls.

--The Fur Brigade. Reynolds, Dickson, pseud. Fitzgerald, Edmond j., illus. LC 53-6978. 207p. illus. 22cm. 1953. Funk & Wagnalls.

--Gold in Mosquito Creek. Reynolds, Dickson, pseud. Condon, Grattan, illus. LC 46-72098. 192 p. incl. front., illus. 21 cm. 1946. T. Nelson & Sons.

--Karen Presents ... Urbanowich, Evelyn, illus. LC 55-7591. 218p. illus. 22cm. 1955. Funk & Wagnalls.

--Music for Melanie. Stolberg, Doris, illus. LC 58-7279. 220p. illus. 22cm. 1958. Funk & Wagnalls.

--Music for Melanie. Stolberg, Doris, illus. (Illus.). (gr. 7-11). N.D. (ISBN 0-308-80134-2). Funk & W.

--Mystery of the Logging Camp. Reynolds, Dickson, pseud. Condon, Grattan, illus. LC 45-104927. 171 p. incl. front., illus. 21 cm. 1945. T. Nelson & Sons.

--Summer of Surprise. LC 60-6427. 186p. (gr. 7-11). 1960. (ISBN 0-308-80176-8). Funk & W.

--We Chased a Rainbow. Wallace, Lucille, illus. LC 57-6505. 214p. illus. 22cm. 1957. Funk & Wagnalls.

Reynolds, Helen Mary (1874-)

--In Our Back Yard. Hartwell, Marjorie, illus. LC 34-107493. vii, 152 p. illus. 19 cm. c.1934. C. Scribner's Sons.

Reynolds, Jack

--Down on the Farm. Allen, J. C., photos by. LC 35-173. 60p. 1935. Whitman Pub.

Reynolds, James Joseph, ed.

--Modern Poetry for Children. LC 79-125512. v. 20cm. (Granger Poetry Library). N.D. (ISBN 0-89609-167-8). Granger Book Co.

--Modern Poetry for Children: Book 6. LC 30-10164. Repr. of 1928 ed (Pub. by Noble). (Granger Poetry Library). (gr. 3). 1976. (ISBN 0-89609-041-8). Granger Bk.

Reynolds, Jamie

--The Football Dragon. Reynolds, Al, illus. LC 80-66029. (Illus.). 52p. (gr. k-3). 1981. (ISBN 0-936774-00-2). Bozo Pr.

Reynolds, Jane L.

--Sing to the Earth. 84p. (gr. k-4). 1978. (ISBN 0-932320-00-7). Solar Studio.

Reynolds, John Murray (1901-)

--Bugles at Midnight. Wright, Cameron, illus. LC 31-570833. ix, 270, 1 p. front., illus. 19 1/2 cm. 1931. D. Appleton and Company.

--The Guns of Yorktown. Lee, Manning De Villeneuve (1894-1980), illus. LC 32-5031. ix, 274, 1 p. front., illus. 19 1/2 cm. 1932. D. Appleton and Company.

--Men of Morgan. Lee, Manning De Villeneuve (1894-1980), illus. LC 33-4811. vi p., 2 l., 279, 1 p. front., illus. 19 1/2 cm. 1933. D. Appleton and Company.

Reynolds, Joyce

--The Prince & the Pauper. (Orig.). (gr. 4-8). 1979. (ISBN 0-88243-102-1). Gospel Pub.

Reynolds, Julie, ed. see Dranow, Ralph.

Reynolds, Kay, ed. see Pini, Wendy & Pini, Richard.

Reynolds, Louis Bernard (1917-) & Paddock, Charles Lee (1891-)

--Little Journeys into Storyland: Stories That Will Live and Lift. LC 47-20367. 235, 1 p. col. front., illus. (incl. ports.) 24 cm. 1947. Southern Publishing Association.

Reynolds, Malvina (1900-1978)

--Cheerful Tunes for Lutes & Spoons. Robbins, Jodi, illus. LC 76-120781. (Illus.). 42p. (gr. 1-8). 1970. (ISBN 0-915620-01-4). Schroeder Music.

--Morningtown Ride. Leeman, Michael, illus. (Illus.). 20p. (ps-4). 1984. (ISBN 0-931793-00-9). Turn The Page.

--Tweedles & Foodles for Young Noodles. Robbins, Jodi, illus. LC 73-80670. (Illus.). 42p. (gr. k-4). 1961. (ISBN 0-915620-00-6). Schroeder Music.

Reynolds, Marjorie Harris (1903-)

--Cabin on Ghostly Pond. (Illus.). (Harper Trophy Ser.). (gr. 3-6). 1966. (ISBN 0-06-440060-3, Trophy). Har-Row.

--Cabin on Ghostly Pond. Bjorklund, Lorence F. (1913-1978), illus. LC 62-794335. (Illus.). (gr. 5 up). 1962. (ISBN 0-06-024931-5, HarpJ). Har-Row.

--Dark Horse Barnaby. Biegel, Peter, illus. LC 67-15546. (Illus.). 151 p. 22cm. 1967. Macmillan.

--A Horse Called Mystery. Dennis, Wesley (1903-1966), illus. (Illus.). 205 p. 21cm. 1964. Harper & Row.

--Keep a Silver Dollar. Lyne, Michael, illus. LC 66-11496. (Illus.). (gr. 3-7). 1966. (ISBN 0-06-024946-3, HarpJ). Har-Row.

--Ride the Wild Storm. Bjorklund, Lorence F. (1913-1978), illus. LC 69-11305. (Illus.). 169 p. 22cm. 1969. Macmillan.

--Sire Unknown. Bjorklund, Lorence F. (1913-1978), illus. LC 68-20608. (Illus.). 153 p. 22cm. 1968. Macmillan.

Reynolds, Pamela (1923-)

--A Different Kind of Sister. LC 68-27704. 192 p. 22cm. 1968. Lothrop, Lee & Shepard.

--Earth Times Two. LC 79-121823. 160 p. 22cm. 1970. Lothrop, Lee & Shepard Co.

--Horseshoe Hill. Berson, Harold (1926-), illus. LC 65-220346. (Illus.). 224p. (gr. 4-6). 1965. (ISBN 0-688-41056-1). Lothrop.

--Will the Real Monday Please Stand Up. LC 74-23494. 184 p. 22cm. 1975. (ISBN 0-688-41694-2). (ISBN 0-688-51694-7). Lothrop, Lee & Shepard Co.

Reynolds, R. G., ed. see Hultz, Helen Lorraine.

Reynolds, Suzanne (1951-1962)

--Snowy: The Little White Horse. Studio Brambilla, Milan, illus. LC 65-29939. (Illus.). 26 p. 33cm. 1965. Golden Press.

Reynolds, William Jensen, jt. ed. see Crowder, Nettie Lou.

Reznik, Ruth, ed. see Omer, Devorah.

Reznik, Ruth, tr. see Banai, Margalit.

Reznik, Ruth, tr. see Omer, Devorah.

Reznikoff, Dominique see Mido, pseud.

Reznikoff, Dominique (1927-)

--A Dog's Life. Mido, pseud. Gerda, illus. LC 66-4156. 1 v. unpaged. col. ill. 21cm. (A Golden Read-it Yourself Book). 1966, c.1964. Golden Press.

Rhea, Carolum

--A Child's Life Is Cong. Dugan, William J., illus. LC 64-10054. 63p. col. illus. 25cm. c.1964. Broadman.

Rhead, Louis (1857-1926), ed. see Swift, Jonathan.

Rhead, Louis John (1857-1926)

--Bold Robin Hood and His Outlaw Band: Their Famous Exploits in Sherwood Forest. LC 12-232040. xi, 1 p., 1 l., 285, 1 p. incl. front., illus., plates, map. 23 cm. 1912. Harper & Brothers.

--Robin Hood. (Illus.). (Rhead's Illustrated Juveniles). N.D. Harper & Brothers Trade-List.

--Tom Brown's School Days. (Illus.). (Rhead's Illustrated Juveniles). N.D. Harper & Brothers Trade-Lst.

Rhead, Louis John (1857-1926), illus.

--The Arabian Nights' Entertainments. LC 16-220779. 6 p. l., 429, 1 p. incl. front., illus., plates. 23 cm. 1916. Harper & Brothers.

Rhie, Schi-Zhin (1936-)

--Soon-Hee in America. Rhie, Schi-Zhin (1936-), photos by. LC 77-81780. (Illus.). 36p. (gr. k-3). 1977. (ISBN 0-930878-00-0). Hollym Intl.

Rhinehart, Susan Oneacre (1938-)

--Something Old, Something New. Lobel, Arnold Stark (1933-), illus. LC 61-12068. (Illus.). 32p. (gr. k-3). 1961. (ISBN 0-06-024985-4). Har-Row.

Rhiner, Gladys

--Jimmie Goes to Church. Smalley, Janet (1893-), illus. LC 57-63274. (Illus.). (ps). 1957. (ISBN 0-8054-4105-0). Broadman.

--Jimmy Goes Camping. Peterson, John Lawrence (1924-), illus. LC 78-113038. (Illus.). 32 p. 24cm. c.1978. (ISBN 0-8054-4255-3). Broadman Press.

--Jimmy Goes to the Country. LC 81-66558. (gr. k-2). 1981. (ISBN 0-8054-4273-1). Broadman.

Rhoades, Cornelia Harson see Rhoades, Nina, pseud.

Rhoades, Nina, pseud., see Rhoades, Cornelia Harson.

Rhoades, Nina, pseud., see Rhodes, Cornelia Harson.

Rhoades, Nina, pseud. (1863-)

--The Adventures of Joan. Rhoades, Cornelia Harson. Withington, Elizabeth R., illus. LC 25-3850. 237 p. front., plates. 19 cm. c.1924. Lothrop, Lee & Shepard Co.

--Brave Little Peggy. Rhoades, Cornelia Harson. Hoxie, Bertha Davidson, illus. LC 8-17832. 4 p. l., 7-264 p. front., 7 pl. 19 cm. 1908. Lothrop, Lee & Shepard Co.

--The Children on the Top Floor. Rhoades, Cornelia Harson. Davidson, Bertha G., illus. LC 4-22663. 219 p. front., 7 pl. 19 cm. 1904. Lee and Shepard.

--Dorothy Brown. Rhoades, Cornelia Harson. (Books for Older Girls). N.D. Lothrop, Lee & Shepard.

--Dorothy Brown: A Story for Girls. Rhoades, Cornelia Harson. Rhoades, Elizabeth, illus. LC 9-16443. 20 cm. 416p. 1909. Lothrop, Lee & Shepard.

--Four Girls of Forty Years Ago. Rhoades, Cornelia Harson. Weeden, Eleanor G., illus. LC 20-20005. 281 p. front., plates. 19 cm. c.1920. Lothrop, Lee & Shepard Co.

--The Girl from Arizona. Rhoades, Cornelia Harson. Withington, Elizabeth R., illus. LC 13-17253. 4 p. l., 358 p. front., plates. 19 1/2 cm. $1.0. 1913. Lothrop, Lee & Shepard Co.

--How Barbara Kept Her Promise. Rhoades, Cornelia Harson. LC 5-17591. 5p 1 (7) 245p front, 7 pl 19". (The Brick House Books). 1905. Lothrop, Lee & Shepard.

--The Independence of Nan. Rhoades, Cornelia Harson. Withington, Elizabeth R., illus. LC 16-170676. 373 p. front., plates. 20 cm. $1.2. 1916. Lothrop, Lee & Shepard Co.

--The Little Girl Next Door. Rhodes, Cornelia Harson. Davidson, Bertha G., illus. LC 2-19390. 248 p. front., plates. 19 cm. 1902. Lee and Shepard.

--Little Miss Rosamond. Rhoades, Cornelia Harson. Davidson, Bertha G., illus. LC 6-16300. 260 p. front., 7 pl. 19 cm. 1906. Lothrop, Lee & Shepard Co.

--Little Queen Esther. Rhoades, Cornelia Harson. (The Gentle and Brave Library). N.D. Frederick Warne & Co.

--Little Queen Esther. Rhoades, Cornelia Harson. Withington, Elizabeth R., illus. LC 12-15812. 286 p. front., plates. 19 cm. $1.0. 1912. Lothrop, Lee & Shepard Co.

--Maisie's Merry Christmas. Rhoades, Cornelia Harson. Withington, Elizabeth R., illus. LC 11-5996. 311 p. front., plates. 19 cm. $1.0. 1911. Lothrop, Lee & Shepard Co.

--Making Mary Lizzie Happy. Rhoades, Cornelia Harson. Withington, Elizabeth R., illus. LC 14-14543. 5 p. l., 9-292 p. front., plates. 19 cm. $1.0. 1914. Lothrop, Lee & Shepard Co.

--Marion's Vacation. Rhoades , Cornelia Harson. Davidson, Bertha G., illus. LC 7-23304. vii, 299 p. front., 7 pl. 19 cm. 1907. Lothrop, Lee & Shepard Co.

--Nora's Twin Sister. Rhoades, Cornelia Harson. Bickford, Nana French, illus. LC 19-157404. 250 p. front., plates. 19 cm. c.1919. Lothrop, Lee & Shepard Co.

--Only Dollie: A Story for Girls. Rhoades, Cornelia Harson. Davidson, Bertha G., illus. LC 1-15318. 12 cm. 213p. 1901. Lothrop, Lee & Shepard.

--The Other Sylvia. Rhoades, Cornelia Harson. Withington, Elizabeth R., illus. LC 10-25830. 19 cm. 242p. (The Brick House Books). 1910. Lothrop,Lee & Shepard.

--Plucky Little Patsy. Rhoades, Cornelia Harson. Bickford, Nana French, illus. LC 17-23652. 322 p. incl. front. plates. 19 cm. $1.0. 1917. Lothrop, Lee & Shepard Co.

--Polly's Predicament: A Story. Rhoades, Cornelia Harson. Copeland, Charles, illus. LC 6-30461. 341 p. front., 4 pl. 19 1/2 cm. c.1906. W. A. Wilde Company.

--Priscilla of the Doll Shop. Rhoades, Cornelia Harson. Davidson, Bertha G., illus. LC 7-15112. 5 p. l., 9 284 p. front., 7 pl. 19 cm. 1907. Lothrop, Lee & Shepard Co.

--Puzzling Pepita. Rhoades, Cornelia Harson. Withington, Elizabeth R., illus. LC 23-124382. 325 p. front., plates. 19 cm. c.1923. Lothrop, Lee & Shepard Co.

--A Real Cinderella. Rhoades, Cornelia Harson. Withington, Elizabeth R., illus. LC 15-15953. 276 p. incl. front. plates. 19 cm. $1.0. 1915. Lothrop, Lee & Shepard Co.

--Ruth Campbell's Experiment: A Story. Rhoades, Cornelia Harson. Stecher, William Frederick (1864-), illus. LC 4-24570. 288 p. front., 3 pl. 19 1/2 cm. 1904. W. A. Wilde Company.

--Silver Linings. Rhoades, Cornelia Harson. Eckerson, Margaret, illus. LC 3-23600. 5 p. l., 347 p. front., 3 pl. 20 cm. 1903. McClure, Phillips & Co.

--That Preston Girl: A Story. Rhoades, Cornelia Harson. Stecher, William Frederick (1864-), illus. LC 5-26923. (Illus.). 20 cm. 340p. c.1905. W. A. Wilde & Co.

--Victorine's Book. Rhoades, Cornelia Harson. Withington, Elizabeth R., illus. LC 11-21862. 3 p. l., 339 p. front., plates. 19 cm. $1.2. 1911. Lothrop, Lee & Shepard Co.

--When Gretel Was Fifteen. Rhoades, Cornelia Harson. Withington, Elizabeth R., illus. LC 22-260518. 327 p. front., plates. 19 1/2 cm. 1921. Lothrop, Lee & Shepard Co.

--Winifred's Neighbors. Rhoades, Cornelia Harson. 224p. N.D. Lothrop, Lee & Shepard.

Rhoads, Bert

--Bickie's Cow College. Baerg, Harry John (1909-), illus. LC 62-14170. 123 p. illus. 22 cm. 1962. Review and Herald Pub. Association.

Rhoads, Dorothy Mary (1895-)

--The Bright Feather and Other Maya Tales. Houser, Lowell, illus. LC 32-24546. xv, 196 p. incl. illus., plates. col. front. 21 cm. 1932. Doubleday, Doran and Company, Inc.

--The Corn Grows Ripe. Charlot, Jean (1898-1979), illus. LC 56-13799. 88p. illus. 26cm. 1956. (ISBN 0-670-24168-7). Viking Press. **Award: (JNM).**

Rhoads, Marie P.

--Paul, the Hunchback. Rhoads, Marie P., illus. (Illus.). (gr. k-12). N.D. (ISBN 0-932806-01-5). IEM-HOTEP.

Rhode, H. & Coon, B.

--Cha-Ki-Shi. N.D. Charles Scribner's Sons.

Rhoden, Emily

--Taming a Tomboy. (The Rugby Series for Boys). N.D. A. L. Burt Company.

--Taming a Tomboy. (Illus.). (The Wellesley Series for Girls). N.D. A. L. Burt.

Rhoden, Emma von, pseud., see Friedrich, Emmy Friederike Charlotte Kuhne.

Rhodes, Bertha Marilda

--Eagle Ranch. (The Little American Ser.). N.D. Reilly & Lee Co.

--Engine Company No. Twenty-Five. (The Little American Ser.). N.D. Reilly & Lee Co.

--Flag to the Front. (The Little American Ser.). N.D. Reilly & Lee Co.

--Just Tom. (The Little American Ser.). N.D. Reilly & Lee Co.

--Little American Books. Hubbard, Eleanore Mineah, illus. LC 36-19093. (Junior Press Books). 6 v. illus. (part col.) 19 1/2 cm. 1936. A. Whitman & Co.

--Signals. (The Little American Ser.). N.D. Reilly & Lee Co.

--Spotted Deer's Party. (The Little American Ser.). N.D. Reilly & Lee Co.

Rhodes, Cornelia Harson see Rhoades, Nina, pseud.

Rhodes, Daniel D. & Allen, Mathews F., Jr.

--He Taught by Parables. Bahler, Mary A., illus. (Illus., Orig.). (gr. 7-9). 1967. (ISBN 0-8042-9373-2). John Knox.

Rhodes, Dorothy

--Someone for Maria. Bromhall, Winifred, illus. LC 63-7226. (Illus.). 32 p. 1964. Golden Gate Junior Books.

Rhodes, Geneva Linebaugh

--Moonlight and Rainbow: A Story of Navajo Indians. LC 39-9534. 69, 2 p. illus. (part col.) 26 1/2 cm. c.1939. McKnight & McKnight.

Rhodes, Gerald P (1904-)

--Tales from Ransom Valley: Animal Adventures for Little Folk. 1st ed. Przondak, Catherine, illus. LC 53-7372. 90p. illus. 23cm. 1953. Exposition Press.

Rhodes, Irma G

--In Quest of Treasure: New Poems for Young People, with Study Guides. LC 79-164866. 71 p. 22cm. (Exposition-banner book). 1971. (ISBN 0-682-47321-9). Exposition Press.

Rhodes, Irma G & Peschel, Enid Rhodes (1943-)

--Flashbacks: Poems for Children. limited 1st. McKesson, Malcolm F, illus. LC 78-106002. (Illus.). 62 p. (p. 61 blank). 22cm. (Living poets series ; no. 19). c.1978. Dragon's Teeth Press.

Rhodes, James

--The Way of Charles Speaks Soft. LC 78-160107. 112 p. 22cm. 1972. (ISBN 0-200-71852-5). Criterion Books.

Rhodes, Nelson, jt. auth. see Arrowsmith, Donald Pogue.

Rhodes, Neva E.

--Jimbo, the Monkey. Foster, Celeste K., illus. LC 70-94999. 32p. col. illus. 29cm. c.1970. T. S. Denison.

Rhodes, Rhoda J.

--Mrs. Classandruzzi Reads a Story. N.D. Carlton Press Inc.

Rhodin, Eric Nolan (1916-)

--The Good Greenwood. LC 72-150382. 123 p. 21cm. 1971. (ISBN 0-664-32495-9). Westminster Press.

--Hideout at Winter House. LC 74-110083. 144 p. 21cm. 1970. Westminster Press.

--The Sinister Affair. LC 73-1955. 160 p. 22cm. 1973. (ISBN 0-664-32530-0). Westminster Press.

Rhoscomyl, Owen

--A Scout's Story. (Illus.). N.D. Dana Estes & Co.

Rhymes-Yannotta, Judy

--Adventure in Bear Country. 59p. (gr. 6-8). 1978. Dorrance.

Rhys, Brian, tr. see Guillot, Rene.

Rhys, Ernest, ed. see Abbott, Jacob.

Rhys, Ernest, ed. see Alcott, Louisa May.

Rhys, Ernest, ed. see Andersen, Hans Christian.

Rhys, Ernest, ed. see Canton, William.

Rhys, Ernest, jt. ed. see Dalgliesh, Alice.

Rhys, Ernest, ed. see Dickens, Charles John Huffam.

Rhys, Ernest, ed. see Dodge, Mary Elizabeth Mapes, Mrs.

Rhys, Ernest, ed. see Ewing, Juliana Horatia Gatty, Mrs.

Rhys, Ernest, ed. see Hughes, Thomas.

Rhys, Ernest, ed. see Jefferies, Richard.

Rhys, Ernest, jt. ed. see Kingsley, Charles.

Rhys, Ernest, ed. see Kingston, William Henry Giles.

Rhys, Ernest, ed. see Lamb, Charles (1775-1834) & Lamb, Mary Ann.

Rhys, Ernest, ed. see Marryat, Frederick.

Rhys, Ernest, ed. see Reid, Thomas Mayne.

Rhys, Ernest, ed. see Verne, Jules.

Rhys, Ernest, ed. see Wyss, Johann David Von.

Rhys, Ernest, ed. see Yonge, Charlotte Mary.

Rhys, Ernest (1859-1946), ed.

--Aesop Fables. L'Estrange, Roger, tr. N.D. P. Dutton & Co.

--AEsop's Fables: An Anthology of the Fabulists of All Countries. xxiv, 231, 1 p. 17 cm. (Half-title: Everyman's library, ed. by Ernest Rhys. For young people. no. 657). 1913. J. M. Dent & Sons, Ltd.

--The English Fairy Books. Witney, Frederic C., illus. 21 cm. 318p. 1916. F. A. Stokes & Company.

--Fairy Gold: A Book of Old English Fairy Tales. LC 77-114912. (Illus.). xiv, 303 p. 23cm. (Library of Old English and medieval literature). 1970. Books for Libraries Press.

--Fairy Gold: A Book of Old English Fairy Tales. xiv p., 1 l., 305. 1 p. incl. illus., plates. 17 1/2 cm. (Half-title: Everyman's library, ed. by Ernest Rhys. For young poeple). 1907. J. M. Dent & Co.

--Fairy-Gold: A Book of Old English Fairy Tales. Cole, Herbert, illus. LC 7-35196. xvi, 474 p., 1 l. col. front., illus., plates (part col.) 20 cm. 1906. J. M. Dent & Co,.

--The New Golden Treasury of Songs and Lyrics. 17 cm. 329p. 1914. E. P. Dutton.

Rhys, Ernest (1859-1946) & Rhys, Grace Little, Mrs. (1865-1929)

--English Fairy Tales. Tilney, Frederick Colin, ed. Cole, Herbert & Bell, R. Anning, illus. 18 cm. 128p. (Tales for Children from Many Lands). 1916. E. P. Dutton.

Rhys, Grace Little, Mrs., jt. auth. see Rhys, Ernest.

Rhys, Grace Little, Mrs. (1865-1929), ed.

--A Children's Garland of Verse. N.D. E. P. Dutton & Co.

--The Children's Garland of Verse. Robinson, Charles (1870-1937), illus. LC 79-51958. (Illus.). xxi, 296 p., 7 leaves of plates. 20cm. (Granger Poetry Library). 1979. (ISBN 0-89609-200-3). Granger Book Co.

--The Children's Garland of Verse. Robinson, Charles (1870-1937), illus. LC 21-26989. xxi p., 1 l., 296 p. 8 col. pl. (incl. front.) 20 cm. 1921. J. M. Dent & Sons Ltd.

--Cradle Songs and Nursery Rhymes. LC 1-12530. xxiii, 275 p. 14 1/2 cm. (Half-title: The Canterbury poets). 1894. W. Scott, Limited.

--In Wheelabout and Cockalone. Tarrant, Margaret Winifred (1888-) & Rhys, Megan, illus. 238p. 1918. Frederick A. Stokes.

Rhys, Mimpsy

--Mr. Hermit Crab: A Tale for Children by a Child. Sewell, Helen Moore (1896-1957), illus. Barnicle, Mary Elizabeth, intro. by. LC 29-22917. xv p., 1 l., 190 p. incl. illus., plates. col. front. 22 cm. 1929. The Macmillan Co.

Ribbons, Ian (1924-)

--Monday, Twenty-One October Eighteen-Five: The Day of Trafalgar. Ribbons, Ian (1924-), illus. LC 75-353176. (Illus.). 80p. 1968. Oxford University Press.

Ribianszky, Alexandra, tr. see Kormos, Istvan.

Ricchiuti, Paul Burton (1925-)

--Elijah Jeremiah Phillip's Great Journey. Larkin, Howard C., illus. (Illus.). 34p. 23cm. 1975. Pacific Press Pub. Association.

--General Lee. (Uplook Ser.). 1978. (ISBN 0-8163-0198-0). Pacific Pr Pub Assn.

--I Found a Feather. Larkin, Howard C., illus. LC 67-24371. (Illus.). 1 v. 23cm. 32p. 1967. Pacific Press Pub. Association.

--Jimmy & the Great Balloon. (Uplook Ser.). 1978. (ISBN 0-8163-0204-9). Pacific Pr Pub Assn.

--Let's Play Make-Believe. Larkin, Howard C., illus. (Illus.). 33p. 23cm. 1975. Pacific Press Pub Association.

--Mandy. (Uplook Ser.). 1978. (ISBN 0-8163-0206-5). Pacific Pr Pub Assn.

--Mike. (Uplook Ser.). 1978. (ISBN 0-8163-0207-3). Pacific Pr Pub Assn.

--Up in the Air. Larkin, Howard C., illus. (ps-k). N.D. Pacific Pr Pub Assn.

--When You Open Your Bible. Larkin, Howard C., illus. LC 67-18008. 1 v. (unpaged) col. illus. 23 cm. 1967. Pacific Press Pub. Association.

--Whose House Is It?. (Hello World Ser.). 1967. (ISBN 0-8163-0308-8). Pacific Pr Pub Assn.

Ricciuti, Edward Raphael (1938-)

--An Animal for Alan. Eaton, Tom (1940-), illus. LC 74-105460. (Illus.). 5 7/8 x 8 1/2. 64p. (18 pt.). (Nature I Can Read Bks.). (gr. k-3). 1970. (ISBN 0-06-024987-0, HarpJ). Har-Row.

--Catch a Whale by the Tail. Moss, Geoffrey, illus. LC 72-77938. (Illus.). 5 7/8 x 8 1/2. 64p. (18 pt.). (Nature I Can Read Bks.). (gr. k-3). 1969. (ISBN 0-06-024989-7, HarpJ). Har-Row.

--Donald & the Fish That Walked. Hoff, Sydney (1912-), illus. LC 74-2609. (Illus.). 5 7/8 x 8 1/2. 64p. (18 pt.). (Nature I Can Read Bks.). (gr. k-3). 1974. (ISBN 0-06-024998-6, HarpJ). (ISBN 0-06-024997-8). Har-Row.

Rice, Alice Caldwell Hegan, Mrs. (1870-1942)

--Captain June. LC 7-29097. 5 p. l., 3-120 p. incl. 8 pl. front. 20 cm. 1907. The Century Co.

--Mrs. Wiggs of the Cabbage Patch. 153p. N.D. Cassell & Co.

--Mrs. Wiggs of the Cabbage Patch. (Illus.). ca. 250p. (Thrushwood Bks.). (gr. 5-11). 1970. (ISBN 0-448-02523-X). G&D.

--Mrs. Wiggs of the Cabbage Patch. Repr. of 1901 ed. (gr. 7-9). 1935. Hawthorn.

--Mrs. Wiggs of the Cabbage Patch. Brindl, Helen M., ed. (Appleton Modern Literature Se.). 1935. Appleton-Century-Crofts.

Rice, Alice Hamilton

--Lois and Her Children. 228p. N.D. Pilgrims Press.

--The Story Hour Series, 6 vols. N.D. Pilgrims Press.

--The Story of Jesus as Told by Grandfather John. LC 1-29232. 264p. c.1900. R. R. Donnelley & Sons Co.

Rice, Alice R.

--The Goodship Friendship. (gr. 3-6). 1981. (ISBN 0-86653-031-2). Good Apple.

Rice, Anna L, jt. auth. see Ketchum, Irma A.

Rice, Arthur Leslie (1890-)

--The Magic Glasses: A Children's Fantasy. LC 52-13888. 63p. 23cm. 1953. Vantage Press.

Rice, Carrie Shaw

--In Childland Straying. 3d ed. LC 34-3799. 3 p. l., 11-70 p. front. (port.) 20 1/2 x 17 1/2 cm. 1895. Vaughan & Morrill Printing Co.

Rice, Charles Duane (1910-1971)

--The Little Dog Who Wore Earmuffs. Saxon, Charles D., illus. LC 57-100727. unpaged. illus. 24cm. 1957. Dodd, Mead.

--Minty's Magic Garden. Saxon, Charles D., illus. LC 54-9233. unpaged. illus. 24cm. 1954. Dodd, Mead.

Rice, Dorothy

--The Gypsy Laddie. Rice, Dorothy, illus. LC 75-156794. (Illus.). 32 p. 24cm. 1st U.S. edition. 1972. Atheneum.

Rice, Earle, Jr.

--The Animals. LC 78-72323. (Illus.). (Pacesetters Ser.). (gr. 4 up). 1979. (ISBN 0-516-02181-8). Childrens.

--The Animals. Sanford, Jim, illus. LC 78-72323. (Illus.). 58 p. 18cm. (Pacemaker bestellers book). c.1979. (ISBN 0-8224-5361-4). Fearon Pitman Publishers.

--Death Angel. Porcuna, Ramon, illus. LC 80-65913. (Illus.). 73 p. 18cm. (TaleSpinners I). (Pacemaker book). c.1981. (ISBN 0-8224-6729-1). Fearon Education.

--Fear on Ice. LC 80-82984. (Illus.). 64p. (SporTellers Ser.). (gr. 4 up). 1981. (ISBN 0-516-02262-8). Childrens.

--Tiger, Lion, Hawk. LC 77-81595. (Illus.). 64p. (Pacesetters Ser.). (gr. 4 up). 1978. (ISBN 0-516-02173-7). Childrens.

Rice, Edward

--Mother India's Children. 1971. (ISBN 0-394-82036-3). Pantheon Books.

Rice, Elizabeth (1913-)

--Benje, the Squirrel Who Lost His Tail. Rice, Elizabeth (1913-), illus. LC 79-82115. (Illus.). 32 p. 25cm. 1969. (ISBN 0-516-03417-0). Childrens Press.

--Henry and Benjamin. Rice, Elizabeth (1913-), illus. LC 77-110692. (Illus.). 32 p. 24cm. 1970. Steck-Vaughn.

--I'm Alvin. Rice, Elizabeth (1913-), illus. LC 67-1512. (Illus.). 32 p. 24cm. 1967. Steck-Vaughn Co.

--Jacki. Rice, Elizabeth (1913-), illus. LC 72-82116. (Illus.). 32 p. 25cm. 1969. Childrens Press.

--Who-Oo-Oo!. Rice, Elizabeth (1913-), illus. LC 78-176069. (Illus.). 32 p. 24cm. 1972. (ISBN 0-8114-7741-X). Steck-Vaughn Co.

--Yippy. Rice, Elizabeth (1913-), illus. LC 77-139287. (Illus.). 32 p. 25cm. 1971. (ISBN 0-8114-7718-5). Steck-Vaughn Co.

Rice, Ethel M

--Wiggle and Waggle: The Story of the Cuddley Kitten and Pedigreed Pup. Kay, Albert, illus. LC 42-332360. 28 p. illus. (part col.) 28 1/2 cm. 1939. S. Gabriel Sons & Company.

Rice, Eve Hart (1951-), adapted by see Aesopus.

Rice, Eve Hart (1951-)

--Benny Bakes a Cake. Rice, Eve Hart (1951-), illus. LC 80-17313. p. cm. c.1981. (ISBN 0-688-80312-1). (ISBN 0-688-84312-3). Greenwillow Books. **Award: (ALA).**

--Ebbie. Rice, Eve Hart (1951-), illus. LC 75-11688. p. cm. 1975. (ISBN 0-688-80017-3). (ISBN 0-688-84017-5). Greenwillow Books.

--Ebbie. Rice, Eve Hart (1951-), illus. LC 77-12313. (Illus.). 32 p. (Picture puffin). 1978, c.1975. (ISBN 0-14-050273-4). Penguin Books.

--Goodnight, Goodnight. Rice, Eve Hart (1951-), illus. LC 79-17253. (Illus.). 31 p. 26cm. 1980. (ISBN 0-688-80259-1). (ISBN 0-688-84254-2). Greenwillow Books. **Award: (ALA).**

--Goodnight, Goodnight. Rice, Eve Hart (1951-), illus. LC 83-61188. p. cm. 1983. (ISBN 0-14-050386-2). Puffin Books.

Rideout, Jacob Barzilla, Mrs.
--Early Western Life. LC 12-38090. 208 p. front., plates. 18 cm. c.1887. Presbyterian Board of Publication and Sabbath-School Work.
Rider, Alex
--A La Ferme: At the Farm. Seltzer, Isadore, illus. (gr. 2-5). 1962. (ISBN 0-385-06520-5). Doubleday.
Rider, Brett, pseud., see Gooden, Arthur Henry.
Rides At The Door, pseud. & Blackfeet Heritage Program
--Napi Stories. Davis, Darnell. De Marce, Roxanne, ed. LC 79-54097. (Illus.). 38 p. 22cm. c.1979. Blackfeet Heritage Program.
Ridge, Antonia Florence, jt. auth. see Bouhuys, Mies.
Ridge, Antonia Florence (0000-1981)
--Jan and His Clogs. Freeman, Barbara Constance (1906-), illus. LC 51-14800. unpaged. illus. 22 x 28 cm. 1952. Roy Publishers.
--Never Run from the Lion, and Another Story. LC 59-16368. 67p. illus. 22cm. 1959. H. Z. Walck.
--Rom-Bom-Bom, and Other Stories. Thompson, Ralph, illus. LC 64-1010. 90 p. illus. 20 cm. (Puffin books, PS203). 1963, c.1946. Penguin Books.
Ridge, Antonia Florence (0000-1981) & Bouhuys, Mies
--Hurray for a Dutch Birthday. Willett, Jillian, illus. (Illus.). (ps-5). N.D. (ISBN 0-571-06025-0). Faber & Faber.
--The Little Red Pony. Wilde, Dick, illus. 1962. Bobbs Merrill.
--Little Red Pony. Wilde, Dick, illus. (Illus.). (gr. 3-5). 1962. (ISBN 0-8382-0469-4). Hale.
--Melodia: The Dutch Street-Organ. Wood, Leslie (1920-), illus. (Illus.). (ps-5). N.D. (ISBN 0-571-08721-3). Faber & Faber.
Ridge, Delores F., ed. see Matanah.
Ridge, Lola
--Sun Up. N.D. B W Huebsch.
Ridgway, Marion V.
--First Steps. Hopkins, Hildegarde L., illus. LC 43-17318. 24p. col. ill. 15 x 19cm. 1943. Howell Soskin.
--How Far?. Smith, Helen, illus. LC 45-5084. (Illus.). 39p. (gr. k-3). 1945. David McKay Co.
--What's Coming. Paflin, Roberta, pseud. (1903-), illus. Petty, Roberta Harris Pfaflin. LC 44-322. 21 p. col. illus. 18cm. 1944. Howell Soskin.
Ridle, Julia Brown (1923-)
--Hog Wild. Shortall, Leonard W., illus. LC 61-12089. 232p. 21cm. 1961. Harper & Row.
--Hog Wild!. Shortall, Leonard W., illus. (Illus.). 232 p. 22cm. (Harper Trophy book). 1975. (ISBN 0-06-440068-9). Harper & Row.
--Mohawk Gamble. LC 63-8003. 209 p. illus. 22 cm. 1963. Harper & Row.
Ridley, Annie E.
--Bible Pictures and Stories for Little Folks. (Illus.). N.D. Cassell, Petter, Galpin.
Ridley, M. L.
--The Three Chums. N.D. Thomas Whittaker.
--Walter Alison: His Friends and Foes. N.D. Thomas Whittaker.
Ridlon, Marci, pseud., see Balterman, Marci Ridlon.
Ridlon, Marci, pseud. (1942-)
--A Frog Sandwich: Riddles & Jokes. Balterman, Marci Ridlon. Dypold, Pat, illus. LC 73-81994. (Illus.). 30 p. 21cm. (Follett Beginning to Read Book. Level 3). 1973. (ISBN 0-695-80417-0). (ISBN 0-695-80417-0). Follett.
--The Strange Hotel: Five Ghost Stories. Balterman, Marci Ridlon. Sumichrast, Jozef (1948-), illus. LC 74-83609. (Illus.). 32 p. 21cm. (Follett Beginning-to-Read Book). c.1975. (ISBN 0-695-40517-9). (ISBN 0-695-30517-4). Follett Pub. Co.
--That Was Summer. Balterman, Marci Ridlon. Carpenter, Mia, illus. LC 69-10256. (Illus.). 80 p. 21cm. 1969. Follett Pub. Co.
--Woodsey Log Library. Balterman, Marci Ridlon, 4 bks. Szekeres, Cyndy (1933-), illus. (Illus.). 128p. (ps-1). 1981. Boxed Set. (ISBN 0-394-84911-6). Random.
Ridyard, David
--Grandpa Loves Us. north american ed. Gully, Jim, photos by. LC 85-17357. p. cm. (Growing up). c.1985. (ISBN 0-918831-17-2). (ISBN 0-918831-40-7). Gareth Stevens Pub.
--Sometimes I Have to. north american ed. Gully, Jim, photos by. LC 85-17356. p. cm. (Growing up). 1985. (ISBN 0-918831-44-X). (ISBN 0-918831-16-4). Gareth Stevens Pub.
Riedel, Gustav
--Blind William, 1 of 6, Vol. 4. (American Youth's Library). N.D. Claxton, Remsen, & Haffelfinger.
Riegel, Mary E
--The Adventures of Bo. N.D. Carlton Press.
Rienow, Leona Train (1903-1983)
--The Bewitched Caverns. Pope, Allen, illus. LC 48-6252. 151 p. illus. 21 cm. 1948. C. Scribner's Sons.
--The Dark Pool. Pope, Allen, illus. LC 49-7766. 149 p. illus. 21 cm. 1949. C. Scribner's Sons.
Ries, Vera see Lear, Edward.
Riesenberg, Felix, Jr. (1913-1962)
--Balboa, Swordsman and Conquistador;. Rojankovsky, Feodor Stepanovich (1891-1970), illus. LC 56-9466. 178p. illus. 22cm. (World landmark books, W-25). 1956. Random House.
--Bob Graham at Sea. Cartwright, Charles E., illus. LC 25-17065. viii, 337 p. front., illus. 21 cm. c.1925. Harcourt, Brace and Company.
--The Crimson Anchor: A Sea Mystery. LC 48-6373. 207 p. 21 cm. (A Junior Red badgemystery). 1948. Dodd, Mead.
--Full Ahead!. A Career Story of the American Merchant Marine. LC 41-19636. ix p., 1 l., 276 p. 21 cm. (Career books). 1941. Dodd, Mead & Company.
--Galapagos Bound!. Smuggling in the Tuna Fleet. LC 47-2148. 5 p. l., 161 p. 21 cm. 1947. Dodd, Mead & Company.
--The Man on the Raft. LC 45-7646. 4 p. l., 192 p. plans on fold. 1. 19 cm. 1945. Dodd, Mead & Company.
--The Mysterious Sailor: A Sea Adventure. LC 49-10276. 210 p. 21 cm. (Junior Red badge mysterie). 1949. Dodd, Mead.
--The Phantom Freighter. LC 44-3824. vii, 2 180 p. illus. (map) 20 1/2 cm. 1944. Dodd, Mead & Company.
--Salvage: A Modern Sea Story. LC 42-19435. vii p., 1 l., 220 p. 20 1/2 cm. 1942. Dodd, Mead & Company.
--The Undercover Sloop. LC 62-11994. 176p. 21cm. 1962. Westminster Press.
--The Vanishing Steamer. LC 58-5556. 224 p. 21cm. 1958. Westminster Press.
Riesner, Charles Francis
--Little Inch-High People. Wolfe, George, illus. LC 38-4096. 9 p. l., 7-97 p. illus., col. plates. 26 cm. c.1937. Junior Progress, Inc.
Rietci, Rita Krohne see Ritchie, Rita, pseud.
Rietveld, Jane Klatt (1913-)
--A B C Molly. (gr. 3-5). N.D. G&D.
--ABC Molly. Rietveld, Jane Klatt (1913-), illus. LC 66-107802. 89p. illus. 23cm. c.1966. Norton.
--Great Lakes Sailor. Rietveld, Jane Klatt (1913-), illus. LC 52-12805. 188p. illus. 21cm. 1952. Viking Press.
--Monkey Island. Rietveld, Jane Klatt (1913-), illus. (Illus.). (gr. k-3). 1963. (ISBN 0-670-48614-0). (ISBN 0-670-48615-9). Viking Pr.
--Nicky's Bugle. Rietveld, Jane Klatt (1913-), illus. LC 47-24294. 56 p. illus. 26 cm. 1947. Viking Press.
--Rocky Point Campers. Rietveld, Jane Klatt (1913-), illus. LC 50-10310. 94p. illus. 24cm. 1950. Viking Press.
--Roly & Poly. N.D. E. M. Hale & Co.
--Roly and Poly. Rietveld, Jane Klatt (1913-), illus. LC 56-4069. (Illus.). 26 cm. 44p. 1956. Viking Press.
--To Hide, to Seek. LC 57-14112. 251p. 22cm. 1957. Viking Press.
--Wild Dog. LC 53-12935. 189p. illus. 23cm. 1953. Wilcox and Follett.
Rieu, Emile Victor (1887-)
--The Flattered Flying Fish and Other Poems. 1st ed. Shepard, Ernest Howard (1879-1976), illus. LC 62-18691. (Illus.). 101 p. 20cm. 1962. Dutton.
Rieu, Nelly
--The Reckless Seven. Burns, Eloise (1904-), illus. LC 30-20166. 6 p. l., 299 p. incl. col. front., illus., plates. 19 cm. 1930. The Macmillan Company.
Riffel, Maria, tr. see Carver, Marjorie Reineman.
Rifkin, Natalie, ed. see LaBastille, Anne.
Rigby, Douglas
--Moustachio. 1947. E M Hale.
--Moustachio. Duvoisin, Roger Antoine (1904-1980), illus. 31 p. col. illus. 27 cm. 1947. Harper.
Rigby, Reginald
--The Absurd Story of James. (Illus.). N.D. Frederick A. Stokes.
--Mother Goose Cooked. (Illus.). 1900. John Lane.
Rigby, Shirley Lincoln
--Smaller Than Most. Carter, Debby L., illus. LC 85-42636. p. cm. c.1985. (ISBN 0-06-025027-5). (ISBN 0-06-025028-3). Harper & Row.
Rigg, H. K., ed.
--Tales from the Skipper. (Illus.). 256p. 1968. (ISBN 0-8271-6808-X). Barre Publishers.
Riggs, Constance Kakavecos
--Sam Shue and the Seven Satchels. Seymour, Gabriel (1958-), illus. LC 76-1480. (Illus.). 64 p. 22cm. (ps-4). 1977, c.1976. (ISBN 0-915998-02-5). Lime Rock Press.
Riggs, Dorothy A.
--Henry. (gr. 4-7). N.D. Carlton.
Riggs, Eleanor
--Stories from Lands of Sunshine. LC 4-16265. 4 p. l., 11-155 p. illus. 20 cm. 1904. University Publishing Company.
Riggs, Frances, jt. auth. see Means, Florence Crannell, Mrs.
Riggs, G. C. Mrs. see Wiggin, Kate Douglas Smith.
Riggs, G. C. Mrs. see Wiggin, Kate Douglas Smith (1856-1923) & Wilkins, Mrs.
Riggs, G. C. Mrs. see Smith, Nora Archibald (1859-1934) & Wiggin, Kate Douglas Smith.
Riggs, G. C. Mrs. see Wiggin, Kate Douglas Smith (1856-1923) & Smith, Nora.
Riggs, G. C. Mrs. see Wiggin, Kate Douglas Smith (1856-1923) & Smith, Nora Archibald.
Riggs, Ida Berry
--Little Champion. Merwin, Decie (1894-1961), illus. LC 44-9753. v, 7-144 p. illus. 21 1/2 cm. 1944. The Macmillan Company.
Riggs, Rene C.
--Animal Stories From Eskimo Land. N.D. Frederick A. Stokes.
--Igloo Tales From Eskimo Land. N.D. Frederick A. Stokes.
Riggs, Sidney Noyes
--Arrows and Snakeskin. LC 62-9327. 192p. illus. 21cm. 1962. Lippincott.
Riggs, Strafford, ed.
--The Story of Beowulf: Retold from the Ancient Epic. Pitz, Henry Clarence (1895-1976), illus. LC 33-32232. 5 p. l., 84 p. incl. front., illus. (part col.) 25 x 22 cm. c.1933. D. Appleton-Century Company, Incorporated.
Righter, Linwood Layton (1881-)
--Chatt Roland: A Story of American Fish Pirates. Lee, Manning De Villeneuve (1894-1980), illus. LC 29-9996. N.D. Doubleday, Doran & Company, Inc.
--Five Fathoms of Silver. LC 31-30704. viii p., 1 l., 306 p. incl. pl. front. 21 cm. (windmill books). 1931. Doubleday, Doran & Company, Inc.
--Junior Starke, Poundman: An Adventure Story of the American Fish Pounds. Lee, Manning De Villeneuve (1894-1980), illus. LC 28-21824. viii p., 1 l., 306 p. incl. plan, diagr. col. front. 21 cm. 1928. Doubleday, Doran & Company, Inc.
Rigney, Francis Joseph (1882-), ed.
--What's the Joke?. Stories Boys Like. Salg, Bert N. & Neill, John Rea (1878-1943), illus. LC 32-23283. 126 p. incl. front., illus. 22 cm. c.1932. D. Appleton and Company.
Rigney, William J.
--Tiny and Her Vanity. LC 44-11922. 16p. illus. 24 1/2cm. (Fairy Tale Ser.). c.1892. McLoughlin Bros.
Rigsby, Howard (1909-)
--Voyage to Leandro. LC 39-23981. 4 p. l., 242 p. incl. plates (part double) front. 22 cm. 1939. Harper & Brothers.
Rigway, Marion V.
--Night-Night. N.D. Houghton Mifflin Co.
Riha, Bohumil (1907-)
--Ryn, the Wild Horse. 1st ed. Hanak, Mirko, illus. LC 76-86648. (Illus.). 102 p. 23cm. 1971, c.1966. Doubleday.
Rihbany, Abraham Mitrie
--A Far Journey. N.D. Houghton Mifflin.
--The Hidden Treasure of Rasmola. N.D. Houghton Mifflin Co.
Riis, Jacob August (1849-1914)
--Hero Tales of the Far North. 20 cm. 328p. (Macmillan's Juvenile Library). 1915. The Macmillan Co.
Rikhoff, J.
--The Quixote Anthology. N.D. (ISBN 0-448-00120-9, Universal Library). Grosset & Dunlap.
Riley, A. Lila
--Ruby;. Or, A Heart of Gold. 96 p. illus. 22 x 17 cm. c.1899. D. C. Cook Publishing Company.
Riley, Alice Cushing Donaldson, jt. auth. see Gaynor, Jessie Love Smith, Mrs.
Riley, Alice Cushing Donaldson, Mrs. (1867-)
--Let's Pretend: Four Half Hour Plays for Young People. LC 34-255483. 144 p. diagr. 20 cm. c.1934. Walter H. Baker Company.
--The Play's the Thing, for Children. LC 32-5738. ix, 131 p. col. illus. 20 cm. c.1932. The John C. Winston Company.
--The Voyage of the Wishbone Boat. Bridgman, Lewis Jesse (1857-1931), illus. LC 7-23466. 3 p. l., 11-205 p. col. front., plates (partly col.) 23 cm. c.1907. H. M. Caldwell Company.
--The Wishbone Boat. Bridgman, Lewis Jesse (1857-1931), illus. LC 2-260268. 11-205p. front., 5pl. 19cm. c.1906. H. M. Caldwell.
Riley, James Whitcomb (1849-1916)
--Afterwhiles. LC 3-14538. (Illus.). 19 cm. 1892. Bowen-Merrill Co.
--Afterwhiles: Poetry. LC 78-74511. Repr. of 1898 ed. (Children's Literature Reprint Ser.). (gr. 6 up). 1979. (ISBN 0-8486-0011-8). Core Collection.
--Armazindy. (Illus.). 19 cm. viii, 169p. 1894. Bowen-Merrill Co.
--Baby Ballads. New ed. Cotton, William, illus. 1915. Bobbs-Merrill.
--Book of Joyous Children. Vawter, Will, illus. LC 2-24265. (Illus.). 19 cm. xiv, 176p. 1902. Bobbs-Merrill Co.
--The Book of Joyous Children. Vawter, Will, illus. LC 79-98085. (Illus.). xiv, 176 p. 21cm. (Granger index reprint series). 1969. Books for Libraries Press.
--The Boy Lives on Our Farm. Betts, Ethel Franklin, illus. (Illus.). 29x26 cm. 18p. 1908. Bobbs-Merrill Co.
--The Boys of the Old Glee Club. Vawter, Will, illus. Booth, Franklin, designed by. (Illus.). 24cm. 27p. N.D. Bobbs-Merrill Co.
--A Child-World. LC 6-24741. (Illus.). 19 cm. 209p. 1897. Bowen-Merrill Co.
--A Defective Santa Claus. Relyea, Charles M. & Vawter, Will, illus. LC 4-35316. (Illus.). 20 cm. 77p. 1904. Bobbs-Merrill Co.
--A Defective Santa Claus. Vawter, Will & Relyea, Charles M., illus. 1915. Bobbs-Merill.
--A Defective Santa Claus: A Christmas Poem. Vawter, Will & Relyea, Charles M., illus. 1905. Bobbs-Merrill Co.
--A Discouraging Model. Christy, Howard Chandler (1873-1952), illus. N.D. Bobbs-Merrill Co.
--Doc Sifers. N.D. Bobbs-Merrill Co.
--Early Poems. N.D. Bobbs-Merrill Co.
--The Flying Islands of the Night. LC 3-16435. 19 cm. 88p. 1892. Bowen-Merrill Co.
--The Flying Islands of the Night. Franklin Booth ed. Booth, Franklin, illus. LC 13-22235. 26cm. 124p. 1913. Bobbs- Merrill Co.
--Fugitive Pieces. N.D. Bobbs-Merrill Co.
--The Girl I Loved. Christy, Howard Chandler (1873-1952) & Armstrong, Margaret, illus. LC 10-19397. (Illus.). 22 cm. 49p. 1910. Bobbs-Merrill Co.
--The Gobble-Uns 'll Git You If You Don't Watch Out!. James Whitcomb Riley's Little Orphant Annie. 1st ed. Schick, Joel (1945-), illus. LC 74-23110. (Illus.). 40 p. 23cm. 1975. (ISBN 0-397-31621-6). Lippincott.
--The Gobble-Uns'll Git You If You Don't Watch Out!. Schick, Joel (1945-), illus. LC 74-23110. (gr. 3-5). 1975. (ISBN 0-397-31621-6, JBL-J). Har-Row.
--The Golden Year. N.D. Bobbs-Merrill Co.
--Good-Bye, Jim. Christy, Howard Chandler (1873-1952) & Stuart, Bertha, illus. LC 14-2781. (Illus.). 20cm. 33p. 1913. Bobbs-Merrill Co.
--Green Fields and Running Brooks. LC 6-24742. 19 cm. 224p. 1893. Bobbs-Merrill Co.
--His Pa's Romance. Vawter, Will & Clay, John Cecil, illus. LC 3-29650. 18 cm. 168p. 1903. Bobbs-Merrill Co.
--Home Again with Me. Christy, Howard Chandler (1873-1952) & Booth, Franklin, illus. LC 8-26007. (Illus.). 22 cm. 49p. N.D. Bobbs-Merrill Co.
--Home-Folks. LC 6695. 19 cm. 106p. 1900. Bowen-Merrill Co.
--A Host of Children. Betts, Ethel Franklin, illus. LC 20-22863. (Illus.). 24 cm. 188p. 1920. Bobbs-Merrill Co.
--If You Don't Watch Out. Betts, Ethel Franklin, illus. 1915. Bobbs-Merrill.
--Joyful Poems for Children. Geer, Charles Hand (1922-) & Tate, Sally, illus. LC 60-14663. (Illus.). 157 p. 24cm. 1960. Bobbs-Merrill.
--Joyful Poems for Children. Tate, Sally, illus. LC 47-363. 138, 4 p. col. front., illus. col. plates. 22 1/2 cm. 1946. The Bobbs-Merrill Company.
--Little Orphant Annie. Betts, Ethel Franklin, illus. 1915. Bobbs-Merrill.
--Little Orphant Annie. Stanley, Diane (1943-), illus. LC 82-415. p. cm. 1983. (ISBN 0-399-20904-2). Putnam.
--Morning. N.D. Bobbs-Merrill Co.
--Neighborly Poems and Dialect Sketches. LC 10-1968. 20 cm. 219p. 1897. Bobbs-Merrill Co.
--Old-Fashioned Roses. LC 15-17456. 16 cm. 1889. Bobbs-Merrill Co.
--An Old Sweetheart of Mine. Christy, Howard Chandler (1873-1952) & Keep, Virginia, illus. LC 33-18546. (Illus.). 22 cm. 59p. 1902. Bobbs-Merrill Co.
--An Old Sweetheart of Mine. Christy, Howard Chandler (1873-1952) & Keep, Virginia, illus. LC 2-28774. (Illus.). 22 cm. 58p. 1922. Bobbs-Merrill Co.
--The Orphant Annie Book. Betts, Ethel Franklin, illus. LC 8-26008. 30 x 27cm. 30p. 1908. Bobbs-Merrill Co.
--Out to Old Aunt Mary's. LC 30-82654. 1903. Bobbs-Merrill Co.
--Out to Old Aunt Mary's. Christy, Howard Chandler (1873-1952) & Armstrong, Margaret, illus. LC 4-34548. 23cm. 50p. 1904. Bobbs-Merrill Co.
--Pipes of Pan at Zekesbury. LC 3-15990. (Illus.). 19 cm. 1891. Bobbs-Merrill Co.
--Poems Here at Home. N.D. Bobbs-Merrill Co.
--Poems Here at Home. Kemble, Edward Windsor (1861-1933), illus. LC 12-38035. (Illus.). 17 cm. 187p. 1893. Century Co.
--Poems of Childhood. Shinn, Everett (1876-1953), illus. N.D. Grosset & Dunlap.

Ritchie, Barbara Gibbons
--The Ghost That Haunted the House That Culpepper Built. Powers, Richard M. Gorman (1921-), illus. LC 68-16066. (Illus.). 64 p. 26cm. 1968. Viking Press.
--Ramon Makes a Trade. (Illus.). (gr. 2-4). 1959. (ISBN 0-8382-0690-5). Hale.
--Ramon Makes a Trade. Thollander, Earl Gustave (1922-), illus. LC 59-13838. (Illus.). 48p. (gr. 3-8). 1959. (ISBN 0-395-28055-9). Parnassus.
--To Catch a Mongoose. Thollander, Earl Gustave (1922-), illus. (Illus.). (gr. 3-6). 1964. Parnassus.
Ritchie, Eileen, retold by.
--Little Red Riding Hood. Serkin, Amalia, illus. LC 49-2005. 21 p. col. illus. 27 cm. (Chanticleer junior book). c.1948. Chanticleer Press.
--Little Red Riding Hood. Serkin, Amalia, illus. N.D. Garden City Publishing Co.
Ritchie, Jean
--Apple Seeds & Soda Straws. Bolognese, Donald Alan (1934-), illus. (Illus.). (gr. 4-6). 1965. (ISBN 0-8098-2043-9). Walck.
Ritchie, Jean, compiled by.
--Jean Ritchie's Swapping Song Book. Pickow, George, photos by. LC 52-9433. (Illus.). (gr. 4-7). 1964. (ISBN 0-8098-2374-8). Walck.
--The Swapping Song Book. Pickow, George, photos by. 1952. Oxford University Press.
Ritchie, Jean, compiled by see Tripp, Edward.
Ritchie, Jean, compiled by see Tripp, Edward & Fossner, A. K.
Ritchie, Jo-An
--Jonie and Her Soldier. Wheeler, Gerald, ed. LC 85-2473. 128p. (Orion Ser.). c.1985. (ISBN 0-8280-0249-5). Review and Herald Pub. Association.
--Jonie Goes to Academy. LC 78-21271. 124 p. 17cm. c.1979. (ISBN 0-8127-0193-3). Southern Pub. Association.
--Jonie Graduates. LC 78-27431. 128 p. 17cm. (Orion). c.1979. (ISBN 0-8127-0201-8). Southern Pub. Association.
--Jonie in Alaska. Wheeler, Gerald, ed. 128p. (Orig.). (Banner Ser.). 1985. (ISBN 0-8280-0250-9). Review & Herald.
--Jonie's Direct Line. LC 75-44644. 96 p. 21cm. (Crown book). c.1976. (ISBN 0-8127-0110-0). Southern Pub. Association.
Ritchie, Lily Munsell
--Adventures of Chicken Little Jane. Hubbard, Charles D., illus. (Chicken Little Jane Ser.). N.D. Barse & Hopkins.
--Chicken Little Jane. LC 18-18002. 306 p. incl. front., illus. plates. 20 cm. c.1918. Britton Publishing Company.
--Chicken Little Jane. LC 19-140851. 4 p. l., 11-390 p. incl. front., illus. plates. 20 cm. c.1919. Britton Publishing Company.
--Chicken Little Jane Comes to Town. Hubbard, Charles D., illus. (Chicken Little Jane Ser.). N.D. Barse & Hopkins.
--Chicken Little Jane in the Rockies. (Chicken Little Jane Ser.). N.D. Barse & Co.
--Chicken Little Jane on the "Big John". Hubbard, Charles D., illus. (Chicken Little Jane Ser.). N.D. Barse & Hopkins.
Ritchie, Rita, pseud., see Reitci, Rita Krohne.
Ritchie, Rita, pseud., see Rietci, Rita Krohne.
Ritchie, Rita, pseud. (1930-)
--The Enemy at the Gate. Reitci, Rita Krohne. 1st. ed. Bjorklund, Lorence F. (1913-1978), illus. LC 59-11500. 250p. 21cm. 1959. (ISBN 0-525-29318-3). Dutton.
--The Golden Hawks of Genghis Khan. Reitci, Rita Krohne. 1st ed. Bjorklund, Lorence F. (1913-1978), illus. LC 58-9567. (Illus.). 191 p. 22cm. 1958. Dutton.
--Ice Falcon. Reitci, Rita Krohne. LC 63-7987. (Illus.). 240 p. 21cm. 1963. Norton.
--Night Coach to Paris. Reitci, Rita Krohne. LC 70-99455. 247 p. 21cm. 1970. Norton.
--Pirates of Samarkand. Reitci, Rita Krohne. 1st ed. Jacques, Robin (1920-), illus. LC 67-5798. (Illus.). 158 p. 21cm. 1967. W. W. Norton.
--Rogue Whaler. Reitci, Rita Krohne. LC 66-2679. 300p. 21cm. c.1966. Norton.
--Secret Beyond the Mountains. Rietci, Rita Krohne. 1st. ed. LC 60-11862. (gr. 6-9). 1960. (ISBN 0-525-38958-X). Dutton.
--The Year of the Horse. Rietci, Rita Krohne. 1st ed. Bjorklund, Lorence F. (1913-1978), illus. LC 57-8965. 191p. illus. 21cm. 1957. (ISBN 0-525-43463-1). Dutton.
Ritchie, Ruth see Juline, Ruth Bishop, pseud.
Ritchie, Ruth (1900-)
--The Chewing Gum Trees. Juline, Ruth Bishop, pseud. Dickinson, Harlyn, illus. LC 50-11132. 122 p. col. illus. 21 cm. 1950. Lothrop, Lee & Shepard.
--The Lost Indian Treasure. Juline, Ruth Bishop, pseud. Hessemer, Betty, illus. LC 60-6627. 143p. illus. 21cm. 1960. Westminster Press.
--A Place for Johnny Bill. Juline, Ruth Bishop, pseud. Helms, Georgeanne, illus. LC 61-5553. 143p. illus. 21cm. 1961. Westminster Press.
Riter, Dorris
--Edge of Violence. (gr. 7-11). 1964. (ISBN 0-679-25040-9). McKay.
Ritson, Joseph (1752-1803), ed.
--The Adventures of Robin Hood. Browne, Gordon Frederick (1858-1932), illus. N.D. George Routledge & Sons.
--Gammer Gurton's Garland: Or, the Nursery Parnassus : a Choice Collection of Pretty Songs and Verses, for the Amusement of All Little Good Children Who Can Neither Read nor Run. LC 78-1736. 46 p. 23cm. 1978. (ISBN 0-8414-7389-7). Folcroft Library Editions.
--Gammer Gurton's Garland: Or, The Nursery Parnassus, a Choice Collection of Pretty Songs and Verses, for the Amusement of All Little Good Children, Who Can Neither Read nor Run. LC 73-22095. p. 1973. (ISBN 0-88305-562-7). Norwood Editions.
--Robin Hood's Adventures. N.D. David McKay.
Ritson, Joseph (1752-1803) & Lees, Jim, eds.
--Robin Hood: A Collection of all the Ancient Poems, Songs and Ballads. (Illus.). 240p. Repr. of 1823 ed. 1972. (ISBN 0-87471-101-0). Rownan and Littlefield.
Ritt, William & Gray, Clarence
--Brick Bradford in the City Beneath the Sea. (Adapted from the Newspaper Adventure Strip). 152 p. front., illus. (incl. map) 15 cm. c.1934. The Saalfield Publishing Company.
Rittenhouse, Constance & Vinton, Iris
--Abbie Higgins, Young Group Executive. LC 50-10890. 280p. (Dod, Mead Career Bks.). 1950. Dodd, Mead & Co.
Rittenhouse, Dicie M.
--The Two of Us. N.D. Fleming H. Revell Co.
Rittenhouse, Laura J.
--Mamma's Stories for Little People. 100p. N.D. National Temperance Society.
Ritter, Elizabeth Hart, Mrs. (1897-)
--Parasols Is for Ladies. MacKnight, Ninon (1908-), illus. Ninon, pseud. LC 41-258315. 5 p. l., 96, 1 p. illus., (part col.) 27 cm. c.1941. The John C. Winston Company.
--You Never Can Tell. Holland, Marion (1908-), illus. LC 47-2867. 28p. (A Story Parade Picture Book). 1947. Grosset & Dunlap.
Ritter, Mathilde, illus.
--In the Mouse's House. N.D. Laidlaw Bros.
Ritzinger, Wallie
--One Christmas Eve. Lyons, Dave, illus. LC 52-31436. 22p. N.D. Pageant Press, Inc.
Rivenburgh, Viola K.
--Tales of the Menehune, the Little Pixie Folk of Hawaii. Raleigh, Amanda E., illus. LC 80-128981. (Illus.). 48p. 1980. (ISBN 0-918146-19-4). (ISBN 0-918146-19-4). Peninsula WA.
Rivera, Carlos, tr. see Geisel, Theodor Seuss.
Rivera, Carlos, tr. see Gurney, Nancy Jack (1915-1973) & Gurney, T. Eric.
Rivera, Carlos, tr. see Lofting, Hugh John.
Rivera, Carlos, tr. see Palmer, Helen Marion.
Rivera, Carlos, tr. see Perkins, Albert Rogers.
Rivera, Edith Vonnegut
--Nora's Tale. LC 73-11744. (Illus.). 59 p. 28cm. 1973. (ISBN 0-87777-048-4). R. W. Baron.
Rivera, Geraldo
--Miguel Robles-So Far. 1st ed. Rivera, Edith Vonnegut, illus. LC 72-88172. (Illus.). 30 p. 22cm. 1973. (ISBN 0-15-253900-X). Harcourt Brace Jovanovich.
Rivers-Coffey, Rachel
--A Horse Like Mr. Ragman. LC 77-9241. 149 p. 22cm. c.1977. (ISBN 0-684-15167-7). Scribner.
Rivers, Jack, ed. see Durian, Wolf.
Rivers, Jim
--Roy Rogers and the Enchanted Canyon: An Original Story Featuring Roy Rogers, King of the Cowboys, the Famous Motion Picture, Radio, and Television Star, As the Hero. Authorized Ed. Schroeder, Roy, illus. LC 55-21028. 282p. illus. 21cm. c.1954. Whitman Pub. Co.
Rivers, Kay McClanahan (1944-)
--Jill Wins a Friend. Sommers, Linda, illus. LC 76-16021. (Illus.). 32 p. 25cm. (Kids in sports). c.1976. (ISBN 0-913778-59-1). Child's World.
Rivers, Laurel
--Little Dandy. LC 13-253274. 2 p. l., 7-35 p. 21 cm. 1913. Rex Publishing Co.
Rivers-Moore, Marion
--Farmer Baker. N.D. Transatlantic Arts, Inc.
Rivers, Tim
--Metaphysical Stories for Children. Rivers, Tim, illus. LC 73-128599. 101 p. illus. 23cm. c.1969. Saturn Press.
Rives, Amelie
--The Ghost Garden. N.D. Grosset & Dunlap.
Rives, Elsie
--Abraham, Man of Faith. McPheeters, William N., illus. LC 76-382767. (Illus.). 48 p. 24cm. (Biblearn series). c.1976. Broadman Press.
Rives, Hallie Erminie (1876-)
--The Child's Books of Dickens Stories. N.D. Bobbs-Merrill Co.
--Dickens Retold for Children. N.D. Bobbs-Merrill Co.
Rives, Hallie Erminie (1876-) & Forbush, Gabrielle Elliot
--The John Book. N.D. Beechhurst Press.
Rivkin, Ann
--The Time to Choose. (gr. 7-11). 1977. (ISBN 0-590-10347-4, Schol Trade Pap). Schol Bk Serv.
Riwkin-Brick, Anna (1908-1970)
--Eva Visits Noriko-San. LC 57-14080. (Illus.). unpaged. illus. 26cm. 1957. Macmillan.
Riwkin-Brick, Anna (1908-1970) & Lindgren, Astrid (1907-)
--Duck Lives in Holland. Riwkin-Brick, Anna (1908-1970), photos by. LC 63-1561. 22p. 22cm. 1963. Macmillan.
--Lilibet, Circus Child. Riwkin-Brick, Anna (1908-), photos by. LC 61-2476. unpaged. illus. 22cm. 1961. Macmillan,.
--Noy Lives in Thailand. (Illus.). 48 p. 22cm. (Children of the world books). 1967. Macmillan.
--Randi Lives in Norway. LC 65-20181. 1 v. (unpaged) illus. 23cm. c.1965. Macmillan.
Rizzato, Sergio, illus.
--Chinese Fairy Tales. Ponsot, Marie Birmingham, tr. LC 61-163012. 154p. illus. 35cm. (Deluxe golden book). c.1960. Golden Press.
--Chinese Fairy Tales. Ponsot, Marie Birmingham, tr. from Chinese. (Illus.). (gr. 4-6). 1974. (ISBN 0-307-66820-7, Golden Pr). Western Pub.
--Tales of India. Ponsot, Marie Birmingham, tr. 1961. Golden Press.
Rizzo, Jeff, jt. auth. see Landes, William-Alan.
Rizzoto, Flora M., jt. auth. see Streiber, William R.
Roa, Annia
--Peter Pelican-Pedro Pelicano. Henry, William, illus. LC 64-22715. (Illus.). (gr. k-4). 1974. (ISBN 0-87208-006-4). Island Pr.
Roach, Marilynne Kathleen (1946-), adapted by see Horatius Flaccus, Quintus.
Roach, Marilynne Kathleen (1946-)
--Encounters with the Invisible World: Being Ten Tales of Ghosts, Witches, & the Devil Himself in New England. Roach, Marilynne Kathleen (1946-), illus. LC 76-22186. (Illus.). 131 p. 21cm. c.1977. (ISBN 0-690-01277-2). Crowell.
--Encounters with the Invisible World: Being Ten Tales of Ghosts, Witches and the Devil Himself in New England. Roach, Marilynne Kathleen (1946-), illus. 1977. Harper.
--The Mouse and the Song. Low, Joseph (1911-), illus. LC 73-13877. (Illus.). 42 p. 24cm. 1974. (ISBN 0-8193-0721-1). (ISBN 0-8193-0721-1). Parents' Magazine Press.
--Presto: Or, The Adventures of a Turnspit Dog. Roach, Marilynne Kathleen (1946-), illus. LC 79-11746. (Illus.). vi, 148 p. 22cm. 1979. (ISBN 0-395-28269-1). Houghton Mifflin.
Roadknight, Mrs., selected by.
--Old-Fashioned Rhymes. LC 7-35197. 1906. Longmans Green & Co.
Roam, Pearl Sovern (1920-)
--Lost Herd. LC 64-15552. 90 p. 21 cm. 1964. Zondervan Pub House.
--Return of Spotted Eagle. LC 63-1853. 87 p. 21 cm. 1962. Zondervan Pub. House.
--Spotted Eagle. LC 60-2720. 89p. 20cm. 1960. Zondervan Pub. House.
Robb, Brian (1913-)
--Last of the Centaurs. (Illus.). (gr. k-4). 1979. (ISBN 0-233-97000-2). Andre Deutsch.
--My Grandmother's Djinn. Robb, Brian (1913-), illus. LC 77-351988. (Illus.). 32 p. 26cm. 1976. (ISBN 0-233-96779-6). Deutsch.
--My Grandmother's Djinn. Robb, Brian (1913-), illus. LC 77-22646. (Illus.). 32 p. 26cm. 1978, c.1976. (ISBN 0-8193-0917-6). (ISBN 0-8193-0918-4). Parents' Magazine Press.
--Twelve Adventures of the Celebrated Baron Munchausen. Robb, Brian (1913-), illus. (Illus.). (gr. 2 up). 1979. (ISBN 0-233-97019-3). Andre Deutsch.
Robb, Charles F. & Getz, Carl H.
--Red O'Leary Wins Out: The True Story of a Real Boy Detective. LC 27-211341. 287 p. incl. front., illus., plates. 20 cm. c.1927. J. H. Sears & Company, Inc.
Robbie, Dorothy & Hand, Desmond
--Alice in Wonderland. (The Adaptation Ser.). N.D. (ISBN 0-912262-19-2). Proscenium.
Robbins, Alan
--The Secret of the Gold Jaguar: A Solve-the-Puzzles Adventure Tale. LC 84-18344. (Illus.). 128 p. 24cm. c.1985. (ISBN 0-399-51116-4). Putnam.
Robbins, Eliza (1786-1853), ed.
--Class-Book of Poetry: For Use of Schools or Private Instruction. LC 40-37449. viii, 9-252 p. illus. 19 cm. 1852. D. Appleton and Company.
Robbins, Grace A
--High Take at Low Tide. LC 46-2188. 5 p. l., 3-242 p. incl. front. 19 cm. 1946. Rinehart & Company, Inc.
Robbins, Ken
--City Country: A Car Trip in Photographs. Robbins, Ken, illus. LC 85-40165. (Illus.). 32 p. 26cm. 1985. (ISBN 0-670-80743-5). Viking Kestrel.
--Views from a Car. LC 84-6048. p. cm. c.1984. Four Winds Press.
Robbins, Maria, retold by.
--My Favorite Teeny Tiny Strawberry Animal Story Library, 6 bks. Dawson, Diane, illus. LC 77-90037. (Illus.). (ps). 1978. Set. (ISBN 0-88470-077-1, Pub by One Strawberry). Larousse.
--My Very First Teeny Tiny Strawberry Paperback Library: Six Delightful and Charming Tales. Dawson, Diane, illus. LC 76-1502. (Illus.). 6 pamphlets (in case). 11cm. (Tiny Strawberry books). c.1976. One Strawberry, Inc. : Distributed by Larousse & Co.
Robbins, Orison (1878-)
--A Boy of the Old French West. Stecher, William Frederick (1864-), illus. LC 27-19316. 284 p. front., plates. 20 cm. c.1927. Lothrop, Lee & Shepard Co.
--Escaping the Mohawks: The Story of a Young Noble of New France. Stecher, William Frederick (1864-), illus. LC 29-194591. 352 p. front., plates. 20 cm. c.1929. Lothrop, Lee & Shepard Co.
Robbins, Richard S.
--Bible Stories in Action for Children. 1981. CSS Pub.
Robbins, Ruth (1917-)
--The Emperor & the Drummer Boy. Sidjakov, Nicolas (1924-), illus. LC 62-14073. (Illus.). (gr. 2-6). 1962. (ISBN 0-87466-043-2). (ISBN 0-87466-011-4). Parnassus. **Awards: (NYT); (ALA).**
--Harlequin & Mother Goose: Or, The Magic Stick. Sidjakov, Nicolas (1924-), illus. LC 65-22429. 1 v. (unpaged) col. illus. 26 cm. 1965. Parnassus Press.
--Ishi Last of His Tribe. (Illus.). 1964. (ISBN 0-87466-049-1). Parnassus Press.
--Taliesin and King Arthur. Robbins, Ruth (1917-), illus. LC 75-129540. (Illus.). 32 p. 21cm. 1970. Parnassus Press.
Robbins, Ruth (1917-), adapted by.
--Baboushka and the Three Kings. Sidjakov, Nicolas (1924-), illus. Sanks, Mary Clement, contrib. by. LC 60-15036. (Illus.). 28 p. c.1960. (ISBN 0-395-27673-X). Parnassus Press. **Awards: (RCM); (NYT); (ALA).**
--How the First Rainbow Was Made: An American Indian Tale. Robbins, Ruth (1917-), illus. 1980. Houghton.
--How the First Rainbow Was Made: An American Indian Tale. Robbins, Ruth (1917-), illus. LC 80-16482. (Illus.). 41 p. 24cm. 1980. (ISBN 0-395-29082-1). Parnassus Press.
Robbins, Sarah Stuart, Mrs. (1817-)
--Antonio and His Angel. (Illus.). N.D. Methodist Book Concern.
--Bab: Faithfulness, 1 of 6 vols. N.D. Set. Bradley & Woodruff.
--Babbette: Or, Faithfullness. LC 12-38115. 203 p. front. 18 cm. (Half-title: The Gillettes. v). c.1886. R. Carter and Brothers.
--Ben Philbrick Learning to be Helpful, 1 of 6 vols. (Illus.). (Rock Cove Ser.). N.D. Set. Methodist Bk Concern.
--Ben Philbrick Learning to Be Helpful. LC 12-381221. 215 p. front. 18 cm. (Half-title: Rock Cove series ... ii). c.1889. R. Carter and Brothers.
--Bert, the Enterprising, 1 of 6 vols. N.D. Set. Bradley & Woodruff.
--Bert, the Enterprising Boy. LC 12-38114. 230 p. front. 18 cm. (Half-title: The Gillettes. iv). c.1886. R. Carter and Brothers.
--Brentford Parsonage. LC 12-38101. 455 p. front. 18 cm. (The Highland Series, v. 4). 1876. R. Carter and Brothers.
--Brentwood Parsonage, 1 of 10 vols. (Illus.). (Dale & Hillside Stories Ser.). N.D. Set. Methodist Bk Concern.
--Busy Bees: Ledgeside Ser, 1 of 6 vols. N.D. Set. Bradley & Woodruff.
--Busy Bees: Or, Winter Evenings in Margaret Russel's School. LC 12-38132. vi. 7-391 p. front., plates. 18 cm. (Ledgeside series, iii). 1870. R. Carter & Brothers.
--Butterfly at Mount Mansfield, 1 of 6 vols. (Illus.). 181p. (Butterfly's Flights Ser.). N.D. Set. Robert Carter & Brothers.
--Butterfly at Niagara, 1 of 6 vols. (Illus.). 230p. (Butterfly's Flights Ser.). N.D. Set. Robert Carter & Brothers.
--Butterfly at Saratoga, 1 of 6 vols. (Illus.). 224p. (Butterfly's Flights Ser.). N.D. Set. Robert Carter & Brothers.
--Butterfly at the Seaside, 1 of 6 vols. (Illus.). 224p. (Butterfly's Flights Ser.). N.D. Set. Robert Carter & Brothers.
--Butterfly in Philadelphia, 1 of 6 vols. (Illus.). 220p. (Butterfly's Flights Ser.). N.D. Set. Robert Carter & Brothers.
--Butterfly's Trip to Montreal, 1 of 6 vols. (Illus.). 237p. (Butterfly's Flights Ser.). N.D. Set. Robert Carter & Brothers.
--Christie: Or, Where the Tree Fell, 1 of 4 vols. (Aunty May's Children). N.D. Set. Methodist Bk Concern.
--Clifton Rice. N.D. Alfred Martien.

AUTHOR INDEX ROBERTS, JACK

--Clifton Rice: Or, Thou God Seest Me. LC 76-371849. (Illus.). 278 p., 3 leaves of plates. 16cm. 1865. J. S. Claxton.
--Comfort Strong, 1 of 10 vols. (Illus.). (Dale & Hillside Stories Ser.). N.D. Set. Methodist Bk Concern.
--Comfort Strong. LC 12-38102. 381 p. front. 18 cm. (The Highland Series, v. 5). 1876. R. Carter and Brothers.
--Conant Farm, 1 of 6 vols. (Ledgeside Ser.). N.D. Set. Bradley & Woodruff.
--Conant Farm. LC 12-38133. 345 p. front., plates. 18 cm. (Publisher's lettering: Ledgeside series. v). 1871. R. Carter and Brothers.
--Dan the Missionary, 1 of 6 vols. (The Gillette Ser.). N.D. Bradley & Woodruff.
--Dave Philbrick: The Boy with His Foot in the Stirrup, 1 of 6 vols. (Illus.). (Rock Cove Ser.: Vol. 4). N.D. Set. Methodist Bk Concern.
--Dick, Captain of the Family Ship. (Illus.). N.D. Methodist Book Concern.
--Dick, the Captain of the Family Ship. LC 12-381113. 199 p. front. 18 cm. (Half-title: The Gillettes. i). c.1885. R. Carter and Brothers.
--Doors Outward, 1 of 10 vols. (Illus.). (Dale & Hillside Stories Ser.). N.D. Set. Methodist Bk Concern.
--Doors Outward. A Tale. LC 12-38103. vi, 7-404 p. front. 18 cm. (The highland series, v. 3). 1875. R. Carter and Brothers.
--Dorothy Ottley: Winning by Love, 1 of 6 vols. (Illus.). (Rock Cove Ser.: Vol. 3). N.D. Set. Methodist Bk Concern.
--Dorothy Ottley Winning by Love. LC 12-381238. 222 p. front. 18 cm. (Half-title: Rock Cove series ... iii). c.1889. R. Carter and Brothers.
--Down the Steps, 1 of 6 vols. (Ledgeside Ser.). N.D. Set. Bradley & Woodruff.
--Down the Steps. LC 12-38134. 409 p. front., plates. 18 cm. (Publisher's lettering: Ledgeside series. vi). 1871. R. Carter and Brothers.
--Edged Tools. (Green Mountain Stories: Vol. 5). N.D. Robert Carter & Brothers.
--Ernest: Or, No Humbug, 1 of 4 vols. (Aunty May's Children Ser.). N.D. Set. Methodist Bk Concern.
--Faith, the Cripple, 1 of 4 vols. (Aunty May's Children). N.D. Set. Methodist Bk Concern.
--Faith Thurston's Work, 1 of 10 vols. (Illus.). (Dale & Hillside Stories Ser.). N.D. Set. Methodist Bk Concern.
--Faith Thurston's Work and How She Did It, 1 of 6 vols. LC 12-38104. v, 6-329 p. 19 cm. 1884. R. Carter & Brothers.
--Faithful and True: Or, The Evans Family. LC 12-381304. 368 p. front., plates. 18 cm. (The Win and Wear Series, v. 3). 1864. R. Carter & Brothers.
--Girding on the Armor. (Illus.). 362p. 1905. American Tract Society.
--Gladys Philbrick: How She was Made Great, 1 of 6 vols. (Illus.). (Rock Cove Ser.: Vol. 1). N.D. Set. Methodist Bk Concern.
--Gladys Philbrick: How She Was Made Great. LC 12-381211. 204 p. front. 28 cm. (Half-title: Rock cove series, i). c.1889. R. Carter and Brothers.
--Grandfather's Nell, 1 of 6 vols. (Ledgeside Ser.). N.D. Set. Bradley & Woodruff.
--Grandfather's Nell: Or, What Hapened at the Toll-Gate. 2 p. l., 7-363 p. front., plates. 18 cm. (Ledgeside series. iv). 1869. R. Carter and Brothers.
--Hester Trueworthy, 1 of 10 vols. (Illus.). (Dale & Hillside Stories Ser.). N.D. Set. Methodist Bk Concern.
--Hester Trueworthy's Royalty. LC 12-38105. 337 p. front. 18 cm. 1880. R. Carter and Brothers.
--Huldah Brent's Will. LC 12-381188. 358 p. front., plates. 20 cm. c.1891. Bradley & Woodruff.
--Jack, Who Persevered. LC 12-38113. 196 p. front. 18 cm. (Half-title: The Gillettes. iii). c.1886. R. Carter and Brothers.
--Jerry Downer: Whose School of Courtesy Turned Out Good Pupils. LC 12-38126. 207 p. front. 20 cm. (Half-title: Rock Cove series ... vi). 1890. Leonard Publishing Company.
--Jerry Downer, Whose School of Courtesy Turned out Good Pupils, 1 of 6 vols. (Illus.). (Rock Cove Ser.: Vol. 6). N.D. Set. Methodist Bk Concern.
--Jessie a Pilgrim, 1 of 5 vols. (Jessie Bks). N.D. Set. Methodist Bk Concern.
--Jessie Ross, 1 of 5 vols. (Jessie Bks). N.D. Set. Methodist Bk Concern.
--Jessie Says So, 1 of 5 vols. (Jessie Bks). N.D. Set. Methodist Bk Concern.
--Jessie's Golden Rule, 1 of 5 vols. (Jessie Bks). N.D. Set. Methodist Bk Concern.
--Jessie's Place, 1 of 5 vols. (Jessie Bks). N.D. Set. Methodist Bk Concern.
--Kitty's Dream, 1 Vol. (Illus.). N.D. Methodist Book Concern.
--Kitty's Dream, & Other Stories. (Illus.). N.D. Methodist Bk Concern.
--Little Fish Peddler, 1 Vol. (Illus.). N.D. Methodist Book Concern.
--The Little Seabird. (Illus.). N.D. Methodist Bk Concern.
--Mabel Hazard's Thoroughfare, 1 of 10 vols. (Illus.). (Dale & Hillside Stories Ser.). N.D. Set. Methodist Bk Concern.
--Mabel Hazard's Thoroughfare. LC 12-38106. 334 p. front. 18 cm. (The Highland Series, v. 2). 1874. R. Carter & Brothers.
--Mabel's Step-Mother. LC 12-38107. 426 p. front. 18 cm. 1882. R. Carter & Brothers.
--Mabel's Stepmother, 1 of 10 vols. (Illus.). (Dale & Hillside Stories Ser.). N.D. Set. Methodist Bk Concern.
--Margaret Russell's School, 1 of 6 Vols. (Ledgeside Ser.). N.D. Set. Bradley & Woodruff.
--Margaret Russell's School. LC 12-38128. 389 p. front., plates. 18 cm. (Ledgeside Series, ii) 1869. R. Carter & Brothers.
--Miss Ashton's New Pupil. (Illus.). (The Wellesley Series for Girls). N.D. A. L. Burt.
--Miss Ashton's New Pupil. LC 12-38119. 263p. front., pl. 1892. Bradley & Woodruff.
--Miss Ashton's New Pupil: A School Girls Story. (The Girl Comrades Ser.). N.D. A. L. Burt Company.
--Moore's Forge, 1 of 10 vols. (Illus.). (Dale & Hillside Stories Ser.). N.D. Set. Methodist Bk Concern.
--Moore's Forge. A Tale. LC 12-381082. 381 p. front. 18 cm. (The highland series, v. 6). 1878. R. Carter and Brothers.
--My New Home. 383 p. front., plates, 18 cm. (Publisher's lettering: Win & Wear Series. v. 5). 1865. R. Carter and Brothers.
--Ned's Motto: Or, Little by Little, 1 of 6 vols. LC 76-371852. (Illus.). 339 p., 4 leaves of plates. 18cm. (The Win and Wear Ser.). 1864. R. Carter.
--One Happy Winter: Or, A Visit to Florida. LC 12-38129. 240 p. illus. 19 cm. 1878. Lockwood, Brooks and Company.
--Paul's Angel. LC 35-32649. 143 p. front., plates. 18 cm. 1891. Bradley & Woodruff.
--Rachel: Or, The City Without Walls, 1 of 4 vols. (Aunty May's Children Ser.). N.D. Set. Methodist Bk Concern.
--Robert Graham's Promise. A Story for Boys. LC 12-38109. viii, 9-332 p. 20 cm. 1885. R. Carter & Brothers.
--Robert Linton. (Illus.). 395p. 1905. American Tract Society.
--Robert Linton, and What Life Taught Him. LC 12-38120. viii, 9-395 p. front., plates. 18 cm. (Green Mountain Series, v. 2). 1868. R. Carter and Brothers.
--Squire Downing's Heirs, 1 of 6 vols. (Ledgeside Ser.). N.D. Set. Bradley & Woodruff.
--Squire Downing's Heirs. LC 12-38137. 358 p. front., plates. 18 cm. (Ledgeside Series, i). 1868. R. Carter & Brothers.
--Sue Downer: What Selfishness Did for Her, 1 of 6 vols. (Illus.). (Rock Cove Ser.: Vol. 5). N.D. Set. Methodist Bk Concern.
--Tony Starr's Legacy: Or, Trust in a Covenant-Keeping God, 1 of 6 vols. (Illus.). 338p. (The Win & Wear Ser.). N.D. Set. R Carter & Brothers.
--Turning a New Leaf: Or, The Story of Charles Terry. LC 12-38138. ix, 10-355 p. front., plates. 18 cm. (Publisher's lettering: Win & Wear Series, v. 6). 1866. R. Carter & Brothers.
--Walter & Nellie: Or, The Shadow of the Rock. N.D. Methodist Bk Concern.
--Weighed in the Balance. LC 12-38127. 1 p. l., v-vi, 7-402 p. front., plates. 18 cm. (Green Mountain Series, v. 3). 1868. R. Carter and Brothers.
--Who Won?, 1 of 10 vols. (Illus.). (Dale & Hillside Stories Ser.). N.D. Set. Methodist Bk Concern.
--Who Won. LC 12-38110. vi, 7-402 p. front., plates. 18 cm. (The Highland Series, v. 1). 1873. R. Carter and Brothers.
--Will: Honesty, 1 of 6 vols. N.D. Set. Bradley & Woodruff.
--Willie Books: Containing; Willie's Lesson, Willie Trying to be Manly, Willie Trying to beThorough, Willie Wishing to be Useful, Willie Seeking to be Christian, 5 Vols. (Illus.). N.D. Publications of the Methodist Book Concern.
--Willie Seeking to be a Christian, 1 of 5 vols. (Illus.). (Willie Bks). N.D. Set. Methodist Bk Concern.
--Willie Trying to be Manly, 1 of 5 vols. (Illus.). (Willie Bks). N.D. Set. Methodist Bk Concern.
--Willie Trying to be Thorough, 1 of 5 vols. (Illus.). (Willie Bks). N.D. Set. Methodist Bk Concern.
--Willie Wishing to be Useful, 1 of 5 vols. (Illus.). (Willie Bks). N.D. Set. Methodist Bk Concern.
--Willie's Lesson, 1 of 5 vols. (Illus.). (Willie Bks). N.D. Set. Methodist Bk Concern.
--Win and Wear. LC 49-4039. 298 p. plates. 18 cm. (Her Win & Wear series). 1866. R. Carter.
Roberson, Margaret Murray
--Shenac's Work at Home, 1 of 6 Vols. 410p. (The Glen Elder Library: Vol. 4). N.D. American Sunday-School Union.
Roberson, Rick James, jt. ed. see Engdahl, Sylvia Louise.
Robert, Adrian
--The Awful Mess Mystery. Harvey, Paul (1926-), illus. LC 84-8724. (Illus.). 48p. (gr. 2-4). 1985. (ISBN 0-8167-0402-3). (ISBN 0-8167-0403-1). Troll Assocs.
--Broderick the Great & the Rockaway Raiders. LC 83-15897. 128p. (Escapade Ser.). (gr. 4-6). 1985. (ISBN 0-689-31382-9). Atheneum.
--Ellen Ross, Private Detective. Garcia, T. R., illus. LC 84-8744. (Illus.). 48p. (gr. 2-4). 1985. (ISBN 0-8167-0414-7). (ISBN 0-8167-0415-5). Troll Assocs.
--My Grandma, the Witch. Fiammenghi, Gioia (1929-), illus. LC 84-8742. (Illus.). 48p. (gr. 2-4). 1985. (ISBN 0-8167-0422-8). (ISBN 0-8167-0423-6). Troll Assocs.
--Secret of the Haunted Chimney. Trivas, Irene, illus. LC 84-8763. (Illus.). 48p. (gr. 2-4). 1985. (ISBN 0-8167-0408-2). (ISBN 0-8167-0409-0). Troll Assocs.
--Secret of the Old Barn. Carter, Penny, illus. LC 84-8743. (Illus.). 48p. (gr. 2-4). 1985. (ISBN 0-8167-0412-0). (ISBN 0-8167-0413-9). Troll Assocs.
Robert, Mary E.
Johnny Hop's Adventure. 47p. (Children's Picture Bks.). N.D. T. S. Denison & Co.
Robert, Mati see Hoberg, Marielis, pseud.
Robert, Mati (1909-)
--One summer on Majorca. Hoberg, Marielis, pseud. Lenzen, Georg Hans, illus. Hollingdale, R J, tr. LC 61-5953. 192p. 1962. Abelard Schuman.
--The Voyage to Africa. Bartsch, Jochen (1906-), illus. LC 61-13157. 175 p. illus. 21 cm. 1961. Abelard-Schuman.
Roberton, E. Jean, ed. see Andersen, Hans Christian.
Roberts
--Seven Bears. (gr. 3-5). N.D. (ISBN 0-590-05413-9, Schol Pap). Scholastic Inc.
Roberts, Bethany
--Waiting-for-Spring Stories. Joyce, William, illus. LC 83-49486. (Illus.). 32p. (ps-3). 1984. (ISBN 0-06-025061-5). (ISBN 0-06-025062-3). HarpJ.
Roberts, Bruce Stuart, jt. auth. see Roberts, Nancy Correll.
Roberts, Bruce Stuart (1930-) & Roberts, Nancy Correll (1924-)
--America's Most Haunted Places. Roberts, Bruce Stuart (1930-), photos by. LC 75-23188. (Illus.). 95p. 1976. (ISBN 0-385-09964-9). (ISBN 0-385-09965-7). Doubleday.
--Ghosts & Specters: Ten Supernatural Stories. Roberts, Bruce Stuart (1930-), photos by. LC 73-20909. (Illus.). 93 p. 24cm. 1974. (ISBN 0-385-07231-7). (ISBN 0-385-07231-7). (ISBN 0-385-00698-5). Doubleday.
--Ghosts of the Wild West. Roberts, Bruce Stuart (1930-), photos by. LC 76-2813. (Illus.). 81 p. 24cm. c.1976. (ISBN 0-385-11298-X). (ISBN 0-385-11299-8). Doubleday.
Roberts, Charles George Douglas, Sir (1860-1943)
--Around the Camp Fire. Copeland, Charles, illus. (Illus.). (Crowell's Young People Ser.). 1896. Thomas Y. Crowell.
--The Cruise of the Yacht "Dido". A Tale of the Tide Country. LC 6-14227. 145 p. incl. plates. front. 19 cm. (Cosy corner series). 1906. L. C. Page & Company.
--The Feet of the Furtive. Bransom, Paul (1885-), illus. N.D. Macmillan.
--Haunters of the Pine Gloom: A Lynx Story. Bull, Charles Livingston (1874-1932), illus. LC 4-22283. (The Cosy Corner Ser.). 1905. L C Page & Co.
--Hoof and Claw. Bransom, Paul (1885-), illus. LC 14-15050. 1914. Macmillan.
--In the Deep of the Snow. Fink, Denman, illus. 1907. Crowell.
--Jim; the Story of a Backwoods Police Dog. LC 19-632554. 216 p. 20 cm. 1919. The Macmillan Company.
--The King of the Mamozekel: A Moose Story. Bull, Charles Livingston (1874-1932), illus. LC 4-22282. (The Cosy Corner Ser.). 1905. L C Page & Co.
--Kings in Exile. Bransom, Paul (1885-) & Bull, Charles Livingston (1874-1932), illus. 1910. Macmillan.
--Little People of the Sycamore: A Racoon Story. Bull, Charles Livingston (1874-1932), illus. LC 5-22365. (The Cosy Corner Ser.). 1906. L C Page & Co.
--The Lord of the Air: An Eagle Story. Bull, Charles Livingston (1874-1932), illus. LC 4-22280. (The Cosy Corner Ser.). 1905. L C Page & Co.
--Red Fox: The Story of His Adventurous Career in the Ringwaak Wilds, and of His FinalTriumph over His Enemies. Bull, Charles Livingston (1874-1932), illus. 1905. Page.
--The Return to the Trails: A Bear Story. Bull, Charles Livingston (1874-1932), illus. LC 5-22364. (The Cosy Corner Ser.). 1905. L C Page & Co.
--Reube Dare's Shad Boat: A Tale of the Tide Country. 1895. Hunt and Eaton.
--The Secret Trails. Bransom, Paul (1885-) & Reynolds, Warwick (1880-), illus. LC 16-23022. 1916. Macmillan.
--The Watchers of the Camp-Fire: A Panther Story. Bull, Charles Livingston (1874-1932), illus. LC 4-22281. (The Cosy Corner Ser.). 1904. L C Page & Co.
--The Young Acadian: Or, the Raid from Beausejour. McManus, Blanche, illus. LC 7-22817. 4 p. l., 7-139 p. front., 5 pl. 19 cm. (Cosy corner series). 1907. L. C. Page & Company.
Roberts, Cliff
--The Dot. LC 60-13162. (Illus.). 28cm. 1960. F. Watts.
--The Hole. LC 62-8429. (Illus.). 22 x 27cm. 1962, c.1961. F. Watts.
--Start With a Dot. LC 68-6312. (Illus.). Orig. Title: The Dot; 1960. 1968, c.1960. F. Watts.
Roberts, David Stuart (1943-)
--Deborah: A Wilderness Narrative. LC 76-134663. (Illus.). (gr. 7-12). 1970. (ISBN 0-8149-0677-X). Vanguard.
Roberts, David (1926-)
--Adventure at Murray's: A Strange Shopping Trip. Gadbois, Robert, illus. LC 77-1646. (Illus.). 31 p. 25cm. (Books by children for children). c.1977. (ISBN 0-87191-611-8). Creative Education.
--The Spear Thrower: A Story of Early Man. Caswell, Leslie & Edwards, Brian (1936-), illus. LC 73-153501. (Illus.). 38 p. (Origami story book). 1972. (ISBN 0-528-82676-X). Rand McNally.
Roberts, David (1926-), retold by.
--Brave Warrior: A Japanese Legend. Tourret, Gwen & Tourret, Shirley, illus. LC 73-151718. (Original author: Robert Mather). (Illus.). 38 p. (Origami story book). 1972. (ISBN 0-528-82674-3). Rand McNally.
--Thunderbird: An Indian Legend. Harley, Donald, illus. LC 73-152573. (Original author: Edward Thorneycroft). (Illus.). 38 p. (Origami story book). 1972. (ISBN 0-528-82675-1). Rand McNally.
Roberts, Doreen, jt. auth. see Moss, Elaine Dora.
Roberts, Edith Elizabeth Kneipple see Van Deusen, Elizabeth Kneipple, pseud.
Roberts, Edith Elizabeth Kneipple, Mrs. (1902-)
--Monkey Stories. Van Deusen, Elizabeth Kneipple, pseud. Hyde, Helen H., illus. LC 26-21874. (Illus.). 61p. 19 cm. 245p. 1926. B. Humphries, Inc.
--Tales of Borinquen: Porto Rico. Van Deusen, Elizabeth Kneipple, pseud. LC 29-582. (Illus.). 19 cm. 294p. 1928. Silver Burdett & Co.
--Tropical Tales: Porto Rico. Van Deusen, Elizabeth Kneipple, pseud. LC 29-19183. (Illus.). 19 cm. 240p. 1929. Silver Burdett & Co.
Roberts, Edward Barry, jt. auth. see Woodward, Elspeth.
Roberts, Eleanor
--Once Upon a Summertime: A Story with Lyrics for Children. LC 51-11864. 137 p. 23 cm. 1951. Exposition Press.
Roberts, Elisabeth
--Jumping Jackdaws: Here Comes Simon. Seward, Prudence, illus. LC 74-32044. (Illus.). 192 p. 23cm. 1975, c.1973. (ISBN 0-528-82097-4). (ISBN 0-528-82098-2). Rand McNally.
Roberts, Elizabeth Madox (1886-1941)
--Under the Tree. 1930. Viking Press.
--Under the Tree. Bedford, Francis Donkin (1864-1950), illus. (Illus.). (gr. k-3). 1922. (ISBN 0-670-73950-2). Viking Pr.
Roberts, Helen M (1896-)
--Mission Tales. Lawrence, Muriel, illus. LC 62-11254. 7 v. illus. 22 cm. 1963, c.1948. Set. (ISBN 0-87015-107-X). Pacific Books.
Roberts, Helen R, Mrs.
--Under the Sugar-Plum Tree. LC 41-8957. 3 p. l., 9-26 p. 15 cm. c.1940. Walker, Evans & Cogswell Co.
Roberts, Irma
--The Jungle Twins. Wiese, Kurt (1887-1974), illus. LC 51-12698. 127 p. illus. 21 cm. 1951. Coward-McCann.
Roberts, Isabel J
--The Little Girl from Back East. LC 11-9150. 132 p. front. 18 cm. 1911. Benziger Brothers.
--Polly Day's Island. Roberts, Jack, illus. LC 14-5822. 234 p. front. 19 cm. 1914. Benziger Brothers.
Roberts, Jack
--Bumpy-Bobs: The Little Pink Hippo. Roberts, Jack, illus. N.D. Duffield.
--Bumpy Bobs, the Pink Hippo. Roberts, Jack, illus. N.D. Dodd, Mead & Co.
--The Wonderful Adventures of Ludo, The Little Green Duck. Roberts, Jack, illus. N.D. Dodd, Mead & Co.
--The Wonderful Adventures of Ludo, the Little Green Duck. Roberts, Jack, illus. LC 25-26027. 48 p. col. illus. 19 x 19 cm. c.1924. Duffield & Company.

Roberts, Jane (1929-)

--Emir's Education in the Proper Use of Magical Powers. Cherry, Lynne (1952-), illus. (Illus.). 1979. (E Friede). Delacorte.

Roberts, Jim

--Free at Last. Roberts, Jim, illus. (Illus.). 12p. (Action Bks.). (ps-3). 1975. (ISBN 0-570-07106-2). Concordia.

--Little David & the Giant. Roberts, Jim, illus. (Illus.). 12p. (Action Bk. Ser.). (ps-2). N.D. Concordia.

--The Man with the Long Hair. Roberts, Jim, illus. (Illus.). 12p. (Action Bks.). (ps-3). 1975. (ISBN 0-570-07105-4). Concordia.

--The Original Floating Zoo. Roberts, Jim, illus. (Illus.). 12p. (Action Bks). (ps-3). 1975. (ISBN 0-570-07107-0). Concordia.

--Someone Who Cared. Roberts, Jim, illus. (Illus.). 12p. (Action Bks.). (ps-3). 1975. (ISBN 0-570-07104-6). Concordia.

Roberts, Jim, jt. auth. see McCall, Yvonne Holloway.

Roberts, Jim & Scheck, Joann

--Bible Pop-O-Rama Books, 2 vols. Roberts, Jim, illus. Incl. The Brightest Star. (ISBN 0-8066-1601-6, 10-0915); When Jesus Was a Boy. (ISBN 0-8066-1602-4, 10-7064). (Illus.). (gr. 3 up). 1978. Augsburg.

Roberts, Kay

--Bobby Bunnyfly. Unwin, Nora Spicer (1907-), illus. LC 47-122171. 33 p. illus. 16 cm. 1947. R. Welch Pub. Co.

Roberts, Linda

--Pepi. Leonard, Deborah, illus. (Illus.). 32p. (gr. 4-6). 1977. Dorrance.

Roberts, Martha Gaby

--Honeymaid: The Story of Silver Dollar Tabor. LC 77-363995. 112 p. 22cm. c.1977. (ISBN 0-87315-064-3). Golden Bell Press.

Roberts, Mary Duffy (1925-)

--Dons Great Discovery. (Illus.). N.D. David McKay Company.

--Don's Great Discovery. Voute, Kathleen (1892-), illus. LC 59-9372. 134p. illus. 21cm. 1959. I. Washburn.

--Get With It, Joan. LC 61-6976. 179p. 21cm. 1961. Washburn.

--The Ghost of the Fifth Door. Hall, H. Tom, illus. LC 68-18806. (Illus.). 125 p. 21cm. 1968. Macrae Smith.

--The Hurricane Mystery. Porter, Jean Macdonald (1906-), illus. LC 60-711072. 114p. illus: 21cm. 1960. I. Washburn.

--Promises to Keep. 1st ed. LC 62-12685. 150p. 21cm. 1962. Duell, Sloan and Pearce.

--The Trailmakers. Voute, Kathleen (1892-), illus. LC 61-12755. 116p. illus. 21cm. 1961. Washburn.

Roberts, Mary E.

--Johnny Hop's Adventure. Lee, Carvel Bigham (1910-), illus. LC 60-12613. unpaged. illus. 29cm. 1960. T. S. Denison.

--Selected Plays. 104p. N.D. Northwestern Press.

--Selected Plays. 104p. N.D. T. S. Denison & Co.

--Snappy Plays. 133p. N.D. Northwestern Press.

--Snappy Plays. 133p. N.D. T. S. Denison & Co.

--Treasure of Lone Pine. LC 43-16892. 95 p. 18 1/2 cm. 1943. The Wartburg Press.

Roberts, Mrs.

--Rose & Emily: Or, Sketches of Youth. LC 45-499552. 2 p. l., 3-176 p. front. 10 cm. (On cover: Young ladies cabinet, vol. II). 1823. D. Hogan.

Roberts, Nancy Correll, jt. auth. see Roberts, Bruce Stuart.

Roberts, Nancy Correll (1924-)

--Appalachian Ghosts. LC 77-76263. (gr. 3-7). 1978. Doubleday.

--Sense of Discovery: the Mountain. Roberts, Bruce Stuart (1930-), photos by. LC 79-76424. (Illus.). 90 p. 28cm. 1969. (ISBN 0-8042-2946-5). John Knox Press.

Roberts, Nancy Correll (1924-) & Roberts, Bruce Stuart (1930-)

--Ghosts & Specters of the Old South: Ten Supernatural Stories. LC 84-14153. p. cm. 1984, c.1974. (ISBN 0-87844-058-5). Sandlapper Pub.

Roberts, Olavine Moe

--Happy Days. Roberts, Olavine Moe, illus. LC 56-13101. 14p. illus. 22cm. (Pan Press young folks book). c.1956. Pan Press.

Roberts, P. D. T

--The Banquet of the Flowers: A Tale for Little Folks. Roberts, P. D. T., illus. LC 19-16418. 32 p. col. front., col. pl. 19 cm. c.1919. The Union Press.

Roberts, Peg (1917-)

--Mr. Rumpletop's Gift. Aven, Debra, illus. LC 82-71439. (gr. k-3). 1984. (ISBN 0-8054-4161-1). Broadman.

Roberts, Rachel Sherwood

--Crisis at Pemberton Dike. Converse, James, illus. 152p. 1984. (ISBN 0-8361-3350-1). Herald Pr.

Roberts, Ralph, jt. auth. see Strang, Ruth.

Roberts, Ruby Altizer

--The Story of Buzzy Bee. Barley, Jeanne Altizer, illus. LC 81-90592. (Illus.). 29 p. 26cm. c.1982. R.A. Roberts.

Roberts, Sarah

--The Adventures of Big Bird in Dinosaur Days. Schulman, Janet, ed. Mathieu, Joseph (1945-), illus. LC 83-61891. (Illus.). 32p. (Sesame Street Mini-Storybooks Ser.). (ps-3). 1984. (ISBN 0-394-85926-X). Random.

--Bert & the Missing Mop Mix-Up. Mathieu, Joseph (1945-), illus. LC 82-22971. (Illus.). 40p. (Sesame Street Start-to-Read Bks.). (ps-2). 1983. (ISBN 0-394-85752-6). (ISBN 0-394-95752-0). Random.

--Don't Cry, Big Bird. Leigh, Tom, illus. LC 81-4075. p. cm. (Sesame Street Start-to-Read Books). 1981. (ISBN 0-394-84868-3). (ISBN 0-394-94868-8). Random House.

--Ernie's Big Mess. Mathieu, Joseph (1945-), illus. LC 81-2464. (Illus.). 40p. (Sesame Street Start-to-Read Bks.). (gr. k-2). 1981. (ISBN 0-394-84847-0). (ISBN 0-394-94847-5). Random.

--I Want to Go Home. Mathieu, Joseph (1945-), illus. LC 84-11725. (Illus.). 40p. (Sesame Street Start-to-Read Bks.). (ps-3). 1985. (ISBN 0-394-97027-6, BYR). (ISBN 0-394-87027-1). Random.

--Nobody Cares About Me!. Featuring Jim Henson's Sesame Street Muppets. Henson, Jim, pseud. (1946-), created by Henson, James Maury. Mathieu, Joseph (1945-), illus. Children's Television Workshop LC 81-15913. (Illus.). 35 p. 24cm. (A Sesame Street Start-to-Read Book). c.1982. (ISBN 0-394-95177-8). Random House/Children's Television Workshop.

Roberts, Suzanne Fleisher see Marath, Sparrow, pseud.

Roberts, Suzanne Fleisher (1931-)

--Gracie. Marath, Sparrow, pseud. Miller, Marilyn Jean (1925-), illus. LC 65-198905. 143p. illus. 22cm. (Signal bks.). c.1965. Doubleday.

--Holly Andrews, Nurse in Alaska. LC 67-2669. 190 p. 21cm. (Career romance for young moderns.). 1967. Messner.

Roberts, Terence, pseud., see Sanderson, Ivan Terence.

Roberts, Terence, pseud. (1911-1973)

--Mystery Schooner. Sanderson, Ivan Terence. Sanderson, Ivan Terence (1911-1973), illus. LC 44-8906. 271 p. illus. 21 cm. 1944. The Viking Press.

Roberts, Theodore Goodridge

--Tom Akerley: His Adventure in Tall Timber at Gaspard's Clearings on the Indian River. Bull, Charles Livingston (1874-1932), illus. N.D. L. C. Page.

Roberts, Thomas Sacra (1940-)

--The Barn: Story. Fiammenghi, Gioia (1929-), illus. LC 74-23499. (Illus.). 40 p. 22cm. 1975. (ISBN 0-07-053130-7). McGraw-Hill.

--The Magical Mind Adventure of Hannah and Coldy Coldy. 1st ed. Mack, Stanley (1935-), illus. LC 73-151847. (Illus.). 82 p. 24cm. 1971. (ISBN 0-394-92164-X). Knopf.

--Pirates in the Park. 1st ed. Berson, Harold (1926-), illus. LC 72-92383. (Illus.). 48 p. 1973. (ISBN 0-517-50257-7). Crown Publishers.

Roberts, Tom, pseud., see Thomas, Robert Murray.

Roberts, Tom, pseud. (1921-)

--Java Raids. Thomas, Robert Murray. (gr. 7-11). 1964. (ISBN 0-679-20078-9). McKay.

Roberts, Ursula Wyllie, Mrs. (1887-), ed.

--Childhood in Verse and Prose. LC 24-11578. xxiii, 408 p. 20 cm. 1923. H. Milford, Oxford University Press.

Roberts, Virginia Keller & Mackay, Mary L., eds.

--Songs for Young Children: A Collection of Songs for Seasons of the Year. 98p. illus. 25cm. 1962, c.1961. Denison.

Roberts, Walter Charles

--Just for Fun: Rhymes. Selle, Catherine G., illus. LC 31-2679. 3 p. l., 58 p. illus. 19 cm. c.1931. Row, Peterson and Company.

Roberts, Willo Davis (1928-)

--Baby-Sitting Is a Dangerous Job. LC 84-20445. 161 p. 22cm. 1985. (ISBN 0-689-31100-1). Atheneum.

--Don't Hurt Laurie!. 1st ed. Sanderson, Ruth, illus. LC 76-46569. (Illus.). 166 p. 22cm. 1977. (ISBN 0-689-30571-0). Atheneum.

--Eddie & the Fairy Godpuppy. Morrill, Leslie H., illus. LC 83-15678. (Illus.). 136p. (gr. 3-7). 1984. (ISBN 0-689-31021-8). Atheneum.

--Elizabeth. 368p. (gr. 7 up). 1984. (ISBN 0-590-33136-1, Sunfire). Scholastic Inc.

--The Girl with the Silver Eyes. LC 80-12391. p. cm. 1980. Atheneum.

--House of Fear. 192p. (Orig.). (gr. 7 up). 1983. (ISBN 0-590-32537-X, Windswept). Scholastic Inc.

--The Minden Curse. 1st ed. Streeter, Sherry, illus. LC 77-24433. (Illus.). 226 p. 22cm. 1978. (ISBN 0-689-30603-2). Atheneum.

--More Minden Curses. Streeter, Sherry, illus. LC 79-22670. (Illus.). 234 p. 22cm. 1980. (ISBN 0-689-30759-4). Atheneum.

--No Monsters in the Closet. LC 83-3905. p. cm. (Escapade). 1983. (ISBN 0-689-31376-4). Atheneum.

--The Pet-Sitting Peril. 1st ed. LC 82-13757. 167 p. 22cm. 1983. (ISBN 0-689-30963-5). Atheneum.

--The View from the Cherry Tree. 1st ed. LC 75-6759. 181 p. 25cm. 1975. (ISBN 0-689-30483-8). Atheneum.

Robertshaw, James Denis see Gaunt, Michael, pseud.

Robertson, Alden

--The Wild Horse Gatherers. Robertson, Alden, illus. (Illus.). (gr. 7 up). 1978. (ISBN 0-684-15591-5, ScribJ, ScribJ). Scribner.

Robertson, Barbara Anne, jt. ed. see Downie, Mary Alice Dawe.

Robertson, Barbara Anne (1931-)

--The Wind Has Wings: Poems from Canada. Downie, Mary Alice Dawe (1934-), ed. Cleaver, Elizabeth Mrazik (1939-), illus. LC 79-308081. (Illus.). 95 p. 25cm. 1978, c.1968. (ISBN 0-19-540287-1). Oxford University Press.

Robertson, Beatrice

--Rodney the Red Rooster & Other Stories. (gr. 4-7). N.D. Carlton.

Robertson, Beth

--Bluebonnet Children: A Book of Children's Verse. Porter, Jean Macdonald (1906-), illus. LC 46-745. 5 p. l., 76 p. front., illus. 21 1/2 cm. 1945. The Paebar Company.

Robertson, Dale

--The Son of the Phantom. authorized. Falk, Lee Harrison (1915-) & Moore, Ray (1905-1984), created by. LC 46-799429. 2 p. l., 9-248 p. illus. 20 1/2 cm. 1946. Whitman Publishing Company.

Robertson, Dorothy Lewis (1912-), retold by.

--Fairy Tales from the Philippines. Burns, Howard M., illus. LC 76-132626. (Illus.). 127 p. 24cm. 1971. (ISBN 0-396-06276-8). Dodd, Mead.

--Fairy Tales from Viet Nam. Mars, Witold Tadeusz J. (1912-), illus. LC 68-12810. (Illus.). 93 p. 24cm. 1968. Dodd, Mead.

Robertson, Frances C.

--The Dudley Duck Family & Other Stories for Children. 1978. (ISBN 0-533-03535-X). Vantage.

Robertson, Frank Chester (1890-1969)

--The Fall of Buffalo Horn. LC 28-2810. v, 232, 1 p. front. 20 cm. 1928. D. Appleton and Company.

--On the Trail of Chief Joseph. LC 27-17796. 8 p. l., 229, 1 p. front. 19 1/2 cm. 1927. D. Appleton and Company.

--Sagebrush Sorrel. Townsend, Lee (1895-), illus. LC 53-72431. 186p. illus. 22cm. 1953. T. Nelson.

--Where Desert Blizzards Blow. Townsend, Lee (1895-), illus. LC 52-10882. 186 p. 21 cm. 1952. T. Nelson.

Robertson, Graeme (1947-)

--The Battle of Bongerhoohoo. Szmid, Gordon, illus. LC 79-11855. p. cm. c.1979. (ISBN 0-672-52592-5). Bobbs-Merill.

Robertson, Helen Gray (1900-)

--Bognor. 1st ed. LC 52-6268. (Illus.). 65p. 21cm. 1951. Pageant Press.

Robertson, Jennifer Sinclair (1942-)

--Circle of Shadows. LC 76-27079. vii, 104 p. 20cm. 1977, c.1975. (ISBN 0-8066-1555-9). Augsburg Pub. House.

--The Easter Story. Parry, Alan, illus. (Illus.). 32p. 1st U.S. edition. Repr (Pub. by Ark Publishing). (Ladybird Bible Ser.). (ps-4). 1980. (ISBN 0-310-42860-2). Zondervan.

--The Encyclopedia of Bible Stories. 1st ed. King, Gordon (1939-), illus. LC 74-1081. (Illus.). 268 p. 32cm. 1974. (ISBN 0-87981-036-X). Holman.

--Fior, Son of the King. LC 76-27080. 122 p. 20cm. 1977, c.1974. (ISBN 0-8066-1559-1). Augsburg Pub. House.

--Jesus in Danger. Parry, Alan, illus. LC 80-22826. p. cm. (Ladybird Bible Series). 1980, c.1978. (ISBN 0-310-42870-X). Zondervan Pub. House.

--Jesus, the Storyteller. Parry, Alan, illus. LC 80-23031. p. cm. (Ladybird Bible Series). 1980. (ISBN 0-310-42840-8). Zondervan Pub. House.

--King in a Stable. Bewley, Sheila, illus. (Illus.). 1st U.S. edition. (gr. 2-5). 1977. (ISBN 0-87239-123-X). Standard Pub.

--The Ladybird Bible Storybook. Parry, Alan, illus. LC 83-16832. (Illus.). 377. 1983. (ISBN 0-310-44440-3). Zondervan Pub. House.

--The Ladybird New Testament. Parry, Alan, illus. LC 81-13061. p. cm. 1981. (ISBN 0-310-44450-0). Zondervan.

--Paul the Traveler. Parry, Alan, illus. (Illus.). 32p. 1st U.S. edition. Repr (Pub. by Ark Publishing). (Ladybird Bible Ser.). (ps-4). 1980. (ISBN 0-310-42890-4). Zondervan.

Robertson, Jenny see Robertson, Jennifer Sinclair.

Robertson, Jenny Sinclair see Robertson, Jennifer Sinclair.

Robertson, Keith Carlton (1914-)

--The Crow and the Castle. Greiner, Robert, illus. LC 57-13885. 219p. illus. 21cm. 1957. (ISBN 0-670-24899-1). Viking Press.

--The Dog Next Door. Dennis, Morgan (1891-1960), illus. LC 50-64843. (Illus.). 222 p. 22cm. 1950. Viking Press.

--Henry Reed, Inc. McCloskey, John Robert (1914-1969), illus. LC 58-4758. (Illus.). 239 p. 22cm. 1958. Viking Press. **Award: (ALA).**

--Henry Reed's Baby-Sitting Service. McCloskey, John Robert (1914-1969), illus. LC 66-11908. 204p. illus. 22cm. c.1966. (ISBN 0-670-36825-3). Viking.

--Henry Reed's Big Show. McCloskey, John Robert (1914-1969), illus. LC 76-123026. (Illus.). 206 p. 22cm. 1970. (ISBN 0-670-36839-3). Viking Press.

--Henry Reed's Journey. McCloskey, John Robert (1914-1969), illus. LC 63-8522. (Illus.). 220 p. 22cm. 1963. Viking Press.

--Ice to India. Weaver, Jack (1925-), illus. LC 55-1060. (Illus.). 224 p. 22cm. 1955. Viking Press.

--If Wishes Were Horses. 1st ed. Kennedy, Paul Edward (1929-), illus. LC 58-5841. 246p. illus. 22cm. 1958. (ISBN 0-06-440052-2). Harper.

--In Search of a Sandhill Crane. Cuffari, Richard (1925-1978), illus. LC 79-15056. (Illus.). 201 p. 20cm. 1979, c.1973. (ISBN 0-14-031259-5). Puffin Books.

--In Search of a Sandhill Crane. Cuffari, Richard (1925-1978), illus. LC 72-9910. (Illus.). 201 p. 23cm. 1973. (ISBN 0-670-39662-1). Viking Press.

--The Lonesome Sorrel. 1st ed. Oughton, Taylor (1925-), illus. LC 52-5491. (Illus.). 214 p. 22cm. 1952. Winston.

--Mascot of the Melroy. Weaver, Jack (1925-), illus. LC 53-8726. (Illus.). 256 p. 22cm. 1953. Viking Press.

--The Missing Brother: A Mystery Story for Older Boys. Busoni, Rafaello (1900-1962), illus. LC 50-10388. (Illus.). 220 p. 22cm. 1950. Viking Press.

--The Money Machine. Porter, George, illus. LC 79-85874. (Illus.). 220 p. 22cm. 1969. Viking Press.

--The Mystery of Burnt Hill. Busoni, Rafaello (1900-1962), illus. LC 52-12806. (Illus.). 224 p. 21cm. 1952. Viking Press.

--Outlaws of the Sourland. Kashiwagi, Isami (1925-), illus. LC 53-3268. 224p. illus. 21cm. 1953. Viking Press.

--The Phantom Rider. Weaver, Jack (1925-), illus. LC 55-4106. 222p. illus. 21cm. 1955. Viking Press.

--The Pilgrim Goose. Best, Allena Champlin, Mrs. (1892-1974), illus. Berry, Erick, pseud. LC 56-2010. (Illus.). 80 p. 25cm. 1956. Viking Press.

--The Pinto Deer. Kashiwagi, Isami (1925-), illus. Berry, Erick, pseud. LC 56-14124. 220p. illus. 21cm. 1956. Viking Press.

--Tales of Myrtle the Turtle. 1st ed. Parnall, Peter (1936-), illus. LC 73-22483. (Illus.). 138 p. 23cm. 1974. (ISBN 0-670-69167-4). Viking Press.

--Three Stuffed Owls. Weaver, Jack (1925-), illus. LC 54-12165. (Illus.). 198 p. 21cm. 1954. Viking Press.

--Ticktock and Jim. (Famous Horse Stories). N.D. Grosset & Dunlap.

--Ticktock and Jim. Dennis, Wesley (1903-1966), illus. LC 48-544242. 240 p. illus. 22 cm. 1948. J. C. Winston Co.

--Ticktock and Jim, Deputy Sheriffs. 1st ed. Stahl, Everret, illus. LC 49-485791. v, 215 p. illus. 22 cm. 1949. Winston Co.

--Wreck of the Saginaw. Weaver, Jack (1925-), illus. (Illus.). (gr. 7 up). 1954. (ISBN 0-670-79060-5). Viking Pr.

--The Year of the Jeep. Mars, Witold Tadeusz J. (1912-), illus. LC 68-16074. (Illus.). 254 p. 22cm. 1968. Viking Press.

Robertson, Lida Bestor

--Jakie's Christmas. LC 37-1667. 3 p. l., 9-69 p. front., plates. 21 cm. c.1936. Birmingham Printing Company.

--Jakie's Christmas. LC 27-18541. 54 p. incl. front., plates. 21 cm. c.1927. The Christopher Publishing House.

Robertson, Lilian

--Picnic Woods. Robertson, Lilian, illus. LC 49-5055. 32 p. illus. (part col.) 25 cm. 1949. Harcourt, Brace.

--Runaway Rocking Horse. Robertson, Lilian, illus. LC 48-921449. 32 p. illus. (part col.) 21 x 27 cm. 1948. Harcourt, Brace.

Robertson, Margaret Murray

--Christie: Or,The Way Home, 2 vols. LC 12-38083. 2 v. fronts., plates. 17 cm. c.1866. American Sunday-School Union.

--The Inglises: Or, How the Way Opened. N.D. A. D. F. Randolph.

--Janet's Love & Service. N.D. Lentlehon & Co.

--The Little House in the Hollow, 1 of 6 vols. LC 12-38084. 1 p. l., 5-227 p. front., plates. 17 cm. (The Glen Elder Library). c.1868. American Sunday-School Union.

--The Orphans of Glen Elder, 1 of 7. (The Glen Elder Library). N.D. American Sunday-School Union.
--Stephen Grattan's Faith, 1 of 7. (The Glen Elder Library). N.D. American Sunday-School Union.
--Story of Little Gabriel, 1 of 6 Vols. 178p. (The Glen Elder Library: No. 5). N.D. American Sunday-School Union.
Robertson, Mary Elsie (1937-)
--Jemimalee. Brown, Judith Gwyn (1933-), illus. LC 77-78761. (Illus.). 122 p. 22cm. c.1977. (ISBN 0-07-053162-5). (ISBN 0-07-053163-3). McGraw-Hill.
--Tarantula and the Red Chigger. LC 80-17487. 172 p. 21cm. c.1980. (ISBN 0-316-75115-4). Little, Brown.
Robertson, O. J., jt. auth. see Bottom, Raymond.
Robertson, Primrose McPherson see Primrose, pseud.
Robertson, Primrose McPherson, illus.
--Little Red Ridinghood. LC 50-23550. 28 p. col. illus. 22 cm. (Bonnie book). 1949. John Martin's House.
--Little Red Ridinghood. Primrose, pseud. LC 50-22399. (Illus.). 24p. 20cm. (The Television Bonnie Bks.). 1950, c.1949. John Martin's House.
Robertson, Thomas L.
--The Leather Greatcoat. Rice, Elizabeth (1913-), illus. LC 59-653859. 158p. illus. 21cm. 1959. Steck Co.
--The Yellow Canes. Knapp, Bill, illus. LC 56-6471. 170p. illus. 22cm. 1956. Steck Co.
Robertson, Thorburn Brailsford (1884-)
--The Universe and the Mayonnaise and Other Stories for Children. Clausen, K., illus. LC 14-190841. 125 p. col. front., illus., col. plates. 22 x 18 cm. 1914. John Lane.
Robertson, Wilfrid (1892-)
--Dunkirk Dunes to Libyan Sand. Kay, B., illus. LC 43-1372. vii, 248 p. col. front., illus. 19 cm. 1941. Oxford University Press.
Robertson, William Webb
--The Peepie-Winkies. Williams, Bernice S., illus. LC 35-8469. 24 p. col. front., illus. 19 cm. c.1935. C. J. Creller.
Robeson, Kenneth
--Death in Silver. (Doc Savage Adventure Book). (gr. 7 up). 1975. (ISBN 0-307-02376-1, Golden Pr). Western Pub.
--The Ghost Legion. A Superhero Adventure. (Illus.). 210 p. 20cm. (His The fantastic adventures of Doc Savage, 3). 1975, c.1961. (ISBN 0-307-02377-X). Golden Press.
--Man of Bronze. A Superhero Adventure. (Illus.). 211 p. 20cm. (His the fantastic adventures of Doc Savage, 1). 1975, c.1963. (ISBN 0-307-02379-6). Golden Press.
--Quest of Qui. (Doc Savage Adventure Book). (gr. 7 up). 1975. (ISBN 0-307-02378-8, Golden Pr). Western Pub.
--The Sargasso Ogre. (Doc Savage Adventure Book). (gr. 7 up). 1975. (ISBN 0-307-02380-X, Golden Pr). Western Pub.
--Secret in the Sky. (Doc Savage Adventure Book). (gr. 7 up). 1975. (ISBN 0-307-02375-3, Golden Pr). Western Pub.
Robichaud, Marjorie W.
--Michelle & Dock & the Magic Clock. (Illus.). 48p. (gr. k-5). 1985. (ISBN 0-89962-454-5). Todd & Honeywell.
Robichaux, R. G.
--The Hinkety-Dinkety Club. N.D. Carlton.
Robida, Albert (1848-1926)
--Treasure of Carcassonne. Lathrop, Dorothy Pulis (1891-1980), illus. Cooper, Frederic Taber (1864-1937), tr. LC 28-245102. 213 p. incl. illus., plates. col. front. 20 cm. 1928. Longmans, Green and Co.
Robin, G, ed. see Willet, Billie M.
Robin, Suni (1951-)
--The Fiddler, the Fire, and Feast. Robin, Suni (1951-), illus. LC 79-16641. (Illus.). 29 p. 21cm. c.1979. (ISBN 0-89742-022-5). (ISBN 0-89742-017-9). Dawne-Leigh Publications.
Robinet, Harriette Gillem (1931-)
--Jay and the Marigold. Scott, Trudy, illus. LC 76-8551. p. cm. 48p. 1976. (ISBN 0-516-03514-2). Childrens Press.
--Ride the Red Cycle. Brown, David (1926-), illus. LC 79-24905. (Illus.). 34 p. 23cm. 1980. (ISBN 0-395-29183-6). Houghton-Mifflin.
Robinette, Joseph
--ABC (America Before Columbus). 40p. (gr. k-8). 1984. (ISBN 0-88680-212-1). I E Clark.
Robinette, Vivien
--Mr. Tipps: The Story of a Cat. Robinette, Viview, illus. LC 57-20029. 60p. illus. 21cm. c.1956. Triangle Pub. Co.
Robins
--My Father Spoke of His Riches. N.D. The Swallow Press.
Robins, E. P., tr. see Grousset, Paschal.
Robins, Edward (1862-)
--A Boy in Early Virginia: Or, Adventures with Captain John Smith. Betts, John Henderson, illus. LC 1-24979. (Illus.). 12cm. 285p. 1901. G. W. Jacobs & Co.
--Chasing an Iron Horse: Or, A Boy's Adventures in the Civil War. LC 2-19880. 5 p., 1 l., 7-293 p. front., plates. 21 cm. 1902. G. W. Jacobs & Co.
--With Thomas in Tennessee. LC 3-24216. 318 p. front., 4 pl. 21 cm. 1903. G. W. Jacobs & Co.
--With Washington in Braddock's Campaign. LC 6957. 253 p. front., plates. 19 cm. c.1900. G. W. Jacobs & Co.
Robins, Eleanor
--Lost Dog Mystery. Heidinger, Herb, illus. Bd. with Look Alike Mystery; Bank Robber's Map; Hub Cap Mystery; Old Book Mystery. (Illus.). 48p. (Orig.). (Meg Parker Mysteries Ser.: Set 1). (gr. 4-8). 1984. (ISBN 0-87879-439-5, 439-5, High Noon Books). Acad Therapy.
Robins, Elizabeth
--Two Stories. N.D. Frederick A. Stokes.
Robins, Elizabeth & Wilberforce, Octavia
--Prudence and Peter, and Their Adventures with Pots and Pans. Lenski, Lois (1893-1974), illus. N.D. William Morrow & Co.
Robins, Joan
--Addie Meets Max. Truesdell, Susan G., illus. LC 84-48329. (Illus.). 32p. (Early I Can Read Bk.). (ps-3). c.1985. (ISBN 0-06-025063-1). (ISBN 0-06-025064-X). HarpJ.
--My Brother, Will. Hafner, Marylin (1925-), illus. LC 85-9852. (Illus.). 9 7/8 x 8. 24p. (14 pt.). (ps-3). 1986. (ISBN 0-688-05222-3). (ISBN 0-688-05223-1). Greenwillow.
Robins, Louise Mary, jt. ed. see Stone, Ruth.
Robins, Mary Ellis
--Moon-Stories. Robins, Mary Ellis, illus. LC 15-4664. 3 p. l., 9-118, 1 p. illus. 18 cm. c.1914. Maverick Press.
Robins, Patricia
--Any Time at All. Rix, Lauretta, illus. LC 64-23947. 57 p. illus. 21 cm. 1964. St. Martin's Press.
Robinson, pseud., see Scott, Theresa Ann.
Robinson, ed. see Hughes, Thomas.
Robinson, A. A.
--Wage Earning Boy. N.D. Association Press.
Robinson, Adjai (1932-)
--Femi and Old Grandaddie. Pinkney, Jerry (1939-), illus. LC 72-76688. (Illus.). 48 p. 28cm. 1972. Coward, McCann & Geoghegan.
--Kasho and the Twin Flutes. Pinkney, Jerry (1939-), illus. LC 72-94144. (Illus.). 48 p. 27cm. 1973. (ISBN 0-698-30517-5). (ISBN 0-698-20265-1). (ISBN 0-698-20265-1). Coward, McCann & Geoghegan.
--Three African Tales. Byard, Carole M, illus. LC 78-13927. p. cm. 1979. (ISBN 0-399-20656-6). Putnam.
Robinson, Adjai (1932-), retold by.
--Singing Tales of Africa. Price, Christine Hilda (1928-1980), illus. LC 73-1378. (Illus.). 50p. (gr. 2-6). 1974. (ISBN 0-684-13683-X, ScribJ). Scribner.
Robinson, Ann (1920-)
--Joshua. Robinson, Ann (1920-), illus. LC 68-16500. (Illus.). 166 p. 20cm. 1968. Roy Publishers.
Robinson, Anna, adapted by.
--Harry's Temptation: Or, Christmas in Canada. Davidson, Bertha G., illus. LC 6-34794. (Illus.). (Christmas in Many Lands Ser.). 1906. Dana Estes & Co.
Robinson, Anna, ed. see Chatterbox.
Robinson, Anna, adapted by see Clarke, Mary Cowden, Mrs.
Robinson, Anna De Knight
--Stories of Adventure for Friday Afternoons. Dedicated to the Boys and Girls of the Pittsburgh Public Schools. Robinson, Anna DeKnight, illus. LC 6-130. 4 p. l., 13-116 p. front., illus. 21 cm. c.1905. Eichbaum Co.
Robinson, Anne Mathilde
--Little Miss April. Paynter, Grace M. & Von Bernuth, Lecian, illus. LC 31-962023. 80 p. illus. 21 cm. c.1931. Oglethorpe University Press.
Robinson, Annie Douglas Green see Douglas, Marian, pseud.
Robinson, Annie Douglas Green, Mrs. (1842-)
--In the Poverty Year: A Story of Life in New Hampshire in 1816. Douglas, Marian, pseud. LC 1-23078. 3 p. l., 5-79 p. front. 19 cm. 1901. T. Y. Crowell & Co.
--Peter and Polly: Or, Home-Life in New England a Hundred Years Ago. Douglas, Marian, pseud. LC 16-3399. 1 p. l., 5-268 p. 16 cm. 1876. J. R. Osgood and Company.
--Picture Poems for Young Folks. Douglas, Marian, pseud. Robinson, Annie Douglas Green, Mrs. (1842-), illus. Douglas, Marian, pseud. LC 15-8690. vi p., 1 l., 104 p. illus. 20 cm. 1872. J. R. Osgood and Company.
Robinson, Barbara Webb (1927-)
--Across from Indian Shore. Ness, Evaline Michelow, Mrs. (1911-), illus. LC 61-11921. 153p. illus. 24cm. 1962. Lothrop, Lee and Shepard.
--The Best Christmas Pageant Ever. 1st ed. Brown, Judith Gwyn (1933-), illus. LC 72-76501. (Illus.). 80 p. 21cm. 1972. (ISBN 0-06-025043-7). (ISBN 0-06-025043-7). Harper & Row.
--The Fattest Bear in the First Grade. Szekeres, Cyndy (1933-), illus. LC 73-87821. (Illus.). 32p. 24cm. 1969. Random House.
--Temporary Times, Temporary Places. LC 81-47732. p. cm. (A Charlotte Zolotow Book). c.1982. (ISBN 0-06-025043-7). (ISBN 0-06-025042-9). Harper & Row. **Award: (ALA).**
--Trace Through the Forest. LC 65-13388. 219p. 22cm. c.1965. Lothrop.
Robinson, Benelle H.
--Citizen Pablo. Porter, Jean Macdonald (1906-), illus. LC 59-6719. (Illus.). 128p. (gr. 4-6). 1959. (ISBN 0-381-99719-7). John Day.
Robinson, C.
--Treasury of Best Loved Rhymes. N.D. (ISBN 0-531-05111-0). Franklin Watts.
Robinson, Celia Myrover
--Rowena's Happy Summer. Dunlap, Hope, illus. LC 12-10819. 104 p. col. front., col. pl. 19 1/2 cm. $0.60. c.1912. Rand, McNally & Company.
Robinson, Chaille Howard Payne see Robinson, Kathleen, pseud.
Robinson, Chaille Howard Payne (1892-)
--Designed by Suzanne. Robinson, Kathleen, pseud. LC 67-12596. 127 p. 22cm. 1968. Lothrop, Lee & Shepard Co.
--When Debbie Dared. Robinson, Kathleen, pseud. LC 63-17831. 216 p. 20 cm. 1963. Whitman Pub. Co.
--When Sara Smiled. Robinson, Kathleen, pseud. Korach, Mimi (1922-), illus. LC 62-15251. 216 p. 20 cm. (Teen novel). 1962. Whitman Pub. Co.
Robinson, Charles, jt. auth. see Sachs, Marilyn Stickle.
Robinson, Charles Henry (1843-)
--Hawk: The Young Osage. Avery Studio, illus. LC 13-20584. (The American Boy's Library). 1913. L. C. Long & Co.
--Longhead: The Story of the First Fire. Bull, Charles Livingston (1874-1932), illus. LC 13-17063. 1913. Page Co.
Robinson, Charles (1931-)
--The Black Cat Book. Robinson, Charles (1931-), illus. (Illus.). N.D. Frederick A. Stokes Co.
--New Kid in Town. 1st ed. Robinson, Charles (1931-), illus. LC 75-8870. (Illus.). 32 p. 23cm. 1975. (ISBN 0-689-30484-6). Atheneum.
--Yuri and the Mooneygoats. Robinson, Charles (1931-), illus. LC 70-86948. (Illus.). 39 p. 23cm. 1969. Simon and Schuster.
Robinson, Charles (1931-), ed.
--The Big Book of Nursery Rhymes. Robinson, Charles (1931-), illus. (Illus.). (ps-2). N.D. (ISBN 0-88388-024-5). Bellerophon Bks.
--The Book of Nursery Rhymes. Robinson, Charles (1931-), illus. LC 76-383474. (Illus.). 80 p. 26cm. c.1975. (ISBN 0-85636-016-3). Minerva.
Robinson, Dorothy Clapp
--The Mystery of Contrary House. 1st. ed. LC 56-12196. 86p. 21cm. 1956. Vantage Press.
Robinson, Dorothy W
--The Legend of Africania. Temple, Herbert, illus. LC 74-4781. (Illus.). 32 p. (Ebony Jr! book). 1974. (ISBN 0-87485-037-1). Johnson Pub. Co. **Award: (CSKA).**
Robinson, Earl, jt. auth. see Arkin, David.
Robinson, Earl Hawley (1910-), ed.
--Young Folks Song Book. Seeger, Peter R. (1919-), intro. by. 1963. (ISBN 0-671-84081-9, Fireside). S&S.
Robinson, Edith (1858-)
--The Captain of the School. Stephens, Alice Barber (1858-1932), illus. LC 1-20302. 3 p. l., 258 p. front., plates. 20 cm. 1901. Little, Brown & Company.
--Forced Acquaintances: A Book for Girls. LC 20-16479. 394 p. 19 1/2 cm. 1887. Ticknor and Company.
--A Little Daughter of Liberty. Sacker, Amy M., illus. LC 99-4303. (Cosy Corner Ser.). 1899. L. C. Page & Co.
--A Little Puritan Bound Girl. Barry, Etheldred Breeze (1870-), illus. LC 3-25409. 88 p. incl. front., illus., plates. 18 1/2 cm. (Cosy corner series). 1904. L. C. Page & Company.
--A Little Puritan Cavalier. Barry, Etheldred Breeze (1870-), illus. LC 5-20770. 19cm. 132p. (Cosy Corner Ser.). 1905. L. C. Page & Co.
--A Little Puritan Pioneer. Sacker, Amy M., illus. LC 1-23079. (Illus.). 74p. (The Cosy Corner Ser.). 1901. The Page Company.
--A Little Puritan Rebel. Sacker, Amy M., illus. LC 98-101. 131p. (Cosy Corner Ser.). 1898. L. C. Page & Co.
--Little Puritan Stories. New ed. Barry, Etheldred Breeze, et al. (1870-), illus. LC 32-7816. 387 p. incl. illus., plates. front. 20 cm. 1931. L. C. Page & Company.
--A Little Puritan's First Christmas. Sacker, Amy M., illus. 94p. (Cosy Corner Ser.). 1900. L. C. Page & Co.
--A Loyal Little Maid. Sacker, Amy M., illus. LC 12-38081. 4 p. l., 79 p. incl. front., illus., 2 pl. 18 1/2 cm. (Charming juvenile series). 1897. Joseph Knight Company.
--A Loyal Little Maid. Sacker, Amy M., illus. (Cosy Corner Ser.). 1897. L. C. Page & Co.
--The Outsider at St. Agatha's. LC 17-242081. 3 p. l., 121 p. front., pl. 19 cm. c.1917. The Pilgrim Press.
--Penhallow Tales. LC 99-33. 184p. 1896. Copeland & Day.
--A Puritan Knight Errant. Bridgman, Lewis Jesse (1857-1931), illus. 280 p. front., plates. 20 1/2 cm. (Princess series). (Cosy Corner Ser.). 1903. L. C. Page & Company.
Robinson, Edward, adapted by.
Count of Monte Cristo. Greene, Hamilton, illus. (A Golden Picture Classic). 1958. Golden Press.
Robinson, Edwin Arlington (1869-1935)
--Slumber Song. N.D. Bruce Humphries.
Robinson, Ella M.
--Stories of My Grandmother. (gr. 7 up). N.D. Southern Pub.
Robinson, Emma Amelia (1863-)
--Toto and Sundri: From a Heathen Home to Christian Service. N.D. Abingdon Press.
Robinson, Evangeline, jt. auth. see Peel, Arthur J.
Robinson, Florine
--Ed & Ted. 1st ed. Davis, Omar, illus. LC 65-29735. (Illus.). (ps-3). 1965. (ISBN 0-682-43103-6). Exposition.
--Friends Together: A Story About Two Boys Who Became Friends. Davis, Omar, illus. LC 65-29735. (Illus.). 59p. (gr. 2-5). 1967. (ISBN 0-682-45716-7). Exposition.
Robinson, Frank Malcolm, jt. auth. see Scortia, Thomas Nicholas.
Robinson, Gail, retold by.
--Raven, the Trickster: Legends of the North American Indians. Troughton, Joanna Margaret (1947-), illus. LC 82-4017. (Illus.). 125 p. 22cm. 1982. (ISBN 0-689-50247-8). Atheneum.
Robinson, Gail & Hill, Douglas Arthur (1935-), eds.
--Coyote, the Trickster: Legends of the North American Indians. McCallum, Graham (1943-), illus. LC 76-7248. (Illus.). 124 p. 23cm. c.1976. (ISBN 0-8448-0923-3). Crane Russak.
Robinson, Geraldine
--Three Kittens in a Boat. Robison, Geraldine, illus. LC 58-9085. unpaged. illus. 14x19cm. 1958. F. Warne.
Robinson, Gertrude (1876-)
--Bringing up Raffles. Latimer, Glenna M. (1898-), illus. LC 40-139806. 51, 1 p. illus. 26 x 20 1/2 cm. 1940. E. P. Dutton & Co., Inc.
--Catch a Falling Star. Carman, Albert, illus. LC 42-16188. 251 p. incl. plan. col. front. 21 cm. 1942. E. P. Dutton and Company, Inc.
--Chee-Chee's Brother. 1st ed. Latimer, Glenna M. (1898-), illus. LC 37-18110. (Illus.). 40p. 26cm. 1937. E.P. Dutton.
--Father and the Mountains. Morse, Dorothy Bayley (1906-1979), illus. LC 50-6923. 209p. (gr. 7-11). 1950. Oxford University Press.
--Fox Fire. Ishmael, Woodi (1914-), illus. LC 44-668347. 245 p. illus. 21 cm. 1944. E. P. Dutton and Company, Inc.
--In a Scout's Books. White, Ralph, illus. LC 57-12651. 135p. illus. 21cm. 1957. (ISBN 0-8114-7635-9). Steck Co.
--The Mooring Tree: A Story of Jamestown. LC 57-12319. 168p. 22cm. 1957. Oxford University Press.
--Mother Penny. Babcock, Cathie, illus. LC 46-460860. 56 p. illus. 26 1/2 x 20 1/2 cm. 1946. E. P. Dutton & Co., Inc.
--Peter Snow, Surgeon. Ishmael, Woodi (1914-), illus. LC 43-7871. 215 p. illus. 21 cm. 1943. E. P. Dutton and Company, Inc.
--Robeen. 1st ed. Brazelton, Julian, illus. LC 38-21855. 2 p. l., 9-258 p. front., illus. (incl. map) 21 1/2 cm. 1938. E. P. Dutton & Co., Inc.
--Sachim Bird. LC 36-18136. 1 p. l., 15-216 p. illus. 21 1/2 cm. c.1936. E. P. Dutton & Co.
--The Sign of the Golden Fish. Chapman, Frederick Trench (1887-), illus. (Land of the Free Ser.). 1952. Holt, Rinehart and Winston.
--The Sign of the Golden Fish: A Story of the Cornish Fishermen in Maine. Chapman, Frederick Trench (1887-), illus. LC 49-8795. ix, 207 p. illus., maps. 22 cm. (Land of the Free Series). 1949. J. C. Winston Co.
--Smoking Hoof. Burchard, Peter Duncan (1921-), illus. LC 51-12502. (Illus.). 220 p. 21cm. 1951. Oxford University Press.
--Sons of Liberty. Ishmael, Woodi (1914-), illus. LC 41-10153. 248 p. incl. illus., plates (1 double) 21 cm. 1941. E. P. Dutton and Company.
--Spindleshanks. Burchard, Peter Duncan (1921-), illus. LC 54-5710. (Illus.). 187 p. 21cm. (Oxford books for boys and girls). 1954. Oxford University Press.

--White Heron Feather. Best, Allena Champlin, Mrs. (1892-1974), illus. Berry, Erick, pseud. LC 30-24626. 8 p. l., 299, 1 p. incl. front., illus., plates. 19 1/2 cm. c.1930. Harper & Brothers.
--Winged Feet: Scouting for George Washington. Brazelton, Julian, illus. LC 39-20725. xiv, 311 p. incl. front., illus. maps. 21 cm. 1939. E. P. Dutton & Co., Inc.
Robinson, Helen M., ed. see Monroe, Marion (1898-) & Artley, Stern.
Robinson, Helen Ring, adapted by see Stowe, Harriet Elizabeth Beecher, Mrs.
Robinson, Henry Morton
--The Enchanted Grindstone and Other Poems. 1952. Simon and Schuster.
Robinson, Hugh Laughlin, jt. auth. see Huggins, Alice Margaret.
Robinson, Ian Paul (1957-), retold by.
--Cinderella. Embleton, Gerry, illus. LC 79-51469. p. cm. (Derrydale Fairy Tale Library). 1979. (ISBN 0-517-28807-9). Derrydale Books.
--Goldilocks. Embleton, Gerry, illus. LC 79-51470. p. cm. (Derrydale Fairy Tale Library). 1979. (ISBN 0-517-28808-7). Derrydale Books.
Robinson, Irene Bowen (1891-) & Robinson, William Wilcox, Mrs. (1891-)
--Picture Book of Animal Babies. Robinson, Irene Bowen (1891-), illus. LC 47-3617. 40 p. illus. (part col.) 26 x 21 cm. 1947. The Macmillan Company.
Robinson, J. E.
--Three Friends. LC 50-56016. (Illus.). 32. (A Cozy Corner Bk.). 1950. Whitman.
Robinson, Jackie
--Breadthrough To The Big League. 1965. (ISBN 0-8382-0115-6, Cadmus Books). E. M. Hale and Company.
Robinson, Jan M. (1933-)
--The December Dog. 1st ed. Sandin, Joan (1942-), illus. LC 73-82407. (Illus.). 64 p. 23cm. 1969. Lippincott.
--The Story of Warple. Jewell, Jack, illus. LC 77-15907. (Illus.). 32 p. c.1978. (ISBN 0-87695-209-0). Aurora Publishers.
Robinson, Jean O. (1934-)
--Francie. Daley, Joann, illus. LC 70-118960. (Illus.). 182 p. 23cm. 1970. (ISBN 0-695-80171-6). Follett Pub. Co.
--The Mystery of Lincoln Detweiler and the Dog Who Barked Spanish. Fiammenghi, Gioia (1929-), illus. LC 76-46027. (Illus.). 128 p. 23cm. c.1977. (ISBN 0-695-80713-7). (ISBN 0-695-40713-9). Follett Pub. Co.
--The Secret Life of T. K. Dearing. Robinson, Charles (1931-), illus. LC 72-90083. (Illus.). 126 p. 21cm. 1973. (ISBN 0-8164-3096-9). Seabury Press.
--The Strange, but Wonderful, Cosmic Awareness of Duffy Moon. Di Fiori, Lawrence, illus. LC 73-15526. (Illus.). 142 p. 20cm. 1974. (ISBN 0-8164-3115-9). Seabury Press.
Robinson, Joan Mary Gale Thomas see Thomas, Joan Gale, pseud.
Robinson, Joan Mary Gale Thomas (1910-)
--About Teddy Robinson. Robinson, Joan Mary Gale Thomas (1910-), illus. (Illus.). 121 p. 20cm. (A Young Puffin). 1975, c.1959. (ISBN 0-14-030752-4). Penguin Books.
--Charley. Seward, Prudence, illus. LC 78-103869. (Illus.). 251 p. 21cm. 1st U.S. edition. 1970, c.1969. Coward-McCann.
--The Dark House of the Sea Witch. LC 79-10845. 128 p. 22cm. 1979. (ISBN 0-698-20494-8). Coward, McCann & Geoghegan.
--Dear Teddy Robinson. Robinson, Joan Mary Gale Thomas (1910-), illus. LC 66-31473. (Illus.). 105 p. 20cm. (Puffin books, PS272). 1966, c.1960. Penguin Books.
--Mary-Mary Stories. Robinson, Joan Mary Gale Thomas (1910-), illus. LC 68-15610. (Illus.). 96 p. 21cm. 1st U.S. edition. 1968. Coward-McCann.
--More About Teddy Robinson. 1970. (ISBN 0-14-030441-X, Puffin). Penguin.
--When Marnie Was There. LC 68-23868. 255 p. 22cm. 1968, c.1967. Coward-McCann.
Robinson, John (1921-)
--The Adventures of QBert. LC 83-12181. p. cm. c.1983. (ISBN 0-910313-12-1). Parker Bros.
Robinson, Kathleen, pseud., see Robinson, Chaille Howard Payne.
Robinson, Leora B.
--The House with Spectacles. N.D. G P Putnam's Sons.
Robinson, Lincoln Fay
--Goldie and Yellowhammer. Robinson, Lincoln Fay, illus. LC 49-10699. 32 p. illus. 21 x 28 cm. 1949. Viking Press.
--Jack's House. Robinson, Lincoln Fay, illus. LC 33-33264. vi, 258 p. incl. front., illus. 21 cm. 1933. The Viking Press.
--Two Boys. Robinson, Lincoln Fay, illus. LC 32-30789. 4 p. l., 3-134 p., 1 l. col. front., illus. 21 cm. 1932. Doubleday, Doran & Co.
Robinson, Louise
--Behind the Big Glass Window. 277p. N.D. Little,.
--The Goose Quill. N.D. Silver Burdett & Co.
Robinson, Lucy, jt. auth. see Brandreth, Gyles Daubeney.
Robinson, Lucy Catlin Bull, Mrs. (1861-1903)
--A Child's Poems from October to October, 1870-1871. LC 21-22142. 2 p. l., vii, 9-171 p. front. (port.) 16 1/2 cm. 1872. Case, Lockwood & Brainard Priv. Print.
Robinson, Lucy M.
--Skyward and Back Again, for First and Second Grade. LC 12-38089. (School education helps, v.1, no. 8-10.). 18 1/2cm. 46p. 1894. School education company.
--Skyward and Back: Stories of Natural Phenomena for First and Second Grade. Robinson, Lucy M., illus. LC 34-38290. 101 p. illus. 18 1/2 cm. 1895. School Education Company.
Robinson, Mabel Louise (1874-1962)
--All by Ourselves. Wright, Mary Sherwood, illus. LC 24-157598. 7 p. l., 254 p. incl. front., illus., plates. 20 cm. c.1924. E. P. Dutton & Company.
--Back-Seat Driver. Shortall, Leonard W., illus. LC 49-11437. 68 p. illus. 22 cm. 1949. Random House.
--Blue Ribbon Stories: The/Best Magazine Stories for Boys and Girls... LC 29-22205. 22cm. 1929. MacMillan.
--Bright Island. (Illus.). (gr. 7-9). 1937. (ISBN 0-394-90986-0). Random. **Award: (JNM).**
--Dr. Tam O'Shanter. LC 21-12356. 6 p. l., 3-174 p. front., plates. 19 1/2 cm. c.1921. E. P. Dutton & Company.
--King Arthur and His Knights. Gorsline, Douglas Warner (1913-1985), illus. LC 53-6268. (Illus.). 174 p. 22cm. (World landmark books, W-5). 1953. Random House.
--Little Lucia. LC 22-21774. 314 p. incl. pl. front. 19cm. c.1922. E. P. Dutton.
--Little Lucia and Her Puppy. LC 23-133347. 7 p. l., 124 p., 1 l. incl. front., plates. 20 cm. c.1923. E. P. Dutton & Company.
--Little Lucia's Island Camp. LC 24-24690. 5 p. l., 117 p. front., illus., plates. 20 cm. c.1924. E. P. Dutton & Company.
--Little Lucia's School. Balcom, Sophia T., illus. LC 26-14626. 5 p. l., 138 p., front., plates. 19 1/2 cm. c.1926. E. P. Dutton & Company.
--Riley Goes to Obedience School. Shortall, Leonard W., illus. LC 56-9467. 80p. illus. 22cm. 1956. (ISBN 0-394-81543-2). Random House.
--Robin and Angus. Wilkin, Eloise Burns (1904-), illus. LC 31-12977. 6 p. l., 186 p. incl. illus., plates (1 double) col. front. 20 1/2 cm. 1931. The Macmillan Company.
--Robin and Heather. Vibberts, Eunice, illus. LC 32-25313. 5 p. l., 214 p. incl. illus., plates. col. front. 20 1/2 cm. 1932. The Macmillan Company.
--Robin and Tito. Wilkin, Eloise Burns (1904-), illus. LC 30-24623. 5 p. l., 192 p. incl. illus., plates. col. front. 20 1/2 cm. 1930. The Macmillan Company.
--Runner of the Mountain Tops. Ward, Lynd Kendall (1905-1985), illus. 1939. Random House. **Award: (JNM).**
--Sarah's Dakin. Brown, Julie, illus. LC 27-14895. 6 p. l., 3-271 p. illus. 20 cm. c.1927. E. P. Dutton & Company.
--Skipper Riley, the Terrier Sea Dog. Shortall, Leonard W., illus. LC 55-6064. 90p. illus. 22cm. 1955. (ISBN 0-394-81638-2). Random House.
--Strong Wings. Ward, Lynd Kendall (1905-1985), illus. LC 51-11807. (Illus.). 249 p. 21cm. 1951. Random House.
Robinson, Mabel Louise (1874-1962), ed.
--Blue Ribbon Stories. N.D. Appleton Century Co.
--Second Book of Blue Ribbon Stories. N.D. Appleton Century Co.
Robinson, Marileta (1942-)
--The Big Bicycle Race. Morrill, Leslie H., illus. LC 83-26261. (Illus.). 40p. (Cabbage Patch Kids Ser.). (gr. 1-5). 1984. (ISBN 0-910313-29-6). (ISBN 0-910313-29-6). Parker Bro.
--Mr. Goat's Bad Good Idea: Three Stories. Getz, Arthur, illus. LC 77-26601. (gr. 1-4). 1979. (ISBN 0-690-03862-3, TYC-J). (ISBN 0-690-03864-X). Har-Row.
Robinson, Martha
--The Twins at Thatchem Quickett. Geer, Charles Hand (1922-), illus. LC 62-18469. 186p. illus. 21cm. 1962. Washburn.
--Wheaton Book of Animal Stories. (Illus.). (gr. 9-12). N.D. (ISBN 0-08-026421-2). Pergamon.
Robinson, Mary B.
--The Story of Susie Pig. (Illus.). (gr. 1-3). 1951. (ISBN 0-7232-0436-5). Warne.
Robinson, Mary Dummett Nauman see Nauman, Mary D.
Robinson, Mary Stephens
--A Household Story of the American Conflict. LC 2-2049. 3 v. in 1. front., pl. 15 1/2 cm. 1868. N. Tibbals.
Robinson, Mary V., ed.
--Stories for Christmas. Smith, Bruce, illus. (Illus.). 1967. (ISBN 0-8042-2570-2). John Knox.
Robinson, Mary Yandes (1864-)
--Songs of the Trees. Robinson, Mary Yandes (1864-), illus. (Music by Josephine Robinson). 1915. Bobbs-Merrill.
--The Songs of the Trees: Pictures, Rhymes and Tree Biographies. Robinson, mary Yandes (1864-), illus. LC 3-27220. (Music by Josephine Robinson). 6 p. l., 7-125, 1 p. col. illus., col. plates. 29 1/2 cm. 1903. The Bobbs-Merrill Company.
Robinson, Matthew (1937-)
--Giveaway Gibson. Myers, Lou, illus. LC 70-158393. (Illus.). 31 p. 23cm. (Gordon of Sesame Street tells a story). 1971. (ISBN 0-394-82326-5). Random House.
--A Lot of Hot Water. Mack, Stanley (1935-), illus. LC 78-158395. (Illus.). 31 p. 23cm. (Gordon of Sesame Street tells a story). 1971. (ISBN 0-394-82327-3). Random House.
--Matt Robinson's Gordon of Sesame Street Storybook: No More Milk. Koren, Edward (1935-) & Mathieu, Joseph, illus. LC 76-37409. (Illus.). 64 p. 29cm. 1972. (ISBN 0-394-82406-7). (ISBN 0-394-92406-1). Random House.
--The Pecan Tree. Velde, Robert, illus. LC 74-158394. (Illus.). 31 p. 23cm. (Gordon of Sesame Street tells a story). 1971. (ISBN 0-394-82328-1). Random House.
--The Six-Button Dragon. Brumsic, Brandon, Jr., illus. LC 77-158392. (Illus.). 31 p. 23cm. (Gordon of Sesame Street tells a story). 1971. (ISBN 0-394-82329-X). Random House.
Robinson, Nancy K., jt. auth. see Miller, Marvin.
Robinson, Nancy Konheim (1942-)
--Jungle Laboratory. (Illus.). (gr. 2-5). 1974. (ISBN 0-8038-3710-0). Hastings.
--Just Plain Cat. LC 82-18258. 119 p. 22cm. 1983, c.1981. (ISBN 0-590-07876-3). Four Winds Press.
--Mom, You're Fired!. Arno, Ed, illus. (Illus.). 112p. (Orig.). (gr. 4-6). 1983. (ISBN 0-590-32951-0, Apple Paperbacks). Scholastic Inc.
--Oh Honestly, Angela!. LC 85-2102. 114 p. 22cm. 1985. (ISBN 0-590-32983-9). Scholastic.
--Veronica, the Show-off. Greenwald, Sheila, pseud. (1934-), illus. Green, Sheila Ellen. LC 82-18277. 119 p. 22cm. c.1982. (ISBN 0-590-07877-1). Four Winds Press.
--Veronica, the Show-off. Greenwald, Sheila, pseud. (1934-), illus. Green, Sheila Ellen. LC 85-4483. p. cm. 1985, c.1982. (ISBN 0-02-777360-4). Four Winds Press.
--Wendy and the Bullies. Fetz, Ingrid (1915-), illus. LC 80-13366. p. cm. c.1980. (ISBN 0-8038-8097-9). Hastings House.
Robinson, Peter
--Susan Perl's Color Wheel. Perl, Susan (1922-1983), illus. (Illus.). (A Cricket Book). (gr. k-2). 1978. (ISBN 0-448-46529-9). Platt.
Robinson, R. N.
--The Queen's Navee. May, Walter W., illus. N.D. Brentano's Publications.
Robinson, Richard Gavin
--Captain Sintar. Maitland, Antony Jasper (1935-), illus. LC 69-20306. (Illus.). 156 p. 21cm. 1969, c.1967. Dutton.
Robinson, Roland E., ed.
--Wandjina, Children of the Dreamtime: Aboriginal Myths & Legends. Shaw, Roderick, illus. LC 73-384644. (Illus.). 112 p. 28cm. 1968. Jacaranda.
Robinson, Sandra C.
--The Last Bit-Bear: A Fable. Ditzler, Ellen, illus. (Illus.). (gr. k-6). 1984. (ISBN 0-911797-09-2). HR&W.
Robinson, Sondra T.
--Almansor. 1974. (ISBN 0-8402-1322-0). Nash Pub.
Robinson, Thomas Pendleton (1878-)
--Buttons. Bacon, Peggy, pseud. (1895-), illus. Bacon, Margaret Frances. LC 38-13327. 63 p. illus. 31 cm. 1938. The Viking Press.
--Greylock and the Robins. Lawson, Robert (1892-1957), illus. LC 46-25280. 31, 1 p. incl. col. front., col. illus. 26 x 20 cm. 1946. The Viking Press.
--In and Out. De Angeli, Marguerite Lofft, Mrs. (1889-), illus. LC 43-13707. 140 p. illus. (part col.) 24 cm. 1943. The Viking Press.
--Lost Dog Jerry. Dennis, Morgan (1891-1960), illus. LC 52-12234. (Illus.). 190 p. 22cm. 1952. Viking Press.
--Mr. Red Squirrel. 1st ed. Wiese, Kurt (1887-1974), illus. LC 43-13572. 32 p. incl. col. front., col. illus. 26 x 20 cm. 1943. The Viking Press.
--Pete. Dennis, Morgan (1891-1960), illus. LC 41-3124. 4 p. l., 13-139 p. illus. 22 1/2 cm. 1941. The Viking Press.
--Trigger John's Sons. LC 35-27094. vi, 270 p. front. 21 cm. 1934. The Viking Press.
--Trigger John's Sons. McCloskey, John Robert (1914-1969), illus. LC 49-10455. 284 p. illus. 22 cm. 1949. Viking Press.
Robinson, Thomas Pendleton (1878-), ed.
--The Player's Shakespeare. 140p. N.D. Viking Press.
Robinson, Tom D.
--An Eskimo Birthday. Coalson, Glo (1946-), illus. LC 74-23750. (Illus.). 39 p. 24cm. 1975. Dodd, Mead.
Robinson, Veronica (1926-)
--David in Silence. Ambrus, Victor G., pseud. (1935-), illus. Ambrus, Gyozo Laszlo. (gr. 5-7). 1965. Harper & Row.
--David in Silence. Ambrus, Victor G., pseud. (1935-), illus. Ambrus, Gyozo Laszlo. LC 66-10900. (Illus.). 126 p. 21cm. 1966, c.1965. Lippincott. **Award: (ALA).**
--Delos. LC 80-65667. 128 p. 21cm. 1980. (ISBN 0-233-97259-5). A. Deutsch.
Robinson, Virginia (1931-)
--Maggie's Champion. LC 57-6004. 187 p. 22cm. 1957. Lothrop, Lee & Shepard.
Robinson, W. A.
--Little Chicken Thieves, 1 of 25 vols. (Selected Bks for Sunday School: The/Clifton Library). N.D. Set. Methodist Bk Concern.
Robinson, Wanda Veronica see Robinson, Veronica.
Robinson, Warren F
--The G-Man's Son at Porpoise Island. LC 37-5833. 3 p. l., 11-251 p. 19 1/2 cm. c.1937. The Goldsmith Publishing Company.
--The Phantom Whale. LC 37-5829. 4 p. l., 15-249 p. 19 1/2 cm. c.1937. The Goldsmith Publishing Co.
Robinson, William Heath (1872-1944)
--The Adventures of Uncle Lubin. Robinson, William Heath (1872-1944), illus. LC 25-24044. 7 p. l., 114 p., 2 l. col. front., illus. 21 cm. 1925. Frederick A. Stokes Company.
--The Adventures of Uncle Lubin. Robinson, William Heath (1872-1944), illus. LC 76-377206. (Illus.). xiv, 117 p. 20cm. (Young puffin). 1975. (ISBN 0-14-030756-7). Puffin Books.
--Bill the Minder. Robinson, William Heath (1872-1944), illus. LC 25-130013. 7 p. l., 254, 2 p. mounted col. front., illus., mounted col. plates. 23 1/2 cm. 1924. George H. Doran Company.
--Bill the Minder. Robinson, William Heath (1872-1944), illus. xiv, 11, 254, 11 p. illus., 15 col. pl. (incl. front.) 25 cm. 1912. H. Holt & Co.
Robinson, William Heath (1872-1944) & Stratton, Helen (1832-1915), illus.
--The Arabian Nights. N.D. Dodge Publishing Company.
Robinson, William Henry (1867-)
--The Golden Palace of Neverland. Davidson, Clara D., illus. LC 7-21222. vii, 307 p. col. front., 5 col. pl. 20 cm. 1907. E. P. Dutton & Company.
Robinson, William Powell (1910-)
--Where the Panther Screams. 1st ed. Bjorklund, Lorence F. (1913-1978), illus. LC 61-6653. 179p. illus. 21cm. 1961. World Pub. Co.
Robinson, William Wilcox, Mrs., jt. auth. see Robinson, Irene Bowen.
Robinson, William Wilcox (1891-)
--At the Seashore. Robinson, Irene Bowen, Mrs. (1891-), illus. LC 42-9902. 40 p. ill. part. col. 32cm. 1942. Macmillan Co.
--Beasts of the Tar Pits: Tales of Ancient America. rev. text and illus. ed. Robinson, Irene Bowen, Mrs. (1891-), illus. LC 61-11590. (Illus.). 48 p. 1961. Ward Ritchie Press.
--Big Boy. Robinson, Irene Bowen, Mrs. (1891-), illus. LC 44-4991. 55, 1 p. incl. front., illus. 23 1/2 x 18 1/2 cm. 1944. The Macmillan Company.
--On the Farm. Robinson, Irene Bowen, Mrs. (1891-), illus. LC 39-9818. (Illus.). 40p. 31cm. 1939. The Macmillan Company.
Robison, Bonnie (1924-)
--Killer, the Outrageous Hawk. Sprattler, Rob, illus. Zillmer, Rolf, designed by. LC 74-8445. (Illus.). 61 p. 24cm. 1974. (ISBN 0-516-07630-2). Childrens Press.
Robison, Deborah
--Anthony's Hat. Robison, Deborah, illus. (gr. k-3). 1977. (ISBN 0-590-00297-X, Schol Pap). Scholastic Inc.
--Bye-Bye, Old Buddy. Robison, Deborah, illus. LC 83-5149. c.1983 (Clarion Bks.). (ISBN 0-89919-183-5). Houghton Mifflin.
--No Elephants Allowed. Robison, Deborah, illus. LC 80-21404. (Illus.). 32 p. c.1981. (ISBN 0-395-30078-9). Houghton Mifflin/Clarion Books.
--The Porcupine Book of Verse. Robison, Deborah, illus. LC 75-310930. (Illus.). 48 p. 26cm. 1974. (ISBN 0-570-06995-5). Concordia Pub. House.
Robison, Deborah & Perez, Carla
--Your Turn, Doctor. Robison, Deborah, illus. LC 81-68778. (Illus.). 32 p. c.1982. (ISBN 0-8037-9780-X). (ISBN 0-8037-9788-5). Dial Press.

--Savez-Vous Planter les Choux?. And Other French Songs. Rockwell, Anne F. (1934-) & Hopkins, Marjorie (1911-), illus. LC 79-827697. (Illus.). 64 p. 26cm. 1969. World Pub. Co.
--The Stolen Necklace: A Picture Story from India. Rockwell, Anne F. (1934-), illus. Jatakas LC 68-14681. 1 v. col. illus. 26cm. 32p. 1968. World.
--The Three Bears & Fifteen Other Stories. Rockwell, Anne F. (1934-), illus. LC 74-5381. (Illus.). 116 p. 21cm. 1975. (ISBN 0-690-00597-0). (ISBN 0-690-00597-0). Crowell.
--The Three Bears & Fifteen Other Stories. Rockwell, Anne F. (1934-), illus. LC 74-5381. (Illus.). 128p. (gr. k-5). 1975. (ISBN 0-690-00597-0, TYC-J). (ISBN 0-690-00598-9). Har-Row.
--The Three Bears & Fifteen Other Stories. Rockwell, Anne F. (1934-), illus. LC 75-5381. (Illus.). 128p. (A Trophy Bk.). (ps-3). 1984. (ISBN 0-06-440142-1, Trophy). Har-Row.
--When the Drum Sang: An African Folktale. Rockwell, Anne F. (1934-), illus. LC 77-101837. (Illus.). 32 p. 26cm. 1970. (ISBN 0-8193-0424-7). (ISBN 0-8193-0425-5). Parents' Magazine Press.
--The Wolf Who Had a Wonderful Dream: A French Folktale. Rockwell, Anne F. (1934-), illus. LC 78-184984. (Illus.). 34 p. 21cm. 1973. (ISBN 0-690-89723-5). (ISBN 0-690-89723-5). Crowell.

Rockwell, Anne F (1934-) & Rockwell, Harlow
--Blackout. Rockwell, Anne F. (1934-) & Rockwell, Harlow, illus. LC 78-12185. (Illus.). 63 p. 23cm. (Ready-to-read). c.1979. (ISBN 0-02-777610-7). Macmillan.
--Can I Help?. Rockwell, Anne F. (1934-) & Rockwell, Harlow, illus. LC 82-15375. (Illus.). 24 p. 17cm. (My World). c.1982. (ISBN 0-02-777720-0). (ISBN 0-02-777720-0). Macmillan.
--Happy Birthday to Me. Rockwell, Anne F. (1934-) & Rockwell, Harlow, illus. LC 81-3738. (Illus.). 24 p. 17cm. (My World). c.1981. (ISBN 0-02-777680-8). (ISBN 0-02-777680-8). Macmillan.
--Head to Toe. Rockwell, Anne F. (1934-) & Rockwell, Harlow, illus. 40p. (ps-1). 1973. Doubleday.
--How My Garden Grew. Rockwell, Anne F. (1934-) & Rockwell, Harlow, illus. LC 81-17145. (Illus.). 24 p. 17cm. (My World). c.1982. (ISBN 0-02-777710-3). (ISBN 0-02-777660-3). Macmillan.
--I Love My Pets. Rockwell, Anne F. (1934-) & Rockwell, Harlow, illus. LC 82-15188. (Illus.). 24 p. 17cm. (My World). c.1982. (ISBN 0-02-777710-3). (ISBN 0-02-777710-3). Macmillan.
--I Play in My Room. Rockwell, Anne F. (1934-) & Rockwell, Harlow, illus. LC 81-2634. p. cm. (My World). c.1981. (ISBN 0-02-777670-0). Macmillan.
--Molly's Woodland Garden. Rockwell, Anne F. (1934-) & Rockwell, Harlow, illus. LC 79-121097. 32 p. (chiefly col. illus. 22cm. 1971. Doubleday.
--My Baby-Sitter. Rockwell, Anne F. (1934-) & Rockwell, Harlow, illus. LC 85-5000. (Illus.). 24 p. 17cm. (My World Ser.). c.1985. (ISBN 0-02-777780-4). Macmillan.
--My Back Yard. Rockwell, Anne F. (1934-) & Rockwell, Harlow, illus. LC 83-18717. 24p. (My World Ser.). (ps). 1984. (ISBN 0-02-777740-5). (ISBN 0-02-777690-5). Macmillan.
--My Barber. Rockwell, Anne F. (1934-) & Rockwell, Harlow, illus. LC 80-24496. (Illus.). 24 p. c.1981. (ISBN 0-02-777630-1). Macmillan.
--Nice & Clean. Rockwell, Anne F. (1934-) & Rockwell, Harlow, illus. LC 84-3945. (Illus.). 24p. (ps-1). 1984. (ISBN 0-02-777290-X, Collier). Macmillan.
--The Night We Slept Outside. Rockwell, Anne F. (1934-) & Rockwell, Harlow, illus. LC 82-17963. p. cm. (Ready-to-Read). c.1983. (ISBN 0-02-777450-3). Macmillan.
--Olly's Polliwogs. Rockwell, Anne F. (1934-) & Rockwell, Harlow, illus. LC 74-82146. (Illus.). 57 p. 27cm. 1970. Doubleday.
--Out to Sea. Rockwell, Anne F. (1934-) & Rockwell, Harlow, illus. LC 80-12520. (Illus.). 47 p. 23cm. (Ready-to-read). c.1980. (ISBN 0-02-777620-4). Macmillan.
--Sick in Bed. Rockwell, Anne F. (1934-) & Rockwell, Harlow, illus. LC 81-15637. (Illus.). 24 p. (My World). c.1982. (ISBN 0-02-777730-8). Macmillan.
--The Supermarket. Rockwell, Anne F. (1934-) & Rockwell, Harlow, illus. LC 79-11411. (Illus.). (ps-1). 1979. (ISBN 0-02-777580-1). Macmillan.
--Thruway. Rockwell, Anne F. (1934-) & Rockwell, Harlow, illus. LC 70-156842. (Illus.). 24 p. 1972. Macmillan.
--Toad. 1st ed. LC 78-16000880. 29 p. col. ill. 22cm. c.1972. Doubleday.
--When I Go Visiting. Rockwell, Anne F. (1934-) & Rockwell, Harlow, illus. LC 83-17586. (Illus.). 24p. (ps-k). 1984. (ISBN 0-02-777740-5). (ISBN 0-02-777740-5). MacMillan.

Rockwell, Carey
--Danger in Deep Space. Ley, Willy (1906-1964), ed. Rockwell, Carey, illus. LC 53-8503. 209p. illus. 20cm. (His A Tom Corbett space cadet adventure. 2). 1953. (ISBN 0-448-08502-X). Grosset & Dunlap.
--On the Trail of the Space Pirates. Ley, Willy, ed. Rockwell, Carey, illus. (gr. 6-10). N.D. (ISBN 0-448-08503-8). G&D.
--The Revolt on Venus. Ley, Willy (1906-1969), ed. Rockwell, Carey, illus. LC 54-856150. 213p. illus. 20cm. (His A Tom Corbett space cadet adventure 5). 1954. (ISBN 0-448-08505-4). Grosset & Dunlap.
--The Robot Rocket. Ley, Willy (1906-1969), ed. Rockwell, Carey, illus. LC 56-136428. 181p. illus. 20cm. (A Tom Coerbett Space Cadet Adventure: No. 8). 1956. (ISBN 0-448-08508-9). Grosset & Dunlap.
--Sabotage in Space. Ley, Willy (1906-1969), ed. Rockwell, Carey, illus. LC 55-119656. 212p. illus. 20cm. (His A Tom Corbett space cadet advanture 7). c.1955. (ISBN 0-448-08507-0). Grosset & Dunlap.
--The Space Pioneers. Ley, Willy (1906-1969), ed. Rockwell, Carey, illus. LC 53-3911. 210p. illus. 20cm. (His A Tom Corbett space cadet adventure 4). 1953. (ISBN 0-448-08504-6). Grosset & Dunlap.
--Stand by for Mars!. Rockwell, Carey, illus. LC 52-14369. 216 p. illus. 20 cm. (Tom Corbett space cadet adventure). 1952. Grosset & Dunlap.
--Treachery in Outer Space. Ley, Willy (1906-1969), ed. Rockwell, Carey, illus. LC 54-4974. 210p. illus. 20cm. (His A Tom Corbett space cadet adventure 6). 1954. (ISBN 0-448-08506-2). Grosset & Dunlap.

Rockwell, Ethel Theodora
--Children of Old Carolina. LC 25-7306. 63 p. plates. 23 cm. (North Carolina. University University extension division. University of North Carolina extension bulletin. vol. IV, no. 12). c.1925. The University of North Carolina Press.

Rockwell, Harlow
--The Compost Heap. Rockwell, Harlow, illus. LC 73-10544. 32p. (ps-1). 1974. Doubleday.
--I Did It. Rockwell, Harlow, illus. LC 73-19059. (Illus.). 64p. (Ready-to-Read Ser.). (gr. 1-4). 1974. (ISBN 0-02-777550-X). Macmillan.
--My Dentist. Rockwell, Harlow, illus. LC 75-6974. (Illus.). 32p. (ps-3). 1975. (ISBN 0-688-80011-4). (ISBN 0-688-84004-3). Greenwillow.
--My Doctor. Rockwell, Harlow, illus. 1973. Macmillan.
--My Kitchen. Rockwell, Harlow, illus. LC 79-15929. (Illus.). 24 p. c.1980. (ISBN 0-688-80236-2). (ISBN 0-688-84236-4). Greenwillow Books. **Award: (ALA).**
--My Nursery School. Rockwell, Harlow, illus. LC 75-25871. (Illus.). 24p. (gr. k-3). 1976. (ISBN 0-688-80025-4). (ISBN 0-688-84025-6). Greenwillow.
--My Nursery School. Rockwell, Harlow, illus. LC 84-3370. 1984, c.1976. (ISBN 0-14-050478-8). Puffin Books.
--Our Garage Sale. Rockwell, Harlow, illus. LC 80-16704. p. cm. c.1981. (ISBN 0-688-80278-8). (ISBN 0-688-84278-X). Greenwillow Books.
--The Vacant Lot. Rockwell, Harlow, illus. LC 79-23086. p. cm. 1980. (ISBN 0-688-80259-1). (ISBN 0-688-84259-3). Greenwillow Books.

Rockwell, Harlow, jt. auth. see Rockwell, Anne F.

Rockwell, Molly, jt. auth. see Rockwell, Norman Percevel.

Rockwell, Norman Percevel (1894-1978) & Rockwell, Molly
--Norman Rockwell's Christmas Book. Rockwell, Norman Percevel (1894-1978), illus. LC 77-7087. p. cm. 1977. (ISBN 0-8109-1583-9). H. N. Abrams.
--Norman Rockwell's Christmas Book. Rockwell, Norman Percevel (1894-1978), illus. LC 79-14125. p. cm. (Fireside book). 1979, c.1977. (ISBN 0-671-25040-X). Simon and Schuster.

Rockwell, Thomas (1933-)
--Hey, Lover Boy. LC 80-68739. 155 p. 22cm. c.1981. (ISBN 0-440-03583-X). Delacorte Press.
--Hiding Out. Molina, Charles, illus. LC 73-94113. (Illus.). 79 p. 22cm. 1974. (ISBN 0-87888-069-0). Bradbury Press.
--How to Eat Fried Worms. McCully, Emily Arnold (1939-), illus. LC 73-4262. (Illus.). xi, 115 p. 21cm. 1973. (ISBN 0-531-02631-0). F. Watts.
--How to Eat Fried Worms, and Other Plays. Schick, Joel (1945-), illus. LC 78-72854. (Illus.). 142 p. 21cm. (gr. 4-7). c.1980. (ISBN 0-440-03498-1). (ISBN 0-440-03499-X). Delacorte Press.
--Humph!. Batherman, Muriel (1926-), illus. LC 74-153974. (Illus.). 32 p. 26cm. 1971. (ISBN 0-394-82116-5). (ISBN 0-394-92116-X). Pantheon Books.
--The Neon Motorcycle. Horen, Michael, illus. LC 72-10350. (Illus.). 40 p. 26cm. 1973. (ISBN 0-531-02561-6). Watts.
--Norman Rockwell's Hometown. Rockwell, Norman Percevel (1894-1978), illus. LC 78-130217. (Illus.). 45 p. 31cm. (Library). 1970. Windmill Books.
--Oatmeal Is Not for Mustaches. Christelow, Eileen (1943-), illus. LC 84-9081. c.1984. (ISBN 0-03-063653-1). Holt, Rhinehart and Winston.
--The Portmanteau Book. 1974. Little Brown and Company.
--Rackety-Bang & Other Verses. Rockwell, Gail, illus. LC 69-13462. (Illus.). 64p. (gr. 3-6). 1969. (ISBN 0-394-81461-4). Pantheon.
--Squawwwk!. Rockwell, Gail, illus. LC 73-189262. (Illus.). 147 p. 20cm. 1972. (ISBN 0-316-75339-4). Little, Brown.
--The Thief. Rockwell, Gail, illus. LC 76-19380. p. cm. 83p. 1977. (ISBN 0-440-08774-0). (ISBN 0-440-08775-9). Delacorte Press.
--Tin Cans. Lambert, Saul (1928-), illus. LC 75-890. (Illus.). 70 p. 22cm. 1975. (ISBN 0-87888-077-1). Bradbury Press.

Rockwell, Vera Cober
--The New Pioneers. LC 40-34110. 277 p. front. 20 cm. c.1940. W. A. Wilde Company.
--The New Pioneers. N.D. Wilcox & Follett Co.

Rockwood, Harry
--Harry Sharpe, the New York Detective. (The Eureka Detective Story). N.D. J. S. Ogilvie Co.

Rockwood, Joyce (1947-)
--Enoch's Place. LC 79-20090. 207 p. 22cm. c.1980. (ISBN 0-03-054846-2). Holt, Rinehart and Winston.
--Groundhog's Horse. Kalin, Victor, illus. LC 77-22676. (Illus.). 115 p. 22cm. c.1978. (ISBN 0-03-021526-9). Holt, Rinehart, and Winston.
--Long Man's Song. LC 74-14937. xv, 208 p. 22cm. 1975. (ISBN 0-03-013671-7). Holt, Rinehart and Winston.
--The Midnight Horse. 128p (Pub. by Holt, Rinehart & Winston). (gr. 3-7). 1980. (ISBN 0-590-31305-3). Scholastic Inc.
--To Spoil the Sun. LC 76-10568. (Illus.). p. cm. 24 cm. 180p. c.1976. (ISBN 0-03-018066-X). Holt, Rinehart and Winston. **Award: (ALA).**

Rockwood, Roy, pseud., see Stratemeyer Syndicate.

Rockwood, Roy, pseud.
--Adrift on the Pacific: Or, The Secret of the Island Cave. Stratemeyer Syndicate. Nuttall, Charles, illus. vi, 248 p. front., plates. 19 1/2 cm. Reissue of 1908 ed. (The Sea Treasure Ser: Vol. 1). c.1908. Grosset & Dunlap.
--Adrift on the Pacific: Or, The Secret of the Island Cave. Stratemeyer Syndicate. Nuttall, Charles, illus. LC 8-14520. 20 cm. vi, 248p. (The Deep Sea Ser.: Vol. 3). 1908. Grosset & Dunlap.
--Bomba the Jugle Boy. Stratemeyer Syndicate. Rogers, Walter S., illus. Repr. of 1926 ed (Pub. by Cupples & Leon Co) (Bomba the Jungle Boy Ser.: Vol. 1). 1953. Grosset & Dunlap.
--Bomba the Jungle Boy. Stratemeyer Syndicate. Rogers, Walter S., illus. LC 77-84109. 180 p. 20cm. Repr. of 1926 ed (Pub. by Cupples & Leon Co). (Bomba the Jungle Boy Ser.: Vol. 1). c.1978. (ISBN 0-448-14701-7). Grosset & Dunlap.
--Bomba the Jungle Boy. Stratemeyer Syndicate. Rogers, Walter S., illus. Repr. of 1926 ed (Pub. by Cupples & Leon Co). (Bomba the Jungle Boy Ser.: Vol. 1). N.D. McLoughlin Brothers - Clover Books.
--Bomba the Jungle Boy Among the Pygmies: Or, Battling with Stealthy Foes. Stratemeyer Syndicate. Suk, A., illus. LC 31-14332. 2 p. l., 212 p. front. 19 1/2 cm. (Bomba the Jungle Boy Ser.: Vol. 12). c.1931. Cupples & Leon Company.
--Bomba the Jungle Boy Among the Slaves: Or, Daring Adventures in the Valley of Skulls. Stratemeyer Syndicate. Hastings, Howard Livingston (1887-), illus. LC 29-11399. 2 p. l., 210 p. front. 19 1/2 cm. (Bomba the Jungle Boy Ser.: Vol. 8). c.1929. Cupples & Leon Company.
--Bomba the Jungle Boy Among the Slaves. Stratemeyer Syndicate. Repr. of 1929 ed (Pub. by Cupples & Leon Co). (Bomba the Jungle Boy Ser.: Vol. 8). 1953. Grosset & Dunlap.
--Bomba the Jungle Boy Among the Slaves. Stratemeyer Syndicate. Hastings, Howard Livingston (1887-), illus. Repr. of 1929 ed (Pub. by Cupples & Leon Co). (Bomba the Jungle Boy Ser.: Vol. 8). N.D. McLoughlin Brothers - Clover Books.
--Bomba the Jungle Boy and the Cannibals: Or, Winning Against Native Dangers. Stratemeyer Syndicate. Hastings, Howard Livingston (1887-), illus. LC 32-13781. 2 p. l., 207 p. front. 19 1/2 cm. (Bomba the Jungle Boy Ser.: Vol. 13). c.1932. Cupples & Leon Company.
--Bomba the Jungle Boy and the Hostile Chieftain: Or, A Hazardous Trek to the Sea. Stratemeyer Syndicate. Hastings, Howard Livingston (1887-), illus. LC 34-6197. 2 p. l., 212 p. front. 19 cm. (Bomba the Jungle Boy Ser.: Vol. 16). c.1934. Cupples & Leon Company.
--Bomba the Jungle Boy and the Lost Explorers: Or, A Wonderful Revelation. Stratemeyer Syndicate. Hastings, Howard Livingston (1887-), illus. LC 30-168946. 2 p. l., 210 p. front. 19 1/2 cm. (Bomba the Jungle Boy Ser.: Vol. 10). c.1930. Cupples & Leon Company.
--Bomba the Jungle Boy and the Lost Explorers. Stratemeyer Syndicate. Hastings, Howard Livingston (1887-), illus. Repr. of 1930 ed (Pub. by Cupples & Leon Co) (Bomba the Jungle Boy Ser.: Vol. 10). 1953. Grosset & Dunlap.
--Bomba the Jungle Boy and the Painted Hunters: Or, A Long Search Rewarded. Stratemeyer Syndicate. Hastings, Howard Livingston (1887-), illus. LC 32-137909. 2 p. l., 206 p. front. 19 1/2 cm. (Bomba the Jungle Boy Ser.: Vol. 14). c.1932. Cupples & Leon Company.
--Bomba the Jungle Boy and the River Demons: Or, Outwitting the Savage Medicine Man. Stratemeyer Syndicate. Hastings, Howard Livingston (1887-), illus. 2 p. l., 209 p. front. 19 1/2 cm. (Bomba the Jungle Boy Ser.: Vol. 15). c.1933. Cupples & Leon Company.
--Bomba the Jungle Boy at the Giant Cataract: Or, Chief Nascanora and His Captives. Stratemeyer Syndicate. Rogers, Walter S., illus. (Bomba the Jungle Boy Ser.: Vol. 3). 1926. Cupples & Leon Co.
--Bomba the Jungle Boy at the Giant Cataract. Stratemeyer Syndicate. Rogers, Walter S., illus. Repr. of 1926 ed (Pub. by Cupples & Leon Co). (Bomba the Jungle Boy Ser.: Vol. 3). 1953. Grosset & Dunlap.
--Bomba the Jungle Boy at the Giant Cataract. Stratemeyer Syndicate. Rogers, Walter S., illus. Repr. of 1926 ed (Pub. by Cupples & Leon Co). (Bomba the Jungle Boy Ser.: Vol. 3). N.D. McLoughlin Brothers - Clover Books.
--Bomba the Jungle Boy at the Moving Mountain: Or, the Mystery of the Caves of Fire. Stratemeyer Syndicate. Rogers, Walter S., illus. (Bomba the Jungle Boy Ser.: Vol. 2). 1926. Cupples & Leon Co.
--Bomba the Jungle Boy at the Moving Mountain. Stratemeyer Syndicate. Rogers, Walter S., illus. Repr. of 1926 ed (Pub. by Cupples & Leon Co). (Bomba the Jungle Boy Ser.: Vol. 2). 1953. Grosset & Dunlap.
--Bomba the Jungle Boy at the Moving Mountain. Stratemeyer Syndicate. Rogers, Walter S., illus. Repr. of 1926 ed (Pub. by Cupples & Leon Co). (Bomba the Jungle Boy Ser.: Vol. 2). N.D. McLoughlin Brothers - Clover Books.
--Bomba the Jungle Boy in a Strange Land: Or, Facing the Unknown. Stratemeyer Syndicate. Hastings, Howard Livingston (1887-), illus. LC 31-14331. 2 p. l., 209 p. front. 19 1/2 cm. (Bomba the Jungle Boy Ser.: Vol. 11). c.1931. Cupples & Leon Company.
--Bomba the Jungle Boy in the Abandoned City: Or, A Treasure Ten Thousand Years Old. Stratemeyer Syndicate. Rogers, Walter S., illus. (Bomba the Jungle Boy Ser.: Vol. 5). 1927. Cupples & Leon Co.
--Bomba the Jungle Boy in the Abandoned City. Stratemeyer Syndicate. Rogers, Walter S., illus. Repr. of 1927 ed (Pub. by Cupples & Leon Co). (Bomba the Jungle Boy Ser.: Vol. 5). 1953. Grosset & Dunlap.
--Bomba the Jungle Boy in the Abandoned City. Stratemeyer Syndicate. Rogers, Walter S., illus. Repr. of 1927 ed (Pub. by Cupples & Leon Co). (Bomba the Jungle Boy Ser.: Vol. 5). N.D. McLoughlin Brothers - Clover Books.
--Bomba the Jungle Boy in the Land of Burning Lava: Or, Outwitting Superstitious Natives. Stratemeyer Syndicate. Hastings, Howard Livingston (1887-), illus. LC 36-89769. 2 p. l., 206 p. front. 19 cm. (Bomba the Jungle Boy Ser.: Vol. 18). c.1936. Cupples & Leon Company.
--Bomba the Jungle Boy in the Perilous Kingdom: Or, Braving Strange Hazards. Stratemeyer Syndicate. Hastings, Howard Livingston (1887-), illus. LC 37-360955. iii, 208 p. front. 19 cm. (Bomba the Jungle Boy Ser.: Vol. 19). c.1937. Cupples & Leon Company.
--Bomba the Jungle Boy in the Steaming Grotto: Or, Victorious Through Flame and Fury. Stratemeyer Syndicate. Hastings, Howard Livingston (1887-), illus. LC 38-17381. iv, 209 p. front. 19 cm. (Bomba the Jungle Boy Ser.: Vol. 20). c.1938. Cupples & Leon Company.

--The Boy with the U. S. Survey. LC 9-24020. 381p. front. 20 1/2cm. (U. S. Service Ser.). 1909. Lothrop, Lee & Shepard Co.
--The Boy with the U. S. Trappers. LC 19-17885. 388p. front. 20 1/2cm. (U. S. Service Ser.). c.1919. Lothrop, Lee & Shepard.
--The Boy with the U.S Life Savers. LC 15-18115. 336p. (U.S. Service Ser.). 1915. Lothrop, Lee & Shepard.
--The Boy with the U.S Marines. LC 26-20330. iv, 259p. front., pl. 20cm. (U.S service Ser.). 1926. Lothrop, Lee & Shepard.
--The Finder of Fire. LC 27-6549. 3 p. l., 272, 1 p. front. 19 1/2 cm. 1927. D. Appleton and Company.
--The Gem-Hunters. Federer, Charles A., illus. LC 24-11572. 362 p. front., plates. 20 1/2 cm. (His Museum series). c.1924. Lothrop, Lee & Shepard Co.
--The Heroes of the Ruins. (Round the World With the Boy Journalists). N.D. A. L. Burt. Co.
--Heroes of the Ruins. Federer, Charles A., illus. LC 22-20539. ix p., 1 l., 13-256 p. col. front., plates. 20 cm. (His Round the world with the boy journalists: III). c.1922. George H. Doran Company.
--Hunters of Ocean Depths. LC 25-8112. 303p. (The Museum Books). 1925. Lothrop,Lee & Shepard.
--Hunting Hidden Treasure in the Andes. (Round the World with the Boy Journalists). N.D. A. L. Burt. Co.
--Hunting Hidden Treasure in the Andes. Federer, Charles A., illus. LC 22-1945. vi p., 2 l., 11-309 p. col. front., plates. 20 cm. (Half-title: Round the world with the boy journalists:II)). c.1921. George H. Doran Company.
--In the Days Before Columbus. Federer, Charles A., illus. LC 22-1974. xiv p., 1 l., 17-334 p. col. front., plates, maps. 20 cm. (Half-title: Romance-history of America: I)). c.1921. George H. Doran Company.
--The Magic Makers of Morocco. (Round the World With the Boy Journalists). N.D. A. L. Burt Co.
--The Magic-Makers of Morocco. Federer, Charles A., illus. LC 24-9668. vi p., 2 l., 11-232 p. col. front., plates. 20 1/2 cm. (His Round the world with the young journalists. V)). c.1924. George H. Doran Company.
--The Monster Hunters. (The Museum Books). N.D. Lothrop, Lee & Shepard.
--The News-Hunters. LC 26-105632. ix, 321 p. front., plates, ports. 20 1/2 cm. (His Museum series). c.1926. Lothrop, Lee & Shepard Co.
--Plotting in Pirate Seas. (Round the World With the Boy Journalists). N.D. A. L. Burt Co.
--Plotting in Pirate Seas. Federer, Charles A., illus. LC 22-194468. vi p., 2 l., 11-251 p. col. front., plates. 20 cm. (Half-title: Round the world with the boy journalist: I)). c.1921. George H. Doran Company.
--The Polar Hunters. LC 17-13187. 6 p. l., 369 p. front., plates, port. 20 1/2 cm. (His The Museum books). 1917. Lothrop, Lee & Shepard Co.
--The Pyramid Builder. LC 29-19458. 3 p. l., 247, 1 p. front. 19 1/2 cm. 1929. D. Appleton and Company.
--The Quest of the Western World. Federer, Charles A., illus. viii p., 1 l., 11-314 p. col. front., plates, maps. 20 cm. (Half-title: Romance-history of America: II)). c.1921. George H. Doran Company.
--The Sahara Hunters. LC 23-9672. 329 p. front., plates. 20 1/2 cm. (His The Museum series). c.1923. Lothrop, Lee & Shepard Co.
--The Tamer of Herds. LC 28-4065. 3 p. l., 241 p. front. 19 1/2 cm. 1928. D. Appleton & Company.
--A Toreador of Spain. (Round the World with Boy Journalists). N.D. A. L. Burt Co.
--A Toreador of Spain. Federer, Charles A., illus. LC 23-13313. vi p., 2 l., 11-268 p. col. front., plates. 20 1/2 cm. (His Round the world with the young journalists: IV). c.1923. George H. Doran Company.
--The Tusk-Hunters. LC 27-10465. 2 p. l., 3-308 p. front., plates. 20 1/2 cm. (His Museum series). c.1927. Lothrop, Lee & Shepard Co.
--The Wonder of War at Sea. LC 19-6767. xi, 376 p. front., plates. 20 1/2 cm. 1919. Lothrop, Lee & Shepard Co.
--The Wonder of War in the Air. LC 17-30275. xii p., 1 l., 347 p. front., illus., plates. 20 1/2 cm. c.1917. Lothrop, Lee & Shepard Co.
--The Wonder of War in the Holy Land. LC 19-15229. 6 p. l., 368 p. front., plates. 20 cm. (His Museum series). c.1919. Lothrop, Lee & Shepard Co.
--The Wonder of War on Land. LC 18-17244. viii, 3, 372 p. front., plates. 20 1/2 cm. c.1918. Lothrop, Lee & Shepard Co.
--The Wreck-Hunters. LC 22-7207. 359 p. front., plates. 21 cm. c.1922. Lothrop, Lee & Shepard Co.

Romaine, Florence
--The Flute Boy of the Navajos. Hogner, Nils (1893-1970), illus. LC 35-14581. 4 p. l., 11-80 p. incl. front., illus. 19 1/2 cm. (Our changing world). 1935. T. Nelson and Sons.
--Whistling Bill. Tousey, Thomas Sanford, illus. LC 37-30895. 61 p. incl. front., illus. 19 1/2 cm. (Our changing world). 1937. T. Nelson and Son.

Romanek, Enid Warner
--Teddy. Romanek, Enid Warner, illus. LC 78-23177. (Illus.). 32 p. 26cm. c.1978. (ISBN 0-684-15811-6). Scribner.

Romano, Louis G., jt. auth. see Georgiady, Nicholas P.

Romaunt, Christopher
--The Island Home: The Young Castaways. 1874. D. Lothrop & Co.

Rombola, John, illus.
--The Little Disaster. LC 70-107086. (Illus.). 31 p. 17cm. (Bill Martin instant reader). 1970. (ISBN 0-03-084598-X). Holt, Rinehart and Winston.

Romm, J. Leonard (1946-)
--The Swastika on the Synagogue Door. Marks, Kathleen F., illus. LC 83-27263. (A Lazarus Family Mystery). c.1984. (ISBN 0-940646-53-6). Rossel Books.

Gay, Romney, pseud., see Britcher, Phyllis.

Gay, Romney, pseud. 1900-) & Piatti, Celestino (1922-), illus.
--Children's Story Book: More Than Sixty Famous Stories with New Illustrations. Britcher, Phyllis. LC 35-33162. 1 p. l., 7-285 p. col. front., illus. 29 1/2 cm. c.1934. Whitman Publishing Company.

Romriell, Gerri
--Charlie Chicken and Mr. Worm. LC 75-13416. (Illus.). 27 p. 29cm. (Gotalott series). c.1969. Imed.

Romskaug, Brenda, tr. see Romskaug, Brenda & Romskaug, Reidar.

Romskaug, Brenda & Romskaug, Reidar, eds.
--Norwegian Fairy Tales. Pettersen, Ivar, illus. Romskaug, Brenda & Romskaug, Reidar, trs. LC 63-18002. (Illus.). 128p. N.D. Dufour Editions.

Romskaug, Reidar, jt. ed. see Romskaug, Brenda.

Romskaug, Reidar, tr. see Romskaug, Brenda & Romskaug, Reidar.

Ronald, James (1905-)
--She Got What She Asked for. LC 41-22360. 286 p. 21 cm. c.1941. J. B. Lippincott Company.

Ronalds, Mary Teresa (1946-)
--The Eyewitness: The Testimony of John. Bozeman, Nancy, illus. 320 p. 24cm. 1967. (ISBN 0-687-12511-1). Abingdon Press.

Ronan, Eve, jt. auth. see Ronan, Margaret.

Ronan, Margaret (1918-)
--The Dynamite Book of Ghosts & Haunted Houses. 96p. (Orig.). (gr. 3 up). 1980. (ISBN 0-590-30622-7, Schol Pap). Scholastic Inc.
--House of Evil & Other Strange Unsolved Mysteries. (gr. 7 up). 1977. (ISBN 0-590-11857-9). Scholastic Inc.
--Master of the Dead, & Other Strange Unsolved Mysteries. (gr. 7-12). 1980. (ISBN 0-590-30005-9). Scholastic Inc.
--Strange Unsolved Mysteries. (gr. 7-12). 1975. (ISBN 0-590-01654-7, Schol Pap). Scholastic Inc.

Ronan, Margaret (1918-) & Ronan, Eve
--Curse of the Vampires. (gr. 7-12). 1980. (ISBN 0-590-30062-8). Scholastic Inc.

Ronay, Nadja
--Ginger: A Story. Accardo, Anthony, illus. LC 82-170230. (Illus.). 61 p. 37cm. c.1981. Magnolia Publications.

Rongen, Bjorn (1906-)
--Anna of the Bears. Paton, Jane Elizabeth (1934-), illus. Ramsden, Evelyn, tr. LC 67-2663. 118 p. illus. 21 cm. (an ariel book. 1967, c.1965. Farrar, Straus & Giroux.
--Anna of the Bears. Paton, Jane Elizabeth (1934-), illus. LC 66-8129. 124 p. illus. 19 cm. (Pied Piper book). 1965. Methuen.
--Olaf and the Echoing Cave. Pinto, Ralph & Ramsden, Evelyn, illus. Ramsden, Evelyn, tr. (Illus.). 128 p. 24cm. 1968, c.1962. McGraw-Hill.

Roo, Anne Louise de see De Roo, Anne Louise.

Rood, Henry Edward (1867-)
--In Camp at Bear Pond. Mears, W. E., illus. LC 4-31052. 3 p. l., 262, 1 p. front., 3 pl. 19 cm. 1904. Harper & Brothers.

Rood, Ronald N (1920-)
--How Do You Spank a Porcupine?. LC 69-17070. (Illus.). 160 p. 21cm. 1969. Trident Press.
--Hundred Acre Welcome: Story of Cinchoteague Pony. N.D. (ISBN 0-8289-0058-2). Stephen Greene Press.
--The Loon in My Bathtub: Nature for the Family. N.D. Stephen Greene Press.

Roodkapje & Bruna, Dick (1927-)
--Dick Bruna's Little Red Riding Hood. Bruna, Dick (1927-), illus. LC 67-801. (Illus.). 28 p. 17cm. 1966. Follett Pub. Co.

Rook, David
--Neeka the Kestrel. Rook, David, illus. LC 68-26543. (Illus.). 40 ils. drawings. 72p. 1st U.S. edition. (gr. 5 up). 1968. (ISBN 0-8027-6044-9). Walker & Co.
--Run Wild, Run Free. 205p. Orig. Title: The White Colt. (gr. 7 up). 1969 (StarLine). Schol Bk Serv.

Rooke, Daphne Marie (1914-)
--Twins in Australia. Miret, Gil, illus. LC 56-8267. 183p. illus. 22cm. 1956. Houghton Mifflin.
--Twins in South Africa. Lorraine, Walter Henry (1929-), illus. LC 55-5218. (Illus.). 171 p. 21cm. 1955. Houghton Mifflin.

Roome, Doris Hardfinger
--The Secret Friend and the Blue-eyed Bunny: Two Stories for Children. 1st ed. Rene, Jo Anne Nicol, illus. LC 56-7472. (Illus.). 44p. 21cm. 1956. Exposition Press.

Rooney, Ruth, jt. ed. see Simons, Barbara Brooks.

Roop, Peter
--The Cry of the Conch. Patric, illus. LC 84-4232. (Illus.). (Treasury of Children's Hawaiian Stories). (gr. 3-5). 1984. (ISBN 0-916630-39-0). Pr Pacifica.
--Natosi: Strong Medicine. 32p. (gr. 3-8). 1984. (ISBN 0-89992-390-9). (ISBN 0-89992-090-X). Coun India Ed.
--Sik-Ki-Mi. 32p. (Indian Culture Ser.). (gr. 3-6). 1984. (ISBN 0-89992-391-7). (ISBN 0-89992-091-8). Coun India Ed.

Roop, Peter, et al.
--Go Hog Wild: Jokes from down on the Farm. Hanson, Joan (1938-), illus. LC 84-5662. (Illus.). 32p. (Make Me Laugh! Joke Bks.). (gr. 1-4). 1984. (ISBN 0-8225-0982-2). Lerner Pubns.
--Out to Lunch: Jokes about Food. Hanson, Joan (1938-), illus. LC 84-4416. (Illus.). 32p. (Make Me Laugh! Joke Bks.). (gr. 1-4). 1984. (ISBN 0-8225-0983-0). Lerner Pubns.
--Space Out: Jokes about Outer Space. Hanson, Joan (1938-), illus. LC 84-5650. (Illus.). 32p. (Make Me Laugh! Joke Bks.). (gr. 1-4). 1984. (ISBN 0-8225-0984-9). Lerner Pubns.

Rooper, Miss
--The Pic-Nic. 64p. (Prize Story Book ser.). N.D. De Witt Publishing House.
--The Sand Cave. 64p. (Prize Story Book Ser.). N.D. De Witt Publishing House.

Roorbach, Harriet A.
--I Learn About Sharing. Kurek, Sarah C., illus. N.D. (ISBN 0-687-18516-5). Abingdon Press.

Roos, Ann
--The Royal Road: Father Serra and the California Missions. Stewart, George, illus. LC 51-11178. (Illus.). 243 p. 21cm. 1951. Lippincott.

Roos, Ann, et al., eds. see Girl Scouts of the U. S. A.

Roos, Audrey Kelley (1912-1982) & Roos, Stephen Kelley (1945-)
--The Incredible Cat Caper. Coville, Katherine (1939-), illus. LC 85-1626. (Illus.). 136 p. 22cm. c.1985. (ISBN 0-385-29408-5). Delacorte Press.

Roos, Audrey Kelley (1912-1982) & Roos, William (1911-)
--The Mystery Next Door. LC 72-501. (Illus.). 121 p. 22cm. 1972. (ISBN 0-684-12949-3). Scribner.

Roos, Kelley see Roos, Audrey Kelley (1912-1982) & Roos, Stephen Kelley.

Roos, Mathilda
--At Eventide. C. A. W. , tr. from Swedish. N.D. Augustana Book Concern.
--Elsie in the Uplands. N.D. Augustana Book Concern.
--In Budding Time: Five Stories for Boys and Girls. LC 24-1976. 96 p. illus., pl. 19 cm. c.1923. Covenant Book Concern.
--Two Little Friends and the Secret of Love: With Other Stories for Little Folks. (Illus.). 1905. Augustana Book Concern.

Roos, Stephen Kelley, jt. auth. see Roos, Audrey Kelley.

Roos, Stephen Kelley (1945-)
--My Horrible Secret. Newsom, Carol, illus. LC 82-14954. 119 p. 22cm. c.1983. (ISBN 0-440-03788-3). Delacorte Press.
--My Secret Admirer. Newsom, Carol, illus. LC 84-5010. (Illus.). 112p. (gr. 4-6). 1984. (ISBN 0-385-29342-9). (ISBN 0-385-29343-7). Delacorte.
--The Terrible Truth: Secrets of a Sixth-Grader. Newsom, Carol, illus. (gr. 5-7). 1983. (ISBN 0-385-29306-2). Delacorte.

Roos, William, jt. auth. see Roos, Audrey Kelley.

Roosevelt, Anna Eleanor (1884-1962)
--Christmas, A Story. Kredel, Fritz (1900-1973), illus. LC 40-84735. 1940. Knopf.
--Scamper: The Bunny Who Went to the White House. Flack, Marjorie (1897-1958), illus. LC 34-5291. 72 p. incl. col. front., illus., col. plates (part double) 21 x 19 cm. 1934. The Macmillan Company.
--Scamper's Christmas: More About the White House Bunny. Flack, Marjorie (1897-1958), illus. LC 34-38910. 71 p. incl. col. front., illus., col. plates (part double) 21 x 19 cm. 1934. The Macmillan Company.

Roosevelt, Michele Chopin
--Spring Is Here!. LC 81-80764. (Illus.). 8 p. 16cm. c.1982. (ISBN 0-394-84971-X). Random House.
--Zoo Animals. Roosevelt, Michele Chopin, illus. 1983. Random.

Roosevelt, Wyn (1870-)
--The Frontier Boys in Colorado: Or, Captured by Indians. Schneider, Sophie, illus. LC 8-19094. 2 p. l., 9-260 p. front., plates. 20 cm. c.1908. Chatterton-Peck Company.
--The Frontier Boys in Hawaii. (Illus.). (The Frontier Boys). N.D. A. L. Chatterton Co.
--The Frontier Boys in Hawaii: Or, The Mystery of the Hollow Mountain. Schneider, Sophie, illus. LC 9-18590. 19cm. 256p. 1909. Chatterton-Peck Co.
--The Frontier Boys in Mexico. (Illus.). (The Frontier Boys). N.D. A. L. Chatterton Co.
--The Frontier Boys in the Grand Canyon. (Illus.). (The Frontier Boys). N.D. A. L. Chatterton Co.
--The Frontier Boys in the Rockies. (Illus.). (The Frontier Boys). N.D. A. L. Chatterton Co.
--The Frontier Boys in the Rockies: Or, A Winter in the Big Canyon. LC 9-17210. 20cm. 245p. 1909. Chatterton-Peck Co.
--The Frontier Boys in the Saddle. Mencl, Rudolf, illus. LC 10-11873. 2 p. l., 9-260 p. front., plates. 20 cm. c.1910. A. L. Chatterton Co.
--The Frontier Boys in the Sierras. (Illus.). (The Frontier Boys). N.D. A. L. Chatterton Co.
--The Frontier Boys in the Sierras: Or, The Lost Mine. Schneider, Sophie, illus. LC 9-18593. 19cm. 259p. 1909. Chatterton-Peck Co.
--The Frontier Boys in the South Seas. Mencl, Rudolf, illus. LC 12-213267. 2 p. l., 9-258 p. front., plates. 20 cm. c.1912. A. L. Chatterton Co.
--The Frontier Boys on the Coast. (Illus.). (The Frontier Boys). N.D. A. L. Chatterton.
--The Frontier Boys on the Coast: Or, In the Pirate's Power. Schneider, Sophie, illus. LC 9-17209. 20cm. 252p. 1909. Chatterton-Peck & Co.
--The Frontier Boys on the Overland Trail. Schneider, Sophie, illus. LC 8-15884. 2 p. l., 9-258 p. front., plates. 20 cm. c.1908. Chatterton-Peck Company.

Root, Betty
--My Kitten. Mynott, Pat, illus. (Illus.). 10p. (ps). 1973. Rand.
--My Teddy Bear. Murphy, Jill (1949-), illus. (Illus.). 10p. (ps). 1973. Rand.

Root, Charlet
--The Feast of Lamps: A Story of India. Duvoisin, Roger Antoine (1904-1980), illus. LC 38-29543. 2 p. l., 9-75 p. incl. col. front., illus. (part col.) 24 cm. 1938. A. Whitman & Co.

Root, Harvey Woods (1876-)
--Tommy with the Big Tents. Skinner, T., illus. LC 24-5804. 5 p. l., 202 p. front., plates. 20 cm. c.1924. Harper & Brothers.

Root, Phyllis
--Hidden Places. San Souci, Daniel, illus. LC 83-8615. 32p. (Adventure Diaries). (gr. 3-6). 1983. (ISBN 0-940742-30-6, Pub. by Carnival Press). (ISBN 0-940742-23-3). Raintree Pubs.
--Moon Tiger. Young, Ed (1931-), illus. LC 85-7572. (Illus.). 32 p. c.1985. (ISBN 0-03-000042-4). Holt, Rinehart, and Winston.

Root, Phyllis & Marron, Carol A.
--Gretchen's Grandma. Ray, Deborah (1940-), illus. LC 83-8608. c.1983. (ISBN 0-940742-16-0). Raintree Publishers.

Root, Shelton L., jt. ed. see Arbuthnot, May Hill.

Rootham, Helen, ed.
--Kossovo: Heroic Songs of the Serbs. Rosandic, Toma, illus. LC 78-74518. Repr. of 1920 ed. (Children's Literature Reprint Ser.). 1979. (ISBN 0-8486-0221-8). Core Collection.

Ropes, E. Mary
--Bel's Baby. (Young Folks Ser, Number Three). N.D. Set. Fleming H. Revell Co.
--Made Clear at Last. (Illus.). 80p. (The Rosebud Ser.). N.D. Fleming H. Revell Co.
--Susie Wood Charge. (Illus.). 80p. (The Rosebud Ser.). N.D. Fleming H. Revell Co.

Ropner, Pamela
--The Golden Impala. Thompson, Ralph, illus. LC 58-878836. 159p. illus. 22cm. 1958. Criterion Books.
--The Guardian Angel. Bewley, Sheila, illus. LC 67-9010. 159 p. illus. 21 cm. 1967, c.1966. Coward-McCann.
--The House of the Bittern. Williams, Kathleen M., illus. (Illus.). 127 p. 22cm. 1st U.S. edition. 1967, c.1965. Coward-McCann.
--The Sea Friends. LC 75-88875. 190 p. 21cm. 1969, c.1968. Coward-McCann.

Roquette-Buisson, Vicomtesse, tr. see Spitteler, Carl Friedrich George.

Rorem, Melva, tr. see Wiemer, Rudolf Otto.

Rosenberg, Ethel Clifford, et al. (1915-1978)
--War Paint and Wagon Wheels: Stories of Indians and Pioneers. Fay, Leo Charles, et al. (1920-), eds. Kinney, David & Harris, Bill, illus. LC 67-17749. (Illus.). 192 p. 25cm. 1968. David-Stewart Pub. Co.
Rosenberg, Ethel Clifford (1915-1978)
--A Bear Before Breakfast. Clifford, Eth, pseud. Oechsli, Kelly (1918-), illus. LC 62-8006. unpaged. illus. 29cm. 1962. Putnam.
--A Bear Can't Bake a Cake for You. Lacy, Jacqueline, illus. LC 62-22168. (Illus.). 24cm. (Reading-go-Round Bks.). 1962. E. C. Seale.
--The King Who Was Different. Clifford, Eth, pseud. 1st ed. Webb, Francoise, illus. LC 69-12436. (Illus.). 48 p. 24cm. (gr. 1-3). 1969. Bobbs-Merrill.
--Mommies Are for Loving. Penn, Ruth Bonn, pseud. Emberley, Edward Randolph (1931-), illus. LC 62-12029. unpaged. illus. 16x21cm. (gr. k-3). 1962. (ISBN 0-399-60468-5). Putnam.
--Pigeons Don't Growl and Bears Don't Coo. Clifford, Eth, pseud. Friend, Esther, illus. LC 63-21736. (Illus.). 31 p. 23cm. 1963. E. C. Seale.
--Red Is Never a Mouse. Clifford, Eth, pseud. Heckler, Bill, illus. LC 60-7169. unpaged. illus. 29cm. N.D. Bobbs-Merrill.
--Search for the Crescent Moon. Clifford, Eth, pseud. Holmes, Bea, illus. LC 72-13582. (Illus.). x, 207 p. 22cm. 1973. (ISBN 0-395-16035-9). Houghton Mifflin.
--Simply Silly. Penn, Ruth Bonn, pseud. Reisner, Joe, illus. LC 64-22146. (Illus.). 31 p. 24cm. 1964. E. C. Seale.
--Why Is an Elephant Called an Elephant?. Clifford, Eth, pseud. 1st ed. Lacy, Jacqueline, illus. LC 66-18599. 1 v. (unpaged) illus. (part col.) 27 cm. 1966. Bobbs-Merrill.
--The Witch that wasn't. Clifford, Eth, pseud. Kauper, Jean Dorion, illus. LC 64-18133. 24cm. 32p. 1964. E. C. Seale & Co.
--The Year of the Second Christmas. Clifford, Eth, pseud. 1st ed. Learner, Stan, illus. LC 59-14301. unpaged. illus. 21x26cm. c.1959. Bobbs-Merrill.
--The Year of the Three-Legged Deer. Clifford, Eth, pseud. Cuffari, Richard (1925-1978), illus. LC 75-185435. (Illus.). ix, 164 p. 22cm. 1972. (ISBN 0-395-13724-1). Houghton Mifflin.
Rosenberg, Ethel Clifford (1915-1978) & Clifford, David, pseud.
--No Pigs, No Possums, No Pandas. Clifford, Eth, pseud. Rosenberg, David. LC 61-15074. unpaged. illus. 29cm. c.1961. Putnam.
Rosenberg, Jeanne see Matthews, Ann.
Rosenberg, Lesley
--Child Star and the Sun Cakes. Murray, Mark C, illus. LC 78-31409. (Illus.). 32 p. c.1979. (ISBN 0-89742-020-9). (ISBN 0-89742-007-1). Dawne-Leigh Publications.
Rosenberg, Melrich Vonelm (1905-)
--With Sword & Song. Blaisdell, Elinore (1904-), illus. LC 37-291651. 5 p. l., 210 p. incl. col. front. double col. plates. 22 cm. 1937. Houghton Mifflin Company.
Rosenberg, Nancy Sherman see Sherman, Nancy.
Rosenberg, Sondra
--Are There Any More at Home Like You?. Vasiliu, Mircea (1920-), illus. LC 72-89429. (Illus.). 138 p. 22cm. 1973. St. Martin's Press.
--Will There Never Be a Prince?. Vasiliu, Mircea (1920-), illus. LC 70-94353. (Illus.). 136 p. 22cm. 1970. St. Martin's Press.
Rosenblatt, Arthur S
--The Care Bears Battle the Freeze Machine. Ewers, Joe, illus. LC 83-24955. (Illus.). 44 p. 29cm. (A Tale from the Care Bears). c.1984. (ISBN 0-910313-15-6). Parker Bros.
--Keep on Caring. LC 84-26610. p. cm. (A Tale from the Care Bear Cousins). c.1985. (ISBN 0-910313-84-9). Parker Bros.
--Smarty. LC 81-12412. p. cm. c.1981. (ISBN 0-316-75720-9). Little, Brown.
--Strawberry Shortcake & the Deep, Dark Woods. Sustendal, Pat, illus. (Illus.). 40p. (Strawberry Shortcake Ser.). (ps-3). 1983. (ISBN 0-910313-07-5). Parker Bros.
Rosenblatt, Suzanne Mavis (1937-)
--Everyone Is Going Somewhere. Rosenblatt, Suzanne Maris (1937-), illus. LC 75-35920. (Illus.). 32 p. 26cm. c.1976. (ISBN 0-02-777700-6). Macmillan.
Rosenbloom, Joseph (1928-)
--Biggest Riddle Book in the World. Behr, Joyce (1929-), illus. LC 76-1165. (Illus.). 272 p. 22cm. c.1976. (ISBN 0-8069-4532-X). (ISBN 0-8069-4533-8). Sterling Pub. Co.
--Daffy Definitions. Behr, Joyce (1929-), illus. LC 82-19323. (Illus.). 128 p. 21cm. 1983, c.1977. Sterling Pub. Co.
--Daffy Dictionary: Funabridged Definitions from Aardvark to Zuider Zee. Behr, Joyce (1929-), illus. LC 76-51173. (Illus.). 256 p. 22cm. 1977. (ISBN 0-8069-4542-7). Sterling Pub. Co.
--Deputy Dan and the Bank Robbers. Raglin, Tim, illus. LC 84-15969. p. cm. (Step into Reading Book. A Step 3 Book). 1985. (ISBN 0-394-87045-X). (ISBN 0-394-97045-4). Random House.
--Deputy Dan Gets His Man. Raglin, Tim, illus. LC 85-1686. p. cm. (Step into reading. A Step 3 book). 1985. (ISBN 0-394-87045-X). (ISBN 0-394-97045-4). Random House.
--The Funniest Riddle Book Ever!. Wilhelm, Hans (1945-), illus. LC 84-16192. (Illus.). 24 p. 22cm. c.1985. (ISBN 0-8069-4698-9). (ISBN 0-8069-4699-7). Sterling Pub. Co.
--Gigantic Joke Book. LC 77-93310. (Illus.). (gr. 2 up). 1978. (ISBN 0-8069-4590-7). (ISBN 0-8069-4591-5). Sterling.
--How Do You Make an Elephant Laugh? & Six Hundred Ninety-Nine Other Zany Riddles. Behr, Joyce (1929-), illus. LC 79-65074. (Illus.). (gr. 3 up). 1979. (ISBN 0-8069-4604-0). (ISBN 0-8069-4605-9). Sterling.
--Knock-Knock! Who's There. Hoffman, Sanford, illus. LC 84-8617. p. cm. 128p. 1984. (ISBN 0-8069-4696-2). (ISBN 0-8069-4697-0). Sterling Pub. Co.
--Laughs, Hoots & Giggles. Behr, Joyce (1929-) & Hoffman, Sanford, illus. LC 84-8911. (Illus.). 480 p. 22cm. 1984. (ISBN 0-8069-5530-9). (ISBN 0-8069-5531-7). Sterling Pub. Co.
--The Looniest Limerick Book in the World. Hoffman, Sanford, illus. LC 81-85034. (Illus.). 128 p. 22cm. c.1982. (ISBN 0-8069-4660-1). (ISBN 0-8069-4661-X). Sterling.
--Mad Scientist: Riddles, Jokes, Fun. Hoffman, Sanford, illus. LC 82-50555. (Illus.). 128 p. 22cm. c.1982. (ISBN 0-8069-4662-8). (ISBN 0-8069-4663-6). Sterling Pub. Co.
--Maximilian Does It Again. LC 82-18204. 128p. 1983. (ISBN 0-525-67142-0). Lodestar Bks.
--Maximilian, You're the Greatest. LC 80-20517. 142 p. 21cm. c.1980. (ISBN 0-525-66705-9). Elsevier/Nelson Books.
--Maximilian, You're the Greatest. (Illus.). 1979. Lodestar.
--Maximillian You're the Greatest. (gr. 3-6). 1979. (ISBN 0-448-17023-X, G&D). Putnam Pub Group.
--Monster Madness: Riddles, Jokes, Fun. Behr, Joyce (1929-), illus. LC 80-52339. (Illus.). 127 p. 22cm. c.1980. (ISBN 0-8069-4634-2). (ISBN 0-8069-4635-0). Sterling Pub. Co.
--The Official Wild West Joke Book. Hoffman, Sanford, illus. LC 82-19537. (Illus.). 128 p. 22cm. c.1983. (ISBN 0-8069-4666-0). (ISBN 0-8069-4667-9). Sterling Pub.
--Ridiculous Nicholas Haunted House Riddles. Behr, Joyce (1929-), illus. LC 83-9148. p. cm. c.1983. (ISBN 0-8069-4678-4). (ISBN 0-8069-4679-2). Sterling Pub. Co.
--Ridiculous Nicholas Pet Riddle Book. Behr, Joyce (1929-), illus. 1982. Sterling.
--Ridiculous Nicholas Pet Riddles. Behr, Joyce (1929-), illus. LC 81-8744. p. cm. c.1981. (ISBN 0-8069-4654-7). (ISBN 0-8069-4655-5). Sterling Pub. Co.
--Ridiculous Nicholas Riddle Book. Behr, Joyce (1929-), illus. LC 81-50988. (Illus.). 64 p. 22cm. c.1981. Sterling.
--Silly Verse (and Even Worse). Behr, Joyce (1929-), illus. LC 78-66322. (Illus.). 128 p. 22cm. c.1979. (ISBN 0-8069-4600-8). (ISBN 0-8069-4601-6). Sterling Pub. Co.
--Snappy Put-Downs & Funny Insults. Behr, Joyce (1929-), illus. LC 80-54348. (Illus.). 128 p. 22cm. c.1981. (ISBN 0-8069-4646-6). (ISBN 0-8069-4647-4). Sterling.
--Sports Riddles. 1st ed. Weissman, Sam Q., illus. LC 81-7232. (Illus.). 64 p. 21cm. 1982. Harcourt Brace Jovanovich.
--Wacky Insults and Terrible Jokes. Hoffman, Sanford, illus. LC 83-4718. (Illus.). 128 p. 22cm. c.1983. (ISBN 0-8069-4674-1). (ISBN 0-8069-4675-X). Sterling Pub. Co.
--Wild West Riddles & Jokes. Hoffman, Sanford, illus. LC 85-2632. (Illus.). 128 p. 22cm. c.1985. (ISBN 0-8069-4704-7). (ISBN 0-8069-4705-5). (ISBN 0-8069-7996-8). Sterling Pub. Co.
--The Zaniest Riddle Book in the World. Hoffman, Sanford, illus. LC 83-18102. (Illus.). 128 p. c.1984. (ISBN 0-8069-4680-6). Sterling Pub. Co.
Rosenbluth, Rosalyn
--Why Won't the Dragon Roar?. Davidson, Rosalie (1921-), illus. LC 76-30610. (Illus.). 45 p. 23cm. (Imagination book). c.1977. (ISBN 0-8116-4407-3). Garrard Pub. Co.
Rosendall, Betty (1916-)
--The Number Ten Duckling. Dunnington, Tom, illus. LC 72-1463. (Illus.). 31 p. 25cm. 1972. (ISBN 0-516-03553-3). Childrens Press.
Rosenfeld, Friedrich see Feld, Friedrich, pseud.
Rosenfeld, Friedrich (1902-)
--Engine Fourteen-Fourteen. Feld, Friedrich, pseud. Rettich, Rolf, illus. Koenig, Marion, tr. LC 65-23882. (Illus.). 63 p. 21cm. 1965. (ISBN 0-8075-2057-8). A. Whitman.
--Mystery of the Musical Umbrella. Feld, Friedrich, pseud. Jackson, Doris, illus. Holmes, William Kersley (1882-), tr. from Ger. LC 62-7885. (Illus.). 83 p. 24cm. (The Random House easy to read library, R-24). (gr. 2-4). 1962. (ISBN 0-394-90124-X). Random House.
--The Parrot of Isfahan. Feld, Friedrich, pseud. Schmischke, Kurt, illus. Holmes, William Kersley (1882-), tr. LC 70-8989. (Illus.). 94 p. 21cm. 1964. A. Whitman.
Rosenfield, James
--The Lion and the Lily. LC 72-3153. (Illus.). 209 p. 21cm. 1972. (ISBN 0-396-06644-5). Dodd, Mead.
Rosenheim, Lucile G
--The Dancing Heart. LC 51-9817. 183 p. 21 cm. 1951. Messner.
--Kathie, the New Teacher. LC 49-6146. 195 p. 21 cm. 1949. J. Messner.
--Sunny, the New Camp Counselor. LC 52-12746. 179 p. 21cm. 1952. Messner.
Rosenmiller, D. P., tr. see Hoffmann, Franz.
Rosenquist, Fingal (1907-)
--Nipper Shiffer's Donkey. Bileck, Marvin (1920-), illus. LC 55-6408. 141p. illus. 21cm. 1955. Harper.
Rosenthal, Bert
--Isiah Thomas: Pocket Magic. LC 83-10080. (Illus.). 48p. (Sportsstars Ser.). (gr. 2-8). 1983. (ISBN 0-516-04334-X). (ISBN 0-516-44334-8). Childrens.
Rosenthal, Harriet S.
--Olga the Octopus. N.D. Vantage.
Rosenthal, Jules M. (1924-)
--Alice, the Cat Who Was Hounded. Rosenthal, Jules M., illus. LC 65-11733. 1 v. (unpaged) illus. 21 cm. 1965. Whitman.
Rosenthal, M. L., tr. see Lorenzini, Carlo.
Rosenwasser, Dorothy Eckmann (1917-)
--Everett the Elephant. Rosenwasser, Dorothy Eckmann (1917-), illus. LC 62-10028. unpaged. illus. 29cm. 1962. Bobbs-Merrill.
Roser, Bill & Hotchner, Katherine Feingold
--Dorothy and the Wizard of Oz: A Participation Musical. LC 83-460001. 51 p. 18cm. c.1979. Dramatic Pub. Co.
Roser, Wiltrud
--Everything About Easter Rabbits. Mayer, Eva L., tr. LC 72-7430. (Illus.). 32p. 26cm. c.1972. (ISBN 0-690-27156-5). (ISBN 0-690-27157-3). Crowell.
--Everything About Easter Rabbits. Roser, Wiltrud, illus. LC 72-7430. (Illus.). (ps-3). 1979. (ISBN 0-690-27156-5, TYC-J). (ISBN 0-690-27157-3). Har-Row.
--Everything about Easter Rabbits. Roser, Wiltrud, illus. Mayer, Eva L., tr. from Ger. LC 72-7430. (Illus.). 32p. (Trophy Picture Bk.). (ps-2). 1983. (ISBN 0-06-443038-3, Trophy). Har-Row.
--Everything about Easter Rabbits. Roser, Wiltrud, illus. 1973. Harper.
Rosetti
--Poems for Children. N.D. Educational Publishing Co.
Rosevear, Marjorie
--The Secret Cowboy. Geer, Charles Hand (1922-), illus. LC 55-9864. 155p. illus. 22cm. 1955. Messner.
Rosholt, Malcolm & Rosholt, Margaret
--The Child of Two Mothers. Larson, Lynn, illus. LC 83-63177. (Illus.). 108p. (gr. 4 up). 1983. (ISBN 0-910417-03-2). Rosholt Hse.
Rosholt, Margaret, jt. auth. see Rosholt, Malcolm.
Roskey, William
--Fifth Gospel: The Odyssey of a Time Traveler in First Century Palestine. LC 83-81189. 240p. 1984. (ISBN 0-9612112-0-2). Elghund Pub.
Rosman, Alice Grant
--Jock the Scot: The Adventures of the Dog of the House Who Gave up Town Life to Run a Country Estate. Esley, Joan, illus. LC 31-26111. 6 p. l., 204 p. col. front., illus., col. plates. 24 cm. c.1930. Minton, Balch & Company.
Rosman, Alice Grant, tr. see Genevoix, Maurice Charles-Louis.
Rosmer, Jean, pseud., see Alcanter de Brahm, Jeanne Ichard.
Rosmer, Jean, pseud.
--In Secret Service. Alcanter de Brahm, Jeanne Ichard. Lawson, Robert (1892-1957), illus. Olcott, Virginia, tr. Hoffherr, Frederic Georges, frwd. by. LC 37-18106. (Illus.). 21cm. 226p. 1937. J. B. Lippincott.
--The Princess and the Gypsy. Alcanter de Brahm, Jeanne Ichard. De Angeli, Marguerite Lofft, Mrs. (1889-), illus. Olcott, Virginia, tr. 252p. N.D. J. B. Lippincott.
Rosmond, Babette (1921-), ed.
--Prize Stories from Seventeen: Fiction Contest Winners, 1959-1968. LC 68-8950. xiii, 300 p. 21cm. (Seventeen books). 1968. (ISBN 0-02-605110-9). Macmillan.
--Seventeen from Seventeen: An Anthology of Stories. (gr. 8-10). 1967. (ISBN 0-02-605100-1). Macmillan.
--Seventeen's Stories. (gr. 6-10). 1971. Pyramid Pubns.
Rosner, Ruth
--Rhinos Don't Climb!. LC 83-47708. (Illus.). 32p. (ps-3). 1984. (ISBN 0-06-025068-2). (ISBN 0-06-025069-0). HarpJ.
Rosner, Ruth, jt. auth. see Durrell, Julie.
Rosner, Sara, ed.
--Look Back in Love: Ten Bittersweet Stories of American Life. (gr. 7-12). 1974. (ISBN 0-590-04844-9, Starline). Schol Bk Serv.
Rosny, J H, pseud., see Boex, J. H. H..
Rosny, J H, pseud. (1856-1940)
--The Giant Cat. Boex, J. H. H.. N.D. Robert M McBride.
--The Quest for Fire: A Novel of Prehistoric Times. Boex, J. H. H.. Bercher, J. O., illus. Talbott, Harold, tr. LC 67-142273. 193p. illus. 22cm. 1967. Pantheon.
Ross, Abram Bunn (1866-)
--Five Going on Six. Curtis, Elizabeth & Choate, Florence, illus. LC 28-6997. 107 p. illus. 21 cm. c.1927. The John C. Winston Company.
Ross, Andrea
--Seymour & Juvenile Skits. LC 82-70225. 60p. (gr. 3-5). 1982. (ISBN 0-9603118-8-2). Davenport.
Ross, Clinton (1861-1920)
--Adventures of Three Worthies. N.D. Putman & Sons.
Ross, Dave see Ross, David.
Ross, David (1896-1975), ed.
--The Illustrated Treasury of Poetry for Children. Burris, Burmah, illus. LC 76-86680. (Illus.). xiv, 338 p. 26cm. 1970. Grosset & Dunlap.
Ross, David (1935-)
--Letters from Foxy. Valpy, Judith, illus. LC 68-12652. 103p. illus. (pt. col. 24cm. 1st U.S. edition. 1968, c.1966. Pantheon.
Ross, David (1949-)
--Baby Bear's Christmas. Ross, David (1949-), illus. LC 85-2918. (Illus.). 32 p. 18cm. c.1985. (ISBN 0-688-05765-9). (ISBN 0-688-05766-7). W. Morrow.
--A Book of Hugs. LC 79-7896. (Illus.). 32 p. 26cm. c.1980. (ISBN 0-690-04011-3). Crowell.
--Gorp & the Jelly Sippers. Ross, David (1949-), illus. (Illus.). 32p. (gr. 2-5). 1982. (ISBN 0-8027-6473-8). Walker & Co.
--Gorp & the Space Pirates. Ross, David (1949-), illus. LC 82-62864. (Illus.). 32p. (gr. 1-3). 1983. (ISBN 0-8027-6494-0). Walker & Co.
--How to Prevent Monster Attacks. Ross, David (1949-), illus. LC 83-26536. (Illus.). 63 p. 22cm. 1984. (ISBN 0-688-03790-9). W. Morrow.
--More Hugs!. LC 83-46167. (Illus.). 32. c.1984. (ISBN 0-690-04406-2). (ISBN 0-690-04407-0). Crowell.
--Mummy Madness: Jokes, Riddles, Things to Do. LC 79-13494. (Illus.). 71 p. 23cm. 1979. (ISBN 0-531-04094-1). F. Watts.
--Space Monster. Ross, David (1949-), illus. LC 80-54705. (Illus.). 32 p. 22cm. 1981. (ISBN 0-8027-6415-0). Walker.
--Space Monster Gorp & the Runaway Computer. Ross, David (1949-), illus. LC 83-40392. 32p. 1984. (ISBN 0-8027-6524-6). Walker & Co.
Ross, David (1949-) & Kinzel, Dotti
--Rat Race and Other Rodent Jokes. Ross, David (1949-), illus. LC 82-14330. p. cm. 1983. (ISBN 0-688-01878-5). Morrow.
Ross, David (1949-) & Wilson, Jeanne (1954-)
--Mr. Terwilliger's Secret. LC 80-21835. (Illus.). 32 p. 22cm. (Easy-read story book). 1981. (ISBN 0-531-04191-3). F. Watts.
Ross, Diana, see Denney, Diana.
Ross, Diana (1910-)
--Ebenezer the big balloon. N.D. Transatlantic Arts, Inc.
--I Love My Love with an A. Wood, Leslie (1920-), illus. (Illus.). 32p. (ps-5). 1972. (ISBN 0-571-09340-X). Faber & Faber.
--Little Red Engine & the Rocket. (gr. k-2). N.D. (ISBN 0-571-05256-8). Transatlantic.
--Little Red Engine & the Taddlecombe Outing. Wood, Leslie (1920-), illus. (gr. 1-3). 1969. (ISBN 0-571-08697-7). Transatlantic.
--Little Red Engine Gets a Name. (Illus.). (gr. k-2). N.D. (ISBN 0-571-06439-6). Transatlantic.
--Little Red Engine Goes Carolling. (gr. 1-3). 1971. (ISBN 0-571-09775-8). Transatlantic.
--Little Red Engine Goes Home. (Illus.). (gr. k-2). 1959. (ISBN 0-571-03362-8). Transatlantic.
--Little Red Engine Goes to Be Mended. (gr. k-2). N.D. (ISBN 0-571-06589-9). Transatlantic.
--Little Red Engine Goes to Market. (Illus.). (gr. k-2). N.D. (ISBN 0-571-06330-6). Transatlantic.
--Little Red Engine Goes to Town. (Illus.). (gr. k-2). N.D. (ISBN 0-571-06420-5). Transatlantic.
--Little Red Engine Goes Travelling. (Illus.). (gr. k-2). N.D. (ISBN 0-571-06111-7). Transatlantic.
--Old Perisher. Ardizzone, Edward Jeffrey Irving (1900-1979), illus. (Illus.). 32p. (ps-5). 1965. (ISBN 0-571-06162-1). Faber & Faber.

--The Story of the Little Red Engine. (Illus.). (gr. k-2). N.D. (ISBN 0-571-06421-3). Transatlantic.
--William and the Lorry. N.D. Transatlantic Arts.
Ross, Elizabeth
--The Three Little Pigs. (Illus.). (ps-1). 1973. (ISBN 0-307-61544-8, Golden Pr). Western Pub.
Ross, Ellen, Mrs.
--Dora's Boy. (Crowell's Library For Young People). N.D. Thomas Y. Crowell & Co.'s Catalogue.
Ross, Eulalie Steinmetz (1910-), compiled by.
--The Blue Rose: A Collection of Stories for Girls. Arno, Enrico (1913-1981), illus. LC 66-11207. (Illus.). 21cm. 186p. (gr. 3-7). 1966. (ISBN 0-15-209182-3). HarBraceJ.
--The Buried Treasure and Other Picture Tales. 1st ed. Cellini, Joseph (1924-), illus. LC 58-7532. (Illus.). 187 p. 22cm. 1958. Lippincott.
--The Lost Half-Hour: A Collection of Stories. Arno, Enrico (1913-1981), illus. LC 63-17006. 191p. illus. 21cm. c.1963. Harcourt.
Ross, Frances, jt. ed. see Kerr, Mildred Lewis.
Ross, Frances & Mohne, Wilhelmina., eds.
--Magic Tales. Griffith, Arthur & Osborn, Helen, illus. LC 47-1302. 126 p. illus. 21 1/2 cm. 1946. Charles E. Merrill Co., Inc.
Ross, Frank Xavier see Frank, R., pseud.
Ross, Gail J., jt. auth. see Erickson, Carol A.
Ross, George Maxim
--The Pine Tree. Ross, George Maxim, illus. LC 66-7119. (Illus.). 38 p. 23cm. 1966. Dutton.
--The River. 1967. E.P. Dutton & Co.
--Teckel. LC 60-15075. unpaged. illus. 21x28cm. 1960. Vanguard Press.
--What Did the Rock Say?. LC 78-102435. (Illus.). 62 p. 17cm. 1970. Holiday House.
--When Lucy Went Away. 1st ed. Fetz, Ingrid (1915-), illus. LC 75-33246. (Illus.). 32 p. 22cm. c.1976. Dutton.
Ross, Geraldine
--The Elf Who Didn't Believe in Himself. Werth, Kurt (1896-), illus. LC 66-12932. 32p. (gr. k-2). 1966. (ISBN 0-8114-7515-8). Steck-V.
--Scat, the Witch's Cat. Werth, Kurt (1896-), illus. LC 58-11191. (Illus.). 26cm. 30p. (gr. k-3). 1958. (ISBN 0-07-053844-1). McGraw.
--Stop It, Moppit. (Illus.). (gr. 1-3). 1959. (ISBN 0-8382-0798-7). Hale.
--Stop It, Moppit. Werth, Kurt (1896-), illus. (Illus.). (gr. k-3). 1959. (ISBN 0-07-053841-7). McGraw.
--Stop it, Moppit!. Werth, Kurt (1896-), illus. LC 59-8528. (Illus.). 31p. 26cm. 1959. Whittlesey House.
Ross, H. L.
--Wonderful Window Word Book. DeJohn, Marie, illus. LC 79-1910. (Illus.). (ps-k). 1979. (Gingerbread Bks). Dutton.
Ross, Harriet, compiled by.
--Great Adventure Stories. Bolle, Frank, illus. LC 60-6579. (Illus.). 160p. 1982. (ISBN 0-87460-180-0). (ISBN 0-87460-181-9). Lion Bks.
--Great Detective Stories. Bolle, Frank, illus. LC 64-24881. (Illus.). 160p. 1981. (ISBN 0-87460-186-X). (ISBN 0-87460-187-8). Lion Bks.
--Great Horror Stories. new ed. Bolle, Frank, illus. LC 64-24882. (Illus.). 160p. 1982. (ISBN 0-87460-188-6). (ISBN 0-87460-189-4). Lion Bks.
--Great Mystery Stories. Bolle, Frank, illus. LC 60-6578. (Illus.). 160p. (The Lion Classics Ser). 1981. (ISBN 0-87460-194-0). (ISBN 0-87460-195-9). Lion Bks.
--Great Short Stories. (gr. 4-9). N.D. (ISBN 0-685-14216-7). Lion Bks.
--Great Stories About Horses. new ed. Bolle, Frank, illus. LC 63-18759. (Illus.). 160p. 1972. (ISBN 0-87460-202-5). (ISBN 0-87460-203-3). Lion Bks.
--Great Story Poems: A Collection. (Illus.). 160p. 1981. (ISBN 0-686-69773-1). Lion Bks.
--Great Suspense Stories. new ed. Bolle, Frank, illus. LC 61-5152. (Illus.). 160p. 1981. (ISBN 0-87460-206-8). (ISBN 0-87460-207-6). Lion Bks.
--Myths & Legends of Many Lands. new ed. Bolle, Frank, illus. (Illus.). 160p. (gr. 5 up). 1984. Lion Bks.
Ross, Helen
--The Adventures of Dip & Dee Darrow. 1984. (ISBN 0-533-05987-9). Vantage.
Ross, J. K, adapted by see Dickens, Charles John Huffam.
Ross, Jan (1932-)
--Dogs Have Paws. Masheris, Robert, illus. LC 82-1568. (Illus.). 32 p. 21cm. c.1982. (ISBN 0-695-41670-7). (ISBN 0-695-31670-2). Follett.
Ross, Jessica
--Fanona the Beautiful. Ross, Jessica, illus. LC 70-141008. 32p. (ps-3). 1971. (ISBN 0-03-086235-3). (ISBN 0-03-086236-1). HR&W.
--Ms. Klondike. Perle, Ruth Lerner, ed. Hefter, Richard (1942-), illus. LC 77-4649. 34p. col. ill. 20 x 24cm. 1977. (ISBN 0-670-49510-7). Viking Press.
Ross, Katharine (1950-)
--The Baby Animals Party. McCue, Lisa, illus. LC 84-43177. p. cm. c.1986. (ISBN 0-394-97355-0). Random House.
Ross, Laura, pseud., see Mincielli, Rose Laura.
Ross, Laura, pseud. (1912-)
--Pulcinella: Or, Punch's Merry Pranks. Mincielli, Rose Laura. Low, Joseph (1911-), illus. LC 60-5508. (Illus.). 34 p. 26cm. 1960. Knopf.
--Puppet Shows: Using Poems and Stories. Mincielli, Rose Laura. Ross, Frank Xavier, Jr. (1914-), illus. LC 75-121822. (Illus.). 192 p. 24cm. 1970. Lothrop, Lee and Shepard.
Ross, Louis
--The Bear Under the Bed. Disalvo-Ryan, DyAnne, illus. (Illus.). (ps-2). 1980. (Gingerbread). Dutton.
--In the Peanut Butter Colony. Apple, Margot, illus. LC 79-51982. (Illus.). 31cm. 20p. c.1979. Gingerbread House.
--Martin & the Math Mumps. Mulkey, Kim, illus. (Illus.). (gr. 1-4). 1980. (Gingerbread). Dutton.
--Puddle Duck. Schories, Patricia, illus. LC 79-1947. (Illus.). 20 p. 31cm. c.1979. (ISBN 0-525-69020-4). (ISBN 0-525-69021-2). Gingerbread House.
Ross, Margaret Isabel (1897-)
--Back of Time. Wiese, Kurt (1887-1974), illus. LC 32-29767. viii p., 3 l., 271 p. incl. illus., plates. front. 22 cm. 1932. Harper & Brothers.
--The Dawn Hill Brand: A Story of Australia. Orr, Forrest W., illus. LC 39-30364. 4 p. l., 226, 1 p. incl. front., illus. 22 cm. 1939. Houghton Mifflin Company.
--A Farm in the Family. Shenton, Edward (1895-), illus. LC 43-16887. 4 p. l., 261 p. incl. front., illus., plates. 21 cm. 1943. Harper & Brothers.
--A Gift for Ibn Diab. DeMuth, Flora Nash (1888-), illus. LC 41-21723. vii p., 1 l., 308 p. incl. front., illus. 21 cm. c.1941. Harper & Brothers.
--Green Treasure. 1st ed. Peck, Anne Merriman (1884-), illus. LC 48-7169. 173 p. illus. 21 cm. 1948. Harper.
--Greentree Downs. Richards, George Mather (1880-), illus. LC 37-19884. 4 p. l., 197 p., 1 l. incl. front., illus. plates. 22 cm. 1937. Houghton Mifflin Company.
--Kaga's Brother: A Story of the Chippewas. 4 p. l., 221 p., 1 l. incl. map. col. front. 21 cm. 1936. Harper & Brothers.
--Land of Williwaws: A Story of Adventure in Patagonia and the Falkland Islands. Richards, George Mather (1880-), illus. LC 34-11038. 6 p. l., 207 p. front., plates. 20 cm. 1934. Houghton Mifflin Company.
--Morgan's Fourth Son. Daugherty, James Henry (1889-1974), illus. LC 40-33283. vi p., 3 l., 252 p. incl. front., illus., plates. 21 cm. c.1940. Harper & Brothers.
--South of Zero: The Journal of John Hale Meredith While with the Clark-Jamison Antarctic Expedition of 191- to 191-. Whiting, John Downes (1884-), illus. LC 31-32955. xiv p., 1 l., 280 p. col. front., illus. 22 cm. 1931. Harper & Brothers.
--White Wind: An Account of the Oates Land Party of the Biggers' Antarctic Expedition of 193- to 193-. Quinn, Paul, illus. LC 37-39258. 5 p. l., 240 p. col. front., illus. 21 cm. 1937. Harper & Brothers.
--Wilderness River: Adventure in the Fur Trapping Country. LC 52-6281. 214 p. 22cm. 1952. Harper.
Ross, Marvin, illus.
--The Jackal at Jericho. (Illus., Orig.). (Little Talker Ser.). N.D. (ISBN 0-89293-097-7). Beta Bk.
--The Lion in the Den. (Little Talkers Ser.). N.D. (ISBN 0-89293-098-5). Beta Bk.
Ross, Nancy Wilson (1905-)
--Thor's Visit to the Land of the Giants. Watson, Aldren Auld (1917-), illus. LC 59-9742. 51p. illus. 22cm. (Legacy books Y-6). 1959. Random House.
Ross, Neville
--The Children's Snowstorm. (Illus.). N.D. Frederick A. Stokes.
Ross, Pat
--Gloria and the Super Soaper. 1st ed. Paradis, Susan, illus. LC 81-19323. (Illus.). 59 p. 22cm. c.1982. (ISBN 0-316-75751-9). Little, Brown.
--Hi Fly. 1st ed. Wallner, John C. (1945-), illus. LC 73-89362. 32 p. of illus. 1974. (ISBN 0-517-51425-7). Crown Publishers.
--M and M and the Bad News Babies. 1st ed. Hafner, Marylin (1925-), illus. LC 81-18714. p. cm. (An I Am Reading Book). c.1983. (ISBN 0-394-84532-3). (ISBN 0-394-94532-8). Pantheon Books.
--M & M and the Bad News Babies. Hafner, Marylin (1925-), illus. LC 84-16557. (Illus.). 46 p. 20cm. 1985, c.1983. (ISBN 0-14-031851-8). Puffin Books.
--M & M & the Big Bag. Hafner, Marylin (1925-), illus. LC 80-23299. (Illus.). 48p. (I Am Reading Book). (gr. 1-4). 1981. (ISBN 0-394-84340-1). (ISBN 0-394-94340-6). Pantheon.
--M and M and the Big Bag. Hafner, Marylin (1925-), illus. LC 84-16565. p. cm. 1985. (ISBN 0-14-031852-6). Puffin Books.
--M and M and the Haunted House Game. Hafner, Marylin (1925-), illus. LC 79-27678. p. cm. (I am reading book). c.1980. (ISBN 0-394-84185-9). (ISBN 0-394-94185-3). Pantheon Books.
--M & M and the Mummy Mess. Hafner, Marylin (1925-), illus. LC 85-73264. p. cm. 1986, c.1985. (ISBN 0-14-032084-9). Puffin Books.
--M & M and the Mummy Mess. Hafner, Marylin (1925-), illus. LC 84-20847. (Illus.). 40 p. 22cm. 1985. (ISBN 0-670-80548-3). Viking Kestrel.
--M & M and the Santa Secrets. Hafner, Marylin (1925-), illus. LC 84-21018. (Illus.). 41 p. 22cm. 1985. (ISBN 0-670-80624-2). Viking Kestrel.
--Meet M and M. Hafner, Marylin (1925-), illus. LC 79-190. (Illus.). 41 p. 24cm. (I am reading book). c.1980. (ISBN 0-394-84184-0). (ISBN 0-394-94184-5). Pantheon Books.
--Molly and the Slow Teeth. Milord, Jerry, illus. LC 79-28644. (Illus.). 43 p. 22cm. c.1980. (ISBN 0-688-41962-3). Lothrop, Lee & Shepard Books.
--What Ever Happened to the Baxter Place?. Duvoisin, Roger Antoine (1904-1980), illus. LC 75-22251. (Illus.). 48p. (gr. 1-5). 1976. (ISBN 0-394-93178-5). Pantheon.
Ross, Patricia Font (1901-)
--The Hungry Moon: Mexican Nursery Tales. Merida, Carlos (1898-), illus. LC 46-7681. 4 p. l., 3-72, 2 p. col. illus., col. plates. 26 cm. (Borzoi books for young people). 1946. A. A. Knopf.
--In Mexico They Say. Pitz, Henry Clarence (1895-1976), illus. LC 42-8284. 5 p. l., 3-211 p., 1 l. incl. col. front., illus. col. plates. 22 cm. 1942. A. A. Knopf.
--The Magic Forest. 1st ed. Merida, Carlos (1898-), illus. LC 48-7505. 128 p. col. illus. 23 cm. 1948. A. A.Knopf.
Ross, Raleigh E
--Tom and Bert at a Century of Progress. LC 33-140234. 256 p. 20 cm. c.1933. The White House Publishers.
Ross, Ramon Royal
--Prune. Sarabasha, Susan, illus. LC 84-3018. (Illus.). 192p. (gr. 3 up). 1984. (ISBN 0-689-31056-0). Atheneum.
Ross, Ramon Royal, jt. auth. see Fay, Leo Charles.
Ross, Robert, jt. auth. see Woodhouse, Martin.
Ross, Roselle
--Mother & Baby Friendly Animal Stories. Kolada, Paul & Godal, Eric, illus. LC 50-13344. 72 p. col. illus. 32 cm. (Maxton books for little people). c.1949. Maxton Publishers.
Ross, Roselle, ed. see Lorenzini, Carlo.
Ross, Rosslyn
--Mr. McKenzie. Lambone, Raymond, illus. LC 68-792606. 31p. col. illus. 24cm. 1966. Tri-Ocean.
Ross, Sutherland, pseud., see Callard, Thomas Henry.
Ross, Sutherland, pseud. (1912-)
--Freedom Is the Prize. Callard, Thomas Henry. LC 64-23995. 192p. 24cm. (Companion bk. ser.). c.1964. Walker.
Ross, Tony, jt. auth. see Lewis, Naomi.
Ross, Tony (1938-)
--The Boy Who Cried Wolf. Ross, Tony (1938-), illus. LC 84-23273. p. cm. 1985. (ISBN 0-8037-0193-4). Dial Books for Young Readers.
--The Greedy Little Cobbler. Ross, Tony (1938-), illus. LC 79-56766. (Illus.). 28 p. 22cm. 1980, c.1979. (ISBN 0-8120-5389-3). Barron's.
--Hugo & Oddsock. Ross, Tony (1938-), illus. (Illus.). (gr. 1-3). 1978. (ISBN 0-695-80959-8). (ISBN 0-695-40959-X). Follett.
--Hugo and the Man Who Stole Colors. Ross, Tony (1938-), illus. LC 77-152990. (Illus.). 22 p. 24cm. c.1977. (ISBN 0-695-80774-9). (ISBN 0-695-40774-0). Follett Pub. Co.
--Hugo & the Wicked Winter. Ross, Tony (1938-), illus. (Illus.). N.D. (ISBN 0-8464-0498-2). Beekman Pubs.
--I'm Coming to Get You. Ross, Tony (1938-), illus. LC 84-5831. (Illus.). (ps-2). 1984. (ISBN 0-8037-0119-5). (ISBN 0-8037-0119-5). Dial Bks for Young Readers.
--Jack and the Beanstalk. Ross, Tony (1938-), illus. LC 80-67493. (Illus.). 32 p. 28cm. 1981, c.1980. (ISBN 0-440-04168-6). (ISBN 0-440-04174-0). Delacorte Press.
--Naughty Nicky. Ross, Tony (1938-), illus. LC 82-21265. (Illus.). 24 p. 24cm. 1st U.S. edition. 1983, c.1982. (ISBN 0-03-063522-5). Holt, Rinehart, and Winston.
--Puss in Boots: The Story of a Sneaky Cat. Ross, Tony (1938-), illus. LC 81-2181. p. cm. 1981. (ISBN 0-440-07122-4). (ISBN 0-440-07157-7). Delacorte Press.
--The Three Pigs. Ross, Tony (1938-), illus. LC 83-2356. p. cm. 1983. (ISBN 0-394-86143-4). (ISBN 0-394-96143-9). Pantheon Books.
--Towser & Sadie's Birthday. Ross, Tony (1938-), illus. LC 83-15126. (Illus.). 32p. (ps-1). 1984. (ISBN 0-394-86539-1). (ISBN 0-394-96539-6). Pantheon.
--Towser & the Terrible Thing. Ross, Tony (1938-), illus. (Illus.). 32p. (ps-1). 1984. (ISBN 0-394-86541-3). (ISBN 0-394-96541-8). Pantheon.
--Towser and the Water Rats. Ross, Tony (1938-), illus. LC 83-17392. (Illus.). 16cm. 32p. (ps-1). 1984. (ISBN 0-394-86540-5). (ISBN 0-394-96540-X). (ISBN 0-394-96540-X). Pantheon.
Ross, Tony (1938-), retold by.
--The Enchanted Pig: An Old Rumanian Tale. Ross, Tony (1938-), illus. LC 83-71162. p. cm. 1983. (ISBN 0-911745-00-9). (ISBN 0-911745-00-9). Peter Bedrick Books.
--The Pied Piper of Hamelin. Ross, Tony (1938-), illus. LC 77-24056. (Illus.). 14 p. 23cm. 1978, c.1977. (ISBN 0-688-41824-4). (ISBN 0-688-51824-9). Lothrop, Lee & Shepard Co.
Ross, Uta V. O.
--The Boy Who Wanted to Be a Missionary. Dienemann, Debbie, illus. 48p. (Orig.). 1984. (ISBN 0-687-03910-X). Abingdon.
Ross, Zola Helen, jt. auth. see McDonald, Lucile Saunders, Mrs.
Ross, Zola Helen (1912-) & McDonald, Lucile Saunders (1898-)
--The Sunken Forest. LC 68-12865. 119 p. 22cm. 1968. Weybright and Talley.
Ross (1938-)
--A Noisy Book. LC 75-174721. (Illus.). 32 p. 25cm. 1973, c.1971. Scroll Press.
Rossel, Seymour (1945-), ed. see Rosenberg, Amye & Mason, Patrice G.
Rossetti, Christina Georgina, jt. auth. see Richards, Laura Elizabeth Howe, Mrs.
Rossetti, Christina Georgina (1830-1894)
--Adding: A Poem. Balet, Jan Bernard (1913-), illus. LC 64-15428. (Illus.). 17 x 24cm. 1964. Holt, Rinehart and Winston.
--Commonplace and Other Stories. N.D. Robert Brothers.
--Doves & Pomegranates. Powell, David, ed. Gill, Margery Jean (1925-), illus. Lewis, N., intro. by. LC 74-146624. (Illus.). 25 drawings. index. note. 96p. 1st U.S. edition. (gr. 5 up). 1971. (ISBN 0-02-777760-X). Macmillan.
--Goblin Market. Gershinowitz, George, illus. LC 81-47329. p. cm. 1981. (ISBN 0-87923-400-8). D.R. Godine.
--Goblin Market. Rackham, Arthur (1867-1939), illus. LC 72-92555. (Illus.). 42 p. 22cm. 1969. F. Watts.
--Goblin Market. Rackham, Arthur (1867-1939), illus. N.D. J. B. Lippincott.
--Goblin Market. Raskin, Ellen (1928-1984), illus. LC 76-115984. (Illus.). 30 p. 1970. E. P. Dutton.
--Maude. N.D. Duffield & Co.
--Sing-Song. Repr. Of 1872 Ed. Bd. with Speaking Likenesses. Repr. of 1874 ed; Goblin Market. Repr. of 1893 ed. LC 75-32176. (Illus.). (Classics of Children's Literature, 1621-1932: Vol. 39). 1977. (ISBN 0-8240-2288-2). Garland Pub.
--Sing Song. (Pocket Classics). N.D. MacMillan.
--Sing-Song. Davis, Marguerite (1889-), illus. (Illus.). (New Little Library Series). (gr. k-3). 1952. (ISBN 0-02-777830-4). Macmillan.
--Sing-Song. Hughes, Arthur (1832-1915), illus. LC 67-412. (Illus.). x, 130 p. 22cm. (Legacy library facsimile). 1966. University Microfilms.
--Sing-Song ; Speaking Likenesses ; Goblin Market. Hughes, Arthur (1832-1915) & Housman, Laurence (1865-1959), illus. Taylor, R. Loring, pref. by. LC 75-32176. (Illus.). 328 p. in various pagings. 19cm. (Classics of Children's Literature, 1621-1932). 1976. (ISBN 0-8240-2288-2). Garland Pub.
--Sing Song: A Nursery Rhyme Book. Hughes, Arthur (1832-1915), illus. (Illus.). 130p. 1872. (ISBN 0-486-22107-5). Dover Books.
--Sing-Song: A Nursery Rhyme Book. Hughes, Arthur (1832-1915), illus. LC 68-55822. (Illus.). x, 129 p. 21cm. 1968. Dover Publications.
--Sing-Song: A Nursery Rhyme Book. Hughes, Arthur (1832-1915), illus. 1969. Dover.
--What Is Pink: A Poem. Aruego, Jose (1932-), illus. LC 71-152289. (Illus.). color ils. 32p. (ps-3). 1971. (ISBN 0-685-00251-9). Macmillan.
--What is Pink?. A Poem. Soucheck, Margaret A., illus. LC 63-15204. (Illus.). 17 x 24cm. (A Little Owl Book). 1963. Holt, Rinehart and Winston.
Rossetti, Christina Georgina (1830-1894) & Hughes, Arthur (1832-1915)
--Sing-Song: A Nursery Rhyme Book. N.D. Robert Brothers.

Rossini, Gioacchino Antonio (1792-1868) see Johnston, Johanna.
Rossini, Gioacchino Antonio (1792-1868)
--Cinderella. Montresor, Beni (1926-), adapted by. Montresor, Beni (1926-), illus. LC 72-9562. (Illus.). 32 p. 1973, c.1965. (ISBN 0-394-82619-1). Random House.
--Cinderella. Cinderella. Montresor, Beni (1926-), adapted by. Montresor, Beni (1926-), illus. LC 65-21556. 1. v. (unpaged) col. illus. 21 x 26 cm. 1965. Knopf.
--William Tell. Mizusawa, Hiroshi, illus. (Pictorial Fantasia Ser). (gr. 3-6). 1969. Silver.
Rossiter, Don, jt. auth. see Rossiter, Gretchen.
Rossiter, Gretchen & Rossiter, Don
--Rocket on the Road. 1 st ed. LC 62-12176. 136p. illus. 21cm. 1962. Duell, Sloan and Pearce.
Rossiter, Harriet
--The Twin's Birthday Surprise. LC 53-12154. 40p. 1954. Vantage Press.
Rossman, George Parker (1919-)
--Pirate Slave. LC 76-43989. p. cm. c.1976. (ISBN 0-8407-6517-7). T. Nelson.
Rossman, Parker see Rossman, George Parker.
Rossman, Vern
--Between Yesterday and Tomorrow. 1957. Friendship Press.
--Drum, Hammer & Cross. (gr. 9 up). 1967. (ISBN 0-377-80021-X). Friend Pr.
Rossow, Robert
--Tex Rains: Culver Trooper. LC 53-5469. 248p.21cm. 1953. Dodd, Mead.
Ross Williamson, Hugh (1901-1978)
--Guy Fawkes. Stobbs, William (1914-), illus. LC 66-11191. 160p. illus. 21cm. 1966, c.1964. Roy.
Rostand, Edmond Eugene Alexis (1868-1918)
--The Far Princess. N.D. Bruce Humphries.
--The Far Princess. N.D. Dresser, Chapman & Grimes Inc.
--The Story of Chanticleer. Hann, Florence Yates, adapted by. Shepherd, J. A., illus. LC 13-22822. vii p., 1 l., 144 p. col. front., col. illus., col. plates. 21 cm. 1913. Frederick A. Stokes Company.
Rosten, Norman (1914-)
--The Wineglass: A Passover Story. Zemach, Kaethe (1958-), illus. LC 77-16758. (Illus.). 30 p. 22cm. c.1978. (ISBN 0-8027-6318-9). (ISBN 0-8027-6319-7). Walker.
Rostiser, Leila Brechnser
--Mascot Mike of Notre Dame. LC 49-49309. 64 p. illus. 21 cm. (Dunne's mascot series). 1949. Dunne Press.
--Mascot Peruna. LC 51-13678. 67 p. illus. 23 cm. 1951. Naylor Co.
Rostler, William
--It's Your Move. (Orig.). (gr. 5 up). 1984. (ISBN 0-671-54716-X). Archway.
Roston, Murray, tr. see Barash, Asher.
Rostron, Hilda L
--Stories about Jesus the friend. 1961. Christian Literature Crusade.
--Stories about Jesus the helper. (Ladybird Series). 1961. Christian Literature Crusade.
--Story about Children of the Bible. (Ladybird Ser.). 1962. Christian Literature Crusade.
Rostron, Richard
--The Sorcerer's Apprentice. Lieberman, Frank Joseph (1910-), illus. LC 41-12912. (Illus.). 41p. (gr. 3-7). 1941. William Morrow & Co.
Rosvall, Toivo David
--The Very Stupid Folk: A Finnish Tale for Children. Gergely, Tibor (1900-1978), illus. LC 38-14374. 51, 2 p. illus. 19 cm. 1938. E. P. Dutton & Co., Inc.
Rotch, Francis (1885-)
--The Blue-Eyed God. Clymer, John F., illus. LC 38-7064. 311, 1 p. incl. illus., plates. col. front. 22 cm. 1938. The Caxton Printers, Ltd.
Roth, Arnold (1929-)
--A Comick Book of Pets. Encore ed. LC 76-15593. (Illus.). 65p. (Encore Ed.). (gr. 3 up). 1976. (ISBN 0-684-17398-0, ScribJ). Scribner.
Roth, Arthur Joseph see Pomeroy, Pete, pseud.
Roth, Arthur Joseph (1925-)
--Avalanche. (gr. 7 up). 1979. (ISBN 0-590-05728-6, Schol Pap). Scholastic Inc.
--The Caretaker. LC 80-66249. p. cm. c.1980. (ISBN 0-590-07631-0). Four Winds Press.
--The Castaway. 112p. (Orig.). (gr. 5 up). 1983. (ISBN 0-590-31241-3). Scholastic Inc.
--Crash Landing!. Febland, David, illus. (Illus.). 96p. (Orig.). (Twistaplot Bks.: No. 6). (gr. 7 up). 1983. (ISBN 0-590-32726-7). Scholastic Inc.
--Great Spy Stories. (gr. 7 up). N.D. (ISBN 0-590-31393-2). Scholastic Inc.
--The Iceberg Hermit. Pomeroy, Pete, pseud. LC 74-7435. 201 p. 22cm. 1974. (ISBN 0-590-07301-X). Four Winds Press.
--The Iceberg Hermit. 1974. Scholastic.
--The Mallory Burn. Pomeroy, Pete, pseud. LC 70-153922. 169 p. 21cm. (gr. 5up). 1971. (ISBN 0-448-21415-6). (ISBN 0-448-26185-5). Grosset & Dunlap.
--Scissors, Paper, Rock. Pomeroy, Pete, pseud. LC 76-10270. p. cm. c.1976. (ISBN 0-590-07454-7). Four Winds Press.
--The Secret Lover of Elmtree. LC 76-10270. (gr. 7 up). 1976. (ISBN 0-590-07454-7, Four Winds). Schol Bk Serv.
--Two for Survival: A Novel. Pomeroy, Pete, pseud. LC 76-13632. 169 p. 22cm. c.1976. (ISBN 0-684-14721-1). Scribner.
--Wipeout!. Pomeroy, Pete, pseud. Roth, Arthur Joseph. LC 68-12391. 156 p. 22cm. 1968. Four Winds Press.
--The Yucky Monster. Pomeroy, Pete, pseud. O'Sullivan, Tom, illus. LC 78-72112. (Illus.). 29 p. 23cm. c.1979. (ISBN 0-89799-066-8). Dandelion Press.
Roth, Charles Edmund (1934-)
--Walking Catfish & Other Aliens. LC 72-7436. (Illus.). index. 176p. (gr. 6 up). 1973. (ISBN 0-201-06528-2, A-W Childrens). A-W.
Roth, David (1940-)
--Best of Friends. LC 82-23378. 200 p. 22cm. 1983. (ISBN 0-395-33889-1). Houghton Mifflin.
--The Girl in the Grass. LC 81-18091. 224p. (gr. 7 up). 1982. (ISBN 0-8253-0086-X). Beaufort Bks NY.
--The Hermit of Fog Hollow Station. LC 80-22241. 96 p. 22cm. c.1980. (ISBN 0-8253-0012-6). Beaufort Books.
--River Runaways. LC 81-6271. p. cm. 1981. (ISBN 0-395-31678-2). Houghton Mifflin.
--The Winds of Summer. LC 74-160106. 192 p. 22cm. (Criterion books). 1972. Abelard-Schuman.
--A World for Joey Carr. LC 81-3879. p. cm. 1981. (ISBN 0-8253-0058-4). Beaufort Books.
Roth, Edward, tr. see Verne, Jules.
Roth, Mary Jane
--His Majesty, the Frog. Cellini, Joseph (1924-), illus. LC 79-119843. (Illus.). 47 p. 20cm. 1971. Morrow.
--The Pretender Princess. Greenwald, Sheila, pseud. (1934-), illus. Green, Sheila Ellen. LC 67-451. (Illus.). 48 p. 20cm. 1967. (ISBN 0-688-31702-2). W. Morrow.
Roth, Naema see Ylval, pseud.
Roth, Naema (1869-)
--Luz Star-Eye's Dream Journey to the Isles of the Southern Sea: A Story for Children. Ylval, pseud. Roth, Naema (1869-), illus. Ylval, pseud. LC 12-26747. 1 p. l., 137 p. front., illus. 21 cm. c.1912. The Aryan Theosophical Press.
Roth, Richard (1835-1915)
--Prince Frederick and the Dawn of the Reformation. Ireland, Mary Eliza Haines, Mrs. (1834-1927), illus. LC 14-2136. 167, 1 p. 18 cm. (Reformation series, vol. iv). 1913. The German Literary Board.
Roth, Susan L., jt. auth. see Phang, Ruth.
Rothberg, Abraham (1922-)
--The Boy and the Dolphin. 1st ed. Gobbato, Imero (1923-), illus. LC 68-22726. (Illus.). 85 p. 22cm. 1969. Norton.
Rothberg, Michael
--The Cat's-Eye. 16p. (Orig.). 1980. (ISBN 0-938370-00-6). Wildflower.
Rothberg, Muriel W, retold by see Little Red Riding Hood & Perrault, Charles.
Rothberg, Muriel W, retold by see Perrault, Charles.
Rothe, Fenella
--Mr. Bear's House. McKinley, Clare, illus. LC 53-295858. unpaged. illus. 21cm. (Rand McNally book-elf book, 475). c.1953. Rand McNally.
--Mr. Bear's House. McKinley, Clare, illus. LC 58-10173. unpaged. illus. 33cm. (A Rand McNally Giant Book). 1958, c.1953. Rand McNally.
Rothenberg, Lillian, jt. auth. see Liebers, Ruth.
Rothgiesser, Ruben
--The Ship of Hope. N.D. Harlem Book Co.
Rothman, Joel (1938-)
--I Can Be Anything You Can Be. Perl, Susan (1922-1983), illus. LC 72-90694. (Illus.). 32p. (gr. k-4). 1973. (ISBN 0-87592-024-1). Scroll Pr.
--Joel Rothman's the Antcyclopedia. Freshman, Shelley, illus. LC 74-12667. (Illus.). 32 p. 22cm. 1974. Phinmarc Books.
--Night Lights. Lasker, Joseph Leon (1919-), illus. LC 74-188434. (Illus.). 40p. (ps-3). 1972. (ISBN 0-8075-5628-9). A Whitman.
--Once There Was a Stream. Roberts, Bruce Stuart (1930-), photos by. LC 72-90692. (Illus.). 32p. (gr. k-4). 1973. (ISBN 0-87592-038-1). Scroll Pr.
Rothman, Joel (1938-) & Palacios, Argentina
--This Can Lick a Lollypop: Body Riddles for Kids. Ruben, Patricia, photos by. LC 77-80911. (ps-3). 1979. Doubleday.
Rothmund, Toni Ludemann, Mrs. (1877-)
--The Amber Bead. Kutzer, Ernst (1880-), illus. Katzin, Winifred, tr. LC 30-20354. vii p., 1 l., 175 p. col. front., illus., col. plates. 24 cm. 1930. Longmans, Green and Co.
Rothrock, Thomas, jt. auth. see Gulick, Bill.
Rothschild, Alice
--Bad Trouble in Miss Alcorn's Class: A Story. Rosenhouse, Irwin, illus. LC 58-9558. 100p. illus. 23cm. (Young Scott Books). 1959. Scott.
--Fruit Is Ripe for Timothy. Woodward, Hildegard (1898-), illus. LC 63-19195. 1 v. (unpaged) col. illus. 21 x 25 cm. 1963. Young Scott Books.
Rothwell, John H., jt. auth. see Weatherwax, Rudd B.
Rotkappchen
--Little Red Cap. Crawford, Elizabeth D, tr. Zwerger, Lisbeth, illus. LC 83-61776. (Original Authors: The Grimm Brothers). (Illus.). 24 p. c.1983. (ISBN 0-907234-48-8). Picture Book Studio USA : Distributed by Alphabet Press.
Rotsler, William (1926-)
--The A-Team, No. 2: The Danger Maze. Arico, Diane, ed. 128p. (Orig.). (Plot It Yourself Ser.). (gr. 8-12). 1984. (ISBN 0-671-52761-4). Wanderer Bks.
--The A-Team Number One: Defense Against Terror. Barish, Wendy, ed. LC 83-16190. 1983. (ISBN 0-671-49608-5). Simon & Schuster.
--The A-Team Number One: Defense Against Terror. Barish, Wendy, ed. 128p. (Orig.). (Plot-It-Yourself Adventure Stories). 1983. (ISBN 0-671-49608-5). Wanderer Bks.
--Goonies, Cavern of Horror. LC 85-5086. p. cm. (Plot-It-Yourself Adventure Stories). c.1985. (ISBN 0-671-60135-0). Wanderer Books.
--Joanie Loves Chachi: A Test of Hearts, No. 2. Schneider, Meg, ed. LC 82-13608. 160p. (Orig.). (gr. 3-7). 1982. (ISBN 0-671-46011-0). Wanderer Bks.
--Joanie Loves Chachi: Secrets, No. 1. Barish, Wendy, ed. LC 82-10867. 160p. (gr. 3-7). 1982. (ISBN 0-671-46010-2). Wanderer Bks.
--Love Boat Number One: The Love Boat. Barish, Wendy, ed. LC 83-14786. 128p. (Orig.). (Plot-Your-Own-Adventure Stories). (gr. 3-7). 1983. (ISBN 0-671-49802-9). Wanderer Bks.
--Magnum, P. I. Number One: Maui Mystery. Barish, Wendy, ed. 128p. (Plot-It-Yourself Adventure Stories Ser.). 1983. (ISBN 0-671-49607-7). Wanderer Bks.
--Mr. Merlin: Episode Number One. LC 81-14772. (Based on characters created by Larry Tucker and Larry Rosen). p. cm. 1981. (ISBN 0-671-44479-4). (ISBN 0-671-44479-4). Wanderer Books.
--Mr. Merlin: Episode Number Two. LC 81-16625. (Based on characters created by Larry Tucker and Larry Rosen). 160 p. 19cm. c.1981. (ISBN 0-671-44480-8). (ISBN 0-671-44480-8). Simon & Schuster.
--Plot-Your-Own-Adventure: Distress Call. Barish, Wendy, ed. (Illus., Orig.). (Star Trek II). (gr. 3-7). 1982. (ISBN 0-671-46389-6). Wanderer Bks.
--Star Trek II: Biographies. Barish, Wendy, ed. LC 82-17621. 160p. (gr. 3-7). 1982. (ISBN 0-671-46391-8). Wanderer Bks.
--The Star Trek II Gift Set, 3 vols. N.D. Boxed Set. (ISBN 0-317-12429-3). Wanderer Bks.
--Star Trek II: Short Stories. Barish, Wendy, ed. LC 82-17558. 160p. (gr. 3-7). 1982. (ISBN 0-671-46390-X). Wanderer Bks.
--Star Trek III: Plot-It-Yourself Adventure Stories, the Vulcan Treasure. Barish, Wendy, ed. LC 84-3529. 19cm. 128p. (Orig.). (gr. 3 up). 1984. (ISBN 0-671-50138-0). Wanderer Bks.
--Star Trek III Short Stories. Barish, Wendy, ed. 160p. (Orig.). (gr. 3 up). 1984. (ISBN 0-671-50139-9). Wanderer Bks.
--Staying Alive. LC 83-10334. 152 p. 20cm. (Plot-your-own-adventure stories). c.1983. (ISBN 0-671-49541-0). Wanderer Books.
Rotsler, William (1926-) & Farrant, Trevor
--The Pirate Movie. LC 82-8453. (Illus.). 191 p., 8 leaves of plates. 19cm. c.1982. (ISBN 0-671-45999-6). Wanderer Books.
Rotsler, William (1926-) & Finkleman, Ken
--Grease 2: A Novel. LC 82-4800. (Illus.). 192 p., 4 leaves of plates. 19cm. c.1982. (ISBN 0-671-45576-1). Wanderer Books.
Rough Rock Demonstration School. Board of Education see Callaway, Sydney M. & Witherspoon, Gary.
Roughsey, Dick (1921-)
--The Giant Devil Dingo. Roughsey, Dick (1921-), illus. LC 75-14210. (Illus.). 38 p. 26cm. 1975, c.1973. (ISBN 0-02-777840-1). Macmillan.
Rouke, Eve, retold by.
--Robinson Crusoe. Correas, Jose, illus. LC 65-24738. (Original author: Daniel Defoe (1660-1731)). 1 v. (unpaged) col. illus. 24 cm. (Holly story book library). 1965. World Pub. Co.
Rouke, Eve, ed. see Grimm, Jakob Ludwig Karl (1785-1863) & Grimm, Wilhelm Karl.
Rouke, Eve, retold by see Lorenzini, Carlo.
Rouke, Eve, ed. see Wilde, Oscar Fingal O'Flahertie Wills.
Roulet, Mary F Nixon, Mrs.
--The Blue Lady's Knight. LC 1156. 127 p. 18 cm. c.1899. B. Herder.
--Japanese Folk Stories and Fairy Tales. LC 8-17694. 191 p. incl. front., illus. 19 cm. (On cover: Electic readings). c.1908. American Book Company.
--Japanese Folk Stories and Fairy Tales. Ramsey, Eloise, pref. by. LC 37-4398. 191 p. incl. front., illus. 19 cm. c.1937. American Book Company.
--Our Little Alaskan Cousin. LC 7-20707. 6 p. l., 138 p. front., 5 pl. 20 cm. (On verso of half-title: The Little cousin series). 1907. L. C. Page & Company.
--Our Little Australian Cousin. Horne, Diantha W., illus. LC 8-29330. 1 p. l., v p., 2 l., 131 p. front., 5 pl. 20 cm. (On verso of half-title: The Little cousin series). 1908. L. C. Page & Company.
--Our Little Brazilian Cousin. De Meserac, Louis, illus. LC 7-31213. vi p., 2 l., 127 p. front., 5 pl. 20 cm. (On verso of half-title: The little cousin series). 1907. L. C. Page & Company.
--Our Little Grecian Cousin. Horne, Diantha W., illus. LC 8-23099. 6 p. l., 141 p. front., 5 pl. 20 cm. (On verso of half-title: The Little cousin series). 1908. L. C. Page & Company.
--Our Little Hungarian Cousin. Goss, John, illus. LC 9-283988. 6 p. l., 138 p. front., 5 pl. 20 cm. (On verso of half-title: The Little cousin series). 1909. L. C. Page & Company.
--Our Little Spanish Cousin. McManus, Blanche, illus. LC 6-26189. 6 p. l., 125 p. front., 5 pl. 20 cm. (On verso of half-title: The Little cousin series). 1906. L. C. Page & Company.
--The Waif of Rainbow Court. LC 12-22250. 4 p. l., 141 p. 19 cm. 1912. B. Herder.
Roulstone, John (0000-1822)
--Mary Had a Little Lamb. Gavrilavicz, Stella, illus. Gavy, pseud. LC 55-8199. (Illus.). 17cm. (A Rand McNally Junior Elf Bk.). 1955. Rand McNally.
--Mary's Little Lamb. LC 22-24183. (Illus.). 18cm. 1920. The Merrymount Press.
Round, Dora, tr. see Rutgers van der Loeff-Basenau, Anna Maria Margarethe.
Round, Graham, illus.
--Elijah & the Great Drought. (Illus.). 16p (Pub. by Lion Publishing). 1982. (ISBN 0-86683-662-4). Winston Pr.
--Miriam & the Princess of Egypt. (Illus.). 16p (Pub. by Lion Publishing). 1982. (ISBN 0-86683-659-4). Winston Pr.
--Naaman & the Little Servant Girl. (Illus., Pub. by Lion Publishing). 1982. (ISBN 0-86683-660-8). Winston Pr.
Round, William M. F., jt. auth. see Clarke, Rebecca Sophia.
Round, William Marshall Fitts, et al. (1845-1906)
--Winter Evening Library: Containing "Ned and his Engine", "Torn and Mended", "Little Blind May" and "Loved into Shape", 5 vols. N.D. Set. D. Lothrop & Co.
Round, William Marshall Fitts (1845-1906)
--Child Marian Abroad. LC 8-1663. 3 p. l., 9-158 p. front., plates. 18 cm. 1878. Lee and Shepard.
--Child Marian Abroad. LC 5-33646. (Illus.). 19cm. 158p. (American Girl's Ser.). 1905. Lee & Shepard.
--Hal: The Story of Clodhopper. vii, 263 p. 19 cm. 1880. Lee and Shepard.
--Torn and Mended. A Christmas Story. LC 8-1665. iv, 7-187 p. front., pl. 18 x 14 cm. c.1877. D. Lothrop & Co.
Rounds, Glen Harold (1906-)
--Beaver Business. Rounds, Glen Harold (1906-), illus. 1960. (ISBN 0-8382-0064-8, Cadmus Books). E. M. Hale and Company.
--The Blind Colt. Rounds, Glen Harold (1906-), illus. N.D. E . M . Hale and co.
--The Blind Colt. Rounds, Glen Harold (1906-), illus. LC 41-51997. 80 p. col. front., illus., col. plates. 25 cm. c.1941. Holiday House.
--The Blind Colt. Rounds, Glen Harold (1906-), illus. LC 60-2171. unpaged. illus. 25cm. 1960. Holiday House.
--Blind Outlaw. Rounds, Glen Harold (1906-), illus. LC 80-15848. p. cm. c.1980. (ISBN 0-8234-0423-4). Holiday House.
--The Boll Weevil. Rounds, Glen Harold (1906-), illus. LC 67-249331. (Illus.). 48 p. 1967. Golden Gate Junior Books.
--Buffalo Harvest. Rounds, Glen Harold (1906-), illus. LC 52-13433. (Illus.). 141 p. 21cm. 1952. Holiday House.
--Casey Jones: The Story of a Brave Engineer. Rounds, Glen Harold (1906-), illus. LC 68-22390. (Illus.). 48p. (ps-5). 1968. (ISBN 0-516-08806-8, Golden Gate). Childrens.
--The Day the Circus Came to Lone Tree. Rounds, Glen Harold (1906-), illus. LC 73-78458. (Illus.). 39 p. 1973. (ISBN 0-8234-0232-0). Holiday House.
--The Farmer's Friends. Rounds, Glen Harold (1906-), illus. N.D. Holiday House.
--Hunted Horses. Rounds, Glen Harold (1906-), illus. LC 51-12853. (Illus.). 154 p. 20cm. 1951. Holiday House.

--Lone Muskrat. Rounds, Glen Harold (1906-), illus. LC 53-12623. (Illus.). 124p. (gr. 4-7). 1953. (ISBN 0-8234-0071-9). Holiday.
--Lumbercamp. Rounds, Glen Harold (1906-), illus. LC 37-28494. (Illus.). 21 cm. 116p. N.D. Holiday House.
--The Morning the Sun Refused to Rise: An Original Paul Bunyan Tale. Rounds, Glen Harold (1906-), illus. LC 83-49033. (Illus.). 48p. (ps-6). 1984. (ISBN 0-8234-0514-1). (ISBN 0-8234-0514-1). Holiday.
--Mr. Yowder and the Giant Bull Snake. Rounds, Glen Harold (1906-), illus. LC 77-24136. (Illus.). 48 p. c.1978. (ISBN 0-8234-0311-4). Holiday House. **Award: (ALA).**
--Mr. Yowder and the Lion Roar Capsules. Rounds, Glen Harold (1906-), illus. LC 75-35607. (Illus.). 47 p. c.1976. (ISBN 0-8234-0272-X). Holiday House.
--Mr. Yowder and the Steamboat. Rounds, Glen Harold (1906-), illus. LC 76-43089. p. cm. 1976. (ISBN 0-8234-0294-0). Holiday House.
--Mr. Yowder and the Train Robbers. Rounds, Glen Harold (1906-), illus. LC 81-2198. p. cm. c.1981. (ISBN 0-8234-0394-7). Holiday House. **Award: (ALA).**
--Mr. Yowder and the Windwagon. Rounds, Glen Harold (1906-), illus. LC 83-6183. p. cm. c.1983. (ISBN 0-8234-0499-4). Holiday House.
--Mr. Yowder, the Peripatetic Sign Painter: Three Tall Tales. Rounds, Glen Harold (1906-), illus. LC 79-18387. (Illus.). 126 p. 24cm. c.1980. (ISBN 0-8234-0370-X). Holiday House.
--Ol' Paul, the Mighty Logger. Rounds, Glen Harold (1906-), illus. LC 49-9464. (Illus.). 173p. (gr. 4-6). 1949. (ISBN 0-8234-0082-4). Holiday.
--Ol' Paul, the Mighty Logger: Being a True Account of the Seemingly Incredible exploits and Inventions of the Great Paul Bunyan. Rounds, Glen Harold (1906-), illus. LC 36-19227. 132p. front. illus. 19 1/2cm. 1936. Holiday House.
--Ol' Paul, the Mighty Logger: Being a True Account of the Seemingly Incredible Exploits and Inventions of the Great Paul Bunyan. 40th anniversary ed. Rounds, Glen Harold (1906-), illus. LC 75-22163. (Illus.). 93 p. 25cm. 1976. (ISBN 0-8234-0269-X). Holiday House.
--Once We Had a Horse. Rounds, Glen Harold (1906-), illus. LC 76-151758. (Illus.). 63 p. 17cm. 1971. (ISBN 0-8234-0193-6). Holiday House.
--Pay Dirt. Rounds, Glen Harold (1906-), illus. 1938. Holiday House.
--Rodeo. Rounds, Glen Harold (1906-), illus. N.D. Holiday House.
--The Snake Tree. Rounds, Glen Harold (1906-), illus. LC 66-8498. 95 p. illus. 25 cm. 1966. World Pub. Co.
--Stolen Pony. Rounds, Glen Harold (1906-), illus. 1948. E M Hale.
--Stolen Pony. Rounds, Glen Harold (1906-), illus. LC 48-8402. 154 p. illus. 20 cm. 1948. Holiday House.
--Stolen Pony. Rounds, Glen Harold (1906-), illus. LC 71-3445. (Illus.). 96 p. 25cm. 1969. Holiday House.
--The Strawberry Roan. Rounds, Glen Harold (1906-), illus. LC 79-119066. (Illus.). 48 p. 1970. (ISBN 0-87464-160-8). Golden Gate Junior Books.
--Sweet Betsy from Pike. Rounds, Glen Harold (1906-), illus. LC 72-94228. (Illus.). 46 p. 1973. (ISBN 0-516-08855-6). Children's Press.
--Washday on Noah's Ark: A Story of Noah's Ark According to Glen Rounds. Rounds, Glen Harold (1906-), illus. LC 84-22380. (Illus.). 32 p. c.1985. (ISBN 0-8234-0555-9). Holiday House.
--The Whistle Punk of Camp Fifteen: Being the Life and Good Times of the New Whistle Punk of Camp Fifteen up Horse Crick Way. Rounds, Glen Harold (1906-), illus. LC 59-16484. (Illus.). 116 p. 21cm. 1959. Holiday House.
--Whitey and Jinglebob. Rounds, Glen Harold (1906-), illus. LC 46-731426. 28 p. incl. col. front., illus. (part col.) 28 x 21 cm. (Story parade picture book). 1946. Grosset and Dunlap.
--Whitey and the Blizzard. Rounds, Glen Harold (1906-), illus. LC 52-9568. 1952. Holiday House.
--Whitey and the Colt-Killer. Rounds, Glen Harold (1906-), illus. LC 81-20502. (Illus.). 90 p. 19cm. (Avon/Camelot Book). 1982, c.1962. (ISBN 0-380-57158-7). Avon Books.
--Whitey & the Colt-Killer. Rounds, Glen Harold (1906-), illus. LC 62-2117. 90p. illus. 21cm. 1962. Holiday House.
--Whitey and the Rustlers. Rounds, Glen Harold (1906-), illus. LC 51-10677. (Illus.). 21 cm. 32p. 1951. Holiday House.
--Whitey & the Wild Horse. Rounds, Glen Harold (1906-), illus. LC 58-147357. 90p. illus. 21cm. 1958. Holiday House.
--Whitey Looks for a Job. Rounds, Glen Harold (1906-), illus. LC 44-47951. 28 p. incl. col. front., illus. (part col.) 24 1/2 x 21 cm. (Story parade picture book). 1944. Grosset and Dunlap.
--Whitey Ropes & Rides. Rounds, Glen Harold (1906-), illus. N.D. E. M. Hale & Co.
--Whitey Ropes & Rides. Rounds, Glen Harold (1906-), illus. LC 56-14274. (Illus.). 90 p. 21cm. 1956. Holiday House.
--Whitey Takes a Trip. Rounds, Glen Harold (1906-), illus. LC 54-28221. 87p. illus. 21cm. 1954. Holiday House.
--Whitey's First Round-Up. Rounds, Glen Harold (1906-), illus. LC 42-6767. (Illus.). 25 x 21 cm. 28p. (A Story Parade Picture Book). 1942. Grosset & Dunlap.
--Whitey's First Roundup. Rounds, Glen Harold (1906-), illus. LC 81-20501. (Illus.). 94 p. 19cm. (Avon/Camelot Book). 1982, c.1960. (ISBN 0-380-57141-2). Avon Books.
--Whitey's First Roundup. Rounds, Glen Harold (1906-), illus. LC 60-510075. 94p. illus. 21cm. 1960. (ISBN 0-8234-0141-3). Holiday House.
--Whitey's New Saddle. Rounds, Glen Harold (1906-), illus. LC 81-20487. (Illus.). 92 p. 20cm. (Avon/Camelot Book). 1982, c.1963. (ISBN 0-380-57125-0). Avon Books.
--Whitey's New Saddle. Rounds, Glen Harold (1906-), illus. LC 63-6460. 92 p. illus. 21 cm. 1963. Holiday House.
--Whitey's Sunday Horse. Rounds, Glen Harold (1906-), illus. LC 43-8181. 28 p. incl. col. front., illus. (part col.) 24 x 21 cm. (Story parade picture book). c.1943. Grosset & Dunlap.
--Wild Appaloosa. Rounds, Glen Harold (1906-), illus. LC 82-48751. p. cm. c.1983. (ISBN 0-8234-0482-X). Holiday House.
--Wild Horses of the Red Desert. Rounds, Glen Harold (1906-), illus. LC 77-2897. (Illus.). 48 p. 1969. Holiday House.
--Wild Orphan. Rounds, Glen Harold (1906-), illus. LC 61-65004. unpaged. illus. 25cm. 1961. Holiday House.

Rounds, Margaret, tr. see Lederer, Joe.

Rounds, Ruth
--It Happened to Hannah. Morse, Dorothy Bayley (1906-1979), illus. LC 54-5062. (Illus.). 122 p. 21cm. 1954. Dutton.
--Saint Santa Claus. Woodbury, Mabel Jones, illus. LC 51-6889. (Illus.). 128 p. 21cm. 1951. Dutton.

Rountree, Harry & Hamer, S. H.
--Archibald's Amazing Adventure, 12 vols. (Illus.). 80p. (The Menagerie Books Ser.). 1905. Set. Cassell & Co.
--Cheepy the Chicken: Being an Account of Some of His Most Wonderful Doings, 12 vols. (Illus.). 80p. (The Menagerie Books Ser.). 1905. Set. Cassell & Co.

Rountree, Lynda
--Me and Jimmy. Rountree, Harry (1878-1950), illus. (The Cosy Corner Ser.). N.D. Frederick Warne & Co.
--Ronald, Rupert and Reg. Rountree, Harry (1878-1950), illus. (The Cosy Corner Ser.). N.D. Frederick Warne & Co.

Rourke, Constance
--Audubon. 1936. Harcourt Brace and Janovich. **Award: (JNM).**

Rouse, Adelaide Louise (0000-1912)
--Almost a Genius. (Illus.). (The Wellesley Series for Girls). N.D. A. L. Burt.
--Almost a Genius. LC 8-1666. 314 p. front., plates. 19 cm. c.1895. Congregational Sunday School and Publishing Society.
--Almost a Genius. 314p. N.D. Pilgrim Press.
--Almost a Genius. 314p. N.D. Sunday-School Library.
--Almost a Genius: A Story for Girls. (The Girl Comrades Ser.). N.D. A. L. Burt Company.
--Annice Wynkoop, Artist. (Illus.). 325p. N.D. A. I. Bradley & Co.'s Pub.
--Annice Wynkoop, Artist. (Illus.). (The Wellesley Series for Girls). N.D. A. L. Burt.
--Annice Wynkoop, Artist. Barry, Etheldred Breeze (1870-), illus. LC 98-786. 1 p. l., 5-294 p. front., plates. 20 cm. c.1898. A. I. Bradley & Co.
--The Deane Girls. (Illus.). 406p. N.D. A. I. Bradley & Co.'s Pub.
--The Deane Girls. (Illus.). (The Meade Series for Girls). N.D. A. L. Burt.
--The Deane Girls. (Illus.). (The Wellesley Series for Girls). N.D. A. L. Burt.
--The Deane Girls: A Home Story. (The Girl Comrades Ser.). N.D. A. L. Burt Company.
--Frontier and City, or, Winnie at Clark's Corners. Or, Winnie at Clark's Corners. LC 8-1667. 294 p. front., plates. 19 cm. 1889. American Tract Society.
--Frontier and City: Or, Winnie at Clark's Corners, 1 of 50 vols. 294p. (Library of Best Authors). 1905. Set. American Tract Society.
--Helen Beaton, College Woman. LC 5129. 292 p. front., pl. 20 cm. c.1900. A. I. Bradley & Co.
--Helen Beaton, College Woman. (The Girl Comrades Ser.). N.D. A. L. Burt Company.
--Helen Beaton, College Woman. (The Girl Comrades Ser.). N.D. A. L. Burt.
--Helen Beaton, College Woman. (Illus.). (The Wellesley Series for Girls). N.D. A. L. Burt.
--Her Father's Family. (Illus.). 266p. 1905. American Tract Society.
--Stephen Vane's Trust. LC 8-1668. 393 p. front., plates. 19 cm. c.1890. American Tract Society.
--Wendover House. LC 8-16698. 1 p. l., 5-269 p. 19 cm. c.1892. The American Sunday School Union.

Rouse, C. C
--Montana Bullwhacker. LC 69-17694. (Illus.). 125 p. 22cm. (Destiny book, D-124). 1969. Pacific Press Pub. Association.

Rouse, Lydia L., Mrs. (1844-1932)
--Angus Leslie's Daughter, 1 of 25 vols. 232p. (Selected Bks for Sunday School: No. 18). N.D. Set. Methodist Bk Concern.
--Changed Lives. LC 8-1671. 362p. front. 17 1/2cm. (Changed Lives Ser.). c.1886. American Sunday School Union.
--Duncan Kennedy's New Home. LC 8-1671. 324 p. front., plates. 19 cm. c.1885. American Tract Society.
--Duncan Kennedy's New Home. (Illus.). 324p. 1905. American Tract Society.
--Ebb & Flow, 1 of 20 vols. 329p. (Selected Bks for Sunday School: No. 19). N.D. Set. Methodist Bk Concern.
--Honest Wullie. LC 8-1672. 316 p. front., plates. 19 cm. c.1884. American Tract Society.
--Honest Wullie. (Illus.). 316p. 1905. American Tract Society.
--Honest Wullie. (Illus.). (Sunday-Hour Lib.). N.D. American Tract Society.
--Jim Bentley's Resolve. LC 8-167321. 175 p. front., plates. 18 cm. c.1882. American Tract Society.
--Jim Bentley's Resolve, 1 of 25 vols. 175p. (Golden Rod Library). 1905. American Tract Society.
--Kathie's Margaret. 304p. N.D. Sunday-School Publications.
--Lady Marion's Answer. (Illus.). 227p. 1905. American Tract Society.
--Only Judith. N.D. Methodist Bk Concern.
--Rolled Away. 256p. N.D. Sunday-School Publications.
--Sandy's Faith. (Illus.). 136p. (Popular Ser.). N.D. American Tract Society.
--Sandy's Faith. A Tale of Scottish Life. 136 p. front., pl. 18 cm. c.1881. American Tract Society.

Rouse, William Henry Denham (1863-)
--The Talking Thrush. N.D. E P Dutton.

Rouse, William Henry Denham (1863-), intro. by.
--The Arabian Nights. Paget, Walter, illus. LC 9-35173. 328 p. incl. illus., plates. col. front., 4 col. pl. 21 1/2 cm. 1907. E. Nister.

Roussel, Napoleon (1805-1878)
--Adolphus: Or, Vanity Cured. With Other Sketches. LC 8-1675. 180 p. 16 cm. 1852. Massachusetts Sabbath School Society.

Rousselet, Louis (1845-1929)
--The Ocean Rovers: Or, Two Cabin Boys. LC 8-1677. 3 p. l., 9-359 p. incl. front., illus., plates. 19 cm. c.1892. C. E. Brown and Company.
--Ralph the Drummer Boy: A Story of the Days of Washington. Gordon, William John, tr. LC 2-13335. xii, 307 p. incl. front., illus. plates. 19 cm. 1884. H. Holt and Company.

Rousselot, Norman W
--Horses and Horses. LC 66-9565. (Illus.). 27 p. 20cm. 1966. Naylor Co.

Routh, Jonathan
--The Nuns Go East. LC 73-1754. (Illus.). 32 p. 29cm. 1973, c.1972. (ISBN 0-672-51837-6). Bobbs-Merrill.
--The Nuns Go to Africa. LC 72-75886. (gr. 4-8). 1972. (ISBN 0-672-51727-2). Bobbs.
--The Nuns Go to Penguin Island. LC 72-75887. 32p. (gr. 4-8). 1971. (ISBN 0-672-51728-0). Bobbs.
--The Nuns Go West. LC 73-2439. (Illus.). 32 p. 29cm. 1972. (ISBN 0-672-51838-4). Bobbs-Merrill.

Routledge, Edmund, compiled by.
--Riddles and Jokes. (Routledge's Cheap Ser.). N.D. George Routledge & Sons.

Routledge, William
--The Musical Cinderlla. Crane, Walter (1845-1915), illus. Parker, Louis N., contrib. by. (Music by Louis N. Parker). N.D. George Routledge & Sons.
--The Singing Lancers. (Illus.). N.D. George Routledge.
--The Singing Quadrille: An Illustrated Colored Picture Book for Children Nursery Rhymes set to quadrille music. N.D. George Routledge.

Rouze, Michel
--The Mystery of Mont Saint-Michel. 1st ed. Spier, Peter Edward (1927-), illus. LC 55-10576. (Illus.). 190 p. 21cm. (Holt books for young people). 1955. Holt.

Rovira, Francesc, jt. auth. see Delgado, Eduard.

Rowan, Jean
--Rufus the New Forest Pony: A New Forest Pony. Eyles, Derek, illus. LC 67-20245. b&w ils. 144p. (gr. 4-7). 1968. Warne.

Rowand, Phyllis (1915-)
--The Cats Who Stayed for Dinner. Burchard, Peter Duncan (1921-), illus. LC 51-28015. (Illus.). 41p. 21cm. 1951. Wonder Books.
--The Day After Yesterday. Rowand, Phyllis (1915-), illus. LC 53-7300. 54p. illus. 24cm. 1953. Little, Brown.
--Every Day in the Year. Rowand, Phyllis (1915-), illus. 1953. Little, Brown.
--Every Day in the Year. Rowand, Phyllis (1915-), illus. LC 59-9108. (Illus.). 27cm. 26p. (A book full of Christmas.). (ps). 1959. (ISBN 0-316-75958-9). Little.
--George. 1st ed. Rowand, Phyllis (1915-), illus. LC 56-8458. illus. 26cm. 42p. 1956. (ISBN 0-316-75959-7). Little, Brown and Co.
--George Goes to Town. 1st ed. LC 58-8491. (Illus.). 41p. 26cm. 1958. Little, Brown.
--It Is Night. LC 53-8551. unpaged. illus. 26cm. 1953. Harper.
--Watch the Birdie!. Rowand, Phyllis (1915-), illus. LC 47-30816. (Illus.). 40p. 25cm. (Young Scott Bks.). 1947. W. R. Scott.
--Who Does Baby Look Like?. Rowand, Phyllis (1915-), illus. LC 50-8339. (Illus.). 40p. 21cm. (A Wonder Book for Children). 1950. Wonder Books.

Rowbotham, Frances Jameson, ed. see Plutarchus.

Rowbotham, Francis Jameson, ed.
--Stories from Plutarch. (Illus.). (Children's Favorite Classics). N.D. Thomas Y. Crowell.

Rowcroft, Charles
--The Australian Crusoes, 1 of 50 vols. (Illus.). (The Norwood Ser.: No. 36). 1900. Lee & Shepard.

Rowe, Anne (1937-)
--The Little Knight. Ruth, Rod (1912-), illus. LC 76-155749. (Illus.). 24 p. 24cm. 1971. Lothrop, Lee & Shepard Co.

Rowe, Dorothy (1898-)
--The Begging Deer and Other Stories of Japanese Children. Ward, Lynd Kendall (1905-1985), illus. LC 28-14308. xiii p., 1 l., 109 p. col. front., illus. col. plates. 20 cm. 1928. The Macmillan Company.
--The Moon's Birthday and Other Stories of Chinese Children. K'o Shuang Shou & Ma Tzu-Yu, illus. LC 27-219423. 7 p. l., 124 p. col. front., illus., col. plates. 20 cm. 1927. The Macmillan Company.
--The Rabbit Lantern, and Other Stories of Chinese Children. Ling Jui Tang, illus. Portier, Lucius Chapin, intro. by. LC 25-16128. xiii p., 3 l., 98 p. col. front., illus., col. plates. 21 cm. 1925. The Macmillan Company.
--Traveling Shops: Stories of Chinese Children. Ward, Lynd Kendall (1905-1985), illus. LC 29-21676. 6 p. l., 109 p. incl. illus., plates. col. front., col. plates. 20 cm. 1929. The Macmillan Company.

Rowe, John Gabriel (1874-)
--Crusoe Island. (Adventure Stories for Boys). N.D. Cupples & Leon Co.
--The Island Treasure. (Adventure Stories for Boys). N.D. Cupples & Leon Co.
--The Lightship Pirates: A Thrilling Tale of Peril and Adventure on the Texas Coast. LC 28-16177. vi p., 1 l., 390 p. incl. col. front., plan. plates. 20 cm. (His Sea stories for boys). c.1928. Cupples & Leon Company.
--The Mystery of the Derelict. (Adventure Stories for Boys). N.D. Cupples & Leon Co.
--The Secret of the Golden Idol: A Story of the Thrilling Adventures of Two American Boys on Tropical Islands. LC 28-16176. vi p., 1 l., 300 p. incl. col. front., maps. plates. 20 cm. (His Sea stories for boys). c.1928. Cuples & Leon Company.
--Sergeant Dick of the Royal Mounted Police: A Thrilling Story of the Canadian Woods. by john g. rowe ... ed. LC 29-11403. 4 p. l., 296 p. col. front., plates. 20 cm. c.1929. Cupples & Leon Company.

Rowe, Nellie Marie
--The Crystal Locket. Enright, Elizabeth (1909-1968), illus. LC 35-258361. 8 p. l., 19-143 p. incl. col. front., ilus., col. plates. 24 cm. 1935. A. Whitman & Co.
--My Magic Storyland. Breuer, Matilda, illus. LC 29-30235. 125, 1 p. incl. front., illus. (part col.) 24 cm. (Red and gold library). c.1929. A. Whitman & Co.

Rowe, Richard
--A Child's Corner Book: Stories for Boys and Girls, 1 of 4 Vols. (Lucky Bag Library Ser.). N.D. Set. T. Whittaker.
--A Holiday Book: Stories for the Young, 1 of 5 Vols. (Hero Library Ser.). N.D. Set. T. Whittaker.
--The Lucky Bag: Stories for the Young, 1 of 4 Vols. (Lucky Bag Library Ser.). N.D. Set. T. Whittaker.
--The Tower On the Top: A Tale for Boys, 1 of 5 Vols. (Hero Library Ser.). N.D. Set. T. Whittaker.

Rowe, Susan, illus.
--Tales for a Winter's Night. (Illus.). 132p. 1984. (ISBN 0-905895-86-X, Pub. by Salem Hse Ltd). Merrimack Pub Cir.
Rowe, Viola Carson (1903-1969)
--Freckled and Fourteen. Tomes, Jacqueline, illus. LC 65-18509. (Illus.). 223 p. 22cm. 1965. Morrow.
--Girl in a Hurry. O'Sullivan, Tom, illus. LC 56-7868. 180p. 22cm. 1956. Longmans, Green.
--Oh, Brother. 1 st. ed. Genia, pseud. (1930-), illus. Wennerstrom, Genia Katherine. LC 55-6733. 214p. illus. 21cm. 1955. Longmans, Green.
--Practically Twins. Giacomini, Olindo, illus. LC 63-10433. (Illus.). 216. 20cm. (A Teen Novel). 1963. Whitman Pub. Co.
--Promise to Love. LC 60-6707. 182p. 21cm. 1960. Longmans, Green.
--True to You. LC 64-14754. 216 p. 20 cm. (Whitman teen novels). 1964. Whitman Pub. Co.
--A Way with Boys. 1st ed. McGee, Millard, illus. LC 57-10521. (Illus.). 132 p. 21cm. 1957. Longmans, Green.
Rowell, Adelaide Corinne (1887-)
--Touchdown. Ishmael, Woodi, illus. LC 41-26746. 256 p. illus. 21 cm. 1942. E. P. Dutton & Company, Inc.
Rowell, Mary C.
--Thorndyke Manor. (Illus.). (Scribner-Blackie Series of Books for Young People). N.D. Charles Scribner's Sons.
Rowland, Albert Lindsay (1882-), ed. see Alcott, Louisa May.
Rowland, Eva Eickemeyer
--In and Out of the Nursery. Eickemeyer, Rudolf, Jr. (1862-1932), illus. LC 5817. 82 p. front., illus. 24 x 36 cm. 1900. R. H. Russell.
Rowland, Florence Wightman (1900-)
--Amish Boy. Payson, Dale (1943-), illus. LC 71-110314. (Illus.). 45 p. 23cm. (See and read beginning to read book). 1970. Putnam.
--Amish Wedding. Payson, Dale (1943-), illus. LC 79-127007. (Illus.). 60 p. 23cm. (See and read beginning to read storybook). 1971. Putnam.
--The Austrian Colt. Cirlin, Edgar, illus. LC 50-9831. (Illus.). 39 p. 26cm. (Colonial House Book). 1950. Macrae-Smith.
--Eo of the Caves. Pictures. Krigstein, Bernard (1919-), illus. LC 59-15224. 160p. illus. 21cm. 1959. H. Z. Walck.
--Jade Dragons. LC 58-14242. 128p. illus. 21cm. 1954. H. Z. Walck.
--Jade Dragons. Gorsline, Douglas Warner (1913-1985), illus. LC 54-100115. 128p. illus. 21cm. 1954. Oxford University Press.
--Juddie. Geer, Charles Hand (1922-), illus. LC 57-13171. 158p. illus. 21cm. 1958. Oxford University Press.
--Little Sponge Fisherman. Funai, Mamoru R. (1932-), illus. LC 69-11473. (Illus.). 45p. 23cm. 1969. Putnam.
--Pasquala of Santa Ynez Mission. Geer, Charles Hand (1922-), illus. LC 61-9957. 111p. illus. 21cm. 1961. (ISBN 0-8098-2351-9). H. Z. Walck.
--Robbie of the Kirkhaven Team. David, Brian, illus. LC 72-80122. (Illus.). 23 p. 20cm. (Magic circle book). c.1973. (ISBN 0-663-25491-4). Ginn.
--School for Julio: A See and Read Storybook. Thollander, Earl Gustave (1922-), illus. LC 68-24545. (Illus.). 46 p. 23cm. (See and read beginning to read book). 1968. (ISBN 0-399-60558-4). Putnam.
--The Singing Leaf. Thollander, Earl Gustave (1922-), illus. LC 65-20713. 48p. col. illus. 23cm. (See and read beginning to read bk.). c.1965. Putnam.
Rowland, Jasper M (1910-)
--Billy Bunny. Hood, Egon, illus. LC 47-15790. 40 p. col. illus. 28 1/2 x 21 1/2 cm. (His Chipper series, no. 1). c.1945. The American Crayon Company.
--Chipper. Hood, Egon, illus. LC 46-22546. 40 p. col. illus. 28 x 21 1/2 cm. (His Chipper series, no. 2). c.1946. The American Crayon Company.
Rowland, John T.
--North to Adventure. 1963. Norton Company.
Rowland, Pamela
--What Should I Wear?. Axeman, Lois, illus. LC 75-11633. (Illus.). 29 p. 26cm. 1975. (ISBN 0-516-03666-1). Childrens Press.
Rowlandson, G. D.
--The Conceited Princess. Warne, Winifred M, illus. (Skimble Skamble). N.D. Frederick Warne & Co.
--Periwinkle & the Fairies. Warne, Winifred M, illus. (Skimble Skamble). N.D. Frederick Warne & Co.
Rowlandson, G. D., illus.
--Tabbykins and His Friends. (The Cosy Corner Ser.). N.D. Frederick Warne & Co.
--Timmy and His Friends. (The Cosy Corner Ser.). N.D. Frederick Warne & Co.
Rowlett, Margaret (1897-)
--D is for Daddy. 1st ed. LC 47-25010. (Illus.). 32p. 27cm. (Borzoi Books for Young People). 1947. A. A. Knopf.
--When Cricket Was Little. Rowlett, Margaret (1897-), illus. LC 48-10018. 46 p. col. illus. 17 x 26 cm. 1948. Aladdin Books.
Rowley, Anthony (1920-)
--A Sunday in Autumn. Quackenbush, Robert Mead (1929-), illus. LC 67-1902. (Illus.). 31 p. 29cm. (Carousel book). c.1967. L. W. Singer Co.
Rowley, Clara G
--The Wonder Bird and Other Stories. LC 36-6898. 65 p. incl. col. front., illus. 21 cm. c.1934. B. Humphries, Inc.
Rowman, James P, ed. see Hamsa, Bobbie.
Rowntree, Lester
--Denny and the Indian Magic. Moynihan, Roberta, illus. LC 59-16390. 128p. illus. 22cm. 1959. Viking Press.
--Little Turkey. Bennett, Richard Michael (1899-), illus. LC 55-14926. 191p. illus. 21cm. 1955. Viking Press.
--Ronnie. Perceval, Don Louis (1908-), illus. LC 52-8098. (Illus.). 188 p. 22cm. 1952. Viking Press.
--Ronnie and Don. Perceval, Don Louis (1908-), illus. LC 53-340092. 160p. illus. 22cm. 1953. Viking Press.
Rowse, Alfred Leslie (1903-)
--Brown Buck: A Californian Fantasy. Ward, John (1917-), illus. LC 76-373212. (Illus.). 72 p. 23cm. 1976. (ISBN 0-7181-1456-6). Joseph.
Rowsell, Mary C.
--The Boys of Fairmead. (Warne's Adventure Library). N.D. Frederick Warne & Co.
--Honor Bright, 1 of 15 vols. (Illus.). (Dainty Ser. of Choice Gift Bks: No. 5). 1905. Set. Henry Altemus Co.
--Saint Nicholas Eve, and Other Tales. N.D. E P Dotton.
--Traitor or the Patriot. (Illus.). (Scribner-Blackie Series of books for young people). N.D. Charles Scribner's Sons.
Rox, Henry
--Banana Circus. LC 40-826447. 48 p. incl. front., illus. 24 x 19 cm. c.1940. G. P. Putnam's Sons.
Roy, Anne
--A Bear for All Seasons. LC 84-9391. p. cm. 1984. (ISBN 0-911745-77-7). P. Bedrick Books.
--School Bear Days. LC 84-9386. p. cm. 1984. (ISBN 0-911745-78-5). P. Bedrick Books.
Roy, C.
--Sunshine Country. N.D. Christian Lit.
Roy, Cal
--Bubble, the Birds, & the Noise. Roy, Cal, illus. (Illus.). (gr. k-4). 1968. (ISBN 0-8392-3069-9). Astor-Honor.
--The Legend and the Storm. Roy, Cal, illus. LC 75-17931. (Illus.). 211 p. 21cm. 1975. (ISBN 0-374-34367-5). Farrar, Straus and Giroux.
--The Painter of Miracles. LC 73-90967. (Illus.). 131 p. 22cm. 1974. (ISBN 0-374-35728-5). Farrar, Straus and Giroux.
--What Every Young Wizard Should Know. Roy, Cal, illus. LC 63-12380. (Illus.). 43. 27cm. (An Astor Bk.). 1963. (ISBN 0-8392-3043-5). I. Oblensky.
Roy, Cal, retold by.
--The Serpent & the Sun: Myths of the Mexican World. Roy, Cal, illus. LC 72-81487. (Illus.). 96p. (gr. 4 up). 1972. (ISBN 0-374-36742-6). FS&G.
Roy, Claude (1915-)
--The Very Obliging Flowers. Le Foll, Alain, illus. LC 67-31516. (Illus.). 38 p. 1968. Grove Press. **Award: (NYT).**
Roy, Helen M.
--Archie the Chipmunk. 1970. Vantage.
Roy, Jessie Hailstalk (1896-)
--Pioneers of Long Ago. Jones, Lois Mailou, illus. LC 52-25663. 316 p. illus. 20 cm. 1951. Associated Publishers.
Roy, Just Jean Etienne (1794-1870)
--Lucille: Or, The Young Flower-Maker. LC 8-1678. 140 p. front. 16 cm. 1873. D. & J. Sadlier & Co.
Roy, Kristina
--The Three Comrades. Lukesh, Charles, illus. LC 57-52243. 130p. 30cm. 1957, c.1941. Loizeaux Bros.
Roy, Lee
--The Fish Who Was All Alone. N.D. Carlton Press.
Roy, Lillian Elizabeth Becker, Mrs. (1868-1932)
--The Adventures of Snooki and Snak. Merritt, Hale, illus. LC 28-13322. 127 p. incl. front., plates. 21 cm. c.1928. Grosset & Dunlap.
--The Adventures of Sonny and Sue. Merritt, Hale, illus. LC 28-133212. 128 p. incl. front., plates. 22 cm. c.1928. Grosset & Dunlap.
--Alice in Beeland. Greene, Julia, illus. N.D. Cupples & Leon Co.
--The Blue Birds at Happy Hills. (The Blue Bird Ser.). N.D. A. L. Burt Co.
--The Blue Birds at Happy Hills. LC 74-180524. 258 p. 21cm. (Her The blue bird series). c.1919. Platt & Nourse.
--The Blue Birds of Happy Times. (The Blue Bird Ser.). N.D. Nourse.
--The Blue Birds of Happy Times Nest. (The Blue Bird Ser.). N.D. A. L. Burt.
--The Blue Birds of Happy Times Nest. 21cm. 320p. (The Blue Bird Ser.). 1914. Platt & Pecker Co.
--The Blue Birds' Uncle Ben. (The Blue Bird Ser.). N.D. A. L. Burt co.
--The Blue Birds' Uncle Ben. LC 17-28330. 320 p. front., plates. 21 cm. c.1917. The Platt & Nourse Co.
--The Blue Birds' Winter Nest. (The Blue Bird Ser.). N.D. A. L. Burt Co.
--The Blue Birds' Winter Nest. (The Blue Bird Ser.). N.D. Nourse.
--Five Little Starrs. (The Five Little Starrs Ser.). N.D. A. L. Burt Co.
--Five Little Starrs. (The Five Little Starrs Ser.). N.D. Nourse.
--Five Little Starrs in Alaska. (The Five Little Starrs Ser.). N.D. A. L. Burt Co.
--Five Little Starrs in Alaska. (The Five Little Starrs Ser.). N.D. Nourse.
--Five Little Starrs in an Island Cabin. (The Five Little Starrs Ser.). N.D. A. L. Burt Co.
--Five Little Starrs in an Island Cabin. (The Five Little Starrs Ser.). N.D. Nourse.
--Five Little Starrs in Canadian Forest. (The Five Little Starrs Ser.). N.D. Nourse.
--Five Little Starrs in Hawaii. (The Five Little Starrs Ser.). N.D. A. L. Burt Co.
--Five Little Starrs in Hawaii. LC 68-2649. (The Five Little Starrs Ser.). 1919. Nourse.
--Five Little Starrs in the Canadian Forest. (The Five Little Starrs Ser.). N.D. A. L. Burt Co.
--Five Little Starrs on a Canalboat. (The Five Little Starrs Ser.). N.D. A. L. Burt Co.
--Five Little Starrs on a Canalboat. (The Five Little Starrs Ser.). N.D. Nourse.
--Five Little Starrs on A Motor Tour. (The Five Little Starrs Ser.). N.D. A. L. Burt Co.
--Five Little Starrs on a Motor Tour. (The Five Little Starrs). N.D. Nourse.
--Five Little Starrs on a Ranch. (The Five Little Strrs Series). N.D. A. L. Burt Co.
--Five Little Starrs on a Ranch. (The Five Little Starrs Ser.). N.D. Nourse.
--Girl Scouts in Arizona and New Mexico. LC 23-10906. 2 p. l., 236 p. front. plates. 20 cm. (Girl scouts mountain series). c.1923. G. Sully & Company.
--Girl Scouts in Arizona & New Mexico. (The Girl Scouts). N.D. Grosset & Dunlap.
--Girl Scouts in Dandelion Camp. (The Girl Scouts). N.D. Grosset & Dunlap.
--Girl Scouts in Glacier Park. Barbour, H. S., illus. LC 28-13220. 3 p. l., 210 p. front., plates. 20 cm. (Her Girl scout series). c.1928. Grosset & Dunlap.
--The Girl Scouts in the Adirondacks. (Girls Scouts Mountain Ser.). 1921. George Sully & Co.
--Girl Scouts in the Adirondacks. (The Girl Scouts). N.D. Grosset & Dunlap.
--The Girl Scouts in the Magic City. (Girl Scout Ser.). N.D. Grosset & Dunlap.
--Girl Scouts in the Redwoods. (Girl Scout Ser.). N.D. Grosset & Dunlap.
--The Girl Scouts in the Rockies. (Girl Scouts Mountain Ser.). 1921. George Sully & Co.
--Girl Scouts in the Rockies. (The Girl Scouts). N.D. Grosset & Dunlap.
--The Girl Scouts of Dandelion Camp. (Girl Scouts Mountain Ser.). 1921. George Sully & Co.
--Janet: A Stock-Farm Scout. 235 p. front. 19 cm. (Her Girl scouts country life series). c.1925. A. L. Burt Company.
--The Little Washingtons. (Little Washingtons Bks.). N.D. Grosset & Dunlap.
--The Little Washingtons at School. (Little Washington Bks.). N.D. Grosset & Dunlap.
--The Little Washingtons' Holidays. LC 25-10062. 144 p. front. 20 cm. (Her Little Washington books). c.1925. Grosset & Dunlap.
--The Little Washingtons' Relatives. (Little Washington Bks.). N.D. Grosset & Dunlap.
--The Little Washingtons' Travels. (Little Washington Bks.). N.D. Grosset & Dunlap.
--Little Woodcrafter's Book. LC 17-29176. xi p., 1 l., 15-323 p. front., illus. (incl. music) plates. 20 cm. c.1917. George H. Doran Company.
--Little Woodcrafters' Fun on the Farm. Rogers, Walter S., illus. LC 28-134937. 224 p. front., plates. 20 cm. c.1928. Grosset & Dunlap.
--Natalie: A Garden Scout. (Girl Scout Country Life Ser.). N.D. A. L. Burt Co.
--Natalie: A Garden Scout. LC 23-144028. 311 p. front. 20 cm. (Her Girl scout country life series). c.1921. The Nourse Company.
--Norma: A Flower Scout. LC 25-720272. 231 p. front. 19 cm. (Her Girl scouts country life series). c.1925. A. L. Burt Company.
--Polly and Carola. Barbour, H. S., illus. LC 30-131139. 3 p. l., 238 p. front., plates. 20 cm. c.1930. Grosset & Dunlap.
--Polly and Carola at Ravenswood. Tandy, Russell H., illus. LC 31-12246. 3 p. l., 240 p. front., plates. 20 cm. (Her Polly Brewster books). c.1931. Grosset & Dunlap.
--Polly & Eleanor. (The Polly Brewster Books). N.D. Grosset & Dunlap.
--Polly and Her Friends Abroad. (The Polly Brewster Bks.). N.D. Grosset & Dunlap.
--Polly in Alaska. (The Polly Brewster Bks). N.D. Grosset & Dunlap.
--Polly in Egypt. Barbour, H. S., illus. LC 28-13219. 3 p. l., 212 p. front., plates. 20 cm. (Her Polly Brewster series). c.1928. Grosset & Dunlap.
--Polly in New York. (The Polly Brewster Bks.). N.D. Grosset & Dunlap.
--Polly in South America. (The Polly Brewster Bks.). N.D. Grosset & Dunlap.
--Polly in the Orient. (The Polly Brewster Bks). N.D. Grosset & Dunlap.
--Polly in the Southwest. Barbour, H. S., illus. LC 25-4770. 3 p. l., 276 p. front., plates. 20 cm. (Her Polly Brewster series). c.1925. Grosset & Dunlap.
--Polly Learns to Fly. Tandy, Russell H., illus. LC 32-12764. 3 p. l., 216 p. front., plates. 20 cm. (Her Polly Brewster books). c.1932. Grosset & Dunlap.
--Polly of Pebbly Pit. (The Polly Brewster Books). N.D. Grosset & Dunlap.
--Polly's Business Adventure. (The Polly Brewster Bks.). N.D. Grosset & Dunlap.
--Polly's New Friend. Barbour, H. S., illus. LC 29-11013. 2 p. l., 268 p. front., plates. 20 cm. (Lettered on cover: The Polly Brewster series). c.1929. Grosset & Dunlap.
--Polly's Southern Cruise. (The Polly Brewster Bks.). N.D. Grosset & Dunlap.
--The Seedlings Harvest. LC 10-23740. (Illus.). 247p. 1910. Wessels & Bissell Co.
--Woodcraft Boys in the Rockies. LC 28-14832. 252 p. incl. front. plates. 20 cm. c.1928. Grosset & Dunlap.
--The Woodcraft Girls at Camp. LC 16-20590. 343 p. front., plates. 20 cm. 1916. George H. Doran Company.
--The Woodcraft Girls Camping in Maine. Barbour, H. S., illus. LC 28-13494. 224 p. front., plates. 20 cm. c.1928. Grosset & Dunlap.
Roy, Lillian Elizabeth Becker, Mrs. (1868-1932) & Hoisington, May Folwell, Mrs. (1874-)
--Woodcraft Boys at Sunset Island. LC 19-83195. ix p., 1 l., 13-269 p. incl. front. plates. 20 cm. c.1919. George H. Doran Company.
Roy, Ronald (1940-)
--Avalanche!. 1st ed. MacLean, Robert (1926-), illus. LC 81-2224. p. cm. (Unicorn book). c.1981. (ISBN 0-525-26060-9). Dutton.
--Awful Thursday. Hoban, Lillian (1925-), illus. LC 78-14049. (Illus.). 38 p. 24cm. (I am reading book). c.1979. Pantheon Books.
--Breakfast with My Father. Howell, Troy, illus. LC 80-12963. (Illus.). 32 p. c.1980. Houghton Mifflin/Clarion Books.
--The Chimpanzee Kid: A Novel. LC 85-3755. 151 p. 22cm. c.1985. (ISBN 0-89919-364-1). Clarion Books.
--Frankie Is Staying Back. Kessell, Walter, illus. LC 80-28257. p. cm. c.1981. (ISBN 0-395-31025-3). Houghton Mifflin/Clarion Books.
--The Great Frog Swap. Chess, Victoria (1939-), illus. LC 79-21966. 46 p. 22cm. c.1981. (ISBN 0-394-84432-7). (ISBN 0-394-94432-1). Pantheon Books.
--I Am a Thief. 1st ed. Williges, Mel, illus. LC 81-22079. p. cm. c.1982. (ISBN 0-525-45114-5). E.P. Dutton.
--Million Dollar Jeans. 1st ed. Dos Santos, Joyce Audy, illus. LC 82-18320. p. cm. (A Unicorn bk.). c.1983. (ISBN 0-525-44047-X). Dutton.
--Move over, Wheelchairs Coming Through. Hausherr, Rosemarie, illus. LC 84-14314. (Illus.). 96p. (gr. 4-7). 1985. (ISBN 0-89919-249-1, Clarion). HM.
--Nightmare Island. 1st ed. MacLean, Robert (1926-), illus. LC 80-23526. p. cm. (Unicorn book). c.1981. (ISBN 0-525-35905-2). Dutton.
--Old Tiger, New Tiger. Bargielski, Pat, illus. LC 78-51997. (Illus.). 32 p. 26cm. c.1978. (ISBN 0-687-28809-6). Abingdon.
--A Thousand Pails of Water. Vo-Dinh, Mai (1933-), illus. LC 78-3275. (Illus.). 28 p. 22cm. c.1978. (ISBN 0-394-83752-5). Pantheon.
--Three Ducks Went Wandering. Galdone, Paul (1914-), illus. LC 78-12629. (Illus.). 32 p. 23cm. c.1979. (ISBN 0-8164-0416-X). Seabury Press.
--Where's Buddy?. Howell, Troy, illus. LC 81-12257. (Illus.). 95 p. 21cm. c.1982. (ISBN 0-89919-076-6). Clarion Books.
Roy, S. Waukley
--The Little Washingtons. (The Little Washington Ser.). 1921. Nourse.
--The Little Washingtons. LC 21-16861. 158 p. front. 18 cm. c.1918. The Platt & Nourse Co.
--The Little Washingtons at School. (The Little Washington Ser.). 1921. Nourse.

--Danger on Shadow Mountain. Rosier, Lydia, illus. LC 74-95710. (Illus.). 160 p. 23cm. 1970. Morrow.
--Devil's Doorstep. Mars, Witold Tadeusz J. (1912-), illus. LC 66-11234. (Illus.). (gr. 3-7). 1966. (ISBN 0-688-21235-2). Morrow.
--High Country Adventure. Cellini, Joseph (1924-), illus. LC 67-292. (Illus.). 159 p. 23cm. 1967. W. Morrow.
--Lion on the Run. Lewin, Ted (1935-), illus. LC 72-7880. (Illus.). 159 p. 23cm. 1973. (ISBN 0-688-20063-X). (ISBN 0-688-20063-X). W. Morrow.
--Lost in the Desert. Rosier, Lydia, illus. LC 72-142993. (Illus.). 159 p. 23cm. 1971. Morrow.
--Seal of Frog Island. Johnson, Eugene Harper, illus. LC 61-5271. (Illus.). (gr. 1-5). 1961. (ISBN 0-688-31673-5). Morrow.
--Shipwreck Bay. Goldstein, Nathan (1927-), illus. LC 66-18151. (Illus.). (gr. 3-7). 1966. (ISBN 0-688-21722-2). Morrow.

Runa, pseud., see Beskow, Elizabeth Maria.

Rundell, Joseph Benjamin, retold by.
--Aesop's Fables. Griset, Ernest, illus. N.D. D. Appleton & Co.

Rundell, Joseph Benjamin, ed. see Aesopus.

Rungachary, Santha
--Tales for All Times. Khemraj, P., illus. (Illus.). (Nehru Library for Children). (gr. 1-9). 1979. (ISBN 0-89744-187-7). Auromere.

Runk, Wesley T.
--Angel Voices: The Messengers of Christmas. (Orig.). (gr. 1-3). 1977. CSS Pub.
--Parables of Jesus. 1971. CSS Pub.

Running, Corinne
--When Coyote Walked the Earth. Bennett, Richard Michael (1899-), illus. 80p. (gr. 3-7). N.D. Henry Holt & Co.

Runyan, Esther L
--Quellen Queel and the Prince. LC 52-9689. 50p. illus. 23cm. c.1952. Vantage Press.

Runyan, John, pseud., see Palmer, Bernard Alvin.

Runyan, John, pseud. (1914-)
--Biff Norris and the Clue Midnight Stage. Palmer, Bernard Alvin. 125p. 1963. Moody Press.
--Biff Norris and the Clue of the Angry Fisherman. Palmer, Bernard Alvin. (The Biff Norris Ser.). 1966. Moody.
--Biff Norris and the Clue of the Disappearing Wolf. Palmer, Bernard Alvin. (The Biff Norris Ser.). 1967. Moody.
--Biff Norris and the Clue of the Gold Ring. Palmer, Bernard Alvin. (The Biff Norris Ser.). 1965. Moody.
--Biff Norris and the Clue of the Golden Ram. Palmer, Bernard Alvin. 125p. 1962. Moody Press.
--Biff Norris and the Clue of the Half-Burned Book. Palmer, Bernard Alvin. (The Biff Norris Ser.). 1969. Moody.
--Biff Norris and the Clue of the Lavender Mink. Palmer, Bernard Alvin. (The Biff Norris Ser.). 1964. Moody.
--Biff Norris and the Clue of the Lonely Landing Strip. Palmer, Bernard Alvin. (Biff Norris Ser.). 1962. Moody.
--Biff Norris and the Clue of the Midnight Stage. Palmer, Bernard Alvin. (The Biff Norris Ser.). 1963. Moody.
--Biff Norris and the Clue of the Mysterious Letter. Palmer, Bernard Alvin. (The Biff Norris Ser.). 1968. Moody.
--Biff Norris and the Clue of the Nervous Stranger. Palmer, Bernard Alvin. (The Biff Norris Ser.). 1962. Moody.
--Biff Norris and the Clue of the Worn Saddle. Palmer, Bernard Alvin. (The Biff Norris Ser.). 1962. Moody.
--Tom Barnes and the Substitute Second Baseman. Palmer, Bernard Alvin. 64p. (The Tom Barnes Ser.). 1964. Moody.
--Tom Barnes, Blocking Back. Palmer, Bernard Alvin. 64p. (The Tom Barnes Ser.). 1966. Moody.
--Tom Barnes, Forward. Palmer, Bernard Alvin. (The Tom Barnes Ser.). 1968. Moody.

Runyon, Catherine (1947-)
--All Wrong Mrs. Bear. Runyon, Catherine (1947-), illus. (Illus.). (ps-2). 1972. (ISBN 0-8024-0140-6). Moody.
--Too-Soon Mr. Bear, and Other Stories. Runyon, Catherine (1947-), illus. LC 79-23404. (Illus.). 30 p. 21cm. c.1979. (ISBN 0-8024-8788-2). Moody Press.

Runyon, Leilah
--I Learn to Read About Jesus. Deist, June K., illus. (Illus.). (Basic Bible Readers Ser.: Primer). (gr. k-1). 1962. (ISBN 0-87239-257-0). Standard Pub.

Ruppert, Donna (1943-)
--The Dragon's Path. Ruppert, Donna (1943-), illus. LC 79-17169. (Illus.). 58 p. 21cm. c.1979. (ISBN 0-89742-023-3). (ISBN 0-89742-014-4). Dawne-Leigh Publications.

Rupprecht, Maureen, illus.
--Cabbage Patch Kids King-Size Activity & Coloring Book. (Illus.). 128p. (Cabbage Patch Kids Ser.). 1984. (ISBN 0-910313-34-2). Parker Bro.

Rusch, Althea Randolph Bedle, Mrs. (1871-)
--Jeannie's Journal: Or, First Year at Boarding School. Pancoast, Charles W., illus. LC 8-30703. 3 p. l., 177 p. front., 3 pl. 21 cm. 1908. Bonnell, Silver and Company.
--Jeannie's Journal: Or, Two Years at Boarding School. LC 14-14569. 2 p. l., 177, 138 p. front., plates. 21 cm. c.1914. The H. W. Gray Co., Sole Agents for Novello & Co.

Rush, Allison
--The Last of Danu's Children. LC 82-2981. (gr. 7 up). 1982. (ISBN 0-395-32270-7). HM.

Rush, Anne Kent (1945-)
--Greta Bear Goes to Yellowstone National Park. LC 84-80077. 1984. Greta Bear Enterprises.

Rush, Caroline
--Eight Tales of Mr. Pengachoosa. Strandquest, Dominique Michele (1951-), illus. LC 72-96419. (Illus.). 66 p. 22cm. 1974, c.1971. (ISBN 0-517-50312-3). Crown Publishers.
--Further Tales of Mr. Pengachoosa. Strandquest, Dominique Michele (1951-), illus. LC 72-96418. (Illus.). 88 p. 22cm. 1973. (ISBN 0-517-50311-5). Crown.
--Scarecrow. Lawson, Carol, illus. LC 68-26074. (Illus.). (gr. k-3). 1968. St Martin.
--Tales of Mr. Pengachoosa. Strandquest, Dominique Michele (1951-), illus. LC 72-93464. (Illus.). 56 p. 22cm. 1973. (ISBN 0-517-50301-8). Crown Publishers.

Rush, Earl Marvin
--Nothing but Dogs. LC 47-11210. 56 p. col. illus. 24 cm. 1947. Grosset & Dunlap.

Rush, Elizabeth
--House at the End of the Lane. Wilson, Suzy, illus. (Illus., Orig.). 1982. (ISBN 0-914676-64-4, Star & Eleph Bks). Green Tiger Pr.

Rush, Emmy Matt
--My Garden of Roses. LC 25-19531. 18 cm. 64p. 1925. Four Seas.

Rush, Hannah
--Dog and Butterfly: A Play-Along Story. Rinciari, Ken, illus. LC 65-165027. 1v. (unpaged) illus. (pt. col.)26cm. (Rutledge bk.). c.1965. Nelson.
--The Peek-a-Boo Book of Animals. Seiden, Art, illus. LC 65-22518. 1 v. (chiefly col. illus.) 14 x 24 cm. 1965. T. Nelson.
--The Peek-a-Boo Book of Puppies & Kittens. Haley, Gail Einhart (1939-), illus. LC 65-6861. 1 v. (chiefly col. illus.) 14 x 24 cm. 1965. T. Nelson.

Rush, Peter (1937-)
--Travellers' Tales. Rush, Peter (1937-), illus. (Illus.). 86p. 1st U.S. edition. (gr. 3-5). 1984. (ISBN 0-7182-5085-0, Pub. by Kaye & Ward). David & Charles.

Rush, Philip (1908-)
--The Castle & the Harp. Keeping, Charles William James (1924-), illus. LC 64-22973. 20cm. 223p. 1964. McGraw.
--Frost Fair. Gough, Philip (1908-), illus. LC 67-1583. (Illus.). 191 p. 20cm. 1967, c.1965. Roy Publishers.
--He Sailed With Dampier. Ogle, Richard B., illus. 1947. Boardman.
--He Went with Dampier. Jobson, Patrick (1919-), illus. 184p. illus. 21cm. 1958. Roy Publishers.
--The Minstrel Knight. Krush, Joe (1918-), illus. LC 56-14523. 21cm. 236p. 1956. Bobbs Merrill.
--My Brother Lambert: A Story of the Simnel Rebellion. Walsh, David, illus. LC 57-696618. 143p. illus. 21cm. (Pageant of history books). 1957. Roy Publishers.

Rush, Sarah
--Hucket-a-Bucket Again. Lamson, Harold K., illus. LC 67-15702. (Illus.). 31 p. 26cm. 1967. Lerner Publications Co.
--Hucket-a-Bucket Down the Street. Kodner, Howard, illus. LC 64-8403. 1 v. (unpaged) col. illus. 26 cm. 1965. Lerner Publications Co.

Rush, William Marshall see Layton, Mark, pseud.

Rush, William Marshall (1887-1950)
--Duff: The Story of a Bear. Christensen, Gardell Dano (1907-), illus. LC 50-96591. (Illus.). 149 p. 22cm. 1950. Longmans, Green.
--Forest Ranger. LC 45-8204. 4 p. l., 245 p. 21 cm. 1945. M. S. Mill Co., Inc.
--Gold Prospector. 1st ed. Harper, Arthur, illus. LC 48-414264. 232 p. illus. 21 cm. 1948. Longmans, Green.
--Lumberman's Dog. 1st ed. Lambo, Donald W. (1903-1966), illus. LC 55-6734. 244p. illus. 21cm. 1955. Longmans, Green.
--Red Fox of Kinapoo: A Tale of the Nez Perce Indians. Wilson, Charles Banks (1918-), illus. 279p. 1949. Longmans, Green & Co.
--Red Fox of the Kinapoo. Wilson, Charles Banks (1918-), illus. (Illus.). (gr. 6-9). N.D. McKay.
--Rocky Mountain Ranger. 1st ed. Bennett, Richard Michael (1899-), illus. LC 44-7519. 3 p. l., 223 p. illus. 21 cm. 1944. Longmans, Green and Co.
--Silver Spurs: The Story of a Montana Cattle Ranch. Layton, Mark, pseud. LC 47-18108. 4 p. l., 216 p. 21 cm. 1947. M. S. Mill Company.
--Wheat Rancher. Habersack, Ernest R., illus. LC 46-609673. 3 p. l., 247 p. illus. 21 cm. 1946. Longmans, Green and Co.
--Wild Horses of Rainrock. Ray, Ralph (1920-1952), illus. 1951. E M Hale.
--Wild Horses of Rainrock. 1st ed. Ray, Ralph (1920-1952), illus. LC 51-11623. v, 236 p. 22cm. 1951. Longmans, Green.
--Yellowstone Scout. Ray, Ralph (1920-1952), illus. LC 45-891860. 4 p. l., 184 p. illus. 21 cm. 1945. Longmans, Green & Co., Inc.

Rushmore, Helen (1898-)
--Bigfoot Wallace and the Hickory Nut Battle. Wilde, George A., illus. LC 74-103064. (Illus.). 45 p. 23cm. (A Reading shelf book). 1970. Garrard Pub. Co.
--Chief Takes Over. Geer, Charles Hand (1922-), illus. LC 56-10738. (Illus.). (gr. 3-6). 1956. (ISBN 0-15-216789-7). HarBraceJ.
--Cowboy Joe of the Circle S. LC 50-9425. (Illus.). 21cm. 147p. (Voyager bk.: AVB29). c.1950. Harcourt.
--Ghost Cat. 1 st. ed. Lonette, Reisie Dominee (1924-), illus. LC 54-5156. (Illus.). 21cm. 150p. (gr. 2-6). 1954. (ISBN 0-15-230751-6). HarBraceJ.
--Ghost Dance on Coyote Butte. Vestal, Herman B., illus. LC 78-151989. (Illus.). 47 p. 23cm. (Reading shelf book). (American Folk Tales). 1971. (ISBN 0-8116-4030-2). Garrard Pub. Co.
--Gib Morgan: Fantastic Driller. Wilde, George A., illus. LC 79-103959. (Illus.). 64 p. 24cm. (A Reading shelf book). 1970. Garrard Pub. Co.
--Look Out for Hogan's Goats. Korach, Mimi (1922-), illus. LC 69-11773. (Illus.). 62 p. 24cm. (Reading shelf book). 1969. Garrard Pub. Co.
--The Lost Treasure Box. 1st ed. Glanzman, Louis S. (1922-), illus. LC 49-10607. 184 p. illus. 21 cm. 1949. Harcourt, Brace.
--The Magnificent House of Man Alone: An Osage Indian Story. Vaughn, Frank E., illus. LC 68-13594. (Illus.). (American Folk Stories). (gr. 2-5). 1968. (ISBN 0-8116-4009-4). Garrard.
--Old Billy Solves a Mystery. Korach, Mimi (1922-), illus. LC 73-17101. p. 1974. (ISBN 0-8116-4041-8). Garrard Pub. Co.
--Ponca, Cowpony. 1st ed. Burchard, Peter Duncan (1921-), illus. LC 52-6909. (Illus.). 175 p. 21cm. 1952. Harcourt, Brace.
--Sancho, the Homesick Steer. Hearne, Jack, illus. LC 72-190356. (Illus.). 62 p. 24cm. 1972. (ISBN 0-8116-4257-7). Garrard Pub. Co.
--The Shadow of Robbers' Roost. 160p. (gr. 4-6). 1969 (StarLine). Schol Bk Serv.
--The Shadow of Robbers' Roost. 1st ed. Orbaan, Albert F. (1913-), illus. LC 60-72004. 186p. illus. 22cm. 1960. World Pub. Co.

Ruskay, Sophie
--Discovery at Aspen. LC 60-10204. (Illus.). 21cm. 210p. (Wonderful World Book Series). 1960. A. S. Barnes & Co, Inc.

Ruskin
--Queen of Air, 1 of 88 vols. popular ed. (Handy Volume Classics). N.D. T. Y. Crowell & Co.

Ruskin, John, et al. (1819-1900)
--The King of the Golden River, and Other Wonder Stories. 98 p. 18 cm. (Riverside literature series. no. 126). c.1898. Houghton, Mifflin and Company.

Ruskin, John, jt. auth. see Amicis, Edmondo de.

Ruskin, John, jt. auth. see Browning, Robert.

Ruskin, John, ed. see Grimm, Jakob Ludwig Karl (1785-1863) & Grimm, Wilhelm Karl.

Ruskin, John (1819-1900), ed. see Sharpe, Richard Scrafton (0000-1852) & Pearson, Mrs.

Ruskin, John (1819-1900)
--Dame Wiggins of Lee and Her Seven Wonderful Cats. N.D. Charles E. Merrill Co.
--Dame Wiggins of Lee and her Seven Wonderful Cats. Broomfield, Robert (1930-), illus. 1963. McGraw-Hill Book Co.
--Dame Wiggins of Lee & Her Seven Wonderful Cats. Broomfield, Robert (1930-), illus. (gr. k-4). N.D. (ISBN 0-07-008121-2). McGraw.
--Dame Wiggins of Lee and Her Seven Wonderful Cats. Chadwick, Mara Louise Pratt, Mrs., ed. Marshall, Francesca, contrib. by. N.D. David McKay Co.
--Dame Wiggins of Lee and Her Seven Wonderful Cats. Greenaway, Kate (1846-1901), illus. N.D. E. P. Dutton & Co.
--King of the Golden River. (Illus.). (The Wellesley Series for Girls). N.D. A. L. Burt.
--King of the Golden River. (The Elm Ser.). N.D. Barse & Hopkins.
--The King of the Golden River. (Illus.). (Editha Ser.). N.D. Caldwell.
--King of the Golden River. (Illus.). (Children's Classics Ser.). N.D. Dana Estes and Company.
--King of the Golden River. N.D. David McKay Co.
--King of the Golden River. (Illus.). (Children's Hour Series.). N.D. Dodge Publishing Co.
--King of the Golden River. N.D. Educational Publishing Company.
--The King of the Golden River. LC 75-32165. (Illus.). 247 p. in various pagings. 23cm. (Classics of Children's Literature, 1621-1932). 1976. (ISBN 0-8240-2278-5). Garland Pub.
--The King of the Golden River. N.D. Grosset & Dunlap.
--The King of the Golden River. LC 6-33582. 83 p. front. 14 cm. c.1906. H. M. Caldwell Co.
--The King of the Golden River. (Little Classics). N.D. James R Osgood & Co.
--King of the Golden River, 1 of 3 Vols. (Illus.). (Little Jacket Ser.). N.D. Lee & Shepard.
--King of the Golden River. N.D. Lothrop, Lee & Shepard.
--The King of the Golden River. 1952. Macmillan.
--King of the Golden River. (Illus.). 1910. Putman.
--The King of the Golden River. (Literary Gem Second Ser.: No. 2). N.D. Putman & Sons.
--The King of the Golden River. LC 3-1772. 20cm. 75p. 1900. Roycrofters.
--King of the Golden River. (Illus.). (Crowell's Child Life Series.). 1915. T Y Crowell.
--The King of the Golden River. (Illus.). (The Cosy Corner Ser.). N.D. The Page Company.
--King of the Golden River. (Illus.). (The Sunshine Library for Young People). N.D. Thomas Y. Crowell.
--The King of the Golden River. Bates, Katharine Lee (1859-1929), ed. Johansen, John C., illus. LC 3-16816. 18cm. 82p. (Canterbury Classics). 1903. Rand McNally & Co.
--The King of the Golden River. Dalziel, Edward (1817-1905), illus. (Cosy Corner Ser.). N.D. L. C. Page & Co.
--The King of the Golden River. Doyle, Richard (1824-1883), illus. (Cosy Corner Ser.). N.D. L. C. Page & Co.
--The King of the Golden River. Doyle, Richard (1824-1883), illus. LC 67-411. (Illus.). 24cm. 64p. (Legacy lib. facsim.). 1966. University Microfilms.
--King of the Golden River. Ginn, ed. (Classics for Children). N.D. Ginn and Company.
--The King of the Golden River. 1st ed. Kredel, Fritz (1900-1973), illus. Becker, May Lamberton, Mrs. (1873-1958), intro. by. LC 46-25119. 3 p. l., 5-111, 2 p., 1 l. col. front., illus., col. plates 22 cm. (Half-title: Rainbow classics). 1946. The World Publishing Company.
--King of the Golden River. O'Shea, Michael Vincent (1866-1932), ed. (Heath's Home and School Classics.). 1910. Heath & Co.
--The King of the Golden River. Rackham, Arthur (1867-1939), illus. LC 32-28180. 47, 1 p. col. front., illus., col. plates. 23 cm. 1932. J. B. Lippincott Co.
--The King of the Golden River. Thorndike, Edward Lee (1874-), ed. O'Keeffe, Neil, illus. LC 36-3142. 5 p. l., 3-45 p. incl. front., illus. 20 cm. (Thorndike library). c.1936. D. Appleton-Century Company, Incorporated.
--The King of the Golden River. Wolf, Ben, illus. LC 45-10476. 48 p. incl. col. front., illus. (part col.) 27 1/2 cm. 1945. The Hyperion Press, Distributed by Duell, Sloan and Pearce.
--The King of the Golden River: A Legend of Stiria. Doyle, Richard (1824-1883), illus. N.D. Joseph Knight Co.
--The King of the Golden River: A Legend of Stiria. Schmidt, Austin Guildford (1883-), ed. Doyle, Richard (1824-1883), illus. LC 18-20422. 71 p. illus. 19 cm. (Loyola English classics). c.1918. Loyola University Press.
--The King of the Golden River: A Legend of Styria, 36 vols. (Illus.). (St. Nicholas Ser.). 1905. Set. A L Burt Co.
--The King of the Golden River: A Story. Turska, Krystyna Zofia (1933-), illus. LC 77-22976. (Illus.). 40 p. 29cm. 1978. (ISBN 0-688-80122-6). (ISBN 0-688-84122-8). Greenwillow Books.
--The King of the Golden River and "Coure", 2 Vols in 1. Thorndike, Edward Lee (1874-), ed. Amicis, Edmondo de & O'Keeffe, Neil, illus. (The Thorndike Library). N.D. Appleton-Century-Crofts.
--The King of the Golden River, and Dame Wiggins of Lee & Her Seven Wonderful Cats. N.D. Charles E Merrill.
--King of the Golden River & Dame Wiggins of Lee & Her Seven Wonderful Cats. 1900. Maynard Merrill & Co.
--The King of the Golden River, and Dame Wiggins of Lee and Her Seven Wonderful Cats. Kirk, Maria Louise (1860-), illus. LC 21-6627. 5 p. l., 3-72 p. col. front., col. plates. 20 cm. 1921. J. B. Lippincott Company.

AUTHOR INDEX RUSSO, SUSAN

--The King of the Golden River, and Dame Wiggins of Lee and Her Seven Wonderful Cats. Merchant, Elizabeth Lodor, ed. Greene, Julia, illus. LC 30-527831. x, 69 p. col. front., illus., col. pl. 21 cm. (child's garden of charming books). c.1929. The John C. Winston Company.
--The King of the Golden River: Or, the Black Brothers, a Legend of Stiria. Doyle, Richard (1824-1883), illus. LC 44-449361. 5 p. l., 9-53 p. incl. front., illus. 18 cm. 1885. Ginn & Company.
--The King of the Golden River: Or, the Black Brothers, a Legend of Stiria. Fisher, Elizabeth M., illus. LC 27-19605. 125 p. incl. col. front., col. illus., col. plates. 21 cm. ("A just right book"). c.1927. A. Whitman & Company.
--The King of the Golden River: Or, the Black Brothers, a Legend of Stiria. O'Shea, Michael Vincent (1866-1932), ed. Gallagher, Sears (1869-1955), illus. LC 6304. xiv, 58 p. incl. front., illus., plates. 19 cm. (On cover: Heath's home and school classics. The story book series. no. 7). 1900. D. C. Heath & Co.
--The King of the Golden River: Or, the Black Brothers, a Legend of Stiria. O'Shea, Michael Vincent (1866-1932), ed. Gallagher, Sears (1869-1955), illus. LC 42-470856. xiv, 57, 1 p. incl. front., illus., plates. 19 1/2 cm. c.1900. D. C. Heath & Co.
--The King of the Golden River: Or, the Black Brothers. LC 26-16145. 4 p. l., 3-120 p. incl. illus., plates. front. 17 cm. (On cover: The little library). 1926. The Macmillan Company.
--The King of the Golden River: Or, the Black Brothers. Stewart, Charles William (1915-), illus. LC 59-5886. 60p. illus. 22cm. 1958. Watts.
--The King of the Golden River: Or, the Black Brothers. Stewart, Charles William (1915-), illus. LC 59-5882. 60p. illus. 22cm. 1967, c.1958. Watts.
--Ruskin's Selections. Ginn, ed. (Classics for Children). N.D. Ginn and Company.

Ruskin, John (1819-1900) & Pearson, Mrs.
--Dame Wiggins of Lee and Her Seven Wonderful Cats. Brewster, Patience, ed. Sharpe, Richard Scrafton (0000-1852), illus. LC 79-7901. p. cm. c.1980. (ISBN 0-690-03915-8). (ISBN 0-690-03916-6). Crowell.

Rusling, Albert
--The Mouse & Mrs. Proudfoot. LC 84-17871. p. cm. 1st U.S. edition. 1984. (ISBN 0-13-604265-1). Prentice-Hall.

Russ, Joanna (1937-)
--Kittatinny: A Tale of Magic. 1st ed. Li, Loretta, illus. LC 77-94981. (Illus.). 92 p. 28cm. c.1978. (ISBN 0-913780-24-3). Daughters Pub. Co.

Russ, Lavinia (1819-1900)
--Alec's Sand Castle. Stevenson, James Walker (1929-), illus. LC 72-82893. (Illus.). 30 p. 27cm. 1972. (ISBN 0-06-020149-5). (ISBN 0-06-020149-5). Harper & Row.
--The April Age. LC 74-18194. 119 p. 22cm. 1975. (ISBN 0-689-30431-5). Atheneum.
--Over the Hills & Far Away. LC 68-13371. (gr. 5-9). 1968. (ISBN 0-15-258946-5, HJ). HarBraceJ.

Russ, Lavinia (1819-1900) & Russ, Liza, eds.
--Forever England: Poetry & Prose About England & the English. Ambrus, Victor G., pseud. (1935-), illus. Ambrus, Gyozo Laszlo. LC 75-82638. (Illus.). line drawings. (gr. 7-12). 1969. (ISBN 0-15-228976-3). HarBraceJ.

Russ, Liza, jt. ed. see Russ, Lavinia.

Russ, Richard Patrick
--Beasts Royal. 84p. N.D. G P Putnam's Sons.
--Caesar: The Life Story of a Panda Leopard. Rountree, Harry (1878-1950), illus. LC 31-22564. vii, 1, 87, 1 p. col. front., plates. 21 x 16 cm. 1930. G. P. Putnam's Sons.

Russan, Ashmore & Boyle, Frederick
--The Orchid Seekers. (Illus.). (Boys' Presentation Library). N.D. Frederick Warne & Co.

Russcol, Margalit, pseud., see Banai, Margalit.

Russell, Alice Dyar
--Strangers in the Desert. Rankins, James F., illus. LC 38-32228. xii p., 1 l., 234 p. incl. front., illus., plates. 22 cm. 1938. Harper & Brothers.

Russell, Amy
--Five Ponies for Princess. LC 64-15675. 152 p. 22 cm. 1964. Bobbs-Merrill.

Russell, Anna Virginia
--A Story Told by Pins. Polley, Frederick, illus. LC 8-11707. 64 p. incl. front., illus. 19 cm. 1908. The Neale Publishing Company.

Russell, Anne
--Seabiscuit: Wild Pony of the Outer Banks. rev. ed. Halpin, Diane R., illus. (Illus.). 32p. (Orig.). (The Lost Colony Collection). (gr. k-6). 1984. (ISBN 0-935326-51-0). Gallopade Pub Group.

Russell, Arthur, pseud., see Goode, Arthur Russell.

Russell, Arthur Joseph (1861-)
--Stony Lonesome. Hallock, Ruth Mary (1876-), illus. 3 p. l., 166 p. illus. 18 cm. 1903. Rand, McNally & Company.

Russell, B. A & Sanders, Charles Walton (1805-1889), eds.
--The Robin Red Breast: A New Juvenile Singing Book. 199p. 1856 (Co. Pub by S. C Griggs & Co). Ivison & Phinney.

Russell, Betty
--Big Store, Funny Door. Gehr, Mary, illus. LC 55-7786. unpaged. illus. 22cm. 1955. A. Whitman.
--Chick-Chick Here. Claffy, Cecile, illus. LC 57-7920. unpaged. illus. 22cm. 1957. A. Whitman.
--Funny Boots. Gehr, Mary, illus. LC 51-14194. (Illus.). unpaged. 21cm. 1951. A. Whitman.
--Run Sheep, Run. Gehr, Mary, illus. LC 52-14410. unpaged. illus. 21 cm. 1952. A. Whitman.

Russell, Charles
--The True Robinson Crusoes: Stories of Adventure, 1 of 4. (Album Library). N.D. Colby and Rich.

Russell, Charles, tr. see Denis, F. & Charnier, V.

Russell, Charles, tr. see Denis, L. & Charnier, V.

Russell, Donald Bert (1899-)
--Adam Bradford, Cowboy. Ranft, Max, illus. LC 73-91289. (Illus.). 64 p. 23cm. (Americans all cowboy series). 1970. Benefic Press.
--Cowboy Marshal. Herrington, Roger, illus. LC 71-112729. (Illus.). 94 p. 23cm. (Cowboys of many races). 1970. Benefic Press.
--Cowboy on the Trail. Ranft, Max, illus. LC 71-94372. (Illus.). 95 p. 23cm. (Cowboys of many races). 1970. Benefic Press.
--Cowboy Soldier. Ranft, Max, illus. LC 73-103699. (Illus.). 95 p. 23cm. (Cowboys of many races). 1970. Benefic Press.

Russell, Dorothy Kendall, Mrs. (1897-)
--Betty's Diary. (Illus.). N.D. Dodge Publishing Co.
--The Secret Passage. LC 19-170778. 4 p. l., 183 p. col. front., col. plates. 22 x 17 cm. 1918. Frederick A. Stokes Company.

Russell, Dorothy Kendall, Mrs. (1897-) & Horton, Edith Kendall, Mrs. (1898-)
--Ride 'em Cowboy. Polly, illus. LC 39-14608. 162 p. illus., col. double plates. 21 cm. c.1939. Lithographed by H. H. Boelter, Inc.

Russell, Emmet
--Lilac Time. LC 55-27081. 134p. 20cm. c.1954. Van Kampon Press.

Russell, Eric Frank (1909-)
--Men, Martians And Time Machines. N.D. Berkley Books.

Russell, Florence Kimball, Mrs.
--Born to the Blue: A Story of the Army. Elwell, R. Farrington, illus. LC 6-245781. 5 p. l., 245 p. front., 7 pl. 20 cm. 1906. L. C. Page & Company.
--From Chevrons to Shoulder-Straps: A Story of West Point. Goss, John, illus. LC 14-16942. vi p., 2 l., 324 p. front., illus., plates. 21 cm. (Her The boys' story of the army series). 1914. The Page Company.
--In West Point Gray As Plebe and Yearling. Bonnar, James K., illus. LC 8-32339. 4 p. l., 401 p. front., 5 pl. 21 cm. (On verso of half-title: The boys' story of the army series). 1908. L. C. Page & Company.

Russell, Frank Alden, jt. auth. see Raile, Vilate.

Russell, Franklin Alexander (1926-)
--At the Pond, Vols. 1-3. Cuffari, Richard (1925-1978), illus. Incl. Vol. 1. Corvus the Crow. LC 72-182120. (ISBN 0-590-07169-6); Vol. 2. Lotor the Raccoon. LC 73-189140. (ISBN 0-590-07170-X); Vol. 3. Datra the Muskrat. LC 72-77813. (ISBN 0-590-07234-X). (ISBN 0-590-07234-X). (Illus.). (gr. 5-9). 1972 (Four Winds). Schol Bk Serv.
--Corvus the Crow. Cuffari, Richard (1925-1978), illus. LC 72-182120. (Illus.). 116 p. 24cm. (His At the pond, v. 1). 1972. Four Winds Press.
--The Frightened Hare. Sweney, Fredric, illus. LC 65-14148. (Illus.). 60p. (gr. 4-6). 1966. (ISBN 0-03-057445-5). (ISBN 0-03-057450-1). HR&W.
--Hawk in the Sky. (gr. 4-6). 1977. (ISBN 0-590-11853-6, Schol Pap). Schol Bk Serv.
--The Honeybees. Portal, Colette (1936-), illus. LC 67-8838. (Illus.). 1 v. (unpaged). 26cm. 1967. Knopf: Distributed by Random House. Award: (NYT).
--Lotor the Raccoon. Cuffari, Richard (1925-1978), illus. LC 73-189140. (Illus.). 92 p. 24cm. (His At the pond, v. 2.). 1972. Four Winds Press.
--Searchers At the Gulf. 1970. (ISBN 0-393-06373-9). Norton & Co.
--Season on the Plain. 1974. (ISBN 0-88349-024-2). Readers Digest Dr.
--The Secret Islands. Russell, Franklin Alexander (1926-), illus. 1966. (ISBN 0-393-07381-5). Norton & Co.

Russell, Geraldine
--Rocket Trip to the Moon. 32p. 1st U.S. edition. (ps-1). 1970. (ISBN 0-307-12170-4, Golden Pr). Western Pub.

Russell, Hattie Sandford, Mrs. (1843-)
--What Christmas Brought to Tom and Nell. 32p. N.D. Cochrane Publishing Co.

Russell, Issac
--The Pilot or the Skylark. (Illus.). 348p. 1910. W. A. Wilde & Co.

Russell, Ivy Ethel Southern (1909-)
--Debbie. Horn, Joyce, illus. LC 58-11769. 151p. illus. 21cm. 1958. F. Warne.

Russell, Joseph P., ed. see Ingram, Kristen J.

Russell, Keith
--The Young Birdmen Across the Continent: Or, the Coast-to-Coast Flight of the Night Mail. Rodgers, Richard H. (1876-1953), illus. LC 30-10381. vi p., 1 l., 241 p. front., plates. 20 cm. (His The Young birdman books). 1930. Sears Publishing Company, Inc.
--The Young Birdmen on the Wing: Or, the Rescue at Greenly Island. Rodgers, Richard H. (1876-1953), illus. LC 29-17822. vi p., 1 l., 248 p. front., plates. 20 cm. (Young birdmen books). c.1929. J. H. Sears & Company, Inc.
--The Young Birdmen up the Amazon: Or, Secrets of the Tropic Jungle. Rodgers, Richard H. (1876-1953), illus. LC 30-19281. vii, 248 p. front., plates. 20 cm. (His The Young birdmen books). c.1930. Sears Publishing Company, Inc.

Russell, Marie see Browning, James, pseud.

Russell, Marie see Cobb, Andy, pseud.

Russell, Marie
--The Busy Bulldozer. Browning, James, pseud. Grider, Dorothy (1915-), illus. LC 52-33989. unpaged. illus. 21cm. (Rand McNally book-elf book, 459). c.1952. Rand McNally.
--Cowboy Dan. Cobb, Andy, pseud. Phillips, Katherine L., illus. LC 51-20937. (Illus.). 17cm. 33p. (A Rand McNally Book Elf Junior). 1950. Rand McNally.
--Cowboy Dan. Cobb, Andy, pseud. Phillips, Katherine L., illus. LC 57-10609. unpaged. illus. 27cm. (Rand McNally storytime book). 1957, c.1950. Rand McNally.
--My First Zoo Book. Phillips, Katherine L., illus. LC 53-31786. unpaged. illus. 17cm. (Rand McNally book-elf junior, 677). c.1952. Rand McNally.
--Sparky the Fire Dog. Browning, James, pseud. N.D. Rand McNally & Co.
--Sparky, the Fire Dog. Browning, James, pseud. Chase, Mary Jane, illus. LC 54-11040. unpaged. illus. 21cm. (Rand McNally book-elf book, 495). c.1954. Rand McNally.

Russell, Martha Stockton, Mrs.
--Sing, Swing, Play: How to do it. LC 38-29032. (Illustrated with Fifty-Eight Folk Songs). 93 p., 1 l. diagrs. 26 cm. 1938. The Viking Press.

Russell, Mary Annette Beauchamp Russell (1866-1941)
--The April Baby's Book of Tunes: With the Story of How They Came to Be Written. Greenaway, Kate (1846-1901), illus. LC 6713. 3 p. l., 74, 1 p. col. front., col. illus., col. pl. 18 x 19 cm. 1900. The Macmillan Company.

Russell, Mary K., Mrs.
--Lydia and Her Sisters. LC 32-6106. vi p., 1 l., 352 p. front., plates. 21 cm. 1931. Yale University Press.

Russell, Mary McSorley (1881-)
--Skeet. Manget, Jeanne C., illus. LC 54-8305. 55p. illus. 21cm. 1954. Little, Brown.

Russell, Maurice
--Told to Burmese Children. Walker, Monica, illus. LC 57-5063. 80p. 20cm. 1957. Roy Publishers.

Russell, Nellie Holland
--The Bonnie New World: The Adventures of Jimmie Holland of the Carolina Colony. 1 st. ed. LC 57-140946. 241p. 21cm. 1957. Exposition Press.

Russell, Nellie Naomi (1862-1911)
--Gleanings from Chinese Folklore. Porter, Mary H., compiled by. N.D. Gale Reprint.

Russell, Ota Lee
--Jackknife Summer. (Illus.). 139p. (gr. 7-8). 1958. (ISBN 0-87178-454-8). Brethren.
--Wilderness Boy. Monomachov, Ludmilla, illus. LC 56-34984. 147p. illus. 21cm. 1956. Brethren Pub. House.

Russell, Patrick, pseud., see Sammis, John.

Russell, Patrick, pseud. (1942-)
--Going, Going, Gone. Sammis, John. 1st ed. Guzzi, George, illus. LC 67-17270. (Illus.). 144 p. 22cm. (Doubleday signal books). 1967. Doubleday.

Russell, Peggy
--Peter the Petulant Penguin and Other Poems. LC 39-17505. 27 p. illus. 25 cm. 1935. Printed for Peggy Russell by R. A. Burnett and R. Kline.

Russell, Ruth W., ed.
--Stories You Can Tell. LC 64-10850. 159p. 21cm. 1964, c.1963. Judson.

Russell, Sandra Joanne
--A Farmer's Dozen. 1st ed. Russell, Sandra Joanne, illus. LC 81-47739. (Illus.). 31 p. c.1982. (ISBN 0-06-025143-3). (ISBN 0-06-025144-1). Harper & Row.

Russell, Solveig Paulson (1904-)
--About Bananas. Rogers, Carol, illus. (Illus.). 30 p. 24cm. (Melmont look, read, learn). 1968. Melmont Publishers.
--Bible ABC Book. Pallarito, Don, illus. LC 67-27153. (Illus.). 1 v. (unpaged. 26cm. 1967. Concordia Pub. House.
--Four-Legged Helpers. Wills, Jan, illus. LC 67-7747. (Illus.). 1 v. (unpaged. 21cm. 1967. Broadman Press.
--How Shall We Ride Away. Hawkinson, John Samuel (1912-), illus. LC 66-11632. (Illus.). (gr. k-3). 1966. (ISBN 0-516-08619-7). Melmont.
--If You Were a Cat. Rice, Elizabeth (1913-), illus. LC 67-1965. (Illus.). 48 p. 22cm. 1967. Childrens Press.
--Indian Big and Indian Little. Kessler, Leonard P. (1921-), illus. LC 64-15653. 40 p.col. illus. 19 x 24 cm. 1964. Bobbs-Merrill.
--Like & Unlike. (Illus.). 1973. (ISBN 0-8098-1209-6). Walck.
--Motherly Smith & Brother Bimbo. Perl, Susan (1922-1983), illus. LC 77-127375. (Illus.). 64 p. 1971. (ISBN 0-687-27239-4). Abingdon Press.
--The Mushmen. Gobbato, Imero (1923-), illus. LC 68-12302. (Illus.). 94 p. 22cm. 1968. Dodd, Mead.
--Rozy Dozy. Leder, Dora, illus. LC 74-23567. (Illus.). 32 p. 24cm. 1975. (ISBN 0-687-36624-0). Abingdon Press.
--Spring, Fall, and in Between. Pallarito, Don, illus. LC 68-14636. (Illus.). 28 p. 26cm. 1968. Concordia Pub. House.
--Up Down and All Around. 1967. Lutheran Publications.
--Up Down and All Around. Pallarito, Don, illus. LC 67-27152. (Illus.). 1 v. 26cm. 30p. 1967. Concordia Pub. House.
--What Good Is a Tail?. 1st ed. Keats, Ezra Jack (1916-1983), illus. LC 62-18097. unpaged. illus. 29cm. 1962. Bobbs- Merrill.
--Which Is Which?. Haley, Gail Einhart (1939-), illus. LC 66-116974. 30p. illus. (pt. col.) 27cm. 1966. Prentice.
--A White Sweater Must Be White. Seiden, Art, illus. LC 67-23806. (Illus.). 42 p. 24cm. 1967. Grosset & Dunlap.

Russell, Sophia
--Loving Kindness: or, The Ashdown Flower Show. N.D. E. P. Dutton.

Russell, Vera
--Friendly Workers Visit Larry. Spiegel, Lawrence M., illus. (Illus.). (Third Grade Bk.). (gr. 3-4). N.D. Denison.
--Up and Down Main Street. Griffin, Ruth, illus. LC 56-3941. 31p. illus. 20 x 24cm. 1956. Melmont Pub.

Russell, Violet
--Heroes of the Dawn. Elvery, Beatrice, illus. 21cm. 251p. 1914. Maunsel & Co.

Russell, Walter Bowman (1871-)
--The Age of Innocence. Russell, Walter Bowman (1871-), illus. LC 4-33125. ix, 1, 272 p. incl. illus. 40 pl. col. front. 22 cm. 1904. Dodd, Mead & Company.
--The Sea Children. LC 2-1059. x, 260 p. front., illus. 25 cm. 1901. R. H. Russell.

Russell, Ward
--The Worm Turns: A Humorous Story of College Days. LC 26-21464. 249 p. 20 cm. c.1926. Hall & Lathrop.

Russell, Willey
--Our Day Out. 56p. 1984. (ISBN 0-413-54870-8, Pub. by Eyre Methuen England). Methuen Inc.

Russell, William Clark (1844-1911)
--Captain Jackman: Or, A Tale of Two Tunnels. 240p. 1899. F. M. Buckles & Co.
--Master Rockafellar's Voyage. Browne, Gordon Frederick (1858-1932), illus. LC 13-2327. viii, 272 p. incl. front., illus., plates. 19 cm. 1891. T. Whittaker.
--The Wreck of the Grosvenor. Schaeffer, Mead (1898-1980), illus. N.D. Dodd Mead & Co.

Russell, William F. (1945-), ed.
--Classics to Read Aloud to Your Children. LC 84-7033. viii,311. c.1984. (ISBN 0-517-55404-6). Crown.

Russian War Relief Inc, jt. auth. see Kennell, Ruth Epperson.

Russman, Penny & Wright, Sheila
--Changing Bodies, Changing Goals & Other Youth Soccer Stories. Woog, Dan, ed. Wright, Curt, photos by. LC 84-71345. (Illus.). 96p. (Orig.). (gr. 5-9). 1984. (ISBN 0-9613538-0-5). Ascot Pr.

Russo, Susan (1947-)
--Joe's Junk. Russo, Susan (1947-), illus. LC 81-13228. (Illus.). 32 p. 24cm. c.1982. (ISBN 0-03-061264-0). Holt, Rinehart and Winston.

Russo, Susan (1947-), selected by.
--The Ice Cream Ocean and Other Delectable Poems of the Sea. Russo, Susan (1947-), illus. LC 83-16195. (Illus.). 48p. (gr. k-3). 1984. (ISBN 0-688-02122-0). (ISBN 0-688-02123-9). Lothrop.
--The Moon's the North Wind's Cooky: Night Poems. 1st ed. Russo, Susan (1947-), illus. LC 78-32178. (Illus.). 36 p. 18cm. c.1979. (ISBN 0-688-41879-1). (ISBN 0-688-51879-6). Lothrop, Lee & Shepard.

Rust, Doris Dibblin
--The Animals at Number Eleven. Hughes, Shirley (1929-), illus. N.D. Transatlantic Arts.
--The Animals at Rose Cottage. Hughes, Shirley (1929-), illus. LC 59-12803. 74p. illus. 21cm. (Wonderful world book). 1959. A. S. Barnes.
--A Dog Had a Dream. Elgee, Cecil, illus. N.D. Transatlantic Arts.
--Donkey Tales. Elgee, Cecil, illus. (Illus.). (ps-5). N.D. (ISBN 0-571-09867-3). Faber & Faber.
--A Melon for Robert and South Seas Tales. Elgee, Cecil, illus. (Illus.). (gr. 1-4). N.D. Transatlantic.
--Mixed-Muddly Island. Hughes, Shirley (1929-), illus. N.D. Transatlantic Arts.
--Simple Tales for the Very Young. Elgee, Cecil, illus. (Illus.). (ps-5). 1960. (ISBN 0-571-03842-5, Pub. by Faber & Faber). Merrimack Pub Cir.
--A Story a Day. (Illus.). (gr. k-2). 1955. Transatlantic.
--Tales from the Australian Bush. Elgee, Cecil, illus. (Illus.). (ps-5). N.D. (ISBN 0-571-08358-7, Pub. by Faber & Faber). Merrimack Pub Cir.
--Tales of Magic from Far & Near. Elgee, Cecil, illus. (Illus.). (ps-5). N.D. (ISBN 0-686-24625-X, Pub. by Faber & Faber). Merrimack Pub Cir.
Rutgers van der Loeff-Basenau, Anna Maria Margarethe (1910-)
--Avalanche!. Schrotter, Gustav, illus. Round, Dora, tr. LC 58-5253. (Illus.). 219 p. 22cm. (Morrow junior books). 1958, c.1957. (ISBN 0-688-21055-4). Morrow.
--Great Day in Holland: The Skating Race. Nix, Robert, illus. Anthony, Henrietta, tr. from Dutch. LC 65-13612. 1v. (unpaged) illus. (pt. col.) 23cm. c.1965. Abelard.
--Oregon at Last. Geer, Charles Hand (1922-), illus. Edwards, Roy (1922-), tr. from Dutch. LC 62-9866. 22cm. 220p. 1962. Morrow.
--They're Drowning Our Village. Inckel, A. E., illus. Edwards, Roy, tr. from Dutch. LC 60-12174. (Illus.). 168 p. 22cm. 1960, c.1959. F. Watts.
--Vassilis on the Run. Mocniak, George, illus. LC 69-10248. (Illus.). 192 p. 23cm. 1969, c.1965. (ISBN 0-695-49025-7). Follett Pub. Co.
Ruth, Babe, pseud., see Ruth, George Herman.
Ruth, Eddie
--How Do the Ducks Know. (Illus.). 28p. (Orig.). (gr. 1-4). 1980. (ISBN 0-911826-18-1). Am Atheist.
--I Didn't Eat the Apple. (Illus.). 28p. (Orig.). (gr. 1-4). 1981. Am Atheist.
--A Tale of Eternal Life. Fernandez, Oscar, illus. (Illus.). 28p. (Orig.). (gr. 1-4). 1981. Am Atheist.
Ruth, George Herman see Ruth, Babe, pseud.
Ruth, George Herman (1894-)
--The "Home-Run King". Or, How Pep Pindar Won His Title. Ruth, Babe, pseud. LC 22-4749. 3 p. l., 240 p. front. 19 cm. c.1920. A. L. Burt Company.
Ruth, Nicki
--Animal Fantasies. N.D. Carlton Press.
Ruth, Rod (1912-), illus.
--Humpty Dumpty & Other Nursery Rhymes. 32p. (Tell-a-Tale Reader). (ps-3). 1980. (ISBN 0-307-68415-6, Golden Pr). Western Pub.
Rutherford, Anworth (1877-)
--The Bottle of Dust. Wilson, Helen Hughes, illus. LC 40-12423. 244 p. col. front., illus. 22 cm. 1940. The Caxton Printers, Ltd.
--Hidden Island. Irish, William S., illus. 261p. N.D. Caxton Printers.
--Hidden Island. Irish, William S., illus. LC 27-20266. 5 p. l., 3-241 p. front., plates. 19 1/2 cm. 1927. Little, Brown, and Company.
--Sandlappers. Cram, L. D. (1898-), illus. LC 35-22659. 233 p. front., illus., plates. 19 1/2 cm. 1935. The Caxton Printers, Ltd.
--Squawberry Canyon. Pierce, Harry, illus. LC 32-20303. 203 p., 1 l. front., plates. 19 1/2 cm. 1932. The Caxton Printers, Ltd.
Rutherford, Bill, jt. auth. see Rutherford, Bonnie.
Rutherford, Bill, ed. see Mother Goose.
Rutherford, Bill, jt. ed. see Rutherford, Bonnie.
Rutherford, Bonnie, ed. see Mother Goose.
Rutherford, Bonnie & Rutherford, Bill
--Good, Good Morning. Rutherford, Bonnie & Rutherford, Bill, illus. (Illus.). 16p. (Golden Board Book). (ps). 1971. (ISBN 0-307-11250-0, Golden Pr). Western Pub.
--How to Love a Boy and How to Love a Puppy. Rutherford, Bonnie & Rutherford, Bill, illus. LC 67-29314. (Illus.). 28 p. 19cm. 1968. C. R. Gibson Co.
--How to Love a Kitten and How to Love a Girl. Rutherford, Bonnie & Rutherford, Bill, illus. LC 68-31181. (Illus.). 1 v. (unpaged. 19cm. (Stardust books). 1968. C. R. Gibson Co.
--How to Love a Puppy and How to Love a Boy. Rutherford, Bonnie & Rutherford, Bill, illus. (Illus.). (Stardust Book Ser). (ps). 1969. (ISBN 0-8378-1906-7). Gibson.
--Long Ago and Far Away Stories. Rutherford, Bonnie & Rutherford, Bill, illus. LC 62-52255. 61p. illus. 29cm. 1962. Grosset & Dunlap.
Rutherford, Bonnie & Rutherford, Bill, eds.
--Stardust Mother Goose. Rutherford, Bonnie & Rutherford, Bill, illus. (Illus.). 25 p. 19cm. (Stardust books). 1968. C. R. Gibson Co.
Rutherford, Bonnie & Rutherford, Bill, illus.
--The Gingerbread Man. 32p. (ps-3). 1972. (ISBN 0-307-10460-5, Golden Pr). (ISBN 0-307-60460-8). Western Pub.
--Mother Goose. (ps-1). 1973. (ISBN 0-307-68970-0, Golden Pr). Western Pub.
--Three Little Pigs. LC 61-134904. 28 p. illus. 25 cm. (Early fun-to-read classic). 1961. Platt & Munk.
Rutherford, Emily see Noble , Emily.
Rutherford, Frank (1911-)
--All the Way to Pennywell: Children's Rhymes of the North East. LC 72-187067. (Illus.). 145 p. 19cm. 1971. (ISBN 0-903380-00-5). University of Durham Institute of Education.
Rutherford, Gay, pseud.
--Maine Interlude. Gifford, James Noble. Rutherford, Gay, pseud. LC 54-7485. 216p. 20cm. 1954. Arcadia House.
Rutherford, Gay see Rutherford, Gay.
Rutherford, Mildred Lewis (1852-1928)
--Mannie Brown,That School Girl, and Edward Kennedy, That College Boy: That School Girl, and Edward Kennedy, That College Boy. LC 12-38332. 4 p. l., 148 p. front. 18 cm. 1896. The Peter Paul Book Company.
Rutherford, Montgomery
--Husky: Co-Pilot of the Pilgrim. Landau, Jacob (1917-), illus. 271p. (gr. 6-9). N.D. Henry Holt & Co.
Rutherford, Pamela J.
--Calico Caterpillars & Other Clever Creatures. Backus, Joyce, illus. LC 78-65998. (Illus.). 1980. (ISBN 0-533-04133-3). Vantage.
Rutherford, Russell H.
--Tom: The History of a Very Little Boy. N.D. Pott, Young & Co.
Rutherford, Warren see Warren, Howard.
Rutherland, Ross
--Freedom Is the Prize. (gr. 5-8). N.D. (ISBN 0-8027-6025-2). Walker & Co.
Ruthin, Margaret, pseud., see Catherall, Arthur.
Ruthin, Margaret, pseud. (1906-)
--Katrina of the Loneley Isles. Catherall, Arthur. 1st American ed. LC 65-24573. 162p. 22cm. 1965, c.1964. Ariel Books.
--Katrina of the Lonely Isles. Catherall, Arthur. Gibson, Gwen, illus. LC 65-24573. 162p. 22cm. 1st U.S. edition. (Ariel bk.). 1965, c.1964. Farrar.
--The Ring of the Prophet. Catherall, Arthur. 1953. Warne.
--The Secret Pagoda. Catherall, Arthur. 1960. Warne.
--Strange Safari. Catherall, Arthur. 1955. Warne.
--White House of hungary. Catherall, Arthur. 1954. Warne.
Ruthstrom, Dorotha (1936-)
--The Big Kite Contest. Hoban, Lillian (1925-), illus. LC 79-26903. (Illus.). 48p. (An I Am Reading Book). (gr. 1-3). 1980. (ISBN 0-394-84430-0). (ISBN 0-394-94430-5). Pantheon.
--The Blue Ribbon Idea. Hoban, Lillian (1925-), illus. LC 79-26903. p. cm. (I am reading book). c.1980. (ISBN 0-394-84430-0). Pantheon Books.
Ruthven, Eleanor Coker
--The House That Had No Stairs. Jicha, Jon, illus. LC 81-114828. (Illus.). 45 p. 22cm. c.1980. R.L. Bryan Co.
Rutledge, Archibald Hamilton (1883-1973)
--Bolio and Other Dogs. LC 30-19494. 3 p. l., 248, 1 p. 19 1/2 cm. 1930. Frederick A. Stokes Company.
--Tom and I on the Old Plantation. Rosenmeyer, Bernard J., illus. LC 72-4643. (Illus.). 214 p. 22cm. (The Black Heritage Library Collection). 1972. (ISBN 0-8369-9124-9). Books for Libraries Press.
--Tom and I on the Old Plantation. Rosenmeyer, Bernard J., illus. LC 18-172433. 6 p. l., 214 p. front., plates. 19 1/2 cm. c.1918. Frederick A. Stokes Company.
Rutley, C. B.
--Colin and Patricia in Canada. N.D. St. Martin's Press.
--Colin and Patricia in South Africa. N.D. St. Martin's Press.
Ruttan, Robert A
--The Adventures of Oolakuk. Berger, Vivian, illus. LC 72-76571. (Illus.). 95 p. 22cm. 1969. Prentice-Hall.
Rutter, Eileen Joyce see Chant, Joy, pseud.
Rutter, Liliana
--Adventures of the Blueberry Bear. N.D. (ISBN 0-8062-2386-3). Carlton.
Rutz, Viola Larkin (1932-)
--Little Tree and His Wish. 1966. Lutheran Publications.
--Little Tree and His Wish. Roberts, Jim, illus. LC 66-15866. 1 v. (unpaged) col. illus. 27 cm. 1966. Concordia Pub. House.
Ruxton, George Frederick Augustus (1820-1848), ed.
--Captives Among the Indians. (Adventure Library). N.D. Macmillan.
Ruy-Vidal, Francois
--The Secret Journey of Hugo the Brat. Claveloux, Nicole, illus. LC 68-18198. (Illus.). 32 p. 24cm. 1969, c.1968. Harlin Quist. **Award: (NYT).**
Ryan, Betsy, pseud., see Ryan, Elizabeth Anne.
Ryan, Betsy, pseud. (1943-)
--Love Dreams. Ryan, Elizabeth Anne. (gr. 7-12). 1977. (ISBN 0-590-10405-5, Schol Pap). Schol Bk Serv.
--Search the Silence: Poems of Self-Discovery. Ryan, Elizabeth Anne. (Illus.). (gr. 10-12). 1975. (ISBN 0-590-09828-4, Schol Pap). Scholastic Inc.
Ryan, Betsy, pseud. (1943-), ed.
--Sounds of Silence. Ryan, Elizabeth Anne. (Illus.). (gr. 9-12). 1972. (ISBN 0-590-03166-X, Schol Trade Pap). Schol Bk Serv.
Ryan, Betty Hogan
--Porpy. Van Scozza, Peter, illus. LC 46-7993. 34 p. col. illus. 23 1/2 x 21 cm. c.1946. Ziff-Davis Publishing Company.
Ryan, Betty Molgard
--Sally Alligator. Lindberg, Howard E., illus. (Illus.). (Nature & Science Bk.). (gr. k-6). N.D. Denison.
--Sally Alligator. Lindberg, Howard E., illus. LC 60-12622. unpaged. illus. 29cm. 1960. T. S. Denison.
--Socks. Winship, Florence Sarah, illus. LC 49-5075. 32 p. col. illus. 17 cm. (Tell-a-tale books). c.1949. Whitman Pub. Co.
Ryan, Cheli Duran
--Hildilid's Night. Lobel, Arnold Stark (1933-), illus. (Illus.). 30 p. 1971. Macmillan. **Awards: (ALA); (RCM).**
--Hildilid's Night. Lobel, Arnold Stark (1933-), illus. LC 75-146627. 1974. Macmillan.
--Paz. Hogrogian, Nonny (1932-), illus. LC 73-139444. (Illus.). 37 p. 20cm. 1971. Macmillan.
Ryan, Elizabeth Anne see Ryan, Betsy, pseud.
Ryan, Elizabeth McCarley
--Higgledy-Piggledy Room. LC 49-49574. 24 p. col. illus. 18 x 21 cm. 1948. Shady Hill Press.
--What all That Boy Wont Think of Next: A Nostalgic Story Set in A Mississippi Farming Community Dduring the Horse and Buggy Days. (Illus.). N.D. (ISBN 0-8111-0421-4). The Naylor Company.
Ryan, Ginny
--Margo, the Horse Who Wouldn't Stay on the Merry-Go-Round. Poling, Sugar, illus. LC 41-1364. 31, 1 p. incl. col. front., col. illus. 28 cm. c.1938. B. Humphries, Inc.
--Margo, the Horse Who Wouldn't Stay on the Merry-Go-Round. Poling, Sugar, illus. LC 46-5469. 31, 1 p. incl. col. front., col. illus. 27 1/2 cm. c.1945. The Dietz Press, Inc.
Ryan, Jeanette Mines
--Reckless. LC 83-3854. p. cm. (Avon/Flare book). c.1983. (ISBN 0-380-83717-X). Avon Books.
Ryan, Jessica
--The Malibu Monster. 1st ed. Galdone, Paul (1914-), illus. LC 57-12859. 168p. illus. 22cm. 1957. Bobbs-Merrill.
--The Mystery of Arroyo Seco. 1st ed. Stone, David Karl (1922-), illus. LC 62-19336. 187p. illus. 22cm. 1962. (ISBN 0-672-50398-0). Bobbs- Merrill.
Ryan, Joan & Snell, Gordon, eds.
--Land of Tales: Stories of Ireland for Children. LC 83-5618. (Illus.). 160p. 1983. (ISBN 0-8023-1276-4). Dufour.
Ryan, John D. see Ernest, pseud.
Ryan, John Gerald Christopher (1921-)
--Captain Pugwash. Ryan, John Gerald Christopher (1921-), illus. 1957. S.G.Phillips Inc.
--Captain Pugwash: A Pirate Story. Ryan, John Gerald Christopher (1921-), illus. LC 57-12279. unpaged. illus. 26cm. 1957. Criterion Books.
--Captain Pugwash & the Midnight Feast. Ryan, John Gerald Christopher (1921-), illus. (Illus.). 48p. (gr. k-5). 1984. (ISBN 0-370-30978-2, Pub. by the Bodley Head). Merrimack Pub Cir.
--Captain Pugwash & the Wreckers. Ryan, John Gerald Christopher (1921-), illus. (Illus.). 48p. 1st U.S. edition. (gr. k-5). 1984. (ISBN 0-370-30977-4, Pub. by the Bodley Head). Merrimack Pub Cir.
--The Captain Pugwash Cartoon Book. Ryan, John Gerald Christopher (1921-), illus. (Illus.). 32p. 1st U.S. edition. (gr. 1 up). 1979. (ISBN 0-370-30030-0, Pub. by Chatto Bodley Jonathan). Merrimack Pub Cir.
--Captian Pugwash & the Mutiny. Ryan, John Gerald Christopher (1921-), illus. (Illus.). 48p. 1982. (ISBN 0-370-30453-5, Pub. by Chatto-Bodley-Jonathan). Merrimack Pub Cir.
--Pugwash Aloft. Ryan, John Gerald Christopher (1921-), illus. (Illus.). 32p. (gr. 1-4). 1980. (ISBN 0-370-00692-5, Pub. by Chatto Bodley Jonathan). Merrimack Pub Cir.
--Pugwash Aloft: A Pirate Story. Ryan, John Gerald Christopher (1921-), illus. LC 59-613353. unpaged. illus. 26cm. 1959, c.1958. Criterion Books.
--Pugwash & the Ghost Ship. Ryan, John Gerald Christopher (1921-), illus. (Illus.). 32p. (gr. 1-4). 1980. (ISBN 0-370-00719-0, Pub. by Chatto Bodley Jonathan). Merrimack Pub Cir.
--Pugwash & the Ghost Ship. Ryan, John Gerald Christopher (1921-), illus. LC 68-23218. (Illus.). color photos. 32p. (gr. k-3). 1968. (ISBN 0-87599-146-7). S G Phillips.
--Pugwash & the Sea Monster. Ryan, John Gerald Christopher (1921-), illus. (Illus.). 32p. (gr. 1-4). 1980. (ISBN 0-370-10793-4, Pub. by Chatto Bodley Jonathan). Merrimack Pub Cir.
--Pugwash & the Smuggler. Ryan, John Gerald Christopher (1921-), illus. (Illus.). 32p. (gr. 1-4). 1980. (ISBN 0-370-10786-1, Pub. by Chatto, Bodley Head & Jonathan). Merrimack Pub Cir.
--Pugwash in the Pacific. Ryan, John Gerald Christopher (1921-), illus. LC 73-929. (Illus.). 32 p. 27cm. 1973. (ISBN 0-87599-199-8). S. G. Phillips.
Ryan, Marah Ellis
--The Treasure Trail. N.D. Grosset & Dunlap.
Ryan, Mary E.
--Dance a Step Closer. LC 84-4309. 192p. (gr. 7 up). 1984. (ISBN 0-385-29350-X). Delacorte.
Ryan, Patricia
--George and Other Parables. (Illus.). 1 v. (unpaged. 23cm. 1972. Argus Communications.
Ryan, Roberta
--Who? Me?. LC 60-9542. 62p. illus. 19cm. (960 foreign mission graded series, primary). 1960. Convention Press.
Ryan, Walter Anthony (1878-)
--Childhood Verse. LC 4-452. 62 p. illus. 20 1/2 cm. 1903. Ohio Book Publishing Company.
Rybakov, A.
--The Bronze Bird. 211p. 1975. (ISBN 0-8285-1118-7, Pub. by Progress Pubs USSR). Imported Pubns.
Ryck, Francis
--Undesirable Company. LC 74-80463. 1974. (ISBN 0-8128-1709-5). Stein & Day.
Ryckman, John
--Ginger's Upstairs Pet. Merkling, Erica, illus. LC 78-161025. (Illus.). 40 p. 23cm. 1971. (ISBN 0-8116-6717-0). Garrard Pub. Co.
Ryckman, John & McInnes, John
--Wish Me Well. Hauge, Carl & Hauge, Mary, illus. LC 72-157848. (Illus.). 40 p. 23cm. 1971. (ISBN 0-8116-6714-6). Garrard Pub. Co.
Rydberg, Ernest Emil see Rydberg, Ernie, pseud.
Rydberg, Ernie, pseud., see Rydberg, Ernest Emil.
Rydberg, Ernie, jt. auth. see Rydberg, Louisa Hampton.
Rydberg, Ernie, pseud. (1901-)
--Bright Summer. Rydberg, Ernest Emil. 1st ed. Neville, Vera (1900-1978), illus. LC 53-8761. 131p. illus. 22cm. 1953. Longmans, Green.
--Conquer the Winds. Rydberg, Ernest Emil. 1st ed. Johnson, Avery Fischer (1906-), illus. LC 57-709034. 153p. illus. 21cm. 1957. Longmans, Green.
--The Dark of the Cave. Rydberg, Ernest Emil. Kidwell, Carl (1910-), illus. LC 65-14131. 118p. illus. 22cm. c.1965. McKay.
--The Day the Indians Came. Rydberg, Ernest Emil. Cram, L. D. (1898-), illus. LC 64-19406. vi, 133 p. illus. 21 cm. 1964. D. McKay Co.
--Footsy. Rydberg, Ernest Emil. Shaw, Charles (1941-), illus. LC 72-88756. (Illus.). 143 p. 19cm. 1973. Bobbs-Merrill.
--Footsy. Rydberg, Ernest Emil. Shaw, Charles (1941-), illus. LC 73-8522. (Illus.). 180 p. 25cm. 1973. (ISBN 0-8161-6118-6). G. K. Hall.
--The Golden Window. Rydberg, Ernest Emil. LC 56-7869. 143 p. 21cm. 1956. Longmans, Green.
--The Mystery in the Jeep. Rydberg, Ernest Emil. 1st ed. Voorhies, Stephen J., illus. LC 59-12753. 156p. 21cm. 1959. Longmans, Green.
--The Silver Fleet. Rydberg, Ernest Emil. 1st ed. Thomas, Allan (1901-), illus. LC 55-673590. 150p. illus. 22cm. 1955. Longmans, Green.
--Sixteen Is Special. Rydberg, Ernest Emil. McGee, Millard, illus. LC 54-7683. (gr. 6-9). 1954. (ISBN 0-679-20181-5). McKay.
--The Yellow Line. Rydberg, Ernest Emil. LC 71-91015. 124 p. 21cm. 1969. Meredith Press.
Rydberg, Louisa Hampton (1908-)
--Marni. LC 57-11163. 181p. 21cm. 1957. Longmans, Green.
Rydberg, Louisa Hampton (1908-) & Rydberg, Ernie, pseud. (1901-)
--The Shadow Army. Rydberg, Ernest Emil. LC 76-6115. 160 p. 21cm. c.1976. (ISBN 0-8407-6493-6). T. Nelson.

Rydberg, Viktor

--The Christmas Tomten. Jennings, Linda M, adapted by. Wiberg, Harald Albin (1908-), illus. Blecher, Lone Thygesen & Blecher, George, trs. from Swedish LC 81-3225. (Illus.). 32 p. c.1981. (ISBN 0-698-20528-6). Coward, McCann & Geoghegan.

Ryder, Annie H.

--Margaret Regis and Some other Girls. (Illus.). N.D. Lothrop Pub. Co.

Ryder, Annie H., selected by.

--New Every Morning. N.D. D. Lothrop Co.

Ryder, Donald G. (1946-)

--The Inside Story: Living and Learning Through Life's Storms. LC 85-27780. p. cm. c.1985. (ISBN 0-935973-38-9). Ryder Pub. Co.

Ryder, Eileen

--Horace the Helicopter. Ryan, John Gerald Christopher (1921-), illus. LC 59-12809. (Illus.). 25cm. 47p. c.1958. A. S. Barnes & Company, Inc.

Ryder, Joanne

--Beach Party. Stanley, Diane (1943-), illus. LC 81-19857. (Illus.). 48 p. c.1982. (ISBN 0-7232-6198-9). F. Warne.

--Fireflies. Bolognese, Donald Alan (1934-), illus. LC 76-58695. (Illus.). 5 7/8 x 8 1/2. 64p. (18 pt.). (Nature I Can Read Bks.). (gr. k-3). 1977. (ISBN 0-06-025153-0). (ISBN 0-06-025154-9). Har-Row.

--Fog in the Meadow: A Story. 1st ed. Owens, Gail, illus. LC 77-25650. (Illus.). 32 p. 23cm. c.1979. (ISBN 0-06-025148-4). (ISBN 0-06-025149-2). Harper and Row.

--The Incredible Space Machines. Daly, Gerry, illus. (Illus.). 32p. (A Three-Two-One Contact Bk.). (gr. 4-7). 1982. (ISBN 0-394-85201-X). Random.

--Inside Turtle's Shell, and Other Poems of the Field. Bonners, Susan, illus. LC 84-833. p. cm. c.1985. (ISBN 0-02-778010-4). Macmillan.

--The Night Flight. Schwartz, Amy (1954-), illus. LC 85-4482. (Illus.). 32 p. 27cm. c.1985. (ISBN 0-02-778020-1). Four Winds Press.

--Simon Underground. Schoenherr, John Carl (1935-), illus. LC 74-20397. (Illus.). 32 p. 24cm. c.1976. (ISBN 0-06-025156-5). (ISBN 0-06-025157-3). Harper & Row.

--The Snail's Spell. Cherry, Lynne (1952-), illus. LC 80-24737. p. cm. c.1981. (ISBN 0-7232-6197-0). F. Warne.

--A Wet and Sandy Day. Carrick, Donald (1929-), illus. LC 76-18401. (Illus.). 32 p. 22cm. c.1977. (ISBN 0-06-025158-1). (ISBN 0-06-025159-X). Harper & Row.

Ryder, Joanne & Feinberg, Harold S.

--Snail in the Woods. Polseno, Jo, illus. LC 78-22157. (Illus.). 5 7/8 x 8 1/2. 64p. (18 pt.). (Nature I Can Read Bks.). (gr. k-3). 1979. (ISBN 0-06-025169-7). Har-Row.

Ryder, Marion Dayton Crowell, Mrs. (1893-)

--Scuttle Watch. Raymond, Alexander Gillespie (1909-1956), illus. LC 41-12026. 5 p. l., 3-286 p., 1 incl. front., illus. 21 1/2 cm. 1941. A. A. Knopf.

--Scuttle Watch. Raymond, Alexander Gillespie (1909-1956), illus. LC 79-91988. (Illus.). 286 p., 1 leaf of plates. 21cm. c.1941. (ISBN 0-88492-034-8). W.S. Sullwold.

Ryder, Milton P, adapted by.

--The Smallest Christmas Tree. LC 81-163387. (Original Author: Masahiro Kasuya(1937)). (Illus.). 27 p. 25cm. c.1981. (ISBN 0-8170-0921-3). Judson Press.

Ryder, Shirley

--Let's Pretend It's a Birthday. Bartlett, Henrietta, illus. LC 58-7686. unpaged. illus. 26cm. c.1958. Lothrop, Lee & Shepard Co.

Rydingsvard, Anna Maria (1856-), tr. see Segerstedt, Albrekt Julius.

Rydingsvard, Anna Maria Von (1856-), tr. see Segerstedt, Albrekt Julius.

Rye, Karen, tr. see Mathiesen, Egon.

Ryland, Cally Thomas (1871-)

--The Taming of Betty. Picknell, George W., illus. LC 4-21996. (Illus.). 228. 19cm. 1904. Lee and Shepard.

Ryland, Hobart (1901-)

--Prof and Easy: The Story of Two Dogs. LC 40-10379. viii, 11-127 p. 19 1/2 cm. c.1940. The Christopher Publishing House.

Rylant, Cynthia

--A Blue-Eyed Daisy. LC 84-21554. p. cm. 112p. 1985. (ISBN 0-02-777960-2). Bradbury Press. **Award: (ALA).**

--Every Living Thing. Schindler, Steven D., illus. 81p. 1985. (ISBN 0-02-777200-4). Bradbury.

--Miss Maggie. 1st ed. Di Grazia, Thomas (0000-1983), illus. LC 82-18206. p. cm. c.1983. (ISBN 0-525-44048-8). Dutton.

--The Relatives Came. Gammell, Stephen, illus. LC 85-10929. 32p. 1985. (ISBN 0-02-777220-9). Bradbury Press. **Awards: (NYT); (ALA); (RCM).**

--This Year's Garden. Szilagyi, Mary, illus. LC 84-10974. c.1984. (ISBN 0-02-777970-X). Bradbury Press.

--Waiting to Waltz, a Childhood: Poems. Gammell, Stephen, illus. LC 84-11030. (Illus.). 45 p. 24cm. c.1984. (ISBN 0-02-778000-7). Bradbury Press. **Award: (ALA).**

--When I Was Young in the Mountains. Goode, Diane (1949-), illus. LC 81-5359. p. cm. c.1982. (ISBN 0-525-42525-X). Dutton. **Awards: (ALA); (RCM).**

Rymer, Alta May (1925-)

--Beep-Bap-Zap-Jack. rev. version. ed. Rymer, Alta May (1925-), illus. LC 74-20428. (Illus.). 37 p. 26cm. 1974. (ISBN 0-9600792-0-3). Rymer.

--Captain Zomo. Rymer, Alta May (1925-), illus. LC 79-67651. (Illus.). 48p. (Orig.). (Tales of Planet Artembo Ser.: Bk. 2). (gr. 4-6). N.D. (ISBN 0-9600792-2-X). Rymer Bks.

--Stars of Obron: Chambo Returns. Rymer, Alta May (1925-), illus. (Illus.). 48p. (Orig.). (Tales of Planet Artembo Ser.: Bk. 3). (gr. 4-6). N.D. (ISBN 0-9600792-3-8). Rymer Bks.

Ryniker, Alice Durland

--Eagle Feather for a Crow. Ryniker, Alice Durland, illus. LC 80-83763. (Illus.). 71 p. 26cm. c.1980. (ISBN 0-932154-07-7). Persimmon Hill, National Cowboy Hall of Fame.

Rynning-Tonnesen, Olaf

--Secret Transmitter. (gr. 6-9). 1965. (ISBN 0-672-50486-3). Bobbs.

Rypins, Senta Jones, tr. see Seidlin, Oskar.

Ryss, Evgenii Samoilovich

--Search Behind the Lines. Carey, Bonnie, tr. LC 74-6553. 222 p. 22cm. 1974. (ISBN 0-688-21831-8). (ISBN 0-688-21831-8). W. Morrow.

S. G.

--Dickie Winton: Or, Between Gate & Front Door. N.D. Thos Nelson & Sons.

S. T. C.

--Little Doorkeeper: Or, Patience & Peace, 1 of 20 vols. (Illus.). 225p. (Selected Bks for Sunday School: No. 22). N.D. Set. Methodist Bk Concern.

S. W. L., ed.

--Selections for Little Folks. LC 16-3874. viii, 9-112 p. 15 1/2 cm. c.1870. Eldredge & Brother.

Saari, Kaye

--The Kidnapping of the Coffee Pot. Galeron, Henri, illus. LC 74-6874. (Illus.). 32 p. 27cm. 1975, c.1974. (ISBN 0-8252-0114-4). (ISBN 0-8252-0115-2). Harlin Quist. **Award: (ALA).**

Saarinen, Lilian Swann

--Who Am I?. LC 46-8127. 31 p. illus. (part. col.) 20 1/2 x 26 cm. c.1946. Reynal & Hitchcock.

Saavedra, Miguel De Cervantes see Cervantes Saavedra, Miguel de

Sabin, Belle Carpenter & Huleatt, Blanche Carpenter

--Uncle Sam's Rhymes for Santa Claus Times. Huleatt, Blanche Carpenter, illus. LC 1-29115. 119 p. col. illus. 24 1/2 cm. c.1900. Monarch Book Company.

Sabin, Edwin Legrand (1870-1952)

--Adventuring With Carson and Fremont. Stephens, Charles H., illus. N.D. J. B. Lippincott.

--Bar B Boys: Or, The Young Cow-Punchers. LC 9-25392. 4 p. l., 386 p. front., 7 pl. 20 1/2 cm. c.1909. T. Y. Crowell & Co.

--Beaufort Chums. Copeland, Charles, illus. LC 5-29532. iii, 281 p. front., plates. 19 1/2 cm. c.1905. T. Y. Crowell & Co.

--The Boy Settler: Or, Terry in the New West. LC 16-24923. 3 p. l., 301 p. front., plates. 20 1/2 cm. $1.00. c.1916. Thomas Y. Crowell Company.

--Buffalo Bill and the Overland Trail. (The Trail Blazers Ser.). N.D. J. B. Lippincott Co.

--Circle K: Or, Fighting for the Flock. Rowe, Clarence H., illus. (Crowell's American Boys and Girls Library). N.D. Thomas Y. Crowell Company.

--General Crook and the Fighting Apaches: Treating Also of the Part Borne by Jimmie Dunn in the Days 1871-1886. Stephens, Charles H., illus. LC 18-21823. 301, 1 p. col. front., plates, port., map. 20 cm. (On cover: Trail blazers series). 1918. J. B. Lippincott Company.

--Gold Seekers of '49 ... Stephens, Charles H., illus. LC 15-20910. 335, 1 p. col. front., plates, maps. 20 cm. (Lippincott Juniors). 1915. J. B. Lippincott Company.

--The Great Pike's Peck Rush: Or, Terry in the New Gold Fields. (Great Western Ser.). N.D. Thomas Y. Crowell Company.

--In the Ranks of Old Hickory. Eltonhead, Frank, illus. LC 27-210182. 351, 1 p. col. front., plates, port., maps. 20 cm. (Lettered on cover: Trail blazers series). (Lippincott Juniors). c.1927. J. B. Lippincott Company.

--Into Mexico with General Scott. Stephens, Charles H., illus. LC 20-20317. 316, 1 p. incl. col. front. plates, maps. 19 1/2 cm. (On cover: Trail blazers series). 1920. J. B. Lippincott Company.

--Klondike Pardners. Justis, Lyle, illus. LC 29-28054. 286 p. incl. illus., plates (part col.) col. front. 19 1/2 cm. (The American trail blazers). 1929. J. B. Lippincott Company.

--Lost with Lieutenant Pike. Stephens, Charles H., illus. LC 19-18644. 314, 1 p. col. front., plates, port., map. 20 cm. (On cover: Trail blazers series). 1919. J. B. Lippincott Company.

--Mississippi River Boy. Gallagher, M. J., illus. LC 32-23721. 317 p. incl. col. front., illus. (1 col.) 21 cm. c.1932. J. B. Lippincott Company.

--Old Four-Toes: Or, Hunters of the Peaks. LC 12-21922. ix, 350 p. incl. front. plates. 20 1/2 cm. c.1912. Thomas Y. Crowell Company.

--Old" Jim Bridger on the Moccasin Trail: A Tale of the Beaver West and of the Men Who Opened the Mountains. LC 28-21420. xii p., 1 l., 316 p. col. front., col. plates. 20 1/2 cm. c.1928. Thomas Y. Crowell Company.

--On the Overland Stage: Or, Terry as a King Whip Cub. (Great Western Ser.). N.D. Thomas Y. Crowell Company.

--On the Plains with Custer. (The Trail Blazers Ser.). N.D. J. B. Lippincott.

--Opening the Iron Trail: Or, Terry As a "U. Pay." Man (a Semi-Centennial Story). Stephens, Charles H., illus. LC 19-15732. vi p., 1 l., 273 p. front., plates. 20 1/2 cm. c.1919. Thomas Y. Crowell Company.

--Opening the West with Lewis and Clark: By Boat, Horse and Foot up the Great River Missouri, Across the Stony Mountains and on to the Pacific, When in the Years 1804, 1805, 1806, Young Captain Lewis, the Long Knife, and His Friend Captain Clark, the Red Head Chief, Aided by Sacajawea, the Bird-Woman, Conducted Their Little Band of Men Tried and True Through the Unknown New United States. LC 17-24688. 3 p. l., 5-278 p. col. front., plates, ports., fold. map. 19 1/2 cm. (On cover: Trail blazers series). 1917. J. B. Lippincott Company.

--Pirate Waters. Ward, Lynd Kendall (1905-1985), illus. N.D. J. B. Lippincott.

--Pluck on the Long Trail: Or, Boy Scouts in the Rockies. Rowe, Clarence H., illus. LC 12-21404. xiii, 321 p. incl. front., illus. plates. 19 1/2 cm. (The boy scout series). c.1912. Thomas Y. Crowell Company.

--Pluck on the Long Trial. (Illus.). (Crowell's Boy Scout Library). 1915. T Y Crowell.

--Range and Trail: Or, the Bar B's Great Drive. LC 10-17992. vii, 445 p. front., plates. 20 1/2 cm. c.1910. T. Y. Crowell & Co.

--Scarface Ranch: Or, the Young Homesteaders. LC 14-14803. vii p., 1 l., 297 p. incl. col. front. plates. 20 1/2 cm. c.1914. Thomas Y. Crowell Company.

--Treasure Mountain. Or, the Young Prospector. Rowe, Clarence H., illus. (Crowell's American Boys and Girls Library). N.D. Thomas Y. Crowell Company.

--When You Were a Boy. Steele, Frederic Dorr, illus. 1905. Baker & Taylor Co.

--With Carson and Fremont. (The Trail Blazers Ser.). N.D. J. B. Lippincott.

--With George Washington into the Wilderness. Thomson, William T., illus. LC 24-27997. 297, 1 p. col. front., plates, ports., map. 20 cm. (The American trail blazers). 1924. J. B. Lippincott Company.

--With Lieutenant Pike. Stephens, Charles H., illus. (Lippincott Juniors Ser.). N.D. J. B. Lippincott.

--With Sam Houston in Texas. Stephens, Charles H., illus. LC 16-19421. 319, 1 p. col. front., plates, port., maps. 19 1/2 cm. (On cover: Trail blazers series). 1916. J. B. Lippincott Company.

Sabin, Eldridge Hosmer (1865-1934)

--Dollie's Big Dream. new ed. Abbott, Elenore Plaisted & Knipe, Helen Alden, illus. 1930. A. Whitman & Co.

--The Magical Man of Mirth. Abbott, Elenor Plaisted & Knipe, Helen Alden, photos by LC 10-16392. 283 p. col. front., col. plates 23 cm. 1910. G. W. Jacobs & Company.

--Prince Trixie: Or, Baby Brownie's Birthday. Beem, Frances M., illus. 24cm. 142p. 1914. Rand McNally & Co.

--The Queen of the City of Mirth. (Illus.). N.D. Hurst & Co.

--The Queen of the City of Mirth. Abbott, Elenore Plaisted & Knipe, Helen Alden, illus. LC 17-23896. (Illus.). 23cm. 164p. 1911. George W Jacobs.

--Stella's Adventures in Starland. Rev ed. Brown, Edith, illus. LC 7-7519. 4 p. l., 210 p. illus., 9 pl. 21 1/2 cm. 1907. Small, Maynard & Co.

Sabin, Francene

--The Magic String. Snyder, Joel, illus. LC 81-4076. p. cm. c.1981. (ISBN 0-89375-547-8). (ISBN 0-89375-548-6). Troll Associates.

Sabin, Francene & Sabin, Louis (1930-)

--The Great Easter Egg Mystery. Trivas, Irene, illus. LC 81-7610. p. cm. (A Troll Easy-to-Read Mystery). c.1982. (ISBN 0-89375-604-0). (ISBN 0-89375-605-9). Troll.

--The Great Santa Claus Mystery. Trivas, Irene, illus. LC 81-7530. p. cm. (A Troll Easy-to-Read Mystery). c.1982. (ISBN 0-89375-602-4). (ISBN 0-89375-603-2). Troll Associates.

--Mystery at the Jellybean Factory. Trivas, Irene, illus. LC 81-10388. p. cm. (A Troll Easy-to-Read Mystery). c.1982. (ISBN 0-89375-600-8). (ISBN 0-89375-601-6). Troll Associates.

--Secret of the Haunted House. Trivas, Irene, illus. LC 81-8751. p. cm. (A Troll Easy-to-Read Mystery). c.1982. (ISBN 0-89375-598-2). (ISBN 0-89375-599-0). Troll Associates.

Sabin, Frances Ellis (1870-) & Magoffin, Ralph V. D. (1874-1942)

--Classical Myths That Live Today. (gr. 8 up). 1958. Silver.

Sabin, Louis, jt. auth. see Sabin, Francene.

Sabin, Louis (1930-)

--Birthday Surprise. Magine, John (1921-), illus. LC 81-2632. (Illus.). 32p. (gr. k-2). 1981. (ISBN 0-89375-527-3). (ISBN 0-89375-528-1). Troll Assocs.

--Paul Bunyan. Smolinski, Dick, illus. LC 84-2747. (Illus.). 26 p. 24cm. c.1985. (ISBN 0-8167-0254-3). (ISBN 0-8167-0255-1). Troll Associates.

Saccaro, Margherita, jt. auth. see Turin, Adela.

Saccuzzo, Santo

--Slow Foot: The Story of an Indian Boy of Long Ago. LC 61-17891. 56 p. illus. 21 cm. c.1961. Greenwich Book Publishers.

Sachar, Louis (1954-)

--Johnny's in the Basement. LC 81-65064. p. cm. (Avon flare book). c.1981. (ISBN 0-380-78782-2). Avon Books.

--Sideways Stories from Wayside School. Hockerman, Dennis, illus. LC 78-3213. (Illus.). 141 p. 23cm. c.1978. (ISBN 0-695-80964-4). (ISBN 0-695-40964-6). Follett Pub. Co.

Sachs, Elizabeth Ann see Sachs, Elizabeth-Ann.

Sachs, Elizabeth-Ann (1946-)

--Just Like Always. Sugarman, Tracy (1921-), illus. LC 81-2289. p. cm. 1981. (ISBN 0-689-30859-0). Atheneum.

--Shyster. Brown, Judith Gwyn (1933-), illus. LC 85-7943. (Illus.). 99 p. 22cm. 1985. (ISBN 0-689-31161-3). Atheneum.

--Where Are You, Cow Patty?. LC 84-2950. 156p. (gr. 5-8). 1984. (ISBN 0-689-31057-9). Atheneum.

Sachs, Marilyn Stickle (1927-)

--Amy and Laura. Sugarman, Tracy (1921-), illus. LC 66-8827. (Illus.). 189 p. 22cm. 1966. Doubleday.

--Amy Moves In. 1st ed. Brown, Judith Gwyn (1933-), illus. LC 64-11697. (Illus.). 191 p. 22cm. 1964. Doubleday.

--Beach Towels. 1st ed. Spence, Jim, illus. LC 82-5056. p. cm. (Skinny book). c.1982. (ISBN 0-525-44003-8). Dutton.

--The Bear's House. Glanzman, Louis S. (1922-), illus. Ellen, Fran, created by. LC 76-157621. (Illus.). 1971. (ISBN 0-385-03363-X). (ISBN 0-385-06632-5). Doubleday and Company.

--Bus Ride. Rowen, Amy, illus. LC 79-23596. (Illus.). 107 p. 22cm. (Skinny book). c.1980. (ISBN 0-525-27325-5). (ISBN 0-525-45048-3). Dutton.

--Call Me Ruth. LC 82-45208. 134 p. 22cm. 1982. (ISBN 0-385-17607-4). Doubleday.

--Class Pictures. LC 80-390. 138 p. 22cm. c.1980. (ISBN 0-525-27985-7). E. P. Dutton.

--A December Tale. LC 76-7697. p. cm. c.1976. (ISBN 0-385-12314-0). (ISBN 0-385-11019-7). Doubleday.

--Dorrie's Book. Sachs, Anne, illus. LC 74-33688. (Illus.). 136 p. 22cm. 1975. (ISBN 0-385-03350-8). (ISBN 0-385-03213-7). Doubleday.

--The Fat Girl. 1st ed. LC 83-11697. p. cm. c.1983. (ISBN 0-525-44076-3). E.P. Dutton.

--Fourteen. LC 82-18209. p. cm. c.1983. (ISBN 0-525-44044-5). Dutton.

--Hello- Wrong Number. Johnson, Pamela, illus. LC 81-3281. p. cm. (Skinny book). c.1981. (ISBN 0-525-31629-9). Dutton.

--Laura's Luck. 1st ed. Ohlsson, Ib (1935-), illus. LC 65-19905. 181 p. illus. 22 cm. 1965. Doubleday.

--Laura's Luck. Ohlsson, Ib (1935-), illus. 1956. (ISBN 0-8382-0425-2, Cadmus Books). E. M. Hale And Company.

--Marv. 1st ed. Glanzman, Louis S. (1922-), illus. LC 73-116250. (Illus.). 160 p. 22cm. 1970. Doubleday.

--Matt's Mitt. 1st ed. Knight, Hilary (1926-), illus. LC 74-10932. (Illus.). 32 p. 1975. (ISBN 0-385-00260-2). (ISBN 0-385-00260-2). (ISBN 0-385-00260-2). Doubleday.

--Peter and Veronica. 1st ed. Glanzman, Louis S. (1922-), illus. LC 69-12226. (Illus.). 174 p. 22cm. 1969. Doubleday.

--A Pocket Full of Seeds. 1st ed. Stahl, Ben F., illus. LC 73-79708. (Illus.). 137 p. 22cm. 1973. (ISBN 0-385-06091-2). (ISBN 0-385-06091-2). Doubleday. **Award: (ALA).**

--A Secret Friend. LC 77-25606. p. cm. c.1978. (ISBN 0-385-13569-6). (ISBN 0-385-13570-X). Doubleday.
--A Summer's Lease. LC 78-12486. 124 p. 22cm. c.1979. (ISBN 0-525-40480-5). Dutton.
--Thunderbird. Spence, Jim, illus. LC 84-21252. (Illus.). 79 p. 22cm. (Skinny book). c.1985. (ISBN 0-525-44163-8). E.P. Dutton.
--The Truth About Mary Rose. 1st ed. Glanzman, Louis S. (1922-), illus. LC 72-89128. (Illus.). 159 p. 22cm. 1973. (ISBN 0-385-09448-5). (ISBN 0-385-09448-5). Doubleday.
--Underdog. 1985. (ISBN 0-385-17609-0). Doubleday.
--Veronica Ganz. 1st ed. Glanzman, Louis S. (1922-), illus. LC 68-11813. (Illus.). 156 p. 22cm. 1968. Doubleday. **Award: (ALA).**

Sachs, Marilyn Stickle (1927-) & Robinson, Charles (1931-)
--Fleet-Footed Florence. 1st ed. Robinson, Charles (1931-), illus. LC 76-56330. (Illus.). 48 p. 27cm. c.1981. (ISBN 0-385-12745-6). (ISBN 0-385-12746-4). Doubleday.

Sachs, Rosa, tr. see Helm, Clementine.

Sacife, Roger Livingston (1875-)
--What Daddies Do: Old Fashioned Rhymes for New Fangled Kiddies. LC 29-1579. vii, 1, 118, 1 p. incl. illus., plates. 19 cm. c.1929. Houghton Mifflin Company.

Sackett, Bert (1891-1947)
--Everglade Gold. Werth, Kurt (1896-), illus. LC 48-628442. 249 p. illus. 21 cm. 1948. Random House.
--Hurricane Treasure: The Secret of Injun Key. Knight, Clayton (1891-1969), illus. LC 45-6556. 6 p. l., 3-296 p. plates, double map. 21 cm. 1945. Random House.
--Sponger's Jinx. Knight, Clayton (1891-1969), illus. LC 43-15770. 5 p. l., 3-210 p. plates. 21 cm. 1943. Random House.

Sackett, Rose McLaughlin
--The Cousin from Clare. De Angeli, Marguerite Lofft, Mrs. (1889-), illus. LC 32-10336. 6 p. l., 270 p. front., plates. 20 cm. 1932. The Macmillan Company.
--Penny Lavender. Voute, Kathleen (1892-), illus. LC 47-5873. vi, 249 p. illus. 32 cm. 1947. Macmillan Co.
--Three Tunes for a Flute. Bennett, Richard Michael (1899-), illus. LC 38-25348. 5 p. l., 293 p. incl. front., illus. (incl. music.) 21 1/2 cm. 1938. The Macmillan Company.

Sackett, Samuel John (1928-)
--Cowboys & the Songs They Sang. LC 66-17571. 72p. (gr. 3 up). 1967. (ISBN 0-201-09165-8, A-W Childrens). A-W.

Sacre, Marie-Jose
--Anna's Dream House. Sacre, Marie-Jose, illus. Clements, Andrew (1949-), tr. from Ger. LC 83-8201. (Illus.). 28p. Orig. Title: Das Redenede Bildnis. (gr. 4 up). 1983. (ISBN 0-907234-44-5, Pub. by Picture Bk Studio USA). Neugebauer Pr.

Saddler, Allen, pseud., see Richards, Ronald Charles William.

Saddler, Allen, pseud. (1923-)
--The Archery Contest. Richards, Ronald Charles William. Wright, Joe, illus. (Illus.). 32p. (The King & Queen Ser.). (ps). 1983. (ISBN 0-19-279760-3, Pub by Oxford U Pr Childrens). Merrimack Pub Cir.
--The Fishing Competition. Richards, Ronald Charles William. Wright, Joe, illus. (Illus.). 32p. (The King & Queen Ser.). (ps-k). 1983. (ISBN 0-19-279774-3). Oxford U Pr.
--The King & the Invisible Dwarf. Richards, Ronald Charles William. Wright, Joe, illus. LC 83-670214. (Illus.). 32p. (The King & Queen Ser.). (ps-k). 1983. (ISBN 0-19-279776-X). (ISBN 0-19-279776-X). Oxford U Pr.
--The King Gets Fit. Richards, Ronald Charles William. Wright, Joe, illus. (Illus.). 32p. (The King & Queen Ser.). (ps). 1983. (ISBN 0-19-279761-1, Pub by Oxford U Pr Childrens). Merrimack Pub Cir.

Saddler, Allen & Wright, Joe
--The King at Christmas. (Illus.). 32p. (gr. k-3). 1984. (ISBN 0-19-279775-1, Pub. by Oxford U Pr Childrens). Merrimack Pub Cir.
--The Queen's Painting. (Illus.). 32p. (gr. k-3). 1984. (ISBN 0-19-279777-8, Pub. by Oxford U Pr Childrens). Merrimack Pub Cir.

Sadler, Catherine Edwards, retold by.
--Heaven's Reward: Fairy Tales from China. Cheng, Judith, illus. LC 84-21532. (Illus.). ix, 37 p. 24cm. 1985. (ISBN 0-689-31127-3). Atheneum.
--Treasure Mountain: Folktale from Southern China. Yun, Cheng Mung, illus. (gr. 4-6). 1982. Atheneum.

Sadler, Doris
--Wainy Waindwop. 1965. Exposition Press.

Sadler, Glenn Edward, jt. auth. see Leech, Bryan Jeffery.

Sadler, James, Mrs.
--Bessie Conway: Or, The Irish Girl in America. N.D. P. J. Kennedy.

Sadler, Marilyn (1942-)
--Alistair in Outer Space. Bollen, Roger (1942-), illus. LC 84-4896. (Illus.). 48p. (gr. k-3). 1984. (ISBN 0-13-022369-7). P-H.
--It's Not Easy Being a Bunny. Bollen, Roger (1942-), illus. (Illus.). 48p. (Beginner Bks.: No.68). (gr. k-3). 1983. (ISBN 0-394-86102-7). (ISBN 0-394-96102-1). Random.
--The Very Bad Bunny. Bollen, Roger (1942-), illus. LC 84-3319. (Illus.). 41 p. 24cm. c.1984 (Beginner Books). (ISBN 0-394-86861-7). (ISBN 0-394-96861-1). Random.

Sadler, R. K & Hayllar, T. A. S.
--Bring the House Down. LC 78-300527. (Illus.). 192 p. 25cm. c.1976. (ISBN 0-471-02128-8). J. Wiley.
--Exit, Pursued by a Bear: A Drama Experience for Form One. LC 73-5280. (Illus.). 192 p. 1973. (ISBN 0-471-74843-9). J. Wiley & Sons Australasia.
--Smile on the Face of the Tiger. LC 76-366724. (Illus.). 200 p. 25cm. (Language and literature experience ; book 1). c.1975. (ISBN 0-471-74849-8). J. Wiley.

Sadler, Richard, tr. see Grimm, Jakob Ludwig Karl (1785-1863) & Grimm, Wilhelm Karl.

Sadler, Richard, tr. see Konner, Alfred.

Sadler, Samuel Whitchurch (0000-1890)
--The Adventurous Voyage of the Polly, and other Yarns. N.D. E & J B Young.
--African Cruiser. (Illus.). (The Starlight Library). N.D. E. P. Dutton & Co.
--The African Cruiser. N.D. George Routledge & Sons.
--The African Cruiser: A Midshipman's Adventures on the West Coast. LC 42-26785. 4 p. l., 197 p. front., 2 pl. 17 cm. N.D. E. P. Dutton.

Sadley, Marie Christine
--Mamma's Angel Child in Toyland. Ross, M. T. Penny, illus. 22cm. 115p. 1915. Rand, McNally & Co.

Sadlier, Anna Theresa (1854-)
--Arabella. LC 7-40799. 177 p. 20 cm. 1907. B. Herder.
--How Frank Did It, "That Worthless Land" and Littke John: Three Stories. 63 p. 15 cm. (Catholic library. v. 28). 1898. C. Wildermann.
--The Man From Nowhere. N.D. Benziger Brothers.
--Mary Tracy's Fortune. 169 p. incl. front. 17 1/2 cm. (On verso of t.-p.: Benziger's juvenile series). c.1902. Benziger Brothers.
--The Mysterious Doorway. LC 1-29116. 125 p. incl. front. 17 cm. 1900. Benziger Brothers.
--The Mystery of Hornby Hall. N.D. Benziger Bros.
--Pauline Archer. N.D. Benziger Brothers.
--A Summer at Woodville. N.D. Benziger Brothers.
--The Talisman. 186 p. front. 18 1/2 cm. 1903. Benziger Brothers.
--Wayward Winifred. LC 5-36924. 230p. 19cm. 1905. Benziger Bros.

Sadlier, James, Mrs., pseud. (1820-1908), tr. see Walsh, Joseph Alexis.

Sadlier, Mary Ann Madden, Mrs. (1820-1903)
--The Babbler: A Drama in One Act for Boys. N.D. D. & J. Sadlier.
--The Elder Brother: A Drama in two Acts for Boys. N.D. D. & J. Sadlier.
--Father Sheehy. (Catholic Youth's Library). N.D. D. & J. Sadlier.
--The Invisible Hand: A Drama in two Acts for Boys. N.D. D. & J. Sadlier.
--The Secret: A Drama in one Act for Girls. N.D. D. & J. Sadlier.
--The Talisman: An Original Drama in one Act for Young Ladies. N.D. D. & J. Sadlier.

Sadlier, Mary Ann Madden, Mrs. (1820-1903), tr.
--Benjamin: Or, The Pupil of the Christian Brothers. (Catholic Youth's Library). N.D. D. & J. Sadlier.
--The Castle of Rousillon. (Sadlier's Fireside Library). N.D. D. & J. Sadlier.
--The Exile of Tadmore, and Other Tales. (Catholic Youth's Library). N.D. D. & J. Sadlier.
--Idleness: The Double Lesson and Other Tales. (Catholic Youth's Library). N.D. D. & J. Sadlier.
--Julia: The Gold Thimble. N.D. D. & J. Sadlier.
--The Orphan of Moscow: The Young Governess. (Sadlier's Fireside Library). N.D. D. & J. Sadlier.
--The Poachers, and Other Tales. (Catholic Youth's Library-Second Ser.). N.D. D. & J. Sadlier.
--The Pope's Niece, and Other Tales. (Catholic Youth's Library). N.D. D. & J. Sadlier.
--Selim: The Pacha of Salonica. (Catholic Youth's Library-Second Ser.). N.D. D. & J. Sadlier.
--The Vendetta, and Other Tales. (Catholic Youth's Library). N.D. D. & J. Sadlier.

Sadowski, Karen
--Where's Hodgey?. Gadbois, Robert, illus. LC 77-1999. (Illus.). 31 p. 25cm. (Books by children for children). c.1977. (ISBN 0-87191-610-X). Creative Education.

Sadowsky, Ethel S (1927-)
--Francois and the Langouste: A Story of Martinique. 1st ed. Danska, Herbert (1928-), illus. LC 69-10664. (Illus.). 60 p. 22cm. 1969. (ISBN 0-316-76601-1). Little, Brown.

Safford, Mary Joanna
--Lorelei, and Other Stories. (Waldorf Series.). N.D. Merriam Co.

Safford, Mary Joanna (0000-1916), tr. see Kremnitz, Marie Charlotte Von Bardeleben.

Safford, Mary Joanna, tr. see Lorenzini, Carlo.

Safford, Mary Joanna, tr. see Nordau, Max Simon.

Saffron, Robert
--By-Line for Josie. LC 49-11238. 182 p. port. 21 cm. 1949. Viking Press.

Safier, Daniel Edwin
--The Listening Book. Gillerman, Skippy, illus. LC 52-5210. 160p. 1952. Caxton Printers.

Sage, Agnes Carolyn (1854-)
--Christmas Elves: Or, the Tales of the Day Fairies. Shepherd, illus. 1888. R Worthington.
--The Jolly Ten and Their Year of Stories. (The Girl Chum Ser.). N.D. A. L. Burt Company.
--The Jolly Ten, and Their Year of Stories. (Illus.). (The Wellesley Series for Girls). N.D. A. L. Burt.
--The Jolly Ten and Their Year of Stories. LC 12-38334. 299 p. front., plates. 19 1/2 cm. c.1888. Congregational Sunday-School and Publishing Society.
--A Little Colonial Dame. Humphrey, Mabel L. (1859-), illus. (Illus.). (Popular Ser. for Young People). N.D. Frederick A. Stokes Co.
--A Little Colonial Dame: A Story of Old Manhattan Island. Humphrey, Mabel L. (1859-), illus. LC 98-1263. 5 p. l., 197 p. front., plates. 21 1/2 cm. c.1898. Frederick A. Stokes Company.
--A Little Daughter of the Revolution. (Illus.). (Popular Ser. for Young People). N.D. Frederick A. Stokes Co.
--A Little Daughter of the Revolution: A Story of the Boys and Girls of '76. Humphrey, Mabel L. (1859-), illus. LC 99-5324. 4 p. l., 203 p. front., plates. 21 cm. c.1899. Frederick A. Stokes Company.
--Two Girls of Old New Jersey: A School-Girl Story of '76. Connah, Douglas John, illus. LC 12-18012. 3 p. l., v-vi p., 2 l., 195 p. front., plates. 21 1/2 x 17 1/2 cm. $1.3. 1912. Frederick A. Stokes Company.

Sage, Alison
--The Ogre's Banquet. Calvi, Gian, illus. LC 77-18648. (Illus.). 31 p. 30cm. 1st U.S. edition. c.1978. (ISBN 0-385-14360-5). Doubleday.

Sage, Betty, pseud., see Goodwin, Elizabeth Sage.

Sage, Jacquelyn Ilya, retold by.
--Many Furs: A Grimm's Fairy Tale. Sage, Jacquelyn Ilya, illus. LC 81-947. (Illus.). 32 p. 29cm. c.1981. (ISBN 0-89742-041-1). Celestial Arts.

Sage, James
--The Boy and the Dove. Doisneau, Robert, photos by. Derlon, Pierre, contrib. by. LC 77-18427. (Illus.). 64 p. c.1978. (ISBN 0-89480-030-2). Workman Pub. Co.

Sage, Juniper, pseud., see Hurd/Edith Thacher & Brown, Margaret Wise.

Sage, Juniper, pseud. & Brown, Margaret Wise (1910-1952)
--The Man in the Manhole. Hurd, Edith Thacher & Brown, Margaret Wise. Ballantine, Bill, pseud. (1911-), illus. Ballantine, William Oliver. (Juniper Sage is the joint pseud. of Edith Thatcher Hurd (1910-) and Margaret Wise Brown (1910-1952)). 48p. (Young Scott Bks.). 1955. W. R. Scott, Inc.
--The Man in the Manhole and the Fix-It Man. Hurd, Edith Thacher & Brown, Margaret Wise. Ballantine, Bill, pseud. (1911-), illus. Ballantine, William Oliver. LC 46-8592. (Juniper Sage is the joint pseud. of Edith Thatcher Hurd (1910-) and Margaret Wise Brown (1910-1952)). 40 p. col. illus. 25 x 20 1/2 cm. c.1946. W. R. Scott, Inc.

Sage, Lee
--The Last Rustler. N.D. Grosset & Dunlap.

Sage, Michael
--Careful Carlos. Spilka, Arnold (1917-), illus. LC 67-3680. (Illus.). 32p. (gr. k-2). 1967. (ISBN 0-8234-0022-0). Holiday.
--Deep in a Haystack. Spilka, Arnold (1917-), illus. LC 66-7757. 1v. (unpaged) illus. 11 x 13 cm. 1966. (ISBN 0-670-26607-8). Viking.
--Dippy Dos & Don'ts. Spilka, Arnold (1917-), illus. LC 67-20961. (Illus.). 1 v. (unpaged. 1967. Viking Press.
--If You Talked to a Boar. Spilka, Arnold (1917-), illus. 32p. 1960. J. B. Lippincott.
--One Good Friend. LC 68-22454. 124 p. 24cm. 1968. Cobble Hill Press.
--The Tree and Me. Spilka, Arnold (1917-), illus. LC 70-109127. (Illus.). 29 p. 24cm. 1970. H. Z. Walck.

Sage, Michael, jt. auth. see Lang, Don.

Sage, Sidney
--Adventures of Alice in Wonderland. LC 35-180. 32cm. 14p. 1934. Saalfield Publishing Co.
--The Tale of Peter Rabbit. LC 35-181. 32cm. 14p. 1934. The Saalfield Publishing Co.

Sagendorf, Bud, pseud., see Sagendorf, Forrest Cowles.

Sagendorf, Bud, pseud. (1915-)
--Popeye. Sagendorf, Forrest Cowles. LC 55-42196. (Illus.). 21cm. (gr. k-3). 1955. (ISBN 0-448-00667-7). Wonder Treasure Books.

Sagendorf, Forrest Cowles see Sagendorf, Bud, pseud.

Sagendorph, Kent
--Beyond the Amazon. LC 38-17389. vi, 208 p. front. 19 1/2 cm. (His Dan Perry adventure stories). c.1938. Cupples & Leon Company.
--Radium Island. LC 38-173887. vi, 208 p. front. 19 1/2 cm. (His Dan Perry adventure stories). c.1938. Cupples & Leon Company.
--Sin-Kiang Castle. LC 38-173909. vi, 208 p. front. 19 1/2 cm. (His Dan Perry adventure stories). c.1938. Cupples & Leon Company.

Sainsbury, Noel Everingham see Lawton, Charles, pseud.

Sainsbury, Noel Everingham, Jr. (1884-)
--Billy Smith, Exploring Ace. (The Great Ace Ser.). N.D. Cupples & Leon Co.
--Billy Smith, Exploring Ace: Or, Into the Heart of Savage New Guinea by Airplane. LC 28-24950. 247 p. 19 1/2 cm. 1928. R. M. McBride & Company.
--Billy Smith, Mystery Ace: Or, Airplane Discoveries in South America. LC 32-13779. 3 p. l., 199 p. front. 19 1/2 cm. (His Great Ace Series). c.1932. Cupples & Leon Company.
--Billy Smith, Secret Service Ace: Or, Airplane Adventures in Arabia. LC 32-13780. 2 p. l., 212 p. front. 19 1/2 cm. (His Great Ace Series). c.1932. Cupples & Leon Company.
--Billy Smith, Shanghaied Ace: Or, Malay Pirates and Solomon Island Cannibals. LC 34-6601. 3 p. l., 206 p. front. 19 1/2 cm. (His Great ace series). c.1934. Cupples & Leon Company.
--Billy Smith, Trail Eater Ace: Or, Into the Wilds of Northern Alaska by Airplane. LC 33-9283. 3 p. l., 209 p. front. 19 1/2 cm. (The Great Ace Series). c.1933. Cupples & Leon Company.
--Clarkville's Battery: Or, "Baseball Versus Gangsters". LC 38-38060. iii, 293 p. front. 20 cm. (His champion sport stories). c.1937. Cupples & Leon, Company.
--Cracker Stanton. LC 34-6602. 3 p. l., 302 p. front. 20 cm. (His Champion sport stories). c.1934. Cupples & Leon Company.
--The Fighting Five. LC 34-25925. 3 p. l., 201 p. front. 20 cm. (His Champion sport stories). c.1934. Cupples & Leon Company.
--Gridiron Grit. LC 34-259265. 3 p. l., 202 p. front. 20 cm. (His Champion sport stories). c.1934. Cupples & Leon Company.
--Home Run Hennessey: Or, "Winning the All-Star Game,". Lawton, Charles, pseud. LC 41-6041. iv, 210 p. front. 20 cm. (His Champion sport stories). c.1941. Cupples & Leon Company.
--Ros Hackney, Halfback: Or, "How Clarkville's Captain Made Good". Lawton, Charles, pseud. LC 38-38059. iii, 206 p. front. 20 cm. (His Champion sport stories). c.1937. Cupples & Leon Company.
--Touchdown to Victory: Or, the Touchdown Express Makes Good. Lawton, Charles, pseud. LC 42-21063. iv, 207 p. front. 20 cm. (His Champion sport stories). 1942. Cupples & Leon Company.
--The Winning Forward Pass: Or, "Onward to the Orange-Bowl Game". Lawton, Charles, pseud. LC 40-10195. iii, 206 p. front. 20 cm. his champion sport stories. (Champion Sport Stories). N.D. C.

St. Catherine's Convent,New York
--Poems for Catholics & Convents: And Plays for Catholic Schools. LC 13-24606. xii, 282 p. 19 cm. 1873. Stereotyped and Printed at the New York Catholic Protectory.

St. Nicholas Magazine
--Aviation Stories,. Retold from St. Nicholas. LC 31-26076. vii, 197 p. front., plates. 19 1/2 cm. 1930. London, The Century Co.
--Bird Stories: Retold from St. Nicholas. LC 24-20974. 5 p. l., 3-181 p. front., plates, maps. 19 1/2 cm. c.1924. The Century Co.
--Civil War Stories: Retold from St. Nicholas. LC 5-34175. 5 p. l., 3-201 p. incl. illus., plates, ports. front. (port.) 19 1/2 cm. 1905. The Century Co.
--Colonial Stories: Retold from St. Nicholas. LC 5-34179. viii, 194 p. incl. illus., plates, ports. front. 19 1/2 cm. 1905. The Century Co.
--Courageous Girls: Retold from St. Nicholas. LC 18-17644. 7 p. l., 3-208 p. incl. front., plates. 19 1/2 cm. (On verso of half-title: Hero stories retold from St. Nicholas magazine). 1918. The Century Co.
--Elephant Stories,. Retold from St. Nicholas. LC 19-13139. 5 p. l., 3-188 p. incl. plates. front., pl. 19 1/2 cm. 1919. The Century Co.

--Pro Fever. Snyder, Paul (1923-), illus. LC 73-23112. (Illus.). 32 p. 24cm. (His Four seasons at Lakeview). 1974. EMC Corp.
--Rescue by Fire. Bergeron, Joseph R., illus. LC 73-396. (Illus.). 48 p. 23cm. ("Tromp it" series). 1973. (ISBN 0-912022-61-2). (ISBN 0-912022-61-2). EMC Corp.
--A Ride to Remember. Bergeron, Joseph R., illus. LC 72-13770. (Illus.). 47 p. 23cm. ("Tromp it" series). 1973. (ISBN 0-912022-51-5). (ISBN 0-912022-42-6). EMC Corp.
--Rip's Ups and Downs. Snyder, Paul (1923-), illus. LC 74-550. (Illus.). 34 p. 24cm. (His Four seasons at Lakeview). 1974. (ISBN 0-88436-073-3). EMC Corp.
--The Sixth Man. Snyder, Paul (1923-), illus. LC 73-23084. (Illus.). 34 p. 24cm. (His Four seasons at Lakeview). 1974. (ISBN 0-88436-075-X). (ISBN 0-88436-075-X). EMC Corp.
--The Tough Decision. LC 73-8190. (Illus.). 29 p. 24cm. (His Red Line Blue Line Ice Hockey Adventures). 1973. (ISBN 0-912022-13-2). Amecus Street.
--The Tough Decision. 1973. (ISBN 0-516-05143-1). Childrens Press.
--The Two That Count. LC 73-8192. (Illus.). 28 p. 24cm. (His Red Line Blue Line Ice Hockey Adventures). 1973. (ISBN 0-912022-14-0). Amecus Street.
--The Two that Count. 1973. (ISBN 0-516-05144-X). Childrens Press.
--The Unlikely Hero. Snyder, Paul (1923-), illus. LC 73-23065. (Illus.). 34 p. 24cm. (His Four seasons at Lakeview). 1974. (ISBN 0-88436-071-7). EMC Corp.

Saintsbury, George, intro. by see Balzac, Honore De.

Saintsbury, George Edward Bateman (1845-1933), ed.
--National Rhymes of the Nursery. Browne, Gordon Frederick (1858-1932), illus. N.D. E. & J. B .Young & Co.
--National Rhymes of the Nursery. Browne, Gordon Frederick (1858-1932), illus. (Fine Art Juvenile Ser.). N.D. Frederick A Stokes Co.

St. Vincent, Isobel
--The Fatal Necklace: The Story of Marie Antoinette of France. LC 57-11148. 158p. illus. 21cm. 1957cm. N.D. Roy Publishers.
--Young Marie: The Story of Madame Tussaud. LC 56-9176. 169p. illus. 21cm. N.D. Roy Publishers.

Saint Simon, Mrs., tr. see Hoffmann, Ernst Theodor Amadeus.

Saito, Michiko (1946-)
--Jenny's Journey. Saito, Michiko, pseud. (1946-), illus. Fujiwara, Michiko. LC 74-2086. (Illus.). 48 p. 22cm. 1974. (ISBN 0-07-054461-1). (ISBN 0-07-054461-1). McGraw-Hill.

Sakade, Florence
--Japanese Twins' Lucky Day: A Picture Play. Koyano, Hanji, illus. (ps-3). N.D. (ISBN 0-8048-0322-6). C E Tuttle.
--Kintaro's Adventures & Other Stories. Hayashi, Yoshio, illus. (Illus.). (gr. 1-5). 1958. (ISBN 0-8048-0343-9). C E Tuttle.
--Little One-Inch & Other Stories. (Illus.). (gr. 1-5). 1958. (ISBN 0-8048-0384-6). C E Tuttle.
--Origami Storybook: Japanese Paper-Folding Play. Sono, Kazuhiko, illus. LC 60-10952. (gr. 1-3). N.D. (ISBN 0-8048-0457-5). C E Tuttle.
--Peach Boy & Other Stories. Kurosaki, Yoshisuke, illus. (Illus.). (gr. 1-5). 1958. (ISBN 0-8048-0469-9). C E Tuttle.
--Urashima Taro & Other Stories. (Illus.). (gr. 1-6). 1958. (ISBN 0-8048-0609-8). C E Tuttle.

Sakade, Florence, ed.
--Japanese Children's Favorite Stories. 2d ed. rev. Kurosaki, Yoshisuke, illus. LC 58-11620. (Illus.). 120 p. 1958. C. E. Tuttle Co.
--Japanese Children's Stories. 2nd ed. Hayashi, Yoshio, illus. LC 58-11621. 120p. illus. (part col.) 21x22cm. 1959. (ISBN 0-8048-0285-8). C. E. Tuttle Co.

Sakade, Florence & Sono, Kazuhiko
--Fold-And-Paste Origami Storybook. LC 64-22899. 27cm. 31p. (gr. 1-4). 1964. (ISBN 0-8048-0189-4). C E Tuttle.

Saki, pseud., see Munro, Hector Hugh.

Saki, pseud. (1870-1916)
--The Story-Teller: Thirteen Tales by Saki. Munro, Hector Hugh. 1st ed. Titherington, Jeanne, illus. LC 82-3149. 103 p. 23cm. 1982. (ISBN 0-87923-445-8). D.R. Godine.

Salaff, Alice
--Words Are Funny: A Riddle Book. Newmann, Vera, illus. 1952. Doubleday & Co.

Salaman, Nina Ruth Davis, Mrs. (1876-1925), ed.
--Apples and Honey. LC 22-26034. xix, 347, 1 p. incl. front. 19 cm. 1922. Doubleday, Page & Company.
--Apples & Honey: A Gift-Book for Jewish Boys and Girls. LC 27-12789. xix, 1, 260 p. incl. front. 19 1/2 cm. 1927. Bernard G. Richards Co., Inc.

Salamanca, Lucy
--Lost in the Everglades. Polseno, Jo, illus. LC 70-142151. (Illus.). 192 p. 24cm. 1971. Golden Press.
--Tommy Tiger of the Seminoles. Peterson, Russell Francis, illus. LC 61-5593. 133p. illus. 21cm. 1961. F. Watts.

Salander, Eric L.
--Gary & Larry Gopher & Their Friends: Adventures in the Wilderness. Salander, Carol, illus. LC 62-419. (Illus.). 52p. (Orig.). (Bk. 1). (gr. 3-6). 1982. (ISBN 0-943472-00-8). Delgren Bks.
--Gary & Larry Gopher & Their Friends: Sad & Happy Tales about Their Friends. (Illus.). 60p. (Orig.). (Bk. 13). (gr. 4-8). 1982. (ISBN 0-943472-02-4). Delgren Bks.
--Gary & Larry Gopher & Their Friends: The Legend of Sir Swen Squirrel. Salander, Carol, illus. (Illus.). 48p. (Orig.). (Bk. 2). (gr. 3-6). 1982. (ISBN 0-943472-01-6). Delgren Bks.

Salas, Nichole
--Night of the Kachina. LC 78-16066. (Illus.). (Pacesetters Ser.). (gr. 4 up). 1978. (ISBN 0-516-02157-5). Childrens.

Salassi, Otto Russell (1939-)
--And Nobody Knew They Were There. LC 83-16487. 192p. (gr. 7up). 1984. (ISBN 0-688-00940-9). (ISBN 0-688-00940-9). Greenwillow.
--On the Ropes. LC 80-20399. 248 p. 22cm. c.1981. (ISBN 0-688-80313-X). (ISBN 0-688-84313-1). Greenwillow Books.

Salat, Barbara
--Fritzel & the Musical Band. 1977. (ISBN 0-918912-01-6). Well Being.
--Fritzel & the Spineless Grozoo. 1977. (ISBN 0-685-85773-5). Well Being.
--Fritzel the Mouse & His Friend Fat Freddy. 1977. (ISBN 0-918912-02-4). Well Being.

Salata, Estelle
--Mice at Center Ice. LC 85-27740. p. cm. (Schoolhouse Novels). 1986, c.1984. (ISBN 0-8086-0311-6). Schoolhouse Press.

Salaz, Ruben D.
--Cosmic Reader of the Southwest: For Young People. Aragon, Loretta, illus. (Illus.). (gr. 4 up). 1976. (ISBN 0-932492-00-2). Fineline Pubns.

Salazar, Violet
--Squares Are Not Bad. Rockwell, Harlow, illus. LC 67-8239. (Illus.). 25 p. 22cm. 1967. Golden Press.

Salder, Doris
--A Girl Dog's Diary. 1965. Exposition Press.

Saldinger, Frances, jt. auth. see Disney, Walt, Productions.

Sale, Elizabeth
--Recitation from Memory. LC 43-15070. 4 p. l., 3-298 p. 20 1/2 cm. 1943. Dodd, Mead & Company.

Saleh, Harold J
--Even Tiny Ants Must Sleep. Pinkney, Jerry (1939-), illus. LC 67-13905. (Illus.). 31p. 1967. McGraw-Hill.

Salem, Mary Miller
--The Three Story Book: Three Complete Books in One. LC 51-12242. 1 v. illus. 28 cm. 1951. Childrens Press.

Salisbury, Claude L
--Why the Sun Was Put in the Middle of Things. LC 70-11529. (Illus.). 30 p. 25cm. 1969. Art Directors Studio Press.

Salisbury, Helen Wright (1895-)
--The Church Nursery School and Bible Stories for the Very Young. N.D. Cowman Publications, Inc.
--Finger Fun: Songs and Rhythms for the Very Young. LC 55-31000. (Illus.). 56 p. 29cm. 1955. Cowman Publications.

Salisbury, Kent
--Funny Fingers. new ed. Allen, Joan, illus. (Illus.). color ils. 1st U.S. edition. (ps-1). 1971. (ISBN 0-307-13537-3, Golden Pr). Western Pub.
--Funny Fingers. Allen, Joan, illus. (Golden Tall Funny Books). 1974. (ISBN 0-307-13537-3, Golden Pr). Western Pub.
--Let's Take a Trip. Kirby, Beverly, illus. (Illus.). 14p. (Golden Tall Funny Bks.). (ps-2). 1975. (ISBN 0-307-13531-4, Golden Pr). Western Pub.
--Ookpik Visits the U.S.A. Edwards, Beverly, illus. LC 70-5917. (Illus.). 22 p. 33cm. (Golden magnetic storybook). 1968. Golden Press.
--Tell-a-Tall-Tale. Zanazania, Adrina, illus. (Illus.). (gr. 4-9). 1966. (ISBN 0-307-13533-0, Golden Pr). Western Pub.

Salkey, Andrew see Salkey, Felix Andrew Alexander.

Salkey, Felix Andrew Alexander (1928-)
--Earthquake. Papas, William (1927-), illus. LC 69-13413. (Illus.). 123 p. 23cm. 1969, c.1968. Roy Publishers.
--Hurricane. LC 79-317572. 89 p. 21cm. 1979. Oxford University Press.
--Jonah Simpson. Craig, Gerry, illus. LC 70-99447. (Illus.). 168 p. 23cm. 1970, c.1969. Roy Publishers.

Sallis, Susan
--Only Love. LC 79-2686. p. cm. c.1980. (ISBN 0-06-025174-3). (ISBN 0-06-025175-1). Harper & Row.
--An Open Mind. LC 77-25678. (gr. 7 up). 1978. (ISBN 0-06-025162-X, HarpJ). (ISBN 0-06-025163-8). Har-Row.
--Secret Places of the Stairs. LC 83-48442. 160p. (A Charlotte Zolotow Bk.). (gr. 7 up). 1984. (ISBN 0-06-025142-5, HarpJ). (ISBN 0-06-025147-6). Har-Row.
--A Time for Everything. LC 78-22496. p. cm. c.1979. (ISBN 0-06-025172-7). (ISBN 0-06-025173-5). Harper & Row.

Salmon, Annie Elizabeth see Martin, Nancy, pseud.

Salmon, Douglas
--Legends from the Living Sea. Vallentine, J. Manson, illus. LC 66-13159. (Illus.). (gr. 2-5). 1974. (ISBN 0-87208-013-7). Island Pr.

Salome, Mary, Mother
--Goosy Gander: Author of "Told in the Twilight", 1 of 6 Vols. (Illus.). (The Art Gem Ser.: Vol.4). N.D. E. P. Dutton & Co.
--Holly Boughs, 1 of 6 Vols. (Illus.). (The Art Gem Ser.). N.D. E. P. Dutton & Co.
--Little Pickle, 1 of 6 Vols. (The Art Gem Ser.: Vol. 6). N.D. E. P. Dutton & Co.
--Our Pussy Cat, 1 of 6 Vols. (Illus.). (The Art Gem Ser.: Vol. 3). N.D. E. P. Dutton & Co.
--Tens and Elevens, 1 of 6 Vols. (Illus.). (The Art Gem Ser.: Vol. 5). N.D. E. P. Dutton & Co.
--Told in the Twilight. LC 12-3600. 1912. Benziger Brothers.
--Twilight Tales, 1 of 6 Vols. (Illus.). (The Art Gem Ser.: Vol. 2). N.D. E. P. Dutton & Co.

Salome, Sr., jt. auth. see Weilert, Augustine, Sr.

Salop, Byrd Kalish
--The Kiddush Cup Who Hated Wine. Goldstein, Lil, illus. LC 58-1390. unpaged. illus. 28cm. c.1957. David Co.
--The Kiddush Cup Who Hated Wine. Goldstein, Lil, illus. 32p. (gr. 1 up). 1981. (ISBN 0-8246-0265-X). Jonathan David.

Salot, Lorraine (1914-)
--Tippy Finds Some Friends. Foster, Celeste K., illus. LC 74-125163. (Illus.). 31 p. 29cm. 1971. (ISBN 0-513-00495-5). Denison.

Salsbury, Juniata
--The Purple Hyacinth: A Fairy Story. LC 44-31056. 110 p. illus. 20 x 15 1/2 cm. 1895. The Transatlantic Publishing Company.
--Timothy Dole. (Illus.). N.D. Joseph Knight Co.
--Timothy Dole. (Illus.). (Gift Book Ser.). N.D. L. C. Page & Co.

Salsbury, Rebecca & Allen, William Harvey (1874-)
--Liberty the Giant Killer. Hogan, Inez (1895-), illus. LC 20-138225. 3 p. l., 96 p. illus. 19 1/2 cm. c.1919. Institute for Public Service.

Salt, Harriet
--Young Hawk and His Pony. Hogan, Inez (1895-), illus. LC 21-29421. 89 p. col. front., illus., col. plates. 21 x 20 cm. c.1931. Macrae Smith Company.

Salten, Felix, pseud., see Salzmann, Siegmund.

Salten, Felix, jt. auth. see Disney, Walt, Productions.

Salten, Felix, pseud. (1869-1945)
--Bambi. Salzmann, Siegmund. Cooney, Barbara (1917-), illus. 112p. Repr. 1981. (ISBN 0-89967-032-6). Harmony & Co.
--Bambi. Salzmann, Siegmund. Galsworthy, J., frwd. by. (gr. k-3). 1964. (ISBN 0-448-04751-9, Tempo). G&D.
--Bambi. Salzmann, Siegmund. Goodenow, Girard, illus. 134p. Repr. 1981. (ISBN 0-89966-358-3). Buccaneer Bks.
--Bambi. Salzmann, Siegmund. Goodenow, Girard, illus. LC 56-2046. 190p. illus. 22cm. 1956. Junior Deluxe Editions.
--Bambi. Salzmann, Siegmund. Pinner, Erna (1896-), illus. (Illus.). ca. 250p. (Thrushwood Bks.). (gr. k-3). 1969. (ISBN 0-448-02518-3, G&D). Putnam Pub Group.
--Bambi: A Life in the Wood. Salzmann, Siegmund. 1935. Simon & Schuster.
--Bambi: A Life in the Wood. Salzmann, Siegmund. Wiese, Kurt (1887-1974), illus. Chambers, David Whitaker (1901-1961), tr. Galsworthy, John (1867-1933), intro. by. LC 28-17486. 1928. Simon and Schuster.
--Bambi: A Life in the Woods. Salzmann, Siegmund. Cooney, Barbara (1917-), illus. LC 74-124383. (Illus.). 190 p. 24cm. 1970 (Wanderer Bks.). Simon and Schuster.
--Bambi's Children. Salzmann, Siegmund. N.D. Bobbs-Merrill Co.
--Bambi's Children. Salzmann, Siegmund. Bartlett, William, illus. LC 69-17259. (Adapted and Abridged from Felix Salten's Famous Story). (Illus.). 20 p. 29cm. (Silver dollar). 1969, c.1951. Grossett & Dunlap.
--Bambi's Children. Salzmann, Siegmund. Chaffee, Allen, ed. Erickson, Phoebe (1907-), illus. LC 50-10616. (Illus.). 63 p. 29cm. 1950. Random House.
--Bambi's Children. Salzmann, Siegmund. Erickson, Phoebe (1907-), illus. LC 48-6199. (Based on the Original Story). 32 p. illus. (part col.) 22 cm. 1948. Grosset and Dunlap.
--Bambi's Children: The Story of a Forest Family. Salzmann, Siegmund. Johnson, Elice, illus. Stillman, Clara Gruening, tr. LC 77-353404. (Illus.). 315 p. 21cm. 1976, c.1939. (ISBN 0-285-62244-7). Souvenir Press.
--Felix Salten's Favorite Animal Stories. Salzmann, Siegmund. Eichenberg, Fritz (1901-), illus. LC 48-9045. ix, 243 p. illus. 22 cm. 1948. J. Messner.
--Fifteen Rabbits. Salzmann, Siegmund. Chambers, David Whitaker (1901-1961), tr. N.D. Simon & Schuster.
--Fifteen Rabbits. Salzmann, Siegmund. Eichenberg, Fritz (1901-), illus. 240p. 1976. Delacorte.
--The Hound of Florence. Salzmann, Siegmund. Wiese, Kurt (1887-1974), illus. Paterson, Huntley, tr. LC 30-15343. (Illus.). 21cm. 236p. 1930. Simon & Schuster.
--Jibby, the Cat. Salzmann, Siegmund. LC 48-7229. (Illus.). +mcm. 117p. N.D. Julian Messner, Inc.
--Perri. Jungnickel, Ludwig Heinrich, illus. Mussey, June Barrows, tr. LC 38-27967. (Illus.). 228p. 21cm. 1938. Bobbs-Merrill.
--Samson and Deliah. Salzmann, Siegmund. Chambers, David Whitaker (1901-1961), tr. 1931. Simon and Schuster.
--Walt Disney's Bambi. Salzmann, Siegmund. LC 82-3080. (Illus.). 96 p. (Disney Read-Aloud Film Classic). c.1982. (ISBN 0-517-54462-8). (ISBN 0-517-54463-6). Harmony Books.

Salten, Felix, pseud. (1869-1945), ed.
--Fairy Tales from Near and Far. Salzmann, Siegmund. Johnson, Elice, illus. Stillman, Clara Gruening, tr. LC 49-1725. 141 p. illus. (part col.) 26 cm. 1945, c.1946. Philosophical Library.

Salter, Mary Turner, jt. auth. see Gates, Josephine Scribner, Mrs.

Salter-Mathieson, Nigel Cedric Stephen (1932-)
--Little Chief Mischief. Gruen, Chuck, illus. LC 62-18799. (Illus.). (An Astor Bk.). (gr. 2-7). 1962. (ISBN 0-8392-3020-6). Astor-Honor.

Saltler, Helen Roney (1921-)
--The Day the Empire State Went Visiting. Stevens, Mary E. (1920-1966), illus. LC 58-10335. unpaged. illus. 26cm. 1958. Dodd, Mead.

Saltykov, Mikhail Evgrafovich (1826-1889)
--Fables. LC 74-14115. p. cm. 1976. (ISBN 0-8371-7790-1). Greenwood Press.

Saltzberg, Barney
--It Must Have Been the Wind. LC 81-47722. (Illus.). 30 p. 23cm. c.1982. (ISBN 0-06-025176-X). (ISBN 0-06-025177-8). Harper & Row.
--What to Say to Clara. LC 83-15567. (Illus.). 32p. (gr. k up). 1984. (ISBN 0-689-31041-2). Atheneum.
--The Yawn. Saltzberg, Barney, illus. LC 85-7950. (Illus.). 28 p. 1985. (ISBN 0-689-31073-0). Atheneum.

Saltzman, Mark
--No One Knows Where Gobo Goes. Elwell, Peter, illus. LC 84-6616. (Illus.). (ps-2). 1984. (ISBN 0-03-000713-5). HR&W.

Salus, Naomi Panush
--My Daddy's Mustache. De Paola, Tomie, pseud. (1934-), illus. De Paola, Thomas Anthony. LC 78-68363. (Illus.). 32 p. 22cm. c.1979. (ISBN 0-385-13188-7). (ISBN 0-385-13189-5). Doubleday.

Salway, Lance
--A Nasty Piece of Work & Other Ghost Stories. Ford, Jeremy, illus. LC 84-17641. (Illus.). 128p. 1st U.S. edition. (gr. 4-8). 1985. (ISBN 0-89919-360-9, Clarion). HM.

Salway, Lance, tr. see Evenhuis, Gertie.

Salzberg, Doris Thorner
--Raggedy Granny Stories. Gruelle, John Barton (1880-1938) & Gruelle, Worth, illus. LC 77-6113. p. cm. 41p. 1977. (ISBN 0-672-52354-X). Bobbs-Merrill.

Salzburg, Jacob Louis
--The Dancing Mule. DeMuth, Flora Nash (1888-), illus. LC 42-24041. 31, 1 p. illus. 19 cm. 1942. Harper & Brothers.
--The Singing Cobbler. Lazarus, Sidney, illus. LC 39-24724. 5 p. l., 3-133 p. front., illus. 21 cm. 1939. Harper & Brothers.

Salzer, L. E., pseud., see Wilson, Lionel.

Salzer, L. E., pseud. (1924-)
--Haunted House Mysteries. Wilson, Lionel. LC 78-10951. (Illus.). 47 p. 24cm. c.1979. (ISBN 0-89547-070-5). C.P.I.

Salzman, Yuri
--Hope You're Feeling Better. LC 77-25655. (Illus.). 32 p. 20cm. c.1979. (ISBN 0-06-025164-6). (ISBN 0-06-025165-4). Harper & Row.

Salzmann, Siegmund see Salten, Felix, pseud.

--Rootabags Stories. Petersham, Maud Sylvia Fuller, Mrs. (1890-1971) & Petersham, Miska (1889-1960), illus. LC 68-5198. 21cm. 218p. 1923. Harcourt Brace.
--The Sandburg Treasury: Prose and Poetry for Young People. Bacon, Paul (1913-), illus. LC 79-120818. (Illus.). 480 p. 25cm. 1970. Harcourt Brace Jovanovich.
--The Wedding Procession of the Rag Doll and the Broom Handle and Who Was in It. 1st ed. Pincus, Harriet (1938-), illus. LC 67-2763. (Illus.). 1 v. (unpaged). 32p. 1967. Harcourt, Brace & World.
--The Wedding Procession of the Rag Doll and the Broom Handle and Who Was in It. Pincus, Harriet (1938-), illus. LC 78-7912. p. cm. (Voyager/HBJ book). N.D. (ISBN 0-15-695487-7). Harcourt Brace Jovanovich.
--Wind Song. Smith, William Arthur (1918-), illus. LC 60-10248. (Illus.). (gr. 5 up). 1960. (ISBN 0-15-297497-0, HJ). HarBraceJ.
--Wind Song. Smith, William Arthur (1918-), illus. LC 60-10248. (Illus.). (gr. 5 up). 1965. (ISBN 0-15-697096-1, VoyB). HarBraceJ.

Sandburg, Carl August (1878-1967), ed.
--American Songbag. LC 28-681. (Illus.). (gr. 10 up). 1927. (ISBN 0-15-106287-0). HarBraceJ.

Sandburg, Helga (1918-)
--Anna and the Baby Buzzard. 1st ed. Turkle, Brinton Cassaday (1915-), illus. LC 76-81712. (Illus.). 48 p. 24cm. 1970. Dutton.
--Blueberry. LC 63-10919. 158 p. 22 cm. 1963. Dial Press.
--Bo and the Old Donkey. 1st. ed. Morton, Marian (1918-), illus. LC 64-22790. 1 v. (unpaged) col. illus. 26 cm. 1965. Dial Press.
--Gingerbread. Geer, Charles Hand (1922-), illus. LC 64-14325. 192 p. illus. 22 cm. 1964. Dial Press.
--Joel and the Wild Goose. Daly, Thomas, illus. LC 63-17886. 1 v. (unpaged) col. illus. 20 x 27 cm. 1963. Dial Press.
--Owl's Roost. (gr. 1-4). 1962. (ISBN 0-8037-6794-3). Dial.
--The Unicorns. (Illus.). 96p. 1965. (ISBN 0-8037-9225-5). Dial Press.

Sandeau, Leonard Sylvain Jules (1811-1883)
--Sea-Gull's Rock. N.D. Benziger Brothers.

Sanderlin, Owenita Harrah (1916-)
--Jeanie O'Brien: A Novel. LC 65-216505. 144p. 24cm. c.1965. (ISBN 0-531-01702-8). Watts.
--Match Point. (gr. 3 up). 1979. (ISBN 0-307-21518-0, Golden Pr). Western Pub.
--Tennis Rebel. Freedman, Chuck, photos by. LC 77-21135. (Illus.). 95 p. 22cm. (Triumph book). 1978. (ISBN 0-531-01466-5). F. Watts.

Sanders, Anna Pearl Goodman (1935-)
--The Library Mice. Fern, Eugene A. (1919-), illus. LC 62-146450. unpaged. illus. 23cm. 1962. Ariel Books.

Sanders, Charles Walton, jt. ed. see Russell, B. A.

Sanders, Charlotte
--Holidays at Home: Written for the Amusement of Young Persons. 268 p. 18 cm. 1804. Printed by J. Swaine, For T. H. Burnton, No. , Broad-Way, Opposite the City Hotel.

Sanders, D. Johnson De Santa
--Arnis, the Little Star That Couldn't Shine: A Space Tale. Sanders, Krister H., illus. (Illus.). 47p. (gr. 2-6). 1972. (ISBN 0-682-47554-8). Exposition.

Sanders, Jean Elsie
--Tales from Old Judea. N.D. Allan Pub.

Sanders, John Edward (1930-)
--A Firework for Oliver. 1965. Walker and Company.

Sanders, Margaret Webb
--The Year of the Mintie May. Henneberger, Robert G. (1921-), illus. LC 54-9860. 182p. illus. 22cm. 1954. Putnam.

Sanders, Margaret Webb, jt. auth. see Meg, Elisabeth.

Sanders, Martha
--Alexander and the Magic Mouse. Fix, Philippe, illus. LC 71-83819. (Illus.). 42 p. 27cm. 1969. American Heritage Press.

Sanders, Peter, jt. auth. see Stokes, Bill.

Sanders, Ruby Wilson
--Winding Canyon. Joslin, Charles H., illus. LC 57-5251. 166p. illus. 22cm. 1958. Caxton Printers.

Sanders, Scott Russell (1945-), retold by.
--Hear the Wind Blow: American Folksongs. Goembel, Ponder, illus. LC 85-4160. p. cm. 1985. (ISBN 0-02-778140-2). Bradbury Press.

Sanders, Sheila
--Beast Goes Camping. Oelerich, Majorie L, ed. LC 85-18523. p. cm. (Adventures of beast). c.1985. (ISBN 0-914867-14-8). Baker Street Productions.
--Beast Has Too Much to Do. Oelerich, Marjorie L, ed. LC 85-17077. p. cm. (Adventures of Beast). c.1985. (ISBN 0-914867-15-6). Crestwood House.
--It's Too Bad, Beast. Oelerich, Marjorie L, ed. LC 85-15790. p. cm. (adventures of beast). c.1985. (ISBN 0-914867-12-1). Baker Street Productions.
--Ugly Beast. Oelerich, Majorie L, ed. LC 85-18496. p. cm. (Adventures of beast). c.1985. (ISBN 0-914867-13-X). Baker Street Productions.

Sanders, Stella
--Flying Horseshoe Ranch. Latham, Barbara (1896-), illus. LC 55-148785. 87p. illus. 26cm. 1955. Viking Press.

Sandersen, L. W.
--Chickadee-Dee & His Friends. N.D. Frederick A Stokes Co.

Sanderson, Ivan Terence see Roberts, Terence, pseud.

Sanderson, Ivan Terence (1911-1973)
--Animal Tales. 1946 (Borzoi Books). Alfred A Knopf.
--John and Juan in the Jungle. Covarrubias, Miguel (1904-1957), illus. LC 52-12973. (Illus.). 64 p. 26cm. 1953. Dodd, Mead.

Sanderson, Margaret Love
--The Camp Fire Girls at Driftwood Heights. (The Camp Fire Girls Ser.). N.D. Reilly & Lee.
--The Camp Fire Girls at Hillside. Roberts, Hazel, illus. LC 14-2138. 264 p. front., plates. 20 cm. (Half-title: The camp fire girls series). c.1913. The Reilly & Britton Co.
--The Camp Fire Girls at Lookout Pass. Carsey, Alice, illus. LC 19-832214. 288 p. front., plates. 20 cm. (Her Camp fire girls series). c.1917. The Reilly & Britton Co.
--The Camp Fire Girls at Pine-Tree Camp. Adams, Pauline Batchelder (1897-), illus. (Camp Fire Girls Ser.). 1916. The Reilly & Britton Co.
--The Camp Fire Girls at Top O' the World. Trapp, Bernice C., illus. LC 16-18328. 248 p. front., plates. 20 cm. (Half-title: Camp Fire Girls Series). c.1916. The Reilly & Britton Co.
--The Camp Fire Girls on a Yacht. LC 20-17182. 207 p. front. 20 cm. (Her Camp fire girls series). c.1920. The Reilly & Lee Co.
--The Camp Fire Girls on Hurricane Island. (The Camp Fire Girls Ser.). N.D. Reilly & Lee.
--Captain Becky's Masquerade. LC 12-17299. 240 p. front. 20 cm. (Her The Captain Becky Series). c.1912. The Reilly & Britton Co.
--Captain Becky's Winter Cruise. LC 12-17298. 259 p. front. 20 cm. $0.60. (Her The Captain Becky series). c.1912. The Reilly & Britton Co.

Sanderson, Ruth, illus.
--The Pudgy Bunny Book. (Illus.). 16p. (Pudgy Bks.). (gr. k). 1984. (ISBN 0-448-10210-2, G&D). Putnam Pub Group.

Sanderson, Ruth, jt. auth. see Talbot, Charlene Joy.

Sanderson, William Elwood (1903-)
--Horses are for Warriors. Crowell, Pers (1910-), illus. LC 52-11881. 183p. illus. 22cm. 1954. Caxton Printers.
--Nez Perce Buffalo Horse. Crowell, Pers (1910-), illus. LC 77-137771. (Illus.). (gr. 8-10). 1972. (ISBN 0-87004-212-2). Caxton.

Sandford, D. P., Mrs.
--May to Christmas at Thorne Hill. (Illus.). N.D. E P Dutton.

Sandham, Elizabeth
--More Trifles!. For the Benefit of the Rising Generation. LC 21-835781. 106 p. 14 cm. 1814. Published by Paraclete Potter. P. & S. Potter, Printers.
--The Twin Sisters,. Or, The Advantages of Religion. 2d ed. LC 8-4784. iv, 5-215 p. 14 1/2 cm. 1815. Print and Published by William Slade, Jun.

Sandifer, Shannon, ed. see Coltharp, Barbara.

Sandin, Joan (1912-)
--The Long Way to a New Land. Sandin, Joan (1912-), illus. LC 80-8942. p. cm. (An I Can Read History Book). (ps-3). c.1981. (ISBN 0-06-025193-X). (ISBN 0-06-025194-8). Harper & Row. **Award: (ALA).**

Sandman Lilius, Irmelin (1936-)
--Gold Crown Lane. Ionicus, illus. Helweg, Marianne, tr. LC 79-2103. (Illus.). 100 p. 21cm. (Her The Sola trilogy ; pt. 1). 1980, c.1976. (ISBN 0-440-04231-3). (ISBN 0-440-04232-1). Delacorte Press/S. Lawrence.
--The Goldmaker's House. Ionicus, illus. Tate, Joan (1922-), tr. LC 79-2104. (Illus.). 85 p. 21cm. (Fru Sola. English ; pt. 2.). (The Sola Trilogy: Pt. 2). 1980. (ISBN 0-440-04200-3). (ISBN 0-440-04201-1). Delacorte Press/S. Lawrence.
--Horses of the Night. Ionicus, illus. Tate, Joan (1922-), tr. LC 79-2105. (Illus.). 136 p. 21cm. (Fru Sola. English ; pt. 3.). (The Sola Trilogy: Pt. 3). 1980. (ISBN 0-440-04451-0). Delacorte Press/S. Lawrence.

Sandmel, Frances Fox
--All on the Team. Roman, Sylvia, illus. LC 59-11189. 125p. illus. 21cm. 1959. (ISBN 0-687-01039-X). Abingdon Press.

Sando, Anne, jt. auth. see Hall-Guest, Olga.

Sando, Anne, jt. auth. see Hall-Quest, Edna Olga Wilbourne, Mrs.

Sandor, Bortnyik
--Tatters and Scraps: Two Paper Dolls in Toyland. 22 x 20cm. 41p. 1933. Albert Whitman & Co.

Sandoz, Edouard Marcel (1881-)
--The Squire of Ravensmark. LC 49-817787. 217 p. illus. 22 cm. 1949. Houghton Miffin Co.
--Twice Besieged. Sandoz, Edouard Marcel (1918-), illus. LC 47-309157. (Illus.). 224 p. illus. 21 cm. 1947. Oxford Univ. Press.

Sandoz, Mari Susette (1901-1966)
--The Horsecatcher. LC 56-8429. (Illus.). 192 p. 22cm. 1957. Westminster Press. **Award: (JNM).**
--Santa Mouse. N.D. (ISBN 0-448-04213-4). Grosset & Dunlap.
--The Story Catcher. McCorkell, Elsie Jane, illus. LC 63-10929. 175 p. illus. 23 cm. 1963. Westminster Press.

Sandries, ed.
--Call of the Wild. (Original Author Jack London (1876-1916)). (gr. 7-8). N.D. Lothrop.

Sandrus, Mary Yost
--Adventures with Animals. (gr. 7-9). N.D (Pub. by Scott F). Lothrop.
--Adventures with Animals. Orloff, Gregory, illus. LC 58-1548. 301p. illus. 22cm. 1958. Scott, Foresman.
--Eight Treasured Stories. Moderow, Gertrude (1900-1973) & Noyes, Ernest, eds. Kredel, Fritz (1900-1973), illus. LC 50-6722. v, 287 p. illus. 22 cm. 1950. Scott, Foresman.

Sandstead, Jewell
--Skippy's Adventure. (gr. 2-4). 1970. Vantage.

Sandwell, Helen B
--The Valley of Color-Days. Preston, Alice Bolam (1889-), illus. LC 24-233042. vi p., 1 l., 299 p. col. front., col. plates. 22 1/2 cm. 1924. Little, Brown, and Company.

Sandys, E. V, retold by.
--Beowulf. Klep, Rolf, illus. LC 41-27326. 5 p. l., 3-93 p. incl. front., plates. 26 cm. 1941. Thomas Y. Crowell Company.

Sandys, E. V, retold by see Ibsen, Henrik Johan.

Sanford, A. P., ed. see Hobbs, Mabel.

Sanford, Agnes Mary White (1897-)
--Melissa & the Little Red Book. Heinen, Sandy, illus. (Illus.). (gr. 1-6). N.D. (ISBN 0-910924-81-3). Macalester.
--A Pasture for Peterkin. 1st ed. Sanford, Ted, illus. LC 57-20927. 136p. illus. 23cm. 1956. Macalester Park Pub. Co.

Sanford, Anne Putnam, Mrs., ed.
--American Patriotic Plays: Ten New Plays. LC 37-3787. v, 321 p. 19 cm. 1937. Dodd, Mead & Company.
--Little Plays for Everybody: Short Plays for Grammar and High Schools. LC 32-819237. vi, 342 p. 19 1/2 cm. 1932. Dodd, Mead and Company.
--New Plays for Christmas. LC 35-17528. 1935. Dodd Mead & Co.
--Outdoor Plays for Boys and Girls. LC 30-8630. viii, 323 p. 19 1/2 cm. 1930. Dodd, Mead and Company.
--Plays for Autumn and Winter Holidays. LC 38-9869. vi p., 2 l., 3-259 p. 19 1/2 cm. c.1938. Dodd, Mead & Company.
--Plays for Civic Days: Citizenship Plays for Community Centers. LC 31-22269. vi, 297 p. 19 1/2 cm. 1931. Dodd, Mead and Company.
--Plays for Graduation Days. LC 30-8626. vii p., 4 l., 5-322 p. 19 1/2 cm. 1930. Dodd, Mead and Company.
--Plays for Spring and Summer Holidays. LC 38-27154. iv, 283 p. 19 1/2 cm. c.1938. Dodd, Mead & Company.

Sanford, Anne Putnam, Mrs. & Schauffler, Robert Haven (1879-), eds.
--Little Plays for Little People. LC 29-20547. xi, 361 p. 19 1/2 cm. 1929. Dodd, Mead and Company.

Sanford, D. P., jt. auth. see Cheney, Emma C.

Sanford, D. P., Mrs.
--Aunt Sophy's Boys and Girls. LC 12-38373. iv, 5-212 p. front., illus., plates. 21 1/2 x 18 cm. 1879. E. P. Dutton and Company.
--Captain's Children. (Illus.). N.D. E. P. Dutton & Co.
--Carl's First Days: Easy Reading for the Little Ones, by the Author of "The Rose Dale Books.". LC 42-27105. iv, 7-164 p. illus., plates. 16 x 18 cm. 1879. E. P. Dutton & Company.
--Easy Reading for the Little Ones. (The Rose Dale Books). N.D. E. P. Dutton.
--Eunice Somers: A Learner in Life's School. 238p. N.D. E. P. Dutton.
--Five Happy Children: Easy Reading for the Dear Little Ones. LC 12-38376. 252 p. front., illus., plates. 17 1/2 cm. (The Rose Dale Bks.: No. 3). 1872. E. P. Dutton and Company.
--Frisk and His Flock. LC 76-365095. (Illus.). vi, 184 p., 33 leaves of plates. 22cm. 1876. Dutton.
--A Houseful of Children. Hobbs, Mabel, intro. by. LC 44-36614. 210 p. front., illus., plates. 21 cm. 1877. E. P. Dutton & Company.
--Ida and Baby Bell: Easy Reading for the Dear Little Ones. LC 12-383753. 262 p. front., illus., plates. 17 1/2 cm. (The Rose Dale Bks.: No.2). 1872. E. P. Dutton and Company.
--The Little Brown House and the Children Who Live in It. LC 44-36613. vi. 7-212 p. incl. front., illus. plates. 21 cm. 1878. E. P. Dutton and Company.
--Little Folks at Brookside. Richards, Harriet Roosevelt, illus. N.D. E. P. Dutton & Co.
--Little Frank's Story Book. N.D. E. P. Dutton.
--Little Nell's Story Book. (Illus.). N.D. E. P. Dutton.
--Mark the Fisher Boy, 1 of 3 Vols. (Illus.). (The Gift Library: Vol. 2). N.D. Set. E. P. Dutton Co.
--Mark the Fisher-Boy and Other Stories. LC 44-39863. 150 p. front., plates. 15 1/2 cm. 1872. E. P. Dutton and Company.
--Mother Holda Stories. (Illus.). N.D. E. P. Dutton & Co.
--Pussy Tip-Toes Family. New & Improved. N.D. E. P. Dutton.
--Rose, Tom, and Ned. Easy Reading for the Dear Little Ones. LC 12-38374. 246 p. front., illus., plates. 17 1/2 cm. (The Rose Dale Bks.: No.1). 1872. E. P. Dutton and Company.
--The Sunday Evening Hour. (Illus.). N.D. E. P. Dutton & Co.
--Under the Skylight, and Other Stories for Christmas. LC 44-33368. lll p. front., pl. 15 1/2 cm. 1872. Gen. Port. Episcopal Sunday-School Union and Church Book Society.
--Young Laymen: Or, the Boy Workers of Wiltham Parish. N.D. E. P. Dutton.

Sanford, David E
--My Village, My World. Nebel, Gustave E., illus. LC 75-75075. (Illus.). 190 p. 22cm. 1969. Crown Publishers.

Sanford, M. Malonia Ray
--A Visit to El-Fay-Gno-Land. LC 44-316240. 106 p. incl. front., illus. 17 1/2 x 14 cm. (On cover: Enchanted library for young folks). 1879. The Authors' Publishing Company.

Sanford, Mabel Adelina Fairclough, Mrs. (1882-)
--Joseph's City Beautiful: A Story of "Old Nauvoo" on the Mississippi. LC 40-1705. 207 p. 20 cm. c.1939. Herald Publishing House.

Sanford-Norris, Mary Ann
--Squirrel Baby. 1978. (ISBN 0-533-03030-7). Vantage.

Sanford, Sara L.
--Jake's Late. Bukovcik, Onalee, illus. (Illus.). 32p. (gr. 1-3). 1983. (ISBN 0-943944-01-5). Sneak-A-Peek Bks.
--Smirk Smiles. Flake, Gary, intro. by. LC 50-332. (Illus.). 24p. 1983. (ISBN 0-943944-00-7). Sneak-A-Peek Bks.

Sanford, Wendy (1925-) & Mendoza, George (1934-)
--The Puma and the Pearl. Forberg, Ati, pseud. (1925-), illus. Forberg, Beate Gropius. LC 62-19515. unpaged. illus. 16 x 24 cm. 1962. Walker.

Sanford, William R, jt. auth. see Green, Carl R.

Sanford, William & Green, Carl
--Black Friday. Schroeder, Howard, ed. LC 84-27444. (Illus.). 48p. (Movie Monsters Ser.). (gr. 3-5). 1985. (ISBN 0-89686-258-5). Crestwood Hse.
--Bride of Frankenstein. Schroeder, Howard, ed. LC 84-17539. (Illus.). 48p. (Movie Monsters Ser.). (gr. 3-5). 1985. (ISBN 0-89686-259-3). Crestwood Hse.
--Dracula's Daughter. Schroeder, Howard, ed. LC 84-27462. (Illus.). 48p. (Movie Monsters Ser.). (gr. 3-5). 1985. (ISBN 0-89686-260-7). Crestwood Hse.
--The Mole People. Schroeder, Howard, ed. (Illus.). 48p. (Movie Monsters Ser.). (gr. 3-5). 1985. (ISBN 0-89686-262-3). Crestwood Hse.
--The Raven. Schroeder, Howard, ed. LC 84-19866. (Adapted from a Screenplay by Garrett Fort). (Illus.). 48p. (Movie Monsters Ser.). (gr. 3-5). 1985. (ISBN 0-89686-263-1). Crestwood Hse.
--Tarantula. Schroeder, Howard, illus. (Adapted from a Screenplay by Martin Berkeley). (Illus.). 48p. (Movie Monsters Ser.). (gr. 3-5). 1985. (ISBN 0-89686-264-X). Crestwood Hse.
--Werewolf of London. Schroeder, Howard, ed. (Illus.). 48p. (Movie Monsters Ser.). (gr. 3-5). 1985. (ISBN 0-89686-265-8). Crestwood Hse.

San Francisco. Public Library. Friends, jt. auth. see Alden, Richard.

Sanger, Frances, pseud., see Lau, Josephine Sanger.

Sanger, Frances Ella
--The Wooden Mug. Larer, Marian, illus. 1950. Westminster Press.

Sanger, Marjory Bartlett (1920-)
--Billy Bartram and His Green World. (Illus.). 256p. 1972. (ISBN 0-374-30707-5). Farrar, Straus and Giroux.
--The Bird Watchers. Price, Christine Hilda (1928-1980), illus. LC 57-8980. 1957. E. P. Dutton & Co.
--Greenwood Summer. 1st ed. Price, Christine Hilda (1928-1980), illus. LC 58-9572. 160p. illus. 21cm. 1958. Dutton.

Sarton, Elizabeth Mary (1912-)

--The Poet and the Donkey. Martin, Stefan (1936-), illus. LC 72-80024. (Illus.). 126 p. 22cm. 1969. (ISBN 0-393-08590-2). W. W. Norton.

--A Private Mythology. 1966. (ISBN 0-393-04175-1). Norton & Co.

--Punch's Secret. 1st ed. Knotts, Howard Clayton, Jr. (1922-), illus. LC 73-14337. (Illus.). 30 p. 24cm. 1974. (ISBN 0-06-025191-3). (ISBN 0-06-025191-3). Harper & Row.

--A Walk Through the Woods. Mizumura, Kazue, illus. LC 75-25413. (Illus.). 30 p. c.1976. (ISBN 0-06-025189-1). (ISBN 0-06-025190-5). Harper & Row.

Sarton, May see Sarton, Elizabeth Mary.

Sartorius, Ina Craig, Mrs., jt. auth. see Hurley, Beatrice Jane Davis.

Sarver, Hannah, pseud., see Nielsen, Jean Sarver.

Sarver, Hannah, pseud., see Nielson, Jean Sarver.

Sarver, Hannah, pseud. (1922-)

--Square Peg. Nielson, Jean Sarver. (gr. 7-11). 1962. (ISBN 0-308-80172-5). Funk & W.

Sasaki, Isao

--Snow. (gr. k-3). 1982. Viking.

Sasaki, Tazu (1932-)

--The Golden Thread: Japanese Stories for Children. Suzuki, Etsuro, illus. Mayer, Fanny H., tr. LC 68-13865. (Illus.). 64 p. 23cm. 1968. C. E. Tuttle Co.

Sass, Herbert Ravenel

--Gray Eagle. LC 27-241802. 4 p. l., 3-269 p. front. 20 1/2 cm. 1927. Minton, Balch & Company.

Sasse, Alma Benecke

--The Mystery of the Chinese Box. Hamer, Alan, illus. LC 39-11259. 4 p. l., 252 p. illus. 20 1/2 cm. 1939. Thomas Y. Crowell Company.

--Terry Carvel's Theater Caravan. LC 43-15759. 6 p. l., 238 p. 20 1/2 cm. 1943. Doubleday, Doran and Company, Inc.

Sato, Satoru (1928-), adapted by.

--Coppelia. Murakami, Tsutomu, illus. Brannen, Ann, tr. LC 72-94813. (Original By Ernst Theodor Amadeus Hoffman with Music by Leo Delibes). (Illus.). color line drawings. 26p. (Fantasia Pictorial Ser). (gr. k-8). 1970. Japan Pubns.

Satow, Fiona

--My Friend Krow. 1979. (ISBN 0-89191-141-3). Cook.

Satterfield, C. W., adapted by see Disney, Walter Elias (1901-1966) & Strebe, Dorothy.

Satterlee, Walter, jt. auth. see Herman, R. L.

Sattler, Helen Roney (1921-)

--Annie. Monroe, Katherine, illus. LC 61-7930. 183p. c.1961. Dodd, Mead.

--Morgan the Mule. Flint, Russ, illus. (Illus.). N.D. (ISBN 0-516-09116-6). Childrens.

--Morgan the Mule. Flint, Russ, illus. (Illus.). 16p. (gr. k-6). 1982. (ISBN 0-8249-8981-3). Ideals.

--No Place for a Goat. Weissman, Bari, illus. LC 80-26558. (Illus.). 32 p. c.1981. (ISBN 0-525-66723-7). Elsevier/Nelson Books.

--Shadow Across the Campus. LC 56-11977. 245 p. 22cm. 1957. Dodd, Mead.

--The Smallest Witch. 1st ed. Goldsborough, June (1923-), illus. LC 81-2202. (Illus.). 32 p. 24cm. c.1981. (ISBN 0-525-66747-4). Elsevier/Dutton.

--Train Whistles. rev. ed. LC 84-11279. (Illus.). 32p. (ps-2). 1985. (ISBN 0-688-03978-2). (ISBN 0-688-03980-4). Lothrop.

--The Young Barbarians. LC 47-1834. 4 p. l., 212 p. 21 cm. 1947. W. Morrow and Company.

Saturday Evening Post Editors

--The Saturday Evening Post Christmas for Children Book. LC 81-65816. (Illus.). 112p. (ps up). 1981. (Co-Pub by Sat Eve Post). Curtis Pub Co.

Sauer, G. Selma

--The Patchy Zoo. LC 31-22803. 44 p. col. illus. 28 1/2 cm. c.1931. F. Warne and Co., Inc.

Sauer, I.

--Eve's Little Friends. 1981. (ISBN 0-07-054830-7). McGraw.

Sauer, Julia Lina (1891-1985)

--Fog Magic. Ward, Lynd Kendall (1905-1985), illus. LC 43-14784. (First Published September 1943). 7 p. l., 107 p. illus. 22 cm. 1943. The Viking Press. **Award: (JNM).**

--The Light at Tern Rock. Schreiber, Georges (1904-1977), illus. LC 51-13389. (Illus.). 62 p. 26cm. 1951. Viking Press. **Award: (JNM).**

--Mike's House. N.D. E. M. Hale & Co.

--Mike's House. Freeman, Don (1908-1978), illus. LC 54-8562. (Illus.). 31 p. 26cm. 1954. Viking Press.

--Radio Roads to Reading: Library Book Talks Broadcast to Girls and Boys. LC 39-17305. 236 p. 20 cm. 1939. The H. W. Wilson Company.

Sauer, Wesley Monroe

--A Book of Fairy Poems. N.D. Christopher Publishing House.

Saul, George Brandon (1901-)

--Candlelight Rhymes for Early-to-Beds. LC 76-28803. 29 p. 21cm. c.1970. Walton Press.

--The Forgotten Birthday. Williams, Robert J., Jr. (1895-), illus. LC 74-29718. (Illus.). 24 p. 22cm. 1971. Walton Press.

--King Noggin. Williams, Robert J., Jr. (1895-), illus. LC 71-30952. (Illus.). 18 p. 22cm. 1971. Walton Press.

--The Wild Queen. 1967. (ISBN 0-910244-45-6). John F. Blair Publisher.

Saulnier, Karen Luczak, jt. auth. see Miller, Ralph R.

Saulsbury, Dotty

--Mr. Doomer. Hitch, Elaine Saulsbury, illus. LC 37-21030. 2 p. l., 1, 16, 16 p. illus. 22 cm. 1937. E. P. Dutton & Co., Inc.

Saunders, Dennis, ed.

--Magic Lights & Streets of Shining Jet. Williams, Terry, photos by. LC 76-20519. (Illus.). 142 p. 22cm. Orig. Title: Fancy Free. 1977, c.1974. (ISBN 0-688-80065-3). (ISBN 0-688-84065-5). Greenwillow Books.

Saunders, Jean (1932-)

--Only Yesterday. (gr. 7-12). 1977. (ISBN 0-590-10410-1, Schol Pap). Schol Bk Serv.

Saunders, John

--The Tempter Behind, 1 of 20 vols. New ed. (Illus.). 350p. (Sunday-School Lib: No. 13). 1895. Set. Lothrop Pub. Co.

--The Tinker's Wig. Matania, F., illus. N.D. Frederick Warne & Co.

Saunders, John Richard see Columbia Record Club.

Saunders, Kathleen

--The Manmade Bear. Woon, Kay, illus. 33p. (gr. 2-5). 1980. (ISBN 0-939666-11-1). Yosemite Natl Hist.

Saunders, Lowell

--The Kitten Who Was Different. Talarczyk, June, illus. LC 66-9567. (Illus.). 1 v. (unpaged). 28cm. 1966. T. S. Denison.

Saunders, Margaret Marshall (1861-1947)

--Alpatok: The Story of an Eskimo Dog. Horne, Diantha W., illus. LC 6-14550. 3 p. l., 51 p. incl. illus., plates. front. 18 1/2 cm. (Cosy corner series). 1906. L. C. Page & Company.

--Beautiful Joe. (The Phoenix Ser.). N.D. George W. Jacobs & Co.

--Beautiful Joe. N.D. Grossett & Dunlap.

--Beautiful Joe. new and enl. ed. Copeland, Charles, illus. Butterworth, Hezekiah, intro. by. LC 7-284567. 399 p. col. front., illus., 8 pl. 20 1/2 cm. 1907. Griffith & Rowland Press.

--Beautiful Joe. modern abridged. MacLean, Robert (1926-), illus. LC 65-11914. 254 p. illus. (part col.) 22 cm. (Whitman classics library). 1965. Whitman Pub. Co.

--Beautiful Joe: An Autobiography. Butterworth, Hezekiah, intro. by. LC 4-16152. 304 p. front., plates. 18 1/2 cm. 1894. American Baptist Publication Society.

--Beautiful Joe: An Autobiography. Butterworth, Hezekiah, intro. by. LC 21-382. 304 p. front. (port.) plates. 18 1/2 cm. 1903. The Judson Press.

--Beautiful Joe's Paradise. N.D. Grosset & Dunlap.

--Beautiful Joe's Paradise: Or, the Island of Brotherly Love; a Sequel to 'Beautiful Joe'. Bull, Charles Livingston (1874-1932), illus. LC 2-21399. 1 p. l., 365 p. front., illus., pl. 19 1/2 cm. 1902. L. C. Page and Company.

--Bonnie Prince Fetlar: The Story of a Pony and His Friends. LC 20-18408. vi p., 1 l., 9-352 p. 19 1/2 cm. $2.00. c.1920. George H. Doran Company.

--Boy: The Wandering Dog. N.D. Grosset & Dunlap.

--Charles and His Lamb: Written for the Little Ones of the Household. LC 12-38345. 73 p. incl. front., illus. 19 1/2 cm. 1895. C. H. Banes.

--Daisy. (Illus.). 57p. N.D. American Baptist Pub. Society.

--Daisy. 57p. N.D. Sunday-School Publications.

--For His Country, and Grandmother and the Crow. Meynelle, Louis, illus. LC 5565. 60 p. incl. front., illus., 4 pl. 18 1/2 cm. (Lettered on cover: Cosy corner series). 1900. L. C. Page & Company.

--For the Other Boy's Sake, and Other Stories: And Other Stories. LC 8-2057. 374 p. front., plates. 20 cm. 1896. C. H. Banes.

--For the Other Boy's Sake, and Other Stories. (Illus.). 374p. N.D. American Baptist Publication Society.

--Golden Dicky: The Story of a Canary and His Friends. LC 19-15020. xi p., 2 l., 280 p. col. front. 19 1/2 cm. c.1919. Frederick A. Stokes Company.

--The House of Armour. 543p. N.D. American Baptist Publication Society.

--Jimmy Gold-Coast: Or, the Story of a Monkey and His Friends. LC 24-19921. 1 p. l., vii-ix, 11-319 p. front., illus. 19 1/2 cm. c.1924. David McKay Company.

--King of the Park. LC 8-2058. (Illus.). 20cm. 226p. (Crowell's Young People Ser.). 1897. Thomas Y. Crowell.

--Nita, the Story of an Irish Setter. Barry, Etheldred H., illus. LC 4-18900. (Illus.). 19cm. 77p. (Cosy Corner Ser.). 1904. L. C. Page & Co.

--Princess Sukey. (A Story of a Pigeon and Her Human Friends). N.D. Abingdon Press.

--Princess Sukey: The Story of a Pigeon and Her Human Friends. LC 5-16120. vi, 336 p. front., 4 pl. 20 1/2 cm. c.1905. Eaton & Mains.

--Princess Sukey: The Story of a Pigeon and Her Human Friends. (Illus.). N.D. Methodist Book Concern.

--Pussy Black-Face: Or, the Story of a Kitten and Her Friends; a Books for Boys and Girls. Horne, Diantha W. & Bull, Charles Livingston (1874-1932), illus. LC 13-9810. vii, 3, 311 p. col. front., illus., plates. 20 1/2 cm. 1913. L. C. Page & Company.

--The Story of the Gravelys: A Tale for Girls. LC 3-25214. 1 p. l., 283 p. front., 5 pl. 20 1/2 cm. (Princess series). 1904. L. C. Page & Company.

--Tilda Jane: An Orphan in Search of a Home; a Story for Boys and Girls. Carleton, Clifford, illus. LC 1-18538. 287 p. front., 9 pl. 19 1/2 cm. 1901. L. C. Page & Company.

--Tilda Jane's Orphans. Goss, John, illus. LC 9-28037. 21cm. 345p. 1909. Page Co.

--The Wandering Dog: Adventures of a Fox-Terrier. LC 16-21075. viii p., 2 l., 13-363 p. front., plates. 20 1/2 cm. c.1916. George H. Doran Company.

Saunders, Marion, tr. see Collin Delavaud, Marie Moreal De Brevans.

Saunders, Marion, tr. see Javal, Lily Leon-Levy.

Saunders, Marshall see Saunders, Margaret Marshall.

Saunders, Roy (1911-)

--Craig of the Welsh Hills. Saunders, Roy (1911-), illus. LC 59-12236. (Illus.). 184 p. 21cm. 1959, c.1958. Sloan and Pearce.

Saunders, Rubie, tr. see Le Paillot, Jean.

Saunders, Susan (1945-)

--Charles Rat's Picnic. 1st ed. Byrd, Robert John (1942-), illus. LC 83-5496. (Illus.). 32 p. 23cm. c.1983. (ISBN 0-525-44067-4). E.P. Dutton.

--Dorothy and the Magic Belt. Rose, David S. (1947-), illus. LC 84-17946. (Illus.). 64 p. 19cm. (A Brand-New Oz Adventure). c.1985. (ISBN 0-394-87067-0). (ISBN 0-394-97067-5). Random House.

--Fish Fry. Schindler, Steven D., illus. LC 82-2567. (Illus.). 32p. 1st U.S. edition. (gr. k-3). 1982. (ISBN 0-670-31664-4). Viking Pr.

--A Sniff in Time. Mariano, Michael, illus. LC 81-10763. (Illus.). 32 p. 1982. (ISBN 0-689-30890-6). Atheneum.

--Wales' Tale. 1st ed. Hirsh, Marilyn (1944-), illus. LC 79-21985. (Illus.). 32 p. 23cm. c.1980. (ISBN 0-670-74870-6). Viking Press.

Saunders, Violette

--Dear Matilda: Letters from Mike to Matilda. 1st ed. Negulesco, Dusty, illus. LC 57-14149. 63p. illus. 21cm. 1957. Exposition Press.

Saunders, Winnie Crandall

--Daughters of Dakota. Peck, Anne Merriman (1884-), illus. LC 60-5627. 184p. illus. 22cm. 1960. Caxton Printers.

Sauro, Regina Calderone (1924-)

--Too-Long Trunk. Petie, Haris, pseud. (1915-), illus. Petty, Roberta. LC 64-10340. (Illus.). (ps-2). 1964. (ISBN 0-8313-0085-X). Lantern.

Sauser-Hall, Frederic see Cendrars, Blaise, pseud.

Sautel, Maureen Ann see McGinn, Maureen, pseud.

Sauter, Edwin Charles Scott, Jr., jt. auth. see Hennessy, Maurice N.

Sauvage, Elie

--The Little Gypsy. Frolich, Lorenz, illus. Luyster, I. M., tr. N.D. Roberts Bros.

Savage, Alma Helen (1900-)

--Eben, the Crane. Keller, Charles, illus. LC 44-403729. 74, 2 p. col. illus. 23 1/2 cm. 1944. Sheed & Ward.

--Holiday in Alaska. Nielsen, Jon (1912-), illus. LC 45-1819. 80 p. incl. col. front., illus. (part col.) 21 cm. (Half-title: New world neighbors). c.1944. D. C. Heath and Company.

--Kulik's First Seal Hunt. McGrath, Anthony A., illus. LC 48-9564. ix, 114 p. illus. 21 cm. 1948. St. Anthony Guild Press.

--Smoozie, the Story of an Alaskan Reindeer Fawn. Keller, Charles, illus. LC 41-19432. 4 p. l., 68, 1 p. incl. front., illus. 23 1/2 cm. 1941. Sheed & Ward.

Savage, Blake, pseud., see Goodwin, Harold Leland.

Savage, Blake, pseud. (1914-)

--Rip Foster Rides the Gray Planet. Goodwin, Harold Leland. Cate, E. Deane, illus. LC 52-4711. 250 p. illus. 21 cm. 1952. Whitman Pub. Co.

Savage, Charles D.

--Chris the Christmas Cricket. Heflin, Mary L., ed. Martin-Meek, Martha S., illus. (Illus.). (ps-3). 1978. (ISBN 0-9602198-0-3). Adolph Green.

Savage, Dennis

--One Man's Moon. 1960. Friendship Press.

Savage, Joan (1922-)

--Hurray for Bobo. Schwartz, Berta (1922-), illus. LC 47-20338. 37 p. illus. (part col.) 19 1/2 x 17 cm. (Star-bright book. S-304). 1947. Childrens Press, Inc.

--Hurray for Bobo. I new ed. Schwartz, Berta (1922-), illus. LC 57-3762. unpaged. illus. 24cm. 1957, c.1947. Childrens Press.

Savage, Josephine

--Daughter of Delaware. LC 63-159216. 189p. 21cm. c.1964. John Day.

--Gunpowder Girl. Orbaan, Albert F. (1913-), illus. LC 58-9708. 192p. illus. 22cm. 1958. J. Day Co.

Savage, Kathleen, jt. auth. see Siewert, Margaret.

Savage, Les

--The Phantom Stallion. McCann, Gerald (1916-), illus. LC 55-5861. 178p. illus. 21cm. 1955. Dodd, Mead.

Savage, Peter, jt. auth. see Swayne, Dick.

Savery, Constance Winifred (1897-)

--Dark House on the Moss. LC 48-53427. 216 p. 21 cm. 1948. Longmans, Green.

--Emeralds for the King. Dowling, Victor J. (1906-), illus. LC 45-3234. vi p., 2 l., 270 p. illus. 21 cm. 1945. Longmans, Green & Co.

--Enemy Brothers. Pitz, Henry Clarence (1895-1976), illus. LC 43-51243. vi, 313 p. illus. 21 cm. 1943. Longmans, Green and Co.

--Flight to Freedom. N.D. Christian Lit.

--The Good Ship Red Lily. Walker, Nedda, illus. LC 44-7071. vii p., 1 l., 197 p. illus. 21 cm. 1944. Longmans, Green and Co.

--Magic in My Shoes. 1st ed. Price, Christine Hilda (1928-1980), illus. LC 58-7331. (Illus.). 152 p. 21cm. 1958. Longmans.

--Moonshine in Candle Street. Birch, Reginald Bathurst (1856-1943), illus. LC 37-16938. vii, 149 p. illus., plates. 20 cm. 1937. Longmans, Green and Co.

--Pippin's House: An East Anglian Story. Bowman, Charlot, illus. LC 31-254182. ix p., 1 l., 207 p. incl. front., illus., plates. 19 1/2 cm. 1931. Longmans, Green and Co.

--The Reb and the Redcoats. 1st ed. Bock, Vera, illus. LC 61-11481. (Illus.). 241 p. 21cm. 1961. Longmans, Green.

--Welcome Santza. Torrey, Helen (1901-), illus. LC 55-8313. 166p. illus. 22cm. 1956. Longmans, Green.

Save the Children Fund, London see Aiken, Joan.

Saville, Frank E, jt. auth. see Burleson, Grey.

Saville, Leonard Malcolm (1901-1982)

--Not Scarlet But Gold. N.D. Transatlantic Arts.

--The Secret of the Ambermere Treasure. Foster, Marcia Lane (1897-), illus. LC 67-11911. (Illus.). 221 p. 22cm. 1967, c.1953. Criterion Books.

--Spy in the Hills. LC 45-889319. 6 p. l., 3-244 p. incl. front. 19 cm. 1945. Farrar & Rinehart, Inc.

--Young's Johnnie Bimbo. N.D. Transatlantic Arts.

Saville, Malcolm see Saville, Leonard Malcolm.

Saviozzi, Adriana, pseud., see Mazza, Adriana.

Saviozzi, Adriana, pseud. (1928-)

--Somebody Saw. Mazza, Adriana. Saviozzi, Adriana, pseud. (1928-), illus. Mazza, Adriana. LC 62-9060. (Illus.). unpaged. 26cm. 32p. 1962. World Pub. Co.

Saviozzi, Adriana, pseud. (1928-), illus.

--Nursery Songs. Mazza, Adriana. Gale, Leah, contrib. by. (Little Golden Book). 1959. Golden Press.

Savitri

--Savitri & Satyavan. Wheaton, Jaya, illus. (Illus.). (gr. 1-9). 1979. (ISBN 0-89744-160-5). Auromere.

Savitri & Dutta, S.

--Shakuntala. Varma, B. G., illus. (Illus.). (gr. 1-9). 1979. (ISBN 0-89744-161-3). Auromere.

Savitt, Sam, jt. auth. see Kraus, Robert.

Savitt, Sam (1917-)

--A Day at the LBJ Ranch. Savitt, Sam (1917-), illus. LC 64-855592. 54p. col. illus. 24cm. c.1965. Random.

--The Dingle Ridge Fox & Other Stories. Savitt, Sam (1917-), illus. LC 78-7739. (Illus.). 22cm. 122p. (gr. 5 up). 1978. Dodd.

--The Dingle Ridge Fox & Other Stories. Savitt, Sam (1917-), illus. 128p. (Orig., Pub. by Dodd, Mead & Co.). (gr. 4-6). 1980. (ISBN 0-590-05733-2). Scholastic Inc.

--A Horse to Remember. Savitt, Sam (1917-), illus. LC 85-43420. p. cm. 1986, c.1984. (ISBN 0-14-032029-6). Puffin Books.

--A Horse To Remember. Savitt, Sam (1917-), illus. LC 83-16655. (Illus.). 128p. (gr. 7-9). 1984. (ISBN 0-670-37920-4, Viking Kestrel). Viking.

--Midnight, Champion Bucking Horse. 1st ed. Savitt, Sam (1917-), illus. LC 57-12026. 118p. illus. 23cm. 1957. Dutton.

--Midnight, Champion Bucking Horse. Savitt, Sam (1917-), illus. LC 74-5490. (Illus.). 118 p. 21cm. 1974, c.1957. (ISBN 0-8193-0745-9). (ISBN 0-8193-0745-9). Parents' Magazine Press.

--Springfellow. (ps-2). 1978. (Windmill). Dutton.

AUTHOR INDEX SAYLER, HARRY

--Step-A-Bit: The Story of a Foal. LC 56-8294. 68p. illus. 24x27cm. 1956. Dutton.
--There Was a Horse. Savitt, Sam (1917-), illus. LC 61-12910. 96p. illus. 24cm. 1961. Dial Press.
--Vicki and the Black Horse. 1st ed. Savitt, Sam (1917-), illus. LC 64-13849. 160 p. illus. 22 cm. 1964. Doubleday.
--Vicki and the Brown Mare. Savitt, Sam (1917-), illus. LC 76-12503. (Illus.). 156 p. 22cm. c.1976. (ISBN 0-396-07362-X). Dodd, Mead.
--Wild Horse Running. Savitt, Sam (1917-), illus. LC 73-2132. (Illus.). 126 p. 24cm. 1973. (ISBN 0-396-06808-1). Dodd, Mead.

Savitz, Harriet May, jt. auth. see Shecktor, M. Caporale.

Savitz, Harriet May (1933-)
--Fly, Wheels, Fly!. LC 71-101161. 90 p. 21cm. 1970. John Day Co.
--The Lionhearted. LC 75-6878. 149 p. 21cm. 1975. (ISBN 0-381-99623-9). John Day Co.
--On the Move. LC 72-12093. 144 p. 21cm. 1973. (ISBN 0-381-99641-7). John Day Co.
--Run, Don't Walk: A Novel. LC 79-14612. 122 p. 22cm. 1979. (ISBN 0-531-02897-6). Watts.

Savitz, Harriet May (1933-) & Shecktor, M. Caporale
--Peter & Other Stories. LC 74-89321. 96p. (gr. 6-9). 1969. (ISBN 0-381-99714-6). John Day.

Savoldi, Gloria Root
--Mystery of the Old Dutch Chest. Brudi, Theresa, illus. LC 65-23590. 22cm. 157p. 1965. Criterion Books.
--Tennessee Boy. LC 76-185927. 159 p. 21cm. 1972. (ISBN 0-664-32513-0). Westminster Press.

Savonarola, Ghirolamo Maria Francesco Matteo, jt. auth. see Cipriani, Charlotte Jane.

Savory, Phyllis
--Congo Fireside Tales. Tolford, Joshua (1909-), illus. (Illus.). (gr. 4-6). 1962. (ISBN 0-8038-1112-8). Hastings.
--Lion Outwitted by Hare & Other African Tales. Altschuler, Franz (1923-), illus. LC 74-126432. (Illus.). line ils. 160p. (Folklore Ser). (gr. 3 up). 1971. (ISBN 0-8075-4556-2). A Whitman.
--The Song of the Golden Birds. Hulme, Jillian, illus. 31 line drawings. 78p. (gr. 2-6). 1971. (ISBN 0-535-00032-4). Tri-Ocean.

Savryn, L., ed.
--Once upon a Cat. Mitchell, Kathy, illus. LC 82-83751. (Illus.). 48p. (ps-3). 1983. (ISBN 0-448-46625-2, G&D). Putnam Pub Group.

Sawitz, Mike, jt. auth. see Ourth, John.

Sawkins, Raymond Harold see Forbes, Colin, pseud.

Sawyer, Astrid Rosing, tr. see Gredsted, Torry.

Sawyer, Edith Augusta (1869-)
--The Christmas Makers' Club. Williamsom, Ada Clendenin, illus. LC 8-22344. 5 p. l., 275 p. front., 5 pl. 20 1/2 cm. 1908. L. C. Page & Company.
--Denise of the Three Pines. Withington, Elizabeth R., illus. LC 22-13123. 20cm. 315p. 1922. Page Co.
--Elsa's Gift Home: Or, More About the Christmas Makers' Club. Nosworthy, Florence England, illus. LC 11-14715. 5 p. l., 229 p. front., plates. 20 1/2 cm. 1911. L. C. Page & Company.
--Jose, Our Little Portuguese Cousin. Horne, Diantha W., illus. LC 11-13983. (The Little Cousin Ser.). 1911. L. C. Page & Co.
--Merin and Shari: A Boy and Girl of Mongolia. Ayer, Margaret (0000-1981), illus. viii, 126, 2 p. incl. col. front., illus. 21 1/2 cm. c.1938. Thomas Y. Crowell Company.

Sawyer, Edith Augusta (1869-) & Walmsley, Alice Freeman
--Madge at Camp Welles: Or, Summer Holidays on a New Hampshire Lake. Kirkpatrick, William, illus. (Illus.). 327p. N.D. W. A. Wilde Co.

Sawyer, Edna, illus.
--The Enchanted Automobile. Safford, Mary Joanna, tr. from Fr. (Illus.). 4tocm. N.D. L. C. Page & Co.

Sawyer, Henry S., jt. auth. see Casey, Beatrice Marie.

Sawyer, Paul
--Mom's New Job. Bostrom, Roald, illus. LC 77-27982. (Illus.). 30 p. 25cm. c.1978. (ISBN 0-8172-1150-0). Childrens Press.
--New Neighbors. Atterberry, Jay P., illus. LC 77-27974. (Illus.). (Moods & Emotions Ser.). (gr. k-3). 1978. (ISBN 0-8172-1156-X). Raintree Pubs.
--There Once Was a Book of Limericks. Redman, Tom, et al., illus. LC 77-27109. (Illus.). 47 p. 25cm. c.1978. (ISBN 0-8172-1168-3). Raintree Childrens Books.

Sawyer, Ruth Estelle (1880-1970)
--Annabel. Sawyer, Ruth Estelle (1880-1970), illus. LC 41-23282. 5 p. l., 9-37 p. col. illus. 28 cm. 1941. Falmouth Publishing House.
--A Child's Yearbook. Sawyer, Ruth Estelle (1880-1970), illus. LC 17-29876. (Illus.). 30p. 1917. Harper & Bros.
--The Christmas Anna Angel. Seredy, Kate (1899-1975), illus. LC 44-933871. 48 p., 1 l. incl. col. front., illus. (part col.) 22 1/2 x 17 1/2 cm. 1944. The Viking Press. **Award: (RCM).**
--A Cottage for Betsy. Bock, Vera, illus. LC 54-8988. 120p. illus. 21cm. 1954. Harper.
--Daddles: The Story of a Plain Hound-Dog. 1st ed. Frankenberg, Robert Clinton (1911-), illus. LC 64-10180. 99 p. illus. 22 cm. c.1964. Little, Brown.
--The Enchanted Schoolhouse. Troy, Hugh (1906-1964), illus. LC 56-12185. (Illus.). 128 p. 25cm. 1956. Viking Press.
--Journey Cake, Ho!. McCloskey, John Robert (1914-1969), illus. LC 77-15996. (Illus.). 45 p. 23cm. (Picture puffin). 1978, c.1953. (ISBN 0-14-050173-0). Puffin Books.
--Journey Cake, Ho!. McCloskey, John Robert (1914-1969), illus. LC 53-3366. 45 p. 27cm. 1953. Viking Press. **Awards: (ALA); (RCM).**
--Journey Cake, Ho!. McCloskey, John Robert (1914-1969), illus. LC 82-4784. (Illus.). 45 p. 27cm. 1982, c.1981. (ISBN 0-670-40943-X). Viking.
--Joy to the World: Christmas Legends. Hyman, Trina Schart (1939-), illus. LC 66-14905. (Illus.). 24cm. 102p. (A book of six Christmas stories gathered and retold by the great storyteller, with accompanying ballads). (gr. 3 up). 1966. (ISBN 0-316-77177-5). Little. **Award: (ALA).**
--The Least One. Politi, Leo (1908-), illus. LC 41-218841. 88, 1 p. illus. (part col.) 25 1/2 cm. 1941. The Viking Press.
--The Little Red Horse. Barnum, Jay Hyde (1888-1962), illus. LC 50-101252. (Illus.). 108 p. 22cm. 1950. Viking Press.
--The Long Christmas. Angelo, Valenti (1897-), illus. LC 41-51959. 200 p. incl. front., illus. 23 1/2 cm. 1941. The Viking Press.
--Maggie Rose: Her Birthday Christmas. 1st ed. Sendak, Maurice Bernard (1928-), illus. LC 52-7882. (Illus.). 151 p. 20cm. 1952. (ISBN 0-06-025201-4). Harper.
--My Spain: A Storyteller's Year of Collecting. (gr. 9 up). 1967. (ISBN 0-670-50110-7). Viking Pr.
--Old Con and Patrick. O'Toole, Cathal, illus. LC 46-11980. 137, 1 p. col. front., illus. 21 1/2 cm. 1946. The Viking Press.
--Oscar. LC 40-4880. 27, 1 p. illus. 27 cm. 1939. Falmouth Publishing House.
--Picture Tales from Spain. Sanchez, Carlos M. (1908-), illus. LC 36-27442. ix p., 1 l., 132 p. incl. illus., plates. 14 x 18 1/2 cm. 1936. Frederick A. Stokes Company.
Picture Tales from Spain. Sanchez, Carlos M. (1908-), illus. 1936. J. B. Lippincott Co.
--Roller Skates. Angelo, Valenti (1897-), illus. LC 36-23268. 4 p. l., 3-186 p. illus. 23 1/2 cm. 1936. The Viking Press. **Award: (JNM).**
--The Tale of the Enchanted Bunnies. LC 23-12521. 4 p. l., ii p., 1 l., 137, 1 p. incl. col. illus., col. plates. 24 cm. c.1923. Harper & Brothers.
--This Is the Christmas: A Serbian Folk Tale. LC 45-9579. 43 p. 17 1/2 cm. 1945. The Horn Book.
--This Way to Christmas. Barney, Maginel Wright, Mrs. (1881-1966), illus. LC 16-20438. 5 p. l., 165, 1 p. front. 19 1/2 cm. 1916. Harper & Brothers.
--This Way to Christmas. Barney, Maginel Wright, Mrs. (1881-1966), illus. LC 24-27648. 7p. 1., 175p. col. front., col. plates. 24cm. 1924. Harper.
--This Way to Christmas. Barney, Maginel Wright, Mrs. (1881-1966), illus. LC 68-808. 175 p. col. illus. 24 cm. c.1952. Harper & Row.
--Tono Antonio. Mora, F. Luis, illus. LC 34-31648. 132 p. incl. illus., plates. 23 cm. 1934. The Viking Press.
--Way of the Storyteller. rev. ed. 1977. (ISBN 0-14-004436-1). Penguin.
--The Year of Jubilo. Shenton, Edward (1895-), illus. LC 40-27712. 266 p. illus. 22 cm. 1940. The Viking Press.
--The Year of the Christmas Dragon. Troy, Hugh (1906-1964), illus. LC 60-5063. (Illus.). 88 p. 24cm. 1960. Viking Press.

Sawyer, Ruth Estelle (1880-1970) & Molles, Emmy, eds.
--Dietrich of Berne and the Dwarf King Laurin: Hero Tales of the Austrian Tirol. Chapman, Frederick Trench (1887-), illus. LC 63-8524. 190 p. illus. 22 cm. c.1963. Viking Press.

Sawyer, Walter Leon see Standish, Winn, pseud.

Sawyer, Walter Leon (1862-1915)
--Captain Jack Lorimer: Or, the Young Athletes of Millvale High. Standish, Winn, pseud. Brown, Arthur William & Gowing, Louis D., illus. 3 p. l., ix-x p., 1 l., 296 p. front., 5 pl 21 cm. (The Jack Lorimer Ser.). 1906. L. C. Page & Company.
--Jack Lorimer, Freshman: Or, From Millvale High to Exmouth. Standish, Winn, pseud. Cue, Harold, illus. LC 12-22555. viii p., 1 l., 302 p. front., plates. 20 1/2 cm. (His The Jack Lorimer series) $1.50). 1912. L. C. Page & Company.
--Jack Lorimer's Champions: Or, Sports on Land and Lake. Standish, Winn, pseud. Bonnar, James K., illus. LC 7-23939. 3 pl., v-x p., 1 l., 300 p. front., 6 pl. 21 cm. (On verso of half-title: The Jack Lorimer series). 1907. L. C. Page & Company.
--Jack Lorimer's Holidays: Or, Millvale High in Camp. Standish, Winn, pseud. Fairbanks, Frank P., illus. LC 8-16516. ix, 1 p., 1 l., 293 p. front., 6 pl. 21 cm. (On verso of half-title: The Jack Lorimer series). 1908. L. C. Page & Company.
--Jack Lorimer's Substitute: Or, the Acting Captain of the Team. Standish, Winn, pseud. Goss, John, illus. LC 9-19037. x p., 1 l., 286 p. front., 5 pl. 21 cm. (The Jack Lorimer Ser.). 1909. L. C. Page & Company.

Saxby, E. M.
--Winnie's Golden Key. (Illus.). 80p. (The Rosebud Ser.). N.D. Fleming H. Revell Co.

Saxby, Jessie Margaret Edmonston (1842-)
--Their First Place. (Illus.). N.D. Society for Promoting Christian Knowledge.
--The Viking Boys. N.D. Thomas Whittaker.

Saxby, Lewis
--The Life of a Wooden Doll. LC 3-26362. 63 p. incl. front., illus. 20 1/2 x 25 cm. 1903. Fox, Duffield & Company.

Saxby, Mrs.
--Breakers Ahead: Or, Uncle Jack's Stories of Great Shipwrecks of Recent Times, 1869 to 1880. (Illus.). N.D. Thos Nelson & sons.

Saxe, John Godfrey (1816-1887)
--Blind Men & the Elephant. Galdone, Paul (1914-), illus. LC 62-20729. (Illus.). (gr. k-3). 1963. (ISBN 0-07-055003-4). McGraw.
--Clever Stories of Many Nations: Rendered in Rhyme. N.D. James R. Osgood.
--Fables and Legends of Many Countries: Rendered in Rhyme. N.D. James R. Osgood.

Saxe, Mary Solace (1875-)
--Our Little Quebec Cousin. Meister, Charles E., illus. LC 19-7822. 3 p. l., v-vii p., 1 l., 122 p. front., plates. 19 1/2 cm. (On verso of half-title: The little cousin series). 1919. The Page Company.

Saxelby, E.
--Coquerico. 1959. Ginn & Co.

Saxon, Carl
--Blackie Thorne at Camp Lenape. LC 31-29020. 211 p. incl. front. 19 cm. c.1931. The Penn Publishing Company.
--Camp Lenape on the Long Trail. Marder, David, illus. LC 35-25385. 224 p. incl. front. 19 cm. c.1935. The Penn Publishing Company.
--The Mystery at Camp Lenape. LC 31-290191. 223 p. incl. front. 19 cm. c.1931. The Penn Publishing Company.

Saxon, Charles D.
--Don't Worry About Poopsie. Saxon, Charles D., illus. LC 58-8400. unpaged. illus. 27cm. 1958. Dodd, Mead.

Saxon, Gladys Relyea see Seyton, Marion, pseud.

Saxon, Gladys Relyea
--All Around the Land. Polseno, Jo, illus. LC 58-6518. (Illus.). 22cm. 127p. 1958. Holt Rinehart & Winston.
--California Camel Adventure. Wilson, Helen Hughes, illus. LC 55-7978. 183p. illus. 22cm. 1955. Caxton Printers.
--Four Proud Days. Fellin, Peter, illus. LC 61-8565. unpaged. illus. 22cm. (Wonderful world book). 1961. Barnes.
--How Fast. Harris, Isabel Sherwin, illus. LC 51-6528. unpaged. illus. 21cm. 1954. Crowell.
--The Night the Storm Came. 1st ed. Maclain, Scott, illus. LC 51-12375. unpaged. illus. 22cm. 1951. Aladdin Books.
--Sea Beach Adventure. Galdone, Paul (1914-), illus. LC 56-10038. (Illus.). 190p. (gr. 4-6). 1956. (ISBN 0-03-032600-1). HR&W.

Saxon, Nancy
--Panky and William. LC 83-2633. p. cm. 1983. (ISBN 0-689-30997-X). Atheneum.
--Panky in the Saddle. Saxon, Charles D., illus. LC 83-15910. (Illus.). 160p. (gr. 3-7). 1984. (ISBN 0-689-31038-2). Atheneum.

Saxon, Nancy & Saxon, Peter
--Panky in Love. Saxon, Charles D., illus. LC 84-21747. (Illus.). 155 p. 22cm. 1985. (ISBN 0-689-31101-X). Atheneum.

Saxon, Peter, jt. auth. see Saxon, Nancy.

Saxton, Josephine Mary (1935-)
--The Hieros Gamos of Sam and an Smith (Pub. by Doubleday). (gr. 9 up). 1972. Curtis.

Say, Allen (1937-)
--The Bicycle Man. Say, Allen (1937-), illus. (Illus.). (gr. k-3). 1982. (ISBN 0-395-32254-5). HM. **Award: (ALA).**
--Dr. Smith's Safari. LC 78-184401. (Illus.). 28 p. 22cm. 1972. (ISBN 0-06-025218-9). (ISBN 0-06-025219-7). Harper & Row.
--The Feast of Lanterns. LC 76-3836. (Illus.). 56 p. 23cm. c.1976. (ISBN 0-06-025213-8). (ISBN 0-06-025214-6). Harper & Row.
--The Ink-Keeper's Apprentice. LC 78-20264. 185 p. 21cm. c.1979. (ISBN 0-06-025208-1). Harper & Row. **Award: (ALA).**
--Once Under the Cherry Blossom Tree: An Old Japanese Tale. 1st ed. Say, Allen (1937-), illus. LC 73-14336. (Illus.). 31 p. 24cm. 1974. (ISBN 0-06-025216-2). (ISBN 0-06-025216-2). Harper & Row.

Sayers, Frances Clarke, Mrs. (1897-1957)
--Bluebonnets for Lucinda. Sewell, Helen Moore (1896-1957), illus. LC 34-230987. 32 p., illus. (part col.) 20 x 20 cm. 1934. The Viking Press.
--Ginny and Custard. Evans, Eileen, illus. LC 51-13570. (Illus.). 128 p. 22cm. 1951. Viking Press.
--Mr. Tidy Paws. Gay, Zhenya (1906-1978), illus. LC 35-19150. 64 p. illus. 23 1/2 cm. 1935. The Viking Press.
--Oscar Lincoln Busby Stokes. 1st ed. Anderson, Gunnar, illus. LC 69-13778. (Illus.). 32 p. 22cm. 1970. Harcourt, Brace & World.
--Sally Tait. Evans, Eileen, illus. LC 48-45232. 126 p. illus. 22 cm. 1948. Viking Press.
--Tag-Along Tooloo. Sewell, Helen Moore (1896-1957), illus. LC 41-187169. 6 p. l., 15-87 p. incl. illus., col. plates. 23 1/2 cm. 1941. The Viking Press.

Sayler, Harry Lincoln see Lamar, Ashton, pseud.

Sayler, Harry Lincoln see Stuart, Gordon, pseud.

Sayler, Harry Lincoln, jt. auth. see Whitney, Elliott.

Sayler, Harry Lincoln (1863-1913)
--The Aeroplane Express: Or, The Boy Aeronaut's Grit. Lamar, Ashton, pseud. Riesenberg, S. H., illus. LC 12-1214. 20cm. 246p. (The Aeroplane Boys Ser.). 1910. Reilly & Britton Co.
--The Air Ship Boys: Or, the Quest of the Aztec Treasure. Lamar, Ashton, pseud. Harper, Frank Robert (1908-), illus. LC 9-15995. 315 p. front., illus. (map) 3 pl. (1 double) 19 1/2 cm. c.1909. The Reilly & Britton Co.
--The Airship Boys Adrift: Or, Saved by an Aeroplane. Lamar, Ashton, pseud. 2nd ed. Smith, J. O., illus. LC 10-1469. vi p., 1 l., 312 p. front., 2 pl., 2 diagr. 19 1/2 cm. (His The airship boys series) $1.00). 1909. The Reilly & Britton Co.
--The Airship Boys as Detective: Or, Secret Service in Cloudland. Lamar, Ashton, pseud. (The Airship Boys). N.D. The Reilly & Britton Co.
--The Airship Boys Due North: Or By Balloon to the Pole. Lamar, Ashton, pseud. Riesenberg, S. H., illus. LC 10-15097. vi p., 1 l., 9-335 p. front., plates. 19 1/2 cm. (His The airship boys series). c.1910. The Reilly & Britton Co.
--The Airship Boys in Finance: Or, The Flight of the Flying Cow. Lamar, Ashton, pseud. Riesenberg, S. H., illus. LC 11-318920. 295 p. front., plates. 19 1/2 cm. (His The airship boys series). c.1911. The Reilly & Britton Co.
--The Airship Boys in The Barren Lands: Or, The Secret of the White Eskimos. Lamar, Ashton, pseud. Harper, Frank Robert (1908-) & Riesenberg, S. H., illus. (The Airship Boys Ser.). N.D. Reilly & Britton Co.
--The Airship Boys in the Great War: Or, The Rescue of Bob Russell. Lamar, Ashton, pseud. (The Airship Boys Ser.). N.D. The Reilly & Britton Co.
--The Airship Boys' Ocean Flyer: Or, New York to London in Twelve Hours. Lamar, Ashton, pseud. Riesenberg, S. H., illus. LC 11-324484. vi p., 1 l., 9-327 p. front., plates. 20 cm. (His The airship boys series)). c.1911. The Reilly & Britton Co.
--Battling the Bighorn: Or, The Aeroplane in the Rockies. Lamar, Ashton, pseud. Nuyttens, Joseph Pierre, illus. LC 11-32425. 20cm. 280p. (The Aeroplane Boys Ser.). 1911. Reilly & Britton Co.
--A Cruise in the Sky: Or, the Legend of the Great Pink Pearl. Lamar, Ashton, pseud. Riesenberg, S. H., illus. LC 11-20879. 218 p. incl. plates. col. front. 19 1/2 cm. (His The aeroplane boys series)). c.1911. The Reilly & Britton Co.
--In the Clouds for Uncle Sam: Or, Morey Marshall of the Signal Corps. Lamar, Ashton, pseud. Riesenberg, S. H., illus. LC 10-6489. 4 p. l., 216 p. incl. plates. col. front. 19 cm. (His The aeroplane boys series). c.1910. The Reilly & Britton Co.
--Johnny Hep: The Soldier Boy. Lamar, Ashton, pseud. Sayler, Harry Lincoln (1863-1913), illus. N.D. Reilly & Britton Co.
--On the Edge of the Arctic: Or, an Aeroplane in Snowland. Lamar, Ashton, pseud. Hall, Norman P., illus. LC 13-24795. 256 p. incl. plates. front. 20 cm. (His The aeroplane boys series)). c.1913. The Reilly & Britton Co.
--Terrible Teddy and Peaceful Bill: Or, The Quest of the Treasure Box. Lamar, Ashton, pseud. Gallup, Francis, illus. LC 8-14516. 19cm. 184p. 1908. Reilly & Britton Co.

--When Scout Meets Scout: Or, The Aeroplane Spy. Lamar, Ashton, pseud. Riesenberg, S. H., illus. LC 12-13901. 249 p. col. front., plates. 19 1/2 cm. (His The aeroplane boys series)). c.1912. The Reilly & Britton Co.

Sayler, Mary Harwell

--Downhill Flats. Wahl, Richard (1939-), illus. LC 81-67373. (Illus.). 96 p. 20cm. c.1982. (ISBN 0-8054-4805-5). Broadman Press.

--Hard-Luck Holly. Wahl, Richard (1939-), illus. LC 82-7229. 1984, c.1983. (ISBN 0-8054-4807-1). Broadman Press.

--Why Are You Home, Dad?. Ham, John, illus. (gr. 1-6). 1983. (ISBN 0-8054-4276-6). Broadman.

Sayles, Arlen A

--The Pied Piper of Heaven. LC 70-163079. (Illus.). vii, 31 p. 22cm. 1971. (ISBN 0-8059-1589-3). Dorrance.

Sayles, Edwin Booth, jt. auth. see Stevens, Mary Ellen.

Sayles, Edwin Booth (1892-) & Stevens, Mary Ellen

--Throw Stone, the First American Boy: Twenty-Five Thousand Years Ago. Wright, Barton, illus. LC 60-12007. 142p. illus. 24cm. 1960. Reilly Lee,.

Sayre, Anne (1923-)

--Never Call Retreat. 192p. 1957. Thomas Y. Crowell Co.

Sayre, Paul (1894-)

--The Adventures of Bozo. LC 40-9822. 4 p. l., 161 p. 24 cm. c.1940. Athens Press.

Sazer, Nina (1949-)

--What Do You Think I Saw?. A Nonsense Number Book. Ehlert, Lois Jane (1934-), illus. LC 75-26643. (Illus.). 32 p. c.1976. (ISBN 0-394-83182-9). (ISBN 0-394-93182-3). Pantheon Books.

Scacheri, Mabel, Mrs., jt. auth. see Scacheri, Mario.

Scacheri, Mario & Scacheri, Mabel, Mrs.

--Winnebago Boy. LC 37-169401. x p. l., 182, 1 p. illus. 24 cm. c.1937. Harcourt, Brace and Company.

Scaduto, Al, jt. auth. see Smoller, Mark H.

Scaife, Roger Livingston see Livingston, Robert, pseud.

Scaife, Roger Livingston (1875-)

--The Land of the Great-Out-of-Doors. Livingston, Robert, pseud. Day, Maurice (1892-), illus. LC 20-17525. 5 p. l., 142, 2 p. col. front., col. plates. 21 cm. $2.0. 1920. Houghton Mifflin Company.

--Muvver and Me: Old-Fashioned Rhymes for New-Fangled Kiddies. Livingston, Robert, pseud. Winter, Milo Kendall (1888-1956), illus. LC 17-25769. vii, 98, 2 p., 1 l. col. front., illus. 19 1/2 cm. 1917. Houghton Mifflin Company.

--What Daddies Do: Old Fashioned Rhymes for New Fangled Kiddies. Livingston, Robert, pseud. Hunt, Alice Ercle, illus. LC 16-22650. vii, 1, 96, 2 p. illus. 19 1/2 cm. 1916. Houghton Mifflin Company.

--What Daddies do: Old Fashioned Rhymes for New Fangled Kiddies. Livingston, Robert, pseud. Hunt, Alice Ercle, illus. LC 29-9015. 19cm. 1929. Houghton Mifflin Co.

Scally, Kevin

--How to Wake a Sleeping Beauty. Scally, Kevin, illus. (Illus.). 32p. (Magic Road Bks.). (ps-3). 1984. (ISBN 0-448-11128-4, G&D). Putnam Pub Group.

--Save the Three Pigs. Scally, Kevin, illus. (Illus.). 32p. (Magic Road Bks.). (ps-3). 1984. (ISBN 0-448-11127-6, G&D). Putnam Pub Group.

--Story of Red Riding Hood. Scally, Kevin, illus. (Illus.). 32p. (Magic Road Bks.). (ps-3). 1984. (ISBN 0-448-11126-8, G&D). Putnam Pub Group.

--The Three Bears. Scally, Kevin, illus. (Illus.). 32p. (Magic Road Bk.). (ps-3). 1984. (ISBN 0-448-11129-2, G&D). Putnam Pub Group.

Scandlin, Christiana

--Hans the Eskimo: A Story of Arctic Adventure. LC 3-7166. 125 p. incl. front., illus., pl. 19 cm. 1903. Silver, Burdett and Company.

Scanlon, Marion Stephany

--Little Johnnie Trout. Spiegel, Lawrence M., illus. LC 62-19896. (Illus.). 20p. (Nature & Science Bk. Ser.). (gr. k-6). 1962. (ISBN 0-513-00364-9). Denison.

--Three Little Clouds. Jones, Catherine O., illus. LC 59-13954. unpaged. illus. 29cm. 1959. T. S. Denison.

Scanlon, Tony

--Cry on a Foggy Night. Boucher, John, illus. LC 68-28963. (Illus.). 59 p. 19cm. (Trend books). 1969. Cheshire.

--Gaye Lizzie. Howell, Elizabeth, illus. LC 68-16548. (Illus.). 74 p. 18cm. (Trend books). 1969. Cheshire.

--The Snowdroppers. Weg, illus. LC 68-16549. (Illus.). 79 p. 19cm. (Trend books). 1969. Cheshire.

Scanlon, Tony, jt. auth. see Bird, Bettina.

Scannell, Edith, jt. auth. see Scannell, Florence.

Scannell, Florence

--The Little Musician: Christmas in Italy. Scannell, Edith M., illus. LC 13-2085. 20cm. 32p. (Christmas in Many Lands' Ser). 1912. Estes & Lauriat's.

Scannell, Florence & Scannell, Edith

--Dulce's Promise: Christmas in England. (Illus.). 20cm. 32p. (Christmas in Many Lands' Series). 1912. Estes & Lauriat's.

--Jean Noel: Christmas in France. (Illus.). 20cm. 32p. (Christmas in Many Lands' Series). 1912. Estes & Lauriat's.

--Lischen and the Fairy: Christmas in Germany. (Illus.). 32p. (Christmas in Many Lands' Ser). 1912. Estes &n Lauriat's.

Scannell, Vernon

--The Dangerous Ones. LC 76-108015. 94 p. 22cm. (The Pergamon English Library). 1970. Pergamon Press.

Scarato, Giorgio & Spaliviero, Franco, illus.

--The Three Bears. LC 84-18689. p. cm. (Upside down books). c.1985. (ISBN 0-88110-250-4). Educational Development Corp.

Scarborough, Alma May C. (1913-)

--I Help Too. Teichman, Dorothy, illus. LC 61-5064. (Illus.). (ps). 1961. (ISBN 0-8054-4121-2). Broadman.

--Sing Me a Bible Song. (ps-3). 1969. (ISBN 0-8054-4149-2). (ISBN 0-8054-4606-0). Broadman.

Scarborough, Mildred

--A Cape Ann Chronicle: Or, Lily's Garden. LC 12-38367. 192 p. front., plates. 19 cm. c.1896. American Baptist Publication Society.

--Dorothy Doremus. LC 12-38368. vi, 7-216 p. incl. front. 19 1/2 cm. c.1891. The American Sunday-School Union.

--Olive's Expiation. 236p. N.D. Sunday-School Publications.

--The Parramore Children. 312p. N.D. American Baptist Publishing Society.

--Tangled Threads: Or, Linda's Awakening. LC 12-383706. 3 p. l., 5-192 p. 18 1/2 cm. c.1891. American Baptist Publication Society.

Scargill, William Pitt (1787-1836)

--Recollections of a Blue-Coat Boy: Or, a View of Christ's Hospital. LC 68-18215. 208p. illus. 16cm. (Early Children's Bks.). 1968. S. R. Publishers.

Scariano, Margaret M.

--Bigfoot & the Timberland Mystery. 96p. (Orig.). (Voyager Ser.). 1982. (ISBN 0-8010-8225-0). Baker Bk.

--To Catch a Mugger. LC 81-22850. (Illus.). 44 p. 18cm. (Perspectives book). c.1982. (ISBN 0-87879-298-8). Academic Therapy Publications.

Scarry, Huck, pseud., see Scarry, Richard Jr..

Scarry, Huck, pseud. (1953-)

--Huck Scarry's Steam Train Journey. Scarry, Richard Jr.. LC 79-11532. (Illus.). 1979. (ISBN 0-529-05538-4, Philomel). (ISBN 0-529-05550-3). Putnam Pub Group.

--Looking into the Middle Ages. Scarry, Richard Jr.. Scarry, Huck (1953-), illus. LC 84-47626. (Illus.). 12p. (ps-12). 1985. (ISBN 0-06-025224-3). HarpJ.

Scarry, Patricia Murphy (1924-)

--The Bunny Book. Scarry, Richard McClure (1919-), illus. LC 55-163223. unpaged. illus. 21cm. (Little golden book, 215). 1955. Simon and Schuster.

--Corky. Wilde, Irma, illus. (Illus.). 24p. (gr. k-3). 1976. (ISBN 0-307-60086-6, Golden Pr). Western Pub.

--Danny Beaver's Secret. Scarry, Richard McClure (1919-), illus. LC 53-3029. 21cm. 28p. (Little golden library, 160). 1953. Simon and Schuster.

--The Golden Story Book of River Bend. Gergely, Tibor (1900-1978), illus. LC 76-81956. (Illus.). 93 p. 29cm. 1969. Golden Press.

--The Jeremy Mouse Book. Knight, Hilary (1926-), illus. LC 74-83817. (Illus.). 64 p. 29cm. 1969. (ISBN 0-07-055043-3). American Heritage Press.

--Just for Fun. Scarry, Richard McClure (1919-), illus. LC 60-1081. 31p. illus. 22cm. (Golden beginning reader, 4008). 1960. Golden Press.

--Little Richard. Szekeres, Cyndy (1933-), illus. LC 74-95737. (Illus.). 94 p. 17cm. 1970. American Heritage Press.

--Little Richard and Prickles. Szekeres, Cyndy (1933-), illus. LC 75-155178. (Illus.). 93 p. 18cm. 1971. (ISBN 0-07-055051-4). American Heritage Press.

--More About Waggy. Szekeres, Cyndy (1933-), illus. LC 72-7927. (Illus.). 91 p. 17cm. 1973. (ISBN 0-07-055052-2). (ISBN 0-07-055052-2). McGraw-Hill.

--More About Waggy and His Friends. Szekeres, Cyndy (1933-), illus. LC 72-4775. p. 1973, c.1972. (ISBN 0-07-055052-2). (ISBN 0-07-055053-0). American Heritage Press.

--My Baby Brother. Wilkin, Eloise Burns (1904-), illus. LC 57-1020. unpaged. illus. 21cm. (Little golden book, 279). c.1956. Simon And Schuster.

--My Baby Sister. Koester, Sharon Smith, illus. LC 68-7849. (Illus.). 24 p. 23cm. (Little golden book, 340). 1958. Golden Press.

--My Kitten. Wilkin, Eloise Burns (1904-), illus. LC 53-2379. 21cm. 28p. (Little golden library, 163). 1953. Simon and Schuster.

--My Pets. Wilkin, Eloise Burns (1904-), illus. (Giant Little Golden Book). 1959. Golden Press.

--My Puppy. Wilkin, Eloise Burns (1904-), illus. LC 55-127682. unpaged. illus. 21cm. (Little golden book, 233). 1955. Simon and Schuster.

--My Snuggly Bunny. Wilkin, Eloise Burns (1904-), illus. LC 56-1862. unpaged. illus. 21cm. (Little golden books, 250). 1956. Simon and Schuster.

--My Teddy Bear. Wilkin, Eloise Burns (1904-), illus. (Little Golden Book). 1954. Golden Press.

--My Teddy Bear. Wilkin, Eloise Burns (1904-), illus. LC 54-1146. unpaged. illus. 21cm. (Little golden book, 168). 1953. Simon and Schuster.

--Patsy Scarry's Bedtime Storybook. Szekeres, Cyndy (1933-), illus. LC 79-5450. (Illus.). 72p. (ps-2). 1980. (ISBN 0-394-83268-X). (ISBN 0-394-93268-4). Random.

--Pierre Bear. Scarry, Richard McClure (1919-), illus. LC 55-1020. unpaged. illus. 21cm. (Little golden book, 212). 1955, c.1954. Simon and Schuster.

--The Sweet Smell of Christmas. Miller, John Parr (1913-), illus. LC 78-119327. (Illus.). 30 p. 24cm. 1970. Golden Press.

--Waggy and His Friends. Szekeres, Cyndy (1933-), illus. LC 78-117365. (Illus.). 123 p. 18cm. 1971, c.1970. (ISBN 0-07-055048-4). American Heritage Press.

--The Wait-for-Me Kitten. Obligado, Lilian Isabel (1931-), illus. (Illus.). (ps-2). 1962. (ISBN 0-307-60643-0, Golden Pr). Western Pub.

Scarry, Richard Jr. see Scarry, Huck, pseud.

Scarry, Richard McClure (1919-), adapted by see La Fontaine, Jean de.

Scarry, Richard McClure (1919-)

--ABC Word Book. Scarry, Richard McClure (1919-), illus. LC 70-158377. (Illus.). 61 p. 33cm. 1971. (ISBN 0-394-82339-7). (ISBN 0-394-92339-1). Random House.

--The Adventures of Tinker and Tanker. Scarry, Richard McClure (1919-), illus. LC 68-29281. (Illus.). 96 p. 29cm. 1968, c.1961. Doubleday.

--At Work. Scarry, Richard McClure (1919-), illus. (Illus.). 24p. (Golden Look-Look Ser.). 1976. (ISBN 0-307-11824-X, Golden Pr). (ISBN 0-307-61824-2). Western Pub.

--The Best Mistake Ever! and Other Stories. Scarry, Richard McClure (1919-), illus. LC 84-2029. (Step into Reading. A Step 2 Book). c.1984. (ISBN 0-394-86816-1). Random House.

--Best Storybook Ever. Scarry, Richard McClure (1919-), illus. LC 68-28867. (Illus.). 288 p. 27cm. 1968. Golden Press.

--Boats. Scarry, Richard McClure (1919-), illus. LC 67-5848. 1 v.(unpaged). col. illus. 24 x 10cm. (A Golden Go-Go Book). 1967. Golden Press.

--The Bunny Book. Scarry, Richard McClure (1919-), illus. LC 66-9492. (Illus.). 24 p. 22cm. (Golden book for kindergarten). c.1965. Golden Press.

--Busy, Busy World. Scarry, Richard McClure (1919-), illus. LC 65-8169. 92p. col. illus., col. maps (on lining papers) 31cm. c.1965. Golden.

--Cars. Scarry, Richard McClure (1919-), illus. LC 67-5847. 1 v. (unpaged). col. illus. 24 x 10cm. (A Golden Go-Go Books). 1967. Golden Press.

--Christmas Mice. Scarry, Richard McClure (1919-), illus. (Illus.). 24p. (First Little Golden Bks.). (ps). 1982. (ISBN 0-307-10125-8, Golden Pr). Western Pub.

--Conejin & Botijon. new ed. (Illus.). 24p. (gr. 4-9). 1969. (ISBN 0-88332-007-X). Larousse.

--Conejin & Botijon in Africa. Scarry, Richard McClure (1919-), illus. (Illus.). 24p. (gr. 4-9). 1969. (ISBN 0-88332-008-8). Larousse.

--Conejin & Botijon in the Far East. new ed. Scarry, Richard McClure (1919-), illus. (Illus.). 24p. (gr. 4-9). 1969. (ISBN 0-88332-012-6). Larousse.

--Conejin & Botijon, the Astronauts. Scarry, Richard McClure (1919-), illus. (Illus.). 24p. (gr. 4-9). 1969. (ISBN 0-88332-009-6). Larousse.

--Conejin & the Pirates. Scarry, Richard McClure (1919-), illus. (Illus.). 24p. (gr. 4-9). 1974. (ISBN 0-88332-010-X). Larousse.

--The Early Bird. Scarry, Richard McClure (1919-), illus. LC 68-23662. (Illus.). 34 p. 23cm. (Random House early bird book). c.1968. Random House.

--The Egg in the Hole Book. Scarry, Richard McClure (1919-), illus. 1967. Golden Press.

--Favorite Storybook. Scarry, Richard McClure (1919-), illus. 1976. Random House.

--Feed the Hippo His ABC's. Scarry, Richard McClure (1919-), illus. (Play & Learn Bk). (ps-1). 1970. (ISBN 0-307-10741-8, Golden Pr). Western Pub.

--Find Your ABC's. Scarry, Richard McClure (1919-), illus. LC 73-2440. (Illus.). 32 p. 21cm. 1973. (ISBN 0-394-82683-3). Random House.

--Funniest Storybook Ever. Scarry, Richard McClure (1919-), illus. LC 72-1586. (Illus.). 58 p. 33cm. 1972. (ISBN 0-394-82432-6). (ISBN 0-394-92432-0). Random House.

--The Golden Happy Book of Animals. LC 64-55982. 1 v. (unpaged). col. illus. 32cm. 1964, c.1963. Golden Press.

--The Great Big Car and Truck Book. Scarry, Richard McClure (1919-), illus. 1951. Golden Press.

--The Great Pie Robbery. Scarry, Richard McClure (1919-), illus. LC 69-19287. (Illus.). 34 p. 1969. Random House.

--The Hickory Dickory Clock. Scarry, Richard McClure (1919-), illus. LC 61-14162. c.1961. Doubleday.

--I Am a Bunny. Scarry, Richard McClure (1919-), illus. (Illus.). (Golden Sturdy Bk.). (gr. k-2). 1967. (ISBN 0-307-12125-9, Golden Pr). Western Pub.

--In My Town. Scarry, Richard McClure (1919-), illus. LC 76-16675. (Illus.). 24 p. 21cm. (Golden look-look book). 1977, c.1976. (ISBN 0-307-11828-2). Golden Press.

--Is This the House of Mistress Mouse?. Scarry, Richard McClure (1919-), illus. (Illus.). (Golden Touch & Feel Bk). (ps-3). 1964. (ISBN 0-307-12029-5, Golden Pr). Western Pub.

--Little Bedtime Book. Scarry, Richard McClure (1919-), illus. LC 78-55298. (Illus.). (Richard Scarry's Best Little Books Ever). (ps-2). 1978. (ISBN 0-394-83967-6, BYR). Random.

--Look-Look Books. Scarry, Richard McClure (1919-), illus. 1976. Golden Press.

--More Adventures of Tinker and Tanker. Scarry, Richard McClure (1919-), illus. LC 72-130202. (Illus.). 96 p. 29cm. 1971, c.1963. Doubleday.

--My House. Scarry, Richard McClure (1919-), illus. (Illus.). (Golden Look-Look Ser.). 1976. (ISBN 0-307-61820-X, Golden Pr). (ISBN 0-307-11820-7). Western Pub.

--My Nursery Tale Book. Scarry, Richard McClure (1919-), illus. LC 64-21034. 1 v. (unpaged) col. ill. 33cm. (A Big Golden Book). 1964, c.1961. Golden Press.

--The Naughty Bunny. Scarry, Richard McClure (1919-), illus. (Little Golden Book). 1960. Golden Press.

--Nursery Tales. Scarry, Richard McClure (1919-), illus. (Giant Little Golden Book). 1958. Golden Press.

--On the Farm. Scarry, Richard McClure (1919-), illus. (Illus.). (Golden Look-Look Ser.). 1976. (ISBN 0-307-61821-8, Golden Pr). (ISBN 0-307-11821-5). Western Pub.

--On Vacation. Scarry, Richard McClure (1919-), illus. (Illus.). (Golden Look-Look Ser.). 1976. (ISBN 0-307-61823-4, Golden Pr). (ISBN 0-307-11823-1). Western Pub.

--Please and Thank You Book. Scarry, Richard McClure (1919-), illus. LC 73-2441. (Illus.). 32 p. 21cm. 1973. (ISBN 0-394-82681-7). Random House.

--Polite Elephant. Scarry, Richard McClure (1919-), illus. 1964. Golden Press.

--Rabbit and His Friends. Scarry, Richard McClure (1919-), illus. LC 53-303052. unpaged. illus. 21cm. (Little golden golden library, 169). c.1953. Simon and Schuster.

--Rabbit & His Friends. Scarry, Richard McClure (1919-), illus. (Illus.). (ps-2). 1953. (ISBN 0-307-60169-2, Golden Pr). Western Pub.

--Richard Scarry's Animal Nursery Tales. Scarry, Richard McClure (1919-), illus. LC 74-24618. (Illus.). 69 p. 31cm. 1975. Golden Press.

--Richard Scarry's Babykins & His Family. Scarry, Richard McClure (1919-), illus. LC 73-76032. (Illus.). 64p. (gr. k-2). 1973. (ISBN 0-307-68006-1, Golden Pr). (ISBN 0-307-18004-2). Western Pub.

--Richard Scarry's Babykins & His Family. rev ed. Scarry, Richard McClure (1919-), illus. (Illus.). 1976. (ISBN 0-307-13765-1, Golden Pr). (ISBN 0-307-63765-4). Western Pub.

--Richard Scarry's Best Christmas Book Ever. Scarry, Richard McClure (1919-), illus. LC 81-5172. p. cm. 1981. (ISBN 0-394-84936-1). (ISBN 0-394-94936-6). Random House.

--Richard Scarry's Best First Book Ever. Scarry, Richard McClure (1919-), illus. LC 79-3900. p. cm. c.1979. (ISBN 0-394-84250-2). (ISBN 0-394-94250-7). Random House.

--Richard Scarry's Best Mother Goose Ever. Scarry, Richard McClure (1919-), illus. LC 71-119328. (Illus.). 92 p. 31cm. (Giant golden book). 1970. Golden Press.

--Richard Scarry's Best Stories Ever. Scarry, Richard McClure (1919-), illus. LC 70-169100. (Illus.). 175 p. 28cm. (His The Look & learn library). 1971. Golden Press.

--Richard Scarry's Best Story Book Ever. Scarry, Richard McClure (1919-), illus. (Illus.). 296p. (gr. 1-5). 1968. (ISBN 0-307-16548-5, Golden Pr). (ISBN 0-307-66548-8). Western Pub.

AUTHOR INDEX

SCHATZ, LETTA

--Richard Scarry's Busiest People Ever. Scarry, Richard McClure (1919-), illus. LC 76-8123. (Illus.). (ps-2). 1976. (ISBN 0-394-93293-5, BYR). (ISBN 0-394-83293-0). Random.
--Richard Scarry's Busy Busy world. Scarry, Richard McClure (1919-), illus. N.D. Golden Press.
--Richard Scarry's Busy Houses. Scarry, Richard McClure (1919-), illus. LC 81-50713. (Illus.). 24 p. 17cm. c.1981. (ISBN 0-394-84937-X). Random House.
--Richard Scarry's Cars and Trucks and Things That Go. Scarry, Richard McClure (1919-), illus. LC 73-88691. (Illus.). 69 p. 31cm. 1974. (ISBN 0-307-15785-7). Golden Press.
--Richard Scarry's Color Book. Scarry, Richard McClure (1919-), illus. LC 75-36465. (Illus.). 13 p. (incl. covers). 20cm. c.1976. (ISBN 0-394-83237-X). Random House.
--Richard Scarry's Favorite Mother Goose Rhymes. Scarry, Richard McClure (1919-), illus. (Illus.). 32p. (gr. k-2). 1976. (ISBN 0-307-12059-7, Golden Pr). (ISBN 0-307-60259-1). Western Pub.
--Richard Scarry's Funniest Storybook Ever. abridged. Scarry, Richard McClure (1919-), illus. LC 82-7555. 42 p. c.1982. (ISBN 0-394-82432-6). Random House.
--Richard Scarry's Going Places. Scarry, Richard McClure (1919-), illus. LC 70-169099. (Illus.). 164 p. 28cm. (His Look & learn library). 1971. Golden Press.
--Richard Scarry's Great Big Air Book. Scarry, Richard McClure (1919-), illus. LC 77-146649. (Illus.). 69 p. 33cm. 1971. (ISBN 0-394-92167-4). Random House.
--Richard Scarry's Great Big Mystery Book. Scarry, Richard McClure (1919-), illus. LC 77-38512. (Illus.). 41 p. 31cm. 1972, c.1969. (ISBN 0-394-82431-8). (ISBN 0-394-92431-2). Random House.
--Richard Scarry's Great Big Schoolhouse. Scarry, Richard McClure (1919-), illus. LC 74-90292. (Illus.). 69 p. 33cm. 1969. Random House.
--Richard Scarry's Great Steamboat Mystery. Scarry, Richard McClure (1919-), illus. LC 75-6237. (Illus.). 32p. (Picturebacks Ser). (ps-1). 1975. (ISBN 0-394-83124-1, BYR). Random.
--Richard Scarry's Hop Aboard, Here We Go. Scarry, Richard McClure (1919-), illus. 48p. (ps-2). 1972. (ISBN 0-307-13756-2, Golden Pr). (ISBN 0-307-63756-5). Western Pub.
--Richard Scarry's Little Bedtime Book. Scarry, Richard McClure (1919-), illus. LC 78-55298. (Illus.). 48 p. 15cm. (Richard Scarry's Best little books ever). c.1978. (ISBN 0-394-83967-6). Random House.
--Richard Scarry's Little Counting Book. Scarry, Richard McClure (1919-), illus. LC 78-55299. (Illus.). 48 p. 15cm. c.1978. (ISBN 0-394-83966-8). Random House.
--Richard Scarry's Lowly Worm Sniffy Book. Scarry, Richard McClure (1919-), illus. LC 77-90054. (Illus.). 22 p. 17cm. (Sniffy book). c.1978. (ISBN 0-394-83778-9). Random House.
--Richard Scarry's Lowly Worm Storybook. 32 p. col. ill. 21cm. c.1977. (ISBN 0-394-83706-1). Random House.
--Richard Scarry's Mix or Match Storybook. Scarry, Richard McClure (1919-), illus. LC 78-64601. (Illus.). (ps-2). 1979. (ISBN 0-394-84150-6, BYR). Random.
--Richard Scarry's Mother Goose. Scarry, Richard McClure (1919-), illus. LC 72-78507. (Illus.). 22 p. 32cm. 1972. Golden Press.
--Richard Scarry's Mr. Fixit and Other Stories. Scarry, Richard McClure (1919-), illus. LC 78-55300. (Illus.). 48 p. 15cm. (Richard Scarry's best little books ever). c.1978. (ISBN 0-394-83965-X). Random House.
--Richard Scarry's Nicky Goes to the Doctor. Scarry, Richard McClure (1919-), illus. LC 76-187503. (Illus.). 32p. (ps-1). 1972. (ISBN 0-307-12056-2, Golden Pr). (ISBN 0-307-62056-5). Western Pub.
--Richard Scarry's Nicky Goes to the Doctor. Scarry, Richard McClure (1919-), illus. (Look-Look Bks.). (gr. k-1). 1978. (ISBN 0-307-61842-0, Golden Pr). (ISBN 0-307-11842-8). Western Pub.
--Richard Scarry's Peasant Pig and the Terrible Dragon: With Lowly Worm the Jolly Jester. Scarry, Richard McClure (1919-), illus. LC 80-5086. (Illus.). 44 p. 28cm. c.1980. (ISBN 0-394-84567-6). (ISBN 0-394-94567-0). Random House.
--Richard Scarry's Pig Will and Pig Won't: A Book of Manners. Scarry, Richard McClure (1919-), illus. LC 83-19177. c.1984. (ISBN 0-394-96585-X). Random House.
--Richard Scarry's Please and Thank You Book. Scarry, Richard McClure (1919-), illus. LC 77-18184. p. cm. (Random House pictureback). 1978, c.1973. Random House.
--Richard Scarry's Postman Pig and His Busy Neighbors. Scarry, Richard McClure (1919-), illus. LC 77-91646. (Illus.). 32 p. 21cm. (Random House pictureback). c.1978. (ISBN 0-394-83898-X). (ISBN 0-394-93898-4). Random House.
--Richard Scarry's Silly Stories. Scarry, Richard McClure (1919-), illus. LC 73-76030. (Illus.). 64p. (gr. k-2). 1973. (ISBN 0-307-68002-9, Golden Pr). (ISBN 0-307-18002-6). Western Pub.
--Richard Scarry's Silly Stories. Scarry, Richard McClure (1919-), illus. (Illus.). (gr. 3-6). 1976. (ISBN 0-307-13769-4, Golden Pr). Western Pub.
--Richard Scarry's Stories to Color: With Lowly Worm & Mr. Paint Pig. Scarry, Richard McClure (1919-), illus. (Illus.). (ps-3). 1978. (ISBN 0-394-83961-7, BYR). Random.
--Richard Scarry's Teeny Tiny Tales. Scarry, Richard McClure (1919-), illus. (Illus.). (ps-2). 1969. (ISBN 0-307-12075-9, Golden Pr). Western Pub.
--Richard Scarry's Tinker & Tanker Tales of Pirates & Knights. Scarry, Richard McClure (1919-), illus. (Illus.). (Kid's Paperback Ser.). (ps-2). 1979. (ISBN 0-307-63436-1, Golden Pr). (ISBN 0-307-13436-9). Western Pub.
--Richard Scarry's Tinker & Tanker Travel Out West & to Africa. Scarry, Richard McClure (1919-), illus. (Illus.). (Kid's Paperback Ser.). (ps-2). 1979. (ISBN 0-307-63437-X, Golden Pr). (ISBN 0-307-13437-7). Western Pub.
--Richard Scarry's to Market, to Market. Scarry, Richard McClure (1919-), illus. (Illus.). (Golden Scratch & Sniff Bks.). (ps-2). 1979. (ISBN 0-307-13543-8, Golden Pr). (ISBN 0-307-64343-8). Western Pub.
--Richard Scarry's Toy Book. Scarry, Richard McClure (1919-), illus. (Illus.). (ps-3). 1978. (ISBN 0-394-83962-5, BYR). Random.
--The Rooster Struts. Scarry, Richard McClure (1919-), illus. LC 63-2141. (A Golden Happy Book). 1963. Golden Press.
--The Santa Claus Book. Scarry, Richard McClure (1919-), illus. 1965. Golden Press.
--Shoe Book. Scarry, Richard McClure (1919-), illus. N.D. Golden Press.
--Short and Tall. Scarry, Richard McClure (1919-), illus. LC 76-16674. (Illus.). 24 p. 22cm. (Golden look-look book). c.1976. (ISBN 0-307-11827-4). Golden Press.
--Six Golden Look-Look Books, 6 bks. Scarry, Richard McClure (1919-), illus. 1977. Set. (ISBN 0-307-15524-2, Golden Pr). Western Pub.
--Storytime. Scarry, Richard McClure (1919-), illus. LC 76-11630. (Illus.). (Richard Scarry's Best Little Books Ever). (ps-1). 1978. (ISBN 0-394-83338-4, BYR). Random.
--The Supermarket Mystery. Scarry, Richard McClure (1919-), illus. LC 69-19288. (Illus.). 34 p. 1969. Random House.
--Teeny Tiny Tales. Scarry, Richard McClure (1919-), illus. 1965. Golden Press.
--Tinker and Tanker. 1st ed. Scarry, Richard McClure (1919-), illus. LC 60-6356. unpaged. illus. 27cm. (Read aloud books). c.1960. Garden City Books.
--Tinker and Tanker and the Pirates. 1st ed. Scarry, Richard McClure (1919-), illus. LC 61-12578. unpaged. illus. 27cm. (Read- aloud books). 1961. Doubleday.
--Tinker and Tanker and Their Space Ship. 1st ed. Scarry, Richard McClure (1919-), illus. LC 60-130748. unpaged. illus. 27cm. (Read-aloud books). 1961. Doubleday.
--Tinker and Tanker in Africa. Scarry, Richard McClure (1919-), illus. LC 62-15923. 1963. Doubleday.
--Tinker & Tanker Journey to Tootletown & Build a Space Ship. Scarry, Richard Mcclure (1919-), illus. (ps-2). 1978. (ISBN 0-307-13435-0, Golden Pr). (ISBN 0-307-63453-1). Western Pub.
--Tinker and Tanker, Knights of the Round Table. 1st ed. Scarry, Richard McClure (1919-), illus. LC 62-15924. (Illus.). unpaged. 27cm. (Read-aloud books). c.1963. Doubleday.
--Tinker and Tanker Out West. 1st ed. Scarry, Richard McClure (1919-), illus. LC 61-5931. unpaged. illus. 27cm. (Read aloud books). 1961. Doubleday.
--Trains. Scarry, Richard McClure (1919-), illus. LC 67-5845. 1 v. (unpaged) col. illus. 24 x 10cm. (A Golden Go-Go Book). 1967. Golden Press.
--What Do People Do All Day. Scarrry, Richard McClure (1919-), illus. LC 68-14489. 25 p. col. illus. 33cm. 1968. Random House.
S.C.D, jt. auth. see D.S.C.
Schaad, Hans P
--Gunpowder Tower. Crawford, Elizabeth D., tr. from Ger. LC 67-2965. 1 v. (unpaged) col. illus. 24 x 33 cm. 1967, c.1966. Harcourt, Brace & World.
--The Rhine Pirates. Crawford, Elizabeth D., tr. from Ger. LC 68-7304. (Illus.). 1 v. (unpaged). 1968. (ISBN 0-15-266680-X). Harcourt, Brace & World.
Schaaf, Paul (1897-)
--The Crane with One Leg. Wilkon, Jozef (1930-), illus. LC 65-100325. 1v. (unpaged) col. illus. 27cm. 1965, c.1964. Warne.
Schaap, Ted (1931-)
--The Magic Pencil. LC 76-14606. (Illus.). 26 p. 29cm. 1977, c.1976. (ISBN 0-684-14822-6). Scribner.
Schabert, Kyrill, tr. see Winterfeld, Henry.
Schaching, O. V.
--The Mad Knight. N.D. Benziger Brothers.
Schachnowitz, Selig
--Avrohom ben Avrohom: The Famous Historical Novel About the Ger Tzedek of Vilna. N.D. (ISBN 0-87306-134-9). Feldheim.
--Light from the West. Leftwich, Joseph (1892-1983), tr. (gr. 7 up). N.D. (ISBN 0-87306-131-1). Feldheim.
Schachtel, Roger (1949-)
--Fantastic Flight to Freedom. Shaw, Charles (1941-), illus. LC 79-23116. (Illus.). 46p. (Quest, Adventure, Survival). (gr. 4-9). 1982. (ISBN 0-8172-2058-5). Raintree Pubs.
Schachtman, Max (1903-1972), tr. see Mader, Friedrich Wilhelm.
Schackne, Stewart
--Rowena the Skating Cow. Eichenberg, Fritz (1901-), illus. LC 40-354289. 61 p. incl. col. illus., col. plates. 26 cm. 1940. C. Scribner's Sons.
Schad, Helen
--What Am I. LC 53-395901. unpaged. illus. 21cm. (Treasure books, 364). c.1953. Treasure Books.
Schaefer, Charles E. (1933-) & Mellor, Kathleen C., eds.
Young Voices. The Poetry of Children. LC 72-156989. viii, 148 p. 24cm. (The Poetry Search Anthology, 1969). 1971. Bruce Pub. Co.
Schaefer, Jack Warner (1907-)
--The Canyon. 1953. Houghton Mifflin.
--First Blood. large type ed. (Keith Jennison Large Type Bks). (gr. 7 up). N.D. (ISBN 0-531-00186-5). Watts.
--Mavericks. Bjorklund, Lorence F. (1913-1978), illus. LC 67-23312. (Illus.). 184 p. 22cm. 1967. Houghton Mifflin.
--Old Ramon. West, Harold, illus. LC 60-5211. (Illus.). 22 cm. 102p. 1960. Houghton Mifflin. **Awards: (ALA); (JNM).**
--Old Ramon. West, Harold, illus. (Illus.). 102 p. 21cm. (Sandpiper Books). 1973, c.1960. (ISBN 0-395-15056-6). Houghton.
--Plainsmen. Bjorklund, Lorence F. (1913-1978), illus. LC 68-7830. (Illus.). 22cm. 262p. (gr. 7 up). 1963. (ISBN 0-395-07088-0). HM.
--Shane. 1949. Houghton Mifflin.
Stubby Pringle's Christmas. Bjorklund, Lorence F. (1913-1978), illus. LC 64-19982. (Illus.). 22cm. 43p. (gr. 4-6). 1964. (ISBN 0-395-07086-4). HM.
Schaeffer, C. W., tr. see Von Bogatozky, C. H.
Schaeffer, Cornelia, tr. see Juchen, Aurel von.
Schaeffer, Cornelia, tr. see Von Juchel, Aurel.
Schaeffer, Cornelia, tr. see Zimnik, Reiner.
Schaeffler, Ursula
--The Thief and the Blue Rose. Crawford, Elizabeth D., tr. from Ger. LC 67-6567. (Illus.). 25 p. 31cm. 1967, c.1963. Harcourt, Brace & World.
Schaeppi, Mary
--The Tale of the Magic Bread. Werner, Gisela, illus. LC 70-112427. (Illus.). 32 p. 27cm. 1970, c.1968. Scroll Press.
Schafer, Lily Rodgers
--Twilight Stories. Setchell, Martha Powell, illus. LC 54-44391. 22cm. 47p. 1954. Bucknell Pub. Co.
Schaff, Louise E.
--Skald of the Vikings. 1966. (ISBN 0-688-41129-0). William Morrow and Company.
--Skald Ofthe Vikings. Ayearst, Patricia, illus. LC 66-13210. 192p. illus. 22cm. c.1966. Lothrop.
Schaffer, Barbara
--Hush, Little Baby. Schaffer, Barbara, illus. (Illus.). 10p. (Platt & Munk Peggy Cloth Squeekum Bks.). (ps). 1982. (ISBN 0-448-46829-8, G&D). Putnam Pub Group.
Schaffer, Ulrich (1942-)
--Zilja's Secret Plan. Shoji, Takashi, illus. LC 78-6404. (Illus.). 32 p. 25cm. 1st U.S. edition. 1978. (ISBN 0-8028-3514-7). Eerdmans.
Schaffner, C. Louise
--Sam: Or, Our Cat Tales. LC 13-23420. 127 p. incl. illus., plates. 18 1/2 cm. $0.3. c.1913. Atkinson, Mentzer & Company.
Schaleben-Lewis, Joy
--The Dentist & Me. Weiss, Murray, photos by. LC 76-46533. (Illus.). (Moods & Emotions Ser.). (gr. k-3). 1977. (ISBN 0-8172-0064-9). Raintree Pubs.
Schalet, Lilian Lee
--Do You Know. Muhlin, Amalia, illus. (Illus.). 39p. 1979. (ISBN 0-533-03765-4). Vantage.
Schalit, Michael, tr. see Hauff, Wilhelm.
Schall, Michaelle D., jt. auth. see Gad, E.
Schantz, Daniel
--Eddie Holds on. Cochran, Wallace, illus. LC 85-2620. (Illus.). 95 p. 19cm. (Adventures with Eddie Ser.). c.1985. (ISBN 0-87239-922-2). Standard Pub.
--Eddie's Impossible Friend. Cochran, Wallace, illus. LC 85-2621. (Illus.). 95 p. 19cm. (Adventures with Eddie Ser.). c.1985. (ISBN 0-87239-923-0). Standard Pub.
--Upside Down Eddie. Cochran, Wallace, illus. LC 85-2689. (Illus.). 95 p. 19cm. (Adventures with Eddie). c.1985. (ISBN 0-87239-921-4). Standard Pub.
Schanz, Frieda, jt. auth. see Lohmeyer, Julius.
Schapp, Tim (1931-)
--The Magic Pencil. Scapa, created by. LC 76-14606. (Illus.). 26p. (Encore Editions). (gr. k-3). 1976. (ISBN 0-684-17399-9, ScribT). Scribner.
Scharbach, Alexander (1794-1858)
--Boy Sailor: Matthew Calbraith Perry. 1 st ed. Laune, Paul Sidney (1899-), illus. LC 55-10895. 20cm. 194p. (The Childhood of Famous Americans Ser.). 1955. Bobbs Merrill.
--The Gold Race. McCann, Gerald (1916-), illus. LC 56-5345. 204p. illus. 22cm. 1956. Dodd, Mead.
--Matthew Calbraith Perry: Boy Sailor. Fiorentino, Al, illus. LC 62-166136. 200p. col. illus. 20cm. (Childhood of famous Amers.). N.D. Bobbs.
Scharen, Beatrix
--Gigin and Till. Scharen, Beatrix, illus. Hoover, Roseanna, tr. LC 69-13535. (Illus.). 27 p. 1969. Atheneum.
--Tillo. (Illus.). 20p. (gr. 2-5). 1974. (ISBN 0-201-06727-7, A-W Childrens). A-W.
Scharff, Robert
--The How and Why Wonder Book of Oceanography. Doremus, Robert (1913-), illus. LC 64-14936. 47 p. illus. (part col). 28cm. 1964. Wonder Books.
--The How and Why Wonder Book of Robots an Electronic Brains. McMains, Denny, illus. LC 63-9532. (Editorial Production by Donald D. Wolf). 48 p. illus. 29cm. 1963. Grossett & Dunlap.
--Look for a Birds Nest. (Illus.). 96p. 1958. G P Putnam's Sons.
Scharfstein, Ben-Ami see Ben-Ami, pseud.
Scharfstein, Ben-Ami (1919-)
--The Jingle-Book for Jewish Children. Ben-Ami, pseud. Forst, Sigmund, illus. LC 53-25465. unpaged. illus. 29cm. 1953, c.1947. Shilo.
--Noah and the Animal Boat. Forst, Sigmund, illus. LC 48-11261. 44 p. col. illus. 29 cm. 1948. Shilo Pub. House.
Scharfstein, Edythe (1922-) & Scharfstein, Sol
--Rhyme-Land. Neigher, Hy, illus. LC 52-19610. 44 p. illus. 26cm. (A Giant Yom Tov Book). 1952, c.1951. Ktav Pub. House.
Scharfstein, Sol, jt. auth. see Scharfstein, Edythe.
Scharmach, Nancy J
--White Thunder. LC 66-29761. 89 p. 21 cm. c.1967. Chilton Books.
Schatell, Brian
--Farmer Goff and His Turkey Sam. Schatell, Brian, illus. 1982. Harper.
--Farmer Goff and His Turkey Sam. Schatell, Brian, illus. LC 81-47756. (Illus.). 32 p. c.1982. (ISBN 0-397-31982-7). (ISBN 0-397-31983-5). Lippincott.
--The McGoonys Have a Party. Schatell, Brian, illus. LC 85-40095. (Illus.). 32 p. 24cm. c.1985. (ISBN 0-397-32123-6). (ISBN 0-397-32124-4). J.B. Lippincott.
--Midge and Fred. 1st ed. LC 82-48540. p. cm. c.1983. (ISBN 0-397-32046-9). (ISBN 0-397-32047-7). Lippincott.
--Sam's No Dummy, Farmer Goff. Schatell, Brian, illus. LC 83-47669. (Illus.). 32p. (ps-3). 1984. (ISBN 0-397-32061-2, JBL-J). (ISBN 0-397-32062-0). Har-Row.
Schatz, Letta
--Banji's Magic Wheel. Grifalconi, Ann (1929-), illus. LC 73-90050. (Illus.). 45 p. 23cm. 1975. (ISBN 0-695-80441-3). (ISBN 0-695-40441-5). Follett Pub. Co.
--Bola and the Oba's Drummers. Feelings, Thomas (1933-), illus. LC 67-24444. (Illus.). 156 p. 23cm. 1967. McGraw-Hill.
--Never-Empty. Selig, Sylvie (1942-), illus. LC 68-13785. (Illus.). 46 p. 1969. Follett.
--No Light for Brightville. Seiden, Art, illus. LC 65-14475. 21cm. 31p. (Follett Beginning-to-Read Books). 1965. Follett Publishing Co.
--Rhinoceros, Preposterous. Emberley, Edward Randolph (1931-), illus. LC 65-12087. (Illus.). 26cm. 32p. (gr. k-3). 1965. (ISBN 0-8114-7553-0). Steck-V.
--So Many Henrys. Kuzich, John, illus. LC 73-153912. (Illus.). 23 p. (Magic circle book). 1972. (ISBN 0-663-22983-9). Ginn.
--Taiwo and Her Twin. Fax, Elton Clay (1909-), illus. LC 64-16491. 128 p. illus. 24 cm. 1964. McGraw-Hill.
--The Troubles of Kings: Two Tales from Africa. Freas, John (1914-), illus. LC 70-125138. (Illus.). 48 p. (Magic circle book). 1971. Ginn.

--When Will My Birthday Be. Bergere, Richard, illus. LC 61-17751. (Illus.). 26cm. 31p. (gr. k-3). 1962. (ISBN 0-07-055180-4). McGraw.

--Whiskers, My Cat. Galdone, Paul (1914-), illus. (Illus.). 32 p. 26cm. 1967. McGraw-Hill.

Schatz, Letta, retold by.

--Extraordinary Tug of War. Burningham, John Mackintosh (1936-), illus. (Illus.). 26cm. 48p. (Picture Books). (ps-3). 1968. (ISBN 0-695-82339-6). Follett.

Schauener, Zita de, tr. see Kastner, Erich.

Schauffler, Grace Leavitt

--Hi Winkie. Schauffler, Grace Leavitt, illus. LC 28-7551. 36 p. incl. col. front., 18 1/2cm. c.1928. T. Nelson & Sons.

Schauffler, Robert Haven, jt. ed. see Sanford, Anne Putnam, Mrs.

Schauffler, Robert Haven (1879-), ed.

--The Junior Poetry Cure: A First Aid Kit For the Young of All Ages. LC 21-25287. N.D. Dodd Mead & Co.

--Little Plays for Little People. Sanford, A. P., compiled by. N.D. Dodd Mead & Co.

Schawe, Louise

--Friendly Dogs, Here, There and Everywhere. Woodbury, Mabel Jones, illus. LC 38-296293. v, 1, 170 p. col. illus. 20 1/2 cm. c.1938. World Book Company.

Schayer, Ernest Richard

--The Good Loser. LC 17-8204. 1 p. l., 59 p. front., double pl. 18 1/2 cm. $0.5. c.1917. D. McKay.

Schealer, John Milton (1920-)

--The Sycamore Warrior: A Mystery of Ancient Egypt. 1st ed. Altman, Elaine Joan, illus. LC 60-6015. 180p. illus. 21cm. 1960. Dutton.

--Zip-Zip and His Flying Saucer. 1st ed. Helweg, Hans H. (1917-), illus. LC 56-6314. 118p. illus. 21cm. 1956. Dutton.

--Zip-Zip and the Red Planet. 1st ed. MacLean, Robert (1926-), illus. LC 61-12457. 128p. illus. 21cm. 1961. Dutton.

--Zip-Zip Goes to Venus. 1st ed. Helweg, Hans H. (1917-), illus. LC 58-9574. 125p. illus. 21cm. 1958. (ISBN 0-525-43691-X). Dutton.

Scheck, Joann

--Bible Pop-O-Rama Books. Roberts, Jim, illus. Incl. God Loves His People. (ISBN 0-8066-1505-2, 10-2580); When Jesus Was a Baby. (ISBN 0-8066-1521-4, 10-7062); Jesus Tells a Story. (ISBN 0-8066-1512-5, 10-3540); Jesus Does Great Things. (ISBN 0-8066-1511-7, 10-3500). (Illus.). 12p. (gr. 3 up). 1976. Augsburg.

--Man Who Couldn't Wait: Story of Peter. (Illus.). color ils. 32p. (Orig.). (Arch Bks: Set 8). (ps-4). 1971. (ISBN 0-570-06056-7). Concordia.

--Man Who Took Seven Baths. (Illus.). 32 full color. 32p. (Orig.). (Arch Bks, Set 7). (ps-3). 1970. (ISBN 0-570-06048-6). Concordia.

--Two Men in the Temple: Luke 18: 9-14 for Children. Roberts, Jim, illus. LC 68-4305. (Illus.). 1 v. (unpaged). 21cm. (Arch books). 1968. Concordia Pub. House.

Scheck, Joann, jt. auth. see Roberts, Jim.

Scheckman, Claudia S.

--The Perfect Chocolate Chip Cookie. LC 80-67918. (Illus.). 44p. 1st U.S. edition. (ps-6). N.D. Double M Pr.

Schecter, Ben (1935-)

--Conrad's Castle. Schecter, Ben (1935-), illus. LC 67-205831. (Illus.). 32 p. 26cm. 1967. Harper & Row.

Scheele, William E. (1920-)

--Ancient Elephants. 1st ed. Scheele, William E. (1920-), illus. LC 58-9421. 64 p. illus. 22cm. 1958. World Pub. Co.

Scheer, George Fabian (1917-), ed. see Mooney, James.

Scheer, George Fabian (1917-), ed.

--Cherokee Animal Tales. Frankenberg, Robert Clinton (1911-), illus. 80p. (gr. 3-5). 1968. (ISBN 0-8234-0027-1). Holiday.

Scheer, James

--Charla's Children. 218p. (Orig.). 1981. (ISBN 0-87123-171-9). Bethany Hse.

Scheer, Julian Weisel (1926-)

--Upside Down Day. Oechsli, Kelly (1918-), illus. LC 68-1779. (Illus.). 32 p. 24cm. 1968. Holiday House.

Scheer, Julian Weisel (1926-) & Bileck, Marvin (1920-)

--Rain Makes Applesauce. Scheer, Julian Weisel (1926-), illus. LC 64-56216. (Illus.). 1 v. (unpaged). 28cm. 1964. Holiday House. **Awards: (NYT); (ALA); (RCM).**

Scheffler, Jean

--Chalkboard Stories. 128p. (Orig.). (gr. 2-8). 1982. (ISBN 0-87879-332-1). Acad Therapy.

Scheib, Ida

--Elephants in the Garden. Scheib, Ida, illus. LC 58-5516. 21cm. 57p. 1958. D. McKay Co.

Scheidlinger, Lucy Prince

--The Little Bus that Liked Home Best. Hill, Homer, illus. LC 56-17283. 21cm. (Magic Talking Book, T-13). 1955. J. C. Winston Co.

Scheier, Michael, jt. auth. see Frankel, Julie.

Scheinert, Carlton A

--Dodo: The Little Wild Duck. Grider, Dorothy (1915-), illus. LC 49-4088. 32 p. col. illus. 17 cm. (Tell-a-tale books, 891). c.1948. Whitman Pub. Co.

Scheitzer, Byrd Baylor, pseud., see Baylor, Byrd.

Scheitzer, Byrd Baylor, pseud.

--One Small Blue Bead. Baylor, Byrd. Shimin, Symeon (1902-), illus. LC 65-15170. (Illus.). 40 p. 27cm. 1965. Macmillan.

Schell, Mildred, ed. see Kasuya, Masahiro.

Schell, Mildred, adapted by see Tolstoy, Leo Nikolaevich.

Schellie, Don (1932-)

--Apache Warriors. 192p. 1973. (ISBN 0-590-17290-5). Four Winds Press.

--Kidnapping Mr. Tubbs. LC 78-6153. 182 p. 22cm. c.1978. (ISBN 0-590-07542-X). Four Winds Press. **Award: (ALA).**

--Maybe Next Summer. LC 79-6338. 244 p. 22cm. c.1980. (ISBN 0-590-07585-3). Four Winds Press.

--Me, Cholay & Co. Apache Warriors. LC 73-76458. (Illus.). 241 p. 22cm. 1973. Four Winds Press.

--Shadow and the Gunner. LC 82-70415. 136 p. 22cm. c.1982. (ISBN 0-590-07643-4). Four Winds Press.

Schemberger, Irene N

--Tom's Big Strike. Stevens, Mary, illus. LC 59-5366. (Illus.). 144 p. 23cm. 1959. Follett Pub. Co.

Schemm, Mildred Walker see Walker, Mildred.

Schempf, Bonnie Winck & Raedel, Margit

--Timpetoo. Proft, Irmhild & Proft, Hilmar, illus. LC 70-103604. (Illus.). 24 p. 24cm. (gr. k-3). 1971. (ISBN 0-87614-010-X). Carolrhoda Books.

Schenk, A & Wilde, Irma, illus.

--The Christmas Surprise Book: Six Pop-up Christmas Scenes, Ten Christmas Stories. LC 50-11713. 26cm. 12p. (Activity Book). 1950. Grosset & Dunlap.

Schenley, Ruth Stewart

--Too Many Kittens. Fleishman, Seymour (1918-), illus. LC 63-20351. 1 v. (unpaged) illus. (part col.) 23 cm. 1963. A. Whitman.

Scher, Paula

--The Brownstone. Mack, Stanley (1935-), illus. LC 73-1397. (Illus.). 32 p. 29cm. 1973. (ISBN 0-394-82487-3). (ISBN 0-394-82487-3). Pantheon Books.

Scherer, Catharine D.

--Ladybug. Legman, Linda C., illus. LC 83-70738. (Illus.). 10p. 1983. (ISBN 0-9611024-0-3). Drum Assocs.

Scherer, James A. B.

--The Tree of Light. Craig, Frank, illus. N.D. Thomas Y. Crowell Company.

Scherf, Margaret (1908-1979)

--The Mystery of the Empty Trunk. Escourido, Joseph, illus. LC 66-15293. 165p. illus. 21cm. c.1966. (ISBN 0-531-01835-0). Watts.

--The Mystery of the Shaky Staircase. LC 64-12127. 142p. 21cm. c.1965. Watts.

--The Mystery of the Velvet Box. Geer, Charles Hand, illus. LC 62-13960. 154 p. illus. 21 cm. 1963. Watts.

Scherman, Katharine (1915-)

--The Sword of Siegfried. Gorsline, Douglas Warner (1913-1985), illus. LC 59-9743. 50p. illus. 22cm. (Legacy Books, Y-7). 1959. Random House.

--William Tell. Schreiber, Georges (1904-1977), illus. LC 60-10022. (Illus.). 51 p. 22cm. (Legacy Books, Y-15). 1960. Random House.

Schermer, Judith

--Mouse in House. LC 78-24406. (Illus.). 32 p. 1979. Houghton Mifflin.

Schermerhorn, James, Jr. (1897-)

--On the Campus, Freshman. LC 25-176981. 4 p. l., 237 p. 19 1/2 cm. 1925. Dodd, Mead and Company.

--The Phantom Ship. LC 36-8943. 2 p. l., 202 p. front. 20 cm. (Adventure and mystery books for boys). c.1936. Cupples & Leon Company.

Scherpelz, Carrie, jt. auth. see Ziegler, Sandra K.

Schertle, Alice (1941-)

--The April Fool. McCully, Emily Arnold (1939-), illus. LC 80-21435. (Illus.). 32 p. 26cm. c.1981. (ISBN 0-688-41990-9). (ISBN 0-688-51990-3). Lothrop, Lee & Shepard Books.

--Bim Dooley Makes His Move. Chess, Victoria (1939-), illus. LC 82-9987. (Illus.). 32p. (gr. k-3). 1984. (ISBN 0-688-02674-5). (ISBN 0-688-02675-3). Lothrop.

--Cathy and Company and Bumper the Bully. Pavia, Cathy J., illus. LC 79-17923. p. cm. (Her Cathy and Company). N.D. (ISBN 0-516-07721-X). Childrens Press.

--Cathy and Company & Hank, the Horse. Pavia, Cathy J., illus. LC 79-19179. p. cm. (Cathy and Company). c.1980. (ISBN 0-516-07725-2). Childrens Press.

--Cathy and Company, and Mean Mr. Meeker. Pavia, Cathy J., illus. LC 79-17707. p. cm. (Cathy and Company). c.1980. (ISBN 0-516-07723-6). Childrens Press.

--Cathy and Company and the Double Dare. Pavia, Cathy J., illus. LC 79-18588. p. cm. (Cathy and Company). c.1980. (ISBN 0-516-07726-0). Childrens Press.

--Cathy and Company and the Green Ghost. Pavia, Cathy J., illus. LC 79-18555. p. cm. (Cathy and Company). c.1980. (ISBN 0-516-07722-8). Childrens Press.

--Cathy and Company and the Nosy Neighbor. Pavia, Cathy J., illus. LC 79-18585. p. cm. (Cathy and Company). c.1980. (ISBN 0-516-07724-4). Childrens Press.

--Goodnight, Hattie, My Dearie, My Dove. Edwards, Linda Strauss, illus. LC 84-12221. (Illus.). 26 p. 26cm. c.1985. (ISBN 0-688-03934-0). (ISBN 0-688-03935-9). Lothrop, Lee & Shepard Books.

--The Gorilla in the Hall. Galdone, Paul (1914-), illus. LC 76-28799. (Illus.). 32 p. 24cm. c.1977. (ISBN 0-688-41781-7). Lothrop, Lee & Shepard Co.

--Hob Goblin and the Skeleton. 1st ed. Coville, Katherine (1939-), illus. LC 80-19521. (Illus.). 32 p. c.1982. (ISBN 0-688-00279-X). Lothrop, Lee & Shepard Books.

--In My Treehouse. Dunham, Meredith, illus. LC 82-10016. (Illus.). 33 p. 26cm. c.1983. (ISBN 0-688-01638-3). (ISBN 0-688-01639-1). Lothrop, Lee & Shepard Books.

--My Two Feet. Dunham, Meredith, illus. LC 84-12192. (Illus.). 32 p. 26cm. c.1985. (ISBN 0-688-02676-1). (ISBN 0-688-02677-X). Lothrop, Lee & Shepard Books.

Schettler, Amanda

--The Adventures of Mike and Fanny: A Story about a Dog. Schettler, Amanda, illus. LC 52-9243. 21cm. 47p. N.D. Exposition Press.

Scheu-Riesz, Helene

--Three Folklore Plays. N.D. Island Workshop Press.

Schhroeder, Binette

--Tuffa & the Ducks. (Illus.). 12p. (Dial Book for Young Readers Ser.). (ps-k). 1983. (ISBN 0-8037-9894-6). Dutton.

Schiagall, Oscar (1901-)

--Laura Jane sees Everything at Hess's. Maas, Julie, illus. LC 66-5314. 1 v. (unpaged) illus. 27cm. 1966. Public Service Syndicate.

Schick, Alice, ed. see Shelley, Mary Wollstonecraft Godwin.

Schick, Alice, ed. see Stoker, Bram.

Schick, Alice (1946-) & Allen, Marjorie N. (1931-)

--The Remarkable Ride of Israel Bissel, As Related by Molly the Cow: Being the True Account of an Extraordinary Post Rider Who Persevered. Schick, Joel (1945-), illus. LC 75-29179. (Illus.). 53 p. 23cm. c.1976. (ISBN 0-397-31676-3). Lippincott.

Schick, Alice (1946-) & Friedman, Sara Ann (1935-)

--Zoo Year. Schick, Joel (1945-), illus. LC 78-4653. (Illus.). (gr. 6-12). 1978. (ISBN 0-397-31813-8, HarpJ). Har-Row.

Schick, Alice (1946-) & Schick, Joel (1945-)

--Just This Once. LC 77-28871. (Illus.). 43 p. 24cm. (Lippincott I-like-to-read book). c.1978. (ISBN 0-397-31803-0). Lippincott.

--Santaberry and the Snard. LC 78-23796. (Illus.). 47 p. 24cm. (Lippincott I-Like-to-Read Book). c.1979. Lippincott.

--Viola Hates Music. LC 76-46566. (Illus.). 48 p. 16cm. c.1977. (ISBN 0-397-31734-4). Lippincott.

Schick, Alice (1946-) & Schick, Joel (1945-), eds.

--Mary Shelley's Frankenstein. Schick, Alice (1946-) & Schick, Joel (1945-), illus. LC 80-385. (Original Author: Mary Wollstonecraft Godwin Shelley (1797-1851)). (Illus.). 46 p. 29cm. c.1980. (ISBN 0-440-02693-8). Delacorte Press.

Schick, Eleanor (1942-)

--Andy. Schick, Eleanor (1942-), illus. LC 79-127468. (Illus.). 32 p. 1971. Macmillan.

--City Green. Schick, Eleanor (1942-), illus. LC 73-8574. (Illus.). 40 p. 21cm. 1974. (ISBN 0-02-781170-0). Macmillan.

--City in the Summer. Schick, Eleanor (1942-), illus. LC 69-11306. (Illus.). 32 p. 1974, c.1969. Collier Books.

--City in the Summer. Schick, Eleanor (1942-), illus. 1969. Macmillan.

--City in the Winter. LC 69-18237. 21x26cm. 32p. 1970. Macmillan.

--City in the Winter. Schick, Eleanor (1942-), illus. LC 69-18237. (Illus.). 1 v. (unpaged. (Collier juvenile paperbacks). 1973, c.1970. Collier Books.

--City Sun. Schick, Eleanor (1942-), illus. LC 74-3311. (Illus.). 40 p. 21cm. 1974. (ISBN 0-02-781200-6). Macmillan.

--The Dancing School. Schick, Eleanor (1942-), illus. LC 66-156807. 32p. illus. 17x19cm. c.1966. Harper.

--Five and Seven B. Schick, Eleanor (1942-), illus. LC 66-9817. (Illus.). 1 v. 32p. 1967. Macmillan.

--Home Alone. Schick, Eleanor (1942-), illus. LC 79-19785. (Illus.). 56 p. 23cm. (Dial easy-to-read). c.1980. (ISBN 0-8037-4256-8). (ISBN 0-8037-4255-X). Dial Press.

--I'm Going to the Ocean. Schick, Eleanor (1942-), illus. LC 66-179036. 1v. (unpaged) illus. 15x22cm. (D.). c.1966. Macmillan.

--Jeanie Goes Riding. Schick, Eleanor (1942-), illus. LC 67-17213. 1 v. (unpaged) col. illus. 26cm. 1967, c.1968. Macmillan.

--Joey on His Own. Schick, Eleanor (1942-), illus. LC 81-68770. (Illus.). 56 p. 22cm. (Dial Easy-to-Read). c.1982. (ISBN 0-8037-4301-7). (ISBN 0-8037-4302-5). Dial Press.

--Katie Goes to Camp. Schick, Eleanor (1942-), illus. LC 68-26432. (Illus.). 1 v. (unpaged). 1968. Macmillan.

--The Little School At Cotton Wood Corners. Schick, Eleanor (1942-), illus. 1965. (ISBN 0-8382-0471-6, Cadmus Books). E. M. Hale And Company.

--The Little School at Cotton Wood Corners. Schick, Eleanor (1942-), illus. LC 65-21017. 1v. (unpaged) illus. 16x21cm. c.1965. (ISBN 0-06-025226-X). Harper.

--Making Friends. Schick, Eleanor (1942-), illus. LC 75-78077. (Illus.). 32 p. 21cm. 1969. Macmillan.

--My Album. Schick, Eleanor (1942-), illus. LC 83-25420. (Illus.). 7 3/8 x 8. 32p. (14 pt.). (gr. k-3). 1984. (ISBN 0-688-03827-1). (ISBN 0-688-03828-X). Greenwillow.

--Neighborhood Knight. Schick, Eleanor (1942-), illus. LC 75-5920. (Illus.). 64 p. 23cm. (Greenwillow read-alone). c.1976. (ISBN 0-688-80000-9). (ISBN 0-688-84000-0). Greenwillow Books.

--One Summer Night. Schick, Eleanor (1942-), illus. LC 76-25199. p. cm. 1977, c.1976. (ISBN 0-688-80072-6). (ISBN 0-688-84072-8). Greenwillow Books.

--Only in the Summer. LC 69-11306. 20x26cncm. 32p. 1969. Macmillan.

--Peggy's New Brother. Schick, Eleanor (1942-), illus. LC 70-99124. (Illus.). 32 p. 24cm. 1970. Macmillan.

--Peter & Mr. Brandon. Carrick, Donald (1929-), illus. LC 75-165105. (Illus.). 32p. (ps-2). 1973. (ISBN 0-02-781120-4). Macmillan.

--A Piano for Julie. Schick, Eleanor (1942-), illus. LC 83-14154. (Illus.). 7 3/8 x 8. 32p. (14 pt.). (gr. k-3). 1984. (ISBN 0-688-01818-1). (ISBN 0-688-01819-X). Greenwillow.

--Rainy Sunday. Schick, Eleanor (1942-), illus. LC 80-11596. (Illus.). 56 p. 22cm. (Dial easy-to-read). c.1981. (ISBN 0-440-77371-7). (ISBN 0-440-77369-5). Dial Press.

--Summer at the Sea. Schick, Eleanor (1942-), illus. LC 77-3026. (Illus.). 56 p. 22cm. (Greenwillow read-alone). 1979, c.1978. (ISBN 0-688-80116-1). (ISBN 0-688-84116-3). Greenwillow Books.

--Surprise in the Forest. Schick, Eleanor (1942-), illus. (Illus.). (gr. k-2). 1964. (ISBN 0-8382-0828-2). Hale.

--Surprise in the Forest: A Trisha Lucy Lassiter Story. Schick, Eleanor (1942-), illus. LC 64-16652. (Illus.). 14cm. 32p. (ps-1). 1964. (ISBN 0-06-025236-7). Har-Row.

Schick, Joel, jt. auth. see Schick, Alice.

Schick, Joel, jt. ed. see Schick, Alice.

Schick, Joel, ed. see Shelley, Mary Wollstonecraft Godwin.

Schick, Joel, ed. see Stoker, Bram.

Schick, Joel (1945-)

--Joel Schick's Christmas Present. LC 77-3236. (Illus.). 32 p. c.1977. (ISBN 0-397-31761-1). Lippincott.

Schickel, Richard Warner (1933-)

--The Gentle Knight. Blake, Quentin (1932-), illus. LC 64-22863. (Illus.). 58 p. 22cm. 1964. Abelard-Schuman.

Schickling, Wanda Gail

--Chipper Picks a Family. (gr. 4-6). 1952. (ISBN 0-8024-1135-5). Moody.

--My Little Chatterbox. LC 51-6021. 111 p. illus. 20 cm. c.1950. Gospel Pub. House.

--Thirty-One Stories to Live by. 96p. (gr. k-3). 1959. (ISBN 0-88207-021-5). Victor Bks.

Schieker, Eva Hearst, tr. see Schieker, Sofie Ebe.

Schieker, Sofie Ebe

--House at the City Wall. Simon, Howard (1903-1979), illus. Schieker, Eva Hearst, tr. LC 55-7506. (Illus.). 24 cm. 92p. (gr. 3-5). 1955. (ISBN 0-695-43830-1). Follett.

Schiele, Henriette, jt. auth. see Orr, Gulielma Day.

Schiever, Shirley & Motley, Ann

--Folk Tales. 15p. (gr. 2-6). 1982. (ISBN 0-88450-201-5). Communication Skill.

Schiff, Bessie

--Pollyanna of Pleasant Valley. LC 55-7506. 22cm. 155p. 1945. The Wartburg Press.

--The Traveling Gallery. Brock, Emma Lillian (1886-1974), illus. LC 36-10944. 163 p. incl. col. front., illus., col. pl. 22 1/2 cm. 1936. A. Whitman & Co.

Schmeiser, Marie Hall
--Marie Fredericka. Schitoskey, Kay, illus. (Illus.). 1974. (ISBN 0-682-47844-X). Exposition Press.
--Pa's Ranch. McCray, Virginia Gould, illus. LC 75-321556. (Illus.). 47 p. 29cm. c.1974. (ISBN 0-533-01482-4). Vantage Press.
Schmeltz, Susan Alton
--Just for You. 1st ed. Caudill-Paye, Judythe (1939-), illus. LC 81-11928. (Illus.). ix, 86 p. 29cm. c.1981. (ISBN 0-9606586-0-2). Quality Books.
--Oh, So Silly!. Cocca-Leffler, Maryann (1958-), illus. LC 84-4998. 1984. (ISBN 0-8193-1128-6). Parent's Magazine Press.
--Pets I Wouldn't Pick. Appleby, Ellen, illus. LC 81-11071. (Illus.). 46 p. 23cm. c.1982. (ISBN 0-8193-1073-5). (ISBN 0-8193-1074-3). Parents Magazine Press.
Schmeltzer, Kurt
--The Axe of Bronze: A Story of Stonehenge. Charlton, Michael Alan (1923-), illus. LC 58-230116. 142p. illus. 21cm. 1958. Sterling Pub. Co.
--The Long Arctic Night. Cobb, David, illus. Brommer, Elizabeth, tr. from Ger. LC 52-11612. (Illus.). 188 p. 22cm. 1952. F. Watts.
Schmid, C.
--One Hundred Stories. 1980. Dghtrs St Paul.
Schmid, Canon, pseud., see Schmid, Christoph Von.
Schmid, Christoph Von see Schmid, Canon, pseud.
Schmid, Christoph Von (1768-1854)
--Angelica. LC 44-15716. 44, 1 p. incl. front', illus. 16 cm. (Half-title: Dunigan's popular library of instruction and amusement). 1848. P. J. Kenedy.
--The Basket of Flowers: Or, Piety and Truth Triumphant. A Tale for the Young. Bedell, Gregory Townsend (1793-1834), tr. from Fr. LC 21-3875. 144 p. front., illus. 16 cm. 1833. H. Perkins.
--The Best Inheritance. LC 44-15717. 95, 1 p. incl. front., illus. 16 cm. (Half-title: Dunigan's popular library of instruction and amusements). 1848. P. J. Kenedy.
--The Black Lady and Robin Red Breast. Schmid, Canon, pseud. (Our Boy' and Girls' Ser.). N.D. Benziger Brothers' Pub.
--The Cake and the Easter Eggs. Schmid, Canon, pseud. (Our Boys' and Girls' Lib.). N.D. Benziger Brothers' Pub.
--The Canary Bird, 1 of 50 bks. (Illus.). (New Primary Lib.). N.D. Set. American Tract Society.
--The Canary Bird. (Schmid's Exquisite Tales Ser.). N.D. Set. Kelly, Piet & Co.
--The Canary Bird. LC 44-15719. 72 p.incl. front., illus. 16 cm. (Half-title: Dunigan's popular library of instruction and amusement). 1848. P. J. Kenedy.
--The Canary Bird and Other Tales. Schmid, Canon, pseud. (Pastime Ser.). N.D. Benziger Brothers' Pub.
--The Carrier Pigeon. (Schmid's Exquisite Tales Ser.). N.D. Set. Kelly, Piet & Co.
--The Carrier Pigeon. LC 44-15720. 69, 1 p. illus. 16 cm. (Half-title: Dunigan's popular library of instruction and amusement). 1848. P. J.Kenedy.
--Clara: Or, Red And White Roses. LC 44-16852. 61, 1 p. incl. front. illus. 16 cm. (Half-title: Dunigan popular library of instruction and amusement). 1848. P. T. Kenedy.
--The Crocus: A Fresh Flower for the Holidays. Hale, Sarah Josepha Buell, Mrs. (1788-1879), ed. LC 15-12448. x, 7-277 p. incl. front., illus., plates. 18 1/2 cm. 1849. E. Dunigan & Brother.
--The Forget-Me-Not. LC 44-16851. 23, 1 p. incl. front., illus. 16 cm. (Half-title: Dunigan's popular library of instruction and amusement). 1848. P. J. Kenedy.
--Godfrey the Hermit. Schmid, Canon, pseud. (Our Boys' and Girls' Ser.). N.D. Benziger Brothers' Pub.
--The Hop Blossoms. Schmid, Canon, pseud. (Our Boys' and Girls' Ser.). N.D. Benziger Brothers' Pub.
--The Madonna. LC 44-16853. 53, 1 p.incl. front., illus. 16 cm. (Half-title: Dunigan's popular library of instruction and amusement). 1848. P. J.Kenedy.
--The Old Robber's Castle, and Other Tales. Schmid, Canon, pseud. (Our Boys' and Girls' Lib.). N.D. Benziger Brothers' Pub.
--One Hundred Tales for Children. Schmid, Canon, pseud. N.D. P. J. Kenedy.
--Overseer of Mahlbourg. Schmid, Canon, pseud. N.D. Benziger Brothers.
--The Oyster of Mahlbourg, and Other Tales. Schmid, Canon, pseud. (Our Boys' and Girls' Ser.). N.D. Benziger Brothers' Pub.
--Rosa Von Tannanburg: A Tale. Archer, Lucie Agens, tr. LC 21-86996. 172 p. front., pl. 19 cm. 1881. J. Scott.
--The Rose Bush. Schmid, Canon, pseud. (Our Boys' and Girls' Ser.). N.D. Benziger Brothers' Pub.
--The Water Pitcher. LC 44-16854. 69 p. incl. front., illus. 16 cm. (Half-title: Dunigan's popular library of instruction and amusement). 1848. P. J.Schmid.
Schmid, Eleonore, jt. auth. see Delessert, Etienne.
Schmid, Eleonore (1939-)
--Cats' Tales. Schmid, Eleonore (1939-), illus. Bell, Anthea, tr. LC 85-7185. (Illus.). 42 p. 32cm. 1985. North-South Books : Distributed in the U.S. by Holt, Rinehart, and Winston.
--Horns Everywhere. Schmid, Eleonore (1939-), illus. LC 67-30314. (Illus.). 1 v. (unpaged). 24cm. 1968. H. Quist.
--Tonia: The Mouse with the White Stone and What Happened on Her Way to See Uncle Tobias. Schmid, Eleonore (1939-), illus. LC 73-88947. (Illus.). 30 p. 29cm. 1974. (ISBN 0-399-20396-6). (ISBN 0-399-20396-6). Putnam.
Schmid, Evan (1920-)
--Master Mozart: A Story of Wolfgang Amadeus Mozart. Majewski, Mary Agnes, illus. LC 54-2986. 96p. illus. 24cm. 1954. Dujarie Press.
Schmidt, Al, ed. see Disney, Walter Elias.
Schmidt, Anna M., jt. auth. see Ashton, Dudley.
Schmidt, Annie M. G
--Pink Lemonade: Poems for Children. Cares, Linda, illus. Ten Harmsel, Henrietta (1921-), tr. from Dutch. LC 81-5591. (Illus.). 64 p. 26cm. c.1981. (ISBN 0-8028-4050-7). Eerdmans.
--Wiplala. Dalenoord, Jenny, illus. Anthony, Henrietta, tr. LC 62-830757. 159p. illus. 21cm. 1962. Abelard-Schuman.
Schmidt, Austin Guildford (1883-), ed. see Ruskin, John.
Schmidt, Eric Von see Von Schmidt, Eric.
Schmidt, Ferdinand (1816-1890)
--Gudrun. Upton, George Putnam (1834-1919), tr. LC 6-36031. ix, 11-134 p. front., 2 pl. 17 cm. (Life stories for young people). 1906. A. C. McClurg & Co.
--Herman and Thusnelda. Upton, George Putnam (1834-1919), tr. LC 7-31226. vi p., 1 l., 9-128 p. front. 17 cm. (Life stories for young people). 1907. A. C. McClurg & Co.
--The Nibelungs. Upton, George Putnam (1834-1919), tr. LC 6-36030. xi, 13-174 p. front., 3 pl. 17 cm. (Life stories for young people). 1906. A. C. McClurg & Co.
Schmidt, Ferdinand (1816-1890) & Becker, Karl Friedrich (1777-1806)
--Gods and Heroes. Upton, George Putnam (1834-1919), tr. LC 12-225511. ix, 1 p., 1 l., 13-123 p. front. 17 cm. (Half-title: Life stories for young people). 1912. A. C. McClurg & Co.
Schmidt, Hans J.
--The Crying Princess & the Golden Goose. (Children's Theatre Playscript Ser.). 1955. (ISBN 0-88020-024-3). Coach Hse.
--The Three Thousand Mice of Dr. Proctor. (Children's Theatre Playscript Ser.). 1963. (ISBN 0-88020-053-7). Coach Hse.
Schmidt, Helene (1919-), tr. see Pesek, Ludek.
Schmidt, Karen, illus.
--The Little Red Hen. (Illus.). 16p. (Pudgy Pals Ser.). (ps). 1984. (ISBN 0-448-10218-8, G&D). Putnam Pub Group.
Schmidt, Kurt
--Annapolis Misfit. LC 73-90313. 224p. (gr. 7 up). 1974. (ISBN 0-517-51435-4). Crown.
Schmidt, Sarah Lindsay (1928-)
--The Hurricane Mystery. LC 43-157834. 6 p. l., 3-243 p. illus. 21 cm. 1943. Random House.
--New Land: A Novel for Boys and Girls. Dobias, Frank (1902-), illus. LC 33-25689. ix p., 1 l., 13-317 p. incl. plates. front. 20 cm. 1933. R. M. McBride & Company. **Award: (JNM).**
--Ranching on Eagle Eye. Laune, Paul Sidney (1899-), illus. LC 36-29838. 20cm. 374p. 1936. Robert M. McBride & Co.
--The Secret of Silver Peak. Kreis, Hans, illus. LC 38-34549. 334 p. incl. front., illus. 21 cm. c.1938. Random House.
--Shadow Over Winding Ranch. Busoni, Rafaello (1900-1962), illus. LC 40-842768. 5 p. l., 298 p. incl. front., illus. 21 cm. c.1940. Random House.
--This Is My Heritage. LC 53-6812. 242p. 22cm. 1953. Abelard Press.
Schmidt, Thusnelda, jt. ed. see Cathon, Laura Elizabeth.
Schmidt, Werner Felix (1923-)
--The Forests of Adventure. Marokvia, Artur F. (1909-), illus. LC 63-7118. 161 p. illus. 22 cm. 1963. Little, Brown.
Schmidt, William
--Star Eye. Monsma, Hester, adapted by. (Voyager Ser.). (gr. 5 up). 1979. (ISBN 0-8010-8166-1). Baker Bk.
--Star Eye. Monsma, Hester, adapted by. LC 61-751. 136p. illus. c.1961. Zondervan Pub. House.
Schmieding, Alfred, jt. ed. see Kramer, William Albert.
Schmitt, Gladys (1909-1972)
--Boris, the Lop-Sided Bear. Kuskin, Karla Seidman (1932-), illus. LC 66-15378. (Illus.). 22cm. 32p. (gr. 1-3). 1966. (ISBN 0-02-781250-2, CCPr). (ISBN 0-02-781240-5, CCPr). Macmillan.
--Heroic Deeds of Beowulf. (Illus.). (Legacy Ser: No.17). (gr. 4-7). 1962. (ISBN 0-394-80167-9). (ISBN 0-394-90167-3). Random.
--The Heroic Deeds of Beowulf. Ferro, Walter, illus. LC 62-14834. 51p. illus. 22cm. (Legacy books, Y-17). 1962. Random House.
Schmitt, H.
--Chips the Hero. (ps-3). N.D. Dghtrs St Paul.
Schmitz, James Henry (1911-)
--The Universe Against Her. 1981. (ISBN 0-8398-2597-8, Gregg). G K Hall.
Schmogner, Walter, jt. auth. see Hacks, Peter.
Schnack, Friedrich (1888-)
--Click and the Toyshop. Holle, Erich, illus. Rapoport, Eileen, tr. from Ger. LC 68-12338. 128p. illus. 22cm. 1967. Abelard.
Schnapp, Charles (1882-)
--Archag: The Little Armenian. Waterman, Margaret P., tr. LC 20-20429. xxi p., 1 l., 268 p. incl. plates. col. front. 19 cm. (On verso of half-title: "Little schoolmates" series, ed. by Florence Converse). c.1920. E. P. Dutton & Company.
Schnapp, Katie
--Children's Rhymes. (Illus.). 1979. (ISBN 0-533-04215-1). Vantage.
Schneideman, Rose
--Radio Plays for Young People to Act. 1st ed. LC 61-5874. 218p. 22cm. 1961. Dutton.
Schneider, Alice, ed. see Mother Goose.
Schneider, Alice (1907-), ed.
--Child's Treasury of Fairy Tales and Legends. Weihs, Erika (1917-), illus. N.D. Grosset & Dunlap.
--Tales of Many Lands: A Treasury of Fairy Tales, Folk Tales and Legends. Weihs, Erika (1917-), illus. Frank, Josette (1893-), intro. by. LC 47-2668. xvi, 303 p. illus. 22 cm. 1946. The Citadel Press.
Schneider, Andrea, jt. auth. see Fingland, Randy.
Schneider, Benjamin
--Winter Patriot. LC 67-20741. 146 p. 21cm. 1967. Chilton Book Co.
Schneider, Erika, illus.
--The Twelve Days of Christmas. LC 84-9489. 1984. (ISBN 0-907234-62-3). Picture Book Studio USA.
Schneider, Estelle B, adapted by see Pyle, Howard.
Schneider, Herman (1905-) & Schneider, Nina (1913-)
--Follow the Sunset. 1st ed. Corcos, Lucille (1908-1973), illus. LC 52-6370. (Illus.). 43 p. 28cm. (Junior books). 1952. Doubleday.
Schneider, Jennifer
--The Daybreak Man. LC 74-20386. 300p. (gr. 7 up). 1975. (ISBN 0-06-025254-5, HarpJ). Har-Row.
Schneider, Meg, ed. see Milton, Hilary Herbert.
Schneider, Meg, ed. see Nash, Bruce Mitchell.
Schneider, Meg, ed. see Rotsler, William.
Schneider, Meg, ed. see Shea, George.
Schneider, Meg, ed. see Sheldon, Ann.
Schneider, Meg, ed. see Solomon, Maury.
Schneider, Meg, ed. see Taylor, Lester Barbour, Jr.
Schneider, Nina, jt. auth. see Schneider, Herman.
Schneider, Nina (1913-)
--Hercules, the Gentle Giant. De Paola, Tomie, pseud. (1934-), illus. De Paola, Thomas Anthony. LC 72-79285. (Illus.). 48 p. (gr. 1-4). 1969, c.1947. Hawthorn Books.
--Hercules, the Gentle Giant. Werth, Kurt (1896-), illus. LC 47-2724. 37, 7 p. illus. (part col.) 26 1/2 x 21 cm. 1947. Roy Publishers.
--Robert and His New Friends. Malvern, Corinne (1905-1956), illus. LC 51-13060. (Little Golden Book: 124). 1951. Simon and Schuster.
--While Susie Sleeps. Wilson, Dagmar (1916-), illus. LC 48-5925. 32 p. illus. (part col.) 26 cm. (Young Scott Books). 1948. W. R. Scott.
Schneider-Reichel, Margaret
--Once There Was a Big Crocodile. N.D. MacMillan.
Schneider, Rex
--The Wide-Mouthed Frog. Schneider, Rex, illus. LC 80-13449. p. cm. 1980. (ISBN 0-916144-58-5). (ISBN 0-916144-59-3). Stemmer House Publishers.
Schnell, Robert Wolfgang
--Bonko. Wilkon, Jozef (1930-), illus. LC 77-99446. (Illus.). 26 p. 28cm. 1970, c.1969. Scroll Press.
Schnittkind, Henry Thomas (1886-)
--Alice and the Stork. N.D. The Stratford Company.
--Alice and the Stork: A Fairy Tale for Workingmen's Children. LC 15-14520. 95 p. 20 cm. c.1915. R. G. Badger; Etc., Etc.
Schnurr, Constance Burke
--The Crazy Lady. LC 69-11601. (Illus.). 48 p. 21cm. 1969. Harcourt, Brace & World.
Schoder, Judith
--The Blood Suckers. (Teens reading on a 2-3rd grade level). (Illus.). 64p. (A Jem Book Ser.). 1981. (ISBN 0-671-43778-X). Messner.
--Funny Bunny. Wasserman, Dan, ed. Reese, Bob, illus. (Illus.). (Ten Word Bks.). (gr. k-1). 1979. (ISBN 0-89868-069-7). (ISBN 0-89868-080-8). ARO Pub.
--The Hides-It. Hockerman, Dennis, illus. 32p. (Beginning-to-Read Ser.). (gr. k-3). 1982. (ISBN 0-695-41669-3, Dist. by Caroline Hse). (ISBN 0-695-31669-9). Modern Curr.
Schoder, Judith & Shebar, Sharon
--The Bell Witch. Morrill, Leslie H., illus. (Illus.). 64p. (Jem High Interest-Low Reading Level). (gr. 7 up). 1983. (ISBN 0-671-44005-5). Messner.
Schoder, Judy, jt. auth. see Shebar, Sharon Sigmond.
Schoen, Barbara (1924-)
--A Place and a Time. 234 p. 21cm. 1967. Crowell.
--A Spark of Joy. LC 69-18666. 228 p. 21cm. 1969. Crowell.
Schoenherr, John Carl, jt. auth. see Harding, Lee John.
Schoenherr, John Carl (1935-)
--The Barn. 1st ed. Schoenherr, John Carl (1935-), illus. LC 68-26992. 40 p. 26cm. 1968 (An Atlantic Monthly Press Book). Little, Brown. **Award: (ALA).**
Schoenoff, Evelyn G
--Tom the Gobbler. Schoenoff, Herbert A., illus. LC 52-67124. unpaged. illus. 22cm. 1952. Erle Press.
Schoepfer, G. R.
--River of Miracles. Schoepfer, Virginia B., ed. Brenes, Irma M., illus. (Illus.). (gr. 1-11). 1978. (ISBN 0-931436-01-X, Children's Books). G R Schoepfer.
Schoepfer, Virginia B., ed. see Schoepfer, G. R.
Schoettle, Lynn
--Grandpa's Long Red Underwear. McCully, Emily Arnold (1939-), illus. LC 72-1082. (Illus.). 32 p. 22cm. 1972. Lothrop, Lee & Shepard.
Schofield, Dennis & Zych, Peg, illus.
--Read & Learn with Tom, the Reporter. (Illus.). (Read & Learn Ser.). (gr. 4-6). N.D. (ISBN 0-675-01057-8). Merrill.
Schofield, Lily
--Tom Cataphus and Potiphar. (Illus.). N.D. Frederick Warne & Co.
Scholastica, Mary, jt. ed. see Armitage, Marie Teresa.
Scholastica, Mary, jt. ed. see Finn, William Joseph.
Scholder, Fritz, jt. auth. see Highwater, Jamake Mamake.
Scholefield, Edmund O., pseud., see Butterworth, William Edmund.
Scholefield, Edmund O, pseud. (1929-)
--Tiger Rookie. Butterworth, William Edmund III. 1st ed. Frame, Paul (1913-), illus. LC 66-13902. 159 p. illus. 21 cm. 1966. World Pub. Co.
Scholey, Arthur (1932-)
--Baboushka. Burrows, Ray & Burrows, Corinne, illus. 22p. (gr. 1-6). 1983. (ISBN 0-89107-281-0, Crossway Bks). Good News.
--The Dicken's Christmas Carol Show. 1979. (ISBN 0-87602-119-4). Anchorage.
--The Discontented Dervishes. Rushton, William, illus. (Illus.). 136p. (gr. 2-5). 1982. (ISBN 0-233-96870-9). Andre Deutsch.
Scholey, Arthur (1932-) & Watts, Anna Bernadette (1942-)
--Sallinka and the Golden Bird. LC 78-6417. p. cm. c.1978. (ISBN 0-13-789487-2). Prentice-Hall.
Scholz, Jackson Volney (1897-)
--Backfield Blues. LC 70-151941. 190 p. 22cm. 1971. Morrow.
--Backfield Buckaroo. LC 67-16370. 192 p. 21cm. 1967. Morrow.
--Base Burglar. LC 55-8842. 221 p. 21cm. (Morrow Junior Books). 1955. Morrow.
--Batter up. LC 46-6225. 3 p. l., 212 p. 20 1/2 cm. (Morrow Junior Books). 1946. W. Morrow and Company.
--Bench Boss. LC 58-7729. 255 p. 21cm. (Morrow Junior Books). 1958. W. Morrow.
--The Big Mitt. LC 68-23913. 190 p. 21cm. 1968. Morrow.
--Center-Field Jinx. LC 61-9725. 220p. 21cm. 1961. Morrow.
--Deep Short. LC 52-8042. 249 p. 21cm. (Morrow Junior Books). 1952. Morrow.
--Dugout Tycoon. LC 63-14203. 254 p. 21cm. 1963. Morrow.
--End Zone. LC 54-7950. 191 p. 21cm. 1954. Morrow.
--Fairway Challenge. LC 64-17611. 224 p. 21 cm. 1964. Morrow.
--Fielder from Nowhere. LC 48-7837. 222 p. 21 cm. (Morrow Junior Books). 1948. W. Morrow.
--A Fighting Chance. LC 56-8481. 222 p. 22cm. (Morrow Junior Books). 1956. Morrow.

--The Red Runners. Hawkins, Seckatary, pseud. Williams, Carll B., illus. LC 22-21204. 4 p. l., xiii-xiv p., 1 l., 336 p. front., illus. 21 cm. c.1922. Stewart Kidd Company.
--Stoner's Boy. Hawkins, Seckatary, pseud. Williams, Carll B., illus. LC 27-501312. 7 p. l., 3-287 p. incl. front., illus. 19 cm. c.1926. R. F. Schulkers.
--Stormie the Dog Stealer. LC 25-515521. vi p., 1 l., 292, 1 p. incl. front. 20 cm. 1925. D. Appleton and Company.
--The Yellow Y. Hawkins, Seckatary, pseud. Williams, Carll B., illus. LC 27-501427. 5 p. l., 3-311 p. incl. front., illus. 19 cm. c.1926. R. F. Schulkers.
Schuller, Margaret
--Fairy Puff Puff. N.D. Carlton Press.
Schulman, Janet, ed. see Boon, Emilie.
Schulman, Janet, ed. see Elliot, Dan.
Schulman, Janet, ed. see Hill, Eric.
Schulman, Janet, ed. see Roberts, Sarah.
Schulman, Janet (1933-), ed. see Sesame Street.
Schulman, Janet, ed. see Wood, Elizabeth.
Schulman, Janet (1933-)
--The Big Hello. Hoban, Lillian (1925-), illus. LC 75-33672. (Illus.). 32 p. 22cm. (Greenwillow Read-Alone). c.1976. (ISBN 0-688-80036-X). (ISBN 0-688-84036-1). Greenwillow Books.
--Camp KeeWee's Secret Weapon. Hafner, Marylin (1925-), illus. LC 78-16742. (Illus.). 63 p. 22cm. (Greenwillow Read-Alone). 1978, c.1979. (ISBN 0-688-80185-4). (ISBN 0-688-84185-6). Greenwillow Books.
--The Great Big Dummy. 1st ed. Hoban, Lillian (1925-), illus. LC 78-27728. (Illus.). 30 p. 22cm. (Greenwillow Read-Alone). c.1979. (ISBN 0-688-80208-7). (ISBN 0-688-84208-9). Greenwillow Books.
--Jack the Bum and the Halloween Handout. Stevenson, James Walker (1929-), illus. LC 76-11032. (Illus.). 55 p. 22cm. c.1977. (ISBN 0-688-80057-2). (ISBN 0-688-84057-4). Greenwillow Books.
--Jack the Bum and the Haunted House. Stevenson, James Walker (1929-), illus. LC 76-21801. (Illus.). 56 p. 22cm. (Greenwillow Read-Alone Books). c.1977. (ISBN 0-688-80067-X). (ISBN 0-688-84067-1). Greenwillow Books.
--Jack the Bum and the UFO. Stevenson, James Walker (1929-), illus. LC 77-20194. (Illus.). 56 p. 22cm. (Greenwillow Read-Alone). c.1978. (ISBN 0-688-80119-6). (ISBN 0-688-84119-8). (ISBN 0-688-84119-8). Greenwillow Books.
--Jenny and the Tennis Nut. Hafner, Marylin (1925-), illus. LC 76-51763. (Illus.). 56 p. 22cm. (Greenwillow Read-Alone). c.1978. (ISBN 0-688-80093-9). (ISBN 0-688-84093-0). Greenwillow Books.
Schulman, Janet (1933-), adapted by.
--The Nutcracker. Chorao, Ann Mckay Sproat (1936-), illus. LC 79-11223. (Original Author: Ernst Theodor Amadeus Hoffmann (1776-1822)). (Illus.). 62 p. 22cm. c.1979. Dutton.
Schulman, Lester Martin (1934-), ed.
--Cracked Looking Glass: Stories of Other Realities. LC 78-138302. color jacket. 252p. (gr. 9 up). 1971. (ISBN 0-02-781400-9). Macmillan.
--Loners: Short Stories About the Young & Alienated. Schulman, Lester Martin (1934-), frwd. by. 256p. (gr. 7 up). 1970. (ISBN 0-02-781390-8). Macmillan.
--Winners & Losers: An Anthology of Great Sports Fiction. LC 68-24106. 256p. (gr. 7up). 1968. (ISBN 0-02-781380-0, Collier). Macmillan.
--Woman's Place. LC 73-8575. notes. 288p. (gr. 8 up). 1974. (ISBN 0-02-781420-3). Macmillan.
--A Woman's Place: An Anthology of Short Stories. LC 74-18079. 411 p. 24cm. 1974. (ISBN 0-8161-6244-1). G. K. Hall.
Schulte, Elaine Louise (1934-)
--Zack and the Magic Factory. LC 76-142. 126 p. 21cm. c.1976. T. Nelson.
Schultz, Barbara (1923-)
--The House on Pinto's Island. LC 68-12989. 192 p. 22cm. 1968. Bobbs-Merrill.
--The Secret of the Pharaohs. LC 66-18605. 231p. map. 22cm. 1966. (ISBN 0-672-50484-7). Bobbs.
Schultz, Edwin W.
--Bobbie's Bedtime Stories. LC 22-24025. (Short Stories for Children). c.1922. Quality Shop Press.
Schultz, Gwendolyn M.
--Big Cowboy Western. Lewis, Richard William (1933-1966), illus. 1956. (ISBN 0-688-51199-6). William Morrow and Company.
--The Blue Valentine. 1956. (ISBN 0-688-21111-9). William Morrow and Company.
--The Blue Valentine. newly illustrated. Coberly, Elizabeth, illus. LC 78-12184. (Illus.). 53 p. 20cm. 1979, c.1965. (ISBN 0-688-22176-9). Morrow.
--The Blue Valentine. Sherman, Theresa (1916-), illus. LC 65-151662. 64p. illus. 20cm. 1965. Morrow.
Schultz, Irene (1927-)
--The Woodland Gang and the Dark Old House. Kahoun, Cindy, illus. LC 84-9199. (Illus.). 128 p. 20cm. (The Woodland Gang Ser.: No. 2). c.1984. (ISBN 0-917457-01-3). Black and White and Read All Over Pub. Co.
--The Woodland Gang and the Hidden Jewels. Kahoun, Cindy, illus. LC 84-9220. (Illus.). 128 p. 20cm. (The Woodland Gang Mysteries: No. 1). c.1984. (ISBN 0-917457-00-5). Black and White and Read All Over Publishing Co.
--The Woodland Gang and the Missing Will. Kahoun, Cindy, illus. LC 84-9210. (Illus.). 128 p. 20cm. (The Woodland Gang Mysteries: No. 4). c.1984. (ISBN 0-917457-03-X). Black and White and Read All Over Pub. Co.
--The Woodland Gang and the Old Gold Coins. Kahoun, Cindy, illus. LC 84-9215. (Illus.). 127 p. 20cm. (The Woodland Gang Ser.: No. 6). c.1984. (ISBN 0-917457-05-6). Black and White and Read All Over Pub. Co.
--The Woodland Gang and the Stolen Animals. Kahoun, Cindy, illus. LC 84-9194. (Illus.). 127 p. 20cm. (The Woodland Gang Ser.: No. 5). c.1984. (ISBN 0-917457-04-8). Black and White and Read All Over Pub. Co.
--The Woodland Gang and the Two Lost Boys. Kahoun, Cindy, illus. LC 84-9204. (Illus.). 128 p. 20cm. (The Woodland Gang Ser.: No. 3). c.1984. (ISBN 0-917457-02-1). Black and White and Read All Over Pub. Co.
Schultz, James Willard (1859-1947)
--Alder Gulch Gold. Henning, Albin, illus. LC 31-25566. 4 p. l., 146, 1 p. front., plates. 20 cm. 1931. Houghton Mifflin Company.
--Apauk: Caller of Buffalo. N.D. Houghton Mifflin Co.
--Blackfeet Tales of Glacier National Park. N.D. Houghton Mifflin Co.
--The Danger Trail. Varian, George, illus. LC 23-98616. 3 p. l., 295, 1 p. front., plates. 20 cm. 1923. Houghton Mifflin Company.
--The Dreadful River Cave: Chief Black Elk's Story. Cue, Harold, illus. LC 20-19375. v p., 2 l., 243 1 p., 1 l. incl. front. plates. 21 cm. 1920. Houghton Mifflin Company.
--Friends and Foes in the Rockies. Mulford, Stockton, illus. LC 33-24539. 4 p. l., 174, 1 p. front., plates, 20 cm. 1933. Houghton Mifflin Company.
--The Gold Cache. N.D. Houghton Mifflin Co.
--Gold Dust. Mulford, Stockton, illus. LC 34-28617. 4 p. l., 243, 1 p. front., plates. 21 cm. 1934. Houghton Mifflin Company.
--In Enemy Country. LC 28-20609. 4 p. l., 234, 1 p. front., plates. 20 cm. 1928. Houghton Mifflin Company.
--In the Great Apache Forest: The Story of a Lone Boy Scout. LC 20-9474. 4 p. l., 224, 2 p. front., plates. 21 cm. 1920. Houghton Mifflin Company.
--Lone Bull's Mistake. N.D. Houghton Mifflin Co.
--The Loud Mouthed Gun. (Indian Culture Ser.). (gr. 4-8). 1984. (ISBN 0-89992-095-0). Coun India Ed.
--On the Warpath. (Riverside Library for Boys and Girls). N.D. Houghton Mifflin Co.
--Plumed Snake Medicine. Varian, George, illus. LC 24-28113. 3 p. l., 244, 1 p. front., plates, 21 cm. 1924. Houghton Mifflin Company.
--The Quest of the Fish-Dog Skin. Bjorklund, Lorence F. (1913-1978), illus. LC 60-9085. (Illus.). 218 p. 20cm. 1960. Houghton Mifflin.
--The Quest of the Fish-Dog Skin. Varian, George, illus. LC 13-357353. 3 p. l., 218, 2 p. front., plates. 21 cm. 1913. Houghton Mifflin Company.
--Questers of the Desert. Schoonover, Frank Earle (1877-1972), illus. LC 25-21772. 3 p. l., 224, 1 p. front., plates. 20 cm. 1925. Houghton Mifflin Company.
--Red Crow's Brother: Hugh Monroe's Story of His Second Year on the Plains. Schoonover, Frank Earle (1877-1972), illus. LC 27-20663. 4 p. l., 208, 1 p. front., plates. 20 cm. 1927. Houghton Mifflin Company.
--Rising Wolf: The Story of a White Blackfoot. N.D. Houghton Mifflin Co.
--Running Eagle. (Indian Culture Ser.). (gr. 2-10). 1984. (ISBN 0-89992-093-4). Coun India Ed.
--Running Eagle: The Warrior Girl. LC 19-5271. 4 p. l., 311 p. front., plates. 20 cm. 1919. Houghton Mifflin Company.
--Sahtaki and I. LC 24-12307. 3 p. l., 305, 1 p. col. front. 20 cm. 1924. Houghton Mifflin Company.
--Seizer of Eagles. N.D. Houghton Mifflin Co.
--Sinopah, the Indian Boy. N.D. Houghton Mifflin Co.
--Skull Head the Terrible. Schoonover, Frank Earle (1877-1972), illus. LC 29-189278. 4 p. l, 207, 1 p. front., plates. 20 cm. 1929. Houghton Mifflin Company.
--A Son of the Navahos. LC 27-7729. 4 p. l., 200, 1 p. front., plates. 19 cm. 1927. Houghton Mifflin Company.
--Stained Gold. Schoonover, Frank Earle (1877-1972), illus. LC 37-21140. 3 p. l, 217 p. front., plates. 22 cm. 1937. Houghton Mifflin Company.
--The Trail of the Spanish Horse. Bjorklund, Lorence F. (1913-1978), illus. LC 60-9084. 212p. illus. 20cm. 1960. (ISBN 0-395-07094-5). Houghton Mifflin.
--The War-Trail Fort. N.D. Houghton Mifflin Co.
--The White Beaver. Thomson, Rodney, illus. LC 30-23191. 4 p. l., 271, 1 p. front, plates. 20 cm. 1930. Houghton Mifflin Company.
--The White Buffalo Robe. Schoonover, Frank Earle (1877-1972), illus. LC 36-18206. 4 p. l., 220, 1 p. front., plates. 21 cm. 1936. Houghton Mifflin Company.
--William Jackson, Indian Scout: His True Story. LC 26-17247. 3 p. l., 200, 1 p. front., plates. 20 cm. 1926. Houghton Company.
--With the Indians in the Rockies. Bjorklund, Lorence F. (1913-1978), illus. LC 60-908354. 227p. illus. 20cm. 1960. Houghton Mifflin.
--With the Indians in the Rockies. Varian, George, illus. LC 12-23115. 227 p. front., plates. 20 1/2cm. 1912. Houghton Mifflin.
--With the Indians of the Rockies. Brett, Harold Matthews (1880-), illus. LC 25-19428. (Illus.). viii, 252p. (River side bookshelf). 1925. Houghton Mifflin Company.
Schultz, Jeanne (1870-)
--Madeleine's Rescue: A Story for Girls and Boys. Tofani, illus. LC 22-14564. v, 176 p. front., illus. 22 cm. 1894. D. Appleton and Company.
--Straight On: A Story for Young and Old. Zier, Edouard, illus. LC 22-14563. 319 p. illus. 22 cm. 1891. D. Appleton and Company.
Schultz, Pearle Henriksen (1918-)
--Generous Strangers. LC 70-134680. (Illus.). 192p. (gr. 6 up). 1976. (ISBN 0-8149-0673-7). Vanguard.
Schultz, Sam
--Make Me Laugh: 100 Monster Jokes, 100 Knock-Knock Jokes, 100 Animal Jokes. 64p. 1984. (ISBN 0-8431-1006-6). Price Stern.
--One Hundred and One Animal Jokes: Guaranteed to Make You Howl. Hanson, Joan (1938-), illus. LC 81-20955. (Illus.). 48 p. (Make Me Laugh!). c.1982. (ISBN 0-8225-0978-4). Lerner Publications Co.
--One Hundred and One Family Jokes: Guaranteed to Make Your Whole Family Giggle. Hanson, Joan (1938-), illus. LC 81-20861. (Illus.). 48 p. 16cm. (Make Me Laugh). c.1982. (ISBN 0-8225-0981-4). Lerner Publications Co.
--One Hundred and One Knock-Knock Jokes: Guaranteed to Make Even a Sourpuss Smile. Hanson, Joan (1938-), illus. LC 81-20954. (Illus.). 48 p. (Make Me Laugh!). c.1982. (ISBN 0-8225-0976-8). Lerner Publications Co.
--One Hundred and One Monster Jokes: Guaranteed to Curl Your Hair. Hanson, Joan (1938-), illus. LC 81-20953. (Illus.). 48 p. (Make Me Laugh!). c.1982. (ISBN 0-8225-0977-6). Lerner Publications Co.
--One Hundred and One School Jokes: Guaranteed to Keep You Awake in Class. Hanson, Joan (1938-), illus. LC 81-20912. (Illus.). 48 p. (Make Me Laugh!). c.1982. (ISBN 0-8225-0979-2). Lerner Publications Co.
--One Hundred and One Sports Jokes: Guaranteed to Make You a Winner. Hanson, Joan (1938-), illus. LC 81-20913. (Illus.). 50 p. (Make Me Laugh!). c.1982. (ISBN 0-8225-0980-6). Lerner Publications Co.
Schultze, Carl Emil see Bunny, pseud.
Schultze, Carl Emil (1866-1939)
--The Many Adventures of Foxy Grandpa: Including All the Merry Pictures Contained in the Two Volumes Entitled "Adventures of Foxy Grandpa" and "Further Adventures of Foxy Grandpa". Bunny, pseud. LC 2-23700. cover-title, 1 p. l., 72 col. pl. 23 x 38 cm. 1902. Foxy Grandpa Company.
Schulz, Charles Monroe, jt. auth. see Bayley, Monica.
Schulz, Charles Monroe (1922-)
--Be My Valentine, Charlie Brown. Schulz, Charles Monroe (1922-), illus. LC 75-7750. (Illus.). 48p. (ps-3). 1976. (ISBN 0-394-83164-0, BYR). (ISBN 0-394-93164-5). Random.
--Bon Voyage, Charlie Brown, and Don't Come Back!!. LC 79-92273. p. cm. 1980. (ISBN 0-394-84415-7). Random House.
--A Boy Named Charlie Brown. LC 79-80346. (Illus.). 143 p. 29cm. 1969. Holt, Rinehart and Winston.
--A Charlie Brown Christmas. LC 66-13149. (Illus.). 42 p. 22cm. 1965. World Pub. Co.
--A Charlie Brown Thanksgiving. (Charlie Brown Ser). (gr. 3 up). 1974. (ISBN 0-394-83047-4, BYR). (ISBN 0-394-93047-9). Random.
--Charlie Brown's All-Stars. LC 66-21127. (Illus.). 48p. (ps up). 1972. (ISBN 0-529-00135-7). Random.
--Dr. Beagle & Mr. Hyde. LC 81-80708. (Orig.). (Peanuts Parade Bk.). 1981. (ISBN 0-03-059862-1, Owl Bks). HR&W.
--Happiness Is a Warm Puppy. Schulz, Charles Monroe (1922-), illus. (Illus.). (gr. 1 up). 1971. (ISBN 0-528-82660-3). Rand.
--Here Comes the April Fool!. 192p. (Orig.). (Peanuts Parade Ser.). 1980. (ISBN 0-03-057981-3). HR&W.
--He's Your Dog, Charlie Brown!. LC 68-26838. (Illus.). 48 p. 22cm. 1968. World Pub. Co.
--Home Is on Top of a Doghouse. (Illus.). 1982. Determined Prods.
--Hooray for You, Charlie Brown. Schulz, Charles Monroe (1922-), illus. (Illus.). (gr. k-4). 1977. (ISBN 0-394-83586-7, BYR). Random.
--Is This Good-Bye, Charlie Brown?. Risom, Ole & Gerver, Jane, eds. Schulz, Charles Monroe (1922-), illus. LC 83-17801. (Illus.). 48p. (Charlie Brown TV Specials Ser.). (gr. 1 up). 1984. (ISBN 0-394-85953-7, BYR). (ISBN 0-394-95953-1). Random.
--It Was a Short Summer, Charlie Brown. (Illus.). 1 v. (unpaged). 18cm. (Starline Edition, T4707). 1973, c.1970. Scholastic.
--It Was a Short Summer, Charlie Brown. LC 77-128486. (Illus.). 48 p. 1970. World.
--It's a Mystery, Charlie Brown. Schulz, Charles Monroe (1922-), illus. (Illus.). 48p. (Charlie Brown Ser.). (gr. 1 up). 1975. (ISBN 0-394-83101-2, BYR). (ISBN 0-394-93101-7). Random.
--It's Another Holiday, Charlie Brown. Schulz, Charles Monroe (1922-), illus. (Illus.). (gr. k-4). 1977. (ISBN 0-394-83587-5, BYR). Random.
--It's Arbor Day, Charlie Brown. LC 76-40450. (Illus.). 46 p. 24cm. c.1977. Random House.
--It's Good to Have a Friend. (8 double-page layouts with pop-up & moveable action mechanics). (Illus.). 20p. (gr. 1 up). 1972. Hallmark.
--It's Magic, Charlie Brown. LC 81-13964. (Illus.). 44 p. 25cm. c.1982. (ISBN 0-394-85088-2). (ISBN 0-394-95088-7). Random House.
--It's the Easter Beagle, Charlie Brown. Schulz, Charles Monroe (1922-), illus. LC 75-35553. (Illus.). 48p. (gr. 1 up). 1976. (ISBN 0-394-83229-9, BYR). (ISBN 0-394-93229-3). Random.
--It's the Great Pumpkin, Charlie Brown. rev. ed. LC 80-10287. p. cm. c.1980. (ISBN 0-394-94460-7). (ISBN 0-394-84460-2). Random House.
--It's the Great Pumpkin, Charlie Brown. LC 67-24470. (Illus.). 48 p. 1967. World Pub. Co.
--It's Your First Kiss, Charlie Brown. LC 78-7460. p. cm. 1978. (ISBN 0-394-83955-2). (ISBN 0-394-93955-7). Random House.
--Letters to the Peanuts Gang. (Illus.). 1982. Determined Prods.
--Life Is a Circus, Charlie Brown. LC 80-28770. p. cm. 1981. (ISBN 0-394-84826-8). (ISBN 0-394-94826-2). Random House.
--Peanuts Revisited: Favorites Old & New. (gr. 5 up). 1970. (ISBN 0-03-029945-4). HR&W.
--Play It Again, Charlie Brown. LC 76-169253. (Illus.). 48 p. 1971. World Pub.
--Race for Your Life, Charlie Brown. LC 77-15208. (Illus.). 126 p. 29cm. c.1978. (ISBN 0-03-042646-4). Holt, Rinehart, and Winston.
--Race for Your Life, Charlie Brown. LC 77-74456. p. cm. 1977. (ISBN 0-394-83588-3). (ISBN 0-394-93588-8). Random House.
--Security Is a Thumb & a Blanket. LC 82-70029. (Illus.). 1982. Determined Prods.
--Security Is a Thumb & a Blanket. Schulz, Charles Monroe (1922-), illus. (gr. 1 up). 1971. (ISBN 0-528-82662-X). Rand.
--She's a Good Skate, Charlie Brown. LC 80-20285. (Illus.). 44 p. 24cm. c.1981. (ISBN 0-394-84495-5). (ISBN 0-394-94495-X). Random House.
--Snoopy & His Sopwith Camel. (gr. 5 up). 1969. (ISBN 0-03-083177-6). HR&W.
--Snoopy & the Twelve Days of Christmas. (gr. 1 up). N.D. (ISBN 0-317-13662-3). Determined Prods.
--The "Snoopy, Come Home" Movie Book. LC 72-82149. (Illus.). 128 p. 29cm. 1972. (ISBN 0-03-002951-1). Holt, Rinehart and Winston.
--Snoopy on Wheels. Schulz, Charles Monroe (1922-), illus. LC 82-60878. (Illus.). 28p. (Chunky Bks.). (ps). 1983. (ISBN 0-394-85630-9). Random.
--Snoopy Trucks & Trailers. 48p. N.D. (ISBN 0-8431-0665-4). Price Stern.
--Snoopy's Secret Life. (8 double-page layouts with pop-up & moveable action mechanics). (Illus.). 20p. (gr. 1 up). 1972. Hallmark.

Schwarz, Jacob D.
--The Story of Chanuko. N.D. Union of American Hebrew Congregation.

Schwarz, Julia O., jt. auth. see Stefansson, Vilhjalmur.

Schwarz, Lieselotte
--The Dreams. (Illus.). 1974. Scroll Pr.
--I Am King Liebel. LC 66-8892. (Illus.). 1 v. (unpaged. 1966. Follett Pub. Co.
--In One Little House. LC 66-8889. (Illus.). 1 v. (unpaged). 1966. Follett Pub. Co.
--Mitzi, the Little Cat. LC 66-8890. (Illus.). 1 v. (unpaged. 1966. Follett Pub. Co.
--A Spoon for the Golden Rooster. LC 66-8891. 1 v. (unpaged) col. illus. 11 x 16 cm. c.1966. Follett.

Schwarzkopf, Chet
--Heart of the Wild. LC 69-11702. 1969. (ISBN 0-87004-128-2). Caxton.

Schwarzkopf, Chet & Alexandroff, Dimitri N., illus.
--Fur, Fin, and Feathers. LC 52-13135. 149 p. illus. 21cm. 1954. Crowell.

Schwatka, Frederick, et al. (1849-1892)
--Stories of Danger and Adventure. LC 19-6564. 366 p. incl. front., illus., plates, port. 19 cm. c.1886. D. Lothrop and Company.

Schwatka, Frederick (1849-1892)
--Children of the Cold. (Illus.). N.D. Cassell & Co.

Schwebell, Gertrude Clorius, retold by.
--The Man Who Lost His Shadow, and Nine Other German Fairy Tales. Barsis, Max (1894-1973), illus. LC 74-78682. (Illus.). 318 p. 22cm. 1974, c.1957. (ISBN 0-486-21151-7). Dover Publications.
--Where Magic Reigns. Barsis, Max (1894-1973), illus. 318p. N.D. Frederick Ungar Publishing Co Inc.
--Where Magic Reigns: German Fairy Tales Since Grimm. Barsis, Max (1894-1973), illus. LC 57-12327. 318 p. illus. 24 cm. 1957. Stephen Daye Press.

Schwebell, Gertrude Clorius, ed. see Fouque, Friedrich De la Motte.

Schwed, Fred, Jr.
--Wacky, the Small Boy. Duncan, Gregor, illus. LC 39-328191. 85, 1 p. incl. illus., plates. 21 cm. 1939. Simon and Schuster.

Schwed, Hermine
--Ted in Mythland. Squire, Maud Hunt (1873-), illus. LC 7-26321. 19cm. 165p. 1907. Moffat, Yard & Co.

Schwedt, Irene
--Anyone for Deep-Sea Fishing?. 1978. (ISBN 0-533-03538-4). Vantage.

Schweikert, H. G., ed. see Bullen, Frank Thomas.

Schweitzer, Albert (1875-1965)
--The Story of My Pelican. Wildikann, Anna (1901-), photos by. Wardenburg, Martha, tr. LC 65-12738. 72p. 1965. Hawthorn Books, Inc.

Schweitzer, Byrd Baylor, pseud., see Baylor, Byrd.

Schweitzer, Byrd Baylor, pseud. (1924-)
--Amigo. Baylor, Byrd. Williams, Garth Montgomery (1912-), illus. (Illus.). 41 p. 23cm. (Collier Juvenile Paperbacks). 1973, c.1963. Collier Books.
--Amigo. Baylor, Byrd. Williams, Garth Montgomery (1912-), illus. LC 63-18124. (Illus.). 41 p. 26cm. 1963. Macmillan.
--The Chinese Bug. Baylor, Byrd. Darwin, Beatrice, illus. (Illus.). (gr. k-3). 1968. (ISBN 0-395-07096-1). (ISBN 0-395-07097-X). HM.
--The Man Who Talked to a Tree. Baylor, Byrd. 1st ed. Shimin, Symeon (1902-), illus. LC 67-20140. (Illus.). 47 p. 26cm. 1968. Dutton.
--One Small Blue Bead. Baylor, Byrd. Shimin, Symeon (1902-), illus. LC 65-15170. (Illus.). 40 p. 27cm. 1965. Macmillan.

Schweitzer, Iris
--Hilda's Restful Chair. Schweitzer, Iris, illus. LC 81-67667. (Illus.). 28 p. 21cm. 1st U.S. edition. 1982, c.1981. (ISBN 0-689-50230-3). Atheneum.
--In a Forest of Flowers. Schweitzer, Iris, illus. LC 73-87216. (Illus.). 32 p. 1974. (ISBN 0-399-60872-9). Putnam.
--Tiglis and the Bird-Machine. LC 78-18146. (Illus.). 62 p. 25cm. (Reading-on-my-own book). c.1980. (ISBN 0-385-12160-1). (ISBN 0-385-12161-X). Doubleday.

Schweninger, Ann (1951-)
--Christmas Secrets. Schweninger, Ann (1951-), illus. LC 83-16983. (Illus.). 32p. (ps). 1984. (ISBN 0-670-22109-0, Viking Kestrel). Viking.
--A Dance for Three. Schweninger, Ann (1951-), illus. LC 78-72197. (Illus.). (ps-2). 1979. Dial.
--Halloween Surprises. Schweninger, Ann (1951-), illus. LC 83-27372. 32 p. 24cm. 1984. (ISBN 0-670-35935-1). Viking.
--The Man in the Moon As He Sails the Sky and Other Moon Verse. Schweninger, Ann (1951-), illus. LC 79-52051. (Illus.). 48 p. 20cm. c.1979. (ISBN 0-396-07741-2). Dodd, Mead.
--On My Way to Grandpa's. Schweninger, Ann (1951-), illus. LC 80-22729. (Illus.). 32 p. 21cm. c.1981. (ISBN 0-8037-6741-2). (ISBN 0-8037-6752-8). Dial Press.

Schweninger, Ann (1951-) & Chorao, Ann Mckay Sproat (1936-)
--The Hunt for Rabbit's Galosh. LC 74-33659. (Illus.). 32 p. 22cm. c.1976. (ISBN 0-385-00130-4). (ISBN 0-385-00274-2). Doubleday.

Schwerin, Doris Halpern (1922-)
--The Tomorrow Book. Gundersheimer, Karen, illus. LC 82-12504. c.1984. (ISBN 0-394-85459-4). Pantheon Books.

Schwerman, Richard D
--Lost in the Forest. Wahl, Richard (1939-), illus. LC 75-35938. (Illus.). 62 p. 21cm. (Career adventure book). c.1976. (ISBN 0-516-03522-3). Children's Press.

Schwimmer, Rosika (1877-)
--Tisza Tales. Pogany, Willy (1882-1955), illus. LC 28-28704. x p., 1 l., 225 p. col. front., illus., plates (part col.) 24 cm. c.1928. Doubleday, Doran and Company, Inc.

Scikels, Dorothy Judd
--Indians, Hunters of the Plains. Lambdin, R. L., illus. LC 41-8635. 20p. illus. pt. col. 34cm. c.1941. Garden City Pub.

Sciller, Justin G., ed. see Bunyan, John.

Sciortino, Anthony, jt. auth. see Sciortino, Joseph.

Sciortino, Joseph & Sciortino, Anthony
--Santa's Search. (gr. k-2). N.D. Carlton.

Scism, Carol K. (1931-)
--Secret Emily. Mackay, Donald A. (1895-), illus. LC 70-158728. (Illus.). 133 p. 22cm. 1972. Dial Press.
--The Wizard of Walnut Street. Alexander, Martha G. (1920-), illus. LC 73-4803. (Illus.). 54 p. 24cm. 1973. Dial Press.

Scofield, Dorothy
--The Shining Road. 1957. McKay.
--The Shining Road. Manget, Jeanne C., illus. LC 57-6619. 186 p. 22cm. 1957. Longmans, Green.

Scofield, Elizabeth, ed.
--A Fox in One Bite, And Other Tasty Tales from Japan. 1st ed. Wakana, Kei, illus. LC 65-191854. (Illus.). 44 p. 22cm. 1965. Kodansha International Distributed Outside Japan by Japan Publications Trading Co., Rutland, Vt.
--Hold Tight, Stick Tight: A Collection of Japanese Folk Tales. 1st. ed. Wakana, Kei, illus. LC 66-23841. 46p. illus. (pt. col.) 22cm. 1966. Kodansha International.

Scoggin, Margaret Clara (1905-1968), ed.
--Battle Stations: True Stories of Men in War. LC 53-7637. 306 p. 22cm. 1953. Knopf.
--Chucklebait: Funny Stories for Everyone. Steinberg, Saul (1914-), illus. 1945. Alfred A. knopf.
--Chucklebait: Funny Stories for Everyone. Steinberg, Saul (1914-), illus. (Illus.). (gr. 7 up). 1947. (ISBN 0-394-91026-5). Knopf.
--The Edge of Danger: True Stories of Adventure. LC 51-11091. 298 p. 22cm. (Borzi books for young people). 1951. Knopf.
--Escape and Rescues. (Illus.). 1960. Borzoi Books.
--Lure of Danger: True Adventure Stories. (gr. 7 up). 1947. (ISBN 0-394-91367-1). Knopf.
--More Chucklebait: Funny Stories for Everyone. Steinberg, Saul (1914-), illus. (Illus.). (gr. 7 up). 1949. (ISBN 0-394-91420-1). Knopf.

Scollard, Clinton (1860-1932)
--A Boy's Book of Rhymes. LC 99-2739. 18cm. 53p. 1896. Copeland & Day.

Scoppettone, Sandra, jt. auth. see Fitzhugh, Louise.

Scoppettone, Sandra (1936-)
--Happy Endings Are All Alike: A Novel. LC 78-2976. 202 p. 21cm. c.1978. (ISBN 0-06-025239-1). (ISBN 0-06-025240-5). Harper & Row.
--The Late Great Me. LC 75-27416. 256 p. 22cm. c.1976. (ISBN 0-399-11620-6). Putnam.
--Long Time Between Kisses. LC 81-47853. 224p. (gr. 7 up). 1982. (ISBN 0-06-025229-4, HarpJ). (ISBN 0-06-025230-8). Har-Row.
--Playing Murder. LC 83-47707. p. cm. 224p. (gr. 7up). 1985, c.1984. (ISBN 0-06-025283-9). (ISBN 0-06-025283-9). (ISBN 0-06-025284-7). Harper & Row.
--Trying Hard to Hear You. LC 74-2611. 264 p. 21cm. 1974. (ISBN 0-06-025247-2). Harper & Row.

Scortia, Thomas Nicholas (1926-) & Robinson, Frank Malcolm (1926-)
--The Prometheus Crisis. LC 74-33689. 336p. 1975. (ISBN 0-385-09653-4). Doubleday.

Scortia, Thomas Nicholas (1926-) & Zebrowski, George (1945-), eds.
--Human-Machines: An Anthology of Stories About Cyborgs. (Orig.). 1975. (ISBN 0-394-71607-8, Vin). Random.

Scotland, Anne de Bonneville
--The Land of Nada: A Fairy Story. LC 44-30308. 115 p. front. 17 cm. 1895. Arena Publishing Company.

Scott, Alma Olivia Schmidt see Travers, Georgia, pseud.

Scott, Alma Olivia Schmidt (1892-)
--The Story of Kattor. Travers, Georgia, pseud. Gag, Flavia (1907-1979), illus. LC 39-29425. 19 1/2 x 24cm. 32p. c.1939. Coward-McCann.
--The Wily Woodchucks. Travers, Georgia, pseud. Gag, Flavia (1907-1979), illus. LC 46-4718. 32 p. col. illus. 19 1/2 x 25cm. 1946. Coward-McCann.

Scott, Ann Herbert (1926-)
--Big Cowboy Western. Lewis, Richard William (1933-1966), illus. LC 65-22023. 1v. (unpaged) col. illus. 26cm. c.1965. Lothrop.
--Let's Catch a Monster. Hall, H. Tom, illus. LC 67-22591. (Illus.). 26cm. 44p. 1967. Lothrop, Lee & Shepard Co.
--Not Just One. Yaroslava, pseud. (1925-), illus. Mills, Yaroslava Surmach. LC 68-14072. (Illus.). 1 v. 26cm. 28p. 1968. Lothrop, Lee & Shepard Co.
--On Mother's Lap. Coalson, Glo (1946-), illus. LC 76-39726. (Illus.). 39 p. 27cm. 1972. (ISBN 0-07-055896-5). (ISBN 0-07-055897-3). McGraw-Hill.
--Sam. Shimin, Symeon (1902-), illus. LC 67-22968. 1967. McGraw.

Scott, Anne (1900-)
--Flower Babies' Book. Ross, M. T. Penny, illus. N.D. Rand McNally.
--George Sampson Brite. LC 39-32045. 154p. 21cm. 1939. Meador Publishing Company.

Scott, Beatrice McGowan
--Art Songs for Children. N.D. Hinds, Hayden & Eldredge.

Scott, Beryl, jt. auth. see Scott, Paul Thomas.

Scott, Beryl & Scott, Paul
--Eliza & the Indian War Pony. Bolognese, Donald Alan (1934-), illus. (Illus.). (gr. 3-7). N.D. Lothrop.

Scott, Beverly A.
--Christmas in America. Davis, Suzi, illus. Greenwald, Gerald J., concept by. LC 75-308791. (Illus.). 45 p. 21cm. 1974. Kreative Kapers for Kids.
--Santa's New Suit Funbook. 1973. (ISBN 0-686-11715-8). B A Scott.

Scott, Bill
--Darkness Under the Hills. (Illus.). (gr. 7 up). 1980. (ISBN 0-19-554274-6). Oxford U Pr.

Scott, Blackie
--It's Fun at Grandmother's House. LC 85-22021. p. cm. c.1985. (ISBN 0-932419-01-1). S. Hunter Publishing.

Scott, Carol J
--Kentucky Daughter. LC 84-12737. 186 p. 24cm. c.1985. (ISBN 0-89919-330-7). Clarion Books.

Scott, Carrie Emma, jt. ed. see Johnson, Edna.

Scott, Cora Annett Pipitone see Annett, Cora, pseud.

Scott, Dan, pseud., see Stratemeyer Syndicate.

Scott, Dan, pseud.
--The Mystery at Blizzard Mesa. Stratemeyer Syndicate. Beeler, Joe, illus. LC 61-65316. 182p. illus. 20cm. (Bret King Mystery Stories: No. 5). 1961. Grosset & Dunlap.
--The Mystery of Bandit Gulch. Stratemeyer Syndicate. Beeler, Joe, illus. LC 64-2157. 179 p. illus. 20 cm. (Bret King Mystery Stories: No. 9). 1964. Grosset & Dunlap.
--The Mystery of Ghost Canyon. Stratemeyer Syndicate. Beeler, Joe, illus. LC 60-517721. 182p. illus. 20cm. (Bret King Mystery Stories: No. 1). 1960. Grosset & Dunlap.
--The Mystery of Rawhide Gap. Stratemeyer Syndicate. Sorrentino, Santo, illus. LC 60-51650. 182p. illus. 20cm. (Bret King Mystery Stories: No. 4). 1960. Grosset & Dunlap.
--The Mystery of the Comanche Caves. Stratemeyer Syndicate. Beeler, Joe, illus. LC 62-133565. (Illus.). 177p. illus. 20cm. (Bret King Mystery Stories: No. 7). 1962. (ISBN 0-448-09807-5). Grosset & Dunlap.
--The Phantom of Wolf Creek. Stratemeyer Syndicate. Beeler, Joe, illus. LC 63-1136. 178 p. illus. 20 cm. (Bret King Mystery Stories: No. 8). 1963. Grosset & Dunlap.
--The Range Rodeo Mystery. Stratemeyer Syndicate. Beeler, Joe, illus. LC 60-51771. 180p. illus. 20cm. (Bret King Mystery Stories: No. 3). 1960. (ISBN 0-448-09803-2). Grosset & Dunlap.
--The Secret of Fort Pioneer. Stratemeyer Syndicate. Beeler, Joe, illus. LC 61-191435. 181p. illus. 20cm. (Bret King Mystery Stories: No. 6). 1961. Grosset & Dunlap.
--The Secret of Hermit's Peak. Stratemeyer Syndicate. Beeler, Joe, illus. LC 60-51725. (Illus.). 181 p. 20cm. (Bret King Mystery Stories: No. 2). 1960. Grosset & Dunlap.

Scott, Dennis
--Sir Gawain & the Green Knight. 1978. (ISBN 0-87602-202-6). Anchorage.

Scott, Dustin C., pseud., see Chute, Verne.

Scott, Ellen Corrigan, Mrs. (1862-)
--Elizabeth Bess: A Little Girl of the Sixties. Beard, Alice, illus. LC 17-24271. 7 p. l., 230 p. front., plates. 20 cm. 1917. The Macmillan Company.
--The Loyalty of Elizabeth Bess. LC 18-17411. 5 p. l., 243 p. front. 20 cm. 1918. The Macmillan Company.

Scott, Eric
--Down the Rivers, Westward Ho!. LC 67-24421. viii, 180 p. 21cm. 1967. Meredith Press.

Scott, Evelyn D., Mrs. (1893-1963)
--Billy, the Maverick. LC 34-28465. 5 p. l., 3-359 p. incl. front., illus. 20 cm. c.1934. H. Holt and Company.
--The Fourteen Bears, Summer and Winter. Parsons, Virginia, illus. LC 72-89616. (Illus.). 60 p. 31cm. 1973. (ISBN 0-307-63579-1). Golden Press.
--Witch Perkins: A Story of the Kentucky Hills. LC 29-18257. 4 p. l., 3-322 p. plates. 21 cm. c.1929. H. Holt and Company.

Scott, Evelyn D., Mrs. (1893-1963) & Wellman, Frederick Creighton (1879-)
--In the Endless Sands: A Christmas Book for Boys and Girls. LC 25-25010. ix p., 1 l., 382 p. col. front., plates. 20 1/2 cm. 1925. H. Holt and Company.

Scott, Everett Deacon
--Third Base Thatcher. (The Christy Mathewson Books for Boys). N.D. Grosset & Dunlap.
--Third Base Thatcher. Crump, Leslie (1894-), illus. LC 23-840241. 5 p. l., 284 o. front., plates. 20 cm. 1923. Dodd, Mead and Company.

Scott, Florence E.
--Across the Continent with Paul and Peggy. (Illus.). N.D. Hurst & Co.
--Here and There With Paul and Peggy. (Illus.). N.D. Hurst & Co.
--Kindergarden Limericks. Wheelock, Lucy, intro. by. Scott, Arthur O., illus. LC 15-13549. 59 p. 1 l. col. front., col. plates. 26 cm. c.1915. Hurst and Company.

Scott, Florence E., intro. by see Boylan, Grace Duffie, Mrs.

Scott, Frances
--Giants Every Where. 32p. (Make a Book Ser.). 1974. (ISBN 0-8467-0013-1). The Two Continents Publishing Group Ltd.
--Maybe I'll Be. 32p. (Make A Book Ser.). 1975. (ISBN 0-8467-0049-2). The Two Continents Publishing Group Ltd.

Scott, Frances Gruse, jt. auth. see Merrill, Jean Fairbanks.

Scott, Gabriel (1874-)
--Kari: A Story of Kari Supper from Lindeland, Norway. D'Aulaire, Edgar Parin (1898-), illus. Barstad, Anvor, tr. LC 31-23461. xi p., 1 l., 242, 1 p. incl. illus., plates. col. front. 21 cm. 1931. Doubleday, Doran & Company, Inc.

Scott, Gertrude Fisher
--Jean Cabot at Ashton. Scott, Arthur O., illus. LC 12-15816. 3 p. l., 361 p. front., plates. 20 cm. 1912. Lothrop, Lee & Shepard Co.
--Jean Cabot at the House with the Blue Shutters. Scott, Arthur O., illus. LC 15-15868. vii p., 2 l., 333 p. front., plates. 20 cm. 1915. Lothrop, Lee & Shepard Co.
--Jean Cabot in Cap and Gown. Scott, Arthur O., illus. LC 14-14544. 4 p. l., 312 p. front., plates. 20 cm. 1914. Lothrop, Lee & Shepard Co.
--Jean Cabot in the British Isles. Scott, Arthur O., illus. LC 13-172524. 4 p. l., 327 p. front., plates. 20 cm. 1913. Lothrop, Lee & Shepard Co.

Scott, Hilda
--Tom Thumb and Thumbelina. Scott, Hilda, illus. N.D. Holiday House.

Scott, Hilda, illus.
--Cinderella: Or, The Little Glass Slipper. LC 39-1829. 41 p. illus. (part col.) 12 1/2 cm. 1938. Holiday House.

Scott, Isabel Hawley
--The Adventures of Jane Adair. Peters, Marion, illus. LC 23-17926. vii p., 1 l., 11-206 p. front., plates . 20 cm. c.1923. Fleming H. Revell Company.
--Billee: The Story of a Little Boy and a Big Bear. Tomlin, Bradley Walker, illus. LC 21-123581. 2 p. l., 9-196 p. front., plates. 20 cm. c.1921. Fleming H. Revell Company.

Scott, J. Denton, jt. auth. see Cooke, Donald Ewin.

Scott, J. Loughran, rev. by.
--Bulfinch's Age of Fable: Or, Beauties of Mythology. New Rev. ed. (Illus.). 524p. 1900. David McKay.

Scott, J. W.
--Arabian Nights. Doyle, H. J., illus. N.D. Herbert B. Turner & Co.

Scott, Jack D.
--Alligator. Sweet, Ozzie, photos by. LC 84-9927. (Illus.). 64p. (gr. 4 up). 1984. (ISBN 0-399-21011-3). Putnam Pub Group.

Scott, James Maurice (1906-)
--Devil You Don't. LC 69-14829. 196p. (gr. 8 up). 1969. (ISBN 0-8019-5446-0). (ISBN 0-8019-5447-9). Chilton.
--Dingo. LC 67-22759. (gr. 1-6). 1967. (ISBN 0-8019-5276-X). Chilton.
--Hudson of Hudson's Bay. Walford, Astrid (1907-), illus. LC 51-10797. 176 p. illus., map (on lining papers) 20 cm. 1951. H. Schuman.

--The Snakesblood Ruby. Lufkin, Raymond H. (1897-), illus. LC 32-307866. 4 p. l., 261 p. front., plates. 20 cm. 1932. Dodd, Mead & Company.

Scrace, Carolyn

--The Spunky Bears by the Sea. Scrace, Carolyn, illus. LC 84-9571. (Illus.). 28 p. 9cm. 1985. (ISBN 0-8037-0156-X). Dial Books for Young Readers.

--The Spunky Bears Go to Play Group. Scrace, Carolyn, illus. LC 84-9572. p. cm. 1985. (ISBN 0-8037-0157-8). Dial Books for Young Readers.

--The Spunky Bears in Winter. LC 84-9573. p. cm. 1985. (ISBN 0-8037-0158-6). Dial Books for Young Readers.

--The Spunky Bears Take a Trip. LC 84-9570. p. cm. 1985. (ISBN 0-8037-0159-4). Dial Books for Young Readers.

Scrase, Leslie, jt. auth. see Head, Jean.

Screen, Robert Martin

--With My Face to the Rising Sun. LC 77-76441. p. cm. c.1977. (ISBN 0-15-298780-0). Harcourt Brace Jovanovich.

Scribbs, Buck

--The Adventures of Herbilee & Harbilee Hitlow. Garner, Sam, ed. 72p. (Orig.). 1980. (ISBN 0-935440-00-3). October Pr.

Scriber, Adelbert M

--Old Jed: A Love and War Romance of the Delaware Valley. LC 27-16586. vi, 326 p. 20 cm. 1927. Republican Watchman.

Scribner, Charles, Jr. (1921-), tr. see Grimm, Jakob Ludwig Karl (1785-1863) & Grimm, Wilhelm Karl.

Scribner, Charles, Jr. (1921-), retold by.

--The Devil's Bridge: A Legend. Ness, Evaline Michelow, Mrs. (1911-), illus. LC 77-12722. (Illus.). 32p. (gr. k-3). 1978. (ISBN 0-684-15034-4, ScribJ). Scribner.

Scribner, Harvey (1850-)

--A Messenger from Santa Claus. Bang, L. & Stine, David L., illus. LC 4-25685. 27cm. 191p. 1904. Franklin Printing and Engraving Co.

Scrimshaw, Nathaniel L. (1959-)

--At the Heart of the Mountain: A BASIC Adventure for the Commodore 64. LC 83-20251. p. cm. c.1984. (ISBN 0-8176-3600-5). Softext.

Scrimsher, Lila Gravatt (1899-1974)

--The Pumpkin Flood at Harpers Ferry. Hutchinson, William Miller (1916-), illus. LC 62-7503. 94p. illus. 22cm. 1962. Reilly & Lee Co.

Scripture Union

--David, the Shepherd Boy. (New Owl Ser.). 1978. (ISBN 0-87508-928-3). Chr Lit.

--Man up a Tree: Zacchaeus. 1978. (ISBN 0-87508-932-1). Chr Lit.

--Moses, the Baby Who Was Kept. 1978. (ISBN 0-87508-927-5). Chr Lit.

--Mr. Noah's Houseboat. 1978. (ISBN 0-87508-926-7). Chr Lit.

--The Wedding Party at Cana. 1978. (ISBN 0-87508-931-3). Chr Lit.

Scriven, Gerard F. (1920-)

--The Wanderings of Wopsy. Elgin, Jill, illus. LC 51-16692. 96 p. illus. 24 cm. 1950. Catechetical Guild Educational Society.

--Wopsy Again: The Further Adventures of a Guardian Angel. Elgin, Jill, illus. LC 47-28820. 103 p. illus. 24 cm. 1947. Catechetical Guild Educational Society.

--Wopsy: The Adventures of a Guardian Angel. Elgin, Jill, illus. LC 46-2403. 94 p. illus. 23 1/2 cm. 1946. Catechetical Guild.

Scriven, Peter

--The Tintookies & Little Fella Bindi. (Illus.). (gr. 1 up). N.D. (ISBN 0-392-04991-0, ABC). Sportshelf.

Scruton, Clive

--Bubble and Squeak. LC 84-11752. p. cm. (Flapperjack book). (Flapperjack book.). 1985. (ISBN 0-394-87101-4). Random House.

--Circus Cow. Scruton, Clive, illus. LC 84-11751. (Illus.). 24p. (Flapperjack Bks.). (ps-1). 1985. (ISBN 0-394-87102-2, BYR). (ISBN 0-394-87101-4). Random.

--Pig in the Air. LC 84-11757. p. cm. (Flapperjack book). (Flapperjack book.). 1985. (ISBN 0-394-87103-0). Random House.

--Scaredy Cat. LC 84-15899. p. cm. (Flapperjack book). 1985. Random House.

Scudder, D. C.

--Stories about the Heathen. 128p. N.D. Lockwood, Brooks, & Co. for American Tract Society.

Scudder, Henry Townsend

--Jeremiah Splinkety-Splunk, and Other Fairy Tales. LC 44-30306. 134 p. 17 1/2 cm. 1896. Crothers & Korth.

Scudder, Horace Elisha (1838-1902), ed. see Aesopus.

Scudder, Horace Elisha (1838-1902), ed. see Longfellow, Henry Wadsworth.

Scudder, Horace Elisha (1838-1902), tr. see Andersen, Hans Christian.

Scudder, Horace Elisha (1838-1902)

--The Bodley Books: Containing: "Doings of the Bodley Family in Town and Country" "The Bodleys Telling Stories" "The Bodleys on Wheels" "The Bodleys Afoot". (Illus.). (First Series). N.D. Houghton, Mifflin & Co.

--The Bodley Books: Containing: "Mr. Bodley Abroad" "The Bodley Grandchildren and their Journey in Holland" "The English Bodley Family" "The Viking Bodleys". (Illus.). (Second Series). N.D. Houghton, Mifflin & Co.

--The Bodley Grandchildren and Their Journey in Holland. LC 12-38440. viii, 9-192 p. incl. front., illus., plates. 22 cm. 1882. Houghton, Mifflin and Company.

--The Bodleys Afoot. LC 7-24033. 202 p. incl. front., illus., plates. 22 x 18 cm. 1880. Houghton, Osgood & Company.

--The Bodleys Afoot. LC 7-23536. 202 p. incl. front., illus., plates. 22 x 18 cm. c.1907. Houghton, Mifflin and Company.

--The Bodleys on Wheels. LC 6-37603. viii, 9-222 p. incl. front., illus., plates. 22 cm. c.1906. Houghton, Mifflin and Company.

--The Bodleys Telling Stories. LC 4-16153. viii, 9-236 p. incl. front., illus., plates. 21 x 18 cm. 1878. Hurd and Houghton.

--The Book of Fables and Folk Stories. illustrated. LC 6-38552. xiii, 162 p., 1 l. incl. front., illus. 20 cm. c.1906. Houghton, Mifflin and Company.

--The Book of Legends Told Over Again. LC 408. iv p., 1 l., 64 p. 4 pl. (incl. front.) 18 cm. 1899. Houghton, Mifflin and Company.

--The Book of Legends Told Over Again. LC 5136. iv p., 1 l., 82 p. 18 cm. (Riverside literature series, no. 144). 1900. Houghton, Mifflin & Co.

--Doings of the Bodley Family in Town and Country. LC 20-16455. viii, 9-250 p. incl. front., illus., plates. 22 x 18 cm. 1880. Houghton, Mifflin and Company.

--Doings of the Bodley Family in Town and Country. LC 37-18326. viii, 9-250 p. incl. front., illus., plates. 22 cm. 1875. Hurd and Houghton.

--Dream Children. (Illus.). 1910. Houghton Mifflin & Co.

--Dream Children. (Scudder's Bks. for Young People). N.D. Hurd & Houghton.

--Dream Children. LC 12-38829. xii p., 1 l. 15-241 p. plates. 17 cm. 1864. Sever and Francis.

--The English Bodley Family. N.D. Houghton Mifflin.

--Fables and Folk Stories. LC 4-12405. xii, 13-200 p. 18 cm. (On cover: Riverside literature series, nos. 47-48). 1890. Houghton, Mifflin and Company.

--Fables and Folk Stories: In Two Parts. 96p. (Riverside Literature Ser: Nos. 47-48). N.D. Houghton, Mifflin and Company.

--Mr. Bodley Abroad. LC 3-19157. 2 p. l., 9-210 p. incl. illus., plates. front. 22 cm. c.1908. Houghton, Mifflin and Company.

--Seven Little People and Their Friends. (Illus.). 1910. Houghton Mifflin & Co.

--Seven Little People and Their Friends. (Scudder's Bks. for Young People). N.D. Hurd & Houghton.

--Stories from My Attic. (Illus.). N.D. Hurd & Houghton.

--Stories from My Attic: For Children. (Illus.). N.D. Houghton Mifflin & Co.

--The Viking Bodleys. N.D. Houghton Mifflin.

Scudder, Horace Elisha (1838-1902), ed.

--The Book of Fables. LC 19-16216. 22cm. 162p. 1919. Houghton Mifflin.

--The Book of Fables: Chiefly From Aesop. (Illus.). N.D. Houghton, Mifflin & Co.

--The Book of Folk Stories. LC 12-38499. 17 1/2cm. 152p. 1887. Houghton Mifflin.

--The Book of Legends. (Illus.). N.D. Houghton Mifflin & Co.

--The Children's Book. LC 4-1054. (A Collection of the Best and Most Famous Stories and Poems in the English Langauge). v. 444 p. front., illus., pl. 26cm. 1890. Houghton Mifflin.

--The Children's Book. Emmet, Rosina, et al., illus. LC 4-901. (A Collection of the Best and Most Famous Stories and Poems in the English Langauge). v, 444 p. col. front., illus. 26 x 22 cm. 1881. Houghton, Mifflin and Company.

--The Children's Book: A Collection of the Best Literature for Children. (Illus.). 1910. Houghton Mifflin & Co.

Scudder, Joseph, Mrs.

--Captain Waltham: A Tale of Southern India. J. W. D., ed. LC 12-88505. 280 p. front., plates. 18 cm. c.1869. Presbyterian-Publication Committee.

Scudder, Mildred Lee see Lee, Mildred.

Scudder, Norma

--Elmo. (Illus.). 33p. 1982. (ISBN 0-942316-03-7). Pueblo Pub Pr.

Scull, Florence Doughty (1905-)

--Bear Teeth for Courage. Lent, Blair (1930-), illus. LC 64-17955. ix, 163p. illus. 22cm. c.1964. Van Nostrand.

Sculley, Bradley, ed. see Crane, Stephen Townley.

Sculley, Bradley, ed. see Twain, Mark.

Scully, Frank (1892-1964), retold by see Mother Goose.

Scully, Frank (1892-1964), retold by.

--Blessed Mother Goose. Luke, Keye, illus. (Illus.). 95p. 1951. Chilton Books.

Seablom, Seth H

--The Great Mukilteo to Friday Harbor Auto Race: A Story Book. LC 75-38037. (Illus.). 32 p. 21cm. c.1976. (ISBN 0-918800-00-5). Seablom Design.

--Rolando's Reward. LC 77-78193. (Illus.). 1978. (ISBN 0-918800-02-1). Seablom.

Seabrook, Katherine Edmondson, Mrs.

--Colette and Baba in Timbuctoo. LC 33-18477. 3 p. l., 168 p. incl. front., illus. 22 cm. c.1933. Coward-McCann, Inc.

--Gao of the Ivory Coast. D'Aulaire, Edgar Parin (1898-) & Lee, Manning de Villeneuve (1894-1980), illus. LC 31-6818. 4 p. l., 3-121 p. incl. illus., plates. col. front. 22 cm. c.1931. Coward-McCann, Inc.

--Gao of the Ivory Coast. D'Aulaire, Edgar Parin (1898-), illus. LC 76-106865. (Illus.). 120 p. 23cm. 1970. (ISBN 0-8371-3487-0). Negro Universities Press.

Seabrooke, Brenda (1941-)

--The Best Burglar Alarm. 1st ed. Lustig, Loretta, illus. LC 78-7455. (Illus.). 32 p. 24cm. 1978. (ISBN 0-688-22165-3). (ISBN 0-688-32165-8). Morrow.

--Home Is Where They Take You in. LC 79-24508. 190 p. 21cm. 1980. (ISBN 0-688-22221-8). (ISBN 0-688-32221-2). Morrow.

Seabury Editors

--What About Me. (gr. 6). N.D (Crossroad Bks). Seabury.

--Who Is the Greatest. (gr. 6). N.D (Crossroad Bks). Seabury.

Seabury, Ruth Isabel, selected by.

--India Picture Stories. LC 41-40541. 19p. 22 1/2cm. 1922. Missionary Education Movement.

Seaby, Allan W.

--Exmoor Lass and Other Pony Stories. (Nature). (MacMillan Bks. for Boys & Girls). (gr. 4-6). N.D. MacMillan Bks.

--Skewbald, the New Forest Pony. (Nature). (MacMillan Bks. for Boys & Girls). (gr. 4-6). N.D. MacMillan Bks.

Seachrest, Effie

--Egyptian Photoplays. Seachrest, Effie, photos by. LC 21-8192. 128 p. illus., col. pl. 20 cm. c.1921. Rand, McNally & Company.

--Greek Photoplays. Blashfield, Edwin Howland, illus. Seachrest, Effie, photos by. LC 16-24448. 152 p. illus. (part col.) 20 cm. c.1916. Rand, McNally & Company.

Seager, Joan

--Mystery at Lynx Lodge. Johnson, Douglas, illus. LC 65-16278. 114 p. illus. 22 cm. 1965. McGraw-Hill Co. of Canada.

--The Vengeance of Wol. Johnson, Douglas, illus. LC 66-20909. 124 p. illus. 21 cm. 1966. McGraw-Hill Co. of Canada.

Seager, Ralph W.

--The Manger Mouse & Other Christmas Poems. Orig. Title: Christmas Chimes in Rhyme. 1977. (ISBN 0-8170-0768-7). Judson.

Seagren, Daniel

--Letters to Cindy from an Older Sister. LC 78-133357. (Illus.). 111 p. 22cm. (Zondervan teen book). 1971. Zondervan Pub. House.

Seale, Nancy

--The Little Princess, Sara Crewe. (Orig.). 1982. (ISBN 0-87602-231-X). Anchorage.

Sealsfield, Charles (1793-1864)

--The Indian Chief: Or, Tokeah and the White Rose. LC 73-158371. 3 v. in 2. 20cm. (Samtliche Werke: Bd. 4-5). 1972. (ISBN 3-487-08016-8). Olms Presse.

Sealy, Shirley

--A Time for Winning. Holdaway, Richard, illus. 148p. (gr. 9-12). 1980. (ISBN 0-934126-10-0). Raymont Pubs.

Seaman, Augusta Huiell, jt. auth. see Miner, Bruce B.

Seaman, Augusta Huiell, Mrs. (1879-1950)

--The Adventure of the Seven Keyholes. LC 26-7443. 5 p. l., 3-150 p. front., plates. 20 cm. c.1926. The Century Co.

--Americans All: Stories to Tell Boys and Girls of Ten to Twelve. LC 19-10470. v, 105 p. 19 cm. 1919. Everyland Press.

--Bitsy Finds the Clue: A Mystery of Williamsburg, Old and New. LC 46-7682. viii p., 1 l., 271 p. 20 1/2 cm. (Young moderns). 1946. Doubleday & Company, Inc.

--Bitsy Finds the Clue: A Mystery of Williamsburg, Old and New. Nurick, Irving, illus. LC 34-23656. viii p., 1 l., 271 p. front. 21 cm. 1934. Doubleday, Doran & Company, Inc.

--Bluebonnet Bend. Relyea, Charles M., illus. LC 35-17937. vii, 253 p. front., plates. 20 cm. c.1925. The Century Co.

--The Boarded-up House. Squires, C. Clyde, illus. LC 15-19190. 6 p. l., 3-217 p. incl. front., plates. 20 cm. 1915. The Century Co.

--A Book of Mysteries: Three Baffling Tales. Wiese, Kurt (1887-1974), illus. LC 29-21925. 4 p. l., 3-224 p. incl. plates. front. 20 cm. 1929. Doubleday, Doran & Company, Inc.

--The Brass Keys of Kenwick. Lee, Manning de Villeneuve (1894-1980), illus. LC 31-31933. 3 p. l., v-vi p., 1 l., 273 p. col. front. 21 cm. c.1931. Doubleday, Doran & Company, Inc.

--The Case of the Calico Crab. N.D. Grosset & Dunlap.

--The Case of the Calico Crab. Lee, Manning de Villeneuve (1894-1980), illus. LC 42-22620. ix, 222 p. incl. front., illus. 20 cm. 1942. D. Appleton-Century Company, Incorporated.

--The Charlemonte Crest: A Mystery of Modern Haiti. Lee, Manning de Villeneuve (1894-1980), illus. LC 30-31184. 5 p. l., 228 p. col. front., 1 illus. 21 cm. 1930. Doubleday, Doran & Company, Inc.

--The Crimson Patch. Relyea, Charles M., illus. LC 20-142152. 4 p. l., 3-226 p. front., plates. 19 cm. 1920. The Century Co.

--The Curious Affair at Heron Shoals. Lee, Manning de Villeneuve (1894-1980), illus. LC 40-32070. x p., 1 l., 20 p. incl. front., illus. 20 cm. 1940. D. Appleton-Century Company Incorporated.

--The Disappearance of Anne Shaw. LC 28-27810. vii p., 1 l., 262 p. front., plates. 20 cm. 1928. Doubleday, Doran & Company, Inc.

--The Disappearance of Anne Shaw. LC 46-7626. vi p., 1 l., 262 p. 20 1/2 cm. (Young moderns). 1946. Doubleday & Co., Inc.

--The Disappearance of Anne Shaw. LC 39-193560. vi p., 1 l., 262 p. front. 21 cm. (Young moderns bookshelf). 1938. The Sun Dial Press, Inc.

--The Dragon's Secret. Relyea, Charles M., illus. LC 21-17548. 5 p. l., 3-253 p. front., plates. 20 cm. 1921. The Century Co.

--The Edge of Raven Pool. Sichel, Harold M. (1881-), illus. LC 24-8799. 5 p. l., 3-242 p. front., plates. 20 cm. c.1924. The Century Co.

--The Figurehead of the "Folly". Tazelaar, Elizabeth C., illus. LC 35-206790. 5 p. l., 264 p. front. 21 cm. 1935. Doubleday Doran & Company, Inc.

--The Girl Next Door. Relyea, Charles M., illus. LC 17-24404. 7 p. l., 3-260 p. incl. front., plates. 20 cm. 1917. The Century Co.

--The Half-Penny Adventure. Haggander, Sylvia, illus. LC 45-981046. ix, 163, 1 p. incl. front., illus. 19 cm. 1945. D. Appleton Century Company, Inc.

--The House in Hidden Lane: Two Mysteries for Younger Girls. Brockman, Ann, illus. LC 31-14058. 5 p. l., 3-206 p. col. front. 20 cm. 1931. Doubleday, Doran & Company, Inc.

--Jaqueline of the Carrier Pigeons. Edwards, George Wharton (1859-1950), illus. N.D. Macmillan.

--Mamselle of the Wilderness. Edwards, George Wharton (1859-1950), illus. N.D. Macmillan.

--Melissa Across-the-Fence. Relyea, Charles M., illus. LC 18-18528. 4 p. l., 3-121 p. front., plates. 20 cm. 1918. The Century Co.

--The Missing Half. Lee, Manning de Villeneuve (1894-1980), illus. LC 41-218850. ix, 245 p. incl. front., illus. 20 cm. 1941. D. Appleton-Century Company, Incorporated.

--The Mystery at Linden Hall. N.D. Grosset & Dunlap.

--The Mystery at Linden Hall. Lee, Manning de Villeneuve (1894-1980), illus. LC 39-21777. xiii p., 1 l., 234 p. incl. front., illus. plates. 20 cm. 1939. D. Appleton-Century Company, Incorporated.

--The Mystery at Number Six. Couse, W. P., illus. LC 27-18894. 5 p. l., 3-254 p. front., plates. 20 cm. 1922. The Century Co.

--The Mystery of the Empty Room. Nurick, Irving, illus. LC 33-25865. vi p., 1 l., 309 p. col. front. 21 cm. 1933. Doubleday, Doran & Company, Inc.

--Mystery of the Folding Key. Lee, Manning de Villeneuve (1894-1980), illus. LC 43-16549. 4 p. l., 208 p. front., illus. 19 1/2 cm. 1943. D. Appleton-Century Company, Incorporated.

--Mystery of the Old Violin. Orig. Title: The Inn of the Twin Anchors. (gr. 4-6). 1972 (Starline). Schol Bk Serv.

--The Mystery of the Other House. LC 47-3748. 5 p. l., 211 p. front. 19 1/2 cm. 1947. Doubleday & Company, Inc.

--The Pine Barrens Mystery. Haywood, Carolyn (1898-), illus. LC 37-24276. 5 p. l., 263 p. col. front. 21 cm. 1937. Doubleday, Doran & Company, Incorporated.

--The Riddle at Live Oaks. LC 50-3299. vi, 250 p. 21 cm. (Young Moderns). 1949, c.1934. Doubleday.

--The Riddle at Live Oaks: Two Mysteries for Youngest Enthusiasts, Both Boys and Girls. Foster, Genevieve Stump (1893-1979), illus. LC 34-23658. vi, 250 p. col. front. 20 cm. 1934. Doubleday, Doran & Company, Inc.

--Riddle of the Lonely House (Pub. by Doubleday). Orig. Title: The Strange Pettingill Puzzle. (gr. 4-6). 1972 (Starline). Schol Bk Serv.

--The River Acres Riddle: A Book of Mysteries. LC 36-10907. 4 p. l., 3-224 p. front., illus. 21 cm. (Young moderns books). 1936. Doubleday, Doran & Company, Inc.

--The River Acres Riddle: A Book of Mysteries. LC 37-232388. 4 p. l., 3-224 p. incl. plates. front. 21 cm. (Young moderns bookself). 1937. The Sun Dial Press, Inc.

--The River Acres Riddle: A Book of Mysteries. LC 42-25898. 4 p. l., 3-224 p. illus. 20 1/2 cm. (Young moderns bookshelf). 1942. The Sun Dial Press.

--Sally Simms Adventures It. Taylor, Ethel C., illus. LC 24-21817. viii, 226 p. incl. front., illus. 20 cm. c.1924. The Century Co.

--The Sapphire Signet. Relyea, Charles M., illus. LC 16-176528. 5 p. l., 3-290 p. incl. plates. front. 20 cm. 1916. The Century Co.

--The Secret of Tate's Beach. Relyea, Charles M., illus. LC 26-18166. 19cm. vii, 306p. N.D. Century Co.

--The Shadow on the Dial. LC 27-22951. ix, 224 p. front., plates. 20 cm. c.1927. The Century Co.

--The Slipper Point Mystery. Relyea, Charles M., illus. LC 19-144768. 5 p. l., 3-207 p. front., plates. 20 cm. 1919. The Century Co.

--The Stars of Sabra. Lee, Manning de Villeneuve (1894-1980), illus. LC 32-246692. viii p., 1 l., 273 p. col. front., map. 21 cm. 1932. Doubleday, Doran & Company, Inc.

--The Strange Pettingill Puzzle: Two Mysteries for Boys and Girls. Foster, Genevieve Stump (1893-1979), illus. LC 36-29608. vi, 272 p. front., illus. 21 cm. 1936. Doubleday, Doran & Company, Inc.

--Three Sides of Paradise Green. Relyea, Charles M., illus. LC 18-18530. 6 p. l., 3-275 p. front., plates. 20 cm. 1918. The Century Co.

--Tranquility House. N.D. Appleton Century Co.

--The Vanderlyn Silhouette. Lee, Manning de Villeneuve (1894-1980), illus. LC 38-29554. xv, 245 p. incl. front., illus. 21 cm. 1938. D. Appleton-Century Company, Incorporated.

--The Vanishing Octant Mystery. 1st ed. Koering, Ursula (1921-), illus. LC 49-10702. 206 p. illus. 20 cm. 1949. Doubleday.

--Voice in the Dark. Lee, Manning de Villeneuve (1894-1980), illus. LC 37-2755. ix, 240 p. incl. front., illus., plates. 20 cm. 1937. D. Appleton-Century Company, Incorporated.

--When a Cobbler Ruled the King. Edwards, George Wharton (1859-1950), illus. N.D. Macmillan.

Seaman, Edward

--The Special Messenger. LC 30-33972. 32. 21cm. (The Maytime Stories). 1930. Fleming H. Revell Company.

Seaman, Louise Hunting (1894-)

--The Brace Bantam. Sewell, Helen Moore (1896-1957), illus. LC 46-493142. 48 p. incl. front., illus. 21 x 18 1/2 cm. 1946. The Macmillan Company.

Seaman, Mary Lott, illus.

--The Golden Goose. LC 28-21042. 42 p. col. illus. 15 cm. (The happy hour books). c.1928. The Macmillan Company.

Searchfield, Emile

--Aim at a Sure End. N.D. Cassell & Co.

--Dolly's Golden Slippers. N.D. Cassell & Co.

--Ella's Golden Year. N.D. Cassell & Co.

--The Heiress of Wyvern Court. N.D. Cassell & Co.

--Her Wilful Way. N.D. Cassell & Co.

--Jacob Winterton's Inheritance. (Illus.). N.D. Methodist Bk Concern.

--The Secret Cave: The Story of Mistress Joan's Ring. N.D. Thomas Nelson & Sons.

Searcy, Margaret Zehmer (1926-), retold by see Swanton, John Reed.

Searcy, Margaret Zehmer (1926-)

--Alli Gator Gets a Bump on His Nose. Wise, Lu Celia, illus. LC 78-61370. (Illus.). 55 p. 29cm. c.1978. (ISBN 0-916620-20-4). Portals Press.

--The Charm of the Bear Claw Necklace: A Story of Stone-Age Southeastern Indians. LC 80-27424. (Illus.). 68 p. 24cm. c.1981. (ISBN 0-8173-0060-0). University of Alabama Press.

--Ikwa of the Temple Mounds. LC 74-2814. (Illus.). 73 p. 24cm. c.1974. University of Alabama Press.

--Wolf Dog of the Woodland Indians. LC 81-19763. p. cm. c.1982. (ISBN 0-8173-0091-0). University of Alabama Press.

Searcy, Margaret Zehmer (1926-), retold by.

--The Race of Flitty Hummingbird and Flappy Crane: An Indian Legend. Wise, Lu Celia, illus. LC 80-126333. (Illus.). 32 p. 29cm. c.1980. (ISBN 0-916620-21-2). Portals Press.

Searing, Annie Eliza Pidgeon, Mrs. (1857-)

--When Granny Was a Little Girl. Justice, Marion T., illus. LC 26-20632. ix p., 2 l., 270 p. incl. illus., plates. col. front. 21 cm. 1926. Doubleday, Page & Company.

--When Granny Was a Little Girl. Justice, Marion T., illus. LC 37-22506. ix p., 2 l., 270 p. incl. 1 illus., plates. col. front. 21 cm. (Young Moderns Bookshelf). 1937. The Sun Dial Press, Inc.

Searle, Chris

--The Black Man of Shadwell. (Illus.). 104p. 1980. (ISBN 0-904613-15-1). Writers & Readers.

Searle, Karen

--Stories for Christmas. LC 76-24335. 72 p. 23cm. c.1976. (ISBN 0-88494-304-6). Bookcraft.

Sears, Jane L

--Surfboard Summer. Rosado, Pat, illus. LC 65-19363. 214p. 20cm. 1965. Whitman Pub.

Sears, Paul McCutcheon (1920-)

--Downy Woodpecker. N.D. E . M. Hale and Co.

--Downy Woodpecker. Latham, Barbara (1896-), illus. (Illus.). 48p. (gr. k-3). 1953. (ISBN 0-8234-0159-6). Holiday.

Seastrand, Pollye

--Red and Silver. N.D. Carlton Press Inc.

Seaton, Judith, jt. auth. see Lohse, Charlotte.

Seaton, Lilian, tr. see Unnerstad, Edith Totterman.

Seaton, Mildred L.

--Space Age Christmas. (gr. k-2). N.D. Carlton.

Seaver, JoAnn Tuttle

--Adam and Eve Name the Animals. Waterfield, Gloria & Seaver, JoAnn Tuttle, illus. Nettis, Joseph (1928-), photos by. LC 72-11100. (Illus.). 32 p. 26cm. 1973. (ISBN 0-8255-8100-1). (ISBN 0-8255-8100-1). Macrae Smith.

Seavy, Marquita & Seavy, Susan

--The Kindling of the Flame: A Novel. LC 80-14639. (Illus.). 240 p. 22cm. 1980. (ISBN 0-531-04161-1). Watts.

Seavy, Susan, jt. auth. see Seavy, Marquita.

Seawell, Lawrie

--Bindi-Eye. Duncan, Judy, illus. LC 68-16547. (Illus.). 88 p. 18cm. (Trend Books). 1969. Cheshire.

--The Dark House and Rabbit Trap. Mason, Heather, illus. LC 68-16542. (Illus.). 60 p. 18cm. (Trend books). 1968. Cheshire.

--Some Trannie That!. Howell, Elizabeth, illus. LC 68-28965. (Illus.). 68 p. 18cm. (Trend Books). 1968. Cheshire.

Seawell, Manon Young McConnell see Young, Gloria, pseud.

Seawell, Manon Young McConnell (1904-)

--Good Morning, Gloria. Young, Gloria, pseud. LC 36-19984. 141, 3 p. 20 cm. c.1936. The Story Book Press.

Seawell, Molly Elliott (1860-1916)

--Betty at Fort Blizzard. Frederick, Edmund, illus. N.D. J. B. Lippincott.

--Betty's Virginia Christmas. N.D. J.B.Lippincott.

Decatur and Somers. LC 4-15638. 3 p. l., 169 p. front., 5 pl. 20 cm. (On cover: Young Heroes of Our Navy). 1894. D. Appleton and Company.

--Francezka. Fisher, Harrison, illus. 5 p. l., 466 p. front., pl. 20 cm. 1902. The Bowen-Merrill Company.

--The Great Scoop. Stecher, William Frederick (1864-), illus. LC 3-16374. (Illus.). 144p. 19cm. 1903. L. C. Page & Company.

--The Great Scoop. New ed. Stecher, William Frederick (1864-), illus. (Illus.). (Cosy Corner Ser.). 1905. L. C. Page & Co.

--The Imprisoned Midshipmen. LC 8-21618. 5 p. l., 245, 1 p. col. front., 3 col. pl. 20 cm. 1908. D. Appleton and Company.

--Laurie Vane, and Other Stories. Copeland, Charles, illus. 152 p. front., 3 pl. 19 cm. c.1901. W. A. Wilde Company.

--Little Jarvis ... LC 4-16154. 64 p. front., plates. 20 cm. (On cover: Young Heroes of Our Navy). 1890. D. Appleton and Company.

--The Lively Adventures of Gavin Hamilton. Edwards, Harry C., illus. LC 99-4993. 4 p. l., 310 p., 1 l. front., 5 pl. 19 cm. 1899. Harper & Brothers.

--Midshipman Paulding. 20cm. 133p. 1891. D. Appleton & Co.

--Paul Jones. LC 4-15639. viii p., 1 l., 166 p. front., 6 pl., port. 20 cm. (On cover: Young heroes of our navy). 1893. D. Appleton and Company.

--Quarterdeck and Fok'sle: Stories of the Sea. LC 8-6865. 272 p. front., 4 pl. 19 cm. c.1895. W. A. Wilde & Company.

--Quarterdeck and Fol'sle: Stories of the Sea. 1910. W. A. Wilde Co.

--The Rock of the Lion. Keller, Arthur I., illus. LC 8-6866. 3 p. l., 333 p. illus. 19 cm. 1898. Harper & Brothers.

--The Son of Columbus. (Illus.). N.D. Harper & Brothers Trade List.

--Through Thick and Thin. (Illus.). N.D. Lothrop Lee & Shepard Co.

--Through Thick and Thin, and The Midshipmen's Mess: A Soldier Story and a Sailor Story. Laskey, H. G. & Mente, Charles, illus. LC 8-68673. 5 p. l., 215 p. incl. front., 12 pl. 20 cm. 1893. D. Lothrop Company.

--A Virginia Cavalier. LC 8-6868. 3 p. l., 349 p. front., 19 pl. 18 cm. 1897. Harper & Brothers.

--A Virginia Cavalier. LC 42-316022. 3 p. l., 349 p. front., plates. 19 cm. 1901. Harper & Brothers.

--A Virginia Cavalier. LC 4-16106. 3 p. l., 349 p. front., 15 pl. 19 cm. 1903. Harper & Brothers.

Seawell, Molly Elliott (1860-1916) & Barnes, James

--Boys on the Railroad. LC 9-24259. 5 p. l., 212 p., 1 l. front., plates. 19 cm. (On cover of t.-p.: Harper's athletic series, iii). 1909. Harper & Brothers.

Sebby, Sam Raymond

--Three Dragons. Lawrence, Judith Ann, illus. LC 68-29447. (Illus.). 91 p. 22cm. 1968. Grove Press.

Sebesta, Sam Leaton, jt. ed. see Ruddell, Robert Byron.

Sebestiakov, Yvonne, tr. see Borska, Ilona & Hoffmann, Ernst Theodor Amadeus.

Sebestyen, Ouida (1924-)

--Far from Home. LC 80-18328. 191 p. 22cm. c.1980. (ISBN 0-316-77932-6). Little, Brown.

--IOU's. LC 82-124. 188 p. 22cm. c.1982. (ISBN 0-316-77933-4). Little, Brown.

--On Fire. Kroupa, Melanie, ed. LC 84-72617. 228p. (gr. 6 up). 1985. (ISBN 0-87113-010-6). Atlantic Monthly.

--Words by Heart. LC 78-27847. p. cm. c.1979. (ISBN 0-316-77931-8). Little, Brown. **Awards: (IRA); (ALA).**

Seccombe, Barbara, tr. see Guillot, Rene.

Seccombe, Captain, illus.

--Naval and Military Drolleries, 1 of 19 Vols. (Aunt Louisa's Choice Books Ser.: Vol. 18). N.D. Scribner & Welford.

Seccombe, Thomas Strong (1840-1899)

--Cinderella. Emrik & Binger, illus. 1882. A. C. Armstrong & Son.

--The Good Old Story of Cinderella: Retold in Rhyme. Seccombe, Thomas Strong (1840-1899), illus. LC 22-25283. 47, 1 p. col. front., illus., col. plates 24 x 21 cm. 1882. F. Warne and Co.

Sechan, Edmond

--The String Bean. Sechan, Edmond, photos by. LC 81-43242. (Illus.). 64p. 1982. (ISBN 0-385-17135-8). Doubleday.

Sechrist, Berniece Sargent (1880-)

--Big Enough. Woolfolk, Josiah Pitts (1840-1971), intro. by. LC 55-43669. 142p. 20cm. c.1955. Nonpareil Press.

Sechrist, Elizabeth Hough, jt. auth. see Woolsey, Janette.

Sechrist, Elizabeth Hough, Mrs. (1903-), ed. see Pitz, Henry Clarence.

Sechrist, Elizabeth Hough, Mrs. (1903-)

--Rufie Had a Monkey!. Janeway, Hestermary, illus. LC 39-74411. 46 p. illus. 25 cm. c.1939. David McKay Company.

Sechrist, Elizabeth Hough, Mrs. (1903-), compiled by.

--Christmas Everywhere. new rev. and enl. ed. 1962. Macrae Smith.

--Heigh-Ho for Halloween. 1948. Macrae Smith.

--Merry Meet Again: Poems for Small Children to Recite. Fry, Guy, illus. LC 77-160908. (Illus.). xvi, 13-186 p. 23cm. (Granger Index Reprint Series). 1971, c.1941. (ISBN 0-8369-6272-9). Books for Libraries Press.

--Merry Meet Again: Poems for Small Children to Recite. Fry, Guy, illus. LC 41-171824. xvi p., 1 l., 13-186 p. illus., col. plates. 21 x 17 cm. c.1941. Macrae-Smith-Company.

--Once in the First Times: Folk Tales from the Philippines. Sheppard, John (1911-), illus. xvi, 215 p. illus., map (on lining-papers) 21 cm. 1949. Macrae Smith Co.

--Once in the First Times: Folk Tales from the Philippines. Sheppard, John (1911-), illus. LC 69-18630. (Illus.). x, 213 p. 21cm. 1969. (ISBN 0-8255-8140-0). (ISBN 0-8255-8141-9). Macrae Smith Co.

--One Thousand Poems For Children. 1946. (ISBN 0-8255-8146-X). Macrae Smith Company.

--Pirates and Pigeons: Famous Stories of Boyhood Years. Hayes, Katharine W., illus. LC 33-12107. 286 p. col. front., plates. 21 cm. c.1933. J. B. Lippincott Company.

--Poems For Red Letter Days. (Illus.). 1951. (ISBN 0-8255-8155-9). (ISBN 0-8255-8154-0). Macrae Smith Company.

--Thirteen Ghostly Yarns. LC 42-14388. x p., 1 l., 13-240 p. incl. plates, illus. 21 x 17 cm. 1942. Macrae-Smith-Company.

--Thirteen Ghostly Yarns. Fry, Guy, illus. LC 32-15771. xiii, 299 p. incl. front., illus., plates. 20 cm. 1932. R. Swain.

--Thirteen Ghostly Yarns. Rev. ed. Michini, Albert, illus. LC 63-20357. 211 p. illus. 21 cm. 1963. Macrae Smith.

Sechrist, Elizabeth Hough, Mrs. (1903-) & Woolsey, Janette (1904-), eds.

--It's Time for Story Hour. McCorkell, Elsie Jane, illus. LC 64-23918. 258p. illus. 24cm. c.1964. Macrae.

Seckar, Alvena V.

--Misko. Merwin, Decie (1894-1961), illus. 160p. 1956. Henry Z. Walck, Inc.

--Misko. Merwin, Decie (1894-1961), illus. LC 56-8011. 159p. illus. 21cm. 1956. Oxford University Press.

--Trapped in the Old Mine. Gotlieb, Jules, illus. LC 53-10538. 63p. illus. 22cm. (Everyday Science Stories). 1953. J. Messner.

--Zuska of the Burning Hills. Voute, Kathleen (1892-), illus. LC 52-6170. (Illus.). 222 p. 21cm. (Oxford Books for Boys and Girls). 1952. Oxford University Press.

Secor, Alson, ed. see Secor, Eugene.

Secor, Eugene (1841-)

--Verse for Little Folks and Others. Secor, Alson, ed. LC 30-10794. 64 p. illus. 23 cm. c.1911. Successful Farming.

Sedgwick, Catharine Maria (1789-1867)

--The Boy of Mount Rhigi... LC 42-27106. 3 p. l., 3-232 p. front. 17 1/2 cm. 1848. C. H. Peirce.

Sedgwick, Jane M., tr. see Balzac, Honore de.

Sedgwick, Kate & Frischkorn, Rebecca

--Children in Art. LC 77-10833. (Illus.). 56 p. 24cm. c.1978. (ISBN 0-03-020896-3). Holt, Rinehart and Winston.

Sedgwick, Miss

--Means and Ends. (Harper's Massachusetts Library, Juvenile Ser.). N.D. Harper & Bros.

--Poor Rich Man and Rich Poor Man. 1882. Harper's Trade-List.

--Stories for Young Persons. 1882. Harper's Trade-List.

--Tales Of Glauber Spa. N.D. Harper & Brothers.

--Wilton Harvey and Other Tales. N.D. Harper & Brothers.

Sedgwick, Modwana (1916-)

The Adventures of Galldora. John, Diana, illus. LC 67-1516. (Illus.). 107 p. 20cm. (Puffin Books, PS277). 1966, c.1960. Penguin Books.

Sedgwick, Rae

--The White Frame House. LC 80-65838. 132 p. 22cm. (gr. 3-6). c.1980. (ISBN 0-440-09018-0). (ISBN 0-440-09019-9). Delacorte Press.

Sedlacek, Hanus (1881-)

--Nursery Rhymes from Bohemia. Mates, Rudolf (1881-), illus. Szalatnay, Rafael D. (1884-), tr. LC 34-21836. 30 1/2cm. 24p. 1929. Robert M. McBride & company.

Sedlaczek, Teresa

Peedy Weed & What's Going on Around Here. (gr. k-3). N.D. Carlton.

See, Ingram

--The Jungle Secret. 1st ed. Floherty, John Joseph, Jr. (1892-1964), illus. LC 61-9757. (Illus.). 141 p. 22cm. (Signal Book). 1961. Doubleday.

See, Sam, pseud., see Platt, Samuel C..

Seebach, Julius Frederick (1869-) & United Lutheran Church in America. Women's Missionary Society

--All God's Children ... Six Stories of Christians in Many Lands. LC 30-249364. 3 p. l., 5-50 p. 19 cm. c.1930. Women's Missionary Society, The United Lutheran Church in America.

Seebach, Julius Frederick (1869-) & Seebach, Margaret Rebecca Himes (1875-)

--The Singing Weaver and Other Stories: Hero Tales of the Reformation. Gillespie, Jessie, illus. LC 17-21643. 7 p. l., 11-287, 1 p. 19 1/2 cm. $1.0. 1917. The Lutheran Publication Society.

Seebach, Margaret Rebecca Himes, jt. auth. see Seebach, Julius Frederick.

Seebach, Margaret Rebecca Himes, Mrs. (1875-)

--The Marigold Horse and Other Stories. LC 24-22823. vii, 9-271 p. 19 1/2 cm. c.1924. Women's Missionary Society, The United Lutheran Church in America.

--The Mystery of Jordan Green. LC 33-30456. 222 p. front., plates. 20 1/2 cm. (John Rung Prize Ser.). c.1933. The Board of Publication of the United Lutheran Church in America.

Seebach, Margaret Rebecca Himes, Mrs. (1875-), ed.

--Other People's Children. LC 14-19847. vii, 9-227 p. 19 cm. c.1914. The Lutheran Publication Society.

Seed, Cecile Eugenie see Seed, Jenny, pseud.

Seed, David

--Stream Runner. LC 78-21769. 185 p. 22cm. c.1979. (ISBN 0-590-07568-3). Four Winds Press.

Seed, Jenny, pseud., see Seed, Cecile Eugenie.

Seed, Jenny, pseud. (1930-)

--The Bushman's Dream: African Tales of the Creation. Seed, Cecile Eugenie. Brett, Bernard (1925-), illus. LC 74-33877. (Illus.). vii, 119 p. 23cm. 1st U.S. edition. 1975, c.1974. (ISBN 0-87888-083-6). Bradbury Press.

--The Great Thirst. Seed, Cecile Eugenie. LC 73-80198. 188 p. 23cm. 1973, c.1971. (ISBN 0-87888-058-5). Bradbury Press.

--The Great Thirst. Seed, Cecile Eugenie. 1974 (Bradbury Press). E.P. Dutton & Co.

--Kulumi the Brave: A Zulu Tale. Seed, Cecile Eugenie. Stubley, Trevor Hugh (1932-), illus. LC 71-82767. (Illus.). 32 p. 29cm. 1st U.S. edition. 1970. World Pub. Co.

--Tombi's Song. Seed, Cecile Eugenie. MacDougall, Donald, illus. LC 68-11645. 47p. col. illus. 21cm. c.1966. Rand McNally.

--Vengeance of the Zulu King. Seed, Cecile Eugenie. Stubley, Trevor Hugh (1932-), illus. LC 78-138546. (Illus.). drawings. 224p. (gr. 6 up). 1971. (ISBN 0-394-92138-0). Pantheon.

--The Voice of the Great Elephant. Seed, Cecile Eugenie. LC 73-77425. (Illus.). 178 p. 22cm. 1969, c.1968. Pantheon Books.

Seeger, Charles Louis., jt. auth. see Seeger, Peter.

Seeger, Elizabeth (1889-1973), adapted by.

--The Five Brothers: The Story of the Mahabharata. Baldridge, Cyrus LeRoy (1889-), illus. 320p. (gr. 6-9). 1948. John Day Books.

--The Five Sons of King Pandu: The Story of the Mahabharata. Laite, Gordon (1925-), illus. Ganguli, Kisari Mohan, tr. LC 67-21797. (Illus.). xix, 340 p. 24cm. 1967. (ISBN 0-201-09183-6, Young Scott Bks.). W. R. Scott.

Seeger, Martin L

--The Day of the Earthquake. Miller, Marilyn Jean (1925-), illus. LC 67-22600. (Illus.). 192 p. 22cm. 1967. Lothrop, Lee & Shepard.

Seeger, Peter (1919-) & Seeger, Charles Louis. (1886-1979)

--The Foolish Frog. Jagr, Miloslav, illus. Deitch, Gene, designed by. LC 73-2121. 1973. (ISBN 0-02-781480-7). Macmillan Publishing Co.

Seeger, Ruth Porter Crawford (1901-)

--American Folk Songs for Children. (gr. 1 up). N.D. Doubleday.

--American Folk Songs for Children in Home, School and Nursery School: A Book for Children, Parents and Teachers. Cooney, Barbara (1917-), illus. LC 48-9384. 190 p. illus. 29 cm. 1948. Doubleday & Co.

--American Folk Songs for Children in Home, School, and Nursery School: A Book for Children, Parents, and Teachers. Cooney, Barbara (1917-), illus. (Illus.). 192p. 1980. (Zephyr). Doubleday.

--American Folk Songs for Christmas. (gr. 1 up). 1953. Doubleday.

--Animal Folk Songs for Children: Traditional American Songs. 1st ed. Cooney, Barbara (1917-), illus. LC 50-11074. (Illus.). 80 p. 29cm. 1950. Doubleday.

Seegmiller, Jean, jt. auth. see Carlson, Renee P.

Seegmiller, Wilhelmina, jt. auth. see Van Sickle, James Hixon, Jr.

Seegmiller, Wilhelmina (1866-1913)

--Little Rhymes for Little Readers. Hallock, Ruth Mary (1876-), illus. LC 3-31978. 81 p. illus. 30 cm. 1903. Rand, McNally and Company.

--A New Garden of Verses for Children. Wickes, Frances Gillespy, ed. LC 25-22484. ix, 154 p. illus. 21 1/2 cm. c.1925. Rand, McNally & Company.

--Sing a Song of Seasons. Seegmiller, Wilhelmina (1866-1913), illus. LC 15-5174. 84 p. illus. (part col.) 23 1/2 cm. c.1914. Rand, McNally & Company.

Seeley, Eva Brunell & Lane, Martha Allen Luther (1862-)

--Chinook and His Family, True Dog Stories. LC 30-19619. x, 316 p. illus. 19 cm. c.1930. Ginn and Company.

Seely, Herman Gastrell

--A Son of the City: A Story of Boy Life. Arting, Fred J., illus. LC 17-25592. 4 p. l., 341 p. front., illus. 19 1/2 cm. $1.3. 1917. A. C. McClurg & Co.

Seely, Howard

--A Ranchman's Stories. N.D. Dodd, Mead & Co.

Seely, Sue, tr. see Stevenson, Robert Louis.

Seeman, Elizabeth Brickel (1904-)

--The Talking Dog & the Barking Man. Flora, James Royer (1914-), illus. LC 59-10961. 186p. illus. 21cm. 1960. F. Watts.

Seeman, William

--Down Goose Creek. N.D. Fleming H. Revell Co.

Seemann, Margarete (1893-1949)

--The Hummel-Book. 7th ed. Hummel, Innocentia, Sr. (1909-), illus. Eytel, Lola Ch., tr. (Secular name of Sr. Innocentia Hummel is Berta Hummel). 64p. illus. (Part col.: p4.50). N.D. W. S. Heinman.

Seers, H. Waddingham

--The Book of Nature Stories. Ford, M. C., illus. 20cm. 256p. 1921. Dodd, Mead & Co.

--Nature Stories to tell to Children. 19cm. 256p. 1918. Dodd, Mead & Co.

Seesner, Henriette Arnold Wesner

--Words and Pictures: A Book for Children. Otteson, Madalene, illus. LC 55-7290. 56p. illus. 21cm. 1955. Exposition Press.

Sefton, Catherine

--The Emma's Dilemma. Bennett, Jill (1947-), illus. LC 83-670188. (Illus.). 96p. (gr. 4-6). 1983. (ISBN 0-571-11841-0). Faber & Faber.

--Ghost & Bertie Boggin. 94p. (gr. 2-6). 1982. (ISBN 0-571-11524-1). Faber & Faber.

--The Haunting of Ellen. (Story of Suspense Ser.). (gr. 5 up). 1977. (ISBN 0-06-440084-0, Trophy). Har-Row.

--The Haunting of Ellen. LC 74-25022. 146 p. 21cm. (A Story of Suspense). 1975. (ISBN 0-06-025256-1). (ISBN 0-06-025257-X). Harper & Row.

--The Haunting of Ellen. by catherine sefton. ed. 146p. 20cm. (Harper Trophy Book). (A Story of Suspense). 1977. (ISBN 0-06-440084-0). Harper and Row.

--In a Blue Velvet Dress. 1st ed. Keith, Eros, illus. LC 72-11243. (Illus.). 160 p. 22cm. 1973. (ISBN 0-06-025262-6). (ISBN 0-06-025262-6). Harper & Row.

--Island of the Strangers. LC 85-5437. (Illus.). 118 p. 22cm. c.1985. (ISBN 0-15-239100-2). Harcourt Brace Jovanovich.

--The Sleepers on the Hill. (gr. 5-9). 1978. (ISBN 0-571-10305-7, Pub. by Faber & Faber). Merrimack Bk Serv.

Segal, David, tr. see Neshamit, Sarah.

Segal, E. A., jt. auth. see Marshak, Ilia Iakovlevich.

Segal, Edith (1902-)

--Be My Friend, and Other Poems for Boys and Girls. Kruckman, Herbert Lincoln (1904-), illus. LC 64-24794. 46p. ill. 22cm. 1964, c.1952. Citadel Press.

--Be My Friend, and Other Poems for Boys and Girls. Kruckman, Herbert Lincoln (1904-), illus. LC 53-20510. 46p. ill. 22cm. 1952. Sylvan Press.

--Come with Me: Poems, Guessing Poems, Dance Poems for Young People. 1st ed. Kamen, Samuel, illus. LC 63-24893. 63 p. illus. 23 cm. 1963. Citadel Press.

Segal, Joyce

--It's Time to Go to Bed. Eaton, Robin, illus. LC 78-20284. (Illus.). 32 p. c.1979. (ISBN 0-385-14034-7). (ISBN 0-385-14035-5). Doubleday.

--The Scariest Witch in Wellington Towers. Apple, Margot, illus. LC 79-12239. (Illus.). 45 p. 22cm. c.1981. (ISBN 0-698-30722-4). Coward, McCann & Geoghegan.

Segal, Lore Groszmann (1928-), ed. see Grimm, Jakob Ludwig Karl (1785-1863) & Grimm, Wilhelm Karl.

Segal, Lore Gruszmann (1928-), tr. see Grimm, Jakob Ludwig Karl (1785-1863) & Grimm, Wilhelm Karl.

Segal, Lore Groszmann (1928-)

--All the Way Home. 1st ed. Marshall, James (1942-), illus. LC 73-82699. (Illus.). 32 p. 19cm. 1973. (ISBN 0-374-30215-4). Farrar, Straus, Giroux.

--The Juniper Tree & Other Tales from Grimm. Sendak, Maurice Bernard (1928-), illus. 1976. (ISBN 0-685-63350-0, Noonday). FS&G.

--The Story of Mrs. Lovewright and Purrless Her Cat. Zelinsky, Paul O., illus. LC 84-25011. (Illus.). 32 p. 27cm. c.1985. (ISBN 0-394-86817-X). (ISBN 0-394-96817-4). Knopf. **Award: (NYT).**

--The Story of Old Mrs. Brubeck & How She Looked for Trouble & Where She Found Him. Sewall, Marcia (1935-), illus. LC 78-31317. (Illus.). 40p. (gr. k-2). 1978. (ISBN 0-394-84039-9). Pantheon. **Award: (NYT).**

--Tell Me a Mitzi. 1st ed. Pincus, Harriet (1938-), illus. LC 69-14980. (Illus.). 40 p. 1970. Farrar, Straus and Giroux.

Segal, Lore Groszmann (1928-) & Wells, Rosemary

--Tell Me a Trudy: Stories. LC 77-24123. p. cm. 1977. (ISBN 0-374-37395-7). Farrar, Straus and Giroux.

Segal, Nelly, tr. see Gutman, Naham.

Segal, Nelly, tr. see Wisler, Israel Menahem.

Segal, Sheila F.

--Joshua's Dream. Paiss, Jana, illus. LC 84-8450. (Illus.). 26 p. 22cm. c.1985. (ISBN 0-8074-0272-9). Union of American Hebrew Congregations.

Segar, Elzie Crisler (1894-1938)

--Popeye. N.D. David McKay Co.

--Popeye Among the White Savages: With "Pop-up" Picture, Drawn. 1 p. l., 5-60 (i.e. 62) p. illus. (1 col.) 13 cm. (On cover: The midget Pop-Up Bks.). c.1934. Blue Ribbon Press.

--Popeye and the Pirates. Wehr, Julian, illus. LC 45-7197. (Illus.). 24p. 27cm. 1945. Duenewald Printing Corp.

--Popeye, the Sailor Man. LC 37-3371. (Illus.). 33p. 27cm. 1937. Grosset & Dunlop.

Segerstedt, Albrekt Julius (1763-1831)

--My Lady Legend. Rydingsvard, Anna Maria (1856-), tr. (Illus.). N.D. Lothrop Pub. Co.

--My Lady Legend, and Other Folk Tales from the North. Rydingsvard, Anna Maria Von (1856-), tr. from Swedish. Segerstedt, Albrekt Julius (1763-1831), intro. by. LC 14-7958. 3 p. l., 297 p. 19 cm. 1891. D. Lothrop Company.

Segovia, Gertrudis (1881-)

--The Spanish Fairy Book (Cuento De Hadas). Quinn, Elisabeth Vernon, tr. LC 78-74519. 321 p. 20cm. Repr. of 1918 ed. Orig. Title: Cuento De Hadas. 1979. (ISBN 0-8486-0222-6). Core Collection Books.

--The Spanish Fairy Book (Cuentos De Hadas). Wood, George W., illus. Quinn, Elisabeth Vernon (1881-), tr. LC 18-201725. 7 p. l., 3-321 p. col. front., col. plates. 21 cm. c.1918. Frederick A. Stokes Company.

Segraves, Kelly Lee (1942-)

--Delicate Deception. LC 78-1847. p. cm. 1978. (ISBN 0-89293-022-5). Beta Books.

--Whaling Through Jonah. (Illus., Orig.). (Young Readers Ser.). (gr. 6-12). 1977. (ISBN 0-89293-077-2). Beta Bk.

Seguin, Alfred

--The Black Crusoe. Meaulle, Fortune Louis, illus. LC 73-38022. (Illus.). 356 p. 23cm. (The Black Heritage Library Collection). 1972. (ISBN 0-8369-8995-3). Books for Libraries Press.

Seguin-Fontes, Martha

--The Cat's Surprise. Beris, Sandra, adapted by. LC 83-5433. p. cm. (A Larousse Thinking Cap Story). c.1983. Larousse.

--Find Me!. Beris, Sandra, adapted by. LC 83-9898. p. cm. c.1983. Larousse.

--Secret Sounds Around the House. Seguin-Fontes, Martha, illus. Beris, Sandra, tr. from Fr. LC 83-14875. (Illus.). 32p. (Thinking Cap Ser.). 1984. (ISBN 0-88332-327-3). Larousse.

--A Wedding Book. Beris, Sandra, adapted by. LC 83-5434. p. cm. (A Larousse Thinking Cap Story). c.1983. Larousse.

Seguin, Lisabeth Gooch Seguin, Mrs.

--Children's Pastime: Pictures and Stories for the Little Ones. (Illus.). N.D. E. P. Dutton & Co.

Segur, Adrienne

--My Big Book of Cat Stories. Hubbard, Eleanore Mineah, illus. LC 67-20160. (Illus.). 108 p. 33cm. (Deluxe golden book). 1967. Golden Press.

Segur, Adrienne, illus.

--The Fairy Tale Book. Ponsot, Marie, tr. (Giant Little Golden Book). 1958. Golden Press.

Segur, Sophie Rostopchine, jt. auth. see Grote.

Segur, Sophie Rostopchine, Mrs. (1799-1874)

--The Adventures of a Donkey. LC 24-16765. 6 p. l., 274 p. incl. front., illus., plates. 18 cm. 1880. The Baltimore Publishing Company.

--The Adventures of a Donkey: From the French of Mme. la Comtesse De Segur. P. S, tr. LC 24-167651. 6 p. l., 274 p. 1 l., incl. front., illus., plates. 19 1/2 cm. 1881. J. P. Piet.

--The Angel Inn. Marriott, Patricia (1920-), illus. LC 76-481227. (Illus.). 231 p. 21cm. Orig. Title: L'auberge De L'ange-Gardien. 1976. (ISBN 0-224-01263-0). J. Cape.

--The Angel Inn. Marriott, Patricia (1920-), illus. Aiken, Joan (1924-), tr. LC 78-12784. p. cm. Orig. Title: L'auberge De L'ange-Gardien. 1978. (ISBN 0-916144-28-3). (ISBN 0-916144-29-1). Stemmer House Publishers.

--At the Inn of the Guardian Angel. Pendleton, Amena, retold by. Freeman, Margaret (1893-), illus. LC 31-30507. x p., 1 l., 256 p. col. front., illus., col. plates. 20 1/2 cm. 1931. Houghton Mifflin Company.

--Forest Of Lilacs. (Harlin Quest Ser.). N.D. Crown Publishers.

--Forest of Lilacs. Claveloux, Nicole, illus. LC 72-84756. (Illus.). 40 p. 28cm. c.1969. Harlin Quist.

--Forest of Lilacs. Claveloux, Nicole, illus. (Illus.). 56p. (gr. 2 up). 1968. (ISBN 0-531-04025-9). (ISBN 0-531-05025-4). Quist.

--French Fairy Tales, 1 of 3 Vols. Didier, Jules, illus. Coleman, Mrs., et al., trs. (Famous Fairy Library). N.D. Porter & Coates.

--Happy Surprises. Olcott, Julia, as told by. Hubbard, Eleanore Mineah, illus. Loiseaux, Louis Aguste, intro. by. LC 29-29526. 5 p. l., 15-163, 1 p. incl. front., illus. col. double pl. 22 1/2 cm. c.1929. A. Whitman & Co.

--The Inn of the Guardian Angel. (Illus.). 1882. Lee & Shepard.

--The Inn of the Guardian Angel. Afoulquier, Jean Antoine Valentin, illus. Adams, H. I. (1822-1896), tr. from Fr. LC 77-360893. (Illus.). vi, 314 p., 31 leaves of plates. 19cm. 1871. Lee and Shepard.

--Old French Fairy Tales. Sterrett, Virginia Frances (1900-), illus. LC 20-19079. 279 p. col. front., illus., col. plates. 29 cm. $5.0. c.1920. The Penn Publishing Company.

--Princess Rosette and Other Fairy Tales. Kutcher, Ben (1895-), illus. Olcott, Virginia, tr. LC 30-28182. 3 p. l., 9-200 p. incl. front., illus., plates. 23 cm. c.1930. Macrae Smith Company.

--Sophie: The Story of a Bad Little Girl. Barney, Maginel Wright, Mrs. (1881-1966), illus. Melcher, Marguerite Fellows, tr. LC 29-181779. 5 p. l., 3-157, 1 p. incl. front., illus. 20 cm. 1929. A. A. Knopf.

--The Story of a Donkey. Welsh, Charles (1850-1914) & Dole, Charles Fletcher (1845-), eds. Saunders, F. H., illus. LC 1-30824. (Illus.). 19 1/2cm. 71p. (Heath's Home and School Classics). 1901. Heath & Co.

--The Story of a Donkey. Willard, James Hartwell (1847-), illus. LC 3-255393. xiv, 15-132 p. incl. front., illus., plates. 19 1/2 cm. (Altermus' Good Time Ser.). 1903. H. Altermus Company.

--The Wise Little Donkey: Memoirs of a Donkey. Brock, Emma Lillian (1886-1974), illus. Loiseaux, Louis Marie Auguste, tr. LC 31-21185. 191 p. col. front., illus., col. plates. 22 1/2 cm. (Translation of Memoires d'un aue.). Orig. Title: Translation of Memoires d'un aue. c.1931. A. Whitman & Co.

Segur, Sophie Rostopchine, Mrs. (1799-1874) & Melcher, Marguerite Fellows

--Memoirs of a Donkey. Ford, Julia Lauren (1891-), illus. LC 24-25127. 7 p. l., 238 p. incl. front., illus. plates. 16 1/2 cm. (Lettered on cover: The Little Library). 1924. The Macmillan Company.

Segur, Sophie Rostopchine, Mrs. (1799-1874) & Welsh, Charles

--Sophie. Prand, Monsieur Eugene, illus. LC 1-12756. vi, 96 p. incl. illus., plates. front. 19 1/2 cm. (On cover: Heath's home and school classics. no. 35). 1901. D. C. Heath & Co.

Segur, Sophie Rostopchine (1799-1874)

--French Fairy Tales. (New Acorn Library). N.D. John C. Winston Co.

Seibel, George (1872-)

--The Stories He Told. LC 47-12387. 167 p. 23 cm. 1947. Gibson Press.

Seibert, Elizabeth G

--The Abrus Necklace. LC 56-10435. 222 p. 21 cm. 1956. Macrae Smith Co.

--Sidonie. 1st ed. Keene, Ray, illus. LC 62-193301. 188p. illus. 22cm. 1962. Bobbs-Merrill.

--White Rose & Ragged Staff. LC 68-11885. (Illus.). 222 p. 22cm. 1968. Bobbs-Merrill.

Seibert, Jerry

--Sacajawea: Guide to Lewis and Clark. Bjorklund, Lorence F. (1913-1978), illus. LC 60-13063. 192p. illus. 22cm. (Piper books). c.1960. Houghton Mifflin.

Seibert, Venita (1875-)

--The Gossamer Thread: Being the Chronicles of Velleda, Who Understood About "the Different World,". Benda, Wladyslaw Theodore (1873-), illus. LC 10-15395. (Being the Chronicles of Velleda, Who Understood About" the Different World".). 6 p. l., 224 p. front., plates. 19 1/2 cm. $1.0. c.1910. Small, Maynard & Company.

Seibold, Frank M. (1914-)

--Tales From The Sonita. (Illus.). N.D. (ISBN 0-8111-0523-7). The Naylor Company.

Seide, Diane see Seidner, Diane, pseud.

Seidel, Heinrich

--The Magic Inkstand. Anderson, Wayne (1946-), illus. Taylor, Elizabeth W., tr. (Illus.). 160p. 1982. (ISBN 0-224-01856-6, Pub. by Chatto-Bodley-Jonathan). Merrimack Pub Cir.

Seidelman, James Edward (1926-) & Mintonye, Grace

--The Fourteenth Dragon. LC 77-73526. (gr. 1 up). 1977. (ISBN 0-8252-2482-9). Quist.

--The Fourteenth Dragon. Anderson, Robert Lindberg, illus. LC 68-29127. (Illus.). 1 v. (unpaged. 1968. (ISBN 0-531-05023-8). (ISBN 0-531-04023-2). H. Quist.

Seiden, Art, ed.

--The Junior Joke Book. (Wonder Play Bks.). N.D. Wonder Books.

--Treasury of Bedtime Stories. Seiden, Art, illus. (Illus.). 160p. (gr. k-3). 1969. (ISBN 0-448-02833-6). G&D.

Seiden, Art, illus.

--Little Bunny Learns Colors. LC 81-80765. (Illus.). 24 p. 23cm. (Happy house bks.). c.1982. (ISBN 0-394-84968-X). Random House.

--My ABC Book. LC 54-151024. unpaged illus. 21cm. (Wonder books, 610). c.1953. Wonder Books.

--Read Aloud Train Stories. LC 57-4244. (Illus.). 160p. 1957. Wonder Books Inc.

--Snow White and the Seven Dwarfs. LC 67-23810. 1 v. (unpaged) col. illus. 29 cm. (Nursery treasure books). N.D. Grosset & Dunlap.

--Snow White and the Seven Dwarfs. LC 55-26938. (Illus.). 21cm. 1955. Treasure Books.

--Tick-Tock. (Illus.). 10p. (Platt & Munk Peggy Cloth Clock Bks.). (ps). 1982. (ISBN 0-448-46828-X, G&D). Putnam Pub Group.

--Train Stories. (Illus.). (Read-Aloud Bks.). (ps). N.D. Wonder.

Seiden, Art, jt. ed. see Glazer, Tom.

Seidler, Ann G., jt. auth. see Slepian, Janice B.

Seidler, Barbara

--The Legend of King Piast. Rosinski, Grzegorz, illus. Kedron, Jane, tr. (Illus.). (Young People's Ser.). (gr. 2-8). 1977. (ISBN 0-917004-08-6). Kosciuszko.

--Queen Wanda & the Wawel Dragon. Kedron, Jane, tr. (Illus.). (Young People's Ser.). 1974. (ISBN 0-917004-06-X). Kosciuszko.

Seidler, Lotte, tr. see Lengstrand, Rolf.

Seidler, Rosalie

--Grumpus and the Venetian Cat. Seidler, Rosalie, illus. LC 64-19565. (Illus.). 39p. 1964. Atheneum.

--Panda Cake. Seidler, Rosalie, illus. LC 78-6109. (Illus.). 33 p. 20cm. c.1978. (ISBN 0-8193-0962-1). Parents' Magazine Press.

Seidler, Tor

--Terpin. LC 82-11734. p. cm. 1982. (ISBN 0-374-37413-9). Farrar, Straus & Giroux.

Seidlin, Oskar, jt. auth. see Plant, Richard.

Seidlin, Oskar (1911-)

--Green Wagons. Cooney, Barbara (1917-), illus. Rypins, Senta Jones, tr. LC 43-6806. 2 p. l., 130, 1 p. illus. 24 cm. 1943. Houghton Mifflin Company.

Seidman, M. S

--Who Woke the Sun?. Kuskin, Karla Seidman (1932-), illus. LC 60-8695. (Illus.). unpaged. 17cm. 1960. Macmillan.

Seidmann-Freud, Tom (1892-1930)

--The Magic Boat. LC 80-83156. (Illus.). 10 p. 22cm. c.1981. (ISBN 0-688-00404-0). Greenwillow Books.

--Peregrin and the Goldfish. LC 30-20057. (Illus.). 25p. 29cm. 1929. Macmillan Co.

Seidner, Diane, pseud., see Seide, Diane.

Seidner, Diane, pseud. (1930-)

--Young Nurse in New York. Seide, Diane. LC 67-16206. x, 113 p. 22cm. 1967. Dial Press.

Seifert, Emma

--Dr. Eckhart's Boys. Ireland, Mary Eliza Haines, Mrs. (1834-1927), tr. LC 10-20053. 120 p. 15 1/2 cm. 1901. U. B. Publishing House.

Seignobosc, Francoise see Francoise, pseud.

Seignobosc, Francoise (1897-1961)

--The Big Rain. Francoise, pseud. Seignobosc, Francoise (1897-1961), illus. Francoise, pseud. LC 61-5786. (Illus.). unpaged. 27cm. (gr. k-2). c.1961. (ISBN 0-684-12400-9). Scribner.

--Biquette, the Little White Goat. Francoise, pseud. Seignobosc, Francoise (1897-1961), illus. Francoise, pseud. LC 53-6106. (Illus.). 26cm. 32p. c.1953. Scribner.

--Chouchou. Francoise, pseud. Seignobosc, Francoise (1897-1961), illus. Francoise, pseud. LC 58-10636. (Illus.). (gr. k-2). c.1958. (ISBN 0-684-13460-8, ScribJ). Scribner. **Award: (NYT).**

--Fanchette and Jeannot. Francoise, pseud. Authorized American. LC 38-11329. (Illus.). 27 x 24cm. 25p. 1937. Grosset & Dunlop.

--The Gay ABC. Francoise, pseud. LC 39-30537. (Illus.). 24cm. 55p. 1939. C. Scribner's Sons, Ltd.

--Jeanne-Marie at the Fair. Francoise, pseud. Seignobosc, Francoise (1897-1961), illus. Francoise, pseud. LC 59-6618. (Illus.). unpaged. 26cm. (gr. k-2). c.1959. (ISBN 0-684-92297-5). Scribner.

--Jeanne-Marie Counts Her Sheep. Francoise, pseud. Seignobosc, Francoise (1897-1961), illus. Francoise, pseud. LC 51-9415. (Illus.). 32 p. 26cm. c.1951. Scribner.

--Jeanne-Marie in Gay Paris. Francoise, pseud. Seignobosc, Francoise (1897-1961), illus. Francoise, pseud. LC 56-6139. unpaged. illus. 26cm. c.1956. (ISBN 0-684-12700-8). Scribner. **Award: (ALA).**

--Minou. Francoise, pseud. Seignobosc, Francoise (1897-1961), illus. Francoise, pseud. LC 62-1705. (Illus.). 1 v. (unpaged. 26cm. c.1962. Scribner.

--Mr. and Mrs. So and So. Francoise, pseud. Seignobosc, Francoise (1897-1961), illus. Francoise, pseud. LC 39-6124. 36 p. col. illus. 27 cm. c.1939. Oxford University Press.

--Noel for Jeanne-Marie. Francoise, pseud. Seignobosc, Francoise (1897-1961), illus. Francoise, pseud. LC 53-12093. (Illus.). 26cm. (gr. k-2). 1953. (ISBN 0-684-13165-X, ScribJ). Scribner.

--Small-Trot. Francoise, pseud. Seignobosc, Francoise (1897-1961), illus. Francoise, pseud. LC 52-7751. (Illus.). unpaged. 24cm. 1952. Scribner.

--Springtime for Jeanne-Marie. Francoise, pseud. Seignobosc, Francoise (1897-1961), illus. Francoise, pseud. LC 55-14216. (Illus.). 27cm. 32p. (ps-1). c.1955. (ISBN 0-684-12719-9). (ISBN 0-684-12633-8). Scribner. **Award: (ALA).**

--The Story of Colette. Francoise, pseud. LC 40-80540. 32p. 28cm. 1940. C. Scribner.

--Thank-You Book. Francoise, pseud. Seignobosc, Francoise (1897-1961), illus. Francoise, pseud. LC 47-30948. (Illus.). 26cm. 32p. (ps-1). 1947. (ISBN 0-684-13176-5). Scribner.

--The Things I Like. Francoise, pseud. LC 60-6337. unpaged. illus. 26cm. c.1960. Scribner.

--What Do You Want to Be?. Francoise, pseud. Seignobosc, Francoise (1897-1961), illus. Francoise, pseud. LC 57-6076. (Illus.). unpaged. 26cm. c.1957. Scribner.

Seiler, Conrad (1897-)

--The Clown Out West: A Comedy for Children in Three Acts. LC 63-48872. 82 p. 19 cm. (Longmans' Play Series). c.1959. Longmans, Green.

Seir, Birte

--Blue Jay and the Monster. Seir, Birte, illus. Campbell, Karel, tr. (Illus.). 40 p. 27cm. 1967. Lerner Publications Co.

Seivwright, Jean

--Castle Secrets. Herrick, Arthur R., illus. LC 31-29813. 4 p. l., 3-245 p. col. front., illus. 20 cm. 1931. Little, Brown, and Company.

Seixas, Judith S. (1922-)

--Junk Food: What it Is, What it Does. Huffman, Tom, illus. LC 83-14135. (Illus.). 6 1/4 x 8 3/8. 48p. (16 pt.). (gr. 1-3). 1984. (ISBN 0-688-02559-5). (ISBN 0-688-02560-9). Greenwillow.

--Vitamins: What They Are, What They Do. Huffman, Tom, illus. LC 85-17761. (Illus.). 6 1/4 x 8 3/8. 56p. (16 pt.). (gr. 1-4). 1986. (ISBN 0-688-06065-X). (ISBN 0-688-06066-8). Greenwillow.

Sejima, Yoshimasa (1913-) & Takeichi, Yasoo

--The Mighty Prince. LC 73-127524. (Illus.). 24 p. 30cm. 1971. Crown Publishers.

Seki, Keigo (1899-), ed.

--Folktales of Japan. Adams, Robert J., tr. 222p. 1963. The University Of Chicago Press.

Seklemian, A. G

--The Golden Maiden and Other Folk Tales and Fairy Stories Told in Armenia. Dolbear, Ella & Geary, Elizabeth, illus. Blackwell, Alice Stone, intro. by. LC 98-188. xxi, 224 p. front., illus. 19 cm. 1898. The Helman-Taylor Company.

Sekorova, Dagmar, compiled by.

--European Fairy Tales. Hanak, Mirko, illus. LC 79-116344. (Illus.). 169 p. 25cm. 1971. Lothrop, Lee & Shepard Co.

Sela, Owen

--The Bengali Inheritance. 1975. (ISBN 0-394-49410-5). Pantheon Books.

--The Kiriov Tapes. 1974. (ISBN 0-394-48534-3). Pantheon Books.

--The Portugese Fragment. (9). 1973. (ISBN 0-394-48824-5). Pantheon Books.

Selarose, Rose

--Once Upon a Time in the Meadow: A "Six Cousins" Story. LC 81-85056. (Illus.). 20 p. 24cm. (Golden Storytime Bk.). c.1982. (ISBN 0-307-11962-9). Golden Press.

Selbert, Ingrid

--Our Changing World. Miller, Andrew, illus. (Illus.). 12p. 1982. (ISBN 0-399-20869-0, Philomel). Putnam Pub Group.

Selby, Angelica

--On Duty: A Story for Girls. (Illus.). N.D. Frederick Warne.

Selby, Judy

--Happy Day You. LC 71-121375. (Illus.). 63 p. 1970. (ISBN 0-670-36077-5). Grossman Publishers.

Selby-Lowndes, Joan

--The Blue Train: The Story of Anton Dolin. LC 58-9112. 253 p. 21cm. 1958. Abelard-Schuman.

--Circus Train. Lewis, Geoffrey Dean, illus. LC 57-5306. 240p. illus. 22cm. 1957. Abelard-Schuman.

Selby, N. Harcourt

--The Real Diary of a Real Girl. LC 4-11525. 187 p. incl. front., plates. 16 cm. 1904. Street & Smith.

Selby-Lowndes, Joan, tr. see Guillot, Rene.

Selden, George see Thompson, George Selden, pseud.

Selden, George (1929-)

--Harry Kitten and Tucker Mouse. Thompson, George Selden, pseud. Williams, Garth Montgomery (1912-), illus. LC 83-16530. p. cm. 1985. (ISBN 0-374-32860-9). Farrar Straus Giroux.

Selden, Neil Roy (1931-)

--The Great Lakeside High Experiment. 192p. (Orig.). (gr. 7 up). 1982. (ISBN 0-590-31709-1, Wishing Star). Scholastic Inc.

Selden, Samuel (1899-1979), ed. see Shakespeare, William.

Selders, Adelbert

--Children's Stories. LC 20-16799. 84 p. front. (port.) 18 cm. 1920. Piedmont Herald.

Seldes, Gilbert Vivian (1893-1970), intro. by see Kent, Jack.

Self, Margaret Cabell (1902-)

--Chitter Chat Stories. Grilley, Virginia, illus. LC 46-5470. 72 p. illus. 23 1/2 cm. 1946. E. P. Dutton & Company, Inc.

--Henrietta. Lee, Eileen Littlefield, illus. LC 66-24003. (Illus.). 60 p. 26cm. 1966. Vanguard Press.

--Ponies on Parade. Self, Margaret Cabell (1902-), illus. LC 45-3504. 87, 1 p. incl. col. front., col. illus. 23 1/2 cm. 1945. E. P. Dutton & Company, Inc.

--The Shaggy Little Burro of San Miguel. Fraser, Betty M., pseud. (1928-), illus. Fraser, Elizabeth Marr. LC 65-230218. 46p. illus. 23cm. 1966, c.1965. Duell.

--The Shaggy Little Burro of San Miguel. Fraser, Betty M., pseud. (1928-), illus. Fraser, Elizabeth Marr. (Illus.). (gr. 2-5). 1967. (ISBN 0-696-79312-1). Hawthorn.

--Sky Rocket: The Story of a Little Bay Horse. Savitt, Sam (1917-), illus. LC 78-111913. (Illus.). x, 270 p. 22cm. 1970. Dodd, Mead.

--Susan and Jane Learn to Ride. Jefferson, Robert Louis (1929-), illus. LC 65-24907. (Illus.). 152 p. 22cm. 1965. Macrae Smith Co.

--Those Smith Kids. Howe, Gertrude Herrick (1902-), illus. LC 44-6675. 185 p. incl. plates. 21 cm. 1944. E. P. Dutton & Company, Inc.

--A Treasury of Horse Stories. Megargee, Edwin, illus. 368p. 1945. A. S. Barnes & Co.

Self, Margaret M., ed. see Fergus, Meryl.

Self, Margaret M. (1917-)

--Betsy & Brian Are Kind. (ps). 1975. (ISBN 0-8307-0394-2). Regal.

--Betsy & Brian Come to Church. (Illus.). 8p. (ps). 1975. (ISBN 0-8307-0382-9). Regal.

--Betsy & Brian Say, "Thank You, God". (ps). 1975. (ISBN 0-8307-0384-5). Regal.

--Betsy & Brian's Christmas. (ps). 1975. (ISBN 0-8307-0385-3). Regal.

--Betsy & Brian's Glad Easter. (ps). 1975. (ISBN 0-8307-0391-8). Regal.

--Betty & Brian Can Help. 8p. (ps). 1975. (ISBN 0-8307-0389-6). Regal.

--Betty & Brian Do Good Things. (ps). 1975. (ISBN 0-8307-0393-4). Regal.

--Betty & Brian Go for a Walk. (ps). 1975. (ISBN 0-8307-0392-6). Regal.

God Helps Betsy & Brian. 8p. (ps). 1975. (ISBN 0-8307-0386-1). Regal.

Selfridge, Barbara, retold by.

--The Brave Prince. Matamoros, Concha, illus. LC 66-140488. 1v. (unpaged) col. illus. 24cm. (Holly Story Book Library__ Q1048). N.D. World.

--Poor Mr. Bear. Molino, illus. LC 66-14047. 1v. (unpaged) col. illus. 24cm. (Holly story bk. lib. Holly bk., Q1047). N.D. World.

--The Timid Dragon: A Folktale from South America. Correas, Jose, illus. LC 65-247377. 1v. (unpaged) col. illus. 24cm. (Holy story bk. lib.). c.1965. World.

--The Viking. Rojas, Riera, illus. LC 65-24740. 1v. (unpaged) col. illus. 24cm. (Holly Story Book Library). c.1965. World.

Selfridge, Oliver G

--Fingers Come in Fives. Tinkelman, Murray (1933-), illus. LC 65-19303. 44p. col. illus. 24cm. c.1966. Houghton.

--Sticks. (Illus.). (gr. k-4). 1967. (ISBN 0-395-07101-1). HM.

--Trouble with Dragons. Hughes, Shirley (1929-), illus. LC 77-22441. (Illus.). 86 p. 25cm. c.1978. (ISBN 0-201-07458-3). Addison-Wesley.

Selig, Sylvie, jt. auth. see Hoban, Russell Conwell.

Selig, Sylvie, jt. auth. see Junne, I. K.

Selig, Sylvie, jt. auth. see Maschler, Fay.

Selig, Sylvie, jt. auth. see Turin, Adela.

Selig, Sylvie (1942-)

--Kangaroo. 42p. (gr. k-1). 1980. (ISBN 0-224-01746-2, Pub. by Chatto Bodley Jonathan). Merrimack Pub Cir.

Seligman, Dorothy Halle

--Run Away Home. Hoffmann, Christine, illus. LC 74-84699. (Illus.). 31 p. 27cm. 1969. Golden Gate Junior Books.

--The Trouble with Horses. Hoffmann, Christine, illus. LC 71-157853. (Illus.). 32 p. 27cm. 1971. (ISBN 0-87464-178-0). (ISBN 0-87464-179-9). Golden Gate Junior Books.

Seligman, Iran L., jt. auth. see Miller, Patricia K.

Seligmann, Jean H., jt. auth. see Levine, Milton I.

Seligmann, Jean & Levine, Milton

--Tommy Visits the Doctor. Scarry, Richard McClure (1919-), illus. (Illus.). (ps-1). 1962. (ISBN 0-307-60480-2, Golden Pr). Western Pub.

Selincourt, Aubrey De see De Selincourt, Aubrey.

Selkirk, Jane, pseud., see Chapman, John Stanton Higham.

Selkirk, Jane, pseud. (1891-1972)

--Blue Smoke Mystery. Chapman, John Stanton Higham. Brown, Paul (1893-1958), illus. LC 43-6457. ix p., 1 l., 270 p. incl. illus., plates (part double) 21 cm. 1943. Dodd, Mead & Comapny.

--Clue of the Cipher Key. Chapman, John Stanton Higham. LC 42-8148. 4 p. 1l., 3-296 p. 21 cm. 1942. Dodd, Mead & Company.

--Green Garnet Mystery. Chapman, John Stanton Higham. LC 46-4465. 4 p. l., 210 p. 19 1/2 cm. 1946. Dodd, Mead & Company.

--Mystery of the Hectic Holidays. Chapman, John Stanton Higham. LC 44-8263. 5 p. l., 222 p. 19 cm. 1944. Dodd, Mead & Company.

--Mystery of the Jasper Jewel Case. Chapman, John Stanton Higham. LC 41-4135. vii, 238 p. illus. 21 cm. 1941. Dodd, Mead & Company.

--Treasure Box Mystery: An Ethridge Acres Mystery. Chapman, John Stanton Higham. LC 51-14195. 307 p. 21 cm. (Junior Red badge mysteries). 1951. Dodd, Mead.

Selkirk, Jane, pseud. (1891-1972) & Chapman, Mary Ilsley

--Mystery of Horseshoe Caves. Chapman, John Stanton Higham. LC 48-11254. (Jane Selkirk is the Joint Pseud. of John Stanton Higham Chapman and Mary Ilsley Chapman). 21cm. vii, 209p. (Junior Red Badge Mysteries). 1948. Dodd, Mead & Company.

Selkowe, Valrie M.

--Spring Green. 1st ed. Bassett, Jeni Crisler, illus. LC 84-11202. (Illus.). 28 p. 21cm. c.1985. (ISBN 0-688-04055-1). (ISBN 0-688-04056-X). Lothrop, Lee & Shepard Books.

Sell, Nancy J

--The Wandering Heart. LC 66-18947. 248p. 23cm. 1966. Zondervan.

Sell, Roger S., ed. see Frost, Robert Lee.

Selleger-Elout, J M & Van Stockum, Hilda Gerarda (1908-)

--Marian and Marion. Midderigh-Bokhorst, B., illus. LC 49-8404. 177 p. illus. 21 cm. 1949. Viking Press.

Sellers, Naomi, pseud., see Flack, Naomi John White.

Sellers, Ronnie (1948-)

--If Christmas Were A Poem. Ackley, Peggy Jo, illus. LC 83-7575. (Illus.). 32p. (ps-3). 1983. (ISBN 0-89845-057-8). (ISBN 0-89845-164-7). Caedmon.

--My First Day at School. Stren, Patti, illus. LC 85-5752. (Illus.). 29 p. 24cm. 1985. (ISBN 0-89845-372-0). (ISBN 0-89845-373-9). Caedmon.

--When Springtime Comes. Ackley, Peggy Jo, illus. LC 83-23988. (Illus.). 1984. (ISBN 0-89845-276-7). (ISBN 0-89845-277-5). Caedmon.

Sellew, Catharine Freeman (1922-)

--Adventures with Abraham's Children. Savage, Steele (1900-), illus. (Illus.). (An introduction to the men of the Old Testament). (gr. 5 up). 1964. (ISBN 0-316-78051-0). Little.

--Adventures with the Giants. 1st ed. Savage, Steele (1900-), illus. LC 50-6633. xi, 132p. col. illus. 21cm. (gr. 1-3). 1950. (ISBN 0-316-78053-7). Little, Brown.

--Adventures with the Gods. Hauman, George (1890-1961) & Hauman, Doris, Mrs. (1897-), illus. LC 45-6154. 6 p. l., 114 p. col. plates. 21 cm. 1945. Little, Brown and Company.

--Adventures with the Heroes. 1st ed. Savage, Steele (1900-), illus. LC 54-5125. 145p. illus. 21cm. 1954. (ISBN 0-316-78055-3). Little, Brown.

Sellew, Rebecca Elisebeth Tucker, Mrs. (1856-), selected by.

--The Silver Shower,and Other Stories for Young Readers. LC 14-14917. 160 p. front., plates. 17 1/2 cm. $0.5. c.1914. W. B. Rose.

Sellier, Charles E., Jr.

--The Life & Times of Grizzly Adams. LC 77-73343. (Illus.). (gr. 4-12). 1977. (ISBN 0-917214-02-1). Schick Sunn.

Sells, E. S., Mrs.

--Amy's Temptation. (Illus.). N.D. Methodist Book Concern.

--Amy's Temptation. N.D. Nelson & Phillips.

Selman, LaRue

--Boots, Two. Jordan, Alton, ed. (Illus.). (Buppet Ser.). (gr. k-3). 1981. (ISBN 0-89868-094-8, Read Res). (ISBN 0-89868-105-7). ARO Pub.

--The Hero, Two. Jordan, Alton, ed. (Illus.). (Buppet Ser.). (gr. k-3). 1981. (ISBN 0-89868-089-1, Read Res). (ISBN 0-89868-100-6). ARO Pub.

--JD & the Bee. Jordan, Alton, ed. (Illus.). (Buppet Ser.). (gr. k-3). 1981. (ISBN 0-89868-093-X, Read Res). (ISBN 0-89868-104-9). ARO Pub.

--Rain Frog. Jordan, Alton, ed. (Illus.). (Buppet Ser.). (gr. k-3). 1981. (ISBN 0-89868-091-3, Read Res). (ISBN 0-89868-102-2). ARO Pub.

--Sammy Skunk Plays the Clown. Jordan, Alton, ed. (Illus.). (Buppet Ser.). (gr. k-3). 1981. (ISBN 0-89868-097-2, Read Res). (ISBN 0-89868-108-1). ARO Pub.

Selous, Edmund

--Tommy Smith Again at the Zoo. N.D. J.B. Lippincott.

--Tommy Smith at the Zoo. N.D. J.B Lippincott.

--Tommy Smith's Animals. (Illus.). N.D. Frederick A. Stokes.

--Tommy's Smith's Other Animals. (Illus.). N.D. Frederick A. Stokes.

Selover, Zabeth, jt. auth. see Bailey, Bernadine Freeman, Mrs.

Selsam, Millicent Ellis (1912-), ed. see Ruchlis, Hyman.

Selsam, Millicent Ellis (1912-)

--Benny's Animals, and How He Put Them in Order. Lobel, Arnold Stark (1933-), illus. LC 66-10725. (Illus.). 60 p. 23cm. (Science I Can Read Book). 1966. Harper & Row.

--The Bug That Laid the Golden Eggs. Kaufmann, John (1931-) & Krieger, Harold, illus. (Illus.). 60, 3 p. 23cm. (Science I can read book). 1967. Harper & Row.

--Egg to Chick. Wolff, Barbara, illus. LC 74-85034. (Illus.). 5 7/8 x 8 1/2. 64p. (18 pt.). (Nature I Can Read Bks.). (gr. k-3). 1970. (ISBN 0-06-025290-1). Har-Row.

--Greg's Microscope. Lobel, Arnold Stark (1933-), illus. LC 63-8002. (Illus.). 64 p. 23cm. (Science I Can Read Bk.). 1963. (ISBN 0-06-025296-0). Harper & Row.

--Hidden Animals. LC 72-85020. (Illus.). 5 7/8 x 8 1/2. 64p. (18 pt.). (Nature I Can Read Bks.). (gr. k-3). 1969. (ISBN 0-06-025281-2). (ISBN 0-06-025282-0). Har-Row.

--Let's Get Turtles. Lobel, Arnold Stark (1933-), illus. (Illus.). (Science I Can Read Bks.). (gr. k-3). 1965. (ISBN 0-06-025311-8, HarpJ). Har-Row.

--More Potatoes!. Shecter, Ben (1935-), illus. LC 78-183167. (Illus.). 5 7/8 x 8 1/2. 64p. (18 pt.). (Nature I Can Read Bks.). (gr. k-3). 1972. (ISBN 0-06-025324-X). Har-Row.

--Nature Detective. N.D. E. M. Hale & Co.

--Plenty of Fish. Blegvad, Erik (1923-), illus. LC 60-5786. 61p. illus. 23cm. (Science I Can Read Bk.). 1960. Harper.

--Terry and the Caterpillars. Lobel, Arnold Stark (1933-), illus. LC 62-13309. 64p. illus. 23cm. (Science I Can Read Bk.). 1962. (ISBN 0-06-025406-8). Harper & Row.

--Tony's Birds. Werth, Kurt (1896-), illus. LC 61-577510. 64p. illus. 23cm. (Science I Can Read Bk.). 1961. Harper.

--When an Animal Grows. Kaufmann, John (1931-), illus. LC 66-7288. (Illus.). 5 7/8 x 8 1/2. 64p. (18 pt.). (Nature I Can Read Bks.). (gr. k-3). 1966. (ISBN 0-06-025460-2). Har-Row.

Seltzer, Adele Szoid, Mrs., tr. see Bonsels, Waldemar.

Seltzer, Adele Szold, tr. see Bonsels, Waldemar.

Seltzer, Adele Szold, Mrs. (1876-), tr. see Bonsels, Waldemar.

Seltzer, Adele Szold, Mrs. (1876-), tr. see Maran, Rene.

Seltzer, Richard Warren, Jr. (1946-)

--The Lizard of Oz. Couture, Christin, illus. LC 74-20172. (Illus.). 128p. (Orig.). 1974. (ISBN 0-915232-01-4). B & R Samizdat.

--Now and Then and Other Tales from Ome. LC 76-12138. (Illus.). 63 p. 23cm. c.1976. (ISBN 0-915232-03-0). (ISBN 0-915232-02-2). B & R Samizdat Express.

Selvage, Annette Marie

--The Bluebird Tales from the Land of By-Lo. 1 st. ed. LC 55-11653. 124p. illus. 21cm. 1956. Vantage Press.

Selway, Bunny

--Midnight Pony. 1982. (ISBN 0-533-05163-0). Vantage.

Selz, Irma

--The Curious Tourist. Selz, Irma, illus. LC 74-86677. (Illus.). 48p. (gr. 1-3). 1969. (ISBN 0-448-02831-X). G&D.

--Flight in a Jet. Selz, Irma, illus. LC 67-23812. (Illus.). 60 p. 25cm. 1967. Grosset & Dunlap.

--Katy, Be Good-. Selz, Irma, illus. LC 61-17690. unpaged. illus. 26cm. c.1962. Lothrop, Lee & Shepard Co.

--Wonderful Nice!. Selz, Irma, illus. LC 59-15442. unpaged. illus. 26cm. c.1960. Lothrop, Lee & Shepard.

Selzer, Joan G. & Boston Children's Medical Center Staff

--No More Diapers. Johnson, John Emil (1929-), illus. LC 70-164845. (Illus.). (ps). 1971. Delacorte.

Semple, Daisy & Reilly, Genevieve

--Tommy and Jane and the Birds. Peat, Fern Bisel, Mrs. (1893-), illus. LC 29-24238. 94 p., 1 l. incl. front., illus. (part col.) 23 1/2 cm. c.1929. The Saalfield Publishing Co.

Semple, Lorenzo

--The Flash Gordon Book. Haney, Lynn (1941-) & Cover, Arthur Byron (1950-), eds. LC 80-22147. (Illus.). 58 p. 29cm. c.1980. (ISBN 0-399-20782-1). G. P. Putnam.

Semrad, Alberita R.

--The Zoo. N.D. Rand McNally & Co.

Sendak, Jack

--Circus Girl. Sendak, Maurice Bernard (1928-), illus. LC 57-9258. unpaged. illus. 25cm. c.1957. Harper.

--The Happy Rain. Sendak, Maurice Bernard (1928-), illus. LC 56-8242. 40 illus. 26. 1956. Harper & Brothers.

--The King of the Hermits, and Other Stories. Zemach, Margot (1931-), illus. LC 67-1291. (Illus.). 105 p. 24cm. 1967. Farrar, Strauss & Giroux.

--The Magic Tears. 1st ed. Miller, Mitchell (1947-), illus. LC 72-157900. (Illus.). 58 p. 21cm. 1971. (ISBN 0-06-025471-8). (ISBN 0-06-025472-6). Harper & Row. **Award: (NYT).**

--Martze. Miller, Mitchell (1947-), illus. LC 68-13680. (Illus.). 70 p. 21cm. 1968. Farrar, Straus & Giroux.

--The Second Witch. Shulevitz, Uri (1935-), illus. LC 65-20255. (Illus.). 94 p. 24cm. 1965. Harper & Row.

Sendak, Maurice Bernard (1928-)

--Chicken Soup with Rice. Sendak, Maurice Bernard (1928-), illus. (Illus.). (ps-3). 1962. (ISBN 0-06-025535-8, HarpJ). Har-Row.

--Chicken Soup with Rice: A Book of Months. Sendak, Maurice Bernard (1928-), illus. (Illus.). 32p. (gr. k-3). 1970. (ISBN 0-590-02954-1). Scholastic Inc.

--Hector Protector. Sendak, Maurice Bernard (1928-), illus. LC 65-21388. (Illus.). (ps-3). 1965. (ISBN 0-06-025485-8, HarpJ). (ISBN 0-06-025486-6). Har-Row.

--Hector Protector, and As I Went Over the Water. Sendak, Maurice Bernard (1928-), illus. LC 65-8256. 1v. (unpaged) col. illus. 19x22cm. c.1965. Harper.

--Higglety Pigglety Pop: Or There Must Be More to Life. Sendak, Maurice Bernard (1928-), illus. LC 67-18553. (Illus.). 18 cm. 69p. 1967. Harper & Row.

--Higglety Pigglety Pop!. Or There Must Be More to Life. Sendak, Maurice Bernard (1928-), illus. (Illus.). 69p. 18cm. 1979, c.1967. (ISBN 0-06-443021-9). Harper & Row.

--In the Night Kitchen. Sendak, Maurice Bernard (1928-), illus. LC 70-105483. (Illus.). 40 p. 29cm. 1970. Harper & Row. **Awards: (NYT); (RCM).**

--Kenny's Window. Sendak, Maurice Bernard (1928-), illus. 1956. (ISBN 0-8382-0402-3, Cadmus Books). E. M. Hale And Company.

--Kenny's Window. Sendak, Maurice Bernard (1928-), illus. LC 56-5148. (Illus.). unpaged. 24cm. 1956. Harper.

--Maurice Sendak's Really Rosie: Starring the Nutshell Kids. Sendak, Maurice Bernard (1928-), illus. LC 75-6301. (Illus.). 64p. (gr. 1-5). 1975. (ISBN 0-06-025537-4, HarpJ). Har-Row.

--Nutshell Library. Sendak, Maurice Bernard (1928-), illus. LC 62-13315. (Illus.). 4 v. 1962. Harper & Row.

--One Was Johnny. Sendak, Maurice Bernard (1928-), illus. (Illus.). (ps-3). 1962. (ISBN 0-06-025540-4, HarpJ). Har-Row.

--Outside Over There. Wong, Jeanyee (1920-) & Sendak, Maurice Bernard (1928-), illus. LC 79-2682. (Calligraphy by Jeanyee Wong). (Illus.). 40 p. c.1981. (ISBN 0-06-025523-4). (ISBN 0-06-025524-2). Harper & Row. **Awards: (BGH); (NYT); (ABA); (ALA); (RCM).**

--Pierre. Sendak, Maurice Bernard (1928-), illus. (Illus.). (ps-3). 1962. (ISBN 0-06-025965-5, HarpJ). Har-Row.

--Seven Little Monsters. Sendak, Maurice Bernard (1928-), illus. LC 77-150022. (Illus.). 8 leaves. c.1977. (ISBN 0-06-025477-7). (ISBN 0-06-025501-3). (ISBN 0-06-025478-5). Harper & Row.

--The Sign on Rosie's Door. Sendak, Maurice Bernard (1928-), illus. LC 60-9451. (Illus.). 46 p. 23cm. 1960. Harper.

--Very Far Away. Sendak, Maurice Bernard (1928-), illus. LC 57-5356. (Illus.). 52 p. 21cm. 1957. Harper.

--Where the Wild Things Are. Sendak, Maurice Bernard (1928-), illus. LC 63-21253. (Illus.). 1 v. (unpaged). c.1963. Harper & Row. **Awards: (RCM); (NYT); (IBBY); (ALA).**

Sendak, Maurice Bernard (1928-) & Matthew, Margolis

--Some Swell Pup: Or, Are You Sure You Want a Dog?. 1st ed. Sendak, Maurice Bernard (1928-), illus. LC 75-42870. (Illus.). 23cm. 32p. 1976. (ISBN 0-374-37134-2). Farrar, Strauss and Giroux.

Sendak, Philip (1894-1970)

--In Grandpa's House. Sendak, Maurice Bernard (1928-), illus. Barofsky, Seymour, tr. LC 85-42625. (Illus.). 42 p. 21cm. c.1985. (ISBN 0-06-025462-9). (ISBN 0-06-025463-7). Harper & Row.

Senje, Sigurd, pseud., see Rasmussen, Sigurd.

Senje, Sigurd

--Escape!. Ramsden, Evelyn, tr. from Norwegian. LC 64-12509. 156 p. 21 cm. 1st U.S. edition. 1964. (ISBN 0-15-226200-8). Harcourt, Brace & World.

Senn, J. A.

--The Deadly Dinner. Verdick, Mary, ed. Noyes, David, illus. (Illus., Orig.). (Pal Paper backs). (Pal Skills 1 Ser.). (gr. 7-12). 1978. (ISBN 0-8374-3525-0). Xerox Ed Pubns.

Senn, Steve (1950-)

--Born of Flame: A Spacebread Story. LC 81-10815. vii, 200 p. 22cm. 1982. (ISBN 0-689-30891-4). Atheneum.

--A Circle in the Sea. LC 81-1397. p. cm. 1981. (ISBN 0-689-30861-2). Atheneum.

--The Double Disappearance of Walter Fozbek. Senn, Steve (1950-), illus. LC 80-23857. p. cm. c.1980. (ISBN 0-8038-1571-9). Hastings House.

--In the Castle of the Bear. LC 85-7951. p. cm. 1985. (ISBN 0-689-31167-2). Atheneum.

--Spacebread. LC 80-18326. (Illus.). 216 p. 22cm. (Argo book). 1981. (ISBN 0-689-30830-2). Atheneum.

Sennott, Robert Francis, jt. auth. see MacIsaac, Janet.

Senogles, Galen D. & Mack, Galen S.

--Suppose You're a Nose. LC 76-9170. (Illus.). 37 p. 24cm. 1969. Slayton Dale Publications.

Senour, Caro Smith, Mrs. (1864-)

--Boots, a Kidnapped Boy. LC 13-40. 157 p. front., pl. 19 1/2 cm. $1.0. 1912. The Shakespeare Press.

--Captain Kidd, Jr. and Sinbad the Sailor: A Tale of Two Kittens. 3 p. l., ix-x p., 1 l., 147 p. incl. front., illus. 23 cm. 1908. C. S. Senour.

--Master St. Elmo: The Autobiography of a Celebrated Dog. LC 4-31318. (Illus.). xi, 153p. 1904. The Juvenile Book Company.

Senseney, Dan

--Austin of the Air Force. 1st ed. Bolle, Frank, illus. LC 62-15489. (Illus.). 142 p. 22cm. (Signal Bk.). 1962. Doubleday.

--Scanlon of the Sub Service. 1st ed. Johnson, Ray (1900-), illus. LC 63-11210. (Illus.). 142 p. 22cm. (Signal book). 1963. Doubleday.

Sentman, George Armor (1913-)

--Drummer of Vincennes: A Story of the George Rogers Clark Expedition. 1st ed. Gretzer, John, illus. LC 52-5435. 181 p. illus. 22 cm. (Winston Adventure Bks.). 1952. Winston.

--Russky. LC 65-17270. 176p. 22cm. c.1965. Doubleday.

Sepia, Riva

--Peter & Jacob. 104p. (gr. 2-6). 1971. (ISBN 0-8181-0206-3). Pageant-Poseidon.

Seredy, Kate (1899-1975), tr. see Gedo, Leopold.

Seredy, Kate (1899-1975)

--A Brand-New Uncle. Seredy, Kate (1899-1975), illus. LC 61-7694. (Illus.). 142 p. 22cm. 1961. Viking Press.

--The Chestry Oak. Seredy, Kate (1899-1975), illus. LC 48-4483. vii, 236 p. illus. 22 cm. 1948. Viking Press.

--The Good Master. Seredy, Kate (1899-1975), illus. LC 35-174873. 210, 1 p. incl. illus., plates. 2 col. pl. (incl. front.) 21 cm. 1935. The Viking Press. **Award: (JNM).**

--Gypsy. Seredy, Kate (1899-1975), illus. LC 51-12377. (Illus.). 62 p. 30cm. 1951. Viking Press.

--Lazy Tinka. Seredy, Kate (1899-1975), illus. LC 62-15445. 56p. illus. 23cm. 1962. Viking Press.

--Listening. Seredy, Kate (1899-1975), illus. LC 36-23267. 157 p. incl. front., illus. 23 cm. 1936. The Viking Press.

--The Open Gate. Seredy, Kate (1899-1975), illus. LC 43-51325. 280 p., 1 l. incl. illus., plates. 21 x 16 cm. 1943. The Viking Press.

--Philomena. Seredy, Kate (1899-1975), illus. LC 55-13596. (Illus.). 93 p. 25cm. 1955. Viking Press.

--The Singing Tree. Seredy, Kate (1899-1975), illus. LC 39-27943. 247 p. incl. illus., plates. col. front., col. pl. 21 cm. 1939. The Viking Press. **Award: (JNM).**

--The Tenement Tree. Seredy, Kate (1899-1975), illus. LC 59-16207. (Illus.). 96 p. 26cm. 1959. Viking Press.

--A Tree for Peter. Seredy, Kate (1899-1975), illus. LC 41-22370. 4 p. l., 102 p. illus. 25 cm. 1941. The Viking Press.

--The White Stag. 1951. Viking.

--The White Stag. Seredy, Kate (1899-1975), illus. LC 79-17074. p. cm. 1979. (ISBN 0-14-031258-7). Puffin Books.

--The White Stag. Seredy, Kate (1899-1975), illus. LC 37-37800. (Illus.). 94, 1 p. 24cm. 1937. The Viking Press. **Award: (JNM).**

Serfozo, Mary

--Welcome, Roberto!. Bienvenido, Roberto!. Serfozo, John, illus. LC 69-15958. (Illus.). 32 p. 24cm. 1969. Follett Pub. Co.

Sergel, Willard John see Willard, Clark, pseud.

Sergel, Willard John (1886-)

--The Adventures of Jimjo and Jipee. Williard, Clark, pseud. LC 40-2563. 156 p. incl. front., illus., plates. 23 1/2 cm. c.1939. The Penn Publishing Company.

--The Adventures of Skip and Scrub. Willard, Clark, pseud. LC 40-347416. 160 p. incl. illus., plates. front. 23 1/2 cm. c.1940. The Penn Publishing Company.

Sergent, Nellie Barney, ed.

--Younger Poets: Verse by High School Boys and Girls. 436p. c.1932. Appleton Century Co.

Serkin, Amalia

--Bedtime Stories. LC 49-173741. 21 p. col. illus. 27 cm. (Chanticleer junior book). c.1948. Chanticleer Press.

Serkin, Amalia, illus.

--Mother Goose Nursery Rhymes. LC 49-1918. 25 p. col. illus. 27 cm. (Chanticleer Junior Bk.). 1948. Chanticleer Press.

Serl, Emma (1876-)

--In Fableland. Wood, Harry E., illus. LC 12-18788. 178 p. illus. 19 1/2 x 15 cm. c.1911. Silver, Burdett & Company.

--In Fairyland. Barnhart, Nancy (1889-), illus. LC 17-227051. 163 p. illus., col. plates. 19 cm. $0.40. c.1917. Newson & Company.

--In Rabbitville. Hallock, Ruth Mary (1876-), illus. 112p. 1930. American Book Co.

Serling, Edward Rodman see Serling, Rod, pseud.

Serling, Rod, pseud., see Serling, Edward Rodman.

Serling, Rod, pseud. (1924-1975)

--Rod Serling's The Twilight Zone. Serling, Edward Rodman. Gibson, Walter Brown (1897-), adapted by. Mayan, Earl E., illus. LC 63-18982. (Illus.). 207 p. 26cm. 1963. Grosset & Dunlap.

Seros, Kathleen (1924-1975), adapted by.

--Sun & Moon: Fairy Tales from Korea. Sibley, Norman & Kraus, Robert (1925-), illus. LC 82-82510. (Illus.). 61p. (gr. 3-9). 1982. (ISBN 0-930878-25-6). Hollym Intl.

Serova, E.

--Hedgehog Gloves. (Illus.). 14p. 1974. (ISBN 0-8285-1157-8, Pub. by Progress Pubs USSR). Imported Pubns.

Serpe, Jerry & Swan, Curt, illus.

--Superman. Penick, Ib LC 78-68791. (Paper Engineering by Ib Penick). (Illus.). 14 p. 24cm. (Pop-up book ; 38). c.1979. (ISBN 0-394-84168-9). Random House.

Serra Deliz, Wenceslao

--Adios Falcon. 1a ed. Marichal, Poli, illus. LC 85-1116. p. cm. (Ninos y Letras). 1985. (ISBN 0-8477-3530-3). Editorial De la Universidad De Puerto Rico.

Serrage, Jane

--Seraphine Went Walking. Hurd, Clement (1908-), illus. LC 41-98860. 30, 3 p. col. illus. 21 1/2 x 25 cm. c.1944. E. P. Dutton and Company, Inc.

Serrailer, Anne, tr. see Chonz, Selina.

Serrailer, Ian, tr. see Chonz, Selina.

Serraillier, Anne, tr. see Chonz, Selina.

Serraillier, Ian Lucien, tr. see Chonz, Selina.

Serraillier, Ian Lucien (1912-)

--The Ballad of St. Simeon. Stern, Simon (1943-), illus. LC 70-113798. (Illus.). 28 p. 29cm. 1970. (ISBN 0-531-01971-3). F. Watts.

--The Bishop and the Devil. Stern, Simon (1943-), illus. LC 70-153859. (Illus.). 32 p. 29cm. 1971. (ISBN 0-7232-6088-5). F. Warne.

--The Challenge of the Green Knight. Ambrus, Victor G., pseud. (1935-), illus. Ambrus, Gyozo Laszlo. LC 67-5173. (Illus.). 56 p. 26cm. 1st U.S. edition. 1967, c.1966. H. Z. Walck.

--The Challenge of the Green Knight. Ambrus, Victor G., pseud. (1935-), illus. Ambrus, Gyozo Laszlo. N.D. Henry Z. Walck Inc.

--The Challenge of the Green Knight. Ambrus, Victor G., pseud. (1935-), illus. Ambrus, Gyozo Laszlo. LC 67-88091. (Illus.). 8, 56 p. 26cm. 1966. Oxford U.P.

--The Clashing Rocks: The Story of Jason. Stobbs, William (1914-), illus. LC 64-131316. (Illus.). 96 p. 20cm. 1st U.S. edition. 1964, c.1963. H. Z. Walck.

--Enchanted Island: Stories from Shakespeare. Farmer, Peter, illus. LC 64-14955. (Illus.). (gr. 8 up). 1964. (ISBN 0-8098-3053-1). Walck.

--Escape From Warsaw. 1963. Scholastic.

--Escape from Warsaw (Pub. by Criterion). Orig. Title: The Silver Sword. (gr. 7-9). 1972. (ISBN 0-590-01516-8). Scholastic Inc.

--A Fall from the Sky: The Story of Daedalus. Stobbs, William (1914-), illus. LC 66-13953. 61p. illus. 21cm. 1st U.S. edition. 1966, c.1965. Walck.

--The Gorgon's Head: The Story of Perseus. Stobbs, William (1914-), illus. LC 62-17972. (Illus.). (gr. 4-7). 1962. (ISBN 0-8098-2361-6). Walck.

--Heracles the Strong. Negri, Rocco (1932-), illus. LC 70-119574. (Illus.). 102 p. 21cm. 1970. (ISBN 0-8098-2071-4). H. Z. Walck.

--Robin and His Merry Men: Ballads of Robin Hood. Ambrus, Victor G., pseud. (1935-), illus. Ambrus, Gyozo Laszlo. LC 70-107382. (Illus.). 64 p. 26cm. 1st U.S. edition. 1970, c.1969. (ISBN 0-8098-3092-2). H.Z. Walck.

--Robin in the Greenwood. Ambrus, Victor G., pseud. (1935-), illus. Ambrus, Gyozo Laszlo. LC 71-437932. (Illus.). 22cm. iii, 76p. 1967. Oxford Univ. Press.

--Robin in the Greenwood: Ballads of Robin Hood. Ambrus, Victor G., pseud. (1935-), illus. Ambrus, Gyozo Laszlo. LC 68-17105. (Illus.). 75 p. 26cm. 1st U.S. edition. 1968. H. Z. Walck.

--The Silver Sword. Hodges, Cyril Walter (1909-), illus. LC 59-6556. (Illus.). 187 p. 22cm. (Criterion Book for Young People). 1959. Criterion Books. **Award: (CMA).**

--The Silver Sword. Hodges, Cyril Walter (1909-), illus. 1959. S G Phillips.

--Suppose You Met a Witch. 1st ed. Emberley, Edward Randolph (1931-), illus. LC 75-105751. (Illus.). 31 p. 1973. Little, Brown.

--The Tale of Three Landlubbers. Briggs, Raymond Redvers (1934-), illus. LC 71-123633. 32 p. (chiefly col. illus. 27cm. 1st U.S. edition. 1971, c.1970. Coward-McCann.

--There's No Escape. Hodges, Cyril Walter (1909-), illus. 1973. Scholastics.

--Thomas and the Sparrow: Poems. Severin, illus. LC 61-37788. 71 p. illus. 29 cm. (Chameleon books, 31). 1951. Oxford University Press.

--Way of Danger: The Story of Theseus. Stobbs, William (1914-), illus. LC 63-10911. (Illus.). 1st U.S. edition. (gr. 4-7). 1963. (ISBN 0-8098-2367-5). Walck.
--The Weather Birds. Serraillier, Ian Lucien (1912-), illus. 1945. Macmillan.
Serraillier, Ian Lucien (1912-), retold by.
--Beowulf the Warrior. Severin, illus. LC 61-12890. (Illus.). (gr. 8 up). 1961. (ISBN 0-8098-3039-6). Walck. **Award: (ALA).**
--The Franklin's Tale. Gough, Philip (1908-), illus. LC 72-79498. (Original Author: Geoffrey Chaucer (1340-1400)). (Illus.). 27 p. 29cm. 1972. Kaye & Ward, New York, F. Warne.
--Havelok the Dane. Raphael, Elaine, pseud. (1933-), illus. Bolognese, Elaine Raphael Chionchio. LC 67-19928. (Illus.). 66 p. 21cm. 1967. H. Z. Walck.
Servello, Joe, jt. auth. see Barrett, John M.
Service, Pamela F
--Winter of Magic's Return. LC 85-7952. 192 p. 25cm. 1985. (ISBN 0-689-31130-3). Atheneum.
Service, Robert William (1874-1958)
--The Shooting of Dan McGrew & the Cremation of Sam McGee. Wells, Rosemary & Jeffers, Susan, illus. LC 74-82268. (Illus.). 3 color ils. 64p. (gr. 5 up). 1969. (ISBN 0-201-09347-2, A W Childrens). A W.
--The Shooting of Dan McGrew, and the Cremation of Sam McGee: The Cremation of Sam McGee. Wells, Rosemary, illus. LC 74-82268. (Illus.). 61 p. 24cm. 1969. Young Scott Bks.
Servien, Gerard F. (1920-)
--Wopsy and the Witch Doctor. Elgin, Jill, illus. LC 51-16793. 96 p. illus. 24cm. 1950. Catechetical Guild Educational Society.
Serwadda, William Moses (1931-)
--Songs and Stories from Uganda. Pantaleoni, Hewitt (1933-), ed. Dillon, Leo (1933-) & Dillon, Diane (1933-), illus. LC 72-7556. (Illus.). 80 p. 1974. (ISBN 0-690-75240-7). Crowell.
Serwer, Blanche Luria (1910-)
--Let's Steal the Moon: Jewish Tales, Ancient and Recent. 1st ed. Hyman, Trina Schart (1939-), illus. LC 71-105750. (Illus.). 88 p. 25cm. 1970. Little, Brown.
Sesame Street
--Bathtime on Sesame Street. Schulman, Janet (1933-), ed. Mathieu, Joseph (1945-), illus. LC 82-80571. (Illus.). 12p. (Little Pops). (ps-3). 1983. (ISBN 0-394-85449-7). Random.
--Big Bird's Busy Book. Lerner, Sharon Ruth (1925-), ed. Gantz, David & Crawford, Mel, illus. LC 74-5521. (Illus.). 96p. (ps-4). 1975. (ISBN 0-394-82904-2, BYR). Random.
--Big Bird's Farm. Barrett, John E., photos by. LC 81-50537. (Illus.). 14p. (Board Bks.). (ps). 1981. (ISBN 0-394-84812-8). Random.
--Big Bird's Rhyming Book. Chartier, Normand (1945-), illus. LC 78-68790. (Illus.). (Sesame Street Pop-up Ser.: No. 13). (ps-3). 1979. (ISBN 0-394-84140-9, BYR). Random.
--Cookie Monster, Where Are You?. Jones, Randy (1950-), illus. LC 75-39342. (Sesame Street Pop-up Ser.: No. 10). (ps-3). 1976. (ISBN 0-394-83257-4, BYR). Random.
--Cookie Monster's Book of Cookie Shapes. Brown, Richard Eric (1946-), illus. (A Tell-a-Tale Reader Ser.). (gr. k-3). 1979. (ISBN 0-307-68403-2, Golden Pr). Western Pub.
--Ernie & Bert's Delivery Service. Smollin, Michael J., illus. LC 82-61011. (Illus.). 16p. (ps-2). 1983. (ISBN 0-394-85761-5). Random.
--Ernie's Rainy Day Book. Smollin, Michael J., illus. (Illus.). (Do-It Cloth Bks.). (ps). 1982. (ISBN 0-394-85405-5). Random.
--Grover's Monster Album. LC 80-50179. (Illus.). 14p. (Board Books). (ps). 1980. (ISBN 0-394-84577-3). Random.
--Grover's New Kitten. Barrett, John E., photos by. LC 81-50538. (Illus.). 14p. (Board Bks.). (ps). 1981. (ISBN 0-394-84872-1). Random.
--Grover's Super Surprise Book. Cooke, Tom, illus. LC 77-93776. (Illus.). (Pop-up Ser.: No. 12). (ps-3). 1978. (ISBN 0-394-83841-6, BYR). Random.
--The King on a Swing. (Illus.). (Sesame Street Pop-up Ser: No. 6). (ps-2). 1972. (ISBN 0-394-82461-X, BYR). Random.
--One Rubber Duckie. Barrett, John E., photos by. LC 81-86375. (Illus.). (Board Bks.). (ps). 1982. (ISBN 0-394-85309-1). Random.
--The Sesame Street Birthday Book. 9p. (Wipe off Bks.). (ps). 1980. (ISBN 0-307-01855-5, Golden Pr). Western Pub.
--Sesame Street Mix or Match Storybook. Mathieu, Joseph (1945-), illus. LC 77-70853. (Illus.). (ps-1). 1977. (ISBN 0-394-83547-6, BYR). Random.
--The Sesame Street Mother Goose. Jones, Randy (1950-), illus. LC 75-39341. (Illus.). (Sesame Street Pop-up Ser.: No. 9). (ps-3). 1976. (ISBN 0-394-83256-6, BYR). Random.
--The Sesame Street Nineteen Seventy-Seven Calendar: A Fairy Tale Collection. (gr. 1 up). 1976. (ISBN 0-394-83322-8). Random.
--Sesame Street Pop-up Riddle Book. Sutherland, David, illus. LC 77-70852. (Illus.). (Sesame Street Pop-up: No. 11). (ps-3). 1977. (ISBN 0-394-83546-8, BYR). Random.
--Sesame Street Storybook. (Illus.). (ps-4). 1971. (ISBN 0-394-82332-X, BYR). (ISBN 0-394-92332-4). Random.
--Sherlock Hemlock: Great Twiddlebug Mystery. Sesame Street, illus. (Illus.). (Tell-a-Tale Readers). (gr. k-3). 1972. (ISBN 0-307-68564-0, Whitman). Western Pub.
--Sweet Dreams on Sesame Street. Schulman, Janet (1933-), ed. Swanson, Maggie, illus. LC 82-80572. (Illus.). 12p. (Little Pops Ser.). (ps-3). 1983. (ISBN 0-394-85448-9). Random.
--Up & Down Book Starring Ernie & Bert. Swanson, Maggie, illus. (Illus.). (A Tell-a-Tale Reader Ser.). (gr. k-3). N.D. (ISBN 0-307-68402-4, Golden Pr). Western Pub.
--What Happens Next. (Illus.). (Sesame Street Pop-up Ser: No. 4). (ps-2). 1971. (ISBN 0-394-82336-2). Random.
--Who Am I?. (Golden Sturdy Bks.). (ps). 1978. (ISBN 0-307-12124-0, Golden Pr). Western Pub.
--Who Are the People in Your Neighborhood?. (Sesame Street Pop-up Ser.: No. 7). (ps). 1974. (ISBN 0-394-82827-3, BYR). Random.
--Your Friends from Sesame Street. Smollin, Michael J., illus. (Illus.). (Cloth Bks). (ps). 1979. (ISBN 0-394-84137-9, BYR). Random.
Sesame Street & Kinglsey, Emily Perl (1940-)
--Cookie Monster's Storybook. Cooke, Tom, illus. LC 79-3914. (Illus.). (Sesame Street Ser.). (ps-2). 1979. (ISBN 0-394-84242-1, BYR). (ISBN 0-394-94242-6). Random.
Sesame Street & Wilcox, Daniel
--The Sesame Street ABC Storybook. LC 74-5522. (Illus.). 72p. 1974. (ISBN 0-394-82921-2, BYR). (ISBN 0-394-92921-7). Random.
Sesame Street see Geiss, Tony.
Sesame Street, jt. auth. see Mathieu, Joseph.
Seskin, Stephen
--The Stone in the Road. Arndt, Ursula, illus. LC 68-19182. (Illus.). 44 p. 23cm. 1968. Van Nostrand.
Sesshu, et al. (1420-1500), illus.
--Cricket Songs: Japanese Haiku. Behn, Harry, tr. LC 64-11489. (Illus.). (gr. 4 up). 1964. (ISBN 0-15-220890-9, HJ). HarBraceJ. **Award: (ALA).**
Sessions, Laura Hooker, Mrs.
--Spruce-Hemlock Valley and other Stories. LC 29-30196. 128 p. front., plates. 20 1/2 cm. c.1929. Meador Publishing Company.
Sessions, Ruth Huntington, Mrs. (1859-)
--The Ups and Downs of Emily. Larkin, Peter (1926-), illus. LC 40-36110. 5 p. l., 334 p. incl. illus., plates. 21 x 16 cm. 1940. Dodd, Mead & Company.
Sessler, Jacob John (1899-)
--Story Talks from Animal Life: 35 Inspiring Tales for Children. LC 56-10896. 128p. 20cm. 1956. Revell.
Seth, Ronald Sydney (1911-)
--Fairy Tales of Greece. Miller, George W., illus. LC 61-65153. unpages. illus. 21 cm. 1961. Dutton.
--Operation Getaway. LC 54-10314. 191p. 21cm. 1st U.S. edition. 1954. J. Day Co.
--The Spy and the Atom Gun: Introducing Captain Geoffrey Martel of the British Secret Service. LC 58-5319. 152 p. 22 cm. (Ariel books). 1958. Farrar, Straus and Cudahy.
Seth-Smith, Elsie K. (1883-)
--The Black Tower. Sayer, Nancy, illus. LC 57-7685. (Illus.). 205 p. 21cm. 1957. Vanguard Press.
--Vagabonds All. Vaughan, Anne (1913-), illus. LC 46-252925. 3 p. l., 282 p. illus. 21 cm. 1946. Houghton Mifflin Company.
Seton, Anya
--The Mistletoe and Sword: A Story of Roman Britain. LC 55-7657. (Illus.). 253 p. 22cm. (Cavalcade books). 1955. Doubleday.
--Smouldering Fires. LC 74-33661. 159 p. 22cm. 1975. (ISBN 0-385-06979-0). (ISBN 0-385-06987-1). Doubleday.
Seton, Ernest Evan Thompson (1860-1946)
--Animal Heroes. N.D. Charles Scribner's Sons.
--Animal Heroes. (Every Boy's Library). N.D. Grosset & Dunlap.
--Bannertail: The Story of a Gray Squirrel. Seton, Ernest Evan Thompson (1860-1946), illus. LC 22-237336. ix p., 2 l., 3-265 p. illus., plates. 20 cm. 1922. C. Scribner's Sons.
--The Biography of a Grizzly. N.D. Appleton Century Co.
--Biography of a Grizzly. (Illus.). (gr. 2-5). N.D. (ISBN 0-448-02372-5). G&D.
--Biography of a Grizzly & Other Stories. Bronson, Clark, illus. (Illus.). (gr. 4-9). 1969. (ISBN 0-528-82252-7). Rand.
--The Biography of a Silver Fox: Or, Domino Reynard of Goldur Town. Seton, Ernest Evan Thompson (1860-1946), illus. 1909. Appleton Century Co.
--Ernest Thompson Seton's Trail and Camp-Fire Stories. Seton, Julia Moss, Mrs. (1889-), ed. LC 40-32443. xvii p., 1 l., 155 p. 19 1/2 cm. 1940. D. Appleton-Century Company, Incorporated.
--Johnny Bear, Lobo, and Other Stories. Seton, Ernest Evan Thompson (1860-1946), illus. LC 35-30059. vii p., 3 l., 3-162 p. front., illus., plates. 19 1/2 cm. (Modern Standard Authors). c.1935. C. Scribner's Sons.
--King of the Grizzlies. Hanak, Mirko, illus. LC 72-192511. (Illus.). 122 4 1, illus. (some col.) 22. (Children's Illustrated Classics Ser). 1972. (ISBN 0-525-33225-1). Dutton.
--King of the Grizzlies. Kunstler, Morton (1927-), illus. (Illus.). (gr. 4-6). 1970. (ISBN 0-590-08786-X). (ISBN 0-590-20750-4). Scholastic Inc.
--King of the Grizzlies. Kunstler, Morton (1927-), illus. Repr. (Starbright Editions). (gr. 4-6). 1973. Schol Bk Serv.
--Krag and Johnny Bear. N.D. Charles Scribner's Sons.
--Lives of the Hunted. Seton, Ernest Evan Thompson (1860-1946), illus. 1901. Scribner.
--Lobo, Rag and Vixen. Seton, Ernest Evan Thompson (1860-1946), illus. (Illus.). N.D. Charles Scribner's Sons.
--Monarch the Big Bear of Tallac. Seton, Ernest Evan Thompson (1860-1946), illus. N.D. Charles Scribner's Sons.
--The Preacher of Cedar Mountain: A Tale of the Open Country. Seton, Ernest Evan Thompson (1860-1946), illus. 1917. Doubleday.
--Rolf in the Woods. (Growing Literature). N.D. Grosset & Dunlap.
--Rolf in the Woods. Seton, Ernest Evan Thompson (1860-1946), illus. N.D. Doubleday Page & Co.
--Sign Talk. N.D. Doubleday Page & Co.
--Trail and Camp-Fire Stories. Seton, Julia Moss (1889-), ed. LC 66-5227. xvii, 156 p. 19 cm. 1965. Seton Village Press.
--The Trail of the Sandhill Stag. Seton, Ernest Evan Thompson (1860-1946), illus. N.D. Charles Scribner's Sons'.
--Trail of the Sandhill Stag & Other Lives of the Hunted. Seton, Ernest Evan Thompson (1860-1946), illus. (Illus.). (Children's Illustrated Classics). (gr. 5-9). N.D. (ISBN 0-525-41447-9). Dutton.
--Two Little Savages. (Illus.). (gr. 4-8). 1903. Dover.
--Two Little Savages. Seton, Ernest Evan Thompson (1860-1946), illus. LC 3-269689. (Being the Adventures of Two Boys Who Lived As Indians and What They Learned With Over Two Hundred Drawings.). xvii, 19-522 p. incl. 29 pl. 21 cm. 1903. Doubleday, Page & Company.
--Two Little Savages. Seton, Ernest Evan Thompson (1860-1946), illus. (Illus.). N.D. (ISBN 0-8446-2909-X). Peter Smith Publisher, Inc.
--Two Little Savages: Being the Adventures of Two Boys Who Lived As Indians and What They Learned. complete and unabridged. Seton, Ernest Evan Thompson (1860-1946), illus. LC 75-110035. (With Over Two Line Drawings). (Illus.). 288 p. 29cm. 1970, c.1969. (ISBN 0-516-04215-7). Childrens Press.
--Two Little Savages: Being the Adventures of Two Boys Who Lived As Indians and What They Learned. Seton, Ernest Evan Thompson (1860-1946), illus. LC 59-6382. (With Over Two Hundred Line Drawings). 416 p. illus. 20 cm. 1959. Doubleday.
--Two Little Savages: Being the Adventures of Two Boys Who Lived as Indians and What They Learned. Seton, Ernest Evan Thompson (1860-1946), illus. LC 28-17934. (With Over Two Hundred Line Drawings). xiv p., 2 l., 19-552 p. incl. plates, illus. 20 1/2 cm. 1911. Grosset & Dunlap.
--The Wild Animal Play. Seton, Ernest Evan Thompson (1860-1946), illus. (Illus.). 4x7 1/2cm. 135p. N.D. Doubleday, Page & Co.
--Wild Animals I Have Known. (Illus.). (gr. 2-5). 1966. (ISBN 0-448-00590-5). G&D.
--Wild Animals I Have Known. (Looking Glass Library). (gr. 3-7). N.D. (ISBN 0-394-80455-4). Random.
--Wild Animals I Have Known. Seton, Ernest Evan Thompson (1860-1946), illus. LC 77-7918. (Illus.). (gr. 5 up). 1977. (ISBN 0-87905-033-0). Peregrine Smith.
--Wild Animals I Have Known, Being the Personal Histories of Lobo, Silverspot, Raggylug, Bingo, The Springfield Fox, The Pacing Mustang, Wully, and Redruff. Seton, Ernest Evan Thompson (1860-1946), illus. 1899. Scribner.
--Woodland Tales. LC 40-32833. 1 p. l., v-xv, 150 p. illus. 19 1/2 cm. 1940. Seton Village Press.
--Woodland Tales. Seton, Ernest Evan Thompson (1860-1946), illus. LC 21-26464. xv, 238 p., 1 l. illus. (incl. music) 20 1/2 cm. 1921. Doubleday, Page & Company.
--Woodmyth & Fables. Seton, Ernest Evan Thompson (1860-1946), illus. LC 5-10178. 181 p. illus. 21 cm. 1905. The Century Co.
Seton, Ernest Evan Thompson (1860-1946), ed.
--Famous Animal Stories. N.D. Dial Press.
--Famous Animal Stories: Animal Myths, Fables, Fairy Tales, Stories of Real Animals. LC 32-321626. xii, 686 p. 22 1/2 cm. c.1932. Brentano's.
Seton, Julia Moss (1889-), ed. see Seton, Ernest Evan Thompson.
Seton, Julia Moss (1889-)
--Indian Creation Stories. Taylor, Marceil, illus. LC 52-9927. 161p. illus. 21cm. 1952. House-Warven
Seton, William
--Rachel's Fate And Other Tales. N.D. The Catholic Publication Society.
Seuberlich, Hertha
--Annuzza: A Girl of Romania. Pallasch, Gerhard, illus. Humphries, Stella, tr. LC 62-12650. 198 illus. 21. (gr. 7-9). 1962. Rand. **Award: (ALA).**

Seufert, Karl Rolf (1923-)
--Caravan in Peril. Humphries, Stella, tr. from Fr. LC 62-142706. 404p. illus. 22cm. 1963. Pantheon.
Seuling, Barbara (1937-)
--The Great Big Elephant and the Very Small Elephant. Seuling, Barbara (1937-), illus. LC 76-48173. (Illus.). 40 p. 26cm. c.1977. (ISBN 0-517-52843-6). Crown Publishers.
--Just Me. Seuling, Barbara (1937-), illus. LC 81-6893. (Illus.). 64 p. 22cm. (A Let Me Read Book). c.1982. (ISBN 0-15-241683-8). Harcourt Brace Jovanovich.
--The Triplets. Seuling, Barbara (1937-), illus. LC 79-18621. (Illus.). 32 p. c.1980. (ISBN 0-395-29107-0). Houghton Mifflin/Clarion Books.
Seuling, Barbara (1937-), retold by.
--The Teeny Tiny Woman: An Old English Ghost Tale. Seuling, Barbara (1937-), illus. LC 77-11131. (Illus.). 32 p. 1978, c.1976. (ISBN 0-14-050266-1). Puffin Books.
--The Teeny Tiny Woman: An Old English Ghost Tale. 1st ed. Seuling, Barbara (1937-), illus. LC 75-22160. (Illus.). 32 p. 19cm. 1976. (ISBN 0-670-69505-X). Viking Press.
Seuss, Dr., pseud., see Geisel, Theodor Seuss.
Seuss, Dr., pseud. (1904-)
--I Can Lick Thirty Tigers Today! & Other Stories. Geisel, Theodor Seuss. LC 71-86940. (Illus.). 64p. (Dr. Seuss Paperback Classics Ser.). (gr. k-3). 1980. (ISBN 0-394-84543-9). Random.
--I Had Trouble in Getting to Solla Sollew. Geisel, Theodor Seuss. LC 65-23994. (Illus.). 64p. (Dr. Seuss Paperback Classics Ser.). (gr. k-3). 1980. (ISBN 0-394-84542-0). Random.
--Oh, the Thinks You Can Think!. Geisel, Theodor Seuss. LC 75-1602. (Illus.). 41 p. 24cm. 1975. (ISBN 0-394-83129-2). (ISBN 0-394-93129-7). Beginner Books.
--On Beyond Zebra!. Geisel, Theodor Seuss. LC 55-9321. (Illus.). 64p. (Dr. Seuss Paperback Classics Ser.). (gr. k-3). 1980. (ISBN 0-394-84541-2). Random.
--Scrambled Eggs Super!. Geisel, Theodor Seuss. LC 53-5013. (Illus.). 64p. (Dr. Seuss Paperback Classics Ser.). (gr. k-3). 1980. (ISBN 0-394-84544-7). Random.
--Thidwick, the Big-Hearted Moose. Geisel, Theodor Seuss. LC 48-8129. (Illus.). 48p. (Dr. Seuss Paperback Classics Ser.). (gr. k-3). 1980. (ISBN 0-394-84540-4). Random.
Sevela, Efraim (1928-)
--Why There Is No Heaven on Earth. Lourie, Richard (1940-), tr. LC 81-47736. p. cm. c.1982. (ISBN 0-06-025502-1). (ISBN 0-06-025503-X). Harper & Row.
Seventeen
--Nineteen from Seventeen: Stories from Seventeen Magazine. Ivens, Bryna, selected by. LC 52-9528. 239 p. 21 cm. 1952. Lippincott.
--The Seventeen Reader: Stories and Articles from Seventeen Magazine. Ivens, Bryna, selected by. LC 51-1421. ix, 310 p. illus. 21 cm. 1951. Lippincott.
--Stories from Seventeen. Ivens, Bryna, selected by. LC 55-6722. 214p. 21cm. 1955. Lippincott.
Severance, Jane
--Lots of Mommies. Jones, Jan M. (1949-), illus. LC 83-81922. (Illus.). 36p. (Orig.). 1983. (ISBN 0-914996-24-X). Lollipop Power.
--When Megan Went Away. Schook, Tea, illus. LC 79-90437. (Illus.). 32 p. 18cm. c.1979. (ISBN 0-914996-22-3). Lollipop Power.
Severance, W. Murray, jt. auth. see Yoder, Dorotha S.
Severance, W. Murray, ed. see Yoder, Dorotha S.
Severance, W. Murray, ed. see Yoder, Dorotha S & Severance, W. Murray.

Severin, Jean (1911-)
--The Star of Les Baux. Cohn, Emma & Spain, Louise, trs. from Fr. LC 70-106597. 160 p. 21cm. 1970. (ISBN 0-15-279390-9). Harcourt Brace Jovanovich.
Severn, David, pseud., see Unwin, David Storr.
Severn, David, pseud. (1918-)
--A Cabin for Crusoe. Unwin, David Storr. Koering, Ursula (1921-), illus. LC 46-3356. 3 p. l., 241, 1 p. plates. 21 cm. 1946. Houghton Mifflin Co.
--Crazy Castle. Unwin, David Storr. Kiddell-Monroe, Joan (1908-), illus. 1952. Macmillan.
--The Cruise of the Maiden Castle. Unwin, David Storr. 1948. Macmillan.
--The Cruise of the Maiden Castle. Unwin, David Storr. LC 49-10613. 213 p. 21 cm. 1949. Macmillan Co.
--The Girl in the Grove: A Story of Suspense. Unwin, David Storr. LC 74-9074. 266 p. 22cm. 1974. (ISBN 0-06-025533-1). (ISBN 0-06-025534-X). Harper & Row.
--Jeff Dickson Cowhand: Cowhand. Unwin, David Storr. (Illus.). (Jet Ser). (gr. 7-11). 1963. Verry.
--Treasure for Three. Unwin, David Storr. Kiddell-Monroe, Joan (1908-), illus. LC 50-7505. 20cm. 212p. 1950. Macmillan.
--Wagon for Five. Unwin, David Storr. Koering, Ursula (1921-), illus. LC 47-30514. 228 p. illus. 21 cm. 1947, c.1944. Houghton Mifflin Co.
--The Wild Valley. Unwin, David Storr. 1st ed. Lamb, Lynton Harold (1907-1977), illus. LC 63-15757. 20cm. 165p. 1963, c.1959. Dutton.
--The Wishing Bone. Unwin, David Storr. LC 82-461055. (Illus.). 109 p. 25cm. 1977. (ISBN 0-04-823141-X). Allen & Unwin.
Severne, Harleigh
--Chums. (Illus.). (The Boy's Own Favorite Ser.). N.D. E. P. Dutton & Co.
Severs, Vesta-Nadine (1935-)
--Lucinda. Molina, Charles, illus. LC 77-20058. (Illus.). 128 p. 24cm. (Midwestern Memories). c.1978. (ISBN 0-570-07805-9). (ISBN 0-570-07800-8). Concordia Pub. House.
Severy, Richard & Haworth, Karen
--Mystery Pig: Julia Macrae Bks. (Illus.). 48p. (gr. 2-8). 1983. (ISBN 0-531-04677-X). Watts.
Sewall, Arthur
--Gay Dashleigh's Academy Days. (The Boys Own Library). N.D. David McKay.
--Gay Dashleigh's Academy Days. LC 964. 235 p. 18 cm. (Medal library, no. 38). 1900. Street & Smith.
Sewall, Frank (1837-1915)
--Angelo, the Circus Boy. 1900. Massachusetts New-Church Union.
Sewall, Marcia (1935-)
--The Cobbler's Song: A Fable. 1st ed. Sewall, Marcia (1935-), illus. LC 82-9438. (Illus.). 31 p. (A Unicorn Bk.). c.1982. (ISBN 0-525-44005-4). Dutton.
--The Little Wee Tyke. Sewall, Marcia (1935-), illus. LC 79-11853. (Illus.). (ps-2). 1979. (ISBN 0-689-30724-1). Atheneum.
--Master of All Masters: An English Folktale. 1st ed. Sewall, Marcia (1935-), illus. LC 72-76290. (Illus.). 28 p. 1972. Little, Brown.
--Ridin' That Strawberry Roan. Sewall, Marcia (1935-), illus. LC 84-21904. (Illus.). 31 p. 24cm. 1985. (ISBN 0-670-80623-4). Viking Kestrel.
--The Wee, Wee Mannie and the Big, Big Coo: A Scottish Folk Tale. 1st ed. Sewall, Marcia (1935-), illus. LC 76-48947. (Illus.). 32 p. c.1977 (Pub. by Atlantic Monthy Pr.). (ISBN 0-316-78180-0). Little, Brown.
Seward, Prudence (1926-), ed.
--Nursery Rhymes. (Illus.). color ils. 48p. (gr. k-3). 1971. (ISBN 0-531-01977-2). Watts.
Sewell, Anna (1820-1878)
--The Adventures of Black Beauty: Beauty Finds a Home. Hanson, Andrea, ed. LC 83-3006. p. cm. 1983. (ISBN 0-394-95901-9). (ISBN 0-394-85901-4). Random House.
--Beauty & Vicky. Hanson, Andrea & Fanelli, Jenny, eds. LC 83-21264. (Illus.). 144p. (The Adventures of Black Beauty Ser.). (gr. 4-7). 1984. (ISBN 0-394-86383-6, BYR). (ISBN 0-394-96383-0). Random.
--Black Beauty, 98 vols. (The Rugby Ser.). 1905. Set. A L Burt Co.
--Black Beauty. N.D. A. L. Burt Co.
--Black Beauty. (The Oxford Ser.). N.D. A. L. Burt Company.
--Black Beauty. (The Manhattan Ser.). N.D. A. L. Burt's Pubs.
--Black Beauty. (Illus.). (The Little Men Ser.). N.D. A. L. Burt's Pubs.
--Black Beauty. (Illus.). (The Rugby Series for Boys). N.D. A. L. Burt's Pubs.
--Black Beauty. (Illus.). (Burt's Young Folks' Library). N.D. A. L. Burt's Pubs.
--Black Beauty. (Illus.). N.D. A. L. Chatterton Co.
--Black Beauty, No. 16. (The Cornell Ser.). N.D. A. L. Burt's Pubs.
--Black Beauty. 1905. American News Co.
--Black Beauty. (Illus.). (Pleasant Hour Ser.). N.D. Barse and Hopkins.
--Black Beauty. (Illus.). (The Rainy Day Ser.). N.D. Barse & Hopkins.
--Black Beauty. N.D. Bruce Humphries.
--Black Beauty. (Illus.). (The Alcazar Classics). N.D. Caldwell.
--Black Beauty. (Heirloom Library). N.D. Chanticleer Bks.
--Black Beauty. N.D. David McKay Co.
--Black Beauty. (Illus.). (The Favorite Lib.). N.D. DeWolfe, Fiske & Co.
--Black Beauty. (Dearborn Ser.). N.D. Donohue, Henneberry & Co.
--Black Beauty. (Advance Ser.). N.D. Donohue, Henneberry & Co.
--Black Beauty. N.D. E P Dutton.
--Black Beauty. N.D. Educational Publishing Company.
--Black Beauty. (Doubleday Classics). N.D. Garden City Books.
--Black Beauty. (Washington Square Classics Ser.). N.D. George W Jacobs.
--Black Beauty. (The Phoenix Ser.). N.D. George W. Jacobs & Co.
--Black Beauty. N.D. Grosset & Dunlap.
--Black Beauty. (The Good Value Books). N.D. Grosset & Dunlap.
--Black Beauty. (Illustrated Junior Library). N.D. (ISBN 0-448-05907-X). (ISBN 0-448-05807-3). Grosset & Dunlap.
--Black Beauty. (Illus.). (The Empyreal Library of Handy Volume Classics). N.D. H. M. Caldwell Co.
--Black Beauty. (Illus.). (The Young Folks Lib.). N.D. H. M. Caldwell Co.
--Black Beauty, 1 of 3 vols. (The Lakeside Series of Handy Volume Classics). N.D. Set. H. M. Caldwell Co.
--Black Beauty. (Altemus' Vademecum Ser.). N.D. Henry Altemus Co.
--Black Beauty. (Illus.). (Young People's Lib.). N.D. Henry Altemus Co.
--Black Beauty. (Illus.). (Beauxarts Ser.). N.D. Henry Altemus Co.
--Black Beauty. Large Type ed. (Illus.). (Petit-Trianon Ser.). N.D. Henry Altemus.
--Black Beauty. (Illus.). (Ever New Books for Young People). N.D. Henry Altemus Company Publications.
--Black Beauty. (Illus.). (Little Men and Women Ser.). N.D. Henry Altemus Co.
--Black Beauty. (Illus.). (Boys and Girls' Classics). N.D. Henry Altemus.
--Black Beauty. (Illus.). (Home Ser.). N.D. Hurst and Company.
--Black Beauty. (Illus.). (Hurst's Half Leather Classics). N.D. Hurst and Company.
--Black Beauty. (Illus.). (The Cambridge Classics). N.D. Hurst and Company.
--Black Beauty. (Illus.). (The Laurelhurst Ser.). N.D. Hurst and Company.
--Black Beauty. (Illus.). (The Cosmos Ser.). N.D. Hurst and Company.
--Black Beauty. (Illus.). (Almonte Library). N.D. Hurst and Company.
--Black Beauty. (Illus.). (Hurst's Fairy Tale Ser.). N.D. Hurst and Company.
--Black Beauty. (Illus.). (The New Argyle Ser.). N.D. Hurst and Company.
--Black Beauty. (Illus.). (Hurst's Presentation Ser.). N.D. Hurst and Company.
--Black Beauty. (Illus.). (Arlington Edition). N.D. Hurst and Company.
--Black Beauty. (Illus.). (The Hawthorne Library). N.D. Hurst and Company.
--Black Beauty. (Illus.). (Alligator Classics). N.D. Hurst & Co.
--Black Beauty. (Illus.). (Knickerbocker Classics). N.D. Hurst & Co.
--Black Beauty. (New Red Letter Ser). N.D. International Books Company.
--Black Beauty. (Illus.). (St. Nicholas Series for Girls). N.D. International Book Co.
--Black Beauty. (Sunset Series). N.D. J. S. Ogilvie.
--Black Beauty. (Sears Juvenile Classics). N.D. J.H.Sears & Co.
--The Black Beauty. (New International Library). N.D. John C. Winston Co.
--Black Beauty. (gr. 4-8). N.D. Lancer.
--Black Beauty. (Illus.). N.D. Lothrop Lee & Shepard Co.
--Black Beauty. (The Phoenix Ser.). N.D. Macrae Smith.
--Black Beauty. (The Washington Square Classics). N.D. Macrae Smith.
--Black Beauty. (The Nelson Classics). N.D. Nelson Bks.
--Black Beauty. 357p. N.D. Nourse.
--Black Beauty. (Illus.). (Young People's Classics). N.D. R. F. Fenno & Co.
--Black Beauty. (Illus.). N.D. Random House Inc.
--Black Beauty. (Illus.). N.D. Rand,McNally & Co.'s.
--Black Beauty. (Twentieth Century Ser.). N.D. Rand, McNally & Co.' s.
--Black Beauty. (New Alpha Library). N.D. Rand, McNally & Co.'s.
--Black Beauty. (The Antique Library). N.D. Rand, McNally & Co.'s.
--Black Beauty. (The Advance Library Ser.: Vol. 27). N.D. Rand, McNally & Co.
--Black Beauty. (Illus.). (The Independent Library Ser.: Vol. 27). N.D. Rand, McNally & Co.
--Black Beauty. (Illus.). (The Junior Library Ser.: Vol. 4). N.D. Rand, McNally & Co.
--Black Beauty, 1 of 24 vols. (Illus.). (Children's Favorite Classics). 1900. T. Y. Crowell & Co.
--Black Beauty. (Illus.). (Children's Home Library). 1915. T Y Crowell.
--Black Beauty. (Illus.). (The Waldorf Lib.). N.D. T. Y. Crowell & Co.
--Black Beauty. (The New Astor Library of Prose). N.D. T. Y. Crowell & Co.
--Black Beauty. (Children's Favorite Classics). N.D. Thomas Y. Crowell & Co.
--Black Beauty. (Standard Literature Ser.: No. 31). N.D. University Publishing Co.
--Black Beauty. LC 4619. 295 p. front., plates. 16 cm. 1900. W. B. Conkey Company.
--Black Beauty. (Illus.). N.D. William Collins Sons & Company Ltd.
--Black Beauty. (Classic Ser.). N.D. World Publishing Co.
--Black Beauty. Beer, John, illus. LC 41-51829. 6 p. l., 3-239 p. front. (port.) plates. 22 1/2 cm. (Great Illustrated Classics). 1941. Dodd, Mead & Company.
--Black Beauty. Bown, Derick, illus. LC 78-3823. p. cm. (Raintree's illustrated classics). 1978. (ISBN 0-8393-6209-9). Raintree Childrens Books.
--Black Beauty. Brown, Paul (1893-1958), illus. LC 52-14140. (Told in Short Form and in Pictures). unpaged. illus. 21 x 25 cm. 1952. Scribner.
--Black Beauty. Claire, Malcolm, as told by. Uncle Mal, pseud. Magnie, Bernice, illus. LC 46-7498. (Illus.). 27cm. 32p. (An Old Faithful Bk.). 1946. Prang Company.
--Black Beauty. Crowell, Pers (1910-), illus. LC 62-53294. 29cm. 60p. (Silver Sollar Library). 1962. (ISBN 0-448-00313-9, Silver Dollar Library). Grosset & Dunlap.
--Black Beauty. Doremus, Robert (1913-), illus. LC 52-1485. 235 p. illus. 21 cm. (Whitman Classic). c.1951. Whitman Pub. Co.
--Black Beauty. Dwoskin, Charles, intro. by. LC 59-11158. 222 p. illus. 23 cm. (Around the world treasures: Great Britain). 1959. F. Watts.
--Black Beauty. Dwoskin, Charles, intro. by. LC 57-18992. 252 p. 21 cm. c.1956. Fine Editions Press.
--Black Beauty. Fraumeni, Thomas G., illus. LC 51-1294. 340 p. illus. 21 cm. 1950, c.1951. Globe Book Co.
--Black Beauty. Gorham, J. C, ed. LC 5-21567. 1 p. l., 109 p. front., illus., plates. 21 cm. c.1905. A. L. Burt Company.
--Black Beauty. Groth, John (1908-), illus. LC 62-18395. (Illus.). 248 p. 24cm. (Macmillan Classics, 32). 1962. Macmillan.
--Black Beauty. Kemp-Welch, Lucy, illus. (Children's Illustrated Classics). 1950. E. P. Dutton & Co.
--Black Beauty. Lee, Edgar, ed. Miller, Harry Lambright, illus. LC 5-39869. (An Adaptation for the Little Folks of Anna Sewell's Autobiography of a Horse). 96 p., 1 l. front., illus. 21 1/2 x 17 cm. c.1905. The Saalfield Publishing Company.
--Black Beauty. Levin, Marcia Lauter Obrasky (1918-), retold by. Martin, Marcia, pseud. Santos, George, illus. LC 53-20024. unpaged. illus. 21 cm. (Wonder books, 595). 1952. Wonder Books.
--Black Beauty. Levin, Marcia Lauter Obrasky (1918-), retold by. Santos, George, illus. LC 53-20024. unpaged. illus. 21 cm. (Wonder books, 595). 1952. Wonder Books.
--Black Beauty. McMann, Jessica S., illus. LC 26-143463. 2 p. l., iii-iv, 244 p. col. front., illus. 25 cm. (Sears Illustrated Juveniles). c.1926. J. H. Sears & Company, Inc.
--Black Beauty. Moseley, Keith, illus. (Picture Story Books). N.D. (ISBN 0-448-02838-7). Grosset & Dunlap.
--Black Beauty. Mozley, Charles (1915-), illus. LC 59-11158. (Illus.). 222 p. 23cm. (Around the World Treasures: Great Britain). 1959. F. Watts.
--Black Beauty. Muheim, Henry, illus. LC 43-153522. 1 p. l., 9-252 p. front., illus. 21 cm. 1943. The Saalfield Publishing Company.
--Black Beauty. complete and unabridged. Rios, Michael, illus. LC 76-79984. (Illus.). 223 p. 29cm. 1969. Childrens Press.
--Black Beauty. Shaw, Edward Richard (1855-1903), ed. LC 8-11255. 217 p. 18 cm. (On cover: Standard Literature Ser. No. 31). 1898. University Publishing Company.
--Black Beauty. Steinel, William, illus. LC 65-11915. 256p. illus. (pt. col.) 22cm. (Whitman classics lib.). c.1965. Whitman Pub.
--Black Beauty. Taylor, Alta Lucretia (1885-), ed. Clinton, Althea L., pseud. Summer, Park, illus. LC 34-20031. 152 p. front., illus. 13 1/2 cm. c.1934. The Saalfield Publishing Company.
--Black Beauty. Taylor, Alta Lucretia (1885-), ed. Clinton, Althea L., pseud. Lawson, George, illus. LC 34-350. 54 p. front., illus. 20 1/2 cm. (Easy-to-Read Books). c.1934. The Saalfield Publishing Company.
--Black Beauty. Thorndike, Edward Lee (1874-), ed. Stoops, Herbert Morton, illus. LC 35-2731. x, 280 p. incl. front., illus. 19 1/2 cm. (Thorndike library). c.1935. D. Appleton-Century Company, Incorporated.
--Black Beauty. Toaspern, H., Jr., illus. (Illus.). (Animal Autobiographical Ser.). N.D. Caldwell.
--Black Beauty, 11 vols. New ed. Toaspern, H., Jr., illus. (Illus.). (Six to Sixteen Ser.: No. 9). 1905. Set. H M Caldwell Co.
--Black Beauty. Vance, Eleanor Graham (1908-), ed. Phoebe, Erickson, illus. LC 49-11994. 62 p. illus. (part col.) 29 cm. c.1949. Random House.
--Black Beauty, and Other Stories: A Collection of Stories Which Are Favorites with Boys and Girls. Brundage, Frances, illus. 109 p. illus. 25 cm. 1930. The Saalfield Publishing Company.
--Black Beauty and the Runaway Horse. Richardson, I. M, adapted by. Milone, Karen, illus. LC 82-7029. p. cm. (Anna Sewell's The Adventures of Black Beauty: Bk. 2). 1982. (ISBN 0-89375-812-4). (ISBN 0-89375-813-2). Troll Assoicates.
--Black Beauty: Anna Sewell's Famous Classic. Brown, Ozni, retold by. Brown, Ozni, illus. LC 56-17285. unpaged. illus. 21cm. (Magic Talking Books, T-11). 1955. J.C. Winston Co.
--Black Beauty Finds a Home. Richardson, I. M., ed. Milone, Karen, illus. LC 82-7024. (Illus.). 32p. (Adventures of Black Beauty Ser.). (gr. 2-5). 1982. (ISBN 0-89375-816-7). (ISBN 0-89375-817-5). Troll Assocs.
--Black Beauty Grows Up. Richardson, I. M., ed. Milone, Karen, illus. LC 82-7075. (Illus.). 32p. (Adventures of Black Beauty Ser.). (gr. 2-5). 1982. (ISBN 0-89375-810-8). (ISBN 0-89375-811-6). Troll Assocs.
--Black Beauty: His Groom and Companions. Austin, Winifred & Toaspern, H., Jr., illus. LC 4-24555. vii, 11-262 p. front., illus., plates. 20 1/2 cm. 1902. L. C. Page & Company.
--Black Beauty: His Groom and Companions. Pyle, Katharine D. (0000-1938), illus. 4 p. l., 239 p. col. front., plates (part col.) 23 cm. 1923. Dodd, Mead and Company.
--Black Beauty: His Groom and Companions. Toaspern, H., Jr., illus. LC 8-11253. (The "Uncle Tom's Cabin" of the Horse.). 200 p. illus. 20 1/2 x 15 cm. c.1894. J. Hovendon & Company.
--Black Beauty: His Grooms and Companions. LC 44-20549. (Illus.). 17cm. iv, 245p. 1891. American Humane Education Society.
--Black Beauty: His Grooms and Summer Companions. LC 8-11252. iv, 5-237, 1 p. 18 cm. 1891. J. F. Murphy.
--Black Beauty: His Grooms & Companions. N.D. Lothrop, Lee & Shepard.
--Black Beauty: His Grooms and Companions. LC 1343. iv, 5-199 p. 18 cm. (On cover: Arrow Library, No. 103). c.1900. Street & Smith.
--Black Beauty: His Grooms and Companions. american ed. LC 44-20549. iv, 5-245, 1 p. illus. 17 cm. N.D. The American Humane Education Society.
--Black Beauty: The Autobiography of a Horse. 5 p. l., 278 p. col. front., col. plates. 22 1/2 cm. $1.5. 1911. Barse & Hopkins.
--Black Beauty: The Autobiography of a Horse. LC 8-11254. viii, 9-199 p. incl. col. front., illus. plates. 16 x 12 cm. (Altemus' Young People's Library). c.1897. H. Altemus.
--Black Beauty: The Autobiography of a Horse. LC 3-23594. 237 p. 2 front. (1 col.) illus., col. plates. 21 cm. c.1903. Hurst and Company.
--Black Beauty: The Autobiography of a Horse. xvii, 238 p. illus. 17 1/2 cm. (Half--title: Everyman's library, ed. by Ernest Rhys. For young people). N.D. J. M. Dent & Sons, Ltd.
--Black Beauty: The Autobiography of a Horse. LC 50-14607. xi, 236 p. illus. 22 cm. (Lippincott Classics). 1950. Lippincott.
--Black Beauty: The Autobiography of a Horse. LC 4-16314. 250 p. col. front., plates. 17 1/2 cm. c.1895. T. Y. Crowell & Company.
--Black Beauty: The Autobiography of a Horse. Aldin, Cecil Charles Windsor (1870-1935), illus. xii, 13-291 p. col. front., col. plates. 28 cm. 1913. F. A. Stokes Co.
--Black Beauty: The Autobiography of a Horse. Blain, Mary E, adapted by. Hofsten, Hugo Von, illus. LC 7-24189. 45 p. col. front., 5 col. pl. 21 cm. (Rainy Day Ser.). c.1907. Brewer, Barse & Co.
--Black Beauty: The Autobiography of a Horse. complete and unabridged. Bown, Derick & Bevins, John, illus. (Illus.). 128 p. 28cm. 1968. Grosset & Dunlap.

Shaffer, Betty
--Lisa. LC 82-72149. 141p. (Orig.). (gr. 8-12). 1982. (ISBN 0-87123-316-9). Bethany Hse.
Shaffer, Grace D.
--Africa's Floating Logs. (Penguin Ser.). (gr. 5-8). 1972. Review & Herald.
Shaffer, Robert
--The Crocodile Tomb. 1st ed. Matulay, Laszlo (1912-), illus. LC 57-11689. 190 p. illus. 21 cm. 1957. Holt.
--The Lost Ones. 1st ed. Marokvia, Artur F. (1909-), illus. LC 56-6233. 223 p. illus. 21 cm. 1956. Holt.
--Skeeter,. The Story of an Arabian Gazelle. Wiese, Kurt (1887-1974), illus. LC 52-8281. 192 p. illus. 21 cm. 1952. Dodd, Mead.
Shaftner, Dorothy (1918-)
--Kim Fashions a Career. LC 68-24550. 190 p. 21cm. 1968. Putnam.
--Kim in Style. LC 72-153995. 191 p. 22cm. 1971. Putnam.
Shah, Amina (1918-)
--Arabian Fairy Tales. Buday, George, pseud. (1907-), illus. Buday, Gyorgy. (gr. 1-4). 1971. (ISBN 0-584-62352-6). Transatlantic.
Shah, Idries Sayed (1924-)
--The Exploits of the Incomparable Mulla Nasrudin. Nasreddin, Hoca (1924-), compiled by. Williams, Richard, illus. LC 67-20796. (Illus.). 158 p. 25cm. 1967, c.1966. Simon and Schuster.
--The Exploits of the Incomparable Mulla Nasrudin. Williams, Richard, illus. (Illus.). 158 p. 18cm. (Dutton paperback, D339). 1972, c.1966. Dutton.
--World Tales: The Extraordinary Coincidence of Stories Told in All Times, in All Places. LC 79-1734. p. cm. 1979. Harcourt Brace Jovanovich.
Shakespeare, William, ed. see Mother Goose.
Shakespeare, William (1564-1616)
--Brandram: Shakespeare for the Young. N.D. J. B. Lippincott CO.
--The Children's Shakespeare: Stories from "As You Like It", "The Tempest", "The Merchant of Venice", "Midsummer Night's Dream". Durden, illus. (Illus.). N.D. George H. Doran.
--Donkey Head. Weil, Lisl (1910-), adapted by. Weil, Lisl (1910-), illus. LC 77-2865. (Illus.). 40 p. 26cm. 1977. (ISBN 0-689-30600-8). Atheneum.
--Hamlet. (Magnum Easy Eye Classic Ser.). (gr. 9 up). N.D. Lancer.
--Hudson and Lamb's Merchant of Venice. Hudson & Lamb, Charles (1775-1834), eds. (Classics for Children). N.D. Ginn and Company.
--Julius Caesar. (gr. 7-12). 1972 (Starline). Schol Bk Serv.
--Julius Caesar. (Keith Jennison Large Type Bks.). (gr. 6 up). N.D. (ISBN 0-531-00209-8). Watts.
--Julius Caesar. Stewart, Diana, adapted by. Shaw, Charles (1941-), illus. LC 80-16486. (Illus.). 48p. (Raintree Short Classics). (gr. 4-12). 1983. (ISBN 0-8172-2013-5). Raintree Pubs.
--Macbeth. Stewart, Diana, adapted by. Shaw, Charles (1941-), illus. LC 81-19273. (Illus.). 48 p. 24cm. c.1982. (ISBN 0-8172-1681-2). Raintree Publishers.
--Macbeth. folio ed. Von, illus. LC 81-43787. (Illus.). 91 p. 26cm. c.1982. (ISBN 0-89480-205-4). Workman.
--A Midsummer Night's Dream. Rackham, Arthur (1867-1939), illus. N.D (-). Doubleday Page & Co.
--A Midsummer Night's Dream. Stewart, Diana, adapted by. Shaw, Charles (1941-), illus. LC 81-19272. (Illus.). 48p. (Raintree Short Classics). (gr. 4-12). 1983. (ISBN 0-8172-2015-1). (ISBN 0-8172-1680-4). Raintree Pubs.
--More Stories from Shakespeare. Lang, Jeanie, Mrs. & Chisholm, Louey, eds. Price, Norman Mills (1877-1951), illus. ix, 118 p. col. front., 7 col. pl. 15 x 12 cm. (Told to the Children Ser.: No. 37). 1910. E P Dutton & Co.
--Romeo & Juliet. (Illus.). 128p. (gr. 7 up). 1970. (ISBN 0-590-02921-5, Schol Pap). Scholastic Inc.
--Romeo & Juliet. Stewart, Diana (1941-), adapted by. Shaw, Charles, illus. LC 79-24465. (Illus.). (Raintree Short Classics). (gr. 4 up). 1980. (ISBN 0-8172-1653-7). Raintree Pubs.
--Romeo and Juliet. Stewart, Diana, adapted by. Shaw, Charles (1941-), illus. LC 79-24465. (Illus.). 48 p. 24cm. c.1980. (ISBN 0-8172-1653-7). Raintree Publishers.
--Romeo & Juliet. Stewart, Diana, adapted by. Shaw, Charles (1941-), illus. LC 79-24465. (Illus.). 48p. (Raintree Short Classics Ser.). (gr. 4-12). 1983. (ISBN 0-8172-2020-8). Raintree Pubs.
--Seeds of Time: Selections from Shakespeare. Grohskopf, Bernice, compiled by. Oechsli, Kelly (1918-), illus. (Illus.). (gr. 5 up). 1963. (ISBN 0-689-20122-2). (ISBN 0-689-20122-2). Atheneum.
--Shake Hands with Shakespeare: Eight Plays for Elementary Schools. Cullum, Albert, adapted by. LC 68-22404. (Illus.). 320 p. 20cm. 1968. Citation Press.
--Shakespeare: Player's Handbook of Short Scenes. Selden, Samuel (1899-1979), ed. (Illus.). (gr. 8 up). 1960. Holiday.
--Shakespeare's Stories Simply Told, 1 of 2 vols. Seymour, Mary Alice Ives, ed. Howard, Frank, illus. (Comedies). N.D. Thos Nelson & Sons.
--Three Children and Shakespeare. White, Anne Terry (1896-), ed. Tobias, Beatrice, illus. LC 38-31823. vi p., 1 l., 266, 1 p. illus. 23 cm. 1938. Harper & Brothers.
--Under the Greenwood Tree: Songs From the Plays. Weisgard, Leonard Joseph (1916-), illus. Weisgard, Leonard Joseph (1916-), selected by. 51p. 1940. Oxford University Press.
--When Daisies Pied, & Violets Blue. Chalmers, Mary Eileen (1927-), illus. (Illus.). 32p. (gr. 1-3). 1974. (ISBN 0-698-20286-4, Coward). Putnam Pub Group.
Shakespeare, William (1564-1616) & Lamb, Charles (1775-1834)
--As You Like It. Gollancz, I., ed. (The Lamb Shakespeare for the Young). N.D. Duffield.
--Complete Tales from Shakespeare. Trewin, ed. (gr. 4-6). N.D. (ISBN 0-531-01930-6). Watts.
--Cymbeline. Gollancz, I., ed. (The Lamb Shakespeare for the Young). N.D. Duffield.
--Macbeth. (The Lamb Shakespeare for the Young). N.D. Duffield.
--The Merchant of Venice. Gollancz, I., ed. (The Lamb Shakespeare for the Young). N.D. Duffield.
--A Midsummer Night's Dream. Gollancz, I., ed. (The Lamb Shakespeare for the Young). N.D. Duffield.
--Romeo and Juliet. Gollancz, I., ed. (The Lamb Shakespeare for the Young). N.D. Duffield.
--The Tempest. Gollancz, I., ed. (The Lamb Shakespeare for the Young). N.D. Duffield.
--Twelfth Night. Gollancz, I., ed. (The Lamb Shakespeare for the Young). N.D. Duffield.
--The Winter's Tale. (The Lamb Shakespeare for the Young). N.D. Duffield.
Shakespeare, William (1564-1616) & Mendelssohn-Bartholdy, Felix (1809-1847)
--Bottom's Dream. Updike, John Hoger (1932-), adapted by. Chappell, Warren (1904-), illus. LC 69-14991. (Illus.). 34 p. 1969. (ISBN 0-394-80854-1). (ISBN 0-394-90854-6). A. A. Knopf.
Shaler, Eleanor
--Gaunt's Daughter. LC 57-4951. 246 p. 21 cm. 1957. Viking Press.
Shaler, Robert
--Boy Scout of the Naval Reserve. (Premier Boy Scout Ser.). N.D. Hurst & Co.
--Boy Scouts and the Prize Pennant. (Premier Boy Scout Ser.). N.D. Hurst & Co.
--The Boy Scouts as Forest Fire Fighters. (Premier Boy Scout Ser.). N.D. Hurst & Co.
--Boy Scouts for City Improvement. (Premier Boy Scout Ser.). N.D. Hurst & Co.
--Boy Scouts in the Great Flood. (Premier Boy Scout Ser.). N.D. Hurst & Co.
--Boy Scouts in the Saddle. (Premier Boy Scout Ser.). N.D. Hurst & Co.
--Boy Scouts of the Field Hospital. (Premier Boy Scout Ser.). N.D. Hurst & Co.
--Boy Scouts of the Flying Squadron. (Premier Boy Scout Ser.). N.D. Hurst & Co.
--The Boy Scouts of the Geological Survey. LC 14-13684. 160 p. 19 cm. $0.3. c.1914. Hurst & Company.
--Boy Scouts of the Life Saving Crew. (Premier Boy Scout Ser.). N.D. Hurst & Co.
--Boy Scouts of the Signal Corps. (Premier Boy Scout Ser.). N.D. Hurst & Co.
--Boy Scouts on Picket Duty. (Premier Boy Scout Ser.). N.D. Hurst & Co.
--Boy Scouts with the Red Cross. (Premier Boy Sout Ser.). N.D. Hurst & Co.
--Boys Scout of Pioneer Camp. (Premier Boy Scout Ser.). N.D. Hurst & Co.
Shalleck, Alan J., jt. ed. see Rey, Margret Elisabeth Waldstein.
Shallenberger, Alice
--Little High Hill. Ludwig, Helen, illus. LC 65-10362. 1 v. (unpaged) col. illus. 28 cm. 1965. Golden Gate Junior Books.
Shane, Harold Gray, jt. auth. see Shane, Ruth.
Shane, Harold Gray (1914-)
--Gulliver's Travels. Clark, William, ed. Eckart, Frances, illus. (Illus.). 16p. (Hero Legends Bk.). (gr. 3-5). 1980. (ISBN 0-89290-083-0). Soc for Visual.
--King Arthur & the Magic Sword. Clark, William, ed. Maltman, Chauncey, illus. LC 68-3547. (Illus.). 16p. (Hero Legends Bk.). (gr. 3-5). 1980. (ISBN 0-89290-079-2). Soc for Visual.
--Robin Hood & Allan-a-Dale. Clark, William, ed. McIntyre, Dorothy, illus. LC 68-3588. (Illus.). 16p. (Hero Legends Bk.). (gr. 3-5). 1980. (ISBN 0-89290-081-4). Soc for Visual.
--William Tell. Clark, William, ed. Winkler, Albert, illus. (Illus.). 16p. (Hero Legends Bk.). (gr. 3-5). N.D. (ISBN 0-89290-078-4). Soc for Visual.
Shane, Ruth & Shane, Harold Gray (1914-)
--The New Baby. Wilkin, Eloise Burns (1904-), illus. LC 79-10844. p. cm. 1979, c.1948. Golden Press.
--The Twins: The Story of Two Little Girls Who Look Alike. Wilkin, Eloise Burns (1904-), illus. LC 55-14362. unpaged. illus. 21cm. (A Little Golden Book, 227). 1955. Simon and Schuster.
Shangold, Helen
--Cloze Stories for Reading Success. (gr. k-3). 1981. (ISBN 0-8027-9124-7). Walker & Co.
Shank, Marcia, jt. auth. see Garnholz, Terry.
Shank, Margarethe Erdahl (1910-)
--The Coffee Train. Lonette, Reisie Dominee (1924-), illus. LC 53-9129. (Illus.). 285 p. 20cm. 1953. Doubleday.
Shank, Merna B.
--Happy Ways: Verses for Children, No. 1. 1982. (ISBN 0-87813-211-2). Park View.
--Thankful Days: Verses for Children, No. 2. 1982. (ISBN 0-87813-212-0). Park View.
Shankar, Alaka
--The Seven Queens. Vyas, Anil, illus. (Illus.). 16p. (Orig.). (gr. k-3). 1980. (ISBN 0-89744-217-2, Pub. by Children's Bk Trust India). Auromere.
--Sonali's Friend. Joshi, Jagadish, illus. (Illus.). 16p. (Orig.). (gr. k-3). 1980. (ISBN 0-89744-218-0, Pub. by Children's Bk Trust India). Auromere.
Shankland, Frank North
--Famous Romances. Hays, Ethel & Turner, Dolly, illus. LC 44-549684. 3 p. l., 9-72 p. illus. 24 cm. c.1943. R. Speller.
--Teen-Age Romances: A Book for Young Folks. MacCracken, Marthena Louise, illus. LC 51-3767. 67 p. illus. 23 cm. 1951. Christopher Pub. House.
Shankman, Sarah & Don Bluth Productions
--Dirk the Daring Saves Princess Daphne. Fontes, Ron, designed by. LC 84-234075. (Illus.). 35 p. 21cm. (Dragon's lair). (A Big-Looker Storybook). c.1984. (ISBN 0-87135-017-3). Magicom.
Shanley, Charles D.
--The Truent Chicken. (The Truent Chicken Ser.). N.D. Hurd & Houghton.
Shannon, George William Bones (1952-)
--Bean Boy. Sis, Peter, illus. LC 83-20764. (Illus.). 40p. (gr. k-3). 1984. (ISBN 0-688-03779-8). (ISBN 0-688-03780-1). Greenwillow.
--Dance Away. Aruego, Jose (1932-) & Dewey, Ariane (1937-), illus. LC 81-6391. (Illus.). 32 p. c.1982. (ISBN 0-688-00838-0). (ISBN 0-688-00839-9). Greenwillow Books.
--The Gang and Mrs. Higgins. Vines, Andrew, illus. LC 80-15957. (Illus.). 47 p. 22cm. (Greenwillow Read-Alone Bks.). c.1981. (ISBN 0-688-80303-2). (ISBN 0-688-84303-4). Greenwillow Books.
--Humpty Dumpty. (Illus., Orig.). 1st U.S. edition. 1980. (ISBN 0-914676-37-7, Star & Eleph Bks). Green Tiger Pr.
--Lizard's Song. 1st ed. Aruego, Jose (1932-) & Dewey, Ariane (1937-), illus. LC 80-21432. (Illus.). 32 p. c.1981. (ISBN 0-688-80310-5). (ISBN 0-688-84310-7). Greenwillow Books.
--The Piney Woods Peddler. Tafuri, Nancy, illus. LC 81-2219. (Illus.). 32 p. c.1981. (ISBN 0-688-80304-0). (ISBN 0-688-84304-2). Greenwillow Books. **Award: (ALA).**
--Stories to Solve: Folktales from Around the World. Sis, Peter, illus. LC 84-18656. (Illus.). 55 p. 23cm. c.1985. (ISBN 0-688-04303-8). (ISBN 0-688-04304-6). (ISBN 0-688-04303-8). (ISBN 0-688-04304-6). Greenwillow Books.
--The Surprise. Aruego, Jose (1932-) & Dewey, Ariane (1937-), illus. LC 83-1434. p. cm. 1983. (ISBN 0-688-02313-4). (ISBN 0-688-02314-2). Greenwillow Books.
Shannon, J. Michael
--Riddles and More Riddles. Magnuson, Diana, illus. LC 82-19765. p. cm. (Laughing Matters). c.1983. (ISBN 0-516-01873-6). Children's Press.
Shannon, Jean, jt. auth. see Colina, Tessa Patterson.
Shannon, Mattie Bayly, jt. auth. see Sipley, Mildred.
Shannon, Monica (1905-1965)
--California Fairy Tales. Millard, C. E., illus. LC 26-23676. 21cm. 298p. 1926. Doubleday, Page & Company.
--California Fairy Tales. Millard, C. E., illus. 311p. N.D. Frederick Ungar Publishing Co Inc.
--California Fairy Tales. Millard, C. E., illus. LC 57-13347. 208 p. illus. 21 cm. 1957, c.1953. Stephen Daye Press.
--Dobry. Katchamakoff, Atanas (1898-), illus. LC 34-36557. 6 p. l., 5-176 p. incl. illus., plates. double col. front. 23 1/2 cm. 1934. The Viking Press. **Award: (JNM).**
--Eyes for the Dark. Millard, C. E., illus. LC 28-23339. x p., 1 l., 311 p. incl. illus., plates. col. front., col. plates. 21 cm. 1928. Doubleday, Doran & Company, Inc.
--Goose Grass Rhymes. Brown, Neva Kanaga, illus. LC 30-29910. xi, 155 p. col. front., illus. 20 1/2 cm. 1930. Doubleday, Doran & Company, Inc.
--More Tales from California. Millard, C. E., illus. LC 35-35690. ix p., 1 l., 311 p. incl. illus., plates. front. 20 1/2 cm. 1935. Doubleday, Doran & Company, Inc.
--More Tales From California. Millard, C. E., illus. 311p. N.D. Frederick Ungar Publishing Co Inc.
--More Tales From California. Millard, C. E., illus. LC 60-13988. 21cm. 311p. 1960. Stephen Daye Press.
--Tawnymore. Charlot, Jean (1898-1979), illus. LC 31-24149. vii p., 2 l., 3-254 p. incl. illus., plates. col. front. 20 1/2 cm. 1931. Doubleday, Doran & Company, Inc.
Shannon, Terry, pseud., see Mercer, Jessie.
Shannon, Terry, pseud.
--And Juan. Mercer, Jessie. Payzant, Charles, illus. LC 61-8776. (Illus.). 42 p. 24cm. 1961. A. Whitman.
--Around the World with Gogo. Mercer, Jessie. Payzant, Charles, illus. LC 64-10546. 1v. (unpaged) col. illus. 22x27cm. c.1964. Golden Gate.
--A Dog Team for Ongluk. Mercer, Jessie. Payzant, Charles, illus. LC 62-7010. (Illus.). 31 p. 25cm. (Look, Read, Learn). 1962. Melmont Publishers.
--Indians of the Past and Present. Mercer, Jessie. Payzant, Charles, illus. N.D. Albert Whitman & Company.
--Kidlik's Kayak. Mercer, Jessie. Payzant, Charles, illus. LC 59-9660. (Illus.). 44 p. 24cm. 1959. A. Whitman.
--Little Wolf, the Rain Dancer. Mercer, Jessie. Payzant, Charles, illus. N.D. Albert Whitman & Co.
--A Playmate for Puna. Mercer, Jessie. Payzant, Charles, illus. LC 63-7014. 31 p. illus. 25 cm. (Look, Read, Learn). 1963. Melmont.
--Red is for Luck. Mercer, Jessie. Payzant, Charles, illus. LC 63-9156. 85 p. illus. 22 cm. 1963. Golden Gate Junior Books.
--Ride the Ice Down!. Mercer, Jessie. Payzant, Charles, illus. 1970. (ISBN 0-516-08843-2). Childrens Press.
--Running Fox, the Eagle Hunter. Mercer, Jessie. Payzant, Charles, illus. LC 57-7755. (Illus.). 46 p. 24cm. 1957. Whitman.
--Tyee's Totem Pole. Mercer, Jessie. Payzant, Charles, illus. LC 55-10587. (Illus.). (gr. 3-5). 1955. (ISBN 0-8075-8189-5). A. Whitman.
--Wakapoo and the Flying Arrows. Mercer, Jessie. Payzant, Charles, illus. LC 63-20352. 47p. illus. (pt. col.) 24cm. c.1963. A. Whitman.
Shannon, Terry, pseud. & Payzant, Charles
--Today Is Story Day: A Tale for Every Day of the Week. Mercer, Jessie. Payzant, Charles, illus. LC 54-951483. unpaged. illus. 28cm. 1954. Aladdin Books.
Shapiro, Arnold
--Kenny's Crazy Kite. (Illus.). (Surprise Bk). (ps-4). 1978. (ISBN 0-8431-0445-7). Price Stern.
Shapiro, Edna
--Windwagon Smith. Aloise, Frank E., illus. LC 69-12924. (Illus.). 35 p. 23cm. (A Reading Shelf Book). 1969. (ISBN 0-8116-4016-7). Garrard Pub. Co.
Shapiro, G. H., jt. auth. see Adshead, Gladys Lucy.
Shapiro, Irwin, jt. auth. see Disney, Walter Elias.
Shapiro, Irwin, ed. see Arabian Nights.
Shapiro, Irwin, as told by see Disney, Walter Elias.
Shapiro, Irwin (1911-), retold by see Disney, Walt, Productions.
Shapiro, Irwin (1911-), ed. see Melville, Herman.
Shapiro, Irwin, jt. ed. see Soifer, Margaret.
Shapiro, Irwin, jt. ed. see Soifer, Margaret K.
Shapiro, Irwin (1911-)
--Casey Jones and Locomotive No. 638. McKay, Donald A. (1895-), illus. LC 44-3476. 53 p. illus. 24 cm. 1944. J. Messner, Inc.
--Circus Boy. Authorized. Anglund, Joan Walsh (1926-), illus. LC 60-29903. unpaged. illus. 21 cm. (Little Golden Bk.200). 1957. Simon and Schuster.
--Cleo. Hurford, Miriam Story, illus. Graybill, Durward B., photos by. LC 56-3079. unpaged. illus. 21 cm. (A Little Golden Book: 287). 1957. Simon and Schuster.
--Dan McCann and His Fast Sooner Hound. Korach, Mimi (1922-), illus. LC 74-28287. (Illus.). 48 p. 23cm. 1975. (ISBN 0-8116-4043-4). Garrard Pub. Co.
--Daniel Boone. Hurford, Miriam Story, illus. LC 56-3079. unpaged. illus. 21cm. (Little golden book, 256). 1956. Simon and Schuster.
--The Gremlins of Lieut. Oggins. McKay, Donald A. (1895-), illus. 1943. Julian Messner.

--Gretchen and the White Steed. Vestal, Herman B., illus. LC 72-1471. (Illus.). 63 p. 23cm. 1972. (ISBN 0-8116-6962-9). Garrard Pub. Co.
--Heroes in American Folklore. McKay, Donald A. (1895-) & Daugherty, James Henry (1889-1974), illus. LC 62-10205. (Illus.). (gr. 5 up). 1962. (ISBN 0-671-32054-8). Messner.
--How Old Stormalong Captured Mocha Dick. McKay, Donald A. (1895-), illus. LC 42-20568. 47, 1 p. col. illus. 24 cm. 1942. J. Messner, Inc.
--The Hungry Ghost Mystery. Hutchinson, William Miller (1916-), illus. LC 78-5841. (Illus.). 63 p. 23cm. (Garrard Mystery Bk.). c.1978. (ISBN 0-8116-6403-1). Garrard Pub. Co.
--J. Fred Muggs. Schmidt, Edwin, illus. LC 55-3178. unpaged. illus. 21cm. (Little Golden Library, 234). 1955. Simon and Schuster.
--Joe Magarac and His U.S.A. Citizen Papers. Daugherty, James Henry (1889-1974), illus. LC 78-66070. (Illus.). 58 p. 23cm. (Pitt paperback ; 148). 1979, c.1962. University of Pittsburgh Press.
--John Henry and the Double Jointed Steam Drill. Daugherty, James Henry (1889-1974), illus. 1945. Julian Messner.
--Jonathan and the Dragon. Vroman, Tom, illus. LC 62-9858. 31 p. illus. 22 cm. (Golden reader). 1962. Golden Press.
--Lassie Finds a Way: A New Story of the Famous Dog. Authorized. Greene, Hamilton, illus. LC 57-3591. unpaged. illus. 33 cm. (Big Golden Bk.456). 1957. Simon and Schuster.
--Paul Bunyan Tricks a Dragon. Burns, Raymond Howard (1924-), illus. LC 74-19059. (Illus.). 48 p. 23cm. 1975. (ISBN 0-8116-4042-6). Garrard Pub. Co.
--Sam Patch, Champion Jumper. Schroeder, Ted (1931-1973), illus. LC 71-169844. (Illus.). 47 p. 23cm. (Reading Shelf Bk.). 1972. (ISBN 0-8116-4033-7). Garrard Pub. Co.
--Steamboat Bill and the Captain's Top Hat. McKay, Donald A. (1895-), illus. LC 43-16228. 48 p. illus. 24 cm. 1943. J. Messner Inc.
--Tall Tales of America. Schmidt, Al, illus. 1959. Golden Press.
--Tall Tales of America. Schmidt, Al, illus. 1961. Golden Press.
--Tall Tales of America. Schmidt, Al, illus. LC 59-19325. (Illus.). 124 p. 23cm. c.1958. Guild Press.
--Twice Upon a Time. Adams, Adrienne (1906-), illus. 1973. (ISBN 0-684-13358-X). Charles Scribner's Sons.
--Twice Upon a Time. Adams, Adrienne (1906-), illus. LC 72-97116. (Weekly Reader Children's Book Club). (Illus.). 40 p. 27cm. 1973. Xerox Family Education Services.
--Uncle Sam's 200th Birthday Parade. Brugos, Frank, illus. LC 74-77047. (Illus.). 45 p. 31cm. 1974. (ISBN 0-307-63745-X). Golden Press.
--Willie's Whizmobile. Frame, Paul (1913-), illus. LC 72-10559. (Illus.). 39 p. 24cm. 1973. (ISBN 0-8116-6726-X). Garrard Pub. Co.
--Yankee Thunder: The Legendary Life of Davy Crockett. Daugherty, James Henry (1889-1974), illus. LC 44-4323. 205 p. incl. front., illus. 22 1/2 cm. 1944. J. Messner, Inc.

Shapiro, Larry
--Adventures of Christopher Cricket. (Illus.). (Surprise Bk). (ps-4). 1978. (ISBN 0-8431-0443-0). Price Stern.
--Pop-up Books. Incl. Pop-up Colors; Pop-up Numbers; Pop-up Opposites; Pop-Up Shapes. (Illus.). (gr. 3-7). 1979. (Pub. by Gingerbread Bks.). Dutton.

Shapiro, Milton J. (1926-)
--Treasury of Sports Humor. LC 75-176383. 192p. (Sports Bks. Ser.). (gr. 7 up). 1972. (ISBN 0-671-32503-5). Messner.

Shapiro, Zeva, tr. see Meir, Mira.

Shappel, Bernice M.
--Harvey Hopper. Brophy, Ruth, illus. LC 66-6196. 1v. (unpaged) col. illus. 29cm. c.1966. Denison.

Sharfman, Amalie
--A Beagle Named Bertram. Palazzo, Tony (1905-1970), illus. LC 54-9152. 116p. illus. 21cm. 1954. Crowell.
--Mr. Peabody's Pesky Ducks. 1st ed. Darling, Louis, Jr. (1916-1970), illus. LC 57-8045. 88 p. illus. 22 cm. 1957. Little, Brown.
--Papa's Secret Chocolate Dessert. Obligado, Lilian Isabel (1931-), illus. LC 77-177319. (Illus.). 95 p. 23cm. 1972. Lothrop, Lee & Shepard Co.

Sharkey, Donald C., jt. auth. see Kelly, Gerald A.

Sharkey, Donald C (1912-)
--The Lost Prince. LC 40-35468. 153 (i.e. 191) p. col. front., col. plates. 19 cm. 1940. Bonziger Brothers, Inc.
--Nicholas, the Boy King. LC 49-13592. 194 p. 21 cm. 1948. Ave Maria Press.

Sharma, B. Jane
--Tell Me a Story. LC 73-79980. (Illus.). 22 p. 22cm. 1973. (ISBN 0-8059-1866-3). Dorrance.

Sharma, Partap (1939-)
--The Surangini Tales. 1st ed. Hitz, Demi (1942-), illus. LC 72-88173. (Illus.). 125 p. 21cm. 1973. (ISBN 0-15-283200-9). Harcourt Brace Jovanovich.

Sharman, Russell
--One of the Least. 143p. N.D. Sunday-School Library.

Sharmat, Marjorie Weinman (1928-)
--Attila the Angry. Hoban, Lillian (1925-), illus. LC 84-15860. (Illus.). 32p. (gr. k-3). 1985. (ISBN 0-8234-0545-1). Holiday.
--Bartholomew the Bossy. Chartier, Normand (1945-), illus. (Illus.). 32p. (ps-3). 1984. (ISBN 0-02-782520-5). Macmillan.
--The Best Valentine in the World. 1st ed. Obligado, Lilian Isabel (1931-), illus. LC 81-13345. (Illus.). 32 p. 23cm. c.1982. (ISBN 0-8234-0440-4). Holiday House.
--A Big Fat Enormous Lie. 1st ed. McPhail, Michael David (1940-), illus. LC 77-15645. (Illus.). 32 p. 25cm. c.1978. (ISBN 0-525-26510-4). Dutton.
--Burton and Dudley. Cooney, Barbara (1917-), illus. LC 75-1091. (Illus.). 48 p. 21cm. 1975. (ISBN 0-8234-0260-6). Holiday House.
--Chasing After Annie. 1st ed. Simont, Marc (1915-), illus. LC 80-7906. (Illus.). 62 p. 20cm. c.1981. (ISBN 0-06-025562-5). (ISBN 0-06-025567-6). Harper & Row.
--Edgemont. Szekeres, Cyndy (1933-), illus. LC 76-113. p. cm. c.1976. (ISBN 0-698-20375-5). (ISBN 0-698-30627-9). Coward, McCann & Geoghegan.
--Fifty-One Sycamore Lane. Weil, Lisl (1910-), illus. LC 73-129754. (Illus.). 122 p. 22cm. 1971. Macmillan.
--Frizzy the Fearful. 1st ed. Wallner, John C. (1945-), illus. LC 82-12093. (Illus.). 32 p. 24cm. c.1983. (ISBN 0-8234-0475-7). Holiday House.
--Getting Something on Maggie Marmelstein. 1st ed. Shecter, Ben (1935-), illus. LC 78-157895. (Illus.). 101 p. 21cm. 1971. (ISBN 0-06-025552-8). Harper & Row.
--Getting Something on Maggie Marmelstein. Shecter, Ben (1935-), illus. LC 78-157895. (Illus.). 101 p. 20cm. (Trophy Book, J33). 1973, c.1971. (ISBN 0-06-440038-7). Harper.
--Gila Monsters Meet You at the Airport. Barton, Byron (1930-), illus. LC 80-12264. (Illus.). 32 p. c.1980. (ISBN 0-02-782450-0). Macmillan.
--Gila Monsters Meet You at the Airport. Barton, Byron (1930-), illus. LC 83-2181. p. cm. 1983. (ISBN 0-14-050430-3). Puffin Books.
--Gladys Told Me to Meet Her Here. Frascino, Edward, illus. LC 78-85019. (Illus.). 31 p. 27cm. 1970. Harper & Row.
--Goodnight, Andrew, Goodnight, Craig. Chalmers, Mary Eileen (1927-), illus. LC 69-10205. (Illus.). 32 p. 18cm. 1969. Harper & Row.
--Griselda's New Year. Chartier, Normand (1945-), illus. LC 79-11375. (Illus.). 63 p. 23cm. (Ready-To-Read). c.1979. (ISBN 0-02-782420-9). Macmillan.
--Grumley the Grouch. Chorao, Ann Mckay Sproat (1936-), illus. LC 79-28290. (Illus.). 32 p. 25cm. c.1980. (ISBN 0-8234-0410-2). Holiday House.
--He Noticed I'm Alive... & Other Hopeful Signs. LC 84-4329. 160p. (gr. 7 up). 1984. (ISBN 0-385-29351-8). Delacorte.
--A Hot Thirsty Day. Wells, Rosemary, illus. LC 70-123130. (Illus.). 32 p. 23cm. 1971. Macmillan.
--How to Meet a Gorgeous Girl. LC 83-14365. (Illus.). 137. c.1984. (ISBN 0-385-29324-0). Delacorte Press.
--I Don't Care. Hoban, Lillian (1925-), illus. LC 76-48251. (Illus.). 32 p. 27cm. c.1977. (ISBN 0-02-782290-7). Macmillan.
--I Saw Him First. LC 82-14839. p. cm. 1983. (ISBN 0-440-03975-4). Delacorte Press.
--I Want Mama. 1st ed. McCully, Emily Arnold (1939-), illus. LC 74-3584. (Illus.). 32 p. 1974. (ISBN 0-06-025554-4). Harper & Row.
--I'm Not Oscar's Friend Anymore. 1st ed. DeLuna, Tony, illus. LC 74-23767. (Illus.). 32 p. 1975. (ISBN 0-525-32537-9). Dutton.
--I'm Terrific. Chorao, Ann Mckay Sproat (1936-), illus. LC 76-9094. (Illus.). vii, 184 p. 29cm. 1976. (ISBN 0-8234-0282-7). Holiday House.
--The Lancelot Closes at Five. Weil, Lisl (1910-), illus. LC 75-31945. (Illus.). 120 p. 22cm. c.1976. (ISBN 0-02-782320-2). Macmillan.
--Little Devil Gets Sick. Hafner, Marylin (1925-), illus. LC 79-7209. (Illus.). 63 p. 24cm. (A Reading-On-My-Own Book). c.1980. (ISBN 0-385-14209-9). (ISBN 0-385-14210-2). Doubleday.
--Lucretia the Unbearable. Stevens, Janet, illus. LC 81-1923. p. cm. c.1981. (ISBN 0-8234-0395-5). Holiday House.
--Maggie Marmelstein for President. Shecter, Ben (1935-), illus. LC 75-6300. (Illus.). 122 p. 21cm. c.1975. (ISBN 0-06-025542-0). (ISBN 0-06-025555-2). Harper & Row.
--Mitchell Is Moving. Aruego, Jose (1932-) & Dewey, Ariane (1937-), illus. LC 85-47782. p. cm. 1985, c.1978. (ISBN 0-02-045260-8). Collier Books.
--Mitchell Is Moving. Aruego, Jose (1932-) & Dewey, Ariane (1937-), illus. LC 78-6816. (Illus.). 47 p. 23cm. (Ready-to-read). c.1978. (ISBN 0-02-782410-1). Macmillan.
--Mooch the Messy. Shecter, Ben (1935-), illus. LC 76-3842. (An I Can Read Book). c.1976. (ISBN 0-06-025531-5). (ISBN 0-06-025532-3). Harper & Row.
--Mooch the Messy Meets Prudence the Neat. Shecter, Ben (1935-), illus. LC 77-29049. (Illus.). 63 p. 22cm. (A Break-Of-Day Book). c.1978. (ISBN 0-698-30703-8). Coward, McCann & Geoghegan.
--Morris Brookside, a Dog. Himler, Ronald Norbert (1937-), illus. LC 73-76797. 19cm. 48p. 1973. Holiday.
--Morris Brookside Is Missing. Himler, Ronald Norbert (1937-), illus. LC 74-5442. (Illus.). 32 p. 19cm. 1974. (ISBN 0-8234-0245-2). Holiday House.
--Mr. Jameson and Mr. Phillips. Degen, Bruce, illus. LC 77-25665. (Illus.). 48 p. 26cm. c.1979. (ISBN 0-06-025528-5). (ISBN 0-06-025529-3). Harper & Row.
--Mysteriously Yours, Maggie Marmelstein. 1st ed. Shecter, Ben (1935-), illus. LC 81-48656. p. cm. c.1982. (ISBN 0-06-025516-1). (ISBN 0-06-025517-X). Harper & Row.
--Nate the Great. Simont, Marc (1915-), illus. LC 75-183552. (Illus.). 60 p. 23cm. (A Break-Of-Day Book). 1972. (ISBN 0-698-20218-X). (ISBN 0-698-20218-X). Coward, McCann & Geoghegan.
--Nate the Great and the Fishy Prize. Simont, Marc (1915-), illus. LC 84-15545. (Illus.). 46 p. 23cm. (Break-of-day book). c.1985. (ISBN 0-698-30745-3). Coward-McCann.
--Nate the Great and the Lost List. Simont, Marc (1915-), illus. LC 76-350105. (Illus.). 48 p. 23cm. (A Break-Of-Day Book). c.1975. (ISBN 0-698-20341-0). (ISBN 0-698-30593-0). Coward, McCann & Geoghegan.
--Nate the Great and the Missing Key. Simont, Marc (1915-), illus. LC 80-13952. (Illus.). 47 p. 23cm. (Break-of-day book). c.1981. (ISBN 0-698-30726-7). Coward, McCann & Geoghegan.
--Nate the Great and the Phony Clue. Simont, Marc (1915-), illus. LC 76-42461. (Illus.). 48 p. 23cm. (A Break Of Day Book). c.1977. (ISBN 0-698-30650-3). Coward, McCann & Geoghegan.
--Nate the Great and the Snowy Trail. Simont, Marc (1915-), illus. LC 81-19539. (Illus.). 47 p. 23cm. (Break-of-day book). c.1982. (ISBN 0-698-30738-0). Coward, McCann & Geoghegan.
--Nate the Great and the Sticky Case. Simont, Marc (1915-), illus. LC 77-17011. (Illus.). 44 p. 23cm. (A Break-Of-Day Book). c.1978. (ISBN 0-698-30697-X). Coward, McCann & Geoghegan.
--Nate the Great Goes Undercover. Simont, Marc (1915-), illus. LC 74-79700. (Illus.). 47 p. 23cm. (A Break-Of-Day Book). 1974. (ISBN 0-698-30547-7). Coward, McCann & Geoghegan.
--Octavia Told Me a Secret. Litzinger, Roseanne, illus. LC 79-10425. (Illus.). 32 p. c.1979. (ISBN 0-590-07605-1). (ISBN 0-590-07558-6). Four Winds Press.
--One Terrific Thanksgiving. Obligado, Lilian Isabel (1931-), illus. LC 85-726. p. cm. 1985. (ISBN 0-8234-0569-9). Holiday House.
--Rex. McCully, Emily Arnold (1939-), illus. LC 67-14075. (Illus.). (gr. k-3). 1967. (ISBN 0-06-025544-7, HarpJ). Har-Row.
--Rich Mitch. Lustig, Loretta, illus. LC 83-5398. (Illus.). 136 p. 21cm. 1983. (ISBN 0-688-02407-6). Morrow.
--Rollo and Juliet, Forever!. Hafner, Marylin (1925-), illus. LC 80-628. (Illus.). 32 p. c.1981. (ISBN 0-385-15784-3). Doubleday.
--Sasha the Silly. Stevens, Janet, illus. LC 83-18357. (Illus.). 32p. (ps-3). 1984. (ISBN 0-8234-0503-6). Holiday.
--Say Hello, Vanessa. Hoban, Lillian (1925-), illus. LC 79-1511. (Illus.). 32 p. 24cm. c.1979. (ISBN 0-8234-0354-8). Holiday House.
--Scarlet Monster Lives Here. 1st ed. Kendrick, Dennis, illus. LC 78-19484. (Illus.). 64 p. 23cm. (An I Can Read Book). c.1979. (ISBN 0-06-025526-9). (ISBN 0-06-025527-7). Harper & Row.
--Sometimes Mama and Papa Fight. Chorao, Ann Mckay Sproat (1936-), illus. LC 79-2018. (Illus.). 30 p. 24cm. c.1980. (ISBN 0-06-025611-7). (ISBN 0-06-025612-5). Harper & Row.
--Sophie and Gussie. Hoban, Lillian (1925-), illus. LC 74-20738. 20cm. 64p. 1975. (ISBN 0-02-045120-2). Collier Books.
--Sophie and Gussie. Hoban, Lillian (1925-), illus. LC 72-85188. (Illus.). 64 p. 22cm. (Ready-To-Read). 1973. Macmillan.
--The Spy in the Neighborhood. Weil, Lisl (1910-), illus. (Illus.). 122 p. 20cm. 1974, c.1971. Collier Books.
--The Story of Bentley Beaver. Hoban, Lillian (1925-), illus. LC 82-47715. (Illus.). 5 7/8 x 8 1/2. 64p. (18 pt.). (I Can Read Ser.). (gr. k-3). 1984. (ISBN 0-06-025512-9). (ISBN 0-06-025513-7). Har-Row.
--Taking Care of Melvin. Chess, Victoria (1939-), illus. LC 79-16751. (Illus.). 32 p. 25cm. c.1980. (ISBN 0-8234-0368-8). Holiday House.
--Thornton, the Worrier. Chorao, Ann Mckay Sproat (1936-), illus. LC 78-1286. 21cm. 322p. 1978. (ISBN 0-8234-0328-9). Holiday House.
--The Three Hundred and Twenty-Ninth Friend. Szekeres, Cyndy (1933-), illus. LC 78-21770. (Illus.). 48 p. c.1979. (ISBN 0-590-07558-6). Four Winds Press.
--The Trip, and Other Sophie and Gussie Stories. Hoban, Lillian (1925-), illus. LC 76-10168. (Illus.). 63 p. 22cm. (Ready-To-Read). c.1976. (ISBN 0-02-782300-8). Macmillan.
--The Trolls of Twelfth Street. Shecter, Ben (1935-), illus. LC 78-31788. (Illus.). (Break-of-Day Bk.). (gr. k-3). 1979. (ISBN 0-698-30716-X, Coward). Putnam Pub Group.
--Twitchell the Wishful. Stevens, Janet, illus. LC 80-16815. (Illus.). 40 p. c.1981. (ISBN 0-8234-0379-3). Holiday House.
--Two Ghosts on a Bench. Langner, Nola (1930-), illus. LC 81-47734. (Illus.). 64 p. 24cm. c.1982. (ISBN 0-06-025518-8). (ISBN 0-06-025519-6). Harper & Row.
--Two Guys Noticed Me- and Other Miracles: A Novel. LC 84-19873. 149 p. 22cm. c.1985. (ISBN 0-385-29394-1). Delacorte Press.
--Uncle Boris and Maude. McLean, Sammis, illus. LC 78-18565. (Illus.). 62 p. 25cm. (A Reading-On-My-Own Book). c.1979. (ISBN 0-385-12946-7). (ISBN 0-385-12947-5). Doubleday.
--A Visit with Rosalind. Weil, Lisl (1910-), illus. LC 79-160071. (Illus.). 133 p. 22cm. 1971, c.1972. Macmillan.
--Walter the Wolf. Oechsli, Kelly (1918-), illus. LC 74-26659. (Illus.). 32 p. 23cm. 1975. (ISBN 0-8234-0253-3). Holiday House.
--What Are We Going to Do About Andrew?. Cruz, Raymond (1933-), illus. LC 79-20535. (Illus.). 32 p. 24cm. 1980. (ISBN 0-02-782440-3). Macmillan.
--Who's Afraid of Ernestine?. Chambliss, Maxie, illus. LC 85-14911. p. cm. c.1985. (ISBN 0-698-30746-1). Coward-McCann.

Sharmat, Marjorie Weinman (1928-) & Sharmat, Mitchell (1927-)
--The Day I Was Born. 1st ed. Durell, Ann, ed. Dawson, Diane, illus. LC 80-16313. (Illus.). 30 p. 26cm. c.1980. (ISBN 0-525-28560-1). Dutton.
--I Am Not a Pest. Dawson, Diane, illus. LC 78-11845. p. cm. c.1979. (ISBN 0-525-32520-4). Dutton.

Sharmat, Mitchell, jt. auth. see Sharmat, Marjorie Weinman.

Sharmat, Mitchell (1927-)
--Come Home, Wilma. Hoffman, Rosekrans (1926-), illus. LC 80-18991. p. cm. (A Concept Book/Level 1). 1980. (ISBN 0-8075-1278-8). A. Whitman.
--Gregory, the Terrible Eater. Aruego, Jose (1932-) & Dewey, Ariane (1937-), illus. LC 79-19172. (Illus.). 32 p. c.1980. (ISBN 0-590-07586-1). Four Winds Press.
--Reddy Rattler and Pictures Easy Eagle. Simont, Marc (1915-), illus. LC 78-20924. (Illus.). 63 p. 24cm. (A Reading-On-My-Own Book). c.1979. (ISBN 0-385-14216-1). (ISBN 0-385-14216-1). Doubleday.
--The Seven Sloppy Days of Phineas. Truesdell, Susan G., illus. 1983. Harcourt.
--The Seven Sloppy Days of Phineas Pig. 1st ed. Truesdell, Susan G, illus. LC 81-6954. p. cm. c.1982. Harcourt Brace Jovanovich.

Sharoff, Victor
--Garbage Can Cat. Watson, Howard N., illus. LC 70-79871. (Illus.). 48 p. 24cm. 1969. Westminster Press.
--The Heart of the Wood. Tripp, Wallace Whitney (1940-), illus. LC 74-132604. (Illus.). 63 p. 22cm. (A Break-Of-Day Book). 1971. Coward, McCann & Geoghegan.

Sharp, Adda Mai Cummings
--Daffy. Rice, Elizabeth (1913-), illus. LC 50-9876. (Illus.). 47 p. 24cm. 1950. Steck Co.
--Gee Whillikins. Rice, Elizabeth (1913-), illus. (gr. 3-4). 1950. (ISBN 0-8114-7519-0). Steck-V.
--Where Is Cubby Bear. Rice, Elizabeth (1913-), illus. LC 50-3817. (Illus.). 21cm. 63p. (gr. 1-2). 1950. (ISBN 0-8114-7569-7). Steck-V.

Sharp, Adda Mai Cummings & Young, Epsie
--Chichi's Magic. Rice, Elizabeth (1913-), illus. (Illus.). (Woodland Frolics Ser.G). (gr. 5-7). 1954. (ISBN 0-8114-3758-2). Steck-V.
--Chippy Chipmunk's Vacation. Rice, Elizabeth (1913-), illus. (Woodland Frolics Ser.G). (gr. 3-5). 1965. (ISBN 0-8114-3756-6). Steck-V.

--Did You Ever. Rice, Elizabeth (1913-), illus. (Illus.). (gr. 1-2). 1957. (ISBN 0-8114-3763-9). Steck-V.
--Downy Duck Grows Up. Rice, Elizabeth (1913-), illus. (Woodland Frolics Ser.G). (gr. 2). 1965. (ISBN 0-8114-3754-X). Steck-V.
--Every Day a Surprise. Rice, Elizabeth (1913-), illus. (Illus.). (Wonder-Wonder Ser.G). (primer 1-2). 1957. (ISBN 0-8114-3762-0). Steck-V.
--Gordo & the Hidden Treasure. Rice, Elizabeth (1913-), illus. (Illus.). (Woodland Frolics Ser.G). (gr. 4-6). 1955. (ISBN 0-8114-3757-4). Steck-V.
--Gordo and the Hidden Treasures. Rice, Elizabeth (1913-), illus. (Woodland Frolics Ser.). N.D. World Publishing Co.
--Heart of the Wild. Rice, Elizabeth (1913-), illus. (Woodland Frolics Ser.G). (gr. 6-8). 1955. (ISBN 0-8114-3759-0). Steck-V.
--Little Lost Bobo. Rice, Elizabeth (1913-), illus. (Woodland Frolics Ser.G). (gr. 2-4). 1965. (ISBN 0-8114-3755-8). Steck-V.
--Rainbow in the Sky. Rice, Elizabeth (1913-), illus. (Illus.). (gr. 2-4). 1957. (ISBN 0-8114-3764-7). Steck-V.
--Secret Places. Rice, Elizabeth (1913-), illus. 1955. The Steck Company.
--Watch Me. Rice, Elizabeth (1913-), illus. (Woodland Frolics Ser.G). (gr. 1). 1965. (ISBN 0-8114-3753-1). Steck-V.
--Whatnot Tales. Rice, Elizabeth (1913-), illus. (Illus.). (gr. 3-5). 1957. (ISBN 0-8114-3765-5). Steck-V.

Sharp, Allen
--Conspiracy of Blood: Can You Prevent the Crime of the Century?. Hart, Celia, illus. LC 83-23922. (Illus.). 44 i.e. 88 p., 2 p. of plates. 19cm. (Storytrails). 1984. (ISBN 0-521-27707-8). Cambridge University Press.
--The Eye of Heaven: Can You Save the Victim of a Web of Mystery. LC 84-19951. (Illus.). 96 p. 19cm. (Storytrails). 1985. (ISBN 0-521-31707-X). Cambridge University Press.
--The Hands of Pablo Santos. LC 84-17511. (Illus.). 96 p. 19cm. (Storytrails). 1985. (ISBN 0-521-31706-1). Cambridge University Press.
--Return of the Undead: Can You Destroy the Vampire of Valdah?. LC 83-25193. (Illus.). 45 i.e. 90 p. 19cm. (Storytrails). 1984. (ISBN 0-521-27709-4). Cambridge University Press.
--The Second Conquest: Can You Change the World's Future. LC 84-19860. (Illus.). 96 p. 19cm. (Storytrails). 1985. (ISBN 0-521-31705-3). Cambridge University Press.
--Shadow Over the Marsh: Can You Discover the Dark Secret Which Threatens Your Very Life?. LC 84-19874. (Illus.). 96 p. 19cm. (Storytrails). 1985. (ISBN 0-521-31704-5). Cambridge University Press.
--The Sicilian Contract: Can You Find the Killer with a "Contract" on Your Life?. LC 83-23924. 95 p. 19cm. (Storytrails). 1984. (ISBN 0-521-27706-X). Cambridge University Press.
--The Unsolved Case of Sherlock Holmes: Can You Solve It?. LC 83-23923. (Illus.). 45 p. 19cm. (Storytrails). 1984. (ISBN 0-521-27708-6). Cambridge University Press.

Sharp, Ann Pearsall
--Little Garden People and What They Do. Bryson, Marion, illus. LC 38-29390. 34 p. illus. (part col.) 30 cm. c.1938. The Saalfield Publishing Company.

Sharp, Annabel
--Peggy Parsons, a Hampton Freshman. (The Peggy Parsons Bks.). N.D. Nourse.
--Peggy Parsons at Prep School. (The Peggy Parsons Bks.). N.D. Nourse.

Sharp, Arthur (1886-)
--The Country Mouse. LC 55-37273. unpaged. illus. 19 x 25 cm. c.1955. Shoestring Press.
--Golly,the Pollywog. LC 54-33880. unpaged. illus. 16 x 24 cm. c.1954. Hand Printed by Silk Screen Process at the Shoestring Press.
--Noah. LC 40-32645. 32 p. illus. 21 x 22 cm. 1940. Vanguard Press.

Sharp, Christopher
--Bad Mouth Christopher. (gr. 1-4). 1980. (ISBN 0-570-03482-5). Concordia.

Sharp, Christopher, tr. see Lebrun, Francoise.

Sharp, Clifford, Mrs., ed. see Nesbitt, E.

Sharp, Dolph (1914-)
--The Other Ark. Hawes, Charles, illus. LC 73-77772. 47 p., col. illus. 23cm. 1969. Putnam.

Sharp, Edith Lambert (1917-)
--Nkwala. 1st ed. Winter, William, illus. LC 58-8492. (Illus.). 125 p. 22cm. 1958. Little, Brown. **Award: (ALA).**

Sharp, Evelyn, jt. auth. see Wilson, Theodora Wilson.

Sharp, Evelyn (1869-)
--All the Way to Fairyland. LC 44-30631. 6 p. l., 3-196 p. col. front., col. plates. 20 1/2 x 16 1/2 cm. 1898. John Lane.
--All the Way to Fairyland. Dearmer, Percy, illus. 1900. John Lane.
--The Children Who Ran Away. Meylan, Paul J., illus. LC 3-24296. 20cm. 319p. (Every Boy's and Every Girl's Ser.). 1903. Macmillan Co.
--The Child's Christmas. Robinson, Charles (1870-1937), illus. (Illus.). N.D. H. M. Caldwell.
--The Hill that Fell Down. Browne, Gordon Frederick (1858-1932), illus. (Illus.). N.D. Caldwell.
--The Making of a Prig. 1900. John Lane.
--The Making of a Schoolgirl, 1 of 6 vols. (The Bodley Booklets Ser.: No. 2). 1900. Set. John Lane.
--The Other Side of the Sun: Fairy Tales. Syrett, Nellie, illus. LC 186. 19cm. 188p. 1900. John Lane.
--Penelope's Secret. N.D. Dodge.
--Round the World to Wympland. Woodward, Alice Bolingbroke (1862-), illus. LC 1-25657. 5 p. l., 235 p. front., plates. 19 1/2 cm. 1902. J. Lane.
--The Story of the Weathercock. Robinson, Charles (1870-1937), illus. (Illus.). N.D. H. M. Caldwell.
--Who was Jane?. A Story for Young People of All Ages. Brock, Charles Edmond (1870-1938), illus. LC 24-5205. 20cm. 305p. 1922. Macmillan.
--Wymps, and Other Fairy Tales. Dearmer, Percy, illus. LC 12-38464. 5 p. l., 3-190 p., 1 l. 8 col. pl. (incl. front.) 20 x 16 1/2 cm. 1897. J. Lane.
--Young James. LC 26-17978. viii, 312 p. front., plates. 20 cm. 1925. Longmans, Green & Co.
--The Youngest Girl in the School. Brock, Charles Edmond (1870-1938), illus. LC 1-24445. ix, 326 p. front., 7 pl. 19 cm. 1901. The Macmillan Company.
--Youngest Girl in the School. Brock, Charles Edmond (1870-1938), illus. (Every Boy's and Every Girl's Ser.). N.D. The Macmillan co.

Sharp, Margery (1905-)
--Bernard into Battle: A Miss Bianca Story. Morrill, Leslie H, illus. LC 78-11332. (Illus.). 87 p. 21cm. c.1978. (ISBN 0-316-78326-9). Little, Brown.
--Bernard the Brave: A Miss Bianca Story. Jaques, Faith (1923-), illus. LC 76-374600. (Illus.). vi, 108 p. 21cm. 1976. (ISBN 0-434-96306-2). Heinemann.
--Bernard the Brave: A Miss Bianca Story. Morrill, Leslie H., illus. LC 76-53829. (Illus.). 128 p. 21cm. c.1977. (ISBN 0-316-78292-0). Little, Brown.
--Lost at the Fair. 1st ed. Fry, Rosalind, illus. LC 65-10587. 57 p. col. illus. 21 cm. 1965. Little, Brown.
--Miss Bianca. Williams, Garth Montgomery (1912-), illus. LC 62-9556. 152 p. illus. 21 cm. 1962. Little, Brown. **Award: (ALA).**
--Miss Bianca and the Bridesmaid. 1st ed. Blegvad, Erik (1923-), illus. LC 72-5508. (Illus.). 123 p. 21cm. 1972. (ISBN 0-316-78299-8). Little, Brown.
--Miss Bianca in the Antarctic. Blegvad, Erik (1923-), illus. LC 75-158484. (Illus.). 134 p. 21cm. 1971. Little, Brown.
--Miss Bianca in the Orient. 1st ed. Blegvad, Erik (1923-), illus. LC 79-119110. (Illus.). 144 p. 21cm. 1970. Little, Brown.
--Miss Bianca in the Salt Mines. 1st ed. Williams, Garth Montgomery (1912-), illus. LC 66-14901. (Illus.). 148 p. 21cm. 1966. Little, Brown.
--The Rescuers. 1st ed. Williams, Garth Montgomery (1912-), illus. LC 59-6477. (Illus.). 149 p. 22cm. 1959. Little, Brown.
--The Turret. Williams, Garth Montgomery (1912-), illus. 1963. Little Brown and Co.

Sharp, Mary
--Bobbi Saves Christmas!. Skar, Cynthia S., illus. (Illus.). 28p. (Orig.). (gr. 1-4). 1981. (ISBN 0-9603200-1-6). Bobbi Ent.

Sharp, Mary & Niemi, Matt
--Bobbi, Father of the Finnish White Tailed Deer. Shappell, Sherry, illus. LC 79-54100. (Illus., Orig.). (gr. 4-6). 1979. (ISBN 0-9603200-0-8). Bobbi Ent.

Sharp, Pat
--Brain Power!. Secret of a Winning Team. Weston, Martha, illus. LC 83-14896. (Illus.). 56p. (gr. 3-5). 1984. (ISBN 0-688-02679-6). (ISBN 0-688-02680-X). Lothrop.

Sharp, Paul (1927-)
--Adventure Stories for Boys. Sharp, Paul (1927-), illus. N.D. Golden Press.
--Paul the Pitcher. Sharp, Paul (1927-), illus. LC 84-7071. (Illus.). 29 p. 18cm. (A Rookie Reader). c.1984. (ISBN 0-516-02064-1). (ISBN 0-516-42064-X). Childrens Press.

Sharp, Richard, jt. auth. see Keevy, Russell.

Sharp, William (1900-)
--Tall Book of Fairy Tales. Sharp, William (1900-), illus. (Illus.). (Tall Book Ser.). (gr. k-3). N.D. (ISBN 0-06-025545-5, HarpJ). (ISBN 0-06-025546-3). Har-Row.

Sharpe, Caroline (1947-)
--Ben and Clementine. LC 76-143250. 25 p. chiefly illus. (some col. 25cm. 1971. (ISBN 0-200-71721-9). Abelard-Schuman.

Sharpe, Caroline (1947-), illus.
--Sindbad the Sailor. (Illus.). 32p. 1974. (ISBN 0-85953-030-2, Pub. by Child's Play England). Playspaces.

Sharpe, Elaine F.
--The Star Book. 64p. (gr. 3-7). 1981. (ISBN 0-671-42534-X). Wanderer Bks.

Sharpe, Richard Scrafton, jt. auth. see Pearson, Mrs.

Sharpe, Richard Scrafton (0000-1852) & Pearson, Mrs.
--Dame Wiggins of Lee and Her Seven Wonderful Cats: A Humorous Tale Written Prinicipally by a Lady of Ninety. Ruskin, John (1819-1900), ed. Broomfield, Robert (1930-), illus. LC 63-17491. (Illus.). 31 p. 1963. McGraw-Hill.

Sharpe, Sara
--Gardener George Goes to Town. Mexley, Susan, illus. LC 82-47577. (Illus.). 40p. (gr. k-3). 1982. (ISBN 0-06-025619-2, HarpJ). (ISBN 0-06-025620-6). Har-Row.

Sharpe, Stella Gentry, Mrs.
--Tobe. Farrell, Charles, illus. 3 p. l., 121 p. illus. 27 1/2 cm. 1939. The University of North Carolina Press.

Shattuck, Harriette Robinson, Mrs. (1850-)
--Little Folks East and West. LC 21-8706. (Comprising: "Prairie Stories", "Mother Goose Stories","Fairy Stories" and "True Stories".). 4 p. l., 3-95 p. front., illus., plates. 19 x 16 cm. 1892. Lee and Shepard.

Shaub, Josephine Emmons (1928-) & Shaub, Paul (1923-)
--Squeaky, the Mechanical Whale: 02297358x. LC 57-6007. unpaged. illus. 26 cm. 1958. Lothrop, Lee and Shepard Co.

Shaub, Paul, jt. auth. see Shaub, Josephine Emmons.

Shaul, Dvora Ben
--Night in the Wadi. Hirsch, Shirley, illus. Braun, Werner, photos by. (gr. 5-8). N.D. (ISBN 0-87631-026-9). Funk & W.

Shaw, Anna Moore
--Pima Indian Legends. Tashquinth, Matt, illus. LC 68-13547. (Illus.). xv, 111 p. 19cm. 1968. University of Arizona Press.

Shaw, Arnold (1909-)
--The Street That Never Slept. (Illus.). 1971. (ISBN 0-698-10355-6). Coward.

Shaw, Barbara B
--Kiki of Kingfisher Cove: A Tale of a Nova Scotia Cat. LC 77-563106. (Illus.). 40 p. 22cm. 1977. (ISBN 0-88999-067-0). Lancelot Press.

Shaw, Byam (1872-1919)
--Old King Cole's Book of Nursery Rhymes. Shaw, Byam (1872-1919), illus. LC 80-23777. p. cm. (Facsimile Classics Ser.). 1980. (ISBN 0-8317-6600-X). Mayflower Books.

Shaw, Catherine
--Hilda: Or, Seeketh not Her Own. N.D. Robert Carter & Brothers.

Shaw, Catherine, ed.
--Suffer Little Children: Or, a Child's Life of Christ. Dudley, Ambrose, illus. (Illus.). N.D. R. F. Fenno & Co.

Shaw, Charles Dannelly (1834-)
--Stories of the Ancient Greeks. (Illus.). 264p. N.D. Dana Estes and Company.
--Stories of the Ancient Greeks. LC 3-31029. xii, 264 p. front., 24 pl. 18 cm. 1903. Ginn & Company.

Shaw, Charles Green (1892-1974)
--The Giant of Central Park. LC 40-32646. 64 p. illus. 24 x 19 1/2 cm. c.1940. W. R. Scott, Inc.
--It Looked Like Spilt Milk. LC 47-30767. 31 p. illus. 27 cm. 1947. Harper.

Shaw, Denis
--The Pakistani Twins. Spence, Geraldine (1931-), illus. LC 65-12043. 155p. illus. 21cm. (Twins Ser.). 1965, c.1960. (ISBN 0-8023-1094-X). Dufour.

Shaw, Edward R., ed. see Martineau, Harriet.

Shaw, Edward Richard (1855-1903), adapted by see Defoe, Daniel.

Shaw, Edward Richard (1855-1903), ed. see Sewell, Anna.

Shaw, Edward Richard (1855-1903), ed.
--Fairy Tales for the Second School Year. LC 99-2156. 102p. (Standard Literature Ser.: No. 39). 1899. University Publishing Co.

Shaw, Evelyn S. (1927-)
--Alligator. Zweifel, Frances, illus. LC 70-183157. (Illus.). 5 7/8 x 8 1/2. 64p. (18 pt.). (Nature I Can Read Bks.). (gr. k-3). 1972. (ISBN 0-06-025556-0). (ISBN 0-06-025557-9). Har-Row.
--Elephant Seal Island. Pape, Cherryl, illus. LC 77-25649. (Illus.). 5 7/8 x 8 1/2. 64p. (18 pt.). (Nature I Can Read Bks.). (gr. k-3). 1978. (ISBN 0-06-025603-6). (ISBN 0-06-025604-4). Har-Row.
--Fish Out of School. Carpentier, Ralph, illus. LC 77-105477. (Illus.). 5 7/8 x 8 1/2. 64p. (18 pt.). (Nature I Can Read Bks.). (gr. k-3). 1970. Har-Row.
--Fish Out of School. Carpentier, Ralph, illus. LC 77-105477. (Illus.). 60 p. 23cm. (A Science I Can Read Book). 1970. Harper & Row.
--A Nest of Wood Ducks. Pape, Cherryl, illus. LC 76-3833. (Illus.). 5 7/8 x 8 1/2. 64p. (18 pt.). (Nature I Can Read Bks.). (gr. k-3). 1976. (ISBN 0-06-025591-9). (ISBN 0-06-025592-7). Har-Row.
--Sea Otters. Pape, Cherryl, illus. LC 79-2017. (Illus.). 5 7/8 x 8 1/2. 64p. (18 pt.). (Nature I Can Read Bks.). (gr. k-3). 1980. (ISBN 0-06-025613-3). (ISBN 0-06-025614-1). Har-Row.

Shaw, Flora L., pseud., see Lugard, Flora Louisa Shaw.

Shaw, Flora L., Lady, pseud. (1852-1929)
--Castle Blair: A Story of Youthful Days. Lugard, Flora Louisa Shaw. N.D. Messrs. Roberts Brothers.
--Hector. 340p. N.D. Little, Brown.
--Phyllis Browne. 385p. N.D. Little, Brown.

Shaw, Frank Hubert (1878-)
--First at the Pole: A Romance of the Artic Adventure. Hodgson, Edward S., illus. LC 10-4047. vi. p., 1 l., 311, 1 p. col. front., 3 p. 21 cm. 1909. Cassell and Company, Limited.
--Sons of the Sea: A Story for Boys. Hodgson, Edward S., illus. LC 16-13319. 4 p. l., 310 p. col. front., col. plates. 21 1/2 cm. 1912. Cassell and Company, Ltd.
--Treasure Trove of the Southern Seas. LC 20-9631. 4 p. l., 311, 1 p. col. front., col. plates. 21 cm. 1919. Cassell and Company, Ltd.
--With Jellicoe in the North Sea. LC 17-22304. vii, 311, 1 p. 4 col. pl. (incl. front.) 21 1/2 cm. 1916. Funk and Wagnalls Company.

Shaw, Hana Muskova, tr. see Charskaia, Lidiia Aleksieevna.

Shaw, James Byrnie (1866-1948)
--The Sky-Blue Butterfly. Good, Peter, illus. Lee, Helen, intro. by. LC 74-183872. (Illus.). 64p. 1st U.S. edition. (gr. 3-6). 1971. (ISBN 0-87106-105-8). Globe Pequot.

Shaw, Jane, retold by see Harris, Joel Chandler.

Shaw, Jennie R.
--Neighbor's house, 1 of 50 vols. (Illus.). 350p. (Sunday-School Lib: No. 14). N.D. Set. Lothrop Pub.
--Our Daughter's Library: Includes "New Commandment," "Mrs. Thorne's Guests," "Neighbor's House," "Strawberry Hill," and "St. Augustine's Ladder.", 5 vols. (Illus.). N.D. Set. D Lothrop.

Shaw, Jennie R., jt. auth. see Fell, Archie.

Shaw, John MacKay (1897-)
--The Things I Want: Poems for Two Children. 50 p. 21cm. 1967. Friends of Florida State University Library.
--Zumpin: More Poems for Two Children. LC 75-10832. (Illus.). 48 p. 24cm. 1969. Friends of Florida State University Library.

Shaw, Kerry
--Swamp Angel. 96p. 1975. (ISBN 0-87695-172-8). Aurora Publishers Inc.
--Swamp Angel. LC 73-93413. 113 p. 22cm. c.1977. Aurora Publishers.

Shaw, Mabel
--A Treasure of Darkness: An Idyll of African Child Life. Sabin, Mama, illus. LC 38-4433. xv, 160 p. col. front., plates. 20 cm. 1936. Longmans, Green and Co.

Shaw, Marian
--Queen Bess: A Story for Girls. (Illus.). N.D. G. P. Putnam's Sons.

Shaw, Ray, retold by see Tchaikovsky, Peter Ilyich.

Shaw, Richard (1923-), ed.
--The Bird Book. LC 74-81672. (Illus.). 48 p. 24cm. 1974. (ISBN 0-7232-6132-6). F. Warne.
--Budd's Noisy Wagon. Galdone, Paul (1914-), illus. (Illus.). 32 p. 1968. F. Warne.
--Call Me Al Raft. LC 75-16313. 128 p. 21cm. 1975. (ISBN 0-8407-6464-2). T. Nelson.
--The Cat Book. LC 73-83101. (Illus.). 48 p. 24cm. 1973. (ISBN 0-7232-6127-X). Warne.
--The Fox Book. LC 78-161068. (Illus.). 47 p. 24cm. 1971. (ISBN 0-7232-6082-6). Frederick Warne.
--The Frog Book. LC 72-83128. (Illus.). 46 p. 24cm. 1972. (ISBN 0-7232-6083-4). F. Warne.
--The Hard Way Home. LC 76-54132. 127 p. 21cm. c.1977. (ISBN 0-8407-6529-0). T. Nelson.
--The Kitten in the Pumpkin Patch. Kahane, Jacqueline, illus. LC 73-83099. (Illus.). 40 p. 1973. (ISBN 0-7232-6099-0). F. Warne.
--The Mouse Book. LC 75-8104. (Illus.). 46 p. 24cm. c.1975. (ISBN 0-7232-6119-9). F. Warne.
--The Owl Book. LC 71-123006. (Illus.). 48 p. 24cm. 1970. F. Warne.
--Shape Up, Burke. LC 76-2530. 142 p. 21cm. c.1976. (ISBN 0-8407-6489-8). T. Nelson.
--Tree for Rent. Fry, Rosalind, illus. LC 72-165821. (Illus.). 32 p. 24cm. 1971. (ISBN 0-8075-8082-1). A. Whitman.
--Who Are You Today?. Werth, Kurt (1896-), illus. LC 77-100340. (Illus.). 32 p. 1970. F. Warne.

--Witch, Witch!. Stories & Poems of Sorcery, Spells & Hocus-Pocus. Arrowood, Clinton McKendrick Lee (1939-), illus. LC 75-8102. (Illus.). 205 p. 24cm. c.1975. F. Warne.

Shaw, Thelma

--Jeepers, There's a Jet. Royt, Kevin, illus. LC 60-8427. unpaged. illus. 25 cm. 1960. A. Whitman.

--Juano and the Wonderful Fresh Fish. Pinkney, Jerry (1939-), illus. LC 69-15798. (Illus.). 32 p. 27cm. 1969. Addison-Wesley.

--My Happy Day, a Word Book. Bruce, Suzanne, illus. LC 51-6019. unpaged, illus. 21 cm. (Rand McNally Book-Elf Bk. 450). c.1951. Rand McNally.

Shaw, Thelma, jt. auth. see Deming, O. T.

Shawn, Rosemary

Look Who I Am. Stolberg, Doris, illus. LC 52-2574. unpaged, illus. 22 cm. c.1952. Hart Pub. Co.

Shay, Myrtle

--The Adventures of Ricky and Chub. Kennedy, Paul Edward (1929-), illus. LC 65-19354. 190p. illus. 21cm. c.1965. Lantern.

--Two on the Trail. 1st ed. Kocsis, James C. (1936-), illus. Paul, James, pseud. (Illus.). 192 p. 22cm. 1967. Bobbs-Merrill.

Shea, Aileen, tr. see Brandenburg, Albert Jacques.

Shea, George (1940-)

--Big Bad Ernie. Williams, Ted C. (1930-), photos by. LC 78-12632. (Illus.). 56 p. 24cm. c.1978. (ISBN 0-87191-679-7). Creative Education.

--I Died Here. Shields, Bill, illus. LC 78-72329. 60 p. ill. 18cm. (A Pacemaker Bestellers Book). c.1979. (ISBN 0-8224-5364-9). Fearon Pitman Publishers.

--Make It to the Superbowl! Panthers vs. Grizzlies. LC 83-10353. 115. 19cm. c.1983. (ISBN 0-671-47611-4). Wanderer Books.

--Make the Play-offs!. Blues vs. Sharks. 117. c.1983. (ISBN 0-671-47609-2). Wanderer Books.

--Nightmare Nina. Hanrahan, Dan, illus. LC 78-71857. (Illus.). 56 p. 24cm. c.1978. (ISBN 0-87191-682-7). Creative Education.

--Strike Two. LC 80-82990. (Illus.). 64p. (SporTellers Ser.). (gr. 4 up). 1981. (ISBN 0-516-02267-9). Childrens.

--What to Do When You Are Bored. Schneider, Meg, ed. Evert, Sally, illus. (Illus.). 64p. (Orig.). (gr. 8-12). 1983. (ISBN 0-671-44426-3). Wanderer Bks.

--What to Do When You're Bored. LC 82-4782. p. cm. 1982. (ISBN 0-671-44426-3). Wanderer Books.

Shea, J. Vernon, ed.

--Black & the White. (gr. 11 up). N.D. Pyramid Pubns.

Shead, Isobel Ann

--The Jago Secret. Friedman, Marvin (1930-), illus. LC 67-21176. (Illus.). 192 p. 23cm. (Merit mystery). 1967, c.1966. Follett.

Shead, Isobel Ann, jt. auth. see Barrett, Charles Leslie.

Sheahan, Henry Beston see Beston, Henry B., pseud.

Sheahan, Henry Beston (1888-1968)

--The Firelight Fairy Book. Beston, Henry B., pseud. Day, Maurice (1892-), illus. LC 19-18335. 4 p. l., 257, 1 p. col. front., illus. (part col.) 22 cm. c.1919. The Atlantic Monthly Press, Inc.

--Five Bears and Miranda. Beston, Henry B., pseud. Dobias, Frank (1902-), illus. LC 39-297192. 60 p. illus. (part col.) 23 1/2 cm. 1939. The Macmillan Company.

--The Sons of Kai: The Story the Indian Told. Beston, Henry B., pseud. LC 26-20426. 5 p. l., 55 p. incl. illus., plates. col. front., col. plates. 16 cm. 1926. The Macmillan Company.

--The Starlight Wonder Book. Beston, Henry B., pseud. Day, Maurice (1892-), illus. LC 23-13421. 6 p. l., 3-262, 3 p. col. front., illus. 22 cm. c.1923. The Atlantic Monthly Press.

Sheard, Virginia Stanton see Sheard, Virna, pseud.

Sheard, Virginia Stanton, Mrs.

--The Golden Apple Tree. Price, Norman Mills (1879-1951), illus. LC 20-23024. 6 p. l., front., pl. 21cm. c.1920. James A. McCann.

Sheard, Virna, pseud., see Sheard, Virginia Stanton.

Sheard, Virna, pseud.

--Trevelyan's Little Daughters. Sheard, Virginia Stanton. Birch, Reginald Bathurst (1856-1943), illus. N.D. Frederick A. Stokes.

Shearer, James F., tr. see Iduaste, Andres.

Shearer, John (1947-)

--Billy Jo Jive and the Case of the Midnight Voices. Shearer, Ted, illus. LC 81-15281. (Illus.). 46 p. 24cm. 1982. (ISBN 0-440-00752-6). (ISBN 0-440-00758-5). Delacorte Press.

--Billy Jo Jive and the Case of the Missing Pigeons. Shearer, Ted, illus. LC 78-50409. (Illus.). 42 p. 24cm. 1979. (ISBN 0-440-00567-1). (ISBN 0-440-00568-X). Delacorte Press.

--Billy Jo Jive and the Walkie Talkie Caper. Shearer, Ted, illus. LC 80-17780. (Illus.). 46 p. 24cm. c.1981. (ISBN 0-440-00791-7). (ISBN 0-440-00792-5). Delacorte Press.

--Billy Jo Jive Super Private Eye: The Case of the Missing Ten Speed Bike. Shearer, Ted, illus. LC 75-43563. (Illus.). 47 p. 24cm. c.1976. (ISBN 0-440-00534-5). Delacorte Press.

--Billy Jo Jive: The Case of the Sneaker Snatcher. Shearer, Ted, illus. LC 76-47242. 24cm. 47p. c.1977. (ISBN 0-440-00546-9). (ISBN 0-440-00548-5). Delacorte Press.

--The Case of the Sneaker Snatcher. Shearer, Ted, illus. LC 76-47242. 24cm. 47p. 1977. (ISBN 0-440-00546-9). Delacorte.

--I Wish I Had an Afro. Shearer, John (1947-), illus. 1970. Cowles.

Shearer, Tony

--Praying Flute. 88p. 1975. (ISBN 0-914172-01-8). Sun Books Sun Publishing.

Shearon, Lillian Nicholson, Mrs.

--The Little Mixer. LC 22-24454. 3.p. l., 55 p. illus. 19 cm. c.1922. The Bobbs-Merrill Company.

--The Little Mixer. LC 45-10490. 62, 1 p. incl. col. front., illus. (part col.) 19 1/2 cm. 1945. The Bobbs-Merrill Company.

--The Other Little Mustard Seed. LC 30-28404. 109 p. 19 1/2 cm. c.1930. The Bobbs-Merrill Company.

Shebar, Jonathan M. & Shebar, Sharon Sigmond (1945-)

--Animal Dads Take Over. Saffioti, Lino, illus. LC 80-25332. (Illus.). 64p. (gr. 3-6). 1981. (ISBN 0-671-34003-4). Messner.

Shebar, Sharon, jt. auth. see Schoder, Judith.

Shebar, Sharon Sigmond, jt. auth. see Shebar, Jonathan M.

Shebar, Sharon Sigmond (1945-)

--Night Monsters. Wasserman, Dan, ed. Reese, Bob, illus. (Illus.). (Ten Word Bks.). (gr. k-1). 1979. (ISBN 0-89868-068-9). (ISBN 0-89868-079-4). ARO Pub.

Shebar, Sharon Sigmond (1945-) & Schoder, Judy

--Groundhog Day. Jordan, Alton, ed. Reese, Bob, illus. (Illus.). (Holdays Ser.). (gr. k-3). 1977. (ISBN 0-89868-027-1, Read Res). (ISBN 0-89868-060-3). ARO Pub.

Shecktor, M. Caporale, jt. auth. see Savitz, Harriet May.

Shecktor, M. Caporale & Savitz, Harriet May (1933-)

--The Moon Is Mine. Robinson, Charles (1931-), illus. LC 68-17569. (Illus.). 61 p. 24cm. 1968. (ISBN 0-381-99715-4). John Day Co.

Shecter, Ben (1935-)

--Across the Meadow. Shecter, Ben (1935-), illus. LC 72-77762. (Illus.). 32 p. 20cm. 1972, c.1973. (ISBN 0-385-06190-0). (ISBN 0-385-06190-0). Doubleday.

--The Discontented Mother. Shecter, Ben (1935-), illus. LC 80-14435. p. cm. c.1980. (ISBN 0-15-223574-4). (ISBN 0-15-223575-2). Harcourt Brace Jovanovich.

--Emily, Girl Witch of New York. Shecter, Ben (1935-), illus. LC 63-17887. 33 p. illus. (part col.) 16 x 24 cm. 1963. Dial Press.

--Game for Demons. LC 72-80369. 193 p. 22cm. 1972. (ISBN 0-06-025578-1). Harper & Row.

--Game for Demons. 193 p. 20cm. (A Harper Trophy Book). 1974, c.1972. Harper & Row.

--Hester the Jester. Shecter, Ben (1935-), illus. LC 76-58706. (Illus.). 5 7/8 x 8 1/2. 32p. (18 pt.). (Early I Can Read Bks.). (ps-3). 1977. (ISBN 0-06-025599-4). (ISBN 0-06-025600-1). Har-Row.

--The Hiding Game. Shecter, Ben (1935-), illus. LC 80-15291. p. cm. 1980, c.1977. (ISBN 0-590-07765-1). Four Winds Press.

--The Hiding Game. Shecter, Ben (1935-), illus. LC 76-18137. (Illus.). 32 p. 23cm. c.1977. (ISBN 0-8193-0856-0). (ISBN 0-8193-0857-9). Parents' Magazine Press.

--If I Had a Ship. 1st ed. Shecter, Ben (1935-), illus. LC 76-101065. (Illus.). 32 p. 22cm. 1970. Doubleday.

--Inspector Rose. Shecter, Ben (1935-), illus. LC 69-10207. (Illus.). 48 p. 24cm. 1969. Harper & Row.

--Jonathan and the Bank Robbers. 1st ed. Shecter, Ben (1935-), illus. LC 64-22791. 32 p. col. illus. 21 x 26 cm. 1964. Dial Press.

--Molly Patch and Her Animal Friends. LC 75-6304. (Illus.). 59 p. 19cm. c.1975. (ISBN 0-06-025586-2). (ISBN 0-06-025589-7). Harper & Row.

--Partouche Plants a Seed. LC 66-18659. 32 p. col. illus. 16 x 21 cm. 1966. Harper & Row.

--The River Witches. LC 75-25397. (Illus.). 180 p. 22cm. c.1979. (ISBN 0-06-026843-3). (ISBN 0-06-026844-1). Harper & Row.

--Someplace Else. LC 77-146003. (Illus.). 167 p. 22cm. 1971. (ISBN 0-06-025577-3). Harper & Row.

--Sparrow Song. LC 79-2689. p. cm. c.1981. (ISBN 0-06-025609-5). (ISBN 0-06-025610-9). Harper & Row.

--The Stocking Child: A Tale. LC 76-7878. (Illus.). 32 p. 18cm. c.1976. (ISBN 0-06-025593-5). (ISBN 0-06-025594-3). Harper & Row.

--Stone House Stories. 1st ed. Shecter, Ben (1935-), illus. LC 72-9865. (Illus.). 47 p. 21cm. 1973. (ISBN 0-06-025582-X). (ISBN 0-06-025583-8). Harper & Row.

--A Summer Secret. LC 76-41512. (Illus.). 32 p. 19cm. c.1977. (ISBN 0-06-025597-8). (ISBN 0-06-025598-6). Harper & Row.

--The Toughest and Meanest Kid on the Block. LC 72-83852. (Illus.). 32 p. 21cm. 1973. (ISBN 0-399-20310-9). (ISBN 0-399-60797-8). Putnam.

--The Whistling Whirligig. Shecter, Ben (1935-), illus. LC 73-5493. (Illus.). 143 p. 22cm. 1974. (ISBN 0-06-025591-9). (ISBN 0-06-025592-7). Harper & Row.

Shedd, Ephraim Cutler

--Our Little Persian Cousin. Horne, Diantha W., illus. LC 9-19833. vii p., 2 l., 165 p. front., 9 pl. 20 cm. (On verso of half-title: The Little cousin series) $0.60). 1909. L. G. Page & Company.

Shedlock, Marie L. (1854-1935)

--Eastern Stories and Legends. Moore, Anne Carroll (1871-1961), illus. LC 20-18410. xxi, 212 p. incl. front. 19 1/2 cm. c.1920. E. P. Dutton & Company.

Sheedy, Alexandra Elizabeth (1962-)

--She Was Nice to Mice: The Other Side of Elizabeth I's Character Never Before Revealed by Previous Historians. Levy, Jessica Ann, illus. LC 75-9960. (Illus.). 95 p. 19cm. 1975. (ISBN 0-07-056515-5). (ISBN 0-07-056516-3). McGraw-Hill.

Sheehan, Arthur T & Sheehan, Elizabeth Odell (1919-)

--Father Damien and the Bells. Fisher, Leonard Everett (1924-), illus. LC 57-8535. 174p. illus. 22cm. (Vision books, 26). 1957. Vision Books.

Sheehan, Elizabeth Odell, jt. auth. see Sheehan, Arthur T.

Sheehan, Elizabeth Winston

--The Conestoga Wagon. Sheehan, Jane Hoskins, illus. LC 45-5983. viii,162p. 21cm. 1945. The Hobson Book Press.

Sheehan, Ethna (1908-), ed.

--Folk and Fairy Tales from Around the World. Vasiliu, Mircea (1920-), illus. LC 73-129955. (Illus.). viii, 151 p. 24cm. 1970. Dodd, Mead.

--A Treasury of Catholic Children's Stories. Gerhard, Mae, illus. LC 63-19654. 319 p. col. illus. 22 cm. 1963. M. Evans; Distributed in Association with Lippincott, Philadelphia.

Sheehan, Nora

--The Little Red Hen: Traditional. LC 78-72321. (Illus.). 32 p. c.1979. (ISBN 0-89799-122-2). (ISBN 0-89799-005-6). Dandelion Press.

Sheehy, Emma Dickson

--Molly and the Golden Wedding. 1st ed. Henneberger, Robert G. (1921-), illus. LC 56-6234. 159 p. illus. 21 cm. 1956. Holt.

Sheeler, Willard D., jt. ed. see Dale, Jean N.

Sheen, Fulton John (1895-1979)

--Jesus, Son of Mary. Busoni, Rafaello (1900-1962), illus. 37p. 1947. Farrar, Straus and Cudahy, Inc.

--Jesus, Son of Mary. De John, Marie, illus. LC 80-19635. (Illus.). 30 p. 24cm. 1980. (ISBN 0-8164-0470-4). Seabury Press.

Shefelman, Janice Jordan (1930-)

--A Paradise Called Texas. Shefelman, Tom & Shefelman, Karl, illus. LC 83-1754. (Stories for Young Americans Ser.). c.1983. (ISBN 0-89015-375-2). Eakin Press.

--Willow Creek Home. LC 85-16189. p. cm. 1985. Eakin Press.

Sheffer, H. R., pseud., see Abels, Harriette Sheffer.

Sheffer, H. R., pseud. (1926-)

--Moto-Cross Monkey. Abels, Harriette Sheffer. Schroeder, Howard, ed. Vista III Design, illus. LC 80-28762. (Illus.). 48p. (Teamates Ser.). (gr. 3 up). 1981. (ISBN 0-89686-106-6). (ISBN 0-89686-116-3). Crestwood Hse.

--Partners on Wheels. Abels, Harriette Sheffer. Schroeder, Howard, ed. LC 80-28428. (Illus.). 48p. (Teamates Ser.). (gr. 3 up). 1981. (ISBN 0-89686-105-8). (ISBN 0-89686-115-5). Crestwood Hse.

--Sarah Sells Soccer. Abels, Harriette Sheffer. Schroeder, Howard, ed. (Illus.). 48p. (Teamates Ser.). (gr. 3 up). 1981. (ISBN 0-89686-100-7). (ISBN 0-89686-110-4). Crestwood Hse.

--Second-String Nobody. Abels, Harriette Sheffer. Schroeder, Howard, ed. Vista III Design, illus. LC 80-28767. (Illus.). 47 p. 22cm. (Team-Mates Ser.). c.1981. (ISBN 0-89686-101-5). (ISBN 0-89686-111-2). Crestwood House.

--Street-Hockey Lady. Abels, Harriette Sheffer. Schroeder, Howard, ed. Vista III Design, illus. LC 80-29531. (Illus.). 48p. (Teamates Ser.). (gr. 3 up). 1981. (ISBN 0-89686-102-3). (ISBN 0-89686-112-0). Crestwood Hse.

--Swim for Pride. Abels, Harriette Sheffer. Schroeder, Howard, ed. Vista III Design, illus. LC 80-28774. (Illus.). 47 p. 22cm. (Team-Mates Ser.). c.1981. (ISBN 0-89686-104-X). (ISBN 0-89686-104-X). Crestwood House.

--Two at the Net. Abels, Harriette Sheffer. Schroeder, Howard, ed. Vista III Design, illus. LC 80-28429. (Illus.). 48p. (Teamates Ser.). (gr. 3 up). 1981. (ISBN 0-89686-108-2). (ISBN 0-89686-118-X). Crestwood Hse.

--Weekend in the Dunes. Abels, Harriette Sheffer. Schroeder, Howard, ed. Vista III Design, illus. LC 80-28624. (Illus.). 48p. (Teamates Ser.). (gr. 3 up). 1981. (ISBN 0-89686-109-0). (ISBN 0-89686-119-8). Crestwood Hse.

--Winner on the Court. Abels, Harriette Sheffer. Schroeder, Howard, ed. Vista III Design, illus. LC 80-28451. (Illus.). 48p. (Teamates Ser.). (gr. 3 up). 1981. (ISBN 0-89686-107-4). (ISBN 0-89686-117-1). Crestwood Hse.

Sheffield, Janet N. (1926-)

--Not Just Sugar and Spice. LC 75-20350. p. cm. 1975. (ISBN 0-688-22048-7). (ISBN 0-688-32048-1). Morrow.

Sheip, Levi C., tr. see Hoffmann, Franz.

Shekerjian, Haig & Shekerjian, Regina, eds.

--Book of Christmas Carols. (Illus.). (gr. 3 up). 1963. (ISBN 0-06-006240-1, HarpT). Har-Row.

Shekerjian, Regina, jt. ed. see Shekerjian, Haig.

Shelby, Annie Blanche, ed.

--The Lullaby Book: Or, Mothers' Love Songs. LC 21-22111. xv p., 1 l., 183 p. col. front. 21 1/2 cm. 1921. Duffield & Company.

Shelby, Kermit

--Big Shake & the Night of Terror. (Voyager Ser.). 1981. (ISBN 0-8010-8209-9). Baker Bk.

--Snowfire. 160p. (gr. 4-6). 1973. (ISBN 0-8024-0123-6). Moody.

Sheldon, Ann, pseud., see Adams, Harriet Stratemeyer.

Sheldon, Ann, pseud., see Stratemeyer Syndicate.

Sheldon, Ann, pseud. (1894-1982)

--The Emperor's Pony. Adams, Harriet Stratemeyer. LC 83-6969. p. cm. (Linda Craig Ser.: No. 9). c.1983. (ISBN 0-671-47558-4). Wanderer Books.

--The Ghost Town Treasure. Adams, Harriet Stratemeyer. LC 81-16043. 191 p. 20cm. Repr. of 1964 ed (Pub. by Doubleday). (Linda Craig Ser.: No. 6). 1982. (ISBN 0-671-44527-8). (ISBN 0-671-44526-X). Wanderer Bks.

--Linda Craig and the Clue on the Desert Trail. Adams, Harriet Stratemeyer. LC 62-17297. 192 p. 22 cm. (Linda Craig Ser.: No. 2). 1962. Doubleday.

--Linda Craig and the Ghost Town Treasure. Adams, Harriet Stratemeyer. LC 64-11384. 187 p. 22 cm. (Linda Craig Ser.: No. 5). 1964. Doubleday.

--Linda Craig and the Mystery in Mexico. Adams, Harriet Stratemeyer. LC 64-11385. 189 p. 22 cm. (Linda Craig Ser.: No. 6). 1964. Doubleday.

--Linda Craig and the Mystery of Horseshoe Canyon. Adams, Harriet Stratemeyer. LC 63-12878. 191 p. 22 cm. (Linda Craig Ser.: No. 4). 1963. Doubleday.

--Linda Craig and the Palomino Mystery. Adams, Harriet Stratemeyer. LC 62-16261. 184 p. 22 cm. (Linda Craig Ser.: No. 1). 1962. Doubleday.

--Linda Craig and the Secret of Rancho Del Sol. Adams, Harriet Stratemeyer. LC 63-12879. 191 p. 22 cm. (Linda Craig Ser.: No. 3). 1963. Doubleday.

--Linda Craig: Search for Scorpio. Adams, Harriet Stratemeyer. Barish, Wendy, ed. 160p. (Orig.). (Linda Craig Ser.). (gr. 3 up). 1984. (ISBN 0-671-53237-5). Wanderer Bks.

--Linda Craig: Secret of the Old Sleigh. Adams, Harriet Stratemeyer. Schneider, Meg, ed. 192p. (Linda Craig Ser.: No. 8). (gr. 3-7). 1983. (ISBN 0-671-46459-0). Wanderer Bks.

--Linda Craig: The Clue on the Desert Trail. Adams, Harriet Stratemeyer. 192p (Pub. by Doubleday). (Linda Craig Ser.: No. 3). (gr. 3-7). c.1981. (ISBN 0-671-42651-6). (ISBN 0-671-42652-4). Wanderer Bks.

--Linda Craig: The Haunted Valley. Adams, Harriet Stratemeyer. Barish, Wendy, ed. 192p. (Linda Craig Ser.: No. 7). (gr. 3-7). 1982. (ISBN 0-671-45551-6). (ISBN 0-671-45550-8). Wanderer Bks.

--Linda Craig: The Mystery in Mexico. Adams, Harriet Stratemeyer. rev. ed. LC 81-2996. 192p. (Orig., Pub. by Doubleday). (Linda Craig Ser.: No. 5). (gr. 3-7). 1981. (ISBN 0-671-42706-7). (ISBN 0-671-42703-2). Wanderer Bks.

--Linda Craig: The Mystery of Horseshoe Canyon. Adams, Harriet Stratemeyer. LC 80-29352. p. cm. Repr. of 1963 ed (Pub. by Doubleday). (Linda Craig Ser.: No. 4). c.1981. (ISBN 0-671-42653-2). (ISBN 0-671-42654-0). Wanderer Bks.

--Linda Craig: The Palamino Mystery. Adams, Harriet Stratemeyer. LC 80-39846. p. cm. Repr. of 1962 ed (Pub. by Doubleday). (Linda Craig Ser.: No. 1). c.1981. (ISBN 0-671-42649-4). (ISBN 0-671-42650-8). Wanderer Books.
--Linda Craig: The Secret of Rancho Del Sol. Adams, Harriet Stratemeyer. LC 80-28122. 192p (Pub. by Doubleday). (Linda Craig Ser.: No. 2). (gr. 3-7). 1981. (ISBN 0-671-42647-8). (ISBN 0-671-42648-6). Wanderer Bks.
--Phantom of Dark Oaks. Stratemeyer Syndicate. Schwartz, Betty, ed. LC 83-16936. 192p. (Orig.). (The Linds Craig Ser.: No. 10). (gr. 3-7). 1984. (ISBN 0-671-49880-0). Wanderer Bks.

Sheldon, Aure (1917-1976)
--Fit for a King. Sweetland, Robert, illus. LC 74-9032. (Illus.). 32 p. 24cm. c.1974. (ISBN 0-87614-048-7). Carolrhoda Books.
--Of Cobblers and Kings. Leake, Donald, illus. LC 77-24725. (Illus.). 36 p. 26cm. c.1978. (ISBN 0-8193-0831-5). (ISBN 0-8193-0832-3). (ISBN 0-8193-0927-3). Parents' Magazine Press.

Sheldon, Charles M.
--Young People's Book of Bible Stories. (gr. 1-5). 1963. (ISBN 0-448-04105-7). G&D.

Sheldon, Denise, tr. see Ichikawa, Satomi.

Sheldon, E. M.
--The Clevelands. 87p. N.D. Hurd & Houghton for American Tract Society.
--The Clevelands. 87p. (Missing Boat Stories). N.D. Lockwood, Brooks, & Co. for American Tract Society.

Sheldon, Louise Patterson, ed. see Mother Goose.

Sheldon, Mary
--One Thousand Men for a Christmas Present. (Illus.). (Every Boy's Library). N.D. Caldwell.
--One Thousand Men for a Christmas Present, 1 of 25 vols. Bridgman, Lewis Jesse (1857-1931), illus. (The Young of Heart Ser.). N.D. Set. Dana Estes & Co.

Sheldon, Walter J. see Walters, Shelley, pseud.

Sheldon, William D., ed. see Drdek, Richard E & Hansen, Mary Lewis.

Sheldon, William Denley, jt. auth. see Mason, George Evan.

Sheldon, William Denley, jt. ed. see Silvaroli, Nicholas J.

Sheldon, William Denley (1915-)
--Beyond the Block. Wheelock, Warren, ed. LC 70-78562. (Illus.). 245 p. 21cm. (Breakthrough). 1969. Allyn and Bacon.
--The House Biter. Dickas, Dan, illus. LC 65-28368. 1 v. (unpaged) col. illus. 17 x 24 cm. (A Little Owl Book, LC26). c.1966. Holt, Rinehart and Winston.

Sheldon, William Denley (1915-), compiled by.
--Arrivals and Departures. Centennial ed. (Illus.). 478 p. 24cm. (Sheldon Basic Reading Series.). 1968. Allyn and Bacon.
--Arrivals and Departures. Pacing ed. LC 72-84036. (Illus.). 477 p. 24cm. (His Sheldon Reading Series.). 1973. Allyn and Bacon.
--Believe and Make Believe. Centennial ed. (Illus.). 446 p. 24cm. (Sheldon Basic Reading Series.). 1968. Allyn and Bacon.
--Believe and Make-Believe. Pacing ed. LC 72-84034. (Illus.). 448 p. 24cm. (His Sheldon Reading Series.). 1973. Allyn and Bacon.
--Story Caravan. Pacing ed. Austin, Mary Carrington, compiled by. LC 72-83070. (Illus.). 292 p. 24cm. (His Sheldon Reading Series.). 1973. Allyn and Bacon.

Sheldon, William Denley (1915-) & Austin, Mary Carrington, eds.
--Magic Windows. Centennial ed. (Illus.). 288 p. 24cm. (Sheldon Basic Reading Series.). 1968. Allyn and Bacon.

Sheldon, William Denley (1915-) & Lyons, Nellie, eds.
--The Reading of Poetry. LC 63-4217. 374 p. illus. 22 cm. 1963. Allyn and Bacon.

Sheldon, William Denley (1915-) & Mills, Queenie Beatrice (1911-)
--At Home. Centennial ed. (Illus.). 63 p. 23cm. (Sheldon Basic Reading Series.). 1968. Allyn and Bacon.
--Here and Away. Centennial ed. Mill, Eleanor, illus. (Illus.). 76 p. 23cm. (Sheldon Basic Reading Series.). 1968. Allyn and Bacon.
--Here and Near. Centennial ed. (Illus.). 71 p. 23cm. (Sheldon Basic Reading Series.). 1968. Allyn and Bacon.

Sheldon, William Denley (1915-) & Wheelock, Warren, eds.
--From the Top. LC 75-11401. (Illus.). 111 p. 21cm. (Breakthrough). c.1976. Allyn and Bacon.
--Out of Sight. LC 71-182081. (Illus.). 113 p. 21cm. (Breakthrough). 1973. Allyn and Bacon.
--Over and Out. LC 75-13062. (Illus.). 119 p. 21cm. (Breakthrough). c.1976. Allyn and Bacon.
--Play It Again. LC 75-11404. (Illus.). 112 p. 21cm. (Breakthrough). c.1976. Allyn and Bacon.
--Prime Time. LC 75-13063. (Illus.). 113 p. 21cm. (Breakthrough). c.1976. Allyn and Bacon.
--Where It's At. LC 79-182083. (Illus.). 115 p. 21cm. (Breakthrough). 1973. Allyn and Bacon.

Sheldon, William Denley (1915-) & Woessner, Nina C. (1933-), eds.
--The Big Ones-2. 2d ed. LC 78-50387. (Illus.). v, 195 p. 21cm. (Breakthrough). c.1978. Allyn and Bacon.
--Busy Signal. LC 78-90577. (Illus.). vi, 183 p. 21cm. (Breakthrough!). c.1978. Allyn and Bacon.
--Point in Time. LC 75-31450. (Illus.). 181 p. 21cm. (Breakthrough). c.1976. Allyn and Bacon.

Shelley, Hugh, tr. see Castex, Pierre Georges.

Shelley, Hugh, tr. see Ezo.

Shelley, Hugh, tr. see Lavolle, L. N.

Shelley, Mary Wollstonecraft Godwin (1797-1851)
--Frankenstein. 272p. (gr. 7-9). 1970. (ISBN 0-590-01553-2). Scholastic Inc.
--Frankenstein. (gr. 3 up). 1978. (ISBN 0-307-21632-2, Golden Pr). Golden Pr. (ISBN 0-307-61632-0). Western Pub.
--Frankenstein. Binder, Otto Oscar (1911-1974), ed. Cruz, Nardo, illus. LC 73-75462. (Illus.). footnotes. 64p. (Orig.). (Now Age Illustrated Ser.). (gr. 5-10). 1973. (ISBN 0-88301-204-9). (ISBN 0-88301-097-6). (ISBN 0-88301-177-8). Pendulum Pr.
--Frankenstein. Schick, Alice & Schick, Joel, eds. LC 80-385. (Illus.). 48p. (gr. 3 up). 1980. Delacorte.
--Frankenstein. Stewart, Diana, adapted by. Kelley, Gary, illus. LC 81-5216. (Illus.). 48p. (Raintree Short Classics). (gr. 4-8). 1983, c.1981. (ISBN 0-8172-2008-9). (ISBN 0-8172-1674-X). Raintree Pubs.
--Frankenstein. Weinberg, Larry, adapted by. Barr, Ken, illus. LC 81-15703. (Illus.). 94 p. 20cm. (Step-up Adventures: No.2). (gr. 2-5). c.1982. (ISBN 0-394-84827-6). (ISBN 0-394-94827-0). Random House.
--Frankenstein, or, the Modern Prometheus. Furth, Janet, contrib. by. LC 80-54132. (Illus.). xi, 244, 48 p. 18cm. (The Silver classics). c.1982. (ISBN 0-382-03440-6). Silver Burdett Co.
--Robert Andrew Parker's Illustrated Frankenstein. 1st ed. Parker, Robert Andrew (1927-), ed. Parker, Robert Andrew, illus. LC 76-18097. (Illus.). 148 p. 28cm. 1976. (ISBN 0-517-51697-7). C. N. Potter.

Shelley, Noreen (1920-), retold by.
--Legends of the Gods: Strange and Fascinating Tales from Around the World. Dick, Astra Lacis, illus. LC 76-46680. (Illus.). 96 p. 25cm. c.1976. (ISBN 0-8448-1040-1). Crane Russak.

Shelton, tr. see Cervantes Saavedra, Miguel de.

Shelton-Cammack
--Hoosier Moppets. LC 74-166381. (Illus.). 32 p. 18cm. 1973. Schoolmaster's Press.

Shelton, Flora Beal
--Folk Tales of Tibet. Forrester, Mary, illus. LC 51-4393. (Illus.). 38 p. 20cm. 1951. Story Book Press.

Shelton, Ingrid
--The Lollipop Dragon & the Writing Contest. Gambill, Henrietta, ed. (Illus.). 80p. (Orig.). (Tiny Tumtum Tales Ser.). (gr. k-4). 1983. (ISBN 0-87239-698-3). Standard Pub.
--The Lollipop Dragon Finds the Missing Teddy Bear. Gambill, Henrietta, ed. (Illus.). 80p. (Orig.). (Tiny Tumtum Tales Ser.). (gr. k-4). 1983. (ISBN 0-87239-697-5). Standard Pub.
--The Lollipop Dragon Helps the Flower Lady. Gambill, Henrietta, ed. (Illus.). 80p. (Orig.). (Tiny Tumtum Tales Ser.). (gr. k-4). 1983. (ISBN 0-87239-696-7). Standard Pub.
--The Lollipop Dragon Plans a Potluck Picnic. Gambill, Henrietta, ed. (Illus.). 80p. (Orig.). (Tiny Tumtum Tales Ser.). (gr. k-4). 1983. (ISBN 0-87239-695-9). Standard Pub.

Shelton, Lola (1903-)
--Witch's Colt. Savitt, Sam (1917-), illus. LC 58-10421. 183 p. illus. 21 cm. 1958. Dodd, Mead.

Shelton, Thomas, tr. see Cervantes Saavedra, Miguel de.

Shelton, William Ray (1919-)
--Stowaway to the Moon: The Camelot Odyssey. LC 73-79709. 360p. (gr. 10 up). 1973. (ISBN 0-385-07435-2). Doubleday.

Shemin, Margaretha Hoeneveld (1928-)
--The Empty Moat. LC 77-86301. 159 p. 22cm. 1969. Coward-McCann.
--The Little Riders. Spier, Peter Edward (1927-), illus. LC 63-15544. (Illus.). 60 p. 21cm. 1963. Coward-McCann.
--Mrs. Herring. Quackenbush, Robert Mead (1929-), illus. LC 67-18039. (Illus.). 192 p. 22cm. 1967. Lothrop, Lee & Shepard.

Shenberf, Yitzhak
--Under the Fig Tree: Palestintian Stories. N.D. (ISBN 0-8052-3274-5). Schocken Books.

Shepard, Annis (1938-)
--The Wrong Kind of Dragon. Laughbaum, J. S., illus. LC 83-6023. 48p. (Orig.). (gr. 1-3). 1983. (ISBN 0-687-46569-9). Abingdon.

Shepard, Birsa (1894-)
--The Cat Next Door. Doane, Pelagie (1906-1966), illus. LC 43-11748. 64 p. incl. front., illus. 21 1/2 cm. 1943. Oxford University Press.

Shepard, Ernest Howard (1879-1976)
--Ben and Brock. Shepard, Ernest Howard (1879-1976), illus. LC 66-10252. 91 p. illus. 20 cm. 1st U.S. edition. 1966. Doubleday.
--Betsy and Joe. 1st ed. Shepard, Ernest Howard (1879-1976), illus. LC 67-16465. (Illus.). 78 p. 22cm. 1967, c.1966. Dutton.

Shepard, Ernest Howard (1879-1976), illus.
--Winnie the Pooh & His Friends. (Illus.). (ps-k). N.D. Platt.

Shepard, Mary see McCluskey, John.

Shepard, Mary L.
--Little Jess and the Circus: Forty Acres. 31p. N.D. (ISBN 0-913678-10-4). New Day Press.

Shepard, Morgan see Martin, John, pseud.

Shepard, Morgan (1865-), adapted by see Aesopus.

Shepard, Morgan (1865-), ed. see Maeterlinck, Maurice.

Shepard, Morgan (1865-), ed. see Morris, William.

Shepard, Morgan (1865-)
--God's Dark, and Other Bedtime Verses and Songs. Martin, John, pseud. LC 27-19771. 32 p. incl. front., illus. 20 1/2 cm. c.1927. George H. Doran Company.
--Jack and Jill. Martin, John, pseud. LC 12-25852. 203, 1 p. col. illus. 14 1/2 cm. (On cover: "The Read Out Loud" Bks.). 1911. Dodd, Mead & Company.
--John Martin's Read Aloud Book. Martin, John, pseud. Drucklieb, Herman L., illus. LC 22-22658. (Being Tales to Be Read to Little Tots by Permission of Mother Goose; Also a Few Happy Jingles). 110 p. illus. 26 cm. $2.50. c.1922. John Martin and Dodd, Mead and Company.
--John Martin's Stories for Children. Martin, John, pseud. Reynolds, Jessie & Royt, Mary, illus. LC 37-2686. 1 p. l., 7-252 p. illus. 19 1/2 cm. c.1936. Whitman Publishing Company.
--Little Boy Blue. Martin, John, pseud. 177, 1 p. col. illus. 14 1/2 cm. (On cover: "The Read Out Loud" Bks.). 1911. Dodd, Mead & Company.
--Mistress Mary. Martin, John, pseud. LC 12-258511. 227 1 p. col. illus. 14 1/2 cm. (On cover: "The Read Out Loud" Boks.). 1911. Dodd, Mead & Company.
--Old King Cole. Martin, John, pseud. LC 12-25848. 183, 1 p. col. illus. 14 1/2 cm. (On cover: "The Read Out Loud" Bks.). 1911. Dodd, Mead & Company.
--Pussy Cat, Pussy Cat. Martin, John, pseud. LC 12-258501. 185 1 p. col. illus. 14 1/2 cm. (On cover: "The Read Out Loud" Bks.). 1911. Dodd, Mead & Company.
--Wags: Or, The Philosophy of a Peaceful Pup. (Illus.). N.D. Wessels & Bissell Co.

Shepard, Ray Anthony
--Sneakers. LC 72-89837. 103 p. 22cm. 1973. (ISBN 0-525-39510-5). Dutton.
--Sneakers. LC 73-9676. 140 p. 25cm. 1973. (ISBN 0-8161-6127-5). G. K. Hall.

Shepard, Ray Anthony, retold by see Chesnutt, Charles Waddell.

Shepard, W.
--Our Young Folks Josephus. N.D. J. B. Lippincott Co.

Shephard, Esther (1891-1975)
--Paul Bunyan. Kent, Rockwell (1882-1971), illus. LC 41-51876. (Illus.). (gr. 7 up). 1941. (ISBN 0-15-259749-2, HJ). HarBraceJ.
--Paul Bunyan. Kent, Rockwell (1882-1971), illus. 233p. 1924. Harcourt Brace Jovanovich.
--Paul Bunyan. slightly rev. ed. Kent, Rockwell (1882-1971), illus. LC 85-5448. (Illus.). xiii, 233 p. 23cm. (Voyager HBJ book). 1985, c.1952. (ISBN 0-15-259749-2). Harcourt Brace Jovanovich.

Shephard, Morgan (1865-), retold by see Raspe, Rudolf Erich.

Shepherd, Charles R
--Lim Yik Choy: The Story of a Chinese Orphan. LC 32-23723. 252 p. 19 1/2 cm. c.1932. Fleming H. Revell Company.

Shepherd, David Gwynne (1924-)
--We Were There at the Battle of the Bulge. Kraynak, George, illus. LC 61-4923. 181 p. illus. 22 cm. (We were there books, 34). 1961. (ISBN 0-448-05034-X). Grosset & Dunlap.
--We Were There at the Driving of the Golden Spike. Plummer, William Kirtman, illus. LC 60-51563. 179 p. illus 22 cm. (We were there books, 31). 1960. (ISBN 0-448-05031-5). Grosset & Dunlap.

Shepherd, Dorothy W.
--Boxes Are Wishes. Shepherd, Dorothy W., illus. LC 59-11212. 24cm. 32p. (gr. k-2). 1959. (ISBN 0-8114-7505-0). Steck-V.

Shepherd, Elizabeth
--Jellyfishes. Berelson, Howard (1940-), illus. LC 69-16815. (Illus.). 64 p. 25cm. 1969. Lothrop, Lee & Shepard Co.

Shepherd, Gene D & Martin, William Ivan, Jr. (1916-)
--Gentle, Gentle Thursday. Maitin, Samuel, illus. LC 70-129129. (Illus.). 32 p. 21cm. (A Bill Martin Freedom Bk.). 1970. Bowmar.

Shepherd, Irana, illus.
--Jack & the Beanstalk. (Illus.). (Carousel Bks.). (ps-2). N.D. (ISBN 0-8431-0904-1). Price Stern.

Shepler, Ida M.
--Callie Burton's Pot of Gold. N.D. United Brethren Publishing House.
--Children of Toil. N.D. United Brethren Publishing House.
--Wako and the Dill Children. N.D. United Brethren Publishing House.

Sheppard, Eli, pseud., see Young, Martha.

Sheppard, Gordon
--The Man Who Gave Himself Away. Rozier, Jacques (1934-), illus. LC 78-141523. (Illus.). 32 p. 1971. (ISBN 0-8252-0059-8). (ISBN 0-8252-0060-1). H. Quist.

Sheppard-Jones, Elisabeth (1920-), as told by.
--Welsh Legendary Tales. 1960. Nelson.

Sheppard, Katya, tr. see Grimm, Jakob Ludwig Karl (1785-1863) & Grimm, Wilhelm Karl.

Sheppard, S.
--Trials of The Kitchen Curtains. N.D. Carlton Press.

Sheppard, William Henry Crispin (1871-)
--Don Hale in the War Zone. Bodine, Hugh A., illus. LC 17-31032. 312 p. front., plates. 19 1/2 cm. 1917. The Penn Publishing Company.
--Don Hale Over There. Bodine, Hugh A., illus. LC 18-229641. 326 p. front., plates. 19 cm. 1918. The Penn Publishing Company.
--Don Hale with the Flying Squadron. Bodine, Hugh A., illus. LC 19-16357. 308 p. front., plates. 19 cm. 1919. The Penn Publishing Company.
--Don Hale With the Yanks. (The Don Hale Ser.). N.D. Penn.
--A Knight of the West Side. LC 9-16420. 20cm. 384p. 1909. Penn Publishing Co.
--A Knight of the West Side. (The Vacation Ser.). N.D. Penn.
--A Knight of the West Side. (The Outdoor Bks.). N.D. Penn Publishing Co.
--A Knight of the West Side. (Illus.). (The Little People's Ser.). N.D. Penn Publishing Co.
--The Rambler Club Afloat. (The Rambler Club Ser.). 1909. Penn.
--The Rambler Club Among the Lumber Jacks. Sheppard, William Henry Crispin (1871-), illus. LC 11-31857. 19cm. 319p. (The Rambler Club Ser.). 1911. Penn.
--The Rambler Club in Panama. Sheppard, William Henry Crispin (1871-), illus. (The Rambler Club Ser.). N.D. Penn.
--The Rambler Club in the Mountains. LC 10-30144. 19cm. 316p. (The Rambler Club Ser.). 1910. Penn.
--The Rambler Club on Circle T Ranch. Sheppard, William Henry Crispin (1871-), illus. (The Rambler Club Ser.). 1911. Penn.
--The Rambler Club on the Texas Border. Sheppard, William Henry Crispin (1871-), illus. LC 15-19807. 320 p. front., plates. 19 cm. $0.50. (The Rambler Club Ser.). 1915. The Penn Publishing Company.
--The Rambler Club with the Northwest Mounted. Sheppard, William Henry Crispin (1871-), illus. LC 14-12209. 312 p. front., plates. 19 cm. $0.50. 1914. The Penn Publishing Company.
--The Rambler Club's Aeroplane. Sheppard, William Henry Crispin (1871-), illus. LC 12-206314. 320 p. front., plates, 19 cm. $0.60. (The Rambler Club Ser.). 1912. The Penn Publishing Company.
--The Rambler Club's Ball Nine. Sheppard, William Henry Crispin (1871-), illus. LC 13-191244. 316 p. front., plates, 19 cm. $0.50. 1913. The Penn Publishing Company.
--The Rambler Club's Football Team. (The Rambler Club Ser.). N.D. Penn.
--The Rambler Club's Gold Mine. Sheppard, William Henry Crispin (1871-), illus. LC 12-124842. 315 p. front., illus. (map) plates. 19 cm. $0.60. 1912. The Penn Publishing Company.
--The Rambler Club's House-Boat. Sheppard, William Henry Crispin (1871-), illus. LC 12-20632. 320 p. front., plates. 19 cm. $0.60. 1912. The Penn Publishing Company.
--The Rambler Club's Motor Car. Sheppard, william Henry Crispin (1871-), illus. LC 13-135362. 308 p. front., plates. 19 cm. $0.50. 1913. The Penn Publishing Company.
--The Rambler Club's Motor Yacht. Sheppard, William Henry Crispin (1871-), illus. (The Rambler Club Ser.). N.D. Penn Publishing Co.
--The Rambler Club's Winter Camp. LC 10-30143. 19cm. 320p. (The Rambler Club Ser.). 1910. Penn.

Sher, Eva
--Life with Farmer Goldstein. 247 p. 22cm. 1967. Funk & Wagnalls.

Sherak, Jackie
--The Silly Green Cat. LC 62-16369. (Illus.). 24cm. 47p. c.1962. Golden, Gate Junior Books.
Sherard, J. L.
--Blueberry Bear. N.D. Thomas Y. Crowell Company.
--Blueberry Bear's New Home. N.D. Thomas Y. Crowell Company.
Sherburne, Zoa Morin (1912-)
--Almost April. LC 56-5295. 224 p. 21cm. (Morrow Junior Bks.). 1956. Morrow.
--Ballerina on Skates. LC 61-6827. 187 p. 21cm. (Morrow Junior Bks.). 1961. Morrow.
--Evening Star. LC 60-5078. 217 p. 21cm. 1960. Morrow.
--Girl in the Mirror. LC 66-14750. 190p. 21cm. N.D. Morrow.
--The Girl Who Knew Tomorrow. LC 78-104736. 190 p. 21cm. 1970. Morrow.
--The High White Wall. LC 57-5072. 220 p. 21 cm. (Morrow Junior Books). 1957. Morrow,.
--Jennifer. LC 59-5055. 192 p. 21cm. (Morrow Junior Bks.). 1959. Morrow.
--Leslie. LC 72-1545. 175 p. 21cm. 1972. (ISBN 0-688-20041-9). (ISBN 0-688-30041-3). Morrow.
--Princess in Denim. LC 58-5052. 248 p. 21 cm. (Morrow Junior Books). 1958. W. Morrow.
--River at Her Feet. LC 65-10262. 189p. 21cm. c.1965. Morrow.
--Stranger in the House. LC 63-738385. 192 p. 21cm. 1963. Morrow.
--Too Bad About the Haines Girl. LC 67-449. 191 p. 21cm. 1967. W. Morrow.
--Why Have the Birds Stopped Singing?. LC 73-17721. 189 p. 20cm. 1974. (ISBN 0-688-20111-3). (ISBN 0-688-30111-8). Morrow.
Sherer, Mary Louise Huston (1901-)
--Ho Fills the Rice Barrel. Greenwood, Marion, illus. LC 57-11029. 127 p. illus. 25cm. 1957. Follett Pub. Co.
--Mystery of the Black Friday Mine. Lewis, Richard William (1933-1966), illus. LC 65-23591. 128 p. illus. 22 cm. 1965. Criterion Books.
--The Secret of Bruja Mountain. Wallace, Beverly Dobrin (1921-), illus. LC 74-185057. (Illus.). 188 p. 23cm. 1972. (ISBN 0-8178-4711-1). Harvey House.
Sheret, Rene Dundee (1933-)
--Dutch. Sheret, Rene Dundee (1933-), illus. LC 75-97750. (Illus.). 3 color pictures. 32p. (gr. k-2). 1970. (ISBN 0-672-50922-9). Bobbs.
--Dutch and the Jewel Robbers. Sheret, Rene Dundee (1933-), illus. LC 72-88754. (Illus.). 24 p. 24cm. 1973. Bobbs-Merrill.
--What If You Heard?. Sheret, Rene Dundee (1933-), illus. LC 79-118200. (Illus.). 30 p. 29cm. 1970. Bobbs-Merrill.
Sheridan, John
--Eric & the Lost Planes. Livingstone, Malcolm, illus. LC 79-7321. (Illus.). (Storybook Ser.). (gr. 5-8). 1979. (ISBN 0-672-52612-3). Bobbs.
--Eric & the Mad Inventor. Livingstone, Malcolm, illus. LC 79-7322. (Illus.). (Storybook Ser.). (gr. 5-8). 1979. (ISBN 0-672-52609-3). Bobbs.
--Eric the Wild Car. Livingstone, Malcolm, illus. LC 78-66366. (Illus.). (Storybook Ser.). (gr. 5-8). 1979. (ISBN 0-672-52565-8). Bobbs.
Sheridan, Solomon Neill (1859-)
--Billy Vanilla: A Story of the Snowbird Country. Cue, Harold, illus. LC 19-17747. 4 p. l., 11-279 p. front., plates. 20 1/2 cm. c.1919. Lothrop, Lee & Shepard Co.
--The Little Spotted Seal. Blaine, Mahlon, illus. LC 29-183194. ix p., 1 l., 192 p., 1 l. col. front., illus., col. plates. 21 1/2 cm. 1929. Harper & Brothers.
Sheriff, Abigail O., Mrs.
--Stories Old and New. LC 22-9472. vi, lll p. illus., pl. 19 cm. c.1922. Ginn and Company.
Sherlock, Hilary, jt. auth. see Sherlock, Philip Manderson, Sir.
Sherlock, Philip Manderson, Sir (1902-)
--The Iguana's Tail: Crick Crack Stories from the Caribbean. Fiammenghi, Gioia (1929-), illus. LC 68-21948. (Illus.). 97 p. 23cm. 1969. Crowell.
--Three Finger Jack's Treasure. Reeves, William, illus. LC 62-612. 176 p. illus. 21cm. 1962, c.1961. Macmillan.
--Three Finger Jack's Treasure. Reeves, William, illus. 1961. St Martin's Press.
--West Indian Folk-Tales. Kiddell-Monroe, Joan (1908-), illus. LC 66-10987. (Illus.). (Myths & Legends Ser). (gr. 4-7). 1966. (ISBN 0-8098-2392-6). Walck.
Sherlock, Philip Manderson, Sir (1902-), as told by.
--Anansi, the Spider Man: Jamaican Folk Tales. Brown, Marcia (1918-), illus. LC 54-5619. 112p. illus. 23cm. 1954. Crowell. **Award: (ALA).**
Sherlock, Philip Manderson, Sir (1902-) & Sherlock, Hilary
--Ears and Tails and Common Sense:. More Stories from the Caribbean. Aliki, pseud. (1929-), illus. Brandenberg, Aliki Liacouras. LC 74-2045. (Illus.). xvii, 121 p. 21cm. 1974. (ISBN 0-690-00450-8). Crowell.
Sherman, Allan (1924-1973)
--Hello Muddah, Hello Fadduh!. Hoff, Sydney (1912-), illus. LC 64-16636. 1 v. (unpaged) col. illus. 24 cm. 1964. Harper & Row.
--I Can't Dance!. Hoff, Sydney (1912-), illus. LC 64-19606. 28 p. col. illus. 24 cm. 1964. Harper & Row.
Sherman, Clifford Leon
--The Dot Book. LC 14-178141. 30 l. illus. 30 cm. $1.00. 1914. Houghton Mifflin Company.
--The Dot Circus. LC 15-187006. 29 l. illus. 30 cm. $1.00. 1915. Houghton Mifflin Company.
Sherman, Dennis Ronald (1934-)
--The Lion's Paw. LC 74-25122. 240p. 1975. Doubleday.
--Old Mali & the Boy. (A novel). (gr. 8 up). 1964. (ISBN 0-316-78547-4). Little.
Sherman, Diane Finn (1928-)
--Little Skater. Grider, Dorothy (1915-), illus. 1959. (ISBN 0-8382-0472-4, Hale Giant Books). E. M. Hale and Company.
--Little Skater. Grider, Dorothy (1915-), illus. LC 65-14638. 1 v. (unpaged) col. illus. 32 cm. 1965, c.1959. Rand McNally.
--My Counting Book. Koester, Sharon Smith, illus. LC 63-11267. 1 v. (unpaged) col. illus. 33 cm. (A Rand McNally Giant Bk.). c.1960. Rand McNally.
--Nancy Plays Nurse. Grider, Dorothy (1915-), illus. LC 72-91708. 33cm. 20p. (Giant Bk.). (gr. k-3). 1965. (ISBN 0-8382-1046-5). Rand McNally.
--Nancy Plays Nurse. Grider, Dorothy (1915-), illus. (Illus.). (ps-k). 1969. (ISBN 0-528-88819-6). Rand.
Sherman, Edith Bishop, Mrs. (1889-)
--Bright College Year. 1950. Doubleday & Co.
--Fighting Muskets. Pitz, Henry Clarence (1895-1976), illus. LC 38-29407. vii p., 1 l., 324 p. illus. (incl. map) 20 1/2 cm. 1938. Longmans, Green and Co.
--Flying Banners. LC 42-236377. 4 p. l., 246 p. illus. 21 cm. 1942. Longmans, Green and Co.
--The Gay Chariot. LC 36-18205. xii p., 1 l., 301 p. incl. front., illus. 20 1/2 cm. 1936. Longmans, Green and Co.
--Mid-Flight. Townsend, Lee (1895-), illus. LC 37-17506. vii, 392 p. incl. front., illus. 20 1/2 cm. 1937. Longmans, Green and Co.
--Milady at Arms: A Story of the Revolutionary Days. De Angeli, Marguerite Lofft, Mrs. (1889-), illus. LC 27-20085. 6 p. l., 330 p. col. front., plates. 20 1/2 cm. 1927. Doubleday, Page & Company.
--Milady at Arms: A Story of the Revolutionary Days. De Angeli, Marguerite Lofft, Mrs. (1889-), illus. LC 37-21035. 5 p. l., 330 p. col. front. 20 1/2 cm. (Young Moderns Bookshelf). 1937. The Sun Dial Press, Inc.
--Mistress Madcap. LC 46-7683. viii, 248 p. 20 1/2 cm. (Young Moderns). 1946. Doubleday & Co., Inc.
--Mistress Madcap. LC 37-21037. viii, 248 p. front. 20 1/2 cm. (Young Moderns Bookshelf). 1937. The Sun Dial Press, Inc.
--Mistress Madcap. Clark, Charles E., illus. LC 25-23370. viii, 248p. 21cm. 1925. Doubleday, Page & Company.
--Mistress Madcap Surrenders. LC 26-21008. 5 p. l., 200 p. col. front. 20 1/2 cm. 1926. Doubleday, Page & Company.
--Mistress Madcap Surrenders: A Rebel Heroine in the Revolution. LC 35-7677. 5 p., l., 260 p. 20 1/2 cm. (Young Moderns Bks.). 1935. Doubleday, Doran & Company, Inc.
--Mistress Madcap Surrenders: A Rebel Heroine in the Revolution. LC 37-21036. 5 p. l., 260 p. col. front. 20 1/2 cm. (Young moderns bookshelf). 1937. The Sun Dial Press, Inc.
--Mystery at High Hedges. LC 37-58327. 3 p. l., 13-251 p. 19 1/2 cm. c.1937. The Goldsmith Company.
--Polly What's-Her-Name. LC 36-411. 3 p. l., 11-250 p. 19 1/2 cm. c.1936. The Goldsmith Publishing Company.
--Upstairs, Downstairs. Owen, Mildred Ann, illus. LC 28-23276. 5 p. l., 312 p. incl. illus., plates. front. 21 cm. 1928. Doubleday, Doran & Company, Inc.
--Upstairs, Downstairs: A Boarding School Mystery for Girls. LC 39-18663. 4 p. l., 312 p. incl. 1 illus., plates. front. 20 1/2 cm. (Young Moderns Bookshelf). 1937. The Sun Dial Press, Inc.
Sherman, Eileen Bluestone
--The Odd Potato: A Chanukah Story. Kahn, Katherine Janns, illus. LC 84-17186. (Illus.). 32 p. 28cm. c.1984. (ISBN 0-930494-36-9). (ISBN 0-930494-37-7). Kar-Ben Copies.
Sherman, Elisabeth (1911-)
--Dateline Central High. LC 58-10183. 220 p. 21cm. 1958. Coward-McCann.
--Let's Look Ahead. Fisher, Lois Jeannette (1909-), illus. N.D. Grosset & Dunlap.
--Merry Music Makers. N.D. Grosset & Dunlap.
Sherman, Fanny Jessop
--Admiral Wags. Brown, Paul (1893-1958), illus. LC 43-7706. 2 p. l., 84 p. illus. (part col.) 25 1/2 x 20 1/2 cm. 1943. Dodd, Mead & Company.
Sherman, Frank Dempster (1860-1916)
--Little-Folk Lyrics. Cowles, Genevieve Almeda (1871-) & Cowles, Maude Alice (1871-1905), illus. LC 4-13836. xi p., 1 l., 15-140 p., 1 l. incl. front., plates. 20 cm. 1897. Houghton, Mifflin and Company.
--Little-Folk Lyrics. Cowles, Maude Alice (1871-1905) & Cowles, Genevieve Almeda (1871-), illus. LC 79-84353. (Illus.). xi, 140 p. 21cm. (Granger Index Reprint Ser.). 1969. Books for Libraries Press.
--Little-Folk Lyrics. Cowles, Maude Alice (1871-1905) & Cowles, Genevieve Almeda (1871-), illus. LC 35-33078. 88 p., 1 l. 16 1/2 cm. 1892. Houghton, Mifflin and Company.
Sherman, Harold Morrow (1898-)
--Bases Full!. Ernie Challenges the World. LC 28-11321. 3 p. l., 250 p. front., plates. 19 1/2 cm. c.1928. Grosset & Dunlap.
--Batter Up: A Story of American Legion Junior Baseball. Townsend, Ernest N., illus. LC 30-13112. 20cm. 304p. (The Home Run Ser.). 1930. Grosset & Dunlap.
--Beyond the Dog's Nose. LC 27-20268. p. l., 230, 1 p. front., map. 19 1/2 cm. 1927. D. Appleton and Company.
--Beyond the Dog's Nose. (Buddy Bks. for Boys) N.D. Grosset & Dunlap.
--Block That Kick!. Rev ed. Schaeffer, Phil, illus. LC 28-22148. 4 p. l., 323 p. front., plates. 19 1/2 cm. c.1928. Grosset & Dunlap.
--Cameron MacBain, Backwoodsman. (Buddy Books for Boys). N.D. Grosset & Dunlap.
--Crashing Through!. Graef, Robert A., illus. LC 32-22561. v, 266 p. front., plates. 21 cm. c.1932. Grosset & Dunlap.
--Ding Palmer, Air Detective. LC 30-13096. 2 p. l., 252 p. front., plates. 19 1/2 cm. c.1930. Grosset & Dunlap.
--Don Rader, Trail Blazer. Schaeffer, Phil, illus. LC 29-10226. 4 p. l., 272 p. front., plates. 19 1/2 cm. c.1929. Grosset & Dunlap.
--Double Play, and Other Baseball Stories. LC 32-224022. 3 p. l., 244 p. front., pl. 19 1/2 cm. c.1932. Grosset & Dunlap.
--Down the Ice, and Other Winter Sport Stories. LC 32-109306. 3 p. l., 13-247 p. 19 1/2 cm. c.1932. The Goldsmith Publishing Company.
--Fight 'em, Big Three. LC 26-15067. 4 p. l., 262, 1 p. front. 19 1/2 cm. 1926. D. Appleton and Company.
--Fight 'em, Big Three. LC 30-12331. 4 p. l., 262, 1 p. front. 19 1/2 cm. 1929. Grosset & Dunlap.
--Flashing Steel. LC 29-281265. 4 p. l., 264 p. front., plates. 19 1/2 cm. c.1929. Grosset & Dunlap.
--Flying Heels, and Other Hockey Stories. LC 30-2687. ix p., 1 l., 238 p. front., plates (1 double) 19 1/2 cm. c.1930. Grosset & Dunlap.
--Get 'em, Mayfield. LC 27-5418. 4 p. l., 253, 1 p. front. 19 cm. 1927. D. Appleton and Company.
--Goal to Go!. Machtey, illus. LC 31-20925. 3 p. l., 250 p. front., plates. 19 1/2 cm. c.1931. Grosset & Dunlap.
--Hit and Run!. LC 29-11682. 4 p. l., 248 p. front., plates (1 double) 19 1/2 cm. c.1929. Grosset & Dunlap.
--Hit by Pitcher. Hastings, Howard Livingston (1887-), illus. LC 28-14242. 4 p. l., 241 p. front., plates. 19 1/2 cm. c.1928. Grosset & Dunlap.
--Hold That Line!. Tandy, Russell H., illus. LC 30-138046. vii, 253 p. front., plates. 19 1/2 cm. c.1930. Grosset & Dunlap.
--Interference, and Other Football Stories. LC 70-178460. 247 p. 21cm. 1971. (ISBN 0-8369-4061-X). Books for Libraries Press.
--Interference, and Other Football Stories. LC 32-114581. 3 p. l., 13-247 p. 19 1/2 cm. c.1932. The Goldsmith Publishing Company.
--It's a Pass!. LC 32-198282. 4 p. l., 13-243 p. 19 1/2 cm. c.1931. The Goldsmith Publishing Co.
--The Land of Monsters. Anderson, Harold N., illus. LC 31-123752. 3 p. l., 249 p. front., plates. 19 1/2 cm. c.1931. Grosset & Dunlap.
--Mayfield's Fighting Five. LC 26-6026. 4 p. l., 264, 1 p. front. 19 1/2 cm. 1926. D. Appleton and Company.
--Number Forty-Four and Other Football Stories. LC 30-118554. 4 p. l., 256 p. front., plates. 19 1/2 cm. c.1930. Grosset & Dunlap.
--Number Froty-Four and Other Football Stories. LC 72-4408. 256 p. 22cm. (Short story index reprint series). 1972. (ISBN 0-8369-4188-8). Books for Libraries Press.
--One Minute to Play. N.D. Grosset & Dunlap.
--Over the Line. LC 29-179209. 3 p. l., 235 p. 19 1/2 cm. c.1929. The Goldsmith Publishing Co.
--Safe!. LC 28-14237. 4 p. l., 308 p. front., plates. 19 1/2 cm. c.1928. Grosset & Dunlap.
--Shoot That Ball! and Other Baseball Stories. LC 30-292516. 4 p. l., 239 p. front. 19 1/2 cm. c.1930. Grosset & Dunlap.
--Slashing Sticks and Other Hockey Stories. LC 31-1924. 3 p. l., 218 p. front., pl. 19 1/2 cm. c.1931. Grosset & Dunlap.
--Strike Him Out!. LC 31-18735. 4 p. l., 7-240 p. 19 1/2 cm. c.1931. The Goldsmith Publishing Co.
--Tahara Among African Tribes. LC 38-33395. 4 p. l., 13-246 p. 19 1/2 cm. c.1933. The Goldsmith Publishing Company.
--Tahara, Boy King of the Desert. LC 38-33396. 4 p. l., 13-250 p. 19 1/2 cm. c.1933. The Goldsmith Publishing Company.
--Tahara, Boy Mystic of India. LC 38-333983. 3 p. l., 11-252 p. 19 1/2 cm. c.1933. The Goldsmith Publishing Company.
--Tahara in the Land of Yucatan. LC 38-333976. 5 p. l., 15-246 p. 19 1/2 cm. c.1933. The Goldsmith Publishing Company.
--The Tennis Terror, and Other Tennis Stories. LC 32-10932. 3 p. l., 13-244 p. 19 1/2 cm. c.1932. The Goldsmith Publishing Company.
--Touchdown!. LC 27-18972. 4 p. l., 229 p. front., plates. 19 1/2 cm. c.1927. Grosset & Dunlap.
--Under the Basket, and Other Basket Ball Stories. 3 p. l., 13-242 p. 19 1/2 cm. c.1932. The Goldsmith Publishing Company.
Sherman, Harold Morrow (1898-) & Daniel, Hawthorne (1890-)
--Cameron MacBain, Backwoodsman. LC 27-17787. 3 p. l., 239, 1 p. front. 19 1/2 cm. 1927. D. Appleton and Company.
Sherman, Ivan
--I Am a Giant. LC 74-22189. (Illus.). 32 p. 27cm. 1975. (ISBN 0-15-237983-5). Harcourt Brace Jovanovich.
--I Do Not Like It When My Friend Comes to Visit. Sherman, Ivan, illus. LC 73-75326. (Illus.). 32 p. 27cm. 1973. (ISBN 0-15-238000-0). Harcourt Brace Jovanovich.
--Robert and the Magic String. LC 72-88174. (Illus.). 32 p. 27cm. 1973. (ISBN 0-15-267820-4). Harcourt Brace Jovanovich.
Sherman, James Woodward
--The Captain of the Clothespins. Wireman, Eugenie M., illus. (Illus.). 19cm. 143p. 1926. Little Brown & Co.
--The Gay Kitchen. Wireman, Eugenie M., illus. x, 143 p. col. front., illus., col. plates. 19 cm. 1926. Little, Brown, and Company.
--Joey Gets the Golf Bug. 1st ed. Nicholas, Frank, illus. LC 61-5330. 171 p. illus. 20 cm. 1961. Little, Brown.
--Out in the Kitchen. Wireman, Eugenie M., illus. x, 133 p. col. front., illus., col. plates. 19 cm. 1925. Little, Brown, and Company.
--A Quart of Moonlight. Gee, John, illus. LC 28-22606. vii, 147, 1 p. front., illus. 19 1/2 cm. 1928. Little, Brown, and Company.
--The Talkative Table. Wireman, Eugenie M., illus. LC 25-25013. x, 133 p. col. front., illus., col. plates. 19 cm. 1925. Little, Brown, and Company.
Sherman, Martha Coleman
--Just a Dream of Childhood Days, and Other Verses. LC 14-188295. 80 p. front., 1 illus. 18 cm. $1.0. 1914. Childhood Publishing House.
Sherman, Nancy (1931-)
--The Boy Who Ate Flowers. Carroll, Nancy, illus. LC 60-8939. (Illus.). unpaged. 27cm. 1960. Platt & Munk Co.
--Gwendolyn and the Weathercock. Sorel, Edward (1929-), illus. LC 63-9389. unpaged. illus. 19 x 26 cm. 1963. Golden Press. **Award: (NYT).**
--Gwendolyn, the Miracle Hen. Sorel, Edward (1929-), illus. LC 61-7372. unpaged. illus. 19x26 cm. c.1961. Golden Press.
--Miss Agatha's Lark. 1st ed. Vasiliu, Mircea (1920-), illus. LC 67-18653. (Illus.). half full color, half b&w. 32p. (gr. 2-6). 1968. (ISBN 0-672-50380-8). Bobbs.
Sherman, Stuart P., ed. see Hawthorne, Nathaniel.
Sherman, V. T
--Capturing a Spy: Or, A New Peril. LC 21-214689. 156 p., 1 l., 7-150 p. incl. front. pl. 19 cm. c.1913. M. A. Donohue & Co.
Shermas, Mildred Walker see Walker, Mildred.
Sherriff, Robert Cedric (1896-1975)
--The Hopkins Manuscript. LC 39-15798. 352 p. 21 cm. 1939. The Macmillan Company.
--King John's Treasure: An Adventure Story. Relf, Douglas, illus. LC 54-13507. 242p. illus. 19cm. 1954. Macmillan.
Sherriffs, Gordon D.
--The Haunted Treasure of the Espectros. 1st ed. LC 62-11158. 175 p. 21 cm. 1962. Chilton Co., Book Division.
Sherrill, Dorothy (1901-)
--The Story of a Little Duck. Sherrill, Dorothy (1901-), illus. LC 34-358829. 42 p. col. illus. 17 cm. c.1934. The Merrill Publishing Co.
--The Story of a Little Gray Mouse. Sherrill, Dorothy (1901-), illus. LC 45-8592. 63 p. col. illus. 17 1/2 cm. 1945. Greenberg.

--The Story of a Little White Teddy Bear Who Didn't Want to Go to Bed. LC 61-9051. unpaged. ill. 18cm. 1961, c.1931. Holt, Rinehart & Winston.
--The Story of a Little White Teddy Bear Who Didnt Want to Go to Bed. Sherrill, Dorothy (1901-), illus. LC 31-28054. 62 p. col. illus. 17 1/2 cm. c.1931. Farrar & Rinehart Incorporated.
--The Story of a Little Yellow Dog and a Little White Bear. Sherrill, Dorothy (1901-), illus. LC 32-23287. 62 p. col. illus. 18 cm. c.1932. Farrar & Rinehart, Incorporated.
--The Story of Roly and Poly, the Santa Claus Bears. Sherrill, Dorothy (1901-), illus. LC 52-8656. unpaged, illus. 16 cm. 1952. Crowell.
--The Story of Sleepy Sally. Sherrill, Dorothy (1901-), illus. LC 35-4529. 56 p. col. illus. 17 1/2 cm. c.1933. Greenberg.
--The Story of Sleepy Sam. Sherrill, Dorothy (1901-), illus. LC 32-222015. 46 p. col. illus. 18 cm. c.1932. Greenberg.
Sherrill, Elizabeth see Wilkerson, David.
Sherrill, John see Wilkerson, David.
Sherrod, David, jt. auth. see Poynter, Margaret.
Sherrod, Jane (1917-) & Thayer, Zel
--Ho-I-Man and His Friends. Singer, Kurt Deutsch (1911-), ed. Spiegel, Lawrence M., illus. LC 62-14147. v. illus. 25 cm. 1962. T. S. Denison.
Sherrow, Victoria
--There Goes the Ghost. Lloyd, Megan, illus. LC 83-49485. (Illus.). 32p. (gr. k-3). c.1985. (ISBN 0-06-025509-9). (ISBN 0-06-025510-2). HarpJ.
Sherry, Dulcie Sylvia (1932-)
--Frog in a Coconut Shell. LC 68-24419. 160p. (gr. 4-6). 1968. (ISBN 0-397-30999-6). Lippincott.
--The Haven-Screamers. LC 77-117240. 139 p. 21cm. 1970. Lippincott.
--The Liverpool Cats. Koehn, Ilse (1929-), illus. LC 69-12009. (Illus.). 153 p. 22cm. 1st U.S. edition. 1969. Lippincott.
--Mat the Little Monkey. Grabianski, Janusz (1928-1976), illus. LC 76-46173. (Illus.). 43 p. 25cm. 1977. (ISBN 0-8448-1046-0). Crane Russak.
--Secret of the Jade Pavilion. Nebel, Gustave E., illus. LC 67-24341. (Illus.). 158 p. 22cm. 1st U.S. edition. 1967, c.1966. Lippincott.
--A Snake in the Old Hut. LC 73-2944. 160 p. 22cm. 1973. T. Nelson.
Sherry, Sylvia see Sherry, Dulcie Sylvia.
Sherwan, Earl
--Bruno, the Bear of Split Rock Island. 1st ed. Sherwan, Earl (1917-), illus. LC 66-10790. 142p. illus. 24cm. c.1966. Norton.
--Mask, the Door Country Coon. Sherwan, Earl (1917-), illus. (gr. 4-6). N.D. G&D.
--The Smart Little Mouse. Phillips, Katherine L., illus. LC 50-12315. 21cm. 23p. (A Rand McNally Giant Bk.). 1956, c.1950. Rand McNally.
Sherwood, ed.
--Sherwood's Juvenile Stories. N.D. R. Worthington.
Sherwood, E. Hugh
--Jack Jingling in Jungleland. LC 19-143838. 80 p. incl. front., illus. (part col.) 18 1/2 by 24 1/2 cm. c.1918. Rand, McNally & Company.
Sherwood, E. Hugh & Budlong, Maud G
--Bobbie Bubbles. N.D. Rand Mcnally.
Sherwood, Henry Mrs. see Sherwood, Mary Martha Butt, Mrs.
Sherwood, M. E. W.
--Sweet Brier. Taylor, illus. (Illus.). N.D. Lothrop Pub Co.
Sherwood, Mary Martha Butt, Mrs. (1775-1851)
--Arzoomund, 1 of 16 Vols. (Mrs. Sherwood's Works: No.8). N.D. Harper & Bros.
--The Birth-Day Present, 1 of 16 Vols, Vol. 8. (Mrs. Sherwood's Works). N.D. Harper & Bros.
--Blanch Gamond. (Waste Not, Want Not Ser.). N.D. N. Tibbals & Sons.
--The Bracelets. (Waste Not, Want Not Ser.). N.D. N. Tibbals & Sons.
--The Butterfly, 1 of 16 Vols, Vol. 7. (Mrs. Sherwood's Works). N.D. Harper & Bros.
--Clever Stories. N.D. Robert Carter & Brothers.
--Duty Is Safety: Or, Troublesome Tom. LC 21-305490. 64 p. incl. front., illus. 14 1/2 x 11 1/2 cm. 1847. G. S. Appleton.
--Emeline, 1 of 16 Vols, Vol. 7. (Mrs. Sherwood's Works). N.D. Harper & Bros.
--The Errand Boy, 1 of 8 Vols, Vol. 8. (Mrs. Sherwood's Works). N.D. Harper & Bros.
--Fairchild Family, 1 of 16 Vols, Vol. 2. (Mrs. Sherwood's Works). N.D. Harper & Bros.
--Flowers of the Forest. (Lily Ser.). N.D. Robert Carter & Brothers.
--Flowers of the Forest, and Other Stories. N.D. Robert Carter & Brothers.
--The Governess, 1 of 16 Vols, Vol. 6. (Mrs. Sherwood's Works). N.D. Harper & Bros.
--The History of Little Henry and His Bearer. LC 76-366237. (Illus.). 69 p. 15cm. 1832. American Sunday School Union.
--The History of Little Henry and His Bearer. 2d american, from the 2d london ed. LC 78-316918. 32 p. 17cm. 1817. Hudson and Co. Printers.
--The History of the Fairchild Family. (Illus.). (Fine Art Juveniles Ser.). N.D. Frederick A. Stokes Co.
--The History of the Fairchild Family. LC 75-32157. p. cm. (Classics of Children's Literature,1621-1932). 1977. (ISBN 0-8240-2271-8). Garland Publishing.
--The History of the Fairchild Family: Or, The Child's Manual. (Illus.). N.D. George Routledge & Sons.
--Jack, the Sailor Boy. N.D. Robert Carter & Brothers.
--Joan, the Trusty. (Lily Ser.). N.D. Robert Carter & Brothers.
--Juliana Oakley. 2d american ed. Anderson, Alexander (1775-1870), illus. LC 21-3057. 105 p. front., illus. 15 1/2 cm. 1833. M. Day.
--Juliana Oakley. 2nd ed. Oakley, Julianna, illus. LC 22-105314. 108 p. front., illus. 14 1/2 cm. 1825. G. C. Morgan, and Wilder and Campbell.
--The Little Beggars, 1 of 16 Vols, Vol. 4. (Mrs. Sherwood's Works). N.D. Harper & Bros.
--Little Beggars. (Lily Ser.). N.D. Robert Carter & Brothers.
--Little Blue Mantle. (Waste Not, Want Not Ser.). N.D. N. Tibbals & Sons.
--Little Forrester. (Waste Not, Want Not Ser.). N.D. N. Tibbals & Sons.
--Little Henry. (Waste Not, Want Not Ser.). N.D. N. Tibbals & Sons.
--Little Henry and His Bearer, 1 of 16 Vols, Vol. 3. N.D. Harper & Bros.
--Little Woodman. (Waste Not, Want Not Ser.). N.D. N. Tibbals & Sons.
--Little Woodman. (Lily Ser.). N.D. Robert Carter & Brothers.
--The Little Woodman, and Other Stories. N.D. Robert Carter & Brothers.
--Lucy Clare, 1 of 16 Vols, Vol. 3. (Mrs. Sherwood's Works). N.D. Harper & Bros.
--My Aunt Kate, 1 of 16 vols, Vol. 7. (Mrs. Sherwood's Works). N.D. Harper & Bros.
--My Uncle Timothy, 1 of 16 Vols, Vol. 6. (Mrs. Sherwood's Works). N.D. Harper & Bros.
--The Orphan Boy, 1 of 16 Vols, Vol. 8. (Mrs. Sherwood's Works). N.D. Harper & Bros.
--Stories on the Church Catechism. N.D. T. Whittaker.
--Susan Gray. (The Ruby Stories). N.D. American News Co.
--Susan Gray. (The Holiday Ser.). N.D. The American News Co.
--Susan Grey. N.D. Scribner, Welford & Armstrong.
--Susan Grey, 1 of 52 Vols. (Illus.). (Warne's Round the Globe Library: Vol. 17). N.D. Scribner & Welford.
--Two Orphans. (Lily Ser.). N.D. Robert Carter & Brothers.
--The Two Sisters, 1 of 16 Vols, Vol. 8. (Mrs. Sherwood's Works). N.D. Harper & Bros.
--Victoria, 1 of 16 Vols, Vol. 8. (Mrs. Sherwood's Works). N.D. Harper & Bros.
--Waste Not, Want Not. (Waste Not, Want Not Ser.). N.D. N. Tibbals & Sons.
--The White Dove. (Waste Not, Want Not Ser.). N.D. N. Tibbals & Sons.
--The Young Forester, 1 of 16 Vols, Vol. 8. (Mrs. Sherwood's Works). N.D. Harper & Bros.
--Young Forester. (Lily Ser.). N.D. Robert Carter & Brothers.
Sherwood, Mary Martha Butt, Mrs. (1775-1851) & Plumer, William Swan (1802-1880)
--Narratives of Little Henry and His Bearer, The Amiable Louisa, and Ann Eliza Williams. LC 44-38249. 105 p. 15 1/2 cm. N.D. The American Tract Society.
Sherwood, Merriam (1892-), tr. see Charlemagne.
Sherwood, Merriam (1892-), tr. see El Cid Campeador.
Sherwood, Rowena, jt. auth. see Swem, Leota.
Shetter, Dede (1931-)
--The Frisky Favorite. LC 48-15210. 56 p. illus. 10 x 13 cm. 1947. Adventure Trails Publications.
Shetter, Stella C.
--Early Candlelight Stories. Gregory, Dorothy Lake, illus. LC 22-194765. 250 p. col. front., illus., col. plates. 19 1/2 cm. c.1922. Rand, McNally & Company.
--Early Candlelight Stories. Gregory, Dorothy Lake, illus. LC 24-276504. 256 p. incl. front., illus. 18 cm. c.1924. Rand, McNally & Company.
--When Grandma Was a Little Girl. Gregory, Dorothy Lake, illus. LC 26-149164. 250 p. col. front., illus., col. plates. 20 cm. c.1926. Rand, McNally & Co.
Shetty, Sharat
--A Hindu Boyhood. 64p. (Two World Ser.). 1970. M.Evans and Company.
Shevrin, Aliza, selected by see Rabinovitch, Sholem.
Shevrin, Aliza, tr. see Rabinovitch, Sholem.
Shibano, Tamizo
--The Old Man Who Made the Trees Bloom. Iguchi, Bunshu, illus. Ooka, D. T., tr. from Japanese. (Illus.). 32p. (Japanese Fairy Tale Ser.: No. 2). 1985. (ISBN 0-89346-247-0). Heian Intl.
Shiefman, Vicky (1942-)
--Mindy. Weil, Lisl (1910-), illus. LC 74-7231. (Illus.). 84 p. 22cm. 1974. Macmillan.
Shields, Brenda Desmond Armstrong (1914-)
--Tezza, the Coral Trout. Derrick, John, illus. LC 62-13668. unpaged. illus. 19x26 cm. 1962. (ISBN 0-910244-29-4). J. F. Blair.
Shields, Cornelia
--Amy Goes to the Moon. (Illus.). (Little Book Ser). (gr. k-6). 1976. (ISBN 0-89409-006-2). Childrens Art.
Shields, Karena
--Three in the Jungle. Petersen, Harold, illus. 5 p. l., 3-216 p. incl. front., illus., plates. 20 1/2 cm. c.1944. Harcourt, Brace and Company.
Shields, Milford E
--Dirty Face. Jackson, Frederica, illus. 48 p. incl. front., illus. 19 cm. 1944. B. Humphries, Inc.
--Static Land. LC 49-4980. 135 p. illus. 21 cm. 1949, c.1947. B. Humphries.
Shields, Rita
--Ceclia's Locket. Funk, Clotilde Embree, illus. LC 61-13104. 147 p. illus. 24 cm. 1961. Longmans, Green.
--Cecilia's Locket. Funk, Clotilde Embree, illus. (Illus.). (gr. 3-7). N.D. McKay.
--Chris Muldoon. Abel, Raymond (1911-), illus. LC 65-149215. (Illus.). 21cm. 160p. (gr. 3-7). c.1965. (ISBN 0-679-25031-X). McKay.
--Mary Kate. O'Sullivan, Tom, illus. LC 63-10490. (Illus.). 120 p. 21cm. 1963. D. McKay Co.
--Norah and the Cable Car. 1960. McKay.
--Norah and the Cable Car. Bennett, Richard Michael (1899-), illus. LC 60-6708. 150 p. illus. 21cm. 1960. Longmans, Green.
Shields, Sarah Annie Frost, Mrs.
--Almost a Man. Frost, Arthur Burdett (1851-1928), illus. LC 12-32403. 288 p. front., plates. 17 1/2 cm. (The Golden Rod Lib.). c.1877. American Tract Society.
--Almost a Woman. LC 12-328591. 414 p. front., plates. 17 1/2 cm. (The Golden Rod Lib). c.1876. American Tract Society.
Shiffrin, Abraham B. see Christopher, Robin, pseud.
Shiffrin, Abraham B. (1902-)
--Dimple Diggers, Thirty Poems. Christopher, Robin, pseud. Ries, Gerta, illus. LC 28-343664. 5 p. l., 3-74 p., 1 l. illus. 21 cm. 1927. Elm-House.
Shigley, Forest Dwight (1930-)
--Randy Raindrop Takes a Trip. Spiegel, Lawrence M., illus. LC 60-11826. (Illus.). (Nature & Science Bk.). (gr. k-6). 1960. Denison.
Shillaber, Benjamin Penhallow see Partington, pseud.
Shillaber, Benjamin Penhallow (1814-1890)
--Cruises with Captain Bob around the Kitchen Fire, 1 of 4 vols. (Illus.). (Ike Partington Stories). 1882. Lee & Shepard.
--Cruises with Captain Bob Around the Kitchen Fire, 1 of 60 vols. (Illus.). (American Boys' Ser.: No. 56). 1900. Lee & Shepard.
--Cruises with Captain Bob on Sea and Land. LC 77-369695. (Illus.). 326 p., 4 leaves of plates. 18cm. 1880, c.1879. Lee and Shepard.
--The Double-Runner Club: Or, The Lively Boys of Rivertown. LC 12-387331. 314 p. front., plates. 17 1/2 cm. (Ike Partington series. 3). 1882. Lee and Shepard.
--The Double-Runner Club: Or, The Lively Boys of Rivertown, 1 of 60 vols. (Illus.). (American Boys' Ser.: No. 57). 1900. Lee & Shepard.
--Ike Partington: Or, The Adventures of a Human Boy and His Friends. 225 p. incl. illus., plates. front. 19 cm. (On cover: American Boys Ser.). c.1906. Lothrop, Lee & Shepard Co.
--Ike Partington: Or, The Humors of a Human Boy and His Friends, 1 of 60 vols. (Illus.). (American Boys' Ser.: No. 58). 1900. Lee & Shepard.
--Ike Partington: Or, The Humors of the Human Boy and His Friends, 1 of 4 vols. (Illus.). (Ike Partington Stories). 1882. Lee & Shepard.
--Ike Partington Stories, 4 vols. (Illus.). 1882. Set. Lee & Shepard.
--Lively Boys! Lively Boys!, Ike Partington: Or, the Adventures of a Human Boy and His Friends. LC 13-939452. 225 p. incl. illus., plates. front. 18 cm. (Ike Partington Ser.,V. 1). 1879. Lee and Shepard.
--Mrs. Partington's Mother Goose. (Illus.). N.D. Lee & Shepard.
Shillaber, Carrie Wheeler see Aunt Carrie, pseud.
Shillaber, Carrie Wheeler, ed.
--Five Little Chickens. Aunt Carrie, pseud, 1 of 4 vols. (Wonderful Globe Ser.). N.D. D. Lothrop.
--Five Little Chickens And Other Songs for Our Little Ones. Aunt Carrie, pseud. LC 16-38715. 1 p. l., 5-224 p. front., illus. 19 cm. c.1885. D. Lothrop and Company.
--New Songs for Our Little Ones. Aunt Carrie, pseud. (Illus.). 144p. N.D. D. Lothrop & Co.
Shilstone, Arthur, ed. see Boys' Life Magazine Editors.
Shimer, Edgar Dubs (1853-)
--Fairy Stories My Children Love Best of All. Perkins, Lucy Fitch, Mrs. (1865-1937), illus. LC 20-1068. 277 p. col. front., illus. 20 cm. $1.25. 1920. L. A. Noble.
--The Fairyland Reader: New Fairy Stories of All Nations. Perkins, Lucy Fitch, Mrs. (1865-1937), illus. LC 38-18283. 277 p. front., illus. 19 1/2 cm. c.1935. Noble and Noble.
Shimin, Symeon (1902-)
--I Wish There Were Two of Me. LC 75-32636. (Illus.). 30 p. 24cm. c.1976. (ISBN 0-7232-6128-8). F. Warne.
--A Special Birthday. LC 76-14777. p. cm. 1976. (ISBN 0-07-056901-0). (ISBN 0-07-056902-9). McGraw-Hill.
Shimizu, Kozo
--The Gift of the Grateful Crane. (Illus.). 26p. (Gakken Picture Story Ser.). (gr. k-5). 1972. (ISBN 0-87040-028-2). Japan Pubns.
Shimoni, S.
--Legends of Abraham the Patriarch. (Illus.). (Biblical Ser.). (gr. 1-5). 1975. (ISBN 0-914080-07-5). Shulsinger Sales.
--Legends of Daniel. (Illus.). (Biblical Ser.). (gr. 1-5). 1975. (ISBN 0-914080-14-8). Shulsinger Sales.
--Legends of Joseph & His Brothers. (Illus.). (Biblical Ser.). (gr. 1-5). 1975. (ISBN 0-914080-11-3). Shulsinger Sales.
--Legends of Joshua. (Illus.). (Biblical Ser.). (gr. 1-5). 1975. (ISBN 0-914080-12-1). Shulsinger Sales.
--Legends of Moses the Law-Giver. (Illus.). (Biblical Ser.). (gr. 1-5). 1975. (ISBN 0-914080-08-3). Shulsinger Sales.
--Legends of Ruth. (Illus.). (Biblical Ser.). (gr. 1-5). 1975. (ISBN 0-914080-10-5). Shulsinger Sales.
--Legends of Samson. (Illus.). (Biblical Ser.). (gr. 1-5). 1975. (ISBN 0-914080-09-1). Shulsinger Sales.
Shine, Deborah see Adams, Edith, pseud.
Shine, Deborah see Bright, Sarah, pseud.
Shine, Deborah, ed. see Haus, Felice.
Shine, Deborah (1932-), ed.
--Strawberry Shortcake's Bathtime Book. Bracken, Carolyn, illus. (Illus.). 5p. (Bathtime Books). (gr. k-2). 1984. (ISBN 0-394-86349-6, BYR). Random.
Shine, Mabel Gifford, Mrs.
--Jacob, a Lad of Nazareth. Cole, Clarence Leonard, illus. LC 15-8426. 342 p. col. front., col. plates. 19 1/2 cm. $1.00. c.1915. Rand, McNally & Company.
Shinn, Alida Visscher
--Sigurdur in Iceland: A Photographic Picture Book. LC 42-25184. 39 p. front., illus. 24 x 18 1/2 cm. 1942. David McKay Company.
Shinn, George W
--Stories for the Happy Days of Christmas Time. (Whittaker's Select Bks). 1888. Thomas Whittaker.
Shipley, Arthur Hayes
--Gray Shadow. Shipley, David B., illus. LC 78-78376. v, 181 p. 23cm. c.1979. (ISBN 0-914330-19-5). Pioneer Pub. Co. : Distributed by Wild Life Books.
Shipley, C. L.
--The Jade Piccolo. 1969. (ISBN 0-689-10251-8). Atheneum Publishers.
Shipley, Mary E
--The Desolate Shore: A Story for Boys. (Illus., Pub. by Society for Promoting Christian Knowledge). N.D. E & J B Young.
--Jessie's Work. 224p. N.D. American Tract Society.
--Jessie's Work. (Faithfulness in Little Things). N.D. D. Appleton & Co.
--Jessie's Work: Faithfulness In Little Things. N.D. Bradley & Woodruff.
--Jessie's Work: Or,Faithfulness in Little Things. N.D. E. P. Dutton.
--True to Herself: A Tale. (Illus.). N.D. Society for Promoting Christian Knowledge.
Shipley, Nancy Sommerville
--The Scarlet Lily. LC 59-8822. 234 p. 22cm. 1959. F. Fell.
Shipman, Dorothy M., ed.
--Stardust & Holly: Poems & Songs of Christmas. LC 32-28093. Repr. of 1932 ed (Pub. by Macmillan). (Granger Poetry Library). 1976. (ISBN 0-89609-050-7). Granger Bk.
Shipman, Helen Barham, Mrs. (1892-)
--Kurly Kew and the Tree-Princess: A Story of the Forest-People, Told for Other-People. LC 30-30234. 5 p. l., 9-200, 1 p. col. front., illus., col. plates. 20 cm. 1930. L. MacVeagh, The Dial Press.
Shippen, Katherine Binney (1892-1980)
--Big Mose. 1st ed. Graham, Margaret Bloy (1920-), illus. LC 52-12997. 90p. illus. 22cm. 1953. Harper.

--Baby Chimp's Chocolate Cake. Clarke, Peter Brian (1932-), illus. LC 80-19167. p. cm. (Acorn magic readers). c.1980. Collier Books.
--Baby Elephant's Yellow Hat. Clarke, Peter Brian (1932-), illus. LC 80-19155. p. cm. (Acorn Magic Readers). c.1980. Collier Books.
--A Bath in the Mud. Clarke, Peter Brian (1932-), illus. LC 80-19264. p. cm. (Acorn magic readers). c.1980. Collier Books.
--First Story. Wasmuth, Eleanor, illus. (Illus.). 48p. (Macmillan Learning Window Book Ser.). (ps-k). 1982. (ISBN 0-02-782580-9). Macmillan.
--Little Lion's New TV. Clarke, Peter Brian (1932-), illus. LC 80-19153. p. cm. (Acorn magic readers). c.1980. Collier Books.
--The Little Red Ducks. Clarke, Peter Brian (1932-), illus. LC 80-19051. p. cm. (Acorn magic readers). c.1980. Collier Books.
--More Very First Stories with Hilary Hippo & Friends. 117p. N.D. Macmillan.
--The Upside-Down Book. Clarke, Peter Brian (1932-), illus. LC 80-19265. p. cm. (Acorn magic readers). c.1980. Collier Books.
--Very First Stories with Pamela Pig & Friends. 121p. 1980 (Collier). Macmillan.

Shreve, Susan Richards (1939-)
--The Bad Dreams of a Good Girl. De'Groat, Diane (1947-), illus. LC 81-8359. (Illus.). 92 p. 22cm. c.1982. (ISBN 0-394-84777-6). (ISBN 0-394-94777-0). Knopf : Distributed by Random House.
--Children of Power. 1979. (ISBN 0-02-610510-1). Macmillan.
--Family Secrets: Five Very Important Series. Cuffari, Richard (1925-1978), illus. LC 78-12471. (Illus.). 56 p. 22cm. c.1979. (ISBN 0-394-83896-3). (ISBN 0-394-93896-8). Knopf : Distributed by Random House. **Award: (ALA).**
--The Flunking of Joshua T. Bates. De Groat, Diane (1947-), illus. LC 83-19636. (Illus.). 96p. (gr. 2-6). 1984. (ISBN 0-394-86380-1). (ISBN 0-394-96380-6). Knopf.
--How I Saved the World on Purpose. Richardson, Suzanne, illus. LC 84-25154. (Illus.). 65 p. 22cm. c.1985. (ISBN 0-03-070456-1). Holt, Rinehart, and Winston.
--Loveletters: A Novel. LC 77-15514. 217 p. 22cm. c.1978. (ISBN 0-394-83707-X). (ISBN 0-394-93707-4). Knopf : Distributed by Random House.
--The Masquerade: A Novel. LC 79-20073. 184 p. 22cm. c.1980. (ISBN 0-394-94142-X). Knopf : Distributed by Random House.
--The Nightmares of Geranium Street. LC 77-4568. 127 p. 22cm. c.1977. (ISBN 0-394-83435-6). (ISBN 0-394-93435-0). Knopf.
--The Revolution of Mary Leary. LC 82-185. 185 p. 22cm. c.1982. (ISBN 0-394-84776-8). (ISBN 0-394-94776-2). Distributed by Random House.

Shrisharani, Krishnalal
--The Adventures of the Upside Down Tree. N.D. Taplinger Publishing Co., Inc.

Shryock, Meredith G.
--Ponyo Finds a Wild One. (Illus.). 62p. (gr. 3-6). 1968. Vantage.

Shtainmets, Leon
--The Story of Ricky, the Royal Dwarf. 1st ed. Shtainmets, Leon, illus. LC 75-21671. (Illus.). 48 p. 24cm. c.1976. (ISBN 0-06-025647-8). Harper & Row.

Shtainmets, Leon, retold by see Andersen, Hans Christian.

Shub, Elizabeth
--Seeing is Believing. Isadora, Rachel, illus. 1979. Greenwillow.
--The White Stallion. Isadora, Rachel, illus. LC 81-20308. p. cm. (Greenwillow Read-Alone Books). c.1982. (ISBN 0-688-01210-8). (ISBN 0-688-01211-6). Greenwillow Books. **Award: (ALA).**

Shub, Elizabeth, adapted by.
--The Adventures of Little Mouk. Laimgruber, Monika (1946-), illus. Shub, Elizabeth, tr. LC 74-4420. (Original Author: William Hauff (1802-1872)). (Illus.). 36 p. 29cm. 1975, c.1974. (ISBN 0-02-743400-1). Macmillan.
--Uncle Harry. Fromm, Lilo (1928-), illus. LC 79-181575. (Original Author:Gerlinde Schneider). (Illus.). 32 p. 1972. (ISBN 0-02-781230-8). Macmillan.

Shub, Elizabeth, adapted by see Bolliger-Savelli, Antonella.
Shub, Elizabeth, adapted by see Grimm, Jakob Ludwig Karl (1785-1863) & Grimm, Wilhelm Karl.
Shub, Elizabeth, adapted by see Konopka, Ursula & Guggenmos, Josef.
Shub, Elizabeth, adapted by see Shulevitz, Uri (1935-) & Rands, William Brighty.
Shub, Elizabeth, tr. see Borchers, Elisabeth.
Shub, Elizabeth, tr. see Du Bois, William Sherman Pene.
Shub, Elizabeth, tr. see Fontane, Theodor.
Shub, Elizabeth, tr. see Grimm, Jakob Ludwig Karl (1785-1863) & Grimm, Wilhelm Karl.
Shub, Elizabeth, tr. see Hasler, Eveline.
Shub, Elizabeth, tr. see Janosch.
Shub, Elizabeth, tr. see Rabinovitch, Sholem.
Shub, Elizabeth, tr. see Singer, Isaac Bashevis.
Shub, Elizabeth, tr. see Vincent, Gabrielle.

Shufen, Li
--Two Lambs. Cheng'an, Jiang, tr. (Illus.). 24. 24p. (Orig.). (gr. 2-4). 1982. (ISBN 0-8351-1202-0). China Bks.

Shuford, Mary Frances
--Midge. LC 29-3974. 4 p. l., 245, 1 p. front. 19 1/2 cm. 1929. D. Appleton & Company.

Shulevitz, Uri (1935-), adapted by see Peretz, Isaac Loeb.
Shulevitz, Uri (1935-), adapted by see Rabinovitch, Sholem.

Shulevitz, Uri (1935-)
--Dawn. Shulevitz, Uri (1935-), illus. LC 74-9761. (Illus.). 32 p. 1974. (ISBN 0-374-31707-0). Farrar, Straus and Giroux. **Award: (IBBY).**
--The Moon in My Room. LC 63-16242. 32p. (ps-1). 1963. (ISBN 0-06-025645-1, HarpJ). (ISBN 0-06-025646-X). Har-Row.
--One Monday Morning. Shulevitz, Uri (1935-), illus. (Illus.). 46 p. 26cm. 1967. Scribner.
--Rain Rain Rivers. Shulevitz, Uri (1935-), illus. LC 73-85370. (Illus.). 32 p. 1969. Farrar, Straus, and Giroux. **Award: (ALA).**
--Rain Rain Rivers. Shulevitz, Uri (1935-), illus. 1967. Scribner's.
--Soldier and Tsar in the Forest: A Russian Tale. 1st ed. Shulevitz, Uri (1935-), illus. Lourie, Richard, tr. LC 72-188254. (Illus.). 32 p. 26cm. 1972. (ISBN 0-374-37126-1). Farrar, Straus, and Giroux.
--The Treasure. Shulevitz, Uri (1935-), illus. LC 78-12952. p. cm. 1979. (ISBN 0-374-37740-5). Farrar, Straus and Giroux. **Awards: (NYT); (ALA).**

Shulevitz, Uri (1935-) & Rands, William Brighty (1823-1882)
--Oh What a Noise!. Shub, Elizabeth, adapted by. Shulevitz, Uri (1935-), illus. LC 72-146629. 32 p. (chiefly col. illus). 26cm. 1971. Macmillan.

Shulman, Alix Kates (1932-)
--Awake or Asleep. Bozzo, Frank, illus. (Illus.). 24 color ils. 48p. (gr. k-2). 1971. (ISBN 0-201-09106-2, A-W Childrens). A-W.
--Bosley on the Number Line. Wennerstrom, Genia Katherine (1930-), illus. Genia, pseud. LC 71-125654. (Illus.). vii, 80 p. 21cm. 1970. McKay.
--Finders Keepers. McCully, Emily Arnold (1939-), illus. LC 71-155997. (Illus.). 3 color halftones. line drawings. 32p. (ps-2). 1971. (ISBN 0-87888-034-8). Bradbury Pr.

Shulman, Milton (1913-)
--Preep & the Queen. Maxey, Dale (1927-), illus. LC 72-136588. (Illus.). color ils. 48p. (gr. k-2). 1971. (ISBN 0-394-82137-8). (ISBN 0-394-92137-2). Random.
--Preep, the Little Pigeon of Trafalgar Square. Maxey, Dale (1927-), illus. LC 63-11947. 42 p. col. illus. 29 cm. 1964. (ISBN 0-394-91526-7). Random House.

Shultz, J. W.
--Bird Woman. N.D. Houghton Mifflin Co.
--Short Bow's Big Medicine. N.D. Houghton Mifflin Co.

Shumaker, Elmer F.
--Adventures of Casper the Cat: Catcher of Communists. N.D. Carlton.
--Casper Goes to The Farm. N.D. Carlton Press.
--Here is Casper. N.D. Carlton Press.

Shumaker, Esther
--Gray Lady, the 'roo & Other Stories. (Illus.). 32p. (gr. 3-6). 1968. Vantage.

Shuman, Ruth Lewis
--Penny and Pete's Surprise. McKinley, Clare, illus. LC 49-10180. 21cm. 32p. N.D. Rand McNally & Co.

Shumate, Aurora M., jt. auth. see Grice, Homer L.

Shumate, Aurora Medford, Mrs. (1880-), compiled by.
--Glad Days. N.D. Broadman Press.
--Songs for the Pre-School Age. N.D. Baptist Sunday School Board.
--Songs for the Pre-School Age. 1941. Broadman Press.

Shumsky, Lou
--First Fight. Barth, Ernest Kurt, illus. LC 62-16178. 21cm. 147p. 1962. Funk & Wagnalls.

Shumsky, Lou & Shumsky, Zena (1926-)
--Problem Father (Pub. by Funk&W). Orig. Title: First Flight. (gr. 4-6). 1972 (Starline). Schol Bk Serv.
--Shutterbug. Collier, Zena. Donahue, Vic, illus. LC 63-15394. 117 p. illus. 22 cm. 1963. Funk & Wagnalls.

Shumsky, Zena, jt. auth. see Shumsky, Lou.
Shumsky, Zena Feldman see Collier, Jane, pseud.

Shumsky, Zena Feldman (1926-)
--A Tangled Web. Collier, Jane, pseud. Korach, Mimi (1922-), illus. LC 67-3910. (Illus.). 127 p. 22cm. 1967. Funk & Wagnalls.

Shumway, Harry Irving (1883-)
--The Wonderful Voyages of Cap'n Pen. Strothmann, F., illus. LC 29-18551. 6 p. l., 3-275 p. front., plates. 20 cm. 1929. Little, Brown, and Company.

Shura, Mary Francis, pseud., see Craig, Mary Francis.

Shura, Mary Francis (1923-)
--Backwards for Luck. CoConis, Ted, pseud., illus. CoConis, Constantinos. LC 67-18591. 133 p. illus. 22 cm. 1967. Knopf.
--The Barkley Street Six-Pack. Sparkman, Gene, illus. LC 79-52043. (Illus.). 159 p. 21cm. c.1979. (ISBN 0-396-07714-5). Dodd, Mead.
--Chester. Swan, Susan Elizabeth (1944-), illus. LC 79-6633. (Illus.). 92 p. 21cm. c.1980. (ISBN 0-396-07800-1). Dodd, Mead.
--Eleanor. Swan, Susan Elizabeth (1944-), illus. LC 82-19795. p. cm. 1983. (ISBN 0-396-08116-9). Dodd, Mead.
--Garret of Greta McGraw. Goldstein, Leslie, illus. (Illus.). illus. 21 cm. 114p. (gr. 4-7). 1961. (ISBN 0-394-91181-4). Knopf.
--The Gray Ghosts of Taylor Ridge. Hampshire, Michael Allen, illus. LC 77-16861. (Illus.). 128 p. 21cm. c.1978. (ISBN 0-396-07526-6). Dodd, Mead.
--Happles and Cinnamunger. Tormey, Bertram M., illus. LC 81-43223. p. cm. 1981. (ISBN 0-396-08002-2). Dodd, Mead.
--Jefferson. Craig, Mary Francis. Swan, Susan Elizabeth (1944-), illus. LC 83-27496. 1984. (ISBN 0-396-08326-9). Dodd.
--Jessica. 368p. (gr. 7 up). 1984. (ISBN 0-590-33242-2, Sunfire). Scholastic Inc.
--Mary's Marvelous Mouse. Adams, Adrienne (1906-), illus. LC 62-9468. (Illus.). 22cm. (Read Alone Bks). (gr. k-3). 1962. (ISBN 0-394-91396-5). Knopf.
--Mister Wolf and Me. Hack, Konrad, illus. LC 78-22432. (Illus.). 126 p. 21cm. c.1979. (ISBN 0-396-07666-1). Dodd, Mead.
--The Nearsighted Knight. Adams, Adrienne (1906-), illus. LC 63-9111. 111 p. illus. 21 cm. 1964. Knopf.
--Pornada. Schachner, Erwin, illus. LC 68-18459. (Illus.). 69 p. 23cm. 1968. Atheneum.
--The Riddle of Raven Hollow. 126p. (Cat's Eye Mysteries Ser.). Orig. Title: The Riddle of Raven's Gulch. (gr. 3-6). 1983. (ISBN 0-590-32784-4). Scholastic Inc.
--Riddle of Raven Hollow. Tamer, Salem, illus (Pub. by Dodd, Mead). (gr. 4-6). 1976. (ISBN 0-590-03568-1, Schol Pap). Scholastic Inc.
--The Riddle of Raven's Gulch. Tamer, Salem, illus. LC 74-25513. (Illus.). 124 p. 21cm. 1975. (ISBN 0-396-07069-8). Dodd, Mead.
--Run Away Home. Spanfeller, James John (1930-), illus. LC 65-11968. 135 p. illus. 21 cm. 1965. A. A. Knopf; Distributed by Random House.
--The Search for Grissi. Lewin, Ted (1935-), illus. LC 84-28624. (Illus.). 128 p. 21cm. c.1985. (ISBN 0-396-08584-9). (ISBN 0-396-08584-9). Dodd, Mead.
--The Season of Silence. 1st ed. Sanderson, Ruth, illus. LC 75-23194. (Illus.). 123 p. 22cm. 1976. (ISBN 0-689-30513-3). Atheneum.
--The Seven Stone. Payson, Dale (1943-), illus. LC 72-80653. (Illus.). 64 p. 23cm. 1972. (ISBN 0-8234-0214-2). Holiday House.
--Shoe Full of Shamrock. Bodecker, Niels Mogens (1922-), illus. LC 65-21712. (Illus.). 26cm. 64p. (gr. 2-6). 1965. (ISBN 0-689-20384-5). (ISBN 0-689-20385-3). Atheneum.
--Simple Spigott. Tomes, Jacqueline, illus. (Illus.). 21cm. 90p. (gr. 2-5). 1960. (ISBN 0-394-81627-7). (ISBN 0-394-91627-1). Knopf.
--A Tale of Middle Length. Parnall, Peter (1936-), illus. LC 66-5714. (Illus.). (gr. 3-7). 1966. (ISBN 0-689-20386-1). (ISBN 0-689-20388-8). Atheneum.
--Top Cat. Robinson, Charles (1931-), illus. (Illus.). (gr. 4-6). 1975. (ISBN 0-590-00068-3, Schol Trade Pap). Schol Bk Serv.
--Topcat of Tam. Robinson, Charles (1931-), illus. LC 71-179096. (Illus.). 63 p. 23cm. 1972. (ISBN 0-8234-0198-7). Holiday House.
--The Valley of the Frost Giants. Keeping, Charles William James (1924-), illus. LC 72-116337. (Illus.). 48 p. 26cm. 1971. Lothrop, Lee & Shepard.

Shurfranz, Vivian
--Danielle. 368p. (gr. 7 up). 1984. (ISBN 0-590-33156-6, Sunfire). Scholastic Inc.

Shurtleff, Bertrand Leslie (1897-)
--Awol,the Rajah. 1st ed. Thorne, Diana (1894-), illus. LC 48-18221. 274 p. illus. 21 cm. 1948. Bobbs-Merrill Co.
--Ten Fathoms by Scuba. 1st ed. Pope, Miller, illus. LC 63-11663. 192 p. illus. 22 cm. 1963. Bobbs-Merrill.

Shute, E. L.
--Jappie Chappie. Shute, E. L., illus. 1887. Frederick Warne & Co.

Shute, Henry Augustus (1856-1943)
--Brite and Fair. Brehm, Worth, illus. LC 20-17526. 4 p. l., 274 p. front., plates. 19 1/2 cm. 1920. Cosmopolitan Book Corporation.
--Brite and Fair. Tudor, Tasha (1915-), illus. LC 68-22886. (Sequel to The Real Diary of a Real Boy). (Illus.). xii, 286 p. 20cm. 1968. Noone House.
--Chadwick and Shute. LC 28-186. 234 p. 19 1/2cm. c.1927. Dorrance & Co.
--A Country Lawyer. Deremeaux, Irma, illus. N.D. Houghton Mifflin.
--Letters to Beany and the Love-Letters of Plupy Shute. LC 5-36118. 1 p. l., 176 p. 16 cm. 1905. The Everett Press.
--The Misadventures of Three Good Boys: That Is to Say, Fairly Good Boys. Gallagher, Sears (1869-1955), illus. LC 14-9084. vi p., 2 l., 280 p., 1 l. front., plates, group of ports. 19 cm. 1914. Houghton Mifflin Company.
--Plupy "the Real Boy". Rockwell, Warren, illus. LC 10-22861. 368 p. incl. illus., plates. front. 19 1/2 cm. 1911. R. G. Badger.
--Real Boys. Gruger, F. R., illus. LC 5-26224. 19cm. 257p. 1905. G W Dillingham.
--Real Boys. Being the Doings of Plupy, Beany, Pewt, Puzzy, Whack, Bug, Skinny, Chick, Pop, Pile, and Some of the Girls. Gruger, F. R., illus. LC 20-18825. 3 p. l., 9-257 p. illus. 19 1/2 cm. 1905. M. A. Donohue & Company.
--The Real Diary of a Real Boy. 12th ed. LC 2-27422. v. 135 p. 16 1/2 cm. 1902. The Everett Press.
--The Real Diary of a Real Boy. 3d. ed. LC 3-7162. v, 154 p. 16 1/2 cm. 1903. The Everett Press.
--The Real Diary of a Real Boy. 12th ed. LC 7-7194. 5 p. l., 5-200 p. front., plates. 20 cm. 1906. The Everett Press Company.
--The Real Diary of a Real Boy. 16th ed. LC 16-3397. 5 p. l., 5-200 p. front., plates, ports, 19 1/2 cm. 1914. The Everett Press Company.
--The Real Diary of a Real Boy. Tudor, Tasha (1915-), illus. LC 67-27745. (Illus.). xiii, 194 p. 20cm. 1967. R. R. Smith Co.
--Sequil: Or, things Whitch Aint Finished in the First. LC 4-35726. 1 p. l., 189 p. 16 1/2 cm. 1904. The Everett Press.
--The Youth Plupy: Or, the Lad with the Downy Chin. Birch, Reginald Bathurst (1856-1943), illus. N.D. Houghton Mifflin.

Shute, Katharine H., ed. see Jewett, Sarah Orne.

Shuten, Doji
--O-E Yama: The Story of General Raiko and the Ogres of O-E Yama. N.D. International Pub.

Shutter, Lilly
--Dorinda's Diamonds. Reed, Veronica, pseud. (1916-), illus. Sherman, Theresa. LC 55-10007. 220p. illus. 21cm. 1955. T. Nelson.

Shuttleworth, Frank Kaylev, jt. ed. see Starbuck, Edwin Diller.
Shuttleworth, Frank Kayley, jt. ed. see Starbuck, Edwin Diller.

Shvarts, Evgenii Livovich
--A Tale of Stolen Time. Hogrogian, Nonny (1932-), illus. Pargment, Lila (1932-) & Titiev, Estelle, trs. LC 66-10817. 1v. (unpaged) col. illus. 16x21cm. c.1966. Prentice.
--Two Brothers. Lisowski, Gabriel (1946-), illus. Hapgood, Elizabeth Reynolds, tr. from Rus. LC 72-9868. (Illus.). 48p. (gr. 1-5). 1973. (ISBN 0-06-025248-0, HarpJ). (ISBN 0-06-025249-9). Har-Row.

Shyer, Marlene Fanta
--Adorable Sunday. LC 82-24049. 182 p. 22cm. c.1983. (ISBN 0-684-17848-6). Scribner.
--Blood in the Snow. Smith, Maggie Kaufman, illus. LC 75-14370. (Illus.). 124 p. 22cm. 1975. (ISBN 0-395-21929-9). Houghton Mifflin.
--Grandpa Ritz and the Luscious Lovelies. LC 85-2332. 170 p. 22cm. c.1985. (ISBN 0-684-18408-7). Scribner.
--My Brother, the Thief. LC 80-343. 138 p. 22cm. c.1980. (ISBN 0-684-16434-5). Scribner.
--Stepdog. Schremer, Judith, illus. LC 83-11649. p. cm. 1983. (ISBN 0-684-17998-9). Scribner.
--Tino. Palmer, Jańice, illus. LC 77-75882. (Illus.). 131 p. 22cm. 1969. Random House.
--Welcome Home, Jellybean. LC 77-17970. 152 p. 22cm. c.1978. (ISBN 0-684-15519-2). Scribner.

Sian-Tek, Lim
--Folk Tales from China. Smith, William Arthur (1918-), illus. 160p. (gr. 6-9). 1944. John Day Books.
--More Folk Tales from China. Smith, William Arthur (1918-), illus. 160p. (gr. 6-9). 1948. John Day Books.

Sibee, Marie
--Dying Saviour and the Gipsy Girl. N.D. Methodist Book Concern.

Siberell, Anne
--Whale in the Sky. LC 82-2483. (Illus.). 32 p. 27cm. c.1982. (ISBN 0-525-44021-6). Dutton.

Sibley, Jacqueline
--Jonathan Mark at Home. (gr. 5-8). N.D. Tyndale.
--Jonathan Mark at the Beach. (gr. 5-8). N.D. (ISBN 0-8423-1954-9). Tyndale.
--Jonathan Mark at the Doctors. (gr. 5-8). N.D. (ISBN 0-8423-1951-4). Tyndale.
--Jonathan Mark in the Kitchen. (gr. 5-8). N.D. (ISBN 0-8423-1953-0). Tyndale.
--Jonathan Mark in the Park. (gr. 5-8). N.D. Tyndale.

Siceloff, David G.
--Boy Settler on the Cherokee Strip. Dunn, C. Alfred, illus. (Illus.). 249p. 1964. Caxton Printers, Ltd.

--The Shores of Tomorrow. LC 76-28486. 1st U.S. edition. (Nelson's Science Fiction Ser). (gr. 7 up). 1976. (ISBN 0-8407-6525-8). Elsevier-Nelson.
--Starman's Quest. LC 58-8767. 185 p. 21 cm. c.1958. Gnome Press.
--Starman's Quest. 2d ed. LC 70-93842. 186 p. 21cm. 1969. Meredith Press.
--The Stochastic Man. LC 75-6378. 236p. 1975. (ISBN 0-06-013868-8, HarpT). Har-Row.
--Strange Gifts: Eight Stories of Science Fiction. LC 75-14036. 192p. (Nelson's Science Fiction Ser.). (gr. 6 up). 1975. (ISBN 0-525-66460-2). Lodestar Bks.
--Sundance and Other Science Fiction Stories. LC 74-3343. 192 p. 22cm. 1974. (ISBN 0-8407-6386-7). T. Nelson.
--Sunrise on Mercury, and Other Science Fiction Stories. LC 74-31021. 175 p. 22cm. 1975. (ISBN 0-8407-6445-6). T. Nelson.
--Sunrise on Mercury & Other Science Fiction Stories: A Science Fiction Anthology. LC 74-31021. 224p. 1975. (ISBN 0-525-66445-9). Lodestar Bks.
--Thorns. LC 69-13671. 222 p. 22cm. 1969, c.1967. Walker.
--Three Survived. LC 69-11814. 117 p. 22cm. 1969. Holt, Rinehart and Winston.
--Time of the Great Freeze. 1st ed. LC 64-14345. 192 p. 22cm. 1964. Holt, Rinehart and Winston.
--Tomorrow's Worlds: Ten Stories of Science Fiction. (gr. 7 up). 1969. (ISBN 0-696-83764-1). Hawthorn.
--Trips in Time: Nine Stories of Science Fiction. LC 77-24213. (Nelson Science Fiction Ser.). (gr. 7 up). 1977. (ISBN 0-525-66574-9). Lodestar Bks.
--World's Fair, Nineteen Ninety-Two. new ed. Endewelt, Jack, illus. LC 76-85947. (Illus.). frontispiece. 224p. (gr. 7 up). 1970. (ISBN 0-695-80089-2). (ISBN 0-695-40089-4). Follett.
--Worlds of Maybe: Seven Stories of Science Fiction. LC 73-123115. 1970. (ISBN 0-8407-6104-X). Nelson.

Silver Dollar City, Inc., ed. see Wiskur, Darrell D.

Silverman, Althea Osber
--Habibi and Yow: A Little Boy and His Dog. Robinson, Jessie Berkowitz, illus. LC 46-6386. 108 p. illus. 26 x 20 1/2 cm. 1946. (ISBN 0-8197-0257-9). Bloch Publishing Company.
--Habibi's Adventures in the Land of Israel. Robinson, Jessie Berkowitz, illus. LC 51-766. 202 p. illus. 22 cm. 1951. Bloch Pub. Co.
--The Harp of David. (gr. 3-7). N.D. (ISBN 0-87677-135-5). Prayer Bk.

Silverman, Maida
--Anna & the Seven Swans. Frumin, Natasha, retold by. Small, David (1945-), illus. LC 83-27296. (Illus.). 32p. (ps-3). 1984. (ISBN 0-688-02755-5, Morrow Junior Books). (ISBN 0-688-02756-3). Morrow.
--The Get Along Gang & the Bad Loser. Chandler, Jean (1927-), illus. (Illus.). 32p. (Orig.). (Get Along Gang Ser.). (ps-2). 1984. (ISBN 0-590-33189-2). Scholastic Inc.

Silverman, Melvin Frank (1931-1966)
--Ciri-Biri-Bin. Silverman, Melvin Frank (1931-1966), illus. LC 57-9466. 40p. 1957. World Pub. Co.
--Good-for-Nothing Burro. Silverman, Melvin Frank (1931-1966), illus. LC 58-11153. (Illus.). unpaged. 24cm. 1958. World Pub. Co.
--Hymie's Fiddle. Silverman, Melvin Frank (1931-1966), illus. 48p. 1960. The World Publishing Co.

Silverman, Stanley H.
--Dexter. Daly, George, illus. 1941. Golden Press.
--Dexter. Daly, George, illus. LC 41-22779. 63 p. illus. (part. col.) 22 x 17 cm. c.1941. Simon and Schuster.

Silverpen, pseud., see Meteyard, Eliza.

Silvers, Earl Reed (1891-)
--At Hillsdale High. LC 22-18162. 4 p. l., 269, 1 p. front. 19 1/2 cm. 1922. D. Appleton and Company.
--Barry and Budd. LC 25-196228. 4 p. l., 247, 1 p. front. 19 1/2 cm. 1925. D. Appleton and Company.
--Barry Goes to College. LC 28-10864. 4 p. l., 245, 1 p. front. 19 1/2 cm. 1928. D. Appleton & Company.
--Barry the Undaunted. LC 24-7951. 4 p. l., 262, 1 p. front. 19 1/2 cm. 1924. D. Appleton and Company.
--Carol of Cranford High. LC 30-52461. 4 p. l., 243, 1 p. front. 19 1/2 cm. 1930. D. Appleton & Company.
--Carol of Highland Camp. LC 27-171201. 5 p. l., 3-277 p. front. 19 1/2 cm. 1927. D. Appleton & Company.
--Code of Honor. Warren, Ferdinand E., illus. LC 32-944325. vii, 1 p., 1 l., 245, 1 p. front., illus. 19 1/2 cm. 1932. D. Appleton & Company.
--Dick Arnold of Raritan College. LC 20-7921. 4 p. l., 258, 1 p. col. front. 19 1/2 cm. 1920. D. Appleton and Company.
--Dick Arnold of the Varsity. LC 21-15889. vii, 257, 1 p. col. front. 19 1/2 cm. 1921. D. Appleton & Company.
--Dick Arnold Plays the Game. LC 20-171840. vii, 249, 1 p. col. front. 19 1/2 cm. 1920. D. Appleton and Company.
--The Glory of Glenwood. Hall, T. Victor, illus. LC 31-5061. 5 p. l., 269, 1 p. front., illus. 19 1/2 cm. 1931. D. Appleton & Company.
--The Hillsdale High Champions. LC 25-7197. 4 p. l., 273 p. 19 1/2 cm. 1925. D. Appleton and Company.
--Jackson of Hillsdale High. LC 23-13886. 4 p. l., 250, 1 p. front. 19 1/2 cm. 1923. D. Appleton & Company.
--The Menlo Mystery. LC 26-16047. 4 p. l., 206 p. front. 19 1/2 cm. 1926. D. Appleton & Company.
--Ned Beals, Freshman. 4 p. l., 237, 1 p. front. 19 1/2 cm. 1922. D. Appleton & Company.
--Ned Beals Works His Way. LC 23-732286. 4 p. l., 242, 1 p. front. 19 1/2 cm. 1923. D. Appleton & Company.
--The Red-Headed Halfback. LC 29-17262. vii, 1 p., 1 l., 275, 1 p. front 19 1/2 cm. 1929. D. Appleton and Company.
--The Scarlet of Avalon. LC 30-213299. 6 p. l., 3-266, 1 p. front., illus. 20 cm. 1930. D. Appleton & Company.
--The Spirit of Menlo: A Story of the Heart of a Boy. LC 26-67381. viii p., 2 l., 3-258 p. front. 19 1/2 cm. 1926. D. Appleton & Company.
--Team First. LC 29-795725. 4 p. l., 247, 1 p. front. 19 1/2 cm. 1929. D. Appleton & Company.

Silvers, Vicki (1941-)
--Sing a Song of Sound. Ehlert, Lois Jane (1934-), illus. LC 72-90695. (Illus.). 32p. (ps-2). 1973. (ISBN 0-87592-046-2). Scroll Pr.

Silverstein, Ruth
--Kirby Koala Visits Grandma. Garris, Norma, et al., illus. (Illus.). 22p. (Kirby Koala Ser.). (ps-3). 1984. (ISBN 0-89954-275-1). Antioch Pub Co.

Silverstein, Sara Malka Solomon
--Every Day Poems for the Jewish Child. LC 82-112500. (Illus.). 39 p. 26cm. 1980. (ISBN 0-89655-050-8). B'Ruach HaTorah Publications.

Silverstein, Shel see Silverstein, Shelby

Silverstein, Shel see Uncle Shelby, pseud.

Silverstein, Shel (1932-)
--A Light in the Attic. Uncle Shelby, pseud. 1st ed. Silverstein, Shelby (1932-), illus. Uncle Shelby, pseud. LC 80-8453. p. cm. c.1981. (ISBN 0-06-025673-7). (ISBN 0-06-025674-5). Harper & Row. **Award: (ALA).**

Silverstein, Shelby see Uncle Shelby, pseud.

Silverstein, Shelby (1932-)
--The Giving Tree. Silverstein, Shelby (1932-), illus. LC 64-11840. (Illus.). 57 p. 23cm. 1964. Harper & Row.
--The Missing Piece. Silverstein, Shelby (1932-), illus. LC 75-37408. (Illus.). 105 p. 23cm. c.1976. (ISBN 0-06-025671-0). Harper & Row.
--The Missing Piece Meets the Big O. Silverstein, Shelby (1932-), illus. LC 80-8721. (Illus.). 98 p. 22cm. c.1981. (ISBN 0-06-025657-5). (ISBN 0-06-025658-3). Harper & Row.
--Uncle Shelby's "A Giraffe and a Half". Silverstein, Shelby (1932-), illus. 1964. (ISBN 0-8382-1059-7, Cadmus Books). E. M. Hale and Company.
--Uncle Shelby's "A Giraffe & a Half. Uncle Shelby, pseud. Silverstein, Shelby (1932-), illus. Uncle Shelby, pseud. LC 64-19709. (Illus.). (gr. k-3). 1964. (ISBN 0-06-025655-9, HarpJ). (ISBN 0-06-025656-7). Har-Row.
--Uncle Shelby's ABZ Book: A Primer for Tender Young Minds. Silverstein, Shelby (1932-), illus. LC 61-15128. unpaged illus. 28 cm. 1961. Simon and Schuster.
--Uncle Shelby's Story of Lafcadio, the Lion Who Shot Back. LC 62-13320. (Illus.). (gr. 1-5). 1963. (ISBN 0-06-025675-3, HarpJ). (ISBN 0-06-025676-1). Har-Row.
--Uncle Shelby's Zoo: Don't Bump the Glump!. Uncle Shelby, pseud. Silverstein, Shelby (1932-), illus. Uncle Shelby, pseud. LC 64-12513. 62 p. col. illus. 23 cm. 1964. Simon and Schuster.
--Where the Sidewalk Ends. Silverstein, Shelby (1932-), illus. LC 73-105486. (Illus.). 176p. (gr. k-3). 1974. (ISBN 0-06-025667-2, HarpJ). (ISBN 0-06-025668-0). Har-Row.
--Who Wants a Cheap Rhinoceros?. Uncle, Shelby, pseud. rev. and expanded. Silverstein, Shelby (1932-), illus. Uncle Shelby, pseud. LC 82-23945. (Illus.). 56 p. c.1983. (ISBN 0-02-782690-2). Macmillan.

Silverstein, Solomon, jt. auth. see Malka, Sora.

Silverstone, Marilyn & Miller, Luree (1926-)
--Bala: Child of India. Silverstone, Marilyn, photos by. LC 68-13445. (Illus.). 44 photos. 48p. 1st U.S. edition. (Children Everywhere Ser.: No. 4). (gr. 2-4). 1968, c.1962. (ISBN 0-8038-0670-1). Hastings.

Silverthorne, Elizabeth (1930-)
--The Ghost of Padre Island. Anderson, Dennis, illus. LC 74-13180. (Illus.). 174 p. 23cm. 1975. (ISBN 0-687-14221-0). Abingdon Press.
--I, Heracles. Osborne, Billie Jean, illus. LC 78-1811. (Illus.). 128 p. 21cm. c.1978. (ISBN 0-687-18459-2). Abingdon.

Silvester, M. Genevieve
--Stories New and Old. LC 37-154671. 345 p. col. front., col. illus. 20 1/2 cm. c.1930. Whitman Publishing Co.

Silvester, M. Genevieve & Peter, Edith Marshall
--Happy Hour Stories. LC 22-409733. 112 p. col. illus. 19 cm. c.1921. American Book Company.

Silvis, Craig
--Rat Stew. Gusman, Annie, illus. LC 78-24815. (Illus.). 31 p. 1979. (ISBN 0-395-27803-1). Houghton Mifflin.

Sim, Margo
--Five Australian Native Animal Stories. 1984. (ISBN 0-533-06068-0). Vantage.

Simak, Clifford Donald, jt. auth. see Benford, Gregory Albert.

Simak, Clifford Donald (1904-)
--Goblin Reservation. 192p. (gr. 7 up). 1968. Putnam.

Simbari, Nicola (1927-)
--Gennarino. Simbari, Nicola (1927-), illus. LC 62-52099. (Illus.). unpaged. 30cm. 1962. Lippincott. **Award: (NYT).**

Simenon, Georges (1903-)
--Inspector Maigret & the Burglar's Wife. (Inspector Maigret Ser.: No.1). (gr. 8-12). 1970. Curtis.
--Inspector Maigret & the Killers. (Inspector Maigret Ser.: No. 3). (gr. 8-12). 1970. Curtis.
--Inspector Maigret & the Strangled Stripper. 133p (Pub. by Doubleday). (Inspector Maigret Ser.). (gr. 6-12). N.D. Curtis.
--Maigret Pickpocket. 200p. 1971. Curtis.
--Maigret's Boyhood Friend. 200p. 1971. Curtis.
--The Short Cases of Inspector Maigret (Pub. by Doubleday). (Inspector Maigret Ser. No. 4). (gr. 7-12). 1971. Curtis.
--Versus Inspector Maigret (Pub. by Doubleday). (Inspector Maigret: No. 4). (gr. 9-12). 1971. Curtis.

Simeons, Albert T. W. (1900-)
--Ramlal. Shore, Robert (1924-), illus. LC 65-217227. (Illus.). 22cm. 176p. (gr. 6 up). 1965. (ISBN 0-689-20392-6). (ISBN 0-689-20393-4). Atheneum.

Simhoni, S, ed.
--Legends of Ruth: Retold for Jewish Youth. Luizada, A., illus. Lask, I. M., tr. from Hebrew. LC 67-15344. 63 p. illus. 24 cm. c.1962. Shulsinger.
--Legends of Samson: Retold for Jewish Youth. Luizada, A., illus. Lask, I. M., tr. from Hebrew. LC 65-111736. 64 p. illus. 25 cm. c.1963. Shulsinger Bros.

Simister, Florence Parker (1913-)
--Daniel and Drum Rock. Coe, Lloyd (1899-1976), illus. LC 62-221231. 128p. illus. 22cm. c.1963. Hastings.
--Girl with a Musket. LC 59-7464. 116 p. illus. 22 cm. 1959. Hastings House.
--Pewter Plate. Coe, Lloyd (1899-1976), illus. LC 57-107354. (Illus.). (gr. 3-6). 1957. (ISBN 0-8038-5705-5). Hastings.

Simkins, Wallis
--The Little Cockalorum. Dunkelberger, Ralph, illus. LC 22-19166. 317 p. front., plates 19 1/2 cm. 1922. The Penn Publishing Company.
--The Little Cockalorum Crows Again. Dunkelberger, Ralph, illus. LC 23-14119. 340 p. front., plates. 19 1/2 cm. 1923. The Penn Publishing Company.
--The Little Cockalorum Finds Romance. Dunkelberger, Ralph, illus. LC 25-19909. v, 297 p. front., plates. 19 1/2 cm. 1925. The Penn Publishing Company.
--The Little Cockalorum on Her Own. Dunkelberger, Ralph, illus. LC 24-231715. 336 p. front., plates. 19 1/2 cm. 1924. The Penn Publishing Company.

Simko, Michael V
--The White Birch Mystery. LC 27-5941. iii, 275 p. 19 cm. c.1926. P. J. Kenedy & Sons.

Simmerman, Naoma, jt. auth. see Schuyler, Ruby.

Simmonds, William see Aimwell, Walter, pseud.

Simmons, Anthony (1922-)
--The Optimists of Nine Elms. Stahl, Ben F., illus. LC 74-15298. (Illus.). 62 p. 24cm. 1975, c.1974. (ISBN 0-394-83086-5). (ISBN 0-394-93086-X). Pantheon Books.

Simmons, Barbara
--The Noisy Number Robots. Brannon, Charles, illus. (Illus.). 48p. (Texas Instruments Magic Wand Speaking Library). (ps-3). 1982. (ISBN 0-89512-060-7). Tex Instr Inc.
--Zany Zingers: Texas Instruments Magic Wand Speaking Library. Yamada, Jane, illus. (Illus.). 49p. (ps-3). 1983. (ISBN 0-89512-086-0). Tex Instr Inc.

Simmons, Dawn Langley see Hall, Gordon Langley, pseud.

Simmons, Diane (1939-)
--Joanna, the Crowing Hen of Bethel: A Little Peasant Girl Meets the Boy Jesus and Follows His Advice. LC 78-12726. (Illus.). 56 p. 23cm. c.1979. (ISBN 0-570-07976-4). Concordia Pub.

Simmons, Ellie
--Cat. Simmons, Ellie, illus. LC 68-20184. (Illus.). 32p. (gr. k-1). 1968. (ISBN 0-679-20036-3). McKay.
--Dog: A Book You Can Read Before You Know How. LC 67-19908. 32 p. (chiefly illus. 14cm. 1967. McKay.
--Family. LC 79-97806. 26 p. (chiefly illus. 14cm. (Book you can read before you know how). 1970. D. McKay Co.
--Mary Changes Her Clothes. LC 60-6284. unpaged. illus. 25 cm. N.D. D. McKay Co.
--Mary, the Mouse Champion. Simmons, Ellie, illus. LC 62-20010. unpaged. illus. 24 cm. 1963. D. McKay Co.
--Wheels. Simmons, Ellie, illus. LC 69-13785. (Illus.). 24 p. 15cm. (Book you can read before you know how). 1969. McKay.

Simmons, F. J., adapted by see Asbjornsen, Peter Christen (1812-1885) & Moe, Jorgen Engebretsen.

Simmons, Henry Bradford
--The Jingle Jangle Rhyme Book. LC 98-797. 21 x 28cm. 18p. 1898. F. A. Stokes.

Simmons, Margaret Irwin, pseud., see Lansing, Elisabeth Carleton Hubbard.

Simmons, Margaret Irwin
--Kay Allen on Overseas Mission. 256p. 1945. Thomas Y. Crowell.

Simmons, Peter, tr. see Coleno, Alice.

Simmons, Peter, tr. see Isserlis, H. & Auroy, J.

Simmons, Willard B
--Elmer Elf. Giardini, Albert, illus. LC 52-35365. unpaged. illus. 19 cm. 1952. School of the Museum of Fine Arts Press.

Simms, Mary Jane (1868-)
--Lady Shepp and Her Friends. 3 p. l., 74 p. illus. 20 cm. 1906. The Democrat Press.

Simon
--Far Out Tales. (gr. 4-6). N.D. (ISBN 0-590-10126-9, Starline). Schol Bk Serv.

Simon, Bobby
--Just Like Daddy. Dart, Eleanor, illus. LC 52-40858. unpaged. illus. 21 cm. (Two-in-one Wonder book, 580). 1952. Wonder Books.

Simon, Charlie May, pseud., see Fletcher, Charlie May Hogue.

Simon, Charlie May, Mrs., pseud. (1897-)
--Arkansas Stories. Fletcher, Charlie May Hogue. 1st ed. Hagen, Lyman B, ed. O'Reilly, Susan, illus. LC 81-65366. (Illus.). 84 p. 24cm. 1981. (ISBN 0-935304-22-3). (ISBN 0-935304-47-9). August House.
--Bright Morning. Fletcher, Charlie May Hogue. Simon, Howard (1903-1979), illus. LC 39-6274. 241 p. illus. 20 1/2 cm. 1939. E. P. Dutton & Co., Inc.
--Christmas Every Friday, and Other Christmas Stories. Fletcher, Charlie May Hogue. Hagen, Lyman B., ed. O'Reilly, Susan, illus. LC 81-65364. (Illus.). 67 p. 24cm. 1981. (ISBN 0-935304-21-5). (ISBN 0-935304-46-0). August House.
--The Faraway Trail. Fletcher, Charlie May Hogue. Simon, Howard (1903-1979), illus. LC 40-336437. 212, 1 p. illus. 21 cm. 1940. E. P. Dutton and Company, Inc.
--Green Grows the Prairie: Arkansas in the 1890's. Fletcher, Charlie May. 1st ed. Crichlow, Ernest T. (1914-), illus. LC 56-5480. 192p. illus. 21cm. (American heritage series). 1956. Aladdin Books.
--Joe Mason, Apprentice to Audubon. Fletcher, Charlie May Hogue. Pitz, Henry Clarence (1895-1976), illus. LC 46-485418. 215 p. illus. 21 cm. 1946. E. P. Dutton and Company.
--The Long Hunt. Fletcher, Charlie May Hogue. 1st ed. Anderson, Rus, illus. LC 52-10037. (Illus.). 152 p. 21cm. 1952. Dutton.
--Lonnie's Landing. Fletcher, Charlie May Hogue. Simon, Howard (1903-1979), illus. LC 41-278894. 175, 1 p. illus. 21 cm. 1942. E. P. Dutton and Company, Inc.
--Lost Corner. Fletcher, Charlie May Hogue. Simon, Howard (1903-1979), illus. LC 35-14238. 6 p. l., 15-201, 1 p. illus. 19 1/2 cm. 1935. E. P. Dutton & Co., Inc.
--Popos Miracle. Fletcher, Charlie May Hogue. Simon, Howard (1903-1979), illus. LC 38-27325. 222, 1 p. col. front., illus., col. plates. 21 cm. 1938. E. P. Dutton & Co., Inc.
--Razorbacks Are Really Hogs. Fletcher, Charlie May Hogue. Vestal, Herman B., illus. LC 74-182272. (Illus.). 48 p. 23cm. 1972. (ISBN 0-8116-4034-5). Garrard Pub. Co.
--Robin on the Mountain. Fletcher, Charlie May Hogue. Simon, Howard (1903-1979), illus. LC 34-23273. 178 p. incl. illus., plates. 19 1/2 cm. c.1934. E. P. Dutton & Co., Inc.
--Roundabout. Fletcher, Charlie May Hogue. Simon, Howard (1903-1979), illus. LC 41-232127. 204, 1 p. illus. 21 cm. 1941. E. P. Dutton & Company, Inc.

--The Royal Road. Fletcher, Charlie May Hogue. 1st ed. Pitz, Henry Clarence (1895-1976), illus. LC 48-4141. 152 p. illus. 22 cm. 1948. E. P. Dutton.

--Secret on The Congo. Fletcher, Charlie May Hogue. (Ginn Book-Length Stories). 1955. Ginn & Co.

--Tenny Gay. Fletcher, Charlie May Hogue. Simon, Howard (1903-1979), illus. LC 36-27395. 207 p. illus. 21 cm. c.1936. E. P. Dutton & Co., Inc.

--Younger Brother: A Cherokee Indian Tale. Fletcher, Charlie May Hogue. Simon, Howard (1903-1979), illus. LC 42-18291. 182, 1 p. illus. 21 cm. 1942. E. P. Dutton and Company, Inc.

Simon, Ellen

--The Critter Bk. Simon, Ellen, illus. N.D. Holiday House.

Simon, George Thomas (1912-)

--Don Watson Starts His Band. Simon, George Thomas (1912-), photos by. LC 40-33458. xii p., 1 l., 306 p. 21 cm. 1940. Dodd, Mead & Company.

Simon, Henry A.

--Treasury of Christmas Songs & Carols. Busoni, Rafaello (1900-1962), illus. (O.s.i.). (Illus.). (gr. 7 up). 1955. (ISBN 0-395-08191-2). HM.

Simon, Iris, illus.

--This Is the House That Jack Built: Traditional. LC 78-72322. (Illus.). 32 p. 23cm. 1979. (ISBN 0-89799-139-7). (ISBN 0-89799-006-4). Dandelion Press.

Simon, Iris Illus. by see Millett, Esther Lee.

Simon, John Ivan (1925-), ed.

--Fourteen for Now: A Collection of Contemporary Short Stories. LC 68-24320. 22cm. xvi, 316p. (gr. 6 up). 1969. (ISBN 0-06-025680-X). Har-Row.

Simon, John O., jt. ed. see Kennedy, Sarah.

Simon, Kia

--Toddler. Simon, Kia, illus. (Illus.). 28p. (Orig.). (gr. 3-6). 1976. (ISBN 0-917744-20-9). Aldebaran Rev.

--The Wise Queen. (Illus.). (Children's Work Ser.). (gr. 2-8). 1979. (ISBN 0-915288-31-1). Shameless Hussy.

Simon, Leonard (1922-) & Bendick, Jeanne

--The Day the Numbers Disappeared. Bendick, Jeanne (1919-), illus. LC 62-21573. 45p. col. illus. 26cm. c.1963. Whittlesey-McGraw.

Simon, Lorena Cotts (1897-)

--Children's Story Hour. LC 60-16904. (Illus.). 22cm. 42p. 1961. Naylor.

Simon, Lucy, ed.

--The Lobster Quadrille and Other Poems for Children. Bennett, Susan, illus. LC 70-84927. (Illus.). 42 p. 1969. CBS Records, Lancelot Press.

Simon, Madeleine

--Isle of Illusion. Holloway, Jim, illus. LC 83-51038. (Illus.). 157 p. c.1983. (ISBN 0-88038-068-3). TSR.

Simon, Marcia L (1939-)

--A Special Gift. LC 78-4329. p. cm. c.1978. (ISBN 0-15-277865-9). Harcourt Brace Jovanovich.

Simon, Mina Lewiton (1904-1970)

--Beasts of Burden. N.D. E . M. Hale and Co.

--Candita's Choice. N.D. E . M. Hale and Co.

--Candita's Choice. Simon, Howard (1903-1979), illus. LC 59-5793. (Illus.). (gr. 3-6). 1959. (ISBN 0-06-023821-6, HarpJ). Har-Row.

--The Divided Heart. LC 47-30300. (Illus.). 214p. 21cm. 1947. D. McKay Co.

--Elizabeth and the Young Stranger: A Novel for Young Adults. LC 61-13469. 133 p. 21cm. 1961. D. McKay Co.

--Especially Humphrey. Simon, Howard (1903-1979), illus. LC 67-19767. (Illus.). 56 p. 24cm. 1967. Delacorte Press.

--First Love. Simon, Howard (1903-1979), illus. LC 52-12663. (Illus.). 166 p. 21cm. 1952. (ISBN 0-679-20052-5). D. McKay Co.

--Humphrey on the Town. Simon, Howard (1903-1979), illus. LC 76-101999. (Illus.). 72 p. 21cm. 1971. Delacorte Press.

--If You Were an Eel, How Would You Feel?. Simon, Howard (1903-1979), illus. LC 63-8832. (Illus.). 34cm. 31p. (ps-3). 1963. (ISBN 0-695-84100-9). (ISBN 0-695-44100-0). Follett.

--Is Anyone Here?. 1st ed. Simon, Howard (1903-1979), illus. LC 67-189935. 1 v. (unpaged) col. illus. 29cm. 1967. Atheneum.

--Penny's Acres. LC 55-8995. 214 p. 21cm. 1955. D. McKay Co.

--Rachel. LC 54-5948. (Illus.). 185 p. 20cm. 1954. F. Watts.

--Rachel and Herman. LC 57-5189. 202 p. illus. 20 cm. 1957. F. Watts.

--That Bad Carlos. Simon, Howard (1903-1979), illus. LC 64-12972. (Illus.). 175 p. 20cm. 1964. Harper & Row.

--Who Knows When Winter Goes. Simon, Howard (1903-1979), illus. (Illus.). (ps-3). 1965. (ISBN 0-695-49320-5). Follett.

--Who Knows When Winter Goes?. Simon, Howard (1903-1979), illus. LC 65-12311. 31p. col. illus. 30cm. c.1966. Follet.

Simon, Morris

--Castle in the Clouds. LC 84-50625. 80p. (Fantasy Forest Adventures Ser.). (gr. 2-5). 1984. (ISBN 0-394-72782-7, Pub. by BYR). Random.

--The Youngest Samurai. LC 84-51000. 160p. (Dungeons & Dragons Endless Quest Bks.). (gr. 5 up). N.D. (ISBN 0-394-72789-4, Pub. by BYR). Random.

Simon, Norma Feldstein (1927-)

--The Baby House. Adams, Adrienne (1906-), illus. LC 55-9505. unpaged. illus. 24cm. N.D. Lippincott.

--My Beach House. Haley, Velma, illus. LC 58-5615. (Illus.). 22cm. 1958. Lippincott.

--Benjy's Bird. Lasker, Joseph Leon (1919-), illus. LC 65-15104. (Illus.). 1 v. (unpaged. 23cm. 1965. A. Whitman.

--The Daddy Days. Graboff, Abner (1919-), illus. LC 58-5201. unpaged. illus. 27 cm. 1958. Abelard-Schuman. **Award: (NYT).**

--A Day at the County Fair. LC 60-6756. unpaged. illus. 24 cm. 1960. Lippincott.

--Elly, the Elephant. LC 62-8320. (Illus.). unpaged. 24cm. 1962. St. Martin's Press.

--Elly the Elephant. Bleifield, Stanley, illus. LC 81-23990. 1982. (ISBN 0-8075-1970-7). Whitman.

--Go Away, Warts!. Lexa, Susan, illus. LC 79-28534. (Illus.). 32 p. 24cm. (Concept books level 2). c.1980. (ISBN 0-8075-2970-2). A. Whitman.

--How Do I Feel?. Lasker, Joseph Leon (1919-), illus. LC 77-126430. 40 p. (chiefly illus., part col. 24cm. 1970. (ISBN 0-8075-3414-5). A. Whitman.

--I Know What I Like. Leder, Dora, illus. LC 76-165822. (Illus.). 32 p. 24cm. 1971. (ISBN 0-8075-3507-9). A. Whitman.

--I Was So Mad!. Leder, Dora, illus. LC 73-22425. (Illus.). 40p. (Concept Bks.). (gr. k-2). 1974. (ISBN 0-8075-3520-6). A Whitman.

--I Wish I Had My Father. Zeldich, Arieh (1949-), illus. LC 83-1287. p. cm. 1983. (ISBN 0-8075-3522-2). A. Whitman.

--I'm Busy, Too. Leder, Dora, illus. LC 79-18374. p. cm. (Concept book/level 1). 1979. (ISBN 0-8075-3464-1). A. Whitman.

--Nobody's Perfect, Not Even My Mother. Leder, Dora, illus. LC 81-520. (Illus.). 32 p. 24cm. (Concept books/level 1). c.1981. (ISBN 0-8075-5707-2). A. Whitman.

--Oh, That Cat!. Leder, Dora, illus. LC 85-15546. p. cm. 1985. (ISBN 0-8075-5919-9). A. Whitman.

--Our First Sukkah. Gordon, Ayala, illus. (Illus.). (Festival Series of Picture Story Books). (ps-k). 1959. (ISBN 0-8381-0703-6). United Syn Bk.

--Ruthie. 1st ed. Eaglin, Tom, illus. LC 68-22070. (Illus.). 180 p. 21cm. 1968. Meredith Press.

--See the First Star. Lasker, Joseph Leon (1919-), illus. LC 68-22196. (Illus.). 1 v. (unpaged. 24cm. 1968. A. Whitman.

--A Tree for Me. Stone, Helen (1904-), illus. LC 56-927105. unpaged. illus. 24cm. 1956. Lippincott.

--Up and Over the Hill. MacKenzie, Garry (1921-), illus. LC 57-10864. unpaged. illus. 21 cm. c.1957. Lippincott.

--We Remember Philip. Sanderson, Ruth, illus. LC 78-11691. (Illus.). 32 p. 24cm. (Concept books). c.1979. (ISBN 0-8075-8709-5). A. Whitman.

--The Wet World. Miller, Jane Judith (1925-), illus. LC 54-810410. unpaged. illus. 24cm. 1954. Lippincott. **Award: (NYT).**

--What Do I Do?. Lasker, Joseph Leon (1919-), illus. LC 74-79544. (Illus.). 40 p. 24cm. 1969. A. Whitman.

--What Do I Do: English - Spanish Edition. Lasker, Joseph Leon (1919-), illus. LC 74-79544. (Illus.). ils, some color. 40p. (Concept Bks.). (ps-2). 1969. (ISBN 0-8075-8823-7). A Whitman.

--What Do I Say?. Lasker, Joseph Leon (1919-), illus. (Illus.). 40 p. 24cm. 1967. A. Whitman.

--Where Does My Cat Sleep?. Leder, Dora, illus. LC 82-10872. p. cm. 1982. (ISBN 0-8075-8926-8). A. Whitman.

Simon, Patty

--Just Like Mommy. Cummings, Alison, illus. LC 52-40859. unpaged. illus. 21 cm. (Two-in-one Wonder book, 589). c.1952. Wonder Books.

Simon, R. E., Jr., jt. auth. see Deer, Ada.

Simon, Romain (1915-), illus.

--Forest Animals. LC 62-13379. (Illus.). 30cm. 92p. 1962, c.1960. Grosset & Dunlap.

Simon, Romain (1915-) & Faucher, Paul (1898-)

--The Hare and the Tortoise. Simon, Romain (1915-), illus. Hirsch, Constance, tr. LC 66-4012. 1v. (unpaged) col. illus. 19x22cm. (Pere Castor bk; 62083). 1966. Golden Pr.

Simon, Ruth Corabel Shimer (1918-)

--A Castle for Tess. LC 67-7413. 208 p. 23cm. (Merit mystery). 1967. Follet Pub. Co.

--Mat and Mandy and the Big Dog, Bigger. Weil, Lisl (1910-), illus. LC 54-9153. 93p. illus. 21cm. 1954. Crowell.

--Mat and Mandy and the Little Old Car. Weil, Lisl (1910-), illus. LC 52-7864. 110p. 1952. Thomas Y. Crowell.

Simon, Samuel Sylvan (1910-), ed.

--Easily Staged Plays for Girls: Nine New Non-Royalty Plays. LC 37-15454. viii, 147 p. 19 1/2 cm. 1937. S. French.

--Easliy Staged Plays for Boys: Nine New Non-Royalty Plays. LC 37-4750. viii, 149 p. 19 cm. 1936. S. French.

Simon, Seymour (1931-)

--Chip Rogers Computer Whiz. Miller, Steve, illus. LC 84-6663. 96p. (gr. 2-5). 1984. (ISBN 0-688-03855-7, Morrow Junior Books). Morrow.

--Einstein Anderson Goes to Bat. Winkowski, Fred, illus. LC 81-16106. (Illus.). 73 p. 22cm. (Einstein Anderson, Science Sleuth: No. 5). 1982. (ISBN 0-670-29068-8). Viking Press.

--Einstein Anderson Lights up the Sky. 1st ed. Winkowski, Fred, illus. LC 82-2689. (Illus.). 73 p. 22cm. (Einstein Anderson Science Slenth: No. 6). 1982. (ISBN 0-670-29066-1). Viking Press.

--Einstein Anderson Makes up for Lost Time. Winkowski, Fred, illus. LC 80-28117. (Illus.). 73 p. 22cm. (Einstein Anderson, Science Sleuth: No. 3). 1981. (ISBN 0-670-29067-X). Viking Press.

--Einstein Anderson, Science Sleuth. Winkowski, Fred, illus. LC 80-5514. p. cm. ((His). (Einstein Anderson, Science Sleuth: No. 1). 1980. (ISBN 0-670-29070-X). Viking Press.

--Einstein Anderson, Science Sleuth. Winkowski, Fred, illus. LC 81-4605. p. cm. (Einstein Anderson, Science Sleuth: No. 1). 1981. (ISBN 0-671-43168-4). (ISBN 0-671-43168-4). Wanderer Books.

--Einstein Anderson Sees Through the Invisible Man. Winkowski, Fred, illus. LC 83-3500. p. cm. (Einstein Anderson Science Sleuth: No. 7). 1983. (ISBN 0-670-29065-3). Viking Press.

--Einstein Anderson Shocks His Friends. 1st ed. Winkowski, Fred, illus. LC 80-15786. (Illus.). 73 p. 22cm. (Einstein Anderson, Science Sleuth: No. 2). c.1980. (ISBN 0-670-29070-X). Viking Press.

--Einstein Anderson Shocks His Friends. Winkowski, Fred, illus. LC 81-4573. p. cm. (Einstein Anderson, Science Sleuth: No. 2). 1981. (ISBN 0-671-43169-2). Wanderer Books.

--Einstein Anderson Tells a Comet's Tale. Winkowski, Fred, illus. LC 81-2352. p. cm. (Einstein Anderson, Science Sleuth: No. 4). 1981. (ISBN 0-670-29071-8). Viking Press.

--Ghosts. Gammell, Stephen, illus. LC 75-37520. (Illus.). 79 p. 23cm. (Eeric series). c.1976. (ISBN 0-397-31664-X). (ISBN 0-397-31665-8). Lippincott.

--Shadow Magic. Ormai, Stella, illus. LC 84-4433. (Illus.). 48p. (ps-3). 1985. (ISBN 0-688-02681-8). (ISBN 0-688-02682-6). Lothrop.

--Silly Animal Jokes and Riddles. Kendrick, Dennis, illus. LC 80-19030. (Illus.). 61 p. (Let's-try-it-out). c.1980. (ISBN 0-07-057397-2). McGraw-Hill.

--Space Monsters From Movies, TV & Books. LC 77-3566. (Eerie series (er)). (gr. 4 up). 1977. (ISBN 0-397-31765-4, HarpJ). (ISBN 0-397-31766-2). Har-Row.

Simon, Shirley Schwartz, jt. auth. see Stadtler, Bea.

Simon, Shirley Schwartz (1921-)

--Best Friend. Lonette, Reisie Dominee (1924-), illus. LC 64-14439. (Illus.). 191 p. 22cm. 1964. Lothrop, Lee & Shepard.

--Cousins at Camm Corners. Lonette, Reisie Dominee (1924-), illus. LC 62-16567. 192 p. illus. 22 cm. c.1963. Lothrop, Lee and Shepherd Co.

--Libby's Step-Family. Lonette, Reisie Dominee (1924-), illus. LC 66-82364. 191p. illus. 22cm. 1966. Lothrop.

--Molly and the Rooftop Mystery. Werth, Kurt (1896-), illus. LC 60-53424. 190 p. illus. 22 cm. 1961. Lothrop, Lee & Shepard Co.

--Molly's Cottage. Werth, Kurt (1896-), illus. LC 59-13156. 223 p. illus. 22 cm. 1959. Lothrop, Lee & Shepard.

Simon, Sidney Blair (1927-)

--The Armadillo Who Had No Shell. (gr. k-3). N.D. (ISBN 0-448-21207-2). (ISBN 0-448-25895-1). G&D.

--The Armadillo Who Had No Shell. 1st ed. Lorraine, Walter Henry (1929-), illus. LC 66-107885. 32p. col. illus. 19x24cm. 1966. Norton.

--Henry, the Uncatchable Mouse. Langner, Nola (1930-), illus. LC 64-17531. 1 v. (unpaged) illus. 19 x 24 cm. 1964. Norton.

Simon, Solomon (1895-1970)

--More Wise Men of Helm and Their Merry Tales. Goodman, Hannah, ed. Kraft, Stephen, illus. LC 65-14594. 119p. illus. 23cm. 1965. Behrman.

--The Wandering Beggar. N.D. Behrman House Inc.

Simon, Tony (1921-)

--Ripsnorters & Ribticklers. 64p. (gr. 4-6). 1969 (StarLine). Schol Bk Serv.

Simond, Ada D.

--Let's Pretend: Mae Dee & Her Family & the First Wedding of the Year. Shannon, Sarochin, illus. LC 78-62432. (Illus.). (National History Ser.). (gr. 3 up). 1979. (ISBN 0-89482-003-6). (ISBN 0-89482-004-4). (ISBN 0-89482-016-8). Stevenson Pr.

--Let's Pretend: Mae Dee & Her Family Go to Town. LC 77-82126. (Illus.). (National History Ser.). (gr. 3 up). 1977. (ISBN 0-89482-009-5). (ISBN 0-89482-002-8). (ISBN 0-89482-015-X). Stevenson Pr.

--Let's Pretend: Mae Dee & Her Family in the Merry, Merry Season. Shannon, Sarochin, illus. LC 77-88603. (Illus.). (National History Ser.). (gr. 3 up). 1978. (ISBN 0-89482-005-2). (ISBN 0-89482-006-0). (ISBN 0-89482-017-6). Stevenson Pr.

--Let's Pretend: Mae Dee & Her Family Join the Juneteenth Celebration. LC 77-88604. (Illus.). (National History Ser: USA). (gr. 3 up). 1978. (ISBN 0-89482-027-3). (ISBN 0-89482-028-1). (ISBN 0-89482-020-6). Stevenson Pr.

--Let's Pretend: Mae Dee & Her Family on a Weekend in May. LC 77-20629. (Illus.). (National History Ser.). (gr. 3 up). 1977. (ISBN 0-89482-010-9). (ISBN 0-89482-011-7). (ISBN 0-89482-018-4). Stevenson Pr.

--Let's Pretend: Mae Dee & Her Family Ten Years Later. Shannon, Sarochin, illus. LC 78-62431. (Illus.). (National History Ser.). (gr. 5 up). 1982. (ISBN 0-89482-012-5). (ISBN 0-89482-013-3). Stevenson Pr.

Simond, William A. (1822-1859)

--A Boy with Edison. N.D. Doubleday Doran.

--Oscar: Or, The Boy Who Had His Own Way. LC 43-27480. 3 p. l., v-xiii, 1, 15-313 p. front., illus. (incl. map) 18 cm. (His The Aimwell stories). 1858. Gould and Lincoln.

Simonds, Esther L.

--Searching for Christmas. (Illus.). 10 color ils. 24p. (Childrens Ser). (gr. 3 up). 1969. (ISBN 0-911718-26-5). Malter-Westerfield.

Simonds, Peter

--Maple Leaf Up, Maple Leaf Down. N.D. Island Press Cooperative, Inc.

Simonds, William see Aimwell, Walter, pseud.

Simonetta, Linda, jt. auth. see Simonetta, Sam.

Simonetta, Sam (1936-) & Simonetta, Linda (1948-)

Trappers, Trains & Mining Claims: Colorado History Stories for the Elementary Level. LC 75-9515. vii, 231 ill. 23. 1975. (ISBN 0-87108-089-3). (ISBN 0-87108-194-6). Pruett Pub. Co.

Simons-Ailes, Sandra, illus.

--Mrs. Ortiz Makes Fry Bread. (Illus.). 30p. (Orig.). 1st U.S. edition. (ps-7). 1979. (ISBN 0-915347-06-7). Pueblo Acoma Pr.

Simons, Barbara Brooks (1934-)

--A Visit to the Forest. 1st ed. Lowenheim, Alfred (1947-), illus. LC 78-5439. (Illus.). 64 p. 27cm. (Adventures in Nature). c.1978. (ISBN 0-916392-22-8). (ISBN 0-916392-21-X). Oak Tree Publications.

--A Visit to the Mountains. Lowenheim, Alfred (1947-), illus. LC 78-13562. p. cm. (Adventures in Nature). c.1978. (ISBN 0-916392-31-7). (ISBN 0-916392-30-9). Oak Tree Publications.

--A Visit to the Ocean. 1st ed. Lowenheim, Alfred (1947-), illus. LC 78-4602. (Illus.). 64 p. 27cm. (Adventures in Nature). c.1978. (ISBN 0-916392-24-4). (ISBN 0-916392-23-6). Oak Tree Publications.

--A Visit to the Prairie. 1st ed. Lowenheim, Alfred (1947-), illus. LC 78-13738. p. cm. (Adventures in Nature). c.1978. (ISBN 0-916392-33-3). (ISBN 0-916392-32-5). Oak Tree Publications.

Simons, Barbara Brooks (1934-) & Rooney, Ruth, eds.

--All-Time Favorites. LC 75-314319. (Illus.). 128 p. 28cm. (Their Treasured tales of childhood ; 4). 1974. Southwestern Co.

--Fables & Nursery Rhymes. LC 75-314052. (Illus.). 128 p. 28cm. (Their Treasured tales of childhood ; 1). 1974. Southwestern Co.

--Stories About Animals. LC 75-314049. (Illus.). 128 p. 28cm. (Their Treasured tales of childhood ; 2). 1974. Southwestern Co.

--Stories About People. LC 75-314050. (Illus.). 128 p. 28cm. (Their Treasured tales of childhood ; 3). 1974. Southwestern Co.

--Treasured Tales of Childhood. LC 75-314051. (Illus.). v. 28cm. N.D. Southwestern Co.

Simons, Dorothy M

--The Red-Headed Elf, and Other Stories. 1 st. ed. LC 55-7171. 82p. illus. 21cm. 1955. Vantage Press.

Simons, Evelyn see Irish, Marie, pseud.
Simons, Evelyn, et al.
--Thirty New Christmas Dialogues and Plays. Irish, Marie, pseud. LC 9-29614. 175 p. 18 cm. 1909. A. Flanagan Company.
Simons, Hannah
--Elihu the Musical Gnu. Kinsley, Molly, illus. LC 58-59595. unpaged. illus. 22 x 26 cm. 1958. Platt & Munk Co.
--Something New: at the Circus. Bradfield, Margaret, illus. LC 60-6813. unpaged. illus. 19 x 23 cm. 1960. Abingdon Press.
Simons, Jeff
--Starships. Tatman, Bruce, illus. (Illus.). 24p. (gr. 4-7). 1983. (ISBN 0-89954-222-0). Antioch Pub Co.
--Teddy Bears Care Enough. Kinarney, Tom, illus. (Illus.). 24p. (Teddy Bears Are Ser.). (gr. 1-6). 1984. (ISBN 0-89954-283-2). Antioch Pub Co.
--Whisper's Mysterious Adventure. Wilson-Heaney, Katherine, illus. (Illus.). 24p. (Whisper the Winged Unicorn Ser.). (gr. 2-6). 1984. (ISBN 0-89954-280-8). Antioch Pub Co.
Simons, Joan
--High Jumps and Dumbbells. 1st ed. Bond, Joyce L., illus. LC 79-55024. (Illus.). x, 140 p. 23cm. 1979. (ISBN 0-931866-04-9). Alpine Publications.
Simons, Susan, ed. see Zumwalt, Wanda.
Simons, Traute
--Paulino. Bohdal, Susi (1951-), illus. (Illus.). (gr. 1-3). 1978. (ISBN 0-88776-110-0). Tundra Bks.
Simons, Wendy
--Harper's Mother. LC 80-17308. 220 p. 22cm. 1980. (ISBN 0-13-383984-2). Prentice-Hall.
Simonson, Mary Jane, pseud., see Wheeler, Mary Jane.
Simonson, Mary Jane, pseud.
--Cowboy on the Mountain. Wheeler, Mary Jane. Reedstrom, Ernest Lisle (1928-), illus. LC 78-94371. (Illus.). 64 p. 23cm. (Cowboys of many races). 1970. Benefic Press.
--Cowboy Without a Horse. Wheeler, Mary Jane. Reedstrom, Ernest Lisle (1928-), illus. LC 75-87129. (Illus.). 46 p. 23cm. (Cowboys of many races). 1970. Benefic Press.
Simont, Marc, jt. auth. see Zolotow, Charlotte Shapiro.
Simont, Marc (1915-), tr. see Garcia Lorca, Federico.
Simont, Marc (1915-)
--The Contest at Paca. LC 59-7623. (Illus.). 60 p. 23cm. 1959. Harper.
--How Come Elephants. Simont, Marc (1915-), illus. (Illus.). (ps-1). 1965. (ISBN 0-06-025691-5). Har-Row.
--The Lovely Summer. LC 52-7876. (Illus.). unpaged. 26cm. 1952. Harper.
--Mimi Picture and Story. Simont, Marc (1915-), illus. LC 54-8991. 21cm. 55p. 1954. Harper & Brothers.
--The Plumber Out of the Sea. LC 55-8592. 39p. illus. 24cm. 1955. Harper.
--Polly's Oats. LC 51-11666. (Illus.). unpaged. 26cm. 1951. Harper.
Simont, Marc (1915-), illus.
--The Castle in the Silver Wood and Other Scandinavian Fairy Tales. LC 39-9935. xii, 181 p. incl. front., illus. 21 cm. 1939. Dodd, Mead and Company.
Simpkins, Thomas V.
--Loudly and Whispers and Rhymes of the Ring. N.D. Vantage Press INc.
Simple Simon
--The History of Simple Simon. Galdone, Paul (1914-), illus. LC 65-277753. 1v. (unpaged) col. illus. 19x26cm. c.1966. McGraw.
Simpson, Ben E. (1939-)
--Start with the Sun. LC 75-33676. 135 p. 21cm. 1975. (ISBN 0-374-37233-0). Farrar Straus Giroux.
Simpson, Claude Mitchell (1910-1976), ed. see Dreiser, Theodore Herman Albert.
Simpson, David Penistan (1917-)
--A Nice Day in the City. LC 83-49478. (Illus.). 48p. (gr. 1-4). 1984. (ISBN 0-06-025641-9). (ISBN 0-06-025644-3). (ISBN 0-06-025644-3). HarpJ.
Simpson, Dorothy
--Honest Dollar. Morse, Dorothy Bayley (1906-1979), illus. (Illus.). (gr. 4-6). 1957. (ISBN 0-397-30393-9). Lippincott.
--Island in the Bay. 1 st. ed. LC 55-11808. 184p. 21cm. c.1956. Lippincott.
--A Lesson for Janie. Morse, Dorothy Bayley (1906-1979), illus. LC 58-8679. 189 p. illus. 21 cm. 1958. Lippincott.
--Matter of Pride. Morse, Dorothy Bayley (1906-1979), illus. LC 59-9221. (Illus.). (gr. 4-6). 1959. (ISBN 0-397-30461-7). Lippincott.
--New Horizons. Morse, Dorothy Bayley (1906-1979), illus. LC 61-11736. (Illus.). (gr. 7-9). 1961. (ISBN 0-397-30581-8). Lippincott.
--Visitor from the Sea. LC 65-13435. 188 p. 21 cm. 1965. Lippincott.
Simpson, Elizabeth
--Prince Melody in Music Land. Repr. 1927. Alfred A. Knopf.
--Prince Melody in Music Land: Musical Fairy Tales for Musical Children. Martin, Mary Virginia, illus. LC 18-26166. 6 p. l., 17-183 p. incl. plates. front., illus. (incl. music) 20 1/2 cm. 1917. A. A. Knopf.
Simpson, Helen De Guerry (1897-1940)
--Mumbudget. McArthur, Molly, illus. LC 29-22375. xi, 199, 1 p. col. front., col. plates. 20 1/2 cm. 1929. Doubleday, Doran & Company, Inc.
Simpson, J. M. see Ashmore, Annie, pseud.
Simpson, J. M., Mrs.
--The Smugglers Cave: Or, Who Shall be the Heir?. Ashmore, Annie, pseud. LC 1-9992. 16cm. 215p. (Leather-Clad Tales). 1890. F. F. Lovell & Company.
--Warren Haviland. Ashmore, Annie, pseud. LC 37-18324. 3 p. l., 5-313 p. incl. front. 19 cm. (Half-title: Leather clad tales. no. 41). 1891. United States Book Company.
Simpson, John Thomas
--Hidden Treasure: The Story of a Chore Boy Who Made the Old Farm Pay. Suydam, E. H., illus. LC 19-106886. 303 p. col. front., plates. 19 1/2 cm. c.1919. J. B. Lippincott.
Simpson, Lesley Byrd, jt. auth. see Jessup, Marie Hendrick.
Simpson, Norman T., ed.
--Once Told Tales of Old New England. Will, Alan, illus. LC 74-76047. (Illus.). 32p. (Orig.). (gr. 3-6). 1974. (ISBN 0-912944-15-3). Berkshire Traveller.
Simpson, Phyllis
--Michael the Magnificent. Pruett, Rose Marie, illus. (Illus.). 32 p. 1967. Steck-Vaughn Co.
Simpson, Sally
--Who Ever Saw?. Rhymes. Emmons, Marion, illus. LC 49-1247. 32 p. col. illus. 28 cm. c.1948. John Martin's House.
Sims, A. E., ed.
--Shakespeare Birthday Book for Boys and Girls. N.D. Thomas Y. Crowell Company.
Sims, Judy & Chesse, Bruce K., eds.
--Puppets for Dreaming & Scheming: A Puppet Source Book. Sims, Judy, intro. by. LC 77-76175. (Illus.). (gr. 1-6). 1978. Early Stages.
Sims, R. George
--Nellie's Prayer. (Illus.). N.D. Raphael Tuck & Sons.
Sims, W. Hines, jt. ed. see Rice, Lillian Moore.
Sinatra, Stephen, et al.
--All About Me, "Hercules the Heart". N.D. (ISBN 0-8062-1504-6). Carlton.
Sinclair, Andrew
--Inkydoo, the Wild Boy. Roy, Jeroo, illus. LC 77-356941. (Illus.). 96 p. 21cm. 1976. (ISBN 0-200-72441-X). Abelard-Schuman.
Sinclair, Bertha Muzzy see Bower, B. M., pseud.
Sinclair, Catherine (1800-1864)
--Holiday House. LC 75-32159. xi, xii, 354 p. 19cm. (Classics of Children's Literature, 1621-1932). 1976. (ISBN 0-8240-2273-4). Garland Pub.
--Holiday House. N.D. Thomas Whittaker.
--Holiday House: A Book for the Young. LC 51-48702. 320 p. illus. 20 cm. N.D. Ward, Lock.
Sinclair, Cecelia, jt. auth. see Barker, William Henry.
Sinclair, Dorothy S.
--Sayings and Doings in Fairy Land. Hardy, Paul (1862-), illus. (The Story Book House). N.D. Dana Estes and Company.
--Sayings and Doings in Fairyland. Hardy, Paul (1862-), illus. (Little People's Ser.). N.D. Dana Estes and Company.
--Sayings and Doings in Fairyland: Or, Old Friends with New Faces. N.D. E P Dutton & Co.
Sinclair, J. M
--Mary Cloudsdale: A Story for Girls. (Illus.). N.D. E & J B Young.
Sinclair, James R.
--Fairy Stories from the Little Mountain. (Illus.). 29p. N.D. Publications of A. Wessels Co.
Sinclair, Janet
--The Childrens'a Bazaar and Robin's Birthday. N.D. Thomas Whittaker.
Sinclair, Kenneth L (1910-)
--Lost City of the Sun. Mays, Lewis Victor, Jr. (1927-), illus. LC 55-11099. 265p. illus. 22cm. 1955. Funk & Wagnalls.
--Mystery Mine. Quinn, Sidney, illus. LC 51-13748. 209 p. illus. 22 cm. 1951. Winston.
--Thunder Mountains Mine. Cisneros, Jose, illus. LC 53-6977. 364p. illus. 22cm. 1953. Funk & Wagnalls.
Sinclair, Lewis, jt. auth. see Disney, Walter Elias.
Sinclair, Michael
--Sonntag. 1971. (ISBN 0-399-10755-X). G. P. Putnam's Sons.
Sinclair, Miss
--Be Ye Ready, 1 of 12 bks. (Illus.). (Stories from the Proverbs Ser.). N.D. Set. Thos Nelson & Sons.
--Lending to the Lord, 1 of 12 bks. (Illus.). (Stories from the Proverbs Ser.: No. 3). N.D. Set. Thos Nelson & Sons.
--Mark Lambert, 1 of 12 bks. (Illus.). (Stories from the Proverbs Ser.: No. 2). N.D. Set. Thos Nelson & Sons.
--The Runaway, 1 of 12 bks. (Illus.). (Stories from the Proverbs: No. 1). N.D. Set. Thosmas Nelson & Sons.
Sinclair, Mrs. Bertha Muzzy see Bower, B. M., pseud.
Sinclair-Stevenson, Christopher (1939-), ed.
--A Parade of Princes. Wegner, Fritz (1924-), illus. LC 66-31704. x, 228 p. illus. 25 cm. 1966, c.1964. W. W. Norton.
Sinclair, Tom
--Tales of a Wandering Warthog. Levine, Abby, ed. Wallner, John C. (1945-), illus. LC 84-19621. (Illus.). 134p. (gr. 4 up). 1984. (ISBN 0-8075-7754-5). A Whitman.
Sinclair, Upton Beall see Fitch, Ensign Clarke, pseud.
Sinclair, Upton Beall see Garrison, Lieut Frederick, pseud.
Sinclair, Upton Beall (1878-1968)
--Clif, the Naval Cadet: Or, Exciting Days at Annapolis. LC 3-17008. 3 p. l., ii, 7-272 p. front. 19 cm. (Boys' own library). 1903. Street & Smith.
--From Port to Port: Or, Clif Faraday in Many Waters. LC 3-13931. 3 p. l., ii, 7-250 p. front. 19 1/2 cm. 1903. Street & Smith.
--The Gnomobile: A Gnice Gnew Gnarrative with Gnonsense, but Gnothing Gnaughty. Cosgrave, John O'Hara, II (1908-1968), illus. LC 36-19100. 5 p. l., 3-181 p. incl. illus., pl. 21 cm. c.1938. Farrar & Rinehart, Incorporated.
--The Gnomobile: A Gnice Gnew Gnarrative with Gnonsense, but Gnothing Gnaughty. Tillard, Marcel, illus. LC 62-19325. 191 p. illus. 22 cm. 1962. Bobbs-Merilll.
--Off for West Point: Or, Mark Mallory's Struggle. LC 3-16998. 3 p. l., ii, 7-251 p. front. 19 cm. 1903. Street & Smith.
Sindall, Marjorie A
--Three Cheers for Charlie. Gill, Margery Jean (1925-), illus. LC 68-15237. (Illus.). 64 p. 22cm. 1st U.S. edition. 1968, c.1966. Criterion Books.
Sindbad the Sailor
--The Adventures of Sindbad the Sailor: A Wonder Tale for All Children. Housman, Laurence (1865-1959), retold by. Blaine, Mahlon, illus. LC 44-111608. (A Wonder Tale for All Children). 85 p. incl. front., illus., double plates. 22 cm. c.1936. The Three Sirens Press.
--The Seven Voyages of Sindbad the Sailor. Mathers, Edward Powys (1892-), tr. from Fr. Wilson, Edward Arthur (1886-), illus. Forester, Cecil Scott (1899-1966), intro. by. LC 49-10251. (Literally Rendered from the Arabic into French). 124 p. illus. (part col.) 29 cm. 1949. Limited Editions Club.
--The Seven Voyages of Sindbad the Sailor. Reed, Philip G. (1908-), illus. LC 62-8023. 57 p. illus. 22 cm. 1962. Atheneum.
--The Seven Voyages of Sindbad the Sailor from the Arabian Nights Entertainment. Reed, Philip G. (1908-), illus. LC 39-27770. 2 p. l., 71, 1 p. col. illus. 16 1/2 cm. 1939. Printed by the Broadside Press for Holiday House of New York City.
--Sindbad, the Sailor. Benchley, Nathaniel Goddard (1915-1981), retold by. O'Sullivan, Tom, illus. LC 60-10166. 53 p. illus. 23 cm. (Legacy books, Y-14). 1960. Random House.
Sindelar, Joseph Charles (1885-)
--Father Thrift and His Animal Friends. Hodge, Helen Geraldine, illus. (Illus.). 20cm. 128p. 1918. Beckley Corby Co.
--Nixie Bunny in Holiday-Land. Hodge, Helen Geraldine, illus. LC 44-20550. 158 p. 1 l. incl. col. front., col. illus. 19 1/2 cm. (Half-title: The Primary social studies series). c.1915. Beckley-Cardy Company.
--Nixie Bunny in Manners-Land. Hodge, Helen Geraldine, illus. LC 12-23067. 144 p. incl. col. front., col. illus. 19 1/2 cm. (Half-title: The Nixie Bunny series). c.1912. Beckley-Cardy Company.
--Nixie Bunny in Workaday-Land. Hodge, Helen Geraldine, illus. LC 41-104662. 144 p. incl. col. front., col. illus. 19 1/2 cm. (Half-title: The primary social studies series). c.1941. Beckely-Cardy Company.

Sinding, Franey, tr. see Bernhardsen, Einar Christian Rosenvinge.

Singer, Bill
--The Fox with Cold Feet. Kendrick, Dennis, illus. LC 80-10288. p. cm. 1980. (ISBN 0-8193-1021-2). (ISBN 0-8193-1022-0). Parents Magazine Press.

Singer, Caroline (1888-) & Baldridge, Cyrus Le Roy (1889-)
--Boomba Lives in Africa. LC 72-4556. (Illus.). 63 p. 22cm. (The Black Heritage Library Collection). 1972. (ISBN 0-8369-9125-7). Books for Libraries Press.
--Boomba Lives in Africa. LC 35-18845. 64 p. col. illus. 26 cm. 1935. Holiday House.
Singer, Caroline (1888-) & Baldrige, Cyrus LeRoy (1889-)
--Ali Lives in Iran. 71, 1 p. illus. (part col.) 26 cm. 1937. Holiday House.
Singer, Frank, jt. auth. see Anthony, Anthony B.
Singer, Isaac Bashevis, tr. see Du Bois, William Sherman Pene.
Singer, Isaac Bashevis (1904-)
--Alone in the Wild Forest. Zemach, Margot (1931-), illus. Singer, Isaac Bashevis (1904-) & Shub, Elizabeth, trs. from Yiddish LC 78-161372. (Illus.). 79 p. 24cm. (Ariel book). 1971. (ISBN 0-374-30238-3). Farrar, Straus & Giroux.
--A Day of Pleasure: Stories of a Boy Growing up in Warsaw. LC 70-95461. (Illus.). photos. 160p. (gr. 7 up). 1969. (ISBN 0-374-31749-6). (ISBN 0-374-51367-8). FS&G. **Awards: (NBA); (ALA).**
--The Fearsome Inn. Hogrogian, Nonny (1932-), illus. Singer, Isaac Bashevis (1904-) & Shub, Elizabeth, trs. from Yiddish LC 67-23693. (Illus.). 1 v. (unpaged). 23cm. 1967. Scribner. **Award: (JNM).**
--The Fools of Chelm and Their History. Shulevitz, Uri (1935-), illus. Singer, Isaac Bashevis (1904-) & Shub, Elizabeth, trs. from Yiddish LC 73-81500. (Illus.). 57 p. 23cm. 1973. (ISBN 0-374-32434-4). Farrar, Straus and Giroux.
--The Golem. Shulevitz, Uri (1935-), illus. LC 82-12028. p. c. c.1982. (ISBN 0-374-32741-6). Farrar, Straus, Giroux. **Award: (ALA).**
--Joseph and Koza: Or, The Sacrifice to the Vistula. Shimin, Symeon (1902-), illus. Singer, Isaac Bashevis (1904-) & Shub, Elizabeth, trs. from Yiddish LC 78-106398. (Illus.). 38 p. 31cm. 1970. (ISBN 0-374-33795-0). Farrar, Straus and Giroux.
--Mazel & Shlimazel: Or, the Milk of a Lioness. Zemach, Margot (1931-), illus. LC 67-19887. (Illus.). 48p. (ps-3). 1967. (ISBN 0-374-34884-7). FS&G.
--Naftali the Storyteller and His Horse, Sus, and Other Stories. Zemach, Margot (1931-), illus. LC 76-26917. (Illus.). 129 p. 24cm. 1976. (ISBN 0-374-35490-1). Farrar, Straus, Giroux. **Award: (ALA).**
--The Power of Light: Eight Stories for Hanukkah. 1st ed. Lieblich, Irene, illus. LC 80-20263. (Illus.). 86 p. 24cm. 1980. (ISBN 0-374-36099-5). Farrar, Straus, Giroux.
--Stories for Children. LC 84-13612. 337 p. 24cm. 1984. (ISBN 0-374-37266-7). Farrar, Straus, Giroux. **Award: (ALA).**
--The Topsy-Turvy Emperor of China. Du Bois, William Sherman Pene (1916-), illus. Singer, Isaac Bashevis (1904-) & Shub, Elizabeth, trs. from Yiddish LC 71-121805. (Illus.). 32 p. 24cm. 1971. (ISBN 0-06-025678-8). Harper & Row.
--When Shlemiel Went to Warsaw & Other Stories. Zemach, Margot (1931-), illus. Singer, Isaac Bashevis (1904-) & Shub, Elizabeth, trs. from Yiddish LC 68-30932. (Illus.). 115 p. 24cm. 1968. Farrar, Straus and Giroux. **Awards: (ALA); (JNM).**
--Why Noah Chose the Dove. Carle, Eric (1929-), illus. Shub, Elizabeth, tr. from Yiddish. LC 73-87426. (Illus.). 32p. (ps-3). 1974. (ISBN 0-374-38420-7). FS&G.
--The Wicked City. Fisher, Leonard Everett (1924-), illus. LC 72-175144. (Illus.). 40p. (gr. 4 up). 1972. (ISBN 0-374-38426-6). FS&G. **Award: (ALA).**
--Zlateh the Goat and Other Stories. Sendak, Maurice Bernard (1928-), illus. Singer, Isaac Bashevis (1904-) & Shub, Elizabeth, trs. from Yiddish LC 66-81142. xi, 90p. illus. 24cm. 1966. (ISBN 0-06-025698-2). (ISBN 0-06-025699-0). Harper. **Awards: (NYT); (ALA); (JNM).**
Singer, Isaac Bashevis (1904-), retold by.
--Elijah the Slave. 1st ed. Frasconi, Antonio (1919-), illus. Singer, Isaac Bashevis (1904-) & Shub, Elizabeth, trs. from Yiddish LC 70-125146. (Illus.). 31 p. 27cm. 1970. Farrar, Straus and Giroux.
Singer, Isaac Bashevis (1904-) & Lieblich, Irene
--A Tale of Three Wishes. LC 75-43632. (Illus.). 27 p. 21cm. c.1975. (ISBN 0-374-37370-1). Farrar, Straus and Giroux.
Singer, Isaac Singer (1904-), intro. by see Aesopus.
Singer, Jane Sherrod see Sherrod, Jane (1917-) & Thayer, Zel.
Singer, Jane Sherrod (1917-) & Singer, Kurt Deuisch (1911-)
--Folk Tales of Mexico. LC 77-82459. (Illus.). 110 p. 25cm. 1969. T. S. Denison.
Singer, Janet
--Cheer Leader. LC 39-105314. 3 p. l., 13-251 p. 19 1/2 cm. c.1934. The Goldsmith Publishing Company.
Singer, Kurt Deuisch, jt. auth. see Singer, Jane Sherrod.
Singer, Kurt Deutsch (1911-), ed. see Sherrod, Jane (1917-) & Thayer, Zel.

Skelton, Red (1913-)
--Gertrude & Heathcliffe. (Illus.). 64p. (gr. 2-6). 1974. (ISBN 0-684-14000-4). Scribner.
--Red Skelton's Favorite Ghost Stories. 192p. Orig. Title: A Red Skelton in Your Closet. (gr. 9-12). 1968. (ISBN 0-448-04882-5, Tempo). G&D.
Skelton, Richard Bernard see Skelton, Red.
Skelton, Zan
--To Be Somebody. LC 67-31812. 121 p. 22cm. 1967. Moody Press.
Skerry-Olsen, Eva
--Pim. Anderson, Marvin, illus. LC 48-4218. 75p. 1948. Coslett Publishing Co.
Skertchley, J. A.
--In Quest of Sheba's Treasure. (Warne's Adventure Library). N.D. Frederick Warne & co.
Skeyhill, Tom
--Sergeant York: Or, Last of the Long Hunters. 240p. N.D. John C. Winston Co.
Skidmore, Hubert Standish (1911-)
--Hill Doctor. 1st ed. Spruance, Benton, illus. LC 40-944724. 4 p. l., 307 p. front. 20 1/2 cm. 1940. Doubleday, Doran & Company, Inc.
--Hill Lawyer. Bennett, Richard Michael (1899-), illus. LC 42-19562. 3 p. l., 301 p. 21 cm. 1942. Doubleday, Doran & Company, Inc.
--River Rising!. Spruance, Benton, illus. LC 39-27692. 4 p. l., 298 p. front. 20 1/2 cm. 1939. (ISBN 0-385-07469-7). Doubleday, Doran & Company, Inc.
Skinner, Ada Maria, jt. ed. see Dickinson, Asa Don.
Skinner, Ada Maria, jt. ed. see Skinner, Eleanor Louise.
Skinner, Ada Maria (1878-)
--The Tale of Tibby and Tabby. N.D. Duffield.
Skinner, Ada Maria (1878-), ed.
--Christmas Stories and Plays. LC 25-15942. x, 362 p. 19 cm. c.1925. Rand McNally & Company.
--Little Folks' Christmas Stories and Plays. LC 15-135619. x, 276 p. col. front 19 1/2 cm. c.1915. Rand, McNally & Company.
Skinner, Ada Maria (1878-) & Skinner, Eleanor Louise (1872-), eds.
--A Child's Book of Country Stories. Smith, Jessie Willcox (1863-1935), illus. LC 25-24611. 6 p. l., 3-265 p. col. front., col. plates. 24 cm. 1925. Duffield and Company.
--A Child's Book of Modern Stories. N.D. Dodd Mead & Co.
--A Child's Book of Modern Stories. Smith, Jessie Willcox (1863-1935), illus. LC 20-15344. 7 p. l., 3-341 p. col. front., col. plates. 24 1/2 cm. 1920. Duffield and Company.
--The Emerald Story Book: Stories and Legends of Spring, Nature and Easter. LC 15-10954. viii, 5 p., 1 l., 371 p. col. front. 19 1/2 cm. 1915. Duffield & Company.
--The Garnet Story Book: Tales of Cheer Both Old and New. LC 20-3194. 3 p. l., iii, 290 p. col. front. 19 1/2 cm. the jewel series $1.7. 1920. Duffield and Company.
--A Little Child's Book of Stories. Smith, Jessie Willcox (1863-1935), illus. 6 p. l., 258 p. col. front., col. pl. 24 cm. 1922. Duffield and Company.
--The Pearl Story Book: Stories and Legends of Winter, Christmas, and New Year's Day. LC 19-3498. 5 p. l., 377 p. col. front. 19 1/2 cm. the jewel series. (The Jewel Ser.). 1919. Duffield & Company.
--The Topaz Story Book: Stories and Legends of Autumn, Hallowe'en, and Thanksgiving. LC 17-24878. 6 p. l., 381 p. col. front. 19 cm. (On verso of half-title: The jewel series) $1.50). 1917. Duffield & Company.
--The Turquoise Story Book: Stories and Legends of Summer and Nature. LC 18-17254. 8 p. l., 3-409 p. col. front. 19 1/2 cm. (On verso of half-title: The jewel series). 1918. Duffield & Company.
--A Very Little Child's Book of Stories. Smith, Jessie Willcox (1863-1935), illus. N.D. Dodd, Mead & Co.
--A Very Little Child's Book of Stories. Smith, Jessie Willcox (1863-1935), illus. LC 23-15034. xiv, 232 p. col. front., col. plates. 24 cm. 1923. Duffield and Company.
Skinner, Ada Maria (1878-) & Wickes, Frances Gillespy, Mrs., eds.
--A Child's Own Book of Verse: Book One -Three. Petersham, Maud Sylvia Fuller, Mrs. (1890-1971) & Petersham, Miska (1889-1960), illus. LC 17-21861. 3 v. illus. 19 cm. 1917. The Macmillan Company.
Skinner, Charles Montgomery (1852-1907)
--American Myths & Legends. LC 3-28288. (Illus.). 2 vols. 8 cm. 1903. J.B. Lippincott.
--Myths & Legends Beyond Our Borders. LC 98-943. (Illus.). 18 cm. 319p. 1899. J.B. Lippincott.
--Myths & Legends of Flowers, Trees, Fruits, and Plants in All Ages and in All Climes. LC 99-5884. (Illus.). 18 cm. 354p. 1900. J.B. Lippincott.
--Myths & Legends of Our New Posessions & Protectorate. N.D. J.B. Lippincott.
--Myths & Legends of Our Own Land. LC 4-4060. (Illus.). 2 vols. 18 cm. 1896. J.B. Lippincott.
Skinner, Constance Lindsay (0000-1939)
--Andy Breaks Trail. LC 28-21187. 4 p. l., 199 p. col. front., illus. 19 1/2 cm. 1928. The Macmillan Company.
--Becky Landers: Frontier Warrior. LC 63-22983. 182 p. 20 cm. (Acorn books, AB23). 1963, c.1958. Macmillan.
--Becky Landers Frontier Warrior. (gr. 4-6). 1967. (ISBN 0-02-782810-7). (ISBN 0-686-66480-9). Macmillan.
--Becky Landers: Frontier Warrior. LC 26-19729. v, 234 p. col. front. 19 1/2 cm. 1926. The Macmillan Company.
--Debby Barnes: Trader. Rae, John (1882-1963), illus. LC 32-115648. vi p., 1 l., 244 p. col. front., illus. 20 1/2 cm. 1932. The Macmillan Company.
--The Ranch of the Golden Flowers. LC 28-27801. vii p., 1 l., 182 p. col. front., illus. 20 1/2 cm. 1928. The Macmillan Company.
--Red Man's Luck. Granger, Caroline Gibbons, illus. LC 30-246299. 251 p. illus. 21 1/2 cm. 1930. Coward-McCann, Inc.
--Rob Roy: The Frontier Twins. LC 34-372522. 4 p. l., 218 p. front., illus. 19 1/2 cm. 1934. The Macmillan Company.
--Roselle of the North. Schoonover, Frank Earle (1877-1972), illus. LC 27-22475. vii p., 1 l., 256 p. 20 1/2 cm. 1927. The Macmillan Company.
--Silent Scot: Frontier Scout. LC 25-19623. 4 p. l., 234 p. front., plates. 19 1/2 cm. 1925. The Macmillan Company.
--The Tiger Who Walks Alone. LC 27-19315. viii p., 1 l., 211 p. col. front., illus. 19 1/2 cm. 1927. The Macmillan Company.
--The White Leader. Schuyler, Remington (1884-1955), illus. LC 26-162642. 5 p. l., 219 p. front. (port.) plates. 19 1/2 cm. 1926. The Macmillan Company.
Skinner, Cornelia Otis, jt. auth. see Kimbrough, Emily.
Skinner, Eleanor Louise, jt. ed. see Skinner, Ada Maria.
Skinner, Eleanor Louise (1872-), ed.
--Nursery Tales from Many Lands. Wright, Blanche Fisher (1878-), illus. LC 17-17068. viii, 136 p. incl. col. front., illus. 19 cm. c.1917. C. Scribner's Sons.
--Nursery Tales from Many Lands. Wright, Blanche Fisher (1878-), illus. LC 35-7033. viii, 136 p. incl. col. front., illus. 19 1/2 cm. c.1935. C. Scribner's Sons.
--Tales and Plays of Robin Hood. LC 15-17807. 236 p. incl. col. front., illus. (part col.) 19 1/2 cm. c.1915. American Book Company.
Skinner, Eleanor Louise (1872-) & Skinner, Ada Maria (1878-), eds.
--Children's Plays. Pogany, Willy (1882-1955), illus. LC 19-1207. xiii, 269, 1 p. col. front., col. illus. 19 1/2 cm. 1919. D. Appleton and Company.
--Happy Tales for Story Time. LC 18-132895. 180 p. incl. col. front., illus. (part col.) 19 cm. c.1918. American Book Company.
--Merry Tales. LC 15-16897. 232 p. incl. col. front., illus., col. pates. 20 cm. c.1915. American Book Company.
Skinner, Joseph Osmun, jt. ed. see Skinner, Mary Budd, Mrs.
Skinner, Mary Budd, Mrs. & Skinner, Joseph Osmun, eds.
--St. Nicholas Book of Verse. Berger, William Merritt (1872-), illus. LC 23-13567. 5 p. l., 430 p. incl. plates. 21 cm. 1923. The Century Co.
Skinner, Peg
--What's a Deemie?. 1980. (ISBN 0-8062-1456-2). Carlton.
Skinner, Richard (1939-)
--Kate the Skate. Millar, Pete, illus. LC 79-5201. (Illus.). 24 p. 28cm. (Cable Car children's story). c.1979. (ISBN 0-934360-00-6). Carson Press.
Skipper, G. C (1939-)
--The Ghost at Manor House. Dunnington, Tom, illus. LC 77-17270. (Illus.). 48 p. 21cm. c.1978. (ISBN 0-516-03472-3). Childrens Press.
--The Ghost in the Church. Schindler, Steven D., illus. LC 75-35921. (Illus.). 46 p. 21cm. c.1976. (ISBN 0-516-03468-5). Childrens Press.
--A Night in the Attic. Wahl, Richard (1939-), illus. LC 76-8818. p. cm. 46p. 1976. (ISBN 0-516-03469-3). Childrens Press.
Skipper, Mervyn
--The Fooling of King Alexander. Chapman, Gaynor (1935-), illus. LC 67-13862. (Illus.). 30 p. 27cm. 1st U.S. edition. 1967, c.1930. Atheneum.
--The Jungle Meeting-Pool. Coulter, R. W., illus. LC 29-19794. x, 157 p. illus. 21 1/2 cm. 1929. Frederick A. Stokes Company.
Skirrow, Desmond
--The Case of the Silver Egg. Jacques, Robin (1920-), illus. LC 68-29283. (Illus.). 239 p. 22cm. 1st U.S. edition. 1968. Doubleday.
Skjonsberg, Gunnar
--Journey to the End of the Earth. Ware, Kay (1916-) & Sutherland, Lucille, eds. Rapp, Rita, illus. LC 62-21766. 1 v. (unpaged) col. illus. 23 cm. (Read for fun series). 1963, c.1961. Webster Pub. Co.
Skofield, James
--All Wet! All Wet!. 1st ed. Stanley, Diane (1943-), illus. LC 82-47713. p. cm. c.1984. (ISBN 0-06-025751-2). (ISBN 0-06-025752-0). Harper & Row.
--Nightdances. Gundersheimer, Karen, illus. LC 80-8943. p. cm. c.1981. (ISBN 0-06-025741-5). (ISBN 0-06-025742-3). Harper & Row.
--Snow Country. 1st ed. Allen, Laura Jean, illus. LC 82-48856. p. cm. 1983. (ISBN 0-06-025784-9). (ISBN 0-06-025787-3). Harper & Row.
Skofield, James, tr. see Korschunow, Irina.
Skold, Betty Westrom (1923-)
--Lord, I Have a Question: Story Devotions for Girls. LC 79-50079. (gr. 3-6). 1979. (ISBN 0-8066-1718-7). Augsburg.
Skolsky, Mindy Warshaw
--Carnival and Kopeck and More About Hannah. Weinhaus, Karen Ann, illus. LC 77-25643. (Illus.). 74 p. 23cm. c.1979. (ISBN 0-06-025686-9). (ISBN 0-06-025692-3). Harper & Row.
--Hannah and the Best Father on Route Nine-W. Weinhaus, Karen Ann, illus. LC 80-8940. p. cm. c.1982. (ISBN 0-06-025743-1). (ISBN 0-06-025744-X). Harper & Row.
--Hannah Is a Palindrome. 1st ed. Weinhaus, Karen Ann, illus. LC 79-2009. (Illus.). 124 p. 23cm. c.1980. (ISBN 0-06-025726-1). Harper & Row.
--The Whistling Teakettle and Other Stories About Hannah. 1st ed. Weinhaus, Karen Ann, illus. LC 76-21395. (Illus.). 70 p. 23cm. c.1977. (ISBN 0-06-025688-5). (ISBN 0-06-025689-3). Harper & Row.
Skorpen, Liesel Moak (1935-)
--All The Lassies. Scott, Bruce Martin, illus. (Illus.). 32p. 1969. (ISBN 0-8037-0184-5). (ISBN 0-8037-0185-3). Dial Press.
--All the Lassies. Scott, Bruce Martin, illus. LC 69-18224. (Illus.). 32 p. 1970. Dial Press.
--Bird. Sandin, Joan (1942-), illus. LC 75-25399. (Illus.). 39 p. 23cm. c.1976. (ISBN 0-06-025693-1). (ISBN 0-06-025694-X). Harper & Row.
--Charles. Alexander, Martha G. (1920-), illus. LC 72-129857. (Illus.). 32 p. 18cm. 1971. (ISBN 0-06-025712-1). Harper & Row.
--Elizabeth. Alexander, Martha G. (1920-), illus. LC 76-105490. (Illus.). 32 p. 18cm. 1970. Harper & Row.
--Grace. LC 83-49472. 128p. (gr. 5 up). 1984. (ISBN 0-06-025798-9). (ISBN 0-06-025799-7). HarpJ.
--His Mother's Dog. Mullin, Mary Ellen, illus. LC 76-58707. (Illus.). 46 p. 23cm. c.1978. (ISBN 0-06-025722-9). (ISBN 0-06-025723-7). Harper & Row.
--If I Had a Lion. Landshoff, Ursula (1908-), illus. LC 67-18555. (Illus.). 32 p. 1967. Harper & Row.
--Kisses and Fishes. 1st ed. Kellogg, Steven (1941-), illus. LC 73-14332. (Illus.). 32 p. 24cm. 1974. (ISBN 0-06-025716-4). Harper & Row.
--Mandy's Grandmother. Alexander, Martha G. (1920-), illus. LC 74-20383. (Illus.). 32 p. 23cm. 1975. (ISBN 0-8037-4962-7). (ISBN 0-8037-4963-5). Dial Press.
--Michael. Sandin, Joan (1942-), illus. LC 74-20391. (Illus.). 40 p. 23cm. c.1975. (ISBN 0-06-025718-0). (ISBN 0-06-025719-9). Harper & Row.
--Old Arthur. 1st ed. Tripp, Wallace Whitney (1940-), illus. LC 72-76515. (Illus.). 46 p. 23cm. 1972. (ISBN 0-06-025714-8). Harper & Row.
--Outside My Window. Mayer, Mercer (1943-), illus. LC 68-10372. (Illus.). 32 p. 18cm. 1968. Harper & Row.
--Phipps. Burn, Doris (1923-), illus. LC 77-180915. (Illus.). 47 p. 24cm. 1972. Coward, McCann & Geoghegan.
--Plenty for Three. Tomes, Margot Ladd (1917-), illus. LC 78-145908. (Illus.). 48 p. 1971. Coward, McCann & Geoghegan.
--That Mean Man. McCully, Emily Arnold (1939-), illus. LC 68-24334. (Illus.). 32 p. 27cm. 1968. Harper & Row.
--We Were Tired of Living in a House. Burn, Doris (1923-), illus. LC 79-79485. (Illus.). 47 p. 1969. Coward-McCann.
Skorseth, Theresa (1951-)
--The Birds of Storm Hill. LC 81-17572. 143 p. 23cm. c.1982. (ISBN 0-687-03547-3). Abingdon.
Skrebitskii, Georgii Alekseevich (1903-)
--Forest Echo. White, Anne Terry (1896-), tr. from Russian. LC 66-219745. 71p. col. illus. 24cm. (Venture bk.). 1967. (ISBN 0-8076-0414-3). Braziller.
--In the Forest and on the Marsh. White, Anne Terry (1896-), tr. from Russian. LC 66-15752. viii, 163p. illus. 23cm. (Venturebk.). (A Venture Bk.). 1966. (ISBN 0-8076-0357-0). Braziller.
--White Birds Island. Pitz, Henry Clarence (1895-1976), illus. Voynow, Zina, tr. from Russian. LC 48-7491. 84 p. illus. 22 cm. 1948. Knopf.
Skrine, Francis Henry, ed. see Banerjea, S. B.
Skulicz, Matthew V. (1944-)
--Right on, Shane. LC 70-166993. 119 p. 21cm. 1972. Putnam.
Skulsky, Shelomoh (1913-), ed.
--Legends of Abraham the Patriarch: Retold for Jewish Youth. Luizada, A., illus. Lask, I. M., tr. LC 65-967846. 63 p. illus. 24 cm. c.1961. Shulsinger.
--Legends of Bar Kochba. (Illus.). (Jewish History Ser.). (gr. 5-10). 1975. (ISBN 0-914080-20-2). Shulsinger Sales.
--Legends of Joseph and His Brothers: Retold for Jewish Youth. Luizada, A., illus. Lask, I. M., tr. LC 65-967856. 63 p. illus. 24 cm. c.1961. Shulsinger.
--Legends of Judah the Maccabee. (Illus.). (Jewish History Ser.). (gr. 5-10). 1975. (ISBN 0-914080-19-9). Shulsinger Sales.
--Legends of King David. (Illus.). (Biblical Ser.). (gr. 5-10). 1975. (ISBN 0-914080-16-4). Shulsinger Sales.
--Legends of King Solomon. (Illus.). (Biblical Ser.). (gr. 5-10). 1975. (ISBN 0-914080-17-2). Shulsinger Sales.
--Legends of Moses the Law-Giver: Retold for Jewish Youth. Luizada, A., illus. Lash, I . M., tr. LC 65-967865. 64 p. illus. 24 cm. c.1961. Shulsinger.
Skurzynski, Gloria Joan (1930-)
--Caught in the Moving Mountains. Thompson, Ellen M., illus. LC 84-4371. (Illus.). 144p. (gr. 4-8). 1984. (ISBN 0-688-01635-9). Lothrop.
--Honest Andrew. 1st ed. Wiesner, David, illus. LC 79-23516. (Illus.). 32 p. 22cm. (let me read book). c.1980. (ISBN 0-15-235672-X). (ISBN 0-15-642152-6). Harcourt Brace Jovanovich.
--In a Bottle with a Cork on Top. Coalson, Glo (1946-), illus. LC 75-29466. (Illus.). 39 p. 22cm. c.1976. (ISBN 0-396-07277-1). Dodd, Mead.
--Lost in the Devil's Desert. Scrofani, Joseph, illus. LC 81-13667. p. cm. (Mountain West Adventure Ser.). 1982. (ISBN 0-688-00898-4). Lothrop, Lee & Shepard Books.
--The Magic Pumpkin. Negri, Rocco (1932-), illus. LC 76-161011. (Illus.). 47 p. 1971. Four Winds Press.
--Manwolf. LC 80-22393. p. cm. c.1981. (ISBN 0-395-30079-7). Clarion Books/Houghton Mifflin.
--Martin by Himself. Munsinger, Lynn (1951-), illus. LC 79-11748. (Illus.). 36 p. 21cm. 1979. (ISBN 0-395-28271-3). Houghton Mifflin.
--The Poltergeist of Jason Morey. LC 74-25516. 178 p. 21cm. 1975. (ISBN 0-396-07088-4). Dodd, Mead.
--The Remarkable Journey of Gustavus Bell. Hildebrandt, Tim (1939-) & Hildebrandt, Greg (1939-), illus. LC 72-6168. (Illus.). 63 p. 24cm. 1973. (ISBN 0-687-36122-2). Abingdon Press.
--Swept in the Wave of Terror. Skurzynski, Gloria Joan (1930-), illus. LC 85-4278. (Illus.). 159 p. 22cm. (Mountain West Adventures Ser.). c.1985. (ISBN 0-688-05820-5). Lothrop, Lee & Shepard Books.
--The Tempering. LC 82-9602. p. cm. 1983, c.1982. (ISBN 0-89919-152-5). Clarion Books.
--Trapped in the Slickrock Canyon. San Souci, Daniel, illus. LC 83-14988. (Illus.). 123 p. 22cm. (Mountain west adventure). c.1984. (ISBN 0-688-02688-5). Lothrop, Lee & Shepard.
--What Happened in Hamelin. LC 79-15233. p. cm. c.1979. (ISBN 0-590-07625-6, Four Winds Press). Scholastic.
Skurzynski, Gloria Joan (1930-), retold by.
--Two Fools and a Faker: Three Lebanese Folk Tales. Papas, William (1927-), illus. LC 77-5775. (Illus.). 39 p. c.1977. (ISBN 0-688-41806-6). (ISBN 0-688-51806-0). Lothrop, Lee & Shepard.
Slaatten, Evelyn
--The Good, the Bad, and the Rest of Us. LC 80-15595. 157 p. 21cm. 1980. (ISBN 0-688-22251-X). (ISBN 0-688-32251-4). Morrow.
--In the Captain's Shoes. LC 78-1986. 122 p. 22cm. 1978. (ISBN 0-531-02215-3). Watts.

--The Amiable Giant. Slobodkin, Louis (1903-1975), illus. LC 55-13694. 33p. illus. 26cm. 1955. Macmillan.
--Bixxy and the Secret Message. Slobodkin, Louis (1903-1975), illus. LC 49-11317. 94 p. illus. 21 cm. 1949. Macmillan Co.
--Bixxy and the Secret Message. Slobodkin, Louis (1903-1975), illus. 1966. Macmillan Company.
--Circus, April First. LC 53-13049. (Illus.). 89p. 21cm. 1953. Macmillan.
--Clear the Track. Slobodkin, Louis (1903-1975), illus. (gr. k-3). 1967. (ISBN 0-02-783680-0). Macmillan.
--Clear the Track for Michael's Magic Train. Slobodkin, Louis (1903-1975), illus. LC 45-35231. 48 p. col. illus. 19 x 22 1/2 cm. 1945. The Macmillan Co.
--Colette and the Princess. Slobodkin, Louis (1903-1975), illus. LC 65-21293. 46p. col. illus. 27cm. c.1965. Dutton.
--Dinny & Danny. Slobodkin, Louis (1903-1975), illus. LC 51-12244. (Illus.). (gr. k-2). 1951. Macmillan.
--Excuse Me Certainly. Slobodkin, Louis (1903-1975), illus. LC 59-15200. N.D. (ISBN 0-8149-0403-3). Vanguard Press.
--The Friendly Animals. Slobodkin, Louis (1903-1975), illus. LC 44-9409. 25 p. col. illus. 23 1/2 x 28 cm. c.1944. The Vanguard Press.
--Gogo, the French Sea Gull. Slobodkin, Louis (1903-1975), illus. LC 60-11819. unpaged. illus. 27 cm. 1960. Macmillan.
--A Good Place to Hide. Slobodkin, Louis (1903-1975), illus. LC 61-14713. (Illus.). 29 p. 24cm. 1961. Macmillan.
--The Horse with the High-Heeled Shoes. Slobodkin, Louis (1903-1975), illus. LC 54-11527. (Illus.). 30p. (ps-3). 1954. (ISBN 0-8149-0653-2). Vanguard.
--Hustle and Bustle. Slobodkin, Louis (1903-1975), illus. LC 48-7866. 40 p. col. illus. 19 x 26 cm. 1948. Macmillan Co.
--The Late Cuckoo. Slobodkin, Louis (1903-1975), illus. LC 62-19106. unpaged. illus. 26 cm. 1962. Vanguard Press.
--The Little Mermaid Who Could Not Sing. Slobodkin, Louis (1903-1975), illus. LC 56-10629. 38 p. illus. 26 cm. 1956. Macmillan.
--Luigi and the Long-Nosed Soldier. Slobodkin, Louis (1903-1975), illus. LC 63-17088. 32, 8 p. illus. (part col.) 27 cm. 1963. Macmillan.
--Magic Michael. (Illus.). 1 v. (unpaged. (Collier juvenile paperbacks). 1973, c.1944. Collier Books.
--Magic Michael. Slobodkin, Louis (1903-1975), illus. LC 44-684045. 48 p. incl. col. front., col. illus. 19 x 23 cm. 1944. The Macmillan Company.
--Melvin, the Moose Child. LC 67-4382. (Illus.). 32 p. 26cm. 1967, c.1957. Vanguard Press.
--Melvin the Moose Child. Slobodkin, Louis (1903-1975), illus. LC 57-11096. 32 p. illus. 26 cm. 1957. Macmillan.
--Millions and Millions and Millions!. Slobodkin, Louis (1903-1975), illus. LC 55-11892. (Illus.). unpaged. 28cm. 1955. (ISBN 0-8149-0406-8). Vanguard Press.
--Mister Petersand's Cats. (Illus.). (gr. 1-3). 1954. (ISBN 0-8149-0398-3). Vanguard.
--Moon Blossom and the Golden Penny. Slobodkin, Louis (1903-1975), illus. LC 63-24766. unpaged illus. (part col.) 23 cm. 1963. Vanguard Press.
--Mr. Mushroom. Slobodkin, Louis (1903-1975), illus. LC 50-7615. (Illus.). 32 p. 16cm. 1950. Macmillan.
--Mr. Petersand's Cats and Kittens. LC 66-5567. 63 p. illus. (part col.) 23 cm. 1966, c.1954. Vanguard Press.
--Mr. Petersand's Cats and Kittens. Slobodkin, Louis (1903-1975), illus. LC 54-128399. 63p. illus. 22cm. 1954. Macmillan.
--Nomi and the Lovely Animals. Slobodkin, Louis (1903-1975), illus. LC 60-15071. unpaged. illus. 22 cm. 1960. Vanguard Press.
--One Is Good but Two Are Better. Slobodkin, Louis (1903-1975), illus. LC 56-12038. unpaged. illus. 27cm. 1956. Vanguard Press.
--Our Friendly Friends. Slobodkin, Louis (1903-1975), illus. LC 51-8263. (Illus.). (gr. 1-4). 1951. (ISBN 0-8149-0407-6). Vanguard.
--Picco, the Sad Italian Pony. N.D. E. M. Hale & Co.
--Picco, the Sad Italian Pony. Slobodkin, Louis (1903-1975), illus. LC 61-15480. (Illus.). unpaged. 27cm. 1961. Vanguard Press.
--The Polka-Dot Goat. Slobodkin, Louis (1903-1975), illus. LC 64-20782. (Illus.). 34 p. 26cm. 1964. Macmillan.
--Read About the Busman. Slobodkin, Louis (1903-1975), illus. LC 67-1925. (Illus.). 70 p. 23cm. 1967. F. Watts.
--Read About the Fireman. Slobodkin, Louis (1903-1975), illus. LC 67-10228. (Illus.). 71 p. 23cm. 1967. F. Watts.
--Round Trip Space Ship. Slobodkin, Louis (1903-1975), illus. LC 68-110074. 167p. illus. 21cm. c.1968. Macmillan.
--The Seaweed Hat. Slobodkin, Louis (1903-1975), illus. LC 47-11033. 48 p. col. illus. 28 cm. 1947. Macmillan Co.
--The Space Ship in the Park. Slobodkin, Louis (1903-1975), illus. LC 70-187799. (Illus.). 167 p. 21cm. 1972. Macmillan.
--The Space Ship Returns to the Apple Tree. Slobodkin, Louis (1903-1975), illus. LC 58-11080. (Illus.). 127 p. 21cm. 1958. Macmillan.
--The Space Ship Under the Apple Tree. Slobodkin, Louis (1903-1975), illus. 1952. E M Hale.
--The Space Ship Under the Apple Tree. Slobodkin, Louis (1903-1975), illus. LC 52-14184. (Illus.). 114 p. 21cm. 1952. Macmillan.
--Thank You--You're Welcome. LC 57-122596. unpaged. illus. 21x27cm. 1957. Vanguard Press.
--The Three-Seated Space Ship. LC 62-11357. (gr. 3-5). 1972. (ISBN 0-02-045020-6, Collier). Macmillan.
--The Three-Seated Space Ship: The Latest Model of the Space Ship Under the Apple Tree. LC 62-11357. 126 p. illus. 21 cm. 1962. (ISBN 0-02-785480-9). Macmillan.
--Trick or Treat. Slobodkin, Louis (1903-1975), illus. LC 59-11304. (Illus.). 29 p. 27cm. 1959. Macmillan.
--Up High and Down Low. Slobodkin, Louis (1903-1975), illus. LC 60-8575. (Illus.). 32 p. 26cm. 1960. Macmillan.
--The Wide-Awake Owl. Slobodkin, Louis (1903-1975), illus. LC 58-6732. unpaged. illus. 26 cm. 1958. Macmillan.
--Wilbur the Warrior. Slobodkin, Louis (1903-1975), illus. LC 79-175537. (Illus.). 42 p. 27cm. 1972. Vanguard Press.
--Yasu and the Strangers. Slobodkin, Louis (1903-1975), illus. LC 65-316845. 34p. illus. (pt. col.) 20x26cm. c.1965. Macmillan.

Slobodkina, Esphyr (1908-)
--Behind the Dark Window Shade. Slobodkina, Esphyr (1908-), illus. LC 58-5821. unpaged. illus. 24 cm. c.1958. Lothrop, Lee and Shepart Co.
--Billie. Wohlberg, Meg (1905-), illus. LC 58-14498. (Illus.). unpaged. 26cm. 1959. Lothrop, Lee and Shepard.
--Billy, the Condominium Cat. Slobodkina, Esphyr (1908-), illus. LC 79-23402. (Illus.). 48 p. 18cm. c.1980. (ISBN 0-201-09204-2). Addison-Wesley.
--Boris and His Balalaika. Bobri, V., pseud. (1898-), illus. Bobritsky, Vladimir V.. LC 64-12745. 42 p. col. illus. 26 cm. 1964. Abelard-Schuman.
--Caps for Sale. Slobodkina, Esphyr (1908-), illus. LC 40-33530. (Illus.). cover-title, 43 p. c.1940. W. R. Scott, Inc.
--Caps for Sale: A Tale of a Peddler, Some Monkeys, and Their Monkey Business. LC 85-902. p. cm. (Young Scott Books). 1985, c.1947. (ISBN 0-201-09147-X). (ISBN 0-06-025778-4). Harper & Row.
--Caps for Sale: A Tale of a Peddler, Some Monkeys & Their Monkey Business. Slobodkina, Esphyr (1908-), illus. LC 47-29233. 42 p. col. illus. 23 cm. c.1947. W. R. Scott.
--The Clock. Slobodkina, Esphyr (1908-), illus. LC 56-10679. unpaged. illus. 27cm. c.1956. Abelard-Schuman.
--The Flame, the Breeze, and the Shadow. Slobodkina, Esphyr (1908-), illus. LC 69-13185. (Illus.). 62 p. 24cm. 1969. Rand McNally.
--Jack and Jim. Slobodkina, Esphyr (1908-), illus. LC 61-7138. (Illus.). unpaged. 26cm. c.1961. Abelard-Schuman.
--The Little Dinghy. Slobodkina, Esphyr (1908-), illus. LC 58-8607. unpaged. illus. 27 cm. 1958. Abelard-Schuman.
--Little Dog Lost, Little Dog Found. Slobodkina, Esphyr (1908-), illus. LC 56-5899. (Illus.). unpaged. 27cm. 1956. Abelard-Schuman.
--Little Dog Lost: Little Dog Found. Slobodkina, Esphyr (1908-), illus. N.D. E. M. Hale & Co.
--The Long Island Ducklings. Slobodkina, Esphyr (1908-), illus. LC 61-12779. (Illus.). unpaged. 23cm. c.1961. Lantern Press.
--Moving Day for the Middlemans. Slobodkina, Esphyr (1908-), illus. LC 60-7500. unpaged. illus. 26 cm. c.1960. Abelard-Schuman.
--Pezzo the Peddler and the Circus Elephant. LC 67-23073. (Illus.). 41 p. 27cm. 1967. Abelard-Schuman.
--Pezzo the Peddler and the Thirteen Silly Thieves. Slobodkina, Esphyr (1908-), illus. LC 78-105260. (Illus.). 42 p. 27cm. 1970. (ISBN 0-200-71675-1). Abelard-Schuman.
--Pinky and the Petunias. Slobodkina, Esphyr (1908-), illus. LC 59-12312. (Illus.). unpaged. 26cm. 1959. Abelard-Schuman.
--Pinky and the Petunias. Slobodkina, Esphyr (1908-), illus. 1959. E M Hale.
--Wonderful Feast. Slobodkina, Esphyr (1908-), illus. (Illus.). (gr. k-2). 1955. (ISBN 0-8382-0980-7). Hale.
--The Wonderful Feast. Slobodkina, Esphyr (1908-), illus. LC 54-120298. unpaged. illus. 24cm. c.1955. Lothrop, Lee & Shepard Co.

Slocombe, Edwin M., jt. auth. see Fernald, Helen Clark.

Slocum, Joshua
--Sailing Alone Around the World. 272p. (Century Seafarers Ser.). (gr. 6up). 1984. (ISBN 0-7126-0338-7). Hippocrene Bks.

Slocum, Rosalie
--Breakfast with the Clowns. LC 37-285272. 32 p. col. illus. 23 cm. 1937. The Viking Press.

Slonim, Elsie
--Mousie Longtail: The Mouse Who Rose to Fame. 1979. (ISBN 0-533-03622-4). Vantage.

Slosson, Annie Trumbull, Mrs. (1838-)
--Puzzled Souls. LC 16-2135. 130 p. front. 18 1/2 cm. 1915. The Sunday School Times Company.

Slote, Alfred (1926-)
--The Biggest Victory. LC 76-37389. 154 p. 21cm. 1972. (ISBN 0-397-31252-0). (ISBN 0-397-31210-5). Lippincott.
--Clone Catcher. 1st ed. Slote, Elizabeth, illus. LC 82-47761. (Illus.). 154 p. 22cm. c.1982. (ISBN 0-397-32017-5). (ISBN 0-397-32018-3). Lippincott.
--C.O.L.A.R. Kramer, Anthony, illus. LC 80-8723. (Illus.). 160p. (gr. 2-5). 1981. (ISBN 0-397-31936-3, JBL-J). (ISBN 0-397-31937-1). Har-Row.
--C.O.L.A.R. A Tale of Outer Space. 1st ed. Kramer, Anthony, illus. LC 80-8723. (Illus.). 145 p. 21cm. c.1981. (ISBN 0-397-31936-3). (ISBN 0-397-31937-1). Lippincott.
--The Devil Rides with Me and Other Fantastic Stories. LC 79-23092. 83 p. 22cm. c.1980. (ISBN 0-416-30141-X). Methuen.
--Gargan's Boy. 1975. Harper.
--Hang Tough, Paul Mather. (gr. 4-7). 1973. Harper & Row.
--Hang Tough, Paul Mather. LC 72-11531. 156 p. 22cm. 1973. (ISBN 0-397-31451-5). Lippincott.
--The Hotshot. LaCrosse, William, photos by. LC 76-19781. p. cm. 87p. (A Triumph Bk.). 1977. (ISBN 0-531-00330-2). Watts.
--Jake. 1971. Harper.
--Jake. LC 72-151469. 155 p. 21cm. 1971. Lippincott.
--Love and Tennis. LC 79-14914. p. cm. c.1979. (ISBN 0-02-785870-7). Macmillan.
--Matt Gargan's Boy. LC 74-26669. 159 p. 21cm. 1975. (ISBN 0-397-31617-8). Lippincott.
--Moon in Fact & Fancy. LC 73-144781. (Illus.). (gr. 4-9). N.D. (ISBN 0-529-01224-3). Collins-World.
--My Father, the Coach. LC 72-1816. 157 p. 21cm. 1972. (ISBN 0-397-31413-2). Lippincott.
--My Robot Buddy. 1st ed. Schick, Joel (1945-), illus. LC 75-9922. (Illus.). 92 p. 21cm. 1975. (ISBN 0-397-31641-0). Lippincott.
--My Trip to Alpha One. Berson, Harold (1926-), illus. LC 78-6463. (Illus.). 94 p. 21cm. c.1978. (ISBN 0-397-31810-3). Lippincott.
--Omega Station. Kramer, Anthony, illus. LC 82-48461. (Illus.). 147 p. 21cm. c.1983. (ISBN 0-397-32035-3). (ISBN 0-397-32036-1). Lippincott.
--The Princess Who Wouldn't Talk. 1st ed. Arndt, Ursula, illus. LC 64-25320. 48 p. col. illus. 27 cm. c.1964. Bobbs-Merrill.
--Rabbit Ears. 1982. Harper.
--Rabbit Ears. LC 81-47760. 110 p. 21cm. c.1982. (ISBN 0-397-31988-6). (ISBN 0-397-31989-4). Lippincott.
--Stranger on the Ball Club. LC 70-117241. 172 p. 21cm. 1970. Lippincott.
--Tony and Me. 1974. Harper.
--Tony and Me. LC 74-5182. 156 p. 21cm. 1974. (ISBN 0-397-31507-4). Lippincott.
--The Trouble on Janus. Watts, James (1955-), illus. LC 85-40099. p. cm. c.1985. (ISBN 0-397-32158-9). (ISBN 0-397-32159-7). Lippincott.

Slote, Gil & Hurd, Danny
--Songs for All Year Long, and Gosh, What a Wonderful World!. Rosenhouse, Irwin, illus. Asch, Moses, designed by. LC 64-2764. 2 v. in 1. illus. (pt. col.) 31cm. 1964, c.1955. Oak Pubns.

Slung, Michele B, ed.
--Crime on Her Mind: Fifteen Stories of Female Sleuths Form the Victorian Era to the Forties. 1975. (ISBN 0-394-48533-5). Pantheon Books.

Sly, William James (1867-)
--More World Stories Retold: Two Hundred Stories for Retelling and Dramatization. LC 37-17674. (Illus.). 19 1/2 cm. 297p. 1937. Judson Press.
--World Stories Retold. N.D. George W. Jacobs & Co.
--World Stories Retold. N.D. Macrae Smith.

Slye, Leonard Franklin see Rogers, Roy, pseud.

Small, David (1945-)
--Eulalie and the Hopping Head. LC 81-20699. (Illus.). 32 p. 18cm. c.1982. (ISBN 0-02-786010-8). Macmillan.
--Imogene's Antlers. LC 84-12085. (Illus.). 30 p. 24cm. c.1985. (ISBN 0-517-55564-6). Crown Publishers.

Small, Ernest, pseud., see Lent, Blair.

Small, Ernest, pseud. (1930-)
--Baba Yaga. Lent, Blair. Lib. ed. Lent, Blair (1930-), illus. Baba-Iaga LC 66-12098. 48p. col. illus. 28cm. c.1966. (ISBN 0-395-16975-5). Houghton.

Small, Kenneth John
--Colour the Wind: Poems for Junior Secondary School Students. LC 79-320423. xi, 116 p. c.1976. (ISBN 0-471-02497-X). J. Wiley & Sons.

Small, Mary
--And Alice Did the Walking. (Illus.). 1st U.S. edition. (gr. 1-3). 1979. (ISBN 0-19-550564-6). Oxford U Pr.

Small, Richard Loring
--Alphonse-the-Swordfish and Willie-the-Wisp. 1st ed. Oechsli, Kelly (1918-), illus. LC 63-11647. 130 p. illus. 24 cm. 1963. (ISBN 0-672-50208-9). Bobbs-Merrill.

Small, Ruth
--Fatsy Patsy. (Illus.). 64p. 1983. (ISBN 0-89962-329-8). Todd & Honeywell.

Small, Sidney Herschel
--Dangerous Duty. Anderson, Rus, illus. LC 54-5709. (Illus.). 218 p. 21cm. 1954. Oxford University Press.

Small, William J
--Mary Jane Ellen McCling. Gehr, Mary, illus. LC 56-13376. (Illus.). unpaged. 25cm. 1956. A. Whitman.

Smalley, Janet (1893-)
--The Animals Came in. LC 30-232301. 88 p. col. illus. 20 1/2 cm. c.1930. W. Morrow & Co.
--The Animals Came In. 96p. 1933. William Morrow & Co.
--How It All Began. LC 32-22547. 94, 2 p. col. illus. 22 cm. c.1932. W. Morrow and Company, Inc.
--Now and Then, Here and There Around the States with Johnny Bear. LC 31-22908. 2 p.l., 8-91 p. col. illus. 20 1/2 cm. c.1931. W. Morrow & Company.
--Plum to Plum Jam and Still More Picture Tales of How Things Come to Be. LC 29-18029. 87 p. col. illus. 20 1/2 cm. c.1929. W. Morrow & Co.
--Rice to Rice Pudding and Other Picture Tales of How Things Come to Be. LC 28-20422. 85 p. col. illus. 20 1/2 cm. c.1928. W. Morrow & Co.
--Rice to Rice Pudding, and Other Picture Tales of How Things Come to Be. LC 42-197162. 85 p. col. illus. 20 1/2cm. 1942. W. Morrow & Co.
--This Is the Book That the Author Made, That Tells the Tale of Toil and Trade, from the Orange Grove to the Marmalade, from the Cotton Boll to the Trimming Braid, Things That Are Handled by Man and Maid, in Every House That Jack Built. LC 42-16716. 2 p. l., 79 p. illus. 21 1/2 cm. 1929. B. Blackwell.

Smarananda, Swami
--The Story of Ramakrishna. Chakravarty, Biswaranjan, illus. (Illus., Orig.). (gr. k-5). 1976. (ISBN 0-87481-168-6). Vedanta Pr.

Smaridge, Norah Antoinette (1903-)
--Big Tidy-Up. 1963. Bruce Publishing Company.
--Big Tidy-Up. Gray, Leslie, illus. (ps-1). 1970. (ISBN 0-307-60877-8, Golden Pr). Western Pub.
--Impatient Jonathan. Locke, Margo, illus. LC 64-10153. (Illus.). (gr. k-3). 1964. (ISBN 0-687-18703-6). Abingdon Press.
--Lee's Dad. Smith, Phil (1930-), illus. LC 68-58305. (Illus.). 48 p. 29cm. (A Carousel Bk.). 1969. L. W. Singer Co.
--Litterbugs Come in Every Size. Bracke, Charles, illus. (Illus.). 32p. (Big Golden Bk). (ps-3). 1972. (ISBN 0-307-10455-9, Golden Pr). (ISBN 0-307-60455-1). Western Pub.
--Little Lulu & the Pet Parade. Baker, Darrell, illus. (Golden Play & Learn Bk). 1974. (ISBN 0-307-10732-9, Golden Pr). Western Pub.
--Ludi, the Little St. Bernard. Vianney, M. John, Sr., illus. LC 57-420. unpaged. illus. 21 cm. (Christian Child's Stories, 10). 1956. Bruce Pub. Co.
--The Mysteries in the Commune. Handville, Robert, illus. LC 82-45389. (Illus.). 238 p. 22cm. 1982. (ISBN 0-396-08076-6). Dodd, Mead.
--The Mystery at Greystone Hall. Handville, Robert, illus. LC 79-52045. (Illus.). 160 p. 22cm. c.1979. (ISBN 0-396-07733-1). Dodd, Mead.
--The Mystery in the Old Mansions. Handville, Robert, illus. LC 81-43235. p. cm. 1981. (ISBN 0-396-07980-6). Dodd, Mead.
--Nando of the Beach. Korn, Elizabeth P., illus. LC 58-11351. unpaged. illus. 21 cm. 1958. Bruce Pub. Co.
--Neatos & Litterbugs: Mystery of the Missing Ticket. Bracke, Charles, illus. (Illus.). 24p. (ps-2). 1952. (ISBN 0-307-60515-9, Golden Pr). Western Pub.

AUTHOR INDEX SMITH, CHARLOTTE

--Only Silly People Waste. Carrithers, Mary, illus. LC 75-15623. (Illus.). 32 p. 23cm. c.1976. Abingdon Press.
--Peter's Tent. Turkle, Brinton Cassaday (1915-), illus. LC 65-18146. (Illus.). 32 p. 21cm. 1965. (ISBN 0-670-55043-4). Viking Press.
--Raggedy Andy: The I Can Do It, You Can Do It Book. Goldsborough, June (1923-), illus. LC 73-82467. (Illus.). 20 p. 32cm. (Golden book). 1973. Golden Press.
--Raggedy Ann: A Thank You, Please & I Love You Book. Goldsborough, June (1923-), illus. (Illus.). 32p. (ps-1). 1970. (ISBN 0-307-10487-7, Golden Pr). (ISBN 0-307-60487-X). Western Pub.
--Scary Things. Van Sciver, Ruth (1915-), illus. LC 60-10615. (Illus.). 40 p. 22cm. 1960. (ISBN 0-687-36922-3). Abingdon Press.
--The Secret of the Brownstone House. Hampshire, Michael Allen, illus. LC 77-6504. (Illus.). 128 p. 22cm. c.1977. (ISBN 0-396-07474-X). Dodd, Mead.
--Sunday Best. 1959. Bruce Pub Co.
--Teacher's Pest. 1st ed. Nebel, Gustave E., illus. LC 68-26122. (Illus.). 32 p. 24cm. 1968. Hawthorn Books.
--Watch Out!. Perl, Susan (1922-1983), illus. LC 65-107244. (Illus.). 1 v. (unpaged). 23cm. 1965. Abingdon Press.
--Watch Out!. Perl, Susan (1922-1983), illus. 1965. E M Hale.
--What a Silly Thing to Do. Perl, Susan (1922-1983), illus. LC 67-7568. (Illus.). 40 p. 23cm. 1967. Abingdon Press.
--Where Did Everybody Go: Funny Rhymes About Place Words. Buckett, George (1936-), illus. (Illus.). 20p. (Preschool Learning Bk.). (ps). 1971. (ISBN 0-307-12176-3, Golden Pr). Western Pub.
--You Know Better Than That. Perl, Susan (1922-1983), illus. LC 72-7033. (Illus.). 32 p. 23cm. 1973. (ISBN 0-687-46744-6). Abingdon Press.
--Your Five Gifts. Tingle, Dolli, pseud. (1920-), illus. Brackett, Esther M.. LC 69-12371. (Illus.). 25 p. 19cm. (Stardust Bks.). 1969. C. R. Gibson Co.
Smaridge, Norah Antoinette (1903-) & Martin, Ron (1947-)
--School Is Not a Missile Range. LC 76-27745. (Illus.). 32 p. 22cm. c.1977. (ISBN 0-687-36925-8). Abingdon.
Smart, Adam, pseud., see Sutro, Alfred.
Smart, Christopher (1722-1771)
--For I Will Consider My Cat Jeoffry. McNully, Emily Arnold (1939-), illus. LC 83-15660. (Illus.). 32p. (ps up). 1984. (ISBN 0-689-31026-9). Atheneum.
Smart, James Dick (1906-1982)
--A Promise to Keep. Swanson, J. M., illus. (Illus.). (gr. 5-7). 1949. (ISBN 0-664-46302-9). Westminster.
Smath, Jerry
--But No Elephants. LC 79-16136. p. cm. 1979. (ISBN 0-8193-1007-7). (ISBN 0-8193-1008-5). Parents Magazine Press.
--Elephant Goes to School. Smath, Jerry, illus. LC 83-23823. (Illus.). 23cm. 48p. (ps-3). 1984. (ISBN 0-8193-1126-X). Parents.
--The Housekeeper's Dog. LC 80-10580. p. cm. 1980. (ISBN 0-8193-1023-9). (ISBN 0-8193-1024-7). Parents Magazine Press.
--Up Goes Mr. Downs. Smath, Jerry, illus. LC 84-1199. (Illus.). 34 p. 23cm. 1984. (ISBN 0-8193-1137-5). Parents Magazine Press.
Smeaton, O.
--A Mystery of the Pacific. (Illus.). (Scribner-Blackie Series of books for young people). N.D. Charles Scribner's Sons.
Smedley, Constance, pseud., see Armfield, Anne Constance Smedley.
Smedley, Constance, pseud.
--An April Princess. Armfield, Anne Constance Smedley. N.D. Dodd, Mead & Co.
Smedley, Francis Edward (1818-1864)
--Frank Fairlegh. (The Young People's Library). N.D. William Collins Co.
Smedts, Joske, tr. see Van Iterson, Siny Rose.
Smeltzer, Patricia & Smeltzer, Victor
--Thank You for a Book to Read. (Illus.). 24p (Pub. by Lion Publishing). (gr. k-6). 1983. (ISBN 0-86683-719-1). Winston Pr.
--Thank You for a Pair of Jeans. (Illus.). 24p (Pub. by Lion Publishing). (gr. k-6). 1983. (ISBN 0-86683-718-3). Winston Pr.
Smeltzer, Victor, jt. auth. see Smeltzer, Patricia.
Smiley, Lavinia
--Come Shopping. N.D. Transatlantic Arts.
--Hugh the Dragon Killer. N.D. Transatlantic Arts, Inc.
--Mister Snodgrass's Holiday. (Illus.). (gr. 1-4). 1959. Transatlantic.
--Robin In Danger. N.D. Transatlantic Arts.
Smiley, Minerva Jenson (1883-)
--Billy's Search for Florida Undersea Treasure. 1st ed. Smiley, Russ, illus. LC 55-20538. (Illus.). 42p. 26cm. 1954. Mercury Pub. Co.
Smiley, Virginia Kester (1923-)
--The Buzzing Bees. Hodgell, Bob, illus. LC 57-5205. unpaged. illus. 22 cm. 1957. Abelard-Schuman.
--A Horse for Matthew Allen. Hopkins, Bryan, photos by. LC 70-153911. (Illus.). 21 p. 23cm. (A Magic Circle Bk.). 1972. (ISBN 0-663-22980-4). Ginn.
--Little Boy Navajo. Two Arrows, Tom, illus. LC 54-10215. unpaged. illus. 23cm. 1954. Abelard-Schuman.
--Swirling Sands. LC 58-10989. 179 p. 21 cm. 1958. Dodd, Mead.
Smith
--Prince of Argolis, a Story of the Old Greek Fairy Times. 1900. Hurst & Co.
Smith, ed. see La Fontaine, Jean de.
Smith, Abbie Nora (1856-)
--Dolly Days and Dolly Ways: Dolly's Record Book. LC 17-196. 4 p. l., v-xi, 1, 47, 1 p. incl. front., illus., plates. 22 cm. c.1916. P. Elder and Company.
--King Gobbler. LC 6-46351. 6 p., 1 l., 11-178 p. incl. illus., plates. 20 cm. c.1906. The Educational Publishing Co.
Smith, Adah E.
--Grace and Her Stepmother. (Illus.). 256p. N.D. Sunday School Publications.
Smith, Agnes
--The Bluegreen Tree. Thomas, J. Sharkey, illus. LC 76-50105. (Illus.). 108p. (Orig.). 1977. (ISBN 0-87012-271-1). Westwind Pr.
--Edge of the Forest. Moynihan, Roberta, illus. (Illus.). (gr. 7 up). 1959. (ISBN 0-670-28900-0). Viking Pr.
--An Edge of the Forest. Thomas, J. Sharkey, illus. (Illus.). 202p (Pub. by Viking Press). (gr. 7 up). 1974. (ISBN 0-87012-171-5). Westwind Pr.
Smith, Albert
--The Adventures of Mr. Ledbury. N.D. George Routledge & Sons.
--Christopher Tadpole. N.D. George Routledge & Sons.
--The Scattergood Family. N.D. George Routledge & Sons.
Smith, Albert Richard (1816-1860)
--Beauty and the Beast. Crowquill, Alfred, pseud. (1804-1872), illus. Forrester, Alfred Henry. LC 16-5957. 64 p. incl. col. front., col. illus. 14 1/2 cm. 1845. Burgess, Stringer, & Co.
--Beauty and the Beast. Crowquill, Alfred, pseud. (1804-1872), illus. Forrester, Alfred Henry. LC 45-424036. 64 p. incl. illus., pl. 19 cm. N.D. Manhattan Publishing Company.
Smith, Alfred E.
--In Calico and Crinoline. Bischoff, Ilse Marthe (1903-), illus. N.D. Viking Press.
Smith, Alicia Kay (1913-)
--Over the Moon's Edge. LC 39-31679. viii p., 2 l., 3-79 p. incl. plates. 23 cm. c.1938. C. A. A. Parker.
Smith, Alison (1932-)
--Help! There's a Cat Washing in Here!. 1st ed. Rowen, Amy, illus. LC 80-25522. (Illus.). 152 p. 21cm. c.1981. (ISBN 0-525-31630-2). Dutton.
--Reserved for Mark Anthony Crowder. LC 78-6460. 123 p. 22cm. c.1978. (ISBN 0-525-38199-6). Dutton. **Award: (IRA).**
Smith, Amanda Smith, Mrs. (1845-)
--Grandma's Country Life Stories for the Children. LC 14-10759. 62, 1 p. incl. front., illus., plates, ports. 23 1/2 cm. c.1914. Press of the Methodist Book Concern.
Smith, Angela, ed.
--The Children's Poem Book, Vol. II. Newton, B. L., intro. by. 1981. (ISBN 0-686-30171-4). Great Nat Soc Poet.
--A Collection of Religious Poems, Vol. III. Newton, B. L., intro. by. 1981. (ISBN 0-686-30172-2). Great Nat Soc Poet.
Smith, Anna B. Jewett
--Pup Tent. 1959. Exposition Press.
Smith, Anna Harris
--Four-Footed Friends: Stories of Animals and Children. LC 13-820. x, 172 p. incl. front., illus. 19 cm. c.1912. Ginn and Company.
Smith, Anna Marion
--Mother Goose and What Happened Next. Birch, Reginald Bathurst (1856-1943), illus. LC 9-17233. 22cm. 140p. 1909. E. P. Dutton & Co.
Smith, Anna Mary see Mary Marguerite, Sr.
Smith, Anne Warren (1938-)
--Blue Denim Blues. LC 82-1744. 126 p. 22cm. 1982. (ISBN 0-689-30942-2). Atheneum.
Smith, Annette Klein
--Terror in Cairo. 1st ed. Wilson, George Davis, illus. LC 79-87528. p. cm. (A Handy B k.). c.1979. (ISBN 0-15-284812-6). Harcourt Brace Jovanovich.
Smith, Annie Swan, Mrs. (1859-)
--Arlie's Mission. Russell, Lillian, illus. N.D. Methodist Book Concern.
--Bonnie Jean. (Illus.). (The Dolphin Ser.: Vol. 6). N.D. Fleming H. Revell Co.
--For Lucy's Sake, 1 of 6 Vols. (Illus.). 96p. (The Young Folks Series.). N.D. Set. F H Revell.
--Freedom's Sword. Stainland, C. J., illus. (Illus.). 256p. (The Cross and Crown Ser.). N.D. Cassell & Co.'s Pubs.
--Grandmother's Child, 1 of 6 Vols. (Illus.). 96p. (The Young Folk Series). N.D. F H Revell.
--Jack's Year of Trial. (Illus.). N.D. Thos Nelson & Sons.
--Saint Veda's: Or, The Pearl of Orr's Haven. (Illus.). N.D. Methodist Bk Concern.
--The Strait Gate: A New series of books for Boys and Girls, 1 of 4 Vols. (Illus.). (The Eaglehurst Ser.). N.D. White & Allen.
--Thankful Rest. N.D. Thos Nelson & Sons.
--Wilful Winnie. N.D. Thos Nelson & Sons.
Smith, Arthur Douglas Howden (1887-)
--Allen Breck Again. Crawford, Will, illus. 1934. Coward-McCann, Inc.
--A Cadet of Belgium: An American Boy in the Great War. Jones, Bayard, illus. LC 15-4808. 286 p. front., plates. 19 1/2 cm. (His Boys at the front in the great war). c.1915. George H. Doran Company.
--Grey Maiden: The Story of a Sword Through the Ages. Pitz, Henry Clarence (1895-1976), illus. LC 29-18317. ix p., 1 l., 306 p. col. front., illus. 21 cm. 1929. Longmans, Green and Co.
--In Defence of Paris: An American Boy in the Trenches. Jones, Bayard, illus. LC 15-7999. 256 p. front., plates. 19 1/2 cm. (His Boys at the front in the great war). c.1915. George H. Doran Company.
--Porto Bello Gold. N.D. Brentano's.
--Swain's Saga. Sanchez, Carlos M. (1908-), illus. LC 31-29829. ix, 236 p. incl. illus., geneal. tab. col. front., plates. 20 1/2 cm. 1931. The Macmillan Company.
Smith, Arthur L.
--Mildred the Rain Cloud. 1963. Golden, Gate Junior Books.
--Mildred the Rain Cloud. Berwick, Jean Shepherd (1929-), illus. LC 63-7533. (Illus.). (gr. k-3). 1963. (ISBN 0-516-08729-0, Golden Gate). Childrens.
Smith, Beatrice Schillinger
--The Case of the Lost Dogs. Overlie, George, illus. LC 75-39145. (Illus.). 32 p. 16cm. (Carolrhoda Mini-Mystery). c.1976. (ISBN 0-87614-053-3). Carolrhoda Books.
--The Case of the Missing Bills. Overlie, George, illus. LC 75-39146. (Illus.). 32 p. 16cm. (A Carolrhoda Mini-Mystery). c.1976. (ISBN 0-87614-054-1). Carolrhoda Books.
--Don't Mention Moon to Me. LC 74-10280. 126 p. 21cm. 1974. (ISBN 0-8407-6397-2). T. Nelson.
--The Fish Creek Mystery. Overlie, George, illus. LC 75-39148. (Illus.). 32 p. 16cm. (A Carolrhoda Mini-Mystery). c.1976. (ISBN 0-87614-055-X). Carolrhoda Books.
--The Ghost in the Park. Overlie, George, illus. LC 75-39149. (Illus.). 32 p. 16cm. (A Carolrhoda Mini-Mystery). c.1976. (ISBN 0-87614-056-8). Carolrhoda Books.
--The Mystery of the Green Gloves. Overlie, George, illus. LC 75-39150. (Illus.). 32 p. 16cm. (A Carolrhoda Mini-Mystery). c.1976. (ISBN 0-87614-057-6). Carolrhoda Books.
--The Road to Galveston. LC 72-7657. 127 p. 23cm. 1973. (ISBN 0-8225-0755-2). Lerner Publications Co.
--Voices from the Haunted House. Overlie, George, illus. LC 75-39151. (Illus.). 32 p. 16cm. (A Carolrhoda Mini-Mystery). c.1976. (ISBN 0-87614-058-4). Carolrhoda Books.
Smith, Bernice Driskell
--Bonny Squirrel & Mrs. Boyette. (Illus.). 1980. (ISBN 0-533-03079-X). Vantage.
--Company for Thanksgiving. 1st ed. Pomerantz, Norman, illus. LC 66-15457. (Illus.). 24 p. 23cm. 1967. Greenwich Book Publishers.
--Pink Satin. 1st ed. LC 63-9229. 44p. 23cm. 1963. Greenwich Book Publishers.
--Shellbby Rumford: The Story of a Happy Rabbit. (Illus.). 64p. 1984. (ISBN 0-682-40177-3). Exposition Pr FL.
Smith, Bertha Whitridge, Mrs.
--Only a Dog: A Story of the Great War. LC 17-5815. ix p., 1 l., 111 p. front., illus. 19 cm. c.1917. E. P. Dutton & Co.
Smith, Betty Wehner (1898-1972)
--A Tree Grows in Brooklyn. Allen, Virginia F., ed. 224p. 1967. (ISBN 0-685-18910-4). Bowmar-Noble.
Smith, Blanche H.
--The Brown Paper Box: Three Stories. (Illus.). 36p. 1977. Dorrance.
Smith, Bob
--Old African Tales Told Again. Jungles, Dorothy, illus. (Illus.). (gr. 2-5). 1977. (ISBN 0-915864-99-1). Academy Chi Pubs.
Smith, Bob B., illus.
--My First Book. (Little Golden Book). 1942. Golden Press.
Smith, Bonnie Sours (1942-)
--Dorrie & the Mystery of Angell Swamp. 128p. (Pennypincher Ser.). (gr. 5-9). 1984. (ISBN 0-89191-949-X). Cook.
--A Dream for Dorrie. LC 85-7746. 127 p. 18cm. (Dorrie Whitfield series ; bk. 3). c.1985. (ISBN 0-89191-739-X). Chariot Books.
Smith, Bradford (1909-1984)
--Dan Webster, Union Boy. Goldstein, Nathan (1927-), illus. LC 62-16595. 200 p. illus. 20 cm. (Childhood of famous Americans). c.1962. Bobbs-Merrill.
--Dan Webster, Union Boy. 1st ed. John, Charles V., illus. LC 54-6063. 192p. illus. 20cm. (Childhood of famous American series 79). 1954. Bobbs-Merrill.
--Stephen Decatur, Gallant Boy. 1st ed. Burns, Raymond Howard (1924-), illus. LC 55-6829. 192p. illus. 20cm. (Childhood of famous Americans series 90). 1955. Bobbs-Merrill Co.
--Stephen Decatur: Gallant Boy. Goldstein, Nathan (1927-), illus. LC 62-16613. 200 p. illus. 20 cm. (Childhood of famous Americans). c.1962. Bobbs-Merrill.
--William Bradford, Pilgrim Boy. 1st ed. Busch, Paul, illus. LC 53-5240. (Illus.). 192 p. 20cm. (Childhood of famous Americans Ser.). 1953. Bobbs-Merrill.
--With Sword and Pen: The Adventures of Captain John Smith. 1st ed. Hunt, David, illus. LC 56-5196. 192 p. illus. 21 cm. (American heritage series). 1956. Aladdin Books.
Smith, C. P.
--Fairy Story for My Grandchildren. N.D. Carlton.
Smith, C. Ross, tr. see Noel, Bernard.
Smith, Cara Lockhart
--Riding to Canonbie: Poems. Smith, Cara Lockhart, illus. LC 72-83412. (Illus.). 56 p. 28cm. 1st U.S. edition. 1972. (ISBN 0-87888-054-2). Bradbury Press.
Smith, Carl W
--The Lone Wolf and the Hidden Empire. authorized. Vance, Louis Joseph, created by. Vallely, Henry E., illus. LC 48-11262. (An Original Story Featuring the Famous Character Created by Louis Joseph Vance). 248 p. illus. 21 cm. 1947. Whitman Pub. Co.
--Quiz Kids and the Crazy Question Mystery. authorized. Read, Isobel, illus. LC 46-7941. 2 p. l., 9-248 p. illus. 20 1/2 cm. 1946. Whitman Publishing Company.
--Red Ryder and the Secret of the Lucky Mine. authorized. Harman, Fred (1902-1982), created by. LC 48-17791. (Based on the Famous Newspaper Strip by Fred Harman). 248 p. illus. 21 cm. c.1947. Whitman Pub. Co.
Smith, Carole, jt. auth. see Hooker, Ruth.
Smith, Carole (1935-)
--Danger at the Golden Dragon. De John, Marie, illus. LC 83-1278. p. cm. 1983. (ISBN 0-8075-1449-7). A. Whitman.
--The Hit & Run Connection. Fuhs, Pat, ed. DeJohn, Marie, illus. LC 81-12920. (Illus.). 128p. (Pilot Bks.). (gr. 4-9). 1981. (ISBN 0-8075-3317-3). A Whitman.
--Stealing Isn't Easy. Tucker, Kathleen, ed. Marstall, Bob, illus. (Illus.). 128p. (High-Low Mysteries Ser.). (gr. 4-9). 1984. (ISBN 0-8075-7621-2). A Whitman.
--Who Burned the Hartley House?. Dickson, Glenn, illus. LC 85-682. p. cm. 1985. (ISBN 0-8075-8993-4). A. Whitman.
Smith, Catherine C. see Smith, Kay.
Smith, Catherine E.
--Enchanted Ground (Pub. by Society for Promoting Christian Knowledge). N.D. E. & J. B. Young & Co.
--Friend and Foe (Pub. by Society for Promoting Christian Knowledge). N.D. E. & J. B. Young & Co.
--In Humble Dales (Pub. by Society for Promoting Christian Knowledge). N.D. E. & J. B. Young & Co.
--Real and Unreal (Pub. by Society for Promoting Christian Knowledge). N.D. E. & J. B. Young & Co.
--Trust Tries. (Illus.). N.D. Society for Promoting Christian Knowledge.
Smith, Catriona Mary, jt. auth. see Smith, Raymond Kenneth.
Smith, Charles A. (1809-1879), tr. see Hoffman, Franz.
Smith, Charles A., tr. see Hoffmann, Franz.
Smith, Charles Adam (1809-1879), tr. see Hoffmann, Franz.
Smith, Charlotte Curtis
--Bob Knight's Diary at Poplar Hill School. Knight, Bob, illus. LC 3107. iii, 248 p. illus. 21 1/2 cm. c.1900. E. P. Dutton & Company.
--Bob Knight's Diary Camping Out. Knight, Bob, illus. LC 2-23831. (Illus.). 232p. 1902. E P Dutton.
--Bob Knight's Diary on a Farm. Knight, Bob, illus. LC 11-25010. 2 p. l., 304, 1 p. illus. 21 1/2 cm. c.1911. E. P. Dutton & Company.
--Bob Knight's Diary with the Circus. Knight, Bob, illus. LC 8-21921. 2 p. l., 219 p. illus. 21 1/2 cm. c.1908. E. P. Dutton & Company.
--The Girls of Pineridge. Ruyl, Beatrice Baxter (1879-), illus. LC 6-34816. 4 p. l., 287 p. front., 5 pl. 19 cm. 1906. Little, Brown, and Company.
Smith, Charlotte Helen see Charims, pseud.

Smith, Charlotte Helen (1905-)
--Inky & Pinky. Charims, pseud. LC 36-17314. 28 p. illus. (part col.) 20 1/2 x 20 cm. c.1936. Grosset & Dunlap, Inc.
--Surprise: The Story of Molly and Mops. Charims, pseud. LC 35-5044. 32 p. col. illus. 21 cm. c.1935. Whitman Publishing Co.
Smith, Charlton Lyman
--Bab Haskins in Southern Seas. LC 22-186520. xvi, 288 p. 19 1/2 cm. c.1922. The Cornhill Publishing Company.
--Gus Harvey. N.D. Small,Maynard & Co.
--Gus Harvey, the Boy Skipper of Cape Ann. N.D. Hale, Cushman & Flint.
--Gus Harvey, the Boy Skipper of Cape Ann Town. N.D. Marshall Jones.
Smith, Cicely Fox
--Painted Ports. Hodges, Cyril Walter (1909-), illus. 212p. (gr. 3-8). 1948. Oxford University Press.
--The Ship Aground: A Tale of Adventure. Hodges, Cyril Walter (1909-), illus. LC 41-51981. 221 p. illus. 22 cm. 1941. Oxford University Press.
--The Valiant Sailor. Dear, Neville, illus. LC 57-520292. 186p. illus. 22cm. 1957. Criterion Books.
--Valiant Sailor. Dear, Neville, illus. (Illus.). (gr. 6-10). 1957. (ISBN 0-87599-105-X). S G Phillips.
Smith, Clarence H.
--Camille the Camel. 1959. Exposition Press.
Smith, Claude Clayton (1944-)
--The Stratford Devil. LC 84-19684. (Walker's American History Series for Young People). 1984. (ISBN 0-8027-6544-0). Walker.
Smith, Dale R., et al., eds. see Tucker, Bettie C.
Smith, Deane S
--Criss-Cross Vacation. Fay, Herman B., Jr., illus. LC 56-77072. 127p. illus. 21cm. 1956. Sterling Pub. Co.
Smith, Dee
--A Black Velvet Story. Flack, Marjorie (1897-1958), illus. LC 40-301927. 56 p. illus. 21 1/2 cm. 1940. Frederick A. Stokes Company.
Smith, Dennis (1940-)
--The Little Fire Engine That Saved the City. Kraus, Robert (1925-), ed. Barbaresi, Nina, illus. (Illus.). 32p. (gr. k-3). N.D. (ISBN 0-671-45564-8). Windmill Bks.
Smith, Dodie, pseud., see Smith, Dorothy Gladys.
Smith, Donald
--Adam the Astronaut: Alphabet Book. (Illus.). 32p. (ps-1). 1984. (ISBN 0-241-11048-3, Pub by Hamish Hamilton). David & Charles.
Smith, Doris Buchanan (1934-)
--Dreams & Drummers. LC 77-26590. 180 p. 21cm. c.1978. (ISBN 0-690-01381-7). (ISBN 0-690-03843-7). Crowell.
--The First Hard Times. 1st ed. LC 82-60084. 137 p. 22cm. 1983. (ISBN 0-670-31571-0). Viking Press. **Award: (ALA).**
--Kelly's Creek. Tiegreen, Alan, illus. LC 75-6761. (Illus.). 69 p. 21cm. 1975. (ISBN 0-690-00731-0). Crowell.
--Kick a Stone Home. LC 74-4209. 152 p. 24cm. 1974. (ISBN 0-690-00535-0). Crowell.
--Kick a Stone Home. (gr. 6-9). 1983. Harper & Row.
--Last Was Lloyd. LC 80-29468. 124 p. 22cm. 1981. (ISBN 0-670-41921-4). Viking Press.
--Laura Upside-Down. LC 84-3689. 48 p. 1984. (ISBN 0-670-41998-2). Viking Kestrel.
--Moonshadow of Cherry Mountain. LC 82-70416. 154 p. 22cm. c.1982. (ISBN 0-590-07829-1). Four Winds Press.
--Moonshadow of Cherry Mountain. LC 85-5004. (Illus.). 154 p. 22cm. 1985, c.1982. (ISBN 0-02-785850-2). Four Winds Press.
--Salted Lemons. LC 80-66250. p. cm. c.1980. (ISBN 0-590-07666-3). Four Winds Press.
--A Taste of Blackberries. Robinson, Charles (1931-), illus. LC 72-7558. (Illus.). 58 p. 21cm. 1973. (ISBN 0-690-80511-X). (ISBN 0-690-80511-X). Crowell. **Award: (ALA).**
--Tough Chauncey. Eagle, Michael (1942-), illus. LC 73-16375. (Illus.). 222 p. 22cm. 1974. (ISBN 0-688-20112-1). (ISBN 0-688-20112-1). Morrow. **Award: (BGH).**
--Up and Over. LC 75-45468. 224 p. 22cm. 1976. (ISBN 0-688-22066-5). (ISBN 0-688-32066-X). Morrow.
Smith, Doris Susan (1949-)
--The Country Life of J. B. Rabbit. Smith, Doris Susan (1949-), illus. LC 83-47682. (Illus.). (ps-4). 1983. (ISBN 0-448-16586-4, G&D). (ISBN 0-448-16586-4). Putnam Pub Group.
--The Tortoise & the Hare. Smith, Doris Susan (1949-), illus. LC 78-12525. (Illus.). (A Goodnight Bk.). (ps-1). 1979. (ISBN 0-394-84102-6). Knopf.
--The Travels of J.B. Rabbit. Smith, Doris Susan (1949-), illus. LC 82-80876. (Illus.). 40 p. 29cm. c.1982. (ISBN 0-448-16585-6). Grosset & Dunlap.
Smith, Dorothy Gladys see Smith, Dodie, pseud.
Smith, Dorothy Gladys (1896-)
--The Hundred and One Dalmatians. Smith, Dodie, pseud. Grahame Johnstone, Anne & Grahame Johnstone, Janet, illus. LC 57-13886. (Illus.). 199 p. 22cm. 1957. Viking Press.
--The Hundred and One Dalmations. Smith, Dodie, pseud. Grahame Johnstone, Anne & Grahame Johnstone, Janet, illus. LC 57-23223. (Illus.). 190 p. 22cm. 1956. Heinemann.
--The Starlight Barking. Smith, Dodie, pseud. Grahame Johnstone, Anne & Grahame Johnstone, Janet, illus. LC 68-16145. 156p. illus. 22cm. 1967. (ISBN 0-671-65012-2). S&S.
Smith, Dorothy Hall, jt. ed. see Govoni, Ilse Hayes.
Smith, Dorothy Hall & Espenscheid, Gertrude Elliott, eds.
--The Tall Book of Christmas. LC 54-9002. (Illus.). 96p. (Tall Bks.). (gr. k-3). 1980. (ISBN 0-06-025700-8, HarpJ). (ISBN 0-06-025701-6). Har-Row.
--The Tall Book of Christmas. LC 54-9002. 92p. illus. 31x14cm. 1954. Harper.
Smith, Dorothy Johnson (1898-)
--Muddy Paws. Neville, Vera (1900-1978), illus. LC 48-2108. 216 p. illus. 22 cm. 1948. T. Y. Crowell Co.
--The Secret of the Lighthouse. Porter, Jean Macdonald (1906-), illus. LC 50-10092. (Illus.). 244 p. 21cm. 1950. Crowell.
Smith, Dorothy Stafford see Smith, Sarah Stafford, pseud.
Smith, Dwight Laurence
--Hiram and Other Cats. Cook, Gladys Emerson, illus. N.D. Grosset & Dunlap.
Smith, Edesse Peery
--The Pokes of Gold. LC 58-9900. 207 p. 21 cm. 1958. Dodd, Mead.
Smith, Edgar W., ed. see Doyle, Arthur Conan, Sir.
Smith, Edith Freelove
--Trading East. Pitz, Henry Clarence (1895-1976), illus. LC 30-25737. (Story based on Hakluyt's Voyages to Russia Turkeman, and Persia). viii p., 2 l., 3-284, 1 p. incl. illus., plates. front. 21 1/2 cm. 1930. Little, Brown, and Company.
Smith, Eilzabeth Thomasina Meade see Meade, L. T., pseud.
Smith, Eleanor (1858-), ed.
--Song Devices and Jingles. Young, Florence Liley, illus. LC 21-3999. xi, 65 p. col. front., 5 col. pl. 24 x 19 1/2 cm. c.1920. Lothrop, Lee & Shepard Co.
--Songs For Little Children, Part 1. N.D. Milton Bradley.
--Songs for Little Children, Part 2. N.D. Milton Bradley.
Smith, Elias Darby (1840-)
--On Hurley Hills and Other Verse. N.D. Sherman, French & Co.
Smith, Elizabeth
--The Christmas Mice. 1979. (ISBN 0-8062-1287-X). Carlton.
Smith, Elizabeth A. see Faralone, pseud.
Smith, Elizabeth A.
--One of the Billingses: Or, Edith's Mistake. (Illus.). 246p. (Selected Bks for Sunday School: No. 23). N.D. Set. Methodist Bk Concern.
--Stories of Childhood. Faralone, pseud. LC 99-5943. 160p. 19cm. 1899. E. A. Cook.
Smith, Elizabeth Oakes Prince, Mrs. (1806-1893)
--The Dandelion. LC 24-9833. 157 p. incl. front., illus. 11 1/2 cm. (Half-title: Stories, not for good children, nor bad children, but for real children ... no. 2). 1846. Saxton and Kelt.
Smith, Elizabeth Thomasina Meade see Meade, L. T, pseud.
Smith, Elizabeth Thomasina Meade see Meade, L. T., pseud.
Smith, Elizabeth Thomasina Meade, Mrs. (1854-1914)
--Bashful Fifteen. Meade, L. T., pseud. LC 8-9638. iv, 326 p. 19 cm. c.1892. Cassell Publishing Company.
--Betty: A Schoolgirl. Meade, L. T., pseud. Rev ed. Hopkins, Everard, illus. LC 8-10180. iii p., 1 l., 297 p. front., plates. 19 cm. c.1894. The Cassell Publishing Co.
--A Bevy of Girls. LC 8-346074. iv, 427 p. front., plates. 18 1/2 cm. 1905. Stitt Publishing Company.
--A Bunch of Cherries. Meade, L. T., pseud. LC 41-40538. vi, 288 p. front., plates. 19 cm. N.D. The Mershon Company.
--Catalina: Art Student. Meade, L. T., pseud. Boucher, W. (0000-1906), illus. LC 8-10181. 320 p. front., plates. 19 1/2 cm. 1897. J. B. Lippincott Company.
--The Children of Wilton Chase. Meade, L. T., pseud. Hopkins, Everard, illus. LC 8-10182. 5 p. l., 275 p. front., plates. 19 1/2 cm. c.1891. Cassell Publishing Company.
--The Colonel's Conquest. Meade, L. T., pseud. LC 7-29156. viii p., 1 l., 309 p. front., 5 pl. 20 1/2 cm. 1907. G. W. Jacobs & Company.
--Daddy's Boy. Meade, L. T., pseud. Troubridge, Laura, illus. LC 67-121415. (Illus.). vi, 334. 19cm. 1889. White and Allen.
--The Daughter of a Soldier, a Colleen of South Ireland. Meade, L. T., pseud. Wrenn, Charles L., illus. LC 16-15131. (Illus.). 331p. 20cm. 1915. Hurst & Company.
--Deb and the Duchess: A Story for Boys and Girls. Meade, L. T., pseud. Edwards, Mary Ellen, illus. LC 67-121425. (Illus.). v, 399. 21cm. 1889. White & Allen.
--The Doctor's Children. Meade, L. T., pseud. Boyd, A. S., illus. LC 67-121412. (Illus.). 296p. 20cm. 1911. Lippincott.
--Four on an Island: A Book for the Little Folks. Meade, L. T., pseud. LC 8-10183. 4 p. l., 262 p. front., plates. 19 cm. c.1892. Cassell Publishing Company.
--Four on an Island: A Book for the Little Folks. Meade, L. T., pseud. LC 29-30765. 2 p. l., 262 p. front. 19 1/2 cm. 1910. Grosset & Dunlap.
--A Girl of High Adventure. Meade, L. T., pseud. New copyright ed. Wrenn, Charles L., illus. LC 14-14573. 3 p. l., iii-iv, 387 p. fronts., plates. 20 cm. $0.6. c.1914. Hurst & Company.
--Girls New and Old. Meade, L. T., pseud. Williamson, J., illus. LC 8-10184. iii, 348 p. front., plates. 18 cm. c.1895. The Cassell Publishing Co.
--The Girls of Merton College. Smith, Elizabeth Thomasina Meade. Meade, L. T., pseud. N.D. Hurst & Co.
--The Girls of Mrs. Pritchard's School. Meade, L. T., pseud. LC 4-24505. iii, 313 p. front., plates. 19 cm. c.1904. The Mershon Company.
--Girls of the True Blue. Meade, L. T., pseud. LC 26-7507. 1 p. l., 310 p. front. 19 1/2 cm. 1912. Grosset & Dunlap.
--Heart of Gold. Meade, L. T., pseud. authorized. 218 p. 19 cm. (Lovell's International Series, No. 120). c.1890. United States Book Company, Successors to J. W. Lovell Company.
--Kitty O'Donovan. Meade, L. T., pseud. Lewis, Martin, illus. LC 12-206356. iii p., 1 l., 330 p. front., plates. 19 1/2 cm. c.1912. Hurst & Company.
--The Lady of the Forest. Meade, L. T., pseud. LC 67-123601. (Illus.). 318p. 19cm. 1889. F. Warne.
--The Lady of the Forest: A Story for Girls. Meade, L. T., pseud. LC 26-7506. 2 p. l., 317 p. front. 19 1/2 cm. N.D. A. L. Burt Company.
--The Little School Mothers. A Story for Girls. Meade, L. T., pseud. LC 7-21231. 2 p. l., 294 p. front., plates. 19 1/2 cm. c.1907. D. McKay.
--A Madcap. Copping, Harold (1863-1932), illus. LC 4-28206. 19cm. 260p. 1904. Mershon Co.
--The Manor School. Meade, L. T., pseud. LC 3-27221. iv, 337 p. 18 1/2 cm. c.1903. The Mershon Company.
--Me and My Dolls: The Story of the Joys and Troubles of Miss Bo-Peep and Her Doll Family, to Which Is Added the Strange Adventures of Mopsy and Hans. Meade, L. T., pseud. LC 12-38718. 4 p. l., 7-121 p. front., plates. 17 cm. c.1898. Lothrop Publishing Company.
--Merry Girls of England. Meade, L. T., pseud. Stacey, W. S., illus. LC 2-6296. vi p., 1 l., 9-288 p. front., plates. 19 1/2 cm. 1897. A. I. Bradley & Co.
--A Modern Tomboy. Meade, L. T., pseud. LC 26-7498. 2 p. l., 320 p. front. 19 1/2 cm. N.D. Grosset & Dunlap.
--Out of the Fashion. Meade, L. T., pseud. LC 8-101861. 1 p. l., 270 p. front. (port.) plates. 19 cm. c.1892. Cassell Publishing Company.
--The Palace Beautiful: A Story for Girls. Meade, L. T., pseud. LC 52-25500. 410 p. illus. 20 cm. N.D. A. L. Burt Co.
--Peggy from Kerry. Meade, L. T., pseud. Lewis, Martin, illus. LC 12-206341. iii p., 1 l., 330 p. 19 1/2 cm. $0.6. c.1912. Hurst & Company.
--The Queen of Joy. Meade, L. T., pseud. Wrenn, Charles L., illus. LC 14-14572. 4 p. l., 372 p. front., plates. 20 cm. $0.6. c.1914. Hurst & Company.
--Red Rose and Tiger Lily: Or, In a Wider World. Meade, L. T., pseud. LC 8-10188. 2 p. l., 284 p. front., plates. 19 cm. c.1894. The Cassell Publishing Co.
--A Ring of Rubies. Meade, L. T., pseud. LC 8-10187. 1 p. l., 292 p. front., plates. 18 cm. c.1892. Cassell Publishing Company.
--The School Queens. Meade, L. T., pseud. LC 26-75057. 1 p. l., 179 p. 18 1/2 cm. (Our girls books series). 1910. The New York Book Company.
--A Sweet Girl Graduate. Meade, L. T., pseud. LC 10-13850. 320 p. front., illus. 19 1/2 cm. c.1910. Hurst and Company.
--A Sweet Girl Graduate. Smith, Elizabeth Thomasina Meade. Meade, L. T., pseud. N.D. New York Book Co.
--The Time of Roses: A Story for Girls. Meade, L. T., pseud. LC 26-7502. 1 p. l., 364 p. 19 1/2 cm. N.D. A. L. Burt Company.
--Turquoise and Ruby. Meade, L. T., pseud. LC 6-39726. iii, 380 p. front., plates. 19 cm. c.1906. Chatterton-Peck Company.
--A Very Naughty Girl. Meade, L. T., pseud. N.D. J.B. Lippincott.
--A Very Naughty Girl. Meade, L. T., pseud. Rainey, William R. I. (1852-1936), illus. LC 42-332379. 330 p. 19 cm. N.D. Hurst and Company.
--A World of Girls: The Story of a School. Meade, L. T., pseud. Edwards, Mary Ellen, illus. LC 42-26413. v, 7-288 p. front., plates. 19 1/2 cm. N.D. The Mershon Company.
--A Young Mutineer: A Story for Girls. Meade, L. T., pseud. Browne, Gordon Frederick (1858-1932), illus. LC 26-7504. 4 p. l., 299 p. front., plates. 19 1/2 cm. N.D. A. L. Burt.
--A Young Mutineer: A Story for Girls. Meade, L. T., pseud. Browne, Gordon Frederick (1858-1932), illus. LC 26-7503. 187 p. front. (port.) 19 cm. 1893. Hurst & Company.
Smith, Elmer Boyd (1860-1843), ed. see Mother Goose.
Smith, Elmer Boyd (1860-1943)
--After They Came Out of the Ark. Smith, Elmer Boyd (1860-1943), illus. LC 18-220316. 46, 2 p. col. illus. 21 1/2 x 26 1/2 cm. c.1918. G. P. Putnam's Sons.
--Chicken World. Smith, Elmer Boyd (1860-1943), illus. 28 p. incl. col. front., col. illus. 22 1/2 x 28 1/2 cm. c.1910. G. P. Putnam's Sons.
--The Circus and All About It. Smith, Elmer Boyd (1860-1943), illus. LC 9-27959. (Illus.). 22x28 cm. 62p. 1909. Frederick A. Stokes.
--The Country Book. Smith, Elmer Boyd (1860-1943), illus. LC 24-22117. 30 p. illus., col. plates. 21 1/2 x 28 cm. 1924. Frederick A. Stokes Company.
--The Early Life of Mr. Man Before Noah. LC 14-21199. 50 p., 1 l. col. illus. 21 1/2 x 28 1/2 cm. $2.0. 1914. Houghton Mifflin Company.
--The Farm Book: Bob and Betty Visit Uncle John. Smith, Elmer Boyd (1860-1943), illus. Bader, Barbara, intro. by. LC 82-12021. (Illus.). 55 p. 1982, c.1938. (ISBN 0-395-32951-5). Houghton Mifflin.
--Fun in the Radio World. Smith, Elmer Boyd (1860-1943), illus. LC 23-13006. 30 p. illus., col. plates. 21 1/2 x 28 1/2 cm. 1923. Frederick A. Stokes Company.
--In the Land of Make Believe. Smith, Elmer Boyd (1860-1943), illus. LC 16-214012. 28 p. illus., col. plates. 20 1/2 x 26 cm. 1916. H. Holt and Company.
--Lions 'n' Elephants 'n' Everything. Smith, Elmer Boyd (1860-1943), illus. LC 29-18359. 32 p. col. plates, illus. 22 x 23 1/2 cm. c.1929. G. P. Putnam's Sons.
--The Railroad Book: Bob and Betty's Summer on the Railroad. LC 83-8505. p. cm. 1983, c.1913. (ISBN 0-395-34832-3). Houghton Mifflin.
--The Railrodd Book: Bob and Betty's summer on the railroad. Smith, Elmer Boyd (1860-1943), illus. LC 13-23213. 28 p, l l. illus. col. pl. 20 1/2 x 26cm. 1913. Houghton Mifflin.
--Santa Claus and All About Him. Smith, Elmer Boyd (1860-1943), illus. LC 8-193. (Illus.). 28x21 cm. 62p. 1908. Frederick A. Stokes.
--The Seashore Book. Smith, Elmer Boyd (1860-1943), illus. LC 84-24483. (Illus.). 55 p. 1985. (ISBN 0-395-38015-4). Houghton Mifflin.
--The Seashore Book: Bob and Betty's Summer with Captain Hawes. LC 12-221386. 30 p. illus., col. plates. 20 1/2 x 25 1/2 cm. 1912. Houghton Mifflin Company.
--The Story of Noah's Ark. Smith, Elmer Boyd (1860-1943), illus. LC 5-34691. 56 p. col. illus. 21 1/2 x 29 cm. 1905. Houghton, Mifflin and Company.

Smith, Elva Sophronia, jt. ed. see Hazeltine, Alice Isabel.

Smith, Elva Sophronia (1871-1965)
--Pioneering in a Conestoga Wagon. Sherman, Larry, illus. (Illus.). 32p. (gr. 1-6). 1976. (ISBN 0-682-48468-7). Exposition.

Smith, Elva Sophronia (1871-1965), ed.
--Adventure Calls: True Stories and Some That Might Have Been True. LC 53-9770. 281p. 22cm. 1953. Lothrop, Lee & Shepard.
--A Book of Lullabies. LC 73-4883. (Granger index reprint series). 1973. (ISBN 0-8369-6421-7). Books for Libraries Press.
--A Book of Lullabies. N.D. Lothrop,Lee & Shepard.
--Good Old Stories for Boys and Girls. LC 19-6769. 320 p. col. front., col. plates. 20 1/2 cm. 1919. Lothrop, Lee & Shepard Co.
--More Mystery Tales for Boys and Girls. Bridgman, Lewis Jesse (1857-1931), illus. LC 22-26982. 392 p. front., illus. 20 cm. c.1922. Lothrop, Lee & Shepard Co.
--Mystery Tales for Boys and Girls. Bridgman, Lewis Jesse (1857-1931), illus. LC 17-23758. 5 p. l., 388 p. front., illus. 20 cm. 1917. Lothrop, Lee & Shepard Co.

--Robbie's Bible Stories, 1 of 21 vols. (Illus.). (Boys & Girls Booklovers Ser.: No. 17). 1905. Set. Henry Altemus Co.
--Robbies Bible Stories. N.D. Sherwood Publishing Co.
--The Roggie and Reggie Stories. Squire, Maud Hunt (1873-) & Mars, Ethel (1876-), illus. LC 6841. v p., 1 l., 95 p. col. front., col. plates. 21 1/2 x 18 cm. 1900. Harper & Brothers.
--The Stories of Peter and Ellen. Squire, Maud Hunt (1873-) & Mars, Ethel (1876-), illus. LC 3-228162. 5 p. l., 3-137, 1 p. col. front., 14 col. pl. 22 x 17 1/2 cm. 1903. Harper & Brothers.
--Ten Little Comedies: Tales of the Troubles of Ten Little Girls Whose Tears Were Turned into Smiles. LC 12-38734. 5 p. l., 256 p. 10 pl. (incl. front.) 19 cm. 1897. Little, Brown, and Company.
--When Roggie and Reggie Were Five. Adams, Henrietta S., illus. LC 9-27968. 5 p. l., 3-168 p. 1 l., col. front., 7 col. pl. 22 cm. $1.3. 1909. Harper & Brothers.
--The Wonderful Stories of Jane and John. N.D. Dodd Mead & Co.
--The Wonderful Stories of Jane & John. N.D. Small,Maynard & Co.
--The Wonderful Stories of Jane and John. Woods, Alice, illus. (Illus.). N.D. Duffield & Co.
--The Wonderful Stories of Jane and John. Woods, Alice, illus. LC 99-589087. 3 p. l., v-vii, 74 p., 1 l., col. front., col. plates. 23 cm. 1899. H. S. Stone & Company.

Smith, Gilbert
--The Green Mountain Boys Ride. N.D. Appleton Century Co.

Smith, Glanville Wynkoop (1901-)
--The Adventures of Sir Ignatius Tippitolio: Better Known to the World As Tippy, Proprietor of Tippitolio's Grand Imperial Hotel Oriella. Eichenberg, Fritz (1901-), illus. LC 45-352301. 5 p. l., 162 p. incl. front., illus. 21 1/2 cm. 1945. Harper & Brothers.
--The Adventures of Tippy. Eichenberg, Fritz (1901-), illus. (gr. 2). N.D. Harper & Bros.

Smith, Glen, jt. ed. see Smith, Louisa.

Smith, Glenna C.
--The Little Mouse Was a Grouch. Jordan, Alton, ed. (Illus.). (Buppet Series). (gr. k-3). 1981. (ISBN 0-89868-095-6, Read Res). (ISBN 0-89868-106-5). ARO Pub.
Smith, Goldie C.
--Sleepy Time Rhymes. (ps-k). 1970. (ISBN 0-528-88817-X). Rand.
Smith, Gregory Jay, jt. ed. see Howes, Barbara.
Smith, Guy N., ed.
--Sleeping Beauty. LC 79-89578. (Illus.). (Disney Classics Ser.). (gr. k-4). 1980. (ISBN 0-448-16108-7, G&D). Putnam Pub Group.
Smith, H. O., jt. auth. see Lucas, Edward Verrall.
Smith, Hannah Merriam, jt. auth. see Sargent, Shirley.
Smith, Harriet Lummis, Mrs.
--The Friendly-Terrace Quartette: How Peggy and Priscilla and Amy and Ruth Did Their Share on the Farm and in the Shop. O'Brien, Harriet, illus. LC 21-379447. 4 p. l., 319 p. front., plates. 20 1/2 cm. (Her The Friendly Terrace Series). 1920. The Page Company.
--The Girls of Friendly Terrace: Or, Peggy Raymond's Success. Goss, John, illus. LC 12-101389. 4 p. l., 347 p. front. plates. 20 1/2 cm. 1912. L. C. Page & Company.
--Pat and Pal. Tyng, Griswold, illus. LC 28-25483. 4 p. l., 291 p. front., illus. plates. 19 1/2 cm. 1928. L. C. Page & Company.
--Peggy Raymond at "The Poplars". (The Peggy Raymond Ser.). N.D. A L Burt Co.
--The Peggy Raymond Ser. N.D. A L Burt Co.
--Peggy Raymond's Friendly Terrace Quartette: How Peggy and Priscilla and Amy and Ruth Did Their Share on the Farm and in the Shop. Taylor, H. Weston & Goss, John, illus. (The Peggy Raymond Ser.). N.D. L. C. Page.
--Peggy Raymond's School Days. (The Peggy Raymond Ser.). N.D. A L Burt Co.
--Peggy Raymond's School Days: Or, Old Girls and New. Taylor, H. Weston, illus. LC 16-18334. 4 p. l., 313 p. front., plates. 20 1/2 cm. (Her The Friendly-Terrace Series). 1916. The Page Company.
--Peggy Raymond's Success. (The Peggy Raymond Ser.). N.D. A L Burt Co.
--Peggy Raymond's Success: Or, The Girls of Friendly Terrace. (The Peggy Raymond Ser.). N.D. Page Co.
--Peggy Raymond's Vacation. (The Peggy Raymond Ser.). N.D. A L Burt Co.
--Peggy Raymond's Vacation: Or, Friendly Terrace Transplanted. Goss, John, illus. LC 13-13962. 4 p. l., 324 p. front., plates. 20 1/2 cm. (Her The Friendly Terrace Series). 1913. L. C. Page & Company.
--Peggy Raymond's Way: Or, Blossom Time at Friendly-Terrace. Merrill, Frank Thayer (1848-), illus. LC 22-188559. 4 p. l., 324 p. col. front., plates. 19 1/2 cm. (Her Friendly Terrace Series). 1922. The Page Company.
--Polly and the Milk Route. LC 13-25442. 62 p. incl. plates. 17 1/2 cm. $0.1. c.1913. David C. Cook Publishing Co.
--Pollyanna of the Orange Blossems. (The Pollyanna Bks.). N.D. Grosset & Dunlap.
--Pollyanna of the Orange Blossoms: The Third Glad Book. Taylor, H. Weston, illus. (The Pollyanna Bks.). N.D. Page Co.
--Pollyanna's Debt of Honor. (The Pollyanna Bks.). N.D. Grosset & Dunlap.
--Pollyanna's Debt of Honor: The Fifth Glad Book. Taylor, H. Weston, illus. (The Pollyanna bks.). N.D. L. C. Page.
--Pollyanna's Jewels. (The Pollyanna Bks.). N.D. Grosset & Dunlap.
--Pollyanna's Jewels: The Fourth Glad bk. Taylor, H. Weston, illus. (The Pollyanna bks.). N.D. L. C. Page.
--Pollyanna's Western Adventure. (The Pollyanna Bks.). N.D. Grosset & Dunlap.
--Pollyanna's Western Adventure: The Sixth Glad bk. Taylor, H. Weston, illus. (The Pollyanna bks.). N.D. L. C. Page.
Smith, Harriet Theresa see Comstock, Harriet Theresa Smith, Mrs.
Smith, Harry
--Children's Sunday Series. N.D. Fleming H. Revell Co.
Smith, Harry, ed. see Mother Goose.
Smith, Harry Allen (1907-1976)
--Don't Get Personal with a Chicken. LC 77-23991. p. cm. 1977, c.1959. (ISBN 0-8128-2363-X). Stein and Day.
--Write Me a Poem, Baby. LC 77-23994. (Illus.). 142 p. 21cm. 1977, c.1956. (ISBN 0-8128-2361-3). (ISBN 0-8128-2360-5). Stein and Day.
Smith, Harry L., illus.
--Mother Goose: Her Book. LC 7-10592. (Illus.). 48p. 25 x 21cm. 1906. Duffield & Company.
Smith, Harry W.
--Michael and the Mary Day. 1st ed. Smith, Harry W., illus. LC 78-66734. (Illus.). 59 p. 29cm. c.1979. (ISBN 0-89272-046-8). Down East Magazine.
Smith, Helen Catherine Snyder & Swetnam, George
--Hannah's Town. Smith, Helen Catherine Snyder, illus. LC 73-84564. (Illus.). 113 p. 24cm. 1973. (ISBN 0-913228-06-0). Dillon Liederbach.
Smith, Helen R., ed.
--Laughing Matter. Wiese, Kurt (1887-1974), illus. LC 49-11540. (Illus.). 166 p. 21cm. 1949. Scribner's Sons.
Smith, Helen Vosburgh
--A Child's Book of Birds in Rhymes and Pictures. (Illus.). 1959. Exposition Press.
Smith, Henry Justin (1875-)
--Senor Zero. Glanckoff, Samuel (1894-), illus. LC 31-25228. 3 p. l., 3-337 p. incl. illus., plates. front. 22 cm. c.1931. Harcourt, Brace and Co.
--Young Phillips, Reporter. 269p. (gr. 9). N.D. Harcourt, Brace & Co.
Smith, Henry Nash, ed. see Cooper, James Fenimore.
Smith, Herbert Huntington (1851-1919)
--His Majesty's Sloop, Diamond Rock. LC 4-28417. viii, p., 2 l., 431, 1 p. front., 3 pl. 20 cm. 1904. Houghton Mifflin and Company.
Smith, Hessie, jt. auth. see Boyd, Lilyth Watson.
Smith, Holly
--Pidgey & P. J. 1981. (ISBN 0-8062-1670-0). Carlton.
Smith, Hopkinson F.
--Colonel Carter of Cartersville. N.D. Houghton Mifflin Co.
Smith, Howard Everett, Jr., jt. auth. see Norris, Louanne.
Smith, Howard Everett, Jr. (1927-)
--The Animal Olympics. 1st ed. Lane, John (1932-), illus. LC 78-60302. (Illus.). 48 p. 27cm. c.1979. (ISBN 0-385-14354-0). (ISBN 0-385-14355-9). Doubleday.
Smith, Howden A. D.
--Porto Bello Gold. N.D. Grosset & Dunlap.
Smith, Imogene Henderson (1922-)
--Egg on Her Face. LC 63-9864. 190 p. 21 cm. 1963. Lippincott.
--Time on Her Hands. LC 65-13420. 189p. 21cm. c.1965. Lippincott.
Smith, Inge, tr. see Havrevold, Finn.
Smith, Ingrid, jt. auth. see Koehler-Broman, Mela.
Smith, Irene (1903-)
--Down the Road with Johnny. Wiese, Kurt (1887-1974), illus. LC 51-13392. 64 p. illus. 22 cm. 1951. Whittlesey House.
--Hubbub in the Hollow. rev. ed. Palazzo, Tony (1905-1970), illus. LC 52-8331. 48p. 1952. Whittlesey House.
--Lucky Days for Johnny. Tyng, Griswold & Wiese, Kurt, illus. LC 50-923691. (Illus.). 64 p. 22cm. 1950. Whittlesey House.
--The Santa Claus Book. Depper, Hertha, illus. (gr. 2-6). N.D. Franklin Watts Inc.
Smith, Ivan
--Death of a Wombat. Pugh, Clifton, illus. (Illus.). 96p. (gr. 4 up). 1973. (ISBN 0-684-13538-8). Scribner.
Smith, J. Manton
--Essex Lad, 1 of 50 vols. (The Golden Rod Lib.). N.D. Set. American Tract Society.
Smith, James, ed. see Bogatsky, C. H. V.
Smith, James Cruickshanks (1867-), compiled by.
--Book of Ballads for Boys and Girls. Soutar, George N.D. Oxford University Press.
--A Book of Verse for Boys and Girls. LC 17-23319. 3 pt. in 1 v. 19 cm. 1915. Clarendon Press.
Smith, James Fletcher (1897-), adapted by see Gilbert, William Schwenck, Sir (1836-1911) & Sullivan, Sir Arthur Seymour, Sir.
Smith, James Steel
--James Steel Smith's City Song. Hervert, Fuka, illus. LC 75-109202. (Illus.). 32 p. 17cm. (Bill Martin instant reader). c.1970. (ISBN 0-03-084584-X). Holt, Rinehart & Winston.
Smith, Jane S. & Carlson, Betty (1919-)
--A Surprise for Bellevue. 1972. (ISBN 0-89107-131-8). Good News.
Smith, Janet Adam, ed.
--The Faber Book of Children's Verse. 1962. (ISBN 0-571-05273-8). Faber & Faber.
--The Faber Book of Children's Verse. 412p. 1963. (ISBN 0-571-05457-9). Faber & Faber.
--The Faber Book of Children's Verse. (Illus.). (gr. 4-7). 1954. (ISBN 0-571-05273-8). Transatlantic.
--The Looking Glass Book of Verse. Joerns, Consuelo, illus. LC 59-13337. 408 p. illus. 20 cm. (Looking glass library, 8). 1959. Looking Glass Library; Distributed by Random House.
Smith, Janet Patton
--The Ghost in the Swing. LC 72-10011. 216 p. 22cm. 1973. (ISBN 0-8114-7752-5). Steck-Vaughn Co.
Smith, Janice Lee (1949-)
--The Kid Next Door & Other Headaches: Stories about Adam Joshua. Gackenbach, Dick, illus. LC 83-47689. (Illus.). 160p. (gr. 1-4). 1984. (ISBN 0-06-025792-X, HarpJ). (ISBN 0-06-025793-8). Har-Row.
--The Monster in the Third Dresser Drawer and Other Stories About Adam Joshua. Gackenbach, Dick, illus. LC 81-47109. p. cm. c.1981. (ISBN 0-06-025739-3). (ISBN 0-06-025739-3). Harper & Row.
Smith, Jean Pajot (1945-)
--Li'l Tuffy & His ABC's. Smith, Jean Pajot (1945-), illus. (Illus.). 64p. (Ebony Jr. Bk). (ps-4). N.D. (ISBN 0-87485-063-0). Johnson Chi.
Smith, Jean Shannon, jt. auth. see Gardner, Mercedes.
Smith, Jeanie Oliver Davidson, Mrs.
--Stories of Fido and Hunter. LC 12-38732. 61 p. front. 16 cm. 1896. Press of J. J. Little & Co.
Smith, Jeannette (1896-)
--Tula: A Little Pueblo Girl. LC 40-7293. 1 p. l., 5-96 p. illus. 20 cm. c.1940. McKnight & McKnight.
Smith, Jessie Willcox, jt. auth. see Kingsley, Charles.
Smith, Jessie Willcox (1863-1935), selected by.
--A Child's Book of Old Verses. Smith, Jessie Willcox (1863-1935), illus. ix, 124p. illus., col. plates. 22cm. 1952. Dodd, Mead.
--A Child's Book of Old Verses. Smith, Jessie Willcox (1863-1935), illus. LC 10-23655. ix, 2, 124 p. col. front., col. plates. 24 1/2 cm. 1910. Duffield & Company.
--The Jessie Willcox Smith Little Mother Goose. Smith, Jessie Willcox (1863-1935), illus. (Illus.). (gr. k-3). 1971. (ISBN 0-396-06352-7). Dodd.
Smith, Jessie Willcox (1863-1935), illus.
--A Child's Book of Country Stories. N.D. Dodd Mead & Co.
--A Child's Book of Modern Stories. N.D. Dodd Mead & Co.
Smith, Jim (1920-)
--Alphonse & the Stonehenge Mystery. Smith, Jim (1920-), illus. (Illus.). 32p. (The Frog Band Ser.). (gr. 1-3). 1980. (ISBN 0-316-80162-3). Little.
--The Frog Band and Durrington Dormouse. LC 77-10549. p. cm. 1978. (ISBN 0-316-80155-0). Little, Brown.
--The Frog Band and the Mystery of Lion Castle. LC 78-61426. (Illus.). 32 p. 30cm. c.1978. (ISBN 0-316-80161-5). Little, Brown.
--The Frog Band and the Mystery of the Lion Castle. Smith, Jim (1920-), illus. 1979. Little Brown.
--The Frog Band and the Onion Seller. Smith, Jim (1920-), illus. LC 76-27177. (Illus.). 32 p. 30cm. 1980, c.1976. (ISBN 0-316-80006-6). Little, Brown.
--The Frog Band and the Owlnapper. LC 80-82784. (Illus.). 32 p. 30cm. c.1980. (ISBN 0-316-80163-1). Little, Brown.
--Nimbus & the Crown Jewels. (Illus.). 32p. (gr. 1 up). 1982. (ISBN 0-316-80167-4). Little.
--Nimbus the Explorer. Smith, Jim (1920-), illus. (Illus.). 32p. (gr. 1 up). 1982. (ISBN 0-316-80168-2). Little.
Smith, Joan
--The Gift of Umtal. LC 82-60928. 144p. (Julia MacRae Ser.). (gr. 5 up). 1983. (ISBN 0-531-04580-3, MacRae). Watts.
Smith, John, jt. ed. see Seymour, William Kean.
Smith, John Charles (1924-), compiled by.
--My Kind of Verse. Shulevitz, Uri (1935-), illus. LC 68-20609. (Illus.). xix, 235 p. 24cm. 1968. Macmillan.
Smith, John Frederick, tr. see Hoffmann, Franz.
Smith, John Moyr, ed.
--Tales of Old Thule. Smith, John Moyr, illus. LC 44-31057. 3 p. l., 199 p. front., illus. 19 cm. 1879. J. B. Lippincott & Co.
Smith, John Talbot, jt. ed. see Mabie, Hamilton Wright.
Smith, John Talbot (1855-1923)
--The Boy Who Came Back. LC 21-19392. 218 p. 19 cm. 1921. B. Benziger & Co., Inc.
--The Boy Who Looked Ahead. LC 20-18303. 186 p. 19 1/2 cm. 1920. B. Benziger & Co., Inc.
Smith, Josephine M.
--Three Secrets. N.D. Macmillan.
Smith, Joyce M.
--Giants, Lions & Fire. 1981. (ISBN 0-8423-1022-3). Tyndale.
--Young Disciples. (gr. 7-11). 1983. (ISBN 0-8423-8599-1). Tyndale.
Smith, Julie P.
--Widow Goldsmith's Daughters. (Julie P. Smith Novels). N.D. G. W. Carleton & Co.
Smith, Juliet
--Airport. LC 80-52521. (Starters Ser.). N.D. (ISBN 0-382-06488-7). Silver.
Smith, Juliet B.
--One Little Rebel. (Illus.). N.D. Methodist Bk Concern.
Smith, Kate, pseud., see Smith, Kathryn Elizabeth.
Smith, Kate, pseud. (1910-)
--Kate Smith Stories of Annabelle. Smith, Kathryn Elizabeth. Martin, Bill & Martin, Bernard Herman (1912-), illus. LC 51-31790. (Based on the original Annabelle Stories by Jane Gale). unpaged. illus. 28 cm. c.1951. Tell-Well Press.
Smith, Katherine Eunice Young see Smith, Eunice Young.
Smith, Katherine Eunice Young (1902-)
--Denny's Story. Smith, Katherine Eunice Young (1902-), illus. LC 52-11338. unpaged. illus. 25 cm. 1952. A. Whitman.
--High Heels for Jennifer. Smith, Katherine Eunice Young (1902-), illus. LC 64-253213. 225p. illus. 22cm. c.1964. Bobbs.
--The House with the Secret Room. Smith, Katherine Eunice Young (1902-), illus. LC 56-10536. 114p. illus. 26cm. 1956. Bobbs-Merrill.
--Jennifer Dances. Smith, Katherine Eunice Young (1902-), illus. LC 54-9497. (Illus.). 250 p. 23cm. 1954. Bobbs-Merrill.
--The Jennifer Gift. Smith, Katherine Eunice Young (1902-), illus. LC 50-6951. (Illus.). 256 p. 22cm. 1950. Bobbs-Merrill.
--Jennifer Is Eleven. Smith, Katherine Eunice Young (1902-), illus. LC 52-10279. (Illus.). 206 p. 23cm. 1952. Bobbs-Merrill.
--The Jennifer Prize. 1st ed. Smith, Katherine Eunice Young (1902-), illus. LC 51-13149. (Illus.). 263 p. 23cm. 1951. Bobbs-Merrill.
--The Knowing One. LC 67-24427. (Illus.). 107 p. 24cm. 1967. Meredith Press.
--The Little Red Drum. Smith, Katherine Eunice Young (1902-), illus. LC 61-8778. unpaged. illus. 23 cm. 1961. A. Whitman.
--Sam's Big Worry. LC 53-2854. unpaged. illus. 24cm. 1953. A. Whitman.
--Shoon: Wild Pony of the Moors. LC 65-17704. 177p. 22cm. c.1965. Bobbs.
--To Each a Season. LC 65-26518. 278p. 22cm. c.1965. Bobbs.
--Where To, Tillie Turtle?. Smith, Katherine Eunice Young (1902-), illus. LC 64-15678. 29cm. 32p. (gr. k-3). 1964. (ISBN 0-672-50576-2). Bobbs.
Smith, Kathryn Elizabeth see Smith, Kate, pseud.
Smith, Kay (1929-)
--Parakeets and Peach Pies. Aruego, Jose (1932-), illus. LC 77-117563. (Illus.). 32 p. 27cm. 1970. Parents' Magazine Press.
Smith, Ken
--The Phool and I. LC 55-13887. 271p. 21cm. 1955. Christopher Pub. House.
Smith, L. A., tr. see Grousset, Paschal.
Smith, L. H, jt. auth. see Nicholson, Joyce Thorpe.
Smith, Langford Wheaton Mrs. see Leetch, Dorothy Lyman.
Smith, Laura Irene Ivory (1903-)
--Mawal: Jungle Boy of French Indo-China. LC 47-12145. 24cm. 60p. 1947. Moody Press.
Smith, Laura Rountree see June, Caroline Silver, pseud.

AUTHOR INDEX SMITH, MARY

Smith, Laura Rountree (1876-1924)
--Animal Tales. LC 41-418540. 80 p. illus. 18 1/2 cm. 1920. March Brothers.
--Brownie Mew. (The Easy Library). N.D. A. Whitman & Co.
--The Bunny and Bear Book. Dulio, Dorothy & Stearus, Fred, illus. LC 68-129765. 19cm. 128p. 1923. Flanagan Co.
--Bunny-Be-Glad. June, Caroline Silver, pseud. (The Easy Library). N.D. A. Whitman & Co.
--Bunny-Be-Glad and The Fifty Fairy Flower Legends. June, Caroline Silver, pseud. Walsh, Haidee Zack, illus. 128p. (gr. 2-4). N.D. A. Whitman & Co.
--Bunny Boy and Grizzly Bear. (The Children's Hour Bks.). N.D. Grosset & Dunlap.
--Bunny Boy and Grizzly Bear. Smith, Laura Roundtree (1876-1924), illus. LC 6-749. 112 p. illus. 18 cm. c.1905. A. Flanagan Company.
--Bunny Bright Eyes. 94 p. illus. 19 cm. c.1906. A. Flanagan Company.
--Bunny Cotton-Tail, Jr. LC 12-27192. (A Sequel to the Tale of Bunny Cotton-Tail). 1 p. l., 7-128 p. col. front., illus. 17 1/2 cm. $0.30. c.1912. A. Flanagan Company.
--Children of Many Lands. LC 24-294252. 3 p. l., 5-142 p. illus. 19 cm. 1924. A. Flanagan Company.
--Circus Animals in Funland. Scannell, Mae Herrick, et al., illus. LC 28-15822. 245 p. incl. col. front., illus. (part col.) 21 cm. (Just right books). c.1928. A. Whitman & Company.
--The Circus Book. (The Children's Hour Bks.). N.D. Grosset & Dunlap.
--The Circus Cotton Tails. (The Children's Hour Bks.). N.D. Grosset & Dunlap.
--The Cotton Tails in Toyland. (The Children's Hour Bks.). N.D. Grosset & Dunlap.
--The Fairy Babies. (The Children's Hour Bks.). N.D. Grosset & Dunlap.
--The Fairy Babies. Dulin, Dorothy, illus. LC 24-19716. (Illus.). 124p. 18cm. 1924. A. Flanagan.
--Father Bunny and His Birds. Ross, M. T. Penny, illus. LC 22-22651. 128 p. col. front., illus. (part col.) col. plates. 20 cm. 1922. C. H. Van Vliet Co.
--Fifty Famous Sky Stories: A Child's Book of Familiar Sky Legends. June, Caroline Silver, pseud. LC 26-1844. 126 p. incl. col. front., illus. (part col.) 18 1/2 cm. ("Just right books"). c.1925. Albert Whitman Company.
--Fifty Funny Animal Tales. Mora, Joseph Jacinto (1876-), illus. LC 30-1376. 126, 1 p. incl. col. front., illus. (part col.) 18 1/2 cm. (just right book). c.1923. Albert Whitman Company.
--Flora and Fred in Flower Land. LC 23-16049. 192 p. col. front., col. plates. 20 cm. c.1923. Stanton & Van Vliet Co.
--Flora and Fred Play Housekeeping. LC 23-16043. 157 p. col. plates. 20 cm. c.1923. Stanton & Van Vliet Co.
--Flora and Fred Pretend. Burd, Clara Miller, illus. LC 23-16385. 186 p. col. front., col. plates. 20 cm. c.1923. C. H. Van Vliet Co.
--Flora's Fairy Forget Me Not. LC 23-15587. 20cm. 182p. 1923. Stanton & Van Vliet Co.
--Four Little Cotton-Tails in Vacation. LC 43-29023. 31 p. incl. illus., plates. 18 1/2 cm. (Instructor library books. 270). c.1917. Hall & McCreary Company.
--Good Night Stories. Burd, Clara Miller & Higgins, Violet Moore, illus. LC 21-18315. 120 p. col. front., illus., col. plates. 23 1/2 x 14 cm. c.1921. Stanton and Van Vliet Co.
--Healthy Bunny. Ross, M. T. Penny, illus. LC 22-22652. 127 p. col. front., illus. (part col.) col. plates. 20 cm. c.1922. C. H. Van Vliet Co.
--Jolly Polly and Curly Tail. (The Easy Library). N.D. A. Whitman & Co.
--The Like-to-Do Stories. Deal, L. Kate, illus. LC 22-3978. 136 p. col. front., illus. 19 1/2 cm. c.1920. Beckley-Cardy Company.
--Little Bear. LC 9-15205. 126 p. illus. 18 cm. c.1908. A. Flanagan Company.
--Little Bear. (The Children's Hour Bks.). N.D. Grosset & Dunlap.
--Little Folks from Etiquette Town. June, Caroline Silver, pseud. Lyon, Mildred & Jones, Marguerite M., illus. LC 28-6527. 91, 1, 7-111 p. incl. col. front., illus. (part col.) 21 cm. ("A just right book"). c.1927. Albert Whitman Company.
--Little Folks from Spotless Town. Lyon, Mildred & Jones, Marguerite M., illus. LC 28-16720. 4 p. l., 7-109, 9-123 p. col. front., illus. (part col.) 21 cm. (Just right books). c.1928. A. Whitman & Company.
--Little Sandman and The Fifty Famous Sky Stories. June, Caroline Silver, pseud. New ed. 128p. (gr. 2-4). N.D. A. Whitman & Co.
--Mother Bunny and Her Flowers. Ross, M. T. Penny, illus. LC 22-226532. 128 p. col. front., illus. (part col.) col. plates. 20 cm. c.1922. C. H. Van Vliet Co.
--Mother Goose Stories in Prose. LC 7-30843. 1 p. l., 5-110 p. illus. 20 1/2 cm. c.1907. A. Flanagan Company.
--New Gingerbread Boy. (The Easy Library). N.D. A. Whitman & Co.
--The Pixie in School. Wilson, Clara Powers, illus. LC 19-16212. 3 p. l., 137 p. col. front., col. plates. 21 1/2 cm. $1.50. 1919. A. C. McClurg & Co.
--The Pixie in School. Wilson, Clara Powers, illus. LC 25-21056. 1 p. l., 144 p. col. front., col. plates. 20 cm. 1925. A. Flanagan Company.
--The Pixie in the House. Wilson, Clara Powers, illus. LC 15-233672. 3 p. l., 137 p. col. front., col. illus. 21 1/2 cm. 1915. A. C. McClurg & Co.
--The Pixie in the House. Wilson, Clara Powers, illus. LC 25-21055. 3 p. l., 130 p. col. illus. 20 cm. 1925. A. Flanagan Company.
--The Pixie on the Farm. Wilson, Clara Powers, illus. LC 25-21053. 1 p. l., 144 p. col. front., col. plates. 20 cm. 1925. A. Flanagan Company.
--The Pixie Out Doors. Wilson, Clara Powers, illus. N.D. A. C. McClurg.
--The Pixie Out-Doors. Wilson, Clara Powers, illus. LC 25-210540. 1 p. l., 128 p. col. front., col. plates. 20 cm. 1925. A. Flanagan Company.
--Polite Bunny. Ross, M. T. Penny, illus. LC 22-226542. 127 p. col. front., illus. (part col.) col. plates. 20 cm. c.1922. C. H. Van Vliet Co.
--Rosy-Face Twins: The Adventure Book of Health. June, Caroline Silver, pseud. Lyon, Mildred, illus. LC 24-25184. 109 p. incl. col. front., col. illus. 18 1/2 cm. (Just right book). c.1924. Albert Whitman Company.
--The Runaway Bunny. Dulin, Dorothy, illus. LC 30-1317. 128 p. col. illus. 18 1/2 cm. 1923. A. Flanagan Company.
--The Singing Twins. New ed. Higgins, Violet Moore, illus. 128p. (gr. 2-5). 1930. A. Whitman & Co.
--The Social Twins: The Dainty Book of Etiquette. June, Caroline Silver, pseud. Jones, Marguerite M., illus. LC 24-25185. 111 p. incl. col. front., illus. (part col.) 18 1/2 cm. (Just right book). c.1924. A. Whitman & Company.
--Story Time Tales. LC 41-40540. 71 p. illus. 18 1/2 cm. 1920. March Brothers.
--The Tale of Bunny Cotton-Tail. LC 5-30266. 45 p. incl. front., illus. 19 cm. c.1904. A. Flanagan Company.
--The Tale of Bunny Cotton Tail. (The Children's Hour Bks.). N.D. Grosset & Dunlap.
--The Tale of Bunny Cotton-Tail. Dulin, Dorothy, illus. LC 25-545. 128 p. incl. col. front., col. illus. 18 1/2 cm. 1922. A. Flanagan Company.
--The Tale of Curly Tail. Scannell, Mae Herrick, illus. 96 p. incl. col. front., illus. (part col.) 18 1/2 cm. (Just Right Books). c.1923. Albert Whitman Company.
--Three Little Cotton Tails. LC 7-25507. 1 p. l., 5-98 p. illus. 18 cm. c.1907. A. Flanagan Company.
--The Tiddly Winks. Walsh, Haidee Zack, illus. 94, 1 p. incl. col. front., col. illus. 18 1/2 cm. (just right book). c.1923. Albert Whitman Company.
--Treasure Twins. (The Easy Library). N.D. A. Whitman & Co.

Smith, Laurence Dwight
--Adirondack Adventure. Johnson, Gwen B., illus. LC 45-10240. 286 p. incl. front., illus. 20 1/2 cm. 1945. S. Curl, Inc.
--The G-Men in Jeopardy. (The G-Men Stories). N.D. Grosset & Dunlap.
--The G-Men Trap the Spy Ring. Laune, Paul Sidney (1899-), illus. LC 39-19892. 3 p. l., 218 p. front., illus. (plan) 19 1/2 cm. c.1939. Grosset & Dunlap.
--The Mystery of the Yellow Tie. Laune, Paul Sidney (1899-), illus. LC 39-21496. iii, 220 p. front. 19 1/2 cm. (Spotlight Books for Boys). c.1939. Grosset & Dunlap.

Smith, Laurence & Harrison, Gregory
--Catch the Light. (Illus.). 48p. (gr. 5-8). 1983. (ISBN 0-19-276050-5, Pub. by Oxford U Pr Childrens). Merrimack Pub Cir.

Smith, Lawrence
--The Deeds of Doyly McPurr. (Illus.). 1974. State Mutual Bk.

Smith, Lawrence Beall (1909-)
--A Garland of Fairy Tales. Smith, Lawrence Beall (1909-), illus. LC 64-14942. 125p. illus. (pt. col.) 29cm. (Rutledge bk.). 1965, c.1964. Doubleday.

Smith, Leonard K
--Boy Scouts to the Rescue. Bryant, Samuel Hanks, illus. LC 39-301792. 4 p. l., 3-290 p. front., plates. 21 cm. 1939. Little, Brown and Company.
--Corey Takes the Scout Trail. rev. ed. LC 30-11613. 6 p. l., 259, 1 p. incl. front., illus., plates. 19 1/2 cm. 1930. D. Appleton & Company.
--Forty Days to Santa Fe. Elwell, R. Farrington, illus. LC 38-32417. 5 p. l., 3-325 p. incl. front., plates. 21 cm. 1938. Little, Brown and Company.
--Scouting on Mystery Trail. Carlson, George L., illus. LC 37-19449. vi p., 3 l., 295 p. incl. front., illus. 21 cm. 1937. The Macmillan Company.

Smith, Leonore Rose, ed.
--First Nursery Songs. Littlejohn, Fini R. (1914-), illus. LC 48-40130. 46 p. col. illus. 28 cm. c.1945. Garden City Pub. Co.

Smith, Linell Nash see Chenault, Nell, pseud.

Smith, Linell Nash (1932-)
--The Auction Pony. 1st ed. Bacon, Peggy, pseud. (1895-), illus. Bacon, Margaret Frances. LC 65-10584. (Illus.). 117 p. 21cm. 1965. Little, Brown.
--Miranda and the Cat. 1st ed. Bacon, Peggy, pseud. (1895-), illus. Bacon, Margaret Frances. LC 63-13466. 43 p. illus. 22 cm. 1963. Little, Brown.
--Molly's Miracle. 1st ed. Smith, Linell Nash (1932-), illus. LC 59-9109. 98 p. illus. 22 cm. 1959. Little, Brown.

Smith, Lloyd E., retold by see Perrault, Charles.

Smith, Louisa & Smith, Glen, eds.
--The Not Like Any Other Children's Book, Book. Smith, Glen, illus. (Illus.). 40p. (Orig.). 1st U.S. edition. (gr. 2 up). 1982. (ISBN 0-9609230-0-4). Smith & Smith Pub.

Smith, Lucia B. (1943-)
--My Mom Got a Job. Johnson, Cynthia, illus. LC 79-1494. p. cm. 1979. (ISBN 0-03-048321-2). Holt, Rinehart and Winston.
--A Special Kind of Sister. Hall, Chuck, illus. LC 78-14096. (Illus.). 32 p. 24cm. c.1979. (ISBN 0-03-047121-4). Holt, Rinehart, and Winston.

Smith, M. L. G.
--Minnie Weston. (Illus.). 188p. N.D. Sunday-School Publications.

Smith, Mabell Shippie Clarke, Mrs. (1864-)
--Enterprising Ethel. LC 31-19418. 3 p. l., 9-249 p. illus. 19 1/2 cm. c.1931. The World Syndicate Publishing Company.
--Ethel Morton and the Christmas Ship. LC 17-935054. 2 p. l., 9-246 p. front., illus., plates. 19 1/2 cm. (Her The Ethel Morton books). c.1915. The New York Book Company.
--Ethel Morton at Chautauqua. LC 17-9351. 2 p. l., 9-250 p. front., illus., plates. 19 1/2 cm. (Her The Ethel Morton books). c.1915. The New York Book Company.
--Ethel Morton at Rose House. LC 17-9352. 2 p. l., 9-248 p. front., illus., plates. 19 1/2 cm. (Her The Ethel Morton books). c.1915. The New York Book Company.
--Ethel Morton at Rose House. (Ethel Morton Ser.). N.D. World Publishing Co.
--Ethel Morton at Sweetbrier Lodge. LC 17-935350. 2 p. l., 9-247 p. front., illus., plates. 19 1/2 cm. (Her The Ethel Morton books). c.1915. The New York Book Company.
--Ethel Morton at Sweetbrier Lodge. (Ethel Morton Ser.). N.D. World Publishing Co.
--Ethel Morton's Enterprise. LC 17-935417. 2 p. l., 9-249 p. front., illus., plates. 19 1/2 cm. (Her The Ethel Morton books). c.1915. The New York Book Company.
--Ethel Morton's Enterprise. (Ethel Morton Ser.). N.D. World Publishing Co.
--Ethel Morton's Holidays. LC 17-935554. 2 p. l., 9-246 p. front., illus., plates. 19 1/2 cm. (Her The Ethel Morton books). c.1915. The New York Book Company.
--Ethel Morton's Holidays. (Ethel Morton Ser.). N.D. World Publishing Co.

Smith, Madeline Babcock
--The Lemon Jelly Cake. LC 52-9065. 240 p. 21cm. 1952. Little, Brown.

Smith, Mamie
--Sally Anne. 2nd ed. Eulalie, pseud. (1896-), illus. Banks, Eulalie M.. LC 33-19066. (Illus.). 26p. 28cm. 1932. Suttonhouse.

Smith, Margaret, ed. see Bronte, Charlotte.

Smith, Marion Howell (1906-)
--A Chariot for Beppi. LC 50-1387. 59 p. illus. 24 cm. 1949. Bellevue Books.

Smith, Marion Jaques (1899-)
--A Mother Bear's Troubled Trip, on the Way North. LC 67-28219. (Illus.). 1976. (ISBN 0-87027-093-1). Cumberland Pr.
--On the Way North: A Mother Bear's Troubled Trip. Smith, Marion Jaques (1899-), illus. (Illus.). 80 p. 28cm. 1967. Bond Wheelwright Co.
--Pokey and Timothy of Stonehouse Farm. Smith, Marion Jaques (1899-), illus. LC 73-80612. (Illus.). 67 p. 28cm. 1973. (ISBN 0-87027-129-6). Bond Wheelwright Co.

Smith, Martha, jt. auth. see Gaines, Edith.

Smith, Martha see McCluskey, John.

Smith, Martin (1942-)
--Canto for a Gypsy. 1972. (ISBN 0-399-11024-0). G. P. Putnam's Sons.
--Gypsy in Amber. 1971. (ISBN 0-399-10386-4). G. P. Putnam's Sons.

Smith, Mary E., ed. see Brooklyn. Public School 48 & Brooklyn. Public School 173.

Smith, Mary Estella (1863-)
--Eskimo Stories. Brown, Howard V., illus. LC 2-29252. 190 p. front., illus. 20 cm. 1902. Rand, McNally & Company.
--Holland Stories. Butler, Bonnibel, illus. LC 13-13534. (Illus.). xi, 159. 20cm. 1913. Rand, McNally & Company.
--Holland Stories. Butler, Bonnibel, illus. LC 32-23578. xi, 162 p. col. front., illus., col. plates. 20 cm. c.1932. Rand, McNally & Company.

Smith, Mary Prudence Wells see Thorne, P., pseud.

Smith, Mary Prudence Wells, Mrs. (1840-1930)
--The Boy Captive in Canada. Becher, Arthur E., illus. LC 5-32678. xiv p., 1 l., 352 p. front., 6 pl. 19 cm. 1905. Little, Brown, and Company.
--The Boy Captive of Old Deerfield. LC 53-27782. 233p. 20cm. 1953. J. W. Haigis, Jr.
--The Boy Captive of Old Deerfield. LC 74-25163. (Illus.). 233 p., 5 leaves of plates. 23cm. 1974. Rivercity Press.
--The Boy Captive of Old Deerfield. Bridgman, Lewis Jesse (1857-1931), illus. LC 4-24567. x p., 1 l., 304 p., 1 l. front., illus., plates. 19 cm. 1904. Little, Brown, and Company.
--The Boy Captive of Old Deerfield. Schoonover, Frank Earle (1877-1972), illus. LC 29-26908. x p., 3 l., 3-295 p. front., illus. (plan) col. plates. 22 1/2 cm. (Beacon Hill bookshelf). 1929. Little, Brown, and Company.
--Boys and Girls of Seventy-Seven. Grunwald, Ch., illus. LC 9-25388. x p., 1 l., 315 p. front., 3 pl. 19 cm. (Her The old Deerfield series). 1909. Little, Brown, and Company.
--Boys of the Border. LC 54-31854. 249p. 21cm. 1954. J. W. Haigis, Jr.
--Boys of the Border. Grunwald, Ch., illus. LC 7-31225. viii, 2 p., 1 l., 379 p. front., illus. (plan) 4 pl., map. 19 cm. (On verso of half-title: The Old Deerfield series. v. 3). 1907. Little, Brown, and Company.
--The Browns. 266p. (The "Jolly Good Times" Stories). N.D. Little, Brown.
--The Browns. LC 12-38749. viii, 266 p. incl. front. 17 1/2 cm. 1884. Roberts Brothers.
--Five in a Ford. Goss, John, illus. LC 18-18542. viii p., 2 l., 292 p., 1 l. front., plates. 19 cm. (Her The summer vacation series) $1.35.). 1918. Little, Brown, and Company.
--Four on a Farm. McConnell, Emlen, illus. LC 1-24851. 5 p. l., 309 p. front., 1 illus. (plan) 5 pl. 19 cm. 1901. Little, Brown & Company.
--A Jolly Good Summer. 319p. (The "Jolly Good Times" Stories). N.D. Little, Brown.
--A Jolly Good Summer. (Illus.). (The Boys' and Girls' Books). N.D. Little, Brown and Company.
--A Jolly Good Summer. LC 12-387501. 3 p. l., iii-iv p., 1 l., 7-319 p. 17 1/2 cm. (Her Jolly good times series. v. 8). 1895. Roberts Brothers.
--Jolly Good Times at Hackmatack. LC 4-16155. iv,7-347. 17cm. (Jolly Good Times Ser.). 1891. Roberts Brothers.
--Jolly Good Times at Hackmatack. Thorne, P., pseud. Grose, Helen Mason, illus. LC 4-17533. iv p., 1 l., 7-347 p. front., illus. (plan) pl. 19 cm. 1903. Little, Brown, and Company.
--Jolly Good Times at School. Also, Some Times Not Quite So Jolly. Thorne, P., pseud. LC 4-18939. 281 p. 2 pl. (incl. front.) 19 cm. (jolly good times series, v. 2). 1903. Little, Brown, and Company.
--Jolly Good Times at School. Also, Some Times Not Quite So Jolly. Thorne, P., pseud. Grose, Helen Mason (1880-), illus. LC 5-34512. 281 p. front., pl. 19 cm. (Her Jolly good times series. v. 2). 1904. Little, Brown, and Company.
--Jolly Good Times at School: Also, Some Times Not Quite So Jolly. Grose, Helen Mason (1880-), illus. LC 28-19247. 6 p. l., 3-302 p. incl. plates. col. front. 21 cm. (Her Jolly good times stories, no. 2). 1928. Lttle, Brown, and Company.
--Jolly Good Times: Child-Life on a Farm. Grose, Helen Mason (1880-), illus. LC 27-183267. ix p., 2 l., 297 p. incl. plates. col. front. 21 cm. (Her Jolly good times stories, no. 1). 1927. Little, Brown, and Company.
--Jolly Good Times: Or, Child-Life on a Farm. LC 3-21294. 277 p. incl. front. pl. 19 cm. (Her Jolly good times series, v. 1). 1902. Little, Brown, and Company.
--Jolly Good Times: Or, Child-life on a Farm. Thorne, P., pseud. LC 44-29963. 277p. 18cm. 1875. Roberts Brothers.
--Jolly Good Times To-Day. 281p. (The "Jolly Good Times" Stories). N.D. Little, Brown.
--Jolly Good Times to-Day. LC 20-19318. 4 p. l., 7-281 p. 2 pl. (incl. front.) 17 1/2 cm. 1894. Roberts Brothers.
--More Good Times at Hackmatack. (Illus.). (The Jolly Good Times Story). N.D. Little Brown & Co.
--More Good Times at Hackmatack. LC 12-38751. 1 p. l., vi, 7-277 p. front., pl. 17 1/2 cm. 1892. Roberts Brothers.

--Their Canoe Trip. LC 12-38748. 260 p. front., plates, map. 17 1/2 cm. (Her Jolly good times series. v. 4). 1889. Roberts Brothers.
--Their Canoe Trip. N.D. Robert Brothers.
--Three in a Camp. LC 16-21402. 5 p. l., 276 p. front., plates. 19 cm. (Her The summer vacation series). 1916. Little, Brown, and Company.
--Two in a Bungalow. Grose, Helen Mason (1880-), illus. LC 14-17095. 5 p. l., 302 p., 1 l. front., plates. 19 cm. $1.2. (Her The summer vacation series). 1914. Little, Brown, and Company.
--The Young and Old Puritans of Hatfield. Day, Bertha Corson (1875-1968), illus. LC 58317. x p., 1 l., 352 p. front., illus., 5 pl. 19 cm. (young Puritans series. v. 4). 1900. Little, Brown, and Company.
--The Young Puritans in Captivity. Smith, Jessie Willcox (1863-1935), illus. LC 99-53327. ix p., 2 l., 323 p. front., 5 pl. 19 cm. (Young Puritans series). 1899. Little, Brown and Company.
--The Young Puritans in King Philip's War. Bridgman, Lewis Jesse (1857-1931), illus. LC 98-1083. viii p., 2 l., 373 p. front., plates. 19 cm. (Young Puritans series...II). 1898. Little, Brown and Company.
--The Young Puritans of Old Hadley. Bridgman, Lewis Jesse (1857-1931), illus. LC 12-38757. 2 p., 1 l., 345 p. front., plates. 19 cm. (Young Puritan series). 1897. Roberts Brothers.

Smith, Mary Rowell
--Of Course You Can: A Book of Rhymes for the Young. 1st ed. Hitt, George, illus. LC 53-563854. 62p. illus. 21cm. 1953. Exposition Press.

Smith, Mary (1930-) & Smith, Robert Alan (1927-)
--Crocodiles Have Big Teeth All Day. LC 72-118918. (Illus.). 30 p. 21cm. 1970. (ISBN 0-695-80141-4). Follett Pub. Co.
--Long Ago Elf. LC 69-10268. (Illus.). 47 p. 1968. Follett Pub. Co.

Smith-Masters, Margaret Melville see LeFevre, Felicite, pseud.

Smith-Masters, Margaret Melville (1869-)
--Fiddle Diddle Dee. LeFevre, Filicite, pseud. Rev. ed. Barney, Maginel Wright (1877-), illus. LC 28-19677. (Illus.). 63p. 19cm. 1928. Greenberg.
--The Little Grey Goose. LeFevre, Felicite, pseud. Rev ed. Derrick, Freda (1892-), illus. LC 25-19536. 50 p. illus., col. plates. 19 1/2 cm. 1925. Macrae Smith Company.
--The Little Grey Goose. Lefreve, Felicite, pseud. Derrick, Freda (1892-), illus. LC 65-8306. 95p. illus. (pt. col.) 21cm. 1966. Richards Pr.
--Little Henry and the Tiger. LeFevre, Felicite, pseud. Rev ed. Best, Allena Champlin, Mrs. (1892-1974), illus. Berry, Erick, pseud. LC 31-25974. 41 p. col. front., col. illus. 21 1/2 cm. 1931. Harper & Brothers.
--Papa Peacock: A Truly Tempting Tale. LeFevre, Felicite, pseud. Rev ed. Gagarin, Sonia, illus. LC 31-29832. 2 p. l., 19 p. col. illus. 16 x 23 1/2 cm. 1931. Brewer, Warren & Putnam.
--Soldier Boy. Lefevre, Felicite, pseud. Sarg, Tony, pseud. (1882-1942), illus. Sarg, Anthony Frederick. LC 26-10570. (Illus.). 64p. 1926. Greenberg, Inc.
--Topsy Turvy. LeFevre, Felicite, pseud. Rev ed. Thomas, Dorothy Gay, illus. LC 28-12195. 3 p. l., 1, 95 p. illus. (part col.) 20 cm. 1928. Macrae Smith Company.

Smith-Masters, Margaret Melville (1869-), retold by.
--The Cock, the Mouse and the Little Red Hen. Lefevre, Felicite, pseud. J. L. G, illus. LC 20-20551. (Illus.). 64p. 14cm. 1920. Henry Altemus Co.
--The Cock, the Mouse and the Little Red Hen. LeFevre, Felicite, pseud. Unrevised. Peat, Fern Bisel, Mrs. (1893-), illus. LC 46-39313. 40 p. col. front., illus. (part col.) 28 cm. 1931. The Saalfield Publishing Company.
--The Cock, the Mouse, and the Little Red Hen. Peat, Fern Bisel, Mrs. (1893-), illus. LC 33-1. (Illus.). 20p. 22cm. (Calico Classics). 1932. The Saalfield Publishing Co.
--The Cock, the Mouse and the Little Red Hen: An Old Tale. LeFevre, Felicite, pseud. Sarg, Tony, pseud. (1882-1942), illus. Sarg, Anthony Frederick. LC 45-37894. 96 p. incl. col. front., col. illus. 22 cm. 1945. Macrae Smith Company.
--The Cock, the Mouse, and the Little Red Hen: An Old Tale. Lefreve, Felicite, pseud. Sarg, Tony, pseud. (1882-1942), illus. Sarg, Anthony Frederick. LC 66-4565. 102p. illus. (pt. col.) 20cm. 1966. Richards Pr.

Smith, Mattie Sampson (1840-)
--Miss Claire's Pupils. LC 6-20359. 3 p. l., 9-311 p. 20 cm. c.1905. The National Baptist Publishing House.

Smith, Minna Caroline (1860-1929), tr. see Nodier, Charles.

Smith, Minna Caroline (1860-)
--Boys of Cary Farm. (Illus.). N.D. D. Lothrop Co.
--Red Top Ranch: A Story of Ranch Life in Wyoming. LC 7-29004. 4 p. l., 213 p. front., 5 pl. 21 1/2 cm. 1907. E. P. Dutton & Company.

Smith, Minna Josephine (1882-)
--Llewellyn's Tower. Woodward, Hildegard (1898-), illus. LC 38-101218. 5 p. l., 170 p. illus. 21 cm. 1938. The Macmillan Company.

Smith, Moyne Rice
--Plays & How to Put Them on. Bolognese, Donald Alan (1934-), illus. LC 61-9958. 169 p. illus. 25 cm. 1961. H. Z. Walck.
--Seven Plays and How to Produce Them. Bolognese, Donald Alan (1934-), illus. LC 68-11232. (Illus.). 148 p. 24cm. 1968. H. Z. Walck.

Smith, Myrtle
--The Cat's Meow. N.D. Pageant Press Inc.

Smith, Nancy, jt. auth. see Bijur, Hilda.

Smith, Nancy Covert (1935-)
--The Falling-Apart Winter. LC 82-70071. 128p. (gr. 4-7). 1982. (ISBN 0-8027-6461-4). (ISBN 0-8027-6464-9). Walker & Co.
--Josie's Handful of Quietness. Forberg, Ati, pseud. (1925-), illus. Forberg, Beate Gropius. LC 74-5024. (Illus.). 143 p. 23cm. 1975. (ISBN 0-687-20560-3). Abingdon Press.

Smith, Nancy Woollcott (1915-)
--A Den for Tony. Robinson, Jessie Berkowitz, illus. LC 53-8940. 87p. illus. 21cm. 1953. Coward- McCann.
--Ghostly Trio. 128p. (gr. 4-6). 1969. (ISBN 0-590-08047-4, Schol Trade Pap). Schol Bk Serv.
--The Ghostly Trio. Marino, Dorothy Bronson (1912-), illus. LC 54-8714. 182p. illus. 20cm. 1954. Coward- McCann.
--Hurricane Mystery. Low, Vaike, illus. LC 58-7009. 221 p. illus. 20 cm. 1958. Coward-McCann.
--The Riddle of Split Rock. Low, Vaike, illus. LC 55-10788. (Illus.). 185 p. 20cm. 1955. Coward-McCann.

Smith, Nellie Standish
--Childhood's Precious Years. LC 72-85423. (Illus.). 18 p. 22cm. (Contemporary poets of Dorrance series). 1972. (ISBN 0-8059-1735-7). Dorrance.

Smith, Neville, jt. auth. see Smith, Virginia.

Smith, Nila Banton, et al., eds.
--Bobbs-Merrill Best of Children's Literature. LC 60-12936. v. illus. 24 cm. c.1960. Bobbs-Merrill.

Smith, Nila Banton & Hart, Hazel C., eds.
--Beyond the Horizon. N.D. Bobbs-Merrill Co.
--Foolish and Wise. N.D. Bobbs-Merrill Co.
--Fun All Around. N.D. Bobbs-Merrill Co.
--Shining Hours. N.D. Bobbs-Merrill Co.
--Sunny and Gay. N.D. Bobbs-Merrill Co.
--Time for Adventure. N.D. Bobbs-Merrill Co.

Smith, Nora, jt. ed. see Wiggin, Kate Douglas Smith.

Smith, Nora Archibald, ed. see Porter, Jane.

Smith, Nora Archibald, jt. ed. see Wiggin, Kate Douglas Smith.

Smith, Nora Archibald (1859-1934)
--Action Poems and Plays for Children. Peck, Anne Merriman (1884-), illus. 169p. N.D. Thomas Y. Crowell Co.
--The Adventures of a Doll. Groesbeck, Dan Sayre, illus. LC 8-277. 5 p. l., 3-64 p. col. front., 3 col. pl. 21 x 16 1/2 cm. 1907. The McClure Company.
--Bee of the Cactus Country. Best, Allena Champlin, Mrs. (1892-1974), illus. Berry, Erick, pseud. LC 32-13056. 5 p. l., 131, 1 p. col. front., illus. 21 cm. 1932. Houghton Mifflin Company.
--Boys and Girls of Bookland. Smith, Jessie Willcox (1863-1935), illus. N.D. Collins.
--Boys and Girls of Bookland. Smith, Jessie Willcox (1863-1935), illus. LC 23-13281. 5 p. l., 100 p. col. front., col. plates. 31 1/2 cm. 1923. Cosmopolitan Book Corporation.
--Boys and Girls of Bookland. Smith, Jessie Willcox (1863-1935), illus. N.D. David McKay Co.
--Children of the Lighthouse. LC 24-22121. 4 p. l., 101, 1 p. incl. front., illus. 19 1/2 cm. 1924. Houghton Mifflin Company.
--The Christmas Child, and Other Verse for Children. LC 20-19659. xii p., 2 l., 154 p., 1 l. front., plates. 20 cm. 1920. Houghton Mifflin Company.
--Nelson the Adventurer: A Story for Boys. LC 6-36047. 3 p. l., 121, 1 p. front., illus. 19 1/2 cm. 1906. Houghton, Mifflin and Company.
--Old, Old Tales from the Old, Old Book. N.D. Doubleday Page & Co.
--Plays, Pantomimes and Tableaux for Children. LC 17-28179. 6 p. l., 3-257 p. 19 1/2 cm. 1917. Moffat, Yard & Company.
--Three Little Marys. LC 2-23087. 3 p. l., 120 p., 1 l. front., pl. 19 1/2 cm. 1902. Houghton, Mifflin and Company.
--A Truly Little Girl. LC 27-21884. 4 p. l., 168 p. col. front., illus., plates. 21 cm. 1927. Houghton Mifflin Company.
--Under the Cactus Flag: A Story of Life in Mexico. N.D. Houghton Mifflin.

Smith, Nora Archibald (1859-1934) & Wiggin, Kate Douglas Smith (1856-1923), eds.
--Golden Numbers: A Book of Verse. 1902. McClure.
--Twilight Stories: More Tales for the Story Hour. Draper, Kayren, illus. LC 25-17938. xii, 228 p. incl. plates. front. 19 1/2 cm. 1925. Houghton Mifflin Company.

Smith, Oswald J
--The Adventures of Andy McGinnis: A Story for Boys and Girls. LC 46-447634. 4 p. l., 7-67 p. 20 cm. 1945. Zondervan Publishing House.

Smith, Paula J., ed.
--Spring Is in the Air. Paley, Joan, illus. LC 72-125133. (Illus.). 24 p. (Magic circle book). 1971. Ginn.

Smith, Pauline
--The Little Karoo. Bennett, Arnold, intro. by. 190p. 1978. (ISBN 0-224-60699-9, Pub. by Chatto Bodley Jonathan). Merrimack Pub Cir.

Smith, Pauline Coggeshall (1908-)
--Brush Fire!. LC 78-14768. 96 p. 21cm. c.1979. (ISBN 0-664-32639-0). Westminster Press.
--Hold Yourself Dear. LC 65-21616. 190p. 21cm. c.1965. Messner.

Smith, Peery
--The Hidden Place. LC 62-7834. 156 p. illus. 21 cm. 1962. Dutton.

Smith, Peter (1943-)
--Jenny's Baby Brother. Graham, Bob, illus. (Illus.). 28p. 1983. (ISBN 0-00-184345-1, Pub. by W Collins Australia). Intl Schol Bk Serv.
--Jenny's Baby Brother. Graham, Bob, illus. LC 83-23350. (Illus.). 31 p. 22cm. (ps-2). 1984, c.1981. (ISBN 0-670-40636-8). Viking.

Smith, Ralph see Paxton, S. H., pseud.

Smith, Ralph (1901-)
--The Dragon in New Albion. Paxton, S. H., pseud. 1st ed. LC 53-7307. 213p. illus. 21cm. 1953. Little, Brown.

Smith, Raymond Kenneth (1949-) & Smith, Catriona Mary (1948-)
--The Long Dive. LC 78-66614. (Illus.). 24 p. 1979, c.1978. (ISBN 0-689-30672-5). Atheneum. **Award: (NYT).**
--The Long Slide. LC 77-449. p. cm. 1977. (ISBN 0-689-30576-1). Atheneum Publishers.

Smith, Reva
--Jolly & Folly. (Sunshine Ser.). 1981. (ISBN 0-8163-0423-8). Pacific Pr Pub Assn.

Smith, Riley K
--Manachar and Munachar: Two Celtic Tales. 1st ed. Smith, Riley K., illus. LC 76-50516. (Illus.). 64 p. 22cm. c.1977. (ISBN 0-385-12435-X). (ISBN 0-385-12436-8). Doubleday.

Smith, Robert Alan, jt. auth. see Smith, Mary.

Smith, Robert Everett (1910-), illus.
--Baby's Book. LC 42-254799. 42 p. illus. (part col.) 20 1/2 x 17 1/2 cm. (On cover: The Little golden library, 10). 1942. Simon and Schuster, Inc.

Smith, Robert Gordon (1910-)
--The Boys' Entertainment Book: A Collection of Snappy Skits, Shorties, Stunts, Games, Dramatized Songs and Ghost Stories Written for Boy Scouts, Cub Scouts, Church and School Youth Groups, Boys' Clubs, and Even Girls' Clubs, Who Are Seeking New Material and Ideas for All Types of Entertainments, Amateur Shows, Special Programs, Parties and Campfires. LC 57-9455. (Illus.). 367 p. 22cm. 1957. T. S. Denison.

Smith, Robert Kimmel (1930-)
--Chocolate Fever. Fiammenghi, Gioia (1929-), illus. LC 73-181327. (Illus.). 93 p. 19cm. 1972. Coward, McCann & Geoghegan.
--Jelly Belly. Jones, Bob (1926-), illus. LC 80-23898. (Illus.). 155 p. 22cm. c.1981. (ISBN 0-440-04186-4). (ISBN 0-440-04190-2). Delacorte Press.
--The War with Grandpa. Lauter, Richard, illus. LC 83-14366. (Illus.). 128p. (gr. 4-8). 1984. (ISBN 0-385-29312-7). (ISBN 0-385-29314-3). Delacorte.

Smith, Robert Miller (1905-)
--Football Twins. LC 53-902196. 192p. 20cm. (Barnes junior sports novel series). 1953. A. S. Barnes.
--Little League Catcher. LC 52-119119. 156p. 20cm. (Barnes junior sports novel). c.1953. A. S. Barnes.

Smith, Robert Paul (1915-1977)
--Jack Mack. Blegvad, Erik (1923-), illus. LC 60-12496. unpaged. illus. 21 cm. 1960. Coward-McCann.
--Nothingatall, Nothingatall, Nothingatall. Cober, Alan Edwin (1935-), illus. LC 65-11455. 1v. (unpaged) col. illus. 27cm. c.1965. Harper.
--When I Am Big. Hoban, Lillian (1925-), illus. LC 64-12815. 32p. col. illus. 22cm. 1965. Harper.

Smith, Robert Tighe (1926-)
--Make a Wish Come True. (Creative Education Bks). (gr. 1-6). 1973. (ISBN 0-516-05113-X). Childrens.
--Make a Wish Come True. LC 72-89459. 32p. (gr. 5-12). 1973. (ISBN 0-87191-224-4). Creative Ed.
--A New Day. (Creative Education Bks). (gr. 1-6). 1973. (ISBN 0-516-05112-1). Childrens.
--Put Them in Cages. 1973. (ISBN 0-516-05114-8). Childrens Press.
--White Buses Can Fly. 32p. (gr. 5-12). 1973. (ISBN 0-87191-225-2). Creative Ed.
--Whites Buses Can Fly. (Creative Education Bks). (gr. 1-6). 1973. (ISBN 0-516-05111-3). Childrens.

Smith, Roger
--Gordon Goes To School. (Illus.). 32p. (Umbrella Book Ser.). (gr. k-3). 1984. (ISBN 0-19-278202-9, Pub. by Oxford U Pr Childrens). Merrimack Pub Cir.
--Greta the Green Cow. (Illus.). 30p. (Umpbrella Books). (ps). 1983. (ISBN 0-19-278200-2, Pub by Oxford U Pr Childrens). Merrimack Pub Cir.

Smith, Ronald Douglas
--December King. LC 82-70368. c.1983. (ISBN 0-8054-4516-1). Broadman Press.

Smith, Rosemary
--The Circus Book. Fleur, Anne Elizabeth (1901-), illus. Sari, pseud. LC 46-224459. 32 p. illus. (part col.) 22 1/2 x 19 cm. c.1946. John Martin's House, Inc.

Smith, Ruel Perley (1869-1937)
--Jack Harvey's Adventures: Or, The Rival Campers Among the Oyster Pirates. Gowing, Louis D., illus. LC 8-32390. (Illus.). 21 cm. 200p. (The Rival Campers Ser.). 1908. Page Co.
--The Rival Campers Afloat: Or, the Prize Yacht Viking. Gowing, Louis D., illus. LC 6-30462. 4 p. l., 351 p. front., 5 pl. 21 cm. 1906. L. C. Page & Company.
--The Rival Campers Ashore: Or, the Mystery of the Mill. Gowing, Louis D., illus. LC 7-30991. (Illus.). 21 cm. 297p. (The Rival Campers Ser.). 1907. Page Co.
--The Rival Campers: Or, the Adventures of Henry Burns. Shute, A. Burnham, illus. LC 5-24189. (Illus.). 21 cm. 338p. (The American Boy's Library). 1905. L. C. Page & Co.

Smith, Rukshana
--Rainbows of the Gutter. 156p. (Orig.). 1st U.S. edition. (gr. 6 up). 1984. (ISBN 0-370-30526-4, Pub. by the Bodley Head). Merrimack Pub Cir.
--Sumitra's Story. LC 82-19794. p. cm. 1983. (ISBN 0-698-20579-0). Coward, McCann.

Smith, Russell Duryee (1861-)
--The Indian Canoe. LC 25-8739. 2 p. l., vii-viii p., 2 l., 3-319 p. front., plates. 20 cm. c.1925. The Century Co.
--The Wild White Woods: A Winter Camp on the Canada Line. new ed. N.D. E. P. Dutton & Co.

Smith, Ruth Leslie (1902-)
--Hurry! Dinner Is at Six!. 1st ed. Tallon, Robert (1935-), illus. LC 69-12438. (Illus.). 143 p. 22cm. 1969. Bobbs-Merrill.

Smith, S. Jennie
--Madge, a Girl in Earnest. N.D. Lothrop, Lee & Shepard.

Smith, S. S., pseud., see Williamson, Thames Ross.

Smith, S. S., pseud. (1894-)
--The Feud Mystery: A Boys' Story of Wild Sardinia. Williamson, Thames Ross. LC 34-4566. ix, 303 p. incl. front., illus., plates. 22 cm. c.1934. Harcourt, Brace and Company.

Smith, S. T.
--The Violin Maker. N.D. Benziger Brothers.

Smith, Sam
--Rover's Regatta Day. LC 77-82647. (Illus.). 30 p. c.1977. (ISBN 0-385-13623-4). (ISBN 0-385-13624-2). Doubleday.
--Rover's Regatta Day. LC 78-304726. (Illus.). 30 p. 1977. (ISBN 0-385-13623-4). E. Benn.

Smith, Samuel Francis (1808-1895)
--Knights and Sea Kings. N.D. D. Lothrop Co.
--Mythology and Early Greek History: Or, Myths and Heroes. LC 18-12330. 3 p. l., 7-324 p. front., plates. 19 cm. c.1887. D. Lothrop and Company.

Smith, Sarah Stafford, pseud., see Smith, Dorothy Stafford.

Smith, Sarah Stafford, pseud. (1905-)
--The Ink-Bottle Club. Smith, Dorothy Stafford. Linton, Anne, illus. LC 67-5525. (Illus.). 175 p. 21cm. 1967. F. Watts.
--The Ink-Bottle Club Abroad. Smith, Dorothy Stafford. Phillips, Douglas, illus. LC 69-16892. (Illus.). 144 p. 21cm. 1969. F. Watts.

Smith, Sarah Storer (1905-)
--The Glacier Mystery: A Boy's Story of the Tyrolese Alps. Balmer, Clinton, illus. LC 82-24065. 7 p. l., 3-301 p. incl. front., illus., plates. 22 cm. c.1932. Harcourt, Brace and Company.

AUTHOR INDEX SNEDEKER, CAROLINE

Smith, Sidney
--The Gumps. (C. & L. Famous Comics in Book Form: Bk. 2). N.D. Cupples & Leon Co.
--The Gumps. (C. & L. Famous Comics in Book Form: Bk. 1). N.D. Cupples & Leon Co.
--The Gumps: C & L Famous Comics in Book Form. 48p. (Bk. 6). N.D. Cupples & Leon Co.
Smith, Stephanie A.
--Snow-Eyes. LC 85-7953. p. cm. 1985. (ISBN 0-689-31129-X). Atheneum.
Smith, Steven Philip
--American Boys. 1975. (ISBN 0-399-11462-9). G. P. Putnam's Sons.
Smith, Susan
--My First Animal Book. Daste, Larry, illus. (Illus.). 49p. (Texas Instruments Magic Wand Speaking Library). (gr. 3). 1983. (ISBN 0-89512-085-2). Tex Instr Inc.
Smith, Susan Cowles Grant, Mrs. (1885-)
--The Christmas Tree in the Woods. Sewell, Helen Moore (1896-1957), illus. 35p. N.D. G P Putnam's Sons.
--The Christmas Tree in the Woods. Sewell, Helen Moore (1896-1957), illus. LC 32-30930. (Illus.). 38p. 19cm. 1932. Minton, Balch & Company.
--Tranquillina's Paradise. Handforth, Thomas Schofield (1897-1948), illus. LC 31-5206. 34, 1 p. incl. illus., col. plates. 30 cm. c.1930. Minton, Balch & Company.
Smith, Susan Mathias (1950-)
--The Night Light. Wickart, Terry L., illus. LC 81-4095. (Illus.). 31 p. 21cm. c.1981. (ISBN 0-695-41627-8). (ISBN 0-695-31627-3). Follett Pub. Co.
--No One Should Have Six Cats!. Friedman, Judith (1935-), illus. 32p. (Beginning-to-Read Ser.). (gr. k-3). 1982. (ISBN 0-695-41673-1, Dist. by Caroline Hse). (ISBN 0-695-31673-7). Follett.
Smith, Susie K.
--Patrick Finds a Home. (gr. 2-5). 1970. Vantage.
Smith, Terry (1894-)
--Reprieve from Little Big Horn: A Novel of General Custer's Cavalry. LC 58-14510. 229 p. 21 cm. 1957. Exposition Press.
Smith, Theresa Kalab
--Bimbo, a Little Kinkajou. Smith, Theresa Kalab, illus. LC 74-110694. (Illus.). 32 p. 24cm. 1970. Steck-Vaughn Co.
--Dilly Dally. Smith, Theresa Kalab, illus. LC 61-8168. (Illus.). 48 p. 22cm. 1961. Tex.,Steck Co.
--Fog Is Secret. (Illus.). (gr. k-3). 1966. (ISBN 0-8382-0259-4). Hale.
--The Fog Is Secret. Smith, Theresa Kalab, illus. LC 66-12569. 1v. (unpaged) illus. 26cm. 1966. Prentice.
--Kokwa: A Little Koala Bear. LC 39-23753. 29 p. incl. front., illus. 24 cm. 1939. Longmans, Green and Co.
--The Littlest Skunk. 1964. Simon and Schuster.
--The Littlest Skunk. Smith, Theresa Kalab, illus. LC 64-14877. (Illus.). 48p. 24cm. 1964. Steck Co.
--No Home for a Kitten. Smith, Theresa Kalab, illus. LC 69-11092. (Illus.). 32 p. 24cm. 1969. Steck-Vaughn Co.
--Peppy. Smith, Theresa Kalab, illus. LC 65-12086. 39p. col. illus. 22x25cm. c.1965. Steck.
--Poncho & the Pink Horse. Smith, Theresa Kalab, illus. LC 51-8073. (Illus.). 23p. (gr. k-2). 1951. (ISBN 0-8114-7548-4). Steck-V.
--Sleepy Squirrel. Smith, Theresa Kalab, illus. LC 62-11502. (Illus.). 48p. (gr. k-3). 1962. (ISBN 0-8114-7559-X). Steck-V.
--Up a Tree. Smith, Theresa Kalab, illus. LC 56-10795. (Illus.). 48p. (gr. 1-2). 1956. (ISBN 0-8114-7567-0). Steck-V.
--Wags. Smith, Theresa Kalab, illus. (Illus.). 1967. Steck.
--Watching for Winkie. LC 42-21972. 47 p. illus. 26 x 21 cm. 1942. Longmans, Green & Co.
--Wiki of Walpi. Smith, Theresa Kalab, illus. LC 54-6832. 44p. (gr. 1-4). 1954. (ISBN 0-8114-7570-0). Steck-V.
Smith, Thorne (1893-1934)
--Lazy Bear Lane. Shanks, George, illus. LC 31-33552. x p., 1 l., 240 p. incl. illus., plates. col. front. 21 cm. 1931. Doubleday, Doran & Company, Inc.
Smith, Vesta Henderson, jt. auth. see Smith, Garry Van Dorin.
Smith, Vian Crocker (1920-1969)
--Come Down the Mountain. LC 68-10598. 212 p. 22 cm. 1967. Doubleday.
--The Lord Mayor's Show. LC 73-97629. N.D. Doubleday.
--Martin Rides the Moor. Houlihan, Ray, illus. LC 65-19049. 181p. illus. 22cm. 1st U.S. edition. 1965. Doubleday.
--A Second Chance. LC 66-11174. 279p. 22cm. 1966, c.1965. Doubleday.
--Tall and Proud. Stivers, Don, illus. LC 67-29. (Illus.). 159 p. 22cm. 1st U.S. edition. 1966. Doubleday.
--The Wind Blows Free. LC 67-13785. N.D. Doubleday.
Smith, Viola B.
--Touch of Spring. Michel, Sandra Seaton (1935-), ed. Keane, Marie, illus. (Illus.). (gr. k up). 1976. (ISBN 0-917178-02-5). Lenape Pub.
Smith, Virginia
--Not Here and Never Was. Smith, Virginia, illus. LC 68-28794. (Illus.). 43 p. 28cm. 1968. Harvey House.
Smith, Virginia & Smith, Neville
--Little Janie's Christmas. LC 46-17220. 20 p. col. illus. 22 1/2 x 19 cm. c.1946. Wilcox & Follett Co.
Smith, Vivian Brian (1933-)
--Snowmobile Kid. Stahl, Harry, illus. LC 72-108187. (Illus.). 87 p. 23cm. (The Snowmobile Ser.). 1969. Story House Corp.
--Snowmobile Escape. Kalnins, Sigrid, ed. Stahl, Harry, illus. 88p. (gr. 4-9). 1971. Story House.
Smith, W. Hovey, jt. auth. see Farnagle, A. E.
Smith, Walter Burges
--Looking for Alice. Howard, C. M., illus. LC 4-28953. 196 p. front., illus., 11 pl. 22 cm. c.1904. Lothrop Publishing Company.
--Looking for Alice. Howard, C. M., illus. (The Pansy Books). N.D. Lothrop Lee & Shepard Co.
Smith, Wanda VanHoy
--Ash Brooks, Super Ranger. Owens, Gail, illus. LC 84-13912. (Illus.). 128p. (gr. 3-5). 1984. (ISBN 0-684-18222-X, ScribJ). (ISBN 0-684-18222-X). Scribner.
Smith, Wendy
--Haddock McCraddock: A Picture Story. LC 78-7136. (Illus.). 38 p. 28cm. c.1978. (ISBN 0-385-14656-6). (ISBN 0-385-14657-4). Doubleday.
--Timothy Turtle Learns About Love. (Illus.). (ps-4). 1977. De Vorss.
Smith, William Bradford (1909-)
--William Bradford, Pilgrim Boy. Doremus, Robert (1913-), illus. LC 62-16610. (Illus.). 200p. 20cm. (Childhood of Famous Americans). 1963. Bobbs-Merrill.
Smith, William J., tr. see Hellsing, Lennart.
Smith, William Jay, jt. ed. see Bogan, Louise.
Smith, William Jay, ed. see Chukovsky, Kornei Ivanovich.
Smith, William Jay (1918-), tr. see Beskow, Elsa Maartman.
Smith, William Jay (1918-)
--Around My Room and Other Poems. Madden, Donald B. (1927-), illus. LC 79-84921. (Illus.). 24 p. 16cm. 1969, c.1955. Lancelot Press.
--Boy Blue's Book of Beasts: Poems. 1st ed. Kepes, Juliet Appleby (1919-), illus. LC 57-8046. 58 p. illus. 22 cm. 1957. Little, Brown.
--Grandmother Ostrich and Other Poems. Madden, Donald B (1927-), illus. LC 72-84922. (Illus.). 24 p. 16cm. 1969, c.1955. Lancelot Press.
--Ho for a Hat. 1st ed. Chermayeff, Ivan (1932-), illus. LC 63-7683. (Illus.). 32cm. 47p. 1964. Little, Brown and Co.
--If I Had a Boat. Bolognese, Donald Alan (1934-), illus. LC 65-201736. 1 v. (unpaged) col. illus. 16x22cm. c.1966. (ISBN 0-02-786000-0). Macmillan.
--Laughing Time. Kepes, Juliet Appleby (1919-), illus. LC 55-8095. (Illus.). 22cm. 54p. (Poems for Young Readers). (gr. k-3). 1955. (ISBN 0-316-80148-8, Pub. by Atlantic Monthly Pr). Little Brown.
--Laughing Time and Other Poems. Madden, Donald B. (1927-), illus. LC 75-84920. (Illus.). 24 p. 15cm. 1969, c.1955. Lancelot Press.
--Laughing Time: Nonsense Poems. Krahn, Fernando (1935-), illus. LC 80-65839. (Illus.). 96p. 1980. Delacorte.
--Laughing Time. Poems. 1st ed. Kepes, Juliet Appleby (1919-), illus. LC 55-80954. (Illus.). 54 p. 22 cm. 1955. Little, Brown.
--Little Dimity. 1963. Macmillan.
--Mr. Smith & Other Nonsense. Bolognese, Donald Alan (1934-), illus. LC 67-19774. (Illus.). 61 p. 24cm. 1968. (ISBN 0-440-05893-7, Sey lawerence). (ISBN 0-440-05894-5). Delacorte Press.
--My Little Book of Big and Little. Bolognese, Donald Alan (1934-), illus. 1963. Macmillan.
--Puplents and Pebbles. Kepes, Juliet Appleby (1919-), illus. 1959. Little, Brown.
--Puptents and Pebbles; a Nonsense ABC. 1st ed. Kepes, Juliet Appleby (1919-), illus. LC 59-5276. (Illus.). 32p. 27cm. 1959. Little, Brown.
--Typewriter Town. 1960. Dutton.
--What Did I See?. Almquist, Don (1929-), illus. LC 62-21356. unpaged. illus. 30 cm. (Modern masters book for children). 1962. Crowell-Collier Press.
Smith, William Jay (1918-), ed.
--Poems from France. Duvoisin, Roger Antoine (1904-1980), illus. (gr. 4 up). 1967. (ISBN 0-690-63507-9). T Y Crowell.
--Poems from Italy. Raphael, Elaine, pseud. (1933-), illus. Bolognese, Elaine Raphael Chionchio. 1972. Crowell.
Smith, William John (1936-)
--It Rains, It Shines. Lichterman, Shelley, illus. LC 67-17063. 37p. col. illus. 21 x 26cm. 1967. Harvey House.
Smith, William Joseph (1899-)
--The Spirit of Jogues. Lord, Daniel A., intro. by. LC 32-17674. xii, 177 p. front. 19 cm. 1932. Benziger Brothers.
Smith, William W.
--The Pig Book for Boys & Girls. N.D. J.B. Lippincott.
Smith, Winsome
--Elephant in the Kitchen. Nicklaus, Carol, illus. (Illus.). 128p. 1st U.S. edition. (gr. 3-6). 1983. (ISBN 0-590-32470-5). Scholastic Inc.
Smither, Ethel Lisle (1887-1974)
--Early Old Testament Stories. Wiese, Kurt (1887-1974), illus. (Illus.). (gr. 3-5). N.D. (ISBN 0-687-11382-2). Abingdon.
--First to Be Called Christians. Wiese, Kurt (1887-1974), illus. LC 55-14818. 80p. illus. 21cm. 1955. Abingdon Press.
--Later Old Testament Stories. Wiese, Kurt (1887-1974), illus. (Illus.). (gr. 3-5). N.D. (ISBN 0-687-21193-X). Abingdon.
--Stories of Jesus. Wiese, Kurt (1887-1974), illus. N.D. Abingdon Press.
Smithers, Leonard C., ed.
--Tartarian Tales. (Illus.). N.D. H. M. Caldwell & Co.
Smithies, Richard Hugo Ripman (1936-) & Cavanagh, Maura
--The Yeggs and the Yahbuts. Ellis, Deborah, illus. LC 72-90289. (Illus.). 77 p. 22cm. 1969. Random House.
Smithson, Isabel & Barnes, George Foster
--About Giants and Other Wonder People. LC 44-30311. 87 p. incl. illus., plates. 18 1/2 cm. 1888. D. Lothrop Company.
Smits, Peteris, compiled by.
--Latvian Folk Fairy Tales and Legends, 15 vols. 8000p. N.D. (ISBN 0-87908-025-6). Rota Press.
Smitt, Elizabeth
--Don't You Remember the Dragon?. Smitt, Elizabeth, illus. LC 75-107598. (Illus.). 40 p. 17cm. 1970. Random House.
Smock, Nell Stolp
--Have You Ever Seen?. Jingles and Pictures. Smock, Nell Stolp, illus. LC 43-2344. 62 p. illus. (part col.) 17 x 13 cm. c.1942. Rand McNally & Company.
--Little and Big. LC 47-30408. 24 p. col. illus. 17 x 20 cm. 1947. Abingdon-Cokesbury Press.
--White Tail, the King of the Forest. LC 39-6847. (Illus.). 23 cm. 48p. 1938. Platt & Munk.
--Wilderness Pet: The Story of a Boy and a Young Deer. LC 65-16803. (Illus.). 44 p. 24cm. 1965. Platt & Munk.
Smola, Hedwig, ed.
--Tales from the Arabian Nights. Grabianski, Janusz (1928-1976), illus. (Illus.). (gr. 4-8). N.D. (ISBN 0-696-82299-7). Hawthorn.
Smola, Hedwig, ed. see Arabian Nights.
Smolinski, Richard, ed. see Verdick, Mary Peyton.
Smoller, Mark H. & Scaduto, Al
--Hurray I Went to the Dentist Today. (Illus.). 1969. (ISBN 0-682-47005-8). Exposition.
Smollin, Michael J.
--The Alligator's ABC. Smollin, Michael J., illus. LC 80-85418. (Illus.). 28p. (Chunky Bks.). (ps). 1981. (ISBN 0-394-84897-7). Random.
--The Alligator's Color Book. Smollin, Michael J., illus. LC 80-85419. (Illus.). 28p. (Chunky Bks.). (ps). 1981. (ISBN 0-394-84935-3). Random.
--Meet Strawberry Shortcake & Her Friends. Smollin, Michael J., illus. (Illus.). 8p. (Strawberry Shortcake Bk.). (ps). 1980. (ISBN 0-394-84389-4, BYR). Random.
--Santa's Workshop. Smollin, Michael J., illus. LC 80-53051. (Illus.). 9 p. 16cm. (Happy house). c.1981. (ISBN 0-394-84702-4). Random House.
--The Sesame Street Players Present Mother Goose. LC 81-52979. (Illus.). 32p. (ps-1). 1982. (ISBN 0-394-95223-5). (ISBN 0-394-85223-0). Random.
--The Sweet Smell of Strawberryland: A Strawberry Shortcake Book. Smollin, Michael J., illus. LC 79-66563. (Illus.). 24p. (Sniffy Bks.). (ps). 1980. (ISBN 0-394-84387-8, BYR). Random.
Smucker, Barbara Claassen (1915-)
--Cherokee Run. Eitzen, Allan (1928-), illus. LC 57-12988. 123 p. illus. 22 cm. N.D. Herald Press.
--Cherokee Run. Eitzen, Allan (1928-), illus. 123p. illus. 20cm. 1966, c.1957. Moody.
--Henry's Red Sea. Eitzen, Allan (1928-), illus. LC 55-7810. 108p. illus. 22cm. 1955. Herald Press.
--Runaway to Freedom. Lilly, Charles, illus. LC 77-11834. (Illus.). 110p. (gr. 4-8). 1979. (ISBN 0-06-440106-5, Trophy). Har-Row.
--Runaway to Freedom: A Story of the Underground Railway. Lilly, Charles, illus. LC 77-11834. (Illus.). 154 p. 21cm. 1st U.S. edition. 1978, c.1977. (ISBN 0-06-025724-5). (ISBN 0-06-025725-3). Harper & Row.
--Susan. Orig. Title: Wigwam in the City. (gr. 4-6). 1972 (Starline). Schol Bk Serv.
--Wigwam in the City. 1st ed. Miret, Gil, illus. LC 66-6677. 154p. illus. 22cm. 1966. (ISBN 0-525-42724-4). Dutton.
Smyth, Gillespie, Mrs., ed.
--Children's, Bible Stories. (New Acorn Library). N.D. John C. Winston Co.
--Children's Bible Stories. (Illus.). 1882. Porter & Coates.
Smyth, Gwenda
--A Pet for Mrs. Arbuthnot. James, Ann, illus. LC 84-1863. (Illus.). 32p. (ps-2). 1984. (ISBN 0-517-55434-8). Crown.
Smyth, Lindley, Jr.
--Thrilling Adventures Among the Americans. (The Challenge Ser.). N.D. John C. Winston.
Smythe, Patricia Rosemary (1928-)
--Jacqueline Rides for a Fall. (Illus.). N.D. A. S. Barnes & Co.
--Pony Problems. Hughes, Fiona (1954-), illus. LC 79-148622. (Illus.). 63 p. 22cm. 1971. (ISBN 0-8289-0131-7). S. Greene Press.
--Three Jays Against the Clock: The Second Adventure of the Three Jays. McConnell, J. E., illus. LC 58-12784. 180 p. illus. 21 cm. (Her Three Jays series). 1958. Barnes.
--Three Jays Lend a Hand. 1st ed. Money, Keith (1935-), illus. LC 62-12686. 149 p. illus. 21 cm. 1962, c.1961. Duell, Sloan and Pearce.
--Three Jays on Holiday: The Third Adventure of the Three Jays. McConnell, J. E., illus. LC 59-8011. 182 p. illus. 21 cm. 1st U.S. edition. 1959, c.1958. Barnes.
Snake, Sam, as told by.
--The Adventures of Nanabush: Ojibway Indian Stories. Kagige, Francis, illus. Coatsworth, Emerson S. & Coatsworth, David, compiled by. LC 83-460068. (Illus.). 85 p. 24cm. 1st U.S. edition. 1980, c.1979. (ISBN 0-689-50162-5). Atheneum.
Snavely, Bessie R
--Home on the Ranch: Animal Stories for Boys and Girls. 1st ed. Zornow, L., illus. LC 55-118337. 45p. illus. 21cm. 1956. Exposition Press.
Snavely, Ellen Bartow (1910-)
--Shoes for Angela. Shortall, Leonard W., illus. LC 62-15672. (Illus.). 29 p. 21cm. (The Follett Beginning-To-Read Series). 1962. Follett Pub. Co.
Snead, Charles S.
--The Kind Kingdom. (Illus.). 1980. (ISBN 0-89962-016-7). Todd & Honeywell.
Snedden, Genevra Sisson, Mrs. (1873-)
--Docas, Indian of Santa Clara. Bateman, Jane, illus. LC 42-164572. ix p., 2 l., 3-194 p. illus. (part col.) 21 cm. 1942. D. C. Heath and Company.
--Docas, Indian of Santa Clara. Bateman, Jane, illus. LC 58-1479. 192 p. illus. 24 cm. 1958. Heath.
--Docas: The Indian Boy of Santa Clara. LC 90-3412. x, 150 p. incl. front., illus. 19 cm. 1899. Heath & Co.
Snedeker, Caroline Dale Parke, Mrs. (1871-1956)
--The Beckoning Road. Lee, Manning De Villeneuve (1894-1980), illus. LC 29-11251. x p., 1 l., 326 p. col. front., illus. 21 cm. 1929. Doubleday, Doran & Company, Inc.
--The Black Arrowhead: Legends of Long Island. Lee, Manning De Villeneuve (1894-1980), illus. viii p., 2 l., 279 p. incl. illus., plates. col. front. 21 cm. 1929. Doubleday, Doran & Company, Inc.
--The Coward of Thermopylae. 1911. Doubleday.
--Downright Dencey. Maginel, Wright Barney, illus. (gr. 3-7). 1927. (ISBN 0-385-07284-8). Doubleday. **Award: (JNM).**
--The Forgotten Daughter. LC 33-31759. viii p., 1 l., 309 p. incl. illus., plates. col. front. 21 cm. 1933. Doubleday, Doran & Company, Inc. **Award: (JNM).**
--The Forgotten Daughter. Lathrop, Dorothy Pulis (1891-1980), illus. LC 66-13480. viii, 279p. 22cm. 1966, c.1929. Doubleday.
--Luke's Quest. 1st ed. Unwin, Nora Spicer (1907-), illus. LC 47-11184. xii, 208 p. front. 21 cm. 1947. Doubleday.
--Lysis Goes to the Play. Lonette, Reisie Dominee (1924-), illus. LC 61-15449. 61 p. illus. 25 cm. 1962. (ISBN 0-688-41047-2). Lothrop, Lee & Shepard.
--The Perilous Seat. 1923. Doubleday Page & Co.
--The Perilous Seat. (Windmill Bks.). N.D. Doubleday Doran & Co.
--The Spartan. 1912. Doubleday Page & Co.
--Theras and His Town. Davis, Dimitris (1905-), illus. LC 61-13330. 237 p. illus. 22 cm. 1961. Doubleday.
--Theras and His Town. Haring, Mary Whitson, illus. LC 24-10212. x p., 2 l., 252 p. incl. plates. front. 22 cm. 1924. Doubleday, Page & Company.

--The Town of the Fearless. Lee, Manning de Villeneuve (1894-1980), illus. N.D. Doubleday Doran.
--A Triumph for Flavius. Rogers, Cedric (1915-), illus. LC 55-7031. (Illus.). 25 cm. 87p. (gr. 4-6). 1955. (ISBN 0-688-41045-6). Lothrop.
--Uncharted Ways. Lee, Manning De Villeneuve (1894-1980), illus. LC 35-274398. 6 p. l., 3-340 p. front., plates. 22 cm. 1935. Doubleday, Doran & Company, Inc.
--The White Isle. Kredel, Fritz (1900-1973), illus. LC 40-33284. 7 p. l., 271 p. incl. illus., plates. front. 22 cm. 1940. Doubleday, Doran & Co., Inc.

Sneider, Vernon John (1916-1981)
--West of the North Star. LC 72-159850. (Illus.). 188 p. 21cm. 1971, c.1972. Putnam.

Snell, Ada L., ed.
--First Noel. (gr. 7-9). N.D. Twayne.
--Joyful Songs: Carols of the Nativity. (gr. 7-9). N.D. Twayne.

Snell, Gordon, jt. ed. see Ryan, Joan.

Snell, LeRoy W.
--The Carcajou: A Mystery of the Northwest. Hastings, Howard Livingston (1887-), illus. LC 31-14417. 5 p. l., 302 p. col. front., plates. 20 cm. c.1931. Cupples & Leon Company.
--The Challenge of the Yukon: A Story of the Northwest. LC 35-18695. 2 p. l., 204 p. front. 20 cm. c.1935. Cupples & Leon Company.
--The Lead Disk: A Story of the Northwest. LC 34-25924. 2 p. l., 203 p. front. 20 cm. c.1934. Cupples & Leon Company.
--The Phantom of the Rivers: A Story of the Northwest. LC 36-179505. 2 p. l., 208 p. front. 20 cm. c.1936. Cupples & Leon Company.
--The Shadow Patrol: A Story of the Northwest. LC 34-259216. 2 p. l., 203 p. front. 20 cm. c.1934. Cupples & Leon Company.
--The Spirit of the North: A Story of the Northwest. LC 35-186965. 3 p. l., 204 p. front. 20 cm. c.1935. Cupples & Leon Company.
--The Wolf Cry: A Story of the Northwest. LC 34-25922. 2 p. l., 211 p. front. 20 cm. c.1934. Cupples & Leon Company.

Snell, Nigel Edward Creagh (1936-)
--Clare's New Baby Brother. (Illus.). 32p. (ps-1). 1982. (Pub. by Hamish Hamilton England). David & Charles.
--Danny Is Afraid of the Dark. (Illus.). 32p. (ps-1). 1982. (Pub. by Hamish Hamilton England). David & Charles.
--David's First Day at School. (Illus.). 32p. 1st U.S. edition. (ps-1). 1981. (Pub. by Hamish Hamilton England). David & Charles.
--Jane Has Asthma. (Illus.). 32p. 1st U.S. edition. (ps-1). 1981. (Pub. by Hamish Hamilton England). David & Charles.
--Kate Visits the Doctor. (Illus.). 32p. 1st U.S. edition. (ps-1). 1981. (Pub. by Hamish Hamilton England). David & Charles.
--Lucy Loses Her Tonsils. (Illus.). 1980. (Pub. by Hamish Hamilton England). David & Charles.
--Paul Gets Lost. (Illus.). 32p. (ps-1). 1982. (Pub. by Hamish Hamilton England). David & Charles.
--Peter Gets a Hearing Aid. (Illus.). 32p. 1980. (Pub. by Hamish Hamilton England). David & Charles.
--Sally Moves House. (Illus.). 32p. 1st U.S. edition. (ps-1). 1981. (Pub. by Hamish Hamilton England). David & Charles.
--Tom Visits the Dentist. (Illus.). 32p. 1st U.S. edition. 1980. (Pub. by Hamish Hamilton England). David & Charles.

Snell, Roy Judson see Craig, James, pseud.

Snell, Roy Judson see O'Hara, david, pseud.

Snell, Roy Judson (1878-)
--Arctic Stowaways: A Mystery Story for Younger Boys and Girls, Ages 7 to 12. LC 35-56642. 3 p. l., 11-189 p. 20 cm. c.1935. The Reilly & Lee Co.
--The Arrow of Fire. LC 30-12305. 3 p. l., 11-289 p. 20 cm. (His Mystery stories for boys). c.1930. The Reilly & Lee Co.
--The Black Schooner. LC 23-114445. 250 p. front. 20 cm. (His Mystery stories for boys). c.1923. The Reilly & Lee Co.
--The Blue Envelope. LC 22-13122. 258 p. incl. front. 20 cm. (Adventure stories for girls). c.1922. The Reilly & Lee Co.
--By Bursting Flash Bulbs. O'Hara, David, pseud. Warren, Ferdinad E., illus. LC 41-7317. (Illus.). vi, 214. 19cm. (A Jimmy Drury Mystery). 1941. Grosset and Dunlop.
--Captain Kituk. (Eskimo Stories). N.D. Reilly & Lee Co.
--Captain Kituk. Kerr, George F., illus. LC 18-157822. 4 p. l., 225 p. front., plates. 20 cm. 1918. Little, Brown, and Company.
--Caught by the Camera. O'Hara, David, pseud. Warren, Ferdinand E., illus. LC 40-2317. vi p., 1 l., 214 p. front. 20 cm. (A Jimmie Drury Mystery). c.1939. Grosset & Dunlap.
--The Circus of the O'Moo. (Adventure Stories for Girls). N.D. Reilly & Lee.
--The Crimson Flash. LC 22-10169. 238 p. incl. front. 20 cm. (His Mystery stories for boys). c.1922. The Reilly & Lee Co.
--The Crimson Thread. LC 25-149471. 303 p. front. 20 cm. (Adventure stories for girls). c.1925. The Reilly & Lee Co.
--The Cruise of the O Moo. LC 22-252299. 240 p. front. 20 cm. (Adventure stories for girls). c.1922. The Reilly & Lee Co.
--The Crystal Ball. LC 36-92249. 3 p. l., 11-285 p. 20 cm. (His Mystery stories for girls). c.1936. The Reilly & Lee Co.
--Curlie Carson Listens in. LC 23-2032. 238 p. incl. front. 20 cm. (His Radio-phone boys stories). c.1922. The Reilly & Lee Co.
--Dark Treasure. Craig, James, pseud. LC 27-8785. 3 p. l., 9-221 p. 19 cm. (His Radio phone boys stories). c.1926. The Reilly & Lee Co.
--The Desert Patrol. Craig, James, pseud. LC 23-11447. 213 p. incl. front. 20 cm. (His Radio-phone boys stories). c.1923. The Reilly & Lee Co.
--The Dinner That Was Always There. Smith, Sarah K., illus. LC 23-15038. 95 p. incl. col. front., illus. (part col.) 19 cm. (Just right books). c.1923. A. Whitman and Company.
--Eskimo Island and Penguin Land. Shinn, Cobb X., illus. LC 28-15619. (Illus.). 128p. 21cm. (Just Right Bks.). 1928. A. Whitman.
--An Eskimo Robinson Crusoe. Kerr, George F., illus. LC 17-28598. ix, 147 p. col. front., plates. 20 cm. 1917. Little, Brown, and Company.
--An Eskimo Robinson Crusoe. Kerr, George F., illus. LC 31-29958. ix, 197 p. col. front., plates. 20 cm. c.1931. The Reilly & Lee Co.
--The Firebug. LC 25-149482. 284 p. front. 20 cm. (His Mystery stories for boys). c.1925. The Reilly & Lee Co.
--The Flying Sub. LC 25-15124. 282 p. incl. front. 20 cm. (His Radio-phone boys stories). c.1925. The Reilly & Lee Co.
--Forbidden Cargoes. LC 27-191974. 3 p. l., 9-282 p. 20 cm. (His Mystery stories for boys). c.1927. The Reilly & Lee Co.
--The Galloping Ghost. 3 p. l., 11-316 p. 20 cm. (His Mystery stories for boys). c.1933. The Reilly & Lee Co.
--The Golden Circle. LC 31-122489. 3 p. l., 11-299 p. 20 cm. (His Mystery stories for girls). c.1931. The Reilly & Lee Co.
--The Gray Shadow. LC 31-122474. 3 p. l., 11-281 p. 20 cm. (His Mystery stories for boys). c.1931. The Reilly & Lee Co.
--Green Arrow. N.D. Reilly & Lee Co.
--Green Eyes. LC 30-123061. 3 p. l., 11-265 p. 20 cm. (His Mystery stories for girls). c.1930. The Reilly & Lee Co.
--Gypsy Flight. LC 35-5660. 3 p. l., 11-252 p. 20 cm. (His Mystery stories for girls). c.1935. The Reilly & Lee Co.
--The Gypsy Shawl. LC 29-209834. 3 p. l., 11-270 p. 20 cm. (His Mystery stories for girls). c.1929. The Reilly & Lee Co.
--The Hidden Trail. LC 24-179660. 3 p. l., 9-284 p. front. 20 cm. (His Mystery stories for boys). c.1924. The Reilly & Lee Co.
--Hour of Enchantment. LC 33-147946. 3 p. l., 11-252 p. 20 cm. (His Mystery stories for girls). c.1933. The Reilly & Lee Co.
--Ice Bound in the South Polar Seas. Lofts, Olive, illus. LC 26-24567. 4 p. l., 13-253 p. incl. illus., plates (part col.) 19 cm. ("Just right" book). c.1925. A. Whitman & Co.
--Icebound in the South Polar Seas. (Adventure Bks. for Boys). N.D. A. Whitman & Co.
--The Invisible Wall. LC 28-11921. 3 p. l., 9-297 p. 20 cm. (His Radio Phone boys stories). c.1928. The Reilly & Lee Co.
--Jane Withers and the Phantom Violin. authorized. Vallely, Henry E., illus. LC 43-22702. (An Original Story Featuring Jane Withers, Famous Motion Picture Star, As the Heroine). 3 p. l., 11-248 p. illus. 20 1/2 cm. 1943. Whitman Publishing Company.
--The Jet Plane Mystery. N.D. Wilcox & Follett Co.
--Jimmie Drury: Candid Camera Detective. O'Hara, david, pseud. Rev ed. Warren, Ferdinand E., illus. LC 38-7574. v p., 1 l., 213 p. front. 20 cm. c.1938. Grosset & Dunlap.
--Johnny Longbow. LC 28-20762. 3 p. l., 11-310 p. 20 cm. (His Mystery stories for boys). c.1928. The Reilly & Lee Co.
--Little Boy France. Frazee, Hazel, illus. LC 23-17188. 3 p. l., 13-66, 1 p. col. front., illus. (part col.) 22 cm. c.1919. A. Whitman and Company.
--Little Red Pony Auto. (The Easy Library). N.D. A. Whitman & Co.
--Little White Fox and His Arctic Friends. (Eskimo Stories). N.D. Reilly & Lee Co.
--Little White Fox and His Arctic Friends. Kerr, George F., illus. LC 16-17917. ix, 130 p. col. front., col. plates. 19 cm. 1916. Little, Brown, and Company.
--Lost in the Air. LC 20-17180. 271 p. incl. front. (port.) 20 cm. (His Mystery stories for boys). c.1920. The Reilly & Lee Co.
--The Magic Curtain. LC 32-131991. 3 p. l., 11-298 p. 20 cm. (His Mystery stories for girls). c.1932. The Reilly & Lee Co.
--Monkeyland: Betty and Billy Visit Monkeys in the Tropics. LC 41-22674. 127 p. illus. 22 cm. c.1941. The Reilly & Lee Co.
--Mystery Wings. LC 35-5659. 3 p. l., 11-233 p. 20 cm. (His Mystery stories for boys). c.1935. The Reilly & Lee Co.
--Norma Kent of the WACS. Meixner, Hedwig Jo, illus. LC 43-22706. 2 p. l., 9-252 p. illus. 20 1/2 cm. (Fighters for freedom series). 1943. Whitman Publishing Company.
--On the Yukon Trail. (The Radio-Phone Boys' Stories). N.D. Reilly & Lee.
--Panther Eye. LC 21-680035. 237 p. front. 20 cm. (His Mystery stories for boys). c.1921. The Reilly & Lee Co.
--The Phantom Violin. LC 34-9206. 3 p. l., 11-273 p. 20 cm. (His Mystery stories for girls). c.1934. The Reilly & Lee Co.
--The Purple Flame. LC 24-17967. 258 p. front. 20 cm. (Adventure stories for girls). c.1924. The Reilly & Lee Co.
--Red Dynamite. LC 36-922534. 3 p. l., 11-254 p. 20 cm. (His Mystery stories for boys). c.1936. The Reilly & Lee Co.
--The Red Lure. LC 27-878653. 3 p. l., 9-263 p. 19 cm. (His Mystery stories for boys). c.1926. The Reilly & Lee Co.
--Riddle of the Storm. LC 32-13240. 3 p. l., 11-300 p. 20 cm. (His Mystery stories for boys). c.1932. Reilly & Lee Co.
--The Rope of Gold. LC 29-104381. 3 p. l., 11-278 p. 20 cm. (His Mystery stories for boys). c.1929. The Reilly & Lee Co.
--Sally Scott of the WAVES. Meixner, Hedwig Jo, illus. LC 43-22705. 3 p. l., 11-248 p. illus. 20 1/2 cm. (Fighters for freedom series). 1943. Whitman Publishing Company.
--The Seagoing Tank. LC 24-186730. 3 p. l., 9-264 p. front. 20 cm. (Radio-phoneBboys Stories). c.1924. The Reilly & Lee Co.
--The Seal of Secrecy: A Mystery Story for Boys and Girls. LC 37-598567. 3 p. l., 11-236 p. 20 cm. c.1937. The Reilly & Lee Co.
--The Secret Mark. LC 23-11443. 245 p. front. 20 cm. (Adventure stories for girls). c.1923. The Reilly & Lee Co.
--The Shadow Passes. LC 38-758198. 3 p. l., 11-238 p. 21 cm. (His Mystery stories for boys). c.1938. The Reilly & Lee Co.
--Sign of the Green Arrow. LC 39-237473. 3 p. l., 11-215 p. 20 cm. c.1939. Reilly & Lee.
--The Silent Alarm. LC 27-866523. 3 p. l., 9-273 p. 19 cm. (His Adventure stories for girls). c.1926. The Reilly & Lee Co.
--Ski Patrol. LC 40-14501. 253 p. incl. front., illus. col. pl. 21 cm. c.1940. M. A. Donohue & Company.
--Skimmer the Daring. 3rd ed. (Adventure Bks. for Boys). N.D. A. Whitman & Co.
--Smoky Moon: A Mystery Story for Young Boys and Girls, Ages 7 to 12. LC 34-344250. 3 p. l., 11-205 p. 20 cm. c.1934. The Reilly & Lee Co.
--Soolook, Wild Boy. (Eskimo Stories). N.D. Reilly & Lee Co.
--Soolook: Wild Boy. Bull, Charles Livingston (1874-1932), illus. LC 20-19183. 4 p. l., 232 p. front., plates. 20 cm. 1920. Little, Brown, and Company.
--Sparky Ames of the Ferry Command. Darwin, Erwin L., illus. LC 44-370. 3 p. l., 11-248 p. illus. 20 1/2 cm. (Fighters for freedom series). 1943. Whitman Publishing Company.
--Third Warning. LC 38-7580. 3 p. l., 11-254 p. 21 cm. (His Mystery stories for girls). c.1938. The Reilly & Lee Co.
--The Thirteenth Ring. LC 27-14061. 3 p. l., 9-295 p. 20 cm. (His Mystery stories for girls). c.1927. The Reilly & Lee Co.
--A Ticket to Adventure: A Mystery Story for Girls. LC 37-5986. 3 p l., 11-248 p. 20 cm. c.1937. The Reilly & Lee Co.
--Told Beneath the Northern Lights: A Book of Eskimo Legends. Hoopes, Florence J., illus. LC 25-17411. 5 p. l., 3-238 p. col. front., illus. 21 cm. 1925. Little, Brown, and Company.
--Triple Spies. LC 20-17181. 243 p. front. 20 cm. (His Mystery stories for boys). c.1920. The Reilly & Lee Co.
--Under the Chewing Gum Tree: A Mystery Story for Young Boys and Girls, Ages 7 to 12. LC 36-9226. 3 p. l., 11-186 p. 20 cm. c.1936. The Reilly & Lee Co.
--What the Dark Room Revealed. O'Hara, David, pseud. Warren, Ferdinand E., illus. LC 39-2058. vi p., 1 l., 204 p. front., plates. 20 cm. (A Jimmie Drury Mystery). c.1939. Grosset & Dunlap.
--Whispering Isles. LC 27-14208. 3 p. l., 11-268 p. 20 cm. (His Radio-phone boys stories.). c.1927. The Reilly & Lee Co.
--Whispers at Dawn: Or, the Eye. LC 34-9205. 4 p. l., 11-247 p. 20 cm. (His Mystery stories for boys). c.1934. The Reilly & Lee Co.
--White Fire. LC 22-15209. 238 p. incl. front. 20 cm. (His Mystery stories for boys). c.1922. The Reilly & Lee Co.
--Wings for Victory. LC 42-24279. 251 p. col. front. 21 cm. 1942. M. A. Donohue & Company.
--Wings Over England. vi p., 1 l., 241 p. incl. front., plates. 21 cm. c.1941. M. A. Donohue & Company.
--Witches Cove. LC 28-11920. 3 p. l., 11-268 p. 20 cm. (His Mystery stories for girls). c.1928. The Reilly & Lee Co.

Snelling, Lois (1893-)
--Secret of the Red Gourd. LC 61-6815. 22cm. 245p. (gr. 7-11). 1961. Funk & W.
--Strange Case at Willowood. LC 59-80327. 246 p. illus. 22 cm. 1959. Funk & Wagnalls.
--Strange Night and Other Stories. Hocut, Carron Bain, illus. Hagen, Lyman B, intro. by. LC 82-72147. (Illus.). 68 p. 24cm. 1983. (ISBN 0-935304-49-5). (ISBN 0-935304-48-7). August House.
--Treasure in the Valley. LC 58-7278. 243 p. 22 cm. 1958. Funk & Wagnalls.
--The Yellow Cup Mystery. LC 63-15395. 216p. 1963. Funk & Wagnalls.

Snelling, Vera M.
--Little Star. Stowell, Gordon, illus. (Illus.). 24p. 1st U.S. edition. (gr. k-2). 1969. (ISBN 0-8192-2044-2). Morehouse.

Snelling, William J. see Goodrich, Samuel Griswold.

Snellings, M. L.
--Jessie Strikes Louisiana Gold. 1969. (ISBN 0-685-08181-8). Claitors.

Sneve, Virginia Driving Hawk (1933-)
--Betrayed. LC 74-7574. (Illus.). 125 p. 22cm. 1974. (ISBN 0-8234-0243-6). Holiday House.
--The Chichi Hoohoo Bogeyman. Agard, Nadema (1948-), illus. LC 75-10797. (Illus.). 63 p. 23cm. 1975. (ISBN 0-8234-0266-5). Holiday House.
--High Elk's Treasure. Lyons, Oren, illus. LC 72-75600. (Illus.). 96 p. 23cm. 1972. (ISBN 0-8234-0212-6). Holiday House.
--Jimmy Yellow Hawk. Lyons, Oren, illus. LC 78-179095. (Illus.). 76 p. 24cm. 1972. (ISBN 0-8234-0197-9). Holiday House.
--Three Lakota Grandmother Stories: Health Lessons for Young Readers. LC 76-24676. 1975. (ISBN 0-686-24338-2). Assn Am Indian.
--When Thunders Spoke. Lyons, Oren, illus. LC 73-78453. (Illus.). 93 p. 22cm. 1974. (ISBN 0-8234-0230-4). Holiday House.

Snitslaar, L., tr. see De Vries, P. J. Cohen.

Snitzlaar, L., tr. see De Vries, P. J. Cohen.

Snow, Charles Horace (1877-)
--Stocky of Lone Tree Ranch. N.D. Grosset & Dunlap.
--Stocky of Lone Tree Ranch. Pott, M. H., illus. LC 32-28976. 3 p. l., 9-274 p. incl. front., plates. 20 cm. c.1932. Macrae Smith Company.

Snow, Donald Clifford see Fall, Thomas, pseud.

Snow, Donald Clifford (1917-)
--Canalboat to Freedom. Fall, Thomas, pseud. Cellini, Joseph (1924-), illus. LC 66-16741. 215p. illus. 21cm. c.1966. Dial. **Award: (ALA).**
--Dandy's Mountain. Fall, Thomas, pseud. Barberis, Juan Carlos, illus. LC 67-16205. 200p. illus. 21cm. 1967. (ISBN 0-8037-1656-7). Dial.
--Eddie No-Name. Fall, Thomas, pseud. Prohaska, Ray (1901-), illus. LC 63-8505. (Illus.). 45 p. 25cm. 1963. Pantheon Books.
--Eddie No-Name. Fall, Thomas, pseud. Prohaska, Ray (1901-), illus. (gr. 4-6). 1974. (ISBN 0-590-09907-8, Schol Pap). Schol Bk Serv.
--Edge of Manhood. Fall, Thomas, pseud. (Illus.). (gr. 6-10). 1964. (ISBN 0-8382-0218-7). Hale.
--Edge of Manhood. Fall, Thomas, pseud. new ed. (gr. 4-6). 1977. (ISBN 0-590-08617-0, Schol Pap). Schol Bk Serv.
--Edge of Manhood. Fall, Thomas, pseud. 1st ed. Pitz, Henry Clarence (1895-1976), illus. LC 64-20483. 91 p. illus. 21 cm. 1964. (ISBN 0-8037-2225-7). Dial Press.
--Emily & the Killer Hawk. Fall, Thomas, pseud. Gordon, Louise, illus. (gr. 4-6). 1976. (ISBN 0-590-10125-0, Schol Trade Pap). Schol Bk Serv.
--My Bird Is Romeo. 1st ed. Gordon, Louise, illus. LC 64-12293. 96 p. illus. 21 cm. 1964. Dial Press.
--Wild Boy. Fall, Thomas, pseud. (Illus.). (gr. 5-8). 1965. (ISBN 0-8382-0957-2). Hale.
--Wild Boy. Fall, Thomas, pseud. 1st ed. Pitz, Henry Clarence (1895-1976), illus. LC 65-15325. 105 p. illus. 21 cm. 1965. (ISBN 0-8037-9545-9). Dial Press.

Snow, Dorothea Johnston (1909-)
--The Charmed Circle. Korach, Mimi (1922-), illus. LC 62-15253. 216 p. 20 cm. (Teen novel). 1962. Whitman Pub. Co.
--Come, Chucky, Come. Tolford, Joshua (1909-), illus. LC 52-5915. (Illus.). 45 p. 21cm. 1952. Houghton Mifflin.
--A Doll for Lily Belle. Walker, Nedda, illus. LC 60-5209. 52 p. illus. 22 cm. 1960. Houghton Mifflin.

--Donald Duck on Tom Sawyer's Island. Strobel & Mattinson, illus. (Illus.). (Tell-a-Tale Readers). (gr. k-3). 1978. (ISBN 0-307-68409-1, Whitman). Western Pub.
--Eli Whitney: Boy Mechanic. Fiorentino, Al, illus. LC 60-7708. 200p. col. illus. 20cm. (Childhood of famous Americans Series). 1962. Bobbs.
--Eli Whitney: Boy Mechanic. John, Charles V., illus. LC 48-8226. 187 p. illus. 20 cm. (The Childhood of Famous American Series). 1948. Bobbs-Merrill Co.
--Jeb and the Flying Jenny. Tolford, Joshua (1909-), illus. LC 54-9049. (Illus.). 41 p. 22cm. 1954. Houghton Mifflin.
--John Paul Jones: Salt Water Boy. 1st ed. Laune, Paul Sidney (1899-), illus. LC 50-14873. 195 p. illus. 20 cm. (Childhood of famous Americans series). 1950. Bobbs-Merrill.
--John Paul Jones: Salt-Water Boy. Moyers, William (1916-), illus. LC 62-12693. 200p. col. illus. 20cm. (Childhood of famous Americans Series). c.1962. Bobbs.
--Lassie and the Mystery at Blackberry Bog. Sawyer, Ken, illus. 1959. Golden Press.
--Love's Dream Remembered. 1979. (ISBN 0-685-90722-8, Avalon). Bouregy.
--The Mystery of Ghost Burro Canyon. Stone, David Karl (1922-), illus. LC 62-10030. 191 p. illus. 22 cm. 1962. Bobbs-Merrill.
--No-Good, the Dancing Donkey. Friend, Esther, illus. LC 44-6676. 61 p. illus. (part col.) 17 cm. 1944. Rand McNally & Company.
--On the Farm. N.D. Wilcox Follett Co.
--Peter: The Lonesome Hermit. Snow, Dorothea Johnston (1909-), illus. LC 49-135917. 32 p. col. illus. 17 cm. (Tell-a-tale books, 884). c.1948. Whitman Pub. Co.
--Playtime. N.D. Wilcox & Follett Co.
--Puddlejumper. Snow, Dorothea Johnston (1909-), illus. LC 49-7204. 33 p. col. illus. 17 cm. (Rand McNally book, 626). c.1948. Rand McNally.
--Raphael Semmes: Tidewater boy. 1st ed. Laune, Paul Sidney (1899-), illus. LC 52-10698. 192 p. illus. 20 cm. (Childhood of famous Americans Series). 1952. Bobbs-Merrill.
--Raphael Semmes: Tidewater Boy. Ponter, James J., illus. LC 62-16609. 200 p. illus. 20 cm. (Childhood of famous Americans Series). 1962. Bobbs-Merril.
--Samuel Morse: Inquisitive boy. 1st ed. Morse, Dorothy Bayley (1906-1979), illus. LC 55-6828. 190p. illus. 20cm. (Childhood of famous Americans series). 1955. Bobbs-Merrill.
--Samuel Morse: Inquisitive Boy. Reed, Walt, illus. LC 59-14002. 192 p. illus. 20 cm. (Childhood of famous Americans Series). 1960. Bobbs-Merrill.
--The Secret of the Stone Frog. 1st ed. Burns, Raymond Howard (1924-), illus. LC 59-10208. 215 p. illus. 21 cm. 1959. Bobbs-Merrill.
--Sequoyah,. Young Cherokee Guide. Giacoia, Frank, illus. LC 60-8881. 192p. illus. 20cm. (Childhood of Famous Americans Series). c.1960. Bobbs-Merrill.
--A Sight of Everything. Guthrie, Vee, illus. LC 62-12264. 63 p. illus. 22 cm. 1963. Houghton Mifflin.
--That Certain Girl. Wilde, Carol (1938-), illus. LC 64-20791. 216p. 20cm. (Whitman Teen Novels). 1964. Whitman Pub. Co.
--Tomahawk Claim. LC 68-11886. (Illus.). 190 p. 22cm. 1968. Bobbs-Merrill.
--The Whistling Mountain Mystery. 1st ed. Todd, Robert, illus. LC 54-6064. 237p. illus. 21cm. 1954. (ISBN 0-672-50579-7). Bobbs-Merrill.

Snow, Jack (1907-)
--The Magical Mimics in Oz. Kramer, Frank, illus. Baum, Lyman Frank (1856-1919), created by. LC 46-6891. 6 p. l., 17-242, 1 p. incl. front., illus. 23 1/2 cm. 1946. The Reilly & Lee Co.
--The Shaggy Man of Oz. Kramer, Frank, illus. Baum, Lyman Frank (1856-1919), created by. LC 49-49190. (Founded on and continuing the Famous Oz Stories by L. Frank Baum). 254 p. illus. 24 cm. 1949. Reilly & Lee.

Snow, Jack (1907-) & Wagglebug, H. M.
--Who's Who in Oz. Gringhuis, Richard H. (1918-1974) & Neill, John Rea (1878-1943), illus. Dirk, pseud. LC 54-38447. 277p. illus. 24cm. 1954. Reilly Lee Co.

Snow, Louise
--Turnovers: Or, Lesser Leaves; Some Little Stories from Real Life for Little Folk. LC 14-2272. 137 p. 20 cm. c.1914. Broadway Publishing Co.

Snow, Paul
--Iron Horse to Diesel. Pious, Robert, illus. LC 61-190524. 91 p. illus. 24 cm. (Whitman badger book). 1961. Whitman Pub. Co.

Snow, Pegeen
--Mrs. Periwinkle's Groceries. Warshaw, Jerry (1929-), illus. LC 80-22140. p. cm. 1981. (ISBN 0-516-03558-4). Children's Press.
--A Pet for Pat. Dunnington, Tom, illus. LC 83-23159. (Prepared Under the Direction of Robert Hillerich; 1927-). (Illus.). 30 p. 19cm. (A Rookie Reader). c.1984. (ISBN 0-516-02049-8). (ISBN 0-516-02049-8). (ISBN 0-516-42049-6). Childrens Press.

Snow, Richard Folger (1947-)
--Freelon Starbird. Stahl, Ben F., illus. LC 75-43901. (Being a Narrative of the Extroidinary Hardships Suffered by an Accidental Soldiar in a Beaten Army During the Autumn and Winter of 1776.). (Illus.). 209 p. 22cm. 1976. (ISBN 0-395-24275-4). Houghton Mifflin.

Snow, Sophia P.
--Annie and Willie's Prayer. LC 12-32766. (Illus.). 28p. 21cm. 1885. E.P. Dutton.
--Annie and Willie's Prayer. LC 13-23441. (Illus.). 8p. 25cm. 1878. Globe Printing Co.
--Annie's and Willie's Christmas Prayer. Torsch, illus. LC 17-1324. (Illus.). 10p. 14cm. 1879. F. Nolen.

Snow, Sophia P. & Floy, Henry
--Christmas Stories About Santa Claus. (Illus.). N.D. Methodist Book Concern.
--Christmas Stories About Santa Claus. (Illus.). N.D. Nelson & Phillips.

Snow, Toni A.
--Abigull. LC 80-82792. (Illus.). 48p. (Orig.). (gr. 2-6). 1980. (ISBN 0-932384-12-9). Tashmoo.

Snow-White and Rose-Red
--Snow-White and Rose-Red. Taylor, Ethel Bonney, illus. LC 38-16688. 62 p. incl. col. front., illus. (part col.) 17 cm. c.1938. Whitman Publishing Company.
--Snow White and Rose Red: A Favorite Fairy Tale. Tenggren, Gustaf (1896-1970), illus. LC 55-2055. unpaged. illus. 21cm. (A Little Golden Book, 228). 1955. Simon and Schuster.
--Snow-White and Rose-Red: Another Story, About a Different Snow-White. Biers, Clarence & Dunlap, Hope (1880-), illus. LC 38-127416. 32 p. col. illus. 17 cm. c.1938. Rand McNally & Company.

Snow-White and the Seven Dwarfs
--Snow-Drop and the Seven Dwarfs. Anderson, Anne, illus. LC 28-8656. 35 p. incl. col. front., col. illus. 18 cm. 1928. T. Nelson and Sons.
--Snow-White and the Seven Dwarfs. Livings, Bess, illus. LC 37-36387. 62 p. illus. (part col.) 17 cm. c.1937. Rand, McNally & Company.
--Snow White and the Seven Dwarfs. Seiden, Art, illus. LC 55-26938. unpaged. illus. 2ucm. (Treasure books, 896). 1955. Treasure Books.
--Snow White and the Seven Dwarfs. Stearns, Sharon (1912-), illus. LC 46-5159. 36 p. col. illus. 25 1/2 x 20 1/2 cm. 1946. Wilcox & Follett Co.

Snowdon, Lynda, compiled by
--Baa, Baa, Black Sheep & Other Rhymes. Mostyn, David, illus. (Illus.). 12p. (First Nursery Rhyme Bks.). (ps-1). 1981. Crown.
--Doctor Foster & Other Rhymes. Mostyn, David, illus. (Illus.). 12p. (First Nursery Rhyme Bks.). (ps-1). 1981. Crown.
--Hey Diddle Diddle & Other Rhymes. Cousins, Lynne, illus. (Illus.). 12p. (First Nursery Rhyme Bks.). (ps-1). 1981. Crown.
--Jack & Jill & Other Rhymes. Mostyn, David, illus. (Illus.). 12p. (First Nursery Rhyme Bks.). (ps-1). 1981. Crown.

Snurleson, Snorri
--Foosersnooser. McMurray, Chuck, illus. LC 77-82723. (Illus.). (ps-3). 1977. (ISBN 0-930366-01-8). Northcountry Pub.
--Once Upon a Moose in Minnesota: A Tall Tale. McMurray, Chuck, illus. LC 77-85629. (Illus.). 30 p. 21cm. c.1977. (ISBN 0-930366-02-6). Northcountry Pub. Co.

Snyder, Alice K
--The Three Bears. LC 51-6888. unpaged. illus. 23 x 32 cm. (Open-door book). 1951. Garden City Books.

Snyder, Anne (1922-)
--Fifty Thousand Names for Jeff. Carty, Leo (1931-), illus. (Illus.). 70 p. 20cm. (Holt Owlet Book). 1973, c.1969. (ISBN 0-03-005736-1). Holt.
--First Step. LC 75-4867. 128p. (gr. 5-10). 1975. (ISBN 0-03-014651-8). HR&W.
--My Name Is Davy-I'm an Alcoholic. LC 76-28457. (Illus.). 128 p. 22cm. c.1977. (ISBN 0-03-017841-X). Holt, Rinehart & Winston.
--Nobody's Family. 1st ed. De Groat, Diane (1947-), illus. LC 74-10616. (Illus.). 117 p. 24cm. 1975. (ISBN 0-03-013256-8). Holt, Rinehart and Winston.
--The Old Man and the Mule. Lazarevich, Mila (1942-), illus. LC 77-24442. (Illus.). 32. c.1978. (ISBN 0-03-022571-X). Holt, Rinehart and Winston.

Snyder, Carol (1941-)
--The Great Condominium Rebellion. Kramer, Anthony, illus. LC 81-65491. p. cm. c.1981. (ISBN 0-440-03062-5). (ISBN 0-440-03063-3). Delacorte Press.
--Ike and Mama and the Block Wedding. Robinson, Charles (1931-), illus. LC 78-11702. (Illus.). 80 p. 21cm. c.1979. (ISBN 0-698-20461-1). Coward, McCann & Geoghegan.
--Ike and Mama and the Once-a-Year Suit. Robinson, Charles (1931-), illus. LC 77-21429. (Illus.). 47 p. 21cm. c.1978. (ISBN 0-698-20436-0). Coward, McCann & Geoghegan.
--Ike & Mama and the Once-in-a-Lifetime Movie. Robinson, Charles (1931-), illus. LC 80-27374. (Illus.). 95 p. 22cm. 1981. (ISBN 0-698-20501-4). Coward, McCann & Geoghegan.
--Ike and Mama and the Seven Surprises. Robinson, Charles (1931-), illus. LC 84-17077. (Illus.). 160 p. 22cm. c.1985. (ISBN 0-688-03732-1). Lothrop, Lee & Shepard Books.
--Ike and Mama and Trouble at School. Robinson, Charles (1931-), illus. LC 82-12557. p. cm. 1983. (ISBN 0-698-20570-7). Coward, McCann & Geoghegan.
--Memo to Myself (When and If I Have a Teenage Child). LC 82-25506. p. cm. 1983. (ISBN 0-698-20588-X). Coward-McCann.

Snyder, Charles McCoy (1859-)
--The Bandit Bunny Alphabet. Brill, George Reiter (1867-), illus. LC 2-1244. 22cm. 32p. 1901. E. Stern & Co.
--Bandit Bunny Alphabet and Other Stories. Brill, George Reiter (1867-), illus. LC 2-1241. 32p. 1901. American Book and Bible House.
--Runaway Robinson. Brill, George Reiter (1867-), illus. LC 1-19482. 238p. 1901. D. Biddle.
--Snap Shots. Brill, George Reiter (1867-), illus. LC 7-25234. 18 x 8cm. 54p. 1907. E. Stern & Co.

Snyder, Dick
--One Day at the Zoo. Snyder, Dick, photos by. LC 60-12611. (Illus.). 22x27 cm. (gr. k-3). 1960. (ISBN 0-684-13482-9). Scribner.
--Talk to Me Tiger. (Illus.). (gr. 3 up). 1965. (ISBN 0-87464-091-1). Golden Gate.

Snyder, Don E
--Danny's Glider Ride. Murakami, Tsutomu, illus. (Illus.). 28 p. 21cm. (Follett beginning to read book). 1968. Follett Pub. Co.

Snyder, Fairmont
--Rhymes for Kindly Children: Modern Mother Goose Jingles. Gruelle, John Barton (1880-1938), illus. LC 17-7036. 95 p. col. illus. 24 cm. c.1916. P. F. Volland & Co.

Snyder, Harvey Albert
--Boys of the Bible. (Illus.). 1929. Holt, Rinehart & Winston.
--Girls of the Bible. LC 30-13686. 106p. (gr. 2-4). 1930. (ISBN 0-03-034380-1). HR&W.

Snyder, Maude Alexander
--Tales and Tangles. N.D. Christopher Publishing House.

Snyder, Pearl Daru (1914-)
--Shadow: The "All-American" Dog. Snyder, Pearl Daru (1914-), illus. LC 48-3642. 29 p. col. illus., col. map (on lining-papers) 24 x 25 cm. 1946. Prang Co.
--Too Little. Snyder, Pearl Daru (1914-), illus. LC 47-20170. 32 p. col. illus. 23 1/2 x 25 cm. 1947. Prang Company.

Snyder, Phillip C.
--Pa Pong: A Siamese Kitty. Mohrman, Janet S., illus. 28p. (ps-1). 1981. Custom Hse.
--Poochie. Mohrman, Janet S., illus. 28p. (Orig.). (ps). 1982. (ISBN 0-940560-04-6). Custom Hse.

Snyder, Robin
--Gobots On Earth. Ditko, Steve, illus. (Illus.). 24p. (Golden Super Adventure Bks.). (gr. 4). 1985. (ISBN 0-317-13975-4, Pub. by Golden Bks). Western Pub.
--War of the Gobots. Ditko, Steve, illus. (Illus.). 24p. (Golden Super Adventure Bks.). (gr. 4). 1985. (ISBN 0-317-13974-6, Pub. by Golden Bks). Western Pub.

Snyder, Zilpha Keatley (1927-)
--And All Between. 1st ed. Raible, Alton Robert (1918-), illus. LC 75-29315. (Illus.). 216 p. 22cm. 1976. (ISBN 0-689-30514-1). Atheneum.
--Below the Root. 1st ed. Raible, Alton Robert (1918-), illus. LC 74-19489. (Illus.). 231 p. 22cm. 1975. (ISBN 0-689-30457-9). Atheneum. **Award: (ALA).**
--The Birds of Summer. 1st ed. LC 82-13756. 195 p. 22cm. 1983. (ISBN 0-689-30967-8). Atheneum.
--Black and Blue Magic. LC 66-12850. 21cm. 186p. (A16). 1972, c.1966 (Aladdin). Atheneum.
--Black and Blue Magic. Holtan, Gene, illus. LC 66-12850. 186 p. illus. 22 cm. 1966. Atheneum.
--Blair's Nightmare. LC 83-15677. 204p. (gr. 3-7). 1984. (ISBN 0-689-31022-6). Atheneum.
--The Changeling. 1st ed. Raible, Alton (1918-), illus. LC 79-115075. (Illus.). 220p. 23cm. 1970. Atheneum.
--The Changeling. Raible, Alton Robert (1918-), illus. LC 79-115075. (Illus.). 220 p. 21cm. (Aladdin Book, A23). 1973, c.1970. Atheneum.
--The Changing Maze. Mikolaycak, Charles (1937-), illus. LC 85-5009. (Illus.). 32 p. 27cm. c.1985. (ISBN 0-02-785900-2). Macmillan.
--Come On, Patsy. Zemach, Margot (1931-), illus. LC 81-10814. p. cm. 1982. (ISBN 0-689-30892-2). Atheneum.
--The Egypt Game. 1st ed. Raible, Alton Robert (1918-), illus. LC 67-2717. (Illus.). 215 p. 22cm. 1967. Atheneum. **Award: (JNM).**
--Eyes in the Fishbowl. 1st ed. Raible, Alton Robert (1918-), illus. LC 68-12229. (Illus.). 168 p. 22cm. 1968. Atheneum.
--A Fabulous Creature. LC 80-18977. 252p. (gr. [illegible]
--The Famous Stanley Kidnapping Case. 1982. (ISBN 0-689-70754-1, Aladdin). Atheneum.
--The Famous Stanley Kidnapping Case: Kidnapping Italian Style. LC 79-12308. p. cm. 1979. (ISBN 0-689-30728-4). Atheneum.
--The Headless Cupid. 1st ed. Raible, Alton Robert (1918-), illus. LC 78-154763. (Illus.). 203 p. 22cm. 1971. Atheneum. **Awards: (IBBY); (ALA); (JNM).**
--The Princess and the Giants. 1st ed. Darwin, Beatrice, illus. LC 72-86949. (Illus.). 47 p. 1973. (ISBN 0-689-30103-0). Atheneum.
--Season of Ponies. Raible, Alton Robert (1918-), illus. LC 64-11892. 133 p. illus. 22 cm. 1964. Atheneum. **Award: (ALA).**
--Today Is Saturday. 1st ed. Arms, John, illus. LC 69-13534. (Illus.). 56 p. 25cm. 1969. Atheneum.
--The Truth About Stone Hollow. 1st ed. Raible, Alton Robert (1918-), illus. LC 73-84836. (Illus.). 211 p. 22cm. 1974. (ISBN 0-689-30147-2). Atheneum.
--Until the Celebration. 1st ed. Raible, Alton Robert (1918-), illus. LC 76-40984. (Illus.). 214 p. 22cm. 1977. (ISBN 0-689-30572-9). Atheneum.
--The Velvet Room. Raible, Alton Robert (1918-), illus. LC 65-10474. 216 p. illus. 22 cm. 1965. Atheneum.
--The Witches of Worm. 1st ed. Raible, Alton Robert (1918-), illus. LC 72-75283. (Illus.). 183 p. 22cm. 1972. Atheneum. **Awards: (ALA); (JNM).**

So-Un, Kim
--Story Bag: A Collection of Korean Folk Tales. Eui-Hwan, Kim, illus. Higashi, Setsu, tr. LC 55-13738. (Illus.). (gr. 2-5). 1955. (ISBN 0-8048-0548-2). C E Tuttle.

Soans, Richard G.
--John Gilbert Yeoman. (The Treasure Library). N.D. Frederick Warne & Co.

Sobersides, Solomon
--A Pretty New Year's Gift: Or, Entertaining Histories. the 2d worcester ed. LC 28-201021. 135 p. incl. front., illus. 11 cm. 1796. Printed by Thomas, Son & Thomas, and Sold at Their Bookstore.

Sobin, Gustaf
--The Tale of the Yellow Triangle. Meyer, Jolaine, illus. LC 73-75711. (Illus.). 35 p. 26cm. 1973. (ISBN 0-8076-0686-3). G. Braziller.

Soble, Mae Stein
--Bible Plays for Children. LC 22-3507. 136 p. 20 cm. 1919. J. T. White & Co.

Sobol, Donald J. (1924-)
--Angie's First Case. Owens, Gail, illus. LC 80-70011. p. cm. 1981. (ISBN 0-590-07564-0). Four Winds Press.
--Angie's First Case. Owens, Gail, illus. (Illus.). 144p. (gr. 3-6). 1982. (ISBN 0-590-32420-9, Apple Paperbacks). Scholastic Inc.
--The Best of Encyclopedia Brown, 4 vols. Ohlsson, Ib (1935-) & Shortall, Leonard W., illus. (Illus.). (gr. 4-6). N.D. Boxed Set. (ISBN 0-590-00662-2, Apple Paperbacks). Scholastic Inc.
--The Double Quest. Rethi, Lili (1894-), illus. LC 57-5670. 240p. illus. 22cm. 1957. F. Watts.
--Encyclopedia Brown and the Case of the Dead Eagles. 1975. Lodestar.
--Encyclopedia Brown and the Case of the Midnight Visitor. 1977. Lodestar.
--Encyclopedia Brown and the Case of the Midnight Visitor. 1st ed. Brandy, Lillian Bradi, illus. LC 77-22159. 21cm. 96p. (America's Sherlock Holmes in Sneakers: No. 12). c.1977. (ISBN 0-8407-7221-1). T. Nelson.
--Encyclopedia Brown & the Case of the Secret Pitch. (Illus.). (Encyclopedia Brown Ser.: No. 2). (gr. 2-6). 1965. (ISBN 0-525-67202-8). (ISBN 0-525-67808-5). Lodestar Bks.
--Encyclopedia Brown and the Case of the Secret Pitch: Ten All-New Mysteries. Shortall, Leonard W., illus. LC 65-19640. 96p. illus. 21cm. c.1965. (ISBN 0-8407-7203-3). Nelson.
--Encyclopedia Brown: Boy Detective. LC 63-9632. (Illus.). (Encyclopedia Brown Ser.: No. 1). (gr. 2-6). 1963. (ISBN 0-525-67200-1). (ISBN 0-525-67800-X). Lodestar Bks.
--Encyclopedia Brown, Boy Detective. (Illus.). 1963. Lodestar.

--Encyclopedia Brown: Boy Detective. 80p. (gr. 4-6). 1969. (ISBN 0-590-08037-7, Schol Trade Pap). Schol Bk Serv.
--Encyclopedia Brown, Boy Detective. Shortall, Leonard W., illus. LC 63-9632. (Illus.). 88 p. 21cm. 1963. T. Nelson.
--Encyclopedia Brown Carries on. Ohlsson, Ib (1935-), illus. LC 79-6340. (Illus.). 72 p. 22cm. c.1980. (ISBN 0-590-07562-4). Four Winds Press.
--Encyclopedia Brown Eleven and the Case of the Exploding Plumbing & Other Mysteries. Shortall, Leonard W., illus (Pub. by Thomas Nelson). (Encyclopedia Brown Ser.: No. 11). (gr. 4-6). 1976. (ISBN 0-590-01412-9). Scholastic Inc.
--Encyclopedia Brown Finds the Clues. (Illus.). 1966. Lodestar.
--Encyclopedia Brown Finds the Clues. Shortall, Leonard W., illus. LC 66-6191. 96 p. illus. 21 cm. 1966. T. Nelson.
--Encyclopedia Brown Gets His Man. 1966. Lodestar.
--Encyclopedia Brown Gets His Man. Shortall, Leonard W., illus. LC 67-24666. (Illus.). 96 p. 21cm. 1967. T. Nelson.
--Encyclopedia Brown Keeps the Peace. 1973. Lodestar.
--Encyclopedia Brown Keeps the Peace. Shortall, Leonard W., illus. LC 73-82912. (Illus.). 96 p. 21cm. (His Encyclopedia Brown books). 1969. T. Nelson.
--Encyclopedia Brown Lends a Hand. Shortall, Leonard W., illus. LC 74-10281. (Illus.). 96 p. 22cm. 1974. (ISBN 0-8407-7218-1). T. Nelson.
--Encyclopedia Brown Saves the Day. Shortall, Leonard W., illus. LC 71-117149. (Illus.). 96p. (Encyclopedia Brown Ser: No. 7). (gr. 2-6). 1970. (ISBN 0-525-67210-9). (ISBN 0-525-67807-7). Lodestar Bks.
--Encyclopedia Brown Saves the Day: Ten All-New Mysteries. Shortall, Leonard W., illus. LC 71-117149. (Illus.). 96 p. 21cm. 1970. T. Nelson.
--Encyclopedia Brown Sets the Pace. Ohlsson, Ib (1935-), illus. LC 81-69511. (Illus.). 89 p. 22cm. c.1982. (ISBN 0-590-07563-2). Four Winds Press.
--Encyclopedia Brown Shows the Way. 1971. Lodestar.
--Encyclopedia Brown Shows the Way. LC 72-2911. (Illus.). 96p. 1st U.S. edition. (Encyclopedia Brown Ser.: No. 9). (gr. 2-6). 1972. (ISBN 0-525-67216-8). (ISBN 0-525-67809-3). Lodestar Bks.
--Encyclopedia Brown Shows the Way: Ten All-New Mysteries. Shortall, Leonard W., illus. LC 72-2911. (Illus.). 96 p. 22cm. 1972. (ISBN 0-8407-7216-5). (ISBN 0-8407-7216-5). T. Nelson.
--Encyclopedia Brown Solves Them All. Shortall, Leonard W., illus. LC 68-22746. (Illus.). 96 p. 21cm. 1968. T. Nelson.
--Encyclopedia Brown Strikes Again. (gr. 4-6). 1973. (ISBN 0-590-01650-4, Schol Trade Pap). Schol Bk Serv.
--Encyclopedia Brown Takes the Case. 1971. Lodestar.
--Encyclopedia Brown Takes the Case. Shortall, Leonard W., illus. LC 73-6443. (Illus.). 96p. (Encyclopedia Brown Ser.: No. 10). (gr. 2-6). 1973. (ISBN 0-525-66318-5). (ISBN 0-525-67811-5). Lodestar Bks.
--Encyclopedia Brown Takes the Case: Ten All-New Mysteries. 1st ed. Shortall, Leonard W., illus. LC 73-6443. (Illus.). 96 p. 22cm. (His Encyclopedia Brown books). 1973. (ISBN 0-8407-6318-2). (ISBN 0-8407-6318-2). T. Nelson.
--Encyclopedia Brown Tracks Them Down. Shortall, Leonard W., illus. LC 77-160147. (Illus.). drawings. 96p. 1st U.S. edition. (Encyclopedia Brown Ser: No. 8). (gr. 2-6). 1971. (ISBN 0-525-67214-1). (ISBN 0-525-67812-3). Lodestar Bks.
--Encyclopedia Brown Tracks Them Down: Ten All-New Mysteries. Shortall, Leonard W., illus. LC 77-160147. (Illus.). 96 p. 21cm. 1971. (ISBN 0-8407-7214-9). (ISBN 0-8407-7215-7). T. Nelson.
--Encyclopedia Brown's Book of Wacky Crimes. Enik, Ted, illus. LC 82-9683. (Illus.). 112 p. 21cm. c.1982. (ISBN 0-525-66786-5). Dutton.
--Encyclopedia Brown's Book of Wacky Sports. Enik, Ted, illus. LC 82-84250. 128p. (gr. 3-7). 1983. (ISBN 0-688-03884-0, Morrow Junior Books). Morrow.
--Encyclopedia Browns's Book of Wacky Spies. Enik, Ted, illus. (gr. 4-7). 1984. (ISBN 0-688-02744-X). Morrow.
--Great Sea Stories. (gr. 4-6). 1977. (ISBN 0-590-10336-9). Scholastic Inc.
--Greta the Strong. Hyman, Trina Schart (1939-), illus. LC 72-85946. (Illus.). 158 p. 24cm. 1970. Follett Pub. Co.
--Lock Stock and Barrel. Smith, Edward John, illus. 1965. (ISBN 0-664-32346-4). Westminster Press.
--Lost Dispatch. (Illus.). (gr. 6 up). 1958. (ISBN 0-8382-0484-8). Hale.
--The Lost Dispatch: A Story of Antietam. Palumbo, Anthony, illus. LC 58-9786. 178 p. illus. 21 cm. 1958. F. Watts.
--Milton, the Model A. Drescher, Joan Elizabeth (1939-), illus. LC 70-159977. (Illus.). 45 p. 27cm. 1971. (ISBN 0-8178-4831-2). Harvey House.
--More Two-Minute Mysteries. (gr. 7-12). 1972. (ISBN 0-590-03454-5). Scholastic Inc.
--More Two Minute Mysteries. 128p. Repr. (gr. 5 up). 1974 (Schol Trade Pap). Schol Bk Serv.
--Secret Agents Four. Shortall, Leonard W., illus. LC 67-23548. (Illus.). 142 p. 20cm. 1967 (Four Winds Press). Scholastic.
--Still More Two-Minute Mysteries. (gr. 7-12). 1976. (ISBN 0-590-09987-6). Scholastic Inc.
--True Sea Adventures. LC 75-20425. 96p. (gr. 3 up). 1975. (ISBN 0-525-66454-8). Lodestar Bks.
--Two-Minute Mysteries. 160p. (gr. 7-12). 1969. (ISBN 0-590-08111-X). Scholastic Inc.
--Two-Minute Mysteries. Repr. (Starbright Editions). (gr. 7-12). 1973. Schol Bk Serv.

Sobol, Donald J. (1924-), ed.
--The Best Animal Stories of Science Fiction and Fantasy. LC 79-5099. p. cm. 1979. (ISBN 0-7232-6169-5). F. Warne.
--The Strongest Man in the World: Stories. Schule, Clifford H., illus. LC 67-18016. 208p. illus. 23cm. 1967. Westminister.

Sobol, Donald J. (1924-) & Andrews, Glenn
--Encyclopedia Brown Takes the Cake!. Ohlsson, Ib (1935-), illus. (Illus.). 128p. (gr. 4-6). 1984. (ISBN 0-590-32858-1, Apple Paperbacks). Scholastic Inc.
--Encyclopedia Brown Takes the Cake!. A Cook and Case Book. Ohlsson, Ib (1935-), illus. LC 82-21142. (Illus.). 121 p. 22cm. c.1983. Four Winds Press.

Sobol, Donald J. (1924-) & Shortall, Leonard W.
--Encyclopedia Brown and the Case of the Dead Eagles. LC 75-15911. (Illus.). 96 p. 21cm. (Encyclopedia Brown books). (America's Sherlock Holmes in Sneakers: No. 12). 1975. (ISBN 0-8407-7220-3). T. Nelson.

Sobol, Harriet Langsam (1936-)
--Cosmo's Restaurant. Agre, Patricia, photos by. LC 78-9685. (Illus.). 51 p. c.1978. Macmillan.
--My Other-Mother, My Other-Father. Agre, Patricia, photos by. LC 78-24165. (Illus.). 48p. (gr. 3-7). 1979. (ISBN 0-02-785960-6). Macmillan.
--Pete's House. Agre, Patricia, photos by. LC 77-12564. (Illus.). (gr. 3-6). 1978. (ISBN 0-02-785980-0). Macmillan.
--We Dont't Look Like Our Mom & Dad. Agre, Patricia, photos by. (Illus.). 32p. (gr. 4-7). 1984. (ISBN 0-698-20608-8, Coward). Putnam Pub Group.

Sobol, Rose (1931-)
--Woman Chief. LC 76-2289. p. cm. c.1976. (ISBN 0-8037-9655-2). Dial Press.

Society of Brothers
--Behold That Star: A Christmas Anthology: A Collection of Fifteen Christmas Stories. Maendel, Maria Arnold, illus. LC 65-28550. (Illus.). 1966. (ISBN 0-87486-003-2). Plough.
--Behold that Star: A Collection of Fifteen Christmas Stories. 3rd ed. Maendel, Maria Arnold, illus. LC 65-28550. (Illus.). 1974. (ISBN 0-87486-003-2). Plough.

Society of the Holy Child Jesus
--Jack. LC 6-25692. vii, 122 front 17 1/2. 1916. Benziger Brothers.

Society for Promoting Christian Knowledge see Ewing, Juliana Horatia Gatty, Mrs.

Society Of Brothers see Swinger, Marlys.

Sockman, Ralph Washington (1889-1970)
--Easter Story for Children. Laite, Gordon (1925-), illus. (Illus.). (gr. 2-5). 1966. (ISBN 0-687-11507-8). Abingdon.

Soderhjelm, Kai
--Free Ticket To Adventure. Kaufmann, John (1931-), illus. MacMillan, Annabelle, pseud. (1922-), tr. from Swedish. Quick, Annabelle. 1964. (ISBN 0-8382-0269-1, Cadmus Books). E. M. Hale and Company.
--Free Ticket to Adventure. Kaufmann, John (1931-), illus. MacMillan, Annabelle, pseud. (1922-), tr. Quick, Annabelle. LC 64-14440. 192 p. illus. 22 cm. 1964. Lothrop, Lee & Shepard.

Soderstrom, Lori, jt. auth. see Hubbard, Irene.

Soderstrom, Mary (1942-)
--Maybe Tomorrow I'll Have a Good Time. Wein, Charlotte Epstein, illus. LC 80-25357. p. cm. 1981. Human Sciences Press.

Soe, Robert C. Du see Du Soe, Robert C.

Soele, Jeffrey Owen
--Onion the Grunion. Soele, Jeffrey Owen (1931-), illus. LC 67-7702. 1 v. (chiefly illus.) 23 x 29 cm. 1965. Blotter Press.

Soelen, Philip Van see Van Soelen, Philip.

Soemer, Cecelia
--The Story of Maximilian: The Mouse Who Went to School. Krinsky, Marjorie, illus. LC 56-997270. unpaged. illus. 24cm. c.1956. D. McKay Co.

Sofer, Barbara
--The Holiday Adventures of Achbar. Gaelen, Nina, illus. LC 83-6. p. cm. 1983. (ISBN 0-930494-20-2). (ISBN 0-930494-22-9). KAR-BEN COPIES.

Softly, Barbara Frewin (1924-)
--Hippo, Potta & Muss. Veale, Tony, illus. LC 71-88586. (Illus.). color ils. 48p. (gr. k-3). 1969. (ISBN 0-8178-4541-0). Harvey.
--A Lemon-Yellow Elephant Called Trunk. Veale, Tony, illus. LC 71-115818. (Illus.). 42 p. 1st U.S. edition. 1971, c.1970. Harvey House.
--Magic People. 1st ed. Edwards, Gunvor, illus. LC 67-3080. (Illus.). 1 v. (unpaged. 22cm. (Book to begin on). 1967, c.1966. Holt, Rinehart and Winston.
--Magic People: A Book to Begin On. Edwards, Gunvor, illus. LC 67-10237. (Illus.). 48p. (Books to Begin on Ser.). (gr. 1-4). 1967. (ISBN 0-03-062430-4). HR&W.
--Magic People Around the World: A Book to Begin On. Bock, Vera, illus. LC 71-98923. (Illus.). 2 color ils. 48p. (gr. 1-4). 1970. (ISBN 0-03-084266-2). (ISBN 0-03-084267-0). HR&W.
--Place Mill. Hughes, Shirley (1929-), illus. LC 63-13667. 190 p. illus. 21 cm. 1962. St. Martin.
--Plain Jane. Hughes, Shirley (1929-), illus. LC 62-18040. 256 p. illus. 21 cm. 1962, c.1961. St. Martin's Press.
--Ponder and William. John, Diana, illus. LC 66-72784. 126 p. illus. 20 cm. (B66-5795). (Puffin Books). 1966. Penguin.
--Ponder and William on Holiday. John, Diana, illus. LC 75-3052. (Illus.). 106 p. 20cm. (A Young Puffin Original). 1968. Penguin Books.
--A Stone in a Pool. Hughes, Shirley (1929-), illus. LC 64-24564. 215p. illus., map. 21cm. c.1964. Macmillan.
--Stone in a Pool. Hughes, Shirley (1929-), illus. LC 64-24564. (Illus.). 21cm. 215p. (gr. 1up). 1964. St Martin.

Sohl, Frederic John (1916-)
--His Majesty's Wonderful Nose: Which Young Folk May Dramatize Freely. Creasman, Ralph, illus. LC 67-2818. (Illus.). 50 p. 21cm. 1967. Reilly & Lee Co.

Sohn, Monte
--Elsie and the Looking Club. Early, Walter, illus. LC 46-4406. 1 p. l., 61, 1 p. col. illus. 19 1/2 cm. 1946. The American Crayon Company.
--Elsie the Cow. Early, Walter, illus. LC 42-12307. 1 p. l., 61 p. col. illus. 23 cm. 1942. Dodd, Mead & Company.

Sohrab, Mirza Ahmad (1891-) & Chanler, Julie, Mrs. (1881-1966)
--Silver Sun. Barney, Marginel Wright, illus. LC 39-19007. 102 p. illus. 25 cm. 1939. Universal Publishing Co.

Soi, Elijah K.
--The Peacock and the Snake. Moore, Beryl, illus. LC 76-980820. (Illus.). 22cm. 36p. (Basic English readers). 1976. East African Pub. House.

Soifer, Margaret K
--With Puppets, Mimes and Shadows. LC 36-35197. 2 p. l., 132 p. 20 cm. c.1936. The Furrow Press.

Soifer, Margaret K, ed. see Arabian Nights.

Soifer, Margaret K. & Shapiro, Irwin (1911-), eds.
--Golden Tales From the Arabian Nights. Tenggren, Gustaf (1896-1970), illus. 1964. Golden Press.

Soifer, Margaret & Shapiro, Irwin (1911-), eds.
--Golden Tales from the Arabian Nights. Tenggren, Gustaf (1896-1970), illus. (Giant Golden Book). 1957. Golden Press.

Sokol, Bill, pseud., see Sokol, William.

Sokol, Bill, pseud. (1925-)
--The Fable of Profitt the Fox. Sokol, William. Sokol, Bill, pseud. (1925-), illus. Sokol, William. LC 64-11628. (gr. 2-4). 1964. (ISBN 0-03-043935-3). (ISBN 0-03-043940-X). HR&W.
--A Lion in the Tree. Sokol, William. Sokol, Bill, pseud. (1925-), illus. Sokol, William. LC 61-16228. unpaged. illus. 31 cm. 1961. Pantheon.

Sokol, Camille
--La Pluche. 1st ed. Sokol, Bill., pseud. (1925-), illus. Sokol, William. LC 63-17125. unpaged. illus. 18 x 24 cm. 1963. Holt, Rinehart and Winston.

Sokol, William see Sokol, Bill, pseud.

Sol, pseud., see Perrins, Glen Warner.

Solasko, Fainna, tr. see Gyulnazaryan, Hadjak.

Solasko, Fainna, tr. see Obruchev, Vladimir Afanasevich.

Solasko, Fianna, tr. see Nosov, Nikolai Nikolaevich.

Solberg, Charles Orrin (1869-)
--Oliver Nidson: An Orphan's Struggles and Victories. LC 28-12878. 167 p. 20 cm. c.1927. Augsburg Publishing House.

Solbert, Romaine (1925-), tr. see Johnson, Elizabeth.

Solbert, Romaine G. see Solbert, Ronni, pseud.

Solbert, Ronni, pseud., see Solbert, Romaine G..

Solbert, Ronni, ed. see Issa.

Solbert, Ronni, pseud. (1925-)
--The Song That Sings Itself. Solbert, Romaine G.. LC 72-79801. (Illus.). 32 p. 24cm. 1972. Bobbs-Merrill.
--Thirty Two Feet of Insides. Solbert, Romaine G.. Solbert, Ronni, pseud. (1925-), illus. Solbert, Romaine G.. LC 79-117455. (Illus.). color ils. 32p. (gr. 7 up). 1970. (ISBN 0-394-90445-1). Pantheon.

Sole-Vendrell, Carme (1944-)
--Jon's Moon. Sole-Vendrell, Carme (1944-), illus. LC 81-84109. (Illus.). 32p. 1st U.S. edition. (gr. k-8). 1982. (ISBN 0-8052-3797-6). Schocken.

Solem, Elizabeth K. (1922-), ed.
--Encyclopaedia Britannica Picture Stories. World's Children Series. LC 47-5781. 12 v. illus. 20 x 26 cm. 1947. Encyclopaedia Britannica Press.

Soley, James Russell
--The Sailor Boys of '61. (Illus.). (Little People's Ser.). N.D. Dana Estes and Company.

Solis-Cohen, Emily, Jr.
--David the Giant Killer and Other Tales of Grandma Lopez. N.D. Harlem Book Co.

Solis-Cohen, Emily (1886-), tr. see Steinberg, Judah.

Sollers, Allan A
--A Fox Story. Reusswig, William, illus. LC 63-9582. 25 p. col. illus. 29 cm. (Young owl book). c.1963. Holt Rinehart and Winston.

Solley, Charles Marion (1925-)
--Peterkin: An Educational Fable. Mitchell, Jane, illus. LC 72-77604. (Illus.). 95 p. 24cm. (Focus books). 1972. (ISBN 0-8185-0034-4). Brooks/Cole Pub. Co.

Solman, Alfred
--Daddy Long Legs: Fun Songs. 68 p., 1 l. col. illus. 33 cm. c.1900. M. Witmark & Sons.

Solomon, Evelyn
--The Big Flood. Sparks, Judith, ed. (Illus.). 24p. (A Happy Day Book). (gr. k-2). 1980. (ISBN 0-87239-407-7). Standard Pub.

Solomon, Evi, compiled by.
--Holidays. Axeman, Lois, illus. LC 84-9429. (Illus.). 32p. (Shape of Poetry Ser.). (gr. k-3). 1984. (ISBN 0-89565-266-8). Childs World.

Solomon, Jack (1927-) & Solomon, Olivia (1937-)
--Zickary Zan: A Collection of the Lore of Child-Children and Adults Including: Folk Games, Jump-Rope, Rhymes, Counting-Out Rhymes, Taunts, Nonsense Verse, Parodies, Autograph Verse, School Diaries, and Folksay from Central and Southeastern Alabama. Brewton, Mark, illus. LC 79-1117. p. cm. c.1979. (ISBN 0-8173-0012-0). University of Alabama Press.

Solomon, Joan (1930-)
--Bobbi's New Year. (Illus.). (ps-3). 1980. (Pub. by Hamish Hamilton England). David & Charles.
--A Day by the Sea. (Illus.). (ps-3). 1978. (Pub. by Hamish Hamilton England). David & Charles.
--Kate's Party. (Illus.). (ps-3). 1978. (Pub. by Hamish Hamilton England). David & Charles.
--News for Dad. (Illus.). (ps-3). 1980. (Pub. by Hamish Hamilton England). David & Charles.
--Shabnam's Day Out. (Illus.). (ps-3). 1980. (Pub. by Hamish Hamilton England). David & Charles.
--Spud Comes to Play. (Illus.). (ps-3). 1978. (Pub. by Hamish Hamilton England). David & Charles.
--Wedding Day. (Illus.). (ps-3). 1981. (Pub. by Hamish Hamilton England). David & Charles.

Solomon, Louis
--T V Doctors. (Illus.). (gr. 7 up). 1974. (ISBN 0-590-09836-5, Starline). Schol Bk Serv.

Solomon, Maury
--Create-&-Color Storybook One: Fairy Tales to Illustrate Yourself. Hart, Laura, illus. (Illus.). 64p. (Orig.). (Create-&-Color Storybook Ser.). 1981. (ISBN 0-671-43156-0). Wanderer Bks.
--Fairy Tales to Illustrate Yourself. Schneider, Meg, ed. Hart, Laura, illus. (Illus.). 64p. (Create & Color Storybook Ser.: No. 2). (gr. 8-12). 1982. (ISBN 0-671-43157-9). Wanderer Bks.

Solomon, Olivia, jt. auth. see Solomon, Jack.

Solomon, Ruth Freeman (1908-)
--The Eagle and the Dove. 1971. (ISBN 0-399-10227-2). G. P. Putnam's Sons.
--The Ultimate Triumph. 1975. (ISBN 0-399-11225-1). G. P. Putnam's Sons.

Solonevich, George (1915-), tr. see Kovalik, Vladimir (1928-) & Kovalik, Nada.

Solotaroff, Lynn, tr. see Bykov, Vasilii Vladimirovich.

Somerset, Henry see Somerset, Isabella Caroline Somers-Cocks, Lady.

Somerset, Isabella Caroline Somers-Cocks, Lady (1851-1921)
--In An Old Garden (Pub. by Society for Promoting Christian Knowledge). (Miss Marian's Story). N.D. E. & J. B. Young & Co.

Somerville, Elizabeth
--The History of Little Phoebe, and the Reclaimed Child. LC 21-17593. (Illus.). 30 p. 10cm. N.D. Printed by Sheldon & Goodwin. Stereotyped by J. F. & C. Starr.
Somerville, Ralph
--The New House that Jack Built. (Illus.). (The Little Ones' Library Ser.). N.D. Frederick A. Stokes Co.
Sommer-Bodenburg, Angela
--My Friend the Vampire. Glienke, Amelie, illus. LC 83-23930. (Illus.). 160p. (gr. 3-5). 1984. (ISBN 0-8037-0045-8). (ISBN 0-8037-0046-6). (ISBN 0-8037-0046-6). Dial Bks for Young Readers.
--The Vampire Moves In. Glienke, Amelie, illus. LC 84-7068. (Illus.). (gr. 3-6). 1985, c.1982. (ISBN 0-8037-0077-6). (ISBN 0-8037-0078-4). Dial Bks Young.
Sommer, E. Van
--By Uphill Paths: Or, Waiting and Winning. N.D. Thos Nelson & Sons.
Sommer, Oskar H., tr. see Andersen, Hans Christian.
Sommer, Susan (1947-)
--And I'm Stuck with Joseph. Moon, Ivan, illus. LC 84-611. 1984. (ISBN 0-8361-3356-0). Herald Press.
Sommerfelt, Aimee (1892-)
--Miriam. Iversen, Pat Shaw, tr. LC 63-10425. 160 p. 22cm. (Criterion book for young people). 1963. (ISBN 0-200-71991-2). Criterion Books.
--My Name Is Pablo. Dahl, Hans N., illus. (Illus.). (gr. 3-7). 1965. (ISBN 0-200-71395-7). Criterion Bks.
--My Name Is Pablo. Dahl, Norman, illus. Crampton, Patricia, tr. LC 65-235926. 143p. illus. 21cm. 1966, c.1965. Criterion.
--No Easy Way. Brudi, Theresa, illus. Crampton, Patricia, tr. LC 67-23451. (Illus.). 159 p. 22cm. 1968, c.1967. Criterion Books.
--The Road to Agra. Aas, Ulf, illus. LC 61-12805. 191 p. illus 22 cm. (Criterion book for young people). 1961. Criterion Books.
--The Road to Agra. Aas, Ulf, illus. (Illus.). 20cm. 156p. 1964, c.1961. Scholastic.
--White Bungalow. (Illus.). (gr. 5-7). 1963. (ISBN 0-8382-0943-2). Hale.
--The White Bungalow. Aas, Ulf, illus. Ramdsen, Evelyn, tr. LC 64-12007. (Illus.). 22cm. 126p. (gr. 5-9). 1964. Criterion Bks. **Award: (ALA).**
Sommers, Jane R
--Heavenward Led: Or, The Two Bequests. (Illus.). N.D. Porter & Coates.
--The Two Bequests: Or, Heavenward Led. (Roundabout Lib.). N.D. Henry T. Coates & Co.
--The Two Bequests: Or, Heavenwoo Led. N.D. John C. Winston.
Sondergaard, Arensa & Reed, Mary Maud (1880-1960)
--Fun for Fidelia. Henderson, Doris & Henderson, Marion, illus. LC 51-8049. (Illus.). 32p. 21cm. (Our Animal Story Bks.). 1951, c.1950. Heath.
Sondheimer, Ilse
--The Boy Who Could Make His Mother Stop Yelling. DeRosa, Dee, illus. LC 81-86219. (Illus.). 32 p. 24cm. c.1982. (ISBN 0-943156-00-9). Rainbow Press.
Song of the Circus. Phonodisc, jt. auth. see Geis, Darlene Stern.
Sonneborn, Ruth Cantor (1899-1974)
--Friday Night Is Papa Night. 1st ed. McCully, Emily Arnold (1939-), illus. LC 75-102918. (Illus.). 31 p. 22cm. 1970. Viking Press.
--I Love Gram. 1st ed. Carty, Leo (1931-), illus. LC 78-136821. (Illus.). 31 p. 24cm. 1971. (ISBN 0-670-39064-X). Viking Press.
--The Lollipop Party. Turkle, Brinton Cassaday (1915-), illus. LC 67-20956. 1 v. (unpaged) col. illus. 21 cm. 32p. 1967. Viking Press.
--Seven in a Bed. Freeman, Don (1908-1978), illus. LC 68-27564. (Illus.). 31 p. 21cm. 1968. Viking Press.
--Someone Is Eating the Sun. Gurney, J. Eric (1910-), illus. LC 74-2543. (Illus.). 32 p. 21cm. (Random House pictureback). 1974. (ISBN 0-394-82917-4). Random House.
Sonnenblick, Carol, jt. auth. see Friedman, Judith.
Sonnleitner, A. Th., pseud., see Tluchor, Alois.
Sono, Kazuhiko, jt. auth. see Sakade, Florence.
Sootin, Laura
--Let's Go to a Zoo. Doremus, Robert (1913-), illus. (Illus.). (Let's Go Ser). (gr. 1-3). 1959. (ISBN 0-399-60416-2). Putnam.
Soper, Eileen Alice (1905-)
--Dormouse Awake. 1948. Macmillan.
--Sail Away Shrew. 1949. Macmillan.
Soper, Eunice
--The Mannerly Twins. (gr. 1-3). N.D. Southern Pub.
--Pets and Pranks. Stout, Ron, illus. LC 58-10582. 61 p. illus. 24 cm. 1958. Pacific Press Pub. Association.
--Red Wagons and Billy Goats. Baerg, Harry John (1909-), illus. LC 68-22289. (Illus.). 63 p. 24cm. 1968. Review and Herald Pub. Association.
Soper, Gill, jt. auth. see Stuart, Monica.
Sophie, May, pseud., see Clark, Rebecca Sophie.
Sophie, May, pseud. (1833-1906)
--Flaxie Frizzle. Clark, Rebecca Sophie, 1 of 6 vols. (Illus.). (Flaxie Frizzle Stories). 1882. Lee & Shepard.
Sophrin, Alan D
--The Newcomer. LC 68-20709. 223 p. 21cm. 1968. John Day Co.
--Quiet Rebel. LC 67-25564. 191 p. 21cm. 1967. John Day Co.
Sopko, Eugen
--Townsfolk and Countryfolk. Sopko, Eugen, illus. LC 82-11824. p. cm. 1982. (ISBN 0-571-12515-8). Faber and Faber.
Sorensen, Edna Jennings
--Felipe's Long Journey. A Story of the Andes. LC 61-9742. 117 p. illus. 21 cm. 1961. F. Watts.
Sorensen, Robert
--Shadow of the Past. Uhlich, Richard, ed. (Illus., Orig.). (Bluejeans Paperback Ser.). (gr. 7-12). 1978. (ISBN 0-8374-0042-2). Xerox Ed Pubns.
Sorensen, Virginia Eggertsen (1912-)
--Around the Corner. 1st ed. Weaver, Robert (1924-), illus. LC 78-158005. 186 p. 22cm. 1971. (ISBN 0-15-204000-5). Harcourt Brace Jovanovich.
--Companions of the Road. 1978. Atheneum.
--Curious Missie. 1st ed. Miller, Marilyn Jean (1925-), illus. LC 53-7872. 208 p. illus. 21 cm. 1953. Harcourt, Brace.
--Friends of the Road. LC 77-17293. (Illus.). 180 p. 22cm. (Margaret K. McElderry Bks.). 1978. (ISBN 0-689-50093-9). Atheneum.
--The House Next Door: Utah, 1896. Rev ed. Cassel, Lili, pseud. (1924-), illus. Wronker, Lili Cassel. LC 54-11824. 223p. illus. 21cm. (Strength of the Union). 1954. Scribner.
--Lotte's Locket. 1st ed. Rocker, Fermin (1907-), illus. LC 64-17087. 253 p. illus. 20 cm. 1964. Harcourt, Brace & World.
--Miracles on Maple Hill. 1st ed. Krush, Joe (1918-) & Krush, Beth (1918-), illus. LC 56-8358. 180p. illus. 22cm. 1956. (ISBN 0-15-660440-X). Harcourt, Brace. **Awards: (JNM); (ALA).**
--Plain Girl. 1st ed. Geer, Charles Hand (1922-), illus. LC 55-8681. (Illus.). 151 p. 21cm. 1955. Harcourt, Brace.
Sorenson, Edna Jennings
--Felipe's Long Journey: A/Story of the Andes. Keats, Ezra Jack (1916-1983), illus. LC 61-9742. (Illus.). 117p. 21cm. 1961. F. Watts.
Sorenson, Grace
--Christmas Plays for Boys and Girls. 96p. N.D. T. S. Denison & Co Inc.
--The Elusive Aunt Laura. 62p. N.D. T. S. Denison & Co.
--Holiday Plays for Young Actors. 176p. N.D. T. S. Denison & Co.
--Humorous Plays for Children. LC 25-14487. 190 p. 18 1/2 cm. c.1925. T. S. Denison & Company.
--Juvenile Comedies. LC 26-18742. 196 p. 18 1/2 cm. 1926. T. S. Denison & Company.
--Lively Plays for Boys and Girls. 172p. N.D. Northwestern Press.
--Lively Plays for Boys and Girls. 172p. N.D. T. S. Denison & Co.
--Merry Little Plays for Children. Patten, Cora Mel (1869-), notes by. LC 31-25176. 208 p. 19 1/2 cm. c.1931. Walter H. Baker Company.
--The Mysterious Friends. 47p. N.D. T. S. Denison & Co.
--Peppy Plays for Boys and Girls: A Collection of Suitable Plays for Pupils of the Upper Grades. LC 41-2167. 94 p. 18 1/2 cm. 1939. The Northwestern Press.
Sorenson, Jane
--Boy Friend. LC 85-2597. 144 p. 19cm. (Jennifer book ; 5). c.1985. (ISBN 0-87239-931-1). Standard Pub.
--Fifteen Hands. LC 85-2594. p. cm. (Jennifer book ; 7). c.1985. (ISBN 0-87239-933-8). Standard Pub.
--In Another Land. LC 85-2595. 144 p. 19cm. (Jennifer book ; 8). c.1985. (ISBN 0-87239-934-6). Standard Pub.
--It's Me Jennifer. 128p. (Orig.). (Jennifer Bks.). (gr. 5-9). 1984. (ISBN 0-87239-771-8). Standard Pub.
--It's Your Move, Jennifer. LC 84-216. 128p. (Orig.). (Jennifer Bks.). (gr. 5-9). 1984. (ISBN 0-87239-772-6). Standard Pub.
--Jennifer Says Good-Bye. LC 84-218. p. cm. 1984, c.1983. (ISBN 0-87239-774-2). Standard Pub.
--Jennifer Says Goodbye. 128p. (Orig.). (Jennifer Bks.). (gr. 5-9). 1984. (ISBN 0-87239-774-2). Standard Pub.
--Jennifer's New Life. LC 84-219. 128 p. 20cm. 128p. (Orig.). (Jennifer Bks.). (gr. 5-9). 1984. (ISBN 0-87239-773-4). Standard Pub.
--Once Upon a Friendship. LC 85-2600. 128 p. 19cm. (Jennifer book ; 6). c.1985. (ISBN 0-87239-932-X). Standard Pub.
Sorenson, Stephen
--Growing up Isn't Easy, Lord: Story Devotions for Boys. LC 79-50080. (gr. 3-6). 1979. (ISBN 0-8066-1713-6). Augsburg.
--Lord, Teach Me Your Ways. Cox, Charles T (1937-), illus. LC 81-20671. (Illus.). 96 p. 25cm. c.1982. (ISBN 0-687-22660-0). Abingdon.
Sorine, Stephanie Riva (1954-)
--Our Ballet Class. Sorine, Daniel S., photos by. LC 80-28927. (Illus.). 48p. (gr. k-3). 1981. (ISBN 0-394-94821-1). (ISBN 0-394-85041-6). Knopf.
Sorrells, Dorothy C.
--The Little Shell Hunter. Rogers, Carol, illus. 1961. Simon and Schuster.
--The Little Shell Hunter. Rogers, Carol, illus. LC 61-12386. (Illus.). 40p. 24cm. 1961. Steck Co.
Sorrentino, Angela A.
--Freddie the Sled. 1978. (ISBN 0-533-03604-6). Vantage.
Sortor, June Elizabeth see Sortor, Toni, pseud.
Sortor, Toni, pseud., see Sortor, June Elizabeth.
Sortor, Toni, pseud. (1939-)
--Adventures of B. J., the Amateur Detective. Sortor, June Elizabeth. Eitzen, Allan (1928-), illus. LC 75-1265. (Illus.). 94 p. 23cm. 1975. (ISBN 0-687-00884-0). Abingdon Press.
Sothern, Jean
--Thumbs up. Egri, Ted, illus. LC 41-25432. 3 p. l., 65, 1 p. col. illus. 24 x 20 cm. c.1941. Musette Publishers, Inc.
Sotomayor, Antonio (1902-)
Khasa Goes to the Fiesta. Sotomayor, Antonio (1902-), illus. LC 66-10968. (Illus.). 57 p. 29cm. 1967. Doubleday.
Soule, Gardner Bosworth (1913-)
--The Maybe Monsters. (Illus.). (gr. 5 up). 1963. (ISBN 0-399-60457-X). Putnam Pub Group.
--The Mystery Monsters. LC 65-13313. 191 p. illus., ports. 21 cm. (Rare Creatures of Land and Sea). 1965. Putnam.
Soule, Jean Conder (1919-)
--Lenny's Twenty Pennies. Richards, Ken, illus. LC 62-13578. unpaged. illus. 30 cm. 1962. Parents' Magazine Press.
--Never Tease a Weasel. Hampson, Denman, illus. LC 64-12353. 26cm. 48p. (gr. k-3). 1964. (ISBN 0-8193-0095-0, Four Winds). Scholastic Inc.
Soule, Jean Conder (1919-) & Soule, Nancy
--Scuttle, the Stowaway Mouse. Remington, Barbara, illus. LC 68-21083. (Illus.). 41 p. 1969. Parents' Magazine Press.
Soule, Nancy, jt. auth. see Soule, Jean Conder.
Sousa, John Philip (1854-1932)
--Pipetown Sandy. Hinton, Charles Louis (1869-), illus. LC 5-26226. 5 p. l., 383 p. front., 12 pl. 19 1/2 cm. c.1905. The Bobbs-Merrill Company.
Soussaint, Samat M.
--Stories of the Crusades. (gr. 7 up). 1970. World Pub.
Southall, Ivan Francis (1921-)
--Ash Road. LC 77-15063. 184 p. 22cm. 1978, c.1965. (ISBN 0-688-80135-8). (ISBN 0-688-84135-X). Greenwillow Books.
--Ash Road. Seale, Clem, illus. LC 66-146365. (Illus.). 154 p. 22cm. 1966, c.1965. St. Martin's Press. **Award: (ALA).**
--Benson Boy. Fetz, Ingrid (1915-), illus. LC 72-81058. (Illus.). 21cm. 137p. 1973. (ISBN 0-02-786070-1). Macmillan.
--Bread & Honey. (gr. 7 up). 1970. St Martin.
--Chinaman's Reef Is Ours. LC 78-103144. 160 p. 22cm. 1970. St. Martin's Press.
--The Curse of Cain: Bible Stories. Kiddell-Monroe, Joan (1908-), illus. LC 68-26080. (Illus.). 120p. (gr. 6-9). 1968. St Martin.
--Finn's Folly. LC 72-84216. 158 p. 23cm. 1969. St. Martin's Press.
--The Fox Hole. Ribbons, Ian (1924-), illus. LC 67-25670. (Illus.). 125 p. 22cm. 1967. St. Martin's Press.
--Head in the Clouds. Kennedy, Richard (1910-), illus. LC 72-85189. (Illus.). 106 p. 21cm. 1st U.S. edition. 1973, c.1972. Macmillan.
--Hills End. LC 73-18369. 215 p. 21cm. 1974. (ISBN 0-02-786120-1). Macmillan.
--Hills End. LC 63-15002. 174 p. illus. 22 cm. 1963, c.1962. St Martin's Press. **Award: (ALA).**
--Josh. LC 75-187795. 192p. (gr. 7 up). 1972. (ISBN 0-02-786080-9). Macmillan. **Awards: (ALA); (CMA).**
--King of the Sticks. LC 79-10473. 177 p. 22cm. c.1979. (ISBN 0-688-80224-9). (ISBN 0-688-84224-0). Greenwillow Books.
--Let the Balloon Go. LC 84-5984. 136 p. 22cm. 1985, c.1968. (ISBN 0-02-786220-8). Bradbury Press.
--Let the Balloon Go. Ribbons, Ian (1924-), illus. LC 68-26076. (Illus.). 141 p. 22cm. 1968. St. Martin's Press.
--The Long Night Watch. 160p. 1984. (ISBN 0-374-34644-5). FS&G.
--Matt and Jo. LC 73-581. 113 p. 22cm. 1973. (ISBN 0-02-786110-4). Macmillan.
--Seventeen Seconds. 1974. MacMillan Publishing Company.
--Sly Old Wardrobe. Greenwood, Edward Alister (1930-), illus. LC 67-28104. (Illus.). color ils. 40p. (gr. k-3). 1969. St Martin.
--The Sword of Esau. Kiddell-Monroe, Joan (1908-), illus. (Illus.). 116 p. 22cm. 1968. St. Martin's Press.
--To the Wild Sky. Tuckwell, Jennifer, illus. LC 72-193470. (Illus.). 224 p. 19cm. (Puffin books). 1970. Penguin Books.
--To the Wild Sky. Tuckwell, Jennifer, illus. LC 67-13163. (Illus.). 184 p. 22cm. 1967. St. Martin's Press.
--Walk a Mile and Get Nowhere. LC 70-122472. 118 p. 22cm. 1970. (ISBN 0-13-944322-3). Bradbury Press.
--What About Tomorrow. LC 76-45637. p. cm. 1977, c.1976. (ISBN 0-02-786170-8). Macmillan.
Southall, Ivan Francis (1921-), adapted by.
--The Golden Goose. LC 80-52047. p. cm. c.1981. (ISBN 0-688-00608-6). (ISBN 0-688-00609-4). Greenwillow Books.
Southcott, Ethel Stewart
--The Missing Heirloom. LC 36-16498. 90p. 17cm. 1936. Augustana Book Concern
Southern Baptist Convention. Sunday School Board
--Once Upon a Time: A Collection of Interesting Stories for Children. LC 36-33961. 5 p. l., 9-185 p. 19 cm. c.1936. Broadman Press.
Southey, Robert (1774-1843)
--The Three Bears. Moyers, William (1916-), illus LC 49-1260. 39 p. col. illus. 31 cm. (The Evergreen Tales; Or, Tales for the Ageless). 1949. Limited Editions Club.
Southgate, Vera
--Story of Cricket. Matthew, Jack (1911-), illus. (Illus.). (gr. 3-4). N.D. (ISBN 0-7214-0075-2). Merry Thoughts.
Southgate, Vera, ed.
--Beauty & the Beast. Winter, Eric, illus. (Illus.). (gr. 3). 1968. (ISBN 0-7214-0219-4). Merry Thoughts.
--Cinderella. Winter, Eric, illus. (Illus.). (gr. 3). N.D. (ISBN 0-7214-0077-9). Merry Thoughts.
--Elves & the Shoemaker. Lumley, Robert, illus. (Illus.). (gr. 1). N.D. (ISBN 0-7214-0078-7). Merry Thoughts.
--Jack & the Beanstalk. Winter, Eric, illus. (Illus.). (gr. 3). N.D. (ISBN 0-7214-0080-9). Merry Thoughts.
--Little Red Hen. Lumley, Robert, illus. (Illus.). (gr. 1). N.D. (ISBN 0-7214-0084-1). Merry Thoughts.
--Princess & the Pea. Winter, Eric, illus. (Illus.). (gr. 1). N.D. (ISBN 0-7214-0085-X). Merry Thoughts.
--Three Little Pigs. Lumley, Robert, illus. (Illus.). (gr. 1). N.D. (ISBN 0-7214-0081-7). Merry Thoughts.
Southwart, Elizabeth
--The Password to Fairyland. N.D. Frederick A. Stokes.
Southwick, David
--Jack Wheeler. (The Boys Own Library). N.D. David McKay.
--Jack Wheeler. (Illus.). (St. Nicholas Series for Boys). N.D. International Book Co.
Southwold, Stephen (1887-)
--Happy Families. LC 29-222081. viii, 182 p. col. front., illus., col. plates. 19 cm. $1.40. 1929. Longmans, Green and Co.
--In Between Stories. Millar, Harold Robert (1869-1939), illus. LC 23-163904. viii, 9-155 p., 1 l. col. front., illus., col. pl. 19 cm. $1.25. 1923. Longmans, Green and Co.
--Listen, Children!. Drinkwater, John, frwd. by. LC 26-14799. 255 p. 19 1/2 cm. 1926. Dodd, Mead and Company.
--Man's Great Adventure: Thirty Stories of Mankind from the Dawn Man to the Man of to-Day. Gee, L., illus. LC 29-190894. 256 p. incl. col. front., illus., col. plates. 19 cm. 1929. Longmans, Green and Co.
--True Tales of an Old Shellback. Bestall, A. E., illus. LC 30-30717. xii, 178, 2 p. incl. col. front., illus. (part col.) 19 cm. 1930. Longmans, Green and Co.
Southwold, Stephen (1887-), as told by.
--The Book of Animal Tales. Appleton, Honor C., illus. LC 35-169616. 286, 2 p. col. front., illus., col. plates. 23 cm. 1929. Thomas Y. Crowell Company.
--The Children's Play-Hour Book. LC 27-12372. (Illus.). 163p. 25cm. 1927. Longmans, Green and Co.
Southworth, A. S., Mrs.
--Our Charlie: Or, The Little Teacher. 125p. (Gay Cottage Stories). N.D. Lockwood, Brooks, & Co. for American Tract Society.
--Our Charlie: The Little Teacher. 125p. N.D. Hurd & Houghton for American Tract Society.
Souvestre, Emile
--Peronnique: A Celtic Folk Tale from Brittany. Michael-Dansac, Monique (1806-1854), illus. LC 78-98618. (Illus.). 32 p. 1970, c.1969. Atheneum.

Souza, Paul, illus.
--Roy Rogers and Dale Evans in Big Toppers. LC 56-56517. unpaged. illus. 22cm. c.1956. Whitman Pub.
Sowerby, Githa, jt. auth. see Joan, Natalie.
Sowerby, Githa, jt. auth. see Sowerby, Millicent.
Sowerby, Katherine Githa
--Bumbletoes. Sowerby, Millicent, illus. (Illus.). N.D. Duffield & Co.
--Cinderella. Sowerby, Millicent, illus. N.D. George H Doran.
--The Dainty Book. Sowerby, Millicent, illus. N.D. George H Doran & Co.
--Little Plays for Little People. Sowerby, Millicent, illus. N.D. George H Doran.
--Little Plays for Little People. Sowerby, Millicent, illus. 21cm. 90p. N.D. Hodder & Stoughton.
--Little Stories for Little People. Sowerby, Millicent, illus. N.D. JUV. George H Doran & Co.
--The Merry Book: A Dainty Little Book of Verse and Pictures. Sowerby, Millicent, illus. N.D. George H Doran.
--My Birthday: The Fortune of the Day in Picture and Rhyme. Sowerby, Millicent, illus. N.D. George H Doran.
--Poems of Childhood. Sowerby, Millicent, illus. N.D. George H Doran.
--The Pretty Book. Sowerby, Millicent, illus. N.D. George H Doran.
--The Quaint Book. Sowerby, Millicent, illus. N.D. George H Doran.
Sowerby, Katherine Githa, retold by see Grimm, Jakob Ludwig Karl (1785-1863) & Grimm, Wilhelm Karl.
Sowerby, Katherine Githa & Joan, Natalie
--The Gay Book. Sowerby, Millicent, illus. LC 35-28727. (Illus.). 29p. 21cm. 1935. Artists and Writers Guild.
Sowerby, Katherine Githa & Sowerby, Millicent
--Children of Yesterday. (Illus.). N.D. Duffield & Co.
Sowerby, Millicent, jt. auth. see Sowerby, Katherine Githa.
Sowerby, Millicent & Sowerby, Githa
--Childhood. (Illus.). N.D. Duffield & Co.
Sowers, Phyllis Ayer, jt. auth. see Bothwell, Jean.
Sowers, Phyllis Ayer, Mrs.
--Carlos and Lola: A Boy and Girl of the Philippines. Ayer, Margaret (0000-1981), illus. LC 35-15910. 150 p. incl. col. front., illus. (part col.) 21 1/2 cm. c.1935. Thomas Y. Crowell Company.
--Dhan of the Pearl Country. Ayer, Margaret (0000-1981), illus. LC 39-23038. 6 p. l., 17-124, 1 p. incl. illus. (part col.) map. col. front. 23 1/2 cm. 1939. A. Whitman & Co.
--Elephant Boy of the Teak Forest. LC 49-106584. iv. 169 p. illus. 22 cm. 1949. J. Messner.
--Lin Foo and Lin Ching: A Boy and Girl of China. Ayer, Margaret (0000-1981), illus. LC 32-22195. 4 p. l., 3-121 p. incl. front., illus. 22 cm. c.1932. Thomas Y. Crowell Company.
--The Lotus Mark: A Story of Siam. Ayer, Margaret (0000-1981), illus. LC 35-16046. 5 p. l., 110 p. front., illus. 22 cm. 1935. The Macmillan Company.
--Nam and Deng: A Boy and Girl of Siam. Ayer, Margaret (0000-1981), illus. LC 33-21525. 4 p. l., 3-138 p. incl. front., illus. 22 cm. c.1933. Thomas Y. Crowell Company.
--Our Little Corinthian Cousin of Long Ago: Being the Story of Timon and the Golden Age of Greece. Cue, Harold, illus. LC 37-30932. 5 p. l., 93 p. front., plates. 19 1/2 cm. (little cousins of long ago series). c.1937. L. C. Page & Company.
--Our Little Mongolian Cousin. LC 36-17326. viii p., 2 l., 122 p. front., illus. (map) plates. 19 1/2 cm. c.1936. L. C. Page & Company.
--Sons of the Dragon. Ayer, Margaret (0000-1981), illus. LC 42-9592. 285 p. col. front., illus., col. plates. 23 cm. 1942. A. Whitman & Company.
--Swords and Sails in the Philippines. Ayer, Margaret (0000-1981), illus. LC 44-3051. 127, 1 p. incl. col. front., illus. (part col.) 23 1/2 x 18 1/2 cm. 1944. A. Whitman & Company.
--Under the Japanese Moon. Ayer, Margaret (0000-1981), illus. LC 37-30934. 5 p. l., 303 p. front., illus. 20 1/2 cm. c.1937. L. C. Page & Company.
--Yasu-Bo and Ishi-Ko: A Boy and Girl of Japan. Ayer, Margaret (0000-1981), illus. LC 34-32561. 5 p. l., 3-142, 1 p. col. front., illus. (part col.) 22 cm. c.1934. Thomas Y. Crowell Company.
Sowers, Phyllis Ayer, Mrs., jt. auth. see Bothwell, Jean.
Soya, Carl Erik Martin (1896-)
--Grandmother's House. Hansen, Agnes Camilla, tr. 1966, c.1943. (ISBN 0-8008-3600-6). Taplinger Publishing Company.
Soyer, Abraham (1867-1940)
--The Adventures of Yemima, and Other Stories. 1st ed. Soyer, Rebecca S. & Soyer, Raphael (1899-), illus. Beagle, Rebecca S., tr. Beagle, Peter Soyer (1939-) LC 78-26017. (Illus.). viii, 70 p. 24cm. 1979. (ISBN 0-670-10616-X). Viking Press.
Spain, Louise, tr. see Severin, Jean.
Spain, Pleasant De see De Spain, Pleasant.
Spalding, Arthur Whitefield
--Five-Finger Stories. Nye, Vernon Paul, illus. LC 52-681115. (Illus.). 24cm. 126p. 1952. Review and Herald Publishing Assn.
Spalding, Henry Stanislaus (1865-)
--Arrows of Iron. LC 34-2149. 230 p. front., plates. 19 cm. 1934. Benziger Brothers.
--At the Foot of the Sand-Hills. LC 17-28762. 199 p. front., plates. 19 cm. 1917. Benziger Brothers.
--At the Gate of Stronghold. LC 29-16433. 224 p. front., plates. 19 cm. 1929. Benziger Brothers.
--The Camp by Copper River. LC 15-25699. 192 p. front., plates. 19 cm. $0.85. 1915. Benziger Brothers.
--The Cave by the Beech Fork: A Story of Kentucky-1815. LC 1-81235. (Illus.). 19 cm. v, 232p. 1901. Benziger Bros.
--Held in the Everglades. LC 19-15233. 234 p. front. 19 cm. 1919. Benziger Brothers.
--In the Wilds of the Canyon. LC 23-13103. 192 p. front. 19 cm. 1923. Benziger Brothers.
--The Indian Gold-Seeker. LC 27-117231. 207 p. front., plates, map. 19 cm. 1927. Benziger Brothers.
--The Marks of the Bear Claws. LC 8-17246. 2 p. l., 3-229 p. front. 19 1/2 cm. 1908. Benziger Brothers.
--The Old Mill on the Withrose. LC 10-25678. (Illus.). 19cm. 244p. 1910. Benziger Bros.
--The Race for Copper ISland. LC 3-14964. (Illus.). 19 cm. 303p. 1905. Benziger Bros.
--Signals from the Bay Tree. LC 21-18250. (Illus.). 19 cm. 208p. 1921. Benziger Bros.
--Stranded on Long Bar. LC 25-22988. 174 p. front., map. 19 cm. 1925. Benziger Brothers.
--The Sugar-Camp and After. LC 12-25386. 233 p. front., plates. 19 cm. $0.85. 1912. Benziger Brothers.
Spalding, Maud Wolcott
--Babes and Cradles, Just Outside the Door. Parkhurst, Anita & Marsh, Lucille Patterson, illus. LC 48-21617. 61 p. illus. 18 x 24 cm. 1948. Southern Pub. Assn.
Spalding, Rebecca Wentworth
--A Dryad's Colophon;. A/Story of the Dryads and the Hurricane. LC 41-15928. (Illus.). 37p. 23cm. 1941. The Standard Printing Company.
Spamer, Claribel
--Juvenile Treasure Chest. 87 p. 19 cm. c.1956. Baker's Plays.
Spang, Gunter (1926-)
--Clelia and the Little Mermaid. Ott, Pepperl, illus. LC 68-11721. (Illus.). 28 p. 34cm. 1967. Abelard-Schuman.
--Horse in the Hotel. Heinen, Anton, illus. Rapoport, Eileen, tr. LC 64-10282. (Illus.). 21 cm. 175p. (gr. 4-6). 1963. Abelard.
--House in Sunflower Street. Tripp, Franz Josef, illus. LC 64-22553. (Illus.). (gr. k-3). 1964. (ISBN 0-8098-1102-2). Walck.
--The Soap Bubble Millionaire. Siegfried, Oelk, illus. Rapoport, Eileen, tr. LC 63-7035. 160p. 1962. Obelard-Schumann.
Spangenberg, Judith Dunn see Dunn, Judy, pseud.
Spangler, Wanda L.
--Marantha: The Mouse in the Tomb. N.D. (ISBN 0-8062-2500-9). Carlton.
Spanner, Helmut & Fechner, Amrei
--I Am a Little Cat. (Little Animal Miniatures Ser.). (ps). 1984. (ISBN 0-8120-5587-X). Barron.
Spanoghe, Ann & Disney, Walt, Productions
--The Strongest Man in the World. LC 77-374252. (Illus.). 128 p., 4 p. of plates. 18cm. 1976. (ISBN 0-450-02827-5). New English Library.
Spar, Jerome (1918-)
--Willy: A Story of Water. Connor, Bil, illus. LC 66-11438. 32p. illus. (pt. col.) 26cm. 1966, c.1965. Oddo.
--Willy: A Story of Water. Connor, Bil, illus. LC 68-56819. (Illus.). 32 p. 26cm. (Wonderful world of children's books). 1968. Oddo Publishing.
Sparenberg, David
--Goliath. N.D. (ISBN 0-8283-1594-9). Braden Press.
Sparhawk, Frances Campbell (1847-)
--A Chronicle of Campbell. N.D. Lothrop Pub. Co.
--Dorothy Brooke Across the Sea. Merrill, Frank Thayer (1848-), illus. LC 13-174112. vii, 359 p. front., plates. 10 1/2 cm. $1.5. c.1913. Thomas Y. Crowell Company.
--Dorothy Brooke at Ridgemore. Merrill, Frank Thayer (1848-), illus. LC 12-228611. vii, 409 p. front., plates 20 1/2 cm. $1.5. c.1912. Thomas Y. Crowell Company.
--Dorothy Brooke's Experiments. Merrill, Frank Thayer (1848-), illus. LC 11-20820. (Crowell's American Boy and Girl Library). 1911. Thomas Y. Crowell Company.
--Dorothy Brooke's School Days. Merrill, Frank Thayer (1848-), illus. LC 9-24328. vii, 358 p. front., 7 pl. 20 1/2 cm. $1.5. c.1909. T. Y. Crowell & Co.
--Dorothy Brooke's Vacation. Merrill, Frank Thayer (1848-), illus. LC 10-154801. 4 p. l., 331 p. front., plates. 20 1/2 cm. $1.50. c.1910. T. Y. Crowell & Co.
--Little Polly Blatchley. (Illus.). N.D. Lothrop Pub. Co.
Spark, Muriel Sarah (1918-)
--The Very Fine Clock. Gorey, Edward St. John (1925-), illus. LC 68-22247. (Illus.). 32 p. 1968. Knopf.
Sparks, Asa Howard (1937-)
--Hope for the Frogs: A Story. Dick, JoAnn, illus. LC 78-72061. (Illus.). 48 p. 24cm. c.1979. (ISBN 0-915190-17-6). Jalmar Press.
Sparks, Beatrice Mathews (1918-), ed.
--Jay's Journal. LC 78-19612. ix, 179 p. 22cm. c.1979. (ISBN 0-8129-0801-5). Times Books.
Sparks, Charles Elmer (1875-)
--Paths in the Wilderness: A Story of Lutheran Pioneers in Georgia. Nortenheim, William S., illus. LC 23-17768. 171 p. front., plates. 19 cm. c.1923. The United Lutheran Publication House.
Sparks, Enid
--Children of the Four Winds. Padgett, Jim, illus. LC 72-93954. (Illus.). 133 p. 21cm. 1969. Southern Pub. Association.
--Dana's Date with Troubles. (gr. 7-9). N.D. Southern Pub.
--Judy and Terry, the Golden Rule Children. Torrey, Helen (1901-), illus. LC 73-94883. (Illus.). 141 p. 21cm. 1969. Southern Pub. Association.
--Through the Week with Jesus. Padgett, Jim, illus. LC 68-3129. (Illus.). 128 p. 22cm. 1968. Southern Pub. Association.
Sparks, George Robert (1858-)
--The Man with the Wooden Leg and the Adventures of Doris, Bobbie and Joan in Washington Park, Chicago. St. John, J. Allen & Kaufman & Fabry Co., illus. LC 21-22101. 4 p. l., 66 p. front., 1 illus., plates. 17 cm. 1921. M. A. Donohue & Co.
Sparks, Jeff
--Nursery Rhymes for the Times: Ecology and Mother Goose. Sparks, Jeff, illus. LC 76-161204. (Illus.). 55 p. 29cm. 1971. Malcolm & Hayes.
Sparks, Jody, ed.
--Baby Jesus ABC Storybook. Lamb, Cecile, illus. (Illus.). 24p. (Happy Day Bk.). (gr. k-3). 1979. (ISBN 0-87239-354-2). Standard Pub.
Sparks, John
--Moe Takes the Cake. Larrecq, John Maurice (1926-1980), illus. (Illus.). (ps-3). 1970. (ISBN 0-87466-005-X). Parnassus.
Sparks, Judith, ed. see Bennett, Marian.
Sparks, Judith, ed. see Crandall, Ruth.
Sparks, Judith, ed. see Gambill, Henrietta.
Sparks, Judith, ed. see LeFevre, G. L.
Sparks, Judith, ed. see O'Rourke, Robert.
Sparks, Judith, ed. see Patterson, Yvonne.
Sparks, Judith, ed. see Solomon, Evelyn.
Sparks, Judith Ann, ed. see Maschke, Ruby.
Sparks, Lyle Weaver
--Anna-Marie and The Village of the Whole Wide World: Stories of Little and Grown-up Children. LC 15-248871. 3 p. l., 9-67 p. 19 cm. $0.50. c.1915. El-Es Pub. Co.
Sparks, Richard W.
--A Candle Opera. Acheson, Robert B., illus. (Illus.). 54p. (gr. 1-10). 1983. (ISBN 0-9614185-0-8). S J F Co.
Sparks, Ted
--Hot Lead & Cold Feet. (gr. 4-6). 1979. (ISBN 0-590-12094-8). Scholastic Inc.
Sparks, Ted, jt. auth. see Conway, Tim.
Spath, Margaret
--The Adventures of Pecky. (Illus.). (gr. k-3). N.D. Vantage.
Spaulding, Francis Trow, jt. ed. see Spaulding, Susan Thompson.
Spaulding, Frank Ellsworth, ed. see Page, Thomas Nelson.
Spaulding, Susan Thompson & Spaulding, Francis Trow (1896-1950), eds.
--Open Gates: A Book of Poems for Boys and Girls of Junior High School Age. LC 78-128158. 384 p. 21cm. (Granger index reprint series). 1970, c.1924. Books for Libraries Press.
Spavin, Don, ed.
--Chippewa Dawn: Legends of an Indian People. Kraywinkle, Jack, illus. LC 80-106276. (Illus.). 55 p. 24cm. 1977. (ISBN 0-89658-004-0). Voyageur Press.
Spayd, Barbara Grace, ed. see Garland, Hannibal Hamlin.
Spear, Sarah Foster Prince see Keene, S. F., Mrs., pseud.
Spear, Sarah Foster Prince, Mrs.
--The Academy Boys in Camp. 264p. N.D. Congregational Sunday-School and Publishing Society.
--The Artist's Children: Or, A Year Here and There. Keene, Mrs. S. F., pseud. LC 66-46222. (Illus.). 256p. 18cm. 1869. Cong. Sabbath School and Pub. Society.
--The Island Home. 318p. N.D. Congregational Sunday-School And Publishing Society.
Speare, Elizabeth George (1902-)
--The Bronze Bow. LC 61-10640. 255 p. 22 cm. 1961. Houghton, Mifflin. **Awards: (JNM); (IBBY); (ALA).**
--Calico Captive. Mars, Witold Tadeusz J. (1912-), illus. LC 57-9017. (Illus.). 274 p. 22cm. 1957. Houghton Mifflin.
--The Sign of the Beaver. LC 83-118. 135 p. 22cm. c.1983. (ISBN 0-395-33890-5). Houghton Mifflin. **Awards: (ALA); (JNM); (SOA).**
--The Witch of Blackbird Pond. LC 58-11063. 249 p. 22cm. 1958. Houghton Mifflin. **Awards: (JNM); (IBBY); (ALA).**
Spearing, Judith Mary Harlow (1922-)
--Ghosts Who Went to School. 160p. (gr. 4-6). 1970. (ISBN 0-590-02256-3). Scholastic Inc.
--Ghosts Who Went to School. Glass, Marvin, illus. LC 66-12856. 183p. illus. 22cm. c.1966. (ISBN 0-689-20410-8). (ISBN 0-689-20411-6). Atheneum.
--The Museum House Ghosts. 1st ed. Glass, Marvin, illus. LC 69-18957. (Illus.). 181p. 22cm. 1960. Atheneum.
Spearman, Frank Hamilton, et al. (1859-)
--Making Good: Stories of Golf and Other Outdoor Sports. LC 10-11297. 4 p. l., 212 p., 1 l. front., illus., plates. 18 1/2 cm. (On verso of t.-p.: Harper's athletic series, IV). 1910. Harper & Brothers.
Spearman, Frank Hamilton (1859-)
--The Mountain Divide. N.D. Charles Scribner's Sons.
Spears, Raymond Smiley (1876-)
--Camping on the Great Lakes. LC 13-21740. (Illus.). 371p. 19cm. (Harper's Camp-Life Ser.). 1913. Harper & Bros.
--Camping on the Great River: The Adventures of a Boy Afloat on the Mississippi. LC 12-245591. 4 p. l., 401, 1 p. front., plates. 19 1/2 cm. $1.5. 1912. Harper & Brothers.
--Driftwood. Avison, George F. (1885-), illus. LC 21-15252. 6 p. l., 6-283 p. incl. plates. front. 19 1/2 cm. N.D. The Century Co.
Specking, Inez (1890-1960)
--The Awakening of Edith: A Boarding School Story. LC 24-277461. 217 p. front., plates. 19 cm. 1924. Benziger Brothers.
--Boy: The Story of Missy's Brother. LC 25-5968. 164 p. front. 19 cm. 1925. Benziger Brothers.
--Martha Jane--Sophomore. Mann, Hortense, illus. LC 29-9008. 3p. l., 204 p. incl. front., plates. 191-612 cm. 1929. B. Herder Book Co.
--Martha Jane: A Western Boarding School Story. LC 25-200297. 192 p. front., plates. 19 cm. 1925. Benziger Brothers.
--Martha Jane at College. LC 26-19732. 183 p. front. 18 1/2 cm. 1926. Benziger Brothers.
--Mirage: A Novel. LC 25-229894. 223 p. 19 cm. 1925. Benziger Brothers.
--Missy: The Heart Story of a Child. LC 24-22682. 188 p. front. 19 cm. 1924. Benziger Brothers.
--A Shakespeare for Children. N.D. Vantage Press.
Specter, Otto
--Fables in Pictures. (Illus.). 1888. Porter & Coates.
--One Hundred Picture Fables. Dalziel, Edward (1817-1905) & Dalziel, George (1815-1902), illus. Hey, F., tr. from Ger. N.D. George Routledge & Sons.
Spector, Robert Melvyn (1926-)
--Greatest Rebel. LC 69-16475. 272p. (gr. 7 up). 1969. (ISBN 0-8098-3079-5). Walck.
--Salt Water Guns. LC 78-100710. (Illus.). 216 p. 21cm. 1970. (ISBN 0-8098-3089-2). H. Z. Walck.
Spector, Shushannah (1903-)
--Five Young Heroes of Israel. Shevo, Aharon, illus. LC 70-115117. (Illus.). 53 p. 24cm. 1970. Shengold.
--The Seder That Almost Wasn't. Wettenstein, Raphael, illus. LC 67-31080. (Illus.). 48 p. 26cm. c.1967. Shengold Publishers.
Speed, Belle Tevis, Mrs., compiled by.
--Stories of Patriotism & Devotion. Speed, Belle Tevis, tr. from Fr. (Illus.). N.D. Methodist Bk Concern.
--Stories of Patriotism and Devotion. For Young People. Speed, Belle Tevis, Mrs., tr. from Fr. LC 12-39155. 325 p. front., plates. 17 1/2 cm. 1883. Walden and Stowe.
Speed, Eric, pseud., see Stratemeyer Syndicate.
Speed, Eric, pseud.
--Dead Heat at Le Mans. Stratemeyer Syndicate. LC 76-24708. 179 p. 20cm. (Wynn and Lonny Racing Ser.: Vol. 5). c.1977. (ISBN 0-448-12807-1). (ISBN 0-448-13409-8). Grosset & Dunlap.

--Gold Cup Rookies. Stratemeyer Syndicate. LC 75-17388. 180 p. 20cm. (Wynn and Lonny Racing Ser.: Vol. 4). c.1976. (ISBN 0-448-12166-2). (ISBN 0-448-13329-6). Grosset & Dunlap.
--GT Challenge. Stratemeyer Syndicate. LC 75-17390. 180 p. 20cm. (Wynn and Lonny Racing Ser.: Vol. 3). c.1976. (ISBN 0-448-12167-0). (ISBN 0-448-13330-X). Grosset & Dunlap.
--The Mexicali One Thousand. Stratemeyer Syndicate. LC 74-1898. (Illus.). 182p. (Wynn and Lonny Racing Ser.: Vol. 1). (gr. 3-6). 1975. (ISBN 0-448-11790-8). (ISBN 0-448-13220-6). Grosset & Dunlap.
--The Midnight Rally. Stratemeyer Syndicate. LC 77-89962. 180 p. 20cm. (Wynn and Lonny Racing Ser.: Vol. 6). c.1978. (ISBN 0-448-14558-8). Grosset & Dunlap.
--Road Race of Champions. Stratemeyer Syndicate. LC 74-1899. 180 p. 20cm. (Wynn and Lonny Racing Ser.: Vol. 2). 1975. (ISBN 0-448-11791-6). (ISBN 0-448-13221-4). Grosset & Dunlap.
Speed, Flora & Speed, Lancelot
--The Adventures of King Kebole. (Illus.). N.D. Frederick Warne & Co.
Speed, James (1866-)
--Billy and Jane: Explorers. Rev ed. Speed, James (1886-), photos by. LC 22-21787. 2 v. illus. 17 cm. N.D. D. C. Heath & Co.
--Jack and Nell in Field and Forest. LC 6-32111. 192 p. 17 1/2 cm. 1906. Public-School Publishing Co.
Speed, Lancelot, jt. auth. see Speed, Flora.
Speed, Lancelot (1860-1931)
--The Red Fairy Book. LC 67-28307. (Illus.). 367 p. 23cm. 1967. McGraw-Hill.
Speed, Nell (1878-1913)
--At Boarding School With the Tucker Twins. (The Tucker Twins Ser.). N.D. A. L. Burt Co.
--At Boarding School with the Tucker Twins. Scott, Arthur O., illus. LC 15-13839. 4 p., 1 l., 5-313 p. front., plates. 20 cm. $0.6. c.1915. Hurst & Company.
--Back at School with the Tucker Twins. (The Tucker Twins Ser.). N.D. A. L. Burt Co.
--The Carter Girls. (The Carter Girls Ser.). N.D. A. L. Burt Co.
--The Carter Girls. Scott, Arthur O., illus. LC 18-13640. 3 p. l., 5-315 p. front., plates. 20 cm. c.1918. Hurst & Co., Inc.
--The Carter Girls' Mysterious Neighbors. (The Carter Girls Ser.). N.D. A. L. Burt Co.
--The Carter Girls of Carter House. (The Carter Girls Ser.). N.D. A. L. Burt Co.
--The Carter Girls' Week-End Camp. (The Carter Girls Ser.). N.D. A. L. Burt Co.
--A House Party with the Tucker Twins. (The Tucker Twins Ser.). N.D. A. L. Burt Co.
--A House Party with the Tucker Twins. Scott, Arthur O., illus. LC 27-7309. 301 p. incl. front. plates. 19 1/2 cm. c.1921. Hurst & Company.
--In New York with the Tucker Twins. (The Tucker Twins Ser.). N.D. A. L. Burt Co.
--Molly Brown of Kentucky. (The Molly Brown Ser.). N.D. A. L. Burt Co.
--Molly Brown of Kentucky. Scott, Arthur O., illus. LC 18-13641. 4 p., 1 l., 5-314 p. front., plates. 20 cm. c.1918. Hurst & Co., Inc.
--Molly Brown's College Friends. (The Molly Brown Ser.). N.D. A. L. Burt Co.
--Molly Brown's Freshman Days. (The Molly Brown Ser.). N.D. A. L. Burt Co.
--Molly Brown's Freshman Days. (Illus.). (Molly Brown Ser.). N.D. Hurst & Co.
--Molly Brown's Freshman Days. Wrenn, Charles L., illus. LC 12-14402. 4 p., 1 l., 5-301 p. front. plates. 20 1/2 cm. $0.6. c.1912. Hurst & Company.
--Molly Brown's Junior Days. (The Molly Brown Ser.). N.D. A. L. Burt Co.
--Molly Brown's Junior Days. (Molly Brown Ser.). N.D. Hurst & Co.
--Molly Brown's Junior Days. Wrenn, Charles L., illus. LC 12-16434. 4 p., 1 l., 5-301 p. front., plates. 20 1/2 cm. c.1912. Hurst & Company.
--Molly Brown's Orchard Home. (The Molly Brown Ser.). N.D. A. L. Burt Co.
--Molly Brown's Orchard Home. Wrenn, Charles L., illus. LC 15-107244. 4 p., 1 l., 5-309 p. front., plates. 20 cm. $0.6. c.1915. Hurst & Company.
--Molly Browns Post-Graduate Days. (The Molly Brown Ser.). N.D. A. L. Burt Co.
--Molly Brown's Post-Graduate Days. Wrenn, Charles L., illus. LC 14-6289. 4 p., 1 l., 5-307 p. front., plates. 20 cm. $0.6. c.1914. Hurst & Company.
--Molly Brown's Senior Days. (The Molly Brown Ser.). N.D. A. L. Burt Co.
--Molly Brown's Senior Days. Wrenn, Charles L., illus. LC 13-10541. 4 p., 1 l., 5-304 p. front., plates 20 1/2 cm. $0.6. c.1913. Hurst & Company.
--Molly Brown's Sophomore Days. (The Molly Brown Ser.). N.D. A. L. Burt Co.
--Molly Brown's Sophomore Days. Wrenn, Charles L., illus. LC 12-144596. 4 p., 1 l., 5-309 p. front., plates. 20 1/2 cm. $0.6. c.1912. Hurst & Company.
--Tripping with the Tucker Twins. (The Tucker Twins Ser.). N.D. A. L. Burt Co.
--Vacation with the Tucker Twins. (The Tucker Twins Series). N.D. A. L. Burt Co.
Speer, Bonnie Stahlman
--Errat's Garden. Palm, Mary Ellen, illus. LC 70-88717. (Illus.). 31 p. 1969. Reilly & Lee Books.
Speevack, Yetta
--The Spider Plant. Watson, Wendy McLeod (1942-), illus. LC 65-10476. (Illus.). 154 p. 22cm. 1965. Atheneum.
Speicher, Helen Ross Smith, jt. auth. see Borland, Kathryn Kilby.
Speicher, Helen Ross Smith (1915-) & Borland, Kathryn Kilby (1916-)
--Southern Yankees. Fetz, Ingrid (1915-), illus. LC 60-14549. 192 p. illus. 22 cm. 1960. Bobbs-Merrill.
Speiser, Jean
--River in the Dark: A Novel. LC 60-6913. 189 p. 21 cm. (Your=fair-land series). 1960. J. Day Co.
Spellman, John Willard (1934-), ed.
--The Beautiful Blue Jay, and Other Tales of India. 1st ed. Pinkney, Jerry (1939-), illus. LC 67-17294. (Illus.). xii, 101 p. 24cm. 1967. Little, Brown.
Spelman, Mary see Towne, Mary, pseud.
Spence, Eleanor Rachel (1928-)
--A Candle for Saint Anthony. LC 77-9976. 139 p. 23cm. 1977. (ISBN 0-19-271415-5). Oxford University Press.
--The Devil Hole. LC 77-909. 215 p. 22cm. 1977, c.1976. (ISBN 0-688-41798-1). (ISBN 0-688-51798-6). Lothrop, Lee & Shepard.
--The Green Laurel. Spence, Geraldine (1931-), illus. LC 65-10802. v, 181p. illus. 23cm. 1965, c.1963. Roy.
--Jamberoo Road. Roberts, Doreen (1922-), illus. LC 76-90929. 23cm. 162p. 1969. Roy.
--Lillipilly Hill. Einzig, Susan (1922-), illus. LC 63-16200. 176 p. illus. 23 cm. 1963, c.1960. Roy Publishers.
--The Nothing Place. Spence, Geraldine (1931-), illus. LC 73-5494. (Illus.). 228 p. 22cm. 1st U.S. edition. 1973. (ISBN 0-06-025732-6). (ISBN 0-06-025732-6). Harper & Row.
--The Nothing-Place. Spence, Geraldine (1931-), illus. LC 73-179068. (Illus.). 5, 137 p. 23cm. 1972. (ISBN 0-19-271335-3). Oxford University Press.
--The Switherby Pilgrims. Gray, Corinna (1940-), illus. LC 74-465310. (Illus.). 22cm. vii, 170p. 1967. Oxford Univ.Press.
--The Switherby Pilgrims. Gray, Corinna (1940-), illus. LC 67-25636. (Illus.). v, 170 p. 22cm. 1967. Roy Publishers.
--The Year of the Currawong. Floyd, Gareth (1940-), illus. LC 65-24274. 170 p. illus. 23 cm. 1965. Roy Publishers.
Spence, Elizabeth Isabella (1768-1832)
--The Spanish Guitar. A Tale; for the Use of Young Persons. LC 22-105337. 69 p. illus. 13 cm. N.D. Printed by Munroe, Francis & Parker.
Spence, Marie Hays
--Jamie's Jingle Book. Spence, Marie Hays, photos by. LC 40-132778. 1 p. l., 68 p., 2 l. illus. 19 1/2 cm. 1940. The Naylor Company.
Spencer, Alice
--Little Folks' Story of the Apostles. LC 47-24758. 91 p. illus. 20 cm. 1947. Wm. B. Eerdmans Publishing Company.
Spencer, Brenda
--The Friends of Van. N.D. Transatlantic Arts, Inc.
Spencer, Brenda, jt. auth. see Dowd, J. H.
Spencer, Catherine
--Pennies for a Penny. N.D. Macmillan.
Spencer, Chris
--Mystery at Hawktowers, and Other Stories. LC 85-19862. p. cm. (Lion paperback). 1985. (ISBN 0-85648-819-4). Lion Pub.
--Starforce Red Alert. LC 84-71418. 144p (Pub. by Lion Pubs). (gr. 9-12). 1984. (ISBN 0-89107-321-3, Crossway Bks). Good News.
Spencer, Cornelia, pseud., see Yankey, Grace Sydenstricker.
Spencer, Cornelia, pseud. (1899-)
--Land of the Chinese People. Yankey, Grace Sydenstricker. rev. ed. (Illus.). (Portraits of the Nations Ser). (gr. 7-9). 1964. Lippincott.
Spencer, Dick
--Tales of Demon Dick and Bunker Bill. LC 34-41985. 1 p. l., 7-77 p. illus. 18 x 26 1/2 cm. c.1934. Whitman Publishing Co.
Spencer, Doris, jt. auth. see Spencer, Ric.
Spencer, Edna Earle Cole
--The Good Samaritan and Other Biblical Stories. Wagner, Harold, illus. xiii, 14-126 p. front., 3 pl. 19 1/2 cm. c.1915. Doran.
Spencer, Katherine Smith (1855-)
--The Soldier Boy She Lost. LC 19-16370. 34p. 18cm. 1919. Burdick-Allen-Dietas Co.
Spencer, Pat
--Hustler's Gold. (gr. 9 up). N.D. Soccer.
Spencer, Philip (1925-)
--Day of Glory: The Guns at Lexington and Concord. Lluothated by Pete- Bulha-D. 1st ed. LC 55-5885. 192p. illus. 21cm. (American heritage). 1955. Aladdin Books.
Spencer, Ric & Spencer, Doris
--Snickle-Fritz Goes Camping. 1982. (ISBN 0-533-05128-2). Vantage.
Spencer, Sharon Dougherty (1933-)
--Breaking the Bonds: A Novel About the Peace Corps. Leone, Sergio, illus. LC 63-3236. 184 p. illus. 22 cm. 1963. Grosset & Dunlap.
Spencer, Zane Ann, jt. auth. see Leech, Jay.
Spencer, Zane Ann (1935-) & Leech, Jay (1931-)
--Branded Runaway. LC 80-80. 89 p. 21cm. c.1980. (ISBN 0-664-32662-5). Westminster Press.
--Cry of the Wolf. LC 76-56450. 144 p. 21cm. c.1977. (ISBN 0-664-32611-0). Westminster Press.
Spender, Brenda Elizabeth (1884-)
--On'y Tony: The Adventures of Three Ponies and a Little Boy. Turner, Barbara, illus. LC 36-30338. 4 p. l., 11-96 p. incl. front., illus. 21 cm. 1935. C. Scribner's Sons.
--On'y Tony's Circus. Turner, Barbara, illus. LC 37-8006. viii, 9-63 p. front., plates. 21 cm. 1937. C. Scribner's Sons.
Spender, Constance
--The Gilroy Family. N.D. Macmillan.
--Lion Hearts. N.D. Macmillan.
Spender, Stephen Harold (1909-)
--The Magic Flute. Montresor, Beni (1926-), illus. LC 66-9616. (Illus.). 1 v. (unpaged). 1966. G. P. Putnam's Sons. **Award: (NYT).**
Spenner, Helmut
--I am a Little Cat. Kimber, Robert, tr. from Ger. (Illus.). 24p. 1st U.S. edition. (Little Animal Stories Ser.). 1983. (ISBN 0-8120-5513-6). Barron.
Spenser, Edmund, jt. auth. see Chaucer, Geoffrey.
Spenser, Edmund (1552-1599)
--The Adventures of the Redcrosse Knight. Mary Charitina, ed. Wong, Jeanyee (1920-), illus. LC 45-11148. (The First of Spenser's Fairie Queene retold for Children). 9 p. l., 109, 1 p. col. illus. 24 cm. 1945. Sheed and Ward.
--Faerie Queene, 1 of 2 Bks, Bks. I. New Ed. ed. Kitchin, G. W., notes by. (Clarendon Press Ser.). N.D. Set. MacMillan.
--Faerie Queene, 1 of 2 bks, Bk. II. 7th ed. Kitchin, G. W., notes by. (Clarendon Press Ser.). N.D. Set. MacMillan.
--The Faerie Queene. Nolan, Walter K., ed. (Book 1). 1968. Barron.
--The Faery Queen and Her Knights. Church, Alfred John (1829-1912), retold by. LC 9-274168. vii, 309 p. col. front., 7 col. pl. 19 1/2 cm. 1909. The Macmillan Company.
--Saint George and the Dragon: Being the Legend of the Red Cross Knight from the Faerie Queene. Warburg, Sandol Stoddard, ed. Baynes, Pauline Diana (1922-), illus. LC 63-7323. (Illus.). 25 cm. 132p. 1963. Houghton Mifflin. **Award: (ALA).**
--Spenser's Faerie Queene. 1900. Maynard Merrill & Co.
--Spenser's Faerie Queene. Kitchen, G. W., illus. N.D. Clarendon Press.
--Stories from the Faerie Queen. Lang, Jeanie, Mrs., as told by. Le Queene, Rose, illus. ix, 115 p. 8 col. pl. (incl. front.) 15 cm. (Told to the Children Ser.). 1905. E P Dutton.
--The Story of the Faerie Queene. Brooks, Edward, Dr. (1831-1912), ed. 2 p. l., 9-418 p. incl. front., illus., pl. 19 1/2 cm. (Classic Stories Ser. for Boys and Girls). 1902. The Penn Publishing Company.
--The Story of the Red Cross Knight. (Illus.). N.D. Thos Nelson & Sons.
--Tales Chosen from the Fairie Queene. Maclehose, Sophia H., ed. N.D. MacMillan.
Spenser, Edmund (1552-1599) & Malory, Thomas Sir
--The Courteous Knight, & Other Tales from Spenser & Malory. Edwardson, E., ed. 1900. Thomas Nelson & Sons.
Sperandio, Guido
--Vanuk Vanuk. 1st ed. Ventura, Piero Luigi (1937-), illus. Murgo, Jane, tr. LC 73-79711. (gr. k-3). 1973. (ISBN 0-385-01161-X). (ISBN 0-385-07382-8). Doubleday.
Sperber, Ann, adapted by.
--The Ugly Duckling. Sperber, Ann & Obligado, Lilian Isabel (1931-), illus. LC 78-12523. (Original Author: Hans Christian Andersen). (Illus.). 17cm. 18p. (A Goodnight Bk.). (ps-1). 1979. (ISBN 0-394-84103-4). Knopf.
Sperber, Ann, tr. see La Fontaine, Jean De (1621-1695) & Aesopus.
Spero, James, adapted by.
--Rackham's Fairy Tale Coloring Book: Seventeen Stories from the Brothers Grimm. Rackham, Arthur (1867-1939) & Sibbett, Ed, Jr., illus. LC 79-51257. (Original Authors: Jakob Ludwig Kal Grimm, 1785-1863 and Wilhelm Karl Grimm, 1786-1859). (Illus.). 64 p. 28cm. 1979. (ISBN 0-486-23844-X). Dover Publications.
Sperry, Armstrong W. (1897-1976)
--All Sail Set: A Romance of the Flying Cloud. Sperry, Armstrong W. (1897-1976), illus. 1982. Godine.
--All Sail Set: Or, a Romance of the Flying Cloud. Sperry, Armstrong W. (1897-1976), illus. McFee, William, intro. by. LC 35-12196. 244p. 1936. John C. Winston Co.
--All Sails Set: A Romance of the "Flying Cloud". Sperry, Armstrong W. (1897-1976), illus. LC 84-47650. (Illus.). xvi, 175 p. 23cm. (Nonpareil books ; #35). 1984, c.1935. (ISBN 0-87923-523-3). D.R. Godine.
--Bamboo, the Grass Tree. Sperry, Armstrong W. (1897-1976), illus. LC 42-18846. 47 p. col. illus. 21 1/2 cm. 1942. The Macmillan Company.
--Black Falcon. Sperry, Armstrong W. (1897-1976), illus. LC 49-11410. (Illus.). 218p. (gr. 5-9). 1949. (ISBN 0-03-035970-8). HR&W.
--Black Falcon: A Story of Piracy and Old New Orleans. 1st ed. Sperry, Armstrong W. (1897-1976), illus. LC 49-11410. v, 218 p. illus. 22 cm. 1949. J. C. Winston Co.
--Call It Courage. Sperry, Armstrong W. (1897-1976), illus. LC 40-4229. 95 p. illus. 23 1/2 cm. 1940. The Macmillan Company. **Award: (JNM).**
--Call it Courage. Sperry, Armstrong W. (1897-1976), illus. 1936. Winston.
--Coconut, the Wonder Tree. Sperry, Armstrong W. (1897-1976), illus. LC 42-18845. 47) p. col. illus. 21 1/2 cm. 1942. The Macmillian Company.
--Danger to Windward. 1st ed. Sperry, Armstrong W. (1897-1976), illus. LC 47-11070. 241 p. illus. 22 cm. 1947. J. C. Winston Co.
--Frozen Fire. 1st ed. Sperry, Armstrong W. (1897-1976), illus. LC 56-10773. 192 p. illus. 22 cm. 1956. Doubleday.
--Hull-Down for Action. Sperry, Armstrong W. (1897-1976), illus. LC 45-35200. 4 p. l., 213 p. illus. 20 1/2 cm. 1945. Doubleday, Doran & Company, Inc.
--Little Eagle: A Navago Boy. Sperry, Armstrong W. (1897-1976), illus. LC 38-31824. 102 2 p. incl. col. front., illus. (part col. incl. music) 23 1/2 cm. c.1938. The John C. Winston Company.
--Lost Lagoon. Sperry, Armstrong W. (1897-1976), illus. (Illus.). (gr. 7-11). 1959. (ISBN 0-385-07388-7). Doubleday.
--Lost Lagoon: A Pacific Adventure. Sperry, Armstrong W. (1897-1976), illus. LC 39-28951. v p., 1 l., 277 p. col. front., illus. 22 1/2 cm. 1939. Doubleday, Doran & Co., Inc.
--No Brighter Glory. Sperry, Armstrong W. (1897-1976), illus. 1942. Macmillan.
--One Day with Jambi in Sumatra. Sperry, Armstrong W. (1897-1976), illus. LC 34-27235. 65 p. illus. (part col.) 20 cm. c.1934. The John C. Winston Company.
--One Day with Manu. Sperry, Armstrong W. (1897-1976), illus. LC 33-12230. 64 p. illus. (part col.) 26 cm. c.1933. The John C. Winston Company.
--One Day with Tuktu: An Eskimo Boy. Sperry, Armstrong W. (1897-1976), illus. LC 35-248935. 66 p. illus. (part col.) 26 cm. 1935. The John C. Winston Company.
--River of the West: The Story of the Boston Men. 1st ed. Pitz, Henry Clarence (1895-1976), illus. LC 52-8967. 182 p. illus. 22 cm. (winston adventure books). (Winston Adventure Bks.). 1952. (ISBN 0-03-065690-7). Winston.
--South of Cape Horn: A Saga of Nat Palmer and Early Antartic Exploration. 1st ed. Sperry, Armstrong W. (1897-1976), illus. LC 58-5677. 180 p. illus. 22 cm. 1958. J. C. Winston Co.
--Storm Canvas. Sperry, Armstrong W. (1897-1976), illus. LC 44-5270. (Illus.). 301p. (gr. 5-9). 1944. (ISBN 0-03-043145-X). HR&W.
--Storm Canvas. Sperry, Armstrong W. (1897-1976), illus. N.D. John C. Winston.
--The Rain Forest. Sperry, Armstrong W. (1897-1976), illus. LC 47-1835. 190 p. incl. col. front., col. illus. 22 1/2 cm. 1947. (ISBN 0-02-786230-5). The Macmillan Company.
--Thunder Country. Sperry, Armstrong W. (1897-1976), illus. LC 52-9410. 150 p. illus. 22 cm. 1952. Macmillan.
--The Voyages of Christopher Columbus. Sperry, Armstrong W. (1897-1976), illus. LC 50-11712. 186 p. col. illus. 22 cm. (Landmark Bks.: No. 1). 1950. Random House.
--Wagons Westward: The Old Trail to Santa Fe. Sperry, Armstrong W. (1897-1976), illus. 1936. Winston.

Sperry, Armstrong W. (1897-1976), ed.
--Story Parade: A Collection of Modern Stories for Boys and Girls, 5 Vols. LC 37-36658. 2 p. l., iii-ix, 1, 363 p. illus. 23 1/2 cm. 1938. The John C. Winston Company.
Sperry, Charlotte Grace
--Teddy Sunbeam: Little Fables for Little Housekeepers. LC 5-32472. (Illus.). 23cm. 45p. 1905. P. Elder & Co.
Sperry, J. E., pseud., see Eisenstat, Jane Sperry.
Sperry, J. E., pseud. (1920-)
--The Challenge of Aab. Eisenstat, Jane Sperry. Sperry, J. E., pseud. (1920-), illus. Eisenstat, Jane Sperry. LC 62-7309. (Illus.). 21cm. 216p. 1962. Harper.
Sperry, Margaret (1905-), adapted by see Ewald, Carl.
Sperry, Margaret (1905-), adapted by see Topelius, Zakarias.
Sperry, Margaret (1905-)
--The Magician's Cloak. Cooke, Dorothea, illus. LC 38-11064. 4 p. l., 45 p. illus., col. plates. 27 1/2 cm. c.1938. H. Holt and Company.
Sperry, Margaret (1905-), retold by.
--The Hen That Saved the World, and Other Norwegian Folk Tales. Rev ed. Beckman, Per (1913-), illus. LC 52-9611. 63 p. illus. 24 cm. 1952. John Day Co.
--Scandinavian Stories. Williams, Jenny (1939-), illus. LC 70-117746. (Illus.). 287 p. 25cm. 1971. (ISBN 0-531-01982-9). F. Watts.
Sperry, Portia Howe & Donaldson, Lois
--Abigail. Selover, Zabeth, illus. LC 38-25508. 7 p. l., 19-196 p. incl. col. front., illus., plates (part col.) 21 1/2 cm. 1938. A. Whitman & Co.
Sperry, Raymond, pseud., see Garis, Howard Roger.
Sperry, Raymond, pseud. (1873-1962)
--Larry Dexter and the Land Swindlers: Or, Queer Adventures in a Great City. Garis, Howard Roger. LC 27-13657. 1 p. l., v-vi, 313 p. 19 cm. (His Larry Dexter series--no. 2). 1926. Garden City Publishing Co., Inc.
--Larry Dexter at the Big Flood: Or, the Perils of a Reporter. Garis, Howard Roger. LC 27-7334. iv, 311 p. 19 cm. (On cover: Larry Dexter series No. 1). 1926. Garden City Publishing Co., Inc.
Sperry, Raymond, J ., pseud., see Stratemeyer Syndicate.
Sperry, Raymond, J ., pseud.
--The White Ribbon Boys of Chester: Or, The Old Tavern Keeper's Secret. Stratemeyer Syndicate. Rogers, Walter S., illus. (The White Ribbon Boys Ser.: Vol. 1). 1915. Cupples & Leon Co.
Sperzel, Florence E
--Fairyland. LC 37-39259. 42 p. front., plates. 19 1/2 cm. c.1937. The Christopher Pub House.
Speyer, Wilhelm (1887-)
--Galahads and Pussy-Cats. Gay, Zhenya (1906-1978), illus. Budicky, Margaret Mary Juers (1905-), tr. LC 29-23364. 2 p. l., 224 p. front., illus. 23 1/2 cm. c.1929. J. Cape and H. Smith.
Spice, Marjorie Davis (1924-)
--Miraca of Paraguay. Escourido, Joseph, illus. LC 61-7955. 22cm. 96p. (gr. 2-6). 1961. (ISBN 0-8272-2302-1). Bethany Pr.
Spicer, Dorothy Gladys
--Forty Six Days of Christmas. Jauss, Anne Marie (1907-), illus. (Illus.). (gr. 3-6). 1960. (ISBN 0-698-30091-2, Coward). Putnam Pub Group.
--Humming Top. LC 68-31176. 192p. (gr. 7-11). 1968. (ISBN 0-87599-147-5). S G Phillips.
--The Kneeling Tree, and Other Folktales from the Middle East. Morrow, Barbara, illus. LC 78-106931. (Illus.). 121 p. 24cm. 1971. Coward McCann.
--Long Ago in Serbia. large type ed. Ominsky, Linda, illus. (Illus.). (gr. 3-7). 1968. (ISBN 0-664-32414-2). Westminster.
--Thirteen Devils. Sofia, pseud. (1926-), illus. Zeiger, Sophia. LC 68-863. (Illus.). 127 p. 27cm. 1967. Coward-McCann.
--Thirteen Dragons. Sofia, pseud. (1926-), illus. Zeiger, Sophia. LC 72-94130. (Illus.). 157 p. 27cm. 1974. (ISBN 0-698-20254-6). (ISBN 0-698-20254-6). Coward, McCann & Geoghegan.
--Thirteen Ghosts. Sofia, pseud. (1926-), illus. Zeiger, Sophia. LC 65-20385. (Illus.). (gr. 3-6). 1965. (ISBN 0-698-30357-1, Coward). Putnam Pub Group.
--Thirteen Giants. Sofia, pseud. (1926-), illus. Zeiger, Sophia. LC 66-8432. (Illus.). 127p. illus. 27cm. (gr. 3-6). 1966. (ISBN 0-698-30358-X, Coward). Putnam Pub Group.
--Thirteen Goblins. Sofia, pseud. (1926-), illus. Zeiger, Sophia. LC 68-23863. (Illus.). 127 p. 27cm. 1969. Coward-McCann.
--Thirteen Jolly Saints. Sofia, pseud. (1926-), illus. Zeiger, Sophia. LC 79-88876. (Illus.). 127 p. 27cm. 1970. Coward-McCann.
--Thirteen Monsters. Sofia, pseud. (1926-), illus. Zeiger, Sophia. LC 64-17992. 127 p. illus. 27 cm. 1964. Coward-McCann.
--Thirteen Rascals. Sofia, pseud. (1926-), illus. Zeiger, Sophia. LC 76-166590. (Illus.). 127 p. 27cm. 1972, c.1971. Coward, McCann & Geoghegan.
--Thirteen Witches, Two Wizards: Stories. Sofia, pseud. (1926-), illus. Zeiger, Sophia. LC 63-10172. 93 p. illus. 26 cm. 1963. Coward-McCann.
--Thirteen Witches, Two Wizards, the Devil, and a Pack of Goblins. Sofia, pseud. (1926-), illus. Zeiger, Sophia. LC 63-10172. (Illus.). 26cm. 1963. Coward-McCann.
--Thirteen Witches, Two Wizards, the Devil & a Pack of Goblins. Sofia, pseud. (1926-), illus. Zeiger, Sophia. (Illus.). (gr. 3-6). 1970. (ISBN 0-698-30363-6, Coward). Putnam Pub Group.
Spicer, Dorothy Gladys, compiled by.
--The Owl's Nest: Folktales from Friesland. Wadowski-Bak, Alice, illus. LC 68-18824. (Illus.). 124 p. 24cm. 1968. Coward-McCann.
Spicer, Jesse
--String: The Story of a Lonesome Worm. LC 39-6269. 47, 1 p. col. illus. 23 1/2 cm. c.1939. Oquage Press.
Spicer, Robert A., jt. auth. see Goodman, Robert B.
Spicer, Robert A., jt. ed. see Goodman, Robert B.
Spicer, Venetia
--The Adventures of Chatrat. Spicer, Venetia, illus. LC 81-17741. (Illus.). 48 p. 1981. (ISBN 0-7043-2269-2). Quartet Books.
Spicer-Zerner, Jessie & Brooks, Andrea, illus.
--One Hundred Years Ago. (Illus.). 96p. 1983. (ISBN 0-448-81691-1, G&D). Putnam Pub Group.
Spiegel, Doris (1901-)
--Danny and Company Ninety-Two. LC 48-3220. 32 p. col. illus. 13 x 20 cm. 1945. Coward-McCann.
Spiegel, Marshall
--Cycle Jumpers. 176p. (gr. 5 up). 1974 (Starbright). Schol Bk Serv.
Spiegel, Richard, jt. ed. see Fisher, Barbara.
Spiegel, Richard Alan, jt. ed. see Fisher, Barbara.
Spiegelberg, Flora, Mrs.
--Grandma Flora's Animal Stories for Little Folk. LC 10-31006. (Illus.). 64p. 20 x 17cm. 1906. Educational Publishing Co.
--Princess Goldenhair and the Wonderful Flower. Winter, Milo Kendall (1888-1956), illus. LC 16-5185. 176 p. incl. col. front., illus. col. plates. 23 1/2 cm. c.1915. Rand, McNally & Company.
--Princess Goldenhair and the Wonderful Flower. Winter, Milo Kendall (1888-1956), illus. LC 33-16069. 3 p. l., 11-176 p. illus. 20 1/2 cm. 1915. The World Syndicate Publishing Company.
Spiegelman, Judith M
--Ali of Turkey. Bimen, Levent (1944-), illus. LC 69-10720. (Illus.). 63 p. 23cm. 1969. J. Messner.
Spiegler, Charles G. (1911-), ed.
--Against the Odds. Seward, James E., illus. LC 68-4256. (Illus.). v, 119 p. 23cm. (Merrill mainstream book). 1967. C. E. Merrill Pub. Co.
Spielberg, Steven (1947-) & Columbus, Chris
--The Goonies Storybook. LC 85-194475. (Based on the Motion Picture from Warner Bros.,Inc.: Story by Steven Spielberg : Screenplay by Chris Columbus.). (Illus.). 57 p. 29cm. c.1985. (ISBN 0-671-60134-2). Little Simon.
Spielhagen, Frederick
--What the Swallow Sang. (Leisure Hour Ser.). N.D. Henry Holt & Co.
Spielman, M. H.
--Margery Redford and Her Friends. Browne, Gordon Frederick (1858-1932), illus. N.D. Frederick A. Stokes.
Spielmann, M. H.
--Littledom Castle and Other Tales. N.D. E P Dutton.
--The Rainbow Book. Rackham, Arthur (1867-1939), illus. (Illus.). 1910. Frederick Warne & Co.
Spier, Peter Edward (1927-), tr. see Revius, Jacobus.
Spier, Peter Edward (1927-)
--And So My Garden Grows. Spier, Peter Edward (1927-), illus. LC 68-25599. (Illus.). 44 p. (Mother Goose library). 1969. Doubleday.
--Bill's Service Station. 1st ed. LC 80-1842. (Illus.). 8 p. (Peter Spier's Village Books). c.1981. (ISBN 0-385-15727-4). Doubleday.
--Bored-Nothing to Do!. Spier, Peter Edward (1927-), illus. LC 77-20726. (Illus.). 44 p. c.1978. (ISBN 0-385-13177-1). (ISBN 0-385-13178-X). Doubleday.
--Crash! Bang! Boom. LC 70-157625. (Illus.). (ps-1). 1972. Doubleday.
--The Erie Canal. Spier, Peter Edward (1927-), illus. LC 70-102055. (Illus.). 27cm. 36p. (Zephyr Book). 1973, c.1970. Doubleday.
--Fast-Slow, High-Low: A Book of Opposites. LC 72-76207. (Illus.). 44 p. 1972. (ISBN 0-385-06781-X). (ISBN 0-385-06781-X). Doubleday.
--Fire House: Hook & Ladder Company Number Twenty-Four. LC 80-1843. (Illus.). 11 p. 23cm. (Peter Spier's Village Books). c.1981. (ISBN 0-385-15728-2). Doubleday.
--The Fox Went Out on a Chilly Night. Spier, Peter Edward (1927-), illus. LC 60-7139. (Illus.). (gr. 1-3). 1961. Doubleday. **Awards: (ALA); (RCM).**
--Gobble, Growl, Grunt. LC 79-144300. (Illus.). 44 p. 1971. Doubleday.
--Hurrah, We're Outward Bound!. 1st ed. Spier, Peter Edward (1927-), illus. LC 68-12836. (Illus.). 41 p. (Mother Goose library). 1968. Doubleday.
--The Legend of New Amsterdam. LC 78-6032. (Illus.). 32p. (ps-3). 1979. Doubleday.
--London Bridge Is Falling Down!. Spier, Peter Edward (1927-), illus. LC 67-17695. (Illus.). 41 p. (Mother Goose library). 1967. Doubleday. **Award: (BGH).**
--My School. LC 80-1845. (Illus.). 14 p. 23cm. (Peter Spier's Village Books). c.1981. (ISBN 0-385-15732-0). Doubleday.
--Noah's Ark. 1st ed. Spier, Peter Edward (1927-), illus. LC 76-43630. (Illus.). 46 p. c.1977. (ISBN 0-385-09473-6). (ISBN 0-385-12730-8). Doubleday. **Awards: (NYT); (IBBY); (RCM).**
--Noah's Ark. Spier, Peter Edward (1927-), illus. 48p. (ps). 1981. (Zephyr). Doubleday. **Award: (ABA).**
--Oh, Were They Ever Happy!. Spier, Peter Edward (1927-), illus. LC 77-78144. (Illus.). 42 p. c.1978. (ISBN 0-385-13175-5). Doubleday. **Award: (ALA).**
--The Pet Store. LC 80-1846. (Illus.). 11 p. 23cm. (Peter Spier's Village Books). c.1981. (ISBN 0-385-15730-4). Doubleday.
--Peter Spier's Christmas!. Spier, Peter Edward (1927-), illus. LC 80-2875. (Illus.). 40p. (ps up). 1983. (ISBN 0-385-13183-6). (ISBN 0-385-13184-4). (ISBN 0-385-13184-4). Doubleday.
--Peter Spier's Little Cats. LC 82-45494. (Illus.). 14p. (Peter Spier's Little Animals Ser.). (ps-1). 1984. (ISBN 0-385-18197-3). (ISBN 0-385-18197-3). Doubleday.
--Peter Spier's Little Dogs. LC 82-45493. (Illus.). 14p. (ps-1). 1984. (ISBN 0-385-18196-5). (ISBN 0-385-18196-5). Doubleday.
--Peter Spier's Little Ducks. Spier, Peter Edward (1927-), illus. LC 82-45492. (Illus.). 14p. (Doubleday Balloon Books). (ps-1). 1984. (ISBN 0-385-18199-X). (ISBN 0-385-18199-X). Doubleday.
--Peter Spier's Little Rabbits. Spier, Peter Edward (1927-), illus. LC 82-45491. (Illus.). 14p. (gr. k-1). 1984. (ISBN 0-385-18198-1). Doubleday.
--Peter Spier's Rain. Spier, Peter Edward (1927-), illus. LC 81-43056. (Illus.). 36 p. 27cm. (ps-1). c.1982. (ISBN 0-385-15484-4). Doubleday. **Award: (ALA).**
--Tin Lizzie. Spier, Peter Edward (1927-), illus. LC 74-1510. (Illus.). 42 p. c.1975. (ISBN 0-385-09470-1). (ISBN 0-385-09470-1). Doubleday.
--To Market! To Market!. Spier, Peter Edward (1927-), illus. LC 67-18664. (Illus.). 41 p. (Mother Goose library). 1967. Doubleday.
--To Market! To Market!. Spier, Peter Edward (1927-), illus. LC 67-18664. (Illus.). 1 v. (unpaged). (Zephyr Book). (The Mother Goose Library). 1973, c.1967. Doubleday.
--The Toy Shop. LC 80-1847. (Illus.). 11 p. 23cm. (Peter Spier's Village Books). c.1981. (ISBN 0-385-15729-0). Doubleday.
Spier, Peter Edward (1927-), retold by.
--The Book of Jonah. Spier, Peter Edward (1927-), illus. 35p. 1985. (ISBN 0-385-19334-3). Doubleday.
Spies, Victor C
--Sun Dance and the Great Spirit. Bjorklund, Lorence F. (1913-1978), illus. LC 54-10100. (Illus.). 128 p. 25cm. 1954. (ISBN 0-695-48376-5). Follett.
Spilhaus, Athelstan Frederick (1911-)
--Turn to the Sea. Daly, Eileen, adapted by. Armstrong, Bill H., illus. LC 62-8163. (Illus.). 59p. 22cm. (A Whitman Learn About Bk.). 1962. Whitman Pub. Co.
Spilka, Arnold (1917-)
--Aloha from Bobby. Spilka, Arnold (1917-), illus. LC 62-16643. (Illus.). 23cm. 32p. (gr. k-3). 1962. (ISBN 0-8098-1084-0). Walck.
--And the Frog Went "Blah!" and Other Poems. LC 72-502. (Illus.). 40 p. 25cm. 1972. (ISBN 0-684-12991-4). Scribner.
--A Lion I Can Do Without. (Illus.). (gr. k-2). 1964. (ISBN 0-8382-0441-4). Hale.
--A Lion I Can Do Without. Spilka, Arnold (1917-), illus. LC 64-21122. (Illus.). 26cm. 40p. (gr. k-3). 1964. (ISBN 0-8098-1103-0). Walck.
--Little Birds Don't Cry. LC 65-18144. 1 v. (unpaged) illus. 11 x 13 cm. 1965. Viking Press.
--Once Upon a Horse. LC 66-13954. 1v. (unpaged) illus. (pt. col.) 21x25cm. c.1966. Walck.
--Paint All Kinds of Pictures. LC 63-17187. 1 v. (unpaged) illus. (part col.) 21 x 27 cm. c.1963. H. Z. Walck.
--A Rumbudgin of Nonsense. LC 70-120364. (Illus.). 32 p. 25cm. 1970. Scribner.
--Whom Shall I Marry?. Spilka, Arnold (1917-), illus. LC 60-50952. 36p. 1960. Holiday House.
Spillane, Frank Morrison see Spillane, Mickey, pseud.
Spillane, Frank Morrison (1918-)
--The Day the Sea Rolled Back. Spillane, Mickey, pseud. 1st ed. Maroto, illus. LC 78-7855. (Illus.). 138 p. 22cm. c.1979. (ISBN 0-525-61589-X). Windmill Books.
Spillane, Mickey, pseud., see Spillane, Frank Morrison.
Spiller, Burton Lowell (1886-)
--Northland Castaways. 1st ed. Moyers, William (1916-), illus. LC 57-12856. 228p. illus. 21cm. 1957. Bobbe-Merrill.
Spillmann, Joseph (1842-1905)
--Blessed Are the Merciful: A Tale of the Negro Uprising in Haiti. Gray, Mary Richards, tr. LC 7-986. 135 p. 17 1/2 cm. (Added t.-p.: Tales of foreign lands ... vol. X). 1906. B. Herder.
--The Cabin Boys. Gray, Mary Richards, tr. from Ger. LC 7-41589. 137p. (Tales of Foreign Lands: Vol. 12). 1907. B. Herder.
--Children of Mary: A/Tale of the Caucasus. Long, Helena, Miss, tr. LC 12-38944. 122p. 17cm. (Tales of Foreign Lands). Orig. Title: Ger. 1896. B. Herder.
--The Chiquitan Festival of Corpus Christi Day: A Tale of the Old Missions of South America. Gray, Mary Richards, tr. LC 7-987. 129p. 17cm. (Tales of Foreign Lands). Orig. Title: Ger. 1906. B. Herder.
--Love Your Enemies. A Tale of the Maori-Insurrections in New Zealand. 2d ed. Long, Helena, tr. LC 8-28102. 117 p. 17 1/2 cm. (Added t.-p.: Tales of foreign lands ... vol. I). 1897. B. Herder.
--Love Your Enemies. A Tale of the Maori-Insurrections in New Zealand. Long, Helena, tr. LC 8-28103. 2 p. l., 86 p. plates. 17 cm. 1895. St. Aemilianus' Orphan Asylum.
--The Pirate's Prisoner. 135p. 17cm. (Tales of Foreign Lands). Orig. Title: Ger. 1930. Mission Press.
--The Queen's Nephew. An Historical Narration from the Early Japanese Mission. Long, Helena, tr. LC 8-28101. 149 p. 17 1/2 cm. (Added t.-p.: Tales of foreign lands ... vol. V). 1896. B. Herder.
--The Shipwreck: A Story for the Young. Gray, Mary Richards, tr. LC 7-449. 126 p. 17 1/2 cm. (Added t.-p.: Tales of foreign lands ... vol. VII). 1906. B. Herder.
--The Slaves of the Sultan: A Story of Constantinople in the 17th Century. LC 31-7. 2 p. l., 7-140 p. 17 cm. (Tales of foreign lands ... vol. XVII). 1930. Mission Press.
--The Trip to Nicaragua: A Tale of the Days of the Conquistadores. Gray, Mary Richards, tr. LC 7-41590. 148 p. 17 1/2 cm. (Added t.-p.: Tales of foreign lands ... vol. XI). 1907. B. Herder.
--The Yang Brothers: An Unforgettable Story of the Boxer Uprising. Rogan, James Watkyn (1915-), adapted by. Armstrong, George Douglas (1927-), illus. LC 51-38459. 120 p. illus. 17 cm. (Tales of valor series). 1951. Mission Press.
--The Yang Brothers and the Boxers: A Story from the Chinese Missions. Frommelt, Horace A., tr. LC 31-4. 2 p. l., 7-132 p. 17 cm. (Tales of foreign lands ... vol. XIII). 1930. Mission Press.
Spina, Paul
--A Tree Grew and Birds Flew. Spina, Paul, illus. LC 67-30316. (Illus.). 40 p. 1967. H. Quist; Distributed by Crown Publishers.
Spinelli, Eileen (1942-)
--Thanksgiving at the Tappletons'. Cocca-Leffler, Maryann (1958-), illus. LC 84-40793. p. cm. 1985, c.1982. (ISBN 0-201-15892-2). Lippincott.
Spinelli, Eileen (1942-) & Atherton, Lisa
--The Giggle and Cry Book. Spence, Jim, illus. LC 81-5654. p. cm. 1981. (ISBN 0-916144-88-7). Stemmer House Publishers.
Spinelli, Jackaline
--Queenie. (Stars on Ice Ser.). (gr. 9-12). 1972. (ISBN 0-8091-6532-5). Paulist Pr.
--Two Different Worlds. (Stars on Ice Ser.). (gr. 9-12). 1972. (ISBN 0-8091-6534-1). Paulist Pr.
Spinelli, Jerry (1941-)
--Night of the Whale. LC 85-10119. 147 p. 21cm. c.1985. (ISBN 0-316-80718-4). Little, Brown.
--Space Station Seventh Grade. LC 82-4676. p. cm. c.1982. (ISBN 0-316-80709-5). Little, Brown and Co.
--Who Put That Hair in My Toothbrush?. LC 83-20716. (gr. 5-9). 1984. (ISBN 0-316-80712-5). Little.
Spink, Michael
--One Two Three Frieze. (Illus.). (ps-1). 1969. (ISBN 0-525-36439-0). Dutton.
Spink, Reginald, tr. see Danielsson, Bangt Emmerick.

--Heidi. (Shirley Temple Edition. Illustrations from the photoplay starring Shirley Temple). 19 1/2cm. 404p. c.1937. Saalfield Pub. Co.
--Heidi. (Illus.). (Children's Favorite Classics). 1915. Thomas Y Crowell.
--Heidi. (Honor Bks.). N.D. Thomas Nelson & Sons.
--Heidi. (Handy Volume Classics). N.D. Thomas Y. Crowell & Co.
--Heidi. (Read-Aloud Bks.). (gr. 4-6). N.D. (ISBN 0-685-02427-X). Wonder.
--Heidi. (Classic Ser.). N.D. World Publishing Co.
--Heidi. Brooks, Louise, tr. LC 59-10876. (Shirley Temple Edition. Illustrations from the motion picture featuring Shirley Temple). (Illus.). 29cm. 252p. 1959. Random House.
--Heidi. Brown, Kay (1943-), ed. Embleton, Gerry, illus. LC 79-23514. p. cm. c.1979. (ISBN 0-517-30779-0). Derrydale Books.
--Heidi. Brundage, Frances, illus. LC 25-2769. 2 p. l., 307 p. col. front., illus. 23 cm. (Lettered on cover: Companion series). c.1924. The Saalfield Publishing Company.
--Heidi. Cohen, Vincent O., illus. 1950. Dutton.
--Heidi. Cohen, Vincent O., illus. LC 52-8405. 320p. illus. 21cm. (Children's illustrated classics). 1952. E. P. Dutton.
--Heidi. Dole, Helen James Bennett, tr. from German. (Illus.). 363p. N.D. Ginn & Co. Trade Dept.
--Heidi. Dole, Helen James Bennett, Mrs. (1857-1944), tr. (Thrushwood Bks.). N.D. Grosset & Dunlap.
--Heidi. Elgaard, Greta, illus. LC 62-18396. 284 p. illus. 24 cm. (Macmillan classics, 34). 1962. Macmillan.
--Heidi. Elgaard, Greta, illus. 1962. Western.
--Heidi. Goldsborough, June (1923-), illus. LC 35-32768. 1 p. l., 7-284 p. col. front., illus. 29 1/2 cm. c.1934. Whitman Publishing Company.
--Heidi. Goldsborough, June (1923-), illus. Rosembaum, tr. LC 65-11921. 252p. col. illus. 22cm. (Whitman classics lib. 2707). c.1965. Whitman Pub.
--Heidi. Gregory, Dorothy Lake & Winter, Milo Kendall (1888-1956), illus. Allen, Philip Schuyler (1871-), tr. Bates, Katherine Lee LC 25-2467. (A Story for Children and Those Who Love Children). 404 p. incl. front., illus. 18 1/2 cm. c.1925. Rand, McNally & Company.
--Heidi. Hayes, Florence Sooy (1895-), adapted by. Weihs, Erika (1917-), illus. LC 47-223. 64 p. illus. (part col.) 28 x 21 1/2 cm. c.1946. Random House.
--Heidi. Heal, Edith (1903-), ed. Rodgers, Richard S., tr. LC 31-15417. (Adapted for Story-Teller's House). 64 p. incl. front., illus. 20 1/2 cm. 1931. T. S. Rockwell Company.
--Heidi. world wide ed. Higgins, Violet Moore, illus. Abbott, Mabel, tr. LC 24-21075. 284 p. incl. col. front., col. illus. 23 1/2 cm. (Just right book). c.1924. A. Whitman & Co.
--Heidi. Hill, Deborah, ed. Clarke, Grace Dalles, illus. LC 56-14163. 96p. illus. 27cm. (Golden picture classics, CL-105-69). 1956. Simon and Schuster.
--Heidi. Howell, Troy, illus. LC 81-16053. p. cm. 1982. (ISBN 0-671-43790-9). Wanderer Books.
--Heidi. Jameson, Arthur, illus. LC 45-5181. 2 p. l., 9-234 p. illus. 21 cm. c.1944. Whitman Publishing Co.
--Heidi. Kirk, Maria Louise (1860-), illus. Stork, Elisabeth Pausinger, Mrs., tr. Stork, Charles Wharton, intro. by. 318, 1 p. col. front., col. plates. 21 cm. $1.25. 1915. J. B. Lippincott Company.
--Heidi. gift. ed. Kirk, Maria Louise (1860-), illus. Stork, Elisabeth Pausinger, Mrs., tr. LC 19-18302. 318, 1 p. col. front., col. plates. 24 cm. 1919. J. B. Lippincott Company.
--Heidi. 1st ed. Knight, Susan, illus. LC 52-6374. (A World-Famous Classic Simply Told). 121 p. illus. 22 cm. (Winston pixie books). 1952. Winston.
--Heidi. Lawson, George, illus. LC 33-21127. (A Child's Story of Life in the Alps). 2 p. l., 404 p. col. front., plates. 21 cm. c.1933. The Saalfield Publishing Company.
--Heidi. Leone, Sergio, illus. Dole, Helen B., tr. LC 63-6888. (Illus.). 20cm. 304p. (Companion Library). 1963. Grosset Dunlap.
--Heidi. Leslie, Cecil, illus. Brooks, Louise, tr. LC 72-175659. (Illus.). 238 p. 19cm. (Puffin books). 1971. (ISBN 0-14-030097-X). Penguin Books.
--Heidi. Malvern, Corinne (1905-1956), illus. LC 54-2639. (Adapted from the Original Story). unpaged. illus. 21cm. (Little golden books, 192). 1954. Simon and Schuster.
--Heidi. Melcon, H. A., tr. from Ger. (Illus.). (The Meade Series for Girls). N.D. A. L. Burt.
--Heidi. Melcon, H. A., tr. (Illus.). (The Wellesley Series for Girls). N.D. A. L. Burt.
--Heidi. Mozley, Charles, illus. Law, Joy, tr. LC 59-11160. 23cm. 256p. (The Around the World Treasures). 1959. F. Watts.
--Heidi. Osborne, Helen, illus. LC 43-95369. 1 p. l., 9-252 p. front., illus. 21 cm. 1943. The Saalfield Publishing Company.
--Heidi. Petersham, Maud Sylvia Fuller, Mrs. (1890-1971) & Petersham, Miska, pseud. (1889-1960), illus. Petreszelyem, Mihaly. LC 32-182377. 5 p. l., 319 p. col. front., col. plates. 22 1/2 cm. c.1932. Garden City Publishing Company, Inc.
--Heidi. Rhead, Louis John (1857-1926), illus. LC 25-17414. 5 p. l., 333 p. incl. illus., plates. col. front. 23 1/2 cm. c.1925. Harper & Brothers.
--Heidi. Sanderson, Ruth, illus. LC 84-47647. p. cm. 1984. (ISBN 0-394-53820-X). Knopf.
--Heidi. Sharp, William (1900-), illus. Dole, Helen James Bennett, Mrs. (1857-1944), tr. LC 46-1680. vi, 326 p. col. front., illus., col. plates. 21 cm. (Illustrated junior library). 1945. Grosset & Dunlap, Inc.
--Heidi. Shoemaker, Edna Cooke, illus. Watkins, Shirley, tr. LC 25-28590. 3 p. l., 11-305 p. col. front., col. plates. 20 cm. (The Washington square classics). c.1925. Macrae Smith Company.
--Heidi. Smalley, Janet (1893-), illus. LC 55-38185. 284p. illus. 21cm. (Whitman famous classics, 1607). 1955. Whitman Pub. Co.
--Heidi. Smith, Jessie Willcox (1863-1935), illus. (A Scribner illustrated classic). N.D. Charles Scribner's Sons.
--Heidi. Smith, Jessie Willcox (1863-1935), illus. (McKaky's Illustrated Classics). N.D. David McKay Co.
--Heidi. Tait, Agnes (1897-), illus. Patri, Angelo, intro. by. LC 48-329949. xiii, 337 p. illus. (part col.) 23 cm. (Lippincott classics). 1948. J. B. Lippincott Co.
--Heidi. Tenggren, Gustaf (1896-1970), illus. LC 23-17346. 356 p. col. front., illus., col. plates. 22 cm. (Riverside bookshelf). 1923. Houghton Mifflin Company.
--Heidi. Thorndike, Edward Lee (1874-), ed. Woodward, Hildegard (1898-), illus. LC 35-2781. vii, 360 p. incl. front., illus. 19 1/2 cm. (Thorndike library). c.1935. D. Appleton-Century Company, Incorporated.
--Heidi. Thorne, Jenny, illus. LC 78-5489. p. cm. (Raintree's illustrated classics). 1978. (ISBN 0-8393-6206-4). Raintree Childrens Books.
--Heidi. Weisgard, Leonard Joseph (1916-), illus. LC 46-3854. 334 p., 1 l. col. front., illus., col. plates. 22 cm. (Half-title: Rainbow classics). 1946. The World Publishing Company.
--Heidi. Welling, Gertrude, illus. LC 26-143452. 3 p. l., 243 p. col. front., illus. 25 cm. (Sears illustrated juveniles). c.1926. J. H. Sears & Company, Inc.
--Heidi. White, Helene Schimmelfenning, tr. LC 2-18734. 2 p. l., 338 p. col. front., plates. 17 1/2 cm. c.1902. T. Y. Crowell & Co.
--Heidi. White, Helene Schimmelfenning, tr. LC 13-21709. 3 p. l., 433 p. col. front., col. plates. 21 1/2 cm. c.1913. Thomas Y. Crowell Co.
--Heidi. Whittemore, Constance, illus. LC 27-16233. ix p., 2 l., 433 p. col. front., col. plates. 22 1/2 cm. c.1927. Thomas Y. Crowell Company.
--Heidi. Wilcox, Jesse, illus. LC 58-14965. 24cm. (The Scribner illustrated Classics). 1958. Scribner.
--Heidi. Zachert, Adeline Beth (1877-), ed. Burd, Clara Miller, illus. LC 25-213877. xiii, 7-290 p. col. front., illus., col. plates. 21 cm. (Lettered on cover: The Winston clear-type popular classics). c.1924. The John C. Winston Company.
--Heidi. Zachert, Adeline Beth (1877-), intro. by. LC 57-12788. 278 p. illus 22 cm. (ChildrenS classics). N.D. Winston.
--Heidi: A Little Swiss Girl's City and Mountain Life. centennial ed. Davis, Marguerite (1889-), illus. Dole, Helen James Bennett, Mrs. (1857-1944), tr. LC 27-20820. vi, 410 p. col. front., illus., col. plates. 19 1/2 cm. c.1927. Ginn and Company.
--Heidi: A Story for Children. MacDonald, Roberta, illus. Brooks, Louise, tr. LC 54-4891. 315p. illus. 22cm. 1954. Doubleday Classic.
--Heidi: A Story for Children and Those That Love Children. Dole, Helen James Bennett, Mrs. (1857-1944), tr. LC 99-5746. (A Story for Children and Those That Love Children). vii p., 1 l., 363 p. front., illus. 18 cm. (On cover: Home and school library). 1899. Ginn & Company.
--Heidi: A Story for Children and Those Who Love Children. Enright, Maginel Wright, illus. Allen, Philip Schuyler (1871-), tr. LC 21-14704. (A Story for Children and Those Who Love Children). viii, 368 p. col. front., col. plates. 23 1/2 cm. (Windermere series). c.1921. Rand, McNally & Company.
--Heidi: A Story for Girls. Watson, J. Davis, illus. Melcon, H. A., tr. from Ger. LC 1-16990. iv, 367 p. front., plates. 19 cm. c.1901. A. L. Burt.
--Heidi: Child of the Mountains. Lerch, Steffie E. (1908-), illus. LC 50-4747. (Adapted and abridged from the famous story.). 40 p. col.illus. 21 cm. (Wonder books). N.D (Wonder Books). Grosset & Dunlap.
--Heidi: Child of the Mountains. Sutton, Felix, retold by. LC 54-23321. (Wonder Play Books: 2301). N.D. Wonder Books.
--Heidi Grows Up. Tritten, Charles, tr. (Thrushwood Bks.). N.D. Grosset & Dunlap.
--Heidi, Her Years of Wandering and Learning: A Story for Children and Those Who Love Children. Brooks, Louise, tr. from Ger. 269p. 1884. Cupples, Upham & Co.
--Heidi's Children. (Deluxe Illustrated Classics Ser.). 1977. (ISBN 0-307-12221-2, Golden Pr). Western Pub.
--Heidi's Children. Tritten, Charles, tr. (Thrushwood Bks.). N.D. Grosset & Dunlap.
--Heidi's Friends. Leone, Sergio, illus. LC 65-18972. (A Sequel of Heidi. Adapted from Orig. Stories by Johanna Spyri). 181p. illus. 22cm. 1965. Grosset.
--Heimatlos. Richardson, Frederick (1862-1937), illus. Hopkins, Emma Stelter (1870-), tr. LC 12-217257. (Two Stories for Children, and for Those Who Love Children). vi, 231 p. illus. 17 1/2 cm. $0.40. c.1912. Ginn and Company.
--In the Swiss Mountains. Dole, Helen James Bennett, Mrs. (1857-1944), tr. LC 29-12056. 4 p. l., 288 p. col. front., col. plates. 21 cm. c.1929. Thomas Y. Crowell Company.
--Jo, the Little Machinist. Dole, Helen James Bennett, Mrs. (1857-1944), tr. LC 23-15033. 3 p. l., 76 p. col. front 20 1/2 cm. c.1923. Thomas Y. Crowell Company.
--Jorli: The Stauffer Mill. Kirk, Maria Louise (1860-), illus. (The Children's Classics). N.D. J. B. Lippincott.
--Jorli; the Story of a Swiss Boy. Clayton, Francis Treadway & Wunderli, Olga, trs. LC 24-8258. xii p., 1 l., 111 p. incl. front., illus., plates 18 1/2 cm. c.1924. B. H. Sanborn & Co.
--The Little Alpine Musician. Dole, Helen James Bennett, Mrs. (1857-1944), tr. LC 24-12433. 4 p. l., 345 p. col. front., col. plates. 20 1/2 cm. c.1924. Thomas Y. Crowell Company.
--Little Curly Head: The Pet Lamb. Dole, Helen James Bennett, Mrs. (1857-1944), tr. LC 19-15739. 2 p. l., 9-77 p. col. front. 20 1/2 cm. c.1919. Thomas Y. Crowell Co.
--Little Miss Grasshopper. Dole, Helen JamesBennett (1857-1944), tr. LC 18-19298. 76 p. col. front., col. plates. 20 1/2 cm. c.1918. Thomas Y. Crowell Company.
--A Little Swiss Boy. Brundage, Frances, illus. Coumbe, Clement W., tr. 251 p. incl. front., illus. 18 1/2 cm. (Half-title: Every child's library). c.1926. The Saalfield Publishing Company.
--Maxa's Children. Brundage, Frances, illus. Coumbe, Clement W., tr. LC 27-335. 244 p. incl. front., illus. 18 1/2 cm. (Half-title: Every child's library). c.1926. The Saalfield Publishing Company.
--Mazli. N.D. Grosset & Dunlap.
--Mazli. Stork, Elisabeth Pausinger, Mrs., tr. N.D. A L Burt Co.
--Mazli: A Story of the Swiss Valleys. gift. ed. Kirk, Maria Louise (1860-), illus. Stork, Elisabeth Pausinger, Mrs., tr. LC 23-15473. 319, 1 p. col. front., illus., col. plates. 24 cm. c.1923. J. B. Lippincott Company.
--Mazli; a Story of the Swiss Valleys: A Story of the Swiss Valleys. Kirk, Maria Louise (1860-), illus. Stork, Elisabeth Pausinger, Mrs., tr. LC 21-21761. 320 p. col. front., col. plates. 21 cm. 1921. J. B. Lippincott Company.
--Moni, the Goat Boy. (The Children's Classics). N.D. J. B. Lippincott.
--Moni, the Goat Boy. Brundage, Frances, illus. Coumbe, Clement W., tr. LC 27-8242. 90, 1 p. incl. col. front., illus. 20 cm. (John Newberry series). c.1926. The Saalfield Publishing Company.
--Moni the Goat Boy. Dole, Helen James Bennett, Mrs. (1857-1944), tr. LC 14-13882. 3 p. l., 43 p. col. front., col. plates. 19 1/2 cm. 1914. Thomas Y. Crowell Co.
--Moni the Goat Boy. Kirk, Maria Louise (1860-), illus. Stork, Elisabeth Pausinger, Mrs., tr. Stork, Charles Wharton, intro. by. LC 16-23094. 72 p. col. front., col. plates. 19 1/2 cm. $0.50. 1916. J. B. Lippincott Company.
--Moni the Goat Boy. Kunz, Edith F., tr. from German. (Illus.). 208p. (Once Upon a Time Ser.). N.D. Ginn & Co. Trade Dept.
--Moni, the Goat-Boy and Other Stories. Dole, Helen James Bennett, Mrs. (1857-1944), tr. LC 38-27696. v. 229 p. col. front. 21 cm. c.1923. Grosset & Dunlap.
--Moni the Goat Boy, and Other Stories. Kunz, Edith F., tr. from Ger. LC 6-3513. viii, 211 p. incl. front., illus. 17 1/2 cm. c.1906. Ginn & Company.
--Moni the Goat Boy, Mazli, Cornelli: Three Stories. Merrill, Anna Darby, adapted by. Bennett, Juanita C., illus. LC 36-48850. 237 p. illus. 20 cm. c.1935. Whitman Publishing Company.
--The New Year's Carol. Wesson, Grace Edwards, illus. Goodwin, Alice Howland Goodwin, Mrs. (1835-), tr. LC 24-28119. 3 p. l., 34 p. col. front., illus., plates. 19 1/2 cm. c.1924. Houghton Mifflin Company.
--Peppino. Greer, Blanche (1884-), illus. Stork, Elisabeth Pausinger, Mrs., tr. LC 27-16975. 114 p. incl. col. front. col. plates. 19 1/2 cm. 1926. J. B. Lippincott Company.
--The Pet Lamb, and Other Swiss Stories. Ross, Michael, illus. Clathrop, M. E. & Popper, E. M., trs. from Ger. LC 56-8295. 244p. illus. 20cm. 1956. E. P. Dutton.
--Red-Letter Stories. Wheelock, Lucy, tr. from Ger. LC 8-28096. 94 p. front., plates. 17 cm. c.1884. D. Lothrop & Co.
--Red-Letter Stories: Swiss Tales. Wheelock, Lucy, tr. from Ger. 94p. 1885. D. Lothrop & Co.
--Renz and Margritli. N.D. Grosset & Dunlap.
--Renz and Margritli. Dole, Helen James Bennett, Mrs. (1857-1944), tr. LC 31-20918. vi p., 1 l., 351 p. col. front., col. plates. 20 1/2 cm. c.1931. Thomas Y. Crowell Company.
--Rico and Wiseli, 8. N.D. T. Y. Crowell Co.
--Rico and Wiseli. Brooks, Louise, tr. LC 4-18035. 2 v. in 1. front. 18 1/2 cm. c.1885. De Wolfe, Fiske & Co.
--Rico and Wiseli. Brooks, Louise, tr. from Ger. LC 23-2034. 5 p. l., 7-509 p. col. front., col. plates. 20 cm. 1922. Thomas Y. Crowell Company.
--The Rose Child. Dole, Helen James Bennett, Mrs. (1857-1944), tr. LC 16-15320. 5 p. l., 9-62 p. col. front., col. plates. 19 1/2 cm. c.1916. Thomas Y. Crowell Co.
--Shirley Temple in Heidi. LC 37-375877. 2 p. l., 404 p. plates. 21 cm. c.1937. The Saalfield Publishing Company.
--Stories of Swiss Children. Dole, Helen James Bennett, Mrs. (1857-1944), tr. LC 27-150103. vii, 425 p. col. front., col. plates. 22 cm. 1926. Thomas Y. Crowell Company.
--Stories of Swiss Children. Stork, Elisabeth Pausinger, Mrs., tr. LC 38-27698. 5 p. 1 l., 11-318, 1 p. col. front. 21 1/2 cm. 1938. Grosset & Dunlap.
--The Story of Heidi. Vernon, Ethel S., illus. LC 34-31802. 1 p. l., 7-92 p. illus. 29 1/2 cm. c.1934. Whitman Publishing Company.
--The Story of Rico. Boll, Helene H., tr. 163p. N.D. Beacon Press.
--The Story of Rico. Boll, Helene H., tr. LC 22-190. xi p., 1 l., 163 p. col. front., col. plates. 21 cm. c.1921. The Boston Press.
--Swiss Stories for Children and for Those Who Love Children. Wheelock, Lucy, tr. LC 8-28095. 119, 7-94 p. 18 1/2 cm. c.1887. D. Lothrop Company.
--Tiss: A Little Alpine Waif. Carlson, George L., illus. Dole, Helen James Bennett, Mrs. (1857-1944), tr. LC 22-193. 4 p. l., 7-78 p. col. front. 20 1/2 cm. c.1921. Thomas Y. Crowell Company.
--Toni, the Little Wood-Carver. Dole, Helen James Bennett, Mrs. (1857-1944), tr. LC 20-15071. 78 p. col. front. 20 cm. c.1920. Thomas Y. Crowell Co.
--Toni; the Little Wood-Carver: And Other Stories. Dole, Helen James Bennett, Mrs. (1857-1944), tr. LC 38-27699. v. 196 p. col. front. 21 1/2 cm. 1938. Grosset & Dunlap.
--Trini, the Little Strawberry Girl. Dole, Helen James Bennet, Mrs. (1857-1944), tr. N.D. Thomas Y. Crowell Co.
--Uncle Titus. Wheelock, Lucy, tr. LC 8-28094. (A Story for Children and for Those Who Love Children). 2 p. l., 201 p. 18 1/2 cm. c.1886. D. Lothrop and Company.
--Uncle Titus. Wheelock, Lucy, tr. (Illus.). (Mountain Ser.). N.D. Lothrop Pub. Co.
--Uncle Titus and His Visit to the Country. Brooks, Louise, tr. N.D. Thomas Y. Crowell Co.
--Uncle Titus in the Country. Brundage, Frances, illus. Coumbe, Clement W., tr. LC 27-334. 245 p. incl. front., illus. 18 1/2 cm. (Half-title: Every child's library). c.1926. The Saalfield Publishing Company.
--Veronica. N.D. Grosset & Dunlap.
--Veronica, and Other Friends. Brooks, Louise, tr. N.D. De Wolfe, Fiske & Co.
--Veronica and Other Friends. Brooks, Louise, tr. LC 26-14759. 2 p. l., 9-248 p. col. front., col. plates. 20 1/2 cm. c.1924. Thomas Y. Crowell Company.
--Vinzi. N.D. Grosset & Dunlap.
--Vinzi. Stork, Elisabeth Pausinger, Mrs., tr. N.D. A L Burt Co.
--Vinzi: A Story of the Swiss Alps. Kirk, Maria Louise (1860-), illus. Stork, Elisabeth Pausinger, Mrs. (1860-), tr. LC 23-186130. 296, 1 p. col. front., col. plates. 21 cm. (On verso of half-title: Stories all children love). 1923. J. B. Lippincott Company.
--What Sami Sings with the Birds. Dole, Helen James Bennett, Mrs. (1857-1944), tr. LC 17-18593. 5 p. l., 9-90 p. col. front., col. plates. 20 1/2 cm. $0.50. c.1917. Thomas Y. Crowell Company.

Spyri, Johanna Heusser (1827-1901) & Carroll, Lewis, pseud. (1832-1898)
--Heidi and Alice in Wonderland, 2 Bks in 1. Dodgson, Charles Lutwidge. N.D. World Publishing Co.

Spyri, Johanna Heusser (1827-1901) & Tritten, Charles
--Heidi's Children: A Sequel to Heidi Grows Up. Goldsborough, June (1923-), illus. LC 67-16754. 254p. col. illus. 22cm. (Golden Pr. Classics lib.). 1967. Golden Pr.

Squance, Herbert S.
--Miss Mackerell Skye. (Illus.). N.D. E. P. Dutton & Co.

Squier, Emma Lindsay (1892-)
--The Bride of the Sacred Well and Other Tales of Ancent Mexico. Allen, James E., illus. LC 28-11210. xi p., 3 l., 275 p. front., plates. 19 1/2 cm. 1928. Cosmopolitan Book Corporation.
--Children of the Twilight: Folk-Tales of Indian Tribes. LC 26-8129. 5 p. l., 257 p. 19 1/2 cm. 1926. Cosmopolitan Book Corporation.
--On Autumn Trails, and Adventures in Captivity. Bransom, Paul (1885-), illus. LC 23-132829. 239 p. front., plates. 20 cm. 1923. Cosmopolitan Book Corporation.
--The Wild Heart. Bransom, Paul (1885-), illus. Porter, Geneva Grace Stratton (1863-1924), intro. by. LC 22-711712. 2 p. l., 220 p. illus. 20 cm. 1922. Cosmopolitan Book Corporation.

Squillace, Albert, jt. auth. see Myrus, Donald Richard.

Squire, Roger, retold by.
--Wizards & Wampum: Legends of the Iroquois. Keeping, Charles William James (1924-), illus. LC 71-156584. (Illus.). line drawings. 128p. (gr. 3 up). 1972. (ISBN 0-200-71820-7). Abelard.

Squires, Edith Lombard, Mrs. (1884-)
--Eleven Plays for Little Children. 115 p. 19 cm. (Playhouse plays). c.1931. Fitzgerald Publishing Corporation.
--Ten Little Plays for Little Tots. LC 30-15653. 93 p. 19 cm. c.1930. Walter H. Baker Company.

Squires, Elizabeth Briggs
--David's Silver Dollar. Austin, Margot, Mrs., illus. LC 40-82780. 86 p. col. front., col. illus. 23 1/2 x 19 1/2 cm. c.1940. The Platt & Munk Co., Inc.

Squires, Grace
--Little Mildred's Secret. Ruyl, Beatrice Baxter (1879-), illus. LC 5-20778. 313 p. front., 5 pl. 19 cm. (Pleasant street series. New ed. v. 8). c.1905. H. M. Caldwell Co.
--Merle and May: A Story of Girlhood Days. LC 6-39753. v, 364 p. front., 5 pl. 21 1/2 cm. 1906. E. P. Dutton & Company.
--Peaseblossom and Mustardseed. Horne, Diantha W., illus. LC 6-23703. 3 p. l., 11-237 p. 19 cm. c.1906. D. Estes & Company.
--Tom, Nadine and Snuffles. (Illus.). (Six to Sixteen Series.). N.D. Dodge Publishing Co.
--Tom, Nadine and Snuffles. Horne, Diantha W., illus. (Illus.). (Six to Sixteen Ser.). N.D. Caldwell.

Sroda, George
--Life Story of TV Star & Celebrity Herman the Worm. Hughes, Janet, illus. (Illus.). 189p. 1979. (ISBN 0-9604486-1-6). (ISBN 0-9604486-2-4). G Sroda.

Staab, Jane, adapted by.
--The Fairy Tale Book. Mars, Witold Tadeusz J. (1912-), illus. LC 76-52895. (Illus.). 72 p. 26cm. (Kid's paperback). c.1977. (ISBN 0-307-13432-6). Golden Press.

Staar, Helen
--The Junior High Variety Book. 126p. N.D. T. S. Denison & Co.

Staats, Sara Rader
--Big City ABC. Keys, Robert, illus. LC 67-17283. (Illus.). 30 p. 22cm. 1968. Follett Pub. Co.

Stabilis, Vincent (1884-)
--Children Playing School. Stabilis, Vincent, illus. LC 43-5900. 95 p. illus. 22 cm. c.1941. House of Field, Inc.

Stables, Gordon see Stables, William Gordon.

Stables, William Gordon see Stables, William Gordon.

Stables, William Gordon (1840-1910)
--Artic Sea Adventures, 1 of 5 vol. set. (Illus.). N.D. International Book Co.
--As We Sweep Through the Deep: A Story of the Stirring Times of Old. (Illus.). N.D. Thomas Nelson & Sons.
--Battle and Breeze. N.D. E. P. Dutton & Co.
--Born to Command. A Tale of the Sea and of Sailors. Overend, W. H., illus. LC 8-7679. 533 p. front., plates. 18 1/2 cm. 1892. E. & J. B. Young and Co.
--By Sea and Land: A Story of the Blue and Scarlet. (Illus.). N.D. Frederick Warne.
--Captain Jack. N.D. E & J B Young.
--Courage, True Hearts. (Illus.). (Scribner-Blackie Series of books for young people). N.D. Charles Scribner's Sons.
--The Cruise of the Snow-Bird. (St. Nicholas Series for Boys). N.D. International Book Co.
--Every Inch a Sailor, 98 vols. (The Rugby Ser.). 1905. Set. A L Burt Co.
--Every Inch A Sailor. (Illus.). (The Round Table Ser.). N.D. A. L. Burt's Pubs.
--Every Incha Sailor. (The Rugby Series for Boys and Girls). N.D. A. L. Burt Company.
--Exiles of Fortune. N.D. E. P. Dutton & Co.
--Exiles of Fortune: A Tale of a Far North Land. N.D. Pott & Co.
--Fighting for Cuba. LC 30-9744. 8 p., 1 l., 13-329 p. 19 1/2 cm. (A just right book). 1928. A. Whitman & Company.
--For Cross or Crescent. N.D. E. P. Dutton & Co.
--Frank Hardinge: Or, From Torried Zones to Regions of Perpetual Snow. Cowell, Sydney, illus. (Illus.). 352p. N.D. A. I. Bradley & Co.'s Pub.
--From Greenland's Icy Mountains (Pub. by Society for Promoting Christian Knowledge). N.D. E. & J. B. Young & Co.
--From Squire to Squatter. N.D. Pott & Co.
--Hearts of Oak. N.D. E. P. Dutton & Co.
--How Jack Mackenzie Won His Epaulettes, 98 vols. (The Rugby Ser.). 1905. Set. A L Burt Co.
--How Jack Mackenzie Won His Epaulettes. (Illus.). (The Round Table Ser.). N.D. A. L. Burt's Pubs.
--In Search of Fortune. N.D. E. P. Dutton & Co.
--Jack Locke: A Tale of the War and the Wave. (Warne's Home Circle Library). N.D. Frederick Warne & Co.
--Jack Locke: A Tale of the War and the Wave. (Illus.). (The Home and Enterprise Library Ser.). N.D. Frederick Warne & Co.
--Jungle, Peak and Plain. (Illus.). 192p. N.D. Cassell, Petter, Galpin.
--Life at Sea. (Illus.). (St. Nicholas Series for Boys). N.D. International Book Co.
--Life on the Ocean Wave: Or, The Cruise of the Good Ship. (Illus.). N.D. E. P. Dutton & Co.
--Little Gypsy Lass. (Illus.). 304p. N.D. J B Lippincott.
--A Naval Cadet. (Illus.). (Scribner-Blackie Series of books for young people). N.D. Charles Scribner's Sons.
--Old England on the Sea. N.D. E. P. Dutton & Co.
--On to the Rescue. N.D. E. P. Dutton & Co.
--Sable and White. N.D. E. P. Dutton & Co.
--Shireen and Her Friends: The Autobiography of a Persian Cat. Reitz, Hans, illus. (Books For Young People Ser.). N.D. L. C. Page & Co.
--Stanley Grahame: A Tale of the Dark Continent. (Illus.). N.D. A. C. Armsrong & Sons.
--Stanley Grahame: A Tale of the Dark Continent. (Illus.). (St. Nicholas Series for Boys). N.D. International Book Co.
--To Greenland and the Pole. (Illus.). (The Round Table Ser.). N.D. A. L. Burt's Pubs.
--To Greenland and the Pole: A Story of the Arctic Regions. (The Rugby Series for Boys and Girls). N.D. A. L. Burt Company.
--To Greenland and to the Pole. (Illus.). (Scribner-Blackie Series of Books for young people). N.D. Charles Scribner's Sons.
--Travels by the Fireside. (Warne's Adventure Library). N.D. Frederick Warne & Co.
--Twixt Daydawn and Light. N.D. E. P. Dutton & Co.
--Westward with Columbus. (Illus.). (Scribner-Blackie Series of books for young people). N.D. Charles Scribner's Sons.
--Wild Adventures around the Pole. (Illus.). (St. Nicholas Series for boys). N.D. International Book Co.
--Wild Adventures in Wild Places. (Illus.). N.D. Cassell, Petter, Galpin.

Stachen, Lee Garland
--Abraham the Patriarch. LC 63-1779. 64 p. illus. 21 cm. (Know your Bible program). 1963. N. Doubleday.

Stack, Jerome
--The Adventures of Little and Big Whiskers: Two Rats in LCase You Didn't Know. Billups, Jack, illus. LC 76-55083. (Illus.). 153 p. 22cm. c.1976. Reward Books.

Stack, Nicolette Meredith see Hill, Eileen, pseud.

Stack, Nicolette Meredith see Meredith, Nicolete.

Stack, Nicolette Meredith McGuire (1896-)
--Corky's Hiccups. O'Sullivan, Tom, illus. (Illus.). 24p. (ps-4). 1968. (ISBN 0-307-60513-2, Golden Pr). Western Pub.
--Pierre of the Island. Williamson, Gertrude M., illus. LC 54-9338. 96p. illus. 21cm. 1954. Bruce Pub. Co.
--Rainbow Tomorrow. Pollard, George, illus. LC 56-7045. 148p. illus. 22cm. 1956. Bruce Pub. Co.
--Two to Get Ready. Williamson, Gertrude M., illus. LC 53-10250. 179p. illus. 22cm. 1953. Caxton Printers.

Stack, Peggy
--Six and Twenty Tales. N.D. Transatlantic Arts.

Stackpole, Edouard Alexander (1903-)
--Dead Man's Gold. LC 58-11495. 212 p. illus. 21 cm. 1958. Washburn.
--Madagascar Jack: The Story of a Nantucket Whaler, Being the Account of Obed C. Folger, Thirteen Years of Age, Who Went to the South Seas with Whalemen, and Found There Many Adventures As Well As Sperm Whales. Grant, Gordon H. (1875-1962), illus. LC 35-150462. ix, 1, 308 p. incl. illus., plates. col. front. 21 cm. 1935. W. Morrow & Company.
--Mutiny at Midnight: The Adventures of Cyrus Hussey of Nantucket Aboard the Whaleship Globe in the South Pacific, from 1822 to 1826 ... LC 39-19006. viii, 245 p. 21 cm. 1939. W. Morrow and Company.
--Privateer Ahoy!, A Story of the War of 1812. LC 37-20195. x, 310 p. incl. front., illus. 21 cm. 1937. W. Morrow & Co.
--Smuggler's Luck. 320p. 1931. William Morrow & Co.
--You Fight for Treasure. Pitz, Henry Clarence (1895-1976), illus. N.D. William Morrow & Co.
--You Fight for Treasure!. Rodgers, Richard H. (1876-1953), illus. N.D. William Morrow & Co.

Stacpoole, Henry De Vere (1865-)
--The Cruise of the Kingfisher. 4 p. l., 307 p. front., plates. 19 1/2 cm. 1927. L. C. Page & Company.
--The First Cruise of the King Fisher. N.D. Duffield.
--Poppyland. Pearce, Leighton, illus. LC 14-19362. viii p., 3 l., 3-219 p. col. front., col. plates. 26 cm. 1914. John Lane.

Stacy, Donald L. (1925-)
--The Runaway Dot. LC 69-12437. (Illus.). 31 p. 1969. Bobbs-Merrill.

Staden, Ann
--Pepper Face & Other Stories. Dinan, Carolyn, illus. (Illus.). (ps-5). N.D. (ISBN 0-686-24619-5). Faber & Faber.

Stadler, John
--Animal Cafe. Stadler, John, illus. LC 80-15072. p. cm. 1980. (ISBN 0-87888-166-2). Bradbury Press.
--Cat at Bat. Stadler, John, illus. LC 78-12651. (Illus.). 30 p. 25cm. (A Fat Cat Book). c.1979. Dutton.
--Gorman and the Treasure Chest. Stadler, John, illus. LC 82-9583. p. cm. 32p. 1982. (ISBN 0-87888-207-3). (ISBN 0-87888-207-3). Bradbury Press.
--Gorman & the Treasure Chest. Stadler, John, illus. LC 82-9583. (Illus.). 32p. 1st U.S. edition. (ps-2). 1984. Bradbury Pr.
--Hector, the Accordian-Nosed Dog. LC 81-7713. p. cm. 1981. (ISBN 0-87888-191-3). Bradbury Press.
--Hector, the Accordion-Nosed Dog. Stadler, John, illus. LC 81-7713. (Illus.). 32p. (ps-2). 1983. (ISBN 0-02-786680-7). Bradbury Pr.
--Rodney & Lucinda's Amazing Race. Stadler, John, illus. LC 80-39848. (Illus.). 32p. 1st U.S. edition. (ps-2). 1981. (ISBN 0-02-786670-X). Bradbury Pr.
--Rodney and Lucinda's Amazing Race. Stadler, John, illus. LC 80-39848. p. cm. 1981. (ISBN 0-87888-179-4). Bradbury Press.
--Rodney and Lucinda's Amazing Race. Ungerer, Tomi, pseud. (1931-), illus. Ungerer, Jean Thomas. 1981. Bradbury Pr.
--Snail Saves the Day. LC 85-47539. (Illus.). 32 p. 24cm. c.1985. (ISBN 0-690-04468-2). (ISBN 0-690-04469-0). Crowell.

Stadtler, Bea (1921-)
--The Adventures of Gluckel of Hameln. Sharon, Paul, illus. LC 67-18814. 135 p. illus. 22cm. 1967. (ISBN 0-8381-0731-1). United Synagogue.

Stadtler, Bea (1921-) & Simon, Shirley Schwartz (1921-)
--Once Upon a Jewish Holiday. Stories. Giacalone, Bill, illus. LC 65-291923. 125p. col. illus. 26cm. 1966, c.1965. KTAV.

Stadtler, Ben
--The Story of Dona Garcia Mondes. Shevo, Aharon, illus. LC 70-83166. x, 136 p. illus. 23cm. 1969. United Synagogue Commission on Jewish Education.

Staffelbach, Elmer Hubert (1893-)
--For Texas and Freedom. Wiley, Hugh, illus. LC 53-7801. 271p. illus. 22cm. (Long rifle series). 1953. Harr Wagner Pub. Co.
--For Texas and Freedom. Wiley, Hugh, illus. LC 48-7064. 271 p. illus. 21 cm. 1948. Macrae, Smith Co.
--Long Rifle Vanguard. Merritt, Warren Chase, illus. LC 53-7802. 330p. illus. 22cm. (Long rifle series). 1953. H. Wagner Pub. Co.
--Towards Oregon. Hargens, Charles, Jr. (1893-), illus. LC 53-20938. 353p. illus. 22cm. (Long rifue series). 1953. H. Wagner Pub. Co.
--Towards Oregon. Hargens, Charles, Jr. (1893-), illus. LC 46-22916. 3 p. l. 353 p. illus. 21 1/2cm. 1946. Macrae-Smith.

Stafford, Alphonso Orenzo (1871-)
--Animal Fables from the Dark Continent. LC 7-2065. 128 p. illus. 19 cm. (On cover: Eclectic readings). c.1906. American Book Company.

Stafford, Ann
--Five Proud Riders. Bobri, V., pseud. (1898-), illus. Bobritsky, Vladimir V.. LC 38-9512. 4 p. l., 3-290, 1 p. illus. 21 cm. 1st U.S. edition. 1938. A. A. Knopf.
--Pony for Sale. Bobri, V., pseud. (1898-), illus. Bobritsky, Vladimir V.. LC 39-30536. 4 p. l., 3-271, 1 p. incl. front., illus. 21 cm. 1939. A. A. Knopf.

Stafford, Jean (1915-1979), ed. see Arabian Nights.

Stafford, Jean (1915-1979)
--Elephi. Blegvad, Erik (1923-), illus. LC 62-14500. 76 p. illus. 20 cm. (Artel books). 1962. Farrar, Straus & Cudahy.

Stafford, Kay
--Ling Tang and the Lucky Cricket. Zibold, Louise, illus. LC 44-9410. 79, 1 p. incl. front., illus. (part col.) 26 cm. 1944. Whittlesey House, McGraw-Hill Book Company, Inc.

Stafford, Linda
--Mind Invaders. (gr. 9-12). 1982. Victor Bks.

Stafford, Marie Peary (1893-)
--Muskox: Little Tooktoo's Friend. Rev ed. Wiese, Kurt (1887-1974), illus. LC 31-2448. 64 p. col. front., illus., col. plates. 23 cm. 1931. W. Morrow & Co.

Stagg, James
A Castle for the Kopcheks. LC 64-15458. 201 p. 22 cm. 1964. Macmillan.

Stahl, Benjamin (1910-)
--Blackbeard's Ghost. Stahl, Ben F., illus. LC 65-110223. (Illus.). 184 p. 25cm. 1965. Houghton Mifflin.
--Blackbeard's Ghost & the Secret of Red Skull. (gr. 4-6). N.D. HM.
--The Secret of Red Skull. Stahl, Ben F., illus. LC 78-135134. (Illus.). 243 p. 24cm. 1971. (ISBN 0-395-12372-0). Houghton Mifflin.

Stahl, Hilda Ann
--Elizabeth Gail and the Dangerous Double. LC 79-55754. 126 p. 18cm. (Elizabeth Gail Ser.: No. 4). c.1980. (ISBN 0-8423-0723-0). Tyndale House.
--Elizabeth Gail & the Music Camp Romance. 128p. (Elizabeth Gail Ser.: No. 14). (gr. 3-7). 1983. (ISBN 0-8423-0708-7). Tyndale.
--Elizabeth Gail and the Mystery at the Johnson Farm. LC 78-66373. 128 p. 18cm. (Elizabeth Gail series ; no. 1). c.1978. (ISBN 0-8423-0720-6). Tyndale House.
--Elizabeth Gail and the Secret Box. LC 78-63097. 124 p. 18cm. (Elizabeth Gail series ; no. 2). c.1979. (ISBN 0-8423-0720-6). Tyndale House.
--Elizabeth Gail & the Secret Love. (Elizabeth Gail Ser.: No. 16). (gr. 3 up). 1983. (ISBN 0-8423-0706-0). Tyndale.
--Elizabeth Gail & the Strange Birthday Party. (Elizabeth Gail Ser.: No. 6). (gr. 4-6). 1980. (ISBN 0-8423-0724-9). Tyndale.
--Elizabeth Gail & the Teddy Bear Mystery. (Elizabeth Gail Ser.: No. 3). 1979. (ISBN 0-8423-0722-2). Tyndale.
--Elizabeth Gail & the Terrifying News. (Elizabeth Gail Ser.: No.7). (gr. 4-8). 1980. (ISBN 0-8423-0725-7). Tyndale.
--Elizabeth Gail & the Time for Love. (Elizabeth Gail Ser.: No. 18). (gr. 3 up). 1983. (ISBN 0-8423-0732-X). Tyndale.
--Melody of Love. LC 75-26683. p. cm. 1975. (ISBN 0-8024-6509-9). Moody Press.
--Teddy Jo & the Abandoned House. LC 83-50991. 128p. (Orig.). (The Teddy Jo Ser.: No. 7). (gr. 2-8). 1984. (ISBN 0-8423-6949-X). Tyndale.
--Teddy Jo & the Kidnapped Heir. 128p. (Teddy Jo Ser.). (gr. 7-12). 1984. (ISBN 0-8423-6951-1). Tyndale.
--Teddy Jo & the Ragged Beggars. 128p. (Teddy Jo Ser.). (gr. 6-8). 1984. (ISBN 0-8423-6950-3). Tyndale.
--Teddy Jo & the Stolen Ring, No. 3. 128p. 1982. (ISBN 0-8423-6945-7). Tyndale.
--Teddy Jo & the Strange Medallion, No. 5. (gr. 4-7). 1983. (ISBN 0-8423-6947-3). Tyndale.
--Teddy Jo & the Strangers in the Pink House, No. 4. (gr. 4-7). 1983. (ISBN 0-8423-6946-5). Tyndale.

Stahl, Le Roy
--Peppy Puppet Plays. 96p. N.D. T. S. Denison & Co.

Stahl, P. J., pseud. (1814-1886), tr.
--Little Chatterbox. Hetzel, Pierre Jules. N.D. D. Appleton & Co.

Stahlmann, Catherine
--Bunny Blue. Van Tellingen, Ruth Thompson, illus. N.D. Rand McNally & Co.
--Jack Jingle's Wish. Mitchell, Ben & Monaco, Arto, illus. LC 53-6151. 17cm. (Rand McNally Book-Elf Giant Book). 1953. Rand McNally & Co.

--Peter Pat and the Policeman. Grider, Dorothy (1915-), illus. LC 49-7203. 33 p. col. illus. 17 cm. (Rand McNally book, 625). c.1948. Rand McNally.
--Puppies. Wilde, Irma, illus. LC 52-36200. 52 p. illus. 20cm. (A Rand McNally book-elf junior). c.1952. Rand McNally.

Stainer, J, jt. ed. see Metcalfe, J Powell.

Stalder, Valerie, retold by.
--Even the Devil Is Afraid of a Shrew: A Folktale of Lapland. Brown, Richard Eric (1946-), illus. Broekel, Ray, pseud. (1923-), adapted by Broekel, Rainer Lothar. LC 70-177415. 40 p. of col. illus. 27cm. 1972. (ISBN 0-201-07188-6). Addison-Wesley.

Stall, Dorothy
--Chukchi Hunter. Mason, George Frederick (1904-), illus. LC 46-20797. 224 p. incl. illus., plates. 21 cm. (Morrow junior books). 1946. W. Morrow & Company.

Stallings, Ethel Wiley
--Cabin on the Trail: A Story of the Revolution for Boys and Girls Based on Actual Events. 1st Ed. 1 st. ed. LC 56-10302. 152p. 21cm. 1956. Exposition Press.

Stallman, Birdie (1911-)
--Learning About Dragons. Halverson, Lydia, illus. LC 81-4746. p. cm. (Learning about series). c.1981. (ISBN 0-516-06531-9). Childrens Press.

Stallybrass, Oliver George Weatherhead (1925-), tr. see Docker, Rolf.

Stallybrass, Oliver George Weatherhead (1925-), tr. see Jensen, Niels.

Stalns, Katherine Berle
--Thimble Bells Tinkle. LC 56-26471. 52 p. illus. 20cm. 1956, c.1955. Story Book Press.

Stamaty, Mark Alan (1947-)
--Minnie Maloney & Macaroni. LC 76-2281. (Illus.). 38 p. 20cm. c.1976. (ISBN 0-8037-5588-0). (ISBN 0-8037-5589-9). Dial Press.
--Small in the Saddle. LC 74-23244. (Illus.). 32 p. 1975. (ISBN 0-525-61525-3). Windmill Books.
--Where's My Hippopotamus?. Stamaty, Mark Alan (1947-), illus. LC 76-42927. (Illus.). (gr. k-3). 1977. Dial Bks Young.
--Where's My Hippopotamus?. Stamaty, Mark Alan (1947-), illus. LC 76-42927. (Illus.). 32p. (ps-3). 1979. (Pied Piper Book). Dial Bks Young.
--Who Needs Donuts?. LC 73-6020. (Illus.). 40 p. 1973. Dial Press.

Stames, C. Alexander
--Hawaiian Folklore Tales. (Illus.). 1975. (ISBN 0-682-48301-X). Exposition Press.

Stamler, Suzanne, adapted by see Gellek, Nazli.

Stamm, Claus
--The Dumplings and the Demons. Mizumura, Kazue, illus. LC 64-21475. 44 p. col. illus. 23 cm. 1964. Viking Press.
--Three Strong Women: A Tall Tale From Japan. Mizumura, Kazue, illus. (gr. 3-5). 1962. Penguin.
--Three Strong Women: A Tall Tale from Japan. Mizumura, Kazue, illus. (Illus.). 47 p. 20cm. (Viking Seafarer Book). 1974, c.1962. (ISBN 0-670-05095-4). Viking Press.
--Very Special Badgers: A Tale of Magic from Japan. Mizumura, Kazue, illus. LC 60-1641. (Illus.). 26cm. 40p. (gr. k-3). 1960. (ISBN 0-670-74533-2). Viking Pr.

Stamm, Russell
--Invisible Scarlet O'Neil: A New Story Based on the Famous Newspaper Strip. authorized. LC 44-336. 3 p. l., 11-248 p. illus. 20 1/2 cm. 1943. Whitman Publishing Company.

Stamper, J.
--Tales for the Midnight Hour. (gr. 7-12). 1977. (ISBN 0-590-10423-3). Scholastic Inc.

Stamps, Cathy Baker (1925-)
--Story Time in Rhyme: With Tales for Jimmy and His Pals. LC 54-6758. 54p. illus. 20cm. (Contemporary poets of Dorrance, 458). 1954. Dorrance.

Stanchfield, Jo M (1927-)
--Driving Through the Clouds, and Other Stories. Pollard, Susie, illus. LC 72-92846. (Illus.). 83 p. (Her Highway holidays series, book 3). 1973. (ISBN 0-8372-0798-3). Bowmar.
--Out at Home Plate, and Other Stories. Pollard, Susie, illus. LC 73-81512. (Illus.). 86 p. (Her Highway holidays series, book 6). 1973. (ISBN 0-8372-0801-7). Bowmar.
--Pablo, the Bullfighter and Other Stories. Pollard, Susie, illus. LC 72-92848. (Illus.). 79 p. (Her Highway holidays series, book 2). 1973. (ISBN 0-8372-0797-5). Bowmar.
--Watch Out for Alligators and Other Stories. Pollard, Susie, illus. LC 73-81593. (Illus.). 85 p. (Her Highway holidays series, book 5). 1973. (ISBN 0-8372-0800-9). Bowmar.
--A Wild Bus Ride, and Other Stories. Pollard, Susie, illus. LC 73-81511. (Illus.). 85 p. (Her Highway holidays series, book 4). 1973. (ISBN 0-8372-0799-1). Bowmar.
--Wrong-Way Camper, and Other Stories. Pollard, Susie, illus. LC 72-92847. (Illus.). 87 p. (Her Highway holidays series, book 1). 1973. (ISBN 0-8372-0796-7). Bowmar.

Stanchfield, Jo M (1927-) & Granite, Harvey R, eds.
--Tempos. LC 77-83336. (Illus.). 248 p. 23cm. (Vistas). c.1978. (ISBN 0-395-25227-X). Houghton Mifflin.

Standard Educational Corporation
--Child's World, 8 Vols. Beckwith, Yvonne, ed. (gr. 4-6). 1971. Standard Ed.

Standing Bear, Luther (1868-)
--Stories of the Sioux. Stoops, Herbert Morton, illus. LC 34-255251. vi p., 3 l., 3-79 p. front., plates. 21 cm. 1934. Houghton Mifflin Company.

Standish, Burt L., pseud., see Patten, Gilbert.

Standish, Burt L., pseud. (1866-1945)
--Frank Merriwell at Yale. Patten, Gilbert. (The Famous Frank Merriwell Stories). N.D. David McKay.
--Frank Merriwell at Yale. Patten, Gilbert. Rudman, Jack, ed. (The Merriwell Ser.). N.D. (ISBN 0-8373-9309-4). (ISBN 0-8373-9009-5). F Merriwell.
--Frank Merriwell Down South. Patten, Gilbert. (The Famous Frank Merriwell Stories). N.D. David McKay.
--Frank Merriwell Down South. Patten, Gilbert. Rudman, Jack, ed. (The Merriwell Ser.). N.D. (ISBN 0-8373-9305-1). (ISBN 0-8373-9005-2). F Merriwell.
--Frank Merriwell in Camp. Patten, Gilbert. (The Famous Frank Merriwell Stories). N.D. David McKay.
--Frank Merriwell in Europe. Patten, Gilbert. Rudman, Jack, ed. (The Merriwell Ser.). N.D. (ISBN 0-8373-9308-6). (ISBN 0-8373-9008-7). F Merriwell.
--Frank Merriwell's Bravery. Patten, Gilbert. (The Famous Frank Merriwell Stories). N.D. David McKay.
--Frank Merriwell's Bravery. Patten, Gilbert. Rudman, Jack, ed. (The Merriwell Ser.). N.D. (ISBN 0-8373-9306-X). (ISBN 0-685-74117-6). F Merriwell.
--Frank Merriwell's Brother. Patten, Gilbert. (The Famous Frank Merriwell Stories). N.D. David McKay.
--Frank Merriwell's Champions. Patten, Gilbert. (The Famous Frank Merriwell Stories). N.D. David McKay.
--Frank Merriwell's Chums. Patten, Gilbert. (The Famous Frank Merriwell Stories). N.D. David McKay.
--Frank Merriwell's Chums. Patten, Gilbert. Rudman, Jack, ed. (The Merriwell Ser.). N.D. (ISBN 0-8373-9302-7). (ISBN 0-8373-9002-8). F Merriwell.
--Frank Merriwell's Courage. Patten, Gilbert. (The Famous Frank Merriwell Stories). N.D. David McKay.
--Frank Merriwell's Cruise. Patten, Gilbert. (The Famous Frank Merriwell Stories). N.D. David McKay.
--Frank Merriwell's Daring. Patten, Gilbert. (The Famous Frank Merriwell Stories). N.D. David McKay.
--Frank Merriwell's Faith. Patten, Gilbert. (The Famous Frank Merriwell Stories). N.D. David McKay.
--Frank Merriwell's False Friend. Patten, Gilbert. (The Famous Frank Merriwell Stories). N.D. David McKay.
--Frank Merriwell's Foes. Patten, Gilbert. (The Famous Frank Merriwell Stories). N.D. David McKay.
--Frank Merriwell's Hunting Tour. Patten, Gilbert. (The Famous Frank Merriwell Stories). N.D. David McKay.
--Frank Merriwell's Hunting Tour. Patten, Gilbert. Rudman, Jack, ed. (The Merriwell Ser.). N.D. (ISBN 0-8373-9307-8). (ISBN 0-8373-9007-9). F Merriwell.
--Frank Merriwell's Lads. Patten, Gilbert. (The Famous Frank Merriwell Stories). N.D. David McKay.
--Frank Merriwell's Loyalty. Patten, Gilbert. (The Famous Frank Merriwell Stories). N.D. David McKay.
--Frank Merriwell's Power. Patten, Gilbert. (The Famous Frank Merriwell Stories). N.D. David McKay.
--Frank Merriwell's Races. Patten, Gilbert. (The Famous Frank Merriwell Stories). N.D. David McKay.
--Frank Merriwell's Return to Yale. Patten, Gilbert. (The Famous Frank Merriwell Stories). N.D. David McKay.
--Frank Merriwell's Reward. Patten, Gilbert. (The Frank Merriwell Stories). N.D. David McKay.
--Frank Merriwell's School Days. Patten, Gilbert. (The Famous Frank Merriwell Stories). N.D. David McKay.
--Frank Merriwell's Secret. Patten, Gilbert. (The Famous Frank Merriwell Stories). N.D. David McKay.
--Frank Merriwell's Set-Back. Patten, Gilbert. (The Famous Frank Merriwell Stories). N.D. David McKay.
--Frank Merriwell's Skill. Patten, Gilbert. (The Famous Frank Merriwell Stories). N.D. David McKay.
--Frank Merriwell's Sports Afield. Patten, Gilbert. (The Famous Frank Merriwell Stories). N.D. David McKay.
--Frank Merriwell's Sports Afield. Patten, Gilbert. Rudman, Jack, ed. (The Merriwell Ser.). N.D. (ISBN 0-8373-9310-8). (ISBN 0-8373-9010-9). F Merriwell.
--Frank Merriwell's Trip West. Patten, Gilbert. (The Famous Frank Merriwell Stories). N.D. David McKay.
--Frank Merriwell's Trip West. Patten, Gilbert. Rudman, Jack, ed. (The Merriwell Ser.). N.D. (ISBN 0-8373-9304-3). (ISBN 0-8373-9003-6). F Merriwell.
--Frank Merriwell's Vacation. Patten, Gilbert. (The Famous Frank Merriwell Stories). N.D. David McKay.
--Frank Merriwell's Victories. Patten, Gilbert. (The Famous Frank Merriwell Stories). N.D. David McKay.
--Guarding the Keystone Sack. Patten, Gilbert. (The Big League Ser.). N.D. Barse & Hopkins.
--The Man on First. Patten, Gilbert. (The Big League Ser.). N.D. Barse & Hopkins.

Standish, Carole
--The Mystery Cruise. 192p. (Orig.). (gr. 7 up). 1984. (ISBN 0-590-33105-1, Windswept Bks). Scholastic Inc.
--The Snow's Secret. 192p. (Orig.). (gr. 7 up). 1982. (ISBN 0-590-32362-8, Windswept). Scholastic Inc.
--Someone is Out There. 192p. (Orig.). (gr. 7 up). 1982. (ISBN 0-590-31570-6, Windswept). Scholastic Inc.

Standish, Marilyn, jt. auth. see Landes, William-Alan.

Standish, Winn, pseud., see Sawyer, Walter Leon.

Standley, Elizabeth
--Plays Are Fun. (gr. 1-5). N.D. Carlton.

Standon, Anna Slater (1929-)
--The Hippo Had Hiccups. Standon, Edward Cyril (1926-), illus. LC 64-10207. (Illus.). 1 v. (unpaged). 26cm. 1964. Coward-McCann.
--A Penny Bell. Standon, Edward Cyril (1926-), illus. LC 77-108909. (Illus.). 32 p. 27cm. 1st U.S. edition. 1970. Harvey House.
--The Singing Rhinoceros. Standon, Edward Cyril (1926-), illus. LC 63-8833. unpaged. illus. 26 cm. 1963. Coward-McCann.
--The Tin Can Tortoise. Standon, Edward Cyril (1926-), illus. LC 65-10971. 1 v. (unpaged) col. illus. 26 cm. 1965. Coward-McCann.

Standon, Anna Slater (1929-) & Standon, Edward Cyril (1926-)
--Bridie the Bantam. Standon, Edward Cyril (1926-), illus. LC 67-149081. 1v. (unpaged) col. illus. 26cm. 32p. 1967. Dial.
--A Flower for Ambrose. LC 67-3385. (Illus.). 48 p. 24cm. 1967, c.1964. Delacorte Press.
--Little Duck Lost. Standon, Edward Cyril (1926-), illus. LC 66-7728. (Illus.). 48 p. 24cm. 1966, c.1965. Delacorte Press.
--Three Little Cats. LC 67-3387. 1 v. (unpaged) illus. 24 cm. 1967. Delacorte Press.

Standon, Edward Cyril, jt. auth. see Standon, Anna Slater.

Stanek, Lou Willett
--Gleanings. LC 85-42622. 184 p. 22cm. c.1985. (ISBN 0-06-025808-X). (ISBN 0-06-025809-8). Harper & Row.
--Megan's Beat. LC 82-45511. p. cm. c.1983. (ISBN 0-8037-5201-6). Dial Press.

Stanek, Muriel Novella (1915-1971)
--Don't Hurt Me, Mama. Cogancherry, Helen, illus. LC 83-16771. p. cm. 1983. (ISBN 0-8075-1689-9). A. Whitman.
--Growl When You Say R. Smith, Phil (1930-), illus. LC 79-171. (Illus.). 32 p. 24cm. (Concept books/level 2). c.1979. (ISBN 0-8075-3074-3). A. Whitman & Co.
--I Know a Dairy Man. Dougherty, Charles L., illus. LC 71-90862. (Illus.). 23cm. 46p. (Community Helper Bk). (gr. 1-3). 1970. (ISBN 0-399-60278-X). Putnam.
--I Won't Go Without a Father. Mill, Eleanor, illus. LC 78-188435. (Illus.). 24cm. 32p. (Concept Bks.). (gr. 1-4). 1972. (ISBN 0-8075-3524-9). A Whitman.
--Left, Right, Left, Right!. Hawkinson, Lucy Ozone (1924-1971), illus. LC 79-79548. (Illus.). 32 p. 24cm. 1969. A. Whitman.
--My Little Foster Sister. Cheng, Judith, illus. LC 81-13006. p. cm. (Concept Books: Level 1). 1981. (ISBN 0-8075-5365-4). A. Whitman.
--New in the City. Brewer, Paul, illus. LC 65-238886. 127p. illus. 22cm. c.1965. (ISBN 0-8075-5576-2). A. Whitman.
--One, Two, Three for Fun. Fleishman, Seymour (1918-), illus. LC 67-26519. (Illus.). 32 p. 24cm. 1967. A. Whitman.
--Starting School. DeLuna, Betty & DeLuna, Tony, illus. LC 81-297. (Illus.). 32 p. 19cm. (Self-starter books). c.1981. (ISBN 0-8075-7617-4). A. Whitman.
--Tall Tina. Hawkinson, Lucy Ozone (1924-1971), illus. LC 79-126436. (Illus.). 32 p. 24cm. 1970. (ISBN 0-8075-7758-8). A. Whitman.
--Who's Afraid of the Dark. Cogancherry, Helen, illus. LC 80-19074. p. cm. (Concept book/level 1). 1980. (ISBN 0-8075-9011-8). A. Whitman.

Stanford, Bedel. S.
--Story of Elizabeth Broad: A Tale of Two Colonies. N.D. E J B Young & Co.

Stanford, Donald Kent (1918-)
--Crash Landing!. Campbell, Stan, illus. LC 59-12385. 218 p. illus. 22 cm. 1959. Funk & Wagnalls.
--The Horsemasters. LC 57-6508. 212p. illus. 22cm. 1957. Funk & Wagnalls.
--The Red Car. Tricogola, George & Hicks, Alan, illus. LC 54-9735. (Illus.). 249 p. 22cm. 1954. Funk & Wagnalls.
--Ski Town!. Campbell, Stan, illus. LC 58-11845. 212 p. 22 cm. 1958. (ISBN 0-308-80169-5). Funk & Wagnalls Co.
--The Treasure of the Coral Reef. LC 56-10705. 193 p. illus. 22 cm. 1956. Funk & Wagnalls.

Stanford, Donald Kent (1918-) & Baker, Vern
--J, Seven-Eleven. Campbell, Stan, illus. (Illus.). (gr. 6-10). 1962. Funk & Wagnalls.
--Must Be Good Riders: Orphans Preferred. Campbell, Stan, illus. LC 62-17765. 220 p. illus. 22 cm. 1962. Funk & Wagnalls.

Stanford, Ernest Elwood (1888-)
--The Mascot Goes Across. Stanford, Ernest Elwood (1888-), photos by. LC 29-7734. ix, 353 p. front., plates. 19 1/2 cm. c.1929. The Century Co.

Stang, Judit see Varga, Judy, pseud.

Stang, Judit see Mother Goose.

Stang, Judit see Stang, Judy.

Stang, Judy (1921-1977)
--Let's Play Nurse and Doctor. Stang, Judy (1921-1977), illus. LC 53-29431. unpaged. illus. 20cm. (Treasure Books). 1953. Treasure Books.
--The Pet in the Jar. Stang, Judy (1921-1977), illus. (Illus.). (Eager Readers Ser.). (gr. k-3). 1975. (ISBN 0-307-60801-8, Golden Pr). Western Pub.

Stang, Judy (1921-1977), illus.
--Mother Goose. (Read-Aloud Bks.). (gr. k-3). N.D. (ISBN 0-448-02003-3). Wonder.

Stang, Wendy, jt. auth. see Richards, Susan.

Stang, Wendy & Richards, Susan (1950-)
--Hubert. The Caterpillar Who Thought He Was a Moustache. Anderson, Robert Lindberg, illus. (Illus.). 32p. (Harlin Quist Bks). (gr. 2-5). 1973. (ISBN 0-8252-0037-7). Dial.
--Hubert. The Caterpillar Who Thought He Was a Moustache. Anderson, Robert Lindberg, illus. LC 67-16284. 1v. (unpaged) illus. (pt. col.) 16cm. 1967. H. Quist; Dist. by Crown. **Award: (NYT).**

Stangeland, Katharina Maria Bech Brondum Michaelis see Michaelis, Karin, pseud.

Stanger, Margaret A
--A Brand New Baby. Doane, Pelagie (1906-1966), illus. LC 42-167107. 132 p. illus. 24 x 21 cm. 1942. The Beacon Press.

Stangl, Jean
--Paper Stories. LC 84-60238. (ps-3). 1984. (ISBN 0-8224-5402-5). Pitman Learning.

Stanish, Bob
--Hippogriff Feathers. (gr. 3-12). 1981. (ISBN 0-86653-009-6). Good Apple.
--I Believe in Unicorns. (gr. 3-8). 1979. (ISBN 0-916456-51-X). Good Apple.
--A Monster's Shoe & the Cat. Stanish, Bob, illus. (Illus.). 44p. (gr. 1-4). 1983. (ISBN 0-88047-018-6). DOK Pubs.
--Sunflowering. (gr. 4-12). 1977. (ISBN 0-916456-12-9). Good Apple.

Stanistreet, Grace Marie, ed.
--Grace Marie Stanistreet's Recitations for Children. LC 78-102251. (Illus.). 289 p. 20cm. 1978. Granger Book Co.
--Grace Marie Stanistreet's Recitations for Children. LC 30-28310. 290 p. incl. front. (port.) 20 cm. c.1930. The Penn Publishing Company.

Stankevich, Boris (1928-)
--Two Green Bars. LC 67-19892. (gr. 5-9). 1967. (ISBN 0-15-291930-9). HarBraceJ.

Stanley
--Ingle Nook Stories. Irwin, Mary Grace (1891-), illus. N.D. Publications of E. P. Dutton & Co.

Stanley, Carol (1946-)
--I've Got a Crush on You. 160p. (Orig.). (gr. 7 up). 1981. (ISBN 0-590-30324-4, Wildfire). Scholastic Inc.
--Take Care of My Girl. (gr. 7 up). 1979. (ISBN 0-590-32203-6, Wildfire). Scholastic Inc.
--The Wrong Boy. 160p. (Orig.). (gr. 7 up). 1982. (ISBN 0-590-32285-0, Wildfire). Scholastic Inc.

Stanley, Charles D.
--The Jolly Bear and His Friends. (The Truant Chicken Ser.). N.D. Hurd & Houghton.
--The Monkey of Porto-Bello. (The Truant Chicken Ser.). N.D. Hurd & Houghton.

Stanley, Chuck, pseud., see Strong, Charles Stanley.

Stanley, Diane, jt. auth. see Johnston, Susan T.

Stanley, Diane see Zuromskis, Diane.

Stavros, Joyce, ed.
--Here We Go 'round the Poetry Bush: A Collection of Poetry by Children. Utah. State Institute of Fine Arts, Salt Lake City & Granite School District LC 74-173585. (Illus.). iv, 95 p. 29cm. N.D. Printed by Lithodyne.
Staw, Flora L
--Hector, 1 of 4 Vols. (Illus.). (Flora Staw's Stories). N.D. Robert Brothers.
Stawell, R., Mrs.
--The Fairy of Old Spain. N.D. E P Dutton.
Stawell, Randolph
--My Days with the Fairies. Dulac, Edmund (1882-1953), illus. N.D. George H Doran & Co.
Staynes, Jill
--Out of That World. LC 79-670152. 138 p. 21cm. 1979. (ISBN 0-571-11302-8). Faber & Faber.
Stead, Richard
--Adventures on Great Rivers. (The Adventure Library). N.D. J. b. Lippincott.
--Adventures on the High Seas. (The Adventure Library). N.D. J. B. Lippincott.
Stead, William Thomas, ed. see AEsopus.
Stead, William Thomas (1849-), ed. see Aladdin.
Stead, William Thomas (1849-), ed. see Grimm, Jakob Ludwig Karl (1785-1863) & Grimm, Wilhelm Karl.
Stead, William Thomas (1849-), ed. see Hawthorne, Nathaniel.
Stead, William Thomas (1849-), ed. see Malory, Thomas, Sir.
Steadman, Eleanor B.
--Nursery School Daze. N.D. Vantage Press Inc.
Steadman, Ralph Idris (1936-)
--The Bridge. Steadman, Ralph Idris (1936-), illus. LC 74-24652. (Illus.). 32 p. 30cm. 1975, c.1972. (ISBN 0-529-05257-1). (ISBN 0-529-05259-8). Collins.
--Jelly Book. LC 73-99918. (Illus.). 32 p. 1970, c.1967. Scroll Press.
--The Little Red Computer. LC 69-17734. (Illus.). 32 p. 30cm. 1969. McGraw-Hill.
Stealy, Jennie
--Little People of The Plaza. N.D. D. Lothrop Co.
Stearns, Albert
--Chris and the Wonderful Lamp. Birch, Reginald Bathurst (1856-1943), illus. LC 12-38973. 4 p. l., xi-xiv p., 1 l., 253 p. incl. front., illus., plates. 20 cm. 1895. The Century Co.
--Sindbad, Smith & Co. Birch, Reginald Bathurst (1856-1943), illus. LC 12-38929. x p., 1 l., 271 p. incl. plates. front. 20 cm. 1896. The Century Co.
Stearns, David M
--Chuckle: The Story of a Woodchuck. Stearns, Sharon (1912-), illus. LC 39-27826. 64 p. illus. 19 cm. c.1939. Farrar and Rinehart, Inc.
--Sleek: The Story of an Otter. Stearns, Sharon, pseud. (1912-), illus. Banigan, Sharon Church. LC 38-357457. 64 p. illus. 19 cm. c.1938. Farrar and Rinehart, Inc.
--Sniffy: The Story of a Skunk. Stearns, Sharon (1912-), illus. LC 40-30723. 64 p. illus. 19 cm. c.1940. Farrar and Rinehart, Inc.
--Whisk: The Story of a Chipmunk. Stearns, Sharon (1912-), illus. LC 41-11118. 62 p. col. illus. 19 cm. c.1941. Farrar and Rinehart, Inc.
Stearns, David M & Stearns, Sharon, Mrs. (1912-)
--Leander the Gander. LC 62-16894. unpaged. illus. 29 x 14 cm. (Read-aloud book). 1962. Follett Pub. Co.
--Leander The Gander and Spunky The Donkey. Banigan, Sharon Church. N.D. Wilcox & Follett Co.
--Spunky the Donkey. LC 62-16895. unpaged, illus. 29 x 14 cm. (a read-aloud book. 1962. Follett Pub. Co.
Stearns, Emily Newlin
--Golden Sentinel: A Story. (Illus.). 64 p. 21cm. 1973. (ISBN 0-682-47618-8). Exposition Pr.
Stearns, John Newton see Merry, Robert, pseud.
Stearns, John Newton (1829-1895)
--Merry's Illustrated Book of Rhymes. Merry, Robert, pseud. Hatchet, Hiram, pseud. LC 44-28597. vi, 7-108 p. illus. 17 1/2 cm. 1859. Bartlett and Miles.
--Merry's Illustrated Book of Rhymes. Merry, Robert, pseud. Hatchet, Hiram, pseud. LC 44-28601. vi, 7-108 p. incl. front., illus. 18 cm. 1861. H. Dayton.
Stearns, Monroe Mather (1913-), tr. see Daveluy, Paule Cloutier.
Stearns, Monroe Mather (1913-)
--Albert and His Adventures. Reidel, Marlene, illus. LC 61-13143. (Based on a Story by Marlene Reidel). unpaged. illus. 31 cm. 1961. Bobbs-Merrill.
--Eric's Journey. Reidel, Marlene, illus. LC 60-50303. (Based of a Story by Marlene Reidel). unpaged. illus. 30 cm. 1960. Lippincott.
--Gabriel & His Magic Wand. Reidel, Marlene, illus. (Illus.). (gr. k-3). 1962. (ISBN 0-397-30600-8). Lippincott.
--Kasimir's Journey. Reidel, Marlene, illus. (Based on a Story by Marlene Reidel). (Illus.). (gr. k-3). 1959. (ISBN 0-397-30450-1). Lippincott. **Award: (NYT).**
--Kasimir's Journey: Verse. Reidel, Marlene, illus. LC 64-55139. 1 v. (unpaged) col. illus. 30 cm. 1957. Lippincott.
--Ring-a-Ling. Verses Adapted from Folk Songs. Zabransky, Adolf (1909-), illus. 116 p. illus. 33 cm. N.D. (ISBN 0-397-31423-X). Lippincott.
--Underneath My Apple Tree: Verses. Zabransky, Adolf (1909-), illus. LC 60-4686. 66 p. illus. 29 cm. 1960. Lippincott.
Stearns, Pamela Fujimoto (1935-)
--The Fool and the Dancing Bear. 1st ed. Strugnell, Ann, illus. LC 78-26965. (Illus.). 167 p. 21cm. c.1979. (ISBN 0-316-81171-8). Little, Brown.
--Into the Painted Bear Lair. Strugnell, Ann, illus. LC 76-20744. (Illus.). 153 p. 21cm. 1976. (ISBN 0-395-24736-5). Houghton Mifflin.
--The Mechanical Doll. Hyman, Trina Schart (1939-), illus. LC 78-24351. p. cm. 1979. Houghton Mifflin.
Stearns, Sharon, Mrs., jt. auth. see Stearns, David M.
Stearns, Sharon (1912-)
--Billy Boy and His Friends. Stearns, Sharon (1912-), illus. LC 50-24481. 18 p. col. illus. 22 cm. (Bonnie book). 1949. John Martin's House.
--The Kitten Book. Stearns, Sharon (1912-), illus. LC 50-235484. 18 p. col. illus. 21 cm. (Bonnie book). 1949. John Martin's House.
--The Puppy Book. Stearns, Sharon (1912-), illus. LC 50-23553. 18 p. col. illus. 22 cm. (Bonnie book). 1949. John Martin's House.
--Where, Oh Where?. Stearns, Sharon (1912-), illus. LC 53-23304. unpaged. illus. 21cm. (Cozy-corner book). 1953, c.1952. Whitman Pub. Co.
Stearns, Sharon (1912-), illus.
--Fuzzy Duckling. LC 53-16720. (Illus.). 17cm. 16p. (Fuzzy Wuzzy Tell a Tales). 1952. Whitman Pub. Co.
--Pancho, the Donkey. LC 50-13866. (Illus.). 22cm. 28p. (Bonnie Book). 1950. John Martin's House.
Stebbing, Grace
--Adventures in Texas. Hardy, Paul (1862-), illus. N.D. Frederick A Stokes.
--Only a Tramp: Or, Golden Links. (Whittaker Select Bks). N.D. Set. Thomas Whittaker.
--Silverdale Rectory: or, the Golden Links. (Whittaker's Select Bks). 1888. Thomas Whittaker's.
--That Bother of a Boy. (Illus.). N.D. E. P. Dutton & Co.
--That Bother of a Boy. Hardy, paul (1862-), illus. (Little People's Ser.). N.D. Dana Estes and Company.
Stebbing, Hilary
--Monty's New House. LC 46-572. 24 p. col. illus. 25 cm. 1944. The Transatlantic Arts Company Limited.
Stebbins, Anna Elizabeth
--Small Flags Waving. Lockwood, Myna, illus. LC 43-9680. 223 p. illus. 21 cm. 1943. E. P. Dutton & Co., Inc.
Stebbins, Charles Maurice, jt. ed. see Frary, Marie Harriette.
Stecher, Miriam Brodie (1917-) & Kandell, Alice S (1938-)
--Daddy and Ben Together. LC 81-4425. (Illus.). 32 p. c.1981. (ISBN 0-688-00735-X). (ISBN 0-688-00736-8). Lothrop, Lee & Shepard Books.
--Max, the Music-Maker. LC 80-10692. (Illus.). 25 p. 1980. (ISBN 0-688-41958-5). (ISBN 0-688-51958-X). Lothrop, Lee & Shepard. **Award: (ALA).**
Steedman, Amy
--Legends and Stories of Italy for Children. Cameron, Katharine, illus. LC 10-2553. 1909. G. P. Putnam's Sons.
--The Madonna of the Goldfinch. Steedman, E. M., illus. LC 19-4521. 4 p. l., 184 p. 8 col. mounted plates (incl. front.) 24 cm. 1918. Frederick A. Stokes Co.
--Nursery Tales. N.D. E P Dutton.
--Nursery Tales, Told to the Children. Woodroffe, Paul Vincent (1875-1945), illus. LC 8-14767. vii, 118 p. 8 col. pl. (incl. front.) 15 cm. (Half-title: Told to the children series, ed. by Louey Chisholm). N.D. T. C. & E. C. Jack.
--Stories from the Arabian Nights. Blaikie, F. M. B., illus. LC 8-3877. 15 x 12cm. 117p. (Told to the Children Ser.). 1907. E. P. Dutton & Co.
--Wild Animals. LC 27-2932. 159 p. col. front., illus., col. plates. 26 cm. 1926. T. Nelson and Sons.
Steedman, Amy, jt. ed. see Chisholm, Louey.
Steedman, Amy, ed. see Grimm, Jakob Ludwig Karl (1785-1863) & Grimm, Wilhelm Karl.
Steedman, Amy, retold by see Kingsley, Charles.
Steel, Flora Annie Webster, Mrs. (1847-1929)
--The Adventures of Akbar. Shaw, Byam (1872-1919), illus. LC 13-22508. 6 p. l., 204 p. col. front., col. plates. 21 cm. c.1913. Frederick A. Stokes Company.
--Tales of the Punjab: Told by the People. Kipling, Joseph Rudyard (1865-1936), illus. Temple, R. C., notes by. LC 1-9724. xvi, 395 p. front., illus. 19 cm. 1894. Macmillan and Co.
--The Tiger, the Brahman, and the Jackal. LC 63-124024. unpaged. illus. 29 cm. (Young owl book). 1963. Holt, Rinehart and Winston.
Steel, Flora Annie Webster, Mrs. (1847-1929), retold by.
--English Fairy Tales. Rackham, Arthur (1867-1939), illus. Fadiman, Clifton, afterword by. LC 62-19429. (Illus.). 256 p. 24cm. (Macmillan classics, 35). 1962. Macmillan.
--English Fairy Tales. Rackham, Arthur (1867-1939), illus. LC 18-20967. ix, 363 p. col. front., illus., 15 col. pl. 21 x 16 cm. 1918. The Macmillan Company.
--English Fairy Tales. Rackham, Arthur (1867-1939), illus. LC 24-26097. ix, 363 p. col. front., illus., 3 col. pl. 20 cm. (The children's classics). 1923. The Macmillan Company.
--Tattercoats: An Old English Tale. Goode, Diane (1949-), illus. LC 76-9947. (Illus.). 32 p. 32cm. c.1976. (ISBN 0-87888-109-3). Bradbury Press.
Steel, Flora Annie Webster, Mrs. (1847-1922) & Temple, R. C., eds.
--Tales of the Punjab. Gentleman, David William (1930-), illus. LC 73-175388. (Illus.). 310p. 1980. (ISBN 0-370-01271-2, Pub. by Chatto, Bodley Head & Jonathan). Merrimack Pub Cir.
Steele, Edwin E
--Growing Pains in Nature Study. Provonsha, Clyde N., illus. LC 56-1624. 112 p. illus. 24 cm. 1956. Southern Pub. Association.
Steele, Francesca Maria, pseud., see Dale, Darley.
Steele, Frederic Dorr, illus.
--Paddy O'Leary and His Learned Pig. N.D. Dodd, Mead & Co.
Steele, Marshall, jt. auth. see Arnold, Paul.
Steele, Mary Quintard Govan see Gage, Wilson, pseud.
Steele, Mary Quintard Govan (1922-)
--Because of the Sand Witches There. Galdone, Paul (1914-), illus. LC 75-5932. (Illus.). 183 p. 22cm. 1975. (ISBN 0-688-80001-7). (ISBN 0-688-84001-9). Greenwillow Books.
--The First of the Penguins. LC 84-21197. 152 p. 22cm. 1985, c.1973. (ISBN 0-688-04801-3). Greenwillow Books.
--The First of the Penguins. Jeffers, Susan, illus. LC 73-1964. (Illus.). 154 p. 22cm. 1973. (ISBN 0-02-786880-X). Macmillan.
--Journey Outside. LC 79-9919. p. cm. 1979. (ISBN 0-14-030588-2). Puffin Books.
--Journey Outside. Negri, Rocco (1932-), illus. LC 69-18263. (Illus.). 143 p. 25cm. 1969. Viking Press. **Awards: (ALA); (JNM).**
--The Life (and Death) of Sarah Elizabeth Harwood. LC 80-11350. p. cm. 1980. (ISBN 0-688-80285-0). Greenwillow Books.
--Mrs. Gaddy and the Ghost. Gage, Wilson, pseud. Hafner, Marylin (1925-), illus. LC 78-16366. (Illus.). 55 p. 22cm. (Greenwillow read-alone). c.1979. (ISBN 0-688-80179-X). (ISBN 0-688-84179-1). Greenwillow Books.
--The Owl's Kiss: Three Stories. LC 78-1983. 128p. (gr. 5-9). 1978. (ISBN 0-688-80174-9). (ISBN 0-688-84174-0). Greenwillow.
--The Secret of Crossbone Hill. Gage, Wilson, pseud. 1st ed. Stevens, Mary, illus. LC 59-5920. 183 p. illus. 21 cm. 1959. World Pub. Co.
--The Secret of Fiery Gorge. Gage, Wilson, pseud. 1st ed. Stevens, Mary, illus. LC 60-7203. 185 p. illus. 21 cm. 1960. World Pub. Co.
--The True Men. LC 76-5482. p. cm. c.1976. (ISBN 0-688-80052-1). (ISBN 0-688-84052-3). Greenwillow Books.
--Wish, Come True. Stock, Catherine, illus. LC 79-10321. p. cm. 1979. (ISBN 0-688-80230-3). (ISBN 0-688-84230-5). Greenwillow Books.
Steele, Mary Quintard Govan (1922-), ed.
--The Fifth Day: Poems. Domanska, Janina, illus. LC 77-26143. (Illus.). xiii, 77 p. 22cm. c.1978. (ISBN 0-688-80146-3). (ISBN 0-688-84146-5). Greenwillow Books.
Steele, Mary Quintard Govan (1922-) & Steele, William Owen (1917-1979)
--The Eye in the Forest. 1st ed. LC 74-23768. (Illus.). 136 p. 22cm. 1975. (ISBN 0-525-29510-0). Dutton.
Steele, Muriel Nixon
--Animal Capers. Smith, Bud, illus. LC 30-14221. 15, 1 p. illus. 22 cm. 1929. Hickman Printing Company.
--Sunland Tales. Smith, Bud, illus. LC 31-103. 3 p. l., 11-44 p., 2 l. incl. illus., plates. 14 cm. c.1930. Wolfer Printing Company.
Steele, Philip, jt. auth. see King, David Clive.
Steele, Philip, ed. see Swallow, Su.
Steele, Phillip
--Going to the Zoo. LC 80-52529. (Starters Ser.). N.D. (ISBN 0-382-06476-3). Silver.
Steele, Robert Reynolds (1860-1944)
--The Story of Alexander. Mason, Fred, illus. LC 67-9487. (Illus.). xiii, 225 p. 22cm. (Legacy Library facsimile). 1966. University Microfilms.
Steele, Robert Reynolds (1860-1944), ed.
--The Russian Garland of Fairy Tales: Being Russian Folk Legends: Translated from a Collection of Chap-Books Made in Moscow. Rev ed. De Rosciszewski, R., illus. LC 17-26975. v p., 1 l., vii-viii, 243, 1 p. col. front., 5 col. pl. 22 cm. 1916. R. M. McBride & Company.
Steele, Rose Yarbrough (1898-)
--Little Toy Dog, and Other Poems. Glass, Wilma Baker, illus. LC 49-87825. 40 p. illus. 22 cm. 1948. Story Book Press.
Steele, Rufus (1877-1935)
--Scar Neck: The Adventurous Story of a Great Nevada Mustang. Stoops, Herbert Morton, illus. LC 30-21438. 3 p. l., 92 p. incl. plates. col. front. 18 cm. (Round Table Ser.). 1930. Harper & Brothers.
Steele, William Owen, jt. auth. see Steele, Mary Quintard Govan.
Steele, William Owen (1917-1979)
--Andy Jackson's Water Well. 1959. (ISBN 0-8382-0043-5, Cadmus Books). E. M. Hale and Company.
--Andy Jackson's Water Well. Ramus, Michael, illus. LC 59-7282. 80 p. illus. 22 cm. 1959. Harcourt, Brace.
--The Buffalo Knife. Galdone, Paul (1914-), illus. LC 52-6460. (Illus.). 177p. (gr. 4-6). 1968. (ISBN 0-15-614750-5, VoyB). HarBraceJ.
--The Buffalo Knife. Galdone, Paul (1914-), illus. LC 52-6460. 177 p. illus. 21 cm. 1952. Harcourt, Brace.
--The Cherokee Crown of Tannassy. LC 77-19997. 1977. (ISBN 0-910244-99-5). Blair.
--Daniel Boone's Echo. 1st ed. Nicolas, pseud. (1911-1973), illus. Mordvinoff, Nicolas. LC 57-9741. 78p. illus. 22cm. 1957. (ISBN 0-15-221980-3). Harcourt, Brace.
--Davy Crockett's Earthquake. 1st ed. Nicolas, pseud. (1911-1973), illus. Mordvinoff, Nicolas. LC 56-6920. 62p. illus. 22cm. 1956. (ISBN 0-15-222696-6). Harcourt, Brace.
--De Soto, Child of the Sun: The Search for Gold. 1st ed. Bjorklund, Lorence F. (1913-1978), illus. LC 55-11907. (Illus.). 190 p. 21cm. (American heritage series). 1956. Aladdin Books.
--The Far Frontier. 1st ed. Galdone, Paul (1914-), illus. LC 59-12905. 185 p. illus. 21 cm. 1959. Harcourt, Brace.
--Flaming Arrows. 1st ed. Galdone, Paul (1914-), illus. LC 57-6791. (Illus.). 178 p. 21cm. 1957. Harcourt, Brace.
--Francis Marion: Young Swamp Fox. 1st ed. Gringhuis, Richard H. (1918-1974), illus. Gringhuis, Dirk, pseud. LC 54-6065. 192p. illus. 20cm. (Childhood of famous Americans series 80). 1954. Bobbs-Merrill.
--Francis Marion: Young Swamp Fox. Nicholas, Frank, illus. LC 62-12703. 200 p. illus. 20 cm. (Childhood of Famous Americans). 1962. Bobbs-Merrill.
--The Golden Root. 1st ed. Kredel, Fritz (1900-1973), illus. LC 51-12378. (Illus.). 76 p. 20cm. 1951. Alladin Books.
--Hound Dog Zip to the Rescue. Korach, Mimi (1922-), illus. LC 73-103960. (Illus.). 62 p. 24cm. (Reading shelf book). 1970. Garrard Pub. Co.
--John Sevier: A Pioneer Boy. 1st ed. James, Sandra, illus. LC 54-6065. 192p. illus. 20cm. (Childhood of famous Americans series). 1953. Bobbs-Merrill.
--John's Secret Treasure. Dennis, R., illus. 1975. Macmillan.
--The Lone Hunt. Galdone, Paul (1914-), illus. LC 56-10074. (Illus.). 176 p. 22cm. 1956. Harcourt, Brace.
--The Lone Hunt. Galdone, Paul (1914-), illus. LC 75-29489. p. cm. (Voyager book ; AVB 101). 1976, c.1956. (ISBN 0-15-652983-1). Harcourt Brace Jovanovich.
--The Magic Amulet. 1st ed. LC 78-20573. 114 p. 21cm. c.1979. (ISBN 0-15-250427-3). Harcourt Brace Jovanovich.
--The Man with the Silver Eyes. 1st ed. LC 76-18850. 147 p. 21cm. c.1976. (ISBN 0-15-251720-0). Harcourt Brace Jovanovich.
--The No-Name Man of the Mountain. 1st ed. Davis, Jack, illus. LC 64-22272. (Illus.). 79 p. 21cm. 1964. Harcourt, Brace & World.
--Over-Mountain Boy. 1st ed. Kredel, Fritz (1900-1973), illus. LC 52-11823. (Illus.). 192 p. 21cm. (American heritage). 1952. Aladdin Books.
--The Perilous Road. Galdone, Paul (1914-), illus. (gr. 5-7). 1954. Harcourt & Brace.
--The Perilous Road. 1st ed. Galdone, Paul (1914-), illus. LC 58-6820. 191 p. illus. 23 cm. 1958. Harcourt, Brace. **Awards: (ALA); (JNM).**

AUTHOR INDEX STEINER, CHARLOTTE

--The Spooky Thing. 1st ed. Coker, Paul, Jr., illus. LC 60-13041. 80 p. illus. 22 cm. 1960. Harcourt,Brace.
--The Story of Daniel Boone. Baumgartner, Warren, illus. LC 53-8124. 175p. illus. 22cm. (Signature books, 15). 1953. (ISBN 0-448-05615-1). Grosset & Dunlap.
--The Story of Leif Ericson. Lape, Pranas (1921-), illus. LC 54-5862. 181p. illus. 22cm. (Signature books, 30). 1954. Grosset & Dunlap.
--Tomahawk Border. Wooten, Vernon, illus. LC 66-14987. (Illus.). 120 p. 24cm. 1966. Colonial Williamsburg; Distributed by Holt, Rinehart and Winston, New York.
--Tomahawks and Trouble. 1st ed. Galdone, Paul (1914-), illus. LC 55-9006. 213p. illus. 21cm. 1955. (ISBN 0-15-289084-X). Harcourt, Brace.
--Trail Through Danger. Beck, Charles, illus. LC 65-25307. 184p. illus. 21cm. c.1965. (ISBN 0-15-289661-9). Harcourt.
--Triple Trouble for Hound Dog Zip. Korach, Mimi (1922-), illus. LC 72-76324. (Illus.). 64 p. 24cm. 1972. (ISBN 0-8116-4037-X). Garrard Pub. Co.
--The War Party. 1st ed. Cauley, Lorinda Bryan (1951-), illus. LC 78-52815. (Illus.). 63 p. 22cm. (Let me read book). c.1978. (ISBN 0-15-294789-2). (ISBN 0-15-694697-1). Harcourt Brace Jovanovich.
--Wayah of the Real People. Barnett, Isa, illus. LC 64-14585. ix, 128 p. illus. 24 cm. 1964. (ISBN 0-03-045220-1). Colonial Williamsburg; Distributed by Holt, Rinehart and Winston, New York.
--We Were There on the Oregon Trail. Polseno, Jo, illus. LC 56-5042. (Illus.). ix, 177 p. 24cm. (We were there books, 1). 1955. Grosset & Dunlap.
--We Were There with the Pony Express. Vaughn, Frank E., illus. LC 56-5889. (Illus.). 182 p. 24cm. (We were there books, 8). 1956. Grosset & Dunlap.
--Westward Adventure: The/True Stories of Six Pioneers. Voute, Kathleen (1892-), illus. (0). 188p. N.D. Harcourt Brace & World Inc.
--Wilderness Journey. 1st ed. Galdone, Paul (1914-), illus. LC 52-11964. 209p. illus. 21cm. 1953. (ISBN 0-15-297318-4). Harcourt, Brace.
--Winter Danger. Galdone, Paul (1914-), illus. LC 54-5157. (Illus.). 183p. (gr. 4-6). 1954. (ISBN 0-15-298034-2, HJ). HarBraceJ.
--The Year of the Bloody Sevens. 1st ed. Beck, Charles, illus. LC 63-16036. 187 p. illus. 21 cm. 1963. Harcourt, Brace & World. **Award: (ALA).**

Steen, Elizabeth K
--Red Jungle Boy. Steen, Elizabeth K., illus. LC 37-28528. 3 p. l., 82, 1 p. col. illus. 23 x 24 cm. c.1937. Harcourt, Brace and Company.

Steen, Shirley & Front, Charles
--A Child's Bible in Colour: The New Testament. Front, Charles, illus. LC 78-51445. (Illus.). 274 p. 19cm. (Piccolo book). 1978. (ISBN 0-8091-2118-2). Paulist Press.

Steers, B. MacDonald
--Stormalong Goes a-Whaling: Fabulous Stories About Stormalong, the Paul Bunyan of the Sea. Soderberg, Yngve Edward, illus. LC 66-22116. vii, 50p. illus. 24cm. c.1966 (Globe Pequot). Pequot Pr.

Stefanik, Alfred T
--Copycat Sam: Developing Ties with a Special Child. Huff, Laura, illus. LC 81-20212. p. cm. 1982. (ISBN 0-89885-058-4). Human Sciences Press.

Stefansson, Evelyn
--Within The Circle. N.D. Charles Scribner's Sons.

Stefansson, Thorsteinn
--The Golden Future. LC 75-304646. (Illus.). 165 p. 23cm. 1974. (ISBN 0-19-271363-9). Oxford University Press.
--The Golden Future. Ambrus, Victor G., pseud. (1935-), illus. Ambrus, Gyozo Laszlo. LC 76-28785. p. cm. c.1976. (ISBN 0-8407-6520-7). T. Nelson.

Stefansson, Vilhjalmur (1879-1962) & Irwin, Violet Mary (1881-)
--Kak, the Copper Eskimo. Richards, George Mather (1880-), illus. LC 24-20561. vii p., 2 l., 3-253 p. incl. plates. col. front., plates. 20 cm. 1924. The Macmillan Company.
--The Mountain Jade. (Fiction). (MacMillan Bks. for Boys & Girls). (gr. 7-9). N.D. MacMillan Bks.
--The Shaman's Revenge. (Fiction). (MacMillan Bks. for Boys & Girls). (gr. 7-9). N.D. MacMillan Bks.

Stefansson, Vilhjalmur (1879-1962) & Schwarz, Julia O.
--Northward Ho!. N.D. MacMillan.

Steffa, Tim, tr. see Hunnas, Mauri.

Steffan, Alice Jacqueline Kennedy see Steffan, Jack, pseud.

Steffan, Alice Jacqueline Kennedy (1907-)
--The Bright Thread: A Novel of St. Clare of Assisi. Steffan, Jack, pseud. LC 62-10955. 190p. 21cm. c.1962. John Day.
--Firm Hand on the Rein. Steffan, Jack, pseud. Laune, Paul Sidney (1899-), illus. LC 61-11305. 182 p. illus. 21 cm. 1961. Longmans, Green.
--The Gift of Wilderness. Steffan, Jack, pseud. LC 60-10946. 188 p. illus. 21 cm. (Your fair land series). 1960. John Day Co.
--Mountain of Fire. Steffan, Jack, pseud. LC 59-11453. 191 p. illus. 21 cm. (Your fair land series). 1959. J. Day Co.

Steffan, Jack, pseud., see Steffan, Alice Jacqueline Kennedy.

Stegall, Carrie Coffey (1908-)
--The Adventures of Brown Sugar: Adventures in Creative Writing. (Illus.). xxii, 86 p. 1967. National Council of Teachers of English.

Stege, Matthew & Christenson, Joyce Francis, illus.
--A St. Croix Valley Story. Independent School District 834 LC 72-89560. (Illus.). xiii, 108 p. 26cm. 1972. Croixside Press.

Stegeman, Janet A. (1923-)
--Last Seen on Hopper's Lane. LC 82-70203. p. cm. c.1982. (ISBN 0-8037-4970-8). Dial Press.

Steger, Hans U
Travelling to Tripiti. Crawford, Elizabeth D., tr. from Ger. LC 68-1203. (Illus.). 48p. 1968, c.1967. Harcourt, Brace & World.

Steichen, Edward, jt. auth. see Martin, Mary Steichen, Mrs.

Steig, William (1907-)
--Abel's Island. 1st ed. Steig, William (1907-), illus. LC 75-35918. (Illus.). 117 p. 23cm. 1976. Farrar, Straus and Giroux. **Awards: (ALA); (JNM)**
--The Amazing Bone. Steig, William (1907-), illus. LC 76-26479. p. cm. 1976. Farrar, Straus and Giroux. **Awards: (ALA); (BGH); (RCM).**
--The Amazing Bone. Steig, William (1907-), illus. LC 77-21948. p. cm. 1977, c.1976. (ISBN 0-14-050247-5). Puffin Books.
--Amos and Boris. Steig, William (1907-), illus. LC 72-165403. (Illus.). 32 p. 1971. (ISBN 0-374-30278-2). Farrar, Straus and Giroux. **Awards: (NYT); (ALA).**
--Amos & Boris. Steig, William (1907-), illus. LC 77-21946. p. cm. 1977, c.1971. (ISBN 0-14-050229-7). Puffin Books.
--The Bad Island. Steig, William (1907-), illus. LC 70-86945. (Illus.). 32 p. 32cm. 1969. Windmill Books.
--C D B!. Steig, William (1907-), illus. 1968. Simon and Schuster.
--C D C!. Steig, William (1907-), illus. LC 84-48515. (Illus.). 64p. (gr. k up). 1984. (ISBN 0-374-31015-7). FS&G.
--Caleb and Kate. Steig, William (1907-), illus. LC 77-4947. 27cm. 32p. 1977. (ISBN 0-374-31016-5). Farrar, Straus and Giroux.
--Doctor De Soto. Steig, William (1907-), illus. LC 82-15701. p. cm. 1982. (ISBN 0-374-31803-4). Farrar, Straus, and Giroux. **Awards: (ABA); (IBBY); (ALA); (JNM).**
--Dominic. Steig, William (1907-), illus. LC 70-188272. (Illus.). 146p. 1972. (ISBN 0-374-31822-0). (ISBN 0-374-41826-8). FS&G. **Award: (ALA).**
--An Eye for Elephants. Steig, William (1907-), illus. LC 76-130203. (Illus.). 48 p. 18cm. 1970. Windmill Books.
--Farmer Palmer's Wagon Ride. Steig, William (1907-), illus. LC 74-9949. (Illus.). 32 p. 27cm. 1974. (ISBN 0-374-32288-0). Farrar, Straus, Giroux.
--Farmer Palmer's Wagon Ride. Steig, William (1907-), illus. LC 77-29063. p. cm. 1978, c.1974. (ISBN 0-14-050267-X). Puffin Books.
--Gorky Rises. Steig, William (1907-), illus. LC 80-68068. (Illus.). 32 p. 28cm. 1980. (ISBN 0-374-32752-1). Farrar, Straus, Giroux. **Award: (NYT).**
--The Real Thief. Steig, William (1907-), illus. LC 73-77910. (Illus.). 58 p. 24cm. 1973. (ISBN 0-374-36217-3). Farrar, Straus and Giroux. **Award: (ALA).**
--Roland, the Minstrel Pig. Steig, William (1907-), illus. LC 68-14923. (Illus.). 32 p. 32cm. 1968. Windmill Books; Distributed by Harper & Row.
--Roland, the Minstrel Pig. Steig, William (1907-), illus. LC 77-26812. p. cm. 1978. Windmill Books.
--Rotten Island. rev. ed. Bierhorst, Jane B., ed. Steig, William (1907-), illus. (gr. 6 up). 1984. (ISBN 0-87923-526-8). S&S.
--Rotten Island. Steig, William (1907-), illus. LC 84-40475. (Illus.). 32 p. 29cm. 1984, c.1969. (ISBN 0-87923-526-8). D.R. Godine.
--Solomon the Rusty Nail. Steig, William (1907-), illus. 30p. 1985. (ISBN 0-374-37131-8). Farrar.
--Sylvester and the Magic Pebble. Steig, William (1907-), illus. (Illus.). 1973. E.P. Dutton & Co.
--Sylvester and the Magic Pebble. Steig, William (1907-), illus. (Illus.). 1969. Simon & Schuster Inc.
--Tiffky Doofky. Steig, William (1907-), illus. LC 78-19657. p. cm. 1978. (ISBN 0-374-37542-9). Farrar, Straus, and Giroux.
--Yellow and Pink. Steig, William (1907-), illus. (Illus.). 32p. 1984. (ISBN 0-374-38670-6). FS&G.

Stein, A.
--Little Anna, 1 of 4 vols. (Illus.). (The Cheerful Heart Library). 1900. Set. Lee & Shepard.

Stein, Charlotte M.
--The Stained Glass Window. N.D. Double M Pr.

Stein, Elizabeth Ogle
--Jack's Visit to Cherryville. LC 53-10310. 22cm. 30p. 1953. Vantage Press Books.

Stein, Evaleen (1863-1923)
--Child Songs of Cheer. Inglis, Antoinette, illus. LC 18-174689. 3 p. l., 5-120 p. col. front., col. plates. 20 cm. c.1918. Lothrop, Lee & Shepard
--Children's Stories. Warren, Elizabeth B., illus. LC 27-18. (Illus.). 20cm. 175p. 1926. Page Co.
--The Christmas Porringer. Everhart, Adelaide, illus. LC 14-1568. 5 p. l., 190 p. front., plates. 20 cm. 1914. The Page Company.
--The Circus Dwarf Stories. Howe, Gertrude Herrick, (1902-), illus. LC 27-183221. 5 p. l., 222 p. front., plates. 20 cm. c.1927. L. C. Page & Company.
--Gabriel and the Hour Book. Everhart, Adelaide, illus. LC 6-25606. 5 p. l., 173 p. col. front., 5 col. pl. 20 cm. (Roses of St. Elizabeth series). 1906. L. C. Page & Company.
--The Little Count of Normandy: Or, The Story of Raoul. Goss, John, illus. LC 11-278088. 5 p. l., 300 p. front., plates. 20 cm. 1911. L. C. Page & Company.
--A Little Shepherd of Provence. Marlowe, Diantha W. Horne, illus. (The Roses Ser.). 1910. L. C. Page.
--A Little Shepherd of Provence. Marlowe, Diantha W. Horne, illus. LC 11-35102. (Illus.). 20cm. 210p. 1910. Page Co.
--Our Little Celtic Cousin of Long Ago: Being the Story of Ferdiad, a Boy of Ireland, in the Time of Brian Boru. Goss, John, illus. LC 18-22446. xii p., 2 l., 125 p. col. front., plates. 20 cm. (little cousins of long ago series). 1918. The Page Company.
--Our Little Crusader Cousin of Long Ago: Being the Story of Hugh, Page to King Richard of England, in the Third Crusade. Meister, Charles E., illus. LC 21-4906. xiv p., 2 l., 144 p. col. front., plates, 20 cm. (little cousins of long ago series). 1921. The Page Company.
--Our Little Frankish Cousin of Long Ago: Being the Story of Rainolf, a Boy at the Court of Charlemagne. Meister, Charles E. & Von Landau, Helena, illus. LC 17-21796. viii, p., 2 l., 116 p. col. front., plates. 20 cm. (little cousins of long ago series). 1917. The Page Company.
--Our Little Norman Cousin of Long Ago: Being a Story of Normandy in the Time of William the Conqueror. Goss, John, illus. LC 15-18276. 5 p. l., ix-x, 117 p. col. front., 5 pl. 20 cm. (little cousins of long ago series). 1915. The Page Company.
--Pepin: A Tale of Twelfth Night. Matsubara, T., illus. LC 24-244601. 6 p. l., 186, 1 p. incl. front., plates, 20 cm. 1924. L. C. Page & Company (Incorporated.
--Rosechen and the Wicked Magpie. Bridgman, Lewis Jesse (1857-1931) & Goss, John, illus. LC 17-11792. 193 p. incl. col. front., illus. 21 cm. c.1917. Lothrop, Lee & Shepard Co.
--When Fairies Were Friendly. Gooch, Thelma, illus. LC 23-2978. 6 p. l., 3-190 p. front., plates. 20 cm. 1922. The Page Company.

Stein, Gertrude (1874-1946)
--The World ... Is Round. Hurd, Clement (1908-), illus. LC 39-31266. 2 p. l., 67 p. illus. 27 cm. c.1939. W. R. Scott, Inc.
--The World Is Round. Hurd, Clement (1908-), illus. LC 66-14571. (Illus.). 94 p. 28cm. 1966, c.1939. Young Scott Books.
--The World Is Round. Rose, Francis Cyril, Sir (1909-), illus. LC 65-15900. 61 p. illus. 24 cm. 1965. Haskell House.

Stein, Hazel
--The Wise Men's Camel Boy. Sanden, Howard A., illus. LC 66-476. 32 p. col. illus. 22 cm. 1965. Augsburg Pub. House.

Stein, Mini
--Puleng of Lesotho. Traill, Ian, illus. LC 75-81393. (Illus.). 64 p. 23cm. 1969. J. Messner.

Stein, Monte see Johnathan, pseud.

Stein, Monte
--Daddy and Me. Johnathan, pseud. Babcock, lisa, illus. LC 47-2540. 32 p. illus. 22 1/2 x 20 1/2 cm. 1946. C. Scribner's Sons.

Stein, R. Conrad see Stein, Richard Conrad.

Stein, Richard Conrad (1937-)
--Me and Dirty Arnie. LC 81-84216. 132 p. 21cm. c.1982. (ISBN 0-15-253141-6). Harcourt Brace Jovanovich.
--Steel Driving Man: The Legend of John Henry. Wiskur, Darrell D., illus. LC 70-85959. (Illus.). 29 p. 25cm. 1969. Childrens Press.

Steinbach, Alexander Alan
--Sabbath Queen. N.D. Behrman House Inc.

Steinbeck, John Ernst (1902-1968)
--Grapes of Wrath. large type ed. (Keith Jennison Bks). (gr. 7 up). N.D. (ISBN 0-531-00193-8). Watts.
--Red Pony. (Keith Jennison Large Type Bks). (gr. 9 up). 1966. (ISBN 0-531-00271-3). Watts.
--The Red Pony. reissue ed. Dennis, Wesley (1903-1966), illus. (Illus.). (gr. 7 up). 1959. (ISBN 0-670-59184-X). Viking Pr.

Steinberg, Barbara Hope
--The Magic Millstones and Other Japanese Folk Stories. Eve, Esme, illus. LC 74-18696. (Illus.). 24cm. 64p. 1969. Oxford Univ. Press.

Steinberg, Fannie
--Birthday in Kishinev. 1st ed. Hanuschak, Luba, illus. LC 78-56546. (Illus.). 79 p. 22cm. 1978. (ISBN 0-8276-0111-5). Jewish Publication Society of America.

Steinberg, Judah (1863-1908)
--The Breakfast of the Birds: An Other Stories from the Hebrew of Judah Steinberg. Solis-Cohen, Emily (1886-), tr. LC 18-33659. 175 p. col. front., col. plates. 27 cm. 1917. The Jewish Publication Society of America.

Steinberg, Phillip Orso (1921-)
--George: The Discontented Giraffe. Lee, Carvel Bigham (1910-), illus. LC 57-12702. unpaged. illus. 29 cm. 1957. T. S. Denison Co.
--George, the Discontented Giraffe. Moline, Earl Warren, Jr., illus. LC 57-127027. unpaged. illus. 29cm. 1957. T. S. Denison Co.
--Porkadot, the City-Bred Pig. Lee, Carol, illus. LC 59-14410. unpaged. illus. 29 cm. (Children's Picture Bks.). 1959. T. S. Denison.

Steiner, Alexis
--All My Horses. Jaruska, Wilhelm, illus. LC 64-8402. (Foreign Land Bks). (gr. k-5). 1965. (ISBN 0-8225-0353-0). Lerner Pubns.
--Kriki and the Fox. Jaruska, Wilhelm, illus. Hurd, E., tr. LC 60-12370. 63 p. illus. 24 cm. 1961. Watts.
--Kriki, the Wild Duck. Jaruska, Wilhelm, illus. Hurd, E., tr. LC 61-6550. 62 p. illus. 24 cm. 1960. Watts.

Steiner, Barbara A, jt. auth. see Cloven, George.

Steiner, Barbara Annette (1934-)
--But Not Stanleigh. Cloven, George & Cloven, Ruth, illus. LC 81-9265. (Illus.). 32p. (gr. k-4). 1980. (ISBN 0-516-03454-5). Childrens.
--Oliver Dibbs to the Rescue!. Christelow, Eileen (1943-), illus. LC 85-42801. p. cm. c.1985. (ISBN 0-02-787890-2). Four Winds.
--The Searching Heart. 144p. (Orig.). (gr. 7 up). 1982. (ISBN 0-590-32361-X, Wildfire). Scholastic Inc.
--Secret Love. 158p. (Orig.). (gr. 7 up). 1982. (ISBN 0-590-32002-5, Wildfire). Scholastic Inc.
--The Secret of the Dark. 176p. (Orig.). (gr. 7-12). 1984. (ISBN 0-590-33252-X, Windswept Bks). Scholastic Inc.
--Stanleigh's Wrong-Side-Out Day. Cloven, George & Cloven, Ruth, illus. LC 82-9711. (Illus.). 32 p. 28cm. c.1982. (ISBN 0-516-03619-X). Childrens Press.

Steiner, Charlotte
--Annie's ABC Kitten. Steiner, Charlotte, illus. LC 65-21558. (Illus.). 31 p. 27cm. 1965. Knopf.
--The Big Laughing Book. Steiner, Charlotte, illus. LC 49-11564. 58 p. illus. (part col.) 30 cm. c.1949. Grosset & Dunlap.
--Bobby Follows the Butterfly. LC 59-9307. unpaged. illus. 23 cm. 1959. Macmillan.
--The Charlotte Steiner Theater Book. Steiner, Charlotte, illus. N.D. Sam'l Gabriel Sons & Co.
--Daddy Comes Home. Babcock, Lisa, illus. LC 44-8542. 24 p. illus. (part col.) 20 1/2 x 22 cm. c.1944. Doubleday, Doran & Company, Inc.
--The Fitfiddles Keep Fit. Steiner, Charlotte, illus. LC 63-10822. unpaged. illus. 27 cm. 1963. Knopf.
--A Friend Is "Amie.". LC 56-8902. (Illus.). unpaged. 27cm. 1956. Knopf.
--Giddy-Ap, Giddy-Ap!. 1 st. ed. LC 51-12484. unpaged. illus. 20 x 23 cm. (Junior Books). 1951. Doubleday.
--Good Day. Which Way?. LC 60-5505. unpaged. illus. 26 cm. 1960. Knopf.
--The Hungry Book. LC 67-3599. (Illus.). 1 v. (unpaged. 26cm. 1967. Knopf.
--I Am Andy. Steiner, Charlotte, illus. LC 61-6055. 29 p. (chiefly illus.). 22cm. (You-tell-a-story book). 1961. (ISBN 0-394-91269-1). Knopf.
--I'd Rather Stay with You. LC 65-16542. 1v. (chifly col. illus.) 20cm. c.1965. Seabury.
--Jack Is Glad, Jack is Sad. Steiner, Charlotte, illus. LC 62-14765. unpaged. illus. 23 cm. 1962. (ISBN 0-394-91279-9). Knopf.
--Karoleena. LC 57-8091. 90 p. illus. 25 cm. 1957. Doubleday.
--Karolena's Red Coat. 1st ed. Steiner, Charlotte, illus. LC 60-10554. 38 p. illus. 25 cm. 1960. (ISBN 0-385-07894-3). Doubleday.
--Kiki and Muffy. LC 43-15295. 26 p. illus. (part col.) 21 x 22 cm. c.1943. Doubleday, Doran & Company, Inc.

--Kiki Dances. LC 49-11028. 31 p. col. illus. 21 x 23 cm. (Junior books). 1949. Doubleday.
--Kiki Goes to Camp. LC 53-9141. (Illus.). unpaged. (Junior books). c.1953. Doubleday.
--Kiki Is an Actress. LC 58-7161. unpaged. illus. 24 cm. 1958. Doubleday.
--Kiki Is An Actress. 1958. (ISBN 0-8382-1022-8, Cadmus Books). E. M. Hale And Company.
--Kiki Loves Music. LC 54-8912. (Illus.). unpage. (Junior books). c.1954. Doubleday.
--Kiki Skates. LC 50-9427. (Illus.). 32 p. (Junior books). 1950. Doubleday.
--Kiki's Play House. LC 61-11143. unpaged. illus. 22 x 27 cm. 1962. Doubleday.
--Let Her Dance!. Steiner, Charles, illus. LC 70-80105. (Illus.). 32 p. 18cm. 1969. Lothrop, Lee & Shepard Co.
--Listen to My Seashell. LC 59-5038. unpaged. illus. 21 x 26 cm. 1959. Knopf.
--Little John Little. Steiner, Charlotte, illus. LC 52-8235. unpaged. illus. 21 cm. c.1951. Wonder Books.
--The Little Train That Saved the Day. LC 47-11188. 25 p. illus. (part col.) 18 x 34 cm. 1947. Grossett & Dunlap.
--The Little Train That Saved the Day. Steiner, Charlotte, illus. LC 52-37329. unpaged. illus. 21 cm. (Wonder books, 571). 1952. Wonder Books.
--The Littlest Mother Goose. (Illus.). (Mail-Me Book). (ps-2). 1964. Random.
--Lolly's Pony Ride. 1st ed. Steiner, Charlotte, illus. LC 59-5900. unpaged. illus. 22 x 27 cm. c.1959. Doubleday.
--Look What Tracy Found. LC 72-168996. (Illus.). 32 p. 26cm. 1972. (ISBN 0-394-82305-2). (ISBN 0-394-92305-7). Knopf.
--Lulu. LC 39-30368. 19 l. col. illus. 21 x 26 cm. 1939. Doubleday, Doran & Company, Inc.
--Lulu Meets Peter. LC 42-25583. 25 p. illus. (part col.) 21 1/2 x 21 1/2 cm. 1942. Doubleday, Doran & Co., Inc.
--Lulu's Play School. LC 48-8222. 32 p. col. illus. 21 x 23 cm. (Junior books). 1948. Doubleday.
--Make-Believe Puppy. N.D. E. M. Hale & Co.
--Make-Believe Puppy. Heller, Helen, photos by. LC 52-13639. unpaged. illus. 29 cm. 1952. Lothrop, Lee and Shepard.
--My Bunny Feels Soft. LC 58-6495. unpaged. illus. 21 x 26 cm. (Borzoi Book). 1958. Knopp.
--My Slippers Are Red. LC 57-9194. unpaged. illus. 21 x 26 cm. 1957. Knopf.
--Now That You Are Five. Steiner, Charlotte, illus. LC 63-7237. 57 p. illus. 21 cm. 1963. Association Press.
--Patsy's Pet. LC 55-9009. unpaged. illus. 21 x 23cm. 1955. Doubleday.
--Pete & Peter. LC 41-20737. 26 p. illus. (part col.) 22 x 22 cm. 1941. Doubleday, Doran & Co., Inc.
--Pete's Puppets. LC 52-11000. (Illus.). unpaged. 23cm. (Junior books). 1952. Doubleday.
--Polka Dot. LC 47-5780. 34 p. col. illus. 20 x 23 cm. c.1947. Doubleday.
--Red Ridinghood Goes Sledding. LC 62-8151. 26 p. illus. 24 cm. 1962. Macmillan.
--Red Ridinghood's Little Lamb. LC 63-21812. 1 v. (unpaged) col. illus. 27 cm. c.1964. Knopf.
--The Sleepy Quilt. LC 45-378681. 16 p. col. illus. 18 1/2 x 19 1/2 cm. 1945. Doubleday, Doran & Co., Inc.
--Square Bear and Cousin Bear. LC 66-31575. 1 v. (unpaged) col. illus. 27cm. c.1967. Seabury.
--Surprise Mrs. Bunny. Steiner, Charlotte, illus. LC 53-29593. unpaged. illus. 21cm. N.D. Wonder Books.
--Ten in a Family. LC 60-11420. unpaged. illus. 26 cm. 1960. Knopf.
--Terry Writes a Letter. LC 58-9948. unpaged. illus. 23 cm. 1958. Macmillan.
--Tim and Tom Play Ball. LC 61-12190. unpaged. illus. 26 cm. 1961. Macmillan.
--Timmy Needs a Thinking Cap. LC 61-7061. (Illus.). unpaged. 27cm. 1961. Macmillan.
--Tomboy's Doll. LC 69-14334. (Illus.). 31 p. 26cm. 1969. Lothrop, Lee & Shepard Co.
--Wake up! Wake up!. LC 47-577. 25 p. illus. (part col.) 17 x 23 cm. 1946. Grosset & Dunlap.
--What Do You Love: A Little Picture Book. LC 68-15321. (Illus.). 32 p. 22cm. 1968. Knopf.
--What's the Hurry, Harry?. LC 68-14070. (Illus.). 1 v. (unpaged. 26cm. 1968. Lothrop, Lee & Shepard Co.
--Where Are You Going?. LC 48-1017. 24 p. col. illus., 21 x 22 cm. 1946. Doubleday.
--Whose Baby?. LC 50-14308. 19cm. 31p. (gr. k-1). 1950. Thomas Y. Crowell Co.

Steiner, Charlotte, compiled by.
--Happy Birthday Book: An Anthology of Verses and Stories. Steiner, Charlotte, illus. LC 53-12216. 45 p. illus. 32cm. N.D. Garden City Books.

Steiner, Charlotte, jt. auth. see Hall, William Norman.

Steiner, Charlotte, ed. see Mother Goose.

Steiner, Charlotte & Burlingham, Mary
--The Climbing Book. LC 43-8542. 20 p. col. illus. 16 x 15cm. 1943. Vanguard Press.
--The Second Climbing Book: A Pull-Out Book. LC 44-85567. cover-title, 20 p. col. illus. 17 1/2 x 15 cm. 1944. Vanguard Press, Inc.

Steiner, Charlotte & Hoff, Virginia
--The Copycat Colt. N.D. Wonder Books.
--Frisky the Black Colt. N.D (Wonder Books). Grosset & Dunlap.

Steiner, Claude (1935-)
--A Warm Fuzzy Tale. Dick, Joann, illus. Freed, Alvyn M. (1913-), intro. by. LC 77-77981. (Illus., Orig.). 1st U.S. edition. (ps-3). 1977. (ISBN 0-915190-08-7). Jalmar Pr.

Steiner, Edward Alfred (1866-)
--Uncle Joe's Lincoln. LC 19-350. 9, 13-171 p. front. pl. 19 1/2cm. c.1918. Fleming H. Revell.

Steiner, Heiri, jt. auth. see Ehmcke, Susanne.

Steiner, Jorg (1930-)
--The Bear Who Wanted to Be a Bear. Muller, Jorg (1930-), illus. Tashlin, Frank (1913-1972), created by. LC 76-29355. (Illus.). 34 p. 26cm. 1977. (ISBN 0-689-50079-3). Atheneum.
--Rabbit Island. Muller, Jorg (1930-), illus. LC 84-18503. p. cm. 1985. (ISBN 0-930267-00-1). Bergh Pub. Group.
--Rabbit Island. Muller, Jorg (1930-), illus. Lammers, Ann Conrad, tr. from Ger. LC 78-1512. p. cm. 1978. (ISBN 0-15-265034-2). Harcourt Brace Jovanovich. **Award: (MLB).**

Steiner, Lewis Henry (1827-1892), tr. see Hoffmann, Franz.

Steiner, Pat, compiled by.
--Green Andrew Green. LC 84-2402. (Illus.). 79 p. 21cm. c.1984. (ISBN 0-664-32714-1). Westminster Press.

Steiner, Rudolf, jt. auth. see Von Goethe, Johann W.

Steiner, Rudolf (1861-1925)
--And It Came to Pass: An Old Testament, Reader for Children. 1973. (ISBN 0-87968-556-5). Krishna Pr.

Steiner, Stan, jt. auth. see Babin, Maria Teresa.

Steiner, Stanley (1925-)
--The Last Horse. Yazz, Beatien, illus. LC 61-9781. 71 p. illus. 24cm. 1961. Macmillan.

Steinhorn, Harriet (1929-) & Lowy, Edith
--Shadows of the Holocaust: Plays, Readings, and Program Resources. Wikler, Madeline, illus. LC 83-14887. p. cm. 1983. (ISBN 0-930494-25-3). Kar-Ben Copies.

Steinman, Beatrice
--This Railroad Disappears. LC 58-10943. 181 p. illus. 21 cm. 1958. F. Watts.

Steinmann-Brunner, Elsa (1901-)
--Lia and the Red Carnations. Gruger, Johannes, illus. Winston, Richard (1917-1979) & Winston, Clara, trs. from Ger. LC 60-7027. 221 p. illus. 21 cm. 1960. Pantheon Books.
--The Son of the Gondolier. Winston, Richard & Winston, Clara, trs. LC 58-8006. (Illus.). 191 p. 22cm. 1958. Pantheon.

Steinmetz, Leon
--Clocks in the Woods. LC 77-11859. (Illus.). 32 p. 26cm. c.1979. (ISBN 0-06-025649-4). (ISBN 0-06-025650-8). Harper & Row.
--Pip Stories. Steinmetz, Leon, illus. (Illus.). 48p. (gr. k-2). 1980. (ISBN 0-316-78738-8). Little.

Steinorth, Karl, jt. auth. see Spitzing, Gunter.

Steinour, Marcus
--Dudley Smithwright & the Phantom Voice. Davenport, May, illus. LC 82-71048. (Illus.). 96p. (Dudley Smithwright Ser.). (gr. 3-5). 1982. (ISBN 0-943864-09-7). (ISBN 0-943864-04-6). Davenport.

Stelzer, Theodore
--Child's Garden of Song. 81p. N.D. Concordia Publishing House.
--A Child's Garden of Song. 81p. 1949. Lutheran Publications.

Stem, Linda J.
--The Secret Witch. Tio, Valerie P., illus. Bd. with They Caught the Who-Ever-It-Was. LC 79-84579. (Illus.). (gr. 5-8). 1979. (ISBN 0-934816-02-6). Metis Pr Inc.

Stemp, Robin Jenniver Pamela (1944-)
--Guy and the Flowering Plum Tree. Dinan, Carolyn, illus. LC 80-67029. (Illus.). 32 p. 26cm. 1st U.S. edition. 1981, c.1980. (ISBN 0-689-50188-9). Atheneum.

Stempel, Hans & Ripkins, Martin
--Andromedar SR 1. Edelmann, Heinz, illus. LC 71-141524. (Illus.). 28 p. 33cm. (Here-and-there book from Harlin Quist). 1971. (ISBN 0-8252-0061-X). (ISBN 0-8252-0062-8). H. Quist.

Stenberg-Masolle, Aina, illus.
--Cinderella. LC 39-15202. 16 p. incl. col. front., col. illus. 24 1/2 cm. c.1939. Grosset & Dunlap.

Steneman, Shep, jt. auth. see Lucas, George.

Steneman, Shep, adapted by see Disney, Walt, Productions.

Steneman, Shep (1945-)
--Superman's Book of Superhuman Achievements. Andru, Ross & Orlando, Joe, illus. LC 79-5572. (Illus.). 96p. (gr. 3-7). 1981. (ISBN 0-394-94410-0). (ISBN 0-394-84410-6). Random.

Stengel, Hansgeorg
--Busy Builders: A Counting Picture Book. Meyer-Rey, Ingeborg & Schultz-Debowski, Rudolf, illus. LC 70-83470. 27 p. col. illus. 27cm. 1969. Childrens Press.

Stephan, Hanna (1902-)
--The Quest. 1st ed. Maitland, Antony Jasper (1935-), illus. Goodall, Daphne Machin, tr. LC 68-15390. (Illus.). viii, 216 p. 21cm. 1968, c.1967. (ISBN 0-316-81280-3). Little, Brown.

Stephane, Nelly (1921-)
--Roland. Francois, Andre (1915-), illus. LC 58-9750. unpaged. illus. 31 cm. 1958. Harcourt, Brace. **Award: (NYT).**

Stephen, David (1910-)
--Rory the Roebuck. Higgins, Don (1928-), illus. LC 68-54815. (Illus.). 75 p. 21cm. 1969, c.1961. Funk & Wagnalls.
--String Lug the Fox. 1st ed. Langley, Nina Scott, illus. LC 52-5005. (Illus.). 174 p. 21cm. 1952. Little, Brown.

Stephens, Annabel Wiseman
--Pancho, the Monkey. LC 54-9166. 57p. 21cm. 1954. Pageant Press.
--Told by a Dog. Chase, Rhoda Campbell, illus. LC 35-23322. vii p., 1 l., 182 p. illus. 20 cm. c.1935. Johnson Publishing Company.

Stephens, Charles Asbury (1845-1931)
--The Ark of 1803: A Story of Louisiana Puchase Times. Burgess, H., illus. LC 4-12774. vi p., 1 l., 340, 1 p. 9 pl. 19 cm. 1904. A. S. Barnes & Company.
--A Busy Year at the Old Squire's. LC 34-27230. 3 p. l., 313 p. front. 20 cm. 1934. The Old Squire's Bookstore.
--Camping Out. (C. A. Stephens Ser.). N.D. Hurst & Co.
--Camping Out. (Roundabout Library). (Camping Out Ser.). N.D. John C. Winston Co.
--Camping Out. New ed. (C. A. Stephens' Books for Boys). N.D. John C. Winston Co.
--Camping Out, 1 of 6 vols. (Illus.). (Roundabout Lib.). (Camping Out Ser.). N.D. Porter and Coates.
--Charles Adams Tales. the story-teller's ed. LC 73-84136. (Illus.). 184 p. 24cm. 1973. C. A. Stephens Collection, Brown University.
--Fox Hunting. (Charles Stephens Ser.). N.D. Hurst & Co.
--Fox Hunting. (Camping Out Ser.). 1873. James Osgood.
--Fox Hunting. (Roundabout Library). (Camping Out Ser.). N.D. John C. Winston Co.
--Fox Hunting. New ed. (C. A. Stephens' Books for Boys). N.D. John C. Winston Co.
--Fox Hunting, 1 of 6 vols. (Illus.). (Roundabout Lib.). (Camping Out Ser.). N.D. Porter and Coates.
--Grandfather's Broadaxe. 224p. (gr. 7 up). 1967. (ISBN 0-201-09203-4, Young Scott Bks). A-W.
--Grandfather's Broadaxe, and Other Stories of a Maine Farm Family. Moriarty, Jerome B., illus. LC 66-17575. (Illus.). 222 p. 23cm. 1967. W. R. Scott.
--A Great Year of Our Lives at the Old Squire's. LC 12-219238. vii p., 1 l., 313 p. front., plates. 20 cm. c.1912. The Old Squire's Bookstore.
--A Great Year of Our Lives at the Old Squire's. LC 34-27231. vii, 313 p. front. 20 cm. 1934. The Old Squire's Bookstore.
--Haps and Mishaps at the Old Farm. LC 34-27232. 6 p. l., 7-236 p. front. (port.) 20 cm. 1934. The Old Squire's Bookstore.
--Katahdin Camps. Abbott, Jacob Bates (1803-1879), illus. LC 28-117083. 5 p. l., 254 p. front., illus., plates. 20 cm. 1928. Houghton Mifflin Company.
--The Knockabout Club Alongshore: The Adventures of a Party of Young Men on a Trip from Boston to the Land of the Midnight Sun. LC 27-27539. (Illus.). 22cm. 240p. (The Famous Knockabout Club Ser.). 1883. Estes & Lauriat's.
--The Knockabout Club in the Tropics: The Adventures of a Party of Young Men in New Mexico, Mexico, and Central America. LC 4-30133. (Illus.). 22cm. 240p. (The Famous Knockabout Club Ser.). N.D. Dana Estes and Company.
--The Knockabout Club in the Woods. (Illus.). (The Famous Knockabout Club Ser). N.D. Estes & Lauriat's.
--Left on Labrador: Or, The Cruise of the Schooner Yacht "Curlew". (C. A. Stephens Ser.). N.D. Hurst & Co.
--Left On Labrador: Or, The Cruise of the Schooner Yacht "Curlew", 1 of 6 vols. (Roundabout Library). (Camping Out Ser.). N.D. John C. Winston Co.
--Left on Labrador: Or, The Cruise of the Schooner Yacht "Curlew". New ed. (C. A.Stephens' Books for Boys). N.D. John C. Winston Co.
--Left on Labrador: Or, The Cruise of the Schooner Yacht "Curlew", 1 of 6 vols. (Illus.). (Roundabout Lib.). (Camping Out Ser.). N.D. Porter and Coates.
--Little Big-Heart and Other Stories. the story-teller's ed. LC 74-24790. (Illus.). 192 p. 24cm. 1974. C. A. Stephens Collection, Brown University.
--Lynx Hunting. (Charles Asbury Stephens Ser.). N.D. Hurst & Co.
--Lynx Hunting, 1 of 6 vols. (Roundabout Library). (Camping Out Ser.). N.D. John C. Winston Co.
--Lynx Hunting. New ed. (C. A. Stephens' Books for Boys). N.D. John C. Winston Co.
--Lynx Hunting, 1 0f 6 vols. (Illus.). (Roundabout Lib.). (Camping Out Ser.). N.D. Porter and Coates.
--Molly's Baby: A Little Heroine of the Seas. story-teller's ed. LC 74-12633. (Illus.). 301 p. 20cm. 1969. C. A. Stephens Collection, Brown University.
--Molly's Baby: A Little Heroine of the Seas. LC 34-27233. 4 p. l., 301 p. front. 20 cm. 1934. The Old Squire's Bookstore.
--My Folks in Maine. LC 72-3380. vi, 304 p. 22cm. (Short story index reprint series). 1972. (ISBN 0-8369-4161-6). Books for Libraries Press.
--My Folks in Maine. LC 34-15304. vi p., 1 l., 304 p. 20 cm. c.1934. The Old Squire's Bookstore.
--Off to the Geysers. (Charles Asbury Stephens Ser.). N.D. Hurst & Co.
--Off To The Geysers: Or, The Young Yachers in Iceland, 1 of 6 vols. (Roundabout Library). (Camping Out Ser.). N.D. John C. Winston Co.
--Off to the Geysers: Or, The Young Yachters in Iceland, 1 of 6 vols. (Illus.). (Roundabout Lib.). (Camping Out Ser.). N.D. Porter and Coates.
--On the Amazon. (Charles Asbury Stephens Ser.). N.D. Hurst & Co.
--On the Amazon. New ed. (Charles Asbury Stephens Books for Boys). N.D. John C. Winston Co.
--On The Amazon: Or, The Cruise of the "Rambler". (Roundabout Library). (Camping Out Ser.). N.D. John C. Winston Co.
--On the Amazon: Or, The Cruise of the "Rambler", 1 of 6 vols. (Illus.). (Roundabout Lib.). (Camping Out Ser.). N.D. Porter and Coates.
--On the Amazons. (Camping Out Ser.). 1873. James R. Osgood.
--Pioneer Boys Afloat on the Mississippi: A Story of Louisiana Purchase Times. Burgess, H., illus. LC 7-41588. vi p., 1 l., 240 p., 1 l. 9 pl. 19 cm. 1907. A. S. Barnes & Company.
--Stories of My Home Folks. LC 26-19260. 3 p. l., 231 p. front. (port.) 17 cm. c.1926. Perry Mason Company.
--Under the Sea in the Salvador. story-teller's ed. LC 75-10422. (Illus.). 146 p. 24cm. 1969. C. A. Stephens Collection, Brown University.
--When Life Was Young at the Old Farm in Maine. LC 12-3602. viii p., 1 l., 420 p. front., plates, fold. map. 20 cm. c.1912. The Old Squire's Bookstore.
--When Life Was Young at the Old Farm in Maine. LC 34-27234. viii p., 1 l., 420 p. incl. front. 20 cm. 1934. The Old Squire's Bookstore.
--The Young Moose Hunters. (Illus.). N.D. Dana Estes and Company.
--The Young Moose Hunters. (Juvenile Classics). 1874. Henry L. Shepard & Co.
--The Young Moose Hunters. New ed. 1945. L. C. Page.
--The Young Moose Hunters. A Backwoods-Boy's Story. LC 12-38876. 288 p. front., illus., plates. 21 cm. 1882. Estes and Lauriat.
--The Young Moose Hunters: A Backwoods-Boy's Story. Merrill, Frank Thayer (1848-), illus. LC 30-123089. 288 p. incl. front. illus. 20 cm. 1874. H. L. Shepard & Co.

Stephens, Charles Asbury (1845-1931), ed.
--Camping Out: As Recorded by "Kit.". LC 12-389680. viii, 261 p. front., plates. 19 cm. (Our young yachters' series. vol. 1). 1872. J. R. Osgood and Company.
--Left on Labrador: Or, the Cruise of the Schooner-Yacht "Curlew." As Recorded by "Wash.". LC 12-38947. viii, 256 p. front., plates. 18 cm. (Our young yachter's series. vol. ii). 1872. J. R. Osgood and Company.
--Lynx-Hunting: From Notes by the Author of "Camping Out.". LC 12-38969. 283 p. incl. front. plates. 19 cm. (camping series. vol. iv). 1873. J. R. Osgood and Company.
--Off to the Geysers: Or, the Young Yachters in Iceland. LC 12-31389. vii, 238 p. front., plates. 19 cm. (Our young yachter's series, vol. iii). 1872. J. R. Osgood and Company.
--On the Amazons: Or, the Cruise of "the Rambler". As Recorded by Wash. LC 12-389708. 6, 2, 7-258 p. incl. front. plates. 19 cm. (camping-out series. vol. vi). 1874. J. R. Osgood and Company.

Stephens, David
--Rory the Roebuck. Higgins, Don (1928-), illus. LC 68-54815. (Illus.). 11 ils. 80p. (gr. 2-7). 1969. (ISBN 0-308-80070-2). Funk & W.

--Printer's Devil. 1st ed. Burchard, Peter Duncan (1921-), illus. LC 52-11824. 192 p. illus. 21 cm. (American heritage). 1952. Aladdin Books.
--Walt Dinsey's Perri. Broun, Emily, pseud. (Deluxe Edition). 1958. Golden Press.
--We Live to Be Free. N.D. Farrar & Rinehart.
--White Swallow. Potter, Edna, illus. N.D. Dodd Mead & Co.
--White Swallow. Potter, Edna, illus. LC 27-22953. 6 p. l., 3-158 2 p. col. front., illus. 22 cm. 1927. Duffield and Company.

Sterne, Emma Gelders, Mrs. (1894-1971), retold by.
--All About Peter Pan. Gooch, Thelma, illus. LC 30-1386. (Original Story by Sir James Matthew Barrie, 1860-). (Illus.). 48p. 14cm. (The All About Ser.). 1924. Cupples and Leon Company.

Sterne, Emma Gelders, Mrs. (1894-1971) & Lindsay, Barbara, eds.
--King Arthur and the Knights of the Round Table. Tenggren, Gustaf (1896-1970), illus. LC 62-52839. 140p. col. illus. 27cm. (Golden illus. classic). 1962. Golden.

Sterne, G. M., Miss
--Aunt Margaret's Visit. N.D. George Routledge & Sons.

Sterne, Noelle
--Tyrannosaurus Wrecks. Chess, Victoria (1939-), illus. LC 78-22499. (Illus.). 32p. (A Trophy Picture Bk.). (gr. 1-4). 1983. (ISBN 0-06-443043-X, Trophy). Har-Row.
--Tyrannosaurus Wrecks: A Book of Dinosaur Riddles. Chess, Victoria (1939-), illus. LC 78-22499. (Illus.). (gr. 1-4). 1979. (ISBN 0-690-03959-X, TYC-J). (ISBN 0-690-03960-3). Har-Row.

Sterns, Emerson E.
--The Jingles and Riddles of Mother Hen. LC 17-1859. 8 p. 25 1/2cm. c.1883. American News Co.

Sterrett, Cliff, ed.
--Polly and Her Pals on the Farm: Adapted from the Newspaper Comic Strip. LC 34-35. 152 p. front., illus. 15 cm. c.1934. The Saalfield Publishing Company.

Sterrett, Frances Roberta (1869-)
--Mary Rose of Mifflin. (Growing Literature Ser.). N.D. Grosset & Dunlap.
--Rusty of the High Towers. Oldham, Marion Mildred, illus. LC 29-186988. 314 p. front., plates. 20 cm. c.1929. The Penn Publishing Company.
--Rusty of the Meadow Lands. Oldham, Marion Mildred, illus. LC 31-30603. 4 p. l., 7-331 p. front., plates. 20 cm. c.1931. The Penn Publishing Company.
--Rusty of the Mountain Peaks. Oldham, Marion Mildred, illus. LC 30-256223. 312 p. front., plates. 20 cm. c.1930. The Penn Publishing Company.
--Rusty of the Tall Pines. Gardiner, Florence, illus. LC 28-238762. 298 p. front., plates. 20 cm. 1928. The Penn Publishing Company.

Stertz, Eda (1921-)
--Katie's Treasure. LC 80-139180. 123 p. 21cm. (Pathfinder novel ; 12). c.1980. (ISBN 0-310-37921-0). Zondervan Pub. House.

Steurt, Majorie Rankin (1888-)
--A Kingdom for Mimus. (Illus.). 1964. Golden, Gate Junior Books.

Steven, Hugh
--Danger in the Blue Lagoon. LC 79-5117. (Illus.). 37 p. 22cm. c.1979. Good Life Productions.
--Din Be Still. LC 79-113770. (Illus.). 27 p. 22cm. c.1979. Good Life Productions.

Stevens, Alden Gifford (1886-)
--Lion Boy: A Story of East Africa. Watson, Eva Auld, illus. LC 38-27673. xviii, 233, 1 p. incl front., plates. 21 cm. 1938. Frederick A. Stokes Company.
--Lion Boy's White Brother. Frankenberg, Robert Clinton (1911-), illus. LC 51-10232. (Illus.). 241 p. 21cm. 1951. Lippincott.
--The Way of a Lion. Mason, George Frederick (1904-), illus. LC 39-27880. (Illus.). 22cm. 144p. 1939. J. B. Lippincott.

Stevens, Alden Gifford (1886-) & Kendall, Patricia
--Mark of the Leopard. 1st ed. Vernam, Roger, illus. LC 47-31075. 6 l., 3-278 p. illus. 21 cm. 1947. J. B. Lippincott Co.

Stevens, Ann
--The Romper Room Birthday Word Book. Gantz, David, illus. LC 83-20757. 1984. (ISBN 0-385-19004-2). Doubleday.

Stevens, Bryna, ed.
--Borrowed Feathers, and Other Fables. Wright, Freire & Foreman, Michael (1938-), illus. LC 77-79844. (Illus.). 32 p. 21cm. (Random House pictureback). c.1977. (ISBN 0-394-93730-9). Random House.

Stevens, Carla McBride (1928-)
--Anna, Grandpa, and the Big Storm. Tomes, Margot Ladd (1917-), illus. LC 81-10252. (Illus.). 59 p. 21cm. c.1982. (ISBN 0-89919-066-9). Clarion Books.
--Bear's Magic & Other Stories. Lee, Robert J. (1921-), illus. (gr. k-3). 1977. (ISBN 0-590-01506-0). (ISBN 0-590-20800-4). Scholastic Inc.
--The Birth of Sunset's Kittens. Stevens, Leonard A., photos by. LC 69-14569. (Illus.). maps. photos. 48p. (gr. k-5). 1969. (ISBN 0-685-21698-5, A-W Childrens). A-W.
--Catch A Cricket. 1961. (ISBN 0-8382-0156-3, Cadmus Books). E. M. Hale and Company.
--Hooray for Pig!. Bennet, Rainey (1907-), illus. (gr. k-2). 1974. Houghton Mifflin.
--Hooray for Pig!. Bennett, Rainey (1907-), illus. LC 73-17074. (Illus.). 48 p. 21cm. 1974. (ISBN 0-8164-3114-0). Seabury Press.
--How to Make Possum's Honey Bread. Kent, Jack, pseud. (1920-), illus. Kent, John Wellington. LC 75-28183. (Illus.). 40 p. c.1975. (ISBN 0-8164-3166-3). Seabury Press.
--Magic Carrot Seed. Kent, Jack, pseud. (1920-), illus. Kent, John Wellington. (gr. k-3). 1976. (ISBN 0-590-10271-0, Schol Pap). Scholastic Inc.
--Pig and the Blue Flag. Bennett, Rainey (1907-), illus. 1977. Houghton.
--Pig and the Blue Flag. Bennett, Rainey (1907-), illus. LC 76-58384. p. cm. c.1977. (ISBN 0-8164-3192-2). Seabury Press.
--Rabbit & Skunk & the Big Fight (Pub. by Scott). (gr. k-3). 1976. (ISBN 0-590-01311-4). Scholastic Inc.
--Rabbit & Skunk & the Big Fight. Kraus, Robert (1925-), illus. LC 61-24400. 72p. (ps-1). 1964 (Young Scott Bks). A-W.
--Rabbit and Skunk and the Scary Rock. Kraus, Robert, illus. unpaged. illus. 19 x 23 cm. (Young Scott book). 1962. W. R. Scott.
--Rabbit & Skunk & the Spook. Kraus, Robert (1925-), illus. (Illus.). (gr. 2-3). N.D. (ISBN 0-590-08087-3). (ISBN 0-590-20612-5). Scholastic Inc.
--Rabbit on Bear Mountain. Joerns, Consuelo, illus. (Illus.). 48p. 1980. (ISBN 0-590-31257-X). Scholastic Inc.
--Sara & the Pinch. Wallner, John C. (1945-), illus. (Illus.). 48p. (gr. k-3). 1980. (ISBN 0-395-29435-5, Clarion). HM.
--Stories from a Snowy Meadow. Rice, Eve Hart (1951-), illus. LC 76-3542. (Illus.). 48 p. 22cm. c.1976. (ISBN 0-8164-3161-2). Seabury Press.
--Trouble for Lucy. Himler, Ronald Norbert (1937-), illus. LC 79-10445. p. cm. (gr. 4-6). c.1979. (ISBN 0-8164-3240-6). Seabury Press.
--Wonderful Stories from the New Testament: For Young and Old. N.D. Cupples & Leon Company.
--Wonderful Stories From the Old Testament: For Young and Old. N.D. Cupples & Leon Company.

Stevens, Cat, pseud., see Georgin, Steven Demetre.

Stevens, Cat, pseud. (1948-)
--Teaser and the Firecat. Georgin, Steven Demetre. Stevens, Cat, pseud. (1948-), illus. Georgin, Steven Demetre. LC 74-3119. (Illus.). 40 p. 25cm. 1974, c.1972. Four Winds Press.

Stevens, Clifford J (1928-)
--Wild Dogs of Chongdo. McIlrath, James, illus. LC 79-84745. (Illus.). 79 p. 21cm. c.1979. (ISBN 0-87973-301-2). Our Sunday Visitor.

Stevens, Dinah
--Tomboy. Scott, Arthur O., illus. LC 30-21330. 3 p. l., 277, 1 p. front., illus. 20 cm. 1930. D. Appleton and Company.

Stevens, E. Mary
--Here Comes Joe. Julian-Ottie, Vanessa, illus. 1984. Faber and Faber.

Stevens, Eden Vale
--Abba. LC 62-10251. (Illus.). 21cm. 116p. 1962. Atheneum.
--Abba. 1st ed. Stevens, Anthony, illus. LC 62-10251. 93 p. illus. 21 cm. 1957. Judson Press.
--The Piper. LC 63-10377. 85 p. illus. 24 cm. 1964. Atheneum.

Stevens, Elizabeth Welty
--Ann of Bar Ton Ranch. Suba, Susanne (1913-), illus. LC 38-27674. 5 p. l., 3-196 p. illus. 21 cm. 1938. A. A. Knopf.

Stevens, Harry
--Who's That?. LC 83-80437. (Illus.). 16 p. c.1983. (ISBN 0-88332-294-3). Larousse.

Stevens, James F. (1892-1971)
--Paul Bunyan. 1925. Alfred A. Knopf.
--Paul Bunyan. Lewis, Allen, illus. (Illus.). (gr. 7 up). 1948. (ISBN 0-394-44005-6). Knopf.
--Paul Bunyan's Bears. LC 47-11588. 7 l., 1-129 p. illus. 28 cm. 1947. F. McCaffrey Publishers.
--Tree Treasure, a Conservation Story. A Conservation Story. Norling, Ernest Ralph (1892-), illus. LC 50-11508. (Illus.). 83 p. 29cm. 1950. Binfords & Mort.

Stevens, Janet, adapted by.
--Animal Fair. Stevens, Janet, illus. LC 80-8809. (Illus.). 32 p. 24cm. c.1981. (ISBN 0-8234-0388-2). Holiday House.
--The House that Jack Built: A Mother Goose Nursery Rhyme. Stevens, Janet, illus. LC 84-15832. (Illus.). 32p. (ps-2). 1985. (ISBN 0-8234-0548-6). Holiday.
--The Tortoise & the Hare: An Aesop Fable. Stevens, Janet, illus. LC 83-18668. (Original Author: Aesop). (Illus.). 32p. (ps-3). 1984. (ISBN 0-8234-0510-9). Mar. 1985. (ISBN 0-8234-0564-8). Holiday.

Stevens, Janet, adapted by see Andersen, Hans Christian.

Stevens, Kathleen
--The Beast in the Bathtub. north american ed. Bowler, Ray, illus. LC 85-12691. (Illus.). 30 p. 1985. (ISBN 0-918831-15-6). G. Stevens.
--Molly, McCullough, & Tom the Rogue. Zemach, Margot (1931-), illus. LC 82-45584. (Illus.). 32p. (gr. 2-6). 1983. (ISBN 0-690-04295-7, TYC-J). (ISBN 0-690-04296-5). Har-Row.

Stevens, Leonard A. (1920-)
--Old Pepperass: The Locomotive That Climbed Mount Washington. Kramer, Frank, illus. LC 59-10567. 233 p. illus. 21 cm. 1959. Dodd, Mead.

Stevens, Lillian O., ed. see Malory, Thomas, Sir.

Stevens, Lucile Vernon (1899-)
--The Redbird Affair. LC 75-305291. 189 p. 21cm. 1974. Avalon Books.

Stevens, Margaret M.
--Stepping Stones for Little Feet. Stevens, David S., illus. (Illus.). 31p. 1st U.S. edition. (gr. 4-6). 1975. De Vorss.
--Stepping Stones Three. Stevens, David S., illus. (Illus.). 32p. (gr. 1-8). 1983. (ISBN 0-87516-518-4). De Vorss.
--When Grandpa Died. Ualand, Kenneth, illus. LC 78-12360. p. cm. 1979. (ISBN 0-516-02025-0). Childrens Press.

Stevens, Mark, adapted by see Forrest, Hal.

Stevens, Mary C.
--Marjory with the Chamorros. LC 7-12000. 3 p. l., 5-73 p. front., illus. 19 1/2cm. c.1907. American Tract Society.

Stevens, Mary E. (1920-1966), ed. see Tatham, Julie Campbell.

Stevens, Mary Ellen, jt. auth. see Sayles, Edwin Booth.

Stevens, Mary Ellen & Sayles, Edwin Booth (1892-)
--Little Cloud and the Great Plains Hunters: Fifteen Thousand Years Ago. Wright, Barton, illus. LC 62-7502. 155 p. illus. 24 cm. 1962. Reilly & Lee.

Stevens, Norma Young (1927-)
--Go Out with Joy. LC 66-19905. 126p. 20cm. 1966. Broadman.

Stevens, Peter
--The Noisy Baby Animals. Thomas, Glen, illus. LC 55-268098. (Illus.). unpaged. 21cm. (Magic talking books, T-7). 1955. Winston.

Stevens, Reba Mahan, Mrs.
--Old Town Clock and Other Stories. Young, Florence Liley, illus. LC 31-24066. 157 p. col. front., illus. 22 cm. c.1931. Lothrop, Lee & Shepard Co.

Stevens, Richard M
--Zipper the Zany: The Little Cat Who Tried to Write a Book. Stevens, Richard M., illus. LC 45-106431. 47 p. incl. front., illus. 20 x 19 cm. c.1945. Wm. Penn Publishing Corp.

Stevens, Robley D., jt. auth. see Manger, Maryland.

Stevens, S. K., jt. auth. see Wallower, Lucille.

Stevens, S. S.
--Red Ryder and the Secret of Wolf Canyon. Harman, Fred, created by. LC 41-186213. 3 p. l., 11-220 p. incl. 1 illus., plates. 21 cm. c.1941. Whitman Publishing Company.

Stevens, Thomas
--Children of the World, from A to Z. Collins, Alice Hesslien (1907-), illus. LC 3-23864. 56 p. 26 col. pl. 28 1/2cm. 1903. R. H. Russell.

Stevens, William Oliver (1878-1955)
--Drummer Boy of Burma. Stevens, William Oliver (1878-1955), illus. LC 43-91919. 5 p. l., 277 p. illus. (incl. map) 21 cm. 1943. Dodd, Mead & Company.
--Messmates: Midshipman "Pewee" Clinton's First Cruise. Thomson, William T., illus. LC 13-210602. 364 p. incl. front. plates. 20 cm. 1913. J. B. Lippincott Company.
--Pewee" Clinton, Plebe: A Story of Annapolis. Pullinger, Herbert, illus. LC 12-24239. 310, 1 p. front., plates. 20 cm. 1912. J. B. Lippincott Company.

Stevens, William Oliver (1878-1955) & Barclay, McKee
--The Young Privateersman. LC 10-217521. vii, 1 p., 2 l., 311, 1 p. col. front., col. plates. 20 cm. 1910. D. Appleton and Company.

Stevenson, Augusta (1869-1976)
--Abe Lincoln, Frontier Boy. Funk, Clotilde Embree, illus. LC 53-723. 186p. illus. 20cm. (The Childhood of Famous Americans series). 1953. Bobbs-Merrill.
--Abe Lincoln, Frontier Boy. Funk, Clotilde Embree, illus. LC 32-23559. 186, 1 p. illus. 20 cm. c.1932. The Bobbs-Merrill Company.
--Abe Lincoln, Frontier Boy. Robinson, Jerry, illus. LC 59-13991. 192 p. illus. 20 cm. (Childhood of Famous Americans). 1959. Bobbs-Merrill.
--An Indian Boy's Pet, and Other Plays. (Children's Classics in Dramatic Form: Bk. I). N.D. Houghton Mifflin Co.
--Andy Jackson, Boy Soldier. Laune, Paul Sidney (1899-), illus. LC 52-3870. 196 p. illus. 20 cm. (Childhood of Famous Americans Series). 1952. Bobbs-Merrill.
--Andy Jackson, Boy Soldier. Laune, Paul Sidney (1899-), illus. LC 42-187212. 6 p. l., 11-196 p. illus. 20 cm. (The Boyhood of Famous Americans Series). 1942. The Bobbs-Merrill Company.
--Andy Jackson, Boy Soldier. Nankivel, Claudine, illus. LC 60-7714. 200 p. illus. 20 cm. (Childhood of Famous Americans). 1962. Bobbs-Merrill.
--Anthony Wayne, Daring Boy. Laune, Paul Sidney (1899-), illus. LC 48-8457. 186 p. illus. 20 cm. (The Childhood of Famous Americans Series). 1948. Bobbs-Merrill Co.
--Anthony Wayne, Daring Boy. Morrow, Gray, illus. LC 62-12705. 200 p. illus. 20 cm. (Childhood of Famous Americans). 1962. Bobbs-Merrill.
--Ben Franklin, Boy Printer. Quigley, Ray, illus. LC 60-7723. 200p. col. illus. 20cm. (Childhood of Famous Americans). 1962. Bobbs.
--Ben Franklin, Printer's Boy. Laune, Paul Sidney (1899-), illus. LC 53-721. 176p. illus. 20cm. (The Childhood of Famous Americans Series). 1953. Bobbs-Merrill.
--The Black Pearl, and Other Plays. (Children's Classics Dramatic Form: Bk. 5). N.D. Houghton Mifflin Co.
--Booker T. Washington, ambitious boy. Bolden, Melvin Reed (1919-), illus. LC 59-13993. 192 p. illus. 20cm. 1960. Bobbs-Merrill.
--Booker T. Washington, Ambitious Boy. 1st ed. John, Charles V., illus. LC 50-14744. 199 p. illus. 20 cm. (The Childhood of Famous Americans series). 1950. Bobbs-Merrill.
--Buffalo Bill: Boy of the Plains. Dreany, E. Joseph, illus. LC 59-13994. 192 p. illus. 20 cm. (Childhood of famous Americans Series). 1959. Bobbs-Merrill.
--Buffalo Bill, Boy of the Plains. 1st ed. Laune, Paul Sidney (1899-), illus. LC 48-5748. 189 p. illus. 20 cm. (The Childhood of Famous Americans Series). 1948. Bobbs-Merrill Co.
--Clara Barton, Girl Nurse. Giacoia, Frank, illus. LC 62-9247. 200 p. illus. 20 cm. (Childhood of famous Americans). 1962. Bobbs-Merrill.
--Daniel Boone: Boy Hunter. Doremus, Robert (1913-), illus. LC 60-7709. 200 p. illus. 20 cm. (Childhood of famous Americans Ser.). c.1961. Bobbs-Merrill.
--Daniel Boone, Boy Hunter. Laune, Paul Sidney (1899-), illus. LC 43-13936. 194 p. illus. 19 1/2 x 15 1/2 cm. (The Childhood of famous Americans series). 1943. The Bobbs-Merrill Company.
--Francis Scott Key, Maryland Boy. Morrow, Gray, illus. LC 60-14835. 192 p. illus. 20 cm. (Childhood of Famous Americans). c.1960. Bobbs-Merrill.
--George Carver, Boy Scientist. Funk, Clotilde Embree, illus. LC 52-3871. 202 p. illus. 20 cm. (Childhood of Famous Americans Series). 1952. Bobbs-Merrill.
--George Carver, Boy Scientist. Wood, Wallace, illus. LC 59-13995. (Illus.). 192 p. 20cm. (Childhood of Famous Americans). 1959. Bobbs-Merrill.
--George Custer, Boy of Action. Fiorentino, Al, illus. LC 63-1312. (Illus.). 200 p. 20cm. (Childhood of Famous Americans). 1963. Bobbs-Merrill.
--George Washington: Boy Leader. Dreany, E. Joseph, illus. LC 59-12852. 200 p. illus. 20 cm. (Childhood of famous Americans Series). 1959. Bobbs-Merrill.
--George Washington, Boy Leader. Dresser, Lawrence T., illus. LC 53-722. 184p. illus. 20cm. (The Childhood of Famous Americans Series). 1953. Bobbs-Merrill.
--George Washington, Boy Leader. Dresser, Lawrence T., illus. LC 42-21760. ix p., 1 l., 13-184 p. illus. 20 cm. (The Boyhood of Famous Americans Series). 1942. The Bobbs-Merrill Company.
--The Hole in the Dike, and Other Plays. (Children's Classics in Dramatic Form: Bk. 2). N.D. Houghton Mifflin Co.
--Israel Putnam, Fearless Boy. Robinson, Jerry, illus. LC 59-12853. (Illus.). 192 p. 20cm. (Childhood of Famous Americans). 1959. Bobbs-Merill.
--Kit Carson: Boy Trapper. Doremus, Robert (1913-), illus. LC 62-9252. 200 p. illus. 20 cm. (Childhood of famous Americans Series). 1962. Bobbs-Merrill.
--Kit Carson, Boy Trapper. Laune, Paul Sidney (1899-), illus. LC 45-6320. 195 p. illus. 20 cm. (The Childhood of Famous Americans Series). 1945. The Bobbs-Merrill Company.

Stevenson, Peter (1953-)
--Braithwaite's Original Brass Band. LC 80-18065. (Illus.). 32 p. 26cm. 1981. (ISBN 0-7232-6193-8). F. Warne.
Stevenson, Peter (1953-), illus.
--My Big Book of Nursery Rhymes. LC 82-81486. (Illus.). 127 p. 29cm. c.1982. (ISBN 0-88332-284-6). Larousse.
Stevenson, Ralph L, Jr.
--Sam's Stamp Store. Wolgamott, Elizabeth, illus. O'Neil, Greg, intro. by. (Illus.). 28p. (Orig.). (ps-2). 1983. (ISBN 0-9610762-0-8). Sirius Leag.
Stevenson, Richard.
--Wilderness Road Virginia. Clugston, Katharine Thatcher, adapted by. Laune, Paul Sidney (1899-), illus. LC 37-7080. viii p., 1 l., 309, 1 p. incl. front., illus., plates. 20 1/2 cm. c.1937. Blue Ribbon Books, Inc.
Stevenson, Robert Louis, et al. (1850-1894)
--Monster Masterpieces, 3 bks. 1980. (ISBN 0-307-13621-3, Golden Pr). Western Pub.
Stevenson, Robert Louis, jt. auth. see Lindskoog, Kathryn Ann.
Stevenson, Robert Louis, jt. auth. see Radnor, Marvin.
Stevenson, Robert Louis (1850-1894)
--An Inland Voyage and Travels with a Donkey. LC 13-22445. 278p. (Everymnan's Library). c.1913. E. P. Dutton & Co.
--Black Arrow. N.D. David McKay Co.
--Black Arrow. N.D. Grosset & Dunlap.
--The Black Arrow. Carlin, Jerome (1913-) & Christ, Henry Irving (1915-), eds. LC 47-29673. (Illus.). 21cm. 263p. 1947. Globe Book Co.
--The Black Arrow. Edwards, Lionel Dalhousie Robertson (1878-), illus. (Illus.). 21 cm. 278p. (Children's Illustrated Classics). 1958. E. P. Dutton & Co.
--The Black Arrow. Irwin, Don, illus. LC 78-110033. (Illus.). 256 p. 29cm. 1970, c.1969. Childrens Press.
--The Black Arrow. Low, Will & Brennan, Alfred, illus. N.D. Charles Scribner's Sons.
--The Black Arrow. Wyeth, Newell Convers (1882-1945), illus. (The Scribner Illustrated Classics). 1955. Charles Scribner's Sons.
--Catriona. Matthew, Jack (1911-), illus. 326p. 1947. Oxford University Press.
--A Chil'd Garden of Verses. (Nelson Classics). N.D. Thomas Nelson & Sons.
--A Child is Garden of Verses. LC 9-2513. 76p. 1909. C. Scribners' & Son.
--A Child's Garden of Verse. Owens, Annie, illus. LC 85-12389. 1985. (ISBN 0-517-55823-8). C. N. Potter: Dist. by Crown Publishers.
--A Child's Garden of Verse. Pease, Bessie Collins, illus. (Illus.). 21 cm. 113p. (Brown Book Ser.). 1905. Dodge.
--A Child's Garden of Verse. Shilabeer, Mary Eleanor (1904-) & Stevenson, Robert Louis (1850-1894), illus. (Illus.). 21 cm. 127p. (Children's Illustrated Classics: 47). N.D. E. P. Dutton & Co.
--A Child's Garden of Verse. Squire, Maud Hunt (1873-) & Mars, Ethel (1876-), illus. N.D. R. H. Russell.
--A Child's Garden of Verse and Other Poems. (Illus.). 127 p. 21cm. (Classics to grow on). 1966, c.1964. Parents' Magazine's Cultural Institute.
--A Child's Garden Of Verses. (The Sue Seeley Edition). N.D. A. Whitman & Co.
--A Child's Garden of Verses. (Embassy Ser.). N.D. Barse & Hopkins.
--A Child's Garden of Verses. (Traymore Ser.). N.D. Barse & Hopkins.
--A Child's Garden of Verses. (Savoy Ser.). N.D. Barse & Hopkins.
--A Child's Garden of Verses. (Blackstone Ser.). N.D. Barse & Hopkins.
--A Child's Garden of Verses. LC 40-28546. 17 cm. 92p. N.D. Barse & Hopkins.
--A Child's Garden of Verses. (Illus.). 20cm. (Commodore Ser.). N.D. Barse & Hopkins.
--A Child's Garden of Verses. (Illus.). (Netherland Ser.). N.D. Barse and Hopkins.
--A Child's Garden of Verses. (Illus.). (The Golden Books). N.D. Barse and Hopkins.
--A Child's Garden of Verses. (Illus.). (Biltmore Ser.). N.D. Barse and Hopkins.
--A Child's Garden of Verses. (Illus.). (Regis Ser.). N.D. Barse and Hopkins.
--A Child's Garden of Verses. (Illus.). (New Retlaw Ser.). N.D. Barse and Hopkins.
--A Child's Garden of Verses. (Illus.). (New Relyea Classics). N.D. Barse and Hopkins.
--A Child's Garden of Verses. (Illus.). (New Drexel Ser.). N.D. Barse and Hopkins.
--A Child's Garden of Verses. (Illus.). (Aberdeen Ser.). N.D. Barse and Hopkins.
--A Child's Garden of Verses. (Illus.). (Blenheim Ser.). N.D. Barse and Hopkins.
--A Child's Garden of Verses. (Illus.). (Knickerbocker Ser.). N.D. Barse and Hopkins.
--A Child's Garden of Verses. (Illus.). (Elberon Ser.). N.D. Barse and Hopkins.
--A Child's Garden of Verses. (Illus.). (Pleasant Hour Ser.). N.D. Barse and Hopkins.
--A Child's Garden of Verses. (Dagonet Ser.). N.D. Barse & Hopkins.
--A Child's Garden of Verses. (Illus.). (The Rainy Day Ser.). N.D. Barse & Hopkins.
--A Child's Garden of Verses. Author's ed. LC 1-10090. ix, 101 p. 19 cm. 1885. C. Scribner's Sons.
--A Child's Garden of Verses. LC 13-22845. 20cm. 113p. 1913. C. Scribner's Sons.
--A Child's Garden of Verses. (Illus.). (The Alcazar Classics). N.D. Caldwell.
--A Child's Garden of Verses. 1974. (ISBN 0-8098-1902-3). David McKay.
--A Child's Garden of Verses. (The Rose Ser.). N.D. Dodge Publishing Company.
--A Child's Garden of Verses. (Illus.). N.D. George W Jacobs & Co.
--A Child's Garden of Verses. LC 2-20656. (Illus.). 164p. (Altemus' Young People's Library). 1902. H. Altemus Co.
--A Child's Garden of Verses, 25 vols. (Illus.). (The Editha Ser.: No. 7). 1905. Set. H M Caldwell Co.
--A Child's Garden of Verses. (Illus.). (The Empyreal Library of Handy Volume Classics). N.D. H. M. Caldwell Co.
--A Child's Garden of Verses. (Illus.). (The Young Folks Lib.). N.D. H. M. Caldwell Co.
--A Child's Garden of Verses. (Illus.). (The Exquisite Ser.). N.D. H. M. Caldwell Co.
--A Child's Garden of Verses. (Illus.). (The Chateau Series). N.D. H. M. Caldwell Co.
--A Child's Garden of Verses. (Harper's Selected Juveniles). N.D. Harper & Brothers.
--A Child's Garden of Verses. (Illus.). 17 cm. 164p. (Altemus' Young People's Library). 1902. Henry Altemus Company.
--A Child's Garden of Verses. 20 cm. 141p. (Altemus' Illustrated Boys' and Girls' Classics). N.D. Henry Altemus Company.
--A Child's Garden of Verses. (Altemus' Wyncote Ser.). N.D. Henry Altemus Co.
--A Child's Garden of Verses. (Illus.). (Altemus Vademecum Ser.). N.D. Henry Altemus Co.
--A Child's Garden of Verses. (Illus.). (Boys' and Girls' Classics). N.D. Henry Altemus Co.
--A Child's Garden of Verses. (Illus.). (Petit-Trainon). N.D. Henry Altemus Co.
--A Child's Garden of Verses. (Illus.). (Beauxarts Ser.). N.D. Henry Altemus Co.
--A Child's Garden of Verses. (The Child's Garden of Charming Bks.). N.D. J. C. Winston Co.
--A Child's Garden of Verses. (The Children's Classics). N.D. J.B. Lippincott.
--A Child's Garden of Verses. (Sears Juvenile Classics). N.D. J.H.Sears & Co.
--A Child's Garden of Verses. (Cosy Corner Ser.). N.D. L. C. Page & Co.
--A Child's Garden of Verses. N.D. Parents' Magazine Press.
--A Child's Garden of Verses. (Popular Story Ser.). N.D. Platt & Munk Co.
--A Child's Garden of Verses. LC 4-31123. 18 x 10cm. 87p. (Old World Ser.). 1899. T. B. Mosher.
--A Child's Garden of Verses. (Illus.). (Children's Home Library). 1915. T Y Crowell.
--A Child's Garden of Verses. (The Treasury Series for Children). N.D. Thomas Y. Crowell Co.
--A Child's Garden of Verses. N.D. William Collins Sons & Co Ltd.
--A Child's Garden of Verses. (Classic Ser.). N.D. World Publishing Co.
--A Child's Garden of Verses. Adams, Will & Drake, John, eds. Le Mair, Henriette Willebeek (1889-1966), illus. Myers, Helen Elizabeth (1910-), contrib. by. LC 40-29659. (A Talking book directed by John Drake and Will Adams, with Original Music by Helen Myers, as sung by Josephine Therese, recorded by R. C. A.). 1 p. l., 1, 16, 1 p. col. illus. 27 x 26 cm. c.1940. David McKay Company.
--A Child's Garden of Verses. Barry, Etheldred Breeze (1870-), illus. LC 1-29124. 19cm. 107p. (Cosy Corner Ser.). 1900. L. C. Page & Co.
--A Child's Garden of Verses. Barry, Etheldred Breeze (1870-), illus. (Illus.). 181/2cm. 107p. (Cosy Corner Ser.). 1930. L. C. Page & Co.
--A Child's Garden of Verses. Bennett, Juanita C., illus. (Illus.). 21x24 cm. 24p. c.1938. Grosset & Dunlap.
--A Child's Garden of Verses. Blegvad, Erik (1923-), illus. 1978. Random.
--A Child's Garden of Verses. Brice, Tony, illus. LC 42-17479. 2 p. l., 7-63 p. col. illus. 17 cm. 1942. Rand McNally & Company.
--A Child's Garden of Verses. Brundage, Frances, illus. LC 25-3335. 306p. (The Companion Ser.). c.1924. The Saalfield Pub. Co.
--A Child's Garden of Verses. Comstock, Frances Bassett & Comstock, Enos Benjamin (1879-1945), illus. LC 9-16209. 26 x 22cm. 91p. c.1909. McLoughlin Brothers Co.
--A Child's Garden of Verses. Davis, Marguerite (1889-), illus. LC 27-22677. 17cm. 121p. 1927. The Macmillan Co.
--A Child's Garden of Verses. Duvoisin, Roger Antoine (1904-1980), illus. 112p. N.D. Heritage Press.
--A Child's Garden of Verses. Eulalie, pseud. (1896-), illus. Banks, Eulalie M.. LC 29-25765. 19cm. 85p. c.1929. Platt & Munk Co.
--A Child's Garden of Verses. Eulalie, pseud. (1896-), illus. Banks, Eulalie M.. (Illus.). 19 cm. 84p. c.1932. Platt & Munk Co.
--A Child's Garden of Verses. Foreman, Michael (1938-), illus. LC 85-13173. (Illus.). 124 p. 24cm. c.1985. (ISBN 0-385-29430-1). Delacorte Press.
--A Child's Garden of Verses. Fujikawa, Gyo, illus. LC 57-13979. (Illus.). 31 cm. 104p. c.1957. Grosset & Dunlap.
--A Child's Garden of Verses. Fujikawa, Gyo, illus. LC 64-56675. 3 v. illus. (part col.) 12 cm. 1964. Grosset & Dunlap.
--A Child's Garden of Verses. Fujikawa, Gyo, illus. 1957. Putnam.
--A Child's Garden of Verses. Hallock, Ruth Mary (1876-), illus. LC 19-13565. 27cm. 96p. 1919. Rand, McNally & Co.
--A Child's Garden of Verses. Hix, Melvin, selected by. LC 10-22286. 20cm. 97p. (Golden Hour Ser.). c.1910. Educational Publilshing Co.
--A Child's Garden of Verses. Kirk, Maria Louise (1860-), illus. LC 19-15777. 21cm. 191p. 1919. J. B. Lippincott Co.
--A Child's Garden of Verses. Le Mair, Henriette Willebeek (1889-1966), illus. LC 27-1490. 89p. c.1926. David McKay Co.
--A Child's Garden of Verses. Le Mair, Henriette Willebeek (1889-1966), illus. (Illus.). 21 cm. 127p. c.1930. David McKay Co.
--A Child's Garden of Verses. Lerch, Steffie E. (1908-), illus. LC 48-6651. 32 p. illus. (part col.) 25 cm. 1948. Wilcox & Follett Co.
--A Child's Garden of Verses. McCracken ed. McCracken, James, illus. Seely, Sue, tr. (Illus.). 21 cm. 127p. c.1930. A. Whitman & Co.
--A Child's Garden of Verses. Mars, Ethel (1876-) & Squire, Maud Hunt (1873-), illus. LC 6102. 31 x 30cm. 115p. 1900. R. H. Russell.
--A Child's Garden of Verses. Mars, Ethel (1876-) & Squire, Maud Hunt (1873-), illus. LC 2-14131. 20cm. 93p. 1902. Rand McNally & Co.
--A Child's Garden of Verses. Merrill, Frank Thayer (1848-), illus. LC 18-21384. 18cm. 87p. c.1918. Thomas Y. Crowell.
--A Child's Garden of Verses. Noe, Eva, illus. LC 26-14413. 25cm. 243p. (Sears Illustrated Juveniles). c.1926. J. H. Sears & Co.
--A Child's Garden of Verses. O'Reilly, E. Dorothy, illus. LC 9-4559. 20cm. 131p. c.1908. A. Flanagan Co.
--A Child's Garden of Verses. O'Reilly, E. Dorothy, illus. LC 23-1011. 20cm. 130p. 1923. A. Flanagan Co.
--A Child's Garden of Verses. Owen, Annie LC 85-12101. p. cm. 1985. (ISBN 0-517-55855-6). C.N. Potter : Distributed by Crown Publishers.
--A Child's Garden of Verses. Pease, Bessie Collins, illus. LC 5-26237. 21cm. 113p. 1905. Dodge Publishing Co.
--A Child's Garden of Verses. Provensen, Alice (1918-) & Provensen, Martin (1916-), illus. LC 65-7407. (Illus.). 68 p. 29 cm. 1964, c.1951. Golden Press.
--A Child's Garden of Verses. Provensen, Alice (1918-) & Provensen, Martin (1916-), illus. LC 57-13979. (Illus.). 104 p. 31cm. 1973, c.1957. Grosset & Dunlap.
--A Child's Garden of Verses. Provensen, Alice (1918-) & Provensen, Martin (1916-), illus. LC 51-11454. 76 p. illus. 29 cm. 1951. Simon and Schuster.
--A Child's Garden of Verses. Robinson, Charles (1870-1937), illus. LC 6-30280. 20cm. 136p. 1894. C. Scribner's Sons.
--A Child's Garden of Verses. Robinson, Charles (1870-1937), illus. LC 1-10091. 32 p. illus. 20 cm. 1895. C. Scribner's Sons.
--A Child's Garden of Verses. Robinson, Charles (1870-1937), illus. LC 75-300509. (Illus.). 136 p., 1 leaf of plates. 20cm. 1895. Scribner.
--A Child's Garden of Verses. Robinson, Charles (1870-1937), illus. LC 78-65435. (Illus.). xiv, 136 p. 19cm. 1979. (ISBN 0-394-73686-9). Shambhala.
--A Child's Garden of Verses. Shillabeer, Mary (1904-) & Stevenson, Robert Louis (1850-1894), illus. LC 60-52206. (Illus.). 21cm. 127p. (Children's Illustrated Classics: No.47). 1960. Dutton.
--A Child's Garden of Verses. Smith, Jessie Willcox (1863-1935), illus. LC 5-33663. 25cm. 124p. 1905. C. Scribner's Sons.
--A Child's Garden of Verses. Smith, Jessie Willcox (1863-1935), illus. (Illus.). 24 cm. 105p. (The Scribner Illustrated Classics). N.D. Charles Scribner's Sons.
--A Child's Garden of Verses. Smith, Jessie Willcox (1863-1935) LC 85-12766. (Illus.). viii, 118 p., 8 p. of plates. 25cm. 1985. (ISBN 0-517-48924-4). Children's Classics ; Distributed by Crown Publishers.
--A Child's Garden of Verses. Sowerby, Millicent, illus. 23cm. 125p. (St. Martin's Library of Standard Authors). 1908. C. Scribner's Sons.
--A Child's Garden of Verses. Storer, Florence Edith, illus. LC 9-29816. 22cm. 115p. 1909. C. Scribner's Sons.
--A Child's Garden of Verses. Tapper, Thomas, ed. Barry, Etheldred Breeze (1870-), illus. LC 18-14499. 114p. (The Cosy Corner Ser.). 1918. The Page Co.
--A Child's Garden of Verses. Tudor, Tasha (1915-), illus. LC 59-8079. (Starling Burgess legally changed name to Tasha Tudor). 118 p. illus. 22 cm. 1959, c.1947. H. Z. Walck.
--A Child's Garden of Verses. Tudor, Tasha (1915-), illus. LC 47-30858. (Starling Burgess legally changed name to Tasha Tudor). 118 p. illus. (part col.) 22 cm. 1947. Oxford Univ. Press.
--A Child's Garden of Verses. Tudor, Tasha (1915-), illus. LC 81-7317. (Starling Burgess legally changed name to Tasha Tudor). p. cm. 1981. (ISBN 0-528-82401-5). (ISBN 0-528-80073-6). Rand McNally.
--A Child's Garden of Verses. Weekes, Blanche Ethel, intro. by. Russell, Dorothy E., illus. LC 28-14274. 21cm. 122p. c.1928. The John C. Winston Co.
--A Child's Garden of Verses, 1 cass, Vol. II. Wickwire, Nancy, read by. Incl. The Unseen Playmate; My Ship & I; My Kingdom; Armies in the Fire; The Little Land. (Includes the verses listed plus other). N.D (SAC 6035). Spoken Arts.
--A Child's Garden of Verses. Wiedenbeck, Emilie Agnes (1896-), illus. Mabie, Peter, pseud. LC 46-224467. 28 p. col. illus. 24 1/2 x 20 1/2 cm. 1946. James & Jonathan Co.
--A Child's Garden of Verses. Wildsmith, Brian Lawrence (1930-), illus. LC 66-11213. (Illus.). 29cm. 96p. 1966. F. Watts.
--A Child's Garden of Verses. Wildsmith, Brian Lawrence (1930-), illus. LC 66-78512. (Illus.). 96 p. 29cm. 1966. Oxford U.P.
--A Child's Garden of Verses. Wildsmith, Brian Lawrence (1930-), illus. LC 66-11213. 96p. col. illus. 29cm. 1966. Watts. **Award: (ALA).**
--A Child's Garden of Verses. Wilkin, Eloise Burns (1904-), selected by. Wilkin, Eloise Burns (1904-), illus. LC 57-1222. unpaged. illus. 21cm. (Little Golden Bk, 289). 1957. Simon and Schuster.
--A Child's Garden of Verses. Wilson, Joyce Lancaster, illus. LC 1-29124. ix p., 1 l., 107 p. incl. illus., plates. front. 19 cm. (On cover: Cosy Corner Ser.). 1900. L. C. Page & Company.
--A Child's Garden of Verses, and Other Poems. LC 64-15711. (Illus.). 21cm. 127p. 1964. Parent's Magazine Cultural Institute.
--A Child's Garden of Verses and Other Poems. Robinson, Charles (1870-1937), illus. 127p. 1966. Parents' Magazine Press.
--A Child's Garden of Verses and Underwoods. (Illus.). N.D. Herbert B. Turner & Co.
--A Child's Garden of Verses and Underwoods. N.D. Small Maynard & Co.
--A Child's Garden of Verses and Underwoods. medallion. Harvey, Alexander (1868-), illus. LC 6-42417. lxiii, 101 p., 3 l., 5-134 p. front. (port.) 17 cm. 1906. Current Literature Publishing Co.
--A Child's Garden of Verses: Selected Poems. Kalish, Lionel, illus. LC 63-9162. 1v. (unpaged) col. illus. 22cm. (Harlin Quist bk.). 1965, c.1964. Delacorte Pr., Dist. Dial.
--A Child's Garden of Verses: Selections from Robert L. Stevenson. Provensen, Alice (1918-) & Provensen, Martin (1916-), illus. (gr. 3-6). 1975. (ISBN 0-307-10873-2, Golden Pr). Western Pub.
--A Child's Garden of Verses Underwoods Ballads. LC 5-30076. 18cm. 317p. (The Bibliographical Edition of the Works of Robert Louis Stevenson). 1905. C. Scribner's Sons.
--A Child's Garden of Verses: With Nine Poems Not Published in Prior Editions. Wilson, Joyce Lancaster, illus. Smith, Janet Adam, intro. by. LC 77-92195. (Illus.). 114 p. 26cm. 1978. (ISBN 0-915918-04-8). Press in Tuscany Alley.
--A Child's Garden Verses. Shillabeer, Mary Eleanor (1904-), illus. (Children's Illustrated Classics). N.D. E. P. Dutton & Co.
--A Child's Garden Verses. Wilkin, Eloise Burns (1904-), illus. (Little Golden Book). 1957. Golden Press.
--The Complete Poems of Robert Louis Stevenson. LC 23-17137. 528. 1923. C. Scribner's Sons.
--Daisies from Stevenson's Child's Garden Verse. (Flower and Gem Ser.). N.D. DeWolfe, Fiske & Co.

--Doctor Jekyll & Mister Hyde & Other Stories. (gr. 8 up). N.D. (ISBN 0-590-08525-5, Schol Pap). Scholastic Inc.
--A Dog of Flanders. (Illus.). (McKay's Young People's Classics). N.D. David McKay.
--Dr. Jekyll and Mr. Hyde. (Burt's Home Library). N.D. A L Burt Co.
--Dr. Jekyll and Mr. Hyde. (Christmas Classics). N.D. Barse & Hopkins.
--Dr. Jekyll & Mr. Hyde. (gr. 3 up). 1978. (ISBN 0-448-41110-5, G&D). Putnam Pub Group.
--Dr. Jekyll & Mr. Hyde. Elias, Horace Jay (1910-), adapted by. (Illus.). (gr. 5 up). 1976. (ISBN 0-06-465053-7, PBN). B&N Imports.
--Dr. Jekyll & Mr. Hyde. new ed. Platt, Kin (1911-), ed. Redondo, Nestor, illus. LC 73-75457. (Illus.). footnotes. 64p. (Orig.). (New Age Illustrated Ser.). (gr. 4-12). 1979. (ISBN 0-88301-202-2). (ISBN 0-88301-096-8). (ISBN 0-88301-176-X). Pendulum Pr.
--Escape at Bedtime and Other Poems. O'Reilly, E. Dorothy, illus. LC 24-234. 32 p. illus. 18 cm. (On cover: The little classic Ser.). 1922. A. Flanagan Company.
--I Have a Little Shadow" "My Shadow" and Other Selections from A Child's Garden of Verses. LC 29-15317. (Illus.). 32cm. 34p. 1929. C. L. Graham & Co.
--In the South Seas & Island Nights' Entertainments. 339p. (Everyman's Library). 1925. E. P. Dutton.
--Island Nights' Entertainments. (Nelson Classics). N.D. Thomas Nelson & Sons.
--Kidnapped. N.D. A. L. Burt Co.
--Kidnapped. (Illus.). 1st U.S. edition. Repr. of 1960 ed. (Childrens Illustrated Classics Ser.). 1974. (ISBN 0-460-05015-1, Pub. by J. M Dent England). Biblio Dist.
--Kidnapped. N.D. David McKay Co.
--Kidnapped. (Great Illustrated Classics). N.D. Dodd, Mead & Co.
--Kidnapped. N.D. Garden City Publishing Co.
--Kidnapped. (Washington Square Classics Ser.). N.D. George W Jacobs.
--Kidnapped. (Every Boy's Library). N.D. Grosset & Dunlap.
--Kidnapped. (Illus.). (Boys' and Girls' Classics). N.D. Henry Altemus Co.
--Kidnapped. (Fiction). (MacMillan Bks. for Boys & Girls). (gr. 7-9). N.D. MacMillan Bks.
--Kidnapped. (The Washington Square Classics). N.D. Macrae Smith.
--Kidnapped. 318p. (The Lake English Classics). N.D. Scott Foresman & Co.
--Kidnapped. (The Nelson Classics). N.D. Thomas Nelson & Sons.
--Kidnapped. DuBois, Gaylord, adapted by. Schmidt, Al, illus. (A Golden Reading Adventure). 1960. Golden Press.
--Kidnapped. Godwin, Frank (1889-), illus. Kaufmann, Myrtle S., intro. by. (The Children's Book-Shelf). N.D. J. C. Winston Co.
--Kidnapped. Irwin, Don, illus. LC 74-79989. (Illus.). 29cm. 224p. 1969. Children's Press.
--Kidnapped. Oakley, George, illus. (Children's Illustrated Classics). N.D. E. P. Dutton & Co.
--Kidnapped. Pulliam, Roy Avron (1902-) & Darby, Oscar Nolan, eds. Rice, Elizabeth (1913-), illus. LC 50-12563. 207 p. illus. (part col.)23 cm. (Teasure Book). 1949. Steck Co.
--Kidnapped. Rhead, Louis John (1857-1926) & Schoonover, Frank Earle (1877-1972), illus. (Rhead's Illustrated Juveniles). N.D. Harper & Bros.
--Kidnapped. Rice, Elizabeth (1913-), illus. Pulliam, R. A., adapted by. LC 50-12563. (Illus.). 23cm. 207p. 1949. Steck Co.
--Kidnapped. Sutton, Felix (1910-), abridged by. Glanzman, Louis S. (1922-), illus. LC 60-5164. 60 p. illus. 29 cm. 1960. Grosset & Dunlap.
--Kidnapped. 1st ed. White, Daniel D., illus. LC 74-79989. (Illus.). 224 p. 29cm. 1969. Childrens Press.
--Kidnapped. Wyeth, Newell Convers (1882-1945), illus. 1941. Scribner.
--Kidnapped. Wyeth, Newell Convers (1882-1945), illus. LC 73-169458. (Being Memoirs of the Adventures of David Balfour in the Year 1751). (Illus.). 289 p. 23cm. (Scribner Library). (The Scribner Illustrated Classics). 1973, c.1913. (ISBN 0-684-20951-9). (ISBN 0-684-13418-7). Scribner.
--Kidnapped: A World Famous Classic Simply Told. White, Daniel D., illus. LC 52-13680. 121p. illus. 22cm. (Pixie books). 1953. Winston.
--Kidnapped & Dr. Jekyll & Mr. Hyde. (Sears Juvenile Classics). N.D. J.H.Sears & Co.
--The Master of Ballantrae, 1 of 5 vols. (Robert Louis Stevenson's Wks.). N.D. Set. A. L. Burt's Pubs.
--The Master of Ballantrae. (Sears Juvenile Classics). N.D. J.H.Sears & Co.
--The Merry Men and Other Tales. (The Nelson Classics). N.D. Thomas Nelson & Sons.
--The Merry Men, and other tales and Fables. N.D. Charles Scribner.
--The Merry Men and Other Tales and Fables. N.D. Hurst & Co.
--The Merry Men and other Tales and Fables. (Illus.). (The Royal Ser.). N.D. The American News Co.
--The Moon. Saldutti, Denise, illus. (gr. k-2). 1984. Harper.
--Mother Goose Rhymes. (Illus.). (McKay's Young People's Classics). N.D. David McKay.
--My Shadow, and other Poems. O'Reilly, E. Dorothy, illus. 27 p. illus. 18cm. (The Little Classic Ser.). 1922. Flanagan Co.
--My Ship and I, and other Poems. O'Reilly, E. Dorothy, illus. LC 24-236. 31 p. ill. 18cm. (The Little Classic Ser.). 1922. Flanagan Co.
--My Treasure, and other Poems. O'Reilly, E. Dorothy, illus. LC 24-237. 31 p. ill. 18cm. (The Little Classic Ser.). 1922. A. Flanagan Co.
--New Arabian Nights. (The Nelson Classics) N.D. Thomas Nelson & Sons.
--The Nurnberg Stove. (Illus.). (McKay's Young People's Classics). N.D. David McKay.
--Nursery Tales. (Illus.). (McKay's Young People's Classics). N.D. David MCKay.
--Poems of Robert Louis Stevenson. Plotz, Helen, ed. Atterbery, Charles, illus. LC 72-78282. (Illus.). index. 128p. (Poets Ser.). (gr. 7 up). 1973. (ISBN 0-690-64395-0, TYC-J). Har-Row.
--A Provence Rose. (Illus.). (McKay's Young People's Classics). N.D. David McKay.
--Robert Louis Stevenson's A Child's Garden of Verses. Sanderson, Ruth, illus. LC 76-40721. (Illus.). 18 p. 32cm. (Cricket Book). c.1977. (ISBN 0-8228-6511-4). Platt and Munk.
--Selections from A Child's Garden of Verses. Ehrlich, Elizabeth, illus. LC 78-72100. (Illus.). 32 p. 23cm. 1979. (ISBN 0-89799-134-6). (ISBN 0-89799-055-2). Dandelion Press.
--Songs with Music: From 'A Child's Garden of Verses'. Tarrant, Margaret Winifred (1888-), illus. Crawford, Thomas (1860-), contrib. by. LC 37-18286. (Music by Rev. Thomas Crawford). 3 p. l., 9-55 p. illus. (part col.) 27 cm. 1936. T. Nelson & Sons.
--St. Ives: Being the Adventures of a French Prisoner in England. LC 5-30060. (Being the Adventures of a French Prisoner in England). xxvi, 528 p. 18 cm. (Half-title: The Biographical Edition of the Works of Robert Louis Stevenson). 1905. C. Scribner's Sons.
--Stevenson: Great Tales of Mystery & Adventure. (Great Writers Collection). (gr. 7 up). 1965. Platt.
--Stevenson's Poems, 1 of 88 vols. Oak Leaf ed. (Handy Volume Classics). N.D. T. Y. Crowell & Co.
--Stevenson's Poems, 1 of 56 vols. (Illus.). (The Faience Lib.). N.D. T. Y. Crowell & Co.
--Stevenson's Poems, 1 of 16 vols. (Illus.). (The Copley Ser.). N.D. T. Y. Crowell & Co.
--Stevenson's Stories for Boys. N.D. Cupples & Leon.
--Strange Case of Doctor Jekyll & Mister Hyde & Other Stories. (Illus.). 1961. (ISBN 0-399-20040-1). Putnam Pub Group.
--Strange Case of Dr. Jekyll & Mr. Hyde & Other Famous Tales. (Illus.). (Great Il. Classics). (gr. 9 up). 1979. Dodd.
--The Strange Case of Dr. Jekyll & Mr. Hyde. (Keith Jennison Large Type Bks). (gr. 6 up). N.D. (ISBN 0-531-00285-3). Watts.
--The Strange Case of Dr. Jekyll & Mr. Hyde. (gr. 3 up). 1981. (ISBN 0-307-21633-0, Golden Pr). Golden Pr. (ISBN 0-307-61633-9). Western Pub.
--Strange Case of Dr. Jekyll & Mr. Hyde. Schreiter, Rick (1936-), illus. (Illus.). (Illustrated Editions). (gr. 7 up). 1967. (ISBN 0-531-01081-3). Watts.
--The Suicide Club & Other Stories. (gr. 7-12). 1975. (ISBN 0-590-09829-2, Schol Pap). Schol Bk Serv.
--The Touchstone. Shulevitz, Uri (1935-), illus. LC 76-3412. 22cm. 47p. 1976. (ISBN 0-688-80051-3). (ISBN 0-688-84051-5). Greenwillow Books.
--Treasure Island. N.D. A. L. Burt Co.
--Treasure Island. (Illus.). (The Rugby Series for Boys). N.D. A. L. Burt's Pubs.
--Treasure Island. (Heirloom Library). N.D. Chanticleer Bks.
--Treasure Island. 310p. (Merrill's English Texts). N.D. Charles E Merrill.
--Treasure Island. (Scribner English Texts). N.D. Charles Scribner's Sons.
--Treasure Island. (Heath's English Classics Ser.). N.D. D C Heath.
--Treasure Island. 20cm. 280p. (The Golden Books for Children). 1917. D. McKay.
--Treasure Island. (Illus.). (McKay's Young People's Classics). N.D. David McKay.
--Treasure Island. N.D. Garden City Publishing Co.
--Treasure Island. (Washington Square Classics Ser.). N.D. George W Jacobs.
--Treasure Island. LC 71-186809. (Illus.). 28cm. 87p. 1971. (ISBN 0-8212-0469-6). Graphic Society.
--Treasure Island. (The Good Value Books). N.D. Grosset & Dunlap.
--Treasure Island. (Illus.). (The Young Folks Lib.). N.D. H. M. Caldwell Co.
--Treasure Island. N.D. Harper & Bros.
--Treasure Island. (English Readings Ser.). N.D. Henry Holt.
--Treasure Island. (Illus.). (Boys' and Girls' Classics). N.D. Henry Altemus Co.
--Treasure Island. LC 62-6064. 212 p. illus. 22 cm. (Riverside literature series, R4). 1962. Houghton Mifflin.
--Treasure Island, 1 of 64 vols. (Young America Library: No. 46). 1900. Set. Hurst & Co.
--Treasure Island. (Sears Juvenile Classics). N.D. J.H.Sears & Co.
--Treasure Island. (The Winston Clear-Type Popular Classics). N.D. John C. Winston.
--Treasure Island. (Longmans' English Classics). N.D. Longmans Green & Co.
--Treasure Island. (The Washington Square Classics). N.D. Macrae Smith.
--Treasure Island. N.D. Modern Library.
--Treasure Island. LC 71-186809. (Illus.). 87 p. 28cm. 1972. (ISBN 0-8212-0469-6). New York Graphic Society.
--Treasure Island. 18cm. 224p. 1966. Pyramid.
--Treasure Island. (Illus.). (Young People's Classics). N.D. R. F. Fenno & Co.
--Treasure Island. (Illus.). (The Junior Library Ser.: Vol. 17). N.D. Rand, McNally & Co.
--Treasure Island. 269p. (The Lake English Classics). N.D. Scott Foresman & Co.
--Treasure Island. (Children's Home Library). 1915. T Y Crowell.
--Treasure Island. (Children's Favorite Classics). N.D. Thomas Y. Crowell Company.
--Treasure Island. (Classic Ser.). N.D. World Publishing Co.
--Treasure Island. Boas, F., ed. Brock, Henry Matthew (1875-1960), illus. (Scholar's Library). N.D. St. Martin's Press.
--Treasure Island. 1st ed. Bolden, Joseph, illus. LC 52-6375. (Illus.). 22cm. 121p. (Winston Pixie Books). 1952. Winston.
--Treasure Island. Bown, Derick, illus. LC 78-3553. p. cm. (Raintree's illustrated classics). 1978. (ISBN 0-8393-6211-0). Raintree Childrens Books.
--Treasure Island. New ed. Burne, Harry H. A., illus. (The Father and Son Library). N.D. Sears Publishing Co.
--Treasure Island. Davenport, Basil, intro. by. (Great Illustrated Classics). N.D. Dodd, Mead & Co.
--Treasure Island. Dulac, Edmund (1882-1953), illus. LC 79-62919. (Illus.). 191 p. 32cm. 1979. (ISBN 0-913870-78-1). Abaris Books.
--Treasure Island. Gilles, Chuck, illus. LC 84-5249. p. cm. c.1984. (ISBN 0-671-52760-6). Wanderer Books.
--Treasure Island. Godwin, Frank (1889-), illus. (The Children's Bookshelf). N.D. John C. Winston.
--Treasure Island. Hogarth, Grace (1905-) & Ward, Lynd Kendall (1905-1985), illus. LC 71-106514. (Illus.). 216 p. 22cm. (Lifetime library). 1970. American Education Publications.
--Treasure Island. complete and unabridged. Irwin, Don, illus. LC 68-31323. (Illus.). 248 p. 29cm. 1968. Childrens Press.
--Treasure Island. Johnston, Johanna (1914-1982), abridged by. Frankenberg, Robert Clinton (1911-), illus. (Illus.). 88 p. 32cm. (Doubleday picture classic). 1960. Doubleday.
--Treasure Island. Kelsey, Charles W., illus. (Sears Illustrated Juveniles). N.D. Sears Publishing Co.
--Treasure Island. Law, Frederick H., ed. (Appleton English Classics). N.D. D. Appleton & Co.
--Treasure Island. McCann, Gerald (1916-), illus. LC 63-6900. (Illus.). 20 cm. 263p. (Companion Library). N.D. Grosset & Dunlap.
--Treasure Island. Newbolt, Henry (1911-), ed. (The Nelson Classics). N.D. Thomas Nelson & Sons.
--Treasure Island. a limited. Paget, Walter, illus. LC 78-105397. (Illus.). 302 p., 1 leaf of plates. 24cm. (The Collector's Library of the World's Best-Loved Books). 1978. Franklin Library.
--Treasure Island. Poskanzer, Susan Cornell, ed. LC 80-54133. (Illus.). 234, g48 p., 1 p. of plates. 18cm. (A Silver Classic). c.1982. (ISBN 0-382-03436-8). Silver Burdett Co.
--Treasure Island. Reid, Stephen (1873-1934), illus. 320p. N.D. Thomas Y. Crowell Co.
--Treasure Island. Rhead, Louis John (1857-1926) & Schoonover, Frank Earle (1877-1972), illus. (Rhead's Illustrated Juveniles). N.D. Harper & Bros.
--Treasure Island. Richards, E. B., intro. by. (The Winston Companion Classics). N.D. J. C. Winston Co.
--Treasure Island. Schmid, Eleonore (1939-), illus. LC 76-46293. (Illus.). 87 p., 7 leaves of plates. 26cm. 1977. (ISBN 0-679-20393-1). D. McKay Co.
--Treasure Island. Van Abbe, Salaman (1883-1955), illus. (Children's Illustrated Classics). N.D. E. P. Dutton & Co.
--Treasure Island. West, Michael, ed. Paget, Walter, illus. LC 52-503339. 160 p. illus. 19 cm. 1937. Longmans, Green.
--Treasure Island. White, Anne Terry (1896-), abridged by. Greene, Hamilton, illus. LC 56-14164. 96p. col. illus., col. maps. 27cm. (Golden picture classics, CL-101-69). 1956. Simon and Schuster.
--Treasure Island. Wilson, Charles Banks (1918-), illus. (The Lippincott Classics). 1948. J. B. Lippincott Co.
--Treasure Island. Wilson, Edward Arthur (1886-), illus. 304p. N.D. Heritage Press.
--Treasure Island. Winter, Milo Kendall (1888-1956) & Dulac, Edmund (1882-1953), illus. LC 85-17457. p. cm. 1986, c.1985. Children's Classics.
--Treasure Island. Winter, Milo Kendall (1888-1956), illus. (Windermere Ser.). N.D. Rand McNally.
--Treasure Island. Wyeth, Newell Convers (1882-1945), illus. 1939. Scribner.
--Treasure Island. Anniversary ed. Wyeth, Newell Convers (1882-1945), illus. LC 81-8788. p. cm. 1981. (ISBN 0-684-17160-0). Scribner.
--Treasure Island. Wyeth, Newell Convers (1882-1945), illus. LC 73-169457. (Illus.). 251 p. 23cm. (Scribner Library). (The Scribner Illustrated Classics). N.D. Scribner.
--Treasure Island. A World-Famous Classic Simply Told. 1st ed. Rolden, Joseph, illus. LC 52-6375. 121 p. illus. 22 cm. (Winston Pixie Books). 1952. Winston.
--Treasure Island and Kidnapped. (The People's Library). N.D. Funk & Wagnalls.
--Treasure Island and Kidnapped. 652p. N.D. J. C. Winston Co.
--Underwoods. N.D. Thomas B Mosher.

Stevenson, Robert Louis (1850-1894), ed.
--Grimm's Fairy Tales. (Original Author: Grimm/Jakob Ludwig Karl; 1785-1863). (Illus.). (McKay's Young People's Classics). N.D. David McKay.

Stevenson, Robert Louis (1850-1894) & Peake, Mervyn Laurence (1911-1968)
--Treasure Island. LC 78-74610. (Illus.). 222 p. 20cm. 1979, c.1976. (ISBN 0-8052-0620-5). Schocken Books.
--Treausre Island. LC 78-27432. p. cm. 1979. (ISBN 0-8052-3707-0). (ISBN 0-8052-0620-5). Schocken Books.

Stevenson, William (1925-)
--The Bushbabies. Ambrus, Victor G., pseud. (1935-), illus. Ambrus, Gyozo Laszlo. LC 65-22509. 278 p. illus., map. 22 cm. 1965. Houghton Mifflin. **Award: (ALA).**

Steveson, Florence & Murray, Patricia Hagen
--Bianca. N.D. New American Company.

Steward, James Jean (1921-)
--So High the Wall. A Book-Length Story. LC 55-41410. 152p. 20cm. 1955, c.1954. White Pub. House & Press.

Steward, Ray M.
--The Surprising Adventures of the Man in the Moon ... Bridgman, Lewis Jesse (1857-1931), illus. LC 3-19671. v, 142 p. col. front., illus., col. plates. 25 1/2 cm. 1903. Lee and Shepard.

Stewart, Agnes Charlotte
--The Boat in the Reeds. Brooker, Christopher, illus. LC 79-104337. (Illus.). 92 p. 22cm. 1st U.S. edition. 1970, c.1960. Bradbury Press.
--Dark Dove. LC 74-14814. 191 p. 22cm. 1974. (ISBN 0-87599-203-X). S. G. Phillips.
--Elizabeth's Tower. LC 72-4063. 222 p. 22cm. 1972. (ISBN 0-87599-193-9). S. G. Phillips.
--Ossian House. LC 76-9645. 179 p. 22cm. 1976, c.1974. (ISBN 0-87599-219-6). S. G. Phillips.
--The Quarry Line Mystery. LC 73-6445. 192 p. 21cm. 1973. (ISBN 0-8407-6340-9). T. Nelson.
--Silas and Con. LC 77-23318. 119 p. 23cm. 1977. (ISBN 0-689-50086-6). Atheneum.

Stewart, Agnes M.
--Lady Amabel and the Shepherd Boy. (Catholic Youth's Library). N.D. D. & J. Sadlier.
--Stories on the Seven Virtues. N.D. Catholic Publication Society.

Stewart, Allan (1939-)
--Dangerous Hideaway Assignment. 1983. (ISBN 0-8423-5872-2). Tyndale.
--The Phantom Ship. LC 63-1849. 119 p. 21 cm. c.1962. Zondervan Pub. House.
--Rick Shannon & the Case of the Missing Pilot. 144p. (Fingerprint Mystery Ser.). (gr. 8-12). 1984. (ISBN 0-8423-0212-3). Tyndale.
--Shark Bait. (Teen Bks.). (gr. 8 up). 1969. Moody.
--Storm Wind. 128p. (Teen Bks.). (gr. 7 up). 1970. Moody.
--Thunder Rock. LC 60-4685. 117 p. 20 cm. 1960. Zondervan Pub. House.

Stewart, Anna Bird (1880-)
--Bibi, the Baker's Horse. Richter, Catherine M., illus. LC 42-36331. 190 p., 1 l. col. front., illus., col. plates. 21 cm. 1942. J. B. Lippincott Company.
--The Candy Box. Hambridge, Ruth, illus. LC 29-22352. x, 57 p. incl. front., illus. 22 cm. 1929. R. M. McBride & Company.

--The Gentlest Giant, and Other Pleasant Persons: Poems from the Enchanting Realm of When We Were Young. Walker, Dugald Stewart (1888-1937), illus. LC 29-14402. 148, 2 p. incl. front., illus. 22 cm. 1929. R. M. McBride & Company.
--The Gentlest Giant, and Other Pleasant Persons: Poems from the Enchanting Realm of When We Were Little. Walker, Dugald Stewart (1888-1937), illus. LC 15-25260. 142, 2 p. incl. col. front., col. illus., col. plates. 24 cm. 1915. The Wayne Publishing Company (Incorporated).
--Little Brother Goose. Fouse, Dorothea, illus. LC 28-28896. xi p., 2 l., 17-107 p. incl. front., illus. 22 cm. 1928. R. M. McBride & Company.
--Rex, and Other New and Old Selected Verses For Boys and Girls. LC 41-14436. xi, 147, 1 p. illus. 21 cm. 1941. St. Anthony Guild Press.
--Three White Cats of Avignon. Joyce, Robert, illus. LC 29-18032. 4 p. l., 167 p. col. front., illus. 19 cm. 1929. Doubleday, Doran & Company, Inc.
--Three White Cats of Avignon. Joyce, Robert, illus. LC 47-18440. 4 p. l., 167 p. col. front., illus. 19 cm. 1946. Printed by St. Anthony Guild Press.
--Two Young Corsicans: A Boy and His Colt. Richter, Catherine M., illus. LC 44-8267. 261 p. col. front., illus., plates (part col.) 21 cm. 1944. J. B. Lippincott Company.
--Young Miss Burney. Stone, Helen (1904-), illus. LC 47-31369. 21cm. 270p. 1947. J. B. Lippincott Co.

Stewart, Anne (1946-), adapted by see Andersen, Hans Christian.

Stewart, Archie S.
--John Clothespin and the Witch: A Child's Medley of Fairy and Folk Lore. LC 56-11653. 234p. illus. 21cm. (A Bookland Juvenile). 1956. Comet Press Books.

Stewart, Calvin E.
--Uncle Josh Weathersby's Punkin Centre Stories. LC 3-19679. (Illus.). 23cm. 170p. 1903. Regan Printing House.

Stewart, Christine & Yager, Julie
--Six horses and a caravan. 156p. 1963. Tri-Ocean Books.
--Six Horses and a Caravan. 1st ed. Fuller, Roseanne, illus. LC 64-868565. 156p. col. illus. 23cm. 1965, c.1964. U. Smith.

Stewart, Diana, adapted by see Austen, Jane.
Stewart, Diana, adapted by see Bronte, Charlotte.
Stewart, Diana, adapted by see Chaucer, Geoffrey.
Stewart, Diana, adapted by see Doyle, Arthur Conan, Sir.
Stewart, Diana, adapted by see Homerus.
Stewart, Diana, adapted by see Hugo, Victor Marie.
Stewart, Diana, adapted by see James, Henry.
Stewart, Diana, adapted by see Poe, Edgar Allan.
Stewart, Diana, adapted by see Shakespeare, William.
Stewart, Diana, adapted by see Shelley, Mary Wollstonecraft Godwin.
Stewart, Diana, adapted by see Twain, Mark.
Stewart, Doug, jt. auth. see Lamb, Eleanor.

Stewart, Doug & Thomson, Linda H.
--Star Child. (gr. 7-12). 1981. (ISBN 0-912085-00-2). Ensign Prods.

Stewart, Ed, ed.
--A Window to Eternity: Twelve Short Stories of Fantasy and Fiction Based on the Sayings of Christ. Killian, Ted, illus. LC 85-11739. (Illus.). 136 p. 21cm. c.1985. (ISBN 0-8307-1052-3). Regal Books.

Stewart, Elizabeth Laing (1907-)
--Billy Buys a Dog. LC 50-10977. (Illus.). 30 cm. 44p. (An Easy to Read Photograph Book for Children). 1950. Reilly Lee Co.
--Funny Squirrel. LC 53-16716. (Illus.). 28cm. 47p. (ps-3). 1952. Reilly & Lee.
--Kim the Kitten. LC 61-7940. unpaged. illus. 29 cm. 1961. Reilly & Lee Co.
--The Lion Twins. 1964. (ISBN 0-8382-0442-2, Cadmus Books). E. M. Hale And Company.
--The Lion Twins. Perkins, Marlin & Perkins, Carol Morse, photos by LC 64-11897. (Illus.). 30 p. 24cm. 1964. Atheneum.
--Little Dog Tim. LC 59-14181. 32 p. illus. 29cm. 1959. Reilly & Co.
--Mogul Finds a Friend. Perkins, Carol Morse & Perkins, Marlin, illus. LC 62-16303. unpaged. illus. 29 cm. 1962. Reilly & Lee.
--Patch, You just be You. LC 54-205. 30 p. ill. 28cm. 1953. Reilly & Lee.
--See Our Pony Farm. LC 60-7654. (Illus.). 32p. 29cm. 1960. Reilly & Lee Co.
--Taxco Tommy. Lyons, Dave, illus. LC 54-6663. (Illus.). 21 cm. 31p. 1954. Pageant Press, Inc.

Stewart, Grace Bliss
--The Good Fairy. LC 30-20196. 7 p. l., 3-128 p. col. front., illus., col. plates. 23 cm. c.1930. The Reilly & Lee Co.
--In and Out of the Jungle. Stinemetz, Morgan, illus. LC 22-19736. viii, 165 p. front., illus. 19 cm. c.1922. D. C. Heath & Co.
--In the Jungle with Cheerups and the Quixies. LC 24-9575. viii p., 1 l., 165 p. front., plates. 20 cm. 1923. Little, Brown, and Company.
--Jumping into the Jungle. Stinemetz, Morgan, illus. LC 23-16318. viii p., 1 l., 165 p. front., plates. 20 cm. 1923. Little, Brown, and Company.

Stewart, Harriet L., jt. auth. see Heavey, Regina.

Stewart, Jim
--Joey's Horse. Siculan, Daniel (1922-), illus. LC 62-20662. unpaged. illus. 29cm. c.1962. Encyclopedia Britannica Presss: Distributed with Meredith Press.

Stewart, Jo
--Run from Danger. Pierce, Diane, illus. LC 80-26611. p. cm. (Prime Time Adventures). 1981. (ISBN 0-516-02109-5). Childrens Press.

Stewart, John
--The Circus is Coming. 1973. (ISBN 0-664-32533-5). Westminster Press.

Stewart, John Allan see Stewart, Allan.

Stewart, John William (1920-)
--The Key to the Kitchen. Quackenbush, Robert Mead (1929-), illus. LC 78-116341. (Illus.). 32 p. 26cm. 1970. Lothrop, Lee & Shepard Co.

Stewart, K. K.
--God Made Me Special. Mahany, Patricia, ed. LC 82-62731. (Illus.). 24p. (Happy Day Bks.). (ps-2). 1983. (ISBN 0-87239-635-5). Standard Pub.

Stewart, Margery S. & Buck, Eunice V.
--Strange Babies. Wilson, Helen Hughes, illus. LC 56-5039. 109p. illus. 22cm. 1956. Caxton Printers.

Stewart, Mary
--Once Upon a Time Tales. McClure, Griselda Marshall, illus. LC 12-29050. 3 p. l., 5-275 p. col. front., col. plates. 21 cm. c.1912. Fleming H. Revell Company.
--The Shepard of us all. LC 14-1985. 21cm. 255p. 1913. Fleming H. Revell Co.
--Tell Me a Hero Story. Palmer, Samuel M., illus. N.D. Fleming H. Revell Co.
--Tell Me a Noah's Ark Story. N.D. Fleming H. Revell Co.
--Tell Me a Story I Never Heard Before: From the Story-Tellers of Long Ago for the Story-Tellers of to-Day. Field, Rachel Lyman (1894-1942), illus. LC 19-18968. 6 p. l., 9-283 p. illus. 21 cm. c.1919. Fleming H. Revell Company.
--Tell Me a Story of Bunny Blew. Beekman, Henry R., illus. LC 31-332273. 182 p. col. front., illus., col. plates 21 cm. c.1931. Fleming H. Revell Company.
--Tell Me a Story of Jesus. N.D. Fleming H. Revell Co.
--The Way to Wonderland. Smith, Jessie Willcox (1863-1935) & Barton, Helen M., illus. LC 17-29990. 7 p. l., 3-194 p. col. front., illus., col. plates. 24 cm. c.1917. Dodd, Mead & Company.

Stewart, Mary, compiled by.
--Tell Me a True Story. Schauffler, A. F., intro. by. 253p. (Pub. by Fleming H. Revell Co. N.Y. & London). 1980. (Telegraph). Dynamic Learn Corp.

Stewart, Mary Florence Eleanor (1916-)
--The Little Broomstick. Hughes, Shirley (1929-), illus. LC 77-168476. (Illus.). 192 p. 22cm. 1972, c.1971. Morrow.
--Ludo and the Star Horse. D'Achille, Gino, illus. LC 74-26662. (Illus.). 191 p. 22cm. 1975, c.1974. (ISBN 0-688-22017-7). (ISBN 0-688-32017-1). Morrow.
--A Walk in Wolf Wood: A Tale of Fantasy and Magic. Schongut, Emanuel, illus. LC 80-13010. (Illus.). 148 p. 24cm. 1st U.S. edition. 1980. (ISBN 0-688-03679-1). Morrow.

Stewart, Mrs.
--Story of a Boy's Adventures, and How He Rose in the World. (The Popular Library). N.D. The American News Co.

Stewart, Neil
--The Red Lion. Cellini, Joseph (1924-), illus. LC 60-12538. 190 p. illus. 22 cm. 1960. Putnam.

Stewart, Ora Pate (1910-)
--Mopey the Mop. LC 56-17886. 74p. illus. 20cm. 1955. Naylor Co.
--West Wind Song. Palmer, Adell Reese, illus. LC 68-75900. 94 p. illus. 29 cm. c.1964. Paragon Press.

Stewart, Pat, jt. auth. see Potter, Helen Beatrix.
Stewart, Rachel (1917-), tr. see Rodrian, Fred.

Stewart, Robert
--The Daddy Book. Madden, Donald B. (1927-), illus. LC 72-20. (Illus.). 48 p. 27cm. 1972. (ISBN 0-07-061347-8). (ISBN 0-07-061348-6). American Heritage Press.

Stewart, Ruby
--The Legend of the Grey Castle. N.D. Vantage Press.

Stewart, Ruth Weeden, ed.
--Harvest of Holidays. LC 61-17994. 129 p. illus. 25 cm. (Collier's Junior Classics Ser.). 1962. Crowell-Collier Pub. Co.

Stewart, Sylvia
--Jessica of the Camerons. LC 24-29641. 336 p. front., pl. 19 cm. c.1924. The Union Press.

Steyle, Mary B.
--East Side, West Side. LC 38-10118. 4 p. l., 13-160 p. illus. 20 cm. 1938. William B. Eerdmans Publishing Co.

Stickney, J. H. (1840-), ed. see Kingsley, Charles.
Stickney, Jennie H. (1840-), ed. see Aesopus.
Stickney, Jennie H. (1840-), ed. see Andersen, Hans Christian.
Stickney, Jennie H. (1840-), ed. see Wyss, Johann David Von.

Stickter, Jim
--Barco Goes to Peru. Stickter, Jim, illus. (Illus.). (Barco Bks.: No. 1). (gr. 1). 1977. (ISBN 0-930770-05-6). Hemisphere Hse.

Stieff, Frederick Philip
--Unleash the Dogs of War: A Story. Lundean, Louis, illus. LC 44-40383. 3 p. l., 9-227 p. incl. plates. 21 1/2 cm. 1944. R. M. McBride & Co.

Stifter, Adelbert
--Rock Crystal: A Christman Tale. Scharl, Josef (1896-1954), illus. Mayer, Elizabeth & Moore, Marianne Craig (1887-1972), trs. from Ger. (Illus.). (gr. 3 up). 1965. (ISBN 0-394-81558-0). (ISBN 0-394-91558-5). Pantheon.

Stiles, Alice E.
--Short Stories for Children. (gr. 3-7). 1983. (ISBN 0-8062-1934-3). Carlton.

Stiles, Karen
--Kirby Koala Happy Day Rhymes. Garris, Norma & Garris, Dan, illus. (Illus.). 22p. (Kirby Koala Ser.). (ps-2). 1983. (ISBN 0-89954-210-7). Antioch Pub Co.
--Whisper the Winged Unicorn. Wilson-Heaney, Katherine, illus. (Illus.). 24p. (Whisper the Winged Unicorn Ser.). (gr. 2-6). 1983. (ISBN 0-89954-220-4). Antioch Pub Co.

Stiles, Martha Bennett
--Darkness Over the Land. LC 66-9625. (Illus.). ix, 269 p. 22cm. 1966. Dial Press.
--Dougal Looks for Birds. Schweitzer, Iris, illus. LC 77-182108. (Illus.). 40 p. 1972. Four Winds Press.
--One Among the Indians. LC 62-15396. 187p. illus. 22cm. c.1962. Dial.
--The Star in the Forest: A Mystery of the Dark Ages. LC 78-22284. (Illus.). xiv, 206 p., 1 leaf of plates. 22cm. c.1979. (ISBN 0-590-07537-3). Four Winds Press.
--The Strange House at Newburyport. Werth, Kurt (1896-), illus. LC 63-16425. 128 p. illus. 22 cm. 1963. Dial Press.
--Tana and the Useless Monkey. LC 79-4655. 85 p. 21cm. c.1979. Elsevier/Nelson Books.

Stiles, Martha Bennett, retold by.
--James, the Vine Puller: A Brazilian Folktale. Thomas, Larry, illus. LC 74-9031. (Illus.). 32 p. 24cm. c.1974. (ISBN 0-87614-047-9). Carolrhoda Books.

Stiles, Norman
--The Count's Number Parade. Veno, Joseph, illus. (Illus.). 24p. (ps-4). 1977. (ISBN 0-307-68876-3, Golden Pr). Western Pub.
--The Ernie & Bert Book. Mathieu, Joseph (1945-), illus. (Illus.). (Sesame Street Shape Bks.). (ps-1). 1977. (ISBN 0-307-68879-8, Golden Pr). Western Pub.
--Farmer Grover. Cooke, Tom, illus. (Illus.). 24p. (ps-4). 1977. (ISBN 0-307-68878-X, Golden Pr). Western Pub.
--Grover's Little Red Riding Hood. Mathieu, Joseph (1945-), illus. (Illus.). (gr. k-2). 1976. (ISBN 0-307-68934-4, Golden Pr). Western Pub.
--I'll Miss You, Mr. Hooper. Mathieu, Joseph (1945-), illus. LC 83-27013. (Based on the Sesame Street Television Script). (Illus.). 24p. (Sesame Street Bks.). (ps-3). 1984. (ISBN 0-394-86600-2, Pub. by BYR). (ISBN 0-394-96600-7). Random.

Stiles, Norman, jt. auth. see Moss, Jeffrey.
Stiles, Norman, jt. auth. see Wilcox, Daniel.

Stiles, Norman & Wilcox, Daniel
--Grover and the Everything in the Whole Wide World Museum. Mathieu, Joseph (1945-), illus. LC 73-18736. (Illus.). 32 p. 21cm. 1974. (ISBN 0-394-82707-4). Random House.

Still, Dorris Shelton
--Sue in Tibet. N.D. Cupples & Leon Co.
--Sue in Tibet. Smith, William Arthur (1918-), illus. LC 42-11250. (Illus.). 22cm. 159p. 1942. John Day Books.

Still, James (1906-)
--Jack and the Wonder Beans. Tomes, Margot Ladd (1917-), illus. LC 77-7982. (Illus.). 31 p. 24cm. c.1977. (ISBN 0-399-20498-9). Putnam. **Award: (NYT).**
--Sporty Creek: A Novel About an Appalachian Boyhood. McCaffery, Janet, illus. LC 76-47538. (Illus.). 125 p. 21cm. c.1977. (ISBN 0-399-20577-2). Putnam.
--The Wolfpen Rusties: Appalachian Riddles & Gee-Haw Whimmy-Diddles. McCaffery, Janet, illus. (Illus.). (gr. 4 up). 1975. (ISBN 0-399-20460-1). Putnam Pub Group.

Stilley, Frank
--One Hundred Thousand Dollar Rat: And Other Animal Heroes for Human Health. (Illus.). 1975. (ISBN 0-399-20441-5). G. P. Putnam's Sons.

Stillman, Albert Leeds (1883-)
--Drums Beat in Old Carolina. Fogarty, Thomas, Jr. (1873-) & Fogarty, Thomas, Jr. (1873-), illus. LC 39-23412. 4 p. l., 244 p. col. front., illus., plates. 22 1/2 cm. c.1939. The John C. Winston Company.
--Jungle Haven: Being a True and Wondrous Account of Three Outcasts and Their Adventures in the Wilds of the Upper Amazon. Pitz, Henry Clarence (1895-1976), illus. LC 42-19349. viii p., 1 l., 321 p. col. front., illus. 22 1/2 cm. 1942. The John C. Winston Company.

Stillman, Beatrice, tr. see Chukovsky, Kornei Ivanovich.
Stillman, Clara Gruening, tr. see Salten, Felix.

Stillman, Dorothea
--When the New Year Came in March. Walker, Nedda, illus. LC 44-3155. 3 p. l., 11-139 p. illus. 21 cm. 1944. E. P. Dutton & Co.

Stillman, Mildred Whitney, Mrs. (1890-)
--The Mermaid and the Little Fish. Baker, Mary (1897-), illus. LC 32-31296. 63, 1 p. incl. illus., plates. col. front. 24 cm. c.1932. Duffield & Green.
--A Present for Santa Claus. LC 30-30777. 31, 1 p. 16 1/2 cm. 1930. Duffield and Company.

Stillwell, S. M.
--The Church Farm. (Illus.). N.D. E & J B Young.

Stilwell, Alison
--Chin Ling, the Chinese Cricket. LC 47-119809. 48 p. illus. (part col.) 26 cm. 1947. Macmillan Co.
--Chin Ling, the Chinese Cricket. 3rd ed. LC 81-90045. (Illus.). 48 p. 26cm. 1981, c.1947. (ISBN 0-9605862-0-2). Stilwell Studio.

Stimson, Frederic J., jt. auth. see Wheelwright, John Tyler.

Stinar, Virginia
--From Earth to the Moon with Sparty Spaceman. (Illus.). (gr. 2-5). 1969. (ISBN 0-682-47050-3). Exposition.

Stinchcomb, Eleanor
--A Goose and Some Geese: A Jolly Mother Goose Play. N.D. March Brothers.

Stine, ed.
--Weird Worlds, No. 3. (gr. 7-12). 1980. (ISBN 0-590-30036-9). Scholastic Inc.

Stine, Catherine J.
--The Great Escape. 1984. (ISBN 0-8062-1994-7). Carlton.

Stine, George Harry see Correy, Lee, pseud.

Stine, George Harry (1928-)
--Rocket Man. Correy, Lee, pseud. 1st ed. Wagoner, William J., illus. LC 55-10566. 224p. illus. 21cm. 1955. Holt.
--Starship Through Space. Correy, Lee, pseud. Llewellyn, Bill, illus. LC 54-5736. 241p. illus. 22cm. 1954. Holt.

Stine, H. William, jt. auth. see Stine, Megan.
Stine, H. William, ed. see Karman, Janice & Bagdasarian, Ross.
Stine, H. William, jt. ed. see Stine, Megan.
Stine, Jane, jt. auth. see Stine, Jovial Bob.
Stine, Jovial Bob, pseud., see Stine, Robert Lawrence.

Stine, Jovial Bob, pseud. (1943-)
--Bananas Looks at TV. Stine, Robert Lawrence. Viviano, Sam, illus. (Illus.). 48p. (Orig.). 1981. (ISBN 0-590-31851-9, Schol Pap). Scholastic Inc.
--Dynamite's Funny Book of the Sad Facts of Life. Stine, Robert Lawrence. Lee, Jared D., illus. 80p. (gr. 3 up). 1980. (ISBN 0-590-30620-0, Schol Pap). Scholastic Inc.
--Gnasty Gnomes. Stine, Robert Lawrence. Lippman, Peter J (1936-), illus. LC 80-5752. (Illus.). 62 p. 22cm. c.1981. (ISBN 0-394-94686-3). Random House.
--The Great Superman Movie Book. Stine, Robert Lawrence. (gr. 3-7). N.D. (ISBN 0-590-32524-8). Scholastic Inc.
--How to Wash a Duck-and How to Do Everything Else. Stine, Robert Lawrence. Rose, Larry, illus. LC 81-16054. p. cm. 1983. (ISBN 0-671-43965-0). Wanderer Books.
--The Pigs' Book of World Records. Stine, Robert Lawrence. Lippman, Peter J. (1936-), illus. LC 79-5239. (Illus.). 95 p. 21cm. c.1980. (ISBN 0-394-84402-5). (ISBN 0-394-94402-X). Random House.

Stine, Jovial Bob, pseud. (1943-) & Stine, Jane
--The Sick of Being Sick Book. Stine, Robert Lawrence. Durrell, Ann, ed. Nicklaus, Carol, illus. (Illus.). 96p. (gr. 7 up). 1982. (ISBN 0-590-32119-6). Scholastic Inc.
--The Sick of Being Sick Book. Stine, Robert Lawrence. Nicklaus, Carol, illus. LC 79-20248. (Illus.). 80p. (F/Hu/J). (gr. 3-7). 1980. Dutton.

Stine, Megan, ed. see Karman, Janice & Bagdasarian, Ross.

AUTHOR INDEX STOCKTON, FRANK

Stine, Megan & Stine, H. William
--The Case of the Weeping Coffin. Hulsey, John, illus. LC 84-63443. (Illus.). 128p. (Find Your Fate Mystery Ser.: No. 1). (gr. 4-7). 1985. (ISBN 0-394-96725-9, BYR). (ISBN 0-394-96725-9, BYR). Random.
--The Formula for Trouble. Febland, David, illus. (Illus.). 96p. (Orig.). (Twistaplot Bks.: No. 3). (gr. 7 up). 1983. (ISBN 0-590-32638-4). Scholastic Inc.
--Journey to Vernico Five. Roper, Robert, illus. (Illus.). 96p. (Orig.). (Twistaplot Bks.: No. 12). (gr. 4 up). 1984. (ISBN 0-590-33213-9). Scholastic Inc.
--Race into the Past. Klein, David, illus. (Illus.). 96p. (Orig.). (Twistaplot Bks.). (gr. 7 up). 1984. (ISBN 0-590-32868-9). Scholastic Inc.
Stine, Megan & Stine, H. William, eds.
--A Chipmunk Christmas. Cole, Corny, illus. LC 85-1840. (Based on a TV Special written by Janice Karman and Ross Bagdasarian). p. cm. 1985. (ISBN 0-394-87512-5). Random House.
Stine, Robert Lawrence see Stine, Jovial Bob, pseud.
Stine, Robert Lawrence see Stine, Jovial Bob, pseud.
Stine, Robert Lawrence
--The Golden Sword of Dragonwalk. Stine, Jovial Bob, pseud. Febland, David, illus. (Illus.). 96p. (Orig.). (Twistaplot Bks.: No. 4). (gr. 7 up). 1983. (ISBN 0-590-32724-0). Scholastic Inc.
--Horrors of the Haunted Museum. Stine, Jovial Bob, pseud. (Illus.). 96p. (Orig.). (Twistaplot Bks.). (gr. 7 up). 1984. (ISBN 0-590-32930-8). Scholastic Inc.
--Instant Millionaire. Stine, Jovial Bob, pseud. Woodman, Jowill, illus. (Illus.). 96p. (Orig.). (Twistaplot Ser.: No. 14). (gr. 4 up). 1984. (ISBN 0-590-33231-7). Scholastic Inc.
--The Time Raider. Stine, Jovial Bob, pseud. Febland, David, illus. (Illus.). 96p. (Orig.). (Twistaplot Bks.: No. 1). (gr. 7 up). N.D. (ISBN 0-590-32637-6). Scholastic Inc.
Stinetorf, Louise Allender (1900-)
--The Bears of Sansur. Escourido, Joseph, illus. LC 69-17366. (Illus.). 160 p. 22cm. 1969. John Day Co.
--A Charm for Paco's Mother. Escourido, Joseph, illus. LC 65-19739. (Illus.). 127 p. 24cm. 1965. John Day Co.
--Children of South Africa. 1st ed. Watson, Eva Auld, illus. LC 45-7580. 175 p. incl. front. plates. 21cm/. 1945. J. B. Lippincott.
--Elephant Outlaw. LC 56-10723. 173 p. illus. 21 cm. 1956. Lippincott.
--Manuel and the Pearl. Escourido, Joseph, illus. LC 66-5577. 125p. illus. 24cm. 1966. John Day.
--Musa The Shoemaker. N.D. E . M. Hale and Co.
--Musa, the Shoemaker. 1st ed. Johnson, Eugene Harper, illus. LC 58-59936. 182 p. illus. 21 cm. 1959. Lippincott.
--The Secret of Bireh. LC 73-2588. 124 p. 21cm. 1973. (ISBN 0-664-32528-9). Westminster Press.
--The Shepherd of Abu Kush. LC 63-7956. 127 p. 21cm. 1963. John Day Co.
--Tomas and the Hermit. Escourido, Joseph, illus. LC 68-13244. (Illus.). 112 p. 24cm. 1968. John Day Co.
--The Treasure of Tolmec. Grifalconi, Ann (1929-), illus. LC 67-23063. (Illus.). 116 p. 22cm. 1967. John Day Co.
--White Witch Doctor. McDonough, Don, illus. (Illus.). (gr. 7 up). 1950. (ISBN 0-664-30034-0). Westminster.
Stinson, Jeanette Hinshaw
--The Victorious Heart. LC 67-11621. 153 p. 21cm. 1967. Zondervan Pub. House.
Stinton, Judith
--Boo to a Goose. Duchesne, Janet (1930-), illus. (Illus.). 48p. (Blackbird Bks.). (gr. k-3). 1982. (ISBN 0-531-04355-X, MacRae). Watts.
--Tom's Tale. Duchesne, Janet (1930-), illus. (Illus.). N.D. (ISBN 0-686-89154-6, A Julia Macrae BlackBird Book). Watts.
Stirling, Betty Rutledge (1923-)
--Brush Valley Adventure. Munson, Harold W. (1920-), illus. LC 52-13415. 143p. illus. 21cm. 1952. Pacific Press Pub. Association.
--Julie Otis, Student Nurse. LC 56-10343. 205 p. illus. 21 cm. 1956. Pacific Press Pub. Association.
--Ned of the Navajos. Converse, James, illus. LC 62-19057. 136 p. illus. 23 cm. 1962. Pacific Press Pub. Association.
--Neil and Pam, Teachers of Tomorrow. Locke, Vance, illus. LC 58-13779. 179 p. illus. 24 cm. (Careers for Christ). 1958. Pacific Press Pub. Association.
--Polly's D Day. Riedel, Boris, illus. LC 54-9984. 107p. illus. 19cm. 1954. Pacific Press Pub. Association.
--Redwood Pioneer. Koering, Ursula (1921-), illus. LC 55-749186. 157p. illus. 23cm. 1955. (ISBN 0-695-47560-6). Follett Pub. Co.
--This Is How It Happened. Munson, Harold W. (1920-), illus. LC 56-133215. 103p. illus. 23cm. 1956. Pacific Press Pub. Association.
--This Is Where They Went. Maniscalco, Joseph (1926-), illus. LC 59-13497. 122 p. illus. 23 cm. 1959. Pacific Press Pub. Association.
Stirling, Helen, tr. see Von Wiese, Ursula.
Stirling, Helen, tr. see Wiese und Kaiserswaldau, Ursula Renate Von.
Stirling, Helen, tr. see Wise, Ursula Von.
Stirling, Lilla Mary Elderkin (1902-)
--Jockie: A Story of Prince Edward Island. Meyers, Robert William (1919-), illus. LC 51-10317. (Illus.). 202 p. 21cm. 1951. Scribner.
--The Jolly Season. Felt, Sue (1924-), illus. LC 48-114711. 204 p. illus. 20 cm. 1948. C. Scribner's Sons.
--The Pipe Organ in the Parlor. Geer, Charles Hand (1922-), illus. LC 60-7286. 95 p. illus. 23 cm. 1960. Nelson.
--The Stowaway Piper. Werth, Kurt (1896-), illus. LC 61-13830. 128 p. illus. 23 cm. 1961. Nelson.
Stirling, Monica (1916-)
--The Cat from Nowhere. 1st ed. Blegvad, Erik (1923-), illus. LC 69-18628. (Illus.). 47 p. 22cm. 1969. Harcourt, Brace & World.
--The Little Ballet Dancer. Stone, Helen (1904-), illus. LC 52-14573. (Illus.). 61 p. 25cm. c.1952. Lothrop, Lee & Shepard.
Stirling, Nora Bromley (1900-)
--Up from the Sea: The Story of Salvage Operations. 1st ed. Vestal, Herman B., illus. LC 62-7073. 128 p. illus. 24 cm. 1963. Doubleday.
--You Would If You Loved Me. LC 70-88697. 160 p. 22cm. 1969. M. Evans; Distributed by Lippincott, Philadelphia.
Stirling, Yates, Jr. (1872-)
--A United States Midshipman Afloat. Boyer, Ralph L., illus. LC 8-15723. 382 p. front., 6 pl. 19 1/2 cm. (United States Midshipman Ser.). 1908. The Penn Publishing Company.
--A United States Midshipman, in China. Boyer, Ralph L., illus. LC 9-12881. 356 p. front., illus. (map) 6 pl. 19 1/2 cm. 1909. The Penn Publishing Company.
--A United States Midshipman, in Japan. Boyer, Ralph L., illus. LC 11-139797. 396 p. front., plates. 19 1/2 cm. 1911. The Penn Publishing Company.
--A United States Midshipman, in the Philippines. Boyer, Ralph L., illus. LC 10-12172. 382 p. front., plates. 19 1/2 cm. 1910. The Penn Publishing Company.
--A United States Midshipman, in the South Seas. Boyer, Ralph L., illus. LC 13-21021. 402 p. front., plates. 19 1/2 cm. $1.0. 1913. The Penn Publishing Company.
Stirnweis, Shannon (1931-), illus.
--Here, Boy: Lots of Stories for Everyone Who Likes Dogs. LC 66-16546. 156 p. col. illus. 22 cm. (A Whitman Tween-Age Bk.). 1966. Whitman Pub. Co.
Stirrup Associates Inc.
--My Jesus Pocketbook of Li'l Critters. Phillips, Cheryl M., ed. Sherman, Erin, illus. LC 82-63139. (Illus.). 32p. (Orig.). 1983. (ISBN 0-937420-05-0). Stirrup Assoc.
--My Jesus Pocketbook of Noah & the Floating Zoo. Harvey, Bonnie C. & Phillips, Cheryl M., eds. Fulton, Ginger A., illus. LC 83-51680. (Illus.). 32p. (My Jesus Pocketbook Ser.). (ps). 1984. (ISBN 0-937420-10-7). Stirrup Assoc.
Stites, Theodore William (1902-)
--Beaver Island: A Children's Story in Pictures and Verse. LC 43-3879. 47 p. illus. 23 1/2 cm. 1942. Dorrance and Company.
Stitt, Edward Walmsley (1862-) & Goldberg, David S.
--Let's Act. viii, 228 p. plates 19 cm. c.1925. Silver, Burdett and Company.
Stitz-Ulrici, Rolf (1922-)
--Kai Conquers Brixholm. Schramm, Ulrik (1912-), illus. LC 63-19009. 159 p. illus. 22 cm. c.1963. Bobbs-Merrill.
Stobbs, Joanna (1914-)
--One Sun, Two Eyes, & a Million Stars. Stobbs, William (1914-), illus. (Illus.). 32p. (ps). 1983. (ISBN 0-19-279747-6, Pub by Oxford U Pr Childrens). Merrimack Pub Cir.
Stobbs, William (1914-), retold by see Perrault, Charles.
Stobbs, William (1914-)
--A Car Called Beetle. Stobbs, William (1914-), illus. (Illus.). 30p. 1st U.S. edition. (gr. 1-3). 1979. (ISBN 0-370-11144-3, Pub. by Chatto Bodley Jonathan). Merrimack Pub Cir.
--A Gaping Wide-Mouthed Waddling Frog. Stobbs, William (1914-), illus. (Illus.). N.D. (ISBN 0-7207-0849-4, Pub. by Michael Joseph). Merrimack Pub Cir.
--The Golden Goose: A Picture Book. Stobbs, William (1914-), illus. (Illus.). 31 p. 1967. McGraw-Hill.
--Gregory's Dog. Stobbs, William (1914-), illus. LC 84-245259. (Illus.). 16 p. 22cm. c.1984. (ISBN 0-19-272141-0). Oxford University Press.
--Gregory's Garden. Stobbs, William (1914-), illus. (Illus.). 16p. (ps). 1984. (ISBN 0-19-272140-2, Pub. by Oxford U Pr Childrens). Merrimack Pub Cir.
--The Hare and the Frogs: An Aesop Fable. Stobbs, William (1914-), illus. LC 79-322434. (Illus.). 29 p. 1978. (ISBN 0-370-30098-X). Bodley Head.
--Henny-Penny: A Picture Book. Stobbs, William (1914-), illus. LC 70-93810. (Illus.). 26 p. 1970, c.1968. Follett Pub. Co.
--The House That Jack Built. Stobbs, William (1914-), illus. (Illus.). 32p. (ps-1). 1983. (ISBN 0-19-279751-4). Oxford U Pr.
--Jack and the Beanstalk. Stobbs, William (1914-), illus. LC 66-7403. (Illus.). 1 v. (unpaged). 24cm. 1966, c.1965. Delacorte Press.
--Jack & the Beanstalk: A Picture Book. Stobbs, William (1914-), illus. (Illus.). (gr. k-3). 1969. Delacorte.
--Jake. Stobbs, William (1914-), illus. 32p. 1975. (ISBN 0-7207-0768-4, Pub. by Michael Joseph). Merrimack Pub Cir.
--Johnny Cake. Stobbs, William (1914-), illus (Pub. by Viking Pr). (Viking Seafarer Ser.). (gr. 1-3). N.D. (ISBN 0-670-05098-9, Puffin). Penguin.
--Johnny-Cake: A Picture Book. Stobbs, William (1914-), illus. (Illus.). 32p. (gr. k-3). 1973. (ISBN 0-670-40826-3). Viking Pr.
--Little Tiger. Stobbs, William (1914-), illus. 32p. 1975. (ISBN 0-7207-0769-2, Pub. by Michael Joseph). Merrimack Pub Cir.
--A Rolls Called Ark. Stobbs, William (1914-), illus. (Illus.). 26p. (gr. 1-4). 1980. (ISBN 0-370-02033-2, Pub. by Chatto, Bodley Head & Jonathan). Merrimack Pub Cir.
--Round & Round the Garden. Stobbs, William (1914-), illus. (Illus.). 32p. (ps). 1983. (ISBN 0-370-30497-7, Pub. by The Bodley Head). Merrimack Pub Cir.
--Sophie. Stobbs, William (1914-), illus. 32p. 1974. (ISBN 0-7207-0769-2, Pub. by Michael Joseph). Merrimack Pub Cir.
--There's a Hole in My Bucket. Stobbs, William (1914-), illus. (Illus.). 30p. (Umbrella Books). (ps). 1983. (ISBN 0-19-279755-7, Pub by Oxford U Pr Childrens). Merrimack Pub Cir.
--This Little Piggy. Stobbs, William (1914-), illus. 32p. N.D. (ISBN 0-370-30428-4, Pub. by Chatto-Bodley-Jonathan). Merrimack Pub Cir.
Stobbs, William (1914-), retold by.
--The Country Mouse & Town Mouse. Stobbs, William (1914-), illus. (Illus.). 24p. 1976. (ISBN 0-7207-0828-1, Pub. by Michael Joseph). Merrimack Pub Cir.
--Old Mother Goose & the Golden Egg. Stobbs, William (1914-), illus. (Illus.). 28p. (gr. 1-2). 1980. (ISBN 0-370-30005-X, Pub. by Chatto Bodley Jonathan). Merrimack Pub Cir.
--Old Mother Goose and the Golden Egg: A Bodley Head Picture Book. Stobbs, William (1914-), illus. LC 80-670111. (Illus.). 27 p. 1977. (ISBN 0-370-30005-X). Bodley Head.
--One, Two, Buckle My Shoe. Stobbs, William (1914-), illus. LC 84-246015. (Illus.). 26 p. 1984. (ISBN 0-370-30587-6). Bodley Head.
--Puss in Boots. Stobbs, William (1914-), illus. LC 74-25152. (Illus.). 32. 25cm. 1975. (ISBN 0-07-061582-9). (ISBN 0-07-061581-0). McGraw-Hill.
--The Story of the Three Bears. Stobbs, William (1914-), illus. (Illus.). (gr. k-3). 1965. (ISBN 0-07-061576-4, GB). McGraw.
--The Story of the Three Little Pigs. Stobbs, William (1914-), illus. (Illus.). (gr. k-3). 1965. (ISBN 0-07-061578-0). McGraw.
--The Story of the Three Little Pigs. Stobbs, William (1914-), illus. LC 65-25144. 30 p. col, illus. 19 x 26 cm. 1965. Whittlesey House.
Stobbs, William (1914-) & Jacobs, Joseph, eds.
--Guleesh: A Picture Story from Ireland. Stobbs, William (1914-), illus. LC 77-165545. (Illus.). 32p. 27cm. 1972, c.1971. (ISBN 0-695-40036-3). (ISBN 0-695-80036-1). Follett Pub. Co.
Stobo, Edward John
--The O'erturn O' Botany Bay: Or, Dipper Folk Idyls. LC 1-31589. 270 p. illus. 19 cm. 1901. American Baptist Publication Society.
Stock, Catherine
--Emma's Dragon Hunt. Stock, Catherine, illus. LC 83-25109. (Illus.). 32p. (gr. k up). 1984. (ISBN 0-688-02696-6). (ISBN 0-688-02698-2). Lothrop.
--Sampson: The Christmas Cat. Stock, Catherine, illus. LC 84-9946. (Illus.). 32p. (ps-3). 1984. (ISBN 0-399-21002-4, Putnam). (ISBN 0-399-21002-4). Putnam Pub Group.
--Sophie's Bucket. 1st ed. Stock, Catherine, illus. LC 84-15461. (Illus.). 32p. (gr. k up). 1985. (ISBN 0-688-04224-4). (ISBN 0-688-04225-2). Lothrop.
Stock, Elliot E
--Jim Crow: Musical Plays in One Act for Children. (Music by Ernest Brumleu). N.D. E P Dutton & Co.
--The Magic Chest: Musical Plays in One Act for Children. (Incidental music by Ernest Brumleu). N.D. E P Dutton & Co.
--The Pied Piper: Musical Plays in One Act for Children. N.D. E P Dutton.
Stock, George Chadwick, jt. auth. see Stock, Lucy Gould.
Stock, Lucy Gould (1873-) & Stock, George Chadwick
--Songs of the Seasons. 1910. W. A. Wilde Co.
Stockdale, Alice Boyd see Proudfoot, Alice-Boyd, pseud.
Stockdale, Alice Boyd
--The Animals Go to the Supermarket. Proudfoot, Alice-Boyd, pseud. Grastorf, Marilyn, illus. LC 77-79693. (Illus.). 40 p. 22cm. c.1977. (ISBN 0-8448-1098-3). Crane, Russak.
Stockdale, Bill, jt. auth. see Butterworth, Ben
Stockham, Peter
--Chapbook ABC'S. Stockham, Peter, illus. LC 74-75263. vi. 120 p. ill. 15cm. 1974. (ISBN 0-486-23076-7). (ISBN 0-486-23075-9). Dover Pub.
Stockham, Peter, ed.
--Chapbook Riddles: Reprints of Six Rare and Charming Early Juveniles. LC 74-75262. (Illus.). viii, 84 p. 15cm. 1974. (ISBN 0-486-23078-3). (ISBN 0-486-23077-5). Dover Publications.
Stocking, Jay Thomas (1870-1936)
--The City That Never Was Reached and other Stories for Children. LC 11-23709. vii, 163 p. col. front. 20 1/2 cm. $1.00. c.1911. The Pilgrim Press.
--The Golden Goblet and Other Stories. LC 15-153001. vii p., 1 l., 3-154 p. col. front., col. plates. 20 1/2 cm. c.1914. The Pilgrim Press.
--Mr. Friend-O'-Man. Ives, Sarah Noble, illus. LC 20-12950. 3 p. l., v-vi, 130 p. front., illus. (incl. music) 19 1/2 cm. c.1920. Pub. Jointly by Council of Women for Home Missions and Interchurch World Movement of North America.
--Query Queer Stories. LC 27-70. 7 p. l., 3-183 p. col. front., col. plates. 20 cm. c.1926. The Pilgrim Press.
--Stocking Tales: A Book of Stories for Children. Bromhall, Winifred, illus. LC 37-1869. v p., 2 l., 3-119 p. front. (port.) illus. 20 cm. c.1937. The Pilgram Press.
Stockton, Francis Richard see Stockton, Frank Richard.
Stockton, Frank Richard (1834-1902)
--The Bee-Man of Orn. Sendak, Maurice Bernard (1928-), illus. LC 64-13399. (Illus.). 21cm. 44p. (gr. 3-7). 1964. (ISBN 0-03-044810-7). (ISBN 0-03-080114-1). HR&W. **Award: (ALA).**
--The Bee-Man of Orn, and Other Fanciful Tales. N.D. Charles Scribner.
--Captain Chap: Or, The Rolling Stones, 1 of 11 vols. (Popular Bks for Boys). 1900. Set. J B Lippincott.
--Captain Chap: Or, The Rolling Stones. Stephens, Charles H., illus. LC 4-16465. 298 p. front., illus., plates. 20 cm. 1897. J. B. Lippincott Company.
--The Casting Away of Mrs. Lecks and Mrs. Aleshine. Richards, George Mather (1880-), illus. 1933. Appleton.
--The Clocks of Rondaine and Other Stories. Blashfield, Edwin Howland & Rogers, W. A., illus. LC 8-15533. x, 174 p. incl. front., illus., plates. 21 1/2 cm. 1892. C. Scribner's Sons.
--Fanciful Tales. Langworthy, Julia Elizabeth, ed. Burt, Mary Elizabeth (1850-1918), intro. by. LC 4-35679. xiii, 135 p. 4 pl. (incl. front.) 19 cm. 1894. C. Scribner's Sons.
--Fanciful Tales. Langworthy, Julia Elizabeth, ed. Burt, Mary Elizabeth (1850-1918), intro. by. LC 4-18940. xiii, 135 p. 4 pl. (incl. front.) 19 cm. (On verso of half-title: Scribner's Series of School Reading). 1904. C. Scribner's Sons.
--The Floating Prince and Other Fairy Tales. Birch, Reginald Bathurst (1856-1943), illus. LC 4-16156. 6 p., 1 l., 190 p. incl. front., illus. 21 x 18 cm. 1881. C. Scribner's Sons.
--The Griffin and the Minor Canon. 1st ed. Sendak, Maurice Bernard (1928-), illus. LC 63-10792. 55 p. illus. 21 cm. 1963. Holt, Rinehart and Winston. **Award: (ALA).**
--A Jolly Fellowship. LC 4-16466. x p., 1 l., 298 p. incl. front., illus. 19 1/2 cm. 1880. C. Scribner's Sons.
--A Jolly Fellowship. LC 75-301689. (Illus.). x, 298 p., 1 leaf of plates. 20cm. 1893, c.1880. Scribner.
--A Jolly Fellowship: Adventures in Southern Seas. (The Boy's Library of Pluck and Action). N.D. Charles Scribner's Sons.
--A Jolly Fellowship: Adventures in Southern Seas. (Illus.). N.D. Grosset & Dunlap.
--The Lady or the Tiger. N.D. Charles Scribner's Sons.
--The Lady or The Tiger, and Other Stories. N.D. Charles Scribner Sons.
--Mrs. Cliff's Yacht. (Illus.). N.D. Charles Scribner's Sons.

--Old Pipes and the Dryad. Hanley, Catherine, illus. LC 69-10018. (Illus.). 46 p. 23cm. 1968, c.1969. Watts.
--The Poor Count's Christmas. N.D. J. B. Lippincott.
--The Poor Count's Christmas. Bensell, Edmund B., illus. LC 27-27700. 80 p. incl. plates, col. front. 21 1/2 cm. 1927. Frederick A. Stokes Company.
--The Queen's Museum and Other Fanciful Tales. Richardson, Frederick (1862-1937), illus. LC 6-397603. viii, 219 p. illus. 10 col. pl. 24 1/2 cm. 1906. C. Scribner's Sons.
--The Reformed Pirate: Stories from The Floating Prince, Ting-a-Ling Tales & The Queen's Museum. Birch, Reginald Bathurst (1856-1943), illus. Davis, Mary Gould, frwd. by. LC 36-26516. vi p., 2 l., 342 p. incl. plates. col. front. 21 cm. 1936. C. Scribner's Sons.
--Round-About Rambles in Lands of Fact and Fancy. LC 8-15532. 1 p. l., 371 p. front., illus. 22. c.1872. Scribner, Armstrong & Co.
--Roundabout Rambles in Lands of Fact and Fancy. (Illus.). N.D. Charles Scribner's & Sons.
--The Story of Viteau. LC 4-183282. 3 p. l., 193 p. front., 15 pl. 19 1/2 cm. 1884. C. Scribner's Sons.
--The Storyteller's Pack. Bryson, Bernarda (1905-1977), illus. 1968. Trade Publications.
--The Storyteller's Pack: A Frank R. Stockton Reader. Bryson, Bernarda (1905-1977), illus. LC 67-23694. (Illus.). xxiv, 358 p. 24cm. 1968. Scribner.
--Tales Out of School. LC 35-28565. 2 p. l., iii-iv, 325 p. front., illus. 22 1/2 cm. 1876. Scribner, Armstrong & Co.
--Tales Out of School. new ed. Floethe, Richard (1901-), illus. 1 p. l., iv, 325 p. front., illus. 21 cm. 1903. C. Scribner's Sons.
--Ting-a-Ling. Bensell, Edmund B., illus. LC 4-16467. 2 p. l., 187 p. incl. illus., plates. 18 cm. 1882. C. Scribner's Sons.
--Ting-a-Ling. Bensell, Edmund B., illus. LC 45-40833. 2 p. l., 187 p. incl. illus., plates. 20 1/2 cm. 1870. Hurd and Houghton.
--Ting-a-Ling Tales. Floethe, Richard (1901-), illus. LC 55-10144. (Illus.). 21cm. 161p. (Willow Leaf Library Edition Ser). 1955. (ISBN 0-684-20954-3). Scribner.
--What Might Have been Expected. LC 2-28759. vi, 9-202 p. front. 19cm. 1898. Dodd, Mead & Co.
--What Might Have Been Expected. Eytinge, Sol & Sheppard, illus. LC 72-3103. (Illus.). 292 p. 22cm. (The Black Heritage Library Collection). 1972. (ISBN 0-8369-9080-3). Books for Libraries Press.
--What Might Have Been Expected. Eytinge, Sol & Sheppard, illus. LC 28-4341. vi, 9-292 p. front., plates. 18 cm. c.1874. Dodd & Mead.
--The Young Master of Hyson Hall. Rev ed. Davisson, Virginia & Stephens, Charles H., illus. LC 99-5138. vii p., 1 l., 7-287 p. front., plates. 19 1/2 cm. 1900. J. B. Lippincott Company.

Stockton, Frank Richard (1834-1902) & Dickens, Charles John Huffam (1812-1870)
--The Griffin and the Minor Canon: Also The Magic Fishbone. Gentleman, David William (1930-), illus. LC 64-7839. 80p. illus. 20cm. c.1965. Dufour.

Stockton, Frank Richard (1834-1902) & Langworthy, Julia Elizabeth, eds.
--Fanciful Tales. Burt, Mary Elizabeth (1850-1918), intro. by. LC 45-263412. xiii, 130 p. front., plates. 18 1/2 cm. 1914. C. Scribner's Sons.

Stockum, Hilda Van see Pothast-Gimberg, C. E.
Stockum, Hilda Van see Van Iterson, Siny Rose.
Stockum, Hilda Van see Van Stockum, Hilda Gerarda.
Stockum, Hilda Van, tr. see Van Iterson, Siny Rose.

Stockwell, E. C., Mrs.
--Stories for All the Year. N.D. Judson Press.

Stockwell, Grace
--The Mysterious Little Girl. Nelson, Ralph Lewis, illus. LC 24-21584. vii, 292 p. front plates. 19 1/2 cm. $1.7. c.1924. The Century Co.

Stoddard, Anne Glen, Mrs.
--Bingo Is My Name. Hader, Berta Hoerner (1890-1976) & Hader, Elmer Stanley (1889-1973), illus. LC 31-24491. 58 p. col. front., illus. (part col.) 21 1/2 cm. c.1931. The Century Co.
--A Good Little Dog. Hader, Berta Hoerner (1890-1976) & Hader, Elmer Stanley (1889-1973), illus. LC 30-251901. 59 p. incl. col. front., illus (part col.) 21 1/2 cm. c.1930. The Century Co.
--Here, Bingo!. Hader, Berta Hoerner (1890-1976) & Hader, Elmer Stanley (1889-1973), illus. LC 32-20866. 61 p. col. front., illus. (part col.) 21 1/2 cm. c.1932. The Century Co.
--Tony Sarg's Alphabet: Verses. Sarg, Tony, pseud. (1882-1942), illus. Sarg, Anthony Frederick. LC 27-6842. 28 l. col. illus. 23 1/2 cm. 1926. Greenberg Inc.

Stoddard, Darrell
--The Hero. Jordan, Alton, ed. Reese, Bob, illus. (Illus.). (I Can Read Underwater Bks.). (gr. k-3). 1974. (ISBN 0-89868-001-8). (ISBN 0-89868-034-4). ARO Pub.

Stoddard, Elizabeth Drew Barstow see Stoddard, R. H., pseud.
Stoddard, R. H., pseud., see Stoddard, Elizabeth Drew Barstow.

Stoddard, R. H., Mrs., pseud. (1823-1902)
--Lolly Dinks' Doings. Stoddard, Elizabeth Drew Barstow. N.D. William F. Gill.

Stoddard, Richard Henry, retold by see Little Red Riding Hood.

Stoddard, Richard Henry (1825-1903)
--Adventures in Fairy Land. (Illus.). N.D. James Miller.
--Adventures in Fairy Land. Oertel, et al., illus. (Illus.). N.D. Thomas R. Knox & Co.

Stoddard, Richard Henry (1825-1903), retold by.
--Little Red Riding Hood. Fredericks, Alfred, illus. N.D. Hurd & Houghton.

Stoddard, Sandol see Warburg, Sandol Stoddard.

Stoddard, Sandol (1927-)
--Bedtime for Bear. Munsinger, Lynn (1951-), illus. LC 85-5259. (Illus.). 32 p. c.1985. (ISBN 0-395-38811-2). Houghton Mifflin.
--Bedtime Mouse. Munsinger, Lynn (1951-), illus. LC 81-4078. p. cm. 1981. (ISBN 0-395-31609-X). Houghton Mifflin.
--Children's Bible Stories. LC 82-45340. 1983. (ISBN 0-385-18521-9). Doubleday.
--Curl up Small. Hyman, Trina Schart (1939-), illus. LC 64-10725. (Illus.). 32 p. 24cm. 1964. Houghton Mifflin.
--Five Who Found the Kingdom: New Testament Stories. 1st ed. Sabin, Robert (1949-), illus. LC 80-1663. (Illus.). 119 p. 22cm. c.1981. (ISBN 0-385-17169-2). Doubleday.

Stoddard, W O, jt. auth. see Mighels, Philip Verrill.
Stoddard, William Osborn, jt. auth. see Tilford, Tilden.

Stoddard, William Osborn (1835-1925)
--Ahead of the Army. Emerson, C. Chase, illus. LC 3-14855. vi p., 2 l., 11-302 p. front., 3 pl. 19 1/2 cm. 1903. Lothrop Publishing Company.
--Among the Lakes. LC 8-16107. v, 321 p. 18 1/2cm. 1883. C. Scribner's Sons.
--Among the Lakes. LC 41-351618. v, 321 p. 18 1/2 cm. 1890. C. Scribner's Sons.
--The Battle of New York: A Story for All Young People. 3 p. l., 248 p. col. front., plates. 20 cm. 1892. D. Appleton and Company.
--Boys of Bunker Academy. LC 2-28760. 383 p. front., plates 20 1/2 cm. 1902. G. W. Jacobs & Co.
--Boys of Bunker Academy. (Pastime and Academy Ser.). N.D. George W. Jacobs.
--The Captain's Boat. LC 76-365096. (Illus.). 272 p., 8 leaves of plates. 20cm. c.1894. Merriam.
--Chris, the Model Maker: A Story of New York. Clinedinst, B. West, illus. LC 8-16106. iii p., 1 l., 287 p. front., 5 pl. 20 cm. 1894. D. Appleton and Company.
--Chuck Purdy: The Story of a New York Boy. LC 8-16104. v, 7-318 p. front., plates. 18 1/2 cm. 1891. D. Lothrop Company.
--Chumley's Post, 1 of 11 vols. (Popular Bks for Boys). 1900. Set. J B Lippincott.
--Crowded Out O' Crofield: Or, The Boy Who Made His Way. LC 8-16105. 261 p. illus. 20 cm. 1890. D. Appleton and Company.
--Dab Kinzer: A Story of a Growing Boy. LC 4-161577. vi p., 1 l., 321 p. 18 1/2 cm. 1881. C. Scribner's Sons.
--Dab Kinzer: A Story of a Growing Boy. LC 9-6845. vi p., 1 l., 321 p. 18 1/2 cm. 1909. C. Scribner's Sons.
--Dan Monroe, a Story of Bunker Hill. Kennedy, J. W. Ferguson (1905-), illus. LC 5-23022. 4 p. l., 329 p. front., 7 pl. 19 1/2cm. (Revolutionary Ser.). N.D. Lothrop Pub. Co.
--The Despatch Boat of the Whistle: A Story of Santiago. Merrill, Frank Thayer (1848-), illus. LC 99-1494. 319 p. front., illus., plates 19 1/2 cm. c.1899. Lothrop Publishing Company.
--Elinors' Chase, 1 of 8. (Frank Leslie's Boys' Library Ser.). N.D. American News Co.
--The Errand Boy of Andrew Jackson: A War Story of 1814. Crawford, Will, illus. LC 2-13259. 327 p. front., plates. 19 1/2 cm. 1902. Lothrop Publishing Company.
--The Fight for the Valley: A Story of the Siege of Fort Schuyler and the Battle of Oriskany in the Burgoyne Campaign of 1777. LC 4-17225. vi p. 2 l., 250 p. col. front., 3 pl. 19 1/2 cm. 1904. D. Appleton and Company.
--The First Cruiser Out. Carter, F. A., illus. N.D. Duffield.
--The First Cruiser Out: A Cuban War Story; Visitors at Grampus Island; and, The Tale of an Oar. 3 p. l., 291 p., 1 l. front., plates. 19 1/2 cm. 1898. H. S. Stone and Company.
--Gid Granger: The Story of a Country Boy. N.D. Lothrop Pub. Co.
--Gid Granger: The Story of a Rough Boy. LC 8-16103. 258 p. incl. front., plates 18 1/2 cm. c.1891. D. Lothrop Company.
--Guert Ten Eyck: A Hero Story. Merrill, Frank Thayer (1848-), illus. LC 8-34321. 3 p. l., 3-258 p. incl. plates. front. 20 1/2 cm. 1893. D. Lothrop Company.
--In the Open: Stories of Outdoor Life. LC 8-32332. 4 p. l., 3-191, 1 p. front., 7 pl. 18 1/2 cm. $0.6. 1908. Harper & Brothers.
--Jack Morgan: A Boy of 1812. Crawford, Will, illus. 4 p. l., 11-353 p. front., plates. 19 1/2 cm. 1901. Lothrop Publishing Company.
--Little Smoke: A Tale of the Sioux. Dellenbaugh, Frederic S., illus. LC 4-16468. 1 p. l., 295 p. front., 13 pl. 20 1/2 cm. 1891. D. Appleton and Company.
--Long Bridge Boys: A Story of 1861. Hazleton, Isaac Brewster, illus. LC 4-22837. 5 p. l., 9-344 p. incl. front. 3 pl. 19 1/2 cm. 1904. Lothrop Publishing Company.
--The Lost Gold of the Montezumas: A Story of the Alamo. Stephens, Charles H., illus. LC 8-34320. 5 p. l., 7-309 p. front., plates. 20 cm. 1898. J. B. Lippincott Company.
--Mart Satterlee Among the Indians. LC 8-28492. 2 p. l., 7-238 p. 19 cm. (On cover: The popular series no. 3). 1891. R. Bonner's Sons.
--Ned, the Son of Webb: What He Did. Rev ed. Searles, Victor A., illus. LC 5160. 4 p. l., 11-333 p. front., plates. 19 cm. 1900. D. Estes & Company.
--The Noank's Log: A Privateer of the Revolution. Crawford, Will, illus. LC 3572. 337 p. front., plates. 19 1/2 cm. 1900. Lothrop Publishing Company.
--On the Old Frontier: Or, The last of the Iroquois. Murphy, H. D., illus. LC 4-164693. 340 p. front. 9 pl. 20cm. 1893. D. Appleton & Co.
--The Partners: The Story of an Every-Day Girl and Boy and How They Helped Along. Cox, Arthur Scott, illus. LC 8-16102. 1 p. l., 5-302 p. incl. plates. front. 20 cm. 1895. Lothrop Publishing Company.
--The Quartet. LC 4-16158. (A Sequel to Dab Kinzer, a story of a Growing Boy). v, 332 p. 18 1/2 cm. 1881. C. Scribner's Sons,.
--The Railroad Cut. (Illus.). (Every Boy's Library). N.D. Caldwell.
--The Red Mustang: A Story of the Mexican Border. LC 4-16159. viii, 9-284 p. incl. front. 16 pl. 16 1/2 cm. (Harper's Young People Series). 1890. Harper & Brothers.
--The Red Patriot: A Story of the American Revolution. Clinedinst, B. West, illus. LC 8-34319. 4 p. l., 275 p. front., plates. 20 cm. 1897. D. Appleton and Company.
--Saltillo Boys. LC 12-38989. iv p., 1 l., 362 p. 18 1/2 cm. 1882. C. Scribner's Sons.
--The Spy of Yorktown: A Story of Arnold and Washington in the Last Year of the War of Independence. Clinedinst, B. West, illus. LC 3-20587. vii, 229 p. col. front., 5 pl. 20 cm. 1903. D. Appleton and Company.
--Success Against Odds: Or, How a Boy Made His Way. Clinedinst, B. West, illus. 4 p. l., 273 p. front., plates. 20 cm. 1898. D. Appleton and Company.
--The Swordmaker's Son. Varian, George, illus. LC 8-16101. (Illus.). 280p. 1896. The Century Co.
--The Talking Leaves. N.D. Grosset & Dunlap.
--Talking Leaves. (Harper's Young People's Ser.). N.D. Harper & Bros.
--The Talking Leaves: An Indian Story. LC 4-35673. vi, 336 p. incl. front., plates. 17 cm. 1882. Harper & Brothers.
--The Talking Leaves: An Indian Story. LC 4-18941. vi, 336 p. incl. front., plates. 17 1/2 cm. 1903. Harper & Brothers.
--The Talking Leaves: An Indian Story. (Illus.). (Harper's Young People Ser.). N.D. Harper & Brothers.
--Tamed. (Illus.). (Editha Ser.). N.D. Caldwell.
--Tom and the Monkey King. (Illus.). N.D. Merriam Company.
--Two Arrows: A Story of Red and White. LC 4-16470. 239 p. front., plates. 16 1/2 cm. (Harper's young people series). 1886. Harper & Brothers.
--Two Cadets with Washington. Kennedy, J. W. Ferguson, illus. LC 6-16299. 3 p. l, 341 p. front, 7 pl. 19 1/2 cm. (Revolutionary Ser.). 1906. Lothrop, Lee & Shepard Co.
--Ulric the Jarl. Tobin, George T., illus. N.D. Methodist Book Concern.
--The Village Champion. LC 3-24209. 394 p. front., 4 pl. 20 1/2cm. 1903. G. W. Jacobs & Co.
--The Village Champion. (Pastime and Adventure Series.). N.D. George W. Jacobs.
--The Voyage of the Charlemagne. Kennedy, J. W. Ferguson, illus. LC 2-18091. (Illus.). 20cm. 285p. (The Boys Own Authors Ser.). N.D. Dana Estes & Co.
--Walled In. (Illus.). N.D. Rand, McNally & Co.'s.
--The White Cave. LC 8-16099. 3 p. l., 254 p. incl. plates. front. 19 1/2 cm. 1893. The Century Co.
--The Windfall. Clinedinst, B. West, illus. LC 8-16098. 3 p. l., 288 p. incl. plates. front. 20 cm. 1896. D. Appleton and Company.
--Winter Fun. LC 8-16097. v, p., 1 l, 273 p. 18 1/2 cm. 1885. C. Scribner's Sons.
--With the Black Prince. LC 98-289. 4 p. l., 240 p. front., plates 20 cm. 1898. D. Appleton and Company.
--The Wreck of the Sea Lion. LC 1-31927. 272 p. front., plates. 19 cm. (Adventure Stories Ser.). 1901. The Penn Publishing Company.
--The Young Financier. (Vacation Ser.). N.D. Penn Publishing Co.
--The Young Financier. Rev ed. Betts, John Henderson, illus. LC 3-3962. 269 p. incl. front., illus., plates. pl. 19 cm. (Adventure Stories Ser.). 1900. The Penn Publishing Company.
--Zeb, a New England Boy. LC 4-25112. 21cm. 388p. (Pastime and Adventure Ser.). 1904. George W. Jacobs.

Stoddard, William Osborn (1835-1925), adapted by.
--The Story Without an End: And, Noemi. Pickard, J. C. & Wheelock, Lucy, trs. from Ger. & Fr. 48p. N.D. Lothrop Publishing Co.

Stoddard, William Osborn, Jr. (1873-)
--The Captain of the Cat's Paw. LC 14-15177. 4 p. l. 207, 1 p. front., plates, diagr. 19 1/2 cm. $1.0. 1914. Harper & Brothers.
--The Farm That Jack Built: Making Good on the Farm. Varian, George, illus. LC 16-7499. 4 p. l., 311, 1 p. col. front., col. plates. 19 cm. $1.3. 1916. D. Appleton and Company.
--Longshore Boys. Pullinger, Herbert, illus. LC 9-27027. 3 p. l., 5-292 p. col. front., 3 col. pl. 19 1/2 cm. $1.5. 1909. J. B. Lippincott Company.
--Making Good in the Village. Varian, George, illus. LC 16-7662. 4 p. l., 287, 1 p. col. front., col. plates. 19 1/2 cm. $1.3. 1916. D. Appleton and Company.
--Making Good with an Invention. Varian, George, illus. LC 16-22593. 5 p. l. 300, 1 p. col. front., col. plates. 19 1/2 cm. $1.3. 1916. D. Appleton and Company.

Stoddart, Gabrielle, et al.
--One Two Number Zoo. (Illus.). 26p. (ps-k). 1984. (ISBN 0-340-26435-7, Pub. by Hodder & Stoughton UK). David & Charles.

Stoebener, Harry G. (1917-)
--Where the Trees Never End. LC 72-110447. 199 p. 21cm. 1970. Chilton Book Co.

Stoeckicht, Louisa
--The Story of Ricky the Raccoon. LC 73-83672. 60 p. (chiefly illus. 22cm. 1969, c.1967. Schocken Books.
--The Story of the Little Fox. LC 77-83673. 48 p. (chiefly illus. 22cm. 1969, c.1967. Schocken Books.

Stoff, Barbara J. Raport
--Ring Around San Francisco. Stoff, Barbara J. Raport, illus. LC 78-71594. (Illus.). 43 p. 22cm. c.1978. (ISBN 0-933376-00-6). (ISBN 0-933376-01-4). Joy Pub. Co.

Stoiber, Rudolf Maria (1925-)
--Mystery on the Floating Hotel. Rev ed. Candea, Romulus, illus. LC 57-12086. 216 p. illus. 22 cm. 1958. Houghton Mifflin.
--Secret of Channel Six. Lang, Dorothy, tr. LC 61-15716. 200 p. 21 cm. 1961. Abelard-Schuman.

Stokely, Edith Keeley
--Bubbleloon. Porter, J. Erwin, illus. LC 26-161642. 201 p. col. front., illus., col. plates 26 cm. c.1926. George H. Doran Company.
--Pantaloon. Kay, Gertrude Alice (1884-1939), illus. LC 27-19780. 5 p. l., 9-168 p. col. front., illus., col. plates. 24 1/2 cm. c.1927. George H. Doran Company.

Stoker, Abraham see Stoker, Bram.

Stoker, Bram (1847-1912)
--Dracula. (gr. 9 up). N.D. (ISBN 0-396-06069-2). Dodd.
--Dracula. N.D. Doubleday Doran & Co.
--Dracula. Farr, Naunerle, ed. Redondo, Nestor, illus. LC 73-75460. (Illus.). footnotes. 64p. (Orig.). (Now Age Illustrated Ser.). (gr. 5-10). 1973. (ISBN 0-88301-203-0). (ISBN 0-88301-100-X). (ISBN 0-88301-175-1). Pendulum Pr.
--Dracula. Schick, Alice (1946-) & Schick, Joel (1945-), eds. LC 80-13619. (Illus.). 48p. (gr. 3 up). 1980. Delacorte.
--Dracula. Spence, Jim, illus. LC 81-15867. (Illus.). 94 p. 20cm. (Step-up Adventures Ser.). 1982. (ISBN 0-394-84828-4). (ISBN 0-394-94828-9). (ISBN 0-394-94828-9). Random House.
--The Jewel of Seven Stars. (gr. 7-9). 1973 (Starline). Schol Bk Serv.
--Under the Sunset. Fitzgerald, William & Cockburn, W. V., illus. LC 80-19564. p. cm. 1st U.S. edition. 1980. Borgo Press.
--Under the Sunset. Fitzgerald, William & Cockburn, W. V, illus. LC 78-113034. (Illus.). ix, 190 p., 5 leaves of plates. 22cm. 1st U.S. edition. (Newcastle Forgotten Fantasy Library Vol.17). 1978. (ISBN 0-87877-116-6). Newcastle Pub. Co.

--Page Boy of Camelot. Busoni, Rafaello (1900-1962), illus (Pub. by Follett). Orig. Title: Page Boy for King Arthur. (gr. 4-6). 1972 (Starline). Schol Bk Serv.
--Robin Hood's Arrow. Busoni, Rafaello (1900-1962), illus. LC 48-9388. (Being an Account of Dan of the Mill and His Adventures with Robin Hood and the Merry Men of Sherwood Forest.). 161 p. illus. 25 cm. 1948. (ISBN 0-695-47770-6). Wilcox & Follett Co.
--Sagebrush Filly. 1st ed. Mayan, Earl E., illus. LC 50-10130. (Illus.). 184 p. 25cm. 1950. Knopf.
--Secret of the Bog. Price, Christine Hilda (1928-1980), illus. LC 48-8890. 217 p. illus. 20 cm. 1948. Holiday House.
--Squire for King Arthur. Busoni, Rafaello (1900-1962), illus. LC 55-113789. (Illus.). 25cm. 108p. (gr. 3-5). 1955. (ISBN 0-695-48260-2). Follett.
--Tall Sails to Jamestown. LC 67-27066. 190 p. 22cm. 1967. Macrae Smith.

Stone, Evelyn (1879-1971), ed.
--Bedtime Mother Goose. Himler, Ronald Norbert (1937-), illus. (Illus.). 24p. (Orig.). (Look-Look Ser.). (ps). 1980. (ISBN 0-307-11855-X, Golden Pr). Western Pub.

Stone, Gene, pseud., see Stone, Eugenia.

Stone, George
--A Legend of Wolf Song. Kramer, Dick, illus. 1975. (ISBN 0-448-11879-3). Grosset & Dunlap.

Stone, Helen V.
--Pablo the Potter. Petie, Haris, pseud. (1915-), illus. Petty, Roberta. LC 69-13202. (Illus.). 32 p. 24cm. 1969. Lantern Press.

Stone, Idella Purnell (1901-)
--Little Yusuf, the Story of a Syrian Boy. McCreery, James L., illus. LC 31-6490. (Illus.). 122p. 22cm. 1931. The Macmillan Company.
--Lost Princess of Yucatan. LC 31-23586. 6 p. l., 3-188 p. 20 cm. c.1931. H. Holt and Company.
--Pedro the Potter. Hogner, Nils (1893-1970), illus. LC 35-13167. vii p., 1 l., 13-144 p. incl. front., illus., plates. 20 cm. 1935. T. Nelson and Sons.

Stone, Idella Purnell (1901-) & Weatherwax, John M.
--Why the Bee is Busy and Other Rumanian Fairy Tales: Told to Little Marcu by Baba Maritza. Smith, Helen, illus. LC 30-28190. (Illus.). 134p. 19cm. 1930. The Macmillan Company.

Stone, Irving (1903-)
--The Great Adventure of Michelangelo. Abr. and Illus. ed. Cellini, Joseph (1924-), illus. LC 65-10617. xii, 297p. illus. 25cm. Orig. Title: The Agony and the Estacy. 1965. Doubleday.

Stone, Isabel Scott
--The Little Crusaders. LC 1-30191. 294 p. 20 1/2 cm. c.1900. The Abbey Press.

Stone, Jon (1931-) & Children's Television Workshop
--Big Bird in China: Ta Niao Tsai Chung-Kuo. DiNapoli, Victor, illus. LC 82-62383. (Illus.). 61 p. 28cm. c.1983. (ISBN 0-394-85645-7). (ISBN 0-394-95645-1). Random House.
--Furry Old Grover's Resting Places. Smollin, Michael J., illus. LC 83-21087. (Illus.). 32p. (Picturebacks Ser.). (ps-3). 1984. (ISBN 0-394-86056-X, BYR). Random.
--The Monster at the End of This Book. Smollin, Michael J., illus. (Illus.). (gr. k-2). 1976. (ISBN 0-307-60316-4, Golden Pr). Western Pub.
--The Monster at the End of This Book: Featuring Grover, a Jim Henson Muppet, As Performed on Sesame Street by Frank Oz. Smollin, Michael J., illus. LC 77-1695. (Illus.). 23 p. 32cm. c.1977. (ISBN 0-307-10506-7). (ISBN 0-307-60506-X). Western Pub. Co.
--Would You Like to Play Hide & Seek in This Book with Lovable, Furry Old Grover?. Featuring Jim Henson's Muppet. Smollin, Michael J., illus. LC 76-8120. (Illus.). 36 p. 21cm. (A Random House Pictureback). c.1976. (ISBN 0-394-83292-2). Random House.

Stone, Jon (1931-) & Bailey, Joseph A.
--Christmas Eve on Sesame Street. Matthieu, Joseph (1945-), illus. LC 81-50247. p. cm. 1981. (ISBN 0-394-84733-4). (ISBN 0-394-94733-9). Random House.

Stone, Jon (1931-) & Henson, James Maury (1936-)
--Lovable Furry Old Grover's Resting Places: Featuring Grover, a Jim Henson Sesame Street Muppet. Smollin, Michael J., illus. LC 83-21087. (A Random House Pictureback). c.1984. (ISBN 0-394-86056-X). Random House.

Stone, Josephine Rector, pseud., see Dixon, Jeanne.

Stone, Josephine Rector, pseud. (1936-)
--Green Is for Galanx. Dixon, Jeanne. LC 79-23290. 170 p. 22cm. (An Argo Bk.). 1980. (ISBN 0-689-30737-3). Atheneum.
--The Mudhead. Dixon, Jeanne. LC 80-11982. p. cm. 1980. (ISBN 0-689-30787-X). Atheneum.
--Praise All the Moons of Morning. Dixon, Jeanne. LC 78-12633. 172 p. 22cm. (An Argo Bk.). 1979. (ISBN 0-689-30697-0). Atheneum.
--Those Who Fall from the Sun. Dixon, Jeanne. Luber, Mal, illus. LC 78-5139. 153 p. 22cm. 1978. (ISBN 0-689-30615-6). Atheneum.

Stone, Judith
--In the Jaws of Death. Hutchins, Beth, illus. LC 79-21916. (Illus.). 46p. (Quest, Adventure, Survival). (gr. 4-9). 1982. (ISBN 0-8172-2062-3). Raintree Pubs.
--Minutes to Live. Sauber, Rob, illus. LC 79-26068. (Illus.). 46p. (Quest, Adventure, Survival). (gr. 4-9). 1982. (ISBN 0-8172-2065-8). Raintree Pubs.

Stone, Karen, adapted by see Gellek, Nazli.

Stone, Kathleen P., Mrs.
--The Four-Year-Old's Story-Book. Young, Florence Liley, illus. LC 27-19175. 159 p. col. front., 1 illus., col. plates. 20 cm. c.1927. Lothrop, Lee & Shepard Co.
--The Six-Year-Old's Story-Book. Young, Florence Liley, illus. LC 29-198811. 191 p. col. front., col. plates. 20 cm. c.1929. Lothrop, Lee & Shepard Co.

Stone, Laura, adapted by.
--The Chipmunks & the Little Lost Dog. Williams, A. O., illus. LC 84-17982. (Illus.). 32p. (Picturebacks Ser.). (gr. k-3). 1985. (ISBN 0-394-87204-5, BYR). Random.

Stone, Laura, ed. see Bagdasarian, Ross & Karman, Janice.

Stone, Lydia
--Pink Donkey Brown. Dwyer, Mary E., illus. LC 25-13539. 80 p. incl. col. front., illus. (part col.) 20 cm. c.1925. Rand, McNally & Company.

Stone, Mary, adapted by.
--Children's Stories That Never Grow Old: A Selection of the Best Children's Classics. Neill, John Rea (1878-1943), illus. LC 8-21617. 3 p. l., 11-312 p. incl. col. front., col. illus. 20 cm. c.1908. The Reilly and Britton Co.

Stone, Nancy Young (1925-)
--Dune Shadow. LC 80-18798. 180 p. 22cm. 1980. (ISBN 0-395-29860-1). Houghton Mifflin.
--Whistle up the Bay. Beeby, Betty (1923-), illus. LC 65-28564. 219 p. illus. 24 cm. 1966. W. B. Eerdmans Pub. Co.
--The Wooden River. Beeby, Betty (1923-), illus. LC 73-9677. (Illus.). 192 p. 24cm. 1973. (ISBN 0-8028-4061-2). Eerdmans.

Stone, Patti (1926-)
--Judy George, Student Nurse. LC 66-14015. 21cm. 192p. (Career Romance for Young Moderns). (gr. 7 up). 1966. (ISBN 0-671-74425-9). Messner.
--Nina Grant, Pediatric Nurse. LC 60-7050. 191 p. 22cm. (A Career-Romance for Young Moderns). 1960. J. Messner.
--Sandra, Surgical Nurse. LC 61-6366. 192 p. 21 cm. (A Career Romance for Young Moderns). 1961. J. Messner.

Stone, Raymond, pseud., see Stratemeyer Syndicate.

Stone, Raymond, pseud.
--Tommy Tiptop and His Baseball Nine: Or, The Boys of Riverdale and Their Good Times. Stratemeyer Syndicate. Repr. of 1912 ed (Pub. by Graham & Matlack). (The Tommy Tiptop Ser.: Vol. 1). 1917. C. E. Graham Co.
--Tommy Tiptop and His Baseball Nine: Or, The Boys of Riverdale and Their Good Times. Stratemeyer Syndicate. LC 12-15743. (Illus.). 23cm. 126p. (The Tommy Tiptop Ser.: Vol. 1). 1912. Graham & Matlack.
--Tommy Tiptop and His Boat Club: Or, The Young Hunters of Hemlock Island. Stratemeyer Syndicate. Repr. of 1914 ed (Pub. by Graham & Matlack). (The Tommy Tiptop Ser.: Vol. 4). 1917. C. E. Graham Co.
--Tommy Tiptop and His Boat Club: Or, The Young Hunters of Hemlock Island. Stratemeyer Syndicate. (Illus.). (The Tommy Tiptop Ser.: Vol. 4). 1914. Graham & Matlack.
--Tommy Tiptop and His Boy Scouts: Or, The Doings of the Silver Fox Patrol. Stratemeyer Syndicate. Repr. of 1915 ed (Pub. by Graham & Matlack). (The Tommy Tiptop Ser.: Vol. 5). 1917. C. E. Graham Co.
--Tommy Tiptop and His Boy Scouts: Or, The Doings of the Silver Fox Patrol. Stratemeyer Syndicate. Mencl, Rudolf, illus. (The Tommy Tiptop Ser.: Vol. 5). 1915. Graham & Matlack.
--Tommy Tiptop and His Football Eleven: Or, A Great Victory and How it Was Won. Stratemeyer Syndicate. Repr. of 1912 ed (Pub. by Graham & Matlack). (The Tommy Tiptop Ser.: Vol. 2). 1917. C. E. Graham Co.
--Tommy Tiptop and His Football Eleven: Or, A Great Victory and How it Was Won. Stratemeyer Syndicate. LC 12-16328. (Illus.). 126 p. incl. front., plates. 23 cm. (The Tommy Tiptop Ser.: Vol. 2). 1912. Graham & Matlack.
--Tommy Tiptop and His Great Show: Or, Raising Some Money that Was Needed. Stratemeyer Syndicate. Owen, Robert Emmett (1878-), illus. (The Tommy Tiptop Ser.: Vol. 6). 1917. C. E. Graham Co.
--Tommy Tiptop and His Winter Sports: Or, Jolly Times on the Ice and in Camp. Stratemeyer Syndicate. Repr. of 1912 ed (Pub. by Graham & Matlack). (The Tommy Tiptop Ser.: Vol. 3). 1917. C. E. Graham Co.
--Tommy Tiptop and His Winter Sports: Or, Jolly Times on the Ice and in Camp. Stratemeyer Syndicate. LC 12-16329. (Illus.). 23cm. 126p. (The Tommy Tiptop Ser.: Vol. 3). 1912. Graham & Matlack.

Stone, Richard H., pseud., see Stratemeyer Syndicate.

Stone, Richard H., pseud.
--Adrift Over Hudson Bay: Or, Slim Tyler in the Land of Ice. Stratemeyer Syndicate. LC 31-144140. (Illus.). 2 p. l., 212 p. front. 19 1/2 cm. (Slim Tyler Air Stories: Vol. 4). c.1931. Cupples & Leon Company.
--An Air Cargo of Gold: Or, Slim Tyler, Special Bank Messenger. Stratemeyer Syndicate. LC 30-158424. (Illus.). 2 p. l., 208 p. front. 19 1/2 cm. (Slim Tyler Air Stories: Vol. 3). c.1930. Cupples & Leon Company.
--An Airplane Mystery: Or, Slim Tyler on the Trail. Stratemeyer Syndicate. LC 31-14415. (Illus.). 2 p. l., 206 p. front. 19 1/2 cm. (Slim Tyler Air Stories: Vol. 5). c.1931. Cupples & Leon Company.
--Aviation Stories for Boys. Stratemeyer Syndicate. (A Four-in-one reprint. Includes: "Sky Riders of the Atlantic"; "Lost over Greenland"; "An Air Cargo of Gold"; and "Adrift over Hudson Bay" from the series, "Slim Tyler Air Stories"). 1936. Cupples & Leon Company.
--Lost Over Greenland: Or, Slim Tyler's Search for Dave Boyd. Stratemeyer Syndicate. LC 30-15843. (Illus.). 2 p. l., 208 p. front. 19 1/2 cm. (Slim Tyler Air Stories: Vol. 2). c.1930. Cupples & Leon Company.
--Secret Sky Express: Or, Slim Tyler Saving a Fortune. Stratemeyer Syndicate. LC 32-136840. (Illus.). 2 p. l., 210 p. front. 19 1/2 cm. (Slim Tyler Air Stories: Vol. 6). c.1932. Cupples & Leon Company.
--Sky Riders of the Atlantic: Or, Slim Tyler's First Trip in the Clouds. Stratemeyer Syndicate. LC 30-15844. (Illus.). 2 p. l., 206 p. front. 19 1/2 cm. (Slim Tyler Air Stories: Vol. 1). c.1930. Cupples & Leon Company.

Stone, Rosetta
--Because a Little Bug Went Ka-Choo!. Frith, Michael K, illus. LC 75-1605. p. cm. 1975. (ISBN 0-394-83130-6). (ISBN 0-394-93130-0). Beginner Books.

Stone, Ruth (1915-) & Robins, Louise Mary, eds.
--Golden Grove: Adult Poems for Children. 1965. The Dial Press, Inc.

Stone, Stuart Basham (1880-)
--The Kingdom of Why. Newell, Peter (1862-1924), illus. LC 13-22823. (Being the Strange Story of Lucile's Adventures with Sapient Sage, the Foolish Ideas,the Striped Jester, and Other Folk, Creatures, Kings, Beasts, Bogies, Wizards and Witches Who Dwell in That Wonderful Land.). 5 p. l., 275 p. front., illus., plates. 23 1/2 cm. $1.2. c.1913. The Bobbs-Merrill Company.

Stone, William Standish (1907-1973)
--Pepe Was the Saddest Bird. Mordvinoff, Nicolas (1911-1973), illus. Nicolas, pseud. LC 44-8832. 62 p. illus. 28 1/2 x 18 cm. 1944. A. A. Knopf.
--The Ship of Flame: A Saga of the South Seas. Mordvinoff, Nicolas (1911-1973), illus. Nicolas, pseud. LC 45-9583. 4 p. l., 5-164, 2 p. incl. col. front., illus. 20 cm. 1945. A. A. Knopf.
--Teri Taro from Bora Bora. Sperry, Armstrong W. (1897-1976), illus. LC 40-10197. 5 p. l., 3-133, 2 p. incl. front., illus. col. plates. 21 1/2 cm. 1940. A. A. Knopf.
--Thunder Island. Mordvinoff, Nicolas (1911-1973), illus. Nicolas, pseud. LC 42-3784. 4 p. l., 3-104, 1 p. incl. col. front., illus. plates (part col.) 21 1/2 cm. 1942. A. A. Knopf.

Stoneley, Jack
--Scruffy. LC 78-20723. 157 p. 22cm. c.1979. (ISBN 0-394-84161-1). (ISBN 0-394-94161-6). Random House.

Stoner, Burton
--Jim Crow Tales. Williams, Carll B., illus. LC 5-20921. 149 p. front., illus., plates. 23 1/2 x 20 cm. c.1905. The Saalfield Publishing Co.
--Squeaks and Squawks from Far Away Forests: A Sequel to Jim Crow Tales. Bull, Charles Livingston (1874-1932), illus. LC 6-42926. 172 p. incl. col. front., illus. plates (partly col.) 23 1/2 x 20 cm. c.1906. The Saalfield Publishing Company.

Stoner, Kathleen & Stoner, Michael
--Kitty Claus, the Christmas Cat. Zann, Nicky, illus. (Illus.). (gr. k-3). N.D. (ISBN 0-918806-01-1). T V Music.

Stoner, Mabel Allen (1892-)
--Little Lost Laddie and Other Stories. Kilgore, Al, illus. LC 53-12647. (Illus.). 21 cm. 27p. 1953. Pageant Press, Inc.

Stoner, Michael, jt. auth. see Stoner, Kathleen.

Stones, Elizabeth, ed. see Aesopus.

Stoney, T. Butler, illus.
--Old Man Who Lived in a Wood. N.D. E. P. Dutton & Co.

Stong, Philip Duffield (1899-1957)
--A Beast Called an Elephant. Wiese, Kurt (1887-1974), illus. LC 55-8584. 123p. illus. 22cm. 1955. Dodd, Mead.
--Captain Kidd's Cow. Wiese, Kurt (1887-1974), illus. LC 41-6803. 4 p. l., 122 p 1 l. col. illus., col. plates (2 double. 1941. Dodd, Mead & Company.
--Censored, The Goat. Wiese, Kurt (1887-1974), illus. LC 45-10470. (Illus.). 25cm. 78p. 1945. Dodd, Mead & Co.
--Cowhand Goes to Town. Wiese, Kurt (1887-1974), illus. LC 39-24306. 6 p. l., 3-85 p. incl col front., illus. (part col.) 26 cm. 1939. Dodd, Mead & Company.
--Edgar: The Seven Fifty-Eight. Lenski, Lois (1893-1974), illus. LC 38-9972. (Illus.). 20cm. 101p. 1938. Farrar & Rinehart.
--Farm Boy: A Hunt for Indian Treasure. Wiese, Kurt (1887-1974), illus. LC 34-39940. 80 p. incl. col. front., illus. (part col.) 26 cm. 1934. Doubleday, Doran & Company, Inc.
--High Water. Wiese, Kurt (1887-1974), illus. LC 37-28530. 79, 1 p. incl. col. front., illus. (part col.) plates (part col.) 26 cm. 1937. Dodd, Mead & Company.
--The Hired Man's Elephant. Lee, Doris Emrick (1905-1983), illus. LC 39-5589. 4 p. l., 8-149 p. illus 22 1/2 cm. 1939. Dodd, Mead and Company.
--Hirum, the Hillbilly. Wiese, Kurt (1887-1974), illus. LC 51-14201. (Illus.). 104 p. 22cm. 1951. Dodd, Mead.
--Honk: the Moose. Wiese, Kurt (1887-1974), illus. LC 35-27382. 80 p. incl. col. front., illus. (part col.) 26 cm. 1935. (ISBN 0-396-07358-1). Dodd, Mead & Company.
--Honk, the Moose. Special ed. Wiese, Kurt (1887-1974), illus. (Illus.). 80p. Repr. of 1935 ed. 1956. E M Hale.
--Mike: The Story of a Young Circus Acrobat. Wiese, Kurt (1887-1974), illus. LC 57-9751. 126p. illus. 22cm. 1957. Dodd, Mead.
--Mississippi Pilot: With Mark Twain on the Great River. Wiese, Kurt (1887-1974), illus. LC 54-7670. 253 p. 22cm. (Cavalcade Bks.). 1954. Doubleday.
--Missouri Canary. Wiese, Kurt (1887-1974), illus. LC 43-16085. 4 p. l., 77, 1 p. incl. col. front., illus. (part col.) 25 x 20 cm. 1943. Dodd, Mead & Company.
--No-Sitch, the Hound. Wiese, Kurt (1887-1974), illus. LC 56-19991. 79, 1 p. incl. col. front., illus. (part col.) 26 cm. 1936. Dodd, Mead & Company.
--Phil Stong's Big Book: Farm Boy, High Water and No-Sitch, the Hound. Wiese, Kurt (1887-1974), illus. LC 61-12920. 159 p. illus. 24 cm. 1961. Dodd, Mead.
--Positive Pete!. Wiese, Kurt (1887-1974), illus. LC 47-31057. 64 p. illus. (part col.) 25 cm. 1947. Dodd, Mead.
--The Prince and the Porker. Wiese, Kurt (1887-1974), illus. LC 50-10180. (Illus.). 67 p. 25cm. 1950. Dodd, Mead.
--Way Down Cellar. Wiese, Kurt (1887-1974), illus. LC 42-12310. 4 p. l., 159 p. col illus. 23 cm. 1942. Dodd, Mead & Company.
--Way Down Cellar. Wiese, Kurt (1887-1974), illus. 1942. E M Hale.
--Young Settler. Wiese, Kurt (1887-1974), illus. LC 38-19937. 80 p. incl. col front., illus. (part col.) 26 cm. 1938. Dodd, Mead & Company.

Stooke, Eleanor H.
--Little Maid Marigold. (Illus.). 223p. 1905. American Tract Society.

Stopes, Marie Charlotte Carmichael (1880-)
--A Road to Fairyland. Rackham, Arthur (1867-1939), illus. LC 28-8523. 5 p. l., 219 p. col. front. 20 1/2 cm. 1926. G. P. Putnam's Sons, Ltd.
--A Road to Fairyland. Rackham, Arthur (1867-1939), illus. LC 27-4669. xi, 171 p. col. front. 20 cm. 1927. G. P. Putnam's Sons.

Stophlet, Janis
--Boo-Boo: The Elephant Who Couldn't Remember How Not to Forget. Miller, Russell L., illus. (Illus.). 16p. (ps-4). 1985. (ISBN 0-918747-03-1). AZ Hse Pub.

AUTHOR INDEX STOUTENBURG, ADRIEN

--An Inch Worm Named Thad: He Would Not Add. Miller, Russell L., illus. (Illus.). 16p. (ps-4). N.D. (ISBN 0-918747-04-X). AZ Hse Pub.

Stopple, Libby
--A Box of Peppermints. Bell, Martha, illus. LC 75-20957. (Illus.). 96p. (gr. 2-10). 1975. (ISBN 0-913632-08-2). (ISBN 0-913632-07-4). Am Univ Artforms.

Storch, Florence
--Santa's Rocket Sleigh. Webbe, Elizabeth, illus. LC 56-13193. unpaged. illus. 21cm. (A Rand McNally Elf Bk. 568). c.1957. Rand McNally.

Storey, Estelle
--Stell. (Illus.). (gr. 4-8). N.D. Vantage.

Storey, Margaret (1926-)
--Ask Me No Questions. LC 74-23926. 142 p. 22cm. 1975, c.1974. (ISBN 0-525-25972-4). E. P. Dutton.
--The Double Wizard. Jackson, June, illus. LC 79-670153. (Illus.). 113 p. 21cm. 1979. (ISBN 0-571-11265-X). Faber & Faber.
--The Family Tree. Hughes, Shirley (1929-), illus. LC 73-10040. (Illus.). 204 p. 22cm. 1st U.S. edition. 1973. (ISBN 0-8407-6330-1). T. Nelson.
--The Mollyday Holiday. Ede, Janina (1937-), illus. (Illus.). (ps-5). N.D. (ISBN 0-571-09590-9). Faber & Faber.
--Pauline. Ambrus, Victor G., pseud. (1935-), illus. Ambrus, Gyozo Laszlo. LC 67-15378. 210p. illus. 22cm. 1st U.S. edition. 1967, c.1965. Doubleday.
--A Quarrel of Witches. Roberts, Doreen (1922-), illus. (Illus.). (ps-5). 1970. (ISBN 0-571-09416-3). Faber & Faber.
--The Stone Wizard. Stewart, Charles William (1915-), illus. (Illus.). 84p. 1979. (ISBN 0-571-11328-1). Faber & Faber.
--A War of Wizards. Ede, Janina (1937-), illus. (Illus.). (ps-5). N.D. (ISBN 0-686-24629-2, Pub. by Faber & Faber). Merrimack Pub Cir.
--Wrong Gear. (gr. 5 up). N.D. (ISBN 0-571-10151-8, Pub. by Faber & Faber). Merrimack Pub Cir.

Storey, Victoria Carolyn see Martin, Vicky, pseud.

Stork, Elisabeth Pansinger, Mrs., tr. see Beyrich, Clementine Helm.

Stork, Elisabeth Pausinger, tr. see Spyri, Johanna Heusser.

Stork, Elisabeth Pausinger, Mrs., tr. see Spyri, Johanna Heusser.

Stork, Elizabeth Pausinger, Mrs., tr. see Spyri, Johanna Heusser.

Storm, Dan
--Picture Tales from Mexico. Storm, Mark, illus. LC 41-51877. ix p., 1 l., 122 p. illus. 13 1/2 x 18 1/2 cm. 1941. Frederick A. Stokes Company.
--Picture Tales from Mexico. Storm, Mark, illus. N.D. J. B. Lippincott.

Storm, John
--Faraway Tree. McVicker, George, illus. LC 48-6057. 24cm. 70p. 1948. Lothrop Bks.
--Malcolm MacBeth. Alston, Charles, illus. LC 46-11875. 148 p. incl. illus., plates. 20 cm. 1946. Lothrop, Lee & Shepard Co.

Storm, Mark
--Gruyo of the Flying H. Storm, Mark, illus. LC 56-4243. 95p. illus. 24cm. 1956. Childrens Press.

Storman, Suzanne
--Dance of the Wooden Doll. N.D. Vantage Press Inc.

Storr, Catherine Cole (1913-)
--The Adventures of Polly and the Wolf. Watts, Marjorie-Ann, illus. LC 71-113383. (Illus.). 94 p. 22cm. 1970, c.1957. M. Smith Co.
--The Adventures of Polly and the Wolf. Watts, Marjorie-Ann, illus. N.D. Transatlantic Arts, Inc.
--The Chinese Egg. LC 75-11575. 302 p. 21cm. 1975. (ISBN 0-07-061794-5). (ISBN 0-07-061795-3). McGraw-Hill.
--Clever Polly and the Stupid Wolf. N.D. Transatlantic Arts, Inc.
--Clever Polly & the Stupid Wolf. Watts, Marjorie-Ann, illus. Repr. (gr. 1-4). 1968. (ISBN 0-14-030312-X, Puffin). Penguin.
--Cold Marble and Other Ghost Stories. LC 85-10319. 101 p. 21cm. 1985. (ISBN 0-571-13582-X). Faber and Faber.
--February Yowler. Floyd, Gareth (1940-), illus. LC 82-670154. (Illus.). 76 p. 21cm. 1982. (ISBN 0-571-11854-2). Faber and Faber.
--The First Easter. Molan, Christine, illus. LC 83-13917. (Illus.). 32p. (People of the Bible Ser.). (gr. 1-2). 1983. (ISBN 0-8172-1987-0, Raintree Childrens Books Belitha Press Ltd. London). (ISBN 0-8172-1987-0). Raintree Pubs.
--The Freedom of the Seas. Fortnum, Peggy, pseud. (1919-), illus. Nuttall-Smith, Margaret Emily Noel. LC 65-24864. 64 p. illus. 25 cm. 1965, c.1962. Duell, Sloan and Pearce.
--The Good Samaritan. Crompton, Paul, illus. LC 83-11136. (Illus.). 32p. (People of the Bible Ser.). 1983. (ISBN 0-8172-1988-9, Raintree Childrens Books Belitha Press Ltd. - London). (ISBN 0-8172-1988-9). Raintree Pubs.
--Jesus Begins His Work. Molan, Christine, illus. LC 82-9037. p. cm. (People of the Bible). c.1982. (ISBN 0-8172-1978-1). Raintree Childrens Books.
--Joseph and His Brothers. Molan, Christine, illus. LC 82-9087. p. cm. (People of the Bible). c.1982. (ISBN 0-8172-1976-5). Raintree Childrens Books.
--Joseph the Dream Teller. Molan, Christine, illus. LC 83-13932. (Illus.). 32p. (People of the Bible Ser.). (gr. 1-2). 1983. (ISBN 0-8172-1989-7, Raintree Children's Books Belitha Press Ltd. - London). (ISBN 0-8172-1989-7). Raintree Pubs.
--Kate & the Island. Floyd, Gareth (1940-), illus. (Illus.). 87p. 1978. (ISBN 0-571-10119-4). Faber & Faber.
--Lessing Fables. N.D. Longmans, Green & Co.
--Lucy. De Larrea, Victoria, illus. LC 68-19836. (Illus.). 72 p. 19cm. 1968, c.1961. Prentice-Hall.
--Lucy. De Larrea, Victoria, illus. (Illus.). 72 p. 21cm. 1974, c.1961. Prentice-Hall.
--Lucy Runs Away. De Larrea, Victoria, illus. LC 75-81385. (Illus.). 67 p. 20cm. 1969. Prentice-Hall.
--The Magic Drawing Pencil. Watts, Marjorie-Ann, illus. LC 60-12797. 191 p. illus. 21 cm. (A Wonderful World Bk.). 1960. Barnes.
--Marianne & Mark. Watts, Marjorie-Ann, illus. (Illus.). 1st U.S. edition. (Faber Fanfare Ser.). (gr. 6-9). 1979. (ISBN 0-571-11336-2). Faber & Faber.
--Marianne Dreams. rev. ed. Watts, Marjorie-Ann, illus. LC 64-4963. 203 p. illus. 19 cm. (Puffin books). 1964. Penguin Books.
--Marianne Dreams. Watts, Marjorie-Ann, illus. N.D. Transatlantic Arts.
--Noah and His Ark. Russell, Jim (1933-), illus. LC 82-7712. p. cm. (People of the Bible). c.1982. (ISBN 0-8172-1975-7). Raintree Childrens Books.
--The Painter & the Fish. Howard, Alan (1922-), illus. (Illus.). 32p. (ps-5). 1975. (ISBN 0-571-10475-4). Faber & Faber.
--Polly, The Giant's Bride. N.D. Transatlantic Arts.
--Rufus. Dower, Walter (1912-), illus. LC 69-17744. (Illus.). 130 p. 20cm. 1969. Gambit.
--The Story of the Terrible Scar. Rose, Gerald Hembdon Seymour (1935-), illus. (Illus.). 70p. (gr. 2-5). 1970. (ISBN 0-571-10996-9). Faber & Faber.
--The Sword in the Stone. Hunter, Susan, illus. LC 84-18293. p. cm. (Raintree stories). 1985. (ISBN 0-8172-2113-1). Raintree Childrens Books.
--Tales of Polly & the Hungry Wolf. (Illus.). 96p. (gr. 2-5). N.D. (ISBN 0-571-11585-3). Faber & Faber.
--Thursday. LC 72-76524. 274 p. 21cm. 1972. (ISBN 0-06-026067-X). (ISBN 0-06-026068-8). Harper & Row.
--The Trojan Horse. Codd, Michael, illus. LC 84-18292. (Illus.). 32 p. 25cm. (Raintree stories). c.1985. (ISBN 0-8172-2114-X). Raintree Childrens Books.
--Winter's End. LC 78-19488. 206 p. 21cm. c.1979. (ISBN 0-06-026069-6). (ISBN 0-06-026072-6). Harper & Row.

Storr, Catherine Cole (1913-), retold by.
--Dick Whittington. LC 85-16904. p. cm. 1985. (ISBN 0-8172-2507-2). (ISBN 0-8172-2515-3). Raintree Childrens Books.
--The Flying Dutchman. LC 85-16711. p. cm. 1985. (ISBN 0-8172-2501-3). (ISBN 0-8172-2509-9). Raintree Childrens Books.
--King Midas. Codd, Michael, illus. LC 84-18307. (Illus.). 32 p. 25cm. (Raintree stories). 1985. (ISBN 0-8172-2112-3). Raintree Childrens Books.
--King Midas and His Gold. Codd, Michael, illus. LC 85-28900. p. cm. (Great Tales from Long Ago). 1986, c.1985. (ISBN 1-550-01022-0). Torstar Books.
--Miracles by the Sea. Molan, Christine, illus. LC 82-23022. (Illus.). 32p. (People of the Bible). (gr. 1-2). 1983. (ISBN 0-8172-1983-8). Raintree Pubs.
--Moses of the Bullrushes. Russell, Jim (1933-), illus. (Illus.). 32p. (People of the Bible Ser.). (gr. 1-2). 1983. (ISBN 0-8172-1990-0, Raintree Children's Books Belitha Press Ltd. - London). Raintree Pubs.
--Moses of the Bulrushes. Russell, Jim (1933-), illus. LC 83-11121. (People of the Bible). 1984. (ISBN 0-8172-1990-0). Raintree Children's Books.
--The Pied Piper of Hamelin. Dzierzek, Anna, illus. LC 84-26971. (Illus.). (Raintree Stories Clippers Ser.). (gr. k-4). 1984. (ISBN 0-8172-2107-7). (ISBN 0-8172-2238-3). (ISBN 0-8172-2251-0). pap. 23.95g incl. cassette; (ISBN 0-8172-2266-9); cassette 14.00. Raintree Pubs.
--The Pied Piper of Hamelin. Dzierzek, Anna, illus. LC 85-28859. p. cm. (Great Tales from Long Ago). 1986, c.1984. (ISBN 1-550-01010-7). Torstar Books.
--The Prodigal Son. Rowe, Gavin, illus. LC 82-23011. (Illus.). 32p. (People of the Bible). (gr. 1-2). 1983. (ISBN 0-8172-1982-X). Raintree Pubs.
--Rip Van Winkle. Wingham, Peter, illus. LC 83-26996. (Original Author: Washington Irving,1783-1859). (Illus.). 32p. (Raintree Stories Clippers Ser.). (gr. k-4). 1984. (ISBN 0-8172-2108-5). (ISBN 0-8172-2252-9). (ISBN 0-8172-2236-7). pap. 23.95g incl. cassette; (ISBN 0-8172-2267-7); cassette only 14.00. Raintree Pubs.
--Rip Van Winkle. Wingham, Peter, illus. LC 85-28889. (Original Author: Washington Irving,1783-1859). p. cm. (Great Tales from Long Ago). 1986, c.1985. (ISBN 1-550-01020-4). Torstar Books.

Storr, Francis (1839-1919), ed.
--Half a Hundred Hero Tales of Ulysses and the Men of Old. Pape, Frank Cheyne (1878-), illus. LC 11-1346. vii p., 1 l., 384 p. front., 7 pl. 21 cm. $1.35. 1911. H. Holt and Company.

Storr, Francis (1839-1919) & Turner, Hawes, eds.
--Canterbury Chimes: Or, Chaucer Tales Retold for Children. (Original Author: Chaucer/Geoffry). N.D. E P Dutton & Co.
--Canterbury Chimes: Or, Chaucer Tales Retold For Children. (Original Author: Chaucer/Geoffry). (Illus.). N.D. Messrs. Roberts Brothers.

Stortz, Diane
--My Thank You Book. Rev. ed. Miller, Marjorie, ed. Hook, Frances Arnold (1912-), illus. (Illus.). 28p. (Orig.). (ps-3). N.D. (ISBN 0-87239-558-8). Standard Pub.

Story, Bettie Wilson
--The Other Side of the Tell: Adventure on an Archaeological Dig in the Desert of Israel. Fleishman, Seymour (1918-), illus. LC 76-1548. (Illus.). 150 p. 18cm. c.1976. (ISBN 0-912692-92-8). D. C. Cook Pub. Co.
--River of Fire. 1978. (ISBN 0-89191-170-7). Cook.
--Summer of Jubilee. Kohn, Arnold, illus. LC 77-71908. (Illus.). 132 p. 18cm. c.1977. (ISBN 0-89191-071-9). D. C. Cook Pub. Co.
--Under the Eye of the Blazing Sun. 1982. (ISBN 0-686-34603-3). Caroline Hse.
--Under the Eye of the Blazing Sun. 1981. (ISBN 0-89191-532-X). Cook.
--Under the Eye of the Blazing Sun: Two Adventure Novels and a Romance. LC 81-18139. (Illus.). 455 p. 19cm. c.1981. (ISBN 0-89191-532-X). Chariot Books.

Story, Elisabeth Pausinger, tr. see Spyri, Johanna Heusser.

Story Parade Magazine
--Adventure Stories from Story Parade: Outstanding Stories of Adventure. LC 50-6686. 314 p. illus. 24 cm. 1950. Winston.
--Animal Story Parade: Favorite Stories of Animals. LC 51-8074. (Illus.). 28cm. 68p. 1951. Garden City Books.
--Story Parade: A Collection of Modern Stories for Boys and Girls. LC 37-27028. ix, 1 331 p. illus. 23 1/2 cm. c.1936. The John C. Winston.
--Story Parade Mystery Book. Parker, Lockie, ed. LC 53-8208. 255p. illus. 21cm. 1953. Abelard.

Story, Walter Scott
--Boy Heroes of the Sea. Clarke, William Wallace, illus. LC 28-20761. 6 p. l., 3-274 p. front., plates. 19 1/2 cm. 1928. The Century Co.
--Skinny Harrison, Adventurer. N.D. Lothrop,Lee & Shepard.
--The Uncharted Island. Lee, Manning De Villeneuve (1894-1980), illus. LC 26-15716. v p., 2 l., 3-325 p. front., plates. 19 1/2 cm. 1926. The Century Co.
--The Young Crusader, How Richard of Devon Served Richard the Lion-Hearted. Merrill, Frank Thayer (1848-), illus. LC 23-12448. 336 p. front., plates. 19 1/2 cm. c.1923. Lothrop.

The, Storytellers' Magazine
--The Storytellers. Wood, Harry, illus. LC 15-15700. (Six Months with the Storytellers' Magazine; with Numerous Illustrations). xi, 1, 370 p. incl. front., illus. 23 cm. $1.60. 1915. The Storytellers Company.

Stott, Rowena
--The Hedgehog Feast. Holden, Edith, illus. LC 78-54668. (Illus.). 18p. (gr. 1 up). 1978. (ISBN 0-671-96193-4). Windmill Bks.

Stott, Rowena, jt. auth. see Holden, Edith.

Stottle, Burr S
--Hunting the Tango: A Novel. Wood, Harry, illus. LC 16-14636. 218 p. incl. front. 20 cm. c.1916. Burton Publishing Company.

Stoughton Holbourn, Ian Bernard (1872-1935)
--The Child of the Moat: A Story for Girls. 1557 A.D. LC 16-24926. 5 p. l., 408 p. incl. illus., pl. 19 1/2 cm. 1916. G. A. Shaw.

Stout, Bert, jt. auth. see Reed, Alan.

Stout, Robert T.
--Children's Favorite Story of Santa Claus. Stout, Robert T., illus. (Illus.). 32p. (ps-6). 1982. (ISBN 0-911049-08-8). (ISBN 0-911049-04-5). Yuletide Intl.
--The Noorps Are Coming. Stout, Robert T., illus. (Illus.). 32p. (ps-6). 1982. (ISBN 0-911049-05-3). Yuletide Intl.
--The Original Story of Santa Claus. Stout, Robert T., illus. (Illus.). 56p. (ps-8). 1981. (ISBN 0-911049-00-2). Yuletide Intl.
--The Secret of Halloween. Stout, Robert T., illus. (Illus.). 24p. (Orig.). (ps-6). 1982. (ISBN 0-911049-02-9). Yuletide Intl.

Stout, S. J, jt. auth. see Holt, Roy D.

Stoutenberg, Adrien Pearl see Arden, Barbi, pseud.

Stoutenberg, Adrien Pearl see Minier, Nelson, pseud.

Stoutenburg, Adrien Pearl see Kendall, Lace, pseud.

Stoutenburg, Adrien Pearl, et al. (1916-)
--Everygirls Sports Stories. Furman, Abraham Loew (1902-), ed. LC 56-12152. 221p. illus. 21cm. (Everygirls library). 1956. Lantern Press.

Stoutenburg, Adrien Pearl (1916-)
--American Tall Tale Animals. Powers, Richard M. Gorman (1921-), illus. (Illus.). 128 p. 26cm. 1968. Viking Press.
--American Tall Tales. Powers, Richard M. Gorman (1921-), illus. LC 76-28350. p. cm. (Puffin books). 1976. (ISBN 0-670-12032-4). (ISBN 0-670-05027-X). Penguin Books.
--American Tall Tales. Powers, Richard M. Gorman (1921-), illus. LC 65-13352. (Illus.). 112 p. 26cm. 1966. Viking Press.
--The Blue-Eyed Convertible. LC 61-5570. 157 p. 21cm. 1961. Westminster Press.
--A Cat Is. Katzoff, Sy, illus. LC 77-134658. (Illus.). 48 p. 27cm. 1971. (ISBN 0-531-01969-1). F. Watts.
--The Crocodile's Mouth: Folk-Song Stories. Rounds, Glen Harold (1906-), illus. LC 66-7040. 64p. illus. 26cm. 1966. Viking.
--Fee, Fi, Fo, Fum: Friendly and Funny Giants. Negri, Rocco (1932-), illus. LC 74-85870. (Illus.). 126, 1 p. 26cm. 1969. (ISBN 0-670-31127-8). Viking Press.
--Four on the Road. LC 59-9089. 175 p. 21 cm. 1959. Westminster Press.
--Good-by: Cindrella. LC 60-5616. 173 p. 21 cm. 1960. Westminster Press.
--Haran's Journey. Kubinyi, Laszlo (1937-), illus. LC 75-153733. (Illus.). 118 p. 24cm. 1971. Dial Press.
--Honeymoon. LC 58-7702. 160 p. 21 cm. 1958. Westminster Press.
--In This Corner. LC 57-8072. 191 p. 22 cm. 1957. Westminster Press.
--Little Smoke. Kendall, Lace, pseud. Savitt, Sam (1917-), illus. LC 61-5889. unpaged. illus. 24 cm. (gr. 1-4). 1961. (ISBN 0-698-30224-9). Coward-McCann.
--The Model Airplane Mystery. LC 43-16231. 1 p. l., v-vi p., 1 l., 249 p. 20 1/2 cm. 1943. Doubleday, Doran & Co., Inc.
--The Mud Ponies. Kendall, Lace, pseud. Fern, Eugene A. (1919-), illus. LC 63-10169. (Based on a Pawnee Indian Myth). 62 p. illus. 25 cm. 1963. Coward-McCann.
--Out There. LC 77-150118. 222 p. 25cm. 1971. (ISBN 0-670-53269-X). Viking Press.
--Rain Boat. Kendall, Lace, pseud. Kaufmann, John (1931-), illus. LC 65-13287. 159p. illus. 23cm. c.1965. Coward.
--River Duel. LC 56-7100. 188p. 21cm. 1956. Westminster Press.
--The Secret Lions. Kendall, Lee, pseud. Howland, Douglas, illus. LC 62-7999. (Illus.). 48p. 1962. Coward-McCann.
--The Silver Trap. LC 53-9211. 205p. 22cm. 1954. Westminster Press.
--Stranger on the Bay. LC 55-7808. 176 p. 21cm. 1955. Westminster Press.
--The Things That Are. Lostutter, Robert, illus. LC 64-20523. 55 p. col. illus. 24 cm. 1964. Reilly & Lee Co.
--Timber Line Treasure. Turkle, Brinton Cassaday (1915-), illus. LC 51-12725. 218 p. illus. 22 cm. 1951. Westminster Press.
--A Time for Dreaming. LC 63-8202. 173 p. 21cm. 1963. Westminster Press.
--Walk into the Wind. LC 64-10801. 174 p. 21 cm. 1964. Westminster Press.
--Where to Now, Blue?. LC 78-4336. (Illus.). 186 p. 22cm. c.1978. (ISBN 0-590-07518-7). Four Winds Press.
--Window on the Sea. LC 62-7250. 159 p. 22 cm. 1962. Westminster Press.

--Rex. Wilson, Joyce Muriel Judson. 224p. 1968. (ISBN 0-670-59720-1). Viking Press.
--The Wind on the Dragon. Wilson, Joyce Muriel Judson. 192p. 1969. Viking Press.
--Zara. Wilson, Joyce Muriel Judson. 224p. 1970. (ISBN 0-670-79633-6). Viking Press.

Strasser, Todd
--Angel Dust Blues. LC 78-31735. 1979. (ISBN 0-698-20485-9, Coward). Putnam Pub Group.
--Angel Dust Blues: A Novel. LC 78-31735. 203 p. 22cm. c.1979. (ISBN 0-698-20485-9). Coward, McCann & Geoghegan.
--The Complete Computer Popularity Program. LC 84-5000. 137p. (gr. 4-6). 1984. (ISBN 0-385-29352-6). Delacorte.
--Friends till the End: A Novel. LC 80-68738. 199 p. 22cm. c.1981. (ISBN 0-440-02750-0). Delacorte Press.
--Rock 'N' Roll Nights. 11 x 12 1/2. 232p. Repr. of 1982 ed (Pub. by Delacorte). (15 pt.). (gr. 8-10). N.D. Am Printing Hse.
--Rock 'n' Roll Nights: A Novel. LC 81-12618. 217 p. 22cm. c.1982. (ISBN 0-440-07407-X). Delacorte.
--Turn It up!. A Novel. LC 83-20915. 177 p. 22cm. c.1984. (ISBN 0-385-29282-1). Delacorte Press.
--A Very Touchy Subject. LC 84-16963. 180 p. 22cm. c.1985. (ISBN 0-385-29378-X). Delacorte.
--Workin' for Peanuts. LC 82-14070. 196 p. 22cm. c.1983. (ISBN 0-440-09401-1). Delacorte Press.

Stratemeyer, Edward L. see Abbott, Manager Henry, pseud.
Stratemeyer, Edward L. see Alger, Horatio, pseud.
Stratemeyer, Edward L. see Bell, Emerson, pseud.
Stratemeyer, Edward L. see Bonehill, Captain Ralph, pseud.
Stratemeyer, Edward L. see Bowie, Jim, pseud.
Stratemeyer, Edward L. see Daly, Jim, pseud.
Stratemeyer, Edward L. see Henty, D. T., pseud.
Stratemeyer, Edward L. see James, Captain Lew, pseud.
Stratemeyer, Edward L. see Pad, Peter, pseud.
Stratemeyer, Edward L. see St. Meyer, Ned, pseud.
Stratemeyer, Edward L. see Strayer, E. Ward, pseud.
Stratemeyer, Edward L. see Ward, Tom, pseud.
Stratemeyer, Edward L. see Winfield, Arthur M., pseud.
Stratemeyer, Edward L. see Woods, Nat, pseud.
Stratemeyer, Edward L. see Zimmy, pseud.
Stratemeyer, Edward L., jt. auth. see Adams, William Taylor.
Stratemeyer, Edward L., jt. auth. see Charles, Louis.

Stratemeyer, Edward L. (1862-1930)
--The Aircraft Boys of Lakeport: Or, Rivals of the Clouds. Boehm, H. Richard, illus. LC 12-22134. viii p. 1 l., 320 p. incl. front. plates. 19 cm. (The Lakeport Ser.: Vol. 6). 1912. Lothrop, Lee & Shepard Co.
--At the Fall of Montreal: Or, A Soldier Boy's Final Victory. Shute, A. Burnham, illus. LC 3-19437. 19cm. 312p. (The Colonial Ser.: No. 3). 1903. Lothrop, Lee & Shepard.
--At the Fall of Port Arthur: Or, A Young American in the Japanese Navy. Shute, A. Burnham, illus. LC 5-10449. x p., 1 l., 281 p. fornt., 7 pl. 19 cm. (Soldiers of Fortune Ser.: Vol. 3). 1905. Lothrop, Lee and Shepard.
--The Automobile Boys of Lakeport: Or, A Run for Fun and Fame. Goss, John, illus. LC 10-25829. 19cm. 315p. (The Lakeport Ser.: Vol. 5). 1910. Lothrop,Lee & Shepard.
--The Baseball Boys of Lakeport: Or, The Winning Run. Klepper, Max F., illus. LC 8-17828. viii p. 1 l., 315 p. front., 5 pl. 19 cm. Repr. of 1905 ed (Pub. by A. S. Barnes). (The Lakeport Ser.: Vol. 2). Orig. Title: The Winning Run; Or, The Baseball Boys of Lakeport. c.1908. Lothrop, Lee & Shepard Co.
--Between Boer and Briton: Or, Two Boys' Adventures in South Africa. Repr. of 1900 ed (Pub. by Lee & Shepard). (Stratemeyer Popular Ser.: Vol. 13). N.D. Grosset & Dunlap.
--Between Boer and Briton: Or, Two Boys' Adventures in South Africa. Shute, A. Burnham, illus. LC 4792. vii, 354 p. front., plates. 18 1/2 cm. 1900. Lee and Shepard.
--Between Boer and Briton: Or, Two Boys' Adventures in South Africa. Shute, A. Burnham, illus. Reissue of 1900 ed. (Stratemeyer Popular Ser.: Vol. 13). N.D. Lothrop, Lee & Shepard.
--The Boat Club Boys of Lakeport: Or, The Water Champions. Nuttall, Charles, illus. LC 8-22240. viii p., 1 l., 297 p. front. 7 pl. 19 cm. (The Lakeport Ser.: Vol. 3). 1908. Lothrop, Lee & Shepard Co.
--Bob, the Photographer: Or, a Hero in Spite of Himself. Winfield, Arthur M., pseud. LC 2-27943. 19cm. 325p. 1902. Wessels Co.
--Bob the Photographer: Or, Strictly on the Job. Repr. (The Alger Ser.: No. 123). 1920. Street & Smith.
--Bound to be an Electrician: Or, Franklin Bell's Success. Repr. (Stratemeyer Popular Ser.: Vol. 8). N.D. Grosset & Dunlap.
--Bound to be an Electrician: Or, Franklin Bell's Success. Repr. (The Alger Ser.: No. 105). 1920. Street & Smith.
--Bound to be an Electrician: Or, Franklin Bell's Success. Bridges, M. B. & Puente, H., illus. LC 3-20581. 20cm. 249p. Repr. (Working Upward Ser.: Vol. 2). 1903. Lee & Shepard.
--Bound to be an Electrician: Or, Franklin Bell's Success. Bridges, M. B. & Dupont, G. B., illus. Repr. (Stratemeyer Popular Ser.: Vol. 8). N.D. Lothrop, Lee & Shepard.
--Bound to be an Electrician: Or, Franklin Bell's Success. Bridges, M. B. & Puente, H., illus. Repr. (Working Upward Ser.: Vol. 2). N.D. M. A. Donohue & Co.
--Bound to be an Electrician: Or, Franklin Bell's Success. Bridges, M. B. & Puente, H., illus. (Bound to Win Ser.: Vol. 1). 1897. W. L. Allison Co.
--Bound to be an Electrician: Or, Franklin Bell's Success. Bridges, M. B. & Puente, H., illus. Repr. (Working Upward Ser.: Vol. 2). N.D. W. L. Allison Co.
--Boys of the Fort: Or, True Courage Wins. Repr. of 1901 ed (Pub. by Mershon Co). (The Alger Ser.: No. 120). Orig. Title: Boys of the Fort; Or, A Young Captain's Pluck. 1920. Street & Smith.
--Boys of the Gold Fields: Or, The Nugget Hunters. Repr. of 1900 ed (Pub. by Stitt Publishing Co). (The Alger Ser.: No. 115). Orig. Title: Pioneer Boys of the Gold Fields; Or, The Nugget Hunters of '49. 1920. Street & Smith.
--Boys of the Great Northwest: Or, Across the Rockies. Repr. of 1904 ed (Pub. by Mershon Co). (The Alger Ser.: No. 114). Orig. Title: Pioneer Boys of the Great Northwest; Or, With Lewis and Clark across the Rockies. 1920. Street & Smith.
--Boys of the Wilderness: Or, Down in Old Kentucky. Repr. of 1903 ed (Pub. by Mershon Co). (The Alger Ser.: No. 113). Orig. Title: With Boone on the Frontier; Or, The Pioneer Boys of Old Kentucky. 1920. Street & Smith.
--The Campaign of the Jungle: Or, Under Lawton Through Luzon. Shute, A. Burnham, illus. LC 7-324391. vii, 316 p. front., 7 pl. 19 cm. (The Old Glory Ser.: Vol. 5). 1900. Lee and Shepard.
--Chased Across the Pampas: Or, American Boys in Argentina and Homeward Bound. Goss, John, illus. LC 11-24118. iv, 2 p. 1 l., 320 p. front., plates. 19 cm. (Pan-American Ser.: Vol. 6). 1911. Lothrop, Lee & Shepard Co.
--Comrades in Peril: Or, Afloat on a Battleship. Repr. of 1899 ed (Pub. by Mershon Co). (The Alger Ser.: No. 117). Orig. Title: A Sailor Boy with Dewey; Or, Afloat in the Philippines. 1920. Street & Smith.
--Dave Porter and His Classmates: Or, For the Honor of Oak Hall. Nuttall, Charles, illus. LC 9-9468. vi p., 1 l., 308 p. front., 7 pl. 19 cm. (The Dave Porter Ser.: Vol. 5). 1909. Lothrop, Lee & Shepard Co.
--Dave Porter and His Double: Or, The Disappearance of the Basswood Fortune. Rogers, Walter S., illus. LC 16-20443. 4 p. l., 295 p. fornt. plates. 19 cm. (The Dave Porter Ser.: Vol. 12). 1916. Lothrop, Lee & Shepard Co.
--Dave Porter and His Rivals: Or, The Chums and Foes of Oak Hall. Goss, John, illus. LC 11-6442. vi p. 1 l., 308 p. 19 cm. $1.2. (The Dave Porter Ser.: Vol. 7). 1911. Lothrop, Lee & Shepard Co.
--Dave Porter and the Runaways: Or, Last Days at Oak Hall. Boehm, H. Richard, illus. LC 13-7080. xi p. 1 l., 301 p. front plates 19 cm. $1.2. (The Dave Porter Ser.: Vol. 9). 1913. Lothrop, Lee & Shepard Co.
--Dave Porter at Bear Camp: Or, The Wild Man of Mirror Lake. Rogers, Walter S., illus. LC 15-159548. 4 p. l., 308 p. front., plates., 19 cm. (The Dave Porter Ser.: Vol. 11). 1915. Lothrop, Lee & Shepard Co.
--Dave Porter at Oak Hall: Or, The School Days of an American Boy. Brett, Harold Matthews (1880-), illus. LC 5-32326. 19cm. (The Dave Porter Ser.: Vol. 1). 1905. Lothrop, Lee & Shepard.
--Dave Porter at Star Ranch: Or, The Cowboy's Secret. Hammond, Lyle T., illus. LC 10-162375. vi p. 1 l. 303 p. front. plates 19 cm. (The Dave Porter Ser.: Vol. 6). 1910. Lothrop, Lee & Shepard Co.
--Dave Porter in the Far North: Or, The Pluck of an American Schoolboy. Nuttall, Charles, illus. LC 8-10280. vii, 285 p. front. 7 pl. 19 cm. (The Dave Porter Ser.: Vol. 4). 1908. Lothrop, Lee & Shepard Co.
--Dave Porter in the Gold Fields: Or, The Search for the Landslide Mine. Rogers, Walter S., illus. LC 14-145420. vi p. 1 l., 303 p. front., plates 19 cm. (The Dave Porter Ser.: Vol. 10). 1914. Lothrop, Lee & Shepard Co.
--Dave Porter in the South Seas: Or, The Strange Cruise of the Stormy Petrel. Hazelton, Isaac Brewster, illus. LC 6-28448. 19cm. 286p. (The Dave Porter Ser.: Vol. 2). 1906. Lothrop, Lee & Shepard.
--Dave Porter on Cave Island: Or, A Schoolboy's Mysterious Mission. Boehm, H. Richard, illus. LC 12-8138. vii 300 p. front plates. 19 cm. (The Dave Porter Ser.: Vol. 8). 1912. Lothrop, Lee & Shepard Co.
--Dave Porter Under Fire: Or, A Young Army Engineer in France. Owen, Robert Emmett (1878-), illus. LC 18-17249. viii p. 1 l., 308 p. incl. front. plates 19 cm. (The Dave Porter Ser.: Vol. 14). 1918. Lothrop, Lee & Shepard Co.
--Dave Porter's Great Search: Or, The Perils of a Young Civil Engineer. Rogers, Walter S., illus. LC 17-28763. vi p. 1 l., 309 p. front., plates. 19 cm. (The Dave Porter Ser.: Vol. 13). 1917. Lothrop, Lee & Shepard Co.
--Dave Porter's Return to School. Or, Winning the Medal of Honor. Edge, F. Gilbert, illus. LC 7-12696. vi p. 1 l., 304 p. front., 7 pl. 19 cm. (The Dave Porter Ser.: Vol. 3). 1907. Lothrop, Lee & Shepard Co.
--Dave Porter's War Honors: Or, At the Front with the Fighting Engineers. Owen, Robert Emmett (1878-), illus. LC 19-6768. viii p. 1 l., 308 p. front. plates. 19 cm. (The Dave Porter Ser.: Vol. 15). 1919. Lothrop, Lee & Shepard Co.
--Defending His Flag: Or, a Boy in Blue and a Boy in Gray. Tyng, Griswold, illus. LC 7-27612. x p. 1 l., 431 p. front. 7 pl. 20 1/2 cm. 1907. Lothrop, Lee & Shepard Co.
--Fighting for His Own: Or, The Fortunes of a Young Artist. Repr. (Stratemeyer Popular Ser.: Vol. 10). N.D. Grosset & Dunlap.
--Fighting for His Own: Or, The Fortunes of a Young Artist. Repr. (The Alger Ser.: No. 107). 1920. Street & Smith.
--Fighting for His Own: Or, The Fortunes of a Young Artist. Bridges, M. B. & Dupont, G. B., illus. LC 3-20580. vi. 233 p. front., 3 pl. 19 1/2 cm. Repr. (Working Upward Ser.: Vol. 4). 1903. Lee and Shepard.
--Fighting for His Own: Or, The Fortunes of a Young Artist. Bridges, M. B. & Dupont, G. B., illus. Repr. (Working Upward Ser.: Vol. 4). N.D. M. A. Donohue & Co.
--Fighting for His Own: Or, The Fortunes of a Young Artist. Bridges, M. B. & Dupont, G. B., illus. Repr. (Working Upward Ser.: Vol. 4). N.D. W. L. Allison Co.
--Fighting for His Own: Or, The Fortunes of a Young Artist. Dupont, G. B., illus. Repr. (Stratemeyer Popular Ser.: Vol. 10). N.D. Lothrop, Lee & Shepard.
--Fighting for His Own: Or, the Fortunes of a Young Artist. DuPont, G. B. & Bridges, M. B., illus. LC 13-33881. (Illus.). 19cm. 233p. (Bound to Win Ser.: Vol. 10). 1897. W. L. Allison Co.
--Fighting in Cuban Waters: Or, Under Schley on the Brooklyn. Shute, A. Burnham, illus. 12cm. 344p. (The Old Glory Ser.: Vol. 3). c.1899. Lothrop Lee & Shepard.
--First at the North Pole: Or, Two Boys in the Arctic Circle. Repr. of 1909 ed (Pub. by Lee & Shepard). (Stratemeyer Popular Ser.: Vol. 15). N.D. Grosset & Dunlap.
--First at the North Pole: Or, Two Boys in the Arctic Circle. Nuttall, Charles, illus. LC 9-30119. viii p., 1 l., 314 p. front, 7 pl. 19 cm. $1.25. 1909. Lothrop, Lee & Shepard Co.
--The Football Boys of Lakeport: Or, More Goals Than One. Klepper, Max F., illus. LC 9-22621. viii p., 1 l., 324 p. incl. front. plates. 19 cm. $1.2. (The Lakeport Ser.: Vol. 4). 1909. Lothrop, Lee & Shepard Co.
--For His Country: Or, The Adventures of Two Chums. Repr. of 1899 ed (Pub. by Mershon Co). (The Alger Ser.: No. 116). Orig. Title: When Santiago Fell; Or, The War Adventures of Two Chums. 1920. Street & Smith.
--For the Liberty of Texas. Meynelle, Louis, illus. Repr. of 1900 ed (Pub. by Dana Estes & Co). (The Mexican War Ser.: Vol. 1). 1909. Lothrop, Lee & Shepard Co.
--For the Liberty of Texas. Meynelle, Louis, illus. Repr. of 1900 ed (Pub. by Dana Estes & Co). (The Mexican War Ser.: Vol. 1). 1917. Lothrop, Lee & Shepard Co.
--For the Liberty of Texas. Meynelle, Louis, illus. Repr. of 1900 ed (Pub. by Dana Estes & Co). (The Mexican War Ser.: Vol. 1). 1930. Lothrop, Lee & Shepard Co.
--The Fort in the Wilderness: Or, The Soldier Boys of the Indian Trails. Shute, A. Burnham, illus. (The Colonial Ser.: No. 5). 1905. Lothrop, Lee, & Shepard.
--The Gun Club Boys of Lakeport: Or, The Island Camp. Nuttall, Charles, illus. LC 8-17831. 4 p. l., 321 p. front., 5 pl. 19 cm. Repr. (The Lakeport Ser.: Vol. 1). c.1908. Lothrop, Lee & Shepard Co.
--Joe, the Surveyor: Or, The Value of a Lost Claim. Repr. (Stratemeyer Popular Ser.: Vol. 11). N.D. Grosset & Dunlap.
--Joe the Surveyor: Or, The Value of a Lost Claim. Repr. (The Alger Ser.: No. 108). 1920. Street & Smith.
--Joe the Surveyor: Or, The Value of a Lost Claim. Bridges, M. B. & Dupont, G. B., illus. Repr. (Stratemeyer Popular Ser.: Vol. 11). N.D. Lothrop, Lee & Shepard.
--Joe the Surveyor: Or, The Value of a Lost Claim. Shute, A. Burnham, illus. LC 3-11068. 19cm. 248p. 1903. Lee & Shepard.
--Larry the Wanderer: Or, the Rise of a Nobody. Repr. (Stratemeyer Popular Ser.: Vol. 12). N.D. Grosset & Dunlap.
--Larry the Wanderer: Or, The Rise of a Nobody. Repr. (The Alger Ser.: No. 109). 1920. Street & Smith.
--Larry the Wanderer: Or, The Rise of a Nobody. Shute, A. Burnham, illus. LC 4-22839. x. 263 p. front., 5 pl. 19 1/2 cm. 1904. Lee and Shepard.
--Larry the Wanderer: Or, The Rise of a Nobody. Shute, A. Burnham, illus. Repr. (Stratemeyer Popular Ser.: Vol. 12). N.D. Lothrop, Lee & Shepard.
--The Last Cruise of the Spitfire: Or, Luke Foster's Strange Voyage. Repr. (Stratemeyer Popular Ser.: Vol. 1). N.D. Grosset & Dunlap.
--The Last Cruise of the Spitfire. Or, Luke Foster's Strange Voyage. rev. ed. LC 3281. (Illus.). vi, 5-245 p. front., plates. 19 cm. (Ship and Shore Ser.: Vol. 1). 1900. Lee and Shepard.
--The Last Cruise of the Spitfire: Or, Luke Foster's Strange Voyage. Repr. (The Alger Ser.: No. 98). 1919. Street & Smith.
--The Last Cruise of The Spitfire: Or, Luke Foster's Strange Voyage. (Illus.). (Ship and Shore Ser.: Vol. 1). 1894. The Merriam Co.
--The Last Cruise of the Spitfire: Or, Luke Foster's Strange Voyage. Boutwood, Charles E., illus. Repr. (Stratemeyer Popular Ser.: Vol. 1). N.D. Lothrop, Lee & Shepard.
--Lost in the Land of Ice: Or, Under the Northern Lights. Repr. (The Alger Ser.: No. 122). 1920. Street & Smith.
--Lost in the Orinoco: Or, American Boys in Venezuela. Shute, A. Burnham, illus. Reissue of 1902 ed. (Pan-American Ser.: Vol. 1). 1905. Lothrop, Lee & Shepard.
Lost on the Orinoco: Or, American Boys in Venezuela. Shute, A. Burnham, illus. LC 2-12216. viii p., 1 l., 312 p. front., plates. 18 1/2 cm. (Pan-American Ser.: Vol. 1). 1902. Lee and Shepard.
--Marching on Niagara: Or, The Soldier Boys of the Old Frontier. Shute, A. Burnham, illus. (The Colonial Ser.: No. 2). 1902. Lothrop, Lee & Shepard.
--The Minute Boys of Bunker Hill, 1 of 2 vols. Kennedy, J. W. Ferguson, illus. LC 99-4118. 308 p. incl. front. plates. 19 1/2 cm. (The Minute Boys Ser.: No. 2). 1899. Set. Dana Estes & Co.
--The Minute Boys of Bunker Hill. Kennedy, J. W. Ferguson, illus. Repr. of 1899 ed (Pub. by Dana Estes & Co). (The Minute Boys Ser.: Vol. 9). N.D. L. C. Page & Co.
--The Minute Boys of Lexington, 1 of 2 vols. Shute, A. Burnham, illus. (The Minute Boys Ser.: No. 1). 1898. Set. Dana Estes & Co.
--The Minute Boys of Lexington. Shute, A. Burnham, illus. Repr. of 1898 ed (Pub. by Dana Estes & Co). (The Minute Boys Ser.: Vol. 10). N.D. L. C. Page & Co.
--Oliver Bright's Search: Or, The Mystery of a Mine. Repr. (Stratemeyer Popular Ser.: Vol. 5). N.D. Grosset & Dunlap.
--Oliver Bright's Search: Or, The Mystery of a Mine. Repr. (Working Upward Ser.: Vol. 5). 1903. Lee & Shepard.
--Oliver Bright's Search: Or, The Mystery of a Mine. Repr. (The Alger Ser.: No. 102). 1920. Street & Smith.
--Oliver Bright's Search: Or, the Mystery of a Mine. rev. ed. Boutwood, Charles E., illus. LC 99-216521. iv. 3-242 p. front., plates. 19 cm. (The Bound to Succeed Ser.: Vol. 2). 1899. Lee and Shepard.
--Oliver Bright's Search: Or, The Mystery of a Mine. Boutwood, Charles E., illus. Repr. (Stratemeyer Popular Ser.: Vol. 5). N.D. Lothrop, Lee & Shepard.
--Oliver Bright's Search: Or, The Mystery of a Mine. Boutwood, Charles E., illus. (The Bound to Succeed Ser.: Vol. 2). 1895. Merriam Co.
--On Fortune's Trail: Or, The Heroes of the Black Hills. Repr. of 1902 ed (Pub. by Mershon Co). (The Alger Ser.: No. 121). Orig. Title. With Custer in the Black Hills; Or, A Young Scout among the Indians. 1920. Street & Smith.

--On the Trail of Pontiac: Or, The Pioneer Boys of the Ohio. Shute, A. Burnham, illus. LC 4-21590. x p. 1 l., 311 p. front., 7 pl. 19 cm. (The Colonial Ser.: No. 4). 1904. Lee and Shepard.

--On to Pekin: Or, Old Glory in China. Shute, A. Burnham, illus. LC 6845. vii, 322 p. front., plates 19 cm. (Soldiers of Fortune Ser.: Vol. 1). 1900. Lee & Shepard.

--On to Pekin: Or, Old Glory in China. Shute, A. Burnham, illus. Reissue of 1900 ed. (Soldiers of Fortune Ser.: Vol. 1). N.D. Lothrop, Lee & Shepard.

--Reuben Stone's Discovery: Or, The Young Miller of Torrent Bend. Repr. (Stratemeyer Popular Ser.: Vol. 2). N.D. Grosset & Dunlap.

--Reuben Stone's Discovery: Or, The Young Miller of Torrent Bend. Rev ed. LC 3282. (Illus.). iv, 5-260 p. front., plates 19 cm. (Ship and Shore Ser.: Vol. 2). 1900. Lee and Shepard.

--Reuben Stone's Discovery: Or, The Young Miller of Torrent Bend. Repr. (The Alger Ser.: No. 99). 1919. Street & Smith.

--Reuben Stone's Discovery: Or, The Young Miller of Torrent Bend. Boutwood, Charles E., illus. Repr. (Stratemeyer Popular Ser.: Vol. 2). N.D. Lothrop, Lee & Shepard.

--Reuben Stone's Discovery: Or, The Young Miller of Torrent Bend. Boutwood, Charles E., illus. LC 18-208521. 260 p. incl. front. plates. 20 1/2 cm. (Ship and Shore Ser.: Vol. 2). 1895. The Merriam Co.

--Richard Dare's Venture: Or, Striking Out for Himself. Repr. (Stratemeyer Popular Ser.: Vol. 4). N.D. Grosset & Dunlap.

--Richard Dare's Venture: Or, Striking Out for Himself. Repr. (Working Upward Ser.: Vol. 6). 1903. Lee & Shepard.

--Richard Dare's Venture: Or, Striking Out for Himself. Repr. (The Alger Ser.: No. 101). 1919. Street & Smith.

--Richard Dare's Venture: Or, Striking Out for Himself. rev. ed. Boutwood, Charles E., illus. LC 99-2040. iv. p. 1 l., 5-248 p. front. plate. 19 cm. (The Bound to Succeed Ser.: Vol. 1). 1899. Lee and Shepard.

--Richard Dare's Venture: Or, Striking Out for Himself. Boutwood, Charles E., illus. Repr. (Stratemeyer Popular Ser.: Vol. 4). N.D. Lothrop, Lee & Shepard.

--Richard Dare's Venture: Or, Striking Out for Himself. Boutwood, Charles E., illus. LC 13-338630. 248 p. front. plates. 19 1/2 cm. (The Bound to Succeed Ser.: Vol. 1). 1894. Merriam Co.

--Shorthand Tom: Or, the Exploits of a Young Reporter. DuPont, G. B., illus. LC 13-338707. 259 p. front. plates. 19 cm. (Bound to Win Ser.: Vol. 4). c.1897. W. L. Allison Co.

--Shorthand Tom, the Reporter: Or, The Exploits of a Bright Boy. Repr. (Stratemeyer Popular Ser.: Vol. 9). N.D. Grosset & Dunlap.

--Shorthand Tom the Reporter: Or, The Exploits of a Bright Boy. Repr. (The Alger Ser.: No. 106). 1920. Street & Smith.

--Shorthand Tom, the Reporter: Or, The Exploits of a Bright Boy. Bridges, M. B. & Puente, H., illus. Repr. (Stratemeyer Popular Ser.: Vol. 9). N.D. Lothrop, Lee & Shepard.

--Shorthand Tom, the Reporter: Or, The Exploits of a Bright Boy. Dupont, G. B., illus. LC 3-20583. iv p. 1 l., 5-259 p. front., 3 pl. 19 cm. Repr. (Working Upward Ser.: Vol. 3). 1903. Lee and Shepard.

--Shorthand Tom, the Reporter: Or, The Exploits of a Bright Boy. Dupont, G. B., illus. Repr. (Working Upward Ser.: Vol. 3). N.D. M. A. Donohue & Co.

--Shorthand Tom, the Reporter: Or, The Exploits of a Bright Boy. Dupont, G. B., illus. Repr. (Working Upward Ser.: Vol. 3). N.D. W. L. Allison Co.

--To Alaska for Gold: Or, The Fortune Hunters of the Yukon. Repr. of 1899 ed (Pub. by Lee & Shepard). (Stratemeyer Popular Ser.: Vol. 6). N.D. Grosset & Dunlap.

--To Alaska for Gold: Or, The Fortune Hunters of the Yukon. Repr. of 1899 ed (Pub. by Lee & Shepard). (The Alger Ser.: No. 103). 1920. Street & Smith.

--To Alaska for Gold: Or, The Fortune Hunters of the Yukon. Shute, A. Burnham, illus. LC 99-3687. vi, 1 l., 248 front., plates. 20. (The Bound to Succeed Ser.: Vol. 3). 1899. Lee & Shepard.

--To Alaska for Gold: Or, The Fortune Hunters of the Yukon. Shute, A. Burnham, illus. Reissue of 1899 ed. (Stratemeyer Popular Ser.: Vol. 6). N.D. Lothrop, Lee & Shepard.

--Trail and Trading Post: Or, The Young Hunters of the Ohio. Kennedy, J. W. Ferguson, illus. LC 6-34682. x p. 1 l., 311 p. front. 7 pl. 19 cm. (The Colonial Ser.: No. 6). 1906. Lothrop, Lee & Shepard Co.

--Treasure Seekers of the Andes: Or, American Boys in Peru. Nuttall, Charles, illus. LC 7-26595. viii p., 1 l., 327 p. front. 7 pl. 19 1/2 cm. (Pan-American Ser.: Vol. 5). 1907. Lothrop, Lee & Shepard Co.

--True to Himself: Or, Roger Strong's Struggle for Peace. Repr. (Stratemeyer Popular Ser.: Vol. 3). N.D. Grosset & Dunlap.

--True to Himself: Or, Roger Strong's Struggle for Place. Repr. (The Alger Ser.: No. 100). 1919. Street & Smith.

--True to Himself: Or, Roger Strong's Struggle for Place. Shute, A. Burnham, illus. 280p. (Ship and Shore Ser.: Vol. 3). 1900. Lee & Shepard.

--True to Himself: Or, Roger Strong's Struggle for Place. Shute, A. Burnham, illus. LC 8-30424. vi p., 1 l., 280 p. front., 3 pl. 19 cm. Repr. (Stratemeyer Popular Ser.: Vol. 3). N.D. Lothrop, Lee & Shepard Co.

--Two Young Lumbermen: Or, From Maine to Oregon for Fortune. Repr. of 1903 ed (Pub. by Lee & Shepard). (Stratemeyer Popular Ser.: Vol. 14). N.D. Grosset & Dunlap.

--Two Young Lumbermen: Or, From Maine to Oregon for Fortune. Shute, A. Burnham, illus. LC 3-38960. 19cm. 326p. (Great American Industries Ser.: Vol. 1). 1903. Lee & Shepard.

--Two Young Lumbermen: Or, From Maine to Oregon for Fortune. Shute, A. Burnham, illus. Reissue of 1903 ed. (Stratemeyer Popular Ser.: Vol. 14). N.D. Lothrop, Lee & Shepard.

--Under Dewey at Manila: Or, The War Fortunes of a Castaway. Shute, A. Burnham, illus. 19cm. 282p. (The Old Glory Ser.: Vol. 1). 1898. Lothrop Lee & Shepard.

--Under MacArthur in Luzon: Or, Last Battles in the Philippines. Shute, A. Burnham, illus. ix, 312 p. front., plates 18 1/2 cm. (The Old Glory Ser.: Vol. 6). 1901. Lee and Shepard.

--Under Otis in the Philippines: Or, A Young Officer in the Tropics. Shute, A. Burnham, illus. 1 p. 1., vii, 332 p. pl. 19 cm. (The Old Glory Ser.: Vol. 4). 1899. Lothrop Lee & Shepard.

--Under Scott in Mexico. Mora, Joseph Jacinto (1876-), illus. LC 9-10035. vi, 2 p., 1 l., 11-287 p. front., 7 pl. 19 cm. Repr. of 1902 ed (Pub. by Dana Estes & Co). (The Mexican War Ser.: Vol. 3). c.1909. Lothrop, Lee & Shepard Co.

--Under Scott in Mexico. Mora, Joseph Jacinto (1876-), illus. Repr. of 1902 ed (Pub. by Dana Estes & Co). (The Mexican War Ser.: Vol. 3). 1917. Lothrop, Lee & Shepard Co.

--Under Scott in Mexico. Mora, Joseph Jacinto (1876-), illus. Repr. of 1902 ed (Pub. by Dana Estes & Co). (The Mexican War Ser.: Vol. 3). 1930. Lothrop, Lee & Shepard Co.

--Under the Mikado's Flag: Or, Young Soldiers of Fortune. Shute, A. Burnham, illus. LC 4-33214. viii p., 1 ., 305 p. front., 7 pl. 19 cm. (Soldiers of Fortune Ser.: Vol. 2). 1904. Lee & Shepard.

--Under the Mikado's Flag: Or, Young Soldiers of Fortune. Shute, A. Burnham, illus. Reissue of 1904 ed. (Soldiers of Fortune Ser.: Vol. 2). N.D. Lothrop, Lee & Shepard.

--Under Togo for Japan: Or, Three Young Americans on Land and Sea. Shute, A. Burnham, illus. LC 6-9277. viii p., 1 l., 309 p. front., 7 pl. 19 cm. (Soldiers of Fortune Ser.: Vol. 4). 1906. Lothrop, Lee & Shepard.

--Under Togo for Japan: Or, Three Young Americans on Land and Sea. Shute, A. Burnham, illus. LC 42-48594. 20cm. 300p. (Soldiers of Fortune Series). 1930. Lothrop, Lee & Shepard.

--With Taylor on the Rio Grande. Kennedy, J. W. Ferguson, illus. LC 9-10029. 287 p. front., 7 pl. 19 cm. Repr. of 1901 ed (Pub. by Dana Estes & Co). (The Mexican War Ser.: Vol. 2). c.1909. Lothrop, Lee & Shepard Co.

--With Taylor on the Rio Grande. Kennedy, J. W. Ferguson, illus. Repr. of 1901 ed (Pub. by Dana Estes & Co). (The Mexican War Ser.: Vol. 2). 1917. Lothrop, Lee & Shepard Co.

--With Taylor on the Rio Grande. Kennedy, J. W. Ferguson, illus. Repr. of 1901 ed (Pub. by Dana Estes & Co). (The Mexican War Ser.: Vol. 2). 1930. Lothrop, Lee & Shepard.

--With Washington in the West: Or, a Soldier Boy's Battles in the Wilderness. Shute, A. Burnham, illus. LC 1-23698. viii p. 1 l., 302 p. front., plates. 19 cm. (The Colonial Ser.: No. 1). 1901. Lee and Shepard.

--The Young Auctioneer: Or, The Polishing of a Rolling Stone. Repr. (Stratemeyer Popular Ser.: Vol. 7). N.D. Grosset & Dunlap.

--The Young Auctioneer: Or, The Polishing of a Rolling Stone. Repr. (The Alger Ser.: No. 104). 1920. Street & Smith.

--The Young Auctioneer: Or, The Polishing of a Rolling Stone. Bridges, M. B. & DuPont, G. B., illus. LC 3-20456. 20cm. 310p. Repr. (Working Upward Ser.: Vol. 1). 1903. Lee & Shepard.

--The Young Auctioneer: Or, The Polishing of a Rolling Stone. Bridges, M. B. & Dupont, G. B., illus. Repr. (Working Upward Ser.: Vol. 1). N.D. M. A. Donohue & Co.

--The Young Auctioneer: Or, The Polishing of a Rolling Stone. Bridges, M. B. & Dupont, G. B., illus. Repr. (Working Upward Ser.: Vol. 1). N.D. W. L. Allison Co.

--The Young Auctioneer: Or, The Polishing of a Rolling Stone. Shute, A. Burnham, illus. Repr. (Stratemeyer Popular Ser.: Vol. 7). N.D. Lothrop, Lee & Shepard.

--The Young Auctioneers: Or, The Polishing of a Rolling Stone. DuPont, G. B. & Bridges, M. B., illus. (Bound to Win Ser.: Vol. 7). 1897. W. L. Allison Co.

--The Young Bandmaster: Or, Against Big Odds. Repr. (The Alger Ser.: No. 119). 1920. Street & Smith.

--Young Explorers of the Amazon: Or, American Boys in Brazil. Shute, A. Burnham, illus. LC 4-8275. 1 p. l., viii p., 1 l., 350 p. front., 7 pl. 19 cm. (Pan-American Ser.: Vol. 4). 1904. Lee and Shepard.

--Young Explorers of the Amazon: Or, American Boys in Brazil. Shute, A. Burnham, illus. Reissue of 1904 ed. (Pan-American Ser.: Vol. 4). N.D. Lothrop, Lee & Shepard.

--Young Explorers of the Isthmus: Or, American Boys in Central America. Shute, A. Burnham, illus. LC 3-8338. x p., 1 l., 306 p. front., pl. 19 cm. (Pan-American Ser.: Vol. 3). 1903. Lee and Shepard.

--Young Explorers of the Isthmus: Or, American Boys in Central America. Shute, A. Burnham, illus. Reissue of 1903 ed. (Pan-American Ser.: Vol. 3). N.D. Lothrop, Lee & Shepard.

--The Young Explorers: Or, Adventures above the Arctic Circle. Repr. of 1909 ed (Pub. by Lothrop, Lee & Shepard). (The Alger Ser.: No. 112). Orig. Title: First at the North Pole; Or, Two Boys in the Arctic Circle. 1920. Street & Smith.

--The Young Lumberman: Or, Out for Fortune. Repr. of 1903 ed (Pub. by Lee & Shepard). (The Alger Ser.: No. 111). Orig. Title: Two Young Lumbermen; Or, From Maine to Oregon. 1920. Street & Smith.

--The Young Pearl Hunters: Or, In Hawaiian Waters. Repr. of 1899 ed (Pub. by Mershon Co). (The Alger Ser.: No. 118). Orig. Title: Off for Hawaii; Or, The Mystery of a Great Volcano. 1920. Street & Smith.

--The Young Ranchman: Or, Between Boer and Briton. Repr. of 1900 ed (Pub. by Lee & Shepard). (The Alger Ser.: No. 110). Orig. Title: Between Boer and Briton; Or, Two Boys' Adventures in South Africa. 1920. Street & Smith.

--The Young Volcano Explorers: Or, American Boys in the West Indies. Shute, A. Burnham, illus. LC 2-26352. viii p. 1 l., 132 p. front., pl. 19 cm. (Pan-American Ser.: Vol. 2). 1902. Lee & Shepard.

--The Young Volcano Explorers: Or, American Boys in the West Indies. Shute, A. Burnham, illus. Reissue of 1902 ed. (Pan-American Ser.: Vol. 2). N.D. Lothrop, Lee & Shepard.

--A Young Volunteer in Cuba: Or, Fighting for the Single Star. Shute, A. Burnham, illus. LC 98-1681. vii, 298 p. pl. 18 cm. (The Old Glory Ser.: Vol. 2). 1898. Lee and Shepard.

Stratemeyer, Louis Charles see Charles, Louis, pseud.

Stratemeyer Syndicate see Allen, Captain Quincy, pseud.

Stratemeyer Syndicate see Appleton, Victor, pseud.

Stratemeyer Syndicate see Barnes, Elmer Tracey, pseud.

Stratemeyer Syndicate see Barnum, Richard, pseud.

Stratemeyer Syndicate see Barnum, Vance, pseud.

Stratemeyer Syndicate see Bartlett, Philip A., pseud.

Stratemeyer Syndicate see Barton, May Hollis, pseud.

Stratemeyer Syndicate see Beach, Charles Amory, pseud.

Stratemeyer Syndicate see Carr, Annie Roe, pseud.

Stratemeyer Syndicate see Carson, James, pseud.

Stratemeyer Syndicate see Chadwick, Lester, pseud.

Stratemeyer Syndicate see Chapman, Allen, pseud.

Stratemeyer Syndicate see Cooper, James A., pseud.

Stratemeyer Syndicate see Cooper, John R., pseud.

Stratemeyer Syndicate see Davenport, Spencer, pseud.

Stratemeyer Syndicate see Dawson, Elmer A., pseud.

Stratemeyer Syndicate see Dixon, Franklin W., pseud.

Stratemeyer Syndicate see Duncan, Julia K., pseud.

Stratemeyer Syndicate see Emerson, Alice B., pseud.

Stratemeyer Syndicate see Endicott, Ruth Belmore, pseud.

Stratemeyer Syndicate see Ferris, James Cody, pseud.

Stratemeyer Syndicate see Forbes, Graham B, pseud.

Stratemeyer Syndicate see Gordon, Frederick, pseud.

Stratemeyer Syndicate see Hamilton, Robert W., pseud.

Stratemeyer Syndicate see Hardy, Alice Dale, pseud.

Stratemeyer Syndicate see Hawley, Mabel C., pseud.

Stratemeyer Syndicate see Henderley, Brooks, pseud.

Stratemeyer Syndicate see Hill, Grace Brooks, pseud.

Stratemeyer Syndicate see Holmes, Thomas K., pseud.

Stratemeyer Syndicate see Hope, Laura Lee, pseud.

Stratemeyer Syndicate see Hunt, Francis, pseud.

Stratemeyer Syndicate see Judd, Frances K., pseud.

Stratemeyer Syndicate see Lancer, Jack, pseud.

Stratemeyer Syndicate see Locke, Clinton W., pseud.

Stratemeyer Syndicate see Long, Helen Beecher, pseud.

Stratemeyer Syndicate see Marlowe, Amy Bell, pseud.

Stratemeyer Syndicate see Martin, Eugene, pseud.

Stratemeyer Syndicate see Moore, Fenworth, pseud.

Stratemeyer Syndicate see Morrison, Gertrude W., pseud.

Stratemeyer Syndicate see Penrose, Margaret, pseud.

Stratemeyer Syndicate see Rockwood, Roy, pseud.

Stratemeyer Syndicate see Roe, Harry Mason, pseud.

Stratemeyer Syndicate see Scott, Dan, pseud.

Stratemeyer Syndicate see Sheldon, Ann, pseud.

Stratemeyer Syndicate see Speed, Eric, pseud.

Stratemeyer Syndicate see Sperry, Raymond, Jr. pseud.

Stratemeyer Syndicate see Stokes, Roy Eliot, pseud.

Stratemeyer Syndicate see Stone, Raymond, pseud.

Stratemeyer Syndicate see Stone, Richard H., pseud.

Stratemeyer Syndicate see Thorndyke, Helen Louise, pseud.

Stratemeyer Syndicate see Todd, Burbank L., pseud.

Stratemeyer Syndicate see Warner, Frank A., pseud.

Stratemeyer Syndicate see Webster, Frank V., pseud.

Stratemeyer Syndicate see Wheeler, Janet D., pseud.

Stratemeyer Syndicate see White, Ramy Allison, pseud.

Stratemeyer Syndicate see Young, Clarence, pseud.

Stratford, Philip (1927-)

--Olive, a Dog: Olive, un Chien. Stratford, Philip (1927-), illus. LC 75-17152. (Illus.). 24 p. 12cm. (A Tundra Bk.). 1977. (ISBN 0-912766-27-1). Tundra Books of Northern New York.

--Olive, a Dog: Olive, un Chien. Stratford, Philip (1927-), illus. (Eng., Fr.). (Illus.). (Mini Books for Mini Hands Ser.). (gr. k-3). 1979. (ISBN 0-912766-27-1). (ISBN 0-686-86799-8). Tundra Bks.

Strathdee, Jean

--The House That Grew. Wallace, Jessica, illus. LC 81-453356. (Illus.). 32 p. 24cm. c.1979. (ISBN 0-19-558041-9). Oxford University Pr.

Stratton, Chris

--Benita's Platter Pollution. (The Bugaloos Ser.: No. 3). (gr. 4-12). 1971. Curtis.

--The Bugaloos. (The Bugaloos Ser.: No. 1). (gr. 5-12). 1971. Curtis.

--Getting Together, No. 2. (The Bobby Sherman Show). (gr. 4-12). 1971. Curtis.

--Here Come the Brides. (gr. 6-12). 1969. Curtis.

--Rock City Rebels. (Bugaloos Ser.: No. 2). (gr. 5-12). 1971. Curtis.

Stratton, Clarence, ed. see Hough, Henry Beetle.

Stratton, Clarence (1880-)

--Harbor Pirates. Stevens, Charles K., illus. LC 29-7299. 5 p. l., 265 p. incl. plates. col. front., 19 1/2 cm. 1929. The Macmillan Company.

--In Singapore: The Story of a Strange Search. Cue, Harold, illus. LC 32-23560. 304 p. incl. front., illus. 21 1/2 cm. c.1932. Lothrop, Lee & Shepard Co.

--Paul of France. Pape, Eric (1870-), illus. vii p., 1 l., 292, 1 p. col. front. 19 1/2 cm. 1927. The Macmillan Company.

--Robert the Roundhead. Pitz, Henry Clarence (1895-1976), illus. LC 30-253161. vii p., 2 l., 220 1 p. col. front., illus 22 cm. 1930. Oxford University Press.

--Swords and Statues: A Tale of Sixteenth Century Italy. Lawson, Robert (1892-1957), illus. LC 37-127619. xiii, 254, 1 p. col. front., illus. 22 cm. c.1937. The John C. Winston Company.

--When Washington Danced: A Tale of the American Revolution. Moderow, Gertrude, adapted by. Key, Alexander Hill (1904-1979), illus. v p., 1 l., 835 p. incl. front., illus. 21 1/2 cm. c.1938. Scott, Foresman and Company.

Stratton, David William, jt. auth. see Stratton, Neville Lucille.

Stratton, Elenore

--The Wild Pasture. Yap, Weda, illus. LC 40-6280. 20cm. 32p. 1940. Harper & Bros.

Stratton, George W. (1830-1901) & Stratton, L. L. Laila

--Laila: Juvenile Opera in Three Parts. LC 44-45326. 64 p. 14 1/2 x 23 cm. c.1867. G. W. Stratton.

Stratton, Helen, illus.

--The Lamb Shakespeare for Young Folks: The Tempest. N.D. Dodge Publishing Co.

Stratton, L. L. Laila, jt. auth. see Stratton, George W.

Stratton, Neville Lucille & Stratton, David William

--Wild wings over the marshes. (Illus.). 1964. Golden, Gate Junior Books.

Stratton, W.

--Tutka of the Barren Grounds. Pomerantz, Norman, illus. LC 63-19083. 95 p. illus. 22cm. 1963. Criterion Books.

Straus, Franklin (1915-)

--Destructive David. Bartholomew, illus. LC 79-27663. p. cm. c.1980. (ISBN 0-570-03483-3). Concordia Pub. House.

Straus, Helen Sachs, frwd. by see Okun, Lillian.

Strauss, Ludwig (1892-1953)

--The Magic Kite-Tail, and Other Stories. Parzen, Trude, illus. Wallower, Arthur, tr. LC 67-18061. 103 p. col. illus. 23 cm. 1967. Van Nostrand.

Strauss, Victoria

--The Lady of Rhuddesmere. LC 81-19706. 218 p. 23cm. c.1982. (ISBN 0-7232-6210-1). F. Warne.

--Worldstone. LC 85-42802. p. cm. c.1985. (ISBN 0-02-788380-9). Four Winds Press.

Stravinskii, Igor Fedorovich (1882-1969)

--The Firebird. Manasek, Ludek & Kuthanova, Olga, illus. LC 74-76289. (Illus.). 64 p. 29cm. (Curtain-raiser book). 1970, c.1969. F. Watts.

Strawbridge, Anne West (1883-)

--Samantha. Koomar, John, illus. LC 51-14253. 87 p. illus. 24 cm. 1951. Dorrance.

Strawn, Arthur (1900-)

--The Road to Granada: A Story of Adventure in the Days of the Moorish. Wars in Spain. Torrey, Helen (1901-), illus. LC 31-250452. 3 p. l., 278 p. front.,illus. 20 1/2 cm. 1931. Brewer, Warren & Putnam.

Strayer, E. Ward, pseud., see Stratemeyer, Edward L..

Strayer, E. Ward, pseud. (1862-1930)

--Making Good with Margaret. Stratemeyer, Edward L.. Scott, Arthur O., illus. 1918. George Sully & Co.

Streatfeild, Noel, adapted by see Brande, Marlie.

Streatfeild, Noel (1897-), ed. see Otava, Merja.

Streatfeild, Noel (1897-)

--Ballet Shoes. Floethe, Richard (1901-), illus. LC 37-40818. 4 p. l., 5-294 p. col. plates. 21 cm. c.1937. Random House.

--The Barrow Lane Gang. (Jackanory Ser.). (gr. 1-3). N.D. (ISBN 0-563-07455-8). BBC.

--The Boy Pharaoh. Floethe, Richard (1901-), illus. (Illus.). 128p. (gr. 2-7). 1972. (ISBN 0-7181-0986-4, Pub. by Michael Joseph). Merrimack Pub Cir.

--The Children on the Top Floor. Willett, Jillian, illus. LC 65-11932. (Illus.). 248 p. 22cm. 1965, c.1964. Random House.

--Circus Shoes. LC 39-8343. xi, 401 p. col. plates. 21 cm. c.1939. Random House. **Award: (CMA).**

--Circus Shoes. Floethe, Richard (1901-), illus. LC 80-28761. p. cm. (Gregg Press Children's Literature Ser.). 1981, c.1939. (ISBN 0-8398-2625-7). Gregg Press.

--Dancing Shoes. Floethe, Richard (1901-), illus. LC 58-6196. 273 p. illus. 21 cm. 1958. Random House,.

--The Family at Caldicott Place. Maxey, Betty, illus. LC 68-23654. (Illus.). 177 p. 22cm. 1968, c.1967. Random House.

--Family Shoes. Floethe, Richard (1901-), illus. LC 54-7014. (Illus.). 247 p. 21cm. 1954. Random House.

--Far to Go. Moxley, Charles, illus. LC 77-355461. (Illus.). 158 p. 22cm. 1976. (ISBN 0-00-184246-3). Collins.

--The Magic Summer. Ardizzone, Edward Jeffrey Irving (1900-), illus. LC 67-5354. (Illus.). 270 p. 22cm. 1967. Random House.

--Movie Shoes. Suba, Susanne (1913-), illus. LC 49-8353. (Illus.). 274p. (gr. 7-9). 1949. (ISBN 0-394-90879-1). Random.

--New Shoes. Low, Vaike, illus. LC 60-5590. 314 p. illus. 21 cm. 1960. (ISBN 0-394-80880-0). Random House.

--Osbert. Suba, Susanne (1913-), illus. LC 52-700. (Illus.). 30p. (Slottle Library). 1950. Rand McNally.

--Party Shoes. Zinkeisen, Anna Katrina (1901-), illus. LC 47-4698. vii, 333 p. illus. 21 cm. 1947. Random House.

--The Secret of the Lodge. 1940. Random House.

--Skating Shoes. Floethe, Richard (1901-), illus. LC 51-13118. (Illus.). 245 p. 21cm. 1951. Random House.

--The Stranger in Primrose Lane. Floethe, Richard (1901-), illus. LC 41-19205. 4 p. l., 3-338 p. col. plates. 21 cm. c.1941. Random House.

--Tennis Shoes. Floethe, Richard (1901-), illus. LC 38-27605. 4 p. l., 11-290 p. col. plates. 21 cm. 1938. Random House.

--The Theater Cat. Suba, Susanne (1913-), illus. LC 52-818. (Illus.). 30p. (Slotte Library). 1951. Rand McNally.

--Theater Shoes: Or, Other People's Shoes. Floethe, Richard (1901-), illus. LC 45-9989. 5 p. l., 3-282 p. col. plates. 21 cm. 1945. Random House.

--Theatre Shoes. Floethe, Richard (1901-), illus. LC 84-22937. 288 p. 25cm. 1985, c.1973. (ISBN 0-385-29399-2). Delacorte Press.

--Thursday's Child. Fortnum, Peggy, pseud. (1919-), illus. Nuttall-Smith, Margaret Emily Noel. LC 71-123073. (Illus.). line drawings. 288p. (gr. 4-7). 1971. (ISBN 0-394-82096-7, BYR). (ISBN 0-394-92096-1). Random.

--Traveling Shoes. Lonette, Reisie Dominee (1924-), illus. LC 62-9001. (Illus.). 245 p. 22cm. 1962. Random House.

--When the Sirens Wailed. Brown, Judith Gwyn (1933-), illus. LC 75-38326. (Illus.). 22cm. 176p. (gr. 4-6). 1976. (ISBN 0-394-83147-0, BYR). (ISBN 0-394-93147-5). Random.

Streatfeild, Noel (1897-) & Brande, Marlie (1911-)

--Nicholas. LC 68-10724. (Illus.). 29 p. 1968, c.1967. Follett.

Streatfield, Henrietta S.

--The Mystery of Hope Lodge: Or, The Fortunes of Elsie Norman. N.D. E. & J. B. Young & Co.

--Sandy Jim: The Message of a Rose. (Illus.). 128p. (The Steadfast Ser.). N.D. Fleming H. Revell Co.

--Through Thorns and Briars (Pub. by Society for Promoting Christian Knowledge). N.D. E. & J. B. Young & Co.

Strebe, Dorothy, jt. auth. see Disney, Walter Elias.

Stredder, Eleanor

--Alive in the Jungle: A Story for the Young. N.D. Thomas Nelson & Sons.

--Archie's Find. N.D. Thomas Nelson & Sons.

--Doing and Daring: A New Zealand Story. (Illus.). N.D. Thomas Nelson & Sons.

--The Hermit Princes: A Tale of Adventure in Japan. (Illus.). N.D. Thomas Nelson & Sons.

--Jack and His Ostrich. N.D. Thos Nelson & Sons.

--The Merchant's Children. N.D. Thomas Nelson & Sons.

Street, Annie M.

--Mother Goose's Ball. (Illus.). N.D. Lothrop Pub. Co.

Street, James Howell (1903-1954)

--The Biscuit Eater. Fuller, Arthur, illus. LC 41-217311. 4 p. l., 88 p. illus. 23 1/2 cm. 1941. The Dial Press.

--Goodbye, My Lady. LC 54-9416. 21cm. 222p. 1954. Lippincott.

Street, Julia Montgomery (1898-)

--Drovers' Gold. Galdone, Paul (1914-), illus. LC 61-5503. 158 p. illus. 24 cm. 1961. Dodd, Mead.

--Dulcie's Whale. D'Adamo, Anthony, illus. LC 63-11653. 154 p. illus. 22 cm. 1963. Bobbs-Merrill.

--Fiddler's Fancy. Sibley, Don (1922-), illus. LC 55-7493. 157p. illus. 28cm. 1955. Follett.

--Moccasin Tracks. Kramer, Frank, illus. LC 58-8708. (Illus.). 236 p. 21cm. 1958. Dodd, Mead.

Street, Julian Leonard (1879-)

--The Goldfish: A Christmas Story for Children Between Six and Sixty. Wireman, Eugenie M., illus. LC 12-239260. 58 p. col. front., plates (partly col.) 19 1/2 cm. 1912. John Lane Company Etc., Etc.

--My Enemy the Motor: A Tale in eight honks and one crash. Taylor, Horace, illus. LC 8-7892. 19cm. 123p. 1908. J. Lane Co.

Street, Julian & Whitten, Mary Street

--Lyrics for Lads and Lasses. N.D. D. Appleton & Co.

Street, Lottie E.

--A Knot of Blue. 365p. N.D. Pilgrims Press.

--A Knot of Blue. (Pilgrim Prize Series). N.D. Set 9.00. Thomas Whittaker.

Street, Nicki, jt. auth. see Durish, Jack.

Streeter, Floyd Benjamin (1888-) & Francis, H. D.

--The Phantom Steer. 1st ed. Leamon, Tom, illus. LC 52-12375. 154p. illus. 21cm. 1953. Ariel Books.

Streeter, James, Jr.

--Home Is Over the Mountains: The Journey of Five Black Children. Hoover, Russell, illus. LC 70-181763. (Illus.). 64p. (Regional American Stories). (gr. 3-6). 1972. (ISBN 0-8116-4256-9). Garrard.

Streiber, William R. & Rizzoto, Flora M.

--Popo: The Adventures of a Mexican Donkey. Ely, Gladys, illus. LC 70-146604. (Illus.). 107 p. 22cm. (A Quest Book for Children). 1971. (ISBN 0-8356-0420-9, Quest). Theosophical Pub. House.

Streich, Corrine, ed.

--Grandparents' Houses: Poems about Grandparents. Hoban, Lillian (1925-), illus. LC 84-1604. (Illus.). 32p. (gr. 1 up). 1984. (ISBN 0-688-03894-8). (ISBN 0-688-03894-8). Greenwillow.

Streit, Jacob

--Animal Stories. Piening, Jacob, tr. from Ger. 36p. 1st U.S. edition. (gr. 3-5). 1974. (ISBN 0-88010-035-4, Pub. by Verlag Walter Keller Switzerland). Anthroposophic.

Stren, Patti

--Hug Me. LC 76-58694. (Illus.). 32 p. 20cm. c.1977. (ISBN 0-06-026080-7). (ISBN 0-06-026081-5). Harper & Row.

--I Was a 15-Year-Old Blimp. LC 83-12621. p. cm. c.1985. (ISBN 0-06-026057-2). (ISBN 0-06-026058-0). Harper & Row.

--I'm Only Afraid of the Dark (at Night!!). LC 81-48653. (Illus.). 48p. (gr. k-3). 1982. (ISBN 0-06-026059-9, HarpJ). (ISBN 0-06-026060-2). Har-Row.

--Mountain Rose. LC 81-7794. p. cm. c.1982. (ISBN 0-525-35228-7). Dutton.

--Sloan and Philamina: Or, How to Make Friends with Your Lunch. LC 78-10377. (Illus.). 42 p. (A Unicorn Bk.). c.1979. (ISBN 0-525-39485-0). Dutton.

--There's a Rainbow in My Closet. LC 78-22490. p. cm. c.1979. (ISBN 0-06-026082-3). (ISBN 0-06-026083-1). Harper & Row.

Strete, Craig Kee

--The Bleeding Man and Other Science Fiction Stories. Hamilton, Virginia, frwd. by. LC 77-4505. ix, 118 p. 27cm. 118p. c.1977. (ISBN 0-688-80118-8). (ISBN 0-688-84118-X). Greenwillow Books.

--Paint Your Face on a Drowning in the River. LC 78-3752. 149 p. 22cm. c.1978. (ISBN 0-688-80175-7). (ISBN 0-688-84175-9). Greenwillow Books.

--When Grandfather Journeys into Winter. 1st ed. Frenck, Hal, illus. LC 78-14830. (Illus.). 86 p. 22cm. c.1979. (ISBN 0-688-80193-5). (ISBN 0-688-84193-7). Greenwillow Books.

Stretton, Barbara

--The Truth of the Matter. LC 83-4305. 256p. 1983. (ISBN 0-394-96144-7). (ISBN 0-394-86144-2). Knopf.

--You Never Lose: A Novel. LC 81-15557. 237 p. 22cm. c.1982. (ISBN 0-394-85230-3). Knopf.

Stretton, Hesba (1832-1911)

--Alone in London, 1 of 4. (The Pilgrim Street Ser.). N.D. American Sunday-School Union.

--The Apprentice. (Illus.). 300p. N.D. A. I. Bradley & Co.'s Pub.

--Brought Home, 1 of 3 Vols. (Thistle Ser.). N.D. Set. Dodd, Mead & Co.

--Brought Home, 1 of 9 vols. N.D. Dodd, Mead & Co.

--Carola, 1 of 8 vols. N.D. Set. Dodd, Mead & Co.

--Cassy. (The Stretton Library). N.D. Dodd & Mead.

--Cassy, 1 of 9 vols. N.D. Set. Dodd, Mead & Co.

--The Children of Cloverly. (Illus.). 364p. N.D. A. I. Bradley & Co.'s Pub.

--Children of Cloverly. (Cloverly Ser.). N.D. Henry Hoyt.

--The Children of Cloverly. 1888. Thomas Whittaker.

--The Collier Boy: or, The Story of Fern's Hollow, 1 of 4. (The Pilgrim Street Ser.). N.D. American Sunday-School Union.

--Cousins at Cloverly: Children of Lake Huron. (Illus.). N.D. Methodist Books Concern.

--The Crew of the Dolphin, 1 of 3 Vols. (Thistle Ser.). N.D. Set. Dodd, Mead & Co.

--The Crew of the Dolphin, 1 of 9 vols. N.D. Set. Dodd, Mead & Co.

--The Crew of the Dolphin. (Illus.). (The Dolphin Ser.: Vol. 1). N.D. Fleming H. Revell Co.

--The Crew of the Dolphin. 1888. Thomas Whittaker.

--The Doctor's Dilemma, 1 of 8 vols. N.D. Set. Dodd, Mead & Co.

--Enoch Roden's Training, 1 of 5 Vols. (Illus.). (Maude Grenville Library). N.D. Set. Methodist Book Concern.

--Enoch Roden's Training. (Maude Grenville Library). N.D. Nelson & Phillips.

--Enoch Roden's Training. 1888. Thomas Whittaker.

--Fishers of Derby Haven, 1 of 4 Vols. (Lyntonville Library). N.D. Set. Methodist Book Concern.

--Fishers of Derby Haven. (Illus.). 288p. N.D. Sunday-School Publications.

--Friends till Death and Other Stories. (Illus.). 1888. Thomas Whittaker.

--Her Only Son and Michel Lorio's Cross, 1 of 9 vols. N.D. Set. Dodd, Mead & Co.

--Jessica's First Prayer. (Illus.). (The Wellesley Series for Girls). N.D. A. L. Burt.

--Jessica's First Prayer, 1 of 4. (The Pilgrim Street Ser.). N.D. American Sunday-School Union.

--Jessica's First Prayer. LC 3-26884. xi, 13-116 p. incl. front., 8 pl. 19 1/2 cm. (Altemus' good times series). c.1903. H. Altemus Company.

--Jessica's First Prayer. (Illus.). (Boys' and Girls' Classics). N.D. Henry Altemus Co.

--Jessica's First Prayer. (Illus.). (Sunshine Library for Young People). 1900. T. Y. Crowell & Co.

--Jessica's First Prayer: By the Author of Fern's Hollow, Etc. LC 60-58011. 83 p. illus. 16 cm. N.D. American Tract Society.

--The King's Servants. (The Stretton Library). N.D. Dodd & Mead.

--Little Meg's Children, 1 of 25 vols. (Illus.). (Intermediate, Primary and Infant Libs.). N.D. A. I. Bradley & Co.'s Pubs.

--Little Meg's Children. (Illus.). 157p. (Popular Ser.). N.D. American Tract Society.

--Little Meg's Children. 157p. (Heart Life Classics). N.D. American Tract Society.

--Little Meg's Children. (Illus.). 215p. N.D. Ira Bradley & Co's.

--Little Meg's Children. 160p. N.D. Sunday-School Publications.

--Little Meg's Children. 1888. Thomas Whittaker.

--Lost Gip. (Illus.). 267p. N.D. A. I. Bradley & Co.'s Pubs.

--Lost Gip, 1 of 9 vols. N.D. Dodd, Mead & Co.

--Lost Gip. (The Cloverly Ser.). N.D. Henry Hoyt.

--Lost Gip and Michael Lorio's Cross. N.D. Dodd, Mead & Co.

--Lost Gip and Michel Lorio. (The Stretton Library). N.D. Dodd & Mead.

--Max Kromer. (The Stretton Library). N.D. Dodd & Mead.

--Max Kromer, 1 of 9 vols. N.D. Set. Dodd, Mead & Co.

--Max Kromer: A Story of the Seige of Strasbourg. N.D. London Religious Tract Society.

--Nelly's Dark Days. N.D. A. D. F. Randolph.

--Nelly's Dark Days. (The Stretton Library). N.D. Dodd & Mead.

--Nelly's Dark Days, 1 of 9 vols. N.D. Set. Dodd, Mead & Co.

--Night and a Day. (Illus.). 128p. (Popular Ser.). N.D. American Tract Society.

--A Night and a Day: with "Apple-Tree Court" & "The Worth of a Baby". 128p. 1877. American Tract Society.

--Peter Killip's King. (The Cloverly Ser.). N.D. Henry Hoyt.

--Peter Killip's King: Or, The Fishers of Derby Haven. (Illus.). 350p. N.D. A. I. Bradley & Co.'s Pubs.

--Pilgrim Street. (Illus.). 294p. N.D. A. I. Bradley & Co.'s Pubs.

--Pilgrim Street, 1 of 4. (The Pilgrim Street Ser.). N.D. American Sunday-School Union.

--Pilgrim Street. (The Cloverly Ser.). N.D. Henry Hoyt.

--Sam Franklin's Savings Bank. new engravings. ed. Whymper, Edward, illus. N.D. Fleming H Revell.

--The Sweet Story of Old: A Sunday Book for Little Ones. 1888. Thomas Whittaker.

--Through a Needle's Eye, 1 of 8 vols. N.D. Set. Dodd, Mead & Co.

--Under the Old Roof. new ed. N.D. Fleming H Revell.

--The Wonderful Life, 1 of 9 vols. N.D. Dodd, Mead & Co.

--The Young Apprentice. (The Cloverly Ser.). N.D. Henry Hoyt.

Strickland, Agnes (1796-1874)

--Stories from History. LC 14-619. 359p. (Agnes Strickland Library). 1943. Porter & Coates.

--Tales from English History. For Children. LC 43-295799. 276 p. front. 19 cm. N.D. Porter & Coates.

Strickland, Catherine Patricia O'Malley see O'Malley, Patricia.

Strickland, Catherine Patricia O'Malley (1900-)

--Faraway Fields: The Career of an Airline Publicity Girl. LC 49-11482. 244p. 21cm. 1949. Dodd, Mead.

--Happy Landings for Ann. LC 56-9008. 241p. 21cm. 1956. Dodd, Mead.

--Leslie Takes the Skyroad. LC 59-12035. 242 p. 21 cm. (Dodd, Mead cCareer books). 1959. Dodd, Mead.

--War Wings for Carol. LC 43-9190. 279. 21cm. 1943. Dodd, Mead.

--Wider Wings. LC 42-15036. (Illus.). 278p. 22cm. 1949. Greystone Press.

--Wider Wings. Laune, Paul Sidney (1899-), illus. N.D. Dodd Mead & Co.

--Winging Her Way. LC 46-8594. (Illus.). 197p. 20cm. 1946. Dodd, Mead.

--Wings for Carol. LC 41-3676. (Illus.). 320p. 21cm. 1941. Greystone Press.

--Wings for Carol. Laune, Paul Sidney (1899-), illus. N.D. Dodd Mead & Co.
Strickland, Harold H.
--Juggernaut of the Rangers. Brown, Paul (1893-1958), illus. LC 46-63946. 6 p. l., 130, 1 p. incl. front., illus. 22 1/2 cm. 1946. Dodd, Mead & Company.
Strickland, Joshua (1896-)
--Aliens on Earth!. Aloise, Frank E., illus. LC 77-71532. (Illus.). 94 p. 25cm. c.1977. (ISBN 0-448-12898-5). (ISBN 0-448-13416-0). Grosset & Dunlap.
Striker, Francis Hamilton (1903-1962)
--The Clue of the Cypress Stump. LC 48-3990. 206 p. 1 illus. 20 cm. (His A Tom Quest Adventure). 1948. Grosset & Dunlap.
--The Inca Luck Piece. LC 56-26171. 182p. (His A Tom Quest adventure, T-7). 1955. McLoughlin.
--The Lone Ranger. Laune, Paul Sidney (1899-), illus. LC 39-13614. (Based on the Famous Character). 3 p. l., 185 p. front. 19 1/2 cm. c.1939. Grosset & Dunlap.
--The Lone Ranger. Tuska, Jon (1942-), intro. by. LC 80-16561. p. cm. (Gregg Press Western Fiction Ser.). 1980, c.1936. (ISBN 0-8398-2676-1). Gregg Press.
--The Lone Ranger and the Bitter Spring Feud. Trendle, George W., created by. LC 53-6959. 203p. illus. 20cm. (The Lone Rangers Ser.). 1953. Grosset & Dunlap.
--The Lone Ranger and the Code of the West. Trendle, George W., created by. LC 54-12302. 180p. illus. 20cm. (His The Lone Ranger stories 16). 1954. Grosset & Dunlap.
--Lone Ranger and the Gold Robbery. N.D. Grosset & Dunlap.
--The Lone Ranger and the Mystery Ranch. Laune, Paul Sidney (1899-), illus. LC 76-9854. p. cm. 1976, c.1938. (ISBN 0-89190-501-4). American Reprint Co.
--The Lone Ranger and the Mystery Ranch. Laune, Paul Sidney (1899-), illus. LC 41-28300. 3 p. l., 199 p. front. 19 1/2 cm. c.1938. Grosset & Dunlap.
--The Lone Ranger and the Outlaw Stronghold. Laune, Paul Sidney (1899-), illus. LC 39-216761. 3 p. l., 214 p. front. 19 1/2 cm. c.1939. Grosset & Dunlap.
--The Lone Ranger and the Silver Bullet. LC 48-7090. 210 p. front. 20 cm. 1948. Grosset & Dunlap.
--The Lone Ranger and the Texas Renegades. Horn, Ted, illus. LC 39-13615. 23 p. incl. col. front., illus. (part col.) 25 cm. c.1938. Grosset & Dunlap.
--The Lone Ranger and the War Horse. authorized. Dreany, E. Joseph, illus. LC 51-40030. unpaged. illus. 21 cm. (Cozy corner book). c.1951. Whitman Pub. Co.
--The Lone Ranger and Tonto. Laune, Paul Sidney (1899-), illus. LC 40-5180. 3 p. l., 214 p. front. 19 1/2 cm. c.1940. Grosset & Dunlap.
--The Lone Ranger at the Haunted Gulch. Laune, Paul Sidney (1899-), illus. LC 41-51517. vi p., 1 l., 216 p. incl. front. 19 1/2 cm. c.1941. Grosset & Dunlap.
--The Lone Ranger: Based on the Famous Character. LC 37-5757. v, 218 p. front. 19 cm. c.1937. Grosset & Dunlap.
--The Lone Ranger in Wild Horse Canyon. LC 50-6609. viii, 212 p. front. 20 cm. 1950. Grosset & Dunlap.
--The Lone Ranger on Gunsight Mesa. (The Lone Ranger Ser.). N.D. Grosset & Dunlap.
--The Lone Ranger on Powderhorn Trail. Trendle, Geoge W., created by. LC 49-4279. viii, 207 p. front. 20 cm. 1949. Grosset & Dunlap.
--The Lone Ranger on Red Butte Trail. Trendle, George W., created by. LC 56-2669. 176 p. illus. 20 cm. (His The Lone Ranger Stories 18). 1956. Grosset & Dunlap.
--The Lone Ranger Rides. Smith, William Arthur (1918-), illus. LC 41-2322. viii, 263 p. illus. 19 1/2 cm. c.1941. G. P. Putnam's Sons.
--The Lone Ranger Rides Again. Weisman, Robert R., illus. LC 43-3404. 3 p. l., 214 p. front. 19 1/2 cm. 1943. Grosset & Dunlap.
--The Lone Ranger Rides North. LC 47-82. 4 p. l., 213 p. 19 1/2 cm. 1946. Grosset & Dunlap.
--The Lone Ranger Traps the Smugglers. Laune, Paul Sidney (1899-), illus. LC 41-232757. vi p., 1 l., 214 p. incl. front. 19 1/2 cm. c.1941. Grosset & Dunlap.
--The Lone Ranger: Trouble on the Santa Fe. Trendle, George W., created by. LC 55-32922. 181p. illus. 20cm. (His The Lone Ranger Stories 17). 1955. Grosset & Dunlap.
--The Lone Ranger West of Maverick Pass. (The Lone Ranger Ser.). N.D. Grosset & Dunlap.
--The Lone Ranger's New Deputy. Shearer, Ted, illus. LC 52-16441. 77 p. illus. 19 cm. (Sandpiper books). 1951. Simon and Schuster.
--Mystery of the Timber Giant. LC 56-26170. 186p. (His A Tom Quest Adventure, T-8). 1955. McLoughlin Bros.
--The Secret of the Lost Mesa. LC 49-39329. 209 p. front. 20 cm. (His A Tom Quest Adventure). 1949. Grosset & Dunlap.
--The Secret of Thunder Mountain. LC 58-10254. (Illus.). 175p. 20cm. (A Tom Quest Adventure). 1958. Grosset & Dunlap.
--Sergeant Preston and Rex. Neebe, William, illus. LC 56-108755. unpaged. illus. 21cm. (Rand McNally Elf Bk. 569). c.1956. Rand McNally.
--Sign of the Spiral. LC 47-111698. vi, 214 p. front. 20 cm. (His A Tom Quest Adventure). 1947. Grosset & Dunlap.
--The Telltale Scar. LC 47-11170. vi, 216 p. front. 20 cm. 1947. Grosset & Dunlap.
Striker, Susan
--The Anti-Coloring Book of Red-Letter Days. (Illus.). 64p. (Orig.). 1981. (ISBN 0-03-057873-6). HR&W.
Strimple, Helen
--Lindy Lou and the Green Umbrella. Strimple, Helen, illus. LC 46-8464. 32 p. illus. (part col.) 24 1/2 x 20 1/2 cm. 1946. Broadman Press.
Strindberg, Gert, selected by.
--Norwegian Fairy Tales. Stindberg, Gert, illus. 1956. Dufour.
--Norwegian Fairy Tales. Stindberg, Gert, illus. LC 58-7704. 96 p. illus. 19 cm. c.1947. Roy Publishers.
--Norwegian Fairy Tales. Strindberg, Gert, illus. LC 68-10493. (Illus.). 96 p. 23cm. (World Fairy Tale Collections). 1968. Follett Pub. Co.
Stringer, Arthur John Arbuthnott (1874-)
--Lonely O'Malley: A Story of Boy Life. Merrill, Frank Thayer (1848-), illus. LC 5-32325. xi, 383, 1 p. front., illus. 19 1/2 cm. 1905. Houghton, Mifflin and Company.
--Lonely O'Malley: A Story of Boy Life. Merrill, Frank Thayer (1848-), illus. LC 24-19664. 4 p. l., viii-xi, 383 p. front., illus. 19 1/2 cm. c.1924. The Bobbs-Merrill Company.
Stringer, Bruce
--Earlihee the Turtle. Harper, Teresa, illus. (Illus.). N.D. (ISBN 0-932298-06-0). Copple Hse.
Stringer, Ruth M.
--Penny. Cooke, Tom, illus. LC 62-16562. 96 p. illus. 24 cm. (Read-By-Yourself Bks.). 1962. Houghton Mifflin.
Striplin, Clara M
--Mother Robin's Family. Maniscalco, Joseph (1926-), illus. LC 54-9985. 82p. illus. 24cm. 1954. Pacific Press Pub. Association.
Striplin, Clara M., ed. see Isaac, Ella M.
Strobel, Marion
--Saturday Afternoon. LC 30-11379. v, 279 p. 19 1/2 cm. c.1930. Farrar & Rinehart Incorporated.
Strobl, Tony, ed. see Disney, Walt, Productions.
Strodder, Chris (1956-)
--A Sky for Henry. Kennedy, Emilie (1951-), illus. LC 85-11997. p. cm. c.1985. (ISBN 0-931093-04-X). (ISBN 0-931093-03-1). Red Hen Press.
Stroebe, Clara see Stroebe, Klara.
Stroebe, Klara (1887-), ed.
--The Danish Fairy Book. Hood, George W., illus. Martens, Frederick Herman (1874-1932), tr. LC 22-18659. vii p., 2 l., 218 p. col. front., col. plates. 21 cm. c.1922. Frederick A. Stokes Company.
--The Norwegian Fairy Book. Hood, George W., illus. Martens, Frederick Herman (1874-1932), tr. LC 22-18658. viii p., 2 l., 304 p. col. front., col. plates. 21 cm. c.1922. Frederick A. Stokes Company.
--The Swedish Fairy Book. Hood, George W., illus. Martens, Frederick Herman (1874-1932), tr. LC 21-18126. 6 p. l., 3-211 p. col. front., col. plates. 21 cm. c.1921. Frederick A. Stokes Company.
Stroeyer, Poul see Stroyer, Poul.
Stroh, R. W
--Adventure in the Lost World. Mulkey, Kim, illus. LC 85-2530. (Illus.). 92 p. 20cm. c.1985. (ISBN 0-8167-0535-6). (ISBN 0-8167-0536-4). Troll Associates.
Stromberg, Rose Marie
--Cowboys and Indians Funbook. Thompson, Marjorie, illus. LC 60-16816. 127 p. illus. 28 cm. 1960. Hart Pub. Co.
Stromberg, Rose Marie, ed.
--Funny Riddles and Rhymes. Berenzy, Roberta, illus. LC 60-8531. 127 p. illus. 28 cm. 1960. Hart Pub. Co.
Strommen, Irene Hugsen
--Rivers to the Sea: A Novel. 1st ed. Wiese, Kurt (1887-1974), illus. LC 55-14102. 266p. 21cm. 1955. Augsburg Pub. House.
Stromstedt, Margareta, jt. auth. see Wiegman, Lies.
Strong, Arline
--Glowing in the Dark. Stong, Arline, illus. LC 75-8874. (Illus.). 47 p. 1975. (ISBN 0-689-30485-4). Atheneum.
Strong, Armour
--Dear Days: A Story of Washington School Life. LC 1-25618. x, 316 p. front., plates. 20 cm. 1901. H. T. Coates & Co.
--Dear Days: A Story of Washington School Life. N.D. John C. Winston Co.
Strong, Bethany
--Murder in the Mirror: Flashes of Fire. LC 83-11225. c.1983. (ISBN 0-917250-07-9). Parable Press.
Strong, Charles Stanley see Stanley, Chuck, pseud.
Strong, Charles Stanley (1906-)
--Bullwhacker. Stanley, Chuck, pseud. LC 54-7482. 224p. 20cm. 1954. Arcadia House.
--The King Ram: A Novel. LC 61-7489. 192 p. illus 21 cm. (The Your-Fair-Land Ser.). 1961. John Day Co.
--The Lost Convoy: Adventure with the Norwegian Underground. LC 60-13368. 194 p. illus 22 cm. 1960. Chilton Co., Book Division.
--Ranger: Sea Dog of the Royal Mounted. Wiese, Kurt (1887-1974), illus. LC 48-1780. vii, 247 p. illus. 22 cm. 1948. J. C. Winston Co.
--Ranger, Seadog of the Royal Mounted. Wiese, Kurt (1887-1974), illus. 1948. Holt Rinehart & Winston.
--Ranger's Arctic Patrol. Wiese, Kurt (1887-1974), illus. LC 52-8978. 214 p. illus. 22 cm. 1952. Winston.
--Rider of Pecos Valley. Stanley, Chuck, pseud. LC 55-102009. 223p. 20cm. 1955. Arcadia House.
--Roll the Red Wagons: A Story of the Volunteer Fire Service. LC 55-9335. 210p. 21cm. 1955. Dodd, Mead.
--Seal Hunters,. A Snow King Story. LC 57-11397. 208 p. 21 cm. 1958. Dodd, Mead.
--Snow King, Herd Dog of Lapland. N.D. Dodd Mead & Co.
--South Pole Husky. LC 50-5526. 295 p. illus. 22 cm. 1950. Longmans, Green.
--We Were There with Byrd at the South Pole. Kaye, Graham, illus. Balchen, Bent (1889-1973), contrib. by. LC 56-5388. 176p. illus. 24cm. (We-Were-There Bks. 4). 1956. (ISBN 0-448-05004-8). Grosset & Dunlap.
--West to Denver. Stanley, Chuck, pseud. LC 54-10732. 222p. 20cm. 1954. Arcadia House.
Strong, Harold, Mrs.
--Bedtime Stories. N.D. Barse & Co.
--My Very Own Book. N.D. Barse & Co.
--Toy land Tales. N.D. Barse & Co.
Strong, Jeremy
--Trouble with Animals. Allen, Jonathan, illus. LC 80-2459. p. cm. 1981. (ISBN 0-690-04116-0). (ISBN 0-690-04117-9). Crowell.
Strong, Joanna, pseud., see Horowitz, Caroline.
Strong, Joanna (1909-) & Hart, Harold (1903-), eds.
--A Treasury of Laughs for Boys & Girls. Leonard, Tom B., pseud. Barreaux, Adolphe, illus. LC 48-6992. 192 p. illus. 24 cm. 1948. Hart Pub. Co.
Strong, Joseph Dwight, jt. auth. see Clark, Mary Latham.
Strong, Joseph Dwight (1823-1907)
--Beauty Benson, 1 of 6 vols. (Illus.). (Gregory Gold Ser.). N.D. D. Lothrop & Co.
--Better Than Gold. (Fair Play Ser.). N.D. D. Lothrop & Co.
--The Blacksmith, 1 of 6 vols. (Illus.). (Gregory Gold Ser.). N.D. D Lothrop.
--Brown Pony, 1 of 6 vols. (Illus.). (Trust and Try Ser.). N.D. D. Lothrop & Co.
--Child Life in Many Lands. (Illus.). (Child Life Ser.). N.D. D. Lothrop Co.
--Fair Play and Other Stories. (Fair Play Ser.). N.D. D. Lothrop & Co.
--Fair Play Ser. (Containing, "Wintergreen Girl," "Kitty Collins," "Susie's Watch."). (Illus.). N.D. D. Lothrop & Co.
--Gregory Gold, 1 of 6 vols. (Illus.). (Gregory Gold Ser.). N.D. D. Lothrop & Co.
--Gregory Gold Ser. (Containing, "Gregory Gold,""Minna's Proud Heart," "Beauty Benson"). N.D. D. Lothrop & Co.
--Little Bertie, 1 of 6 vols. (Illus.). (Trust and Try Ser.). N.D. D. Lothrop & Co.
--Little Bertie's Picture Library: Containing "Little Bertie," "The Lame Beggar," "Minna's Proud Heart," etc, 12 vols. N.D. Set. D. Lothrop & Co.
--Little Nora. (Illus.). N.D. D. Lothrop & Co.
--Minna's Proud Heart, 1 of 6 vols. (Illus.). (Gregory Gold Ser.). 1870. D. Lothrop & Co.
--New Year and Other Stories. (Bill Rigg's Library). N.D. D. Lothrop & Co.
--Snowflake Series for Boys, 10 Vols. (Containing "Westminster Boys," "Brown Pony," "George's Aquarium," "Little Carl,'" "The Patient Blind Boy"). (Illus.). N.D. Set. D. Lothrop & Co.
--Snowflake Series for Girls: Containing "Such a Smart Girl", "Rhodd and Her Rosebud", "Grandpa's Birthday", etc, 10 vols. N.D. Set. D. Lothrop & Co.
--Susie's Watch, and Other Stories. LC 73-176731. (Illus.). 62 p. 14cm. (Fair Play Ser.). c.1870. D. Lothrop.
--The True Story Ser. Containing "The Lame Beggar," "Minna's Proud Heart," "Brown Pony," "Truthful Jenny," etc, 12 vols. N.D. Set. D. Lothrop & Co.
--Truthful Jenny, 1 of 6 vols. (Illus.). (Gregory Gold Ser.). N.D. D. Lothrop & Co.
--Wilful Waste, 1 of 6 vols. (Illus.). (Gregory Gold Ser.). N.D. D Lothrop.
--Wintergreen Girl, and Other Stories. (Fair PLay Ser.). N.D. D. Lothrop & Co.
Strong, Leonard Alfred George (1896-)
--Fortnight South of Skye. Line, Clifton, illus. LC 35-32773. 5 p. l., 9-216, 1 p. incl. front., illus. 20 1/2 cm. (Tales of Action No. 2). c.1935. Loring and Mussey.
--King Richard's Land: A Tale of the Peasants' Revolt. Gay, Zhenya (1906-1978), illus. LC 34-128821. 3 p. l., 3-231, 1 p., 1 l. col. front., illus. 19 1/2 cm. 1934. A. A. Knopf.
--Mr. Sheridan's Umbrella. Hodges, Cyril Walter (1909-), illus. LC 35-30573. vii, 215, 1 p. col. front., illus. 20 1/2 cm. (The Nelsonia Library, edited by John Hampden and Freda Holmdahl). 1935. T. Nelson & Son Ltd.
Strong, Paschal Neilson see Lyons, Kennedy, pseud.
Strong, Paschal Neilson, et al. (1901-)
--Teen-Age Small Boat Stories. Furman, Abraham Loew (1902-), ed. Vaughn, Frank E., illus. LC 59-13372. (Illus.). 255 p. 22cm. 1959. Lantern Press.
Strong, Paschal Neilson (1901-)
--Behind the Great Smokies. Fay, Herman B., Jr., illus. LC 32-29906. 5 p. l., 3-246, 1 p. incl. illus., plates. front. 19 1/2 cm. 1932. Little, Brown, and Company.
--Three Plebes at West Point. Heffron, Walter J., illus. LC 35-16315. viii p., 2 l., 3-242 p. incl. front., illus., plates. 19 1/2 cm. 1935. Little, Brown, and Company.
--Typhoon Gold. Lyons, Kennedy, pseud. Crews, Monte, illus. LC 37-21825. vi p., 2 l., 3-269 p. incl. illus., plates. front. 23 cm. 1937. Little, Brown and Company.
--The Vagabond Scouts: Or, The Adventures of Duncan Dunn. Lyons, Kennedy, pseud. Cue, Harold, illus. LC 31-23582. 4 p. l., 280 p. front., plates. 20 1/2 cm. c.1931. L. C. Page and Company.
--West Point Wins. Avison, George F. (1885-), illus. LC 30-23548. vi, 267 p. col. front., illus. 20 1/2 cm. 1930. Little, Brown, and Company.
--Wings Over Wonder Island. Crews, Monte, illus. LC 40-7022. 5 p. l., 3-263 p. incl. plates. 21 cm. 1940. Little, Brown and Company.
Strong, Patience
--Honey for Tea. Pearce, Susan Beatrice, illus. LC 50-9928. (Illus.). 47. 19cm. Orig. Title: Nursery Versery; England. 1950. Dutton.
Strong, W. M., adapted by see Lecomte, Eva.
Strong, W. M., tr. see Lecomte, Eva.
Strother, Elsie Francis Warmouth Weitzel (1912-)
--Lions 'n' Things. Strother, Elsie Francis Warmouth Weitzel (1912-) & Strothman, F., illus. (Illus.). (ps-3). 1968. Vantage.
--The Royal Cheetah and the Untouchable. LC 73-15550. 172 p. 22cm. 1974. (ISBN 0-664-32544-0). Westminster Press.
Strousse, Flora G. (1897-1974)
--The Friar and the Knight: Bartolome De Ohnedo and Cortez. Wilson, William N., illus. LC 57-10095. 190p. illus. 22cm. (American background Bks.). 1957. P. J. Kenedy.
--The Littlest Christmas Tree. 1st ed. Cooke, Donald Ewin (1916-), illus. LC 53-2801. (Illus.). 24. 29cm. 1953. Morehouse Gorham Co.
Strout, C. W. D., Mrs.
--Slippery Paths: A Temperance Story. (Illus.). N.D. Hoyt, Fogg & Donham.
Stroyer, Poul, jt. auth. see Hellsing, Lennart.
Stroyer, Poul (1923-)
--It's a Deal. Stroyer, Poul (1923-), illus. 24p. 1960. Astor Books.
--It's A Deal. Stroyer, Poul (1923-), illus. 1960. McDowell, Obolensky.
--Second Treasure Chest of Tales. Stroyer, Poul (1923-), illus. (Illus.). 1960. (ISBN 0-8392-3032-X). Astor-Honor.
--Treasure Chest of Tales. Stroyer, Poul (1923-), illus. (Illus.). (gr. 3 up). 1959. (ISBN 0-8392-3039-7). Astor-Honor.
Struble, Virginia (1900-)
--Cactus. Thoele, Lillian, illus. LC 58-9108. unpaged. illus. 21 cm. 1958. Bethany Press.
--The Little Ducks Who Swam Away from Home. Jacks, Flo, illus. LC 61-8568. unpaged. illus. 22 cm. 1961. Barnes.
Strubler, Maria
--Quiet Fancies for the Little Ones. LC 8-279. 47p. 16cm. 1907. Harmegnies & Howell.
Strugatskii, Arkadii Natanovich & Strugatskii, Boris Natanovich
--Prisoners of Power. LC 77-5145. ix, 286 p. 22cm. c.1977. (ISBN 0-02-615170-7). Macmillan.
Strugatskii, Boris Natanovich, jt. auth. see Strugatskii, Arkadii Natanovich.
Struges, Lillian, illus.
--Fairy Tale Princes and Princesses: The Stories Children Like Best. LC 37-313. 165 p. col. front., illus. 21 cm. (Half-title: Old trail series). c.1926. The Saalfield Publishing Company.
Strugnell, Alison
--Fairy Tales. Strugnell, Alison, illus. (Illus.). 170p. (gr. 5 up). 1975. (ISBN 0-571-10703-6). Faber & Faber.

--The Shop in the Mountain. LC 62-11215. 188 p. 21 cm. 1961. Vanguard Press.
--Thunder Over Spain. LC 65-17374. 168p. 22cm. 1965, c.1962. Vanguard.

Styles, Showell see Styles, Frank Showell.

Styron, Rose Burgunder (1928-)
--From Summer to Summer: Poems. Fava, Rita (1932-), illus. LC 65-15110. 64p. illus. 24cm. c.1965. Viking.

Suba, Susanne (1913-)
--The Man with the Bushy Beard & Other Tales. Suba, Susanne (1913-), illus. LC 69-13073. (Illus.). 35 p. 1969. Viking Press.
--The Monkeys & the Pedlar. 1st ed. Suba, Susanne (1913-), illus. LC 71-123014. (Illus.). 32 p. 1970. Viking Press.

Suba, Susanne (1913-), illus.
--Moon Uncle, Moon Uncle: Rhymes from India. 1st ed. Cassedy, Sylvia (1930-) & Thampi, Parvathi Menon, trs. LC 72-178836. (Illus.). 32p. (gr. k-3). 1973. (ISBN 0-385-07761-0). (ISBN 0-385-02963-2). Doubleday.

Suben, Eric
--Elves & the Shoemaker. Bloom, Lloyd, illus. LC 82-82287. (Original Author: Jakob Ludwig Grimm, 1785-1863). (Illus.). 24p. (Little Golden Bk.). (ps-2). 1983. (ISBN 0-307-03076-8, Golden Pr). (ISBN 0-307-60203-6). Western Pub.
--Jungle Noises. Michelini, Carlo A. & Vanetti, Giorgio, illus. (Illus.). 16p. (Golden Magical Places Ser.). (ps-k). 1984. (ISBN 0-307-17102-7, Golden Bks). Western Pub.

Subin, Louis see Brandt, Keith, pseud.

Sublett, Lucille B
--Follow Me. Bonniwell, Zita Welch, illus. LC 28-7875. 32 p. col. illus. 23 cm. c.1928. Children's Publishing House.

Sudbery, Rodie (1943-)
--The Silk and the Skin. LC 77-350231. (Illus.). 144 p. 21cm. 1976. (ISBN 0-233-96816-4). Deutsch.
--A Sound of Crying. (gr. 5-8). 1970. (ISBN 0-525-39710-8). Dutton.
--A Sound of Crying. LC 71-104126. 149 p. 22cm. 1970. (ISBN 0-8415-2005-4). McCall Pub. Co.

Suddaby, Donald (1900-1964)
--Bell in the Forest. (gr. 7-11). 1964. (ISBN 0-685-20954-7). Verry.
--Fresh News From Sherwood. Stobbs, William (1914-), illus. LC 61-8566. 150p. illus. 21cm. (Wonderful World Bk.). 1961. A. S. Barnes.

Suddeth, Ruth Elgin & Morenus, Constance Gay
--Tales of the Western World: Folk Tales of the Americas. Hunter, Warren, illus. LC 52-11190. 281p. illus. 23cm. 1953. Steck Co.

Suder, Henry
--Song-Roundels and Games. 2nd ed. LC 7-2090. ix, 9-76 p. illus. 22 1/2 cm. c.1906. Press of Rogers & Hall Co.

Suetake, Kunihiro, tr. see Cassedy, Sylvia (1930-) & Okamura, Koson.

Sueur, Meridel Le see Le Sueur, Meridel.

Sueyeshi, Akiko
--Ladybird on a Bicycle. Allbright, Viv, illus. LC 83-1501. (Illus.). 40p. (gr. 2-6). 1983. (ISBN 0-571-11802-X). (ISBN 0-571-11802-X). Faber & Faber.

Suffling, R. E.
--Afloat in a Gipsy Van: Books of Adventure for Boys. Hardy, Paul (1862-), illus. N.D. Frederick A Stokes Co.

Sugano, Yoshikatsu (1915-)
--The Kitten's Adventure. LC 78-99205. 24 p. of col. illus. 25cm. 1971, c.1968. McGraw-Hill.

Sugarman, Tracy, jt. auth. see Beim, Jerrold.

Sugden, Marian
--The So Safe Place. LC 66-14530. 32p. illus. 19x26cm. 1966, c.1965. McGraw.

Sugden, Marianne Cookson, Mrs. (0000-1908), ed. see Arabian Nights.

Sugimoto, Etsu Inagaki & Austen, Nancy Virginia
--With Taro and Hana in Japan. Hood, George W., illus. LC 26-180020. 3 p. l., 120 p. col. front., col. illus. 20 cm. 1926. Frederick A. Stokes Company.

Sugita, Yutaka see Reed, Kit, pseud.

Sugita, Yutaka (1930-)
--Angel. LC 80-112848. (Illus.). 26 p. 25cm. 1979, c.1978. (ISBN 0-89742-009-8). Dawne-Leigh Publications.
--Blackie, the Bird Who Could!. LC 74-26581. (Illus.). 26 p. 25cm. 1975, c.1972. (ISBN 0-07-061778-3). (ISBN 0-07-061779-1). McGraw-Hill.
--Caspar & the Rainbow Bird. Aoki, Hisako, tr. LC 77-92135. (Barron's Juvenile Ser.). (gr. k-6). 1978. (ISBN 0-8120-5253-6). Barron.
--The Flower Family. LC 75-20082. 1975. (ISBN 0-07-061768-6). (ISBN 0-07-061769-4). McGraw-Hill.
--Good Night 1, 2, 3. LC 76-149045. 24 p. of illus. 25cm. 1971. Scroll Press.
--Helena the Unhappy Hippopotamus. LC 73-6665. p. 1973. (ISBN 0-07-061762-7). (ISBN 0-07-061763-5). McGraw-Hill.
--The Mouse's Feast. (Illus.). (ps-6). 1980. (ISBN 0-8120-5370-2). Barron.
--My Friend Little John. Sugita, Yutaka (1930-), illus. LC 72-8799. (Illus.). 32p. (gr. k-2). 1973. (ISBN 0-07-062459-3, GB). McGraw.
--My Friend Little John and Me. LC 72-8799. (Illus.). 24 p. 25cm. 1973, c.1972. (ISBN 0-07-062458-5). McGraw-Hill.
--Wake up, Little Tree: A Christmas Fantasy. Thomas Nelson, Inc, tr. LC 73-116581. (Illus.). 32 p. 26cm. N.D. T. Nelson.
--When We Dream. Reed, Kit, pseud. 1st English ed. Sugita, Yutaka (1930-), illus. LC 67-1284. (Illus.). 22p. 25cm. 1966, c.1965. Hawthorn Books.

Sugita, Yutaka (1930-) & Aoki, Hisako
--Fly Hoops Fly. LC 74-92136. (Barron's Juvenile Ser.). (gr. k-6). 1978. (ISBN 0-8120-5254-4). Barron.

Suhl, Yuri (1908-)
--The Man Who Made Everyone Late. Di Fiori, Lawrence, illus. LC 74-7482. (Illus.). 39 p. 1974. (ISBN 0-590-07223-4). Four Winds Press.
--The Merrymaker. Di Grazia, Thomas (0000-1983), illus. LC 74-13182. (Illus.). 45 p. 23cm. 1975. (ISBN 0-590-07346-X). Four Winds Press.
--On the Other Side of the Gate: A Novel. LC 74-13452. 149 p. 21cm. 1975. (ISBN 0-531-02792-9). F. Watts.
--The Purim Goat. Zemach, Kaethe (1958-), illus. LC 79-6551. (Illus.). 58 p. 23cm. c.1980. (ISBN 0-590-07658-2). Four Winds Press.
--Simon Boom Gets a Letter. Krahn, Fernando (1935-), illus. LC 76-15574. (Illus.). 37 p. 21cm. c.1976. (ISBN 0-590-07434-2). Four Winds Press.
--Simon Boom Gives a Wedding. Zemach, Margot (1931-), illus. LC 70-161015. (Illus.). 47 p. 1972. Four Winds Press. **Awards: (NYT).**
--Uncle Misha's Partisans. LC 73-76459. 211 p. 22cm. 1973. Four Winds Press.

Suire, Diane Dow (1954-)
--Adventures. Connelly, Gwen, illus. LC 83-25212. (Illus.). 32 p. 26cm. (The Shape of Poetry). 1984. (ISBN 0-89565-265-X). Child's World.
--Animals. Dunnington, Tom, illus. LC 83-25213. (Illus.). 32 p. 27cm. (The Shape of Poetry). c.1984. (ISBN 0-89565-264-1). Child's World.

Sukus, Jan
--My Little Circus. Wood, JoAnne, illus. (Put & Play Ser.). (ps). 1981. (ISBN 0-307-05101-3, Golden Pr). Western Pub.
--The Raggedy Ann & Andy Book. Ruhman, Ruth M., illus. (Illus.). (ps-1). 1973. (ISBN 0-307-68942-5, Golden Pr). Western Pub.

Sulkey, Andrew
--Earthquake. Papas, William (1927-), illus. LC 69-13413. 123p. 23cm. 1969, c.1968. Roy Publishers.
--Jonah Simpson. Craig, Gerry, illus. LC 70-90447. (Illus.). 168p. 23cm. 1970, c.1969. Roy Publishers.

Sulkin, Edith, ed. see Goldszmit, Henryk.

Sulkin, Sidney, ed. see Goldszmit, Henryk.

Sulkowski, Ann E.
--Witch Who Used a Six Shift Vacuum Cleaner. (gr. 2-4). 1970. Vantage.

Sullivan, Adair Reynaud
--Secret of the Beach. Hutchinson, William MIller (1916-), illus. LC 60-9879. 181 p. illus. 21 cm. 1960. Longmans, Green.

Sullivan, Alan (1868-)
--Brother Blackfoot. Berger, William Merritt (1872-), illus. LC 27-188493. 3 p. l., 3-300 p. front., illus., plates. 19 1/2 cm. 1927. The Century Co.
--Brother Eskimo. Avison, George F. (1885-), illus. LC 21-17085. 5 p. l., 3-249 p. front., plates. 19 1/2 cm. 1921. The Century Co.

Sullivan, Arthur Seymour, Sir, jt. auth. see Gilbert, William Schwenck, Sir.

Sullivan, Arthur Seymour, Sir, jt. auth. see Wells, Rosemary.

Sullivan, Edward, Sir (1852-), retold by see Scott, Walter, Sir.

Sullivan, Edward, Sir (1852-), ed.
--Tales from Scott. (Illus.). (Six to Sixteen Ser.). N.D. Caldwell.

Sullivan, Francis John see Sullivan, Frank.

Sullivan, Frank (1892-1976)
--A Moose in the Hoose. Prince, George, illus. LC 59-10819. 54 p. illus. 24 cm. 1959. Random House.
--Night the Old Nostalgia Burned Down. N.D. Grosset & Dunlap.

Sullivan, George
--Return of the Battleship. (Illus.). (gr. 7 up). 1983. (ISBN 0-396-08174-6). Dodd.

Sullivan, Joan
--Round is a Pancake. Lamacchia, Frank, illus. LC 63-15205. (Illus.). 26. 24cm. (A Little Owl Bk.). 1963. Holt, Rinehart and Winston.

Sullivan, John F., Jr.
--Songs After Sundown. N.D. Bruce Humphries, Inc.

Sullivan, John Joseph (1903-)
--The Legends of French Island: Adventures of the Riverview Boys. LC 41-12312. viii p., 1 l., 237 p. 19 1/2 cm. c.1941. The Bruce Publishing Company.
--The Monkey & the Pumpkin. Molloy, Eideen, illus. 1978. (ISBN 0-533-03077-3). Vantage.

Sullivan, Margaret M. Reynolds (1902-)
--Judy of Honeycomb Tower. LC 43-5431. 235 p. 17 1/2 cm. 1943. The Ave Maria Press.
--The Mystery of Lady Ridge. LC 38-29967. 220 p. 17 1/2 cm. 1938. The Ava Maria Press.

Sullivan, Martha H.
--The Little Boy Who Had Two Birthdays. (Illus.). 16p. (gr. 1-4). N.D. St Anthony.

Sullivan, Mary Ann
--Child of War. LC 84-47832. 144p. (gr. 5 up). 1984. (ISBN 0-8234-0537-0). Holiday.

Sullivan, Mary Wilson (1907-)
--Bluegrass Iggy. LC 75-15912. p. cm. 1975. (ISBN 0-8407-6475-8). T. Nelson.
--Brian-Foot-in-the-Mouth. LC 77-29130. 95 p. 21cm. c.1978. (ISBN 0-8407-6595-9). T. Nelson.
--Earthquake 2099. LC 82-7128. 119 p. 22cm. c.1982. (ISBN 0-525-66761-X). Lodestar Books.
--The Indestructible Old-Time String Band. LC 74-34391. 123 p. 21cm. 1975. (ISBN 0-8407-6426-X). T. Nelson.
--The VW Connection. LC 80-22730. p. cm. 1980, c.1981. (ISBN 0-525-66701-6). Elsevier/Nelson Books.
--What's This About Pete?. LC 76-2528. 125 p. 21cm. c.1976. (ISBN 0-8407-6496-0). T. Nelson.

Sullivan, Monica
--Slipping Through the Jelly Line. LC 81-52144. 264p. (Orig.). (gr. 9-12). 1981. (ISBN 0-941228-00-2). Rubenstein.

Sullivan, Pat
--Felix the Cat. LC 54-16669. unpaged. illus. 21cm. (Treasure Bks. 872). c.1953. Treasure Books.

Sullivan, Peggy Anne (1929-)
--Many Names for Eileen. Wood, Muriel, illus. LC 68-10485. (Illus.). 32 p. 23cm. (Wonderland books). 1969. Follett Pub. Co.
--The O'Donnells. Stevens, Mary E. (1920-1966), illus. LC 56-9869. 160p. illus. 25cm. 1956. (ISBN 0-695-46440-X). Follett Pub. Co.

Sullivan, Scott (1952-), illus.
--Hello Kitty Can Count!. LC 82-80922. (Illus.). 16 p. 19cm. (Hummingbird). c.1982. (ISBN 0-394-85433-0). Random House.
--Hello Kitty on the Go. LC 82-80668. (Illus.). 24 p. 15cm. c.1982. (ISBN 0-394-85152-8). Random House.

Sullivan, Silky
--The B Street Five. Axeman, Lois, illus. LC 81-38468. (Illus.). 31 p. 24cm. (Henry and Melinda Sports Stories). c.1982. (ISBN 0-516-01918-X). (ISBN 0-516-41918-8). Childrens Press.
--Henry and Melinda. Axeman, Lois, illus. LC 81-12283. (Illus.). 31 p. 24cm. (Henry and Melinda Sports Stories). c.1982. (ISBN 0-516-01916-3). (ISBN 0-516-41916-1). Childrens Press.
--Henry and Melinda Team up. Axeman, Lois, illus. LC 81-12250. (Illus.). 31 p. 24cm. (Henry and Melinda Sports Stories). c.1982. (ISBN 0-516-01917-1). (ISBN 0-516-41917-X). Childrens Press.
--Kings on Court. Axeman, Lois, illus. LC 81-12251. (Illus.). 31 p. 24cm. (Henry and Melinda Sports Stories). c.1982. (ISBN 0-516-01919-8). (ISBN 0-516-41919-6). Childrens Press.
--Mystery at the Basketball Game. Axeman, Lois, illus. LC 81-12252. (Illus.). 31 p. 24cm. (Henry and Melinda Sports Stories). c.1982. (ISBN 0-516-01921-X). (ISBN 0-516-41921-8). Childrens Press.
--Roller Skates. Axeman, Lois, illus. LC 81-12299. (Illus.). 31 p. 24cm. (Henry and Melinda Sports Stories). c.1982. (ISBN 0-516-01920-1). (ISBN 0-516-41920-X). Childrens Press.

Sullivan, Sir Arthur Seymour, Sir, jt. auth. see Gilbert, William Schwenck, Sir.

Sullivan, Tom
--Common Senses. Reinert, Rick, illus. 48p. (gr. k-6). 1981. (ISBN 0-8249-8022-0). Ideals.

Sumer, Mine, jt. auth. see Walker, Barbara Kerlin.

Sumera, Annabelle
--Silly Goose and the Holidays. Winik, Leon & Barber, Ray, illus. LC 73-109195. (Illus.). 32 p. 17cm. (Bill Martin instant reader). 1970. Holt, Rinehart and Winston.
--What Lily Goose Found. Cauley, Lorinda Bryan (1951-), illus. (Illus.). (Young Reader Ser.). (gr. k-3). 1979. (ISBN 0-307-60163-3, Golden Pr). Western Pub.

Sumiko
--My Baby Brother Ned. (Illus.). 32p. 1st U.S. edition. (ps-1). 1983. (ISBN 0-434-96533-2, Pub. by W. Heinemann). David & Charles.

Sumiko & Wilkinson, Barry, illus.
--Storytime. 94p. 1974. (ISBN 0-00-138180-6). Collins & World.

Summerfield, Geoffrey
--Welcome & Other Poems. Usbourne, Karen, illus. (Illus.). 96p. (gr. 7-11). 1983. (ISBN 0-233-97528-4). Andre Deutsch.

Summerfield, Geoffrey, ed.
--First Voices. LC 71-158144. (Illus.). 4 v. 22cm. 1971, c.1970. Knopf; Distributed by Random House.
--Junior Voices. LC 72-22659. (Illus.). 21cm. (Penguin Education). 1970. (ISBN 0-14-080067-0). Penguin.

Summers, Bob (1942-)
--Me the Flunkie: Yearbook of a School for Failures. LC 79-121141. (Illus.). 175 p. 18cm. (Fawcett Premier Bk.T478). 1970. Fawcett Publications.

Summers, Hollis Spurgeon, Jr. (1916-)
--Someone Else: Sixteen Poems About Other Children. Miller, Jane Judith (1925-), illus. LC 62-162959. 39 p. illus. 25 cm. 1962. Lippincott.

Summers, James Levingston (1910-)
--The Amazing Mr. Tenterhook. LC 64-15359. 159 p. 21 cm. 1964. Westminster Press.
--The Cardiff Giants. LC 64-11191. 176 p. 21 cm. 1964. Westminster Press.
--Change of Focus. LC 70-187504. 173 p. 21cm. 1972. (ISBN 0-664-32514-9). Westminster Press.
--Cumash Summer. Lambo, Donald W. (1903-1966), illus. LC 67-17531. (gr. 8-10). 1967. (ISBN 0-679-25035-2). McKay.
--Don't Come Back a Stranger. LC 72-126129. 186 p. 21cm. 1970. (ISBN 0-664-32482-7). Westminster Press.
--Gift Horse. LC 61-5564. 190 p. 21 cm. 1961. Westminster Press.
--Girl Trouble. LC 52-11785. 215 p. 22cm. 1953. Westminster Press.
--Girl Trouble. Shostak, Jerome, ed. LC 57-4083. 262p. illus. 22cm. (Teen-Age Bookshelf). 1957. Oxford Book Co.
--Heartbreak Hot Rod. LC 57-10466. 208 p. 22 cm. 1958. Doubleday.
--The Iron Doors Between. LC 68-15010. 206 p. 21cm. 1968. Westminster Press.
--The Karting Crowd. LC 61-10300. 172 p. 21 cm. 1961. Westminster Press.
--The Limit of Love. LC 59-11052. 192 p. 21 cm. 1959. Westminster Press.
--The Long Ride Home. LC 66-5500. 170p. 22cm. c.1966. Westminster.
--The Lucky Suzuki. Lambo, Donald W. (1903-1966), illus. LC 68-25826. (Illus.). 154 p. 21cm. 1968. D. McKay Co.
--Muscle Boy. LC 62-7393. 176 p. 21 cm. 1962. Westminster Press.
--Off the Beam. LC 56-7102. 219 p. 22 c. 1956. Westminster Press.
--Open Season. LC 51-10771. 182 p. 21 cm. 1951. Doubleday.
--Operation ABC. LC 55-5760. 190 p. 22cm. 1955. Westminster Press.
--Prom Trouble. LC 54-6432. 222 p. 22cm. 1954. Westminster Press.
--Ring Around Her Finger. LC 57-8073. 206 p. 21 cm. 1957. Westminster Press.
--Senior Dropout. LC 65-16495. 174p. 22cm. c.1965. Westminster.
--The Shelter Trap. LC 68-15774. 128 p. 18cm. 1967. G. A. Pflaum.
--The Shelter Trap. LC 62-11516. 160 p. 21 cm. 1962. Westminster Press.
--Sons of Montezuma. LC 58-6119. 192p. 21cm. 1958. Westminster Press.
--This Random Sky. LC 60-6187. 192 p. 21 cm. 1960. Westminster Press.
--Tiger Terwilliger. LC 63-13355. 170 p. 21cm. 1963. Westminster Press.
--Tougher Than You Think. LC 59-569566. 224 p. 21cm. 1959. Westminster Press.
--Trouble on Hogback Hill. LC 60-8636. 186 p. 21 cm. 1960. Westminster Press.
--Trouble on the Run. LC 56-5173. 216p. 21cm. c.1956. Westminster Press.
--The Trouble with Being in Love. LC 63-8203. 174 p. 21cm. 1963. Westminster Press.
--Wait for Private Black. LC 58-9947. 188 p. 21 cm. 1958. Westminster Press.
--Wild Buggy Jordan. LC 65-19278. 180 p. 22cm. 1965. D. McKay Co.
--The Wonderful Time. LC 57-5434. 192 p. 22 cm. 1957. Westminster Press.
--You Can't Make It by Bus. LC 70-78480. 174 p. 21cm. 1969. Westminster Press.

Summers, Jester
--Joseph the Forgiver. Sloan, Michael, illus. LC 76-383002. (Illus.). 48 p. 24cm. (Biblearn Ser.). c.1976. (ISBN 0-8054-4224-3). Broadman Press.

Summers, JoAn (1943-)
--Fruitbasket Friends. LC 75-7481. (Illus.). 89 p. 21cm. c.1975. (ISBN 0-88270-121-5). Logos International.
--Happy Faces: Animals Tell Their Favorite Bible Stories. (Illus.). (gr. k-3). 1971. (ISBN 0-88243-720-8). Gospel Pub.

Suteyev, Vladimir Grigorevich, ed.
--The Chick & the Duckling. Aruego, Jose (1932-) & Dewey, Ariane (1937-), illus. Ginsburg, Mirra, tr. from Russian. LC 74-188773. (Translated from the Russian of V. Suteyev). (ps-k). 1972. (ISBN 0-02-735940-9). Macmillan.
Suteyev, Vladimir Grigorevich, jt. auth. see Polushkin, Maria.
Sutherland, Dora D., ed.
--Children's Heart Throbs: A Compilation of Fifth Grade Poetry and Prose. LC 31-161182. 68 p. port. 20 cm. c.1930. Mayes Printing Company.
Sutherland, Efua Theodora (1924-)
--Playtime in Africa. Bell, Willis E, photos by. LC 62-7368. (Illus.). 56 p. 24cm. 1962. Atheneum.
--Vulture! Vulture!. Two Rhythm Plays. 1970. Panther House.
Sutherland, Louis
--Magic Bullets. 1956. Little, Brown and Company.
Sutherland, Lucille, jt. auth. see Ware, Kay.
Sutherland, Lucille, ed. see Beattie, Janet.
Sutherland, Lucille, ed. see Beim, Jerrold.
Sutherland, Lucille, ed. see Falk, Ann Mari.
Sutherland, Lucille, ed. see Hallqvist, Britt G.
Sutherland, Lucille, adapted by see Hellsing, Lennart (1919-) & Stroyer, Poul.
Sutherland, Lucille, ed. see Hertz, Grete Janus.
Sutherland, Lucille, ed. see Lindgren, Astrid Ericsson.
Sutherland, Lucille, ed. see Peterson, Hans.
Sutherland, Lucille, ed. see Proysen, Alf.
Sutherland, Lucille, ed. see Sigsgaard, Jens.
Sutherland, Lucille, ed. see Skjonsberg, Gunnar.
Sutherland, Lucille, jt. ed. see Ware, Kay.
Sutherland, Margaret (1941-)
--Hello, I'm Karen. Paton, Jane Elizabeth (1934-), illus. LC 75-25614. (Illus.). 92 p. 20cm. 1st U.S. edition. 1976, c.1974. (ISBN 0-698-20371-2). Coward, McCann & Geoghegan.
Sutherland, Philip
--It Happened to Tip. Sutherland, Philip, illus. LC 77-155143. (Illus.). 129 p., 5 leaves of plates. 17cm. (The Beanville Series). c.1977. Press at Diamond Hill.
Sutherland, Robert D.
--Sticklewort and Feverfew. Sutherland, Robert D., illus. LC 79-92898. (Illus.). 355 p. 27cm. c.1980. (ISBN 0-936044-00-4). (ISBN 0-936044-01-2). Pikestaff Press.
Sutherland, Zena Bailey (1915-), compiled by.
--Nursery Rhymes, Songs & Stories. (Illus.). (J/Sf). (gr. k-4). 1980. (ISBN 0-525-66707-5). Lodestar Bks.
Sutherland, Zena Bailey (1915-) & Livingston, Myra Cohn (1926-), eds.
--The Scott, Foresman Anthology of Children's Literature. LC 83-17194. (Illus.). xxxi, 1002 p. c.1984. (ISBN 0-673-15527-7). Scott Foresman.
Sutphin, Florence E
--An Autobiography by Chucky Woodchuck. LC 67-20568. (Illus.). 63 p. 23cm. 1967. Christopher Pub. House.
Sutro, Alfred see Smart, Adam, pseud.
Sutro, Alfred (1869-1933)
--Prehistoric Beasts Discovered for His Grandchildren. Smart, Adam, pseud. LC 37-4768. 24 l. illus. 23 1/2 x 29 cm. c.1937. Printed by Grabhorn Press.
--Words at Play. Smart, Adam, pseud. Davenport, W. R., illus. LC 39-2148. 24 l. illus. 32 1/2 x 22 1/2 cm. c.1939. Printed at the Grabhorn Press.
Suttler, Thomas Reid
--The Three Fleas. N.D. Vantage Press.
Suttles, Shirley Smith see Conger, Lesley, pseud.
Suttles, Shirley Smith see Conger, Marion, pseud.
Sutton, Adah Louise (1865-)
--A Little Maid in Toyland. Russell, Alfred, illus. LC 9-2769. 24 x 21cm. 210p. 1908. Saalfield Publishing Co.
--Mr. Bunny, his book. Fry, W. H., illus. 4cm. 106p. 1900. Saalfield Publishing Co.
--Mushroom Fairies. LC 12-9601. (Illus.). 23 x 31cm. 159p. 1910. Saalfield Publishing Co.
--Teddy Bears. Schaefer, A. J., illus. LC 7-21532. 154 p. col. front., illus., 5 col. pl. 23 1/2 x 20 1/2 cm. c.1907. The Saalfield Publishing Co.
Sutton, Ann Livesay (1923-) & Sutton, Myron
--Exploring With The Bartrams. 1963. (ISBN 0-8382-0236-5, Cadmus Books). E. M. Hale and Company.
Sutton, Clifford E
--Bobby Brown and the Space Ship. Sutton, Frances Dee, illus. LC 80-67719. (Illus.). 48 p. 28cm. c.1980. Sutton.
Sutton, Edith F
--Granny's Dreams. LC 27-1989. vi p.,1 l., 9-104 p. front. 20 cm. c.1926. J. F. Rowny Press.
Sutton, Edith Gideon, Mrs.
--To a Little Child. Terlesky, Vitalie Z., illus. LC 41-307495. 89 p. incl. front. 19 1/2 cm. c.1931. B. Humphries, Inc.
Sutton, Eric, tr. see Kastner, Erich.
Sutton, Eugenia Geneva Hansen see Sutton, Jean, pseud.
Sutton, Evelyn Mary (1906-)
--My Cat Likes to Hide in Boxes. Dodd, Lynley Stuart (1941-), illus. LC 73-12854. (Illus.). 32 p. 20cm. 1974, c.1973. (ISBN 0-8193-0752-1). (ISBN 0-8193-0752-1). Parents' Magazine Press.
Sutton, Felix (1910-), adapted by see Clemens, Samuel Langhorne.
Sutton, Felix (1910-), abridged by see Knight, Eric Mowbray.
Sutton, Felix (1910-), adapted by see Melville, Herman.
Sutton, Felix (1910-), abridged by see Stevenson, Robert Louis.
Sutton, Felix (1910-), adapted by see Terhune, Albert Payson.
Sutton, Felix (1910-), ed. see Wyss, Johann David Von.
Sutton, Felix (1910-)
--Adventures of the Range Rider. Glanzman, Louis S. (1922-), illus. LC 56-19721. 64 p. illus. 21 cm. (Wonder Bks. 2528). 1955, c.1956. Wonder Books.
--The City Under the Sea: An Ace Cooper Adventure. LC 60-128509. 146 p. 21 cm. 1961. Duell, Sloan and Pearce.
--Dangerous Safari: Big Game Hunting in Africa. Aitken, Russell B., frwd. by. LC 58-8217. 191 p. illus. 22 cm. (A Young American Adventure Bk.). 1958. Young America Books.
--Hot Rock of Hondo: Prospecting for Uranium in the Western Badlands. Merritt, Phillip L., frwd. by. LC 58-8218. 190 p. illus. 22 cm. (Young American Adventure Book). 1958. Young American Books.
--Let's Take a Trip in Our Car. Schucker, James, illus. Farwell, Byron E. (1921-), created by. LC 55-164902. unpaged. illus. 21cm. (The Treasure Book Parade, 890). 1954. Treasure Books.
--The Magic Clown. Schucker, James, illus. LC 54-2456. unpaged. illus. 21cm. (The Treasure Book Parade, 876). 1954. Treasure Books.
--Mighty Mouse. Chad, illus. LC 53-29594. unpaged. illus. 21cm. (Treasure Bks. 860). 1953. Treasure Books.
--Mighty Mouse and the Sacred Scarecrow. N.D (Wonder Books). Grosset & Dunlap.
--Mighty Mouse and the Sacred Scarecrow. Chad, illus. LC 54-32787. unpaged. illus. 21cm. (Treasure Books, 884). (A Terry-Toon Book). 1954. Treasure Books.
--Mighty Mouse: Dinky Learns to Fly. N.D (Wonder Books). Grosset & Dunlap.
--Mighty Mouse: Dinky Learns to Fly. Chad, illus. LC 54-16667. unpaged. illus. 21cm. (Treasure Bks. 866). 1953. Treasure Books.
--Mighty Mouse: Santa's Helper. N.D (Wonder Books). Grosset & Dunlap.
--Mighty Mouse, Santa's Helper. Chad, illus. LC 55-565171. unpaged. illus. 21cm. (Treasure Bks. 896). 1955. Treasure Books.
--Mighty Mouse to the Rescue. N.D (Wonder Books). Grosset & Dunlap.
--The Nine Friendly Dogs. Goldsborough, June (1923-), illus. LC 55-24399. unpaged. illus. 21cm. (Wonder Bks. 622). 1954. Wonder Books.
--The Picture Story of Davy Crockett. Vestal, Herman B., illus. LC 55-288328. 64p. illus. 21cm. (Wonder Playbooks for Children, 2525). c.1955. Wonder Books.
--Skin Diving for Sunken Treasure. Robikoff, Dimitri, frwd. by. LC 57-12496. 194 p. illus. 22 cm. (A Young America Adventure Bk.). c.1957. Young America Books.
--The Terry Bears Win the Cub Scout Badge. Moore, J. Robert, illus. LC 56-197202. unpaged. illus. 21cm. (A Terry-Toon Book). 1955. Treasure Books.
--We Were There at Pearl Harbor. Kitts, Willard A., ed. Vaughn, Frank E., illus. LC 57-10106. 177 p. illus. 24 cm. (We Were There Books 15). 1957. Grosset & Dunlap.
--We Were There at the Battle of Lexington and Concord. Miers, Earl Schenck, ed. Vestal, Herman B., illus. LC 58-12567. 182 p. illus. 22 cm. (We Were There Books, 20). 1958. Grosset & Dunlap.
--We Were There at the First Airplane Flight. Leoning, Grover (1912-), ed. Matulay, Laszlo (1912-), illus. LC 60-51913. 179 p. illus. 22 cm. (We Were There Books, 28). 1960. Grosset & Dunlap.
--Wild Bill Hickok. Nielsen, Jon (1912-), illus. LC 57-67. unpaged. illus. 21 cm. (Wonder Books, 649). 1957, c.1956. Wonder Books.
Sutton, Felix (1910-) & Jason, Leon
--The Terrytoons Playhouse. Chad, et al., illus. LC 58-4243. unpaged. illus. 29 cm. (TerryToons Story Bk.). 1958. Grosset & Dunlap.
Sutton, Jane (1950-)
--Confessions of an Orange Octopus. 1st ed. Spence, Jim, illus. LC 83-8850. p. cm. c.1983. (ISBN 0-525-44068-2). Dutton.
--Gabie's Christmas Shopping Disaster. Gerberg, Mort, illus. LC 84-1578. p. cm. c.1984. (ISBN 0-525-44110-7). Dutton.
--Me and the Weirdos. 1981. Harcourt.
--Me and the Weirdos. Kossin, Sandy (1926-), illus. LC 80-26584. (Illus.). 117 p. 22cm. c.1981. (ISBN 0-395-30447-4). Houghton Mifflin Co.
--Not Even Mrs. Mazursky. Drescher, Joan Elizabeth (1939-), illus. LC 83-20678. (Illus.). 96p. (gr. 3-5). 1984. (ISBN 0-525-44083-6). (ISBN 0-525-44083-6). Dutton.
--What Should a Hippo Wear?. Munsinger, Lynn (1951-), illus. LC 78-24005. p. cm. 1979. Houghton Mifflin.
Sutton, Jean, pseud., see Sutton, Eugenia Geneva Hansen.
Sutton, Jean, jt. auth. see Sutton, Jefferson Howard.
Sutton, Jean, pseud. & Sutton, Jefferson Howard (1913-1979)
--The Beyond. Sutton, Eugenia Geneva Hansen. LC 67-24175. 223 p. 21cm. 1968, c.1967. Putnam.
--The Boy Who Had the Power. Sutton, Eugenia Geneva Hansen. LC 71-151222. 189 p. 22cm. 1971. Putnam.
--Lord of the Stars. Sutton, Eugenia Geneva Hansen. LC 71-77769. 220 p. 21cm. 1969. Putnam.
--The Programmed Man. Sutton, Eugenia Geneva Hansen. LC 68-15082. (Illus.). 192 p. 21cm. 1968. Putnam.
Sutton, Jeff see Sutton, Jean, pseud. & Sutton, Jefferson Howard.
Sutton, Jeff see Sutton, Jefferson Howard (1913-1979) & Sutton, Jean.
Sutton, Jefferson Howard, jt. auth. see Sutton, Jean.
Sutton, Jefferson Howard (1913-1979)
--Beyond Apollo. LC 66-7398. 21cm. 223p. (gr. 9 up). 1966. (ISBN 0-399-20016-9). Putnam.
Sutton, Jefferson Howard (1913-1979) & Sutton, Jean, pseud.
--Alien from the Stars. Sutton, Euginia Geneva Hansen. LC 74-113507. 223 p. 21cm. 1970. Putnam.
Sutton, Larry
--The Case of the Smiley Faces. Blumer, Patt, illus. LC 80-69288. (Illus.). 32 p. 16cm. (A Carolrhoda Mini-Mystery). c.1981. (ISBN 0-87614-133-5). Carolrhoda Books.
--The Case of the Trick Note. Blumer, Patt, illus. LC 80-69287. (Illus.). 32 p. 16cm. (A Carolrhoda Mini-Mystery). c.1981. (ISBN 0-87614-134-3). Carolrhoda Books.
--Ghost Plane Over Hartley Field. Blumer, Patt, illus. LC 80-69286. (Illus.). 30 p. 16cm. (A Carolrhoda Mini-Mystery). c.1981. (ISBN 0-87614-135-1). Carolrhoda Books.
--The Mystery of the Blue Champ. Blumer, Patt, illus. LC 80-69289. (Illus.). 30 p. 16cm. (A Carolrhoda Mini-Mystery). c.1981. (ISBN 0-87614-137-8). Carolrhoda Books.
--The Mystery of the Late News Report. Blumer, Patt, illus. LC 80-69285. (Illus.). 30 p. 16cm. (A Carolrhoda Mini-Mystery). c.1981. (ISBN 0-87614-136-X). Carolrhoda Books.
--Taildragger's High. 161p. 1985. (ISBN 0-374-37372-8). Farrar Strauss.
Sutton, Lee
--Venus Boy. Floethe, Richard (1901-), illus. LC 54-7882. 182p. illus. 22cm. 1955. Lothrop, Lee &Shepard.
Sutton, Margaret Beebe, Mrs. (1903-)
--Baby's Day in Rhymes and Pictures. Doane, Pelagie (1906-1966), illus. LC 38-18524. 28 p. col. illus. 21 1/2 cm. c.1938. Grosset & Dunlap.
--The Black Cat's Clue. LC 52-8143. 210 p. illus. 20 cm. (Her A Judy Bolton Mystery 23). 1952. Grosset & Dunlap.
--The Clue in the Patchwork Quilt. Doane, Pelagie (1906-1966), illus. LC 41-7698. vii, 214 p. incl. front. 19 1/2 cm. (Her Judy Bolton Mystery Stories). c.1941. Grosset & Dunlap.
--The Clue in the Ruined Castle. LC 55-22545. 176p. illus. 20cm. (Her a Judy Bolton Mystery 26). c.1955. Grosset & Dunlap.
--The Clue of the Broken Wing. LC 58-782. 182 p. illus. 20 cm. (Her A Judy Bolton Mystery 29). 1958. Grosset & Dunlap.
--The Clue of the Stone Lantern. LC 76-47656. p. cm. 1976, c.1950. (ISBN 0-88411-712-X). Aeonian Press.
--The Clue of the Stone Lantern. LC 50-6610. x, 210 p. front. 20 cm. (Her A Judy Bolton Mystery). 1950. Grosset & Dunlap.
--The Discovery at the Dragon's Mouth. LC 60-1101. 182 p. illus. 20 cm. (Her A Judy Bolton Mystery 31). 1960. Grosset & Dunlap.
--The Forbidden Chest. LC 53-6960. 210p. illus. 20cm. (Her A Judy Bolton Mystery 31). 1953. Grosset & Dunlap.
--Gail Gardner, Junior Cadet Nurse. LC 45-9777. viii, 239 p. 19 cm. 1945. Dodd, Mead & Company.
--Gail Gardner Wins Her Cap. LC 44-718897. 5 p. l., 243 p. 19 cm. 1944. Dodd, Mead & Company.
--The Ghost Parade. Doane, Pelagie (1906-1966), illus. LC 33-8152. vi, 217 p. front., plates. 19 1/2 cm. (Her Judy Bolton Mystery Series). c.1933. Grosset & Dunlap.
--The Haunted Apartment. Dillon, Corinne Boyd, illus. LC 47-215. 5 p. l., 195 p. illus. 19 1/2 cm. 1946. Dodd, Mead & Company.
--The Haunted Attic. Doane, Pelagie (1906-1966), illus. LC 76-47657. p. cm. 1976, c.1967. (ISBN 0-88411-715-4). Aeonian Press.
--The Haunted Attic. Doane, Pelagie (1906-1966), illus. LC 32-13344. viii, 212 p. front., plates. 19 1/2 cm. (Her Judy Bolton Mystery Stories). c.1932. Grosset & Dunlap.
--The Haunted Fountain. LC 57-136256. 180p. illus. 20cm. (Her A Judy Bolton Mystery 28). 1957. Grosset & Dunlap.
--The Haunted Road. LC 54-856313. 181p. illus. 20cm. (Her A Judy Bolton Mystery 25). 1954. Grosset & Dunlap.
--The Hidden Clue. LC 64-2156. x, 167 p. illus. 20 cm. (Her A Judy Bolton Mystery, 35). 1964. Grosset & Dunlap.
--The Invisible Chimes. Doane, Pelagie (1906-1966), illus. LC 76-47629. p. cm. 1976, c.1967. (ISBN 0-88411-716-2). Aeonian Press.
--The Invisible Chimes. Doane, Pelagie (1906-1966), illus. LC 32-13343. viii, 213 p. front., plates 19 1/2 cm. (Her Judy Bolton Mystery Stories). c.1932. Grosset & Dunlap.
--Jemima, Daughter of Daniel Boone. Hazelton, Isaac Brewster, illus. LC 42-194408. xi, 251 p. incl. front., illus. 21 1/2 cm. 1942. C. Scribner's Sons.
--Juneau, the Sleigh Dog. N.D. Grosset & Dunlap.
--The Living Portrait. Doane, Pelagie (1906-1966), illus. LC 47-11171. viii, 208 p. front. 20 cm. (Her A Judy Bolton Mystery). 1947. Grosset & Dunlap.
--Lollypop: The True Story of a Little Dog. Doane, Pelagie (1906-1966), illus. LC 39-18655. 24 p. col. illus. 22 cm. c.1939. Grosset & Dunlap.
--The Magic Makers and the Bramble Bush Man. Doane, Pelagie (1906-1966), illus. LC 36-1854. 4 p. l., 3-114 p. front., illus. 23 cm. c.1936. Grosset & Dunlap.
--The Magic Makers and the Golden Charm. Doane, Pelagie (1906-1966), illus. LC 36-185585. 4 p. l., 3-118 p. front., illus. 28 cm. c.1936. Grosset & Dunlap.
--The Magic Makers in Backwards Land. Doane, Pelagie (1906-1966), illus. LC 36-29311. 4 p. l., 3-111 p. front., illus. 23 cm. c.1936. Grosset & Dunlap.
--The Mark on the Mirror. Doane, Pelagie (1906-1966), illus. LC 42-3785. vii p., 1 l., 206 p. incl. front. 19 1/2 cm. 1949. Grosset & Dunlap.
--The Midnight Visitor. Doane, Pelagie (1906-1966), illus. v, 249 p. front. 19 1/2 cm. (Her Judy Bolton Mystery). c.1939. Grosset & Dunlap.
--The Mysterious Half Cat. Doane, Pelagie (1906-1966), illus. LC 36-1049. vii, 215 p. front. 19 1/2 cm. (Her Judy Bolton Mystery Stories). c.1936. Grosset & Dunlap.
--The Mystic Ball. Doane, Pelagie (1906-1966), illus. LC 34-14230. viii, 212 p. front. 19 1/2 cm. (Her Judy Bolton Mystery Stories). c.1934. Grosset & Dunlap.
--The Name on the Bracelet. Doane, Pelagie (1906-1966), illus. LC 40-7530. vii, 216 p. incl. front. 19 1/2 cm. (Her Judy Bolton Mystery Stories). c.1940. Grosset & Dunlap.
--Palace Wagon Family: A True Story of the Donner Party. 1st ed. Stevens, Mary (1907-), illus. LC 57-9204. 210p. illus. 22cm. 21 cm. 1957. Knopf.
--The Phantom Friend. LC 59-16068. 174 p. illus. 20 cm. (Her a Judy Bolton Mystery 80). 1959. Grosset & Dunlap.
--The Pledge of the Twin Knights. LC 65-13772. x, 172p. illus. 20cm. (Her Judy Bolton Mystery, 36). c.1965. Grosset.
--The Puzzle in the Pond. LC 63-1032. 170 p. illus. 20 cm. (Her A Judy Bolton Mystery). 1963. Grosset & Dunlap.
--The Rainbow Riddle. Doane, Pelagie (1906-1966), illus. LC 76-47626. p. cm. 1976, c.1946. (ISBN 0-88411-711-1). Aeonian Press.
--The Rainbow Riddle. Doane, Pelagie (1906-1966), illus. LC 46-2309. 3 p. l., ix-x p., 1 l., 200 p. incl. front 19 1/2 cm. (Her Judy Bolton Mystery). 1946. Grosset & Dunlap.
--The Riddle of the Double Ring. Doane, Pelagie (1906-1966), illus. LC 37-1016. vii, 216 p. front., plates. 19 cm. (Her Judy Bolton Mystery Stories). c.1937. Grosset & Dunlap.
--The Search for the Glowing Hand. (gr. 4-8). N.D. (ISBN 0-448-09637-4). G&D.
--The Secret of Sand Castle. (gr. 5-10). N.D. (ISBN 0-448-09638-2). G&D.
--The Secret of the Barred Window. Doane, Pelagie (1906-1966), illus. LC 43-16039. vii p., 1 l., 207 p. incl. front. 19 1/2 cm. (Her Judy Bolton Mystery Stories). 1943. Grosset & Dunlap.

--Going into Business. LC 3-31031. 243 p. front., plates. 19 1/2 cm. 1903. The Pilgrim Press.
--Grandfather's Tales of Colonial Days. LC 7-28455. 190 p. incl. illus., plates. col. front. 19 1/2 cm. c.1907. McLoughlin Brothers.
--Grandmamma's Tales of Colonial Days. LC 7-28448. 191 p. incl. illus. pl. col. front 19 1/2cm. c.1907. McLoughlin Brothers.
--Hobby Camp. LC 5-32689. 20cm. 808p. 1905. Pilgrim Press.
--Lee, a Mountain Hero. 12cm. 145p. 1900. Westminster Press.
--Rufe and Ruth: A Partnership. LC 2-25166. 20cm. 234p. 1902. Pilgrim Press.
--Stories of the Blue and Gray. Ives, Sarah Noble, illus. LC 7-30456. 188 p. col. front., illus., col. plates. 19 1/2 cm. c.1907. McLoughlin Brothers.

Sweet, May MacDaniel, Mrs. (1865-), tr. see Fanciulli, Giuseppe.

Sweet, May McDaniel, Mrs. (1865-), tr. see Lorenzini, Carlo.

Sweeter, Kate Dickinson (0000-1939)
--Micky of the Alley. Williams, George Alfred (1875-), illus. LC 3-22511. 20cm. 176p. 1903. D. Appleton & Co.

Sweetkind, Morris (1898-)
--Wonderful World: A Book of Poems for Children. Wilson, Sol, illus. LC 67-9538. (Illus.). 32x28 cm. 36p. 1967. W. J. Mack Co.

Sweetser, Kate Dickinson (0000-1939)
--Boys and Girls from Thackeray. Williams, George Alfred (1875-), illus. LC 7-28978. (Illus.). 25 cm. 355p. 1907. Harper & Brothers.
--Micky of the Alley and Other Youngsters. Williama, George Alfred, illus. LC 3-22511. ix, 176 p. front., 3pl., 19 1/2cm. 1903. D. Appleton & Co.
--Peggy's Prize Cruise. LC 25-185841. 313 p. front., plates. 20 cm. c.1925. Barse & Hopkins.
--Teddy Baird's Luck. Williams, George Alfred (1875-), illus. LC 4-25382. 20cm. 172p. 1904. D. Appleton & Co.
--Ten Boys from Dickens. N.D. Harper & Brothers.
--Ten Girls from Dickens. N.D. Harper & Bros.
--Ten Great Adventures. N.D. Harper & Bros.

Sweetser, Mary Chisholm (1894-)
--The Extra Gift. Hall, H. Tom, illus. LC 70-87985. (Illus.). 29 p. 26cm. 1969. Macrae Smith.

Swem, Leota & Sherwood, Rowena
--A Primer of Nursery Rhymes. LC 9-16409. 1 p. l., 124, 2 p. illus. 19 1/2 cm. $0.3. N.D. Houghton Mifflin Company.

Swenson, Mary
--The Adventures of the Get Along Gang. McPheeters, Neal, illus. (Illus.). 48p. (Orig.). (Get Along Gang Ser.). (ps-3). 1984. (ISBN 0-590-33186-8). Scholastic Inc.
--Milton and His Magic Motorcycle: A Drug Abuse Prevention Program. Herring, Lee, illus. LC 74-165325. (Illus.). v. 22cm. c.1972. Printed by Tane Press.
--Milton and His Magic Motorcycle: Plays. LC 72-81156. v. 22cm. N.D. Printed by Tane Press.

Swenson, May (1919-)
--More Poems to Solve. 1970. (ISBN 0-684-12325-8). Charles Scribner's Sons.
--Poems to Solve. LC 66-275169. 1 v. (unpaged. 22cm. 1966. Scribner.

Swetman, Norman A. (1921-)
--The Witches of Hucklebee County. LC 74-6149. (Illus.). 86 p. 21cm. 1969. Vantage Press.

Swetnam, Evelyn Frances (1919-)
--Yes, My Darling Daughter. Harden, Laurie, illus. LC 77-85134. (Illus.). 166 p. 23cm. c.1978. Harvey House.

Swetnam, George, jt. auth. see Smith, Helen Catherine Snyder.

Swett, Sophia Miriam (1858-1912)
--Bilberry Boys and Girls: Their Adventures and Misadventures, Their Trials and Triumphs. Barry, Etheldred Breeze (1870-), illus. LC 12-392734. 326 p. incl. front. plates. 19 1/2 cm. 1898. Lothrop Pub. Co.
--The Boy from Beaver Hollow. LC 6717. 139p. 1900. Westminster Press.
--A Cape Cod Boy. (The Outdoor Bks.). N.D. Penn Publishing Co.
--A Cape Cod Boy. (Adventure Stories Ser.). N.D. Penn Publishing Co.
--A Cape Cod Boy. (Illus.). (The Little People's Ser.). N.D. Penn Publishing Co.
--A Cape Cod Boy. Hoyt, P. L., illus. LC 1-7828. (Illus.). 12 cm. 311p. (The Vacation Ser.). 1901. Penn.
--Cap'n Thistletop: A Story for Girls and Boys. LC 12-39274. 266 p. front., plates. 19 1/2 cm. c.1895. W. A. Wilde & Company.
--Captain Polly. LC 12-39250. 1 p. l., vii)-viii 9-306 p. front. plates. 16 1/2 cm. 1889. Harper & Brothers.
--Flying Hill Farm: A Story. LC 12-392521. vi, 263 p. incl. front. plates. 19 cm. 1892. Harper & Brothers.
--How the Pennypackers Kept the Light. LC 12-187943. 208 p. incl. front. plates. 19 1/2 cm. $0.7. c.1912. D. Estes & Company.
--The Lion-Tamer's Little Girl. Merrill, Frank Thayer (1848-), illus. LC 7-38903. 154 p. incl. front. 11 pl. 18 1/2 cm. (Her Billy Boy Brown series). 1903. S. E. Cassino.
--The Littlest One of the Browns. LC 3579. 102 p. incl. front., plates. 19 cm. 1900. D. Estes and Company.
--The Lollipops' Vacation and Other Stories. Barry, Etheldred Breeze, et al. (1870-), illus. LC 12-392727. viii p., 1 l., 260 p. incl. front. illus. plates. 20 cm. c.1896. Estes and Lauriat.
--Long Tom and How They Got Him,. Merrill, Frank Thayer (1848-), illus. LC 7-38902. 132 p. incl. front. 11 pl. 18 1/2 cm. (Her Billy Boy Brown series). 1903. S. E. Casino.
--Mary Augusta's Price. LC 3-26372. vii p., 2 l., 13-112 p. incl. front., 2 pl. 18 cm. 1903. H. Altemus Company.
--Mary Augusta's Price, 1 of 21 vols. (Illus.). (Boys & Girls Booklovers Ser.: No. 16). 1905. Set. Henry Altemus Co.
--The Mate of the "Mary Ann". A Story. LC 12-392767. 2 p. l., 235 p. front., plates. 19 cm. 1894. Harper & Brothers.
--Peaseblossom's Lion. Merrill, Frank Thayer (1848-), illus. LC 7-38901. 156 p. incl. front. 11 pl. 18 1/2 cm. (Her billy Boy Brown series). 1903. S. E. Cassino.
--Polly and the Other Girl. Strehlan, Carl A., illus. LC 6-34640. ix p., 1 l., 13-121 p. incl. front., illus. plates. 18 1/2 cm. c.1906. H. Altemus Company.
--The Ponkaty Branch Road and Other Stories for Young People. Bodfish, W. Parker, illus. LC 28-1648. 233 p. incl. front. pates. 19 1/2 cm. 1896. Lothrop Publishing Company.
--Princess Wisla. Merrill, Frank Thayer (1848-), illus. LC 8-30702. viii, 256 p., 1 l., incl. illus., plates. front. 19 1/2 cm. 1908. Little, Brown, and Company.
--Sarah the Less. LC 2-12743. 174 p. incl. front. plates. 19 1/2 cm. 1902. THe Westminster Press.
--The Six Little Pennypackers: Or, From Little Bear Lighthouse to London. Merrill, Frank Thayer (1848-), illus. LC 11-32447. 20cm. 200p. 1911. Dana Estes & Co.
--Sonny Boy. LC 4-30949. 18cm. 102p. 1904. H. Altemus Co.
--Sonny Boy, 1 of 21 vols. (Illus.). (Boys & Girls Booklovers Ser.: No. 11). 1905. Set. Henry Altemus Co.
--Tom Pickering of "Scutney: His Experiences and Perplexities. Young, H. D., illus. LC 12-39275. 282 p. front., 3 pl. 19 1/2 cm. c.1897. Lothrop Publishing Company.
--The Wonder-Ship. LC 2-215862. iii, 83 p. front. 19 1/2 cm. (The golden hour series). 1902. T. Y. Crowell & Company.
--The Yellow-Capped Monkey. Merrill, Frank Thayer (1848-), illus. LC 7-38900. 125 p. incl. front. 11 pl. 18 1/2 cm. (Her Billy Boy Brown series). 1903. S. E. Cassino.
--The Young Shipbuilder. (The Outdoor Bks.). N.D. Penn Publishing Co.
--The Young Shipbuilder. (Illus.). (The Little People's Ser.). N.D. Penn Publishing Co.
--The Young Shipbuilder. Betts, John Henderson, illus. LC 2-17554. (Illus.). 19 cm. 354p. (The Vacation Ser.). 1902. Penn.
--The Young Shipbuilder. Betts, John Henderson, illus. (Adventure Stories Ser.). N.D. Penn Publishing Co.

Swett, Sophie see Swett, Sophia Miriam.

Swiderska, Barbara
--The Fisherman's Bride. Swiderska, Barbara, illus. LC 78-148051. (Illus.). 31 p. 26cm. 1971. Scroll Press.

Swift, Edd, pseud., see Swift, Edward.

Swift, Edd, pseud. (1943-)
--Ted and Priscilla. Swift, Edward. Swift, Edd, pseud. (1943-), illus. Swift, Edward. LC 74-158883. (Illus.). 31 p. 26cm. 1971. Hawthorn Books.

Swift, Edward see Swift, Edd, pseud.

Swift, Fletcher Harper (1876-)
--Joseph: A Drama for Children, in One Act and Three Scenes. LC 20-13730. 1 p. l, 5-31 p. 19 cm. c.1907. W. B. Harison.
--The Most beautiful thing in the world. Williams, George Alfred (1875-), illus. LC 14-22571. 1914. American Tract Society.
--The Most Beautiful Thing in the World. Williams, George Alfred, illus. LC 5-32783. v. 57 p. 4pl. 19 1/2cm. 1905. E. P. Dutton.

Swift, Helen Miller (1914-)
--Adventure in Store. 1st ed. LC 55-8314. 242p. 21cm. 1955. Longmans, Green.
--Chocolate Soda. 1st ed. LC 56-10109. 216 p. 22cm. 1956. Longmans, Green.
--First Semester. 1960. David McKay Company.
--First Semester. 1st ed. LC 60-10213. 210 p. 22 cm. 1960. Longmans, Green.
--Head Over Heels. LC 67-19771. 182 p. 21cm. 1968. Delacorte Press.
--Second Semester. Abel, Raymond (1911-), illus. LC 61-13105. 244 p. illus. 21 cm. 1961. Longmans, Green.

Swift, Hildegarde Hoyt, Mrs. (1890-1977)
--House by the Sea. Ward, Lynd Kendall (1905-1985), illus. LC 36-27889. 9 p. l., 3-245 p. incl. front. illus, plates. 22 cm. c.1938. Harcourt, Brace and Company.
--Little Blacknose: The Story of a Pioneer. Ward, Lynd Kendall (1905-1985), illus. LC 29-20428. 6 p. l., 3-149 p. col. front., illus., col. plates. 19 1/2 cm. c.1929. Harcourt, Brace and Company. **Award: (JNM).**
--North Star Shining: A Pictorial History of the American Negro. Ward, Lynd Kendall (1905-1985), illus. (Illus.). 1947. (ISBN 0-688-21904-7). Morrow.
--The Railroad to Freedom: A Story of the Civil War. Daugherty, James Henry (1889-1974), illus. LC 32-258412. xix, 364 p. incl. front, illus., plates. 24 cm. c.1932. Harcourt, Brace and Company. **Award: (JNM).**
--The Railroad to Freedom: A Story of the Civil War. Daugherty, James Henry (1889-1974), illus. 1960. Harcourt.

Swift, Hildegarde Hoyt, Mrs. (1890-1977) & Ward, Lynd Kendall (1905-1985)
--The Little Red Lighthouse and the Great Gray Bridge. LC 42-36286. 56 p. col. illus. 21 1/2 x 18 cm. 1942. Harcourt, Brace and Company.
--The Little Red Lighthouse and the Great Gray Bridge. LC 73-12861. (Illus.). 56 p. 22cm. (A Voyager Book, AVB 89). 1974, c.1942. (ISBN 0-15-652840-1). Harcourt Brace Jovanovich.

Swift, Jonathan (1667-1745)
--The Adventures of Captain Gulliver: In a Voyage to the Islands of Lilliput & Brobdingnag. LC 21-3059. 1 p. l., 7-119 p. front., illus. 10 1/2 cm. 1794. Printed and Sold by S. Hall, No. , Cornhill.
--Gulliver's Travel. (Illus.). 223p. Repr. of 1952 ed. (Children's Illustrated Classics). 1975. (ISBN 0-460-05018-4, Pub. by J. M. Dent England). Biblio Dist.
--Gulliver's Travel. N.D. William Collins Sons & Co Ltd.
--Gulliver's Travels. (Famous Bks. for Young Americans). N.D. A. L. Burt Co.
--Gulliver's Travels. 1925. Alfred A. Knopf.
--Gulliver's Travels. N.D. American News Co.
--Gulliver's Travels. N.D. D. C. Heath & Co.
--Gulliver's Travels. N.D. Garden City Publishing Co.
--Gulliver's Travels. Presentation Edition ed. (Routledge's Presentation Poets). N.D. George Routledge & Sons.
--Gulliver's Travels. World-Wide Edition ed. (Illus.). (Routledge's World-Wide Library). N.D. George Routledge & Sons.
--Gulliver's Travels. N.D. Grosset & Dunlap.
--Gulliver's Travels, 12 vols. (Illus.). 446p. (Juvenile Classics Ser.). N.D. Set. H M Caldwell Co.
--Gulliver's Travels. 1900. Hurst & Co.
--Gulliver's Travels. N.D. J. B. Lippincott.
--Gulliver's Travels. (Sears Juvenile Classics). N.D. J.H.Sears & Co.
--Gulliver's Travels. (The Children's Bookshelf). N.D. John C. Winston.
--Gulliver's Travels. (The Winston Clear-Type Popular Classics). N.D. John C. Winston.
--Gulliver's Travels, 4. (The Children's Favorites). N.D. Leavitt & Allen Bros.
--Gulliver's Travels. N.D. Longmans Green & Co.
--Gulliver's Travels. (The Washington Square Classics). N.D. Macrae Smith.
--Gulliver's Travels. (World-Famous Fiction). N.D. Porter & Coates.
--Gulliver's Travels. (The Youth's Cabinet of Popular Standard Bks.). N.D. Pott, Young, & Co.
--Gulliver's Travels. (Treasure Books Ser.). N.D. Steck Co.
--Gulliver's Travels, 1 of 15 vols. (Illus.). (Star Ser.). N.D. T. Y. Crowell.
--Gulliver's Travels. N.D. The Steck Co.
--Gulliver's Travels. LC 31-23587. 64 p. incl. front. illus. 20 1/2 cm. 1931. Thomas S. Rockwell Company.
--Gulliver's Travels. (Children's Favorite Classics). N.D. Thomas Y. Crowell Company.
--Gulliver's Travels. (Classic Ser.). N.D. World Publishing Co.
--Gulliver's Travels. Bellew, Patrick, adapted by. Bellew, Patrick, illus. LC 45-10639. 56 p. incl. col. front., illus. (part col.) 27 1/2 cm. 1945. The Hyperion Press, Distributed by Duell, Sloan and Pearce.
--Gulliver's Travels. Bown, Derick, illus. LC 78-3394. p. cm. (Raintree illustrated classics). 1978. (ISBN 0-8393-6207-2). Raintree Childrens Books.
--Gullivers Travels. Browne, Gordon Frederick (1858-1932), illus. (Scribner-Blackie Series of books for young people). N.D. Charles Scribner's Sons.
--Gulliver's Travels. Cole, Herbert, illus. N.D. John Lane.
--Gulliver's Travels. Colum, Padraic (1881-1972), ed. Pogany, Willy (1882-1955), illus. 1917. Macmillan.
--Gulliver's Travels. Colum, Padraic (1881-1972), retold by. Pogany, Willy (1882-1955), illus. Fadiman, Clifton Paul, afterword by. LC 62-19431. 260 p. illus. 24 cm. (Macmillian classics, 87). 1962. Macmillan.
--Gulliver's Travels. Craig, Henry & Brock, Charles Edmund (1870-1938), illus. (Crandford Series). N.D. Macmillian & Co.
--Gulliver's Travels. Dennis, G. R., ed. (Bohn's Popular Library). N.D. Harcourt Brace & Co.
--Gulliver's Travels. Eichenberg, Fritz (1901-), illus. 352p. N.D. Heritage Press.
--Gullivers Travels. Eimerl, Sarel Henry (1925-), adapted by. Maraja, pseud., illus. Maraja, Libico. LC 62-12869. (Illus.). 27 cm. 155p. (A Golden Illustrated Classic). 1962. Golden Press.
--Gulliver's Travels. Irwin, Don, illus. LC 74-110032. (Illus.). 29cm. 192p. 1962. Childrens Press.
--Gulliver's Travels. Klots, Allen, Jr., intro. by. (Great Illustrated Classics). N.D. Dodd Mead & Co.
--Gulliver's Travels. Morten, illus. 400p. N.D. Cassel Petter & Galpin.
--Gulliver's Travels. Abridged. Moss, Elaine, ed. Baltzer, Hans (1900-), illus. LC 63-20600. 175 p. col. illus. 21 cm. (Splendor books). 1963, c.1961. Duell, Sloan and Pearce.
--Gulliver's Travels. Naish, Theodore, illus. N.D. Penguin Books.
--Gulliver's Travels. Rackham, Arthur (1867-1939), illus. N.D. David McKay Co.
--Gulliver's Travels. Rackham, Arthur (1867-1939), illus. (Children's Illustrated Classics). N.D. E. P. Dutton & Co.
--Gulliver's Travels. Rhead, Louis (1857-1926), ed. (Illus.). N.D. Harper & Brothers Trade-List.
--Gulliver's Travels. Rich, Edwin Gile, ed. N.D. Houghton Mifflin Co.
--Gulliver's Travels. Sherburn, George, intro. by. (Harper's Modern Classics). N.D. Harper & Brothers.
--Gulliver's Travels. Small, David (1945-), illus. LC 83-1033. (Illus.). 1983. (ISBN 0-688-02045-3). Morrow.
--Gulliver's Travels. Rev. and slightly abridged for readers of our time. Watson, Aldren Auld (1917-), illus. LC 47-310829. 306 p. illus., col. plates. 21 cm. (Illustrated junior library). 1947. Grosset & Dunlap.
--Gulliver's Travels. Deluxe ed. Watson, Aldren Auld (1917-), illus. LC 47-27066. (Rev. & Slightly Abridged for Readers of Our Time). (Illus.). 24cm. 331p. (Illustrated Junior Library). 1947. Grosset & Dunlop.
--Gulliver's Travels. Winter, Milo Kendall (1888-1956), illus. (Windermere Ser.). N.D. Rand McNally.
--Gulliver's Travels: A Voyage to Lilliput. Kirk, Maria Louise (1860-), illus. (The Children's Classics). N.D. J. B. Lippincott.
--Gulliver's Travels: A Voyage to Lilliput. Supple, Elizabeth, ed. 54 p. front., illus. 20 1/2 cm. (Easy-to-read books). c.1934. The Saalfield Publishing Company.
--Gulliver's Travels: Among the Giants. N.D. Educational Publishing Company.
--Gulliver's Travels: By Lemuel Gulliver, First a Surgeon, and Then a Captain of Several Ships. Jacques, Robin (1920-), illus. LC 57-3103. 195p. illus. 22cm. 1955. Oxford University Press.
--Gulliver's Travels: Edited for Young Readers. Weisgard, Leonard Joseph (1916-), illus. LC 54-42474. 272p. illus. 22cm. 1954. Junior Deluxe Editions.
--Gulliver's Travels in Lilliput and Brobdingnag. Lang, John, retold by. Blaikie, F. M. B., illus. LC 6-35315. ix, 116 p. 8 col. pl. (inc. front.) 15 cm. (Half-title: Told to the children series...). 1906. T. C. & E. C. Jack.
--Gulliver's Travels: Including A Voyage to Lilliput, A Voyage to Brobdingnag, A Voyage to Laputa, A Voyage to the Country of the Houyhnhnms. Hess, Erwin L., illus. LC 42-2898. 2 p. l., 9-237 p. illus. 21 cm. c.1940. Whitman Publishing Company.
--Gulliver's Travels into Several Remote Nations of the World. N.D. Colby and Rich.
--Gulliver's Travels: Into Several Remote Nations of the World. (Royal Illuminated Library). N.D. Lee & Shepard.
--Gulliver's Travels into Several Remote Nations of the World: Arranged in Three Parts from the Original of Jonathan Swift. Holmes, Mabel Dodge (1883-), ed. Prittie, Edwin John, illus. LC 30-201619. xi p., 1 l., 274 p. col. front. illus. col. plates. 22 1/2 cm. c.1930. The John C. Winston Company.
--Gulliver's Travels into Several Remote Regions of the World: In Words of One Syllable. LC 99-4119. 157 p. incl. front., 54 illus. 19 1/2 cm. (On verso of t.-p.: Altemus' illustrated one syllable series v. 7). 1899. H. Altemus.
--Gulliver's Travels into Some Strange Parts of the World. Andrews, Leonora De Lima, ed. LC 40-6698. 245 p. illus. 19 cm. c.1940. McLoughlin Bros., Inc.

--The Edge of Nowhere. 1st ed. Abel, Raymond (1911-), illus. LC 72-75285. (Illus.). 211 p. 24cm. 1972. Atheneum.

--The Spell of the Northern Lights. Abel, Raymond (1911-), illus. LC 74-19310. (Illus.). 251 p. 24cm. 1975. (ISBN 0-689-30460-9). Atheneum.

--The Turnabout Year. 1st ed. Abel, Raymond (1911-), illus. LC 76-4922. (Illus.). v, 216 p. 24cm. 1976. (ISBN 0-689-30546-X). Atheneum.

Sypherd, Wilbur Owen

--The Book of Books. Dwiggins, W. A., illus. 1944. A. A. Knopf.

Syred, Celia M. (1911-)

--Hebe's Daughter. LC 76-372235. 207 p. 23cm. 1976. (ISBN 0-340-20699-3). Hodder & Stoughton.

Syrett, Netta

--The Fairy Doll and Other Plays for Children. LC 23-26061. 4 p.l., 3-88 p. 16 cm. 1922. Dodd, Mead and Company.

--The Old Miracle Plays of England. Thorp, Helen, illus. vii, 118 p. col. front., col. pl. 20 cm. 1911. A. R. Mowbray & Co., Ltd.

--Rachel and the Seven Wonders. Mercer, Joyce, illus. LC 24-131. 3 p.l., 9-172 p. incl. illus., plates. col. front., col. plates. 22 cm. 1923. Frederick A. Stokes Company.

--Robin Goodfellow and Other Fairy Plays for Children. LC 18-3780. 4 p. l., vii-viii, 139 p. 17 cm. 1918. John Lane.

--Six Fairy Plays for Children. N.D. Dodd Mead & Co.

--Six Fairy Plays for Children. LC 3-24269. 166 p. 17 1/2 cm. 1904. J. Lane.

--Tinkelly Winkle. N.D. Dodd Mead & Co.

Syson, Michael, jt. auth. see Bulla, Clyde Robert.

Szalatnay, Rafael D. (1884-), tr. see Kozisek, Josef.

Szalatnay, Rafael D. (1884-), tr. see Sedlacek, Hanus.

Szambelan-Strevinsky, Christine

--Dark Hour of Noon. 1st ed. LC 81-48601. 215 p. 21cm. c.1982. (ISBN 0-397-32013-2). (ISBN 0-397-32014-0). Lippincott.

Szasz, Frank

--The Golden Storytime Book of Animal Stories. Szasz, Frank, illus. 1957. Golden Press.

Szecsi, Katalin

--Hide-&-Seek. Reich, Karoly, illus. (gr. k-6). N.D. (ISBN 9-6313-0515-5). Newbury Bks.

Szekely, Edmond B.

--Brother Tree. Matinez, Antonielena C., illus. (Illus.). 32p. 1977. (ISBN 0-89564-074-0). IBS Intl.

Szekely, Sari

--Marika. Gabor, Barbara, illus. LC 39-74401. 64 p. incl. col. front., illus. (part col.) "junior press books. 1939. A. Whitman & Co.

Szekeres, Cyndy, jt. auth. see Bailey, Carolyn Sherwin.

Szekeres, Cyndy, jt. auth. see Johnston, Susan T.

Szekeres, Cyndy (1933-)

--Baby Bear's Surprise. Szekeres, Cyndy (1933-), illus. LC 83-83282. (Illus.). 14 p. 22cm. c.1984. (ISBN 0-307-12200-X). Golden Book.

--Long Ago. Szekeres, Cyndy (1933-), illus. LC 76-56113. (Illus.). 45 p. c.1977. (ISBN 0-07-062665-0). McGraw-Hill.

--Puppy Too Small. Szekeres, Cyndy (1933-), illus. LC 83-83353. (Illus.). 14 p. 21cm. c.1984. (ISBN 0-307-12201-8). Golden Book.

--Scaredy Cat. Szekeres, Cyndy (1933-), illus. LC 83-83283. (Illus.). 14 p. 22cm. c.1984. (ISBN 0-307-12202-6). Golden Book.

Szekeres, Cyndy (1933-), illus.

--A Child's First Book of Poems. LC 81-80484. (Illus.). 44 p. 29cm. c.1981. (ISBN 0-307-15812-8). (ISBN 0-307-65812-0). Golden Press.

Szenes, Andre see Dugo, Andre, pseud.

Szenes, Andre (1895-)

--Jon the Bluejay, and Carl the Cardinal. Dugo, Andre, pseud. 1st ed. LC 51-13535. 32 p. illus. 26cm. 1951. Holt.

--Pete, the Crow. Dugo, Andre, pseud. Szenes, Andre (1895-), illus. Dugo, Andre, pseud. LC 49-484111. 32 p. col. illus. 26 cm. 1949. Viking Press.

--Tom's Magic TV. Dugo, Andre, pseud. (Illus.). (gr. 2-4). 1953. (ISBN 0-8382-0882-7). Hale.

--Tom's Magic TV. Dugo, Andre, pseud. 1st ed. Szenes, Andre (1895-), illus. Dugo, Andre, pseud. LC 53-8964. unpaged. illus. 20cm. c.1953. Holt.

Szent-Gyorgyi, Albert

--The Crazy Ape. N.D. (ISBN 0-448-00256-6). Grosset & Dunlap.

Szilagyi, Mary

--Thunderstorm. Szilagyi, Mary, illus. LC 84-24570. (Illus.). 32p. (ps-2). 1985. (ISBN 0-02-788580-1). Bradbury Pr.

Szyk, Arthur (1894-1951), illus.

--The Arabian Nights Entertainments, 2 vols. Burton, Richard, Sir (1821-1890), tr. from Arabic. N.D. Heritage Press.

Taback, Simms

--Joseph Had a Little Overcoat. Taback, Simms, illus. LC 76-47343. (Illus.). 34 p. 22cm. c.1977. (ISBN 0-394-83251-5). Random House.

Tabak, May Natalie

--Fish Is Not a Pet. Tabak, May Natalie, illus. (Illus.). (gr. k-3). 1959. (ISBN 0-8382-0250-0). Hale.

Taber, Gladys Bagg (1899-1980)

--Daisy and Dobbin: Two Little Seahorses. Wiese, Kurt (1887-1974), illus. LC 48-8614. 62 p. illus. (part col.) 22 cm. 1948. Macrae-Smith Co.

Taber, Ralph Graham

--Chained Lightening: A Story of Adventure in Mexico. Taber, Ralph Graham & Ravelle, M., photos by LC 15-21415. 6 p. l., 273 p. front., plates. 20 cm. 1915. The Macmillan Comapny.

Tabor, Becky

--Kiddidears of the Long Ago. Collings, Ruth Elizabeth, illus. LC 25-6529. 76 p. incl. illus., plates (part col.) 24 cm. 1925. The Knickerbocker Press.

Tabor, Grace

--Wonderdays and Wonderways Through Flowerland: A Summer Adventure of Once Upon a Time. Chase, Rhoda Campbell, illus. LC 16-25124. 6 p. l., 267 p. col. front., illus., col. plates. 22 cm. 1916. R. M. McBride & Company.

Tabor, Tommie

--Cowboy Jack: The Sheriff. Battaglia, Aurelius (1910-), illus. LC 53-395859. unpaged illus. 21cm. (Jolly books, 223). 1953. Jolly Books.

Tabrah, Ruth, ed. see Buffet, Guy & Buffet, Pam.

Tabrah, Ruth, ed. see Buffet, Pam & Buffet, Guy.

Tabrah, Ruth, ed. see Mui, Shan.

Tabrah, Ruth Milander (1921-), ed. see Springer, Philipo.

Tabrah, Ruth Milander (1921-), ed. see Suyeoka, George.

Tabrah, Ruth Milander (1921-)

--Emily's Hawaii. Hall, Pat, illus. LC 85-30071. p. cm. 1985, c.1964. (ISBN 0-916630-45-5). Press Pacifica.

--Hawaiian Heart. LC 64-20348. 191 p. 23 cm. 1964. Follett Pub. Co.

--The Old Man & the Astronauts. LC 75-16524. (Illus.). (gr. 1-7). 1975. (ISBN 0-89610-015-4). Island Her.

--The Red Shark. LC 78-121410. 224 p. 23cm. 1970. Follett Pub. Co.

Tabrah, Ruth Milander (1921-), ed.

--Issunboshi. Suyeoka, George, illus. LC 74-80514. (Illus.). (gr. 1-7). 1974. (ISBN 0-89610-004-9). Island Her.

--Momotaro: Peach Boy. Suyeoka, George, illus. LC 72-86744. (Illus.). 64 p. 26cm. (Island heritage book). c.1972. (ISBN 0-8348-3004-3). J. Weatherhill.

Taffy, pseud., see Llewellyn, David William Alun.

Taffy, pseud. (1903-)

--Lost on the Moor. Llewellyn, David William Alun. N.D. Thomas Whittaker.

Tafuri, Nancy

--All Year Long. Tafuri, Nancy, illus. LC 82-9275. (Illus.). 8 x 9 7/8. 32p. (40 pt.). (ps-1). 1983. (ISBN 0-688-01414-3). (ISBN 0-688-01416-X). Greenwillow.

--All Year Long. Tafuri, Nancy, illus. LC 84-3475. 1984. (ISBN 0-14-050479-6). Puffin Books.

--Early Morning in the Barn. Tafuri, Nancy, illus. LC 83-1436. p. cm. 1983. (ISBN 0-688-02328-2). (ISBN 0-688-02329-0). Greenwillow Books.

--Have You Seen My Duckling?. Tafuri, Nancy, illus. LC 83-17196. (Illus.). 8 x 9 7/8. 24p. (28 pt.). (ps-1). 1984. (ISBN 0-688-02797-0). (ISBN 0-688-02798-9). Greenwillow. **Awards: (ALA); (RCM).**

--Rabbit's Morning. Tafuri, Nancy, illus. LC 84-10229. (Illus.). 9 7/8 x 8. 24p. (16 pt.). (ps-1). 1985. (ISBN 0-688-04063-2). (ISBN 0-688-04064-0). Greenwillow.

--Who's Counting?. LC 85-17702. (Illus.). 9 7/8 x 8. 24p. (96 pt.). (ps-1). 1986. (ISBN 0-688-06130-3). (ISBN 0-688-06131-1). Greenwillow.

Taggard

--Twenty Grand. (gr. 7 up). 1975. (ISBN 0-590-08909-9). Scholastic Inc.

Taggard, Ernestine, ed.

--Here We Are. N.D. Robert M. McBride & Co.

Taggart, George H.

--Jesus Cares for Me. (ps-k). N.D. Review & Herald.

--Jesus Says Remember. (gr. 1-4). N.D. Review & Herald.

--Jesus Thinks of Me. (ps-k). N.D. Review & Herald.

--Psalms for Tiny Tots. (ps-2). N.D. Review & Herald.

Taggart, Marion Ames (1866-), adapted by see May, Karl Friedrich.

Taggart, Marion Ames, jt. auth. see Nixon-Roulet, Mary F.

Taggart, Marion Ames (1866-)

--At Aunt Anna's. Jacobs, W. L., illus. LC 3-22110. xi, 271 p. front., 3 pl. 19 1/2 cm. 1903. D. Appleton and Company.

--At Greenacres. (The Jack-in-the-Box Books). N.D. A. L. Burt Co.

--At Greenacres. Peck, Anne Merriman (1884-), illus. LC 21-15429. ix p., 1 l., 13-253 p. col. front., plates. 19 1/2 cm. (Her The Jack-in-the-box Bks.). c.1921. George H. Doran Company.

--Beth of Old Chilton. Stecher, William Frederick (1864-), illus. LC 17-11096. 348 p. col. front., plates. 19 1/2 cm. c.1916. W. A. Wilde Company.

--Beth's Old Home. Stecher, William Frederick (1864-), illus. LC 16-2880. 345 p. front., plates. 19 1/2 cm. c.1915. W. A. Wilde Company.

--Beth's Wonder-Winter: A Story. Stecher, William Frederick (1864-), illus. LC 15-1631. 349 p. col. front., plates. 19 1/2 cm. c.1914. W. A. Wilde Company.

--Betty Gaston--The Seventh Girl. Stecher, William Frederick (1864-), illus. LC 10-27860. 20cm. 152p. (Six Girls Ser.). 1910. W. A. Wilde.

--The Blissylvania Post-Office: A Story. LC 8-20106. 152 p. 17 cm. 1897. Benziger Brothers.

--The Bottle Imp. Peck, Anne Merriman (1884-), illus. LC 21-15431. ix p., 1 l., 13-241 p. col. front., plates. 19 1/2 cm. (Her The Jack-in-the-box Bks.). 1921. George H. Doran Company.

--By Branscome River. LC 8-20105. 165 p. 17 cm. (American Author Ser.). 1897. Benziger Brothers.

--Captain Sylvia. Burd, Clara Miller, illus. LC 18-5503. ix, 350 p. front., plates. 19 1/2 cm. 1918. Doubleday, Page & Company.

--Daddy's Daughters. Breck, G. William, illus. 3 p. l., v-vi, 322 p. front., 3 pl. 19 1/2 cm. 1906. H. Holt and Company.

--The Daughters of the Little Grey House. N.D. Doubleday Page & Co.

--The Daughters of the Little Grey House. LC 7-33202. 5 p. l., 3-333 p. 19 1/2 cm. 1907. The McClure Company.

--The Dearest Girl: A Story for Girls. LC 24-23736. 231 p. front., plates. 19 cm. 1924. Benziger Brothers.

--The Doctor's Little Girl. Rand, Amy Carol, illus. LC 7-30163. 5 p. l., 296 p. front., 7 pl. 20 1/2 cm. 1907. L. C. Page and Company.

--Her Daughter Jean. (Illus.). 340p. N.D. W. A Warne Co.

--Her Daughter Jean: A Story. Stecher, William Frederick (1864-), illus. LC 13-26561. 332 p. col. front., plates. 19 1/2 cm. c.1913. W. A. Wilde Company.

--Hollyhock House: A Story for Girls. Rogers, Frances (1888-1974), illus. LC 16-5584. 6 p. l., 3-321, 1 p. front., plates. 19 1/2 cm. 1916. Doubleday, Page & Company.

--In the Days of King Hal. LC 2-24724. 172 p. incl. illus., plates. 20 1/2 cm. 1902. Benziger Brothers.

--The Little Aunt. Bingham, Ruth, illus. LC 14-4066. 318 p. incl. front. plates. 19 1/2 cm. c.1913. M. A. Donohue & Co.

--The Little Grey House. Betts, Ethel Franklin, illus. LC 4-25104. 4 p. l., 267 p. col. front. 20 cm. 1904. McClure, Phillips & Co.

--The Little Grey House: A Gay Story for Girls. Betts, Ethel Franklin, illus. LC 37-23239. 3 p. l., 3-267 p. front. 20 1/2 cm. (Young moderns bookshelf). 1937. The Sun Dial Press, Inc.

--The Little Women Club, 1 of 21 vols. Nagel, Eva M., illus. LC 5-38485. vii, 9-176 p. incl. front., 3 pl. 18 cm. (Boys and Girls Booklovers Ser.: No.21). c.1905. H. Altemus Company.

--The Little Women Club. Nagel, Eva M., illus. (Illus.). (Illustrated Cherrycroft Ser.). N.D. Henry Altemus Co.

--Loyal Blue and Royal Scarlet. A Story of Seventy-Six. LC 94-5007. 233 p. 19 1/2 cm. 1899. Benziger Brothers.

--Miss Lochinvar: A Story for Girls. Jacobs, W. L. & Jones, Bayard F., illus. LC 2-214094. ix, 261 p. front., pl. 20 1/2 cm. 1902. D. Appleton and Company.

--Miss Lochinvar's Return. LC 6-32358. 4 p. l., 310 p. col. front., 3 col. pl. 20 1/2 cm. 1906. D. Appleton and Company.

--Nancy and the Coggs Twins. Goss, John, illus. LC 14-17164. 5 p. l., 362 p. front., plates. 20 1/2 cm. (Her The doctor's little girl series). 1914. The Page Company.

--Nancy Porter's Opportunity. O'Brien, Harriet, illus. LC 12-17667. 5 p. l., 314 p. front., illus., plates. 20 1/2 cm. (Her The doctor's little girl Ser.). 1912. L. C. Page and Company.

--Nancy, the Doctor's Little Partner. Barry, Etheldred Breeze (1870-), illus. LC 11-180637. 5 p. l., 283 p. front., illus., plates. 20 1/2 cm. (Her The doctor's little girl series). 1911. L. C. Page and Company.

--Nut-Brown Joan: A Story for Girls. Ostertag, Blanche, illus. LC 5-9275. 3 p. l., 314 p. front. 19 1/2 cm. 1905. H. Holt and Company.

--Pamela's Legacy: A Sequel to "The Dearest Girl". LC 25-19910. 4 p. l., 7-270 p. front., plates. 19 cm. 1925. Benziger Brothers.

--A Pilgrim Maid: A Story of Plymouth Colony in 1620. The, Donaldsons, illus. LC 20-5775. xi, 319, 1 p. front., plates. 19 1/2 cm. 1920. Doubleday, Page & Company.

--Poppy's Pluck. (The Jack-in-the-Box-Books). N.D. A. L. Burt Co.

--Poppy's Pluck. Peck, Anne Merriman (1884-), illus. LC 21-15432. ix p., 1 l., 13-252 p. col. front., plates. 19 1/2 cm. (Her The Jack-in-the-box Bks.). (The Jack-in-the-Box Books). c.1921. George H. Doran Company.

--Pussy-Cat Town. Chase, Rebecca, illus. LC 6-34815. 5 p. l., 245 p. col. front., illus., col. plates. 20 x 15 1/2 cm. (roses of St. Elizabeth series). 1906. L. C. Page & Company.

--The Queer Little Man. (The Jack-in-the-Box Books). N.D. A. L. Burt Co.

--The Queer Little Man. Peck, Anne Merriman (1884-), illus. LC 21-15430. ix p., 1 l., 13-252 p. col. front., plates. 19 1/2 cm. (Her The Jack-in-the-box Bks.). c.1921. George H. Doran Company.

--Six Girls and Betty: A Story. Stecher, William Frederick (1864-), illus. LC 11-296648. 320 p. front., plates. 19 1/2 cm. (Six Girls Ser.). c.1911. W. A. Wilde Company.

--Six Girls and Bob: A Story of Patty-Pans and Green Fields. Stecher, William Frederick (1864-), illus. LC 6-30459. 330 p. front., 4 pl. 20 cm. (Six Girls Ser.). c.1906. W. A. Wilde Company.

--Six Girls and the Seventh One: A Story. Stecher, William Frederick (1864-), illus. LC 9-25969. 358 p. front., 4 pl. 20 cm. $1.5. (Six Girls Ser.). c.1909. W. A. Wilde Company.

--Six Girls and the Tea Room: A Story. Stecher, William Frederick (1864-), illus. LC 7-26963. 319 p. front., 4 pl. 19 1/2 cm. (Six Girls Ser.). c.1907. W. A. Wilde Company.

--Six girls Growing Older. Stecher, William Frederick (1864-), illus. LC 8-31460. (Illus.). 331p. (Thel Six Girls Ser.). 1908. W. A. Wilde Co.

--Six Girls Grown up: A Story. Stecher, William Frederick (1864-), illus. LC 12-21314. 343 p. front., plates. 20 cm. (Six Girls Ser.). c.1912. W. A. Wilde Company.

--Sweet Nancy: Or, More About the Doctor's Little Girl. Barry, Etheldred Breeze (1870-), illus. LC 9-26807. ix, 309 p. front., 7 pl. 20 1/2 cm. 1909. L. C. Page and Company.

--Three Girls and Especially One. LC 8-201039. 2 p. l., 3-150 p. 17 cm. (American Author Ser.). 1897. Benziger Brothers.

--Who Is Sylvia?". Clere, Vera, illus. LC 22-21184. 6 p. l., 285 p. front., plates. 19 1/2 cm. 1922. Doubleday, Page & Company.

--The Wyndham Girls. Relyea, Charles M., illus. LC 2-22478. 5 p. l., 303 p. incl. pl. front. 19 1/2 cm. 1902. The Centruy Co.

Taggart, Marion Ames (1866-), adapted by.

--Jack Hildreth on the Nile. rev ed. LC 2656. (Adapted from the original of C. May). 250p. front. pl. 19 1/2cm. 1900. Benziger Bros.

--The Treasure of Nugget Mountain. LC 8-20102. 231 p. 19 1/2 cm. (At head of Title: Jack Hildreth among the Indians). (Jack Hildreth Among the Indians Ser.). 1898. Benziger Brothers.

--Winnetou, the Apache Knight. 223 p. 19 1/2 cm. (At head of title: Jack Hildreth among the Indians). 1898. Benziger Brothers.

Tagore, Rabindranath, pseud., see Thakura, Ravindranatha.

Tagore, Rabindranath, Sir, pseud. (1861-1941)

--Moon, for What Do You Wait. Thakura, Ravindranatha. Lewis, Richard (1935-), ed. Bryan, Ashley F. (1923-), illus. (Illus.). (gr. k-4). 1967. (ISBN 0-689-20228-8). Atheneum.

Tague, Lola F (1896-)

--Melissa and the Valley Belle. Barrer-Russell, Gertrude (1921-), illus. LC 65-138249. 64p. illus. 24cm. c.1965. Lothrop.

--The Wonderful Merry-Go-Round. Werth, Kurt (1896-), illus. LC 60-12084. (Illus.). 25cm. 46p. (gr. 4-6). 1961. (ISBN 0-688-51130-9). Lothrop.

Taines, Gerald

--The Crow and the Snow. Anderson, Peter, illus. LC 63-3870. (Illus.). 31p. 29cm. (Gerry Tales). 1963. Artist Pub. Co.

Tait, Dorothy see Fairbairn, Ann, pseud.

Tait, Douglas, jt. auth. see Kroeber, Theodora Kracaw.

Tait, George Edward (1910-)

--The Saddle of Carlos Perez. Tait, George Edward (1910-), illus. LC 50-6854. 87p. illus. 21cm. 1950. Westminster Press.

Tait, James Selwin (1846-1917)

--Wayne and His Friends. LC 12-15063. 2 p. l., iii, 3-214 p. front., plates. 20 1/2 cm. c.1895. J. S. Tait & Sons.

Takahashi, Hiroyuki (1923-)
--The Foxes of Chironupp Island. Takahashi, Hiroyuki, illus. Herring, Ann King (1923-), tr. LC 76-9033. (Illus.). 48 p. 24cm. 1976. (ISBN 0-525-61544-X). Windmill Books.
Takai, Teiji (1911-)
--Henry and the Red Glove. Takai, Teiji (1911-), illus. LC 59-12324. unpaged. illus. 36 cm. 1959. Pennington Press.
Takeichi, Yasoo, jt. auth. see Sejima, Yoshimasa.
Taklender, Sharon
--Cartoon Cookbook for Kids. Taklender, Sharon, illus. (Illus.). 32p. (Orig.). (gr. 2-8). 1982. (ISBN 0-9608526-0-3). Folksmedia Pub.
Talanda, Susan
--Dad Told Me Not To. Wheeler, Cindy (1955-), illus. LC 83-8628. p.1983. (ISBN 0-940742-13-6). Raintree Publishers.
Talarczyk, June
--Mr. and Mrs. Bear Counting Book. Talarczyk, June, illus. LC 75-88063. (Illus.). 29 p. 29cm. 1969. T. S. Denison.
Talbert, Marc (1953-)
--Dead Birds Singing. LC 85-147. 170 p. 22cm. c.1985. (ISBN 0-316-83125-5). Little, Brown.
Talbot, Anne Richardson
Bobby und Bobbinette, 10 vols. Ruyl, Beatrice Baxter (1879-), illus. (Illus.). (Pleasant Street Ser.: No. 7). 1905. Set. H M Caldwell Co.
Talbot, Charlene Joy (1928-)
--A Home with Aunt Florry. LC 74-75572. 22cm. 200p. 1974. (ISBN 0-689-30419-6). Atheneum.
--An Orphan for Nebraska. LC 78-12179. 208 p. 22cm. 1979. (ISBN 0-689-30698-9). Atheneum.
--The Sodbuster Venture. LC 81-8051. 194 p. 22cm. 1982. (ISBN 0-689-30893-0). Atheneum.
--Tomas Takes Charge. Lonette, Reisie Dominee (1924-), illus. LC 66-14611. 191p. illus. 22cm. c.1966. Lothrop.
Talbot, Charlene Joy & Sanderson, Ruth
--The Great Rat Island Adventure. LC 77-1055. (Illus.). 164 p. 22cm. 1977. (ISBN 0-689-30596-6). Atheneum.
Talbot, Charles Remington see Brownjohn, John, pseud.
Talbot, Charles Remington see Merriweather, Magnus, pseud.
Talbot, Charles Remington, jt. auth. see Lothrop, Harriet Mulford Stone, Mrs.
Talbot, Charles Remington (1851-1891)
--A Double Masquerade: A Romance of the Revolution. LC 21-870714. 307 p. incl. front., plates, map. 18 cm. 1885. D. Lothrop and Company.
--The Impostor, a Football and College Romance: With Other Stories for Young People. Barnes, Hiram Putnam, illus. LC 21-8703. 405 p. incl. front., plates. 19 1/2 cm. 1895. Lothrop Publishing Company.
--Little Miss Muslin of Quintillion Square: Her Fortunes and Misfortunes. Brownjohn, John, pseud. Hopkins, L., illus. LC 16-3870. 28 p. front., illus. 24 x 19 1/2 cm. c.1878. D. Lothrop & Co.
--A Midshipman at Large: A Story of Newport and Ocean Yachting. LC 12-39293. 394 p. incl. front., plates. 18 1/2 cm. c.1887. D. Lothrop Company.
--Miltiades Peterkin Paul. His Adventures. Brownjohn, John, pseud. Hopkins, L., illus. LC 16-3869. 30 p. front., illus. 24 x 19 1/2 cm. c.1877. D. Lothrop & Co.
--Romulus and Remus: A Dog Story. Merrill, Frank Thayer (1848-), illus. LC 20-19339. vi, 7-217 p. front., plates. 18 1/2 cm. 1888. D. Lothrop Company.
--Royal Lowrie's Last Year at St. Olave's. Merriweather, Magnus, pseud. LC 12-39292. 292 p. incl. front., illus., plates. 18 1/2 cm. c.1879. D. Lothrop and Company.
--The Story of Honor Bright. Merriweather, Magnus, pseud. Shirlaw, Walter, illus. LC 12-39291. vi, 9-404 p. incl. front., illus., plates. 18 1/2 cm. c.1881. D. Lothrop & Company.

Talbot, Eleanor W
--The Mother Goose Goslings. Talbot, Eleanor, illus. LC 17-1320. 22 l. col. illus. 24 1/2 x 20 1/2 cm. c.1882. Cassell, Petter, Galpin & Co.

Talbot, Ella V.
--The Perseverance of Chryssa Arkwright. N.D. Methodist Bk Concern.
--The Preseverance of Chryssa Arkwright: A Lesson in Self-Help. LC 21-8704. 266 p. 19 cm. 1890. Hunt & Eaton.

Talbot, Ethel M.
--Anne of Queen Annes. N.D. Frederick Warne & Co.
--At School with Morag. (The Crown Library for Boys & Girls). N.D. Frederick Warne & Co.
--Nancy New Girl. (The Magnet Library). N.D. Frederick Warne & Co.
--Skipper & Co. (The Magnet Library). N.D. Frederick Warne & Co.
Talbot, Ethelbert (1848-1928)
--Tim: The Autobiography of a Dog. LC 14-178109. 3 p. l., 80, 1 p. front. 18 cm. $0.5. 1914. Harper & Brothers.
Talbot, Gladys Mary
--Little Lost Lamb. (Illus.). (ps). N.D. (ISBN 0-8024-4797-X). Moody.
Talbot, Gladys Mary, ed.
--Forty Stories for You to Tell. LC 52-4450. 192 p. 20 cm. 1952. Moody Press.
--Stories I Love To Tell. 156p. 1949. Moody Press.
Talbot, Louisa Agnes, jt. auth. see Armfield, Anne Constance Smedley, Mrs.
Talbot, Nathan, jt. auth. see Arthur, Catherine.
Talbot, Toby (1928-), tr. see Manuel, Don Juan.
Talbot, Toby (1928-)
--Away Is So Far. Strandquest, Dominique Michele (1951-), illus. LC 73-88072. (Illus.). 91 p. 19cm. 1974. Four Winds Press.
--A Bucketful of Moon. Gobbato, Imero (1923-), illus. LC 75-26818. (Illus.). 47 p. 22cm. c.1976. (ISBN 0-688-41727-2). (ISBN 0-688-51727-7). Lothrop, Lee and Shepard Co.
--Dear Greta Garbo: A Novel. LC 77-14383. 91 p. 23cm. c.1978. (ISBN 0-399-20613-2). Putnam.
--I Am Maria. 1st ed. Mill, Eleanor, illus. LC 72-87084. (Illus.). 28 p. 24cm. 1969. Cowles Book Co.
--My House Is Your House. Weaver, Robert (1924-), illus. LC 73-104357. (Illus.). 46 p. 25cm. 1970. Cowles Book Co.
--The Night of the Radishes. Grifalconi, Ann (1929-), illus. LC 72-75959. (Illus.). 57 p. 22cm. 1972. (ISBN 0-399-20263-3). (ISBN 0-399-20263-3). Putnam.
--Once Upon a Truffle. 1st ed. Horen, Michael, illus. LC 78-118914. (Illus.). 47 p. 25cm. 1970. Cowles.
--The Rescue. Dodson, Bert, illus. LC 72-83408. (Illus.). 62 p. 22cm. 1973. (ISBN 0-399-20299-4). (ISBN 0-399-20299-4). Putnam.
--Two by Two, Dos Por Dos. Angel, Marie (1923-), illus. (Illus.). 1974. (ISBN 0-695-80484-7). (ISBN 0-695-40484-9). Follett Co.
Talbot, Toby (1928-), ed.
--Coplas:. Folk Poems in Spanish and English. Negri, Rocco (1932-), illus. LC 77-182116. (Illus.). 79 p. 24cm. 1972. Four Winds Press.
Talbot, Winifred
--Denny's Friend Rags. Brophy, Ruth, illus. LC 64-239725. (Illus.). (A Third Grade Bk.). (gr. 3-4). 1965. Denison.
--Happy Hospital Surprises. Spiegel, Lawrence M., illus. LC 61-15234. unpaged. illus. 29 cm. 1961. T. S. Denison.
Talbott, Addison (1882-)
--Pack Jack Trail. Thomas, SanfordTousey, illus. LC 42-22992. 234p. illus. 21cm. 1942. Macrae-Smith Co.
--Pack Jack Trail. Tousey, Thomas Sanford, illus. LC 42-22862. 284 p. illus. 21 cm. 1942. Macrae-Smith-Company.
Talbott, Harold, tr. see Rosny, J. H.
Talcott, Anna, jt. auth. see Tucker, Edith S.
Taliaferro, Al, adapted by see Disney, Walt, Productions.
Taliaferro, Margaret
--Real Reason for Christmas. LC 76-55080. 128p. 1982. (Galilee). Doubleday.
Tallant, Edith
--Danny and Prue. Freund, Rudolf (1915-1969), illus. LC 38-326111. 143 p. incl. front., illus. double col. plates. 24 cm. c.1938. Thomas Y. Crowell Company.
--David and Patience. Morse, Dorothy Bayley (1906-1979), illus. 166 p. col. front., illus. 23 1/2 cm. c.1940. J. B. Lippincott Company.
--The Girl Who Was Marge. Morse, Dorothy Bayley (1906-1979), illus. LC 39-117468. 6 p. l., 11-267 p. incl. illus., plates. col. front. 21 cm. c.1939. J. B. Lippincott Company.
Tallant, Robert
--Evangeline & the Acadians. (gr. 5-6). 1957. (ISBN 0-394-80374-4, BYR). Random.
Tallarico, Anthony, jt. ed. see Weigle, Oscar.
Tallarico, Tony
--Giant Apes Joke Book. Tallarico, Tony, illus. LC 76-19662. (Illus.). 48 p. 28cm. (Elephant books). c.1976. (ISBN 0-448-12724-5). Grosset & Dunlap.
--Gobble, Gobble. Tallarico, Tony, illus. (Illus.). 24p. (gr. 3-8). 1982. (ISBN 0-448-03872-2, G&D). Putnam Pub Group.
--Let's Take a Trip. Tallarico, Tony, illus. (Illus.). 12p. (Tote Bks.). (gr. 3-8). 1982. (ISBN 0-89828-305-1). Tuffy Bks.
--Monster Hunt. Tallarico, Tony, illus. (Illus.). 16p. 1st U.S. edition. (Video Game Bk.). (gr. 3-8). 1982. (ISBN 0-89828-327-2). Tuffy Bks.
--Rocket Attack. Tallarico, Tony, illus. (Illus.). 16p. (Video Game Bk.). (gr. 3-8). 1982. (ISBN 0-89828-326-4). Tuffy Bks.
--Seasons. (Illus.). 12p. 1st U.S. edition. (Tote Bks.). 1982. (ISBN 0-89828-301-9). Tuffy Bks.
--Star Jokes. Duenewald, Doris, ed. Tallarico, Tony, illus. LC 78-54178. (Illus.). (Elephant Books Ser.). (gr. 1-7). 1978. (ISBN 0-448-14819-6). G&D.
--Super Jokes. Tallarico, Tony, illus. LC 79-51214. (Illus.). (gr. 2-6). 1980. (ISBN 0-448-16564-3, G&D). Putnam Pub Group.
--Wacky Sports. Tallarico, Tony, illus. (Illus.). 128p. (Orig.). 1981. (ISBN 0-590-31588-9). Scholastic Inc.
Talley, Naomi
--The New-Cut Road. LC 72-137463. 151 p. 22cm. 1971. Hawthorn Books.
Tallman, Jane
--Thanksgiving for All. Lee, Julian, pseud. (1902-) & Swarthout, Elwyn, eds. Latham, Jean Lee. Orig. Title: The Pompion Pie. 1932. Dramatic Publishing Company.
Tallon, Robert (1935-)
--The Alligator's Song. Tallon, Robert (1935-), illus. LC 80-19522. (Illus.). 48 p. 24cm. c.1981. (ISBN 0-8193-1043-3). (ISBN 0-8193-1044-1). Parents Magazine Press.
--Fish Story. Tallon, Robert (1935-), illus. LC 76-23092. (Illus.). 32 p. 23cm. c.1977. (ISBN 0-03-017526-7). Holt, Rinehart and Winston.
Flea Story. Tallon, Robert (1935-), illus. LC 77-3168. p. cm. c.1977. (ISBN 0-03-021531-5). Holt, Rinehart and Winston.
--Handella. LC 72-75885. (Illus.). 56 p. 29cm. 1972. Bobbs-Merrill.
--Latouse My Moose. Tallon, Robert (1935-), illus. LC 82-23397. p. cm. 1983. (ISBN 0-394-86017-9). (ISBN 0-394-96017-3). Knopf.
--Little Cloud. Tallon, Robert (1935-), illus. LC 78-11061. (Illus.). 32 p. 24cm. c.1978. (ISBN 0-8193-0981-8). (ISBN 0-8193-0982-6). Parents' Magazine Press.
--Mooseberry and the Fuzzo Makers. Tallon, Robert (1935-), illus. LC 83-16214. p. cm. 1984. (ISBN 0-394-86505-7). Knopf.
--Rhoda's Restaurant. Tallon, Robert (1935-), illus. LC 73-1756. (Illus.). 58 p. 29cm. 1973. Bobbs-Merrill.
--Rotten Kidphabets. Tallon, Robert (1935-), illus. LC 75-5502. p. cm. 1975. (ISBN 0-03-014431-0). Holt, Rinehart and Winston.
--The Things in Dolores' Piano. Tallon, Robert (1935-), illus. LC 76-117335. (Illus.). 48 p. 29cm. 1970. Bobbs-Merrill.
--Worm Story. Tallon, Robert (1935-), illus. LC 77-10709. (Illus.). 32 p. 24cm. c.1978. (ISBN 0-03-021536-6). Holt, Rinehart and Winston.
--ZAG: A Search Through the Alphabet. Tallon, Robert (1935-), illus. LC 76-8549. p. cm. c.1976. (ISBN 0-03-017531-3). Holt, Rinehart and Winston.
--Zoophabets. Tallon, Robert (1935-), illus. LC 71-156107. (Illus.). 30 p. 29cm. 1971. Bobbs-Merrill.
Talmadge, Marian & Gilmore, Iris (1900-)
--Emma Edmonds: Nurse & Spy. LC 78-92823. (Illus.). bibl. index. 128p. (Spies of the World Ser). (gr. 5-8). 1970. (ISBN 0-399-60152-X). Putnam.
--Pony Express Boy. LC 56-9314. 213p. illus. 21cm. 1956. Dodd, Mead.
--Six Great Horse Rides. Mawicke, Tran (1911-), illus. (Illus.). (gr. 5-9). 1967. (ISBN 0-399-60584-3). Putnam.
--Wings for Peace: A Story of Cadet Frank Barton of the Air Force Academy. Briggs, James E., frwd. by. LC 59-9619. 268 p. 21 cm. 1959. Dodd, Mead.
--Wings of Tomorrow: The Adventures of a Cadet at the Air Force Academy. Briggs, James E., frwd. by. LC 58-5334. 270 p. 21 cm. 1958. Dodd, Mead.
Talman, Thrace
--The Red Bridge, 1 of 4 vols. (The Red Bridge Ser.). N.D. National Temperance Society.
Tamar, Erika
--Blues for Silk Garcia. LC 82-25259. p. cm. c.1983. (ISBN 0-517-54671-X). Crown Publishers.
--Good-Bye, Glamour Girl. LC 83-49493. 218 p. 22cm. c.1984. (ISBN 0-397-32087-6). (ISBN 0-397-32088-4). Lippincott.
Tamarin, Alfred, jt. auth. see Glubok, Shirley Astor.
Tamas, George
--The Adventures of Wonder Worm. Lopez, Richard, illus. LC 80-80926. (Illus.). 37p. (gr. k-8). 1980. (ISBN 0-939478-01-3). Calif Irvine.
Tamburine, Jean (1930-)
--Almost Big Enough. Tamburine, Jean (1930-), illus. LC 65-10811. (Illus.). (gr. k-2). 1963. (ISBN 0-687-01089-6). Abingdon.
--Almost Big Enough. Tamburine, Jean (1930-), illus. (Illus.). (gr. k-2). 1963. (ISBN 0-8382-0028-1). Hale.
--How Now Brown Cow. Tamburine, Jean (1930-), illus. LC 67-17381. (Illus.). 62 p. 29cm. 1967. Abingdon Press.
--I Think I Will Go to the Hospital. Tamburine, Jean (1930-), illus. LC 65-14093. (Illus.). 48 p. 28cm. 1965. Abingdon Press.
Tamchina, Jurgen
--Dominique & the Dragon. Petrides, Heidrun (1944-), illus. Crawford, Elizabeth D., tr. from Ger. LC 68-59618. (Illus.). (gr. 3-6). 1969. (ISBN 0-15-223972-3, HJ). HarBraceJ.
Tamchina, Jurgen, jt. auth. see Crawford, Elizabeth D.
Tamulaitis, Vytas (1913-)
--Nimblefoot the Ant: Her Adventures. Mills, Clark & Lape, Pranas (1921-), illus. Baranauskas, Albinas, tr. from Lithuanian. LC 65-21429. 183p. illus. 22cm. c.1965. Manylands Bks.
Tanager, Paul
--Two Pipers. Gaudriault, Monique & Rozier, Jacques (1934-), illus. LC 77-73524. (Illus.). 24 p. 30cm. c.1977. (ISBN 0-8258-8402-7). Harlin Quist.
Tanaka, Beatrice, retold by.
--The Tortoise and the Sword: A Vietnamese Legend. Tanaka, Beatrice, illus. LC 71-177320. (Illus.). 46 p. 26cm. 1972. Lothrop, Lee & Shepard Co.
Tanaka, Hideyuki
--The Happy Dog. Tanaka, Hideyuki, illus. LC 82-72248. (Illus.). 23 p. 22cm. 1st U.S. edition. (ps-2). 1983. c.1981. (ISBN 0-689-50259-1). Atheneum.
Tandy, J. M.
--Old Barnaby's Treasure. N.D. Pott, Young & Co.
Tandy, Sophia
--Aunt Margery's Maxims. (Illus.). N.D. Methodist Book Concern.
--The Harleys of Chelsea Place: Or, In Union Is Strength. (Star of Hope Series for Girls). N.D. Leavitt & Allen Bros.
--The Harleys of Chelsea Place: Or, In Union is Strength, 1 of 25 vols. (Illus.). 245p. (Selected Bks for Sunday School: No. 18). N.D. Set. Methodist Bk Concern.
--The Little Doorkeeper: Or, Patience & Peace. (Illus.). N.D. Methodist Bk Concern.
Taneyhill, M. Ellen
--Young Folks of Renfrew, 1 of 25 vols. (Illus.). 229p. (Selected Bks for Sunday School: No. 24). N.D. Set. Methodist Bk Concern.
Tangye, Derek
--Somewhere a Cat Is Waiting. 1976. (E Friede). Delacorte.
Taniguchi, Kazuko (1946-)
--Monster Mary, Mischief Maker. Taniguchi, Kazuko (1946-), illus. LC 75-40472. (Illus.). 41 p. 22cm. c.1976. (ISBN 0-07-062868-8). McGraw-Hill.
Taniuchi, Kota (1947-)
--The North Star Man. Taniuchi, KOta (1947-), illus. Fujita, Tamao (1905-), tr. LC 70-110721. (Illus.). 25 p. 25cm. (Watts international picture book). 1970, c.1969. (ISBN 0-531-01935-7). Watts.
--Trolley. Taniuchi, Kota (1947-), illus. LC 72-110719. (Illus.). 25 p. 26cm. (Watts international picture book). 1971, c.1969. (ISBN 0-531-01937-3). F. Watts.
--Up on a Hilltop. Taniuchi, Kota (1947-), illus. LC 77-110720. (Illus.). 25 p. 26cm. (Watts international picture book). 1971, c.1969. (ISBN 0-531-01938-1). F. Watts.
--Who's Calling Me?. Taniuchi, Kota (1947-), illus. LC 73-4589. (Illus.). 23 p. 26cm. 1973. (ISBN 0-8098-1211-8). H. Z. Walck.
Tannen, Mary (1943-)
--Huntley Nutley and the Missing Link. Sauber, Rob, illus. LC 82-18651. p. cm. 1983. (ISBN 0-394-95759-8). Knopf.
--The Lost Legend of Finn. LC 81-15599. (Illus.). 144 p. 22cm. c.1982. (ISBN 0-394-85211-7). (ISBN 0-394-95211-1). Knopf : Distributed by Random House.
--The Twits. Burgoyne, John, illus. LC 80-18410. (Illus.). 96p. (ps-5). 1981. (ISBN 0-394-84599-4). (ISBN 0-394-94599-9). Knopf.
--The Wizard Children of Finn. Burgoyne, John, illus. Gregory, Isabella Augusta Persse, Lady (1852-1932), created by. LC 80-20955. (Illus.). 214 p. 22cm. c.1981. (ISBN 0-394-94744-4). (ISBN 0-394-84744-X). Knopf.
Tannenbaum, D. Leb
--A Visit to the Doctor. Leder, Dora, illus. (Illus.). 64p. (New Feelings Activity Bks.). (ps-2). 1981. (ISBN 0-671-43205-2, Little Simon). S&S.
Tannenforst, Ursula, pseud., see Tilghman, Emily.
Tannenforst, Ursula, pseud. (1844-)
--Heroines of a School-Room. Tilghman, Emily. (Illus.). c.1907. John C. Winston.
Tanner, Dorothy
--Legends from the Red Man's Forest. Tanner, Dorothy, illus. LC 12-39314. 128 p. illus. 19 1/2 cm. (On cover: The Teacher's helper. vol. II, no. 5). c.1895. A. Flanagan.
Tanner, Edwin Platt (1874-)
--Yesterday's Children. Glackens, Louis M., illus. LC 27-4665. 216 p. col. front., illus. 18 1/2 cm. c.1927. Rand, McNally & Company.

Tanner, Louise Stickney (1922-)
--Reggie and Nilma: A New York City Story. LC 75-140938. 183 p. 21cm. (An Ariel Bk.). 1971. (ISBN 0-374-36244-0). Farrar, Straus and Giroux.

Tanner, Maude Muller
--Billy Forget-Me-Not. Snow, Dorothea Johnston (1909-), illus. LC 40-1416. 54, 1 p. incl. front., illus. 23 1 2 cm. c.1939. Follett Publishing Company.

Tanner, Ruben
--The Teddy Bears' Picnic: A Counting Book. Goodman, Joan E., illus. LC 79-1867. (Illus.). 20 p. 32cm. c.1979. (ISBN 0-525-69000-X). (ISBN 0-525-69001-8). Gingerbread House.
--Too Many Wheels. Bracken, Carolyn, illus. LC 79-1909. (Illus.). 20 p. 32cm. c.1979 (Gingerbread House). (ISBN 0-525-69014-X). (ISBN 0-525-69015-8). Dutton.

Tanner, Suzy-Jane
--Grow up, Mom. Tanner, Suzy-Jane, illus. (Illus.). 32p. (Gorilla Bks.). (gr. 1-4). 1985. (ISBN 0-915677-12-1). Roundtable Pub.
--My Uncle Lancelot. Tanner, Suzy-Jane, illus. (Illus.). 32p. (Gorilla Bks.). (gr. 1-4). 1985. (ISBN 0-915677-13-X). Roundtable Pub.

Tanobe, Miyuki (1937-)
--Children of Quebec. Tanobe, Miyuki (1937-), illus. (Illus.). (gr. k-3). N.D. (ISBN 0-912766-86-7). Tundra Bks.

Tanous, Helen Nicol (1917-) & Tanous, Henry
--What If?. Miller, John Parr (1913-), illus. LC 51-13063. unpaged. illus. 21 cm. (Little golden library, 130). 1951. Simon and Schuster.

Tanous, Henry, jt. auth. see Tanous, Helen Nicol.

Tanvykuliev, K.
--The Boy & the Camel. 16p. 1979. (ISBN 0-8285-1113-6, Pub. by Progress Pubs USSR). Imported Pubns.

Tanz, Christine
--An Egg Is to Sit on. Hoffman, Rosekrans (1926-), illus. LC 77-90534. (Illus.). 32 p. 18cm. c.1978. (ISBN 0-688-41811-2). (ISBN 0-688-51811-7). Lothrop, Lee & Shepard Co.

Tapio, Pat Decker (1937-)
--The Lady Who Saw the Good Side of Everything. Galdone, Paul (1914-), illus. LC 75-4610. (Illus.). 30 p. 1975. (ISBN 0-8164-3145-0). Seabury Press.

Tapley, Caroline (1934-)
--John Come Down the Backstay. Cuffari, Richard (1925-1978), illus. LC 73-84839. (Illus.). x, 182 p. 22cm. 1974. (ISBN 0-689-30149-9). Atheneum.

Taplinger, Richard, jt. auth. see Dhotre, Damoo.

Tapp, Kathy Kennedy
--Mothkin Magic. Chessare, Michele (1921-), illus. LC 83-2782. p. cm. 1983. (ISBN 0-689-50288-5). Atheneum.

Tappan, Eva March, jt. auth. see Chaucer, Geoffrey.

Tappan, Eva March, jt. ed. see Bergstrom, Richard.

Tappan, Eva March (1854-1930)
--Dixie Kitten. N.D. Houghton Mifflin.
--Ella, a Little Schoolgirl of the Sixties: A Book for Children and for Grown-ups Who Remember. Best, Ruth J., illus. LC 23-17272. 4 p. l., 174 p. col. front., plates. 19 1/2 cm. 1923. Houghton Mifflin Company.
--The Farmer and His Friends. N.D. Houghton Mifflin Co.
--The House with the Silver Door. LC 13-191201. 5 p. l., 3-184, 2 p. col. front., col. plates. 20 cm. 1913. Houghton Mifflin Company.
--Letters from Colonial Children. LC 8-23916. xii p., 1 l., 318, 2 p. front., illus. 22 x 17 1/2 cm. 1908. Houghton Mifflin Company.
--An Old, Old Story-Book. N.D. Houghton Mifflin.
--The Prince from Nowhere, and Other Tales. LC 28-21214. 206p. 20cm. 1928. Houghton Mifflin Company.
--Robin Hood: His Book. Harding, Charlotte (1873-), illus. LC 3-26880. xiv, 267 p. col. front., illus., 5 col. pl. 21 cm. 1903. Little, Brown & Company.
--When Knights Were Bold. N.D. Houghton Mifflin Co.

Tappan, Eva March (1854-1930), ed.
--The Book of Humor. LC 17-877. xiii, 1, 527, 1 p., 1 l. col. front., plates. 19 1/2 cm. (children's hour. vol. XIII). 1916. Houghton Mifflin Company.
--The Book of Humor. LC 30-8362. (Illus.). xiii,507. 22cm. (The Children's Hour). 1929. Houghton Mifflin.
--Folk Stories and Fables. 1st ed. LC 7-31223. (Illus.). xxix, 529. 22cm. (The Children's Hour). 1907. Houghton Mifflin.
--Folk Stories and Fables. LC 30-9139. (Illus.). xxvii, 399. 22cm. (The Children's Hour). 1929. Houghton Mifflin.
--The Little Lady in Green and Other Tales. LC 25-19645. (Originally by Richard Bergstrom (1828-1893)). 6 p. l., 226 p. incl. front., plates. 20 1/2 cm. 1925. Houghton Mifflin Company.
--Modern Stories. LC 7-31216. xi, 1, 485, 1 p., 1 l. front., 12 pl. 22 cm. (Half-title: The children's hour ... vol. x). 1907. Houghton, Mifflin & Company.
--Myths from Many Lands. LC 7-31218. xiii, 1, 509, 1 p., 1 l. front., 12 pl. 22 cm. (Half-title: The Children's hour ... vol. ii). 1907. Houghton, Mifflin & Company.
--Myths from Many Lands. LC 30-9139. (Illus.). xiii,334. 22cm. (The Children's Hour). 1929. Houghton Mifflin.
--Old Fashioned Stories & Poems. LC 7-31214. xvi p., 1 l., 477, 1 p., 1 l. front., 15 pl. 22 cm. (Half-title: The children's hour ... vol. vi). 1907. Houghton, Mifflin & Company.
--The Out-of-Door Book. LC 7-31219. xiii, 1, 516, 2 p. front., 11 pl. 22 cm. (Half-title: The children's hour ... vol. vii). 1907. Houghton Mifflin & Company.
--The Out-of-Door Book. LC 30-9137. (Illus.). xiii, 516. 22cm. (The Children's Hour). 1929. Houghton Mifflin.
--The Out-of-Door Book. Robinson, Mark, illus. LC 36-35623. (Illus.). 22cm. xiii, 516p. (Riverside Bookshelf). 1935. Houghton Mifflin Company.
--Poems & Rhymes. LC 7-31222. xxii p., 2 l., 3-514, 2 p. front., 14 pl. 22 cm. (Half-title: The Children's hour ... vol. ix). 1907. Houghton, Mifflin & Company.
--Stories from Seven Old Favorites. LC 30-8361. (Illus.). xiii,441. 22cm. (The Children's Hour). 1929. Houghton Mifflin.
--Stories from Seven Old Favorities. LC 7-31217. xiii, 1, 441, 1 p., 1 l. front., 13 pl. 22 cm. (Half-title: The Children's hour ... vol. v). 1907. Houghton, Mifflin & Company.
--Stories from the Classics. LC 7-31215. xvii, 1, 495, 1 p., 1 l. front., 12 pl. 22 cm. (children's hour. vol. iii). 1907. Houghton, Mifflin & Company.
--Stories from the Classics. LC 30-10343. (Illus.). xiii, 358. 22cm. (The Children's Hour). 1929. Houghton Mifflin.
--Stories of Legendary Heroes. LC 7-31220. xii p., 1 l., 474, 2 p. front., 12 pl. 22 cm. (Half-title: The children's hour ... vol. iv). 1907. Houghton, Mifflin & Company.
--Stories of Legendary Heroes. LC 30-10344. (Illus.). xii, 370. (The Children's Hour). 1929. Houghton Mifflin Company.

Tappan, Eva March (1854-1930), tr. from Swedish.
--The Golden Goose and Other Fairy Tales. LC 5-35790. 4 p. l.. 3-240 p., 1 l. illus. 19 1/2 cm. 1905. Houghton, Mifflin Company.

Tapper, Thomas, ed. see Stevenson, Robert Louis.

Tapsell, Alan, tr. see Bergman Sucksdorff, Astrid.

Tapsell, Alan, tr. see Wilcke, Ella.

Tarbox, Increase Niles (1815-1888)
--The Old Meeting-House, 1 of 4 Vols. (Uncle George's Stories). N.D. Set. Congregational Publishing Society.
--Rambles in Old Pathways, 1 of 4 Vols, Pt. 2. (Uncle George's Stories). N.D. Set. Congregational Publishing Society.
--Uncle George's Stories, 1 of 4 Vols. (Uncle George's Stories). N.D. Set. Congregational Publishing Society.

Tarcov, Edith
--A Train for Tommy. Moore, Lilian, ed. Russell, William, illus. (Easy Readers Ser.). (gr. 1-2). N.D. Wonder.
--A Train for Tommy. Russell, William, illus. LC 62-52426. (Editoral Consultant: Lillian Moore). 61 p. illus. 22cm. 1962. Grosset & Dunlap.

Tarcov, Edith, retold by.
--Rumpelstiltskin: A/Tale Told Long Ago. Gorey, Edward St. John (1925-), illus. LC 74-2139. (Original Story by the Brothers Grimm). (Illus.). 48p. 21cm. 1974, c.1973. Four Winds Press.
--Three Famous Stories. Rainey, illus. (gr. 2-3). 1975. (ISBN 0-590-10156-0). Scholastic Inc.

Tarcov, Edith, retold by see Grimm, Jakob Ludwig Karl (1785-1863) & Grimm, Wilhelm Karl.

Tardi, Jacques, illus.
--The Enchanted Pig: Rumanian Fairy Tale. american ed. LC 83-71175. (Illus.). 40 p. 23cm. c.1984. (ISBN 0-87191-953-2). Creative Education.

Tardzhemanov, D.
--Shuktugan. 16p. 1975. (ISBN 0-8285-1226-4, Pub. by Progress Pubs USSR). Imported Pubns.

Tarkington, Booth see Tarkington, Newton Booth.

Tarkington, Kate
--Rex Goes to the Rodeo. Tarkington, Kate, illus. LC 56-227241. 88p. illus. 20cm. c.1955. Naylor Co.

Tarkington, Newton Booth (1869-1946), adapted by see Walker, Stuart & Strange, Hubert S.

Tarkington, Newton Booth (1869-1946)
--Penrod. (Illus.). ca. 250p. (Thrushwood Bks.). (gr. 5-11). 1970. (ISBN 0-448-02524-8). G&D.
--Penrod & Sam. (Growing Literature Ser.). N.D. Grosset & Dunlap.
--Penrod and Sam. Grant, Gordon H. (1875-1962), illus. LC 57-41976. 220p. illus. 22cm. N.D. Junior Deluxe Editions.
--Penrod, His Complete Story. LC 31-28239. (gr. 4-9). 1931. Doubleday.
--Penrod Jashber. N.D. GRosset & Dunlap.
--Seventeen. (Growing Literature). N.D. Grosset & Dunlap.
--Seventeen. Eaton, Harold T., intro. by. (Harper's Modern Classics). N.D. Harper & Brothers.

Tarlton, Gillian Leigh
--The Two Worlds of Coral Harper. 1st ed. LC 82-48758. 150 p. 22cm. c.1983. (ISBN 0-15-292371-3). Harcourt Brace Jovanovich.

Tarn, William Woodthorpe (1869-)
--The Treasure of the Isle of Mist. Lawson, Robert (1892-1957), illus. LC 20-1903. v p., 1 l., 192 p. 19 cm. 1920. G. P. Putnam's Sons.
--The Treasure of the Isle of Mist. Lawson, Robert (1892-1957), illus. LC 34-27187. 6 p. l., 184 p. incl. illus., plates. front. 22 cm. c.1934. G. P. Putnam's Sons.

Tarrant, Margaret Winifred (1888-)
--The Margaret Tarrant Christmas Book. Tarrant, Margaret Winifred (1888-), illus. N.D. Hale Cushman & Flint.
--The Margaret Tarrant Nursery Rhyme Book. Tarrant, Margaret Winifred (1888-), illus. (Illus.). N.D. E. P. Dutton & Co.
--Margaret Tarrant's Fairy Tales. Tarrant, Margaret Winifred (1888-), illus. LC 78-7086. (Illus.). (gr. 4 up). 1978. (ISBN 0-690-03919-0, TYC-J). (ISBN 0-690-03920-4). Har-Row.
--Margaret Tarrant's Nursery Rhymes. Tarrant, Margaret Winifred (1888-), illus. LC 78-7087. (Illus.). (ps up). 1978. (ISBN 0-690-03921-2, TYC-J). (ISBN 0-690-03922-0). Har-Row.

Tarrant, Margaret Winifred (1888-), ed.
--Mother Goose Nursery Tales. Tarrant, Margaret Winifred (1888-), illus. N.D. Frederick A. Stokes.

Tarrant, Margaret Winifred (1888-), illus.
--Rhymes of Old Times. N.D. Hale Cushman & Flint.
--Rhymes of Old Times. Medici Society Tarrant, Margaret Winifred (1888-), illus. LC 26-18282. 5 p. l., 108 p. incl. illus. (part col.) col. mounted plates. col. mounted front. 22 cm. 1925. The Medici Society.

Tarrant, Margaret Winifred (1888-) & Dutton, Lewis
--Joan in Flowerland. Tarrant, Margaret Winifred (1888-), illus. LC 36-131376. 59, 1 p. incl. col. front., illus., col. plates. 32 cm. 1935. F. Warne & Co., Ltd.

Tarry, Ellen (1906-)
--Hezekiah Horton. Harrington, Oliver, illus. LC 42-18466. 24cm. 39p. 1942. Viking Press.
--Janie Belle. Sheldon, Myrtle, illus. LC 40-32966. (Illus.). 30. 26 x 20cm. 1940. Garden City Publishing Co. Inc.
--The Runaway Elephant. Harrington, Oliver, illus. (Sequel to "Hezikiah Horton"). 40p. 1950. Viking Press.

Tarry, Ellen (1906-) & Ets, Marie Hall (1893-)
--My Dog Rinty. Alland, Alexander & Alland, Alexandra, illus. LC 46-4736. 48 p. incl. front., illus. 24 1/2 x 19 1/2 cm. 1946. The Viking Press.

Tarshis, Elizabeth Kent, Mrs. (1913-)
--The Village That Learned to Read. N.D. E . M. Hale and Co.
--The Village That Learned to Read. Haydon, Harold (1909-), illus. LC 41-8636. 4 p. l., 158, 2 p. col. front., illus. 25 1/2 x 19 1/2 cm. 1941. Houghton Mifflin Company.
--Young Sailors of Sidon: A Story of Long Ago Phoenicia. Holberg, Richard A. (1889-1942), illus. LC 38-35985. xiii, 162 p. incl. front., illus. 21 1/2 cm. c.1938. L. C. Page & Company.

Tarsky, Sue
--I Can. Sleight, Katy, illus. LC 84-11663. (Illus.). 28 p. 18cm. (Early bird book Chatterbox). 1985. (ISBN 0-394-86698-3). Random House.
--Open the Door. Ward, Deborah, illus. LC 84-17730. (Illus.). 28 p. 18cm. (Early bird book. Chatterbox). 1985. (ISBN 0-394-86699-1). Random House.
--Who Goes Splash?. Sleight, Katy, illus. LC 84-17731. (Illus.). 28 p. 18cm. (Early bird book. Chatterbox). 1985. (ISBN 0-394-86701-7). Random House.

Tashjian, Virginia A. (1921-), retold by see Toumanian, Hovhannes.

Tashjian, Virginia A. (1921-)
--The Miller-King. Ameijide, Ray, illus. LC 74-125139. (Illus.). 28 p. 22cm. (A Magic Circle Book). 1971. Ginn.

Tashjian, Virginia A. (1921-), ed.
--Juba This and Juba That: Story Hour Stretches for Large or Small Groups. 1st ed. De Larrea, Victoria, illus. LC 69-10666. (Illus.). xi, 116 p. 22cm. 1969. (ISBN 0-316-83230-8). Little, Brown.
--Three Apples Fell from Heaven: Armenian Tales. 1st ed. Hogrogian, Nonny (1932-), illus. LC 70-129903. (Illus.). x, 76 p. 24cm. 1971. Little, Brown.
--With a Deep Sea Smile: Story Hour Stretches for Large or Small Groups. 1st ed. Wells, Rosemary, illus. LC 72-8874. (Illus.). xii, 132 p. 22cm. 1974. (ISBN 0-316-83216-2). Little, Brown.

Tashlin, Frank (1913-1972)
--The Bear That Wasn't. Tashlin, Frank (1913-1972), illus. LC 62-4936. unpaged. illus. 22 cm. 1962, c.1946. Dover Publications.
--The Bear That Wasn't. Tashlin, Frank (1913-1972), illus. LC 46-1683. 55 p. illus. 26 cm. 1946. E. P. Dutton & Co., Inc.
--The 'Possum that Didn't. Tashlin, Frank (1913-1972), illus. LC 50-9357. (Illus.). 31. 26cm. 1950. Farrar, Strauss.

Tasker, James (1908-)
--African Treehouse. Elgin, Kathleen (1923-), illus. LC 73-79450. (Illus.). 64 p. 26cm. 1973. (ISBN 0-8178-5101-1). (ISBN 0-8178-5101-1). Harvey House.

Taslitt, Israel Isaac
--At the Walls of Jericho. Taslitt, Israel Isaac, illus. LC 60-53265. 196p. illus. c.1961. Bloch Pub. Co.
--Thunder Over Tabor: A Novel Based on the Biblical Story of Deborah. Elron, Baruch, illus. LC 75-103111. (Illus.). 167 p. 22cm. 1969. (ISBN 0-87631-022-6). Sabra Books.
--Young Samson: The Strongest Boy Who Ever Lived. Luizada, A., illus. LC 68-55547. (Illus.). 191 p. 22cm. (Sabra book). 1968. Funk and Wagnalls.

Taslitt, Israel Isaac, tr. see Ofek, Uriel.

Taslitt, Israel Isaac, tr. see Omer, Devorah.

Tassell, A.
--Wild Gwen: A Story of School Life. N.D. E. & J. B. Young & Co.

Tassin, Algernon De Vivier (1869-)
--The Rainbow String. Brewster, Anna Richards, illus. LC 21-19155. 6 p. l., 114 p. incl. illus., plates. col. front. 19 cm. 1921. The Macmillan Company.

Tassinari, G., rev. by see Lorenzini, Carlo.

Tate
--The Fathers. N.D. The Swallow Press.

Tate, tr. see Faber, Peter.

Tate, Carole, ed.
--Rhymes and Ballads of London. Tate, Carole, illus. LC 72-90691. (Illus.). 27 p. 1973, c.1971. Scroll Press.
--Strawberry Fair. Tate, Carole, illus. (Illus.). (gr. k-4). 1975. (ISBN 0-00-195762-7). Collins-World.

Tate, Eleanora Elaine (1948-)
--Just an Overnight Guest. LC 80-12970. p. cm. c.1980. (ISBN 0-440-74225-0). (ISBN 0-440-74223-4). Dial Press.

Tate, Elizabeth
--The Little Flower Girl. Stone, Helen (1904-), illus. LC 56-6332. unpaged. illus. 25 cm. 1956. Lothrop, Lee & Shepard Co.
--Little Teddy and the Big Sea. 1954. E M Hale and Company.
--Little Teddy and the Big Sea. Werth, Kurt (1896-), illus. LC 53-6733. unpaged. illus. 28cm. c.1954. Lothrop, Lee & Shepard.

Tate, Joan (1922-), tr. see Beckman, Gunnel.

Tate, Joan (1922-), tr. see Frick, Lennart.

Tate, Joan (1922-), tr. see Hagerup, Inger.

Tate, Joan (1922-), tr. see Herrmanns, Ralph.

Tate, Joan (1922-), tr. see Lorentzen, Karin.

Tate, Joan (1922-), tr. see Malmgren, Ulf.

Tate, Joan (1922-), tr. see Sandman Lilius, Irmelin.

Tate, Joan (1922-), tr. see Svend, Otto Sorensen.

Tate, Joan (1922-)
--Ben and Annie. Brown, Judith Gwyn (1933-), illus. LC 73-9048. (Illus.). 78 p. 22cm. 1st U.S. edition. 1974. (ISBN 0-385-08570-2). (ISBN 0-385-08570-2). Doubleday.
--Grandpa and My Sister Bee. American ed. Wood, Leslie (1920-), illus. LC 75-40402. (Illus.). 24 p. 21cm. (Stepping Stones). 1976, c.1973. (ISBN 0-516-03581-9). Childrens Press.
--Jock and the Rock Cakes. american ed. Dinan, Carolyn, illus. LC 75-40357. p. cm. 1976, c.1973. (ISBN 0-516-03584-3). Childrens Press.
--Luke's Garden and Gramp: Two Novels. LC 80-8445. p. cm. 1981. (ISBN 0-06-026139-0). (ISBN 0-06-026144-7). Harper & Row.
--The Next-Doors & the Silver Grill. (gr. 7 up). 1977. (ISBN 0-590-09857-8, Schol Pap). Schol Bk Serv.
--Not the Usual Kind of Girl. (gr. 7-12). 1975. (ISBN 0-590-09818-7, Schol Pap). Scholastic Inc.
--Ring on My Finger. (gr. 7 up). 1977. (ISBN 0-590-10318-0, Schol Pap). Scholastic Inc.

--The Runners. Tate, Joan (1922-), illus. (Illus.). 96p. (gr. 4-8). 1975. David & Charles.
--Sam & Me. LC 69-12666. 94 p. 22cm. 1969, c.1968. Coward-McCann.
--Tina and David. LC 73-4382. 95 p. 21cm. 1973. T. Nelson.
--Wild Boy. Jeschke, Susan (1942-), illus. LC 73-5495. (Illus.). 100 p. 22cm. 1st U.S. edition. 1973. (ISBN 0-06-026096-3). (ISBN 0-06-026096-3). Harper & Row.

Tate, Sally
--Fluffy, the Pink Bunny. Tate, Sally, illus. LC 43-8951. 20 p. col. illus. 23 x 18 cm. 1943. Cupples and Leon Company.

Tate, Sally, retold by.
--The Gingerbread Man. Tate, Sally, illus. LC 44-8660. 28 p. col. illus. 28 1/2 cm. c.1944. Whitman Publishing Co.

Tate, Sally, retold by see Mother Goose.

Tate, Zetta C
--Susan and Little Black Boy. Long, Stanley E., illus. LC 52-14714. unpaged. illus. 24cm. 1952. Pacific Press Pub. Association.

Tatham, Julie Campbell
--Behind the White Veil. LC 51-1373. vii, 214p. illus. 20cm. (The Vicki Barr Flight Stewardess Ser.). 1951. Grosset & Dunlap.
Cherry Ames at Spencer. LC 49 3929. vii, 213 p. front. 20 cm. 1949. (ISBN 0-448-09713-3). Grosset & Dunlap.
--Cherry Ames, Clinic Nurse. LC 52-10255. 208p. illus. 20cm. (The Cherry Ames Stories). 1952. (ISBN 0-448-09713-3). Grosset & Dunlap.
--Cherry Ames, Country Doctor's Nurse. LC 55 1360. 214p. illus. 20cm. (The Cherry Ames Stories 16). c.1955. (ISBN 0-448-09713-3). Grosset & Dunlap.
--Cherry Ames, Dude Ranch Nurse. LC 53-2323. 210p. 20cm. (The Cherry Ames Stories). 1953. (ISBN 0-448-09714-1). Grosset & Dunlap.
--Cherry Ames, Mountaineer Nurse. LC 51-4230. 212p. front. 20cm. (Her The Cherry Ames Stories 12). 1951. (ISBN 0-448-09712-5). Grosset & Dunlap.
--Cherry Ames, Night Supervisor. LC 50-4001. vii, 209p. illus. 20cm. (The Cherry Ames Stories). 1950. (ISBN 0-448-09711-7). Grosset & Dunlap.
--Cherry Ames, Rest Home Nurse. LC 54-65640. 214p. illus. 20cm. (Her The Cherry Ames Stories 15). 1954. (ISBN 0-448-09715-X). Grosset & Dunlap.
--The Clue of the Broken Blossom. LC 50-5645. 211p. front. 20cm. (The Vicki Barr Flight Stewardess Ser.). 1950. (ISBN 0-448-09405-3). Grosset & Dunlap.
--Ginny Gordon and the Lending Library. Wesley, Margaret, illus. LC 54-4377. 282p. illus. 20cm. 1954. Whitman Pub. Co.
--Ginny Gordon and the Missing Heirloom. Jervis, Margaret, illus. LC 50-8331. 249p. illus. 21cm. 1950. Whitman.
--Ginny Gordon and the Mystery at the Old Barn. Jervis, Margaret, illus. LC 51-6063. 250p. illus. 21cm. 1951. Whitman Pub. Co.
--Ginny Gordon and the Mystery of the Disappearing Candlesticks. authorized. Jervis, Margaret, illus. LC 49-3810. 248 p. illus. 21 cm. 1948. Whitman Pub. Co.
--The Mongrel of Merryway Farm. Megargee, Edwin, illus. LC 52-8422. 232 p. illus. 21 cm. 1952. World Pub. Co.
--The Mystery at Hartwood House. LC 52-7176. 210p. illus. 20cm. (Vicki Barr flight stewardess series 7). 1952. Grosset & Dunlap.
--Rin Tin Tin's Rinty: An Original Story Featuring Rinty, Son of the Famous Movie Dog, Rin Tin Tin. Authorized. Martin, Rene (0000-1977), illus. LC 54-33177. 282p. illus. 20cm. 1954. Whitman Pub. Co.
--To Nick from Jan. LC 57-12203. 223p. 21cm. 1957. Coward-McCann.
--Trixie Belden and the Gatehouse Mystery. Stevens, Mary E. (1920-1966), illus. LC 51-6062. 250p. illus. 21cm. 1951. Whitman Pub. Co.
--Trixie Belden and the Mysterious Visitor. Stevens, Mary E. (1920-1966), ed. LC 54-3747. (Illus.). 282 p. 21cm. 1954. Whitman Pub. Co.
--Trixie Belden and the Red Trailer Mystery. Stevens, Mary E. (1920-1966), ed. LC 50-8332. 248p. illus. 21cm. 1950. Whitman.
--Trixie Belden and the Secret of the Mansion. authorized. Stevens, Mary E. (1920-1966), ed. LC 49-3808. 248 p. illus. 21 cm. 1948. Whitman Pub. Co.

Tatlock, Jessie May (1878-)
--Greek & Roman Mythology. N.D. Appleton-Century-Crofts.

Taubner, Cheryl
--Fun with the Fraggles. Yeagle, Dean, illus. (Illus.). (Fraggle Rock Bks.). (ps-1). 1984. (ISBN 0-03-000709-7). HR&W.

Tauer, Roi (1941-), created by see Merrick, Donna & Clark, Ginnie.

Taurman, Mary Lawrence
--The Great Heart: A Christmas Story. Jones, Elmo, illus. 1959. The Dietz Press.

Taves, Isabella (1915-)
--Not Bad for a Girl. LC 70-179090. 95 p. 22cm. 1972. M. Evans.
--True Ghost Stories. Deas, Michael, illus. (gr. 5-7). 1978. Watts.

Tavo, Gus, pseud., see Ivan, Martha Miller Pfaff.

Tavo, Gus, pseud.
--Trail to Lone Canyon. Ivan, Martha Miller Pfaff. Walker, Gil, illus. LC 64-20171. (Gustavo is the joint pseud. for Martha Miller Pfaff Ivan, 1909-, and Gustave E. Ivan). 212 p. illus. 22 cm. 1964. Knopf.

Tavo, Gus, pseud. & Ivan, Gustave E.
--The Buffalo Are Running. Ivan, Martha Miller Pfaff. Miller, E. F., illus. LC 60-11421. (Gustavo is the joint pseud. for Martha Miller Pfaff Ivan, 1909-, and Gustave E. Ivan). 215 p. illus. 22 cm. 1960. Knopf.
--Hunt the Mountain Lion. Ivan, Martha Miller Pfaff. Turkle, Brinton Cassaday (1915-), illus. LC 59-10026. (Gustavo is the joint pseudonym for Martha Miller Pfaff Ivan, 1909-, and Gustave E. Ivan). 209 p. illus. 22 cm. 1959. Knopf.
--Ride the Pale Stallion. Ivan, Martha Miller Pfaff. Bjorklund, Lorence F. (1913-1978), illus. LC 68-11171. (Gustavo is the joint pseud. for Martha Miller Pfaff Ivan, 1909-. and Gustave E. Ivan). 180 p. 22cm. 1968. Knopf.
--Track the Grizzly Down. Ivan, Martha Miller Pfaff. 1st ed. Goldstein, Leslie, illus. LC 63-9105. (Gustavo is the joint pseudonym for Martha Miller Pfaff Ivan, 1909-, and Gustave E. Ivan). 209 p. illus. 22 cm. 1963. Knopf.

Taylor, Allan (1897-)
Morgan's Long Rifles. Orbaan, Albert F. (1913-), illus. LC 65-13306. (Illus.). 253 p. 22cm. 1965. Putnam.

Taylor, Alta Lucretia see Clinton, Althea L., pseud.

Taylor, Alta Lucretia (1885-), ed. see Asbjornsen, Peter Christen (1812-1885) & Moe, Jorgen Engebretsen.

Taylor, Alta Lucretia (1885-), ed. see Defoe, Daniel.

Taylor, Alta Lucretia (1885-), ed. see Sewell, Anna.

Taylor, Alta Lucretia (1885-)
--Billy Whiskers in Mischief: Continuing the Famous Billy Whiskers Series. Brundage, Frances, illus. LC 27-650. 3 p. l., 11-157 p. col. front., illus., col. plates. 23 cm. (The Billy Whiskers series. v. 28). c.1926. The Saalfield Publishing Company.

Taylor, Alta Lucretia (1885-), ed.
--The Big Story Book: Short Stories and Verse Selected for Boys and Girls. Taylor, Alta Lucretia (1885-), illus. LC 30-18655. 376 p. col. front., illus. 25 cm. c.1930. The Saalfield Publishing Company.
--Kitty-Cat Stories. Clinton, Althea L., pseud. Bailey, Bill & Taylor, Alta Lucretia (1885-), illus. Clinton, Althea L., pseud. 44 p. incl. col. front., col. illus. 24 1/2 cm. c.1930. The Saalfield Publishing Company.
--The Little Red Hen and Other Stories. Clinton, Althea L., pseud. Bailey, Bill & Taylor, Alta Lucretia (1885-), illus. Clinton, Althea L., pseud. 44 p. incl. col. front., col. illus. 24 1/2 cm. c.1930. The Saalfield Publishing Company.
--Puppy-Dog Stories. Clinton, Althea L., pseud. Bailey, Bill & Taylor, Alta Lucretia (1885-), illus. Clinton, Althea L., pseud. 44 p. incl. col front., col. illus. 24 1/2 cm. c.1930. The Saalfield Publishing Company.
--The Tale of Peter Rabbit and Other Stories. Clinton, Althea L., pseud. Bailey, Bill, illus. 44 p. incl col. front., col. illus. 24 1/2 cm. c.1930. The Saalfield Publishing Company.
--The Treasure Book of Best Stories. Clinton, Althea L., pseud. Madsen, Eleanora & Peat, Fern Bisel, Mrs. (1893-), illus. Clinton, Althea L., pseud. LC 39-12104. 3 p. l., 11-92 p. col. front., illus., col. plates. 30 1/2 cm. c.1939. The Saalfield Publishing Company.
--The Treasure Book of Best Stories. Clinton, Althea L., pseud. Peat, Fern Bisel, Mrs. (1893-), illus. LC 33-18662. 3 p. l., 11-92 p. col. front., illus., col. plates. 30 1/2 cm. c.1933. The Saalfield Publishing Company.
--Wide-Awake Stories. Clinton, Althea L., pseud. Bailey, Bill & Taylor, Alta Lucretia (1885-), illus. Clinton, Althea L., pseud. LC 30-31912. 187 p. incl. col. front., illus. (part col.) 24 1/2 cm. c.1930. The Saalfield Publishing Company.

Taylor, Ann
--My Mother. N.D. Thomas Nelson & Sons.

Taylor, Annie Elizabeth
--Sweetheart and Bob. LC 8-2108. 82 1 p. 17 x 14 cm. 1902. W. J. McClure, Book and Job Printer.

Taylor, Arthur Raymond (1936-)
--Mr. Fizbee & the Little Troup. Taylor, Arthur Raymond (1936-), illus. LC 62-14820. (Illus.). 48p. (gr. k-4). 1962. (ISBN 0-03-035490-0). (ISBN 0-03-035520-6). HR&W.

Taylor, Audilee Boyd
--Where Did My Feather Pillow Come from?. 1st ed. Dillon, Sharon Saseen, illus. LC 81-71027. (Illus.). 32 p. 24cm. c.1982. (ISBN 0-942250-00-1). Castlemarsh Publications.

Taylor, B L
--A Penny Whistle. N.D. Knopf.

Taylor, Barbara J (1927-)
--I Can Do. Andrus, Fay Ping, illus. Taylor, Dee R., photos by. LC 73-190411. (Illus.). 32 p. 26cm. 1972. (ISBN 0-8425-0500-8). Brigham Young University Publications.

Taylor, Bayard (1825-1878)
--Arabian Night's Entertainments, 1 vol. Lane, William Edward, tr. (Illus.). N.D. David McKay.
--Beauty and the Beast and Tales of Home. N.D. G. P. Putnam's Sons.
--Boys of Other Countries. Enl. ed. Coburn, Frederick Simpson, et al. (1871-), illus. LC 12-23512. vi, 260 p. col. front, plates (part col.) 21 1/2 cm. 1912. G. P. Putnam's Sons.
--Boys of Other Countries. New ed. Ives, Sarah Noble, et al., illus. LC 1-24944. v, 166 p. front., plates. 20 cm. 1901. G. P. Putnam's Sons.
--Boys of Other Countries. New ed. Ives, Sarah Noble, et al., illus. LC 4-32666. v, 166 p. front., 1 illus., 7 pl. 20 cm. (On cover: The Knickerbocker series). 1904. G. P. Putnam's Sons.
--Boys of Other Countries: Stories for American Boys. LC 19-11366. 2 p. l., 164 p. incl. illus., plates. 20 cm. 1876. G. P. Putnam's Sons.

Taylor, Benjamin F.
--Old-Time Pictures and Sheaves of Rhyme. N.D. S. C. Griggs & Co.

Taylor, Bert Leston (1866-1921)
--The Well in the Wood. Cory, Fanny Young, illus. LC 4-23765. 7 p. l., 191, 1 p. col. front., col. illus. 20 1/2 cm. 1904. The Bobbs-Merrill Company.

Taylor, Bess
--Witch in the Shrouds: A Voyage in Miniature. 148p. (gr. 4-6). 1980. Dorrance.

Taylor, Beulah
--Nickie and Sue: Two Lovable Parakeets. Robison, Guerin, illus. 43p. col. illus. 29cm. 1962, c.1961. Pageant.

Taylor, C. W., retold by see Wang Pao-Chuan.

Taylor, Casey
--Game Plan. LC 75-6830. 256p. (gr. 9 up). 1975. (ISBN 0-689-30486-2). Atheneum.

Taylor, Charles Keen
--Billy, His Summer Awakening. Gallagher, Sears (1869-1955), illus. LC 11-24119. 6 p. l., 3-283 p. front., plates. 20 cm. $1.50. (On cover: The Billy series). 1911. Little, Brown, and Company.

Taylor, Daphne
--The Pompous Parrot and Other West Indian Tales. 1947. St Martin's Press.
--The Pompous Parrot and Other West Indian Tales. Richards, Nan, illus. N.D. Macmillan.

Taylor, Deems, jt. auth. see Kennedy, Mary.

Taylor, Don Alonzo
--Old Sam and the Horse Thieves. Bjorklund, Lorence F. (1913-1978), illus. LC 67-4550. (Illus.). 160 p. 23cm. 1967. Follett Pub. Co.
--Old Sam Thoroughbred Trotter. Bjorklund, Lorence F. (1913-1978), illus. LC 55-750383. 160p. illus. 24cm. 1955. (ISBN 0-695-46510-4). Follett Pub. Co.

Taylor, Dorothy Loring
--Abigail's New Home. Schimmel, Beth, illus. LC 82-238196. (Illus.). 20p. (Valley View Farm Tales). (gr. k-3). 1982. (ISBN 0-9610640-0-5). D L Taylor.

Taylor, Doug
--At the Circus. Taylor, Doug, illus. LC 84-17531. p. cm. (Sunny-bunny book). c.1985. (ISBN 0-517-55568-9). Crown.
--The Best Time for a Hug: Featuring the Kiddiewinks. Taylor, Doug, illus. LC 83-23233. (Illus.). 10. (Kiddiewinks Books). c.1984. (ISBN 0-517-55290-6). Crown.
--Funny's Lost Key. Taylor, Doug, illus. LC 84-17530. p. cm. (Sunny-bunny book). c.1985. (ISBN 0-517-55571-9). Crown.
--How Do You Feel?. Taylor, Doug, illus. LC 83-15110. (Illus.). 32. (Kiddiewinks Books). c.1984. (ISBN 0-517-55289-2). Crown.
--Pac-Baby's ABC. Taylor, Doug, illus. (Illus.). 1983. (ISBN 0-686-43029-8). Crown.
--Pac-Baby's Colors. Taylor, Doug, illus. (Illus.). (ps). 1983. (ISBN 0-517-55018-0). Crown.
--Pac-Baby's Shapes. Taylor, Doug, illus. (ps). 1983. (ISBN 0-517-55020-2). Crown.
--Ways to Say I Love You: Featuring the Kiddiewinks. Taylor, doug, illus. LC 83-23906. (Illus.). 14 p. 15cm. (Kiddiewinks books). c.1984. (ISBN 0-517-55291-4). Crown.

Taylor, E M
--Teddy and Mickey at the Seaside. 28p. N.D. Pitman Publishing Corporation.
--Teddy and Mickey's Adventure at Brighton. 28p. N.D. Pitman Publishing Corporation.

Taylor, Edgar, tr. see Grimm, Jakob Ludwig Karl (1785-1863) & Grimm, Wilhelm Karl.

Taylor, Edward C
--Ted Strong's Saddle Pard: Or, A Desperate Dash. LC 27-1992. 276 p. 17 1/2 cm. (His The Western story library--no. 45). c.1927. Street & Smith Corporation.

Taylor, Edward John, tr. see Basile, Giovanni Battista.

Taylor, Eliza Dean
--Loving Service Stories ... Drummond, Henry (1851-1897), illus. LC 12-32321. 159 p. incl. front., pl. 19 cm. 1894. J. Pott & Company.

Taylor, Elizabeth Buchanan, tr. see Nickl, Peter.

Taylor, Elizabeth W., tr. see Seidel, Heinrich.

Taylor, Elizabeth (1912-1975)
--Mossy Trotter. Acs, Laszlo Bela (1931-), illus. LC 67-17158. 160 p. illus. 21 cm. 1st U.S. edition. 1967. (ISBN 0-15-255705-9). Harcourt, Brace & World.

Taylor, Emily Goddard
--Our Little West Indian Cousin. Withington, Elizabeth R., illus. LC 22-95703. 3 p. l., v-xi, 1 p., 2 l., 95 p. front., plates. 19 1/2 cm. (little cousin series). 1922. The Page Company.

Taylor, Ethel Bonney, illus.
--Favorite Story Book. LC 41-22363. 2 p. l., 9-253 p. illus. (part col.) 26 1/2 cm. c.1941. Whitman Publishing Company.

Taylor, Eugene Jackson (1913-1978)
--Goose Eggs. Taylor, Eugene Jackson (1913-1978), illus. LC 84-905. (Illus.). 32 p. 24cm. (Biscuit, Buttons & Pickles ser.). c.1984. (ISBN 0-394-86832-3). (ISBN 0-394-96832-8). Knopf : Distributed by Random House.
--Ivy Cottage. Taylor, Eugene Jackson (1913-1978), illus. LC 84-900. (Illus.). 32p. (Biscuit, Buttons, & Pickles Ser.). (ps-4). c.1984. (ISBN 0-394-96831-X). (ISBN 0-394-86831-5). Knopf.
--Rag Doll Press. Taylor, Eugene Jackson (1913-1978), illus. LC 84-20122. p. cm. (Biscuit, Buttons & Pickles Ser.). c.1985. (ISBN 0-394-86834-X). (ISBN 0-394-96834-4). Knopf : Distributed by Random House.
--The Thorn Witch. Taylor, Eugene Jackson (1913-1978), illus. LC 84-12533. (Illus.). 204p. (Biscuit, Button, & Pickles Ser.). (ps-3). 1985. (ISBN 0-394-86833-1). (ISBN 0-394-96833-6). Knopf.

Taylor, Fannie J
--Adolph, and How He Found the "Beautiful Lady". Toerring, Helen, illus. LC 12-39371. 85 p. incl. front., illus., 3 pl. 19 1/2 cm. 1896. Fleming H. Revell Company.

Taylor, Florance Walton, Mrs.
--Ball Two!. Overlie, George, illus. LC 76-165317. (Illus.). 32 p. 23cm. (Felipe adventure story). 1971. (ISBN 0-8225-0143-0). Lerner Publications Co.
--Carrier Boy. Fisher, Leonard Everett (1924-), illus. LC 56-12323. 160 p. illus. 22 cm. 1956. Abelard-Schuman.
--Corn Festival. Overlie, George, illus. LC 78-165320. (Illus.). color ils. 32p. (Felipe Adventure Stories Ser). (gr. 2-4). 1971. (ISBN 0-8225-0146-5). Lerner Pubns.
--From Texas to Illinois. Overlie, George, illus. LC 79-165315. (Illus.). 32 p. 23cm. (Felipe adventure story). 1971. (ISBN 0-8225-0141-4). Lerner Publications Co.
--Gold Dust and Bullets. Granstaff, William (1925-), illus. LC 62-13171. 176 p. illus. 22 cm. 1962. A. Whitman.
--Jim Long-Knife. Gringhuis, Richard H. (1918-1974), illus. Gringhuis, Dirk, pseud. LC 59-9656. 174 p. illus. 22 cm. 1959. A. Whitman.
--Navy Wings of Gold. Stein, Harve (1904-), illus. LC 44-6746. 5 p. l., 15-232 p. incl. plates (part col.) col. front. 23 cm. 1944. A. Whitman & Company.
--Owen of the Bluebird. Stein, Harve (1904-), illus. LC 42-9471. 6 p. l., 15-246 p. incl. col. front., illus., plates (part col.) 23 cm. (Young America books). 1942. A. Whitman & Company.
--A Plane Ride. Overlie, George, illus. LC 71-165321. (Illus.). 32 p. 23cm. (Felipe adventure story). 1971. (ISBN 0-8225-0147-3). Lerner Publications Co.
--School Picnic. Overlie, George, illus. LC 70-165318. (Illus.). color ils. 32p. (Felipe Adventure Stories Ser). (gr. 2-4). 1971. (ISBN 0-8225-0144-9). Lerner Pubns.
--Towpath Andy. Wuerfel, Lillian B., illus. LC 38-326167. 249 p. incl. col. front., illus., plates (part col.) 21 1/2 cm. 1938. A. Whitman & Co.
--Vermilion Clay. Young, Eleanor Mussey, illus. LC 37-23780. 5 p. l., 17-163 p. incl. illus., plates. col. front., col. pl. 22 1/2 cm. c.1937. A. Whitman & Co.
--What Is a Migrant?. Overlie, George, illus. LC 72-165316. (Illus.). color ils. 32p. (Felipe Adventure Stories Ser.). (gr. 2-4). 1971. (ISBN 0-8225-0142-2). Lerner Pubns.
--Where's Luis?. Overlie, George, illus. LC 73-165319. (Illus.). 32 p. 23cm. (Felipe adventure story). 1971. (ISBN 0-8225-0145-7). Lerner Publications Co.

--With Fife and Drum. Young, Eleanor Mussey, illus. LC 36-11051. 3 p. l., 9-129 p. incl. col. front., illus., col. pl. 22 1/2 cm. 1936. A. Whitman & Co.

Taylor, Florence Marian Tompkins (1892-)
--Good News to Tell. Lear, John, illus. LC 49-108353. 49 p. illus. (part col.) 17 x 23 cm. (Children's hour library). 1949. Westminster Press.
--Growing Pains. Marsh, Lucille Patterson, illus. LC 48-2107. 48 p. illus. (part col.) 17 x 23 cm. 1948. Westminster Press.

Taylor, Frances Lillian (0000-1931)
--Two Indian Children of Long Ago. Deal, L. Kate, illus. LC 22-12087. 160 p. col. front., illus. 19 1/2 cm. c.1920. Beckley-Cardy Company.

Taylor, Frances Lillian (0000-1931), adapted by.
--Nursery Tales: The Little Blue Pig, Goody Twoshoes, Four and Twenty Blackbirds. Taylor, Frances Lillian (0000-1931), illus. LC 43-29022. 32 p. illus. 18 1/2 cm. (Instructor library books. 140). N.D. Hall & McCreary Company.

Taylor, George B.
--Claiborne. (The Oakland Stories). N.D. Sheldon & Co.
--Cousin Guy. (The Oakland Stories). N.D. Sheldon & Co.
--Gustave. (The Oakland Stories). N.D. Sheldon & Co.
--Kenney. (The Oakland Stories). N.D. Sheldon & Co.

Taylor, Gladys King
--Paddy. Munson, Harold W. (1920-), illus. LC 53-5464. unpaged. illus. 23cm. 1953. Pacific Press Pub. Association.

Taylor, Grant
--Guns of Salvation Valley. N.D. J. B. Lippincott.
--Whip Ryder's Way. N.D. J. B. Lippincott.

Taylor, Harold, tr. see De Coster, Charles T.

Taylor, Helen L.
--Christiana. N.D. Wells, Gardner, Darton & Co.'s.
--Little Pilgrim's Progress. N.D. (ISBN 0-686-13759-0). Believers Bkshelf.
--Little Pilgrim's Progress. (gr. 2-6). N.D. (ISBN 0-8024-0003-5). Moody.
--Out-of-the-Way. N.D. Wells. Gardner, Darton & Co.'s.

Taylor, Henry D
--On Board the Rescue. A Story for Boys. LC 10-1512. 95 p. 19 cm. 1889. Haynes & Co.

Taylor, Jane, et al. (1783-1824)
--Meddlesome Matty and Other Poems for Infant Minds. Adelaide, pseud. Payne, Wyndham, illus. Sitwell, Edith, Dame (1887-1964), intro. by. xii, 1, 54, 1 p. col. illus. 22 cm. 1926. The Viking Press.
--Original Poems. Adelaide, pseud. Cooper, James Davis (1823-1904), illus. LC 22-830608. xiv, 15-190 p. incl. front., illus. 20 1/2 cm. 1868. G. Routledge & Sons.
--The "Original Poems" and Others. Lucas, Edward Verrall (1868-1938), ed. Bedford, Francis Donkin (1864-1950), illus. LC 21-16047. xl, 414, 1 p. incl. illus., ports., plates. col. front. 21 cm. (Fine Art Juveniles). 1905. Frederick A. Stokes company.
--Original Poems for Infant Minds. Adelaide, pseud. LC 21-3876. 1 p. l., iv, 5-208 p. col. front., illus. 15 cm. 1864. J. Miller.
--Original Poems, for Infant Minds. Adelaide, pseud. LC 21-6404. 4 p. l., 7-112 p. 14 cm. 1806. Printed and Sold by Kimber, Conrad, & Co. No. , Market Street, and No. , South Second Street.

Taylor, Jane, jt. auth. see Edgeworth, Maria.

Taylor, Jane, jt. auth. see Gilbert, Ann Taylor, Mrs.

Taylor, Jane (1783-1824)
--Pleasures of Taste and Other Stories. (Harper's Massachusetts School Library, Juvenile Ser.). N.D. Harper & Bros.
--The Pleasures of Taste and Other Stories. Hale, Sarah J., Mrs., selected by. LC 8-25961. (Selected from the Writing of Miss Jane Taylor: with a Sketch of Her Life). 288 p. front. 16 cm. 1839. Marsh, Capen, Lyon, and Webb.

Taylor, Jane (1783-1824) & Gilbert, Ann Taylor
--Hymns for Infant Minds. N.D. American Sunday-School Union.
--Hymns for Infant Minds. 109p. N.D. Hurd & Houghton for American Tract Society.
--Hymns for Infant Minds. 109p. N.D. Lockwood, Brooks, & Co. for American Tract Society.
--Hymns for Infant Minds. N.D. Robert Carter & Brothers.
--Little Ann and Other Poems. Greenaway, Kate (1846-1901), illus. N.D. Frederick Warne & Co.
--Little Ann and Other Poems. Greenaway, Kate (1846-1901), illus. LC 12-32708. 64 p. incl. col. front., col. illus. 23 1/2 cm. 1883. G. Routledge & Sons.
--Meddlesome Mattie, 1 of 6 Vols. (Illus.). (Aunt Mattie Ser.: Vol. 3). N.D. Set. Porter & Coates.
--Meddlesome Matty, 1 of 50 Vol. (Primary Class Library: Vol. 10). N.D. Sunday-School Publications.
--Meddlesome Matty, 1 of 10 Vol. (Louise's Little Library: Vol. 8). N.D. Set. Sunday-School Publciations.
--Original Poems. (Carters' Fireside Library). N.D. Robert Carter & Brothers.
--Original Poems for Infant Minds. LC 12-393630. 180 p. illus. 16 cm. 1840. H. F. Anners.
--Original Poems for Infant Minds. N.D. John C. Winston.
--Original Poems for Infant Minds. N.D. Nichols & Hall.
--Original Poems, for Infant Minds. LC 14-7867. 15cm. 180p. N.D. Published by West and Richardson, No. , Cornhill, . E. G. House, Printer, Court Street.
--Original Poems for Infant Minds and Rhymes for the Nursery, 2 Vols. LC 75-32151. p. cm. 1976. (ISBN 0-8240-2265-3). Garland Pub.
--Rhymes for Children. Hix, Melvin, ed. LC 7-19576. 184 p. 13 cm. (Golden hour series). c.1907. Educational Publishing Company.
--Rhymes for the Nursery. LC 25-21123. 64 p. illus. 14 1/2 x 12 cm. 1851. G. S. Appleton.

Taylor, Jefferys
--Boy Crusoes. (St. Nicholas Series for Boys). N.D. International Book Co.
--Harry's Holiday. (Illus.). N.D. E. P. Dutton & Co.
--The Young Islanders: Or, School-boy Crusoes. N.D. J. B. Lippincott & Co.
--Young Islanders: The School Boy Crusoes. N.D. Nichols & Hall.

Taylor, John
--Volcano in Our Yard. Taylor, John, illus. (Illus.). (gr. 2-5). 1975. (ISBN 0-686-11663-1). Thompson's.

Taylor, John Edward, tr. see Basile, Giovanni Battista.

Taylor, Joye
--Verses for Children. Paterson, Elizabeth, illus. LC 41-1479. 45, 1 p. incl. illus., pl. 23 cm. 1939. Whitcombe & Tombs, Limited.

Taylor, Judy (1932-)
--Sophie and Jack. Gantner, Susan, illus. LC 82-13279. c.1982. (ISBN 0-399-20947-6). Philomel.
--Sophie and Jack Help Out. Gantner, Susan, illus. LC 83-13302. p. cm. 1983. (ISBN 0-399-21059-8). Philomel Books.

Taylor, Kamala Purnaiya see Markandaya, Kamala, pseud.

Taylor, Katharine Haviland
--Nursery Nights. Merwin, Decie (1894-1961), illus. LC 42-20279. 93, 2 p. incl. col. front., illus. (part col.) 24 1/2 cm. 1942. J. B. Lippincott Company.
--Real Stuff. N.D. Harcourt Brace & Co.

Taylor, Katharine (1888-) & Greene, Henry Copley (1871-)
--The Shady Hill Play Book. Shurtleff, Harold R., illus. LC 28-25646. xxvi p., 1 l., 168 p. illus., diagrs. 20 1/2 cm. 1928. The Macmillan Company.

Taylor, Kathryn, illus.
--ABC. LC 45-51208. 53 p. illus. (part col.) 17 cm. (On cover: Story hour series). c.1944. Whitman Publishing Company.

Taylor, Kenneth Nathaniel (1917-)
--Lost on the Trail. (gr. 4-8). 1980. (ISBN 0-8423-3843-8). Tyndale.

Taylor, Kenneth Nathaniel (1917-), ed.
--Great Stories for Children. DeVelasco, Joe E., illus. LC 77-123029. (Illus.). 376 p. 26cm. 1971. (ISBN 0-8423-1180-7). Tyndale House Publishers.
--Romans for the Children's Hour. 251p. 1959. Moody.
--Stories for the Children's Hour. rev. ed. Doares, Robert G., illus. LC 68-26408. (Illus.). 189 p. 24cm. 1968. Moody Press.
--Stories for the Children's Hour. Frazier, Beth Conrad, illus. LC 53-271064. 190p. illus. 24cm. 1953. Moody Press.
--Taylor's Bible Story Book. LC 76-123034. (Illus.). 476 p. 27cm. 1971, c.1970. (ISBN 0-8423-6700-4). Tyndale House Publishers.

Taylor, Lester Barbour, Jr. (1932-)
--Haunted Houses. Schneider, Meg, ed. LC 82-20145. 124 p. 19cm. (The Chiller Series). c.1983. (ISBN 0-671-46282-2). Wanderer Books.

Taylor, Loren E., ed.
--Stunts and Skits. LC 65-771579. i, 112p. illus. 23cm. (Children's dramatics ser., 4) Bibl.). c.1965. Burgess.

Taylor, Lucy
--Going on Pilgrimage. N.D. Thos Nelson & Sons.

Taylor, Malcolm
--Knight of the Air. Pope, Allen, illus. LC 39-5014. 248 p. incl. front. plates. 21 1/2 cm. 1938. Houghton Mifflin Company.
--PX. Kidder, Harvey, illus. LC 43-4645. 4 p. l., 230, 1 p. front., plates. 21 1/2 cm. 1943. Houghton Mifflin Co.

Taylor, Margaret Stewart see Collier, Margaret, pseud.

Taylor, Margaret (1917-)
--Jasper, the Drummin' Boy. Taylor, Margaret (1917-), illus. LC 47-30242. 63 p. illus. 24 cm. 1947. The Viking Press.

Taylor, Margaret (1917-), ed.
--Did You Feed My Cow?. Rhymes and Games from City Streets and Country Lanes. Galdone, Paul (1914-), illus. LC 56-9798. 85 p. illus. 23 cm. 1956. Crowell.

Taylor, Mark, jt. ed. see Arbuthnot, May Hill.

Taylor, Mark (1927-)
--The Best Prize of All. LC 85-514. p. cm. (A Tale from the Care Bear Cousins). c.1985. (ISBN 0-910313-86-5). Parker Bros.
--Bobby Shafto's Gone to Sea. Booth, Graham Charles (1935-), illus. LC 76-119068. (Illus.). 48 p. 1970. Golden Gate Junior Books.
--The Bold Fisherman. Booth, Graham Charles (1935-), illus. LC 67-4401. (Illus.). 1 v. (unpaged). 26cm. 1967. Golden Gate Junior Books.
--The Case of the Missing Kittens. 1st ed. Booth, Graham Charles (1935-), illus. LC 78-4908. (Illus.). 48 p. 1978. (ISBN 0-689-30627-X). Atheneum.
--The Case of the Purloined Compass. Booth, Graham Charles (1935-), illus. LC 84-21517. (Illus.). 46 p. (Secret life of Angus). 1985. (ISBN 0-689-31104-4). Atheneum.
--The Great Rescue. Brett, Jan (1949-), illus. LC 83-25113. (Illus.). 44 p. 29cm. (Cabbage Patch Kids). c.1984. (ISBN 0-910313-28-8). Parker Bros.
--Henry Explores the Jungle. 1st ed. Booth, Graham Charles (1935-), illus. LC 68-18461. 1 v. (chiefly col. illus. 24cm. 1968. Atheneum.
--Henry Explores the Mountains. Booth, Graham Charles (1935-), illus. LC 74-19315. (Illus.). 48 p. 1975. (ISBN 0-689-30461-7). Atheneum.
--Henry, the Castaway. 1st ed. Booth, Graham Charles (1935-), illus. LC 72-75287. (Illus.). 47 p. 1972. (ISBN 0-689-30070-0). Atheneum.
--Henry, the Explorer. 1st ed. Booth, Graham Charles (1935-), illus. LC 66-9534. (Illus.). 1 v. (unpaged. 1966. Atheneum.
--Jennie Jenkins. 1st ed. Rounds, Glen Harold (1906-), illus. LC 74-16155. (Illus.). 43 p. 25cm. 1975. (ISBN 0-316-83357-6). Little, Brown.
--Lamb, Said the Lion, I Am Here. Siberell, Anne, illus. LC 75-157854. (Illus.). 48 p. 1971. (ISBN 0-87464-182-9). Golden Gate Junior Books.
--Lamb, Said the Lion, I Am Here. Siberell, Anne, illus. LC 75-157854. (Illus.). 48. 22 x 27cm. 1971. (ISBN 0-87464-182-9). Golden Gate Junior Books.
--Mr. Pepper Stories. Kincade, Nancy, illus. LC 83-15654. (Illus.). 96p. (gr. 1-4). 1984. (ISBN 0-689-31023-4). Atheneum.
--Old Blue: You Good Dog You. Holtan, Gene, illus. LC 72-97823. (Illus.). color ils. 48p. (gr. k up). 1970. (ISBN 0-516-08838-6, Golden Gate). Childrens.
--The Old Woman and the Pedlar. Booth, Graham Charles (1935-), illus. LC 69-15399. (Illus.). 47 p. 26cm. 1969. Golden Gate Junior Books.
--The Shyest Kid in the Patch. Munsinger, Lynn (1951-), illus. (Illus.). 40p. (Cabbage Patch Kids Ser.). (gr. 1-5). 1984. (ISBN 0-910313-30-X). Parker Bro.
--A Time for Flowers. Booth, Graham Charles (1935-), illus. LC 67-24935. (Illus.). 1 v. (unpaged. 26cm. 31p. 1967. Golden Gate Junior Books.
--The Winds' Child. 1st ed. Blegvad, Erik (1923-), illus. LC 72-86952. (Illus.). 47 p. 21cm. 1973. (ISBN 0-689-30121-9). Atheneum.
--Young Melvin and Bulger. 1st ed. Brett, Jan (1949-), illus. LC 79-7118. (Illus.). 44 p. 24cm. c.1981. (ISBN 0-385-15190-X). Doubleday.

Taylor, Mark (1927-), retold by
--The Fisherman and the Goblet: A Vietnamese Folk Tale. Yashima, Taro, pseud. (1908-), illus. Iwamatsu, Jun Atsushi. LC 70-120604. (Illus.). 30 p. 1971. (ISBN 0-87464-152-7). Golden Gate Junior Books.

Taylor, Marvin Merchant (1860-)
--Captain Rudder's Voyage, 36 vols. (Illus.). (St. Nicholas Ser.). 1905. Set. A L Burt Co.
--Captain Rudder's Voyage. (The Rugby Series for Boys and Girls). N.D. A. L. Burt.
--The Mogfoots. Very, Marjorie, illus. LC 21-970. 46 p., 1 l., col. front., illus., col. plates. 20 cm. c.1920. The Four Seas Company.

Taylor, Mary Imlay (0000-1938)
--Little Mistress Good Hope and Other Fairy Tales. Smith, Jessie Willcox (1863-1935), illus. LC 2-23834. 186 p., 1 l. incl. col. front., col. illus. 19 1/2 cm. 1902. A. C. McClurg and Company.

Taylor, Mildred D.
--Let the Circle Be Unbroken. LC 81-65854. 394 p. 22cm. c.1981. (ISBN 0-8037-4748-9). Dial Press. **Awards: (CSKA); (ALA).**
--Roll of Thunder, Hear My Cry. Pinkney, Jerry (1939-), illus. LC 76-2287. (Illus.). 276 p. 22cm. c.1976. (ISBN 0-8037-7473-7). Dial Press. **Awards: (JNM); (ALA); (BGH).**
--Song of the Trees. Pinkney, Jerry (1939-), illus. LC 74-18598. (Illus.). 48 p. 22cm. 1975. (ISBN 0-8037-5452-3). (ISBN 0-8037-5453-1). Dial Press.

Taylor, Molly
--Pepe from Flying Saucer Land & Pepe Makes a Friend. 1982. (ISBN 0-533-04839-7). Vantage.

Taylor, Morgan
--The Thrings of the Dark Mountain. Larson, Irene Mullen & Sichel, Harold M. (1881-), illus. LC 24-23138. 122 1 p. col. front., illus. 20 cm. 1924. Minton, Balch & Company.

Taylor, Norman Burke (1885-), retold by see Virgilius Maro, Publius.

Taylor, Patricia
--My Bedtime Book of Magic Carpet Stories from Many Lands. (gr. k-3). N.D. (ISBN 0-448-04108-1). G&D.
--Shaggy Finds His Collar. Sharpe, Caroline (1947-), illus. LC 74-184443. (Illus.). 18 p. (Whitman scratch-and-sniff book). 1972. Western Pub. Co.

Taylor, Paul Bartlett
--King Scramble. Taylor, Paul Bartlett, illus. LC 31-22914. (Illus.). 21.5 cm. 14p. 1931. Henry Holt & Co.
--Tippletappleteven Town. Taylor, Paul Bartlett, illus. LC 31-22800. (Illus.). 21.5 cm. 12p. 1931. Henry Holt & Co.

Taylor, Paul L., illus.
--Magic Riddle Book. (Illus.). pop-ups. acetates. 24p. (gr. k-3). 1969. (ISBN 0-394-81171-2). Random.

Taylor, Phoebe Atwood (1909-1976)
--The Deadly Sunshade: An Asey Mayo Mystery. LC 41-37. 297 p. 19 1/2 cm. c.1940. W. W. Norton & Co., Inc.

Taylor, Reginald
--Circus Triumphant. Weare, Tony, illus. LC 58-6445. 253 p. illus. 22 cm. (Criterion book for young people). 1958. Criterion Books.
--Circus Triumphant. Weare, Tony, illus. 1958. S G Phillips Inc.
--My Friend, My Enemy. LC 66-151651. 190p. 23cm. 1966, c.1965. Criterion.

Taylor, Ronald Ditz (1948-)
--The Book Where Michael Meets the Royal Street Elves and Learns About Whales and Whale Oil, the Electric Light, the Ostrich, and the Two-Headed Sea Serpent. Turner, Ellen, illus. LC 78-55985. (Illus.). 69 p. 26cm. c.1978. (ISBN 0-931604-00-1). Curbstone Press.

Taylor, Ross McLaury (1909-1977)
--We Were There on the Chisholm Trail. Vestal, Stanley, ed. Wilson, Charles Banks (1918-), illus. LC 57-10105. 176 p. illus. 24 cm. (We were there books, 14). 1957. Grosset & Dunlap.
--We Were There on the Santa Fe Trail. Webb, Walter Prescott (1913-), ed. Orbaan, Albert F. (1913-), illus. LC 60-16157. 176 p. illus. 22 cm. (We were there books, 29). 1960. (ISBN 0-448-05029-3). Grosset & Dunlap.

Taylor, Sally
--Mountain Express. Carr, Ed., illus. LC 81-52499. (Illus.). 28 p. 21cm. (Starters Stories.: Blue, No. 5). c.1981. (ISBN 0-382-06574-3). Silver Burdett Co.

Taylor, Sydney Brenner (1904-1978)
--All-of-a-Kind Family. John, Helen, illus. LC 72-204159. (Illus.). 188 p. 25cm. 1965, c.1951. Follett Pub. Co.
--All-of-a-Kind Family. John, Helen, illus. LC 51-13398. (Illus.). 192 p. 25cm. 1951. Wilcox and Follett.
--All-of-a-Kind Family Downtown. Krush, Beth (1918-) & Krush, Joe (1918-), illus. LC 70-184789. (Illus.). 187 p. 25cm. 1972. (ISBN 0-695-80308-5). (ISBN 0-695-80308-5). Follett.
--All-of-a-Kind Family Uptown. Stevens, Mary E. (1920-1966), illus. LC 58-7734. (Illus.). 160 p. 25cm. 1958. Follett Pub. Co.
--Danny Loves a Holiday. 1st ed. Owens, Gail, illus. LC 80-17065. p. cm. c.1980. (ISBN 0-525-28510-5). Dutton.
--Dog Who Came to Dinner. Johnson, John Emil (1929-), illus. (Illus.). (Beginning-to-Read Ser.). (gr. 1-3). 1966. (ISBN 0-695-42086-0, Dist. by Caroline Hse). (ISBN 0-695-32086-6). Modern Curr.
--Ella of All of a Kind Family. 1st ed. Owens, Gail, illus. LC 77-26991. (Illus.). 133 p. 24cm. c.1978. (ISBN 0-525-29238-1). Dutton.
--Mister Barney's Beard. Geer, Charles Hand (1922-), illus. LC 61-8811. (Illus.). (Follett beginning-to-read book). (gr. 1-3). 1961. (ISBN 0-695-86015-1). (ISBN 0-695-46015-3). Follett.
--More All-of-a-Kind Family. Stevens, Mary E. (1920-1966), illus. LC 54-10104. (Illus.). 159 p. 25cm. 1954. Follett Pub. Co.
--Now That You Are Eight. Fetz, Ingrid (1915-), illus. LC 63-7240. 56 p. illus. 21 cm. 1963. Association Press.
--A Papa Like Everyone Else. Porter, George, illus. LC 66-16942. (Illus.). 159 p. 23cm. 1966. Follett Pub. Co.

Taylor, T., Miss
--Cross in the Heart. (Illus.). N.D. Methodist book Concern.
--John Richmond: Or, A Sister's Love. (Illus.). N.D. Methodist Book concern.
--Marguerite: Or, the Huguenot Child. LC 12-39345. 188 p. 17 cm. 1870. Hitchcock and Walden.
--Marguerite: Or, The Huguenot Child. (Illus.). N.D. Methodist Book Concern.
--Marguerite: Or, the Huguenot Child. 188p. N.D. Nelson & Phillips.
Taylor, T. William
--The Christmas Donkey. Brooks, Andrea, illus. LC 83-82200. (Illus.). 24 p. 20cm. (Little Golden book). c.1984. (ISBN 0-307-04600-1). (ISBN 0-307-60242-7). Western Pub. Co.
Taylor, Talus, jt. auth. see Tison, Annette.
Taylor, Theodore, jt. auth. see Irigaray, Louis.
Taylor, Theodore (1922-)
--The Cay. LC 69-15161. 137 p. 22cm. 1969. Doubleday. **Award: (ALA).**
--The Children's War. LC 73-144304. 166 p. 22cm. 1971. Doubleday.
--The Maldonado Miracle. LC 74-180113. 189 p. 22cm. 1973. (ISBN 0-385-08456-0). (ISBN 0 385 08456 0). Doubleday.
--The Odyssey of Ben O'Neal. A Sequel to Teetoncey and Ben O'Neal and the Third Novel of a Cape Hatteras Trilogy by the Author of "The Cay". 1st ed. Cuffari, Richard (1925-1978), illus. LC 76-23800. (Illus.). 208 p. 22cm. c.1977. (ISBN 0-385-00166-5). (ISBN 0-385-00289-0). Doubleday.
--Sweet Friday Island. 160p. (gr. 7 up). 1984. (ISBN 0 590 33171 1, Point). Scholastic Inc.
--Teetoncey. 1st ed. Cuffari, Richard (1925-1978), illus. LC 73-13097. (Illus.). 153 p. 22cm. 1974. (ISBN 0-385-09584-8). (ISBN 0-385-09584-8). Doubleday.
--Teetoncey and Ben O'Neal. 1st ed. Cuffari, Richard (1925-1978), illus. LC 74-4875. (Illus.). 185 p. 22cm. 1975. (ISBN 0-385-06688-0). (ISBN 0-385-04504-2). Doubleday.
--The Trouble with Tuck. LC 81-43139. p. cm. 1981. (ISBN 0-385-17774-7). Doubleday.
Taylor, Tinker
--Uzz, Fuzz and Buzz. (Roundabout Ser.). N.D. D. Appleton & Co.
Taylor, Turney Allan, jt. auth. see Dwight, Allan.
Taylor, W. L.
--Dear Little Marchioness: The Story of a Child's Faith and Love. Taylor, W. L., illus. N.D. Thomas Crowell & Co.
Taylor, William M.
--The Lost Found and the Wanderer. New Ed. ed. N.D. Charles Scribner.
Taylor, Winifred
--Labors of Love: Or, The Story of Lucy's Work & What Came of It. (Illus.). N.D. Methodist Bk Concern.
--Loyal to Duty: A Tale for Girls. N.D. Henry A. Young.
Taymond, Walter
--A Tangled Web. 5x7 1/2cm. 342p. N.D. Doubleday, Page & Co.
Tazewell, Charles (1900-1972)
--Deluxe Littlest Angel. Reinert, Rick, illus. (Illus.). 48p. (gr. k-6). 1984. (ISBN 0-8249-8071-9). Ideals.
--I'm a Fridgit!. 1st ed. Langelier, Joyce, illus. LC 68-4241. (Illus.). 1 v. (unpaged. 29cm. 1963. Rolton House Publishers.
--The Littlest Angel. Evans, Katherine Floyd (1901-1964), illus. LC 47-214. 28 p. col. illus. 24 cm. 1946. Childrens Press.
--The Littlest Angel. Leone, Sergio, illus. LC 62-51371. unpaged. illus. 31 cm. 1962. Grosset & Dunlap.
--The Littlest Angel. Svensson, Borje, illus. Dudley, Dick, designed by. LC 85-158243. (Illus.). 10 p. 28cm. 1985, c.1964. (ISBN 0-8249-8098-0). Ideals Pub. Corp.
--The Littlest Snowman. Authorized. DeSantis, George, illus. Coronet LC 67-23811. 1v. (unpaged) col. illus. 29cm. 1967, c.1956. (ISBN 0-448-04225-8). Grosset.
--Littlest Stories. 1st ed. Langelier, Joyce, illus. LC 61-18008. unpaged. illus. 29 cm. 1962. Rolton House Publishers.
--The Littlest Stork. Evans, Katherine Floyd (1901-1964), illus. LC 53-11700. unpaged. illus. 17cm. (Family Bk.). 1953. Childrens Press.
--The Small One. Whitman, Franklin J., Jr., illus. 1947. Holt Rinehart & Winston.
--The Small One. Whitman, Franklin J., Jr., illus. LC 47-12453. 21cm. 32p. 1947. John C. Winston Co.
Tchaika, Florence Esther Matthews, Mrs. (1894-)
--Trouble at Beaver Dam. Rojankovsky, Feodor Stepanovich (1891-1970), illus. LC 53-10514. 63p. illus. 22cm. (Everyday science stories). 1953. J. Messner.
Tchaika, Florence Esther Matthews, Mrs. (1894-) & Coffin, Rebecca Jane, eds.
--City Stories Told by City Children As They Go Exploring in New York. Columbia University. Teachers College. Lincoln School Carter, Helene (1887-1960), illus. LC 28-27758. xi p., 1 l., 101 p. incl. front., illus., plates. 21 1/2 cm. 1928. The Macmillan Company.
Tchaikovsky, Peter Ilich (1840-1893)
--Nutcracker. Hori, Fumiko (1918-), illus. (Pictorial Fantasia Ser). (gr. 3-6). 1969. Silver.
--The Nutcracker: The Ballet. Shaw, Ray, retold by. Shaw, Ray, photos by. LC 78-114686. (Illus.). 32 p. 24cm. 1970. Prentice-Hall.
--Swan Lake. Hatsuyama, Shigeru, illus. (Pictorial Fantasia Ser). (gr. 3-6). 1969. Silver.
Tchaikovsky, Peter Ilich (1840-1893) & Hoffmann, Ernst Theodor Amadeus (1776-1822)
--P. I. Tchaikovsky's The Nutcracker. Kushida, Magoichi (1915-), ed. Hori, Fumiko (1918-), illus. Herring, Ann King (1918-), tr. LC 75-94811. (Illus.). 28 p. (Fantasia pictorial, 8). 1971. Gakken.
Tchaikovsky, Peter Ilyich, jt. auth. see Bednar, Kamil.
Tchaikovsky, Peter Ilyich, jt. auth. see Chappell, Warren.
Tchakmakian, Pascal
--Breezy, the Rebel Bird: A Fairy Tale for All Ages. (ps up). 1971. (ISBN 0-682-47261-1). Exposition.
Tchudi, Stephen N
--The Burg-O-Rama Man. LC 82-14075. 184 p. 22cm. c.1983. (ISBN 0-440-00833-6). Delacorte Press.
Teachers & Writers Collaborative
--Five Tales of Adventure: A Collection of Stories by Children. (Orig.). 1975. (ISBN 0-915924-04-8). Tchrs & Writers Coll.
Teague, Bob, pseud., see Teague, Robert.
Teague, Bob, pseud. (1929-)
--Adam in Blunderland. Teague, Robert. 1st ed. Sowell, Floyd (1929-), illus. LC 76-144231. (Illus.). 118 p. 25cm. 1971. Doubleday.
--Agent K-Thirteen, the Super Spy. Teague, Robert. Moss, Geoffrey, illus. LC 73-19486. p. 1974. (ISBN 0-385-08704-7). (ISBN 0-385-08704-7). (ISBN 0-385-08704-7). Doubleday.
--Super-Spy K-Thirteen in Outer Space. Teague, Robert. 1st ed. McLean, Sammis, illus. LC 79-7213. (Illus.). 48 p. 27cm. c.1980. (ISBN 0-385-14314-1). (ISBN 0-385-14315-X). Doubleday.
Teague, Elizabeth
--A Book of Teddy Bears, Brown Bears, White Bears, Gruff Bears, Kind Bears, He-Bears, She-Bears & Very Little Furry Bears. (gr. 1-3) 1976. (ISBN 0-8277-4660-1). British Bk Ctr.
Teague, Kathleen (1937-)
--What Happened to Hector?. Del Rossi, Ric, illus. LC 73-22078. (Illus.). 32 p. 23cm. 1974. (ISBN 0-8116-6050-8). Garrard Pub. Co.
Teague, Robert see Teague, Bob, pseud.
Teahan, James T, jt. auth. see Collodi, Carlo.
Teal, Evelyn Dangberg
--Riding the Danger Trail. Lantz, Paul (1908-), illus. LC 61-8573. 133 p. illus. 21 cm. (Wonderful World Bk.). 1961. Barnes.
--Whirling Riatas: A Story of Early California Near the End of the Spanish Period. Teal, Evelyn Dangberg, illus. LC 57-36780. 141 p. illus. 20 cm. 1957. Naylor Co.
Teal, Mildred
--Bird of Passage. 1st ed. Lewin, Ted (1935-), illus. LC 76-54278. (Illus.). 109 p. 22cm. c.1977. (ISBN 0-316-83452-1). Little, Brown.
--The Flight of the Kite Merriweather. 1st ed. Van De Bovenkamp, Valli, illus. LC 68-26670. (Illus.). 87 p. 18cm. 1968. Atheneum.
Teal, Thomas, tr. see Ericson, Stig.
Teal, Thomas, tr. see Jansson, Tove.
Teal, Valentine M. (1903-)
--Angel Child. Doane, Pelagie (1906-1966), illus. LC 65-15344. 1 v. (unpaged) col. illus. 33 cm. 1965. R. MacNally.
--Angel Child. Doane, Pelagie (1906-1966), illus. LC 46-8468. (Illus.). 40p. 2cm. 1946. Rand McNally & Company.
--The Little Woman Wanted Noise. Lawson, Robert (1892-1957), illus. LC 43-43736. 40p. illus. 24cm. 1967, c.1943. Rand McNally.
Teale, Edwin Way (1899-1980)
--Lost Dog. (Illus.). (gr. 4-6). 1961. (ISBN 0-8382-0485-6). Hale.
--The Lost Dog. Lantz, Paul (1908-), illus. 63p. 1961. Dodd, Mead & Co.
Teall, Edna A. W., Mrs.
--The Batter and Spoon Fairies. Whittemore, Constance, illus. LC 29-4324. xii p., 1 l., 279, 1 p. incl. front., illus., plates. 21 1/2 cm. 1929. Harper & Brothers.
Teasdale, Sara (1884-1933)
--Stars To-Night. Lathrop, Dorothy Pulis (1891-1980), illus. (Illus.). (gr. 4-6). 1930. (ISBN 0-02-789090-2). Macmillan.
Teasdale, Sara (1884-1933), ed.
--Rainbow Gold: Poems Old and New Selected for Boys and Girls. Walker, Dugald Stewart (1888-1937), illus. LC 73-4877. p. (Granger index reprint series). 1973. (ISBN 0-8369-6422-5). Books for Libraries Press.
--Rainbow Gold: Poems Old and New Selected for Boys and Girls. Walker, Dugald Stewart (1888-1937), illus. LC 78-74828. (Illus.). 267 p., 1 leaf of plates. 20cm. (Granger Poetry Library). 1979. (ISBN 0-89609-148-1). Granger Book Co.
--Rainbow Gold: Poems Old and New Selected for Boys and Girls. Walker, Dugald Stewart (1888-1937), illus. LC 22-18833. 3 p. l., 5-267 p. incl. illus., plates, col. front. 21 cm. 1922. The Macmillan Company.
Tashranchian, Hassan, adapted by.
--Kaliiah and Dimnah: Fables fron the Ancient East. Ur, Anatole, illus. 1985 (Harmony). Crown.
Tedder, Elizabeth, illus.
--Litle Red Riding Hood. LC 38-18602. 16 p. illus. (part col.) 27 x 25 cm. c.1938. Grosset & Dunlap.
--Little Red Riding Hood. LC 38-18602. (Illus.). 26 x 24cm. 16p. 1938. Grosset & Dunlop.
Tedford, Jack
--Complete Book of Family Fun & Games. King, Robin, pseud. (1919-), illus. Raleigh-King, Robin Victor Lethbridge. (Illus.). (gr. 7 up). 1958. (ISBN 0-531-01645-5). Watts.
Tedrick, W. R.
--Operation Groundhog. N.D. Carlton Press.
Tee-Van, Helen Damrosch (1893-1976)
--Red Howling Monkey: The Tale of a South American Indian Boy. Tee-Van, Helen Damrosch (1893-1976), illus. LC 26-15971. (Illus.). 21cm. 142p. 1926. Macmillan.
Teegarden, George M
--Stories, Old and New. Teegarden, George M., illus. LC 8-25960. 2 p. l., 223 p. illus. 24 cm. 1896. Printed at the Institution for the Deaf.
Teen
--The Bananas Yearbook Nineteen-Seventynine. N.D. (ISBN 0-590-12078-6, Schol Pap). Scholastic Inc.
Teeters, Helen, jt. auth. see Hardy, Marjorie.
Tefft, Bess Hagaman (1915-1977)
--Ken of Centennial Farm. Marsh, William, illus. LC 59-10272. 127 p. illus. 23 cm. 1959. Follett Pub. Co.
--Merrie Maple. Tefft, Bess Hagaman (1915-1977), illus. LC 58-5235. 187 p. illus. 21 cm. 1958. Dutton.
Tegner, Esais, jt. auth. see Ragozin, Zenaide Alexeievna.
Teibl, Margaret
--Davey Come Home. Smith, Jacqueline Bardner, illus. LC 78-22477. (Illus.). 60 p. 21cm. c.1979. (ISBN 0-06-026135-8). (ISBN 0-06-026136-6). Harper & Row.
Teicher, Elizabeth
--April's Year. N.D (W. W. Norton Juveniles For Children). Grosset & Dunlap Pub.
--April's Year. LC 66-107921. 174p. 21cm. c.1966. Norton.
--The Loves of April. (gr. 9-12). 1974. (ISBN 0-88451-053-0). Edco-Vis Assoc.
Teichner, Miriam
--The Knitting Grasshopper. Cooke, Dorothea, illus. LC 37-25340. 3 p. l., 3-144 p., 1 l. col. illus. 21 cm. c.1937. H. Holt and Company.
Teichner, Miriam, jt. auth. see Hoke, Helen L., Mrs.
Teilhet, Darwin Le Ora see Fisher, Cyrus, pseud.
Teilhet, Darwin Le Ora see Fisher, Cyrus T., pseud.
Teilhet, Darwin Le Ora (1904-)
--The Avion My Uncle Flew. Fisher, Cyrus, pseud. Floethe, Richard (1901-), illus. LC 46-25154. (Illus.). xi,244. 20cm. 1946. Appleton-Century Company Inc.
--The Hawaiian Sword. Fisher, Cyrus T., pseud. LC 56-10704. 198 p. illus. 22 cm. (gr. 7-11). 1956. Funk & Wagnalls.
Teilhet, Darwin Le Ora (1904-) & Teilhet, Hildegarde Tolman
--Skwee-Gee. Gramatky, Hardie (1907-1979), illus. LC 40-32787. 40 p. illus. (part col.) 26 1/2 x 21 cm. 1940. Doubleday, Doran & Company, Inc.
Teilhet, Hildegarde Tolman, jt. auth. see Teilhet, Darwin Le Ora.
Teitelbaum, Michael
--The Cave of the Lost Fraggle. Elwell, Peter, illus. LC 84-18939. (Illus.). 32 p. 22cm. c.1985. (ISBN 0-03-004554-1). Holt, Rinehart, and Winston.
--Gremlins: To Catch a Gremlin. Dominguez, Luis, illus. LC 83-83379. (Illus.). (ps). 1984. (ISBN 0-307-11373-6, Golden Bks). Western Pub.
Teixeira de Mattos, Alexander Louis (1863-1921), tr. see Fabre, Jean Henri Casimir.
Teixeira De Mattos, Alexander Louis (1865-1921), tr. see Maeterlinck, Maurice.
Teixeira De Mattos, Alexander Louis (1865-1921), tr. see Ewald, Carl.
Teixeria de Mattos, Alexander Louis (1865-1921), tr. see Ewald, Carl.
Telefriend Inc., illus.
--Bang...Bang...You're Not Really Dead. (Living Skills Bks.: No. 008). N.D. (ISBN 0-685-86217-8). Word Bks.
--Tattletale. (Living Skills Books: 002). N.D. (ISBN 0-685-86213-5). Word Bks.
Telemaque, Eleanor Wong (1934-)
--It's Crazy to Stay Chinese in Minnesota. LC 78-14054. 118 p. 21cm. c.1978. (ISBN 0-8407-6613-0). T. Nelson.
Tell, Sharon
--Mini Value Plays. (gr. 2-3). 1977. (ISBN 0-933892-07-1). Child Focus Co.
Tellenback, Margrit H. see Haubensak-Tellenback, Margrit.
Teller, Thomas, pseud., see Tuttle, George.
Teller, Thomas, pseud. (1804-1872), ed.
--Stories about Whale Catching. Tuttle, George. LC 5-32990. 15 x 11cm. 64p. (Teller's Instructive and Entertaining Tales). 1845. S. Babcock.
Temes, Roberta
--The Empty Place. 50p. (gr. 1-6). 1984. (ISBN 0-8290-1345-8). Irvington.
Temkin, Sara Anne Schlossberg (1913-) & Hovell, Lucy A. (1916-)
--Jimmy Williams: Library Assistant. LC 62-10199. (Career Romance Ser.). (gr. 7 up). 1962. (ISBN 0-671-74070-9). Messner.
Temko, Florence
--Come to My House, No. 7236. Lawrence, Leslie & Weingartner, Ronald, eds. Denis, Sandra, illus. (Illus.). 32p. (Bright Beginnings II Ser.). (gr. k-4). 1982. (ISBN 0-88049-003-9). Milton Bradley Co.
--Let's Go for a Ride, No. 7236. Lawrence, Leslie & Weingartner, Ronald, eds. Denis, Sandra, illus. (Illus.). 32p. (Bright Beginnings II Ser.). (gr. k-4). 1982. (ISBN 0-88049-002-0). Milton Bradley Co.
Tempest, Margaret Mary (1892-1982) & Fryer, Kathleen
--Favourite Bible Stories. Brock, Charles Edmond (1870-1938) & Brock, Henry Matthew (1875-1960), illus. (gr. 2-4). N.D. (ISBN 0-00-135151-6). W Collins.
Temple, Crona
--Dick's Water-Lilies and other Stories (Pub. by Society for PromotingChristian Knowledge). N.D. E. & J. B. Young & Co.
--The Ferryman's Boy & Other Stories. (Illus.). N.D. Thomas Nelson & Sons.
--Kristy's Prince. N.D. E J B Young & Co.
--Nobody Cares. (Illus.). N.D. D Lothrop & Co.
--Wavie, the Foundling. (Illus.). (Child Life Ser.). N.D. D. Lothrop Co.
Temple, Crona, jt. auth. see Smith, Frances Burge, Mrs.
Temple, Crona, jt. auth. see Smith, Frances Burge, Mrs.
Temple, Peggy (1913-)
--The Admiral and Others. Pyke, Eliza, illus. Adcock, St. John, frwd. by. LC 27-4382. x, 138 p. illus. 19 1/2 cm. c.1927. E. P. Dutton & Company.
Temple, R. C., jt. ed. see Steel, Flora Annie Webster, Mrs.
Temple, Shirley (1928-), selected by.
--Shirley Temple Treasury. PAtterson, Robert (1899-), illus. LC 59-9739. (Illus.). 29cm. 202p. (gr. 1-7). 1959. (ISBN 0-394-80759-6). Random.
--Shirley Temple's Bedtime Book. Miller, John Parr (1913-), illus. LC 62-7889. 91p. col. illus. 33cm. c.1962. (ISBN 0-394-80757-X). Random.
--Shirley Temple's Nursery Tales. Miller, John Parr (1913-), illus. LC 61-15089. unpaged. col. illus. 33cm. c.1961. Random House.
--Shirley Temple's Storytime Favorites. Miller, John Parr (1913-), illus. LC 62-7892. unpaged. illus. 33 cm. 1962. (ISBN 0-394-80682-4). Random House.
Temple, Willard Henry (1912-)
--The Drip Dried Tourist. 1969. (ISBN 0-399-10225-6). G. P. Putnam's Sons.
--Pitching for Pawling. Gilmore, H. H., illus. LC 40-100854. 6 p. l., 3-267 p. illus. 19 1/2 cm. c.1940. Farrar & Rinehart, Inc.
--The Rebel of Pawling. Robison, Robert S., illus. LC 39-305353. 7 p. l., 3-274 p. illus. 19 1/2 cm. c.1939. Farrar & Rinehart, Inc.
--Web Adams. Logan, Dwight, illus. LC 43-3657. 4 p. l., 199 p. illus. 22 cm. 1943. C. Scribner's Sons.
Templeton, Faith, pseud., see Barber, Harriet Boomer.
Templeton, Faith, pseud.
--Wrecked, Not Lost. Barber, Harriet Boomer. (The Happy Library). N.D. Thomas Nelson & Sons.
Templeton, June
--Tales of Singing Brook Hill. Templeton, June, illus. LC 62-12277. 55 p. illus. 21 cm. 1962. Christopher Pub. House.

Templeton, Larry D.
--The Stars of Childsland. Templeton, Larry D., illus. (Illus.). 22p. (gr. k-3). 1982. (ISBN 0-9608914-0-4). Templeton.

Templeton, Lee
--Columbus' Cabin Boy. (Illus.). 192p. 1983. (ISBN 0-89015-372-8). Eakin Pubns.
--The Mountain Boy. 115p. 1983. (ISBN 0-89015-370-1). Eakin Pubns.

Tempski, Armine von (1899-)
--Born in Paradise. LC 84-27345. 342p (Pub. by Hawthorn Books Inc.). 1985. (ISBN 0-918024-34-X). Ox Bow.
--Judy of the Islands: A Story of the South Seas. Burger, Carl Victor (1888-1967), illus. LC 41-16069. (Illus.). 21 x 16cm. 1941. Dodd, Mead.
--Pam's Paradise Ranch: A/Story of Hawaii. Brown, Paul (1893-1958), illus. LC 40-14201. (Illus.). 333p. 21 x 16cm. 1940. Dodd, Mead.

Tenaille, Marie, jt. auth. see Bergeret, Annie.

Ten Boom, Corrie see Boom, Corrie Ten.

Tench, Mary F. A.
--Madge and Her Friends: Or, Living unto Others, 1 of 6 vols. (Illus.). 230p. (The Evening Hour Library). N.D. Cassell, Petter, Galpin.

Tene, Benjamin
--In the Shade of the Chestnut Tree. Sigberman, Richard, illus. (gr. 6-9). 1981. Jewish Publication Society.

Ten Eyck, Mary Dodge
--College Days at the Manor. LC 30-10610. 284 p. front. 19 cm. 1930. Benziger Brothers.
--Daughters of the Manor. LC 29-226871. 175 p. front. 19 cm. 1929. Benziger Brothers.
--Li'l' Black Judy. LC 30-32138. 223 p. 17 cm. 1930. The Mission Press.

Tenfjord, Jo, pseud., see Tenfjord, Johanne Marie Giaever.

Tenfjord, Johanne Marie Giaever see Holm, Hanneho, pseud.

Tenfjord, Johanne Marie Giaever see Tenfjord, Jo, pseud.

Tenfjord, Johanne Marie Giaever (1918-)
--Beauty Queen. Holm, Hannebo, pseud. Crampton, Patricia, tr. LC 61-15711. 159 p. 21 cm. 1962, c.1961. Abelard-Schuman.
--A Husband for Hannah. Holm, Hannebo, pseud. Crampton, Patricia, tr. LC 63-8231. 159 p. 21 cm. 1963. Abelard-Schuman.
--Olav's Potato Field. Tenfjord, Jo, pseud. Vestal, Herman B., illus. LC 68-13062. (Illus.). 32 p. 27cm. (Our world of people series, Norway). 1968. Silver Burdett Co.

Tenggren, Gustaf (1896-1970)
--Bedtime Stories. Tenggren, Gustaf (1896-1970), illus. (Re-issued) (1959) Little Golden Book). Reissue of 1955 ed. (Little Golden Book). N.D. Golden Press.
--Bedtime Stories. Tenggren, Gustaf (1896-1970), illus. LC 42-24230. 42 p. illus. (part col.) 20 1/2 x 17 1/2 cm. (On cover: The Little golden library. 2). 1942. Simon and Schuster, Inc.
--Five Bedtime Stories. Tenggren, Gustaf (1896-1970), illus. (Giant Little Golden Book). 1957. Golden Press.
--Tenggren's Three of a Kind. Tenggren, Gustaf (1896-1970), illus. LC 73-76031. (Illus.). 64p. (gr. k-2). 1973. (ISBN 0-307-68003-7, Golden Pr). (ISBN 0-307-18003-4). Western Pub.

Tenggren, Gustaf (1896-1970), ed.
--The Good Dog Book: About Rab, Patrasche, Stickeen, Scally, Barry, and Other Dogs. Tenggren, Gustaf (1896-1970), illus. LC 24-23305. 4 p. l., 3-264 p. col. front., illus., col. plates. 22 cm. (Riverside bookshelf). 1924. Houghton Mifflin Company.
--New Illustrated Book of Favorite Hymns. Tenggren, Gustaf (1896-1970), illus. N.D. Garden City Publishing Co.
--The Tenggren Mother Goose. Tenggren, Gustaf (1896-1970), illus. (Illus.). (Reissue). (ps up). 1956. (ISBN 0-316-83723-7). Little.
--Tenggren's Folk Tales. Tenggren, Gustaf (1896-1970), illus. (Illus.). 64p. (gr. k-2). 1973. (ISBN 0-307-68005-3, Golden Pr). (ISBN 0-307-18005-0). Western Pub.
--Tenggren's Jack and the Beanstalk. Tenggren, Gustaf (1896-1970), illus. (Little Golden Book: 179). 1954. Simon and Schuster.
--Tenggren's Story Book. Tenggren, Gustaf (1896-1970), illus. (Big Golden Book). 1955. Golden Press.
--Tenggren's Story Book. Tenggren, Gustaf (1896-1970), illus. LC 49-5038. (Illus.). 67p. 29cm. (A Big Golden Bk.). 1949, c.1948. Simon and Schuster.
--Tenggren's Story Book: Favorite Stories from Arabian Nights, Dr. Doolittle, Gulliver's Travels, Heidi, Rip Van Winkle, Robin Hood, Robinson Crusoe, Rootabaga Stories, Tom Sawyer, Treasure Island, and Uncle Remus. Tenggren, Gustaf (1896-1970), illus. LC 44-6799. 87, 2 p. illus. (part col.) 33 x 26 cm. 1944. Simon and Schuster.

Ten Harmsel, Henrietta (1921-), tr. see Schmidt, Annie M. G.

Tennant, Kylie, pseud., see Rodd, Kylie Tennant.

Tennant, Kylie, pseud. (1912-)
--All the Proud Tribesmen. Rodd, Kylie Tennant. Seale, Clem, illus. LC 60-8982. (Illus.). 159 p. 21cm. 1960. St. Martin's Press.

Tennant, Veronica (1947-)
--On Stage, Please: A Story. Briansky, Rita, illus. LC 79-4819. (Illus.). 176 p. 22cm. 1979, c.1977. (ISBN 0-03-049306-4). Holt, Rinehart, and Winston.

Tenniel, John, Sir, jt. auth. see Dodgson, Charles Lutwidge.

Tenniel, John, Sir (1820-1914), illus.
--Mother Goose's Complete Melodies. (Illus.). 288p. N.D. Donohue, Henneberry & Co.

Tennis, M. H.
--Santa at the Zoo. 1st ed. McLmyre, John G., illus. LC 53-13120. unpaged. illus. 29cm. N.D. Pageant Press.

Tenny, Dixie
--Call the Darkness Down. LC 83-15484. 204p. (gr. 7up). 1984. (ISBN 0-689-50289-3, McElderry Bks). Atheneum.

Tennyson, Alfred Lord (1809-1892)
--Christmas Eve. (Illus.). (Golden Thoughts Series- Silk Vellum). N.D. BArse and Hopkins.
--Idylls of the King. 1939. Macmillan.
--The Lady of Shalott. Watts, Anna Bernadette (1942-), illus. LC 70-736. (Illus.). 32 p. 26cm. 1968. F. Watts.
--The Story of the Idylls of the King. McFee, Inez Nellie Canfield, Mrs., ed. Kirk, Maria Louise (1860-), illus. N.D. Frederick A. Stokes.
--Tales from Tennyson. N.D. A. L. Burt's Pubs.
--Tales from Tennyson, 11 vols. New ed. Bellew, Molly K., ed. Campbell, H. S., illus. (Illus.). (Six to Sixteen Ser.: No. 3). 1905. Set. H M Caldwell Co.
--Tales from Tennyson. Bellew, Molly K., ed. Campbell, H. S., illus. LC 2-22851. 155 p. incl. front., illus. 20cm. 1902. Jamieson-Higgins Co.
--The Young People's Tennyson. Rolfe, William James (1827-1920), ed. LC 29-27733. (Illus.). 17cm. 118p. (The Student's Series of Standard Poetry). 1886. Ticknor & Co.

Tennyson, Alfred Lord (1809-1892) & Malory, Thomas, Sir (0000-1471)
--The Children's King Arthur. (Stories from Tennyson and Malory). (Illus.). N.D. George H. Doran.

Tennyson, Margaret
--The Silver Secret. Sweet, Valerie, illus. LC 59-8060. 223 p. illus. 21 cm. (New venture library). 1959. F. Warne.

Tennyson, Noel, illus.
--Christmas Carols: A Treasury of Holiday Favorites with Words & Pictures. LC 83-60412. (Illus.). 24p. (gr. 1-5). 1983. (ISBN 0-394-86125-6). Random.
--Santa Is Coming. LC 80-54768. (Illus.). 24p. (Shape Bks.). (ps-k). 1981. (ISBN 0-394-84797-0). Random.

Tenpas, Margaret Susan Lyon (1923-)
--The Bridge to Blue Hill. Inderieden, Nancy, illus. LC 76-171067. (Illus.). 32 p. 1972. (ISBN 0-87614-030-4). Carolrhoda Books.

Tensen, Ruth Marjorie
--Come to See the Clowns. Dengel, Dianne, illus. (Illus.). 1963. (ISBN 0-8092-8776-5). (ISBN 0-685-19806-5). Contemp Bks.
--Come to the City. (Illus.). (ps-3). 1951. (ISBN 0-8092-8797-8). Contemp Bks.
--Come to the Farm. (Illus.). (ps-3). 1949. (ISBN 0-8092-8795-1). Contemp Bks.
--Come to the Zoo. (Illus.). (ps-3). 1948. (ISBN 0-8092-8793-5). Regnery.

Terban, Marvin
--Eight Ate: A Feast of Homonym Riddles. Maestro, Giulio (1942-), illus. LC 81-12203. (Illus.). 64 p. 24cm. c.1982. (ISBN 0-89919-067-7). Clarion Books.
--Poochie & Guff. Gantz, David, illus. (Illus.). 16p. (Golden Fuzzy Shape Bks.). (ps). 1983. (ISBN 0-307-25793-2, Golden Pr). Western Pub.
--Poochie & Slomo. Williams, A., illus. (Illus.). 16p. (Golden Fuzzy Shape Bks.). (ps). 1983. (ISBN 0-307-25795-9, Golden Pr). Western Pub.
--Poochie-Balloon Ride. Gantz, David, illus. (Illus.). 16p. (Golden Fuzzy Shape Bks.). (ps). 1983. (ISBN 0-307-25794-0, Golden Pr). Western Pub.
--Too Hot to Hoot: Funny Palindrome Riddles. Maestro, Giulio (1942-), illus. LC 84-14942. (Illus.). 64 p. 24cm. c.1985. (ISBN 0-89919-319-6). Clarion Books.

Teresah, pseud., see Ubertis-Gray, Corinna Teresa.

Ter Haar, Jaap see Haar, Jaap Ter.

Terhune, Albert Payson, jt. auth. see Thorne, Diana.

Terhune, Albert Payson (1872-1942), ed. see London, Jack.

Terhune, Albert Payson (1872-1942)
--The Best-Loved Dog Stories. 274 p. 20cm. 1954, c.1957. (ISBN 0-448-00970-6). Grosset & Dunlap.
--Bruce. LC 20-767455. 5 p. l., 204 p. 19 1/2cm. c.1920. E. P. Dutton & Company.
--Bruce. N.D. Grosset & Dunlap.

--Buff; a Collie and Other Dog Stories. LC 21-14546. vii p., 1 l., 11-341 p. front. 19 1/2cm. c.1921. George H. Doran Company.
--Buff: a Collie and other Dog-Stories. (Illus.). 341 p. 20cm. 1961, c.1921. (ISBN 0-448-00971-4). Grosset & Dunlap.
--Collie to the Rescue. (Illus.). 215 p. 20cm. 1952, c.1940. Grosset & Dunlap.
--The Critter and Other Dogs. 352 p. 20cm. 1961, c.1936. Grosset & Dunlap.
--A Dog Named Chips. LC 31-5062. 5 p. l., 267 p. 19 1/2cm. 1931. Harper & Brothers.
--A Dog Named Chips: The Life and Adventures of a Mongrel Scamp. 267 p. 20cm. 1961, c.1931. Grosset & Dunlap.
--Dog of the High Sierras. (Illus.). 210 p. 20cm. 1961, c.1924. Grosset & Dunlap.
--Dog Stories Every Child Should Know. LC 42-10323. 3 p. l., 13-341 p. col. front. 19 1/2cm. (What every child should know library. 3d ser.). N.D. Pub. by Doubleday, Doran & Co., Inc., for the Parent's Institute, Inc.
--Dogs. Wiese, Kurt (1887-1974), illus. LC 40-14816. 2 p. l., 9-60. 1 p. col. front., illus. 28 x 22 1/2cm. c.1940. The Saalfield Publishing Company.
--Faith of a Collie. N.D. Grosset & Dunlap.
--Further Adventures of Lad. (Illus.). 341 p. 20cm. 1961, c.1922. Grosset & Dunlap.
--Further Adventures of Lad. Bull, Charles Livingston (1874-1932), illus. LC 22-26765. 341 p. col. front. 19 1/2cm. c.1922. George H. Doran Company.
--Gray Dawn. (Illus.). 246 p. 20cm. 1961, c.1927. Grosset & Dunlap.
--Gray Dawn. LC 27-4668. 6 p. l., 369 p. front., col. plates. 19 1/2cm. 1927. Harper & Brothers.
--Gray Dawn. 216 p. 18cm. (Perennial library. P69A). 1965, c.1927. Harper & Row.
--The Heart of a Dog. Goodenow, Girard, illus. LC 57-2508. (Illus.). 224 p. 22cm. 1957. Junior Deluxe Editions.
--The Heart of a Dog. Kirmse, Marguerite (1885-1954), illus. LC 47-235862. 5 p. l., 221 p., 1 l. illus. 20 1/2 cm. (Young moderns). 1947, c.1924. Doubleday & Company, Inc.
--The Heart of a Dog. Kirmse, Marguerite (1885-1954), illus. LC 34-9214. 249 p., 1 l. incl. col. front., illus., col. plates. 22 1/2cm. 1933. Garden City Publishing Company, Incorporated.
--The Heart of a Dog. Kirmse, Marguerite (1885-1954), illus. LC 24-221441. 249 p., 1 l. incl. mounted col. front., illus., mounted col. plates. 23 1/2cm. c.1924. George H. Doran Company.
--The Heart of a Dog. Kirmse, Marguerite (1885-1954), illus. LC 37-14578. 249 p., 1 l. incl. col. front., illus. col. plates. 21 1/2cm. 1937. The Sun Dial Press, Inc.
--Highland Collie. N.D. (ISBN 0-448-00979-X). G&D.
--His Dog. LC 22-8429. 5 p. l., 183 p. front. 19 1/2cm. c.1922. E. P. Dutton & Company.
--Lad. LC 19-7304. 5 p. l., 349 p. front. 19 1/2cm. c.1919. E. P. Dutton & Company.
--Lad. 189p. Repr. 1981. (ISBN 0-89967-022-9). Harmony & Co.
--Lad. Dickey, Robert Livingston (1861-), illus. LC 26-19754. ix p., 1 l., 371 p. front., illus., plates. 21 cm. 1926. E. P. Dutton & Company.
--Lad, a Dog. Koral, Bella, adapted by. Bartlett, William & Elgin, Kathleen (1923-), illus. LC 53-2573. unpaged, illus. 34 cm. (Big treasure books). c.1953. Grosset & Dunlap.
--Lad, a Dog. Anniversary ed. Savitt, Sam (1917-), illus. LC 59-16396. 286 p. illus. 21 cm. 1959. Dutton.
--Lad: A Dog. Savitt, Sam (1917-), illus. (Anniversary ed.). (Illus.). (gr. 6 up). 1967. Dutton.
--Lad, a Dog. Sutton, Felix (1910-), adapted by. Bartlett, William & Elgin, Kathleen (1923-), illus. LC 57-14076. 61 p. illus. 29 cm. c.1957. Grosset & Dunlap.
--Lad of Sunnybank. N.D. Grosset & Dunlap.
--Lad of Sunnybank. LC 29-18203. 5 p. l., 322 p., 1 l. front. 19 1/2cm. 1929. Harper & Brothers.
--Lochinvar Luck. (Illus.). 309 p. 20cm. 1961, c.1923. Grosset & Dunlap.
--Lochinvar Luck. Stinemetz, Morgan, illus. LC 23-3458. 309 p. col. front. 19 1/2cm. c.1923. George H. Doran Company.
--My Friend the Dog. (Illus.). 317 p. 20cm. 1961, c.1926. Grosset & Dunlap.
--My Friend the Dog. Kirmse, Marguerite (1885-1954), illus. LC 26-19286. 6 p. l., 3-317 p. col. mounted front., illus., col. mounted plates. 24cm. 1926. Harper & Brothers.
--Rags. (Famous Dog Stories). N.D. Grosset & Dunlap.
--Real Tales of Real Dogs. Thorne, Diana (1894-), illus. LC 35-17388. 3 p. l., 11-92 p. front., plates. 30 1/2cm. c.1935. The Saalfield Publishing Company.
--Sunnybank: Home of Lad. N.D. Grosset & Dunlap.
--The Terhune Omnibus. Herzberg, Max, ed. N.D. Harper & Bros.

--Treve. LC 24-4361. 312 p. front. 19 1/2cm. c.1924. George H. Doran Company.
--Treve. (Illus.). 312 p. 20cm. 1961, c.1924. Grosset & Dunlap.
--The Way of a Dog: Being the Further Adventures of Gray Dawn and Some Others. LC 51-54219. 334 p. illus.20 cm. 1934, c.1932. Grosset & Dunlap.
--The Way of a Dog: Being the Further Adventures of Gray Dawn and Some Others. LC 32-7812. 5 p. l., 334 p. col. front., illus. 19 1/2cm. 1932. Harper & Brothers.
--Wolf. LC 25-10497. vii p., 1 l., 11-236 p. 19 1/2cm. c.1925. George H. Doran Company.
--Wolf. N.D. Grosset & Dunlap.

Terhune, Mary Virginia Hawes see Harland, Marion, pseud.

Terhune, Mary Virginia Hawes, Mrs. (1830-1922)
--The Christmas Holly. Harland, Marion, pseud. LC 21-3526. (Illus.). 22cm. 86p. 1867. Sheldon & Co.
--An Old-Field School Girl. Harland, Marion, pseud. N.D. Charles Scribner's Sons.
--When Grandmamma Was Fourteen. Harland, Marion, pseud. Barry, Etheldred Breeze (1870-), illus. LC 5-21569. (Illus.). 20cm. 399p. 1905. Lothrop Lee & Shepard Co.
--When Grandmamma Was New: The Story of a Virginia Childhood. Harland, Marion, pseud. LC 99-3091. 305 p. front, illus., plates. 19 1/2 cm. c.1899. Lothrop Publishing Company.
--When Grandmamma Was New: The Story of a Virginia Girlhood in the "Forties". Harland, Marion, pseud. (Illus.). N.D. Lothrop Lee & Shepard Co.

Terlouw, Jan Cornelis (1931-)
--How to Become King. LC 77-12471. (Illus.). 128 p. 24cm. 1977, c.1971. (ISBN 0-8038-3039-4). Hastings House.
--Winter in Wartime. LC 75-41345. (Illus.). 197 p. 21cm. 1976. (ISBN 0-07-063504-8). McGraw-Hill.

Terman, Douglas (1933-)
--By Balloon to the Sahara. Granger, Paul, illus. LC 81-2298. p. cm. (Choose Your Own Adventure). 1981, c.1979. (ISBN 0-13-109652-4). Prentice-Hall.

Terrel, Mary Field, Mrs.
--Bird-House to Let. Terrel, Mary Field, Mrs., illus. LC 31-234739. 8 p. l., 146 p. illus. 19 cm. 1931. Frederick A. Stokes Company.

Terrett, Courtenay (1901-)
--The White Cheyenne. Reynolds, E. Evan, illus. LC 49-119403. 311 p. illus. 21 cm. 1949. Dodd, Mead.

Terris, Danny
--Wildest Horse in America. LoMele, William, illus. (Illus.). Repr. of 1974 ed. (Little Book Ser). (gr. k-6). 1974. (ISBN 0-89409-003-8). Childrens Art.

Terris, Susan (1937-)
--Amanda, the Panda, and the Redhead. 1st ed. McCully, Emily Arnold (1939-), illus. LC 74-4898. (Illus.). 48 p. 27cm. 1975. (ISBN 0-385-08215-0). (ISBN 0-385-08215-0). Doubleday.
--Baby-Snatcher. LC 84-48472. 169 p. 22cm. 1984. (ISBN 0-374-30473-4). Farrar, Straus, Giroux.
--The Backwards Boots. 1st ed. Casalini, Rino, illus. LC 77-137014. (Illus.). 62 p. 27cm. 1971. Doubleday.
--The Chicken Pox Papers. Rockwell, Gail, illus. LC 76-12625. (Illus.). 124 p. 22cm. 1976. (ISBN 0-531-00332-9). F. Watts.
--The Drowning Boy. LC 72-76211. 189 p. 22cm. 1972. (ISBN 0-385-03981-6). (ISBN 0-385-03981-6). Doubleday.
--No Boys Allowed. 1st ed. Cuffari, Richard (1925-1978), illus. LC 74-23348. (Illus.). 47 p. 25cm. 1975. (ISBN 0-385-04887-4). (ISBN 0-385-05749-0). Doubleday.
--No Scarlet Ribbons. LC 80-28501. 153 p. 22cm. c.1981. (ISBN 0-374-35532-0). Farrar Straus Giroux.
--Octopus Pie. 1st ed. LC 83-11517. p. cm. 1983. (ISBN 0-374-35571-1). Farrar Straus Giroux.
--On Fire. LC 77-171323. 119 p. 22cm. 1972. Doubleday.
--The Pencil Families. LC 75-10597. 185 p. 22cm. 1975. (ISBN 0-688-80018-1). (ISBN 0-688-84018-3). Greenwillow Books.
--Pickle. Coconis, Ted, pseud., illus. CoConis, Constantinos. LC 73-77540. (Illus.). 154 p. 21cm. 1973. Four Winds Press.
--Plague of Frogs. LC 73-79720. 180 p. 22cm. 1973. (ISBN 0-385-01916-5). (ISBN 0-385-01916-5). Doubleday.
--Stage Brat. LC 80-14065. p. cm. c.1980. (ISBN 0-590-07683-3). Four Winds Press.
--Tucker and the Horse Thief. LC 79-12810. 188 p. 22cm. c.1979. (ISBN 0-590-07626-4). Four Winds Press.
--Two P's in a Pod. LC 77-8488. 181 p. 22cm. c.1977. (ISBN 0-688-80107-2). (ISBN 0-688-84107-4). Greenwillow Books.

--The Upstairs Witch and the Downstairs Witch. 1st ed. Cole, Olivia H. H., illus. LC 78-112902. (Illus.). 48 p. 22cm. 1970. Doubleday.
--Whirling Rainbows. LC 73-14224. 153 p. 22cm. 1974. (ISBN 0-385-00938-0). (ISBN 0-385-00938-0). Doubleday.
--Wings and Roots. LC 82-2553. p. cm. c.1982. (ISBN 0-374-38451-7). Farrar Straus Giroux.

Terry, Anna Marie
--Terri Tales for Tots. (Illus.). (ps-2). N.D. Vantage.

Terry, Maranell, tr. see Tsugawa, Shuichi.

Terry, Martha Best, Mrs.
--The Children's Sunshine Book. Dailey, Anne Emily, illus. 100 p. incl. illus., plates. 24 x 18 cm. 1903. The Reed Publishing Company

Terry, R. Harold
--Young Children Sing. (Illus.). (ps). 1967. Augsburg.

Terry, Richard Runciman, Sir (1865-1938)
--More Old Rhymes with New Tones. Pippet, Gabriel Joseph (1880-), illus. LC 25-24310. 32 p. incl. front., illus. 28 1/2 cm. 1925. Longmans, Green and Co.
--Still More Old Rhymes with New Tunes. Pippet, Gabriel Joseph (1880-), illus. LC 29-13079. 32 p. incl. front., illus. 29 x 22 1/2 cm. 1927. Longmans, Green and Co.

Tersac, Helene
--The Animals' Ball. Clement, Frederic, illus. Theobald, John & Bryant, Paula, trs. (Illus.). 35p. 1st U.S. edition. (Star & Elephant Ser.). N.D. (ISBN 0-914676-95-4). Green Tiger Pr.

Terzian, James P (1915-)
--Pete Cass: Scrambler. 1st ed. Shields, Bill, illus. LC 68-17815. (Illus.). 143 p. 22cm. (Doubleday signal books). 1968. Doubleday.

Tessin, Marion Von
--The Long-haired Elephant Child. Tessin, Marion Von, illus. LC 58-8265. (Illus.). 48p. 27cm. 1958. Pantheon.

Tessler, Stephanie Gordon & Enderle, Judith A.
--Andrea Whitman: Pediatrics. LC 83-6949. 192p. (Bayshore Medical Center Ser.). (gr. 6-9). 1983. (ISBN 0-8027-6507-6). Walker & Co.
--Elizabeth Hones, Emergency. LC 83-40405. (Bayshore Medical Center Ser.: Bk. 3). 1984. (ISBN 0-8027-6538-6). Walker.
--Gabriella Ortiz, Crisis Center Hot Line. LC 83-40406. (Bayshore Medical Center Ser.: Bk. 4). N.D. (ISBN 0-8027-6539-4). Walker.
--Monica Ross: Maternity. LC 83-5842. 192p. (gr. 6-9). 1983. (ISBN 0-8027-6506-8). Walker & Co.

Testa, Fulvio
--If You Seek Adventure. Testa, Fulvio, illus. LC 83-20920. (Illus.). 32p. (ps-2). 1984. (ISBN 0-8037-0073-3). (ISBN 0-8037-0073-3). Dial Bks for Young Readers.
--If You Take a Paint Brush. Testa, Fulvio, illus. LC 82-45512. p. cm. 1983. (ISBN 0-8037-3829-3). Dial Press.
--If You Take a Pencil. Testa, Fulvio, illus. LC 82-1505. p. cm. c.1982. (ISBN 0-8037-4023-9). Dial Press.
--The Land Where the Ice Cream Grows. Testa, Fulvio, illus. Burgess, Anthony, pseud. (1917-), as told by Wilson, John Anthony Burgess. LC 78-14714. p. cm. 1979. (ISBN 0-385-15022-9). (ISBN 0-385-15023-7). Doubleday.
--Leaves. Testa, Fulvio, illus. LC 83-71163. 1983, c.1980. (ISBN 0-911745-01-7). Bedrick Books: Dist. by Harper & Row.
--Never Satisfied. Testa, Fulvio, illus. LC 82-11825. p. cm. 1980. (ISBN 0-571-12513-1). Faber and Faber in Association with Nord-Sud Verlag.
--Never Satisfied. Testa, Fulvio, illus. 1982. Faber.
--A Short Step. Testa, Fulvio, illus. LC 78-26375. p. cm. 1979. (ISBN 0-8317-7775-3). Mayflower Books.

Testa, Fulvio & Baumann, Kurt
--The Paper Airplane. Testa, Fulvio, illus. LC 81-8358. (Illus.). 27 p. 30cm. 1st U.S. edition. c.1981. (ISBN 0-316-08389-5). (ISBN 0-316-08389-5). Little, Brown.

Tester, Sylvia Root, jt. auth. see Aldridge, Melanie.

Tester, Sylvia Root (1939-)
--Bad & Naughty Twins. 1977. (ISBN 0-913778-91-5). Childs World.
--Billy's Basketball. Sommers, Linda, illus. LC 76-15632. (Illus.). 31 p. 25cm. (Kids in sports). c.1976. (ISBN 0-913778-57-5). Child's World.
--Carla-Too-Little. Sommers, Linda, illus. LC 76-16020. (Illus.). 32 p. 25cm. (Kids in sports). c.1976. (ISBN 0-913778-56-7). Child's World.
--Chase!. Hauge, Carl & Hauge, Mary, illus. LC 80-14509. p. cm. (Easy-read book). 1980. (ISBN 0-89565-157-2). The Child's World.
--A Day of Suprises. Hook, Frances Arnold (1912-), illus. LC 78-23263. p. cm. c.1979. (ISBN 0-89565-022-3). Child's World.
--Family!. Hauge, Carl & Hauge, Mary, illus. LC 80-12373. p. cm. c.1980. (ISBN 0-89565-156-4). Child's World.
--Feeling Angry. Haag, Peg Roth, illus. LC 76-13631. (Illus.). (A Values Ser.). (ps-3). 1976. (ISBN 0-913778-49-4). Childs World.
--The Great Big Boat. Masheris, Robert, illus. LC 79-12176. (Illus.). (Bible Story Books). (ps-3). 1979. (ISBN 0-89565-087-8). Childs World.
--Learning About Ghosts. Stasiak, Krystyna, illus. LC 81-7697. p. cm. (The Learning About Series). c.1981. (ISBN 0-516-06533-5). Childrens Press.
--The Loud-Noisy, Dirty-Grimy, Bad & Naughty Twins: Synonyms. Keely, John, illus. (Illus.). 32p. (Using Words Ser.). (gr. k-3). 1977. (ISBN 0-516-06132-1). Childrens.
--Magic Monsters Around the Year. Fleishman, Seymour (1918-), illus. LC 78-23800. p. cm. (Magic Monsters Series). c.1979. (ISBN 0-89565-059-2). Child's World ; Chicago . Distributed by Childrens Press.
--Magic Monsters Halloween. Bowman, Patricia, illus. LC 79-25183. (Magic Monster Ser.). (gr. k-3). 1980. (ISBN 0-89565-121-1). Childs World.
--Magic Monsters Learn About Safety. Magine, John (1921-), illus. LC 78-24365. (Illus.). (Magic Monster Ser.). (ps-3). 1979. (ISBN 0-89565-060-6). Childs World.
--Melinda. Altschuler, Franz (1923-), illus. LC 76-30615. (Illus.). 32 p. 25cm. c.1977. (ISBN 0-913778-73-7). Child's World.
--Mr. & Mrs. Opposite. (Illus.). 32p. (Concept Bks.). (ps-4). 1977. (ISBN 0-516-05941-6). Childrens.
--Never Monkey with a Monkey: Homographic Homophones. Keely, John, illus. (Illus.). 32p. (Using Words Ser.). (gr. k-3). 1977. (ISBN 0-516-06130-5). Childrens.
--One Unicorn: A Counting Book. Gruter, Arnold, illus. LC 76-57993. (Illus.). 32 p. 25cm. (Counting book). c.1977. (ISBN 0-913778-78-8). Child's World.
--Parade!. Hauge, Carl & Hauge, Mary, illus. LC 80-12389. (Illus.). 32p. (Picture Word Bks.). (ps-1). 1980. (ISBN 0-89565-155-6). Childs World.
--The Parade of Shapes. Fudala, Rose-Mary, illus. LC 76-15629. (Illus.). 32 p. 25cm. (Concept book). c.1976. (ISBN 0-913778-54-0). Child's World.
--Paula's Feeling Angry. Haag, Peg Roth, illus. (Illus.). 1979. (ISBN 0-89565-076-2). Child's World.
--Rover, Jr.'s Baseball Career. Gilbert, Howard, illus. LC 76-15631. (Illus.). 32 p. 25cm. (Kids in sports). c.1976. (ISBN 0-913778-59-1). Child's World.
--Sandy's New Home. Sester, Sher, illus. LC 79-15923. p. cm. (Handling Difficult Times). c.1979. (ISBN 0-89565-098-3). Child's World.
--Sometimes I'm Afraid. Hook, Frances Arnold (1912-), illus. LC 78-23262. (Illus.). 30 p. 27cm. c.1979. (ISBN 0-89565-021-5). Child's World.
--Tell Me a Tale About Trolls. Taber, Ed, illus. LC 76-18098. (Illus.). 32 p. c.1976. (ISBN 0-913778-43-5). Child's World.
--That Big Bruno. Endres, Helen Elise, illus. LC 76-13627. (Illus.). 31 p. 25cm. (Learning about living). 1978, c.1976. (ISBN 0-913778-47-8). Child's World.
--Traffic Jam!. Hauge, Carl & Hauge, Mary, illus. LC 80-16303. (Illus.). 32p. (Picture Word Bks.). (ps-2). 1980. (ISBN 0-516-06442-8). Childrens.
--We Laughed a Lot, My First Day of School. Hook, Frances Arnold (1912-), illus. LC 78-10900. (Illus.). 32 p. 27cm. c.1979. (ISBN 0-89565-020-7). Child's World.
--What is a Monster?. Fleishman, Seymour (1918-), illus. LC 78-23642. (Illus.). 32p. (Magic Monsters Ser.). (ps-3). 1979. (ISBN 0-516-06189-5). Childrens.
--A World of Color. Siculan, Daniel (1922-), illus. LC 76-13629. (Illus.). 32 p. 25cm. (Concept books). c.1976. (ISBN 0-913778-55-9). The Child's World.
--You Dance Like an Ostrich!. Similes. Keely, John, illus. (Illus.). 32p. (Using Words Ser.). (gr. k-3). 1978. (ISBN 0-516-06134-8). Childrens.

Tether, Cynthia Graham (1950-)
--Fudge Dream Supreme. Kock, Carl, illus. LC 73-16815. (Illus.). 32p. (ps-2). 1975. (ISBN 0-87955-109-7). O'Hara.
--Skunk and Possum. McQueen, Lucinda, illus. LC 79-12007. (Illus.). 32 p. 1979. (ISBN 0-395-28270-5). Houghton Mifflin.

Tether, Graham see Tether, Cynthia Graham.

Tetlow, jt. ed. see Kingsley, Charles.

Tetzner, Lisa (1894-)
--Hans Sees the World. Goldsmith, Margaret, tr. LC 34-31982. 15cm. 252p. 1934. Covici Friede Bks.

Teuffel, Blanche Willis Howard Von (1847-1898), tr. see Gross, Theobald.

Teuffel, Blanche Willis Howard Von (1847-1898)
--A Battle and a Boy. LC 8-25964. 285p. 19cm. 1901. Street & Smith.
--A Battle and a Boy: A Story for Young People. LC 8-25964. 285p. 19cm. 1892. Tait, Sons & Co.
--No Heroes. Walcott, Jessie McDermott, illus. LC 8-25963. (Illus.). 97p. 19cm. 1893. Houghton, Mifflin and Company.

Texas Alcohol Narcotics Education, ed. see Brittain, Grady.

Tezel, Naki, jt. auth. see Walker, Barbara Kerlin.

Thacher, Alida McKay (1951-)
--Perilous Journey to the Top. Van Severen, Joe, illus. LC 79-22159. (Illus.). 46p. (Quest, Adventure, Survival). (gr. 4-9). 1982. (ISBN 0-8172-2068-2). Raintree Pubs.

Thacher, Lucy W. S., Mrs., ed.
--The Listening Child: A Selection from the Stories of English Verse, Made for the Youngest Readers and Hearers. LC 79-50851. xxix, 408 p. 20cm. (Granger Poetry Library). 1979. (ISBN 0-89609-171-6). Granger Book Co.
--The Listening Child: A Selection from the Stores of English Verse, Made for the Youngest Readers and Hearers. LC 99-5141. xxix, 408 p. front. 20 cm. 1899. The Macmillan Company.

Thacher, Lucy W. S., Mrs. & Wilkinson, Marguerite Ogden Bigelow, Mrs. (1883-1928), eds.
--The Listening Child: A Selection from the Stores of English Verse, Made for the Youngest Readers and Hearers. Barnhart, Nancy (1889-), illus. Higginson, Thomas Wentworth (1822-1911), intro. by. LC 24-28251. xxxvii, 405 p. incl. illus., plates. col. front. 19 1/2 cm. (The Macmillan children's classics). 1924. The Macmillan Company.

Thackeray, William Makepeace, jt. auth. see Dickens, Charles John Huffam.

Thackeray, William Makepeace (1811-1863)
--The Adventures of Philip, 2. N.D. J. B. Lippincott.
--The Awful History of Bluebeard. Scott, Temple, intro. by. Thackery, William Makepeace (1811-1863), illus. LC 75-308266. (Illus.). 32p. 23cm. 1924. J. Kern.
--Henry Esmond. Smith, Arthur D. Howden, intro. by. (Illus.). (Great Il. Classics). (gr. 9 up). N.D. (ISBN 0-396-02606-0). Dodd.
--The Rose and the Ring. Preston, Phyllis, ed. LC 27-26095. (Illus.). 191p. 15cm. 1926. E. P. Dutton and Company.
--The Rose & the Ring. Preston, Phyllis, ed. Thackeray, William Makepeace (1811-1863), illus. LC 27-260954. 2 p. l., 7-191, 1 p. incl. front. (port.) illus. 15 1/2 cm. (Half-title: The Kings treasuries of literature; general editor: Sir A. T. Quiller Couch). 1926. J. M. Dent & Sons, Ltd.
--The Rose and the Ring. Thackeray, William Makepeace (1811-1863), illus. N.D. Brentano's.
--The Rose and the Ring. Thackeray, William Makepeace (1811-1863), illus. N.D. Frederick A. Stokes Co.
--The Rose and the Ring. Thackeray, William Makepeace (1811-1863), illus. (Folk Lore And Fairy Tales). N.D. MacMillan Bks.
--The Rose and the ring. Thackeray, William Makepeace (1811-1863), illus. N.D. St Martin's Press.
--The Rose and the Ring: Or, Prince Giglio and Prince Bulo. Thackeray, William Makepeace (1811-1863) & Gilbert, John, illus. LC 59-3057. (Bound with Charles Dickens' The Magic Fishbone). (Illus.). 179p. 20cm. (The Children's Illustrated Classics). 1959. Dutton.
--The Rose and the Ring: Or, The History of Prince Giglio and Prince Bulbo. A Fireside Pantomime for Great and Small Children. Falls, Charles Buckles (1874-1960) & Thackeray, William Makepeace (1811-1863), illus. N.D. Wessels & Bissell Co.
--The Rose and the Ring: Or, The History of Prince Giglio and Prince Bulbo. A Fireside Pantomime for Great and Small Children. Thackeray, William Makepeace (1811-1863), illus. (Illus.). (Every Boy's Library). N.D. Caldwell.
--The Rose and the Ring: Or, The History of Prince Giglio and Prince Bulbo. A Fireside Pantomime for Great and Small Children. Thackeray, William Makepeace (1811-1863), illus. N.D. Estes & Lauriat's.
--Rose and the Ring: Or, The History of Prince Giglio and Prince Bulbo/A Fireside Pantomime for Great and Small Children. Thackeray, William Makepeace (1811-1863), illus. (Illus.). (The Young Folks Lib.). N.D. H. M. Caldwell Co.
--The Rose and the Ring: Or, The History of Prince Giglio and Prince Bulbo. A Fireside Pantomime for Great and Small Children. Thackeray, William Makepeace (1811-1863), illus. (Illus.). N.D. Putman.
--The Rose and the Ring: Or, the History of Prince Giglio and Prince Bulbo; a Fire-Side Pantomime for Great and Small Children. Thackeray, William Makepeace (1811-1863), illus. LC 67-28169. (Illus.). vi, 128 p. 21cm. (Legacy library facsimile). 1967. University Microfilms.
--Vanity Fair. (International Classics). N.D. Dodd Mead & Co.

Thackeray, William Makepeace (1811-1863) & Dickens, Charles John Huffam (1812-1870)
--The Rose & the Ring With the Magic Fish-bone: Or, the History of Prince Giglio and Prince Bulbo with the Magic Fish-bone. Thackeray, William Makepeace, et al. (1811-1863), illus. LC 59-3057. 179 p. illus. 20 cm. (Children's illustrated classics). 1959. Dent.

Thackray, Patricia
--Big Bird Gets Lost. Nicklaus, Carol, illus. LC 77-93657. (Illus.). 25cm. 28p. (A Golden scratch & sniff bk.). c.1978. (ISBN 0-307-13524-1). Western Pub. Co.
--Raggedy Ann at the Carnival. Bottner, Barbara (1943-), illus. LC 76-54417. (Illus.). 24 p. 21cm. (Golden look-look books). c.1977. (ISBN 0-307-11830-4). Golden Press.
--Raggedy Ann's Sweet & Dandy, Sugar Candy. Nicklaus, Carol, illus. LC 76-18728. (Illus.). 25cm. 27p. (Golden Scratch & Sniff Bk.). (gr. 3-6). 1977. (ISBN 0-307-13542-X, Golden Pr). (ISBN 0-307-65342-0). Western Pub.
--What Ernie & Bert Did on Their Summer Vacation: Sesame Street. Mathieu, Joseph (1945-), illus. LC 76-52807. (Illus.). (Kids Paperbacks). (ps-4). 1977. (ISBN 0-307-62356-4, Golden Pr). (ISBN 0-307-12356-1). Western Pub.

Thaddeus, M., Sr., compiled by.
--A World to Unite. McHale, Richard E., et al., compiled by. LC 78-14584. (Illus.). 551 p. 24cm. (Christian child reading series). 1969. Reardon, Baer.

Thakura, Ravindranatha see Tagore, Rabindranath, pseud.

Thal, Samuel (1903-)
--Okinpochee Bird Family. Thal, Samuel (1903-), illus. LC 55-10159. (Limited Signed Ed.). (Illus.). 23cm. 32p. (gr. 3 up). N.D. (ISBN 0-8283-1153-6). Branden.

Thaler, Mike (1936-)
--The Chocolate Marshmelephant Sundae. LC 78-58566. (Illus.). 96 p. 23cm. 1978. (ISBN 0-531-02244-7). Watts.
--Clown's Smile. Thaler, Mike (1936-), illus. LC 62-7578. (Illus.). (ps-3). 1962. (ISBN 0-06-026090-4, HarpJ). Har-Row.
--Funny Bones: Cartoon Monster Riddles. Thaler, Mike (1936-), illus. LC 76-16190. (Illus.). 95 p. 22cm. 1976. (ISBN 0-531-00349-3). F. Watts.
--Funny Side up!. How to Create Your Own Riddles. LC 85-2214. p. cm. c.1985. (ISBN 0-590-33288-0). Scholastic.
--How Far Will a Rubber Band Stretch?. Joyner, Jerry (1938-), illus. LC 73-23052. (Illus.). 32 p. 1974. (ISBN 0-8193-0766-1). (ISBN 0-8193-0766-1). Parents' Magazine Press.
--It's Me, Hippo!. LC 82-48848. (Illus.). 5 7/8 x 8 1/2. (18 pt.). (I Can Read Bks.). (gr. k-3). 1983. (ISBN 0-06-026153-6). (ISBN 0-06-026154-4). Har-Row.
--It's Me, Hippo!. 1st ed. Chambliss, Maxie, illus. LC 82-48848. p. cm. (An I Can Read Book). c.1983. (ISBN 0-06-026153-6). (ISBN 0-06-026154-4). Harper & Row.
--The King's Flower. Thaler, Mike (1936-), illus. LC 63-15063. 1 v. (unpaged) illus. (part col.) 22 x 23 cm. 1963. Orion Press.
--Madge's Magic Show. Nicklaus, Carol, illus. LC 77-17288. (Illus.). 32 p. 22cm. (Easy-read story book). 1978. (ISBN 0-531-01450-9). F. Watts.
--Magic Boy. Thaler, Mike (1936-), illus. LC 61-15135. (Illus.). (ps-1). 1961. (ISBN 0-06-026095-5). Har-Row.
--Magic Letter Riddles. Thaler, Mike (1936-), illus. (gr. k-3). 1974. (ISBN 0-590-09925-6, Schol Pap). Schol Bk Serv.
--The Moon and the Balloon. Fishman, Madeleine, illus. LC 82-15450. p. cm. c.1982. (ISBN 0-8038-4744-0). Hastings House Publishers.
--Moonboy. Thaler, Mike (1936-), illus. LC 64-12809. 32 p. illus. (part col.) 20 x 21 cm. 1964. Harper & Row.
--Moonkey. Maestro, Giulio (1942-), illus. LC 76-58716. (Illus.). 32p. (ps-3). 1981. (ISBN 0-06-026124-2, HarpJ). (ISBN 0-06-026125-0). Har-Row.
--Moonkey. Mitsuhashi, Yoko, illus. LC 76-58716. p. cm. c.1977. (ISBN 0-06-026124-2). (ISBN 0-06-026125-0). Harper & Row.
--The Moose Is Loose. Gaffr, Toni, illus. (Illus.). 32p. (Orig.). (ps-3). 1981. (ISBN 0-590-31291-X, Schol Pap). Scholastic Inc.
--My Little Friend. Levin, Arnie, illus. LC 76-148482. (Illus.). 32 p. 26cm. 1971. Lothrop, Lee & Shepard.

--My Puppy. Fishman, Madeleine, illus. LC 79-2681. (Illus.). 32 p. 21cm. c.1980. (ISBN 0-06-026078-5). (ISBN 0-06-026079-3). Harper & Row.
--Never Tickle a Turtle: Cartoons, Riddles & Funny Stories. Thaler, Mike (1936-), illus. (Illus.). (gr. 4-6). 1977. (ISBN 0-531-00386-8). Watts.
--Owly. Wiesner, David, illus. LC 81-47727. (Illus.). 32 p. 21cm. c.1982. (ISBN 0-06-026151-X). (ISBN 0-06-026152-8). Harper & Row.
--Penny Pencil: The Story of a Pencil. Thaler, Mike (1936-), illus. LC 62-14317. (Illus.). unpaged. c.1963. Harper & Row.
--The Prince and the Seven Moons. Arndt, Ursula, illus. LC 66-11582. 1v. (unpaged) illus. (pt. col.) 22cm. c.1966. Macmillan.
--The Rainbow. Leake, Donald, illus. LC 67-16286. 1v. (unpaged) illus. (pt. col.) 15 x 22cm. 1967. H. Quist, Dist. Crown.
--Riddle Riot. Thaler, Mike (1936-), illus. (gr. 4-6). 1976. (ISBN 0-590-03594-0, Schol Pap). Scholastic Inc.
--The Smiling Book. Levin, Arnie, illus. LC 79-116336. (Illus.). 36 p. 26cm. 1971. Lothrop, Lee & Shepard Co.
--Soup with Quackers: Funny Cartoon Riddles. Thaler, Mike (1936-), illus. LC 76-10308. (Illus.). 96p. (gr. 4 up). 1976. (ISBN 0-531-00344-2). Watts.
--The Staff. Schindelman, Joseph (1923-), illus. LC 70-118703. (Illus.). 40 p. 24cm. 1971. (ISBN 0-394-92058-9). Knopf.
--Stuffed Feet. LC 83-10009. p. cm. (Avon/Camelot book). c.1983. (ISBN 0-380-84673-X). Avon Books.
--There's a Hippopotamus Under My Bed. Cruz, Raymond (1933-), illus. LC 77-23457. (Illus.). 32 p. 22cm. (Easy-read story book). 1977. (ISBN 0-531-01339-1). (ISBN 0-531-01318-9). F. Watts.
--What Can a Hippopotamus Be?. Grossman, Robert (1940-), illus. LC 74-30104. (Illus.). 27cm. 33p. (gr. k-3). 1975. (ISBN 0-8193-0809-9, Four Winds). (ISBN 0-8193-0810-2). Scholastic Inc.
--What's up Duck. Thaler, Mike (1936-), illus. LC 77-20807. (Illus.). (gr. 4 up). 1978. (ISBN 0-531-01479-7). Watts.
--Wuzzles. Thaler, Mike (1936-), illus. (gr. k-3). 1976. (ISBN 0-590-10164-1). Scholastic Inc.
--The Yellow Brick Toad: Funny Frog Cartoons, Riddles, and Silly Stories. Thaler, Mike (1936-), illus. LC 77-27719. p. cm. 1978. (ISBN 0-385-14254-4). (ISBN 0-385-14255-2). Doubleday.

Thaler, Susan (1936-)
--Rosaria. Genia, pseud. (1930-), illus. Wennerstrom, Genia Katherine. (Illus.). (gr. 7-9). 1967. (ISBN 0-679-25123-5). McKay.

Thalman, Marilynn, jt. ed. see Thalman, Norman.

Thalman, Norman & Thalman, Marilynn, eds.
--Songs of Joy Through the Church Year. (Illus.). (ps-9). 1963. Fortress.

Thamer, Katie, illus.
--The Song of Songs: King James Version. McClasky, Stephen (Illus.). 40p. Orig. Title: Song of Solomon. 1982. (ISBN 0-914676-46-6, Star & Eleph Bks). Green Tiger Pr.

Thampi, Parvathi Menon, jt. tr. see Cassedy, Sylvia.

Thampi, Parvathi Menon (1925-)
--Geeta and the Village School. 1st ed. Solbert, Ronni, pseud. (1925-), illus. Solbert, Romaine G.. LC 60-7140. 63 p. illus. 25 cm. 1960. Doubleday.

Thane, Adele see Thane, Lillian Adele.

Thane, Elswyth (1900-)
--Dawn's Early Light. new abridged. Finlayson, Ann (1925-), adapted by. LC 70-135857. 244 p. 22cm. 1971. Hawthorn Books.
--Homing. (gr. 7-9). 1943. (ISBN 0-8015-3552-2). Hawthorn.
--Kissing Kin. (gr. 7-9). 1948. (ISBN 0-8015-4320-7). Hawthorn.
--Potomac Squire. (Illus.). (gr. 10-12). 1963. Hawthorn.
--Tryst. (gr. 7-9). 1939. Hawthorn.
--Virginia Colony. LC 69-16488. (Illus.). maps. photos. bibl. index. 144p. (Forge of Freedom Ser). (gr. 5-8). 1969. (ISBN 0-02-789180-1, CCPr). Macmillan.

Thane, Lillian Adele (1904-)
--Gilbert & Sullivan Operettas Adapted for Half-Hour Performance. (gr. 5-12). 1977. (ISBN 0-8238-0188-8). Plays.
--Plays from Famous Stories & Fairy Tales. LC 83-23039. (gr. 4-7). 1983. (ISBN 0-8238-0262-0). Plays.
--Plays from Famous Stories and Fairy Tales: Royalty-Free Dramatizations of Favorite Children's Stories. LC 67-16952. v, 463 p. 22cm. 1967. Plays, Inc.

Thanet, Octave
--We All. N.D. D. Appleton and Company.

Tharau, Hans, pseud., see Weling, Fraulin Von.

Tharau, Hans, pseud.
--The Fellow-Students. Weling, Fraulin Von. (Illus.). 262p. 1905. American Tract Society.

Tharp, Louise Marshall Hall, Mrs. (1898-)
--Champlain, Northwest Voyager. Wilson, Charles Banks (1918-), illus. LC 44-8471. viii, 250 p., 2 l. incl. illus., plates. 21 cm. 1944. Little, Brown and Company.
--Company of Adventurers. Wilson, Charles Banks (1918-), illus. (A story of the men who built the Hudson's Bay Company). (gr. 7-10). 1946. (ISBN 0-316-83908-6). Little.
--Down to the Sea. N.D. Robert M. McBride & Co.
--Lords and Gentlemen. John, Charles V., illus. LC 40-4669. 2 p. l., 188 p. illus. 23 1/2 cm. 1940. Thomas Y. Crowell Company.
--Sixpence for Luck. Howe, Gertrude Herrick (1902-), illus. LC 41-18717. 4 p. l., 284 p. front., illus. 22 cm. 1941. Thomas Y. Crowell Company.
--A Sounding Trumpet. N.D. Robert M. McBride & Co.
--Tory Hole. 1957. Little, Brown.
--Tory Hole. Robinson, Jessie Berkowitz, illus. LC 40-30718. 3 p. l., 202 p. illus. 23 1/2 cm. 1940. Thomas Y. Crowell Company.

Thatcher, A & Hogarth, C. J.
--The Happy Dragon and Other Stories. Rowlands, Constance E., illus. LC 26-3360. viii, 222 p. col. front., illus., col. plates. 21 cm. 1925. Brentano's.

Thatcher, Dora Fickling (1912-)
--Ferryboat Tommy. Biro, Val, pseud. (1921-), illus. Biro, Balint Stephen. (Illus.). (gr. k-3). 1965. (ISBN 0-685-21120-7). Verry.
--Henry the Helicopter. (Illus.). (gr. k-3). 1964. Verry.

Thaxter, Celia Laighton, Mrs. (1835-1894)
--Poems for Our Darlings. LC 11-30753. 80 p. incl. front., illus. 24 x 20 cm. 1877. D. Lothrop & Co.
--Stories and Poems for Children. LC 73-167486. (Illus.). vii, 257 p. 21cm. (Granger index reprint series). 1971. (ISBN 0-8369-6291-5). Books for Libraries Press.
--Stories and Poems for Children. LC 3-195251. vii, 257 p. front. 19 1/2 cm. 1895. Houghton, Mifflin and Company.

Thayer, Bert Clark
--Jinny: The Story of a Filly. Thayer, Bert Clark, illus. N.D. Farrar & Rinehart.

Thayer, E. S., jt. auth. see Preston, Annie A, Mrs.

Thayer, Ernest Lawrence (1863-1940)
--The Annotated Casey at the Bat. Gardner, Martin (1863-1940), intro. by. 206p. 1967 (Potter). Crown.
--Casey at the Bat. Bachaus, Ken, illus. LC 84-9891. (Illus.). 31 p. 25cm. c.1985. (ISBN 0-8172-2121-2). Raintree Childrens Books.
--Casey at the Bat. 1st Book ed. Fisher, Leonard Everett (1924-), illus. Stengel, Casey, intro. by. LC 64-17788. (Illus.). 23 cm. 32p. 1964. F. Watts. **Award: (NYT).**
--Casey at the Bat. Frame, Paul (1913-), illus. LC 64-13248. 32 p. illus. (part col.) 30 cm. 1964. Prentice-Hall.
--Casey at the Bat. Hull, Jim, illus. LC 76-48575. (Illus.). viii, 56 p. 25cm. 1977. Dover Publications.
--Casey at the Bat: A Ballad of the Republic, Sung in the Year Eighteen-Eighty-Eight. Tripp, Wallace Whitney (1940-), illus. LC 77-21199. (Illus.). 32 p. 24cm. 1978. (ISBN 0-698-20457-3). Coward, McCann & Geoghegan.

Thayer, Harriet Maxon
--The Genial Sultan the Princess Who Could Not See, Late for the Coronation. Thayer, Harriet Maxon, illus. LC 23-6270. 80 p. col. front., illus. 19 cm. c.1923. Dorrance.

Thayer, Jane, pseud., see Woolley, Catherine.

Thayer, Jane, pseud. (1904-)
--Andy & His Fine Friends. Woolley, Catherine. Wohlberg, Meg (1905-), illus. (Illus.). (gr. k-3). 1960. Morrow.
--Andy & Mister Cunningham. Woolley, Catherine. Wohlberg, Meg (1905-), illus. (Illus.). (ps-3). 1969. (ISBN 0-688-31024-9). Morrow.
--Andy & the Runaway Horse. Woolley, Catherine. Wohlberg, Meg (1905-), illus. (Illus.). (ps-3). 1963. (ISBN 0-688-31026-5). Morrow.
--Andy & the Wild Worm. Woolly, Catherine. Darwin, Beatrice, illus. LC 72-1981. (Illus.). 48p. (ps-3). 1973. (ISBN 0-688-21837-7). (ISBN 0-688-31837-1). Morrow.
--The Blueberry Pie Elf. Woolley, Catherine. Fleishman, Seymour (1918-), illus. LC 61-5012. (Illus.). (gr. k-3). 1961. (ISBN 0-688-31112-1). Morrow.
--A Contrary Little Quail. Woolley, Catherine. Wohlberg, Meg (1905-), illus. LC 68-10121. (Illus.). ca. 30 color ils. 32p. (gr. k-3). 1968. (ISBN 0-688-31184-9). Morrow.
--A Drink for Little Red Diker. Woolley, Catherine. Mars, Witold Tadeusz J. (1912-), illus. (Illus.). (gr. k-3). 1963. Morrow.
--Emerald Enjoyed the Moonlight. Woolley, Catherine. Fleishman, Seymour (1918-), illus. (Illus.). (gr. k-3). 1964. (ISBN 0-688-21266-2). Morrow.
--Gus & the Baby Ghost. Woolley, Catherine. Fleishman, Seymour (1918-), illus. LC 76-161874. (Illus.). 32p. (ps-3). 1972. (ISBN 0-688-31369-8). Morrow.
--Gus Was a Christmas Ghost. Woolley, Catherine. Fleishman, Seymour (1918-), illus. LC 77-101707. (Illus.). color ils. 32p. (ps-3). 1970. (ISBN 0-688-21370-7). (ISBN 0-688-31370-1). Morrow.
--Gus Was a Friendly Ghost. Woolley, Catherine. Fleishman, Seymour (1918-), illus. (Illus.). (ps-3). 1962. (ISBN 0-688-31368-X). Morrow.
--The Horse with the Easter Bonnet. Woolley, Catherine. Barnum, Jay Hyde (1888-1962), illus. (Illus.). (ps-3). 1953. (ISBN 0-688-31694-8). Morrow.
--A Little Dog Called Kitty. Woolley, Catherine. Fleishman, Seymour (1918-), illus. 1961. Morrow.
--Mister Turtle's Magic Glasses. Woolley, Catherine. Funai, Mamoru R. (1932-), illus. LC 74-118284. (Illus.). (ps-3). 1971. (ISBN 0-688-21650-1). Morrow.
--Mrs. Perrywinkle's Pets. Woolley, Catherine. Galdone, Paul (1914-), illus. (gr. k-3). 1955. William Morrow & Co.
--The Part-Time Dog. Wolley, Catherine. Fleishman, Seymour (1918-), illus. (Illus.). (gr. k-3). 1965. (ISBN 0-688-21642-0). Morrow.
--The Puppy Who Wanted a Boy. Woolley, Catherine. Fleishman, Seymour (1918-), illus. (Illus.). (ps-3). 1958. (ISBN 0-688-31631-X). Morrow.
--Quiet on Account of Dinasaur. Woolley, Catherine. Fleishman, Seymour (1918-), illus. (Illus.). (ps-3). 1964. (ISBN 0-688-31632-8). Morrow.
--Sandy & the Seventeen Balloons. Woolley, Catherine. Wohlberg, Meg (1905-), illus. (Illus.). (gr. k-3). 1955. Morrow.
--Timothy & Madam Mouse: A Non-ABC Book. Woolley, Catherine. Madden, Donald B. (1927-), illus. LC 77-135785. (Illus.). color ils. 48p. (ps-1). 1971. (ISBN 0-688-21972-1). Morrow.
--Try Your Hand. Woolley, Catherine. Schick, Joel (1945-), illus. LC 79-18608. (Illus.). 32p. (gr. k-3). 1980. (ISBN 0-688-22215-3). (ISBN 0-688-32215-8). Morrow.
--What's a Ghost Going to Do. Woolley, Catherine. Fleishman, Seymour (1918-), illus. (Illus.). (ps-3). 1966. (ISBN 0-688-31643-3). Morrow.
--Where Is Squirrel?. Woolley, Catherine. Weissman, Bari, illus. LC 78-31611. (Illus.). 32p. (gr. k-3). 1979. (ISBN 0-688-22192-0). (ISBN 0-688-32192-5). Morrow.
--Where's Andy. Woolley, Catherine. Wohlberg, Meg (1905-), illus. (gr. k-3). 1954. William Morrow & Co.

Thayer, Julie & Thayer, Ruth Hubley
--The Lamb Who Went to Paris. LC 79-27041. (Illus.). 61 p. 26cm. c.1980. C. N. Potter : Distributed by Crown.

Thayer, Marjorie
--The April Foolers. Freeman, Don (1908-1978), illus. LC 77-15958. (Illus.). 32p. (Holiday Play Bks.). (gr. k-4). 1978. (ISBN 0-516-08883-1, Golden Gate). Childrens.
--The Christmas Strangers. Freeman, Don (1908-1978), illus. LC 75-38575. (Illus.). 45 p. 22cm. c.1976. (ISBN 0-516-08719-3). Childrens Press.
--The First Day of School. Burgeson, Marjorie, illus. LC 77-6281. (Illus.). (Holiday Play Books). (gr. k-4). 1977. (ISBN 0-516-08882-3, Golden Gate). Childrens.
--The Halloween Witch. Burgeson, Marjorie, illus. LC 76-8533. (Illus.). 32p. (Holiday Play Books). (gr. k-4). 1976. (ISBN 0-516-08727-4, Golden Gate). Childrens.
--A Mother for Mother's Day. Burgeson, Marjorie, illus. LC 79-22802. (Illus.). 32p. (Holiday Play Bks.). (gr. k-4). 1980. (ISBN 0-516-08878-5, Golden Gate). Childrens.
--The Valentine Box. Burgeson, Marjorie, illus. LC 76-46543. (Illus.). 30 p. c.1977. (ISBN 0-516-08746-0). Childrens Press.
--The Youngest. Payson, Dale (1943-), illus. LC 82-2554. (Illus.). 143 p. 20cm. c.1982. (ISBN 0-396-08047-2). Dodd, Mead.

Thayer, Marjorie & Emanuel, Elizabeth
--Climbing Sun: The Story of a Hopi Indian Boy. Siberell, Anne, illus. LC 80-13743. (Illus.). 96p. (gr. 5 up). 1980. Dodd.

Thayer, Peter, pseud., see Wyler, Rose.

Thayer, Peter, pseud. (1909-)
--Orphans of Big Swamp. Wyler, Rose. N.D. (ISBN 0-8283-1621-X). Branden Press.

Thayer, Ruth Hubley, jt. auth. see Thayer, Julie.

Thayer, Wildie
--Flower Fancies from Fairyland. Thayer, Wildie, illus. LC 12-7618. 6 p. l., 78 p. illus. 16 1/2 cm. $0.50. c.1911. The C. M. Clark Publishing Co.

Thayer, William Makepeace (1820-1898)
--Fort Pillow to the End. (Illus.). (St. Nicholas Series for Boys). N.D. International Book Co.
--Fort Sumter to Roanoke Island. (Illus.). (St. Nicholas Series for Boys). N.D. International Book Co.
--Good Girl and True Woman. (Crowell's Library For Young People). N.D. Thomas Y. Crowell & Co.' Catalogue.
--Murfreesboro to Fort Pillow. (Illus.). (St. Nicholas Deries for Boys). N.D. International Book Co.
--Nelson: Or, how a Country Boy Made his Way in the City. LC 44-398511. 1 p. l., 5-327 p. 17 1/2 cm. (Crowell's Sunday-School Library No. 6). 1878. T. Y. Crowell.
--The Poor Boy and Merchant Prince: Or, Elements of Success Drawn From the Life and Character, of Amos Lawrence; a Book for Youth. LC 11-26706. 17cm. 349p. 1857. Gould & Lincoln.
--Roanoke Island to Murfreesboro. (Illus.). (St. Nicholas Series for Boys). N.D. International Book Co.

Thayer, Zel, jt. auth. see Sherrod, Jane.

Thayne, Emma Lou (1924-)
--Never Past the Gate. LC 75-33580. 250p. 1st U.S. edition. 1975. (ISBN 0-87905-047-0). Peregrine Smith.

The, Christian Science Monitor see Beston, Henry B.

The, Green Tiger Press see Swann, Brian.

The, Koehne Studios, Inc. see Mother Goose.

The, Meadley Harpers, jt. auth. see Cooke, Muriel.

The, Reader's Digest see Sideman, Belle Becker.

The, Youth's Companion see Harper, Wilhelmina.

Thebaud, A. J.
--Twit-Twats. (Illus.). N.D. The Catholic Publication Society.

Theed, M. F.
--What She Did with Her Life. N.D. George Routledge & Sons.

Theen, Olive Ireland
--Christmas Storybook. LC 54-10441. (Illus.). 21cm. 128p. 1954. Bruce Publishing Co.

Theesfeld, Nola
--Silver Linings. Theesfeld, Nola, illus. LC 29-23884. 96 p. illus. 18 cm. c.1929. Augustana Book Concern.

Theis, Dan
--The Education of Steven Bell. Frank, Ken, illus. LC 76-54277. (Illus.). 80 p. 19cm. c.1977. (ISBN 0-8172-0807-0). (ISBN 0-8172-0806-2). Raintree Editions.

Theisen, William Walter (1886-) & Bond, Guy Loraine (1904-), eds.
--Journeys in Storyland. Pitz, Henry Clarence (1895-1976), illus. LC 45-3927. vii, 1 376 p. incl. front., illus. 21 cm. (Half-title: Living literature for supplementary reading). 1945. The Macmillan Company.
--Story Friends on Parade. Annand, George, illus. LC 45-4145. vii, 1, 440 p. incl. front., illus. 21 cm. (Half-title: Living literature for supplementary reading). 1945. The Macmillan Company.

Theiss, Lewis Edwin (1878-1963)
--Aloft in the Shenandoah II: How Lew Heinsling Earned the Right to Fly in Uncle Sam's Newest Dirigible. Merrill, Frank Thayer (1848-), illus. LC 26-212982. 1 p. l., 5-322 p. front. 19 cm. c.1926. W. A. Wilde Company.
--A Champion of the Foothills. Howitt, John Newton, illus. LC 18-6693. vii, 345, 1 p. incl. front. plates. 19 1/2 cm. 1918. Doubleday, Page & Company.
--Flood Mappers Aloft: How Ginger Hale and the Scouts of the Bald Eagle Patrol Surveyed the Watershed of the Susquehanna. Burkard, Albert M., illus. LC 37-24838. 5 p. l., 5-311 p. front., plates. 21 cm. c.1937. W. A. Wilde Company.
--The Flume in the Mountains: The Story of the Building of a Great Power-Plant. Merrill, Frank Thayer (1848-), illus. LC 26-2454. 316 p. col. front. 19 1/2 cm. c.1925. W. A. Wilde Company.
--The Flying Explorer: How a Mail Pilot Penetrated the Basin of the Amazon. Burkard, Albert M., illus. LC 36-73. 304 p. front. 19 1/2 cm. c.1935. W. A. Wilde Company.
--Flying for Uncle Sam: A Story of Civilian Pilot Training. LC 42-22693. 314 p. front., plates. 21 cm. 1942. W. A. Wilde Company.
--Flying Reporter. N.D. WILcox & Follett Co.
--The Flying Reporter. Cue, Harold, illus. LC 30-31492. 312 p. front. 19 1/2 cm. 1930. W. A. Wilde Company.
--Flying the U.S. Mail to South America: How Pan American Airships Carry on in Sun and Storm Above the Rolling Caribbean. Cue, Harold, illus. LC 34-24237. 303 p. front. 19 1/2 cm. c.1933. W. A. Wilde Company.

Thomas, Emma A., Mrs., jt. auth. see Brewster, Frances Stanton.

Thomas, Estelle Webb (1899-)
--Gift of Laughter. LC 67-1803. 208 p. 21cm. 1967. Westminster Press.
--The Torch Bearer. Savitt, Max, illus. LC 59-5261. 184 p. illus. 21 cm. 1959. F. Watts.

Thomas, Gary
--Best of the Little Books. LC 79-56010. (Illus.). 96p. (Little Book Ser.). (gr. 1-4). 1980. (ISBN 0-8178-5170-4). Harvey.

Thomas, George Ernest, as told to see Barton, Bob.

Thomas, Gertrude Ellen Ickler (1895-)
--Land O' Nod: The Story of Denny's Adventures. Brown, Theodora, illus. LC 51-12313. 106 p. illus. 23 cm. 1951. Exposition Press.
--Peter Makes Good, and Stories of Other Dogs. Saunders, Dorothy, illus. LC 30-15028. 187 p. col. illus. 19 1/2 cm. c.1929. Beckley-Cardy Company.

Thomas, Gladys, ed. see Marryat, Frederick.

Thomas, Gwyn (1936-) & Crossley-Holland, Kevin (1941-)
--Tales from the Mabinogion. Jones, Margaret, illus. LC 84-14777. (Illus.). 88 p. 29cm. 1985. (ISBN 0-87951-987-8). Overlook Press.

Thomas, H. C., pseud., see Keating, Lawrence A..

Thomas, Harlan C, pseud., see Keating, Lawrence A..

Thomas, Harlan C, pseud. (1903-1966)
--A Boy Fighter with Andrew Jackson. Keating, Lawrence A.. Vallely, Henry E., illus. LC 46-7936. 2 p. l., 9-249 p. illus. 20 1/2 cm. 1946. Whitman Publishing Company.
--A Boy Sailor with John Paul Jones. Keating, Lawrence A.. Vallely, Henry E., illus. LC 47-190138. 2 p. l., 9-250 p. illus. 20 1/2 cm. 1946. Whitman Publishing Company.
--Red Ryder and the Adventure at Chimney Rock. Keating, Lawrence A.. Thomas, Harlan C., illus. Harman, Fred (1902-1982), created by. LC 46-7935. 2 p. l., 9-249 p. illus. 20 1/2 cm. 1946. Whitman Publishing Company.

Thomas, henry see Schnittkind, Henry Thomas.

Thomas, Henry (1886-)
--Giuseppe, and Laughter Wins: Fairy Tales for Working Men's Children. (Author's Name Originally: Henry Thomas Schnittkind). 61p. 61cm. 1914. Stratford Pub. Co.

Thomas, Ianthe (1951-)
--Eliza's Daddy. 1st ed. Barnett, Moneta (1922-1976), illus. LC 75-41343. (Illus.). 64 p. 22cm. (Let me read book). c.1976. (ISBN 0-15-225400-5). (ISBN 0-15-255401-7). Harcourt Brace Jovanovich.
--Hi, Mrs. Mallory!. Toulmin-Rothe, Ann, illus. LC 78-3013. (Illus.). 48 p. 22cm. c.1979. (ISBN 0-06-026128-5). (ISBN 0-06-026129-3). Harper & Row.
--Lordy, Aunt Hattie. 1st ed. Di Grazia, Thomas (0000-1983), illus. LC 72-9857. (Illus.). 23 p. 1973. (ISBN 0-06-026114-5). (ISBN 0-06-026114-5). Harper & Row.
--My Street's a Morning Cool Street. McCully, Emily Arnold (1939-), illus. LC 74-2629. (Illus.). 24p. (gr. k-3). 1976. (ISBN 0-06-026112-9, HarpJ). (ISBN 0-06-026113-7). Har-Row.
--The Time Junkie. LC 78-52821. (gr. 7 up). N.D. (ISBN 0-15-288191-3). HarBraceJ.
--Walk Home Tired, Billy Jenkins. 1st ed. Di Grazia, Thomas (0000-1983), illus. LC 73-5497. (Illus.). 24 p. 22cm. 1974. (ISBN 0-06-026108-0). (ISBN 0-06-026109-9). Harper & Row.
--Willie Blows a Mean Horn. 1st ed. Toulmin-Rothe, Ann, illus. LC 74-2637. p. cm. c.1978. (ISBN 0-06-026106-4). (ISBN 0-06-026107-2). Harper & Row.
--Willie Blows a Mean Horn. Toulmin-Rothe, Ann, illus. 1981. Harper.

Thomas, Isaiah, ed. see Mother Goose.

Thomas, Jane Resh (1936-)
--The Comeback Dog. Howell, Troy, illus. LC 80-12886. (Illus.). 62 p. 21cm. c.1981. (ISBN 0-395-29432-0). Houghton Mifflin/Clarion Books.
--Courage at Indian Deep. LC 83-14404. (Illus.). 128p. (gr. 3-7). 1984. (ISBN 0-89919-181-9, Clarion). HM.
--Elizabeth Catches a Fish. Duffy, Joseph (1949-), illus. 1977. Houghton.
--Elizabeth Catches a Fish. Duffy, Joseph (1949-), illus. LC 76-28318. 32 p. 26cm. c.1977. (ISBN 0-8164-3181-7). Seabury Press.

Thomas, Jeannette Grise see Grise, Jeannette, pseud.

Thomas, Jessie, et al.
--The Birthday Pie: Animated Cartoon Musical Playlet, One Act. LC 45-47992. (Book and Lyrics by Florence Crocker Comfort, Music by Jessie Thomas, Dances by Georgia Jesseph; Vocal Score Contains Songs, Piano Acc. and Full Directions.). 1 p. l., xi, 2-34 p. diagr. 26 cm. c.1941. The Willis Music Company.

Thomas, Jessie G.
--Katydid. Lyons, Dave, illus. LC 53-20509. 21cm. 47p. 1952. Pageant Press, Inc.

Thomas, Joan Gale, pseud., see Robinson, Joan Mary Gale Thomas.

Thomas, Joan Gale, pseud. (1910-)
--A is for Angel. Robinson, Joan Mary Gale Thomas. Thomas, Joan Gale, pseud. (1910-), illus. Robinson, Joan Mary Gale Thomas. LC 53-6737. 1953. Lothrop, Lee & Shepard.
--If I'd Been Born in Bethlehem. Robinson, Joan Mary Gale Thomas. Roman Catholic ed. Thomas, Joan Gale, pseud. (1910-), illus. Robinson, Joan Mary Gale Thomas. LC 54-12596. unpaged. illus. 21cm. 1954. Lothrop, Lee & Shepard Co.
--If Jesus Came to My House. Robinson, Joan Mary Gale Thomas. Thomas, Joan Gale, pseud. (1910-), illus. Robinson, Joan Mary Gale Thomas. (Illus.). (gr. k-3). 1951. (ISBN 0-688-40981-4). (ISBN 0-688-50981-9). Lothrop.
--One Little Baby: A Christmas Counting Book. Robinson, Joan Mary Gale Thomas. Thomas, Joan Gale, pseud. (1910-), illus. Robinson, Joan Mary Gale Thomas. LC 56-11403. unpaged. illus. 22cm. c.1956. Lothrop, Lee & Shepard Co.
--Our Father. Robinson, Joan Mary Gale Thomas. Thomas, Joan Gale, pseud. (1910-), illus. Robinson, Joan Mary Gale Thomas. N.D. Lothrop, Lee & Shepard.
--Where Is God?. Robinson, Joan Mary Gale Thomas. Thomas, Joan Gale, pseud. (1910-), illus. Robinson, Joan Mary Gale Thomas. LC 59-13154. unpaged. illus. 21 cm. 1959. Lothrop, Lee & Shepard Co.

Thomas, Joyce Carol
--Marked by Fire. LC 81-66479. 172 p. 18cm. (Avon/Flare book). 1982. (ISBN 0-380-79327-X). Avon Books. **Award: (ABA).**

Thomas, Karen
--The Good Thing ... the Bad Thing. Yaroslava, pseud. (1925-), illus. Mills, Yaroslava Surmach. LC 79-9201. p. cm. c.1979. (ISBN 0-13-360354-7). Prentice-Hall.

Thomas, Kathleen
--The Gleanie Bird. Atkinson, Leslie, illus. LC 56-14392. 117 p. illus. 22 cm. 1956. F. Warne.
--Goats Are Better Than Worms. Abrams, Kathie, illus. LC 83-25341. (Illus.). 160p. (gr. 3-6). 1984. (ISBN 0-396-08328-5). (ISBN 0-396-08328-5). Dodd.
--Nifkin. Learmont, Judith, illus. LC 82-45375. p. cm. 1982. (ISBN 0-396-08089-8). Dodd, Mead.
--Out of the Bug Jar. O'Sullivan, Tom, illus. LC 81-43217. (Illus.). 125 p. 21cm. c.1981. (ISBN 0-396-07992-X). Dodd, Mead.

Thomas, Kathy (1930-)
--The Angel's Quest. Seitz, Jacqueline (1936-), illus. LC 83-17503. p. cm. c.1983. (ISBN 0-914544-99-3). Kateri Books.

Thomas, Leslie D.
--The Story of the Willow Plate. Thomas, Leslie D., illus. LC 40-11022. 48p. 1940. William Morrow & Co.

Thomas, Leslie D., ed.
--The Story on the Willow Plate: Adapted from the Chinese Legend. Thomas, Leslie D., illus. LC 69-14802. (Illus.). 47 p. 21cm. 1969, c.1968. Schocken Books.

Thomas, Lida Larrimore Turner see Larrimore, Lida, pseud.

Thomas, Lida Larrimore Turner, Mrs. (1897-)
--The Blossoming of Patricia-the-Less. Larrimore, Lida, pseud. Price, Harriet Longstreet (1891-), illus. LC 24-23177. 253 p. incl. col. front., illus. col. plates. 22 cm. 1924. The Penn Publishing Company.

Thomas, Lowell Jackson (1892-1981)
--Tall Stories. 256p. 1931. Funk & Wagnalls Co.

Thomas, Lynda K., jt. auth. see Hakes, Thomas L.

Thomas, Margaret Loring, Mrs.
--The Burro's Moneybag. LC 31-20657. 123 p. front., illus. 21 cm. c.1931. The Abingdon Press.
--The Burro's Moneybag. Carsey, Alice, illus. LC 47-30204. 128 p. illus. 21 cm. 1947. Abingdon-Cokesbury Press.
--Carlos: Our Mexican Neighbor. Lohse, William R., illus. LC 38-24564. 189 p. incl. front., illus. plates. 21 cm. c.1938. The Bobbs-Merrill Company.
--Carmelita Sings: A Bolivan Story. LC 35-18844. 112 p. front., illus. 21 cm. c.1935. The Abingdon Press.
--The Pack Train Steamboat. LC 32-23422. 239 p. illus., plates. 20 1/2 cm. c.1932. The Bobbs-Merrill Company.
--Paulo in the Chilean Desert. Lohse, William R., illus. LC 34-37238. 190 p. incl. front., illus. 20 1/2 cm. c.1934. The Bobbs-Merril Company.

Thomas, Marlo
--Free to Be ... You and Me. Thomas, Marlo (1943-), concept by. Hart, Carole, et al., eds. Ms. Foundation LC 73-14784. (Illus.). 143 p. 28cm. 1974. (ISBN 0-07-064223-0). (ISBN 0-07-064223-0). McGraw-Hill.

Thomas, Mary Roenah, ed.
--The Young Folks' Book of Mirth: A Collection of the Best Fun in Prose and Verse. LC 75-38604. 327 p. 21cm. (Granger index reprint series). 1972. (ISBN 0-8369-6336-9). Books for Libraries Press.
--The Young Folks' Book of Mirth: A Collection of the Best Fun in Prose and Verse. LC 79-51961. 327 p. 20cm. (Granger Poetry Library). 1979. (ISBN 0-89609-197-X). Granger Book Co.
--The Young Folks' Book of Mirth: A Collection of the Best Fun in Prose and Verse. LC 24-8388. 327 p. 20 1/2 cm. c.1924. Lothrop, Lee & Shepard Co.

Thomas, Matilda Edith (1854-1925)
--New Verses. Humphrey, Maud (1868-), illus. (Babes of the Year Ser.). N.D. Frederick A. Stokes Co.

Thomas, Maud May
--Wait Long, Wait Still. LC 54-7481. 224 p. 20cm. 1954. Arcadia House.

Thomas, Maude Morgan
--Sing in the Dark: A Story of the Welsh in Pennsylvania. 1 st. ed. Schule, Clifford H., illus. LC 53-7340. (Illus.). 22cm. 203p. (Land of the Free Ser.). (Land of the Free Ser). (gr. 5-7). 1954. (ISBN 0-03-034465-4). HR&W.

Thomas, Maurice Walton, ed. see Marryat, Frederick.

Thomas, Patricia J. (1934-)
--Stand Back, Said the Elephant, "I'm Going to Sneeze!". Tripp, Wallace Whitney (1940-), illus. LC 70-135294. (Illus.). color ils. 32p. (ps-3). 1971. (ISBN 0-688-51136-8). Lothrop.
--There Are Rocks in My Socks! Said the Ox to the Fox. 1st ed. Gerstein, Mordicai, illus. LC 78-16632. (Illus.). (ps-3). 1979. (ISBN 0-688-41851-1). (ISBN 0-688-51851-6). Lothrop.

Thomas, Patty
--Let's Go All Around the Neighborhood. Rao, Anthony, illus. LC 81-83363. (Illus.). 24 p. 16cm. (First little golden book). c.1982. (ISBN 0-307-10113-4). (ISBN 0-307-68113-0). Golden Press.

Thomas, Paul, pseud., see Oakes, Donald Thomas.

Thomas, Piri (1928-)
--Stories from El Barrio. LC 78-3287. viii, 141 p. 22cm. c.1978. (ISBN 0-394-93568-3). Knopf.

Thomas, Robert Murray see Roberts, Tom, pseud.

Thomas, Robert Murray (1921-)
--The Java Raids. Roberts, Tom, pseud. Ayer, Margaret (0000-1981), illus. LC 64-12929. (Illus.). 247 p. 21cm. 1964. D. McKay Co.

Thomas, Ruth H.
--Brush Goat, Milk Goat. N.D. E. M. Hale & Co.
--Brush Goat, Milk Goat. Kriva, illus. LC 57-8760. 127 p. illus. 21 cm. 1957. Sterling Pub. Co.

Thomas, Sharon K. & Siegal, Marjorie
--No Baths for Tabitha. Robison, Don, illus. LC 84-52561. (Illus.). 24 p. 22cm. (Predictable Reading Books). c.1985. (ISBN 0-87406-002-8). Willowisp Press.

Thomas, Terry
--At Least We Were Married. 156p. Repr. (gr. 10 up). 1973. (ISBN 0-310-36932-0). Zondervan.

Thomas, Ulrich (1917-)
--Applemouse. Thomas, Ulrich (1917-), photos by. LC 78-185433. (Illus.). 40 p. 24cm. (Terra magica children's book). 1972. (ISBN 0-8090-2005-X). Hill and Wang.

Thomas, Vernon
--Arabian Nights, 2 Vols. (Illus.). N.D. Harper & Brothers'.
--Arabian Nights. (Argyle Ser). N.D. Hurst & Company.
--Arabian Nights. Chapman, E. O., ed. (Illus.). 416p. (School Library: No. 3). N.D. Educational Publishing Company.
--Stories from the Arabian Nights. Basu, pseud., illus. Bose, R. K.. (Illus.). 1979. (ISBN 0-89744-142-7). Auromere.

Thomas, Vernon, ed.
--Fairy Tales from India. (Illus.). (gr. 1-9). 1979. (ISBN 0-89744-137-0). Auromere.
--More Stories from the Arabian Nights. Basu, pseud., illus. Bose, R. K.. (Illus.). 135p. (gr. 1 up). 1981. (ISBN 0-89744-232-6, Pub. by Hemkunt India). Auromere.

Thomas, William Edward (1942-)
--The New Boy Is Blind. LC 80-349. (Illus.). 64p. (gr. 3-6). 1980. (ISBN 0-671-33094-2). Messner.

Thomas, William Jenkyn
--More Welsh Fairy & Folk Tales. (Illus.). (gr. 5 up). 1957. Verry.
--The Welsh Fairy Book. (Fairy Ser.). N.D. Frederick A. Stokes.
--The Welsh Fairy Book. Pogany, Willy (1882-1955), illus. (Illus.). (gr. 3-7). 1950. Dufour.
--The Welsh Fairy Book. Pogany, Willy (1882-1955), illus. (Illus.). (gr. 5 up). 1957. Verry.

Thomas Nelson, Inc, tr. see Sugita, Yutaka.

Thomason, Caroline Wasson
--Plays for Children in French and English. Donovan, Mary Rose, illus. LC 22-23318. 165 p. 5 pl., diagrs. 22 1/2 cm. 1922. The Penn Publishing Company.

Thomasset, M. P.
--The Fairy Spectacles. N.D. Macmillan.
--Princess Crystal. N.D. Macmillan.

Thomes, W. H.
--A Slaver's Adventures on Sea and Land. (Ocean Life Ser.). N.D. Lee & Shepard.

Thompson, illus.
--Animals' Trip to Sea. N.D. E. P. Dutton & Co.

Thompson, Adele Eugenia (1849-)
--American Patty: A Story of Eighteen-Twelve. Kennedy, J. W. Ferguson, illus. LC 9-17257. 5 p. l., 9-306 p. front., 5 pl. 19 cm. (Brave heart series). 1909. Lothrop, Lee & Shepard Co.
--Beck's Fortune. N.D. Lothrop, Lee & Shepard.
--Betty Seldon, Patriot. True, Lilian Crawford, illus. LC 1-17626. 246 p. front., pl. 18 1/2 cm. 1901. Lee and Shepard.
--Brave Heart Elizabeth: A Story of the Ohio Frontier. True, Lilian Crawford, illus. LC 2-19581. 1 p. l., 5 p., 1 l., 7-286 p. front., plates 19 cm. (Brave heart series). 1902. Lee and Shepard.
--A Lassie of the Isles. Kennedy, J. W Ferguson, illus. 6 p., 1 l., 7-269 p. front., 7 pl. 19 cm. (Brave heart series). 1903. Lee and Shepard.
--Nobody's Rose: Or, the Girlhood of Rose Shannon. Learned, A. G., illus. LC 12-15810. 304 p. front., plates. 19 cm. 1912. Lothrop, Lee & Shepard Co.
--Polly of the Pines: A Patriot Girl of the Carolinas. Roth, Henry, illus. LC 6-24159. 313 p. front., 5 pl. 19 cm. (Brave heart series). 1906. Lothrop, Lee & Shepard Co.

Thompson, Ames
--The Adventure Boys and the Island of Sapphires. LC 29-114061. 2 p. l., 212 p. front. 19 1/2 cm. (His Jewel series). c.1929. Cupples & Leon Company.
--The Adventure Boys and the Lagoon of Pearls. (The Jewel Ser.). N.D. Cupples & Leon Co.
--The Adventure Boys and the River of Emeralds. (The Jewel Ser.). N.D. Cupples & Leon Co.
--The Adventure Boys and the Temple of Rubies. LC 28-161754. 2 p. l., 206 p. front. 19 1/2 cm. (His Jewel series). c.1928. Cupples & Leon Company.
--The Adventure Boys and the Valley of Diamonds. (The Jewel Ser.). N.D. Cupples & Leon Co.
--Strange Adventure Stories for Boys. LC 35-6463. 3 p. l., 211 p., 2 l., 210 p., 2 l., 206 p., 2 l., 206 p. front. 21 cm. (His Jewel series). c.1935. Cupples & Leon Co.

Thompson, Arthur Ripley (1872-)
--Gold-Seeking on the Dalton Trail. Avison, George F. (1885-), illus. LC 25-159864. 5 p. l., 327 p. col. front., col. plates. 22 1/2 cm. (Beacon hill bookshelf). 1925. Little, Brown, and Company.
--Gold-Seeking on the Dalton Trail: Being the Adventures of Two New England Boys in Alaska and the Northwest Territory. LC 5169. xii p., 1 l., 352 p., 1 l. front., plates, map. 21 cm. 1900. Little, Brown and Company.
--Gold-Seeking on the Dalton Trail: Being the Adventures of Two New England Boys in Alaska and the Northwest Territory. LC 4-23364. xii p., 1 l., 352 p., 1 l. 10 pl. (incl. front.) map. 21 cm. (Beacon Hill Bookshelf). 1902. Little, Brown, and Company.
--Lizy Ann, and Other Rhymes. Hitchcock, Helen M., illus. LC 42-202. (Illus.). 44. 28cm. 1941. Woodstock Publishing Co.
--Shipwrecked in Greenland. LC 5-29105. x, p., 1 l., 310 p., 1 l. front., 9 pl(photos) 19 1/2cm. 1905. Little, Brown, and Company.
--Sunny Rhymes for Rainy Times. Bjorvand, Helen Hitchcock, illus. LC 43-346. ix, 11-87 p. illus. 20 cm. 1942. The Christopher Publishing House.

Thompson, Augustus Charles (1812-1901)
--Our Little One, the Little Shoe: Little Feet, Little Footsteps. LC 27-7257. xii, 13-112 p. 17 cm. 1867. Gould and Lincoln.

Thompson, Blanche Jennings (1887-)
--The Golden Trumpets. Torrey, Helen (1901-), illus. LC 27-25943. viii, p., 1 l., 163 p. incl. col. front., col. illus. 19 1/2 cm. 1927. Macmillan Company.
--St. Elizabeth's Three Crowns. Rethi, Lili (1894-), illus. LC 58-5113. 189 p. illus. 22 cm. vision books, 31. 1958. Vision Books.

Thompson, Blanche Jennings (1887-), ed.
--All the Silver Pennies: Combining Silver Pennies and More Silver Pennies. Arndt, Ursula, illus. LC 67-4508. (Illus.). xvi, 224 p. 24cm. 1967. (ISBN 0-02-789330-8). Macmillan.
--More Silver Pennies. Doane, Pelagie (1906-1966), illus. xiii, 155 p. illus. 19 cm. 1957. Macmillan.
--Silver Pennies. Bromhall, Winifred, illus. 1961. Macmillan.

Thompson, Norman, ed. see Persaud, Pat.
Thompson, Pat, jt. auth. see Campbell, Carolyn.
Thompson, Pat, selected by see Ormerod, Jan.
Thompson, Paul (1938-) & Kuklin, Susan
--The Hitchhikers. LC 79-21971. (Illus.). 83 p. 22cm. (Triumph book). 1980. (ISBN 0-531-04173-5). F. Watts.
Thompson, Ruth Plumly (1893-1976)
--Captain Salt in Oz. Neill, John Rea (1878-1943), illus. Baum, Lyman Frank (1856-1919), created by. LC 36-9381. 5 p. l., 17-306 p., 1 l. front., illus. 23 1/2 cm. c.1936. The Reilly & Lee Co.
--Comrades of the Desert: A Story for Boys. LC 21-147952. 176 p. incl. pl. 18 cm. 1921. H. Wagner Publishing Co.
--The Cowardly Lion of Oz. Neill, John Rea (1878-1943), illus. Baum, Lyman Frank (1856-1919), created by. LC 23-112177. 5 p. l., 15-291 p. col. front., illus., col. plates. 24 cm. c.1923. The Reilly & Lee Co.
--The Curious Cruise of Captain Santa. Neill, John Rea (1878-1943), illus. LC 26-17470. 2 p. l., 11-124 p. col. front., col. illus. 24 1/2 cm. c.1926. The Reilly & Lee Co.
--The Giant Horse of Oz. Neill, John Rea (1878-1943), illus. Baum, Lyman Frank (1856-1919), created by. LC 28-13881. 5 p. l., 15-288 p. col. front., illus., col. plates. 23 1/2 cm. c.1928. The Reilly & Lee Co.
--The Gnome King of Oz. Neill, John Rea (1878-1943), illus. Baum, Lyman Frank (1856-1919), created by. LC 27-10969. 6 p. l., 15-282 p. col. front., illus., col. plates. 23 1/2 cm. c.1927. The Reilly & Lee Co.
--Grampa in Oz. Neill, John Rea (1878-1943), illus. Baum, Lyman Frank (1856-1919), created by. LC 24-180912. 6 p. l., 15-271 p. incl. front., illus. col. plates. 23 1/2 cm. c.1924. The Reilly & Lee Co.
--Handy Mandy in Oz. Neill, John Rea (1878-1943), illus. Baum, Lyman Frank (1856-1919), created by. LC 37-5402. 6 p. l., 17-246 p., 1 l. incl. front., illus. 23 1/2 cm. c.1937. The Reilly & Lee Co.
--The Hungry Tiger of Oz. Neill, John Rea (1878-1943), illus. Baum, Lyman Frank (1856-1919), created by. LC 26-17314. 5 p. l., 15-261 p., 1 l. col. front., illus., col. plates. 23 1/2 cm. c.1926. The Reilly & Lee Co.
--Jack Pumpkinhead of Oz. Neill, John Rea (1878-1943), illus. Baum, Lyman Frank (1856-1919), created by. LC 29-124672. 6 p. l., 17-252 p., 1 l. col. front., illus., col. plates. 23 1/2 cm. c.1929. The Reilly & Lee Co.
--Kabumpo in Oz. Neill, John Rea (1878-1943), illus. Baum, Lyman Frank (1856-1919), created by. LC 22-12114. 5 p. l., 15-297 p., 1 l. col. front., illus., col. plates. 24 cm. c.1922. The Reilly & Lee Co.
--King Kojo. Marge, illus. LC 38-33404. 239 p. col. front., illus., col. plates. 23 1/2 cm. c.1938. David McKay Company.
--The Lost King of Oz. Neill, John Rea (1878-1943), illus. Baum, Lyman Frank (1856-1919), created by. LC 25-17663. 5 p. l., 13-280 p. col. front., illus., col. plates. 23 1/2 cm. c.1925. The Reilly & Lee Co.
--Ojo in Oz. Neill, John Rea (1878-1943), illus. Baum, Lyman Frank (1856-1919), created by. 6 p. l., 17-304 p. col. front., illus., col. plates. 23 1/2 cm. c.1933. The Reilly & Lee Co.
--Ozoplaning with the Wizard of Oz. Neill, John Rea (1878-1943), illus. Baum, Lyman Frank (1856-1919), created by. LC 39-21292. 6 p. l., 17-272 p. illus. 23 1/2 cm. c.1939. Reilly & Lee.
--The Princess of Cozytown. Scott, Janet Laura, illus. LC 22-20755. 93 p. col. illus. 23 1/2 cm. c.1922. P. F. Volland Company.
--The Purple Prince of Oz. Neill, John Rea (1878-1943), illus. Baum, Lyman Frank LC 32-12600. 5 p. l., 17-281 p. col. front., illus., col. plates. 23 1/2 cm. c.1932. The Reilly & Lee Co.
--The Silver Princess in Oz. Neill, John Rea (1878-1943), illus. Baum, Lyman Frank (1856-1919), created by. LC 38-7474. 6 p. l., 17-255 p. illus. 24 cm. c.1938. The Reilly & Lee Co.
--Speedy in Oz. Neill, John Rea (1878-1943), illus. Baum, Lyman Frank (1856-1919), created by. LC 34-11670. 6 p. l., 17-298 p. col. front., illus., col. plates. 23 1/2 cm. c.1934. The Reilly & Lee Co.
--The Wishing Horse of Oz. Neill, John Rea (1878-1943), illus. Baum, Lyman Frank (1856-1919), created by. LC 35-67237. 6 p. l., 17-298 p. col. front., illus., col. plates. 23 1/2 cm. c.1935. The Reilly & Lee Co.
--The Wonder Book: Stories, Pictures, Games, Puzzles, Hero Tales, Animal Lore, Plays, Fun and Fancy. LC 29-19879. 217 p. col. front., illus., col. plates. 26 cm. c.1929. The Reilly & Lee Co.
--Yankee in Oz. Martin, Dick (1927-), illus. Baum, Lyman Frank (1856-1919), created by. LC 73-160461. (Illus.). 94 p. 28cm. 1972. International Wizard of Oz Club.
--The Yellow Knight of Oz. Neill, John Rea (1878-1943), illus. Baum, Lyman Frank (1856-1919), created by. 6 p. l., 17-275 p. col. front., illus., col. plates. 23 1/2 cm. c.1930. The Reilly & Lee Co.
Thompson, Ruth Plumly (1893-) & Baum, Lyman Frank (1856-1919)
--Pirates in Oz. Neill, John Rea (1878-1943), illus. LC 31-14626. 6 p. l., 17-280 p. col. front., illus., col. plates. 23 1/2 cm. c.1931. The Reilly & Lee Co.
Thompson, Stith (1885-1976), ed.
--One Hundred Favorite Folk Tales. LC 68-27355. 442p. 456p. (Midland Bks.: No. 172). 1968. (ISBN 0-253-15940-7). (ISBN 0-253-20172-1). Ind U Pr.
--Tales of the North American Indians. Thompson, Stith (1885-1976), annotations by. N.D. (ISBN 0-8446-5088-9). Peter Smith Publisher, Inc.
Thompson, Stith (1855-1976) & Balys, Jonas, eds.
--Oral Tales of India. LC 66-22898. 412p. (Folklore Ser.). 1966. (ISBN 0-253-35650-4). (ISBN 0-253-20091-1). Indiana University Press.
Thompson, Susan L
--One More Thing, Dad. Leder, Dora, illus. LC 79-27887. (Illus.). 32 p. 19cm. (Self-starter books). c.1980. (ISBN 0-8075-6095-2). A. Whitman.
Thompson, Sylvia Elizabeth Afiola, jt. auth. see Luling, Elizabeth.
Thompson, Sylvia Elizabeth Afiola (1902-)
--The Rough Crossing. LC 21-20620. 3 p. l., 9-247, 1 p. 19 1/2 cm. 1921. Houghton Mifflin Company.
Thompson, T. J.
--Ten Red Rods. Thompson, T. J., illus. LC 80-83135. (Illus.). 16p. (Orig.). (ps-1). 1980. (ISBN 0-915676-02-8). Ed Sys Pub.
Thompson, Thomas E, jt. auth. see Thompson, John G.
Thompson, Thomas (1880-)
--The 'Flying Spray. LC 45-8512. 256 p. front., 1 illus. 20 cm. 1943. F. Warne and Co. Ltd.
Thompson, Vance (1863-1925)
--The Mouse-Colored Road. Herford, Oliver (1863-1935), illus. LC 13-21057. 7 p. l., 3-91, 1 p. incl. front., plates. 20 cm. 1913. D. Appleton and Company.
Thompson, Vivian Laubach (1911-)
--Ah See and the Spooky House. Walter, Frances, illus. LC 63-7221. unpaged. illus. 27 cm. 1963. Goldon Gate Junior Books.
--Aukele the Fearless: A Legend of Old Hawaii. Thollander, Earl Gustave (1922-), illus. LC 70-181807. (Illus.). 79 p. 25cm. 1972. (ISBN 0-87464-186-1). (ISBN 0-87464-187-X). Golden Gate Junior Books.
--Camp-in-the-Yard. Turkle, Brinton Cassaday (1915-), illus. LC 61-65035. unpaged. illus. 23 cm. c.1961. Holiday House.
--Faraway Friends. Greenwood, Marion, illus. LC 63-24952. 58 p. col. illus. 23 cm. 1963. Holiday House.
--Hawaiian Legends of Tricksters and Riddlers. Selig, Sylvie (1942-), illus. LC 70-8785. (Illus.). 103, 1 p. 23cm. 1969. Holiday House.
--Hawaiian Myths of Earth, Sea, and Sky. Weisgard, Leonard Joseph (1916-), illus. LC 66-320653. (Illus.). 83, 1 p. 23cm. 1966. Holiday House.
--Hawaiian Tales of Heroes and Champions. Kane, Herbert Kawainui, illus. LC 72-151757. (Illus.). 128 p. 24cm. 1971. (ISBN 0-8234-0192-8). Holiday House.
--The Horse That Liked Sandwiches. Aliki, pseud. (1929-), illus. Brandenberg, Aliki Liacouras. LC 62-8718. unpaged. illus. 24 cm. 1962. Putnam.
--Keola's Hawaiian Donkey. Thollander, Earl Gustave (1922-), illus. LC 66-9095. (Illus.). 1 v. (unpaged. 29cm. 1966. Golden Gate Junior Books.
--Kimo Makes Music. Walter, Frances, illus. LC 62-13801. (Illus.). 26cm. 32p. (gr. k-3). 1962. (ISBN 0-87464-129-2). Golden Gate.
--Maui-Full-of-Tricks: A Legend of Old Hawaii. Thollander, Earl Gustave (1922-), illus. LC 75-119065. (Illus.). 94 p. 25cm. 1970. (ISBN 0-87464-162-4). Golden Gate Junior Books.
--Meet the Hawaiian Menehunes. 1st ed. LC 59-10979. 47p. illus. 21cm. 1952. Pageant Press.
--Meet the Hawaiian Menehunes. Lyons, Dave, illus. 1967. Pageant Press, Inc.
--Sad Day, Glad Day. Obligado, Lilian Isabel (1931-), illus. LC 62-6936. unpaged. illus. 20 cm. c.1962. Holiday House.
Thompson, William (1865-)
--Wigwan Wonder Tales. Boog, Carle Michel, illus. LC 19-14898. (Illus.). 19 cm. 156p. 1919. Charles Scribner's Sons.
Thompson, Wilma
--That Barbara. Seuling, Barbara (1937-), illus. LC 67-19760. (Illus.). 170 p. 21cm. 1969. Delacorte Press.
Thoms, William John see Merton, Ambrose, pseud.
Thoms, William John (1803-1885)
--Gammer Gurton's Famous Histories of Sir Guy of Warwick, Sir Bevis of Hampton, Tom Hickathrift, Friar Bacon, Robin Hood, and The King and the Cobbler. Merton, Ambrose, pseud. LC 43-20228. 118 p. incl. front., plates. 17 1/2 cm. 1843, c.1843. Wiley and Putnam.
Thomsen, Adolf
--Beelzebub and the Sea Nymph. LC 56-12337. 116 p. 21 cm. (Nobel book). 1956. Comet Press Books.
Thomsen, Frede, jt. auth. see Wahlenberg, Anna.
Thomsen, Gudrun Thorne, tr. see Christensen, Haaken.
Thomsen, Halvard J., jt. auth. see Barstad, Glenna.
Thomson, Andrew Kilpatrick, ed.
--The Four Corners: An Anthology of Poetry. Horseman, Mollie, illus. LC 73-473795. (Illus.). 304 p. 27cm. 1968. Jacaranda.
--The Four Corners: An Anthology of Poetry. school ed. Horseman, Mollie, illus. LC 78-556136. (Illus.). 2 v. 26cm. 1969, c.1968. (ISBN 0-7016-0296-1). (ISBN 0-7016-0297-X). Jacaranda.
Thomson, David Robert Alexander (1914-)
--Danny Fox. Edwards, Gunvor, illus. (Illus.). 120 p. 20cm. (Young Puffin original). 1967, c.1966. Penguin Books.
--Danny Fox at the Palace. Edwards, Gunvor, illus. LC 76-374370. (Illus.). 125 p. 20cm. (Young puffin original). 1976. (ISBN 0-14-030834-2). Puffin Books.
--Danny Fox Meets a Stranger. Edwards, Gunvor, illus. LC 76-2389. (Illus.). 119 p. 20cm. (Puffin books PS365). (A Young Puffin Original). 1968. Penguin Books.
Thomson, Edward
--Funny Bunnies. Tourane, Jean, illus. LC 77-78939. (Illus.). 28 p. 32cm. 1969. Platt & Munk.
Thomson, Edward William (1849-)
--Smoky Days. (Illus.). (The Sunshine Library for Young People). N.D. Thomas Y. Crowell.
--Walter Gibbs, the Young Boss. Copeland, Charles, illus. N.D. T. Y. Crowell & Co.
--The Young Boss. (Illus.). (Sunshine Library for Young People). 1900. T. Y. Crowell & Co.
Thomson, Elizabeth Gile
--The Real Princess. Warren, Elizabeth B., illus. LC 25-3946. 293 p. front., plates. 19 1/2 cm. c.1924. Lothrop, Lee & Shepard Co.
Thomson, John Stuart (1869-)
--Bud and Bamboo. LC 12-217748. 3 p. l., 96 p. illus. 19 cm. (On verso of half-title: Stories of primitive life for primary grades)). c.1912. D. Appleton and Company.
--Fil and Filippa: Story of Child Life in the Phillipines. Petersham, Maud Sylvia Fuller (1889-1971) & Petersham, Miska (1889-1960), illus. LC 17-25848. vii, 75 p. incl. front., illus. col. plates. 19 cm. 1917. The Macmillan Company.
Thomson, Leonard S.
--The White Snake: An Authentic Chinese Fairy Tale. Pomerantz, Norman, illus. LC 60-9151. (Illus.). 45p. 21cm. 1960. Greenwich Book Publishers.
Thomson, Linda H.
--Saturday's Warrior. 226p. (gr. 7-12). 1982. (ISBN 0-912085-01-0). Ensign Prods.
Thomson, Linda H., jt. auth. see Stewart, Doug.
Thomson, Lucy Gertsch
--Little Steppingstones. Young, Erla, illus. LC 56-27618. 80 p. illus. 24 cm. 1956. Deseret Book Co.
Thomson, Peter (1913-)
--Cougar. Lynch, Brendan, illus. LC 68-10475. (Illus.). 192 p. 23cm. 1968. Follett Pub. Co.
--Longhorns to Abilene. Mocniak, George, illus. LC 65-20064. 191 p. 23 cm. 1965. Follet Pub. Co.
--Rookie Reservist. LC 58-12014. 201 p. 21 cm. (Career books). 1958. Dodd, Mead.
--Sierra Ranger. LC 54-7756. 212p. 21cm. 1954. Dodd, Mead.
--Ski Ranger. LC 57-5412. 215p. 21cm. 1957. Dodd, Mead.
Thomson, Riley, adapted by see Lantz, Walter (1900-) & Bedford, Annie North.
Thomson, Riley & Armstrong, Sam, eds.
--Woody Woodpecker's peck of trouble. Walter Lantz Studio, illus. LC 51-8909. (Adapted from the story "Now everybody loves Waldo", Original Author: Walter Lantz). unpaged. illus. 17cm. (Tell-a-tale Books). c.1951. Whitman Pub. Co.
Thomson, Ruth
--Peabody All at Sea. Kirkwood, Ken, illus. LC 78-17930. (Illus.). 32 p. 25cm. c.1978. (ISBN 0-688-41862-7). (ISBN 0-688-51862-1). Lothrop, Lee & Shepard Co.
--Peabody's First Case. Kirkwood, Ken, illus. LC 78-17931. (Illus.). 32 p. 25cm. c.1978. (ISBN 0-688-41861-9). (ISBN 0-688-51861-3). Lothrop, Lee & Shepard Co.
Thoorens, Leon
--Golden Compass. Armour-Chelu, Ian, illus. (Illus.). (gr. 7 up). 1965. Roy.
Thor, Mabel Nelson
--Happy Days. Holmer, Edvin K., illus. LC 49-50438. (Illus.). 20 cm. 64p. 1949. Augustana Book Concern.
Thoreau, Henry David (1817-1862)
--What Befell at Mrs. Brook's. Overlie, George, illus. LC 72-13329. (Illus.). 32p. (Seedling Bks.). (gr. 2-6). 1974. (ISBN 0-8225-0284-4). Lerner Pubns.
Thorn, Alice Green, jt. auth. see Coleman, Satis Narrona Barton, Mrs.
Thorn, Alice Green, jt. auth. see Coleman, Satis Narrona, Mrs.
Thorn, Alice Green (1890-1942)
--Music for Younger Children. LC 29-3788. (Illus.). 19 cm. 158p. (Half-Title: Series on Childhood education). 1929. Charles Scribner's Sons.
Thorn, Alice Green (1890-1942), ed.
--Singing Words. Stern, Marie Simchow (1909-), illus. Masha, pseud. LC 79-38605. (Illus.). 71 p. 27cm. (Granger index reprint series). 1972, c.1941. (ISBN 0-8369-6337-7). Books for Libraries Press.
--Singing Words. Stern, Marie Simchow (1909-), illus. Masha, pseud. LC 41-21727. 71 p. illus. (part col.) 26 cm. 1941. C. Scribner's Sons.
Thorn, Ismay
--A Flock of Four. (Illus.). (The Little Men Ser.). N.D. A. L. Burt' Pubs.
--A Flock of Four. (Illus.). (The Rugby Ser.). N.D. A. L. Burt.
--A Flock of Four. Browne, Gordon Frederick (1858-1932), illus. N.D. Pott & Co.
--Geoff and Jim. (The Rugby Series for Boys and Girls). N.D. A. L. Burt Company.
--Phil and His Father, 36 vols. (Illus.). (St. Nicholas Ser.). 1905. Set. A L Burt Co.
--Phil and his Father. (Illus.). (The Rugby Series). 1915. A L Burt & Co.
--Quite Unexpected. (Illus.). N.D. Pott & Co.
--Sister Sue. N.D. Thomas Whittaker.
Thornbury, Walter, tr. see La Fontaine, Jean de.
Thorndike, Edward Lee, jt. auth. see Defoe, Daniel.
Thorndike, Edward Lee (1874-), ed. see Andersen, Hans Christian.
Thorndike, Edward Lee (1874-), ed. see Brooks, Elbridge Streeter.
Thorndike, Edward Lee (1874-), ed. see Dodge, Mary Elizabeth Mapes, Mrs.
Thorndike, Edward Lee (1874-), ed. see Hawthorne, Nathaniel.
Thorndike, Edward Lee (1874-), ed. see Kingsley, Charles.
Thorndike, Edward Lee (1874-), ed. see Lorenzini, Carlo.
Thorndike, Edward Lee (1874-), ed. see Ruskin, John.
Thorndike, Edward Lee (1874-), ed. see Sewell, Anna.
Thorndike, Edward Lee (1874-), ed. see Spyri, Johanna Heusser.
Thorndike, Edward Lee (1874-), ed.
--The Arabian Nights. Artzybasheff, Boris Mikhailovich (1899-1965), illus. LC 36-3141. (Edited to Fit the Interests and Abilities of Young Readers). vii, 402 p. incl. front., illus. 19 cm. (Thorndike library). c.1936. D. Appleton-Century Company, Incorporated.
Thorndike, Russell B., ed. see Buchanan, William.
Thorndike, Susan (1944-), ed.
--The Electric Radish and Other Jokes. 1st ed. Cruz, Raymond (1933-), illus. LC 75-183615. (Illus.). 48 p. 22cm. 1973. (ISBN 0-385-04770-3). (ISBN 0-385-04770-3). Doubleday.
Thorndyke
--My Family and I. N.D. Grosset & Dunlap.
Thorndyke, Helen Louise, pseud., see Stratemeyer Syndicate.
Thorndyke, Helen Louise, pseud.
--Honey Bunch and Norman. Stratemeyer Syndicate. Dillon, Corinne Boyd, illus. LC 57-4383. viii, 181 p. illus. 20 cm. (The Honey Bunch and Norman Ser.: Vol. 1). 1957. Grosset & Dunlap.
--Honey Bunch and Norman and the Painted Pony. Stratemeyer Syndicate. LC 62-13364. 175 p. illus. 20 cm. (The Honey Bunch and Norman Ser.: Vol. 11). 1962. Grosset & Dunlap.
--Honey Bunch and Norman and the Paper Lantern Mystery. Stratemeyer Syndicate. LC 61-1805. 182 p. illus. 20 cm. (The Honey Bunch and Norman Ser.: Vol. 10). 1961. Grosset & Dunlap.
--Honey Bunch and Norman and the Walnut Tree Mystery. Stratemeyer Syndicate. LC 63-1128. 20cm. 174p. (The Honey Bunch and Norman Ser.: Vol. 12). (gr. 1-4). 1963. (ISBN 0-448-08112-1). Grosset & Dunlap.
--Honey Bunch and Norman in the Castle of Magic. Stratemeyer Syndicate. LC 59-16127. 184 p. illus. 20 cm. (The Honey Bunch and Norman Ser.: Vol. 8). 1959. Grosset & Dunlap.

Thornton, Nell (1895-)
--The Little Rhymer: Quaint Verses, with Pictures, for the Little Tot. Thornton, Nell (1895-), illus. LC 12-21726. (Dedication verses by Glenn McClanghry). (Illus.). 19 x 15 cm. 59p. (The Cosy Corner Ser.). 1912. L C Page & Co.

Thorp, Charles Nicholas (1870-)
--Story Sermons for Boys and Girls. LC 35-14990. 19 cm. 175p. 1935. Cokesbury Press.

Thorpe, Benjamin (1782-1870) & Keightley, Thomas (1789-1872), eds.
--Tales on the North Wind: Old Fairy Tales. LC 56-9660. 125p. illus. 20cm. 1956. Roy Publishers.

Thorpe, Betty (1911-)
--Fioretta: Or, Cessate De Piagarmi. Blanding, Don (1894-), illus. LC 24-5347. 63 p. front. (port.) illus. 20 1/2 cm. 1922. Advertiser Publishing Co., Ltd.

Thorpe, Minerva
--Pierre and his Dog Jock. LC 98-2031. 210p. 1898. Kenyon Press.
--Two Chums: Or, A Boy and His Dog, 1 of 5 vols. (Illus.). (Sterling Stories for Boys & Girls Ser.). 1901. Set. Laird & Lee.

Thorpe, Rose Hartwick, Mrs. (1850-1939)
--The Chester Girls. LC 12-35162. 256p. 18cm. 1887. American Baptist Publication Society.
--Chester Girls. (Illus.). 256p. N.D. Sunday-School Publications.
--The Fenton Family: Or, For Mother's Sake. LC 41-35162. 2 p. l., 3-317 p. front., plates. 17 1/2 cm. 1884. American Baptist Publication Society.
--Fenton Family: Or, For Mother's Sake. (Illus.). 317p. N.D. Sunday-School Publications.
--Fred's Dark Days. (Illus.). (The Dolphin Ser.: Vol. 5). N.D. Fleming H. Revell Co.
--Nina Bruce: Or, A Girl's Influence. LC 12-39530. 3 p.l., 5-319 p. front., plates. 18 1/2 cm. c.1886. American Baptist Publication Society.
--Nina Bruce: Or, A Girl's Influence. (Illus.). 319p. N.D. Sunday-School Publications.
--The Year's Best Days: For Boys and Girls. LC 44-398500. 202 p. front., plates. 17 1/2 x 13 1/2 cm. 1889. Lee and Shepard.

Thorsmark, Thora
--In Reindeer Land. Orloff, Gregory, illus. LC 42-6279. 333 p. incl. col. front., illus. (part col.) 19 x 14 1/2 cm. 1942. Row, Peterson and Company.

Thorson, Charles
--Keeko. LC 47-11595. (Illus.). 17p. 31cm. 1947. Wilcox & Follet.
--Keeko. Thorson, Charles, illus. LC 52-2418. (Illus.). 31cm. 32p. (ps-3). 1952. (ISBN 0-695-44830-7). Follett.
--The Story of the Three Bears. Thorson, Charles, illus. LC 46-22548. (Illus.). 22cm. 32p. 1946. John Martin's House.

Thorton, Nell
--Little Rhymer: With Dedication Verses. LC 12-21726. 59 p. front., col. illus., pl. 19 1/2 x 15 cm. 1912. R. R. Donnelley & Sons Co.

Thorvall, Kerstin (1925-)
--And Leffe Was Instead of a Dad. De Kiefte, Kees, illus. Miro, Francine Lee, tr. from Swedish. LC 74-81694. (Illus.). 131 p. 22cm. 1974, c.1971. (ISBN 0-87888-103-4). Bradbury Press.
--Girl in April. MacMillan, Annabelle, pseud. (1922-), tr. from Swedish. Quick, Annabelle. LC 63-11692. 158 p. 21cm. 1st U.S. edition. 1963. Harcourt, Brace & World.
--Gunnar Scores a Goal. Hollerbach, Serge, illus. Parker, Anne, tr. from Swedish. LC 68-26000428. (Illus.). 45 p. 23cm. 1st U.S. edition. 1968. Harcourt, Brace & World.

Thrasher, Crystal Faye (1924-)
--Between the Dark and the Daylight. LC 79-12423. p. cm. 1979. (ISBN 0-689-50150-1). Atheneum.
--The Dark Didn't Catch Me. LC 74-18193. 182 p. 22cm. 1975. (ISBN 0-689-50025-4). Atheneum. **Award: (ALA).**
--End of a Dark Road. LC 82-3958. 228p. (gr. 3-7). 1982. (ISBN 0-689-50250-8, McElderry Bk). Atheneum.
--Julie's Summer. LC 81-3479. p. cm. 1981. (ISBN 0-689-50209-5). Atheneum.
--A Taste of Daylight. LC 84-2967. 228p. (gr. 7 up). 1984. (ISBN 0-689-50313-X, McElderry Bk). Atheneum.

The, Three Bears
--Goldilocks & the Three Bears. new ed. Carruth, Jane, retold by. Embleton, Elisabeth & Embleton, Gerry, illus. LC 72-75173. 32p. (Illustrated Classic Tales Ser.). (gr. k-3). 1972. (ISBN 0-529-04695-4). (ISBN 0-529-04699-7). World Pub.
--Goldilocks and the Three Bears. The Illustrated Pop-Up. Cloud, Claude Carey (1899-) & Lentz, Harold B., illus. LC 35-5. 18 p. incl. front., illus. (part col.) 23 1/2 cm. c.1934. Blue Ribbon Press.
--Goldilocks and the Three Bears. Lowe, Edith May Kovar (1905-), adapted by. Windsor, Mary, pseud. Smith, Marion, illus. LC 66-17137. (Illus.). 16 p. (Read-Aloud Picture Book). 1967, c.1966. Follett Pub. Co.
--Goldilocks and the Three Bears. Obligado, Lilian Isabel (1931-), illus. LC 80-50141. (Illus.). 20 p. 24cm. (Golden Storytime Book). c.1980. (ISBN 0-307-11980-7). Golden Press.
--Goldilocks and the Three Bears. Palazzo, Tony (1905-1970), retold by. Palazzo, Tony (1905-1970), illus. LC 59-7578. unpaged. illus. 27cm. (Tony Palazzo Nursery Classic). c.1959. Garden City Books.
--Goldilocks and the Three Bears. Watts, Anna Bernadette (1942-), retold by. Watts, Anna Bernadette (1942-), illus. LC 85-7192. (Illus.). 26 p. 30cm. 1985. North-South Books : Distributed in the U.S. by Holt, Rinehart, and Winston.
--The Story of the Three Bears. Brooke, Leonard Leslie (1862-1940), illus. 24 p. illus. (part col.) 26 cm. (On cover: Leslie Brooke's children's books). N.D. F. Warne & Co., Ltd.
--The Story of the Three Bears: A Picture Book. Stobbs, William (1914-), illus. LC 64-8142. 32p. col. illus. 29x25cm. 1965, c.1964. Whittlesey-McGraw.
--The Three Bears: A Family Story. Divinsky, Beatrice & Kallen, Miriam, illus. LC 34-37988. 31 p. col. illus. 20 x 24 cm. 1934. Lothrop, Lee & Shepard Company.
--The Three Bears. Cameron, Mary, illus. LC 42-21768. (Illus.). 23 x 19cm. 28p. 1942. Random House.
--The Three Bears. Galdone, Paul (1914-), retold by. Galdone, Paul (1914-), illus. LC 78-158833. (Illus.). 32 p. 27cm. 1972. Seabury Press.
--The Three Bears. Hillert, Margaret (1920-), retold by. Wilde, Irma, illus. LC 63-9614. (Illus.). 27 p. 21cm. (Follett just beginning-to-read series). 1963. Follett Pub. Co.
--The Three Bears. Pavel, Frances K. (1907-), adapted by. LC 61-5353. 26 p. illus. 24 cm. (Read it myself book). 1961. Holt,Rinehart and Winston.
--The Three Bears. Rowland, Helen, illus. LC 53-242585. unpaged. illus. 17cm. (Tell-a-tale books). 1953, c.1952. Whitman Pub. Co.
--The Three Bears. Sharp, Gene (1923-), illus. (Illus.). 24p. (gr. k-2). 1976. (ISBN 0-307-69058-X, Golden Pr). Western Pub.
--The Three Bears. Suzanne, illus. LC 55-405254. unpaged. illus. 17cm. (Tell-a-tale books, 2512). c.1955. Whitman Pub. Co.
--The Three Bears. Tedder, Elizabeth, illus. LC 38-18603. 18 p. incl. front., illus. (part col.) 26 1/2 x 24 1/2 cm. c.1938. Grosset & Dunlap.
--The Three Bears. Wadsworth, Wallace Carter (1894-1933), retold by. Brice, Tony, illus. LC 42-3779. 61 p. illus. (part col.) 17 cm. 1942. Rand McNally & Company.
--The Three Bears. Winokur, Joan Gelman (1935-), retold by. Ramirez, Pablo, illus. LC 66-14054. 1v. (unpaged) col. illus. 24cm. (Holly story bk. lib. Q1054). 1966. World.
--The Three Bears: A Rebus Story in Words and Pictures. LC 54-44356. unpaged. illus. 20cm. (Bonnie rebus book, 4183). 1953. S. Lowe Co.

The, Three Bears & Cauley, Lorinda Bryan (1951-)
--Goldilocks and the Three Bears. 1st Peppercorn Paperback ed. Cauley, Lorinda Bryan (1951-), illus. LC 80-26253. (Illus.). 32 p. 24cm. 1981. (ISBN 0-399-20794-5). (ISBN 0-399-20795-3). Putnam.

The, Three Bears & Tolstoy, Leo Nikolaevich (1828-1910)
--The Three Bears. Vasnetsov, Y., illus. (Illus.). 16p. 1976. (ISBN 0-8285-1244-2, Pub. by Progress Pubs USSR). Imported Pubns.

The, Three Bears & Winokur, Joan Gelman (1935-)
--The Three Bears. Ramirez, Pablo, illus. LC 66-14054. 1 v. (unpaged) col. illus. 34 cm. (Holly story book library). 1966. World Pub. Co.

Three Little Bears
--The Three Little Bears. Wadsworth, Wallace Carter (1894-1933), ed. Price, Margaret Evans, Mrs. (1888-1973), illus. N.D. Rand McNally.

Three Little Kittens
--The Three Little Kittens. Merrill, Marion & Protas, Julius, eds. LC 46-22349. 24 p. illus. (part col.) 26 x 21 cm. 1946. The Citadel Press.

Three Little Pigs
--The Animated Three Little Pigs. Merrill, Marion & Protas, Julius, eds. LC 46-223582. 24 p. col. illus. 26 x 21 cm. 1946. The Citadel Press.
--The Story of the Three Little Pigs: A Picture Book. Stobbs, William (1914-), illus. LC 65-25144. 1v. (unpaged) col. illus. 19x26cm. 1965. Whittlesey-McGraw.
--The Three little Kittens. 16 p. col. illus. 33 cm. c.1941. Whitman Publishing Company.
--Three Little Pigs. LC 42-44987. (Illus.). 30cm. 16p. c.1923. Platt & Munk.
--Three Little Pigs. LC 42-44988. (Illus.). 30cm. 16p. c.1934. Platt & Munk.
--The Three Little Pigs. 12 p. col. illus. 23 x 31 cm. (White house animated books). c.1933. The White House Publishers.
--The Three Little Pigs. Barbaresi, Nina, illus. LC 80-84778. (Illus.). 20 p. 24cm. (Golden storytime book). c.1981. (ISBN 0-307-11955-6). Golden Press.
--The Three Little Pigs. Bendel, Ruth, illus. LC 56-8344. unpaged. illus. 17cm. (Rand McNally Junior Elf Bk. 695). N.D. Rand McNally.
--The Three Little Pigs. Benstead, Vivienne, adapted by. Cameron, Mary, illus. LC 42-21772. 28 p. illus. (part col.) 23 1/2 x 19 cm. c.1942. Random House.
--The Three Little Pigs. Brice, Tony, illus. LC 41-2941. 47 p. illus. (part col.) 17 x 14 cm. c.1941. Rand McNally & Company.
--The Three Little Pigs. Galdone, Paul (1914-), retold by. Galdone, Paul (1914-), illus. LC 75-115780. (Illus.). 41 p. 21cm. 1970. Seabury Press.
--The Three Little Pigs. Grace, Eileen, illus. LC 80-27483. p. cm. c.1981. (ISBN 0-89375-462-5). (ISBN 0-89375-463-3). Troll Associates.
--The Three Little Pigs. Jordan, Susan, illus. LC 34-186. 48 p. col. illus. 19 1/2 x 21 1/2 cm. c.1933. Whitman Publishing Co.
--The Three Little Pigs. Peller, Jackie, illus. LC 54-19836. (Bound with Little Red Riding Hood. Little Red Riding Hood, 1954.). unpaged. illus. 21cm. (Two-in-one wonder book, 609). c.1954. Wonder Books.
--The Three Little Pigs. Piper, Watty, pseud. (1870-1945), retold by Bragg, Mabel Caroline. Wilson, Eulalie Banks, illus. Eulalie, pseud. LC 45-559783. 22 p. incl. col. front., illus. (part col.) 21 x 16 1/2 cm. (Never grow old series). 1945. The Platt & Munk Co. Inc.
--Three Little Pigs. Winokur, Joan Gelman (1935-), retold by. Ramirez, Pablo, illus. LC 66-14055. 1v. (unpaged) col. illus. 24cm. (Holly story bk. lib. O1055). 1966. World.
--The Three Little Pigs and Little Red Riding Hood: Two Complete Stories. Tamburine, Jean (1930-) & Peller, Jackie, illus. LC 68-29307. 1 v. (unpaged) col. illus. 30 cm. (Nursery treasure books). c.1954. Grosset & Dunlap.

Three Little Pigs & Disney, Walt, Productions
--Three Little Pigs. Disney, Walt, Productions, illus. LC 34-4570. 62, 2 p. incl. col. front., illus. (part col.) 26 cm. c.1933. Blue Ribbon Books, Incorporated.
--Who's Afraid of the Big Bad Wolf?. Disney, Walt, Productions, illus. LC 33-35700. 31 p. illus. 21 1/2 cm. 1933. David McKay Company.

Three Little Pigs & Kundrat, Theodore V.
--The Three Little Pigs. 1978. (ISBN 0-88020-092-8). Coach Hse.

Throckmorton, Peter, jt. auth. see Chapin, Henry.

Throop, Frances, ed. see Asbjornsen, Peter Christen.

Throop, Frances, tr. see Asbjornsen, Peter Christen.

Throssel, Richard
--Blue Thunder. 32p. (Indian Culture Ser.). (gr. 6-12). 1976. (ISBN 0-89992-046-2). MT Coun Indian.

Thruelsen, Richard
--Voyage of the Vagabond. (Illus.). (gr. 7 up). 1965. (ISBN 0-15-294490-7). HarBraceJ.

Thrum, Thomas George (1843-), compiled by.
--Hawaiian Folk Tales: A Collection of Native Legends. LC 7-9782. (Illus.). 23 cm. 284p. 1907. A C McClurg.
--More Hawaiian Folk Tales: A Collection of Native Legends & Traditions. LC 24-640. (Illus.). 23 cm. 323p. 1923. A C McClurg.

Thruston, Lucy Meacham Kidd, Mrs. (1862-)
--Jack and His Island: A/Boy's Adventures Along the Chesapeake in the War of 1812. De Land, Clyde O., illus. LC 2-23303. (Illus.). 304p. 19cm. 1902. Little, Brown, and Company.

Thulstrup, T. De see Klenova, Varia & Lamprey, Louise.

Thum, Marcella
--Anne of the Sandwich Islands. LC 67-14089. 244 p. 21cm. 1967. Dodd, Mead.
--Librarian with Wings. LC 67-26150. 207 p. 22cm. 1967. Dodd, Mead.
--Mystery at Crane's Landing. LC 64-12472. 21cm. 211p. 1964. Dodd,Mead & Co.
--Secret of the Sunken Treasure. LC 69-16202. 248 p. 21cm. 1969. Dodd, Mead.
--Treasure of Crazy Quilt Farm. Jaeger, Elinor, illus. LC 65-21641. 209p. illus. 21cm. c.1965. (ISBN 0-531-01914-4). Watts.

Thun, Roderich
--The Magic Jewel. English Language ed. Kiem, Edith, illus. LC 60-4373. (Illus.). 46p. 27cm. 1960. Viking Press.

Thurber, James Grover (1894-1961)
--The Great Quillow. 1984. Peter Smith.
--The Great Quillow. Lee, Doris Emrick (1905-1983), illus. LC 44-8406. 3 p. l., 3-54 p. col. illus. 22 x 18 cm. 1944. (ISBN 0-15-232541-7). Harcourt, Brace and Company.
--The Great Quillow. Lee, Doris Emrick (1905-1983), illus. LC 75-6613. (Illus.). 54 p. 21cm. (Voyager book ; AVB 99). 1975, c.1944. (ISBN 0-15-636490-5). Harcourt Brace Jovanovich.
--Many Moons. Chorpenning, Charlotte Lee Barrows (1872-1955), adapted by. 1946. Dramatic Publishing Company.
--Many Moons. Reed, Philip G. (1908-), illus. LC 59-103. (Illus.). 32p. 24cm. 1958. A.M. & R.W. Roe.
--Many Moons. Reed, Philip G. (1908-), illus. LC 59-103. 32 p. col. illus. 24 cm. 1958. Printed by A. M. & R. W. Roe.
--Many Moons. Slobodkin, Louis (1903-1975), illus. LC 43-512506. 47 p. col. illus. 25 1/2 x 21 1/2 cm. 1943. Harcourt, Brace and Company. **Award: (RCM).**
--Many Moons. Slobodkin, Louis (1903-1975), illus. 1944. Harcourt.
--Many Moons. Slobodkin, Louis (1903-1975), illus. (Illus.). 1 v. (unpaged). 23cm. (Voyager book). 1972, c.1971. (ISBN 0-15-656980-9). Harcourt.
--The Secret Life of Walter Mitty. Higashi, Sandra, illus. LC 83-71786. (Illus.). 32 p. 23cm. (Creative Classic Series). c.1983. (ISBN 0-87191-961-3). Creative Education.
--The Thirteen Clocks. Simont, Marc (1915-), illus. LC 50-11076. (Illus.). 124 p. 22cm. 1950. (ISBN 0-671-72100-3). Simon and Schuster.
--The White Deer. Thurber, James Grover (1894-1961) & Freeman, Don (1908-1978), illus. LC 45-35191. 5 p. l., 3-115 p. illus., col. plates (1 double) 21 cm. 1945. Harcourt, Brace and Company.
--The Wonderful O. Simont, Marc (1915-), illus. LC 57-7942. 72 p. illus. 22 cm. 1957. Simon and Schuster.
--The Wonderful O. Simont, Marc (1915-), illus. (Illus.). 72 p. 21cm. (Fireside book). 1976, c.1957. (ISBN 0-671-22423-9). Simon and Schuster.

Thurber, Robert Bruce (1882-)
--From the Ant to the Elephant. LC 37-25037. 191 p. incl. front., illus. 21 cm. c.1937. Review and Herald Publishing Association.

Thurman, A. R., pseud., see Mann, Arthur William.

Thurman, Evelyn
--Christmas in Kentucky with Little Bernel. Carpenter, Marci, illus. LC 77-355851. (Illus.). 25 p. (p. 25 blank). 18cm. c.1976. S.N.

Thurman, Judith (1946-)
--Flashlight, and Other Poems. Rubel, Reina, illus. LC 75-29442. (Illus.). 34 p. 21cm. 1976. (ISBN 0-689-30515-X). Atheneum. **Award: (ALA).**
--I Became Alone: Five Women Poets, Sappho, Louise Labe, Ann Bradstreet, Juana Ines De la Cruz, Emily Dickinson. McCrea, James Craig, Jr. (1920-) & McCrea, Ruth Pirman (1921-), illus. LC 75-9589. 140 p. 22cm. 1975. (ISBN 0-689-30487-0). Atheneum.
--I'd Like to Try a Monster's Eye. Rubel, Reina, illus. LC 76-47630. (Illus.). 36 p. 1977. (ISBN 0-689-30574-5). Atheneum.
--Lost and Found. 1st ed. Rubel, Reina, illus. LC 77-21037. (Illus.). 39p. 21 x 6cm. 1978. (ISBN 0-689-30611-3). Atheneum.
--To See the World Afresh. Moore, Lilian, compiled by. LC 73-84831. index. 120p. (gr. 6 up). 1974. (ISBN 0-689-30141-3). Atheneum.

Thurman, Wallace (1902-1934)
--Blacker the Berry. Larson, Charles Raymond, ed. O'Daniel, Therman Benjamin (1908-), intro. by. 260p. (African-American Library). (gr. 11 up). 1970. (ISBN 0-02-054750-1, Collier). Macmillan.

Thurn-Taxis, Mary
--The Tea Party of Miss Moon: From GrandMama's Tales. Thurn-Taxis, Mary, illus. (Illus.). 23p. 1st U.S. edition. (gr. 1-4). 1984. (ISBN 0-233-97483-0, Pub. by A Deutsch England). David & Charles.

Thurston, Clara Bell
--Cheerful Chestnut Children. Thurston, Clara Bell, illus. N.D. George H Doran.
--The Jingle of a Jap. Thurston, Clara Bell, illus. LC 6-29765. (Illus.). 33p. 1906. Caldwell.

Thurston, Elizabeth A.
--The Little Wrinkled Old Man. N.D. Colby and Rich.
--The Little Wrinkled Old Man: A Christmas Extravaganza, and Other Trifles. 124p. N.D. Lee & Shepard.

Tillstrom, Burr

--The Kuklapolitan Players Present the Dragon Who Lived Downstairs. Small, David (1945-), illus. LC 83-17285. (Illus.). 48 p. 24cm. 1984. (ISBN 0-688-02734-2). (ISBN 0-688-02735-0). Morrow.

Tilney, Frederick Colin, ed.

--Fairy Tales from Spain. Matthews, W., illus. 18cm. 126p. (Tales for Children from Many Lands). 1913. E. P. Dutton & Co.

Tilney, Frederick Colin, adapted by see Aesopus.

Tilney, Frederick Colin, ed. see Andersen, Hans Christian.

Tilney, Frederick Colin, ed. see Defoe, Daniel.

Tilney, Frederick Colin, ed. see Rhys, Ernest (1859-1946) & Rhys, Grace Little, Mrs.

Tilney, Frederick Colin, tr. see La Fontaine, Jean De.

Tilton, Rafael

--The Immortal Dragon of Sylene and Other Faith Tales. Howell, Troy, illus. LC 81-50549. (Illus.). ix, 113 p. 22cm. c.1982. (ISBN 0-86683-656-X). Winston Press.

Tilton, Stephen Willis see Uncle Willis, pseud.

Tilton, Stephen Willis

--Songs for Our Darlings. Uncle Willis, pseud. (Illus.). 1900. Lee & Shepard.

Tilton, Theodore (1835-1907)

--The Fly. (Illus.). N.D. Sheldon & Co.

--Golden-Haired Gertrude: A Story for Children. Stephens, Henry Louis (1824-1882), illus. LC 6-8355. 40 p. front., plates. 19 cm. 1865. Tibbals & Whiting.

Timlow, Elizabeth Westyn (1861-)

--The April-Fool Twins: Further Adventures of Dorothy Dot. LC 8-24874. 236 p. front., 4 pl. 19 1/2 cm. c.1908. E. P. Dutton & Company.

--Cricket. Richards, Harriet Roosevelt, illus. (Illus.). (The Cricket Ser.). N.D. Dana Estes & Co .

--Cricket, 1 of 3 vols. Richards, Harriet Roosevelt, illus. (Criket Ser.: No. 1). N.D. Estes & Lauriat's.

--Cricket at the Seashore. Richards, Harriet Roosevelt, illus. (Illus.). (The Cricket Ser.). N.D. Dana Estes & Co.

--Cricket at the Seashore, 1 of 3 vols. Richards, Harriet Roosevelt, illus. LC 12-39532. 6 p., 2 l., 11-367 p. incl. 7 pl. front. 17 cm. (Cricket Ser.: No. 2). c.1896. Estes and Lauriat.

--Dorothy Dot. Rev ed. Richards, Harriet Roosevelt, illus. LC 98-42. vii, 7-320 p. front., illus., plates. 19 1/2 cm. 1898. E. P. Dutton and Company.

--Eunice and Cricket. Richards, Harriet Roosevelt, illus. (Illus.). (The Cricket Ser.). N.D. Dana Estes & Co.

--Eunice and Cricket, 1 of 3 vols. Richards, Harriet Roosevelt, illus. LC 12-39531. 311 p. incl. 7 pl. front. 17 1/2 cm. (Cricket Ser.: No. 3). c.1897. Estes and Lauriat.

--A Nest of Girls: Or, Boarding School Days. LC 1-11802. 412p. 1901. E. P. Dutton & Co.

--What Came to Winifred. (Illus.). (Editha Ser.). N.D. Caldwell.

--What Came to Winifred. Barry, Etheldred Breeze (1870-), illus. LC 1-12872. 86p. 1901. D. Estes & Co.

Timm, Peter Gerald

--The Attack of the Cat. Meents, Len W, illus. LC 80-27359. (Illus.). 59 p. 21cm. (Prime time adventures). c.1981. (ISBN 0-516-02101-X). Childrens Press.

Timm, Stephen A

--The Dragon and the Mouse. Lalo, illus. LC 80-134845. (Illus.). 36 p. c.1980. (ISBN 0-939728-03-6). Timm.

--The Dragon & the Mouse: The Dream. Lalo, illus. (Illus.). 45p. 1982. (ISBN 0-939728-05-2). (ISBN 0-939728-06-0). Touchstone Ent ND.

--The Dragon & the Mouse: Together Again. Lalo, illus. (Illus.). 46p. (Orig.). (ps-8). 1981. (ISBN 0-939728-03-6). (ISBN 0-939728-04-4). Touchstone Ent ND.

Timmermans, Felix

--St. Nicholas in Trouble. Wenz-Victor, Else, illus. Flashner, Amy, tr. from Ger. LC 30-26058. (Illus.). 20p. 23cm. 1929. Harper & Brothers.

Timmermans, Gommaar (1930-)

--The Great Balloon Race. LC 74-9771. p. cm. 1974. (ISBN 0-201-09330-8). Addison-Wesley.

--The Little White Hen and the Emperor of France. LC 74-9759. p. cm. 1974. (ISBN 0-201-09332-4). Addison-Wesley.

Timmons, Bonnie

--Orville's Outing. 1st ed. LC 83-1742. (Illus.). 24 p. 26cm. c.1983. (ISBN 0-525-44065-8). Dutton.

Timmons, Christine, compiled by.

--The Just-for-Fun Book. LC 75-316086. (Illus.). 44 p. 25cm. (Britannica discovery library ; 12). 1974. (ISBN 0-85229-298-8). Encyclopaedia Britannica.

Timoney, Francis (1938-), adapted by.

--The Three Talking Trees: A Story for Children. McIlrath, James, illus. LC 74-18902. (Original Author: Helen Frazee-Bower). (Illus.). 27 p. 29cm. 1974. (ISBN 0-87973-788-3). (ISBN 0-87973-388-8). Our Sunday Visitor.

Timpanelli, Gioi, retold by.

--Tales from the Roof of the World: Folktales of Tibet. Lockwood, Elizabeth Kelly, illus. LC 83-19826. (Illus.). 64p. (gr. 3-7). 1984. (ISBN 0-670-71249-3, Viking Kestrel). Viking.

Tinbergen, Nikolaas (1907-)

--Kleew. LC 47-30878. (Illus.). 41p. 22cm. 1947. Oxford University Press.

Tindall, Gillian (1938-)

--The Israeli Twins. Acheson, Joseph, illus. (Illus.). (gr. 1-5). 1963. (ISBN 0-685-21257-2). Verry.

Tingle, Dolli, pseud., see Brackett, Esther M..

Tingle, Dolli, pseud. (1920-)

--Little Apple Tree. Brackett, Esther M.. Tingle, Dolli, pseud. (1920-), illus. Brackett, Esther M.. LC 68-21793. (Illus.). 26p. (Stardust Book Ser). (ps). 1968. (ISBN 0-8378-1911-3). Gibson.

Tingley, Katherine A. Westcott (1852-), ed. see Malpas, Philip Alfred.

Tinkelman, Murray (1933-)

--Little Britches Rodeo. LC 84-13710. (Illus.). 48p. (gr. 3-9). 1985. (ISBN 0-688-04261-9). (ISBN 0-688-04262-7). Greenwillow.

Tinkelman, Murray (1933-), illus.

--Who Says Who?. (A Golden Happy Book). 1963. Golden Press.

Tinker, Jack, pseud., see Tinker, John Hepburn.

Tinker, Jack, pseud.

--Barefoot and the Friendly Road. Tinker, John Hepburn. Tinker, Jack, pseud., illus. Tinker, John Hepburn. LC 38-31245. (Illus.). 24cm. 1938. Viking Press.

--The Old Woman and Her Pig: Titty Mouse and Tatty Mouse. Tinker, John Hepburn. Tinker, Jack, pseud., illus. Tinker, John Hepburn. LC 39-8917. (Illus.). 41p. 13cm. 1939. Holiday House.

--The Small and Tall Man. Tinker, John Hepburn. Tinker, Jack, pseud., illus. Tinker, John Hepburn. LC 30-27814. 26 p. incl. col. front., illus. (part col.) 23 1/2 cm. 1930. J. B. Lippincott Company.

Tinker, John Hepburn see Tinker, Jack, pseud.

Tinling, Christine Isabel (1869-)

--It is Written: Bible Stories for Boys and Girls. LC 16-10702. 22cm. 60p. 1916. National Woman's Christian Temperance Union.

Tinney, Ethel

--The Talking Clock. 1st ed. LC 40-29881. (Illus.). 44p. 1940. Fortuny's.

Tipper, Una

--The Tin Can Factory. LC 77-87411. (gr. k-6). 1978. (ISBN 0-8283-1709-7). Branden.

Tippett, Irene Cowan

--Child Problem Plays. LC 38-22681. 56 p. 19 cm. c.1937. Eldridge Entertainment House, Incorporated.

Tippett, James Sterling (1885-1958)

--Christmas Magic. Sewell, Helen Moore (1896-1957), illus. LC 44-47940. 1944. Grosset & Dunlap.

--Counting the Days. Wolcott, Elizabeth Tyler (1892-), illus. LC 27-23173. (Illus.). 14 cm. 49p. 1927. Harper & Bros.

--Counting the Days. 1st ed. Wolcott, Elizabeth Tyler (1892-), illus. LC 40-32847. (Illus.). 66p. 14cm. 1940. Harper & Bros.

--Crickety Cricket!. The Best-Loved Poems of James S. Tippett. Chalmers, Mary Eileen (1927-), illus. LC 73-5498. (Illus.). x, 83 p. 19cm. 1973. (ISBN 0-06-026118-8). (ISBN 0-06-026118-8). Harper & Row.

--Henry and the Garden. Torrey, Helen (1901-), illus. LC 38-37700. (Illus.). 21 cm. 45p. 1938. Grosset & Dunlap.

--I Go a-Traveling. Wolcott, Elizabeth Tyler (1892-), illus. LC 29-11496. vi, 2, 61, 1 p. illus. 14 1/2 cm. (nursery series). c.1929. Harper and Brothers.

--I Know Some Little Animals. DeMuth, Flora Nash (1888-), illus. LC 41-151968. 3 p. l., 40,2 p. illus. 19 cm. c.1941. Harper & Brothers.

--I Live in a City. (Nursery Ser.). N.D. Harper & Bros.

--I Live in a City. Wolcott, Elizabeth Tyler (1892-), illus. LC 27-23173. (Illus.). 49p. 14cm. (The Nursery Ser.). 1927. Harper & Brothers.

--I Spend the Summer. Wolcott, Elizabeth Tyler (1892-), illus. LC 30-11419. vii, 2, 63, 1 p. illus. 14 1/2 cm. (nursery series). c.1930. Harper and Brothers.

--Search for Sammie. Krush, Beth (1918-), illus. LC 54-11968. (Illus.). 47p. (gr. k-3). 1954. (ISBN 0-687-37128-7). Abingdon.

--Shadow and the Stocking: A True Story. Dennis, Morgan (1891-1960), illus. LC 37-35653. 4 p. l., 50, 2 p. front., illus. 14 1/2 cm. 1937. Harper & Brothers.

--Stories About Henry. Torrey, Helen (1901-), illus. LC 40-23561. (Illus.). 21cm. 93p. 1938. Grosset & Dunlap.

--Tools for Andy. N.D. E. M. Hale & Co.

--Tools for Andy. Draper, Kay, illus. LC 51-12135. (Illus.). 47p. 22cm. 1951. Abingdon-Cokesbury Press.

--A World to Know. Wolcott, Elizabeth Tyler (1892-), illus. LC 33-28599. vii, 71 p. incl. front., illus. 14 1/2 cm. c.1933. Harper and Brothers.

Tireman, Loyd Spencer (1896-)

--Baby Jack and Jumping Jack Rabbit. Yrisarri, Evelyn, adapted by. Douglass, Ralph (1895-), illus. LC 44-24564. 47 p. illus. (part col.) 20 1/2 cm. (Mesaland series. Book 1). 1943. The University of New Mexico Press.

--Cocky: Stories. Yrisarri, Evelyn, adapted by. Douglass, Ralph (1895-), illus. LC 46-42894. 46 p. illus. (part col.) 21 cm. (Mesaland series). 1946. The University of New Mexico Press.

--Dumbee: Stories. Yrisarri, Evelyn, adapted by. Douglass, Ralph (1895-), illus. LC 45-10693. 46 p. illus. (part col.) 21 x 16 cm. (Mesaland series. Book 3). 1945. The University of New Mexico Press.

--Hop-a-Long: Stories. Yrisarri, Evelyn, adapted by. Douglass, Ralph (1895-), illus. LC 44-51042. 46 p. illus. (part col.) 21 cm. (Mesaland series. Book 2). 1944. The University of New Mexico Press.

--Quills: Stories. Yrissarri, Evelyn, adapted by. LC 48-11089. 21cm. 47p. (Mesaland Series). 1948. University of New Mexico Press.

Tireman, Loyd Spencer (1896-), illus.

--Big Fat. N.D. University of New Mexico Press.

Tirler, Hermann

--Sloth in the Family. (Illus.). (gr. 5 up). 1967. (ISBN 0-8027-6065-1). Walker & Co.

Tisna, Udayana Pandji, jt. auth. see Last, Jef.

Tisna, Udayana Pandji & Last, Jef, pseud. (1898-1972)

--Bamboo School in Bali. Last, Josephus Carel Franciscus. Orbaan, Albert F. (1913-), illus. Moskin, Marietta Dunston (1928-), tr. (Illus.). 192p. (gr. 2-5). 1969. (ISBN 0-381-99689-1). John Day.

Tison, Annette & Taylor, Talus

--Adventures of the Three Colors. LC 74-146809. (Illus.). color ils. 18p. 1st U.S. edition. (gr. k-3). 1971. (ISBN 0-529-01238-3). Collins-World.

--The Adventures of the Three Colors. LC 77-3162. p. cm. 1977, c.1971. (ISBN 0-529-01238-3). (ISBN 0-529-01239-1). Collins.

--The Adventures of the Three Colors. LC 74-146809. (Illus.). 18 p. 28cm. 1971. World Pub. Co.

--Adventures of Three Colors. LC 80-132764. (Illus.). 36 p. 28cm. (Color Magic Series). c.1980. (ISBN 0-675-01044-6). C. E. Merrill Pub. Co.

--Animal Hide-and-Seek. Tison, Annette & Taylor, Talus, illus. LC 71-184035. (Illus.). 24. 28cm. 1972. (ISBN 0-529-04452-8). (ISBN 0-529-04543-5). World Pub.

--Animals in Color Magic. LC 80-132773. (Illus.). 32 p. 28cm. (Color Magic Series). c.1980. (ISBN 0-675-01046-2). C.E. Merrill Pub. Co.

--Barbapapa. LC 79-118775. (Illus.). 32 p. 1970. (ISBN 0-8098-1171-5). H. Z. Walck.

--Barbapapa's Ark. (gr. k-3). 1979. (ISBN 0-590-11827-7, Schol Pap). Scholastic Inc.

--Barbapapa's New House. LC 72-10920. (Illus.). 32 p. 1973, c.1972. (ISBN 0-529-05042-0). (ISBN 0-529-05043-9). World Pub.

--Barbapapa's School. (gr. k-3). 1979. (ISBN 0-590-05445-7, Schol Pap). Scholastic Inc.

--Barbapapa's Theatre. (gr. k-3). 1979. (ISBN 0-590-05447-3). Scholastic Inc.

--Barbapapa's Voyage. LC 78-184846. (Illus.). color ils. 32p. (gr. k-3). 1972. (ISBN 0-529-05042-0). (ISBN 0-529-04456-0). Collins-World.

--Barbapapa's Voyage. (gr. k-3). 1979. (ISBN 0-590-05444-9, Schol Pap). Scholastic Inc.

--Barbapapa's Voyage: Barbapapa, the Animal Who Can Change His Shape, and His Friends Francois and Cindy, Search for a Barbamam. LC 78-184846. (Illus.). 32 p. 1972. (ISBN 0-529-04456-0). World Pub.

--Inside and Outside. LC 80-132774. (Illus.). 36 p. 28cm. (Color Magic Series). c.1980. (ISBN 0-675-01047-0). C.E. Merrill Pub. Co.

--Inside and Outside. LC 78-184034. (Illus.). 24 p. 28cm. 1972. (ISBN 0-529-04453-6). (ISBN 0-529-04453-6). World Pub.

Titchenell, Elsa Brita (1915-)

--Once Round the Sun. Gruelle, Justin C., illus. LC 50-4319. 56 p. illus. (part col.) 24 cm. (Challenger book). 1950. Theosophical University Press.

--Once Round the Sun. Gruelle, Justin C., illus. LC 81-52615. (Illus.). 56 p. 25cm. 1981. (ISBN 0-911500-61-8). Theosophical University Press.

Titcomb, Margaret (1891-)

--The Voyage of the Flying Bird. Feher, Joseph (1908-), illus. LC 74-94023. (Illus.). viii, 236 p. 20cm. 1970. C. E. Tuttle Co.

--The Voyage of the Flying Bird. Feher, Joseph (1908-), illus. LC 62-17928. 236 p. illus. 24 cm. 1963. Dodd, Mead.

Titherington, Jeanne

--Big World, Small World. Titherington, Jeanne, illus. LC 84-4140. (Illus.). 24 p. 23cm. (ps-1). c.1985. (ISBN 0-688-04022-5). (ISBN 0-688-04023-3). Greenwillow Books.

--Pumpkin Pumpkin. LC 84-25334. (Illus.). 9 7/8 x 8. 24p. (24 pt.). (ps-1). 1986. (ISBN 0-688-05695-4). (ISBN 0-688-05696-2). Greenwillow.

Titiev, Estelle, adapted by.

--How the Moolah Was Taught a Lesson & Other Tales from Russia. Cruz, Raymond (1933-), illus. Pargment, Lila (1888-), tr. LC 75-9200. (Illus.). 53 p. c.1976. (ISBN 0-8037-5744-1). (ISBN 0-8037-5746-8). Dial Press. **Award: (ALA).**

Titiev, Estelle, tr. see Shvarts, Evgenii Livovich.

Titler, Dale Milton (1926-)

--Haunted Treasures: True Tales of Ghosts & Gold. Jenney, Robert, illus. (Illus.). (Treehouse Bks.). (gr. 4-8). 1981. (ISBN 0-13-384230-4). P-H.

Titra, Stephen

--Be Nice to Spiders, Be Kind to Snakes & Twenty-Six Other Songs. LC 72-83031. (Illus.). 64p. (gr. 4-9). 1973. (ISBN 0-528-88097-7). (ISBN 0-528-88578-2). Rand.

Titterington, Sophie Bronson, Mrs. (1846-)

--The Angel of Poverty Row, 1 of 15 vols. (Illus.). 80p. (Little Pilgrim Ser.). N.D. Set. American Baptist Pub. Society.

--Christmas at Eden, 1 of 10 vols. (Illus.). (Little Pilgrim Ser.). N.D. Set. American Baptist Pub. Society.

--Dick Denny's Deliverance. (Illus.). (Little Pilgrim Ser.). N.D. Set. American Baptist Pub. Society.

--Divided, 1 of 10 vols. (Illus.). 80p. (Little Pilgrim Ser.). N.D. Set. American Baptist Pub. Society.

--Fortune Gulch: A Story of the Mines, 1 of 60 vols. LC 12-395273. 2 p. l., 3-176 p. front., plates. 18 1/2 cm. (Crescent Lib.). c.1892. Set. American Baptist Publication Society.

--Fortune Gulch: A Story of the Mines. 176p. N.D. Sunday-School Publications.

--Grandfather Grey's Quartette. 256p. N.D. Sunday-School Publications.

--A Growing Girl, 1 of 10 vols. (Illus.). 80p. (Little Pilgrim Ser.). N.D. Set. American Baptist Pub. Society.

--The House that Jerry Built, 1 of 10 vols. (Illus.). 80p. (Little Pilgrim Ser.). N.D. Set. American Baptist Pub. Society.

--Joe Nelson's Problem. LC 3293. 96 p. front., pl. 18 cm. (junior library). 1900. American Baptist Publication Society.

--The Juniors of Wild Rose Hollow. LC 3294. 92 p. front., pl. 18 cm. (junior library). 1900. American Baptist Publication Society.

--The King's Partners. LC 3295. 124 p. front., plates. 19 cm. (junior library). 1899. American Baptist Publication Society.

--Little Pilgrim, 1 of 10 vols. (Illus.). (Little Pilgrim Ser.). N.D. Set. American Baptist Pub. Society.

--Mable Livingston. (Fern Glen Ser.). N.D. D. Lothrop Co.

--The Mission of a Song, 1 of 10 vols. (Illus.). 80p. (Little Pilgrim Ser.). N.D. Set. American Baptist Pub. Society.

--A New Endeavor. LC 12-39521. iv, 5-394 p. front., plates. 19 cm. c.1891. American Tract Society.

--Prince Goldenrod, 1 of 10m vols. (Illus.). 80p. (Little Pilgrim Ser.). N.D. Set. American Baptist Pub. Society.

--Rachel Hastings' Girls. LC 12-39522. 2 p. l., 3-300 p. front., plates. 19 cm. c.1886. American Baptist Publication Society.

--Rob's Baby, 1 of 15 vols. (Illus.). 80p. (Little Pilgrim Ser.). N.D. Set. American Baptist Pub. Society.

--Soldier Jack. LC 3296. 98 p. front., pl. 19 cm. (junior library). 1900. American Baptist Publication Society.

--The Tropic Land Series, 10 Vols. N.D. Sunday-School Publications.

--Uncle Billy's Class. LC 3297. 103 p. front., pl. 19 cm. (junior library). 1900. American Baptist Publication Society.

--Wonder Library, 10 Vols. N.D. Sunday-School Publications.

Tittle, Sharon, ed. see James, William.

Tittle, Yelberton Abraham (1926-) & Liss, Howard (1922-)

--Pro Quarterback. LC 63-19850. 192 p. 21 cm. (Argonaut all-star sports series). 1963. Argonaut Books.

Tituerington, Jean

--The Chronicles of Pantouflia: Prince Prigio & Prince Ricardo of Pantouflia. Lang, Andrew (1844-1912), retold by. Tituerington, Jean LC 80-83965. (Illus.). 212p. (gr. 2 up). 1981. (ISBN 0-87923-358-3). Godine.

Tituerington, Jean see Tituerington, Jean.

Titus, Eve see Lord, Nancy, pseud.

--Smith of Wootton Major. Baynes, Pauline Diana (1922-), illus. (Illus.). 61 p. 17cm. 1967. Houghton Mifflin.
--The Two Towers. 352p. fold. map. 23cm. 1960. Houghton Mifflin.
--The Two Towers. 2nd ed. 352p. map. (His Lord of the rings, 2). 1967. Houghton Mifflin.

Tolkien, Ronald Reuel (1892-1973) & Gordon, E. V.
--Sir Gawain and the Green Knight. 240p. 1925. Oxford University Press.

Tolle, Jean Bashor
--The Great Pete Penney. LC 79-14603. 90 p. 22cm. 1979. (ISBN 0-689-50145-5). Atheneum.

Tolles, Martha (1921-)
--Katie & Those Boys. Weil, Lisl (1910-), illus. (Illus.). (gr. 4-6). 1976. (ISBN 0-590-09810-1, Schol Pap). Scholastic Inc.
--Katie for President. (gr. 4-6). 1976. (ISBN 0-590-10270-2). Scholastic Inc.
--Katie's Babysitting Job. LC 85-10780. p. cm. c.1985. (ISBN 0-590-33810-2). Scholastic.
--Too Many Boys. Frame, Paul (1913-), illus. LC 65-12532. 158p. illus. 22cm. c.1965. Nelson.
--Who's Reading Darci's Diary?. 128p. (gr. 4-6). 1984. (ISBN 0-525-67153-6). Lodestar Bks.
--Who's Reading Dardi's Diary?. 1984. Dutton.

Tolliver, Ruby Changos (1922-)
--Decision at Sea. LC 80-65972. (gr. 9-12). 1980. (ISBN 0-8054-7314-9). Broadman.
--More Than One Decision. LC 80-69521. 1981. (ISBN 0-8054-7316-5). Broadman.
--A Question of Doors. LC 83-27317. 1984. (ISBN 0-8054-7321-1). Broadman.
--The Summer of Decision. LC 78-74499. 1979. (ISBN 0-8054-7310-6). Broadman.

Tolman, Albert Walter (1866-)
--Jim Spurling, Fisherman: Or, Making Good. LC 18-10172. 6 p. l., 290 1 p. front., illus., plates. 19 cm. 1918. Harper & Brothers.
--Jim Spurling, Leader: Or, Ocean Camp. LC 26-16204. 6 p. l., 288 p. front. 19 1/2 cm. c.1926. Harper & Brothers.
--Jim Spurling, Millman. Salg, Bert N., illus. LC 21-20040. 6 p. l., 307, 1 p. front., plates. 19 1/2 cm. c.1921. Harper & Brothers.
--Jim Spurling, Trawler: Or, Fishing with Cap'n Tom. LC 27-155230. ix p., 1 l., 279 p. front., plates. 19 1/2 cm. c.1927. Harper & Brothers.

Tolman, Newton F.
--Quick Tunes & Good Times. 1972. (ISBN 0-87233-018-4). Bauhan.

Tolstoy, Aleksei Nikolaevich (1882-1945)
--Emelya & the Pike. 1983. (ISBN 0-8285-2644-3, Pub. by Malysh Pubs USSR). Imported Pubns.
--The Great Big Enormous Turnip. Oxenbury, Helen (1938-), illus. LC 69-10277. (Illus.). 34 p. 20cm. 1968. F. Watts.
--The Great Big Enormous Turnip. Oxenbury, Helen (1938-), illus. LC 69-10277. (Illus.). color ils. 44p. (gr. k-3). 1969. (ISBN 0-531-01684-6). Watts.
--A Prince of Outlaws. 1927. Alfred A. Knopf.
--Russian Tales for Children. Kouznetsov, K., illus. Schimanskaya, Evgenia, tr. LC 47-3902. x, 194 p. illus. 21 cm. 1947. Dutton.
--Teryosha. 24p. 1976. (ISBN 0-8285-1242-6, Pub. by Progress Pubs USSR). Imported Pubns.
--The Turnip. 16p. 1978. (ISBN 0-8285-1251-5, Pub. by Progress Pubs USSR). Imported Pubns.
--Vampires: Stories of the Supernatural. Fowler, Mel, illus. Nikanov, Fedor, tr. LC 69-12958. (Illus.). 4 woodcuts. footnotes. 160p. (gr. 5 up). 1969. Hawthorn.

Tolstoy, Leo Nikolaevich, jt. auth. see The, Three Bears.

Tolstoy, Leo Nikolaevich (1828-1910)
--The Fool. (Illus.). 1981. Schoken.
--How Varinka Grew up in a Single Night. Litvinov, Ivy L., illus. Abrahams, Hilary, intro. by. (gr. k-3). 1970. (ISBN 0-531-01854-7). Watts.
--Ivan the Fool & Other Tales of Leo Tolstoy. Asmussen, Des, illus. Daniels, Guy (1919-), tr. (Illus.). 21 cm. 151p. (gr. 5-8). 1966. Macmillan.
--The Lion & the Dog. 12p. 1975. (ISBN 0-8285-1183-7, Pub. by Progress Pubs USSR). Imported Pubns.
--Little Stories. LC 78-129025. 23p. (gr. k-3). 1971. (ISBN 0-87695-113-2). Aurora Pubs.
--Little Stories. Klein, Erika, illus. LC 78-129025. (Illus.). 24 p. 25cm. 1971. (ISBN 0-87695-113-2). Aurora.
--The Long Exile and Other Stories for Children. Dole, Nathan Haskell, tr. N.D. Thomas Y. Crowell & Co.'s Catalogue.
--Martin the Cobbler. Budd, Billy, illus. (Illus.). 32p. (gr. k-12). 1982. (ISBN 0-86683-638-1). Winston Pr.
--Nikolenka's Childhood. Sendak, Maurice Bernard (1928-), illus. Maude, Louise Shanks & Maude, Alymer (1855-1939), trs. LC 63-15485. (Illus.). (gr. 5 up). 1963. (ISBN 0-394-81448-7). Pantheon.
--Papa Panov's Special Day. Vilain, Nathalie, illus. Holder, Mig, adapted by. (Illus.). (gr. 1-4). 1978. (ISBN 0-89191-139-1). Cook.
--Russian Stories & Legends. Alexeieff, Alexander A. (1901-), illus. Maude, Alymer (1858-1938) & Maude, Louise Shanks (1855-1939), trs. (Illus.). (gr. 5 up). 1967. (ISBN 0-394-91614-X). Pantheon.
--The Shoemaker's Dream. Schell, Mildred, adapted by. Kasuya, Masahiro (1937-), illus. LC 82-128770. (Original Author: Leo Tolstoy (1828-1910)). (Illus.). 26 p. 26cm. c.1982. (ISBN 0-8170-0945-0). Judson Press.
--Stories for Children. Pakhomov, Alexei, illus. Guralsky, Jacob, tr. (Illus.). (ps-3). 1977. (ISBN 0-8285-8974-7, Pub. by Progress Pubs USSR). Imported Pubns.
--Tolstoi for the Young: Select Tales from Tolstoi. Sevier, Michael, illus. Townsend, R. S., Mrs., tr. LC 17-181689. 4 p. l., 200 p. col. front., col. plates. 19 1/2 cm. 1916. K. Paul,Trench, Trubner & Co., Ltd.
--Twentytwo Russian Tales for Children. Eros, Keith, illus. Morton, Miriam (1918-), tr. LC 70-84139. 57p. 1969. Simon Schuster Inc.

Tolstoy, Serge
--The Gold Fairy Book. Espenscheid, Gertrude Elliott, illus. LC 62-7886. (Illus.). 29cm. 1962. Random House.

Tom, Mr.
--Fuzzy Buzzard. (Illus.). (ps-2). 1978. (ISBN 0-89508-051-6). Rainbow Bks.
--Fuzzy Buzzard. Bretlinger, Ted, illus. (Illus.). (gr. 2-4). 1978. Oddo.
--Gilly the Goose. (Illus.). (ps-2). 1978. (ISBN 0-89508-024-9). Rainbow Bks.
--Gilly the Goose. Bonnett, Niki, illus. (Illus.). 32p. (gr. 2-4). 1978. Oddo.
--The Little Computer. (Illus.). (ps-2). 1978. (ISBN 0-89508-050-8). Rainbow Bks.
--The Little Computer. Spivey, Elvera, illus. (Illus.). (gr. 2-4). 1978. Oddo.
--Queen Fussy. Spivey, Elvera, illus. LC 76-376456. (Illus.). 41 p. 32cm. 1973. Ten Publications.

Tom Thumb
--The History of Tom Thumb. LC 35-27247. 63 p. illus. 8 1/2 x 9 cm. 1934. Printing by Helen and B. Gentry.
--The Life and Death of Tom Thumb, the Little Giant... LC 21-3878. 1 p. l., 13 p. illus. 10 cm. 1813. Printed by N. Coverly, Jun. Milk-Street.-.
--Tom Thumb. 10p. col. illus. 24cm. (Kriss Kringle Ser.). c.1897. McLoughlin Bros.
--Tom Thumb. Fleur, Anne Elizabeth (1901-), illus. Sari, pseud. LC 42-1753. 59 p. incl. col. front., illus. (part col.) 17 cm. (Little color classics). c.1942. McLoughlin Bros, Inc.

Tom Thumb & Grimm, Jakob Ludwig Karl (1785-1863)
--Grimm Tom Thumb. Bell, Anthea, tr. Otto, Svend (1916-), illus. LC 75-42774. (Illus.). 25 p. 26cm. 1976. (ISBN 0-88332-043-6). Larousse.

Tomaino, Sarah F
--Persephone, Bringer of Spring. Forberg, Ati, pseud. (1925-), illus. Forberg, Beate Gropius. LC 71-87160. (Illus.). 40 p. 26cm. 1971. (ISBN 0-690-61448-9). Crowell.

Tomalin, Ruth
--The Daffodil Bird. Wildsmith, Brian Lawrence (1930-), illus. LC 60-12800. 157 p. illus. 21 cm. (Wonderful world book). 1960, c.1959. Barnes.
--Gone Away. LC 79-670253. 158 p. 21cm. 1979. (ISBN 0-571-11342-7). Faber & Faber.
--A Green Wishbone. Rowe, Gavin, illus. (Illus.). (ps-5). N.D. (ISBN 0-571-10664-1). Faber & Faber.
--Little Nasty. Scullard, Sue, illus. LC 84-28797. (Illus.). 78 p. 21cm. 1985. (ISBN 0-571-13420-3). Faber and Faber.
--The Sea Mice. Rose, Sheila, illus. (Illus.). N.D. (ISBN 0-571-05213-4, Pub. by Faber & Faber). Merrimack Pub Cir.
--The Snake Crook. Hughes, Shirley (1929-), illus. (Illus.). (ps-5). N.D. (ISBN 0-571-10824-5, Pub. by Faber & Faber). Merrimack Pub Cir.
--The Spring House. N.D (Pub. by Faber & Faber). Merrimack Pub Cir.
--A Stranger Thing. Jacques, Robin (1920-), illus. (Illus.). N.D. (ISBN 0-571-10748-6, Pub. by Faber & Faber). Merrimack Pub Cir.

Tomelty, Roma, jt. auth. see Allen, Sybil.

Tomerlin, John (1930-)
--The Fledgling. LC 68-24729. 188 p. 21cm. 1968. Dutton.
--The Magnificent Jalopy. LC 67-2041. 156 p. 21cm. 1967. Dutton.
--The Nothing Special. LC 69-13371. 191 p. 22cm. 1969. Dutton.
--Prisoner of the Iroquois. LC 65-12185. 189p. illus. 22cm. c.1965. Dutton.
--The Sky Clowns. LC 72-78089. 184 p. 22cm. 1973. (ISBN 0-525-39450-8). Dutton.

Tomes, Margot Ladd, jt. auth. see St. George, Judith.

Tomkins, Jane see McConnell, Jane Tompkins.

Tomkins, Jane Harrison see Harrison, Jennie, pseud.

Tomkins, Jane Harrison (1841-1912)
--Autumn Leaves. Harrison, Jennie, pseud, 1 of 12 vols. (The Morning Glory Ser.). 1877. Dodd, Mead.
--Choir Boys of Cheswick: Or, Marty and the Mite Boxes. Harrison, Jennie, pseud. (Illus.). N.D. E. P. Dutton & Co.
--Doctor Will: The Boy from Downstairs. Harrison, Jennie, pseud. Rev ed. LC 12-32953. 208 p. front., plates. 17 cm. c.1880. American Tract Society.
--Elmer's Morning Glory. Harrison, Jennie, pseud. (The Morning Glory Library). N.D. A. D. F. Randolph.
--Elmer's Morning Glory. Harrison, Jennie, pseud, 1 of 12. (The Morning Glory Ser.). 1877. Dodd, Mead.
--A Fisherman's Daughter. Harrison, Jennie, pseud. LC 12-34678. 248 p. front., plates. 19 cm. (The Star Lib.). c.1891. American Tract Society.
--Fisherman's Daughter. Harrison, Jennie, pseud, 1 of 50 vols. 248p. (Library of Best Authors). 1905. American Tract Society.
--Fisherman's Daughter. (Illus.). 101p. (Popular Ser.). N.D. American Tract Society.
--Fisherman's Daughter. (Illus.). (The Star Lib.). N.D. American Tract Society.
--Girls of St. Andrews. Harrison, Jennie, pseud. (Illus.). N.D. Publications of E. P. Dutton & Co.
--Jean Macdonald's Work. Harrison, Jennie, pseud. LC 12-32954. 384 p. front., plates. 19 cm. c.1885. American Tract Society.
--Little Boots. Harrison, Jennie, pseud, 1 of 5 vols. (The Cumberstone Library). N.D. Dodd, Mead.
--Little Boots. Harrison, Jennie, pseud. (Popular Stories). N.D. Dodd, Mead & Company.
--Little Boots. Harrison, Jennie, pseud, 1 of 3 Vols. (The Cumberstone Library). N.D. Set. E P Dutton & Co.
--Little Buds. Harrison, Jennie, pseud, 1 of 12 vols. (The Morning Glory Ser.). 1877. Dodd, Mead.
--The Morning Glory. Harrison, Jennie, pseud. N.D. A. D. F. Randolph.
--The Old Back Room. Harrison, Jennie, pseud, 1 of 10 vols. (Popular Stories). N.D. Dodd, Mead & Co.
--The Old Back Room. Harrison, Jennie, pseud, 1 of 3 Vols. (The Cumberstone Library). N.D. Set. E P Dutton & Co.
--On the Ferry-Boat. Harrison, Jennie, pseud. N.D. Hurd & Houghton.
--On the Ferryboat. Harrison, Jennie, pseud. N.D. Houghton, Osgood & Co.
--The Right Way. Harrison, Jennie, pseud. N.D. A. D. F. Randolph.
--Roger Dunham's Choice. Harrison, Jennie, pseud. LC 12-32952. 270 p. front, plates. 19 cm. c.1887. American Tract Society.
--Roger Dunham's Choice. Harrison, Jennie, pseud, 1 of 50 vols. 270p. (Library of Best Authors). 1905. Set. American Tract Society.
--Uncle Jerry's Blossom. Harrison, Jennie, pseud, 1 of 12 vols. (The Morning Glory Ser.). N.D. Dodd, Mead.
--Up Stairs. Harrison, Jennie, pseud. 271p. N.D. American Tract Society.
--Wayside Flower. Harrison, Jennie, pseud, 1 of 12 vols. (The Morning Glory Ser.). 1877. Dodd, Mead.
--A White Rose. Harrison, Jennie, pseud, 1 of 12 vols. (The Morning Glory Ser.). 1877. Dodd, Mead.
--Whose Fault?. Harrison, Jennie, pseud. LC 25-7196. 356 p. 19 cm. 1890. E. P. Dutton & Company.

Tomkins, Jasper, pseud., see Batey, Tom.

Tomkins, Jasper, pseud.
--The Catalog. Batey, Tom. (Illus.). 56p. 1981. (ISBN 0-914676-54-7, Star & Eleph Bks). Green Tiger Pr.
--The Hole in the Ocean. Batey, Tom. Tomkins, Jasper, pseud., illus. Batey, Tom. (Illus.). 87p. (Star & Elephant Ser.). 1984. (ISBN 0-914676-73-3). Green Tiger Pr.
--Nimby: A Remarkable Cloud. Batey, Tom. Tomkins, Jasper, pseud., illus. Batey, Tom. (Illus.). 60p. (Orig.). 1st U.S. edition. (Star & Elephant Ser.). 1983. (ISBN 0-914676-83-0, Star & Eleph Bks). Green Tiger Pr.

Tomkinson, Grace
--Her Own People: A Novel. LC 45-9931. 3 p. l., 3-248 p., 1 l. 21 cm. 1945. I. Washburn, Inc.

Tomkinson, Julia Redford
--Doris, a Mount Holyoke Girl. LC 14-154952. 179 p. front. (port.) plates. 19 cm. $1.0. c.1913. American Tract Society.

Tomlins, William L., ed.
--The Child's Garden of Song. 1895. Lovell, Coryell & Co.

Tomlins, William L. & Tomlins, William L., eds.
--The Child's Garden of Song. Ricketts, Ella, illus. N.D. A. C. McClurg & Co.

Tomlinson, Everett Titsworth (1859-1931)
--The Boy Officers of Eighteen-Twelve. LC 12-12209. 335 p. front., plates. 19 1/2 cm. (War of 1812 series. (v. 3)). 1896. Lee and Shepard.
--The Boy Sailors of Eighteen-Twelve: A Story of Perry's Victory on Lake Erie in Eighteen-Thirteen. Wood, Stanley, illus. LC 13-17250. 4 p. l., 13-389 p. front., plates. 19 cm. (His War of 1812 Ser.). 1913. Lothrop, Lee & Shepard Co.
--The Boy Soldiers of 1812. Wood, Stanley L. (1866-1928), illus. LC 8-28255. 2 p. l., 3-319 p. front., 7 pl. 19 cm. (War of 1812 series (v. 2)). c.1895. Lee and Shepard.
--Boys of Old Monmouth: A Story of Washingtons Campaign in New Jersey in Seventeen-Seventy-Eight. LC 98-811. (Illus.). 20cm. 427p. (Riverside Library for Boys and Girls). 1898. Houghton Mifflin Co.
--Boys of the Mohawk. (The Rugby Series for Boys and Girls). N.D. A. L. Burt Company.
--The Boys with Old Hickory. LC 98-1094. 352 p. front., 7 pl. 19 1/2 cm. (War of 1812 series. (v. 6)). 1898. Lee and Shepard.
--The Camp-Fire of Mad Anthony. LC 7-29723. xii p., 1 l., 391, 1 p. front., 3 pl. 20 cm. 1907. Houghton, Mifflin and Company.
--Camping on the St. Lawrence: Or, on the Trail of the Early Discoverers. LC 99-4776. 412p. (The St. Lawrence Ser.). 1809. Lothrop, Lee & Shepard.
--Captain Dan Richards. (The Tomlinson Ser.). N.D. Barse & Hopkins.
--Carl Hall of Tait. (The Tomlinson Ser.). N.D. Barse & Hopkins.
--Carl Hall of Tait. LC 14-17815. 282 p. front., plates. 20 1/2 cm. 1914. The Griffith & Rowland Press.
--The Champion of the Regiment: A Story of the Siege of Yorktown. LC 11-250907. viii p., 1 l., 377, 1 p. front., plates. 20 cm. 1911. Houghton Mifflin Company.
--Cruising on the St. Lawrence: Or, A Summer Vacation in Historic Waters. LC 2-19727. 442p. (The St. Lawrence Ser.: No. 3). 1902. Lothrop, Lee & Shepard.
--For the Stars and Stripes. Smith, Frank Vining, illus. LC 9-22619. 415 p. front. 5 pl. 19 1/2 cm. (His War for the Union series. v. 1). 1909. Lothrop, Lee & Shepard Co.
--The Fort in the Forest. 341p. (The Colonial Ser.). 1910. W. A. Wile Co.
--The Fort in the Forest: A Story of the Fall of Fort William Henry in 1757. Emerson, C. Chase, illus. LC 4-24573. 341 p. front., 4 pl. 20 cm. (On cover: The colonial series). 1904. W. A. Wilde Company.
--Four Boys and a Fortune: Why they Went to England, and What they Found. (Our Own Land Ser.). N.D. Grosset & Dunlap.
--Four Boys and a Fortune: Why They Went to England, and What They Found. Newman, George A., illus. LC 10-9258. viii p., 1 l., 370 p. front., plates. 19 1/2 cm. c.1910. Lothrop, Lee & Shepard Co.
--Four Boys in the Land of Cotton: Where they went, what they Saw, and What they Did. (Our Own Land Ser.). N.D. Grosset & Dunlap.
--Four Boys in the Land of Cotton: Where They Went, What They Saw, and What They Did. Edwards, Harry C., illus. LC 7-264577. 415 p. front., 5 pl. 19 1/2 cm. c.1907. Lothrop, Lee & Shepard Co.
--Four Boys in the Yellowstone: How they Went and What they Saw. (Our Own Land Ser.). N.D. Grosset & Dunlap.
--Four Boys in the Yellowstone: How They Went and What They Did. Edwards, Harry C., illus. LC 6-26190. 2 p. l., 3-399 p. front., 5 pl. 19 1/2 cm. c.1906. Lothrop, Lee & Shepard Co.
--Four Boys in the Yosemite. (Our Own Land Ser.). N.D. Grosset & Dunlap.
--Four Boys in the Yosemite. Newman, George A., illus. LC 11-18837. 2 p. l., 3-405 p. front., plates. 19 1/2 cm. 1911. Lothrop, Lee & Shepard Co.
--Four Boys on Pike's Peak: or, Where they Went, What they Did, and What they Saw. (Our Own Land Ser.). N.D. Grosset & Dunlap.
--Four Boys on Pike's Peak: Where They Went, What They Did, What They Saw. Avison, George F. (1885-), illus. LC 12-168542. 2 p. l., 3-401 p. front., plates. 19 1/2 cm. (Our own land series $1.50). 1912. Lothrop, Lee & Shepard.
--Four Boys on the Mississippi: Where they Went, What they Did, and What they Saw. (Our Own Land Ser.). N.D. Grosset & Dunlap.
--Four Boys on the Mississippi: Where They Went, What They Did, and What They Saw. Edwards, Harry C., illus. LC 8-17829. 2 p. l., 3-385 p. front., 5 pl. 19 1/2 cm. (On verso of half-title: Our own land series. v. 3). c.1908. Lothrop, Lee & Shepard.

--The Penguin Twins. Wiese, Kurt (1887-1974), illus. LC 39-278283. x p., 1 l., 116 p. incl. front., illus., 21 1/2 cm. 1939. Frederick A. Stokes Company.
--The Penguin Twins. Wiese, Kurt (1887-1974), illus. N.D. J. B. Lippincott.
--Polar Bear Twins. 1937. E M Hale.
--The Polar Bear Twins. Wiese, Kurt (1887-1974), illus. LC 37-226337. ix p., 1 l., 106 p. incl. front., illus., plates. 21 1/2 cm. 1937. Frederick A. Stokes Company.
--The Polar Bear Twins. Wiese, Kurt (1887-1974), illus. N.D. J. B. Lippincott.
--The Raccoon Twins. Wiese, Kurt (1887-1974), illus. LC 42-19441. 126, 1 p. illus. 21 1/2 x 16 1/2 cm. 1942. Frederick A. Stokes Company.
--The Raccoon Twins. Wiese, Kurt (1887-1974), illus. N.D. J. B. Lippincott.
--The Snowshoe Twins. Wiese, Kurt (1887-1974), illus. LC 41-519037. ix, 113 p. illus. 21 1/2 cm. c.1941. Frederick A. Stokes Company.
--The Snowshoe Twins. Wiese, Kurt (1887-1974), illus. N.D. J. B. Lippincott.
--The Storks Fly Home. 1st ed. Gergely, Tibor (1900-1978), illus. LC 43-13014. 3 p. l., 58 p. col. front., illus. 21 cm. 1943. Frederick A. Stokes Company.
--The Storks Fly Home. Gergely, Tibor (1900-1978), illus. N.D. J. B. Lippincott.

Tompkins, John
--Invitation to the Zoo. Rona, Emy (1904-), illus. (Illus.). (gr. k-2). 1967. (ISBN 0-87460-027-8). Lion.

Tompkins, Juliet Wilbor
--Diantha. N.D. Bobbs-Merrill Co.

Tompkins, Kathleen Burns (1934-)
--The Alphabet Kids. Epstein, Reppy, illus. LC 77-26364. (Illus.). (ps-2). N.D. (ISBN 0-915248-15-8). Vermont Crossroads.

Tompkins, Walker A. (1909-)
--CQ Ghost Ship!. LC 60-9185. 191 p. 22 cm. 1960. Macrae Smith.
--CQ Ghost Ship. LC 77-177595. 191 p. 21cm. 1971. (ISBN 0-87905-502-2). Sagamore Books.
--DX Brings Danger. LC 62-10287. 207 p. illus. 22 cm. 1962. Macrae Smith.
--It Brings Danger. LC 70-177596. 206p. 21cm. 1971. (ISBN 0-87905-501-4). Sagamore Books.
--SOS at Midnight. LC 57-6639. 223p. 22cm. 1957. Macrae Smith Co.
--SOS at Midnight. LC 73-177594. 223 p. 21cm. 1971. (ISBN 0-87905-500-6). Sagamore Books.

Toner, Raymond John (1908-)
--Gamble of the Marines. Merryweather, Jack & Toner, Raymond John (1908-), illus. LC 62-19561. (A Condensed Rev. for Young Readers.). 208p. 22cm. c.1963. Whitman.
--Meeheevee; Being an Account of the Commerce-Raiding Cruise of the United States Frigate Essex into the South Pacific Seas: Being an Account of the Commerce-Raiding Cruise of the United States Frigate Esses into the South Pacific Seas. Toner, Raymond John (1908-), illus. LC 40-334599. 319 p. incl. front., illus., plates. 23 cm. 1940. A. Whitman & Company.
--Midshipman Davy Jones. Toner, Raymond John (1908-), illus. LC 38-31834. 328 p. incl. illus., col. plates, col. front., col. pl. 22 1/2 cm. c.1938. A. Whitman & Co.

Tongue, Ruth L.
--The Chime Child: Somerset Singers. LC 68-77292. 102p. Repr. of 1967 ed. 1968. (ISBN 0-7100-2967-5, Gale Reprints). Routledge & K. Paul.

Tongug, Ruth L., ed. see Briggs, Katharine Mary.

Tonn, Maryjane Hooper (1927-), ed.
--Easter Stories for Children. (gr. 4-6). 1975. Ideals.
--The Happy Christmas Story Book. 1974. Ideals.
--Jolly Old Santa Claus. 32p. 1972. Ideals.
--Religious Christmas Stories for Children. (gr. 2-5). 1974. Ideals.
--Stories Children Love. new ed. 80p. (gr. 1-7). 1975. Ideals.
--Stories for a Rainy Day. (gr. 1-7). 1975. (ISBN 0-685-54744-2). Ideals.
--Storybook Favorites. 1974. Ideals.

Tood, Joan Marlow, adapted by.
--A Child's Swiss Family Robinson. Diserens, Violette, illus. LC 78-105151. (Original Author: Johann David Van Wyss (1743-1818)). (Illus.). 95 p. 22cm. c.1978. (ISBN 0-8055-1263-2). Hart Pub. Co.

Tooke, Louise Mathews see Mathews, Louise.

Tooke, Louise Mathews see Mathews, Louise (1950-) & Bassett, Jeni.

Tooke, Mary E.
--Hand in Hand with the Wise Men. (Illus.). 12cm. 112p. (The Wise Men Ser.). 1899. Williams & Rogers.

Tooker, Dorothy
--Beatrice Perry, X-Ray Technician. LC 52-8990. 250 p. 21 cm. (Career books). 1952. Dodd, Mead.

Tooker, Richard (1902-)
--The Dawn Boy. Snyder, Harold E., illus. LC 32-32416. 2 p. l., 7-284 p. front. 19 1/2 cm. c.1932. Penn Publishing Company.
--Inland Deep. Hansen, Melvin, illus. LC 36-22180. 267 p. incl. front. 20 cm. c.1936. The Penn Publishing Company.

Tool, Richard Arthur
--A Boy's Day and Other Stories. 1975. (ISBN 0-682-48275-7). Exposition Press.

Toole, Fred
--Dennis the Menace. Paplow, Bob, illus. LC 56-9426. unpaged. illus. 21cm. (Rand McNally elf book, 541). c.1956. Rand McNally.
--Dennis the Menace Camps Out. Ketcham, Hank, pseud., illus. Ketcham, Henry King. LC 58-6559. 22cm. (Tip-Top Elf Bk.). 1958. Rand, McNally.

Toomey, Elizabeth, ed. see Dickens, Charles John Huffam.

Toomey, Elizabeth, ed. see Dumas, Alexandre.

Toomey, Elizabeth, jt. ed. see O'Hare, Katherine.

Toon, Gladys E
--The Animal Story Book. Burd, Clara Miller, illus. Trace, Margaret A., frwd. by. LC 28-30112. 3 p. l., 9-63 p. col. front., col. plates. 30 1/2 cm. c.1928. The Saalfield Publishing Company.

Toor, Frances
--A Treasury of Mexican Folkways. Merida, Carlos (1898-), illus. 566p. N.D. Crown Pub Inc.

Toothaker, Roy Eugene (1928-)
--A Wild Goose Chase. Dunnington, Tom, illus. LC 75-11753. p. cm. 1975. (ISBN 0-13-959510-4). Prentice-Hall.

Tooze, Ruth Anderson (1892-1972)
--The Dragon Tree. Escourido, Joseph, illus. LC 69-10819. (Illus.). 71 p. 24cm. 1969. John Day Co.
--Nikkos and the Pink Pelican. Domanska, Janina, illus. LC 64-22967. 64 p. illus. (part col.) 25 cm. 1964. Viking Press.
--Our Rice Village in Cambodia. Keats, Ezra Jack (1916-1983), illus. 1963. (ISBN 0-670-53164-2). Viking Press.
--Policeman Mike's Brass Buttons. Rev. ed. Gay, Zhenya (1906-1978), illus. LC 64-16790. (Illus.). 63p. 21cm. (A New Everyday Adventure Story). Orig. Title: Tim and the Brass Buttons, 1951. 1964. Melmont Publishers.
--Silver from the Sea. rev. ed. Wiese, Kurt (1887-1974), illus. LC 62-9623. (Illus.). (gr. 2-5). 1962. (ISBN 0-670-64535-4). Viking Pr.
--Storytelling. LC 59-7803. 268 p. 22 cm. 1959. Prentice-Hall.
--Telephone Wires Up!. Rev. ed. Hutchinson, William Miller (1916-), illus. LC 64-16792. (Illus.). 64p. 21cm. (A New Everyday Adventure Story). Orig. Title: Wires Up!, 1952. 1964. Melmont Publishers.
--Tim and the Brass Buttons. Gay, Zhenya (1906-1978), illus. LC 51-13155. 63 p. illus. 22 cm. (Everday adventure story). 1951. J. Messner.
--Wire up!. Hutchinson, William Miller (1916-), illus. LC 52-13609. 64 p. illus. 22 cm. (Everyday adventure story). 1952. Messner.

Tooze, Ruth Anderson (1892-1972), retold by.
--Monkey See Monkey Do. Moyers, William (1916-), illus. LC 52-16191. unpaged. illus. 21cm. (Wonder books, 521). 1949. Grosset & Dunlap.
--The Story World. LC 74-12278. 26cm. 200p. (The Child's World). 1974, c.1971. Standard Educational Corp.
--Three Tales of Monkey: Ancient Folk Tales from the Far East. Schmidt, Rosalie Petrash, illus. (Illus.). 72 p. 24cm. 1967. (ISBN 0-381-99687-5). John Day Co.
--Three Tales of Turtle: Ancient Folk Tales from the Far East. Schmidt, Rosalie Petrash, illus. (Illus.). 64 p. 24cm. 1968. John Day Co.
--The Wonderful Wooden Peacock Flying Machine and Other Tales of Ceylon. Schmidt, Rosalie Petrash, illus. LC 69-15734. (Illus.). 126 p. 24cm. 1969. (ISBN 0-381-99684-0). John Day Co.

Tope, Hildred
--Whoa, Ginger!. Stolberg, Doris, illus. LC 45-9808. 191 p. illus. 20 1/2 cm. 1945. W. Morrow & Company.

Topelius, Zakarias (1818-1898)
--Canute Whistlewinks and Other Stories. Olcott, Frances Jenkins (1872-1963), ed. McIntosh, Frank, illus. Foss, Claude William (1855-1935), tr. McIntosh, Frank, illus. LC 27-19561. x p., 1 l., 271, 1 p. incl. illus., plates. col. front., col. plates. 21 cm. 1927. Longmans, Green and Co.
--Four Fairy Plays. N.D. Branden Press.
--The Old Cabin and the Red Shoes. E. H., tr. (Illus.). 1905. Augustana Book Concern.
--Stories for Children, 3 vols. Foss, Claude William (1855-1935), tr. (Illus.). (Vol. 1). 1905. Set. Augustana Book Concern.
--Stories for Children, 3 vols. Foss, Claude William (1855-1935), tr. (cb). (Illus.). (Vol. 2). 1905. Set. Augustana Book Concern.
--Stories for Children, 3 vols. Foss, Claude William (1855-1935), tr. (Illus.). (Vol. 3). 1905. Set. Augustana Book Concern.
--Two Times Two Is Four. Himes, Vera C, adapted by. Dewey, Katherine, illus. LC 31-15094. 64 p. incl. col. front., col. illus. 20 x 22 cm. c.1931. Thomas Y. Crowell Co.
--Where Stories Grow: Tales from Finland. Sperry, Margaret (1905-), adapted by. Karma, Maija, illus. LC 77-797. (Illus.). 94 p. 25cm. c.1977. Crane Russak.

Topelius, Zakarias (1818-1898) & Krohn, Julius Leopold Frederik (1835-1888)
--Top-of-the-World Stories for Boys and Girls. Poulsson, Anne Emilie (1853-1939) & Poulsson, Laura Elizabeth (1851-), trs. LC 16-17491. 2 p. l., 3-206 p. col. front., col. plates. 20 cm. c.1916. Lothrop, Lee & Shepard Co.

Topper, Frank
--Mystery at the Bike Race. Rogers, Jackie, illus. LC 84-16452. (Illus.). 128p. (Solve-It-Yourself Ser.). (gr. 3-7). 1985. (ISBN 0-8167-0454-6). (ISBN 0-8167-0455-4). Troll Assocs.

Torah Umesorach; National Society for Hebrew Day Schools, jt. auth. see Gans, Manfred.

Torbert, Ruth
--Snail Mail. LC 58-8275. 32 p. 22 cm. 1958. Hastings House.

Torchio, illus.
--Three Favorite Fairy Tales. (Illus.). (gr. k-3). 1964. (ISBN 0-307-12070-8, Golden Pr). Western Pub.

Tord, Bijou Le see Le Tord, Bijou.

Torga, Miguel
--The Blackbird and Other Stories. Prieto, Gregorio, illus. Brass, Denis, tr. N.D. Arts, Inc.

Torgersen, Don Arthur (1934-)
--The Angry Giants of Troll Mountain. Dunnington, Tom, illus. LC 80-12515. p. cm. 1980. (ISBN 0-516-03409-X). Childrens Press.
--The Girl Who Tricked the Troll. Dunnington, Tom, illus. LC 77-17198. p. cm. 1978. (ISBN 0-516-03465-0). Childrens Press.
--Huff and Puff and the Troll Hole. Dunnington, Tom, illus. LC 81-15503. (Illus.). 31 p. 25cm. (The Gnomes of Pepper Tree Forest). c.1982. (ISBN 0-516-03744-7). Childrens Press.
--The Last Days of Gorlock the Dragon. Dunnington, Tom, illus. LC 81-38551. (Illus.). 31 p. 25cm. (The Gnomes of Pepper Tree Forest). c.1982. (ISBN 0-516-03743-9). (ISBN 0-516-43743-7). Childrens Press.
--The Scariest Night in Troll Forest. Dunnington, Tom, illus. LC 78-13563. (Illus.). 31 p. 25cm. c.1979. (ISBN 0-516-03613-0). Childrens Press.
--Torrek and the Elfin Girl. Dunnington, Tom, illus. LC 81-10047. p. cm. (The Gnomes of Pepper Tree Forest). 1981. (ISBN 0-516-03741-2). (ISBN 0-516-43741-0). Childrens Press.
--The Troll Who Lived in the Lake. Dunnington, Tom, illus. LC 78-3592. p. cm. 1978. (ISBN 0-516-03631-9). Childrens Press.
--The Troll Who Went to School. Dunnington, Tom, illus. LC 79-10036. p. cm. c.1979. (ISBN 0-516-07685-X). Childrens Press.
--The Wicked Witch of Troll Cave. Dunnington, Tom, illus. LC 80-12043. p. cm. c.1980. (ISBN 0-516-03672-6). Childrens Press.

Torjesen, Elizabeth Fraser (1907-)
--Captain Ramsay's Daughter. Adams, Adrienne (1906-), illus. LC 53-6754. 223p. illus. 23cm. 1953. Lothrop, Lee & Shepard Co.
--Comet Over Nantucket: Maria Mitchell and Her Island: the Story of America's First Woman Astronomer. LC 84-80194. c.1984. (ISBN 0-913408-86-7). Friends United Press.

Tornborg, Pat
--A Sesame Street Christmas: Featuring Jim Henson's Sesame Street Muppets. Cooke, Tom, illus. Children's Television Workshop LC 82-81123. (Illus.). 41 p. 26cm. c.1982. (ISBN 0-307-15817-9, Golden). Western Pub. Co., in Conjunction with Children's Television Workshop.
--Spring Cleaning. Stevenson, Nancy W, illus. Henson, Jim (1936-), created by. Children's Television Workshop LC 80-51508. (Illus.). 26 p. 27cm. c.1980. (ISBN 0-307-23117-8). Western Pub. Co. in Conjunction with Children's Television Workshop.

Toronto. Public Libararies. Boys and Girls Division see Vries, Leonard De.

Torre, Lillian De La see De La Torre, Lillian.

Torre, Vincent
--The Enchanted Forest. Torre, Vincent, illus. LC 77-154260. (Illus.). 73 p. 27cm. c.1977. Inkwell Press.
--The Leaping Knight. Torre, Vincent, illus. LC 75-314510. (Illus.). 45 p. 27cm. 1974. Inkwell Press.
--The Prince and the Stable Boy. Torre, Vincent, illus. LC 76-366963. (Illus.). 42 p. 27cm. c.1975. Inkwell Press.

Torre, Vincent, selected by see Aesopus.

Torrey, Marjorie, pseud., see Chanslor, Marjorie Torrey Hood.

Torrey, Therese Von Hohoff see Hohoff, Tay, pseud.

Torriani, Aimee, jt. auth. see Ellis, Patsy.

Torriani, Aimee (1900-) & Ellis, Patsy
--Rag-a-Tag and Other Fairy Tales. LC 46-599. 3 p. l., 78 p. illus. 20 cm. 1945. The Grail.

Toth, Marian Davies, as told by.
--Tales from Thailand. Pasutanavin, Supee, illus. LC 77-125563. (Illus.). 183 p. 24cm. 1971. (ISBN 0-8048-0563-6). Tuttle.

Totheroh, Dan
--David Hotfoot. Deny, Maurice (1892-), illus. LC 26-16202. viii p., 2 l., 13-246 p. incl. plates, col. front. 21 cm. c.1926. George H. Doran Company.
--The Last Dragon. Eadie, Eleanor Osborn, illus. LC 27-19563. 186 p. col. front., illus., col. plates. 23 1/2 cm. c.1927. George H. Doran Company.

Totten, Bob, ed. see Disney, Walt, Productions.

Tottle, John
--Benjamim Franklin: First Great American. Stein, Harve (1904-), illus. LC 58-13692. (Illus.). 192p. 22cm. (Piper Bks.). 1958. Houghton Mifflin.

Toumanian, Hovhannes (1869-1923)
--The Master & the Labourer: Nazar the Brave. (Illus.). 32p. (gr. k-3). 1983. (ISBN 0-8285-2237-5). Imported Pubns.
--Once There Was and Was Not: Armenian Tales. 1st ed. Tashjian, Virginia A. (1921-), retold by. Hogrogian, Nonny (1932-), illus. LC 66-11000. ix, 83p. illus. (pt. col.) 24cm. 1966. Little. **Award: (ALA).**

Tourison, Eleanor, ed. see Pyle, Howard.

Tourjee, Eben, ed.
--Happy Songs For Our Darlings. (Illus.). N.D. D. Lothrop & Co.

Tourneur, Dina-Kathelin (1934-)
--Buddy Paints a Picture. Tourneur, Dina-Kathelin (1934-), illus. (Buddy Books Ser.). (ps). 1978. (ISBN 0-89191-124-3). Cook.
--Buddy Plants a Seed. (Buddy Books Ser.). (ps). 1978. (ISBN 0-89191-125-1). Cook.
--Caspar Finds a Friend. LC 80-505331. (Illus.). 21 p. 20cm. (Caspur Story Books). 1980. (ISBN 0-222-00774-5). Burke Books.
--Caspar Loses His Dog. LC 80-514349. (Illus.). 20 p. 20cm. (Caspar Story Books). 1980. (ISBN 0-222-00777-X). Burke Books.
--Caspar Plants a Seed. Tourneur, Dina-Kathelin (1934-), illus. LC 80-505329. (Illus.). 20 p. 20cm. (Caspar Storybooks). 1980. (ISBN 0-222-00776-1). Burke Books.

Tournier, Michel
--Friday and Robinson: Life on Esperanza Island. 1 st. ed. Martin, David Stone (1913-), illus. Manheim, Ralph (1907-), tr. LC 78-39598. (Illus.). 118 p. 24cm. 1972. (ISBN 0-394-82414-8). (ISBN 0-394-92414-2). Knopf.

Tourtel, Mary
--A Horse Book. (Illus.). (Dumpy Book for Children Ser.). N.D. Frederick A. Stokes Co.

Tousey, Sanford see Tousey, Thomas Sanford.

Tousey, Thomas Sanford
--Airplane Andy. LC 42-51252. 2 p. l., 43, 1 p. incl. col. front., illus. (part col.) 23 1/2 cm. 1942. Doubleday, Doran & Company, Inc.
--Bill and the Circus. Tousey, Thomas Sanford, illus. LC 47-4515. 31, 1 p. illus. (part col.) 25 cm. 1947. A. Whitman.
--Bob and the Railroad. LC 42-112. 1 p. l., 53, 1 p. illus. (part col.) 23 1/2 cm. 1941. Doubleday, Doran & Company, Inc.
--Chinky Joins the Circus. LC 38-34796. 56 p. illus. (part col.) 18 1/2 x 23 1/2 cm. 1938. Doubleday, Doran & Company, Inc.
--Chinky, the Banker Pony. LC 37-36927. 56 p. illus. (part col.) 19 x 23 cm. 1937. Doubleday, Doran & Company, Inc.
--Cowboy Tommy. LC 32-191972. 56 p. illus. (part col.) 18 1/2 x 24 1/2 cm. 1932. Doubleday, Doran & Company, Inc.
--Cowboy Tommy. Special ed. (Illus.). unpaged. 17x 22cm. 1956, c.1934. E. M. Hale & Co.
--Cowboy Tommy's Roundup. LC 34-37245. 56 p. illus. (part col.) 18 1/2 x 24 1/2 cm. 1934. Doubleday, Doran & Company, Inc.
--Cub Scout. Tousey, Thomas Sanford, illus. LC 51-13270. (Illus.). 25cm. 45p. 1952. Farrar, Straus & Cudahy.
--Dick and the Canal Boat. LC 43-16232. 41 p. illus. (part col.) 23 1/2 cm. 1943. Doubleday, Doran & Company, Inc.
--Fisherman Tommy. LC 40-34736. 47, 1 p. illus., (part col.) 25 cm. 1940. Houghton Mifflin Company.
--Fred and Brown Beaver Ride the River. LC 44-8965. 41 p. illus. (part. col.) 23 x 17 1/2 cm. 1944. Doubleday, Doran & Company, Inc.
--Horseman Hal. Tousey, Thomas Sanford, illus. LC 50-9226. (Illus.). 24 cm. 45p. (Junior Books.). 1950. Doubleday & Co.
--Jack Finds Gold. LC 47-31368. 41 p. illus. (part col.) 23 cm. (Junior books). 1947. Doubleday.
--Jerry and the Pony Express. LC 36-192203. 56 p. illus. (part col.) 18 1/2 x 23 cm. 1936. Doubleday, Doran & Company, Inc.
--Jim Bridger, American Frontiersman. Tousey, Thomas Sanford, illus. LC 52-1181. (Illus.). 48p. 24cm. (Pioneer Bks.). 1952. A. Whitman.

--Kit Carson: American Scout. LC 49-48410. 48 p. illus. (part col.) 24 cm. (His The pioneer books). 1949. A. Whitman.
--Kit Carson, American Scout. Tousey, Thomas Sanford, illus. LC 49-48410. (Illus.). 48p. 24cm. (The Pioneer Bks.). 1949. A. Whitman.
--Little Bear's Pinto Pony. Tousey, Thomas Sanford, illus. LC 43-15765. 29, 3 p. incl. col. front., illus. (part. col.) 24 x 18 1/2 cm. 1943. A. Whitman & Company.
--Lumberjack Bill. LC 43-4372. 7 1 p. illus. (part col.) 26 cm. 1943. Houghton Mifflin Company.
--Ned and the Rustlers. LC 41-175842. 30, 2 p. incl. col. front., illus. (part col.) 24 x 19 cm. 1941. A. Whitman & Company.
--Old Blue. Tousey, Thomas Sanford, illus. LC 42-51970. 32 p. incl. col. front., illus. (part col.) 24 x 18 1/2 cm. 1942. A. Whitman & Comapny.
--Pete and the Old Ford. LC 54-5201. (Illus.). 45p. 25cm. 1954. Ariel Books.
--Pete and the Old Ford. Tousey, Thomas Sanford, illus. 25cm. 48p. 1954. Farrar, Straus & Cudahy.
--A Pony for the Boys. LC 50-6652. (Illus.). 25 cm. 45p. 1950. Houghton Mifflin Co.
--Stagecoach Sam. LC 40-30541. 1 p. l., 53, 1 p. illus. (part col.) 23 1/2 cm. 1940. Doubleday, Doran & Company, Inc.
--Steamboat Billy. LC 35-20110. 56 p. illus. (part col.) 18 1/2 x 24 1/2 cm. 1935. Doubleday, Doran & Company, Inc.
--Ted and Trapper Joe. LC 48-3297. 41 p. illus. (part col.) 23 cm. (Junior books). 1945. Doubleday, Doran.
--Tinker Tim. LC 46-22595. 40, 1 p. illus. (part col.) 23 1/2 cm. 1946. Doubleday & Company, Inc.
--Treasure Cave. Tousey, Thomas Sanford, illus. LC 46-7972. 32 p. incl. col. front., illus. (part col.) 24 1/2 cm. 1946. A. Whitman & Company.
--Trouble in the Gulch. Tousey, Thomas Sanford, illus. LC 44-543010. 32 p. incl. col. front., illus. (part col.) 23 1/2 x 19 cm. 1944. A. Whitman & Company.
--The Twin Calves. Tousey, Thomas Sanford, illus. LC 40-9448. 30, 2 p. incl. col. front., illus. (part col.) 24 x 19 cm. 1940. A. Whitman & Co.
--Val Rides the Oregon Trail. LC 39-30177. 56 p. illus. (part col.) 23 1/2 cm. 1939. Doubleday, Doran & Company, Inc.
--White Prince: The Arabian Horse. LC 48-3809. 32 p. illus. (part col.) 24 cm. 1945. A. Whitman.

Toussaint-Samat, Jean
--Shoes That Had Walked Twice. N.D. J. B. Lippincott.

Touster, Irwin (1921-) & Curtis, Richard Alan (1937-)
--The Perez Arson Mystery. Cuffari, Richard (1925-1978), illus. LC 74-158729. (Illus.). 184 p. 22cm. (Case book mystery). 1972. Dial Press.
--The Runaway Bus Mystery. Cuffari, Richard (1925-1978), illus. LC 72-713. (Illus.). 165 p. 22cm. (Case book mystery series). 1972. Dial Press.

Tovatt, Anthony, jt. auth. see Carlsen, George Robert.

Toverud, Constance Ford, tr. see Paulsson, Bjern Konow.

Tovey, Doreen Evelyn (1918-)
--Raining Cats and Donkeys. Wilson, Maurice Charles John (1914-), illus. LC 68-20825. 156p. illus. 22cm. 1968, c.1967. Norton.

Tower, Caroline
--Four Foot Town: A Story for Youngsters, and Their Parents, About the Day When the Circus Animals Decided to Escape and Live Just Like Human Beings. 1st. Ed. LC 57-7076. 60p. 22cm. 1957. Greenwich Book Publishers.

Towers, Alton, ed.
--A Child's Aesop. (Illus.). (The Little Ones' Library Ser.). N.D. Frederick A. Stokes Co.

Towers, Alton, ed. see Andersen, Hans Christian.

Towle, Calvin K., tr. see Ionesco, Eugene.

Towle, Faith M., retold by.
--The Magic Cooking Pot: A Folk Tale of India. Towle, Faith M., illus. LC 74-20761. (Illus.). 48p. (gr. k-3). 1975. (ISBN 0-395-20273-6). HM.

Towle, George M, tr. see Verne, Jules.

Towne, Belle Kellog
--Around the Ranch, 1 of 18 vols. (Library of Romance Ser). N.D. Lothrop Pub.

Towne, Charles Hanson (1877-)
--Pretty Girls Get There. Busoni, Rafaello (1900-1962), illus. LC 41-4136. 7 p. l., 5-201, 1 p. front., illus. 19 cm. 1941. D. Appleton-Century Company Incorporated.

Towne, Ellis, et al.
--Lill's Travels in Santa Claus Land, and Other Stories. May, Sophie, pseud. (Illus.). N.D. D. Lothrop & Co.

Towne, Mary, pseud., see Spelman, Mary.

Towne, Mary, pseud. (1934-)
--Boxed In. Spelman, Mary. LC 81-43875. 160p. (gr. 4-6). 1982. (ISBN 0-690-04239-6, TYC-J). (ISBN 0-690-04240-X). Har-Row.
--First Serve. Spelman, Mary. Sanderson, Ruth, illus. LC 76-100. (Illus.). 214 p. 22cm. 1976. Atheneum.
--The Glass Room. Spelman, Mary. Cuffari, Richard (1925-1978), illus. LC 70-149220. (Illus.). 121 p. 21cm. (Ariel book). 1971. (ISBN 0-374-32652-5). Farrar, Straus & Giroux.
--Goldenrod. Spelman, Mary. LC 77-1578. 180 p. 22cm. 1977. (ISBN 0-689-30597-4). Atheneum.
--Paul's Game: A Novel. Spelman, Mary. LC 82-72750. 186 p. 22cm. c.1983. (ISBN 0-440-07039-2). Delacorte Press.
--Supercouple. LC 84-16961. 183 p. 22cm. c.1985. (ISBN 0-385-29379-8). Delacorte Press.

Towne, Robert D
--The Teddy Bears at School. Bray, J. R., illus. (The Teddy Bears Bks.). 1910. Reilly & Britton Co.
--The Teddy Bears at the Circus. Bray, J. R., illus. (The Teddy Bears Bks.). 1910. Reilly & Britton Co.
--The Teddy Bears Come to Life. Bray, J. R., illus. (The Teddy Bears Bks.). 1910. Reilly & Britton Co.
--The Teddy Bears go Fishing. Bray, J. R., illus. (The Teddy Bears Bks.). 1910. Reilly & Britton Co.
--The Teddy Bears in a Smashup. LC 44-15606. 16 p. col. illus. 17 c. (His The Teddy bear books). 1907. The Reilly & Britton Co.
--The Teddy Bears in Hot Water. Bray, J. R., illus. (The Teddy Bears Bks.). 1910. Reilly & Britton Co.
--The Teddy Bears on a Lark. LC 43-445450. 16 p. col. illus. 18 cm. (His The Teddy bear books). 1907. The Reilly & Britton Co.
--The Teddy Bears on a Toboggan. Bray, J. R, illus. (The Teddy Bears Bks.). 1910. Reilly & Britton Co.

Towne, Tracy
--The Best Ornament. (Illus.). N.D. D. Lothrop & Co.
--The Best Way. (Illus.). N.D. D. Lothrop & Co.
--Pet's Christmas Honor. (Illus.). N.D. D. Lothrop & Co.

Townend, Jack
--Railroad ABC. Budd, Denison M. (1898-), illus. LC 44-53446. 57 p. col. illus. 10 1/2 x 13 1/2 cm. 1944. F. Watts, Inc.

Townesend, Stephen Chapman Tyler (1860-1914)
--A Thorough-Bred Mongrel: The Tale of a Dog, Told by a Dog to Lovers of Dogs. Shepherd, J. A., illus. Burnett, Frances Hodgson, Mrs. (1849-1924), pref. by. LC 1-31795. iv, vii, vii-x, 175 p. incl. front., illus., plates. 20 cm. c.1901. Frederick A. Stokes Company.

Townley, Robert, illus.
--The Time Stone. 144p. 1981. (ISBN 0-905478-82-7, Pub. by Andersen & Hutchinson England). State Mutual Bk.

Townsend, Cyrus
--The Southerners. Wright, George, illus. N.D. Charles Scribner's Sons.
--Under Tops'ls and Tents. N.D. Charles Scribner's Sons.

Townsend, Doris McFerran see McFerran, Ann, pseud.

Townsend, Edward Waterman (1855-)
--Beaver Creek Farm. LC 7-29726. vii p., 1 l., 236 p. col. front., 3 col. pl. 19 1/2 cm. 1907. D. Appleton and Company.

Townsend, Elisabeth
--Johnny and His Wonderful Bed. Busoni, Rafaello (1900-1962), illus. LC 46-6178. 2 p. l., 55 p. illus. (part. col.) 26 cm. 1946. S. Daye.

Townsend, Elizabeth W. Haydock, Mrs.
--The White Dove, and Other Poems for Children. LC 81-17975. 128 p. front., 3 pl. 17 1/2 cm. 1855. J. C. Derby.

Townsend, Eric
--The Bell of Santadino. Brock, Charles Edmond (1870-1938), illus. LC 38-32024. 255 p. incl. illus., plates. col. front. 20 cm. 1938. David McKay Company.

Townsend, Frances Eliza Hodgson see Burnett, Frances Hodgson, Mrs.

Townsend, Frank S.
--Hugh Graham: A Tale of the Pioneers. N.D. Abingdon Press.

Townsend, George Fyler, tr. see Aesopus.

Townsend, George Fyler (1815-1900), rev. by.
--Arabian Nights, 1 of 8 Vols. New ed. (Illus.). (Warne's Victoria Gift Books Ser.). N.D. R. Worthington.
--Arabian Nights, 1 of 6 vols. (Illus.). (Warne's Lansdowne Fairy Library Ser.: No. 3). N.D. R. Worthington.
--Arabian Nights. Revised. (Warne's Lansdowne Fairy Library). N.D. Scribner, Welford, & Armstrong.
--Arabian Nights. Rev. ed. (Illus.). (Warne's Favorite Fairy Tales). N.D. Scribner, Welford & Armstrong.
--Arabian Nights, 1 of 16 Vols. (Illus.). (Warne's Victoria Gift Books). N.D. Scribner & Welford.
--Arabian Nights, 1 of 7 Vols. (Illus.). (Warne's Lansdowne Fairy Library: No. 3). N.D. Scribner & Welford.
--The Arabian Nights. New Ed. ed. McIlvaine, Thomas, illus. N.D. Frederick A Stokes Co.
--The Arabian Nights Entertainments. (Illus.). N.D. Frederick Warne & Co's.
--Arabian Nights' Entertainments, 1 of 7 vols. New ed. Houghton, Archibald Boyd & Dalziel, George (1815-1902), illus. N.D. Houghton, Osgood & Co.

Townsend, Jacob David (1888-)
--The Cats Stand Accused. Shortall, Leonard W., illus. LC 61-6946. 122 p. illus. 22 cm. 1961. Houghton Mifflin.
--The Five Trials of the Pansy Bed. Hyman, Trina Schart (1939-), illus. LC 67-16481. (Illus.). 58 p. 22cm. 1967. Houghton Mifflin.
--Miss Clafooty & the Demon. Gorey, Edward St. John (1925-), illus. LC 76-116338. (Illus.). 48p. 18cm. (gr. 2-5). 1971. (ISBN 0-688-30005-7). (ISBN 0-688-35005-4). (ISBN 0-688-41367-6). (ISBN 0-688-51367-0). Lothrop.

Townsend, Janet Elizabeth (1925-)
--The Comic Book Mystery. Cuffari, Richard (1925-1978), illus. LC 73-1902. (Illus.). 147 p. 22cm. 1973. (ISBN 0-394-82663-9). (ISBN 0-394-82663-9). Pantheon Books.

Townsend, Jessie Gertrude
--Annie, Bridget & Charlie. Pienkowski, Jan (1936-), illus. (Illus.). (gr. k-2). 1967. Pantheon.

Townsend, John Rowe (1922-)
--Cloudy-Bright. LC 83-49491. 215 p. 22cm. c.1984. (ISBN 0-397-32089-2). (ISBN 0-397-32089-2). (ISBN 0-397-32090-6). Lippincott.
--The Creatures. LC 79-2405. p. cm. c.1979. (ISBN 0-397-31864-2). (ISBN 0-397-31865-0). Lippincott.
--Dan Alone. 1st ed. LC 82-49051. p. cm. c.1983. (ISBN 0-397-32053-1). (ISBN 0-397-32054-X). Lippincott.
--Forest of the Night. McDermott, Beverly Brodsky (1941-), illus. LC 74-23890. (Illus.). 111 p. 21cm. 1st U.S. edition. 1975. (ISBN 0-397-31620-8). Lippincott.
--Good-Bye to the Jungle. LC 67-2765. (Illus.). 184 p. 22cm. 1967, c.1965. Lippincott.
--Good Night, Prof, Dear. LC 71 141445. 156 p. 21cm. 1971, c.1970. Lippincott.
--Gumble's Yard. Hart, Dick (1920-), illus. (Illus.). 140 p. 18cm. (Puffin books, PS299). 1967, c.1961. Penguin Books.
--Hell's Edge. LC 69-14318. 223 p. 22cm. 1969. Lothrop, Lee & Shepherd.
--Hell's Edge. 189 p. 19cm. 1974, c.1968. Puffin Books.
--The Intruder. Phelan, Joseph A., illus. LC 79-101903. (Illus.). 220 p. 22cm. 1970, c.1969. Lippincott. **Awards: (BGH); (CMA).**
--The Islanders. LC 81-47105. 256p. (gr. 7 up). 1981. (ISBN 0-397-31940-1, JBL-J). (ISBN 0-397-31959-2). Har-Row.
--Kate and the Revolution. LC 81-48605. 219 p. 22cm. 1st U.S. edition. c.1982. (ISBN 0-397-32015-9). (ISBN 0-397-32016-7). Lippincott.
--Noah's Castle. 1976. Harper.
--Noah's Castle. LC 75-30709. 256 p. 21cm. c.1975. (ISBN 0-397-31654-2). Lippincott. **Award: (ALA).**
--Pirate's Island. LC 68-14619. (Illus.). 159 p. 22cm. 1968. Lippincott. **Award: (ALA).**
--The Summer People. LC 72-3270. 223 p. 21cm. 1972. (ISBN 0-397-31421-3). Lippincott. **Award: (ALA).**
--Top of the World. Jones, Nikki, illus. LC 77-364811. (Illus.). 5, 72 p. 23cm. 1976. (ISBN 0-19-271388-4). Oxford University Press.
--Top of the World. Wallner, John C. (1945-), illus. 1977. Harper.
--Top of the World. Wallner, John C. (1945-), illus. LC 76-48219. (Illus.). 94p. 21cm. 1977. (ISBN 0-397-31728-X). Lippincott.
--Trouble in the Jungle. Mars, Witold Tadeusz J. (1912-), illus. LC 69-12003. (Illus.). 158 p. 22cm. 1969, c.1961. Lippincott. **Award: (ALA).**
--The Visitors. LC 77-7197. 221 p. 21cm. c.1977. (ISBN 0-397-31752-2). Lippincott.
--The Xanadu Manuscript. Ritchie, Paul, illus. LC 78-303879. (Illus.). 170p. 23cm. 1977. Oxford University Press.

Townsend, John Rowe (1922-), ed.
--Modern Poetry. Pfeffer, Barbara, photos by. LC 73-7736. 224p. (gr. 7 up). 1974. (ISBN 0-397-31477-9, HarpJ). Har-Row.

Townsend, Kenneth
--Felix, the Bald-Headed Lion. Townsend, Kenneth, illus. LC 68-14980. (Illus.). 23cm. 32p. 1st U.S. edition. 1968, c.1967. Delacorte Press.

Townsend, Lenora
--Hoppy. Harlan, Warren, illus. (Illus.). 23p. 1981. (ISBN 0-533-04863-X). Vantage.

Townsend, M. E
--Steffan's Angel, and Other Stories. (Illus.). N.D. E & J B Young.

Townsend, Marvin
--Laugh It up. McCarthy, Patricia, ed. (Illus., Orig.). (Pal Paperbacks Ser.: Kit A). (gr. 7-12). 1974. (ISBN 0-8374-3474-2). Xerox Ed Pubns.

Townsend, Maryann & Stern, Ronnie
--Pop's Secret. LC 80-13007. (Illus.). 32p. (gr. k-3). 1980. (ISBN 0-201-07707-8, A-W Childrens). A-W.

Townsend, Olga
--Blueprint of a Dream. LC 50-9839. 224 p. 22 cm. 1950. Whittlesey House.
--The White-Tailed Deer. Hogner, Nils (1893-1970), illus. LC 51-5638. (Illus.). 21 cm. 224p. 1951. Whittlesey House.

Townsend, R. S., Mrs., tr. see Tolstoy, Leo Nikolaevich

Townsend, Ralph M
--A Journey to the Garden Gate. Winter, Milo Kendall (1888-1956), illus. LC 19-16030. 5 p. l., 127, 1 p., 1 l. col. front., col. plates. 24 cm. $2.0. 1919. Houghton Mifflin Company.

Townsend, Reginald Townsend (1890-), ed.
--An Old-Fashioned Christmas: A/Collection of Stories Full of the Cheerful Yuletide Spirit from Country Life. LC 27-24272. 19cm. 1927. Doubleday, Page & Company.

Townsend, Thomas
--The Home Afloat: Or, The Boy Trappers of the Hackensack. LC 9-22179. 313 p. 19 1/2 cm. c.1908. Athenia Publishing Company.

Townsend, Virginia Frances see Cousin, Virginia, pseud.

Townsend, Virginia Frances (1836-1920)
--Amy Deane, 31 vols. (Illus.). (Famous Books for Girls Ser.: No. 1). 1905. Set. H M Caldwell Co.
--The Boy from Bramley. LC 8-29712. 2 p. l., 3-195 p. pl. 18 cm. (Breakwater series). c.1868. Loring.
--Christmas Stocking. Cousin Virginia, pseud. N.D. Hurst & Company.
--The Christmas Stocking. Cousin Virginia, pseud. LC 8-29711. 155 p. front., plates. 17 1/2 cm. 1869. Wilcox & Rockwell, Successors to Blelock & Co.
--Darryl Gap: Or, Whether it Paid. LC 3-24515. 20cm. 456p. 1894. Lee & Shepard.
--Deerings of Medbury, 1 of 30 vols. (American Girls' Ser.: No. 4). 1900. Set. Lee & Shepard.
--The Deerings of Medbury. N.D. Loring.
--Dorothy Draycott's to-Morrows. LC 8-29710. iv, 383 p. 19 1/2 cm. 1897. Lee and Shepard.
--Dorothy Draycott's Todays,. LC 99-748. vi, 323 p. 19 1/2 cm. Orig. Title: Sirs! Only Seventeen. 1899. Lee and Shepard.
--The Hollands. LC 96-417. 412 p. 19 1/2 cm. c.1897. Lee and Shepard.
--The Hollands, 1 of 30 vols. (American Girls' Ser.: No. 6). 1900. Set. Lee & Shepard.
--The Hollands. LC 8-297099. 412 p. 18 1/2 cm. c.1869. Loring.
--Hope Darrow. A Little Girl's Story. LC 8-29708. 2 p. l., 3-188 p. 18 cm. (Breakwater series). c.1869. Loring.
--Joanna Darling: Or, the Home at Breakwater. LC 8-29707. 2 p. l., 3-176 p. plates. 18 cm. (Breakwater series). c.1868. Loring.
--Margery Keith, 31 vols. (Illus.). (Famous Books for Girls Ser.: No. 14). 1905. Set. H M Caldwell Co.
--Margery Keith, 5 vols, Vol. 5. (The Breakwater Ser.). N.D. Loring.
--Max Meredith's Millennium. LC 8-29706. 2 p. l., 3-218 p. front., pl. 18 cm. (Breakwater series). c.1870. Loring.
--Mills of Tuxbury, 1 of 30 vols. (American Girls' Ser.: No. 13). 1900. Set. Lee & Shepard.
--The Mills of Tuxbury. Merrill, Frank Thayer (1848-), illus. LC 8-29700. 363 p. front., plates. 17 cm. c.1871. Loring.
--Only Girls. LC 8-29701. 3 p. l., 9-230 p. front., plates. 17 1/2 cm. (The Girlhood Ser.). 1872. Lee and Shepard.
--Only Girls. LC 9-17258. 19cm. 230p. 1900. Lee & Shepard.
--Sirs, Only Seventeen. vi, 323 p. 19 1/2 cm. c.1894. Lee and Shepard.
--Six in All, 1 of 30 vols. (American Girls' Ser.: No. 21). 1900. Set. Lee & Shepard.
--Six in All. LC 9-17450. 19 cm. 447p. (American Girls Ser.). 1901. Loring.
--Temptation and Triumph, with Other Stories. Rev. ed. N.D. Methodist Bk Concern.
--That Queer Girl. LC 8-297037. 2 p. l., 7-299 p. plates. 17 1/2 cm. (maidenhood series). 1875. Lee and Shepard.

--That Queer Girl. LC 2-22402. 20cm. 299p. 1902. Lee & Shepard.
--The Well in the Rock, and Other Tales. LC 8-29704. 278 p. front., plates. 18 cm. 1863. J. Miller (Successor to C. S. Francis & Co.
--While It Was Morning, 31 vols. (Illus.). (Famous Books for Girls Ser.: No. 27). 1905. Set. H M Caldwell Co.

Townson, B
--Easy German Stories. N.D. Longmans,Green & Co.

Towry, H. M., ed.
--Spenser for Children. Morgan, Walter J., illus. N.D. Scribner & Welford.

Towsley, Lena
--At the Beach. LC 38-25694. (Illus.). 19x21cm. 63p. 1938. Farrar & Rinehart.
--Five Little Kittens. LC 38-25694. 63 p. illus. 19 x 21 1/2 cm. c.1938. Farrar & Rinehart, Inc.
--Peggy and Peter: What They Did Today. LC 31-28042. 111 p. illus. 23 1/2 x 23 1/2 cm. c.1931. Farrar & Rinehart, Incorporated.
--Sally and Her Friends: How They Played with Peggy and Peter. LC 32-29352. 127 p. illus. 24 x 23 1/2 cm. c.1932. Farrar & Rinehart, Incorporated.

Toye, William Eldred, jt. auth. see Newfeld, Frank.

Toye, William Eldred (1926-)
--How Summer Came to Canada. Cleaver, Elizabeth Mrazik (1939-), illus. LC 73-82683. (Illus.). 32 p. 27cm. 1969. H. Z. Walck.
--How Summer Came to Canada. Cleaver, Elizabeth Mrazik (1939-), illus. LC 72-175662. 32 p. (chiefly col. illus. 27cm. 1969. Oxford University Press.
--The Loon's Necklace. Cleaver, Elizabeth Mrazik (1939-), illus. (Illus.). 1977. (ISBN 0-19-540278-2). Oxford U Pr. **Award: (AFH).**
--The Mountain Goats of Temlaham. Cleaver, Elizabeth Mrazik (1939-), illus. LC 77-82684. (Illus.). 32 p. 27cm. 1969. H. Z. Walck.
--The Mountain Goats of Temlaham. Cleaver, Elizabeth Mrazik (1939-), illus. LC 72-175661. (Illus.). 32 p. 27cm. 1969. Oxford University Press.

Toye, William Eldred (1926-), retold by.
--The Fire Stealer. Cleaver, Elizabeth Mrazik (1939-), illus. LC 79-67169. (Illus.). 28cm. 24p. (ps-3). 1980. (ISBN 0-19-540321-5). Oxford U Pr.

Tozer, Katharine
--Here Comes Mumfie. (Illus.). (gr. 2-6). 1964. (ISBN 0-685-21176-2). Verry.
--Mumfie the Admiral. (Illus.). (gr. 2-6). 1957. (ISBN 0-685-21359-5). Verry.
--Mumfie's Magic Box. (Illus.). (gr. 2-6). 1957. (ISBN 0-685-21360-9). Verry.
--Mumfie's Uncle Samuel. (Illus.). (gr. 2-6). 1964. (ISBN 0-685-21361-7). Verry.
--Wanderings of Mumfie. (Illus.). (gr. 2-6). 1958. (ISBN 0-685-21654-3). Verry.

Tozer, Mary
--The King's Beard. (Illus.). (ps-3). 1979. (ISBN 0-15-242924-7, HJ). HarBraceJ.
--Sing a Song of Sixpence. LC 77-357291. (Illus.). 32 p. 1976. (ISBN 0-437-79417-2). World's Work.

Tracey, Hugh Travers (1903-1977), as told by.
--The Lion on the Path and Other African Stories. Byrd, Eric, illus. LC 68-30936. (Illus.). xiv, 127 p. 24cm. 1968, c.1967. Praeger.

Trachsel, Myrtle Jamison, Mrs.
--Elizabeth of the Mayflower. Godwin, Stephani & Godwin, Edward Fell (1912-), illus. LC 50-10584. ix, 207 p. illus. 22 cm. 1950. Macmillan.
--The Garden of the Little Lame Princess. Bridgman, Lewis Jesse (1857-1931), illus. LC 27-10468. 1 p. l., 7-259 p. col. front., illus. 20 1/2 cm. c.1927. Lothrop, Lee & Shepard Co.
--Linda and Dick of Colonial Williamsburg. Blaisdell, Elinore (1904-), illus. LC 38-237702. 6 p. l., 254 p. incl. illus., plates. 21 cm. 1938. Dodd, Mead and Company.
--Mistress Jennifer and Master Jeremiah: A Story of the Building of Old Ironsides. Sperry, Armstrong W. (1897-1976), illus. LC 37-17502. xi, 217 p. incl. front., illus., plates. 21 cm. 1937. Dodd, Mead & Company.
--Sally Sue Visits Old Natchez. Lee, Manning de Villeneuve (1894-1980), illus. LC 39-30370. viii p., 1 l., 303 p. illus. 21 cm. 1939. Dodd, Mead & Company.

Tracy, Donald Fiske (1905-1976)
--The Duck That Flew Backwards. Sandford, LLoyd, illus. LC 50-10052. 49 p. illus. (part col.) 24 cm. 1950. Dial Press.
--No Trespassing. LC 61-5996. 255 p. 21 cm. 1961. Lippincott.
--Second Try. LC 54-7472. 189p. 22cm. 1954. Westminster Press.

Tracy, Edward B
--Great Horse of the Plains. LC 54-6257. 215p. 21cm. 1954. Dodd, Mead.
--Great Husky: The Story of a Boy and a Dog of the North. Dowling, Victor J. (1906-), illus. LC 49-8737. viii, 273 p. illus. 21 cm. 1949. Dodd, Mead.
--King of the Stallions. Broen, Paul, illus. LC 47-112754. x, 241 p. illus. 21 cm. 1947. Dodd, Mead.
--Paddles: The Story of a Sea Lion. Nelson, Ralph Lewis, illus. LC 42-8281. 113 p. incl. front., illus. 29 cm. 1942. G. P. Putnam's Sons.
--Sons of the Wilderness. McCann, Gerald (1916-), illus. LC 58-6225. 184 p. illus. 21 cm. 1958. Dodd, Mead.

Tracy, Louis
--The Wings of the Morning. (Thrushwood Bks.). N.D. Grosset & Dunlap.
--The Wings of the Morning. (The Winston Clear-Type Popular Classics). N.D. John C. Winston.
--The Wings of the Morning. Schaeffer, Mead (1898-1980), illus. (The Children's Book-Shelf). N.D. J. C. Winston Co.

Tracy, Olive Gertrude (1908-)
--Mysterious Passage: An Adventure Story of India for Boys and Girls. LC 52-425. 93 p. 20 cm. 1951. Zondervan Pub. House.

Tracy, Ray Palmer
--Fighting Sheepman. 1951. Little, Brown & Co.

Trager, Carolyn
--Moving Time. Krenitsky, Nicholas, illus. LC 78-7722. (Illus.). (gr. 5-8). 1978. (ISBN 0-531-02219-6). Watts.

Trager, Helen Gibson, jt. auth. see Htin Aung, U.

Trahey, Jane (1923-)
--The Magic Yarn. LC 60-15309. (Illus.). 27cm. 1960. Random Thoughts Pub. Co.

Traice, Elizabeth C.
--Wee Doggie: The Lives and Adventures. N.D. Thomas Nelson & Sons.

Traill, Catherine Parr Strickland, Mrs. (1802-1899)
--Stories of Canadian Forest: Little Mary and Her Nurse. N.D. Nichols & Hall.

Tralle, Bertha Baldwin, Mrs.
--Mother Nature's Secrets. Kennedy, A. E., illus. LC 30-20270. 72 p. incl. col. front., illus., col. plates. 24 cm. c.1930. S. Gabriel Sons & Company.
--Stories New and Stories True, and How to Tell Them. Tralle, Henry Edward (1867-), intro. by. LC 27-4647. 172 p. 19 1/2 cm. c.1927. Fleming H. Revell Company.

Tramer, Erwin, tr. see Ferdinand, Raimund.

Trammell, Shirley
--Upside Over. Crawford, Mel (1925-), illus. LC 73-81958. (Illus.). 191 p. 21cm. 1969. Golden Press.

Tran Khanh Tuyet
--The Little Weaver of Thai-Yen Village: Co Beth-det Lang Thai-Yen. Hom, Nancy, illus. Jenkins, Christopher N. H. & Tran Khanh Tuyet, trs. LC 77-78105. (Illus.). (Fifth World Tales Ser.). (gr. k-6). c.1977. (ISBN 0-89239-013-1, Imprenta de Libros Infantiles). Childrens Book Pr.

Tran Khanh Tuyet, tr. see Tran Khanh Tuyet.

Tranter, Nigel Godwin (1909-)
--Border Riding. Kennedy, Richard (1910-), illus. (Illus.). (gr. 3-6). 1959. (ISBN 0-685-20970-9). Verry.
--Smoke Across the Highlands: A Junior Mystery. LC 64-18261. 207 p. illus. 20 cm. 1964. Platt & Munk.

Trapp Family
--Trapp-Family Book of Christmas Songs. Wasner, F., ed. Trapp, A., illus. (Illus.). (gr. 4 up). 1950. (ISBN 0-394-81763-X). Pantheon.

Trask, Margaret Pope (1907-)
--At the Sign of the Rocking Horse. Berson, Harold (1926-), illus. LC 64-16535. 178 p. illus. 21 cm. 1964. Crowell.
--Three for Treasure. Frame, Paul (1913-), illus. LC 62-7746. 115 p. illus. 21 cm. 1962. Crowell.

Trask, Willard Ropes (1900-), tr. see Ley, Madeleine.

Traudi, pseud., see Flaxman, Traudi.

Trauermantel, tr. see Koch, Rosalie.

Trauermantel, tr. see Nieritz, Karl Gustav (1795-1876) & Franz, Agnes.

Travaglini, Barbara Carlson
--Henry Hippo. (Illus.). 47 p. 21cm. 1973. (ISBN 0-533-00524-8). Vantage.
--The Kelly Green Cow. Hammond, Kathleen, illus. LC 50-17827. (Illus.). 16. 29cm. 1949. Open Seseme.

Traveller Bird, pseud., see Tsisghwana.

Traveller Bird, pseud. (1930-)
--The Path to Snowbird Mountain: Cherokee Legends. Tsisghwana. LC 70-183741. (Illus.). v, 87 p. 21cm. 1972. (ISBN 0-374-35757-9). Farrar, Straus and Giroux.

Traven, B (0000-1969)
--The Creation of the Sun and the Moon. 1st ed. Beltran, Alberto (1923-), illus. LC 68-30765. (Illus.). 65 p. 22cm. 1968. Hill and Wang.

Travers, Georgia, pseud., see Scott, Alma Olivia Schmidt.

Travers, Georgia
--The Wild Woodchucks. Gag, Flavia (1907-1979), illus. 32p. N.D. Coward-McCann.

Travers, Pamela Lyndon, jt. auth. see Disney, Walt, Productions.

Travers, Pamela Lyndon (1906-)
--About the Sleeping Beauty. Keeping, Charles William James (1924-), illus. LC 75-12893. (Illus.). 111 p. 22cm. 1975. (ISBN 0-07-065123-X). (ISBN 0-07-065122-1). McGraw-Hill.
--The Complete Mary Poppins, 4 vols. Shepard, Mary Eleanor (1909-) & Sims, Agnes, illus. 1976. (ISBN 0-15-619810-X, VoyB). HarBraceJ.
--The Fox at the Manger. 1st ed. Bewick, Thomas (1753-1828), illus. LC 62-19905. 75 p. illus. 20 cm. 1962. Norton.
--Friend Monkey. LC 70-161389. 283 p. 22cm. 1971. (ISBN 0-15-229555-0). Harcourt, Brace Jovanovich.
--The Gingerbread Shop: A Mary Poppins Story. Elliott, Gertrude, illus. (Little Golden Book: 126). 1951. Simon and Schuster.
--The Gingerbread Shop: A Story from "Mary Poppins.". Elliott, Gertrude, illus. LC 52-9933. unpaged. illus. 21 cm. (Little golden library, 126). 1952. Simon and Schuster.
--Happy Ever After. Shepard, Mary Eleanor (1909-), illus. LC 41-310. (Illus.). 19cm. 1940. Reynal & Hitchcock.
--The Magic Compass: A Story from 'Mary Poppins.'. Authorized. Elliott, Gertrude, illus. LC 53-8215. unpaged. illus. 21cm. (Little golden library, 146). 1953. Simon and Schuster.
--Mary Poppins. Shepard, Mary Eleanor (1909-), illus. 1934. Harcourt.
--Mary Poppins. Shepard, Mary Eleanor (1909-), illus. LC 62-53589. 206 p. illus. 20 cm. c.1962. Harcourt, Brace & World.
--Mary Poppins. rev. ed. Shepard, Mary Eleanor (1909-), illus. LC 81-7273. (Illus.). 206 p. 20cm. c.1981. (ISBN 0-15-252408-8). (ISBN 0-15-252409-6). Harcourt Brace Jovanovich.
--Mary Poppins. Shepard, Mary Eleanor (1909-), illus. LC 85-5435. p. cm. (Voyager/HBJ book). 1985, c.1934. (ISBN 0-15-657680-5). Harcourt Brace Jovanovich.
--Mary Poppins. Shepard, Mary Eleanor (1909-), illus. LC 34-28306. 3 p. l., ix-xii, 200 p. incl. front., illus. 19 1/2 cm. c.1934. Reynal & Hitchcock.
--Mary Poppins and Mary Poppins Comes Back. LC 37-388607. ix, 349p. col. pl. front., illus., col. plates. 24cm. c.1937. Reynal & Hitchcock.
--Mary Poppins and Mary Poppins Comes Back. Shepard, Mary Eleanor (1909-), illus. 350p. 1955. Harcourt Brace Jovanovich.
--Mary Poppins; and Mary Poppins Comes Back. Shephard, Mary, illus. LC 64-6824. (Illus.). vii, 350. 25cm. 1964, c.1963. Harcourt, Brace & World.
--Mary Poppins and Mary Poppins Comes Back. Shephard, Mary Eleanor (1909-), illus. LC 37-88890. (Illus.). ix, 349. 24cm. 1937. Reynal & Hitchcock.
--Mary Poppins Comes Back. Shepard, Mary Eleanor (1909-), illus. LC 62-53587. (Illus.). 268p. 20cm. 1962, c.1935. Harcourt, Brace & World.
--Mary Poppins Comes Back. Shepard, Mary Eleanor (1909-), illus. LC 74-17258. p. cm. (Voyager book, AVB 93). 1975, c.1963. Harcourt Brace Jovanovich.
--Mary Poppins Comes Back. Shepard, Mary Eleanor (1909-), illus. LC 36-27038. xi p., 1 l., 268 p. incl. front., illus. 19 1/2 cm. c.1935. Reynal & Hitchcock.
--Mary Poppins from A to Z. 1st ed. Shepard, Mary Eleanor (1909-), illus. LC 62-15629. (Illus.). unpaged. 20cm. 1962. Harcourt, Brace & World.
--Mary Poppins in Cherry Tree Lane. Shepard, Mary Eleanor (1909-), illus. LC 82-71383. p. cm. 1982. (ISBN 0-440-05137-1). (ISBN 0-440-05153-3). Delacorte Press.
--Mary Poppins in the Park. Shepard, Mary Eleanor (1909-), illus. LC 52-10066. (Illus.). 235 p. 20cm. 1952. Harcourt, Brace.
--Mary Poppins in the Park. Shepard, Mary Eleanor (1909-), illus. LC 62-53588. 235 p. illus. 20 cm. 1962, c.1952. Harcourt, Brace & World.
--Mary Poppins in the Park. Shepard, Mary Eleanor (1909-), illus. LC 75-30526. p. cm. (Voyager book ; AVB 102). 1976, c.1952. (ISBN 0-15-657690-2). Harcourt Brace Jovanovich.
--Mary Poppins Opens the Door. Shepard, Mary Eleanor (1909-), illus. LC 62-53590. 239 p. illus. 20 cm. 1962, c.1943. Harcourt, Brace & World.
--Mary Poppins Opens the Door. Shepard, Mary Eleanor (1909-) & Sims, Agnes, illus. LC 75-30697. p. cm. (Voyager book ; AVB 103). 1976, c.1943. (ISBN 0-15-657692-9). Harcourt Brace Jovanovich.
--Mary Poppins Opens the Door. Shepard, Mary Eleanor (1909-) & Sims, Agnes, illus. LC 43-17570. xi, 2, 239 p. illus. 19 1/2 cm. 1943. Reynal & Hitchcock.
--Mr. Wigg's Birthday Party: A Story from "Mary Poppins.". Elliott, Gertrude, illus. LC 52-10821. unpaged. illus. 21 cm. (Little golden library, 140). 1952. Simon and Schuster.
--Stories from Mary Poppins. Elliott, Gertrude, illus. LC 52-9519. (Selected and Abridged from Original Mary Poppin Stories). unpaged. illus. 29 cm. (Big golden book, 565). 1952. Simon and Schuster.

Travers, Pamela Lyndon (1906-), adapted by.
--Two Pairs of Shoes. Dillon, Leo (1933-) & Dillon, Diane (1933-), illus. LC 78-3386. p. cm. 1980. (ISBN 0-670-73677-5). Viking Press. **Award: (ALA).**

Travers, Pamela Lyndon (1906-) & Moore-Betty, Maurice
--Mary Poppins in the Kitchen. Rev ed. Shepard, Mary Eleanor (1909-), illus. LC 77-17764. (Illus.). (gr. 1 up). 1978. (ISBN 0-15-657688-0, VoyB). HarBraceJ.
--Mary Poppins in the Kitchen: A Cookery Book with a Story. Shepard, Mary Eleanor (1909-), illus. LC 75-10131. (Illus.). 128p. (gr. k up). 1975. (ISBN 0-15-252898-9, HJ). HarBraceJ.

Travis, Dempsey
--Don't Stop Me Now. LC 73-107497. (Illus.). photos, 1 color. 64p. (Open Door Bks). (gr. 5 up). 1970. (ISBN 0-516-14812-5). Childrens.

Travis, Falcon
--Super Sleuth: Mini-Mysteries for You to Solve. LC 84-26814. (Illus.). 128 p. 22cm. c.1985. (ISBN 0-8069-4700-4). (ISBN 0-8069-4701-2). Sterling Pub. Co.

Travis, Gretchen
--The Cottage. 1973. (ISBN 0-399-11068-2). G. P. Putnam's Sons.
--Too Old to Die. 1968. (ISBN 0-399-10805-X). G. P. Putnam's Sons.

Travis, Lucille
--A Summer's Growth. 96p. (Orig.). (Voyager Ser.). 1982. (ISBN 0-8010-8866-6). Baker Bk.

Travis, Tom
--Silver Hair: Or, the Trail of the Red Fox. (Champion Stories). 1877. C. T. DeWitt.

Traylor, Sarah M. (1908-)
--The Red Wind. LC 77-3532. (Illus.). 176 p. 23cm. c.1977. (ISBN 0-687-35881-7). Abingdon.

Trdez, Denise see Trez, Denise, pseud.

Treadgold, Mary (1910-)
--Journey from the Heron. 160p. (gr. 5 up). 1983. (ISBN 0-224-01970-8, Pub by Jonathan Cape). Merrimack Pub Cir.
--Left Till Called for. Floethe, Richard (1901-), illus. LC 41-19206. vii p., 1 l., 304 p. incl. plates. col. front. 20 1/2 cm. 1941. Doubleday, Doran & Company, Inc. **Award: (CMA).**
--Maids' Ribbons. (gr. 3-5). 1967. (ISBN 0-8407-6197-X). Nelson.
--Maid's Ribbons. Holden, Susannah, illus. LC 67-139225. 62p. illus. 18cm. (Salamander bks.). 1967, c.1965. Nelson.
--The Mystery of the Polly Harris. Marriott, Patricia (1920-), illus. LC 51-10769. 247 p. illus. 22 cm. 1951. Doubleday.
--No Ponies. Gervis, Ruth S. (1894-), illus. (Illus.). 290p. (gr. 5-9). 1981. (ISBN 0-224-01753-5, Pub. by Chatto-Bodley-Jonathan). Merrimack Pub Cir.
--The Polly Harris. Marriott, Patricia (1920-), illus. LC 70-123117. (Illus.). 192 p. 21cm. 1970. T. Nelson.
--We Couldn't Leave Dinah. (gr. 4-6). N.D. (ISBN 0-14-030224-7, Puffin). Penguin.
--We couldn't Leave Dinah. Grant, Elisabeth, illus. LC 65-756. 222 p. illus. 18cm. 1964, c.1941. Penguin Books.
--The Weather Boy. Geary, Robert, illus. LC 65-25533. 112p. illus. 23cm. 1965, c.1964. (ISBN 0-442-08593-1). VanNostrand.
--Winter Princess. Falconer, Pearl, illus. LC 64-25951. (Illus.). 23cm. 112p. (gr. 4-6). 1902. (ISBN 0-442-08591-5). Van Nos Reinhold.

Treadway, Charles F & Treadway, Ruby Peeples
--Fifty Character Stories. LC 74-87729. x, 174 p. 21cm. 1969. Broadman Press.

Treadway, Jerry, ed. see Joyce, Joy.

Treadway, Ruby Peeples, jt. auth. see Treadway, Charles F.

Trease, Geoffrey see Trease, Robert Geoffrey.

Trease, Robert Geoffrey (1909-)
--The Barons' Hostage. LC 75-11638. 160 p. 21cm. 1975. (ISBN 0-8407-6434-0). T. Nelson.
--Bent Is the Bow. Keeping, Charles William James (1924-), illus. (Illus.). 60 p. 18cm. (Salamander books). 1967, c.1965. Nelson.
--Black Banner Abroad. N.D. Frederick Warne & Co.
--Bows Against the Barons. LC 36-3550. 3 p. l., 152 p. front., illus. 19 cm. 1934. International Publishers.
--Bows Against the Barons. Rev. ed. Hodges, Cyril Walter (1909-), illus. LC 67-20861. (Illus.). v, 154 p. 21cm. 1st U.S. edition. 1967, c.1966. Meredith Press.
--Cue for Treason. Grant, Louis F., illus. LC 42-16180. 281 p. incl. front., illus., plates. 21 1/2 cm. 1941. The Vanguard Press.

--Escape to King Alfred. LC 58-9224. 251 p. 22cm. 1958. Vanguard Press.

--Follow My Black Plume. LC 63-13784. 253p. 2cm. 22cm. c.1963. Vanguard.

--Horsemen on the Hills. N.D. (ISBN 0-8149-0728-8). The Vanguard Press.

--Message to Hadrian: An Adventure Story of Ancient Rome. LC 55-12182. 256p. 22cm. c.1955. (ISBN 0-8149-0429-7). Vanguard Press.

--No Boats on Bannermere. LC 65-11013. 21cm. 252p. (gr. 4-6). N.D. (ISBN 0-448-25939-7). G&D.

--No Boats on Bannermere. Kennedy, Richard (1910-), illus. LC 65-11013. 252p. illus. 21cm. 1st U.S. edition. 1965. Norton.

--The Phoenix and the Flame. N.D. (ISBN 0-670-55228-3). Viking Press.

--Popinjay Stairs: An Historical Adventure About Samuel Pepys. LC 74-30873. (gr. 3-6). 1982. (ISBN 0-8149-0758-X). Vanguard.

--The Red Towers of Granada. Keeping, Charles William James (1924-), illus. LC 67-18646. (Illus.). 185 p. 22cm. 1967, c.1966. Vanguard Press.

--The Secret Fiord. Krush, Joe (1918-), illus. LC 50-9132. (Illus.). 241 p. 21cm. 1st U.S. edition. 1950. Harcourt, Brace.

--Seven Kings of England. N.D. (ISBN 0-8149-0431-9). Vanguard Press.

--The Seven Queens of England. N.D. (ISBN 0-8149-0430-0). Vanguard Press.

--Shadow of the Hawk. Krush, Joe (1918-), illus. LC 49-100534. 236 p. illus. 21 cm. 1949. Harcourt, Brace.

--The Silken Secret. LC 54-11525, 189 p. 22cm. 1954. Vanguard Press.

--A Thousand for Sicily. LC 66-16981. (Illus.). 181 p. 22cm. c.1964. (ISBN 0-8149-0054-2). Vanguard Press.

--Trumpets in the West. Krush, Joe (1918-), illus. LC 47-31021. vii, 239 p. illus. 21 cm. 1947. Harcourt, Brace.

--Victory at Valmy. LC 60-15072. 255 p. 22 cm. 1961, c.1960. Vanguard Press.

--Web of Traitors: An Adventure Story of Ancient Athens. LC 52-11124. 189 p. 22cm. 1952. (ISBN 0-8149-0433-5). Vanguard Press.

--The White Nights of St. Petersburg. Stobbs, William (1914-), illus. LC 67-29447. (Illus.). 199 p. 22cm. 1967. Vanguard Press.

--A Wood by Moonlight and Other Stories. LC 82-670078. 126 p. 21cm. 1981. (ISBN 0-7011-2575-6). Chatto & Windus.

--Word to Caesar. LC 67-5649. 270p. 20cm. (Caravan Bks.). 1965. St. Martin's Press.

Treasure Trails
--Treasure Trails Parade: Stories, Verse, and the Carnival of Fun from Treasure Trails, the Magazine of the Children's Hour. Barrows, Ruth Marjorie (1892-1983), ed. LC 58-246. 418 p. illus. 25 cm. 1958. Spencer Press; Distributed by Grosset & Dunlap, New York.

The, Treasure Book of Children's Verse & Quiller-Couch, Lillian M., eds.
--Treasure Book of Children's Verse. Gray, M. Etheldreda, illus. N.D. Doubleday Doran & Co.

Treat, Lawrence (1903-)
--Crime & Puzzlement: Twenty-Four Solve-Them-Yourself Picture Mysteries. Cabarga, Leslie (1954-), illus. LC 81-47331. p. cm. 1981. (ISBN 0-87923-405-9). D.R. Godine.

--You're the Detective!. Twenty-Four Solve-Them-Yourself Picture Mysteries. Borowik, Kathleen, illus. LC 82-49346. (Illus.). 96p. (Orig.). (gr. 2-7). 1983. (ISBN 0-87923-478-4). Godine.

Treat, Roger L
--Boy Jockey. LC 52-11913. 160p. 20cm. (Barnes junior sports novel). c.1953. A. S. Barnes.

--Duke of the Bruins. LC 50-9605. 168 p. 21 cm. 1950. Messner.

Tredez, Denise see Trez, Denise, pseud.

Tree, Carolyn
--The Meddlesome Penguin. LC 39-6270. 10p. 22cm. 1939. Suttonhouse.

Treece, Henry (1911-1966)
--The Centurion. 1st ed. Russon, Mary Georgina (1937-), illus. LC 67-16509. (Illus.). viii, 113 p. 24cm. 1967. Meredith Press.

--The Dream Time. Keeping, Charles William James (1924-), illus. LC 68-26335. (Illus.). 114 p. 21cm. 1st U.S. edition. 1968. Meredith Press.

--The Further Adventures of Robinson Crusoe. Nickless, Will (1902-), illus. Defoe, Daniel (1660-1731), created by. LC 58-9623. 190 p. illus. 22 cm. (Criterion book for young people). 1958. Criterion Books.

--The Golden One. Stobbs, William (1914-), illus. LC 62-11419. 191 p. illus. 22 cm. (Critierion book for young people) 1962, c.1961. Criterion Books.

--Horned Helmet. Keeping, Charles William James (1924-), illus. LC 63-19079. 118 p. illus. 21 cm. (Criterion book for young people). c.1963. Criterion Books.

--The Invaders: Three Stories. Keeping, Charles William James (1924-), illus. LC 70-186814. (Illus.). 120 p. 22cm. 1972. Crowell.

--The Last Viking. Keeping, Charles William James (1924-), illus. LC 66-12456. 146 p. illus., map. 22 cm. 1966, c.1964. Pantheon Books.

--Man with a Sword. LC 79-319640. (Illus.). vii, 182 p. 21cm. (New Oxford library). 1979. (ISBN 0-19-277084-5). Oxford University Press.

--Man With a Sword. 1964. (ISBN 0-394-81392-8). Pantheon Books.

--Man with a Sword: An Historical novel of strife-torn England at the time of William the Conqueror. Stobbs, William (1914-), illus. LC 64-18737. 211 p. illus. 22cm. 1964, c.1962. Pantheon Books.

--Men of the Hills. Price, Christine Hilda (1928-1980), illus. LC 58-5448. 182 p. illus. 22 cm. (Criterion book for young people). 1958. Criterion Books.

--Perilous Pilgrimage. Price, Christine Hilda (1928-1980), illus. LC 59-6131. 158 p. illus. 22 cm. (Criterion book for young people). 1959. Criterion Books.

--Perilous Pilgrimage. Price, Christine Hilda (1928-1980), illus. 1959. S G Phillips.

--The Queen's Brooch. LC 67-24177. 159 p. 23cm. 1967. Putnam.

--Ride into Danger. Price, Christine Hilda (1928-1980), illus. LC 59-12203. 253 p. illus. 22 cm. (Criterion book for young people). 1959. Criterion Books.

--Ride into Danger. Price, Christine Hilda (1928-1980), illus. 1959. S G Phillips.

--The Road to Miklagard. Price, Christine Hilda (1928-1980), illus. LC 57-12280. 254 p. illus. 22 cm. (Criterion book for young people). 1957. Criterion Books.

--The Road to Miklagard. Price, Christine Hilda (1928-1980), illus. 1957. S G Phillips Inc.

--Splintered Sword. Keeping, Charles William James (1924-), illus. vi, 135p. illus. 21cm. 1st U.S. edition. 1966, c.1965. (ISBN 0-696-80617-7). Duell Dist. Meredith.

--Swords from the North. Keeping, Charles William James (1924-), illus. LC 67-14232. 240p. illus., map 22cm. 1967. Pantheon.

--Viking's Dawn. Price, Christine Hilda (1928-1980), illus. LC 56-9962. 252 p. illus. 22 cm. 1956. Criterion Books.

--Viking's Sunset. Price, Christine Hilda (1928-1980), illus. LC 61-7196. 182 p. illus. 22 cm. 1st U.S. edition. (Criterion book for young people). 1961. Criterion Books.

--War Dog. Payne, Roger, illus. LC 63-12461. 120p. illus. 21cm. (Criterion bk. for young people). 1963, c.1962. Criterion.

--Westward to Vinland. Stobbs, William (1914-), illus. LC 67-22812. (Illus.). 192 p. 22cm. 1967. S. G. Phillips.

--The Windswept City: A Novel of the Trojan War. Jaques, Faith (1923-), illus. (Illus.). xii, 110 p. 21cm. 1st U.S. edition. 1968, c.1967. Meredith Press.

Treece, Henry (1911-1966), adapted by.
--The Burning of Njal. Njala Blatch, Bernard, illus. LC 64-22141. 191 p. illus. 22 cm. 1964. Criterion Books.

Treffinger, Carolyn
--Jimmy's Shoes. Collings, Ruth C., illus. LC 34-36088. 219 p. front., illus., plates. 19 1/2 cm. c.1934. The Penn Publishing Company.

--Li Lun: Lad of Courage. Wiese, Kurt (1887-1974), illus. LC 47-30406. 96 p. illus. 28 cm. 1947. (ISBN 0-687-21693-1). Abingdon-Cokesbury Press. Award: (JNM).

--Rag-Doll Jane: Her Story. Peat, Fern Bisel, Mrs. (1893-), illus. LC 30-182971. 2 p. l., 11-59 p. col. front., col. plates. 31 cm. c.1930. The Saalfield Publishing Company.

--Rag-Doll Jane: Her Story. Peat, Fern Bisel, Mrs. (1893-), illus. LC 35-17090. 34 p. col. illus. 30 1/2 cm. c.1935. The Saalfield Publishing Company.

Treffinger, Eldred Ruffner
--Sage of the Headwater Country. 1st ed. LC 54-12338. 127p. illus. 21cm. 1954. Pageant Press.

Tregarthen, Enys (1851-1923)
--The Doll Who Came Alive. Unwin, Nora Spicer (1907-), illus. 1972. Harper.

--The Doll Who Came Alive. Unwin, Nora Spicer (1907-), illus. LC 70-179780. (Illus.). 75 p. 1972. John Day Co.

--The Doll Who Came Alive. Yates, Elizabeth (1905-), ed. Unwin, Nora Spicer (1907-), illus. LC 42-214402. 75, 1 p. illus. (part col.) 19 1/2 x 19 1/2 cm. 1942. The John Day Company.

--The White Ring. Yates, Elizabeth (1905-), ed. Unwin, Nora Spicer (1907-), illus. LC 49-7971. 65 p. illus. 22 cm. 1949. Harcourt, Brace.

Tregear, Cynthia May Madden (1867-)
--My Blind Children's Fairy Tales. LC 7-40044. (Illus.). 62. 19cm. 1907. Sunshine Home for Blind Babies.

Treider, Ingrid Kittelsen (1890-)
--The Family Under the Living Room Floor. LC 64-2079. 34 p. illus. 21 cm. c.1963. Vantage Press.

--Little Kari. MacKnight, Ninon (1908-), illus. Ninon, pseud. Poulsson, Emilie, tr. from Norwegian. LC 38-186082. xii p., 1 l., 15-149 p. incl. front., illus., plates. 21 1/2 cm. 1938. Lothrop, Lee and Shepard Company.

Treinen, Carmen
--Oink-y: The Little Pig That Cried and Cried. Nossett, Stan, illus. LC 74-165174. (Illus.). 31 p. 28cm. c.1973. Modern Binding Corp.

Trelawny, Edward John
--Adventures of a Younger Son. (Bohn's Popular Library). N.D. Harcourt Brace & Co.

Trelawny, John Edward
--Adventures of a Younger Son. Garnett, Edward, intro. by. (Illus.). (The Adventure Ser.). N.D. MacMillan.

Trell, Max, adapted by see Foster, Harold Rudolf.

Trell, Max (1900-)
--Tom and Mot. McMahon, Jo (1883-), illus. LC 30-23203. vi p., 1 l., 177, 1 p. illus. 21 cm. 1930. Cosmopolitan Book Corporation.

Trella, Phyllis
--Butterflies Have Grandparents, Too. Trella, Phyllis, illus. LC 82-73691. (Illus.). 48p. (Grandparents Ser.). N.D. (ISBN 0-914201-02-6). Cheeruppet.

--Les Duit at the Olympics...& Bea Strong. Trella, Phyllis, illus. (Illus.). 48p. (Les Bea Proud Americans Ser.). N.D. (ISBN 0-914201-01-8). Cheeruppet.

--A Peek at Occupations. Trella, Phyllis, illus. LC 82-73692. (Illus.). 48p. (The P.A.O. Adventures Ser.). N.D. (ISBN 0-914201-03-4). Cheeruppet.

Treloar, Bruce
--Bumble's Island. LC 84-246031. (Illus.). 32p. (ps-k). 1984. (ISBN 0-370-30961-8, Pub. by the Bodley Head). Merrimack Pub Cir.

Tremain, Ruthven (1922-)
--Summer Diary. Tremain, Ruthven (1922-), illus. (Illus.). peel-off stickers. drawings. 128p. (gr. 5 up). 1970. (ISBN 0-02-789410-X). Macmillan.

Tremaine, Dewey F. (1919-)
--Little White Nose. Kenyon, Darl B., Jr., illus. LC 53-8613. 21cm. 32p. 1953. G. P. Putnam's Sons.

Tremblay, Laurence
--Happytown Tales. Newman, Arnold, illus. LC 44-41881. 63, 1 p. illus. 20 cm. 1944. Parker Art Printing Association.

Tremble, Freda B. (1894-)
--Modoc. Mars, Witold Tadeusz J. (1912-), illus. LC 72-83129. (Illus.). 30 p. 24cm. 1972. F. Warne.

Tremper, Andra & Diebert, Linda
--What's New at the Zoo, Kangaroo?. (ps-6). 1982. (ISBN 0-86653-083-5). Good Apple.

Trent, Gregory, pseud., see Williamson, Thames Ross.

Trent-Johns, Altona
--Play Songs of the Deep South. Porter, James A., illus. 36p. N.D. Associated Pub.

Trent, Margaret
--Crossed Trails. LC 32-12524. 256 p. front. 19 cm. (Her The American adventure series). c.1932. A. L. Burt Company.

--The Hills of Home. LC 32-12626. 256 p. front. 19 cm. (Her The American adventure series). c.1932. A. L. Burt Company.

--Hollywood Ho!. LC 32-125252. 251 p. front. 19 cm. (Her The American adventure series). c.1932. A. L. Burt Company.

--Valerie Duval:. Somewhere in France. Wrenn, Charles L., illus. LC 18-12209. (The "Somewhere" Ser.). 1918. Barse & Hopkins.

Trent, Martha
--Alice Blythe: Somewhere in England; a War Time Story. Wrenn, Charles L., illus. LC 18-12211. 215 p. incl. plates. front. 19 1/2 cm. (Her The Somewhere Ser. 3). c.1918. Barse & Hopkins.

--Helen Carey: Somewhere in America; a War Time Story. Wrenn, Charles L., illus. LC 18-122101. 217 p. incl. plates. front. 19 1/2 cm. (Her The Somewhere Ser.1). c.1918. Barse & Hopkins.

--Lucia Rudini: Somewhere in Italy. Wrenn, Charles L., illus. LC 18-122108. 220 p. incl. plates. front. 19 1/2 cm. (Her The Somewhere Ser. 5). c.1918. Barse & Hopkins.

--Marieken De Bruin: Somewhere in Belgium. Wrenn, Charles L., illus. LC 18-122107. 224 p. incl. plates. front. 19 1/2 cm. (Her The Somewhere Ser. 2). c.1918. Barse & Hopkins.

--Phoebe Marshal: Somewhere in Canada. Wrenn, Charles L., illus. LC 19-11152. 6 p. l., 9-221 p. incl. front., plates. 19 cm. c.1919. Barse & Hopkins.

--Valerie Duval: Somewhere in France. Wrenn, Charles L., illus. LC 18-122092. 213 p. incl. plates. front. 19 1/2 cm. (Her The somewhere series. 4). c.1918. Barse & Hopkins.

Trent, Robbie (1894-)
--The Boy's Lunch. Simon, Howard (1903-1979), illus. LC 64-10154. 32p. illus. 21cm. 1964. (ISBN 0-687-03939-8). Abingdon.

--Cubby's World: Story of a Baby Bear. Locke, Margo, illus. LC 66-16997. 46p. col. illus. 25cm. 1966. (ISBN 0-687-10054-2). Abingdon.

--First Christmas. Simont, Marc (1915-), illus. LC 48-8892. (Illus.). (ps-1). 1948. (ISBN 0-06-026121-8, HarpJ). Har-Row.

--The Little Old Lady. LC 58-5416. unpaged. illus. 21 cm. c.1958. Broadman Press.

--Star Shone. large type ed. Ayer, Margaret (0000-1981), illus. LC 66-16997. (Illus.). (ps). 1948. (ISBN 0-664-46121-2). Westminster.

--Susan. Waite, Esther (1899-), illus. LC 44-20041. 127 p. illus. 22 cm. 1944. The Viking Press.

--Susan. Waite, Esther (1899-), illus. LC 72-7183. (Illus.). 152 p. 23cm. 1969, c.1944. Word Books.

Trent, Virginia
--Solomon Snow-Man. 3d ed. LC 20-6579. 67 p. incl. front., illus. (part col.) 15 1/2 cm. 1919. Go-Hawks Happy Tribe.

Trent, W. P., ed. see Ewing, Juliana Horatia Gatty, Mrs.

Trento, Florence
--The Geese That Sang. Pellicer, Joseph Luis, illus. LC 60-5720. 48 p. illus. 22 cm. 1960. Morrow.

Trepeck, Conalee
--Fun at the Hospital. N.D. Carlton Press.

Tress, Arthur (1940-) & Minahan, John (1933-)
--The Dream Collector. Tress, Arthur (1940-), photos by. LC 72-88362. (Illus.). 1 v. (unpaged). 29cm. 1972. (ISBN 0-87858-032-8). Westover Pub. Co.

Tressel, Amalia (1879-)
--Three Kerchiefs and Other Stories for Boys and Girls to Live by. LC 55-4379. 191p. 20cm. 1955. Wartburg Press.

Tressel, Oscar Mrs. see Tressel, Amalia.

Tresselt, Alvin R. (1916-), tr. see Baba, Noburo.

Tresselt, Alvin R. (1916-), tr. see Guggenmos, Josef.

Tresselt, Alvin R. (1916-), tr. see Hamada, Hirosuke.

Tresselt, Alvin R. (1916-), tr. see Maeda, Mieko.

Tresselt, Alvin R., tr. see Maiyagawa, Yasue.

Tresselt, Alvin R. (1916-), tr. see Niklewiczowa, Maria.

Tresselt, Alvin R. (1916-), tr. see Nishimaki, Kayako & Nakamura, Shigeo.

Tresselt, Alvin R. (1916-), tr. see Yoda, Junichi.

Tresselt, Alvin R. (1916-)
--Autumn Harvest. Duvoisin, Roger Antoine (1904-1980), illus. 1951. (ISBN 0-688-51155-4). William Morrow and Company.

--Autumn Harvest. Hafner, Marylin (1925-), illus. LC 51-8824. unpaged. illus. 26 cm. c.1951. Lothrop, Lee & Shepard.

--The Beaver Pond. Duvoisin, Roger Antoine (1904-1980), illus. 1970. Lothrop.

--The Beaver Pond. Duvoisin, Roger Antoine (1904-1980), illus. 1970. (ISBN 0-688-41123-1). William Morrow and Company.

--Bonnie Bess, the Weathervane Horse. Blegvad, Erik (1923-), illus. LC 75-99136. (Illus.). 40 p. 1970. Parents' Magazine Press.

--Bonnie Bess: The Weathervane Horse. Hafner, Marylin (1925-), illus. LC 49-8828. 25 p. col. illus. 26 cm. c.1949. Lothrop, Lee & Shepard Co.

--A Day with Daddy. Heller, Helen, photos by. LC 53-6730. unpaged (chiefly illus.) 29cm. 1953. Lothrop, Lee & Shepard.

--The Dead Tree. Robinson, Charles (1931-), illus. 1972. Parents' Magazine.

--Follow the Road. Duvoisin, Roger Antoine (1904-1980), illus. LC 53-6736. (Illus.). unpaged. 26cm. c.1953. Lothrop, Lee & Shepard Co.

--Follow the Wind. Duvoisin, Roger Antoine (1904-1980), illus. LC 50-10974. (Illus.). (gr. k-3). 1950. (ISBN 0-688-51156-2). Lothrop.

--The Fox Who Travelled. Sears, Nancy, illus. (Illus.). 61 p. 22cm. 1968. Grosset & Dunlap.

--The Fox Who Travelled. Sears, Nancy, illus. 1968. Grosset and Dunlop.

--The Frog in the Well. Duvoisin, Roger Antoine (1904-1980), illus. LC 58-11819. unpaged. illus. 26 cm. 1958. Lothrop, Lee & Shepard Co.

--Helpful Mr. Bear. Kakimoto, Kozo (1915-), illus. 1968. Parent's Magazine Press.

--Hi, Mister Robin. Duvoisin, Roger Antoine (1904-1980), illus. LC 50-7904. (Illus.). (gr. k-3). 1950. (ISBN 0-688-51168-6). Lothrop.

--Hi Mr. Robin. Duvoisin, Roger Antoine (1904-1980), illus. 1950. (ISBN 0-688-51168-6). William Morrow and Company.

--Hide and Seek Fog. Duvoisin, Roger Antoine (1904-1980), illus. LC 65-14087. (Illus.). 32 p. 25cm. 1965. Lothrop, Lee & Shepard. **Awards: (NYT); (ALA); (RCM).**

--I Saw the Sea Come in. Duvoisin, Roger Antoine (1904-1980), illus. LC 54-12395. (Illus.). unpaged. 26cm. c.1954. Lothrop, Lee & Shepard Co.

--It's Time Now!. Duvoisin, Roger Antoine (1904-1980), illus. LC 69-14313. (Illus.). 32 p. 26cm. 1969. Lothrop, Lee & Shepard.

--Johnny Maple-Leaf. Duvoisin, Roger Antoine (1904-1980), illus. LC 48-9592. 28 p. col. illus. 26 cm. c.1948. Lothrop, Lee & Shepard Co.

--The Little Lost Squirrel. Weisgard, Leonard Joseph (1916-), illus. LC 50-12277. 34cm. 26p. (Big Treasure Books). 1950. Grosset & Dunlap.

--The Little Mouse Who Tarried. Kakimoto, Kozo (1915-), illus. LC 72-153794. (Illus.). 32 p. 27cm. 1971. (ISBN 0-8193-0504-9). Parents' Magazine Press.

--Ma Lien and the Magic Brush. Wakana, Kei, illus. (Original Version by Kimishima Hisake). (Illus.). 32 p. 27cm. 1968. Parents' Magazine Press.

--The Old Man and the Tiger. Aquino, Albert, illus. LC 65-215072. (Illus.). 22cm. 60p. (Wonder Bks. Easy Reader). 1965. Grosset.

--Old Man & the Tiger. Aquino, Albert, illus. (Illus.). (Easy Readers Ser.). (gr. k-3). N.D. Wonder.

--The Rabbit Story. Weisgard, Leonard Joseph (1916-), illus. LC 57-599673. unpaged. illus. 26cm. 1957. Lothrop, Lee and Shepard.

--Rain Drop Splash. Weisgard, Leonard Joseph (1916-), illus. LC 46-118781. 29 p. incl. col. front., col. illus. 26 1/2 x 23 cm. c.1946. Lothrop. **Award: (RCM).**

--The Smallest Elephant in the World. Glaser, Milton (1929-), illus. LC 59-10022. unpaged. illus. 26 cm. 1959. Knopf.

--A Sparrow's Magic. Yamanaka, Fuyuji, illus. 1970. Parent's Magazine Press.

--Sun up. Duvoisin, Roger Antoine (1904-1980), illus. LC 49-502425. 25 p. col. illus. 26 cm. c.1949. Lothrop, Lee & Shepard.

--A Thousand Lights and Fireflies. Moodie, John (1916-), illus. LC 65-11652. 1 v. (unpaged) col. illus. 20 x 27 cm. 1965. Parents Magazine Press.

--Thousand Lights & Fireflies. Moodie, John, illus. LC 65-11652. (Illus.). (gr. k-3). 1965. (ISBN 0-8193-0123-X, Four Winds). (ISBN 0-8193-0124-8). Scholastic Inc.

--Timothy Robbins Climbs The Mountain. N.D. E. M. Hale & Co.

--Timothy Robbins Climbs the Mountain. Duvoisin, Roger Antoine (1904-1980), illus. LC 58-10714. unpaged. illus. 26 cm. 1960. Lothrop, Lee & Shepard Co.

--Under the Trees & Through the Grass. Duvoisin, Roger Antoine (1904-1980), illus. (Illus.). (ps-3). 1962. Lothrop.

--Wake up, City!. Duvoisin, Roger Antoine (1904-1980), illus. LC 56-9153. unpaged. illus. 24 cm. c.1957. Lothrop, Lee & Shepard.

--Wake Up, Farm!. Duvoisin, Roger Antoine (1904-1980), illus. LC 55-10441. (Illus.). 24cm. 1955. Lothrop, Lee and Shepard Co.

--Wake up, Farm!. Duvoisin, Roger Antoine (1904-1980), illus. LC 55-10441. (Illus.). unpaged. 24cm. 1966. Lothrop, Lee & Shepard Co.

--What Did You Leave Behind?. 1st ed. Duvoisin, Roger Antoine (1904-1980), illus. LC 77-90604. (Illus.). 32 p. 26cm. c.1978. (ISBN 0-688-41829-5). (ISBN 0-688-51829-X). Lothrop, Lee & Shepard.

--White Snow, Bright Snow. Duvoisin, Roger Antoine (1904-1980), illus. LC 47-11601. 33 p. col. illus., 27 cm. c.1947. Lothrop, Lee & Shepard Co. **Award: (RCM).**

--The Wind and Peter. MacKenzie, Garry (1921-), illus. LC 48-5536. (Illus.). 32p. 18cm. 1948. Oxford University Press.

--The World in the Candy Egg. Duvoisin, Roger Antoine (1904-1980), illus. LC 67-3799. (Illus.). 1 v. (unpaged). 1967. Lothrop, Lee & Shepard.

Tresselt, Alvin R. (1916-), ed.

--Humpty Dumpty's Bedtime Stories. Oechsli, Kelly (1918-), illus. LC 79-136997. (Illus.). color ils. 72p. (gr. k-3). 1971. (ISBN 0-8193-0502-2, Four Winds). (ISBN 0-8193-0503-0). Scholastic Inc.

--Humpty Dumpty's Holiday Stories. Oechsli, Kelly (1918-), illus. LC 72-8116. (Illus.). 72p. (gr. k-3). 1973. (ISBN 0-8193-0644-4, Four Winds). (ISBN 0-8193-0645-2). Scholastic Inc.

--Humpty Dumpty's Storybook. Szekeres, Cyndy (1933-), illus. LC 66-10096. (Illus.). (gr. k-3). 1966. (ISBN 0-8193-0137-X). Parents.

--The Mitten. Mills, Yaroslava Surmach (1925-), illus. 1964. (ISBN 0-688-41053-7). William Morrow and Company.

--The Mitten, an Old Ukranian Folktale. Yaroslava, pseud. (1925-), illus. Mills, Yaroslava Surmach. LC 64-14436. 1v.(unpaged) col. illus. 26cm. 1964. Lothrop.

--Stories from the Bible. Ward, Lynd Kendall (1905-1985), illus. LC 72-132597. (Illus.). 60 p. 32cm. 1971. (ISBN 0-698-30329-6). Coward, McCann & Geoghegan.

--Wishing Penny & Other Fantasy Stories. Lobel, Arnold Stark (1933-), illus. (Illus.). (gr. k-3). 1967. (ISBN 0-8193-0199-X). (ISBN 0-8193-0200-7). Parents.

--Wonder-Fish from the Sea. LC 78-148165. (Original Authors: Josef Guggenmos and Irmgard Lucht). (Illus.). 25 p. 28cm. 1971. (ISBN 0-8193-0483-2). Parents' Magazine Press.

Tresselt, Alvin R. (1916-) & Cleaver, Nancy, pseud. (1906-)

--The Legend of the Willow Plate. Mathews, Evelyn Craw. Low, Joseph (1911-), illus. LC 68-11666. (Illus.). 42p. 1968. Parents' Magazine Press.

Tresselt, Alvin R. (1916-) & Wheaton, Wilbert

--An Elephant Is Not a Cat. Vroman, Tom, illus. LC 62-13577. 1 v. (unpaged) col. illus. 23 cm. c.1962. Parents' Magazine Press.

Tresselt, Alvin R. (1916-) & Zistel, Era

--Treasury of Cat Stories. N.D. Grosset & Dunlap.

Tretiak, Susie

--Good-Bye Daddy. (Illus.). 52p. (gr. k-6). 1982. (ISBN 0-938594-04-4). Spec Lit Pr.

Treuhardt, Beverly Huie & Murdock, Marie

--Sam Bass. LC 58-7014. 140 p. illus. 21 cm. 1958. Steck Co.

Trevathan, Robert E (1925-)

--Longhorns for Fort Sill. LC 62-8951. 192 p. 22 cm. 1962. Criterion Books.

Treville, Stan De see De Treville, Stan.

Trevino, Elizabeth Borton De see De Trevino, Elizabeth Borton.

Trevor, Elleston, pseud., see Dudley-Smith, Trevor.

Trevor, Elleston, pseud. (1920-)

--Badger's Beech. Dudley-Smith, Trevor. Atkinson, Leslie, illus. LC 71-128455. (Illus.). 151 p. 23cm. 1970. (ISBN 0-87695-109-4). Aurora Publishers.

--Badger's Beech. Dudley-Smith, Trevor. Atkinson, Leslie, illus. LC 78-18487. (Illus.). 151 p. 21cm. (Woodlander Ser.). c.1978. (ISBN 0-8202-5015-5). (ISBN 0-8202-5005-8). Sherbourne.

--Badger's Moon. Dudley-Smith, Trevor. (Illus.). (gr. k-3). 1978. (ISBN 0-8202-0201-0). Sherbourne.

--Badger's Moon. Dudley-Smith, Trevor. Atkinson, Leslie, illus. LC 78-18484. (Illus.). 156 p., 4 leaves of plates. 21cm. (Woodlander Ser.). c.1978. (ISBN 0-8202-5016-3). (ISBN 0-8202-5006-6). Charter House.

--Badger's Wood. Dudley-Smith, Trevor. Atkinson, Leslie, illus. LC 59-12199. 147 p. illus. 22 cm. (Criterion Book for Young People). 1959. Criterion Books.

--Badger's Wood. Dudley-Smith, Trevor. Atkinson, Leslie, illus. 1959. S G Phillips.

--Deep Wood. Dudley-Smith, Trevor. Voorhies, Stephen J., illus. LC 47-31268. 282 p. illus. 22 cm. 1st U.S. edition. 1947. Longmans, Green.

--Heather Hill. Dudley-Smith, Trevor. 1st ed. Voorhies, Stephen J., illus. LC 48-7219. 261 p. illus. 21 cm. 1948. Longmans, Green.

--Mole's Castle. Dudley-Smith, Trevor. Atkinson, Leslie, illus. LC 78-18489. (Illus.). 167 p., 4 leaves of plates. 21cm. (Woodlander Ser.). c.1978. (ISBN 0-8202-5017-1). (ISBN 0-8202-5007-4). Charter House.

--Sweethallow Valley. Dudley-Smith, Trevor. Atkinson, Leslie, illus. LC 78-18490. (Illus.). 222 p., 4 leaves of plates. 21cm. (Woodlander Ser.). c.1978. (ISBN 0-8202-5008-2). Charter House Publishers.

--Wizard of the Wood. Dudley-Smith, Trevor. (Illus.). (gr. k-3). 1978. (ISBN 0-685-81582-X). (ISBN 0-685-20688-2). Sherbourne.

Trevor, Lucy Meriol (1919-)

--The Midsummer Maze. Marshall, Hugh, illus. LC 66-2699. (Illus.). 183p. 21cm. 1964. St. Martin's Press.

--The Other Side of the Moon. Thomas, Martin, illus. LC 57-101895. 179p. illus. 21cm. N.D. (ISBN 0-8362-0096-9). Sheed and Ward.

--The Rose Round. LC 64-21277. 176 p. 22 cm. 1964, c.1963. Dutton.

--Sun Slower, Sun Faster. Ardizzone, Edward Jeffrey Irving (1900-1979), illus. LC 57-605201. 217p. illus. 21cm. 1957, c.1955. (ISBN 0-8362-0206-6). Sheed & Ward.

Trevor, Meriol see Trevor, Lucy Meriol.

Trew, Cecil Gwendolen (1897-)

--Asido: The Story of a Mexican Pony. Trew, Cecil Gwendolen (1897-), illus. LC 36-4471. x p., i 1., 139 p. incl. front., illus., plates. 22 cm. 1935. C. Scribner's Sons.

Trewin, ed. see Shakespeare, William (1564-1616) & Lamb, Charles.

Trez, Alain, jt. auth. see Trez, Denise.

Trez, Denise, pseud., see Tredez, Denise.

Trez, Denise, pseud. (1930-) & Trez, Alain, pseud. (1926-)

--The Butterfly Chase. Tredez, Denise. Tredez, Alain. LC 60-11460. unpaged. illus. 29 cm. 1960. World Pub. Co.

--Circus in the Jungle. Trdez, Denise. Tredez, Alain. LC 58-11916. unpaged. illus. 29 cm. 1958. World Pub. Co.

--Fifi. Tredez, Denise. Tredez, Alain. LC 59-11548. unpaged. illus 29 cm. 1959. World Pub. Co.

--Good Night, Veronica. Tredez, Denise. Tredez, Alain. Trex, Denise, pseud. (1930-) & Trez, Alain, pseud. (1926-), illus. Tredez, Denise. Trez, Alain. LC 68-18121. (Illus.). 32 p. 29cm. 1968. Viking Press.

--The Little Knight's Dragon. Tredez, Denise. Tredez, Alain. Trez, Denise, pseud. (1930-) & Trez, Alain, pseud. (1926-), illus. Tredez, Denise. Tredez, Alain. LC 63-8910. unpaged. illus. 23 x 27 cm. 1963. World Pub. Co.

--The Magic Paintbox. Tredez, Denise. Tredez, Alain. LC 62-10242. unpaged. illus. 29 cm. 1962. World Pub. Co.

--Maila and the Flying Carpet. Tredez, Denise. Tredez, Alain. Trez, Denise, pseud. (1930-) & Trez, Alain, pseud. (1926-), illus. Tredez, Denise. Tredez, Alain. McKee, Douglas, tr. LC 78-85863. (Illus.). 32 p. 29cm. 1969. Viking Press.

--Rabbit Country. Tredez, Denise. Tredez, Alain. Trez, Denise, pseud. (1930-) & Trez, Alain, pseud., illus. Tredez, Denise. Tredez, Alain. McKee, Douglas, tr. LC 66-6371. 32p. col. illus. 24cm. 1966. (ISBN 0-670-58646-3). (ISBN 0-670-58647-1). Viking.

--The Royal Hiccups. Tredez, Denise. Tredez, Alain. Trez, Denise, pseud (1930-) & Trez, Alain, pseud. (1926-), illus. Tredez, Denise. Tredez, Alain. McKee, Douglas, tr. LC 65-18152. 1v. (unpaged) col. illus. 29cm. c.1965. Viking.

--The Smallest Pirate. Trez, Alain (1926-) & Trez, Denise (1930-), illus. McKee, Douglas, tr. LC 75-123015. (Illus.). 32 p. 24cm. 1970. Viking Press.

--Sophie. Tredez, Denise. Tredez, Alain. LC 63-14774. 62 p. col. illus 17 cm. 1964. World Pub. C.

--The Three Little Mermaids. Tredez, Denise. Tredez, Alain. LC 69-11165. (Illus.). 32 p. 29cm. 1969. World Pub. Co.

Tribble, Evelyn H., jt. auth. see Feder, Joseph Marvin.

Trice, Edward

--Storm Nelson & the Sea Leopard. (gr. 6 up). N.D. (ISBN 0-392-05476-0, LTB). Sportshelf.

Trick, Edgar Harold

--Adventures of Tommy Tad and Polly Wog. LC 51-54224. 143 p. illus. 18 cm. (True-to-nature series). 1919. Rand McNally.

--More Adventures of Tommy Tad and Polly Wog. LC 51-542251. 155 p. 18 cm. (True to nature series). c.1919. Rand McNally.

--Shellhouse the Turtle. (True to Nature Ser.). N.D. Rand McNally.

Trickey, Edna Butler

--Billy Celebrates. Hyman, Trina Schart (1939-), illus. LC 64-14500. 1 v. (unpaged) col. illus. 21 cm. 1964. United Church Press.

--Billy Finds Out. Hyman, Trina Schart (1939-), illus. (Illus.). 48 p. 21cm. 1966, c.1964. United Church Press.

Trier, Walter (1890-)

--Dandy in the Circus. LC 50-8797. (Illus.). 14x22cm. 48p. 1950. Dodd, Mead & Co.

--Dandy, The Donkey. N.D. Dodd, Mead & Co.

Trigg, Roberta

--Haworth Idyll, a Fantasy. Dashiell, Margaret, illus. LC 47-24302. (Illus.). 88p. 23cm. 1946. Whittet & Shapperson.

Triggs, Lovell Beall, Mrs.

--Rosalita. Yap, Weda (1894-), illus. LC 32-29898. xi, 179 p. incl. col. front., illus. 21 cm. c.1932. The Century Co.

Trigoboff, Joseph (1947-)

--Abu. LC 74-30070. 120 p. 22cm. 1975. (ISBN 0-688-41696-9). Lothrop, Lee & Shephard.

Trilling, Lionel (1905-1975), ed. see Twain, Mark.

Trim, Marj

--Nivek & Nala from Sirch. Schmidt-Fajlik, Ludo (1939-), illus. LC 77-472109. (Illus.). 40 p. 29cm. c.1976. (ISBN 0-919994-01-6). Hoot Productions.

Trim, Marye

--A Million Times Glad. LC 73-102119. (Illus.). 128p. 22cm. (Penguin Ser.). 1970. Review and Herald Pub. Association.

Trimby, Elisa (1948-)

--Mr. Plum's Oasis. LC 80-17662. (Illus.). 32 p. 26cm. 1981. (ISBN 0-688-41991-7). (ISBN 0-688-51991-1). Lothrop, Lee & Shepard Books.

--Mr. Plum's Paradise. LC 76-55731. (Illus.). 32 p. 26cm. 1977, c.1976. (ISBN 0-688-41797-3). (ISBN 0-688-51797-8). Lothrop, Lee & Shepard Co.

Trimby, Elisa (1948-), illus.

--The Christmas Story. LC 84-7836. p. cm. 1984. (ISBN 0-688-02444-0). Lothrop, Lee and Shepard Books.

Trimingham, Ann, jt. auth. see Perkins, Clella Lester.

Trimmer, Ellen McKay

--The Cup. 54p. N.D. Zondervan Publishing House.

--Tiny Tales 'n Tunes. 55p. 1963. Moody.

Trimmer, Marilyn

--Nancy, the Littlest Cowgirl & Other Stories. (gr. 3-4). 1970. Vantage.

Trimmer, Sarah Kirby, Mrs. (1741-1810)

--Fabulous Histories. LC 75-32147. p. cm. (Classics of Children's Literature, 1621-1932). 1977. (ISBN 0-8240-2261-0). Garland Pub.

--The History of the Robins. Hale, Edward Everett (1822-1900), ed. Howard, C. M., illus. LC 3-6458. ix, 90 p. incl. front., illus. 19 cm. (Heath's home and school classics. The story book series, no. 29). 1901. D. C. Heath & Co.

--Mrs. Trimmer's Little Library: Containing "Leading Strings", "Little Fox", and "Honey Blossoms", 3 vols. (Illus.). N.D. James Miller.

--The Robins. 64. (Prize Story Book Ser.). N.D. De Witt Publishing House.

--The Story of the Robins, 1 of 12 vols. New ed. (Illus.). (Good Time Ser.: No. 2). 1905. Set. Henry Altemus Co.

--The Story of the Robins. 1875. Scribner, Welford, & Armstrong.

--The Story of the Robins, 1 of 23 Vols. (Illus.). (Warne's Golden Links Ser.: No. 18). N.D. Scribner & Welford.

--The Story of the Robins. Willard, James Hartwell (1847-), ed. LC 3-25538. xii, 13-132 p. incl. front., illus., plates. 19 1/2 cm. (Altemus' good times series). 1903. H. Altemus Company.

Trimpey, Alice Kent, Mrs.

--The Story of My Dolls. Scott, Janet Laura, illus. LC 35-14392. 5 p. l., 15-76 p. incl. front., illus. 27 1/2 cm. 1935. Whitman Publishing Company.

Trinca, Rod & Argent, Kerry (1960-)

--One Woolly Wombat. Argent, Kerry (1960-), illus. LC 84-21854. (Illus.). 33 p. 29cm. 1985, c.1982. (ISBN 0-916291-00-6). Kane/Miller Book Publishers.

Tring, Stephen, pseud., see Meynell, Laurence Walter.

Trinidad, Angel, jt. auth. see Hawthorne, Nathaniel.

Trinka, Zena Irma

--Jenik and Marenka: A Boy and Girl of Czechoslovakia. Ayer, Margaret (0000-1981), illus. LC 37-20611. 151, 1 p. incl. col. front., illus. (part col.) 21 1/2 cm. c.1937. Thomas Y. Crowell Company.

Tripp, Edward

--From Fair to Fair: Folk Songs of the British Isles. Ritchie, Jean, compiled by. Pickow, George, photos by. LC 66-14766. (Piano Arrangements by Edward Tripp). 93p. illus. 24cm. c.1966. Walck.

--The New Tuba. Reed, Veronica, pseud. (1916-), illus. Sherman, Theresa. 104p. 1955. Henry Z. Walck, Inc., Publishers.

--The New Tuba. Reed, Veronica, pseud. (1916-), illus. Sherman, Theresa. LC 55-8692. (Illus.). 103 p. 21cm. 1955. Oxford University Press.

--The Tin Fiddle. LC 54-8727. (Illus.). unpaged. (Oxford books for boys and girls). 1954. Oxford University Press.

--The Tin Fiddle. Sendak, Maurice Bernard (1928-), illus. 40p. 1954. Henry Z. Walck, Inc.

Tripp, Edward & Fossner, A. K.

--Jean Ritchie's Swapping Song Book. Ritchie, Jean, compiled by. Pickow, George, photos by. LC 64-7776. (Piano Arrangements by Edward Tripp and A.K. Fossner). 93p. illus. 24cm. 1964, c.1952. Walck.

Tripp, John see Moore, John Travers.

Tripp, Paul, jt. auth. see Kleinsinger, George.

Tripp, Paul (1916-)

--The Little Red Flower. Hyman, Trina Schart (1939-), illus. LC 68-22474. (Illus.). 49p. 1968. Doubleday.

--The Strawman Who Smiled by Mistake. 1st ed. Watson, Wendy McLeod (1942-), illus. LC 67-19122. (Illus.). 40 p. 1967. Doubleday.

--The Tail That Went Looking. 1st ed. Lewis, Tim, illus. LC 77-148678. (Illus.). 32 p. 1971. Doubleday.

--Tubby, the Tuba. Chad, illus. LC 54-62932. unpaged. illus. 21cm. (Treasure Bks. 873). 1954. Treasure Books.

--The Vi-Daylin Book of Minnie the Mump, and Other Stories. Hyman, Trina Schart (1939-), illus. LC 70-81775. (Illus.). 46 p. 27cm. 1970. Ross Laboratories.

Tripp, Wallace Whitney (1940-), adapted by see Jerome, Jerome Klapka.

Tripp, Wallace Whitney (1940-)

--Marguerite, Go Wash Your Feet. Tripp, Wallace Whitney (1940-), illus. LC 85-7616. (Illus.). 48 p. 29cm. 1985. (ISBN 0-395-35392-0). Houghton Mifflin.

--My Nose Is Green, Yours Is Blue & Other Rhymes Without Reason. (Illus.). (gr. 4-12). 1976. Little.

--Sir Toby Jingle's Beastly Journey. LC 75-10455. (Illus.). 32p. 24cm. 1976. (ISBN 0-698-20340-2). Coward, McCann & Geoghegan.

Tripp, Wallace Whitney (1940-), compiled by.
--Granfa' Grig Had a Pig & Other Rhymes Without Reason. 1st ed. Tripp, Wallace Whitney (1940-), illus. LC 76-25234. (Illus.). 28cm. 96p. (gr. 4-12). 1976. (ISBN 0-316-85282-1). (ISBN 0-316-85284-8). Little. **Awards: (BGH); (ALA).**
--A Great Big Ugly Man Came up and Tied His Horse to Me: A Book of Nonsense Verse. 1st ed. Tripp, Wallace Whitney (1940-), illus. LC 74-189265. (Illus.). 46 p. 26cm. 1973. (ISBN 0-316-85280-5). Little, Brown. **Award: (ALA).**
--The Tale of a Pig: A Caucasian Folktale. Tripp, Wallace Whitney (1940-), illus. (Illus.). 32 p. 26cm. 1968. (ISBN 0-07-065194-9). (ISBN 0-07-065193-0). McGraw-Hill.

Tritten, Charles
--Heidi Grows up. Coquillot, Jean, illus. Spyri, Johanna Heusser, Mrs. (1827-1901), created by. LC 38-7798. 7 p. l., 9-212 p. col. front., illus., plates. 21 cm. c.1938. Grosset & Dunlap.
--Heidi Grows up. Coquillot, Jean, illus. Spyri, Johanna Heusser, Mrs. (1827-1901), created by. LC 66-31779. 190 p. col. illus. 22 cm. (Whitman Classics Library). 1966. Whitman Pub. Co.
--Heidi's Children. Doane, Pelagie (1906-1966), illus. Spyri, Johanna Heusser (1827-1901), created by. LC 40-3257. 6 p. l., 9-217 p. col. front., illus. 21 cm. c.1939. Grosset & Dunlap.
--Heidi's Children. Goldsborough, June (1923-), illus. LC 67-16754. (Illus.). 254p. 22cm. (The Golden Press Classics Library). 1967. Golden Press.

Tritten, Charles, jt. auth. see Spyri, Johanna Heusser.

Tritten, Charles, tr. see Spyri, Johanna Heusser.

Trivelpiece, Laurel
--During Water Peaches. LC 78-14393. 160 p. 21cm. c.1979. (ISBN 0-397-31831-6). Lippincott.

Trivers, James
--Hamburger Heaven. LC 73-13914. (Illus.). 32cm. c.1976. (ISBN 0-13-372185-X). Prentice-Hall.
--I Can Stop Anytime I Want. Davis, Allen, illus. LC 74-8105. (Illus.) 154 p. 22cm. 1974. (ISBN 0-13-444927-4). Prentice-Hall.
--The Red Fire Book. Millman, David, illus. (Illus.). 1974. (ISBN 0-13-769505-5). P-H.

Trobisch, David see Pimplehuber, pseud.

Trobisch, David & Trobisch, Walter (0000-1979), eds.
--The Adventures of Pumpelhoober. Pimplehuber, pseud. Bruchmann, Eva, illus. Trobisch, Ingrid, Mrs. (1926-), tr. (Illus.). 64p. (gr. 1-3). 1971. (ISBN 0-570-03411-6). Concordia.

Trobisch, Ingrid, Mrs. (1926-), tr. see Trobisch, David & Trobisch, Walter.

Trobisch, Walter, jt. ed. see Trobisch, David.

Troelstra, Sjoukje see Van Hichtum, Ninka, pseud.

Troelstra, Sjoukje
--Afke's Ten. Van Hichtum, Ninka, pseud. Van Stockum, Hilda Gerarda (1908-), illus. Pidgeon, Marie Kiersted, tr. from Dutch. LC 36-28518. 255 p. incl. illus., plates. col. front. 21 cm. c.1936. J. B. Lippincott Company.

Trofimuk, Ann
--Babushka and the Pig. Pinkney, Jerry (1939-), illus. LC 69-14727. (Illus.). 40 p. 24cm. 1969. Houghton Mifflin.

Trollope, Anthony (1815-1882)
--Malachi's Cove. 1st ed. Brockman, Chris, ed. Green, Ken, illus. LC 80-82127. (Illus.). 41 p. 23cm. c.1978. Marigold Press.

Trombetta, Louis M.
--The Christmas Elf. N.D. Carlton.

Troop, Miriam (1917-), ed.
--Limerick Book. Troop, Miriam (1917-), illus. (Illus.). (gr. 4-6). 1964. (ISBN 0-448-02954-5). G&D.

Trosclair
--Cajun Night Before Christmas. Jacobs, Howard (1908-), ed. Rice, James (1934-), illus. LC 74-151725. (Illus.). 48 p. 29cm. 1973. (ISBN 0-88289-002-6). Pelican Pub. Co.

Trotman, Felicity, retold by.
--The Sorcerer's Apprentice. LC 85-12449. p. cm. 1985. (ISBN 0-8172-2505-6). (ISBN 0-8172-2513-7). Raintree Childrens Books.

Trott, Harold Williams, Dr. (1900-)
--Santa Claus in Santa Land. Rueby, Ben R., illus. LC 42-50591. 3 p. l., 95 p. col. illus. 21 cm. 1942. Crosset & Williams.

Trott, Josephine, jt. auth. see Ewing, Ruth.

Trott, Susan (1937-)
--Mr. Privacy. 1st ed. Guminski, Marsha, illus. LC 70-182255. (Illus.). 152 p. 22cm. 1972. (ISBN 0-316-85300-3). Little, Brown.
--The Sea Serpent of Horse. 1st ed. Burns, Irene, illus. LC 73-10204. (Illus.). ix, 117 p. 22cm. 1973. (ISBN 0-316-85301-1). Little, Brown.

Trotta, John (1936-), illus.
--How Many Elephants Are There?. Penick, Ib Children's Television Workshop LC 72-388. 18 p. (on double leaves) (chiefly col. illus. 24cm. (Sesame Street Pop-Up, 5). 1972. (ISBN 0-394-82462-8). Random House.

Trotter, Grace Violet see Paschal, Nancy, pseud.

Trotter, Grace Violet (1900-)
--Clover Creek. Paschal, Nancy, pseud. Carsey, Alice, illus. LC 46-3695. 272 p. illus. 21 cm. 1946. T. Nelson.
--Emeralds on Her Hand. Paschal, Nancy, pseud. LC 65-10655. 211p. 22cm. (Ariel Bks.). (gr. 7-11). c.1965. (ISBN 0-374-32145-0). Farrar.
--HillView House. Paschal, Nancy, pseud. LC 63-19199. 1963. (ISBN 0-664-32318-9). Westminster Press
--Make Way for Lauren. Paschal, Nancy, pseud. LC 63-7094. 229 p. 21 cm. 1963. Westminster Press.
--Name the Day. Paschal, Nancy, pseud. LC 59-5090. 204 p. 21 cm. c.1959. Westminster Press.
--No More Good-Bys. Paschal, Nancy, pseud. LC 62-7172. 191 p. 21 cm. 1962. Westminster Press.
--Portrait by Sheryl. Paschal, Nancy, pseud. LC 58-5128. 205 p. 21cm. 1958. Westminster Press.
--Promise of June. Paschal, Nancy, pseud. LC 55-100058. 189p. 21cm. 1955. T. Nelson.
--Someone to Care. Paschal, Nancy, pseud. LC 57-55707. 206p. 22cm. 1957. Westminster Press.
--Song of the Heart. Paschal, Nancy, pseud. LC 61-5176. 218 p. 21 cm. 1961. Westminster Press.
--Spring in the Air. Paschal, Nancy, pseud. Knight, Susan, illus. LC 53-9309. (Illus.). 192 p. 21cm. 1953. Viking Press.
--Sylvan City. Paschal, Nancy, pseud. Morse, Dorothy Bayley (1906-1979), illus. LC 50-9597. 254 p. illus. 21 cm. 1950. Viking Pr.

Trotter, Melvin E.
--Jimmy Moore of Bucktown. N.D. Fleming H. Revell Co.

Troughton, Joanna Margaret (1947-)
--Spotted Horse. Troughton, Joanna Margaret (1947-), illus. 1978. (ISBN 0-8277-5440-X). British Bk Ctr.

Troughton, Joanna Margaret (1947-), retold by.
--Mouse-Deer's Market. Troughton, Joanna Margaret (1947-), illus. LC 84-11049. (Illus.). 28 p. 26cm. (Folk tales of the world). 1984. (ISBN 0-911745-63-7). Bedrick/Blackie.
--Sir Gawain and the Loathly Damsel. 1st ed. Troughton, Joanna Margaret (1947-), illus. LC 70-186297. (Illus.). 32 p. 26cm. 1972. (ISBN 0-525-39380-3). Dutton.
--Who Will Be the Sun?. Troughton, Joanna Margaret (1947-), illus. LC 85-15074. p. cm. 1986, c.1985. (ISBN 0-87226-038-0). P. Bedrick Books.

Troughton, Joanna Margaret (1947-), illus.
--The Little Mohee: An Appalachian Ballad. LC 70-124307. (Illus.). 32 p. 27cm. 1971. (ISBN 0-525-33830-6). E. P. Dutton.

Trout, John M. (1938-)
--The Road to Meroe. Trout, John M. (1938-), illus. LC 83-1863. 1983. (ISBN 0-914970-44-5). Conch Magazine.
--The Whispering Waters. Trout, John M. (1938-), illus. LC 84-12681. (Illus.). 166 p. 21cm. (Princess Fanisha: Bk.2). 1984. (ISBN 0-914970-49-6). (ISBN 0-914970-43-7). Conch Magazine.

Trowbridge, Catherine Maria (1818-)
--Archie's Keys. N.D. Alfred Martien.
--Changing Places. (Illus.). (Sunday-Hour Lib.). N.D. American Tract Society.
--A Crown of Glory, 1 of 25 vols. 200p. (Golden Rod Library). 1905. American Tract Society.
--Fred Wilder: Or, The Golden Rule. 228p. N.D. Congregational Sunday-School and Publishing Society.
--The Gold Dollar. N.D. Alfred Martien.
--Mistakes. 242p. N.D. Congregational Sunday-School and Publishing Society.
--Two Friends. N.D. Alfred Martien.
--Will and Will Not. (Illus.). N.D. American Sunday-School Union.

Trowbridge, Gertrude Mary Sherman, Mrs. (1867-)
--Those Wilson Children: A Tale of Harum-Scarum Days. Chase, Joseph Cummings, illus. LC 25-212590. 4 p. l., 11-185 p. front., illus. 19 1/2 cm. c.1925. Fleming H. Revell Company.

Trowbridge, John Townsend, jt. auth. see Alcott, Louisa May.

Trowbridge, John Townsend (1827-1916)
--The Adventures of David Vane and David Crane. LC 12-39548. 3 p. l., 9-204 p. incl. 3 pl. front., 2 pl. 18 1/2 cm. c.1889. D. Lothrop Company.
--Biding His Time: Or, Andrew Hapnell's Fortune. LC 12-39542. 190 p. incl. front., illus. 7 pl. 16 1/2 cm. (Start in life series. v. 2). 1889. Lee and Shepard.
--Bound in Honor, 1 of 6 vols. (Illus.). (The Silver Medal Ser.). 1882. Lee & Shepard.
--Bound in Honor: Or, a Harvest of Wild Oats. LC 20-164942. 328 p. plates. 17 1/2 cm. (On cover: Our lucky series). 1878. Lee and Shepard; Etc., Etc.
--Bound in Honor: Or, A Harvest of Wild Oats. LC 5-33628. 19cm. Repr. of 1878 ed. (Silver Medal Stories: No. 4). 1905. Lothrop, Lee & Shepard Co.
--Boys Will Be Boys. (Illus.). N.D. Lee & Shepard.
--The Bright Hope Series, 5 Vols. N.D. Sheldon & Co.
--Burr Cliff. (The Bright Hope Ser.). N.D. Sheldon & Co.
--A Chance for Himself (A Sequel to "Jack Hazard and His Fortunes"). N.D. James R. Osgood.
--A Chance for Himself. (Jack Hazard Ser.). N.D. John C. Winston.
--A Chance For Himself, 1 of 6 Vols. (Illus.). (Jack Hazard Ser.: No. 2). N.D. Set. Porter & Coates.
--A Chance for Himself: Or, Jack Hazard and His Treasure. LC 3-11141. iv p., 1 l., 7-266 p. front., illus., plates. 19 cm. (On cover: Jack Hazard series). c.1900. H. T. Coates & Co.
--Coupon Bonds. (John Townsend Trowbridge Ser.). 1910. Hurst & Co.
--Coupon Bonds. N.D. Lothrop Lee & Shepard.
--Coupon Bonds, and Other Stories. LC 13-9392. v p., 1 l., 411 p. front., plates. 19 1/2 cm. 1873. J. R. Osgood and Company
--Cudjo's Cave. (The Rugby Series for Boys and Girls). N.D. A. L. Burt Company.
--Cudjo's Cave. (John Townsend Trowbridge Ser.). 1910. Hurst & Co.
--Cudjo's Cave. LC 11-20582. 504 p. 19 1/2 cm. 1982, c.1891. Lothrop, Lee & Shepard Co.
--Cudjo's Cave. N.D. Wm. F. Gill & Co.
--Doing His Best. 1873. James R. Osgood.
--Doing His Best. (Jack Hazard Ser.). N.D. John C. Winston.
--Doing His Best. (Illus.). 1888. Porter & Coates.
--Doing His Best, 1 of 6 Vols. (Illus.). (Jack Hazard Ser.: No. 3). 1901. Set. Porter & Coates.
--The Drummer Boy. (Illus.). (The Rugby Series.). 1915. A L Burt & Co.
--The Drummer Boy. (John Townsend Trowbridge Ser.). 1910. Hurst & Co.
--The Drummer Boy. LC 12-39543. 2 p. l., 3-334 p. front., 2 pl. 19 cm. c.1891. Lee and Shepard.
--The Electrical Boy: Or, the Career of Richard Greatman and Greathings. LC 12-395401. iv, 11-390 p. front., illus., plates. 17 1/2 cm. 1891. Roberts Brothers.
--The Electrical Boy: Or, The Career of Richard Greatman and George Greathings. N.D. Little, Brown.
--Farnell's Folly. LC 12-395477. 1 p. l., 469 p. 19 cm. 1885. Lee and Shepard.
--Fast Friends. LC 20-19341. iv, 5-282 p. front., illus., plates. 18 cm. 1875. J. R. Osgood and Company.
--Fast Friends. (The Jack Hazard Ser.). N.D. John C. Winston Co.
--Fast Friends. (Illus.). 1888. Porter & Coates.
--Fast Friends, 1 of 6 Vols. (Illus.). (Jack Hazard Ser.: No. 4). N.D. Set. Porter & Coates.
--Father BrightHopes: Or, An Old Clergyman's Vacation. (John Townsend Trowbridge Ser.). N.D. Hurst & Co.
--Father Brighthopes: Or, an Old Clergyman's Vacation. New and Rev. ed. LC 12-39636. (Autobiographic Preface). 2 p. l., iii-xiv, 15-264 p. front., plates. 17 1/2 cm. (The Toby Trafford Ser.). 1892. Lee and Shepard.
--Father Brighthopes: Or, An Old Clergyman's Vacation, 1 of 5 Vols. (The Bright Hope Ser.). N.D. Set. Sheldon & Co.
--The Fortune of Toby Trafford. (Illus.). (The Toby Trafford Ser). N.D. Lee & Shepard.
--The Fortunes of Toby Trafford. LC 12-39637. 2 p. l., iii-v, 7-315 p. front., plates. 17 1/2 cm. 1893. Lee and Shepard.
--Hearts and Faces. (The Bright Hope Ser.). N.D. Sheldon & Co.
--His One Fault. LC 12-39549. 1 p. l., 7-275 p. plates. 17 1/2 cm. 1887. Lee and Shepard.
--His One Fault, 1 of 6 vols. (Illus.). (The Tide Mill Stories). N.D. Set. Lee & Shepard.
--His Own Master, 1 of 6 vols. (Illus.). (The Silver Medal Ser.). 1882. Lee & Shepard.
--His Own Master. LC 5-33626. 1 p. l., 7-805 p. front., plates. 19 cm. (His Silver medal stories). 1905. Lothrop, Lee & Shepard Co.
--Iron Thorpe. (The Bright Hope Ser.). N.D. Sheldon & Co.
--Jack Hazard and His Fortunes. iv, 254 p. front., illus., pl. 19 1/2 cm. (On cover: Jack Hazard series). c.1899. H. T. Coates & Co.
--Jack Hazard and His Fortunes. N.D. James R. Osgood.
--Jack Hazard and His Fortunes. (Jack Hazard Ser.). N.D. John C. Winston.
--Jack Hazard and His Fortunes, 1 of 6 Vols. (Illus.). (Jack Hazard Ser.). N.D. Set. Porter & Coates.
--Jack Hazard Series, 6 Vols. (Illus.). N.D. Porter & Coates.
--The Jolly Rover. LC 12-39546. 1 p. l., 7-292 p. front., illus., plates. 18 cm. (Silver medal stories. 6). 1883. Lee and Shepard.
--The Kelp Gatherers. (The Start in Life Stories). N.D. Lothrop, Lee & Shepard.
--The Kelp-Gatherers: A Story of the Maine Coast. LC 12-39641. 2 p. l., 9-157 p. front., plates. 16 1/2 x 13 1/2 cm. 1891. Lee and Shepard.
--Lawrence's Adventures. (Jack Hazard Ser.). N.D. John C. Winston.
--Lawrence's Adventures, 1 of 6 vols. (Illus.). (Jack Hazard Ser.: No. 6). N.D. Set. Porter & Coates.
--Lawrence's Adventures among the Ice-Cutters, Glass-Makers, Coal-Miners, Iron-Men, and Ship-Builders. LC 5-25151. (Illus.). 18 1/2cm. 243p. 1871. James R. Osgood.
--Lawrence's Adventures Among the Ice Cutters,Glass Makers, Glass Makers Coal Miners, Iron Men and Ship Builders, 1 of 6 Vols. (Illus.). (Jack Hazard Ser.). N.D. Set. Porter & Coates.
--The Little Master. LC 12-39550. 1 p. l., vii-viii, 9-230 p. plates. 17 1/2 cm. 1887. Lee & Shepard.
--The Little Master, 1 of 6 vols. (Illus.). (The Tide Mill Stories). N.D. Set. Lee & Shepard.
--The Lost Earl. (Illus.). N.D. D. Lothrop Co.
--The Lottery Ticket. LC 12-39544. 202 p. incl. front. 7 pl. 16 1/2 cm. 1896. Lee and Shepard.
--Lucy Arlyn. (John Townsend Trowbridge Ser.). N.D. Hurst & Co.
--Martin Merrivale. N.D. Wm. F. Gill & Co.
--Neighbor Jackwood. (The Rugby Series for Boys and Girls). N.D. A. L. Burt Company.
--Neighbor Jackwood. Rev. ed. LC 13-9383. vi, 459 p. front. (port.) pl. 19 1/2 cm. 1895. Lee and Shepard.
--Neighbor Jackwood. N.D. Wm. F. Gill & Co.
--The Old BattleGround, 1 of 5 Vols. (The Bright Hope Ser.). N.D. Set. Sheldon & Co.
--A Pair of Madcaps. Merrill, Frank Thayer (1848-), illus. LC 9-4962. 359 p. incl. front. 7 pl. 19 1/2 cm. 1909. Lothrop, Lee & Shepard Co.
--Peter Budstone, 1 of 6 vols. (Illus.). (The Tide Mill Stories). N.D. Set. Lee & Shepard.
--Peter Budstone: The/Boy Who Was Hazed. LC 12-39551. 1 p. l., 7-187 p. front., 8 pl. 17 1/2 cm. 1888. Lee and Shepard.
--Phil and His Friends. LC 12-396355. 1 p. l., 7-235 p. front., plates. 18 cm. 1884. Lee and Shepard.
--Phil & His Friends. (The Tide Mill Stories). N.D. Lothrop,Lee & Shepard.
--The Pocket Rifle, 1 of 6 vols. LC 12-39644. (Illus.). 18cm. 274p. (The Silver Medal Ser.). 1882. Lee & Shepard.
--The Prize Cup. Relyea, Charles M., illus. LC 12-39552. ix p., 1 l., 234 p. incl. 10 pl. front. 19 1/2 cm. 1896. The Century Co.
--The Resolute Mr. Pansy: An Electrical Story for Boys. Searles, Victor A., illus. LC 12-39554. 206 p. front., plates. 17 1/2 cm. 1897. Roberts Brothers.
--The Satin-Wood Box. Old Lady Hemenway's Legacy. LC 13-9390. 170 p. incl. front. plates. 17 1/2 cm. 1894. Lee and Shepard.
--The Satin-Wood Box: Old Lady Hemenway's Legacy, 1 of 6 vols. (Illus.). (The Tide Mill Stories). N.D. Set. Lee & Shepard.
--The Scarlet Tanager and Other Bipeds. LC 13-938239. 2 p. l., 9-181 p. front., plates. 16 1/2 x 12 1/2 cm. 1892. C. T. Dillingham.
--The Scarlet Tanager and Other Bipeds. (Illus.). (The Start in Life Ser.). N.D. Lee & Shepard.
--The Silver Medal, 1 of 6 vols. (Illus.). (The Silver Medal Ser.). 1882. Lee & Shepard.
--The Silver Medal. LC 8-22544. 287 p. incl. front. plates. 19 cm. (His Silver medal stories, v. 1). c.1908. Lothrop, Lee & Shepard Co.
--The Silver Medal Series, 4 vols. (Illus.). 1882. Set. Lee & Shepard.
--A Start in Life: A Story of the Genesee Country. LC 12-39545. 1 p. l., 5-163 p. front., 7 pl. 16 1/2 cm. (Start in life stories. 1). 1889. Lee and Shepard.
--The Story of a Wireless Telegraph Boy. LC 8-26832. 3 p. l., 218, 2 p. front. 19 1/2 cm. 1908. Houghton Mifflin Company.
--Three Boys on an Electrical Boat. LC 12-395417. 2 p. l., 215 p. 18 cm. 1894. Houghton, Mifflin and Company.
--The Three Scouts. (The Rugby Series for Boys and Girls). N.D. A. L. Burt Company.
--The Three Scouts. (John Townsend Trowbridge Ser.). N.D. Hurst & Co.
--The Three Scouts. LC 13-939176. 383 p. 19 cm. 1894. Lee and Shepard.
--The Three Scouts. LC 11-17973. 383 p. 19 1/2 cm. c.1892. Lothrop, Lee & Shepard Co.
--The Three Scouts. N.D. Wm. F. Gill & Co.
--The Tinkham Brothers' Tide Mill. (The Tidemill Stories). N.D. Lothrop, Lee & Shepard.

--The Tinkham Brothers' Tidemill. LC 13-9393. iv, 9-326 p. front., plates. 18 cm. 1884. Lee and Shepard.
--Two Biddicut Boys and Their Adventures with a Wonderful Trick-Dog. LC 98-294823. vii p., 1 l., 286 p. incl. front., plates. 19 1/2 cm. 1898. The Century Co.
--Vagabond. (Illus.). (Knickerbocker Classics). N.D. Hurst & Co.
--The Vagabonds. Darley, Felix Octavius Carr (1822-1888), illus. N.D. Hurd & Houghton.
--Woodie Thorpe's Pilgrimage and Other Stories. LC 12-39553. vii p., 1 l., 269 p. front., 6 pl. 17 1/2 cm. (The Toby Trafford series). 1893. Lee and Shepard.
--Young Joe, and Other Boys. LC 7-23637. 2 p. l., 9-302 p. front., plates. 19 cm. (His Silver medal stories, v. 6). c.1907. Lothrop, Lee & Shepard Co.
--The Young Surveyor, 1 of 6 Vols. (Illus.). (Jack Hazard Ser.: No. 5). N.D. Set. Porter & Coates.
--The Young Surveyor: Or, Jack on the Prairies. LC 3-11140. iv p., 1 l., 7-290 p. front., illus., plates. 19 1/2 cm. (On cover: Jack Hazard series). c.1903. H. T. Coates & Co.
--The Young Surveyor: Or, Jack on the Prairies. (Jack Hazard Ser.). 1875. James R. Osgood.
--The Young Surveyor: Or, Jack on the Prairies. LC 3-11140. 20cm. 290p. (Jack Hazard Ser.). N.D. John C. Winston.

Trowbridge, Lydia Jones
--Betty of the Consulate: A Little American Girl's Adventures in Old China. Rumely, Louise Clasper, illus. LC 29-23111. x p., 1 l., 205 p. incl. illus., plates. col. front. 19 1/2 cm. 1929. Doubleday, Doran and Company, Inc.

Troxell, Eleanor
--Pammy and His Friends. LC 28-6393. viii p., 1 l., 83 p. illus. 19 1/2 cm. c.1928. C. Scribner's Sons.

Troxell, Eleanor & Dudley, Dessalee Ryan, Mrs.
--On Shining Rails: Stories About Trains. Jameson, Arthur, illus. LC 39-19005. iv, 115 p. illus. 18 1/2 cm. c.1939. C. Scribner's Sons.

Troy, Hugh (1906-1964)
--The Chippendale Dam. LC 41-17952. 45 p., 1 l. incl. col. front., illus. (part col.) 20 cm. c.1941. Oxford University Press.
--Five Golden Wrens. Troy, Hugh (1906-1964), illus. LC 43-2262. 47 p. illus. 25 cm. 1943. Oxford University Press.
--Maud for a Day. Troy, Hugh (1906-1964), illus. LC 40-32223. 55, 1 p. illus. 21 1/2 cm. c.1940. Oxford University Press.

Troy, Katherine
--Roseheath. (gr. 9 up). N.D. McKay.

Truax, Rhoda see Wyngard, Rhoda, pseud.

Truax, Rhoda
--Winds of Change: Ohio in the Eighteen-Fifties. Wyngard, Rhoda, pseud. 1st ed. Kredel, Fritz (1900-1973), illus. LC 55-5887. 191p. illus. 21cm. (American Heritage Ser.). 1955. Aladdin Books.

Truchot, Theresa (1891-)
--Charcoal Wagon Boy. Winkler, M. Vols, illus. LC 52-12978. (Illus.). 133 p. 22cm. 1952. Binfords & Mort.

Trudeau, Garry B. (1948-), ed. see Caniff, Milton Arthur, et al.

True, Barbara & Henry, Marguerite
--Their First Igloo. N.D. E. M. Hale & Co.
--Their First Igloo on Baffin Island. Blackwood, Gladys Rourke, illus. LC 43-953751. 28 p. illus. (part col.) 26 x 21 cm. (gr. 2-4). 1943. (ISBN 0-8075-7844-4). A. Whitman & Company.

True, John Preston (1859-1933)
--The Iron Star and What It Saw on Its Journey Through the Ages from Myth to History. True, Lilian Crawford, illus. LC 99-5904. vi p., 1 l., 146 p. front., illus., plates. 21 cm. 1899. Little, Brown & Company.
--The Iron Star and What It Saw on Its Journey Through the Ages from Myth to History. True, Lilian Crawford, illus. LC 4-18942. vi p., 1 l., 146 p. front., illus., plates. 19 1/2 cm. 1902. Little, Brown, & Company.
--Morgan's Men: Containing Adventures of Stuart Schuyler, Captain of Cavalry During the Revolution. True, Lilian Crawford, illus. LC 1-24497. viii p., 1 l., 342 p. front., plates. 19 cm. 1901. Little, Brown and Company.
--On Guard!. Against Tory and Tarleton; Containing Adventures of Stuart Schuyler, Major of Cavalry During the Revolution. True, Lilian Crawford, illus. viii p., 1 l., 802 p. front., 5 pl. 19 cm. 1902. Little, Brown, and Company.
--Scouting for Light Horse Harry: Containing Adventures of Thomas Ludlow, Captain of Cavalry During the Revolution, Including Certain Experiences from Bunker Hill to Hobkirk's Hill. True, Lilian Crawford, illus. LC 11-24117. ix, 334 p., 1 l. front., plates. 19 cm. (His The Stuart Schuyler series). 1911. Little, Brown, and Company.
--Scouting for Washington: A Story of the Days of Sumter and Tarleton. De Land, Charles O., illus. LC 5172. 3 p. l., iii-iv p., 1 l., 311 p. front. 5 pl. 19 cm. 1900. Little, Brown & Company.
--Shoulder Arms. N.D. Abingdon Press.
--Shoulder Arms: Or, the Boys of Wild Lake School. LC 12-39555. 328 p. incl. front. 18 1/2 cm. 1889. Hunt & Eaton.
--Shoulder Arms: Or, The Boys of Wild Lake School. (Illus.). N.D. Methodist Bk Concern.
--Their Club and Ours. LC 12-394555. viii, 7-212 p. incl. front., illus., plates. 18 1/2 cm. c.1883. D. Lothrop and Company.

True, Louise
--Number Men. Owens, Lillian, illus. LC 48-4336. (Illus.). 25p. 20 x 24cm. 1948. Children's Press.
--Number Men. Owens, Lillian, illus. 1962. (ISBN 0-516-03051-5). Childrens Press.
--Number Men. Owens, Lillian, illus. N.D. Grosset & Dunlap.

Truepeney, Charlotte
--Zephyr: The Story of a Vervet Monkey. Truepeney, Charlotte, illus. (Illus.). (gr. 4-6). 1964. Scribner.

Truffin, Terry, ed. see Gurley, Jayne.

Truher, Helen, jt. auth. see Brown, Charles Manley.

Truitt, Gloria A. (1939-)
--Cheerful Chad and Other Children of God. Jones, Dennis, illus. LC 84-23038. (Illus.). 24 p. 25cm. c.1985. (ISBN 0-570-04111-2). Concordia Pub. House.

Trulen, Cheryl
--The Angel with Her Tongue Sticking Out. LC 73-84646. 169 p. 18cm. 1974. Xerox Education Publications.

Trullinger, Florence Wildman, Mrs.
--Dog Days: the Adventures of Nicki and Angus. Day, Doris, illus. LC 36-29810. 128 p. incl. front., illus. 22 cm. c.1936. Thomas Y. Crowell Company.

Trullinger, Theo C.
--The Robin Who Could Not Sing. 1978. (ISBN 0-533-02988-0). Vantage.

Truman, Jessie
--Gently Bend the Tender Twig. LC 74-15187. (Illus.). 96 p. 22cm. 1975, c.1974. (ISBN 0-8059-2079-X). Dorrance.

Trumbull, Jane
--Shirley Takes a Chance. Gregory, Dorothy Lake, illus. LC 27-18321. 377 p. illus., col. pl. 19 1/2 cm. c.1927. Rand, McNally & Company.

Truse, Kenneth Philip (1946-)
--Benny's Magic Baking Pan. Morrison, Bill (1935-), illus. LC 73-22077. (Illus.). 32 p. 23cm. 1974. (ISBN 0-8116-6062-1). Garrard Pub. Co.

Truss, Jan (1925-)
--Bird at the Window. LC 79-1999. p. cm. 1980, c.1974. (ISBN 0-06-026137-4). (ISBN 0-06-026138-2). Harper & Row.
--Jasmin. LC 81-8114. 196 p. 22cm. 1982. (ISBN 0-689-50228-1). Atheneum.

Trussell, Tait & Hencke, Paul, eds.
--Dear NASA, Please Send Me a Rocket. U.S. National Aeronautics and Space Administration Ungerer, Tomi, pseud. (1931-), illus. Ungerer, Jean Thomas. Von Braun, Werner, frwd. by. LC 64-215186. 95p. illus. 15cm. c.1964. Dutton.

Trusta, H., pseud., see Phelps, Elizabeth Stuart.

Tsai, Christiana
--Queen of the Dark Chamber. 192p. 1966. Moody Press.

Tsarelka, Lisa
--Stay Away from My Lawnmower. Tripp, Wallace Whitney (1940-), illus. LC 65-22510. 117p. illus. 22cm. c.1965. (ISBN 0-395-07128-3). Houghton.

Tschantre, E., Jr., jt. auth. see Kasson, Gracia.

Tschiffely, Aime Felix (1895-)
--The Tale of Two Horses. 1934. Golden Press.
--The Tale of Two Horses. Wiese, Kurt (1887-1974), illus. Graham, Robert Bontine Cunninghame (1852-1936), pref. by. LC 36-8061. 2 p. l., iii-viii p., 1 l., 220 1 p. illus. 22 1/2 cm. 1935. Simon and Schuster.

Tsisghwana see Traveller Bird, pseud.

Tsow, Ming
--A Day with Ling. (Illus.). 32p. 1st U.S. edition. (gr. 1-3). 1982. (ISBN 0-241-10833-0, Pub. by Hamish Hamilton England). David & Charles.

Tsugawa, Shuichi, ed.
--Japanese Children's Songs. (Illus.). 32p. N.D. International Pub.
--Japanese Children's Songs. Fujishiro, Seiji, illus. Niwa, Tamako (1922-) & Terry, Maranell, trs. 31p. col. illus. 31cm. 1963, c.1959. Fuji Pub. Co., Dist. Rutland, Vt., Japan Pubns.

Tsultim, Yeshe
--The Mouse King: A Story from Tibet. Ralla, Kusho, illus. Hyde-Chambers, Frederick, tr. from Tibetan. (Illus.). (Puffin Folktales of the World Ser.). (gr. 3-6). 1979. (ISBN 0-14-030804-0, Puffin). Penguin.

Tsutsui, Keisuke, ed.
--Joey the Clown. Watanabe, Saburo, illus. Herring, Ann K., tr. LC 74-100673. 14 color ils. 26p. (Fantasia Pictorial Ser). (gr. k-8). 1970. Japan Pubns.

Tuasaki, Chichero
--Momoko & the Pretty Bird. (ps-3). 1973. (ISBN 0-695-80404-9). Follett.

Tubbs, Rhoda, jt. auth. see U. S. Bureau of Indian Affairs.

Tubby, I. M., pseud., see Kraus, Robert.

Tubby, I. M., pseud. (1925-)
--I'm a Little Airplane. Kraus, Robert. (Illus.). 10p. (Tubby Bks.). (ps). 1982. (ISBN 0-671-45565-6). Windmill Bks.
--I'm a Little Choo-Choo. Kraus, Robert. (Shaped Tubby Bks.). (ps). 1982. (ISBN 0-671-44568-5, Pub. by Windmill). S&S.
--I'm a Little Fish. Kraus, Robert. LC 81-51113. (Illus.). 10p. (Tubby Bks). (ps up). N.D. (ISBN 0-671-44435-2). Windmill Bks.
--I'm a Little House. Kraus, Robert Tubby, I. M., pseud. (1925-), illus. Kraus, Robert. (Illus.). 10p. (Tubby Bks.). (ps). 1982. (ISBN 0-671-45566-4). Windmill Bks.
--I'm a Little Tugboat. Kraus, Robert. LC 81-51114. (Illus.). 10p. (Tubby Bks.). (ps up). N.D. (ISBN 0-671-44434-4). Windmill Bks.

Tubby, Ruth Peckham, tr. see Chardon, Jeanne.

Tucci, Al B.
--The Dragon Who Was Different. N.D. Carlton.

Tucci, Niccolo (1908-) & Koffler, Camilla (0000-1955)
--Tico-Tico. 1st ed. Ylla, pseud. Pontabry, Robert, designed by. LC 50-10668. (Illus.). 40 p. 29cm. 1950. Harper.

Tucker, Annie
--Through the Gates: A Tale for the Home. N.D. Thomas Nelson & Sons.

Tucker, Bettie C.
--The Children's Rhyming Bible. Smith, Dale R., et al., eds. (Illus.). 300p. (Orig.). (gr. k-12). 1982. (ISBN 0-9608780-0-9). Rainbows End.

Tucker, Charlotte Maria see A. L. O. E, pseud.

Tucker, Charlotte Maria (1821-1893)
--The A. L. O. E. Picture Story Book. A. L. O. E. , pseud. N.D. Thomas Nelson & Sons.
--A. L. O. E. Ser. Containing "Claudia," "Triumph over Midian," and "Rescued from Egypt". A. L. O. E, pseud, 3 vols. (Illus.). N.D. D. Lothrop & Co.
--A. L. O. E.'s Beautiful Villa Series. A. L. O. E, pseud, 8 Vols. (Illus.). N.D. Set. Thomas Nelson & Sons.
--A. L. O. E.'s Home Circle Library. A. L. O. E, pseud, 6 Vols. (Illus.). N.D. Thomas Nelson & Sons.
--A. L. O. E.'S Picture Story Book. A. L. O. E, pseud. (Illus.). N.D. Thomas Nelson and Sons.
--Adopted Son. A. L. O. E. , pseud. (First Ser.). (Carters' Fireside Library). N.D. Robert Carter & Bros.
--Adopted Son. A. L. O. E. , pseud. (The Little Gipsy Ser.). N.D. The American News Co.
--The Adopted Son. Tucker, Charlotte Maria. A. L. O. E, pseud. (ALOE Select Lib.). 1888. Thomas Whittaker.
--The Adopted Son. A. L. O. E, pseud, 1 of 10 Vols. (Illus.). (The Garland Ser.). N.D. Set. Thomas Nelson & Sons.
--Albert's Adventures. A. L. O. E, pseud, 1 of 12 Vols. (A. L. O. E.'S Fireside Tales). N.D. Set. Thomas Nelson and Sons.
--Albert's Adventures. A. L. O. E. , pseud, 1 of 12 Vols. (Friend and Foe Ser.). N.D. Set. Thomas Whittaker.
--Alfred and Bernard. A. L. O. E, pseud, 1 of 12 Vols. (A. L. O. E.'S Fireside Tales). N.D. Set. Thomas Nelson and Sons.
--An Heir of Heaven. A. L. O. E, pseud, 1 of 12 vols. (Conqueror Ser.). N.D. Set. Thomas Whittaker.
--Angus Tarlton. A. L. O. E. , pseud. (The Little Gipsy Ser.). N.D. The American News Co.
--Augustine Strecker. A. L. O. E. , pseud. (The Gipsey Ser.). N.D. The American News Co.
--Augustine Streeker. A. L. O. E. , pseud. (The Little Gipsey Ser.). N.D. American News Co.
--Australian Uncle. A. L. O. E, pseud, 1 of 12 Vols. (A. L. O. E.'S Fireside Tales). N.D. Set. Thomas Nelson and Sons.
--The Backward Swing. A. L. O. E, pseud, 1 of 8 Vols. (Illus.). (A. L. O. E. Library). (The Victory Ser.). N.D. Set. Thomas Nelson and Sons.
--The Battle of Life. A. L. O. E, pseud. (The Claremont Ser.). N.D. Fleming H. Revell Co.
--Bearing Burdens. A. L. O. E, pseud, 1 of 12 bks. (Illus.). (Stories by A. L. O. E. Packet "B": No. 1). N.D. Set. Thos Nelson & Sons.
--The Beautiful Garment and Other Stories. A. L. O. E. pseud. LC 27-21409. 96 p. plates. 18 cm. c.1927. Augustana Book Concern.
--The Beautiful Villa. A. L. O. E, pseud, 1 of 8 Vols. (A. L. O. E.'S Story Box). N.D. Set. Thomas Nelson and Sons.
--Ben Stone. A. L. O. E, pseud, 1 of 12 Vols. (Friend and Foe Ser.). N.D. Set. Thomas Whittaker.
--Beyond the Black Waters. A. L. O. E, pseud. N.D. Thos Nelson & Sons.
--Blacksmith of Boniface Lane. A. L. O. E, pseud, 1 of 103 vols. (The Pearl Library: No. 7). 1900. Hurst & Co.
--The Blacksmith of Boniface Lane. A. L. O. E, pseud. N.D. Thos Nelson & Sons.
--A Braid of Cords. A. L. O. E, pseud, 1 of 4 Vols. (Illus.). (The Braid of Cords Library). N.D. Set. George Routledge & Sons.
--A Braid of Cords. A. L. O. E. , pseud. (A. L. O. E. Presentation Library). N.D. Potts, Young, & Co.
--Braid of Cords. A. L. O. E. , pseud. (First Ser.). (Carters' Fireside Library). N.D. Robert Carter & Bros.
--Broken Bread. A. L. O. E, pseud, 1 of 12 Vols. (A. L. O. E.'S Fireside Tales). N.D. Set. Thomas Nelson and Sons.
--Broken Chain. A. L. O. E, pseud. N.D. Robert Carter.
--The Brother's Return. A. L. O. E, pseud, 1 of 8 Vols. (Illus.). (A. L. O.. E. Library). (The Victory Ser.). N.D. Set. Thomas Nelson and Sons.
--The Brother's Return. A. L. O. E, pseud, 1 of 14 Vols. (Illus.). (Tales for the Young Ser.). N.D. Set. Thomas Nelson & Sons.
--The Chief's Daughter. A. L. O. E. , pseud. (First Ser.). (Carters' Fireside Library). N.D. Robert Carter & Bros.
--The Children's Garland. A. L. O. E, pseud. (Illus.). N.D. Thomas Nelson & Sons.
--Children's Posey. A. L. O. E, pseud. Large Type ed. (Illus.). N.D. Thomas Nelson & Sons.
--Children's Treasury. A. L. O. E. , pseud. (First Ser.). (Carters' Fireside Library). N.D. Robert Carter & Bros.
--The Children's Treasury. A. L. O. E. , pseud. N.D. Thomas Nelson & Sons.
--Christian Conquests. A. L. O. E, pseud. (The Claremont Ser.). N.D. Set. Fleming H. Revell Co.
--Christian Love and Loyalty. A. L. O. E, pseud, 1 of 4 Vols. (Illus.). (The Braid of Cords Library). N.D. Set. George Routledge & Sons.
--The City of Nocross. A. L. O. E. , pseud. N.D. D. Lothrop & Co.
--City of Nocross. A. L. O. E. , pseud. 1875. Henry Hoyt.
--The City of Nocross and Its Famous Physician. A. L. O. E. , pseud. N.D. Thomas Nelson & Sons.
--The Claremont Tales. A. L. O. E, pseud. (The Claremont Ser.). N.D. Set. Fleming H. Revell Co.
--Claremont Tales. A. L. O. E. , pseud. (First Ser.). (Carters' Fireside Library). N.D. Robert Carter & Sons.
--Claremont Tales. A. L. O. E. , pseud. (The Claremont Library). N.D. The American News Co.
--Claudia. A. L. O. E. , pseud. (A. L. O. E. Ser.). 1870. D. Lothrop & Co.
--Claudia. A. L. O. E. , pseud. (First Ser.). (Carters' Fireside Library). N.D. Robert Carter & Bros.
--Claudia: A Tale. A. L. O. E. , pseud. N.D. Thomas Nelson & Sons.
--Clouds and Sunshine. A. L. O. E, pseud, 1 of 12 Vols. (Illus.). (The Diamond Ser.). N.D. Thomas Nelson and Sons.
--A Conqueror. A. L. O. E, pseud, 1 of 12 Vols. (Conqueror Ser.). N.D. Set. Thomas Whittaker.
--The Convict's Child. A. L. O. E. , pseud. (The Little Children's A. L. O. E. Library). N.D. American News Co.
--The Convict's Child. A. L. O. E, pseud, 1 of 12 Vols. (Friend and Foe Ser.). N.D. Set. Thomas Whittaker.
--The Convicts's Child. A. L. O. E, pseud, 1 of 6 Vols. (Illus.). (A. L. O. E.'s Home Circle Library). N.D. Set. Thomas Nelson & Sons.
--Cords of Affection. A. L. O. E, pseud, 1 of 12 Vols. (A. L. O. E.'S Fireside Tales). N.D. Set. Thomas Nelson and Sons.
--Cords of Life. A. L. O. E, pseud, 1 of 12 Vols. (A. L. O. E.'S Fireside Tales). N.D. Set. Thomas Nelson and Sons.
--The Cords of Love. A. L. O. E. , pseud. (The Little Children's A. L. O. E. Library). N.D. American News Co.
--Cords of Love. A. L. O. E, pseud, 1 of 12 Vols. (A. L. O. E.'S Fireside Tales). N.D. Set. Thomas Nelson and Sons.
--The Cords of Sin. A. L. O. E. , pseud. (The Little Children's A. L. O. E. Library). N.D. American News Co.
--Cortley Hall. A. L. O. E. , pseud. (First Ser.). (Carters' Fireside Library). N.D. Robert Carter & Bros.
--Courage and Candor. A. L. O. E, pseud, 1 of 8 Vols. (A. L. O. E.'S Story Box). N.D. Set. Thomas Nelson and Sons.
--Courage and Candor. A. L. O. E, pseud, 1 of 8 Vols. (Illus.). (A. L. O. E.'s Beautiful Villa Ser.). N.D. Set. Thomas Nelson & Sons.

--A Son of Israel. A. L. O. E. , pseud. (The Little Children's A. L. O. E. Library). N.D. American News Co.
--A Son of Israel. A. L. O. E, pseud, 1 of 6 Vols. (Illus.). (A. L. O. E.'s Home Circle Library). N.D. Set. Thomas Nelson & Sons.
--A Son of Israel. A. L. O. E, pseud, 1 of 12 Vols. (Friend and Foe Ser.). N.D. Set. Thomas Whittaker.
--Sophy Claymore. A. L. O. E, pseud, 1 of 12 Vols. (Friend and foe Ser.). N.D. Set. Thomas Whittaker.
--The Spanish Cavalier. A. L. O. E. , pseud. 1875. Robert Carter & Brothers.
--The Spanish Cavalier: A Story of Seville. A. L. O. E. , pseud. N.D. Thomas Nelson & Sons.
--The Stolen Child. A. L. O. E, pseud, 1 of 12 Vols. (A. L. O. E.'S Fireside Tales). N.D. Set. Thomas Nelson and Sons.
--Straight Road. A. L. O. E. , pseud. N.D. E. P. Dutton.
--Straight Road. A. L. O. E. , pseud. (Fourth Ser.). (Carter's Fireside Library). N.D. Robert Carter & Bros.
--The Straight Road. A. L. O. E, pseud, 1 of 25 Vols. (Illus.). (Warne's Crofton Cousins Ser.). N.D. Scribner & Welford.
--Sunday Chaplet of Stories. A. L. O. E, pseud, 1 of 4 vols. (Illus.). (The Chaplet Ser.). N.D. Set. Thomas Nelson & Sons.
--Tales Illustrative of the Parables. A. L. O. E, pseud. (The Claremont Ser.). N.D. Fleming H. Revell Co.
--Tales Illustrative of the Parables. A. L. O. E. , pseud. (The Claremont Library). N.D. The American News Co.
--Tales of the Sea. A. L. O. E, pseud, 1 of 4 Vols. (Illus.). (The Braid of Cords Library). N.D. Set. George Routledge & Sons.
--A Thankful Guest. A. L. O. E, pseud, 1 of 12 Vols. (Conqueror Ser.). N.D. Set. Thomas Whittaker.
--The Thorn in the Conscience. A. L. O. E, pseud, 1 of 12 Vols. (Illus.). (The Diamond Ser.). N.D. Thomas Nelson and Sons.
--Thorns and Flowers, 1 of 4 bks. (Illus.). (The Little Sower and Other Stories). N.D. Thos Nelson & Sons.
--The Tiny Red Night Cap. A. L. O. E, pseud, 1 of 8 Vols. (Illus.). (The Victory Ser.). N.D. Set. Thomas Nelson and Sons.
--The Tiny Red Night Cap. A. L. O. E, pseud, 1 of 14 Vols. (Illus.). (Tales for the Young Ser.). N.D. Set. Thomas Nelson & Sons.
--Tiny Red Night-Cap. A. L. O. E, pseud, 1 of 8 vols. (Illus.). (A. L. O. E. Library). N.D. Set. Thos Nelson & Sons.
--Treasury of Old Favorite Tales. A. L. O. E, pseud, 1 of 4 Vols. (Illus.). (The Silver Keys Library). N.D. Set. George Routledge & Sons.
--Triumph Over Midian. Tucker, Charlotte Maria. A. L. O. E. , pseud. (A. L. O. E. Ser.). 1870. D. Lothrop & Co.
--The Triumph Over Midian. A. L. O. E. , pseud. N.D. N. Tibbals & Sons.
--Triumph over Midian. A. L. O. E, pseud. N.D. Robert Carter.
--The Truant Kitten. A. L. O. E, pseud, 1 of 14 Vols. (Illus.). (Tales for the Young Ser.). N.D. Set. Thomas Nelson & sons.
--Truant Kitten. A. L. O. E, pseud, 1 of 8 vols. (Illus.). (A. L. O. E. Library). N.D. Thos Nelson & Sons.
--The Truant's Return. A. L. O. E, pseud, 1 of 8 Vols. (Illus.). (The Victory Ser.). N.D. Set. Thomas Nelson and Sons.
--True Heroism. A. L. O. E. , pseud. (Fourth Ser.). (Carters' Fireside Library). N.D. Robert Carter & Bros.
--True Heroism. A. L. O. E. , pseud. (The Little Gipsey Ser.). N.D. The American News.
--Trusted and Trusty. A. L. O. E, pseud, 1 of 4 bks. (Illus.). (The Little Sower and Other Stories). N.D. Thos Nelson & Sons.
--Try Again. A. L. O. E. , pseud. (First Ser.). (Carters' Fireside Library). N.D. Robert Carter & Bros.
--Two Paths. A. L. O. E. , pseud. (Fourth Ser.). (Carters' Fireside Library). N.D. Robert Carter & Bros.
--The Two Sons. A. L. O. E, pseud, 1 of 6 bks. (Illus.). (Stories Illustrating the Proverbs: No. 4). N.D. Set. Thos Nelson & Sons.
--The Victory. A. L. O. E, pseud, 1 of 8 Vols. (Illus.). (The Victory Ser.). N.D. Set. Thomas Nelson and Sons.
--The Victory. A. L. O. E, pseud, 1 of 14 Vols. (Illus.). (Tales for the Young Ser.). N.D. Set. Thomas Nelson & Sons.
--The Wages of Sin. A. L. O. E, pseud, 1 of 12 Vols. (Illus.). (The Diamond Ser.). N.D. Thomas Nelson and Sons.
--Walter Binning. A. L. O. E. , pseud. (Fourth Ser.). (Carters' Fireside Library). N.D. Robert Carter & Bros.
--The Wanderer of Africa. A. L. O. E. , pseud. (The Claremont Library). N.D. American News Co.
--War and Peace. A. L. O. E, pseud, 1 of 4 Vols. (Illus.). (The Chaplet Ser.). N.D. Set. Thomas Nelson & Sons.
--The Whirlpool. A. L. O. E, pseud, 1 of 12 Vols. (Friend and Foe Ser.). N.D. Set. Thomas Whittaker.
--A White Lie. A. L. O. E, pseud, 1 of 12 bks. (Illus.). (Stories by A. L. O. E. Packet "A": No. 4). N.D. Set. Thos Nelson & Sons.
--The White Robe. A. L. O. E, pseud, 1 of 4 bks. (Illus.). (The Little Sower and Other Stories). N.D. Thos Nelson & Sons.
--The Wicket Gate. A. L. O. E, pseud, 1 of 12 bks. (Illus.). (Stories Illustrating the Pilgrim's Progress Ser.: No. 2). N.D. Set. Thos Nelson & Sons.
--Wild Rose Hollow. A. L. O. E, pseud, 1 of 12 vols. (Friend and Foe Ser.). N.D. Set. Thomas Whittaker.
--Willie Graham. A. L. O. E, pseud, 1 of 12 Vols. (Conqueror Ser.). N.D. Set. Thomas Whittaker.
--Wings and Stings. A. L. O. E. , pseud. (Fourth Ser.). (Carters' Fireside Library). N.D. Robert Carter & Bros.
--Wings and Stings. A L O E, pseud. (The Bee Hive Ser.). N.D. Thomas Nelson & Sons.
--Wings and Stings: A Tale for the Young. A. L. O. E, pseud. 5 p. l., 9-108 p. front., 4 pl. 17 1/2 cm. 1876. T. Nelson and Sons.
--The Wonderous Sickle. A. L. O. E, pseud. N.D. Robert Carter & Brothers.
--A Wreath of Indian Stories. A. L. O. E. , pseud. 1877. Robert Carter & Bros.
--A Wreath of Smoke. A. L. O. E, pseud. (Illus.). N.D. E & J B Young.
--The Wreath of Smoke. A. L. O. E. , pseud. (The Claremont Ser.). N.D. Fleming H. Revell Co.
--A Wreath of Smoke. A. L. O. E. , pseud. (The Claremont Library). N.D. The American News Co.
--Young Pilgrim. A. L. O. E. , pseud. (First Ser.). (Carters' Fireside Library). N.D. Robert Carter & Bros.
--The Young Pilgrim. A. L. O. E. , pseud. N.D. Thomas Nelson & Sons.
--Young Pilgrim: A Story Illustrative of Pilgrim's Progress. A. L. O. E, pseud. N.D. Methodist Book Concern.
--Zaida's Note Book. A. L. O. E, pseud. N.D. G W Carleton & Co.

Tucker, David
--Something Special. Dauber, Elizabeth, illus. LC 75-131023. (Illus.). 61 p. 22cm. (Easy reader). 1970. Grosset & Dunlap.

Tucker, E. S. see Tucker, Elizabeth S.

Tucker, Edith S. & Talcott, Anna
--A Trip to the Moon. N.D. Estes & Lauriat.

Tucker, Elizabeth S.
--Favorite Pets. Tucker, Elizabeth S., illus. LC 16-3082. (Illus.). 121p. 28cm. 1893. F. A. Stokes.
--Little Columbia's Gowns and Pleasures. (Illus.). N.D. Frederick A Stokes Co.
--Little Grown-Ups. Humphrey, Maud (1868-), illus. LC 44-11971. (With Numerous Full-Page Colour-Plates After Paintings in Water-Colours). 37 l. incl. col. front., illus., col. plates. 23 1/2 x 23 cm. c.1897. Frederick A. Stokes Company.
--The Magic Key. Tucker, Elizabeth S., illus. LC 1-25392. 3 p. l., 9-258 p., 1 l. front., illus, plates. 19 1/2 cm. 1901. Little, Brown & Company.
--Tales and Verses of Long Ago. Moran, F. Perry, illus. LC 12-2706. (Illus.). 1894. Frederick A. Stokes Company.
--A Truly Story of My Dolls. LC 17-1356. 12p. 13 x 12cm. 1899. L. Prang & Co.

Tucker, Ernest Edward (1916-1969)
--Dan Morgan-Rifleman. Merryweather, Jack, illus. 252p. (The American Adventure Ser.). (gr. 4). 1955. Franklin Watts, Inc.
--Dan Morgan, Rifleman. Merryweather, Jack, illus. LC 55-2072. 220 p. illus. 19 cm. (American adventure series). N.D. Wheeler Pub. Co.

Tucker, Gail
--Oscar the Oil Rig Meets Tuckee the Tug. Tucker, Ray, illus. 1982. (ISBN 0-533-05364-1). Vantage.

Tucker, George Fox (1852-1929)
--The Boy Whaleman. Avison, George F. (1885-), illus. LC 24-21074. 4 p. l., 283 p. col. front., col. plates. 22 1/2 cm. (Beacon Hill bookshelf). 1924. Little, Brown, and Company.

Tucker, Kate Marion (1890-)
--The Haunted Ship. Taylor, Ethel Bonney, illus. LC 29-7079. 5 p. l., 180 p. incl. illus., plates. front. 19 1/2 cm. 1929. The Macmillan Company.

Tucker, Kathleen, ed. see Chevalier, Christa.
Tucker, Kathleen, ed. see Christian, Mary Blount.
Tucker, Kathleen, ed. see Delton, Judy.
Tucker, Kathleen, ed. see Freedman, Sally.
Tucker, Kathleen, ed. see Goldman, Susan.
Tucker, Kathleen, ed. see Haas, Dorothy.
Tucker, Kathleen, ed. see Smith, Carole.
Tucker, Kathleen, ed. see Sussman, Susan.
Tucker, Kathleen, ed. see Van Woerkom, Dorothy O'Brien.

Tucker, Kiyoko Iizuka (1940-)
--The Lion's Nose. 1st english-language ed. Kakimoto, Kozo (1915-), illus. LC 67-1235. (Illus.). 25 p. 25cm. 1966, c.1963. Hawthorn Books.
--Mr. Kuma's Rocket. 1st english-language ed. Kitada, Takishi, illus. LC 67-1328. 25 p. col. illus. 25 cm. 1966, c.1964. Hawthorn Books.

Tucker, Kiyoto, tr. see Fujita, Tamao.

Tucker, Nicholas (1936-), ed.
--Mother Goose Abroad. Stubley, Trevor Hugh (1932-), illus. LC 73-2831. p. 1973. (ISBN 0-690-00092-8). (ISBN 0-690-00093-6). Crowell.
--Mother Goose Abroad: Nursery Rhymes. Stubley, Trevor Hugh (1932-), illus. LC 73-2831. (Illus.). (ps-3). 1975. (ISBN 0-690-00093-6, TYC-J). Har-Row.
--Mother Goose Lost: Nursery Rhymes. Stubley, Trevor Hugh (1932-), illus. LC 70-132304. (Illus.). 32 p. 29cm. 1st U.S. edition. 1971. (ISBN 0-690-56355-8). (ISBN 0-690-56354-X). Crowell.

Tuckett, Guin, jt. auth. see Tuckett, Neil.

Tuckett, Neil & Tuckett, Guin
--Just for Fun. N.D. (ISBN 0-8272-1702-1). Bethany Press.

Tudor, Bethany
--Gooseberry Lane. LC 63-12405. (Illus.). 32 p. 1963. Lippincott.
--Samantha's Surprise. LC 64-19060. (Illus.). 31 p. 1964. Lippincott.
--Samuel's Tree House. LC 78-12087. (Illus.). 25 p. 16cm. 1979. (ISBN 0-529-05435-3). (ISBN 0-529-05522-8). Collins.
--Skiddycock Pond. (Illus.). 31 p. 1965. Lippincott.

Tudor, Tasha (1915-)
--A is for Annabelle. LC 60-15911. (Starling Burgess legally changed her name to Tasha Tudor.). illus. 18 x 24 cm. 56p. 1954. H. Z. Walck.
--A is for Annabelle. LC 54-13078. (Illus.). unpaged. 1954. Oxford University Press.
--Alexander the Gander. enl. ed. LC 61-15646. unpaged. illus. 18 cm. 1961, c.1939. H. Z. Walck.
--Alexander the Gander. LC 39-30176. 47 p. col. illus. 12 cm. c.1939. Oxford University Press.
--Amanda and the Bear. LC 51-13381. unpaged. illus. 18 cm. 1951. Oxford University Press.
--Around the Year. LC 60-7419. unpaged. illus. 18 x 24 cm. c.1957. H. Z. Walck.
--Around the Year. LC 57-11451. (Starling Burgess legally changed her name to Tasha Tudor.). (Illus.). unpaged. (Oxford Books for Boys and Girls). 1957. Oxford University Press.
--Becky's Birthday. Tudor, Tasha (1915-), illus. (Illus.). 47 p. 23cm. 1960. Viking Press.
--Becky's Christmas. Tudor, Tasha (1915-), illus. LC 61-11667. (Illus.). 45 p. 26cm. 1961. Viking Press.
--Becky's Christmas. Tudor, Tasha (1915-), illus. 1961. Walck.
--Book of Fairy Tales. Tudor, Tasha (1915-), illus. LC 61-13221. 92 p. illus. 32 cm. 1961. Platt & Munk.
--Corgiville Fair. LC 72-154042. (Illus.). 48 p. 1971. (ISBN 0-690-21791-9). Crowell.
--The County Fair. enl. ed. (Illus.). 52 p. 18cm. 1964, c.1940. H. Z. Walck.
--The County Fair. LC 40-32444. 47 p. col. illus. 12 x 10 1/2 cm. c.1940. Oxford University Press.
--The Doll's Christmas. LC 59-12744. unpaged. illus. 18 cm. 1950. H. Z. Walck.
--The Doll's Christmas. Tudor, Tasha (1915-), illus. 1950. McKay.
--The Doll's Christmas. Tudor, Tasha (1915-), illus. 1950. Oxford University Press.
--Dorcas Porcus. Tudor, Tasha (1915-), illus. 1942. Oxford University Press.
--Dorcas Porkus. enl. ed. (Illus.). 35 p. 17cm. 1963, c.1942. H. Z. Walck.
--Dorcas Porkus. LC 42-17473. 35 p. col. front., col. illus. 12 x 10 cm. 1942. Oxford University Press.
--Edgar Allan Crow. LC 53-12994. unpaged. illus. 18cm. 1953. Oxford University Press.
--First Delights. Tudor, Tasha (1915-), illus. 1966. (ISBN 0-8382-1013-9, Cadmus Books). E. M. Hale and Company.
--First Delights. Tudor, Tasha (1915-), illus. 1966. Platt and Munk.
--First Graces. 1955. (ISBN 0-8098-1953-8). David MCKay Company.
--Linsey Woolsey. LC 46-11879. 43 p. col. illus. 12 x 10 cm. 1946. Oxford University Press.
--One is One. 1956. (ISBN 0-8098-1047-6). David McKay Company.
--One Is One. Tudor, Tasha (1915-), illus. LC 56-11381. unpaged (chiefly illus.) 18 x 24 cm. (Oxford Books for Boys and Girls). 1956. Oxford University Press. **Award: (RCM).**
--Pumpkin Moonshine. LC 58-13228. (Illus.). 18cm. 1958, c.1938. H. Z. Walck.
--Pumpkin Moonshine. enl. ed. unpaged. illus. 18 cm. 1962, c.1938. H. Z. Walck.
--Pumpkin Moonshine. LC 38-27678. 41 p. col. illus. 12 cm. c.1938. Oxford University Press.
--Snow Before Christmas. LC 41-51900. 37 p. col. illus. 17 x 15 1/2 cm. c.1941. Oxford University Press.
--A Tale for Easter. LC 41-5152. (Starling Burgess legally changed her name to Tasha Tudor.). 33 p. col. illus. 17 x 16 cm. c.1941. Oxford University Press.
--A Tale for Easter. (Illus.). 1 v. (unpaged). 17cm. 1973, c.1969. (ISBN 0-8098-1807-8). Walck.
--Tasha Tudor's Bedtime Book. Klimo, Kate, ed. LC 77-85353. (Illus.). 39 p. 32cm. c.1977. (ISBN 0-448-47217-1). (ISBN 0-8228-7217-X). Platt & Munk.
--A Tasha Tudor's Sampler: A Tale for Easter Pumpkin Moonshine and the Dolls' Christmas. Tudor, Tasha (1915-), illus. LC 77-18. (Tasha Tudor is the legal name change for Starling Burgess). (gr. k-3). 1977. (ISBN 0-679-20412-1). McKay.
--Thistly B. 1949. (ISBN 0-679-20231-5). David McKay Company.
--Thistly B. LC 9-10068. 27 p. col. illus. 18 cm. 1949. Oxford Univ. Press.
--The White Goose. LC 43-13837. 27 p. col. illus. 17 x 15 1/2 cm. 1943. Oxford University Press.

Tudor, Tasha (1915-), ed.
--Favorite Stories. LC 65-21668. 131p. illus. (pt. col.) 26cm. c.1965. Lippincott.
--Take Joy!. Tudor, Tasha (1915-), illus. 160p. 1966. (ISBN 0-529-04961-9). (ISBN 0-529-00208-6). Collins & World.
--Tasha Tudor Book of Fairy Tales. Tudor, Tasha (1915-), illus. LC 61-13221. (Illus.). (ps-2). 1961. (ISBN 0-448-44200-0). Platt.
--The Tasha Tudor Christmas Book. Tudor, Tasha (1915-), illus. 1966. Collins.
--Tasha Tudor's Favorite Stories. LC 65-21668. (Illus.). (gr. 4-6). 1965. (ISBN 0-397-30837-X, HarpJ). (ISBN 0-397-30838-8). Har-Row.
--Wings from the Wind: An Anthology of Poems. 1st ed. Tudor, Tasha (1915-), illus. (Illus.). 119 p. 25cm. 1964. Lippincott.
--Wings from the Wind: An Anthology of Poetry. Tudor, Tasha (1915-), illus. LC 64-19059. (gr. k-6). 1964. (ISBN 0-397-30789-6, LBL-J). Har-Row.

Tudor, Tasha (1915-), illus.
--First Poems of Childhood. LC 67-4523. (Illus.). 45 p. 21cm. 1967. Platt & Munk.

Tudyman, Al (1914-) & Groelle, Marvin C.
--About King. LC 73-158306. (Illus.). 64 p. 24cm. (Functional Basic Reading Series). 1972. (ISBN 0-87076-205-2). Stanwix House.

Tuer, Andrew White (1838-1900)
--Old Fashioned Children's Books. (Illus.). N.D. Charles Scribner's Sons.
--Pages and Pictures from Forgotten Children's Books. N.D. Gale Reprint.
--Stories from Old-Fashioned Children's Books. N.D. Gale Reprint.

Tuer, Andrew White (1838-1900), ed.
--Stories from Old-Fashioned Children's Books. LC 75-75059. (Illus.). xv, 439 p. 20cm. 1969. A. M. Kelley.
--Stories from Old-Fashioned Children's Books. LC 4-31672. xv, 1, 439 p. incl. front., illus. (1 col.) 20 cm. 1899. C. Scribner's Sons.
--Stories from Old-Fashioned Children's Books: Brought Together and Introduced to the Reader. LC 68-31438. (Illus.). xv, 439 p. 21cm. 1968. Singing Tree Press.

Tufts, Anne
--As the Wheel Turns. 1st ed. Doremus, Robert (1913-), illus. LC 52-9045. 246 p. illus. 21 cm. 1952. Holt.
--Rails Along the Chesapeake. 1st ed. Anderson, Rus, illus. LC 57-11691. 223 p. illus. 21 cm. 1957. Holt.
--The Super's Daughter. LC 53-8973. (Illus.). 216 p. 21cm. 1953. Holt.

Tufts, Georgia
--Catrina and the Cats. LC 58-11826. unpaged. illus. 26 cm. 1959. Lothrop, Lee & Shepard.
--The Rabbit Garden. LC 60-53423. unpaged. illus. 26 cm. 1961. Lothrop, Lee & Shepard.

Tufui, Jean
--Dolfini: Tales of the South Pacific. Zanoni, Murray, illus. LC 72-164330. 25p. col. illus. 32cm. 1971. (ISBN 0-600-07011-5). Hamlyn.

Tuggle, Diane
--Spencer's Toothbrush. Nicholoson, Karl, illus. Williams, Carlton H., frwd. by. LC 80-54611. (Illus.). 72p. (Orig.). (gr. k-6). N.D. (ISBN 0-932238-08-4). Avant Bks.

Tuggle, Ruth Ashley (1881-)
--Indian Stories for Children. Tuggle, Juliette, illus. LC 7-36091. 24cm. 106p. 1907. La Grange.

Tularski, Lura
--Star of Stony Ridge. McMillan, Kathleen, illus. LC 47-12042. (Illus.). 42p. (gr. 3-7). 1947. (ISBN 0-8323-0162-0). Binfords.

Tull, Clyde, ed. see Stuart, Elizabeth Billings.

Tull, Jewell Bothwell, Mrs.
--The Winning of the Bronze Cross: The Adventures of a Boy Scout. LC 15-7478. 5 p. l., 13-144 p. plates. 20 cm. c.1915. The Educator Supply Co.

Tullis, Dorothy
--Phillip, the Grasshopper. Matulaitis, Anna, illus. LC 50-3503. (Illus.). 24p. 1975. (ISBN 0-686-17329-5). Tullis Prods.

Tully, Jim
--Biddy Brogan's Boy. LC 42-9125. 5 p. l. 300 p. 21 cm. 1942. C. Scribner's Sons.

Tuner, Philip
--Colonel Sheperton's Clock. (Illus.). (gr. 4-9). 1966. (ISBN 0-529-00221-3). Collins-World.

Tung, Shih-Chin (1900-)
--Ah Bow and the Water Buffalo. Hall, H. Tom, illus. LC 60-14697. 124 p. illus. 21 cm. 1961. Dial Press.
--One Small Dog. Lewin, Ted (1935-), illus. LC 74-25525. (Illus.). 160 p. 22cm. 1975. (ISBN 0-396-07122-8). Dodd, Mead.

Tunis, Edwin Burdett (1897-1973)
--Shaw's Fortune: The Picture Story of a Colonial Plantation. Tunis, Edwin Burdett (1897-1973), illus. (Illus.). (gr. k-6). 1966. (ISBN 0-529-04072-7). (ISBN 0-529-04073-5). Collins-World. **Awards: (NYT).**
--Shaw's Fortune: The Picture Story of a Colonial Plantation. Tunis, Edwin Burdett (1897-1973), illus. LC 75-29640. (Illus.). index. 64p. (gr. 2-6). 1976. (ISBN 0-690-01066-4, TYC-J). Har-Row.

Tunis, John Roberts (1889-1975)
--All-American. Walleen, Hans Alex, illus. LC 42-36301. 3 p. l., 3-245 p. incl. plates, front. 21 cm. 1942. Harcourt, Brace and Company.
--Buddy and the Old Pro. Barnum, Jay Hyde (1888-1962), illus. LC 55-8371. (Illus.). 189 p. 21cm. (Morrow junior books). 1955. Morrow.
--Champion's Choice. N.D. World Publishing Co.
--Champion's Choice. Barnum, Jay Hyde (1888-1962), illus. LC 40-14504. 6 p. l. 3-300 p. incl. front., illus., plates (1 double) 22 cm. c.1940. Harcourt, Brace and Company.
--A City for Lincoln. LC 45-35202. 3 p. l., 3-292 p. 21 cm. 1945. Harcourt, Brace and Company.
--The Duke Decides. MacDonald, James, illus. LC 39-27882. 3 p. l, 3-267 p. incl. front., plates. 22 cm. c.1939. Harcourt, Brace and Company.
--Go, Team, Go!. LC 54-5520. 215 p. 22cm. (Morrow junior books). 1954. Morrow.
--Grand National. LC 73-4930. 159 p. 22cm. 1973. (ISBN 0-688-20090-7). (ISBN 0-688-20090-7). Morrow.
--Highpockets. LC 48-5418. 189 p. 21 cm. (Morrow junior books). 1948. W. Morrow.
--His Enemy, His Friend. LC 67-25322. 196 p. 21cm. 1967. Morrow.
--Iron Duke. Bull, Johan, illus. LC 38-27108. 3 p. l., 3-276 p. incl. illus., plates 22 cm. c.1938. Harcourt, Brace and Company.
--Keystone Kids. LC 43-512223. 3 p. l., 3-200 p. 21 cm. 1943. Harcourt, Brace and Company.
--The Kid Comes Back. LC 46-252502. 3 p. l., 245 p. 20 1/2 cm. 1946. W. Morrow & Company.
--The Kid from Tomkinsville. Barnum, Jay Hyde (1888-1962), illus. LC 40-27964. x, 355 p. incl. front., illus., plates (part double) 22 cm. c.1940. Harcourt, Brace and Company.
--The Other Side of the Fence. LC 53-8343. 224 p. 22cm. (Morrow junior books). 1953. Morrow.
--Rookie of the Year. LC 44-3265. 3 p. l., 3-169 p. 20 1/2 cm. 1944. Harcourt, Brace and Company.
--Schoolboy Johnson. (gr. 7-11). 1958. (ISBN 0-688-21730-3). Morrow.
--Silence over Dunkerque. LC 62-15761. 215 p. illus. 21 cm. 1962. (ISBN 0-688-31760-X). Morrow.
--Son of the Valley. 1963. E . M. Hale and Co.
--Son of the Valley. 192 p. col. front. 21 cm. 1949. W. Morrow.
--Two by Tunis: Highpockets and Go, Team, Go!. LC 75-175816. 407 p. 21cm. 1972. (ISBN 0-688-21985-3). (ISBN 0-688-31985-8). Morrow.
--World Series. Barnum, Jay Hyde (1888-1962), illus. LC 41-13402. x 318 p. incl. front., plates (2 double) 21 cm. c.1941. Harcourt, Brace and Company.
--Yea! Wildcats!. LC 44-840844. 4 p. l., 3-257 p. 21 cm. 1944. Harcourt, Brace and Company.
--Young Razzle. LC 49-9796. 21cm. 192p. (gr. 7 up). 1949. (ISBN 0-688-21731-1). Morrow.

Tupper, Edith Sessions, Mrs.
--By Whose Hand?. LC 3390. 187 p. 18 1/2 cm. (On cover: Magnet detective library, no. 134). 1900. Street & Smith.

Turco, Lewis see Court, Wesli, pseud.

Turco, Lewis
--Murgatroyd and Mabel. Court, Wesli, pseud. Michaels, Robert (1926-), illus. LC 79-101735. (Illus.). 40 p. c.1978. (ISBN 0-930000-06-4). Mathom Pub. Co.

Turin, Adela & Bosnia, Nella
--Arthur & Clementine. (Illus.). 32p. (Feminist Fables for Children Ser.). Orig. Title: Arturo E Clementina. 1980. (ISBN 0-904613-19-4). Writers & Readers.
--The Five Wives of Silverbeard. LC 77-82866. p. cm. (Nonsexist Children's Literature). c.1977. (ISBN 0-8467-0390-4). Two Continents Pub. Group.

Turin, Adela & Saccaro, Margherita
--The Breadtime Story. LC 77-82867. p. cm. (Nonsexist Childrens Literature). c.1977. (ISBN 0-8467-0391-2). Two Continents Pub. Group.

Turin, Adela & Selig, Sylvie (1942-)
--Of Cannons and Caterpillars. LC 77-82868. p. cm. (Nonsexist Children's Literature). c.1977. (ISBN 0-8467-0392-0). Two Continents Pub. Group.
--Of Cannons & Caterpillars. (Illus.). 32p. (Feminist Fables for Children Ser.). Orig. Title: Melaracconti. 1980. (ISBN 0-904613-62-3). Writers & Readers.

Turk, Hanne
--Good Night Max. Turk, Hanne, illus. LC 83-61134. (Illus.). 24p. (Max the Mouse Bks). 1983. (ISBN 0-907234-39-0, Picture Bk Studio USA). Neugebauer Pr.
--Happy Birthday Max!. Turk, Hanne, illus. (Illus.). 24p. (Orig.). (Max the Mouse Bks.). 1984. (ISBN 0-907234-42-9, Pub. by Picture Bk Studio USA). Neugebauer Pr.
--Hieronymus. Turk, Hanne, illus. Gadsby, Oliver, tr. LC 82-183704. (Illus.). 26 p. 29cm. c.1981. (ISBN 0-907234-06-2). Neugebauer Press.
--A Lesson for Max. Turk, Hanne, illus. LC 82-61833. (Illus.). 24p. (Max the Mouse Bk.). 1983. (ISBN 0-907234-23-2, Pub. by Picture Bk Studio USA). Neugebauer Pr.
--Max Packs. Turk, Hanne, illus. (Illus.). 24p. (Orig.). (Max the Mouse Bks.). 1984. (ISBN 0-907234-40-2, Pub. by Picture Bk studio USA). Neugebauer Pr.
--Max the Artlover. LC 82-61832. (Illus.). 24p. (Max the Mouse Bk.: No. 6). 1983. (ISBN 0-907234-25-9, Pub. by Picture Bk Studio USA). (ISBN 0-907234-25-9). Neugebauer Pr.
--Max Versus the Cube. Turk, Hanne, illus. (Illus.). 24p. (A Max the Mouse Bk.). 1982. (ISBN 0-907234-19-4, Pub. by Picture Bk Studio USA). Neugebauer Pr.
--Merry Christmas Max. Turk, Hanne, illus. LC 83-61135. (Illus.). 24p. (Max the Mouse Bks). 1983. (ISBN 0-907234-37-2, Pub. by Picture Bk Studio USA). Neugebauer Pr.
--Rainy Day Max. Turk, Hanne, illus. LC 82-61834. (Illus.). 24p. (Max the Mouse Bk.). 1982. (ISBN 0-907234-24-0, Pub. by Picture Bk Studio USA). Neugebauer Pr.
--Raking Leaves with Max. Turk, Hanne, illus. LC 83-61133. (Illus.). 28p. (Max the Mouse Bks). 1983. (ISBN 0-907234-38-0, Pub. by Picture Bk Studio USA). Neugebauer Pr.
--Snapshot Max. Turk, Hanne, illus. (Illus.). 24p. (Orig.). (Max the Mouse Bks.). 1984. (ISBN 0-907234-41-0, Pub. by Picture Bk Studio USA). Neugebauer Pr.
--A Surprise for Max. Turk, Hanne, illus. (Illus.). 28p. (Orig.). (A Max the Mouse Bk.). N.D. (ISBN 0-907234-18-6, Pub. by Picture Bk Studio USA). Neugebauer Pr.

Turkle, Brinton Cassaday, jt. auth. see Kitt, Tamara.

Turkle, Brinton Cassaday (1915-)
--The Adventure of Obadiah. (Illus.). 1v. (unpaged). 19cm. (Viking Seafarer Bk.). 1974, c.1972. (ISBN 0-670-05091-1). Viking.
--The Adventures of Obadiah. LC 75-190713. (Illus.). 39 p. 1972. (ISBN 0-670-10614-3). Viking Press.
--Deep in the Forest. Turkle, Brinton Cassaday (1915-), illus. LC 76-21691. (Illus.). 32 p. (ps-1). c.1976. (ISBN 0-525-28617-9). Dutton. **Award: (ALA).**
--Do Not Open. Turkle, Brinton Cassaday (1915-), illus. LC 80-10289. p. cm. c.1980. (ISBN 0-525-28785-X). Dutton. **Award: (ALA).**
--The Fiddler of High Lonesome. rev. ed. Turkle, Brinton Cassaday (1915-), illus. LC 84-13674. p. cm. c.1984. (ISBN 0-525-44153-0). Dutton.
--The Fiddler of High Lonesome. Turkle, Brinton Cassaday (1915-), illus. LC 68-16071. (Illus.). 44 p. 24cm. 1968. Viking Press.
--It's Only Arnold. LC 73-5139. (Illus.). 48 p. 22cm. 1973. Viking Press.
--It's Only Arnold. (Illus.). 48p. 20cm. (Viking Seafarer Bks.). 1975, c.1973. (ISBN 0-670-05096-2). Viking Press.
--The Magic of Millicent Musgrave. Turkle, Brinton Cassaday (1915-), illus. LC 67-2944. (Illus.). 27cm. 40p. 1967. Viking Press.
--Mooncoin Castle: Or, Skulduggery Rewarded. LC 77-106920. (Illus.). 141 p. 25cm. 1970. (ISBN 0-670-48790-2). Viking Press.
--Obadiah the Bold. Turkle, Brinton Cassaday (1915-), illus. LC 77-4163. p. cm. 1977. (ISBN 0-14-050233-5). Puffin Books.
--Obadiah the Bold. Turkle, Brinton Cassaday (1915-), illus. LC 65-13350. (Illus.). (gr. k-3). 1965. (ISBN 0-670-52001-2). Viking Pr.
--Rachel and Obadiah. LC 77-15661. (Illus.). 31 p. c.1978. (ISBN 0-525-38020-5). Dutton.
--The Sky Dog. LC 79-85866. (Illus.). 31 p. 25cm. 1969. Viking Press.
--Thy Friend, Obadiah. Turkle, Brinton Cassaday (1915-), illus. LC 69-18861. (Illus.). 37 p. 1969. Viking Press. **Awards: (ALA); (BGH); (RCM).**

Turley, Charles
--Godfrey Marten, Schoolboy. Browne, Gordon Frederick (1858-1932), illus. vi p., 1 l. 338 p. front. 7 pl. 20 1/2 cm. 1906. E. P. Dutton & Company.
--Maitland Major and Minor. Browne, Gordon Frederick (1858-1932), illus. LC 6-35303. vi p., 1 l. 319 p. 6 pl. (incl. front.) 20 1/2 cm. 1906. E. P. Dutton and Company, Plymouth Eng. Printed.
--The Playmate. Millar, Harold Robert (1869-1939), illus. 20cm. 306p. 1907. E. P. Dutton & Co.

Turley, Leonard
--That Barton Boy in Kentucky. LC 49-7184. (Illus.). 204p. 20cm. 1940. H. L. Lindquist Publications.

Turnage, Sheila
--Trout the Magnificent. Stevens, Janet, illus. LC 82-15865. (Illus.). 48p. (ps-3). 1984. (ISBN 0-15-290962-1, HJ). HarBraceJ.

Turnbow, Irene
--Through the Years with Henrietta. Fraser, Betty M., pseud. (1928-), illus. Fraser, Elizabeth Marr. LC 66-13716. 110 p. illus. 23 cm. 1966. (ISBN 0-695-48765-5). Follett Pub. Co.

Turnbull, Agnes Sligh, Mrs. (1888-1982)
--Elijah the Fishbite. Wohlberg, Meg (1905-), illus. LC 40-276717. 6 p. l.113, 1 p. incl. front., illus. 21 x 10 cm. 1940. The Macmillan Company.
--George. (Illus.). (gr. 3-5). 1965. (ISBN 0-8382-0281-0). Hale.
--George. Hyman, Trina Schart (1939-), illus. LC 65-11021. (Illus.). 94p. 22cm. 1965. Houghton Mifflin.
--The Golden Journey. 1955. Houghton Mifflin Company.
--Jed, the Shepherd's Dog. Fleur, Anne Elizabeth (1901-), illus. Sari, pseud. LC 57-7202. (Illus.). (gr. 4-6). 1957. (ISBN 0-395-07129-1). HM.
--The White Lark. Goldstein, Nathan (1927-), illus. LC 68-29335. (Illus.). 57 p. 24cm. 1968. Houghton Mifflin.

Turnbull, Ann Christine (1943-)
--The Frightened Forest. 1st ed. Gaze, Gillian, illus. LC 74-19358. (Illus.). 125 p. 22cm. 1975, c.1974. (ISBN 0-8164-3137-X). Seabury Press.
--Maroo of the Winter Caves. LC 84-4327. 144p. (gr. 4-7). 1984. (ISBN 0-89919-304-8, Clarion). HM.
--The Wolf King. LC 75-25513. 141 p. 22cm. 1976, c.1975. (ISBN 0-8164-3163-9). Seabury Press.

Turnbull, E. Lucia, retold by.
--Fairy Tales of India. N.D. E. M. Hale and Co.
--Fairy Tales of India. Cook, Hazel, illus. LC 60-6266. 170 p. illus. 22 cm. (A Criterion Book for Young People). 1960, c.1959. Criterion Books.
--Legends of the Saints. Rethi, Lili (1894-), illus. 128p. 1959. Lippincott.

Turnbull, E. Lucia, jt. ed. see Jacobs, Joseph.

Turnbull, John Reid (1883-)
--Girl of the Crimson Rose: A Story of the Northland. LC 41-4722. 2 p. l., 7-249 p. 19 1/2 cm. c.1940. Zondervan Publishing House.

Turnbull, Margaret
--The Coast Road Murder. LC 34-24485. 305 p. 19 1/2 cm. 1934. J. B. Lippincott Company.
--Looking After Sandy: A Simple Romance. LC 14-15367. 4 p. l., 3-345, 1 p. front., plates. 19 1/2 cm. 1914. Harper & Brothers.
--W.A.G.'s Tale. Turnbull, Margaret, illus. LC 13-4352. vii, 1 p., 1 l., 169, 1 p., 1 l. col. front., illus. 18 cm. 1913. Houghton Mifflin Company.

Turner, Ann Warren (1945-)
--Dakota Dugout. Himler, Ronald Norbert (1937-), illus. LC 85-3084. (Illus.). 32 p. 27cm. c.1985. (ISBN 0-02-789700-1). Macmillan.
--A Hunter Comes Home. LC 80-13199. p. cm. c.1980. (ISBN 0-517-53913-6). Crown Publishers. **Award: (ALA).**
--Tickle a Pickle. Weinhaus, Karen Ann, illus. LC 83-16434. p. cm. 1984. (ISBN 0-590-07906-9). Four Winds Press.
--The Way Home. 1st ed. LC 82-19880. 116 p. 24cm. c.1982. (ISBN 0-517-54426-1). Crown Publishers.

Turner, Audrey
--Betty Starling, Private Secretary. N.D. Lantern Press, Inc.
--Lacy Edwards, Veterinarian. LC 57-8271. 221 p. illus. 21 cm. 1957. Lantern Press.

Turner, Bill, pseud., see Turner, William Price.

Turner, Bill, pseud. (1927-)
--The Jolly Old Cobbler: A Fairyland Biography. Turner, William Price. Fisher, Marilyn, illus. LC 47-731. (Illus.). 41p. 22 x 19cm. 1946. Cupples & Leon.

Turner, Dona M. (1951-)
--My Cat Pearl. LC 79-7402. (Illus.). 32 p. 23cm. c.1980. (ISBN 0-690-03989-1). (ISBN 0-690-03990-5). Crowell.
--My Cat Pearl. Turner, Dona M. (1951-), illus. 1980. Harper.

Turner, Eliza Sproat, Mrs. (1826-1903)
--Out-of-door Rhymes. LC 3-29649. 20cm. 146p. 1903. J. B. Lippincott Co.

Turner, Elizabeth A.
--Easy Stories. LC 1-3173. iii, 152p. 1900. Ginn.
--Short Stories,. Third Reader Grade. LC [illegible] 1897. Ginn & Company.
--Stories for Young Children. LC 12-39575. 1 p. l., 87 p. 17 1/2 cm. 1884. Ginn, Heath, & Co.

Turner, Elizabeth, Mrs.
--The Daisy: Or, Cautionary Stories in Verse Adapted to the Ideas of Children from Four to Eight Years Old. LC 21-38832. pt. illus. 14 cm. 1808. Pub. by Jacob Johnson.

Turner, Ethel see Curlewis, Ethel Sybil Turner.

Turner, F. Bernadette
--Faith of Little Creatures. (gr. 1-3). N.D. (ISBN 0-8315-0138-3). Speller.

Turner, Frances Wright
--Star Dust. LC 30-30428. 2 p. l., 1, 50 p. 21 1/2 cm. c.1930. The Dingley Press, Inc.

Turner, Gerry
--Hide-Out for a Horse. 1st ed. Komoda, Kiyoaki (1937-), illus. LC 67-75. (Illus.). 117 p. 22cm. 1967. Doubleday.
--Magic Night for Lillibet. Turner, Gerry & Owen, Ralph, illus. LC 59-14302. 26cm. 48p. 1959. Bobbs-Merrill Co.
--The Silver Dollar Hoard of Aristotle Gaskin. 1st ed. Friedman, Marvin (1930-), illus. LC 68-10597. (Illus.). 232 p. 22cm. 1968. Doubleday.
--Stormy and the Tree-House Gang. Wind, Betty, illus. LC 66-3653. 138p. illus. 21cm. c.1966. Concordia.
--Stranger from the Depths. LC 67-17275. 205 p. 22cm. 1967. Doubleday.

Turner, Gil, jt. auth. see Garis, Howard Roger.

Turner, Gladys Tressia (1935-)
--Autobiography of Tammy: A Life full of Love and Fun. Finney, Frederick Marshall, illus. LC 78-1317. p. cm. c.1978. (ISBN 0-89421-007-6). (ISBN 0-89421-009-2). Challenge Press/Children's Books.

Turner, Glennette
--Surprise for Mrs. Burns. Siculan, Daniel (1922-), illus. LC 75-126435. (Illus.). 32 p. 24cm. 1971. (ISBN 0-8075-7669-7). A. Whitman.

Turner, Haines, jt. ed. see Starr, Francis.

Turner, Herman Davis (1893-)
--The Story of the Odyssey: Simply Told. LC 53-12162. 23cm. 120p. 1954. Vantage Press.

Turner, Hunter H., Jr.
--The Little Lighthouse. 1983. (ISBN 0-533-05425-7). Vantage.

Turner, Ian
--Cinderella Dressed in Yella. LC 72-446092. 153 p. 26cm. 1969. Heinemann Educational Australia.
--Cinderella Dressed in Yella. LC 74-172085. (Illus.). 153 p. 26cm. 1972, c.1969. (ISBN 0-8008-1585-8). Taplinger Pub. Co.

Turner, James, ed.
--Unlikely Ghosts. LC 71-82688. (gr. 9 up). N.D. (ISBN 0-8008-7940-6). Taplinger.

Turner, Jo Jasper, jt. ed. see Jacobs, Leland Blair.

Turner, John Hastings (1891-)
--Bear, Mouse and Waterbeetle. Lendon, Warwick, illus. LC 39-14947. xi p., 1 l., 217 p. incl. front., illus. 19 1/2 cm. c.1939. E. P. Dutton & Co., Inc.

Turner, Kathleen & Wills, Marguerite
--Mother Goose May Day. LC 30-5414. (Illus.). 23.5 cm. 32p. (Pageants with a Purpose). 1929. A S Barnes & Co.

Turner, Kermit (1936-)
--Rebel Powers: A Novel. LC 79-2429. p. cm. 24 cm. 197p. N.D. (ISBN 0-7232-6171-7). F. Warne.

Turner, Lillian
--Bettie, the Scribe. Greenland, Katherine Hayward, illus. LC 7-19037. 3 p. l., 329 p. front., 3 pl. 20 cm. c.1907. The Saalfield Publishing Co.
--The Lights of Sydney. (Illus.). (Cassell's Popular Library of Fiction). N.D. Cassell & Co.'s Pubs.

Turner, Lois M.
--Monkey's Tail, Rabbit's Cup. Bozzo, Frank, illus. LC 76-162051. (Illus.). 24 p. 21cm. (A Magic Circle Bk.). 1972. (ISBN 0-663-22975-8). Ginn.

Turner, Marianne, tr. see Lengstrand, Rolf & Rolen, Pierre L.

Turner, Marianne, tr. see Lindgren, Astrid Ericsson.

Turner, Marianne, tr. see Peterson, Hans.

Turner, Marianne, tr. see Svinsaas, Ingvald.
Turner, Mary Ellis
--Karen Long: Medical Technician. LC 43-17035. 5 p. l., 211 p. 21 cm. (Career books). 1943. Dodd, Mead & Company.
Turner, Matilda Hutchinson
--The Christmas Boy, and Other Children's Stories. Kilgore, Al, illus. LC 55-121386. 56p. illus. 21cm. 1955. Pageant Press.
Turner, Michael, tr. see Herge.
Turner, Michael, tr. see Remi, Georges.
Turner, Michael C.
--The King Bear. Frankenberg, Robert Clinton (1911-), illus. LC 68-23521. (Illus.). 176 p. 22cm. 1968. Golden Press.
Turner, Morrie (1923-)
--Nipper. LC 77-97161. (Illus.). 40 p. 24cm. 1970. Westminster Press.
--Nipper's Secret Power. LC 77-153128. (Illus.). 41 p. 24cm. 1971. (ISBN 0-664-32498-3). Westminster Press.
Turner, Mrs.
--The Daisy: Or, Cautionary Stories in Verses. (Illus.). (Forgotten Children's Books). N.D. Distributed by Charles Scribner's Sons.
Turner, Nancy Byrd (1880-)
--The Adventures of Ray Coon. Bridgman, Lewis Jesse (1857-1931), illus. N.D. Rand McNally.
--In the Days of Young Washington. Becher, Arthur E., illus. LC 31-29305. 4 p. l., 242 p. col. front., plates. 21 cm. 1931. Houghton Mifflin Company.
--Magpie Lane: Poems. Merwin, Decie (1894-1961), illus. LC 27-23027. x. 88 p. illus. 21 cm. c.1927. Harcourt, Brace & Company.
--Ray Coon to the Rescue. Ward, Keith, illus. LC 31-16582. 80 p. illus. 23 1/2 cm. c.1931. Rand, McNally & Company.
--Sycamore Silver. Dowling, Victor J. (1906-), illus. LC 42-502152. vii, 330 p. illus. 21 cm. 1942. Dodd, Mead & Company.
--When It Rained Cats and Dogs. Gergely, Tibor (1900-1978), illus. LC 46-11811. 32 p. col. illus. 26 cm. 1946. J. B. Lippincott Company.
--When It Rained Cats and Dogs. New ed. Gergely, Tibor (1900-1978), illus. 1956. J. B. Lippincott.
--Zodiac Town: The Rhymes of Amos and Ann. Bromhall, Winifred, illus. LC 21-19408. 5 p. l., 131, 1 p. incl. plates. front. 21 1/2 cm. c.1921. The Atlantic Monthly Press.
Turner, Nancy Byrd (1880-) & Nichols, Gertrude
--The Hopskips. Martin, Philip L., illus. LC 40-32788. 4 p. l., 88 p. illus. 20 cm. 1940. Frederick A. Stokee Company.
--The Hopskips. Martin, Philip L., illus. 1945. J. B. Lippincott.
Turner, Ned
--Ned Turner's Circus Joke Book. N.D. Dick & Fitzgerald.
--Ned Turner's Clown Joke Book. N.D. Dick & Fitzgerald.
Turner, Philip see Chance, Stephen, pseud.
Turner, Philip (1925-)
--Colonel Sheperton's Clock. Gough, Philip (1908-), illus. LC 66-8476. 190p. illus. 23cm. 1st U.S. edition. 1966, c.1964. (ISBN 0-529-00221-3). World.
--Devil's Nob. LC 72-8918. 190 p. 23cm. 1973. (ISBN 0-8407-6270-4). T. Nelson.
--The Grange at High Force. LC 79-261958. (Illus.). 23cm. 220p. 1965. Oxford University Press. **Award: (CMA).**
--The Grange at High Force. Mars, Witold Tadeusz J. (1912-), illus. LC 67-13824. (Illus.). 223 p. 23cm. 1st U.S. edition. 1967. World Pub. Co.
--Sea Peril. Mars, Witold Tadeusz J. (1912-), illus. LC 68-14689. (Illus.). 223 p. 22cm. 1st U.S. edition. 1968. World Pub. Co.
--Steam on the Line. Floyd, Gareth (1940-), illus. LC 68-26978. (Illus.). 192 p. 22cm. 1st U.S. edition. 1968. World Pub. Co.
--Steam on the Line. Ridley, Trevor, illus. LC 75-496085. (Illus.). 23cm. v, 162p. 1968. Oxford Univ. Press.
--War on the Darnel. Mars, Witold Tadeusz J. (1912-), illus. LC 75-82784. (Illus.). 196 p. 23cm. 1969. World Pub. Co.
--Wigwig and Homer. Humphreys, Graham (1945-), illus. LC 73-128521. (Illus.). 92 p. 21cm. 1970, c.1969. World Pub. Co.
Turner, Philip (1925-), ed.
--Brian Wildsmith's Illustrated Bible Stories. Wildsmith, Brian Lawrence (1930-), illus. (Illus.). color ils. 142p. 1st U.S. edition. (gr. k-3). 1969. (ISBN 0-531-01529-7). Watts. **Award: (ALA).**
Turner, Thomas Noel, adapted by see Moore, Clement Clarke.
Turner, Thyra
--Christmas House: The Story of A Visit from St. Nicholas. Gag, Flavia (1907-1979), illus. LC 43-15467. 3 p. l., 25 p. col. illus. 19 1/2 cm. 1943. C. Scribner's Sons.
Turner, Vernon Kitabu (1948-)
--The Secret of Freedom. LC 85-27519. p. cm. c.1985. (ISBN 0-89865-449-1). Donning Co.
Turner, William Price see Turner, Bill, pseud.
Turner, Wilson G.
--Maya Design Coloring Book. Turner, Wilson G., illus. (Illus.). 48p. (Orig.). (gr. 1-6). 1980. Dover.
Turney, Ida Virginia
--Paul Bunyan Marching On. Lyon, Norma Madge, illus. 80p. N.D. Binfords & Mort.
--Paul Bunyan, the Work Giant. (Illus.). (gr. 3 up). 1969. (ISBN 0-8323-0163-9). Binford.
Turngren, Annette (1902-1980)
--The Copper Kettle. Jackson, Polly, pseud. (1918-), illus. Jackson, Pauline. LC 61-9431. 175 p. illus. 21 cm. 1961. N.J., Prentice-Hall.
--The Copper Kettle. Morse, Dorothy Bayley (1906-1979), illus. LC 39-29718. vi p., 1 l., 13-280 p. front., illus. 20 1/2 cm. 1939. T. Nelson and Sons.
--Flaxen Braids: A Chapter from a Real Swedish Childhood. LC 37-15787. ix p., 1 l., 11-249 p. incl. front., illus., plates. 20 1/2 cm. 1937. T. Nelson and Sons.
--Flaxen Braids: A Chapter from a Real Swedish Childhood. Jackson, Polly, illus. LC 59-10004. 197 p. illus. 21 cm. 1959. Prentice-Hall.
--Mystery Clouds the Canyon. LC 61-10720. 183 p. 22cm. 1961. Funk & Wagnalls Co.
--Mystery Enters the Hospital. LC 65-19346. 156 p. 22cm. 1965. Funk & Wagnalls.
--Mystery Haunts the Fair. LC 59-8638. 181 p. 22 cm. N.D. Funk & Wagnalls.
--The Mystery of Hidden Village. LC 51-7285. 223 p. 21 cm. 1951. Nelson.
--Mystery of the Water Witch. Woolhiser, Harvey, illus. LC 64-17466. (Illus.). 153p. (American Girl Library). (gr. 5-9). 1964. (ISBN 0-394-80915-7). (ISBN 0-394-90915-1). Random.
--Mystery Plays a Golden Flute. LC 69-12158. 182 p. 22cm. 1969. Funk & Wagnalls.
--Mystery Rides the River. Bennett, Richard Michael (1899-), illus. LC 43-13708. v p., 1 l., 221 p. illus. 21 cm. 1943. T. Nelson and Sons.
--Mystery Walks the Campus. LC 56-10706. 201 p. 22 cm. 1956. Funk & Wagnalls.
--Steamboat's Coming. 1st ed. Thomas, Allan (1901-), illus. LC 55-7747. 183p. illus. 22cm. 1955. Longmans, Green.
Turngren, Ellen (0000-1964)
--Hearts are the Fields. Bock, Vera, illus. LC 61-14324. 21cm. 183p. 1961. David McKay Company Inc.
--Hearts Are the Fields. Bock, Vera, illus. LC 61-14324. 183 p. 21cm. 1961. Longmans, Green.
--Listen My Heart. Bock, Vera, illus. 194p. 1956. (ISBN 0-679-20095-9). David McKay Company.
--Listen, My Heart. Bock, Vera, illus. LC 56-5841. 194 p. 22cm. 1956. Longmans, Green.
--Shadows into Mist. Bock, Vera, illus. LC 58-8332. 207 p. 21 cm. 1958. Longmans, Green.
Turpin, Edna Henry Lee (1867-), ed. see Andersen, Hans Christian.
Turpin, Edna Henry Lee (1867-), abridged by see Kingsley, Charles.
Turpin, Edna Henry Lee (1867-)
--Echo Hill. Richards, George Mather (1880-), illus. LC 33-8153. ix, 1, 230 p. incl. front., illus. 20 cm. 1933. The Macmillan Company.
--Happy Acres. N.D. Macmillan.
--Honey-Sweet. Beard, Alice, illus. LC 11-244033. vii, 316 p. front., plates. 19 1/2 cm. 1911. The Macmillan Company.
--Littling of Gaywood. Eichenberg, Fritz (1901-), illus. LC 39-18502. 5 p. l., 3-265 p. illus. 19 1/2 cm. c.1939. Random House.
--Lost Covers. Perard, Victor Semon (1870-1957), illus. LC 37-15190. 281, 1 p. illus. 20 cm. c.1937. Random House.
--The Old Mine's Secret. Wright, George, contrib. by. LC 21-18798. 3 p. l., 288 p. col. front. 19 1/2 cm. 1921. The Macmillan Company.
--Peggy of Roundabout Lane. Beard, Alice, illus. LC 17-24817. 4 p. l., 310 p. front., plates. 19 1/2 cm. 1917. The Macmillan Company.
--Three Circus Days. Hauman, George (1890-1961) & Hauman, Doris, Mrs. (1897-), illus. LC 35-12187. 96 p. incl. col. front., col. illus. 19 cm. 1935. The Macmillan Company.
--Treasure Mountain. Amick, Robert, illus. LC 20-16341. 4 p. l., 3-314 p. front., plates. 19 1/2 cm. 1920. The Century Co.
--Whistling Jimps. Summers, Dudley Gloyme, illus. LC 22-17447. 5 p. l., 3-328 p. front., plates. 19 cm. 1922. The Century Co.
--Zickle's Luck. Peters, Marjorie, illus. LC 38-10338. 6 p. l., 91 p. illus. 19 1/2 cm. 1938. The Macmillan Company.
--Zickle's Puppy Dog. Lundborg, Arne, illus. LC 42-36242. 125 p. illus. 20 x 16 cm. 1942. The Greystone Press.
Turpin, Edna Henry Lee (1867-), ed.
--A Child's Book of Poetry. LC 1-27120. (Maynard's English classic series, no. 231-232). c.1901. Maynard, Merrill & Co.
--Classic Fables: Selected and Ed. for Primary Grades. LC 4-2321. 127 p. illus. 19 cm. (Graded supplementary reading series). 1904. Maynard, Merrill, & Co.
--Poems for Reading and Selections for Memorizing in the Seventh Year. LC 7-20846. (Required by the Syllabus for Elementary Schools of the New York State Education Department). iii, 5-78 p. 17 cm. (Maynard's English classic series. no. 245-246). c.1907. Maynard, Merrill, & Co.
Turpin, Lorna (1950-)
--The Sultan's Snakes. Turpin, Lorna (1950-), illus. LC 80-10956. (Illus.). 46 p. 1980, c.1979. (ISBN 0-688-80260-5). (ISBN 0-688-84260-7). Greenwillow Books.
Turska, Krystyna Zofia (1933-)
--The Magician of Cracow. Turska, Krystyna Zofia (1933-), illus. LC 75-8846. (Illus.). 32 p. 29cm. 1975. (ISBN 0-688-80010-6). Greenwillow Books. **Award: (ALA).**
--Pegasus. LC 73-86319. (Illus.). 32 p. 30cm. 1970. F. Watts.
--Tamara and the Sea Witch. LC 70-164896. (Illus.). 32 p. 29cm. 1972, c.1971. (ISBN 0-8193-0530-8). (ISBN 0-8193-0531-6). Parents' Magazine Press.
--The Woodcutter's Duck. Turska, Krystyna Zofia (1933-), illus. LC 72-85763. (Illus.). 32 p. 30cm. c.1972. Macmillan. **Award: (KGM).**
Turvey, Celia
--Folk Tales of the British Isles. LC 73-171443. (Illus.). vii, 101 p. 19cm. (Stories told and retold). 1964. Oxford University Press.
Tusa, Tricia
--Libby's New Glasses. Tusa, Tricia, illus. LC 83-26688. (Illus.). 32p. (ps-3). 1984. (ISBN 0-8234-0523-0). (ISBN 0-8234-0523-0). Holiday.
--Miranda. LC 85-26769. p. cm. 1986, c.1985. (ISBN 0-689-71063-1). Aladdin Books.
--Miranda. LC 84-21764. (Illus.). 30 p. 21cm. c.1985. (ISBN 0-02-789520-3). Macmillan.
Tutela, Dawn
--Jenny Moves. Newberger, Eli, ed. Kramer, Gretchen, illus. (Illus.). (The Jenny Ser.). (gr. 4-9). 1981. Delair.
Tuthill, Louisa Caroline Huggins, Mrs. (1798-1879)
--Anything for Sport. (Mrs. Tuthill's Juvenile Library). N.D. Perkinpine & Higgins.
--Beautiful Bertha. (Tip-Top Story Books for Girls). 1873. Leavitt & Allen Bros.
--Boarding-School Girl. (Mrs. Tuthill's Juvenile Library). N.D. Perkinpine & Higgins.
--Braggadocio. (Tip-Top Story Books for Boys). 1873. Leavitt & Allen Bros.
--Edith: Or, the Backwoods Girl. (Tip-Top Story Books for Girls). 1873. Leavitt & Allen Bros.
--Get Money. (Tip-Top Story Books for Boys). 1873. Leavitt & Allen Bros.
--Noble Aim Series, 6 Vols. N.D. N. Tibbals & Sons.
--Onward, Right Onward. (Mrs. Tuthill's Juvenile Library). N.D. Perkinpine & Higgins.
--Queer Bonnets. (Tip-Top Story Books for Girls). 1873. Leavitt & Allen Bros.
--A Strike for Freedom. (Mrs. Tuthill's Juvenile Library). N.D. Perkinpine & Higgins.
--Tip-Top. (Tip-Top Story Books for Boys). 1873. Leavitt & Allen Bros.
Tutt, Arthur Monroe
--Nano's Garden. LC 41-8963. 2 p. l., 9-105 p. mounted front. 20 cm. c.1940. The Liberty Chronicle.
Tutt, Clara Little (1891-)
--Badger Tales. LC 41-8117. vi p., 1 l., 200 p. illus. (incl. maps) 20 1/2 cm. c.1940. Lyons and Carnahan.
Tutt, Kay Cunningham
--And Now We Call Him Santa Claus. LC 63-16780. 1963. Lothrop, Lee and Shepard.
Tuttle, Florence Piper
--Mother Goose's Poetry Patch. (The Poetry Readers Ser.). N.D. Stephen Daye Press.
--Poetry Patch House. (The Poetry Readers Ser.). N.D. Stephen Daye Press.
--Puppets and Puppet Plays. Overlie, George, illus. LC 61-14504. 80p. illus. 27cm. 1962. Creative Educational Soc.
Tuttle, George see Teller, Thomas, pseud.
Tuttle, George (1804-1872)
--The Pleasant Journey and Scenes in Town and Country. Teller, Thomas, pseud. Anderson, Alexander (1775-1870), illus. LC 22-22196. 64 p. incl. plates. 14 1/2 x 11 1/2 cm. (On cover: Teller's tales. New series, no. 5). 1845. S. Babcock Pref.
Tuttle, Howard Nelson (1935-)
--Fire Night: A Story of Pompeii, August 24, 79 A.D. 1978. (ISBN 0-533-02947-3). Vantage.
Tuttle, Lisa (1952-)
--Catwitch. 1st ed. Woodruff, Una, illus. LC 83-9060. p. cm. c.1983. (ISBN 0-385-18887-0). Doubleday.
Tuttle, Sharon
--My Little Animal Babies. Wood, JoAnne, illus. (Put & Play Ser.). 1981. (ISBN 0-307-05100-5, Golden Pr). Western Pub.
Tuttle, Veryl Broughton
--The Frightened Tree and Other Stories. Joyce, Robert, illus. LC 25-23245. 165 p. incl. plates. col. front. 21 cm. 1925. Frank-Maurice, Inc.
Tutuola, Amos
--The Brave African Huntress. LC 58-8977. (Illus.). 150p. 21cm. 1958. Grove Press.
Tvarochova, Jirina, tr. see Novy, Karel.
Twain, Mark, pseud., see Clemens, Samuel Langhorne.

Twain, Mark, pseud. (1835-1910), tr. see Hoffmann-Donner, Heinrich.

Twain, Mark, pseud. (1835-1910)
--The Adventures of Huckleberry Finn. Clemens, Samuel Langhorne. 187p. Repr. (gr. 4-6). 1983. (ISBN 0-89966-468-7). Buccaneer Bks.
--The Adventures of Huckleberry Finn. Clemens, Samuel Langhorne. (Doubleday Classics). N.D. Garden City Books.
--The Adventures of Huckleberry Finn. Clemens, Samuel Langhorne. holiday ed. (Illus.). Repr. of 1884 ed. N.D. (ISBN 0-06-014376-2, HarpT). (ISBN 0-06-014375-4). Har-Row.
--The Adventures of Huckleberry Finn. Clemens, Samuel Langhorne. 336p. 1980. (ISBN 0-7011-1256-5, Pub. by Chatto Bodley Jonathan). Merrimack Pub Cir.
--Adventures of Huckleberry Finn. Clemens, Samuel Langhorne. 1962. (ISBN 0-393-09506-1). (ISBN 0-393-05324-5). Norton & Co.
--The Adventures of Huckleberry Finn. Clemens, Samuel Langhorne. (Story Books Ser.). (gr. 2-8). 1978. (ISBN 0-14-030080-5, Puffin). Penguin.
--The Adventures of Huckleberry Finn. Clemens, Samuel Langhorne. (Puffin Classics Ser.). (gr. 3-7). 1983. (ISBN 0-14-035007-1, Puffin). Penguin.
--The Adventures of Huckleberry Finn. Clemens, Samuel Langhorne. (Illus.). (Hardy Boys' Favorite Classics). (gr. 6-9). 1978. (ISBN 0-448-14922-2, G&D). Putnam Pub Group.
--The Adventures of Huckleberry Finn. Clemens, Samuel Langhorne. (gr. 7-12). 1972. (ISBN 0-590-02426-4). Scholastic Inc.
--The Adventures of Huckleberry Finn. Clemens, Samuel Langhorne. (Illus.). 414p. (Orig.). (Bambi Classics Ser.). 1981. (ISBN 0-89531-066-X). Sharon Pubns.
--The Adventures of Huckleberry Finn. Clemens, Samuel Langhorne. (Ultratype Eds). (gr. 7 up). 1969. (ISBN 0-531-00402-3). Watts.
--The Adventures of Huckleberry Finn. Clemens, Samuel Langhorne. large type ed. (Keith Jennison Bks). (gr. 7 up). N.D. (ISBN 0-531-00203-9). Watts.
--The Adventures of Huckleberry Finn. Clemens, Samuel Langhorne. Falter, John Philip (1910-), illus. (gr. 7 up). 1962. (ISBN 0-02-789550-5). Macmillan.
--The Adventures of Huckleberry Finn. Clemens, Samuel Langhorne. Hawes, Baldwin, illus. (Illus.). (Rainbow Classics). (gr. 7-9). 1947. (ISBN 0-529-02790-9). World Pub.
--The Adventures of Huckleberry Finn. Clemens, Samuel Langhorne. McKay, Donald A. (1895-) & Polseno, Jo, illus. (Illus.). (gr. 4-6). N.D. (ISBN 0-448-05451-5, G&D). (ISBN 0-448-05800-6). (ISBN 0-448-06000-0). pap. 4.95; (ISBN 0-448-11002-4); 5.95. (ISBN 0-686-85988-X). Putnam Pub Group.
--The Adventures of Huckleberry Finn. Clemens, Samuel Langhorne. Matthews, Brander, intro. by. (Harper Modern Classics). N.D. Harper & Brothers.
--The Adventures of Huckleberry Finn. Clemens, Samuel Langhorne. Powers, Richard M. Gorman (1921-), illus. N.D. Doubleday.
--Adventures of Huckleberry Finn. Clemens, Samuel Langhorne. Sculley, Bradley & Beatty, R. C., eds. 1962. (ISBN 0-393-09506-1). (ISBN 0-393-05324-5). Norton & Co.
--The Adventures of Huckleberry Finn. Clemens, Samuel Langhorne. Trilling, Lionel (1905-1975), ed. 293p. 1948. Rinehart & Co.
--The Adventures of Tom Sawyer. Clemens, Samuel Langhorne. (Famous Bks. for Young Americans). N.D. A. L. Burt.
--The Adventures of Tom Sawyer. Clemens, Samuel Langhorne. (The Winston Clear-Type Popular Classics). N.D. John C. Winston.
--The Adventures of Tom Sawyer. Clemens, Samuel Langhorne. LC 80-54138. (Illus.). 246, 49 p. 18cm. (A Silver classic). c.1982. (ISBN 0-382-03437-6). Silver Burdett Co.
--The Adventures of Tom Sawyer. Clemens, Samuel Langhorne. (Enriched Classic Ser.). N.D. (ISBN 0-671-48151-7). Simon & Schuster (WSP).
--The Adventures of Tom Sawyer. Clemens, Samuel Langhorne. Herzberg, Max J., intro. by. (Harper's Modern Classics). N.D. Harper & Brothers.
--The Adventures of Tom Sawyer. Clemens, Samuel Langhorne. Hodges, Cyril Walter (1909-), illus. 1977. Grosset and Dunlop.

--Mistress Judith. (The Leisure Hour Ser.). N.D. Henry Holt.
Tytler, M. Fraser
--Tales of Many Lands. (Illus.). N.D. R. Worthington.
Tytler, Sarah, pseud., see Laddie, Henrietta.
Tytler, Sarah, pseud., see Leddie, Henriette.
Tyuk, Yi, tr.
--Korean Folk Tales: Ghosts and Fairies. 1971. (ISBN 0-8048-0935-6). Charles E. Tuttle.
U. P. A. Pictures, Inc.
--Mister Magoo Two. 96p. (Orig.). (gr. 3-7). 1981. (ISBN 0-590-31300-2, Schol Pap). Scholastic Inc.
Ubertis-Gray, Corinna Teresa see Teresah, pseud.
Ubertis-Gray, Corinna Teresa (1877-)
--A Doll, Two Children and Three Storks. Teresah, pseud. Reetz, Wilhelm, illus. Emmrich, Dorothy, tr. from Ital. LC 31-30504. 178 p. incl. col. front., illus. 21 cm. c.1931. E. P. Dutton & Co., Inc.
Uchida, Yoshiko (1921-)
--The Best Bad Thing. LC 83-2833. 120 p. 22cm. 1983. (ISBN 0-689-50290-7). Atheneum. **Award: (ALA).**
--The Birthday Visitor. Robinson, Charles (1931-), illus. LC 74-14076. (Illus.). 32 p. 27cm. 1975. (ISBN 0-684-14229-5). Scribner.
--The Forever Christmas Tree. Mizumura, Kazue, illus. LC 63-17610. 1 v. (unpaged) col. illus. 24 cm. 1963. Scribner.
--The Full Circle. Uchida, Yoshiko (1921-), illus. LC 57-6165. (Illus.). 135 p. 21cm. 1957. Friendship Press.
--The Happiest Ending. LC 85-6245. 111 p. 22cm. 1985. (ISBN 0-689-50326-1). Atheneum.
--Hisako's Mysteries. Bennett, Susan, illus. LC 69-17062. (Illus.). 112 p. 22cm. 1969. Scribner.
--Hisako's Mysteries. Bennett, Susan, illus. 1969. Trade Publication.
--In-Between Miya. Bennett, Susan, illus. LC 67-24051. (Illus.). 128 p. 22cm. 1967. Scribner.
--In-Between Miya. Bennett, Susan, illus. 1967. Trade Publication.
--A Jar of Dreams. LC 81-3480. p. cm. 1981. (ISBN 0-689-50210-9). Atheneum.
--Journey Home. 1st ed. Robinson, Charles (1931-), illus. LC 78-8792. (Illus.). 131 p. 22cm. (Margaret K. McElderry Book). 1978. (ISBN 0-689-50126-9). Atheneum.
--Journey to Topaz. (Illus.). (Encore Edition). (gr. 4-6). 1971. (ISBN 0-684-15856-6, ScribJ). Scribner.
--Journey to Topaz: A Story of the Japanese-American Evacuation. Carrick, Donald (1929-), illus. LC 75-162730. (Illus.). viii, 149 p. 22cm. 1971. (ISBN 0-684-12497-1). Scribner.
--Makoto, the Smallest Boy: A Story of Japan. Shirakawa, Akihito, illus. LC 71-94802. (Illus.). 39 p. 23cm. (Stories from Many Lands). 1970. Crowell.
--Mik and the Prowler. 1st ed. Hutchinson, William Miller (1916-), illus. LC 60-13704. 122 p. illus. 21 cm. 1960. Harcourt, Brace.
--New Friends for Susan. Sugimoto, Henry, illus. LC 51-12898. 185 p. illus. 20 cm. 1951. Scribner.
--The Promised Year. Hutchinson, William Miller (1916-), illus. LC 59-9270. 192 p. illus. 21 cm. 1959. Harcourt, Brace.
--Rokubei and the Thousand Rice Bowls. Mizumura, Kazue, illus. LC 62-17733. unpaged. illus. 24 cm. 1962. Scribner.
--The Rooster Who Understood Japanese. Robinson, Charles (1931-), illus. LC 76-13450. (Illus.). 32 p. 26cm. c.1976. (ISBN 0-684-14672-X). Scribner.
--Samurai of Gold Hill. Forberg, Ati, pseud. (1925-), illus. Forberg, Beate Gropius. LC 72-1232. (Illus.). 119 p. 22cm. 1972. (ISBN 0-684-12955-8). Scribner.
--Sumi & the Goat & the Tokyo Express. Mizumura, Kazue, illus. LC 72-85272. (Illus.). 48 p. 24cm. 1969. Scribner.
--Sumi and the Goat and the Tokyo Express. Mizumura, Kazue, illus. 1969. Trade Publication.
--Sumi Special Happening. Mizumura, Kazue, illus. 1966. Trade Publication.
--Sumi's Prize. Mizumura, Kazue, illus. LC 64-19650. (Illus.). 24cm. 48p. (gr. k-4). 1964. (ISBN 0-684-13157-9). Scribner.
--Sumi's Special Happening. Mizumura, Kazue, illus. LC 66-24484. (Illus.). 24cm. (gr. k-4). 1966. (ISBN 0-684-20968-3). Scribner.
--Takao & Grandfather's Sword. 1st ed. Hutchinson, William Miller (1916-), illus. LC 58-5712. (Illus.). 20 cm. 127p. (gr. 2-6). 1958. (ISBN 0-15-284072-9). HarBraceJ.
Uchida, Yoshiko (1921-), retold by.
--The Dancing Kettle & Other Japanese Folk Tales. Jones, Richard C. (1910-), illus. LC 49-8090. (Illus.). 21 cm. 174p. (gr. 4-6). 1949. (ISBN 0-685-11835-5, HJ). HarBraceJ.
--The Magic Listening Cap: More FolK Tales from Japan. (Illus.). (gr. 4-6). 1955. (ISBN 0-8382-0492-9). Hale.
--The Magic Listening Cap: More Folk Tales from Japan. Uchida, Yoshiko (1921-), illus. LC 55-5240. (Illus.). (gr. 4-6). 1955. (ISBN 0-15-250978-X, HJ). HarBraceJ.
--The Magic Listening Cap: More Folk Tales from Japan. Uchida, Yoshiko (1921-), illus. LC 55-5240. (Illus.). 20cm. 146p. (Voyager Bk.: AVB16). 1965, c.1955. (ISBN 0-15-655119-5). Harcourt.
--Magic Listening Cap: More Folk Tales from Japan. Uchida, Yoshiko (1921-), illus. (gr. 4-6). 1983. Harcourt Brace.
--The Magic Listening Cap: More Folk Tales from Japan. Uchida, Yoshiko (1921-), illus. LC 85-16429. p. cm. (Voyager/HBJ book). 1985, c.1955. (ISBN 0-15-655119-5). Harcourt Brace Jovanovich.
--The Sea of Gold, and Other Tales from Japan. Yamaguchi, Marianne Illenberger (1936-), illus. LC 79-17680. (Illus.). 136 p. 24cm. (Gregg Press Children's Literature Ser.). 1980, c.1965. (ISBN 0-8398-2613-3). Gregg Press.
--The Sea of Gold and Other Tales from Japan. Yamaguchi, Marianne Illenberger (1936-), illus. LC 65-213681. 136p. illus. 24cm. c.1965. Scribners.
--The Sea of Gold and Other Tales From Japan. Yamaguchi, Marianne Illenberger (1936-), illus. 1965. Trade Publicaiton.
Uden, Bernard Gilbert Grant see Froissart, Jean.
Uden, Grant, Sir, retold by see Froissart, Jean.
Udry, Janice May (1928-)
--Alfred. 1st ed. Roth, Judith Shuman, illus. LC 60-13633. unpaged. illus. 24 cm. c.1960. A. Whitman.
--Angie. Knight, Hilary (1926-), illus. LC 71-159038. (Illus.). 64 p. 24cm. 1971. Harper & Row.
--Betsy-Back-In-Bed. Taylor, Hope, illus. LC 63-20353. (Illus.). 24cm. (gr. 1-3). 1963. (ISBN 0-8075-0681-8). A Whitman.
--Danny's Pig. Foster, Marian Curtis (1909-1978), illus. Mariana, pseud. LC 59-15436. unpaged. illus. 25 cm. 1960. Lothrop, Lee, and Shepard Co.
--Emily's Autumn. Blegvad, Erik (1923-), illus. LC 73-91743. (Illus.). 38 p. 19cm. 1969. A. Whitman.
--End of the Line. Taylor, Hope, illus. LC 62-18962. unpaged. illus. 24 cm. c.1962. A. Whitman.
--Glenda. Simont, Marc (1915-), illus. LC 69-14443. (Illus.). 24cm. 55p. 1969. Harper & Row.
--How I Faded Away: Or, the Invisible Boy. Rubin, Caroline, ed. De Bruyn, Monica Jean Grembowicz (1952-), illus. LC 75-30863. p. cm. 32p. (Concept Bks.). 1975. (ISBN 0-8075-3416-1). A. Whitman.
--If You're a Bear. Merkling, Erica, illus. LC 67-26520. (Illus.). 19cm. 32p. 1967. A. Whitman.
--Is Susan Here. 1962. (ISBN 0-8382-0370-1, Cadmus Books). E. M. Hale and Company.
--Is Susan Here?. Edwards, Peter William (1934-), illus. LC 62-7563. unpaged. illus. 21 cm. c.1962. Abelard Schuman.
--Let's Be Enemies. (Illus.). (gr. k-2). 1961. (ISBN 0-8382-0431-7, Cadmus Books). Hale.
--Let's Be Enemies. Sendak, Maurice Bernard (1928-), illus. LC 61-5777. (Illus.). (ps-1). 1961. (ISBN 0-06-026130-7, HarpJ). (ISBN 0-06-026131-5). Har-Row.
--Let's Be Enemies. Sendak, Maurice Bernard (1928-), illus. (Illus.). 32p. (gr. k-3). 1969. (ISBN 0-590-08905-6, Schol Pap). Scholastic Inc.
--Little Bear and the Beautiful Kite. Depper, Hertha, illus. LC 56-26468. unpaged. illus. 17 cm. (Tell-A-Tale Bks. 2532). c.1955. Whitman Pub. Co.
--Mary Ann's Mud Day. Alexander, Martha G. (1920-), illus. LC 67-14073. (Illus.). 29 p. 16cm. 1967. Harper & Row.
--Mary Jo's Grandmother. Mill, Eleanor, illus. LC 78-126433. (Illus.). 32 p. 24cm. 1970. (ISBN 0-8075-4984-3). A. Whitman.
--Mean Mouse And Other Mean Stories. 1962. E M Hale.
--The Mean Mouse, and Other Mean Stories. LC 62-7950. unpaged. illus. 16 x 23 cm. 1962. Harper.
--Moon Jumpers. Sendak, Maurice Bernard (1928-), illus. LC 58-7757. (Illus.). (gr. k-2). 1959. (ISBN 0-06-026145-5, HarpJ). (ISBN 0-06-026146-3). Har-Row. **Award: (RCM).**
--Next Door to Laura Linda. Wohlberg, Meg (1905-), illus. LC 65-15105. 1v. (unpaged) illus. (pt. col.) 24cm. c.1965. A. Whitman.
--Oh No, Cat!. Chalmers, Mary Eileen (1927-), illus. LC 75-43750. 17cm. 32p. 1976. (ISBN 0-698-20368-2). Coward, McCann & Geoghegan.
--The Sunflower Garden. Darwin, Beatrice, illus. LC 69-17738. (Illus.). 37 p. 1969. Harvey House.
--Theodore's Parents. Adams, Adrienne (1906-), illus. LC 58-7737. unpaged. illus. 26 cm. 1958. Lothrop, Lee & Shepard.
--Thump and Plunk. Schweninger, Ann (1951-), illus. LC 80-8443. p. cm. c.1981. (ISBN 0-06-026149-8). (ISBN 0-06-026150-1). Harper & Row.
--Tree Is Nice. Simont, Marc (1915-), illus. LC 56-5153. (Illus.). (ps-1). 1956. (ISBN 0-06-026155-2, HarpJ). (ISBN 0-06-026156-0). Har-Row. **Awards: (RCM); (ALA).**
--What Mary Jo Shared. (Illus.). (gr. 1-4). 1966. (ISBN 0-8382-1041-4). Hale.
--What Mary Jo Shared. Mill, Eleanor, illus. LC 66-16082. (Illus.). 40p. (gr. k-2). 1966. (ISBN 0-8075-8842-3). A Whitman.
--What Mary Jo Shared. Mill, Eleanor, illus. (Illus.). 34p. (gr. k-3). 1970. (ISBN 0-590-01539-7). Scholastic Inc.
--What Mary Jo Wanted. Mill, Eleanor, illus. LC 68-9123. (Illus.). 32 p. 24cm. 1968. A. Whitman.
Ueno, Noriko (1940-)
--Elephant Buttons. LC 72-10264. 1 p., 15 l. of illus. 21cm. 1973. (ISBN 0-06-026160-9). (ISBN 0-06-026160-9). Harper & Row.
Uhl, Marion Norris
--The Spiral Horn. 1st ed. Fraser, Betty M., pseud. (1928-), illus. Fraser, Elizabeth Marr. LC 68-22482. (Illus.). 122 p. 25cm. 1968. Doubleday.
Uhl, Melvin John (1915-)
--About Cargo Ships. Otteson, Madalene, illus. LC 62-7007. 31p. illus. 24cm. 1962. Melmont Pub.
--Dexter, a Discontented Dog. Otteson, Madalene, illus. LC 63-7532. unpaged. illus. 24 cm. 1963. Golden Gate Junior Books.
Uhl, Miriam Alma
--To-Day We Smile--to-Morrow We Weep: A Melo-Tragedy. LC 27-9312. 3 p. l., 5-89 p. front., ports. 18 cm. c.1927. Mrs. Anna M. Uhl.
Uhl, Robert
--Treasures in the Depths. LC 55-7322. 217p. illus. 21cm. (Lodestar books). 1955. Prentice-Hall.
Uhlich, Richard
--Twenty Minutes to Live. Uhlich, Richard, ed. Lawn, John, illus. (Illus., Orig.). (Bluejeans Paperback Ser.). (gr. 7-12). 1978. (ISBN 0-8374-0044-9). Xerox Ed Pubns.
Uhlich, Richard, ed. see Carlson, Diane.
Uhlich, Richard, ed. see Hogan, Elizabeth.
Uhlich, Richard, ed. see Otfinoski, Steven.
Uhlich, Richard, ed. see Sorensen, Robert.
Uhrman, Celia (1927-)
--A Pause for Poetry for Children. LC 73-75157. 60 p. 22cm. 1973. (ISBN 0-8059-1834-5). Dorrance.
Uhrowczik, Tedi
--A Computer Summer. Norseth, Mark, illus. LC 84-12131. c.1984. (ISBN 0-88056-318-4). Dilithium Press.
Ullberg, Nena Grigorian, jt. auth. see Coburn, Jewell Reinhart.
Ullman, James Ramsey (1907-1971)
--Banner in the Sky: The Story of a Boy & a Mountain. (gr. 7-9). 1954. (ISBN 0-397-30264-9, HarpJ). Har-Row.
--Banner in the Sky. The Story of a Boy and a Mountain. LC 54-7296. 252 p. 21cm. 1954. Lippincott. **Awards: (ALA); (JNM).**
Ullmann, Frances, ed. see Calling All Girls.
Ulmer, Frederick A., intro. by see Weeks, Morris, Jr.
Ulmer, Louise
--Adam's Story. LC 59-1292. 24p. (Orig.). (Arch Bks.). (gr. k-4). 1985. (ISBN 0-570-06191-1). Concordia.
--Elijah & the Wicked Queen. (Illus.). 32p. (Arch Bks.: Ser.13). (ps-4). 1976. (ISBN 0-570-06101-6). Concordia.
--The Man Who Learned to Give. (Arch Bk.: Ser. 14). (gr. k-2). 1977. (ISBN 0-570-06109-1). Concordia.
--The Son Who Said He Wouldn't. (Arch Bks.: Ser. 18). 1981. (ISBN 0-570-06145-8). Concordia.
--What's the Matter with Job. (Illus.). 32p. (Arch Bks.: Ser. 11). (gr. 1-4). 1974. (ISBN 0-570-06080-X). Concordia.
Ulmer, Louise & Kronberg, Ruthild (1930-)
--For the Bible Tells Me So: Bible Story-Plays with Puppets. Kirchhoff, Art, illus. LC 78-12792. (Illus.). 32 p. c.1979. (ISBN 0-570-03470-1). Concordia Pub. House.
Ulreich, Nura Woodson see Nura, pseud.
Ulreich, Nura Woodson (1899-1950)
--All Aboard, We Are Off. Nura, pseud. Ulreich, Nura Woodson (1899-1950), illus. Nura, pseud. LC 44-6705. (Illus.). 28 x 23cm. 39p. 1944. The Studio Publications.
--The Kitten Who Listened. Nura, pseud. Ulreich, Nura Woodson (1899-1950), illus. Nura, pseud. LC 50-9064. (Illus.). 30p. 28cm. 1950. Harper.
--The Mitty Children Fix Things. Nura, pseud. Nura, pseud. LC 46-39542. 39 p. illus. (part. ocl.) 28 x 23 cm. 1946. American Studio Books.
--Nura's Children Go Visiting. Ulreich, Nura Woodson (1899-1950), illus. LC 43-5894. 37 p. illus. (part col.) 28 x 23 1/2 cm. 1943. The Studio Publications, Inc.
--Nura's Garden of Betty and Booth. Nura, pseud. Ulreich, Nura Woodson (1899-1950), illus. Nura, pseud. LC 35-8479. 28cm. 16p. 1935. Nura: Distributed by Morrow & co.
Ulyatt, Kenneth (1920-)
--Day of the Cowboy. (Orig.). (Explorer Ser.). (gr. 4-8). 1973. (ISBN 0-14-061008-1, Puffin). Penguin.
--The Longhorn Trail. LC 68-21286. 309 p. 22cm. 1968, c.1967. Prentice-Hall.
--North Against the Sioux. (Illus.). (gr. 3-5). 1978. (ISBN 0-14-030406-1, Puffin). Penguin.
--Outlaws. LC 77-10127. (Illus.). 128p. (gr. 4-8). 1978. (ISBN 0-397-31773-5, JBL-J). Har-Row.
Uminski, Sigmund H
--Tales of Early Poland. LC 67-30549. (Illus.). 100 p. 21cm. 1968. Endurance Press.
Umlauf-Lamatsch, Annelies
--The Snowmen. Wallenta, Emanuela, illus. LC 63-7296. unpaged. illus. 24 cm. c.1963. Rand McNally.
Unada, pseud., see Gliewe, Unada Grace.
Unada, pseud. (1927-)
--Andrew's Amazing Boxes. Gliewe, Unada Grace. Unada, pseud. (1927-), illus. Gliewe, Unada Grace. LC 78-133925. (Illus.). 43 p. 23cm. (See and Read Beginning to Read Storybook). 1971. Putnam.
--Ricky's Boots. Gliewe, Unada Grace. Unada, pseud. (1927-), illus. Gliewe, Unada Grace. LC 78-90861. (Illus.). 42 p. 23cm. (See and Read Storybook). 1970. Putnam.
Uncle John
--Simple Addition by a Little Nigger. (Uncle John's Drolleries). 1876. Mcloughlin Bros.
Uncle Charles
--Simple Rhymes and Familiar Conversations for Children. LC 16-493. vii. 88 p. 17 cm. 1851. Southern Bapt. Publication Society.
Uncle Charlie, pseud., see Welsh, Charles.
Uncle Dan, pseud., see Dermody, Daniel Elmer.
Uncle Dick, pseud., see Lamb, Bertram John.
Uncle Foster
--Charlie Bartlett's Adventures. N.D. Bradley & Woodruff's.
Uncle Fred, jt. auth. see Miller, Harriet.
Uncle Herbert, pseud., see Arthur, Timothy Shay.
Uncle Herbert, pseud., see Knipe, Alden Arthur.
Uncle Herbert, pseud.
--The Prattler. Arthur, Timothy Shay. Uncle Herbert, pseud. (1809-1885), illus. Arthur, Timothy Shay. (Illus.). 366p. 1876. J B Lippincott & Co.
Uncle Herbert, pseud. (1809-1885), ed.
--Boys' and Girls' Treasury. Arthur, Timothy Shay. N.D. J. B. Lippincott & Co.
Uncle John (1747-1822)
--The Children's Album, 1 of 4 vols. (Illus.). 368p. (The Children's Album Ser.). N.D. Cassell, Petter, Galpin.
--The Children's Album of Pretty Pictures, with Short Stories, 1 of 4. (Illus.). 367p. (The Album Library Ser.). N.D. Lee & Shepard.
Uncle John (1747-1822) & Aiken, John
--Evenings at Home, in Words of One Syllable. LC 71-298847. (Illus.). 224 p. 19cm. (One Syllable Ser.). 1869. Cassell, Petter, Galpin.
Uncle Lawrence
--The Story of a Mountain. LC 42-437585. 243 p. incl. front., illus., plates 21 1/2 x 17 1/2 cm. 1890. J. B. Lippincott Company.
Uncle Mal, pseud., see Claire, Malcolm.
Uncle Ned
--The Little Chatterer. (Illus.). 96p. N.D. Cassell, Petter, Galpin.
--Little Schoolmates. (Illus.). 98p. N.D. Cassell, Petter, Galpin.
Uncle Phil
--Twenty Thousand Pounds. N.D. E. & J. B. Young & Co.
Uncle Shelby, pseud., see Silverstein, Shelby.
Uncle Shelby, pseud.
--Who Wants a Cheap Rhinoceros!. Silverstein, Shel. LC 64-17931. (Illus.). 24cm. 48p. 1964. Macmillan.
Uncle Solomon, selected by see Mother Goose.
Uncle Thomas
--Christmas Blossoms and New Year's Wreath for 1847-1854. LC 15-12449. 8 v. fronts., plates. 18 1/2 cm. 1847. Phillips & Sampson.
Uncle Willis, pseud., see Tilton, Stephen Willis.
Underhill, Alice Mertie Waterman (1900-1971)
--Dookie, Sookie, and Big Mo. Converse, James, illus. LC 62-7224. 174 p. illus. 23 cm. c.1961. Pacific Press Pub. Association.
--Little Flower and the Princess. Temple, C. V., illus. LC 54-9986. 23cm. 125p. 1954. Pacific Press Pub. Association.
--Sharna and Poggy: Lights Over Lookout. Muth, Don, Jr., illus. LC 58-10583. 159 p. illus. 21 cm. 1958. Pacific Press Pub. Association.

--Sharna of Rocky Bay. Muth, Don, Jr., illus. LC 57-14581. 134 p. illus. 21 cm. 1957. Pacific Press Pub. Association.

Underhill, Andrew Findlay (1859-)

--For Children Only. Sturges, Katharine, illus. LC 39-13612. 32 p. col. illus. 28 cm. c.1939. McLaughlin Bros., Inc.

--The Rhymes of Goocy Goggles and His Pollywog Named "Woggles". Sturges, Katharine, illus. LC 26-86368. 93 p. col. front., col. illus. 24 1/2 cm. c.1926. McLaughlin Bros., Inc.

Underhill, Ruth Murray (1884-)

--Antelope Singer. Koering, Ursula (1921-), illus. LC 61-8260. 280p. c.1961. Coward-McCann.

--Beaverbird: A Story of Indians on the Coast of Washington, Before the Coming of the White Gartland, Robert (1927-), illus. LC 59-5229. 224 p. illus. 22 cm. 1959. Coward-McCann.

--People of the Crimson Evening. Herrera, Velino (1902-), illus. LC 53-61114. 127p. illus. 26cm. (Indian life and customs pamphlets, 7). (U.S. Bureau of Indian Affairs, Indian Life and Customs: 7). 1951. U. S. Indian Service.

Underhill, Zoe Dana, Mrs., ed.

--The Dwarf's Tailor, & Other Fairy Tales. LC 78-74521. Repr. of 1896 ed. (Children's Literature Reprint Ser.). (gr. 4-5). 1979. (ISBN 0-8486-0224-2). Core Collection.

--The Dwarfs' Tailor, and Other Fairy Tales. LC 12-39791. iv p., 1 l., 260 p. front., plates. 19 cm. 1896. Harper & Brothers.

Underwood, Betty see Underwood, Mary Betty.

Underwood, Charlene

--Of Impossible Things. Achning, Esstellyn, illus. LC 39-383979. 51 p. illus. 21 1/2 cm. c.1938. Mathis, Van Nort & Co.

Underwood, Mary Betty (1921-)

--The Forge and the Forest. LC 74-29448. 257 p. 22cm. 1975. (ISBN 0-395-20492-5). Houghton Mifflin.

--The Tamarack Tree. Holmes, Bea, illus. LC 76-161649. (Illus.). 230 p. 22cm. 1971. Houghton Mifflin.

Underwood, Priscilla

--When Christmas Comes Around. Smith, Jessie Willcox (1863-1935), illus. N.D. Duffield.

Underwood, Ralph

--Ask Me Another Riddle. Bonsall, Crosby Barbara Newell (1921-), illus. N.D. (ISBN 0-448-02938-3). Grosset & Dunlap.

--Ask Me Another Riddle. Bonsall, Crosby Barbara Newell (1921-), illus. LC 76-14690. (Illus.). (Elephant Books Ser.). (gr. k-7). 1976. (ISBN 0-448-12689-3, G&D). Putnam Pub Group.

Tell Me Another Joke. Perl, Susan (1922-1983), illus. (Illus.). (gr. 4-6). 1964. (ISBN 0-448-02578-7, G&D). Putnam Pub Group.

Undset, Sigrid (1882-1949)

--Four Stories. 1959 (Borzoi). Alfred A Knopf.

--Happy Times in Norway. Reeves, Norman, illus. (gr. 7-11). 1942. A. A. Knopf.

--Sigurd and His Brave Companions: A Tale of Medieval Norway. Teilman, Gunvor Bull, illus. LC 43-15504. xi, 1, 139 p. 1 l. col. plates (1 double) illus. 20 1/2 cm. 1943. A. A. Knopf.

Undset, Sigrid (1882-1949), compiled by.

--True and Untrue, and Other Norse Tales. Chapman, Frederick Trench (1887-), illus. LC 45-8981. viii p., 1 l., 253, 1 p. illus. 22 cm. 1945. A. A. Knopf.

Unerstad, Edith

--The Saucepan Journey. N.D. E . M. Hale and Co.

Ungelow, Jean (1820-1897)

--Quite Another Story. 1890. Lovell.

Unger, Arthur, ed. see Datebook (New York).

Unger, Stella

--Mary, the Match Girl: Story, Play and Music. Schrack, Joseph Earl (1890-), illus. LC 41-5747. 29, 1 p. incl. col. front., illus. (part col.) 27 1/2 x 21 cm. (Musical fairy tales (book I). c.1940. Musical Fairy Tales, Inc.

Ungerer, Jean Thomas see Ungerer, Tomi, pseud.

Ungerer, Miriam & Ungerer, Tomi, pseud. (1931-)

--Come into My Parlor. Ungerer, Jean Thomas. LC 63-16040. unpaged. illus. 18 x 26 cm. 1963. Atheneum.

Ungerer, Tomi, pseud., see Ungerer, Jean Thomas.

Ungerer, Tomi, jt. auth. see Hazen, Barbara Shook.

Ungerer, Tomi, jt. auth. see Hodeir, Andre.

Ungerer, Tomi, jt. auth. see Ungerer, Miriam.

Ungerer, Tomi, pseud. (1931-)

--Adelaide. Ungerer, Jean Thomas. Ungerer, Tomi, pseud. (1931-), illus. Ungerer, Jean Thomas. LC 58-8161. (Illus.). 28cm. 40p. (gr. k-3). 1959. (ISBN 0-06-026166-8). Har-Row.

--Allumette. Ungerer, Jean Thomas. Ungerer, Tomi, pseud. (1931-), illus. Ungerer, Jean Thomas. LC 73-23055. (Illus.). 40p. (gr. k-3). 1974. (ISBN 0-8193-0730-0, Four Winds). (ISBN 0-8193-0731-9). Scholastic Inc.

--Allumette: A Fable. Ungerer, Jean Thomas. LC 81-69520. (With due respect to Hans Christian Andersen, the Grimm Brothers, and the Honorable Ambrose Bierce). (Illus.). 32 p. 27cm. 1982, c.1974. (ISBN 0-590-07845-3). Four Winds Press.

--Allumette: A Fable. Ungerer, Jean Thomas. LC 73-23055. (With due respect to Hans Christian Andersen, the Grimm Brothers, and the Hoorable Ambrose Bierce.). (Illus.). 32 p. 27cm. 1974. (ISBN 0-8193-0730-0). (ISBN 0-8193-0730-0). Parents' Magazine Press.

--Ask Me a Question. Ungerer, Jean Thomas. LC 67-21571. (Illus.). 32 p. 22cm. 1968. Harper & Row.

--The Beast of Monsieur Racine. Ungerer, Jean Thomas. Ungerer, Tomi, pseud. (1931-), illus. Ungerer, Jean Thomas. LC 74-149216. (Illus.). 32 p. 31cm. 1971. Farrar, Straus and Giroux. **Award: (NYT).**

--Christmas Eve at the Mellops'. Ungerer, Jean Thomas. LC 60-12511. unpaged. illus. 21 x 24 cm. 1960. Harper.

--Crictor. Ungerer, Jean Thomas. LC 58-5288. (Illus.). 32p. (A Trophy Picture Bk.). (ps-3). 1983. (ISBN 0-06-443044-8, Trophy). Har-Row.

--Crictor. Ungerer, Jean Thomas. 32p. (gr. k-3). 1969. (ISBN 0-590-08030-X). (ISBN 0-590-20644-3). Scholastic Inc.

--Crictor. Ungerer, Jean Thomas. Ungerer, Tomi, pseud. (1931-), illus. Ungerer, Jean Thomas. LC 58-5288. 28cm. 32p. 1958. Harper.

--Emile. Ungerer, Jean Thomas. Ungerer, Tomi, pseud. (1931-), illus. Ungerer, Jean Thomas. LC 60-5788. (Illus.). 28cm. 32p. (gr. k-3). 1960. (ISBN 0-06-026191-9, HarpJ). Har-Row.

--The Hat. Ungerer, Jean Thomas. LC 81-69519. (Illus.). 32 p. 27cm. 1982, c.1970. (ISBN 0-590-07844-5). Four Winds Press.

--The Hat. Ungerer, Jean Thomas. Ungerer, Tomi, pseud. (1931-), illus. Ungerer, Jean Thomas. LC 78-99134. (Illus.). 32 p. 29cm. 1970. Parents' Magazine Press.

--I Am Papa Snap and These Are My Favorite No Such Stories. Ungerer, Jean Thomas. LC 70-159043. (Illus.). 32 p. 31cm. (Harpercrest). 1971. (ISBN 0-06-026169-2). (ISBN 0-06-026170-6). Harper & Row.

--The Mellops Go Diving for Treasure. Ungerer, Jean Thomas. LC 57-9257. unpaged. illus. 21x24cm. 1957. Harper.

--The Mellops Go Flying. Ungerer, Jean Thomas. LC 57-5441. unpaged. illus. 21 cm. 1957. Harper.

--The Mellops' Go Spelunking. Ungerer, Jean Thomas. LC 62-13312. unpaged. illus. 21 x 24 cm. 1963. Harper & Row.

--The Mellops Strike Oil. Ungerer, Jean Thomas. Ungerer, Tomi, pseud. (1931-), illus. Ungerer, Jean Thomas. LC 58-5287. (Illus.). 24cm. 32p. (gr. k-3). 1958. (ISBN 0-06-026231-1). Har-Row.

--The Moon Man. Ungerer, Jean Thomas. Ungerer, Tomi, pseud. (1931-), illus. Ungerer, Jean Thomas. LC 66-12135. 40p, 35cm. 1967. Harper.

--No Kiss for Mother. Ungerer, Jean Thomas. Ungerer, Tomi, pseud. (1931-), illus. Ungerer, Jean Thomas. LC 72-76514. (Illus.). 40 p. 25cm. 1973. (ISBN 0-06-026236-2). (ISBN 0-06-026236-2). Harper & Row.

--One, Two, Where's My Shoe. Ungerer, Jean Thomas. Ungerer, Tomi, pseud. (1931-), illus. Ungerer, Jean Thomas. (Illus.). (gr. k-2). 1964. (ISBN 0-8382-0620-4). Hale.

--One, Two, Where's My Shoe. Ungerer, Jean Thomas. Ungerer, Tomi, pseud. (1931-), illus. Ungerer, Jean Thomas. LC 64-12811. (Illus.). (gr. k-1). 1964. (ISBN 0-06-026241-9, HarpJ). Har-Row.

--Orlando, the Brave Vulture. Ungerer, Jean Thomas. LC 66-125322. 31p. col. illus. 28cm. c.1966. Harper.

--Rufus. Ungerer, Jean Thomas. Ungerer, Tomi, pseud. (1931-), illus. Ungerer, Jean Thomas. LC 61-11450. (Illus.). 32cm. 32p. (ps-3). 1961. (ISBN 0-686-77311-X, HarpJ). Har-Row.

--Snail, Where Are You?. Ungerer, Jean Thomas. LC 62-7946. unpaged (chiefly illus.) 23 cm. 1962. Harper.

--The Three Robbers. Ungerer, Jean Thomas. Ungerer, Tomi, pseud. (1931-), illus. Ungerer, Jean Thomas. LC 62-7367. unpaged. illus. 30 cm. 1962. Atheneum. **Award: (NYT).**

--Zeralda's Ogre. Ungerer, Jean Thomas. Ungerer, Tomi, pseud. (1931-), illus. Ungerer, Jean Thomas. LC 67-14069. (Illus.). 1 v. (unpaged). 32cm. 1967. Harper & Row.

Ungerer, Tomi, pseud. (1931-), compiled by

--A Storybook from Tomi Ungerer: A Collection of Stories Old & New. Ungerer, Jean Thomas. Ungerer, Tomi, pseud. (1931-), illus. Ungerer, Jean Thomas. LC 74-3504. (Illus.). 96p. (gr. k-6). 1974. (ISBN 0-531-02742-2). (ISBN 0-531-02741-4). Watts. **Award: (NYT).**

Uniack, John R

Making the Eleven at St. Michael's. LC 26-17770. 155 p. front. 19 cm. 1926. Benziger Brothers.

Union of American Hebrew Congregations see Bialik, Hayyim Nahman.

United Danish Evangelical Lutheran Church in America. Central Committee of Young People's Leagues

--Christmas Chimes. Nelson, Carl A., ed. LC 31-1385. (An Annual Publication, Issued by Central Committee of Young Peopl's Leagues, the United Danish Ev. Lutheran Church). v. illus. (incl. ports.; part col.) 22 1/2 cm. N.D. Danish Lutheran Publishing House.

United Nations Women's Guild

--Ride with the Sun. Courlander, Harold, ed. Duvoisin, Roger Antoine (1904-1980), illus. (gr. 7 up). 1955. (ISBN 0-07-065930-3). McGraw.

U. S. Bureau of Indian Affairs & Tubbs, Rhoda

--Feast Day in Nambe. Brandt, Rose Katherine (1877-), ed. Students of the Art Department, U. S. Indian School, illus. LC 41-23280. (Verse by Indian Children and Rhoda Tubbs). 3 p., l., 38p. illus. 15 1/2cm. 1941. Haskell Institute.

United Church Board for Homeland Ministries., jt. auth. see Trickey, Edna Butler.

United Lutheran Church in America. Board of Publication, jt. auth. see Gearhart, Robert Harris.

United Lutheran Church in America. Women's Missionary Society, jt. auth. see Seebach, Julius Frederick.

United States Committee for UNICEF, jt. auth. see Pellowski, Anne.

United States. John F. Kennedy Center for the Performing Arts, jt. auth. see Noyes, Beppie.

University Society, New York & After School Club of America

--Little Journeys into Bookland. LC 12-16326. 2 v. fronts. (ports.) illus., col. pl. 24 cm. c.1912. The University Society, Inc., for the After School Club of America, Philadelphia.

University Society, New York & After School Club of America, eds.

--Famous Tales and Laughter Stories. LC 12-4829. 2 v. fronts. illus. 24 1/2cm. c.1912. University Society, Inc.

University Society of New York see Mabie, Hamilton Wright (1846-1916) & Smith, John Talbot.

Unkelbach, Kurt (1913-)

--A Cat and His Dogs. Stirnweis, Shannon (1931-), illus. LC 69-15834. (Illus.). 148 p. 22cm. 1969. Prentice-Hall.

--The Dog in My Life. Orig. Title: Thumper of Walden. (gr. 4-6). 1972 (Starline). Schol Bk Serv.

--The Dog in My Life: Thumper of Walden. LC 66-5269. 156p. 20cm. c.1966. Four Winds Dist. Scholastic.

--The Dog Who Never Knew. LC 68-12386. 127 p. 22cm. 1968. Four Winds Press.

--Love on a Leash. (gr. 7 up). 1964. (ISBN 0-13-540872-5). P-H.

--Uncle Charlie's Poodle. Palmer, Heidi (1948-), illus. LC 74-28312. (Illus.). 156 p. 22cm. 1975. (ISBN 0-396-07074-4). Dodd, Mead.

Unnerstad, Edith Totterman (1900-)

--Cats from Summer Island. Obligado, Lilian Isabel (1931-), illus. Lundberg, Holger, tr. from Swedish. LC 63-16136. 23cm. 48p. (gr. 2-4). 1963. (ISBN 0-02-789680-3). Macmillan.

--The Cats from Summer Island. Slobodkin, Louis (1903-1975), illus. Harker, James, tr. 180p. 1951. Macmillan Company.

--The Ditch Picnic. Kallstrom, Ylva, illus. LC 64-17528. 1v. (unpaged) col. illus. 22x28cm. 1965, c.1964. Norton.

--Journey to England. Sundin-Wickman, Ulla, illus. LC 61-15164. 211 p. illus. 21 cm. 1st U.S. edition. 1961. Macmillan.

--Journey with Grandmother. Backstrom, Claes (1927-), illus. Seaton, Lilian, tr. LC 60-13281. (Illus.). 21cm. 197p. (gr. 4-6). 1960. (ISBN 0-02-789750-8). Macmillan.

--Larry Makes Music. (gr. 1-3). N.D. (ISBN 0-448-26106-5). G&D.

--Larry Makes Music. Kallstrom, Ylva, illus. Edwards, Gunvor, tr. LC 78-4232. (Illus.). 55 p. 22cm. 1967. Norton.

--Little O. Slobodkin, Louis (1903-1975), illus. LC 57-7269. 150 p. illus. 21 cm. 1957. Macmillan.

--Mickie. Ohlsson, Ib (1935-), illus. LC 78-161017. (Illus.). 206 p. 21cm. 1971. Four Winds Press.

--Peep-Larssons Go Sailing. Wikland, Ilon (1930-), illus. LC 66-12351. (Illus.). 21cm. 216p. (gr. 4-6). 1966. (ISBN 0-02-789730-3). Macmillan.

--Pysen. Slobodkin, Louis (1903-1975), illus. Boye, Inger, tr. LC 55-14199. (Illus.). 172 p. 21cm. 1955. Macmillan.

--The Saucepan Journey. Slobodkin, Louis (1903-1975), illus. Harker, James (1903-1975), tr. from Swedish. (Illus.). 180 p. 21cm. 1951. Macmillan.

--The Spettecake Holiday. Clante, Iben, illus. Boye, Inger, tr. LC 58-11081. (Illus.). 211 p. 21cm. 1958. Macmillan.

--Two Little Gigglers. Kallstrom, Ylva, illus. LC 68-18486. (Illus.). 30 p. 23cm. 1st U.S. edition. 1968, c.1967. Norton.

Uno, pseud., see Baker, George Melville.

Uno, pseud. (1832-1890)

--Baby Ballads. Baker, George Melville, 1 of 4 vols. (Illus.). (The Baby Ballad Ser.). 1882. Lee & Shepard.

Unrau, Ruth (1922-)

--Buckwheat Summer. LC 62-13715. 143 p. 21 cm. 1962. Herald Press.

--Who Needs an Oil Well?. Gleysteen, Jan, illus. LC 68-15405. (Illus.). 254 p. 24cm. 1968. Abingdon Press.

Unruh, John H.

--Bright Eyes: The Life of a Baby Jack Rabbit. LC 80-18667. (Illus.). 112p. (Orig.). (gr. 4 up). 1980. (ISBN 0-914598-02-3). Padre Prods.

--Ervin and His Friends in Shadyway. LC 76-5754. (Illus.). 116 p. 21cm. c.1976. Faceter's Gem.

Unsworth, Walter (1928-)

--Grimsdyke. LC 76-2522. 155 p. 21cm. 1976, c.1974. (ISBN 0-8407-6491-X). Nelson.

Unterecker, John Eugene (1922-)

--The Dreaming Zoo. Weinheimer, George, illus. LC 65-14367. 1v. (unpaged) illus. (pt. col.) 26cm. c.1965. (ISBN 0-8098-1113-8). Walck.

Untermeyer, Bryna Ivens, jt. ed. see Untermeyer, Louis.

Untermeyer, Bryna Ivens (1909-), ed.

--Tall Tales. Dolesch, Charles, illus. LC 63-24034. 152 p. illus. (part col.) 27 cm. (Golden Treasury of Children's Literature, v. 10). 1963. Golden Press.

Untermeyer, Bryna Ivens (1909-) & Untermeyer, Louis (1885-1977), eds.

--Adventure Stories. LC 74-3983. (Illus.). 256p. 27cm. (Golden Treasure Chest). 1968. Golden Press.

--Adventures All. Laite, Gordon, et al. (1925-), illus. LC 63-2378. (Illus.). 152 p. 27cm. (Golden Treasury of Children's Literature, v. 8). 1963. Golden Press.

--Animal Stories. LC 78-3984. (Illus.). 255p. 27cm. (The Golden Treasure Chest). 1968. Golden Press.

--Beloved Tales. Obligado, Lilian Isabel (1931-), illus. LC 62-4631. 176p. col. illus. 27cm. (Golden Treasury of Childrens Lit., v.2). N.D. Golden Pr.

--Big & Little Creatures. Jones, Elizabeth Orton, et al. (1910-), illus. LC 62-4314. 1962. Golden Press.

--Creatures Wild and Tame. Harper, Charles, illus. LC 63-1832. (Illus.). 152 p. 26cm. (Golden Treasury of Children's Literature, v. 7). 1963. Golden Press.

--Favorite Classics. LC 75-4861. (Illus.). 256p. 27cm. (The Golden Treasure Chest). 1968. Golden Press.

--Fun and Fancy. Obligado, Lilian Isabel (1931-), illus. LC 62-4528. 164p. col. illus. 26cm. (Golden Treasury of Children's Lit.; As You Grow Bks. v.3). c.1962. Golden.

--Legendary Animals. Provensen, Alice (1918-) & Provensen, Martin (1916-), illus. LC 63-445346. 152 p. illus. 27 cm. (Golden Treasury of Children's Literature, v. 9). 1963. Golden Press.

--Old Friends and Lasting Favorites. Dugan, William J., et al., illus. LC 62-510864. 152 p. illus. 26 cm. (Golden Treasury of Children's Literature, v. 4). 1962. Golden Press.

--Stories and Poems for the Very Young. LC 73-81000. (Illus.). 252 p. 27cm. 1973. Golden Press.

--Tales and Legends. LC 68-31177. (Illus.). 256p. 27cm. (The Golden Treasure Chest). c.1968. Golden Press.

--Unfamiliar Marvels. Helweg, Hans H. (1917-), illus. LC 63-194798. 152p. illus. (pt. col.) 27cm. (Golden treasury of children's lit., v.6). 1963, c.1962. Golden.

--Wonder Lands. Winslow, Jean, illus. LC 62-51597. 152 p. illus. 27 cm. (Golden Treasury of Children's Literature, v. 5). 1962. Golden Press.

Untermeyer, Louis (1885-1977), ed. see Aesopus.

Untermeyer, Louis (1885-1977), retold by see Perrault, Charles.

Untermeyer, Louis, jt. ed. see Untermeyer, Bryna Ivens.

Untermeyer, Louis, jt. ed. see Wier, Albert Ernest.

Untermeyer, Louis (1885-1977), tr. see Keller, Gottfried.

Untermeyer, Louis (1885-1977)

--Chip: My Life and Times. Neville, Vera (1900-1978) & Untermeyer, Louis (1885-1977), illus. LC 33-25196. 6 p. l., 3-102 p. incl. front., illus., plates. 19 1/2 x 21 1/2 cm. c.1933. Harcourt, Brace and Company.

--The Donkey of God. Macdonald, James, illus. 300p. (gr. 7). N.D. Harcourt, Brace & Co.

--The Kitten Who Barked. Obligado, Lilian Isabel (1931-), illus. LC 62-12868. (Illus.). 34 p. 1962. Golden Press.

--The Last Pirate. Birch, Reginald Bathurst (1856-1943), illus. 319p. (gr. 5). N.D. Harcourt, Brace & Co.
--One and One and One. Jones, Robert A., illus. LC 62-21520. unpaged. illus. 30 cm. (Modern masters book for children). 1962. Crowell-Collier Press.
--Poems. Anglund, Joan Walsh (1926-), illus. (Illus.). (gr. 3-7). 1968 (Golden Pr). Western Pub.
--The Pursuit of Poetry. (gr. 7 up). 1969. (ISBN 0-671-20409-2). (ISBN 0-671-21373-3). S&S.
--Rainbow in the Sky. Golden Anniversary ed. Birch, Reginald Bathurst (1856-1943), illus. LC 35-27286. xxvii, 498 p. incl. front., illus., pl. 23 1/2 cm. c.1935. Harcourt, Brace and Company.
--Rainbow in the Sky. Golden Anniversary ed. Birch, Reginald Bathurst (1856-1943), illus. LC 84-19306. (Illus.). xxvii, 498 p. 24cm. 1985, c.1935. (ISBN 0-15-265477-1). Harcourt Brace Jovanovich.
--Tales from the Ballet. Provensen, Alice (1918-) & Provensen, Martin (1916-), illus. (Illus.). 98p. (gr. 1-6). 1968. (ISBN 0-307-17852-8, Golden Pr). (ISBN 0-307-67852-0). Western Pub.
--Thanks: A Poem. Victor, Joan Berg (1942-), illus. (Illus.). N.D. (ISBN 0-307-40158-8, Golden Pr). Western Pub.
--This Singing World for Younger Children. N.D. Harcourt Brace & Co.
--The World's Great Stories: Fifty-Five Legends That Live Forever. Gerhard, Mae, illus. LC 61-10082. 256 p. illus. 24 cm. c.1964. Lippincott.
--The World's Great Stories: Fifty-Five Legends That Live Forever. Gerhard, Mae, illus. LC 64-230303. 256 p. illus. 24 cm. 1964. Published by M. Evans, and Distributed in Association with Lippincott, Philadelphia.

Untermeyer, Louis (1885-1977), ed.
--The Book of Living Verse. 609p. (Harbrace Modern Classics). N.D. Harcourt Brace & Co.
--Cat O' Nine Tales. Di Fiori, Lawrence, illus. LC 70-149736. (Illus.). 96 p. 26cm. 1971. (ISBN 0-07-065937-0). American Heritage Press.
--The Firebringer, and Other Great Stories: Fifty-Five Legends That Live Forever. Gerhard, Mae, illus. LC 68-18716. (Illus.). 255 p. 24cm. 1968. M. Evans; Distributed in Association with Lippincott, Philadelphia.
--The Golden Book of Fun and Nonsense. Provensen, Alice (1918-) & Provensen, Martin (1916-), illus. LC 70-99159. (Illus.). 92 p. 31cm. (Giant golden book). 1970. Golden Press.
--The Golden Book of Poems for the Very Young. Anglund, Joan Walsh (1926-), illus. LC 71-142154. (Illus.). 33 p. 32cm. 1971. Golden Press.
--The Golden Treasury of Animal Stories and Poems. LC 79-149567. (Illus.). 324 p. 27cm. 1971. Golden Press.
--The Golden Treasury of Poetry. Anglund, Joan Walsh (1926-), illus. LC 59-4473. (Illus.). 324 p. 27cm. 1959. Golden Press.
--Love Lyrics. N.D. Golden Press.
--Magic Circle: Stories & People in Poetry. Krush, Beth (1918-) & Krush, Joe (1918-), illus. LC 52-6912. (Illus.). 288p. (gr. 7-9). 1952. (ISBN 0-15-250620-9, HJ). HarBraceJ.
--Merry Christmas. N.D. Golden Press.
--Paths of Poetry: Twenty-Five Poets & Their Poems. Raskin, Ellen (1928-1984), illus. (Illus.). (gr. 7 up). 1966. Delacorte.
--Roses. N.D. Golden Press.
--Songs of Joy: Selections from the Book of Psalms. Victor, Joan Berg (1942-), illus. LC 67-13820. (Illus.). (gr. k up). 1967. (ISBN 0-529-00235-3). (ISBN 0-529-00234-5). World Pub.
--Stars to Steer By. Morse, Dorothy Bayley (1906-1979), illus. LC 41-3447. (Illus.). (gr. 7-9). N.D. (ISBN 0-15-279963-X). HarBraceJ.
--This Singing World: Junior Edition. Ivins, Florence Wyman, illus. LC 23-17203. (Illus.). (gr. 7-9). 1926. (ISBN 0-15-286041-X, HJ). HarBraceJ.
--Time for Peace: Verses from the Bible. Victor, Joan Berg (1942-), illus. (Illus.). 64p. (gr. 4 up). 1969. (ISBN 0-529-00747-9). World Pub.
--The Wonderful Adventures of Paul Bunyan. 172p. N.D. Heritage Press.
--Yesterday and Today. 415p. N.D. Harcourt Brace & Co.

Untermeyer, Louis (1885-1977) & Mannes, Clara Damroach, Mrs. (1869-), eds.
--New Songs for New Voices. Bacon, Peggy, pseud. (1895-), illus. Bacon, Margaret Frances. LC 28-27661. vii, 258 p. illus. 32 cm. c.1928. Harcourt, Brace and Company.

Untermeyer, Louis (1885-1977) & Untermeyer, Bryna Ivens (1909-), eds.
--A Galaxy of Verse. LC 78-1255. (Illus.). 224 p. 23cm. c.1978. (ISBN 0-87131-258-1). M. Evans.
--The Golden Treasury of Children's Literature. LC 66-14668. (Illus.). 27cm. 544p. 1966. (ISBN 0-307-16522-1, Golden Pr). (ISBN 0-307-66522-4). Western Pub.

Unwin, David Storr see Severn, David, pseud.

Unwin, David Storr (1918-)
--Dream Gold. Kashiwagi, Isami (1925-), illus. LC 52-12917. 192 p. illus. 21 cm. 1952. Viking Press.

Unwin, June C.
--Little Sandy Sleighfoot. Unwin, James Alan, illus. LC 57-11001. (Lyrics by Philip M. Crane : Music by Joseph E. Savarino). (Illus.). 31cm. 31p. 1957. (ISBN 0-910748-01-2). Hopkins Syndicate Inc.

Unwin, Nora Spicer (1907-)
--Doughnuts and the White Cat. Unwin, Nora Spicer (1907-), illus. . 48p. (gr. 1-4). N.D. Aladdin Bks.
--Doughnuts for Lin. 1st ed. Unwin, Nora Spicer (1907-), illus. LC 50-9669. (Illus.). 18 x 23cm. 46p. 1950. Aladdin Books.
--Joyful the Morning: The Story of an English Family Christmas. Unwin, Nora Spicer (1907-), illus. LC 63-19796. (Illus.). 21cm. 117p. (gr. 3-7). 1963. (ISBN 0-679-20087-8). McKay.
--The Midsummer Witch. Unwin, Nora Spicer (1907-), illus. LC 66-16046. 78p. col. illus. 24cm. 1966. (ISBN 0-679-20114-9). McKay.
--Poquito: The Little Mexican Duck. Unwin, Nora Spicer (1907-), illus. LC 49-5017. unpaged. illus. 18 x 26 cm. c.1959. D. McKay Co.
--Poquito, the Mexican Duck. (Illus.). (gr. 3-5). 1959. (ISBN 0-8382-0674-3). Hale.
--Proud Pumpkin. LC 53-12217. (Illus.). 46 p. 23cm. 1953. Aladdin Books.
--Proud Pumpkin. Unwin, Nora Spicer (1907-), illus. N.D. E. P. Dutton & Co.
--Round the Year. Unwin, Nora Spicer (1907-), illus. N.D. Holiday House.
--Sinbad the Cygnet. LC 69-13407. (Illus.). 48 p. 1970. John Day Co.
--Two Too Many. 1962. E M Hale.
--Two Too Many. Unwin, Nora Spicer (1907-), illus. LC 62-17446. (Illus.). 24cm. 54p. N.D. David McKay Co.
--Way of the Shepherd: A Story of the Twenty-Third Psalm. (Illus.). (gr. 2-4). 1963. McGraw.

UPA Pictures, Inc
--Gay Purr-ee. Memling, Carl (1918-1969), adapted by. White, Al, illus. LC 62-53127. (Based on the UPA motion picture). unpaged. illus. 32cm. c.1962. Golden Press.

Upadhyay, Asha
--Tales from India. Nodjoumi, Nikzad, illus. LC 75-146651. (Illus.). viii, 56 p. 24cm. 1971. (ISBN 0-394-82166-1). Random House.

Upchurch, Boyd see Boyd, John, pseud.

Updegraff, Florence Maule
--Blue Dowry. Doremus, Robert (1913-), illus. LC 48-6049. 271 p. illus. 21 cm. 1948. Harcourt, Brace.
--Coat for a Soldier. Watson, Eva Auld, illus. LC 41-159290. xiv, 294 p. incl. front., plates. 21 cm. c.1941. Harcourt, Brace and Company.
--Traveler's Candle. Watson, Eva Auld, illus. LC 42-36302. 5 p. l., 3-237 p. incl. plates. front. 21 cm. 1942. Harcourt, Brace and Company.

Updegraff, Laura
--Wee Dorothy. (Illus.). (The Cosy Corner Ser.). N.D. The Page Company.
--Wee Dorothy's True Valentine. Eastman, Alfred C., illus. LC 12-39777. 4 p. l., 107 p. front., illus. 18 1/2 cm. (Cosy corner series). 1896. Joseph Knight Company.

Updike, David
--A Midnight Journey. Parker, Robert Andrew (1927-), illus. LC 85-9334. p. cm. c.1985. (ISBN 0-13-582834-1). Prentice-Hall.
--A Winter Journey. Parker, Robert Andrew (1927-), illus. 40p. 1985. (ISBN 0-13-961566-0). Prentice.

Updike, Estelle R (1855-)
--Tourbillon: Or, the King of the Whirlwinds. LC 15-19266. 27 p. illus. 23 1/2 cm. $0.3. c.1915. The Abingdon Press.

Updike, John Hoger (1932-), adapted by see Shakespeare, William (1564-1616) & Mendelssohn-Bartholdy, Felix.

Updike, John Hoger (1932-)
--Child's Calendar. Burkert, Nancy Ekholm (1933-), illus. LC 65-21555. (Illus.). (gr. k-3). 1965. (ISBN 0-394-91059-1). Knopf.

Updike, John Hoger (1932-), ed.
--Magic Flute. Chappell, Warren (1904-), illus. (Illus.). (gr. 1 up). 1962. (ISBN 0-394-91384-1). Knopf.
--Ring. Chappell, Warren (1904-), illus. (Illus.). (gr. 4 up). 1964. (ISBN 0-394-91544-5). Knopf.

Upham, Alfred H.
--Rhyming Round the World. N.D. Bruce Humphries.

Upham, Elizabeth Norine (1904-)
--Little Brown Bear. Brown, Guy J., illus. LC 48-1421. (Illus.). 27cm. 1947. Child Training Assn.
--Little Brown Bear. Cushman, Doug, illus. LC 78-68408. (Illus.). 39 p. 32cm. c.1979. (ISBN 0-448-48991-0). (ISBN 0-448-13621-X). Platt & Munk.
--Little Brown Bear. Hartwell, Marjorie, illus. LC 42-25186. 57 p. incl. col. front., col. illus. 26 x 21 cm. 1942. The Platt & Munk Co., Inc.
--Little Brown Bear and His Friends. Hartwell, Marjorie, illus. LC 52-14329. unpaged. illus. 26cm. 1952. Platt & Munk.
--Little Brown Bear Goes to School. Hartwell, Marjorie, illus. LC 55-12577. unpaged. illus. 26cm. 1955. Platt & Munk Co.
--Little Brown Bear Loses His Clothes. Chartier, Normand (1945-), illus. LC 77-84185. (Illus.). (A Cricket Book). (gr. k-2). 1978. (ISBN 0-448-46523-X). Platt.
--Little Brown Monkey. Hartwell, Marjorie, illus. LC 50-13395. 56 p. col. illus. 26 cm. 1949. Platt & Munk.
--The Merry Adventures of Little Brown Bear. Hartwell, Marjorie, illus. LC 65-260315. 97p. col. illus. 24cm. 1966, c.1965. Platt & Munk.

Upham, Grace Le Baron Locke see Le Baron, Grace, pseud.

Upham, Grace Le Baron Locke, Mrs. (1845-1916)
--The Children of Bedford Court. (Illus.). 1905. Lee and Shepard Company.
--Jessica's Triumph. Brooks, Amy (0000-1931), illus. (Illus.). (Janet Ser.). N.D. Lothrop & Shepard.
--Little Daughter. Le Baron, Grace, pseud. LC 12-363541. 178 p. front., plates. 16 1/2 cm. (Hazelwood stories. v. 2). 1896. Lee and Shepard.
--Little Daughter. New ed. (Illus.). (The Hazelwood Ser). N.D. Lee & Shepard.
--Little Miss Faith: The Story of a Country Week at Falcons-Height. Le Baron, Grace, pseud. LC 12-363538. 2 p. l., iii-vi p., 1 l., 9-174 p. front., plates. 16 1/2 cm. (Hazelwood stories. v. 1). 1894. Lee and Shepard.
--Queer Janet. Le Baron, Grace, pseud. LC 12-36358. xiii, 187 p. front., illus., plates. 16 1/2 cm. 1897. Lee and Shepard.
--The Rosebud Club. Le Baron, Grace, pseud. LC 12-363571. xix, 178 p. front., illus., plates. 16 1/2 cm. (Hazelwood stories. v. 3). 1896. Lee and Shepard.
--Told Under the Cherry Trees: A Book for the Young. Le Baron, Grace, pseud. Brooks, Amy (0000-1931), illus. LC 99-3968. v, 235 p. front., plates. 19 cm. 1899. Lee and Shepard.
--Twixt You and Me. Le Baron, Grace, pseud. Thompson, Ellen Bernard, illus. LC 98-84. 296 p., 1 l. front., illus., plates. 19 cm. 1898. Little, Brown & Co.

Upington, Marion
--The Beautiful Culpeppers. Slobodkin, Louis (1903-1975), illus. LC 63-16922. 113 p. illus. 21 cm. 1963. (ISBN 0-531-01614-5). F. Watts.

Upjohn, Anna Milo
--Friends in Strange Garments. Upjohn, Anna Milo, illus. LC 27-19155. xi, 148 p. col. front., plates (part col.) 21 cm. 1927. Houghton Mifflin Company.

Upton, Bertha Hudson, Mrs. (1849-1912)
--Adventures of Two Dutch Dolls. 1910. Longmans Green & Co.
--The Golliwog at the Sea-side. Upton, Florence Kate (1873-1922), illus. LC 12-37733. (Illus.). 22 x 28cm. 62p. 1897. Longmans, Green & Co.
--The Golliwogg at the Seaside. 1910. Longmans Green & Co.
--The Golliwogg in Holland. Upton, Florence Kate (1873-1922), illus. LC 4-25693. 64 p. illus. (part col.) 22 x 28 1/2 cm. 1904. Longmans, Green & Co.
--The Golliwogg in War. 1910. Longmans Green & Co.
--The Golliwogg in War!. Upton, Florence Kate (1873-1922), illus. LC 99-3222. 64, 1 p. col. illus. 22 x 28 1/2 cm. c.1899. Longmans, Green & Co.
--The Golliwogg's Air-Ship. 1910. Longmans Green & Co.
--The Golliwogg's Air-Ship. Upton, Florence Kate (1873-1922), illus. LC 2-17236. 64 p., 1 l. col. illus. 22 x 28 1/2 cm. c.1902. Longmans, Green & Co.
--The Golliwogg's Auto Go-Cart. 1910. Longmans Green & Co.
--The Golliwogg's Auto-go-cart. Upton, Florence Kate (1873-1922), illus. LC 1-14001. 66p. 1901. Longman's, Green & Co.
--The Golliwogg's Christmas. Upton, Florence Kate (1873-1922), illus. LC 41-38147. 62 (i. e. 66) p. illus. (part col.) col. pl. 22 x 28 cm. 1907. Longmans, Green & Co.
--The Golliwogg's Christmas. Upton, Florence Kate (1873-1922), illus. 1910. Longmans Green & Co.
--The Golliwogg's Circus. Upton, Florence Kate (1873-1922), illus. LC 2-17236. 64 p. col. illus. 22 x 28 cm. 1903. Longmans, Green & Co.
--The Golliwogg's Circus. Upton, Florence Kate (1873-1922), illus. 1910. Longmans Green & Co.
--The Golliwogg's Desert Island. Upton, Florence Kate (1873-1922), illus. LC 7-6799. 22 x 29cm. 68p. 1906. Longman's, Green & Co.
--The Golliwogg's Desert Island. Upton, Florence Kate (1873-1922), illus. 1910. Longmans Green & Co.
--The Golliwogg's Fox Hunt. Upton, Florence Kate (1873-1922), illus. 1910. Longmans Green & Co.
--The Golliwogg's Polar Adventures. 1910. Longmans Green & Co.
--The Golliwogg's Polar Adventures. Upton, Florence Kate (1873-1922), illus. LC 3972. 62 (i. e. 66), 1 p. col. illus. 22 x 28 cm. 1900. Longmans, Green & Co.
--Two Dutch Dogs and a Golliwog. Upton, Florence Kate (1873-1922), illus. (Illus.). N.D. DeWolfe, Fiske & Co.
--The Vege-men's Revenge. 1910. Longmans Green & Co.
--The Vege-men's Revenge. Upton, Florence Kate (1873-1922), illus. LC 12-39732. 22 x 28cm. 66p. 1897. Longman's, Green & Co.

Upton, Bertha Hudson, Mrs. (1849-1912) & Upton, Florence Kate (1873-1922)
--The Adventures of Borbee and the Wisp. LC 15-25628. 67p. col. illus. 25 x 25 1/2 cm. 1908. Longmans, Green & Co.
--Golliwogg in the African Jungle. N.D. Longmans, Green.
--The Golliwogg's Bicycle Club. N.D. Longmans Green & Co.
--Two Dutch Dolls & a Golliwogg. N.D. Longmans,Green & Co.

Upton, Florence Kate, jt. auth. see Upton, Bertha Hudson, Mrs.

Upton, Florence Kate (1873-1922)
--Adventures of Borbee and the Wisp. LC 15-25628. 26cm. 67p. 1908. Longmans Green & Co.
--Little Hearts. (Illus.). N.D. George Routledge & Sons.

Upton, George Putman
--In Music Land. N.D. A. C. McClurg.

Upton, George Putnam (1834-1919), tr. see Becker, Karl Friedrich.

Upton, George Putnam (1834-1919), tr. see Schmidt, Ferdinand.

Upton, George Putnam (1834-1919), tr. see Schmidt, Ferdinand (1816-1890) & Becker, Karl Friedrich.

Upton, George Putnam (1834-1919), tr. see Schmidt, Ferdinand (1816-1890) & Nibelungenlied. Paraphrases, Tables, Etc.

Upton, George Putnam (1834-1919), tr. from Ger.
--The Argonautic Expedition and The Labors of Hercules. LC 12-22548. ix p., 1 l., 13-123 p. front., plates. 17 cm. (Life Stories for Young People). 1912. A. C. McClurg & Co.

Urann, Clara A., jt. auth. see Pringle, Mary Poague.

Urbahns, Estelle
--The Little Red Dragon. 1st ed. Yap, Weda (1894-), illus. LC 47-23976. 64 p. illus. 23 cm. 1947. E. P. Dutton.
--The Tangled Web. Lieberman, Frank Joseph (1910-), illus. LC 43-13576. 64 p. incl. front., illus., plates. 22 1/2 cm. 1943. E. P. Dutton & Co., Inc.

Ure, Jean
--Ballet Dance for Two. Kennedy, Richard (1910-), illus. LC 60-13161. 21cm. 160p. 1960. Franklin Watts, Inc.
--Hi There, Supermouse!. White, Martin, illus. LC 84-18042. (Illus.). 123 p. 18cm. 1985. (ISBN 0-14-031716-3). Puffin Books.
--If It Weren't for Sebastian. LC 84-15568. 185 p. 22cm. 1985, c.1982. (ISBN 0-385-29380-1). Delacorte.
--See You Thursday. LC 83-5217. 211 p. 22cm. c.1981. (ISBN 0-385-29303-8). Delacorte Press.
--Supermouse. Eagle, Ellen, illus. LC 83-22022. 1984. (ISBN 0-688-02742-3). Morrow.
--What If They Saw Me Now?. LC 83-14981. 160p. (gr. 7 up). 1984, c.1982. (ISBN 0-385-29317-8). Delacorte.
--The You-Two. Eagle, Ellen, illus. LC 84-8947. (gr. 4-7). 1984. (ISBN 0-688-03857-3, Morrow Junior Books). Morrow.

Ure, Olive Emma De Gonville (1876-)
--The Rich Little Poor Boy. LC 22-25002. 22 p. 17 1/2 cm. 1922. The Master Press.

Urgo, Michael
--Red Checker. N.D. Carlton Press.

Urmston, Mary (1891-)
--Betsy and the Proud House. 1st ed. Paull, Grace A. (1898-), illus. LC 47-31292. 179 p. illus. 21 cm. 1947. Doubleday.
--Forty Faces. Sawyers, Martha, illus. LC 40-32987. 3 p. l., 298 p. col. front. 20 1/2 cm. 1940. Doubleday, Doran & Co., Inc.

AUTHOR INDEX VAIZEY, JESSIE

--Larry's Luck. 1st ed. Porter, Jean MacDonald (1906-), illus. LC 52-5760. 188 p. illus. 21 cm. 1952. Doubleday.
--Mystery of the Five Bright Keys. Smith, Robert, illus. LC 46-11968. x p., 1 l., 211 p. illus. 20 1/2 cm. 1946. Doubleday & Company, Inc.
--Mystery of the Five Bright Keys. Smith, Robert, illus. (Illus.). (gr. 5-6). 1959. (ISBN 0-385-07417-4). Doubleday.
--Mystery of the Old Barn. Paull, Grace A. (1898-), illus. LC 45-6794. 5 p. l., 180 p. illus. 20 1/2 cm. 1945. Doubleday, Doran and Company, Inc.
--The New Boy. 1st ed. Turkle, Brinton Cassaday (1915-), illus. LC 50-7753. 207 p. illus. 21 cm. 1950. Doubleday.
--Plain Clothes Patricia. LC 44-4096. 3 p. l., 218 p. 20 1/2 cm. 1944. Doubleday, Doran & Co., Inc.
--Quite Contrary. LC 42-24440. 3 p. l., 279 p. 21 cm. 1942. Doubleday, Doran & Company, Inc.
--The Seven and Sam. Paull, Grace A. (1898-), illus. LC 55-9995. 188p. illus. 22cm. 1955. Doubleday.
--Swamp Shack Mystery. 1st ed. Paull, Grace A. (1898-), illus. LC 59-11611. (Illus.). 189 p. 22cm. 1959. Doubleday.
--The Twenty-Five and Ann. 1st ed. LC 53-9136. 192p. 21.m. 1953. Doubleday.

Urquhart, Elizabeth
--Horace. 1st ed. Pastor, Rosita, illus. LC 51-5490. 115 p. illus. 21 cm. 1951. Dutton.

Urquhart, John & Grossberg, Rita
--Nightingale: A Participation Play. (Orig.). 1983. (ISBN 0-87602-245-X). Anchorage.

Urwin, Iris, tr. see Grosman, Ladislav.

U. S. George Washington Bicentennial Commission, jt. auth. see Price, Olive M.

Usher, Alice
--Sunny Hours. Kniffke, Sophie, illus. (Illus.). 48p. (Orig.). 1st U.S. edition. N.D (Star & Eleph Bks). Green Tiger Pr.

Usher, Kerry
--Heroes, Gods and Emperors from Roman Mythology. Sibbick, John, illus. (gr. 5-8). 1984. Schocken.

Usher, Margo Scegge, pseud., see McHarge, Georges.

Usher, Margo Scegge, pseud., adapted by
--Chitty Chitty Bang Bang. McHarge, Georges. (Illus.). color ils. 80p. Repr. (gr. 3-6). 1969 (Golden Pr). Western Pub.

Ushinskii, Konstantin Dmitrievich (1824-1870)
--How a Shirt Grew in the Field. Rudolph, Marguerita (1908-), ed. Yaroslava, pseud. (1925-), illus. Mills, Yaroslava Surmach. LC 67-3119. (Illus.). 30 p. 26cm. (gr. k-3). 1967. McGraw-Hill.

U.S. National Aeronautics and Space Administration see Trussell, Tait & Hencke, Paul.

U. S. Sanitary Commission, jt. auth. see Ludlow, Fitz Hugh.

Utah. State Institute of Fine Arts, Salt Lake City see Stavros, Joyce.

Uttley, Alice Jane Taylor see Uttley, Alison, pseud.

Uttley, Alison, pseud., see Uttley, Alice Jane Taylor.

Uttley, Alison, Mrs., pseud. (1884-1976)
--Adventures of Sam Pig. Uttley, Alice Jane Taylor. Gower, Francis, illus. LC 76-375736. (Illus.). 159 p. 20cm. (Young Puffin). 1976. (ISBN 0-14-030843-1). Puffin Books.
--Adventures of Tim Rabbit. Uttley, Alice Jane Taylor. Kennedy, A. E., illus. (Illus.). (ps-5). 1945. (ISBN 0-571-05676-8). Faber & Faber.
--Best Sam Pig Stories. Uttley, Alison Jane Taylor. Leslie, Cecil, illus. LC 85-4481. p. cm. 1985. (ISBN 0-571-13665-6). (ISBN 0-571-13650-8). Faber and Faber.
--The Country Child. Uttley, Alice Jane Taylor. 240p. (Puffin Story Bks.). (gr. 1 up). 1976. (ISBN 0-14-030302-2, Puffin). Penguin.
--Foxglove Tales. Uttley, Alice Jane Taylor. Meredith, Lucy, selected by. Felts, Shirley (1934-), illus. LC 84-13504. (Illus.). 192p. (gr. 4 up). 1984. (ISBN 0-571-13354-1). (ISBN 0-571-13354-1). Faber & Faber.
--From Spring to Spring: Stories of the Four Seasons. Uttley, Alice Jane Taylor. Lines, Kathleen, selected by. Hughes, Shirley (1929-), illus. LC 79-670056. (Illus.). 131 p. 23cm. 1978. (ISBN 0-571-11144-0). Faber and Faber.
--Fuzzypeg Goes to School. Uttley, Alice Jane Taylor. Tempest, Margaret Mary (1892-1982), illus. 64p. (Little Grey Rabbit Ser.). 1938. (ISBN 0-00-194105-4). Collins & World.
--Fuzzypeg's Brother. Uttley, Alice Jane Taylor. (Illus.). (Little Grey Rabbit Ser.). (ps-3). N.D. (ISBN 0-00-194129-1). (ISBN 0-00-194145-3). Collins-World.
--Grey Rabbit & the Wandering Hedgehog. Uttley, Alice Jane Taylor. Tempest, Margaret Mary (1892-1982), illus. (Illus.). (Little Grey Rabbit Ser.). (ps-3). N.D. (ISBN 0-00-194144-5). (ISBN 0-00-194115-1). Collins-World.
--Grey Rabbit Finds a Shoe. Uttley, Alice Jane Taylor. Tempest, Margaret Mary (1892-1982), illus. (Illus.). (Little Grey Rabbit Ser.). (ps-3). N.D. (ISBN 0-00-194122-4). (ISBN 0-00-194148-8). Collins-World.
--Grey Rabbit's May Day. Uttley, Alice Jane Taylor. (Illus.). (Little Grey Rabbit Ser.). (ps-3). 1963. (ISBN 0-00-194124-0). Collins-World.
--Gypsy Hedgehogs. Uttley, Alice Jane Taylor. Wigglesworth, Katherine, illus. 72p. 1953. British Book Centre Inc.
--Hare & Guy Fawkes. Uttley, Alice Jane Taylor. Tempest, Margaret Mary (1892-1982), illus. (Illus.). (Little Grey Rabbit Ser.). (ps-3). N.D. (ISBN 0-00-194146-1). (ISBN 0-00-194120-8). Collins-World.
--Hare & the Easter Eggs. Uttley, Alice Jane Taylor. Tempest, Margaret Mary (1892-1982), illus. (Illus.). (Little Grey Rabbit Ser.). (ps-3). N.D. (ISBN 0-00-194117-8). (ISBN 0-00-194149-6). Collins-World.
--Hare & the Rainbow. Uttley, Alice Jane Taylor. (Illus.). (Little Grey Rabbit Ser.). (ps-3). N.D. (ISBN 0-00-194160-7). Collins-World.
--Hare Goes Shopping. Uttley, Alice Jane Taylor. Tempest, Margaret Mary (1892-1982), illus. (Illus.). (Little Grey Rabbit Ser.). (ps-3). N.D. (ISBN 0-00-194155-0). Collins-World.
--Hare Joins the Home Guard. Uttley, Alice Jane Taylor. (Illus.). (Little Grey Rabbit Ser.). (gr. k-3). 1941. (ISBN 0-00-194108-9). Collins-World.
--The Knot Squirrel Tied. Uttley, Alice Jane Taylor. (Little Grey Rabbit Ser.). (ps-3). 1937. (ISBN 0-00-194104-6). Collins-World.
--Lavender Shoes: Eight Tales of Disenchantment. Uttley, Alice Jane Taylor. Ede, Janina (1937-), illus. (Illus.). (ps-5). N.D. (ISBN 0-571-09361-2). Faber & Faber.
--Little Grey Rabbit & the Circus. Uttley, Alice Jane Taylor. Tempest, Margaret Mary (1892-1982), illus. (Illus.). (Little Grey Rabbit Ser.). (ps-3). N.D. (ISBN 0-00-194123-2). Collins-World.
--Little Grey Rabbit & the Snow Baby. Uttley, Alice Jane Taylor. (Illus.). (Little Grey Rabbit Ser.). (ps-3). 1975. (ISBN 0-00-194133-X). Collins-World.
--Little Grey Rabbit & the Weasels. Uttley, Alice Jane Taylor. Tempest, Margaret Mary (1892-1982), illus. (Illus.). (Little Grey Rabbit ser.). (gr. 1-4). N.D. (ISBN 0-00-194114-3). Collins-World.
--The Little Grey Rabbit Books. Uttley, Alice Jane Taylor, 15. Tempest, Margaret Mary (1892-1982), illus. 80p. N.D. British Book Centre.
--Little Grey Rabbit Goes to Sea. Uttley, Alice Jane Taylor. Tempest, Margaret Mary (1892-1982), illus. (Illus.). (Little Grey Rabbit Ser.). (ps-3). N.D. (ISBN 0-00-194119-4). Collins-World.
--Little Grey Rabbit Goes to the North Pole. Uttley, Alice Jane Taylor. (Little Grey Rabbit Ser.). (ps-3). 1970. (ISBN 0-00-194127-5). Collins World.
--Little Grey Rabbit Makes Lace. Uttley, Alice Jane Taylor. Tempest, Margaret Mary (1892-1982), illus. (Illus.). (Little Grey Rabbit Ser.). (ps-3). N.D. (ISBN 0-00-194116-X). Collins-World.
--Little Grey Rabbit to the Rescue. Uttley, Alice Jane Taylor. Tempest, Margaret Mary (1892-1982), illus. 64p. (Little Grey Rabbit Ser.). 1945. (ISBN 0-00-194113-5). Collins & World.
--Little Grey Rabbit's Birthday. Uttley, Alice Jane Taylor. Tempest, Margaret Mary (1892-1982), illus. (Illus.). (Little Grey Rabbit Ser). (ps-3). N.D. (ISBN 0-00-194111-9). Collins-World.
--Little Grey Rabbit's Christmas. Uttley, Alice Jane Taylor. Tempest, Margaret Mary (1892-1982), illus. (Illus.). (Little Grey Rabbit Ser.). (ps-3). N.D. (ISBN 0-00-194106-2). Collins-World.
--Little Grey Rabbit's House. Uttley, Alice Jane Taylor. Jaques, Faith (1923-), illus. (Illus.). 32p. (ps-2). 1983. (ISBN 0-399-20943-3, Philomel). Putnam Pub Group.
--Little Grey Rabbit's Paint Box. Uttley, Alice Jane Taylor. Tempest, Margaret Mary (1892-1982), illus. 64p. (Little Grey Rabbit Ser.). 1959. (ISBN 0-00-194121-6). Collins & World.
--Little Grey Rabbit's Pancake Day. Uttley, Alice Jane Taylor. Tempest, Margaret Mary (1892-1982), illus. (Illus.). (Little Grey Rabbit Ser.). (ps-3). N.D. (ISBN 0-00-194126-7). (ISBN 0-00-194143-7). Collins-World.
--Little Grey Rabbit's Party. Uttley, Alice Jane Taylor. Tempest, Margaret Mary (1892-1982), illus. (Illus.). (Little Grey Rabbit Ser.). (ps-3). N.D. (ISBN 0-00-194103-8). (ISBN 0-00-194147-X). Collins-World.
--Little Grey Rabbit's Spring Cleaning Party. Uttley, Alice Jane Taylor. Wigglesworth, Katherine, illus. 64p. (Little Grey Rabbit Ser.). 1972. (ISBN 0-00-194131-3). Collins & World.
--Little Grey Rabbit's Storybook. Uttley, Alice Jane Taylor. Tempest, Margaret Mary (1892-1982), illus. (Illus.). (Little Grey Rabbit Ser.). (ps-3). 1977. (ISBN 0-00-194162-3). Collins-World.
--Little Grey Rabbit's Valentine. Uttley, Alice Jane Taylor. Tempest, Margaret Mary (1892-1982), illus. (Illus.). (Little Grey Rabbit Ser.). (ps-3). N.D. (ISBN 0-00-194118-6). Collins-World.
--Little Grey Rabbit's Washing Day. Uttley, Alice Jane Taylor. Tempest, Margaret Mary (1892-1982), illus. (Illus.). (Little Grey Rabbit Ser.). (ps-3). N.D. (ISBN 0-00-194109-7). (ISBN 0-00-194141-0). Collins-World.
--Little Red Fox and the Wicked Uncle. Uttley, Alice Jane Taylor. Wigglesworth, Katherine, illus. LC 63-11655. (Illus.). 24cm. 62p. 1963. Bobbs-Merrill Co, Inc.
--Magic in My Pocket. Uttley, Alice Jane Taylor. (gr. 3-5). 1972. (ISBN 0-14-030108-9, Puffin). Penguin.
--Moldy Warp the Mole. Uttley, Alice Jane Taylor. Tempest, Margaret Mary (1892-1982), illus. (Illus.). (Little Grey Rabbit Ser.). (ps-3). N.D. (ISBN 0-00-194107-0). Collins-World.
--Mouse Telegrams. Uttley, Alice Jane Taylor. Wigglesworth, Katherine, illus. 68p. 1955. British Book Centre Inc.
--Sam Pig and the Singing Gate. Uttley, Alice Jane Taylor. N.D. Transatlantic Arts.
--Sam Pig Goes to the Seaside. Uttley, Alice Jane Taylor. Kennedy, A. E., illus. LC 61-2726. 21cm. 144p. N.D. Transatlantic Arts.
--The Sam Pig Storybook. Uttley, Alice Jane Taylor. Leslie, Cecil, illus. LC 84-13503. (ps-5). N.D. (ISBN 0-571-06413-2, Pub. by Faber & Faber). (ISBN 0-571-13406-8). Merrimack Pub Cir.
--Snug & Serena Count Twelve. Uttley, Alice Jane Taylor. Wigglesworth, Katherine, illus. LC 62-19331. (Illus.). 24cm. 60p. (gr. k-3). 1962. (ISBN 0-672-50501-0). Bobbs.
--Snug & Serena Go to Town. Uttley, Alice Jane Taylor. Wigglesworth, Katherine, illus. LC 63-19017. (Illus.). 24cm. 64p. (gr. 1-5). 1963. (ISBN 0-672-50503-7). Bobbs.
--Snug and Serena Meet a Queen. Uttley, Alice Jane Taylor. Wigglesworth, Katherine, illus. 72p. 1953. British Book Centre Inc.
--Snug and Serena Park Cowslips. Uttley, Alice Jane Taylor. Wigglesworth, Katherine, illus. 72p. 1950. British Book Centre Inc.
--Snug and the Chimney-Sweeper. Uttley, Alice Jane Taylor. Wigglesworth, Katherine, illus. 72p. 1953. British Book Centre Inc.
--Speckledy Hen. Uttley, Alice Jane Taylor. Tempest, Margaret Mary (1892-1982), illus. (Illus.). (Little Grey Rabbit Ser.). (ps-3). N.D. (ISBN 0-00-194112-7). Collins-World.
--Squirrel Goes Skating. Uttley, Alice Jane Taylor. Tempest, Margaret Mary (1892-1982), illus. 64p. (Little Grey Rabbit Ser.). 1934. (ISBN 0-00-194101-1). Collins & World.
--Squirrel, the Hare and the Little Grey Rabbit. Uttley, Alice Jane Taylor. Tempest, Margaret Mary (1892-1982), illus. 112p. 1929. British Book Centre Inc.
--Stories for Christmas. Uttley, Alice Jane Taylor. Lines, Kathleen, selected by. Rowe, Gavin, illus. LC 77-374142. (Illus.). 128 p. 23cm. 1977. (ISBN 0-571-11074-6). Faber.
--Stories for Christmas. Uttley, Alice Jane Taylor. Rowe, Gavin, illus. 1977. Penguin.
--Tales of the Four Pigs & Brock the Badger. Uttley, Alison Jane Taylor. Buckels, Alec, illus. (Illus.). (ps-5). 1939. (ISBN 0-571-06456-6, Pub. by Faber & Faber). Merrimack Pub Cir.
--Tim Rabbit and Company. Uttley, Alice Jane Taylor. Kennedy, A. E., illus. LC 59-65353. (Illus.). 128p. 21cm. 1959. Transatlantic Arts.
--Tim Rabbit's Dozen. Uttley, Alice Jane Taylor. Hughes, Shirley (1929-), illus. LC 66-2116. 80p. illus. 21cm. 1966, c.1964. Faber & Faber.
--Tim Rabbit's Dozen. Uttley, Alice Jane Taylor. Hughes, Shirley (1929-), illus. (gr. 1-4). N.D. Transatlantic.
--Toad's Castle. Uttley, Alice Jane Taylor. Wigglesworth, Katherine, illus. 72p. 1951. British Book Centre Inc.
--A Traveler in Time. Uttley, Alice Jane Taylor. Price, Christine Hilda (1928-1980), illus. LC 64-21478. (Illus.). 287 p. 21cm. 1964. Viking Press.
--A Traveller in Time. Uttley, Alice Jane Taylor. Bray, Phyllis, illus. (Illus.). 331p. 1st U.S. edition. (gr. 3-7). 1981. (ISBN 0-571-06182-6). Faber & Faber.
--The Washerwoman's Child. Uttley, Alice Jane Taylor. N.D. Transatlantic Arts.
--Water Rat's Picnic. Uttley, Alice Jane Taylor. Tempest, Margaret Mary (1892-1982), illus. (Illus.). (Little Grey Rabbit Ser.). (gr. k-3). N.D. (ISBN 0-00-194110-0). Collins-World.
--Wise Owl's Story. Uttley, Alice Jane Taylor. Tempest, Margaret Mary (1892-1982), illus. (Illus.). (Little Grey Rabbit Ser.). (ps-3). N.D. (ISBN 0-00-194102-X). Collins-World.

Utz, Lois (1932-)
--A Delightful Day with Bella Ballet. Utz, Lois (1932-), illus. LC 75-190267. (Illus.). 32 p. 25cm. 1972. (ISBN 0-87783-056-8). Oddo Pub.
--The Houndstooth Check. Utz, Lois (1932-), illus. LC 79-190268. (Illus.). 32 p. 25cm. 1972. (ISBN 0-87783-057-6). Oddo Pub.
--The King, the Queen, and the Lima Bean. Utz, Lois (1932-), illus. LC 73-93020. (Illus.). 31 p. 25cm. c.1974. Oddo Pub.
--The Pineapple Duck with the Peppermint Bill. LC 68-19231. (Illus.). 29 p. 29cm. 1968. Bobbs-Merrill.
--The Simple Pink Bubble That Ended the Trouble with Jonathan Hubble. Utz, Lois (1932-), illus. LC 78-190273. (Illus.). 32 p. 25cm. 1972. (ISBN 0-87783-062-2). Oddo Pub.

Uysal, Ahmet E., jt. auth. see Walker, Barbara Kerlin.

Uzilevsky, Marcus
--Old Testament Color & Story. Uzilevsky, Marcus, illus. (Illus.). 32p. 1st U.S. edition. 1974. (ISBN 0-912300-41-8). Troubador Pr.

Vaccaro, Michael A.
--The Happy World of Strawberry Shortcake. LC 80-53104. (Illus.). 11 p. 20cm. c.1981. (ISBN 0-394-84734-2). Random House.

Vacheron, Edith & Kahl, Virginia
--Here Is Henri!. LC 59-14326. (Illus.). 60 p. 21cm. 1959. Scribner.
--More About Henri. Kahl, Virginia (1919-), illus. LC 61-16811. (Illus.). 60p. (gr. 1-3). 1961. (ISBN 0-684-82153-2). Scribner.

Vaes, Alain
--The Porcelain Pepper Pot. Vaes, Alain, illus. LC 82-15303. (Illus.). 32p. (gr. k-3). 1982. (ISBN 0-316-89503-2). Little.
--The Wild Hamster. LC 85-5260. p. cm. c.1984. (ISBN 0-316-89504-0). Little, Brown.

Vaeth, Susan, jt. auth. see Crayder, Dorothy.

Vail, Esther C
--Snow King Lookout. Ricketts, Ralph E., illus. LC 65-3436. iii, 179 p. col. illus. 22 cm. (Ginn book-length stories). 1964. Ginn.

Vail, Jane (1913-)
--Becky's Little World: Stories of Becky and Her Friends and Playmates. 1st ed. Rupprecht, Elizabeth, illus. LC 57-9227. (Illus.). 21cm. 48p. 1957. Exposition Press.

Vail, Philip
--The Magnificent Adventures of Alexander MacKenzie. 216p. 1964. Dodd, Mead & Co.

Vaile, Charlotte Marion White, Mrs. (1852-1902)
--The M.M.C. A Story of the Great Rockies. Gallagher, Sears (1869-1955), illus. LC 4-16832. 232 p. front., plates. 19 1/2 cm. 1898. W. A. Wilde & Company.
--The Orcutt Girls: Or, One Term at the Academy. Merrill, Frank Thayer (1848-), illus. LC 4-16475. 316 p. front., 4 pl. 20 cm. 1896. W. A. Wilde & Company.
--Sue Orcutt. New. ed. (Illus.). 335p. 1910. W. A. Wilde Co.
--Sue Orcutt: A Sequel to "The Orcutt Girls". Merrill, Frank Thayer (1848-), illus. LC 4-16476. 335 p. front., 4 pl. 20 cm. 1897. W. A. Wilde & Company.
--The Truth About Santa Claus. LC 3-20455. 1 p. l., 60 p. front., plates. 19 cm. 1903. T. Y. Crowell & Co.
--Truth about Santa Claus. (Illus.). (Twentieth Century Ser.). 1905. Thomas Y. Crowell & Co.
--The Truth About Santa Claus. (Illus.). (The Sunshine Library for Young People). N.D. Thomas Y. Crowell.
--Two & One. LC 1-24905. 4 p. l., 102 p. front. 19 1/2 cm. (Sunshine Library). 1901. T. Y. Crowell & Co.
--Wheat and Huckleberries: Or, Dr. Northmore's Daughters. 336p. 1910. W. A. Wilde Co.
--Wheat and Huckleberries: Or Dr. Northmore's Daughters. Stephens, Alice Barber (1858-1932), illus. LC 99-4846. 336 p. front., plates. 19 1/2 cm. 1899. W. A. Wilde Company.

Vaizey, George de Horne Mrs. see Vaizey, Jessie Bell, Mrs.

Vaizey, Jessie Bell see Mansergh, Jessie, pseud.

Vaizey, Jessie Bell, Mrs. (1857-)
--About Peggy Saville. N.D. G.P. Putnam's Sons.
--Betty Trevor. LC 16-1548. (Illus.). 19.5 cm. 415p. 1916. G.P. Putnam's Sons.
--A College Girl. N.D. G.P. Putnam's Sons.
--The Fortunes of the Farrells. LC 8-22241. 416 p. front., 4 pl. 20 1/2 cm. 1908. G. W. Jacobs & Company.
--Pixie O'Shaughnessy. LC 7-39197. 368 p. front., 4 pl. 20 1/2 cm. 1907. G. W. Jacobs & Company.

--Pixie O'Shaughnessy. LC 7-39197. (Illus.). 20.5 cm. 368p. 1907. Macrae Smith.
--Sisters Three. LC 4747. 4 p. l., 280 p. front., plates. 19 cm. 1900. Cassell and Company.
--Tom and Some Other Girls: A Public School Story. Tarrant, Percy, illus. LC 1-24847. vi p. 2 l., 279 p. front., pl. 19 cm. 1901. Cassell and Company, Limited.

Vajda, Jerry
--Noah & His Animals. Obata Studios, illus. (Illus.). 12p. (Pre-School Children's Ser.). (ps). 1972. (ISBN 0-570-03406-X). Concordia.

Val, James
--The Legend of the Christmas Tree. 1st ed. Russell, Fredalee, illus. LC 73-85612. (Illus.). 32 p. 29cm. 1973. Val Productions.

Vale, Edmund see Vale, Henry Edmund Theodoric.

Vale, Henry Edmund Theodoric (1888-1969)
--Roc: A Dog's Eye View of War. LC 30-33157. xi, 177, 1 p. incl. front., illus., plates. 19 cm. 1930. E. P. Dutton & Co.
--Roc: A Dog's-Eye View of War. LC 43-13673. 213 p. incl. front., illus., plates. 20 1/2 cm. (Young moderns bookshelf). 1943. The Sun Dial Press.
--Roc: A Dog's Eye-View of War. LC 31-7375. 213 p. incl. front., illus., plates. 19 1/2 cm. 1931. W. Morrow & Company.

Valen, Herb
--The Boy Who Could Enter Paintings. 1st ed. Perl, Susan (1922-1983), illus. LC 67-21178. 58p. illus. (pt. col.) 21cm. 1968. Little, Brown.

Valen, Nanine Elisabeth, jt. auth. see Holman, Felice.

Valen, Nanine Elisabeth (1950-)
--The Devil's Tail. McPhail, Michael David (1940-), illus. LC 77-24135. p. cm. 1977. (ISBN 0-684-15292-4). Scribner.

Valencak, Hannelore
--A Tangled Web. LC 78-16715. 189 p. 22cm. 1978. (ISBN 0-688-22169-6). (ISBN 0-688-32169-0). Morrow.
--When Half-Gods Go. LC 76-6140. p. cm. c.1976. (ISBN 0-688-22077-0). Morrow.

Valens, Evans G., Jr. (1920-)
--Cybernaut. 48p. (gr. 10-12). 1968. (ISBN 0-670-25232-8). (ISBN 0-670-25233-6). Viking Pr.
--Me and Frumpet: An Adventure with Size and Science. 1st ed. Valens, Evans G., Jr. (1920-), illus. Teller, Edward (1908-), frwd. by. LC 58-7707. 127 p. illus. 24 cm. 1958. Dutton.
--Wildfire. 1st ed. Hurd, Clement (1908-), illus. LC 63-14772. (Illus.). 30cm. 1963. World Pub. Co.
--Wingfin and Topple. Hurd, Clement (1908-), illus. LC 62-16362. unpaged. illus. 80 cm. 1962. World Publ Co. **Award: (ALA).**

Valentin, Ursula
--Herr Minkepatt and His Friends. Wilkon, Jozef (1930-), illus. Roget, Elizabeth, tr. LC 65-23177. 25p. illus. (pt. col.) 28cm. (Venture Bk.). 1965. Braziller.

Valentine and Orson
--The Book of Fairy Tales: Contains "Jack and the Beanstalk", "Hop o' My Thumb", "Vale ntine and Orson", and "Jack the Giant Killer". Brock, Henry Matthew (1875-1960), illus. N.D. Frederick Warne & Co.
--The History and Adventures of the Renowned Princes Valentine and Orson. LC 16-3408. cover-title, 11 pl. 14 x 11 cm. 1813. W. Charles.
--The History of Valentine and Orson. LC 21-64055. cover-title, 34 p. illus. 14 cm. 1811. Printed and Published by Samuel Avery, at the Juvenile Bookstore, No. Newbury Street.
--Valentine & Orson. Brock, Henry Matthew (1875-1960), illus. LC 16-4885. cover-title, 12 p. illus., col. plates. 28 x 22 cm. (On cover: The Old Fairy Tales). 1916. F. Warne & Co.

Valentine, Grace
--Rollo's Conquest: Smiling Sally. LC 8-441. v p., 2 l., 3-76 p. front., illus., plates. 17 cm. (Her Little good nights). c.1907. The Lagatree Publishing Co.

Valentine, Helen Lachmann, Mrs. (1893-)
--Mary and Marie: Story. Sheldon, Myrtle, illus. LC 38-350124. 32 p. illus. (part col.) 31 cm. c.1938. Grosset and Dunlap.

Valentine, Laura Jewry, Mrs. (0000-1899)
--Aunt Louisa's Book of Animal Stories. (Illus.). 34cm. 94p. 1898. F. Warne & Co.
--Aunt Louisa's Book of Easy Poetry. (Illus.). 24cm. 94p. 1906. F. Warne & Co.
--Aunt Louisa's Book of Fairy Tales. (Illus.). 24cm. 94p. 1906. F. Warne & Co.
--Aunt Louisa's Book of Fairy Tales. LC 77-75700. (Illus.). 94 p. 28cm. c.1977. (ISBN 0-8055-0321-8). (ISBN 0-8055-1226-8). Hart Pub. Co.
--The Brave Days of Old. (Warne's Home Circle Library). N.D. Frederick Warne & Co.
--The Brave Days of Old. (Illus.). (The Home and Enterprise Library Ser.). N.D. Frederick Warne & Co.
--Daring and Doing. (Illus.). (The Home and Enterprise Library Ser.). N.D. Frederick Warne & Co.
--Maidenhood: Or, the Verge of the Stream. (Illus.). (Warne's Standard Gift Books Ser.). N.D. Scribner & Welford.
--Nursery Tales. 1875. Scribner, Welford, & Armstrong.
--Old Old Fairy Tales. (The Fairy Library). N.D. A. L. Burt Co.
--We Three Boys. (Warne's Adventure Library). N.D. Frederick Warne & Co.

Valentine, Laura Jewry, Mrs. (0000-1899), ed.
--Brave Deeds of Old. (Incident and Adventure Library). N.D. Scribner, Welford & Armstrong.
--Daring and Doing. (Incident and Adventure Library). N.D. Scribner, Welford & Armstrong.
--Eastern Tales, 1 of 6 Vols. (Illus.). (Warne's Lansdowne Fairy Library Ser.: Vol. 5). N.D. R. Worthington.
--Eastern Tales. (Warne's Lansdowne Fairy Library). N.D. Scribner, Welford, & Armstrong.
--Eastern Tales. (Illus.). (Warne's Favorite Fairy Tales). N.D. Scribner, Welford & Armstrong.
--The Girls' Home Book. (Illus.). N.D. Scribner & Welford.
--Heroism and Adventure: A Book for Boys, 1 of 15 Vols. (Illus.). (Warne's Hopeful Enterprise Library: Vol. 2). N.D. Scribner & Welford.
--The Merchant of Venice. LC 22-11339. (Original Author: William Shakespeare, 1564-1616). (Illus.). 27 x 22cm. 16p. (Shakespearian Tales in Verse). 1882. McLoughlin Brothers.
--Nursery Rhymes, Tales and Jingles. (Illus.). N.D. Scribner & Welford.
--Old, Old Fairy Tales. (Chandos Classics). N.D. Frederick Warne & Co.
--On Honor's Roll. (Warne's Golden Link Ser.). N.D. Frederick Warne & Co.
--The Taming of the Shrew. LC 22-11340. (Original Author: William Shakespeare, 1564-1616). (Illus.). 27 x 22cm. 16p. (Shakespearian Tales in Verse). 1882. McLoughlin Brothers.
--The Taming of the Shrew. LC 22-11341. (Original Author: William Shakespeare 1564-1616). (Illus.). 28 x 24cm. 17p. (Little Folks Shakespeare Ser.). 1882. P. G. Thomson.
--The Tempest. LC 22-11342. (Original Author: William Shakespeare. 1564-1616). (Illus.). 27 x 22cm. 16p. (Shakespearian Tales in Verse). 1882. McLoughlin Brothers.
--The Tempest. LC 22-11343. (Original Author: William Shakespeare, 1564-1616). (Illus.). 28 x 24cm. 17p. (Little Folks Shakespeare Ser.). 1882. P. G. Thomson.
--A Winter's Tale. LC 22-11344. (Original Author: William Shakespeare, 1564-1616). (Illus.). 27 x 22cm. 16p. (Shakespearian Tales in Verse). 1882. McLoughlin Brothers.
--A Winter's Tales. LC 22-11345. (Original Author: William Shakespeare, 1564-1616). (Illus.). 28 x 22cm. 17p. (Little Folks Shakespeare Ser.). 1883. P. G. Thomson.

Valentine, Louis Chapin (1889-)
--The Lonely Fisherman. Valentine, Louis Chapin (1889-), illus. LC 33-20978. 6 p. l., 11-74 p. col. front., illus., col. plates. 22 cm. c.1933. Thomas Y. Crowell Company.

Valera, Sinead O Flannagain De see De Valera, Sinead O Flannagain.

Valette, Andree De La see De La Valette, Andree.

Valjavac, Matija Kracmanov (1831-1897) & Vipotnik, Cene
--The Magic Ring: A Picture Story from Yugoslavia. Stupica, Marlenka, illus. LC 68-14682. (Illus.). 1 v. (unpaged. 27cm. 1st U.S. edition. 1968, c.1957. (ISBN 0-529-00472-0). World Pub. Co.

Vallario, Jean, jt. auth. see Hawkins, Mark.

Vallejo, Boris
--Boris. Vallejo, Boris, illus. (Illus.). (A Big Golden Picture Bk.). (gr. 6-9). 1979. (ISBN 0-307-13850-X, Golden Pr). Western Pub.
--The Boy Who Saved the Stars. Vallejo, Boris, illus. LC 79-101629. (Illus.). 32 p. c.1978. (ISBN 0-931064-05-8). O'Quinn Studios.

Valley, Elizabeth Frances Le see Le Valley, Elisabeth Frances.

Vallier, Jean, tr. see Lofting, Hugh John.

Vallier, Jean, tr. see Palmer, Helen Marion.

Vallings, Harold
--The Smuggler's of Haven Quay. (The Albion Library). N.D. Frederick Warne & Co.

Valmiki (1890-1936)
--Rama, the Hero of India: Valmiki's "Ramayana" Done into a Short English Version for Boys and Girls. D'Aulaire, Edgar Parin (1898-), illus. Mukerji, Dhan Gopal (1890-1936), tr. LC 30-23246. xv, 219, 2 p. incl. illus., plates. front. 21 cm. c.1930. E. P. Dutton & Co., Inc.

Vamba, pseud., see Bertelli, Luigi.

Van Aarle, Thomas see Aarle, Thomas Van.

Van Aarle, Thomas F.
--The Don't Put Your Cart Before the Horse Race. Barner, Bob (1947-), illus. LC 79-24102. p. cm. 1980. (ISBN 0-395-29095-3). Houghton Mifflin.

Van Aken, Helen
--Tatsu the Dragon. Noguchi, Yoshie, illus. LC 66-20675. (Illus.). 27cm. 191p. (gr. 1-4). 1966. (ISBN 0-8048-0568-7). C E Tuttle.

Van Akooy, Philip see Akooy, Philip Van.

Van Allen, Diane
--Always Alvin. Reilly, Veronica, illus. (Illus., Orig.). (ps). 1984. (ISBN 0-939332-11-6). Pohl Assoc.

Van Allsburg, Chris
--Ben's Dream. Van Allsburg, Chris, illus. LC 81-20029. (Illus.). 31 p. 27cm. 1982. (ISBN 0-395-32084-4). Houghton Mifflin. **Award: (NYT).**
--The Garden of Abdul Gasazi. Van Allsburg, Chris, illus. LC 79-17610. p. cm. 1979. (ISBN 0-395-27804-X). Houghton Mifflin. **Awards: (BGH); (ALA); (NYT); (RCM).**
--Jumanji. Van Allsburg, Chris, illus. LC 80-29632. (Illus.). 31 p. 1981. (ISBN 0-395-30448-2). Houghton Mifflin Co. **Awards: (RCM); (NYT); (ALA); (BGH).**
--The Mysteries of Harris Burdick. Van Allsburg, Chris, illus. LC 84-9006. (Illus.). unpaged. 1984. (ISBN 0-395-35393-9). Houghton Mifflin. **Awards: (BGH); (ALA).**
--The Polar Express. Van Allsburg, Chris, illus. LC 85-10907. (Illus.). 32 p. 1985. (ISBN 0-395-38949-6). Houghton Mifflin. **Awards: (NYT); (ALA); (RCM).**
--The Wreck of the Zephyr. Van Allsburg, Chris, illus. LC 82-23371. (Illus.). 32p. 1983. (ISBN 0-395-33075-0). HM. **Awards: (NYT); (ALA).**

Van Alstine, Lois, jt. auth. see Colle, Alfred.

Van Alstine, Lois, jt. auth. see Thompson, Minna Burnette.

Van Alstyne, Margaret Ware
--Stories of Alphadorus. LC 43-53. cover-title, 91 p. 23 cm. 1942. Printed by Bridge & Byron.

Van Anrooy, Francine see Van Anrooy, Frans, pseud.

Van Anrooy, Frans, pseud., see Van Anrooy, Francine.

Van Anrooy, Frans see Anrooy, Frans Van.

Van Anrooy, Frans, pseud. (1924-)
--The Bird Tree. Van Anrooy, Francine. Tol, Jaap, illus. (Illus.). il. (ps-3). N.D. (ISBN 0-15-207890-8). HarBraceJ.
--Lady of the Sea. Van Anrooy, Francine. Tol, Jaap, illus. LC 79-108013. (Illus.). color ils. 1st U.S. edition. (gr. 2-5). 1971. (ISBN 0-87614-027-4). Carolrhoda Bks.
--Lady of the Sea. Van Anrooy, Francine. Tol, Jaap, illus. (Illus.). (gr. k-5). 1970 (Dist. by Silver). Scroll Pr.
--Sea Horse. Van Anrooy, Francine. Tol, Jaap, illus. (Illus.). (gr. k-3). 1968. (ISBN 0-15-271440-5). HarBraceJ.

Van Aver, Philip, ed.
--Mother Goose: Twenty Nursery Rhymes. Van Aver, Philip, illus. LC 76-359240. (Illus.). 23 leaves. 29cm. 1970. Grabhorn-Hoyem.

Vanbrugh, Allen
--The Field of Senlac. Godfrey, Michael, illus. LC 68-4400. (Illus.). 23cm. 190p. (Merit bk. ed.). 1968, c.1966. Houghton.

Van Buren, Caroline
--Five Little Martins and the Martin House. LC 31-114. vii, 286 p. 19 1/2 cm. c.1930. Marshall Jones Company.

Van Buren, Maud (1869-) & Bemis, Katharine Isabel, eds.
--Christmas in Storyland. LC 27-20264. 5 p. l., 3-328 p. 19 1/2 cm. c.1927. The Century Co.

Vance, Clara, pseud., see Denison, Mary Andrews.

Vance, Clara, et al., pseud. (1826-1911)
--Original Five Hundred Dollar Prize Stories Series, Part First: Containing "Andy Luttrell," "Master and Pupil," "Shining Hours" and "Sabrina Hacket". Denison, Mary Andrews, 4 vols. N.D. Set. D. Lothrop & Co.

Vance, Clara, pseud. (1826-1911)
--Andy Luttrell. Denison, Mary Andrews, 1 of 6 vols. (Author of "Andy Luttrell."). (Illus.). N.D. D. Lothrop & Co.
--Andy Luttrell. Denison, Mary Andrews, 1 of 50 vols. (Illus.). (Young People's Library: No. 1). N.D. Set. Lothrop Publishing Co.
--Barbara. Denison, Mary Andrews, 1 0f 50 vols. (Illus.). 350p. (Sunday-School Lib: No. 14). N.D. Set. Lothrop Pub. Co.
--Grandmother Normandy. Denison, Mary Andrews, 1 of 50 vols. (Illus.). 350p. (Sunday-School Lib: No. 14). N.D. Set. Lothrop Pub. Co.
--Hidden Treasures. Denison, Mary Andrews, 1 of 6 vols. (Author of "Andy Luttrell."). (Illus.). N.D. D. Lothrop & Co.
--Hidden Treasures. Denison, Mary Andrews, 1 of 50 vols. (Illus.). 350p. (Sunday-School Lib: No. 14). N.D. Set. Lothrop Pub. Co.
--Silent Tom. Denison, Mary Andrews, 1 of 6 vols. (Illus.). N.D. D Lothrop.
--Strawberry Hill. Denison, Mary Andrews, 1 of 50 vols. (Illus.). 350p. (Sunday-School Lib: No. 14). N.D. Set. Lothrop Pub. Co.
--The Talbury Girls. Denison, Mary Andrews, 1 of 6 vols. LC 21-15383. (Author of "Andy Luttrell."). (Illus.). 19cm. 487p. (On cover: Household library, no. 11.). 1887. D. Lothrop & Co.
--The Talbury Girls. Denison, Mary Andrews, 1 of 50 vols. (Illus.). 350p. (Sunday-School Lib: No. 14). N.D. Set. Lothrop Pub. Co.

Vance, Eleanor Graham (1908-), ed. see Sewell, Anna.

Vance, Eleanor Graham (1908-)
--Jonathan. Pucci, Albert John (1920-), illus. LC 66-111563. 30p. col. illus. 27cm. c.1966. Follett.
--The Tall Book of Fairy Tales. Sharp, William (1900-), illus. (Illus.). 124p. (Tall Bks.). (gr. k-3). 1980. (ISBN 0-06-025545-5, HarpJ). (ISBN 0-06-025546-3). Har-Row.

Vance, Eleanor Graham (1908-), retold by.
--Adventures of Robin Hood. Barnum, Jay Hyde (1888-1967), illus. Frank, Josette (1893-), contrib. by. LC 53-6291. unpaged. illus. 29cm. c.1953. (ISBN 0-394-80677-8). (ISBN 0-394-90677-2). Random House.
--Bedtime Stories: Cinderella, Snow White, The Emperor's New Clothes, Why the Sea Is Salt. Stern, Marie Simchow (1909-), illus. Masha, pseud. LC 46-7997. 41 p. illus. (part col.) 25 x 19 1/2 cm. 1946. Wonder Books.
--Famous Fairy Tales: Jack and the Beanstalk, the Fisherman and His Wife, The Real Princess, Hansel and Gretel. Jules, Mervin (1912-), illus. LC 46-21746. 42 p. incl. front., illus (part col.) 25 x 19 1/2 cm. c.1946. Wonder Books.
--Favorite Nursery Tales. Graham, Eleanor, pseud. Dixon, Rachel Taft, illus. LC 46-21571. (Illus.). 41p. 25 x 19cm. 1946. Wonder Books.
--From Little to Big: A Parade of Animal Poems. Goldsborough, June (1923-), illus. LC 74-159324. (Illus.). 30 p. 23cm. 1972. (ISBN 0-695-80235-6). (ISBN 0-695-40235-8). Follett.
--The Tall Book of Fairy Tales. Sharp, William (1900-), illus. LC 47-11762. 124 p. illus. (part col.) 31 x 14 cm. 1947. (ISBN 0-06-025545-5). Harper.

Vance, Jack, pseud., see Vance, John Holbrook.

Vance, Jack, pseud. (1920-)
--Vandals of the Void. Vance, John Holbrook. (Winston Science Fiction Ser.). (gr. 7-9). 1952. (ISBN 0-03-034475-1). HR&W.

Vance, John Holbrook see Vance, Jack, pseud.

Vance, Louis Joseph, created by see Smith, Carl W.

Vance, Marguerite (1889-1965)
--The Beloved Friend. Weisgard, Leonard Joseph (1916-), illus. LC 63-19644. 120 p. illus. 24 cm. 1963. Colonial Williamsburg; Distributed by Holt, Rinehart and Winston, New York.
--The Boy on the Road: A Christmas Story. 1st ed. Walker, Nedda, illus. LC 55-8335. 53p. illus. 21cm. 1955. Dutton.
--Courage at Sea. 1st ed. Bjorklund, Lorence F. (1913-1978), illus. LC 63-8600. (Illus.). 86 p. 21cm. 1963. Dutton.
--Elizabeth Tudor, Sovereign Lady. 1st ed. Walker, Nedda, illus. LC 54-8854. 156p. illus. 21cm. 1954. Dutton.
--Esther Wheelwright: Indian Captive. 1st ed. Bjorklund, Lorence F. (1913-1978), illus. LC 64-13918. 96p. illus. 21cm. c.1964. Dutton.
--A Flower From Dinah. Suba, Susanne (1913-), illus. LC 62-7493. 23 cm. 46p. 1962. E. P. Dutton & Co.
--The Jacksons of Tennessee. 1st ed. Walker, Nedda, illus. LC 53-60828. 181p. illus. 22cm. 1953. Dutton.
--Jared's Gift: A Christmas Story. Lonette, Reisie Dominee (1924-), illus. LC 65-21294. (Illus.). 21cm. 42p. (gr. 2-5). 1965. Dutton.
--Jeptha and the New People. MacLean, Robert (1926-), illus. LC 60-6008. 113 p. illus. 22 cm. 1960. Dutton.
--Lady Jane Grey, Reluctant Queen. 1st ed. Walker, Nedda, illus. LC 52-8246. (Illus.). 21cm. 184p. 1952. Dutton.
--Leave It to Linda. 1st ed. Morse, Dorothy Bayley (1906-1979), illus. LC 58-5234. 125 p. illus. 22 cm. 1958. Dutton.
--The Lees of Arlington: The/Story of Mary and Robert E. Lee. 1st ed. Walker, Nedda, illus. LC 49-11012. (Illus.). 21cm. 160p. 1949. E. P. Dutton.
--Marta. Boyle, Mildred, illus. LC 37-391083. 56 p. incl. col. front., col. plates. 16 1/2 cm. 1937. Harper and Brothers.
--Martha, Daughter of Virginia: The Story of Martha Washington. 1st ed. Walker, Nedda, illus. LC 47-6044. 190 p. illus. 21 cm. 1947. E. P. Dutton.
--Patsy Jefferson of Monticello. 1st ed. Walker, Nedda, illus. LC 48-4837. 154 p. illus. 21 cm. 1948. E. P. Dutton.
--Paula. Angelo, Valenti (1897-), illus. LC 39-244390. 4 p. l., 223 p. illus. 22 1/2 cm. 1939. Dodd, Mead & Company.

AUTHOR INDEX VANDE VELDE

--Paula Goes Away to School. Barney, Maginel Wright, Mrs. (1881-1966), illus. LC 40-311207. 4 p. l., 276 p. illus. 21 x 16 cm. 1940. Dodd, Mead & Company.
--A Rainbow for Robin. Longtemps, Kenneth (1933-), illus. LC 66-11388. 88p. illus. 21cm. c.1966. Dutton.
--Secret for a Star. LC 57-5339. (Illus.). 249 p. 21cm. 1957. Dutton.
--Song for a Lute. 1st ed. Pellicer, Joseph Luis, illus. LC 58-9566. (Illus.). 160 p. 21cm. 1958. Dutton.
--Star for Hansi. Paull, Grace A. (1898-), illus. LC 57-11631. (Illus.). 17cm. 30p. (gr. 3-5). 1957. (ISBN 0-525-39894-5). Dutton.
--A Star for Hansi. Paull, Grace A. (1898-), illus. LC 36-21312. 19cm. 30p. 1936. Harper & Bros.
--While Shepherds Watched. Walker, Nedda, illus. (Illus.). (gr. 2-4). N.D. (ISBN 0-525-42610-8). Dutton.
--Willie Joe and His Small Change. N.D. E . M. Hale and Co.
--Willie Joe and His Small Change. 1st ed. MacLean, Robert (1926-), illus. LC 59-5844. 116 p. illus. 21 cm. 1959. Dutton.
--Windows for Rosemary. 1st ed. Doares, Robert G., illus. LC 56-5268. 60 p. illus. 21 cm. 1956. Dutton.
--The World for Jason. 1st ed. MacLean, Robert (1926-), illus. LC 61-5869. 152 p. illus. 21 cm. 1961. Dutton.

Vance, Willowdean Wooten
--The Sad Pol Parrot Who Couldn't, and Other Stories. Normand, Thomas, illus. LC 57-31009. 40p. illus. 20cm. c.1956. American Guild Press.

Van Cleefe, Mark, et al.
--Charlie the Lonesome Cougar. Cassell, Bob, illus. LC 68-12388. (Based on a Walt Disney Screenplay). (Illus.). 78 p. 22cm. 1968. Four Winds Press.

Van Clief, Sylvia Worth, jt. auth. see Heide, Florence Parry.

Vandegriff, Peggy
--Dy-Dee Doll's Days. Fields, Lawson, photos by. LC 37-37804. 63 p. illus. 17 cm. c.1937. Rand, McNally & Company.

Vandegrift, Kate
--Maximilian. LC 71-80281. 188 p. 22cm. 1969. Meredith Press.

Vandegrift, Margaret, pseud., see Janvier, Margaret Thomson.

Vandegrift, Margaret, pseud. (1845-)
--The Absent-Minded Fairy. Janvier, Margaret Thomson. Bensell, Edmund B., illus. LC 11-9376. 25cm. 117p. 1884. Ketterlinus Printing House.
--Clover Beach. Janvier, Margaret Thomson. (Illus.). 8cm. 287p. 1900. W. B. Conkey Co.
--Clover Beach: A Book for Boys and Girls. Janvier, Margaret Thomson. (Illus.). 1888. Porter & Coates.
--Clover Beach for Boys and Girls. Janiver, Margaret Thomson. 287 p. incl. front., illus, pl. 1900. W. B. Conkey.
--The Dead Doll, and Other Poems. Janvier, Margaret Thomson. (Illustrated Quarto Juveniles). N.D. Houghton, Mifflin and Company.
--The Dead Doll and Other Verses. Janvier, Margaret Thomson. (Illus.). 1888. Ticknor & Co.
--Doris and Theodora. Janvier, Margaret Thomson. (Ways and Means Library). N.D. John C. Winston Co.
--Doris and Theodora. Janvier, Margaret Thomson, 1 of 4 vols. LC 12-34621. 381 p. front., plates. 20 cm. (Roundabout Lib.). (Ways & Means Library). c.1884. Porter & Coates.
--Doris and Theodora: A Story for Girls. Janvier, Margaret Thomson. (Illus.). 1888. Porter & Coates.
--Holiday at Home: For Boys and Girls. Janvier, Margaret Thomson. (Illus.). 1888. Porter & Coates.
--Holidays at Home. Janvier, Margaret Thomson. (Illus.). 8cm. 302p. 1900. W. B. Conkey Co.
--Holidays at Home: For Boys and Girls. Janvier, Margaret Thomson. (Illus.). N.D. Porter & Coates.
--Little Helpers. Janvier, Margaret Thomson. (Illustrated Quarto Juveniles). N.D. Houghton, Mifflin and Company.
--Little Helpers. Janvier, Margaret Thomson. (Illus.). 1888. Ticknor & Co.
--Queen's Body Guard. Janvier, Margaret Thomson, 1 of 4 vols. (Roundabout Library). (Ways and Means Library). N.D. John C. Winston Co.
--The Queen's Body Guard. Janvier, Margaret Thomson. (Illus.). c.1888. Porter & Coates.
--The Queen's Body-Guard. Janvier, Margaret Thomson, 1 of 4 vols. (Roundabout Lib.). (Ways & Means Library). 1891. Set. Porter & Coates.
--Under the Dog-star. Janvier, Margaret Thomson. (Illus.). 8cm. 315p. 1900. W. B. Conkey Co.
--Under the Dog Star: For Boys and Girls. Janvier, Margaret Thomson. (Illus.). N.D. Porter & Coates.
--Ways and Means. Janvier, Margaret Thomson, 1 of 4 vols. (Roundabout Library). (Ways and Means Library). N.D. John C. Winston Co.
--Ways & Means. Janvier, Margaret Thomson, 1 of 4 vols. (Roundabout Lib.). (Ways & Means Library). 1891. Set. Porter & Coates.

Van De Hulst, Willem Gerrit (1879-)
--The Big Read-to-Me Story Book. Van De Hulst, Willen Gerrit (1879-), illus. Schooland, Marian, tr. LC 63-20389. 178 p. illus. (part col.) 27 cm. c.1963. Zondervan Pub. House.

Vandenberg, Frank
--Curly. LC 47-28818. 88 p. 21 cm. 1947. W. B. Eerdmans Pub. Co.
--Rusty. LC 42-251834. 88 p. 20 cm. 1942. Wm. B. Eerdmans Publishing Co.

Van Den Honert, Dorry
--Demi, the Baby Sitter. Wohlberg, Meg (1905-), illus. LC 61-5213. unpaged. illus. 26 cm. (Morrow Junior Bks.). 1961. Morrow.

Vander Boom, Mae M
--The Shepherd's Boy. Seitz, Patricia, illus. LC 74-84814. (Illus.). 47 p. 21cm. 1969. Augsburg Pub. House.

Vanderbilt, Sarah Watson Sanderson, Mrs. (1878-)
--Who's Who in the Land of Nod. Winckler, Ruby, illus. LC 15-19263. vii, 1 p. 21, 3-103, 5 p. incl. illus., plates. front. 21 1/2 x 17 1/2 cm. 1915. Houghton Mifflin Company.

Vander Boom, Mae M.
--The Shephard's Boy. 48p. 1969. Lutheran Publications.
--Shepherd's Boy. Seity, Pat, illus. LC 78-84814. (Illus.). ca. 48p. (gr. 7 up). 1969. (ISBN 0-8066-0926-5). Augsburg.

Vandercook, Margaret O'Bannon Womack, Mrs. (1876-)
--The Camp Fire Girls Across the Seas. LC 15-3865. 254 p. incl. front., illus. 19 cm. c.1914. The John C. Winston Co.
--The Camp Fire Girls Amid the Snows. LC 14-5315. 264 p. incl. front., illus. 19 cm. c.1913. The John C. Winston Co.
--The Camp Fire Girls at Half Moon Lake. LC 22-21109. 224 p. incl. front., illus. 18 1/2 cm. c.1921. The John C. Winston Co.
--The Camp Fire Girls at Sunrise Hill. (Illus.). 19cm. 256p. (Stories About Camp Fire Girls). 1913. John C. Winston.
--The Camp Fire Girls at the End of the Trail. LC 19-420. 240 p. incl. front. 19 cm. c.1917. The John C. Winston Co.
--The Camp Fire Girls Behind the Lines. LC 20-8039. 249 p. incl. front., illus. 19 cm. c.1918. The John C. Winston Co.
--The Camp Fire Girls by the Blue Lagoon. LC 23-7012. 1 p. l., 5-240 p. front., illus. 19 cm. c.1921. The John C. Winston Co.
--The Camp Fire Girls' Careers. (Stories About Camp Fire Girls). N.D. John C. Winston.
--The Camp Fire Girls in After Years. LC 15-179771. 249 p. incl. front., illus. 19 cm. c.1915. The John C. Winston Co.
--The Camp Fire Girls in Glorious France. (Stories About Camp Fire Girls). N.D. John C. Winston.
--The Camp Fire Girls in Merrie England. (Stories About Camp Fire Girls). N.D. John C. Winston.
--The Camp Fire Girls in the Outside World. LC 15-3416. 262 p. incl. front., plates. 19 cm. c.1914. The John C. Winston Co.
--The Camp Fire Girls on the Edge of the Desert. LC 19-15483. 274 p. incl. front., illus. 19 cm. c.1917. The John C. Winston Co.
--The Camp Fire Girls on the Field of Honor. LC 20-803854. 272 p. incl. front., illus. 19 cm. c.1918. The John C. Winston Co.
--The Girl Scouts and the Open Road. LC 23-13264. 224 p. incl. front. 19 cm. (Her Girl Scouts Ser.). c.1923. The John C. Winston Company.
--The Girl Scouts in Beechwood Forest. LC 22-10773. v, 7-224 p. front., 19 1/2 cm. (Her Girl Scouts Ser.). c.1921. The John C. Winston Company.
--The Girl Scouts in Mystery Valley. LC 23-132652. 224 p. incl. front 19 cm. (Her Girl Scouts Ser.). c.1923. The John C. Winston Company.
--The Girl Scouts of the Eagle's Wing. LC 22-21110. 224 p. incl. front. 18 1/2 cm. (Her Girl Scouts Ser.). c.1921. The John C. Winston Company.
--The Girl Scouts of the Round Table. LC 22-107722. 239 p. front. 19 1/2 cm. (Her Girl scouts series). c.1921. The John C. Winston Company.
--The Ranch Girls and the Mystery of the Three Roads. Pilsbry, Elizabeth, illus. LC 25-8734. 249 p. front., plates. 19 cm. (Her Ranch Girls Ser.). c.1924. The John C. Winston Company.
--The Ranch Girls at Boarding School. (The Ranch Girls Ser.). N.D. John C. Winston Co.
--The Ranch Girls at Home Again. New ed. (The Ranch Girls Ser.). 1915. John C. Winston Co.
--The Ranch Girls at Rainbow Lodge. (The Ranch Girls Ser.). N.D. John C. Winston Co.
--The Ranch Girls in Europe. Ginther, Mary Pemberton, illus. LC 15-3417. 248 p. front., plates. 19 cm. (Her The Ranch Girls Ser.). c.1914. The John C. Winston Company.
--The Ranch Girls' Pot of Gold. Bodine, Hugh A., illus. LC 12-180134. 296 p. front., plates. 19 1/2 cm. (Her The Ranch Girls Ser.). c.1912. The John C. Winston Company.
--The Red Cross Girls in Belgium. LC 18-152611. 269 p. front., plates. 19 cm. c.1916. The John C. Winston Company.
--The Red Cross Girls in the British Trenches. LC 16-10721. 287 p. front. 19 cm. $0.3. c.1916. The John C. Winston Company.
--The Red Cross Girls in the National. (The "Red Cross Girls" Ser.). N.D. John C. Winston.
--The Red Cross Girls on the French Firing Line. LC 16-10722. (Illus.). 19 cm. 264p. (The Red Cross Girls Ser.). 1916. John C. Winston.
--The Red Cross Girls with Pershing to Victory. LC 19-174801. 267 p. front. 19 cm. c.1919. The John C. Winston Company.
The Red Cross Girls with Pershing to Victory. 207 p. front. 19 cm. 1949. The John C. Winston Company.
--The Red Cross Girls With The Belgium Defenders. (Illus.). (The Red Cross Girl Ser.). N.D. John C. Winston Co.
--The Red Cross Girls with the Italian Army. LC 18-10275. 19cm. 261p. (The Red Cross Girls Ser.). 1917. John C. Winston.
--The Red Cross Girls With the Marines. (The "Red Cross Girls" Ser.). N.D. John C. Winston.
--The Red Cross Girls with the Russian Army. LC 18-11825. 265 p. front. 19 cm. c.1916. The John C. Winston Company.
--The Red Cross Girls with the Stars and Stripes. LC 18-102766. 263 p. front. 19 cm. (Her The Red cross girls series). c.1918. The John C. Winston Company.

Van Der Essen
--The Frog & Three Other Stories. (Illus.). 32p. (Yok-Yok Ser.). (gr. k-3). 1983. (ISBN 0-87191-927-3). Creative Ed.
--The Magician & Three Other Stories. (Illus.). 32p. (Yok-Yok Ser.). (gr. k-3). 1983. (ISBN 0-87191-928-1). Creative Ed.
--The Night & Three Other Stories. (Illus.). 32p. (Yok-Yok Ser.). (gr. k-3). 1983. (ISBN 0-87191-929-X). Creative Ed.
--The Rabbit & Three Other Stories. (Illus.). 32p. (Yok-Yok Ser.). (gr. k-3). 1983. (ISBN 0-87191-930-3). Creative Ed.

Van Der Groen, Bo see Groen, Bo Van Der.

Van Der Haas, Henrietta
--Orange on Top. Wallower, Lucille (1910-), illus. LC 45-28344. 5 p. l., 3-221 p. incl. front., illus., plates. 21 cm. 1945. Harcourt, Brace and Company.
--Victorious Island. Hordyk, Gerald (1899-), illus. LC 47-30517. 4 l., 3-193 p. illus., maps. 21 cm. 1947. Harcourt, Brace.

Vander Heide, Helen
--A Friend for Beanie. LC 52-666. 127 p. illus. 23 cm. 1951. Moody Press.

Van Der Horst, Brian
--Folk Music in America. LC 75-16255. 72p. (First Bks.). (gr. 4-6). 1972. (ISBN 0-531-00767-7). Watts.

Van Der Land, Sipke, retold by.
--Stories from the Bible. Bouman, Bert, illus. Barendrecht, C., tr. from Dutch. LC 79-10049. (gr. 4-6). 1979. (ISBN 0-8028-5010-3). Eerdmans.

Van Der Meer, Atie, jt. auth. see Van Der Meer, Ron.

Van der Meer, Ron (1945-)
--Basil & Boris in London. (ps-3). 1977. (ISBN 0-8277-5411-6). (ISBN 0-8277-5410-8). British Bk Ctr.
--Basil & Boris in New York. (ps-3). 1977. (ISBN 0-8277-5413-2). (ISBN 0-8277-5412-4). British Bk Ctr.
--The Case of the Kidnapped Dog. (Illus.). 12p. (gr. 1-5). 1984. (ISBN 0-333-34220-8, Pub. by Salem Hse Ltd). Merrimack Pub Cir.
--Monster Island. Van der Meer, Atie, illus. LC 82-138644. (Illus.). 10 p. 28cm. c.1981. (ISBN 0-03-059348-4). Holt, Rinehart, and Winston.

Van Der Meer, Ron (1945-) & Van Der Meer, Atie
--Basil & Boris in London. 1979. (ISBN 0-85122-169-6, Pub. by Dinosaur Pubns). Merrimack Pub Cir.
--Basil & Boris in North America. (ps-2). 1979. (ISBN 0-85122-168-8, Pub. by Dinosaur Pubns). Merrimack Pub Cir.
--Funny Fingers. (Illus.). 14p. 1st U.S. edition. (ps). 1983. (ISBN 0-434-97104-9, Pub. by W. Heinemann England). David & Charles.
--I'm Fed up!. (Illus.). 32p. 1st U.S. edition. (ps-3). 1982. (Pub. by Hamish Hamilton England). David & Charles.
--My Brother Sammy. (Illus.). 32p. 1980. (Pub. by Hamish Hamilton England). David & Charles.
--Naughty Sammy. (Illus.). 32p. 1980. (Pub. by Hamish Hamilton England). David & Charles.
--Oh Lord!. LC 79-24493. (Illus.). 32 p. 26cm. 1980, c.1979. (ISBN 0-517-54006-1). Crown.
--Sammy & the Cat Party. (Illus.). 32p. 1st U.S. edition. 1980. (Pub. by Hamish Hamilton England). David & Charles.

Van der Meer, Wybe J.
--The Miracle Pond. Van der Meer, Madge E., illus. (Illus.). 48p. (Orig.). (gr. 1-4). 1979. (ISBN 0-934744-00-9). Vermeer Arts.
--The Miracle Pond. 2nd ed. Van Der Meer, Madge E., illus. (Illus.). 48p. (gr. 1-4). 1980. (ISBN 0-934744-01-7). Vermeer Arts.

Vandersteen, Willy
--The Circus Baron. Lahey, Nicholas J., tr. from Flemish. LC 75-8497. (Illus.). 56p. (Orig.). 1st U.S. edition. (Adventures of Willy & Wanda Ser.). (gr. 3 up). 1976. (ISBN 0-915560-21-6).. Hiddigeigei.
--The Iron Flowerpotters. Lahey, Nicholas J., tr. from Flemish. LC 76-49376. (Illus., Orig.). 1st U.S. edition. (The Adventures of Willy & Wanda). (gr. 3-8). 1977. (ISBN 0-915560-11-9). Hiddigeigei.
--An Island Called Hoboken. Lahey, Nicholas J., tr. from Flemish. LC 75-8496. (Illus.). 56p. (Orig.). 1st U.S. edition. (Adventures of Willy & Wanda Ser.). (gr. 3 up). 1976. (ISBN 0-915560-01-1). Hiddigeigei.
--The King Drinks. Lahey, Nicholas J., tr. from Flemish. LC 77-78696. (Illus., Orig.). 1st U.S. edition. (The Adventures of Willy & Wanda). (gr. 3-8). 1977. (ISBN 0-915560-04-6). Hiddigeigei.
--The Merry Musketeers. Lahey, Nicholas J., tr. from Flemish. LC 75-8495. (Illus.). 56p. (Orig.). 1st U.S. edition. (Adventures of Willy & Wanda Ser.). (gr. 3 up). 1976. (ISBN 0-915560-18-6). Hiddigeigei.
--The Tender-Hearted Matador: Duck, Lambik, or Your Goose Is Cooked!. Lahey, Nicholas J., tr. LC 75-8494. (Illus.). 56p. (Orig.). 1st U.S. edition. (Adventures of Willy & Wanda Ser.). (gr. 3 up). 1976. (ISBN 0-915560-10-0). Hiddigeigei.
--The Zincshrinker. Lahey, Nicholas J., tr. from Flemish. LC 76-49379. (Illus., Orig.). 1st U.S. edition. (The Adventures of Willy & Wanda). (gr. 3-8). 1977. (ISBN 0-915560-03-8). Hiddigeigei.

Van Derveer, Helen R
--The Little Sallie Mandy Story Book. Willis, Bess Goe, illus. LC 30-8180. 3 p. l., 11-63, 1 p. col. front., col. illus. 23 cm. c.1930. Henry Altemus Company.

Van Der Veer, Judy (1912-1982)
--Gray Mare's Colts. Garbutt, Bernard (1900-), illus. (Illus.). 25 drawings. 96p. (gr. 5 up). 1971. (ISBN 0-516-08818-1, Golden Gate). Childrens.
--Higher Than the Arrow. Matthews, F. Leslie, illus. LC 68-22393. (Illus.). 132 p. 22cm. 1969. Golden Gate Junior Books.
--Hold the Rein Free. Garbutt, Bernard (1900-), illus. LC 66-9181. 243 p. illus. 24 cm. 1966. Golden Gate Junior Books.
--Long Trail for Francisco. LC 74-7480. 108 p. 21cm. 1974. Childrens Press.
--To the Rescue. 1st ed. Galdone, Paul (1914-), illus. LC 79-82639. (Illus.). 160 p. 21cm. 1969. Harcourt, Brace & World.
--Wallace the Wandering Pig. 1st ed. Galdone, Paul (1914-), illus. LC 67-17159. (Illus.). 156 p. 21cm. 1967. Harcourt, Brace & World.

Van Derveer, Lettie Cook
--Short Plays for Just Us Fellows: A Collection of Nine Peppy Plays for Boys. 79 p. 19 cm. 1929. Eldridge Entertainment House, Inc.

Vandervelde, Marjorie Mills (1908-)
--Across the Tundra. (Indian Culture Ser.). (gr. 4-12). 1972. (ISBN 0-89992-053-5). MT Coun Indian.
--Could It Be Old Hiari. (Indian Culture Ser.). (gr. 5-9). 1975. (ISBN 0-89992-040-3). MT Coun Indian.
--Sam & the Golden People. (Indian Culture Ser.). (gr. 4-9). 1972. (ISBN 0-89992-027-6). MT Coun Indian.

Van der Voort, Carl
--Monkey Stories. Hyde, Helen H., illus. LC 39-6271. (Illus.). 61p. 20cm. 1938. B. Humphries.

Van Deusen, Elizabeth Kneipple, pseud., see Roberts, Edith Elizabeth Kneipple.

Van Deusen, Elizabeth Kneipple, pseud.
--Stories of Porto Rico. N.D. Silver Burdett & Co.

Vande Velde, Vivian
--A Hidden Magic. Hyman, Trina Schart (1939-), illus. LC 85-16643. p. cm. c.1985. (ISBN 0-517-55534-4). Crown.
--Once upon a Test: Three Light Tales of Love. Fay, Ann, ed. Hearn, Diane Dawson, illus. LC 84-17283. (Illus.). 32p. (gr. 4up). 1984. (ISBN 0-8075-6070-7). A Whitman.

Vandevere, Lillian J.
--A Pet for Peter. Werber, Adele & Laslo, Doris, illus. LC 50-14877. 17cm. 32p. (Rand McNally Book-elf Junior Series). 1950. Rand McNally & Co.

Van De Water, Frederic Franklyn (1890-1968)
--Elmer 'n Edwina. LC 28-5636. 3 p. l., 289 p. 19 1/2 cm. 1928. D. Appleton and Company.

Van De Water, John Ward
--A Rock on the Hudson. LC 84-14398. 116 p. 22cm. c.1984. (ISBN 0-912526-37-8). Empire State Fiction.

Vandewater, Rosalie
--Two Tea Parties. De Meza, Wilson, illus. 256p. N.D. Cassell, Petter, Galpin.

Van De Wetering, Janwillem (1931-)
--Hugh Pine. Munsinger, Lynn (1951-), illus. LC 80-13652. (Illus.). 82 p. 22cm. 1980. (ISBN 0-395-29459-2). Houghton Mifflin.
--Little Owl: An Eightfold Buddhist Admonition. Brown, Marc Tolon (1946-), illus. 1978. (ISBN 0-395-26456-1). HM.

Van Dine, Alan
--Can You Imagine?. Lostutter, Robert, illus. LC 67-20694. (Illus.). 31 p. 26cm. 1967. Reilly & Lee.

Vandivert, Rita Andre (1905-)
--Barnaby. Vandivert, William, photos by. LC 63-14372. (Illus.). 47 p. 26cm. 1963. Dodd, Mead.
--The Porcupine Known As J. R. Vandivert, William, photos by. LC 59-11053. unpaged. illus. 26 cm. 1959. Dodd, Mead.

Van Dolson, Bobbie J., ed. see Degering, Etta Fowler.

Van Dolson, Bobbie J., ed. see Todd, Sharon.

Van Dolson, Bobbie Jane, ed. see Aitken, Dorothy Lockwood.

Van Dolson, Bobbie Jane, ed. see Armistead, Charles.

Van Dolson, Bobbie Jane, ed. see Dewees, Eleanor.

Van Dolson, Bobbie Jane, jt. ed. see Meseraull, Elaine.

Van Doren, Charles L. see Clark, Allen P., pseud.

Van Doren, Charles Lincoln (1926-)
--Growing up in Colonial America. Papin, Joseph (1914-), illus. LC 61-15732. 96 p. illus. 22 cm. 1962, c.1961. Bold Face Books: Distributed by Sterling Pub. Co.
--Growing up in the Great Depression. Papin, Joseph (1914-), illus. LC 63-12582. 128 p. illus. 22 cm. 1963. Hill and Wang.
--Growing up in the Wild West. Papin, Joseph (1914-), illus. LC 61-15733. 96 p. illus. 22 cm. 1962, c.1961. Bold Face Books; Distributed by Sterling Pub. Co.
--Growing up on a Clipper Ship. Patterson, Robert (1899-), illus. LC 64-24834. xiv, 126p. illus. 22cm. 1964. Hill & Wang.

Van Doren, Margaret (1917-)
--Thomas Retires. Van Doren, Margaret (1917-), illus. LC 39-20951. (Illus.). 26 cm. 39p. 1939. Viking Press.

Van Doren, Mark Albert (1894-1972)
--The Careless Clock: Poems About Children in the Family. Peirce, Waldo (1884-1970), illus. LC 47-30404. ix, 114 p. illus. 22 cm. 1947. W. Sloane Associates.
--Dick and Tom in Town. Richards, George Mather (1880-), illus. LC 32-299078. 5 p. l., 80 p. incl. illus., plates. col. front. 21 cm. 1932. The Macmillan Company.
--Dick and Tom: Tales of Two Ponies. Richards, George Mather (1880-) & Van, Doren Margaret (1917-), illus. LC 31-28317. 5 p. l., 68 p. incl. illus., plates. col. front. 21 cm. 1931. The Macmillan Company.
--Somebody Came. Fox, Lorraine (1922-1976), illus. LC 66-9206. (Illus.). 48 p. 22cm. 1966. Harlin Quist; Distributed by Crown Publishers.
--The Transparent Tree. Van Doren, Margaret (1917-), illus. LC 40-7023. 5 p. l., 3-87 p. illus. (part col.) 26 cm. c.1940. H. Holt and Company.

Van Dresser, Jasmine Stone, Mrs. (1878-)
--How to Find Happyland: A Book of Children's Stories. LC 7-16944. 6 p. l., 3-122 p. illus. (part col.) 10 col. pl. 24 cm. 1907. G. P. Putnam's Sons.
--Jimsey. Gregory, Dorothy Lake, illus. LC 25-11005. 21cm. 90p. 1925. Rand McNally.
--The Little Pink Pig. N.D. Rand McNally.
--The Little Pink Pig and the Big Road. Biers, Clarence, illus. N.D. G.P. Putnam's Sons.
--The Story of Silky and the Kitty with the Black Nose: And The Kitty with the Black Nose. Biers, Clarence & Harman, Joan, illus. LC 41-14765. 60 p. illus. (part col.) 14 x 17 cm. 1939. Rand McNally & Company.
--The Wonderful Hammer. Biers, Clarence, illus. N.D. Rand McNally & Co.

Van Dun, Anke, illus.
--My Busy Day. (Illus.). (Peggy Cloth Books). N.D. (ISBN 0-448-46817-4). Platt.

Van Dyke, Henry (1852-1933)
--Once Upon a Time Tales. McClure, Griselda Marshall, illus. N.D. Fleming H. Revell Co.

Van Dyne, Edith, pseud., see Baum, Lyman Frank.

Van Dyne, Edith, pseud. (1856-1919)
--Aunt Jane's Nieces. Baum, Lyman Frank. LC 6-34811. 325 p. incl. front. 5 pl. 19 cm. c.1906. The Reilly & Britton Co.
--Aunt Jane's Nieces Abroad. Baum, Lyman Frank. (The Aunt Jane's Nieces Ser.). N.D. Reilly & Lee.
--Aunt Jane's Nieces and Uncle John. Baum, Lyman Frank. LC 13-1794. 275 p. incl. front. 19 cm. (Her The Aunt Jane Ser.). c.1911. The Reilly & Britton Co.
--Aunt Jane's Nieces at Millville. Baum, Lyman Frank. LC 8-20860. 306 p. incl. front. 19 cm. c.1908. The Reilly & Britton Co.
--Aunt Jane's Nieces at Work. Baum, Lyman Frank. (The Aunt Jane's Niece Ser.). 1909. Reilly & Lee.
--Aunt Jane's Nieces in Society. Baum, Lyman Frank. LC 10-19391. 264 p. incl. front. 19 1/2 cm. c.1910. The Reilly & Britton Co.
--Aunt Jane's Nieces in the Red Cross. Baum, Lyman Frank. LC 15-27765. 256 p. front. 20 cm. (Her "Aunt Jane's Nieces" Ser.). c.1915. The Reilly & Britton Co.
--Aunt Jane's Nieces on the Ranch. Baum, Lyman Frank. LC 13-24794. 276 p. incl. front. 20 cm. (Her The Aunt Jane's Nieces Ser.). c.1913. The Reilly & Britton Co.
--Aunt Jane's Nieces on Vacation. Baum, Lyman Frank. LC 12-13902. 305 p. incl. front., illus. (map) 20 cm. (Her The Aunt Jane's Nieces Ser.). c.1912. The Reilly & Britton Co.
--Aunt Jane's Nieces Out West. Baum, Lyman Frank. LC 14-12631. 316 p. incl. front. 20 cm. (Her Aunt Jane's Nieces Ser.). c.1914. The Reilly & Britton Co.
--The Flying Girl. Baum, Lyman Frank. 1911. The Reilly & Britton Co.
--The Flying Girl and Her Chum. Baum, Lyman Frank. Nuyttens, Joseph Pierre, illus. LC 12-17514. 313 p. front., plates. 20 cm. (Her The Flying Girl Ser.). c.1912. The Reilly & Britton Co.
--Josie O'Gorman. Baum, Lyman Frank. Armstrong, Harry W., intro. by. LC 23-11448. 224 p. front. 20 cm. c.1923. The Reilly & Lee Co.
--Josie O'Gorman and the Meddlesome Major. Baum, Lyman Frank. Mack, Isabel, illus. LC 24-17969. 208 p. front. 20 cm. c.1924. The Reilly & Lee Co.
--Mary Louise. Baum, Lyman Frank. St. John, J. Allen, illus. LC 17-11216. 267 p. incl. front. 20 cm. (Her The Bluebird Bks.). c.1916. The Reilly & Britton Co.
--Mary Louise Adopts a Soldier. Baum, Lyman Frank. (Mary Louise Ser.). 1919. Reilly & Lee.
--Mary Louise and Josie O'Gorman. Baum, Lyman Frank. Armstrong, Harry W., illus. LC 22-15207. 224 p. 20 cm. (Her The Bluebird Bks.). c.1922. The Reilly & Lee Co.
--Mary Louise and the Liberty Girls. Baum, Lyman Frank. (Mary Louise Ser.). 1918. Reilly & Lee.
--Mary Louise at Dorfield. Baum, Lyman Frank. Evers, Maude Martin, illus. LC 20-17405. 224 p. front. 20 cm. c.1920. The Reilly & Lee Co.
--Mary Louise in the Country. Baum, Lyman Frank. St. John, J. Allen, illus. LC 16-21708. 284 p. front. 20 cm. (Her The Bluebird Bks.). c.1916. The Reilly & Britton Co.
--Mary Louise Solves a Mystery. Baum, Lyman Frank. LC 17-21647. 256 p. front. 20 cm. (Her The Bluebird Bks.). c.1917. The Reilly & Britton Co.
--Mary Louise Stands the Test. Baum, Lyman Frank. (Mary Louise Ser.). N.D. Reilly & Lee.

Vane, Lenchen Coleman De see De Vane, Lenchen Coleman.

Van Epps, Margaret T
--Nancy Pembroke, College Maid. LC 30-109875. 256 p. front. 19 1/2 cm. (Her Nancy Pembroke Ser.). c.1930. A. L. Burt Company.
--Nancy Pembroke, College Maid. (Nancy Pembroke Ser.). N.D. World Publishing Co.
--Nancy Pembroke, College Maid and Nancy Pembroke's Vacation in Canada: Two Books in One. N.D. World Publishing Co.
--Nancy Pembroke in New Orleans. LC 30-117225. 248 p. front. 19 1/2 cm. (Her Nancy Pembroke Ser.). c.1930. A. L. Burt Company.
--Nancy Pembroke in New Orleans. (Nancy Pembroke Ser.). N.D. World Publishing Co.
--Nancy Pembroke in Nova Scotia. LC 30-11719. 20cm. 239p. (The Nancy Pembroke Ser.). 1930. A L Burt Co.
--Nancy Pembroke, Junior. LC 30-117210. 242 p. front. 19 1/2 cm. (Her Nancy Pembroke Ser.). c.1930. A. L. Burt Company.
--Nancy Pembroke, Junior. (Nancy Pembroke Ser.). N.D. World Publishing Co.
--Nancy Pembroke, Senior. LC 31-15095. 252 p. front. 19 1/2 cm. (Her Nancy Pembroke Ser.). c.1931. A. L. Burt Company.
--Nancy Pembroke: Sophomore at Roxford. LC 30-117232. 242 p. front. 19 1/2 cm. (Her Nancy Pembroke Ser.). c.1930. A. L. Burt Company.
--Nancy Pembroke, Sophomore at Roxford. (Nancy Pembroke Ser.). N.D. World Publishing Co.
--Nancy Pembroke's Vacation in Canada. LC 30-117201. 255 p. front. 19 1/2 cm. (Her Nancy Pembroke Ser.). c.1930. A. L. Burt Company.
--Nancy Pembroke's Vacation in Canada. (Nancy Pembroke Ser.). N.D. World Publishing Co.

Van Every, Dale (1896-1976)
--The Day the Sun Died. LC 73-135437. (gr. 8 up). 1971. (ISBN 0-316-89620-9). Little.

Van Eyssen, Shirley
--In the Beginning: A New Interpretation of the Old Testament. Claveloux, Nicole, illus. LC 79-140415. (Illus.). 64 p. 34cm. (Here-and-there book from Harlin Quist). c.1970. (ISBN 0-8252-0051-2). (ISBN 0-8252-0052-0). H. Quist.

Van Garrett, Wouter see Garrett, Wouter Van & Eubanks, L. E.

Van Gelder, Richard George (1928-)
--Bats. Dolan, Tom, illus. LC 67-8577. 21cm. 31p. (Follett beginning science books). 1967. Follett Pub. Co.
--Professor & the Mysterious Box. Ginnings, Harriett Wilcoxen. LC 64-7528. 25cm. 46p. (gr. 2-4). 1964. (ISBN 0-8178-3562-8). Harvey.
--The Professor and the Vanishing Flags. Harriett, pseud. (1905-), illus. Ginnings, Harriett Wilcoxen. LC 65-195894. 1v. (unpaged) illus. 25cm. (Sci. parade bk.). c.1965. (ISBN 0-8178-3602-0). Harvey.

Van Gelder, Robert
--The Enemy in the House. LC 40-341132. 3 p. l., 3-223 p. 21 cm. 1940. Dial Press.
--Front Page Story. LC 37-30408. 4 p. l., 243 p. 21 cm. 1937. Dodd, Mead & Company.
--Marjory Fleming: The Youngest Genius. Chacanne, Rose, illus. LC 40-64477. ix, 245 p. illus. 21 cm. 1940. Dodd, Mead and Company.

Van Gelder, Rosalind
--Monkeys Have Tails. Kaplan, Boche (1926-), illus. LC 65-12264. (Illus.). 48 p. 24cm. 1966. (ISBN 0-679-20116-5). D. McKay Co.

Vangeli, Spiridon (1932-)
--Gugutse's Hat. 12p. 1978. (ISBN 0-8285-1576-X, Pub. by Progress Pubns USSR). Imported Pubns.
--Meet Guguze. Hyman, Trina Schart (1939-), illus. Morton, Miriam (1918-), tr. LC 76-50034. p. cm. c.1977. (ISBN 0-201-08056-7). Addison Wesley.

Vanhalewijn, Mariette
--The Little Witch Wanda. Moerman, Jaklien, illus. LC 74-127831. (Illus.). 32 p. 23cm. 1st U.S. edition. 1970. World.
--Princess Penelope's Three Hundred and Sixty-Five Dresses. Moerman, Jaklien, illus. LC 70-127830. (Illus.). 32 p. 24cm. 1st U.S. edition. 1970. World Pub. Co.

Van Heukelom, A. S.
--Arabella, the Heavenly Cat. Van Heukelom, A. S., illus. LC 78-82758. (Illus.). 48 color ils. 96p. (gr. 2-6). 1969. Platt.

Van Hichtum, Ninka, pseud., see Troelstra, Sjoukje.

Van Hille, C. Gaerthe
--Under the Thatched Roof: A Dutch Children's Classic. Kortschak, Kate, tr. (Illus.). 176p. (gr. 4-6). 1973. (ISBN 0-682-48419-9). Exposition.

Van Hoose, William H.
--Tecumseh: An Indian Moses. 244p. (gr. 8 up). 1984. (ISBN 0-938936-24-7). (ISBN 0-938936-25-5). Daring Bks.

Van Horn, Grace
--Little Red Rooster. Perry, Sheila, illus. LC 61-7135. (Illus.). 21cm. 1962, c.1961. Abelard-Schuman.

Van Horn, William
--Harry Hoyle's Giant Jumping Bean. Van Horn, William, illus. LC 77-21112. (Illus.). 32 p. 1978. Atheneum.
--Harry Hoyle's Slippery Shadow. Van Horn, William, illus. 32p. (ps-3). 1981. (ISBN 0-590-31763-6, Schol Pap). Scholastic Inc.
--Twitchtoe the Beastfinder. Van Horn, William, illus. LC 78-3679. p. cm. 1978. (ISBN 0-689-30670-9). Atheneum.
--The Very Special Birthday Present. LC 81-8053. (Illus.). 32 p. 1982. (ISBN 0-689-30895-7). Atheneum.

Van Housen, Nita
--Poogie and Sibella. Brock, Emma Lillian (1886-1974), illus. LC 32-30026. 5 p. l., 81 p. incl. front., illus., col. plates. 23 cm. c.1932. A. Whitman & Co.

Van Iterson, Siny Rose
--The Curse of Laguna Grande. Van Stockum, Hilda Gerarda (1908-), tr. from Dutch. LC 72-11469. 190 p. 21cm. 1973. (ISBN 0-688-20071-0). (ISBN 0-688-20071-0). Morrow.

--In the Spell of the Past. Stockum, Hilda van, tr. from Dutch. LC 74-31022. 192 p. 21cm. (gr. 7up). 1975. (ISBN 0-688-22023-1). (ISBN 0-688-32023-6). Morrow.
--Pulga. Gode, Alexander & Gode, Alison, trs. from Dutch LC 77-143462. (Illus.). 240 p. 22cm. 1971. (ISBN 0-688-31796-0). Morrow. Awards: (MLB); (ALA).
--The Smugglers of Buenaventura. LC 73-17723. 190 p. 21cm. 1974. (ISBN 0-688-20116-4). (ISBN 0-688-20116-4). Morrow.
--The Spirits of Chocamata. Stockum, Hilda Van, tr. from Dutch LC 77-2213. (Illus.). 221 p. 21cm. 1977. (ISBN 0-688-22108-4). (ISBN 0-688-32108-9). Morrow.
--Village of Outcasts. Pitzele, Patricia & Smedts, Joske, trs. from Dutch LC 74-168478. 190 p. 21cm. 1972. (ISBN 0-688-31988-2). Morrow.

Van Kirk, Louise. M
--Stories for the Kindergarten. Clark, G. Minnie, ed. N.D. E Steiger & Co.

Van Laar, Henrietta
--Judy and Sam: A Story for Boys and Girls. LC 46-2405. 85 p., 1 l. 20 cm. 1946. Wm. B. Eerdmans Publishing Company.
--Nora. Weidenaar, Reynold H., illus. LC 44-46346. (Illus.). 19.5 cm. 89p. 1944. Wm. B. Eerdmans Publishing Co.
--Sam and the BFF Club: A Story for Boys and Girls. LC 53-2322. 58p. 20cm. 1953. Moody Press.
--Sam at Dusky Hollow: A Story for Boys and Girls. LC 52-33571. 57 p. 20 cm. 1952. Moody Press.
--Sam in the City: A Story for Boys and Girls. LC 51-11253. 59 p. 20 cm. 1951. Moody Press.

Van Leeuwen, Jean (1937-), ed. see Andersen, Hans Christian.

Van Leeuwen, Jean (1937-)
--Amanda Pig and Her Big Brother Oliver. Schweninger, Ann (1951-), illus. LC 82-1557. (Illus.). 56 p. 23cm. (Dial Easy-to-Read). c.1982. Dial Press. Award: (ALA).
--Benjy and the Power of Zingies. Apple, Margot, illus. LC 82-1513. p. cm. 1982. (ISBN 0-8037-0379-1). (ISBN 0-8037-0380-5). Dial Press.
--Benjy in Business. Apple, Margot, illus. (Illus.). 112p. (Dial Book for Young Readers Ser.). (gr. 2-6). 1983. (ISBN 0-8037-0873-4). (ISBN 0-8037-0865-3). Dutton.
--Benjy the Football Hero. Owens, Gail, illus. LC 84-21459. (Illus.). 167 p. 22cm. c.1985. (ISBN 0-8037-0189-6). (ISBN 0-8037-0190-X). Dial Books for Young Readers.
--The Great Cheese Conspiracy. Gobbato, Imero (1923-), illus. LC 73-75881. (Illus.). 87 p. 22cm. 1969. Random House.
--The Great Christmas Kidnaping Caper. Kellogg, Steven (1941-), illus. LC 75-9201. (Illus.). 133 p. 22cm. 1975. (ISBN 0-8037-5415-9). (ISBN 0-8037-5416-7). Dial Press.
--The Great Rescue Operation. Apple, Margot, illus. LC 81-65851. (Illus.). 167 p. 22cm. c.1982. (ISBN 0-8037-3139-6). (ISBN 0-8037-3140-X). Dial Press.
--I Was a Ninety-Eight Pound Duckling. LC 72-714. 21cm. 102p. 1972. Dial Bks Young.
--More Tales of Amanda Pig. Schweninger, Ann (1951-), illus. LC 84-28775. (Illus.). 56 p. 23cm. (Dial Easy-to-Read). 1985. (ISBN 0-8037-0223-X). (ISBN 0-8037-0224-8). Dial Books for Young Readers.
--More Tales of Oliver Pig. Lobel, Arnold Stark (1933-), illus. LC 80-23289. p. cm. c.1981. (ISBN 0-8037-8713-8). (ISBN 0-8037-8714-6). Dial Press. Award: (ALA).
--One Day in Summer. Fish, Richard, illus. LC 69-13412. (Illus.). 32 p. 27cm. 1969. Random House.
--Seems Like This Road Goes on Forever. LC 78-72201. 214 p. 22cm. c.1979. (ISBN 0-8037-7687-X). Dial Press.
--Tales of Amanda Pig. Schweninger, Ann (1951-), illus. (Illus.). 56p. (Dial Book for Young Readers). (ps-3). 1983. (ISBN 0-8037-8443-0). (ISBN 0-8037-8450-3). Dutton. Award: (ALA).
--Tales of Oliver Pig. Lobel, Arnold Stark (1933-), illus. LC 79-4276. (Illus.). 64 p. 23cm. (Dial Easy-To-Read). c.1979. (ISBN 0-8037-8736-7). (ISBN 0-8037-8737-5). Dial Press.
--Timothy's Flower. Barnett, Moneta (1922-1976), illus. LC 68-401. (Illus.). (ps-3). 1967. (ISBN 0-394-81896-2). (ISBN 0-394-91896-7). Random.
--Too Hot for Ice Cream. Alexander, Martha G. (1920-), illus. LC 74-2877. (Illus.). 40 p. 23cm. 1974. (ISBN 0-8037-6076-0). (ISBN 0-8037-6076-0). Dial Press.

Van Leeuwen, Jean (1937-), adapted by.
--The Emperor's New Clothes. Dalano, Irene (1919-) & Delano, Jack, illus. LC 79-155597. (Original Story by Hans Christian Andersen, 1805-1875). (Illus.). 57p. 27cm. 1971. (ISBN 0-394-82105-X). (ISBN 0-394-92105-4). Random House.
--A Time of Growing. 322 p. 22cm. 1967. Random House.

Van Lhin, Erik, pseud., see Del Rey, Lester.

Varble, Rachel Margaret McBrayer, Mrs.
--Beatrice the Brave. Sturges, Katharine, illus. LC 34-33870. x, 240 p. incl. front., illus., plates. 20 1/2 cm. 1934. Little, Brown and Company.
--Beth and Seth. Reynolds, Doris, illus. LC 59-12652. 22cm. 200p. 1959. Doubleday.
--A Girl from London: A Romance of Old Virginia. with illustrations by beatrice stevens. ed. Stevens, Beatrice (1876-), illus. LC 29-209723. viii p., 2 l., 3-290 p. incl., illus., plates. col. front. 20 1/2 cm. 1929. Little, Brown, and Company.
--Julia Ann. Morse, Dorothy Bayley (1906-1979), illus. LC 39-31531. 3 p. l., v-vi p., 1 l. 309 p. incl. plates. front., ports. 21 cm. 1939. Doubleday, Doran & Co., Inc.
--Marie of the Gypsies. Jackson, Evelina M., illus. LC 31-29627. 5 p. l., 3-268 p. col. front., illus. 20 1/2 cm. 1931. Little, Brown, and Company.
--Pepys' Boy. 1st ed. Werth, Kurt (1896-), illus. LC 55-10520. (Illus.). 253 p. 22cm. 1955. Doubleday.
--The Red Cape. McCLure, Henrietta Adams, illus. LC 28-19290. viii p., 1 l., 248 p., 1 l. col. front., illus. 20 1/2 cm. 1928. Little, Brown, and Company.
--Romance for Rosa. LC 46-21130. (Illus.). 20cm. 278p. 1946. Doubleday & Company.
--Three Against London. Hodges, Cyril Walter (1909-), illus. LC 62-11441. 188 p. illus. 22 cm. 1962. Doubleday.

Vardey, Lucinda, jt. auth. see Bowman, Sarah.

Vardi, Dov, tr. see Zim, Jacob & Ofek, Uriel.

Varga, Judy, pseud., see Stang, Judit.

Varga, Judy, pseud. (1921-1977)
--The Battle of the Wind Gods. Stang, Judit. Varga, Judy, pseud. (1921-1977), illus. Stang, Judit. LC 73-22446. (Illus.). 32 p. 1974. (ISBN 0-688-21783-4). (ISBN 0-688-31783-9). Morrow.
--Circus Cannonball. Stang, Judit. LC 74-26796. (Illus.). 32 p. 27cm. 1975. (ISBN 0-688-32026-0). Morrow.
--The Crow Who Came to Stay. Stang, Judit. Varga, Judy, pseud. (1921-1977), illus. Stang, Judit. LC 67-294. (Illus.). 32 p. 1967. W. Morrow.
--The Dragon Who Liked to Spit Fire. Stang, Judit. Varga, Judy, pseud. (1921-1977), illus. Stang, Judit. LC 61-7793. (Illus.). 1 v. (unpaged. 26cm. 1961. Morrow.
--Janko's Wish. Stang, Judit. Varga, Judy, pseud. (1921-1977), illus. Stang, Judit. LC 69-10484. (Illus.). 32 p. 1969. Morrow.
--The Magic Wall. Stang, Judit. Varga, Judy, pseud. (1921-1975), illus. Stang, Judit. LC 70-88733. (Illus.). 32 p. 1970. Morrow.
--The Mare's Egg. Strang, Judit. LC 72-165131. (Illus.). 32 p. 26cm. 1972. Morrow.
--Miss Lollipop's Lion. Stang, Judit. Varga, Judy, pseud. (1921-1977), illus. Stang, Judit. LC 63-7042. (Illus.). unpaged. 26cm. 1963. Morrow.
--The Monster Behind Black Rock. Strang, Judit. LC 77-124349. (Illus.). 30 p. 1971. Morrow.
--Once-a-Year Witch. Stang, Judit. LC 72-4002. (Illus.). 32 p. 1973. (ISBN 0-688-20060-5). (ISBN 0-688-20060-5). Morrow.
--Pig in the Parlor. Stang, Judit. Varga, Judy, pseud. (1921-1977), illus. Stang, Judit. LC 63-12000. (gr. k-3). 1963. Morrow.
--The Puppy Who Liked to Chew Things. Stang, Judit. Varga, Judy, pseud. (1921-1977), illus. Stang, Judit. LC 68-11484. (Illus.). 32 p. 26cm. 1968. Morrow.
--The Sociable Seal. Stang, Judit. Varga, Judy, pseud. (1921-1977), illus. Stang, Judit. LC 65-10259. 1v. (unpaged) illus. (pt. col.) 26cm. c.1965. Morrow.

Varga, Margaret (1908-)
--Carol Brant, Picture Magazine Reporter. LC 45-7533. viii p., 1 l. 166 p. 19 cm. (Dodd, Mead Career Bks.). 1945. Dodd, Mead & Company.

Varlay, Rene G. (1927-)
--The Lollipop Songs. Owens, Jeanne, illus. LC 62-8088. 48p. col. illus. 21x23cm. c.1962. (ISBN 0-03-034895-1). Holt.

Varley, Dimitry V. (1906-)
--The Whirly Bird. Rojankovsky, Feodor Stepanovich (1891-1970), illus. LC 60-5507. unpaged. illus. 26 cm. 1961. Knopf.

Varley, Susan
--Badger's Parting Gift. Varley, Susan, illus. LC 83-17500. (Illus.). 25p. (gr. k-3). 1984. (ISBN 0-688-02699-0). (ISBN 0-688-02703-2). Lothrop.

Varnado, Jewel Goodgame (1915-)
--Strait Ahead. 1st ed. LC 55-11662. 73p. 21cm. c.1956. Vantage Press.

Varner, Velmer V. (1916-1972)
--The Animal Frolic. Sojo, Toba, illus. (GB). 1967. (ISBN 0-399-60027-2). Putnam Pub Group.

Varney, Joyce
--The Half-Time Gypsy. 1st ed. Hyman, Trina Schart (1939-), illus. LC 68-15631. (Illus.). 239 p. 22cm. 1968. Bobbs-Merrill.
--The Magic Maker. 1st ed. Hyman, Trina Schart (1939-), illus. LC 66-28679. (Illus.). 176 p. 22cm. 1967, c.1966. Bobbs-Merrill.

Varney, Rosemary Leahy (1931-)
--Wispy, the Littlest Witch. Masheris, Robert, illus. LC 76-48097. (Illus.). 32 p. 25cm. c.1977. (ISBN 0-913778-70-2). Child's World.

Varnum, Brooke Minarik
--Play & Sing..It's Christmas!. A Piano Book of Easy-to-Play Carols. McCully, Emily Arnold (1939-), illus. LC 80-15967. (Illus.). 48p. 1980. (ISBN 0-02-791400-3). (ISBN 0-02-045420-1). Macmillan.

Vartanian, Raymond J.
--ABC. Vartanian, Raymond J., illus. LC 52-36196. unpaged. illus. 17 cm. (Tell-a-tale books). c.1952. Whitman Pub. Co.

Vasconcelos, Jose M. De see De Vasconcelos, Jose M.

Vasiliu, Mircea (1920-)
--A Day at the Beach. Vasiliu, Mircea (1920-), illus. LC 76-24169. (Illus.). 32 p. 21cm. (Random House Pictureback). c.1977. (ISBN 0-394-83475-5). Random House.
--Do You Remember?. Vasiliu, Mircea (1920-), illus. LC 66-6130. 1 v. (unpaged) col. illus. 24cm. c.1966. (ISBN 0-381-99677-8). John Day.
--Everything Is Somewhere. LC 59-6720. unpaged. illus. 21 x 24 cm. 1959. J. Day Co.
--The Good Night, Sleep Tight Book. Vasiliu, Mircea (1920-), illus. LC 72-92796. (Illus.). 28 p. 33cm. 1973. Golden Press.
--Hark, the Little Angel. LC 65-221253. 48p. col. illus. 27cm. c.1965. John Day.
--The Merry Wind. LC 67-21729. (Illus.). 48 p. 1967. John Day Co.
--Mortimer, the Friendly Dragon. LC 68-13942. (Illus.). 48 p. 26cm. 1968. John Day Co.
--The Most Beautiful Word. Vasiliu, Mircea (1920-), illus. LC 74-115954. (Illus.). 32 p. 24cm. 1970. John Day Co.
--Once Upon a Pirate Ship. Vasiliu, Mircea (1920-), illus. LC 73-93304. (Illus.). 44 p. 31cm. 44p. 1974. (ISBN 0-307-13747-3). Golden Press.
--One Day in the Garden. LC 69-10589. (Illus.). 32 p. 1968, c.1969. John Day Co.
--What's Happening?. LC 70-89320. (Illus.). 46 p. 29cm. 1969, c.1970. John Day Co.
--The World Is Many Things. LC 67-13867. (Illus.). 48 p. 24cm. 1967. J. Day Co.
--Year Goes Round. Vasiliu, Mircea (1920-), illus. LC 64-10879. (O.s.i.). (Illus.). 24cm. 48p. (gr. k-3). 1964. (ISBN 0-381-99663-8). John Day.

Vassilevskaya, E.
--The Tiger's Nephew. 12p. 1975. (ISBN 0-8285-1247-7, Pub. by Progress Pubs USSR). Imported Pubns.

Vassilissa
--Kiou, the Owl. Simon, Romain (1915-), illus. LC 83-22502. (Illus.). 31 p. 1984, c.1983. (ISBN 0-911745-40-8). P. Bedrick Books.

Vassos, John (1898-)
--Rex and Lobo. Vassos, John (1898-), photos by. LC 46-20796. 62 p., 1 l. illus. 16 x 20 1/2 cm. 1946. E. P. Dutton & Co., Inc.

Vaughan, Agnes Carr (1887-)
--Evenings in a Greek Bazaar. Wood, Harrie (1902-), illus. LC 32-19821. viii, 1 p., 3 1., 3-209 p. incl. front., illus. 19 1/2 cm. 1932. A. A. Knopf.
--Lucian Goes a-Voyaging. Wood, Harrie (1902-), illus. LC 30-10688. 6 p. l., 3-139 p. front., illus. 19 1/2 cm. 1930. A. A. Knopf.

Vaughan, Anne
--Whopper Whale. LC 51-9570. (Illus.). 26p. 25cm. (A Silver Star Bk.). 1951. Children's Press.
--Whopper Whale. N.D. Grosset & Dunlap.

Vaughan, Auriel Rosemary Malet see Malet, Oriel, pseud.

Vaughan, Auriel Rosemary Malet, Lady (1923-)
--Beginner's Luck. Malet, Oriel, pseud. Wegner, Fritz (1924-), illus. LC 53-6420. 252p. illus. 20cm. 1st U.S. edition. 1953. Little, Brown.

Vaughan, Ciba, tr. see Escoula, Yvonne.

Vaughan, Ciba, tr. see Held, Jacqueline.

Vaughan, Ciba, tr. see Ionesco, Eugene.

Vaughan, Eleanor K., jt. auth. see Branley, Franklyn Mansfield.

Vaughan-Jackson, Genevieve
--Carramore. Vaughan-Jackson, Genevieve (1913-), illus. LC 68-25624. 128p. illus. 22cm. 1968. Hastings.

Vaughan, Jennifer
--Anna and the Moon Queen. McLaren, Annabel, ed. Bailey, Barbara, illus. LC 80-52516. (Illus.). 28 p. 21cm. (Starters Stories. Green: No. 2). 1980. (ISBN 0-382-06507-7). Silver Burdett Co.
--Zoo for Sale. Cousins, Lynne, illus. LC 80-52530. (Illus.). 28 p. 21cm. (Starters Stories. Red: No. 1). c.1980. (ISBN 0-382-06494-1). Silver Burdett Co.

Vaughan, Michael, ed. see Braithewaite, Walter.

Vaughan, Samuel S. (1928-)
--New Shoes. 1st ed. Szekeres, Cyndy (1933-), illus. LC 61-8165. unpaged. illus. 25 cm. 1961. Doubleday.
--The Two-Thirty Bird. Ohlsson, Ib (1935-), illus. LC 65-18036. 47p. illus. (pt. col.) 24cm. c.1965. Norton.
--Whoever Heard of Kangaroo Eggs?. Weisgard, Leonard Joseph (1916-), illus. LC 57-809220. unpaged. illus. 27cm. 1957. Doubleday.

Vaughn, Dorothea B., Mrs. & Fleur, Anne Elizabeth (1901-)
--Rollicking Rhymes. Sari, pseud. LC 41-14437. 32 p. incl. col. front., illus. (part col.) 28 x 22 cm. c.1941. McLoughlin Bros., Inc.

Vaughn, Howard Ridgway (1859-)
--A Good Natured Giant, and Other Stories. Cox, George A., frwd. by. LC 34-5176. 2 p. l., vii-xvi, 90 p. 19 cm. 1934. The Colwell Press, Incorporated.

Vaughn, Ruth (1935-)
--More Skits That Win. LC 77-3461. 61 p. 21cm. c.1977. (ISBN 0-310-33671-6). Zondervan Pub. House.

Vault, M. Vere De see Munch, Theodore William (1919-) & De Vault, M. Vere.

Vaupel, Ouise
--Jerry's Adventures in Up-Side-Down Land and at the Top of the World. LC 39-5587. 6 p. l., 124, 120 p. illus. 20 1/2 cm. c.1938. House of Field, Inc.

Vautier, Gerda, ed.
--A Child's Bouquet of Yesterday. LC 46-22694. 56 p. incl. illus., plates. 17 1/2 x 14 1/2 cm. 1946. American Studio Books.

Vautier, Ghislaine, jt. auth. see McLeish, Kenneth.

Vavra, Robert James (1935-)
--Anna & Dula. Vavra, Robert James (1935-), illus. LC 66-8703. (Illus.). (gr. 2 up). 1966. (ISBN 0-15-203570-2, HJ). HarBraceJ.
--Felipe the Bullfighter. 1st ed. Vavra, Robert James (1935-), illus. LC 68-10006. (Illus.). (gr. 4-6). N.D. (ISBN 0-15-227510-X, HJ). HarBraceJ.
--Lion and Blue. Cowles, Fleur, illus. LC 74-10319. (Illus.). 44 p. 29cm. 1974. (ISBN 0-688-61164-8). Reynal.
--Little Egret and Toro. Short, John Fulton, illus. Fulton, John, pseud. LC 75-3288. (Illus.). 60 p. 30cm. 1967, c.1966. Lion Press.
--Milane: The Story of a Hungarian Gypsy Boy. LC 74-8640. (Illus.). 48 p. 30cm. 1969. (ISBN 0-15-254160-8). Harcourt, Brace & World.
--Pizorro. LC 68-59549. (Illus.). 48 p. 30cm. 1968. Harcourt, Brace & World.
--Romany Free. Cowles, Fleur, illus. LC 77-77315. (Illus.). 45 p. c.1977. (ISBN 0-688-61193-1). Reynal.
--The Story of Taou. Vavra, Robert James (1935-), illus. LC 68-28737. (Illus.). 32 p. 29cm. 1969. Dial Press.
--Tiger Flower. Cowles, Fleur, illus. Menuhiu, Yehudi (1916-), pref. by. LC 69-20105. (Illus.). 45 p. 30cm. 1969, c.1968. Reynal.

Vawter, Bessie C.
--Children's Rhymes of Other Climes. Dealey, Edwina Vawter, illus. (Illus.). 23 x 31cm. 32p. N.D. Times-Mirror Printing and Binding House.

Vawter, Clara
--Of Such is the Kingdom. Vawter, William, designed by. (Illus.). N.D. Bowen-Merrill Pub.
--The Rabbit's Ransom. Vawter, Will, illus. LC 4-1816. (Being a New Edition of "Such Is the Kingdom"). xv, 1 p. 3 1, 23-192 p. incl. front., illus, plates, 20 1/2 cm. c.1902. The Bobbs-Merrill Company.

Vaygouny, Margarite
--Greenland Waters. Creekmore, Raymond (1905-), illus. LC 54-12605. 148p. illus. 21cm. 1954. Macmillan.
--Peter the Stork. Hauman, George (1890-1961) & Hauman, Doris, Mrs. (1897-), illus. LC 51-13382. 109 p. illus. 21 cm. 1951. Macmillan.

Veale, E
--Brownies and Other Stories. Cox, Palmer (1840-1924), illus. LC 7-18093. 320 p. illus. 19 cm. 1900. Hurst & Company.

Vedral, Joyce
--I Dare You. 144p. (gr. 7 up). N.D. (ISBN 0-03-061266-7). HR&W.

Veen, Mary
--Merideth Was Afraid. Veen, Mary, illus. LC 77-84934. (Illus.). 30 p. 25cm. 1969. Childrens Press.

Veglahn, Nancy Crary (1937-)
--Dance of the Planets: The Universe of Nicolaus Copernicus. Ulrich, George M., illus. LC 78-8615. (Illus.). 63 p. 22cm. c.1979. (ISBN 0-698-30693-7). Coward, McCann & Geoghegan.
--Fellowship of the Seven Stars. LC 81-1120. p. cm. c.1981. (ISBN 0-687-12927-3). Abingdon.
--Follow the Golden Goose. Johnson, Milton (1932-), illus. LC 78-110348. (Illus.). 171 p. 22cm. 1970. Addison-Wesley.
--Swimmers, Take Your Marks!. Maccabe, Richard D., illus. LC 74-17694. (Illus.). 115 p. 23cm. (Weekly Reader Children's Book Club Edition). 1975. (ISBN 0-88375-205-0). Xerox Weekly Reader Family Books.
--The Tiger's Tail. LC 64-19609. (A Story of America's Great Political Cartoonist Thomas Nast). 211p. illus., ports. 22cm. c.1964. Harper.
--The Vandals of Treason House. (Illus.). 158 p. 22cm. 1974. Houghton Mifflin.
--The Vandals of Treason House. Miller, Marilyn Jean (1925-), illus. LC 73-87818. (Illus.). 158 p. 21cm. 1974. (ISBN 0-88375-200-X). Xerox Family Education Services.

Veitch, Agnes
--Frank Fielding: Or, Debts and Difficulties. 1873. Leavitt & Allen Bros.

Velthuijs, Max, jt. auth. see Stanton, Henry.

Velthuijs, Max (1923-)
--The Little Boy and the Big Fish. Velthuijs, Max (1923-), illus. LC 72-76547. (Illus.). 32 p. 30cm. 1969. Platt & Munk.
--Little Man Finds a Home. LC 85-7247. (Illus.). 26 p. 26cm. 1985. North-South Books : Distributed in the U.S. by Holt, Rinehart, and Winston.
--The Painter and the Bird. LC 74-8807. (Illus.). 32 p. 30cm. 1975, c.1971. (ISBN 0-201-08082-6). Addison-Wesley.
--The Poor Woodcutter and the Dove. Velthuijs, Max (1923-), illus. LC 79-125037. (Illus.). 32p, 30cm. 1971. (ISBN 0-440-06991-2). (ISBN 0-440-06992-0). Delacorte Press.
--What Can You Do with a Dastardly Dragon?. Stanton, Henry B., tr. LC 74-19488. p. cm. 1975, c.1973. (ISBN 0-201-08147-4). Addison-Wesley.

Veltman, Jan
--The Syrup Can. Wilson, Eleanore Hubbard, illus. Olcott, Frances Jenkins (1872-1963), tr. LC 42-24239. xiii, 62 p. col. front., illus. 21 cm. 1942. W. A. Wilde Company.

Velvin, Ellen
--Jack's Visit. (Illus.). N.D. Thomas Nelson & Sons.
--Rataplan, a Rogue Elephant, and Other Stories. Verbeek, Gustave, illus. LC 2-14860. xiii, 15-328 p. incl. col. front., col. pl. 19 cm. 1902. H. Altemus Company.

Venable, Alan Hudson (1944-)
--The Checker Players. 1st ed. Barton, Byron (1930-), illus. LC 73-2883. (Illus.). 40 p. 1973. Lippincott.
--Hurry the Crossing. LC 73-15783. 155 p. 21cm. 1974. (ISBN 0-397-31452-3). Lippincott.

Venable, Clarke see Clarke, Covington, pseud.

Venable, Clarke (1892-)
--Aces up. Clarke, Covington, pseud. LC 29-13026. 3 p. l., 13-262, ix p. 20 cm. c.1929. The Reilly & Lee Co.
--Desert Wings. Clarke, Covington, pseud. LC 30-15336. 288 p. 20 cm. c.1930. The Reilly & Lee Co.
--For Valor. Clarke, Covington, pseud. LC 28-14007. 4 p. l., 13-264 p. viii pl. on 4 l. 20 cm. c.1928. The Reilly & Lee Co.
--The Lost Canyon. Clarke, Covington, pseud. Armstrong, Harry W., illus. LC 25-14946. 3 p. l., 11-269 p. front. 20 cm. c.1925. The Reilly & Lee Co.
--Mosby's Night Hawk. Clarke, Covington, pseud. LC 31-29966. 4 p. l., 7-290 p. 19 1/2 cm. c.1931. The Reilly & Lee Co.
--Mystery Flight of the Q2. Clarke, Covington, pseud. LC 32-24549. 270 p. 19 1/2 cm. c.1932. The Reilly & Lee Co.
--The Phantom of Paradise Valley. Clarke, Covington, pseud. LC 27-8788. 319 p. 20 cm. c.1926. The Reilly & Lee Co.
--Sea Dogs. Clarke, Covington, pseud. LC 27-19202. 3 p. l., 11-342 p. 19 1/2 cm. c.1927. The Reilly & Lee Co.
--Sky Caravan. Clarke, Covington, pseud. LC 31-13800. 296 p. 19 1/2 cm. c.1931. The Reilly & Lee Co.

Venable, William Henry (1836-1920)
--Tom Tad. vi, 287 p. incl. front. p. 19 1/2 cm. 1902. Dodd, Mead & Company.

Venables, Alma
--A Week of Stories: Or, Tall Tales for Small People. Johnson, Frank, illus. LC 64-21450. 64 p. col. illus. 22 cm. 1964. A. S. Barnes.

Venables, Bob
--Farmyard. LC 84-6498. 1984, c.1983. (ISBN 0-911745-67-X). Bedrick-Blackie.

Venedicto, Miguel A.
--The Magic Pencil. Schor, Narca, illus. (Illus.). 1978. (ISBN 0-533-02316-5). Vantage.

Venn, Mary Eleanor see Adrian, Mary, pseud.

Venn, Mary Eleanor (1908-)
--The Firehouse Mystery. Adrian, Mary, pseud. Vaughan, Anne (1913-), illus. LC 50-5673. (Illus.). 115 p. 22cm. 1950. Houghton, Mifflin.
--The Fox Hollow Mystery. Adrian, Mary, pseud. Coe, Lloyd (1899-1976), illus. LC 58-9242. 100 p. illus. 22 cm. 1959. Hastings House.

--Garden Spider. Mary Adrian, pseud. Ray, Ralph (1920-1952), illus. LC 51-12836. (Illus.). 21cm. 38p. (Holiday Easy Science). 1951. Holiday House.
--The Ghost Town Mystery. Lonette, Reisie Dominee (1924-), illus. LC 78-150015. (Illus.). 128 p. 22cm. 1971. (ISBN 0-8038-2645-1). Hastings House.
--Gray Squirrel. Mary Adrian, pseud. Ferguson, Walter (1930-), illus. LC 55-4189. (Illus.). 21cm. 46p. (Life-Cycle Stories). 1955. Holiday House.
--The Hidden Spring Mystery. Adrian, Mary, pseud. Stein, Harve (1904-), illus. LC 54-5203. 122p. illus. 22cm. 1954. Ariel Books.
--Honeybee. Mary Adrian, pseud. Latham, Barbara (1896-), illus. LC 52-13412. (Illus.). 28cm. 40p. (Holiday Easy Science). 1952. Holiday House.
--The Indian Horse Mystery. Adrian, Mary, pseud. Coe, Lloyd (1899-1976), illus. LC 66-11899. 126p. illus. 22cm. c.1966. Hastings.
--The Junior Sheriff Mystery. Adrian, Mary, pseud. Coe, Lloyd (1899-1976), illus. LC 55-9594. 119p. illus. 22cm. 1955. Ariel Books.
--The Kite Mystery. Adrian, Mary, pseud. Coe, Lloyd (1899-1976), illus. LC 67-25609. (Illus.). 125 p. 22cm. (A Double H Keep Reading Bk.). 1968. Hasting House.
--Mystery Nature Stories. Adrian, Mary, pseud. Korn, Elizabeth P., illus. LC 48-3501. 94 p. illus. 26 cm. 1948. Rinehart.
--The Mystery of the Dinosaur Bones. Adrian, Mary, pseud. Coe, Lloyd (1899-1976), illus. LC 64-8119. 126p. illus. 22cm. (Keep reading bk.). c.1965. Hastings.
The Mystery of the Night Explorers. Adrian, Mary, pseud. Coe, Lloyd (1899-1976), illus. LC 62-10087. 117 p. illus. 22 cm. 1962. Hastings House.
--The Rare Stamp Mystery. Coe, Lloyd (1899-1976), illus. LC 60-10582. (Illus.). 126 p. 22cm. 1960. Hastings House.
--Refugee Hero: A Hungarian Boy in America. Adrian, Mary, pseud. Abel, Raymond (1911-), illus. LC 57-10734. 128p. illus. 22cm. 1957. Hastings House.
--The Skin Diving Mystery. Adrian, Mary, pseud. LC 64-13479. (Illus.). 116 p. 22cm. 1964. Hastings House.
--The Tugboat Mystery. Adrian, Mary, pseud. Rev ed. Moyers, William (1916-), illus. LC 52-7200. 123p. illus. 22cm. 1952. Houghton Mifflin.
--The Uranium Mystery. Adrian, Mary, pseud. Coe, Lloyd (1899-1976), illus. LC 56-104077. 109p. illus. 22cm. 1956. Hastings House.

Venning, Sue, illus.
--Jim Henson's Muppet Show Bill. LC 81-52185. (Illus.). 30p. (Muppet Press Bks.). (gr. 1-7). 1982. (ISBN 0-394-85102-1). Random.

Venti, Pamela Richards
--Why Should I?. Ask Jeremy. Speirs, John Hastie (1906-), illus. LC 83-7360. (Illus.). 32. 25cm. c.1983. (ISBN 0-89693-213-3). Dandelion House.

Ventura, Marisa, jt. auth. see Ventura, Piero Luigi.

Ventura, Piero Luigi (1937-)
--The Magic Well. LC 76-8124. (Illus.). 36 p. 29cm. c.1976. (ISBN 0-394-83132-2). (ISBN 0-394-93132-7). Random House.

Ventura, Piero Luigi (1937-) & Ventura, Marisa
--The Painter's Trick. LC 76-54411. (Illus.). 34 p. 29cm. c.1977. (ISBN 0-394-83320-1). (ISBN 0-394-93320-6). Random House.

Venzi
--Little Angel with the Pink Wings. N.D. Dghtrs St Paul.

Ver Beck, Frank, jt. auth. see Bannerman, Helen Brodie Cowan Watson, Mrs.

Ver Beck, Frank see Ver Beck, William Francis.

Ver Beck, Frank (1858-1933)
--The Little Bear Who Ran Away from Bruintown. LC 23-15165. 3 p. l., 120 p. col. front., col. plates. 19 1/2 cm. c.1923. Small, Maynard and Company.
--Little Black Sambo and the Monkey People. Verbeck, Frank (1858-1933), illus. LC 28-1287. 62 p. 1 l. incl. col. front., col. illus. 14 cm. c.1928. Henry Altemus Company.
--Little Black Sambo in the Bears' Den. VerBeck, Frank (1858-1933), illus. LC 30-24467. 60 p., 1 l. incl. col. front., col. illus. 14 1/2 cm. (Altemus' Wee Books for Wee Folks). c.1930. Henry Altemus Company.

Ver Beck, William Francis see Ver Beck, Frank.

Ver Beck, William Francis (1858-)
--Little Black Sambo and the Crocodiles. Ver Beck, William Francis (1858-), illus. LC 39-31808. (Illus.). 14cm. 58p. (Altemus Wee Books for Wee Folks). 1930. Henry Altemus Company.

Verdery, Eleanor
--About Ellie at Longacre. N.D. E P Dutton.

Verdery, Katherine
--A Dixie Doll. Bromhall, Winifred, illus. LC 29-18021. 6 p. l., 15-192 p. incl. front., illus., plates. 21 1/2 cm. c.1929. The Bobbs-Merrill Company.
--A Little Dixie Captain. Bromhall, Winifred, illus. LC 30-24337. 205 p. incl. front., illus. plates. 21 1/2 cm. c.1930. The Bobbs-Merrill Company.

Verdi, Giuseppe (1813-1901)
--Aida. Luckmann, Helmut, illus. (Curtain Raiser Ser.). (gr. 4-6). 1970. (ISBN 0-531-01928-4). Watts.
--The Story of Aida. Stevenson, Florence, retold by. Fisher, Leonard Everett (1924-), illus. Metropolitan Opera Guild LC 65-207109. 61p. illus. (pt. col.) 27cm. 1966, c.1965. Putnam.

Verdick, Mary, ed. see Andrews, Freida.

Verdick, Mary, ed. see Senn, J. A.

Verdick, Mary Peyton (1923-), ed. see Carlson, Diane.

Verdick, Mary Peyton (1923-), ed. see Carlson, Gordon

Verdick, Mary Peyton (1923-), ed. see Otfinoski, Steven.

Verdick, Mary Peyton (1923-)
--A Dream Come True. Mooney, Thomas J., ed. Wenzel, David & Cone, Les, illus. (Illus., Orig.). (Beginning Pal Paperbacks Ser.). (gr. 7-12). 1977. (ISBN 0-8374-3451-3). Xerox Ed Pubns.
--Eight Exciting Adventures. Rich, Harry & Smolinski, Richard, eds. (Illus., Orig.). (Pal Paperbacks Ser., Kit A-Plus). (gr. 7-12). 1976. (ISBN 0-8374-3494-7). Xerox Ed Pubns.
--His Chute Didn't Open. Mooney, Thomas J., ed. Lawn, John, illus. (Illus., Orig.). (Pal Paperbacks, Pal Skills I Ser.). (gr. 7-12). 1978. (ISBN 0-8374-3524-2). Xerox Ed Pubns.
--It's a Funny World. Mooney, Thomas J., ed. Cone, Les, illus. (Illus., Orig.). (Beginning Pal Paperbacks Ser.). (gr. 7-12). 1977. (ISBN 0-8374-3458-0). Xerox Ed Pubns.
--Sky Dive. Mooney, Thomas J., ed. Blickenstaff, Wayne, illus. (Illus., Orig.). (Pal Paperbacks Ser., Kit A-Plus). (gr. 7-12). 1976. (ISBN 0-8374-3503-X). Xerox Ed Pubns.

Verdick, Mary Peyton (1923-), ed.
--Amazing Adventures. Sovek, Charles, illus. (Illus., Orig.). (Pal Paperbacks Ser., Kit A). (gr. 7-12). 1972. (ISBN 0-8374-3468-8). Xerox Ed Pubns.
--The Ghost Ship. Sovek, Charles, illus. (Illus., Orig.). (Pal Paperbacks Ser., Kit A-Plus). (gr. 7-12). 1976. (ISBN 0-8374-3490-4). Xerox Ed Pubns.
--The Magic Bottle. Lawn, John, illus. (Illus., Orig.). (Pal Paperbacks-Pal Skills I Ser.). (gr. 7-12). 1978. (ISBN 0-8374-3526-9). Xerox Ed Pubns.
--Nine Daring Adventures. De Kiefte, Kees, illus. (Illus., Orig.). (Pal Paperbacks Kit B Ser.). (gr. 7-12). 1973. (ISBN 0-8374-3505-6). Xerox Ed Pubns.
--On the Ledge. Rick, Harry, illus. (Illus., Orig.). (Pal Paperbacks Ser., Kit A-Plus). (gr. 7-12). 1976. (ISBN 0-8374-3495-5). Xerox Ed Pubns.
--Real-Life Adventures. Ashmead, Hal, illus. (Illus., Orig.). (Pal Paperbacks Kit B Ser.). (gr. 7-12). 1973. (ISBN 0-8374-3514-5). Xerox Ed Pubns.
--Remember Me?. Vye, Dulcianne (1923-), illus. (Illus., Orig.). (Pal Paperbacks - Pal Skills I Ser.). (gr. 7-12). 1978. (ISBN 0-8374-3523-4). Xerox Ed Pubns.
--Runaway. Maccabe, Richard D., illus. (Illus., Orig.). (Pal Paperbacks Ser., Kit A-Plus). (gr. 7-12). 1976. (ISBN 0-8374-3486-6). Xerox Ed Pubns.
--Summertime Blues. Wenzel, David, illus. (Illus., Orig.). (Pal Paperbacks - Pal Skills I Ser.). (gr. 7-12). 1978. (ISBN 0-8374-3528-5). Xerox Ed Pubns.
--The Switch. Lawn, John, illus. (Illus., Orig.). (Pal Paperbacks Ser., Kit A-Plus). (gr. 7-12). 1976. (ISBN 0-8374-3487-4). Xerox Ed Pubns.
--What Are Friends for?. Smolinski, Dick, illus. (Illus., Orig.). (Pal Paperbacks - Pal Skills I Ser.). (gr. 7-12). 1978. (ISBN 0-8374-3529-3). Xerox Ed Pubns.
--The World Beyond. Noyes, David, illus. (Illus., Orig.). (Pal Paperbacks Ser., Kit A-Plus). (gr. 7-12). 1976. (ISBN 0-8374-3499-8). Xerox Ed Pubns.

Verdy, Violette, tr. see Gautier, Theophile.

Verdy, Violette (1933-), adapted by.
--Giselle: Or, the Wilis. Brown, Marcia (1918-), illus. LC 74-107299. (Original Author: Theophile Gautier, 1811-1872). (Illus.). 50 p. 26cm. 1970. McGraw-Hill.

Verett, Dotty, jt. auth. see Neff, Carolyn.

Vergilius Maro, Publius, jt. auth. see Chandon, G.

Vergilius Maro, Publius (1919-)
--The Aeneid: A Retelling for Young People. Gerdes, Florence Marie, retold by. Holmgren, George Ellen, Sr., pseud. (1930-), illus. Holmgren, Helen Jean. LC 68-26075. (Illus.). 163 p. 21cm. 1969. St. Martin's Press.
--The Aeneid for Boys and Girls. Church, Alfred John (1829-1912), retold by. Karlin, Eugene (1918-), illus. Fadiman, Clifton Paul (1904-), afterword by. LC 62-19424. 172p. illus. 24cm. (Macmillan classics, 9). 1962. Macmillan.
--Aeneid for Boys and Girls. Church, Alfred John, ed. (Folk Lore and Fairy Tales). (MacMillan Books For Boys And Girls). (gr. 4-6). N.D. MacMillan Bks.

Vergue, George Harrison De La see De La Vergne, George Harrison.

Verhoeff, Carolyn
--All About Johnnie Jones. LC 7-10617. 3 p. l., 11-300 p. front., 6 pl. 20 cm. c.1907. Milton Bradley Company.
--Four Little Fosters. LC 9-13. 19cm. xvi, 295p. 1908. Crist, Scott & Parshall.
--Love Me, Love My Dog. Merrill, Frank Thayer (1848-), illus. LC 22-169721. 5 p. l., 346 p. front., plates. 20 cm. 1922. The Page Company.

Verite, Marcelle
Animal Stars of the Circus. Simon, Romain (1915-), illus. LC 79-114027. (Illus.). 49 p. 31cm. (Scroll Press animal book for children). 1970, c.1966. Scroll Press.

Verleyen, Cyriel
--Diogenes & His Lantern. Branton, Henry, illus. (Illus.). color ils. 1st U.S. edition. (Tales from History Ser). (gr. k-3). 1968. (ISBN 0-690-24028-7). (ISBN 0-690-24029-5). T Y Crowell.
--The Egg of Christopher Columbus. Branton, Henry, illus. LC 70-94798. (Illus.). 23 p. (His Tales from history). 1971, c.1970. Crowell.
--The Geese of Rome. Branton, Henry, illus. LC 68-17085. (Illus.). 23 p. (His Tales From History). 1968. T. Y. Crowell Co.

Vermeulen, Marcel
--Oliver, the Page. Dolan, Ellen M, adapted by. Wabbes, Marie, illus. LC 67-5516. 1 v. (unpaged) col. illus. 19 x 21 cm. (Children of other times). 1967. Webster Division, McGraw-Hill.

Verne, Henry
--Bob Moran and the Buccaneer's Hoard. LC 58-5388. 158 p. illus. 20 cm. 1958. Roy Publishers.
--Bob Moran and the Fawcett Mystery. LC 58-5385. 158 p. illus. 19 cm. 1958. Roy Publishers.
--Bob Moran and the Fiery Claw. LC 59-5659. 19cm. 157p. 1960. Roy Pub.
--Bob Moran and the Pirates of the Air. LC 58-5386. 159 p. illus. 19 cm. 1958. Roy Publishers.
--Bob Moran and the Sunken Galley. LC 58-5387. 159 p. illus. 19 cm. 1958. Roy Publishers.
--Bob Moran in the Valley of Hell. LC 59-5660. 160 p. illus. 19 cm. 1960. Phoenix House.
--Bob Moran in the Valley of Hell. N.D. Roy Pub.

Verne, Jules (1828-1905)
--Abandoned. Rhys, Ernest, ed. Kingston, William Henry Giles (1814-1880), tr. from Fr. (Illus.). 18cm. 237p. (Everyman's Library for Young People). 1909. E. P. Dutton & Co.
--Adventures in the Land of the Behemoth. New ed. 1874. Henry L. Shepard & Co.
--The Adventures of Captain Hatteras. 1875. George Routledge & Sons.
--The Adventures of Captain Hatteras: Containing: "A Journey to the North Pole","The Field of Ice", 2 Vols. (Illus.). N.D. George Routledge & Sons.
--All Around the Moon. N.D. David McKay.
--Among the Cannibals, 1 of 6 Vols. (Jules Verne Library). N.D. Set. Dodd, Mead & Co.
--An Antarctic Mystery, 1 of 11 vols. (Popular Bks for Boys). 1900. Set. J B Lippincott.
--Around the Moon. (Illus.). (Childrens Illustrated Classics Ser.). 1970. (ISBN 0-460-05087-7, Pub. by J. M. Dent England). Biblio Dist.
--Around the Moon. Phillipps, W. F., illus. (Illus.). . 12 draws. 4 color plates. 192p. (Children's Illustrated Classics Ser.). (gr. 3-7). 1970. (ISBN 0-525-25905-8). Dutton.
--Around the World in Eighty Days. (Scribner Series for Young People). N.D. Charles Scribner's Sons.
--Around the World in Eighty Days. (Illus.). (Great Illus. Classics). 1956. Dodd.
--Around the World in Eighty Days. (The Roxburghe Classics). N.D. Estes & Laurait's.
--Around the World in Eighty Days. N.D. Grosset & Dunlap.
--Around the World in Eighty Days. N.D. Laird & Lee's Publication.
--Around the World in Eighty Days, 1 of 50 vols. (Illus.). (The Norwood Ser.: No. 46). 1900. Lee & Shepard.
--Around the World in Eighty Days. (Jules Vernes Lib.). 1888. Porter & Coates.
--Around the World In Eighty Days, 1 of 7 Vols. (Illus.). (Jules Verne Library). N.D. Set. Porter & Coates.
--Around the World in Eighty Days. 1952. Scott, Foresman & Co.
--Around the World in Eighty Days. 190p. N.D. Tennyson Neely's Publications.
--Around The World in Eighty Days. (Standard Literature Ser.: No. 34). N.D. University Publishing Co.
--Around the World in Eighty Days. Boucher, Anthony, intro. by. (Illus.). N.D. Dodd, Mead & Co.
--Around the World in Eighty Days. complete and unabridged. Irwin, Don, illus. LC 79-79982. (Illus.). 223 p. 29cm. 1969. Childrens Press.
--Around the World in Eighty Days. Maraja, pseud., illus. Maraja, Libico. Towle, George M., tr. 1962. Golden Press.
--Around the World in Eighty Days. Phillipps, W. F., illus. Baldick, Jaqueline & Baldick, Robert (1927-1972), trs. from Fr. LC 68-112249. (Illus.). vi, 206p. (Childrens' Illustrated Classics). 1968. Dutton.
--Around the World in Eighty Days. Towle, George M., tr. (New Alta Lib.). N.D. Henry T. Coates & Co.
--Around the World in Eighty Days. Standard ed. Towle, George M, tr. (Illus.). c.1962. Porter & Coates.
--Blockade Runners, No.4. (Lakeside Library Ser.). N.D. Donnelley, Loyd & Co.
--Captain at Fifteen. LC 77-364939. 204 p. 20cm. (Golden grasshopper). 1976. (ISBN 0-200-72360-X). (ISBN 0-200-72361-8). Abelard-Schuman.
Captain Nemo's Fantastic Voyage. abr. ed. (gr. 3-5). N.D. (ISBN 0-590-05811-8, Schol Pap). Scholastic Inc.
--Castaways of the Flag. N.D. Grosset & Dunlap.
--Dick Sand. (Illus.). (The Rugby Series for Boys). N.D. A. L. Burt's Pubs.
--Dick Sand, a Captain at Fifteen. LC 1-9785. (Seaside Library: Vol. 21, No. 414). 1878. G. Munro.
--Dick Sand: Or, A Captain of Fifteen. (Jules Verne Ser.). N.D. A. L. Burt Co.
--Dropped from the Clouds. Rhys, Ernest, ed. Kingston, William Henry Giles (1814-1880), tr. (Illus.). 18cm. 240p. (Everyman's Library for Young People). 1909. E. P. Dutton & Co.
--Eight Hundred Leagues on the Amazon. (Jules Verne Ser.). N.D. A. L. Burt Co.
--Eight Hundred Leagues on the Amazon. (Burt's Home Library). N.D. A L Burt Co.
--The Field of Ice. 190p. 1876. George Routledge & Sons.
--Five Weeks in a Balloon, 1 of 11 Vols. (Illus.). (Jules Verne's Stories, Tales, and Romances). N.D. Set. George Routledge & Sons.
--Five Weeks In A Balloon And, Around The World In Eighty Days. Chambers, Arthur & Desages, P., trs. Meiklem, K. B. & Chancellor, C. N.D. E P Dutton.
--Five Weeks in a Balloon and Round the World in Eighty Days. (Everyman's Library). N.D. E. P. Dutton & Co.
--Flight to France. (gr. 5 up). N.D. (ISBN 0-685-28715-7). Assoc Bk.
--A Floating City and the Blockade Runners. 270p. (Scribner Series for Young People). 1876. Charles Scribner's Sons.
--From the Clouds to the Mountains. N.D. Wm. F. Gill & Co.
--From the Earth to the Moon. (Jules Verne Ser.). N.D. A. L. Burt Co.
--From the Earth to the Moon. (Burt's Home Library). N.D. A L Burt Co.
--From the Earth to the Moon. (Illus.). (The Rugby Series for Boys). N.D. A. L. Burt's Pubs.
--From the Earth to the Moon. (Illus.). 192p. 1st U.S. edition. Repr. of 1970 ed. (Childrens Illustrated Classics Ser.). 1975. (ISBN 0-460-05088-5, Pub. by J. M. Dent England). Biblio Dist.
--From the Earth to the Moon. N.D. David McKay.
--From the Earth to the Moon. (gr. 7-12). 1972. (ISBN 0-590-08953-6, Schol Trade Pap). Schol Bk Serv.
--From the Earth to the Moon. Baldick, Robert, ed. Phillipps, W. F., illus. (Illus.). . draws. 4 color plates. 192p. (Children's Illustrated Classics Ser.). (gr. 3-7). 1970. (ISBN 0-525-30256-5). Dutton.
--From the Earth to the Moon. Hoyt, J. K., tr. from Fr. LC 1-9798. 84p. 1869. Newark Printing & Publishing Co.
--From the Earth to the Moon. Roth, Edward, tr. (Illus.). N.D. Catholic Publication Society.
--From the Earth to the Moon & a Trip Around It. 1958. (ISBN 0-397-00088-X). Lippincott.
--From the Earth to the Moon & Round the Moon. (Illus.). (Great Il. Classics). (gr. 7-9). 1962. (ISBN 0-396-04724-6). Dodd.
--From the Earth to the Moon Direct in Nintey-Seven Hours. N.D. Charles Scribner's Sons.
--Journey to the Center of the Earth. 320p. (Blackie Chosen Classics Ser.). (gr. 6 up). 1970. (ISBN 0-216-88508-6, Pub. by Blackie England). Hippocrene Bks.
--A Journey to the Center of the Earth. (gr. 8 up). N.D. Lancer.
--A Journey to the Center of the Earth. (gr. 7-12). 1972. (ISBN 0-590-08552-2, Schol Pap). Scholastic Inc.

--Journey to the Centre of the Earth. (Illus.). 255p. 1st U.S. edition. Repr. of 1970 ed. (Childrens Illustrated Classics Ser.). 1973. (ISBN 0-460-05084-2, Pub. by J. M. Dent England). Biblio Dist.
--A Journey to the Centre of the Earth. (Scribner Series for Young People). N.D. Charles Scribner's Sons.
--Journey to the Centre of the Earth. (Illus.). (Great Il. Classics). (gr. 7-9). 1979. Dodd.
--A Journey to the Centre of the Earth. New ed. 1874. Henry L. Shepard & Co.
--Journey to the Centre of the Earth. Phillipps, W. F., illus. Baldick, Robert, tr. from Fr. (Illus.). . draws. 4 color plates. 256p. (Children's Illustrated Classics Ser.). (gr. 3-7). 1970. (ISBN 0-525-32896-3). Dutton.
--A Journey to the North Pole. (Illus.). N.D. George Routledge & Sons.
--Jules Verne's Wks, 5 vols. N.D. A. L. Burt's Pubs.
--Lighthouse at the End of the World. (The Children's Favorite Ser.). N.D. Grosset & Dunlap.
--The Lighthouse at the End of the World. N.D. Grosset & Dunlap.
--A Long Vacation. LC 67-17996. (Illus.). 224 p. 22cm. 1967. Holt, Rinehart and Winston.
--Master of the World. (Magnum Easy Eye Classic Ser.). (gr. 7-10). N.D. Lancer.
--Michael Strogoff. (Illus.). (The Rugby Series for Boys). N.D. A. L. Burt's Pubs.
--Michael Strogoff. (Magnum Easy Eye Classic Ser.). (gr. 7-12). N.D. Lancer.
--Michael Strogoff. Wyeth, Newell Convers (1882-1945), illus. (Illus.). (Illustrated Classic). (gr. 7-11). 1927. (ISBN 0-684-20972-1, ScribT). Scribner.
--Michael Strogoff, the Courier of the Czar. (Jules Verne Ser.). N.D. A. L. Burt Co.
--Micheal Strogoff; a Courier of the Czar. Wyeth, Newell Convers (1882-1945), illus. (Illustrated Classics). 1955. Scribner.
--The Moon Voyage. N.D. Ward Lock& Bowden.
--The Mysterious Island ... LC 4-17513. 1 p. l., 493 p. front. 19 cm. N.D. A. L. Burt.
--Mysterious Island. (Illus.). (The Rugby Series for Boys). N.D. A. L. Burt's Pubs.
--The Mysterious Island. (The Children's Favorite Ser.). N.D. Grosset & Dunlap.
--The Mysterious Island. (Juvenile Classics). 1874. Henry L. Shepard & Co.
--The Mysterious Island. Osborne, Lloyd, illus. (The Father & Son Library). N.D. Sears Publishing Co.
--Mysterious Island. Wyeth, Newell Convers (1882-1945), illus. (The Scribner Illustrated Classics). 1920. Charles Scribner's Sons.
--Mysterious Island: Includes;"Dropped from the Clouds," "Abandoned," "Secret of the Island", 3. (Everyman's Library). N.D. E. P. Dutton & Co.
--Off on a Comet. N.D. David McKay.
--Round the Moon. Phillipps, D., illus. (Children's Illustrated Classics Ser.). (gr. 6 up). 1970. (ISBN 0-525-38704-8). Dutton.
--In Search of the Castaways. New ed. N.D. J. B. Lippincott.
--The Secret of the Island. Rhys, Ernest, ed. Kingston, William Henry Giles (1814-1880), tr. from Fr. 18cm. 230p. (Everyman's Library for Young People). 1909. E. P. Dutton & Co.
--The Survivors of the Chancellor, and Dr. Ox and Other stories. N.D. James R. Osgood & Co.
--Their Island Home. (The Children's Favorite Ser.). N.D. Grosset & Dunlap.
--To the Sun?. Roth, Edward, tr. N.D. David McKay.
--The Tour of the World. (Illus.). (The Handy Verne Ser.). N.D. Lee and Shepard.
--Tour of the World in Eighty Days. (Jules Verne Ser.). N.D. A. L. Burt Co.
--Tour of the World in Eighty Days. (Illus.). (The Rugby Series for Boys). N.D. A. L. Burt's Pubs.
--Tour of the World in Eighty Days. (Illus.). (The Young Folks Lib.). N.D. H. M. Caldwell Co.
--Tour of the World in Eighty Days. (Illus.). (St. Nicholas Series for Boys). N.D. International Book Co.
--The Tour of the World in Eighty Days. 1873. James R. Osgood.
--Twenty Thousand Leagues Under the Sea, 98 vols. (The Rugby Ser.). 1905. Set. A L Burt Co.
--Twenty Thousand Leagues Under the Sea. (Jules Verne Ser.). N.D. A. L. Burt Co.
--Twenty Thousand Leagues Under the Sea, 1 of 5 vols. (Jules Verne's Wks.). N.D. Set. A. L. Burt's Pubs.
--Twenty Thousand Leagues Under the Sea. (Illus.). (The Rugby Series for Boys). N.D. A. L. Burt's Pubs.
--Twenty Thousand Leagues Under the Sea, No. 167. (The Cornell Ser.). N.D. A. L. Burt's Pubs.
--Twenty Thousand Leagues Under the Sea. (Best Editions). N.D. Belford, Clarke.
--Twenty Thousand Leagues Under the Sea. N.D. Charles Scribner's Sons.
--Twenty Thousand Leagues Under the Sea, Nos. 14-15. (Illus.). (Lakeside Library Ser.). N.D. Donnelley, Loyd & Co.
--Twenty Thousand Leagues Under the Sea. (Everyman's Library). N.D. E. P. Dutton & Co.
--Twenty Thousand Leagues Under the Sea. (The Roxburghe Classics). N.D. Estes & Lauriat's.
--Twenty Thousand Leagues Under the Sea. (Standard Editions). N.D. Estes & Lauriat.
--Twenty Thousand Leagues Under the Sea. (The People's Library). N.D. Funk & Wagnalls.
--Twenty Thousand Leagues Under The Sea. N.D. George Routledge & Sons.
--Twenty Thousand Leagues Under the Sea, 1 of 11 Vols, Pt. 1. (Illus.). (Jules Verne's Stories, Tales, and Romances). N.D. Set. George Routledge & Sons.
--Twenty Thousand Leagues Under the Sea, 1 of 11 Vols, Pt. 2. (Illus.). (Jules Verne's Stories, Tales, and Romances). N.D. Set. George Routledge & Sons.
--Twenty Thousand Leagues Under the Sea, No.84. (Seaside Library). N.D. George Munro: Dist. by American News Co.
--Twenty Thousand Leagues Under the Sea. N.D. Grosset & Dunlap.
--Twenty-Thousand Leagues Under the Sea. (Illus.). (Classics Illus. Ser.). N.D. (ISBN 0-685-74092-7). Guild Bks.
--Twenty Thousand Leagues Under the Sea, 1 of 64 vols. (Illus.). (Young America Library: No. 50). 1900. Set. Hurst & Co.
--Twenty Thousand Leagues Under the Sea. (New Aldine Ser). N.D. International Book Co.
--Twenty Thousand Leagues Under the Sea, 2 of a 2 vol set. (Favorite Series). N.D. International Book Co.
--Twenty Thousand Leagues Under the Sea. (Sunset Ser.). N.D. J. S. Ogilvie.
--Twenty Thousand Leagues Under the Sea. N.D. James R. Osgood.
--Twenty Thousand Leagues Under the Sea. (New International Library). N.D. John C. Winston Co.
--Twenty Thousand Leagues Under The Sea. (New Acorn Library). N.D. John C. Winston & Co.
--Twenty Thousand Leagues Under the Sea. (The Pastime Ser.). N.D. Laird & Lee's Publications.
--Twenty Thousand Leagues Under the Sea. N.D. Lovell, Coryell & Co.
--Twenty Thousand Leagues Under the Sea. 1962. Macmillan Company.
--Twenty Thousand Leagues Under the Sea. 404 p. 21cm. (Classics to Grow on). 1966. Parents' Magazine's Cultural Institute.
--Twenty Thousand Leagues Under the Sea. (Jules Verne Lib.). 1888. Porter & Coates.
--Twenty Thousand Leagues Under the Sea, 1 of 4 Vols. (Library of Travel). N.D. Set. Porter & Coates.
--Twenty Thousand Leagues Under the Sea. (Illus.). N.D. R Worthington.
--Twenty Thousand Leagues Under The Sea. (The Advance Library Ser.: Vol. 315). N.D. Rand, McNally & Co.
--Twenty Thousand Leagues Under the Sea. (Illus.). (The Independent Library Ser.: Vol. 315). N.D. Rand, McNally & Co.
--Twenty Thousand Leagues Under The Sea. N.D. Standard And Holiday.
--Twenty Thousand Leagues Under the Sea. N.D (Standard and Holiday Books). The American News Co.
--Twenty Thousand Leagues Under the Sea. N.D. William Collins Sons & Co Ltd.
--Twenty Thousand Leagues Under the Sea. Amery, Heather, adapted by. LC 76-13133. (Illus.). 102, 1 p., 8 leaves of plates. 25cm. 1976. (ISBN 0-679-20373-7). D. McKay Co.
--Twenty Thousand Leagues Under the Sea. Aylward, William James (1875-), illus. (The Scribner Illustrated Classics). 1925. Charles Scribner's Sons.
--Twenty Thousand Leagues Under the Sea. Burton, Ardis Edwards, adapted by. Fraumeni, Guy, illus. LC 55-12564. (Illus.). 21cm. 196p. 1955. Globe Book Co.
--Twenty Thousand Leagues Under the Sea. Clare, Andrea M, adapted by. Grove, David, illus. LC 73-80399. (Illus.). 92 p. 21cm. (Pacemaker classic). 1973. (ISBN 0-8224-9233-4). Fearon Publishers.
--Twenty Thousand Leagues Under the Sea. Conaway, Judith (1948-), adapted by. D'Achille, Gino, illus. LC 82-12310. p. cm. (Step-up Adventures: No. 6). (gr. 2-5). 1983. (ISBN 0-394-85333-4). (ISBN 0-394-95333-9). Random House.
--Twenty Thousand Leagues Under the Sea. Fischer, Anton Otto (1882-), illus. N.D. John C. Winston Co.
--Twenty Thousand Leagues Under the Sea. Geis, Darlene, adapted by. Auger, Raoul, illus. LC 58-352341. unpaged. illus. 31 cm. c.1958. Grosset & Dunlap.
--Twenty Thousand Leagues Under the Sea. complete and unabridged. Irwin, Don, illus. LC 68-31324. (Illus.). 283 p. 29cm. 1968. Childrens Press.
--Twenty Thousand Leagues Under the Sea. Irwin, Don, illus. LC 70-2032. (Illus.). 283 p. 29cm. (Educator Classic Library, 2). 1968. Classic Press.
--Twenty Thousand Leagues Under the Sea. Moderow, Gertrude, adapted by. N.D. Scott, Foresman & Co.
--Twenty Thousand Leagues Under the Sea. Nordicht, Lillian, adapted by. Butz, Steve, illus. LC 79-23887. p. cm. c.1980. (ISBN 0-8172-1652-9). Raintree Publishers.
--Twenty Thousand Leagues Under the Sea. Rhys, Ernest, ed. Kingston, William Henry Giles (1814-1880), tr. from Fr. 18cm. 288p. (Everyman's Library for Young People). 1908. E. P. Dutton & Co.
--Twenty Thousand Leagues Under the Sea. Winter, Milo Kendall (1888-1956), illus. Allen, Philip Schuyler (1871-), tr. LC 22-19163. x, 495 p. col. front., col. plates. 23 1/2 cm. (Windermere Ser.). c.1922. Rand, McNally & Company.
--Twenty Thousand Leagues Under the Sea: Part 1. N.D. George Routledge & Sons.
--Twenty Thousand Leagues Under the Sea: Part 2. N.D. George Routledge & Sons.
--A Winter in the Ice. (Illus.). (The Handy Verne Ser.). N.D. Lee & Shepard.
--The Wreck of the Chancellor. (The Handy Verne Ser.). N.D. Lee & Shepard.

Vernede, Robert Ernest (1875-1917)
--The Quietness of Dick. Perard, Victor Semon (1870-1957), illus. LC 11-11743. (Illus.). 19cm. 290p. 1911. H. Holt and Company.

Verner, Diana
--Wild Cherry & Other Tales. 32p. (gr. 3 up). 1979. Dorrance.

Verney, John (1913-)
--February's Road. LC 66-6762. (Illus.). 192 p. 21cm. 1966, c.1961. Holt, Rinehart and Winston.
--Friday's Tunnel. Verney, John, Sir (1913-), illus. LC 66-12033. 320p. illus. 21cm. 1966, c.1959. Holt. **Award: (CMA).**
--Ismo. LC 67-1690. (Illus.). 256 p. 21cm. 1967, c.1964. Holt, Rinehart and Winston.
--The Mad King of Chichiboo. LC 63-7340. 1 v. (unpaged) illus. (part col.) 26 cm. 1963. F. Watts.
--Seven Sunflower Seeds. LC 69-11821. (Illus.). 256 p. 22cm. 1969, c.1968. Holt, Rinehart and Winston.

Verney, Peter Vivian Lloyd (1930-)
--Here Comes the Circus. LC 77-13987. (Illus.). 287 p. 26cm. c.1978. (ISBN 0-448-23115-8). Paddington Press : Distributed by Grosset & Dunlap.

Vernham, Katherine E.
--Bab's Baby and Other Stories. N.D. Thomas Whittaker.
--Deborah's Dressing, and Other Stories. N.D. Thomas Whittaker.
--Jo: A Stupid Boy, And Other Stories. N.D. Thomas Whittaker.
--Such a Tomboy. N.D. Thomas Whittaker.
--The Tucker's Turkey. N.D. Thomas Whittaker.
--A Wonderful Christmas. N.D. Thomas Whittaker.

Vernon, Edna Louise Anderson (1914-)
--The Beggars' Bible. McCoy, Jeanie, illus. LC 77-131534. (Illus.). 136 p. 22cm. 1971. (ISBN 0-8361-1628-3). Herald Press.
--Beggars Bible: An Illustrated Historical Fiction of John Wycliffe for the Nine to Fourteen Age-Group. LC 77-131534. (Illus.). 8 color photos. 128p. 128p. (gr. 4-9). 1971. (ISBN 0-8361-1732-8). Herald Pr.
--The Bible Smuggler. Scottdale, Roger Hane, illus. LC 67-15994. 139p. illus. port. 22cm. 1967. Herald Pr.
--Doctor in Rags. Eitzen, Allan (1928-), illus. LC 72-5367. (Illus.). 146 p. 23cm. 1973. (ISBN 0-8361-1697-6). Herald Press.
--A Heart Strangely Warmed. Eitzen, Allan (1928-), illus. LC 75-11767. (Illus.). 125 p. 23cm. 1975. (ISBN 0-8361-1768-9). (ISBN 0-8361-1769-7). Herald Press.
--Ink on His Fingers. Eitzen, Allan (1928-), illus. LC 73-171105. (Illus.). 128 p. 22cm. 1972. (ISBN 0-8361-1660-7). Herald Press.
--Key to the Prison. Eitzen, Allan (1928-), illus. LC 68-11054. (Illus.). 138 p. 22cm. 1968. Herald Press.
--The King's Book. Eitzen, Allan (1928-), illus. LC 80-18998. (Illus.). 127 p. 21cm. 1980. (ISBN 0-8361-1933-9). Herald Press.
--The Man Who Laid the Egg. Eitzen, Allan (1928-), illus. LC 77-24939. (Illus.). 118 p. 22cm. 1977. (ISBN 0-8361-1827-8). (ISBN 0-8361-1828-6). Herald Press.
--Night Preacher. Eitzen, Allan (1928-), illus. LC 73-94378. 22cm. 123p. 1969. Herald Press.
--Peter and the Pilgrims. Dunbebin, Thomas, illus. LC 63-17755. 127 p. illus. 22 cm. c.1963. Review and Herald Pub. Association.
--The Secret Church. Dunbebin, Thomas, illus. LC 68-22286. 22cm. 127p. 1968. Review & Herald.
--The Secret Church. Eitzen, Allan (1928-), illus. LC 67-159887. (Illus.). 128 p. 23cm. 1967. Herald Press.
--Strangers in the Land. McCoy, Jeanie, illus. LC 64-17651. 126 p. illus. 22 cm. 1964. Review and Herald Pub. Association.
--Thunderstorm in Church. Eitzen, Allan (1928-), illus. LC 74-5009. (Illus.). 134 p. 23cm. 1974. (ISBN 0-8361-1739-5). (ISBN 0-8361-1739-5). Herald Press.

Vernon, Louise Anderson see Vernon, Edna Louise Anderson.

Vernon, Thomas
--Arabian Nights. (The Roxburghe Classics). N.D. Estes & Lauriat's.
--Arabian Nights. (Illus.). (Juvenile Classics). N.D. H. M. Caldwell Co.
--Hale's Arabian Nights. Hale, Edward Everett, ed. (Classics for Children). N.D. Ginn and Company.

Vernon Jones, Vernon Stanley, tr. see Aesopus.

Verr, Harry Coe
--Rainbow Brite and the Color Thieves. LC 84-82181. (Illus.). 42 p. 29cm. c.1984. (ISBN 0-307-16003-3). (ISBN 0-307-66003-6). Western Pub. Co.

Verral, Charles, ed. see Doyle, Arthur Conan, Sir.

Verral, Charles Spain, jt. auth. see Disney, Walter Elias.

Verral, Charles Spain, adapted by see Disney, Walter Elias.

Verral, Charles Spain (1904-), adapted by see Disney, Walt, Productions.

Verral, Charles Spain (1904-)
--Annie Oakley, Sharpshooter. Dreany, E. Joseph, illus. LC 57-1087. unpaged. illus. 21 cm. (A Little Golden Bk. 275). 1957, c.1956. Simon and Schuster.
--Brave Eagle. Vanderlaan, Si, illus. (Little Golden Book). 1957. Golden Press.
--Broken Arrow. Crawford, Mel (1925-), illus. (Little Golden Book). 1957. Golden Press.
--Captain of the Ice. LC 53-8424. 151p. 21cm. 1953. Crowell.
--The Case of the Missing Message. Greene, Hamilton, illus. LC 59-4352. 188 p. illus. 21 cm. (A Brains Benton Mystery). 1959. Golden Press.
--Champion of the Court. LC 54-9154. 192 p. 21cm. 1954. Crowell.
--High Danger. Knight, Clayton (1891-1969), illus. LC 55-10369. 192p. illus. 21cm. 1955. Sterling Pub. Co.
--The King of the Diamond. LC 55-7330. 179p. 21cm. 1955. Crowell.
--Lassie and Her Day in the Sun. Crawford, Mel (1925-), illus. (Little Golden Book). 1958. Golden Press.
--Lassie and the Daring Rescue. authorized. LC 57-1088. unpaged. illus. 21 cm. (A Little Golden Bk. 277). 1957, c.1956. Simon and Schuster.
--The Lone Ranger and Tonto. Schmidt, Edwin, illus. (Little Golden Book). 1957. Golden Press.
--Mighty Men of Baseball. Rawson, Maurice, illus. N.D. E. P. Dutton & Co.
--Play Ball!. McCann, Gerald (1916-), illus. (Little Golden Book). 1958. Golden Press.
--Popeye and the Haunted House. LC 80-139141. (Illus.). 20 p. 21cm. c.1980. Wonder Books.
--Popeye Climbs a Mountain. LC 80-140028. (Illus.). 20 p. 25cm. c.1980. (ISBN 0-448-00502-6). Wonder Books.
--Popeye Goes Fishing. (Illus.). 24p. (Wonder Bks.). (ps-1). 1980. (ISBN 0-686-64625-8, G&D). Putnam Pub Group.
--Rin Tin Tin and the Hidden Treasure. Crawford, Mel (1925-), illus. (Big Golden Book). 1958. Golden Press.
--Rin Tin Tin and the Outlaw. Crawford, Mel (1925-), illus. (Little Golden Book). 1957. Golden Press.
--Smokey and His Animal Friends. Crawford, Mel (1925-), illus. (Little Golden Book). 1960. Golden Press.
--The Winning Quarterback. LC 60-6257. 248 p. 21 cm. 1960. Crowell.
--The Wonderful World Series. LC 56-6244. 154 p. 21 cm. c.1956. Crowell.

Verral, Charles Spain (1904-), adapted by.
--Around the World in Eighty Days. Gill, Tom, illus. (An Abridgement of the Novel by Jules Verne). (A Golden Picture Classic). 1957. Golden Press.

Verral, Charles Spain (1904-) & Hill, Monica
--The Adventures of Lassie. Crawford, Mel (1925-) & Dreany, E. Joseph, illus. (Giant Little Golden Book). 1958. Golden Press.

Verrier, Suzanne
--Titus Tidewater. Verrier, Suzanne, illus. LC 70-112636. (Illus.). 41 p. 1970. Doubleday.

--Abigail Adams: Girl of Colonial Days. Ponter, James J., illus. LC 62-12691. 200p. col. illus. 20cm. (Childhood of famous Amers.). 1962. Bobbs.
--The Captive Lad: A Story of Daniel, the Lionhearted. 1st ed. Laune, Paul Sidney (1899-), illus. LC 54-112957. 181p. illus. 23cm. 1954. Bobbs-Merrill.
--Jane Addams: Little Lame Girl. James, Sandra, illus. LC 44-8093. 192 p. illus. 20 cm. (The Childhood of famous Americans series). 1944. The Bobbs-Merrill Company.
--Jane Addams: Little Lame Girl. Morrow, Gray, illus. LC 62-9250. 200p. col. illus. 20cm. (Childhood of famous Amer.). 1962. Bobbs.
--Jessie Fremont: Girl of Capitol Hill. Funk, Clotilde Embree, illus. LC 56-13041. 192p. illus. 20cm. 1956. Bobbs-Merrill.
--Jessie Fremont: Girl of Capitol Hill. Rawson, Maurice, illus. LC 60-7706. 192 p. illus. 20 cm. (Childhood of famous Americans). 1960. Bobbs-Merrill.
--Julia Ward Howe, Girl of Old New York. Funk, Clotilde Embree, illus. LC 45-8460. 214 p. illus. 19 1/2 x 15 cm. (The Childhood of Famous Americans Ser.). 1945. The Bobbs-Merrill Company.
--Julia Ward Howe, Girl of Old New York. Patterson, Robert (1899-), illus. LC 62-12704. (Illus.). 200p. 20cm. (Childhood of Famous Americans Ser.). 1962. Bobbs-Merrill.
--Louisa Alcott, Girl of Old Boston. 1st ed. James, Sandra, illus. LC 43-140889. (Illus.). 185p. 19 x 15cm. 1943. The Bobbs-Merrill Company.
--Louisa Alcott: Girl of Old Boston. Nankivel, Claudine, illus. LC 62-9253. 200 p. illus. 20 cm. (childhood of famous americans. 1962. Bobbs-Merrill.
--Martha Washington: Girl of Old Virginia. Goldstein, Leslie, illus. LC 59-12849. 200 p. illus. 20 cm. (Childhood of famous Americans). 1959. Bobbs-Merrill.
--Martha Washington: Girl of Old Virginia. 1st ed. James, Sandra, illus. LC 47-308449. 196 p. illus. 20 cm. (childhood of famous Americans series). 1947. Bobbs-Merrill Co.
--Martha Washington of Old Virginia. James, Sandra, illus. LC 53-704. (Illus.). 196p. 20cm. (The Childhood of Famous Americans Ser.). 1953. Bobbs-Merrill.
--The Shepherd Lad: A Story of David of Bethlehem. 1st ed. Laune, Paul Sidney (1899-), illus. LC 53-9873. 168p. illus. 23cm. 1953. Bobbs-Merrill.

Wagstaff, Dorothy
--The Little Horse That Never Grew up. Wagstaff, Dorothy, illus. LC 47-30785. 31 p. illus. 20 x 25 cm. (Borzoi books for young people). 1947. A. A. Knopf.

Wagstaff, Hester
--The Adventures of Velvet and Vicky. N.D. Transatlantic Arts.
--The Doings of Dicky Daw. Wagstaff, Hester, illus. LC 40-6907. 45 p. col. illus. 26 cm. c.1940. Coward-McCann, Inc.
--Tales Of the Jolly Robin Family. N.D. Transatlantic Arts.

Wah-Be-Gwo-Nese, pseud., see King, Cheryl N..

Wah-Be-Gwo-Nese, pseud.
--Ojibwa Indian Legends. King, Cheryl N.. (Illus.). 1972. (ISBN 0-918616-05-0). Northern Mich.

Wahl, Jan (1933-)
--Abe Lincoln's Beard. Krahn, Fernando (1935-), illus. LC 75-156045. (Illus.). 23 x 26cm. 25p. 1971. Delacorte Press.
--The Animals' Peace Day. 1st ed. Chess, Victoria (1939-), illus. LC 74-108079. (Illus.). 32 p. 1970. Crown Publishers.
--Anna Help Ginger. Di Fiori, Lawrence, illus. LC 75-128405. (Illus.). 42 p. 22cm. 1971. Putnam.
--Bear, Wolf, and Mouse. Craft, Kinuko Y., illus. LC 74-83610. (Illus.). 31 p. 21cm. (A Follett Beginning-To-Read Bk.). c.1975. (ISBN 0-695-40516-0). (ISBN 0-695-30516-6). Follett Pub. Co.
--Button Eye's Orange. Watson, Wendy McLeod (1942-), illus. LC 80-14429. p. cm. 1980. (ISBN 0-7232-6188-1). F. Warne.
--Cabbage Moon. Adams, Adrienne (1906-), illus. LC 64-13401. (Illus.). 32 p. 1965. Holt, Rinehart and Winston.
--Carrot Nose. Marshall, James (1942-), illus. LC 78-60514. (Illus.). 39 p. 21cm. 1978. (ISBN 0-374-31122-6). Farrar, Straus, Giroux.
--Christmas in the Forest. Schick, Eleanor (1942-), illus. LC 67-17215. (Illus.). 32 p. 1967. Macmillan.
--The Clumpets Go Sailing. Szekeres, Cyndy (1933-), illus. LC 73-23083. (Illus.). 40 p. 1975. (ISBN 0-8193-0770-X). (ISBN 0-8193-0771-8). Parents' Magazine Press.
--Cobweb Castle. 1st ed. Gorey, Edward St. John (1925-), illus. LC 68-17639. (Illus.). 30 p. 21cm. 1968. Holt, Rinehart and Winston.
--Crabapple Night. 1st ed. Kellogg, Steven (1941-), illus. LC 72-141011. (Illus.). 59 p. 24cm. 1971. (ISBN 0-03-086239-6). Holt, Rinehart and Winston.
--Cristobal and the Witch. McCaffery, Janet, illus. LC 79-149331. (Illus.). 41 p. 25cm. 1972. Putnam.
--The Cucumber Princess. Caraway, Caren, illus. LC 80-29077. p. cm. 1981. (ISBN 0-916144-76-3). (ISBN 0-916144-77-1). Stemmer House Publishers.
--Doctor Rabbit. Parnall, Peter (1936-), illus. LC 78-101994. (Illus.). 48 p. 1970. Delacorte Press.
--Doctor Rabbit's Foundling. Szekeres, Cyndy (1933-), illus. LC 76-42460. (Illus.). 28 p. c.1977. (ISBN 0-394-83275-2). (ISBN 0-394-93275-7). Pantheon Books.
--Doctor Rabbit's Lost Scout. Szekeres, Cyndy (1933-), illus. LC 79-945. p. cm. c.1979. (ISBN 0-394-94246-9). Pantheon Books.
--Dracula's Cat. Chorao, Ann Mckay Sproat (1936-), illus. LC 77-27051. (Illus.). 32 p. 24cm. c.1978. (ISBN 0-13-218933-X). Prentice-Hall.
--Drakestail. Barton, Byron (1930-), illus. (Illus.). 55 p. 22cm. (Greenwillow read-alone). c.1978. Greenwillow Books.
--The Fishermen. 1st ed. McCully, Emily Arnold (1939-), illus. LC 69-12588. (Illus.). 47 p. 24cm. 1969. Norton.
--The Five in the Forest. Blegvad, Erik (1923-), illus. (Illus.). 46 p. 20cm. 1974. (ISBN 0-695-80446-4). (ISBN 0-695-80446-4). Follett.
--Follow Me Cried Bee. Wallner, John C. (1945-), illus. LC 75-9925. p. cm. 1975. (ISBN 0-517-52353-1). Crown Publishers.
--Frankenstein's Dog. Chorao, Ann Mckay Sproat (1936-), illus. LC 77-3674. p. cm. c.1977. (ISBN 0-13-330522-8). Prentice-Hall.
--The Furious Flycycle. Krahn, Fernando (1935-), illus. LC 67-12773. (Illus.). 114 p. 24cm. 1968. Delacorte Press.
--Grandmother Told Me. 1st ed. Mayer, Mercer (1943-), illus. LC 78-182257. (Illus.). 32 p. 19cm. 1972. Little, Brown.
--Grandpa Gus's Birthday Cake. Wallner, John C. (1945-), illus. LC 81-7368. p. cm. c.1981. (ISBN 0-13-363325-X). Prentice-Hall.
--Grandpa's Indian Summer. Scribner, Joanne L. (1949-), illus. LC 76-8853. p. cm. c.1976. (ISBN 0-13-363317-9). Prentice-Hall.
--Great-Grandmother Cat Tales. Szekeres, Cyndy (1933-), illus. LC 76-5484. (Illus.). 54 p. 22cm. c.1976. (ISBN 0-394-83278-7). (ISBN 0-394-93278-1). Pantheon Books.
--Hello, Elephant. Ardizzone, Edward Jeffrey Irving (1900-1979), illus. LC 64-13400. (Illus.). 32p. (gr. k-3). 1964. (ISBN 0-03-045805-6). HR&W.
--How the Children Stopped the Wars. Miller, Mitchell (1947-), illus. LC 69-14979. (Illus.). 95 p. 20cm. 1969. Farrar, Straus and Giroux.
--The Howards Go Sledding. 1st ed. Johnson, John Emil (1929-), illus. LC 64-14328. (Illus.). 32 p. 1964. Holt, Rinehart and Winston.
--Jamie's Tiger. 1st ed. De Paola, Tomie, pseud. (1934-), illus. De Paola, Thomas Anthony. LC 77-88969. (Illus.). 48 p. 22cm. c.1978. (ISBN 0-15-239500-8). Harcourt Brace Jovanovich.
--Jeremiah Knucklebones. 1st ed. Zalben, Jane Breskin (1950-), illus. LC 73-22354. (Illus.). 53 p. 1974. (ISBN 0-03-012741-6). Holt, Rinehart and Winston.
--Juan Diego & the Lady-la Dama y Juan Diego. Fisher, Leonard Everett (1924-), illus. (Illus.). 48p. (gr. 2-5). 1974. (ISBN 0-399-60845-1). Putnam Pub Group.
--The Little Blind Goat. 1st ed. Frasconi, Antonio (1919-), illus. LC 81-9429. p. cm. c.1981. (ISBN 0-916144-70-4). Stemmer House.
--Lorenzo Bear & Company. Krahn, Fernando (1935-), illus. LC 76-145456. (Illus.). 41 p. 24cm. 1971. Putnam.
--Magic Heart. Hyman, Trina Schart (1939-), illus. LC 70-171861. (Illus.). 48 p. 22cm. 1972. (ISBN 0-8164-3038-1). Seabury Press.
--Margaret's Birthday. Mayer, Mercer (1943-), illus. LC 73-161013. (Illus.). 45 p. 24cm. 1971. Four Winds Press.
--May Horses. Lent, Blair (1930-), illus. LC 68-20105. (Illus.). 41 p. 24cm. 1969. Delacorte Press.
--Mooga Mega Mekki. Krahn, Fernando (1935-), illus. LC 73-16818. (Illus.). 45 p. 23cm. (A Lead-Off Bk.). 1974. (ISBN 0-87955-111-9). (ISBN 0-87955-111-9). J. P. O'Hara.
--More Room for the Pipkins. Wallner, John C. (1945-), illus. LC 82-21442. p. cm. c.1983. (ISBN 0-13-601146-2). Prentice-Hall.
--The Muffletump Storybook. Szekeres, Cyndy (1933-), illus. LC 73-93552. (Illus.). 127 p. 22cm. 1975. (ISBN 0-695-80477-4). (ISBN 0-695-40477-6). Follett Pub. Co.
--The Muffletumps' Christmas Party. Szekeres, Cyndy (1933-), illus. LC 75-332695. (Illus.). 32 p. 23cm. c.1975. (ISBN 0-695-80617-3). (ISBN 0-695-40617-5). Follett Pub. Co.
--The Muffletumps' Halloween Scare. Szekeres, Cyndy (1933-), illus. LC 77-152997. (Illus.). 32 p. 22cm. c.1977. (ISBN 0-695-80754-4). (ISBN 0-695-40754-6). Follett Pub. Co.
--The Muffletumps: The Story of Four Dolls. Ardizzone, Edward Jeffrey Irving (1900-1979), illus. LC 66-12034. (Illus.). 1 v. (unpaged. (Holt Owlet). 1973, c.1966. (ISBN 0-03-005741-8). Holt.
--Mulberry Tree. Rojankovsky, Feodor Stepanovich (1891-1970), illus. (Illus.). color ils. 48p. (gr. k-3). 1970. G&D.
--The Norman Rockwell Storybook. Rockwell, Norman Percevel (1894-1978), illus. LC 79-14462. (Illus.). 46 p. 31cm. 1979, c.1969. (ISBN 0-671-25102-3). Simon and Schuster.
--The Norman Rockwell Storybook. Rockwell, Norman Percevel (1894-1978), illus. LC 73-86946. (Illus.). 46 p. 32cm. 1969. Windmill Books.
--Old Hippo's Easter Egg. 1st ed. Cauley, Lorinda Bryan (1951-), illus. LC 79-9199. (Illus.). 32 p. 26cm. c.1980. Harcourt Brace Jovanovich.
--Peter & the Troll Baby. Blegvad, Erik (1923-), illus. LC 82-80866. (Illus.). 32p. (ps-2). 1984. (ISBN 0-307-16525-6, Golden Bks). Western Pub.
--The Pipkins Go Camping. Wallner, John C. (1945-), illus. LC 82-7496. (Illus.). 32 p. 24cm. c.1982. (ISBN 0-13-676270-0). Prentice-Hall.
--Pleasant Fieldmouse. Sendak, Maurice Bernard (1928-), illus. LC 64-14684. (Illus.). (gr. k-3). 1964. (ISBN 0-06-026331-8, HarpJ). Har-Row.
--The Pleasant Fieldmouse Storybook. Blegvad, Erik (1923-), illus. 1975. (ISBN 0-87955-212-3). J. Philip O'Hara Inc.
--The Pleasant Fieldmouse Storybook. Blegvad, Erik (1923-), illus. LC 76-44528. (Illus.). 63 p. 22cm. c.1977. (ISBN 0-13-684514-2). Prentice-Hall.
--Pleasant Fieldmouse's Halloween Party. Tripp, Wallace Whitney (1940-), illus. LC 73-88814. (Illus.). 32 p. 20cm. 1974. (ISBN 0-399-20395-8). Putnam.
--Pleasant Fieldmouse's Valentine Trick. Blegvad, Erik (1923-), illus. LC 77-3169. p. cm. 1977. (ISBN 0-525-61566-0). Windmill Books.
--Pocahontas in London. Alcorn, John (1935-), illus. LC 67-19772. (Illus.). 40 p. 29cm. 1967. Delacorte Press.
--The Prince Who Was a Fish. Jacques, Robin (1920-), illus. LC 76-124291. (Illus.). 62 p. 27cm. 1970. Simon and Schuster.
--Push Kitty. Williams, Garth Montgomery (1912-), illus. LC 68-10371. (Illus.). 31 p. 26cm. 1968. Harper & Row.
--Rickety Rackety Rooster. Johnson, John Emil (1929-), illus. LC 68-16146. (Illus.). 39 p. 1968. Simon & Schuster.
--Runaway Jonah & Other Tales. Shulevitz, Uri (1935-), illus. LC 68-12084. 13 pages of 2 color ils. 48p. (ps-3). 1968. (ISBN 0-02-792340-1). Macmillan.
--S. O. S. Bobomobile: Or, the Further Adventures of Melvin Spitznagle and Professor Mickmecki. Krahn, Fernando (1935-), illus. LC 73-7204. (Illus.). 128p. (gr. 2-6). 1973. (Sey Lawr). Delacorte.
--The Screeching Door: Or, What Happened at the Elephant Hotel. Higginbottom, Jeffrey Winslow (1945-), illus. LC 75-9824. (Illus.). 80p. (gr. 2-5). 1975. (ISBN 0-590-07358-3, Four Winds). Scholastic Inc.
--The Six Voyages of Pleasant Fieldmouse. Parnall, Peter (1936-), illus. LC 68-12196. (Illus.). 94 p. 24cm. 1971. Delacorte Press.
--Sylvester Bear Overslept. Lorenz, Lee, illus. LC 79-4095. p. cm. c.1979. (ISBN 0-8193-1003-4). (ISBN 0-8193-1004-2). Parents' Magazine Press.
--The Teeny, Tiny Witches. Tomes, Margot Ladd (1917-), illus. LC 78-15657. (Illus.). 48 p. 23cm. c.1979. (ISBN 0-399-61133-9). Putnam.
--Tiger Watch. 1st ed. Mikolaycak, Charles (1937-), illus. LC 82-964. (Illus.). 31 p. c.1982. (ISBN 0-15-287674-X). Harcourt Brace Jovanovich.
--The Very Peculiar Tunnel. Kellogg, Steven (1941-), illus. LC 77-179025. (Illus.). 64 p. 23cm. 1972. (ISBN 0-399-20264-1). (ISBN 0-399-20264-1). Putnam.
--Who Will Believe Tim Kitten?. Szekeres, Cyndy (1933-), illus. LC 77-12956. p. cm. 1977. (ISBN 0-394-83666-9). (ISBN 0-394-93666-3). Pantheon Books.
--Wolf of My Own. Hoban, Lillian (1925-), illus. LC 69-10501. (Illus.). 17 color ils. 32p. (gr. k-2). 1969. (ISBN 0-02-792330-4). Macmillan.
--The Wonderful Kite. Shulevitz, Uri (1935-), illus. LC 74-118663. (Illus.). 92 p. 27cm. 1971, c.1970. Delacorte Press.
--Youth's Magic Horn: Seven Stories. LC 77-29127. 127 p. 21cm. c.1978. (ISBN 0-8407-6582-7). T. Nelson.

Wahl, Jan (1933-), retold by.
--Needle and Noodle, and Other Silly Stories. Mack, Stanley (1935-), illus. LC 78-27817. p. cm. c.1979. (ISBN 0-394-84170-0). (ISBN 0-394-94170-5). Pantheon Books.
--The Woman with the Eggs. 1st ed. Cruz, Raymond (1933-), illus. LC 74-77481. (Original Author: Hans Christian Andersen,1805-1875). (Illus.). 31 p. 24cm. 1974. (ISBN 0-517-51587-3). Crown Publishers.

Wahl, Jan (1933-) & Le Prince De Beaumont, Marie (1711-1780)
--Crazy Brobobalou. Winter, Paula Cecelia (1929-), illus. LC 72-98129. (Illus.). 48 p. 21cm. 1973. (ISBN 0-399-20357-5). (ISBN 0-399-20357-5). Putnam.

Wahl, Robert (1948-)
--What Will You Do Today, Little Russell?. Shecter, Ben (1935-), illus. LC 79-153994. (Illus.). 32 p. 1972. Putnam.

Wahlenberg, Anna (1858-1933)
--Diamond Bird & Other Tales. Dolesch, Susanne, illus. MacMillan, Annabelle, pseud. (1922-), tr. Quick, Annabelle. LC 69-12359. (Illus.). 14 line cuts. 168p. (gr. 4-7). 1969. Doubleday.

Wahlenberg, Anna (1858-1933) & Thomsen, Frede
--Old Swedish Fairy Tales. Berkowitz, Jeannette, illus. Patterson, Antoinette De Coursey, Mrs., tr. LC 25-16131. 6 p. l., 15-296 p. col. front., illus., col. plates. 25 cm. 1925. The Penn Publishing Company.

Wahlenberg-Kjerman, Anna Maria Lovisa see Wahlenberg, Anna.

Wahlenberg-Kjerman, Anna Maria Lovisa see Wahlenberg, Anna (1858-1933) & Thomsen, Frede.

Wahn, Graham, jt. auth. see Wahn, Julia.

Wahn, Julia & Wahn, Graham
--Edgar, the Runaway Elephant. Wahn, Julia & Wahn, Graham, illus. LC 41-20169. cover-title, 38 p. illus. (part col.) 28 x 23 cm. c.1941. W. R. Scott, Inc.

Waide, Jan (1952-)
--Jennifer. LC 78-12948. p. cm. 1978. (ISBN 0-88319-039-7). Shoal Creek Publishers.
--Weed. LC 80-16604. p. cm. 1980. (ISBN 0-88319-052-4). Shoal Creek Publishers.

Wain, John Barrington (1925-)
--The Free Zone Starts Here. LC 83-14373. 196p. (gr. 7 up). 1984. (ISBN 0-385-29315-1). Delacorte.
--Lizzie's Floating Shop. 224p. (Orig.). (gr. 3-8). 1984. (ISBN 0-370-30906-5, Pub. by the Bodley Head). Merrimack Pub Cir.
--Nuncle and Other Stories. 1961. St Martin's Press.

Wain, Louis (1861-1939)
--Cat Alphabet. (Illus.). (The Happy Child's Library). N.D. Dodge Publishing Co.

Wain, Louis (1861-1939) & Bingham, Clifton
--Dandy Lion. N.D. E. P. Dutton and Co.

Wainer, Nora Roberts
--The Whale with a Jail. Carle, Eric (1929-), illus. LC 68-26423. (Illus.). 33 p. 21cm. 1968. Funk & Wagnalls.

Wainwright, R. B.
--Three Babies & What They Did. 1900. Thomas Nelson & Sons.

Waite, Arthur Edward (1857-)
--The Golden Stairs: Tales from the Wonder-World. LC 34-38304. 109 p. 19 cm. 1893. The Theosophical Publishing Society.

Waite, Esther (1899-)
--Kate Farley, Pioneer. Waite, Esther (1899-), illus. 96p. N.D. Viking Press.

Waite, Gertrude R. Mitchell
--How Tommy Was Cured of Crying And Other Rhymes for the Little Ones. Mackin, Bernice Roberts, illus. LC 1-31077. 2 p. l., 11-55, 1 p. illus., pl. 25 cm. c.1900. The Abbey Press.

Waite, Helen Elmira (1903-)
--Bold of Heart. MacPherson, Jean Jay (1931-), illus. LC 40-32088. 21cm. 200p. (A Mystery Story for Girls). 1940. MaCrae Smith Co.
--Butterfly Takes Command. Wonsetler, John Charles (1900-), illus. LC 44-3687. vi p., 1 l., 11-297 p. illus. 20 cm. 1944. Macrae-Smith-Company.
--How Do I Love Thee?. The Story of Elizabeth Barrett Browning. LC 52-6763. 221 p. 22cm. 1953. Macrae Smith Co.
--The "Icicle" Melts: A Story for Girls. Withington, Elizabeth R., illus. LC 29-195265. 310 p. front., plates. 19 1/2 cm. c.1929. Lothrop, Lee & Shepard Co.
--The Loyal Traitor. Doane, Pelagie (1906-1966), illus. LC 35-21569. 280 p. front., plates. 20 cm. c.1935. Macrae Smith Company.

Waite, Jon
--Soldiers of the Sea. LC 43-164866. v, 207 p. front. 20 cm. (His Warriors of American series). 1943. Cupples & Leon Company.
--The Tanks Are Coming. LC 45-155466. v, 201 p. front. 19 cm. his warriors of american series. c.1944. Cupples & Leon Company.
--Wings Over Europe. LC 44-160. v, 206 p. front. 19 1/2 cm. (His Warriors of American series). 1943. Cupples & Leon Company.

AUTHOR INDEX WALKER, BARBARA

Waitt, Paul
--The Adventures of Mollie, Waddy and Tony. Atwood, Clara E., illus. LC 15-22562. 7 p. l., 3-111 p. col. front., col. plates. 17 1/2 cm. 1915. Little, Brown, and Company.
--Further Adventures of Mollie, Waddy and Tony. Preston, Alice Bolam (1889-), illus. LC 20-167. viii p., 3 l., 3-125 p. col. front., col. plates. 17 1/2 cm. 1919. Little, Brown, and Company.
Waitzkin, L.
--The Witch of Wych Street. N.D. Harvard University Press.
Wakana, Kei, illus.
--Magic Hat. (Illus.). (gr. k-5). 1970 (Dist. by Silver). Scroll Pr.
--The Magic Hat. LC 71-107496. (Illus.). 22p (ps-3). N.D. (ISBN 0-87592-033-0). Scroll Pr.
Wakayama, Shizuko
--Out for a Walk. (Illus.). 22p. 1st U.S. edition. (Fun Time Ser.). (ps-1). 1981. (ISBN 0-89346-196-2). Heian Intl.
Wakefield, Connie, jt. auth. see Jones, Harold Kenneth.
Wakefield, Dan
--All Her Children. LC 75-14845. (Illus.). 182 p., 4 leaves of plates. 22cm. 1976. (ISBN 0-385-11086-3). Doubleday.
--Home Free. 1977. (Sey Lawr). Delacorte.
Wakefield, Joyce
--Ask a Silly Question. Venezia, Mike, illus. LC 78-24248. p. cm. 1979. (ISBN 0-516-03408-1). Childrens Press.
--Wide Awake Timothy. Dunnington, Tom, illus. LC 80-21843. p. cm. 1981. (ISBN 0-516-03650-0). Childrens Press.
Wakefield, Maunsell Clark (1894-)
--Cat Tales. LC 50-14378. v. illus. 20 cm. 1950. Story Book Press.
Walburg, Simon C. see Berry, Rex, pseud.
Walcott, Cynthia K.
--The Gift. Reynolds, Lynn Hutchinson (1940-), illus. LC 76-5476. p. cm. c.1976. (ISBN 0-87743-105-1). Baha'i Pub. Trust.
Wald, Lillian D.
--Windows on Henry Street. 1934. Little, Brown & Co.
Waldeck, JoBesse McElveen, Mrs.
--Little Jungle Village. Von Dombrowski, Katharina, illus. LC 40-13171. 176 p. incl. illus., col. plates. 26 cm. 1940. The Viking Press.
--Little Lost Monkey. Wiese, Kurt (1887-1974), illus. LC 42-25503. 96 p. illus. (part col.) 22 1/2 cm. 1942. The Viking Press.
Waldeck, Theodore J. (1894-)
--The Golden Stallion. Dennis, Wesley (1903-1966), illus. LC 47-30188. 190 p. col. front., illus. 21 cm. 1947. The Viking Press.
--Jamba the Elephant. Wiese, Kurt (1887-1974), illus. LC 42-18469. 224 p. illus. 21 1/2 cm. 1942. The Viking Press.
--Lions on the Hunt. Wiese, Kurt (1887-1974), illus. LC 42-361664. 251 p. illus. 21 1/2 cm. 1942. The Viking Press.
--Treks Across the Veldt. Sanderson, Ivan Terence (1911-1973), illus. 224p. N.D. Viking Press.
--The White Panther. Wiese, Kurt (1887-1974), illus. LC 41-22675. (Illus.). 5 p.l., 193 p. 21cm. 1941. The Viking Press.
Waldemar, Bonsels
--Adventures of Maya the Bee. N.D. Thomas Seltzer : Dist. by Loring & Mussey.
--An Indian Journey. N.D. Thomas Seltzer: Dist. by Loring & Mussey.
Walden, Amelia Elizabeth (1909-)
--All My Love. LC 54-9254. 314p. 21cm. (Morrow junior books). 1954. Morrow.
--Basketball Girl of the Year. LC 74-100807. 224 p. 22cm. 1970. McGraw-Hill.
--A Boy to Remember. LC 60-11368. 188 p. 21cm. 1960. Westminster Press.
--The Case of the Diamond Eye. LC 78-88368. 192 p. 21cm. 1969. Westminster Press.
--Daystar. LC 54-11626. 187p. 21cm. c.1955. Westminster Press.
--Escape on Skis. LC 74-23568. 173 p. 22cm. 1975. (ISBN 0-664-32560-2). Westminster Press.
--Gateway. LC 46-20182. 5 p. l., 307 p. 21 cm. (Morrow Junior Bks.). 1946. W. Morrow & Company.
--A Girl Called Hank. LC 51-12032. 254 p. 21 cm. (Morrow Junior Bks.). 1951. Morrow.
--Go, Phillips, Go!. LC 73-15959. 208 p. 22cm. 1974. (ISBN 0-664-32541-6). Westminster Press.
--Heartbreak Tennis. LC 76-30817. 168 p. 21cm. c.1977. (ISBN 0-664-32607-2). Westminster Press.
--How Bright the Dawn. LC 62-8278. 1962. Westminster Press.
--I Found My Love. LC 56-5116. c.1956. Westminster Press.
--In Search of Ophelia. LC 66-9157. 251 p. 21cm. 1966. McGraw-Hill.
--Marsha on-Stage!. LC 52-5939. 251 p. 21 cm. 1952. Morrow.
--My Dreams Ride High. LC 63-9470. 189 p. 21cm. 1963. Westminster Press.
--My Sister Mike. LC 56-10334. 188p. 21cm. 1956. Whittlesey House.
--My World's the Stage. LC 64-22961. 222 p. 21cm. 1964. Whittlesey House.
--A Name for Himself. LC 67-4855. 190 p. 21cm. 1967. Lippincott.
--Palomino Girl. LC 57-576554. 175p. 21cm. 1957. Westminster Press.
--Play Ball, McGill. LC 72-76437. 191 p. 21cm. 1972. (ISBN 0-664-32516-5). Westminster Press.
--Queen of the Courts. LC 59-5342. 21cm. 174p. (gr. 7-10). 1959. (ISBN 0-664-32209-3). Westminster.
--Race the Wild Wind. LC 65-12100. 185p. 21cm. c.1965. Westminster.
--Same Scene, Different Place. LC 73-82395. 190 p. 22cm. 1969. Lippincott.
--Shadow on Devil's Peak. LC 61-5247. 207 p. 21cm. 1961. Westminster Press.
--Skymountain. LC 50-14377. 224 p. 21 cm. 1950. Morrow.
--So Near the Heart. LC 62-18864. 224 p. 21cm. 1962. Whittlesey House.
--A Spy Called Michel-E. LC 67-14516. 192 p. 23cm. 1967. Westminster Press.
--A Spy Case Built for Two. LC 69-11138. 240 p. 21cm. 1969. Westminster Press.
--The Spy on Danger Island. LC 65-19281. 224p. 22cm. c.1965. Westminster.
--The Spy Who Talked Too Much. LC 68-10318. 204p. 21cm. c.1968. Westminster.
--The Spy with Five Faces. LC 66-181687. 206p. 21cm. 1966. Westminster.
--Stay to Win. LC 77-157510. 192 p. 22cm. 1971. Lippincott.
--Sunnycove. LC 48-7686. 256 p. 21 cm. (Morrow Junior Books). 1948. W. Morrow.
--Three Loves Has Sandy. LC 55-8294. 160p. illus. 21cm. 1955. Whittlesey House.
--To Catch a Spy. LC 64-11048. (gr. 7-10). 1964. (ISBN 0-664-32329-4). Westminster.
--Today is Mine. LC 58-5660. 224p. 21cm. 1958. Westminster Press.
--Valerie Valentine Is Missing. LC 76-152337. 188 p. 21cm. 1971. (ISBN 0-664-32496-7). Westminster Press.
--Victory for Jill. LC 53-8295. 246p. 21cm. (Morrow Junior Books). 1953. Morrow.
--Walk in a Tall Shadow. 190 p. 22cm. 1968. Lippincott.
--Waverly. LC 47-11029. 285 p. 21 cm. (Morrow Junior Books). 1947. W. Morrow.
--What Happened to Candy Carmichael?. LC 76-120138. 175 p. 22cm. 1970. Westminster Press.
--When Love Speaks. LC 61-15916. 221 p. 21cm. 1961. Whittlesey House.
--Where Is My Heart?. LC 60-5205. 201 p. 21cm. 1960. Westminster Press.
--Where Was Everyone When Sabrina Screamed?. LC 72-13458. 160 p. 22cm. 1973. (ISBN 0-664-32525-4). Westminster Press.
Walden, Arthur Treadwell
--Leading a Dog's Life. Ripley, A. L., illus. LC 31-320803. 5 p. l., 278, 2 p. front., illus., plates. 21 cm. 1931. Houghton Mifflin Company.
Walden, Daniel (1922-) & Berson, Harold (1926-)
--The Nutcracker. LC 59-12359. (Illus.). 41 p. 26cm. 1959. (ISBN 0-397-30467-6). Lippincott.
Walden, Jane Brevoort
--Igloo. 211p. (gr. 7). N.D. G P Putnam's Sons.
Walden, Jane Brevoort & Paine, Stuart D. L.
--The Long Whip. 246p. (gr. 8). N.D. G P Putnam's Sons.
Walden, Robert L
--Uncle Levi and the Little Beggars: A Novel About Boys. LC 52-122298. 270 p. 20 cm. 1952. Dorrance.
Walden, Walter
--Boy Scouts Afloat: Or, Scouting on the Mississippi in a House Boat. Wrenn, Charles L., illus. LC 18-12217. 5 p. l. 9-244 p. front, plates, diagrs. 20 cm. (On verse of t.-p.: The boy scout life series). c.1918. Barse & Hopkins.
--The Hidden Islands. LC 20-4013. 5 p. l. 301 p. front. (map) 19 1/2 cm. $1.50. c.1920. Small, Maynard & Company.
--The Voodoo Gold Trail. LC 22-16877. 2 p. l, 290 p. front., map. 19 1/2 cm. c.1922. Small, Maynard & Company.
Walder, Florence Mark (1912-)
--Ditto Mouse in the Washington Monument. Boyer, Irv, illus. LC 55-5166. 53p. illus. 24cm. (A Ditto Mouse story). 1955. Creative Enterprises.
--Ringer. Ruud, Herb, illus. LC 54-9967. unpaged. illus. 24cm. 1954. Creative Enterprises.
Waldman, Dorothy
--Goomer. Nichols, Marie C. (1905-), illus. LC 59-8343. unpaged. illus. 21 cm. 1952. Ariel Books.
Waldman, Frank see Webster, Joe, pseud.
Waldman, Frank (1919-)
--Basketball Scandal. 1st ed. Arthur, Thomas O., illus. LC 52-12376. 152p. illus. 22cm. 1953. Ariel Books.
--Bonus Pitcher. 1st ed. Candy, Robert (1920-), illus. LC 51-12069. (Illus.). 156 p. 22cm. 1951. Houghton Mifflin.
--The Challenger. LC 55-5285. 189 p. 21cm. 1955. World Pub. Co.
--Dodger Doubleheader. Webster, Joe, pseud. 1st ed. LC 52-9054. 180 p. illus. 22 cm. 1952. Ariel Books.
--Dodger Doubleheader. Webster, Joe, pseud. 160p. 1952. Farrar, Strauss and Cudahy Inc.
--Giant Quarterback. Candy, Robert (1920-), illus. LC 50-14489. 153 p. illus. 21 cm. 1950. Houghton Mifflin.
--Glory Boy. 1st ed. [illegible] (1904-), illus. LC 53-7090. 155p. illus. 22cm. 1953. Ariel Books.
--Lucky Bat Boy. 1st ed. Kramer, Frank, illus. LC 56-9255. 1956. World Pub. Co.
--The Rookie from Junction Flats. Webster, Joe, pseud. LC 51-13272. (Illus.). 151 p. 22cm. 1952. Ariel Books.
Waldman, Jeri, jt. auth. see Waldman, Neil.
Waldman, Jeri & Waldman, Neil
--Pitcher in Left Field. LC 74-2327. (Illus.). 63 p. 22cm. c.1979. (ISBN 0-13-676411-8). Prentice-Hall.
Waldman, Marguerite, tr. see Cesbron, Gilbert.
Waldman, Marguerite, tr. see Couppey, Madeleine.
Waldman, Milton
--Joan of Arc. 1935. Little, Brown & Co.
Waldman, Neil, jt. auth. see Waldman, Jeri.
Waldman, Neil & Waldman, Jeri
--Pitcher in Left Field. LC 74-2327. p. cm. 1975. (ISBN 0-13-677625-6). Prentice-Hall.
Waldo, Fullerton Leonard (1877-1933)
--Grenfell: Knight-Errant of the North. N.D. Macrae Smith.
--Rex: A Dog Story for Boys. Wolf, W. H., illus. LC 25-20307. 251 p. plates. 19 cm. c.1925. Macrae Smith Company.
--Rex: The Story of a Dog. (Junior Bks. for Boys and Girls). N.D. Cupples & Leon Co.
Waldo, Fullerton Leonard (1877-1933) & Bartlett, Arthur Charles (1901-)
--Thrilling Stories About Dogs: Three Complete Books in One Volume: Rex The Sea Dog, Here, Tricks, Here!. LC 40-2201. 251 p. 2 l., 9-299 p. 2 l., 3-232 p. incl. front. 21 cm. c.1939. Cupples & Leon Company.

Waldo, Lillian McLean, Mrs., jt. auth. see Harris, Ada Van Stone.

Waldorf, Mary
--Jake McGee and His Feet. Shortall, Leonard W, illus. LC 79-21817. (Illus.). 82 p. 22cm. 1980. (ISBN 0-395-29066-X). Houghton Mifflin.
--Thousand Camps. LC 81-13229. 197 p. 22cm. 1982. (ISBN 0-395-31866-1). Houghton Mifflin.
Waldron, Ann Wood (1924-)
--The Bluebury Collection. LC 80-21846. 121 p. 22cm. c.1981. (ISBN 0-525-26739-5). E. P. Dutton.
--The House on Pendleton Block. Lisker, Sonia O. (1933-), illus. LC 74-28031. (Illus.). 151 p. 22cm. 1975. (ISBN 0-8038-3033-5). Hastings House Publishers.
--The Integration of Mary-Larkin Thornhill. LC 75-15505. 137 p. 22cm. 1975. (ISBN 0-525-32580-8). Dutton. Award: (ALA).
--The Luckie Star. LC 76-30371. (Illus.). 166 p. 22cm. c.1977. (ISBN 0-525-34270-2). Dutton.
--Scaredy Cat. LC 78-18202. 107 p. 22cm. c.1978. Dutton.
Waldron, Malcolm T.
--The Old Man in the Shade: The Bedtime Journeys of Betty and Bobby Through Fairyland. LC 26-20419. (Illus.). 111p. 24cm. 1926. The Times-Mirror Press.
Waldrop, Victor H., ed.
--Ranger Rick's Storybook. LC 83-8060. (Illus.). 96p. 1983. (ISBN 0-912186-47-X). Natl Wildlife.
--Ranger Rick's Wonder Book. Langford, Alton, illus. LC 82-60673. (Illus.). 96p. (gr. 2-7). 1982. (ISBN 0-912186-44-5). Natl Wildlife.
Waldschmidt, Jean
--Mystery of the Old Thorndyke. LC 55-6314. 189p. illus. 21cm. 1955. Nelson.
Wales, Katie, compiled by.
--A Book of Elephants. McKee, David (1935-), illus. LC 76-23139. (Illus.). 64 p. 25cm. 1977. (ISBN 0-8193-0891-9). (ISBN 0-8193-0892-7). Parent's Magazine Press.
Waley, Alison
--Dear Monkey. LC 73-22690. (gr. k-3). 1974. (ISBN 0-672-52002-8). Bobbs.
Waley, Arthur
--The Adventures of Monkey: Adapted from the Translation Made from the Chinese of Wu Cheng-En. Wiese, Kurt (1887-1974), illus. LC 44-8092. 143 p. illus. 20 1/2 cm. 1944. The John Day Company.
Waley, Arthur, tr. see Ch'Eng-En, Wu.
Wali, Charonne, jt. auth. see Grill, Nannette L.
Wali, Charonne & Grill, Nannette
--Mister Abracadabra. Crawford, Richard (1938-) & Mekelburg, David, illus. LC 72-178585. (Illus.). 63 p. 32cm. c.1971. Scarecrow Publications.
Walje, Nina
--The Restless Summer. LC 79-50812. (gr. 8-12). 1979. (ISBN 0-89636-024-5). Accent Bks.
Walker, A. D.
--Mordecai's Tenants, 1 of 20 vols. (Illus.). 142p. (Selected Bks for Sunday School: No. 23). N.D. Set. Methodist Bk Concern.
Walker, A. G., illus.
--The Seven Champions of Christendom. N.D. E J B Young & Co.
Walker, Abbie Phillips, Mrs. (1867-)
--Sandman Christmas Stories. Chase, Rhoda Campbell, illus. LC 18-18096. 4 p. l., 3-149 p. illus. 18 cm. 1918. Harper & Brothers.
--Sandman Tales: Stories for Bedtime. Chase, Rhoda Campbell, illus. LC 17-13956. (Illus.). 116p. 18cm. 1917. Harper & Brothers.
--Sandman Twilight Stories. Chase, Rhoda Campbell, illus. LC 18-17922. 3 p. l., 3-140 p. illus. 18 cm. 1918. Harper & Brothers.
--Sandman's Christmas Stories. N.D. Harper & Bros.
--Sandman's Fairy Stoires. Chase, Rhoda Campbell, illus. LC 22-230879. 5 p. l., 3-146 p. col. front., col. plates. 18 cm. c.1922. Harper & Brothers.
--Sandman's Goodnight Stories. Chase, Rhoda Campbell, illus. LC 21-193935. 3 p. l., 3-155 p. illus. 18 cm. c.1921. Harper & Brothers.
--The Sandman's Hour: Stories for Bedtime. Chase, Rhoda Campbell, illus. LC 17-165445 4 p. l., 3-121 p. illus. 18 cm. $0.50. 1917. Harper & Brothers.
--Sandman's Might-be-so Stories. 1st ed. Chase, Rhoda Campbell, illus. LC 22-23088. (Illus.). 3-157. 18cm. 1922. Harper & Brothers.
--Sandman's Once-Upon-a-Time Stories. Peck, Clara Elsene, illus. LC 25-17623. 5 p. l., 122 p. col. front. col. plates. 18 1/2 cm. c.1925. Harper & Brothers.
--Sandman's Rainy Day Stories. N.D. Harper & Bros.
--Sandman's Stories of Drusilla Doll. Chase, Rhoda Campbell, illus. LC 22-21118. 5 p. l., 3-175, 1 p. illus. 18 cm. 1920. Harper & Brothers.
--Sandman's Stories of Snowed-in Hut. N.D. Harper & Bros.
--Sandman's Stories of Twinkle Eyes. N.D. Harper & Bros.
--Sandman's Three-Minute Stories. Peck, Clara Elsene, illus. LC 25-21213. 5 p. l., 171 p. col. front., col. plates. 18 cm. c.1925. Harper & Brothers.
--Sandman's Twilight Stories. N.D. Harper & Bros.
--Told by the Sandman: Stories for Bedtime. Chase, Rhoda Campbell, illus. LC 16-217102. 4 p. l., 3-97 p. illus. 18 cm. 1916. Harper & Brothers.
Walker, Alice Johnstone
--Little Plays from American History for Young Folks. LC 14-15432. 4 p. l., 3-155 p. 17 1/2 cm. 1914. H. Holt and Company.
Walker, Annie L., Miss (0000-1907)
--Plays for Children. (Illus.). N.D. E P Dutton & Co.
--Plays for Children. 1875. George Routledge & Sons.
Walker, Arthur Leslie
--The Fairy and the Mouse. LC 40-342830. 52 p. illus. (part col.) 28 1/2 x 22 cm. c.1940. W. A. Wilde Company.
Walker, Barbara Kerlin (1921-)
--The Courage of Kazan. McCrea, James Craig, Jr. (1920-) & McCrea, Ruth Pirman (1921-), illus. LC 78-101935. (Illus.). 48 p. 1970. (ISBN 0-690-21934-2). Crowell.
--The Dancing Palm Tree and Other Nigerian Folktales. Siegl, Helen (1924-), illus. LC 68-21085. (Illus.). 112 p. 23cm. 1968. Parents' Magazine Press.
--A Good Fish Dinner. Cumings, Art, illus. LC 78-11152. p. cm. 1979, c.1978. (ISBN 0-8193-0983-4). (ISBN 0-8193-0984-2). Parents' Magazine Press.
--Hilili and Dilili: A Turkish Silly Tale. Barss, William (1916-), illus. LC 65-13270. 32p. col. illus. 26cm. 1965. Follett.
--How the Hare Told the Truth About His Horse. Mikolaycak, Charles (1937-), illus. LC 73-174604. (Illus.). 32 p. 23cm. 1972. (ISBN 0-8193-0561-8). (ISBN 0-8193-0562-6). Parents' Magazine Press.
--I Packed My Trunk. Kock, Carl, illus. LC 69-15982. (Illus.). 32 p. 1969. (ISBN 0-696-44062-8). Follett Pub. Co.
--The Ifrit and the Magic Gifts. Forberg, Ati, pseud. (1925-), illus. Forberg, Beate Gropius. LC 70-161555. (Illus.). 31 p. 23cm. (Wonderland Books). 1972. (ISBN 0-695-80249-6). (ISBN 0-695-40249-8). Follet Pub. Co.

--Just Say Hic!. A Turkish Silly Tale!. Bolognese, Donald Alan (1934-), illus. LC 65-13271. 32p. col. illus. 26cm. 1965. Follett.
--Korolu, the Singing Bandit. Nodjoumi, Nikzad, illus. LC 78-106580. (Illus.). 159 p. 21cm. (Crowell Hero Tales). 1970. T. Y. Crowell Co.
--Laughing Together. LC 77-7789. (Illus.). (gr. 3 up). 1977. (ISBN 0-590-09123-9). US Comm Unicef.
--Pigs and Pirates: A Greek Tale. Berson, Harold (1926-), illus. LC 79-90935. (Illus.). 48 p. 1969. (ISBN 0-87250-429-8). D. White.
--The Round Sultan and the Straight Answer. Henstra, Friso (1928-), illus. LC 71-117559. (Illus.). 38 p. 27cm. 1970. Parents' Magazine Press.
--The Scared Ghost, and Other Stories. LC 75-10950. 24 p. 24cm. 1975. (ISBN 0-07-067812-X). McGraw-Hill.
--Teeny-Tiny and the Witch-Woman. Foreman, Michael (1938-), illus. LC 74-15297. (Illus.). 32 p. 26cm. 1975. (ISBN 0-394-83088-1). (ISBN 0-394-93088-6). Pantheon Books.
--Watermelons, Walnuts and the Wisdom of Allah, and Other Tales of the Hoca. Berson, Harold (1926-), illus. LC 67-18475. 71 p. col. illus. 24 cm. 1967. (ISBN 0-8193-0195-7). Parents' Magazine Press.

Walker, Barbara Kerlin (1921-), ed.
--Ghost Stories. new ed. 128p. (gr. 7-12). 1975. (ISBN 0-07-067812-X, GB). McGraw.
--Laughing Together: Giggles and Grins from Around the Globe. Taback, Simms, illus. LC 77-7789. (Illus.). xiii, 106 p. 24cm. c.1977. (ISBN 0-590-07486-5). Four Winds Press.
--Laughing Together: Giggles & Grins from Around the World. Taback, Simms, illus. LC 77-7789. (Paperback edition available only through the United Nations). (Illus.). 128p. (gr. 3-7). 1977. (ISBN 0-590-07486-5, Four Winds). Scholastic Inc.
--The Little House Diary. LC 84-48754. (Illus.). 160p. (ps up). 1985. (ISBN 0-06-026341-5). HarpJ.
--Once There Was and Twice There Wasn't. Kibbee, Gordon, illus. LC 67-21156. (Turkish Tales collected by Barbara K. Walker). (Illus.). 128 p. 22cm. 1968. Follett.

Walker, Barbara Kerlin (1921-) & Sumer, Mine
--Stargazer to the Sultan. Low, Joseph (1911-), illus. LC 67-18471. (Illus.). 41 p. 26cm. 1967. Parents' Magazine Press.

Walker, Barbara Kerlin (1921-) & Tezel, Naki
--The Mouse and the Elephant. McCully, Emily Arnold (1939-), illus. LC 79-81193. (Illus.). 36 p. 27cm. 1969. Parents' Magazine Press.

Walker, Barbara Kerlin (1921-) & Uysal, Ahmet E.
--New Patches for Old: A Turkish Folktale. Berson, Harold (1926-), illus. LC 73-12951. (Illus.). 41 p. 27cm. 1974. (ISBN 0-8193-0713-0). (ISBN 0-8193-0713-0). Parents' Magazine Press.

Walker, Caroline Burnite, Mrs., ed. see Lippincott, Sara Jane Clarke, Mrs.

Walker, Carrie D
--Our Story Book. LC 31-181428. 4 p. l., 247, 1 p., 1 l., 67 p. illus. 24 1/2 cm. c.1930. Print. by the Coast Dispatch.

Walker, Challis
--Only Three Wishes. N.D. (ISBN 0-8283-1256-7). Branden Press.
--Three and Three. Walker, Challis, illus. LC 40-6336. 64 p. illus. 26 x 22 cm. c.1940. Coward-McCann, Inc.

Walker, Constance W.
--Dee-Dee and the Monkeys. (Illus.). 1959. Exposition Press.

Walker, David
--Geordie. 1950. Houghton Mifflin Company.
--The Storm and Silence. N.D. Houghton Mifflin Company.
--Storms of our Journey and other Stories. 1962. Houghton Mifflin Company.
--Where the High Winds Blow. 1960. Houghton Mifflin Company.
--Winter of Madness. 1964. Houghton Mifflin Company.

Walker, David (1934-), tr. see Perrault, Charles.

Walker, David E. (1907-)
--The Fat Cat Pimpernel. Howard, Alan (1922-), illus. LC 59-12789. (Illus.). 21cm. 1960. A. S. Barnes & Co.
--Pimpernel and the Poodle. Howard, Alan (1922-), illus. LC 60-8356. (Illus.). 21cm. 1960. A. S. Barnes & Co.

Walker, David G. (1926-)
--Rick Goes to Little League. Dick, Mike, illus. Reese, Pee Wei, intro. by. LC 81-17028. (Illus.). 70 p. 23cm. c.1981. Caroline House.
--Rick Heads for Soccer. Dick, Mike, illus. Rote, Kyle, Jr., frwd. by. LC 82-17857. (Illus.). 76 p. 23cm. 1982. (ISBN 0-89803-120-6). Caroline House Publishers.

Walker, David Harry (1911-)
--Big Ben. Ambrus, Victor G., pseud. (1935-), illus. Ambrus, Gyozo Laszlo. LC 74-82477. (Illus.). 134 p. 22cm. 1969. Houghton Mifflin.
--Dragon Hill. Keane, Raymond, illus. LC 62-15242. 140 p. illus. 22 cm. 1962. Houghton Mifflin.
--Pirate Rock. Mays, Lewis Victor, Jr. (1927-), illus. LC 69-19939. (Illus.). 227 p. 22cm. 1969. Houghton Mifflin.
--Sandy was a Soldier's Boy: A Fable. Broadhead, Dobson, illus. 180p. 1957. Houghton, Mifflin.

Walker, Diana (1925-)
--An Eagle for Courage. LC 68-13236. 176 p. 22cm. 1968. (ISBN 0-200-71541-0). Abelard-Schuman.
--The Hundred Thousand Dollar Farm. LC 76-44320. vii, 182 p. 21cm. c.1977. (ISBN 0-200-00170-1). Abelard-Schuman.
--The Hundred Thousand Dollar Farm. 1977. Harper.
--Mother Wants a Horse. LC 77-11553. 186 p. 21cm. c.1978. (ISBN 0-200-00179-5). (ISBN 0-200-00181-7). Crowell.
--Mystery of Black Gut. LC 69-15239. 176p. (gr. 7-12). 1969. (ISBN 0-200-71601-8). Abelard.
--Never Step on an Indian's Shadow. LC 72-12075. 191 p. 22cm. 1973. (ISBN 0-200-71969-6). Abelard-Schuman.
--The Singing Schooner. LC 66-14123. 176p. 22cm. c.1966. Abelard.
--The Skiers of Ste. Celeste. LC 75-105254. 192 p. 22cm. 1970. Abelard-Schuman.
--The Year of the Horse. LC 75-4613. 177 p. 21cm. 1975. (ISBN 0-200-00151-5). Abelard-Schuman.
--The Year of the Horse. 177p. 19cm. (Harper Trophy Book). 1979, c.1975. (ISBN 0-06-440100-6). Harper & Row.

Walker, Dugald Stewart (1883-1937)
--Dream Boats, and Other Stories. LC 18-20536. xii, 219, 1 p. col. front., plates (part col.) 20 cm. 1918. Doubleday, Page and Company.
--Sally's A B C. LC 29-21691. 59 p. col. illus. 29 cm. 1929. Harcourt, Brace and Company.

Walker, Edith B. & Mook, Charles Craig (1887-)
--Tales of the First Animals. Bartley, Jane Banning, illus. LC 30-25393. 24cm. 120p. c.1930. Farrar & Rinehart.

Walker, Edward Ashley, Mrs.
--From Creation to Moses: Bible Stories for Little the Ones. (Illus.). 1910. James Pott & Co.
--From Creation to Moses: Bible Stories for the Little Ones. N.D. Pilgrims Press.
--From Crib to the Cross: Bible Stories for the Little Ones. (Illus.). 1910. James Pott & Co.
--From Joshua to Daniel: Bible Stories for the Little Ones. (Illus.). 1910. James Pott & Co.
--From Joshua To Daniel: Bible Stories for the Little Ones. N.D. Pilgrim Press.
--Pilgrim's Progress for the Little Ones: Bible Stories for the Little Ones. (Illus.). 1910. James Pott & Co.

Walker, Edward Ashley Walker Mrs. see Walker, Katherine Kent Child.

Walker, Emily Malbone
--The Flight of the Swallow. (Illus.). N.D. James Pott & Co.

Walker, Frank
--Banjo. 192p. 1977. (ISBN 0-7181-1593-7, Pub. by Michael Joseph). Merrimack Pub Cir.

Walker, Gertrude Annie (1863-) & Jenks, S. Harriet
--Songs and Games for Little Ones. N.D. E. Steiger & Co.

Walker, Granville, Jr., ed. see Brown, Lynn.

Walker, Gwen (1925-)
--The Golden Stile. Hodges, Cyril Walter (1909-), illus. LC 58-10613. 188 p. illus. 21 cm. 1958. J. Day Co.

Walker, Henry Cragin
--Jimmy Bunn Stories. Hope-Innes, illus. LC 21-170298. x p., 3 l., 3-183 p. incl. plates. front. 19 1/2 cm. $1.50. 1920. The Century Co.

Walker, Holly Beth, pseud., see Bond, Gladys Baker.

Walker, Holly Beth, pseud. (1912-)
--Meg and the Disappearing Diamonds. Bond, Gladys Baker. Schule, Clifford H., illus. LC 68-254. (Illus.). 156 p. 22cm. (Whitman Tween-Age Book.). (A Meg Mystery). 1967. Whitman Pub. Co.
--Meg and the Secret of the Witch's Stairway. Bond, Gladys Baker. Schule, Clifford H., illus. LC 68-142. (Illus.). 156 p. 22cm. (Whitman Tween-Age Book.). (A Meg Mystery). 1967. Whitman Pub. Co.

Walker, Irma (1921-)
--Inherit the Earth. LC 81-2856. 262 p. 22cm. 1981. (ISBN 0-689-30834-5). Atheneum.
--Portal to E're'were. LC 83-2634. p. cm. 1983. (ISBN 0-689-30998-8). Atheneum.

Walker, J. G.
--Charley Ashley: Or, The Adventures of an Orphan Boy. N.D. E. & J. B. Young & Co.
--Charley Ashley: The Adventures of an Orphan Boy. N.D. Alfred Martien.

Walker, Janice
--My Bible Book. N.D. Rand McNally & Co.

Walker, Jerry L., ed.
--Pop-Rock Lyrics, No. 3. (gr. 7-12). 1971. (ISBN 0-590-09197-2, Schol Trade Pap). Schol Bk Serv.
--Pop-Rock Songs of the Earth. (Illus.). (gr. 7-12). 1972 (Starline). Schol Bk Serv.

Walker, John B.
--War in the Air. N.D. Random House.

Walker, Joseph, tr. see Lorenzini, Carlo.

Walker, Katherine Kent Child (1833-), tr. see Hoffmann, Franz.

Walker, Katherine Kent Child (1833-)
--Climbing the Glacier. N.D. A. D. F. Randolph.
--A Little Leaven. N.D. A. D. F. Randolph.
--Margaret at Home. N.D. A. D. F. Randolph.
--Margaret at Home. (Illus.). N.D. Set. Cheap Sunday-School Library.
--Our Little Girls. N.D. A. D. F. Randolph.
--Pet Dayton. N.D. A. D. F. Randolph.
--Two Heaps. N.D. A D F Randolph & Co.
--Watson's Woods. N.D. A. D. F. Randolph.
--Zoe's Story. (Illus.). N.D. Ser. Cheap Sunday-School Library.
--Zoe's Story: Or Old Friends and Foes in Masks. LC 26-3652. 150 p. 17 1/2 cm. 1863. A. D. F. Randolph.

Walker, Kathrine Sorley
--Eyes on the Ballet. (Illus.). (gr. 6-9). 1965. (ISBN 0-381-99658-1). John Day.

Walker, Kenneth Macfarlane (1882-) & Boumphrey, Geoffrey Maxwell (1894-)
--The Log of the Ark. Boumphrey, Geoffrey Maxwell (1894-), illus. LC 60-7024. (Illus.). 214p. 21cm. 1960. Pantheon Books.
--What Happened in the Ark. LC 26-16189. xv p., 1 l., 275 p. incl. front., illus. 20 cm. 1926. E. P. Dutton & Company.

Walker, Lillie
--Toots and Poochie. N.D. Carlton Press Inc.

Walker, Lonnie F.
--To the Circus. Walker, Lonnie F., illus. LC 62-17379. (gr. k-2). 1962. (ISBN 0-8114-7565-4). Steck-V.

Walker, Louise Jean
--Daisy, the Story of a Horse. Beeby, Betty (1923-), illus. LC 68-28856. (Illus.). 109 p. 24cm. 1970. (ISBN 0-8028-4059-0). Eerdmans.
--Woodland Wigwams. MacMullen, Elna L., illus. LC 64-17630. 121 p. illus., maps. 24 cm. 1964. Hillsdale School Supply.

Walker, Major Benson
--Scottie: The True Story of a Dog. LC 29-14676. 5 p. l., 242 p. col. front., col. plates. 20 1/2 cm. c.1929. Thomas Y. Crowell Cpmpany.
--Skipper: The Story of a Dog. LC 30-242346. 6 p. l., 238 p. col. front., col. plates. 20 1/2 cm. c.1930. Thomas Y. Crowell Company.

Walker, Marian
--The Little Red Chair: Stories About Mary and Tommy and Some Other Small Children. LC 32-29763. 3 p. l., 46 p. incl. illus., plates. plates. (1 col.) 26 cm. 1932. The Macmillan Company.

Walker, Mary Alexander
--Maggot. LC 80-12238. p. cm. 1980. (ISBN 0-689-30789-6). Atheneum.
--To Catch a Zombi. LC 79-11968. p. cm. 1979. (ISBN 0-689-30725-X). Atheneum.
--Year of the Cafeteria. LC 79-156109. 144 p. 22cm. 1971. Bobbs-Merrill.

Walker, Mary Spring
--Both Sides of the Street. N.D. Henry Hoyt.

Walker, Mildred (1905-)
--A Piece of the World. 1st ed. Price, Christine Hilda (1928-1980), illus. LC 78-190561. (Illus.). 218 p. 23cm. 1972. Atheneum.
--Winter Wheat. (gr. 10 up). N.D. (ISBN 0-15-197223-0). HarBraceJ.

Walker, Mort (1923-)
--Most. Browne, Dik (1917-), illus. LC 75-148175. (Illus.). 32 p. 31cm. 1971. (ISBN 0-87807-018-4). Windmill Books.

Walker, Mort (1923-) & Browne, Dik
--The Land of Lost Things. LC 70-159157. (Illus.). 32 p. 29cm. 1973, c.1972. (ISBN 0-87807-044-3). Windmill Books.

Walker, Nona
--Kappy Oliver. 1st ed. Reed, Veronica, pseud. (1916-), illus. Sherman, Theresa. LC 56-10039. 256 p. illus. 21 cm. (Holt Books for Young People). 1956. Holt.

Walker, Pamela
--Twyla. 149 p. 18cm. (Berkley Medallion Book). 1976, c.1973. (ISBN 0-425-03076-8). Berkley Publishing Corp.
--Twyla: A Novel. LC 73-6705. 125 p. 22cm. 1973. (ISBN 0-13-935239-2). Prentice-Hall.

Walker, Paul E.
--Peter Panda. Kalab, Theresa, illus. LC 41-238. (Illus.). 47p. 23 x 19cm. 1940. T. Nelson.

Walker, R.
--Tom McGrath of Ranelegh. (MacMillan Bks. for Boys & Girls). (gr. 7-9). N.D. MacMillan Bks.

Walker, Robert Sparks (1878-)
--The Beechblock Circus. LC 35-9705. vi p., 1 l., 159 p. 19 1/2 cm. 1934. Association Press.

Walker, Robert Wayne (1948-)
--Daniel Webster Jackson and the Wrongway Railway. LC 81-9546. p. cm. c.1981. (ISBN 0-916392-81-3). Oak Tree Publications.

Walker, S. Warren, intro. by see Cooper, James Fenimore.

Walker, Stuart
--The King's Great Aunt Sits on the Floor. 1925. Appleton.

Walker, Stuart & Strange, Hubert S.
--Seventeen. Tarkington, Newton Booth (1869-1946), adapted by. 1924. French.

Walker, Ted, jt. auth. see Aldridge, Alan.

Walker, Victoria (1947-)
--The Winter of Enchantment. LC 75-136421. (Illus.). 150 p. 21cm. 1971, c.1969. Bobbs-Merrill.

Walkey, S.
--In Quest of Sheba's Treasure. (The Albion Library). N.D. Frederick Warne & Co.
--Rogues of the Firey Cross. (Illus.). 256p. (The Cross and Crown Ser.). N.D. Cassell & Co.'s Pubs.
--With the Redskins on the Warpath. (Illus.). 384p. (Books for Boys). 1905. Set. Cassell & Co.

Walking Night Bear, pseud.
--Song of the Seven Herbs. Binder, Henryk. Padilla, Stan (1945-), illus. LC 83-14145. p. cm. 1983. (ISBN 0-943986-22-2). (ISBN 0-943986-21-4). Gold Circle Productions.

Walkley, William S
--Three Golden Days: Tan-Bark Tales. LC 21-21368. 168 p. front., illus. 19 1/2 cm. c.1921. Fleming H. Revell Company.

Wall, Dorothy
--Let's Call Him Blinky Bill. (Illus.). 32p. 1970. Tri-Ocean Books.
--The Tale of Bridget and the Bees. Authorized. Wall, Dorothy, illus. LC 36-5821. (Illus.). 45p. 21cm. 1935. Artists and Writers Guild, Inc.

Wall, H.
--The Emigrant's Lost Son. N.D. George Routledge & Sons.

Wall, James M.
--When Zoo and Forest Met. Landry, Melda, illus. LC 41-1935. (Illus.). 16p. 23cm. (The Zoo and Forest Story Bks.). 1932. B. Humphries.

Wall, Roy
--This Was My Valley. (Illus.). 222p. N.D. (ISBN 0-8111-0155-X). The Naylor Company.

Wallace, Archer (1884-)
--The Field of Honor ,and Ninety-Nine Other Stories for Boys. LC 49-11688. 157 p. 20 cm. 1949. Abingdon-Cokesbury Press.
--More Stories of Grit. LC 30-129601. vi, 140 p. 19 1/2 cm. 1930. R. R. Smith, Inc.
--One Hundred Stories for Boys. LC 47-6280. 171 p. 20 cm. 1947. Abingdon-Cokesbury Press.
--Stories of Grit. LC 28-18418. x, 133 p. 19 1/2 cm. 1928. Doubleday, Doran & Company, Inc.

Wallace, Art
--Toby. 1st ed. Walworth, Jane Armstrong, illus. LC 70-166421. (Illus.). 116 p. 22cm. 1971. Doubleday.

Wallace, Barbara Brooks (1922-)
--Andrew, the Big Deal. LC 76-93809. 192p. (gr. 3-7). 1970. (ISBN 0-695-80111-2). (ISBN 0-695-40111-4). Follett.
--The Barrel in the Basement. Wooding, Sharon, illus. LC 84-21521. (Illus.). 127 p. 22cm. 1985. (ISBN 0-689-31105-2). Atheneum.
--Can Do, Missy Charlie. Friedman, Marvin (1930-), illus. LC 73-90054. (Illus.). 224 p. 23cm. 1974. (ISBN 0-695-80444-8). (ISBN 0-695-80444-8). Follett Pub. Co.
--Claudia. LC 69-11992. 192 p. 23cm. 1969. (ISBN 0-695-81422-2). Follett Pub. Co.
--Claudia. LC 82-1512. p. cm. 1982. (ISBN 0-695-41422-4). Follett.
--The Contest Kid & the Big Prize. Kamen, Gloria (1923-), illus. (gr. 4-6). 1978. (ISBN 0-590-11836-6, Schol Pap). Scholastic Inc.
--The Contest Kid Strikes Again. Kamen, Gloria (1923-), illus. LC 79-24197. (Illus.). 160 p. 21cm. c.1980. (ISBN 0-687-09590-5). Abingdon.
--Hawkins. Kamen, Gloria (1923-), illus. LC 76-28319. (Illus.). 144 p. 21cm. c.1977. (ISBN 0-687-16669-1). Abingdon.
--Hawkins and the Soccer Solution. Kamen, Gloria (1923-), illus. LC 80-23016. p. cm. c.1981. (ISBN 0-687-16672-1). Abingdon.
--Hello, Claudia!. LC 82-1538. 157 p. 23cm. c.1982. (ISBN 0-695-41661-8). Follett Pub. Co.
--Julia and the Third Bad Thing. Eagle, Michael (1942-), illus. LC 75-2965. (Illus.). 54 p. 23cm. c.1975. (ISBN 0-695-80590-8). (ISBN 0-695-40590-X). Follett.
--Miss Switch to the Rescue. McCord, Kathleen Garry, illus. LC 81-10916. (Illus.). 158 p. 21cm. c.1981. (ISBN 0-687-27077-4). Abingdon.
--Palmer Patch. DiFiori, Lawrence, illus. LC 76-2185. (Illus.). 128 p. 23cm. c.1976. (ISBN 0-695-40668-X). Follett.
--Peppermints in the Parlor. LC 80-12326. p. cm. 1980. (ISBN 0-689-30790-X). Atheneum.
--The Secret Summer of L. E. B. Cellini, Joseph (1924-), illus. LC 73-93557. (Illus.). 191 p. 23cm. 1974. (ISBN 0-695-80481-2). (ISBN 0-695-40481-4). Follett.

--Which Do You Like Best. Schulte, Michele, illus. (Illus.). (ps). N.D. Hallmark.
--Zany Zoo. Schanzer, Roslyn, illus. (Illus.). (ps-3). 1972. Hallmark.
Walley, Dean, ed.
--Thumbelina. Noel, Arlene, illus. (Illus.). 8p. of color ils. 20p. (gr. k-3). 1970. (ISBN 0-87529-042-6). Hallmark.
Walley, Dean, jt. auth. see Barwick, Stephanie.
Walley, Dean & Cunningham, Ed
--Zoo Parade. Staake, Frieda, illus. (Illus.). 12p. of color ils. 14p. (ps). 1970. (ISBN 0-87529-073-6). Hallmark.
Wallin, Cheryl W.
--The Lane County Kid's Book: Stories to 1900. (Illus.). 96p. 1st U.S. edition. 1982. (ISBN 0-9607040-0-0). Silver Pennies.
Wallin, Luke
--Blue Wings: A Novel. LC 81-21562. 213 p. 22cm. c.1982. (ISBN 0-02-792400-9). (ISBN 0-87888-200-6). Bradbury Press.
--In the Shadow of the Wind. LC 83-19758. 224p. 1984. (ISBN 0-02-792320-7). Bradbury Pr.
--The Redneck Poacher's Son: A Novel. LC 80-26782. 245 p. 24cm. c.1981. (ISBN 0-02-792480-7). (ISBN 0-87888-174-3). Bradbury Press.
--The Slavery Ghosts. LC 83-2679. p. cm. 1983. (ISBN 0-02-792380-0). Bradbury Press.
Wallin, Marie-Louise
--Tangles. Bothmer, Gerry, tr. LC 77-72619. p. cm. c.1977. (ISBN 0-440-08502-0). Delacorte Press/S. Lawrence.
Wallis, Geraldine (1925-)
--Home to Hawaii. LC 67-2451. 174 p. 21cm. 1967. Norton.
Wallis, Jenny
--The Sandman: His Songs and Rhymes. Lyon, Helen F., illus. (The Sandman Ser.). N.D. L. C. Page & Co.
Wallis, Jenny see Morrison, Mary Jane Whitney, Mrs.
Wallner, Alexandra, jt. auth. see Gamerman, Martha.
Wallner, Alexandra (1946-)
--The Adventures of Strawberry Shortcake and Her Friends. Llimona, Mercedes, illus. LC 79-5148. (Illus.). 42 p. 29cm. c.1980. (ISBN 0-394-94319-8). Random House.
--Ghoulish Giggles and Monster Riddles. LC 82-10969. p. cm. 1982. (ISBN 0-8075-2863-3). A. Whitman.
--Munch: Poems. Wallner, Alexandra (1946-), illus. LC 75-20019. (Illus.). 32 p. 24cm. c.1976. (ISBN 0-517-52459-7). Crown Publishers.
--Strawberry Shortcake and the Winter That Would Not End. LC 81-348. p. cm. 1981. (ISBN 0-394-84823-3). (ISBN 0-394-94823-8). Random House.
Wallner, John C, jt. auth. see Aylesworth, Jim.
Wallner, Shirley J.
--Friendly Little Hobo. Wallner, Shirley J., illus. LC 64-25739. (Illus.). 27cm. 48p. (The Wonderful World of Children's Readers). 1964. Oddo Pub.
--Friendly Little Hobo. Wallner, Shirley J., illus. LC 68-56814. (Illus.). (gr. 2-4). 1968. (ISBN 0-87783-013-4). (ISBN 0-87783-092-4). Oddo.
--Hans & The Golden Stirrup. LC 68-56815. (Illus.). (gr. 2-3). N.D. (ISBN 0-87783-016-9). (ISBN 0-87783-093-2). Oddo.
--Hans and the Golden Stirrup. Wallner, Shirley J., illus. LC 65-22299. 48p. col. illus. 27cm. 1965. Oddo.
Wallop, John Douglass, III (1920-)
--Year the Yankees Lost the Pennant. (gr. 7 up). 1964. (ISBN 0-393-21138-X). Norton.
Wallower, Arthur
--The Carousel Word Book. Wallower, Arthur, illus. LC 77-3512. (Illus.). 20cm. 47p. (Carousel Bk.). 1968. I. W. Singer Co.
Wallower, Arthur, tr. see Strauss, Ludwig.
Wallower, Lucille (1910-)
--Chooky. Wallower, Lucille (1910-), illus. LC 43-50. 92 p. illus. (part col.) 25 1/2 cm. 1942. David McKay Company.
--A Conch Shell for Molly. Wallower, Lucille (1910-), illus. LC 40-32074. 62 p. col. front., illus. (part col.) 26 x 21 1/2 cm. c.1940. David McKay Company.
--The Lost Prince: Louis XVII of France. Wallower, Lucille (1910-), illus. LC 63-10487. 116p. illus. 21cm. c.1963. McKay.
--The Roll of Drums. Wallower, Lucille (1910-), illus. LC 45-598030. 111 p. incl. col. front., illus. (part col.) 28 1/2 x 19 cm. 1945. A Whitman & Company.
Wallower, Lucille (1910-), retold by.
--Old Satan: A Pennsylvania Folk Tale. Wallower, Lucille (1910-), illus. LC 56-5380. unpaged. illus. 24 cm. c.1956. D. McKay Co.
Wallower, Lucille (1910-) & Stevens, S. K.
--Your Pennsylvania. LC 53-8127. 252p. illus. 23cm. 1953. Penns Valley Publishers.
Wallqvister, Gun-Britt (1940-)
--My Cat. Aberg, Lars (1940-), illus. LC 81-47725. p. cm. 1st U.S. edition. c.1982. (ISBN 0-06-026351-2). (ISBN 0-06-026352-0). Harper & Row.
--My Cat Has Kittens. Aberg, Lars (1940-), illus. LC 81-47726. p. cm. c.1982. (ISBN 0-06-026353-9). (ISBN 0-06-026354-7). Harper & Row.
Wallworth, Margaret
--Secret of the Painted Idol: A Ime Twist Adventure. LC 85-16574. 128 p. 18cm. c.1985. (ISBN 0-89191-902-3). Chariot Books.
--Secret of the Silver Candlestick. LC 83-26223. 127 p. 18cm. (A Time Twist Adventure). c.1984. (ISBN 0-89191-832-9). Chariot Books.
--The Secret of the Silver Candlestick. 127p. (Pennypincher Ser.). (gr. 5-10). 1984. (ISBN 0-89191-832-9). Cook.
Walmsley, Alice Freeman, jt. auth. see Sawyer, Edith Augusta.
Walmsley, H. M.
--Wild Sports and Savage Life in Zulu Land. (Hopeful Enterprise Library). N.D. R. Worthington & Co.
Walmsley, Leo (1892-1966)
--Foreigners. LC 68-26334. 278 p. 21cm. 1968. Meredith Press.
--Toro of the Little People. LC 27-2995. 250 p. 19 1/2 cm. c.1926. George H. Doran Company.
Walpole
--Little Arthur's History of Greece. (Illus.). (Crowell's Young People Ser.). N.D. Thomas Y. Crowell.
Walpole, A. S., adapted by see Phaedrus.
Walpole, Ellen Wales (1907-)
--Getting Along. 1st ed. Horwitz, Richard, illus. LC 52-8428. 219 p. illus. 21 cm. 1952. World Pub. Co.
--Tell Me. Anderson, Douglas, illus. LC 47-6658. vii, 160 p. col. illus. 29 cm. 1947. Hinds, Hayden & Eldredge.
Walpole, Hugh Seymour, Sir (1884-1941) & Partington, Wilfred, eds.
--Famous Stories of Five Centuries. N.D. Farrar & Rinehart.
Walrath, Jane Dwyer (1939-)
--Here Is a Place: A Story About Color. Winship, Florence Sarah, illus. (Illus.). 20p. (Preschool Learning Books Ser.). (ps). 1972. (ISBN 0-307-12177-1, Golden Pr). Western Pub.
--My Little Book of Horses. Dunnington, Tom, illus. 32p. (Tell-a-Tale Reader). (ps-3). N.D. (ISBN 0-307-68410-5, Golden Pr). Western Pub.
--Toby, the Rock Hound. Bradfield, Roger (1924-), illus. (Illus.). (A Tell-a-Tale Reader Ser.). (gr. k-3). 1979. (ISBN 0-307-68408-3, Golden Pr). Western Pub.
Walrond, Dorothy
--Mopsie: The Story of a London Waif. (Illus.). N.D. Thomas Nelson & Sons.
--These Little Ones. (Illus.). N.D. Thos Nelson & Sons.
Walser, David, adapted by see Perrault, Charles.
Walser, David, tr. see Grimm, Jakob Ludwig Karl (1785-1863) & Grimm, Wilhelm Karl.
Walser, David, tr. see Perrault, Charles.
Walsh, Amanda
--Egrin & the Painted Wizard. LC 73-167079. 24cm. 35p. (Picture Ser.). (gr. 2-6). 1973. (ISBN 0-14-050081-2, Puffin). Penguin.
Walsh, Bill
--David and Goliath. LC 77-21773. p. cm. (Cartoon Bible story). c.1977. (ISBN 0-8362-0729-7). Sheed Andrews and McNeel.
--Jonah and the Whale. LC 76-41009. p. cm. (Cartoon Bible story for children). c.1976. (ISBN 0-8362-0689-4). Sheed Andrews and McMeel.
--Noah & the Ark. Shedd, Charlie, afterword by. (Cartoon Bible Stories Ser.). 1977. (ISBN 0-8362-0697-5). Andrews & McMeel.
--The Prodigal Son. LC 77-1146. p. cm. (Cartoon Bible story). c.1977. (ISBN 0-8362-0693-2). Sheed Andrews and McMeel.
Walsh, Brandon
--Little Annie Rooney. N.D. David McKay Co.
--Little Annie Rooney wishing Book. McClure, Darrel, illus. LC 32-899. 16 p. col. illus. 33 1/2cm. c.1932. McLoughlin Bros.
Walsh, Chad (1914-)
--Garlands for Christmas. 1965. Macmillan Company.
--The Honey and the Gall. 1967. Macmillan Company.
--Nellie and Her Flying Crocodile. Simont, Marc (1915-), illus. LC 56-5149. (Illus.). 21cm. 179p. 1956. Harper.
--Nellie and Her Flying Crocodile. Simont, Marc (1915-), illus. 180p. 19cm. (Harper Trophy Book). 1979, c.1956. (ISBN 0-06-440102-2). Harper & Row.
--The Rough Years. LC 60-12312. 266 p. 21 cm. 1960. Morehouse-Barlow Co.
Walsh, Ellen Stoll (1942-)
--Brunus and the New Bear. Walsh, Ellen Stoll (1942-), illus. LC 78-22361. (Illus.). 32 p. 22cm. c.1979. (ISBN 0-385-14660-4). (ISBN 0-385-14661-2). Doubleday.
--Theodore All Grown up. LC 80-2244. (Illus.). 32 p. 22cm. c.1981. (ISBN 0-385-15868-8). Doubleday.
Walsh, George Ethelbert (1865-1941)
--Bobby Gray Squirrel. Prittie, Edwin John, illus. LC 30-1341. 3 p. l., 9-135 p. col. front., col. plates. 19 cm. (His Twilight animal series). c.1922. The John C. Winston Company.
--Bobby Gray Squirrel's Adventures. Prittie, Edwin John, illus. 3 p. l., 9-135 p. col. front., col. plates. 19 cm. (His Twilight animal series). c.1922. The John C. Winston Company.
--The Boy Vigilantes of Belgium. Bayha, Edwin F., illus. LC 19-14478. 5 p. l., 3-307 p. front., plates. 19 1/2 cm. $1.5. 1919. The Century Co.
--Bumper the White Rabbit. Prittie, Edwin John, illus. 3 p. l., 9-119 p. col. front., col. plates. 19 cm. (His Twilight animal series). c.1922. The John C. Winston Company.
--Bumper the White Rabbit & His Foes. Richardson, Frederick (1862-1937), illus. (Twilight Animal Stories). N.D. John C Winston.
--Bumper the White Rabbit and His Friends. Prittie, Edwin John, illus. 2 p. l., 9-133 p. col. front., col. plates. 19 cm. (His Twilight animal series). c.1922. The John C. Winston Company.
--Bumper the White Rabbit in the Woods. Prittie, Edwin John, illus. 3 p. l., 9-112 p. col. front., col. plates. 19 cm. (His Twilight animal series). c.1922. The John C. Winston Company.
--Buster the Big Brown Bear. Prittie, Edwin John, illus. LC 30-1334. 3 p. l., 9-181 p. col. front., col. plates. 19 cm. (His Twilight animal series). c.1922. The John C. Winston Company.
--Buster the Big Brown Bear's Adventures. (Twilight Animal Stories). N.D. John C Winston.
--The Mysterious Beacon Light: The Adventures of Four Boys in Labrador. Becher, Arthur E., illus. LC 4-24564. 19cm. 354p. 1904. Little, Brown & Co.
--Polly Comes to Woodbine. Young, Florence Liley, illus. LC 15-15952. 256 p. front., plates. 19 cm. 1915. Lothrop, Lee & Shepard Co.
--The Sign of the Cross. Goodnow, G. S., illus. LC 30-9458. 2 p. l., 7-95 p. plates. 19 cm. c.1929. David C. Cook Publishing Co.
--The Strange Cargo of the "Southern Belle,". LC 6-41270. 59 p. illus. 17 1/2 cm. c.1906. D. C. Cook Publishing Company.
--Washer, the Raccoon. Prittie, Edwin John, illus. LC 30-1343. 3 p. l., 9-129 p. col. front., col. plates. 19 cm. (His Twilight animal series). c.1922. The John C. Winston Company.
--White Tail the Deer. (Twilight Animal Stories). N.D. John C Winston.
--White Tail the Deer's Adventures. Prittie, Edwin John, illus. LC 30-1339. (Illus.). 135p. 19cm. (Twilight Animal Ser.). 1922. The John C. Winston Company.

Walsh, Gillian Paton see Walsh, Jill Paton, pseud.

Walsh, Grahame (1945-)
--The Goori Goori Bird: A Legend of the Bidjara People of the Upper Warrego. Morrison, John, illus. LC 84-12997. (Illus.). 52 p. 1984. (ISBN 0-7022-1777-8). University of Queensland Press.
Walsh, Henry H. (1906-)
--Six Plays in American History. MacLean, Robert (1926-), illus. LC 68-18589. (Illus.). viii, 216 p. 23cm. 1969. S. Greene Press.
Walsh, Honor
--The Story-Book House. Kennedy, J. W. Ferguson, illus. LC 3-12811. 320 p. incl. front. 7 pl. 19 1/2 cm. 1903. D. Estes & Company.
Walsh, Jill Paton, pseud., see Walsh, Gillian Paton.

Walsh, Jill Paton, pseud. (1939-)
--Toolmaker. Walsh, Gillian Paton. Roy, Jeroo, illus. LC 73-7126. (Illus.). 23cm. 45p. 1974, c.1973. (ISBN 0-8164-3109-4). Seabury Press.
Walsh, John Herbert
--The Truants, and Other Poems for Children. Ardizzone, Edward Jeffrey Irving (1900-1979), illus. LC 68-12945. (Illus.). 79 p. 21cm. 1968, c.1965. (ISBN 0-528-80434-0). Rand McNally.
Walsh, Joseph Alexis (1782-1860)
--Tales and Stories. Translated from the French of Vicount Walsh. Sadlier, James, Mrs., pseud. (1820-1908), tr. Sadlier, Mary Anne Madden. LC 38-127439. 2 p. l., 9-144 p. front. 15 1/2 cm. (On cover: Catholic youth's library). c.1885. D. & J. Sadlier & Co.
Walsh, Julia C
--Tooralladdy. LC 7-2064. 158 p. incl. front. 17 1/2 cm. 1907. Benziger Brothers.
Walsh, Martin
--Stranger Than Fiction: Weird Stories & Ghostly Happenings. (gr. 7-9). 1974. (ISBN 0-590-04598-9, Schol Pap). Scholastic Inc.
Walsh, Mary Regina (1889-)
--Molly: The Rogue. Pitz, Henry Clarence (1895-1976), illus. LC 44-40116. 60 p. incl. front., illus. 23 1/2 x 18 cm. 1944. A. A. Knopf.
--Molly the Rogue. Pitz, Henry Clarence (1895-1976), illus. 1944. Borzoi.
--The Mullingar Heifer. Pitz, Henry Clarence (1895-1976), illus. LC 46-202411. 61 p. incl. front., illus. 23 1/2 cm. 1946. A. A. Knopf.
--Water, Water Everywhere. Carter, Helene (1887-1960), illus. N.D. Abingdon Press.
--The Widow Woman and Her Goat. Pitz, Henry Clarence (1895-1976), illus. LC 49-7866. 60 p. illus. 24 cm. 1949. A. A. Knopf.
Walsh, Morris
--Hesperus. Parker, Guy, illus. LC 50-3202. (Illus.). 20cm. 24p. (The Television Bonnie Bks.). 1950, c.1949. John Martin's House.
--Hesperus: A Story. Parker, Guy, illus. LC 48-197716. 32 p. col. illus. 23 cm. (A Merry-Go-Round Book). 1947. J. Martin's House.
Walsh, Richard J
--Kiddie-Kar Book. Weber, Sarah Stilwell, illus. N.D. J.B. Lippincott.
Walsh, Stan, ed. see Disney, Walt, Productions.
Walsh, William Shepard (1854-1919)
--The Story of Santa Claus. (Illus.). N.D. Moffat, Yard & Co.
--The Story of Santa Klaus. Angelico, Fra & Hutt, Henry, illus. LC 68-58166. 222p. Repr. of 1909 ed. 1970 (Gale Reprints). Gale Research Co.
Walstedt, Viola
--Travel Alone, Eva. Leupold, Nancy Swenson, tr. from Swedish. LC 66-120351. 158p. 22cm. 1966, c.1949. Holt.
Walston, Octavius Frank, Mrs.
--Angel's Christmas, 1 of 10 Vols. (Illus.). (The Garland Ser.). N.D. Set. Thomas Nelson & Sons.
Walsum-Quispel, J. M. Van
--Tina's Island Home. Leeflang-Oudenaarden, C. S. T. M., illus. LC 71-99920. (Illus.). 35 p. 1970, c.1969. Scroll Press.
Walsum-Quispel, J. M. Van see Van Walsum-Quispel, J. M.
Waltch, Lilla M.
--Cave of the Incas. Komoda, Kiyoaki (1937-), illus. LC 68-21086. (Illus.). 157 p. 22cm. 1968. Parents' Magazine Press.
--Miss Starr's Secret. Matsuda, Shizu, illus. LC 59-12981. 171 p. illus. 21 cm. 1959. Sterling Pub. Co.
--Mystery of the Inca Cave. Orig. Title: Cave of the Incas. (gr. 4-6). 1971. (ISBN 0-590-04481-8, Schol Trade Pap). Schol Bk Serv.
Walt Disney Enterprises, jt. auth. see Disney, Walter Elias.
Walt Disney Pictures see Matthews, Ann.
Walt Disney Production see Maniere, Michel.
Walt Disney Productions see Crume, Vic.
Walt Disney Productions, jt. auth. see Lorenzini, Carlo.
Walt Disney Productions, Ltd., jt. auth. see Andersen, Hans Christian.
Walt Disney Productions Ltd., jt. auth. see Bethell, Jean Frankenberry.
Walt Disney Productions, Ltd. see Crawford, Mel.
Walt Disney, Productions, Ltd., ed. see Andersen, Hans Christian.
Walt Disney Studio, jt. auth. see Werner, Jane.
Walter, David
--Great Adventurers. LC 79-64163. (Adventures in History Ser.). N.D. (ISBN 0-382-06295-7). Silver.
Walter, Dorothy Blake see Blake, Katherine, pseud.
Walter, Edna, ed.
--Mother Goose's Nursery Rhymes. Folkard, Charles James (1878-1963), illus. N.D. Macmillan.
Walter, Frances & Pearson, Violet T.
--Benjie and His Friends. LC 77-87950. (Illus.). 128 p. 19cm. c.1977. (ISBN 0-916406-81-4). Accent Books.
--Benjie & the Flood. LC 78-65063. (Illus.). (Benje Ser.). (gr. 1-6). 1978. (ISBN 0-89636-017-2). Accent Bks.
--Here's Benjie!. A Child's Animal Story Book. LC 76-50297. (Illus.). 128 p. 19cm. c.1976. (ISBN 0-916406-60-1). Accent Books.
Walter, Greg
--A Box, to Begin with. Heugh, James, illus. LC 66-31457. (Illus.). 37 p. 1966. Harvey House.
Walter, Lavinia Edna, ed. see Mother Goose.
Walter, Marion
--Another, Another, Another & More. Walter, Marion, illus. LC 84-71818. (Illus.). (gr. k-3). N.D. (ISBN 0-233-96644-7, Andre Deutsch). Dutton.
--Look at Annette. Haber-Schaim, Navah, illus. LC 77-186592. (Illus.). 31 p. 1972, c.1971. M. Evans; Distributed in Association with Lippincott, Philadelphia.
--Make a Bigger Puddle, Make a Smaller Worm. Walter, Marion, illus. LC 70-186593. (Illus.). 31 p. 1972, c.1971. M. Evans; Distributed in Association with Lippincott, Philadelphia.

AUTHOR INDEX WALTON, OCTAVIUS

Walter, Mildred Pitts
--Because We Are. 1st ed. LC 83-987. 192 p. 22cm. c.1983. (ISBN 0-688-02287-1). Lothrop, Lee & Shepard.
--Brother to the Wind. Dillon, Leo (1933-) & Dillon, Diane (1933-), illus. LC 83-26800. (Illus.). 32 p. 26cm. c.1985. (ISBN 0-688-03811-5). (ISBN 0-688-03812-3). Lothrop, Lee & Shepard Books.
--The Girl on the Outside. LC 82-267. 150p. (gr. 6 up). 1982. (ISBN 0-688-01438-0). Lothrop.
--Lillie of Watts: A Birthday Discovery. Prince, Leonora E., illus. LC 69-18098. (Illus.). 61 p. 27cm. 1969. Ward Ritchie Press.
--Lillie of Watts Takes a Giant Step. Johnson, Bonnie Helene, illus. LC 74-157634. (Illus.). 187 p. 22cm. 1971. Doubleday.
--My Mama Needs Me. 1st ed. Cummings, Pat, illus. LC 82-12654. (Illus.). 32 p. c.1983. (ISBN 0-688-01670-7). (ISBN 0-688-01671-5). Lothrop, Lee & Shepard Books. **Award: (CSKA).**
--Trouble's Child. LC 84-16387. 157 p. 22cm. c.1985. (ISBN 0-688-04214-7). Lothrop, Lee & Shepard Books.
--Ty's One-Man Band. Tomes, Margot Ladd (1917-), illus. LC 80-11224. (Illus.). 40p. (gr. k-3). 1980. (ISBN 0-590-07580-2, Four Winds). Scholastic Inc.
Walter, Nina Willis (1900-)
--Teeny Weeny. Walstad, Chi Chi, illus. LC 70-102748. (Illus.). 32 p. 1971. (ISBN 0-513-00504-8). Denison.
Walter, William Wilfred (1869-)
--The Healing of Pierpont Whitney. LC 13-26567. 221 p. 20 cm. c.1913. W. W. Walter.
Walters, Frank
--The Story of Mrs Virgil Earp: The Earp Brothers of Tombstone. 256p. N.D. Clarkson N. Potter Inc.
Walters, George
--The Snowplow that Tried to Go South. Resko, John, illus. 32p. (gr. 1-4). N.D. Aladdin Bks.
--The Snowplow that Tried to Go South. Resko, John, illus. N.D. E. P. Dutton & Co.
--Steamshovel That Wouldn't Eat Dirt. Duvoisin, Roger Antoine (1904-1980), illus. (Illus.). (gr. k-2). 1948. (ISBN 0-525-39979-8). Dutton.
Walters, Helen B.
--Henry Stanley & His Secret Key. (gr. 5-9). 1963. (ISBN 0-8272-1401-4). Bethany Pr.
--No Luck for Lincoln. LC 80-27164. 160p. (gr. 3-4). 1981. (ISBN 0-687-28030-3). Abingdon.
--Ponies for a King. McMillan, Constance (1949-), illus. LC 63-10904. 82 p. illus. 21 cm. 1963. Reilly & Lee Co.
--When John Wesley Was a Boy. LC 61-13672. 97p. (Valor ser. 6). 1961. Baker Bk. House.
--When John Wesley Was a Boy. LC 61-13672. 97p. 20cm. (Valor ser. 6). 1966. Baker Bk.
Walters, Helen H.
--Bobo. N.D. Vantage Press.
Walters, Hugh, pseud., see Hughes, Walter Llewellyn.
Walters, Hugh, pseud. (1910-)
--Blast-Off at Zero Three Hundred. Hughes, Walter Llewellyn. 187p. 1958. Criterion Books Inc.
--The Blue Aura. Hughes, Walter Llewellyn. 128p. 1st U.S. edition. (gr. 5-8). 1979. (ISBN 0-571-11423-7). Faber & Faber.
--Boy Astronaut. Hughes, Walter Llewellyn. Ridley, Trevor, illus. (gr. 2-7). 1977. (ISBN 0-8277-5396-9). (ISBN 0-8277-5395-0). British Bk Ctr.
--The Caves of Drach. Hughes, Walter Llewellyn. LC 79-670249. 136p. (gr. 8-11). 1979. (ISBN 0-571-11037-1). Faber & Faber.
--The Dark Triangle. Hughes, Walter Llewellyn. 128p. 1st U.S. edition. (gr. 5-12). 1981. (ISBN 0-571-11584-5). Faber & Faber.
--Destination Mars. Hughes, Walter Llewellyn. LC 64-13733. 160 p. 22cm. 1964. Criterion Books.
--Expedition Venus. Hughes, Walter Llewellyn. LC 63-10426. 191 p. 22cm. (Criterion Book for Young People). 1963. Criterion Books.
--First Contact?. Hughes, Walter Llewellyn. LC 73-10047. 174 p. 21cm. 1973. (ISBN 0-8407-6320-4). T. Nelson.
--First on the Moon. Hughes, Walter Llewellyn. LC 60-14138. 192 p. 22cm. 1960. Criterion Books.
--Journey to Jupiter. Hughes, Walter Llewellyn. LC 66-227736. 190p. illus. 22cm. c.1966. Criterion.
--The Last Disaster. Hughes, Walter Llewellyn. LC 79-670357. 128p. (gr. 5-8). 1979. (ISBN 0-571-11153-X). Faber & Faber.
--Menace from the Moon. Hughes, Walter Llewellyn. LC 59-6130. 191 p. 22cm. (Criterion Book for Young People). 1959. Criterion Books.
--Menace From the Moon. Hughes, Walter Llewellyn. 1959. S G Phillips.
--Mission to Mercury. Hughes, Walter Llewellyn. LC 65-24016. (gr. 7 up). 1965. (ISBN 0-200-00125-6). Criterion Bks.
--Mohole Menace. Hughes, Walter Llewellyn. LC 68-15232. 129p. (gr. 7 up). 1968. (ISBN 0-200-00096-9). Criterion Bks.
--Murder on Mars. Hughes, Walter Llewellyn. 1978. (ISBN 0-571-10717-6). Faber & Faber.
--Neptune One Is Missing. Hughes, Walter Llewellyn. LC 79-120956. (gr. 6-8). 1970. (ISBN 0-679-24060-8, Pub. by Washburn). McKay.
--Outpost on the Moon. Hughes, Walter Llewellyn. LC 62-8942. 191 p. 22 cm. (Criterion Book for Young People). 1962. Criterion Books.
--Passage to Pluto. Hughes, Walter Llewellyn. LC 75-15913. p. cm. 1975. (ISBN 0-8407-6457-X). T. Nelson.
--Spaceship to Saturn. Hughes, Walter Llewellyn. (gr. 7 up). 1967. (ISBN 0-200-72000-7). Criterion Bks.
--Terror by Satellite. Hughes, Walter Llewellyn. LC 64-22142. (gr. 7-11). 1964. Criterion Bks.
--Terror by Satellite. Hughes, Walter Llewellyn. 160p. (Fanfares Ser.). (gr. 4 up). 1980. (ISBN 0-571-11492-X). Faber & Faber.
Walters, Jerry
--Walt Disney's Dumbo on Land, on Sea, in the Air. LC 72-7397. (Illus.). 43 p. 25cm. (Disney's wonderful world of reading, 1). 1972. (ISBN 0-394-82518-7). (ISBN 0-394-82518-7). Random House.
Walters, Marguerite
--The City-Country ABC: My Alphabet Walk in the Country, and My Alphabet Ride in the City. Ohlsson, Ib (1935-), illus. LC 66-10671. (Illus.). 20cm. (A Turnabout Bk.). 1966. Doubleday.
--The Real Santa Claus. Wohlberg, Meg (1905-), illus. LC 50-10975. 31p. 1950. Lothrop, Lee & Shepard.
--The Runaway Baby Bird. N.D (Wonder Books). Grosset & Dunlap.
--Small Pond. 1st ed. Martin, Stefan (1936-), illus. LC 66-14684. (Illus.). 32 p. 27cm. 1967. Dutton.
--Up and Down and All Around. LC 60-5587. unpaged. illus. 32 cm. 1960. F. Watts.
Walters, Maude Owens, Mrs. (1891-), selected by.
--A Book of Christmas Stories for Children. Gardner, Mary Ponton, illus. LC 30-27751. 21cm. 206p. 1930. Dodd, Mead & Co.
--Clever and Foolish Tales for Children. Freed, Ted, Mrs., illus. LC 41-4808. viii, 290 p. illus. 21 cm. 1941. Dodd, Mead & Company.
Walters, Shelley, pseud., see Sheldon, Walter J..
Walters, Shelley, pseud. (1917-)
--The Dunes. Sheldon, Walter J.. LC 74-82010. 280p. 1974. (ISBN 0-679-50477-X). McKay.
Walters, Zella Margaret
The Call of the Brave. Stanley, Helen Miller, ed. Williams, Florence White, illus. LC 29-13628. 61 p. col. plates. 19 1/2 cm. c.1928. David C. Cook Publishing Co.
--The Dawn of Faith: A Story of Young Missionaries and Pirates in Tripoli. Higgins, Violet Moore, illus. LC 29-13680. 63 p. plates. 19 1/2 cm. c.1928. David C. Cook Publishing Co.
--The Magic Window: A Story for Boys and Girls from Six to Twelve. LC 15-21142. 56 p. front., plates. 20 cm. c.1915. The Standard Publishing Company.
--The Standard Bearer of Askelon: A Later Crusade Story. LC 29-136812. 96 p. illus. 19 cm. c.1928. David C. Cook Publishing Co.
Walther, Clara M.
--The Little Lamb's First Christmas. 1978. (ISBN 0-533-03430-2). Vantage.
Walther, Gertrud Von
--The Four Seasons. Glauber, Uta Heil (1936-), illus. Crampton, Patricia, tr. LC 68-29185. (Illus.). 26 p. 28cm. 1968. Abelard-Schuman.
Walther, Gertrud Von see Von Walther, Gertrud.
Waltner, Erma see Lee, Lawrent, pseud.
Waltner, Vera, jt. auth. see Lee, Lawrent.
Walton, Amy
--White Lilac. (Illus.). (Scribner-Blackie Series of Books for Young People). N.D. Charles Scribner's Sons.
Walton, Bessye E. Bloom see Bosa, Stera, pseud.
Walton, Bessye E. Bloom, Mrs. (1903-)
--Adventures of Lappy Cushion-Tail. Bosa, Stera, pseud. Latimer, Glenna M. (1898-), illus. LC 36-179382. 180 p. illus. 26 cm. c.1936. E. P. Dutton and Company, Inc.
--Lappy in the Forest. Bosa, Stera, pseud. Latimer, Glenna M. (1898-), illus. LC 39-4383. 140, 1 p. illus. 26 cm. c.1939. E. P. Dutton and Company, Inc.
Walton, Bryce (1918-)
--Cave of Danger. Orban, Paul, illus. LC 67-15405. 264 p. 21cm. 1967. (ISBN 0-690-18277-5). Crowell.
--The Fire Trail. LC 74-5753. (Illus.). 169 p. 21cm. 1974. (ISBN 0-690-00542-3). Crowell.
--Harpoon Gunner. LC 68-21949. 206 p. 21cm. 1968. Crowell.
--Harpoon Gunner. 1970. (ISBN 0-690-37165-9). Thomas Y. Crowell.
--Hurricane Reef. LC 71-101936. 249 p. 21cm. 1970. (ISBN 0-690-42667-4). Crowell.
--Sons of the Ocean Deeps. (Winston Science Fiction Ser.). 1952. John C. Winston Co.
--Sons of the Ocean Deeps. LC 52-8973. 216 p. 22cm. (Science fiction novel). 1952. Winston.
Walton, Eda Lou
--Turquoise Boy and White Shell Girl. Valentine, Louis Chapin (1889-), illus. LC 33-24918. xii, 202 p. col. front., illus. 22 cm. c.1933. Thomas Y. Crowell Company.
Walton, Eleanor G.
--She Who Will Not When She May. New ed. (Illus.). 1905. Henry Altemus Co.
Walton, Elizabeth Cheatham
--A Galleon Sailed. Lonette, Reisie Dominee (1924-), illus. LC 57-6001. 178p. illus. 22cm. 1957. Lothrop, Lee & Shepard.
--Treasure in the Sand. Polseno, Jo, illus. LC 59-15450. 192 p. illus. 22 cm. 1960. Lothrop, Lee & Shepard.
--Voices in the Fog. Hughes, Shirley (1929-), illus. LC 68-13239. (Illus.). 160 p. 22cm. 1968. (ISBN 0-200-71535-6). Abelard-Schuman.
Walton, Ellis
--Tuck-up Songs: A Series of 82 Short Bed-time Songs. (Illus.). N.D. Thomas Nelson & Sons.
Walton, Frank
--The Flying Machine Boys in Deadly Peril: Or, Lost in the Clouds. LC 21-20587. 233 p. front. 19 1/2 cm. (His Flying machine boys series). c.1914. A. L. Burt Company.
--The Flying Machine Boys in Mexico: Or, The Secret of the Crater. (The Flying Machine Boys Ser.). N.D. A. L. Burt Company.
--The Flying Machine Boys in the Frozen North; Or, The Trail in the Snow. (The Flying Machine Boys Ser.). N.D. A. L. Burt Company.
--The Flying Machine Boys in the Wilds: Or, The Mystery of the Andes. LC 21-20588. 256 p. front. 19 1/2 cm. (His Flying machine boys series). c.1913. A. L. Burt Company.
--The Flying Machine Boys on Duty: Or, The Clue Above the Clouds. (The Flying Machine Boys Ser.). N.D. A. L. Burt Company.
--The Flying Machine Boys on Secret Service: Or, The Capture in the Air. (The Flying Machine Boys Ser.). N.D. A. L. Burt Company.
Walton, Gertrude H, jt. auth. see Dunham, Lillian Shackleton.
Walton, Marilyn Jeffers
--Bats Aren't Sweet. Jeschke, Susan (1942-), illus. LC 83-7320. (Illus.). 32p. (Celebration Bks). (gr. k-4). 1983. (ISBN 0-940742-18-7, Pub. by Carnival Press). (ISBN 0-940742-18-7). Raintree Pubs.
--Chameleons' Rainbow. Salzman, Yuri, illus. LC 84-17760. p. cm. 1985. (ISBN 0-940742-45-4). Raintree Publishers.
--Possum Crest's Greatest Christmas Show. Jeschke, Susan (1942-), illus. LC 83-7354. (Illus.). 32p. (Celebration Bks.). (gr. k-4). 1983. (ISBN 0-940742-19-5, Pub. by Carnival Press). (ISBN 0-940742-19-5). Raintree Pubs.
--Sparky's Valentine Victory. Jeschke, Susan (1942-), illus. LC 83-7321. (Illus.). 32p. (Celebration Bks.). (gr. k-4). 1983. (ISBN 0-940742-20-9, Pub. by Carnival Press). (ISBN 0-940742-20-9). Raintree Pubs.
--Tea & Whoppers. Jeschke, Susan, et al. (1942-), illus. LC 83-5713. (Illus.). 32p. (Celebration Bks.). (gr. k-4). 1983. (ISBN 0-940742-11-X, Pub. by Carnival Press). (ISBN 0-940742-11-X). Raintree Pubs.
--Those Terrible Terwilliger Twins. DiSalvo-Ryan, DyAnne, illus. LC 84-17732. (Illus.). 31 p. c.1984. (ISBN 0-940742-39-X). Raintree Publishers.
Walton, Mary Ann
--My First Book of Bible Stories. Ferand, Emmy, illus. (Little Golden Book). 1943. Golden Press.
--My First Book of Bible Stories. Reed, Mary, ed. Ferand, Emmy, illus. (Little Golden Library). 1943. Simon & Schuster.
Walton, Mason A.
--A Hermit's Wild Friends: Or, Eighteen Years in the Woods. (Illus.). N.D. Dana Estes & Co.
Walton, Octavius Frank, Mrs.
--Angel's Christmas. (Illus.). 64p. N.D. Fleming H Revell.
--Angel's Christmas, and Little Dot, 1 of 50 vols. (Illus.). 119p. (Model Library No. 4). 1905. American Tract Society.
--Audrey: Or, The Children of Light. (Illus.). N.D. Fleming H Revell.
--Christie, the King's Servant. N.D. Fleming H. Revell Co.
--Christie's Old Organ. (Illus.). 165p. 1905. American Tract Society.
--Christie's Old Organ, 1 of 6 Vols. (Standard Stories in Dainty Dress: Vol. 6). N.D. American Tract Society.
--Christie's Old Organ. 166p. (Popular Ser.). N.D. American Tract Society.
Christie's Old Organ, 1 of 50 vols. (Illus.). (New Primary Lib). N.D. Set. American Tract Society.
--Christie's Old Organ, 1 of 50 vols. (Heart Life Classics). N.D. American Tract Society.
--Christie's Old Organ. (The Dolphin Ser.). N.D. Fleming H. Revell Co.
--Christie's Old Organ. N.D. Flemington H. Revell Co.
--Christie's Old Organ. (The New Kingship Ser.). N.D. Fleming H. Revell Co.
--Christie's Old Organ. (Illus.). (The Calumet Ser.). N.D. H. M. Caldwell Co.
--Christie's Old Organ. (Illus.). (The Young Folks Lib.). N.D. H. M. Caldwell Co.
--Christie's Old Organ. (Illus.). (Boys' and Girls' Classics). N.D. Henry Altemus Co.
--Christie's Old Organ. (Illus.). (Vademecum Ser.). N.D. Henry Altemus.
--Christie's Old Organ. (Illus.). (Golden Treasury Ser.). N.D. Henry Altemus.
--Christie's Old Organ. Handy Volume, Large Type ed. (Illus.). (Beauxarts Ser.). N.D. Henry Altemus.
--Christie's Old Organ. 124p. N.D. Moody Press.
--Christie's Old Organ: Mrs. O.F. Walton's Famous Victorian Story of a Boy and an Old Man Looking for God. rev. and updated. Wright, Christopher, ed. LC 82-70861. (Illus.). ix, 117 p. 21cm. (A Victorian Classic for Children). c.1982. (ISBN 0-88270-532-6). Bridge Pub.
--Christie's Old Organ: Or, Home, Sweet Home, 36 vols. (Illus.). (St. Nicholas Ser.). 1905. Set. A L Burt Co.
--Christie's Old Organ: Or, Home Sweet Home. (Illus.). (The Wellesley Series for Girls). N.D. A. L. Burt.
--Christie's Old Organ: Or, Home, Sweet Home. LC 75-304971. (Illus.). 165 p., 3 leaves of plates. 16cm. 1883. R. Carter.
--Little Dot. (Illus.). (Books for Everybody). N.D. American Tract Society.
--Little Dot. 64p. (The New Kingship Ser.). N.D. Fleming H. Revell Co.
--Little Dot, and Angel's Christmas. (Illus.). 119p. (Popular Ser.). N.D. American Tract Society.
--Little Faith. (Illus.). 150p. 1905. American Tract Society.
--Little Faith, 1 of 6 Vols. (Standard Stories in Dainty Dress: Vol. 5). N.D. American Tract Society.
--Little Faith, 1 of 50 bks. (Illus.). (New Primary Lib.). N.D. Set. American Tract Society.
--Little Faith. (Illus.). 128p. N.D. Fleming H Revell.
--My Little Corner. (Illus.). 160p. N.D. Fleming H Revell.
--My Mates and I. (Illus.). 160p. N.D. Fleming H Revell.
--The Mysterious House. (Illus.). 128p. N.D. Fleming H Revell.
--Nobody Loves Me, 1 of 50 Vols. 216p. (Golden Rod Library). 1905. American Tract Society.
--Nobody Loves Me, 1 of 50 vols. (Heart Life Classics). N.D. American Tract Society.
--Nobody Loves Me. (The Dolphin Ser.). N.D. Fleming H. Revell Co.
--Nobody Loves Me. (Illus.). (The New Kingship Ser.). N.D. Fleming H. Revell Co.
--Olive's Story. (Illus.). 237p. 1905. American Tract Society.
--Olive's Story, 1 of 50 vols. (Heart Life Classics). N.D. American Tract Society.
--Olive's Story. LC 8-33292. 176p. 1882. Bradley & Woodruff.
--Olive's Story. (Illus.). 192p. N.D. Fleming H Revell.
--Olive's Story. LC 8-33292. 176 p. incl. front., plates. 18 cm. 1882. I. Bradley & Co.
--A Peep Behind the Scenes. (Illus.). 272p. N.D. A. I. Bradley & Co.'s Pubs.
--A Peep Behind the Scenes. (Illus.). (The Dolphin Ser.: Vol. 4). N.D. Fleming H. Revell Co.
--Poppy's Present. (Illus.). 128p. N.D. Fleming H Revell.
--Saved at Sea, 1 of 6 Vols. (Standard Stories in Dainty Dress: Vol. 3). N.D. American Tract Society.
--Saved at Sea. (Illus.). (Books for Everybody). N.D. American Tract Society.
--Saved At Sea. (Illus.). 128p. N.D. Fleming H Revell.
--Saved at Sea: A Light-House Story. (Illus.). N.D. Thomas Nelson & Sons.
--Saved at Sea: An Adventure Story for Children. (Summit Bks). 1977. (ISBN 0-8010-9598-0). Baker Bk.
--Shadows. (Illus.). 308p. N.D. A. I. Bradley & Co.'s Pubs.
--Taken or Left. (Illus.). 128p. N.D. Fleming H Revell.
--Whiter than Snow. (The Dolphin Ser.). N.D. Fleming H. Revell Co.
--Whiter than Snow. (The New Kingship Ser.). N.D. Fleming H. Revell Co.
--Whiter than Snow, and Little Dot. (The Kingship Ser.). N.D. Fleming H Revell.
--Whiter Than Snow and Little Dot. 126p. N.D. Moody Press.

--Winter's Folly. (A Bright Half Dozen Ser.). N.D. American Tract Society.
--Winter's Folly, 1 of 6 Vols. (Standard Sotries in Dainty Dress). N.D. American Tract Society.
--Winter's Folly. (Illus.). 192p. N.D. Fleming H Revell.
Walton, Robert M. (1947-)
--Joel in Tananar. LC 79-26353. p. cm. 1981. (ISBN 0-914598-77-5). Padre Productions.
Walton, Thelma
--Bible Stories for a Little Child ... Mears, Henrietta Cornelia (1890-), ed. LC 45-45159. v. illus. 21 1/2 cm. (Gospel Light Series for Beginners). c.1937. The Gospel Light Press.
Waltrip, Lela Kingston (1904-) & Waltrip, Rufus Charles (1898-)
--Purple Hills. Price, Christine Hilda (1928-1980), illus. LC 61-13106. 154 p. illus. 21 cm. 1961. Longmans, Green.
--Quiet Boy. Smith, Theresa Kalab, illus. LC 61-7882. 120 p. illus. 22 cm. 1961. Longmans, Green.
--White Harvest. Price, Christine Hilda (1928-1980), illus. LC 60-9880. 118 p. illus. 21 cm. 1960. Longmans, Green.
Waltrip, Rufus Charles, jt. auth. see Waltrip, Lela Kingston.
Walworth, Jeannette Ritchie Hadermann (1837-1918)
--Three Brave Girls. N.D. Thomas Whittaker.
Walz, Lila
--The Mysteries of the "Talking" Animals. LC 79-17127. (Unsolved Mysteries of the World Ser.). N.D. (ISBN 0-89547-077-2). Silver.
Walz, Richard, illus.
--The Pudgy Book of Mother Goose. (Illus.). 16p. (Pudgy Bks.). (gr. k). 1984. (ISBN 0-448-10212-9, G&D). Putnam Pub Group.
Wandelmaier, Roy
--The Great Rock 'n' Roll Mystery. Burns, Raymond Howard (1924-), illus. LC 84-8753. (Illus.). 48p. (gr. 2-4). 1985. (ISBN 0-8167-0416-3). (ISBN 0-8167-0417-1). Troll Assocs.
--Mystery at Loch Ness. Mulkey, Kim, illus. LC 85-2532. (Illus.). 99 p. 20cm. c.1985. (ISBN 0-8167-0529-1). (ISBN 0-8167-0530-5). Troll Associates.
--Secret of the Old Museum. Smolinski, Dick, illus. LC 85-2533. (Illus.). 99 p. 20cm. c.1985. (ISBN 0-8167-0531-3). (ISBN 0-8167-0532-1). Troll Associates.
--Shipwrecked on Mystery Island. Pinkney, J. Brian, illus. LC 85-2531. p. cm. c.1985. (ISBN 0-8167-0533-X). (ISBN 0-8167-0534-8). Troll Associates.
Wanderer, Pauline W.
--The Secret at Death's Door. Klapholz, Mel, illus. LC 79-84305. (Illus.). (gr. 7 up). 1979. (ISBN 0-915224-03-8). Pine St Pr.
Wane, Peter, jt. auth. see MacDonald, George.
Wangerin, Walter, Jr. (1944-)
--The Baby God Promised. (Illus.). 32p. (Arch Bks.: No. 13). (ps-4). 1976. (ISBN 0-570-06105-9). Concordia.
--The Bible: Its Story for Children. LC 81-8696. p. cm. 1981. (ISBN 0-528-82060-5). Rand McNally.
--The Book of the Dun Cow. LC 77-25641. ix, 241 p. 21cm. 1978. (ISBN 0-06-026346-6). (ISBN 0-06-026347-4). Harper & Row. **Award: (ALA).**
--The Glory Story. (Illus.). 32p. (Arch Bks.: Set 11). (gr. 1-4). 1974. (ISBN 0-570-06083-4). Concordia.
--My First Book About Jesus. Cummins, James (1914-), illus. LC 82-10218. c.1983. (ISBN 0-528-82403-1). Rand McNally.
--A Penny Is Everything. (Illus.). 32p. (Arch Bks.: Set 11). (gr. 1-4). 1974. (ISBN 0-570-06084-2). Concordia.
--Potter, Come Fly to the First of the Earth. San Souci, Daniel LC 85-5686. (Illus.). 52 p. 27cm. c.1985. (ISBN 0-89191-745-4). Chariot Books.
--Thistle. 1st ed. Sewall, Marcia (1935-), illus. LC 82-47717. p. cm. c.1983. (ISBN 0-06-026351-2). (ISBN 0-06-026352-0). Harper & Row.
Wangerin, Walter, Jr. (1944-) & Jennings, A.
--God, I've Gotta Talk to You. (Illus.). 32p. (Arch Bk.). (gr. k-4). 1974. (ISBN 0-570-06086-9). Concordia.
Wangner, Ellen Diffin (1872-)
--Bobby Lynx of Round-Top. (The Round-Top). N.D. Nourse.
--Busy Beavers of Round-Top. (The Round-Top Nature Story Books). N.D. Nourse.
--Mother Fox of Round-Top. (The Round-Top Nature Story Books). N.D. Nourse.
Wang Pao-Chuan
--Lady Precious Stream. Taylor, C. W., retold by. Hsiung, Shikh-i (1902-), tr. (Illus.). (Oxford Progressive English Readers Ser.). (gr. k-6). 1971. (ISBN 0-19-638235-1). Oxford U Pr.
Wang Yanrong
--The Tiger & the Tortoise. (Illus.). 23p. (Orig.). (gr. 1-3). 1983. (ISBN 0-8351-1297-7). China Bks.
Waniek, Marilyn Nelson, jt. auth. see Espeland, Pamela Lee.
Wanklyn, Joan
--Bobtail Shawn. N.D. Frederick Warne & Co.
--Chequers: Kitty Alone. Wanklyn, Joan, illus. N.D. Frederick Warne & Co.
--Flip: The Story of an Otter. Wanklyn, Joan, illus. LC 51-14532. 162p. illus. 22cm. c.1951. Warne.
Wann, Bonnie Harrell
--Grandma Said. N.D. Vantage Press.
Wannamaker, Bruce, pseud., see Moncure, Jane Belk.
Wannamaker, Bruce, pseud. (1926-)
--John's Choice. Moncure, Jane Belk. (gr. 1-3). 1982. (ISBN 0-89693-207-9, Sonflower Bks). SP Pubns.
--The Kindness Weapon. Moncure, Jane Belk. 32p. 1984. (ISBN 0-89693-219-2). Victor Bks.
--The Kindness Weapon. Moncure, Jane Belk. Lexa, Susan, illus. LC 84-7038. (Illus.). 32p. (gr. 1-2). N.D. (ISBN 0-89693-219-2). Dandelion Hse.
--We Visit the Zoo. Moncure, Jane Belk. Magnuson, Diana, illus. LC 76-15639. (Illus.). (Going Places Ser.). (ps-3). 1976. (ISBN 0-913778-61-3). Childs World.
Wannamaker, Bruce, pseud. (1926-) & McLean, Mina Gow
--We Visit the Farm. Moncure, Jane Belk. McLean, Mina Gow, illus. LC 76-15975. (Illus.). (Going Places Ser.). (ps-3). 1976. (ISBN 0-913778-43-5). Childs World.
Wannon, Bill
--Crooked Mick of the Speewah. (gr. 9 up). N.D. Soccer.
Wansborough, Harold, jt. auth. see Casey, Beatrice Marie.
Wansborough, Harold, jt. auth. see Hartman, Zoe.
Warach, Marie Norkin
--I Like Red. Warach, Marie Norkin, illus. LC 78-72123. (Illus.). 31 p. 1979. (ISBN 0-89799-116-8). (ISBN 0-89799-002-1). Dandelion Press.
Warburg, Sandol Stoddard, ed. see Spenser, Edmund.
Warburg, Sandol Stoddard (1927-)
--Curl up Small. Hyman, Trina Schart (1939-), illus. LC 64-10725. 32 p. col. illus. 24 cm. 1964. Houghton Mifflin.
--Free. Oliver, Jenni (1947-), illus. LC 75-40013. (Illus.). 48 p. 24cm. 1976. (ISBN 0-395-24210-X). Houghton Mifflin.
--From Ambledee to Zumbledee: An A-B-C of Rather Special Bugs. Lorraine, Walter Henry (1929-), illus. LC 68-15718. (Illus.). 48 p. 19cm. 1968. (ISBN 0-395-07174-7). Houghton Mifflin.
--Growing Time. Weisgard, Leonard Joseph (1916-), illus. LC 69-14729. (Illus.). 44 p. 26cm. 1969. Houghton Mifflin.
--Hooray for Us. Chwast, Jacqueline (1932-), illus. LC 76-115452. (Illus.). 48 p. 14cm. 1970. Houghton Mifflin.
--I Like You. Chwast, Jacqueline (1932-), illus. LC 65-11020. 48 p. illus. 14 cm. 1965. Houghton Mifflin.
--Keep It Like a Secret. 1st ed. Chermayeff, Ivan (1932-), illus. LC 62-7107. unpaged. illus. 20 x 26 cm. 1961. Little, Brown.
--My Very Own Special Particular Private and Personal Cat. Charlip, Remy (1929-), illus. LC 63-14520. 40 p. col. illus. 24 cm. 1963. Houghton Mifflin.
--On the Way Home. Stolpe, Dan, illus. LC 73-6578. (Illus.). 137 p. 24cm. 1973. (ISBN 0-395-17510-0). Houghton Mifflin.
--The Thinking Book. 1st ed. Chermayeff, Ivan (1932-), illus. LC 60-9343. unpaged. illus. 21 x 26 cm. 1960. Little, Brown.
Warburton, Geo A.
--Little Phil: Or, The Engineer's Son. N.D. Wilbur B Ketcham.
Warburton, Thomas, tr. see Jansson, Tove.
Ward, Andrew (1946-)
--Baby Bear and the Long Sleep. 1st ed. Walsh, John (1945-), illus. LC 79-21392. (Illus.). 32 p. 24cm. c.1980. (ISBN 0-316-92197-1). Little, Brown.
Ward, Bertha Evans, ed. see Gras, Felix.
Ward, Bryan, illus.
--Around the World With Ant and Bee. 1960. Watts.
Ward, Donald (1930-), ed.
--The German Legends of the Brothers Grimm, 2 vols. Ward, Donald, tr. from Ger. LC 80-24596. (Illus.). (Translations in Folklore Studies Ser.). 1981. Set. (ISBN 0-915980-79-7). Ins Study Human.
Ward, Elaine M.
--A Beautiful Valentine. Young, Monte, illus. (Illus.). 64p. (Orig.). (The Story Tree Ser.). (ps). 1981. (ISBN 0-89505-073-0). Argus Comm.
--A Big Book: Stories from the Bible. Simon, Howard (1903-1979), illus. (Illus.). (gr. 4-7). N.D. (ISBN 0-687-03470-1). (ISBN 0-687-03471-X). Abingdon.
--On Halloween. Henson, Tex, illus. (Illus.). 48p. (Orig.). (The Story Tree Ser.). (ps). 1982. (ISBN 0-89505-070-6). Argus Comm.
--Roots and Wings. Lull, Ruth, illus. LC 83-1593. c.1983. (ISBN 0-377-00130-9). Friendship Press.
--Sean the Bunny: An Easter Story. Henson, Tex, illus. (Illus.). 64p. (Orig.). (ps). 1982. (ISBN 0-89505-074-9). Argus Comm.
--Spinner's Christmas Gift. Young, Monte, illus. (Illus.). 64p. (Orig.). (The Story Tree Ser.). (ps). 1982. (ISBN 0-89505-072-2). Argus Comm.
--Still Being Me. Bell, Giorgetta A., illus. LC 73-127374. (Illus.). 32 p. 1971. (ISBN 0-687-39472-4). Abingdon Press.
--The Thanksgiving Feast. Henson, Tex, illus. (Illus.). 64p. (Orig.). (The Story Tree Ser.). (ps). 1982. (ISBN 0-89505-071-4). Argus Comm.
Ward, Elizabeth Stuart Phelps (1844-1911), ed. see Craik, Dinah Maria Mulock, Mrs.
Ward, Elizabeth Stuart Phelps, Mrs., et al. (1844-1911)
--Little Boy Blue Ser. Containing "A Narrow Escape", "Tim's Partner", "Strangers from the South", "Little Boy Blue", etc, 6 vols. N.D. Set. D. Lothrop & Co.
--A Narrow Escape, 1 of 4 vols. (Illus.). 190p. (Out of School Ser.). N.D. D Lothrop.
Ward, Elizabeth Stuart Phelps, Mrs. (1844-1911)
--The Boys of Brimstone Court. LC 8-34845. 161 p. front., illus., plates. 18 cm. (On cover: Out of school series). 1879. D. Lothrop and Company.
--Ellen's Idol, 1 of 4 Vols. (Tiny Ser.). N.D. Set. Congregational Publishing Society.
--Ellen's Idol. (Tiny's Library). N.D. Henry A. Young.
--Gypsy Breynton. LC 28-4871. 2 p. l., 11-276 p. front., plates. 19 1/2 cm. (Her Gypsy series). 1875. Dodd, Mead & Company.
--Gypsy Breynton. (The Gypsy Ser.). N.D. E. P. Dutton.
--Gypsy Breynton. LC 8-34854. 17cm. x, 276p. (The Gypsy Ser.). N.D. Graves and Young.
--Gypsy Breynton. N.D. Macmillan.
--Gypsy Breynton, 1 of 4 vols. Clark, Mary Fairman, illus. LC 8-34853. 295p. 1894. Set. Dodd Mead & Company.
--Gypsy Breynton, 1 of 4 vols. Weaver, Miss, illus. (Gypsy Ser.). N.D. Dodd, Mead & Co.
--Gypsy Breyton. Rev ed. Clark, Mary Fairman, illus. LC 8-34853. vi, 7-295, 1 p. incl. front., illus., plates. 20 1/2 cm. (Gypsy series). 1894. Dodd, Mead & Company.
--The Gypsy Series. v. 19 1/2 cm. 1875. Dodd, Mead & Company.
--Gypsy Series, 4 vols. Weaver, Miss, illus. N.D. Dodd, Mead & Co.
--Gypsy's Breynton. (The Phoenix Ser.). N.D. Dodd, Mead & Co.
--Gypsy's Cousin Joy. N.D. Dodd Mead & Co.
--Gypsy's Cousin Joy. (The Phenix Ser.). N.D. Dodd, Mead & Co.
--Gypsy's Cousin Joy. (The Gypsy Ser.). N.D. E. P. Dutton.
--Gypsy's Cousin Joy. LC 8-34852. 3 p. l., 9-282 p. 17 cm. (Gypsy series). 1866. Graves and Young.
--Gypsy's Cousin Joy. Clark, Mary Fairman, illus. LC 8-34851. 4 p. l., v-vi, 7-320 p. incl. front., illus., plates. 20 1/2 cm. (Gypsy series). 1895. Dodd, Mead & Company.
--Gypsy's Cousin Joy, 1 of 4 vols. Weaver, Miss, illus. (Gypsy Ser.). N.D. Dodd, Mead & Co.
--Gypsy's Sowing and Reaping. N.D. Dodd Mead & Co.
--Gypsy's Sowing and Reaping. (The Gypsy Ser.). N.D. E. P. Dutton.
--Gypsy's Sowing and Reaping. LC 8-34850. 3 p. l., 9-302 p. 17 cm. (Gypsy series). 1866. Graves and Young.
--Gypsy's Sowing and Reaping. Clark, Mary Fairman, illus. LC 8-34849. vi, 314 p. incl. front., illus., plates. 20 1/2 cm. (Gypsy series). 1896. Dodd, Mead & Company.
--Gypsy's Year at the Golden Crescent, 1 of 4 Vols. (Illus.). (The Gypsy Stories). N.D. Dodd, Mead & Company.
--Gypsy's Year at the Golden Crescent. (The Phenix Ser.). N.D. Dodd, Mead & Co.
--Gypsy's Year at the Golden Crescent. (The Gypsy Ser.). N.D. E. P. Dutton.
--Gypsy's Year at the Golden Crescent. LC 8-34848. 2 p. l., iii-iv, 11-261 p. 17 cm. (Gypsy series). 1868. Graves & Young.
--Gypsy's Year at the Golden Crescent. Clark, Mary Fairman, illus. LC 8-34846. iv, 276 p. incl. illus., plates. front. 20 1/2 cm. (Gypsy series). 1897. Dodd, Mead & Company.
--Hardy and Hunter: A Boy's own Story. Weir, Harrison William (1824-1906), illus. N.D. George Routledge & Sons.
--I Don't Know How, 1 of 4 Vols. (Tiny Ser.). N.D. Set. Congregational Publishing Society.
--I Don't Know How. (Tiny's Library). N.D. Henry A. Young.
--A Little Maid and Her Moods. (Illus.). N.D. D. Lothrop & Co.
--Little Poems for Little People. (Illus.). N.D. D. Lothrop Co.
--A Lost Hero. Merrill, Frank Thayer (1848-), illus. (Illus.). N.D. Robert Brothers.
--Lovliness. LC 99-4706. 20cm. 45p. 1899. Houghton, Mifflin and Company.
--Mercy Giddon's Work. (Illus.). 311p. N.D. A. I. Bradley & Co.'s Pubs.
--Tiny, 1 of 4 Vols. (Tiny Ser.). N.D. Set. Congregational Publishing Society.
--Tiny. LC 8-34847. 198 p. front., plates 15 1/2 cm. c.1869. H. A. Young & Co.
--Tiny. LC 8-34847. 15cm. 198p. 1869. H. A. Young & Co.
--Tiny. (Tiny's Library). N.D. Henry A. Young.
--Tiny's Sunday Nights. (Tiny's Library). N.D. Henry A. Stuart.
--The Trotty Book. 21st ed. LC 8-34862. vi, 118 p. front., illus., plates. 18 cm. c.1897. Houghton, Mifflin and Company.
--The Trotty Book. (Illus.). N.D. Houghton, Mifflin And Co.
--The Trotty Book. LC 8-34861. 118p. 1870. James R. Osgood.
--Trotty's Wedding Tour, and Story-Book. LC 1-20266. iii p., 1 l., 11-224 p. incl. illus. facsim. front., pl. 18 cm. c.1901. Houghton, Mifflin and Company.
--Trotty's Wedding Tour and Story Book. 1910. Houghton & Mifflin.
--Trotty's Wedding Tour, and Story-Book. LC 8-34863. viii, 9-224 p. incl. illus., facsim. front., pl. 18 cm. 1874. J. R. Osgood and Company.
--Trotty's Wedding-Tour and Story-Book. 1873. James R. Osgood.
--Up Hill: Or, life in the Factory. (Illus.). 318p. N.D. A. I. Bradley & Co.'s Pubs.

Ward, Elizabeth Stuart Phelps, Mrs. (1844-1911) & Eytinge, Margaret
--A Narrow Escape, and Other Stories. (Illus.). N.D. D. Lothrop & Co.

Ward, Gene
--Brother and Sister Songs. 79 p. illus., incl. front. 21 cm. 1961. Vantage Press.

Ward, H. D. Mrs. see Ward, Elizabeth Stuart Phelps, Mrs.
Ward, H. D. Mrs. see Ward, Elizabeth Stuart Phelps, Mrs. (1844-1911) & Eytinge, Margaret.
Ward, H. D. Mrs. see Ward, Elizabeth Stuart Phelps, Mrs., et al.
Ward, Herbert Dickinson (1861-1932)
--The Captain of Kittiewink. LC 4-16478. (Illus.). 18cm. 320p. 1892. Roberts Brothers.
--A Dash to the Pole. LC 8-34860. 270 p. front., illus. 19 cm. c.1895. Lovell, Coryell & Company.
--The New Senior at Andover. LC 8-348591. 6 p. l., 11-333 p. incl. illus., plates. front. 18 1/2 cm. c.1891. D. Lothrop Company.
--The White Crown: And Other Stories. N.D. Houghton Mifflin Co.
Ward, Herman Mathew (1914-), ed.
--Poems for Pleasure. 137p. 1963. (ISBN 0-8090-7740-X). (ISBN 0-8090-1318-5). Farrar, Straus and Giroux.
Ward, Hetta Lord Hayes (1815-1842)
--Davy's Jacket. 1873. D. Lothrop & Co.
--Davy's Jacket. (Illus.). (Play and Study Ser.). N.D. D. Lothrop Co.
Ward, Humphry, pseud., see Ward, Mary Augusta Arnold Humphry Ward.
Ward-Jackson, Annis
--One Thousand One Glenwood. Duncan, Thomas, ed. Parker, Edward, illus. Penney-Jacket, Ruth, intro. by. (Illus.). 117p. 1st U.S. edition. (gr. 6 up). 1979. (ISBN 0-686-70396-0). Era Pr NC.
Ward, Jane Shaw
--Tajar Tales. Drucklieb, Herman L., illus. LC 24-21407. 73 p. front., illus. 19 cm. c.1924. John Martin's Book House.
--Tajar Tales. rev. ed. Drucklieb, Herman L., illus. LC 47-16949. 70 p. illus. 19 cm. 1947. The Woman's Press.
Ward, Jeannette W
--I Have a Question, God. Myers, Bill (1940-), illus. LC 80-70521. (Illus.). 32 p. 24cm. c.1981. (ISBN 0-8054-4265-0). Broadman Press.
Ward, John William George (1879-)
--A Rabbit Advises the Clock and Other Stories for Juniors. LC 32-191930. 219 p. 19 1/2 cm. c.1932. The Abingdon Press.
Ward, John William George (1879-), retold by.
--Treasure Trove for Little People. LC 27-24270. 19cm. 208p. 1927. George H. Doran.
Ward, Kate, pseud., see Pollock, Katherine G..
Ward, Keith, illus.
--Little Red Hen. The Story of the Little Red Hen. LC 35-20107. 16 p. illus. 34 cm. c.1935. Whitman Publishing Co.
Ward, Leila
--I Am Eyes: Ni Macho. Hogrogian, Nonny (1932-), illus. LC 78-1314. (Illus.). 32 p. c.1978. (ISBN 0-688-80161-7). (ISBN 0-688-84161-9). Greenwillow Books.

Ward, Lena
--Hettie Whight: Or, Faithful Over a Few Things. (Illus.). 247p. N.D. Sunday-School Publications.
Ward, Lydia Avery Coonley, Mrs. (1845-1924)
--The Melody of Childhood. LC 21-15172. 7 p. l., 166 p. front. (port.) 18 1/2 cm. 1921. James T. White & Co.
--Singing Verses for Children. LC 4-16245. 82 p. illus. 21 1/2 x 28 1/2 cm. 1897. The Macmillan Company.
Ward, Lynd Kendall, jt. auth. see Swift, Hildegarde Hoyt, Mrs.
Ward, Lynd Kendall (1905-1985)
--The Biggest Bear. Ward, Lynd Kendall (1905-1985), illus. LC 52-8730. (Illus.). 84 p. 28cm. 1952. Houghton Mifflin. **Award: (RUM).**
--The Biggest Bear. Ward, Lynd Kendall (1905-1985), illus. (Illus.). 80 p. 21cm. (Sandpiper Books). 1973, c.1952. (ISBN 0-395-15024-8). Houghton.
--The Biggest Bear. Ward, Lynd Kendall (1905-1985), illus. 70p. 1965. Pitman Publishing Corporation.
--Nic of the Woods. Ward, Lynd Kendall (1905-1985), illus. 1965. E M Hale.
--Nic of the Woods. Ward, Lynd Kendall (1905-1985), illus. LC 65-233280. (Illus.). 95 p. 28cm. 1965. Houghton Mifflin.
--The Silver Pony: A Story in Pictures. Ward, Lynd Kendall (1905-1985), illus. LC 72-5402. (Illus.). 174 p. 24cm. 1973. (ISBN 0-395-14753-0). Houghton Mifflin. **Awards: (NYT); (BGH).**
Ward, Marcus, compiled by.
--The Carrier Crow. Ward, Marcus, illus. (Royal Illuminated Nursery Rhymes). N.D. Colby and Rich.
--The Carrier Crow. Ward, Marcus, illus. (Royal Illuminated Nursery Rhymes). N.D. D. Appleton & Co.
--The Carrier Crow. Ward, Marcus, illus. (Royal Illuminated Nursery Rhymes). N.D. Lee & Shepard.
--The Carrier Crow. Ward, Marcus, illus. (Royal Illuminated Nursery Rhymes). N.D. R. Worthington & Co.
--The Fayre One with the Golden Locks. (Marcus Ward's Royal Illuminated Legends). N.D. Scribner, Welford & Armstrong.
--The Fayre One with the Golden Locks. Ward, Marcus, illus. (Royal Illuminated Library). N.D. Lee & Shepard.
--Four Nursery Rhymes. (Royal Illuminated Nursery Rhymes). N.D. George Routledge & Sons.
--Four Nursery Rhymes. Ward, Marcus, illus. (Royal Illuminated Nursery Rhymes). N.D. Colby and Rich.
--Four Nursery Rhymes. Ward, Marcus, illus. (Royal Illuminated Nursery Rhymes). N.D. D.Appleton & co.
--Four Nursery Rhymes. Ward, Marcus, illus. (Royal Illuminated Nursery Rhymes). N.D. Lee & Shepard.
--Jack and Gill. Ward, Marcus, illus. (Royal Illuminated Nursery Rhymes). N.D. Colby and Rich.
--Jack and Gill: Little Man and His Little Gun. Ward, Marcus, illus. (Royal Illuminated Nursery Rhymes). N.D. D. Appleton & co.
--Jack and Gill: Little Man and His Little Gun. Ward, Marcus, illus. (Royal Illuminated Nursery Rhymes). N.D. Lee & Shepard.
--Jack and Jill: A Little Man and His Little Gun. Ward, Marcus, illus. (Royal Illuminated Nursery Rhymes). N.D. R. Worthington & Co.
--King Alfred and Othere: The Discoverer of the North Cape. Ward, Marcus, illus. (Royal Illuminated Library). N.D. Lee & Shepard.
--Little Bo-Peep. Ward, Marcus, illus. (Royal Illuminated Nursery Rhymes). N.D. Colby and Rich.
--Little Bo-Peep. Ward, Marcus, illus. (Royal Illuminated Nursery Rhymes). N.D. D. Appleton & Co.
--Little Bo-Peep. Ward, Marcus, illus. (Royal Illuminated Nursery Rhymes). N.D. Lee & Shepard.
--Little Man and His Little Gun. Ward, Marcus, illus. (Royal Illuminated Nursery Rhymes). N.D. Colby and Rich.
--The Little Market Woman. Ward, Marcus, illus. (Royal Illuminated Nursery Rhymes). N.D. Colby and Rich.
--The Little Market Woman. Ward, Marcus, illus. (Royal Illuminated Nursery Rhymes). N.D. D. Appleton & Co.
--The Little Market Woman. Ward, Marcus, illus. (Royal Illuminated Nursery Rhymes). N.D. Lee & Shepard.
--The Little Market Woman. Ward, Marcus, illus. (Royal Illuminated Nursery Rhymes). N.D. R. Worthington & Co.
--Ye Marquis of Carabas: Or, Puss in Boots. Ward, Marcus, illus. N.D. Lee & Shepard.
--Mother Hubbard and Her Dog. Ward, Marcus, illus. (Royal Illuminated Nursery Rhymes). N.D. Colby and Rich.
--Mother Hubbard and Her Dog. Ward, Marcus, illus. (Royal Illuminated Nursery Rhymes). N.D. D. Appleton & Co.
--Mother Hubbard and Her Dog. Ward, Marcus, illus. (Royal Illuminated Nursery Rhymes). N.D. Lee & Shepard.
--Ye Pathetic Ballad of Lady Ouncebella and Lord Lovelle. (Marcus Ward's Royal Illuminated Legends: 3). N.D. Scribner, Welford & Armstrong.
--Pocahontas: a Tale of Old Virginie. Ward, Marcus, illus. (Royal Illuminated Legends). N.D. Lee & Shepard.
--Simple Simon. Ward, Marcus, illus. (Royal Illuminated Nursery Rhymes). N.D. Colby and Rich.
--Simple Simon. Ward, Marcus, illus. (Royal Illuminated Nursery Rhymes). N.D. D. Appleton & Co.
--Simple Simon. Ward, Marcus, illus. (Royal Illuminated Nursery Rhymes). N.D. Lee & Shepard.
--Sing a Song of Sixpence. Ward, Marcus, illus (Royal Illuminated Legends). N.D. Colby and Rich.
--Sing a Song of Sixpence. Ward, Marcus, illus. (Royal Illuminated Nursery Rhyme). N.D. D. Appleton & Co.
--Sing a Song of Sixpence. Ward, Marcus, illus. (Royal Illuminated Nursery Rhymes). N.D. Lee & Shepard.
--The Sleeping Beauty: Or, The Enchanted Palace. Ward, Marcus, illus. (Royal Illuminated Legends). N.D. Lee & Shepard.
Ward, Marion B.
--Boat Children of Canton. Sewell, Helen Moore (1896-1957), illus. LC 44-4095. (gr. 3-7). N.D. David McKay Co.
Ward, Martha Eads (1921-)
--The Bug Man. Oechsli, Kelly (1918-), illus. LC 70-140154. (Illus.). 112 p. 24cm. 1972. (ISBN 0-687-04034-5). Abingdon Press.
--Ollie, Ollie, Oxen-Free. McDonald, Ralph J., illus. LC 69-16941. (Illus.). 128 p. 22cm. 1969. (ISBN 0-687-28834-7). Abingdon Press.
Ward, Mary Augusta Arnold Humphry Ward see Ward, Humphry, pseud.
Ward, Mary Augusta Arnold Humphry Ward, Mrs. (1851-1920)
--Milly and Olly. (Illus.). N.D. Macmillan & Co.
--Milly and Olly. Ward, Humphry, pseud. New Rev. ed. Hallock, Ruth Mary (1876-), illus. LC 7-37712. viii p., 3 l., 3-302 p. front., 7 pl. 20 1/2 cm. 1907. Doubleday, Page & Co.
Ward, Mary Frances
--Fast As the Wind: A Story of Curtin Village in the 1860's. Straley, Nancy H, illus. LC 78-105162. (Illus.). vi, 42 p. 23cm. 1978. Roland Curtin Foundation for the Preservation of Eagle Furnace.
Ward, Mary O., Mrs.
--Songs for the Little Ones at Home. LC 41-26719. 288 p. incl. front., illus. 16 1/2 cm. c.1852. American Tract Society.
--Songs for the Little Ones at Home. enl. ed. LC 11-27060. 1 p. l., 7-288 p. front., illus., plates. 19 1/2 cm. c.1884. American Tract Society.
Ward, Mrs H. D. see Ward, Elizabeth Stuart Phelps, Mrs.
Ward, Muriel
--The Little Pond in the Woods. Gergely, Tibor (1900-1978), illus. LC 48-1918. 42 p. illus. (part col.) 21 cm. (The Little Golden Library: No. 43). 1948. Simon and Schuster.
Ward, Nanda Weedon (1932-)
--The Black Sombrero. Ward, Lynd Kendall (1905-1985), illus. LC 52-8342. unpaged. illus. 21 cm. 1952. Ariel Books.
--Hi Tom. Ward, Lynd Kendall (1905-1985), illus. LC 62-10085. (Illus.). 48 p. 26cm. 1962. Hastings House.
--The High Flying Hat. Ward, Lynd Kendall (1905-1985), illus. LC 56-5989. unpaged. illus. 21 cm. 1956. Ariel Books.
--Mister Mergatroid. Haynes, Bob, illus. LC 60-11315. 154 p. illus. 22 cm. 1960. Hastings House.
--Mr. Meadowlark. Haynes, Bob, illus. N.D. Hasting House Publishers Inc.
--Wellington and the Witch. Haynes, Bob, illus. LC 59-7466. 54 p. illus. 26 cm. 1959. Hastings House.
Ward, Nanda Weedon (1932-) & Haynes, Bob
--Beau. LC 57-7161. unpaged. illus. 28 cm. 1957. Ariel Books.
--The Elephant That Ga-lumphed. N.D. E. M. Hale & Co.
--The Elephant That Ga-Lumphed. LC 58-5418. unpaged. illus. 22 x 26 cm. 1959. Ariel Books.
Ward, Nick
--Giant. (Illus.). 30p. (Umbrella Books). (ps). 1983. (ISBN 0-19-278201-0, Pub by Oxford U Pr Childrens). Merrimack Pub Cir.
--Junk. (Illus.). 32p. (ps-1). 1984. (ISBN 0-19-278203-7, Pub. by Oxford U Pr Childrens). Merrimack Pub Cir.
Ward, Patricia
--The Secret Pencil. Hornby, Nicole, illus. LC 60-5591. 276 p. illus. 21 cm. 1960, c.1959. Random House.
Ward, Philip C. (1932-)
--Tony's Steamer. 1st ed. Armstrong, James (1934-), illus. LC 68-11116. (Illus.). 104 p. 21cm. 1968. Little, Brown.
Ward, Richard Elmer
--Hot Leather. 1st ed. LC 56-5527. 108p. 21cm. 1956. Vantage Press.
Ward, Sheila A.
--Dippitidy Doo: Songs & Activities for Children. (Illus.). 32p. (English As a Second Language Bk.). (gr. 1-5). 1980. (ISBN 0-582-51005-8). (ISBN 0-582-51004-X). (ISBN 0 582 51006 6), record 13.50x (ISBN 0-582-51007-4). Longman.
Ward-Thomas, Evelyn Bridget Patricia Stevens see Anthony, Evelyn, pseud.
Ward, Thomas Playfair (1895-)
--The Right to Live. 1st ed. LC 53-10072. 249p. 21cm. 1953. Pageant Press.
Ward, Tom, pseud., see Stratemeyer, Edward L..
Ward, Tom, pseud. (1862-1930)
--The Stable Gang's Last Battle: Or, Killed for Revenge. Stratemeyer, Edward L.. (New York Five Cent Library: No. 13). 1892. Street & Smith.
Ward, Verna Olive
--Egg-sistence. LC 18-1015. 38p. 19cm. 1917. The Maestro Co.
Ward, Winifred Louise (1884-)
--Theatre for Children. xv, 335 p. front. (port.) illus., plates. 21 1/2 cm. 1939. D. Appleton-Century Company, Incorporated.
--Theatre for Children. rev. ed. Vance, Charles, illus. LC 50-46692. xv, 317 p. illus., port. 22 cm. 1950. Childrens Theatre.
--Theatre for Children. 3d ed., rev. Vance, Charles, illus. LC 58-31567. 378 p. illus. 22 cm. 1958. Childrens Theatre.
Ward, Winifred Louise (1884-), ed.
--Stories to Dramatize. LC 52-11569. 389 p. 24cm. c.1952. Childrens Theatre.
Warde, Beatrice
--The Crystal Goblet. N.D. World Publishing Co.
Warde, Margaret, pseud., see Dunton, Edith Kellogg.
Warden, Florence, pseud., see James, Florence Alice Price Mrs..
Warden, Florence, pseud. (1857-)
--My Child and I. James, Florence Alice Price Mrs.. N.D. J. B. Lippincott.
Warden, Gertude
--Her Fairy Prince. N.D. J. B. Lippincott.
Warden, J. K.
--The Archimage. LC 80-85388. 180p. (Orig.). (gr. 7-12). 1981. (ISBN 0-939152-00-2). Grayling.
Wardenburg, Martha, tr. see Schweitzer, Albert.
Wardrop, Marjory, tr.
--Georgian Folk Tales, Vol.1. (Grimm Library). N.D. Charles Scribner's Sons.
Ware, Christine
--The Boy Who Lost His Name. LC 21-381393. 122 p. 19 cm. c.1921. The Abingdon Press.
Ware, Eugene F.
--Rhymes of Ironquill. 10th ed. 344p. N.D. Crane & Co.
Ware, Kay, ed. see Beattie, Janet.
Ware, Kay, ed. see Beim, Jerrold.
Ware, Kay, ed. see Falk, Ann Mari.
Ware, Kay, ed. see Hallqvist, Britt G.
Ware, Kay, ed. see Hertz, Grete Janus.
Ware, Kay, ed. see Lindgren, Astrid Ericsson.
Ware, Kay, ed. see Peterson, Hans.
Ware, Kay, ed. see Proysen, Alf.
Ware, Kay, ed. see Sigsgaard, Jens.
Ware, Kay, ed. see Skjonsberg, Gunnar.
Ware, Kay (1916-) & Sutherland, Lucille
--Timothy's Christmas Visit. (Read For Fun Ser.). 1964. (ISBN 0-07-068254-2). McGraw Hill Book Company.
Ware, Kay (1916-) & Sutherland, Lucille, eds.
--Benjamin has a Birthday. (Read for Fun Ser.). 1964. (ISBN 0-07-068246-1). McGraw HIll Book Company.
--Benjamin Has a Birthday. Wiberg, Harold Albin (1908-), illus. LC 64-6417. (Original Story by Hans Peterson). (Illus.). 23cm. (The Read for Fun Ser.). 1964. Webster Division, McGraw-Hill.
--Grandfathers Old Straw Hat. (Read for Fun Ser.). 1964. (ISBN 0-07-068250-X). McGraw Hill Book Company.
--Grandfather's Straw Hat. Struwer, Ardy, illus. LC 64-7023. (Original Author: Grete Janus Hertz (1915)). 1 v. (unpaged) col. illus. 23cm. (The Read for fun Ser.). 1964. McGraw-Hill.
--Greek and Roman Myths. Miller, Edward (1905-1974), illus. LC 52-32078. 138 p. illus. 21 cm. (Junior everyreaders). 1952. Webster Pub. Co.
--The New House. (Read for Fun Ser.). 1964. (ISBN 0-07-068255-0). McGraw HIll Book Company.
--The Old Man and the Bird. (Read for Fun Ser.). 1964. (ISBN 0-07-068248-8). McGraw HIll Book Company.
--The Town that Forgot it Was Christmas. Stodberg, Nils, illus. LC 61-59875. (Original Story by Alf Proysen.). (Illus.). 23cm. 1961. Webster Pub. Co.
--A Visit to Birdland. (Read For Fun Ser.). 1964. (ISBN 0-07-068252-6). McGraw Hill Book Company.
Ware, Leon Vernon (1909-1976)
--Crazy Dog. Dennis, Morgan (1891-1960), illus. LC 44-8722. 2 p. l., 67 p. incl. front., illus. 25 1/2 cm. 1944. Whittlesey House, McGraw-Hill Book Company, Inc.
--Delta Mystery. LC 74-6441. 224 p. 22cm. 1974. (ISBN 0-664-32553-X). Westminster Press.
--The Jade Monkey Mystery. LC 69-14820. 185 p. 21cm. 1969. Westminister Press.
--The Mystery of Twenty-Two East. N.D. (ISBN 0-685-56328-6, Tempo). G&D.
--The Mystery of Twenty-Two East. LC 65-14038. 183 p. 22 cm. (gr. 7-10). 1965. (ISBN 0-664-32353-7). Westminster Press.
--The Phantom of the Bridge. LC 54-6429. 206p. 21cm. 1954. Westminster Press.
--The Rebellious Orphan. Hamilton, Bill, illus. LC 64-11639. 217 p. illus. 23 cm. 1964. Westminster Press.
--Shifting Winds. Chapman, Frederick Trench (1887-), illus. LC 48-6493. 188 p. illus. 21 cm. 1948. Whittlesey House.
--The Threatening Fog. LC 62-12789. (Illus.). 235 p. 21cm. 1962. Westminster Press.
Ware, Linda Jacobs (1943-)
--God, Why Is She the Way She Is?. Hackett, Michael, illus. LC 79-12241. p. cm. c.1979. (ISBN 0-570-03621-6). Concordia Pub. House.
Ware, Richard Darwin (1869-1931)
--Rollo's Journey to Washington. Seaver, Robert, illus. LC 19-7721. (A Narrative of Contemporaneous Travel and Adventure, with Descriptions of Episodes Occurring During a Sojourn in the Capital City of Our Country in Time of War, Particularly Adapted to the Perusal of Youthful Persons of Any Age). 5 p. l., 170 p. front., plates. 19 1/2 cm. 1919. The Page Company.
Warfel, Diantha
--On Guard. LC 61-14523. 175 p. 21 cm. 1961. Dodd, Mead.
--The Violin Case Case. LC 77-19049. 151 p. 22cm. c.1978. (ISBN 0-525-41992-6). Dutton.
Waring, Gilchrist
--The City of Once Upon a Time. Jones, Elmo, illus. 1946. The Dietz Press.
--Three Ships Come Sailing. Jones, Elmo, illus. (Illus.). (gr. 2-7). N.D (Pub. by Dietz Pr.). Williamsburg.
Waring, Jean
--The Fluffy Lions. N.D. A. S. Barnes & Co.
Waring, Marty B.
--Blake, the Snake. 1978. (ISBN 0-533-02984-8). Vantage.
Waring, P. Alston (1895-)
--The Peacock Country. Bock, Vera, illus. LC 48-53196. xi, 100 p. illus. 25 cm. 1948. J. Day Co.
Waring, Susie M.
--Diamonds and Rubies: or, The Home of Santa Claus. N.D. E. P. Dutton.
--Little Mirabel's Fair. (Illus.). N.D. Publications of E. P. Dutton & Co.
Warmington, E.
--Recitations, Rhymes, for Kindergarten. N.D. E. Steiger& Co.
Warner
--Love Comes to Anne. (gr. 7 up). 1980. (ISBN 0-590-30027-X, Wildfire). Scholastic Inc.
Warner, Ann Spence
--Days of Gold. King, Ruth, illus. N.D. Grosset & Dunlap.
--Days of Gold. King, Ruth, illus. LC 31-23360. 295 p. front., illus., plates. 20 cm. c.1931. The Bobbs-Merrill Company.
--Gold Is Where You Find It. King, Ruth, illus. N.D. Grosset & Dunlap.
--Gold Is Where You Find It. King, Ruth, illus. LC 32-23427. 301 p. incl. illus., plates. front. 19 1/2 cm. c.1932. The Bobbs-Merrill Company.
--Narcissa Whitman, Pioneer Girl. 1st ed. Davis, Bette J. (1923-), illus. LC 53-9871. (Illus.). 12p. 20cm. (The Childhood of Famous Americans Ser.). 1953. Bobbs-Merrill.
--Narcissa Whitman, Pioneer Girl. Sampson, Katherine, illus. LC 59-13999. 192 p. illus. 20 cm. (Childhood of famous Americans). 1959. Bobbs-Merrill.
--Sidesaddle Ranch. King, Ruth, illus. N.D. Grosset & Dunlap.
--Sidesaddle Ranch. King, Ruth, illus. LC 30-220272. 288 p. front., illus., plates. 19 1/2 cm. c.1930. The Bobbs-Merrill Company.
Warner, Anna Bartlett see Lothrop, Amy, pseud.
Warner, Anna Bartlett, jt. auth. see Warner, Susan Bogert.
Warner, Anna Bartlett (1827-1915)
--A Bag of Stories. 238p. 1905. American Tract Society.
--A Bag of Stories. (Sunday-Hour Lib.). N.D. American Tract Society.

--A Bag of Stories, 1 of 50 vols. 61/2x4 1/2cm. (Heart Life Classics). N.D. American Tract Society.
--A Bag of Stories. LC 2-53474. 238 p. front., pl. 17 1/2 cm. 1883. R. Carter & Brothers.
--Blue Flag and Cloth of Gold. LC 8-33473. 359 p. front. 17 1/2 cm. 1880. R. Carter & Brothers.
--Blue Flag and Cloth of Gold. N.D. Thomas Whittaker.
--Casper. Lothrop, Amy, pseud. LC 3-33472. 2 p. l., 7-262 p. 17 1/2 cm. (Added t.-p.: Ellen Montgomery's book shelf. Vol IV). 1856. G. P. Putnam & Co.
--Casper and His Friends, 1 of 5 Vols. (Ellen Montgomery's Book-Shelf). N.D. Robert Carter & Brothers.
--Cross Corners. LC 8-33471. 358 p. 19 1/2 cm. c.1887. R. Carter and Brothers.
--Fresh Air: A Story of the Slums. 4 p. l., 5-161 p. incl. front., illus. 19 1/2 cm. c.1899. American Tract Society.
--Little Jack's Four Lessons. (Illus.). 109p. N.D. American Tract Society.
--Little Jack's Four Lessons. 109 p. front., plates. 17 1/2 cm. 1869. R. Carter and Brothers.
--Miss Muff and Little Hungry. Lothrop, Amy, pseud. LC 16-10103. 40 p. incl. col. front., col. plates. 20 cm. c.1866. Presbyterian Publication Committee.
--The Star Out of Jacob. Lothrop, Amy, pseud. LC 8-34340. 391 p. front., illus., plates. 19 cm. (The Word series). c.1891. Hurst & Company.
--Stories of Vinegar Hill. 6 v. fronts., plates. 15 1/2 cm. 1872. R. Carter and Brothers.
--Three Little Spades. LC 8-33467. vii, 9-268 p. 17 1/2 cm. 1868. Harper & Brothers.
--Three Little Spades. Repr. 1882. Harper's Trade-List.
--Yours and Mine. LC 8-33466. 378 p. 19 1/2 cm. c.1889. R. Carter & Brothers.

Warner, Anne (1869-)
--Second Love. LC 63-8068. 171 p. 22 cm. 1963. Westminster Press.

Warner, Brook (1819-1885)
--Willow Brook. (Illus.). 346p. N.D. A. I. Bradley & Co.'s Pubs.

Warner, Charles Dudley (1829-1900)
--Being a Boy. LC 14-1627. 1 p. l., v-xi, 244 p. front. (port.) illus. 18 1/2 cm. (Riverside school library). c.1896. Houghton, Mifflin & Company.
--Being a Boy. Champ, pseud. (1843-1903), illus. Champney, James Wells. (Illus.). N.D. Houghton, Osgood & Co.

Warner, Donald W.
--Short Stories for Children. 1983. (ISBN 0-8062-2205-0). Carlton.

Warner, Edythe Records (1916-)
--Cabin for Ducks. Warner, Edythe Records (1916-), illus. LC 58-3547. (Illus.). 23p. 32cm. 1958. Viking Press.
--The Fishing River. Warner, Edythe Records (1916-), illus. 61 p. illus. 24 cm. 1962. Viking Press.
--The Little Dark-House. Warner, Edythe Records (1916-), illus. LC 60-4439. 55 p. illus. 24 cm. 1960. Viking Press.
--Siamese Summer. Warner, Edythe Records (1916-), illus. LC 64-126371. 61 p. illus. 26 cm. 1964. Viking Press.

Warner, Ellen E. Kenyon
--Nonsense Dialogues. Curtis, Eliza, illus. (Everychild's Ser.). 1912. Macmillan.

Warner, Esther S., pseud., see Dendel, Esther Sietman Warner.

Warner, Esther S., pseud. (1910-)
--Seven Days to Lomaland. Dendel, Esther Sietman Warner. (gr. 10 up). N.D. Pyramid Pubns.

Warner, Fannie
--Hetty Homer: Or, Tried but True, and Other Tales. 142 p. 15 1/2 cm. 1870. P. F. Cunningham.

Warner, Frances Lester (1888-), ed. see Alcott, Louisa May.

Warner, Frances Lester (1888-)
--Ragamuffin Marionettes. Freeman, Margaret (1893-), illus. 1932. Houghton Mifflin Co.

Warner, Frank A., pseud., see Stratemeyer Syndicate.

Warner, Frank A., pseud.
--Bob Chase after Grizzly Bears. Stratemeyer Syndicate. Randolph, David, illus. (Bob Chase Big Game Ser.: Vol. 2). 1929. Barse & Co.
--Bob Chase After Grizzly Bears. Stratemeyer Syndicate. Randolph, David, illus. Repr. of 1929 ed (Pub. by Barse & Co). (Bob Chase Big Game Ser.: Vol. 2). N.D. Grosset & Dunlap.
--Bob Chase in the Tiger's Lair. Stratemeyer Syndicate. Randolph, David, illus. LC 29-11680. 216 p. incl. front. 19 1/2 cm. (Bob Chase Big Game Ser.: Vol. 3). c.1929. Barse & Co.
--Bob Chase in the Tiger's Lair. Stratemeyer Syndicate. Randolph, David, illus. Repr. of 1929 ed (Pub. by Barse & Co). (Bob Chase Big Game Ser.: Vol. 3). N.D. Grosset & Dunlap.
--Bob Chase with the Big Moose Hunters. Stratemeyer Syndicate. Randolph, David, illus. LC 29-57027. 216 p. incl. plates. front. 19 1/2 cm. (Bob Chase Big Game Ser.: Vol. 1). c.1929. Barse & Co.
--Bob Chase with the Big Moose Hunters. Stratemeyer Syndicate. Randolph, David, illus. Repr. of 1929 ed (Pub. by Barse & Co). (Bob Chase Big Game Ser.: Vol. 1). N.D. Grosset & Dunlap.
--Bob Chase with the Lion Hunters. Stratemeyer Syndicate. Randolph, David, illus. LC 30-8271. 214 p. incl. front. 19 1/2 cm. (Bob Chase Big Game Ser.: Vol. 4). c.1930. Barse & Co.
--Bob Chase with the Lion Hunters. Stratemeyer Syndicate. Randolph, David, illus. Repr. of 1930 ed (Pub. by Barse & Co). (Bob Chase Big Game Ser.: Vol. 4). N.D. Grosset & Dunlap.
--Bobby Blake and His School Chums: Or, The Rivals of Rockledge. Stratemeyer Syndicate. Owen, Robert Emmett (1878-), illus. (The Bobby Blake Ser.: Vol. 4). 1916. Barse & Hopkins.
--Bobby Blake and His School Chums: Or, The Rivals of Rockledge. Stratemeyer Syndicate. Owen, Robert Emmett (1878-), illus. Repr. of 1916 ed (Pub. by Barse & Hopkins). (The Bobby Blake Ser.: Vol. 4). N.D. Barse & Co.
--Bobby Blake and His School Chums: Or, The Rivals of Rockledge. Stratemeyer Syndicate. Owen, Robert Emmett (1878-), illus. Repr. of 1916 ed (Pub. by Barse & Hopkins). (The Bobby Blake Ser.: Vol. 4). N.D. Grosset & Dunlap.
--Bobby Blake at Bass Cove: Or, The Hunt for the Motor Boat Gem. Stratemeyer Syndicate. Repr. of 1915 ed (Pub. by Barse & Hopkins). (The Bobby Blake Ser.: Vol. 2). N.D. Whitman Publishing Co.
--Bobby Blake at Bass Cove: Or, The Hunt for the Motor Boat Gem. Stratemeyer Syndicate. Owen, Robert Emmett (1878-), illus. (The Bobby Blake Ser.: Vol. 2). 1915. Barse & Hopkins.
--Bobby Blake at Bass Cove: Or, The Hunt for the Motor Boat Gem. Stratemeyer Syndicate. Owen, Robert Emmett (1878-), illus. Repr. of 1915 ed (Pub. by Barse & Hopkins). (The Bobby Blake Ser.: Vol. 2). N.D. Barse & Co.
--Bobby Blake at Bass Cove: Or, The Hunt for the Motor Boat Gem. Stratemeyer Syndicate. Owen, Robert Emmett (1878-), illus. Repr. of 1915 ed (Pub. by Barse & Hopkins). (The Bobby Blake Ser.: Vol. 2). N.D. Grosset & Dunlap.
--Bobby Blake at Rockledge School: Or, Winning the Medal of Honor. Stratemeyer Syndicate. Repr. of 1915 ed (Pub. by Barse & Hopkins). (The Bobby Blake Ser.: Vol. 1). N.D. Whitman Publishing Co.
--Bobby Blake at Rockledge School: Or, Winning the Medal of Honor. Stratemeyer Syndicate. Owen, Robert Emmett (1878-), illus. (The Bobby Blake Ser.: Vol. 1). 1915. Barse & Hopkins.
--Bobby Blake at Rockledge School: Or, Winning the Medal of Honor. Stratemeyer Syndicate. Owen, Robert Emmett (1878-), illus. Repr. of 1915 ed (Pub. by Barse & Hopkins). (The Bobby Blake Ser.: Vol. 1). N.D. Barse & Co.
--Bobby Blake at Rockledge School: Or, Winning the Medal of Honor. Stratemeyer Syndicate. Owen, Robert Emmett (1878-), illus. Repr. of 1915 ed (Pub. by Barse & Hopkins). (The Bobby Blake Ser.: Vol. 1). N.D. Grosset & Dunlap.
--Bobby Blake at Snowtop Camp: Or, Winter Holidays in the Big Woods. Stratemeyer Syndicate. Owen, Robert Emmett (1878-), illus. (The Bobby Blake Ser.: Vol. 5). 1916. Barse & Hopkins.
--Bobby Blake at Snowtop Camp: Or, Winter Holidays in the Big Woods. Stratemeyer Syndicate. Owen, Robert Emmett (1878-), illus. Repr. of 1916 ed (Pub. by Barse & Hopkins). (The Bobby Blake Ser.: Vol. 5). N.D. Barse & Co.
--Bobby Blake at Snowtop Camp: Or, Winter Holidays in the Big Woods. Stratemeyer Syndicate. Owen, Robert Emmett (1878-), illus. Repr. of 1916 ed (Pub. by Barse & Hopkins). (The Bobby Blake Ser.: Vol. 5). N.D. Grosset & Dunlap.
--Bobby Blake in the Frozen North: Or, The Old Eskimo's Last Message. Stratemeyer Syndicate. Rogers, Walter S., illus. LC 23-78342. 3 p. l., 9-250 p. front., plates. 19 1/2 cm. (The Bobby Blake Ser.: Vol. 11). c.1923. Barse & Hopkins.
--Bobby Blake in the Frozen North: Or, The Old Eskimo's Last Message. Stratemeyer Syndicate. Rogers, Walter S., illus. Repr. of 1923 ed (Pub. by Barse & Hopkins). (The Bobby Blake Ser.: Vol. 11). N.D. Barse & Co.
--Bobby Blake in the Frozen North: Or, The Old Eskimo's Last Message. Stratemeyer Syndicate. Rogers, Walter S., illus. Repr. of 1923 ed (Pub. by Barse & Hopkins). (The Bobby Blake Ser.: Vol. 11). N.D. Grosset & Dunlap.
--Bobby Blake on a Cruise: Or, The Castaways of Volcano Island. Stratemeyer Syndicate. Owen, Robert Emmett (1878-), illus. (The Bobby Blake Ser.: Vol. 3). 1915. Barse & Hopkins.
--Bobby Blake on a Cruise: Or, The Castaways of Volcano Island. Stratemeyer Syndicate. Owen, Robert Emmett (1878-), illus. Repr. of 1915 ed (Pub. by Barse & Hopkins). (The Bobby Blake Ser.: Vol. 3). N.D. Barse & Co.
--Bobby Blake on a Cruise: Or, The Castaways of Volcano Island. Stratemeyer Syndicate. Owen, Robert Emmett (1878-), illus. Repr. of 1915 ed (Pub. by Barse & Hopkins). (The Bobby Blake Ser.: Vol. 3). N.D. Grosset & Dunlap.
--Bobby Blake on a Plantation: Or, Lost in the Great Swamp. Stratemeyer Syndicate. Rogers, Walter S., illus. LC 22-136022. 248 p. incl. front. plates. 19 1/2 cm. (The Bobby Blake Ser.: Vol. 10). c.1922. Barse & Hopkins.
--Bobby Blake on a Plantation: Or, Lost in the Great Swamp. Stratemeyer Syndicate. Rogers, Walter S., illus. Repr. of 1922 ed (Pub. by Barse & Hopkins). (The Bobby Blake Ser.: Vol. 10). N.D. Barse & Co.
--Bobby Blake on a Plantation: Or, Lost in the Great Swamp. Stratemeyer Syndicate. Rogers, Walter S., illus. Repr. of 1922 ed (Pub. by Barse & Hopkins). (The Bobby Blake Ser.: Vol. 10). N.D. Grosset & Dunlap.
--Bobby Blake on a Ranch: Or, The Secret of the Mountain Cave. Stratemeyer Syndicate. Owen, Robert Emmett (1878-), illus. (The Bobby Blake Ser.: Vol. 7). 1918. Barse & Hopkins.
--Bobby Blake on a Ranch: Or, The Secret of the Mountain Cave. Stratemeyer Syndicate. Owen, Robert Emmett (1878-), illus. Repr. of 1918 ed (Pub. by Barse & Hopkins). (The Bobby Blake Ser.: Vol. 7). N.D. Barse & Co.
--Bobby Blake on a Ranch: Or, The Secret of the Mountain Cave. Stratemeyer Syndicate. Owen, Robert Emmett (1878-), illus. Repr. of 1918 ed (Pub. by Barse & Hopkins). (The Bobby Blake Ser.: Vol. 7). N.D. Grosset & Dunlap.
--Bobby Blake on an Auto Tour: Or, The Mystery of the Deserted House. Stratemeyer Syndicate. Wrenn, Charles L., illus. (The Bobby Blake Ser.: Vol. 8). 1920. Barse & Hopkins.
--Bobby Blake on an Auto Tour: Or, The Mystery of the Deserted House. Stratemeyer Syndicate. Wrenn, Charles L., illus. Repr. of 1920 ed (Pub. by Barse & Hopkins). (The Bobby Blake Ser.: Vol. 8). N.D. Barse & Co.
--Bobby Blake on an Auto Tour: Or, The Mystery of the Deserted House. Stratemeyer Syndicate. Wrenn, Charles L., illus. Repr. of 1920 ed (Pub. by Barse & Hopkins). (The Bobby Blake Ser.: Vol. 8). N.D. Grosset & Dunlap.
--Bobby Blake on Mystery Mountain. Stratemeyer Syndicate. Williams, Oriet, illus. (The Bobby Blake Ser.: Vol. 12). 1926. Barse & Hopkins.
--Bobby Blake on Mystery Mountain. Stratemeyer Syndicate. Williams, Oriet, illus. Repr. of 1926 ed (Pub. by Barse & Hopkins). (The Bobby Blake Ser.: Vol. 12). N.D. Barse & Co.
--Bobby Blake on Mystery Mountain. Stratemeyer Syndicate. Williams, Oriet, illus. Repr. of 1926 ed (Pub. by Barse & Hopkins). (The Bobby Blake Ser.: Vol. 12). N.D. Grosset & Dunlap.
--Bobby Blake on the School Eleven: Or, Winning the Banner of Blue and Gold. Stratemeyer Syndicate. Dinsmore, E. J., illus. (The Bobby Blake Ser.: Vol. 9). 1921. Barse & Hopkins.
--Bobby Blake on the School Eleven: Or, Winning the Banner of Blue and Gold. Stratemeyer Syndicate. Dinsmore, E. J., illus. Repr. of 1921 ed (Pub. by Barse & Hopkins). (The Bobby Blake Ser.: Vol. 9). N.D. Barse & Co.
--Bobby Blake on the School Eleven: Or, Winning the Banner of Blue and Gold. Stratemeyer Syndicate. Dinsmore, E. J., illus. Repr. of 1921 ed (Pub. by Barse & Hopkins). (The Bobby Blake Ser.: Vol. 9). N.D. Grosset & Dunlap.
--Bobby Blake on the School Nine: Or, The Champions of Monotook Lake League. Stratemeyer Syndicate. Owen, Robert Emmett (1878-), illus. (The Bobby Blake Ser.: Vol. 6). 1917. Barse & Hopkins.
--Bobby Blake on the School Nine: Or, The Champions of Monotook Lake League. Stratemeyer Syndicate. Owen, Robert Emmett (1878-), illus. Repr. of 1917 ed (Pub. by Barse & Hopkins). (The Bobby Blake Ser.: Vol. 6). N.D. Barse & Co.
--Bobby Blake on the School Nine: Or, The Champions of Monotook Lake League. Stratemeyer Syndicate. Owen, Robert Emmett (1878-), illus. Repr. of 1917 ed (Pub. by Barse & Hopkins). (The Bobby Blake Ser.: Vol. 6). N.D. Grosset & Dunlap.

Warner, Gertrude Chandler (1890-1979)
--Benny Uncovers a Mystery. Cunningham, David (1938-), illus. LC 76-15222. (Illus.). 128 p. 21cm. (Pilot books). c.1976. (ISBN 0-8075-0644-3). A. Whitman.
--Bicycle Mystery. Cunningham, David (1938-), illus. LC 79-126428. (Illus.). 127 p. 22cm. (Albert Whitman pilot books). 1970. (ISBN 0-8075-0708-3). A. Whitman.
--Blue Bay Mystery. Gringhuis, Richard H. (1918-1974), illus. Gringhuis, Dirk, pseud. LC 61-15230. (Illus.). 157 p. 22cm. 1961. A. Whitman.
--The Box-Car Children. Gregory, Dorothy Lake, illus. 146p. N.D. Rand McNally & Co.
--The Boxcar Children. Deal, L. Kate, illus. LC 42-1418. 156 p. illus. 22 cm. c.1942. Scott, Foresman and Company.
--The Boxcar Children. Deal, L. Kate, illus. LC 50-12678. 156 p. illus. 22 cm. 1950. Scott, Foresman.
--Bus Station Mystery. Cunningham, David (1938-), illus. LC 74-8293. (Illus.). 127 p. 21cm. (Pilot books series). 1974. (ISBN 0-8075-0975-2). A. Whitman.
--Caboose Mystery. Cunningham, David (1938-), illus. LC 67-112. (Illus.). 128 p. 22cm. (Her The boxcar children mysteries). 1966. A. Whitman.
--Children of the Harvest. Smalley, Janet (1893-), illus. LC 40-6553. 95, 1 p. incl. front., illus. 23 1/2 cm. c.1940. Friendship Press.
--The House of Delight. Warner, John A. Carpenter, photos by. LC 16-176538. xiii, 101 p. front., plates. 20 cm. $1.25. c.1916. The Pilgrim Press.
--Houseboat Mystery. Cunningham, David (1938-), illus. LC 67-26521. 128 p. illus. 22 cm. (Boxcar children mysteries). 1967. Whitman.
--Lighthouse Mystery. Cunningham, David (1938-), illus. LC 63-20354. (Illus.). 128p. (Boxcar Children Mysteries-Pilot Bk.). (gr. 3-7). 1963. (ISBN 0-8075-4545-7). A Whitman.
--Mike's Mystery. Gringhuis, Richard H. (1918-1974), illus. Gringhuis, Dirk, pseud. LC 60-8428. (Illus.). 128 p. 22cm. 1960. A. Whitman.
--Mountain Top Mystery. Cunningham, David (1938-), illus. LC 64-7722. (Illus.). 128 p. 22cm. (Her The boxcar children mysteries). 1964. A. Whitman.
--Mystery Behind the Wall. Cunningham, David (1938-), illus. LC 72-13356. (Illus.). 127 p. 21cm. (Her The Alden family mysteries). 1973. (ISBN 0-8075-5364-6). A. Whitman.
--Mystery in the Sand. Cunningham, David (1938-), illus. LC 70-165823. (Illus.). line drawings. 128p. 128p. (Boxcar Children Mysteries-Pilot Bk.). (gr. 3-7). 1971. (ISBN 0-8075-5373-5). A Whitman.
--Mystery Ranch. Gringhuis, Richard H. (1918-1974), illus. Gringhuis, Dirk, pseud. LC 58-9953. (Illus.). 127 p. 22cm. 1958. A. Whitman.
--Peter Piper, Missionary Parakeet. (Illus.). (gr. 4 up). N.D. Zondervan.
--Schoolhouse Mystery. Cunningham, David (1938-), illus. LC 65-23889. (Illus.). 128 p. 22cm. 1965. A. Whitman.
--Snowbound Mystery. Cunningham, David (1938-), illus. LC 68-9124. (Illus.). 128 p. 22cm. (Pilot books). 1968. A. Whitman.
--Surprise Island. Gehr, Mary, illus. LC 49-49618. 181 p. illus. 22 cm. 1949. Scott, Foresman.
--Tree House Mystery. Cunningham, David (1938-), illus. LC 77-91744. (Illus.). 127 p. 22cm. (Pilot books). 1969. A. Whitman.
--The Woodshed Mystery. Cunningham, David (1938-), illus. LC 62-19726. (Illus.). 159 p. 22cm. 1962. A. Whitman.
--The World in a Barn. Young, Florence Liley, illus. LC 27-143466. 4 p. l., 120 p. col. front., illus., col. pl. 18 1/2 cm. c.1927. Friendship Press.
--The World on a Farm. Adams, Adrienne (1906-), illus. LC 31-15091. 5 p. l., 83, 1 p. incl. front., illus. 18 1/2 cm. c.1931. Friendship Press.
--The Yellow House Mystery. Gehr, Mary, illus. LC 53-13243. (Illus.). 191 p. 22cm. 1953. A. Whitman.

Warner, Hannah
--The Easter Story Retold: Or, How the Flower Fairies Heard the Story. (Illus.). 12p. N.D. Pilgrim Press.

Warner, Helen Garnie see Harcourt, Helen, pseud.

Warner, John H.
--Jungle Maid. N.D. Exposition Press.

Warner, Keith Q., tr. see Zobel, Joseph.

Warner, Laverne & Berry, Paulette
--Tunes for Tots. (ps-2). 1982. (ISBN 0-86653-077-0). Good Apple.

Warner, Lucille Schulberg
--Goodbye, Pretty One. 176p. (Orig.). (gr. 7 up). 1982. (ISBN 0-590-31252-9, Wildfire). Scholastic Inc.

Warren, Robert Penn (1905-)
--The Gods of Mount Olympus. Moyers, William (1916-), illus. LC 59-6143. 52 p. 23 cm. (Legacy books, Y-1). 1959. (ISBN 0-394-90151-7). Random House.
Warren, Rosanna Phelps
--The Joey Story. McKie, Roy, illus. LC 64-23496. 57 p. illus. 21 cm. 1964. Random House.
Warren, S. J., Mrs.
--Children's Picture-Book. 96p. N.D. Lockwood, Brooks & Co. for American Tract Society.
Warren, Samuel
--Tittlebat Titmouse. Brady, Cyrus Townsend, ed. 464p. N.D. Funk & Wagnalls.
Warren, Sheila
--Miss Lorena's Cousin. LC 31-163359. 2 p. l., 9-167 p. 19 1/2 cm. c.1931. The World Syndicate Publishing Co.
--Rusty and Tracy. (The Girl's World Ser.). N.D. World Publishing Co.
Warren, Wilda
--Tejana, a Story of Life with the Comanche Indians. LC 41-26747. 5 p. l., 92, 1 p. illus. 19 1/2 cm. c.1941. Mathias, Van Nort & Company.
Warren, William E (1941-)
--Footsteps in the Fog: Still More Not-So-Scary Stories. Frascino, Edward, illus. LC 85-9396. (Illus.). 106 p. 22cm. c.1985. (ISBN 0-13-324807-0). Prentice-Hall.
--The Graveyard and Other Not-So-Scary Stories. Frascino, Edward, illus. LC 83-23125. (Illus.). 86 p. 22cm. c.1984. (ISBN 0-13-363623-2). Prentice-Hall.
--The Thing in the Swamp and More Not-So-Scary Stories. Frascino, Edward, illus. LC 84-6769. (Illus.). 98 p. 22cm. c.1984. (ISBN 0-13-917196-7). Prentice-Hall.
Warren, William Stephen see Warren, Billy, pseud.
Warren, William Stephen (1882-1968)
--Black Lobo. Warren, Billy, pseud. Garbutt, Bernard (1900-), illus. LC 67-21224. (Illus.). 154 p. 22cm. 1967. Golden Gate Junior Books.
--The Golden Palomino. Warren, Billy, pseud. Warren, William Stephen (1882-1968), illus. Warren, Billy, pseud. LC 51-12083. 190 p. illus. 22 cm. 1951. McKay.
--Headquarters ranch. Warren, Billy, pseud. Warren, William Stephen (1882-1968), illus. Warren, Billy, pseud. LC 54-9547. 120p. ill. 22cm. 1954. D. McKay.
--Ride, Cowboy, Ride!. Warren, Billy, pseud. Warren, William Stephen (1882-1968), illus. Warren, Billy, pseud. LC 46-22499. 187 p. illus. 22 1/2 cm. 1946. Reynal & Hitchcock.
--Ride West into Danger. Warren, Billy, pseud. Warren, William Stephen (1882-1968), illus. Warren, Billy, pseud. LC 53-7537. 218p. illus. 23cm. 1953. D. McKay Co.
--Saddles up! Ride 'em High. Warren, Billy, pseud. Warren, William Stephen (1882-1968), illus. Warren, Billy, pseud. LC 48-8281. 224 p. illus. 22 cm. 1948. D. McKay Co.
--Silver Spurs. Warren, Billy, pseud. Warren, William Stephen (1882-1968), illus. Warren, Billy, pseud. LC 50-10053. 185 p. illus. 22 cm. 1950. McKay.
--Tony Gay on the Longhorn Trail. Warren, Billy, pseud. Warren, William Stephen (1882-1968), illus. Warren, Billy, pseud. LC 49-11529. 205 p. illus. 22 cm. 1949. McKay Co.
Warrener
--A Picnic for Bunnykins. Hayward, Walter, illus. LC 83-23532. (Illus.). 24 p. 23cm. 1984. (ISBN 0-670-55361-1). Viking Kestrel.
--Picnic for Bunnykins. Hayward, Walter, illus. LC 83-23532. (Illus.). 24p. (ps-3). 1985. (ISBN 0-670-80052-X, Viking Kestrel). Viking.
--Two Bunnykins Out to Sea. Corkery, Glenys, illus. LC 83-23531. (Illus.). 24p. (ps-3). 1985. (ISBN 0-670-80053-8, Viking Kestrel). Viking.
--Two Bunnykins Out to Tea. Hayward, Walter, illus. LC 83-23531. (Illus.). 24 p. 24cm. 1984. (ISBN 0-670-73619-8). Viking Kestrel.
Warrick, La Mar Sheridan
--Yesterday's Children. LC 43-51148. 3 p. l., 202 p. 21 cm. 1943. Thomas Y. Crowell Company.
Warrick, Patricia Scott (1925-)
--The New Awareness: Religion Through Science Fiction. Greenberg, Martin Harry (1941-), ed. LC 74-22631. p. cm. 1975. (ISBN 0-440-05989-5). Delacorte Press.
Wartenegg, Hanna, illus.
--Carmen. LC 69-11379. (Illus.). 48 p. 29cm. (Curtain raiser book). 1969. F. Watts.
Warth, Julian, pseud., see Parsons, Julia Warth.
Warth, Julian, pseud.
--Dorothy Thorn of Thornton. Parsons, Julia Warth, 1 of 18 vols. (Library of Romance). N.D. Lothrop Pub. Co.
Wartski, Maureen Crane (1940-)
--A Boat to Nowhere. 1st ed. Teicher, Dick, illus. LC 79-28139. (Illus.). 191 p. 21cm. c.1980. (ISBN 0-664-32661-7). Westminster Press.
--The Lake Is on Fire. LC 81-11678. 131 p. 22cm. c.1981. (ISBN 0-664-32687-0). Westminster Press.
--A Long Way from Home. LC 80-19247. 155 p. 21cm. c.1980. (ISBN 0-664-32674-9). Westminster Press.
--My Brother Is Special. LC 78-23999. 153 p. 21cm. c.1979. (ISBN 0-664-32644-7). Westminster Press.
Warwick, Dolores (1936-)
--Learn to Say Goodbye. LC 75-157925. 179 p. 21cm. (Ariel Book). 1971. (ISBN 0-374-34375-6). Farrar, Straus & Giroux.
Wasasier, Harry C.
--The Cookie Jar. (Illus.). (gr. 4-7). N.D. Vantage.
Washburn, Bradford Henry, Jr. (1910-)
--Among the Alps With Bradford. 1927. G. P. Putnam Sons.
--Bradford on Mount Fairweather. 1930. G. P. Putnam Sons.
--Bradford on Mount Washington. 1928. G. P. Putnam Sons.
Washburn, Janice (1926-)
--The Secret of the Spanish Treasure. Van Severen, Joe, illus. LC 79-57212. 144 p. 18cm. (Chariot Books). c.1980. (ISBN 0-89191-245-2). D. C. Cook Pub. Co.
Washburn, May Murray
--Clorinda Clementine. McCain, Susan, illus. LC 62-18926. unpaged. illus. 16 x 24 cm. c.1962. E. C. Seale.
Washburn, Stanley, Jr.
--Nimbo. Stember, Clara Jo, illus. LC 53-7345. 26cm. 39p. 1954. Holt Rinehart & Winston.
Washburne, Carleton Wolsey (1889-), ed. see Harshaw, Ruth Hetzel, Mrs.
Washburne, Heluiz Chandler, Mrs. (1892-1970)
--Fridl, a Mountain Boy. Floethe, Richard (1901-), illus. LC 39-31674. v, 266 p. col. front., illus. 22 1/2 cm. c.1939. The John C. Winston Company.
--Letter's to Channy. N.D. G.P. Putnam's Sons.
--Little Elephant Catches Cold. McConnell, Jean (1928-), illus. LC 37-9727. 24cm. 30p. 1937. Albert Whitman & Co.
--Little Elephant Visits the Farm. McConnell, Jean (1928-), illus. LC 41-134076. 32 p. incl. col. front., col. illus. 24 x 10 cm. 1941. A. Whitman & Company.
--Little Elephant's Christmas. McConnell, Jean (1928-), illus. LC 38-328545. 30, 2 p. incl. col. front., col. illus. 21 cm. 1938. A. Whitman & Co.
--Little Elephant's Picnic. McConnell, Jean (1928-), illus. LC 39-16104. 30, 2 p. front., illus. 24 cm. 1939. A. Whitman & Co.
--Rhamon, a Boy of Kashmir. Duvoisin, Roger Antoine (1904-1980), illus. LC 39-29717. 6 p. l., 17-127 p. col. front., illus. (part col.) 24 cm. 1939. A. Whitman & Co.
--Tomas Goes Trading. 1959. E . M. Hale and Co.
--Tomas Goes Trading. Porter, Jean MacDonald (1906-), illus. LC 59-5457. (Illus.). 127 p. 21cm. 1959. J. Day Co.
Washburne, Marion Foster, Mrs. (1863-), ed. see Craik, Dinah Maria Mulock, Mrs.
Washburne, Marion Foster, Mrs. (1863-), retold by see Hood, Thomas.
Washington, Anthony
--Young Run Away. Adoma, Afua, illus. (Illus., Orig.). (gr. 3-6). 1984. (ISBN 0-9613078-2-X). Detroit Black.
Washington, Miss
--Helena's Cloud with the Silver Lining. N.D. Methodist Book concern.
--How Marjorie Watched. (Illus.). N.D. Methodist Book concern.
--How Marjorie Watched. N.D. Nelson & Phillips.
Washington, Nina
--Ethel's Pearls. N.D. American Tract Society.
Waskow, Arthur, et al.
--Before There Was a Before. LC 84-11177. (Illus.). 80p. (gr. 1-6). 1984. (ISBN 0-915361-08-6, Dist. by Watts). Adama Pubs Inc.
Wasmuth, Eleanor
--An Alligator Day. (Illus.). 32p. (Ready Readers). (gr. 1-3). 1983. (ISBN 0-448-21703-1, G&D). Putnam Pub Group.
--Look at the Seashore. (Illus.). 14p. (ps). 1982. (ISBN 0-448-12309-6, G&D). Putnam Pub Group.
--The Picnic Basket. (Illus.). 32p. (Ready Readers). (gr. 1-3). 1983. (ISBN 0-448-21704-X, G&D). Putnam Pub Group.
--What's That Noise?. Wasmuth, Eleanor, illus. (Illus.). 10p. (ps-3). 1981. (ISBN 0-448-46825-5, G&D). Putnam Pub Group.
Wasner, F., ed. see Trapp Family.
Wason, Robert Alexander
--Happy Hawkins. N.D. Grosset & Dunlap.
Wass De Czege, Albert (1908-) & Boner, Leonoir, eds.
--Selected Hungarian Folk Tales. Petry, Bela, illus. De Czege, Elizabeth M. Wass, tr. LC 72-81238. (Illus.). 135 p. 27cm. (Hungarian Heritage Books, V. 4). c.1972. (ISBN 0-87934-007-X). Danubian Press.
Wass De Czege, Albert, jt. ed. see Wass De Czege, Elizabeth M.
Wass De Czege, Elizabeth M. & Wass De Czege, Albert, eds.
--Hungarian Legends & Folk Tales. Petry, Bela, illus. LC 69-19410. (Illus.). 268p. (Hungarian Heritage Bks.: Vol. 4). (gr. 6 up). 1969. Danubian.
Wasserberg, Esther, jt. auth. see Finfer, Celentha.
Wasserman, Dan, ed. see Cox, Mike, et al.
Wasserman, Dan, ed. see Cox, Mike & Cox, Kris.
Wasserman, Dan, ed. see Reese, Bob.
Wasserman, Dan, ed. see Schoder, Judith.
Wasserman, Dan, ed. see Shebar, Sharon Sigmond.
Wasserman, Dan, ed. see Willoughby, Alana.
Wasserman, Dan, ed. see Winder, Jack.
Wasserman, Jack, jt. auth. see Wasserman, Selma Ginsberg.
Wasserman, Selma Ginsberg (1929-) & Wasserman, Jack (1921-)
--Sailor Jack's new friend. Loeble, Don, illus. LC 60-9014. 64p. illus. 23cm. 1960. Benefic Press.
Wassermann, Jack, jt. auth. see Wassermann, Selma Ginsberg.
Wassermann, Selma Ginsberg (1929-) & Wassermann, Jack (1921-)
--Moonbeam. Rohrer, George, illus. LC 67-27419. (Illus.). 48 p. 23cm. (Moonbeam Books). 1967. Benefic Press.
--Moonbeam and Sunny. Rohrer, George, illus. LC 67-17423. (Illus.). 94 p. 23cm. (Moonbeam Books). 1967. Benefic Press.
--Moonbeam and the Captain. Rohrer, George, illus. LC 68-18211. (Illus.). 48 p. 23cm. (Moonbeam Books). 1968. Benefic Press.
--Moonbeam Is Lost. Rohrer, George, illus. LC 74-94370. (Illus.). 64 p. 23cm. (Moonbeam Books). 1970. Benefic Press.
Wassner, Selig O. (1923-), ed.
--Treasury of Russian Short Stories. Wassner, Selig O. (1923-), tr. (gr. 7 up). 1968. (ISBN 0-8119-0165-3). Fell.
Wasson, Mildred, Mrs.
--Bill and Nancy. Howe, Gertrude Herrick (1902-), illus. LC 40-34114. 5 p. l., 3-323 p. col. front., illus., col. pl. 23 cm. 1940. Liveright Publishing Corporation.
--Miss Nancy Prentiss. Beebe, Robb (1891-), illus. LC 34-619840. 5 p. l., 298 p., 1 l. incl. illus., plates. col. front. 21 cm. 1934. Harper & Brothers.
--Nancy, a Story of the Younger Set. LC 32-18435. vii p., 1 l., 198 p. incl. illus., plates. front. 21 1/2 cm. 1832. Harper & Brothers.
--Nancy Sails. Best, Allena Champlin, Mrs. (1892-1974), illus. Berry, Erick, pseud. LC 36-17529. 5 p. l., 295 p. incl. illus., plates. front. 20 1/2 cm. 1936. Harper & Brothers.
Wasson, Valentina Pavlovna (1901-1959)
--The Choosen Baby. Woodward, Hildegard (1898-), illus. LC 39-11565. 48p. illus. 18 1/2 x 21 1/2cm. c.1939. Carrick & Evans.
--The Chosen Baby. Woodward, Hildegard (1898-), illus. LC 50-12794. (Illus.). 46p. 1950. Lippincott.
Wasson, Valentina Pavlovna (1901-1959) & Coalson, Glo (1946-)
--The Chosen Baby. rev. ed. LC 76-41391. (Illus.). 46 p. 24cm. 1977. (ISBN 0-397-31738-7). Lippincott.
Watanabe, Ryuhei
--Jack & the Beanstalk. Herring, Ann, illus. LC 79-182363. (Illus.). 23p. (Gakken Picture Bks). (gr. k-4). N.D. (ISBN 0-87040-099-1). Japan Pubns.
Watanabe, Shigeo (1928-)
--Daddy, Play with Me. Otomo, Yasuo, illus. LC 84-14818. p. cm. 1985. (ISBN 0-399-21211-6). Philomel Books.
--Get Set! Go!. Otomo, Yasuo, illus. LC 80-22373. p. cm. (I can do it all by myself book ; 3). 1981, c.1980. (ISBN 0-399-20780-5). (ISBN 0-399-61175-4). Philomel Books.
--How Do I Put It on?. Otomo, Yasuo, illus. LC 79-12714. p. cm. (I can do it all by myself book). 1979. (ISBN 0-529-05555-4). (ISBN 0-529-05557-0). Collins. **Award: (ALA).**
--I Can Build a House!. Otomo, Yasuo, illus. LC 82-22386. p. cm. (I can do it all by myself book ; 7.). c.1983. (ISBN 0-399-20950-6). Philomel Books.
--I Can Ride It. Otomo, Yasuo, illus. LC 81-17792. p. cm. (I can do it all by myself book ; #5). c.1982. (ISBN 0-399-20867-4). (ISBN 0-399-61194-0). Philomel Books.
--I Can Take a Walk!. Ohtomo, Yasuo, illus. LC 83-17397. (An I Can Do It All by Myself Book: No. 8). 1984. (ISBN 0-399-21044-X). Putnam.
--I'm the King of the Castle. Ohtomo, Yasuo, illus. LC 81-15865. (Illus.). 32p. (I Can Do It All By Myself Bks.). 1982. (ISBN 0-399-20868-2, Philomel). (ISBN 0-399-61195-9). Putnam Pub Group.
--What a Good Lunch!. Ohtomo, Yasuo, illus. LC 79-19535. (Illus.). 28p. (I Can Do It All by Myself Bks.). (ps). 1980. (ISBN 0-399-20811-9, Philomel). (ISBN 0-399-61181-9). Putnam Pub Group.
--What a Good Lunch!. Eating. Otomo, Yasuo, illus. LC 79-19535. (Illus.). 28 p. 23cm. (I can do it by myself book ; 2). 1980. (ISBN 0-529-05579-1). W. Collins Publishers.
--Where's My Daddy?. Ohtomo, Yasuo, illus. LC 79-19347. (Illus.). 32p. (I Can Do It All by Myself Bks.). 1982. (ISBN 0-399-20899-2, Philomel). Putnam Pub Group.
Waterbury, E. A., jt. auth. see Brown, F. W.
Waterhouse, Alfred James
--Lays for Little Chaps. (Children's Poetry). (Illus.). N.D. Barse & Hopkins.
--Lays for Little Chaps. LC 2-29409. ix, 148 p., 1 l. front., illus. 20 cm. 1902. New Amsterdam Book Company.
Waterhouse, Keith Spencer (1929-) & Hall, Willis (1929-)
--The Irish Adventures of Worzel Gummidge. LC 84-139301. 158 p. 21cm. 1984. (ISBN 0-7278-0979-2). Severn House.
Waterloo, Stanley (1846-), adapted by see Nida, William Lewis.
Waterloo, Stanley (1846-1913)
--The Story of Ab. N.D. Doubleday Dovan & Co.
--These are my jewels. LC 2-23842. 9-232p. 22cm. 1902. Coolidge & Waterloo.
Waterman, Carl
--Adventures of Sammy Sassafras. Spencer, Hugh, illus. LC 19-14701. ix p., 1 l., 160 p. incl. front., plates. 19 cm. c.1919. E. P. Dutton & Company.
Waterman, Charles Elmer (1858-)
--The White Fawn: A Tale of the Land of Molechunkamunk. LC 31-307061. 3 p. l., 9-97 p. 18 1/2 cm. 1931. Chapple Publishing Co., Ltd.
Waterman, Jill
--Harry's Spots. Waterman, Jill, illus. LC 80-506841. (Illus.). 32 p. 27cm. 1979. (ISBN 0-222-00739-7). Burke Books.
Waterman, Margaret P., tr. see Schnapp, Charles.
Waterman, Mary Bissell (1836-1889)
--Tangletop: Or, A Year with the Girls at Locust Hill. LC 12-40202. 1 p. l., 5-351 p. 19 1/2 cm. 1889. American Sunday-School Union.
Waterman, Mary Reddick
--Sagebrush and Pitchwomen. LC 68-28359. vii, 169 p. 22cm. 1968. Naylor Co.
Waterman, Paul
--Great Adventures of the Old Testament. (Activity Book Ser.). (ps-2). N.D. Vol. 1. (ISBN 0-87123-751-2). Vol. 2. (ISBN 0-87123-769-5). Bethany Hse.
Waters, John Frederick (1930-)
--Neighborhood Puddle. Mizumura, Kazue, illus. LC 74-161067. (Illus.). 40 p. 22cm. 1971. F. Warne.
--Saltmarshes and Shifting Dunes. Petie, Haris, pseud. (1915-), illus. Petty, Roberta. LC 72-89779. (Illus.). 45 p. 25cm. (Science parade series). 1970. Harvey House.
--Seal Harbor. Quackenbush, Robert Mead (1929-), illus. (Illus.). 48p. (Marine Life Story Books). (gr. 1-5). 1973. (ISBN 0-7232-6103-2). Warne.
--Summer of the Seals. Eagle, Michael (1942-), illus. LC 78-6712. p. cm. 1978. (ISBN 0-7232-6155-5). F. Warne.
--Victory Chimes. LC 75-32638. 159 p. 22cm. c.1976. (ISBN 0-7232-6130-X). F. Warne.
Waters, Richard D.
--Dangerfield Newby Moves Uptown. 1968. (ISBN 0-377-80001-5). Friend Pr.
Waters, Udell
--Mother O'Possum's Recipe. 1980. (ISBN 0-8062-1494-5). Carlton.
Waterton, Betty Marie (1923-)
--Pettranella. Blades, Ann Sager (1947-), illus. LC 80-52829. (Illus.). 28 p. 25cm. c.1980. (ISBN 0-8149-0844-6). Vanguard Press.
--A Salmon for Simon. Blades, Ann Sager (1947-), illus. 1978. Atheneum. **Award: (AFH).**
Waterton, Betty Marie (1923-) & Blades, Ann Sager (1947-)
--A Salmon for Simon. LC 79-55187. (Illus.). 28 p. 24cm. 1st U.S. edition. 1980, c.1978. (ISBN 0-689-50169-2). Atheneum. **Award: (CCCL).**
Waterworth, E. M.
--Lady Betty's Twins. 117p. 1910. A. W. Wilde.
Watherwax, Richard, jt. auth. see Bissell, LeClair.
Watkin, Lawrence Edward (1901-)
--Marty Markham. Kuhn, Bob, illus. LC 42-21063. 5 p. l., 166 p. incl. illus., plates (1 double) 19 1/2 cm. 1942. H. Holt and Company.
--Thomas Jones and His Nine Lives. Holland, Janice (1913-1962), illus. LC 41-18358. 102, 1 p. incl. front., plates (part double) 23 cm. c.1941. Harcourt, Brace and Company.
Watkins, Dwight Everett (1878-1940) & Raymond, Charles H., eds.
--Best Dog Stories. LC 25-22488. vi, 322 p. col. front., illus. 19 cm. c.1925. Rand McNally & Company.
Watkins, Hope Brister
--The Cunning Fox and Other Tales. (gr. 3-7). 1943. A. A. Knopf.

Watkins, Hope Brister, adapted by.
--The Proud Emperor. Minton, Harold, illus. LC 32-12202. x p., 1 l., 179 p. incl. front., illus., plates. 16 1/2 cm. the little library. 1932. The Macmillan Company.
Watkins, Hope Brister, adapted by see Herodotus.
Watkins, Julia A.
--Royal Echoes: Or, Our Children Among the Poets. revised. LC 11-30759. (Containing Choice Poetical Selections for Children, From the Works of the Best and Most Popular Writers.). 304 p. incl. front., illus., plates, ports. 25 1/2 x 20 cm. 1891. Laird & Lee.
Watkins, Laban Arthur (1884-)
--Rhumbo. Landau, Jacob (1917-), illus. N.D. Grosset & Dunlap.
--Rhumbo. Landau, Jacob (1917-), illus. LC 37-29655. 208 p. incl. plates. 23 1/2 cm. c.1937. Macrae-Smith Company.
Watkins, Lillian, jt. ed. see Loban, Walter.
Watkins, Lucy
--Sophy: Or, The Punishment of Idleness and Disobedience. A Moral Tale. LC 21-6408. 16 p. col. front., 3 col. pl. 13 cm. 1819. Published & Sold by Wm. Charles, No. , South Third Street.
Watkins, Peter
--Tom's Tales. Duchesne, Janet (1930-), illus. (Illus.). 48p. (Julia Macrae Blackbird Bks.). (gr. k-3). N.D. (ISBN 0-531-04606-0). Watts.
Watkins-Pitchford, Denys James see BB, pseud.
Watkins-Pitchford, Denys James (1905-)
--Brendon Chase. BB, pseud. Watkins-Pitchford, Denys James (1905-), illus. LC 45-9401. 6 p. l., 235, 1 p. front., illus. 22 1/2 cm. 1945. C. Scribner's Sons.
--Forest of the Railway. BB, pseud. Watkins-Pitchford, Denys James (1905-), illus. 1957. Dodd Mead.
--The Little Grey Men. BB, pseud. Watkins-Pitchford, Denys James (1905-), illus. LC 49-11210. 249 p. illus. 22 cm. 1949. Scribner's Sons.
--The Little Grey Men: A Story for the Young in Heart. Watkins-Pitchford, Denys James (1905-), illus. 1942. Scribner. **Award: (CMA).**
--Manka, The Sky Gipsy. BB, pseud. Watkins-Pitchford, Denys James (1905-), illus. 1939. Scribner.
--Wild Lone. BB, pseud. Watkins-Pitchford, Denys James (1905-), illus. 1938. Scribner.
Watkins, Richard
--Crocodile Crew. 1st ed. Darling, Lois MacIntyre (1917-), illus. LC 49-10992. 248 p. illus. 21 cm. 1949. Harcourt, Brace.
--Hurricane's Secret. 1st ed. Darling, Lois MacIntyre (1917-), illus. LC 50-9403. (Illus.). 244 p. 21cm. 1950. Harcourt, Brace.
--Milliken's Ark. Dines, Harry Glen (1925-), illus. LC 56-6467. 125p. illus. 23cm. 1956. T. Nelson.
--The Mystery of Willet. Spier, Peter Edward (1927-), illus. LC 59-10494. 167 p. illus. 21 cm. 1959. T. Nelson.
--Sailor Rudd. Watkins, Richard, illus. LC 55-631623. 191p. illus. 21cm. 1955. Nelson.
--Thunder Beach. LC 54-590531. 189p. 21cm. 1954. T. Nelson.
--Venture West. 1st ed. Bjorklund, Lorence F. (1913-1978), illus. LC 51-12531. 238 p. illus. 21 cm. 1951. Harcourt, Brace.
Watkins, Richard Howells
--Partners of the Air. Beebe, Robb (1891-), illus. LC 30-22434. v, 1 p., 1 l., 284, 1 p. front., illus. 19 1/2 cm. 1930. D. Appleton and Company.
Watkins, Shirley
--Georgina Finds Herself. N.D. Macrae Smith.
--Georgina Finds Herself. Grose, Helen Mason (1880-), illus. LC 22-221541. 330 p. front., plates. 19 cm. c.1922. G. W. Jacobs & Company.
--Jane Lends a Hand. Grose, Helen Mason (1880-), illus. LC 23-176842. 334 p. front., plates. 19 cm. c.1923. G. W. Jacobs & Company.
--Jane Lends a Hand. Grose, Helen Mason (1880-), illus. N.D. Macrae Smith.
--Nancy of Paradise Cottage. N.D. Macrae Smith.
--Nancy of Paradise Cottage. Grose, Helen Mason (1880-), illus. LC 21-184751. 307 p. incl. front. 19 cm. c.1921. G. W. Jacobs & Company.
Watkins, Shirley, tr. see Spyri, Johanna Heusser.
Watkins, Sylvestre C. (1911-), ed. see Mother Goose.
Watkins, Sylvestre Cornelius (1911-)
--Jeeps: A Dog for Defense. Rev ed. Nelson, Don, illus. LC 44-51327. 32 p. col. illus. 24 cm. 1944. Wilcox & Follett Co.
Watkins, Tudor
--The Spanish Galleon: An/Adventure Story. 1st American ed. Matthews, Jack, illus. LC 47-3782. (Illus.). 21cm. 176p. 1947, c.1946. Coward-McCann.
Watkins, William Jon (1942-)
--A Fair Advantage. LC 74-3011. vii, 95 p. 22cm. 1975. (ISBN 0-13-623108-X). Prentice Hall.
Watson
--Animal Legends. (Animal Story Bks.). (gr. k-4). 1982. (ISBN 0-86020-673-4, Usborne-Hayes). (ISBN 0-88110-094-3). (ISBN 0-86020-672-6). EDC.
Watson, jt. auth. see Price.
Watson, A. H., ed.
--Nursery Rhymes. Watson, A. H., illus. (Illus.). 1st U.S. edition. Repr. of 1958 ed. (Childrens Illustrated Classics Ser). 1975. (ISBN 0-460-05041-9, Pub. by J. M. Dent England). Biblio Dist.
--Nursery Rhymes. Watson, A. H., illus. LC 58-4595. (Illus.). 22cm. 240p. (Children's Illustrated Classics). (ps-1). 1958. (ISBN 0-525-36240-1). Dutton.
Watson, Aldren Auld (1917-)
--The River: A Story Told in Pictures. LC 63-9572. (Illus.). 17 x 24cm. 25p. (A Little Owl Bk.). 1963. Rinehart and Winston.
Watson, Anna M.
--Trapped!. Auffet, Sharon K., illus. (Illus.). 24p. (ps-5). 1981. (ISBN 0-89323-017-0). BMA Pr.
Watson, Annah Walker Robinson, Mrs. (1848-)
--On the Field of Honor. LC 2-30409. 226 p. pl., ports. 16 1/2 cm. c.1902. The Sprague Publishing Co.
Watson, Clyde, jt. auth. see Watson, Wendy McLeod.
Watson, Clyde (1947-)
--Applebet: An ABC. Watson, Wendy McLeod (1942-), illus. LC 81-19399. p. cm. 1982. (ISBN 0-374-30384-3). Farrar, Straus, Giroux.
--Catch Me & Kiss Me & Say It Again. Watson, Wendy McLeod (1942-), illus. LC 78-17644 p. cm. c.1978. (ISBN 0-529-05436-1). (ISBN 0-529-05438-8). Collins.
--Catch Me and Kiss Me and Say it Again. Watson, Wendy McLeod (1942-), illus. 1983. Putnam.
--Father Fox's Feast of Songs. Watson, Wendy McLeod (1942-), illus. LC 83-2967. (Illus.). 32p. 1983. (ISBN 0-399-20886-0, Philomel). (ISBN 0-399-20928-X). Putnam Pub Group.
--Father Fox's Penny-Rhymes. Watson, Wendy McLeod (1942-), illus. 1971. Harper.
--Father Fox's Pennyrhymes. Watson, Wendy McLeod (1942-), illus. LC 71-146291. (Illus.). 56 p. 24cm. 1971. (ISBN 0-690-29213-9). Crowell. **Award: (ALA).**
--Hickory Stick Rag. Watson, Wendy McLeod (1942-), illus. LC 75-6607. (Illus.). 32 p. 24cm. c.1976. (ISBN 0-690-00959-3). (ISBN 0-690-00960-7). Crowell.
--How Brown Mouse Kept Christmas. Watson, Wendy McLeod (1942-), illus. LC 80-18532. (Illus.). 32 p. 17cm. 1980. (ISBN 0-374-33494-3). Farrar, Straus, Giroux.
--Midnight Moon. Natti, Susanna (1948-), illus. LC 78-26376. p. cm. 1979. (ISBN 0-529-05526-0). (ISBN 0-529-05527-9). Collins.
--Quips and Quirks. Watson, Wendy McLeod (1942-), illus. 1975. Harper.
--Tom Fox and the Apple Pie. Watson, Wendy McLeod (1942-), illus. LC 74-171010. (Illus.). 46 p. 1972. (ISBN 0-690-82783-0). (ISBN 0-690-82784-9). Crowell.
--Tom Fox and the Apple Pie. Watson, Wendy McLeod (1942-), illus. 1972. Harper.
Watson, Colin (1920-1983)
--It Shouldn't Happen to a Dog. LC 76-45534. 1977. (ISBN 0-399-11881-0). Putnam Pub Group.
Watson, E. Elaine
--I Wish, I Wish. Mahany, Patricia, ed. LC 82-62733. (Illus.). 24p. (Happy Day Bks.). (ps-2). 1983. (ISBN 0-87239-637-1). Standard Pub.
Watson, E Weir
--Jimmy Clark and His Rocket Train. Rienstra, Richard, illus. LC 58-59785. 148 p. illus. 22 cm. 1958. Eardmans.
Watson, Elizabeth
--The Story of Bread. Daugherty, James Henry (1889-1974), illus. LC 27-9267. (Illus.). 19 1/2cm. 18p. (City and Country Ser.). 1927. Harper & Brothers.
--The Story of Milk and How It Came About. Daugherty, James henry (1889-1974), illus. LC 27-9264. 3 p. l., 37 p. illus., col. plates. 19 1/2 cm. (City and country series). 1927. Harper & Brothers.
Watson, Elizabeth E.
--God Didn't Put Elephants in Trees. Watson, Elizabeth E., illus. LC 81-65800. (gr. k-3). 1981. (ISBN 0-8054-4267-7). Broadman.
--Pigs Oink, Yes, They Do. Watson, Elizabeth E., illus. LC 83-73372. (gr. k-2). 1984. (ISBN 0-8054-4212-X). Broadman.
Watson, Elizabeth Webster
--Gift Wrap, Please. 1966. Broadman Press.
Watson, Evelyn
--The House by the Red Pump. LC 4-34935. 19cm. 153p. 1904. Becktold Printing and Book Manufacturing Co.
Watson, Frederick
--Muckle John. Stewart, Allan (1865-), illus. (Fiction). (MacMillan Bks. for Boys & Girls). (gr. 7-9). N.D. MacMillan Bks.
Watson, Helen Orr (1892-1978)
--Beano, Circus Dog. 1st ed. Nichols, Marie C. (1905-), illus. LC 53-7088. 177p. illus. 22cm. 1953. Ariel Books.
--Black Horse of Culver. Garbutt, Bernard (1900-), illus. LC 50-10096. (Illus.). 22cm. 186p. 1950. Houghton Mifflin.
--Chanco: The Story of a U. S. Army Homing Pigeon. 1938. Harper & Bros.
--Fools Over Horses. Dennis, Wesley (1903-1966), illus. LC 52-5911. 237 p. 22 cm. 1952. Houghton Mifflin.
--High Stepper. Lee, Manning De Villeneuve (1894-1980), illus. LC 46-8269. 3 p. l., 196, 1 p. plates. 21 cm. 1946. Houghton Mifflin Company.
--Shavetail Sam. Garbutt, Bernard (1900-), illus. LC 44-9758. 20cm. 163p. 1944. Houghton Mifflin Co.
--Top Kick, U.S. Army Horse. Garbutt, Bernard (1900-), illus. LC 42-228631. 3 p. l., 216, 1 p. illus. 22 cm. 1942. Houghton Mifflin Co.
--Trooper: U.S. Army Dog. Garbutt, Bernard (1900-), illus. LC 43-16553. 21cm. 173p. 1943. Houghton Mifflin Co.
--White Boots. Nichols, Marie C. (1905-), illus. LC 48-8676. 180 p. illus. 22 cm. 1948. Houghton Mifflin Co.
Watson, Henry Clay (1831-1869)
--Six Nights in a Block-House. (Illus.). Repr. (St. Nicholas Series for Boys). N.D. International Book Co.
Watson, Ina
--Story of Larry the Seagull. (gr. 2-5). N.D (Pub. by Cowman). Tri-Ocean.
--Story of Silvertail the Lyrebird. (gr. 2-5). N.D (Pub. by Cowman). Tri-Ocean.
Watson, J. Davis, illus.
--The Pilgrim's Progress. (Illus.). N.D. George Routledge & Sons.
--Robinson Crusoe. (Illus.). N.D. George Routledge & Sons.
Watson, James (1936-)
--The Bull Leapers. LC 79-125325. 191 p. 22cm. 1970. Coward-McCann.
--Talking in Whispers. LC 83-17595. p. cm. c.1983. (ISBN 0-394-86538-3). (ISBN 0-394-96538-8). Knopf.

Watson, Jane Werner see Bedford, Annie North, pseud.
Watson, Jane Werner see Bedford, Annie North, pseud.
Watson, Jane Werner see Hill, Monica, pseud.
Watson, Jane Werner see Jasner, W. K., pseud.
Watson, Jane Werner see Jasner, W. K., pseud.
Watson, Jane Werner see Nast, Elsa Ruth, pseud.
Watson, Jane Werner see Nast, Elsa Ruth, pseud.
Watson, Jane Werner see Werner, Jane, pseud.
Watson, Jane Werner, jt. auth. see Brown, Margaret Wise.
Watson, Jane Werner see Disney, Walter Elias.
Watson, Jane Werner, jt. auth. see Disney, Walt, Productions.
Watson, Jane Werner see Disney, Walt, Productions & Werner, Jane.
Watson, Jane Werner see Grimm, Jakob Ludwig Karl (1785-1863) & Grimm, Wilhelm Karl.
Watson, Jane Werner see Werner, Elsa Jane.
Watson, Jane Werner see Werner, Jane.
Watson, Jane Werner, rev. by see Bennett, Dorothy Agnes.
Watson, Jane Werner, ed. see Disney, Walter Elias.
Watson, Jane Werner (1915-), retold by see Disney, Walt, Productions.
Watson, Jane Werner (1915-), ed. see Disney, Walt, Studio.
Watson, Jane Werner (1915-), adapted by see Homer.
Watson, Jane Werner (1915-), ed. see Homerus.
Watson, Jane Werner (1915-), adapted by see Irving, Washington.
Watson, Jane Werner (1915-), as told to see Norris, Kenneth Stafford.
Watson, Jane Werner see Werner, Jane.
Watson, Jane Werner (1915-)
--Albert's Zoo: A Stencil Book. Scarry, Richard McClure (1919-), illus. LC 51-39072. unpaged. illus. 21cm. (Little golden library, 112). 1951. Simon and Schuster.
--Animal Friends. Rev ed. Williams, Garth Montgomery (1912-), illus. LC 52-12327. unpaged. illus. 21cm. (Little golden library, 167). 1953. Simon and Schuster.
--The Case of the Semi-Human Beans. LC 78-24320. 144 p. 22cm. c.1979. (ISBN 0-698-20476-X). Coward, McCann & Geoghegan.
--The Case of the Vanishing Spaceship. LC 81-12661. 109 p. 22cm. c.1982. (ISBN 0-698-20547-2). Coward, McCann & Geoghegan.
--Chatterly Squirrel and Other Animal Stories. Miller, John Parr (1913-), illus. LC 50-8343. (Illus.). 125p. 19cm. (A Golden Story Bk.). 1950. Simon and Schuster.
--Christopher Bunny and Other Animal Stories. Scarry, Richard McClure (1919-), illus. LC 49-48939. (Illus.). 124p. 19cm. (A Golden Story Bk.). 1949. Simon and Schuster.
--Dale Evans and the Lost Gold Mine. Hill, Monica, pseud. Crawford, Mel (1925-), illus. (Little Golden Book). 1955. Golden Press.
--Dale Evans and the Lost Gold Mine. Hill, Monica, pseud. Crawford, Mel (1925-), illus. LC 55-1596. unpaged. illus. 21cm. (Little golden book, 213). 1955, c.1954. Simon and Schuster.
--Dance to a Happy Song. Cary, Louis Favreau (1915-), illus. Cary, pseud. LC 72-10602. (Illus.). 36 p. 24cm. c.1973. (ISBN 0-8116-6730-8). Garrard Pub. Co.
--Disney's Numbers Are Fun. Disney, Walt, Productions, illus. LC 77-71148. (Illus.). 72 p. 26cm. (Kid's paperback). c.1977. (ISBN 0-307-13430-X). Golden Press.
--A Farm Story. Nast, Elsa Ruth, pseud. 1st ed. Stern, Marie Simchow (1909-), illus. Masha, pseud. LC 46-7543. 40 p. incl. col. front., illus. (part col.) 28 x 22 1/2 cm. 1946. Harper & Brothers.
--First Bible Stories. Wilkin, Eloise Burns (1904-), illus. (Little Golden Book. 198). 1954. Simon and Schuster.
--Fun with Decals. Nast, Elsa Ruth, pseud. Malvern, Corinne (1905-1956), illus. LC 53-2460. unpaged. illus. 21cm. (Little golden library, 139). 1953, c.1952. Simon and Schuster.
--The Fuzzy Duckling. Provensen, Alice (1918-) & Provensen, Martin (1916-), illus. LC 64-9732. (Illus.). 25p. 33cm. (A Big Golden Bk.). 1963, c.1949. Golden Press.
--The Fuzzy Duckling. Provensen, Alice (1918-) & Provensen, Martin (1916-), illus. LC 49-8904. (Illus.). 28. (The Little Golden Library). 1949. Simon and Schuster.
--Gene Autry and Champion. Hill, Monica, pseud. Bolle, Frank, illus. LC 57-13505. unpaged. illus. 21cm. (Little golden book, 267). 1956. Simon and Schuster.
--Giant Golden Book of Dinosaurs and Other Pre-historic Reptiles. Zallinger, Rudolph F., illus. 1960. Golden Press.
--A Giant Little Golden Book of Birds. Wilkin, Eloise Burns (1904-), illus. LC 58-3952. 55 p. illus. 21 cm. (Giant little golden book, 5011). 1958. Simon and Schuster.
--How to Have a Happy Birthday: A Party Cut-Out Book. Nast, Elsa Ruth, pseud. Worcester, Retta, illus. LC 53-236. unpaged. illus. 21cm. (Little golden library, 123). 1952. Simon and Schuster.
--Lassie Shows the Way. Hill, Monica, pseud. Authorized. Ames, Lee Judah (1921-), illus. LC 56-301619. unpaged. illus. 21 cm. (Little golden book, 255). 1956. Simon and Schuster.
--The Lion's Paw: A Tale of African Animals. Tenggren, Gustaf (1896-1970), illus. LC 60-777. unpaged. illus. 33 cm. (Big golden book, 355). 1960. Golden Press.
--The Magic Wish and Other Johnny and Jane Stories. Nast, Elsa Ruth, pseud. Malvern, Corinne (1905-1956), illus. LC 49-486575. 125 p. col. illus. 18 cm. (Golden Story Bks.). 1949. Simon and Schuster.
--The Marvelous Merry Go-Round. Miller, John Pearse (1943-), illus. LC 50-13053. (Illus.). 21cm. 42p. (The Little Golden Library). 1950. Simon and Schuster.
--Mr. Noah and His Family. Provensen, Alice (1918-) & Provensen, Martin (1916-), illus. LC 48-7806. (Illus.). 28p. 21cm. (Little Golden Library). 1948. Simon and Schuster.
--The Mysterious Gold and Purple Box. Cary, Louis Favreau (1915-), illus. Cary, pseud. LC 72-3803. (Illus.). 64 p. 23cm. 1972. (ISBN 0-8116-6971-8). Garrard Pub. Co.
--Oklahoma!. Paper Doll Story Book. Cummings, Alison, illus. (Big Golden Book). 1956. Golden Press.
--Our Puppy. Nast, Elsa Ruth, pseud. Rojankovsky, Feodor Stepanovich (1891-1970), illus. LC 49-8169. 28 p. col. illus. 21 cm. (Little golden library, 56). 1949, c.1948. Simon and Schuster.
--Our Puppy. Nast, Elsa Ruth, pseud. Rojankovsky, Feodor Stepanovich (1891-1970), illus. LC 60-26339. unpaged. illus. 21 cm. (Little golden book, 292). 1957. Simon and Schuster.
--Rin Tin Tin and Rusty. Hill, Monica, pseud. Authorized. Crawford, Mel (1925-), illus. LC 55-13909. unpaged. illus. 21cm. (Little golden book, 246). 1955. Simon and Schuster.
--Rin Tin Tin and the Lost Indian. Greene, Hamilton, illus. (Little Golden Book). 1956. Golden Press.
--Rin Tin Tin and the Lost Indian. Hill, Monica, pseud. Authorized. Greene, Hamilton, illus. LC 57-13506. unpaged. illus. 21cm. (Little golden book, 276). 1956. Simon and Schuster.

--Roy Rogers and the New Cowboy. Bedford, A. N., pseud. Helweg, Hans H. (1917-) & Crawford, Mel (1925-), illus. LC 53-4351. (Illus.). 21cm. (A Little Golden Bk.). 1953. Simon and Schuster.
--Smokey the Bear. Rojankovsky, Feodor Stepanovich (1891-1970), illus. (Big Golden Book: 429). 1955. Simon and Schuster.
--Smokey, the Bear. Scarry, Richard McClure (1919-), illus. LC 55-14368. unpaged. illus. 21cm. (Little golden book, 224). 1955. Simon and Schuster.
--Smokey the Bear. Scarry, Richard McClure (1919-), illus. (Illus.). (ps-3). 1955. (ISBN 0-307-60481-0, Golden Pr). Western Pub.
--Stories from Nature. Muller, Gerda Maria, illus. 144p. (gr. 2-5). 1973. (ISBN 0-307-16822-0, Golden Pr). (ISBN 0-307-66818-5). Western Pub.
--Tanya and the Geese. Goldsborough, June (1923-), illus. LC 74-7360. (Illus.). 63 p. 23cm. 1974. (ISBN 0-8116-6977-7). Garrard Pub. Co.
--Tex and His Toys. Nast, Elsa Ruth, pseud. Malvern, Corinne (1905-1956), illus. LC 52-8416. (Illus.). 21cm. (The Little Golden Library). 1952. Simon and Schuster.
--The True Story of Smokey the Bear. Rojankovsky, Feodor Stepanovich (1891-1970), illus. LC 55-149905. (Authorized and Approved by the State Foresters and by the Forest Service, U. S. Dept. of Agriculture, in Cooperation with the Advertising Council, Inc.). unpaged. illus. 33cm. (Big golden book, 429). 1955. Simon and Schuster.
--True Story of Smokey the Bear. Rojankovsky, Feodor Stepanovich (1891-1970), illus. (Illus.). (gr. 1-3). 1955. (ISBN 0-307-10429-X, Golden Pr). (ISBN 0-307-60429-2). Western Pub.
--Uncle Mistletoe. Malvern, Corinne (1905-1956), illus. LC 53-3514. (Illus.). 21cm. (A Little Golden Bk.). 1953. Simon and Schuster.
--Walt Disney Presents Legends of America. Bedford, Annie North, pseud. Crawford, Mel (1925-) & Disney, Walt, Productions, illus. LC 79-7375. (Illus.). 46 p. 30cm. 1969. Golden Press.
--Which Is the Witch?. Jasner, W. K., pseud. Chess, Victoria (1939-), illus. LC 78-31407. p. cm. (I am reading book). c.1979. (ISBN 0-394-83978-1). (ISBN 0-394-93978-6). Pantheon Books.
--A Woods Story. Nast, Elsa Ruth, pseud. Masha, pseud. (1909-), illus. Stern, Marie Simchow. LC 45-5275. (Illus.). 40. 1945. Harper.

Watson, Jane Werner (1915-), ed.
--Castles in Spain. LC 72-132850. (Illus.). (Myths & Legends Ser.). (gr. 4-7). 1971. (ISBN 0-8116-4207-0). Garrard.
--Frosty the Snow Man: Adapted from the Song of The Same Name. Bedford, Annie North, pseud. Malvern, Corinne (1905-1956), illus. LC 51-13064. unpaged. illus. 21cm. (Little golden library, 142). 1951. Simon and Schuster.
--The Giant Golden Book of Elves and Fairies, With Assorted Pixies, Mermaids, Brownies, Witches, and Leprechauns. Williams, Garth MOntgomery (1912-), illus. LC 64-9340. (Illus.). 76p. 33cm. 1951. Golden Press.
--The Giant Golden Book of Elves and Fairies, with Assorted Pixies, Mermaids, Brownies, Witches and Leprechauns. Williams, Garth MOntgomery (1912-), illus. LC 51-13747. (Illus.). 76. 33cm. (A Giant Golden Bk.). 1951. Simon and Schuster.
--The Golden Book of Nursery Tales. Gergely, Tibor (1900-1978), illus. LC 48-7238. 146 p. illus. (part col.) 29 cm. (Big golden book). 1948. Simon and Schuster.
--The Golden Book of Poetry. Elliott, Gertrude, illus. LC 49-4976. (Illus.). 22cm. 67p. (A Big Golden Bk.). 1949. Simon and Schuster.
--The Golden Mother Goose: 367 Childhood Favorites. Provensen, Alice (1918-) & Provensen, Martin (1916-), illus. LC 48-9054. 96 p. col. illus. 33 cm. (A Giant Golden Book, 555). 1948. Simon and Schuster.
--The Iliad and the Odyssey: The Heroic Story of the Trojan War and the Fabulous Adventures of Odysseus. Provensen, Alice (1918-) & Provensen, Martin (1916-), illus. LC 56-14219. (Adapted from the Greek Classics). 96p. illus. 33cm. (Giant golden book. 756. De luxe ed.). 1956. Simon and Schuster.
--Little Steps: Children's Poems of Thanks. Nast, Elsa Ruth, pseud. Doane, Pelagie (1906-1966), illus. LC 47-4013. 36 p. illus. (part col.) 24 x 20 1/2 cm. c.1947. Grosset & Dunlap.
--Nursery Tales. Gergely, Tibor (1900-1978), illus. LC 63-4454. 96p. illus. 27cm. (Golden storytime bk.). 1964, c.1957. Golden.
--Old MacDonald had a Farm. Tenggren, Gustaf (1896-1970), illus. (Little Golden Book). 1960. Golden Press.
--Rama of the Golden Age: An Epic of India. Frame, Paul (1913-), illus. LC 70-126415. (Original Author: Valmiki, 1890-1936). (Illus.). 96 p. 24cm. (A Readings shelf book). 1971. (ISBN 0-8116-4206-2). Garrard Pub. Co.
--The Tall Book of Make-Believe. Williams, Garth Montgomery (1912-), illus. LC 50-6582. 92 p. illus. (part col.) 32 x 14 cm. 1950. Harper.
--Walt Disney's Snow White and the Seven Dwarfs. Disney, Walt, Studio & Grant, Campbell, illus. LC 52-9930. (Illus.). 34cm. (A Big Golden Bk.). 1952. Simon and Schuster.

Watson, Jane Werner (1915-) & Artists and Writers Guild, eds.
--Noah's Ark. Gergely, Tibor (1900-1978), illus. LC 43-14284. (Illus.). 21cm. 34p. 1943. Grosset & Dunlop.

Watson, Jane Werner (1915-) & Chaneles, Sol
--The Golden Book of the Mysterious. Lee, Alan, illus. (Illus.). (gr. 7 up). 1976. (ISBN 0-307-67862-8, Golden Pr). Western Pub.

Watson, Jane Werner (1915-) & Switzer, Robert E. (1927-)
--Sometimes I Get Angry. Hoffmann, Hilde (1927-), illus. LC 74-100334. (Illus.). 32 p. 24cm. (A Read-Together Book for Parents and Children). 1971. Golden Press.
--Sometimes I'm Afraid. Hoffmann, Hilde (1927-), illus. LC 77-100332. (Illus.). 32 p. 24cm. (A Read-Together Book for Parents and Children). 1971. Golden Press.

Watson, Jean, ed. (1936-)
--The Family Library Series, 3 bks. Wane, Peter, illus. Incl. The Pilgrim's Progress in Modern English. Bunyan, John Watson, Jean, tr. Wane, Peter, illus. (Illus.). (ISBN 0-310-38810-4); The Princess & Curdie. MacDonald, Georg; The Princess & the Goblin. MacDonald, Georg. (gr. 3 up). 1980. Set. (ISBN 0-310-42718-5). Zondervan.

Watson, Jean, ed. see MacDonald, George.

Watson, Jean (1936-), abridged by see MacDonald, George (1824-1905) & Wane, Peter.

Watson, Jean L.
--Round the Grange Farm: Or, Good Old Times. N.D. Nelson & Phillips.

Watson, Jenny, retold by.
--Favourite Stories from Thailand. (Favourite Stories Ser.). 1976. (ISBN 0-686-60428-8). Heinemann Ed.
--Favourite Stories from Thailand. bilingual ed. (Orig.). (The Favourite Stories Ser.). 1981. (ISBN 0-686-73755-5). Heinemann Ed.

Watson, Jenny, jt. ed. see Monteiro, Irene-Anne.

Watson, Joseph
--Father Gander's Chimes. LC 16-10113. 1 p. l., 97, 1 p. illus. 15 1/2 x 12 1/2 cm. 1882. Press of the Photo-Engraving Company.

Watson, Junius
--Joe Jacoby. LC 70-122141. 185 p. 22cm. 1970. (ISBN 0-8415-0030-4). McCall Pub. Co.

Watson, Katherine Williams, Mrs. (1889-), retold by.
--Once Upon a Time: Children's Stories Retold for Broadcasting. LC 42-6008. 263 p. 20 cm. 1942. H. W. Wilson Company.
--Radio Plays for Children. LC 47-31139. 8 l., 13-281 p. 21 cm. 1947. H. W. Wilson Co.
--Tales for Telling. LC 50-11281. 267 p. 20 cm. 1950. H.W. Wilson Co.
--Their Way. Wallower, Lucille (1910-), illus. LC 45-10642. 160 p. col. front., illus. 23 1/2 x 18 1/2 cm. 1945. A. Whitman & Company.

Watson, Margery
--Ruffles and Danny. (The Girl's World Ser.). N.D. World Publishing Co.

Watson, Marjorie R., ed. see Hoffmann, Ernst Theodor Amadeus.

Watson, Marquerite Lee
--Cottontail Capers. Watson, Marquerite, illus. LC 45-1558. 72 p. incl. illus., plates. 23 x 31 cm. 1944. Pelican Publishing Company.

Watson, Nancy Dingman
--Annie's Spending Spree. N.D. E. M. Hale & Co.
--Annie's Spending Spree. Watson, Aldren Auld (1917-), illus. LC 57-13818. (Illus.). 45 p. 26cm. 1957. Viking Press.
--The Birthday Goat. Watson, Wendy McLeod (1942-), illus. LC 73-3389. (Illus.). 40 p. 1974. (ISBN 0-690-00145-2). (ISBN 0-690-00146-0). Crowell.
--Blueberries Lavender: Songs of the Farmers' Children : Poems. Blegvad, Erik (1923-), illus. LC 76-18226. (Illus.). 48 p. 25cm. (gr. 6-8). c.1977. (ISBN 0-201-08568-2). Addison-Wesley Pub. Co.
--Carol to a Child: And a Christmas Pageant. Watson, Aldren Auld (1917-), illus. LC 73-82770. (Illus.). 31 p. 22cm. 1969. World Pub. Co.
--Fairy Tale Picture Book. Watson, Aldren Auld (1917-), illus. N.D. Doubleday.
--The Fairy Tale Picturebook. Watson, Aldren Auld (1917-), illus. LC 57-9855. 91 p. illus. 32 cm. 1957. Garden City Books.
--Katie's Chickens. Watson, Aldren Auld (1917-), illus. LC 65-22003. 1v. (unpaged) col. illus. 20x26cm. c.1965 (Borzoi Bks.). Knopf.
--Muncus Agruncus, a Bad Little Mouse. 1st ed. Watson, Wendy McLeod (1942-), illus. LC 74-17103. (Illus.). 32 p. 22cm. c.1976. (ISBN 0-307-12540-8). Golden Press.
--New Under the Stars. Watson, Aldren Auld (1917-), illus. LC 78-91231. (Illus.). 121 p. 21cm. 1970. Little, Brown.
--Puppy Dog Tales. Watson, Aldren Auld (1917-), illus. LC 59-10982. unpaged. illus. 27 cm. c.1961. Doubleday.
--Sugar on Snow. Watson, Aldren Auld (1917-), illus. LC 64-21474. (Illus.). 43 p. 1964. Viking Press.
--Toby and Doll. 1st ed. Watson, Aldren Auld (1917-), illus. LC 55-7538. 125p. illus. 23cm. 1955. Bobbs-Merrill.
--Tommy's Mommy's Fish. 1st ed. Watson, Aldren Auld (1917-), illus. LC 77-164016. (Illus.). 32 p. 23cm. 1971. (ISBN 0-670-71926-9). Viking Press.
--What Does A Begin with?. Watson, Aldren Auld (1917-), illus. LC 56-8901. (Illus.). unpaged. 1956. Knopf.
--When Is Tomorrow?. Watson, Aldren Auld (1917-), illus. LC 55-8939. unpaged. illus. 21x26cm. 1955. Knopf.
--Whose Birthday Is It?. Watson, Aldren Auld (1917-), illus. LC 54-8205. unpaged. illus. 24cm. 1954. Knopf.

Watson, Nancy Dingman, ed.
--Cat Tales. Watson, Aldren Auld (1917-), illus. LC 59-10983. unpaged. illus. 27 cm. c.1961. Doubleday.
--Pig Tales, from Old English Nursery Rhymes. Watson, Aldren Auld (1917-), illus. LC 59-10984. unpaged. illus. 27 cm. c.1961. Doubleday.
--Pony Tales from Old English Nursery Rhymes. Watson, Aldren Auld (1917-), illus. LC 59-10985. unpaged. illus. 27 cm. c.1961. Doubleday.

Watson, Nancy Dingman, ed. see Arabian Nights.

Watson, Pauline (1925-)
--Curley Cat Baby-Sits. Cauley, Lorinda Bryan (1951-), illus. LC 77-1589. (Illus.). 32 p. 22cm. (Let Me Read Book). c.1977. (ISBN 0-15-221110-1). (ISBN 0-15-622700-2). Harcourt Brace Jovanovich.
--Days with Daddy. Scribner, Joanne L. (1949-), illus. LC 77-3501. p. cm. c.1977. (ISBN 0-13-196907-2). Prentice-Hall.
--My Turn, Your Turn. Payson, Dale (1943-), illus. LC 77-25306. p. cm. c.1978. (ISBN 0-13-608703-5). Prentice-Hall.
--A Surprise for Mother. Scribner, Joanne L. (1949-), illus. LC 75-9999. p. cm. 1975. (ISBN 0-13-877902-3). Prentice-Hall.
--The Walking Coat. treehouse pbk. ed. De Paola, Tomie, pseud. (1934-), illus. De Paola, Thomas Anthony. LC 81-7395. p. cm. 1981. (ISBN 0-13-944314-2). Prentice-Hall.
--The Walking Coat. De Paola, Tomie, pseud. (1934-), illus. De Paola, Thomas Anthony. LC 78-64629. p. cm. 1979. (ISBN 0-8027-6350-2). (ISBN 0-8027-6351-0). Walker.
--What Would You Do?. Weissman, Sam Q., illus. LC 79-16296. p. cm. c.1979. (ISBN 0-13-955252-9). Prentice-Hall.
--Wriggles: The Little Wishing Pig. Galdone, Paul (1914-), illus. LC 78-5855. (Illus.). (gr. k-3). 1978. (ISBN 0-395-28828-2, Clarion). HM.
--Wriggles, the Little Wishing Pig. Galdone, Paul (1914-), illus. LC 78-5855. p. cm. c.1978. (ISBN 0-8164-3216-3). Seabury Press.

Watson, Sally Lou (1924-)
--Highland Rebel. 1st ed. McClain, Scott, illus. LC 54-10390. 212p. illus. 21cm. 1954. (ISBN 0-03-066190-0). Holt.
--The Hornet's Nest. LC 67-17721. (Illus.). 246 p. 22cm. 1968. Holt, Rinehart and Winston.
--Jade. LC 69-10242. 270 p. 22cm. 1969. Holt, Rinehart and Winston.
--Lark. LC 64-18258. 223 p. 22 cm. 1964. Holt, Rinehart and Winston.
--Linnet. LC 76-157952. 224 p. 22cm. 1971. (ISBN 0-525-33695-8). Dutton.
--Magic at Wychwood. Bozzo, Frank, illus. LC 76-82752. (Illus.). 127 p. 21cm. 1970. Knopf.
--Mistress Malapert. Genia, pseud. (1930-), illus. Wennerstrom, Genia Katherine. LC 55-7704. (Illus.). 218 p. 21cm. 1955. Holt.
--The Mukhtar's Children. LC 68-12360. 248 p. 22cm. 1968. Holt, Rinehart and Winston.
--Other Sandals. LC 66-12037. 223 p. 22cm. 1966. Holt, Rinehart and Winston.
--Poor Felicity. 1st ed. Summers, Leo, illus. LC 61-12599. (Illus.). 209 p. 22cm. 1961. Doubleday.
--To Build a Land. 1st ed. Cassel, Lili, pseud. (1924-), illus. Wronker, Lili Cassel. LC 57-5748. 255p. illus. 22cm. 1957. Holt.
--To Build a Land. Cassel, Lili, pseud. (1924-), illus. Wronker, Lili Cassel. LC 57-5748. (Illus.). 255p. (gr. 5-7). 1966. (ISBN 0-03-057425-0). HR&W.
--Witch of the Glens. Werner, Barbara, illus. LC 62-17071. 275 p. illus. 21 cm. 1962. (ISBN 0-670-77635-1). Viking Press.

Watson, Simon
--No Man's Land. LC 75-30698. (Illus.). 190 p. 22cm. 1976, c.1975. (ISBN 0-688-80032-7). (ISBN 0-688-84032-9). Greenwillow Books.
--The Partisan. LC 74-20582. 143 p. 22cm. 1975, c.1973. (ISBN 0-333-15583-1). Macmillan.

Watson, Sydney
--In the Twinkling of an Eye. LC 18-209672. 1 l., v-vii p., 1 l., 11-250 p. 19 cm. c.1918. The Biola Book Room, Bible Institute of Los Angeles.
--The Mark of the Beast. N.D. Fleming H. Revell Co.

Watson, Virginia Cruse (1872-), adapted by see Lorenzini, Paolo.

Watson, Virginia Cruse (1872-)
--Flags Over Quebec: A Story of the Conquest of Canada. 1st ed. Stein, Harve (1904-), illus. LC 41-19637. 3 p. l., 3-217 p. illus. 21 cm. 1941. Coward-McCann, Inc.
--Ginevra: A Romance. Lederer, Charlotte Bacskay, Mrs. (1872-), illus. LC 29-15129. 4 p. l. 3-321 p. incl. front., illus. 21 cm. c.1929. E. P. Dutton & Co., Inc.
--Through Many Waters. Robinson, Jessie Berkowitz, illus. LC 44-95858. vii p., 1 l. 150 p. illus. 21 cm. 1944. Harper & Brothers.
--The Trail of Courage. Brown, Marcia (1918-), illus. LC 48-4402. 181 p. illus. 22 cm. 1948. Coward-McCann.
--With Cortes the Conqueror. Schoonover, Frank Earle (1877-1972), illus. LC 18-4159. 332 p. col. front., illus. (incl. map) col. plates. 24 1/2 cm. 1917. The Penn Publishing Company.
--With La Salle, the Explorer. Pitz, Henry Clarence (1895-1976), illus. LC 22-192131. vii, 366 p. col. front., illus., plates. 22 1/2 cm. 1922. H. Holt & Company.

Watson, Wendy Mcleod (1942-)
--The Bunnies' Christmas Eve. Watson, Wendy McLeod (1942-), illus. LC 82-22267. p. cm. c.1983. (ISBN 0-399-20968-9). Philomel Books.
--Has Winter Come?. Watson, Wendy Mcleod (1942-), illus. LC 77-18863. (Illus.). 28 p. c.1978. (ISBN 0-529-05439-6). (ISBN 0-529-05441-8). Collins.
--Jamie's Story. Watson, Wendy McLeod (1942-), illus. LC 80-26676. p. cm. c.1981 (Philomel Bks.). (ISBN 0-399-20789-9). (ISBN 0-399-61177-0). Putnam.
--Lollipop. Watson, Wendy McLeod (1942-), illus. LC 75-26642. p. cm. 1976. (ISBN 0-690-00768-X). Crowell.
--Lollipop. Watson, Wendy McLeod (1942-), illus. LC 77-28340. (Illus.). 31 p. 23cm. (Picture puffin). 1978, c.1976. (ISBN 0-14-050264-5). Puffin Books.
--Moving. Watson, Wendy McLeod (1942-), illus. LC 77-11557. (Illus.). 24 p. 17cm. c.1978. (ISBN 0-690-01326-4). (ISBN 0-690-01327-2). Crowell.
--Very Important Cat. Watson, Wendy McLeod (1942-), illus. LC 58-10779. 53 p. illus. 24 cm. 1958. Dodd, Mead.
--Winter Night. Watson, Wendy McLeod (1942-), illus. LC 77-3307. p. cm. 1977. (ISBN 0-690-01384-1). (ISBN 0-690-01385-X). Crowell.

Watson, Wendy McLeod (1942-) & Grimm, Jakob Ludwig Karl (1785-1863)
--The Hedgehog and the Hare. Watson, Wendy McLeod (1942-), illus. LC 73-82762. (Illus.). 30 p. 1969. World Pub. Co.

Watson, Wendy McLeod (1942-) & Watson, Clyde (1947-)
--Fisherman Lullabies. Watson, Wendy McLeod (1942-), illus. LC 68-26968. (Illus.). color ils. 64p. (gr. k-3). 1968. World Pub.

Watson & Price
--Magical Animals. (Animal Story Bks.). (gr. k-4). 1982. (ISBN 0-86020-671-8, Usborne-Hayes). (ISBN 0-88110-095-1). (ISBN 0-86020-670-X). EDC.

Watt, Lois, jt. auth. see Fine, Janice.

Watt, Violet, jt. auth. see Mercer, Anne.

Watters, Eugene
--The Story of a Hedgeschool Master. 97p. (gr. 6 up). 1974. (ISBN 0-85342-436-5, Pub. by Mercier Pr Ireland). Irish Bk Ctr.

Watters, Lorrain E. (1899-)
--The Magic of Music. Aliki, et al., pseud. (1929-), illus. Brandenberg, Aliki Liacouras. LC 65-1603. vii, 216p. col. illus. 29cm. c.1965. Ginn.
--The Magic of Music: Bk. 4. DeCoste, Robert, illus. LC 65-1603. 208p. illus., music. 26cm. 1967. Ginn.
--The Magic of Music: Primer. Cooke, Tom, illus. 47p. col. illus. 19x24cm. c.1966. Ginn.

Watts, Anna Bernadette see Bernadette, pseud.

Watts, Anna Bernadette, jt. auth. see Scholey, Arthur.

Watts, Anna Bernadette (1942-), retold by see Grimm, Jakob Ludwig Karl (1785-1863) & Grimm, Wilhelm Karl.

Watts, Anna Bernadette (1942-), retold by see The, Three Bears.

Watts, Anna Bernadette (1942-), tr. see Grimm, Jakob Ludwig Karl (1785-1863) & Grimm, Wilhelm Karl.

AUTHOR INDEX WEATHERLEY, FREDERICK

Watts, Anna Bernadette (1942-)
--Brigitte & Ferdinand: A Love Story. Bernadette, pseud. Watts, Anna Bernadette (1942-), illus. Bernadette, pseud. LC 76-9034. (Illus.). 1st U.S. edition. (gr. 1-4). 1976. (ISBN 0-13-081919-0). P-H.
--David's Waiting Day. Bernadette, pseud. Watts, Anna Bernadette (1942-), illus. Bernadette, pseud. LC 77-6461. (Illus.). 1st U.S. edition. (ps-2). 1978. (ISBN 0-13-197178-6). P-H.
--Hans the Miller Man. Bernadette, pseud. Watts, Anna Bernadette (1942-), illus. Bernadette, pseud. LC 69-17735. (Illus.). 32p. (gr. k-3). 1969. (ISBN 0-07-004898-3). (ISBN 0-07-004899-1). McGraw.
--Mother Holly. LC 73-168998. (Adaptation of the Brothers Grimm Story Frau Holle). (Illus.). 32p. 33cm. 1972. Oxford University Press.
--The Proud Crow. Watts, Anna Bernadette (1942-), illus. Bernadette, pseud. LC 75-28404. (Illus.). 32p. (gr. k-2). 1975. (ISBN 0-8075-6640-3). A Whitman.
--Varenka. Bernadette, pseud. Watts, Anna Bernadette (1942-), illus. Bernadette, pseud. LC 79-172527. (Illus.). 32 p. 30cm. 1972, c.1971. (ISBN 0-399-20241-2). Putnam.

Watts, Charles Edwin (1929-)
--Alexander Fiddlewhistle. Watts, charles Edwin (1929-), illus. LC 60-15627. unpaged. illus. 30 cm. 1960. Helicon Press.

Watts, Frances B.
--Tales of Mr. Cinnamon. LC 81-65813. (Illus.). 96p. (The Saturday Evening Post Read-to-Me Ser.). (ps up). 1981. (Co-Pub by Sat Eve Post). Curtis Pub Co.
Watts, Franklin Mowry (1904-1978)
--Oranges. Ulm, Robert (1934-1977), illus. LC 77-16045. (Illus.). 31 p. 25cm. c.1978. Childrens Press.
Watts, Isaac see Bunyan, John.
Watts, Isaac (1674-1748)
--Childhood Songs of Long Ago. McManus, Blanche, illus. N.D. Wessels & Bissell Co.
--Divine and Moral Songs for Children. LC 22-22219. 11 1/2cm. 47p. 1834. American Tract Society.
--Divine and Moral Songs for Children. Gaskin, Arthur, Mrs., illus. (Illus.). Repr. N.D. L. C. Page & Co.
--Songs for Children in Easy Language. Cope, Charles West (1811-1890) & Thompson, John, illus. LC 4-32901. x, 94 p. illus. 23 cm. 1892. J. H. Earle.
Watts, John G.
--Life and Adventures of a Little Bird. Juv ed. (Illus.). N.D. Cassell & Co.
--Martin Noble. Or, A London boy's Life, 13 of 15 Vols. (Illus.). (Warne's Hopeful Enterprise Library). N.D. Scribner & Welford.
Watts, Mabel, jt. auth. see Werth, Kurt.
Watts, Mabel Pizzey, jt. auth. see Hunter, Virginia.
Watts, Mabel Pizzey see Lynn, Patricia, pseud.
Watts, Mabel Pizzey (1906-)
--Around and About Buttercup Farm. Lynn, Patricia, pseud. Rev ed. Kane, Wilma & Miloche, Hilda, illus. LC 52-16194. 1 v. (unpaged) col. illus. 17 cm. (tell-a-tale books. 1951. Whitman Pub. Co.
--The Basket That Flew Over the Mountain. Petie, Haris, pseud. (1915-), illus. Petty, Roberta. LC 74-188765. (Illus.). 31 p. 24cm. 1972. Lantern Press.
--The Bed of Thistledown. Perry, Sheila, illus. LC 62-17044. unpaged. illus. 21 cm. c.1962. Abelard-Schuman.
--Bedtime Stories. Clyne, Barbara, illus. LC 55-8186. unpaged. illus. 21cm. (Rand McNally Elf Book, 499). c.1955. Rand McNally.
--The Boy Who Listened to Everyone. Metzl, Ervine (1899-), illus. LC 63-8178. 1 v. (unpaged) col. illus. 26 cm. 1963. Parents' Magazine Press.
--Busy Bill. Lynn, Patricia, pseud. Rev ed. Clement, Charles (1921-), illus. LC 55-20870. 1 v. (unpaged) col. illus. 21 cm. (Cozy-Corner Book, 2443). c.1954. Whitman Pub. Co.
--Come Play with Me. LC 64-9322. (Illus.). 1 v. (unpaged. 33cm. (Whitman juveniles). 1964, c.1963. Whitman Pub. Co.
--A Cow in the House. Evans, Katherine Floyd (1901-1964), illus. LC 54-5190. (Illus.). 31p. 1956, c.1954. Follet Pub. Co.
--Cub Scout. Timmins, William Frederick, illus. (Illus.). (gr. k-2). 1964. (ISBN 0-8382-0190-3). Hale.
--Cub Scout. Timmins, William Frederick, illus. LC 66-14020. 1 v. (unpaged) col. illus. 33cm. (Rand McNally Giant Bk.). 1966, c.1964. Rand McNally.
--Daniel, the Cocker Spaniel. Grider, Dorothy (1915-), illus. LC 55-8190. unpaged. illus. 21cm. (Rand McNally Elf Book, 505). c.1955. Rand McNally.
--Day It Rained Watermelons. Albertson, Lee, illus. (Illus.). (gr. 1-3). 1964. (ISBN 0-8382-0197-0). Hale.
--Day It Rained Watermelons. Albertson, Lee, illus. LC 64-15171. (Illus.). 24cm. 32p. (ps-2). 1964. (ISBN 0-8313-0101-5). Lantern.
--Digger Dan. Lynn, Patricia, pseud. Frankel, Simon, illus. LC 53-37578. 1 v. (unpaged) col. illus. 17 cm. (Tell-A-Tale Books). 1953. Whitman Pub. Co.
--Dozens of Cousins: Story. Duvoisin, Roger Antoine (1904-1980), illus. LC 50-6487. (Illus.). 46 p. 26cm. 1950. Whittlesey House.
--The Elephant That Became a Ferryboat. Petie, Haris, pseud. (1915-), illus. Petty, Roberta. LC 79-168447. (Illus.). 30 p. 24cm. 1971. Lantern Press.
--Everyone Waits. Hofbauer, Imre, illus. LC 59-5414. unpaged. illus. 26 cm. 1959. Abelard-Schuman.
--Famous Folk Tales to Read Aloud. (Read-Aloud Bks.). (gr. k-3). N.D. Wonder.
--Farm ABC. Lynn, Patricia, pseud. Michell, Gladys Turley, illus. LC 55-17929. 1 v. (unpaged col. illus. 17 cm. (Tell-A-Tale Books, 965). 1954. Whitman Pub. Co.
--Feathered Friends. Opitz, Marge, illus. LC 57-9956. (Illus.). 19cm. (A Rand McNally Junior Elf Bk.). 1957. Rand McNally.
--Getting Ready for Roddy. Lynn, Patricia, pseud. Helweg, Hans H. (1917-), illus. LC 56-26169. (Illus.). 17cm. (Tell-Tale Bks.). 1955. Whitman Pub. Co.
--Goody Naughty Book: The Goody Side and The Naughty Side. Prickett, Helen, illus. LC 56-11564. 2v. in 1. illus. 21cm. (Rand McNally Elf Book, 572). c.1956. Rand McNally.
--Handy Andy. Lynn, Patricia, pseud. Dreany, E. Joseph, illus. LC 54-15485. 1 v. (unpaged) col. illus. 17 cm. (Tell-A-Tale Books). 1953. Whitman Pub. Co.
--Henrietta and the Hat. Miller, Jane Judith (1925-), illus. LC 62-12944. 1 v. (unpaged) col. illus. 27 cm. c.1962. (ISBN 0-8193-0002-0). (ISBN 0-8193-0003-9). Parents' Magazine Press.
--Hide-Away Animals. Chase, Mary Jane, illus. LC 57-9955. unpaged. illus. 19cm. (Rand McNally Junior Elf Book, 604). c.1957. Rand McNally.
--Hiram's Red Shirt. Battaglia, Aurelius (1910-), illus. LC 80-85027. (Illus.). 24p. (Little Golden Bks.). (ps). 1981. (ISBN 0-307-02076-2, Golden Pr). (ISBN 0-307-60276-1). Western Pub.
--I'm for You, and You're for Me. Foreman, Michael (1938-), illus. LC 67-13611. (Illus.). 32 p. 1967. Abelard-Schuman.
--The King and the Whirlybird. Berson, Harold (1926-), illus. LC 69-12605. (Illus.). 40 p. 24cm. 1969. Parents' Magazine Press.
--Knights of the Square Table. Petie, Haris, pseud. (1915-), illus. Petty, Roberta. LC 73-81263. (Illus.). 32 p. 24cm. 1973. Lantern Press.
--The Light Across Piney Valley. Barker, Carol Minturn (1938-), illus. LC 65-12663. 1 v. (chiefly illus., part col.) 26 cm. 1965. Abelard-Schuman.
--Little Campers. Grider, Dorothy (1915-), illus. LC 64-17039. 1 v. (unpaged) col. illus. 32 cm. 1964, c.1963. Rand McNally.
--A Little from Here, a Little from There. LC 62-9064. (Illus.). unpaged. 21cm. c.1962. Abelard-Schuman.
--Little Horseman. 1960. (ISBN 0-8382-0453-8, Hale Giant Books). E. M. Hale and Company.
--Little Horseman. Grider, Dorothy (1915-), illus. LC 63-11261. (Illus.). 21 p. 33cm. (Rand McNally Giant Book). 1964, c.1961. Rand McNally.
--Little Red Riding Hood. Gray, Leslie, illus. (Illus.). 24p. Repr. of 1972 ed. (ps-3). 1977. (ISBN 0-307-60232-X, Golden Pr). Western Pub.
--The Narrow Escapes of Solomon Smart. Johnson, John Emil (1929-), illus. LC 66-9352. (Illus.). 1 v. (unpaged). 1966. Parents' Magazine Press.
--Over the Hills to Ballybog. 1st ed. Pitz, Henry Clarence (1895-1976), illus. LC 54-61563. unpaged. illus. 23cm. 1954. Aladdin Books.
--Over the Hills to Ballybog. Pitz, Henry Clarence (1895-1976), illus. N.D. E. P. Dutton & CO.
--The Patchwork Kilt. 1st ed. Bromhall, Winifred, illus. LC 54-927615. unpaged. illus. 22cm. 1954. Aladdin Books.
--The Patchwork Kilt. Bromhall, Winifred, illus. N.D. E. P. Dutton & Co.
--The Patchwork Kilt. Bromhall, Winifred, illus. (Illus.). (gr. 1-3). 1954. (ISBN 0-8382-0632-8). Hale.
--Something for You, Something for Me. Graboff, Abner (1919-), illus. LC 60-13923. unpaged. illus. 27 cm. c.1960. Abelard, Schuman.
--The Story of Zachary Zween. Hafner, Marylin (1925-), illus. LC 67-9365. (Illus.). 43 p. 27cm. 1967. Parents' Magazine Press.
--Trumpet. Lynn, Patricia, pseud. Myers, Bernice, illus. LC 54-21576. 1 v. (unpaged) col. illus. 17 cm. (Tell-A-Tale, 931). 1953. Whitman Pub. Co.
--Weeks and Weeks. Graboff, Abner (1919-), illus. LC 62-9066. unpaged. illus. 26 cm. c.1962. Abelard-Schuman.
--Where Is the Keeper?. Seiden, Art, illus. (Illus.). (Tell-a-Tale Readers). (gr. k-3). 1979. (ISBN 0-307-68469-5, Whitman). Western Pub.
--While the Horses Galloped to London. Mayer, Mercer (1943-), illus. LC 72-8096. (Illus.). 40 p. 25cm. 1973. (ISBN 0-8193-0652-5). (ISBN 0-8193-0652-5). Parents' Magazine Press.
--Yin Sun and the Lucky Dragon. Hall, H. Tom, illus. LC 69-12300. (Illus.). 46 p. 24cm. 1969. Westminister Press.
--Zoo Friends Are at Our School Today!. Brewer, Sally King (1947-), illus. (A Tell-a-Tale Reader Ser.). (gr. k-3). 1979. (ISBN 0-307-68423-7, Golden Pr). Western Pub.
Watts, Marjorie-Ann
--Crocodile Medicine. Watts, Marjorie-Ann, illus. LC 78-52992. (Illus.). 32 p. 25cm. 1978, c.1977. (ISBN 0-7232-6154-7). F. Warne.
--Crocodile Plaster. Watts, Marjorie-Ann, illus. (Illus.). (gr. k-3). N.D. (ISBN 0-233-96962-4, Andre Deutsch). Dutton.
--The Dragon Clock. Watts, marjorie-Ann, illus. (Illus.). 128p. (gr. 4-8). 1975. David & Charles.
--Mulroy's Magic. Watts, Marjorie Ann, illus. LC 76-377538. (Illus.). 109 p. 20cm. 1975. (ISBN 0-14-030791-5). Puffin Books.
--Zebra Goes to School. Watts, Marjorie-Ann, illus. LC 80-2688. (Illus.). 32p. (ps-2). 1981. (ISBN 0-233-97241-2). Andre Deutsch.
Watts, Marjorie Seymour
--Do You Remember?. Babbitt, Lorena E., illus. LC 27-14200. 29 p. incl. front., illus. 24 cm. c.1927. The Four Seas Company.
Watts, Robert A
--Who Are Billy's Friends?. Dugan, William J., illus. LC 64-10813. 32 p. illus. (part col.) 21 cm. 1964. Broadman Press.
Waugh, Arthur, jt. auth. see Nicholson, William, Sir.
Waugh, Carol-Lynn Rossel (1947-)
--My Friend Bear. 1st ed. Meddaugh, Susan (1944-), illus. LC 81-15600. (Illus.). 32 p. 22cm. c.1982. (ISBN 0-316-92636-1). Little, Brown.
Waugh, Charles, jt. auth. see McSherry, Frank David, Jr.
Waugh, Charles G, jt. auth. see Asimov, Isaac.
Waugh, Charles G. & Greenberg, Martin Harry (1941-), eds.
--The Newbery Award Reader. LC 83-22592. c.1984. (ISBN 0-15-257034-9). Harcourt Brace Javonovich.
Waugh, Dorothy (1896-)
--Muriel Saves String. Waugh, Dorothy (1896-), illus. LC 56-5379. 82 p. illus. 22 cm. 1956. D. McKay Co.
Waugh, Frederick Judd (1861-1940)
--The Clan of Munes. LC 16-23140. 4 p. l., 56, 2 p. incl. col. front. illus. (part col.) 24 1/2 x 32 1/2 cm. $2.5. 1916. C. Scribner's Sons.
Waugh, Ida
--Holly Berries. (Illus.). N.D. Publications of E. P. Dutton & Co.
--Little Chicks and Baby Tricks: Author of "Holly Berries". N.D. E. P. Dutton & Co.
--When Mother Was A Little Girl. N.D. E. P. Dutton & Co.
Waugh, Julia Nott (1888-)
--The Silver Cradle. (Illus.). 160p. 1955. University Of Texas Press.
Wavle, Ardra Soule, as told by.
--Here They Are. Disney, Walt, Studio, illus. LC 40-6908. 2 p. l., 56 p. col. illus. 22 cm. c.1940. D. C. Heath and Company.
Way, Frederick, Jr.
--The Log of the Betsy Ann. N.D. Robert M. McBride & Co.
Way, Irene (1924-)
--Armada Quest. LC 78-26401. 102 p. 21cm. (Pathfinder Ser.). 1979, c.1976. (ISBN 0-310-37841-9). Zondervan Pub. House.
Way, Lula R (1912-) & Wooldridge, Elizabeth T. (1908-)
--Let's Play 'rithmetic: Children's Stories About Ancient Figures and Figuring. Woolbridge, Elizabeth T., illus. LC 59-16448. 59 p. illus. 21 cm. 1959. Exposition Press.
Way, Robert Bernard (1890-)
--The Ian Allan Book of Trains. Way, Robert Bernard (1890-), illus. LC 60-50895. unpaged. illus. 25 cm. 1960. I. Allan; Stamped: Distributed by Sportshelf, New Rochelle, N.Y. N.Y.
Waybill, Marjorie Ann (1929-)
--Chinese Eyes. Cutrell, Pauline, illus. LC 74-5751. (Illus.). 34 p. 1974. (ISBN 0-8361-1738-7). Herald Press.
Wayland, R. S.
--The Legend of Maiden Rock. N.D. J. B. Lippincott.
Wayman, Joe, jt. auth. see Mitchell, Don.
Wayman, Joe & Mitchell, Don
--Anything Can Happen Book. (gr. k-8). 1976. (ISBN 0-916456-06-4). Good Apple.
--Imagination & Me Book. (gr. k-8). 1976. (ISBN 0-916456-02-1). Good Apple.
Wayman, Vivienne
--Panchit's Secret. Broude, Susan, illus. (gr. 4-7). 1976. (ISBN 0-8277-4742-X). British Bk Ctr.
Wayman & Plum
--Secrets & Surprises. (gr. k-8). 1977. (ISBN 0-916456-13-7). Good Apple.
Wayne, Anne Jenifer (1917-1982)
--Kitchen People. Shortall, Leonard W. & Palmer, Margaret, illus. LC 64-253226. 156p. illus. 22cm. 1965, c.1964. Bobbs.
--Sprout. Owens, Gail, illus. LC 75-41341. p. cm. 1976. (ISBN 0-07-068695-5). McGraw-Hill.
--Sprout and the Dogsitter. Owens, Gail, illus. LC 76-56109. (Illus.). 89 p. 21cm. 1977, c.1972. (ISBN 0-07-068696-3). McGraw-Hill.
--Sprout and the Helicopter. Owens, Gail, illus. LC [illegible]. (Illus.). 88 p. 21cm. 1977. (ISBN 0-07-068698-X). McGraw-Hill.
--Sprout and the Magician. Owens, Gail, illus. LC 77-78763. p. cm. 1977. (ISBN 0-07-068705-6). McGraw-Hill.
--Sprout's Window Cleaner. Owens, Gail, illus. LC 75-41342. p. cm. 1976. (ISBN 0-07-068697-1). McGraw-Hill.
Wayne, Bennett, ed.
--Adventurers in Buckskin. Wayne, Bennett, illus. LC 72-6741. (Illus.). index. 168p. (Target Ser.). (gr. 5-12). 1973. (ISBN 0-8116-4900-8). Garrard.
Wayne, Donald, pseud., see Dodd, Wayne Donald.
Wayne, Donald, pseud. (1930-)
--The Adventures of Little White Possum. Dodd, Wayne Donald. Neely, Linda, illus. LC 75-110315. (Illus.). 46 p. 22cm. 1970. Putnam.
Wayne, Elaine
--Bucky Bear, Who Would Not Take His Nap. Weisgard, Leonard Joseph (1916-), illus. LC 44-2811. 41 p. col. illus. 17 1/2 x 16 1/2 cm. 1944. Lothrop, Lee & Shepard Co.
Wayne, Harry Randolph
--Here Comes Jimmy. Here Comes Jimmy's Dog!. Cary, Louis Favreau (1915-), illus. Cary, pseud. LC 63-9566. unpaged. illus. 24 cm. (little owl book). 1963. (ISBN 0-03-036000-5). Holt, Rinehart, and Winston.
Wayne, Jenifer see Wayne, Anne Jenifer.
Wayne, Kyra Petrovskaya see Petrovskaya, Kyra.
Wayne, Kyra Petrovskaya (1918-)
--The Awakening. LC 72-75789. 185 p. 21cm. (Thistle Book). 1972. (ISBN 0-448-21450-4). Grosset & Dunlap.
--The Witches of Barguzin. LC 75-2143. 188 p. 21cm. 1975. (ISBN 0-8407-6429-4). T. Nelson.
Wayne, Mel
--The Horse on Ben Ave. Kennedy, Richard (1910-), illus. LC 62-85526. (Illus.). 23cm. 182p. 1962, c.1961. Duell, Sloan and Pearce.
Wayne, Richard, pseud., see Decker, Duane Walter.
Wayside Publications
--Legend of Sleepy Hollow. Bradley, Will, compiled by. N.D. R. H. Russell.
--Rip Van Winkle. Bradley, Will, compiled by. N.D. R. H. Russell.
Wead, Frank Wilber (1895-)
--Our Greatest Story-Teller: The Story of Talking Pictures. Laune, Paul Sidney (1899-), illus. LC 36-3996. vi, 7-62, 1 p. incl. front., illus. 19 1/2 cm. (Our changing world). 1936. T. Nelson and Sons.
Weales, Gerald Clifford (1925-)
--Miss Grimsbee Is a Witch. 1st ed. Scheel, Lita, illus. LC 57-5521. (Illus.). (What Happens To Those Who Don't Believe in Witches). (gr. 3-7). 1957. (ISBN 0-316-92674-4, Pub. by Atlantic Monthly Pr). Little.
--Miss Grimsbee Takes a Vacation. 1st ed. Scheel, Lita, illus. LC 65-10588. (Illus.). 102 p. 20cm. 1965. Little, Brown.
Wear, George W
--Uncle Billy Stories. LC 31-772. 83 p. 20 1/2 cm. 1930. Meador Publishing Company.
Wear, Ted, pseud., see Wear, Theodore Graham.
Wear, Ted, pseud. (1902-)
--Brownie Makes the Headlines. Wear, Theodore Graham. Ravielli, Louis, illus. LC 53-10516. 63p. illus. 22cm. (Everyday Adventure Story). 1953. J. Messner.
Wear, Theodore Graham see Wear, Ted, pseud.
Weatherall, Maria, tr. see Capek, Karel (1890-1938) & Capek, Josef.
Weatherall, Marie, tr. see Capek, Karel.
Weatherall, Robert, tr. see Capek, Karel.
Weatherall Robert, tr. see Capek, Karel (1890-1938) & Capek, Josef.
Weatherill, Stephen
--Goosey Goosey Gander. Weatherill, Stephen, illus. (Illus.). 12p. (ps-1). 1983. (ISBN 0-688-01939-0). Greenwillow.
--Humpty Dumpty. Weatherill, Stephen, illus. LC 82-82916. (Illus.). 12p. (ps-1). 1983. (ISBN 0-688-01940-4). Greenwillow.
Weatherley, Frederick Edward (1848-1929)
--Elsie's Expedition. N.D. Scribner, Welford & Armstrong.

Weatherly

--Children's Birthday Book. Greenaway, Kate (1846-1901), illus. N.D. Frederick Warne & Co.

Weatherly, Frederic Edward (1848-1929)

--The Book of Gnomes. Hardy, E. Stuart, illus. 26 x 31cm. 36p. 1907. E. P. Dutton & Co.

--Come and Go: A Book of Changing Pictures. LC 67-8159. 1 v. (unpaged) illus. (part col.) 25 cm. N.D. Dutton.

--Here and There: A/Book of Transformation Pictures. LC 73-170110. (Illus.). 26cm. 14p. 1893. Dutton.

--Out of Town. Wilson, Ernest & Watt, Linnie, illus. LC 16-5300. 64 p. incl. col. front., illus. (part col.) 23 x 19 cm. 1884. E. P. Dutton & Co.

--Songs for Michael. Crowle, Pigeon, illus. LC 29-8680. 72 p. incl. pl. 19 1/2 cm. 1928. Longmans, Green and Co.

Weatherly, Frederic Edward (1848-1929), intro. by.

--Peeps into Fairland: A/Panorama Picture Book of Fairy Stories. LC 74-160495. (Illus.). 28 x 36cm. 28p. 1896. Dutton.

Weatherly, George

--The Little Folks. Weatherly, George, illus. viii, 9-80 p. ill. 22cm. N.D. Cassell, Petter calpin & Co.

--Little Folks' Illuminating Book. (Illus.). N.D. Cassell, Petter, Galpin.

Weatherwax, John M., jt. auth. see Purnell, Idella.

Weatherwax, John M., jt. auth. see Stone, Idella Purnell.

Weatherwax, Rudd B. & Rothwell, John H.

--The Story of Lassie. 1951. Duell Sloan & Pearce.

Weaver, Anna

--Eyes for Benny. 1984. (ISBN 0-318-01331-2). Rod & Staff.

Weaver, Annie Vaughan (1905-)

--Boochy's Wings. Weaver, Annie Vaughan (1905-), illus. LC 31-21898. 122, 2 p. incl. col. front., illus. (part col.) plates (part col.) 14 x 18 1/2 cm. 1931. Frederick A. Stokes Company.

--Boochy's Wings. Weaver, Annie Vaughan (1905-), illus. N.D. J. B. Lippincott.

--Frawg. Weaver, Annie Vaughan (1905-), illus. LC 30-249451. 128 p. incl. col. front., illus. (part col.) 14 cm. 1930. Frederick A. Stokes Company.

--Frawg. Weaver, Annie Vaughan (1905-), illus. N.D. J. B. Lippincott.

--Pappy King. Weaver, Annie Vaughan (1905-), illus. LC 32-242801. 5 p. l., 3-81 p. incl. col. front., col. illus. 14 x 18 1/2 cm. 1932. Frederick A. Stokes Company.

Weaver, Burnley

--Ten Little Pickaninnies. Weaver, Burnley, illus. LC 34-374. 22 p. col. illus. 11 x 18 cm. 1933. The Gollifox Press.

Weaver, E P

--The Search: A Story of the Old Frontier. LC 4-32324. vi. 2, 9-224 p. front., plates. 19 cm. (The East and West series). 1904. A. S. Barnes & Company.

Weaver, Eli Witner (1862-1922)

--Paul's Trip with the Moon. LC 99-588. 45p. 1899. Charles E. Merrill Co.

Weaver, Emily

--My Lady Nell. (Pilgrim Prizes Series.). N.D. Set. 9.00. Thomas Whitaker.

--The Rabbi's Sons. 381p. N.D. Sunday-School Library.

Weaver, Florence Stratton

--Spark: The Story of a Little Child's Faith and what came from it. LC 2910. 24cm. 115p. 1899. F. M. Barton.

Weaver, Gertrude (1904-)

--The Emperor's Gift. Unada, pseud. (1927-), illus. Gliewe, Unada Grace. LC 69-16194. (Illus.). 127 p. 23cm. 1969. T. Nelson.

Weaver, Gustine Nancy Courson, Mrs. (1873-)

--Hop-Run: And Six Other Pageants. LC 28-18957. 91 p. front. (ports.) illus. 19 1/2 cm. c.1927. Powell & White.

--The House a Jap Built. LC 9-19413. 19cm. 32p. 1909. Reilly & Britton & Co.

--Santa's Cotton Doll Farm. McGonagill, Dorothy, illus. LC 30-31720. 45, 1 p. incl. front., illus. 19 cm. c.1930. Bethany Press.

Weaver, Harriett E. (1908-)

--There Stand the Giants: The Story of the Redwood Trees. Weaver, Harriet (1908-), illus. LC 60-14383. 70 p. illus. 24 cm. (Sunset Junior Book). 1960. Lane Book Co.

Weaver, Marilou

--The Secret Cave. LC 75-26675. 126 p. 18cm. 1976. (ISBN 0-8024-3829-6). Moody Press.

Weaver, Robert Glenn (1920-)

--Nice Guy, Go Home. LC 68-10212. 180 p. 22cm. 1968. Harper & Row.

Weaver, Sarah Harbine

--The Doings of Jane. LC 20-209479. 3 p. l., 125 p. 19 cm. 1920. The Stratford Company.

Weaver, Sarah Minier Sanborne (1886-)

--The White Buck. N.D. Naylor Company.

Weaver, Stella

--A Poppy in the Corn. LC 61-7463. 319 p. 22cm. 1961, c.1960. Pantheon Books. **Award: (ALA).**

--The Stranger. Vaughan-Jackson, Genevieve (1913-), illus. LC 56-8098. 251 p. illus. 22 cm. 1956. Pantheon Books.

Weaverson, Brownie Rathbone

--The Brownie Girls. LC 99-4612. 54 p. front. (port.) illus. 21 1/2 x 18 1/2 cm. c.1899. F. Weaverson & Co.

Webb, Addison

--Song of the Seasons. Ripper, Charles Lewis (1929-), illus. 127p. (gr. 1-5). 1950. William Morrow & Co.

Webb, B Ethel, ed.

--Cinderella, Jack the Giant Killer, Little Red Riding-Hood and Other Favorite Fairy Tales. Webb, Ethel, illus. LC 28-14545. x, 102 p. col. front., illus., col. pl. 21 cm. c.1928. The John C. Winston Company.

Webb, Barbara, jt. auth. see Cundiff, Ruby Ethel.

Webb, Barbara (1898-)

--Mother Goose Secrets. King, Joe (1909-1979), illus. LC 25-20435. (Illus.). 145p. 23cm. 1925. Small, Maynard & Co.

Webb, Christopher, pseud., see Wibberley, Leonard Patrick O'Connor.

Webb, Christopher, pseud., see Wibberly, Leonard Patrick O'Connor.

Webb, Christopher, pseud. (1915-)

--The Ann and Hope Mutiny. Wibberley, Leonard Patrick O'Connor. LC 66-12585. 192p. 22cm. c.1966. Funk & Wagnalls.

--Eusebius, the Phoenician. Wibberley, Leonard Patrick O'Connor. LC 69-15432. 188 p. 22cm. 1969. Funk & Wagnalls.

--Mark Toyman's Inheritance. Wibberley, Leonard Patrick O'Connor. LC 60-6429. 184 p. 22 cm. 1960. Funk & Wagnalls.

--Matt Tyler's Chronicle. Wibberley, Leonard Patrick O'Connor. LC 58-11363. 216 p. 22cm. 1958. Funk & Wagnalls.

--Quest of the Otter. Wibberly, Leonard Patrick O'Connor. LC 63-15396. 180 p. 22 cm. 1963. Funk & Wagnalls.

--The River of Pee Dee Jack. Wibberley, Leonard Patrick O'Connor. LC 62-11884. 186 p. 22 cm. 1962. Funk & Wagnalls.

Webb, Clifford Cyril (1895-1972)

--Animals from Everywhere. new and rev. ed. Webb, Clifford Cyril (1895-1972), illus. LC 51-9535. 64 p. illus. (part col.) 29 cm. 1950. F. Warne.

--Butterwick Farm. Webb, Clifford Cyril (1895-1972), illus. LC 33-27377. 75 p. incl. col. plates. 23 x 22 cm. 1933. F. Warne and Co. Ltd.

--The Friendly Place. Webb, Clifford Cyril (1895-1972), illus. LC 62-18909. unpaged. illus. 20 x 30 cm. 1962. Warne.

--A Jungle Picnic. Webb, Clifford Cyril (1895-1972), illus. LC 35-1483. 75 p. incl. col. front., col. plates. 24 cm. N.D. F. Warne & Co.

--A Jungle Picnic. Webb, Clifford Cyril (1895-1972), illus. LC 53-12682. 53p. illus. 22cm. 1953. Warne.

--Magic Island. Webb, Clifford Cyril (1895-1972), illus. LC 56-140826. 53p. illus. 22cm. 1956. Warne.

--The North Pole Before Lunch. Webb, Clifford Cyril (1895-1972), illus. LC 37-83120. 63, 1 p. incl. illus., col. plates. 23 x 21 1/2 cm. c.1936. (ISBN 0-7232-0521-3). F. Warne & Co., Ltd.

--The Story of Noah. Webb, Clifford Cyril (1895-1972), illus. LC 33-7386. 57 p. illus. (part col.) 20 x 28 cm. 1932. F. Warne & Co., Inc.

--The Thirteenth Pig. Webb, Clifford Cyril (1895-1972), illus. LC 66-10485. 46p. illus. (pt. col.) 25cm. 1966, c.1965. Warne.

Webb, Clifford Cyril (1895-1972) & Webb, Jennifer

--Animals from Everywhere. Webb, Clifford Cyril (1895-1972), illus. LC 39-17111. 63, 1 p. illus. (part col.) 28 1/2 cm. 1938. F. Warne & Co., Ltd.

Webb, David Maryland

--The Little Seed. Harris, Janet Barnes, illus. LC 79-67086. (Illus.). 38 p. 23cm. c.1979. (ISBN 0-935054-00-6). Webb-Newcomb Greeting Co.

--The Old Woman & the Bird. LC 79-55781. (Illus.). 45p. (gr. 3-8). 1983. (ISBN 0-935054-04-9). Webb-Newcomb.

Webb, Doris, jt. auth. see Webb, Elizabeth Carman.

Webb, Elizabeth Carman & Webb, Doris

--The Littlest Fairy. Clements, Ruth Sypherd, illus. 1910. Dodge.

Webb, Etta

--Yesterday's Girl. LC 37-19006. 7 p. l., 3-272 p. incl. front., illus., plates. 20 1/2 cm. 1937. The Vanguard Press.

Webb, Francoise

--King Didi the Eighth. Webb, Francoise, illus. LC 69-13169. (Illus.). 40 p. 27cm. 1969. Walker.

Webb, J. B., Mrs.

--Helen Mordaunt: or, The Standard of Life. N.D. George Routledge & Sons.

--Ishmael, the Yezidee. N.D. George Routledge & Sons.

Webb, James Plimell (1903-)

--Riley Dawson. LC 50-6980. 245 p. 21 cm. 1950. Dodd, Mead.

Webb, Jean Francis, jt. auth. see Webb, Nancy Bukeley.

Webb, Jean Francis, III (1910-)

--Bride of Cairngore. LC 74-81605. 224p. 1974. (ISBN 0-679-50514-8). McKay.

--The Empty Attic. 192p. (Orig.). (gr. 7 up). 1983. (ISBN 0-590-32445-4, Windswept). Scholastic Inc.

Webb, Jennifer, jt. auth. see Webb, Clifford Cyril.

Webb, Joan

--Hornswoggled. Dawson, Cathy, illus. LC 77-155179. (Illus.). 26. c.1977. J. Horne Co.

--Let's Play Peek-a-Boo. Mulkey, Kim, illus. (Illus.). (First Little Golden Bks.). (ps). 1981. (ISBN 0-307-10109-6, Golden Pr). (ISBN 0-307-68109-2). Western Pub.

--Poochie & the Four Seasons Fair. Sanderson, Ruth, illus. (Illus.). 32p. (ps). 1983. (ISBN 0-307-15819-5, Golden Pr). Western Pub.

Webb, Kate Cope

--Arthur in Shadow and Sunshine. White, Will, illus. LC 12-25206. 49, 1 p. illus. 21 cm. $0.7. 1912. R. J. Orozco.

Webb, Kaye, ed. see Aiken, Joan.

Webb, Margaret

--Marty the Marlin. 28p. 1984. (ISBN 0-533-05929-1). Vantage.

Webb, Marion St. John Adcock, Mrs. (1840-1930)

--The Littlest One. Tarrant, Margaret Winifred (1888-), illus. N.D. Frederick A. Stokes Co.

--The Littlest One, His Book. Watson, A. H., illus. LC 29-16084. 161, 1 p. incl. front., ilus. 19 1/2 cm. 1927. Thomas Y. Crowell Company.

Webb, Mrs.

--Helen Mordaunt: Author of "Naomi". (Illus.). (Routledge's Welcome Series of Girls' Books). N.D. George Routledge & Sons.

--The Stitch in Time, 3 of 25 Vols. (Illus.). (Warne's Crofton Cousins Ser.). N.D. Scribner & Welford.

Webb, Myra Churchill Holmes, Mrs.

--Angie's Uprising. LC 31-3184. 305 p. 20 1/2 cm. c.1931. The Christopher Publishing House.

Webb, Nancy Bukeley (1915-)

--Aguk of Alaska. Webb, Nancy Burkeley (1915-), illus. LC 63-15342. 62 p. illus. 22 cm. p-h junior research books. 1963. (ISBN 0-13-020693-8). Prentice-Hall.

--Makema of the Rain Forest. Webb, Nancy Bukeley (1915-), illus. LC 64-17195. 64p. col. illus., col. map. 22cm. (P-H jr. res. bks.). 1964. Prentice.

--Marcia Blake: Publicity Girl. LC 56-58379. 224 p. 21 cm. 1956. Avalon Books.

Webb, Nancy Bukeley (1915-) & Webb, Jean Francis (1910-)

--Golden Feathers. Cooper, Mario (1905-), illus. LC 54-13192. 192 p. illus. 21 cm. c.1954. Bouregy & Curl.

--Kaiulani: Crown Princess of Hawaii. 256p. 1962. Viking Press.

Webb, P.

--Arabella Duck. N.D. Carlton.

Webb, Robert N.

--The Story of Dan Bear. Kinstler, Everett Raymond (1926-), illus. LC 58-5703. 181 p. illus. 22 cm. (Signature Books, 43). 1953. (ISBN 0-448-05643-7). Grosset & Dunlap.

--Trapped on North Island. LC 61-6914. 151 p. illus. 21 cm. 1961. Duell, Sloan and Pearce.

--We Were There at the Boston Tea Party. Ward, Edmund F., illus. LC 56-5387. (Historical Consultant: Louis L. Snyder). 173 p. illus. 24 cm. (We Were There Books, 3). 1956. (ISBN 0-448-05003-X). Grosset & Dunlap.

--We Were there on the Nautilus. Vaughn, Frank E., illus. LC 61-66511. (Historical Consultant: William R. Anderson). 178 p. illus. 22 cm. (We Were There Books, 35). 1961. (ISBN 0-448-05035-8). Grosset & Dunlap.

--We Were There with Caesar's Legions. Zaccone, Fabian, illus. LC 60-16089. (Historical Consultant: Courtney Whitney). 177 p. illus. 22 cm. (We were there books, 27). 1960. Grosset & Dunlap.

--We Were There with Ethan Allen and the Green Mountain Boys. Pious, Robert, illus. LC 56-10690. (Historical Consultant: Chilton Williamson). 182 p. illus. 24 cm. (We Were There Books, 10). 1956. (ISBN 0-448-05010-2). Grosset & Dunlap.

--We Were There with Florence Nightingale in the Crimea. Copelman, Evelyn, illus. LC 58-12566. (Historical Consultant: Louis L. Snyder). 179 p. illus. 22 cm. (We Were There Books, 21). 1958. (ISBN 0-448-05021-8). Grosset & Dunlap.

--We Were There with Richard the Lionhearted in the Crusades. Vosburgh, Leonard W. (1912-), illus. LC 57-10104. (Historical Consultant:Andre A. Beaumont). 182 p. illus. 24 cm. (We Were There Books, 16). 1957. (ISBN 0-448-05016-1). Grosset & Dunlap.

--We Were There with the Mayflower Pilgrims. Andres, Charles J., illus. LC 56-5890. (Historical Consultant: George F. Willison). 178 p. illus. 24 cm. (We Were There Books, 7). 1956. (ISBN 0-448-05007-2). Grosset & Dunlap.

Webb, Ruth Enid Borlase Morris see Morris, Ruth.

Webb, Sharon

--Earthchild. LC 82-1791. 216p. 1982. (ISBN 0-689-30945-7, Argo). Atheneum.

--Ram Song. LC 84-2918. 228p. (gr. 9 up). 1984. (ISBN 0-689-31058-7, Argo). Atheneum.

Webb, Walter Prescott (1913-), ed. see Taylor, Ross McLaury.

Webb, Wheaton Phillips (1911-)

--The Twelve Labors of Wimpole Stout. Savage, Steele (1900-), illus. LC 72-83708. (Illus.). 176 p. 24cm. 1970. Abingdon Press.

--Uncle Swithin's Inventions. Rounds, Glen Harold (1906-), illus. LC 48-6349. 114 p. illus. 25 cm. 1947. Holiday House.

Webb, Zeff A.

--Book of Legends. (World Legends Ser.). (gr. 3-6). 1982. (ISBN 0-86020-618-1, Usborne Hayes). EDC.

Webb & Amery

--Ulysses. (World Legends Ser.). (gr. 3-6). 1981. (ISBN 0-86020-568-1, Usborne-Hayes). (ISBN 0-88110-058-7). (ISBN 0-86020-567-3). EDC.

Webbe, Elizabeth, illus.

--The Rand McNally Book of Favorite Nature Stories. LC 63-11275. 108 p. col. illus. 33 cm. c.1961. Rand McNally.

--The Rand McNally Book of Favorite Read-Aloud Stories. LC 63-11277. 110 p. col. illus. 33 cm. N.D. Rand McNally.

--Sleeping Beauty. (Illus.). (gr. k-2). 1959. (ISBN 0-8382-0763-4). Hale.

--Sleeping Beauty. LC 61-11898. (Illus.). 33cm. (A Rand McNally giant book). (ps-k). 1961, c.1959. (ISBN 0-528-88849-8). Rand.

--Three Bears. (Illus.). (gr. k-2). 1959. (ISBN 0-8382-0859-2). Hale.

--The Three Bears. (Illus.). (ps-k). 1962. (ISBN 0-528-88853-6). Rand.

--The Three Bears. LC 62-12361. (Illus.). 32cm. (A Rand McNally Giant Bk.). 1962, c.1959. Rand McNally.

Webbe, Gale Dudley see Cole, Stephen, pseud.

Webbe, Gale Dudley (1909-)

--The Growing Season. Cole, Stephen, pseud. LC 66-11706. 22cm. 150p. 1966. Ariel Books.

Webber, Andrew Lloyd, jt. auth. see Rice, Tim.

Webber, Frank Martin

--Peter Painter. Neville, Vera (1900-1978), illus. LC 40-29056. 24cm. 32p. (The Peter Painter Bks.). (gr. 1-3). 1940. David McKay Co.

--Peter Painter and the Holidays. Neville, Vera (1900-1978), illus. LC 43-3405. 82 p. illus. (part col.) 23 1/2 cm. c.1942. David McKay Company.

--Peter Painter's Merry-Go-Round. Neville, Vera (1900-1978), illus. LC 46-20551. 32 p. illus. (part col.) 23 1/2 x 18 1/2 cm. 1946. David McKay Company.

Webber, Helen

--Good-Night, Night. Webber, Helen, illus. LC 65-23420. 1 v. (unpaged) illus. (pt. col.) 19cm. 1968. (ISBN 0-8392-3054-0). Astor-Honor.

--Good Night, Night. Webber, Helen, illus. (gr. k-3). N.D. G&D.

--How Long Is Long Ago & Other Poems. Webber, Helen, illus. (Illus.). (gr. k-6). 1968. (ISBN 0-8392-3068-0). Astor-Honor.

--My Kite Is the Magic Me. Webber, Helen, illus. LC 65-25031. (Illus.). (gr. k-6). 1968. (ISBN 0-8392-3055-9). Astor-Honor.

--My Kite is the Magic Me. Webber, Helen, illus. (gr. k-3). N.D. G&D.

--The Sea Is My Blanket. Webber, Helen, illus. LC 65-25032. (Illus.). 28 p. 19cm. 1968, c.1965. I. Obolensky.

--Summer Sun. Webber, Helen, illus. LC 65-25030. 1v. (unpaged) illus. (pt. col.) 19cm. 1968. Astor-Honor.

--Summer Sun. Webber, Helen, illus. LC 77-2838. (Illus.). 23 p. 19cm. 1968. I. Obolensky.

--Webber Quartet, 4 Vols. Webber, Helen, illus. (gr. k-6). N.D. Set. (ISBN 0-8392-3070-2). Astor-Honor.

--What Is Sour? What Is Sweet?. A Book of Opposites. Webber, Helen, illus. LC 67-9542. 1 v. of col. illus. 29 cm. (Kin/Der owl book, KR9). 1967. Holt, Rinehart and Winston.

--Working Wheels: What Do These Wheels Do?. Webber, Helen, illus. LC 67-9544. 1 v. of illus. 29cm. (Kin Der Owl Book, KS8). 1967. Holt, Rinehart and Winston.

Webber, James Plaisted (1878-1930) & Webster, Hanson Hart (1877-), eds.

--One-Act Plays. N.D. Houghton Mifflin.

--Short Plays For Junior High Schools. 1925. Houghton Mifflin.

--Short Plays for Young People. 1925. Houghton Mifflin.
--Typical Plays for Young People. 3 p. l., 291 p. 19 1/2 cm. 1930. Houghton Mifflin Company.
Webber, Malcolm (1895-)
--Jimco and Harry at the Rocking H. Mull, Virginia, illus. LC 47-27090. 247 p. illus. 21 cm. 1947. Wilcox & Follett Co.
Weber, Alfons (1921-)
--Elizabeth Gets Well. Blass, Jacqueline, illus. LC 78-120996. (Illus.). 28 p. 1970. (ISBN 0-690-25839-9). Crowell.
Weber, Alice
--The Clock on the Stairs, 36 vols. (Illus.). (St. Nicholas Ser.). 1905. Set. A L Burt Co.
--The Clock on the Stairs. (The Rugby Series for Boys and Girls). N.D. A. L. Burt Company.
--The Clock on the Stairs. (Illus.). (The Wellesley Series for Girls). N.D. A. L. Burt.
--When I'm a Man: Or, Little Saint Christopher. (Illus.). 189p. N.D. E. P. Dutton and Co.
Weber, Ane
--In the Land of the Music Machine. Pendergrass, Mark, illus. (Illus., Orig.). (Early Readers Ser.). (gr. 1-4). 1984. (ISBN 0-89191-835-3). (ISBN 0-89191-784-5). Cook.
--Return to the Land of the Music Machine. Pendergrass, Mark, illus. (Illus.). (Early Readers Ser.). (gr. 1-4). 1984. (ISBN 0-89191-836-1). (ISBN 0-89191-785-3). Cook.
Weber, Bruce (1942-)
--The Funniest Moments in School. Callahan, Kevin, illus. LC 73-88721. (Illus.). 128p. (gr. 4 up). 1974. (ISBN 0-87131-134-8). (ISBN 0-87131-153-4). M Evans.
Weber, Carl M.
--Invitation to the Dance. Iwasaki, Chihiro (1918-1974), illus. (Pictorial Fantasia Ser). (gr. 3-6). 1969. Silver.
Weber, Judith E.
--Lights, Camera, Cats!. Porter, Patricia Grant, illus. LC 78-17083. (Illus.). 22cm. 127p. (gr. 3-7). 1978. (ISBN 0-688-41867-8). (ISBN 0-688-51867-2). Lothrop.
Weber, Kathryn (1945-)
--Midnite and Mark. Hamilton, Sandi, illus. LC 83-8622. p. cm. 1983. (ISBN 0-88100-021-3). Ranch House Press.
Weber, Lenora Mattingly, Mrs. (1895-1971)
--Angel in Heavy Shoes: A Katie Rose Story. LC 68-13589. 201 p. 21cm. 1968. T. Y. Crowell Co.
--Beany and the Beckoning Road. LC 52-7645. 243 p. 21cm. 1952. Crowell.
--Beany Has a Secret Life. LC 55-5839. 262 p. 21cm. c.1955. Crowell.
--Beany Malone. N.D. Berkley Books.
--Beany Malone. LC 48-1943. 186 p. front. 21 cm. 1948. T. Y. Crowell Co.
--A Bright Star Falls. LC 57-9242. 260 p. 21 cm. 1959. Crowell.
--A Bright Star Falls. LC 59-11398. 260 p. 21cm. 1959. Crowell.
--Come Back, Wherever You Are. LC 69-13643. 288p. (Beany Malone Ser). (gr. 7 up). 1969. (ISBN 0-690-20123-0, TYC-J). Har-Row.
--Don't Call Me Katie Rose. LC 64-13909. 302 p. 21cm. 1964. Crowell.
--The Gygsy Bridle. Wiese, Kurt (1887-1974), illus. LC 39-235493. 5 p. l., 3-275 p. incl. illus., plates. col. front. 20 1/2 cm. 1930. Little, Brown, and Company.
--Happy Birthday, Dear Beany. LC 57-9242. 244p. 21cm. 1957. Crowell.
--Happy Landing. Simon, Howard (1903-1979), illus. LC 41-5683. 4 p. l., 3-287 p. incl. illus., plates. 20 cm. 1941. Thomas Y. Crowell Company.
--Hello My Love, Goodbye. LC 77-132306. 224p. (Stacy Belford Story Ser.). (gr. 6 up). 1971. (ISBN 0-690-37697-9, TYC-J). Har-Row.
--How Long Is Always?. LC 75-101937. 226 p. 21cm. 1970. Crowell.
--I Met a Boy I Used to Know. LC 66-31715. 294 p. 21cm. 1967. Crowell.
--Leave It to Beany!. LC 50-6613. (Illus.). 239 p. 21cm. 1950. Crowell.
--Make a Wish for Me. LC 56-9735. 250 p. 21cm. 1956. Crowell.
--Meet the Malones. Howe, Gertrude Herrick (1902-), illus. LC 43-124531. 3 p. l., 218 p. illus. 21 cm. 1943. (ISBN 0-690-52999-6). Thomas Y. Crowell Company.
--The More the Merrier. LC 58-8911. 201 p. 21 cm. 1958. Crowell.
--Mr. Gold and Her Neighborhood House. 1933. Little, Brown & Co.
--My True Love Waits. LC 52-13133. 262p. 21cm. 1953. Crowell.
--A New and Different Summer. LC 66-11951. 299p. 21cm. c.1966. Crowell.
--Pick a New Dream. LC 66-10488. 245 p. 21 cm. 1961. Crowell.
--Podgy and Sally, Co-Eds. Foster, John M., illus. LC 30-236581. 314 p. incl. front. plates. 20 cm. c.1930. Barse & Co.
--Riding High. Howe, Gertrude Herrick (1902-), illus. LC 46-5237. 4 p. l. 295 p. incl. front., illus. 21 cm. 1946. Thomas Y. Crowell Company.
--Rocking Chair Ranch. Stahley, Joseph, illus. LC 36 182083. 6 p. l., 210 p. front., plates. 22 cm. 1936. Houghton Mifflin Company.
--Sing for Your Supper. MacKnight, Ninon (1908-), illus. Ninon, pseud. LC 41-20170. 4 p. l., 3-216 p. col. front., 1 illus., plates (part col.) 22 cm. 1941. Thomas Y. Crowell Company.
--Something Borrowed, Something Blue. LC 63-15098. 301 p. 21cm. 1963. Crowell.
--Sometimes a Stranger: A Stacy Belford Story. LC 74-158702. 240 p. 22cm. 1972. (ISBN 0-690-75115-X). Crowell.
--Tarry Awhile. LC 62-16550. 247 p. 21 cm. 1962. Crowell.
--Welcome, Stranger. LC 60-9162. 248 p. 21 cm. 1960. Crowell.
--Wind on the Prairie. Wiese, Kurt (1887-1974), illus. LC 29-21301. 5 p. l., 3-276 p. incl. illus., plates. col. front. 20 1/2 cm. 1929. Little, Brown, and Company.
--Winds of March. LC 65-14907. (gr. 5 up). 1965. (ISBN 0-690-89493-7). T Y Crowell.
--Wish in the Dark. Strothmann, F., illus. LC 31-29959. 6 p. l., 3-287 p. incl. illus., plates. col. front. 20 1/2 cm. 1931. Little, Brown, and Company.
Weber, Lou
--The Bird in the Cowboy Hat Freddie, the Frog, & Tillie, the Turtle. 1978. (ISBN 0-533-03363-2). Vantage.
--M for Marcie. 1st U.S. edition. 1979. (ISBN 0-533-03923-1). Vantage.
Weber, Mary Bond
--The Children of Hill Crest. Patterson, Frances, illus. LC 51-11879. (Illus.). 23cm. 92p. 1951. Exposition Press.
Weber, Sarah Stilwell
--The Musical Tree. N.D. Penn.
Webster, Albert L.
--Caleb: Or, Curious and Diverting Adventures with Friendly Animals Beyond the Hills of Night. Webster, Albert L., illus. LC 28-25020. 5 p. l., 67, 1 p. front., illus. (incl. music) plates. 20 x 23 1/2 cm. 1928. Duffield and Company.
Webster, Alice Jane Chandler see Webster, Jean, pseud.
Webster, Barbara
--Nick, Nac, Nob and Nibble. Webster, Barbara, illus. LC 30-28184. 100, 1 p. incl. front., illus., col. double plates. 23 1/2 cm. c.1930. Macrae Smith Company.
Webster, David (1930-)
--Snow Stumpers. Webster, David (1930-), illus. LC 68-22481. 95p. illus., map. 24cm. 1968. Pub. for Amer. Mus. of Natural Hist. by Natural Hist. Pr.
Webster, Don
--Annie. Webster, Don, illus. LC 45-20313. 27cm. 20p. 1945. Binfords & Mort.
--Tugboat Annie. N.D. Binfords & Mort.
Webster, Elisabeth
--The Magic Cane. 1st ed. Brevannes, Maurice (1904-), illus. LC 53-1809. unpaged. illus: 23cm. 1953. Aladdin Books.
--Red Wing's White Brother: A Real Story of a Michigan Boy and His Life with the Chippewas. LC 56-358234. 64p. 21cm. 1956. W. B. Eerdmans Pub. Co.
Webster, Ethelyn Mae Wing see Wing, Quan, pseud.
Webster, Ethelyn Mae Wing, Mrs. (1875-)
--A B C Ethics from Life's Storybook. Wing, Quan, pseud. Webster, Ethelyn Mae Wing, Mrs. (1875-), illus. LC 34-35136. v. illus. 20 cm. c.1934. The Christopher Publishing House.
Webster, Frank V., pseud., see Stratemeyer Syndicate.
Webster, Frank V., pseud.
--Airship Andy: Or, The Luck of A Brave Boy. Stratemeyer Syndicate. Richards, Dick, illus. 20cm. 201p. (The Webster Ser.: Vol. 14). 1911. Cupples & Leon Company.
--Ben Hardy's Flying Machine: Or, Making a Record for Himself. Stratemeyer Syndicate. Rogers, Walter S., illus. (The Webster Ser.: Vol. 18). N.D. Cupples & Leon.
--Bob Chester's Grit: Or, From Ranch to Riches. Stratemeyer Syndicate. Repr. of 1911 ed (Pub. by Cupples & Leon Co). (The Webster Ser.: Vol. 13). 1938. Saalfield Publishing Co.
--Bob Chester's Grit: Or, From Ranch to Riches. Stratemeyer Syndicate. Richards, Dick, illus. (The Webster Ser.: Vol. 13). 1911. Cupples & Leon Company.
--Bob the Castaway: Or, The Wreck of the Eagle. Stratemeyer Syndicate. Repr. of 1909 ed (Pub. by Cupples & Leon Co). (The Webster Ser.: Vol. 5). 1938. Saalfield Publishing Co.
--Bob the Castaway: Or, The Wreck of the Eagle. Stratemeyer Syndicate. Nuttall, Charles, illus. 20cm. 203p. (The Webster Ser.: Vol. 5). 1909. Cupples & Leon Company.
--The Boy from the Ranch: Or, Roy Bradner's City Experiences. Stratemeyer Syndicate. Nuttall, Charles, illus. LC 9-24452. 2 p. l., 200 p. front., plates 19 1/2 cm. $0.3. (The Webster Ser.: Vol. 3). 1909. Cupples & Leon Company.
--The Boy Pilot of the Lakes: Or, Nat Morton's Perils. Stratemeyer Syndicate. Nuttall, Charles, illus. 20cm. 201p. (The Webster Ser.: Vol. 8). 1909. Cupples & Leon Company.
--The Boy Scouts of Lenox: Or, The Hike Over Big Bear Mountain. Stratemeyer Syndicate. Rogers, Walter S., illus. LC 43-28878. 2 p. l., 212 p. 19 1/2 cm. (The Webster Ser.: Vol. 21). 1915. Cupples & Leon Company.
--The Boys of Bellwood School: Or, Frank Jordan's Triumph. Stratemeyer Syndicate. Repr. of 1910 ed (Pub. by Cupples & Leon Co). (The Webster Ser.: Vol. 12). 1938. Saalfield Publishing Co.
--The Boys of Bellwood School: Or, Frank Jordan's Triumph. Stratemeyer Syndicate. Nuttall, Charles, illus. (The Webster Ser.: Vol. 12). 1910. Cupples & Leon Company.
--The Boys of the Wireless: Or, A Stirring Rescue from the Deep. Stratemeyer Syndicate. Repr. of 1912 ed (Pub. by Cupples & Leon Co). (The Webster Ser.: Vol. 19). 1938. Saalfield Publishing Co.
--The Boys of the Wireless: Or, A Stirring Rescue from the Deep. Stratemeyer Syndicate. Rogers, Walter S., illus. LC 12-185079. 2 p. l., 202 p. front., plates. 19 1/2 cm. (The Webster Ser.: Vol. 19). c.1912. Cupples & Leon Company.
--Comrades of the Saddle: Or, The Young Rough Riders of the Plains. Stratemeyer Syndicate. Repr. of 1910 ed (Pub. by Cupples & Leon Co). (The Webster Ser.: Vol. 11). 1938. Saalfield Publishing Co.
Comrades of the Saddle. Or, The Young Rough Riders of the Plains. Stratemeyer Syndicate. Nuttall, Charles, illus. (The Webster Ser.: Vol. 11). 1910. Cupples & Leon.
--Cowboy Dave: Or, The Round Up at Rolling River. Stratemeyer Syndicate. Repr. of 1915 ed (Pub. by Cupples & Leon Co). (The Webster Ser.: Vol. 23). 1938. Saalfield Publishing Co.
--Cowboy Dave: Or, The Round Up at Rolling River. Stratemeyer Syndicate. Rogers, Walter S., illus. (The Webster Ser.: Vol. 23). 1915. Cupples & Leon Company.
--Darry the Life Saver: Or, The Heroes of the Coast. Stratemeyer Syndicate. Repr. of 1911 ed (Pub. by Cupples & Leon Co). (The Webster Ser.: Vol. 16). 1938. Saalfield Publishing Co.
--Darry the Life Saver: Or, the Heroes of the Coast. Stratemeyer Syndicate. Boehm, H. Richard, illus. (The Webster Ser.: Vol. 16). 1911. Cupples & Leon Company.
--Dick the Bank Boy: Or, The Missing Fortune. Stratemeyer Syndicate. Boehm, H. Richard, illus. (The Webster Ser.: Vol. 17). 1911. Cupples & Leon Company.
--Harry Watson's High School Days: Or, The Rivals of Rivertown. Stratemeyer Syndicate. Rogers, Walter S., illus. LC 12-180597. 2 p. l., 200 p. front., plates. 19 1/2 cm. $0.4. (The Webster Ser.: Vol. 20). 1912. Cupples & Leon Company.
--The High School Rivals: Or, Fred Markham's Struggles. Stratemeyer Syndicate. Richards, Dick, illus. (The Webster Ser.: Vol. 15). N.D. Cupples & Leon Company.
--Jack of the Pony Express: Or, The Young Rider of the Mountain Trails. Stratemeyer Syndicate. Repr. of 1915 ed (Pub. by Cupples & Leon Co). (The Webster Ser.: Vol. 25). 1938. Saalfield Publishing Co.
--Jack of the Pony Express: Or, The Young Rider of the Mountain Trails. Stratemeyer Syndicate. Rogers, Walter S., illus. (The Webster Ser.: Vol. 25). 1915. Cupples & Leon Company.
--Jack the Runaway: Or, On the Road with a Circus. Stratemeyer Syndicate. Repr. of 1909 ed (Pub. by Cupples & Leon Co). (The Webster Ser.: Vol. 10). 1938. Saalfield Publishing Co.
--Jack the Runaway: Or, On the Road with a Circus. Stratemeyer Syndicate. Nuttall, Charles, illus. LC 9-24453. 2 p. l., 201 p. front., plates. 19 1/2 cm. $0.3. (The Webster Ser.: Vol. 10). 1909. Cupples & Leon Company.
--The Newsboy Partners: Or, Who Was Dick Box. Stratemeyer Syndicate. Nuttall, Charles, illus. 20cm. 203p. (The Webster Ser.: Vol. 7). 1909. Cupples & Leon Company.
--Only a Farm Boy: Or, Dan Hardy's Rise in Life. Stratemeyer Syndicate. Nuttall, Charles, illus. LC 9-18438. 20cm. 200p. (The Webster Ser.: Vol. 1). 1909. Cupples & Leon Company.
--Tom Taylor at West Point: Or, The Old Army Officer's Secret. Stratemeyer Syndicate. Rogers, Walter S., illus. (The Webster Ser.: Vol. 22). 1915. Cupples & Leon Company.
--Tom the Telephone Boy: Or, The Mystery of a Message. Stratemeyer Syndicate. Nuttall, Charles, illus. 2 p. l., 204 p. front., plates. 19 1/2 cm. $0.3. (The Webster Ser.: Vol. 2). 1909. Cupples & Leon Company.
--Two Boy Gold Miners: Or, Lost in the Mountains. Stratemeyer Syndicate. Repr. of 1909 ed (Pub. by Cupples & Leon Co). (The Webster Ser.: Vol. 9). 1938. Saalfield Publishing Co.
--Two Boy Gold Miners: Or, Lost in the Mountains. Stratemeyer Syndicate. Nuttall, Charles, illus. (The Webster Ser.: Vol. 9). 1909. Cupples & Leon Company.
--Two Boys of the Battleship: Or, For the Honor of Uncle Sam. Stratemeyer Syndicate. Rogers, Walter S., illus. (The Webster Ser.: Vol. 24). N.D. Cupples & Leon Company.
--The Young Firemen of Lakeville: Or, Herbert Dare's Pluck. Stratemeyer Syndicate. Repr. of 1909 ed (Pub. by Cupples & Leon Co). (The Webster Ser.: Vol. 6). 1938. Saalfield Publishing Co.
--The Young Firemen of Lakeville: Or, Herbert Dare's Pluck. Stratemeyer Syndicate. Nuttall, Charles, illus. 2 p. l., 204 p. front., plates. 19 1/2 cm. (The Webster Ser.: Vol. 6). 1909. Cupples & Leon Company.
--The Young Treasure Hunter: Or, Fred Stanley's Trip to Alaska. Stratemeyer Syndicate. Repr. of 1909 ed (Pub. by Cupples & Leon Co). (The Webster Ser.: Vol. 4). 1938. Saalfield Publishing Co.
--The Young Treasure Hunter: Or, Fred Stanley's Trip to Alaska. Stratemeyer Syndicate. Nuttall, Charles, illus. LC 9-20666. 20cm. 204p. (The Webster Ser.: Vol. 4). 1909. Cupples & Leon Company.
Webster, Frederick Amesley Michael (1886-)
--The Boy from the Blue. (The Treasure Library). N.D. Frederick Warne & Co.
--Holding Their Own. N.D. Frederick Warne & Co.
--The Ivory Talisman. (The Treasure Library). N.D. Frederick Warne & Co.
--Lost City of Light. N.D. Frederick Warne & Co.
Webster, H. T. & Calhoun, Philo
--Who Dealt this Mess?. Goren, Charles H., frwd. by. N.D. Doubleday & Co.
Webster, Hanson Hart, jt. ed. see Webber, James Plaisted.
Webster, Henry Kitchell see Webster, Kitchell, pseud.
Webster, J. Provand
--The Oracle of Baal: A Narrative of Some Curious Events in the Life of Professor Horatio Carmichael. Goble, Warwick, illus. 1900. J B Lippincott.
Webster, Jean, pseud., see Webster, Alice Jane Chandler.
Webster, Jean, pseud. (1876-1916)
--Daddy-Long-Legs. Webster, Alice Jane Chandler. (Illus.). ca. 250p. (Thrushwood Bks.). (gr. 5-11). 1969. (ISBN 0-448-02520-5) G&D.
--Daddy-Long-Legs. Webster, Alice Jane Chandler. Ardizzone, Edward Jeffrey Irving (1900-1979), illus. LC 67-30959. 192p. (gr. 4-8). 1967. (ISBN 0-8015-1890-3). Hawthorn.
--Daddy-Long-Legs. Webster, Alice Jane Chandler. Carter, Roy Cecil, ed. 1937. Appleton Century Co.
--Dear Enemy. Webster, Alice Jane Chandler. Webster, Jean, pseud. (1876-1916), illus. Webster, Alice Jane Chandler. Flowers, Ann A., intro. by. LC 79-18128. p. cm. (Gregg Press Children's Literature Series). 1979, c.1915. Gregg Press.
Webster, Joanne
--Gypsy Gift. LC 81-20823. p. cm. 1982, c.1981. (ISBN 0-525-66763-6). Lodestar Books.
--The Love Genie. 125 p. 21cm. 1980, c.1978. Elsevier-Nelson Books.
Webster, Joe, pseud., see Waldman, Frank.
Webster, Joe, pseud. (1919-)
--Rookie from Junction Flats. Waldman, Frank. Hartman, C. L., illus. 160p. 1952. Farrar, Straus and Cudahy, Inc.
Webster, Kitchell, pseud., see Webster, Henry Kitchell.
Webster, Kitchell, Jr., pseud.
--Pass in Review: The Story of a Culver Cadet. Webster, Henry Kitchell. LC 35-2336. 287 p. front., plates. 20 1/2 cm. c.1935. The Bobbs-Merrill Company.
Webster, Lawrence, jt. ed. see Moore, Lilian.
Webster, Leigh
--Another Girl's Experience: A Story for Girls. McDermott, Jessie, illus. N.D. Robert Brothrers Publication.
--Rich Enough. Pitman, Elizabeth S., illus. 3 p. l., 5-242 p. front., 4 pl. 19 cm. 1897. Roberts Brothers.
Webster, Marion Aldrich
--Jangled Bells: A Story of Puerto Rico. LC 50-58105. 152 p. 21 cm. 1950. Christopher.
Webster, Mary C
--The Wonderful Christmas Tree!. A Story in Rhyme. 4 p. l., 11-95 p. front., illus. 17 1/2 cm. 1882. American Publishing Company.
Webster, Paul Francis, jt. auth. see Churchill, Frank E.
Webster, Polly
--My Private Life. (Illus.). (gr. 6-10). N.D. (ISBN 0-8313-0104-X). Lantern.

Webster, Samuel Charles
--The King Gives a Party. Webster, Samuel Charles, illus. LC 47-30680. 110 p. illus. 22 cm. 1947. H. Holt.
Wechsberg, Joseph (1907-)
--The Pantheon Story of Music for Young People. LC 67-20221. (Illus.). 144 p. 29cm. 1968. Pantheon Books.
Wechter, Nell Wise (1913-)
--Betsy Dowdy's Ride. LC 60-15718. 173 p. 20 cm. 1960. J. F. Balir.
--Swamp Girl. Faries, Patsy, illus. LC 79-156456. (Illus.). 214 p. 21cm. 1971. (ISBN 0-910244-59-6). J. F. Blair.
--Taffy of Torpedo Junction. Sparks, Mary Walker, illus. LC 57-9312. (Illus.). 21cm. 134p. N.D. J. F. Blair.
--Teach's Light. Tucker, Bruce, illus. LC 74-75753. (Illus.). xiii, 144 p. 21cm. 1974. (ISBN 0-910244-78-2). J. F. Blair.
Weddle, Ethel Harshbarger (1897-)
--Alvin C. York, Young Marksman. Goldstein, Nathan (1927-), illus. LC 67-26334. (Illus.). 200 p. 20cm. (Childhood of Famous Americans). 1967. Bobbs-Merrill.
--Walter Chrysler: Boy Machinist. Fiorentino, Al, illus. LC 60-8883. 192 p. illus. 20 cm. (Childhood of Famous Americans). 1960. Bobbs-Merrill.
Weddle, Ferris (1922-)
--Blazing Mountain. Micale, Albert (1913-), illus. LC 61-5082. 119 p. illus. 21 cm. 1961. Watts.
--Blizzard Rescue. Savitt, Sam (1917-), illus. LC 59-114830. 117 p. illus. 21 cm. 1959. Watts.
--Tall Like a Pine. Irvin, Fred M. (1914-), illus. LC 74-17072. (Illus.). 126 p. 22cm. (Leader Book). 1974. (ISBN 0-8075-7757-X). A. Whitman.
--Wilderness Renegades. Savitt, Sam (1917-), illus. LC 62-744620. 161 p. illus. 21 cm. 1962. F. Watts.
Wedekind, Frank
--Princess Russalka. N.D. (ISBN 0-8283-1420-9). Branden Press.
Wedel, Lois
--Pioneer Tales of a Great City. LC 45-12229. 64 p. 18 mc. 1944. The Wartburg Press.
Wedgwood, Henry Allen (1799-1885) & Raverat, Gwendolen Mary Darwin (1885-1957)
--The Bird Talisman: An Eastern Tale. LC 65-9027. v, 69p. illus. (pt. col.) 22cm. 1965. Van Nostrand.
Wee Wisdom Editors
--Bedtime Favorites from Wee Wisdom. Wee Wisdom Editors, illus. (ps-3). 1964. Unity Bks.
--Young Adventurers. Wee Wisdom Editors, illus. LC 66-8320. 255p. illus. 20cm. 1966. Unity Bks.
Weechees
--Cou-Yan-Nai: Comanchee Indian Story for Children. 32p. (gr. 4-9). 1983. (ISBN 0-686-44422-1). MT Coun Indian.
Weed, Clarence Moores (1864-) & Weed, Margaret Aber
--Over and Over Stories, New and Old. LC 29-13474. (Illus.). 20cm. 1929. J. B. Lippincott.
Weed, Margaret Aber, jt. auth. see Weed, Clarence Moores.
Weedon, L. L., jt. auth. see Bland, Edith Nesbit, Mrs.
Weedon, L. L., tr. see Grimm, Jakob Ludwig Karl (1785-1863) & Grimm, Wilhelm Karl.
Weedon, Lucy L., retold by.
--Bible Stories. N.D. E P Dutton.
--Children's Guest: Or, The Trial of Paul's Faith. (Illus.). N.D. E. P. Dutton.
--Fairy Tales from Grimm, 1 of 4 Vols. Hardy, E. Stuart, illus. (Little People's Story Box). N.D. Dodge.
--Fairy Tales from Grimm, 1 of 4 vols. Hardy, E. Stuart, illus. (Little People's Story Box). N.D. Dutton.
--Lamb Tales, 1 of 4 Vols. (Little People's Natural History Box). N.D. Dodge.
--Lamb Tales, 1 of 4 Vols. (Little People's Natural History Box). N.D. Dutton.
--Nursery Tales, 1 of 4 vols. Hardy, E. Stuart, illus. (Little People's Story Box). N.D. Dutton.
--Story of Joseph and His Brethren. N.D. E. P. Dutton & Co.
Weedon, Lucy L. & Fletcher, Evelyn
--All Round the Farm. N.D. E. P. Dutton & Co.
Weekes, Blanche E., ed. see De la Ramee, Marie Louise.
Weekes, Blanche E, ed. see Kingsley, Charles.
Weekes, Blanche Ethel, ed. see Aesopus.
Weekes, Blanche Ethel, intro. by see Ewing, Juliana Horatia Gatty, Mrs.
Weekes, Blanche Ethel, intro. by see Stevenson, Robert Louis.
Weekes, Mary, Mrs.
--Painted Arrows. Lowell, Orson (1871-), illus. LC 41-2094. 1 p. l., v-ix, 262 p. illus. (incl. music) 22 1/2 cm. 1941. T. Nelson & Sons.
Weeks, Alyn Dawson
--Lin and the Awakening Tiger. LC 56-5821. 68 p. 21 cm. 1956. Vantage Press.
Weeks, Annie Florence (1882-), compiled by.
--The World Friendship Room. Weeks, Annie Florence (1882-), illus. LC 40-5746. 83 p. incl. front., illus., diagrs. 19 cm. c.1939. Broadman Press.
Weeks, Arland Deyett (1871-)
--Children of the Pines. LC 74-191578. (Illus.). 302 p. 20cm. c.1926. Lyons and Carnahan.
--Play Days on Plum Blossom Creek. Carr, Warner, illus. N.D. Rand McNally.
--Squaw Point. LC 19-16143. 4 p. l., 238 p. front., plates. 19 1/2 cm. 1919. H. Holt and Company.
Weeks, Helen C., pseud., see Campbell, Helen Stuart.
Weeks, Helen C., pseud. (1839-)
--Grandpa's House. Campbell, Helen Stuart. (The Ainslee Ser. for Young People). N.D. Hurd & Houghton.
--White and Red. Campbell, Helen Stuart. (The Ainslee Ser. for Young People). N.D. Hurd & Houghton.
Weeks, Jack
--The Hard Way. LC 53-8303. 192p. 21cm. (Barnes sports novels). 1953. A. S. Barnes.
--The Take-Charge Guy. LC 55-5104. 192 p. 20cm. (Barnes sports novel). 1955. Barnes.
Weeks, Morris, Jr.
--Inside the Zoo. Faulkner, Douglas & Williamson, Franklin, photos by Ulmer, Frederick A., intro. by. LC 70-101894. (Illus.). (gr. 3 up). 1970. (ISBN 0-671-65116-1, Juveniles). S&S.
Weeks, Nan F
--Chopstick Children. Saunders, Mary Leslie, illus. LC 48-9589. 46 p. illus. 19 x 25 cm. 1948. Broadman Press.
--Little Black Sunday. N.D. Broadman Press.
--Neighbors We'd Like to Know. N.D. Broadman Press.
--The Topsy Tursy Twins. N.D. Broadman Press.
Weeks, Nan F., jt. auth. see Pruitt, Anna Seward.
Weeks, Ramona see Maher, Ramona.
Weeks, Ramona (1934-)
--The Blind Boy and the Loon, and Other Eskimo Myths. LC 69-14859. (Illus.). 158 p. 24cm. 1969. John Day Co.
--The Glory Horse: A Story of the Battle of San Jacinto, and Texas in 1836. Gammell, Stephen, illus. LC 74-79699. (Illus.). 61 p. 27cm. c.1974. (ISBN 0-698-20294-5). Coward, McCann & Geoghegan.
--Mystery of the Stolen Fish Pond. LC 78-91274. 210 p. 21cm. 1969. Dodd, Mead.
--When Windwagon Smith Came to Westport. Maher, Ramona, pseud. Allen, Thomas Burt (1928-), illus. LC 77-442. 26cm. 48p. 1977. (ISBN 0-698-20407-7). Coward, McCann & Geoghegan.
Weeks, Rupert (1918-)
--Pachee Goyo: History and Legends from the Shoshone. Weeks, Rupert (1918-) & Weeks, Violet, illus. Bean, Greg & Fleck, Richard, photos by LC 82-41. (Illus.). xvii, 110 p. 21cm. c.1981. (ISBN 0-936204-16-8). Jelm Mountain Press.
Weeks, Sara
--Tales of a Common Pigeon. Von Schmidt, Eric (1931-), illus. LC 59-7477. 121 p. illus. 22 cm. 1960. Houghton Mifflin.
Weelen, Guy
--The Little Red Train. Funai, Mamoru R. (1932-), illus. LC 66-13216. (Illus.). 26cm. 1966. Lee and Shepard.
--The Little Red Train. Funai, Mamoru R. (1932-), illus. LC 66-13216. 1 v. (unpaged) col. illus. 26cm. c.1966. Lothrop.
Weems, jt. auth. see Horry.
Weems, John Edward, Jr. (1924-)
--Death Song: The Last of the Indian Wars. LC 74-33668. (Illus.). bibl. index. 336p. 1976. (ISBN 0-385-00728-0). Doubleday.
Weems, John Edward, Jr. (1924-), ed.
--A Texas Christmas. Cisneros, Jose & Whitehead, Barbara, illus. (Illus.). 169p. 1983. (ISBN 0-939722-19-4). Pressworks.
Wees, Frances Shelley (1902-)
--Mystery in Newfoundland. Bisset, Douglas, illus. LC 65-22823. 158p. illus. 22cm. 1965. Abelard.
--Mystery in Newfoundland. Bisset, Douglas, illus. (Illus.). (gr. 5-8). 1965. (ISBN 0-8382-0570-4). Hale.
--The Treasure of Echo Valley. Linton, Anne, illus. LC 64-23028. 159 p. illus. 21 cm. 1964. Abelard-Schuman.
Weese, Thomas Eugene de see DeWeese, Gene.
Weesner, Henriette Arnold
--Words and Pictures: A Book for Children. 1st ed. Otteson, Madalene, illus. LC 55-7290. (Illus.). 21cm. 56p. 1955. Exposition Press.
Wefer, Marion
--The Door Opens: Everybody Welcome!. 1952. Friendship Press.
Wegefarth, William Dayton (1885-)
--The True Story of "Bum". Clement, W. N., illus. LC 15-24875. 3-44. 17cm. 1915. Sully and Kleinteich.
Wegen, Ronald
--Balloon Trip. Wegen, Ronald, illus. LC 80-25902. p. cm. c.1981. (ISBN 0-395-30370-2). Houghton Mifflin/Clarion Books.
--Billy Gorilla. 1st ed. Wegen, Ronald, illus. LC 82-17934. (Illus.). 32 p. 26cm. c.1983. (ISBN 0-688-01985-4). (ISBN 0-688-01986-2). Lothrop, Lee & Shepard Books.
--The Halloween Costume Party. Wegen, Ronald, illus. LC 83-2069. 32p. (gr. k-3). 1983. (ISBN 0-89919-184-3, Clarion). HM.
--Sand Castle. Wegen, Ronald, illus. LC 75-30707. 32p. (gr. k-3). 1977. (ISBN 0-688-80033-5). (ISBN 0-688-84033-7). Greenwillow.
--Sky Dragon. Wegen, Ronald, illus. LC 81-7219. p. cm. c.1982. (ISBN 0-688-01144-6). (ISBN 0-688-01146-2). Greenwillow Books.
--What's Wrong, Ralph?. Wegen, Ronald, illus. LC 83-19933. p. cm. c.1984. (ISBN 0-688-02706-7). Lothrop, Lee & Shepard Books.
Wehen, Joy De Weese (1926-)
--The Silver Cricket. LC 66-14954. 184p. 21cm. c.1966. Duell Dist. Meredith.
--So Far from Malabar. LC 70-102422. x, 180 p. 22cm. 1970. Hawthorn Books.
--Stairway to a Secret. Genia, pseud. (1930-), illus. Wennerstrom, Genia Katherine. LC 53-6087. (Illus.). 220 p. 21cm. 1953. Dutton.
--Stranger at Golden Hill. LC 61-6912. 182 p. 21 cm. 1961. Duell, Sloan and Pearce.
--The Tower in the Sky. 1st. LC 55-8322. 192p. 22cm. 1955. Dutton.
Wehnert, Edward H. & Watson, J. D., illus.
--Grimm's Fairy Tales, Andersen's fairy Tales, and the Arabian Nights, 1 Vol. (Young People's Library). N.D. George Routledge & Sons.
Wehr, Julian, illus.
--Animated Nursery Tales. LC 62-52254. unpaged. illus. 27 cm. 1962. McLoughlin Bros.
--Noah's Ark. N.D. Grosset & Dunlap.
--Nursery Tales. 27cm. 24p. (Animated Book Ser). (ps). 1943. G&D.
--Puss in Boots. LC 45-1391. (Illus.). 18p. 22 x 17cm. 1944. Duenewald Printing Corp.
--Snow White and the Seven Dwarfs. LC 49-13597. (Illus.). 22cm. 22p. 1949. Duenwald Print Corp.
Wehren, Kate
--Penny's Bargain Horse. LC 54-7540. 1954. Dodd Mead & Co.
--Poconada. Schule, Clifford H., illus. LC 63-19671. (Illus.). 22cm. 180p. 1963. Macrae Smith Co.
Weidling, Carl Philip (1905-)
--Secret of the Old Bridge. Liberovsky, Paul, illus. LC 63-10492. 149 p. illus. 21 cm. 1963. D. McKay Co.
--The Secret of the Old Bridge. Liberovsky, Paul, illus. 150p. 1963. (ISBN 0-87482-044-8). Wake Brook House.
Weigall, Constance E. C.
--The Red Light. Patterson, Malcolm, illus. (Illus.). N.D. Cassell & Co.
--Stories for Sunday Afternoons (Pub. by Society for Promoting Christian Knowledge). N.D. E. & J. B. Young & Co.
Weigl, Vally
--Songs for a Child. Ninon, pseud. (1908-), illus. MacKnight, Ninon. LC 62-15408. 64p. col. illus. 29cm. c.1962. Westminster.
Weigle, Oscar, adapted by.
--Good Night Fairy Tales. N.D (Wonder Books). Grosset & Dunlap.
--Great Big Joke & Riddle Book. Bonsall, Crosby Barbara Newell (1921-) & Huehnergarth, John, illus. Bonsall, Crosby, pseud. LC 79-129734. (Illus.). 224p. (gr. 1-5). 1981. (ISBN 0-448-02584-1, G&D). (ISBN 0-448-03167-1). Putnam Pub Group.
--The Joke Book. Rutherford, Bill & Rutherford, Bonnie, illus. LC 63-2101. 60 p. illus. 29 cm. 1963. Grosset & Dunlap.
--Jokes & Riddles. Zemsky, Jessica, illus. (Illus.). 128p. (Elephant Activity Bks.). (gr. k-3). 1975. (ISBN 0-448-11884-X, G&D). Putnam Pub Group.
--Jokes, Riddles and Funny Stories. Wilson, Dagmar (1916-), illus. N.D. Grosset & Dunlap.
--Jokes, Riddles, Funny Stories. Bonsall, Crosby Barbara Newell (1921-), illus. LC 59-16408. 105 p. illus. 28 cm. 1959. Grosset & Dunlap.
--The Riddle Book. Huehnergarth, John, illus. LC 67-23804. (Illus.). 45 p. 29cm. 1967. Grosset & Dunlap.
--Short Tales for Sleepyheads. LC 78-54177. (Illus.). (Elephant Books Ser.). (gr. k-3). N.D. (ISBN 0-448-16165-6, G&D). Putnam Pub Group.
--Songs to Sing and Play. Wood, Ruth, illus. (Illus.). unpaged. 21cm. (Wonder bks.: No. 753). c.1960. Wonder Books, Dist. by Grosset.
--The Story of Noah's Ark. Seiden, Art, illus. LC 57-3487. unpaged. illus. 31cm. c.1957. Grosset & Dunlap.
--A Treasury of Bedtime Stories. Dauber, Elizabeth, illus. LC 69-17269. (Illus.). 154 p. 28cm. 1969. Grosset & Dunlap.
--A Treasury of Mother Goose. Berson, Harold (1926-), illus. LC 67-23808. (Illus.). 41 p. 29cm. 1967. Grosset & Dunlap.
Weigle, Oscar, jt. auth. see Lupatelli, Anthony.
Weigle, Oscar, jt. ed. see Farquhar, Margaret Cutting.
Weigle, Oscar, ed. see O'Brien, John Sherman.
Weigle, Oscar & Tallarico, Anthony, eds.
--Disney's World of Riddles. Disney, Walt, Productions, illus. LC 78-71307. (Illus.). 64 p. 29cm. c.1979. (ISBN 0-448-16827-8). Grosset & Dunlap.
Weiher, Joan
--Rush to the Rockies with Sam and Sal. LC 59-11062. unpaged. illus. 22 cm. 1959. Sage Books.
Weihs, Erika (1917-)
--Count the Cats. Weihs, Erika (1917-), illus. LC 75-27321. 24p. (ps-1). 1976. Doubleday.
Weihs, Erika (1917-), illus.
--The Rolling Pancake and Other Nusery Tales. N.D. L. B. Fisher.
Weik, Mary Hays (1898-1979)
--The House at Cherry Hill. Bobri, V., pseud. (1898-), illus. Bobritsky, Vladimir V.. LC 38-32609. 5 p. l., 3-135 p. illus. 21 cm. 1938. A. A. Knopf.
--A House on Liberty Street. Grifalconi, Ann (1929-), illus. LC 72-86950. (Illus.). 69 p. 21cm. 1973, c.1972. Atheneum.
--The Jazz Man. Grifalconi, Ann (1929-), illus. LC 66-5715. 42p. illus. 24cm. c.1966. (ISBN 0-689-30021-2). Atheneum. **Awards: (NYT); (ALA); (JNM).**
--The Jazz Man. Grifalconi, Ann (1929-), illus. LC 66-10417. (Illus.). 1977. (ISBN 0-689-70432-1, Aladdin). Atheneum.
--Scarlet Thread. Remington, Barbara, illus. LC 68-18462. (Illus.). 112p. (gr. 6 up). 1968. (ISBN 0-689-20463-9). (ISBN 0-689-20464-7). Atheneum.
Weikel, Anna Hamlin
--Betty Baird. Brown, Ethel Pennewill, illus. LC 6-29775. 4 p. l., 279 p. front., 3 pl. 20 cm. 1906. Little, Brown, and Company.
--Betty Baird's Golden Year. Brown, Ethel Pennewill, illus. LC 9-25810. vi p., 1 l., 306 p., 1 l. front., 3 pl. 20 cm. (Her Betty Baird series) $1.50). 1909. Little, Brown, and Company.
--Betty Baird's Ventures. Brown, Ethel Pennewill, illus. LC 7-31479. viii p., 1 l., 328 p., 1 l. front., 3 pl. 20 cm. 1907. Little, Brown, and Company.
Weil, Ann Yezner, Mrs. (1908-1969)
--Betsy Ross: Girl of Old Philadelphia. Fiorentino, Al, illus. LC 60-77242. 200 p. illus. 20 cm. (Childhood of famous Americans). 1961. Bobbs-Merrill.
--Betsy Ross, Girl of Old Philadelphia. 1st ed. James, Sandra, illus. LC 54-6067. (Illus.). 20cm. 192p. (The Childhood of Famous Americans Ser.). 1954. Bobbs-Merrill.
--Eleanor Roosevelt: Courageous Girl. Morrow, Gray, illus. LC 65-14814. 200 p. illus. 20 cm. (Childhood of Famous Americans). 1965. Bobbs-Merrill.
--Franklin Roosevelt, Boy of the Four Freedoms. Browne, Syd, illus. LC 47-2099. 200 p. illus. 20 cm. (The Childhood of famous Americans series). 1947. The Bobbs-Merrill Company.
--John Quincy Adams: Boy Patriot. Moyers, William (1916-), illus. LC 62-16623. 200 p. illus. 20 cm. (Childhood of famous Americans). 1963. Bobbs-Merrill.
--My Dear Patsy: A Novel of Jefferson's Daughter. Robinson, Jessie Berkowitz, illus. LC 41-16482. 315 p. incl. front., illus. 20 1/2 cm. c.1941. The Bobbs-Merrill Company.
--Pussycat's Breakfast. Barton, Mary, illus. LC 45-904. 47 p. illus. (part col.) 16 x 24 cm. 1944. Greenberg.
--Red Sails to Capri. Falls, Charles Buckles (1874-1960), illus. LC 52-12816. (Illus.). 156 p. 22cm. 1952. Viking Press. **Award: (JNM).**
--The Silver Fawn. 1st ed. Leon, E., illus. LC 39-21291. 5 p. l., 9-228 p. illus. (1 col.) 22 1/2 cm. c.1939. The Bobbs-Merrill Company.
--The Very First Day. Robinson, Jessie Berkowitz, illus. LC 46-1783. 32 p. incl. col. front., illus. (part col.) 21 cm. 1946. D. Appleton-Century Company, Incorporated.
Weil, Ann (1908-)
--Franklin Roosevelt, Boy of the Four Freedoms. Doremus, Robert (1913-), illus. LC 62-12690. (Illus.). 20cm. 300p. (Childhood of Famous Americans). 1962. Bobbs-Merrill.
Weil, Lisl (1910-), retold by see Respighi, Ottorino.
Weil, Lisl (1910-), adapted by see Shakespeare, William.
Weil, Lisl (1910-)
--Bill the Brave. Weil, Lisl (1910-), illus. LC 48-5721. 32 p. col. illus. 24 cm. 1948. Houghton Mifflin Co.

--The Edge of Fear. Konsterlie, Paul, illus. LC 74-859. (Illus.). 31 p. 23cm. (Her Laurie Newman adventures). 1974. (ISBN 0-87191-338-0). Creative Education; Distributed by Childrens Press, Chicago.
--The Horse Flambeau. Konsterlie, Paul, illus. LC 74-860. (Illus.). 31 p. 23cm. (Her Laurie Newman adventures). 1974. (ISBN 0-87191-335-6). Creative Education; Distributed by Childrens Press, Chicago.
--Howdy!. Hoey, William (1930-), illus. LC 77-176066. (Illus.). 32 p. 1972. (ISBN 0-8114-7735-5). Steck-Vaughn Co.
--Laurie Loves a Horse. Konsterlie, Paul, illus. LC 74-643. (Illus.). 29 p. 23cm. (Her Laurie Newman adventures). 1974. (ISBN 0-87191-352-6). Creative Education; Distributed by Childrens Press, Chicago.
--Little Pup. Rogers, Carol, illus. LC 77-76603. (Illus.). 32 p. 24cm. 1969. Steck-Vaughn Co.
--A Long Distance. Konsterlie, Paul, illus. LC 74-971. (Illus.). 29 p. 23cm. (Her Laurie Newman adventures). 1974. (ISBN 0-87191-333-X). Creative Education; Distributed by Childrens Press, Chicago.
--Men!. Konsterlie, Paul, illus. LC 74-974. (Illus.). 29 p. 23cm. (Her Laurie Newman adventures). 1974. (ISBN 0-87191-336-4). Creative Education; Distributed by Childrens Press, Chicago.
--The New Girl. Konsterlie, Paul, illus. LC 74-824. (Illus.). 31 p. 23cm. (Her Laurie Newman adventures). 1974. (ISBN 0-87191-351-8). Creative Education; Distributed by Childrens Press, Chicago.

Weir, LaVada & Weir, Joan
--Hic Away Henry. Rogers, Carol, illus. (Illus.). 24cm. 32p. (gr. k-2). 1967. (ISBN 0-8114-7527-1). Steck-V.

Weir, Marion Eliza
--Gerald & His Friend Philip, 1 of 25 vols. (Illus.). (Selected Bks for Sunday School: No. 21). N.D. Set. Methodist Bk Concern.
--Rockbourne, 1 of 103 vols. (The Pearl Library: No. 80). 1900. Set. Hurst & Co.

Weir, Mitchell Silas (1829-1914)
--Mr. Kris Kringle. N.D. George W Jacobs.
--Prince Little Boy. 160p. N.D. The Century Co.

Weir, Rosemary Green (1905-)
--Albert & the Dragonettes. Blake, Quentin (1932-), illus. (gr. 3-6). 1977. (ISBN 0-8277-5398-5). (ISBN 0-8277-5397-7). British Bk Ctr.
--Albert the Dragon. Blake, Quentin (1932-), illus. LC 60-12631. 107 p. illus. 21 cm. 1961. Abelard-Schuman.
--Albert the Dragon and the Centaur. Blake, Quentin (1932-), illus. LC 68-14297. (Illus.). 124 p. 22cm. 1968. (ISBN 0-200-71522-4). Abelard-Schuman.
--Blood Royal. Cuffari, Richard (1925-1978), illus. LC 73-75177. (Illus.). 167 p. 21cm. 1973. (ISBN 0-374-30845-4). Farrar, Straus and Giroux.
--The Boy from Nowhere. (gr. 4-6). 1973 (Starline). Schol Bk Serv.
--The Boy from Nowhere. Turner, Dennis, illus. LC 66-73398. 157p. 2llus. 23cm. 1966. Abelard.
--Boy on a Brown Horse. LC 71-136254. 156 p. 22cm. 1971, c.1967. Hawthorn Books.
--Further Adventures of Albert the Dragon. Blake, Quentin (1932-), illus. LC 64-12741. 127 p. illus. 21 cm. 1964. Abelard-Schuman.
--The Heirs of Ashton Manor. LC 66-128376. 150p. front. 22cm. 1966, c.1965. Dial.
--High Courage. Ribbons, Ian (1924-), illus. LC 67-19881. (Illus.). 185 p. 22cm. (Ariel book). 1967. Farrar, Straus & Giroux.
--The Lion and the Rose. LC 73-125152. (Illus.). 167 p. 21cm. (Ariel book). 1970. Farrar, Straus & Giroux.
--Mike's Gang. Pickard, Charles, illus. LC 65-14718. 127 p. illus. 21 cm. 1965. Abelard-Schuman.
--Mystery of the Black Sheep. Ilsley, Velma Elizabeth (1918-), illus. LC 64-14811. 142 p. illus. 21 cm. 1st U.S. edition. 1964, c.1963. Criterion Books.
--No Sleep for Angus. Grant, Elisabeth, illus. LC 71-99510. (Illus.). 144 p. 22cm. 1969. (ISBN 0-200-71627-1). Abelard-Schuman.
--Pyewacket. Pickard, Charles, illus. LC 67-19581. (Illus.). 123 p. 22cm. 1967. Abelard-Schuman.
--Robert's Rescued Railway. LC 60-12515. (Illus.). 178 p. 21cm. 1960, c.1959. F. Watts.
--The Smallest Dog on Earth. Pickard, Charles, illus. LC 63-10717. (Illus.). 127 p. 21cm. 1964. Abelard-Schuman.
--Soap-Box Derby. Biro, Val, pseud. (1921-), illus. Biro, Balint Stephen. LC 65-17040. 128p. illus. 21cm. c.1965. Van Nostrand.
--The Star and the Flame. Stobbs, William (1914-), illus. LC 64-19517. (Illus.). 184 p. 22cm. 1964. Ariel Books.
--The Three Red Herrings. LC 72-1950. 157 p. 22cm. 1972. (ISBN 0-8407-6238-0). T. Nelson.
--Uncle Barney & the Shrink-Drink. Dinan, Carolyn, illus. (gr. 3-7). 1977. (ISBN 0-8277-5401-9). (ISBN 0-8277-5400-0). British Bk Ctr.
--Uncle Barney & the Sleep Destroyer. Dinan, Carolyn, illus. (gr. 2-5). 1976. (ISBN 0-8277-4735-7). British Bk Ctr.

Weir, Ruth Cromer, jt. auth. see Cavanah, Frances.

Weir, Ruth Cromer, jt. ed. see Cavanah, Frances.

Weir, Ruth Cromer (1912-)
--The Great Big Noise. Friend, Esther, illus. LC 48-9408. 24 p. col. illus. 26 cm. c.1948. Wilcox & Follett Co.
--Rags, An Orphan of the Storm. Montgomery, Alice J., illus. LC 47-18439. 23cm. 32p. N.D. Wilcox & Follett Co.
--The Wonderful Plane Ride. Mastri, Fiore & Mastri, Jackie, illus. LC 49-10181. 33 p. col. illus. 21 cm. (Rand McNally book-elf book). (A Rand McNally book-elf Bk.). c.1949. Rand McNally.
--The Wonderful Train Ride. Mastri, Fiore & Mastri, Jackie, illus. LC 47-5946. (Illus.). 21cm. 50p. (A Rand McNally Book-elf book). c.1947. Rand McNally.

Weis, Margaret
--The Endless Catacombs. LC 84-51001. 160p. (A Dungeons & Dragons Endless Quest Bk.). (gr. 5 up). 1984. (ISBN 0-394-72785-1, Pub. by BYR). Random.

Weisgard, Leonard Joseph see Green, Adam, pseud.

Weisgard, Leonard Joseph (1916-)
--Big Book of Nursery Tales. Weisgard, Leonard Joseph (1916-), illus. (Illus.). (Nursery Treasure Bks.). (ps). 1962. (ISBN 0-448-04201-0, G&D). Putnam Pub Group.
--The Big Book of Train Stories. Weisgard, Leonard Joseph (1916-), illus. LC 55-4481. unpaged. illus. 33 cm. (Big Treasure Books). c.1955. Grosset & Dunlap.
--The Big Treasure Book of Nursery Tales. Weisgard, Leonard Joseph (1916-), illus. N.D. Grosset & Dunlap.
--The Clean Pig. Weisgard, Leonard Joseph (1916-), illus. LC 52-8648. 1952. Scribner.
--Down Huckleberry Hill. Weisgard, Leonard Joseph (1916-), illus. LC 47-309497. 31 p. illus. 21 x 27 cm. c.1947. C. Scribner's Sons.
--The Indoor Noisy Book. (The Noisy Book Ser.). 1940. Harper & Row Publishers.
--Just Like Me. LC 54-22396. (Illus.). unpaged. 21cm. 1954. Treasure Books.
--Just Like Me. Weisgard, Leonard Joseph (1916-), illus. LC 57-132. unpaged. illus. 21 cm. (Wonder books, 672). 1957, c.1954. Wonder Books.
--Let's Play Train: A/Story Book Game. LC 54-15103. (Illus.). 21cm. 1953. Treasure Books.
--Louis of New Orleans. Weisgard, Leonard Joseph (1916-), illus. N.D. David McKay Co.
--The Most Beautiful Tree in the World. Weisgard, Leonard Joseph (1916-), illus. LC 56-14259. unpaged. illus. 21 cm. (Wonder books, 653). c.1956. Wonder Books.
--Mr. Peaceable Paints. Weisgard, Leonard Joseph (1916-), illus. LC 56-10261. unpaged. illus. 22x26cm. c.1956. Scribner.
--My First Picture Book. Weisgard, Leonard Joseph (1916-), illus. LC 53-3530. unpaged. illus. 33cm. (Big treasure books). 1953. Grosset & Dunlap.
--My First Picture Book. Weisgard, Leonard Joseph (1916-), illus. LC 53-3530. unpaged col. illus. 30cm. (Nursery treasure bk.). 1964, c.1963. Grosset.
--Nursery Tales. Weisgard, Leonard Joseph (1916-), illus. (Illus.). 32p. (ps-1). 1982. (ISBN 0-448-04244-4, G&D). Putnam Pub Group.
--Pelican Here, Pelican There. Weisgard, Leonard Joseph (1916-), illus. LC 48-9503. 30 p. illus. (part col.) 26 cm. c.1948. C. Scribner's Sons.
--Silly Willy Nilly. Weisgard, Leonard Joseph (1916-), illus. LC 53-6107. unpaged. illus. 26cm. c.1953. Scribner.
--Suki, the Siamese Pussy. LC 37-10497. (Illus.). 32p. 26cm. 1937. T. Nelson and Sons.
--Who Dreams of Cheese?. N.D. E. M. Hale & Co.
--Who Dreams of Cheese?. Weisgard, Leonard Joseph (1916-), illus. LC 50-6025. (Illus.). 32 p. 26cm. 1950. Scribner.
--Whose Little Bird Am I?. Weisgard, Leonard Joseph (1916-), illus. LC 44-7214. 39 p. col. illus. 16 x 13 cm. 1944. Thomas Y. Crowell Company.
--Would You Like to Be a Monkey?. Weisgard, Leonard Joseph (1916-), illus. LC 45-37867. 32 p. illus. 19 1/2 cm. 1945. Thomas Y. Crowell Company.

Weisgard, Leonard Joseph (1916-), retold by.
--Cinderella. Weisgard, Leonard Joseph (1916-), illus. LC 38-35030. 32 p. illus. (part col.) 26 1/2 cm. c.1938. Garden City Publishing Co., Inc.

Weisheit, Eldon (1933-)
--God's Promise for Children. LC 82-70956. 128p. (Orig.). 1982. (ISBN 0-8066-1931-7). Augsburg.
--The Preacher's Yellow Pants. (Illus.). 48p. (gr. k-4). 1973. (ISBN 0-570-03420-5). Concordia.

Weisman, L Donald
--Some Folks went west. 1960. The Steck Company.

Weisner, William (1899-)
--Tom Thumb. 1974. (ISBN 0-8098-1215-0). David McKay Company.

Weiss, Ann Edwards (1943-)
--What's That You Said. Arnosky, Jim (1946-), illus. LC 79-3767. (Illus.). 48p. (Let-Me-Read Ser.). (gr. k-3). 1980. (ISBN 0-15-295525-9, HJ). (ISBN 0-15-696119-9, VoyB). HarBraceJ.

Weiss, Daniel A
--The Mice Who Loved Words. Weiss, Dianne Ewell, illus. LC 68-9478. (Illus.). 32 p. 24cm. 1968. Golden Press.

Weiss, Edna Smith (1916-)
--The Rainbow. Lambo, Donald W. (1903-1966), illus. LC 60-7287. 143 p. illus 23 cm. 1960. Nelson.
--Sally Saucer. Stone, Helen (1904-), illus. LC 56-5545. 179 p. illus. 22 cm. 1956. Houghton Mifflin.
--Truly Elizabeth. Krush, Beth (1918-), illus. LC 57-5880. 178 p. illus. 22 cm. 1957. Houghton Mifflin.

Weiss, Ellen
--The Angry Book Starring Temper Tantrum Turtle. Hefter, Richard (1942-), illus. LC 82-50433. (Illus.). 32p. (Sweet Pickles Mini-Storybooks). (ps-4). 1983. (ISBN 0-394-85541-8). Random.
--Clara, the Fortune-Telling Chicken. Weiss, Ellen, illus. LC 77-26198. (Illus.). 32 p. 26cm. c.1978. Windmill Books.
--Fix It, Please: Featuring Jim Henson's Sesame Street Muppets. Morrison, Bill (1935-), illus. LC 80-67281. (Illus.). 25 p. 27cm. c.1980. (ISBN 0-307-23122-4). Western Pub. Co.
--The Maxx Steele Trap: A Robo Force Adventure. Mones, illus. LC 84-18048. p. cm. 1985. (ISBN 0-394-87143-X). Random House.
--The Messy Book. Hefter, Richard (1942-), illus. LC 82-50432. (Illus.). (Sweet Pickles Mini-Storybooks). (ps-k). 1983. (ISBN 0-394-85545-0). Random.
--Millicent Maybe. Weiss, Ellen, illus. LC 78-13144. (Illus.). 32 p. 22cm. (Easy-read story book). 1979. (ISBN 0-531-02382-6). (ISBN 0-531-02299-4). F. Watts.
--Mokey's Birthday Present. Miles, Elizabeth, illus. LC 84-18908. (Illus.). 32 p. 22cm. c.1985. (ISBN 0-03-004559-2). Holt, Rinehart, and Winston.
--The Muppets on the Road. Cooke, Tom, illus. LC 81-11978. (Illus.). 48p. (Muppet Press Bks.). (gr. 1-6). 1983. (ISBN 0-394-85103-X). Random.
--Pigs in Space: Starring Jim Henson's Muppets. Graham, Alastair, illus. LC 82-16578. (Illus.). 32 p. 21cm. c.1983. (ISBN 0-394-85730-5). Muppet Press/Random House.

Weiss, Ellen & Brown, Richard Eric (1946-)
--The Tool Box: Featuring Jim Henson's Sesame Street Muppets. LC 80-67282. (Illus.). 27cm. 26p. c.1980. (ISBN 0-307-23121-6). Western Pub. Co.

Weiss, Ellen & Henson, James Maury (1936-)
--You Are the Star of a Muppet Adventure: Featuring Jim Henson's Muppets. Alexander, Benjamin, illus. LC 83-4028. (Illus.). 58 p. 20cm. c.1983. (ISBN 0-394-85623-6). Muppet Press/Random House.

Weiss, Evelyn
--Mixups and Fixups: New-Fangled Animal Stories. Elgin, Kathleen (1923-), illus. LC 54-12226. 115p. illus. 22cm. 1954. D. McKay Co.

Weiss, Felix
--Johnny Miller, 1 of 6 vols. (Illus.). (Sunny Days Library). N.D. E P Dutton.

Weiss, George Christian (1910-)
--Joseph and His Brothers. Sponsored by the Benedictine Monks of Belmont Abbey. Weiss, George Christian (1910-), illus. LC 60-3101. 64 p. illus. 21 cm. (Catholic know-your-Bible program). 1960. N. Doubleday.

Weiss, Gertrude S.
--Debbie's Dishes. (gr. k-2). N.D. Carlton.

Weiss, Harvey (1922-)
--The Big Cleanup. Weiss, Harvey (1922-), illus. LC 67-136094. 47p. illus. 26cm. 1967. Etc. Abelard.
--The Expeditions of Willis Partridge. Weiss, Harvey (1922-), illus. LC 60-13919. (Illus.). unpaged. 26cm. c.1960. Abelard-Schuman.
--A Gondola for Fun. Weiss, Harvey (1922-), illus. LC 57-8098. (Illus.). unpaged. 23cm. c.1957. Putnam.
--Horse in No Hurry. Weiss, Harvey (1922-), illus. LC 61-8247. 71 p. illus. 23 cm. 1961. Putnam.
--How to Be a Hero. Weiss, Harvey (1922-), illus. LC 67-18470. (Illus.). 1 v. (unpaged). 24cm. 1968. Parents' Magazine Press.
--How to Ooze and Other Ways of Travelling. Weiss, Harvey (1922-), illus. LC 61-13319. unpaged. illus. 26 cm. 1961. Abelard Schuman.
--My Closet Full of Hats. Weiss, Harvey (1922-), illus. LC 62-7562. unpaged. illus. 26 cm. 1962. Abelard-Schuman.
--Paper, Ink and Roller. 64p. 1958. Young Scott Books.
--Paul's Horse, Herman. Weiss, Harvey (1922-), illus. LC 58-10211. 71 p. illus. 21 cm. 1958. Putnam.
--Twenty-Four and Stanley. Weiss, Harvey (1922-), illus. LC 56-6628. (Illus.). 46 p. 23cm. c.1956. Putnam.
--The Very Private Treehouse. Weiss, Harvey (1922-), illus. LC 64-13724. 60 p. col. illus. 23 cm. 1964. Abelard-Schuman.

Weiss, Harvey (1922-), retold by.
--The Sooner Hound: A Tale from American Folklore. Weiss, Harvey (1922-), illus. LC 59-15015. (Illus.). 46 p. 23cm. 1960, c.1959. Putnam.

Weiss, Hugh
--Week in Daniel's World: France. Weiss, Sabihe, photos by. LC 69-18809. (Illus.). photos. 48p. (Face to Face Bks.). (gr. k-3). 1969. (ISBN 0-685-16355-5, CCPr). (ISBN 0-02-792610-9, CCPr). Macmillan.

Weiss, Jaqueline Schachter
--Young Brer Rabbit, and Other Trickster Tales of the Americas. Arrowood, Clinton McKendrick Lee (1939-), illus. LC 84-26889. p. cm. c.1985. (ISBN 0-88045-037-1). Stemmer House Publishers.

Weiss, Joan Talmage (1928-)
--Dory Boy. Forsberg, Howard, illus. LC 66-9049. (Illus.). 156 p. 22cm. (Whitman Tween-Age Book). 1966. Whitman Pub. Co.
--Home for a Stranger. LC 79-3766. 109 p. 21cm. c.1980. (ISBN 0-15-235224-4). Harcourt Brace Jovanovich.
--Kenny and His Animal Friends. Deluna, Tony, illus. LC 65-21127. (Illus.). 22cm. 156p. (Whitman Tween-Age Bk.). 1965. Whitman Pub.
--The Lemonade Lady: An Easy to Read Children's Book. Brostrom, Eileen, illus. LC 80-50703. (Illus.). 123 p. 21cm. c.1980. (ISBN 0-936822-00-7). Peppertree Pub.

Weiss, Karl, ed.
--The Prison Experience: An Anthology. LC 75-32920. index. 352p. (gr. 6 up). 1976. Delacorte.

Weiss, Leatie (1928-)
--Funny Feet!. Weiss, Ellen, illus. LC 77-11108. (Illus.). 32. 22cm. (Easy-Read Story Book). 1978. (ISBN 0-531-01348-0). F. Watts.
--Heather's Feathers. Weiss, Ellen, illus. LC 76-12624. (Illus.). 32 p. 22cm. (Easy-Read Story Book). 1976. (ISBN 0-531-01204-2). (ISBN 0-531-02475-X). Watts.
--My Teacher Sleeps in School. Weiss, Ellen, illus. LC 85-3663. p. cm. 1985. (ISBN 0-14-050559-8). Puffin Books.
--My Teacher Sleeps in School. Weiss, Ellen, illus. LC 83-10427. 1984. (ISBN 0-7232-6253-5). Warne.

Weiss, Malcolm E. (1928-)
--Far Out Factories. (Illus.). 128p. (gr. 5-9). 1984. (ISBN 0-525-67143-9). Lodestar Bks.
--Gods, Stars, & Computers: Fact & Fancy in Myth & Science. (Illus.). 128p. (gr. 6-8). 1980. Doubleday.
--Solomon Grundy, Born on Oneday: A Finite Arithmetic Puzzle. De Paola, Tomie, pseud. (1934-), illus. De Paola, Thomas Anthony. LC 76-26560. (Illus.). (Young Math Ser.). (gr. k-3). 1977. (ISBN 0-690-01275-6, TYC-J). Har-Row.

Weiss, Nicki (1954-)
--Battle Day at Camp Delmont. Weiss, Nicki (1954-), illus. LC 84-18641. (Illus.). 9 3/4 x 7 1/4. 32p. (14 pt.). (gr. k-3). 1985. (ISBN 0-688-04306-2). (ISBN 0-688-04307-0). Greenwillow.
--Chuckie. Weiss, Nicki (1954-), illus. LC 81-6323. p. cm. c.1982. (ISBN 0-688-00670-1). (ISBN 0-688-00671-X). Greenwillow Books.
--Hank and Oogie. Weiss, Nicki (1954-), illus. LC 81-7136. p. cm. c.1982. (ISBN 0-688-00928-X). (ISBN 0-688-00936-0). Greenwillow Books.
--Maude and Sally. 1st ed. Weiss, Nicki (1954-), illus. LC 82-12003. (Illus.). 32 p. c.1983. (ISBN 0-688-01635-9). (ISBN 0-688-01638-3). Greenwillow Books.
--Menj!. LC 80-15955. (Illus.). 55 p. 22cm. (Greenwillow Read-Alone Books). c.1981. (ISBN 0-688-80306-7). (ISBN 0-688-84306-9). Greenwillow Books.
--Waiting. Weiss, Nicki (1954-), illus. LC 81-242. (Illus.). 32 p. 21cm. c.1981. (ISBN 0-688-00602-7). (ISBN 0-688-00603-5). Greenwillow Books.
--Weekend at Muskrat Lake. Weiss, Nicki (1954-), illus. LC 83-20789. 1984. (ISBN 0-688-03767-4). Greenwillow.

Weiss, Renee Karol (1923-), adapted by see Chuang-Tzu.

--Fluffy Ruffles. Morgan, Wallace, illus. LC 7-37238. 24 x 32cm. 127p. 1907. D. Appleton & Co.
--Folly in Fairyland. Morgan, Wallace, illus. LC 1-26197. 19cm. 261p. 1901. H. Altemus Co.
--Folly in Fairyland. Morgan, Wallace, illus. (Illus.). 261p. (Little Men and Women Ser.). 1901. Henry Altemus & Co.
--Folly in Fairyland. New ed. Morgan, Wallace, illus. 1905. Henry Altemus Co.
--Folly in the Forest. Birch, Reginald Bathurst (1856-1943), illus. LC 2-19882. 19cm. 282p. 1902. H. Altemus Co.
--Folly in the Forest. Birch, Reginald Bathurst (1856-1943), illus. (Illus.). (Little Men and Women Ser.). 1902. Henry Altemus Co.
--Folly in the Forest. New ed. Birch, Reginald Bathurst (1856-1943), illus. 1905. Henry Altemus Co.
--The Happychaps. Cady, Walter Harrison (1877-1970), illus. LC 9-12. (Illus.). 25cm. 140p. 1908. Century Co.
--In the Reign of Queen Dick. Strothmann, W., illus. LC 4-25383. 5 p. l., 228 p. front., 7 pl. 20 1/2 cm. 1904. D. Appleton and Company.
--Jolly Plays for Holidays: A Collection of Christmas Entertainments. LC 14-15818. 148 p. 19 1/2 cm. 1914. W. H. Baker & Co.
--Marjorie at Seacote. Repr. (Happy Books for Happy Girls). (The Marjorie Books). N.D. Grosset & Dunlap.
--Marjorie at Seacote. Bohnert, Herbert F., illus. LC 12-22131. 4 p. l., 288 p. front., plates. 19 1/2 cm. 1912. Dodd, Mead and Company.
--Marjorie in Command. Repr. (Happy Books for Happy Girls). (The Marjorie Books). N.D. Grosset & Dunlap.
--Marjorie in Command. Pratt, Julie Carolyn, illus. LC 10-203862. 4 p. l., 268 p. front., 2 pl. 20 cm. 1910. Dodd, Mead and Company.
--Marjorie's Busy Days. LC 8-28062. 4 p. l., 294 p. front., 3 pl. 20 cm. 1908. Dodd, Mead and Company.
--Marjorie's Busy Days. Repr. (The Marjorie Bks.). N.D. Grosset & Dunlap.
--Marjorie's Maytime. (Happy Books for Happy Girls). (The Marjorie Books). N.D. Grosset & Dunlap.
--Marjorie's Maytime. Bohnert, Herbert F., illus. LC 11-23301. 4 p. l., 241 p. front., plates. 19 1/2 cm. 1911. Dodd, Mead and Company.
--Marjorie's New Friend. Repr. (The Marjorie Bks.). N.D. Grosset & Dunlap.
--Marjorie's New Friend. Bassett, Mary Robertson, illus. LC 9-25663. 4 p. l., 292 p. front., 3 pl. 20 cm. 1909. Dodd, Mead and Company.
--Marjorie's Vacation. LC 7-32326. 5 p. l., 293 p. front., 4 pl. 20 cm. 1907. Dodd, Mead and Company.
--Marjorie's Vacation. Repr. (The Marjorie Bks.). N.D. Grosset & Dunlap.
--The Merry-Go-Round. LC 1-23563. 4 p. l., 152 p. incl. illus., plates. front. 19 1/2 cm. 1901. R. H. Russell.
--Mother Goose's Menagerie. Newell, Peter (1862-1924), illus. LC 1-276913. x, 111 p. col. front., col. plates. 21 1/2 cm. 1901. Noyes, Platt & Company.
--A Nonsense Anthology. 289p. 1902. (ISBN 0-486-20499-5). Dover Books.
--Patty and Azalea. Repr. (The Famous Patty Bks.). N.D. Grosset & Dunlap.
--Patty and Azalea. Caswell, Edward C., illus. LC 19-14356. 5 p. l., 9-302 p. front., plates. 19 1/2 cm. $1.25. 1919. Dodd, Mead and Company.
--Patty at Home. LC 4-23767. vii p., 1 l., 295 p. front., 5 pl. 19 1/2 cm. 1904. Dodd, Mead & Company.
--Patty at Home. (The Famous Patty Bks.). N.D. Grosset & Dunlap.
--Patty Blossom. Caswell, Edward C., illus. LC 17-23977. 295 p. front., plates. 19 1/2 cm. 1917. Dodd, Mead and Company.
--Patty-Bride. Repr. (The Famous Patty Bks.). N.D. Grosset & Dunlap.
--Patty-Bride. Caswell, Edward C., illus. LC 18-18406. 304 p. front., plates. 19 1/2 cm. 1918. Dodd, Mead and Company.
--Patty-Bride. Caswell, Edward C., illus. LC 21-4126. 3 p. l., 9-304 p. front. 19 1/2 cm. 1919. Dodd, Mead and Company.
--Patty Fairfield. LC 1-25446. vii, 247 p. front., plates. 20 cm. 1901. Dodd, Mead & Company.
--Patty Fairfield. (The Famous Patty Bks.). N.D. Grosset & Dunlap.
--Patty in Paris. LC 7-26960. 270 p. front., 5 pl. 19 1/2 cm. 1907. Dodd, Mead and Company.
--Patty in Paris. Repr. (The Famous Patty Bks.). N.D. Grosset & Dunlap.
--Patty in the City. LC 5-28017. ix, 274 p. front., 5 pl. 20 cm. 1905. Dodd, Mead & Company.
--Patty in the City. Repr. (The Famous Patty Bks.). N.D. Grosset & Dunlap.
--Patty's Blossom. Repr. (The Famous Patty Bks.). N.D. Grosset & Dunlap.
--Patty's Butterfly Days. (The Famous Patty Bks.). N.D. Grosset & Dunlap.
--Patty's Butterfly Days. Lewis, Martin, illus. LC 12-21322. 305 p. incl. front. plates. 19 1/2 cm. $1.25. 1912. Dodd, Mead and Company.
--Patty's Fortune. Repr. (The Famous Patty Bks.). N.D. Grosset & Dunlap.
--Patty's Fortune. Caswell, Edward C., illus. LC 16-18025. 294 p. front., plates. 19 1/2 cm. 1916. Dodd, Mead and Company.
--Patty's Friends. LC 8-235469. 283 p. front., 3 pl. 19 1/2 cm. 1908. Dodd, Mead and Company.
--Patty's Friends. Repr. (The Famous Patty Bks.). N.D. Grosset & Dunlap.
--Patty's Motor Car. Repr. (The Famous Patty Bks.). N.D. Grosset & Dunlap.
--Patty's Motor Car. Bunker, Mayo, illus. LC 11-23302. 5 p. l., 9-279 p. front., plates. 19 1/2 cm. 1911. Dodd, Mead and Company.
--Patty's Pleasure Trip. LC 9-24260. 304 p. front., 3 pl. 19 1/2 cm. 1909. Dodd, Mead and Company.
--Patty's Pleasure Trip. Repr. (The Famous Patty Bks.). N.D. Grosset & Dunlap.
--Patty's Romance. Repr. (The Famous Patty Bks.). N.D. Grosset & Dunlap.
--Patty's Romance. Caswell, Edward C., illus. LC 15-18725. 303 p. front., plates. 19 1/2 cm. 1915. Dodd, Mead and Company.
--Patty's Social Season. Repr. (The Famous Patty Bks.). N.D. Grosset & Dunlap.
--Patty's Social Season. Caswell, Edward C., illus. LC 13-193343. 352 p. front., plates. 19 1/2 cm. 1913. Dodd, Mead and Company.
--Patty's Success. LC 10-20385. 292 p. front., 3 pl. 19 1/2 cm. Repr. 1910. Dodd, Mead and Company.
--Patty's Success. Repr. (The Famous Patty Bks.). N.D. Grosset & Dunlap.
--Patty's Suitors. (The Famous Patty Bks.). N.D. Grosset & Dunlap.
--Patty's Suitors. Caswell, Edward C., illus. LC 14-15741. 344p. 1914. Dodd Mead & Co.
--Patty's Summer Days. LC 6-304585. 2 p. l., vii-ix, 296 p. front., 5 pl. 19 1/2 cm. 1906. Dodd, Mead & Company.
--Patty's Summer Days. (The Famous Patty Bks.). N.D. Grosset & Dunlap.
--The Pete & Polly Stories. Cory, Fanny Young, illus. LC 2-23849. viii p., 1 l., 228, 1 p. front., illus., 5 pl. 24 cm. 1902. A. C. McClurg & Company.
--Rubaiyat of a Motor Car. LC 6-16207. (Illus.). 19cm. 60p. 1906. Dodd, Mead & Company.
--The Seven Ages of Childhood. Smith, Jessie Willcox (1863-1935), illus. (Illus.). 12p. (Orig.). 1982. (ISBN 0-914676-98-9, Pub. by Envelope Bks). Green Tiger Pr.
--The Staying Guest. Smith, U. Granville, illus. LC 4-29784. 6 p. l., 3-282 p. incl. illus., plates. front. 20 cm. 1904. The Century Co.
--The Story of Betty. Birch, Reginald Bathurst (1856-1943), illus. LC 99-5017. xii p., 1 l., 260 p. incl. front., plates. 19 1/2 cm. 1899. The Century Co.
--Trotty's Trip. N.D. George W Jacobs.
--Trotty's Trip. Brill, George Reiter (1867-), illus. LC 2-23701. 21cm. 63p. 1902. D. Biddle.
--Two Little Women. (The Two Little Women). N.D. Grosset & Dunlap.
--Two Little Women. Caswell, Edward C., illus. LC 15-196258. 5 p. l., 305 p. front., plates. 19 1/2 cm. 1915. Dodd, Mead and Company.
--Two Little Women and Treasure House. (The Two Little Women). N.D. Grosset & Dunlap.
--Two Little Women and Treasure House. Caswell, Edward C., illus. LC 16-182891. 5 p. l., 270 p. front., plates. 19 1/2 cm. 1916. Dodd, Mead and Company.
--Two Little Women on a Holiday. (The Two Little Women). N.D. Grosset & Dunlap.
--Two Little Women on a Holiday. Caswell, Edward C., illus. LC 17-24705. 5 p. l., 300 p. front. 19 1/2 cm. 1917. Dodd, Mead and Company.
--A Whimsey Anthology. 221p. 1906. (ISBN 0-486-20195-3). Dover Books.

Wells, Carveth (1887-)
--The Jungle Man and His Animals. Sarg, Tony, pseud. (1882-1942), illus. Sarg, Anthony Frederick. Lucas, Frederic Augustus, Dr., intro. by. LC 25-20955. viii, 68 p. col. front., illus., col. plates. 31 1/2 cm. 1925. Duffeld and Company.
--The Jungle Man and His Animals. Sarg, Tony, pseud. (1882-1942), illus. Sarg, Anthony Frederick. Lucas, Frederic Augustus, Dr., intro. by. LC 35-273874. viii, 68 p. col. front., illus., col. plates. 28 1/2 cm. 1935. R. M. McBride & Company.

Wells, Catherine Boot Gannet, Mrs. (1838-)
--Little Dick's Son. LC 1-23100. 80p. 1901. T. Y. Crowell & Co.
--Little Dick's Son. (The "Bimbi" Series of Children's Booklets). N.D. Thomas Y. Crowell.
--Little Dick's Sons. (Illus.). (Crowell's Child Life Series). 1915. T Y Crowell.

Wells, Claudia E. (1938-)
--Whiskers, the Bank Mouse. Shardin, Arthur (1942-), illus. LC 77-10823. p. cm. c.1977. (ISBN 0-930506-00-6). Popcorn Publishers.

Wells, Elizabeth Adams
--My Dog Days and other Animal stories. LC 2-6206. (Illus.). 21cm. 170p. 1901. Herald Publishing Co.

Wells, Elizabeth Neal
--All About Us. Pere, Dorothy H., illus. LC 77-131518. (Illus.). 56 p. 22cm. (Contemporary poets of Dorrance series). 1970. Dorrance.

Wells, Evelyn
--The Gentle Kingdom of Giscomo. LC 52-13373. 375 p. 22cm. 1953. Doubleday.
--I Am Thinking of Kelda. LC 72-89357. 312p. 1974. (ISBN 0-385-00825-2). Doubleday.

Wells, H. G. see Wright, Betty Ren & Wells, Herbert George.

Wells, Helen see Lewis, Francine, pseud.

Wells, Helen (1910-)
--Adam Gimbel: Pioneer Trader. 1955. David McKay Co.
--Behind the White Veil. (gr. 4-8). 1951. (ISBN 0-448-09406-1). G&D.
--The Brass Idol Mystery. LC 64-55767. (Helen Weinstock Legally changed name to Helen Wells). 173 p. illus. 20 cm. (Vicki Barr flight stewardess series, 16). 1964. Grosset & Dunlap.
--Cherry Ames, Army Nurse. LC 44-5096. v, 1 p., 1 l., 214 p. incl. front. 19 1/2 cm. (Her Cherry Ames nurse stories). 1944. Grosset & Dunlap.
--Cherry Ames at Hilton Hospital. LC 59-124488. 180 p. illus. 20 cm. (Cherry Ames stories). 1959. Grosset & Dunlap.
--Cherry Ames, Boarding School Nurse. LC 56-2728. 212 p. illus. 20 cm. (Cherry Ames stories). 1956, c.1955. Grosset & Dunlap.
--Cherry Ames, Camp Nurse. LC 58-14552. 182 p. illus. 20 cm. (Cherry Ames stories). 1958, c.1957. Grosset & Dunlap.
--Cherry Ames, Chief Nurse. LC 44-940444. v, 1 p., 1 l., 213 p. incl. front. 19 cm. (Cherry Ames nurse stories). 1944. Grosset & Dunlap.
--Cherry Ames: Companion Nurse. (Cherry Ames Ser.). (gr. 5-9). 1964. (ISBN 0-448-09724-9). G&D.
--Cherry Ames, Cruise Nurse. LC 48-7092. 216 p. front. 20 cm. (Her Cherry Ames nurse stories). 1948. Grosset & Dunlap.
--Cherry Ames, Department Store Nurse. LC 57-13581. 212 p. illus. 20 cm. (Cherry Ames stories). 1957, c.1956. Grosset & Dunlap.
--Cherry Ames, Flight Nurse. LC 46-129234. v p., 1 l., 215 p. incl. front. 19 cm. (Her Cherry Ames nurse stories). 1945. Grosset & Dunlap.
--Cherry Ames, Island Nurse. LC 60-16094. 184 p. illus. 20 cm. 1960. Grosset & Dunlap.
--Cherry Ames, Jungle Nurse. LC 65-13790. 176p. illus. 20cm. (Her The Cherry Ames nurse stories). c.1965. Grosset.
--Cherry Ames: Mystery in the Doctor's Office. (Cherry Ames Ser.: Vol. 26). (gr. 4-8). 1966. (ISBN 0-448-09726-5). G&D.
--Cherry Ames: Mystery of Rogue's Cave, No. 3. (gr. 4-8). 1972 (Tempo). G&D.
--Cherry Ames: Mystery of Rogue's Cave. (Illus.). 184 p. 21cm. (Cherry Ames stories). 1972, c.1960. (ISBN 0-448-05554-6). Grosset.
--Cherry Ames, Private Duty Nurse. LC 46-8595. 4 p. l., 216 p. 19 1/2 cm. (Her Cherry Ames nurse stories). 1946. Grosset & Dunlap.
--Cherry Ames, Rural Nurse. LC 61-3010. (Illus.). 181. 20cm. (The Cherry Ames Stories). 1961. Grosset & Dunlop.
--Cherry Ames: Rural Nurse. (Cherry Ames Ser.: Vol. 22). (gr. 4-8). 1961. (ISBN 0-448-09722-2, G&D). Putnam Pub Group.
--Cherry Ames, Senior Nurse. LC 44-739. v, 217 p. incl. front. 19 1/2 cm. (Her Cherry Ames nurse stories). 1944. Grosset & Dunlap.
--Cherry Ames, Staff Nurse. LC 62-52094. 177 p. illus. 20 cm. (Cherry Ames Nurse Stories, 23). 1962. Grosset & Dunlap.
--Cherry Ames, Student Nurse. LC 43-16365. v, 213 p. incl. front. 19 1/2 cm. (Her Cherry Ames nurse stories). 1943. Grosset & Dunlap.
--Cherry Ames: The Case of the Dangerous Remedy. (gr. 6 up). 1978. (ISBN 0-448-14851-X, G&D). Putnam Pub Group.
--Cherry Ames: The Case of the Forgetful Patient. (gr. 6 up). 1978. (ISBN 0-448-14850-1, G&D). Putnam Pub Group.
--Cherry Ames, Veterans Nurse. LC 46-2187. v p., 1 l., 216 p. incl. front. 19 cm. (Her Cherry Ames nurse stories). 1946. Grosset & Dunlap.
--Cherry Ames: Veterans' Nurse. (Cherry Ames Ser.: Vol. 6). (gr. 4-8). 1946. (ISBN 0-448-09706-0, G&D). Putnam Pub Group.
--Cherry Ames, Visiting Nurse. LC 47-11172. 216 p. front. 20 cm. (Her Cherry Ames nurse stories). 1947. Grosset & Dunlap.
--A City for Jean. LC 56-7776. 218p. 22cm. 1956. Funk & Wagnalls.
--Clinic Nurse. (Cherry Ames Nurse Stories). N.D. Grosset & Dunlap.
--The Clue of the Carved Ruby. LC 62-2252. 179 p. illus. 20 cm. (Vicki Barr flight stewardess series14). 1961. Grosset & Dunlap.
--The Clue of the Gold Coin. LC 58-395452. 183 p. illus. 20 cm. (Vicki Barr flight stewardess series 12). 1958. Grosset & Dunlap.
--Doctor Betty. LC 70-87831. 190 p. 21cm. (Career romance for young moderns). 1969. (ISBN 0-671-32187-0). Messner.
--Escape by Night: A Story of the Underground Railway. 1st ed. Connelly, George L., illus. LC 53-7414. 182p. illus. 23cm. (Winston adventure books). 1953. Winston.
--A Flair for People. LC 55-6930. 192p. 21cm. (Romance for young moderns). 1955. J. Messner.
--The Ghost at the Waterfall. LC 57-13582. 214p. illus. 20cm. (Vicki Barr flight stewardess series 11). 1957, c.1956. Grosset & Dunlap.
--The Girl in the White Coat. LC 53-105371. 184p. 21cm. (Romance for young moderns). 1953. J. Messner.
--The Hidden Valley Mystery. LC 48-5449. v, 218 p. front. 20 cm. (Her The Vicki Barr flight stewardess series). 1948. Grosset & Dunlap.
--Introducing Patti Lewis, Home Economist. LC 56-6797. 190 p. 21 cm. (Romance for young moderns). 1956. Messer.
--King Kindness and the Witch: And Other Stories. Shrimpton, Louise A., illus. LC 1-29603. 3-118 p. illus. 18 1/2 cm. 1900. C. W. Bardeen.
--Mountaineer Nurse. (Cherry Ames Nurse Stories). N.D. Grosset & Dunlap.
--The Mystery at Hartwood. (The Vicki Barr Flight Stewardess Stories). N.D. Grosset & Dunlap.
--The Mystery of Flight 908. LC 62-511231. 179 p. illus. 20 cm. (Vicki Barr flight stewardess series). 1962. Grosset & Dunlap.
--The Mystery of the Vanishing Lady. LC 54-856582. 214p. illus. 20cm. (Vicki Barr flight stewardess series 9). 1954. Grosset & Dunlap.
--Night Supervisor Julie. N.D. (ISBN 0-448-09711-7). Grosset & Dunlap.
--Peril Over the Airport. LC 53-6964. 212p. illus. 20cm. (Vicki Barr flight stewardess series 8). 1953. Grosset & Dunlap.
--The Search for the Missing Twin. LC 55-1061. 216p. illus. 20cm. (Her The Vicki Barr flight stewardess series 10). c.1954. Grosset & Dunlap.
--The Secret of Magnolia Manor. vii, 213 p. front. 20 cm. (Her The Vicki Barr flight stewardess series). 1949. Grosset & Dunlap.
--The Silver Ring Mystery. LC 60-317. 180 p. illus. 20 cm. (Vicki Barr flight stewardess series 13). 1960. Grosset & Dunlap.
--Silver Wings for Vicki. LC 47-222351. vii p., 1 l., 210 p. incl. front. 19 1/2 cm. (The Vicki Barr flight stewardess series_1). 1947. Grosset & Dunlap.
--Ski Nurse Mystery. LC 67-20841. (Illus.). 176 p. 20cm. (Cherry Ames nurse story, 27). 1968. Grosset & Dunlap.
--Vicki Finds the Answer. LC 47-221723. v p., 1 l., 211 p. incl. front. 19 1/2 cm. (Her The Vicki Barr flight stewardess series). 1947. Grosset & Dunlap.

Wells, Henry Parkhurst
--City Boys in Woods: Or, A Trapping Venture in Maine. LC 12-40097. (Harper's Selected Juveniles.). 1890. Harper & Bros.

Wells, Herbert George, jt. auth. see Wright, Betty Ren.

Wells, Herbert George (1866-1946)
--The Adventures of Tommy. N.D. Grosset & Dunlap.
--The Adventures of Tommy. authorized american. LC 67-19480. (Illus.). 31 p. 1967. Knopf.
--The Adventures of Tommy. Wells, Herbert George (1866-1946), illus. LC 29-21557. 47 p. col. illus. 30 cm. 1929. Frederick A. Stokes Company.
--The Desert Daisy. Ray, Gordon N., intro. by. LC 57-11161. xix p., facsim.: vi, 79, 17 p. illus., port. 23 cm. 1957. Beta Phi Mu.
--The Empire of the Ants & Other Stories. (gr. 7-12). N.D. (ISBN 0-590-11845-5, Schol Pap). Scholastic Inc.
--Famous Short Stories of H. G. Wells. N.D. Garden City Publishing Co.
--The First Men in the Moon. (gr. 7-10). N.D. Lancer.
--The Food of the Gods. Fago, John Norwood, adapted by. Caravana, Anton, illus. LC 78-51554. (Illus.). 62 p. 21cm. (Now age books illustrated). c.1978. (ISBN 0-88301-326-6). (ISBN 0-88301-314-2). Pendulum Press.
--The Invisible Man. (Magnum Easy Eye Classic Ser). (gr. 7-12). N.D. Lancer.
--The Invisible Man. (gr. 7-9). 1972. (ISBN 0-590-01381-5, Schol Pap). Scholastic Inc.
--The Invisible Man. N.D. William Collins Sons & Co.
--The Island of Dr. Moreau. (gr. 7 up). 1978. (ISBN 0-590-11864-1). Scholastic Inc.

--Hector, the Dog Who Loves Fleas. Wende, Philip (1939-), illus. LC 67-5985. (Illus.). 24 p. (Carousel Book). 1967. L. W. Singer Co.

Wenden, Nadine

--The Freckle-Faced Bear. Wenden, Nadine, illus. LC 36-202519. 64 p. illus. (part col.) 17 cm. 1936. Frederick A. Stokes Company.

--The Freckle-Faced Bear. Wenden, Nadine, illus. N.D. J. B. Lippincott.

Wender, Dorothea, jt. auth. see Polese, Marcia Ann.

Wendy, jt. auth. see Cathy.

Weng, Virginia, jt. ed. see Jagendorf, Moritz Adolf.

Wengrov, Charles (1925-)

--The Story of Shavuot. (Illus.). (Holiday Ser.). (gr. k-7). 1965. (ISBN 0-914080-55-5). Shulsinger Sales.

--Tales of King Saul. (Illus.). (Biblical Ser.). (gr. 5-10). 1969. (ISBN 0-914080-21-0). Shulsinger Sales.

--Tales of Noah & the Ark. (Illus.). (Biblical Ser.). (gr. 5-10). 1969. (ISBN 0-914080-23-7). Shulsinger Sales.

--Tales of the Prophet Samuel. (Illus.). (Biblical Ser.). (gr. 5-10). 1969. (ISBN 0-914080-22-9). Shulsinger Sales.

Wenig, Adolf

--Beyond the Giant Mountains: Tales from Bohemia. Wenig, Josef, illus. Mokreja, Lillian F., tr. LC 23-17716. 4 p. l., 3-88, 2 p. illus. 22 cm. 1923. Houghton Mifflin Company.

Wenjing, Yan

--Favorite Children's Stories from China. (Illus.). 270p. (gr. 5-7). 1983. (ISBN 0-8351-1064-8). China Bks.

Wenk, Richard

--The Great Baseball Championship. Gothard, David, illus. (Illus.). 64p. (Orig.). (Pick-a-Path Bks.: No. 3). (gr. 3-6). 1983. (ISBN 0-590-32813-1). Scholastic Inc.

--The Super Trail Bike Race. Gothard, David, illus. (Illus.). 64p. (Orig.). (Pick-a-Path Bks.: No. 5). (gr. 3-6). 1983. (ISBN 0-590-32927-8). Scholastic Inc.

Wennerstrom, Genia Katherine (1930-)

--Pooka the Penthouse Cat. Wennerstrom, Genia Katherine (1930-), illus. LC 72-144021. (Illus.). 32 p. 26cm. 1971. I. Washburn.

Wenning, Elisabeth

--Christmas Mouse. Remington, Barbara, illus. LC 59-12733. (Illus.). 48p. (gr. k-3). 1983, c.1959. (ISBN 0-03-015066-3). (ISBN 0-03-015066-3). HR&W.

Wensell, Ulises

--Come to Our House. Herman, Charlotte & Haas, Dorothy, eds. Wensell, Ulises, illus. LC 78-57836. (Illus.). 60 p. 29cm. c.1978. (ISBN 0-528-82442-2). Rand McNally.

Wentink, Andrew Mark see Balanchine, George.

Wentworth, Helen Clark, Mrs.

--Sunnyside Children. Brown, Marcia Foutz, illus. Clark, Glenn, frwd. by. LC 41-6941. vi, 146 p. illus. 20 cm. c.1940. Macalester Park Publishing Company.

Wentworth, Ruth Starbuck

--The First Nantucket Tea Party. Brenizer, Meredith Marshall, ed. Curtis, Mary Thomas, illus. LC 78-62476. (Illus.). 63 p. c.1978. (ISBN 0-88492-022-4). W. S. Sullwold Pub.

Wentworth, Walter

--The Drifting Island: Or, The Slave-Hunters of the Congo. A Sequel to Kibboo Ganey... LC 12-40489. 2 p. l., 7-33 p. front., plates. 17 1/2 cm. 1890. Roberts Brothers.

--Kibboo Ganey: Or, The Lost Chief of the Copper Mountain. LC 72-3007. (Illus.). 364 p. 22cm. (The Black Heritage Library Collection). 1972, c.1889. (ISBN 0-8369-9091-9). Books for Libraries Press.

--Kibboo Ganey: Or, The Lost Chief of the Copper Mountain. A Story of Travel and Adventure in the Heart of Africa. Merrill, Frank Thayer (1848-), illus. LC 12-40200. 364 p. incl. front. plates. 17 1/2 cm. 1889. Roberts Brothers.

Werlin, Marvin

--Shadow Play. LC 75-23338. 256p. 1st U.S. edition. 1976. (ISBN 0-688-02980-9). Morrow.

Wernecke, Herbert Henry (1895-), ed.

--Christmas Songs & Their Stories. (gr. 7 up). 1957. (ISBN 0-664-20206-3). Westminster.

--Christmas Stories from Many Lands. (gr. 7 up). 1961. (ISBN 0-664-20359-0). Westminster.

--Tales of Christmas from Near & Far. (gr. 7 up). 1963. (ISBN 0-664-20455-4). Westminster.

Werner, Carl

--The Land of Make Believe. N.D. Dodge.

Werner, Elsa Jane see Watson, Jane Werner.

Werner, Elsa Jane (1915-)

--The Golden Book of Words. DeWitt, Cornelius Hugh (1905-), illus. 1949. Simon & Schuster.

--Pat-a-Cake: A Baby's Mother Goose. Battaglia, Aurelius (1910-), illus. LC 49-4193. 28 p. col. illus. 21 cm. (Little golden library, 54). 1948. Simon and Schuster.

--Pets for Peter. Battaglia, Aurelius (1910-), illus. LC 50-10653. (Illus.). 12p. 21cm. (Little Golden Library). 1950. Simon and Schuster.

Werner, Elsa Jane (1915-), ed.

--Nursery Rhymes. Elliot, Gertrude, illus. (Little Golden Library). 1949. Simon and Shuster.

Werner, Herman see Cowen, Eve, pseud.

Werner, Jadwiga

--Squirrel Redcoat. Grabianski, Janusz (1928-1976), illus. Paczynells, Maria, tr. LC 61-66479. (Illus.). 43p. 25cm. 1961. Watts.

Werner, Jane, jt. auth. see Disney, Walter Elias.

Werner, Jane, jt. auth. see Disney, Walt, Productions.

Werner, Jane see Watson, Jane Werner.

Werner, Jane, adapted by see Disney, Walter Elias.

Werner, Jane (1915-), adapted by see Disney, Walt, Productions.

Werner, Jane (1915-), retold by see Grimm, Jakob Ludwig Karl (1785-1863) & Grimm, Wilhelm Karl.

Werner, Jane (1915-)

--Big Golden Book of Poetry. 1974. (ISBN 0-307-60463-2, Golden Pr). Western Pub.

--Chatterly Squirrel and Other Animal Stories. Miller, John Parr (1913-), illus. LC 50-8343. 125 p. col. illus. 19 cm. (Golden story book, 13)). 1950. Simon and Schuster.

--Christopher Bunny and Other Animal Stories. LC 49-48939. 124 p. col. illus. 18 cm. (Golden story book, 3). 1949. Simon and Schuster.

--Elves & Fairies. Williams, Garth Montgomery (1912-), illus. 1964. Golden Press.

--First BIble Stories. Wilkin, Eloise Burns (1904-), illus. (Little Golden Book). 1954. Golden Press.

--The Fuzzy Duckling. Watson, Jane Werner. Provensen, Alice (1918-) & Provensen, Martin (1916-), illus. LC 49-8904. 28 p. illus. 21 cm. (Little golden library, 78). 1949. Simon and Schuster.

--Giant Golden Mother Goose. Provensen, Alice (1918-) & Provensen, Martin (1916-), illus. (Illus.). (ps-1). 1948. (ISBN 0-307-15547-1, Golden Pr). (ISBN 0-307-60555-8). Western Pub.

--Good Morning and Good Night. Wilkin, Eloise Burns (1904-), illus. LC 49-8905. 42 p. illus. (part col.) 21 cm. (Little golden library). 1949, c.1948. Simon and Schuster.

--Jolly Barnyard. Gergely, Tibor (1900-1978), illus. (Little Golden Library). 1950. Simon and Shuster.

--Joseph and His Brethren. Jackson, Pauline (1918-), illus. LC 47-30634. 34 p. illus. (part col.) 21 cm. 1947. Grosset & Dunlap.

--The Marvelous Merry-Go-Round. Miller, John Parr (1913-), illus. (Little Golden Library). 1950. Simon & Schuster.

--Mr. Noah and His Family. Provensen, Alice (1918-) & Provensen, Martin (1916-), illus. LC 48-78067. 28 p. col. illus. 21 cm. (Little golden library, 49). 1948. Simon and Schuster.

--Noah's Ark. Gergely, Tibor (1900-1978), illus. LC 43-142843. 34 p. illus. (part col.) 21 x 19 cm. 1943. Grosset & Dunlap.

--Smokey the Bear. Scarry, Richard McClure (1919-), illus. LC 76-4900. (Illus.). 24 p. 22cm. 1968, c.1955. Golden Press.

--The Tall Book of Make-Believe. Williams, Garth Montgomery (1912-), illus. (Illus.). 92p. (Tall Bks.). (gr. k-3). 1980. (ISBN 0-06-026505-1, HarpJ). (ISBN 0-06-026506-X). Har-Row.

--The True Story of Smokey the Bear. Scarry, Richard McClure (1919-), illus. (Illus.). 24p. (gr. k-3). 1976. (ISBN 0-307-10429-X, Golden Pr). (ISBN 0-307-60429-2). Western Pub.

--Uncle Mistletoe. Malvern, Corinne (1905-1956), illus. LC 53-3514. unpaged. illus. 21cm. (Little golden book, 175). 1953. Simon and Schuster.

--Walt Disney's Bunny Book. Disney, Walt, Studio, illus. (Illus.). 32p. (ps-3). 1972. (ISBN 0-307-10424-9, Golden Pr). Western Pub.

--Walt Disney's Mar y Poppins. Grant, Campbell (1909-), illus. 1964. Golden Press.

--Walt Disney's The Living Desert. Campbell, Grant & Walt Disney Studio, illus. 1956. Golden Press.

--A Woods Story. Stern, Marie Simchow (1909-), illus. LC 45-5275. 40 p. incl. col. front., illus (part col.) 29 x 23 cm. c.1945. Harper and Brothers.

Werner, Jane (1915-), adapted by.

--Bible Stories for Boys and Girls. Dixon, Rachel Taft & Hartwell, Marjorie, illus. (Little Golden Book). 1953. Golden Press.

--Bible Stories for Boys and Girls. Dixon, Rachel Taft & Hartwell, Marjorie, illus. LC 53-3747. unpaged. illus. 21cm. (Little golden book, 174). 1953. Simon and Schuster.

--The Christmas Story. Wilkin, Eloise Burns (1904-), illus. (Little Golden Book). 1952. Golden Press.

--The Giant Golden Book of Elves and Fairies with Assorted Pixies, Mermaids, Brownies, Witches, and Leprechauns. Williams, Garth Montgomery (1912-), illus. LC 51-13747. 76p. illus. 33cm. (Giant golden book, 561). 1951. Simon and Schuster.

--The Golden Book of Nursery Tales. Watson, Jane Werner. Gergely, Tibor (1900-1978), illus. 128p. (Big Golden Book). 1952. Golden Press.

--The Golden Book of Nursery Tales. Rev. ed. Gergely, Tibor (1900-1978), illus. (Big Golden Book: 505). 1952. Simon and Schuster.

--The Golden Book of Poetry. Elliott, Gertrude, illus. LC 47-11438. 97 p. illus. (part col.) 29 cm. 1947. Simon and Schuster.

--The Golden Book of Poetry. Elliott, Gertrude, illus. LC 49-4976. 67 p. illus. (part col.) 29 cm. (Big golden book). 1949. Simon and Schuster.

--The Little Golden Book of Hymns. Malvern, Corinne (1905-1956), illus. (Little Golden Library). 1947. Simon and Shuster.

--The Little Golden Book of Poetry. Malvern, Corinne (1905-1956), illus. (Little Golden Book: 38). 1947. Simon and Schuster.

--The Merry Piper. Watson, Jane Werner. Rockwell, Harlow, illus. (Golden Story Book). 1949. Golden Press.

--Nursery Tales. (A Golden Storytime Book). 1957. Golden Press.

Werner, Mary Kathleen (1948-)

--A Child's Thoughts in Poetry. 1st ed. LC 59-10001. (Illus.). 23cm. 31p. 1959. Greenwich Book Publishers.

Werner, Pat

--How Many Angels in the Sky. Johnson, William R., illus. LC 66-302. 1 v. (unpaged) illus. 22 x 27 cm. 1965. Augsburg Pub. House.

Werner, Vivian L. (1921-)

--Timmie in London. 1st ed. Piquet, Elise, illus. LC 66-8239. 128p. illus. (pt. col.) 25cm. 1966. Doubleday.

--Timmie in Paris. 1st ed. Piquet, Elise, illus. LC 65-19937. 128 p. illus. (part col.) 24 cm. 1965. Doubleday.

Wersba, Barbara (1932-)

--Amanda Dreaming. 1st ed. Mayer, Mercer (1943-), illus. LC 72-75290. (Illus.). 31 p. 26cm. 1973. (ISBN 0-689-30073-5). Atheneum.

--The Boy Who Loved the Sea. Tomes, Margot Ladd (1917-), illus. LC 61-589367. (Illus.). unpaged. 24cm. 1961. Coward-McCann.

--The Brave Balloon of Benjamin Buckley. LC 63-10373. 66 p. illus. 24 cm. 1963. Atheneum.

--Brave Balloon of Benjamin Buckley. 1963. (ISBN 0-8382-1055-4, Cadmus Books). E. M. Hale and Company.

--The Carnival in My Mind. LC 81-48640. 210 p. 21cm. c.1982. (ISBN 0-06-026409-8). (ISBN 0-06-026410-1). Harper & Row.

--The Country of the Heart. LC 75-6947. 115 p. 22cm. 1975. (ISBN 0-689-30469-2). Atheneum.

--The Crystal Child. Diamond, Donna (1950-), illus. LC 81-48643. (Illus.). 48p. (A Charlotte Zolotow Bk.). (gr. 5 up). 1982. (ISBN 0-06-026392-X, HarpJ). (ISBN 0-06-026393-8). Har-Row.

--Do Tigers Ever Bite Kings?. 1st ed. Rivoli, Mario (1943-), illus. LC 66-595093. 1 v. unpaged illus. part col. 25 cm. 1966. Atheneum.

--The Dream Watcher. LC 68-28750. 171 p. 22cm. 1968. Atheneum. **Award: (ALA).**

--The Land of Forgotten Beasts. Tomes, Margot Ladd (1917-), illus. LC 64-19566. 88p. illus. 24cm. c.1964. Atheneum.

--Let Me Fall Before I Fly. Mayer, Mercer (1943-), illus. LC 78-157312. (Illus.). 31 p. 24cm. 1971. Atheneum.

--Run Softly, Go Fast. LC 70-115089. 205 p. 23cm. 1970. (ISBN 0-689-20579-1). Atheneum.

--A Song for Clowns. Rivoli, Mario (1943-), illus. LC 65-217174. 100p. illus. 25cm. c.1965. (ISBN 0-689-20474-4). Atheneum.

--Tunes for a Small Harmonica: A Novel. LC 75-25411. 178 p. 22cm. c.1976. (ISBN 0-06-026372-5). (ISBN 0-06-026373-3). Harper & Row.

Werstein, Irving, adapted by see Disney, Walter Elias.

Werstein, Irving (1914-1971)

--Civil War Sailor. Orbaan, Albert F. (1913-), illus. LC 62-11436. 144p. (Signal bk.). c.1962. Doubleday.

--Danger at Dry Creek: Tales of Wells Fargo. Authorized. Schmidt, Al, illus. LC 59-4411. 188 p. illus 21 cm. 1959. Golden Press.

--The General Slocum Incident: Story of an Ill-Fated Ship. 160p. 1965. John Day & Co.

--Jack Wade, Fighter for Liberty. 1st ed. Orbaan, Albert F. (1913-), illus. LC 63-8729. (Illus.). (gr. 7-9). 1963. (ISBN 0-385-05104-2). Doubleday.

--The Long Escape. 1964. Charles Scribner's Sons.

Wertenbaker, Lael, jt. auth. see Gleaves, Suzanne.

Werth, Kurt (1896-), adapted by.

--The Cobbler's Dilemma: An Italian Folktale. Werth, Kurt (1896-), illus. LC 67-3141. (Illus.). 32 p. 26cm. 1967. (ISBN 0-07-069451-6). McGraw-Hill.

--King Thrushbeard. Werth, Kurt (1896-), illus. LC 68-27567. (Illus.). 32 p. 26cm. 1968. (ISBN 0-670-41326-7). Viking Press.

--Lazy Jack. 1st ed. Werth, Kurt (1896-), illus. LC 78-123021. (Illus.). 32 p. 24cm. 1970. Viking Press.

--The Monkey, the Lion, and the Snake. Gesta Romanorum Werth, Kurt (1896-), illus. LC 67-2492. (Illus.). 31 p. 24cm. 1967. Viking Press.

--The Valiant Tailor. Werth, Kurt (1896-), illus. LC 65-18153. 30p. col. illus. 21cm. c.1965. Viking.

Werth, Kurt (1896-) & Watts, Mabel Pizzey

--Molly and the Giant. Werth, Kurt (1896-), illus. LC 72-6076. (Illus.). 40 p. 24cm. 1973. (ISBN 0-8193-0638-X). (ISBN 0-8193-0638-X). Parents' Magazine Press.

Wertheim, Alexander

--Humorous Tales and Ghost Stories. LC 4-14146. 19cm. 246p. 1904. Broadway Publishing Co.

Wesche, Alice M.

--Runs Far, Son of the Chichimecs. (gr. 3-7). 1982. (ISBN 0-89013-133-3). Museum NM Pr.

Wescott, Edward N.

--David Harum. Parks, Carrie Belle, ed. N.D. D. Appleton-Century Co., Inc.

Wescott, Glenway, jt. auth. see Aesopus.

Wescott, Schluep

--Fun With Timothy Triangle. 64p. N.D. Oddo Publishing Inc.

Wesker, Arnold (1932-)

--Fatlips: A Story for Children. Zarate, Oscar, illus. LC 78-109064. (Illus.). 93 p. 21cm. c.1978. (ISBN 0-06-026388-1). (ISBN 0-06-026389-X). Harper & Row.

Wesley, Dennis, ed. see McGivern, Maureen Daly.

Wesley, Elizabeth, pseud., see McElfresh, Adeline.

Wesley, Mary (1912-)

--Speaking Terms. Morrill, Leslie H., illus. LC 71-137018. (Illus.). 160 p. 22cm. 1971. Gambit.

Wesley-Smith, Peter

--The Ombley-Gombley. Fielding, David, illus. LC 75-115082. (Illus.). 48 p. 24cm. 1st U.S. edition. 1971, c.1969. (ISBN 0-689-20643-7). Atheneum.

Wesselhoeft, Elizabeth Foster Pope see Wesselhoeft, Lily F., pseud.

Wesselhoeft, Elizabeth Foster Pope, Mrs. (1840-1919)

--The Diamond King and the Little Man in Gray. Wesselhoeft, Lily F., pseud. Atwood, Clara E., illus. LC 7-30454. vi, 2, 255 p. front., illus., 3 pl. 19 cm. 1907. Little, Brown & Co.

--Doris and Her Dog Rodney. Wesselhoeft, Lily F., pseud. LC 4633. 3 p. l., 338 p. front., plates. 19 cm. 1900. Little, Brown and Company.

--Fairy Folk of Blue Hill. Wesselhoeft, Lily F., pseud. Repr. N.D. L. C. Page & Co.

--The Fairy-Folk of Blue Hill. Wesselhoeft, Lily F., pseud. Eastman, Alfred C., illus. LC 12-39916. xiii, 240 p. incl. front., illus. 20 cm. 1895. Joseph Knight Company.

--The Fairy Folk of Blue Hill: A Story of Folklore. Wesselhoeft, Lily F., pseud. Eastman, Alfred C., illus. (Illus.). (Gift Book Ser.). N.D. L. C. Page & Co.

--Flipwing the Spy. Wesselhoeft, Lily F., pseud. 277p. N.D. Little, Brown.

--Flipwing, the Spy. A Fable for Children. Wesselhoeft, Lily F., pseud. Plympton, Almira George (1852-1939), illus. LC 12-39917. vi, 7-277 p. incl. front., illus. 17 1/2 cm. 1889. Roberts Brothers.

--Foxy the Faithful. Wesselhoeft, Lily F., pseud. Ireland, H. C., illus. LC 2-22666. (Illus.). 19cm. 312p. Repr. 1902. Little, Brown and Company.

--Frowzle the Runaway. Wesselhoeft, Lily F., pseud. 312p. N.D. Little, Brown.

--Frowzle the Runaway. A Fable for Children. Wesselhoeft, Lily F., pseud. McDermott, Jessie, illus. LC 4-34772. 312 p. front., illus., plates. 17 1/2 cm. 1895. Roberts Brothers.

--High School Days in Harbortown. Wesselhoeft, Lily F., pseud. Ireland, H. C., illus. LC 1-24910. (Illus.). 12cm. 387p. N.D. Little, Brown and Company.

--Jack, the Fire Dog. Wesselhoeft, Lily F., pseud. Ashley, Clifford Warren (1881-), illus. LC 3-23477. 3 p. l., 284 p. front., 5 pl. 19 cm. 1903. Little, Brown, and Company.

--Jerry the Blunderer. Wesselhoeft, Lily F., pseud. (Illus.). (The Boys' and Girls' Books). N.D. Little, Brown and Company.

--Jerry the Blunderer. A Fable for Children. Wesselhoeft, Lily F., pseud. LC 12-39918. 3 p. l., 9-255 p. front., plates. 17 1/2 cm. 1896. Roberts Brothers.

--Laddie, the Master of the House. Wesselhoeft, Lily F., pseud. Withington, Elizabeth R., illus. LC 13-21030. 4 p. l., 323 p. front., plates. 18 1/2 cm. 1913. Little, Brown, and Company.

--Madam Mary of the Zoo. Wesselhoeft, Lily F., pseud. LC 99-5358. 4 p. l., 248 p. front., plates. 19 cm. 1899. Little, Brown & Co.

West, M., adapted by see Haggard, Henry Rider, Sir.

West, Marvin, pseud., see Goldfrap, John Henry.

West, Michael
--Clair De Lune, and Other Troubadour Romances. Paul, Evelyn, illus. Mereer, Alfred, contrib. by. LC 43-35772. 2 p. l., 137, 3 p. illus. (part mounted, part col.) col. plates. 24 1/2 cm. 1913. Brentano's.

West, Michael, ed. see Stevenson, Robert Louis.

West, Nick, pseud., see Lynds, Dennis.

West, Nick, pseud. (1924-)
--Alfred Hitchcock and the Three Investigators in The Mystery of the Coughing Dragon. Lynds, Dennis. Kane, Harry, illus. LC 74-117549. (Based on characters created by Robert Arthur Feder, 1909-1969). (Illus.). viii, 181 p. 22cm. (Alfred Hitchcock Mystery Ser.: Vol. 14). 1970. Random House.
--Alfred Hitchcock and the Three Investigators in The Mystery of the Nervous Lion. Lynds, Dennis. Kane, Harry, illus. LC 78-158379. (Based on characters created by Robert Arthur Feder, 1909-1969). (Illus.). 150 p. 22cm. (Alfred Hitchcock Mystery Ser.: Vol. 16). 1971. (ISBN 0-394-92308-1). Random House.

West, Nick, pseud. (1924-) & Arthur, Robert, pseud. (1909-1969)
--Alfred Hitchcock and the Three Investigators in The Mystery of the Coughing Dragon. Lynds, Dennis. Feder, Robert Arthur. LC 80-18982. (Based on characters created by Robert Arthur Feder, 1909-1969). p. cm. (Alfred Hitchcock Mystery Ser.: Vol. 14). 1981, c.1970. Random House.
--Alfred Hitchcock and the Three Investigators in The Mystery of the Nervous Lion. Lynds, Dennis. Feder, Robert Arthur. LC 80-18981. (Based on characters created by Robert Arthur Feder, 1909-1969). 143 p. 20cm. (Alfred Hitchcock Mystery Ser.: Vol. 16). 1981, c.1971. (ISBN 0-394-84665-6). Random House.
--The Mystery of the Coughing Dragon. Lynds, Dennis. Feder, Arthur Robert. LC 80-18982. (Based on characters created by Robert Arthur Feder, 1909-1969). 176p. (Three Investigators Ser.). (gr. 4-7). 1981. (ISBN 0-394-84666-4). Random.
--The Three Investigators in The Mystery of the Nervous Lion. Lynds, Dennis. rev. ed. Feder, Robert Arthur. LC 83-22997. (Based on characters created by Robert Arthur Feder, 1909-1969). 143 p. 20cm. (The Three Investigators Mystery Series: No. 16). 1984, c.1971. (ISBN 0-394-86416-6). Random House.

West, Patricia M. & Otero, George G.
--Hispanic Folk Songs of the Southwest: An Introduction (Part I). updated. 33p. (Orig.). (Bilingual-Bicultural Foreign Language Ser.). (gr. k-3). 1982. (ISBN 0-943804-11-6). U of Denver Teach.

West, Paul Clarendon, jt. auth. see Denslow, William Wallace.

West, Paul Clarendon (1871-1918)
--Just Boy. Birch, Reginald Bathurst (1856-1943), illus. LC 12-24813. vii, 3-249 p. front., plates. 19 1/2 cm. $1.20. c.1912. George H. Doran Company.

West, Wallace
--The Amazing Inventor from Laurel Creek. Hodges, David, illus. LC 67-1295. (Illus.). 158 p. 21cm. 1967, c.1966. Putnam.

West, Wallace, ed. see Dodgson, Charles Lutwidge.

Westall, Robert Atkinson (1929-)
--Break of Dark: Stories. LC 81-7237. 244 p. 22cm. c.1982. (ISBN 0-688-00875-5). Greenwillow Books.
--The Cats of Seroster. LC 84-4177. 320p. (gr. 7 up). 1984. (ISBN 0-688-03944-8). (ISBN 0-688-02965-5). Greenwillow.
--The Devil on the Road. LC 79-10427. 248 p. 22cm. 1979, c.1978. (ISBN 0-688-80227-3). (ISBN 0-688-84227-5). Greenwillow Books.
--The Devil on the Road. 1978. Macmillan. Award: (CMA).
--Fathom Five. LC 80-11223. p. cm. 1980, c.1979. (ISBN 0-688-80286-9). (ISBN 0-688-84286-0). Greenwillow Books.
--Futuretrack Five. LC 83-14183. 288p. (gr. 7up). 1984. (ISBN 0-688-02598-6). Greenwillow.
--The Haunting of Chas McGill and Other Stories. LC 83-1654. p. cm. 1st U.S. edition. 1983. (ISBN 0-688-02393-2). Greenwillow Books.
--The Machine Gunners. LC 76-13630. p. cm. 1976, c.1975. (ISBN 0-688-80055-6). Greenwillow Books. Awards: (BGH); (CMA).
--The Scarecrows. LC 81-2052. p. cm. 1981. (ISBN 0-688-00612-4). (ISBN 0-688-00613-2). Greenwillow Books. Award: (CMA).
--The Watch House. LC 77-19088. 218 p. 22cm. c.1977. (ISBN 0-688-80149-8). (ISBN 0-688-84149-X). Greenwillow Books.
--The Wind Eye. LC 77-5162. (Illus.). 213 p. 22cm. 1977, c.1976. (ISBN 0-688-80114-5). (ISBN 0-688-84114-7). Greenwillow Books.

--The Wind Eye. LC 77-355575. (Illus.). 6, 212 p. 21cm. 1976. (ISBN 0-333-21187-1). Macmillan.

Westbrook, Bill & Hale, Thomas (1936-)
--Where Have All the Horses Gone?. Hale, Thomas (1936-), illus. LC 73-169819. (Illus.). 57 p. 24cm. 1973. (ISBN 0-87858-037-9). Westover Pub. Co.

Westbrook, Dante
--Daxius. Crumpler, Dewey, illus. LC 77-83857. (Illus.). 23 p. 25cm. (Fifth world tales). c.1977. (ISBN 0-89239-014-X). Children's Book Press.

Westbury, Victoria
--Treela. (gr. 2-6). N.D. (ISBN 0-8181-0288-8). Pageant-Poseidon.

Westcott, Alvin M.
--Billy Lump's Adventure. LC 68-56817. (Illus.). (gr. 2-4). 1968. (ISBN 0-87783-002-9). Oddo.
--Rockets and Crackers. Le Blanc, Lee, illus. LC 75-108729. (Illus.). 80 p. 25cm. 1970. Oddo Pub.

Westcott, Alvin M., jt. auth. see Symons, Catherine.

Westcott, Alvin M. & Symons, Catherine
--Whispering River. Pearson, Jeanne & Pearson, Charles, illus. LC 78-108727. (Illus.). 25cm. 48p. (gr. 3-5). 1970. (ISBN 0-87783-049-5). (ISBN 0-87783-116-5). Oddo.

Westcott, Jan Vlachos (1912-)
--Set Her on a Throne. 240p. (gr. 5 up). 1972. (ISBN 0-316-93126-8). Little.
--The Tower and the Dream. 1974. (ISBN 0-399-11128-X). G. P. Putnam's Sons.

Westcott, Nadine Bernard
--The Giant Vegetable Garden. Westcott, Nadine Bernard, illus. LC 80-29261. (Illus.). 32 p. 26cm. c.1981. (ISBN 0-316-93129-2). (ISBN 0-316-93130-6). Little, Brown.

Westcott, Nadine Bernard, retold by.
--I Know an Old Lady Who Swallowed a Fly. 1st ed. Westcott, Nadine Bernard, illus. LC 79-24728. p. cm. 1980. (ISBN 0-316-93128-4). Little, Brown.

Westcott, Nadine Bernard, retold by see Andersen, Hans Christian.

Westdyk, Roxanne H., jt. auth. see Derrig, Leslie A.

Westen, Percy F.
--On The Wings of the Wind. (The Aviation Library). N.D. Dodge Pub. Co.

Westerberg, Christine (1950-)
--A Little Lion. Westerberg, Christine (1950-), illus. LC 74-20894. (Illus.). 32 p. 22cm. 1975. (ISBN 0-13-537779-X). Prentice-Hall.

Westerberg, Christine (1950-), adapted by.
--The Cap That Mother Made. Westerberg, Christine (1950-), illus. LC 76-48301. (Illus.). 32 p. 22cm. c.1977. (ISBN 0-13-113365-9). Prentice-Hall.

Westergaard, A. C
--Henry and His Travels. Dodge, Daniel Kilham (1867-), tr. LC 23-144073. vi p., 1 l., 292, 1 p. front. 19 1/2 cm. 1923. D. Appleton and Company.

Westerman, Percy Francis (1876-1959)
--Annesley's Double. (MacMillan Bks. for Boys & Girls). (gr. 7-9). 1926. MacMillan Bks.
--The Scouts of Seal Island. (MacMillan Bks. for Boys & Girls). (gr. 7-9). 1922. MacMillan Bks.
--The Sea Scouts of the Petrel. (MacMillan Bks. for Boys & Girls). (gr. 7-9). 1924. MacMillan Bks.
--The Secret Channel and Other Stories. 1919. Macmillan.

Westermann, Paul, jt. auth. see Bischoff, David Frederick.

Western, Alan
--Desert Hawk. LC 45-32784. 288 p. col. front. 20 cm. (The Treasure library). 1937. F. Warne and Co. Ltd.
--The Sargasso Secret. LC 46-401694. 256 p. col. front., illus. (map) 19 1/2 cm. 1939. F. Warne & Co. Ltd.

Western Printing and Lithographing Company
--The Story of Honey Bear. Williams, Ben, illus. LC 54-21755. unpaged. 21cm. 1953. Honey Bear Farm.

Western Writers of America
--Hound Dogs and Others: A Collection of Stories. Kjelgaard, James Arthur (1910-1959), ed. Brown, Paul (1893-1958), illus. LC 72-122734. (Illus.). 245 p. 20cm. (Short story index reprint series). 1970, c.1958. Books for Libraries Press.
--Hound Dogs and Others: A Collection of Stories. Kjelgaard, James Arthur (1910-1959), ed. Brown, Paul (1893-1958), illus. LC 58-13131. 245 p. illus. 21 cm. 1958. Dodd, Mead.
--A Saddlebag of Tales: A Collection of Stories. Montgomery, Rutherford George (1896-), ed. Savitt, Sam (1917-), illus. LC 79-38727. (Illus.). 239 p. 23cm. (Short story index reprint series). 1972, c.1959. (ISBN 0-8369-4140-3). Books for Libraries Press.
--A Saddlebag of Tales: A Collection of Stories. Montgomery, Rutherford George (1896-), ed. Savitt, Sam (1917-), illus. LC 59-9579. 239 p. illus. 21 cm. 1959. Dod, Mead.

--Search for the Hidden Places: A Collection of Stories. Mygatt, Emmie D., ed. Weiss, Emil (1896-1965), illus. LC 63-13178. 241 p. illus. 21 cm. 1963. D. McKay Co.
--Trails of Adventure: A Collection of Stories. Mygatt, Emmie D., ed. LC 61-15930. 274 p. illus. 21 cm. 1961. Dodd, Mead.
--The Wild Horse Roundup. Kjelgaard, James Arthur (1910-1959), ed. Brown, Paul (1893-1958), illus. LC 74-3404. p. cm. (Short story index report series). 1974, c.1957. (ISBN 0-8369-4270-1). Books for Libraries Press.
--The Wild Horse Roundup: A Collection of Stories. Kjelgaard, James Arthur (1910-1959), ed. Brown, Paul (1893-1958), illus. LC 57-13310. 275 p. illus. 21 cm. 1957. Dodd, Mead.

Westervelt, Josephine Hope
--The Quest of the Hidden Ivory: A/Story of Adventure in Tropical Africa. LC 24-23598. (Illus.). 1924. Fleming H. Revell Company.

Westervelt, William D.
--Ghosts of the Hilo Hills. 16p. 1968. (ISBN 0-912180-02-1). The Petroglyph Press.
--Hawaiian Legends of Ghosts and Ghost Gods. N.D. (ISBN 0-8048-0238-6). Charles E. Tuttle.

Westheimer, David
--The Avila Gold. 1974. (ISBN 0-399-11466-1). G. P. Putnam's Sons.

Westlake, Donald Edwin (1933-)
--Philip. Dobrin, Arnold (1928-), illus. LC 67-15406. (Illus.). 46 p. 26cm. 1967. Crowell.

Westlund, P. R.
--Three Rode As One. 256p. (Orig.). N.D. (ISBN 0-918747-02-3). AZ Hse Pub.

Westman, Barbara
--Anna's Magic Broom. Westman, Barbara, illus. LC 77-4831. p. cm. 1977. (ISBN 0-395-25783-2). Houghton Mifflin.

Weston, Christine Goutiere (1904-1980)
--Bhimsa: The Dancing Bear. Duvoisin, Roger Antoine (1904-1980), illus. LC 45-37869. 3 p. l., 120 p. illus. (part col.) 21 cm. 1945. C. Scribner's Sons. Award: (JNM).

Weston, D. C., Mrs.
--Old Testament Stories. (Illus.). N.D. E P Dutton.

Weston, John (1932-)
--The Boy Who Sang the Birds. Diamond, Donna (1950-), illus. LC 75-27706. (Illus.). 106 p. 21cm. c.1976. (ISBN 0-684-14534-0). Scribner.

Weston, Martha
--Poeny's Rainbow. Weston, Martha, illus. LC 80-28505. (Illus.). 33 p. 26cm. c.1981. (ISBN 0-688-00540-3). (ISBN 0-688-00541-1). Lothrop, Lee & Shepard Books.

Weston, May Forth
--The Great Pathfinder: The Story of Jedediah Smith. Lundean, Louis, illus. LC 44-8680. 212 p. incl. front., 1 illus., plates. 21 1/2 cm. 1944. R. M. McBride & Company.

Weston, W. H., retold by.
--Plutarch's Lives for Boys and Girls. Rainey, William R. I. (1852-1936), illus. LC 27-20610. (Illus.). vi, 300. 21cm. 1926. T. Nelson and Sons.

Westover, Russell Channing (1896-1966)
--Tillie the Toiler. (C. & L. Famous Comics in Book Form: Bk. 1). N.D. Cupples & Leon Co.
--Tillie the Toiler. 48p. (C & L Famous Comics in Book Form: No. 5). N.D. Cupples & Leon Co.
--Tillie the Toiler and the Masquerading Duchess: Based on the Famous Newspaper Strip. authorized. LC 43-227031. 3 p. l., 11-248 p. illus. 20 1/2 cm. 1943. Whitman Publishing Company.

Westphal, Clarence (1904-)
--Folk Tales of Korea. Lindberg, Howard E., illus. LC 70-108934. (Illus.). 94 p. 25cm. 1970. Denison.
--Mooney, the Pet Lion. Spiegel, Lawrence M., illus. LC 62-17847. 29cm. 1963. T. S. Denison.

Westphal, Wilma Ross
--Jeanie. (gr. 7 up). N.D. Review & Herald.
--Jeanie Goes to the Mission Field. Collins, Fred, illus. LC 65-18678. 287 p. illus. 22 cm. 1966. Review and Herald Pub. Association.

Westrate, Edwin Victor & Beecher, Elizabeth
--Ranger of '76. LC 61-10635. 216p. 22cm. 1961. Houghton Mifflin.

Westreich, Alice & Westreich, Budd
--Uncle Morgan's Ghost. Miller, Marilyn Jean (1925-), illus. LC 72-97807. (Illus.). x, 148 p. 21cm. 1970. McKay.

Westreich, Budd
--The Day It Rained Sidneys. LC 65-12130. viii, 181p. illus. 21cm. c.1965. McKay.
--Lance Todd at Mystery House. Prezio, Victor, illus. LC 59-7418. 223 p. illus. 21 cm. 1959. Lantern Press.
--Lance Todd at Mystery Island. Lewis, Richard William (1933-1966), illus. LC 59-13373. 224 p. illus. 21 cm. 1959. Lantern Press.
--Please Stand Clear of the Apache Arrows. LC 69-13787. viii, 152 p. 21cm. 1969. D. McKay Co.

Westreich, Budd, jt. auth. see Westreich, Alice.

Westrup, Emily
--A Hunting ABC: Nursery Rhymes for Doggy Times. N.D. Dodge Publishing Co.

Westwood, Gwen (1915-)
--Narni of the Desert. Warner, Peter (1939-), illus. LC 68-11648. 93p. illus. 21cm. 1968. (ISBN 0-528-80413-8). Rand McNally.

Westwood, Jennifer (1940-), abridged by see Wilde, Oscar Fingal O'Flahertie Wills.

Westwood, Jennifer (1940-), retold by.
--Gilgamesh & Other Babylonian Tales. Charlton, Michael Alan (1923-), illus. LC 71-105576. (Illus.). 96 p. 23cm. 1st U.S. edition. 1970, c.1968. Coward-McCann.
--Going to Squintum's:. A Foxy Folktale. French, Fiona (1944-), illus. 28p. 1985. (ISBN 0-8037-0015-6). Dial.
--Medieval Tales. Baynes, Pauline Diana (1922-), illus. LC 68-15657. (Illus.). 147 p. 24cm. 1968, c.1967. Coward-McCann.
--Stories of Charlemagne. LC 74-12435. 153 p. 22cm. 1976, c.1972. (ISBN 0-87599-213-7). S. G. Phillips.
--Tales and Legends. Baynes, Pauline Diana (1922-), illus. LC 77-129179. (Illus.). 123 p. 24cm. 1st U.S. edition. 1971. Coward, McCann & Geoghegan.

Wetherbee, Holden
--The Wonder Ring: A Fantasy in Silhouette. LC 77-16955. (Illus.). ca. 150 p. 22cm. 1979, c.1978. (ISBN 0-385-13263-8). (ISBN 0-385-13262-X). Doubleday.

Wetherby, Alfred
--The Hand in the Dark. N.D. Methodist Bk Concern.
--The Hand in the Dark. LC 12-40214. 1 p. l., 270 p. front. 17 1/2 cm. 1883. Walden and Stowe.
--A Happy Life. LC 12-40217. 227 p. 19 cm. 1885. Cranston & Stowe.
--A Happy Life. N.D. Methodist Bk Concern.

Wetherell, Elizabeth, pseud., see Warner, Susan Bogert.

Wetherell, Elizabeth, pseud. (1819-1885)
--The Christmas Stocking. Warner, Susan Bogert. 1 of 12 vols. New ed. (Illus.). (Good Time Ser.: No. 4). 1905. Set. Henry Altemus Co.
--The Christmas Stocking. Warner, Susan Bogert. (Illus.). 64p. (Ogilvie's Books for Boys and Girls). N.D. J. S. Ogilvie.
--Queechy. Warner, Susan Bogert, 31 vols, No. 20. (Illus.). (Famous Books for Girls Ser.). 1905. Set. H M Caldwell Co.
--Queechy. Warner, Susan Bogert. (Illus.). 1900. J B Lippincott.
--The Wide, Wide World. Warner, Susan Bogert. (Illus.). (Famous Books for Girls Ser.: No. 25). 1905. Set. H M Caldwell Co.
--The Wide, Wide World. Warner, Susan Bogert. (Illus.). 1900. J B Lippincott.
--The Wide, Wide World. Warner, Susan Bogert. (The Young People's Library). N.D. William Collins Co.

Wetherfield, Edith
--The Little Cobbler and the North Wind. 1st ed. LC 56-8089. 64 p. illus. 21 cm. 1956. Vantage Press.

Wetherill, Fred V
--Boys and Buoys. Welsh, Louise & Cash, W. E., Jr., illus. LC 28-21275. 151, 1 p. illus. 17 1/2 cm. 1928. Wetherill Publishing Company.

Wetmore, Claude Hazeltine (1863-)
--Bedtime Stories. Bailey, Mildred L. & Jones, Theresa Jessel, illus. LC 14-17812. 6 p. l., 15-120 p. col. illus. 27 1/2 cm. $1.00. 1914. The Macaulay Company.
--Fighting Under the Southern Cross. (Illus.). 333p. 1910. W. A. Wilde Co.
--In a Brazilian Jungle. (Illus.). 315p. 1910. W. A. Wilde.
--Incaland. (Illus.). 309p. 1910. W. A. Wilde.
--Queen Magi's Little People. Bailey, Mildred L. & Jones, Theresa Jessel, illus. LC 13-19946. 127, 1 p. col. illus., col. plates. 25 cm. 1913. Con. P. Curran Printing Co.
--Queen Tiny's Little People. Bailey, Mildred L. & Jones, Theresa Jessel, illus. LC 14-17811. 105 p. incl. col. illus., pl. 27 1/2 cm. $1.00. 1914. The Macaulay Company.
--Sweepers of the Sea. Coffin, G. A., illus. N.D. Bowen-Merrill.

Wetmore, Marge C.
--Sugar: The Clumsy Colt. 1983. (ISBN 0-8062-2132-1). Carlton.

Wetterer, Margaret K
--The Giant's Apprentice. 1st ed. Primavera, Elise, illus. LC 81-10810. (Illus.). 40 p. 21cm. 1982. (ISBN 0-689-50229-X). Atheneum.
--The Mermaid's Cape. Primavera, Elise, illus. LC 80-20338. (Illus.). 32 p. 21cm. 1981. (ISBN 0-689-50197-8). Atheneum.
--Patrick and the Fairy Thief. 1st ed. Arno, Enrico (1913-1981), illus. LC 79-22576. (Illus.). 31 p. 21cm. 1980. Atheneum.

Wettlin, Margaret, tr. see Gorky, Maxim.

Wettlin, Margaret, tr. see Nosov, Nikolai Nikolaevich.

Wheeler, William Adolphus (1833-1874), ed.
--Mother Goose's Melodies for Children. Moulton, Charles, illus. N.D. Houston Mifflin Co.
Wheeling, Lynn
--When Is That?. Wheeling, Lynn, illus. LC 64-18032. 47 p. col. illus. 19 x 23 cm. 1964. Putnam.
--Who's There?. Wheeling, Lynn, illus. LC 75-92825. (Illus.). 32 p. 21cm. 1970. Putnam.
Wheelock, Effie E, Mrs.
--Little Poems for Little People. LC 30-724. 3 p. l., 11-128 p. front. (port.) 16 cm. c.1930. "Church of God" Publishing House.
Wheelock, Elizabeth M
--Stories of Wagner Operas for Children. New ed. (Illus.). N.D. Bobbs-Merrill.
Wheelock, Gertrude Mercia
--The Dawn Garden: A Fairy Story for Little Girls. LC 22-16174. 119 p. col. front. 19 cm. c.1922. Dorrance.
Wheelock, John Hall (1886-1978), tr. see Dalgliesh, Alice.
Wheelock, John Hall (1868-1978)
--In Love & Song. Martin, Stefan (1936-), illus. LC 75-158886. (Illus.). wood engravings. 128p. (Encore Edition). (gr. 7 up). 1971. (ISBN 0-684-15861-2, ScribT). Scribner.
Wheelock, Lucy, ed.
--The Allan Books. (Illus.). N.D. Set. A. W. Wilde.
--The Marjorie Books. (Illus.). 1910. A. W. Willde.
--Songs with Music. LC 21-1047. vii, 1 p., 1 l., 142 p. col. front., illus. 20 cm. (Half-title: The kindergarten children's). (Vol. 5). c.1920. Houghton, Mufflin Company.
Wheelock, Lucy, tr. from German.
--Red Letter Stories. N.D. Lothrop Pub Co.
--Uncle Titus. N.D. D. Lothrop Co.
--Uncle Titus. N.D. Pilgrim Press.
Wheelock, Lucy, ed. see May, Georgiana Marion Craik.
Wheelock, Lucy, intro. by see Scott, Florence E.
Wheelock, Lucy, jt. tr. see Pickard, J. C.
Wheelock, Lucy, tr. see Spyri, Johanna Heusser.
Wheelock, Lucy, tr. see Stoddard, William Osborn.
Wheelock, Sarah
--The Little Warrens at Breezy Hollow: A Story of Real Boys and Girls. LC 37-22497. x p., 1 l., 206 p. illus. 21 cm. 1937. Frederick A. Stokes Company.
--The Three Little Warrens. Lawson, Marie Abrams (1894-1956), illus. N.D. J. B. Lippincott.
--The Three Little Warrens: A Story of Real Boys and Girls. xi, 227 p. incl. front., illus. 21 cm. 1935. Frederick A. Stokes Company.
Wheelock, Warren, ed.
--Beyond the Block, Vol. 2. 2d ed. Sheldon, William Denley (1915-), illus. LC 77-90628. (Illus.). v, 127 p. 21cm. (Breakthrough!). c.1978. Allyn and Bacon.
Wheelock, Warren, jt. ed. see Sheldon, William Denley.
Wheelock, Warren, jt. ed. see Woessner, Nina C.
Wheelright, John T.
--A Bad Penny. Attwood, Francis G. & Bird, E. B., illus. (Gift Book Ser.). N.D. L. C. Page & Co.
Wheelwright, Jere H.
--Gentlemen, Hush!. Ray, Ralph (1920-1952), illus. 1948. Charles Scribner's Sons.
Wheelwright, John Tyler (1856-1925)
--War Children. Rae, John (1882-1963), illus. 4 p. l., 308 p. front., 3 pl. 20 cm. 1908. Dodd, Mead & Company.
Wheelwright, John Tyler (1856-1925) & Stimson, Frederic J.
--Rollo's Journey to Cambridge. Attwood, Francis G., illus. 1926. Houghton Mifflin Co.
Whelan, Gloria Ann (1923-)
--A Clearing in the Forest. LC 78-3608. 126 p. 22cm. c.1978. (ISBN 0-399-20639-6). Putnam.
--The Pathless Woods. 1st ed. Kessell, Walter, illus. LC 80-8725. (Illus.). 181 p. 21cm. c.1981. (ISBN 0-397-31931-2). (ISBN 0-397-31930-4). Lippincott.
--A Time to Keep Silent. LC 79-11608. 127 p. 22cm. c.1979. (ISBN 0-399-20693-0). Putnam.
Whelen, Mignonette Violett, Mrs.
--Romances of Fanland: Or, Stories Told to Violett. 164 p. 20 1/2 cm. 1906. Griffith and Rowland Press.
Whelpton, Barbara, ed. see Chandon, G & Peron, Rene.
Whelpton, Barbara, ed. see Chandon, G & Vergilius Maro, Publius.
Whelpton, Barbara, tr. see Chandon, G & Peron, Rene.
Whelpton, Barbara, tr. see Chandon, G & Vergilius Maro, Publius.
Whelpton, Barbara, tr. see Desmurger, Marguerite.
Whelpton, Barbara Crocker (1910-), tr. see Grimal, Pierre Antoine.
Whetsel, Charles W.
--The Story of Maudie and Toddy. (Illus.). (gr. k-2). N.D. Vantage.
Whilden, Ellen A
--Hearts and Hands: Or, Maggie's and Ruby's Way. LC 12-40219. 3 p. l., 5-173 p. front., plates. 18 1/2 cm. c.1892. American Baptist Publication Society.
--Hearts and Hands: Or, Maggie's and Ruby's Way. 173p. N.D. Sunday-School Publications.
Whipple, Dorothy (1893-)
--Pinky Winky Kitty Book. N.D. Four Seas.
--The Smallest Tortoise of All. Williams, Hubert, illus. LC 65-10018. 1v. (unpaged) illus. 22cm. 1964. Warne.
--Smallest Tortoise of All. Williams, Hubert, illus. LC 65-10018. (Illus.). (gr. k-2). 1965. Warne.
--The Tale of a Very Little Tortoise. Williams, Hubert, illus. LC 62-12502. unpaged. illus. 22 cm. 1962. F. Warne.
Whipple, Mary Anne & Heizer, Nancy E.
--The First Californians. 2d rev. ed. Seeger, Virginia, illus. LC 75-165582. (Illus.). xi, 83 p. 23cm. 1971. Peek Publications.
Whipple, Wayne (1856-) & Aaron, Samuel Francis (1862-1942)
--Bill Brown Listens in. LC 22-24687. 254 p. front. 19 cm. c.1922. Hurst & Company.
--Bill Brown's Radio. LC 22-192165. 238 p. front. 19 1/2 cm. c.1922. Hurst & Company.
Whishaw, Fred
--Lost in African Jungles. (The Albion Library). N.D. Frederick Warne & Co.
Whisman, Molly
--My Hideout. Kessler, Leonard P. (1921-), illus. LC 69-10210. (Illus.). 32 p. 25cm. 1969. Harper & Row.
Whistler, Charles Watts (1856-1913)
--Dragon Osmund: A Story of Athelstan and of Brunanburn. 5 p. l., 7-368 p. col. front., col. plates. 21 cm. 1914. T. Nelson and Sons.
--Gerald the Sheriff: A Story of the Sea in the Days of William Rufus. Speed, Lancelot, illus. LC 20-1278. ix, 294 p. front., 7 pl. 19 1/2 cm. 1906. F. Warne and Co.
--Havelok the Dane: A Legend of Old Grimsby and Lincoln. LC 20-12777. 1 p. l., vii-xii, 11-393 p. col. front 19 1/2 cm. 1899. T. Nelson and Sons.
--Havelok the Dane: A Legend of Old Grimsby & Lincoln. Margetson, W. H., illus. 1900. Thomas Nelson & Sons.
--A Prince Errant: The Story of Prince Horn and the Princess Rymenhild, As Told by Athulf, Horn's Foster-Brother. LC 20-1279. x p., 1 l., 13-304 p. col. front., col. pl. 19 1/2 cm. 1908. T. Nelson and Sons.
--A Prince of Cornwall. (The Treasure Library). N.D. Frederick Warne & Co.
--A Sea-Queen's Sailing. LC 20-123331. 368 p. col. front., 3 col. pl. 19 1/2 cm. (Lettered on cover: Nelson's girls' library). 1911. T. Nelson and Sons.
--A Thane of Wessex. (Illus.). (Scribner-Blackie Series of Books for young people). N.D. Charles Scribner's Sons.
--Wulfric the Weapon Thane. (Illus.). (Scribner-Blackie Series of books for young people). N.D. Charles Scribner's Sons.
Whistler, Reginald John see Whistler, Rex, pseud.
Whistler, Rex, pseud., see Whistler, Reginald John.
Whistler, Rex, pseud. (1905-1944), illus.
--Hans Andersen. Whistler, Reginald John. LC 79-302846. (Illus.). 470p. 1st U.S. edition. 1979. (ISBN 0-370-01038-8, Pub. by Chatto Bodley Jonathan). Merrimack Pub Cir.
Whitaker, Christine D.
--Poems for Children. N.D. Exposition Press.
--The Singing Teakettle: Poems for Children. 1st ed. LC 55-118382. 40p. 21cm. 1956. Exposition Press.
Whitaker, David (1930-) & Dr. Who (Television Program)
--Doctor Who In An Exciting Adventure with the Daleks. Schwartzman, Arnold, illus. LC 66-553. 157p. illus. 21cm. (Based on the BBC Television Serial of Dr. Who by Terry Nation by Arr. with the BBC.). 1966, c.1964. F. Muller.
--Dr. Who & the Daleks. (Illus.). (gr. 7 up). N.D. (ISBN 0-392-02707-0, LTB). Soccer.
Whitaker, E. W.
--Uncle William's Charges: Or, The Broken Trust. Juv. ed. Garland, C. T., illus. N.D. Cassell & Co.
Whitaker, Ellis
--The Little Bitty Frogs. 1981. (ISBN 0-8062-1752-9). Carlton.
Whitaker, Evelyn
--Baby John. 114 p. 17 cm. 1892. Roberts Brother.
--Baby John Zoe, and For the Fourth Time of Asking. LC 91. 7-382. 17cm. 1899. Little, Brown and Company.
--Belle. 236p. 1898. Little, Brown & Co.
--Dear. LC 5-41092. 312 p. front. 17 cm. 1892. Roberts Brothers.
--Don. 332p. 1895. Roberts Brothers.
--Gay. Tarrant, Percy, illus. 351p. 1903. Little Brown & Co.
--Gilly Flower. (Illus.). (The Wellesley Series for Girls). N.D. A. L. Burt's.
--Gilly Flower. N.D. E & J B Young.
--Honor Bright: Or, Four-Leaved Shamrock. (Illus.). (The Meade Series for Girls). N.D. A. L. Burt.
--Laddie. (Illus.). (Savoy Ser.). N.D. Barse and Hopkins.
--Laddie. (Illus.). (The Golden Bks.). N.D. Barse & Hopkins.
--Laddie. (Relyea Classics). N.D. Barse & Hopkins.
--Laddie. (Dagonet Ser.). N.D. Barse & Hopkins.
--Laddie. (Illus.). (Every Boy's Library). N.D. Caldwell.
--Laddie. (Illus.). (Every Boy's Library). N.D. Dodge Publishing Co.
--Laddie. N.D. E. P. Dutton & Co.
--Laddie, 25 vols. (Illus.). (The Editha Ser.: No. 5). 1905. Set. H M Caldwell Co.
--Laddie, 1 of 12 vols. New ed. (Illus.). (Good Time Ser.: No. 5). 1905. Set. Henry Altemus Co.
--Laddie. (Illus.). (Belles-Lettres Ser.). N.D. Henry Altemus.
--Laddie. (Laddie Ser.). N.D. Henry Altemus Co.
--Laddie. LC 31-35228. 52 p. 18 1/2 cm. 1894. T. Y. Crowell & Co.
--Laddie. 52p. 1894. T. Y. Crowell & Co.
--Laddie. (Illus.). (Sunshine Library for Young People). 1900. T. Y. Crowell & Co.
--Laddie. LC 508328. 76 p. front., plates. 16 cm. 1900. W. B. Conkey Company.
--Laddie and Miss Toosey's Mission. (Illus.). (Altemus' Vademecum Ser.). N.D. Henry Altemus Co.
--Laddie and Miss Toosey's Mission. (Illus.). (Boys' and Girls' Classics). N.D. Henry Altemus Co.
--Laddie and Miss Toosey's Mission. (Illus.). (Golden Treasury Ser.). N.D. Henry Altemus Co.
--Laddie and Miss Toosey's Mission. Handy Volume, Large Type ed. (Illus.). (Petit-Trianon Ser.). N.D. Henry Altemus.
--Laddie and Miss Toosey's Mission. Handy Volume, Large Type ed. (Illus.). (Beauxarts Ser.). N.D. Henry Altemus.
--Larry's Luck. (Illus.). (The Rugby Ser.). N.D. A. L. Burt.
--Lassie. LC 1-20950. 135p. 17cm. 1901. Little, Brown and Company.
--Miss Toosey, 25 vols. (Illus.). (The Editha Ser.: No. 6). 1905. Set. H M Caldwell Co.
--Miss Toosey and Laddie. (Illus.). (The Alcazar Ser.). N.D. Caldwell.
--Miss Toosey and Laddie. (Illus.). (The Young Folks Lib.). N.D. H. M. Caldwell Co.
--Miss Toosey and Laddie, 1 of 156 vols. (Illus.). (The Empyreal Library of Handy Volume Classics). N.D. H. M. Caldwell & Co.
--Miss Toosey and Laddie. (The Golden Counsel Ser.). N.D. H. M. Caldwell & Co.
--The "Miss Toosey" Books. (Illus.). N.D. Little, Brown and Company.
--Miss Toosey's Mission. (Illus.). (The Golden Bks.). N.D. Barse & Hopkins.
--Miss Toosey's Mission. (Relyea Classics). N.D. Barse & Hopkins.
--Miss Toosey's Mission. (Dagonet Ser.). N.D. Barse & Hopkins.
--Miss Toosey's Mission. (Illus.). (Every Boy's Library). N.D. Caldwell.
--Miss Toosey's Mission. (Illus.). N.D. E. P. Dutton & Co.
--Miss Toosey's Mission. 122p. (Altemus' Good Times Ser.). 1903. H. Altemus Co.
--Miss Toosey's Mission, 1 of 12 vols. New ed. (Illus.). (Good Time Ser.: No. 8). 1905. Set. Henry Altemus Co.
--Miss Toosey's Mission. (Illus.). (Belles-Lettres Ser.). N.D. Henry Altemus.
--Miss Toosey's Mission. (Laddie Ser.). N.D. Henry Altemus Co.
--Miss Toosey's Mission. (Illus.). (The Children's Friend Ser.). N.D. Little, Brown and Company.
--Miss Toosey's Mission. (Illus.). (Sunshine Library for Young People). 1900. T. Y. Crowell & Co.
--Miss Toosey's Mission. N.D. Thomas Y. Crowell Co.
--Miss Toosey's Mission and Laddie, 36 vols. (Illus.). (St. Nicholas Ser.). 1905. Set. A L Burt Co.
--Miss Toosey's Mission and Laddie. (Illus.). (The Wellesley Series for Girls). N.D. A. L. Burt.
--Miss Toosey's Mission and Laddie. (Illus.). 157p. N.D. American Tract Society.
--Miss Toosey's Mission and Laddie, 1 of 50 vols. (Heart Life Classics). N.D. American Tract Soceity.
--Miss Toosey's Mission and Laddie. (Illus.). N.D. E. P. Dutton & Co.
--Miss Toosey's Mission and Laddie. (Illus.). N.D. Little, Brown and Company.
--Miss Toosey's Mission, Laddie and Pris. 244p. 1899. Little Brown & Co.
--One of a Covey. (Illus.). (The Wellesley Series for Girls). N.D. A. L. Burt.
--Pomona. Barnes, Robert, illus. LC 20-16480. iv, 5-296 p. front., plates. 17 cm. 1894. Roberts Brothers.
--Rob and Kit. LC 98-1650. vi, 275. 17cm. 1898. Little, Brown, and Company.
--Tip Cat. LC 52-56006. 287 p. 17 cm. 1884. Roberts Bros.
--Tom's Boy. Tarrant, Percy, illus. LC 6330. vi, 342 p., 1 l., front., plates. 17 1/2 cm. 1900. Little, Brown and Company.
--Tom's Opinion. (Illus.). (The Rugby Ser.). N.D. A. L. Burt.
Whitchurch, Mrs.
--Cherry pie: Or, Pictures Bright for Our Pet's Delight. Claudius, W., illus. (Illus.). N.D. Worthington Company.
Whitcomb, Adah Frances, ed. see Mother Goose.
Whitcomb, Carrie Gates Niles, Mrs. (1861-)
--The Autobiography of Jeremy L., the Actor Dog. LC 10-16975. (Illus.). 28p. 20cm. 1910. F. A. Bassette Co.
Whitcomb, Edna Pearle Osborne, Mrs.
--We Five. Brockman, Ann, illus. LC 28-156283. 6 p. l., 240 p. col. front. 21 cm. 1926. Doubleday, Doran & Company, Inc.
Whitcomb, Ida Prentice (1843-1931)
--Carol in Birdland. Stephenson, Eunice Holmes, illus. LC 24-22145. viii p., 3 l., 77, 1 p. col. front., 11 col. pl. 21 cm. $1.75. 1924. Dodd, Mead and Company.
Whitcomb, Jessie Wright see Wright, Elvirton, pseud.
Whitcomb, Jessie Wright see Wright, Jessie E., pseud.
Whitcomb, Jessie Wright, Mrs.
--His Great Responsibility. LC 4-35336. 64 p. illus. 17 1/2 cm. 1904. D. C. Cook Publishing Company.
--An Odd Little Lass: A Story for Girls. Waugh, Ida, illus. LC 12-404138. v, 7-361 p. incl. front. plates. 19 cm. 1898. The Penn Publishing Company.
--Philip Leicester. LC 12-404159. 264 p. front., plates. 19 cm. c.1894. W. A. Wilde & Company.
Whitcomb, Jon (1906-)
--Pom-Pom's Christmas. Whitcomb, Jon (1906-), illus. LC 60-123216. unpaged. illus. 27 cm. 1960. Holt, Rinehart and Winston.
Whitcomb, Mary Burg
--Tee-Bo & the Persnickety Prowler. (Tee-Bo Bks.). (gr. 4 up). 1978. (ISBN 0-307-21583-0, Golden Pr). Western Pub.
--Tee-Bo in the Great Hort Hunt. (Tee-Bo Bks.). (gr. 4 up). 1978. (ISBN 0-307-21584-9, Golden Pr). Western Pub.
--Tee-Bo the Talking Dog on the Trail of the Persnickety Prowler. Stone, David Karl (1922-), illus. LC 75-316452. (Illus.). 138 p. 20cm. 1975. (ISBN 0-307-01583-1). Western Pub. Co.
Whitcomb, Russell
--Comrades Courageous: A Story of Two Youths and the 'Frisco Earthquake. LC 7-36917. 3 p. l., 5-190 p. front. 19 1/2 cm. 1907. R. G. Badger.
--Skimming the Skies. LC 9-2042. 3 p. l., 250 p. front., 3 pl. 19 1/2 cm. (Comrades courageous series). 1909. R. G. Badger.
Whitcup, Pauline
--Grandma's Rhymes and Stories. 48p. N.D. (ISBN 0-87559-137-X). P. Shalom Publications, Inc.
White, ed. see Irving, Washington.
White, Al
--The Mickey Mouse Book. Disney, Walt, Studio, illus. (ps-1). 1965. (ISBN 0-307-68914-X, Golden Pr). Western Pub.
--The Winnie-the-Pooh Book. Disney, Walt, Studio, illus. (Illus.). (ps-1). 1965. (ISBN 0-307-68927-1, Golden Pr). Western Pub.
White, Alan
--The Long Summer. LC 75-17601. 192p. 1975. (ISBN 0-15-153079-3). HarBraceJ.
White, Alexina B
--Little-Folk Songs. LC 11-30758. vi, 94 p. illus. 20 cm. 1871. Hurd and Houghton.
--Little-Folk Songs. Ledyard, Addie, et al., illus. (Illus.). N.D. Estes & Lauriat's.
White, Alice Margaret Geddes & Tobitt, Janet Evelyn
--Dramatized Ballads. 1st ed. Danielson, Barbara, illus. LC 37-10321. 191, 1 p. incl. front., illus. 19 cm. c.1937. E. P. Dutton & Co., Inc.
--The Saucy Sailor and Other Dramatized Ballads. 1st ed. Rawdon, John, illus. LC 40-27622. 185 p. illus. 23 cm. 1940. E. P. Dutton & Company, Inc.
White, Alicen
--Walter in Love. Hoffman, Rosekrans (1926-), illus. LC 72-5141. (Illus.). 32 p. 21cm. 1973. (ISBN 0-688-40040-X). (ISBN 0-688-40040-X). Lothrop, Lee & Shepard Co.
White, Alicen, compiled by.
--A Bouquet of Poems for Choral Speaking. (gr. 2-3). N.D. GS.
--A Bouquet of Poems Selected and Arranged for Choral Speaking. LC 68-104843. 60 p. illus., phonodisc (2 s. 7 in. 33 1/3 rpm.) 19 cm. 1966. Triad Pub. Co.

White, Allen Gould (1827-1915)
--Scrapbook Stories from Ellen G. White's Scrapbooks. Lloyd, ErnestGould Harmon, ed. McMillan, Frank, illus. LC 52-35371. 96 p. illus. 23 cm. 1949. Pacific Press Pub. Association.
White, Alma Bridwell, Mrs. (1862-1946)
--Gems of Life. LC 8-11412. (Illus.). 28cm. 110p. 1907. Pillar of Fire Publishers.
--The Voice of Nature. Clarke, Branford, illus. LC 27-13094. 2 p. l., vii-x, 11-116 p. front., illus., plates (1 col.) ports. 19 1/2 cm. c.1927. Pillar of Fire.
--The Voice of Nature. Clarke, Branford, illus. LC 31-14570. x, 11-120 p. incl. front. illus., plates (1 col.) ports. 19 1/2 cm. 1930. Pillar of Fire.
White, Anna Randall
--The Old, Old Story. (Illus.). 1900. George M Hill Co.
--The Old, Old Story. (Illus.). 330p. N.D. Monarch Book Company.
White, Anne Hitchcock (1902-1970)
--The Adventures of Winnie and Bly. 1st ed. Koering, Ursula (1921-), illus. LC 47-3950. 210 p. illus. 20 cm. 1947. Little, Brown.
--A Dog Called Scholar. Obligado, Lilian Isabel (1931-), illus. LC 63-8533. 158 p. illus. 22 cm. 1963. Viking Press.
--Junket: (No Dogs Allowed). Harris, Aurand (1915-), adapted by. 1959. Children's Theatre Press.
--Junket: The Dog Who Liked Everything "Just So". McCloskey, John Robert (1914-1969), illus. LC 55-14184. 184p. (gr. 4-6). 1969. (ISBN 0-670-05028-8, Seafarer). Viking Pr.
--The Story of Serapina. Palazzo, Tony (1905-1970), illus. LC 51-10800. 128 p. illus. 26 cm. 1951. (ISBN 0-670-67526-1). (ISBN 0-670-67527-X). Viking Press.
--The Uninvited Donkey. Freeman, Don (1908-1978), illus. LC 57-13778. (Illus.). 223 p. 22cm. 1957. Viking Press.
White, Anne Terry, jt. auth. see Aesopus.
White, Anne Terry, jt. auth. see Aladdin.
White, Anne Terry, jt. auth. see Defoe, Daniel.
White, Anne Terry, adapted by see American Heritage.
White, Anne Terry (1906-), ed. see Andersen, Hans Christian.
White, Anne Terry (1896-), ed. see Clemens, Samuel Langhorne.
White, Anne Terry (1896-), ed. see Panova, Vera Fedorovna.
White, Anne Terry (1896-), ed. see Shakespeare, William.
White, Anne Terry (1896-), abridged by see Stevenson, Robert Louis.
White, Anne Terry (1896-), tr. see Bianki, Vitalii Valentinovich.
White, Anne Terry (1896-), tr. see Fedoseev, Grigorii Anisimovich.
White, Anne Terry (1896-), tr. see Kassil, Lev Abramovich.
White, Anne Terry, tr. see Kazakov, Yuri Pavlovich.
White, Anne Terry (1896-), tr. see Pushkin, Alexander Sergeyevich.
White, Anne Terry (1896-), tr. see Skrebitskii, Georgii Alekseevich.
White, Anne Terry (1896-), adapted by.
--Aesop's Fables. (Illus.). 1964. Random House Inc.
--Aladdin and the Wonderful Lamp. (Illus.). 1959. Random House Inc.
--Ali Baba. Abu Kir and Abu Sir. Two Arabian Tales. Frame, Paul (1913-), illus. LC 68-11513. 96p. col. illus. 24cm. 1968. Garrard.
--Ali Baba & the Forty Thieves, Abu Kir & Abu Sir. (Illus.). (gr. 5). 1968. (ISBN 0-8116-4200-3). Garrard.
--Czar of the Water. The Little Humpbacked Horse. Gray, Leslie, illus. White, Anne Terry, tr. from Russian. LC 68-11514. (Illus.). 96 p. 24cm. 1968. (ISBN 0-8116-4201-1). Garrard Pub. Co.
--David the Giantkiller. Thomas, Phero, illus. LC 75-106582. (Illus.). 131 p. 21cm. (Crowell Hero Tales). 1970. Crowell.
--Golden Treasury of Myths & Legends. Provensen, Alice (1918-) & Provensen, Martin (1916-), illus. (Illus.). (Deluxe Ser). (gr. 6 up). 1959. (ISBN 0-307-16747-X, Golden Pr). Western Pub.
--Heidi. Clarke, Grace Dalles, illus. (An abridgement of the novel by Johanna Spyri.). (A Golden Picture Classic). 1956. Golden Press.
--Indians and the Old West: The Story of the First Americans. LC 61-5224. (Adapted from the Pages of American Heritage). 53 p. illus. 24 cm. (Golden library of knowledge). 1961, c.1958. Golden Press.
--Indians and the Old West: The Story of the First Americans. LC 58-59602. (Adapted from the Pages of American Heritage). 56 p. illus. 21 cm. (Golden Library of Knowledge). c.1958. Simon and Schuster.
--Knights of the Table Round. Frame, Paul (1913-), illus. LC 72-92058. (Illus.). 96 p. 24cm. 1970. (ISBN 0-8116-4204-6). Garrard Pub. Co.
--Odysseus Comes Home from the Sea. Homerus Shilstone, Arthur, illus. LC 68-24587. (Illus.). x, 192 p. 21cm. (Crowell Hero Tales). 1968. Crowell.
--Of Beasts, Birds and Men: Fables from Three Lands. Schroeder, Ted (1931-1973), illus. LC 79-94410. (Illus.). 94 p. 24cm. (Reading shelf book). 1970. (ISBN 0-8116-4205-4). Garrard Pub. Co.
--Robinson Crusoe. Rojankovsky, Feodor Stepanovich (1891-1970), illus. 1960. Golden Press.
Robinson Crusoe. Stewart, Norton, illus. (An adaptation from the famous novel by Daniel Defoe.). 48p. (A Golden Stamp Classic). 1956. Golden Press.
--Sindbad the Seaman and The Ebony Horse: Two Arabian Tales. Colabella, Vincent, illus. LC 69-10374. (Illus.). 96 p. 24cm. (Reading Shelf Book). 1969. (ISBN 0-8116-4202-X). Garrard Pub. Co.
--Treasure Island. Greene, Hamilton, illus. (An abridgement of the novel by Robert Louis Stevenson.). (A Golden Picture Classic). 1956. Golden Press.
White, Barbara Anne (1942-)
--Lady Leatherneck. (Dodd, Mead Career Bks.). N.D. Dodd, Mead & Co.
White, Becky
--Bu, the Neanderthal Boy. LC 41-9283. 27 p. col. illus. 26 x 21 cm. 1941. A. Whitman & Company.
--The Dawn Battle. White, Becky, illus. LC 44-161. 64 p. col. illus. 24 by 18 1/2 cm. 1943. A. Whitman & Company.
White, Bessie Felstiner (1892-)
--A Bear Named Grumms. Fleur, Anne Elizabeth (1901-), illus. Sari, pseud. LC 52-11457. 81p. illus. 24cm. 1953. Houghton Mifflin.
--A Bear Named Grumms. Fleur, Anne Elizabeth (1901-), illus. Sari, pseud. LC 66-6350. 81 p. illus. 25 cm. 1966. Houghton Mifflin.
--Carry on, Grumms!. Paull, Grace a. (1898-), illus. LC 56-7277. 110p. illus. 23cm. 1956. Ariel Books.
--On Your Own Two Feet. Tolford, Joshua (1909-), illus. LC 55-59951. 95p. illus. 24cm. 1955. Ariel Books.
--The Strange Man and the Storks. 1st ed. Koering, Ursula (1921-), illus. LC 55-8951. 113p. illus. 21cm. 1955. (ISBN 0-394-91696-4). Knopf.
White, Bettye, jt. auth. see Michels, Barbara.
White, Carol see Stanley, Carol.
White, Catherine Ann (1825-1878), compiled by.
--The Student's Mythology. New & Rev. ed. 1905. A C Armstrong & Sons.
White, Charles Lincoln (1863-)
--The Children of the Lighthouse. Dummer, H. Boylston (1878-), illus. LC 16-13317. (Illus.). vii,84. 19cm. 1916. Association Press.
--Prince and Uncle Billy. Dummer, H. Boylston (1878-), illus. LC 15-2625. 146 p. incl. front., illus. pl. 21 cm. $0.75. c.1914. Fleming H. Revell Company.
White, Charley
--Charley White's Joke Book. N.D. Dick & Fitzgerald.
White, Christopher M.
--Monkey Tricks. 48p. (gr. 6-9). 1984. (ISBN 0-241-11071-8, Pub. by Hamish Hamilton England). David & Charles.
White, Clarence Adam
--Chris'mus' Comin', Honey, and Other Rhymes. N.D. John P. Morton & Co.
White, Constance Mary
--The Ballet School Mystery. LC 52-7597. 213 p. 21 cm. 1952. Dodd,Mead.
--Dancer's Daughter. LC 56-6171. 216 p. 22cm. 1956, c.1955. Dodd, Mead.
White, Dale, pseud., see Place, Marian Templeton.
White, Dale, pseud. (1910-)
--Is Something Up There?. Place, Marian Templeton. LC 68-17081. N.D. Doubleday.
--Young Deputy Smith. Place, Marian Templeton. (Illus.). (gr. 6-9). 1961. (ISBN 0-8382-0995-5). Hale.
White, David Omar (1927-)
--Elizabeth's Shopping Spree. White, David Omar (1927-), illus. LC 66-13776. 1v. (unpaged) col. illus. 27cm. c.1966. (ISBN 0-394-91115-6). Knopf.
--I Know a Giraffe: A Tall Tale. LC 63-14609. 1 v. (unpaged) col. illus. 27 cm. 1965. Knopf.
White, Dori (1919-)
--Sarah and Katie. 1st ed. Hyman, Trina Schart (1939-), illus. LC 75-183169. (Illus.). 168 p. 21cm. 1972. (ISBN 0-06-026402-0). Harper & Row.
White, Doris B.
--Family That Came Back. Huxtable, Grace, illus. (Illus.). (gr. 5-9). 1965. (ISBN 0-685-21117-7). Verry.
White, E. B. see White, Elwyn Brooks.
White, Edgar (1947-)
--Children of Night. McCannon, Dindga, illus. LC 73-13893. (Illus.). 38 p. 24cm. 1974. (ISBN 0-688-41535-0). (ISBN 0-688-41535-0). Lothrop, Lee & Shepard.
--Omar at Christmas. McCannon, Dindga, illus. LC 73-6216. (Illus.). 23 p. 26cm. 1973. (ISBN 0-688-41548-2). (ISBN 0-688-41548-2). Lothrop, Lee & Shepard Co.
--Sati, the Rastifarian. McCannon, Dindga, illus. LC 72-7345. (Illus.). 31 p. 26cm. 1973. Lothrop, Lee & Shepard Co.
White, Eliza Orne (1856-1947)
--The Adventures of Andrew. LC 28-21221. 5 p. l., 162 p. front., plates. 20 1/2 cm. 1928. Houghton Mifflin Company.
--Ann Frances. Sewell, Helen Moore (1896-1957), illus. LC 35-15044. 5 p. l., 126 p. col. front., illus., col. plates. 21 cm. 1935. Houghton Mifflin Company.
--The Blue Aunt. Pyle, Katharine D. (0000-1938), illus. LC 18-18525. 4 p. l., 144 p., 1 l. col. front. 19 1/2 cm. $1.2. 1918. Houghton Mifflin Co.
--A Borrowed Sister. Pyle, Katharine D. (0000-1938), illus. 4 p. l., 150 p., 1 l. front., 3 pl. 19 1/2 cm. 1906. Houghton, Mifflin and Company.
--Brothers in Fur. LC 10-25220. 4 p. l., 117, 1 p. front., plates. 19 1/2 cm. 1910. Houghton, Mifflin Company.
--Diana's Rosebush. Whittemore, Constance, illus. LC 27-22153. 4 p. l., 158 p. front., illus., plates. 19 1/2 cm. 1927. Houghton Mifflin Company.
--Edna, and Her Brothers. Bush-Brown, Margaret, illus. LC 58590. 4 p. l., 143, 1 p. front., 3 pl. 19 1/2 cm. 1900. Houghton, Mifflin and Company.
--The Enchanted Mountain. Ottendorff, E. Pollak, illus. LC 11-274578. 5 p. l., 107, 1 p. front., plates. 19 1/2 cm. 1911. Houghton Mifflin Company.
--The Farm Beyond the Town. Boyle, Mildred, illus. LC 37-33406. 5 p. l., 147 p. col. front., col. illus. 21 cm. 1937. Houghton Mifflin Company.
--The Four Young Kendalls. Hummel, Lisl, illus. LC 32-22199. 3 p. l., 167, 1 p. front., illus. 19 1/2 cm. 1932. Houghton Mifflin Company.
--The Green Door. Hummel, Lisl, illus. LC 30-290167. 4 p. l., 212 p. front., illus. 19 1/2 cm. 1930. Houghton Mifflin Company.
--Helen's Gift House. Blair, Helen (1910-), illus. LC 38-30223. 5 p. l., 146 p. front., plates. 21 cm. 1938. Houghton Mifflin Company.
--The House Across the Way. Maloy, Lois (1902-), illus. LC 40-32446. 5 p. l., 153, 1 p. illus. 24 cm. 1940. Houghton Mifflin Company.
--I, the Autobiography of a Cat. Hutton, Clarke (1898-), illus. LC 41-21732. 4 p. l., 114, 1 p. illus. 25 x 19 1/2 cm. 1941. Houghton Mifflin Company.
--Joan Morse. Benjamin, M. A., illus. LC 26-18097. 5 p. l., 176 p. col. front., col. plates. 19 1/2 cm. 1926. Houghton Mifflin Company.
--Lending Mary. Paull, Grace a. (1898-), illus. LC 34-28616. 4 p. l., 118, 1 p. front., paltes. 21 cm. 1934. Houghton Mifflin Company.
--A Little Girl of Long Ago. LC 4-16479. 3 p. l., 151 p. front., pl. 19 1/2 cm. 1896. Houghton, Mifflin and Company.
--A Little Girl of Long Ago. (Illus.). 1900. Houghton Mifflin & Co.
--Nancy Alden. Boyle, Mildred, illus. LC 36-24405. 4 p. l., 139 p. front., illus. 21 cm. 1936. Houghton Mifflin Company.
--An Only Child. Pyle, Katharine D. (0000-1938), illus. LC 5-24194. 3 p. l., 167, 1 p. front., 3 pl. 19 1/2 cm. 1905. Houghton, Mifflin and Company.
--Patty Makes a Visit. Blair, Helen (1910-), illus. LC 39-23037. 5 p. l., 133 p. front., plates. 21 cm. 1939. Houghton Mifflin Company.
--Peggy in Her Blue Frock. Preston, Alice Bolam (1889-), illus. LC 21-19394. 4 p. l., 149, 1 p. col. front. 19 1/2 cm. c.1921. Houghton Mifflin Co.
--Sally in Her Fur Coat. Hummel, Lisl, illus. LC 29-23735. x p., 1 l., 157, 1 p. front., illus. 20 cm. 1929. Houghton Mifflin Company.
--The Strange Year. Preston, Alice Bolam (1889-), illus. LC 20-190415. 4 p. l., 146 p., 1 l. col. front. 19 1/2 cm. $1.65. c.1920. Houghton Mifflin Co.
--Tony. Preston, Alice Bolam (1889-), illus. LC 24-19026. 4 p. l., 164 p. col. front. 19 1/2 cm. c.1924. Houghton Mifflin Co.
--Training Sylvia. Morse, Dorothy Bayley (1906-1979), illus. LC 42-20282. vii, 1 p., 1 l., 132, 1 p. illus. 25 1/2 cm. 1942. Houghton Mifflin Company.
--When Abigail Was Seven. Hummel, Lisl, illus. LC 31-215358. 4 p. l., 200, 1 p. front., illus. 20 cm. 1931. Houghton Mifflin Company.
--When Esther Was a Little Girl. Moran, Constance Oehler (1898-), illus. LC 44-20853. viii p., 1 l., 141 p. col. front., illus. 21 cm. 1944. Houghton Mifflin Company.
--When Molly Was Six. Pyle, Katharine D. (0000-1938), illus. LC 4-22090. vi, 133 p. front., 2 pl. 19 1/2 cm. c.1894. Houghton, Mifflin and Company.
--When Molly was Six. Pyle, Katharine D. (0000-1938), illus. 1900. Houghton Mifflin & Co.
--Where Is Adelaide?. Sewell, Helen Moore (1896-1957), illus. LC 33-24352. 4 p. l., 154, 1 p. front., illus. 21 cm. 1933. Houghton Mifflin Company.
White, Elwyn Brooks (1899-1985)
--Charlotte's Web. 5 3/8 x 8 13/16. (16-18 pt.). 1986 (Pub. by Lythway Lg Print Bks). G K Hall.
--Charlotte's Web. Williams, Garth Montgomery (1912-), illus. LC 52-9760. (Illus.). 184 p. 21cm. (gr. 4-6). 1952. (ISBN 0-06-026387-3). Harper. **Award: (JNM).**
--E. B. White Boxed Set. Incl. Charlotte's Web. White, Elwyn Brooks (1899-1985; The Trumpet of the Swan. White, Elwyn Brooks (1899-1985; Stuart Little. White, Elwyn Brooks (1899-1985. (Illus.). (gr. 3 up). 1975. (ISBN 0-06-440061-1, Trophy). Har-Row.
--E. B. White Boxed Set. Incl. Charlotte's Web. White, Elwyn Brooks (1899-1985; The Trumpet of the Swan. White, Elwyn Brooks (1899-1985; Stuart Little. White, Elwyn Brooks (1899-1985. (Illus.). (gr. 3 up). N.D. (ISBN 0-686-77171-0, HarpJ). Har-Row.
--A Gift from Maine. LC 83-83102. 160p. 1984. (ISBN 0-930096-57-6). G Gannett.
Second Tree from the Corner. LC 53-11864. 1954. (ISBN 0-06-014590-0, HarpT). Har-Row.
--Stuart Little. Williams, Garth Montgomery (1912-), illus. LC 45-9585. 4 p. l., 131 p. front., illus. 21 cm. 1945. Harper & Brothers.
--Stuart Little. Williams, Garth Montgomery (1912-), illus. LC 75-309606. (Illus.). 131 p. 20cm. (Harper trophy book ; J56). 1973, c.1945. (ISBN 0-06-440056-5). Harper & Row.
--The Trumpet of the Swan. Frascino, Edward, illus. LC 72-112484. (Illus.). 210 p. 22cm. 1970. Harper & Row. **Awards: (IBBY).**
White, Emma Siggins, Mrs. (1857-)
--Tell Me a Story, Grand'Mere: Dedicated to My Grandchildren. Kellogg, Mary Frances, illus. LC 29-5203. (Illus.). 18 x 26cm. 43p. 1928. Kellogg-Baxter Printing Co.
White, Ethel Fairfeild, Mrs.
--Laughing Giraffe, and Other Verses. Hugo, Helen, illus. LC 42-13422. (Illus.). 20cm. 69p. 1942. C. W. Hill Printing Company.
White, Flora
--Peter Pan's A. B. C. (Illus.). N.D. George H Doran.
White, Florence Meiman (1910-)
--How to Lose Your Best Friend. Jenkyns, Chris (1924-), illus. LC 72-84098. (Illus.). 43 p. 1972. W. Ritchie.
--How to Lose Your Lunch Money. Jenkyns, Chris (1924-), illus. LC 73-124601. (Illus.). 47 p. 1970. Ward Ritchie Press.
--My House is the Nicest Place. Lee, Lake W., illus. LC 63-7223. (Illus.). 24cm. 1963. Golden, Gate Junior Books.
White, Frances Hodges (1866-)
--Aunt Nabby's Children. Goldsmith, Wallace, illus. 4 p. l., 130 p. incl. front., illus., pl. 18 1/2 cm. (Cosy Corner Series). 1901. L. C. Page & Co.
--Aunt Nabby's Children. Goldsmith, Wallace, illus. (Illus.). (Goldenrod Library Ser.). 1905. L. C. Page & Co.
--Captain Jinks. Smith, Frank Vining, illus. N.D. Grosset & Dunlap.
--Captain Jinks: The Autobiography of a Shetland Pony. Smith, Frank Vining, illus. LC 9-19187. 3 p. l., 298 p. col. front., 11 pl. 20 1/2 cm. 1909. L. C. Page & Company.
--Helena's Wonderworld. Lawrence, C. A. & Proctor, Ernest L., illus. (Illus.). (Goldenrod Library Ser.). 1905. L. C. Page & Co.
--Helena's Wonderworld. Lawrence, C. A. & Proctor, Ernest L., illus. (Cosy Corner Ser.). N.D. L. C. Page & Co.
--Sea Tales. Proctor, Ernest L., illus. LC 30-28657. 53 p. front., plates. 18 cm. 1898. C. W. Moulton.
--The Stickum-Stamp Family: And Other Stamp Stunts. LC 14-9531. 2 p. l., 7-60 p., 1 l. illus., col. plates. 23 cm. c.1914. Barse and Hopkins.
White, Fred M.
--The Midnight Guest. (Detective Stories for Boys). N.D. Grosset & Dunlap.
White, Frederick (1869-)
--Bill, a Cheerful Dog. White, Frederick (1869-), illus. N.D. Moffat, Yard & Co.
White, G.
--The Toys' Adventures at the Zoo. (True Or Might-Be-True Stories). N.D. MacMillan Bks.
White, Glenn E.
--Folk Tales of Connecticut, Vol. I. Zangari, Rose M., illus. (Illus.). 61p. (Orig.). 1st U.S. edition. (gr. k-12). 1977. (ISBN 0-9611926-0-7). White G E F.

--Folk Tales of Connecticut, Vol. II. Zangari, Rose M., illus. (Illus.). 62p. 1st U.S. edition. (gr. k-12). 1981. (ISBN 0-9611926-1-5). White G E F.

White, Helen C.
--Dust on the King's Highway. N.D. Macmillan.
--Snake Gold. (Fiction). (MacMillan Bks. for Boys & Girls). (gr. 7-9). N.D. MacMillan Bks.

White, Helene Schimmelfenning, tr. see Spyri, Johanna Heusser.

White, Hervey (1866-1944)
--Noll and the Fairies. Keysher, Elizabeth, illus. (Illus.). N.D. Duffield & Co.
--Noll and the Fairies. Krysher, Elizabeth, illus. LC 2-27415. 2 p.l., 221 p., 1 l. front., illus., plates, 16 cm. 1903. H. S. Stone and Company.

White, Hester
--Mar and Lettice (Pub. by Society for Promoting Christian Knowledge). N.D. E. & J. B. Young & Co.

White, James Andrew (1889-)
--Mr. Whittle Invents the Airyoplane: The Terrific Tale of How One Thing Led to Several Others. Alexander, K., illus. LC 38-35742. 95, 1 p. incl. col. front., illus. (part col.) 22 1/2 x 19 1/2 cm. c.1938. Lothrop, Lee & Shepard Company.

White, James Edson, jt. ed. see Waggoner, J. H.

White, James R.
--Let's Broadcast!. N.D. Harper & Bros.
--Three-Way Plays. N.D. Harper & Bros.

White, Jane Neal (1918-)
--Life & Things Like Rocks: A Book of Prayers & Poems for Children. (Illus.). 64p. 1976. (ISBN 0-682-48657-4). Exposition.

White, John Stuart (1847-), ed.
--The Boys' and Girls' Plutareli. LC 11-9133. (Illus.). 27cm. 1883. G. P. Putnam's Sons.

White, John Warren (1939-)
--The Christmas Mice. Torres, Dorothy Benson, illus. LC 84-50927. (Illus.). 31 p. 27cm. (An Angelfood Book). c.1984 (Pub. by Angelfood Bks). (ISBN 0-913299-15-4). Stillpoint Pub.

White, John (1924-)
--The Iron Sceptre. LC 80-36727. p. cm. c.1980. (ISBN 0-87784-589-1). InterVarsity Press.
--The Tower of Geburah: A Children's Fantasy. LC 78-6363. (Illus.). 402 p. 21cm. c.1978. (ISBN 0-87784-560-3). Inter-Varsity Press.

White, Kathleen
--Jimmy, Wopper & Squeaker. (Illus.). (Listen with Mother Ser.). (gr. 1-2). N.D. (ISBN 0-563-10439-2). BBC.

White, Laurence B. & Broekel, Ray, pseud. (1923-)
--The Surprise Book: Seventy-Seven Stupendously Silly Practical Jokes You Can Play on Your Friends. 1st ed. Broekel, Rainer Lothar. Winslow, Will, illus. LC 80-927. (Illus.). vii, 87 p. 24cm. c.1981. (ISBN 0-385-15832-7). (ISBN 0-385-15833-5). Doubleday.

White, Leon Solomon (1919-)
--Patriot for Liberty. LC 74-30451. (Illus.). 192 p. 21cm. 1975. (ISBN 0-397-31619-4). Lippincott.

White, Madge Torence
--Chum, the New Recruit. (The Magnet Library). N.D. Frederick Warne & Co.
--Chum, the New Recruit. (The Star Library). N.D. Frederick Warne & Co.

White, Malcolm, ed.
--Troubador Treasury. LC 78-6269. (Illus., Orig.). (gr. 1-12). 1978. (ISBN 0-912300-86-8). Troubador Pr.

White, Margaret Polly Rossiter, Mrs. (1901-)
--E Ming and E Ru: A Story of Child Life in Old Peking. LC 36-21319. 2 p. l., 3-91 p. incl. front. 19 1/2 cm. c.1936. Fleming H. Revell Company.

White, Margaret Rose, jt. ed. see Martin, Florence Marie.

White, Mary Sue
--Helpers At My Church. 1959. Broadman Press.
--I Know Why We Give Thanks. 1956. Broadman Press.
--See Me Grow. Tamburine, Jean (1930-), illus. LC 66-105746. 1. v. (unpaged) illus. (pt. col.) 18x22cm. c.1966. Abingdon.
--Word Twins. N.D. E. M. Hale & Co.
--Word Twins. Palczak, Stan, illus. LC 61-7049. unpaged. illus. 23 cm. 1961. Abingdon Press.

White, Mary Sue & McDonald, Ruth
--Where I Live. LC 67-2660. (Illus.). 1 v. (unpaged). 27cm. 1967. Abingdon Press.

White, Matthew, Jr. (1857-1940)
--Adventure of a Young Athlete: The Story of how a Boy Saved his father's Name and Fortune. (The Matthew White Ser.). N.D. David McKay.
--Adventures of a Young Athlete. (The Boys Own Library). N.D. David McKay.
--Eric Dane. (The Boys Own Library). N.D. David McKay.
--Eric Dane. (The Matthew White Ser.). N.D. David McKay.
--Eric Dane. (St. Nicholas Series for Boys). N.D. International Book Co.

--Eric Dane: Or, The Football of Fortune. 218 p. incl. front., 3 pl. 17 cm. (On cover: Leather-clad tales, no. 3). c.1889. F. F. Lovell & Company.
--Guy Hammersley. (The Boys Own Library). N.D. David McKay.
--Guy Hammersley: How an Energetic Boy Cleared his name. (The Matthew White Ser.). N.D. David McKay.
--Guy Hammersley: Or, Clearing His Name. LC 1-24778. 243p. 19cm. 1901. Street & Smith.
--Harry Ascott Abroad. LC 26-36544. 94 p. 17 1/2 cm. (Lettered on cover: Enchanted library for young folks). 1879. The Authors' Publishing Company.
--My Mysterious Fortune. (The Boys Own Library). N.D. David McKay.
--My Mysterious Fortune: An Extremly interesting story of Two Hundred Thousand Check. (Matthew White Ser.). N.D. David McKay.
--Tour of A Private Car. (The Boys Own Library). N.D. David McKay.
--The Tour of a Private Car. (Matthew White Ser.). N.D. David McKay.
--Two Boys and a Fortune: Or, The Tyler Will. LC 7-237194. 3 p. l., 250 p. front., plates. 19 cm. c.1907. Chatterton-Peck Company.
--Two Boys and a Fortune: Or, the Tyler Will. (The Enterprise Bks.). N.D. Grosset & Dunlap.
--Two Boys and a Fortune: Or, the Tyler Will. New ed. (Alert Ser.). N.D. Grosset & Dunlap.
--The Young Editor. (The Matthew Ser.). N.D. David McKay.
--The Young Editor. LC 12-1032. 321 p. front., plates. 19 cm. (On cover: Leather clad tales, no. 28). c.1891. United States Book Company.
--The Young Flagman. (Illus.). N.D. Thompson & Thomas.

White, Mosezelle N., ed. see Ransom, Marie D.

White, Nelia Gardner (1894-)
--And Michael. Oldham, Marion Mildred, illus. LC 27-148000. 247 p. front., plates. 20 1/2 cm. c.1927. The Penn Publishing Company.
--Boy of Scott's Corners. Conner, McCauley, illus. LC 38-33569. 251 p. incl. front., plates. 21 cm. c.1938. The Penn Publishing Company.
--The Gift of the King. LC 31-3179. 1 p. 4., 5-78 p. incl. plates. 19 1/2 cm. c.1930. David C. Cook Publishing Co.
--Jen Culliton. LC 27-3940. 4 p. l., 250 1 p. 19 1/2 cm. 1927. D. Appleton and Company.
--Joanna Gray. Willis, Bess Goe, illus. LC 28-24945. 275 p. front., plates. 19 1/2 cm. 1928. The Penn Publishing Company.
--Kristin. Willis, Bess Goe, illus. LC 29-18550. 302 p. front., illus., plates. 19 1/2 cm. c.1929. The Penn Publishing Company.
--Marge. Jones, Susan, illus. LC 26-146277. 224 p. front., plates. 20 cm. c.1926. The Penn Publishing Company.
--Mary. LC 25-153896. 224 p. front. 20 1/2 cm. 1925. The Penn Publishing Company.
--The Mary,Marge & Michael Trio. Pilsbry, Elizabeth, illus. N.D. Penn.
--Toni of Grand Isle. LC 30-234365. 3 p. l., v-viii p., 1, l., 11-299 p. front. 19 1/2 cm. c.1930. The Penn Publishing Company.

White, Oscar A.
--Childhood and Ponyhood Blended. LC 9-28238. (Illus.). 26cm. 48p. 1909. Republican Press.

White, Paul
--Eyes on the Jungle Doctor. (Jungle Doctor Adventure Series). N.D. William B. Eerdmans Publishing Co.
--Hippo Happenings. (Jungle Doctor Ser.). N.D. (ISBN 0-686-13754-X). Believers Bkshelf.
--Janet at School. Finlay, Jeremy, illus. LC 77-26681. (Illus.). (John Day Bk.). (gr. k-4). 1978. (ISBN 0-381-99557-7, TYC-J). Har-Row.
--Jungle Doctor. (Jungle Doctor Adventure Series). N.D. William B. Eerdmans Publishing Co.
--Jungle Doctor and the Whirlwind. (Jungle Doctor Adventure Series). N.D. William B. Eerdmans Publishing Co.
--Jungle Doctor Attacks Witchcraft. (Jungle Doctor Adventure Series). N.D. William B. Eerdmans Publishing Co.
--Jungle Doctor, Cool Pool. (gr. 3-7). N.D. (ISBN 0-8024-4245-5). Moody.
--Jungle Doctor Fables. (Jungle Doctor Ser.). N.D. (ISBN 0-686-13752-3). Believers Bkshelf.
--Jungle Doctor Goes West. (Jungle Doctor Adventure Series). N.D. William B. Eerdmans Publishing Co.
--Jungle Doctor Hunts Big Game. (Jungle Doctor Adventure Series). (gr. 3-6). N.D. Eerdmans.
--Jungle Doctor Looks for Trouble. (Jungle Doctor Adventure Series). N.D. William B. Eerdmans Publishing Co.
--Jungle Doctor Meets a Lion. (Jungle Doctor Adventure Series). (gr. 3-6). 1955. Eerdmans.
--Jungle Doctor Meets a Lion. (gr. 3-7). N.D. (ISBN 0-8024-4206-4). Moody.
--Jungle Doctor on Safari. (Jungle Doctor Ser.). N.D. (ISBN 0-686-13753-1). Believers Bkshelf.

--Jungle Doctor on Safari. (Jungle Doctor Adventure Series.). N.D. William B. Eerdmans Publishing Co.
--Jungle Doctor Operates. (gr. 3-7). N.D. (ISBN 0-8024-4203-X). Moody.
--Jungle Doctor Operates. (Jungle Doctor Adventure Series). N.D. William B. Eerdmans Publishing Co.
--Jungle Doctor to the Rescue. (Jungle Doctor Adventure Series). N.D. William B. Eerdmans Publishing Co.
--Jungle Doctor's Case-Book. (Jungle Doctor Adventure Series). N.D. William B. Eerdmans Publishing Co.
--Jungle Doctor's Enemies. (Illus.). (Jungle Doctor Adventure Series). (gr. 3-6). N.D. Eerdmans.
--Jungle Doctor's Enemies. N.D. William B. Eerdmans Publishing Co.
--Jungle Doctor's Fables. (Illus.). 128p. (Children's Bks). (gr. 3-7). 1971. (ISBN 0-8024-2401-5). Moody.
--Jungle Doctor's Hippo Happenings. (Illus.). 128p. (Children's Bks). (gr. 3-7). 1971. (ISBN 0-8024-2404-X). Moody.
--Jungle Doctor's Monkey Tales. (Illus.). 128p. (Children's Bks). (gr. 3-7). 1971. (ISBN 0-8024-2402-3). Moody.
--Jungle Doctor's Picture Fable: Famous Monkey Last Words. (gr. 3-7). 1973. (ISBN 0-8024-4243-9). Moody.
--Jungle Doctor's Picture Fable: Reflections of Hippo. (gr. 3-7). 1973. (ISBN 0-8024-4244-7). Moody.
--Jungle Doctor's Picture Fables: Monkey & the Eggs. (gr. 1-3). 1975. (ISBN 0-8024-4246-3). Moody.
--Jungle Doctor's Picture Fables: Monkey Crosses the Equator. (Illus.). (gr. 1-3). 1975. (ISBN 0-8024-4247-1). Moody.
--Jungle Doctor's Picture Fables: Monkey in a Lion's Skin. (Illus.). (gr. 1-3). N.D. (ISBN 0-8024-4242-0). Moody.
--Jungle Doctor's Picture Fables: Sweet & Sour Hippo. (gr. 3-7). 1975. (ISBN 0-8024-4248-X). Moody.
--Jungle Doctor's Tug-Of-War. (Illus.). 128p. (Children's Bks). (gr. 3-7). 1971. (ISBN 0-8024-2403-1). Moody.
--Meets a Lion. (Jungle Doctor Ser.). N.D. (ISBN 0-686-13756-6). Believers Bkshelf.
--Monkey Tales. (Jungle Doctor Ser.). N.D. (ISBN 0-686-13755-8). Believers Bkshelf.
--Tug of War. (Jungle Doctor Ser.). N.D. (ISBN 0-686-13757-4). Believers Bkshelf.
--What's Happened to Auntie Jean?. Oram, Peter, illus. (Illus.). 30p. (gr. 1-3). 1976. (ISBN 0-8307-0436-1). Regal.

White, Ramy Allison, pseud., see Stratemeyer Syndicate.

White, Ramy Allison, pseud.
--Sunny Boy and His Big Dog. Stratemeyer Syndicate. Foster, John M., illus. (The Sunny Boy Ser.: Vol. 10). 1927. Barse & Hopkins.
--Sunny Boy and His Big Dog. Stratemeyer Syndicate. Foster, John M., illus. Repr. of 1927 ed (Pub. by Barse & Hopkins). (The Sunny Boy Ser.: Vol. 10). N.D. Barse & Co.
--Sunny Boy and His Big Dog. Stratemeyer Syndicate. Foster, John M., illus. Repr. of 1927 ed (Pub. by Barse & Hopkins). (The Sunny Boy Ser.: Vol. 10). N.D. Grosset & Dunlap.
--Sunny Boy and His Cave. Stratemeyer Syndicate. Foster, John M., illus. LC 30-9460. 210 p. incl. front., plates. 19 1/2 cm. (The Sunny Boy Ser.: Vol. 13). 1930. Barse & Co.
--Sunny Boy and His Cave. Stratemeyer Syndicate. Foster, John M., illus. Repr. of 1930 ed (Pub. by Barse & Co). (The Sunny Boy Ser.: Vol. 13). N.D. Grosset & Dunlap.
--Sunny Boy and His Games. Stratemeyer Syndicate. Hastings, Howard Livingston (1887-), illus. LC 23-7639. 210 p. incl. front., plates. 19 1/2 cm. (The Sunny Boy Ser.: Vol. 6). c.1923. Barse & Hopkins.
--Sunny Boy and His Games. Stratemeyer Syndicate. Hastings, Howard Livingston (1887-), illus. Repr. of 1923 ed (Pub. by Barse & Hopkins). (The Sunny Boy Ser.: Vol. 6). N.D. Barse & Co.
--Sunny Boy and His Games. Stratemeyer Syndicate. Hastings, Howard Livingston (1887-), illus. Repr. of 1923 ed (Pub. by Barse & Hopkins). (The Sunny Boy Ser.: Vol. 6). N.D. Grosset & Dunlap.
--Sunny Boy and His Playmates. Stratemeyer Syndicate. Hastings, Howard Livingston (1887-), illus. (The Sunny Boy Ser.: Vol. 5). 1922. Barse & Hopkins.
--Sunny Boy and His Playmates. Stratemeyer Syndicate. Hastings, Howard Livingston (1887-), illus. Repr. of 1922 ed (Pub. by Barse & Hopkins). (The Sunny Boy Ser.: Vol. 5). N.D. Barse & Co.
--Sunny Boy and His Playmates. Stratemeyer Syndicate. Hastings, Howard Livingston (1887-), illus. Repr. of 1922 ed (Pub. by Barse & Hopkins). (The Sunny Boy Ser.: Vol. 5). N.D. Grosset & Dunlap.

--Sunny Boy At Rainbow Lake. Stratemeyer Syndicate. (The Sunny Boy Ser.: Vol. 14). 1931. Grosset & Dunlap.
--Sunny Boy at the Seashore. Stratemeyer Syndicate. Wrenn, Charles L., illus. (The Sunny Boy Ser.: Vol. 2). 1920. Barse & Hopkins.
--Sunny Boy at the Seashore. Stratemeyer Syndicate. Wrenn, Charles L., illus. Repr. of 1920 ed (Pub. by Barse & Hopkins). (The Sunny Boy Ser.: Vol. 2). N.D. Barse & Co.
--Sunny Boy At the Seashore. Stratemeyer Syndicate. Wrenn, Charles L., illus. Repr. of 1920 ed (Pub. by Barse & Hopkins). (The Sunny Boy Ser.: Vol. 2). N.D. Grosset & Dunlap.
--Sunny Boy at Willow Farm. Stratemeyer Syndicate. Foster, John M., illus. 208 p. incl. front., plates. 19 1/2 cm. (The Sunny Boy Ser.: Vol. 12). c.1929. Barse & Co.
--Sunny Boy At Willow Farm. Stratemeyer Syndicate. Foster, John M., illus. Repr. of 1929 ed (Pub. by Barse & Co). (The Sunny Boy Ser.: Vol. 12). N.D. Grosset & Dunlap.
--Sunny Boy in School and Out. Stratemeyer Syndicate. Hastings, Howard Livingston (1887-), illus. (The Sunny Boy Ser.: Vol. 4). 1921. Barse & Hopkins.
--Sunny Boy In School and Out. Stratemeyer Syndicate. Hastings, Howard Livingston (1887-), illus. Repr. of 1921 ed (Pub. by Barse & Hopkins). (The Sunny Boy Ser.: Vol. 4). N.D. Barse & Co.
--Sunny Boy In School and Out. Stratemeyer Syndicate. Hastings, Howard Livingston (1887-), illus. Repr. of 1921 ed (Pub. by Barse & Hopkins). (The Sunny Boy Ser.: Vol. 4). N.D. Grosset & Dunlap.
--Sunny Boy in the Big City. Stratemeyer Syndicate. Wrenn, Charles L., illus. (The Sunny Boy Ser.: Vol. 3). 1920. Barse & Hopkins.
--Sunny Boy in the Big City. Stratemeyer Syndicate. Wrenn, Charles L., illus. Repr. of 1920 ed (Pub. by Barse & Hopkins). (The Sunny Boy Ser.: Vol. 3). N.D. Barse & Co.
--Sunny Boy In the Big City. Stratemeyer Syndicate. Wrenn, Charles L., illus. Repr. of 1920 ed (Pub. by Barse & Hopkins). (The Sunny Boy Ser.: Vol. 3). N.D. Grosset & Dunlap.
--Sunny Boy in the Country. Stratemeyer Syndicate. Wrenn, Charles L., illus. (The Sunny Boy Ser.: Vol. 1). 1920. Barse & Hopkins.
--Sunny Boy in the Country. Stratemeyer Syndicate. Wrenn, Charles L., illus. Repr. of 1920 ed (Pub. by Barse & Hopkins). (The Sunny Boy Ser.: Vol. 1). N.D. Barse & Co.
--Sunny Boy in the Country. Stratemeyer Syndicate. Wrenn, Charles L., illus. Repr. of 1920 ed (Pub. by Barse & Hopkins). (The Sunny Boy Ser.: Vol. 1). N.D. Grosset & Dunlap.
--Sunny Boy in the Far West. Stratemeyer Syndicate. Hastings, Howard Livingston (1887-), illus. LC 24-15189. 214 p. incl. front., plates. 19 1/2 cm. (The Sunny Boy Ser.: Vol. 7). c.1924. Barse & Hopkins.
--Sunny Boy in the Far West. Stratemeyer Syndicate. Hastings, Howard Livingston (1887-), illus. Repr. of 1924 ed (Pub. by Barse & Hopkins). (The Sunny Boy Ser.: Vol. 7). N.D. Barse & Co.
--Sunny Boy In the Far West. Stratemeyer Syndicate. Hastings, Howard Livingston (1887-), illus. Repr. of 1924 ed (Pub. by Barse & Hopkins). (The Sunny Boy Ser.: Vol. 7). N.D. Grosset & Dunlap.
--Sunny Boy in the Snow. Stratemeyer Syndicate. Foster, John M., illus. LC 28-11409. 208 p. incl. front., plates. 19 1/2 cm. (The Sunny Boy Ser.: Vol. 11). c.1928. Barse & Co.
--Sunny Boy In the Snow. Stratemeyer Syndicate. Foster, John M., illus. Repr. of 1929 ed (Pub. by Barse & Co). (The Sunny Boy Ser.: Vol. 11). N.D. Grosset & Dunlap.
--Sunny Boy on the Ocean. Stratemeyer Syndicate. Hastings, Howard Livingston (1887-), illus. LC 25-10974. 3 p.l., 9-214 p. incl. plates. front. 19 1/2 cm. (The Sunny Boy Ser.: Vol. 8). c.1925. Barse & Hopkins.
--Sunny Boy on the Ocean. Stratemeyer Syndicate. Hastings, Howard Livingston (1887-), illus. Repr. of 1925 ed (Pub. by Barse & Hopkins). (The Sunny Boy Ser.: Vol. 8). N.D. Barse & Co.
--Sunny Boy On the Ocean. Stratemeyer Syndicate. Hastings, Howard Livingston (1887-), illus. Repr. of 1925 ed (Pub. by Barse & Hopkins). (The Sunny Boy Ser.: Vol. 8). N.D. Grosset & Dunlap.
--Sunny Boy with the Circus. Stratemeyer Syndicate. Hastings, Howard Livingston (1887-), illus. LC 26-11043. 3 p. l., 9-214 p. incl. plates. front. 19 1/2 cm. (The Sunny Boy Ser.: Vol. 9). c.1926. Barse & Hopkins.

AUTHOR INDEX WHITEHOUSE, ELIZABETH

--Sunny Boy with the Circus. Stratemeyer Syndicate. Hastings, Howard Livingston (1887-), illus. Repr. of 1926 ed (Pub. by Barse & Hopkins). (The Sunny Boy Ser.: Vol. 9). N.D. Barse & Co.
--Sunny Boy With the Circus. Stratemeyer Syndicate. Hastings, Howard Livingston (1887-), illus. Repr. of 1926 ed (Pub. by Barse & Hopkins). (The Sunny Boy Ser.: Vol. 9). N.D. Grosset & Dunlap.
White, Richardson D. & Longley, Margaret D., eds.
--AESop's Fables in Rhyme for Children. Bull, Charles Livingston (1874-1932), illus. LC 3-24829. 106 p. illus. 31 x 34 1/2 cm. 1908. The Saalfield Publishing Company.
White, Robb (1909-)
--Candy. 1st ed. Howe, Gertrude Herrick (1902-), illus. LC 49-10788. 246 p. illus. 21 cm. 1949. Doubleday.
--Deathwatch. 1st ed. LC 75-157637. 228. 22p.cm. 1972. Doubleday.
--Deep Danger. LC 52-10992. 190 p. 21 cm. 1952. Doubleday.
--Fire Storm: A Novel. LC 78-72186. 111 p. 22cm. (gr. 5-9). c.1979. (ISBN 0-385-14630-2). (ISBN 0-385-14631-0). Doubleday.
--Flight Deck. 1st ed. LC 61-133283. 215 p. 22 cm. 1961. Doubleday.
--The Frogmen. LC 72-76220. 239 p. 22cm. 1973. (ISBN 0-385-03828-3). (ISBN 0-385-03828-3). Doubleday.
--The Haunted Hound. 1st ed. Glanzman, Louis S. (1922-), illus. LC 50-10056. 276 p. illus. 21 cm. 1950. Doubleday.
--The Lion's Paw. Ray, Ralph (1920-1952), illus. LC 46-7386. 5 p. l., 243 p. incl. illus., plates. 20 1/2 cm. 1946. Doubleday & Company, Inc.
--The Long Way Down: A Novel. LC 77-79561. 185 p. 22cm. 1977. (ISBN 0-385-13148-8). Doubleday.
--Midshipman Lee. Fischer, Anton Otto (1882-), illus. LC 38-324154. 6 p. l., 3-249 p. col. front., plates. 21 cm. 1938. Little, Brown and Company.
--Midshipman Lee of the Naval Academy. LC 54-5159. 216p. illus. 21cm. 1954. Random House.
--No Man's Land. LC 70-78712. 263 p. 22cm. 1969. Doubleday.
--The Nub. Wyeth, Andrew Newell (1917-), illus. LC 35-18075. 4 p. l., 3-253 p. incl. plates. front. 21 cm. 1935. Little, Brown, and Company.
--Sail Away. 1st ed. Morse, Dorothy Bayley (1906-1979), illus. LC 48-8771. 243 p. illus. 21 cm. 1948. Doubleday.
--Sailor in the Sun. Shenton, Edward (1895-), illus. LC 41-194242. 4 p. l., 242 p. incl. front., illus. 21 cm. c.1941. Harper & Brothers.
--Secret Sea. 1st ed. Barnum, Jay Hyde (1888-1962), illus. LC 47-11187. viii, 243 p. illus. 21 cm. 1947. Doubleday.
--Silent Ship, Silent Sea. LC 67-1538. 232 p. 22cm. 1967. Doubleday.
--The Smuggler's Sloop. Wyeth, Andrew Newell (1917-), illus. LC 47-6541. 4 l., 3-249 p. illus. 21 cm. (Young moderns). 1947. Doubleday.
--The Smuggler's Sloop. Wyeth, Andrew Newell (1917-), illus. LC 37-3280. 5 p. l., 3-249 p. incl. plates. front. 21 cm. 1937. Little, Brown and Company.
--Surrender. LC 66-7857. 240 p. 22 cm. 1966. Doubleday.
--Survivor. (gr. 8-10). N.D. Doubleday.
--Three Against the Sea. Watson, Aldren Auld (1917-), illus. LC 40-344151. 4 p. l., 216 p. incl.front. (map) plates. 20 1/2 cm. c.1940. Harper & Brothers.
--Torpedo Run: Mutiny and Adventure Aboard a Navy PT Boat During World War II. 1st ed. LC 62-15930. 183 p. illus. 22 cm. (gr. 8-10). 1962. (ISBN 0-385-03451-2). Doubleday.
--Up Periscope. LC 56-9060. 251 p. 22cm. 1956. Doubleday.
White, Robin (1928-)
--The Troll of Crazy Mule Camp. Reiss, Susan, illus. LC 78-72140. (Illus.). 32 p. 23cm. 1979. (ISBN 0-89799-142-7). (ISBN 0-89799-012-9). Dandelion Press.
White, Roy (1896-)
--Sunset for Red Elk. Mays, Lewis Victor, Jr. (1927-), illus. LC 68-12301. (Illus.). viii, 212 p. 21cm. 1967, c.1968. Dodd, Mead.
--Venturing South. (Illus.). 202p. (gr. 7 up). 1958. (ISBN 0-87178-900-0). Brethren.
White, Ruth
--Ollie the Ostrich. N.D. Nelson Bks.
White, Samuel Alexander (1885-)
--Man Scent. White, Samuel Alexander (1885-), illus. LC 36-17731. 286 p. illus. 20 cm. 1936. C. Scribner's Sons.
White, Stephen W., tr. see Hoffmann, Julius.
White, Stewart Edward (1873-1946)
--The Adventures of Bobby Orde. Brehm, Worth, illus. LC 11-27653. vi p., 2 l., 3-340 p. front., plates. 19 1/2 cm. 1911. Doubleday, Page & Company.
--The Blazed Trail. N.D. Doubleday Page & Co.
--The Magic Forest. 1952. Macmillan.
--The Magic Forest: A Modern Fairy Story. 2 p. l., 79 p. 16 1/2 cm. 1903. The Macmillan Company.
--The Magic Forest: A Modern Fairy Story. LC 24-26325. 146 p. incl. 10 pl. illus. 17 cm. (On verso of half-title: The Little library). 1923. The Macmillan Company.
--The Rose Dawn. N.D. Doubleday Page & Co.
--The Shepper-Newfounder. Webster, H. T., illus. LC 31-313385. 3 p. l., 107 p. incl. plates. 19 1/2 cm. 1931. Doubleday, Doran & Company, Inc.
White, Stewart Edward & Adams, Samuel
--The Mystery. N.D. Doubleday Page & Co.
White, Ted, pseud., see White, Theodore Edwin.
White, Ted, pseud. (1938-)
No Time Like Tomorrow. White, Theodore Edwin. LC 71-75074. 152p. 22cm. 1969. Crown Publishers.
--Secret of the Mirauder Satellite. White, Theodore Edwin. LC 67-1411. 171p. 22cm. 1967. Westminster Press.
White, Terence Hanbury (1906-1964)
--The Ill-Made Knight. White, Terence Hanbury (1906-1964), illus. (Revised Edition in the 1958 edition of "The Once and Auture King".). 1940. Putnam.
--The Master: An Adventure Story. 1957. Putnam.
--Mistress Masham's Repose. 1980. (ISBN 0-8398-2615-X, Gregg). G K Hall.
--Mistress Masham's Repose. Eichenberg, Fritz (1901-), illus. 1946. Putnam.
--The Once and Future King. 1958. (ISBN 0-399-10597-2). G. P. Putnam's Sons.
--The Queen of Air and Darkness. (Revised edition in the 1958 edition of "The Once and Future King".). 1940. Collins.
--Sword in the Stone. Bd. with The Once Future King, Part One. 288p. (gr. 7 up). 1963. (LFL). Dell.
--The Sword in the Stone. White, Terence Hanbury (1906-1964), illus. (Illus.). 1939. (ISBN 0-399-10783-5). G. P. Putnam's Sons.
--What Happened to Sherlock Holmes? as Set to Rest In... The Legend of Wilson-The Amazing Athlete. Blackburn, Francis, et al., eds. Meade, Javier & Jamieson, Lindsey, illus. Barton, Hill, intro. by. LC 83-51870. (Illus.). 102p. 1984. (ISBN 0-9612698-0-4). Seagull Pub Co.
--The Witch in the Wood. White, Terence Hanbury (1906-1964), illus. 1939. Putnam.
White, Teri
--Bleeding Hearts. LC 83-63040. c.1984. (ISBN 0-89296-077-9). Mysterious Press.
White, Theodore Edwin see White, Ted, pseud.
White, Theodore Edwin (1938-)
No Time Like Tomorrow. LC 71-75074. 152 p. 22cm. 1969. Crown Publishers.
--Secret of the Marauder Satellite. LC 67-1411. 171 p. 22cm. 1967. Westminster Press.
--Trouble on Project Ceres. LC 77-134205. 157 p. 21cm. 1971. (ISBN 0-664-32489-4). Westminster Press.
White, Trentwell Mason
--The Thing in the Road. LC 30-9728. 5 p. l., 3-178 p. front., plates. 19 1/2 cm. c.1930. Marshall Jones Company.
--Three Rookies at Morton. Pancoast, Morris H., illus. LC 29-209713. 6 p.l., 3-282 p. incl. front., illus., plates. 20 1/2 cm. 1929. Little, Brown and Company.
White, W. C., jt. auth. see Pritchard, Clarence F.
White, Wallace see Nye, Peter, pseud.
White, Wallace (1930-)
--The Storm. Nye, Peter, pseud. LC 82-4852. 92 p. 22cm. (Triumph book). 1982. F. Watts.
White, Wallace (1930-) & Aron, Bill
--One Dark Night. LC 79-10842. (Illus.). 90 p. 22cm. (Triumph book). 1979. (ISBN 0-531-02896-8). F. Watts.
White, William Allen (1868-1944)
--The Court of Boyville. LC 77-116968. (Illus.). xxx, 358 p. 21cm. Repr. (Short story index reprint series). 1970. Books for Libraries Press.
--The Court of Boyville. LC 99-5149. xxx, 358 p. incl. front., illus., plates. 19 1/2 cm. 1899. Doubleday & McClure Co.
White, William C., tr.
--Humpy. N.D. Harper & Bros.
White, William Chapman (1903-), tr. see Ershov, Petr Pavlovich.
White, William Chapman (1903-)
--Made in Russia. Wiren, Georges R., illus. LC 32-24708. (Illus.). viii,41. 20cm. 1932. A. A. Knopf.
--Mouseknees. Johnson, Avery Fischer (1906-), illus. LC 39-19357. 144 p. illus. 19 1/2 cm. c.1939. Random House.
White, William Fletcher (1885-)
--The Duck and its Friends. LC 30-25665. (Illus.). 32p. 25 x 33cm. 1930. Oxford University Press.
White, William Patterson
--The Heart of the Range. N.D. Doubleday Page & Co.
--Hidden Trails. N.D. Doubleday Page & Co.
--Paradise Bend. N.D. Doubleday Page & Co.
White Deer of Autumn
--Ceremony-In the Circle of Life. Wicasta, Sanyan T., illus. (Illus.). 32p. (Orig.). (gr. 2-6). 1982. (ISBN 0-940742-02-0). Carnival Pr.
Whiteford, Andred & Whiteford, Marion
--How Sandy Squirrel Got His Tail. LC 45-2397. 23cm. 32p. 1945. Wilcox & Follett Co.
Whiteford, Marion, jt. auth. see Whiteford, Andred.
Whitehead, Albert Carlton (1875-)
--The Standard Bearer: A Story of Army Life in the Time of Caesar. LC 15-10491. 305 p. incl. col. front., illus. 19 cm. c.1915. American Book Company.
--The Standard Bearer: A Story of Army Life in the Time of Caesar. 305 p. illus. 21 cm. Repr. (Roman life and times series, v. 15). 1962, c.1962. Biblo and Tannen.
Whitehead, Barbara & Lindsey, David L
--The Wonderful Chirrionera and Other Tales from Mexican Folklore. LC 75-318008. (Illus.). 32 p. 32cm. 1974. (ISBN 0-913206-03-2). Heidelberg Publishers.
Whitehead, Edwin Kirby, jt. auth. see Hoosier, A. H. E.
Whitehead, Henry St. Clair (1882-)
--Pinkie at Camp Cherokee. LC 31-349251. vii, 209 p. 20 1/2 cm. 1931. G. P. Putnam's Sons.
Whitehead, Hubert
--Slings and Sandals. N.D. Abingdon Press.
Whitehead, Jane
--Fuzzy Dan. Biers, Clarence, illus. LC 51-25845. (Illus.). 16p. 17cm. (Fuzzy Wuzzy Tell-a-Tales). 1951. Whitman Pub. Co.
Whitehead, Patricia
--Arnold Plays Baseball. Karas, G. Brian, illus. LC 84 8827. (Illus.). 30 p. 24cm. (ABC adventures). ((Series: Whitehead, Patricia.). (ABC adventures.). c.1985. (ISBN 0-8167-0367-1). (ISBN 0-8167-0368-X). Troll Associates.
--Best Halloween Book. Britt, Stephanie, illus. LC 84-8828. p. cm. (ABC Adventures). c.1985. (ISBN 0-8167-0373-6). (ISBN 0-8167-0374-4). Troll Associates.
--Best Thanksgiving Book. Hall, Susan T. (1940-), illus. LC 84-8831. p. cm. (ABC Adventures). c.1985. (ISBN 0-8167-0372-8). (ISBN 0-8167-0371-X). Troll Associates.
--Best Valentine Book. Harvey, Paul (1926-), illus. LC 84-8829. (Illus.). 30 p. 24cm. (ABC adventures). c.1985. (ISBN 0-8167-0369-8). (ISBN 0-8167-0370-1). Troll Associates.
--Christmas Alphabet Book. Borgo, Deborah Colvin, illus. LC 84-8830. p. cm. (ABC Adventures). c.1985. (ISBN 0-8167-0365-5). (ISBN 0-8167-0366-3). Troll Associates.
--Dinosaur Alphabet Book. Snyder, Joel, illus. LC 84-8839. (Illus.). 32p. (ABC Adventures Ser.). (gr. k-2). 1985. (ISBN 0-8167-0363-9). (ISBN 0-8167-0364-7). Troll Assocs.
--Here Comes Hungry Albert. Karas, G. Brian, illus. LC 84-8835. p. cm. (ABC Adventures). c.1985. (ISBN 0-8167-0361-2). (ISBN 0-8167-0362-0). Troll Associates.
--Let's Go to the Farm. Gold, Ethel, illus. LC 84-8834. (Illus.). 30 p. 24cm. (ABC Adventures). c.1985. (ISBN 0-8167-0377-9). (ISBN 0-8167-0378-7). Troll Associates.
--Let's Go to the Zoo. Boyd, Patti, illus. LC 84-8832. p. cm. (ABC Adventures). 1985. (ISBN 0-8167-0376-0). (ISBN 0-8167-0375-2). Troll Asssociates.
--What a Funny Bunny. Page, Don (1946-), illus. LC 84-8833. p. cm. (ABC Adventures). c.1985. (ISBN 0-8167-0361-2). (ISBN 0-8167-0362-0). Troll Associates.
Whitehead, Robert John, jt. auth. see Bamman, Henry A.
Whitehead, Robert John (1928-)
--Some of the Schemes of Columbus Tootle. LC 74-81665. 66 p. 21cm. 1974. (ISBN 0-87133-022-9). Franklin Pub. Co.
Whitehead, Roberta (1905-)
--Five and Ten. Lenski, Lois (1893-1974), illus. LC 43-511504. 41 p. col. illus. 21 cm. (On cover: Nursery books). 1943. Houghton Mifflin Company.
--Peter Opens the Door. Bronson, Mildred, illus. LC 46-25265. 20 p. col. illus. 21 cm. 1946. Houghton Mifflin Company.
--Why Not?. Moyers, William (1916-), illus. LC 51-9283. 92 p. illus. 22 cm. 1951. Houghton Mifflin.
--Wish I May. Moyers, William (1916-), illus. LC 52-5910. 124 p. illus. 22 cm. 1952. Houghton Mifflin.
Whitehead, Ruth
--The Mother Tree. Robinson, Charles (1931-), illus. LC 75-142155. (Illus.). vii, 149 p. 22cm. 1971. Seabury Press.
Whitehill, Dorothy
--Janet, a Twin. (The "Twins" Ser.). N.D. Barse & Hopkins.
--Joy and Gypsy Joe. (The Joyce Payton Ser.). N.D. Barse & Co.
--Joy and Her Chums. Foster, John M., illus. LC 28-108781. 3 p. l., 11-214 p. incl. plates. front. 19 1/2 cm. (Her Joyce Payton Series). 1928. Barse and Co.
--Joy and Pam. (The Joyce Payton Ser.). N.D. Barse & Co.
--Joy and Pam. Wrenn, Thomas N., illus. LC 32-17520. 3 p. l., 11-220 p. incl. plates. front. 19 1/2 cm. N.D. Grosset & Dunlap.
--Joy and Pam a-Sailing. Foster, John M., illus. LC 30-8273. 203 p. front. 19 1/2 cm. (Her Joyce Payton Series). c.1930. Barse & Co.
--Joy and Pam As Seniors. Doane, Pelagie (1906-1966), illus. LC 32-16251. iii, 217 p. front. 19 1/2 cm. (Her Joyce Payton Series). c.1932. Grosset & Dunlap.
--Joy and Pam at Brookside. Foster, John M., illus. 216 p. incl. front., plates. 19 1/2 cm. (Her Joyce Payton series). c.1929. Barse & Co.
--Joyful Adventures of Polly. LC 29-929410. 4 p. l., 11-216 p. incl. plates. front. 19 1/2 cm. (Her Polly series). c.1929. Barse & Co.
--Mary Cinderella Brown. Foster, John M., illus. LC 23-7320. 3 p. l., 236, 1 p. front. 19 1/2 cm. 1923. D. Appleton and Company.
--Phyllis, a Twin. (The "Twins" Ser.). N.D. Barse & Hopkins.
--Polly and Bob. (The "Polly" Ser.). N.D. Barse & Hopkins.
--Polly and Lois. (The "Polly" Ser.). N.D. Barse & Hopkins.
--Polly at Pixie's Haunt. (The "Polly" Ser.). N.D. Barse & Co.
--Polly Polly. (The "Polly" Ser.). N.D. Barse & Hopkins.
--Polly sees the World at War. (The "Polly" Ser.). N.D. Barse & Hopkins.
--Polly's First Year at Boarding School. (The "Polly" Ser.). N.D. Barse & Hopkins.
--Polly's House Party. (The "Polly" Ser.). N.D. Barse & Co.
--Polly's Polly. Foster, John M., illus. LC 25-17412. 5 p. l., 9-215, 1 p. incl. illus., plates. front. 19 1/2 cm. c.1925. Barse & Hopkins.
--Polly's Polly and Priscilla. Tait, Agnes (1897-), illus. LC 32-171515. vi, 203 p. front. 19 1/2 cm. (Her Polly Series). c.1932. Grosset & Dunlap.
--Polly's Polly at Boarding School. Foster, John M., illus. LC 28-14008. iv p., 1 l., 9-218 p. incl. plates. front. 19 1/2 cm. c.1928. Barse & Co.
--Polly's Reunion. (The "Polly" Ser.). N.D. Barse & Hopkins.
--Polly's Reunion. Wrenn, Charles L., illus. LC 24-155026. 3 p. l., 9-222, 1 p. front., plates. 19 1/2 cm. c.1924. Barse & Hopkins.
--Polly's Senior Year at Boarding School. (The "Polly" Ser.). N.D. Barse & Hopkins.
--Polly's Summer Vacation. (The "Polly" Ser.). N.D. Barse & Hopkins.
--The Twins a-Visiting. Foster, John M., illus. LC 30-222112. 2 p. l., 9-220 p. front. 19 1/2 cm. c.1930. Barse & Co.
--The Twins Abroad. Foster, John M., illus. 208 p. incl. plates. front. 19 1/2 cm. (Her The twins series). c.1929. Barse & Co.
--The Twins Adventuring. (The "Twins" Ser.). N.D. Barse & Co.
--The Twins and Tim. Trait, Agnes (1897-), illus. LC 32-17153. v, 185 p. front. 19 1/2 cm. c.1932. Grosset & Dunlap.
--The Twins and Tommy Junior. Gooch, Thelma, illus. LC 22-136018. 214 p. incl. front., plates. 19 1/2 cm. c.1922. Barse & Hopkins.
--The Twins at Camp. Foster, John M., illus. LC 28-140092. 216 p. incl. plates. front. 19 1/2 cm. c.1928. Barse & Co.
--The Twins at Home. LC 25-17624. 211 p. incl. plates. front. 19 1/2 cm. c.1925. Barse & Hopkins.
--The Twins in the South. LC 20-20190. 220 p. incl. front., plates. 19 1/2 cm. c.1920. Barse and Hopkins.
--The Twins in the West. 218 p. incl. plates. front. 19 cm. c.1920. Barse and Hopkins.
--The Twins' Summer Vacation. Gooch, Thelma, illus. LC 21-15999. 5 p. l., 9-214 p. incl. plates. front. 19 1/2 cm. (Her The Dorothy Whitehill series). c.1921. Barse & Hopkins.
--The Twin's Wedding. (The"Twins" Ser.). N.D. Barse & Co.
Whitehouse, Arch, pseud., see Whitehouse, Arthur George Joseph.
Whitehouse, Arthur George Joseph see Whitehouse, Arch, pseud.
Whitehouse, Arthur George Joseph (1895-1979)
--Action in the Sky. Whitehouse, Arch, pseud. (gr. 7-10). 1962. (ISBN 0-696-50109-0). Hawthorn.
--The Laughing Falcon. Whitehouse, Arch, pseud. Orbaan, Albert F. (1913-), illus. LC 68-24554. (Illus.). 157 p. 21cm. 1969. Putnam.
--Scarlet Streamers. Whitehouse, Arch, pseud. Orbaan, Albert F. (1913-), illus. 126 p. 22cm. 1967. Putnam.
--Spies with Wings. Whitehouse, Arch, pseud. Orbaan, Albert F. (1913-), illus. LC 66-31888. (Illus.). 156 p. 21cm. 1967, c.1966. Putnam.
Whitehouse, Elizabeth Scott (1893-1968)
--Bible Stories to Tell. (gr. 1-6). 1967. (ISBN 0-8170-0379-7). Judson.
--Kingdom Stories for Juniors. N.D. Fleming H. Revell Co.

--Victory at Dawson's Glade. Escourido, Joseph, illus. LC 64-15870. (Illus.). 106p. 21cm. 1964. Bethany Press.

Whitehouse, Jeanne see Peterson, Jeanne Whitehouse, pseud.

Whiteley, Mary (1913-)

--How Do You Do? I'm Shelley. LC 64-23092. 157p. illus. 22cm. 1965, c.1964. Collier-Macmillan.

--Wait till September. Saks, Sylvia, illus. LC 53-674643. 185p. illus. 22cm. 1954. Lee & Shepard.

Whitell, Evelyn

--His Heart Was in America. LC 51-25844. 139 p. 21 cm. 1951. Willing Pub. Co.

Whitelock, Louise Clarkson, Mrs. (1865-1928)

--Little Stay-at-Home, and Her Friends. Whitelock, Louise Clarkson (1865-1928), illus. LC 16-3667. 40 pl. col. illus. 23 1/2 x 19 cm. 1879. F. W. Robinson & Co.

Whitelock, William Wallace (1869-)

--When the Heart Is Young. Pennington, Harper, illus. vii, 83 p. front., illus., plates. 19 1/2 cm. 1902. E. P. Dutton & Company.

Whiteman, Edna

--Jane and Jerry. Sommer, Edwin G., illus. LC 29-9093. 4 p. l., 210 p. col. front., illus. 20 1/2 cm. 1929. T. Nelson & Sons.

--Playmates in Print, Verses and Stories for Children. Hurst, Earl Oliver, illus. LC 26-20414. 1 p. l., xi, 122 p. col. front., illus., plates (part col.) 24 cm. c.1926. T. Nelson & Sons.

--The Silver Wand: Folk Fairy Tales Adapted for the Story Teller and the Children. LC 38-172784. xi p., 1 l., 15-121 p. incl. front., plates. 22 1/2 x 19 1/2 cm. 1938. T. Nelson and Sons.

Whiteside, Karen

--Brother Mouky and the Falling Sun. Whiteside, Karen, illus. LC 79-2014. (Illus.). 30 p. c.1980. (ISBN 0-06-026407-1). Harper & Row.

--Lullaby of the Wind. Mizumura, Kazue, illus. (ps-k). 1984. Harper.

Whitfield, Clara S., compiled by.

--Holly Leaves. LC 16-10109. (Illus.). 14 x 20cm. 1884. J. Egginton, Printer.

Whitfield, Raoul (1897-1945)

--Danger Circus. Heaslip, William, illus. LC 33-25677. 5 p. l., 3-191, 1 p. front., illus. 19 1/2 cm. 1933. A. A. Knopf.

--Danger Zone. Dobias, Frank (1902-), illus. LC 31-32068. vii, 209 p. col. front., col. plates. 19 1/2 cm. 1931. A. A. Knopf.

--Death in a Bowl. LC 31-6790. 6 p. l., 3-266 p., 1 l. 19 1/2 cm. 1931. A. A. Knopf.

--Silver Wings. Dobias, Frank (1902-), illus. LC 30-23361. 6 p. l., 3-234 p. incl. col. front., illus. 19 1/2 cm. 1930. A. A. Knopf.

--Wings of Gold. Lee, Manning de Villeneuve, illus. LC 30-21165. 5 p. l., 9-247 p. col. front., plates. 20 cm. c.1930. The Penn Publishing Company.

Whitgift, Andrew

--Cripple Dan: And Other Stories. (Illus.). 330p. N.D. Merrill.

Whitham, G. J.

--Basil the Page. N.D. Dodge.

Whiting, Helen A.

--Negro Folk Tales. Jones, Lois Mailou, illus. 36p. N.D. Associated Pub.

Whiting, John Downes (1884-)

--The Trail of Fire: A Story of the Famous Alabama. Whiting, John Downes (1884-), illus. LC 30-22028. 7 p. l., 17-283, 1 p. front., illus., plates. 21 cm. c.1930. The Bobbs-Merrill Company.

Whiting, Joseph Samuel (1895-)

--Pepper Dot and Jimmie W. Duck. Callahan, Vincent, illus. LC 48-15213. (Illus.). 32p. 28cm. 1947. Valley Pub. Co.

Whiting, Margaret Abott Eaton, Mrs. (1876-), ed.

--Plays and Pageants for Children. LC 25-21669. v. front., illus. (incl. music) 20 cm. c.1925. Educational Publishing Company.

Whiting, May

--Treasure in Shetland. LC 40-34278. 3 p. l., 5, 6-280 p. front. 19 1/2 cm. c.1940. W. A. Wilde Company.

--Treasure in Shetland. N.D. Wilcox & Follett Co.

Whitley, Benjamin

--Looney Limericks. Rudish, Rich, illus. (Illus.). 18p. (ps-2). 1972. Hallmark.

--Topsy-Turvy Town. Fahey, Suzi, illus. (Illus.). 20p. (Hallmark Children's Editions). (ps-2). 1972. Hallmark.

Whitley, Jay, jt. ed. see Felgate, Cynthia.

Whitley, Joy, ed.

--Play School. 64p. (Play School Books Ser.). (gr. k). N.D. (ISBN 0-563-06928-7). BBC.

Whitley, Mary Ann

--A Circle of Light. LC 83-5856. p. cm. 1983. (ISBN 0-8027-6513-0). Walker.

Whitlock, Pamela, ed.

--All Day Long: An Anthology of Poetry for Children. Hassall, Joan (1906-), illus. LC 56-111160. 321p. illus. 21cm. 1954. Oxford University Press.

Whitlock, Pamela, jt. auth. see Hull, Katharine.

Whitman, Bernard, Mrs., jt. auth. see Hale, Lucretia Peabody.

Whitman, Doris

--The Hand of Apollo. Hogarth, Paul (1917-), illus. LC 72-86253. (Illus.). 159 p. 23cm. 1969. Follett Pub. Co.

--When Christmas Comes. Stone, David Karl (1922-), illus. LC 63-9578. (Illus.). 42. 24cm. (A Young Owl Book). 1964. Holt, Rinehart & Winston.

Whitman, Edmund Spurr (1900-)

--Little Pax: The Story of a Boy Who Tried to Change the Name of the World. Ely, Gladys, illus. LC 74-182528. (Illus.). viii, 129 p. 22cm. (Quest Book for Children). 1972. (ISBN 0-8356-0428-4). Theosophical Pub. House.

--Revolt Against the Rain God. Polseno, Jo, illus. LC 65-259245. 143p. illus. 21cm. bibl. c.1965. McGraw.

Whitman, J. Russ

--Loco the Burro & Ali the Jungle Beasts: A Story Poem for Children. Gaber, Susan, illus. (Illus.). (gr. 2-5). 1979. (ISBN 0-682-49255-8). Exposition.

Whitman, Virginia Bruner (1901-)

--Ozark Obie. Hutchinson, William Miller (1916-), illus. LC 61-5502. 160 p. illus. 21 cm. 1961. Broadman Press.

--Secret of the Hidden Ranch. LC 64-11959. 101p. 21cm. 1964. Zondervan Pub. House.

Whitman, Walt (1819-1892)

--I Hear America Singing. Krahn, Fernando (1935-), illus. LC 72-1446. (Illus.). 32p. (ps-3). 1975. (Sey Lawr). (Sey Lawr). Delacorte.

--Leaves of Grass. 1st ed. Cowley, Malcolm, ed. (gr. 7 up). 1959. (ISBN 0-670-42245-2). Viking Pr.

--Miracles: The Wonder of Life. Stone, David Karl (1922-), illus. LC 76-88713. (Illus.). 25 p. 20cm. 1969. (ISBN 0-528-82277-2). Rand McNally.

--Overhead the Sun: Lines from Walt Whitman. 1st ed. Frasconi, Antonio (1919-), illus. LC 69-20284. (Illus.). 37 p. 26cm. 1969. Farrar, Straus and Giroux. **Award: (ALA).**

--Selections from the Leaves of Grass. (gr. 10 up). N.D. Pyramid Pubns.

--There Was a Child Went Forth. Gay, Zhenya (1906-1978), illus. N.D. Harper & Bros.

--Walt Whitman's I Hear America Singing. Krahn, Fernando LC 72-1446. (Illus.). 31 p. 23cm. 1975. (ISBN 0-440-04144-9). Delacorte Presss/S. Lawrence.

Whitman, William, III (1900-)

--Dog Corner Papers. N.D. Houghton Mifflin Co.

--The Giant Sorcerer: Or, The Extraordinary Adventures of Raphael and Cassandra. Boyd, Frank (1893-), illus. LC 27-18996. 5 p. l., 131 p. col. front., illus., plates. 20 1/2 cm. c.1927. Houghton Mifflin Company.

--Navaho Tales. N.D. Houghton Mifflin.

Whitmarsh, C. S., Miss

--Older than Adam. (Summer House Stories). N.D. Thompson, Brown & Co.

--Our Summer House. (Summer House Stories). N.D. Thompson, Brown & Co.

--Rainy Day Stories. (Summer House Stories). N.D. Thompson, Brown & CO.

--Wings and Webs. (Summer House Stories). N.D. Thompson, Brown & Co.

Whitmarsh, Hubert Phelps (1863-)

--The Golden Talisman. 300p. N.D. A. W. Wilde.

--Mysterious Voyage of the Daphne. 305p. N.D. A. W. Wilde.

--The Young Pearl Divers. Burgess, H., illus. (Gift Book Ser.). N.D. L. C. Page & Co.

--The Young Pearl Divers: A Story of Australia Adventure by Land and Sea. Burgess, H., illus. LC 29-253071. vi p., 1 l., 256 p. front., plates. 20 cm. 1896. Joseph Knight Company.

Whitmire, Caroline Steward (1869-)

--Harmony Flats: The Gifts of a Tenement-House Fairy. LC 7-22914. 188 p. 19 1/2 cm. 1907. Benziger Brothers.

Whitmore, Arvella

--You're a Real Hero, Amanda. LC 85-11738. 184 p. 22cm. 1985. (ISBN 0-395-38950-X). Houghton Mifflin.

Whitmore, Carol & Day, Michael E

--Berry Ripe Moon. Whitmore, Carol, illus. LC 77-73264. (Illus.). 54 p. 22cm. c.1977. Tide Grass Press.

Whitmore, Elizabeth B.

--One Step to America. Moyers, William (1916-), illus. LC 58-992022. 165 p. illus. 21 cm. 1958. Broadman Press.

Whitmore, Ken

--Jump!. (Illus.). 144p. (gr. 3-7). 1983. (ISBN 0-19-271461-9, Pub. by Oxford U Pr Childrens). Merrimack Pub Cir.

Whitmore, Lee, jt. auth. see Dennis, Clarence James.

Whitmore, William Henry (1836-1900), intro. by.

--The Original Mother Goose Melody. LC 15-9861. (Illus.). 25cm. 28p. 1889. J. Munsell's Sons.

Whitnall, Harold Orville (1877-1945)

--Hunter of the Caverns. Millard, H. C., illus. LC 39-4586. v, 119 p. illus. 23 cm. 1939. T. Y. Crowell.

--A Parade of Ancient Animals. Millard, H. C., illus. 136p. N.D. Thomas Y. Crowell Co.

Whitney, Adeline Dutton Train, Mrs. (1824-1906)

--The Boys at Chequasset. N.D. Loring.

--Boys at Chequasset: Or, "A Little Leaven". LC 67-118019. (Illus.). 256p. 19cm. 1882. Houghton Mifflin.

--Boys at Chequasset: Or, "A Little Leaven.". LC 8-36251. 258 p. front., plates. 19 1/2 cm. 1890. Houghton, Mifflin and Company.

--The Deacon's Little Maid. LC 12-40094. 32 p. col. front., illus. 25 cm. c.1897. Lothrop Publishing Company.

--Faith Gartney's Girlhood. N.D. A. B. Burt Co.

--Faith Gartney's Girlhood. (Illus.). (The Meade Series for Girls). N.D. A. L. Burt.

--Faith Gartney's Girlhood. (Illus.). (The Wellesley Series for Girls). N.D. A. L. Burt.

--Faith Gartney's Girlhood. (Illus.). N.D. Caldwell.

--Faith Gartney's Girlhood. (The Girls' Own Library). N.D. David McKay.

--Faith Gartney's Girlhood. LC 4-18685. viii, 322 p. 18 cm. 1893. Houghton, Mifflin and Company.

--Faith Gartney's Girlhood. (Alcott and Whitney Series.). N.D. Hurst & Co.

--Faith Gartney's Girlhood. 348 p. 19 cm. 1863. Loring.

--Faith Gartney's Girlhood. LC 8-36250. 348 p. 19 cm. 1865. Loring.

--Faith Gartney's Girlhood. Bush, C. G., illus. LC 4-15178. 348p. 19cm. 1891. Houghton, Mifflin and Company.

--Gayworthys. (Alcott and Whitney Series.). N.D. Hurst & Co.

--The Gayworthys. N.D. Loring.

--Homespun Yarns. LC 72-37570. 394 p. 21cm. (Short story index reprint series). 1972. (ISBN 0-8369-4129-2). Books for Libraries Press.

--Homespun Yearns. LC 8-36248. 2 p. l., 394 p. 19 1/2 cm. 1887. Houghton, Mifflin and Company.

--The Other Girls. LC 1-29608. vi, 463 p. 18 cm. (Real folks series, IV). 1901. Houghton, Mifflin and Company.

--The Other Girls. Harley, J. J., illus. LC 8-36247. vi p., 1 l., 463 p. front., 7 pl. 18 1/2 cm. 1873. J. R. Osgood and Company.

--Patience Strong's Outings. N.D. Loring.

--Real Folks. LC 8-36246. iv, 308 p. front., plates 19 cm. 1879. Houghton, Osgood and Company.

--Real Folks. LC 99-2990. iv, 308 p. 18 cm. (Real folks series, III). 1899. Houghton Mifflin Company.

--Real Folks. LC 26-3643. 1872. J. R. Osgood and Company.

--A Summer in Leslie Goldthwaite's Life. ix p., 1 l., 284 p. 18 1/2 cm. (Half-title: Real folks series, I). 1893. Houghton, Mifflin and Company.

--A Summer in Leslie Goldthwaite's Life. LC 4-15181. ix p., 1 l., 284 p. 18 cm. (Half-title: Real folks series. I...). 1894. Houghton, Mifflin and Company.

--A Summer in Leslie Goldthwaite's Life. (Illus.). N.D. James R Osgood and Company.

--A Summer in Leslie Goldthwaite's Life. Hoppin, Augustus (1828-1896), illus. LC 8-36245. 2 p. l., 230 p. plates. 19 cm. 1867. Ticknor and Fields.

--A Summer in Leslie Goldwaite's Life. (Alcott and Whitney Ser.). N.D. Hurst & Co.

--We Girls: A Home Study. LC 8-34318. iv, 215 p. front., illus. 19 cm. 1870. Fields, Osgood, & Co.

--We Girls: A Home Study. 33d ed. LC 26-23545. iv, 215 p. front. 20 cm. 1887. Houghton, Mifflin and Co.

--We Girls: A Home Study. LC 98-1703. iv, 215 p. illus. 18 cm. (Real folks series, II). 1898. Houghton, Mifflin and Company.

--Zerub Throop's Experiment. N.D. Loring.

Whitney, Alexandra (1922-)

--Once a Bright Red Tiger. Robinson, Charles (1931-), illus. LC 73-7394. (Illus.). 30 p. 1973. (ISBN 0-8098-1212-6). N. Z. Walck.

--Stiff Ears; Animal Folktales of the North American Indian. Whitney, Alexandra (1922-), illus. LC 74-6029. (Illus.). 55 p. 24cm. 1974. (ISBN 0-8098-2103-6). H. Z. Walck.

--Tina, Tiger That Barks: The True Picture Story of Mohan & His Friends. Ecker, Beverly, illus. N.D. (ISBN 0-679-20976-X). McKay.

--Voices in the Wind: Central & South American Legends. new ed. LC 76-12752. (Illus.). (gr. 7 up). 1976. (ISBN 0-679-20364-8). McKay.

Whitney, Alma Marshak (1943-)

--Just Awful. Hoban, Lillian (1925-), illus. LC 73-155227. (Illus.). 32 p. 27cm. 1971. (ISBN 0-201-08625-5). Addison-Wesley.

--Just Awful. Hoban, Lillian (1925-), illus. 1971. Children's Press.

--Just Awful. Hoban, Lillian (1925-), illus. LC 84-43125. p. cm. 1985, c.1971. (ISBN 0-201-08625-5). Harper & Row.

--Leave Herbert Alone. McPhail, Michael David (1940-), illus. LC 72-1526. (Illus.). 32 p. 27cm. 1972. (ISBN 0-201-08623-9). Addison-Wesley.

--Leave Herbert Alone. McPhail, Michael David (1940-), illus. LC 84-43126. p. cm. 1985. (ISBN 0-201-08623-9). Harper & Row.

Whitney, Annie Weston

--The Southern Cousin, 1 of 60 vols. LC 12-40493. 2 p. l., 3-280 p. front., plates. 18 1/2 cm. (Crescent Lib.). c.1892. Set. American Baptist Publication Society.

Whitney, David Charles (1921-)

--Ann's Ann-Imal. Graboff, Abner (1919-), illus. LC 77-77347. (Illus.). 46 p. 23cm. (See and Say Sounds Series). 1969. Watts.

--Blueberry, the Bloodhound. Graboff, Abner (1919-), illus. LC 67-18430. (Illus.). 1 v. (unpaged). 23cm. (See and Say Sounds Series). 1967. Watts.

--Limpy, the Lion. Graboff, Abner (1919-), illus. LC 69-11525. (Illus.). 43 p. 23cm. (See and Say Sounds Series). 1969. F. Watts.

--Skippy the Skunk. Graboff, Abner (1919-), illus. LC 68-24490. (Illus.). 45 p. 23cm. (See and Say Sounds Series). 1968. F. Watts.

--Willie & Winnie & Wilma, the Wicked Witch. Graboff, Abner (1919-), illus. LC 67-18898. (Illus.). 57 p. 23cm. (See and Say Sounds Series). 1967. F. Watts.

Whitney, Elinor, ed. see Minchin, Nydia E.

Whitney, Elinor (1889-)

--The Mystery Club. Siegel, William (1905-), illus. LC 33-24351. xi, 252 p. incl. front., plates. 19 1/2 cm. 1933. Frederick A. Stokes Company.

--Timothy and the Blue Cart. Hader, Elmer Stanley (1889-1973) & Hader, Berta Hoerner (1890-1976), illus. LC 30-243411. 3 p. l., 168 p. col. front., illus. 20 cm. 1930. Frederick A. Stokes Company.

--Tod, of the Fens. LC 28-140039. 6 p. l., 239 p. incl. illus., plates. col. front. 20 1/2 cm. 1928. The Macmillan Company. **Award: (JNM).**

--Try All Ports. Westmacott, Bernard (1887-), illus. LC 31-28242. ix, 246 p. incl. front., illus., plates. 20 1/2 cm. 1931. Longmans, Green and Co.

--Tyke-y, His Book and His Mark. Whitney, Elinor (1889-), illus. LC 25-22396. 78 p. illus. 22 1/2 cm. 1925. The Macmillan Company.

Whitney, Elinor (1889-) & Mahony, Bertha E., eds.

--Realms of Gold in Children's Books. N.D. Doubleday Doran.

Whitney, Elliott

--The Black Fox of Yukon. Armstrong, Harry W., illus. LC 17-22560. 272 p. front., plates. 20 cm. (Half-title: The Boys' Big Game Series)). c.1917. The Reilly & Britton Co.

--The Bobcat of Jump Mountain. Armstrong, Harry W., illus. LC 20-17173. (The Boys Big Game Ser.). 1920. Reilly & Lee.

--The Boss of the Bighorns. Price, Garrett W. (1896-1979), illus. LC 24-17968. 3 p. l., 9-254 p. front. 20 cm. (Half-title: The Boys' Big Game Series). c.1924. The Reilly & Lee Co.

--The Crazy Elk of Terrapin Swamp. (The Boys Big Game Ser.). N.D. Reilly & Lee.

--The Giant Moose. Groesbeck, Dan Sayre (1863-), illus. LC 12-17519. 243 p. front., plates. 20 cm. (Half-title: The Boys' Big Game Series). c.1912. The Reilly & Britton Co.

--The King Condor of the Andes. (The Boys Big Game Ser.). N.D. Reilly & Lee.

--The Pirate Shark. (The Boys Big Game Ser.). N.D. Reilly & Lee.

--The Rogue Elephant. (The Boys Big Game Ser.). N.D. Reilly & Lee.

--The Saber-Tusk Walrus. Price, Garrett W. (1896-1979), illus. LC 23-11443. 249 p. incl. front. 20 cm. (Half-title: The boys' big game series). c.1923. The Reilly & Lee Co.

Whitney, Elliott & Sayler, Harry Lincoln (1863-)

--The Blind Lion of the Congo. Groesbeck, Dan Sayre, illus. LC 12-17521. 266 p. front., plates. 20 cm. (Half-title: The Boys' Big Game Series)). c.1912. The Reilly & Britton Co.

--The King Bear of Kadiak Island. Groesbeck, Dan Sayre, illus. LC 12-17543. 268 p. front., plates. 20 cm. (Half-title: The Boys' Big Game Series)). c.1912. The Reilly & Britton Co.

--The White Tiger of Nepal. Groesbeck, Dan Sayre, illus. LC 12-17520. 255 p. front., plates. 20 cm. (Half-title: The Boys' Big Game Series)). c.1912. The Reilly & Britton Co.

Whitney, Helen Hay, Mrs.

--The Bed-Time Book. Smith, Jessie Willcox (1863-1935), illus. LC 7-25151. 31, 1 p. col. front., illus. (part col.) 5 col. pl. 31 1/2 x 27 1/2 cm. 1907. Duffield and Company.

--The Little Boy Book. Verbeck, Frank (1858-1933), illus. LC 19-43. 30cm. 34p. 1900. R. H. Russell.

--The Punch and Judy Book. Harding, Charlotte (1873-), illus. (Illus.). N.D. Duffield & Co.

--Verses for Jock and Joan. Harding, Charlotte (1873-), illus. LC 5-33917. 32 p. col. front., col. plates. 29 1/2 x 27 1/2 cm. 1905. Fox, Duffield and Company.

AUTHOR INDEX WIBBERLEY, LEONARD

Whitney, Leon Fradley (1894-1973)
--Pigeon City. LC 62-13657. (Illus.). 227p. 20cm. 1962. P. S. Erickson.
--Pigeon City. LC 31-9710. 5 p. l.,227 p. front., illus. 19 1/2 cm. 1931. R. M. McBride & Company.
--That Useless Hound. Hart, Ernest H. (1910-), illus. LC 50-9285. 211 p. illus. 21 cm. 1950. Dodd, Mead.
--That's My Dog!. Hart, Ernest H. (1910-), illus. LC 52-8282. 216 p. illus. 21 cm. 1952. Dodd, Mead.
Whitney, Marion Isabelle
--Juan of Paricutin. LC 53-5659. 168p. illus. 22cm. 1953. Steck Co.
Whitney, Mary Ellen
--Some Little Plays and How to Act Them. Saunders, Dorothy, illus. LC 30-25070. 156 p. incl. front., illus. 19 1/2 cm. (Educational play-book series). c.1927. Beckley-Cardy Company.
Whitney, Myra Ella
--Columbus the Bear and Thomasas the Cat. Goldy-Young, Elsa, illus. LC 38-21547. (Illus.). 20cm. 39p. 1938. Saalfield Publishing Company.
--Rhymes for Jack and Jill. Potter, Edna, illus. LC 30-23914. iii, 1, iv-v p., 1 l., 70 p. illus. (part col.) 19 cm. (Heath supplementary readers). c.1930. D. C. Heath and Company.
Whitney, Phyllis Ayame (1903-)
--Blue Fire. (gr. 7-9). 1961. Hawthorn.
--Creole Holiday. LC 59-9466. 206 p. 21cm. 1959. Westminster Press.
--Ever After. LC 48-8587. 279 p. 22 cm. 1948. Houghton Mifflin Co.
--The Fire And The Gold. 1956. (ISBN 0-690-29923-0). Thomas Y. Crowell.
--The Highest Dream. 1956. (ISBN 0-679-25061-1). McKay.
--The Highest Dream. (gr. 7-12). N.D (StarLine). Schol Bk Serv.
--The Island of Dark Wood. Wishnefsky, Philip, illus. LC 51-10045. 190 p. illus. 22 cm. 1951. Westminster Press.
--Linda's Homecoming. 1949. David McKay Co.
--Linda's Homecoming. LC 54-8248. 250p. 20cm. (Starlight novels for modern girls). 1954, c.1950. Grosset & Dunlap.
--A Long Time Coming: A Novel for Young People. LC 54-1332. 261p. 21cm. 1954. McKay.
--Love Me, Love Me Not. LC 52-1037. 280 p. illus. 22 cm. 1952. Houghton Mifflin.
--Mystery of the Angry Idol. Fiorentino, Al, illus. LC 65-16498. 224p. illus. 23cm. c.1965. Westminster.
--Mystery of the Black Diamonds. 1954. E M Hale.
--Mystery of the Black Diamonds. Gretzer, John, illus. LC 53-8355. 222p. illus. 22cm. 1954. Westminster Press.
--The Mystery of the Crimson Ghost. LC 69-14202. 190 p. 23cm. 1969. Westminster Press.
--Mystery of the Golden Horn. (Illus.). (gr. 5-8). 1962. (ISBN 0-8382-0573-9). Hale.
--Mystery of the Golden Horn. Helms, Georgeanne, illus. LC 62-138749. 240 p. illus. 23 cm. 1962. (ISBN 0-664-32288-3). Westminster Press.
--Mystery of the Green Cat. 192p. (gr. 7-12). 1969. (ISBN 0-590-08571-9, Schol Pap). Scholastic Inc.
--Mystery of the Green Cat. Horwitz, Richard, illus. LC 57-543538. 208 p. illus. 21 cm. 1957. Westminster Press.
--The Mystery of the Gulls. Smalley, Janet (1893-), illus. LC 49-8906. 202 p. illus. 22 cm. 1949. Westminster Press.
--Mystery of the Haunted Pool. (Illus.). (gr. 6-9). 1960. (ISBN 0-8382-0574-7). Hale.
--Mystery of the Haunted Pool. 224p. (gr. 7-12). 1969. (ISBN 0-590-08610-3, Schol Pap). Schol Bk Serv.
--Mystery of the Haunted Pool. Hall, H. Tom, illus. LC 60-9715. (Illus.). 21cm. 223p. (gr. 5-9). 1960. (ISBN 0-664-32241-7). Westminster.
--Mystery of the Hidden Hand. (Illus.). (gr. 5-8). 1963. (ISBN 0-8382-0575-5). Hale.
--Mystery of the Hidden Hand. Hall, H. Tom, illus. (Illus.). (gr. 5-9). 1963. (ISBN 0-664-32313-8). Westminster.
--Mystery of the Scowling Boy. Gretzer, John, illus. LC 72-7272. (Illus.). 189 p. 21cm. 1973. (ISBN 0-664-32523-8). Westminster Press.
--Mystery of the Strange Traveler. Fiorentino, Al, illus. LC 67-16532. 192 p. illus. 21 cm. 1967, c.1951. Westminster Press.
--Mystery on the Isle of Skye. Keats, Ezra Jack (1916-1983), illus. LC 55-11627. 224p. illus. 21cm. c.1955. (ISBN 0-664-32118-6). Westminster Press.
--Nobody Likes Trina. LC 72-12894. 286 p. 25cm. 1973, c.1972. (ISBN 0-8161-6074-0). G. K. Hall.
--Nobody Likes Trina. LC 72-76781. 181 p. 22cm. 1972. (ISBN 0-664-32517-3). Westminster Press.
--A Place for Ann. Blair, Helen (1910-), illus. LC 41-6942. 5 p. l., 211, 1 p. incl. col. front. plates (part col.) 21 1/2 cm. 1941. Houghton Mifflin Company.
--Sea Jade. (gr. 9 up). 1965. (ISBN 0-8015-6624-X). Hawthorn.
--Secret of Goblin Glen. Fiorentino, Al, illus. LC 68-10231. (Illus.). 174 p. 23cm. 1968. Westminster Press.
--Secret of Haunted Mesa. LC 75-4617. 144 p. 21cm. 1975. Westminster Press.
--Secret of the Emerald Star. 1964. E M Hale.
--Secret of the Emerald Star. Stein, Alex, illus. LC 64-16345. (Illus.). 233 p. 23cm. 1964. Westminster Press.
--Secret of the Missing Footprint. Stein, Alex, illus. LC 76-87968. 1970. (ISBN 0-664-32460-6). Westminster Press.
--Secret of the Sammurai Sword. 1958. (ISBN 0-664-32390-1). Westminster Press.
--Secret of the Samurai Sword. LC 58-8800. 1958. E M Hale.
--Secret of the Spotted Shell. Mecray, John, illus. LC 67-14. (Illus.). 256 p. 23cm. 1967. Westminster Press.
--Secret of the Stone Face. LC 77-1261. 144 p. 21cm. c.1977. (ISBN 0-664-32612-9). Westminster Press.
--Secret of the Tiger's Eye. Horowitz, Richard, illus. 1961. E M Hale.
--Secret of the Tiger's Eye. Horwitz, Richard, illus. 1961. (ISBN 0-664-32265-4). Westminster Press.
--Seven Tears for Apollo. (gr. 9 up). 1963. (ISBN 0-8015-6750-5). Hawthorn.
--The Silver Inkwell. Frommholz, Hilda, illus. LC 45-8117. 4 p. l., 272 p. plates. 18 1/2 cm. 1945. Houghton Mifflin Co.
--Spindrift. LC 74-14384. 1975. Doubleday.
--A Star for Ginny. Frommholz, Hilda, illus. LC 42-20281. 5 p. l., 237, 1 p. illus. 22 cm. 1942. Houghton Mifflin Company.
--Step to the Music. LC 53-8425. 256p. 21cm. 1953. Crowell.
--Thunder Heights. (gr. 7-9). 1960. Hawthorn.
--Trembling Hills. (gr. 7-9). 1956. Hawthorn.
--The Vanishing Scarecrow. LC 72-146846. (Illus.). 189 p. 22cm. 1971. (ISBN 0-664-32494-0). Westminster Press.
--Willow Hill. N.D. David McKay Co.
--Willow Hill. LC 47-301654. x p., 1 l., 243 p. 21 1/2 cm. 1947. Reynal & Hitchcock.
--A Window for Julie. Anderson, Jean, illus. LC 43-16007. 5 p. l., 198 p. illus. 21 1/2 cm. 1943. Houghton Mifflin Company.
--Window on the Square. (gr. 7-9). 1962. (ISBN 0-696-87519-5). Hawthorn.
Whitney, Susan
--Dr. Gloom's Outer Space Jokes & Puzzles. Senn, Steve (1950-), illus. (Illus.). 64p. (Dr. Gloom's Activity Ser.). (gr. 4-6). N.D. (ISBN 0-15-224225-2, VoyB). HarBraceJ.
Whitney, Thomas P., tr. see Marshak, Samuil Iakovlevich.
Whitney, Thomas Porter (1917-), tr. see Green, Alexander.
Whitney, Thomas Porter (1917-), tr. see Paustovsky, Konstantin Georgievich.
Whitney, Thomas Porter (1917-)
--Marko the Rich and Vasily the Unlucky. Galanin, Igor, illus. LC 73-6043. (Illus.). 31 p. 27cm. 1974. (ISBN 0-02-792710-5). Macmillan.
--Vasilisa the Beautiful. Hogrogian, Nonny (1932-), illus. LC 73-102971. (Illus.). 32p. col. illus. 24cm. (gr. k-3). 1970. (ISBN 0-02-792540-4). Macmillan.
Whitney, Thomas Porter (1917-), ed.
--The Young Russians: A Collection of Stories About Them. LC 78-185216. (gr. 7up). 1972. (ISBN 0-02-792700-8). Macmillan.
Whitson, Denton
--Savage Heart. 311p. 1959. Chilton Books.
Whitson, Elizabeth
--The Casual Observatory. Whitson, Elizabeth, illus. LC 74-83784. (Illus.). 28 p. 20cm. 1975. (ISBN 0-8378-8002-5). C. R. Gibson Co.
Whitson, George Thomas
--Roaring Wheels. LC 48-1784. 139 p. 20 cm. 1947. Dorrance.
Whitson, John Harvey (1854-1936)
--Campaigning with Tippecanoe. LC 4-26879. 2 p. l., ii, 7-247 p. 19 cm. 1904. The Federal Book Company.
--A Courier of Empire: A Story of Marcus Whitman's Ride to Save Oregon. Emerson, C. Chase, illus. LC 4-25096. 315 p. front., 4 pl. 20 cm. 1904. W. A. Wilde Company.
--With Fremont the Pathfinder: Or, Winning the Empire of Gold. Stecher, William Frederick (1864-), illus. LC 3-22522. 320 p. front., 4 pl. 20 cm. 1903. W. A. Wilde Company.
--The Young Ditch Rider: A Story of the Plains. LC 99-1067. 96 p. illus. 21 1/2 cm. 1899. D. C. Cook Publishing Co.
Whittaker, Daphne, jt. auth. see Kotsky, Cynthia.
Whittaker, Otto, Jr. (1916-)
--The True Story of the Tooth Fairy (and Why Brides Wear Engagement Rings). Goetzman, Anne, illus. LC 68-19790. (Illus.). 34 p. 1968. Droke House; Distributed by Grosset & Dunlap, New York.
Whittaker, Violet
--Puppet People Scripts. 1984. (ISBN 0-8010-9666-9). Baker Bk.
Whitteberry, Caroline
--Pop-O, the Clown. Cummings, Alison, illus. LC 50-4235. (Illus.). 32p. 17cm. (Tell-a-Tale Bks.). 1950. Whitman.
Whittemore, E. M., Mrs.
--Delia, the Blue Bird of Mulberry Bend. N.D. Fleming H. Revell Co.
Whittemore, Maria E
--Flower Fables: An Illustrated Alphabet for Little Folks. LC 16-3872. 80 p. illus. 24 1/2 cm. c.1886. Cassell & Company, Limited.
Whitten, Leslie Hunter (1928-)
--Pinion, the Golden Eagle. Bartlett, William, illus. (Illus.). (gr. 7 up). 1968. (ISBN 0-442-09415-9). Van Nos Reinhold.
Whitten, Mary Street, jt. auth. see Street, Julian.
Whittier, Charles Albert
--In the Michigan Lumber-Camps. LC 4-1645. viii, 9-137 p. front. 19 1/2 cm. (Boys vacation series. Vacation no. 1). 1904. Broadway Publishing Company.
--In the Michigan Lumber Camps. LC 2-110045. viii, 9-137 p. front., plates. 19 cm. (boys' vacation series; first vacation). 1900. F. Tennyson Neely Co.
Whittier, Isabel Mary Skolfield
--Susie, the Naughty Little Rat. 1st ed. LC 56-13132. (Illus.). 18p. 24cm. 1956. Pageant Press.
Whittier, John Greenleaf (1807-1892), ed.
--Barbara Frietchie. Galdone, Paul (1914-), illus. LC 65-16182. 1v. (unpaged) col. illus. 27cm. c.1965. Crowell.
--Child Life: A Collection of Poems. LC 73-128162. (Illus.). xiii, 263 p. 21cm. (Granger index reprint series). 1970. Books for Libraries Press.
--Child Life: A Collection of Poems. LC 6-29122. 2 p. l., vii-xiii, 263 p. front., illus. 19 cm. 1879. Houghton, Osgood and Company.
--Child Life: A Collection of Poems. xiii, 263 p. incl. front., illus. 19 1/2 cm. 1872. J. R. Osgood and Company.
--Child-Life: A Collection of Poems For and About Children. (Illus.). 1900. Houghton Mifflin & Co.
--Child-Life: Collection of Poems For and About Children. 1884. Houghton, Mifflin & Co.
--Child-Life in Prose. 1884. Houghton, Mifflin & Co.
--Child Life in Prose. LC 7-22133. x, 11-301 p. front., illus. 19 1/2 cm. 1874. J. R. Osgood and Company.
--Jack in the Pulpit. Lathbury, Mary Artemisia (1841-1913), illus. 1888. R Worthington.
--Mabel Martin, Cobbler Keezer, Maud Muller and Other Poems. (Riverside Literature Ser.). N.D. Houghton Mifflin Co.
--A Selection from Child Life in Poetry. LC 7-22120. iv, 100 p. 18 cm. (On cover: Riverside literature series. no. 70). 1894. Houghton, Mifflin and Company.
--A Selection from Child Life in Prose. LC 7-22156. 96 p. 18 cm. (On cover: Riverside literature series. no. 71). 1894. Houghton, Mifflin and Company.
--Snowbound and Other Early Poems. (New Pocket Classics). N.D. Macmillan.
--Snowbound & Other Poems. (gr. 10 up). N.D. Pyramid Pubns.
--Whittier and His Snow-Bound, 1 of 12 vols. (Child World Readers Ser.: No. 10). N.D. Set. E L Kellogg & Co.
--Whittier's Snow-Bound, Among the Hills, Songs of Labor, and Other Poems. notes. 96p. (Riverside Literature Ser.: No. 4). N.D. Houghton, Mifflin and Company.
Whittingham, Richard, tr. see Zimnik, Reiner.
Whittington, Dorothy
--Vicky Pageant. 1st ed. LC 59-12238. 148 p. 21 cm. c.1959. Duell, Sloan and Pearce.
Whittington, K. R
--Oswald, the Silly Goose. Escott, Tony, illus. LC 73-89222. (Illus.). 58 p. 24cm. 1st U.S. edition. 1974. (ISBN 0-87888-067-4). Bradbury Press.
Whittington, Richard D. (1423-)
--Dick Whittington and His Cat. Busoni, Rafaello (1900-1962), illus. LC 41-12913. (Illus.). 26cm. 18p. 1941. Grosset & Dunlap.
Whittle, Connie R & Carter, Virginia I
--Happy Scrappy. 1st ed. Duttry, Ray A., illus. LC 56-751705. 47p. illus. 21cm. 1956. Vantage Press.
Whittle, Tyler, pseud., see Tyler-Whittle, Michael Sidney.
Whittle, Tyler, pseud. (1927-)
--Spinning Tops of Naples. Tyler-Whittle, Michael Sydney. (Illus.). (gr. 6-7). 1965. (ISBN 0-8019-1441-8). Chilton.
Whittlesey, Sarah J. C.
Bertha the Beauty. N.D. Claxton, Remsen, & Haffelfinger.
Whittman, Sally
--Plenty of Pelly and Peak. LC 79-3675. p. cm. (I can read book). c.1980. (ISBN 0-06-026564-7). (ISBN 0-06-026563-9). Harper & Row.
Whittum, Lizzie S
--Little Folks of Far-Away Lands. LC 7-20619. 112 p. illus. 18 x 14 cm. (On cover: Choice literature library). c.1907. Educational Publishing Company.
Whitworth, George C., ed.
--Under the Spell of the Nursery Lamp. LC 11-31197. 20cm. 143p. 1911. D. Fitzgerald Inc.
Whydale, Herbert
The Old Mouse's Stocking Basket. N.D. J. B. Lippincott.
Whymper, Alfred
--Taken Up, 1 of 6. (Home and School Reward Ser.: No. 2). N.D. Cassell, Petter, & Galpin.
Whyte, Adam Gowans (1875-)
--The World's Wonder Stories. Brock, T. A., illus. LC 18-298322. xvi p., 1 l., 284 p. front., illus., plates, ports., facsims. 19 cm. 1917. G. P. Putnam's Sons.
Whyte, Christina Gowans
--The Adventures of Merrywink. Wheelhouse, M. V., illus. (Illus.). N.D. Thomas Y. Crowell.
--Nina's Career. LC 7-32567. vii, 314 p. col. front., 5 col. pl. 19 1/2 cm. 1907. The Macmillan Company.
--The Story Book Girls. LC 6-41715. viii p., 1 l., 339 p. 19 1/2 cm. 1906. The Macmillan Company.
Whyte, Jenny Bell
--Adelaide Stories. Prager, Annabelle, illus. LC 72-77767. (Illus.). 76 p. 22cm. 1972. (ISBN 0-671-65194-3). Simon and Schuster.
Whyte, Malcolm Kenneth, Jr. (1933-)
--Fat Cat Coloring & Limerick Bk. Sloan, Donna, illus. 32p. (gr. k-6). 1967. (ISBN 0-912300-04-3). Troubador Pr.
--Love Bug Coloring & Limerick Bk. Sloan, Donna, illus. (Illus.). 32p. (gr. k-6). 1968. (ISBN 0-912300-05-1). Troubador Pr.
Whyte, Malcolm Kenneth, Jr. (1933-), ed.
--Gorey Cats Paper Dolls. Gorey, Edward St. John (1925-), illus. (Illus.). 48p. (Orig.). 1982. (ISBN 0-89844-086-6). Troubador Pr.
--Once Upon a Time. Dunn, Anna, illus. (Illus.). 40p. (gr. 1-8). 1979. (ISBN 0-912300-16-7). Troubador Pr.
Whyte, Ron
--The Flower That Finally Grew. Harrow, Bruce, illus. LC 70-108059. (Illus.). 27 p. 1970. Crown Publishers.
Wiands, Catherine
--Positive Strokes for Little Folks, Vols. 1-7. 2nd ed. Elzbarth, Pat, ed. 32p. (Orig., Pub. by Kingston Hall). (gr. 1-6). N.D. (ISBN 0-943262-00-3). Set of 7. Transitions.
Wibberley, Leonard Patrick O'Connor see O'Connor, Patrick, pseud.
Wibberley, Leonard Patrick O'Connor see Webb, Christopher, pseud.
Wibberley, Leonard Patrick O'Connor (1915-)
--Attar of the Ice Valley. LC 68-13683. 166 p. 21cm. 1968. Farrar, Straus and Giroux.
--The Ballad of the Pilgrim Cat. LC 62-18964. 19cm. 41p. 1962. Washburn.
--The Black Tiger. O'Connor, Patrick, pseud. LC 56-13794. 150 p. illus. 21 cm. 1956. Washburn.
--Black Tiger at Bonneville. O'Connor, Patrick, pseud. LC 60-13323. 135 p. 21cm. 1960. Washburn.
--Black Tiger at Indianapolis. O'Connor, Patrick, pseud. LC 62-19999. 151 p. 21cm. 1962. Washburn.
--A Car Called Camellia. O'Connor, Patrick, pseud. LC 77-107944. 150 p. 21cm. 1970. Washburn.
--The Coronation Book. 192p. (gr. 7-11). 1953. FS&G.
--The Crime of Martin Coverly. LC 79-28538. 167 p. 22cm. c.1980. (ISBN 0-374-31656-2). Farrar Straus Giroux.
--Deadmen's Cave. Leamon, Tom, illus. LC 54-5206. 234 p. illus. 23 cm. 1954. Ariel Books.
--Deadmen's Cave. Leamon, Tom, illus. 192p. 1954. Farrar, Straus & Cudahy.
--Encounter Near Venus. Wadowski-Bak, Alice, illus. LC 67-3797. (Illus.). 214 p. 22cm. 1967. (ISBN 0-374-32178-7). Farrar, Strauss and Giroux.
--The Five-Dollar Watch Mystery. O'Connor, Patrick, pseud. LC 59-8639. 167 p. 21cm. 1959. Washburn.
--Flight of the Peacock. O'Connor, Patrick, pseud. Anderson, Rus, illus. LC 55-203. 179 p. illus. 21 cm. 1954. I. Washburn.
--Flint's Island. LC 70-184127. (Illus.). 165 p. 22cm. 1972. (ISBN 0-374-32331-3). Farrar, Straus & Giroux.
--Gunpowder for Washington. LC 56-59039. 151 p. illus. 21 cm. 1956. Washburn.

--John Treegate's Musket. LC 59-10188. 188 p. 22cm. 1959. Ariel Books.
--John Treegate's Musket. 224p. 1959. (ISBN 0-374-33762-4). Farrar, Straus and Giroux.
--Journey to Untor. LC 74-106291. 188 p. 21cm. (Ariel book). 1970. Farrar, Straus and Giroux.
--Kevin O'Connor and the Light Brigade. LC 57-576662. 186p. 22cm. 1957. Ariel Books.
--Kevin O'Connor and the Light Brigade. 192p. 1957. (ISBN 0-374-34125-7). Farrar, Straus and Giroux.
--The King's Beard. 1st ed. Price, Christine Hilda (1928-1980), illus. LC 51-13273. 198 p. illus. 22 cm. 1952. Ariel Books.
--The King's Beard. Price, Christine Hilda (1928-1980), illus. (Illus.). (gr. 6-10). 1952. (ISBN 0-8382-0407-4). Hale.
--The Last Battle. LC 75-42104. 197 p. 21cm. c.1976. (ISBN 0-374-34349-7). Farrar, Straus and Giroux.
--Leopard's Prey. LC 78-149225. 183 p. 22cm. (Ariel book). 1971. (ISBN 0-374-34378-0). Farrar, Straus and Giroux.
--Little League Family. 1st ed. Cuffari, Richard (1925-1978), illus. LC 77-12887. (Illus.). 189 p. 22cm. c.1978. (ISBN 0-385-12873-8). (ISBN 0-385-12874-6). Doubleday.
--Mexican Road Race. O'Connor, Patrick, pseud. LC 57-13799. (Illus.). 182 p. 21cm. (gr. 7-9). 1957. I. Washburn.
--Perilous Gold. LC 78-7450. 135 p. 22cm. c.1978. (ISBN 0-374-35824-9). Farrar, Straus, Giroux.
--Peter Treegate's War. LC 60-9229. 156 p. 22 cm. 1960. Ariel Books.
--Peter Treegates's War. (gr. 7-11). 1960. (ISBN 0-374-35874-5). FS&G.
--The Raising of the Dubhe. O'Connor, Patrick, pseud. LC 64-14410. vi, 120 p. 21cm. 1964. Washburn.
--Red Pawns. LC 73-82695. 183 p. 22cm. 1973. (ISBN 0-374-36240-8). Farrar, Straus and Giroux.
--Sea Captain from Salem. LC 61-6967. 186p. illus. c.1961. Ariel Books, Farrar, Straus and Cudahy. **Award: (ALA).**
--Seawind from Hawaii. O'Connor, Patrick, pseud. LC 65-20930. 183p. 21cm. (gr. 6-8). c.1965. Washburn Dist. McKay.
--The Secret of the Hawk. 1st ed. Price, Christine Hilda (1928-1980), illus. LC 52-12374. 214 p. illus. 22 cm. c.1953. Ariel Books.
--The Shepherd's Reward: A Christmas Legend. Fisher, Thomas, illus. LC 63-16390. (Illus.). 32 p. 16cm. 1963. I. Washburn.
--The Society of Foxes: A Tale of Adventure. O'Connor, Patrick, pseud. Geary, Clifford N. (1916-), illus. LC 54-9464. 184 p. illus. 21 cm. 1954. I. Washburn.
--The Time of the Lamb. Kredel, Fritz (1900-1973), illus. LC 61-14133. (Illus.). 47 p. 16cm. 1961. Washburn.
--Treegate's Raiders. LC 62-9528. 218 p. 22 cm. 1962. Ariel Books. **Award: (ALA).**
--The Watermelon Mystery. O'Connor, Patrick, pseud. LC 55-14425. 181 p. illus. 21 cm. 1955. I. Washburn.
--The Wound of Peter Wayne. LC 55-9592. 220 p. 22 cm. 1955. Ariel Books.

Wiberg, Harald Albin (1908-)
--Christmas at the Tomten's Farm. Wiberg, Harald Albin (1908-), illus. (Illus.). 92 p. 1968. Coward-McCann.

Wicher, Ernst, Mrs. (1831-1902)
--The Green Gate. Wister, Annie, Mrs. (1830-1908), tr. from German. 1903. J.B. Lippincott.

Wichman, Juliet R.
--Moki Learns to Fish. 1981. (ISBN 0-686-86236-8). Kauai Museum.

Wick, Gordon E.
--Saints in Buckskins. 76p. (gr. 10 up). 1974. (ISBN 0-682-47848-2). Exposition.

Wick, Jean, jt. auth. see Catrevas, Christina.

Wicke, Ernestine (1897-)
--What the Fairies Told Me. LC 36-33984. 3 p. l., 5-32 p. illus. 20 1/2 x 28 cm. c.1936. The Christopher Publishing House.

Wickenden, Dan
--The Amazing Vacation. 1st ed. Blegvad, Erik (1923-), illus. LC 56-8356. 216 p. illus. 21 cm. 1956. Harcourt, Brace.
--The Red Carpet. LC 51-26055. 280 p. 22 cm. 1952. Morrow.

Wickens, Elaine, jt. auth. see Cannon, Calvin.

Wicker, Ireene Seaton, Mrs. (1905-), adapted by see Ershov, Petr Pavlovich.

Wicker, Ireene Seaton, Mrs. (1905-)
--How the Ocelots Got Their Spots. 1st ed. Perrot, Catherine, illus. LC 75-43887. (Illus.). 31 p. c.1976. (ISBN 0-8184-0231-8). L. Stuart.
--The Singing Lady's Favorite Stories. Royt, Mary & Bennett, Juanita C., illus. LC 25-32777. v. mounted col. front., illus. 27 x 29 cm. c.1934. Whitman Publishing Company.
--Sleeping Beauty. LC 46-40929. (Illus.). 16p. 26cm. (ABC Series of Fables with Music). 1941. ABC Music Corporation.
--Young Music Makers. 1961. E M Hale.

Wickes, Frances Gillespy, ed. see Seegmiller, Wilhelmina.

Wickes, Frances Gillespy, Mrs.
--Beyond the Rainbow Bridge. Lupprian, Hildegard (1897-), illus. LC 24-17245. 4 p. l., 309 p. front., plates. 20 cm. c.1924. Milton Bradley Co.
--A Child's Book of Holiday Plays. (Plays). (MacMillan Bks. for Boys & Girls). (gr. 4-6). N.D. MacMillan Bks.
--Happy Holidays. Kay, Gertrude Alice (1884-1939), illus. LC 21-5919. ix, 1, 353 p. incl. front., illus. 18 cm. c.1921. Rand McNally & Company.

Wickes, Frances Gillespy, Mrs., jt. ed. see Skinner, Ada Maria.

Wickes, Martha
--The Mystery of Sun Dial Court. McCollum, Katharine, illus. LC 26-19730. 320 p. front., plates. 19 1/2 cm. 1926. The Penn Publishing Company.

Wicki, Peter & Schroeder, Binette
--Ra Ta Ta Tam: The Strange Story of a Little Engine. Bullock, Michael, tr. from German. (Illus.). 32p. (gr. k-1). 1984. (ISBN 0-224-00974-5, Pub. by Jonathan Cape). Merrimack Pub Cir.

Wickland, Gustaf A
--Tiny Tree: A Christmas Story for Children. Selim, Evelyn, illus. LC 59-107615. unpaged. illus. 22 cm. 1959. Augsburg Pub. House.

Wickman, Mabel
--Animal Tracks. 1965. Exposition Press.

Wicks, Mark
--To Mars Via the Moon: An Astronomical Story. LC 74-16526. (Illus.). 327 p. 21cm. (Science Fiction). 1975. (ISBN 0-405-06318-0). Arno Press.

Wicksteed, Hilda M
--Jerry & Grandpa. LC 30-238841. 3 p. l., 9-145 p. col. front., plates (part col.) 20 1/2 cm. c.1930. Thomas Y. Crowell Company.

Wickstrom, Lois (1948-)
--Ladybugs for Loretta. Mion, Francie & Johnson, Priscilla M., illus. (Illus.). (gr. k-6). 1978. (ISBN 0-916176-04-5). Sproing.
--Oliver. Johnson, Priscilla M., illus. (Illus.). (gr. k-6). 1978. (ISBN 0-916176-03-7). Sproing.

Widdemer, Mabel Cleland (1902-1964)
--Aleck Bell, Ingenious Boy. 1st ed. John, Charles V., illus. LC 62-12698. 200 p. illus. 20 cm. (Childhood of Famous Americans). 1962. Bobbs-Merrill.
--Aleck Bell, Ingenious Boy. Nicholas, Frank, illus. LC 47-30856. 194 p. illus. 20 cm. (Childhood of Famous Americans Series). 1947. Bobbs-Merrill Co.
--The Clue of the Riddle: A Mystery. LC 33-25969. 5 p. l., 3-274 p. front. 19 1/2 cm. c.1933. Farrar & Rinehart, Incorporated.
--De Witt Clinton, Boy Builder. Doremus, Robert (1913-), illus. LC 61-11886. 200 p. illus. 20 cm. (Childhood of Famous Americans). 1961. Bobbs-Merrill.
--Dear Mother Make-Believe. Carpell, Elisie, illus. LC 26-160520. 4 p. l., 299 p. front., plates. 19 1/2 cm. c.1926. Harcourt, Brace and Company.
--Harriet Beecher Stowe, Connecticut Girl. 1st ed. John, Charles V., illus. LC 62-12699. 200 p. illus. 20 cm. (Childhood of Famous Americans series). 1962. Bobbs-Merrill.
--Harriet Beecher Stowe, Connecticut Girl. Patterson, Robert (1899-), illus. LC 49-107111. 196 p. illus. 20 cm. (Childhood of Famous Americans Series). 1949. Bobbs-Merrill Co.
--In the Shadows of the Skyscrapers. Tobin, George T., illus. LC 25-17059. 4 p. l., 3-268 p. front., plates. 19 1/2 cm. c.1925. Harcourt, Brace and Company.
--James Monroe, Good Neighbor Boy. Rawson, Maurice, illus. LC 59-12854. 192 p. illus. 20 cm. (Childhood of famous Americans). 1959. Bobbs-Merrill.
--The Little Green Orchard Mystery. King, Ruth, illus. LC 40-5635. xiii, 1, 238 p. incl. front., illus. 20 cm. 1940. D. Appleton-Century Company, Incorporated.
--The Mystery at Shadylawn. LC 32-19196. 4 p. l., 3-275 p. front. 19 1/2 cm. c.1932. Farrar & Rinehart, Incorporated.
--Peter Stuyvesant, Boy with Wooden Shoes. 1st ed. John, Charles V., illus. LC 62-16597. 200 p. illus. 20 cm. (Childhood of Famous Americans). c.1962. Bobbs-Merrill.
--Peter Stuyvesant, Boy with Wooden Shoes. Pellicer, Joseph Luis, illus. LC 50-6748. 190 p. illus. 20 cm. (Childhood of Famous Americans Series). 1950. Bobbs-Merrill.
--Washington Irving, Boy of Old New York. John, Charles V., illus. LC 62-16619. 200 p. illus. 20 cm. (Childhood of Famous Americans). 1963. Bobbs-Merrill.
--Washington Irving, Boy of Old New York. John, Charles V., illus. LC 46-50026. 204 p. illus. 19 1/2 cm. (The Childhood of Famous Americans Series). 1946. The Bobbs-Merrill Company.
--The Wishing Star: A Mystery of Old Tarrytown. LC 48-3586. 230 p. illus. 21 cm. 1948. Bobbs-Merrill Co.

Widdemer, Margaret (0000-1978), ed. see Macdonald, George.

Widdemer, Margaret (0000-1978)
--Binkie and the Bell Dolls. Price, Harriet Longstreet (1891-), illus. LC 23-14087. 146 p. incl. col. front., illus. col. plates. 22 cm. 1923. The Penn Publishing Company.
--The Great Pine's Son: A Story of the Pontiac War. 1st ed. Savage, Steele (1900-), illus. LC 54-524733. 182p. illus. 22cm. (Winston Adventure Books). 1954. Winston.
--Little Girl and Boy Land: Poems for Children. Zian, Irta I., illus. LC 24-216138. viii, 97 p. illus. 21 cm. c.1924. Harcourt, Brace & Company.
--Marcia's Farmhouse. King, Ruth, illus. LC 39-220323. xi, 258 p. incl. front., illus., plates. 20 cm. 1939. D. Appleton-Century Company, Incorporated.
--Prince in Buckskin: A Story of Joseph Brant at Lake George. 1st ed. Sharp, William (1900-), illus. LC 52-8965. (Illus.). 184 p. 22cm. (Winston Adventure Books). 1952. Winston.
--The Rose-Garden Husband. Biggs, Walter, illus. 1915. J.B. Lippincott.
--Winona of Camp Karonya. (Wohelo Camp Fire Girls Ser.). 1917. A. L. Burt Co.
--Winona of Camp Karonya. Richards, Harriet Roosevelt, illus. LC 17-287997. 318 p. col. front., plates. 19 1/2 cm. 1917. J. B. Lippincott Company.
--Winona of the Camp Fire. (Wohelo Camp Fire Girls Ser.). 1915. A. L. Burt Co.
--Winona of the Camp Fire. Meister, Charles E., illus. LC 15-214357. 336 p. col. front., col. plates. 20 cm. 1915. J. B. Lippincott Company.
--Winona on Her Own. (Wohelo Camp Fire Girls Ser.). 1922. A L Burt Co.
--Winona on Her Own. Pauli, E. Corinne, illus. LC 22-17612. 307 p. col. front., plates. 20 cm. 1922. J. B. Lippincott Company.
--Winona's Dreams Come True. (Wohelo Camp Fire Girls Ser.). 1923. A L Burt Co.
--Winona's Dreams Come True. Pauli, E. Corinne, illus. LC 23-183935. 4 p. l., 7-343 p. col. front., plates. 20 cm. 1923. J. B. Lippincott Company.
--Winona's War Farm. (Wohelo Camp Fire Girls Ser.). 1918. A. L. Burt Co.
--Winona's War Farm. Richards, Harriet Roosevelt, illus. LC 18-10585. 318 p. incl. col. front., plates. 19 1/2 cm. 1918. J. B. Lippincott Company.
--Winona's Way: A Story of Reconstruction. (Wohelo Camp Fire Girls Ser.). 1919. A. B. Burt CO.
--Winona's Way: A Story of Reconstruction. Richards, Harriet Roosevelt, illus. LC 19-183735. 304 p. col. front., plates. 19 1/2 cm. 1919. J. B. Lippincott Company.

Widder, John Arthur, Jr. (1928-)
--Adventures in Black. LC 62-13318. 180p. illus. 22cm. c.1962. Harper.

Widder, Robert B
--Jennie Has a Birthday. LC 72-7661. (Illus.). 32 p. 1974. (ISBN 0-87614-039-8). Carolrhoda Books.

Widell, Helene (1912-)
--The Black Wolf of River Bend. LC 76-165404. 155 p. 21cm. 1971. (ISBN 0-374-30833-0). Farrar, Straus & Giroux.

Widerberg, Siv (1931-)
--I'm Like Me. 1st ed. Backstrom, Claes (1927-), illus. Moberg, Verne, tr. LC 73-521. (Illus.). 63 p. 21cm. 1973. (ISBN 0-912670-08-8). Feminist Press.
--My Best Friend. Held, Fibben, illus. LC 72-114229. (Illus.). 1971. (ISBN 0-399-60481-2). G. P. Putnam's Sons.

Widmayer, Patricia A. Heyndricks
--Spencer, the Smiling Sea Colt. Day, Amie M. & Lindberg, Howard E., illus. LC 64-661212. 1v. (unpaged) col. illus. 29cm. c.1965. (ISBN 0-513-00414-9). Denison.

Widney, Bette Ward
--The Mystery of the Wheat Pirates. Waterhouse, Charles (1924-), illus. LC 68-30262. (Illus.). 191 p. 22cm. 1968. Vanguard Press.

Widney, Gaylord G
--Bunny Snowhite Visits Mr. McDougal's Garden. LC 77-73162. (Illus.). 37 p. 23cm. c.1977. (ISBN 0-913182-89-3). Grossmont Press.

Widney, Stanley A.
--Elevator to the Moon. Goodenow, Earle (1913-), illus. LC 55-7492. 128p. illus. 23cm. N.D. (ISBN 0-695-42170-0). Follett Pub. Co.
--Terry Parks. Stevens, Mary E. (1920-1966), illus. LC 54-10098. 127p. illus. 23cm. 1954. (ISBN 0-695-48470-2). Follett Pub. Co.

Widor, Charles Marie (1845-1937), ed.
--Old Songs and Rounds for Little Children. LC 23-26582. 18, 5-47, 1 p. col. illus. 23 1/2 x 26 cm. c.1912. Duffield & Company.

Wiebe, Gertrude M.
--The Adventures of Pudgy: The Lucky Spaniel. 1st ed. LC 56-12305. 99 p. illus. 21 cm. 1957, c.1956. Vantage Press.
--Adventures of Pudgy the Lucky Spaniel. 1959. Vantage Press,Inc.

Wiedenbeck, Emilie Agnes see Mabie, Peter, pseud.

Wiedenbeck, Emilie Agnes (1896-)
--Chicken Little. Mabie, Peter, pseud. Wiedenbeck, Emilie Agnes (1896-), illus. Mabie, Peter, pseud. 26 p. col. illus. 26 cm. c.1931. Whitman Publishing Company.
--Gingerbread Stories. Mabie, Peter, pseud. Wiedenbeck, Emilie Agnes (1896-), illus. Mabie, Peter, pseud. LC 31-1095. 44 p. illus. (part col.) 23 1/2 x 32 cm. c.1931. Whitman Publishing Company.
--The Little Duck Who Loved the Rain. Mabie, Peter, pseud. Wiedenbeck, Emilie Agnes (1896-), illus. Mabie, Peter, pseud. LC 46-4249. 83 p. illus. (part col.) 25 1/2 x 21 1/2 cm. 1946. Wilcox & Follett Co.
--Old Friends of Ours, Story and Pictures. Mabie, Peter, pseud. Wiedenbeck, Emilie Agnes (1896-), illus. Mabie, Peter, pseud. 30 p. col. illus. 26 cm. (With Chicken Little, Racine, Wis., 1931). c.1931. Whitman Publishing Company.
--The Splendid Zoo. Mabie, Peter, pseud. Wiedenbeck, Emilie Agnes (1896-), illus. Mabie, Peter, pseud. LC 36-18543. 28 p. illus. (part col.) 21 cm. c.1936. Whitman Publishing Company.

Wiederseim, Grace G
--Dolly Drake. N.D. Frederick A. Stokes.
--Fido. (Illus.). N.D. Frederick A. Stokes.
--Grace Wiederseim's Babyskins Bedtime Book. (Illus.). 32p. N.D. Hurst & Co.
--Kitty Puss. (Illus.). N.D. Frederick A. Stokes.
--Nursery Rhymes from Mother Goose. Wiederseim, Grace G, illus. N.D. Charles Scribner's Sons.
--Piggy Wiggy. N.D. Frederick A. Stokes.

Wiegand, Roberta
--The Year of the Comet. LC 84-11004. 144p. (gr. 4-6). 1984. (ISBN 0-02-792720-2). Bradbury Pr.

Wiegman, Lies & Limmer, Hans (1926-)
--My Kangaroo Phoebe. LC 76-113099. (Illus.). 46 p. 24cm. (Terra magica children's book). 1970. Hill and Wang.

Wiegman, Lies & Stromstedt, Margareta (1931-)
--A Legend of Paradise. LC 71-158329. (Illus.). 63 p. 24cm. 1971. St. Martin's Press.

Wiemann, Rudolph, retold by see Busch, Wilhelm.

Wiemer, Rudolf Otto (1905-)
--Animals at the Manger. Pohl, Alfred, illus. Rorem, Melva (1913-) & Denef, Ruth, trs. LC 75-84809. (Illus.). 29 p. 25cm. 1969. Augsburg Pub. House.
--Christmas Story. Herrmann, Reinhard, illus. (Illus.). 24p. 1968. (ISBN 0-8066-9400-9). Augsburg.
--Come Unto Me. Herrmann, Reinhard, illus. (Illus.). 24p. (Children's Bible Picture Bk. Ser). 1968. (ISBN 0-8066-9401-7). Augsburg.
--The Good Robber Willibald. Marcks, Marie, illus. Gollob, Barbara Kowal, tr. LC 68-12233. (Illus.). 65 p. 25cm. 1st U.S. edition. 1968. Atheneum.
--Jonah and the Big Fish. Herrmann, Reinhard & Martinsen, Paul T., illus. 1 v. (unpaged) col. illus.-27cm. c.1967. Augsburg.
--Joseph & His Brothers. Herrmann, Reinhard, illus. (Illus.). 24p. (Children's Bible Picture Bk. Ser). (ps-5). 1968. Augsburg.
--Joseph in Egypt. Hermann, Reinhard, illus. (Illus.). 24p. (Children's Bible Picture Bk. Ser). (ps-5). 1968. (ISBN 0-8066-9405-X). Augsburg.
--Noah's Ark. Herrmann, Reinhard, illus. Martinsen, Paul T., tr. (Illus.). 24 p. 27cm. 1967. Augsburg Pub. House.
--Pete and the Manger Men: A Christmas Story. Marcks, Marie, illus. Hopka, Erich, tr. LC 62-15702. 106 p. illus. 26 cm. 1962. Muhlenberg Press.
--The Prodigal Son. Herrmann, Reinhard, illus. Martinsen, Paul T., tr. LC 67-8420. 1v. (unpaged) col. illus. 27cm. c.1967. Augsburg.
--Prodigal Son. Herrmann, Reinhard, illus. (Illus.). 24p. (Children's Bible Picture Bk. Ser). (ps-3). 1968. (ISBN 0-8066-9407-6). Augsburg.

Wier, Albert Ernest (1879-), ed.
--Songs the Children Love to Sing. (The Whole World Music Ser.). N.D. Appleton Century Co.

Wier, Albert Ernest (1879-) & Untermeyer, Louis (1885-), eds.
--Songs to Sing to Children. LC 35-655725. 128 p. 30 1/2 cm. (singer's music shelf." vol. I). c.1935. Harcourt, Brace and Company.

Wier, Estor Alberti (1910-)

--Action at Paradise Marsh. Blust, Earl R., illus. (Illus.). 127 p. 22cm. (Window books). 1968. Stackpole Books.

--The Barrel. Kidwell, Carl (1910-), illus. LC 66-7752. 136p. 21cm. 1966. (ISBN 0-679-20020-7). McKay. **Award: (ALA).**

--Easy Does It. Mars, Witold Tadeusz J. (1912-), illus. LC 65-17375. (Illus.). 126 p. 22cm. 1965. Vanguard Press.

--Gift of the Mountains. Lewis, Richard William (1933-1966), illus. LC 63-15886. 116 p. illus. 21 cm. 1963. D. McKay Co.

--The Hunting Trail. Cuffari, Richard (1925-1978), illus. LC 74-6030. (Illus.). 104 p. 21cm. 1974. (ISBN 0-8098-3119-8). H. Z. Walck

--King of the Mountain. LC 74-19716. 169 p. 21cm. 1975. (ISBN 0-8098-3126-0). H. Z. Walck.

--The Loner. Price, Christine Hilda (1928-1980), illus. LC 63-9334. (Illus.). 153 p. 21cm. 1963. D. McKay Co. **Awards: (ALA); (JNM).**

--The Long Year. Koering, Ursula (1921-), illus. LC 69-19546. (Illus.). 150 p. 21cm. 1969. D. McKay Co.

--The Partners. Ahl, Anna Maria (1926-), illus. LC 75-183623. (Illus.). 121 p. 22cm. 1972. D. McKay Co.

--The Rumptydoolers. Mars, Witold Tadeusz J. (1912-), illus. LC 64-16260. (Illus.). 159 p. 22cm. 1964. Vanguard Press.

--The Space Hut. Summers, Leo, illus. LC 67-21673. (Illus.). 94 p. 22cm. (Window Books). 1967. Stackpole Books.

--The White Oak. Jauss, Anne Marie (1907-), illus. LC 73-136008. (Illus.). 88 p. 21cm. 1971. McKay.

--The Wind Chasers. Werth, Kurt (1896-), illus. LC 67-15047. (Illus.). 154p. 22cm. 1967. D. McKay Co.

--The Winners. Koering, Ursula (1921-), illus. (Illus.). 179 p. 21cm. 1968, c.1967. D. McKay Co.

Wiersum, Beverly

--The Story of Christmas for Children. (Illus.). 32p. (Christmas Bks.). (gr. k-4). 1983. (ISBN 0-516-09483-1). Childrens.

--The Story of Easter for Children. Kuse, James A., ed. Wells, Lorraine, illus. (Illus.). (ps-3). 1979. (ISBN 0-89542-452-5). Ideals.

Wiesbauer, Marcia

--The Big Green Bean. Hyman, Trina Schart (1939-), illus. LC 73-81592. (Illus.). 24 p. 20cm. (Magic Circle Book). 1974. (ISBN 0-663-25475-2). Ginn.

--Jill. Carreiro, Ron, illus. LC 73-75067. (Illus.). 24 p. 23cm. (Magic circle book). 1974. (ISBN 0-663-25451-5). Ginn.

--Ride, Ride, Ride. Brown, Marc Tolon (1946-), illus. LC 73-81589. (Illus.). 24 p. 20cm. (Magic circle book). 1974. (ISBN 0-663-25449-3). Ginn.

Wiese, Kurt (1887-1974)

--Buddy, the Bear. Wiese, Kurt (1887-1974), illus. LC 36-19453. 32 p. illus. (part col.) 25 cm. 1936. Coward-McCann, Inc.

--The Chinese Ink Stick. Wiese, Kurt (1887-1974), illus. LC 29-19791. vi p., 2 l., 3-199 p. incl. illus., plates (part col.) col. front. 21 cm. 1929. Doubleday, Doran and Company, Inc.

--Cunning Turtle. Wiese, Kurt (1887-1974), illus. LC 56-1170. (Illus.). 26cm. 32p. (gr. k-3). 1956. (ISBN 0-670-25099-6). Viking Pr.

--The Dog, the Fox, and the Fleas. Wiese, Kurt (1887-1974), illus. LC 53-6541. unpaged. illus. 18x26cm. 1953. D. McKay Co.

--Ella, the Elephant. Wiese, Kurt (1887-1974), illus. LC 31-290176. 31 p. illus. (part col.) 24 1/2 cm. 1931. Coward-McCann, Inc.

--Fish in the Air. Wiese, Kurt (1887-1974), illus. (Illus.). (gr. k-3). 1948. (ISBN 0-670-31650-4). Viking Pr. **Award: (RCM).**

--Groundhog & His Shadow. Wiese, Kurt (1887-1974), illus. LC 59-1668. (Illus.). 27cm. 32p. (gr. k-3). 1959. (ISBN 0-670-35554-2). Viking Pr.

--Happy Easter. Wiese, Kurt (1887-1974), illus. N.D. E. M. Hale & Co.

--Happy Easter. Wiese, Kurt (1887-1974), illus. LC 52-8107. (Illus.). 32 p. 25cm. 1952. Viking Press.

--Joe Buys Nails. Wiese, Kurt (1887-1974), illus. LC 31-32082. 56 p. illus. (part col.) 18 1/2 x 24 1/2 cm. 1931. Doubleday, Doran & Company, Inc.

--Karoo, the Kangaroo. Wiese, Kurt (1887-1974), illus. LC 29-20041. 35 p. illus. (part col.) 25 cm. 1929. Coward-McCann, Inc.

--Kurt Wiese's Picture Book of Animals ... Wiese, Kurt (1887-1974), illus. LC 37-23086. 99 p. illus. (part col.) 25 cm. c.1937. Coward-McCann, Inc.

--Liang & Lo. Wiese, Kurt (1887-1974), illus. LC 30-26890. 56 p. col. illus. 18 1/2 x 25 cm. 1930. Doubleday, Doran & Company, Inc.

--Little Boy Lost in Brazil. Wiese, Kurt (1887-1974), illus. LC 42-235971. 56 p. illus. (part col.) 21 x 24 cm. 1942. Dodd, Mead & Company.

--The Parrot Dealer. Wiese, Kurt (1887-1974), illus. 240p. N.D. Coward-McCann.

--The Parrot Dealer. Wiese, Kurt (1887-1974), illus. N.D. Grosset & Dunlap.

--Rabbit Bros. Circus: One Night Only. Wiese, Kurt (1887-1974), illus. (Illus.). 38 p. 1963. Viking Press.

--The Rabbits' Revenge. Wiese, Kurt (1887-1974), illus. LC 40-32789. 48 p. col. illus. 17 x 25 cm. c.1940. Coward-McCann, Inc.

--The Thief in the Attic. Wiese, Kurt (1887-1974), illus. LC 65-18145. 43p. col. illus. 24cm. c.1965. Viking.

--The Three Little Kittens, with New Pictures. Wiese, Kurt (1887-1974), illus. LC 28-21043. (Illus.). 15cm. 42p. (Happy Hour Books). 1928. Macmillan Co.

--Wallie, the Walrus. Wiese, Kurt (1887-1974), illus. LC 30-31017. 31 p. illus. (part col.) 25 cm. 1930. Coward-McCann, Inc.

Wiese und Kaiserswaldau, Ursula Renate Von (1905-)

--Michael and the Elephant. Schreiber, Irene, illus. Stirling, Helen, tr. LC 61-6124. 190 p. illus. 21 cm. 1st U.S. edition. (gr. 3-7). 1961. (ISBN 0-15-253484-9). HarBraceJ.

Wiesner, William (1899-)

--The Constant Little Mouse. Wiesner, William (1899-), illus. LC 77-161014. (Illus.). 29 p. 29cm. 1971. Four Winds Press.

--Funny Questions and Funny Answers. Wiesner, William (1899-), illus. LC 75-93806. 32 p. (chiefly illus., part col.). 23cm. 1970. (ISBN 0-695-80059-0). Follett.

--Grabbit the Rascal. Wiesner, William (1899-), illus. LC 69-13081. (Illus.). 46 p. 24cm. 1969. Viking Press.

--Green Noses. Wiesner, William (1899-), illus. LC 76-81704. (Illus.). 37 p. 1969. Four Winds Press.

--Happy-Go-Lucky. Wiesner, William (1899-), illus. LC 77-97031. (Illus.). 28 p. 1970. Seabury Press.

--How Silly Can You Be?. A Book of Jokes. Wiesner, William (1899-), illus. LC 74-4044. (Illus.). 63 p. 23cm. 1974. (ISBN 0-8164-3123-X). Seabury Press.

--Joco and the Fishbone: An Arabian Nights Tale. Wiesner, William (1899-), illus. 46p. col. illus. 25cm. 1966. (ISBN 0-670-40762-3). Viking.

--Little Sarah and Her Johnny Cake. Wiesner, William (1899-), illus. LC 74-5895. (Illus.). 32 p. 22cm. 1974. (ISBN 0-8098-1222-3). Walck.

--The Magic Slippers. 1st ed. Wiesner, William (1899-), illus. LC 67-1011. (Illus.). 47 p. 27cm. 1967. Norton.

--Magic Tales and Magic Tricks. Wiesner, William (1899-), illus. 1974. (ISBN 0-684-13721-6). Charles Scribner's Sons.

--Moon Stories. Wiesner, William (1899-), illus. LC 72-97772. (Illus.). 32 p. 29cm. 1973. Seabury Press.

--Noah's Ark. 1st ed. Wiesner, William (1899-), illus. LC 66-7870. (Illus.). 27cm. (ps-3). 1966. (ISBN 0-525-36013-1). Dutton.

--Pin, the Reluctant Knight. 1st ed. Wiesner, William (1899-), illus. LC 67-21738. (Illus.). 48 p. 26cm. 1967. W. W. Norton.

--Pocketful of Riddles. Wiesner, William (1899-), illus. (gr. k-2). 1966. (ISBN 0-525-37206-7, Anytime Bks). (ISBN 0-525-45032-7). Dutton.

--Pocketful of Riddles. Wiesner, William (1899-), illus. (Illus.). (gr. k-2). 1977. (Anytime Bks). Dutton.

--The Riddle Pot. Wiesner, William (1899-), illus. LC 73-77461. (Illus.). 120 p. 16cm. 1973. (ISBN 0-525-33860-8). Dutton.

--Sillibill. Wiesner, William (1899-), illus. LC 71-124184. (Illus.). 30 p. 29cm. 1970. Four Winds Press.

--Three Good Friends: An Old Story Retold. Wiesner, William (1899-), illus. LC 46-8525. 31 p. col. illus. 26 x 20 1/2 cm. 1946. Harper & Brothers.

--Tom Thumb. Wiesner, William (1899-), illus. LC 73-15864. (Illus.). 32 p. 22cm. 1974. (ISBN 0-8098-1215-0). H. Z. Walck.

--Too Many Cooks. Wiesner, William (1899-), illus. 32p. 1961. J B Lippincott Company.

--Tops. Wiesner, William (1899-), illus. LC 75-85865. (Illus.). 32 p. 29cm. 1969. Viking Press.

--The Tower of Babel. Wiesner, William (1899-), illus. (Illus.). (ps-1). 1968. (ISBN 0-670-72242-1). (ISBN 0-670-90028-1). (ISBN 0-670-90522-4). Viking Pr. **Award: (ALA).**

--Hansel & Gretel. Wiesner, William (1899-), illus. LC 78-154302. (Original Authors: The Brothers Grimm). (Illus.). color illus. 40p. (gr. k-3). 1971. (ISBN 0-395-28829-0, Clarion). HM.

--Hansel and Gretel: A Shadow Puppet Picture Book. Wiesner, William (1899-), illus. LC 78-154302. (Original Authors: Jakob Ludwig Karl Grimm, 1785-1863 and Wilhelm Karl Grimm, 1786-1859). (Illus.). 40 p. 29cm. 1971. Seabury Press.

--How Silly Can You Be?. A/Book of Jokes. Wiesner, William (1899-), illus. LC 74-4044. (Illus.). 23cm. 63p. (A Clarion Bk.). 1974. Seabury Press.

--Jack & the Beanstalk. Wiesner, William (1899-), illus. Repr. (Starbright Editions). (gr. k-3). 1973. Schol Bk Serv.

--Jack & the Beanstalk. Wiesner, William (1899-), illus. (Illus., Orig.). (gr. 2-3). N.D. (ISBN 0-590-08058-X). (ISBN 0-590-04419-2). Scholastic Inc.

--Plenty of Riddles. abr ed. Wiesner, William (1899-), illus. (Illus., Pub. by Dutton). Orig. Title: A Pocketful of Riddles. (gr. k-3). 1972 (Starline). Schol Bk Serv.

--Turnabout. Wiesner, William (1899-), illus. LC 72-190380. (Illus.). 32 p. 1972. (ISBN 0-8164-3083-7). Seabury Press.

Wiessner, John, Jr.

--Space Bugs: Earth Invasion. (Illus.). 176p. (gr. 5-8). 1983. (ISBN 0-8059-2856-1). Dorrance.

Wiest, Claire & Wiest, Robert

--Down the River Without a Paddle. Wiest, Claire & Weist, Robert, illus. LC 73-6666. (Illus.). 47 p. 24cm. 1973. Childrens Press.

--Some Frogs Have Their Own Rocks. LC 79-131209. (Illus.). 44 p. 22cm. 1970, c.1969. Childrens Press.

--There's One in Every Bunch. LC 78-159786. (Illus.). 48 p. 24cm. 1971. (ISBN 0-516-03625-4). Childrens Press.

Wiest, Robert, jt. auth. see Wiest, Claire.

Wigg, Ristiina, jt. auth. see Carlson, Bernice Wells.

Wiggin, Kate Douglas Smith, ed. see Porter, Jane.

Wiggin, Kate Douglas Smith, jt. ed. see Smith, Nora Archibald.

Wiggin, Kate Douglas Smith (1856-1923)

--The Arabian Nights. Parrish, Frederick Maxfield (1870-1966), illus. 1909. Trade Publication.

--Baby's Friend and Nursery Heroes and Heroines. Hambridge, Ruth & Smith, Nora Archibald (1859-1934), illus. (Pinafore Palace Ser.). N.D. Doubleday Page & Co.

--The Birds' Christmas Carol. LC 9-2672. 67p. 15 x 14cm. 1887. C. A. Murdock & Co.

--Birds' Christmas Carol. 1941. (ISBN 0-8382-0086-9, Cadmus Books). E. M. Hale and Company.

--The Birds' Christmas Carol. N.D. Grosset & Dunlap.

--The Birds' Christmas Carol. LC 4-16481. (Illus.). 67p. 19cm. 1889. Houghton Mifflin and Company.

--The Birds' Christmas Carol. LC 24-22228. 4 p. l., 69 p. incl. front., illus., plates. 20 cm. c.1916. Houghton Mifflin Company.

--The Birds' Christmas Carol. (Riverside Literature Ser.: 232). N.D. Houghton Mifflin Co.

--The Birds' Christmas Carol. Gillespie, Jessie, illus. LC 12-22552. xv, 1, 90, 2 p. incl. col. front., illus. (part col.) plates. 22 x 17 cm. 1912. Houghton Mifflin Company.

--The Birds' Christmas Carol. memorial ed. Gillespie, Jessie, illus. LC 41-52029. 5 p. l., 84, 2 p. incl. col. front., illus. (part col.) 24 1/2 cm. 1941. Houghton, Mifflin Company.

--The Birds' Christmas Carol. Grose, Helen Mason (1880-), illus. LC 4-16481. 67 p. incl. front., illus. plates. 19 1/2 cm. 1889. Houghton, Mifflin and Company.

--The Birds' Christmas Carol. Grose, Helen Mason (1880-), illus. LC 29-22434. 5 p. l., 74 p. col. front., illus., col. plates. 21 cm. 1929. Houghton Mifflin Company.

--The Bird's Christmas Carol. Ingersoll, Helen Frances (1878-), illus. LC 14-19078. (Dramatised Version). 19cm. 103p. 1914. Houghton Mifflin Co.

--The Birds' Christmas Carol. Wireman, Katharine Richardson, illus. LC 9-26720. 67 p. 15 1/2 x 14 1/2 cm. 1887. C. A. Murdock & Co.

--The Bird's Christmas Carol. Wireman, Katharine Richardson, illus. 1912. Houghton Mifflin.

--The Birds' Christmas Carol. Wireman, Katharine Richardson, illus. LC 12-22522. (Illus.). xv, 90p. 22 x 17cm. 1912. Houghton Mifflin Company.

--The Birds' Christmas Carol, and Polly Oliver's Problem. LC 51-7745. 222p. 20cm. (A Thrushwood Bk.). 1951. Grosset & Dunlop.

--Blue Beard: A Musical Fantasy. 1914. Harper.

--Carol Bird's Christmas. (gr. 4-7). 1974. (ISBN 0-590-02978-9, Schol Pap). Scholastic Inc.

--A Cathedral Courtship, and Penelope's English Experiences. Carlton, C., illus. 1893. Houghton Mifflin.

--A Child's Journey with Dickens. 1912. Houghton Mifflin.

--The Diary of a Goose Girl. Shepperson, Claude A., illus. 1902. Houghton Mifflin.

--The Fairy Ring. (Illus.). N.D. E. P. Dutton & Co.

--Half-a-Dozen Housekeepers. New ed. Thompson, Mills, illus. LC 3-21719. 18cm. 142p. 1905. Henry Altemus Co.

--Half-a-Dozen Housekeepers: A Story for Girls in Half-a-Dozen Chapters. Thompson, Mills, illus. LC 3-21719. ix p., 1 l., 13-162 p. incl. front. 5 pl. 18 cm. c.1903. H. Altemus Company.

--An Hour with the Fairies. Smith, Nora Archibald (1859-1934), ed. LC 11-27152. 3 p. l., 3-59 1 p. col. front., plates. 19 1/2 cm. (Pleasant hour series). 1911. Doubleday, Page & Company.

--Mother Carey's Chicken. Crothers, Rachel, illus. LC 25-24497. (Dramatised Version). 20cm. 99p. (French's Standard Library Edition). 1925. Samuel French.

--Mother Carey's Chickens. (Illus.). N.D. Grosset & Dunlap.

--Mother Carey's Chickens. LC 30-30227. iv p., 1 l., 289 p. col. front., illus. (part col.) 22 cm. (Riverside bookshelf). 1930. Houghton Mifflin Company.

--Mother Carey's Chickens. Elliott, Elizabeth Shippen Green, illus. LC 11-23500. v, 1 p., 1 l., 355, 1 p., 1 l. col. front., plates (part col.) 19 1/2 cm. 1911. Houghton Mifflin Company.

--New Chronicles of Rebecca. (Growing Literature Ser.). N.D. Grosset & Dunlap.

--New Chronicles of Rebecca. LC 7-11587. 19cm. 277p. 1907. Houghton Mifflin & Co.

--Nursery Nonsense. Hambridge, Ruth & Smith, Nora Archibald (1859-1934), illus. (Pinafore Palace Ser.). N.D. Doubleday Page & Co.

--The Old Peabody Pew. LC 17 28617. (Dramatised Version). 19cm. 45p. 1917. Samuel French.

--Palace Playtime. Hambridge, Ruth & Smith, Nora Archibald, illus. (Pinafore Palace Ser.). N.D. Doubleday Page.

--Penelope's Irish Experiences. 1901. Houghton Mifflin.

--Penelope's Postscripts: Switzerland, Venice, Wales, Devon, Home. 1915. Houghton Mifflin.

--Penelope's Progress. 1898. Houghton Mifflin.

--Polly Oliver's Problem. LC 12-31367. xvii, 212 p. front. (port.) plates. 18 cm. (Riverside school library). c.1896. Houghton, Mifflin.

--Polly Oliver's Problem: A Story for Girls. LC 4-16482. 212 p. front., 7 pl. 18 cm. 1893. Houghton, Mifflin and Company.

--Polly Oliver's Problem: A Story for Girls. LC 4-31648. 212 p. front., 7 pl. 18 cm. 1894. Houghton, Mifflin and Company.

--Polly Oliver's Problem: A Story for Girls. LC 31-256. 2 p. l., 7-212 p. 18 cm. c.1921. Houghton Mifflin Company.

--Rebecca of Sunnybrook Farm. LC 75-32202. p. cm. (Classics of Children's Literature, 1621-1932). 1976. (ISBN 0-8240-2312-9). Garland.

--Rebecca of Sunnybrook Farm. LC 59-108776. (From the Motion Picture Featuring Shirley Temple. Shirley Temple Ed.). 250 p. illus. 20 cm. 1959. Random House.

--Rebecca of Sunnybrook Farm. (gr. 4-6). 1973. (ISBN 0-590-04487-7). Scholastic Inc.

--Rebecca of Sunnybrook Farm. Goldsborough, June (1923-), illus. LC 65-11925. (Illus.). 254 p. 22cm. (Whitman classics library). 1965. Whitman Pub. Co.

--Rebecca of Sunnybrook Farm. Green, Helen Mason, illus. LC 28-37097. (Illus.). 23cm. (The Riverside Library). 1931. Houghton Mifflin Company.

--Rebecca of Sunnybrook Farm. Grose, Helen Mason (1880-), illus. LC 41-35163. x, 327 p. incl. col. front. 19 1/2 cm. 1910. Grosset & Dunlap.

--Rebecca of Sunnybrook Farm. Grose, Helen Mason (1880-), illus. LC 25-18699. viii p., 1 l., 355 p. col. front., illus., col. plates. 22 cm. (Riverside Bookshelf). 1925. Houghton Mifflin Company.

--Rebecca of Sunnybrook Farm. Smith, Lawrence, illus. LC 31-270719. iii, 1, 341, 1 p. front., 1 illus., plates. 21 1/2 cm. (Riverside library). 1931. Houghton Mifflin Company.

--Rebecca of Sunnybrook Farm. Smith, Lawrence Beall (1909-), illus. LC 62-183972. 301 p. col. illus. 24 cm. (Macmillan classics, 41). 1962. Macmillan.

--Rebecca of Sunnybrook Farm. Thompson, Charlotte, illus. 1910. French.

--Rebecca of Sunnybrook Farm. Thorne, Alice, abridged by. Troop, Miriam (1917-), illus. LC 60-51649. 58 p. illus. 29 cm. N.D. Grosset & Dunlap.

--The Romance of a Christmas Card. Hunt, Alice Ercle, illus. 1916. Houghton Mifflin.

--Rose O'the River. Wright, George, illus. 1905. Houghton Mifflin.

--The Story of Patsy. LC 4-15182. 5 p. l., 68 p. front., illus., plates. 19 1/2 cm. 1889. Houghton, Mifflin and Company.

--The Story of Patsy: A Reminiscence. LC 8-36888. 27 p. 16 x 14 cm. 1883. C. A. Murdock & Co.

--A Summer in a Canon: A California Story. LC 4-16483. iv p., 1 l., 272 p. front., illus. 20 cm. 1889. Houghton, Mifflin and Company.
--A Summer in a Canon: A California Story. LC 8-11029. iv p., 1 l., 272 p. front., illus. 18 cm. 1898. Houghton, Mifflin and Company.
--Susanna and Sue. Stephens, Alice Barber (1858-1932) & Wyeth, Newell Convers (1882-1945), illus. 1909. Houghton Mifflin.
--Timothy's Quest. Herford, Oliver (1863-1935), illus. 201p. 1890. Houghton Mifflin.
--The Writings of Kate Douglas Wiggin, 9 Vols. LC 18-1568. (Illus.). 22cm. 1917. Houghton Mifflin Co.

Wiggin, Kate Douglas Smith (1856-1923) & Smith, Nora Archibald (1859-1934), eds.
--Arabian Nights. Parrish, Frederick Maxfield (1870-1966), illus. (Illus.). (Illustrated Classics Ser). (gr. 2-7). 1909. (ISBN 0-684-20977-2). Scribner.
--Arabian Nights. Parrish, Frederick Maxfield (1870-1966), illus. (Illus.). (Illustrated Library Classics Ser.). (gr. k-3). 1974. (ISBN 0-684-13809-3). Scribner.
--The Arabian Nights: Their Best-Known Tales. Parrish, Frederick Maxfield (1870-1966), illus. LC 9-38132. xii, 339 p. 12 col. pl. 24 cm. 1909. C. Scribner's Sons.
--The Arabian Nights: Their Best-Known Tales. Parrish, Frederick Maxfield (1870-1966), illus. LC 28-486. xii, 329 p. col. plates. 24 cm. 1925. C. Scribner's Sons.
--The Arabian Nights: Their Best-Known Tales. Parrish, Frederick Maxfield (1870-1966), illus. LC 30-10172. xii, 339 p. col. plates. 24 cm. 1929. C. Scribner's Sons.
--The Arabian Nights: Their Best-Known Tales. Parrish, Frederick Maxfield (1870-1966), illus. LC 33-6709. xii, 339 p. col. plates. 24 cm. 1930. C. Scribner's Sons.
--The Arabian Nights: Their Best Known Tales. Parrish, Frederick Maxfield (1870-1966), illus. 1937. Scribner.
--The Arabian Nights: Their Best-Known Tales. Parrish, Frederick Maxfield (1870-1966), illus. LC 74-170396. (Illus.). x, 340 p. 23cm. (Scribner Illustrated Classics). 1974, c.1909. (ISBN 0-684-13809-3). Scribner.
--Baby's Plays and Journeys. Hambridge, Ruth, illus. (Pinafore Palace Ser.). N.D. Doubleday Page & Co.
--Christmas Stories. 1916. Grosset and Dunlap.
--The Fairy Ring. Chappell, Warren (1904-), illus. LC 6-42427. xvii, 445 p. 19 1/2 cm. 1906. McClure, Phillips & Co.
--The Fairy Ring. MacKinstry, Elizabeth (0000-1956), illus. 1910. Doubleday.
--The Fairy Ring. MacKinstry, Elizabeth (0000-1956), illus. LC 35-1698. 21cm. 444p. (Crimson Classics). 1934. Doubleday Page & Co.
--The Fairy Ring. Chappell, Warren (1904-), illus. LC 67-17266. 414p. illus. (pt. col.) 24cm. 1967. Doubleday.
--Fairy Stories Every Child Should Know. LC 42-51972. viii p., 2 l., 317 p. incl. col. front. plates. 19 1/2 cm. (What every child should know library. 4th ser.). 1942. Pub. by Doubleday, Doran & Co., Inc., for the Parents' Institute Inc.
--Fairy Stories Every Child Should Know. MacKinstry, Elizabeth (0000-1956), illus. LC 42-51972. (Illus.). viii, 317 p. 19cm. (What Every Child Should Know Library). Orig. Title: The Fairy Ring, 1906. 1942. Doubleday, Doran & Co. for the Parents' Institute.
--Golden Numbers. N.D. Houghton Mifflin.
--Golden Numbers: A Book of Verse for Youth. N.D. Doubleday Page & Co.
--An Hour with the Fairies. LC 11-27152. (Illus.). 59p. 19cm. (Pleasant Hour Ser.). 1911. Doubleday, Page & Company.
--The Library of Fairy Literature: Containing: The Fairy Ring, Magic Casements, Tales of Laughter, Tales of Wonder, The Talking Beasts, 5 vols. 1906. Set. McClure.
--Magic Casements: A Second Fairy Book. N.D. Doubleday Page & Co.
--Magic Casements: A Second Fairy Book. Repr. of 1907 ed (Pub. by McClure). 1979. (ISBN 0-8492-2990-1). R West.
--Magic Casements; a Second Fairy Book: A Second Fairy Book. LC 7-39995. x p., 2 l., 3-477 p. 20 cm. (On verso of half-title: McClure's library of children's classics). 1907. The McClure Comapny.
--Palace Bedtime. Hambridge, Ruth, illus. (Pinafore Palace Ser.). N.D. Doubleday Page & Co.
--Pinafore Palace: A Book of Rhymes for the Nursery. LC 72-8290. p. (Granger index reprint series). (Series: McClure's Library of Children's Classics.). 1972, c.1907. (ISBN 0-8369-6399-7). Books for Libraries Press.
--Pinafore Palace: A Book of Rhymes for the Nursery. N.D. Doubleday Page & Co.
--Pinafore Palace: A Book of Rhymes for the Nursery. LC 7-30444. 3 p. l., v-x, 6-249 p. 26 cm. (On verso of half-title: McClure's library of children's classics ...). 1907. The McClure Company.
--Pinafore Palace Series, 5 vols. Hambridge, Ruth, illus. 1923. Doubleday.
--Poems Every Child Should Know. LC 42-52197. xvii p., 1 l., 288 p. incl. col. front. 19 1/2 cm. (What every child should know library. 4th ser.). 1942. Pub. by Doubleday, Doran & Co., Inc. for the Parents' Institute, Inc.
--The Posy Ring: A Book of Verse for Children. LC 70-128164. xx, 279 p. 21cm. (Granger index reprint series). 1970. (ISBN 0-8369-6193-5). Books for Libraries Press.
--The Posy Ring: A Book of Verse for Children. N.D. Doubleday Page & Co.
--The Posy Ring: A Book of Verse for Children. LC 3-5775. xx p., 1 l., 279 p. 20 cm. 1903. McClure, Phillips & Co.
--The Posy Ring: Verses and Poems for the Youngest Children. 1 p. l., v-vii, xi-xx p., 2 l., 3-283 p. 18 cm. c.1903. Houghton Mifflin Company.
--The Story Hour. (Illus.). 17cm. 185p. 1899. Houghton, Mifflin & Co.
--The Story Hour. 185p. Repr (Pub. by Houghton Mifflin Co. Boston & N. Y.). 1980. (ISBN 0-8492-8803-7). R West.
--The Story Hour: A Book for the Home and the Kindergarten. LC 14-19353. 185 p. front., plates. 18 cm. 1890. Houghton, Mifflin and Company.
--Tales of Laughter. MacKinstry, Elizabeth (0000-1956), illus. LC 26-21017. xi p., 2 l., 331 p. col. front., illus., plates (part col.) 23 cm. 1926. Doubleday, Page & Company.
--Tales of Laughter. MacKinstry, Elizabeth (0000-1956), illus. LC 38-27976. xi p., 2 l., 331 p. col. front., illus., plates (part col.) 22 1/2 cm. 1938. Garden City Publishing Co., Inc.
--Tales of Laughter: A Third Fairy Book. MacKinstry, Elizabeth (0000-1956), illus. LC 8-31473. xii, 467 p. 20 cm. (On verso of half-title: McClure's Library of Children's Classics). 1908. The McClure Company.
--Tales of Laughter Every Child Should Know. LC 40-9525. xi, 369 p. col. front 19 1/2 cm. (What every child should know library. 2d ser.). c.1939. Pub. by Doubleday, Doran & Co., Inc., for the Parents' Institute, Inc.
--Tales of Wonder: A Fourth Fairy Book. LC 9-25758. xiii, 440 p. 19 1/2 cm. (The Children's crimson classics). 1909. Doubleday, Page & Company.
--Tales of Wonder Every Child Should Know. LC 42-10321. xiii, 364 p. incl. col. front. 19 1/2 cm. (What every child should know library. 3d ser.). N.D. Pub. by Doubleday, Doran & Co., Inc., for the Parents' Institute, Inc.
--The Talking Beasts: A Book of Fable Wisdom. Nelson, Harold, illus. LC 11-29994. xxii, 391 p. col. front., col. plates. 19 1/2 cm. (On verso of half-title: The Children's Crimson Classics). 1911. Doubleday, Page & Company.

Wiggin, Kate Douglas Smith (1856-1923) & Wilkins, Mrs.
--The St. Nicholas Christmas Book. LC 99-4986. viii, 2, 218 p. incl. front., illus. 24 1/2 x 18 1/2 c. 1899. The Century Co.

Wiggin, Maurice (1912-)
--Life With Badger. LC 68-31738. (Illus.). (gr. 8 up). N.D. (ISBN 0-8008-4826-8). Taplinger.

Wiggins, Margaret J
--Black Hills Gold, and Other Tellable Tales. LC 50-3088. 80 p. 22 cm. 1950. Exposition Press.

Wiggins, Walter
--Dreams in Reality of the Undersea Craft. 1st ed. De Vinney, J. E., illus. LC 54-123487. 296p. illus. 21cm. 1954. Pageant Press.

Wight, Emily Carter (1871-1939)
--The Denim Elephant. (Illus.). (The Christmas Stocking Ser.). N.D. Frederick A. Stokes Co.

Wight, Emma Howard
--The Berkleys. LC 7-42016. 134 p. front. 17 1/2 cm. (On verso of t.-p.: Benziger's juvenile series). c.1902. Benziger Brothers.

Wightman, Henry
--The Juvenile Polyanthos: Or, Fireside Companion. LC 31-1359. (Being a Selection of Amusing Stories). 105, 3 p. 14 1/2 cm. 1835. B. Olds.

Wignall, Vera Adell
--Aesop's fables, complete. LC 56-36116. 101p. illus. 20cm. 1956. Pauls Valley.

Wiid, Henry, Mrs.
--East Lynne. (The Good Value Books). N.D. Grosset & Dunlap.

Wiig, Hanna
--The Tale of Tiny Tutak. Skauge, Sven, illus. LC 57-2425. unpaged. illus. 15cm. 1957. Lippincott.

Wike, Hamilton
--Mother Owl. LC 21-19491. 128 p. col. front., illus., col. plates. 19 1/2 cm. $0.5. 1921. National Publishing Co.

Wike, Murlie Burns
--Birds of a Feather Stories: The Cheerful Book of Brave Birds. McIntire, Marjorie Hull, illus. LC 26-4301. 125 p. incl. col. front., illus. (part col.) 18 1/2 cm. (Just right books). c.1925. A. Whitman & Company.

Wikland, Ilon (1930-)
--See What I Can Do!. Wikland, Ilon (1930-), illus. LC 74-3705. (Illus.). (ps). 1974. (ISBN 0-394-82915-8, BYR). Random.

Wilberforce, Bishop
--The Marvellous House: Or, The Bishop's Enigma. A Story for Children. N.D. E J B Young & Co.

Wilberforce, Octavia, jt. auth. see Robins, Elizabeth.

Wilberforce, Samuel (1805-1873)
--Agathos, and other Sunday Stories. N.D. Pott, Young, & Co.
--The Children and the Lion, and Other Sunday Stories. (Illus.). N.D. Methodist Bk Concern.
--Children, and the Lion, and Other Sunday Stories. (Illus.). N.D. Nelson & Phillips.
--The Rocky Island. N.D. Pott, Young, & Co.

Wilbur, C. E., Mrs.
--Annie Barton's Journal: A Story of a Life, 1 of 25 vols. (Selected Bks for Sunday School: The/Clifton Library). N.D. Set. Methodist Bk Concern.

Wilbur, Curtis Dwight (1867-)
--The Bear Family at Home: And How the Circus Came to Visit Them. Lohse, William R., illus. LC 23-14973. 5 p. l., 142 p. front., plates. 23 1/2 cm. c.1923. The Bobbs-Merrill Company.

Wilbur, R. M., Mrs.
--Aleck's Concert, 1 of 10 Vol. (Brookside Library). N.D. Sunday-School Publications.
--Blue Mittens, 1 of 10 Vol. (Brookside Library: No.3). N.D. Sunday-School Publications.
--Company A, Kent's Brigade. 2 p. l., 3-208 p. front., plates. 18 1/2 cm. c.1889. American Baptist Publication Society.
--Company A, Kent's Brigade. 208p. N.D. Sunday-School Publications.
--Dorothy. 2 p. l., 3-192 p. front., plates. 18 1/2 cm. c.1890. American Baptist Publication Society.
--Dorothy. (Illus.). 192p. N.D. Sunday-School Publications.
--Elsie: Or, Do What Good You Can. (Illus.). 204p. N.D. Sunday-School Publications.
--Floy's Reward. 256p. N.D. Sunday-School Publications.
--Floy's Reward: A Sequel to Instead, 1 of 60 vols. 2 p. l., 3-256 p. front., illus., plates. 18 1/2 cm. (Crescent Lib.). c.1892. Set. American Baptist Publication Society.
--Harold's Helps: Or, The Pearl of Prayers. 248p. c.1887. American Baptist Publication.
--Helen and Marguerite. 207 p. front., plates. 18 1/2 cm. c.1895. American Baptist Publication Society.
--Hidden Foes: Or, Roy Hastings Battle. LC 58-53853. 19cm. 250p. c.1889. American Baptist Publication.
--Hitting the Nail on the Head, 1 of 10 Vol. (Brookside Library: No.5). N.D. Sunday-School Publications.
--The Hospital Rose, and Flora's Copy Book. LC 58-53852. 251p. c.1886. American Baptist Publication.
--Instead. LC 58-53851. 250p. c.1892. American Baptist Publication.
--Instead. 250p. N.D. Sunday-School Publications.
--Kitty and the Other Girls. 2 p. l., 3-203 p. front., plates. 18 1/2 cm. c.1891. American Baptist Publication Society.
--The Lassie of Glengarry. 192p. c.1894. American Baptist Publication.
--The Lassie of Glengarry. 192p. N.D. Sunday-School Publications.
--Little Folks' Library, 10 Vols. N.D. Sunday-School Publications.
--Mabel and Joe, 6 of 10 Vol. (Brookside Library). N.D. Sunday-School Publications.
--Mabel and the Foxes. (Brookside Library). N.D. Sunday-School Publications.
--May's Experiment, 1 of 10 Vol. (Brookside Library: No.2). N.D. Sunday-School Publications.
--Mrs. Marshall's Experiment. 252p. c.1893. American Baptist Publication.
--Number Ten, 1 of 10 Vol. (Brookside Library: No.7). N.D. Sunday-School Publications.
--The Palm Tree Club: Or, How Three Girls Grew. 2 p. l., 3-224 p. front., plates. 18 1/2 cm. c.1894. American Baptist Publication Society.
--The Palm Tree Club: Or, How Three Girls Grew. 224p. N.D. Sunday-School Publications.
--Patty Deane: An Old Fashioned Story. 256p. c.1887. American Baptist Publishing Society.
--Patty Deane: An Old Fashioned Story. 256p. N.D. Sunday-School Publications.
--Phil's Ideas, 1 of 10 Vols. (Brookside Library: No.10). N.D. Sunday-School Publications.
--The Princess, 1 of 10 Vol. (Brookside Library: No.4). N.D. Sunday-School Publications.
--Rosebuds for the Little Ones, 10 Vols. N.D. Sunday-School Publications.
--Some Fresh-Air Children, 1 of 10 Vol. (Brookside Library: No.8). N.D. Sunday-School Publications.
--Turtleback Light: A Story of Influence. 239p. c.1893. American Baptist Publication.
--Whatsoever: Or, The Young Stalwarts. 315p. c.1885. American Baptist Publication.
--Wilbur Books, 10 Vols. N.D. Sunday-School Publications.

Wilbur, Richard Purdy (1921-)
--Digging for China: A Poem. Du Bois, William Sherman Pene (1916-), illus. LC 76-83591. (Illus.). 32 p. 19cm. (gr. 7-10). 1970, c.1956. (ISBN 0-385-07768-8). (ISBN 0-385-03587-X). Doubleday.
--Loudmouse. Almquist, Don (1929-), illus. LC 63-17470. 1 v. (unpaged) illus. 30 cm. (Modern masters book for children). 1963. Crowell-Collier Press.
--Loudmouse. 1st ed. Almquist, Don (1929-), illus. LC 68-10360. (Illus.). 1 v. (unpaged. 22cm. 1968. Crowell-Collier Press.
--Loudmouse. Almquist, Don (1929-), illus. LC 82-3081. p. cm. 1982. (ISBN 0-15-249494-4). Harcourt Brace Jovanovich.
--Opposites. Wilbur, Richard Purdy (1921-), illus. LC 78-71154. (Illus.). 1979. (ISBN 0-15-670087-5, VoyB). HarBraceJ.

Wilburr, Harriete, jt. auth. see Lee, Julian.

Wilburr, Harriette (1891-)
--The Gang Goes to Mill. Clarke, William Wallace, illus. LC 24-22817. 372 p. incl. front., illus. col. pl. 19 1/2 cm. c.1924. Rand, McNally & Company.

Wilcke, Ella
--Mona's Island Summer. Tapsell, Alan, tr. LC 61-6073. 21cm. 1962, c.1961. F. Watts.

Wilcox, Daniel, jt. auth. see Sesame Street.

Wilcox, Daniel, jt. auth. see Stiles, Norman.

Wilcox, Daniel (1941-)
--I'm My Mommy ; I'm My Daddy. Crawford, Mel (1925-), illus. LC 75-5654. p. cm. 1975. Western Pub. Co.

Wilcox, Daniel (1941-) & Stiles, Norman
--The Perils of Penelope. Frith, Michael K., illus. LC 73-2767. (Illus.). 46 p. 24cm. 1973. (ISBN 0-394-82697-3). (ISBN 0-394-82697-3). Random House.

Wilcox, Diane L., tr. see Azaad, Meyer.

Wilcox, Don
--Basketball Star. 1st ed. Sibley, Don (1922-), illus. LC 55-8839. (Illus.). 242 p. 20cm. 1955. Little, Brown.
--Castle on the Campus. 1st ed. LC 58-5182. 232 p. 20 cm. 1959. Little, Brown.
--David's Ranch. Zansky, Louis, illus. LC 54-6778. 62p. illus. 22cm. (Everyday science stories). 1954. J. Messner.
--David's Ranch. new ed. Zansky, Louis, illus. LC 65-13673. 62p. illus. 22cm. (New everyday sci. stories). 1965, c.1954. Melmont.
--Joe Sunpool. 1st ed. Houser, Allan C. (1914-), illus. LC 56-8455. 261p. illus. 20cm. c.1956. Little, Brown.

Wilcox, Eleanor Reindollar
--Cornhusk Doll. (Illus.). (gr. 4-7). 1956. (ISBN 0-8382-0182-2). Hale.
--The Cornhusk Doll. McCann, Gerald (1916-), illus. LC 56-5185. 207p. illus. 21cm. 1956. Dodd, Mead.
--Mr. Sims' Argosy. Beck, Charles, illus. LC 58-9698. 201 p. 21cm. 1958. Dodd, Mead.

Wilcox, Ella Wheeler, Mrs. (1855-1919)
--The Beautiful Land of Nod. Mears, Louise M., illus. LC 12-403492. 141, 1 p. front., illus., plates 21 1/2 x 17 1/2 cm. c.1892. Morrill, Higgins & Co.

Wilcox, Jessie
--Pisces Times Two. 160p. (Orig.). (The Zodiac Club Ser.). (gr. 7 up). 1985. (ISBN 0-448-47731-9). Putnam Pub Group.

Wilcox, Tamara
--Mysterious Detectives: Psychics. LC 77-14315. (Illus.). 48p. (Great Unsolved Mysteries Ser.). (gr. 4up). 1983. (ISBN 0-8172-2162-X). Raintree Pubs.

Wilcox, Uthai Vincent
--On Our Block. LC 22-3516. 2 p. l., 3-90 p. illus. 20 cm. 1922. Pacific Press Publishing Assn.

Wilcox, Willis Hamel, jt. auth. see Haslup, Robert Le Roy.

Wild, Jocelyn, jt. auth. see Wild, Robin.

Wild, Laura Hulda (1870-)
--Courageous Adventures: Old Testament Stories for Boys and Girls. 1936. Abingdon-Cokesbury Press.

Wild, Robin & Wild, Jocelyn
--The Bears' ABC Book. 1st American ed. LC 77-73800. (Illus.). 32p. 26cm. c.1977. (ISBN 0-397-31767-0). Lippincott.
--The Bears' Counting Book. LC 78-799. (Illus.). 32 p. 25cm. c.1978. (ISBN 0-397-31808-1). Lippincott.

--Dunmousie Monsters. LC 72-94143. (Illus.). 32 p. 29cm. 1975, c.1974. (ISBN 0-698-20264-3). (ISBN 0-698-30516-7). Coward, McCann & Geoghegan.
--Little Pig and the Big Bad Wolf. LC 71-171615. (Illus.). 46 p. 1972, c.1971. Coward, McCann & Geoghegan.
--The Mouse Who Stole a Zoo. LC 72-76704. (Illus.). 32 p. 27cm. 1972. Coward-McCann & Geoghegan.
--Spot's Dogs and the Alley Cats. LC 78-23836. (Illus.). 32 p. 25cm. c.1979. (ISBN 0-397-31841-3). Lippincott.

Wilde, Arthur L.
--Apache Boy. Christie, Don, et al., photos by (Illus.). photos. 96p. (gr. 5 up). 1969. (ISBN [illegible]

Wilde, George A. & Wilde, Irma
--The Puppy Who Found a Boy. Wilde, George A. & Wilde, Irma, illus. LC 52-27544. unpaged. illus. 21 cm. (Wonder books, 561). c.1951. Wonder Books.
--See--It Goes!. Wilde, George A. & Wilde, Irma, illus. LC 53-242621. unpaged. illus. 17cm. (Tell-a-tale books). 1953. Whitman Pub. Co.

Wilde, Irma
--Big Helpers. Wilde, George A., illus. LC 53-329063. unpaged. illus. 17cm. (Rand McNally Bookshelf Junior, 680). c.1953. Rand McNally.
--The Christmas Puppy. Wilde, Irma, illus. LC 53-430429. unpaged. illus. 21cm. (Wonder Books, 585). 1953 (Wonder Books). Grosset & Dunlap.
--Does Baby Live Here?. LC 53-24261. (Illus.). 21cm. (A Cozy-Corner Bk.). 1953, c.1952. Whitman Pub. Co.
--The Dress-up Parade. Wilde, George A., illus. unpaged. illus. 21cm. (Treasure Books, 861). 1953. Treasure Books.
--The Fixit Man. Wilde, George A., illus. unpaged. illus. 21cm. (Treasure Books, 851). 1952. Treasure Books.
--Fraidy Cat Kitten. Wilde, Irma, illus. N.D. Grosset & Dunlap.
--The Giraffe Who Went To School. N.D (Wonder Books). Grosset & Dunlap.
--Happy Animals. Wilde, Irma, illus. LC 53-16489. (Illus.). 24p. 32cm. (A Blue Angel Picture Bk.). 1954. S. Gabriel Sons.
--The Hide-and-Seek Duck. Wilde, Irma, illus. LC 52-37325. unpaged. illus. 21 cm. (Wonder books, 568). 1952. Wonder Books.
--The Hungry Little Bunny and What He Found Out. Wilde, Irma, illus. LC 50-4746. 21cm. 41p. (Wonder Books: 531). 1950. Grosset & Dunlap.
--Jack & Jill. Wilde, Irma, illus. (Illus.). (Read-Aloud Bks.). (gr. k-3). N.D. Wonder.
--Kitty Black. LC 52-23915. unpaged. illus. 21 cm. (Cosy-corner book). c.1952. Whitman Pub. Co.
--Lucinda, the Little Donkey. Wilde, George A., illus. LC 53-16713. unpaged. illus. 21cm. (Rand McNally book-elf book, 465). c.1952. Rand McNally.
--Mr. Wishing Went Fishing. Wilde, George A., illus. LC 52-38421. unpaged. illus. 21 cm. (Wonder books, 584). 1952. Wonder Books.
--The Snowman's Christmas Present. Wilde, Irma, illus. LC 51-38084. unpaged. illus. 21 cm. (Wonder books, 672). 1951. Wonder Books.
--The Wonderful Treasure Hunt. Wilde, George A., illus. LC 53-20873. unpaged. illus. 21cm. (Treasure Books, 853). 1952. Treasure Books.

Wilde, Irma, jt. auth. see Wilde, George A.

Wilde, Nicholas
--Sir Bertie & the Wyvern: A Tale of Heraldry. LC 84-7779. (Illus.). 64p. (Carolrhoda Good Time Library). (gr. 4 up). 1984. (ISBN 0-87614-273-0). Carolrhoda Bks.

Wilde, Oscar Fingal O'Flahertie Wills (1854-1900)
--Birthday of the Infanta. Bianco, Pamela (1906-), illus. 57p. 1929. MacMillan.
--The Birthday of the Infanta. 2nd ed. Lubin, Leonard B, illus. LC 79-14329. (Illus.). 55 p. 1979. (ISBN 0-670-16974-9). Viking Press.
--The Birthday of the Infanta and Other Tales. Montresor, Beni (1926-), illus. LC 81-1402. p. cm. 1982. (ISBN 0-689-30850-7). Atheneum.
--The Canterville Ghost. N.D. (ISBN 0-8283-1429-2). Branden Press.
--The Canterville Ghost. Payne, Darwin R., retold by. (Children's Theatre Playscript Ser.). 1963. (ISBN 0-88020-021-9). Coach Hse.
--Complete Fairy Tales of Oscar Wilde. Mozley, Charles (1915-), illus. (Illus.). (gr. 4-6). 1960. (ISBN 0-531-01644-7). Watts.
--Fairy Tales. (Illus.). 21cm. 256p. 1913. G. P. Putnam's Sons.
--Fairy Tales. Bock, Vera, illus. LC 47-33798. 16 x 22cm. 87p. N.D. Peter Pauper Press.
--Fairy Tales and Poems in Prose. LC 20-21216. (Illus.). 17cm. 214p. (The Modern Library of the World's Best Bks.). 1918. Boni & Liveright Inc.
--The Happy Prince. N.D. Frederick A. Stokes.
--The Happy Prince. (Illus.). 1910. Putman.
--The Happy Prince. Beckman, Kaj (1913-), illus. LC 77-78348. (Illus.). 28 p. 22 x 27cm. 1977. (ISBN 0-458-92910-7). Methuen.
--The Happy Prince. Claverie, Jean (1946-), illus. LC 80-41046. p. cm. 1980. (ISBN 0-19-279750-6). Oxford University Press.
--The Happy Prince. Claverie, Jean (1946-), illus. 1981. Oxford.
--The Happy Prince. Riswold, Gilbert, illus. LC 65-184933. 1 v. (unpaged) col. illus. 23cm. c.1965. Prentice.
--The Happy Prince. Robinson, Charles (1870-1937), illus. N.D. Brentano's.
--The Happy Prince. Smith, Carol Ann, illus. LC 82-74050. c.1983. (ISBN 0-87191-924-9). Creative Education.
--The Happy Prince and Other Fairy Tales. 217p. 1909. Brentano's.
--The Happy Prince and Other Fairy Tales. N.D. G. P. Putnam's Sons.
--The Happy Prince & Other Stories. Bo, Lars, illus. (gr. 4-7). 1962. (ISBN 0-14-030164-X, Puffin). Penguin.
--The Happy Prince, and Other Stories. Crane, Walter (1845-1915) & Jacomb-Hood, George Percy (1857-1929), illus. LC 68-95987. vi, 154 p. 4 plates, 31 illus. (incl. 4 col.) 22 cm. (Children's illustrated classics, no. 75) 18/-). 1968. Dent.
--The Happy Prince & Other Stories. Fortnum, Peggy, pseud. (1919-), illus. Nuttall-Smith, Margaret Emily Noel. (Illus.). 160p. Repr. of 1968 ed. (Childrens Illustrated Classic). 1977. (ISBN 0-460-05075-3, Pub. by J. M. Dent England). Biblio Dist.
--The Happy Prince & Other Stories. Fortnum, Peggy, pseud. (1919-), illus. Nuttall-Smith, Margaret Emily Noel. LC 68-95987. (Illus.). 48 b&w ils., 4 color plates. 154p. 1st U.S. edition. (Children's Illustrated Classics Series). (gr. 3-7). 1968. (ISBN 0-525-31396-6). Dutton.
--The Happy Prince and Other Stories. Shinn, Everett (1876-1953), illus. N.D. John C. Winston.
--The Happy Prince, and Other Tales. Crane, Walter (1845-1915), illus. N.D. Robert's Brothers.
--The Happy Prince: And Other Tales. Crane, Walter (1845-1915) & Jacomb-Hood, George Percy (1857-1929), illus. (Illus.). 116 p. 20cm. (Legacy library facsimile). 1967. University Microfilms.
--The Happy Prince, and Other Tales. Robinson, Charles (1870-1937), illus. LC 79-3512. p. cm. 1980. (ISBN 0-394-51086-0). (ISBN 0-394-73881-0). Shambhala.
--The Happy Prince and Other Tales and a House of Pomegranets. Claverie, Jean (1946-), illus. LC 75-32193. (Illus.). ix, 116, 157 p. 19cm. (Classics of Children's Literature, 1621-1932). 1977. (ISBN 0-8240-2304-8). Garland Pub.
--Little Hans, the Devoted Friend. Quackenbush, Robert Mead (1929-), illus. LC 69-13104. (Illus.). 48 p. 29cm. 1969. Bobbs-Merrill.
--The Nightingale and the Rose. Foreman, Michael (1938-) & Wright, Freire, illus. LC 80-18511. p. cm. 1981. (ISBN 0-19-520231-7). Oxford University Press.
--The Picture of Dorian Gray. (Magnum Easy Eye Classic Ser.). (gr. 9-12). N.D. Lancer.
--Poems and Fairy Tales. N.D. The Modern Library.
--The Selfish Giant. LC 75-305839. 11p. 20cm. 1932. Egyptian Publications for V. & H.W. Trovillion.
--The Selfish Giant. Durenceau, Andre (1904-), illus. LC 75-302997. (Illus.). 15 p. 20cm. 1932. P. Pauper Press.
--The Selfish Giant. Foreman, Michael (1938-) & Wright, Freire, illus. LC 77-26361. p. cm. 1978. (ISBN 0-458-93420-8). Methuen.
--The Selfish Giant. Isles, Joanna, illus. LC 78-31878. (Illus.). 26 p. 29cm. 1979. (ISBN 0-07-070215-2). McGraw-Hill.
--The Selfish Giant. Quackenbush, Robert Mead (1929-), illus. LC 65-14142. v. (unpaged) col. illus. 24 cm. (Wise owl book, WL09). 1965. Holt, Rinehart and Winston.
--The Selfish Giant. american ed. Reiner, Gertraud & Reiner, Walter, illus. LC 67-27686. (Illus.). 1 v. 72p. 1968, c.1967. Harvey House.
--The Selfish Giant. Rouke, Eve, ed. Ramirez, Pablo, illus. LC 65-24744. 1v. (unpaged) col. illus. 24cm. (Holly story bk. lib.). c.1965. World.
--The Selfish Giant. Zwerger, Lisbeth, illus. 1984. Neugebauer.
--The Selfish Giant. Zwerger, Lisbeth, illus. LC 83-24930. c.1984. (ISBN 0-907234-30-5). Picture Book Studio USA: Dist by Alphabet Press.
--Selfish Giant: A Tale. N.D. P. J. Kennedy & Sons.
--The Selfish Giant: A Tale. LC 75-305839. 11 p. 20cm. 1932. V. & H. W. Trovillion.
--The Star Child. A Fairy Tale. Westwood, Jennifer (1940-), abridged by. French, Fiona (1944-), illus. LC 79-10564. p. cm. c.1979. (ISBN 0-590-07641-8). Four Winds Press.
--The Young King, and Other Fairy Tales. Nardini, Sandro & Bagnoli, Enrico, illus. Updike, John, intro. by. LC 62-5751. (Illus.). 41p. 34cm. 1962. Macmillan.

Wilder, Alec (1907-1980) & Engvick, William, eds.
--Lullabies & Night Songs. Sendak, Maurice Bernard (1928-), illus. LC 65-22880. (Illus.). (ps-3). 1965. (ISBN 0-06-021820-7, HarpJ). (ISBN 0-06-021821-5). Har-Row. **Award: (ALA).**

Wilder, Alexander Lafeyette Chew see Wilder, Alec.

Wilder, Charlotte Frances Felt, Mrs.
--Polly Button's New Year. LC 8-36890. 2 p. l., iii-iv p., 2 l., 137 p. 17 cm. c.1892. T. Y. Crowell & Co.
--Sister Ridnour's Sacrifice, with Other Sketches. LC 8-36891. 269 p. 17 1/2 cm. 1883. Walden and Stowe.

Wilder, Cherry, pseud., see Grimm, Cherry Barbara.

Wilder, Cherry, pseud. (1930-)
--The Luck of Brin's Five. Grimm, Cherry Barbara. LC 77-1590. vii, 230 p. 25cm. 1977. (ISBN 0-689-30601-6). Atheneum.
--The Nearest Fire. Grimm, Cherry Barbara. LC 79-22114. (Illus.). xi, 226 p. 24cm. (Argo Book). 1980. (ISBN 0-689-30762-4). Atheneum.
--A Princess of the Chameln. Grimm, Cherry Barbara. LC 83-15167. (Illus.). 300p. (Rulers of Hylor Ser.). (gr. 8up). 1984. (ISBN 0-689-31025-0, Argo). Atheneum.
--The Tapestry Warriors. Grimm, Cherry Barbara. LC 82-16279. p. cm. 1983. (ISBN 0-689-30966-X). Atheneum.
--Yorath the Wolf. Grimm, Cherry Barbara. LC 84-2976. 192p. (Rulers of Hylor Ser.: Vol. 2). (gr. 8 up). 1984. (ISBN 0-689-31060-9, Argo). Atheneum.

Wilder, Ira & Ballantyne, Robert Michael (1825-1894)
--The Coral Island: An Episode from Robert Michael Ballantyne's Famous Tale of the South Seas. LC 31-2678. 64 p. incl. front., illus., plates. 20 1/2 cm. 1930. Thomas S. Rockwell Company.

Wilder, John Watson
--His Name is Jesus. Penney, Janice, illus. 128p. N.D. Reilly & Lee.

Wilder, Kate Elenor
--Pussy Letters. Wilder, Kate Elenor, illus. LC 29-4807. xiv, 194 p. col. front., illus., col. plates. 24 cm. c.1929. M. A.Donohue & Company.
--Pussy Letters; "How" and "Why" Stories That Will Inspire a Love for Nature and the Great Out-of-Doors. Wilder, Kate Elenor, illus. LC 27-24421. xiv, 194 p. incl. illus., pl. 24 cm. 1927. Kate Elenor Wilder.

Wilder, L. Amelia
--The Twins and Their Texts. N.D. Pilgrims Press.
--The Twins and Their Troubles. LC 12-40222. 225 p. incl. front. pl. 18 cm. c.1896. Congregational Sunday-School and Publishing Society.
--Twins and Their Troubles. 225p. N.D. Pilgrim Press.

Wilder, Laura Ingalls, Mrs. (1867-1957)
--By the Shores of Silver Lake. 1939. (ISBN 0-8382-0138-5, Cadmus Books). E. M. Hale and Company.
--By the Shores of Silver Lake. Williams, Garth MOntgomery (1912-), illus. LC 39-27949. vi p., 1 l., 260 p. incl. illus., plates. col. front. 21 cm. 1939. Harper & Brothers. **Award: (JNM).**
--By the Shores of Silver Lake. newly illustrated, uniform. Williams, Garth Montgomery (1912-), illus. (Illus.). 290 p. 21cm. 1953. Harper.
--Farmer Boy. 1933. (ISBN 0-8382-0245-4, Cadmus Books). E. M. Hale and Co.
--Farmer Boy. Sewell, Helen Moore (1896-1957), illus. LC 33-32922. 5 p. l., 230 p. col. front., illus., 21 1/2 cm. 1933. Harper & Brothers.
--Farmer Boy. newly illustrated, uniform. Williams, Garth Montgomery (1912-), illus. LC 52-7527. (Illus.). 371 p. 21cm. 1953. Harper.
--The First Four Years. Williams, Garth Montgomery (1912-), illus. LC 76-135774. (Illus.). xx, 134 p. 21cm. 1971. (ISBN 0-06-026426-8). Harper & Row.
--Little House Books, 9 vols. Williams, Garth Montgomery (1912-), illus. Incl. Little House in the Big Woods. (ISBN 0-06-440001-8); Little House on the Prairie. (ISBN 0-06-440002-6); Farmer Boy. (ISBN 0-06-440003-4); On the Banks of Plum Creek. (ISBN 0-06-440004-2); By the Shores of Silver Lake. (ISBN 0-06-440005-0); The Long Winter. (ISBN 0-06-440006-9); Little Town on the Prairie. (ISBN 0-06-440007-7); These Happy Golden Years. (ISBN 0-06-440008-5); The First Four Years. (ISBN 0-06-440031-X). (Illus.). (gr. 3-7). 1973. (ISBN 0-06-440040-9, Trophy). Har-Row.
--The Little House in the Big Woods. 1932. (ISBN 0-8382-0454-6, Cadmus Books). E. H. Hale And Company.
--Little House in the Big Woods. Sewell, Helen Moore (1896-1957), illus. LC 32-9672. 5 p. l., 176 p. incl. illus., plates. col. front. 21 1/2 cm. 1932. Harper & Brothers.
--Little House in the Big Woods. newly illustrated, uniform. Williams, Garth Montgomery (1912-), illus. (Illus.). 237 p. 21cm. 1953. Harper.
--Little House in the Big Woods. large type ed. Williams, Garth Montgomery (1912-), illus. LC 68-1409. (Illus.). 237 p. 29cm. N.D. Harper & Row.
--The Little House on the Prairie. 1935. (ISBN 0-8382-0455-4, Cadmus Books). E. M. Hale And Company.
--Little House on the Prairie. Sewell, Helen Moore (1896-1957), illus. LC 35-27325. vi p., 2 l., 200 p., 1 l. col. front., illus. 21 1/2 cm. 1935. Harper & Brothers.
--Little House on the Prairie. newly illustrated, uniform. Williams, Garth Montgomery (1912-), illus. (Illus.). 334 p. 21cm. 1953. Harper.
--Little Town on the Prairie. 1st ed. Sewell, Helen Moore (1896-1957) & Boyle, Mildred, illus. LC 41-23277. (Illus.). vii, 286p. 21cm. 1941. Harper & Bros.
--Little Town on the Prairie. newly illustrated, uniform. Williams, Garth Montgomery (1912-), illus. (Illus.). 304 p. 21cm. 1953. Harper.
--The Long Winter. Sewell, Helen Moore (1896-1957) & Boyle, Mildred, illus. LC 40-33795. vii p., 1 l., 325 p. col. front., illus. 21 cm. c.1940. Harper & Brothers. **Award: (JNM).**
--The Long Winter. newly illustrated, uniform. Williams, Garth Montgomery (1912-), illus. LC 52-7530. (Illus.). 334 p. 21cm. 1953. Harper.
--On the Banks of Plum Creek. 1937. E M Hale.
--On the Banks of Plum Creek. Sewell, Helen Moore (1896-1957) & Boyle, Mildred, illus. LC 37-23640. vi p. 2 l., 239 p. incl. illus., plates. col. front. 21 1/2 cm. 1937. Harper & Brothers. **Award: (JNM).**
--On the Banks of Plum Creek. newly illustrated, uniform. Williams, Garth Montgomery (1912-), illus. LC 52-752826. (Illus.). 338 p. 21cm. 1953. Harper.
--On the Way Home. Lane, Rose W. (1887-1968), ed. LC 62-17966. (Illus.). (gr. 7 up). 1962. (ISBN 0-06-026489-6, HarpJ). (ISBN 0-06-026490-X). Har-Row.
--On the Way Home. Lane, Rose W. (1887-1968), ed. (Illus.). (gr. 7 up). 1962. (ISBN 0-06-440080-8, Trophy). Har-Row.
--These Happy Golden Years. 1943. E M Hale.
--These Happy Golden Years. Sewell, Helen Moore (1896-1957) & Boyle, Mildred, illus. LC 43-51065. 5 p. l., 299, 1 p. col. front., illus. 21 cm. 1943. Harper & Brothers. **Award: (JNM).**
--These Happy Golden Years. newly illustrated, uniform. Williams, Garth Montgomery (1912-), illus. LC 52-753228. (Illus.). 288 p. 21cm. 1953. Harper.

Wilder, Martha L. Thornton, Mrs. (1843-)
--Lonely Hill: A Story for Girls. (The Girl Chums Ser.). N.D. A. L. Burt Company.
--Lonely Hill and Its Possibilities. (Illus.). (The Wellesley Series for Girls). N.D. A. L. Burt.
--Lonely Hill and Its Possibilities: A Story for Out-of-the-Way Places. LC 12-40220. 374 p. front., 2 pl. 19 1/2 cm. c.1893. Congregational Sunday-School and Publishing Society.
--Lonely Hill and Its Possibilities: A/Story for Out-of-the-Way Places. (Illus.). 374p. (The Pilgrim Endeavor Library). N.D. Pilgrims Press.
--Mr. John and His Boys. LC 12-40215. 444 p. 19 cm. c.1888. Presbyterian Board of Publication and Sabbath-School Work.
--Our Girls at Castlewood. LC 12-40242. 334 p. illus. 18 cm. 1887. Presbyterian Board of Publication and Sabbath-School Work.

Wilder, N. W., Mrs.
--Little Graves. N.D. Nelson & Phillips.

Wilder, S. Fannie Gerry, Mrs. (1850-)
--Boston Girls at Home and Abroad. LC 12-40241. 346 p. front., illus., plates. 19 1/2 cm. 1890. J. H. Earle.

Wildermuth, Ottilie Rooschutz (1817-1874)
--Household Stories. Kimmont, Eleanor, tr. from German. 4 v. fronts., plates. 18 cm. 1872. Hitchcock and Walden.
--Household Stories, 1 of 25 vols, Vol. 1. Kinmont, Mary, tr. from Ger. (Illus.). (Selected Bks for Sunday School: The/Auburn Library). N.D. Set. Methodist Bk Concern.
--Leon and Zephie: Or, The Little Wanderers. (Illus.). N.D. E. P. Dutton & Co.
--Ottalie's Stories for the Little Folks. 308p. N.D. E. P.Dutton.
--Stories for the Little Folks. 308p. N.D. E. P. Dutton.
Wildes, Newlin B
--The Best Summer. Micale, Albert (1913-), illus. LC 65-18585. 79 p. illus. 21 cm. 1965. Rand McNally.
--The Horse That Had Everything. Micale, Albert (1913-), illus. LC 66-7292. (Illus.). 128 p. 22cm. 1966. Rand McNally.
Wilding, Suzanne (1917-)
--Big Jump for Robin. Savitt, Sam (1917-), illus. LC 74-5489. (Illus.). 184 p. 22cm. 1974, c.1965. (ISBN 0-8193-0740-8). (ISBN 0-8193-0740-8). Parents' Magazine Press.
--Big Jump for Robin. Savitt, Sam (1917-), illus. LC 65-13565. 22cm. 184p. 1965. St Martin's Press.
--Dream Pony for Robin. Savitt, Sam (1917-), illus. LC 62-12451. (Illus.). 102 p. 22cm. 1962. St. Martin's Press.
--Harlequin Horse. LC 73-90596. 128 p. 22cm. 1969. Van Nostrand Reinhold Co.
--Horse Tales. Savitt, Sam, illus. LC 76-13052. p. cm. 22cm. 201p. c.1976. St. Martin's Press.
--No Love for Schnitzel. Savitt, Sam (1917-), illus. LC 63-9424. 143 p. illus. 22 cm. 1963. St. Martin's Press.
Wildman, George, illus.
--Nancy and Sluggo. Penick, Ib., designed by. LC 80-54575. (Based on Characters Created by Ernie Bushmiller). (Illus.). 16 p. 24cm. c.1981. (ISBN 0-394-84800-4). Random House.
--Popeye. Penick, Ib, designed by. LC 80-52840. (Illus.). 14 p. 24cm. c.1981. (ISBN 0-394-84584-6). Random House.
--The Popeye Mix or Match Storybook: More Than 200,000 Combinations. LC 80-52869. (Illus.). 7 leaves. c.1981. (ISBN 0-394-84585-4). Random House.
Wildman, Marian Warner (1876-)
--Betty's Beautiful Nights. Burd, Clara Miller, illus. LC 16-22258. v, 212 p. front., illus., pl. 21 1/2 cm. c.1916. G. P. Putnam's Sons.
--Loyalty Island. Barry, Etheldred Breeze (1870-), illus. LC 4-22673. 4 p. l., 90 p. incl. illus., plates. front. 18 1/2 cm. (Cosy corner series). 1904. L. C. Page & Company.
--Robin's Nest Ranch. N.D. Dana Estes & Co.
--Theodore and Theodora. (Illus.). (Cosy Corner Ser.). 1905. L. C. Page & Co.
--What Robin Did Then: The Story of a Sierran Home. LC 7-26601. 282 p. front., 7 pl. 21 1/2 cm. c.1907. D. Estes & Company.
Wildsmith, Alan (1937-)
--The Northern Phantom. LC 78-325692. 176 p. 21cm. 1978. (ISBN 0-233-97002-9). Deutsch.
--Snowbound at Forty-Five Acres. Long, Sally, illus. LC 76-383966. (Illus.). 123 p. 23cm. 1976. (ISBN 0-233-96783-4). Deutsch.
Wildsmith, Brain Lawrence (1930-), retold by see Mother Goose.
Wildsmith, Brian Lawrence (1930-)
--Animal Tricks. Wildsmith, Brian Lawrence (1930-), illus. LC 81-112502. (Illus.). 24 p. 1980. (ISBN 0-19-279743-3). Oxford University Press.
--Bear's Adventure. Wildsmith, Brian Lawrence (1930-), illus. LC 81-18814. (Illus.). 32 p. 31cm. c.1981. (ISBN 0-394-85295-8). Pantheon Books.
--Brian Wildsmith's Book of Bedtime Stories. Wildsmith, Brian Lawrence (1930-), illus. LC 84-7795. p. cm. 1985. (ISBN 0-394-86937-0). (ISBN 0-394-96937-5). Pantheon Books.
--Brian Wildsmith's "Circus". Wildsmith, Brian Lawrence (1930-), illus. LC 71-102917. 1 v. (unpaged, chiefly col. illus.). 29cm. 1970. F. Watts.
--Brian Wildsmith's "Mother Goose". Wildsmith, Brian Lawrence (1930-), illus. LC 65-10040. (Illus.). (gr. k-3). 1965. (ISBN 0-531-01535-1). (ISBN 0-531-02372-9). Watts.
--Brian Wildsmith's "The Twelve Days of Christmas". Wildsmith, Brian Lawrence (1930-), illus. LC 71-182554. (Illus.). 32p. (gr. 1 up). 1972. (ISBN 0-531-01555-6). (ISBN 0-531-01554-8). Watts. **Award: (ALA).**
--Brian Wildsmith's "The Twelve Days of Christmas". Wildsmith, Brian Lawrence (1930-), illus. (Illus.). (gr. k-3). 1979. (ISBN 0-531-02386-9). Watts.
--Cat on the Mat. Wildsmith, Brian Lawrence (1930-), illus. (Illus.). 16p. (ps). 1983. (ISBN 0-19-272123-2, Pub by Oxford U Pr Childrens). Merrimack Pub Cir.
--Daisy. Wildsmith, Brian Lawrence (1930-), illus. LC 83-12150. (Illus.). 47 p. 31cm. 1984. (ISBN 0-394-85975-8). (ISBN 0-394-95975-2). Pantheon Books.
--Give a Dog a Bone. Wildsmith, Brian Lawrence (1930-), illus. LC 85-3413. (Illus.). 47 p. 32cm. c.1985. (ISBN 0-394-87709-8). (ISBN 0-394-97709-2). Pantheon Books.
--Hunter and His Dog. Wildsmith, Brian Lawrence (1930-), illus. LC 78-41181. (Illus.). 30 p. 29cm. 1979. (ISBN 0-19-279725-5). Oxford University Press.
--Illustrated Bible Stories. (Brian Wildsmith Bks.). (gr. k-3). 1969. (ISBN 0-531-01529-7). Watts. **Award: (ALA).**
--The Lazy Bear. Wildsmith, Brian Lawrence (1930-), illus. LC 75-323163. (Illus.). 32 p. 1973. (ISBN 0-19-279693-3). Oxford University Press.
--The Lazy Bear. Wildsmith, Brian Lawrence (1930-), illus. LC 73-8398. (Illus.). 32 p. 1974, c.1973. (ISBN 0-531-01559-9). Watts.
--The Lion & the Rat: A Fable by La Fontaine. Wildsmith, Brian Lawrence (1930-), illus. (Illus.). 32p. (ps-1). N.D. (ISBN 0-19-279607-0, Pub. by Oxford U Pr Childrens). Merrimack Pub Cir.
--The Little Wood Duck. Wildsmith, Brian Lawrence (1930-), illus. LC 72-3828. (Illus.). 1 v. (unpaged). 29cm. 1973, c.1972. (ISBN 0-531-02593-4). F. Watts.
--The Little Wood Duck. Wildsmith, Brian Lawrence (1930-), illus. LC 74-154406. (Illus.). 32 p. 29cm. 1972. (ISBN 0-19-279686-0). Oxford University Press.
--The Owl and the Woodpecker. Wildsmith, Brian Lawrence (1930-), illus. LC 74-165476. (Illus.). 32 p. 29cm. 1972, c.1971. (ISBN 0-531-01553-X). F. Watts.
--The Owl and the Woodpecker. Wildsmith, Brian Lawrence (1930-), illus. LC 73-153652. 32 p. (chiefly col. illus.). 29cm. 1971. (ISBN 0-19-279676-3). Oxford University Press.
--Oxford Book of Poetry for Children. Wildsmith, Brian Lawrence (1930-), illus. (Illus.). 178p. N.D. (ISBN 0-19-276031-9, Pub. by Oxford U Pr Childrens). Merrimack Pub Cir.
--Pelican. Wildsmith, Brian Lawrence (1930-), illus. LC 82-12431. p. cm. 1983. (ISBN 0-394-95668-0). Pantheon Books.
--Professor Noah's Spaceship. Wildsmith, Brian Lawrence (1930-), illus. LC 80-40984. (Illus.). 30 p. 31cm. 1980. (ISBN 0-19-279741-7). Oxford University Press.
--Python's Party. Wildsmith, Brian Lawrence (1930-), illus. LC 74-20303. (Illus.). 32 p. 29cm. 1975. (ISBN 0-531-02808-9). Franklin Watts.
--Python's Party. Wildsmith, Brian Lawrence (1930-), illus. LC 75-308681. (Illus.). 29 p. 29cm. 1974. (ISBN 0-19-279705-0). Oxford University Press.
--The True Cross. Wildsmith, Brian Lawrence (1930-), illus. (Illus.). (gr. k-3). 1978. (ISBN 0-531-02482-2). Watts.
--The Trunk. Wildsmith, Brian Lawrence (1930-), illus. (Illus.). 16p. (ps). 1983. (ISBN 0-19-272124-0, Pub by Oxford U Pr Childrens). Merrimack Pub Cir.
--What the Moon Saw. Wildsmith, Brian Lawrence (1930-), illus. (Illus.). (ps-3). 1978. (ISBN 0-19-279724-7). Oxford U Pr.
Wildsmith, Brian Lawrence (1930-), ed.
--The Hare and the Tortoise. Wildsmith, Brian Lawrence (1930-), illus. LC 67-2816. (Based on the Fable by Jean de La Fontaine (1621-1695). 1 v. (chiefly col. illus.). 29cm. 1967, c.1966. F. Watts.
--Maurice Maeterlinck's Blue Bird. Wildsmith, Brian Lawrence (1930-), illus. LC 76-16541. (Illus.). 37 p. 29cm. 1976. (ISBN 0-531-00352-3). Watts.
--The Miller, the Boy, and the Donkey. Wildsmith, Brian Lawrence (1930-), illus. LC 69-16607. (Based on the Fable by Jean de La Fontaine (1621-1695)). (Illus.). 32 p. 29cm. 1969. F. Watts.
--The Miller, the Boy & the Donkey. Wildsmith, Brian Lawrence (1930-), illus. (Based on a Fable by La Fontaine (1621-1695)). (Illus.). 32p. (ps-1). 1984. (ISBN 0-19-272114-3, Pub. by Oxford U Pr Childrens). Merrimack Pub Cir.
Wiles, Irving R., jt. auth. see Gibson, C. D.
Wiles, Julian
--The Tradd Street Follies. Wiles, Julian, illus. LC 76-45729. (Illus.). 101 p. c.1978. (ISBN 0-686-05808-9). Tradd Street Press.
Wiles, Mary J.
--The Alligator with a Toothache. (ps-3). 1978. Dghtrs St Paul.
Wiley, Belle
--Mewanee, the Little Indian Boy. Hubbard, Charles D., illus. LC 12-29313. 101 p. illus. 19 1/2 cm. c.1912. Silver, Burdett & Company.
--Mother Goose Primer. Peck, Anne Merriman (1884-), illus. 1916. Charles E. Merrill Co.
--Rago and Goni. N.D. Appleton-Century-Crofts.
Wiley, Belle & Edick, Grace Willard
--Children of the Cliff. N.D. D. Appleton & Co.
--Lodrix, the Little Lake Dweller. LC 4-33223. 4 p. l., 86 p. front., illus. 19 1/2 cm. 1905. D. Appleton and Company.
Wiley, Karla Hummel (1918-)
--Assignment: Latin America: A Story of the Peace Corps. viii, 240 p. 21cm. 1968. D. McKay Co.
--Styles by Suzy. (gr. 7-11). 1965. (ISBN 0-679-20199-8). McKay.
Wilford, Carol, ed. see Kirby, Mary & Kirby, Elizabeth.
Wilford, Florence
--An Author's Children. (Illus.). N.D. E & J B Young.
--King of the Day. 0 ed. N.D. E & J B Young.
--Little Lives and a Great Love. N.D. Thomas Whittaker.
--Vantage Ground and Other Stories. (Illus.). N.D. E & J B Young.
Wilhelm, Hans (1945-)
--Bunny Trouble. Wilhelm, Hans (1945-), illus. LC 85-191344. (Illus.). 33 p. 24cm. c.1985. (ISBN 0-590-33371-2). Scholastic Inc.
--Don't Give Up, Josephine!. Wilhelm, Hans (1945-), illus. LC 84-24849. (Illus.). 40p. (ps-3). 1985. (ISBN 0-394-97244-9, BYR). (ISBN 0-394-87244-4). Random.
--I'll Always Love You. Wilhelm, Hans (1945-), illus. LC 84-20060. (Illus.). 31 p. c.1985. (ISBN 0-517-55648-0). Crown.
--A New Home, a New Friend. Wilhelm, Hans (1945-), illus. LC 84-18295. (Illus.). 30 p. 28cm. (ps-3). c.1985. (ISBN 0-394-87226-6). (ISBN 0-394-97226-0). Random House.
--Our Christmas, 1985. LC 85-17190. p. cm. c.1985. (ISBN 0-7172-8179-5). Grolier Enterprises.
--Tales from the Land Under My Table. LC 83-4471. p. cm. 1983. (ISBN 0-394-85511-6). (ISBN 0-394-95511-0). Random House.
Wilhelm, Kate (1928-)
--The Killer Thing. 1st ed. 190 p. 22cm. (Doubleday Science Fiction). 1967. Doubleday.
--Where Late the Sweet Birds Sang. LC 75-6379. 260p. 1976. (ISBN 0-06-014654-0, HarpT). Har-Row.
Wilhelm, Kathryn Stephenson (1915-)
--Butterfly Blue. Padgett, Jim, illus. LC 66-2268. 60 p. col. illus. 23 cm. 1966. Southern Pub. Association.
--The Hot Brick, and Other Stories. Padgett, Jim, illus. LC 66-2693. 109 p. illus. 24 cm. 1966. Southern Pub. Association.
--Sally Roses and Other Stories from My Memory Chest. LC 63-18311. (Illus.). 27cm. 91p. 1963. Southern Pub. Assn.
Wilhelm, Richard (1873-1930)
--The Chinese Fairy Book. Hood, George W., illus. Martens, Frederick Herman (1874-1932), tr. LC 21-18125. vi p., 4 l., 329 p. col. front., col. plates. 21 cm. c.1921. Frederick A. Stokes Company.
Wilhelmson, Carl
--Speed of the Reindeer: A Story of Lapland. Busoni, Rafaello (1900-1962), illus. LC 54-4017. (Illus.). 220p. 21cm. 1954. Viking Press.
Wilhoite, Mariel & Horton, Elizabeth
--Bobra of Bali. LC 36-33401. 54 p. incl. col. illus., col. plates. 25 1/2 cm. c.1936. Rand, McNally & Company.
Wilkerson, David
--Beyond the Cross & the Switchblade. Sherrill, John & Sherrill, Elizabeth, intro. by. 192p. 1974. (ISBN 0-912376-08-2). Chosen Bks Inc.
Wilkerson, Don & Manuel, David
--Hell-Bound. LC 78-60735. 199 p. 18cm. c.1978. Rock Harbor Press.
Wilkerson, Jesse
--Come Home, Bill Bailey. LC 56-940. 141p. illus. 20cm. c.1955. Naylor Co.
--Comrades of the Canyons. LC 57-58807. 54 p. illus. 20 cm. 1957. Naylor Co.
Wilkes, Alfred William (1910-)
--Little Boy Black. Ford, George Cephas, Jr., illus. LC 79-158887. (Illus.). 155 p. 22cm. 1971. (ISBN 0-684-12499-8). Scribner.
Wilkes, Defoe
--The Adventures of King Arthur. (Picture Classics Ser.). N.D (Usborne-Hayes). EDC.
--Book of Children's Classic. (Children's Classic Ser.). (gr. 3-6). 1982. (ISBN 0-86020-669-6, Usborne-Hayes). EDC.
--Catching Crooks. (Good Detective Guides Ser.). (gr. 2-5). 1979. (ISBN 0-86020-228-3, Usborne-Hayes). (ISBN 0-88110-040-4). (ISBN 0-86020-227-5). EDC.
--Treasure Island. (Children's Classic Ser.). (gr. 3-6). 1982. (ISBN 0-86020-575-4, Usborne-Hayes). (ISBN 0-88110-063-3). (ISBN 0-86020-574-6). EDC.
Wilkes, Marilyn Z
--C.L.U.T.Z. Ross, Larry (1943-), illus. LC 81-68786. (Illus.). 120 p. 22cm. c.1982. (ISBN 0-8037-1157-3). (ISBN 0-8037-1158-1). Dial Press.
--C.L.U.T.Z. and the Fizzion Formula. Ross, Larry (1943-), illus. LC 84-23311. (Illus.). 136 p. 22cm. c.1985. (ISBN 0-8037-0171-3). (ISBN 0-8037-0179-9). Dial Books for Young Readers.
Wilkes, Mike see Wilks, Michael Thomas.
Wilkie, Katharine Elliott (1904-1980)
--George Rogers Clark: Boy of the Old Northwest. Fiorentino, Al, illus. LC 59-13996. 191 p, illus. 20cm. (Childhoold of famous Americans). 1960. Bobbs-Merrill.
--George Rogers Clark: Boy of the Old Northwest. 1st ed. Laune, Paul Sidney (1899-), illus. LC 57-935531. 192 p. illus. 20 cm. (Childhood of famous Americans series 101). 1958. Bobbs-Merrill.
--John Sevier, Son of Tennessee. LC 58-109384. 192 p. 23 cm. 1958. J. Messner.
--Mary Todd Lincoln: Girl of the Bluegrass. 1st ed. Lees, Harry Hanson, illus. LC 54-9496. 192p. illus. 20cm. (Childhood of famous Americans series 83). 1954. Bobbs-Merrill.
--Mary Todd Lincoln: Girl of the Bluegrasss. Goldstein, Leslie, illus. LC 60-7712. 192 p. illus. 20 cm. (Childhood of famous Americans). 1960. Bobbs-Merill.
--Simon Kenton: Young Trail Blazer. Morrow, Gray, illus. LC 60-8882. 192p. col. illus. 20cm. (Childhood of famous Americans). c.1960. Bobbs-Merrill.
--Will Clark: Boy in Buckskins. 1st ed. Lees, Harry Hanson, illus. LC 53-8879. 192p. illus. (Childhood of famous american Ser.). 1953. Bobbs-Merrill.
--Will Clark: Boy in Buckskins. Moyers, William (1916-), illus. LC 62-16614. 200 p. illus. 20 cm. (Childhood of famous americans). 1963. Bobbs-Merrill.
--William Fargo: Young Mail Carrier. Ponter, James J., illus. LC 62-925777. 200 p. illus. 20 cm. (Childhood of famous Americans). 1962. Bobbs-Merrill.
--Zack Taylor: Young, Rough, and Ready. Sternweiss, Shannon, illus. LC 62-701. 200 p. illus. 20 cm. (Childhood of famous Americans). 1962. Bobbs-Merill.
Wilkie, Katharine Elliott (1904-1980) & Mosley, Elizabeth Robards
--Atlantis. LC 79-473. (Illus.). 191 p. 22cm. c.1979. (ISBN 0-671-32910-3). Messner.
Wilkin, Eloise Burns (1904-), selected by see Stevenson, Robert Louis.
Wilkin, Eloise Burns (1904-)
--Baby Listens. Wilkin, Eloise Burns (1904-), illus. (Little Golden Book). 1960. Golden Press.
--Baby's First Christmas. Wilkin, Eloise Burns (1904-), illus. (Little Golden Book). 1959. Golden Press.
--Baby's First Christmas. Wilkin, Eloise Burns (1904-), illus. LC 80-80710. (Illus.). 14p. (Board Bks.). (ps). 1980. (ISBN 0-394-84575-7). Random.
--Baby's Mother Goose. Wilkin, Eloise Burns (1904-), illus. (Big Golden Book). 1958. Golden Press.
--Eloise Wilkin Four Baby's First Golden Books, 4 bks. Wilkin, Eloise Burns (1904-), illus. (Illus.). (ps). 1981. (ISBN 0-307-13650-7, Golden Pr). Western Pub.
--How Big Is Baby?. Wilkin, Eloise Burns (1904-), illus. (Illus.). 8p. (Baby's First Golden Bks.). (ps). 1980. (ISBN 0-307-10756-6, Golden Pr). Western Pub.
--Ladybug, Ladybug, and Other Nursery Rhymes. Wilkin, Eloise Burns (1904-), illus. LC 79-63899. (Illus.). 24 p. 17cm. c.1979. (ISBN 0-394-84282-0). Random House.
--Linda and Her Little Sister. Wilkin, Eloise Burns (1904-), illus. LC 55-1002. unpaged. illus. 21cm. (Little Golden Book, 214). 1955, c.1954. Simon and Schuster.
--The Little Book. Wilkin, Eloise Burns (1904-), illus. (Illus.). 8p. (Baby's First Golden Bks.). (ps). 1981. (ISBN 0-307-10755-8, Golden Pr). Western Pub.
--My Good Morning Book. Wilkin, Eloise Burns (1904-), illus. LC 82-83789. c.1983. (ISBN 0-307-12271-9). Golden Press.
--My Goodnight Book. Wilkin, Eloise Burns (1904-), illus. (Illus.). 14p. (Golden Sturdy Shape Bk). 1981. (ISBN 0-307-12258-1, Golden Pr). Western Pub.
--Nursery Rhymes. Wilkin, Eloise Burns (1904-), illus. LC 78-64606. (Illus.). 14 p. 20cm. c.1979. (ISBN 0-394-84129-8). Random House.
--Rock-a-Bye Baby. Wilkin, Eloise Burns (1904-), illus. LC 84-60029. (Illus.). (Music Box Ser.). (ps up). 1984. (ISBN 0-394-86798-X, Pub. by BYR). Random.
--Rock-A-Bye, Baby: Nursery Songs & Cradle Games. Wilkin, Eloise Burns (1904-), illus. LC 80-54774. (Illus.). 24p. (Rocking Bks.). (ps). 1981. (ISBN 0-394-84824-1). Random.
Wilkin, Refna (1931-), tr. see Baumann, Hans.

Wilkin, Refna, tr. see Carigiet, Alois.
Wilkins
--The Unwanted Adventure of Harold Greenhouse. (gr. 3-5). N.D. (ISBN 0-590-05410-4, Schol Pap). Scholastic Inc.
Wilkins, Cary, jt. ed. see Lang, Andrew.
Wilkins, Dale
--The Long Trail Boys and the Gray Cloaks: Or, The Mystery of the Night Riders. Pilsbry, Elizabeth, illus. LC 23-13455. 256 p. incl. front. 19 1/2 cm. (Long trail series). c.1923. The John C. Winston Company.
--The Long Trail Boys and the Mystery of the Fingerprint. Oldham, Jean, illus. LC 29-9288. 238 p. incl. front. 19 cm. (long trail series). c.1928. The John C. Winston Company.
--The Long Trail Boys and the Mystery of the Unknown Messenger. Oldham, Jean, illus. LC 29-9289. 250 p. incl. front. 19 cm. (long trail series). c.1928. The John C. Winston Company.
--The Long Trail Boys and the Scarlet Sign. LC 25-232259. 3 p. l., 9-266 p. front. 19 cm. (long trail series). c.1925. The John C. Winston Company.
--The Long Trail Boys and the Vanishing Rider. LC 25-224522. 3 p. l., 9-272 p. front. 19 cm. (long trail series). c.1925. The John C. Winston Company.
--The Long Trail Boys at Sweet Water Ranch: Or, The Mystery of White Shadow. Pilsbry, Elizabeth, illus. LC 23-134561. 248 p. incl. front. 19 1/2 cm. (Long trail series). 1923. The John C. Winston Company.
Wilkins, David Schermerhorn, jt. ed. see Pendleton, Margaret.
Wilkins, Eloise Burns (1904-), illus.
--The Busy ABC. LC 50-39809. 32p. col. illus. 21cm. c.1950. Whitman.
Wilkins, Frances (1923-)
--Wizards and Witches. 1966. E M Hale.
--Wizards and Witches. Wegner, Fritz (1924-), illus. LC 66-14767. 63p. illus. 22cm. (Byways lib.). 1966, c.1965. Walck.
Wilkins, James A.
--Stories in Prose and Rime. N.D. Bruce Humphries, Inc.
Wilkins, Mary Eleanor, Mrs. (1852-1930), compiled by.
--Little Men and Women. (Illus.). 400p. 1900. DeWolfe, Fiske & Co.
Wilkins, Mary Eleanor (1852-1930)
--The Cow With Golden Horns. (Christmas Hearth Library). N.D. D. Lothrop & Co.
--The Cow with Golden Horns, 1 of 5 vols. (Illus.). (Good Fortune Library). N.D. Set. Lothrop Publishing Co.
--Once Upon a Time, and Other Child Verses. Barry, Etheldred Breeze (1870-), illus. N.D. Lothrop Publishing Co.
--Princess Rosetta & the Popcorn Man. Greene, Ellin, retold by. Hyman, Trina Schart (1939-), illus. LC 70-148483. (Illus.). 48p. (gr. k-3). 1971. (ISBN 0-688-51404-9). Lothrop.
Wilkins, Mary Huiskamp see Calhoun, Mary, pseud.
Wilkins, Mrs., jt. auth. see Wiggin, Kate Douglas Smith.
Wilkins, N. G.
--I Am a Duck. 1st U.S. edition. (gr. k-3). 1976. (ISBN 0-590-10292-3). Schol Bk Serv.
Wilkins, Pauline
--Doctor Dan at the Circus. Sampson, Katherine, illus. (Little Golden Book). 1960. Golden Press.
Wilkins, Sarah & Mennella, Roxanna
--Dolls. Fisher, Barbara, ed. Wilkins, Sarah & Mennella, Roxanna, illus. (Illus.). 27p. (Orig.). (gr. 4-6). 1984. (ISBN 0-934830-34-7). Ten Penny.
Wilkins, Sophie, tr. see Fromm, Lilo.
Wilkinson, A. S.
--Famous Fables for Tiny Tots (Pub. by Society for Promoting Christian Knowledge). N.D. E. & J. B. Young & Co.
Wilkinson, Andrews
--Boy Holidays in the Louisiana Wilds. Cue, Harold, illus. LC 17-242841. 4 p. l., 259 p. front., plates. 21 cm. $1.50. 1917. Little, Brown, and Company.
--Plantation Stories of Old Louisiana. Bull, Charles Livingston (1874-1932), illus. LC 14-11727. x, 338 p. col. front., illus., plates. 20 1/2 cm. 1914. The Page Company.
Wilkinson, Barry
--Diverting Adventures of Tom Thumb. Wilkinson, Barry, illus. LC 74-140867. (Illus.). 29p. 1st U.S. edition. (gr. 3-6). 1969. (ISBN 0-15-201620-1, HJ). HarBraceJ.
--The Diverting Adventures of Tom Thumb: A Picture Book. LC 74-2533. (Illus.). 28 p. 1969, c.1967. Harcourt, Brace & World.
--What Can You Do with a Dithery-Do?. Repr. (gr. k-3). 1974. (ISBN 0-590-09882-9, Schol Pap). Schol Bk Serv.
Wilkinson, Barry & Perrault, Charles (1628-1703)
--Puss in Boots. LC 69-18874. (Illus.). 25 p. 1969. World Pub. Co.
Wilkinson, Brenda Scott (1946-)
--Ludell. LC 75-9390. 170 p. 22cm. c.1975. (ISBN 0-06-026491-8). (ISBN 0-06-026492-6). Harper & Row.
--Ludell and Willie. LC 76-18402. 181 p. 22cm. c.1977. (ISBN 0-06-026487-X). (ISBN 0-06-026488-8). Harper & Row.
--Ludell's New York Time. LC 79-3173. 184 p. 22cm. c.1980. (ISBN 0-06-026497-7). (ISBN 0-06-026498-5). Harper & Row.
Wilkinson, Elizabeth Hays
--The Lane to Sleepy Town. LC 11-748. 16cm. 66p. 1910. Reed & Witting.
--Peter and Polly. LC 12-18787. 4 p. l., 3-97 p. incl. col. front., col. illus. 15 cm. $0.50. 1912. Doubleday, Page & Company.
Wilkinson, J. A., ed.
--A Real Robinson Crusoe. LC 12-40212. 339p. 19cm. 1890. D. Lothrop Company.
Wilkinson, Jean (1931-) & Wilkinson, Ned (1930-)
--Come to Work with Us: In ... Hurst, Roy J., illus. Fray, Lee & Roodman, Carl, photos by Levenson, Sam, frwd. by. LC 74-127858. (Illus.). v. 21cm. (Beginning Sextant series). N.D. Sextant Systems.
--Come to Work with Us in a Dairy. (Illus.). glossary. 48p. (Come to Work with Us Books). (gr. 1-4). 1972. (ISBN 0-516-02115-X, Sextant). Childrens.
Wilkinson, Marguerite Ogden Bigelow, Mrs., jt. ed. see Thacher, Lucy W. S., Mrs.
Wilkinson, Ned, jt. auth. see Wilkinson, Jean.
Wilkinson, Nevile Rodwell, Sir (1869-1940)
--Grey Fairy and Titania's Palace. LC 23-3220. xiv, 111, 2 p. col. front., illus. (2 maps, plan) plates (part col.) 25 1/2 cm. 1922. H. Milford.
Wilkinson, Noel Hawtrey, jt. ed. see Wilkinson, William Alexander Chaplin.
Wilkinson, Pamela F.
--Ridin' the Rainbow. Musgrave, Real, illus. LC 81-67744. (Illus.). 40p. 1983. (ISBN 0-931722-10-1). (ISBN 0-931722-09-8). (ISBN 0-931722-11-X). Corona Pub.
Wilkinson, William Alexander Chaplin (1900-) & Wilkinson, Noel Hawtrey (1908-), eds.
--The Dragon Book of Verse. LC 36-10042. viii, 464 p. illus. 19 cm. 1935. The Clarendon Press.
Wilkon, Jozef (1930-) & Bauman, Kurt (1935-)
--The Contest of the Birds. Bell, Anthea, tr. 32p. 1981. (ISBN 0-686-97124-8, Pub. by Andersen-Hutchinson England). State Mutual Bk.
Wilks, Michael Thomas (1947-)
--The Weather Works. 1st ed. LC 82-23306. (Illus.). 32 p. 32cm. c.1983. Holt, Rinehart and Winston.
Wilks, Mike, jt. auth. see Harrison, Sarah.
Will, pseud., see Lipkind, William.
Will, jt. auth. see Nicolas.
Will, Rose Graffe
--The Service Beautiful. LC 26-21296. 4 p. l., 219 p. plates. 17 1/2 cm. 1926. Mission Press, S. V. D.
--The Service Beautiful. LC 48-20924. 237 p. illus. 18 cm. 1948. Mission Press, S. V. D.
Will, pseud. (1904-1974) & Nicolas, pseud. (1911-1973)
--Four-Leaf Clover. Lipkind, William. Mordvinoff, Nicolas. LC 59-8956. (Illus.). 32p. (gr. k-3). 1959. (ISBN 0-15-229140-7, HJ). HarBraceJ.
Willard, Annmary, retold by.
--Pillow-Time Tales: Fourteen Famous Nursery Stories. Dorcas, Couri, illus. LC 53-9335. unpaged. illus. 33cm. (Rand McNally Book-Elf Giant). c.1954. Rand McNally.
Willard, Barbara, tr. see Bolliger, Max.
Willard, Barbara Mary (1909-)
--Augustine Came to Kent. Guggenheim, Hans (1924-), illus. LC 63-16637. 187 p. illus. 22 cm. 1963. Doubleday.
--Charity at Home. Hall, Douglas (1931-), illus. LC 66-7941. (Illus.). 187 p. 21cm. 1st U.S. edition. 1966, c.1965. Harcourt, Brace & World.
--A Cold Wind Blowing. 1st ed. LC 73-77453. 175 p. 22cm. 1973, c.1972. (ISBN 0-525-28125-8). Dutton.
--The Country Maid. LC 79-19002. (Illus.). 184 p. 22cm. 1st U.S. edition. 1980, c.1978. (ISBN 0-688-80256-7). (ISBN 0-688-84256-9). Greenwillow Books.
--A Dog and a Half. Paton, Jane Elizabeth (1934-), illus. LC 73-140076. (Illus.). 128 p. 22cm. 1st U.S. edition. 1971. (ISBN 0-8407-6122-8). T. Nelson.
--Duck on a Pond. Hardy, Mary Rose, illus. LC 69-12457. 174 p. illus. 31 cm. 1969. F. Watts.
--Eight for a Secret. Hart, Lewis, illus. LC 60-11178. 219p. 1960. Franklin Watts.
--The Family Tower. LC 68-14111. 172 p. 21cm. 1st U.S. edition. 1968. Harcourt, Brace & World.
--Flight to the Forest. Floyd, Gareth (1940-), illus. LC 67-17268. (Illus.). 192 p. 22cm. 1st U.S. edition. 1967. Doubleday.
--The Gardener's Grandchildren. King, Gordon (1939-), illus. LC 78-23637. (Illus.). 143 p. 21cm. 1979, c.1978. (ISBN 0-07-070291-8). McGraw-Hill.
--Harrow and Harvest. 1st ed. LC 75-11918. 174 p. 22cm. 1975, c.1974. (ISBN 0-525-31505-5). E. P. Dutton.
--Hetty. Hampshire, Michael Allen, illus. LC 63-15404. (Illus.). (gr. 5-9). 1963. (ISBN 0-15-233815-2). HarBraceJ.
--The House with Roots. Hodgson, Robert, illus. LC 59-13690. 21cm. 183p. 1960. Watts.
--If All the Swords in England. Sax, Robert M., illus. LC 61-7665. 190p. (Clarion books). c.1961. Doubleday.
--The Iron Lily. 1st ed. LC 74-7195. 175 p. 22cm. 1974, c.1971. (ISBN 0-525-[illegible]). Dutton.
--The Lark and the Laurel. LC 74-102442. 207 p. 21cm. 1st U.S. edition. 1970. Harcourt, Brace & World.
--The Miller's Boy. 1st ed. Floyd, Gareth (1940-), illus. LC 76-19058. (Illus.). 143 p. 22cm. 1976. (ISBN 0-525-34970-7). Dutton.
--The Miller's Boy. Floyd, Gareth (1940-), illus. LC 77-354112. (Illus.). 143 p. 21cm. 1976. (ISBN 0-7226-5073-6). Kestrel Books.
--The Penny Pony. Palmer, Juliette (1930-), illus. LC 68-447. (Illus.). 92 p. 20cm. (Puffin books). 1967, c.1961. Penguin Books.
--The Pocket Mouse. Harford-Cross, M., illus. LC 80-85293. (Illus.). 44 p. 21cm. (Blackbird books). 1981. (ISBN 0-531-04070-4). J. MacRae Books.
--The Pocket Mouse. Russon, Mary Georgina (1937-), illus. LC 69-12783. (Illus.). 31 p. 22cm. 1st U.S. edition. (A Read alone book). 1969. Knopf.
--The Richleighs of Tantamount. Hodges, Cyril Walter (1909-), illus. LC 67-16229. (Illus.). 189 p. 21cm. 1st U.S. edition. 1967, c.1966. Harcourt, Brace & World.
--Son of Charlemagne. 1st ed. Weiss, Emil (1896-1965), illus. LC 59-11616. 187 p. illus. 22 cm. (Clarion books). 1959. Doubleday.
--Spell Me a Witch. LC 81-47536. p. cm. 1st U.S. edition. 1981, c.1979. (ISBN 0-15-293822-2). Harcourt Brace Jovanovich.
--The Sprig of Broom. 1st ed. LC 72-78083. viii, 184 p. 22cm. 1972, c.1971. (ISBN 0-525-39805-8). Dutton.
--Storm from the West. Hall, Douglas (1931-), illus. LC 64-17089. (Illus.). 189p. (gr. 7-9). 1964. (ISBN 0-15-280480-3, HJ). HarBraceJ. **Award: (ALA).**
--The Summer with Spike. Linton, Anne, illus. LC 62-7424. 21cm. 195p. 1962, c.1961. Watts.
--Surprise Island. Paton, Jane Elizabeth (1934-), illus. LC 80-28262. p. cm. 1981, c.1969. (ISBN 0-525-66734-2). Elsevier-Dutton Pub. Co.
--Surprise Island. Paton, Jane Elizabeth (1934-), illus. LC 73-93843. (Illus.). 110 p. 21cm. 1st U.S. edition. 1969. Meredith Press.
--Three & One to Carry. Hall, Douglas (1931-), illus. LC 65-179933. (Illus.). 187p. (gr. 4-6). 1965, c.1964. (ISBN 0-15-286380-X). HarBraceJ.
--To London! To London!. Maitland, Antony Jasper (1935-), illus. LC 68-12860. (Illus.). 32 p. 26cm. 1968. Weybright and Talley.
--The Toppling Towers. LC 69-17117. 192 p. 21cm. 1st U.S. edition. 1969. Harcourt, Brace & World.
Willard, Barbara Mary (1909-), ed.
--Happy Families. Turska, Krystyna Zofia (1933-), illus. LC 73-22433. (Illus.). 256 p. 26cm. 1st U.S. edition. 1974. (ISBN 0-02-793010-6). Macmillan.
--Hullaballoo: About Naughty Boys & Girls. Wegner, Fritz (1924-), illus. (gr. 6 up). 1969. (ISBN 0-696-65610-8). Hawthorn.
--Hullabaloo!. About Naughty Boys and Girls. Wegner, Fritz (1924-), illus. LC 71-84911. (Illus.). 207 p. 26cm. 1st U.S. edition. 1969. Meredith Press.
Willard, Barbara Mary (1909-) & Iguchi, Bunshu (1909-)
--Convent Cat. LC 76-3413. (Illus.). 26 p. 25cm. 1976, c.1975. (ISBN 0-07-031703-8). (ISBN 0-07-031704-6). McGraw-Hill.
Willard, Clara A.
--May Chester. 1873. A. D. F. Randolph.
--Nellie Grayson. N.D. A. D. F. Randolph.
Willard, Clark, pseud., see Sergel, Willard John.
Willard, Eleanor Withey, ed.
--Children's Singing Games. 2nd ed. Willard, Eleanor Withey, illus. LC 5-29295. 4 p. l., 7-67 p. illus. 23 x 20 1/2 cm. 1895. F. A. Stokes Company.
--Children's Singing Games. Willard, Eleanor Withey, illus. LC 5-29296. 67 p. illus. 23 1/2 x 21 cm. 1895. The Michigan Trust Company.
Willard, James Hartwell (1847-), ed. see Mother Goose.
Willard, James Hartwell (1847-), ed. see Trimmer, Sarah Kirby, Mrs.
Willard, James Hartwell (1847-)
--Five Kings in a Cave: The Story of a Great Battle. LC 26-23553. 48p. 18cm. (Altemus' Beautiful Stories Ser.). 1906. H. Altemus Company.
Willard, Mary E
--Through the Wilderness. 207 p. front., 3 pl. 18 cm. c.1872. Presbyterian Board of Publication.
Willard, Mildred Wilds (1911-)
--The Ice Cream Cone. Sumichrast, Jozef (1948-), illus. LC 73-81992. (Illus.). 30 p. 21cm. (Follett Beginning-To-Read Book). 1973. (ISBN 0-695-80418-9). (ISBN 0-695-80418-9). Follett Pub. Co.
--The Luck of Harry Weaver. Robinson, Charles (1931-), illus. LC 72-131147. (Illus.). 128 p. 22cm. 1971. (ISBN 0-531-01967-5). F. Watts.
--The Man Who Had to Invent a Flying Bicycle. Cuffari, Richard (1925-1978), illus. LC 67-21674. (Illus.). 126 p. 22cm. (Window books). 1967. Stackpole Books.
Willard, Nancy (1936-)
--All on a May Morning. Shekerjian, Haig & Shekerjian, Regina, illus. LC 75-18769. (Illus.). 32 p. 1975. (ISBN 0-399-20477-6). Putnam.
--The Highest Hit. 1st ed. McCully, Emily Arnold (1939-), illus. LC 77-88970. (Illus.). 115 p. 22cm. c.1978. (ISBN 0-15-234278-8). Harcourt Brace Jovanovich.
--The Island of the Grass King: The Further Adventures of Anatole. McPhail, Michael David (1940-) & O'Connor, John, illus. LC 78-20574. (Illus.). 120 p. 21cm. c.1979. (ISBN 0-15-239082-0). Harcourt Brace Jovanovich.
--The Marzipan Moon. 1st ed. Sewall, Marcia (1935-), illus. LC 80-24221. (Illus.). 48 p. 22cm. c.1981. (ISBN 0-15-252962-4). (ISBN 0-15-252963-2). Harcourt Brace Jovanovich.
--The Merry History of a Christmas Pie: With a Delicious Description of a Christmas Soup. Shekerjian, Haig & Shekerjian, Regina, illus. LC 74-79675. (Illus.). 32 p. 20cm. c.1974. (ISBN 0-399-20421-0). Putnam.
--The Nightgown of the Sullen Moon. 1st ed. McPhail, Michael David (1940-), illus. LC 83-8472. (Illus.). 30 p. c.1983. (ISBN 0-15-257429-8). Harcourt Brace Jovanovich.
--Papa's Panda. 1st ed. Hoban, Lillian (1925-), illus. LC 78-31787. p. cm. c.1979. (ISBN 0-15-259462-0). Harcourt Brace Jovanovich.
--Sailing to Cythera and Other Anatole Stories. McPhail, Michael David (1940-), illus. LC 74-5602. 80p. (gr. k up). 1974. (ISBN 0-15-269960-0, HJ). HarBraceJ.
--Shoes Without Leather. Lydecker, Laura, illus. LC 75-45512. (Illus.). 31 p. 23cm. c.1976. (ISBN 0-399-20499-7). Putnam.
--Simple Pictures are Best. 1st ed. De Paola, Tomie, pseud. (1934-), illus. De Paola, Thomas Anthony. LC 76-4923. (Illus.). 32 p. c.1977. (ISBN 0-15-274958-6). Harcourt Brace Jovanovich.
--Simple Pictures are Best. 1st Voyager/HBJ ed. De Paola, Tomie, pseud. (1934-), illus. De Paola, Thomas Anthony. LC 78-6424. p. cm. (Voyager/HBJ Book). 1978. (ISBN 0-15-682625-9). Harcourt Brace Jovanovich.
--The Snow Rabbit. Lydecker, Laura, illus. LC 75-10675. (Illus.). 32 p. 19cm. c.1975. (ISBN 0-399-20474-1). Putnam.
--Strangers' Bread. 1st ed. McPhail, Michael David (1940-), illus. LC 75-41361. (Illus.). 30 p. 22cm. 1977. (ISBN 0-15-281750-6). Harcourt Brace Jovanovich.
--Uncle Terrible: More Adventures of Anatole. 1st ed. McPhail, Michael David (1940-), illus. LC 82-47940. (Illus.). 120 p. 22cm. c.1982. (ISBN 0-15-292793-X). Harcourt Brace Jovanovich.
--A Visit to William Blake's Inn: Poems for Innocent & Experienced Travelers. Provensen, Alice (1918-) & Provensen, Martin (1916-), illus. LC 80-27403. (Illus.). 44p. 1981. (ISBN 0-15-293822-2, HJ). (ISBN 0-15-293823-0). HarBraceJ. **Awards: (JNM); (ALA); (RCM).**
--The Well-Mannered Balloon. 1st ed. Shekerjian, Haig & Shekerjian, Regina, illus. LC 75-29158. (Illus.). 29 p. 22cm. c.1976. (ISBN 0-15-294985-2). Harcourt Brace Jovanovich.
Willcocks, M. P., tr. see France, Anatole.
Willcox, Kathleen Mary
--Ann and Peter in Switzerland. Toothill, Harry & Toothill, Ilse, illus. LC 65-4801. 144p. illus., map. 19cm. (Kennedys abroad). c.1965. F. Muller.
Willcox, Louise Collier, Mrs. (1865-1929), ed.
--The Torch: A Book of Poems for Boys. Green, Elizabeth Shippen, et al., illus. LC 24-13154. xxiii p., 2 l., 3-514 p. col. front., col. front., col. plates. 24 cm. 1924. Harper & Brothers.
Willems-Treeman, Elizabeth, tr. see Bouhuys, Mies.
Willen, Drenka (1931-), tr. see Kusan, Ivan.
Willenborg, Lee
--The Golden Ram. Willenborg, Lee, illus. LC 38-22137. 201 p. col. front., plates. 21 cm. c.1938. David McKay Company.
--Old Ruddy and Other Forest People. Shepherd, J. Clinton, illus. LC 25-13540. 242 p. illus., col. pl. 19 1/2 cm. c.1935. Rand, McNally & Company.

--Prep Scraps. Clarke, William Wallace, illus. LC 27-18305. vii, 3, 240 p. incl. front., illus. col. pl. 19 1/2 cm. c.1927. Rand, McNally & Company.

Willet, Billie M

--The Adventures of Jenny. Robin, G, ed. N.D. Carlton Press.

Willett, Edward (1923-)

--Around the House. Kendrick, Charles, illus. LC 16-10105. 46 p. col. front., col. illus. 25 x 20 1/2 cm. c.1882. R. Worthington.

--Cats Cradle: Rhymes for Children. New. ed. Kendrick, Charles, illus. LC 17-1327. 25cm. 60p. 1881. Worthington's Sons.

Willett, Franciscus

--Tales of the California Missions. Holland, Cajetan, illus. LC 64-3392. 120 p. illus. 23 cm. 1964. Holy Cross Press.

Willett, John (1932-)

--The Singer in the Stone. LC 80-22771. 86 p. 22cm. 1981. (ISBN 0-395-30374-5). Houghton Mifflin Co.

Willey, Margaret

--The Bigger Book of Lydia. 1st ed. LC 82-48842. p. cm. c.1983. (ISBN 0-06-026485-3). (ISBN 0-06-026486-1). Harper & Row.

Willhelm, Lola Kerr (1882-)

--Prairie Song. 1st ed. Martin, Barry, illus. LC 53-205133. unpaged. illus. 24cm. 1952. Pageant Press.

William, Thomas

--Prince Donkey: A Christmas Story. Gooder, Marty, illus. LC 79-101686. (Illus.). 30 p., 1 leaf of plates. 23cm. c.1977. Dow Publications.

William Andrews Clark Memorial Library, Univ. of California at Los Angeles see Ogilby, John.

Williams, Albert Nathaniel (1914-)

--Simon Peter, Fisher of Men: A Fictionalized Autobiography of the Apostle Peter. 159p. illus. 20cm. (Heroes of God series). 1954. Association Press.

Williams, Alexander (1939-), adapted by see Ali Baba.

Williams, Alexander (1939-), retold by.

--Aesop's Fables. Moffett, John, illus. LC 78-72135. (Illus.). 32 p. 23cm. 1979. (ISBN 0-89799-083-8). (ISBN 0-89799-058-7). Dandelion Press.

Williams, Alice L, compiled by.

--The Children. LC 20-17793. 63, 1 p. front., pl. 18 1/2 cm. 1886. S. E. Cassino.

Williams, Alice Marietta (1901-)

--On Hampton Street. 1st ed. Vaughan, Anne (1913-), illus. LC 47-311115. vii, 183 p. illus. 22 cm. 1947. Longmans, Green.

Williams, Ann Cox

--Emily Jane. Furan, Barbara J., illus. (Illus.). 31 p. 29cm. 1968. T. S. Denison.

Williams, Anne

--National Traits and Fairy-Lore. Custis, Eleanor Parke, illus. Hartwell, S. O., frwd. by. LC 28-6411. xix, p., 3 l., 3-191 p. incl. front., illus. 18 1/2 cm. c.1928. C. Scribner's Sons.

Williams, Anne Sinclair

--Secret of the Round Tower. Kocsis, James C. (1936-), illus. Paul, James, pseud. (Illus.). 87 p. 24cm. 1968. Random House.

Williams, Annie Bowles see J. A. K, pseud.

Williams, Annie Bowles

--The Birchwood Ser. J. A. K, pseud. (Illus.). (8 vols.). N.D. Thomas Y. Crowell & Co.'s Catalogue.

--The Giant Dwarf. J. A. K, pseud. N.D. Thomas Y. Crowell.

--Rolf and His Friends. J. A. K, pseud. N.D. Thomas Y. Crowell & Co.'s Catalogue.

--Scotch Caps. J. A. K, pseud. (Illus.). N.D. Thomas Y. Crowell & Co.'s Catalogue.

Williams, Barbara M. (1925-)

--Albert's Toothache. 1st ed. Chorao, Ann Mckay Sproat (1936-), illus. LC 74-4040. (Illus.). 32 p. 1974. (ISBN 0-525-25368-8). Dutton.

--Brigham Young and Me, Clarissa. 1st ed. LC 77-27721. 80 p. 22cm. c.1978. (ISBN 0-385-14019-3). (ISBN 0-385-14020-7). Doubleday.

--Chester Chipmunk's Thanksgiving. 1st ed. Chorao, Ann Mckay Sproat (1936-), illus. LC 77-20812. (Illus.). 32 p. 24cm. c.1978. (ISBN 0-525-27655-6). Dutton.

--Freddie & the Ten Commandments. 3rd ed. 1978. Crusade Pubs.

--Freddie & the Ten Commandments: Ideal Book for Children. 2nd ed. N.D. Crusade Pubs.

--Gary and the Very Terrible Monster. Axeman, Lois, illus. LC 72-8435. (Illus.). 31 p. 25cm. 1973. Childrens Press.

--Guess Who's Coming to My Tea Party. Salzman, Yuri, illus. LC 77-10548. (Illus.). 32 p. 24cm. c.1978. (ISBN 0-03-021541-2). Holt, Rinehart and Winston.

--Hello, Dandelions!. LC 78-14088. (Illus.). (gr. k-1). 1979. (ISBN 0-03-048326-3). HR&W.

--The Horrible, Impossible Bad Witch Child. LC 81-70558. p. cm. (Avon/Camelot book). (A Snuggle & Read Story Book). c.1982. (ISBN 0-380-80283-X). Avon Books.

--If He's My Brother. De Paola, Tomie, pseud. (1934-), illus. De Paola, Thomas Anthony. LC 75-27480. (Illus.). 32 p. c.1976. (ISBN 0-8178-5422-3). Harvey House.

--Jeremy Isn't Hungry. 1st ed. Alexander, Martha G (1920-), illus. LC 78-4924. (Illus.). 32 p. c.1978. Dutton.

--Kevin's Grandma. 1st ed. Chorao, Ann Mckay Sproat (1936-), illus. LC 74-23713. (Illus.). 32 p. 1975. (ISBN 0-525-33115-8). Dutton.

--Kevin's Grandma. Chorao, Ann Mckay Sproat (1936-), illus. LC 78-103154. (Illus.). 32 p. (Anytime books ; 25). 1978, c.1975. (ISBN 0-525-45039-4). Dutton.

--Mitzi & Frederick the Great. McCully, Emily Arnold (1939-), illus. LC 83-20808. (Illus.). 128p. (gr. 2-4). 1984. (ISBN 0-525-44099-2). (ISBN 0-525-44099-2). Dutton.

--Mitzi and the Elephants. McCully, Emily Arnold (1939-) LC 84-13743. (Illus.). 101 p. 21cm. c.1985. (ISBN 0-525-44158-1). Dutton.

--Mitzi and the Terrible Tyrannosaurus Rex. 1st ed. McCully, Emily Arnold (1939-), illus. LC 81-12665. (Illus.). 102 p. 21cm. c.1982. (ISBN 0-525-45105-6). Dutton.

--Mitzi's Honeymoon with Nana Potts. 1st ed. McCully, Emily Arnold (1939-), illus. LC 83-14086. (Illus.). 104 p. 21cm. c.1983. (ISBN 0-525-44078-X). E.P. Dutton.

--Never Hit a Porcupine. 1st ed. Rockwell, Anne F (1934-), illus. LC 76-50030. (Illus.). 32 p. 18cm. c.1977. (ISBN 0-525-35693-2). Dutton.

--The Secret Name. 1st ed. Perrott, Jennifer, illus. LC 75-187858. (Illus.). 123 p. 21cm. 1972. (ISBN 0-15-272227-0). Harcourt Brace Jovanovich.

--So What If I'm a Sore Loser?. 1st ed. Edwards, Linda Strauss, illus. LC 80-24783. (Illus.). 40 p. 21cm. c.1981. Harcourt Brace Jovanovich.

--Someday, Said Mitchell. 1st ed. Chorao, Ann Mckay Sproat (1936-), illus. LC 75-33247. (Illus.). 32 p. 26cm. c.1976. (ISBN 0-525-39580-6). Dutton.

--Tell the Truth, Marly Dee. 1st ed. LC 82-4997. p. cm. c.1982. (ISBN 0-525-44020-8). Dutton.

--A Valentine for Cousin Archie. 1st ed. Chorao, Ann Mckay Sproat (1936-), illus. LC 80-181. (Illus.). 32 p. 25cm. c.1981. Dutton.

--We Can Jump. Maloney, Mary P. & Fleming, Stanley, illus. LC 72-8346. (Illus.). 31 p. 25cm. 1973. (ISBN 0-516-03664-5). Childrens Press.

--Whatever Happened to Beverly Bigler's Birthday?. 1st ed. McCully, Emily Arnold (1939-), illus. LC 78-20575. (Illus.). 64 p. 22cm. (Let me read book). c.1979. (ISBN 0-15-696083-4). Harcourt Brace Jovanovich.

--Where are You, Angela Von Hauptmann, Now That I Need You?. LC 79-1069. 192 p. 22cm. c.1979. (ISBN 0-03-050606-9). Holt, Rinehart, and Winston.

Williams, Ben, illus.

--A Teeny Tiny Tale. LC 55-40522. (Illus.). 17cm. (Tell a Tale Books: 2513). 1955. Whitman Pub. Co.

Williams, Beulah Bland

--Dude, the White Pony. LC 51-32. 48p. 23cm. 1950. Vantage Press.

Williams, Bill, illus.

--Winnie the Pooh All Year Long. (Illus.). 14p. (Golden Sturdy Shape Bks.). 1981. (ISBN 0-307-12260-3, Golden Pr). Western Pub.

Williams, Blanche Colton, ed.

--A Book of Short Stories. N.D. Appleton-Century-Crofts.

--The Mystery and the Detective. N.D. Appleton-Century-Crofts.

Williams, Charles Wilbur

--It Was All Very Strange. Elgin, Kathleen (1923-), illus. LC 53-10643. 159p. illus. 22cm. 1953. Abelard Press.

--The Rolling Pin. Graboff, Abner (1919-), illus. LC 55-5374. 174p. illus. 22cm. 1955. Abelard-Schuman.

Williams, Chester Sidney, jt. auth. see Disney, Walt, Productions.

Williams, Clara, jt. auth. see Williams, George Alfred.

Williams, Clara A., jt. auth. see Williams, George Alfred.

Williams, Clara Andrews, Mrs. (1882-)

--The Magic Book: Adventures of Jack and Betty. Williams, George Alfred (1875-), illus. LC 13-68957. 1 p. l., 64 p. illus. (part col.) 28 cm. c.1912. Frederick A. Stokes Company.

--Mammy's Li'l' Chilluns. Williams, Clara Andrews (1882-), illus. LC 4-30578. 63 p. col. illus. 23 1/2 cm. 1904. F. A. Stokes Company.

Williams, D. C., ed. see Montgomery, Lucy Maud.

Williams, Dorian (1914-)

--Pancho: The Story of a Horse. Ward, Owen, illus. (Illus.). 126 p. 21cm. 1968, c.1967. Walker.

Williams, Dorothy Jeanne see Williams, J. R., pseud.

Williams, Dorothy Jeanne (1930-)

--The Confederate Fiddle. Williams, J. R., pseud. LC 62-11898. 192 p. 21 cm. 1962. Prentice-Hall.

--Coyote Winter. LC 65-18038. 206p. 21cm. c.1965. Norton.

--Freedom Trail. LC 72-150583. 156 p. 21cm. 1973. (ISBN 0-399-20336-2). (ISBN 0-399-20336-2). Putnam.

--The Horse Talker. Williams, J. R., pseud. LC 60-15129. 177 p. 22cm. 1960. Prentice-Hall.

--Mission in Mexico. Williams, J. R., pseud. LC 59-13100. 186 p. 22cm. 1959. Prentice-Hall.

--New Medicine. LC 75-118076. 159 p. 21cm. 1971. Putnam.

--Oh, Susanna!. Williams, J. R., pseud. Orbaan, Albert F. (1913-), illus. LC 63-15567. 222 p. illus. 21 cm. 1963. Putnam.

--Oil Patch Partners. 1st ed. 179 p. 21cm. 1968. Meredith Press.

--Promise of Tomorrow. LC 59-12770. 192 p. 22cm. 1959. Messner.

--Tame the Wild Stallion. Williams, J. R., pseud. LC 57-12622. 181 p. 22 cm. 1957. Prentice-Hall.

--Tame the Wild Stallion. LC 84-16257. p. cm. 1985, c.1957. (ISBN 0-87565-002-3). (ISBN 0-87565-009-0). Texas Christian University Press.

--To Buy a Dream. LC 58-6010. 102 p. 22 cm. 1958. Messner.

--Winter Wheat. LC 74-21080. 157 p. 21cm. 1975. (ISBN 0-399-20445-8). Putnam.

Williams, E. Harcourt (1880-)

--Tales from Ebony. 167p. N.D. British Book Centre.

--Tales from Ebony. Tunnicliffe, Charles Frederick (1901-), illus. LC 37-20325. xiii p., 1 l., 258 p. col. front., illus., col. plates. 22 cm. c.1935. G. P. Putnam's Sons.

--Three Fairy Plays. LC 26-3909. 30 p. 21 1/2 cm. c.1925. S. French, Ltd.

Williams, E. W., ed. see Forbes, Steven.

Williams, Edward

--Not Like Niggers. LC 78-83396. 190p. (gr. 7-9). 1969. St Martin.

Williams, Edward B.

--The Millionaire Shoemaker. N.D. Dorrance & Co.

Williams, Edward Huntington (1868-1944)

--Animal Autobiographies. LC 30-14222. 123 p. 19 1/2 cm. 1930. The Williams & Wilkins Company.

--Larry of the North. LC 26-16050. 5 p. l., 254 p. front., plates. 19 1/2 cm. c.1926. Harper & Brothers.

--Red Plume. Stinemetz, Morgan, illus. LC 25-17148. 3 p. l., 249 p. front., plates. 19 cm. c.1925. Harper & Brothers.

--Red Plume of the Royal Northwest Mounted. Durant, Charles, illus. LC 28-25635. 20cm. 246p. (Adventure Library). 1928. Harper & Bros.

--Red Plume Returns. Stinemetz, Morgan, illus. LC 27-14799. 5 p. l., 269 p. front., plates. 19 1/2 cm. c.1927. Harper & Brothers.

Williams, Effie M

--A Hive of Busy Bees. Booram, Lucile, illus. LC 31-34929. 94 p. illus. 22 1/2 cm. c.1931. The Warner Press.

Williams, Eleanor Troy

--And a Good Fat Hen. Williams, Eleanor Troy (1907-1979) & Gag, Flavia, illus. LC 39-6474. 47 p. illus. 25 1/2 cm. c.1939. G. P. Putnam's Sons.

Williams, Elizabeth (1850-1922)

--Three Vassar Girls in France. (Illus.). (Mrs. Champney's Famous Vassar Girls Ser). N.D. Estes & Lauriat's.

--Three Vassar Girls in Italy. (Illus.). (Mrs. Champney's Famous Vassar Girls Ser.). N.D. Estes & Lauriat's.

--Three Vassar Girls in Turkey. (Illus.). (Mrs. Champney's Famous Vassar Girls Ser). N.D. Estes & Lauriat's.

--Three Vassar in the Holy Land. (Illus.). (Mrs. Champney's Famous Vassar Girls Ser). N.D. Estes & Lauriat's.

Williams-Ellis, Amabel, Mrs. (1894-), retold by.

--Arabian Nights. Baynes, Pauline Diana (1922-), illus. (gr. 3 up). 1977. (ISBN 0-8277-5368-3). British Bk Ctr.

--Arabian Nights. Baynes, Pauline Diana (1922-), illus. (Illus.). (gr. 4-6). 1957. (ISBN 0-87599-127-0). S G Phillips.

--British Fairy Tales. (ps-5). 1977. (ISBN 0-8277-5366-7). British Bk Ctr.

--Fairies and Enchanters: A New Book of Old English Stories, Providing Also Intelligence of Sundry Giants, Lobs, Mermaids, Witches, Boggarts, Pisgies, Knights, Princesses and Dragons of This Land Whose Histories (Now Carefully Collected) Were Before in Great Danger of Being Forgotten. Hickson, Wilma, illus. LC 34-58994. ix, 301 p. col. front., illus., col. plates. 21 cm. 1934. T. Nelson and Son.

--Fairy Tales from East & West. Stobbs, William (1914-), illus. (ps-5). 1977. (ISBN 0-8277-5419-1). (ISBN 0-8277-5372-1). British Bk Ctr.

--Fairy Tales from East & West. Stobbs, William (1914-), illus. (Illus., Orig.). 1978. (ISBN 0-8467-0535-4, Pub. by Two Continents). Hippocrene Bks.

--Fairy Tales from Everywhere. Stobbs, William (1914-), illus. (ps-5). 1977. (ISBN 0-8277-5417-5). (ISBN 0-8277-5370-5). British Bk Ctr.

--Fairy Tales from Here & There. Stobbs, William (1914-), illus. (ps-5). 1977. (ISBN 0-8277-5416-7). (ISBN 0-8277-5369-1). British Bk Ctr.

--Fairy Tales from Near & Far. Stobbs, William (1914-), illus. (ps-5). 1977. (ISBN 0-8277-5418-3). (ISBN 0-8277-5371-3). British Bk Ctr.

--Fairy Tales from the British Isles. Baynes, Pauline Diana (1922-), illus. LC 64-17125. 344 p. illus. (part col.) 23 cm. 1964, c.1960. Warne.

--Fairy Tales from the British Isles. Baynes, Pauline Diana (1922-), illus. LC 64-17125. (Illus.). 344p. 23cm. 1964, c.1960. Warne.

--The Lassie of Glengarry. 2 p. l., 3-192 p. front., 3 pl. 18 1/2 cm. c.1894. American Baptist Publication Society.

--More British Fairy Tales. 1977. (ISBN 0-8277-5367-5). British Bk Ctr.

--Old World & New World Fairy Tales. Stobbs, William (1914-), illus. LC 67-18015. (Illus.). 359 p. 23cm. 1966. F. Warne.

--Round the World Fairy Tales. Stobbs, William (1914-), illus. LC 66-103139. 303p. illus. (pt. col.) 33cm. 1966, c.1963. Warne.

--Round the World Fairy Tales. Stobbs, William (1914-), illus. (Illus.). (gr. 3-6). 1966. (ISBN 0-7232-6028-1). Warne.

Williams-Ellis, Amabel (1894-), ed. see Arabian Nights.

Williams-Ellis, Amabel, jt. ed. see Budberg, Moura.

Williams-Ellis, Amabel, Mrs. (1894-) & Budberg, Moura, eds.

--Russian Fairy Tales. Nechamkin, Sarah, illus. (Illus.). (gr. 3-6). 1967. (ISBN 0-7232-6025-7). Warne.

Williams-Ellis, Amabel, Mrs. (1894-) & Pearson, Michael, eds.

--Strange Orbits: An Anthology of Science Fiction. LC 76-382972. 3-190 p. 23cm. 1976. Blackie.

Williams, Eustace Leroy

--The Mutineers. Hazelton, Isaac Brewster, illus. LC 3-13817. (Illus.). 20cm. 291p. 1903. Lothrop Lee & Shepard Co.

--The Substitute Quarter-back: Or, The Quality of Mercy. Bridgman, Lewis Jesse (1857-1931), illus. LC 19-226. 12cm. 213p. 1900. Dana Estes & Co.

Williams, Frances J (1935-)

--Red Mouse. Goins, Ellen Haynes (1927-), illus. LC 67-17331. (Illus.). 32 p. 22cm. 1967. Steck-Vaughn Co.

Williams, Frances Leigh (1909-)

--The Shawnee Tomahawk: A True Story of an American Frontier Boy, 1784-1797. 1st ed. Turkle, Brinton Cassaday (1915-), illus. LC 58-6519. (Illus.). 189 p. 21cm. 1958. Holt.

--Welcome to Dunecrest. LC 55-9869. 189p. 21cm. (Romance for young moderns). 1955. Messner.

Williams, Frances Royster

--Cuddles and Tuckie. Williams, Frances Royster, illus. LC 42-11709. 63, 1 p. illus. 23 1/2 cm. 1942. Brown-White-Lowell Press.

--Cuddles and Tuckie Time. Williams, Frances Royster, illus. LC 79-2184. (Illus.). 27cm. 91p. c.1980. (ISBN 0-913504-51-3). Lowell Press.

Williams, Garth Montgomery (1912-)

--The Adventures of Benjamin Pink. Williams, Garth Montgomery (1912-), illus. LC 51-12367. 151 p. illus. 21 cm. 1951. Harper.

--Animal Friends Everywhere!. Williams, Garth Montgomery (1912-), illus. (Illus.). (Golden Storytime Bks.). (ps). 1980. (ISBN 0-307-15514-5, Golden Pr). Western Pub.

--Baby Animals. Williams, Garth Montgomery (1912-), illus. LC 52-12563. unpaged illus. 21 cm. (Golden book, 477). 1952. Simon and Schuster.

--Baby Animals. Williams, Garth Montgomery (1912-), illus. LC 57-1089. (Illus.). 1 v. (unpaged. 21cm. (Little golden book, 274). 1957, c.1956. Simon and Schuster.

--Baby Farm Animals. Williams, Garth Montgomery (1912-), illus. LC 53-3515. 21cm. (Big Golden Book: 481). 1953. Golden Press.

--Baby Farm Animals. Williams, Garth Montgomery (1912-), illus. (Little Golden Book). 1958. Golden Press.

--Baby Farm Animals. Williams, Garth Montgomery (1912-), illus. (Big Golden Book). 1959. Golden Press.

--Baby's First Book. Williams, Garth MOntgomery (1912-), illus. (Little Golden Book). 1959. Golden Press.

--Baby's First Book. Williams, Garth Montgomery (1912-), illus. LC 55-1685. (Illus.). unpage. 21cm. (Golden book, 489). c.1955. Simon and Schuster.

--The Chicken Book. Williams, Garth Montgomery (1912-), illus. LC 46-22690. (Illus.) 21 x 24cm. 31p. 1946. Howell, Soskin.

--The Chicken Book: A Traditional Rhyme. Williams, Garth Montgomery (1912-), illus. LC 69-12504. (Illus.). line drawings. 48p. (ps-3). 1970. Delacorte.

AUTHOR INDEX WILSON, CALVIN

--The Island Mystery. Fleming, Waldo, pseud. 4 p. l., 13-317 p. front., illus. 20 1/2 cm. 1939. Lothrop, Lee and Shepard Company.
--The Lapp Mystery: A Boy's Story of Finnish Lapland. Smith, S. S., pseud. Reid, James (1907-), illus. LC 34-30545. 6 p. l., 3-296 p. incl. illus., plates. front. 22 cm. c.1934. Harcourt, Brace and Company.
--The Last of the Gauchos: A Boys' Tale of Argentine Adventure. Hubbard, Frank, illus. LC 37-190093. 301 p. incl. front., illus. 21 cm. c.1937. The Bobbs-Merrill Company.
--The Lobster War. Orr, Forrest W., illus. LC 35-23310. 6 p. l., 3-334 p. incl. illus., plates. front. 20 1/2 cm. 1935. Lothrop, Lee and Shepard Company.
--The Lost Caravan: A Boys' Story of the Sahara Desert. Fleming, Waldo, pseud. LC 35-14566. 6 p. l., 303 p. front. 20 1/2 cm. 1935. Doubleday, Doran & Company, Inc.
--Messenger to the Pharaoh: A/Story of Ancient Egypt. De Wolfe, Morgan, pseud. 1st ed. O'Brian, William, illus. LC 37-17024. (Illus.). viii, 312. 20cm. 1937. Longmans, Green and Co.
--On the Reindeer Trail. Townsend, Lee ([illegible]), illus. LC 32-17786. ix, 1 p., 2 l., 242, 1 p. front., illus., plates. 21 cm. 1932. Houghton Mifflin Company.
--Opening Davy Jone's Locker: A Boy Explores the Bottom of the Sea. Rogers, Hubert, illus. LC 30-22896. 5 p. l., 309, 1 p. col. front., illus. 21 cm. 1930. Houghton Mifflin Company.
--Pygmy's Arrow. Fleming, Waldo, pseud. Dobias, Frank (1902-), illus. LC 38-32851. 4 p. l., 3-310 p. front., illus. 20 1/2 cm. 1938. Lothrop, Lee and Shepard Company.
--A Riddle in Fez: A Boys' Story of Morocco. Fleming, Waldo, pseud. Dobias, Frank (1902-), illus. LC 37-28565. 5 p. l., 297 p. col. front., illus. 21 cm. 1937. Doubleday, Doran & Co., Inc.
--Saltar, the Mongol. Dragonet, Edward, pseud. Riesenberg, Sidney, illus. LC 38-25696. 6 p. l., 226 p. incl. illus., plates. col. front. 22 cm. 1938. Harper & Brothers.
--The Spy Mystery: A Boys' Story of Soviet Russia. Smith, S. S., pseud. Reid, James (1907-), illus. LC 37-18245. 7 p. l., 3-353 p. incl. illus., plates. front. 22 cm. c.1937. Harcourt, Brace and Company.
--Talking Drums: A Boy's Story of the African Gold Coast. Fleming, Waldo, pseud. Dobias, Frank (1902-), illus. LC 36-179462. 6 p. l., 307 p. col. front., illus. 21 cm. 1936. Doubleday, Doran & Company, Inc.
--A Tamer of Beasts: A Boys' Story of the Early Neolithic Period. Trent, Gregory, pseud. Boog, Carle Michel, illus. LC 38-18121. 7 p. l., incl. illus., plates. front. 22 1/2 cm. c.1938. Harcourt, Brace and Company.
Williard
--The Highest Hit. (gr. 4-6). N.D. (ISBN 0-590-30051-2, Schol Pap). Scholastic Inc.

Willier, Elizabeth Chapman
--Fun and Adventure. 1964. Carlton Press.
--Heroes and Heroines: A Book Containing Only Happy Dog Stories. 1st ed. Martin, Barry, illus. LC 55-12524. 90p. illus. 24cm. c.1955. Pageant Press.
Willing, Jennie Fowler, Mrs. (1834-)
--The Little-Book Man. LC 12-40281. 264 p. front. (port.) 3 pl. 19 1/2 cm. 1894. Cranston & Curts.
--Through the Dark to the Day: A Story. N.D. Methodist Book Concern.
Willington, Louisa Penn & Irving, Washington (1783-1859)
--Aunt Louisa's Rip Van Winkle. LC 77-79198. (Illus.). 24 p. 29cm. c.1977. (ISBN 0-8055-0357-9). Hart Pub. Co.
Willis, Bess Goe & Hoopes, Margaret Campbell, illus.
--The Bedtime Animal Story Book. 60 p., 1 l., incl. col. front., col. illus. 24 1/2 cm. c.1931. Henry Altemus Company.
Willis, Charles Ethelbert (1857-)
--Scouts of '76: A Tale of the Revolutionary War. LC 24-28336. xii p., 1 l., 344 p. col. front., illus. 20 cm. 1924. The Dietz Printing Co.
Willis, Christine, illus.
--Sing a Song of Seasons. LC 79-64439. (Illus.). 12 p. 20cm. (Gingerboard book). c.1979. (ISBN 0-525-69401-3). Dutton.
Willis, Corinne
--Boy Minus Girl. LC 67-23576. 184 p. 21cm. 1967. McKay.
--The Ivory Cage. Lambo, Donald W. (1903-1966), illus. LC 66-20814. 214p. illus. 21cm. 1966. McKay.
--Tilli. Lambo, Don, illus. LC 69-13788. 192p. (gr. 7-9). 1969. McKay.
Willis, Elizabeth Bayley
--Little Bay Creatures. 98p. 1938. Binfords & Mort.
Willis, Elizabeth Powers, Mrs.
--The Bronze Turkey. Hastings, Howard Livingston (1887-), illus. LC 28-7326. 300 p. col. front., col. plates. 20 1/2 cm. c.1928. Thomas Y. Crowell Company.
Willis, Fritz
--Cancan. Willis, Fritz, illus. LC 45-859158. 16 p. illus. 28 x 21 1/2 cm. 1945. A Mistletoe Press Publication; Sole Distributors: The Marcel Rodd Company.
--Clover. LC 46-5288. 21 p. col. illus. 27 1/2 x 22 cm. 1946. The Marcel Rodd Company.
--Jelly and George. LC 46-5289. 23 p. col. illus. 27 1/2 x 22 cm. 1946. The Marcel Rodd Company.
--Jelly and George. Willis, Fritz, illus. N.D. Wilcox & Follett Co.
--Me Too. N.D. Marcel Rodd Co.
--Muffin. LC 48-3292. 28cm. 16p. (Cherokee Press Publication). 1948. Marcel Rodd Co.
--Muffin. N.D. Wilcox & Follett Co.
--The Story of a Good Little Dog, Amber. Willis, Fritz, illus. LC 45-85902. 32 p. illus. (part. col.) 28 x 21 1/2 cm. 1945. A Mistletoe Press Publication The Marcel Rodd Co., Distributors.
--Sugarfoot and The Merry-Go-Round. N.D. Marcel Rodd Co.
--Taffy and the Rose Colored Glasses. N.D. Marcel Rodd Co.
Willis, Irene Cooper
--Florence Nightingale. 276p. N.D. Coward-McCann.
Willis, Irene Jolley, jt. auth. see Willis, Richard.
Willis, Jeanne
--The Tale of Fearsome Fritz. Chamberlain, Margaret, illus. LC 82-23348. p. cm. 1st U.S. edition. 1983, c.1982. (ISBN 0-03-063519-5). Holt, Rinehart, and Winston.
--The Tale of Georgie Grub. Chamberlain, Margaret, illus. LC 81-13194. (Illus.). 26 p. 24cm. 1st U.S. edition. 1982, c.1981. (ISBN 0-03-061222-5). Holt, Rinehart, and Winston.
Willis, Kristine
--The Long-Legged, Long-Nosed, Long-Maned Wolf. Willis, Kristine, illus. (Illus.). 48 p. 27cm. 1968. Steck-Vaughn Co.
Willis, Leydel J.
--Yesterday, Today, & Tomorrow, Bk. 2: Today. new ed. (gr. 8-12). 1977. (ISBN 0-8187-0030-0). Harlo Pr.
Willis, Mary Farley (1901-)
--As It Was on Pa's Farm. LC 79-90024. 22cm. 128p. (A Destiny bk.: D-189). c.1980. (ISBN 0-8163-0393-2). Pacific Press Pub. Association.
Willis, Priscilla D see Adams, Mary Scott, pseud.
Willis, Priscilla D
--Alfred and The Saint. 1st ed. Kidwell, Carl (1910-), illus. LC 52-9669. 179 p. illus. 21 cm. 1952. Longmans, Green.
--Jory and the Buckskin Jumper. Adams, Mary Scott, pseud. Bjorklund, Lorence F. (1913-1978), illus. LC 60-13876. 229 p. illus. 22 cm. 1960. St. Martin's Press.
--The Race Between the Flags. 1st ed. Kidwell, Carl (1910-), illus. LC 55-6736. (Illus.). 177 p. 21cm. 1955. Longmans, Green.
Willis, Richard (1921-) & Willis, Irene Jolley (1929-)
--The Hungry Car. Rev ed. Willis, Robert J., illus. LC 68-31314. (Illus.). 47 p. 24cm. 1968. Childrens Press.
--Rosie's Josie. Willis, Robert J., illus. LC 55-14809. unpaged. illus. 25cm. 1955. Childrens Press.
Willis, Robert J.
--Caesar's Blue Ribbon. Willis, Robert J., illus. LC 56-9864. (Illus.). 64 p. 23cm. 1956. Follett.
--Keefers' Landing. LC 64-20356. 160 p. 22 cm. 1964. Follett Pub. Co.
--Model A Mule. Mays, Lewis Victor, Jr. (1927-), illus. LC 59-10276. (Illus.). 128 p. 23cm. 1959. Follett Pub. Co.
--Molly's Hannibal. Koering, Ursula (1921-), illus. LC 57-11028. 128 p. illus. 23 cm. 1957. Follett Pub. Co.
Willis, Willma
--My Favorite City. Smith, Bob D., illus. LC 67-22723. (Illus.). 43 p. 24cm. 1967. Elk Grove Press.
Willison, George Findlay (1896-1972) & Hessian Hills School Croton-on-Hudson, N.Y, eds.
--Let's Make a Play: Twelve Plays by Children with a Discussion and Explanation of Dramatic Techniques. 1st ed. LC 41-1315. x, 302 p. 21 cm. c.1940. Harper & Brothers.
Williston, Teresa Peirce, retold by.
--Hindu Stories. Squire, Maud Hunt (1873-), illus. LC 25-24141. 111 p. incl. col. front., col. illus. 21 cm. c.1925. New York, Rand, McNally & Company.
--Hindu Tales. Squire, Maud Hunt (1873-), illus. LC 17-139122. 84 p. incl. col. front., col. illus. 19 1/2 cm. c.1917. New York, Rand, McNally & Company.
--Japanese Fairy Tales. Ogawa, Sanchi, illus. LC 4-30140. 88 p. incl. col. front., col., illus. 20 x 16 cm. 1904. Rand, McNally & Co.
--Japanese Fairy Tales. Ogawa, Sanchi, illus. LC 12-30. 96 p. incl. col. front., col. illus. 20x16 cm. c.1911. Rand McNally & Co.
--Japanese Fairy Tales. O'Gawa, Sanchi, illus. LC 49-57555. (Illus.). 84p. 21cm. 1932. Rand, McNally.
Willman, Gordon
--Mary Blount Christian's His Brother's Keeper, Plus Nine Other Stories. Willman, Gordon, illus. LC 77-13648. (Illus.). 125 p. 23cm. (Bro-kee series). c.1978. (ISBN 0-570-07765-6). Concordia Pub. House.
Willman, Gordon, jt. auth. see Puttcamp, Rita.
Willock, Ruth
--I, Victoria Strange. 200p. 1975. (ISBN 0-8015-4138-7). Hawthorn.
Willoughby, [illegible]
--The Little Mouse. Jordan, Alton, ed. Reese, Bob, illus. (Illus.). (I Can Read Underwater Bks). (gr. k-3). 1974. (ISBN 0-89868-007-7, Read Res). (ISBN 0-89868-040-9). ARO Pub.
--My Dolly. Wasserman, Dan, ed. Reese, Bob, illus. (Illus.). (Ten Word Bks.). (gr. k-1). 1979. (ISBN 0-89868-075-1). (ISBN 0-89868-086-7). ARO Pub.
Willoughby, Elaine MacMann see Macmann, Elaine.
Willoughby, Elaine Macmann (1926-)
--Boris and the Monsters. Musinger, Lynn (1951-), illus. LC 79-22603. (Illus.). 32 p. 1980. (ISBN 0-395-29067-8). Houghton Mifflin.
--Mystery of the Lobster Thieves. Keane, Raymond, illus. LC 78-52140. (Illus.). 56 p. 21cm. (Weekly Reader Children's Book Club edition). c.1978. (ISBN 0-88375-217-4). Xerox Education Publications.
--No, No, No, and Yes. Titleman, Lynn, illus. LC 72-5282. (Illus.). 40 p. 23cm. 1973. (ISBN 0-8116-6721-9). Garrard Pub. Co.
--That's How the Ball Bounces. Titleman, Lynn, illus. LC 72-729. (Illus.). 64 p. 23cm. 1972. (ISBN 0-8116-6957-2). Garrard Pub. Co.
Willoughby, F.
--Fairy Guardians: A Book for the Young. N.D. MacMillian.
Willoughby, Jane, jt. auth. see Hamilton, Morris.
Willower, Lucile
--The Morning Star. Willower, Lucile, illus. 1957. David McKay Co.
Wills, Ailsa
--Boy of the Mohawks. N.D. Transatlantic Arts.
Wills, Geoffrey
--A Friend for Frances. Cooke, Tom, illus. LC 83-2235. p. cm. c.1982. (ISBN 0-910313-04-0). Parker Brothers.
Wills, Joany B.
--Who is that Short Chef? Fleetwood, Linda, illus. (Illus.). 132p. (Orig.). 1983. (ISBN 0-938934-04-X). C&M Pubns.
Wills, Jonathan (1947-)
--The Travels of Magnus Pole. Wills, Jonathan (1947-), illus. LC 75-17025. (Illus.). 47 p. 21cm. 1975. (ISBN 0-395-21889-6). Houghton Mifflin.
Wills, Marguerite, jt. auth. see Turner, Kathleen.
Willson, Dixie
--Clown Town. LC 24-23375. 62 p. illus. (part col.) 23 1/2 cm. 1924. Doubleday, Page & Company.
--Hollywood Starlet. LC 42-137373. ix, 1 242 p. plates, ports., forms. 21 cm. (Career books). 1942. Dodd, Mead & Company.
--Honey Bear. Barney, Maginel Wright, Mrs. (1881-1966), illus. 40p. N.D. P. F. Volland Co.
--Hopalong and Lucky at the Bar Q. Carbe, Nino (1909-), illus. LC 50-11918. (Illus.). 40p. 31cm. 1950. Garden City Pub. Co.
--Hostess of the Skyways. (Dodd, Mead Career Bks.). N.D. Dodd, Mead & Co.
--Little Texas. LC 25-17705. viii p., 1 l., 268, 1 p. mounted col. front. 19 1/2 cm. 1925. D. Appleton and Company.
--Mystery in Spangles. LC 50-7795. viii, 230 p. 21 cm. (Junior Red badge mysteries). 1950. Dodd, Mead.
--Mystery of the Scarlet Staircase. LC 46-7635. viii p., 1 l., 198 p. 19 1/2 cm. 1946. Dodd, Mead & Company.
--Pinky Pup: And The Empty Elephant. Best, Allena Champlin, Mrs. (1892-1974), illus. Berry, Erick, pseud. LC 28-17483. 62 p. illus. (part. col.) 25 1/2 cm. c.1928. The P. F. Volland Company.
--Tuffy Good Luck. De Karekjarto, Ilona, illus. LC 27-232798. 39 p. col. illus. 19 cm. (Lettered on cover: Volland "Sunny book" series). c.1927. The P. F. Volland Company.
--The Veiled Mystery. LC 48-9211. viii, 194 p. 21 cm. 1948. Dodd, Mead.
Willson, Dixie, ed.
--Favorite Stories of Famous Children. Millard, C. E., illus. LC 38-31051. viii, 183, 1 p. illus. (incl. ports.) 24 cm. c.1938. H. Holt and Company.
Wilmer, Margaret E.
--The Dumb Traitor, 1 of 4 Vols. N.D. Set. Methodist Book Concern.
--The Glass Cable. 288p. N.D. National Temperance Society Pub.
--The Glass Cable, 1 of 4 Vols. (Glass Cable Ser.). N.D. Set. National Temperance Society.
--Little Girl in Black. 212p. N.D. National Temperance Society.
Wilmot-Buxton, Ethel Mary
--Stories from Old French Romance. N.D. Frederick A. Stokes.
--Stories of Early England. LC 7-22918. xv, 340 p. front., plates. 17 1/2 cm. c.1907. T. Y. Crowell & Co.
--Stories of Norse Heroes. N.D. Thomas Y. Crowell Company.
Wilmot-Buxton, Ethel Mary, retold by.
--The Book of Rustem. Firdausi. Shanama LC [illegible] 19 1/2 cm. c.1907. T. Y. Crowell & Co.
--Stories of Early England, Britain Long Ago. LC 30-10014. xv, 240 p. front., plates. 19 1/2 cm. 1929. Thomas Y. Crowell Company.
Wilner, Isabel, compiled by.
--The Poetry Troupe: An Anthology of Poems to Read Aloud. Wilner, Isabel, illus. LC 77-9439. p. cm. 1977. (ISBN 0-684-15198-7). Scribner.
Wilson, A. E.
--Penny Plain, Two-Pence Coloured. N.D. MacMillan.
Wilson, Adrian, ed. see Wilson, Joyce Lancaster.
Wilson, Albert Frederick
--Higher Than the Wind Can Blow. Schmitt, Carl, illus. LC 34-34434. (Illus.). 184p. 20cm. 1934. Dodd, Mead and Company.
Wilson, Alice
--Life with Tony. (Illus.). 1977. (ISBN 0-533-02918-X). Vantage.
--Poems for Little People. N.D. Harbinger House.
Wilson, Alice & Moloney, Louis
--Flashback!-I Didn't Know That. (Orig.). 1980. (ISBN 0-87602-236-0). Anchorage.
Wilson, Anneliza Carruthers see Wilson, Annie E., pseud.
Wilson, Anneliza Carruthers
--An Ivy Vine, and How it Grew. Wilson, Annie E., pseud. LC 3-1279. 333p. 19cm. 1902. The Presbyterian Committee of Publication.
--Love's Leading Strings. LC 2-19383. 282 p. front., plates. 19 cm. 1902. American Baptist Publication Society.
--True Story of a Jewish Maiden. LC 98-202. 198 p. 19 cm. 1897. Presbyterian Committee of Publication.
Wilson, Annie E., pseud., see Wilson, Anneliza Carruthers.
Wilson, Anthony Clifford (1916-)
--Mystery Tour. LC 55-5840. 163p. 21cm. 1954, c.1953. Crowell.
--Norman and Henry Investigate. Werth, Kurt (1896-), illus. LC 54-55425. 176p. illus. 21cm. 1954, c.1953. Crowell.
--Norman Bones, Detective. Werth, Kurt (1896-), illus. LC 51-5489. 248p. illus. 21cm. 1951. Crowell.
Wilson-Bailey, Eve, Mrs. (1873-)
--Aloysius, the Dragon. LC 40-32790. 46, 1 p. illus. (part col.) 27 1/2 cm. c.1940. Eve Wilson-Bailey.
Wilson, Barbara Ker see Fontannza, Luciennec & Ker Wilson, Barbara.
Wilson, Barbara Ker see Ker Wilson, Barbara.
Wilson, Barbara Ker see Ker Wilson, Barbara (1929-) & Bates, Daisy.

Wilson, Beth
--Little Red Hen. Wilson, Beth, illus. LC 54-22398. unpaged. illus. 17cm. (Tell-a-tale books, 980). c.1953. Whitman Pub. Co.
Wilson, Beth Pierre
--The Great Minu. Pinkney, Jerry (1939-), illus. LC 73-90047. (Illus.). 32 p. 23cm. 1974. (ISBN 0-695-80409-X). (ISBN 0-695-80409-X). Follett Pub. Co.
Wilson, Bettye Dobson
--We Are All Americans. Weiss, Carl K., illus. LC 59-7259. unpaged. illus. 27 cm. 1959. Friendly House Publishers.
Wilson, Bingham Thoburn (1867-1937)
--The Village of Hide and Seek. Dunton, W. Herbert, illus. LC 5-34513. 190 p. 8 col. (incl. front.) 21 cm. 1905. Consolidated Retail Booksellers.
Wilson, Bob
--Stanley Bagshaw & the Twenty-Two Ton Whale. (Illus.). 32p. 1st U.S. edition. (ps-3). 1984. (ISBN 0-241-10812-8, Pub. by Hamish Hamilton England). David & Charles.
Wilson, Calvin Dill (1857-), retold by.
--The Child's Don Quixote. LC 1-13700. 251p. 1901. T. Y. Crowell.
--Don Quixote. (Illus.). (Children's Favorite Classics). 1915. Thomas Y Crowell.
--The Story of the Cid for Young People. Kennedy, J. W. Ferguson, illus. LC 1-118058. 1 p. l., 313 p. front., plates. 19 cm. 1901. Lee and Shepard.
--The Story of the Cid: For Young People. Kennedy, J. W. Ferguson, illus. (Illus.). 300p. 1905. Lee and Shepard Company.

Wilson, Carter (1941-)
--On Firm Ice. Berry, William A., illus. LC 74-78267. (Illus.). 103 p. 24cm. 1969. Crowell.
Wilson, Charles George (1906-)
--Guns in the Wilderness. N.D. McKay.
--Guns in the Wilderness: A Story of Colonial Days. Meyers, Robert William (1919-), illus. LC 51-12252. 191 p. illus. 21 cm. 1951. Washburn.
--Sentry in the Night: A Story of the American Revolution. Murch, Frank J., illus. LC 53-11354. 214p. illus. 21cm. c.1953. Washburn.
--Sword of Francisco. Campbell, Ray Scott, illus. LC 56-115315. 147p. illus. 21cm. 1956. Crowell.
--The Winds Blow Free: A Story of the American Revolution. Busoni, Rafaello (1900-1962), illus. LC 50-7308. 198 p. illus. 21 cm. 1950. I. Washburn.
Wilson, Charles Morrow (1905-1977)
--Butterscotch and the Happy Barnyard. Swanson, Jean D., illus. LC 52-5213. 24cm. 105p. N.D. Caxton Printers.
--Crown Point: The Destiny Road. Vosburgh, Leonard W. (1912-), illus. LC 65-169131. xii, 191p. illus. 21cm. 1965. McKay.
--Ginger Blue. Sheldon, Myrtle, illus. LC 40-690366. 206 p. incl. col. front., illus. 21 1/2 cm. 1940. The Caxton Printers, Ltd.
--The Great Turkey Drive. Vosburgh, Leonard W. (1912-), illus. LC 64-12981. (Illus.). xii, 145 p. 21cm. 1964. McKay.
--The Green Mountain Toymakers. LC 65-215957. v, 149p. 21cm. c.1965. Washburn Dist. McKay.
Wilson, Christopher Bernard
--Growing up with Daddy. Wilson, Dagmar (1916-), illus. LC 57-5997. unpaged. illus. 26 cm. c.1957. Lothrop, Lee & Shepard.
--Hobnob. Wiesner, William (1899-), illus. LC 68-27565. (Illus.). l v. (unpaged. 1968. Viking Press.
--Oliver at Sea. Gobbato, Imero (1923-), illus. LC 69-17139. (Illus.). 57 p. 1969. Norton.
Wilson, Clara Owsley
--Follett Picture-Story of the Tale of a Trailer. LC 38-93062. 1 p. l., 40 p. illus. 21 cm. c.1937. Follet Publishing Company.
Wilson, Clara Owsley & Pennell, Mary Elizabeth (1876-)
--Wiggles a Funny Little Dog. Davis, Marguerite (1889-), illus. LC 36-21699. 47 p. col. illus. 17 x 19 1/2 cm. c.1936. Houghton Mifflin Company.
Wilson, Clifford
--Adventures from the Bay: Men of the Hudson's Bay Company. Scott, Lloyd, illus. LC 62-52619. 159p. illus. (pt. col.) 22cm. (Great stories of Canada, 25). c.1962. St. Martin's.
Wilson, Dagmar (1916-), illus.
--The House that Jack Built. N.D (Wonder Books). Grosset & Dunlap.
--Pollyanna. N.D (Wonder Books). Grosset & Dunlap.
Wilson, Dave & Wilson, Jeanne
--Mr. Terwilliger's Secret. LC 80-21835. (Easy-Read Story Bks.). (gr. k-3). 1979. (ISBN 0-531-04191-3). Watts.
Wilson, David H.
--The Fastest Gun Alive & Other Night Adventures. Mieke, Anne, illus. (Illus.). 96p. (gr. 3-7). 1981. (ISBN 0-7011-2353-2, Pub. by Chatto-Bodley-Jonathan). Merrimack Pub Cir.
Wilson, Dorothy Clarke (1904-)
--The First Book of Christmas Joy. Ronin, Mary, illus. LC 61-11334. 64 p. illus. 23 cm. c.1961. F. Watts.
--The Journey. Bolognese, Donald Alan (1934-), illus. LC 62-7867. (Illus.). (gr. 5-9). 1962. (ISBN 0-687-20605-7). Abingdon.
--That Heaven of Freedom. 1954. Friendship Press.
--The Three Gifts. LC 63-10812. 222 p. 22 cm. 1963. Abingdon Press.
--Where the World Begins. 1960. Friendship Press.
Wilson, Dorothy (1920-)
--Morning, Noon, Night. Plummer, William Kirtman, illus. LC 63-18966. (Illus.). 11cm. 1963. Grosset & Dunlop.
Wilson-Driggs
--The White Indian Boy. N.D. World Book Co.
Wilson, E. M. D., jt. auth. see Fyleman, Rose Amy.
Wilson, Edward Arthur (1886-)
--The Pirate's Treasure: Or, The Strange Adventures of Jack Adams of the Spanish Main. LC 27-821. 96 p. incl. col. illus. 23 1/2 cm. (Volland adventure series). c.1926. The P. F. Volland Company.
Wilson, Edward Arthur (1886-), illus.
--The Seven Voyages of Sinbad the Sailor. Mathers, Edward Powys (1892-), tr. N.D. Heritage Press.
Wilson, Edward B., jt. auth. see Wilson, Lucia S.
Wilson, Eleanore Hubbard, Mrs.
--About Ricco. LC 37-36388. 6 p. l., 17-123 p. col. front., illus. (part col.) 23 1/2 cm. 1937. A. Whitman & Co.
--Adventure Stories in History. (Illus.). 1961. Teachers Publishing Co.
--Flyaway Flippety, a Trip from Holland to Egypt. LC 32-31297. xii, 104 p. incl. col. front., illus. col. plates. 23 1/2 cm. 1932. Harper & Brothers.
--The Magical Jumping Beans. LC 39-19004. 100, 1 p., 1 l. incl. col. front., col. illus. 22 1/2 cm. 1939. E. P. Dutton & Co., Inc.
--Mr. Pumps Goes to Bat. LC 40-3039. 41 p. illus. 18 1/2 x 20 1/2 cm. c.1940. E. P. Dutton and Company, Inc.
--Mr. Pumps, the Popsicle Man. LC 37-147400. 41 p. col. illus. 18 1/2 x 20 1/2 cm. c.1937. E. P. Dutton and Company, Inc.
--Pixie on the Post Road. 212 p., 1 l. incl. front., illus. 21 1/2 cm. 1939. E. P. Dutton & Co., Inc.
--The Secret Three. Wilson, Eleanore Hubbard, illus. LC 51-8306. 21cm. 162p. 1951. Lothrop, Lee & Shepard.
--Treasures Three. LC 41-120273. 213 p. illus. 21 cm. 1941. E. P. Dutton & Co., Inc.
--Wilhelmina's Wish. LC 37-1988. 33 p. illus. (part. col.) 21 cm. c.1937. Rand, McNally & Company.
--Within the Gates of Oxford. LC 40-145426. 4 p. l., 11-177 p. 21 cm. 1940. E. P. Dutton & Co., Inc.
Wilson, Ella Calista Handy, Mrs. (1851-)
--A Royal Hunt, 1 of 6 Vols. (The Beacon Ser.: Vol. 2). N.D. Set. Sunday-School Library.
--A Royal Hunt: A Story of Huguenot Emigration. LC 8-37782. xi, 5-394 p. front., plates. 19 1/2 cm. c.1899. Congregational Sunday-School and Publishing Society.
Wilson, Ellen Janet Cameron, jt. auth. see Agle, Nan Hayden.
Wilson, Ellen Janet Cameron (0000-1976)
--Annie Oakley, Little Sure Shot. Locke, Vance, illus. LC 62-9249. 200 p. illus. 20 cm. (Childhood of famous Americans). 1962. Bobbs-Merrill.
--Annie Oakley, Little Sure Shot. 1st ed. Morse, Dorothy Bayley (1906-1979), illus. LC 58-12911. 191 p. illus. 20 cm. (Childhood of famous Americans series 105). 1958. Bobbs-Merrill.
--Ernie Pyle Boy from Back Home. Dawson, Isabel, illus. LC 62-126974. 200p. 20cm. (Childhood of famous Amers.). 1962, c.1955. Bobbs.
--Ernie Pyle, Boy from Back Home. 1st ed. Laune, Paul Sidney (1899-), illus. LC 55-6826. 192p. illus. 20cm. (Childhood of famous Americans series). 1955. Bobbs-Merrill.
--They Named Me Gertrude Stein. LC 73-76223. (Illus.). (gr. 7 up). 1973. (ISBN 0-374-37467-8). FS&G.
Wilson, Eric H
--Murder on The Canadian. LC 79-1509. p. cm. 1979, c.1976. (ISBN 0-525-66641-9). Elsevier/Nelson Books.
Wilson, Frank
--Cecil the Camel. (Illus.). (ps-1). 1948. (ISBN 0-685-20999-7). Verry.
Wilson, Frank E
--The Hill Billy Kid. LC 27-15521. 290 p. incl. pl. 19 cm. c.1927. Rand, McNally & Company.
Wilson, Gahan (1930-)
--The Bang Bang Family. Wilson, Gahan (1930-), illus. LC 74-11676. (Illus.). 32 p. 24cm. 1974. (ISBN 0-684-13877-8). Scribner.
--Harry and the Sea Serpent. Wilson, Gahan (1930-), illus. LC 75-35008. (Illus.). 127 p. 22cm. c.1976. (ISBN 0-684-14584-7). Scribner.
--Harry, the Fat Bear Spy. Wilson, Gahan (1930-), illus. LC 73-1381. (Illus.). 120 p. 22cm. 1973. (ISBN 0-684-13321-0). Scribner.
Wilson, Gilbert Livingstone (1868-), retold by.
--Myths of the red children. Wilson, Frederick N., illus. LC 7-37546. 154p. incl. front. illus. 19cm. 1907. Ginn & Company.
Wilson, Gina (1943-)
--All Ends Up. LC 83-25300. 160p. (gr. 6 up). 1984. (ISBN 0-571-13196-4). (ISBN 0-571-13196-4). Faber & Faber.
--Cora Ravenwing. LC 79-23259. 161 p. 22cm. 1980. (ISBN 0-689-50170-6). Atheneum.
--The Whisper. LC 83-25298. 160p. (gr. 6 up). 1984. (ISBN 0-571-11930-1). (ISBN 0-571-11930-1). Faber & Faber.
Wilson, Harry Leon (1867-1939)
--Ruggles of Red Gap. N.D. Grosset & Dunlap.
Wilson, Hazel Hutchins, Mrs. (1898-)
--Herbert. 1st ed. Barron, John N., illus. LC 50-6736. 184 p. illus. 22 cm. 1950. Knopf.
--Herbert Again. Barron, John N., illus. LC 51-11075. 168 p. illus. 22 cm. 1951. Knopf.
--Herbert's Homework. 1st ed. Werth, Kurt (1896-), illus. LC 60-13026. 150 p. illus. 22 cm. 1960. (ISBN 0-394-81239-5). (ISBN 0-394-91239-X). Knopf.
--Herbert's Space Trip. Werth, Kurt (1896-), illus. LC 65-21563. (Illus.). (gr. 3-7). 1965. (ISBN 0-394-91232-2). Knopf.
--Herbert's Stilts. 1st ed. Werth, Kurt (1896-), illus. LC 72-2435. (Illus.). 128 p. 22cm. 1972. Knopf.
--His Indian Brother. N.D. E . M. Hale and Co.
--His Indian Brother. Henneberger, Robert G. (1921-), illus. LC 55-14819. 188p. illus. 22cm. 1955. Abingdon Press.
--His Indian Brother. Henneberger, Robert G. (1921-), illus. LC 75-128046. (Illus.). 188 p. 22cm. (Merit book edition). 1970, c.1955. Houghton Mifflin.
--Island Summer. Floethe, Richard (1901-), illus. LC 49-774724. 174 p. illus. 22 cm. 1949. Abingdon-Cokesbury Press.
--Jerry's Charge Account. 1st ed. Geer, Charles Hand (1922-), illus. LC 60-5877. 145 p. illus. 23 cm. 1960. (ISBN 0-316-94483-1). Little, Brown.
--The Little Marquise: Madame Lafayette. 1st ed. Sagsoorian, Paul (1923-), illus. LC 57-9203. 241 p. illus. 22 cm. 1957. Knopf.
--More Fun with Herbert. 1st ed. Barron, John N., illus. LC 54-77109. 150p. illus. 22cm. 1954. Knopf.
--The Owen Boys. Sharp, William (1900-), illus. LC 47-3549. 192 p. illus. 22 cm. 1947. Abingdon-Cokesbury Press.
--The Red Dory. Orr, Forrest, illus. LC 39-23746. 6 p. l., 3-239 p. incl. illus., plates. 21 cm. 1939. Little, Brown and Company.
--The Red Dory. Orr, Forrest W., illus. LC 59-5370. 239 p. illus. 21 cm. 1959. Little, Brown.
--The Story of Lafayette. Legrand, Edy (1893-), illus. LC 52-11071. 182 p. illus. 22 cm. (signature books). 1952. Grosset & Dunlap.
--The Story of Mad Anthony Wayne. Meadowcroft, Enid La Monte (1898-1966), ed. Smith, Lawrence Beall (1909-), illus. LC 52-13750. 179p. illus. 22cm. (Signature books, 24). 1953. Grosset & Dunlap.
--The Surprise of Their Lives. 1st ed. Henneberger, Robert G. (1921-), illus. LC 57-8047. 154p. illus. 22cm. 1957. Little, Brown.
--Tall Ships. 1st ed. Cosgrave, John O'Hara, II (1908-1968), illus. LC 58-5176. 234 p. illus. 21 cm. 1958. Little, Brown.
--Thad, Owen. Sharp, William (1900-), illus. LC 50-8740. 191 p. illus. 22 cm. 1950. Abingdon-Cokesbury Press.
Wilson-Heaney, Katherine, illus.
--Benji & Zax: A Maze Story Book. (Illus.). 24p. (Saturday Morning Bks.). (gr. 2-6). 1983. (ISBN 0-89954-233-6). Antioch Pub Co.
--Teddy Bears Are a Blessing. (Illus.). 24p. (Teddy Bears Are Ser.). (gr. 2-7). 1985. (ISBN 0-89954-331-6). Antioch Pub Co.
Wilson, Helen Finnegan see Wilson, Holly, pseud.
Wilson, Helen Finnegan, Mrs.
--Always Anne. Wilson, Holly, pseud. LC 57-11276. 188 p. 22 cm. 1957. J. Messmer.
--Caroline, the Unconquered. Wilson, Holly, pseud. LC 56-6798. 189 p. 22 cm. 1956. Messner.
--Deborah Todd. Wilson, Holly, pseud. Geer, Charles Hand (1922-), illus. LC 55-6931. 192p. illus. 22cm. 1955. J. Messner.
--Double Heritage. Wilson, Holly, pseud. LC 74-153189. 20cm. 173p. 1971. (ISBN 0-664-32497-5). Westminster Press.
--The Hundred Steps. Wilson, Holly, pseud. LC 58-11491. 190 p. 22 cm. 1958. J. Messner.
--Maggie of Barnaby Bay. Wilson, Holly, pseud. LC 63-8645. 189 p. 22 cm. 1963. J. Messner.
--Snowbound in Hidden Valley. Wilson, Holly, pseud. Morse, Dorothy Bayley (1906-1979), illus. LC 57-6592. 186p. illus. 22cm. 1957. Messner.
--Stranger in Singamon. Wilson, Holly, pseud. Geer, Charles Hand (1922-), illus. LC 59-12771. 192 p. illus. 22 cm. 1959. Messner.
Wilson, Henry, ed. see De Capella, F.
Wilson, Holly, pseud., see Wilson, Helen Finnegan.
Wilson, J. H.
--The King's Message: A Book for the Young. (Illus.). N.D. Thos Nelson & Sons.
--Under the Old Oaks: Or, Won by Love. N.D. Thos Nelson & Sons.
Wilson, Jacqueline
--Nobody's Perfect. 104p. 1st U.S. edition. (gr. 6-10). 1984. (ISBN 0-19-271463-5, Pub. by Oxford U Pr Childrens). Merrimack Pub Cir.
--Waiting for the Sky to Fall. 204p. (gr. 7 up). 1984. (ISBN 0-19-271485-6, Pub. by Oxford U Pr Childrens). Merrimack Pub Cir.
Wilson, Jean B, jt. auth. see Hurd, Marian Kent.
Wilson, Jeanne
--Half Pint. Fayko, Joan, illus. LC 52-7118. 96 p. illus. 20 cm. 1952. Westminster Press.
Wilson, Jeanne, jt. auth. see Ross, David.
Wilson, Jeanne, jt. auth. see Wilson, Dave.
Wilson, John Anthony Burgess see Burgess, Anthony, pseud.
Wilson, John Fleming (1877-1922)
--Scouts of the Desert. LC 20-18932. 3 p. l., 3-179 p. front. 19 1/2 cm. 1920. The Macmillan Company.
--Tad Sheldon, Boy Scout: Stories of His Patrol. 1924. Macmillan.
--Tad Sheldon, Boy Scout: Stories of His Patrol. Dougherty, illus. LC 13-12495. 4 p. l., 3-231 p. front., plates. 19 1/2 cm. $1.00. 1913. Sturgis & Walton Company.
--Tad Sheldon's Fourth of July. N.D. Macmillan.
--Tad Sheldon's Fourth of July: More Stories of His Patrol. Rockwell, Norman Percevel (1894-1978), illus. LC 13-24447. 7 p. l., 3-245 p. front., plates. 19 1/2 cm. $1.00. 1913. Sturgis & Walton Company.
Wilson, Joyce Lancaster
--The Ark of Noah. new ed. Wilson, Adrian, ed. Wilson, Joyce Lancaster, illus. (Illus.). (gr. 1-10). 1975. (ISBN 0-915918-01-3). Pr Tuscany.
--The Four Kings of the Forest ; a Fable. Wilson, Joyce Lancaster, illus. LC 83-460712. (Illus.). 29 p. 25cm. c.1973. Press in Tuscany Alley.
--The Swing. Wilson, Adrian, ed. (Illus.). 1981. (ISBN 0-915918-04-8). Pr Tuscany.
--Tobi. Thiess, Anne, illus. LC 68-13074. (Illus.). 32 p. 26cm. 1968. Funk & Wagnalls.
Wilson, Joyce Muriel Judson see Stranger, Joyce, pseud.
Wilson, Julia (1927-)
--Becky. Wilson, John (1922-), illus. LC 67-3101. (Illus.). 1 v. (unpaged. 27cm. 1967, c.1966. Crowell.
Wilson, Justin & Hadley, Jay (1947-)
--Justin Wilson's Cajun Fables. Troxclair, Errol (1954-), illus. LC 82-18568. p. cm. 1982. (ISBN 0-88289-362-9). Pelican Pub. Co.
Wilson, Karl F
--The Plain and Fancy Mother Goose. Poop, Florence, illus. LC 56-5905. 208 p. illus. 28 cm. 1957. Abelard-Schuman.
Wilson, LaNeil, jt. auth. see Brown, Virginia Pounds.
Wilson, Leisa Graeme
--The Lady Loses Her Hoop: A Gay Little Comedy in One Act. 15 p. pl. 18 1/2 cm. (Drama league junior plays, ed. by Cora M. Patton). c.1934. Walter H. Baker Company.
Wilson, Leon
--This Boy Cody. Koering, Ursula (1921-), illus. LC 50-8808. 234 p. illus. 21 cm. 1950. Watts.
--This Boy Cody and His Friends. Koering, Ursula (1921-), illus. LC 52-12600. (Illus.). 272 p. 21cm. 1952. Watts.
Wilson, Lewis Gilbert (1858-)
--Little Red Wonder Book. 64p. 1915. Beacon Press Inc.
Wilson, Lionel see Ellis, Herbert, pseud.
Wilson, Lionel see Salzer, L. E., pseud.
Wilson, Lionel (1924-)
--Attack of the Killer Grizzly. Bennett, Russell, ed. Zoellick, Scott, illus. LC 79-22057. (Illus.). 46p. (Quest, Adventure, Survival Ser.). (gr. 4-9). 1982. (ISBN 0-8172-1574-3). (ISBN 0-8172-2051-8). Raintree Pubs.
--The Mule Who Refused to Budge: Story. 1st Ed. ed. Berson, Harold (1926-), illus. LC 75-9742. (Illus.). 32 p. 29cm. 1975. (ISBN 0-517-52186-5). Crown Publishers.
--The Mystery of Dracula. LC 78-23283. (Unsolved Mysteries of the World Ser.). N.D. (ISBN 0-89547-065-9). Silver.
--The Mystery of Human Wolves. LC 78-11033. (Unsolved Mysteries of the World Ser.). N.D. (ISBN 0-89547-067-5). Silver.
--The Mystery of the Wax Museum. Ellis, Herbert, pseud. LC 79-19627. (Unsolved Mysteries of the World Ser.). N.D. (ISBN 0-89547-084-5). Silver.
Wilson, Lucia S (1924-) & Wilson, Edward B.
--The Good Old Rule. LC 35-480212. 254 p. plates. 22 cm. 1935. Meador Publishing Company.
Wilson, Margaret (1882-1973)
--The Devon Treasure Mystery. Yap, Weda (1894-), illus. LC 39-22928. 3 p. l., 3-281 p. illus. 19 1/2 cm. c.1939. Randon House.
Wilson, Marjorie
--Children's Rhymes of Travel. 1924. Houghton Mifflin Co.
--Klipper-Klopper and Other Verses for Children. 1922. Houghton Mifflin Co.
--The Twin Umbrellas. Ball, Mary, illus. LC 31-138729. ix, 51, 1 p. col. front., illus., col. plates. 20 1/2 cm. 1930. Houghton Mifflin Company.
Wilson, Mary, jt. auth. see Young, Biloine W.
Wilson, Mike, jt. auth. see Clarke, Arthur Charles.
Wilson, Nena
--Ring: The Story of a St. Bernard. Nelson, Don, illus. LC 31-2832. 64 p. incl. front., illus. 20 1/2 cm. 1930. Thomas S. Rockwell Company.
Wilson, Olivia Lovell, jt. auth. see Burbank, Barbara.
Wilson, Penelope Coker, pseud., see Hall, Penelope Coker.
Wilson, Penelope Coker, pseud. (1930-)
--Fancy and the Cement Patch. Hall, Penelope Coker. Aloise, Frank E., illus. LC 64-22920. 60 p. col. illus. 26 cm. 1964. Reilly & Lee.
--The Wish Bottle. Hall, Penelope Coker. Borja, Corinne (1929-) & Borja, Robert (1923-), illus. LC 64-66128. 1v. (unpaged) illus. (pt. col.) 24cm. 1965. Reilly & Lee.

--Poor but Plucky: Or, The Mystery of a Flood. Stratemeyer, Edward L.. DuPont, G. B., illus. (Bound to Win Ser.: Vol. 8). 1897. W. L. Allison Co.

--Poor but Plucky: Or, The Mystery of a Flood. Stratemeyer, Edward L.. DuPont, G. B., illus. Reissue of 1897 ed. (The Bright and Bold Ser.: Vol. 1). N.D. W. L. Allison Co.

--The Putnam Hall Cadets: Or, Good Times In School and Out. Stratemeyer, Edward L.. Shute, A. Burnham, illus. Repr. of 1901 ed (Pub. by Mershon Co). (Putnam Hall Ser.: Vol. 1). 1907. Chatterton-Peck Co.

--The Putnam Hall Cadets: Or, Good Times In School and Out. Stratemeyer, Edward L.. Shute, A. Burnham, illus. Repr. of 1901 ed (Pub. by Mershon Co). (Putnam Hall Ser.: Vol. 1). 1908. Grosset & Dunlap.

--The Putnam Hall Cadets: Or, Good Times In School and Out. Stratemeyer, Edward L.. Shute, A. Burnham, illus. vi, 263 p. front., plates. 19 cm. Repr. of 1901 ed (Pub. by Mershon Co). (Putnam Hall Ser.: Vol. 1). 1905. Stitt Publishing Co.

--The Putnam Hall Cadets: Or, Good Times In School and Out. Stratemeyer, Edward L.. Shute, A. Burnham, illus. (Putnam Hall Ser.: Vol. 1). 1901. The Mershon Co.

--The Putnam Hall Champions: Or, Bound to Win Out. Stratemeyer, Edward L.. Nuttall, Charles, illus. LC 8-22345. vi. 277 p. front., plates. 19 1/2 cm. (Putnam Hall Ser.: Vol. 3). c.1908. Grosset & Dunlap.

--The Putnam Hall Encampment: Or, the Secret of the Old Mill. Stratemeyer, Edward L.. Nuttall, Charles, illus. LC 12-956714. vi, 288 p. front., plates. 19 1/2 cm. (Putnam Hall Ser.: Vol. 5). c.1910. Grosset & Dunlap.

--The Putnam Hall Mystery: Or, The School Chums' Strange Discovery. Stratemeyer, Edward L.. Nuttall, Charles, illus. LC 11-22326. vi, 280 p. front., plates. 19 1/2 cm. (Putnam Hall Ser.: Vol. 6). c.1911. Grosset & Dunlap.

--The Putnam Hall Rebellion: Or, The Rival Runaways. Stratemeyer, Edward L.. Nuttall, Charles, illus. (Putnam Hall Ser.: Vol. 4). 1909. Grosset & Dunlap.

--The Putnam Hall Rivals: Or, Fun and Sport Afloat and Ashore. Stratemeyer, Edward L.. Angell, Clare, illus. Repr. of 1906 ed (Pub. by Mershon Co). (Putnam Hall Ser.: Vol. 2). 1907. Chatterton-Peck Co.

--The Putnam Hall Rivals: Or, Fun and Sport Afloat and Ashore. Stratemeyer, Edward L.. Angell, Clare, illus. Repr. of 1906 ed (Pub. by Mershon Co). (Putnam Hall Ser.: Vol. 2). 1908. Grosset & Dunlap.

--The Putnam Hall Rivals: Or, Fun and Sport Afloat and Ashore. Stratemeyer, Edward L.. Angell, Clare, illus. Repr. of 1906 ed (Pub. by Mershon Co). (Putnam Hall Ser.: Vol. 2). 1906. Stitt Publishing Co.

--The Putnam Hall Rivals: Or, Fun and Sport Afloat and Ashore. Stratemeyer, Edward L.. Angell, Clare, illus. LC 6-32118. vi, 247 p. front., plates. 19 cm. (Putnam Hall Ser.: Vol. 2). 1906. The Mershon Company.

--The Rebellion at Putnam Hall: Or, The Rival Runaways. Stratemeyer, Edward L.. Nuttall, Charles, illus. Reissue of 1908 ed. (Putnam Hall Ser.: Vol. 3). Orig. Title: The Putnam Hall Rebellion; Or, The Rival Runaways. 1921. Grosset & Dunlap.

--The Rivals of Putnam Hall: Or, Fun and Sport Afloat and Ashore. Stratemeyer, Edward L.. Angell, Clare, illus. Repr. of 1906 ed (Pub. by Mershon Co). (Putnam Hall Ser.: Vol. 6). 1921. Grosset & Dunlap.

--The Rover Boys at Big Bear Lake: Or, The Camps of the Rival Cadets. Stratemeyer, Edward L.. Rogers, Walter S., illus. (The Second Rover Boys' Series for young Americans: Vol. 27). 1923. Grosset & Dunlap.

--The Rover Boys at Big Horn Ranch: Or, The Cowboys' Double Round-up. Stratemeyer, Edward L.. Rogers, Walter S., illus. (The Second Rover Boys' Series for young Americans: Vol. 26). 1922. Grosset & Dunlap.

--The Rover Boys at Colby Hall: Or, The Struggles of the Young Cadets. Stratemeyer, Edward L.. Rogers, Walter S., illus. LC 17-128632. vi, 308 p. front. 19 1/2 cm. (The Second Rover Boys' Series for young Americans: Vol. 21). c.1917. Grosset & Dunlap.

--The Rover Boys at College. Stratemeyer, Edward L.. 312p. Repr. 1980. (ISBN 0-89967-008-3). Harmony & Co.

--Rover Boys at College: Or, The Right Road and the Wrong. Stratemeyer, Edward L.. 191p. Repr. of 1910 ed (Pub. by Grosset & Dunlap). (The Rover Boys' Series for young Americans: Vol. 14). 1981. (ISBN 0-89966-330-3). Buccaneer Bks.

--The Rover Boys at College: Or, The Right Road and the Wrong. Stratemeyer, Edward L.. Repr. of 1910 ed (Pub. by Grosset & Dunlap). (The Rover Boys' Series for young Americans: Vol. 14). N.D. Whitman Publishing Co.

--The Rover Boys at College: Or, The Right Road and the Wrong. Stratemeyer, Edward L.. Nuttall, Charles, illus. LC 10-10700. 19 1/2cm. 292p. (The Rover Boys' Series for young Americans: Vol. 14). 1910. Grosset & Dunlap.

--The Rover Boys at School: Or, The Cadets of Putnam Hall. Stratemeyer, Edward L.. 302p. Repr. of 1899 ed (Pub. by Mershon Co). (The Rover Boys' Series for young Americans: Vol. 1). 1980. (ISBN 0-89967-009-1). Harmony & Co.

--The Rover Boys at School: Or, The Cadets of Putnam Hall. Stratemeyer, Edward L.. Repr. of 1899 ed (Pub. by Mershon Co). (The Rover Boys' Series for young Americans: Vol. 1). N.D. Whitman Publishing Co.

--The Rover Boys at School: Or, The Cadets of Putnam Hall. Stratemeyer, Edward L.. Burch, Stacy & Bridge, W. B., illus. vi, iii-iv, 250 p. incl. front. plates. 19 cm. Repr. of 1899 ed (Pub. by Mershon Co). (The Rover Boys' Series for young Americans: Vol. 1). 1907. Chatterton-Peck Company.

--The Rover Boys at School: Or, The Cadets of Putnam Hall. Stratemeyer, Edward L.. Burch, Stacy & Bridge, W. B., illus. LC 24-20466. 19 1/2cm. 250p. Repr. of 1899 ed (Pub. by Mershon Co). (The Rover Boys' Series for young Americans: Vol. 1). 1908. Grosset & Dunlap.

--The Rover Boys at School: Or, The Cadets of Putnam Hall. Stratemeyer, Edward L.. Burch, Stacy & Bridge, W. B., illus. Repr. of 1899 ed (Pub. by Mershon Co). (The Rover Boys' Series for young Americans: Vol. 1). 1905. Stitt Publishing Co.

--The Rover Boys at School: Or, The Cadets of Putnam Hall. Stratemeyer, Edward L.. Burch, Stacy & Bridge, W. B., illus. LC 99-2627. 20cm. 250p. (The Rover Boys' Series for young Americans: Vol. 1). 1899. The Mershon Co.

--The Rover Boys Down East: Or, The Struggle for the Stanhope Fortune. Stratemeyer, Edward L.. Rogers, Walter S., illus. LC 19-41213. vi, 288 p. front., plates. 19 1/2 cm. (The Rover Boys' Series for young Americans: Vol. 15). c.1911. Grosset & Dunlap.

--The Rover Boys in Alaska: Or, Lost in the Fields of Ice. Stratemeyer, Edward L.. Richards, Dick, illus. LC 14-6990. vi, 285 p. front., plates. 19 1/2 cm. (The Rover Boys' Series for young Americans: Vol. 18). c.1914. Grosset & Dunlap.

--The Rover Boys in Business: Or, the Search for the Missing Bonds. Stratemeyer, Edward L.. Rogers, Walter S., illus. LC 15-8709. 3 p. l., 290 p. front., plates. 19 1/2 cm. (The Rover Boys' Series for young Americans: Vol. 19). c.1915. Grosset & Dunlap.

--The Rover Boys in Camp: Or, The Rivals of Pine Island. Stratemeyer, Edward L.. (Illus.). Repr. of 1904 ed (Pub. by Mershon Co). (The Rover Boys' Series for young Americans: Vol. 8). 1907. Chatterton-Peck Co.

--The Rover Boys in Camp: Or, The Rivals of Pine Island. Stratemeyer, Edward L.. (Illus.). Repr. of 1904 ed (Pub. by Mershon Co). (The Rover Boys' Series for young Americans: Vol. 8). c.1908. Grosset & Dunlap.

--The Rover Boys in Camp: Or, The Rivals of Pine Island. Stratemeyer, Edward L.. (Illus.). Repr. of 1904 ed (Pub. by Mershon Co). (The Rover Boys' Series for young Americans: Vol. 8). 1905. Stitt Publishing Co.

--The Rover Boys in Camp: Or, The Rivals of Pine Island. Stratemeyer, Edward L.. LC 4-23715. (Illus.). 19cm. 263p. (The Rover Boys' Series for young Americans: Vol. 8). 1904. The Mershon Co.

--The Rover Boys in Camp: Or, The Rivals of Pine Island. Stratemeyer, Edward L.. Repr. of 1904 ed (Pub. by Mershon Co). (The Rover Boys' Series for young Americans: Vol. 8). N.D. Whitman Publishing Co.

--The Rover Boys in New York: Or, Saving Their Father's Honor. Stratemeyer, Edward L.. Rogers, Walter S., illus. LC 13-9244. vi, 300 p. front., plates. 19 1/2 cm. (The Rover Boys' Series for young Americans: Vol. 17). c.1913. Grosset & Dunlap.

--The Rover Boys in Southern Waters: Or, The Deserted Steam Yacht. Stratemeyer, Edward L.. Repr. of 1907 ed (Pub. by Mershon Co). (The Rover Boys' Series for young Americans: Vol. 11). N.D. Whitman Publishing Co.

--The Rover Boys in Southern Waters: Or, the Deserted Steam Yacht. Stratemeyer, Edward L.. Nuttall, Charles, illus. LC 7-23467. vi, 247 p. front., plates. 19 cm. Repr. of 1907 ed (Pub. by Mershon Co). (The Rover Boys' Series for young Americans: Vol. 11). c.1907. Chatterton-Peck Company.

--The Rover Boys in Southern Waters: Or, The Deserted Steam Yacht. Stratemeyer, Edward L.. Nuttall, Charles, illus. LC 13-5695. vi, 247 p. front., pl. 19 1/2 cm. Repr. of 1907 ed (Pub. by Mershon Co). (The Rover Boys' Series for young Americans: Vol. 11). c.1908. Grosset & Dunlap.

--The Rover Boys in Southern Waters: Or, The Deserted Steam Yacht. Stratemeyer, Edward L.. Nuttall, Charles, illus. Repr. of 1907 ed (Pub. by Mershon Co). (The Rover Boys' Series for young Americans: Vol. 11). 1907. Stitt Publishing Co.

--The Rover Boys in Southern Waters: Or, The Deserted Steam Yacht. Stratemeyer, Edward L.. Nuttall, Charles, illus. (The Rover Boys' Series for young Americans: Vol. 11). 1907. The Mershon Co.

--The Rover Boys in the Air: Or, From College Campus to Clouds. Stratemeyer, Edward L.. Rogers, Walter S., illus. vi, 288 p. front., plates. 19 1/2 cm. (The Rover Boys' Series for young Americans: Vol. 16). c.1912. Grosset & Dunlap.

--The Rover Boys in the Jungle: Or, Stirring Adventures in Africa. Stratemeyer, Edward L.. Burch, Stacy & Bridge, W. B., illus. Repr. of 1899 ed (Pub. by Mershon Co). (The Rover Boys' Series for young Americans: Vol. 3). 1907. Chatterton-Peck Co.

--The Rover Boys in the Jungle: Or, Stirring Adventures in Africa. Stratemeyer, Edward L.. Burch, Stacy & Bridge, W. B., illus. Repr. of 1899 ed (Pub. by Mershon Co). (The Rover Boys' Series for young Americans: Vol. 3). c.1908. Grosset & Dunlap.

--The Rover Boys in the Jungle: Or, Stirring Adventures in Africa. Stratemeyer, Edward L.. Burch, Stacy & Bridge, W. B., illus. Repr. of 1899 ed (Pub. by Mershon Co). (The Rover Boys' Series for young Americans: Vol. 3). 1905. Stitt Publishing Co.

--The Rover Boys in the Jungle: Or, Stirring Adventures in Africa. Stratemeyer, Edward L.. Burch, Stacy & Bridge, W. B., illus. LC 427. vi, 234 p. front. 18 1/2 cm. (The Rover Boys' Series for young Americans: Vol. 3). 1899. The Mershon Company.

--The Rover Boys in the Land of Luck: Or, Stirring Adventures in the Oil Fields. Stratemeyer, Edward L.. Rogers, Walter S., illus. (The Second Rover Boys' Series for young Americans: Vol. 25). 1921. Grosset & Dunlap.

--The Rover Boys in the Mountains: Or, A Hunt for Fun and Fortune. Stratemeyer, Edward L.. Burch, Stacy & Bridge, W. B., illus. Repr. of 1902 ed (Pub. by Mershon Co). (The Rover Boys' Series for young Americans: Vol. 6). 1907. Chatterton-Peck Co.

--The Rover Boys in the Mountains: Or, A Hunt for Fun and Fortune. Stratemeyer, Edward L.. Burch, Stacy & Bridge, W. B., illus. Repr. of 1902 ed (Pub. by Mershon Co). (The Rover Boys' Series for young Americans: Vol. 6). c.1908. Grosset & Dunlap.

--The Rover Boys in the Mountains: Or, A Hunt for Fun and Fortune. Stratemeyer, Edward L.. Burch, Stacy & Bridge, W. B., illus. Repr. of 1902 ed (Pub. by Mershon Co). (The Rover Boys' Series for young Americans: Vol. 6). 1905. Stitt Publishing Co.

--The Rover Boys in the Mountains: Or, A Hunt for Fun and Fortune. Stratemeyer, Edward L.. Burch, Stacy & Bridge, W. B., illus. LC 2-16918. vi, 244 p. front., pl. 19 cm. (The Rover Boys' Series for young Americans: Vol. 6). 1902. The Mershon Company.

--The Rover Boys on a Hunt: Or, The Mysterious House in the Woods. Stratemeyer, Edward L.. Rogers, Walter S., illus. (The Second Rover Boys' Series for young Americans: Vol. 24). 1920. Grosset & Dunlap.

--The Rover Boys on a Tour: Or, Last Days at Brill College. Stratemeyer, Edward L.. Rogers, Walter S., illus. (The Rover Boys' Series for young Americans: Vol. 20). 1916. Grosset & Dunlap.

--The Rover Boys on Land and Sea: Or, The Crusoes of Seven Islands. Stratemeyer, Edward L.. (Illus.). Repr. of 1903 ed (Pub. by Mershon Co). (The Rover Boys' Series for young Americans: Vol. 7). 1907. Chatterton-Peck Co.

--The Rover Boys on Land and Sea: Or, The Crusoes of Seven Islands. Stratemeyer, Edward L.. (Illus.). Repr. of 1903 ed (Pub. by Mershon Co). (The Rover Boys' Series for young Americans: Vol. 7). c.1908. Grosset & Dunlap.

--The Rover Boys on Land and Sea: Or, The Crusoes of Seven Islands. Stratemeyer, Edward L.. (Illus.). Repr. of 1903 ed (Pub. by Mershon Co). (The Rover Boys' Series for young Americans: Vol. 7). 1905. Stitt Publishing Co.

--The Rover Boys on Land and Sea: Or, The Crusoes of Seven Islands. Stratemeyer, Edward L.. LC 3-19436. (Illus.). (The Rover Boys' Series for young Americans: Vol. 7). 1903. The Mershon Company.

--The Rover Boys on Land and Sea: Or, The Crusoes of Seven Islands. Stratemeyer, Edward L.. Repr. of 1903 ed (Pub. by Mershon Co). (The Rover Boys' Series for young Americans: Vol. 7). N.D. Whitman Publishing Co.

--The Rover Boys on Snowshoe Island: Or, The Old Lumberman's Treasure Box. Stratemeyer, Edward L.. Rogers, Walter S., illus. (The Second Rover Boys' Series for young Americans: Vol. 22). 1918. Grosset & Dunlap.

--The Rover Boys on Sunset Trail: Or, The Old Miner's Mysterious Message. Stratemeyer, Edward L.. Rogers, Walter S., illus. LC 25-4607. vi, 304 p. front., plates. 19 1/2 cm. (The Second Rover Boys' Series for young Americans: Vol. 29). c.1925. Grosset & Dunlap.

--The Rover Boys on the Farm: Or, Last Days at Putnam Hall. Stratemeyer, Edward L.. Nuttall, Charles, illus. LC 8-14519. vi, 235 p. front., plates. 19 1/2 cm. (The Rover Boys' Series for young Americans: Vol. 12). c.1908. Grosset & Dunlap.

--The Rover Boys on the Great Lakes: Or, The Secret of the Island Cave. Stratemeyer, Edward L.. Burch, Stacy & Bridge, W. B., illus. Repr. of 1901 ed (Pub. by Mershon Co). (The Rover Boys' Series for young Americans: Vol. 5). 1907. Chatterton-Peck Co.

--The Rover Boys on the Great Lakes: Or, The Secret of the Island Cave. Stratemeyer, Edward L.. Burch, Stacy & Bridge, W. B., illus. Repr. of 1901 ed (Pub. by Mershon Co). (The Rover Boys' Series for young Americans: Vol. 5). 1905. Stitt Publishing Co.

--The Rover Boys on the Great Lakes: Or, The Secret of the Island Cave. Stratemeyer, Edward L.. Burch, Stacy & Bridge, W. B., illus. LC 1-19475. 19cm. 252p. (The Rover Boys' Series for young Americans: Vol. 5). 1901. The Mershon Co.

--The Rover Boys on the Ocean: Or, A Chase for Fortune. Stratemeyer, Edward L.. Repr. of 1899 ed (Pub. by Mershon Co). (The Rover Boys' Series for young Americans: Vol. 2). N.D. Whitman Publishing Co.

--The Rover Boys on the Ocean: Or, A Chase for Fortune. Stratemeyer, Edward L.. Burch, Stacy & Bridge, W. B., illus. Repr. of 1899 ed (Pub. by Mershon Co). (The Rover Boys' Series for young Americans: Vol. 2). 1907. Chatterton-Peck Co.

--The Rover Boys on the Ocean: Or, A Chase for Fortune. Stratemeyer, Edward L.. Burch, Stacy & Bridge, W. B., illus. LC 24-20467. vi, 248 p. front., plates. 19 1/2 cm. Repr. of 1899 ed (Pub. by Mershon Co). (The Rover Boys' Series for young Americans: Vol. 2). 1908. Grosset & Dunlap.

--The Rover Boys on the Ocean: Or, A Chase for Fortune. Stratemeyer, Edward L.. Burch, Stacy & Bridge, W. B., illus. Repr. of 1899 ed (Pub. by Mershon Co). (The Rover Boys' Series for young Americans: Vol. 2). 1905. Stitt Publishing Co.

--The Rover Boys on the Ocean: Or, A Chase for Fortune. Stratemeyer, Edward L.. Burch, Stacy & Bridge, W. B., illus. LC 428. vi, 248 p. front., plates. 18 cm. (The Rover Boys' Series for young Americans: Vol. 2). c.1899. The Mershon Company.

--The Rover Boys on the Plains: Or, The Mystery of Red Rock Ranch. Stratemeyer, Edward L.. Repr. of 1906 ed (Pub. by Mershon Co). (The Rover Boys' Series for young Americans: Vol. 10). N.D. Whitman Publishing Co.

--The Rover Boys on the Plains: Or, The Mystery of Red Rock Ranch. Stratemeyer, Edward L.. Shute, A. Burnham, illus. Repr. of 1906 ed (Pub. by Mershon Co). (The Rover Boys' Series for young Americans: Vol. 10). 1907. Chatterton-Peck Co.

--The Rover Boys on the Plains: Or, The Mystery of Red Rock Ranch. Stratemeyer, Edward L.. Shute, A. Burnham, illus. Repr. of 1906 ed (Pub. by Mershon Co). (The Rover Boys' Series for young Americans: Vol. 10). c.1908. Grosset & Dunlap.

--The Rover Boys on the Plains: Or, The Mystery of Red Rock Ranch. Stratemeyer, Edward L.. Shute, A. Burnham, illus. Repr. of 1906 ed (Pub. by Mershon Co). (The Rover Boys' Series for young Americans: Vol. 10). 1906. Stitt Publishing Co.

--The Rover Boys on the Plains: Or, The Mystery of Red Rock Ranch. Stratemeyer, Edward L.. Shute, A. Burnham, illus. LC 6-13417. vi, 255 p. front., plates. 19 cm. (The Rover Boys' Series for young Americans: Vol. 10). c.1906. The Mershon Company.

--The Rover Boys on the River: Or, The Search for the Missing Houseboat. Stratemeyer, Edward L.. LC 25-23742. (Illus.). 19 1/2cm. 254p. (The Rover Series for Young Americans). c.1905. Grossert & Dunlap.
--The Rover Boys on the River: Or, The Search for the Missing Houseboat. Stratemeyer, Edward L.. Shute, A. Burnham, illus. Repr. of 1905 ed (Pub. by Stitt Publishing Co). (The Rover Boys' Series for young Americans: Vol. 9). 1907. Chatterton-Peck Co.
--The Rover Boys on the River: Or, the Search for the Missing Houseboat. Stratemeyer, Edward L.. Shute, A. Burnham, illus. LC 20-18846. 3 p. l., 254 p. front., plates. 19 1/2 cm. Repr. of 1905 ed (Pub. by Stitt Publishing Co). (The Rover Boys' Series for young Americans: Vol. 9). c.1908. Grosset & Dunlap.
--The Rover Boys on the River: Or, The Search for the Missing Houseboat. Stratemeyer, Edward L.. Shute, A. Burnham, illus. LC 5-26128. vi, 254 p. front., plates. 19 cm. (The Rover Boys' Series for young Americans: Vol. 9). 1905. Stitt Publishing Company.
--The Rover Boys on Treasure Isle: Or, The Strange Cruise of the Steam Yacht. Stratemeyer, Edward L.. Repr. of 1909 ed (Pub. by Grosset & Dunlap). (The Rover Boys' Series for young Americans: Vol. 13). N.D. Whitman Publishing Co.
--The Rover Boys on Treasure Isle: Or, The Strange Cruise of the Steam Yacht. Stratemeyer, Edward L.. Nuttall, Charles, illus. LC 9-116872. vi, 287 pl front., plates. 19 1/2 cm. (The Rover Boys' Series for young Americans. Vol. 13). c.1909. Grosset & Dunlap.
--The Rover Boys Out West: Or, The Search for a Lost Mine. Stratemeyer, Edward L.. Burch, Stacy & Bridge, W. B., illus. Repr. of 1900 ed (Pub. by Mershon Co). (The Rover Boys' Series for young Americans: Vol. 4). 1907. Chatterton-Peck Co.
--The Rover Boys Out West: Or, The Search for a Lost Mine. Stratemeyer, Edward L.. Burch, Stacy & Bridge, W. B., illus. Repr. of 1900 ed (Pub. by Mershon Co). (The Rover Boys' Series for young Americans: Vol. 4). c.1908. Grosset & Dunlap.
--The Rover Boys Out West: Or, The Search for a Lost Mine. Stratemeyer, Edward L.. Burch, Stacy & Bridge, W. B., illus. Repr. of 1900 ed (Pub. by Mershon Co). (The Rover Boys' Series for young Americans: Vol. 4). 1905. Stitt Publishing Co.
--The Rover Boys Out West: Or, The Search for a Lost Mine. Stratemeyer, Edward L.. Burch, Stacy & Bridge, W. B., illus. vi, 249 p. front., pl. 19. (The Rover Boys' Series for young Americans: Vol. 4). 1900. The Mershon Co.
--The Rover Boys Shipwrecked: Or, A Thrilling Hunt for Pirates' Gold. Stratemeyer, Edward L.. Rogers, Walter S., illus. (The Second Rover Boys' Series for young Americans: Vol. 28). 1924. Grosset & Dunlap.
--The Rover Boys Under Canvas: Or, The Mystery of the Wrecked Submarine. Stratemeyer, Edward L.. Rogers, Walter S., illus. LC 19-15736. vi, 310 p. front., plates. 19 1/2 cm. (The Second Rover Boys' Series for young Americans: Vol. 23). c.1919. Grosset & Dunlap.
--The Rover Boys Winning a Fortune: Or, Strenuous Days Afloat and Ashore. Stratemeyer, Edward L.. Rogers, Walter S., illus. (The Second Rover Boys' Series for young Americans: Vol. 30). 1926. Grosset & Dunlap.
--School Days of Fred Harley. Stratemeyer, Edward L.. Repr. (The Boys' Liberty Ser.: Vol. 15). N.D. M. A. Donohue & Co.
--School Days of Fred Harley: Or, Rivals for All Honors. Stratemeyer, Edward L.. DuPont, G. B., illus. Repr (Pub. by W. L. Allison Co). (The Bright and Bold Ser.: Vol. 2). 1905. M. A. Donohue & Co.
--School Days of Fred Harley: Or, Rivals for all Honors. Stratemeyer, Edward L.. DuPont, G. B., illus. Reissue of 1897 ed. (The Bright and Bold Ser.: Vol. 2). N.D. W. L. Allison Co.
--Schooldays of Fred Harley: Or, Rivals for All Honors. Stratemeyer, Edward L.. DuPont, G. B., illus. LC 13-338710. iv, 5-287 p. front., plates. 19 cm. (Bound to Win Ser.: Vol. 2). c.1897. W. L. Allison Co.
--The Young Bank Clerk. Stratemeyer, Edward L., 39 vols. (Illus.). (Famous Books for Boys Ser.: No. 34). 1905. Set. H M Caldwell Co.
--The Young Bank Clerk: Or, Mark Vincent's Strange Discovery. Stratemeyer, Edward L.. Repr. (The Boys' Own Library). 1902. David McKay.
--The Young Bank Clerk: Or, Mark Vincent's Strange Discovery. Stratemeyer, Edward L.. Repr. (The Boys' Own Library). 1902. Street & Smith.
--The Young Bank Clerk: Or, Mark Vincent's Strange Discovery. Stratemeyer, Edward L.. Repr. (Medal Library: No. 269). 1904. Street & Smith.
--The Young Bridge-Tender. Stratemeyer, Edward L., 39 vols. (Illus.). (Famous Books for Boys Ser.: No. 36). 1905. Set. H M Caldwell Co.
--The Young Bridge-Tender: Or, Ralph Nelson's Upward Struggle. Stratemeyer, Edward L.. Repr. (The Boys' Own Library). 1902. David McKay.
--The Young Bridge-Tender: Or, Ralph Nelson's Upward Struggle. Stratemeyer, Edward L.. LC 2-19725. 20cm. 256p. Repr. (Silver Lake Ser.: Vol. 1). 1902. Street & Smith.
--The Young Bridge-Tender: Or, Ralph Nelson's Upward Struggle. Stratemeyer, Edward L.. Repr. (The Boys' Own Library). 1902. Street & Smith.
--The Young Bridge-Tender: Or, Ralph Nelson's Upward Struggle. Stratemeyer, Edward L.. Repr. (Medal Library: No. 249). 1904. Street & Smith.
--A Young Inventor's Pluck: Or, The Mystery of the Wellington Legacy. Stratemeyer, Edward L.. (Illus.). N.D. Caldwell.
--A Young Inventor's Pluck: Or, The Mystery of the Wellington Legacy. Stratemeyer, Edward L.. LC 1-11762. 235p. 1901. Saalfield Publishing Co.
--A Young Inventor's Pluck: Or, The Mystery of the Wellington Legacy. Stratemeyer, Edward L.. Repr. (The Winfield Ser.: Vol. 2). N.D. Saalfield Publishing Co.

Winfrey, Guy
--Bunny Bearskin. Tessin, Louise D., illus. N.D. Milton Bradley Co.
--Pussy Purr-Mew the Diary of a Kitten. Tessin, Louise D., illus. LC 27-16574. 126 p. illus. (part col.) 21 1/2 cm. c.1927. Milton Bradley Company.

Wing, Camilla
--The Shiny Scoop. Davidson, Harley F., illus. LC 41-11233. 31 p. illus. (part col.) 29 1/2 x 17 1/2 cm. c.1941. Dannie Books.
--The String Bean Horse. Davidson, Harley F., illus. LC 41-11234. 30 p. illus (part col.) 19 1/2 x 17 1/2 cm. c.1941. Dannie Books.

Wing, Francis Marion (1873-)
--Old Forty Dollars. Wing, Francis Marion (1873-), illus. LC 16-22046. 288 p. incl. front., illus. 20 cm. $1.25. c.1916. The Reilly & Britton Co.

Wing, George L
--Tweedle, the Boy Who Wanted to Go Home. 1st ed. Lyons, Dave, illus. LC 57-9943. 66 p. illus. 24 cm. c.1957. Pageant Press.

Wing, Helen
--Billy Whiskers' Twins. Tamburine, Jean (1930-), illus. LC 56-7106. unpaged. illus. 22 cm. (Rand McNally elf book, 538). c.1956. Rand McNally.
--Butterball, the Little Chick. Chase, Mary Jane, illus. LC 55-11976. unpaged. illus. 17cm. (Rand McNally junior elf book). c.1955. Rand McNally.
--Emmett Kelly in Willie the Clown. Timmins, William Frederick, illus. LC 57-7313. (Illus.). 21cm. (A Rand McNally Elf Bk.). 1957. Rand McNally.
--Happy Twins. 1966. (ISBN 0-8382-0319-1, Hale Giant Books). E. M. Hale and Co.
--The Happy Twins. Cooper, Marjorie (1910-), illus. LC 67-6088. (Illus.). 1 v. (unpaged). 33cm. (Rand McNally giant book). 1967, c.1966. Rand McNally.
--Kitten Twins. (Illus.). (gr. k-2). 1960. (ISBN 0-8382-0412-0). Hale.
--The Kitten Twins. Webbe, Elizabeth, illus. LC 61-11901. (ps-k). 1961. (ISBN 0-528-88846-3). Rand.
--The Lazy Lion. 1st ed. Balet, Jan Bernard (1913-), illus. LC 54-7839. (Illus.). 31p. 24cm. (A Concora Bk.). 1953. Rand McNally and Container Corp. of America.
--Little Duckling. Ozone, Lucy, illus. LC 56-12375. unpaged. illus. 17 cm. (Rand McNally junior elf books, 603). c.1956. Rand McNally.
--The Little House on Wheels. Boyer, Irv, illus. LC 55-7768. (Illus.). 27p. 24cm. 1955. Creative Enterprises.
--Playtime Poodles: A Real Live Animal Book. Westelin, Albert G. & Schmidling, Jack, photos by LC 55-8187. unpaged. illus. 21cm. (Rand McNally elf book, 501). c.1955. Rand McNally.
--Rosalinda. Balet, Jan Bernard (1913-), illus. LC 53-31406. 25cm. 30p. (Slottle Library). 1953. Rand McNally & Co.
--The Squirrel Twins. Webbe, Elizabeth, illus. LC 63-11260. (Illus.). 21 p. 33cm. (Rand McNally giant book). c.1961. Rand McNally.
--Super Circus. Timmins, William Frederick, illus. LC 55-8189. unpaged. illus. 21cm. (Rand McNally elf book, 503). c.1955. Rand McNally.
--Teddy Bear Twins. (Illus.). (gr. k-2). 1965. (ISBN 0-8382-0846-0). Hale.
--The Teddy Bear Twins. Cooper, Marjorie (1910-), illus. LC 66-14018. 1v. (unpaged) col. illus. 33cm. (Rand McNally giant bk). 1966, c.1965. Rand McNally.
--Tubby Turtle. (Illus.). (gr. k-2). 1959. (ISBN 0-8382-0901-7). Hale.
--Tubby Turtle. Adler, Helen, illus. LC 61-11900. unpaged. illus. 33 cm. (Rand McNally giant book). 1961, c.1959. Rand McNally.

Wing, Helen, jt. auth. see Seymour, Alta Halverson.

Wing, Henry Ebeneser (1839-1925)
--Raising the Old Boy: Phases of the Life of a New England Country Lad in the Last Mid-Century. LC 23-17469. 92 p. illus. 17 cm. c.1923. The Abingdon Press.

Wing, Henry Ritchet
--Ten Pennies for Candy. Oechsli, Kelly (1918-), illus. LC 63-9567. unpaged. illus. 17 x 24 cm. (a little owl book. 1963. Holt, Rinehart and Winston.
--What is Big?. Carini, Edward (1923-), illus. LC 63-8239. (Illus.). unpaged. 17x24cm. (A Little Owl Bk.). 1963. Holt, Rinehart and Winston.

Wing, Paul (1892-)
--The Unsuccessful Elf. Irvin, Rea (1881-1972), illus. LC 47-18441. 44 p. illus. (part col.) 24 x 28 cm. 1947. Rinehart & Company, Incorporated.

Wing, Quan, pseud., see Webster, Ethelyn Mae Wing.

Wingate, Gifford W (1925-) & Kendrick, Mitch
--How the Chicken Hawk Won the West: A Play for Children. LC 76-366307. (Illus.). 72 p. 19cm. c.1974. (ISBN 0-573-65047-0). S. French.

Wingeier, Carol
--Where the Jungle Meets the Street. Barth, Claire H., ed. (Orig.). (gr. 4-5). 1976. (ISBN 0-377-00049-5). Friend Pr.

Winifred, Austen, illus.
--Baby Mishook: Or, The Adventures of a Siberian Cub, 11 vols. New ed. Golschmann, Leon, tr. from Russian. (Six to Sixteen Ser.: No. 8). 1905. Set. H M Caldwell Co.

Winkler, Bee, jt. auth. see Otchis, Ethel Herberg.

Winkler, Carol Serra, jt. auth. see Carol, Lois.

Winkler, Gershon (1949-)
--The Hostage Torah: A Thrilling Blend of Espionage, Suspense, and Spiritual Confrontation That Stirs the Souls of Three Young Men in the Holyland. Jones, Yochanan, illus. LC 81-81313. (Illus.). 115 p. 23cm. (Judaica Youth Series). 1981. (ISBN 0-910818-33-9). (ISBN 0-910818-34-7) Judaica Press.

Winkler, Louis see Carol, Lois, pseud.

Winkler, R., jt. auth. see Gartner, P.

Winkler, Richard
--Boy Who Saw an Alligator in His Bathtub. Cobb, Betty, illus. LC 61-12387. (Illus.). 26cm. 48p. (gr. k-3). 1961. (ISBN 0-8114-7506-9). Steck-V.

Winkler, Susan D
--Stranger to My Heart. LC 56-58791. 224p. 20cm. 1956. Avalon Books.

Winkowski, Fred
--The Martian Crystal Egg. LC 79-2011. (Illus.). 32 p. c.1980. (ISBN 0-06-026561-2). (ISBN 0-06-026562-0). Harper & Row.

Winky, Pops
--Andy Ant. LC 77-78006. (Illus.). 42 p. 27cm. c.1977. (ISBN 0-918872-01-4). Pacific Pub. House.

Winlow, Anna C
--Our Little Burmese Cousin. LC 31-11368. xi p., 2 l., 157 p. col. front., plates. 19 1/2 cm. (The little cousin series). c.1931. L. C. Page & Company.
--Our Little Chilean Cousin. Leland, Stanley F., illus. LC 28-27612. x p., 2 l., 140 p. col. front., illus. (map) plates. 19 1/2 cm. (The little cousin series). c.1928. L. C. Page & Company.
--Our Little Florentine Cousin of Long Ago, Being the Story of Filippo, a Boy of Renaissance Florence. Merrill, Frank Thayer (1848-), illus. LC 29-19795. ix p., 2 l., 155 p. col. front., plates. 19 1/2 cm. (little cousins of long ago series). c.1929. L. C. Page & Company.
--Our Little Lithuanian Cousin. Foster, John M., illus. LC 26-179918. 2 p. l., vii-viii p., 2 l., 122 p. col. front., illus. (map) plates. 19 1/2 cm. (The little cousin series). c.1926. L. C. Page & Company.

Winlow, Anna C., jt. auth. see Winlow, Clara Vostrovsky, Mrs.

Winlow, Clara Vostrovsky, Mrs. (1876-), tr. see Kozisek, Josef.

Winlow, Clara Vostrovsky, Mrs. (1876-)
--Barbora: Our Little Bohemian Cousin. LC 11-29727. xi p., 2 l., 95 p. front., plates. 19 1/2 cm. (The little cousin series $0.50). 1911. L. C. Page & Company.
--The Kitten That Grew Too Fat. Hogan, Inez (1895-), illus. LC 29-20831. 2 p. l., 1, 93, 1 p. illus. (part col.) 17 x 22 1/2 cm. c.1929. Macrae Smith Company.
--Our Little Bulgarian Cousin. Doseff, Ivan, illus. LC 13-9290. ix p., 1 l., 2, 114 p. col. front., col. plates. 19 1/2 cm. (The Little cousin series $0.60). 1913. L. C. Page & Company.
Our Little Carthaginian Cousin of Long Ago: Being the Story of Hanno, a Boy of Carthage. LC 15-15606. xiv, 127 p. col. front., plates. 19 1/2 cm. (little cousins of long ago series) $0.60). 1915. The Page Company.
--Our Little Czecho-Slovak Cousin. Meister, Charles E., illus. LC 20-6448. viii p., 2 l., 124 p. front., plates. 19 1/2 cm. (On verse of half-title: The little cousin series). 1920. The Page Company.
--Our Little Finnish Cousin. O'Brien, Harriet, illus. LC 18-12017. ix p., 1 l., 98 p. front., plates. 19 1/2 cm. (On verse of half-title: The little cousin series). 1918. The Page Company.
--Our Little Jugoslav Cousin. LC 23-9270. 5 p. l., 106 p. col. front., col. plates. 19 1/2 cm. (The little cousin series). [illegible] L. C. Page and Company (Incorporated.
--Our Little Roumanian Cousin. Meister, Charles E., illus. LC 17-21795. vii p., 2 l., 113 p. front., plates. 19 1/2 cm. (On verse of half-title: The little cousin series). 1917. The Page Company.
--Our Little Servian Cousin. Goss, John, illus. LC 13-22510. vii p., 2 l., 101 p. front., plates, port. 19 1/2 cm. (The little cousin series). 1913. L. C. Page & Company.

Winlow, Clara Vostrovsky, Mrs. (1876-) & Winlow, Anna C.
--Our Little Ukrainian Cousin. Withington, Elizabeth R., illus. LC 25-18294. vi p., 2 l., 131 p. col. front., illus. (map) plates. 19 1/2 cm. (The little cousin series). c.1925. L. C. Page & Company.

Winn, Alison, pseud., see Wharmby, Margot.

Winn, Alison, pseud.
--Aunt Isabella's Umbrella. Wharmby, Margot. Ambrus, Glenys, illus. LC 76-50026. (Illus.). 24 p. 21cm. (Stepping stones). 1977, c.1976. (ISBN 0-516-03579-7). Childrens Press.
--Helter Skelter. Wharmby, Margot. Ede, Janina (1937-), illus. (Illus.). (gr. 1-3). 1966. Verry.
--Swings and Things. Wharmby, Margot. Corbett, Jennie & Fortnum, Peggy, pseud. (1919-), illus. Nuttal-Smith, Margaret Emily Noel. LC 65-10760. (Illus.). 112 p. 21cm. 1965. Rand McNally.

Winn, Chris
--Archie's Acrobats. Winn, Chris, illus. LC 83-10123. 1984. (ISBN 0-8052-3878-6). Schocken Books.

Winn, Chris & Beadle, Jeremy
--Rodney Rootle's Grown-Up Grappler & Other Treasures from the Museum of Outlawed Inventions. Winn, Chris, illus. (Illus.). 32p. (gr. 4-6). 1983. (ISBN 0-316-94752-0, Pub. by Atlantic Monthly Pr.). Little.

Winn, Janet, jt. auth. see Boehm, Bruce Janet.

Winn, Janet Bruce (1928-)
--Home in Flames. Pucci, Albert John (1920-), illus. LC 75-159327. (Illus.). 224p. (gr. 4-8). 1972. (ISBN 0-695-80238-0). (ISBN 0-695-40238-2). Follett.

Winn, Laura Rocke (1902-)
--Margie Asks Why. Padgett, Jim, illus. LC 63-12807. (Illus.). 21cm. 248p. 1963. Southern Pub. Assn.

Winn, Marie (1936-)
--Fisherman Who Needed a Knife: A Story About Why People Need Money. Johnson, John Emil (1929-), illus. LC 72-12429. (Illus.). (ps-3). 1970. (ISBN 0-671-65101-3, Juveniles). (ISBN 0-671-65099-8). S&S.
--The Man Who Made Fine Tops: A Story About Why People Do Different Kinds of Work. Johnson, John Emil (1929-), illus. LC 73-101895. (Illus.). 50 p. 17cm. 1970. Simon and Schuster.
--Shiver, Gobble and Snore: A Story About Why People Need Laws. Darrow, Whitney, Jr. (1909-), illus. 1972. (ISBN 0-671-65180-3). Simon & Schuster.
--The Thief-Catcher: A Story About Why People Pay Taxes. Darrow, Whitney, Jr. (1909-), illus. LC 70-144208. (Illus.). 42 p. 16cm. (Her Concept storybooks). 1972. (ISBN 0-671-65162-5). Simon and Schuster.

Winn, Marie (1936-), ed.
--The Fireside Book of Fun & Game Songs. Darrow, Whitney, Jr. (1909-), illus. Miller, Allan, contrib. by. (Illus.). index. 224p. (gr. 1 up). 1974. (ISBN 0-671-65213-3, Juveniles). S&S.
--What Shall We Do & Allee Galloo: Playsongs & Singing Games for Young Children. Kuskin, Karla Seidman (1932-), illus. LC 72-85039. (Illus.). 96 two color ils. 96p. (ps). 1970. (ISBN 0-06-026537-X, HarpJ). Har-Row.

Winn, Marie (1936-) & Miller, Allan, eds.
--The Fireside Book of Children's Songs. Alcorn, John (1935-), illus. 1965. Simon and Schuster.
--The Fireside Book of Children's Songs. Alcorn, John (1935-), illus. LC 65-17108. (Illus.). 192 p. 29cm. 1966. Simon and Schuster.

Winnick, Karen Beth Binkoff (1946-)
--Patch and the Strings. Winnick, Karen Beth Binkoff (1946-), illus. LC 76-56446. (Illus.). 32 p. 29cm. c.1977. Lippincott.

--Sandro's Dolphin. Winnick, Karen Beth Binkoff (1946-), illus. LC 79-21264. (Illus.). 55 p. 22cm. c.1980. (ISBN 0-688-41944-5). (ISBN 0-688-51944-X). Lothrop, Lee & Shepard Books.

Winnington, Laura, ed.

--The Outlook Fairy Book for Little People. (Illus.). (The Outlook Bks.). N.D. Grosset & Dunlap.

--The Outlook Fairy Book for Little People. N.D. Macmillan.

--The Outlook Fairy Book for Little People. Conacher, J., illus. LC 3-31944. vi p., 1 l., 313 p. front., illus. 25 cm. 1903. The Outlook Company.

--The Outlook Story Book for Little People. new ed. x p., 1 l., 207 p. incl. front., illus. 20 cm. 1911. Macmillan Company.

--The Outlook Story Book for Little People. LC 2-27732. x p., 1 l., 207 p. incl. front., illus., plates. 25 cm. 1902. The Outlook Company.

Winokur, Joan Gelman, jt. auth. see The, Three Bears.

Winokur, Joan Gelman (1935-), retold by see The, Three Bears.

Winokur, Joan Gelman (1935-), retold by see Three Little Pigs.

Winold, Suzie Aiken, Mrs.

--The Jim Family: A Bird Story for Little Folks. LC 12-18789. 41 p. front., illus. 18 cm. c.1911. Jennings & Graham.

Winscom, Jane Anne

--Onward: or,the Mountain Clamberers. 312p. N.D. E. P. Dutton.

--Vineyard Laborers. N.D. Dood & Mead.

Winship, Florence Sarah

--Fuzzy Wuzzy Puppy. Suzanne, illus. LC 54-37046. (Illus.). unpaged. 17cm. (Fuzzy Wuzzy Tell-a-Tales). c.1954. Whitman Pub Co.

Winship, Florence Sarah, illus.

--A B C 1 2 3, and Sounding Rhymes. LC 47-5591. 65 p. col. illus. 29 cm. c.1947. Whitman Pub. Co.

--Fifty Favorite Rhymes of Mother Goose. (Illus.). 24p. (gr. k-1). 1976. (ISBN 0-307-69053-9, Golden Pr). Western Pub.

--Mother Goose. (Illus.). (Golden Cloth Bk). (ps). 1972. (ISBN 0-307-10745-0, Golden Pr). Western Pub.

Winslow, Barbara

--Samantha Goes to Georgetown on the C & O Canal. LC 73-86072. (Illus.). 28 p. 1973. (ISBN 0-87858-048-4). Westover Pub. Co.

Winslow, Helen Maria (1851-)

--Concerning Polly and Some Others. Copeland, Charles, illus. 1902. Lothrop, Lee & Shepard.

Winslow, Janette Dyckman

--Penny Plants Petunias. 1940. Meadow Publishing Co.

Winslow, Joan

--Retch, Romance, and a Riot. 1st ed. LC 83-47993. p. cm. (A Lippincott Page Turner). c.1983. (ISBN 0-397-32063-9). (ISBN 0-397-32064-7). Lippincott.

--Romance Is a Riot. LC 83-47993. 160p. (Lippincott Page-Turner Ser.). (gr. 7 up). 1983. (ISBN 0-397-32063-9, JBL-J). (ISBN 0-397-32064-7). Har-Row.

Winslow, Lucinda, jt. auth. see Hammond, Bruce.

Winslow, Margaret E.

--The Boy Convict of Bermuda. 301p. N.D. Sunday-School Library.

--Cherie's Answered Prayer. A Story of Southern France. LC 12-402751. 285 p. front., 3 pl. 18 cm. c.1886. Presbyterian Board of Publication.

--His Keeper. (Illus.). N.D. Methodist Bk Concern.

--Katie Robertson: A Girl's Story of Factory Life. (The Girl Chum Ser.). N.D. A. L. Burt Co.

--Katie Robertson: A Girl's Story of Factory Life. (Illus.). (The Wellesley Series for Girls). N.D. A. L. Burt.

--Marion: Or, Safe in the Shadow of the Rock. LC 12-40345. 188 p. incl. front., pl. 17 1/2 cm. c.1881. American Sunday-School Union.

--Marion's Temptation: Or, Abiding in Christ. LC 12-40346. 154 p. front., 2 pl. 18 cm. c.1881. Presbyterian Board of Publication.

--Maurizio's Boyhood: Or, All for Christ. A Tale of Modern Martyrdom. LC 12-402665. 272 p. 18 cm. c.1889. Presbyterian Board of Publication and Sabbath-School Work.

--Michal Ellis's Text: A Story for Girls. LC 12-40435. 320 p. front., 3 pl. 18 cm. c.1883. Presbyterian Board of Publication.

--Miss Malcolm's Ten. (Illus.). (The Wellesley Series for Girls). N.D. A. L. Burt.

--Miss Malcolm's Ten: A Story for Girls. LC 26-75202. 3 p. l., 325 p. front. 19 1/2 cm. (On cover: The girl chums series). N.D. A. L. Burt Company.

--Miss Malcolm's Ten: A Story for the King's Daughters. LC 12-402672. 3 p. l., 325 p. front., 2 pl. 19 1/2 cm. c.1892. Congregational Sunday-School and Publishing Society.

--A More Excellent Way: And Other Stories of the Crusade. LC 12-40133. 217 p. front., pl. 17 1/2 cm. 1876. National Temperance Society and Publication House.

--Rescued from the Street. A Story for Boys. LC 12-402683. 280 p. front., 2 pl. 18 cm. c.1887. Presbyterian Board of Publication and Sabbath-School Work.

--Three Years at Glenwood: A Story of School Life. (The Girl Chums Ser.). N.D. A. L. Burt Company.

--Three Years at Glenwood: A Story of School Life. (Illus.). (The Wellesley Series for Girls). N.D. A. L. Burt.

--The West Beach Boys. A Seaside Story. LC 12-40347. 344 p. front., 3 pl. 18 cm. c.1887. Presbyterian Board of Publication.

Winslow, Marjorie

--Mud Pies and Other Recipes. Blegvad, Erik (1923-), illus. LC 61-10336. unpaged. illus. 20 cm. 1961. Macmillan.

Winsor, Frederick

--The Space Child's Mother Goose. Parry, Marian (1924-), illus. 1963. Simon and Schuster.

Winsor, Robert

--A Little Happy Music. Winsor, Robert, illus. LC 77-75192. (Illus.). 32 p. 25cm. 1969. Hawthorn Books.

Winston, Carol, jt. auth. see Preston, Effa Estelle.

Winston, Clara, tr. see Andersen, Hans Christian.

Winston, Clara, tr. see Baumann, Hans.

Winston, Clara, tr. see Benary-Isbert, Margot.

Winston, Clara, tr. see Cervantes Saavedra, Miguel de.

Winston, Clara, tr. see Kastner, Erich.

Winston, Clara, tr. see Kooiker, Leonie.

Winston, Clara, tr. see Linde, Gunnel.

Winston, Clara, tr. see Munchausen.

Winston, Clara, tr. see Steinmann-Brunner, Elsa.

Winston, Clara, tr. see Winterfeld, Henry.

Winston, clara, tr. see Zimnik, Reiner.

Winston, Clare, tr. see Kastner, Erich.

Winston, Nelson W., Mrs., et al.

--Drifting Anchor Ser. Containing "Drifting Anchor," "Percy Raydon," "George Clifford's Loss," and "Gain.", 5 vols. N.D. D. Lothrop & Co.

Winston Press Editorial Staff, ed.

--The Christmas Pageant. De Paola, Tomie, pseud. (1934-), illus. De Paola, Thomas Anthony. (Illus.). 1979. (ISBN 0-03-046356-4). (ISBN 0-86683-605-5). Winston Pr.

Winston, Richard, tr. see Andersen, Hans Christian.

Winston, Richard, tr. see Baumann, Hans.

Winston, Richard, tr. see Benary-Isbert, Margot.

Winston, Richard, tr. see Cervantes Saavedra, Miguel de.

Winston, Richard, tr. see Kastner, Erich.

Winston, Richard, tr. see Kooiker, Leonie.

Winston, Richard, tr. see Linde, Gunnel.

Winston, Richard, tr. see Munchausen.

Winston, Richard, tr. see Steinmann-Brunner, Elsa.

Winston, Richard, tr. see Winterfeld, Henry.

Winston, Richard, tr. see Zimnik, Reiner.

Winston, Richard, Tr, jt. auth. see Frey, Alexander Moriz.

Winter, Ginny Linville (1925-)

--Ballet Book. Winter, Ginny Linville (1925-), illus. (Illus.). (gr. 1-5). 1962. (ISBN 0-8392-3001-X). Astor-Honor.

--What's in My Tree. Winter, Ginny Linville (1925-), illus. (Illus.). ils. 32p. (gr. k-1). 1962. (ISBN 0-8392-3044-3). Astor-Honor.

Winter, Jeanette, retold by.

--The Christmas Visitors: A Norwegian Folktale. Winter, Jeanette, illus. LC 68-24560. (Original Author: Peter Christen Asbjrnsen, 1812-1885). (Illus.). 32 p. 1968. (ISBN 0-394-81207-7). (ISBN 0-394-91207-1). Pantheon Books.

--The Girl & the Moon Man: A Siberian Folktale. Winter, Jeanette, illus. LC 83-19462. 32p. (gr. 1-3). 1984. (ISBN 0-394-86326-7, Pant Bks Young). (ISBN 0-394-96326-1). Pantheon.

Winter, Jeanette, illus.

--Hush Little Baby. LC 83-12182. c.1984. (ISBN 0-394-86325-9). Pantheon Books.

Winter, John Strange, pseud., see Stannard, Henrietta Eliza Vaughan Palmer.

Winter, John Strange, pseud. (1856-1911)

--The Christmas Story. Stannard, Henrietta Eliza Vaughan Palmer. (Illus.). (Dainty Ser.). N.D. Henry Altemus Co.

--Little French Baby. Stannard, Henrietta Eliza Vaughan Palmer. N.D. E. P. Dutton & Co.

--That Little French Baby. Stannard, Henrietta Eliza Vaughan Plamer. (Illus.). (Dainty Ser.). N.D. Henry Altemus Co.

Winter, John Strange, pseud. (1856-1911) & Crompton, Frances Eliza

--The Christmas Fairy. Stannard, Henrietta Eliza Vaughan Palmer. (Illus.). N.D. E. P. Dutton & Co.

--The Christmas Fairy. Stannard, Henrietta Eliza Vaughan Palmer, 1 of 15 vols. (Illus.). (Dainty Ser. of Choice Gift Bks: No. 13). 1905. Set. Henry Altemus Co.

--A Christmas Fairy and Other Stories. Stannard, Henrietta Eliza Vaughan Palmer. Winter, Johns Strange, pseud. 48 p. incl. front., illus. 21 cm. 1900. H. Altemus Company.

--Little Gervaise. Stannard, Henrietta Eliza Vaughan Palmer. N.D. E. P. Dutton & Co.

--Little Gervaise. Stannard, Henrietta Eliza Vaughan Palmer. 48 p. incl. front., illus. 21 cm. N.D. H. Altemus Company.

Winter, Klaus, jt. auth. see Bischoff, Helmut.

Winter, Klaus (1928-) & Bischoff, Helmut

--Happy Owls. Edelberg, Linda R., tr. (gr. 1-4). 1967. (ISBN 0-87460-029-4). Lion.

--Hoppla, Hoppla Farmerman. LC 66-7284. (Illus.). 32 p. 28cm. 1966. Childrens Press.

--King & the Parrot & Other Fables. Winter, Klaus (1928-) & Bischoff, Helmut, illus. LC 69-11544. (Illus.). 32p. (gr. k-3). 1969. Knopf.

Winter, Milo Kendall (1888-1956)

--Billy Popgun. Winter, Milo Kendall (1888-1956), illus. LC 12-25536. vii, 1 p., 1 l., 60 2 p. incl. col. front., illus., col. plates 27 1/2 cm. $2.00. 1912. Houghton Mifflin Company.

Winter, Milo Kendall (1888-1956), illus.

--Arabian Nights. (Windermere Ser.). N.D. Rand McNally & Co.

Winter, Paula Cecelia (1929-)

--The Bear & the Fly. Winter, Paula Cecelia (1929-), illus. (Illus.). (ps-3). 1981. (ISBN 0-590-31568-4). Scholastic Inc.

--The Bear & the Fly: A Story. Winter, Paula Cecelia (1929-), illus. LC 76-2479. (Illus.). (ps-1). 1976. Crown. **Awards: (NYT); (ALA).**

--Sir Andrew. Winter, Paula Cecelia (1929-), illus. LC 80-14069. p. cm. (gr. k-3). c.1980. (ISBN 0-517-53911-X). Crown Publishers.

Winterbotham, Russell Robert (1904-1971)

--Joyce of the Secret Squadron: A Captain Midnight Adventure. Authorized. Darwin, Erwin L., illus. LC 42-226153. 3 p. l., 11-251 p. illus. 21 cm. 1942. Whitman Publishing Company.

--Red Ryder and the Mystery of Whispering Walls. LC 41-18718. 2 p. l., 9-220 p. illus. 20 1/2 cm. c.1941. Whitman Publishing Company.

Winterburn, Florence Hull, Mrs. (1858-)

--Liberty Hall: A Story for Girls. LC 16-17495. 3 p. l., 299, 1 p. front., plates. 19 1/2 cm. $1.25. c.1916. Harper & Brothers.

Winterfeld, Henry (1901-)

--Castaways in Lilliput. Hutchinson, William Miller (1916-), illus. Schabert, Kyrill (1909-1983), tr. from Ger. LC 60-8413. 188 p. illus. 21 cm. 1st U.S. edition. 1960. (ISBN 0-15-214820-5). Harcourt, Brace. **Award: (ALA).**

--Detectives in Togas. Kleinert, Charlotte, illus. Winston, Richard (1817-1979) & Winston, Clara, trs. from Ger. LC 56-6922. (Illus.). (gr. 4-6). 1966. (ISBN 0-15-625315-1, VoyB). HarBraceJ.

--Detectives in Togas. Kleinert, Charlotte, illus. Winston, Richard (1917-1979) & Winston, Clara, trs. from Ger. LC 56-6022. 205 p. illus. 22 cm. 1st U.S. edition. c.1956. Harcourt, Brace.

--Mystery of the Roman Ransom. Biermann, Fritz, illus. McCormick, Edith Joan (1934-), tr. from Germ. LC 71-137759. (Illus.). 186 p. 21cm. 1st U.S. edition. 1971. (ISBN 0-15-256612-0). Harcourt Brace Jovanovich.

--Mystery of the Roman Ransom. Biermann, Fritz, illus. McCormick, Edith Joan (1934-), tr. from Ger. LC 77-3673. p. cm. (Voyager/HBJ book). 1977, c.1971. (ISBN 0-15-662340-4). Harcourt Brace Jovanovich.

--Star Girl. Wegner, Fritz (1924-), illus. Schabert, Kyrill, tr. 191p. 1957. Harcourt, Brace and Co Inc.

--Trouble at Timpetill. Scabert, Kyrill (1909-1983) & Hutchinson, William Miller (1916-), illus. LC 65-12616. 192p. illus. 21cm. 1st U.S. edition. c.1965. Harcourt.

Winteringham, Victoria

--Penguin Day. 1st ed. Winteringham, Victoria, illus. LC 81-47112. (Illus.). 32 p. 23cm. c.1982. (ISBN 0-06-026513-2). (ISBN 0-06-026514-0). Harper & Row.

Winters, Faye

--Norton McNerd. N.D. Carlton Press.

Winters, Jane

--Cornelia's Customers. Parsons, Priscilla, illus. LC 28-20917. vii, 293 p. front., plates. 19 1/2 cm. $1.75. c.1928. The Century Co.

Winters, Mary K., pseud., see Horowitz, Caroline.

Winters, Mary K.

--The Ask-Me Book of Best-Loved Fairy Tales. Flory, Jane Trescott (1917-), illus. LC 50-3999. (Illus.). 26p. 22cm. (Happy Hour Bks.). 1950. Hart.

Winterton, Gayle, pseud., see Adams, William Taylor.

Winterton, Gayle, pseud. (1822-1897)

--The Young Actor. Adams, William Taylor. (The Boys Own Library). N.D. David McKay.

Winterton, Paul see Garve, Andrew, pseud.

Winther, Barbara (1926-)

--Dramatized Folktales of Africa and Asia: One-Act, Royalty-Free Plays for Young People Adapted from the Stories and Legends of Africa and Asia. LC 76-15558. p. cm. c.1976. (ISBN 0-8238-0189-6). Plays, Inc.

Winthrop, Elizabeth, pseud., see Mahony, Elizabeth Winthrop.

Winthrop, Elizabeth, pseud. (1948-)

--Are You Sad, Mama?. Mahony, Elizabeth Winthrop. 1st ed. Diamond, Donna (1950-), illus. LC 77-25661. (Illus.). 24 p. 18cm. c.1979. (ISBN 0-06-026539-6). (ISBN 0-06-026544-2). Harper & Row.

--Being Brave is Best. Mahony, Elizabeth Winthrop. Cooke, Tom, illus. LC 83-23696. (Illus.). 40p. (A Tale from the Care Bears). (ps-3). 1984. (ISBN 0-910313-19-9). Parker Bro.

--Belinda's Hurricane. Mahony, Elizabeth Winthrop. Watson, Wendy McLeod (1942-), illus. LC 84-8028. (Illus.). 64p. (gr. 1-4). 1984. (ISBN 0-525-44106-9). (ISBN 0-525-44106-9). Dutton.

--Bunk Beds. Mahony, Elizabeth Winthrop. 1st ed. Himler, Ronald Norbert (1937-), illus. LC 72-76499. (Illus.). 30 p. 1972. (ISBN 0-06-026531-0). (ISBN 0-06-026531-0). Harper & Row.

--Castle in the Attic. Mahony, Elizabeth Winthrop. Hyman, Trina Schart (1939-), illus. 179p. 1985. (ISBN 0-8234-0579-6). Holiday.

--The Christmas Pageant. Mahony, Elizabeth Winthrop. Wilburn, Kathy, illus. LC 83-83277. (Illus.). 23 p. 15cm. (First Little Golden Book). c.1984. (ISBN 0-307-68150-5). Western Pub. Co.

--Grover Sleeps Over. Mahony, Elizabeth Winthrop. Swanson, Maggie, illus. LC 83-83279. (Illus.). 25 p. 22cm. (A Growing-up Book). c.1984. (ISBN 0-307-12010-4). (ISBN 0-307-62110-3). Published by Western Pub. Co. in Conjunction with Children's Television Workshop.

--I Think He Likes Me. Mahony, Elizabeth Winthrop. Saldutti, Denise, illus. 1979. Harper.

--I Think He Likes Me. Mahony, Elizabeth Winthrop. Saldutti, Denise, illus. LC 78-22478. (Illus.). 32 p. 21cm. c.1980. (ISBN 0-06-026551-5). (ISBN 0-06-026552-3). Harper & Row.

--Journey to the Bright Kingdom. Mahony, Elizabeth Winthrop. Mikolaycak, Charles (1937-), illus. LC 78-23261. (Illus.). 47 p. 25cm. c.1979. (ISBN 0-8234-0357-2). Holiday House.

--Katharine's Doll. Mahony, Elizabeth Winthrop. 1st ed. Hafner, Marylin (1925-), illus. LC 83-1408. (Illus.). 32 p. 24cm. c.1983. (ISBN 0-525-44061-5). E.P. Dutton.

--A Little Demonstration of Affection. Mahony, Elizabeth Winthrop. LC 74-20390. 152 p. 22cm. 1975. (ISBN 0-06-026557-4). (ISBN 0-06-026558-2). Harper & Row. **Award: (ALA).**

--Marathon Miranda. Mahony, Elizabeth Winthrop. LC 78-20615. 155 p. 21cm. c.1979. (ISBN 0-8234-0349-1). Holiday House.

--Miranda in the Middle. Mahony, Elizabeth Winthrop. LC 80-15847. 128 p. 21cm. c.1980. (ISBN 0-8234-0422-6). Holiday Huose.

--Potbellied Possums. Mahony, Elizabeth Winthrop. McClintock, Barbara, illus. LC 76-17829. (Illus.). 32 p. 22cm. c.1977. (ISBN 0-8234-0289-4). Holiday House.

--The Shoelace Box. Mahony, Elizabeth Winthrop. Wilburn, Kathy, illus. LC 83-82197. (Illus.). 24 p. 21cm. (little golden book). 1984. (ISBN 0-307-02054-1). (ISBN 0-307-60233-8). Golden Press.

--Sloppy Kisses. Mahony, Elizabeth Winthrop. Burgess, Anne (1942-), illus. LC 80-13673. (Illus.). 32 p. 17cm. c.1980. (ISBN 0-02-793210-9). Macmillan.

--Sloppy Kisses. Mahony, Elizabeth Winthrop. Burgess, Anne (1942-), illus. LC 83-9446. p. cm. 1983. (ISBN 0-14-050433-8). Puffin Books.

--Strawberry Shortcake & the Big Balloon Race. Mahony, Elizabeth Winthrop. Sustendal, Pat, illus. LC 83-8167. (Illus.). 40p. (Strawberry Shortcake Ser.). (ps-3). 1983. (ISBN 0-910313-08-3). (ISBN 0-910313-08-3). Parker Bro.

--That's Mine. Mahony, Elizabeth Winthrop. McCully, Emily Arnold (1939-), illus. LC 77-73832. (Illus.). 32 p. 21cm. c.1977. (ISBN 0-8234-0308-4). Holiday House.

--Tough Eddie. Mahony, Elizabeth Winthrop. Hoban, Lillian (1925-), illus. LC 84-13664. c.1985. (ISBN 0-525-44164-6). Dutton.

--Walking Away. Mahony, Elizabeth Winthrop. Massena, Noelle, illus. 1973. Harper.

Winthrop, Elizabeth, pseud. (1948-), adapted by

--A Child Is Born: The Christmas Story. Mahony, Elizabeth Winthrop. Mikolaycak, Charles (1937-), illus. LC 82-11728. (Illus.). 32p. (gr. k-3). 1983. (ISBN 0-8234-0472-2). Holiday.

Winthrop, Robert D., jt. auth. see Munch, Theodore William.

AUTHOR INDEX WISE, FRANCIS

Winton, Iris
--Look Out for Pirates!. Vestal, Herman B., illus. LC 61-7790. (Illus.). 63 p. 24cm. (Beginner books, B-22). c.1961. Beginner Books.
Winwar, Frances (1900-)
--Cupid, the God of Love. Mill, Eleanor, illus. LC 59-6140. 54 p. illus. 22 cm. (Legacy books, Y-10). 1959. Random House.
Winward, Irene
--Josephine's Adventures. 127p. 1958. Moody.
Wippern, Adolphus George (1868-), tr. see France, Anatole.
Wire, Edith
--The Enchanted Island: Or, The Adventures of Miss Sassyfras. LC 39-133552. 1 p. l., 51 p. plates. 19 1/2 cm. c.1939. Wire Company.
Wire, Harold Channing
--High Country. N.D. The Westminster Press.
--The Witness Tree. Hastings, Howard Livingston (1887-), illus. xi, 238 p. col. front., col. plates. 20 1/2 cm. c.1930. Thomas Y. Crowell Company.
Wirries, Mary Mabel, Mrs. (1894-)
--The Barrys at Briarhill. LC 31-8808. 160 p. front. 19 1/2 cm. 1931. Benziger Brothers.
Gay Witch April and Other Poems. Hartzell, Edward E., illus. LC 37-810. 73 p. col. illus. 28 cm. 1936. Keddington-Mission Printing Co.
--Juan of San Bruno. Genevieve, Sister, illus. LC 48-17425. 155 p. illus. 21 cm. 1948. Ave Maria Press.
--Mary Rose at Boarding School. LC 24-4867. 141 p. front. 19 cm. 1924. Benziger Brothers.
--Mary Rose at Rose Gables. LC 28-28679. 137 p. front. 19 cm. 1928. Benziger Brothers.
--Mary Rose, Graduate. LC 26-197312. 159 p. front. 19 cm. 1926. Benziger Brothers.
--Mary Rose in Friendville. LC 30-31036. 144, 1 p. front. 19 cm. 1930. Benziger Brothers.
--Mary Rose keeps House. N.D. Benziger Bros.
--Mary Rose, Sophomore. LC 25-3089. 176 p. front. 19 cm. 1925. Benziger Brothers.
--Mary Rose's Sister, Bess. LC 32-305220. 121 p. front. 19 cm. 1932. Benziger Brothers.
--Patsy Goes to the Mountains. LC 34-372401. 173 p. front. 19 cm. 1934. Benziger Brothers.
--Paula of the Drift. LC 29-22332. 161, 1 p. incl. front. 19 cm. 1929. Benziger Brothers.
--Shadows on Cedarcrest. LC 37-18438. 302 p. 17 1/2 cm. c.1937. The Ave Maria Press.
Wirt, Donna Aaron, jt. auth. see Sargent, Susan.
Wirt, Mildred Augustine (1905-)
--Behind the Green Door. LC 40-6308. iv, 211 p. front. 20 cm. (Her Penny Parker mystery stories). c.1940. Cupples and Leon Company.
--Behind the Green Door. LC 58-1322. 211 p. illus. 20 cm. (Her Penny Parker mystery stories). 1958. Cupples and Leon Co.
--The Brownie Scouts and Their Tree House. LC 51-3934. 210 p. front. 20 cm. 1951. Cupples and Leon Co.
--The Brownie Scouts at Silver Beach. LC 52-3113. 215 p. illus. 20 cm. 1952. Cupples and Leon Co.
--The Brownie Scouts at Snow Valley. LC 50-44. 204 p. front. 20 cm. 1949. Cupples and Leon.
--The Brownie Scouts at Windmill Farm. LC 53-3806. 213p. illus. 20cm. 1953. Cupples and Leon Co.
--The Brownie Scouts in the Circus. LC 50-46. 212 p. front. 20 cm. 1949. Cupples and Leon.
--Carolina Castle. LC 36-30706. 224 p. front. 19 cm. c.1936. The Penn Publishing Company.
--The Clock Strikes Thirteen. LC 42-13310. iv. 207 p. front. 20 cm. (Her Penny Parker mystery stories). 1942. Cupples and Leon Company.
--The Clue at Crooked Lane. LC 36-8938. vi, 210 p. incl. front. 20 cm. c.1936. Cupples and Leon Company.
--Clue of the Silken Ladder. LC 41-6804. iv, 207 p. front. 20 cm. (Her Penny Parker Mystery Stories). c.1941. Cupples and Leon Company.
--Connie Carl at Rainbow Ranch. LC 39-22447. 3 p. l., 11-251 p. 21 cm. c.1939. The Goldsmith Publishing Company.
--Courageous Wings. Lea, Frank, illus. LC 37-34669. 217 p. front. 19 cm. c.1937. The Penn Publishing Company.
--The Crimson Cruiser. LC 37-92603. iv. 208 p. front. 19 cm. (Her Trailer books). c.1937. Cupples & Leon Company.
--The Cry at Midnight. LC 47-113567. iv, 207 p. front. 20 cm. (Her Penny Parker mystery stories). 1947. Cupples and Leon Co.
--Dan Carter and the Cub Honor. LC 53-3895. 216p. illus. 20cm. (Her The Dan Carter books). 1953. Cupples and Leon Co.
--Dan Carter and the Great Carved Face. LC 52-37327. 210 p. illus. 20 cm. 1952. Cupples and Leon Co.
--Dan Carter and the Haunted Castle. LC 51-4167. 203 p. front. 20 cm. her the dan carter books. 1951. Cupples and Leon.
--Dan Carter and the Money Box. LC 50-9674. 216 p. front. 20 cm. (Her A Cub Scout book). c.1950. Cupples and Leon.
--Dan Carter, Cub Scout. LC 50-47. 210 p. front. 20 cm. 1949. Cupples and Leon.
--Dan Carter, Cub Scout, and the River Camp. LC 50-106. 213 p. front. 20 cm. 1949. Cupples and Leon Co.
--Danger at the Drawbridge. LC 40-6307. iv, 211 p. front. 20 cm. (Her Penny Parker mystery stories). c.1940. Cupples and Leon Company.
--Danger at the Drawbridge. LC 58-47879. 211 p. illus. 20 cm. (Her Penny Parker mystery stories). 1958. Cupples and Leon Co.
--Dot and Dash at Happy Hollow. LC 38-173833. iii, 209 p. front. 19 1/2 cm. (Her Dot and Dash books). c.1938. Cupples & Leon Company.
--Dot and Dash at the Maple Sugar Camp. LC 38-17382. iii, 210 p. front. 19 1/2 cm. (Her Dot and Dash books). N.D. C.
--Dot and Dash at the Seashore. LC 40 6306. iii, 212 p. front. 19 cm. (Her Dot and Dash books). c.1940. Cupples & Leon Company.
--Dot and Dash in the North Woods. LC 38-17384. iii, 209 p. front. 19 1/2 cm. (Her Dot and Dash books). c.1938. Cupples & Leon Company.
--Dot and Dash in the Pumpkin Patch. LC 39-11080. iii, 210 p. front. 19 1/2 cm. (Her Dot and Dash books). c.1939. Cupples & Leon Company.
--Flash Evans and the Darkroom Mystery. LC 40-10373. iv, 212 p. front. 20 cm. (Her Flash Evans books). c.1940. Cupples & Leon Company.
--Flash Evans: Camera News Hawk. LC 40-103740. iv, 211 p. front. 20 cm. (Her Flash Evans books). c.1940. Cupples & Leon Company.
--Ghost Beyond the Gate. LC 43-16324. 2 p. l., 209 p. front. 20 cm. (Her Penny Parker mystery stories). 1943. Cupples and Leon Company.
--Ghost Gables. LC 39-11048. iii, 205 p. front. 20 cm. c.1939. Cupples and Leon Company.
--Ghost Gables. N.D. World Publishing Co.
--The Girl Scouts at Mystery Mansion. Gayer, Marguerite, illus. LC 57-49156. 218 p. illus. 20 cm. 1957. Cupples and Leon Co.
--The Girl Scouts at Penguin Pass: Or, Trail of the Snowman. LC 55-25863. 218p. illus. 20cm. c.1953. Cupples and Leon Co.
--Girl Scouts at Singing Sands. Gayer, Marguerite, illus. LC 55-129343. 222p. illus. 20cm. 1955. Cupples and Leon Co.
--Guilt of the Brass Thieves. LC 45-22122. 2 p. l., iii-iv, 210 p. front. 19 cm. (Her Penny Parker mystery stories). 1945. Cupples and Leon Company.
--The Hollow Wall Mystery. LC 36-8939. 2 p. l., 209 p. front. 20 cm. c.1936. Cupples and Leon Company.
--Hoofbeats on the Turnpike. LC 45-1417. 2 p. l., 211 p. front. 20 cm. (Her Penny Parker mystery stories). c.1944. Cupples and Leon Company.
--Linda. Rodewald, Fred C., illus. LC 40-6309. v, 278 p. front., plates. 21 1/2 cm. c.1940. Cupples & Leon Company.
--Mystery of the Laughing Mask. LC 40-10376. iii, 203 p. front. 20 cm. c.1940. Cupples and Leon Company.
--The Painted Shield. LC 39-18654. iii, 207 p. front. 20 cm. c.1939. Cupples and Leon Company.
--The Painted Shield. N.D. World Publishing Co.
--Penny Nichols and the Knob Hill Mystery. Rev ed. LC 39-22448. 4 p. l., 15-250 p. 21 cm. c.1939. The Goldsmith Publishing Company.
--Penny Nichols Finds a Clue. LC 36-414. 3 p. l., 11-247 p. 19 1/2 cm. c.1936. The Goldsmith Publishing Company.
--The Phantom Trailer. LC 38-17276. iv, 206 p. front. 19 1/2 cm. (Her Trailer books). c.1938. Cupples & Leon Company.
--Pirate Brig. Lee, Manning De Villeneuve (1894-1980), illus. LC 50-7435. 194 p. illus. 21 cm. 1950. Scribner.
--The Runaway Caravan. LC 37-9471. iv. p., 207 p. front. 19 1/2 cm. (Her Trailer books). c.1937. Cupples & Leon Company.
--Ruth Darrow in the Air Derby: Or, Recovering the Silver Trophy. Foster, John M., illus. LC 30-8181. 216 p. front. 19 1/2 cm. c.1930. Barse & Co.
--Ruth Darrow in the Fire Patrol: Or, Capturing the Redwood Thieves. Foster, John M., illus. LC 30-9323. 215 p. front. 19 1/2 cm. (Her Ruth Darrow flying stories). c.1930. Barse & Co.
--Ruth Darrow in Yucatan. Foster, John M., illus. LC 31-12253. 216 p. front. 19 1/2 cm. (Her Ruth Darrow flying stories). c.1931. Barse & Co.
--Saboteurs on the River. 2 p. l., 211 p. front. 20 cm. (Her Penny Parker Mystery Stories). 1943. Cupples and Leon Company.
--The Secret Pact. LC 41-6805. iv, 208 p. front. 20 cm. (Her Penny Parker mystery stories). c.1941. Cupples and Leon Company.
--The Shadow Stone. LC 37-9256. 2 p. l., 206 p. front. 20 cm. c.1937. Cupples & Leon Company.
--The Sky Racers. Landau, Jacob (1917-), illus. LC 35-25386. 224 p. front. 19 cm. c.1935. The Penn Publishing Company.
--Tale of the Witch Doll. LC 39-11047. iv, 210 p. front. 20 cm. (Her Penny Parker mystery stories). c.1939. Cupples and Leon Company.
--Tale of the Witch Doll. LC 58-4325. 240 p. illus. 20 cm. (Her Penny Parker mystery stories, 1). c.1958. Cupples and Leon Co.
--Through the Moon-Gate Door. LC 38-17386. iii, 206 p. front. 20 cm. c.1938. Cupples and Leon Company.
--Timbered Treasure. iii, 208 p. front. 19 1/2 cm. (Her Trailer books. no. 3). c.1937. Cupples & Leon Company.
--The Twin Ring Mystery. LC 35-6271. 2 p. l., 212 p. front. 20 cm. c.1935. Cupples & Leon Company.
--The Vanishing Houseboat. LC 39-11046. iv, 204 p. front. 20 cm. (Her Penny Parker mystery stories). c.1939. Cupples and Leon Company.
--The Vanishing Houseboat. LC 58-47878. 204 p. illus. 20 cm. (Her Penny Parker mystery stories). 1958. Cupples and Leon Co.
--The Vanishing Houseboat. (Penny Parker Mystery Stories). N.D. Platt & Munk.
Voice from the Cave. iii, 204 p. front. 20 cm. (Her Penny Parker mystery stories). c.1944. Cupples and Leon Company.
--Whispering Walls. LC 46-6430. iv, 212 p. front. 20 cm. (Her Penny Parker Mystery Stories). 1946. Cupples and Leon Company.
--The Wishing Well. LC 42-133113. iv, 206 p. front. 20 cm. (Her Penny Parker mystery stories). c.1942. Cupples and Leon Company.
--The Wooden Shoe Mystery. LC 38-17385. iii, 207 p. front. 20 cm. c.1938. Cupples and Leon Company.
Wirth, Beverly
--Margie and Me. Weinhaus, Karen Ann, illus. LC 82-21075. (Illus.). 48 p. 22cm. c.1983. (ISBN 0-590-07870-4). Four Winds Press.
Wisbeski, Dorothy Gross (1929-)
--Picaro, a Pet Otter. 1st ed. Miller, Edna Anita (1920-), illus. LC 72-111791. (Illus.). 32 p. 1971. Hawthorn Books.
--Picaro, a Pet Otter. treehouse paperback ed. Miller, Edna Anita (1920-), illus. LC 80-18451. (Illus.). 32 p. c.1981. (ISBN 0-13-675702-2). Prentice-Hall.
Wise, Claude Merton, jt. ed. see Diemer, George Willis.
Wise, Daniel see Forrester, Francis, pseud.
Wise, Daniel see Lancewood, Lawrence, pseud.
Wise, Daniel (1813-1898)
--Arthur Ellerslie. Forrester, Francis, pseud. (My Uncle Toby's Library). N.D. Thompson, Brown & Co.
--Arthur's Temptation. Forrester, Francis, pseud. (My Uncle Toby's Library). N.D. Thompson, Brown & Co.
--Arthur's Triumph. Forrester, Francis, pseud. (My Uncle Toby's Library). N.D. Thompson, Brown & Co.
--Aunt Amy. Forrester, Francis, pseud. (My Uncle Toby's Library). N.D. Thompson, Brown & Co.
--Ben Blinker: Or, Maggie's Golden Motto. Forrester, Francis, pseud, 1 of 4 Vols. (Author of "Glen Morris Stories."). (Winwood Cliff Stories). 1882. Lee & Shepard.
--Ben Blinker: Or, Maggie's Golden Motto. Forrester, Francis, pseud, 1 of 4 vols. (Illus.). (Winwood Cliff Ser.). N.D. Set. Methodist Bk Concern.
--Cousin Clara: Or, The Mislaid Jewels. Forrester, Francis, pseud. LC 12-40279. 8, 11-246 p. front., 3 pl. 16 1/2 cm. (Lindendale stories. IV). 1868. H. A. Young & Co.
--Cousin Nellie. Forrester, Francis, pseud. (My Uncle Toby's Library). N.D. Thompson, Brown & Co.
--Dick Duncan. Forrester, Francis, pseud. LC 12-40271. 256 p. incl. front., 4 pl. 17 1/2 cm. (Glen Morris stories. II). 1860. Howe & Ferry.
--Elbert's Return: Or, Foxy at Home Again. Forrester, Francis, pseud. LC 12-40341. 280 p. incl. front., 3 pl. 17 cm. (Hollywood stories. VI). 1874. Perkinpine & Higgins.
--Florence Baldwin's Picnic, and What Came of It. Forrester, Francis, pseud. LC 12-40439. 266 p. incl. front., 3 pl. 17 1/2 cm. (Hollywood stories. II). 1873. Perkinpine & Higgins.
--Florence Baldwin's Picnic, and What Came of It: The Beauty of Right Action Contrasted with the Ugliness of Evil Doing. Forrester, Francis, pseud, 1 of 6 vols. (Illus.). (Hollywood Ser.: Vol. 2). N.D. Set. Methodist Bk Concern.
--Florence Rewarded: Or, Priscilla the Beautiful. Forrester, Francis, pseud. LC 12-40438. 283 p. incl. front., 3 pl. 17 cm. (Hollywood stories. IV). 1873. Perkinpine & Higgins.
--Fretful Lillie. Forrester, Francis, pseud. (My Uncle Toby's Library). N.D. Thompson, Brown & Co.
--Guy Carlton: The Story of a Boy Who Belonged to the "Try Company.". Forrester, Francis, pseud. LC 12-40272. 254 p. incl. front., illus., 3 pl. 17 1/2 cm. (Glen Morris stories. I). 1859. Howe & Ferry.
--The Hollyood Series. Forrester, Francis, pseud, 6 Vols. (Illus.). N.D. Ward & Drummond.
--The Hollywood Ser. Forrester, Francis. Forrester, Francis, pseud, 6 Vols. N.D. N. Tibbals & Sons.
--Jessie Carlton: The Story of a Girl Who Fought with Little Impulse, the Wizard, and Conquered Him. Forrester, Francis, pseud. LC 12-40273. 251 p. incl. front., 4 pl. 17 1/2 cm. (Glen Morris stories. III). 1861. Howe & Ferry.
Lionel's Courage: Or, Clementine's Great Trial. Forrester, Francis, pseud. 291 p. incl. front., 3 pl. 17 cm. (Hollywood stories. III). 1873. Perkinpine & Higgins.
--Louis Sinclair: Or, The Silver Prize Medals. The Story of a Boy Who Escaped from the Hands of a Real Enchanter. Forrester, Francis, pseud. LC 31-195007. 241 p. incl. front., plates. 17 cm. (Lindendale stories). 1867. Graves and Young.
--Minnie Brown. Forrester, Francis, pseud. (My Uncle Toby's Library). N.D. Thompson, Brown & Co.
--Minnie's Pic-Nic. Forrester, Francis, pseud. (My Uncle Toby's Library). N.D. Thompson, Brown & Co.
--Minnie's Play Room. Forrester, Francis, pseud. (My Uncle Toby's Library). N.D. Thompson, Brown & Co.
--Nat and His Chum: Or, The Friendly Rivals. Forrester, Francis, pseud. LC 12-403437. 276 p. incl. front., 3 pl. 17 cm. (Hollywood stories V). 1873. Perkinpine & Higgins.
--Nellie Warren: Or, The Lost Watch. Forrester, Francis, pseud. LC 12-402787. 256 p. front., plates. 16 1/2 cm. (Lindendale stories II). 1866. Graves and Young.
--Peter Clinton: The Story of a Boy. Forrester, Francis, pseud. LC 12-40469. 240 p. front., 3 pl. 17 1/2 cm. (Lindendale stories. V). 1869. H. A. Young & Co.
--Ralph Rattler. Forrester, Francis, pseud. (My Uncle Toby's Library). N.D. Thompson, Brown & Co.
--Redbrook. Forrester, Francis, pseud. (My Uncle Toby's Library). N.D. Thompson, Brown & Co.
--Roderick Ashcourt. Forrester, Francis, pseud, 1 of 4 vols. (Winwood Cliff Stories). 1882. Lee & Shepard.
--Roderick Ashcourt. Forrester, Francis, pseud, 1 of 4 vols. (Illus.). (Winwood Cliff Ser.). N.D. Set. Methodist Bk Concern.
--The Runaway. Forrester, Francis, pseud. (My Uncle Toby's Library). N.D. Thompson, Brown & Co.
--Sidney De Grey: Or, The Rival Schoolboys. Forrester, Francis, pseud. LC 12-402761. 256 p. incl. front. 3 pl. 16 1/2 cm. (Lindendale stories. I). 1865. Graves and Young.
--Stephen and His Tempter: Or, The Children at Hollywood. Forrester, Francis, pseud. LC 12-40344. 254 p. incl. front., 3 pl. 17 cm. (Hollywood stories. (I). 1873. Perkinpine & Higgins.
--Thorncliffe Hall. Forrester, Francis, pseud, 1 of 4 Vols. (Illus.). (Winwood Cliff Ser.: No.4). N.D. Set. Publications of the Methodist Book Concern.
--Thorncliffe Hall: Or, Why Joel Milford Changed His Opinion of Boys Whom He Called "Goody-Goody Fellows.". Forrester, Francis, pseud, 1 of 4 vols. (Illus.). (Winwood Cliff Stories). 1882. Lee & Shepard.
--Walter Sherwood: The Story of an Easy, Good-Natured Boy. Forrester, Francis, pseud. LC 12-402740. 256 p. incl. 4 pl. front. 17 1/2 cm. (Glen Morris stories. IV). 1862. Howe & Ferry.
--Winwood Cliff: Or, Oscar the Sailor's Son. Forrester, Francis, pseud, 1 of 4 vols. (Illus.). (Winwood Cliff Stories). 1882. Lee & Shepard.
--Winwood Cliff: Or, Oscar the Sailor's Son. Forrester, Francis, pseud, 1 of 4 vols. (Illus.). (Winwood Cliff Ser.). N.D. Set. Methodist Bk Concern.
--Winwood Cliff Series. Forrester, Francis, pseud, 4 Vols. (Illus.). N.D. Publciations of the Methodist Book Concern.
--Winwood Cliff Stories. Forrester, Francis, pseud, 4 vols. (Illus.). 1882. Set. Lee & Shepard.
Wise, Francis H. & Wise, Joyce M.
--Bernie, the Saint. new ed. (Illus.). 21p. (Orig.). (Dr. Wise Learn to Read Ser.: No. 20). (gr. 1). 1980. (ISBN 0-915766-41-8). Wise Pub.
--Ike & Mike. (Dr. Wise Learn to Read Ser.). (Illus.). (Phonetic Reader Ser: No. 15). (ps-1). 1975. (ISBN 0-915766-34-5). Wise Pub.
--Jack, The Rabbit. (Illus.). 21p. (Dr. Wise Learn to Read Ser.: 19). (gr. 1). 1976. (ISBN 0-915766-37-X). Wise Pub.

--Jay's Fat Cat. Wise, Joyce M., illus. (Dr. Wise Learn to Read Ser.). (Illus.). 20p. (Phonetic Reader Ser: No. 7). (ps-1). 1974. (ISBN 0-915766-29-9). Wise Pub.
--Kites. (Dr. Wise Learn to Read Ser.). (Illus.). (Learn to Read Ser.: No. 17). (gr. 1). 1977. (ISBN 0-915766-38-8). Wise Pub.
--Park the Car. Wise, Joyce M., illus. (Dr. Wise Learn to Read Ser.). (Illus.). (Phonetic Reader Ser: No. 12). (ps-1). 1975. (ISBN 0-915766-32-9). Wise Pub.
--Red Sail. (Dr. Wise Learn to Read Ser. 18). (Illus.). 1978. (ISBN 0-915766-40-X). Wise Pub.
--Snowman. (Dr. Wise Learn to Read Ser.). (Illus.). (Learn to Read Ser.: No. 16). (gr. 1). 1976. (ISBN 0-915766-37-X). Wise Pub.
--Storybooks. (Illus.). 105p. (Learn to Read Ser. Books 16-20: Vol. 4). (gr. k-1). 1979. (ISBN 0-915766-44-2). Wise Pub.
Wise, John Sergeant (1846-1913)
--Diomed: The Life, Travels and Observations of a Dog. Chapman, J. Linton, illus. (Illus.). N.D. Grosset & Dunlap.
Wise, Joyce M., jt. auth. see Wise, Francis H.
Wise, Lu Celia & Oklahoma State Dept. of Education
--Mini Myths and Legends of Oklahoma Indians. LC 78-623116. (Illus.). 64 p. 29cm. c.1978. The Department.
Wise, Robert A
--The Ghost Town Monster. Snyder, Paul (1923-), illus. LC 74-16076. p. cm. (His Sea Wolf mysteries). 1974. EMC Corp.
--Mystery of Menaloose Island. Williams, Don, illus. (Illus.). 160 p. 21cm. 1967. A. Whitman.
--Mystery of Tanglefoot Island. Snyder, Paul (1923-), illus. LC 74-16077. p. cm. (His Sea Wolf mysteries). 1974. EMC Corp.
--Mystery of Totem Pole Inlet. Snyder, Paul (1923-), illus. LC 74-16078. p. cm. (His Sea Wolf mysteries). 1974. (ISBN 0-88436-138-1). EMC Corp.
--The Treasure of Raven Hill. Snyder, Paul (1923-), illus. LC 74-16079. p. cm. (His Sea Wolf mysteries). 1974. (ISBN 0-88436-140-3). EMC Corp.
Wise, Ursula Von
--Michael and the Elephant. Schreiber, Irene, illus. Stirling, Helen, tr. N.D. Hartcourt Brace & World Inc.
Wise, William (1923-)
--All on a Summer's Day. Binzen, Bill, illus. LC 77-153972. (Illus.). 43 p. 1971. Pantheon Books.
--Cowboy Surprise. Galdone, Paul (1914-), illus. (Illus.). (See & Read Storybooks Ser). (gr. k-3). 1961. (ISBN 0-399-60108-2). Putnam.
--Detective Pinkerton & Mr. Lincoln. Zitzewitz, Hoot Von, illus. N.D. E. P. Dutton & Co.
--Fresh As a Daisy, Neat As a Pin. Leder, Dora, illus. LC 77-99131. (Illus.). 64 p. 24cm. (Stepping-stone book). 1970. Parents' Magazine Press.
--The House with the Red Roof. (Illus.). 48p. 1962. G P Putnum's Sons.
--House with the Red Roof. Polseno, Jo, illus. (Illus.). (See & Read Storybooks Ser). (gr. k-3). 1961. Putnam.
--Jonathan Blake: The Life and Times of a Very Young Man. 1st ed. Simon, Howard (1903-1979), illus. LC 56-8904. (Illus.). 52 p. 24cm. 1956. Knopf.
--The Lazy Young Duke of Dundee. Cooney, Barbara (1917-), illus. LC 78-98425. (Illus.). 47 p. 24cm. 1970. Rand McNally.
--Nanette, the Hungry Pelican. Lubell, Winifred A. Milius (1914-), illus. LC 68-19435. (Illus.). 48 p. 24cm. 1969. (ISBN 0-528-82494-5). Rand McNally.
--Silversmith of Old New York: Myer Myers. Fisher, Leonard Everett (1924-), illus. LC 57-10859. 180 p. illus. 22 cm. (Covenant books). 1958. Farrar, Straus and Cudahy.
--Sir Howard the Coward. Perl, Susan (1922-1983), illus. LC 67-24182. (Illus.). 64 p. 23cm. (See and read beginning to read book). 1968, c.1967. Putnam.
--The Story of Mulberry Bend. Van Zitzewitz, Hoot, illus. LC 63-8593. unpaged. illus. 22 x 26 cm. c.1963. Dutton.
--The Terrible Trumpet. Biro, Val, pseud. (1921-), illus. Biro, Balint Stephen. LC 69-17137. (Illus.). 48 p. 20cm. 1969, c.1966. W. W. Norton.
Wise, William (1923-), retold by.
--Monster Myths of Ancient Greece. Pinkney, Jerry (1939-), illus. LC 80-25530. (Illus.). 45 p. 23cm. 1981. (ISBN 0-399-61143-6). Putnam.
Wise, Winifred Esther (1906-1970)
--Away with the Circus. Brock, Esther, illus. LC 36-31238. 157 p. incl. col. front., illus., plates. 21 cm. 1936. A. Whitman & Co.
--Frances a la Mode. LC 56-10434. 224 p. 21 cm. 1956. Macrae Smith Co.
--Frances by Starlight. LC 58-8727. 201 p. 22 cm. 1958. Macrae Smith Co.
--Minnow Vail. LC 62-15254. 212 p. illus. (on lining papger) 20 cm. (Teen novel). c.1962. Witman Pub. Co.
--The Revolt of the Darumas. Komoda, Beverly (1939-), illus. LC 70-117561. (Illus.). 38 p. 1970. Parents' Magazine Press.
--Swift Walker: A True Story of the American Fur Trade. Wright, Cameron, illus. LC 37-28571. 6 p. l., 3-888 p. incl. front., plates (2 double) 22 cm. c.1937. Harcourt, Brace and Company.
--The Wishing Year. LC 63-19033. 216 p. 20 cm. (Teen novel). 1963. Whitman Pub. Co.
Wiseman, Ann Sayre see Denzer, Ann Wiseman, pseud.
Wiseman, Anne, jt. auth. see McLean, Mollie.
Wiseman, Bernard (1922-)
--Billy Learns Karate. Wiseman, Bernard (1922-), illus. LC 76-8222. p. cm. c.1976. (ISBN 0-03-016601-2). Holt, Rinehart and Winston.
--Bobby and Boo, the Little Spaceman. Wiseman, Bernard (1922-), illus. LC 77-23456. (Illus.). 64 p. 24cm. c.1978. (ISBN 0-03-021546-3). Holt, Rinehart and Winston.
--Cats! Cats! Cats!. Wiseman, Bernard (1922-), illus. LC 83-27288. (Illus.). 23cm. 48p. (ps-3). 1984. (ISBN 0-8193-1127-8). (ISBN 0-8193-1125-1). Parents.
--Christmas with Morris and Boris. 1st ed. Wiseman, Bernard (1922-), illus. LC 83-11962. (Illus.). 40 p. 25cm. c.1983. (ISBN 0-316-94855-1). Little, Brown.
--The Clowns Nose. Wiseman, Bernard (1922-), illus. 1981. Garrard Pub. Co.
--Detective Dog. Wiseman, Bernard (1922-), illus. LC 77-146815. (Illus.). 29 p. 22cm. (Fun-to-learn mystery). 1971. Platt & Munk.
--Doctor Duck & Nurse Swan. Wiseman, Bernard (1922-), illus. LC 83-16528. (Illus.). 32p. (ps-1). 1984. (ISBN 0-525-44095-X). Dutton.
--Don't Make Fun!. Wiseman, Bernard (1922-), illus. LC 82-6240. (Illus.). 32 p. 24cm. 1982. (ISBN 0-395-32086-0). Houghton Mifflin.
--Elmer's Egg. Wiseman, Bernard (1922-), illus. (Illus.). 40p. (Orig.). (ps-3). 1983. (ISBN 0-590-32762-3). Scholastic Inc.
--Halloween with Morris and Boris. Wiseman, Bernard (1922-), illus. LC 75-11577. (Illus.). 48 p. 24cm. 1975. (ISBN 0-396-07189-9). Dodd, Mead.
--The Hat That Grew. Wiseman, Bernard (1922-), illus. (Illus.). (gr. k-2). 1967. (ISBN 0-8382-0320-5). Hale.
--Hats and Coats, Cows and Goats. Wiseman, Bernard (1922-), illus. LC 73-146814. (Illus.). 28 p. 22cm. (Fun-to-learn reader). 1971. Platt & Munk.
--Hooray for Patsy's Oink!. LC 79-21625. (Illus.). 32 p. 23cm. c.1980. (ISBN 0-8116-6079-6). Garrard Pub. Co.
--Iglook's Seal. Wiseman, Bernard (1922-), illus. LC 76-23410. p. cm. 1977. (ISBN 0-396-07396-4). Dodd, Mead.
--Little New Kangaroo. Lopshire, Robert Martin (1927-), illus. LC 72-92444. (Illus.). 40 p. 23cm. (Ready-to-read). 1973. (ISBN 0-02-793220-6). Macmillan.
--Log & Admiral Frog. Wiseman, Bernard (1922-), illus. LC 61-7331. (Illus.). 26cm. 32p. (gr. k-3). 1961. (ISBN 0-06-026546-9, HarpJ). Har-Row.
--The Lucky Runner. Wiseman, Bernard (1922-), illus. LC 79-14215. (Illus.). 48 p. 23cm. (Forreal book). c.1979. (ISBN 0-8116-4313-1). Garrard Pub. Co.
--Morris and Boris: Three Stories. Wiseman, Bernard (1922-), illus. LC 74-6555. (Illus.). 64 p. 24cm. 1974. Dodd, Mead.
--Morris Goes to School. Wiseman, Bernard (1922-), illus. LC 75-77944. (Illus.). 64 p. 23cm. (I can read book). 1970. Harper & Row.
--Morris Has a Birthday Party!. 1st ed. Wiseman, Bernard (1922-), illus. LC 82-22860. (Illus.). 40 p. 25cm. c.1983. (ISBN 0-316-94854-3). Little, Brown.
--Morris Has a Cold. Wiseman, Bernard (1922-), illus. LC 77-12030. (Illus.). 48 p. 24cm. c.1978. (ISBN 0-396-07522-3). Dodd, Mead.
--Morris Is a Cowboy: A Policeman, and a Baby Sitter. Wiseman, Bernard (1922-), illus. LC 60-9460. 64 p. illus. 23 cm. (I can read book). 1960. Harper.
--Morris Is a Cowboy: A Policeman and Baby Sitter. Wiseman, Bernard (1922-), illus. LC 60-9460. (Illus.). (I Can Read Books). (gr. k-3). 1960. (ISBN 0-06-026556-6, HarpJ). Har-Row.
--Morris Tells Boris Mother Moose Stories and Rhymes. Wiseman, Bernard (1922-), illus. LC 79-694. (Illus.). 48 p. 24cm. c.1979. (ISBN 0-396-07693-9). Dodd, Mead.
--Morris Tells Boris Mother Moose Stories & Rhymes. Wiseman, Bernard (1922-), illus. (Illus.). 48p. Repr (Pub. by Dodd, Mead). 1980. (ISBN 0-590-30999-4). Scholastic Inc.
--Morris the Moose. Wiseman, Bernard (1922-), illus. LC 59-10101. unpaged (chiefly illus.) 19 x 22 cm. 1959. Harper.
--Morris the Moose Goes to School. Wiseman, Bernard (1922-), illus. (Illus., Pub. by Har-Row). Orig. Title: Morris Goes to School. (gr. k-3). 1972. (ISBN 0-590-09256-1). (ISBN 0-590-20645-1). Scholastic Inc.
--My Googoo. Wiseman, Bernard (1922-), illus. LC 79-688. p. cm. 1979. (ISBN 0-03-046331-9). Holt, Rinehart and Winston.
--The Nutty Nature Book. Wiseman, Bernard (1922-), illus. LC 74-148200. (Illus.). 28 p. 22cm. (Fun-to learn nature book). 1971. Platt & Munk.
--Oscar Is a Mama!. Wiseman, Bernard (1922-), illus. LC 79-24737. (Illus.). 32 p. 23cm. c.1980. (ISBN 0-8116-6081-8). Gerrard Pub. Co.
--Penny's Poodle Puppy, Pickle. Wiseman, Bernard (1922-), illus. LC 79-26403. (Illus.). 32 p. 23cm. c.1980. (ISBN 0-8116-6080-X). Garrard Pub. Co.
--Quick Quackers. Wiseman, Bernard (1922-), illus. LC 79-14216. (Illus.). 32 p. 23cm. c.1979. Garrard Pub. Co.
--The Silly Science Book. LC 74-148199. (Illus.). 22cm. (A Fun to Learn Science Bk.). 1971. Platt & Munk.
--Tails Are Not for Painting. Wiseman, Bernard (1922-), illus. LC 79-18373. (Illus.). 32 p. 23cm. c.1980. (ISBN 0-8116-7500-9). Garrard Pub. Co.
--Three Stories About Morris & Boris. Wiseman, Bernard (1922-), illus. (Illus.). (gr. k-3). 1976. (ISBN 0-590-09849-7). Scholastic Inc.
Wiseman, Cardinal
--The Lamp of the Sanctuary. (Our Boys' and Girls' Ser.). N.D. Benziger Brothers' Pub.
Wiseman, David (1916-)
--Adam's Common. LC 84-10936. 175 p. 22cm. 1984. (ISBN 0-395-35976-7). Houghton Mifflin Co.
--Blodwen & the Guardians. 176p. (gr. 5up). 1983. (ISBN 0-395-33892-1). HM.
--Jeremy Visick. LC 80-28116. 170 p. 22cm. 1981. (ISBN 0-395-30449-0). Houghton Mifflin. **Award: (ALA).**
--Thimbles: A Novel. LC 81-20280. ix, 134 p. 22cm. 1982. (ISBN 0-395-31867-X). Houghton Mifflin. **Award: (ALA).**
Wiseman, Herbert (1886-)
--The Singing Class. LC 66-29608. (Illus.). xii, 146 p. 20cm. 1967. Pergamon Press.
Wiseman, Nicholas Patrick Stephen, Cardinal (1802-1865)
--The Lamp of the Sanctuary. A Tale. LC 8-30419. 278 p. 15 cm. (On cover: Catholic boys & girls library). 1883. T. B. Noonan & Co.
Wishaw, Fred
--Boris the Bear Hunter: A Tale of Peter the Great and His Times, 98 vols. (The Rugby Ser.). 1905. Set. A L Burt Co.
--Boris the Bear Hunter: A Tale of Peter the Great and His Times. (Illus.). (The Round Table Ser.). N.D. A. L. Burt's Pubs.
Wiskur, Darrell D.
--Mary's Merry Chase. Silver Dollar City, Inc., ed. Wiskur, Darrell, illus. (Illus.). (Silver Dollar City Stories). (ps-1). 1977. (ISBN 0-686-19126-9). Silver Dollar.
--Silver Dollar City's ABC Words & Rhymes. Silver Dollar City, Inc., ed. Wiskur, Darrell D., illus. (Illus.). (Silver Dollar City Stories). (ps-1). 1977. (ISBN 0-686-19127-7). Silver Dollar.
Wisler, Gene Clifton (1920-)
--Buffalo Moon. 144p. (gr. 5-9). 1984. (ISBN 0-525-67146-3). Lodestar Bks.
--The Raid. LC 85-10152. 120 p. 22cm. c.1985. (ISBN 0-525-67169-2). E.P. Dutton.
--Thunder on the Tennessee. 1st ed. LC 82-21057. 154 p. 22cm. c.1983. (ISBN 0-525-67144-7). Dutton.
--Winter of the Wolf. LC 80-21851. 124 p. 21cm. c.1981. (ISBN 0-525-66716-4). Elsevier/Nelson.
Wisler, Israel Menahem see Poochoo, pseud.
Wisler, Israel Menahem (1930-)
--Methuselah's Gang. Poochoo, pseud. Blaustein, Hank, illus. Segal, Nelly, tr. from Hebrew. LC 80-1010. (Illus.). p. cm. 192p. (gr. 3-7). 1980. (ISBN 0-396-07886-9). Dodd, Mead.
Wismer, Donald (1946-)
--Starluck. LC 81-43375. 186 p. 22cm. 1982. (ISBN 0-385-17872-7). (ISBN 0-385-17873-5). Doubleday.
Wissmann, Ruth Leslie
--Fear Waits on Cypress Road. LC 75-14850. 192p. 1975. (ISBN 0-385-11278-5). Doubleday.
--Katy Kelly of Cripple Creek. Morse, Dorothy Bayley (1906-1979), illus. (Illus.). 203 p. 21cm. 1968. Dodd, Mead.
--The Scuba Divers Mystery. LC 66-15767. 141p. 21cm. c.1966. Dodd.
--The Summer Ballet Mystery. LC 62-17931. 127 p. 21 cm. 1962. Dodd, Mead.
Wister, A. L., tr. see Hillern, Wilhelmine von.
Wister, A. L., Mrs.
--The Old Mam'selle's Secret. N.D. J. B. Lippincott Co.
--Seaside and Fireside Fairies. N.D. J. B. Lippincott.
--Why Did He Not Die. N.D. J. B. Lipincott.
Wister, A. L., Mrs., tr.
--German Fairy Tales. N.D. J. B. Lippincott Co.
Wister, Annie Lee (1830-1908), tr. see Lewald-Stahr, Fanny.
Wister, Annie Lee Furness (1830-1905), tr. see Hacklander, Friedrich Wilhelm, Mrs.
Wister, Annie Lee Furness, Mrs. (1830-1905), tr. see Hacklander, Friedrich Wilhelm, Mrs.
Wister, Annie, Mrs. (1830-1908), tr. see Wicher, Ernst, Mrs.
Wister, Owen (1860-1938)
--The Dragon of Wantley, His Rise, His Voracity & His Downfall: A Romance. Stewardson, John, illus. LC 13-20714. 149 p. incl. front., illus., plates. 25 cm. 1892. J. B. Lippincott Company.
--The New Swiss Family Robinson. N.D. Duffield.
--The Virginian. (Thrushwood Bks.). N.D. Grosset & Dunlap.
--The Virginian. Irwin, Don, illus. LC 68-31325. (Illus.). 282 p. 29cm. 1968. Childrens Press.
--The Virginian. Irwin, Don, illus. LC 73-2313. (Illus.). 282 p. 29cm. (Educator classic library, 6). 1968. Classic Press.
Wit, Dorothy May Knowles De see De Wit, Dorothy May Knowles.
With, Karl Henrik (1805-1865)
--The Mouse Story. Fisher, V. T., illus. Behrens, Gerda Frederiksen & Prall, Dorothea, trs. from Danish LC 22-18665. viii p., 2 l., 147 p. col. front., plates. 21 cm. c.1922. Frederick A. Stokes Company.
--The Mouse Story told by an Old Schoolmaster. N.D. J. B. Lippincott.
Witheridge, Elizabeth Plumb (1907-)
--And What of You, Josephine Charlotte?. 1st ed. McGee, Barbara J. (1943-), illus. LC 69-13527. (Illus.). 169 p. 22cm. 1969. Atheneum.
--Dead End Bluff. Geer, Charles Hand (1922-), illus. LC 66-5732. 186p. illus. 22cm. c.1966. Athenum.
--Dead End Bluff. McGee, Barbara J. (1943-), illus. 1969. (ISBN 0-689-20480-9). Atheneum Publishers.
--Jim Penney's Golden Nugget. D'Adamo, Anthony, illus. LC 61-5100. 158 p. illus. 22 cm. 1961. Abingdon Press.
--Just One Indian Boy. LC 73-84841. 218 p. 22cm. 1974. (ISBN 0-689-30151-0). Atheneum.
--Mara Journeys Home. Wallower, Lucille (1910-), illus. LC 57-13933. 127 p. illus. 21 cm. 1957. Abingdon Press.
--Mara of Old Babylon. Wallower, Lucille (1910-), illus. LC 55-142677. 128p. illus. 21cm. 1955. Abingdon Press.
--Never Younger, Jeannie. LC 63-10367. (Illus.). 150 p. 22cm. 1963. Atheneum.
--Never Younger, Jeannie. 1963. E M Hale.
Withers, Carl, jt. ed. see Jablow, Alta.
Withers, Carl A., jt. ed. see Botkin, Benjamin Albert.
Withers, Carl A. (1900-1970), ed.
--Counting Out. Ripley, Elizabeth Blake (1906-1969), illus. LC 46-11924. 46 p. illus. (part col.) 15 1/2 cm. 1946. Oxford University Press.
--Counting-Out Rhymes. Ripley, Elizabeth Blake (1906-1969), illus. LC 77-107664. (Illus.). 46 p. 16cm. 1970, c.1946. Dover Publications.
--Eenie-Meenie-Minie-Mo & Other Counting-Out Rhymes. Ripley, Elizabeth Blake (1906-1969), illus. (Illus.). 48 ils. 44p. 1970. Dover.
--Favorite Rhymes from a Rocket in My Pocket. 48p. (gr. k-3). 1970. (ISBN 0-590-01551-6). Scholastic Inc.
--The Grindstone of God: A Fable. 1st ed. Bryson, Bernarda (1905-1977), illus. LC 70-98912. (Illus.). 32 p. 27cm. 1970. Holt, Rinehart and Winston.
--I Saw a Rocket Walk a Mile: Nonsense Tales, Chants, and Songs from Many Lands. Johnson, John Emil (1929-), illus. LC 65-12425. 160p. illus. 25cm. c.1965. Holt.
--Man in the Moon: Sky Tales from Many Lands. Wilson, Peggy, illus. LC 69-11819. (Illus.). 144p. (gr. k-6). 1969. (ISBN 0-03-076350-9). (ISBN 0-03-076355-X). HR&W.
--Painting the Moon: A Folktale from Estonia. Adams, Adrienne (1906-), illus. LC 73-116888. (Illus.). 29 p. 27cm. 1970. E. P. Dutton.
--A Rocket in My Pocket: The Rhymes and Chants of Young Americans. Suba, Susanne (1913-), illus. LC 48-4881. vi, 214 p. illus. 25 cm. 1948. H. Holt.
--The Tale of a Black Cat. Cober, Alan Edwin (1935-), illus. LC 66-114211. 32p. illus. 15x22cm. c.1966. Holt.
--The Tale of a Black Cat. Cober, Alan Edwin (1935-), illus. LC 66-11421. (Illus.). 1 v. (unpaged). (Holt Owlet). 1973, c.1966. (ISBN 0-03-006501-1). Holt.

--Where Did That Naughty Little Hamster Go?. Hoffman, Rosekrans (1926-), illus. LC 84-40796. p. cm. 1985, c.1974. (ISBN 0-201-14245-7). Lippincott.

Wold, Jo Anne (1938-)

--Gold City Girl. Armstrong, George Douglas (1927-), illus. LC 77-165825. (Illus.). line drawings. 192p. (gr. 5-8). 1971. (ISBN 0-8075-2986-9). A Whitman.

--Well! Why Didn't You Say So?. Unada, pseud. (1927-), illus. Gliewe, Unada Grace. LC 75-8584. (Illus.). 32 p. 19cm. 1975. (ISBN 0-8075-8724-9). A. Whitman.

Wold, Jo Anne (1938-) & Hockerman, Dennis

--Tell Them My Name Is Amanda. LC 77-14297. p. cm. (Concept book). 1977. (ISBN 0-8075-7768-5). Whitman.

Wolde, Gunilla (1939-)

--Betsy and Peter Are Different. LC 78-66265. p. cm. 1979, c.1975. (ISBN 0-394-84210-3). (ISBN 0-394-94210-8). Random House.

--Betsy and the Chicken Pox. LC 76-9323. (Illus.). 23 p. 17cm. (Betsy books). 1976, c.1975. (ISBN 0-394-83328-7). Random House.

--Betsy and the Doctor. LC 78-50057. (Illus.). 23 p. 17cm. (Betsy books). 1978, c.1977. (ISBN 0-394-83782-7). (ISBN 0-394-93782-1). Random House.

--Betsy and the Vacuum Cleaner. LC 78-66266. p. cm. 1979. (ISBN 0-394-84209-X). (ISBN 0-394-94209-4). Random House.

--Betsy's Baby Brother. LC 75-7568. (Illus.). 24 p. 17cm. (Betsy books). 1975, c.1974. (ISBN 0-394-83162-4). (ISBN 0-394-93162-9). Random House.

--Betsy's First Day at Nursery School. LC 76-9322. (Illus.). 24 p. 17cm. (Her Betsy books). 1976. (ISBN 0-394-83327-9). (ISBN 0-394-93327-3). Random House.

--Betsy's Fixing Day. LC 78-50056. (Illus.). 24 p. 17cm. (Betsy books). 1978, c.1977. (ISBN 0-394-83781-9). (ISBN 0-394-93781-3). Random House.

--This Is Betsy. LC 75-7566. (Illus.). 24 p. 1975. (ISBN 0-394-83161-6). (ISBN 0-394-93161-0). Random House.

--Tommy and Sarah Dress up. LC 71-189799. (Illus.). 24 p. 17cm. 1972. (ISBN 0-395-13785-3). Houghton Mifflin.

--Tommy Builds a House. LC 70-157101. (Illus.). 24 p. 17cm. 1971. (ISBN 0-395-12601-0). Houghton Mifflin.

--Tommy Cleans His Room. Wolde, Gunilla (1939-), illus. LC 77-157099. (Illus.). color ils. 24p. (ps-1). 1971. (ISBN 0-395-12602-9). HM.

--Tommy Goes Out. LC 77-157100. (Illus.). 24 p. 17cm. 1971. (ISBN 0-395-12603-7). Houghton Mifflin.

--Tommy Goes to the Doctor. LC 71-189800. (Illus.). 24 p. 17cm. 1972. (ISBN 0-395-13784-5). Houghton Mifflin.

--Tommy Takes a Bath. LC 73-157098. (Illus.). 24 p. 17cm. 1971. (ISBN 0-395-12604-5). Houghton Mifflin.

Woldin, Beth Weiner (1955-)

--Benjamin's Perfect Solution. Woldin, Beth Weiner (1955-), illus. LC 78-12245. (Illus.). 31 p. c.1978. (ISBN 0-7232-6160-1). F. Warne.

--Chipmunk Stew. Woldin, Beth Weiner (1955-), illus. LC 79-21627. (Illus.). 36 p. c.1980. (ISBN 0-7232-6176-8). F. Warne.

--Ellie to the Rescue. LC 79-2428. p. cm. 1979. (ISBN 0-7232-6168-7). F. Warne.

Woldin, Beth Weiner (1955-), illus.

--Puppy Pals. (Illus.). (A Peggy Cloth Book). (ps). 1978. (ISBN 0-448-46832-8). Platt.

Woldum, Thomas

--Harold Sets a Record. Gadbois, Robert, illus. LC 77-1690. (Illus.). 31 p. 25cm. (Books by children for children). c.1977. (ISBN 0-87191-612-6). Creative Education.

Wolf, A., illus.

--Rabbit & the Turtle. (Illus.). (Early Start Pre-School Readers Ser.). (gr. k-1). N.D. Wonder.

Wolf, Aline D.

--A Book about Anna: For Children & Their Parents. Rajpar, Shamin & Wolf, Gerald, illus. LC 80-84874. (Illus.). 56p. (Orig.). 1981. (ISBN 0-9601016-4-0). (ISBN 0-686-77667-4). Parent-Child Pr.

Wolf, Ann, illus.

--Nursery Tales. N.D (Wonder Books). Grosset & Dunlap.

--Read Aloud Nursery Tales. LC 57-4179. (Illus.). 160p. 1957. Wonder Books Inc.

Wolf, Bernard

--Adam Smith Goes to School. (Illus.). 1978. Harper.

--Adam Smith Goes to School. LC 77-17269. (Illus.). 48 p. c.1978. (ISBN 0-397-31764-6). Lippincott.

--Anna's Silent World. LC 76-52943. 1977. (ISBN 0-397-31739-5, HarpJ). Har-Row.

--Cowboy. Wolf, Bernard, illus. LC 84-20541. (Illus.). 80p. (gr. 5 up). 1985. (ISBN 0-688-03877-8, Morrow Junior Books). (ISBN 0-688-03878-6). Morrow.

--Daniel and the Whale Hunters: The Adventures of a Portuguese Boy in a Whaling Town in the Azores. LC 75-37414. (Illus.). 72 p. 1972. (ISBN 0-394-82359-1). (ISBN 0-394-92359-6). Random House.

--Don't Feel Sorry for Paul. Wolf, Bernard, photos by. LC 74-9925. (Illus.). 96p. (gr. 3-6). 1974. (ISBN 0-397-31588-0, HarpJ). Har-Row.

--Dont Feel Sorry For Paul. Wolf, Bernard, photos by. 130p. 1974. J. b. Lippincott Company.

--Jamaica Boy. (Illus.). 48p. (gr. 5-7). 1971. (ISBN 0-402-14151-2). Regnery.

--Little Weaver of Agato. LC 76-87085. (Illus.). (gr. 3-9). 1969. (ISBN 0-8092-8503-7). Regnery.

--Michael & the Dentist. Wolf, Bernard, illus. LC 80-12343. (Illus.). 48p. (ps-3). 1980. (ISBN 0-590-07637-X, Four Winds). Scholastic Inc.

Wolf, Bob

--Uncle Bob's Bible Stories. Lautermilch, John, illus. (Illus.). 108p. (Orig.). (gr. 4-8). 1982. (ISBN 0-89323-028-6). BMA Pr.

Wolf, Carl Umhau (1914-)

--Freddie. Seed, Jim, illus. LC 48-11062. 31 p. illus. 24 cm. 1948. Wartburg Press.

Wolf, Gary K.

--Killerbowl. LC 75-2857. 168p. (Science Fiction Ser.). 1975. (ISBN 0-385-04738-X). Doubleday.

Wolf, Helen

--Not Quite Three. Castagnoli, Martha, illus. LC 54-35675. unpaged. illus. 17cm. (Tell-a-tale books, 962). c.1954. Whitman Pub. Co.

Wolf, Ingrid & Fuchs, Gertraut, eds.

--Pajaro-Cu-Cu: Animal Rhymes from Many Lands. Wolf, Ingrid & Fuchs, Gertraut, illus. LC 67-22420. (Illus.). 1 v. (unpaged. 1967. Atheneum.

Wolf, Janet (1957-)

--The Best Present is Me. Wolf, Janet (1957-), illus. LC 82-48853. c.1984. (ISBN 0-06-026583-3). Harper & Row.

Wolf, Jill

--Cheepers in Special Times to Share. Wright, Wayne, illus. (Illus.). 22p. (Little Shape Bks.). (ps-3). 1984. (ISBN 0-89954-277-8). Antioch Pub Co.

--Felice: God's Little Lamb in Making Friends. Rudegeair, Jean, illus. (Illus.). 22p. (ps-3). 1985. (ISBN 0-89954-333-2). Antioch Pub Co.

--Panda Pals in Outdoor Fun. Garris, Norma, et al., illus. (Illus.). 22p. (Little Shape Bks.). (ps-3). 1984. (ISBN 0-89954-276-X). Antioch Pub Co.

--Teddy Bears Oh No! It's Bedtime. Wilson-Heaney, Katherine & Kinarney, Tom, illus. (Illus.). 22p. (Teddy Bears Are Ser.). (ps-3). 1985. (ISBN 0-89954-328-6). Antioch Pub Co.

--Teddy Bears Take a Vacation. Wilson-Heaney, Katherine & Kinarney, Tom, illus. (Illus.). 24p. (Teddy Bears Are Ser.). (ps-3). 1985. (ISBN 0-89954-329-4). Antioch Pub Co.

Wolf, Jill & Moore, Clement Clarke (1779-1863)

--Teddy Bears Night Before Christmas. Rudegeair, Jean, illus. (Illus.). 24p. (Teddy Bears Are Ser.). (gr. 3-6). 1985. (ISBN 0-89954-330-8). Antioch Pub Co.

Wolf, Lydia

--Cleopatra. (Illus.). 27 p. 26cm. 1966. Story House Corp.

--Cleopatra. LC 66-31459. (Illus.). 26cm. 27p. 1966. Story House Corp.

--Of All Gone Birds and Mixed-up Cats. Wolf, Lydia, ed. Rahmas, Sigrid, illus. LC 65-28836. 1 v. (unpaged) illus. (part col.) 25 cm. 1965. Story House Corp.

--The Way-Out Witch. Wolf, Lydia, illus. LC 65-28835. 1 v. (unpaged) illus. (part col.) 25 cm. 1965. Story House Corp.

Wolf, Susan, jt. auth. see Isenberg, Barbara.

Wolfcheck, Sylvia C

--A Play for Every Holiday: Short Sketches for Class and Assembly in Elementary Schools. 87 p. 19 cm. c.1935. S. French.

Wolfe, Gene, ed. see Disney, Walt, Productions.

Wolfe, Helen Josephine

--Out in the World: Or, A Selfish Life. N.D. Methodist Bk Concern.

Wolfe, Ida Lee

--The Magic Ring and Other Stories for Juniors and Intermediates. LC 41-79425. 196 p. illus. 19 1/2 cm. c.1941. The Standard Publishing Company.

Wolfe, J., ed.

--Jokes & Riddles. (Peter Possum Paperbacks Ser). 1967. (ISBN 0-531-05113-7). Watts.

Wolfe, Linnie Marsh

--John of the Mountains. N.D. Houghton Mifflin Co.

Wolfe, Lloyd E. (1852-), ed. see Hawthorne, Nathaniel.

Wolfe, Louis (1905-)

--Adventures on Horseback. Brown, Paul (1893-1958), illus. 1952. Dodd Mead & Co.

--Indians Courageous. McCann, Gerald (1916-), illus. N.D. Dodd, Mead & Co.

--Journey of the Oceanauts. (gr. 5 up). N.D. (ISBN 0-448-26095-6). G&D.

--Journey of the Oceanauts: Across the Bottom of the Atlantic Ocean on Foot. (Illus.). 263 p. 21cm. 1968. Norton.

Wolfe, Thomas (1900-1938)

--Look Homeward Angel. 1929. (ISBN 0-684-71941-X, ScribT). Scribner.

Wolfe, Warren

--Buck and Tarheel. Very, Marjorie, illus. LC 38-4879. 143 p. incl.=ront., illus. 19 cm. c.1936. B. Humphries, Inc.

Wolfel, Ursula

--Shooting Star. Rothfuchs, Heiner, illus. Bell, Anthea, tr. 96p. 1981. (ISBN 0-905478-52-5, Pub. by Anderson-Hutchinson England). State Mutual Bk.

Wolfert, Jerry

--Brother of the Wind: A Story of The Niagara Frontier. LC 60-12888. 253 p. 21 cm. 1960. John Day Co.

Wolff, Angelika

--Mom! I Broke My Arm!. Glueckselig, Leo, illus. LC 69-18646. (Illus.). 43 p. 27cm. 1969. Lion Press.

--Mom! I Need Glasses!. Hill, Dorothy (1924-), illus. LC 74-112648. (Illus.). 39 p. 27cm. 1970. (ISBN 0-87460-074-X). (ISBN 0-87460-074-X). Lion Press.

Wolff, Angelika, tr. see Blecher, Wilfried.

Wolff, Ann

--The Grand Master Plan: A Novel. LC 84-14636. p. cm. 1985. (ISBN 0-7145-2827-7). Marion Boyars.

Wolff, Ashley

--The Bells of London: With a Story in Pictures. LC 84-13787. p. cm. 1985. (ISBN 0-396-08485-0). (ISBN 0-396-08485-0). Dodd, Mead.

--Only the Cat Saw. LC 85-7031. (Illus.). 32 p. 26cm. c.1985. (ISBN 0-396-08704-3). Dodd, Mead.

--A Year of Birds. (Illus.). 1984. Dodd. **Award: (ALA).**

Wolff, Barbara

--Evening Gray, Morning Red: A Ready-to-Read Handbook of American Weather Wisdom. LC 76-15640. (Illus.). 64 p. 22cm. (Ready-to-read handbook). c.1976. (ISBN 0-02-793320-2). Macmillan.

Wolff, Carolyn

--Three People. Mack, Stanley (1935-), illus. (Illus.). 46 p. 24cm. 1968. Harlin Quist; Distributed by Crown Publishers.

Wolff, Janet Loeb (1924-)

--Let's Imagine Being Places. Owett, Bernard, illus. (Illus.). (Imagination Books). (gr. k-2). 1961. (ISBN 0-525-33487-4). Dutton.

--Let's Imagine Sounds. Owett, Bernard, illus. LC 62-7496. (Illus.). 32 p. (Imagination book). c.1962. Dutton.

--Let's Imagine Thinking up Things. Owett, Bernard, illus. (Illus.). (Imagination Books). (gr. k-2). 1961. (ISBN 0-525-33599-4). Dutton.

Wolff, Robert Jay (1905-1977)

--Feeling Blue. Wolff, Robert Jay (1905-1977), illus. LC 68-12522. (Illus.). 4 color ils. (gr. 1-5). 1968. (ISBN 0-684-12528-5). Scribner.

--Hello, Yellow!. LC 68-29369. (Illus.). 1 v. (unpaged. 21cm. 1968. Scribner.

Wolff, Ruth

--A Crack In the Side Walk. 288p. 1965. John Day & Co.

--A Crack in the Sidewalk. (gr. 7 up). N.D. (ISBN 0-590-03423-5). Scholastic Inc.

--I, Keturah. (gr. 9 up). 1963. John Day.

--Linsey, Herself (Pub. by John Day). Orig. Title: Crack in the Sidewalk. (gr. 7-12). 1972 (Starline). Schol Bk Serv.

Wolfram Von Eschenbach

--The Story of Parzival, the Templar. Sterling, Mary Blackwell, retold by. Chapman, William Ernest, illus. LC 11-28882. xi p., 1 l., 285 p. front., illus., plates. 21 cm. $1.5. c.1911. E. P. Dutton & Company.

Wolfschlager, Irene Hollands

--Moccasined Feet. LC 29-23132. v, 138 p. col. plates. 19 cm. c.1929. Ginn and Company.

Wolfson, Mack, jt. auth. see Fass, Bernie.

Wolfson, Vi

--Nothing Happens to Children in Beverly Hills. 1975. (ISBN 0-399-11516-1). G. P. Putnam's Sons.

Wolfson, Victor (1910-)

--The Eagle on the Plain. 1947. Simon and Schuster.

Wolitzer, Hilma (1930-)

--Introducing Shirley Braverman. LC 75-25872. p. cm. 1975. (ISBN 0-374-33646-6). Farrar, Straus and Giroux.

--Out of Love. LC 76-40983. 160p. (gr. 7 up). 1976. (ISBN 0-374-35675-0). (ISBN 0-374-45685-2). FS&G.

--Toby Lived Here. LC 78-4550. 147 p. 21cm. 1978. (ISBN 0-374-37625-5). Farrar, Straus, Giroux.

--Wish You Were Here. LC 84-10112. 179 p. 22cm. 1984. (ISBN 0-374-38456-8). Farrar, Straus, Giroux.

Wolitzer, Meg (1959-)

--Caribou. LC 84-4142. 176p. (gr. 7 up). 1984. (ISBN 0-688-03991-X). Greenwillow.

Wolkoff, Judie

--Happily Ever After- Almost: A Novel. LC 81-18028. (Illus.). 215 p., 2 leaves of plates. 22cm. 1982. (ISBN 0-87888-199-9). Bradbury Press.

--A Stranger in the Family. 192p. (gr. 4-6). 1984. (ISBN 0-590-32182-X, Apple Paperbacks). Scholastic Inc.

--Wally. LC 77-75364. (Illus.). 199 p. 22cm. c.1977. (ISBN 0-87888-125-5). Bradbury Press.

--Where the Elf King Sings. LC 80-15298. p. cm. 1980. (ISBN 0-87888-169-7). Bradbury Press.

Wolkoff, Judie, jt. auth. see Murphy, Barbara Beasley.

Wolkstein, Diane (1942-)

--The Banza: A Haitian Story. Brown, Marc Tolon (1946-), illus. LC 81-65845. p. cm. c.1981. (ISBN 0-8037-0428-3). (ISBN 0-8037-0429-1). Dial Press.

--The Cool Ride in the Sky. Galdone, Paul (1914-), illus. LC 72-5269. (Illus.). 32 p. 29cm. 1973. (ISBN 0-394-82489-X). (ISBN 0-394-82489-X). Knopf; Distributed by Random House.

--Eight Thousand Stones: A Chinese Folktale. 1st ed. Young, Ed (1931-), illus. LC 71-99466. (Illus.). 27 p. 1972. Doubleday.

--The Magic Orange Tree, and Other Haitian Folk Tales. Henriquez, Elsa, illus. LC 77-15003. ix, 212 p. 24cm. c.1978. (ISBN 0-394-83390-2). (ISBN 0-394-93390-7). Knopf : Distributed by Random House. **Award: (ALA).**

--The Magic Orange Tree, and Other Haitian Folktales. Henriquez, Elsa, illus. LC 79-22787. (Illus.). ix, 212 p. 23cm. 1980, c.1978. (ISBN 0-8052-0650-7). Schocken Books.

--The Magic Wings: A Tale from China. Parker, Robert Andrew (1927-), illus. LC 83-1611. (Illus.). 32 p. 24cm. (A Unicorn Book). c.1983. (ISBN 0-525-44062-3). Dutton.

--The Red Lion: A Persian Story. Young, Ed (1931-), illus. LC 77-3963. 24p. col. ill. 27cm. (gr. k-3). 1977. (ISBN 0-690-01346-9, TYC-J). (ISBN 0-690-01347-7). Har-Row.

--The Visit. Ehlert, Lois Jane (1934-), illus. LC 76-54297. (Illus.). 29 p. 19cm. c.1977. (ISBN 0-394-83449-6). (ISBN 0-394-93449-0). Knopf : Distributed by Random House.

--White Wave: A Chinese Tale. 1st ed. Young, Ed (1931-), illus. LC 78-4781. (Illus.). 32 p. 27cm. c.1979. (ISBN 0-690-03893-3). (ISBN 0-690-03894-1). Crowell. **Award: (ALA).**

Wolkstein, Diane (1942-), retold by.

--The Red Lion: A Tale of Ancient Persia. Young, Ed (1931-), illus. p. cm. 1977. (ISBN 0-690-01347-7). Crowell.

--Squirrel's Song. Hoban, Lillian (1925-), illus. LC 76-5483. p. cm. 1976. (ISBN 0-394-83120-9). (ISBN 0-394-93120-3). Knopf.

Wolkstein, Diane (1942-) & Marshall, James (1942-)

--Lazy Stories. LC 75-25781. (Illus.). 39 p. 24cm. c.1976. (ISBN 0-8164-3135-3). Seabury Press.

Wollaston, Mary A. (1882-)

--The Song Play Book: Singing Games for Children. Crampton, Charles Ward (1877-), ed. LC 19-6772. vii, 61 p. 28 1/2 cm. 1917. The A. S. Barnes Company.

Wolley, Catherine see Thayer, Jane, pseud.

Wollheim, Donald Allen (1914-)

--Mike Mars and the Mystery Satellite. 1st ed. Orbaan, Albert F. (1913-), illus. LC 63-18231. 190 p. illus. 22 cm. 1963. Doubleday.

--Mike Mars Around the Moon. Orbaan, Albert F. (1913-), illus. LC 64-11703. 192 p. illus. 22 cm. 1964. Doubleday.

--Mike Mars, Astronaut. 1st ed. Orbaan, Albert F. (1913-), illus. LC 60-127890. 188 p. illus. 22 cm. 1961. Doubleday.

--Mike Mars at Cape Canaveral. 1st ed. Orbaan, Albert F. (1913-), illus. LC 61-10653. 186 p. illus. 22 cm. 1961. Doubleday.

--Mike Mars Flies the Dyna-Soar. 1st ed. Orbaan, Albert F. (1913-), illus. LC 62-11373. 1962. Doubleday.

--Mike Mars Flies the X-15. 1st ed. Orbaan, Albert F. (1913-), illus. LC 60-14181. 187 p. illus. 22 cm. 1961. Doubleday.

--Mike Mars in Orbit. 1st ed. LC 61-10654. 188 p. illus. 22 cm. 1961. Doubleday.

--Mike Mars, South Pole Spaceman. 1st ed. Orbaan, Albert F. (1913-), illus. LC 62-15868. 190 p. illus. 22 cm. 1962. Doubleday.

--One Against the Moon. 1st ed. LC 59-5328. 220 p. 21 cm. 1956. World Pub. Co.

--The Secret of Saturn's Rings. LC 54-5068. 207 p. 23cm. (Science fiction novel). 1954. Winston.

--The Secret of the Martian Moons: A Science Fiction Novel. LC 55-5741. 206 p. 23cm. (Science Fiction). 1955. Winston.

--The Secret of the Ninth Planet. 1st ed. LC 59-5328. 203 p. 22 cm. (Science Fiction Novel). 1959. Winston.

Wollheim, Donald Allen (1914-), ed.
--Every Boy's Book of Science-Fiction. LC 51-112968. 254 p. 22cm. (Fell's Science Fiction Library.). 1951. Fell.
Wolman, Arnold
--Ho Ho Ho. Wolter, Ted, illus. (Illus.). 36p. (Orig.). (Billy, the Bear Ser.). N.D. (ISBN 0-686-97657-6). Peradam Pub Hse.
--Tickle, the Pickle, Meets God. rev., 2nd ed. (Illus.). 16p. (Orig.). (Tickle, the Pickle Trilogy Ser.). 1975. (ISBN 0-686-97654-1). Peradam Pub Hse.
--Tickle, the Pickle, Meets Marsha, the Mushroom. Wolter, Ted, illus. Duval, Arnaud, tr. from Eng. (Illus.). 24p. (Tickle, the Pickle Trilogy Ser.). 1975. (ISBN 0-686-97653-3). Peradam Pub Hse.
Wolman, Judith
--Bad Willie. Atkinson, Wayne, illus. LC 78-74876. (Illus.). (gr. k-3). N.D. Dandelion Pr.
--The Camping Trip. Sukoneck, Karen, illus. LC 78-73534. (Illus.). (gr. 1-4). N.D. Dandelion Pr.
--David's New Baby. Read, Isobel, illus. LC 78-72116. (Illus.). 32 p. 23cm. 1979. (ISBN 0-89799-016-1). Dandelion Press.
--Duncan McTavish in Paris. Moffett, Robin, illus. LC 78-72111. (Illus.). 32 p. 23cm. c.1979. (ISBN 0-89799-100-1). (ISBN 0-89799-011-0). Dandelion Press.
--Jenny's Birthday Party. Read, Isobel, illus. LC 78-72114. (Illus.). 30 p. 1979. (ISBN 0-89799-117-6). (ISBN 0-89799-014-5). Dandelion Press.
--Lizzie and the Tooth Fairy. Sukoneck, Karen, illus. LC 78-72115. (Illus.). 32 p. 23cm. 1979. (ISBN 0-89799-123-0). (ISBN 0-89799-015-3). Dandelion Press.
Wolman, Judith, adapted by.
--Jesus Performs Miracles. Atkinson, Wayne, illus. LC 78-64419. (Illus.). 32 p. 1979. (ISBN 0-89799-034-X). Dandelion Press.
--Rapunzel. LC 78-74131. (Illus.). (gr. 2-5). N.D. Dandelion Pr.
Wolman, Judith, adapted by see Andersen, Hans Christian.
Wolo
--Amanda. LC 41-20739. (Illus.). 37p. 1941. W. Morrow and Company.
--Friendship Valley. LC 46-217398. 44 p. illus. (part. col.) 26 1/2 x 20 1/2 cm. 1946. W. Morrow & Company.
--The Secret of the Ancient Oak. LC 42-226954. 38, 3 p. illus. (part. col.) 26 1/2 x 20 1/2 cm. 1942. W. Morrow and Company.
--Sir Archibald. LC 44-94030. 37, 4 p. illus. (part col.) 26 1/2 x 20 1/2 cm. 1944. W. Morrow and Company.
--Tweedles, Be Brave!. LC 43-17658. 1 p. l., 31, 8 p. illus. (part col.) 27 x 20 1/2 cm. 1943. W. Morrow and Company.
Wolpin, Harriet, ed. see Grimm, Jakob Ludwig Karl (1785-1863) & Grimm, Wilhelm Karl.
Wolters, Richard A. (1920-)
--Beau, from Both Ends of His Leash. Kuhn, Bob, illus. LC 66-11536. 190p. illus. 21cm. c.1966. Dutton.
Wolverton, Ethel Traugh
--The Elbow Island Mystery. LC 47-4267. 237 p. 21 cm. 1947. Howell, Soskin.
--The Ghost Town Mystery. LC 46-266626. 231 p. 21 cm. (Junior mystery league book). 1946. Howell, Soskin.
--Gold at Hunters' Point. 1st ed. Funk, Clotilde Embree, illus. LC 58-9740. 177 p. illus. 21 cm. 1958. Longmans, Green.
--The House on the Desert. LC 46-266767. 218 p. 21 cm. (Junior mystery league book). 1946. Howell, Soskin.
--House on the Desert. N.D. Lothrop Bks.
--That Missing Deed. Foster, John M., illus. LC 31-226556. 3 p. l., v-vi, 297 p. col. front., illus. (plan) plates, 20 cm. c.1931. F. Warne & Co., Inc.
Wolverton, Sarah Foss
--Adventure Islands: A Mystery Tale of the Caribbean. Wilson, Helen Hughes, illus. LC 45-5770. 320 p. col. front., illus., col. plates. 23 1/2 cm. 1945. The Caxton Printers, Ltd.
Wolvertonian
--School Life. (Illus.). (St. Nicholas Series for Boys). N.D. International Book Co.
Wondriska, William Allen (1931-)
--All by Myself. Wondriska, William Allen (1931-), illus. LC 63-15814. (Illus.). 48p. (gr. k-3). 1963. (ISBN 0-03-036130-3). (ISBN 0-03-041570-5). HR&W.
--All the Animals Were Angry. LC 71-119099. (Illus.). 36 p. 21cm. 1970. Holt, Rinehart and Winston.
--John John Twilliger. LC 66-134620. 1v. (unpaged) illus. (pt. col.) 23x26cm. c.1966. Holt.
--A Long Piece of String. LC 63-10790. unpaged (chiefly illus.) 15 x 24 cm. 1963. Holt, Rinehart and Winston.
--Mr. Brown and Mr. Gray. LC 68-11826. (Illus.). 39 p. 23cm. 1968. Holt, Rinehart and Winston.
--Puff. LC 60-16067. (Illus.). 26cm. 1960. Pantheon.
--The Stop. 1st ed. Wondriska, William Allen (1931-), illus. LC 72-76569. (Illus.). 30 p. 1972. (ISBN 0-03-091982-7). Holt, Rinehart and Winston.
--The Tomato Patch. LC 64-12620. (Illus.). 1 v. (unpaged). 23cm. 1964. Holt, Rinehart and Winston.
--Which Way to the Zoo?. (Illus.). 1962. Holt, Rinehart and Winston, Inc.
Wong, Herbert H., jt. auth. see Vessel, Matthew F.
Wong, Herbert H. & Vessel, Matthew F.
--My Goldfish. Stewart, Arvis L., illus. LC 69-15803. (Illus.). 30p. 21 x 26cm. (Science Series for the Young). 1969. Addison-Wesley.
--Our Terrariums. Watson, Aldren Auld (1917-), illus. LC 69-15805. (Illus.). 31p. 21 x 26cm. (Science Ser. for the Young). 1969. Addison-Wesley.
--Our Tree. Longtemps, Kenneth (1933-), illus. LC 69-15804. (Illus.). 31p. 21 x 26cm. (Science Series for the Young). 1969. Addison-Wesley.
Wong, Jade Snow (1922-)
--Fifth Chinese Daughter. Uhl, Kathryn, illus. LC 50-9710. (Illus.). 1950. (ISBN 0-06-011781-0, HarpT). Har-Row.
Wong, Kat & Lowe, Stephanie
--Don't Put the Vinegar in the Copper. LC 78-59161. (Illus.). (Fifth World Tales Ser.). (gr. k-6). N.D. (ISBN 0-89239-017-4, Imprenta de Libros Infantiles). Childrens Book Pr.
Wong, Olive
From My Window. Bellerose, Mark, illus. LC 73-81587. (Illus.). 16 p. 23cm. (Magic circle book). 1974. (ISBN 0-663-25466-3). Ginn.
--Here Comes Pops. Price, George (1901-), illus. LC 73-82297. (Illus.). 24 p. 20cm. (Magic circle book). 1974. (ISBN 0-663-25465-5). Ginn.
Wonsetler, Adelaide Hill & Wonsetler, John Charles (1900-)
--Liberty for Johanny. 1st ed. Wonsetler, John Charles (1900-), illus. LC 43-15072. ix, 278 p. incl. front., illus. 22 1/2 cm. 1943. Longmans, Green and Co.
--Me and the General. 1st ed. Wonsetler, Adelaide Hill & Wonsetler, John Charles (1900-), illus. LC 41-10471. 5 p. l., 3-299, 1 p. incl. front. (map) illus. col. plates. 21 1/2 cm. 1941. A. A. Knopf.
Wonsetler, John Charles, jt. auth. see Wonsetler, Adelaide Hill.
Wood, Alice M.
--Willie & the Shrog. 1983. (ISBN 0-8062-2202-6). Carlton.
Wood, Audrey
Balloonia. Wood, Audrey, illus. (Illus.). 32p. 1981. (ISBN 0-85953-122-8, Pub. by Child's Play England). Playspaces.
--King Bidgood's in the Bathtub. Wood, Don (1945-), illus. 1985. Harcourt.
--Magic Shoelaces. Wood, Audrey, illus. 32p. 1981. (ISBN 0-85953-109-0, Pub. by Child's Play England). Playspaces.
--Moonflute. Wood, Don (1945-), illus. (Illus.). 36p. 1984. (ISBN 0-914676-44-X). Green Tiger Pr.
--The Napping House. Wood, Don (1945-), illus. LC 83-13035. (Illus.). 32p. 1984. (ISBN 0-15-256708-9). (ISBN 0-15-256708-9). Harcourt Brace. **Awards: (NYT); (ALA).**
--Princess & the Dragon. Wood, Audrey, illus. 32p. 1981. (ISBN 0-85953-150-3, Pub. by Child's Play England). Playspaces.
--Quick As a Cricket. Wood, Don (1945-), illus. (Illus.). 32p. 1982. (ISBN 0-85953-151-1, Pub. by Child's Play England). Playspaces.
--Tugford Wanted to Be Bad. 1st ed. Wood, Audrey, illus. LC 83-318. (Illus.). 32 p. 22cm. (A Let Me Read Book). c.1983. (ISBN 0-15-291083-2). Harcourt Brace Jovanovich.
--Twenty-Four Robbers. Wood, Audrey, illus. (Illus.). 32p. 1981. (ISBN 0-85953-100-7, Pub. by Child's Play England). Playspaces.
Wood, Audrey & Morrison, William (1935-)
--Tickleoctopus. LC 79-22600. (Illus.). 32 p. 21cm. 1980. (ISBN 0-395-29083-X). Houghton Mifflin.
Wood, Beech
--Plucky Jim: The Gang of Thieves. N.D. E. & J. B. Young & Co.
Wood, Charles E.
--Book of Indian Tales. new ed. 166p. 1975. (ISBN 0-8149-0712-1). Vanguard.
Wood, Charles Seely (1845-1912)
--Camp-Fires on the Scioto. 319p. 1910. W. A. Wilde Co.
--On the Frontier With St. Clair. (Illus.). 343p. 1910. W. A. Wilde Co.
--On the Frontier with St. Clair: A Story of the Early Settlement of the Ohio Country. Emerson, C. Chase, illus. LC 2-20983. 343 p. front., plates. 19 1/2 cm. 1902. W. A. Wilde Company.
--The Sword of Wayne. (Illus.). 368p. 1910. W. A. Wilde Co.
--The Sword of Wayne. A Story of the Way He Smote the Indians and Brought Them to Sue for Peace. Emerson, C. Chase, illus. LC 3-22815. 6 p. l., 1-370 p. front., 4 pl. 19 1/2 cm. c.1903. W. A. Wilde Company.
Wood, Christopher
--Happy Nursery Rhyme Book. (The Treasury Series for Children). N.D. Thomas Y. Crowell Co.
Wood, Clement (1888-), ed. see Mother Goose.
Wood, Clement (1888-)
--More Adventures of Huckleberry Finn. Bell, Corydon Whitten (1894-), illus. LC 41-293631. 3 p. l., v-x, 271 p. col. front., illus. 21 cm. (World juvenile library). c.1940. The World Publishing Company.
Wood, Colin
--A Confusion of Time. LC 77-12477. p. cm. 1977, c.1975. (ISBN 0-8407-6553-3). T. Nelson.
Wood, David, Jr. (1901-)
--Phantom Killer of the Flying M. Nenninger, Jerome D., illus. LC 73-137770. (Illus.). 165 p. 22cm. 1971. (ISBN 0-87004-209-2). Caxton Printers.
Wood, David (1944-)
--Flibberty and the Penguin: A Musical Play. LC 75-306675. (Illus.). 5, 68 p. 22cm. (French's Acting Edition). 1974. (ISBN 0-573-05033-3). French.
--The Gingerbread Man: A Musical Play. LC 80-481733. (Illus.). 54 p. 22cm. 1977. (ISBN 0-573-05042-2). S. French.
--Hijack Over Hygenia: A Musical Play for Children. LC 75-310411. (Illus.). 5, 54 p. 22cm. (French's Acting Edition). 1974. (ISBN 0-573-05034-1). French.
--The Plotters of Cabbage Patch Corner: A Musical Play. LC 73-164625. 58 p. 22cm. (French's acting edition). 1972. (ISBN 0-573-05030-9). Samuel French.
Wood, Dorothy, ed.
--This Nation: The Spirit of America in Poems, Speeches, Songs & Documents. McDaniel, Jerry, illus. (Illus.). (gr. 4 up). 1967. (ISBN 0-529-00350-3). (ISBN 0-529-00351-1). World Pub.
Wood, Edgar Allardyce see Wood, Kerry, pseud.
Wood, Eileen
--Airport Summer. Buehr, Walter Franklin (1897-1971), illus. LC 46-11815. 4 p. l., 190 p. illus. 21 cm. 1946. H. Holt and Company.
Wood, Elizabeth
--The Cat Walks. Schulman, Janet, ed. Wood, Elizabeth, illus. LC 83-62360. (Illus.). 12p. (Read-Around Bks.). (gr. k-2). 1984. (ISBN 0-394-86239-2, BYR). Random.
--The Duck Waddles. Schulman, Janet, ed. Wood, Elizabeth, illus. LC 83-62362. (Illus.). 12p. (Read-Around Bks.). (gr. k-2). 1984. (ISBN 0-394-86236-8, BYR). Random.
--The Frog Jumps. Schulman, Janet, ed. Wood, Elizabeth, illus. LC 83-62363. (Illus.). 12p. (Read-Around Bks.). (gr. k-2). 1984. (ISBN 0-394-86234-1, BYR). Random.
--My Favorite Toys. LC 85-2466. p. cm. 1986, c.1985. (ISBN 0-394-87569-9). (ISBN 0-394-97569-3). Random House.
--The Pig Trots. Schulman, Janet, ed. Wood, Elizabeth, illus. LC 83-62364. (Illus.). 12p. (Read-Around Bks.). (gr. k-2). 1984. (ISBN 0-394-86235-X, BYR). (ISBN 0-394-86235-X). Random.
--The Puppy Races. Schulman, Janet, ed. Wood, Elizabeth, illus. LC 83-62361. (Illus.). 12p. (Read-Around Books Ser.). (gr. k-2). 1984. (ISBN 0-394-86237-6). Random.
--The Rabbit Runs. Schulman, Janet, ed. Wood, Elizabeth, illus. LC 83-62359. (Illus.). 12p. (Read-Around Bks.). (gr. k-2). 1984. (ISBN 0-394-86238-4, BYR). (ISBN 0-394-86238-4). Random.
Wood, Elizabeth Lambert, Mrs.
--Cougar Pass. Hosch, Mary Louise, illus. 7 p. l., 3-200 p. incl. front. pl. 20 1/2 cm. 1933. Metropolitan Press.
--Cougar Pass. Husch, Mary Louise, illus. N.D. Binfords & Mort.
--Long Rope. LC 56-1106. 168p. illus. 23cm. 1955. Binfords & Mort.
--Many Horses. LC 54-80. 168p. illus. 23cm. 1953. Binfords & Mort.
--Silver House of Klone Chuck. LC 31-343913. 6 p. l., 186, 1 p. front. 19 1/2 cm. 1931. Metropolitan Press.
--Silver House of Klone Chuck. Husch, Mary Louise, illus. 202p. N.D. Binfords & Mort.
--There Go the Apaches. Price, Harold L. (1912-), illus. LC 42-7377. 2 p. l., 9-227 p. front., pl. 20 1/2 cm. 225p. c.1941. Binfords & Mort.
--The Trail of the Bear. N.D. Binfords & Mort.
--Wolves of the Illahee. N.D. Binfords & Mort.
--Wolves of the Illahee. LC 34-428623. 6 p. l., 3-211 p. incl. front. 20 cm. c.1934. Metropolitan Press.
Wood, Ellen K.
--The Little Green House. N.D. Vantage Press Inc.
Wood, Eric
--The Boy's Book of Adventure. N.D. Funk & Wagnalls.
--Boys' Book of Buccaneers. N.D. Funk & Wagnalls.
--The Boy's Book of the Sea. LC 16-14601. viii, 312 p. col. front., plates (part col.) 21 1/2 cm. 1915. Funk and Wagnalls Company.
--The Flaming Cross of Santa Marta. LC 23-8186. 3 p. l., 256, 1 p. front. 19 1/2 cm. 1923. D. Appleton and Company.
Wood, Eric, jt. auth. see Chaundler, Christine.
Wood, Esther, pseud., see Brady, Esther Wood.
Wood, Esther, pseud. (1905-)
--Belinda Blue. Brady, Esther Wood. 1st ed. Kalab, Theresa, illus. LC 40-31356. 31 p. incl. col. front., illus. (part col.) 26 1/2 cm. c.1940. Longmans, Green and Co.
--Great Sweeping Day. Brady, Esther Wood. Wood, Esther, pseud. (1905-), illus. Brady, Esther Wood. LC 36-17534. 158 p. incl. front., illus, plates. 19 1/2 cm. 1936. Longmans, Green and Co.
--The House in the Hoo. Brady, Esther Wood. 1st ed. Kalab, Theresa, illus. LC 41-19433. 32 p. illus. 24 x 19 1/2 cm. c.1941. Longmans Green and Co.
--Pedro's Coconut Skates. Brady, Esther Wood. Wood, Esther, pseud. (1905-), illus. Brady, Esther Wood. LC 38-27009. 191, 1 p. incl. front., illus. 20 cm. 1938. Longmans, Green and Co.
--Pepper Moon. Brady, Esther Wood. LC 40-27676. 32 p. col. illus. 26 1/2 cm. c.1940. Longmans, Green and Co.
--Silk and Satin Lane. Brady, Esther Wood. Wiese, Kurt (1887-1974), illus. xii p., 1 l., 225 p. incl. front., illus. 19 1/2 cm. 1939. Longmans, Green and Co.
--Silk and Satin Lane. Brady, Esther Wood. Wiese, Kurt (1887-1974), illus. 1939. McKay.
--Silver Widgeon. Brady, Esther Wood. Kalab, Theresa, illus. LC 42-23865. ix p., 1 l., 227 p. incl. illus., plates, map. 21 cm. 1942. Longmans, Green and Co.
Wood, Ethel
--Dolly's Double. Davidson, Bertha G., illus. (Illus.). 1905. Lothrop Lee & Shepard Co.
Wood, Evelyn
--A Stitch in Time. (The Children's Hour Series.). N.D. George H Doran.
Wood, Florence Dorothy
--Long Eye and the Iron Horse: A Biography of Grenville Dodge and the Union Pacific Railroad. LC 66-15170. 208p. illus., map, ports. 22cm. 1966. Criterion.
--Lucky Pocket. LC 51-8907. unpaged. illus. 21 cm. (Cozy-corner book). c.1951. Whitman Pub. Co.
Wood, Frances Elizabeth
--Roy Rogers' Bullet. Authorized. Doe, Bart, illus. LC 53-375426. unpaged. illus. 17cm. (Tell-a-tale books). c.1953. Whitman Pub. Co.
--Yippee! Cowboy. Weisman, Robert R., illus. LC 47-25469. 40 p. col. illus. 22 cm. c.1947. Whitman Pub. Co.
Wood, Frances Hariott
--Rivulet Cottages (Pub. by Society for Promoting Christian Knowledge). N.D. E. & J. B. Young & Co.
--A Storm and a Teapot (Pub. by Society for Promoting Christian Knowledge). N.D. E. & J. B. Young & Co.
--Swallow Castle (Pub. by Society for Promoting Christian Knowledge). N.D. E. & J. B. Young & Co.
--Talitha's Weird Vision (Pub. by Society for Promoting Christian Knowledge). N.D. E. & J. B Young & Co.
Wood, Frank Clifford (1865-)
--Santa Claus Land. McCullough, Eleanor T., illus. LC 28-24508. (Illus.). 28cm. 16p. 1928. Walter-Douglas Co.
Wood, Gilmore
--Johann the Woodcarver. Tarrant, Margaret Winifred (1888-), illus. N.D. Frederick Warne & Co.
Wood, H. J.
--Florence. N.D. George Routledge & Sons.
Wood, Harrie, jt. auth. see Wood, Marni.
Wood, Ivor, jt. auth. see Beresford, Elisabeth.
Wood, Ivor, jt. auth. see Bond, Thomas Michael.
Wood, J. Walter
--Son of the Dine'. (Indian Culture Ser.). (gr. 5-9). 1972. (ISBN 0-89992-023-3). MT Coun Indian.
Wood, James Playsted (1905-)
--Chase Scene. LC 79-11399. 170 p. 21cm. c.1979. (ISBN 0-525-66640-0). Elsevier/Nelson Books.
--The Elephant in the Barn. Kessler, Leonard P. (1921-), illus. (Illus.). 115 p. 23cm. 1961. Harper.
--An Elephant in the Family. Werth, Kurt (1896-), illus. LC 57-7465. 64 p. illus. 26 cm. 1957. T. Nelson.
--The Elephant on Ice. Berson, Harold (1926-), illus. LC 65-16540. 96p. illus. 21cm. N.D. Seabury.

--The Elephant Tells. Rogers, Carol, illus. (Illus.). 92 p. 22cm. 1968. Reilly & Lee.
--Golden Swan. Elgin, Kathleen (1923-), illus. LC 65-165416. (Illus.). (gr. 7-10). 1965. Seabury.
--Kentucky Time. LC 77-4383. 136 p. 23cm. c.1977. (ISBN 0-201-09344-8). Addison-Wesley.
--The Mammoth Parade. Nadler, Robert (1934-), illus. LC 69-13459. (Illus.). 148 p. 22cm. 1969. Pantheon Books.
--The Man with Two Countries. 1st ed. Mars, Witold Tadeusz J. (1912-), illus. LC 67-1018. (Illus.). 168 p. 22cm. 1967. Seabury Press.
--Poetry Is. LC 71-187420. 192p. (gr. 7 up). 1972. (ISBN 0-395-13736-5). HM.
--The Queen's Most Honorable Pirate. Fisher, Leonard Everett (1924-), illus. LC 61-12092. 184p. illus. c.1961. Harper.
--The Queen's Most Honorable Pirate. Fisher, Leonard Everett (1924-), illus. LC 68-72112. 184 p.illus. 21 cm. 1961. Seabury Press.
--Scotland Yard. (gr. 7-9). 1970. (ISBN 0-8015-6588-X). Hawthorn.
--Very Wild Animal Stories. Bartoli, Joseph, illus. LC 65-20666. (Illus.). 116 p. 21cm. 1965. Pantheon Books.
--When I Was Jersey. Greenwald, Sheila, pseud. (1934-), illus. Green, Sheila Ellen. (Illus.). (gr. 5 up). 1967. (ISBN 0-394-81826-1). (ISBN 0-394-91826-6). Pantheon.

Wood, Jean & Armstrong, Nancy M.
--In Our Hogan: Adventure Stories of Navajo Children. (Indian Culture Ser.). (gr. 4-8). 1976. (ISBN 0-89992-058-6). MT Coun Indian.

Wood, Jerline
--Kamra's Christmas Story. Gilbert, Cynthia, illus. (Illus.). 48p. (gr. k-5). 1982. (ISBN 0-910071-00-4). Gneiss Bks.

Wood, JoAnne
--Birds in My Drawer: Funny Alphabet Rhymes. Giacomini, Olindo, illus. (Illus.). 20 p. (A Golden Preschool Learning Book). (ps). 1971. (ISBN 0-307-12175-5, Golden Pr). Western Pub.
--My Little Doll House. Wood, JoAnne, ed. (Put & Play Ser.). (ps). 1981. (ISBN 0-307-05102-1, Golden Pr). Western Pub.
--My Little Farm. Wood, JoAnne, ed. (Put & Play Ser.). (ps). 1981. (ISBN 0-307-05103-X, Golden Pr). Western Pub.

Wood, JoAnne, jt. auth. see Ottum, Bob.

Wood, Joyce (1928-)
--Grandmother Lucy and Her Hats. Francis, Frank, illus. LC 69-10901. (Illus.). 31 p. 27cm. 1st U.S. edition. 1969. Atheneum.
--Grandmother Lucy in Her Garden. Francis, Frank, illus. LC 74-24651. p. cm. 1975. (ISBN 0-529-05238-5). (ISBN 0-529-05239-3). Collins-World.

Wood, Joyce (1928-) & Francis, Frank (1901-)
--Grandmother Lucy Goes on a Picnic. LC 76-80. (Illus.). 32 p. 26cm. 1976, c.1970. (ISBN 0-529-05288-1). Collins.

Wood, Katharine Marie (1910-)
--The Ambitious Elephant. Wood, Katherine Marie (1910-), illus. LC 53-11350. unpaged. illus. 24cm. c.1953. McKay.
--Angels of God. Wood, Katharine Marie (1910-), illus. LC 63-113324. unpaged. col. illus. 29cm. c.1963. Kenedy.
--Browny Bear's Picnic. Wood, Katharine Marie (1910-), illus. (gr. 1). 1951. David McKay Co.
--Browny Bear's Picnic. Wood, Katharine Marie (1910-), illus. LC 51-12163. unpaged. illus. 24 cm. 1951. McKay.
--The Friendly Tiger. Wood, Katharine Marie (1910-), illus. LC 52-12435. unpaged. illus. 24cm. c.1952. D. McKay Co.

Wood, Kay
--Big Bird's Shape Book. LC 75-39343. (Illus.). 26 p. c.1977. (ISBN 0-394-83263-9). Random House.
--Giant in the Universe: Star Trek Pop-up. LC 77-70850. (Illus.). (gr. 1-3). 1977. (ISBN 0-394-83556-5). Random.
--Grover's Favorite Color. LC 75-39346. (Illus.). 26 p. c.1977. (ISBN 0-394-83266-3). Random House.
--Trillions of Trilligs. LC 77-70856. (Illus.). (Star Trek Pop-up). (gr. 1-3). 1977. (ISBN 0-394-83558-1). Random.

Wood, Kenneth (1922-)
--Shining Armour. 144p. (Julia MacRae Bks.). (gr. 7). 1982. (ISBN 0-531-04434-3, MacRae). Watts.

Wood, Kerry, pseud., see Wood, Edgar Allardyce.

Wood, Kerry, pseud. (1907-)
--The Boy and the Buffalo. Wood, Edgar Allardyce. Teather, Audrey, illus. LC 64-10825. 120 p. illus. 19 cm. (Buckskin Books, 9). 1963. St. Martin's Press.
--The Great Chief, Maskepetoon: Warrior of the Crees. Wood, Edgar Allardyce. Hall, John A., illus. LC 58-14530. 160 p. illus. 22 cm. (Great Stories of Canada). 1957. St. Martin's Press.
--The Queen's Cowboy, James McLeod: The Story of the Mounties. Wood, Edgar Allardyce. Rosenthal, Joseph J. (1911-), illus. 1960. St Martin's Press.
--Wild Winter. Wood, Edgar Allardyce. Mays, Lewis Victor, Jr. (1927-), illus. LC 54-9047. (Illus.). 175 p. 22cm. 1954. Houghton Mifflin.

Wood, Lawson (1878-)
--The Bunchy Tail, and his Pic-Nic Tea. (The Rummy Tales). N.D. Frederick Warne & Co.
--The Bushy Tail, and His Good Fortune. (The Rummy Tales). N.D. Frederick Warne & Co.
--The Curly Tail, and How He Reached the North Pole. (The Rummy Tales). N.D. Frederick Warne & Co.
--Noo-Zoo Tales, 6 Bks. N.D. Frederick Warne & Co.
--The Pig Tail, and How It Was Found. (The Rummy Tales). N.D. Frederick Warne & Co.
--Rummy Tales, 6 Bks. Wood, Lawson (1878-), illus. N.D. Frederick Warne & Co.
--The String Tail and How He Gets to the Lord Mayor's Show. N.D. Frederick Warne & Co.
--The Strong Tail, and How He Jumped On to the Moon. (The Rummy Tales). N.D. Frederick Warne & Co.

Wood, Lawson (1878-), illus.
--The Old Nursery Rhymes. N.D. Thomas Nelson & Sons.

Wood, Lucile, jt. auth. see Scott, Louise Binder.
Wood, Lucille, jt. auth. see McLaughlin, Roberta.
Wood, Lucille, jt. ed. see McLaughlin, Roberta.

Wood, Lucille F
--Autumn. Taylor, Paul L., illus. LC 77-139697. (Illus.). 30 p. 21cm. (Rhythms to reading). 1971. Bowmar.
--Halloween. Taylor, Paul L., illus. LC 70-139698. (Illus.). 30 p. 21cm. (Rhythms to reading). 1971. Bowmar.
--The Harbor and the Sea. Taylor, Paul L., illus. LC 71-139702. (Illus.). 30 p. 21cm. (Rhythms to reading). 1971. Bowmar.
--A Springtime Walk. Taylor, Paul L., illus. LC 76-139706. (Illus.). 30 p. 21cm. (Rhythms to reading). 1971. Bowmar.
--A Summer Day on the Farm. Taylor, Paul L., illus. LC 75-139703. (Illus.). 30 p. 21cm. (Rhythms to reading). 1971. Bowmar.
--The Zoo and the Circus. Taylor, Paul L., illus. LC 74-139700. (Illus.). 30 p. 22cm. (Rhythms to reading). 1971. Bowmar.

Wood, Lucille F., jt. auth. see Schubert, Inez.

Wood, Lucille F. & Scott, Louise Binder (1910-)
--More Singing Fun. Miller, Edward (1905-1974), illus. LC 61-276. 77p. col. illus. 28cm. c.1961. Webster Pub. Co.

Wood, M. A.
--Master Deor's Apprentice. 128p. 1981. (ISBN 0-905478-49-5, Pub. by Andersen-Hutchinson England). State Mutual Bk.

Wood, Marni & Wood, Harrie (1902-)
--Something Perfectly Silly. Wood, Harrie (1902-), illus. LC 30-23657. 32 l. col. illus. 25 1/2 cm. 1930. A. A. Knopf.

Wood, Martha C., ed. see Howland, Avia C.

Wood, Mary Buell
--Just Boys: Jangles from the Choir Room. LC 9-22006. 5 p. l., 9-149 p. front., plates. 19 1/2 cm. c.1909. F. H. Revell Company.

Wood, Miriam
--The Snowstorm Jenny Never Forgot. Munson, Harold W. (1920-), illus. LC 77-374023. (Illus.). 80 p. 22cm. c.1976. Review and Herald Pub. Association.

Wood, Nancy (1936-)
--Little Wrangler. 1st ed. Wood, Myron, photos by. LC 66-11176. 49p. illus. 29cm. 1966. (ISBN 0-385-05890-X). Doubleday.
--Many Winters: Prose and Poetry of the Pueblos. Howell, Frank, illus. LC 74-3554. 80p. (gr. 6 up). 1974. Doubleday.

Wood, Nancy (1936-), compiled by.
--Prose and Poetry of the Pueblos. Howell, Frank, illus. 1974. Doubleday.
--War Cry on a Prayer Feather: Prose & Poetry of the Ute Indians. LC 77-76272. (gr. 4 up). 1979. Doubleday.

Wood, Phyllis Anderson (1923-)
--Andy. LC 76-130526. (A High Interest-Low Reading Level Book). (A Hiway Bk). (gr. 9 up). 1971. (ISBN 0-664-32485-1). Westminster.
--A Five-Color Buick and a Blue-Eyed Cat. LC 74-19156. 125 p. 21cm. 1975. (ISBN 0-664-32562-9). Westminster Press.
--Get a Little Lost, Tia. LC 78-17762. p. cm. c.1978. (ISBN 0-664-32636-6). Westminster Press.
--I Think This Is Where We Came in. LC 75-33093. 155 p. 21cm. c.1976. (ISBN 0-664-32582-3). Westminster Press.
--I've Missed a Sunset or Three. LC 72-6399. 144 p. 22cm. 1973. (ISBN 0-664-32519-X). Westminster Press.
--Meet Me in the Park, Angie. LC 83-16937. 118p. 1983. (ISBN 0-664-32710-9). (ISBN 0-664-32710-9). Westminster.
--Night Summer Began. (gr. 10-12). 1976. (ISBN 0-590-10141-2, Schol Pap). Scholastic Inc.
--Pass Me a Pine Cone. LC 82-1870. (Illus.). 160 p. 21cm. c.1982. (ISBN 0-664-32692-7). Westminster Press.
--Song of the Shaggy Canary. 1974. (ISBN 0-664-32543-2). Westminster Press.
--This Time Count Me in. LC 80-15068. 119 p. 21cm. c.1980. (ISBN 0-664-32665-X). Westminster Press.
--Win Me and You Lose. LC 76-44299. 137 p. 21cm. c.1977. (ISBN 0-664-32605-6). Westminster Press.
--Your Bird Is Here, Tom Thompson. LC 78-165016. 125 p. 21cm. 1971, c.1972. (ISBN 0-664-32503-3). Westminster Press.

Wood, Ray, ed.
--The American Mother Goose. Hargis, Ed, illus. Lomax, John A., frwd. by. LC 40-276233. xviii, 109, 1 p. illus. 21 1/2 cm. 1940. Frederick A. Stokes Company, Inc.
--The American Mother Goose. Hargis, Ed, illus. 1939. Lippincott.
--The American Mother Goose. Hargis, Ed, illus. 1940. Lippincott.
--Fun in American Folk Rhymes. Hargis, Ed, illus. LC 52-9530. (Illus.). 109 p. 22cm. 1952. Lippincott.
--Mother Goose in the Ozarks. Hargis, Ed, illus. LC 80-15962. p. cm. c.1980. (ISBN 0-86574-000-3). M. Vance.

Wood, Robert
--What's Next?. Wood, Robert, illus. (ps-2). 1982. (ISBN 0-395-31611-1). HM.

Wood, Robert W.
--How to Tell the Birds from the Flowers. (Illus.). (gr. 4 up). 1959. Dover.

Wood, Rosa Aubrey
--Banjo and Pistols: A Tale of the Blue Ridge. LC 29-20446. 3 p. l., 228 p. incl. front., illus. 19 1/2 cm. 1929. R. M. McBride & Company.

Wood, Ruth C
--Mystery of Gold Hill. Colabella, Vincent, illus. LC 73-159975. (Illus.). 208 p. 22cm. 1971. (ISBN 0-8178-4861-4). Harvey House.
--Mystery of the Absent Neighbors. Koering, Ursula (1921-), illus. LC 68-10712. (Illus.). 199 p. 22cm. 1968. Harvey House.

Wood, Ruzena
--The Palace of the Moon & Other Tales from Czechoslovakia. Turska, Krystyna Zofia (1933-), illus. LC 80-2687. (Illus.). 144p. (gr. 2-7). 1981. (ISBN 0-233-97206-4). Andre Deutsch.

Wood, Samue; see Newbery, F.

Wood, Victor E.
--The Home Front. 1st ed. LC 55-5701. 167p. 21cm. 1955. Vantage Press.

Wood, Violet
--Great is the Company. 176p. 1953. Friendship Press.

Wood, Wendy (1892-)
--Legends of the Borders: Stories for the Young and Not So Young. LC 74-160045. (Illus.). 91 p. 19cm. 1973. (ISBN 0-901311-34-0). Impulse Books.
--The Silver Chanter: Traditional Scottish Tales & Legends. McNaughton, Colin, illus. LC 80-670272. (Illus.). 108p. (gr. 4-7). 1980. (ISBN 0-7011-2448-2, Pub. by Chatto Bodley Jonathan). Merrimack Pub Cir.

Wood, William Hollingsworth (1914-)
--The House in the Sea. Pont, Charles Ernest (1898-), illus. 1954. Little, Brown & Co.
--The House in the Sea: A Story of the First Lighthouse on Eddystone. Pont, Charles Ernest (1898-), illus. LC 54-5102. 229p. illus. 20cm. 1st U.S. edition. 1954. Duell, Sloan and Pearce.

Woodall, Mildred T.
--Sally Sponge and Sammy Seahorse: Two Stories. Ludwig, Helen, illus. LC 54-13318. unpaged. illus. 24cm. c.1955. Greenwich Book Publishers.
--Susie Starfish and Peter Porpoise: Two Stories. Ludwig, Helen, illus. LC 56-16746. unpaged. illus. 24cm. c.1955. Greenwich Book Publishers.

Woodall, Sally Lee
--The Animal ABC. Lasher, Elmer, illus. LC 46-20185. 55 p. illus. 20 1/2 x 15 1/2 cm. 1946. U.S. Camera Publishing Corp.
--Puffy Goes to Sea. Mariinsky, Vaslov, illus. LC 45-35416. 70 p. incl. front. (map) illus. (part col.) 26 cm. c.1944. U.S. Camera.

Woodard, Carol (1929-)
--It's Fun to Have a Birthday. Goldsborough, June (1923-), illus. (Illus.). 24p. (Big Books for Little People Ser). (ps-3). 1970. (ISBN 0-8006-0423-7). Fortress.
--Very Special Baby: A Christmas Story for the Very Young. Forberg, Ati, pseud. (1925-), illus. Forberg, Beate Gropius. (Illus., Orig.). (See & Hear Books Ser). (ps-4). 1969. (ISBN 0-8006-0420-2). Fortress.
--Wet Walk. Ebert, Len, illus. (Illus.). 248p. (Big Books for Little People). (ps-3). 1970. Fortress.

Woodard, F. M.
--Adventures of Kip. 1971. (ISBN 0-87508-641-1). Chr Lit.
--The Clue Chaser. 1972. (ISBN 0-87508-655-1). Chr Lit.

Woodberry, Joan Merle (1921-)
--Come Back, Peter. Tetlow, George (1934-), illus. LC 78-171011. (Illus.). 152 p. 21cm. 1972, c.1968. (ISBN 0-690-20158-3). Crowell.
--Come Back Peter. Tetlow, George (1934-), illus. (Illus.). 112p. 1968. Tri-Ocean Books.

Woodbridge, A. E.
--Summer in the Rockies, 1 of 25 vols. (Selected Bks for Sunday School: The/Auburn Library). N.D. Set. Methodist Bk Concern.

Woodbridge, F. J.
--The Son of Apollo: Themes of Plato. 272p. Repr. of 1929 ed (Pub. by HM). (gr. 7 up). 1972. (ISBN 0-8196-0278-7). Biblo.

Woodbuff, Jane Scott
--Roses of St. Elizabeth. Everhart, Adelaide, illus. N.D. L. C. Page & Co.

Woodburn, Marion Letcher, tr. see Beskow, Elsa Maartman.

Woodbury, Mabel Jones
--The Story of Pamela. Woodbury, Mabel Jones, illus. LC 47-4812. 90, 1 p. illus. 21 cm. 1947. Viking Press.

Woodcock, Louise Phinney, jt. auth. see Skaar, Grace Marion Brown.

Woodcock, Louise Phinney (1892-)
--Guess Who Lives Here. LC 49-9976. 42 p. illus. (part col.) 20 cm. (Little golden library, no. 60). 1949. Simon and Schuster.
--Hi Ho! Three in a Row. Wilkin, Eloise Burns (1904-), illus. LC 54-1145. unpaged. illus. 21cm. (Little golden book, 188). 1954. Simon and Schuster.
--Hiding Places. 24p. N.D. William R. Scott Inc.
--The Kittens Who Hid From Their Mother. Werber, Adele & Laslo, Doris, illus. LC 50-3453. 21cm. 41p. (Wonder Book: 529). 1950. Grosset & Dunlap.
--The Smart Little Boy and His Smart Little Kitty. Bloch, Lucienne (1909-), illus. LC 47-308182. 20 p. col. illus. 21 x 24 cm. c.1947. W. R. Scott.
--Smart Little Boys and His Smart Little Kitty. Bloch, Lucienne (1909-), illus. 1947. E M Hale.
--This Is the Way the Animals Walk. Binney, Ida (1912-), illus. LC 46-226867. 20 p. col. illus. 20 x 24 cm. c.1946. W. R. Scott, Inc.
--Wiggles. Wilkin, Eloise Burns (1904-), illus. LC 53-2863. unpaged. illus. 21cm. (Little golden library, 166). 1953. Simon and Schuster.

Woodford, Peggy (1937-)
--Backwater War. LC 75-8817. viii, 213 p. 21cm. 1975, c.1974. (ISBN 0-374-30477-7). Farrar, Straus, Giroux.
--The Girl with a Voice. 160p. (Orig.). (gr. 9 up). 1984. (ISBN 0-370-30423-3, Pub. by the Bodley Head). Merrimack Pub Cir.
--Looking for Love: Seven Uncommon Love Stories. LC 78-19661. 157 p. 22cm. 1979, c.1977. (ISBN 0-385-14636-1). Doubleday.
--Please Don't Go. LC 72-89840. 187 p. 22cm. 1973, c.1972. (ISBN 0-525-37140-0). Dutton.
--See You Tomorrow. 144p. (gr. 9 up). 1984. (ISBN 0-370-30204-4, Pub. by the Bodley Head). Merrimack Pub Cir.

Woodgate, Arthur G. K.
--Jack and Floss at Sea and at Home. N.D. Thomas Nelson & Sons.

Woodgate, Leslie, compiled by.
--Puffin Song Book. (gr. 1-6). 1972. (ISBN 0-14-030100-3, Puffin). Penguin.

Woodhead, Constance
--The Story of Lazy Bush-Tail. Wanklyn, Joan, illus. LC 53-3441. 42p. illus. 17cm. (The Prettimouse Ser.). 1953. Warne.
--Story of Lazy Bushtail. (Illus.). (gr. 1-3). 1957. (ISBN 0-7232-0437-3). Warne.
--The Story of Three Little Ducklings. (The Prettimouse Ser.). N.D. Frederick Warne & Co.

Woodhouse, Barbara Blackburn (1910-)
--Chica: The Story of a Very Little Dog. N.D. Transatlantic Arts, Inc.

Woodhouse, Martin (1932-)
--Mama Doll. 224p. 1972. (ISBN 0-698-10439-0). Coward.
--Moonhill. LC 74-79679. 1976. (ISBN 0-698-10601-6, Coward). Putnam Pub Group.

Woodhouse, Martin (1932-) & Ross, Robert
--The Medici Emerald. LC 76-11873. 224p. c.1976. (ISBN 0-525-15458-2). E.P. Dutton.

Woodland, Esme Jessie Maud, ed.
--Skipping Susan. Day, Elsa, illus. LC 76-103603. (Illus.). 63 p. 21cm. 1972, c.1966. (ISBN 0-87614-008-8). Carolrhoda Books.

Woodley, Bruce
--Friday Street Fantasy, and Other Stories. LC 75-493505. (Illus.). 19cm. 14p. 1969. Paul Hamlyn.

Woodman, Bill
--Whose Birthday Is It?. LC 79-2776. (Illus.). 42 p. 23cm. c.1980. (ISBN 0-690-04005-9). (ISBN 0-690-04006-7). Crowell.

Woodman, Hannah Rea (1870-)
--The Master's Birthday. A Play for Children, in Three Acts ... 37 p. 20 cm. c.1908. Eldridge Entertainment House.

Woodrich, Mary Neville see Neville, Mary.

Woodright
--Snap Crackle Plots. (Ready to Read Serial Books). (gr. 3-6). N.D. (ISBN 0-686-82485-7). Creative Pubns.

--Murder in Washington: The Body on the Beach. 208p. (Orig.). (Donna Rockford Mystery Ser.). (gr. 7 up). 1982. (ISBN 0-590-32000-9). Scholastic Inc.

--Who Killed Daddy?. (Donna Rockford Ser.). (gr. 7-12). 1980. (ISBN 0-590-32520-5). Scholastic Inc.

Woolfolk, Doug, ed. see Coltharp, Barbara.

Woolford, Sam, et al. (1897-)

--Gulf Coast Adventure. LC 54-8741. 64p. illus. 21cm. 1953. Highland Press.

Woolford, Sarah C.

--Three Stories for Children. 1979. (ISBN 0-533-04011-6). Vantage.

Woolgar, George Jack (1894-)

--Hot on Ice. Irvin, Fred M. (1914-), illus. LC 65-15106. (Illus.). 128p. (Pilot Book Ser). (gr. 3-5). 1965. (ISBN 0-8075-3383-1). A Whitman.

--The Missing Gold Mystery. LC 75-12429. 158 p. 22cm. c.1977. (ISBN 0-8313-0111-2). Lantern Press.

--Mystery in the Desert. LC 67-19633. 192 p. 21cm. 1967. Lantern Press.

--Teen-Age Detective Stories. Furman, Abraham Loew (1902-), ed. LC 68-23983. 192 p. 21cm. (Teen-age library). 1968. Lantern Press.

--Teen-Age Secret Agent Stories. Furman, Abraham Loew (1902-), ed. LC 70-112671. 191 p. 22cm. 1970. Lantern Press.

Woolgar, George Jack (1894-) & Rudnicki, Barbara J.

--Hopi Mysteries. (Indian Culture Ser.). (gr. 5-9). 1974. (ISBN 0-89992-060-8). MT Coun Indian.

Woollcott, Alexander Humphreys (1887-1943)

--Two Gentlemen and a Lady. Edwina, illus. LC 28-24509. 121, 1 p. incl. front., illus., plates. 23 1/2 cm. 1928. Coward-McCann, Inc.

--Verdun Belle. Edwina, illus. LC 35-12199. 121, 1 p. incl. front., illus., plates. 23 1/2 cm. Orig. Title: Two Gentlemen and a Lady. 1934. Grosset & Dunlap.

Woolley, Catherine see Thayer, Jane, pseud.

Woolley, Catherine (1904-)

--Andy and Mr. Cunningham. Wohlberg, Meg (1905-), illus. LC 69-10276. (Illus.). 48 p. 21cm. 1969. Morrow.

--Andy and the Runaway Horse. Wohlberg, Meg (1905-), illus. LC 63-7879. (Illus.). 48 p. 21cm. 1963. Morrow.

--Andy and the Wild Worm. Darwin, Beatrice, illus. LC 72-1981. (Illus.). 48 p. 21cm. 1973, c.1954. (ISBN 0-688-20061-3). (ISBN 0-688-20061-3). Morrow.

--Andy Wouldn't Talk. Thayer, Jane, pseud. Wohlberg, Meg (1905-), illus. LC 57-10588. (Illus.). 46 p. 21cm. (Morrow junior books). 1958. W. Morrow.

--Andy's Square Blue Animal. Thayer, Jane, pseud. Wohlberg, Meg (1905-), illus. LC 62-7019. (Illus.). 46 p. 21cm. 1962. (ISBN 0-688-31028-1). Morrow.

--The Animal Train and Other Stories. Beebe, Robb (1891-), illus. LC 53-7103. 127p. illus. 22cm. 1953. Morrow.

--Applebaums Have a Robot!. Thayer, Jane, pseud. Weissman, Bari, illus. LC 79-28065. (Illus.). 32 p. 1980. (ISBN 0-688-22231-5). (ISBN 0-688-32231-X). Morrow.

--Bunny in the Honeysuckle Patch. Thayer, Jane, pseud. Fleishman, Seymour (1918-), illus. LC 65-10137. 1v. (unpaged) col. illus. 21x24cm. 1965, c.1962. (ISBN 0-688-21132-1). (ISBN 0-688-31132-6). Morrow.

--The Cat That Joined the Club. Fleishman, Seymour (1918-), illus. LC 67-5174. (Illus.). 32 p. 25cm. 1967. Morrow.

--Cathy and the Beautiful People. Frame, Paul (1913-), illus. LC 78-151938. (Illus.). 189 p. 21cm. 1971. Morrow.

--Cathy Leonard Calling. Dauber, Elizabeth, illus. LC 61-6828. (Illus.). 191 p. 21cm. 1961. Morrow.

--Cathy Uncovers a Secret. Almquist, Don (1929-), illus. LC 75-183414. (Illus.). 189 p. 21cm. 1972. Morrow.

--Cathy's Little Sister. Dauber, Elizabeth, illus. LC 64-12041. (Illus.). 190 p. 21cm. 1964. Morrow.

--Charley and the New Car. Barnum, Jay Hyde (1888-1962), illus. LC 57-5033. 48 p. illus. 22 cm. (Morrow junior books). 1957. Morrow.

--The Chicken in the Tunnel. Palazzo, Tony (1905-1970), illus. LC 56-5177. 48 p. illus. 22 cm. (Morrow junior books). 1956. Morrow.

--Chris in Trouble. Frame, Paul (1913-), illus. (Illus.). 192 p. 21cm. 1968. Morrow.

--Clever Raccoon. Thayer, Jane, pseud. Keller, Holly, illus. LC 80-23119. p. cm. 32p. (gr. k-3). 1981. (ISBN 0-688-00238-2). (ISBN 0-688-00239-0). Morrow.

--Curious, Furious Chipmunk. Thayer, Jane, pseud. Fleishman, Seymour (1918-), illus. LC 69-12936. (Illus.). 32 p. 25cm. 1969. (ISBN 0-688-31205-5). Morrow.

--David's Campaign Buttons. Fisher, Leonard Everett (1924-), illus. LC 59-5352. 191 p. illus. 21 cm. (Morrow junior books). 1959. Morrow.

--David's Hundred Dollars. Johnson, Iris Beatty, illus. LC 52-5067. 155 p. illus. 21 cm. 1952. Morrow.

--David's Railroad. N.D. E. M. Hale & Co.

--David's Railroad. Johnson, Iris Beatty, illus. LC 49-9798. 159 p. illus. 21 cm. (Morrow junior books). 1949. W. Morrow.

--Elie's Problem Dog. Koering, Ursula (1921-), illus. LC 55-5749. 159p. illus. 21cm. (Morrow junior books). 1955. Morrow.

--Ginnie and Geneva. Johnson, Iris Beatty, illus. LC 48-3295. 191 p. illus. 21 cm. 1948. W. Morrow.

--Ginnie and Her Juniors. Dauber, Elizabeth, illus. LC 63-8790. (Illus.). 191 p. 21cm. 1963. Morrow.

--Ginnie & the Cooking Contest. Frame, Paul (1913-), illus. LC 66-3960. (Illus.). (gr. 3-7). 1966. (ISBN 0-688-31337-X). Morrow.

--Ginnie and the Mystery Cat. Frame, Paul (1913-), illus. LC 69-18946. (Illus.). 192 p. 22cm. 1969. Morrow.

--Ginnie and the Mystery Doll. Boodell, Patricia, illus. LC 60-5722. 188 p. illus. 21 cm. (Morrow junior books). 1960. Morrow.

--Ginnie and the Mystery House. Koering, Ursula (1921-), illus. LC 57-6081. 191 p. illus. 21 cm. 1957. W. Morrow.

--Ginnie and the Mystery Light. Almquist, Don (1929-), illus. LC 72-11468. (Illus.). 191 p. 21cm. 1973. (ISBN 0-688-20070-2). (ISBN 0-688-20070-2). Morrow.

--Ginnie and the New Girl. Johnson, Iris Beatty, illus. LC 54-7097. (Illus.). 159 p. 21cm. 1954. Morrow.

--Ginnie and the Wedding Bells. Frame, Paul (1913-), illus. LC 67-16371. (Illus.). 187 p. 21cm. 1967. Morrow.

--Ginnie Joins in. Johnson, Iris Beatty, illus. LC 51-11447. (Illus.). 192 p. 21cm. (Morrow junior books). 1951. Morrow.

--Gus and the Baby Ghost. Fleishman, Seymour (1918-), illus. LC 76-161874. (Illus.). 32 p. 25cm. 1972. Morrow.

--Gus Was a Gorgeous Ghost. Thayer, Jane, pseud. Fleishman, Seymour (1918-), illus. LC 77-22203. (Illus.). 32 p. 25cm. (ps-3). 1978. (ISBN 0-688-32133-X). (ISBN 0-688-32133-X). Morrow.

--Gus Was a Mexican Ghost. Thayer, Jane, pseud. Fleishman, Seymour (1918-), illus. LC 73-14587. (Illus.). 32 p. 25cm. (ps-3). 1974. (ISBN 0-688-20104-0). (ISBN 0-688-20104-0). Morrow.

--Gus Was a Real Dumb Ghost. Thayer, Jane, pseud. Dos Santos, Joyce Audy, illus. LC 82-2303. (Illus.). 32 p. 25cm. (gr. k-3). 1982. (ISBN 0-688-01442-9). (ISBN 0-688-01442-9). (ISBN 0-688-01443-7). Morrow.

--Guy Was a Friendly Ghost. Fleishman, Seymour (1918-), illus. LC 62-8857. (Illus.). 32 p. 25cm. 1962. Morrow.

--Holiday on Wheels. Johnson, Iris Beatty, illus. LC 52-12121. (Illus.). 188 p. 21cm. (Morrow junior books). 1953. Morrow.

--I Don't Believe in Elves. Swan, Susan Elizabeth (1944-), illus. LC 74-32045. (Illus.). 32 p. 26cm. 1975. (ISBN 0-688-22030-4). (ISBN 0-688-32030-9). Morrow.

--I Like Trains. Rev. ed. Fonseca, George, illus. LC 65-107274. 1 v. unpaged) col. illus. 17 x 18cm. N.D. Harper.

--I Like Trains. 1st ed. Spiegel, Doris (1901-), illus. LC 44-999847. 32 p. col. illus. 17 x 13 1/2 cm. 1944. Harper & Brothers.

--I'm Not a Cat, Said Emerald. Fleishman, Seymour (1918-), illus. LC 70-85408. (Illus.). 32 p. 25cm. 1970. Morrow.

--Libby Looks for a Spy. Dauber, Elizabeth, illus. LC 65-20952. (Illus.). 191 p. 21cm. 1965. W. Morrow.

--Libby Shadows a Lady. Almquist, Don (1929-), illus. LC 74-2029. (Illus.). 191 p. 21cm. 1974. (ISBN 0-688-21787-7). (ISBN 0-688-21787-7). Morrow.

--Libby's Uninvited Guest. Frame, Paul (1913-), illus. LC 70-108722. (Illus.). 191 p. 21cm. 1970. Morrow.

--The Lighthearted Wolf. Thayer, Jane, pseud. Fleishman, Seymour (1918-), illus. LC 66-10131. 1 v (unpaged) col. illus. 27cm. (gr. k-3). 1966. Morrow.

--The Little Car That Wanted a Garage. Meshekoff, Edward, illus. LC 52-6686. unpaged. illus. 21 cm. (Wonder books, 573). 1952. Wonder Books.

--The Little House: A New Math Story-Game. Madden, Donald B. (1927-), illus. LC 74-188749. (Illus.). 48 p. 26cm. 1972. W. Morrow.

--Little Monkey. Thayer, Jane, pseud. Fleishman, Seymour (1918-), illus. LC 59-5021. unpaged. illus. 26 cm. (gr. k-3). 1959. Morrow.

--Little Mr. Greenthumb. Thayer, Jane, pseud. Fleishman, Seymour (1918-), illus. LC 68-13002. (Illus.). 32 p. 25cm. 1968. Morrow.

--Look Alive, Libby!. Dauber, Elizabeth, illus. LC 62-9321. 191 p. illus. 21 cm. 1962. Morrow.

--Lunch for Lennie. Wohlberg, Meg (1905-), illus. (gr. k-3). 1952. William Morrow & Co.

--Miss Cathy Leonard. Sherman, Theresa (1916-), illus. LC 58-5363. 189 p. illus. 21 cm. 1958. W. Morrow.

--The Mouse on the Fourteenth Floor. Darwin, Beatrice, illus. LC 76-40170. (Illus.). 32 p. 25cm. 1977. (ISBN 0-688-22094-0). (ISBN 0-688-32094-5). Morrow.

--Mr. Turtle's Magic Glasses. Funai, Mamoru R. (1932-), illus. LC 74-118274. (Illus.). 32 p. 23cm. 1971. Morrow.

--The Outside Cat. Thayer, Jane, pseud. Rojankovsky, Feodor Stepanovich (1891-1970), illus. LC 57-6082. unpaged. illus. 27 cm. (Morrow junior books). (gr. k-3). 1957. Morrow.

--Part-Time Dog. Fleishman, Seymour (1918-), illus. LC 65-14066. 1v. (unpaged) col. illus. 25cm. 1965, c.1954. Morrow.

--The Popcorn Dragon. Thayer, Jane, pseud. Barnum, Jay Hyde (1888-1962), illus. LC 53-6661. (Illus.). 48 p. 22cm. (Morrow junior books). (ps-3). 1953. (ISBN 0-688-31630-1). Morrow.

--The Pussy Who Went to the Moon. Fleishman, Seymour (1918-), illus. LC 60-5403. unpaged. illus. 27 cm. (Morrow junior books). 1960. Morrow.

--Quiet on Account of Dinosaur. Fleishman, Seymour (1918-), illus. LC 64-10028. (Illus.). 32 p. 25cm. 1964. Morrow.

--Railroad Cowboy. Johnson, Iris Beatty, illus. LC 51-9399. (Illus.). 160 p. 21cm. (Morrow junior books). 1951. Morrow.

--Rockets Don't Go to Chicago, Andy. Wohlberg, Meg (1905-), illus. LC 67-293. (Illus.). 46 p. 21cm. 1967, c.1965. (ISBN 0-688-21660-9). Morrow.

--A Room for Cathy. Thayer, Jane, pseud. Reed, Veronica, pseud. (1916-), illus. Sherman, Theresa. LC 56-8100. (Illus.). (gr. 3-7). 1956. (ISBN 0-688-31687-5). Morrow.

--Schoolroom Zoo. Johnson, Iris Beatty, illus. LC 50-3998. 191 p. illus. 21 cm. (Morrow Junior books). 1950. Morrow.

--The Second-Story Giraffe. Mars, Witold Tadeusz J. (1912-), illus. LC 59-5774. unpaged. illus. 26 cm. (Morrow junior books). 1959. W. Morrow.

--The Shiny Red Rubber Boots. 32p. 1965. Pitman Publishing.

--Timothy and Madam Mouse: A Non-ABC Book. Madden, Donald B. (1927-), illus. LC 77-135785. (Illus.). 48 p. 26cm. 1971. Morrow.

--Two Hundred Pennies. Neville, Vera (1900-1978), illus. LC 47-30836. 128 p. illus. 23 cm. 1947. W. Morrow.

--What's a Ghost Going to Do?. Fleishman, Seymour (1918-), illus. LC 66-126110. 1 v. (unpaged) col. illus. 25cm. c.1966. Morrow.

--Where's Andy?. LC 54-6259. (Illus.). 46 p. 21cm. 1954. Morrow.

Woolley, Edward Mott (1867-)

--Donald Kirk, the Morning Record Copy-Boy. Varian, George, illus. LC 12-22545. 4 p. l., 273 p. front., plates. 20 cm. $1.20. (His The Donald Kirk series). 1912. Little, Brown, and Company.

--Donald Kirk, the Morning Record Correspondent. LC 13-20206. 4 p. l., 269 p. front., plates. 20 cm. $1.20. (His The Donald Kirk series). 1913. Little, Brown, and Company.

--The Winning Ten. LC 10-21021. vi p., 1 l., 334 p. col. front., 3 coi. pl. 20 cm. $1.50. 1910. D. Appleton and Company.

Woolley, Lazelle Thayer, Mrs. (1872-)

--Faith Palmer at Fordyce Hall. Kromer, A. Edwin, illus. LC 13-19501. 342 p. front., plates. 19 1/2 cm. $1.00. 1913. The Penn Publishing Company.

--Faith Palmer at the Oaks. Kromer, A. Edwin, illus. LC 12-18113. 314 p. front., plates. 19 1/2 cm. 1912. The Penn Publishing Company.

--Faith Palmer in New York. Himmelsbach, Paula B., illus. LC 14-13022. 335 p. front., plates. 19 1/2 cm. $1.00. 1914. The Penn Publishing Company.

--Faith Palmer in Washington. Himmelsbach, Paula B., illus. LC 15-728102. 326 p. front., plates. 19 cm. $1.00. 1915. The Penn Publishing Company.

--The Just Alike Twins. LC 12-19159. 4 p. l., 265 p. front., plates. 19 1/2 cm. $1.00. c.1912. E. P. Dutton & Company.

Woolsey, Janette, jt. ed. see Sechrist, Elizabeth Hough, Mrs.

Woolsey, Janette (1904-) & Sechrist, Elizabeth Hough (1903-)

--It's Time to Give a Play: New Plays for All Occasions. Fry, Guy, illus. LC 55-10732. (Illus.). 307 p. 24cm. 1955. Macrae Smith.

--New Plays for Red Letter Days. Fry, Guy, illus. LC 53-7890. 310 p. 24cm. 1953. Macrae Smith Co.

Woolsey, Maryhale

--Keys & the Candle. Bolognese, Donald Alan (1934-), illus. (Illus.). (gr. 7-10). 1963. (ISBN 0-687-20856-4). Abingdon.

--The Keys and the Candle: The Story of a Boy Scribe in Eleventh Century England. LC 63-7975. 215 p. illus. 22 cm. 1963. Abingdon Press.

Woolsey, Raymond H.

--Flying Doctor of the Philippines. (gr. 5-12). 1972. Review & Herald.

Woolsey, Sarah Chauncey see Coolidge, Susan, pseud.

Woolsey, Sarah Chauncey (1835-1905)

--The Barberry Bush, and Eight Other Stories About Girls for Girls. Coolidge, Susan, pseud. 357 p. incl. front. plates. 18 cm. 1893. Roberts Brothers.

--Clover. Coolidge, Susan, pseud. McCullough, William A., illus. LC 13-357300. 4 p. l., 7-304 p. front., plates. 20 cm. $1.50. (Publisher's lettering: The Katy did series). 1913. Little, Brown, and Company.

--Clover. Coolidge, Susan, pseud. McDermott, Jessie, illus. LC 4-16485. 304 p. incl. front. plates. 18 cm. 1888. Roberts Brothers.

--Cross Patch. Coolidge, Susan, pseud, 1 of 8 Vols. (Illus.). (Popular Story Books Ser.). N.D. Set. Roberts Brothers.

--Cross-Patch and Other Stories. Coolidge, Susan, pseud. Oakford, Eleanor, illus. (Stories for Young People). 1881. Little Brown & Co.

--Cross Patch, and Other Stories. Coolidge, Susan, pseud. Oakford, Eleanor, illus. LC 12-40433. (Adapted from the Myths of Mother Goose). 3 p. l., 9-268 p. illus. 18 cm. 1881. Roberts Brothers.

--Curly Locks. Coolidge, Susan, pseud. LC 99-5152. 1 p. l., 64 p., 1 l. front., illus., 2 pl. 19 cm. 1899. Little, Brown and Company.

--Eyebright. Coolidge, Susan, pseud, 1 of 8 Vols. (Illus.). (Popular Story Books Ser.). N.D. Set. Roberts Brothers.

--Eyebright. A Story. Coolidge, Susan, pseud. LC 12-404321. 2 p. l., 247 p. front., illus., plates. 18 cm. 1879. Roberts Brothers.

--For Summer Afternoons. Coolidge, Susan, pseud. 4 p. l., 336 p. 17 cm. 1890. Roberts Brothers.

--For Summer Afternoons. Coolidge, Susan, pseud. New & enlarged. 1896. Robert Brothers.

--A Guernsey Lily: Or, How the Feud Was Healed. Coolidge, Susan, pseud. LC 9-2778. (A Story for Girls and Boys). 4 p. l., 236 p., 1 l. incl. illus., plates. front. 19 cm. $1.25. c.1908. Little, Brown, & Company.

--A Guernsey Lily: Or, How the Feud Was Healed. Coolidge, Susan, pseud. LC 31-19494. (A Story for Girls and Boys). x p., 1 l., 238 p. incl. front., illus., plates. 22 cm. 1881. Roberts Brothers.

--In the High Valley. Coolidge, Susan, pseud. LC 4-18943. (Being the Fifth and Last Volume of the Katyd Series). 288 p. 4 pl. (incl. front.) 19 cm. 1904. Little, Brown, and Company.

--In the High Valley. Coolidge, Susan, pseud. McCullough, William A., illus. LC 4-35672. (Being the Fifth and Last Volume of the Katy Did Series). 288 p. 4 pl. (incl. front.) 18 cm. 1891. Roberts Brothers.

--In the High Valley. Coolidge, Susan, pseud. McDermott, Jessie, illus. 4 p. l., 7-288 p. front., plates. 20 cm. $1.50. (Publisher's lettering: The Katy did series). 1913. Little, Brown, and Company.

--In the High Valley. Coolidge, Susan, pseud. McDermott, Jessie, illus. (Katy Did Ser.). N.D. Messrs Roberts Brothers.

--Jolly Good Times: Or, Child-Life on a Farm. Coolidge, Susan, pseud. LC 44-299634. 277 p. incl. front. plates. 18 cm. 1875. Roberts Brothers.

--Just Sixteen. Coolidge, Susan, pseud. (Stories for Young People). N.D. Little Brown & Co.

--Just Sixteen. Coolidge, Susan, pseud. LC 12-40431. 304 p. front., plates. 17 1/2 cm. 1889. Roberts Brothers.

--Little Bo-Peep. Coolidge, Susan, pseud. LC 21-20579. 1 p. l., 58 p. front., illus., plates. 19 cm. c.1901. Little, Brown, and Company.

--Little Bo-Peep and Queen Blossom. Coolidge, Susan, pseud. (Illus.). (The Children's Friends Ser.). N.D. Little, Brown and Company.

--A Little Country Girl. Coolidge, Susan, pseud. LC 4-18944. 283 p. front., plates. 19 cm. 1903. Little, Brown, and Company.

--A Little Country Girl. Coolidge, Susan, pseud. LC 4-35671. 283 p. front., plates. 18 cm. 1885. Roberts Brothers.

--A Little Knight of Labor. Coolidge, Susan, pseud. LC 99-5153. 1 p. l., 7-62 p. front., plates. 19 cm. 1899. Little, Brown and Company.

--Little Tommy Tucker. Coolidge, Susan, pseud. LC 6140. 1 p. l., 62 p. front., illus. 19 cm. 1900. Little, Brown & Co.

--Little Tommy Tucker. Coolidge, Susan, pseud. (Illus.). (The Children's Friend Ser.). N.D. Little, Brown and Company.

Worthington, Phoebe & Worthington, Selby
--Teddy Bear Baker. Worthington, Phoebe, illus. LC 79-67181. (Illus.). 16 p. 1979. (ISBN 0-7232-2339-4). F. Warne.
--Teddy Bear Coalman. LC 84-27683. p. cm. 1985. (ISBN 0-14-050498-2). Puffin Books.
--Teddy Bear Coalman. Worthington, Selby, illus. (Illus.). 16p. (ps-k). 1980. (ISBN 0-7232-2052-2). Warne.
--Teddy Bear Coalman: A Story for the Very Young. LC 76-67182. (Illus.). 14 p. 1977. (ISBN 0-7232-2052-2). F. Warne.
--Teddy Bear Postman. (Illus.). (ps-k). 1982. (ISBN 0-7232-2768-3). Warne.
Worthington, Selby, jt. auth. see Worthington, Phoebe.
Worthington, Sophie
--The Summer at Heartsease. (Illus.). N.D. Methodist Bk Concern.
--Under the Apple Trees. N.D. Methodist Bk Concern.
Worthylake, Mary M. (1904-)
--Children of the Seed Gatherers. Luhrs, Henry, illus. LC 64-111152. 46p. col. illus. 22cm. (Melmont Look, Read, Learn). c.1964. Melmont.
Wortis, Avi see Avi, pseud.
Wortis, Joseph (1906-)
--Tricky Dick and His Pals: Comical Stories, All in the Manner of Dr. Heinrich Hoffmann's Der Struwwelpeter. Arkin, David (1906-), illus. LC 73-92230. (Illus.). 28 p. 25cm. 1975, c.1974. (ISBN 0-8129-0445-1). Quadrangle/New York Times Book Co.
Wortman, Arthur, ed.
--There Must Be Magic: First Poems for Children. Overmyer, John, illus. LC 77-102160. (Illus.). 24 p. 18cm. 1970. (ISBN 0-87529-055-8). Hallmark Children's Editions.
--What Should You Do When a Whale Sneezes. Falck, Cheryl, illus. (Illus.). 8p. of color ils. 20p. (gr. k-3). 1970. (ISBN 0-87529-043-4). Hallmark.
Wosmek, Frances see Brailsford, Frances, pseud.
Wosmek, Frances (1917-)
--A Bowl of Sun. Wosmek, Frances (1917-), illus. LC 75-33617. p. cm. 1976. (ISBN 0-516-03412-X). Childrens Press.
--Mystery of the Eagle's Claw. LC 78-12221. 131 p. 21cm. c.1979. (ISBN 0-664-32640-4). Westminster Press.
--Never Mind Murder. LC 77-7950. 140 p. 21cm. c.1977. (ISBN 0-664-32620-X). Westminster Press.
--Sky High. Wosmek, Frances (1917-), illus. LC 50-23975. 28 p. col. illus. 21 cm. (Bonnie Book). 1949. John Martin's House.
--Twinkle Tot Tales. Wosmek, Frances (1917-), illus. N.D. Garden City Publishing Co.
Wotton, Mabel E.
--On Music's Wings. N.D. E. & J. B Young & Co.
--Uncle Tom, The Burglar. (Sunbeam Ser. for Young People). N.D. Penn.
--Uncle Tom the Burglar. (Illus.). (The Little People's Ser.). N.D. Penn Publishing Co.
--Uncle Tom, The Burglar. Waugh, Ida & Brock, H. M., illus. (The Vacation Ser.). N.D. Penn.
Wratislaw, A. H., tr. from Russian.
--Sixty Folk Tales from Exclusively Slavonic Sources. 1900. Houghton Mifflin & Co.
Wratten, Harriet A
--Jo Anne Lives Here. Billings, Edna, illus. LC 35-16049. 64 p. incl. front., illus. 26 1/2 cm. 1935. A Whitman & Co.
Wraxhall, Frederick Charles Lascelles, Sir (1828-1865)
--Golden Hair: A Tale of the Pilgrim Fathers. (Illus.). 1882. Lee & Shepard.
--Golden Hair: A Tale of the Pilgrim Fathers, 1 of 50 vols. (Illus.). (The Norwood Ser.: No. 48). 1900. Lee & Shepard.
--The Prairie Crusoe or Adventures in the Far West, 1 of 50 vols. (Illus.). (The Norwood Ser.: No. 49). 1900. Lee & Shepard.
--Willis the Pilot, 1 of 50. (A Sequel to the Swiss Family Robinson). (Illus.). (The Norwood Ser.: No. 50). 1900. Lee & Shepard.
Wray, Angelina W
--Betty Tucker's Ambition. Young, FLorence Liley, illus. LC 13-172510. 5 p. l., 9-297 p. front., plates. 19 1/2 cm. (Mother Tucker books) $1.00.). 1913. Lothrop, Lee & Shepard Co.
--Mother Tucker's Seven. Withington, Elizabeth R., illus. N.D. Lothrop, Lee & Shepard.
Wraythe, Hope
--Talent in Tatters: Or, Some Vicissitudes in the Life of an English Boy. (Illus.). N.D. E. P. Dutton & Co.
Wriggins, Sally Hovey (1922-), retold by.
--White Monkey King: A Chinese Fable. Solbert, Ronni, pseud. (1925-), illus. Solbert, Romaine G.. Wu, Ch'eng-En, adapted by. LC 76-44281. (Illus.). x, 113 p. 22cm. c.1977. (ISBN 0-394-83450-X). (ISBN 0-394-93450-4). Pantheon Books.
Wright, Adele J., ed. see Andersen, Hans Christian.
Wright, Adele J., retold by see Dodgson, Charles Lutwidge.
Wright, Agnes
--Singing Round the Year: Songs. Potter, Edna, illus. LC 40-324567. 52 p. col. illus. 25 x 21 1/2 cm. c.1940. A. S. Barnes and Company.
Wright, Alan
--Mrs. Bunnykin's Busy Day. LC 21-185300. 1 p. l., 38 p. col. front., illus., col. plates. 20 cm. (Lettered on cover: The Bunnykin books). c.1920. G. W. Jacobs & Company.
--The Story of the Saucy Squirrel. LC 21-185327. 1 p. l., 42 p. col. front., illus., col. plates. 20 cm. (Lettered on cover: The Bunnykin books). c.1920. G. W. Jacobs & Company.
--Tony Twiddler: His Tale. LC 21-18531. 44 p. incl. col. front., illus. col. plates. 20 cm. (Lettered on cover: The Bunnykin books). c.1920. G. W. Jacobs & Co.
Wright, Alice
--Island Holiday. LC 41-570153. xiii p., 2 l., 296 p. illus. 21 1/2 cm. 1941. Frederick A. Stokes Company.
--Island Holiday. Bostelmann, Else, illus. N.D. J. B. Lippincott.
Wright, Anna Maria Rose, Mrs. (1890-1968)
--Barefoot Days. Chapman, Paul, illus. N.D. Grosset & Dunlap.
--The Horse Marines. Koering, Ursula (1921-), illus. LC 58-8165. 193 p. illus. 22 cm. 1958. Houghton Mifflin.
--Hungry Hollow. Grimley, Oliver, illus. LC 51-11814. 135 p. illus. 22 cm. 1951. Friendship Press.
--Land of Silence. Herric, Pru, illus. LC 62-7855. 143 p. illus. 20 cm. 1962. Friendship Press.
--Laughing Gulls. Koering, Ursula (1921-), illus. LC 60-6384. 147 p. illus. 22 cm. 1960. Houghton Mifflin.
--The Life of Hugo, the Horse. Woodruff, Claude W., illus. 32 p. col. illus. 22 x 21 1/2 cm. c.1935. Grosset & Dunlap.
--Offshore Summer. 1957. E M Hale.
--Offshore Summer. Koering, Ursula (1921-), illus. LC 57-7200. 183 p. illus. 22 cm. 1957. Houghton Mifflin.
--Summer at Buckhorn. LC 43-147791. 5 p. l., 243 p. illus. 22 cm. 1943. The Viking Press.
--Whirligig House. LC 51-11786. (Illus.). 280 p. 22cm. 1951. Houghton Mifflin.
Wright, Anna Potter
--Rosa's Quest. 123p. 1904. Moody.
--Rosa's Quest: Or, The Way to the Beautiful Land. 120 p. incl. front., illus., plates. 19 1/2 cm. c.1905. F. H. Revell Company.
--The "True" Mystery Solved. 128p. 1938. Moody.
--The "True" Mystery Solved. LC 39-8340. 128 p. incl. front., illus. 17 1/2 cm. (The Moody Colportage Library). (No. 176). c.1939. The Bible Institute Colportage Ass'n.
Wright, Annie A., ed.
--Fables, Stories and Descriptions. LC 12-402853. 98 p. 20 cm. 1889. A. Flanagan.
Wright, Arthur R. (1890-1948), retold by.
--First Medicine Man: The Tale of Yobaghu-Talyonunh. Yobaghu-Talyonunh Engles, Bill, illus. LC 77-99137. (Illus.). 56 p. 24cm. 1977. (ISBN 0-930766-03-2). (ISBN 0-930766-04-0). O. W. Frost.
Wright, Barbara, jt. auth. see Themerson, Stefan.
Wright, Barbara N.
--Runaway Chick & Freddy the Frog Who Went to School & the Squirrel Friends. N.D. Vantage.
Wright, Betty Ren
--The Cat Who Stamped His Feet. O'Sullivan, Tom, illus. (Illus.). (Eager Readers Ser.). (gr. k-3). 1975. (ISBN 0-307-60806-9, Golden Pr). Western Pub.
--The Day Our TV Broke Down. Bejna, Barbara & Jensen, Shirlee, illus. LC 80-14434. (Illus.). 31 p. 24cm. c.1980. (ISBN 0-8172-1365-1). Raintree Childrens Books.
--The Dollhouse Murders. LC 83-6147. p. cm. c.1983. (ISBN 0-8234-0497-8). Holiday House.
--Getting Rid of Marjorie. LC 81-2623. p. cm. c.1981. (ISBN 0-8234-0429-3). Holiday House.
--Ghosts Beneath Our Feet. LC 84-47835. 144p. (gr. 4-7). 1984. (ISBN 0-8234-0538-9). Holiday.
--Good Morning, Farm. Weinman, Fred, illus. LC 64-6012. 26 p. col. illus. 32 cm. (Whitman giant tell-a-tale book). 1964. Whitman Pub. Co.
--I Like Being Alone. Toht, Don, illus. LC 80-25513. p. cm. c.1981. (ISBN 0-8172-1367-8). Raintree Children Books.
--I Want to Read. Aliki, pseud. (1929-), illus. Brandenberg, Aliki Liacouras. (gr. k-2). 1970. (ISBN 0-307-10879-1, Golden Pr). (ISBN 0-307-60879-4). Western Pub.
--Jim Jump. Stearns, Sharon (1912-), illus. LC 54-33274. unpaged. illus. 17cm. (Tell-a-tale books, 961). c.1954. Whitman Pub. Co.
--Mr. Moggs' Dogs. Frankel, Simon, illus. LC 54-38945. unpaged. illus. 17cm. (Fuzzy Wuzzy Book). c.1954. Whitman Pub. Co.
--My Big Book. Myers, Louise & Myers, Jack, illus. LC 54-33271. unpaged. illus. 20cm. (A Cozy-Corner book, 2422). c.1954. Whitman Pub. Co.
--Poppyseed. Winship, Florence Sarah, illus. LC 55-208669. unpaged. illus. 21cm. (Co2y-corner book, 2441). c.1954. Whitman Pub. Co.
--The Rabbit's Adventure. Swanson, Maggie, illus. (Illus.). (Young Reader Ser.). (gr. k-3). 1979. (ISBN 0-307-60164-1, Golden Pr). Western Pub.
--Roger' Upside-Down Day. Lee, Jared D., illus. 32p. (Tell-a-Tale Reader). (ps-3). 1980. (ISBN 0-307-68481-4, Golden Pr). Western Pub.
--The Secret Window. LC 82-80816. p. cm. c.1982. (ISBN 0-8234-0464-1). Holiday House.
--Snowball. Winship, Florence Sarah, illus. LC 53-16719. (Illus.). 16p. 17cm. (Fuzzy Wuzzy Tell-a-Tales). 1952. Whitman Pub. Co.
--This Room Is Mine. Stang, Judy (1921-1977), illus. LC 8172001670000007. (Illus.). 26 p. 30cm. (Whitman Small World Library Book). c.1966. Whitman Pub. Co.
--This Room Is Mine: A Story About Sharing. Stang, Judy (1921-1977), illus. (Illus.). (Tell-a-Tale Readers). (gr. k-3). 1977. (ISBN 0-307-68643-4, Whitman). Western Pub.
--Train Coming!. Florian, illus. LC 55-22849. unpaged. illus. 17cm. (Tell-a-tale books). c.1954. Whitman Pub. Co.
--Why Do I Daydream?. Glessner, Marc, illus. LC 80-25561. p. cm. c.1981. (ISBN 0-8172-1371-6). Raintree Childrens Books.
--Willy Woo-Oo-Oo. Winship, Florence Sarah, illus. LC 51-34965. unpaged. illus. 17 cm. (tell-a-tale books, 818. c.1951. Whitman Pub. Co.
--The Yellow Cat. Fleur, Anne Elizabeth (1901-), illus. Sari, pseud. LC 53-16401. (Illus.). 17cm. 16p. (Fuzzy Wuzzy Tell-a-Tales). 1952. Whitman Pub. Co.
Wright, Betty Ren, adapted by.
--The Red Badge of Courage. Crane, Stephen (1871-1900) & Shaw, Charles (1941-), illus. LC 81-2611. p. cm. (Short Classics). c.1981. (ISBN 0-8172-1670-7). Raintree Publishers.
Wright, Betty Ren, retold by see Bronte, Emily Jane.
Wright, Betty Ren, ed. see Disney, Walt, Productions.
Wright, Betty Ren, adapted by see Wells, Herbert George.
Wright, Betty Ren & Cogancherry, Helen
--My Sister Is Different. Cogancherry, Helen, illus. LC 80-25508. p. cm. c.1981. (ISBN 0-8172-1369-4). Raintree Childrens Books.
Wright, Betty Ren & Day, Betsy A.
--My New Mom and Me. Day, Betsy A., illus. LC 80-25529. p. cm. c.1981. (ISBN 0-8172-1368-6). Raintree Childrens Books.
Wright, Betty Ren & Wells, Herbert George (1866-1946)
--The Time Machine. Powell, Ivan, illus. LC 81-4097. p. cm. (Raintree Short Classics). c.1981. (ISBN 0-8172-1675-8). Raintree.
Wright, Blanche Fisher (1878-), illus.
--Real Mother Goose. (Illus.). (gr. k-2). 1944. (ISBN 0-8382-0691-3). Hale.
--The Real Mother Goose. LC 16-15134. (Illus.). 132p. (ps-1). 1916. (ISBN 0-528-82322-1). (ISBN 0-528-80177-5). Rand.
--The Real Mother Goose. LC 41-519052. 134, 1 p. incl. col. front., illus. (part col.) 30 1/2 x 25 cm. 1941. Rand McNally & Co.
--The Real Mother Goose. Special anniversary ed. Arbuthnot, May Hill, intro. by. LC 16-151345. 128p. col. illus. 30cm. 1965, c.1916. Rand MacNally.
Wright, Bob
--The Dancing Monkey. Heidinger, Herb, illus. (Illus.). 48p. (Tom & Ricky Mystery Ser.: No. III). (gr. 1-9). 1983. (ISBN 0-87879-360-7, High Noon Books). Acad Therapy.
--The Flying Wheel Mystery. Heidinger, Herb, illus. (Illus.). 48p. 1st U.S. edition. (Tom & Ricky Mystery Ser.: No. III). (gr. 1-9). 1983. (ISBN 0-87879-361-5, High Noon Books). Acad Therapy.
--The Hang Glider Mystery. Heidinger, Herb, illus. Incl. Diamonds in the Sky; The Mystery in the Woods; Ghost at Land's End; The Blue Mouse Mystery. (Illus.). 48p. (Orig.). (Tom & Ricky Mystery Ser.: Set 8). (gr. 4-6). 1984. Set. (ISBN 0-87879-425-5, High Noon Bks). Acad Therapy.
--The Man with the Red Hair. Heidinger, Herb, illus. (Illus.). 48p. 1st U.S. edition. (Tom & Ricky Mystery Ser.: No. III). (gr. 1-9). N.D. (ISBN 0-87879-358-5, High Noon Books). Acad Therapy.
--The Mummy's Crown. Heidinger, Herb, illus. (Illus.). 48p. (Tom & Ricky Mystery Ser.). (gr. 5-9). 1982. (ISBN 0-87879-327-5). Acad Therapy.
--The Mystery of Room Five Hundred-Twelve. Heidinger, Herb, illus. (Illus.). 48p. 1st U.S. edition. (Tom & Ricky Mystery Ser.: No. III). (gr. 1-9). 1983. (ISBN 0-87879-359-3, High Noon Books). Acad Therapy.
--The Red Hot Rod. Heidinger, Herb, illus. (Illus.). 48p. (Orig.). (Tom & Ricky Mystery Ser.). (gr. 5-9). 1982. (ISBN 0-87879-329-1). Acad Therapy.
--The Secret Staircase. Heidinger, Herb, illus. (Illus.). 48p. (Orig.). (Tom & Ricky Mystery Ser.). (gr. 4-9). 1982. (ISBN 0-87879-328-3). Acad Therapy.
--The Siamese Turtle Mystery. Heidinger, Herb, illus. (Illus.). 48p. (Orig.). (Tom & Ricky Mystery Ser.). (gr. 4-9). 1982. (ISBN 0-87879-330-5). Acad Therapy.
--The Tall Man Mystery. Heidinger, Herb, illus. Incl. The Purple Bottle Mystery; The Chinese Vase Mystery; The Persian Cat Mystery; The Junk Car Mystery. (Illus.). 48p. (Orig.). (Tom & Ricky Mystery Ser.: Set 7). (gr. 4-7). 1984. Set. (ISBN 0-87879-419-0, High Noon Books). Acad Therapy.
--Terror in the High Sierras. Heidinger, Herb, illus. LC 81-22899. (Illus.). 44 p. 18cm. (Perspectives book). c.1982. (ISBN 0-87879-300-3). Academic Therapy Publications.
--The Tom & Ricky Map. Heidinger, Herb, illus. (Illus.). (The Tom & Ricky Mystery Ser.: Nos. 1-4). (gr. 1-9). 1983. (ISBN 0-87879-375-5, High Noon Books). Acad Therapy.
--The Tom & Ricky Mystery. Heidinger, Herb, illus. 48p. 1st U.S. edition. (The Tom & Ricky Mystery Ser.: No. III). (gr. 1-9). 1983. (ISBN 0-87879-357-7, High Noon Books). Acad Therapy.
--The Tom & Ricky Mystery Series, 5 vols, No. 2. Heidinger, Herb, illus. (Illus.). 48p. (gr. 4-9). 1983. Set. (ISBN 0-87879-336-4). Acad Therapy.
--The Video Game Spy. Heidinger, Herb, illus. (Illus.). 48p. (Orig.). (Tom & Ricky Mystery Ser.). (gr. 4-9). 1982. (ISBN 0-87879-331-3). Acad Therapy.
Wright, Boyd
--Titan: Story of a Boy & His Heroic Great Dane. 96p. (gr. 5-7). 1971. (ISBN 0-682-47178-X). Exposition.
Wright, Bruce Stanley (1912-1975)
--Black Duck Spring. 1st ed. Teason, James G., illus. LC 66-11550. 191 p. illus. 21 cm. 1966. Dutton.
Wright, Burnaby
--Spunky. Price, Harold L. (1912-), illus. LC 41-154678. 24 p. col. illus. 24 cm. c.1941. Binfords & Mort.
Wright, Caleb E.
--Marcus Blair. (Illus.). N.D. J B Lippincott & Co.
Wright, Christopher, ed. see Walton, Octavius Frank, Mrs.
Wright, Dare (1926-)
--The Doll and the Kitten. Wright, Dare, photos by. LC 60-7141. 55 p. illus. 22 cm. 1960. Doubleday.
--Edith & Big Bad Bill. LC 68-23652. (Illus.). 56 p. 33cm. 1968. Random House.
--Edith & Little Bear Lend a Hand. LC 72-532. (Illus.). 57 p. 33cm. 1972. (ISBN 0-394-82389-3). Random House.
--Edith and Midnight. LC 77-27767. (Illus.). 48 p. 32cm. c.1978. (ISBN 0-385-14155-6). (ISBN 0-385-14156-4). Doubleday.
--Edith & Mister Bear: A Lonely Doll Story. (Illus.). (gr. k-3). 1964. (ISBN 0-394-81109-7). Random.
--Edith and the Duckling. LC 80-1664. (Illus.). 55 p. 32cm. 1981. (ISBN 0-385-17100-5). (ISBN 0-385-17101-3). Doubleday.
--A Gift from the Lonely Doll. LC 66-9785. 1 v. (unpaged) illus. 33 cm. 1966. Random House.
--Holiday for Edith and the Bears. LC 58-9473. (Illus.). unpaged. 32cm. 1958. Doubleday.
--The Kitten's Little Boy. LC 72-161010. (Illus.). 24 p. 29cm. 1971. Four Winds Press.
--The Little One. Wright, Dare, photos by. LC 59-10880. 56 p. illus. 32 cm. 1959. Doubleday.
--Lona: A Fairy Tale. LC 63-7814. 1 v. (unpaged) illus. 33 cm. 1963. Random House.
--The Lonely Doll. Wright, Dare, photos by. LC 57-8093. unpaged. illus. 32 cm. 1957. Doubleday.
--The Lonely Doll Learns a Lesson. LC 61-15088. unpaged. illus. 33 cm. 1961. Random House.
--Look at a Calf. Wright, Dare (1926-), illus. LC 73-17369. (Illus.). 48p. 1974. (ISBN 0-394-92776-1, BYR). Random.
--Look at a Colt. LC 69-17441. (Illus.). 38 p. 29cm. 1969. Random House.
--Take Me Home. LC 65-181651. 1v. (unpaged) illus. 18x12cm. c.1965. Random.
Wright, Elizabeth Le May, ed.
--On with the Show: A Collection of Short Plays for Classroom Reading. Van Riper, Eleanor Wright, illus. LC 37-593. vii, 294 p. illus. diagrs. 21 cm. 1937. D. Appleton-Century Company, Incorporated.
Wright, Elizur, Jr., tr. see La Fontaine, Jean de.
Wright, Elsie (1907-)
--Boys' Book of Famous Fliers. LC 51-39008. 222 p. illus. 20 cm. (Falcon books, A-52). 1951. World Pub. Co.

AUTHOR INDEX WRIGHT, SARAH

--On the Forty-Yard Line. LC 48-116723. 214 p. front. 20 cm. (Falcon books, A-16). 1948. World Pub. Co.
--Patty and Jo, Detectives. LC 33-25675. 222 p. 19 1/2 cm. c.1933. The World Syndicate Publishing Company.
--Patty and Jo, Detectives. LC 48-8930. 215 p. front. 20 cm. (Falcon books, A-30). 1948. World Pub. Co.
--The Scout Patrol Boys at Circle U Ranch. LC 33-30830. 1 p. l., 9-117 p. 19 1/2 cm. 1933. The World Syndicate Publishing Co.
--The Scout Patrol Boys Exploring in Yucatan. LC 33-30829. 1 p. l., 9-117 p. 19 1/2 cm. 1933. The World Syndicate Publishing Co.
Wright, Elvirton, pseud., see Whitcomb, Jessie Wright.
Wright, Elvirton, Mrs., pseud.
--Curly Head. Whitcomb, Jessie Wright. 262p. 1889. The National Temperance Society And Pubn House.
--Freshman and Senior. Whitcomb, Jessie Wright. 452p. N.D. Pilgrim Press.
--Majoribanks: A Girls Story. Whitcomb, Jessie Wright. (The Girl Chums Ser.). N.D. A. L. Burt Company.
--Majoribanks. Whitcomb, Jessie Wright. (Illus.). (The Wellesley Series for Girls). N.D. A. L. Burt.
--Pen's Venture. Whitcomb, Jessie Wright, 36 vols. (Illus.). (St. Nicholas Ser.). 1904. Set. A L Burt Co.
--Pen's Venture. Whitcomb, Jessie Wright. (The Girl Chums Ser.). N.D. A. L. Burt.
--Pen's Venture. Whitcomb, Jessie Wright. (Illus.). (The Wellesley Series for Girls). N.D. A. L. Burt.
--Pen's Venture. Whitcomb, Jessie Wright. (Illus.). 278p. N.D. Pilgrims Press.
Wright, Enid Meadowcroft La Monte see Malkus, Alida Wright Sims, Mrs.
Wright, Enid Meadowcroft La Monte see Meadowcroft, Enid La Monte, Mrs.
Wright, Enid Meadowcroft La Monte see Hickok, Lorena A.
Wright, Enid Meadowcroft La Monte see Gordon, Patricia.
Wright, Enid Meadowcroft La Monte see Graham, Shirley.
Wright, Ernest Vincent (1872-1939)
--The Wonderful Fairies of the Sun. Norman, Cora M, illus. LC 79-128005. (Illus.). xii, 66 p., 1 leaf of plates. 24cm. 1896. Roberts Brothers.
Wright, Ethel Belle (1908-)
--Saturday Ride. 24p. N.D. William R. Scott Inc.
--Saturday Walk. Rose, Richard (1933-), illus. LC 54-6792. 40p. 32p. (ps-2). 1954. (ISBN 0-201-09339-1, A-W Childrens). A-W.
--Saturday Walk. Rose, Richard (1933-), illus. LC 54-67923. unpaged. illus. 19cm. c.1954. W. R. Scott.
Wright, Ethel Belle (1908-) & Rose, Richard
--Saturday Flight. LC 44-4441. cover-title, 20 p. col. illus. 20 x 24 cm. c.1944. W. R. Scott, Inc.
--Saturday Walk: A Cardboard Book for Twos & Threes. LC 41-13242. 20 p. col. illus. 20 1/2 x 24 1/2 cm. c.1941. W. R. Scott, Inc.
Wright, Frances Fitzpatrick (1897-)
--The American Girl Book of Pat Downing Stories. Mocniak, George, illus. LC 63-18282. 179 p. illus. 22 cm. (American girl library, 8). 1963. Random House.
--Bless Your Bones, Sammy. Savage, Steele (1900-), illus. (Illus.). 144 p. 22cm. 1968. Abingdon Press.
--Daybreak at Sampey Place. Ayer, Margaret (0000-1981), illus. LC 54-307628. 125p. illus. 21cm. 1954. Abingdon Press.
--Lucy Ellen. Ullberg, Marjorie Lee, illus. LC 40-6808. 5 p. l., 278 p. illus. 19 1/2 cm. c.1940. Farrar & Rinehart, Inc.
--Lucy Ellen's College Daze. Howe, Gertrude Herrick (1902-), illus. LC 43-13045. 6 p. l., 3-265 p. incl. front., illus. 19 cm. 1943. Farrar & Rinehart, Inc.
--Lucy Ellen's Heyday. Locke, Vance, illus. LC 45-8410. 4 p. l., 3-199 p. front. 19 cm. 1945. Farrar & Rinehart, Inc.
--Medicine for Margery And Other Stories. Henderson, Leslie, illus. LC 26-11851. 64 p. illus., col. plates. 31 cm. (Cokesbury Character Series for Boys and Girls). c.1926. Cokesbury Press.
--Number Eleven Poplar Street. Ayer, Margaret (0000-1981), illus. LC 48-828097. 127 p. illus. 21 cm. 1948. Abingdon-Cokesbury Press.
--Poplar Street Park. Ayer, Margaret (0000-1981), illus. LC 52-3038. 127 p. illus. 21 cm. 1952. Abingdon-Cokesbury Press.
--The Secret of the Old Sampey Place. Ayer, Margaret (0000-1981), illus. LC 46-211299. 127, 1 p. illus. 21 cm. 1946. Abingdon-Cokesbury Press.
--Surprise at Sampey Place. Ayer, Margaret (0000-1981), illus. LC 50-8742. 127 p. illus. 21 cm. 1950. Abingdon-Cokesbury Press.
--Your Loving Sister, Pat Downing. Dodge, Suzanne C., illus. LC 48-10366. 206 p. illus. 20 cm. 1948. Rinehart.
Wright, Freire
--The Adventures of Tom Thumb. (Illus.). 32p. 1st U.S. edition. (ps-1). 1984. (ISBN 0-7182-6090-2, Pub. by Kaye & Ward). David & Charles.
Wright, Freire & Foreman, Michael (1938-)
--Freire Wright & Michael Foreman's Seven in One Blow. LC 77-92379. (Illus.). 36 p. 21cm. (Random House pictureback). (Best book club ever). c.1978. (ISBN 0-394-83805-X). (ISBN 0-394-83804-1). Random House.
--Freire Wright & Michael Foreman's Seven in One Blow. LC 80-19028. (Illus.). 32 p. 21cm. (Random House pictureback). 1981, c.1978. (ISBN 0-394-93805-1). Random House.
--Seven in One Blow. (gr. k-2). 1981. Random.
Wright, Gerald
--North of the Border. LC 61-3124. 119 p. 21 cm. 1961. Zondervan Pub. House.
Wright, Glen, ed.
--Gold of the Gods. LC 81-12864. (Illus.). (Fascinating Tales of the Pacific Ser.). (gr. 4 up). 1982. (ISBN 0-516-02471-X). Childrens.
--Gold of the Gods and Other Fascinating Tales of Old Mexico. LC 81-12864. p. cm. (Fascinating Tales of the Pacific). c.1981. (ISBN 0-89868-120-0). (ISBN 0-89868-113-8). Aro Pub.
--Land Divers of Pentecost. LC 81-81012737. (Illus.). (Fascinating Tales of the Pacific Ser.). (gr. 4 up). 1982. (ISBN 0-516-02472-8). Childrens.
--The Pigeon with Nine Heads. LC 81-12879. (Illus.). (Fascinating Tales of the Pacific Ser.). (gr. 4 up). 1982. (ISBN 0-516-02474-4). Childrens.
--The Pigeon with Nine Heads and Other Fascinating Legendary Tales of Samoa. LC 81-12879. p. cm. (Fascinating Tales of the Pacific). c.1981. (ISBN 0-89868-122-7). (ISBN 0-89868-115-4). Aro Pub.
--Snatched by a Killer Wave. LC 81-12877. (Illus.). (Fascinating Tales of the Pacific Ser.). (gr. 4 up). 1982. (ISBN 0-516-02475-2). Childrens.
Wright, Glen & Murphy, Carol, eds.
--Fascinating Tales of the Pacific, 6 bks. (Illus.). (gr. 3-6). 1981. Set. (ISBN 0-89868-110-3, Read Res). Set. (ISBN 0-89868-117-0, Read Res). ARO Pub.
--A Mountain Blows Its Top. (Illus.). (gr. 3-6). 1981. (ISBN 0-89868-111-1, Read Res). (ISBN 0-89868-118-9, Read Res). ARO Pub.
--Snatched by a Killer Wave. (Illus.). (gr. 3-6). 1981. (ISBN 0-89868-114-6, Read Res). (ISBN 0 89868 121 9, Read Res). ARO Pub.
Wright, Harriet Sabra
--New Plays from Old Tales: Arranged for Boys and Girls. D'Emo, Leon, illus. LC 21-19594. x p., 2 l., 3-180 p. col. front., illus. 19 cm. 1921. The Macmillan Company.
Wright, Helen (1914-) & Rapport, Samuel, eds.
--Great Adventures with Wild Animals. (gr. 7 up). 1967. (ISBN 0-06-026623-6). (ISBN 0-06-026624-4). Har-Row.
Wright, Henrietta Christian (0000-1899)
--Children's Stories in English Literature: From Shakespeare to Tennyson. vi p., 1 l., 454 p. 19 cm. 1907. C. Scribner's Sons.
--Little Folk in Green. Emmet, Lydia F., illus. (Illus.). N.D. White & Stokes.
--Princess Liliwinkins. (Illus.). N.D. Harper & Brothers.
--The Princess of Liliwinkins, and Other Stories. LC 12-40411. 3 p. l., 220 p. front., plates. 19 cm. 1889. Harper & Brothers.
Wright, Henry C.
--A Kiss for a Blow. N.D. Colby & Rich.
--Kiss for a Blow, 1 of 4 vols. (Illus.). (The Rainy Day Ser.). N.D. Set. Lee & Shepard.
--A Kiss for a Blow: Or, A Collection of Stories for Children. 1882. Lee & Shepard.
--A Kiss for a Blow: Or, A Collection of Stories for Children. (Illus.). 1900. Lee & Shepard.
Wright, Isa L
--Trails to Wonderland. Cue, Harold, illus. LC 20-19069. 4 p. l., 157, 1 p. col. front., plates. 20 1/2 cm. $1.75. 1920. Houghton Mifflin Company.
--With the Little Folks. Cue, Harold, illus. 4 p. l., 130 p., 1 l. col. front., plates. 20 1/2 cm. 1919. Houghton Mifflin Company.
Wright, J.
--David, King of Israel. (Reading for the Young). (Illus.). N.D. Macmillan & Co.
Wright, J. McNair, jt. auth. see Hosmer, Margaret Kerr, Mrs.
Wright, Jack (1907-)
--Champs on Ice. N.D. World Publishing Co.
--On the Forty Yard Line. LC 32-22542. 256 p. 19 1/2 cm. 1932. The World Syndicate Publishing Company.
--The Scout Patrol Boys and the Hunting Lodge Mystery. LC 33-30828. 1 p. l., 9-118 p. 19 1/2 cm. c.1933. The World Syndicate Publishing Co.
--The Scout Patrol Boys at Circle U Ranch. (The Scout Patrol Boys Ser.). 1933. World Publishing Co.
--The Scout Patrol Boys Exploring in Yacatan. (The Scout Patrol Boys Ser.). 1933. World Publishing Co.
--The Scout Patrol Boys in the Frozen South. LC 33-30827. 2 p. l., 9-110 p. 10 1/2 cm. c.1933. The World Syndicate Publishing Co.
Wright, Jack (1907-) & Devries, Julian (1904-)
--On the Forty Yard Line and The Strike-Out King, 2 in 1. Devries, Julianne, pseud. (Generates State-of-the-Art Compact System Software). N.D. World Publishing Co.
Wright, James, tr. see Hesse, Hermann.
Wright, James Abell
--The Parade of the Animals: Or, Capers of [illegible] 1/2 cm. c.1934. Whitman Publishing Company.
Wright, James Alfred see Herriot, James, pseud.
Wright, Jean Mary Nelson (1916-)
--Volcano Tales. Ritchings, Joan Drew, illus. LC 50-5589. 64 p. illus. 23 cm. 1950, c.1949. Exposition Press.
Wright, Jessie E., pseud., see Whitcomb, Jessie Wright.
Wright, Jessie E., Mrs., pseud.
--An Odd Little Lass. Whitcomb, Jessie Wright. Waugh, Ida, illus. (Keystone Ser.). N.D. Penn Publishing Co.
--His Best Friend. Whitcomb, Jessie Wright. 295p. N.D. Pilgrim Press.
--Philip Leicester. Whitcomb, Jessie Wright. 264p. 1910. W. A. Wilde.
Wright, Joe, jt. auth. see Saddler, Allen.
Wright, Joseph Lord
--The Adventures of Davy & Bartholomew. Nelson, Rick, illus. LC 78-66284. (Illus., Orig.). (gr. 3-6). 1979. Delanie Way.
Wright, Josephine Lord
--Cotton Cat and Martha Mouse. 1st ed. Johnson, John Emil (1929-), illus. LC 66-11390. 1 v. (unpaged) col. illus. 19 cm. 1966. Dutton.
--Wise Dog. 1st ed. Obligado, Lilian Isabel (1931-), illus. LC 66-11391. 48p. col. illus. 22cm. c.1966. Dutton.
Wright, Judith Arundell (1915-)
--Birds. (Illus.). 48p. 1967. Tri-Ocean Books.
--The Day the Mountains Played. Wrighy, Annette, illus. 48p. 1960. Tri-Ocean Book.
--Range the Mountains High. 142p. illus. 22cm. 1966. Landowne Pr.
Wright, Julia McNair, tr. see Malot, Hector Henri.
Wright, Julia MacNair, Mrs. (1840-1903)
--A Bonnie Boy. 296p. 1905. American Tract Society.
--A Bonnie Boy: A Story of Happy Days. 12cm. 296p. 1899. American Tract Society.
--A Boy of To-Day. 311p. 1905. American Tract Society.
--A Boy of Today. 12cm. 311p. 1898. American Tract Society.
--The Cabin in the Brush. (Illus.). N.D. James Moore.
--The Corner Stall. N.D. Henry Hoyt.
--Fru Dagmar's Son. A Survivor of the "Danmark.". LC 42-27122. vi, 7-348 p. illus. 19 1/2 cm. c.1891. The National Temperance Society and Publication House.
--The Golden Fruit. N.D. Henry Hoyt.
--The Golden Heart. N.D. Henry Hoyt.
--The Golden Life. LC 20-23170. iv, 5-379 p. front., plates. 17 cm. (Added t.-p.: The Sunday-school series of juvenile religious works). 1867. H. Hoyt.
--The Golden Work. N.D. Henry Hoyt.
--The Golden Work. LC 75-300481. (Illus.). 391 p., 2 leaves of plates. 18cm. c.1868. I. Bradley.
--GrahamS Laddie: A Story of God's Providence. LC 12-40416. 334 p. front. (map) 19 cm. 1886. Presbyterian Board of Publication.
--A Million Too Much. (Illus.). (New Alta Lib.). N.D. Porter & Coates.
--Mother Goose for Temperance Nurseries, 8 Vols. King, S. C., illus. 68p. N.D. National Temperance Society.
--Our Chatham-Street Uncle: Or, The Three Golden Balls. 1869. Henry Hoyt.
--Sara Jane: A Girl of One Talent. LC 12-40283. 320 p. front., plates. 18 cm. c.1889. Presbyterian Board of Publication and Sabbath- School Work.
Wright, Katharine O
--Christmas at Thunder Gap. Kirkpatrick, Jaue, illus. LC 54-13317. unpaged. illus. 17cm. 1954. Arrowhead Books.
Wright, Kenneth, pseud., see Del Ray, Lester.
Wright, Kenneth, pseud. (1915-)
--Mysterious Planet. Del Ray, Lester. (gr. 7-9). 1952. (ISBN 0-03-034530-8). HR&W.
--Mysterious Planet. Del Ray, Lester. (Winston Science Fiction Ser.). 1953. John C. Winston Co.
Wright, Lula Esther
--The Magic Boat. Smedley, Dorothy Harewood, illus. LC 27-18009. vii, 156 p. incl. col. front., illus. (part col.) 20 cm. c.1927. Ginn and Company.
Wright, Mabel Osgood, Mrs. (1859-1934)
--Aunt Jimmy's Will. (Every Boy's and Every Girl's Ser.). N.D. Macmillan Co.
--Barbara At the Sign of the Fox. N.D. Macmillan.
--Dogtown: Being Some Chapters from the Annals of the Waddles Family, Set Down in the Language of Housepeople. Wright, Mabel Osgood, Mrs., illus. LC 2-26347. xiii, 405 p. incl. illus., plates. front. 20 cm. 1902. The Macmillan Company.
--The Dream Fox Story Book. LC 6489. 5 p. l., 251 p. illus., plates. 18 1/2 x 15 cm. 1900. The Macmillan Company; Etc., Etc.
--First Reader: Stories of Earth and Sky. Gleeson, Joseph M., illus. LC 4-2142. 19cm. 125p. (The Heart of Nature Ser.). 1904. Macmillan Co.
--Gray Lady & the Birds: Stories of the Bird Year for Home & School. N.D. Macmillan.
--Tommy-Anne, and the Three Hearts. Blashfield, Albert D., illus. (Illus.). N.D. Grosset & Dunlap.
--Tommy-Anne and the Three Hearts. Blashfield, Albert D., illus. LC 3-27280. xvi, 322 p. incl. front., illus., plates. 19 1/2 cm. 1896. The Macmillan Company.
--Wabeno the Magician. Gleeson, Joseph M., illus. (A Sequel to Tommy-Anne and the Three Hearts). (Illus.). N.D. Grosset & Dunlap.
--Wabeno the Magician. Gleeson, Joseph M., illus. LC 99-5155. (The Sequel to "Tommy-Anne and the Three Hearts".). xi, 346 p. front., illus., plates. 19 1/2 cm. 1899. The Macmillan Company.
Wright, Madeline
--Lily & Bojo. 1964. Exposition Press.
--The Wonder Seeds. 1963. Exposition Press.
Wright, Martin, jt. auth. see Moore, John.
Wright, Maud E.
--How Roger Saved His Brother. (Illus.). 80p. (The Rosebud Ser.). N.D. Fleming H. Revell Co.
Wright, Meg, illus.
--Three Stories from India. (Illus.). (gr. 1-8). 1984. (ISBN 0-86508-166-2). BCM Inc.
Wright, Mildred Whatley
--The Elegant Pelican. Rogers, Carol, illus. LC 68-19558. (Illus.). 32 p. 24cm. 1968. Steck-Vaughn Co.
--Henri Goes to the Mardi Gras. Hoff, Sydney (1912-), illus. LC 70-113511. (Illus.). 47 p. 24cm. 1971, c.1970. Putnam.
--Henri LeBear. Kinsey, Carolyn Huff, illus. LC 66-12935. 32p. illus. (pt. col.) 24cm. 1966. Steck-Vaughn.
--Sky Full of Dragons. Dolezal, Carroll, illus. LC 78-76606. 32 color ils. 32p. (gr. 1-2). 1969. (ISBN 0-8114-7658-8). Steck-V.
Wright, Nancy Means
--Down the Strings. LC 82-9637. 183 p. 22cm. c.1982. (ISBN 0-525-66769-5). E.P. Dutton.
Wright, Norman (1927-)
--Chip, Chip. Carbe, Nino (1909-), illus. (Little Golden Book). 1946. Golden Press.
--Chip Chip. Carbe, Nino (1909-), illus. 42 p. illus. (part col.) 20 x 17 cm. (On cover: The Little Golden Library, no. 28). 1947. Simon and Schuster.
Wright, Patricia (1932-)
--A Space of the Heart. LC 74-33669. 360p. 1976. (ISBN 0-385-03648-5). Doubleday.
Wright, Philip Lee
--An Air Express Holdup: Or, How Pilot George Selkirk Carried Through. Randolph, David, illus. LC 30-143941. iii, 202 p. front. 19 1/2 cm. (His The air pilot series). c.1930. Barse & Co.
--The East Bound Air Mail: Or, Fighting Fog, Storm and Hard Luck. Randolph, David, illus. LC 30-8272. 205 p. front. 19 1/2 cm. (His Air pilot series). c.1930. Barse & Co.
Wright, Richard Bruce (1937-)
--Andrew Tolliver. Parker, Lewis, illus. LC 65-27029. 105p. illus. 18cm. (Buckskin bks., no. 11). 1966, c.1965. St. Martin's.
--One John A. Too Many. LC 85-27722. p. cm. (Schoolhouse Novels). 1986, c.1984. (ISBN 0-8086-0312-4). Schoolhouse Press.
Wright, Richard Nathaniel (1908-1960)
--Uncle Tom's Children. N.D. World Publishing.
Wright, Robert, jt. auth. see Collette, Paul.
Wright, Robert Granger, jt. auth. see Hipple, Theodore Wallace.
Wright, Robin S., ed. see Cooper, James Fenimore.
Wright, Robin S, ed. see Scott, Walter, Sir.
Wright, Robin S. (1945-), abridged by see Wallace, Lewis.
Wright, Samuel & Pendergrass, Mark D.
--The Music Machine. LC 79-9200. (A Fantasy Story from Agapeland, (From the Pages of The Ancient Manuscripts)). (Illus.). 142 p. 20cm. c.1979. (ISBN 0-87123-707-5). Bethany Fellowship.
Wright, Sarah K., ed.
--Tales from Grimm. Paflin, Roberta, pseud. (1903-), illus. Petty, Roberta Harris Pfafflin. N.D. E. P. Dutton & Co.
Wright, Sarah K, ed. see Andersen, Hans Christian.

Wright, Sewell Peaslee
--Half Wolf. LC 46-5050. 3 p. l., 9-253 p. incl. front. 19 1/2 cm. 1946. The Westminster Press.
Wright, Sheila, jt. auth. see Russman, Penny.
Wright, Walter L, Mrs.
--Danny Boy, and Other Stories. LC 52-14105. 51 p. 21 cm. 1952. Christopher Pub. House.
Wright, Walter (1937-)
--The Maverick Moon. Wright, Walter, illus. LC 78-19701. p. cm. (Star Wars). c.1979. (ISBN 0-394-84087-9). (ISBN 0-394-94087-3). Random House.
Wright, Zita L.
--Danger on the Ski Trails. (Illus.). 188p. 22cm. (gr. 7-12). 1965. (ISBN 0-688-41182-7). Lothrop.
Wrightson, Patricia (1921-)
--The Dark Bright Water. LC 78-8793. (Illus.). 223 p. 22cm. 1979, c.1978. (ISBN 0-689-50122-6). Atheneum.
--Down to Earth. 1st ed. Horder, Margaret L'Anson (1911-), illus. LC 65-10963. (Illus.). 222 p. 21cm. 1965. Harcourt, Brace & World.
--The Feather Star. Young, Noela, illus. LC 63-7901. (Illus.). (gr. 7 up). 1963. (ISBN 0-15-227501-0, HJ). HarBraceJ. **Award: (ALA).**
--The Ice Is Coming. LC 76-45438. (Illus.). 222 p. 23cm. 1977. (ISBN 0-689-50081-5). Atheneum.
--Journey Behind the Wind. LC 80-25005. p. cm. 1981. (ISBN 0-689-50198-6). Atheneum.
--A Little Fear. LC 83-2784. p. cm. 1983. (ISBN 0-689-50291-5). Atheneum. **Awards: (BGH); (ALA).**
--The Nargun and the Stars. LC 73-85323. (Illus.). 184 p. 22cm. 1974. (ISBN 0-689-30432-3). Atheneum.
--An Older Kind of Magic. Young, Noela, illus. LC 70-167839. (Illus.). 186 p. 21cm. 1st U.S. edition. 1972. (ISBN 0-15-203600-8). Harcourt, Brace, Jovanovich.
--An Older Kind of Magic. Young, Noela, illus. LC 73-164883. (Illus.). 151 p. 21cm. 1972. (ISBN 0-09-111430-6). Hutchinson.
--A Racecourse for Andy. 1st ed. Horder, Margaret L'Anson (1911-), illus. (Illus.). 156 p. 21cm. 1968. Harcourt, Brace & World.
Wrigley, Denis
--The Little Giant James. Wrigley, Denis, illus. (Illus.). (Dinosaur Ser.). (gr. k-3). 1978. (ISBN 0-85122-076-2, Pub. by Dino Pub). Merrimack Pub Cir.
Wrigley, Elsie
--The Tale of the Bookmouse. LC 67-79667. (Illus.). 48 p. 22cm. 1966. F. Warne.
Wrigley, Louise Scott
--Play Poems. LC 55-12232. (Illus.). 21cm. 44p. 1955. Herald House.
--The Shiny Nickel. N.D. Standard Pub.
--The Shiny Nickel, and Other Stories and Poems. LC 55-12320. unpaged. illus. 27cm. (Herald House book). c.1955. Herald Pub. House.
Wriston, Hildreth Tyler
--Andy and the Red Canoe. N.D. E . M. Hale and Co.
--Andy and the Red Canoe. Mars, Witold Tadeusz J. (1912-), illus. LC 60-12641. 149 p. illus. 22 cm. 1960. Ariel Books.
--Camping Down at Highgate. Holbrook, Ruth Langland (1889-), illus. LC 39-30534. viii p., 1 l., 278 p. incl. front., illus., plates. 20 1/2 cm. 1939. Doubleday, Doran & Co., Inc.
--Downstreet with Edith. Paull, Grace a. (1898-), illus. LC 35-20898. 3 p. l., 198 p. incl. illus., plates. col. front. 21 cm. 1935. Doubleday, Doran & Company, Inc.
--Hill Farm. Burchard, Peter Duncan (1921-), illus. LC 56-14068. 191p. illus. 22cm. 1956. Abingdon Press.
--The Oom-Pah Horn. Geer, Charles Hand (1922-), illus. LC 62-11154. 111 p. illus. 22 cm. 1962. Abingdon Press.
--Open Water. Morse, Dorothy Bayley (1906-1979), illus. LC 42-9903. 5 p. l., 274 p. incl. front., illus., plates. 21 cm. 1942. Doubleday, Doran & Company, Inc.
--Putt-Putt Skipper. Orbaan, Albert F. (1913-), illus. LC 58-6976. 222 p. illus. 22 cm. 1958. Ariel Books.
--Show Lamb. N.D. E . M. Hale and Co.
--Show Lamb. Burchard, Peter Duncan (1921-), illus. LC 53-11617. (Illus.). 191 p. 22cm. 1953. Abingdon-Cokesbury Press.
--Susan's Secret. Mars, Witold Tadeusz J. (1912-), illus. LC 57-598606. 126p. illus. 22cm. 1957. Ariel Books.
--A Yankee Musket. Polseno, Jo, illus. LC 59-7500. 190 p. illus. 22 cm. 1959. Abingdon Press.
Wroblewski, Claire L.
--Max Maple. (Illus.). 44p. (Orig.). (gr. k-5). 1983. (ISBN 0-942818-01-6). Sparrow Pub.
--Pork & Bean. (Illus.). 48p. (Orig.). (gr. k-3). 1982. (ISBN 0-942818-00-8). Sparrow Pub.
Wu, Cheng-En, jt. auth. see Morris, Jill.
Wu, Ch'Eng-En Ca (1500-1582)
--The Magic Monkey: Adapted from and Old Chinese Legend. Chan, Christina & Chan, Plato (1931-), eds. Chan, Plato (1931-), illus. LC 44-40172. 50 p. 11. illus (part col.) 23 x 20 cm. 1944. Whittlesey House, McGraw-Hill Book Company, Inc.
--Monkey and the Three Wizards. Foreman, Michael (1938-), illus. Harris, Peter David, tr. LC 76-57800. (Illus.). 40 p. 25cm. 1977. (ISBN 0-87888-110-7). Bradbury Press.
Wulf, Kathleen (1941-)
--I'm Glad I'm Little. Nelson, John (1928-), illus. LC 76-16535. (Illus.). 32 p. 25cm. c.1976. (ISBN 0-913778-53-2). Child's World.
Wulff, Trolli Neutzsky
--The Gipsy Girl. N.D. Zondervan Publications.
--The Secret of Castle Whitenburg: A Charming Story for Boys and Girls. Mueller, Theodore J., adapted by. LC 63-15730. 150 p. 21 cm. 1963. Zondervan Pub. House.
Wunder, Ira, jt. auth. see Darling, Kathy.
Wunderli, Olga, tr. see Spyri, Johanna Heusser.
Wunsch, Josephine Mclean (1914-)
--Class Ring. 176p. (Orig.). (gr. 7 up). 1983. (ISBN 0-590-32359-8, Wildfire). Scholastic Inc.
--Flying Skis. 1st ed. Geer, Charles Hand (1922-), illus. LC 62-7765. 212 p. 21 cm. 1962. D. McKay Co.
--Passport to Russia. (gr. 7-10). 1965. McKay.
--Summer of Decision. LC 68-14126. viii, 184 p. 21cm. 1968. D. McKay Co.
Wunsch, Robert & Albers, Edna, eds.
--Thicker Than Water: Stories of Family Life. N.D. Appleton-Century-Crofts.
Wuorio, Eva-Lis (1918-)
--Code: Polonaise. LC 73-119094. 198 p. 22cm. 1971. (ISBN 0-03-085122-X). (ISBN 0-03-085123-8). Holt, Rinehart and Winston.
--Detour to Danger: A Novel. LC 81-65501. p. cm. c.1981. (ISBN 0-440-01892-7). Delacorte Press.
--Escape If You Can: Thirteen Tales of the Preternautral. LC 77-9053. p. cm. 1977. (ISBN 0-670-29774-7). Viking Press.
--The Happiness Flower. Bolognese, Donald Alan (1934-), illus. LC 68-26973. (Illus.). 78 p. 24cm. 1969. World Pub. Co.
--The Island of Fish in the Trees. 1st ed. Ardizzone, Edward Jeffrey Irving (1900-1979), illus. LC 62-13943. 59 p. illus. 24 cm. 1962. World Pub. Co. **Award: (NYT).**
--Kali & the Golden Mirror. Ardizzone, Edward Jeffrey Irving (1900-1978), illus. (Illus.). (gr. 4-6). 1967. (ISBN 0-529-00249-3). (ISBN 0-529-00250-7). Collins-World.
--The Land of Right up and Down. 1st ed. Ardizzone, Edward Jeffrey Irving (1900-1979), illus. LC 64-12358. 60 p. illus. (part col.) 24 cm. 1964. World Pub. Co.
--October Treasure. 1st ed. Cather, Carolyn, illus. LC 66-11677. 191 p. illus. 21 cm. 1966. Holt, Rinehart and Winston.
--Return of the Viking. Winter, William, illus. 1955. E M Hale.
--Save Alice!. LC 68-23572. (Illus.). 165 p. 21cm. 1968. Holt, Rinehart, and Winston.
--The Singing Canoe. Boker, Irving, illus. LC 71-82775. (Illus.). 56 p. 24cm. 1969. World Pub. Co.
--Tal & the Magic Barruget. Ehrlich, Bettina Bauer (1903-), illus. Bettina, pseud. LC 65-19719. (Illus.). (gr. 2-5). 1965. (ISBN 0-529-03912-5). World Pub.
--To Fight in Silence. LC 78-150031. (Illus.). 216 p. 22cm. 1973. Holt, Rinehart and Winston.
--Venture at Midsummer. (Illus.). 181 p. 21cm. 1967. Holt, Rinehart and Winston.
Wurdemann, A., jt. auth. see Auslander, Joseph.
Wurth, Anne
--Rag Doll Susie: Her Adventures on Laughing Island. Peat, Fern Bisel, Mrs. (1893-), illus. LC 39-16512. 16 p. illus. (part col.) 26 1/2 x 24 cm. c.1939. The Saalfield Publishing Company.
Wurthle, Fritz (1902-)
--The Prince of Fergana. Flora, Paul, illus. Crampton, Patricia, tr. LC 63-7057. 187 p. illus. 21 cm. 1963, c.1962. Abelard-Schuman.
W. W. F, ed.
--The Wreath: Designed As a Token for the Young. LC 15-17156. 6 p. l., 7-160 p. incl. front., illus., plates. 15 1/2 cm. 1836. N. B. Holmes.
Wyatt, Caroline
--Little Mary's Dream. 48p. 1975. (ISBN 0-87482-038-3). Wake Brooke House.
Wyatt, Edgar
--Cochise, Apache Warrior and Statesman. Houser, Allan C. (1914-), illus. LC 53-5193. (Illus.). 192 p. 21cm. 1953. Whittlesey House.
Wyatt, G. E.
--Follow the Right. N.D. Thos Nelson & Sons.
--Lionel Harcourt, the Etonian: Or, "Like Other Follows". N.D. Thos Nelson & Sons.
Wyatt, George
--The Case of the Counterfeit Coin. Greene, Hamilton, illus. LC 61-7966. (Based on the Characters Created by Charles Spain Verral). 183 p. illus. 20 cm. (A Brains Benton Mystery). 1960. Golden Press.
--The Case of the Hunted Hermit. Greene, Hamilton, illus. (A Brains Benton Mystery). 1959. Golden Press.
--The Case of the Painted Dragon. Schmidt, Al, illus. LC 61-9901. 185 p. illus. 20 cm. (His A Brains Benton mystery, 6). c.1961. Golden Press.
--The Case of the Roving Rolls. Schmidt, Al, illus. LC 61-9900. 186 p. illus. 20 cm. (Brains Benton mystery, 4). 1961. Golden Press.
--The Case of the Runaway Skeleton. (A Brains Benton Mystery). 1961. Golden Press.
--The Case of the Stolen Dummy. Dey, Walter, illus. LC 61-7967. 186 p. illus. 20 cm. 1961. Golden Press.
--The Case of the Waltzing Mouse. Schmidt, Al, illus. LC 61-16937. 187 p. illus. 20 cm. (Brains Benton mystery, 5). 1961. Golden Press.
Wyatt, Gladys
--Buffalo Bill. Greene, Hamilton, illus. LC 56-3059. unpaged. illus. 21cm. (Little golden book, 254). 1956. Simon and Schuster.
--Buffalo Bill, Jr. Greene, Hamilton, illus. LC 56-3059. unpaged. illus. 21 cm. (Little golden book, 254). 1956. Simon and Schuster.
--Buffalo Bill, Jr. and the Indian Chief. Greene, Hamilton, illus. (Little Golden Book). 1956. Golden Press.
--Dale Evans and the Coyote. Dreany, E. Joseph, illus. LC 56-3058. unpaged. illus. 21cm. (Little Golden Book, 253p.). 1956. Simon and Schuster.
--Roy Rogers and the Indian Sign. Crawford, Mel (1925-), illus. LC 56-30578. unpaged. illus. 21cm. (Little Golden Book, 259). 1956. Simon and Schuster.
Wyatt, Isabel
--The Dream of King Alfdan: An Old Norse Tale. Kinstler, Everett Raymond (1926-), illus. LC 61-880383. 95 p. illus. 24 cm. 1961. Follett Pub. Co.
--The Golden Stag, and Other Folk Tales from India. Jauss, Anne Marie (1907-), illus. LC 62-157807. (Illus.). 117 p. 21cm. 1962. D. McKay Co.
--King Beetle-Tamer, and Other Lighthearted Wonder Tales. Henning, Amy, illus. LC 79-21245. p. cm. c.1979. (ISBN 0-89742-029-2). (ISBN 0-89742-028-4). Dawne-Leigh Publications.
--King Beetle-Tamer, and Other Lighthearted Wonder Tales. Jauss, Anne Marie (1907-), illus. LC 63-17655. (Illus.). vi, 152. 21cm. 1963. D. McKay.
--Seven-Year-Old Wonder-Book. Rowe, Margaret, illus. LC 78-15817. (ps-3). 1978. (ISBN 0-89742-003-9, Dawne-Leigh). (ISBN 0-89742-004-7). Celestial Arts.
Wyatt, Isabel & Gilbert, Daniel Branden
--The Book of Fairy Princes. Gilbert, Daniel Branden, illus. LC 78-31605. p. cm. c.1978. (ISBN 0-89742-006-3). Dawne-Leigh Publications.
Wyatt, Karen, jt. ed. see Payson, Dale.
Wyatt, Woodrow Lyle (1918-)
--The Exploits of Mr. Saucy Squirrel. Floyd, Gareth (1940-), illus. LC 76-382026. (Illus.). 115 p. 25cm. 1976. (ISBN 0-04-823133-9). Allen & Unwin.
--The Further Exploits of Mr Saucy Squirrel. Floyd, Gareth (1940-), illus. LC 78-300469. (Illus.). 95 p. 25cm. 1977. (ISBN 0-04-823143-6). Allen and Unwin.
Wychoff, Jerome, ed.
--The Golden Grab Bag of Stories, Poems and Songs. Gergely, Tibor (1900-1978), illus. LC 51-12368. (Illus.). 16p. (A Big Golden Bk.). 1951. Simon and Schuster.
Wyckoff, Capwell (1903-)
--In the Camp of the Black Rider. LC 31-12251. 256 p. front. 19 1/2 cm. (Adventure and Mystery Series for Boys). c.1931. A. L. Burt Company.
--The Mercer Boys and the Indian Gold. LC 32-121992. 251 p. front. 19 1/2 cm. (Mercer Boys Ser.). c.1932. A. L. Burt Company.
--The Mercer Boys and the Steamboat Riddle. LC 33-12040. 256 p. front. 19 1/2 cm. (Mercer Boys Ser.). c.1933. A. L. Burt Company.
--The Mercer Boys As First Classmen. LC 30-116197. 254 p. front. 19 1/2 cm. (Mercer Boys Ser.). c.1930. A. L. Burt Company.
--The Mercer Boys at Woodcrest. LC 29-9292. 256 p. front. 19 1/2 cm. (Mercer Boys Ser.). c.1929. A. L. Burt Company.
--The Mercer Boys at Woodcrest. LC 48-11671. 217 p. front. 19 cm. (His The Mercer boys' series). 1948. World Pub. Co.
--The Mercer Boys' Cruise in the Lassie. LC 29-9482. 239 p. front. 19 cm. (Mercer Boys Ser.). c.1929. A. L. Burt Company.
--The Mercer Boys' Cruise in the Lassie. LC 48-4568. 214 p. front. 19 cm. (His The Mercer boys' series). N.D. World Pub. Co.
--The Mercer Boys in Summer Camp. LC 29-12539. 250 p. front. 19 1/2 cm. (Mercer Boys Ser.). c.1929. A. L. Burt Company.
--Mercer Boys in Summer Camp. (Mercer Boys Ser.). N.D. World Publishing Co.
--The Mercer Boys in the Ghost Patrol. LC 51-39073. 198 p. illus. 19 cm. (His The Mercer boys series). 1951. World Pub. Co.
--The Mercer Boys' Mystery Case. LC 29-948494. 256 p. front. 19 1/2 cm. (Mercer Boys Ser.). c.1929. A. L. Burt Company.
--The Mercer Boys' Mystery Case. LC 48-116798. 213 p. front. 19 cm. (His The Mercer boys' series). 1948. World Pub. Co.
--The Mercer Boys on a Treasure Hunt. LC 29-9483. 243 p. front. 19 1/2 cm. (Mercer Boys Ser.). c.1929. A. L. Burt Company.
--The Mercer Boys on a Treasure Hunt. LC 48-11681. 213 p. front. 19 cm. (His The Mercer boys' series). 1948. World Pub. Co.
--The Mercer Boys on the Beach Patrol. LC 29-110144. 256 p. front. 19 1/2 cm. (Mercer Boys Ser.). c.1929. A. L. Burt Company.
--Mercer Boys on the Beach Patrol. (Mercer Boys Ser.). N.D. World Publishing Co.
--The Mercer Boys with the Air Cadets. 254 p. front. 19 1/2 cm. (Mercer Boys Ser.). c.1932. A. L. Burt Company.
--The Mercer Boys with the Coast Guard. N.D. World Publishing Co.
--Mystery at Lake Retreat. (Adventures and Mystery Ser.). c.1931. A. L. Burt Co.
--The Mystery at Lake Retreat. LC 31-130992. 253 p. front. 19 1/2 cm. (Mystery and Adventure Series for Boys). N.D. C.
--The Mystery Hunters at Lakeside Camp. LC 34-804920. 253 p. front. 20 cm. (Mystery Hunters Ser.). c.1934. A. L. Burt Company.
--The Mystery Hunters at Old Frontier. LC 34-804892. 253 p. front. 20 cm. (Mystery Hunters Ser.). c.1934. A. L. Burt Company.
--The Mystery Hunters at the Haunted Lodge. LC 34-804712. 249 p. front. 20 cm. (Mystery Hunters Ser.). c.1934. A. L. Burt Company.
--The Mystery Hunters on Special Detail. LC 36-9236. vi, 7-251 p. front. 20 1/2 cm. (Mystery Hunters Ser.). c.1936. A. L. Burt Company.
--The Mystery of Gaither Cove. LC 32-12201. 253 p. front. 19 1/2 cm. (Mystery and Adventure Series for Boys). c.1932. A. L. Burt Company.
--The North Point Cabin Mystery. LC 32-12203. 256 p. front. 19 1/2 cm. (Mystery and Adventure Series for Boys). c.1932. A. L. Burt Company.
--The Sea Runners' Cache. LC 35-8287. vi p. 1 l., 9-253 p. front. 20 1/2 cm. (The New Adventure and Mystery Ser. for Boys). c.1935. A. L. Burt Company.
--The Search for the City of Ghosts. LC 36-9238. vi. 7-252 p. front. 20 1/2 cm. (New adventure and mystery series for boys). c.1936. A. L. Burt Company.
--The Secret of the Armor Room. LC 30-11618. 256 p. front. 19 1/2 cm. (Mystery and Adventure Series for Boys). c.1930. A. L. Burt Company.
Wyckoff, Charlotte Chandler (1893-1966)
--Jothy: A Story of the South Indian Jungle. Wiese, Kurt (1887-1974), illus. LC 33-219286. xiii, 305 p. incl. front., illus. (incl. music) plates. 20 1/2 cm. 1933. Longmans, Green and Co.
--Kumar. 1st ed. Jacques, Robin (1920-), illus. LC 65-13336. 192 p. illus. 21 cm. 1965. Norton.
Wyckoff, James M. (1918-)
--Kendall of the Coast Guard. 1st ed. Cohen, Gil, illus. LC 61-12607. (Illus.). 141 p. 22cm. (Signal Book). 1961. Doubleday.
Wyckoff, Jerome, ed.
--The Golden Grab Bag. Gergely, Tibor (1900-1978), illus. (Big Golden Book: 559). 1951. Simon and Schuster.
--The Golden Grab Bag of Stories, Poems, and Songs. LC 51-12368. 76 p. illus. 29 cm. (Big golden book). 1951. Simon and Schuster.
Wyckoff, Marjorie Elaine Morrison (1915-) & Artists and Writers Guild
--A Book of Cradle Songs. Masha, pseud. (1909-), illus. Stern, Marie Simchow. LC 44-6137. 36 p. illus. (part col.) 24 x 21 cm. c.1943. Grosset & Dunlap, Distributors.
Wyckoff, Marjorie Elaine Morrison (1915-), compiled by.
--Christmas Carols. Malvern, Corinne (1905-1956), illus. LC 47-346. 41p. (The Little Golden Library: No. 26). 1946. Simon & Schuster.
Wyeth, Betsy James (1921-) & Wyeth, James (1946-)
--The Stray. LC 79-19344. p. cm. 1979. (ISBN 0-374-37280-2). Farrar, Straus and Giroux.
Wyeth, James, jt. auth. see Wyeth, Betsy James.
Wyeth, M. E. C
--Margie Hargrave, and the Percy Children, 1 of 50 vols. LC 74-194093. (Illus.). 200 p. 18cm. (Model Library: No. 3). 1878. Set. American Tract Society.

--Swiss Family Robinson. (New International Library). N.D. John C. Winston Co.

--Swiss Family Robinson. (New Acorn Library). N.D. John C. Winston & Co.

--Swiss Family Robinson. (Illus.). (Winston Series of Books). N.D. John C. Winston & Co.

--Swiss Family Robinson. (The Young People's Library). N.D. John C. Winston.

--Swiss Family Robinson. (The World-Renowned Ser.). N.D. Leavitt & Allen Bros.

--Swiss Family Robinson, 1 0f 6 vols. (Illus.). (Blue Jacket Ser.). N.D. Set. Lee & Shepard.

--Swiss Family Robinson. N.D. MacMillan.

--Swiss Family Robinson. (The Washington Square Classics). N.D. Macrae Smith.

--Swiss Family Robinson. (Crusoe Library). N.D. Mason, Baker & Pratt.

--The Swiss Family Robinson. (The Nelson Classics). N.D. Nelson Bks.

--Swiss Family Robinson. N.D. Nichols & Hall.

--Swiss Family Robinson. (Arabian Nights Library). N.D. Porter & Coates.

--Swiss Family Robinson. (The Youth's Cabinet of A. L. O. E. Presentation Popular Standard Bks.). N.D. Pott, Young, & Co.

--Swiss Family Robinson. N.D. Pott, Young & Co.

--The Swiss Family Robinson. (Hopeful Enterprise Library). N.D. R. Worthington & Co.

--Swiss Family Robinson. (Incident and Adventure Library). N.D. R. Worthington & Co.

--Swiss Family Robinson, 1 of 74 Vols. (The Chandos Classics Ser.). N.D. R. Worthington.

--Swiss Family Robinson, 1 of 163 Vols. (Illus.). (The Cottage Library Ser.). N.D. R. Worthigntion.

--Swiss Family Robinson, 1 of 4 Vols. (Illus.). (Library of Celebrated Books). N.D. R. Worthington.

--Swiss Family Robinson, 1 of 26 Vols. (Illus.). (Warne's Popular Poets Ser.). N.D. R. Worthington.

--Swiss Family Robinson, 1 of 14 Vols. (Warne's Poets and Fiction Ser.). N.D. R. Worthington.

--Swiss Family Robinson, 1 of 8 Vols. (Illus.). (Warne's Victoria Gift Books Ser.). N.D. R. Worthington.

--Swiss Family Robinson. (The Atlantic Library). N.D. Rand, McNally & Co.'s.

--Swiss Family Robinson. (Twentieth Century Ser.). N.D. Rand, McNally & Co.'s.

--Swiss Family Robinson. (The Antique Library). N.D. Rand, McNally & Co.'s.

--Swiss Family Robinson. (Illus.). (The Independent Library Ser.: Vol. 295). N.D. Rand, McNally & Co.

--Swiss Family Robinson. (Illus.). (The Junior Library Ser.: Vol. 13). N.D. Rand, McNally & Co.

--Swiss Family Robinson, 1 of 11 vols. (Warne's National Books Ser.). N.D. Scribner & Welford.

--Swiss Family Robinson, 1 of 16 Vols. (Illus.). (Warne's Victoria Gift Books Ser.). N.D. Scribner & Welford.

--Swiss Family Robinson, 1 of 7 vols. (Including the Sequel). (Illus.). (Warne's Home Sunshine Library). N.D. Scribner & Welford.

--Swiss Family Robinson, 1 of 15 Vols. (Illus.). (Warne's Daring Deeds Library). N.D. Scribner & Welford.

--Swiss Family Robinson, 1 of 16 Vols. (Illus.). (Warne's Incident and Adventure Library: No. 4). N.D. Scribner & Welford.

--Swiss Family Robinson. (Illus.). (Children's Home Library). 1915. T Y Crowell.

--Swiss Family Robinson. (The New Astor Library of Prose). N.D. T. Y. Crowell & Co.

--Swiss Family Robinson. (The Illuminated Ser.). N.D. The American News Co.

--Swiss Family Robinson. N.D. The American Book Co.

--Swiss Family Robinson. (The Nelson Classics). N.D. Thomas Nelson & Sons.

--Swiss Family Robinson. (Standard Literature Ser.: No. 35). N.D. University Publishing Co.

--Swiss Family Robinson. (Classic Ser.). N.D. World Publishing Co.

--The Swiss Family Robinson. Butler, Audrey, ed. Galsworthy, John Gay, illus. LC 78-106513. (Illus.). 182 p. 23cm. (Lifetime library). 1970. American Education Publications.

--The Swiss Family Robinson. Folkard, Charles James (1878-1963), illus. (Children's Illustrated Classics). 1949. E. P. Dutton & Co.

--The Swiss Family Robinson. Folkard, Charles James (1878-1963), illus. viii, 454 p. col. front., illus., col. plates. 20 cm. 1934. J. M. Dent & Sons, Ltd.

--The Swiss Family Robinson. Rev. ed. Gentleman, David William (1930-), illus. (Illus.). xiii, 354 p. 28cm. 1963. Heritage Press.

--The Swiss Family Robinson. Gilbert, John Clitherae, illus. N.D. Clark and Maynard.

--The Swiss Family Robinson. Godwin, Frank (1889-), illus. (The Children's Bookshelf). N.D. John C. Winston.

--The Swiss Family Robinson. Gregori, Leon (1919-), illus. LC 63-6892. (Illus.). vi, 344 p. 20cm. (Companion library). 1963. Grosset & Dunlap.

--The Swiss Family Robinson. Hodgetts, A. Brayley, ed. Finnemore, J., illus. 1900. George M Hill Co.

--Swiss Family Robinson. J. C. G, retold by. (Illus.). (Burt's Series of One Syllable Books). N.D. A. L. Burt's Pubs.

--Swiss Family Robinson. 1st ed. Johnston, Johanna, retold by. Jackson, Polly, pseud. (1918-), illus. Jackson, Pauline. LC 60-13566. 87 p. illus. 32 cm. (Doubleday picture classic). 1961. Doubleday.

--The Swiss Family Robinson. Kingston, William Henry Giles (1814-1880), ed. Irwin, Don, illus. LC 77-2314. (Illus.). 284 p. 29cm. (Educator classic library, 4). 1968. Classic Press.

--The Swiss Family Robinson. Kingston, William Henry Giles (1814-1880), ed. Ward, Lynd Kendall (1905-1985), illus. LC 49-489738. 388 p. illus. (part col.) 24 cm. (Illustrated junior library). 1949. Grosset & Dunlap.

--The Swiss Family Robinson. Kingston, William Henry Giles (1814-1880), ed. Edwards, Jeanne (1921-), illus. LC 47-31091. 366 p. illus. (part col.) 22 cm. (Rainbow Classics). 1947. World Pub. Co.

--Swiss Family Robinson. Memling, Carl (1918-1969), adapted by. Gillin, Denver, illus. LC 61-1438. (Illus.). 23cm. (A Golden Reading Adventure). 1961. Golden Press.

--The Swiss Family Robinson. Milton, Geraldine Edith & Rountree, Harry (1878-1950), illus. LC 26-26579. xi, 307 p. col. front., col. plates. 19 1/2 cm. (The Macmillan children's classics). 1926. The Macmillan Company.

--Swiss Family Robinson. Montolieu, ed. (Illus.). N.D. Houghton, Mifflin And Co.

--Swiss Family Robinson. Montolieu, ed. (New Aldine Ser). N.D. International Book Co.

--Swiss Family Robinson. Montolieu, ed. N.D. Lovell, Coryell & Co.

--Swiss Family Robinson, 1 of 2 vols. Montolieu, ed. (New Oxford Ser: No. 11). N.D. Set. Lovell, Coryell & Co.

--Swiss Family Robinson, 1 of 8 vols. Paul, H. B., Mrs., tr. (Illus.). (Escelsior Gift Books Ser.). N.D. R. Worthington.

--Swiss Family Robinson. Paull, H. B, Mrs., tr. N.D. Frederick Warne.

--Swiss Family Robinson, 1 of14 Vols. Paull, H. B., Mrs., tr. (Illus.). (Warne's Home Presentation Books Ser.). N.D. Scribner & Welford.

--The Swiss Family Robinson. Rhys, Ernest, ed. xiii, 498 p. illus. 17 1/2 cm. (Half-title: Everyman's library). 1910. J. M. Dent & Sons, Ltd.

--The Swiss Family Robinson. Robinson, Thomas Heath (1869-1950), illus. LC 32-21207. xi p., 1 l., 15-436 p. col. front., col. plates. 22 1/2 cm. 1931. Garden City Publishing Company Inc.

--Swiss Family Robinson. Stickney, Jennie H. (1840-), ed. (Classics for Children). N.D. Ginn and Company.

--The Swiss Family Robinson. Sutton, Felix (1910-), ed. Barss, William (1916-), illus. LC 60-51557. 61 p. illus. 29 cm. 1960. Grosset & Dunlap.

--Swiss Family Robinson. Ward, Lynd Kendall (1905-1985) & Gregori, Lee, illus. N.D. Putnam.

--Swiss Family Robinson, 98 vols. Wyss, Jean Rudolf (1781-1830), rev. by. (The Rugby Ser.). 1905. Set. A L Burt Co.

--Swiss Family Robinson. Wyss, Jean Rudolf (1781-1830), rev. by. (Illus.). (Burt's Young Folks' Library). N.D. A. L. Burt's Pubs.

--Swiss Family Robinson, No. 148. Wyss, Jean Rudolf (1781-1830), rev. by. (The Cornell Ser.). N.D. A. L. Burt's Pubs.

--The Swiss Family Robinson. Wyss, Jean Rudolf (1781-1830), rev. by. N.D. (ISBN 0-448-06022-1, Illustrated Junior Library). (ISBN 0-448-05922-3). (ISBN 0-448-05822-7). Grosset & Dunlap.

--The Swiss Family Robinson. Wyss, Jean Rudolf (1781-1830), rev. by. N.D. (ISBN 0-448-05468-X, Companion Library). Grosset & Dunlap.

--Swiss Family Robinson. Wyss, Jean Rudolf (1781-1830), rev. by. N.D. (ISBN 0-448-00302-3, Silver Dollar Library). Grosset & Dunlap.

--Swiss Family Robinson. Wyss, Jean Rudolf (1781-1830), ed. (Illus.). (Boys and Girls Classics). N.D. Henry Altemus.

--Swiss Family Robinson, 1 of 24 vols. Wyss, Jean Rudolf (1781-1830), rev. by. (Illus.). (Children's Favorite Classics). 1900. T. Y. Crowell & Co.

--The Swiss Family Robinson. Wyss, Johann Rudolf (1781-1830), rev. by. LC 29-27456. ix p., 1 l., 11-409 p. col. front., col. plates. 19 1/2 cm. (golden books). 1929. D. McKay.

--The Swiss Family Robinson. Wyss, Johann Rudolf (1781-1830), rev. by. Folkard, Charles James (1878-1963), illus. LC 58-834. 341 p. illus. 21 cm. (Children's illustrated classics). 1958. Dent.

--The Swiss Family Robinson. Wyss, Johann Rudolf (1781-1830), rev. by. Abbott, Elenore Plaisted, illus. Paull, H. B., tr. LC 14-18463. 569 p. col. front., col. plates. 20 cm. (On cover: The Washington square classics). 1914. G. W. Jacobs and Company.

--The Swiss Family Robinson. Rev. ed. Wyss, Johann Rudolf (1781-1830) & Lansing, Jenny H. Stickney, Mrs. (1840-), eds. viii, 364 p. front., illus., plates. 18 1/2 cm. (On cover: Classics for children). 1885. Ginn, Heath, & Co.

--The Swiss Family Robinson. Wyss, Johann Rudolf (1781-1830) & Lansing, Jenny H. Stickney (1840-), eds. Copeland, Charles, illus. LC 15-25468. viii, 417 p. illus. 19 cm. c.1915. Ginn and Company.

--The Swiss Family Robinson. Wyss, Johann Rudolf (1781-1830), rev. by. LC 66-2762. xii, 256 p. 19 cm. (Perennial classic HP 6053 V). 1966. Harper & Row.

--The Swiss Family Robinson. Wyss, Johann Rudolf (1781-1830) & Groth, John Henry, eds. LC 29-13777. xviii p. 1 l., 372 p. incl. front. 18 1/2 cm. (modern readers' series). 1929. The Macmillan Company.

--The Swiss Family Robinson. Wyss, Johann Rudolf (1781-1830) & Holmes, Mabel Dodge (1883-), eds. LC 30-5249. xii, 340 p. col. front., illus., col. plates. 22 cm. c.1929. The John C. Winston Company.

--Swiss Family Robinson. Wyss, Johann Rudolf (1781-1830), rev. by. LC 98-1368. 127 p. illus. 18 1/2 cm. (Standard literature series, no. 35). c.1898. University Publishing Company.

--The Swiss Family Robinson. A New Translation. Wyss, Johann Rudolf (1781-1830) & Kingston, William Henry Giles (1814-1880), eds. LC 12-40142. 3 p. l., ix-xiii, 323, 1 p. incl. front., illus., plates. 21 1/2 cm. c.1882. G. Routledge & Sons.

--The Swiss Family Robinson: A New Version. 1st ed. Wyss, Johann Rudolf (1781-1830), rev. by. Finnemore, J., illus. Hodgetts, Edward Arthur Brayley (1859-), tr. LC 7-1628. 2 p. l., vii-xii, 391 p. incl. front., illus., plates. 26 1/2 cm. c.1897. H. J. Smith & Simon Publishing Co.

--The Swiss Family Robinson. A Translation from the Original German. Kingston, William Henry Giles (1814-1880), ed. Kley, H., illus. 291, 1 p. col. front., Illus., 13 pl. (5 col.) 23 1/2 x 18 cm. 1899. E. Nister.

--Swiss Family Robinson: Adventures of a Father, Mother, and Four Sons, on a Desert Island. N.D. James Miller.

--Swiss Family Robinson in Words of One Syllable. 96p. N.D. Cassell & Co.

--Swiss Family Robinson In Words of One Syllable. Godolphin, Mary, adapted by. (Illus.). N.D. George Routledge & Sons.

--The Swiss Family Robinson: Or, Adventures on a Desert Island. New Ed. ed. Wyss, Johann Rudolf (1781-1830), rev. by. Gilbert, John Clitherae, illus. LC 31-19493. viii, 9-403 p. front., plates. 18 cm. 1865. Hurd and Houghton.

--The Swiss Family Robinson: Or, Adventures on a Desert Island. windermere ed. Wyss, Johann Rudolf (1781-1830), rev. by. Winter, Milo Kendall (1888-1956), illus. LC 17-653768. 441 p. col. front., col. plates. 23 1/2 cm. c.1916. Rand, McNally & Company.

--Swiss Family Robinson: Or, Adventures of a Father and Mother and Four Sons on a Desert Island. (The Caxton Edition). N.D. Belford, Clarke.

--Swiss Family Robinson: Or, Adventures of a Father and Mother and Four Sons on a Desert Island, 1 of 6 Vols. (Illus.). (One-Syllable Books, Cassell's Ser.: No. 2). N.D. Cassell, Petter, Galpin.

--Swiss Family Robinson: Or, Adventures of a Father and Mother and Four Sons on a Desert Island. (Standard Edition). N.D. Estes & Lauriat.

--Swiss Family Robinson: Or, Adventures of a Father and Mother and Four Sons on a Desert Island. (Popular Illustrated). N.D. Fairbanks & Palmer.

--The Swiss Family Robinson: Or, Adventures of a Father and Mother and Four Sons on a Desert Island, 2 vols. (Harper's Boys' and Girls' Library). 1882. Harper's Trade-List.

--Swiss Family Robinson: Or, Adventures of a Father and Mother and Four Sons on a Desert Island, 1 of 64 vols. (Young America Library: No. 39). 1900. Set. Hurst & Co.

--The Swiss Family Robinson: Or, Adventures of a Father and Mother and Four Sons on a Desert Island. from the 7th, lond. ed., greatly improved. 2 v. front. 16 cm. (On cover: Boy's and girl's library of useful and entertaining knowledge, no. III). c.1832. J. & J. Harper.

--Swiss Family Robinson: Or, Adventures of a Father and Mother and Four Sons on a Desert Island. (Victoria Edition). 1882. J B Lippincott.

--Swiss Family Robinson: Or, Adventures of a Father and Mother and Four Sons on a Desert Island, 1 of 50 vols. (Boys' & Girls Library: No. 41). N.D. Set. Lothrop Publishing Co.

--Swiss Family Robinson: Or, Adventures of a Father and Mother and Four Sons on a Desert Island, 3 Vols. (Illus.). (Arabian Nights' Library). N.D. Porter & Coates.

--Swiss Family Robinson: Or, Adventures of a Father and Mother and Four Sons on a Desert Island, 1 of 15 vols. (Illus.). (Star Ser.). N.D. T. Y. Crowell.

--Swiss Family Robinson: Or, Adventures of a Father and Mother and Four Sons on a Desert Island, 1 Vol. (Illus.). N.D. Thomas R. Knox & Co.

--Swiss Family Robinson: Or, Adventures of a Father and Mother and Four Sons on a Desert Island, 1 of 4 vols. (Illus.). (Every Boy's Library). N.D. Thomas Nelson & Sons.

--Swiss Family Robinson: Or, Adventures of a Father and Mother and Four Sons on a Desert Island. (Illus.). N.D. Worthington Company.

--The Swiss Family Robinson: Or, Adventures of a Father and Mother and Four Sons on a Desert Island. from 7th london ed. Wyss, Johann Rudolf (1781-1830), rev. by. LC 40-37554. 1 p. l., ix-x, v-vi, 2, 11-895 p. illus., map. 14 1/2 cm. 1834. Munroe and Francis.

--The Swiss Family Robinson: Or, Adventures of a Shipwrecked Family on a Desolate Island. New and Unabridged. Nodier, Charles (1780-1844), intro. by. (Illus.). N.D. Thomas Nelson and Sons.

--Swiss Family Robinson: Or, Adventures of Father and Mother and Four Sons on a Desert Island. (Illus.). 376p. (Royal Octavo Edition). N.D. Cassell, Petter, Galpin.

--Swiss Family Robinson: Or, The Adventures of a Father and Mother and Four Sons on a Desert Island, 1 Vol. (Illus.). (The Excelsior Edition). N.D. American News Company.

--Swiss Family Robinson: Or, The Adventures of a Father and Mother and Four Sons in a Desert Island. (Illus.). (New Alta Lib.). N.D. Porter & Coates.

--The Swiss Family Robinson: Or, The Adventures of a Shipwrecked Family on an Uninhabited Island ... LC 12-40143. 1 p. l., 7-202 p. front., illus. 16 cm. (Altemus' young people's library). 1896. H. Altemus.

--The Swiss Family Robinson: Or, The Adventures of a Shipwrecked Family on a Desolate Island. LC 4-19037. 2 p. l., 399 p. front. 19 cm. 1899. T. Y. Crowell & Co.

--The Swiss Family Robinson: Or, The Adventures of a Shipwrecked Family on an Uninhabited Isle Near New Guinea. Rhead, Louis John (1857-1926), illus. LC 33-17502. xvii, 601, 1 p. incl. col. front., illus., plates. col. plates, map. 23 1/2 cm. N.D. Harper & Brothers.

--The Swiss Family Robinson: Or, The Adventures of a Shipwrecked Family on an Uninhabited Isle Near New Guinea. Wyss, Johann Rudolf (1781-1830), rev. by. Rhead, Louis John (1857-1926), illus. Paull, Henry H. B., Mrs., tr. LC 9-30111. xvii, 601, 1 p. incl. front. (port.) illus., plates. map. 23 cm. 1909. Harper & Brothers.

--The Swiss Family Robinson: Or, The Adventures of a Shipwrecked Family on an Uninhabited Isle Near New Guinea. Wyss, Johann Rudolf (1781-1830), ed. Hall, Arnold, illus. LC 27-21405. vi, 1, 408 p. illus., col. plates. 24 1/2 cm. c.1927. Minton, Balch & Company.

--The Swiss Family Robinson: Or, The Adventures of a Shipwrecked Family on a Desolate Island. Wyss, Johann Rudolf (1781-1830), ed. LC 99-8719. 1 p. l., 399 p. col. front., plates. 17 cm. c.1899. T. Y. Crowell & Company.

--The Swiss Family Robinson: Retold for Young Children. Wyss, Johann Rudolf (1781-1830) & Aikin, Lucy (1784-1864), eds. LC 14-10424. 5 p. l., 5-181 p. incl. col. front., illus. (part col.) plates (part col.) 19 cm. c.1914. E. P. Dutton & Company.

--The Swiss Family Robinson: The Adventures of a Family Shipwrecked on a Coast Where Human Beings Never Trod Before. Wyss, Johann Rudolf (1781-1830), rev. by. Bennett, Juanita C., illus. 237 p. incl. plates. 20 1/2 cm. c.1935. Whitman Publishing Company.

--Willis the Pilot, 1 of 6. (Crusoe Library: No. 6). N.D. Colby and Rich.

--Willis the Pilot. (Hopeful Enterprise Library). N.D. R. Worthington & Co.

--Willis the Pilot. (Incident and Adventure). N.D. R. Worthington & Co.

--Willis the Pilot, 1 of 15 Vols. (A Sequel to Swiss Family Robinson). (Illus.). (Warne's Daring Deeds Library). N.D. Scribner & Welford.

Yeatman, Linda
--Noah's Ark. Gault, Bob, illus. (Illus.). 12p. (Press-Out Model Bk.). (ps-3). 1984. (ISBN 0-698-20598-7, Coward). Putnam Pub Group.
Yeatman, Linda, ed.
--A Treasury of Animal Stories. Offen, Hilda, illus. LC 83-113193. (Illus.). 155 p. 27cm. c.1982. (ISBN 0-671-45632-6). Little Simon.
--A Treasury of Bedtime Stories. Offen, Hilda, illus. LC 81-82431. (Illus.). 157 p. 27cm. c.1981. (ISBN 0-671-44463-8). Little Simon.
Yeats, John, tr. see Zschokke, Heinrich.
Yeats, William Butler (1865-1939)
--Irish Fairy Tales. (The Fairy Library). N.D. A. L. Burt Co.
--Running to Paradise. Crossley-Holland, Kevin, ed. Valpy, Judith, illus. LC 68-24108. (Illus.). 22 ils. index. 96p. 1st U.S. edition. (gr. 7 up). 1968. (ISBN 0-02-793620-1). Macmillan.
Yeats, William Butler (1865-1939), ed.
--Fairy and Folk Tales of the Irish Peasantry. LC 14-3512. xviii p., 1 l., 326 p. 16 cm. 1888. W. Scott.
--Irish Fairy and Folk Tales. LC 76-42702. xviii, 351 p. 19cm. 1979. (ISBN 0-404-15376-3). AMS Press.
--Irish Fairy and Folk Tales. xviii, 351 p. illus. (music) 17 cm. (On verse of half-title: The modern library of the world's best books). 1918. Boni and Liveright, Inc.
--Irish Fairy and Folk Tales. (Illus.). N.D. Charles Scribner's Sons.
--Irish Fairy and Folk Tales. N.D. Modern Library.
--Irish Folk Stories and Fairy Tales. N.D. (ISBN 0-448-00021-0). Grosset & Dunlap.
--Irish Folk Tales. Friers, Rowel Boyd (1920-), illus. LC 74-154277. (Illus.). xix, 400. 27cm. 1973. Limited Editions Club.
--Irish Folk Tales. Friers, Rowel Boyd (1920-), illus. Limited Editions Club, Inc., New York LC 74-154277. (Illus.). xix, 409 p. 27cm. 1973. Printed for the Members of the Limited Editions Club.
Yechton, Barbara, pseud., see Krause, Lyda Farrington.
Yee, Chiang, pseud., see Chiang, Yee.
Yee, Chiang, pseud. (1903-1977)
--Chin Pao & the Giant Pandas. Chiang, Yee. (Illus.). (gr. 1-5). N.D. Transatlantic.
--Men of the Burma Road. Chiang, Yee. (Illus.). (gr. 4-6). N.D. (ISBN 0-685-20604-1). Transatlantic.
Yee, Ching C. see Crane, Louise, Mrs.
Yektai, Niki
--Sun Rain. Brewster, Patience, illus. LC 83-20792. (Illus.). 32p. 1984. (ISBN 0-590-07886-0). Four Winds Press.
Yellin, Sarah Fell
--Cassie the Cat and Bunny the Rabbit. Nagel, Stina (1918-), illus. (Illus.). 1959. Exposition Press.
Yellow Robe, Rosebud, ed.
--Tonweya and the Eagles, and Other Lakota Indian Tales. Pinkney, Jerry (1939-), illus. LC 78-72470. (Illus.). 118 p. 24cm. c.1979. (ISBN 0-8037-8973-4). (ISBN 0-8037-8974-2). Dial Press. **Award: (ALA).**
Yen, Liang
--Tommy and Dee-dee. Yen, Liang, illus. 32p. 1953. Henry Z. Walck, Inc., Publishers.
Yenni, Julia Truitt
--House for The Sparrow. N.D. Reynal & Hitchcock.
--This is Me, Kathie. N.D. Reynal & Hitchcock.
Yeo, Wilma (1908-)
--Mrs. Neverbody's Recipes. 1st ed. Aliki, pseud. (1929-), illus. Brandenberg, Aliki Liacouras. (Illus.). 34 p. 16cm. 1968. Lippincott.
--The Mystery of the Third Twin. Brown, Judith Gwyn (1933-), illus. LC 72-81824. (Illus.). 186 p. 22cm. 1972. (ISBN 0-671-65202-8). Simon and Schuster.
Yeoman, John, jt. ed. see Blake, Quentin.
Yeoman, John (1934-)
--Alphabet Soup. Blake, Quentin (1932-), illus. LC 71-118958. (Illus.). 31 p. 27cm. 1970, c.1969. (ISBN 0-695-80168-6). Follett.
--The Apple of Youth, and Other Russian Folk Stories. Swiderska, Barbara, illus. LC 68-16601. (Illus.). 63 p. 23cm. 1968, c.1967. F. Watts.
--Apple of Youth & Other Russian Folk Stories. Swiderska, Barbara, illus. (Illus.). 64p. (Folk Stories of the World Ser). (gr. 4-8). 1969. (ISBN 0-531-01612-9). Watts.
--The Bear's Water Picnic. Blake, Quentin (1932-), illus. LC 70-116757. (Illus.). 30 p. 26cm. 1970. Macmillan.
--The Bear's Winter House. Blake, Quentin (1932-), illus. LC 75-85699. (Illus.). 25 p. 27cm. 1969. World Pub. Co.
--Beatrice and Vanessa. Blake, Quentin (1932-), illus. LC 74-13122. (Illus.). 30 p. 27cm. 1st U.S. edition. 1975, c.1974. (ISBN 0-02-793660-0). Macmillan.
--The Boy Who Sprouted Antlers. Blake, Quentin (1932-), illus. LC 66-2302. 44p. illus. (pt. col.) 22cm. 1966, c.1961. Faber & Faber.
--Boy Who Sprouted Antlers. Blake, Quentin (1932-), illus. (Illus.). (gr. 3-5). N.D. Transatlantic.
--A Drink of Water, and Other Stories. Blake, Quentin (1932-), illus. LC 66-2303. 63p. illus. (pt. col.) 22cm. 1966, c.1960. Faber & Faber.
--Drink of Water & Other Stories. Blake, Quentin (1932-), illus. (Illus.). (gr. 3-5). N.D. (ISBN 0-685-20573-8). Transatlantic.
--Mouse Trouble. Blake, Quentin (1932-), illus. LC 74-20586. p. cm. 1975, c.1972. (ISBN 0-02-045610-7). Collier Books.
--Mouse Trouble. Blake, Quentin (1932-), illus. LC 72-85190. (Illus.). 30 p. 26cm. 1973, c.1972. Macmillan.
--Mouse Trouble. Blake, Quentin (1932-), illus. 1976. Macmillan.
--Sixes and Sevens. Blake, Quentin (1932-), illus. LC 79-147893. (Illus.). 29 p. 1974, c.1971. Collier Books.
--The Young Performing Horse. Blake, Quentin (1932-), illus. LC 78-6304. p. cm. 1978, c.1977. (ISBN 0-8193-0970-2). (ISBN 0-8193-0971-0). Parents' Magazine Press.
Yeoman, John (1934-) & Blake, Quentin (1932-)
--The Wild Washerwomen. LC 78-32147. p. cm. c.1979. (ISBN 0-688-80219-2). (ISBN 0-688-84219-4). Greenwillow Books.
Yeomans, Amy
--The Golden Bird. LC 25-18068. 1 p. l., 5-111, 1 p. illus. 20 cm. c.1924. Gospel Publishing House.
--Lucilla. LC 31-3178. 77, 1 p. illus. 19 cm. c.1930. Gospel Publishing House.
Yep, Laurence Michael (1948-)
--Child of the Owl. LC 76-24314. 217 p. 22cm. c.1977. (ISBN 0-06-026739-9). (ISBN 0-06-026743-7). Harper & Row. **Award: (BGH).**
--Dragon of the Lost Sea. LC 81-48644. 213 p. 21cm. c.1982. (ISBN 0-06-026746-1). (ISBN 0-06-026747-X). Harper & Row. **Award: (ALA).**
--Dragon Steel. LC 84-48338. 288p. (gr. 7 up). 1985. (ISBN 0-06-026748-8). (ISBN 0-06-026751-8). HarpJ.
--Dragonwings. LC 74-2625. 248 p. 22cm. c.1975. (ISBN 0-06-026737-2). (ISBN 0-06-026738-0). Harper & Row. **Awards: (IRA); (ALA); (BGH); (JNM).**
--Dragonwings. (gr. 5-9). 1977. Harper & Row.
--Kind Hearts and Gentle Monsters. LC 81-47738. 177 p. 22cm. c.1982. (ISBN 0-06-026732-1). (ISBN 0-06-026733-X). Harper & Row.
--Liar, Liar. LC 83-5432. 165 p. 22cm. 1983. (ISBN 0-688-02417-3). Morrow.
--The Mark Twain Murders. LC 81-69510. vii, 152 p. 22cm. c.1982. (ISBN 0-590-07824-0). Four Winds Press.
--Mountain Light. LC 85-42643. 281 p. 22cm. c.1985. (ISBN 0-06-026758-5). (ISBN 0-06-026759-3). Harper & Row.
--Sea Glass. LC 78-22487. p. cm. c.1979. (ISBN 0-06-026744-5). (ISBN 0-06-026745-3). Harper & Row.
--The Serpent's Children. LC 82-48855. 256p. (gr. 7 up). c.1984. (ISBN 0-06-026809-3, HarpJ). (ISBN 0-06-026812-3). Har-Row.
--Sweetwater. Noonan, Julia (1946-), illus. LC 72-9867. (Illus.). 201 p. 22cm. 1973. (ISBN 0-06-026735-6). (ISBN 0-06-026735-6). Harper & Row.
--The Tom Sawyer Fires. 144p. (gr. 5 up). 1984. (ISBN 0-688-03861-1, Morrow Junior Books). Morrow.
Yerby, Frank (1916-)
--Bride of Liberty. 1st ed. LC 54-7595. 219p. illus. 22cm. (Cavalcade books). 1954. Doubleday.
Yerian, Cameron John & Yerian, Margaret
--Showtime. LC 74-12480. (Illus.). 45 p. 25cm. 1974. (ISBN 0-516-01309-2). Childrens Press.
--The Yawn Book. Flynn, Laurie, illus. LC 75-151704. (Illus.). 32 p. 17cm. 1971. (ISBN 0-8114-7732-0). Steck-Vaughn.
Yerian, Cameron John & Yerian, Margaret, eds.
--Puppets & Shadow Plays. LC 74-12476. (Illus.). index. 48p. (Fun Time Bks.). (gr. 1-6). 1974. (ISBN 0-516-01308-4). Childrens.
Yerian, Margaret, jt. auth. see Yerian, Cameron John.
Yerian, Margaret, jt. ed. see Yerian, Cameron John.
Yershov, Peter
--The Little Humpbacked Horse. 104p. 1980. (ISBN 0-8285-1189-6, Pub. by Progress Pubs USSR). Imported Pubns.
Yezback, Steven A. (1943-)
--Pumpkinseeds. 1st ed. Thompson, Mozelle (1926-), illus. LC 76-77825. (Illus.). 30 p. 29cm. 1969. Bobbs-Merrill.
Ying, Mei
--Immortal Fruit. (Illus.). 63p. (Orig.). 1981. (ISBN 0-8351-0958-5). China Bks.
--Kindhearted Xiawudong. Ying, Mei, illus. (Illus.). 56p. (ps-3). 1984. (ISBN 0-8351-1300-0). China Bks.
Yiqun, Fang
--Two Little Kittens. (Illus.). 22p. (Orig.). (gr. 2-4). 1982. (ISBN 0-8351-1142-3). China Bks.
Ylla, pseud., see Koffler, Camilla.
Ylval, pseud., see Roth, Naema.
Yobaghu-Talyonunh see Wright, Arthur R.
Yoda, Junichi
--Rolling Rice Ball. Watanabe, Saburo, illus. Tresselt, Alvin R. (1916-), tr. LC 70-83383. (Illus.). 32p. 1st U.S. edition. Orig. Title: Omusubi Kororin. (gr. k-3). 1969. (ISBN 0-8193-0299-6). (ISBN 0-8193-0300-3). Parents.
Yoder, Dorotha S
--Bad Little Red Shoes. Fields, Don, illus. LC 69-20226. (Illus.). 41 p. 20cm. 1969. Word Books.
--The Best Gift of All. Severance, W. Murray, ed. McDonald, Ralph J., illus. LC 69-20235. (Illus.). 41 p. 20cm. 1969. Word Books.
--Our Paint-Pot World. Severance, W. Murray, ed. Fields, Don, illus. LC 69-20229. (Illus.). 25 p. 20cm. 1969. Word Books.
Yoder, Dorotha S & Severance, W. Murray
--One-Word Boy. Severance, W. Murray, ed. Fields, Don, illus. LC 69-20227. (Illus.). 26 p. 20cm. 1969. Word Books.
Yoder, Joseph W.
--Rosanna of the Amish. (Illus., Orig.). (gr. 9 up). 1940. (ISBN 0-8361-1424-8). Herald Pr.
Yogesvara, Dasa
--Gopal the Invincible. Jyotirmayi, Devi & Sunita, Devi, illus. LC 82-16396. p. cm. (The Childhood Pastimes of Krishna). c.1982. (ISBN 0-89647-017-2). Bala Productions.
Yogesvara Dasa & Jyotirmayi-Devi
--A Gift of Love: The Story of Sudama the Brahmin. LC 82-8874. (Illus.). 32 p. 24cm. c.1982. (ISBN 0-89647-015-6). Bala Books.
Yokubinas, Gail, jt. auth. see Powell, Meredith.
Yolen, Jane Hyatt, jt. auth. see Huston, Anne.
Yolen, Jane Hyatt (1939-)
--The Acorn Quest. Natti, Susanna (1948-), illus. LC 80-2755. (Illus.). 57 p. 21cm. c.1981. (ISBN 0-690-04106-3). (ISBN 0-690-04107-1). Crowell.
--All in the Woodland Early. Zalben, Jane Breskin (1950-), illus. LC 79-10843. p. cm. c.1979. (ISBN 0-529-05508-2). (ISBN 0-529-05509-0). Collins.
--All in the Woodland Early: An ABC Book. Zalben, Jane Breskin (1950-), illus. (Illus.). (ps-3). 1983. (ISBN 0-399-20969-7, Philomel). Putnam Pub Group.
--The Bird of Time. Mayer, Mercer (1943-), illus. LC 72-139102. (Illus.). 32 p. 27cm. 1971. (ISBN 0-690-14425-3). Crowell.
--The Boy Who Had Wings. Aichinger, Helga (1937-), illus. LC 73-17010. (Illus.). 25 p. 31cm. 1974. (ISBN 0-690-15899-8). (ISBN 0-690-15899-8). Crowell.
--The Boy Who Spoke Chimp. Wiesner, David, illus. LC 79-27259. (Illus.). 120 p. 20cm. (Capers). c.1981. (ISBN 0-394-84467-X). (ISBN 0-394-94467-4). Knopf : Distributed by Random House.
--Brothers of the Wind. Berger, Barbara, illus. LC 80-25562. p. cm. c.1981. (ISBN 0-399-20787-2). Philomel Books.
--Children of the Wolf. LC 83-16979. 144p. (gr. 7 up). 1984. (ISBN 0-670-21763-8, Viking Kestrel). Viking.
--Commander Toad and the Big Black Hole. Degen, Bruce, illus. LC 82-23524. p. cm. 1983. (ISBN 0-698-30741-0). Coward-McCann.
--Commander Toad & the Dis-Asteroid. Degen, Bruce, illus. LC 84-1897. (Illus.). 64 p. 22cm. c.1985. (ISBN 0-698-30744-5). Coward-McCann.
--Commander Toad and the Planet of the Grapes. Degen, Bruce, illus. LC 81-3120. (Illus.). 64 p. 22cm. (Break-of-Day Book). c.1982. (ISBN 0-698-30724-0). Coward, McCann & Geoghegan.
--Commander Toad in Space. Degen, Bruce, illus. LC 79-10467. p. cm. 1980. (ISBN 0-698-30724-0). (ISBN 0-698-20522-7). Coward, McCann & Geoghegan.
--Dragon Night and Other Lullabies. 1st ed. Demi, pseud. (1942-), illus. Hitz, Demi. LC 80-15263. p. cm. (gr. 1-4). c.1980. (ISBN 0-416-30711-6). Methuen.
--Dragon's Blood: A Fantasy. LC 81-69668. xii, 243 p. 22cm. 1982. (ISBN 0-440-02087-5). (ISBN 0-440-02087-5). Delacorte Press.
--Dream Weaver. Hague, Michael R., illus. LC 78-26982. (Illus.). 80 p. 25cm. 1979. (ISBN 0-529-05517-1). Collins.
--The Emperor and the Kite. Young, Ed (1931-), illus. LC 77-27309. p. cm. 1978. (ISBN 0-529-00255-8). Collins & World.
--The Emperor and the Kite. Young, Ed (1931-), illus. LC 67-13816. (Illus.). 31 p. 1967. World Pub. Co. **Award: (RCM).**
--The Giants' Farm. De Paola, Tomie, pseud. (1934-), illus. De Paola, Thomas Anthony. LC 76-58317. p. cm. c.1977. (ISBN 0-8164-3193-0). Seabury Press.
--The Giants Go Camping. De Paola, Tomie, pseud. (1934-), illus. De Paola, Thomas Anthony. LC 78-17928. (Illus.). 46 p. 21cm. c.1979. (ISBN 0-8164-3223-6). Seabury Press.
--The Gift of Sarah Barker. 192p. (gr. 7 up). 1983. (ISBN 0-590-32418-7). Scholastic Inc.
--The Gift of Sarah Barker. LC 80-26443. 155 p. 23cm. c.1981. (ISBN 0-670-64580-X). Viking Press.
--The Girl Who Cried Flowers, and Other Tales. Palladini, David Mario (1946-), illus. LC 73-8903. (Illus.). 55 p. 24cm. 1974. (ISBN 0-690-00216-5). Crowell. **Award: (NYT).**
--The Girl Who Cried Flowers and Other Tales. Palladini, David Mario (1946-), illus. LC 80-26140. p. cm. 1981, c.1974. (ISBN 0-8052-0666-3). Schocken Books.
--The Girl Who Loved the Wind. Young, Ed (1931-), illus. LC 71-171012. (Illus.). 31 p. 26cm. 1972. (ISBN 0-690-33100-2). (ISBN 0-690-33101-0). Crowell.
--Greyling. LC 68-28481. (Illus.). (gr. k-3). 1968. (ISBN 0-529-00543-3, Philomel). Putnam Pub Group.
--Greyling: A Picture Story from the Islands of Shetland. Stobbs, William (1914-), illus. LC 75-22435. p. cm. 1975, c.1968. (ISBN 0-529-00543-3). Collins & World.
--Greyling: A Picture Story from the Island of Shetland. Stobbs, William (1914-), illus. LC 68-28481. (Illus.). color ils. 32p. (Picture Story Books from Around the World Series). (gr. k-3). 1968. (ISBN 0-529-00542-5). (ISBN 0-529-00543-3). World Pub.
--Gwinellen: The Princess Who Could Not Sleep. Renfro, Ed, illus. 1 v. (unpaged) illus. (pt. col.) 26cm. c.1965. Macmillan.
--Hannah Dreaming. LC 77-373214. (Illus.). 32 p. 22cm. 1977. Museum of Fine Arts.
--Heart's Blood. LC 83-14978. 224p. (gr. 7 up). 1984. (ISBN 0-385-29316-X). Delacorte.
--Hobo Toad and the Motorcycle Gang. McCully, Emily Arnold (1939-), illus. LC 75-23028. p. cm. 1975, c.1970. (ISBN 0-529-00883-1). Collins.
--Hobo Toad and the Motorcycle Gang. McCully, Emily Arnold (1939-), illus. LC 70-101843. (Illus.). 62 p. 20cm. 1970. World Pub. Co.
--How Beastly!. A Menagerie of Nonsense Poems. Marshall, James (1942-), illus. 1980. Collins.
--How Beastly!. A Menagerie of Nonsense Poems. Marshall, James (1942-), illus. LC 79-22416. (Illus.). 48p. (gr. 4-6). 1980. (ISBN 0-529-05421-3, Philomel). Putnam Pub Group.
--The Hundredth Dove and Other Tales. Palladini, David mario (1946-), illus. LC 77-1591. p. cm. 1977. (ISBN 0-690-01366-3). Crowell.
--The Hundredth Dove and Other Tales. Palladini, David Mario (1946-), illus. LC 80-13635. (Illus.). 64 p. 23cm. 1980, c.1977. (ISBN 0-8052-0659-0). Schocken Books.
--The Hundreth Dove & Other Tales. Palladini, David Mario (1946-), illus. LC 77-1591. (Illus.). (gr. 3-7). 1977. (ISBN 0-690-01366-3, TYC-J). Har-Row.
--An Invitation to the Butterfly Ball: A Counting Rhyme. Zalben, Jane Breskin (1950-), illus. LC 75-19191. (Illus.). 33 p. 26cm. c.1976. (ISBN 0-8193-0799-8). (ISBN 0-8193-0800-5). Parents' Magazine Press.
--An Invitation to the Butterfly Ball: A/Counting Rhyme. Zalben, Jane Breskin, illus. LC 75-19191. (Illus.). 33p. 26cm. c.1976. (ISBN 0-8193-0799-8). Parents' Magazine Press.
--An Invitation to the Butterfly Ball: A Counting Rhyme. Zalben, Jane Breskin (1950-), illus. LC 82-22462. 1983, c.1976. (ISBN 0-399-20972-7). Philomel Books.
--Inway Investigators: Or, The Mystery at McCracken's Place. Eitzen, Allan (1928-), illus. LC 69-13342. (Illus.). line & wash drawings. 80p. (gr. 3-7). 1969. (ISBN 0-8164-3031-4, Clarion Bk). Seabury.
--Isabel's Noel. Roth, Arnold (1929-), illus. LC 67-25856. (Illus.). 1 v. (unpaged). 26cm. 1967. Funk & Wagnalls.
--It All Depends. Bolognese, Donald Alan (1934-), illus. LC 69-11415. (Illus.). 36 p. 19cm. 1969. Funk & Wagnalls.
--The Little Spotted Fish. Henstra, Friso (1928-), illus. LC 74-14819. (Illus.). 32 p. 1975. (ISBN 0-8164-3134-5). Seabury Press.
--The Longest Name on the Block. Madden, Peter, illus. (Illus.). 32 p. 27cm. (Fun and Frolic Book). 1968. Funk & Wagnalls.
--The Magic Three of Solatia. Noonan, Julia (1946-), illus. LC 74-5010. 172 p. 24cm. 1974. (ISBN 0-690-00532-6). Crowell.
--The Magic Three of Solatia. Noonan, Julia (1946-), illus. 1974. Harper.
--The Mermaid's Three Wisdoms. Rader, Laura, illus. LC 77-18325. (Illus.). 112 p. 24cm. c.1978. (ISBN 0-529-05420-5). Collins.
--The Minstrel and the Mountain: A Tale of Peace. Rockwell, Anne F. (1934-), illus. LC 67-23341. (Illus.). 1 v. (unpaged). 17cm. 1967. World Pub. Co.
--The Moon Ribbon and Other Tales. Palladini, David Mario (1946-), illus. LC 75-34462. (Illus.). 54 p. 23cm. c.1976. (ISBN 0-690-01044-3). Crowell.

--Neptune Rising: Songs and Tales of the Undersea Folk. Wiesner, David, illus. LC 82-5281. p. cm. 1982. (ISBN 0-399-20918-2). Philomel Books.
--No Bath Tonight. Parker, Nancy Winslow (1930-), illus. LC 77-26605. (Illus.). 32 p. c.1978. (ISBN 0-690-03881-X). (ISBN 0-690-03882-8). Crowell.
--No Bath Tonight. Provensen, Alice (1918-) & Provensen, Martin (1916-), illus. 1978. Viking.
--Pirates in Petticoats. Vosburgh, Leonard W. (1912-), illus. LC 63-16693. ix, 118 p. illus. 21 cm. 1963. (ISBN 0-679-20152-1). D. McKay Co.
--Rainbow Rider. Foreman, Michael (1938-), illus. LC 73-19700. (Illus.). 32 p. 27cm. 1974. (ISBN 0-690-00301-3). (ISBN 0-690-00301-3). Crowell.
--The Robot and Rebecca. LC 79-27391. p. cm. (Capers). c.1980. (ISBN 0-394-84488-2). (ISBN 0-394-94488-7). Knopf : Distributed by Random House.
--The Robot and Rebecca and the Missing Owser. LC 81-4870. p. cm. 1981. (ISBN 0-394-84832-2). (ISBN 0-394-94832-7). A. Knopf.
--The Robot & Rebecca: The Mystery of the Code-Carrying Kids. Obrist, Jurg, illus. LC 79-27391. (Illus.). 96p. (Capers Ser.). (gr. 3-6). 1980. (ISBN 0-394-94488-7). (ISBN 0-394-84488-2). Knopf.
--See This Little Line?. 1st ed. Elgin, Kathleen (1923-), illus. LC 63-14216. unpaged. illus. 17 x 25 cm. 1963. D. McKay Co.
--The Seeing Stick. Charlip, Remy (1929-) & Maraslis, Demetra, illus. 1977. Harper.
--The Seventh Mandarin. Young, Ed (1931-), illus. LC 70-115784. (Illus.). 34 p. 29cm. 1970. Seabury Press.
--Shape Shifters: Fantasy and Science Fiction Tales About Humans Who Can Change Their Shapes. LC 77-13646. viii, 182 p. 24cm. c.1978. (ISBN 0-8164-3212-0). Seabury Press.
--Shirlick Holmes and the Case of the Wandering Wardrobe. Rao, Anthony, illus. LC 80-15406. p. cm. 1981. (ISBN 0-698-20498-0). Coward, McCann & Geoghegan.
--Sleeping Ugly. Stanley, Diane (1943-), illus. LC 81-489. p. cm. (Break-of-Day Book). 1981. (ISBN 0-698-30721-6). Coward, McCann & Geoghegan.
--Spider Jane. Bernath, Stefen, illus. LC 77-17193. p. cm. (Break-of-Day). 1978. (ISBN 0-698-30696-1). Coward, McCann & Geoghegan.
--Spider Jane on the Move: Break-of-Day Bk. Bernath, Stefen, illus. (Illus.). (gr. 6-9). 1980. (ISBN 0-698-30714-3, Coward). Putnam Pub Group.
--The Stone Silenus. LC 84-4244. 128p. (gr. 7 up). 1984. (ISBN 0-399-20971-9, Philomel). (ISBN 0-399-20971-9). Putnam Pub Group.
--The Sultan's Perfect Tree. Garrison, Barbara (1931-), illus. LC 76-18096. (Illus.). 33 p. 26cm. c.1977. (ISBN 0-8193-0864-1). Parents' Magazine Press.
--Touch Magic: Fantasy, Faerie & Folklore in the Literature of Childhood. 128p. (gr. 6 up). 1981. (ISBN 0-399-20830-5, Philomel). Putnam Pub Group.
--The Transfigured Hart. Diamond, Donna (1950-), illus. LC 75-2377. (Illus.). 86 p. 24cm. 1975. (ISBN 0-690-00736-1). Crowell.
--Uncle Lemon's Spring. 1st ed. Rounds, Glen Harold (1906-), illus. LC 80-22145. (Illus.). 55 p. 24cm. (Unicorn Book). c.1981. (ISBN 0-525-41830-X). Dutton.
--The Witch Who Wasn't. iv. (chiefly illus. 23cm. 1974, c.1964. Collier Books.
--The Witch Who Wasn't. Roth, Arnold (1929-), illus. LC 64-20730. (Illus.). 34 p. 26cm. 1964. Macmillan.
--The Wizard Islands. Quackenbush, Robert Mead (1929-), illus. LC 73-4474. (Illus.). 115 p. 26cm. 1973. (ISBN 0-690-89671-9). Crowell.
--The Wizard of Washington Square. Cruz, Raymond (1933-), illus. LC 79-82777. (Illus.). 126 p. 20cm. 1969. World Pub. Co.

Yolen, Jane Hyatt (1939-), compiled by.
--Rounds About Rounds. (Illus.). (gr. 4-6). 1977. (ISBN 0-531-00125-3). Watts.
--Zoo Two-Thousand: Twelve Stories of Science Fiction and Fantasy Beasts. LC 72-97773. 224 p. 24cm. (gr. 6up). 1973. (ISBN 0-8164-3103-5). Seabury Press.

Yolen, Jane Hyatt (1939-) & Bernath, Stefen
--Spider Jane on the Move. LC 78-25688. p. cm. 1979. (ISBN 0-698-30714-3). Coward, McCann & Geoghegan.

Yolen, Jane Hyatt (1939-) & Cooney, Gabriel Amadeus
--Milkweed Days. LC 76-10273. p. cm. 1976. (ISBN 0-690-01250-0). (ISBN 0-690-01140-7). Crowell.

Yolen, Jane Hyatt (1939-) & Di Fiori, Lawrence
--Mice on Ice. LC 79-19342. (Illus.). 71 p. 25cm. (Smart Cat Book.). c.1980. (ISBN 0-525-34872-7). E. P. Dutton.

Yolen, Jane Hyatt (1939-) & Furukawa, Mel
--The Seeing Stick. LC 75-6949. p. cm. 1975. (ISBN 0-690-00455-9). (ISBN 0-690-00596-2). Crowell.

Yolen, Jane Hyatt (1939-) & Green, Barbara, eds.
--The Fireside Song Book of Birds & Beasts. Parnall, Peter (1936-), illus. LC 75-175047. (Illus.). (gr. 3-7). 1972. (ISBN 0-671-66540-5, Juveniles). S&S.

Yolen, Jane Hyatt (1939-) & Kent, Jack (1920-)
--The Simple Prince. LC 78-6118. (Illus.). 33 p. 24cm. c.1978. (ISBN 0-8193-0960-5). (ISBN 0-8193-0961-3). Parents' Magazine Press.

Yomen, Ben
--Roberto, the Mexican Boy. Yomen, Ben, illus. LC 47-12229. 71 p. col illus. 24 cm. 1947. A Whitman.

Yonge, Charlotte Mary (1823-1901)
--Adventures of Conrad the Squirrel. (Series of Books for the Young). N.D. MacMillan & Co.
--Afternoon Tea. Sowerby, J. G. & Emmerson, H. H., illus. N.D. R Worthington.
--Aunt Charlotte Nursery Book. (Illus.). 1882. R Worthington.
--Aunt Charlotte Picture Book. 1882. R Worthington.
--Aunt Charlotte's Christmas Box. Nursery Rhymes and Poems. 1882. R Worthington.
--Aunt Charlotte's Stories of Bible History for Children. (Illus.). (The Standard Ser.). 1909. John C. Winston Co.
--Aunt Charlotte's Stories of Bible History for Children. (The Progressive Ser.). N.D. John C Winston.
--Aunt Charlotte's Stories of Bible History. (Illus.). (The Golden Days' Ser.). N.D. John C. Winston & Co.
--Baby Picture Primer. Yonge, Charlotte Mary (1823-1901), illus. (Illus.). (Aunt Charlotte's Picture Book). 1888. R Worthington.
--Baby Rhymes, 1 of 12 Vols. Yonge, Charlotte Mary (1823-1901), illus. (Illus.). (Aunt Charlotte's Picture Book). 1888. R Worthington.
--Beechcroft, 1 of 12 Vols. (Vol. 12). N.D. D. Appleton and Co.
--Ben Sylvester's Word. N.D. D. Appleton.
--Ben Sylvester's Word. (Illus.). N.D. E & J B Young.
--Ben Sylvester's Word. N.D. Publications of E. P. Dutton & Co.
--Ben Sylvester's Word and the Pigeon Pie. N.D. Publications of E. P. Dutton & Co.
--Bk of Golden Deeds, 1 of 103 vols. (The Pearl Library: No. 9). 1900. Hurst & Co.
--Book of Golden Deeds. (Home Series for Girls). N.D. Hurst & Co.
--The Book of Golden Deeds. (The Golden Treasury Ser.). N.D. John Allyn.
--A Book of Golden Deeds, 1 of 4 Vols. (Illus.). (Miss Yonge's Historical Stories). N.D. Lothrop Lee & Shepard Co.
--Book of Golden Deeds. (Series of Books For the Young). N.D. MacMillan & Co.
--A Book of Golden Deeds. LC 29-26910. 1 p. l., iii, 5-480 p. col. front., illus., col. plates. 21 cm. (Honor books). 1929. T. Nelson and Sons.
--A Book of Golden Deeds. LC 29-26910. (Illus.). 480p. 21cm. (Honor Bks.). 1929. T. Nelson.
--A Book of Golden Deeds. LC 15-2599. (Illus.). 314p. 24cm. (Christian Herald Library). 1895. The Christian Herald.
--A Book of Golden Deeds. Burd, Clara Miller, ed. Burd, Clara Miller, illus. LC 27-23172. xiii, 247 p. incl. plates. col. plates. 19 1/2 cm. 1927. Macmillan.
--A Book of Golden Deeds of All Times and All Lands. LC 15-16692. xi,454. 18cm. (Golden Treasury Ser.). 1882. Macmillan and Co.
--A Book of Worthies. (Golden Treasury Ser.). N.D. MacMillan & Co.
--Book of Worthies. (Series of Books for the Young). N.D. MacMillan & Co.
--The Caged Lion, 1 of 12 Vol. N.D. D. Appleton and Co.
--The Caged Lion. New Ed. ed. (Illus.). (Works by Charlotte Yonge). N.D. Macmillian & Co.
--The Carbonels. N.D. Thomas Whittaker.
--Chaplet of Pearls. (Illus.). (Fireside Ser. for Girls). N.D. A. L. Burt's Publications.
--Chaplet of Pearls. (Illus.). (The Wellesley Series for Girls). N.D. A. L. Burt.
--The Chaplet of Pearls. New Ed. ed. (Illus.). N.D. Macmillian & Co.
--The Chaplet of Pearls. (The Days of Chivalry Ser.). N.D. Page Co.
--Chosen People. N.D. Thomas Whittaker.
--The Christmas Mummers, and other Stories. (Illus.). N.D. E & J B Young.
--Cinderella, 1 of 12 Vols. Yonge, Charlotte Mary (1823-1901), illus. (Illus.). (Aunt Charlotte's Picture Book). 1888. R Worthington.
--The Clever Woman of the Family. (Illus.). N.D. MacMillian.
--The Constable's Tower: New Stories. N.D. Set. Thomas Whittaker.
--The Constable's Tower: Or,The Times of Magna Charta. N.D. Thomas Whittaker.
--The Cook and the Captive. N.D. Thomas Whittaker.
--Countess Kate. (Illus.). N.D. E. P. Dutton & Co.
--Countess Kate. N.D. Loring.
--Countess Kate. Raverat, Gwendolen Mary (1885-1957), illus. LC 60-13062. (Illus.). 282 p. 20cm. (Looking glass library, 17). 1960. Looking Glass Library; Distributed by Random House.
--Countess Kate and the Stokesley Secret. (Illus.). N.D. E & J B Young.
--The Cross Roads: Or,A Choice in Life. N.D. Thomas Whittaker.
--The Cunning Woman's Grandson: New Stories. N.D. Set 6.25. Thomas Whittaker.
--The Daisy Chain, 1 of 12 Vol. N.D. D. Appleton and Co.
--The Daisy Chain. (Color Bks.). N.D. DeWolfe, Fiske & Co.
--The Daisy Chain. LC 75-32169. xi, vi, 667 p. 19cm. (Classics of Children's Literature, 1621-1932). 1977. (ISBN 0-8240-2282-3). Garland Pub.
--Daisy Chain. (Illus.). (Series of Works of Fiction). N.D. Macmillan & Co.
--The Daisy Chain. (Illus.). N.D. Thomas Nelson & Sons.
Dove in the Eagle's Nest. (Illus.). (Fireside Ser. for Girls). N.D. A. L. Burt's Publications.
--Dove in the Eagle's Nest. (Burt's Home Lib.). N.D. A. L. Burt's Pubs.
--Dove in the Eagle's Nest. (Illus.). (The Meade Series for Girls). N.D. A. L. Burt.
--Dove in the Eagle's Nest, 1 of 12 Vols. N.D. D. Appleton and Co.
--The Dove in the Eagle's Nest. N.D. Duffield.
--The Dove in the Eagle's Nest. (Illus.). (St. Nicholas Series for Girls). N.D. International Book Co.
--The Dove in the Eagle's Nest. fourth ed. De Angeli, Marguerite Lofft, Mrs. (1889-), illus. N.D. Macmillan & Co.
--Dynevor Terrace. (Illus.). N.D. MacMillian.
--Dynevor Terrace: Or, The Clue of Life, 1 of 12 Vol. N.D. D. Appleton and Co.
--Founded on Paper: Or, Uphill and Downhill Between the Two Jubilees. N.D. Thomas Whittaker.
--Friarswood Post-Office. N.D. D. Appleton & Co.
--Friarswood Post-Office. (Illus.). N.D. E & J B Young.
--Friarswood Post Office. N.D. E P Dutton.
--Heir of Redclyffe. (Illus.). (Fireside Ser. for Girls). N.D. A. L. Burt's Publications.
--Heir of Redclyffe. (Illus.). (The Meade Series for Girls). N.D. A. L. Burt.
--Heir of Redclyffe, 1 of 12 Vol. N.D. D. Appleton and Co.
--The Heir of Redclyffe. New Ed. ed. (Illus.). N.D. Macmillian & Co.
--The Heir of Redclyffe. (Illus.). (The Acme Library). N.D. Rand McNally & Co.
--Henrietta's Wish: Or, Domineering. N.D. E. P. Dutton.
--The Herd Boy and His Hermit. N.D. Thomas Whittaker.
--The History of Sir Thomas Thumb. Blackburn, Jane, illus. LC 78-315554. (Illus.). 142 p. 22cm. 1855. T. Constable.
--Hopes and Fears, 1 of 12 Vol. N.D. D. Appleton and Co.
--Kenneth: or, The Rear Guard of the Grand Army. (Illus.). 1888. E & J B Young.
--Kenneth's Children: A Story for Boys and Girls. (Illus.). N.D. E & J B Young.
--Lads and Lasses of Langley. (Illus.). N.D. E & J B Young.
--Lances of Linwood. (Atlantic Library). N.D. D. Appleton & Co.
--Lances of Lynwood, 1 of 4 Vols. (Illus.). (Miss Yonge's Historical Stories). N.D. Lothrop Lee & Shepard Co.
--The Lances of Lynwood. (Illus.). (Series of Books for the Young). N.D. MacMillan & Co.
--Langley Little Ones. (Illus.). N.D. Publications of E. P. Dutton & Co.
--Langley School. (Illus.). N.D. E. P. Dutton & Co.
--Langley's Adventures. LC 45-53914. vi p., 1 l., 286 p. 16 cm. 1884. E. P. Dutton and Co.
--Little Bo-Peep, 1 of 12 Vols. (Illus.). (Aunt Charlotte's Picture Book). 1888. R Worthington.
--The Little Duke. N.D. Duffield & Co.
--The Little Duke. (Queen's Treasure Ser.). N.D. Harcourt Brace.
--The Little Duke, 1 of 4 Vols. (Illus.). (Miss Yonge's Historical Stories). N.D. Lothrop Lee & Shepard Co.
--The Little Duke. Godfrey, Michael, illus. 163p. illus. (pt. col.) 21cm. (Children's illus. classics 56). 1963. Dent.
--The Little Duke. Lawson, George, illus. LC 32-15195. 3 p. l., 11-250 p. front., illus. 19 cm. (Every child's library). c.1932. The Saalfield Publishing Company.
--The Little Duke. Nesbitt, E., ed. (Illus.). (The Children's Bookcase). N.D. George H. Doran.
--The Little Duke. O'Sullivan, Tom, illus. (Doubleday Junior Classics.). N.D. Doubleday & Co.
--The Little Duke: Or, Richard the Fearless. Rhys, Ernest, ed. Curtis, Dora, illus. 18cm. 232p. (Everyman's Library for Young People). 1910. E. P. Dutton & Co.
--The Little Duke: Richard the Fearless. (Author of "The Heir of Redclyffe."). (Illus.). (Macmillan's Dollar and a Half Series of Books for the Young). N.D. Macmillan & Co.
--The Little Duke: Richard the Fearless. Castellon, Federico (1914-), illus. LC 54-13487. (Illus.). 22cm. 172p. (New Children's Classics). 1954. Macmillan.
--The Little Duke, Richard the Fearless. De Angeli, Marguerite Lofft, Mrs. (1889-), illus. 5 p. l., 188 p. incl. illus., plates col. front., col. plates. 19 1/2 cm. (Macmillan children's classics). 1927. The Macmilan Company.
--Little Lucy's Wonderful Globe. (Illus.). (The Wellesley Series for Girls). N.D. A. L. Burt.
--Little Lucy's Wonderful Globe, 1 of 4 vols. (Wonderful Globe Ser.). 1872. D. Lothrop Co.
--Little Lucy's Wonderful Globe. LC 99-1785. 141 p. incl. illus., plates, maps. pl. 17 1/2 x 13 1/2 cm. c.1898. Educational Publishing Company.
--Little Lucy's Wonderful Globe, 1 of 30 vols. (Illus.). (Morning Glory Ser). N.D. Lothrop Pub. Co.
--Little Lucy's Wonderful Globe. (Illus.). N.D. Macmillan & Co.
--Little Lucy's Wonderful Globe. Peck, Anne Merriman (1884-), illus. LC 27-18543. 4 p. l., 103 p. incl. illus., plates. col front. 17 1/2 cm. 1927. Harper & Brothers.
--Little Lucy's Wonderland Globe. (Illus.). (The Little Women Ser.). N.D. A. L. Burt's Pubs.
--Little Three-Year Old Library, 3 vols. N.D. Set. D. Lothrop & Co.
--Love and Life: A Tale. (Illus.). N.D. Macmillan & Co.
--Magnum Bonum: or, Mother Carey's Brood. (Illus.). N.D. Macmillan & Co.
--More Hannah. N.D. Robert Brothers.
--More Links of the Daisy Chain. N.D. Macmillan & Co.
--Mother Goose. Yonge, Charlotte Mary (1823-1901), illus. (Illus.). (Aunt Charlotte's Picture Book). 1888. R Worthington.
--New Ground. (Illus.). N.D. E. P. Dutton & Co.
--Noah's Ark, 1 of 12 Vols. (Illus.). (Aunt Charlotte's Picture Book). 1888. R Worthington.
--Nuttie's Father. New ed. (Illus.). (Works by Charlotte Yonge). N.D. Macmillian.
--Old Mother Hubbard, 1 of 12 Vols. Yonge, Charlotte Mary (1823-1901), illus. (Illus.). (Aunt Charlotte's Picture Book). 1888. R Worthington.
--Our New Mistress: Or, Changes at Brookfield Earl. N.D. Thomas Whittaker.
--The Patriots of Palestine: A Story of the Maccabees. N.D. Thomas Whittaker.
--The Peasant Tale of Puss and Robin. Frolich, Lorenz, illus. N.D. Macmillan & co.
--Pickle and His Page Boy. (Illus.). N.D. Publications of E. P. Dutton & Co.
--The Pigeon Pie. A Tale of Roundhead Times. LC 42-26786. 172 p. incl. front., illus. 17 1/2 cm. 1869. Roberts Brothers.
--The Pillars of the House, Vols 1-2. New ed. (Illus.). N.D. Macmillian & Co.
--Population of an Old Pear Tree: Or, Stories of Insect Life. (Illus.). N.D. MacMillan & Co.
--The Prince and the Page, 1 of 4 Vols. (Illus.). (Miss Yonge's Historical Stories). N.D. Lothrop Lee & Shepard Co.
--The Prince & the Page. (Prize Library). N.D. Macmillan.
--THe Prince and the Page. (Works for the Young). N.D. Macmillan & Co.
--The Prince & the Page: A Tale of the Last Crusade. New ed. (Illus.). N.D. MacMillan.
--The Princess of Silverland. N.D. Macmillan & Co.
--P's and Q's: Or, the Question of Putting Upon, and Little Lucy's Wonderful Globe. Globe ed. LC 48-35066. xiii, 288 p. illus. 20 cm. 1899. Macmillan.
--Puss in Boots, 1 of 12 Vols. Yonge, Charlotte Mary (1823-1901), illus. (Illus.). (Aunt Charlotte's Picture Book). 1888. R Worthington.
--Red Ridinghood, 1 of 12 Vols. Yonge, Charlotte Mary (1823-1901), illus. (Illus.). (Aunt Charlotte Picture Book). 1888. R Worthington.
--The Runaway. N.D. Macmillan & Co.
--Santa Claus, 1 of 12 Vols. Yonge, Charlotte Mary (1823-1901), illus. (Illus.). (Aunt Charlotte's Picture Book). 1888. R Worthington.
--Sewing and Sowing. (Illus.). N.D. E. P. Dutton & Co.
--Six Cushions. (Illus.). N.D. E & J B Young.
--Six Cushions. (Illus.). N.D. E. P. Dutton.
--The Slaves of Sabinus: New Stories. N.D. Set 6.25. Thomas Whittaker.

--The Stokesley Secret. (Illus.). N.D. E. P. Dutton & Co.
--The Stokesley Secret: Or, How the Pig Paid the Rent. LC 42-267872. 245 p. front., plates. 15 cm. 1862. D. Appleton & Company.
--The Story of Wandering Willie. (Library of Choice Fiction). N.D. Charles Scribner's Sons.
--The Story of Wandering Willie. Paton, Joseph Noel, Sir (1821-1901), illus. N.D. Macmillan & Co.
--The Three Brides, 1 of 12 vols. (NO.7). N.D. D. Appleton and Co.
--The Three Brides. New Ed. ed. (Illus.). N.D. Macmillian & Co.
--Tom Thumb, 1 of 12 Vols. Yonge, Charlotte Mary (1823-1901), illus. (Illus.). (Aunt Charlotte Picture Book). 1888. R Worthington.
--The Treasures in the Marshes. N.D. Thomas Whittaker.
--The Trial, 1 of 12 Vol. N.D. D. Appleton and Co.
--The Two Guardians, 1 of 12 Vols. N.D. D. Appleton and Co.
--Two Guardians or Home in the World. (Illus.). N.D. E. P. Dutton & Co.
--Two Penniless Princesses. McCracken, Elizabeth (1876-), ed. Good, Stafford C. (1890-), illus. LC 31-9631. xiii p., 1 l., 238 p. col. front., illus., col. plates. 19 1/2 cm. (The Green and blue library). 1931. The Macmillan Company.
--Under the Storm: Or, Steadfast's Charge, 1 of 5 Vols. N.D. Set 6.25. Thomas Whittaker.
--Village Children. LC 67-100240. 158 p. 26 1/2 cm. (Gollancz revivals) 15/-). 1967. Gollancz.
--The Wardship of Steepcoombe. N.D. Thomas Whittaker.
--Whittington and his Cat, 1 of 12 Vols. Yonge, Charlotte Mary (1823-1901), illus. (Illus.). (Aunt Charlotte's Picture Book). 1888. R Worthington.
--Young Stepmother, 1 of 12 Vols. (Vol. 8). N.D. D. Appleton and Co.
--Young Stepmother. (Illus.). N.D. MacMillian.

Yonge, Charlotte Mary (1823-1901), ed.
--A Book of Golden Deeds of All Times and All Lands. xi, 466 p. front., plates. 19 cm. 1877. D. Lothrop & Co.
--A Book of Golden Deeds of All Times and All Lands. viii, 367, 1 p. 17 1/2 cm. (Half-title: Everyman's library, ed. by Ernest Rhys. For young people no. 330). 1908. J. M. Dent. & Co.
--A Book of Golden Deeds of All Times and All Lands. LC 15-16692. xi, 454 p. 18 cm. (Half-title: Golden treasury series). 1882. Macmillan and Co.
--A Book of Golden Deeds of All Times and All Lands. LC 16-4522. xi, 466 p. 16 1/2 cm. 1866. Sever and Francis.
--The Book of Golden Deeds of All Times and All Lands ... LC 15-2599. 2 p. l., 13-314 p. 24 cm. (Christian herald librarys). c.1895. The Christian Herald.
--Byewords: A Collection of Tales Old and New. (Illus.). N.D. MacMillian.
--Goody Two Shoes. (First Ser.). (Storehouse of Stories). N.D. Macmillan & Co.
--The Governess. (First Ser.). (Storehouse of Stories). N.D. Macmillan & Co.
--History of Little Jack. (First Ser.). (Storehouse of Stories). N.D. Macmillan & Co.
--Jemima Placid. (First Ser.). (Storehouse of Stories). N.D. Macmillan & Co.
--The Little Queen. (First Ser.). (Storehouse of Stories). N.D. Macmillan & Co.
--The Perambulations of a Mouse. (First Ser.). (Storehouse of Stories). N.D. Macmillan & co.
--A Storehouse of Stories, 1 of 2 ser, Ser. 1. N.D. Set. MacMillan.
--A Storehouse of Stories, 1 of 2 ser, Ser. 2. N.D. Set. MacMillan.
--The Village School. (Storehouse of Stories). N.D. Macmillan & Co.

Yonge, Charlotte Mary (1823-1901) & Dickens, Charles John Huffam (1812-1870)
--The Little Duke, and A Christmas Carol, 2 Vols. in 1. N.D. Appleton-Century-Crofts.

Yonge, Charlotte Mary (1823-1901) & Kingsley, H.
--The Lost Child. N.D. Macmillan & co.

Yonge, Charlotte Mary (1823-1901) & Maguire, J. F.
--Prince Marigold. Waller, S. E., illus. N.D. Macmillan & Co.

Yonge, Charlotte Mary (1823-1901) & Mazini, Linda
--In the Golden Shell: A Story of Palermo. N.D. Macmillan & Co.

Yonge, Charlotte Mary (1823-1901) & Weld, Horatio Hastings (1811-1888)
--Aunt Charlotte's Stories of American History. LC 2-5801. 442 p. illus. 14 1/2 x 18 cm. 1883. D. Appleton and Company.

Yoo, Grace S, pseud., see Yoo, Young Hyun.

Yoo, Grace S, pseud. (1927-)
--Two Korean Brothers: The Story of Hungbu and Nolbu. Yoo, Young Hyun. LC 73-18023. (Illus.). 51 p. (Series: Far Eastern Research and Publications Center.). (Ferpc Ser. of Oriental Stories: No. 7). 1970. Far Eastern Research and Publications Center.

Yoo, Young Hyun see Yoo, Grace S, pseud.

Yoo, Yushin (1940-), retold by.
--Bong Nam and the Pheasants. Demi, pseud. (1942-), illus. Hitz, Demi. LC 79-15749. (Illus.). 22 p. 19cm. c.1979. (ISBN 0-13-079657-3). Prentice-Hall.

Yoon, Francis Taewon, jt. auth. see Yun, Sok-Chung.

Yorgason, Blaine M. (1942-) & Yorgason, Brenton G.
--The Bishop's Horse Race. LC 79-54894. vi, 160 p. 23cm. c.1979. (ISBN 0-88494-385-2). Bookcraft.

Yorgason, Brenton G., jt. auth. see Yorgason, Blaine M.

Yorinks, Arthur see Yaffe, Alan, pseud.

Yorinks, Arthur (1953-)
--It Happened in Pinsk. Yaffe, Alan, pseud. Egielski, Richard (1952-), illus. LC 83-1727. p. cm. 1983. (ISBN 0-374-33651-2). Farrar, Straus & Giroux.
--Louis the Fish. Yaffe, Alan, pseud. Egielski, Richard (1952-), illus. LC 80-16855. (Illus.). 32p. (ps-3). 1980. (ISBN 0-374-34658-5). FS&G.
--Sid and Sol. Yaffe, Alan, pseud. Egielski, Richard (1952-), illus. LC 77-24126. p. cm. 1977. (ISBN 0-374-36904-6). Farrar, Straus and Giroux.

Yorinks, Arthur (1953-) & Andersen, Karen Born
--The Magic Meatballs. Yaffe, Alan, pseud. LC 78-72472. p. cm. 40p. c.1979. (ISBN 0-8037-5139-7). (ISBN 0-8037-5140-0). Dial Press.

York, Carol Beach, jt. auth. see Beach, Mary.

York, Carol Beach (1928-), ed. see Irving, Washington.

York, Carol Beach (1928-)
--Beware of This Shop. LC 77-7085. p. cm. c.1977. (ISBN 0-8407-6549-5). T. Nelson.
--The Blue Umbrella. Sandin, Joan (1942-), illus. (Illus.). 116 p. 21cm. 1968. F. Watts.
--The Christmas Dolls: A Butterfield Square Story. De Larrea, Victoria, illus. LC 67-507794. 100p. illus. 21cm. 1967. Watts.
--Dead Man's Cat: A Mystery. LC 77-181675. 112 p. 21cm. 1972. (ISBN 0-8407-6218-6). (ISBN 0-8407-6219-4). T. Nelson.
--The Doll in the Bakeshop. Turkle, Brinton Cassaday (1915-), illus. LC 65-21642. (Illus.). 98 p. 21cm. 1965. F. Watts.
--Febold Feboldson, the Fix-It Farmer. Trivas, Irene, illus. LC 79-66321. (Illus.). 47 p. 23cm. (Folk Tales of America). c.1980. (ISBN 0-89375-312-2). (ISBN 0-89375-311-4). Troll Associates.
--The Ghost of the Isherwoods. LC 66-12120. 118p. 21cm. c.1966. Watts.
--Good Charlotte: A Butterfield Square Story. De Larrea, Victoria, illus. LC 71-79850. (Illus.). 100 p. 22cm. 1969. (ISBN 0-531-01896-2). Watts.
--Good Day Mice: A Butterfield Square Story. De Larrea, Victoria, illus. (Illus.). line drawings. 108p. (gr. 2-5). 1968. (ISBN 0-531-01682-X). Watts.
--I Will Make You Disappear. LC 74-13995. p. cm. 1974. (ISBN 0-8407-6410-3). T. Nelson.
--The Look-Alike Girl. LC 80-22102. 125 p. 21cm. c.1980. (ISBN 0-8253-0016-9). Beaufort Books.
--The Midnight Ghost. Robinson, Charles (1931-), illus. LC 72-94627. (Illus.). 49, 15 p. 23cm. (Break-of-Day Book). 1973. (ISBN 0-698-20261-9). (ISBN 0-698-20261-9). Coward, McCann & Geoghegan.
--Mike Fink. Parker, Edward, illus. LC 79-66315. (Illus.). 48 p. 23cm. (Folk Tales of America). c.1980. (ISBN 0-89375-302-5). (ISBN 0-89375-301-7). Troll Associates.
--Miss Know It All: A Butterfield Square Story. De Larrea, Victoria, illus. LC 66-186702. 87p. illus. 22cm. c.1966. Watts.
--Miss Know It All Returns: A Butterfield Square Story. De Larrea, Victoria, illus. LC 72-185603. (Illus.). 72 p. 21cm. 1972. (ISBN 0-531-02558-6). Watts.
--Mystery at Dark Wood. Nebel, Gustave E., illus. LC 70-175801. (Illus.). 120 p. 22cm. 1972. (ISBN 0-531-02038-X). Watts.
--The Mystery of the Diamond Cat. Burke, Roseanne, illus. LC 69-11526. (Illus.). 112 p. 21cm. 1969. F. Watts.
--The Mystery of the Spider Doll. Payson, Dale (1943-), illus. LC 72-6073. (Illus.). 90 p. 21cm. 1973. (ISBN 0-531-02601-9). F. Watts.
--Nothing Ever Happens Here. LC 75-106180. 103 p. 22cm. 1970. Hawthorn Books.
--Old Stormalong, the Seafaring Sailor. Harvey, Paul (1926-), illus. LC 79-66322. (Illus.). 45 p. 23cm. (Folk Tales of America). c.1980. (ISBN 0-89375-314-9). (ISBN 0-89375-313-0). Troll Associates.
--Remember Me When I Am Dead. LC 80-13461. 94 p. 21cm. c.1980. (ISBN 0-525-66694-X). Elsevier/Nelson Books.
--Revenge of the Dolls. LC 79-10761. 103 p. 21cm. c.1979. (ISBN 0-525-66632-X). Elsevier-Nelson Books.
--Sam Patch, the Big Time Jumper. Dodson, Bert, illus. LC 79-66318. (Illus.). 46 p. 23cm. (Folk Tales of America). c.1980. (ISBN 0-89375-306-8). (ISBN 0-89375-305-X). Troll Associates.
--The Secret. 192p. (Orig.). (gr. 7 up). 1984. (ISBN 0-590-33098-5, Windswept Bks). Scholastic Inc.
--Sparrow Lake. LC 62-8620. 155 p. 21cm. 1962. Coward-McCann.
--Stray Dog. LC 80-28779. 96 p. 22cm. c.1981. (ISBN 0-8253-0046-0). Beaufort Books.
--Takers and Returners: A Novel of Suspense. LC 72-13123. 123 p. 21cm. 1973. (ISBN 0-8407-6292-5). T. Nelson.
--The Ten O'Clock Club: A Butterfield Square Story. De Larrea, Victoria, illus. LC 76-115775. (Illus.). 120 p. 21cm. 1970. (ISBN 0-531-01944-6). Watts.
--The Tree House Mystery. Lonette, Reisie Dominee (1924-), illus. LC 72-85621. (Illus.). 90 p. 20cm. 1973. (ISBN 0-698-20236-8). (ISBN 0-698-20236-8). Coward, McCann & Geoghegan.
--Until We Fall in Love Again. 141 p. 21cm. 1967. F. Watts.
--When Midnight Comes. LC 79-18617. p. cm. c.1979. (ISBN 0-525-66676-1). Elsevier-Nelson Books.
--Where Love Begins. LC 63-15545. 122 p. 21cm. 1963. Coward-McCann.
--The Witch Lady Mystery. LC 76-146. 86 p. 21cm. c.1976. (ISBN 0-8407-6479-0). T. Nelson.

York, Christopher C.
--The Ram & the Black Sheep. LC 82-84423. (Illus.). 175p. (Daring Relations Involving Families & Their Black Sheep). (gr. 10 up). 1983. (ISBN 0-8187-0050-5). C C York.

York, Judith
--Peek-a-Boo!. York, Judith, illus. (Illus.). (ps). 1979. (Gingerbread). Dutton.

York, Susannah
--Lark's Castle. Balwin, Michael (1934-), illus. LC 76-25761. (Illus.). 112 p. 23cm. 1977, c.1976. (ISBN 0-679-20383-4). D. McKay Co.

Yorke, Anthony, pseud., see Reilly, Bernard James.

Yorke, Zaida, jt. auth. see Bailey, Urania Locke.

Yoseloff, Thomas, tr. see Yoseloff, Thomas (1913-) & Stuckey, Lillien.

Yoseloff, Thomas (1913-)
--The Further Adventures of Till Eulenspiegel. Frank, Jane, illus. Stuckey, Lillien, tr. LC 57-689256. 122p. illus. 24cm. 1957. T. Yoseloff.

Yoseloff, Thomas (1913-) & Stuckey, Lillien, eds.
--The Merry Adventures of Till Eulenspiegel. Brady, William, illus. Yoseloff, Thomas (1913-) & Stuckey, Lillien, trs. LC 44-21949. (Illus.). 145p. 23cm. 1944. B. Ackerman Inc.

Yoshiko Uchida
--The Magic Listening Cap. N.D. E. M. Hale and Co.

Youd, Samuel see Christopher, John, pseud.

Youlin, Frances Cole
--The Wooloo and Lita May. Braley, Margaret Temple, illus. LC 42-21059. 70, 1 p. illus. (part col.) 22 1/2 x 17 1/2 cm. 1942. Cupples & Leon Company.

Youmans, Eleanor Williams, Mrs.
--Cinder. Shields, F. Bernard, illus. LC 33-23354. 3 p. l., 11-132 p. illus. 20 cm. c.1933. The Bobbs-Merrill Company.
--The Forest Road: Two Boys in the Ozarks. Froderstrom, Alma Wentzel, illus. LC 39-21290. 158 p. illus. 21 cm. c.1939. The Bobbs-Merrill Company.
--The Great Adventures of Jack, Jock and Funny. Rannells, Will (1892-), illus. LC 38-24565. 178 p. incl., front., illus., plates. 22 1/2 cm. c.1938. The Bobbs-Merrill Company.
--Little Dog Mack: The Story of a Wirehaired Terrier. Trencck, Van, illus. LC 36-19101. 4 p. l., 13-137 p. incl. illus., plates, front. 20 cm. c.1936. The Bobbs-Merrill Company.
--Mount Delightful: The Story of Ellen Evans and Her Dog Taffy. James, Sandra, illus. LC 44-8260. 155 p. illus. 21 cm. 1944. The Bobbs-Merrill Company.
--Skitter and Skeet. Bennett, Ruth, illus. LC 28-211713. 139, 1 p. illus. 20 cm. c.1928. The Bobbs-Merrill Company.
--Skitter Cat. Bennett, Ruth, illus. LC 25-21401. 3 p. l., 125, 1 p., 1 l., illus. 20 cm. c.1925. The Bobbs-Merrill Company.
--Skitter Cat and Little Boy. Bennett, Ruth, illus. LC 26-15976. 143, 1 p. illus. 20 cm. c.1926. The Bobbs-Merrill Company.
--Skitter Cat and Major. Bennett, Ruth, illus. LC 27-180579. 153, 1 p. illus. 20 cm. c.1927. The Bobbs-Merrill Company.
--The Skitter Cat Book: Containing Skitter Cat, Skitter Cat and Major, Skitter Cat and Little Boy. Taber, J. J., illus. LC 47-6538. 261 p. illus. (part col.) 23 cm. 1947. Bobbs-Merrill Co.
--Teddy Horse: The Story of a Runaway Pony. King, Ruth, illus. LC 30-23595. 136, 1 p. illus. 20 cm. c.1930. The Bobbs-Merrill Company.
--Timmy: The Dog That Was Different. Rannells, Will (1892-), illus. LC 41-17043. 190 p. 1 l., incl. front., illus. plates. 22 1/2 x 17 cm. c.1941. The Bobbs-Merrill Company.

Youmans, Eleanor Williams, Mrs. & Rannells, Will (1892-)
--Waif: The Story of Spe. Rannells, Will (1892-), illus. LC 37-207497. 4 p. l., 3-138 p. col. front., illus., plates. 22 1/2 cm. c.1937. The Bobbs-Merrill Company.

Young, Alida E
--Land of the Iron Dragon. LC 77-16892. (Illus.). 213 p. 22cm. c.1978. (ISBN 0-385-13567-X). (ISBN 0-385-13568-8). Doubleday.

Young, Andrew (1885-1971)
--Quiet As Moss. Hassall, Joan (1906-), illus. 1962. Dufour Editions.

Young, Anne Spottswood, compiled by.
--The Cats of Long Ago: And Other Stories. LC 7-41055. 64 p. incl. front., illus. 16 1/2 cm. c.1907. Eaton & Mains.
--Fairy Worlds: And Other Stories. LC 7-40279. 64 p. incl. front., illus. 16 1/2 cm. c.1907. Eaton & Mains.
--The Home of the Hermit Crab: And Other Stories. LC 7-41578. 64 p. incl. front., illus. 17 cm. c.1907. Eaton & Mains.
--Janie's Valentine: And Other Stories. LC 7-40793. 64 p. incl. front., illus. 17 cm. c.1907. Eaton & Mains.
--The Liberty Bell: And Other Stories. LC 7-41053. 64 p. incl. front., illus. 16 1/2 cm. c.1907. Eaton & Mains.
--Little Builders of the Sea: And Other Stories. LC 7-41054. 63, 1 p. incl. front., illus. 16 1/2 cm. c.1907. Eaton & Mains.
--A Lonesome Dollie: And Other Stories. LC 7-40280. 64 p. incl. front., illus. 16 1/2 cm. c.1907. Eaton & Mains.
--Madcap Cousin: And Other Stories. LC 7-40281. 63, 1 p. incl. front., illus. 16 1/2 cm. c.1907. Eaton & Mains.
--Queen O' the May: And Other Stories. LC 7-40792. 64 p. incl. front., illus. 17 cm. c.1907. Eaton & Mains.
--Seven Times One: And Other Stories. LC 7-40791. 64 p. incl. front., illus. 16 1/2 cm. c.1907. Eaton & Mains.
--Toyland: And Other Stories. LC 7-41052. 64 p. incl. front., illus. 17 cm. c.1907. Eaton & Mains.
--Wahbegwannee, the White Flower, and Other Stories. LC 7-41051. 64 p. incl. front., illus. 17 cm. c.1907. Eaton & Mains.

Young, Barbara (1878-)
--Christopher O!. Barton, Mary, illus. LC 47-31143. 1 v. (unpaged) illus. 21 cm. 1947. D. McKay Co.
--The Puppet Man. Barton, Mary, illus. N.D. David McKay Co.
--The Puppet Man and Other Stories. Barton, Mary, illus. LC 48-3910. 111 p. illus. (part col) 21 cm. 1946. Reynal & Hitchcock.

Young, Beatrice
--Winds, Waves and Wonders. Dowling, Colista, illus. 124p. N.D. Binfords & Mort.

Young, Ben T.
--Rock River Ranger. Hogner, Nils (1893-1970), illus. LC 53-10642. 157p. illus. 22cm. 1953. Abelard Press.

Young, Bennett Henderson (1843-1919)
--Dr. Gander of Youngland. Cobb, Irvin S., frwd. by. LC 22-9071. 3 p. l., 5-170 p. front. (port.) illus., plates (part double) 23 1/2 cm. c.1921. The Standard Printing Co.

Young, Bess Margaret
--Animals We Know. Thomson, J. Murry, illus. LC 27-180603. 96 p. incl. col. front., col. illus. 15 1/2 cm. 1927. T. Nelson and Sons.

Young, Bess Margaret, jt. ed. see Barnes, Emily Ann.

Young, Biloine W. (1926-) & Wilson, Mary (1926-)
--How Carla Saw the Shalako God. Samson, Anne Stringer (1933-), illus. LC 73-160494. (Illus.). 31 p. 24cm. c.1972. (ISBN 0-8309-0088-8). Printed by Independence Press.
--Jennie Redbird Finds Her Friends. Samson, Anne Stringer (1933-), illus. LC 73-161081. (Illus.). 31 p. 24cm. 1973, c.1972. (ISBN 0-8309-0087-X). Independence Press.
--The Medicine Man Who Went to School. Samson, Anne Stringer (1933-), illus. LC 73-161187. (Illus.). 29 p. 24cm. 1973, c.1972. (ISBN 0-8309-0086-1). Independence Press.

Young, Blanche Cowley, retold by.
--How the Manx Cat Lost Its Tail, and Other Manx Folk Stories. Unwin, Nora Spicer (1907-), illus. LC 59-5385. 114 p. illus. 22 cm. 1959. McKay.

Young, Bob, pseud., see Young, Robert William.

Young, Bob, pseud. (1916-1969) & Young, Jan, pseud. (1919-)
--Across the Tracks. Young, Robert William. Young, Janet Randall. LC 58-10924. 192 p. 22cm. 1958. Messner.
--Anza, Hard-Riding Captain. Young, Robert William. Young, Janet Randall. (Illus.). (gr. 7 up). 1967. (ISBN 0-87464-004-0). Golden Gate.
--Good-Bye, Amigos. Young, Robert William. Young, Janet Randall. LC 63-16795. 191 p. 21 cm. 1963. J. Messner.
--One Small Voice. Young, Robert William. Young, Janet Randall. LC 61-6367. 192 p. 22 cm. 1961. J. Messner.
--Run Sheep Run. Young, Robert William. Young, Janet Randall. LC 59-12754. 192 p. 22 cm. 1959. Messner.
--Sunday Dreamer. Young, Robert William. Young, Janet Randall. LC 62-10203. 192 p. 22cm. 1962. Messner.
--Where Tomorrow?. Young, Robert William. Young, Janet Randall. 191 p. 22cm. 1967. Abelard-Schuman.

Young, C. T.
--Black Princess and Other Fairy Tales. (Folk Lore & Fairy Tales). (MacMillan Bks. for Boys & Girls). (gr. 4-6). N.D. MacMillan Bks.

Young, Carol
--What Shall We Be?. Young, Carol, illus. LC 65-161341. (Illus.). unpaged. 28cm. 1965. St. Anthony.

Young, Charles
--Tales of Jack and Jane. Walker, W. H., illus. N.D. John Lane Co.

Young, Chic, pseud., see Young, Murat Bernard Chic.

Young, Clarence, pseud., see Stratemeyer Syndicate.

Young, Clarence, pseud.
--Jack Ranger's Gun Club: Or, From Schoolroom to Camp and Trail. Stratemeyer Syndicate. Nuttall, Charles, illus. 20cm. 288p. (The Jack Ranger Ser.: Vol. 5). 1910. Cupples & Leon Company.
--Jack Ranger's Gun Club: Or, From Schoolroom to Camp and Trail. Stratemeyer Syndicate. Nuttall, Charles, illus. Reissue of 1910 ed. (The Jack Ranger Ser.: Vol. 5). 1915. Cupples & Leon.
--Jack Ranger's Ocean Cruise: Or, The Wreck of the Polly Ann. Stratemeyer Syndicate. Nuttall, Charles, illus. LC 29-307836. 2 p. l., 307 p. front., plates. 19 1/2 cm. (The Jack Ranger Ser.: Vol. 4). 1909. Cupples & Leon Company.
--Jack Ranger's Ocean Cruise: Or, The Wreck of the Polly Ann. Stratemeyer Syndicate. Nuttall, Charles, illus. Reissue of 1909 ed. (The Jack Ranger Ser.: Vol. 4). 1915. Cupples & Leon.
--Jack Ranger's School Days: Or, The Rivals of Washington Hall. Stratemeyer Syndicate. Nuttall, Charles, illus. Reissue of 1907 ed. (The Jack Ranger Ser.: Vol. 1). 1915. Cupples & Leon.
--Jack Ranger's School Victories: Or, Track, Gridiron and Diamond. Stratemeyer Syndicate. Nuttall, Charles, illus. LC 29-30784. 2 p. l., 286 p. front., plates. 19 1/2 cm. (The Jack Ranger Ser.: Vol. 3). 1908. Cupples & Leon Company.
--Jack Ranger's School Victories: Or, Track, Gridiron and Diamond. Stratemeyer Syndicate. Nuttall, Charles, illus. Reissue of 1908 ed. (The Jack Ranger Ser.: Vol. 3). 1915. Cupples & Leon.
--Jack Ranger's Schooldays: Or, The Rivals of Washington Hall. Stratemeyer Syndicate. Nuttall, Charles, illus. LC 7-25163. 2 p. l., 306 p. front., plates. 19 1/2 cm. (The Jack Ranger Ser.: Vol. 1). c.1907. Cupples & Leon Co.
--Jack Ranger's Treasure Box: Or, The Outing of the Schoolboy Yachtsmen. Stratemeyer Syndicate. Nuttall, Charles, illus. LC 29-30782. 2 p. l., 303 p. front., plates. 19 1/2 cm. (The Jack Ranger Ser.: Vol. 6). 1911. Cupples & Leon Company.
--Jack Ranger's Treasure Box: Or, The Outing of the Schoolboy Yachtsmen. Stratemeyer Syndicate. Nuttall, Charles, illus. Reissue of 1911 ed. (The Jack Ranger Ser.: Vol. 6). 1915. Cupples & Leon.
--Jack Ranger's Western Trip: Or, From Boarding School to Ranch and Range. Stratemeyer Syndicate. Nuttall, Charles, illus. 20cm. 302p. (The Jack Ranger Ser.: Vol. 2). 1908. Cupples & Leon Company.
--Jack Ranger's Western Trip: Or, From Boarding School to Ranch and Range. Stratemeyer Syndicate. Nuttall, Charles, illus. Reissue of 1908 ed. (The Jack Ranger Ser.: Vol. 2). 1915. Cupples & Leon Co.
--The Motor Boys Across the Plains: Or, the Hermit of Lost Lake. Stratemeyer Syndicate. Nuttall, Charles, illus. LC 7-24155. 3 p. l., 248 p. front., plates. 19 1/2 cm. (The Motor Boys Ser.: Vol. 4). c.1907. Cupples & Leon Co.
--The Motor Boys Across the Plains: Or, the Hermit of Lost Lake. Stratemeyer Syndicate. Nuttall, Charles, illus. Reissue of 1907 ed. (The Motor Boys Ser.: Vol. 4). 1915. Cupples & Leon.
--The Motor Boys Afloat: Or, The Cruise of the Dartaway. Stratemeyer Syndicate. Nuttall, Charles, illus. Reissue of 1908 ed. (The Motor Boys Ser.: Vol. 5). 1915. Cupples & Leon.
--The Motor Boys Afloat: Or, The Stirring Cruise of the Dartaway. Stratemeyer Syndicate. Nuttall, Charles, illus. LC 8-9524. 3 p. l., 244 p. front., plates. 19 1/2 cm. (The Motor Boys Ser.: Vol. 5). c.1908. Cupples & Leon Company.
--The Motor Boys After a Fortune: Or, The Hut on Snake Island. Stratemeyer Syndicate. Richards, Dick, illus. LC 12-18058. 3 p. l., 248 p. front., plates. 19 cm. (The Motor Boys Ser.: Vol. 13). c.1912. Cupples & Leon Company.
--The Motor Boys in Mexico: Or, The Secret of the Buried City. Stratemeyer Syndicate. Nuttall, Charles, illus. vi, 237 p. front., plates. 19 1/2 cm. (The Motor Boys Ser.: Vol. 3). c.1906. Cupples & Leon Company.
--The Motor Boys in Mexico: Or, The Secret of the Buried City. Stratemeyer Syndicate. Nuttall, Charles, illus. Reissue of 1906 ed. (The Motor Boys Ser.: Vol. 3). 1915. Cupples & Leon.
--The Motor Boys in Strange Waters: Or, Lost in a Floating Forest. Stratemeyer Syndicate. Nuttall, Charles, illus. LC 9-7824. 3 p. l., 248 p. front., plates. 19 1/2 cm. (The Motor Boys Ser.: Vol. 7). c.1909. Cupples & Leon Company.
--The Motor Boys in Strange Waters: Or, Lost in a Floating Forest. Stratemeyer Syndicate. Nuttall, Charles, illus. Reissue of 1909 ed. (The Motor Boys Ser.: Vol. 7). 1915. Cupples & Leon.
--The Motor Boys in the Clouds: Or, A Trip for Fame and Fortune. Stratemeyer Syndicate. Nuttall, Charles, illus. 20cm. 248p. (The Motor Boys Ser.: Vol. 9). 1910. Cupples & Leon Company.
--The Motor Boys on Road and River: Or, Racing to Save a Life. Stratemeyer Syndicate. Rogers, Walter S., illus. LC 15-153028. 3 p. l., 248 p. front., plates. 19 cm. (The Motor Boys Ser.: Vol. 16). c.1915. Cupples & Leon Company.
--The Motor Boys on the Atlantic: Or, The Mystery of the Lighthouse. Stratemeyer Syndicate. Nuttall, Charles, illus. 20cm. 247p. (The Motor Boys Ser.: Vol. 6). 1908. Cupples & Leon Company.
--The Motor Boys on the Atlantic: Or, The Mystery of the Lighthouse. Stratemeyer Syndicate. Nuttall, Charles, illus. Reissue of 1908 ed. (The Motor Boys Ser.: Vol. 6). 1915. Cupples & Leon.
--The Motor Boys on the Border: Or, Sixty Nuggets of Gold. Stratemeyer Syndicate. Richards, Dick, illus. LC 13-7520. 3 p. l., 246 p. front., plates. 19 cm. (The Motor Boys Ser.: Vol. 14). c.1913. Cupples & Leon Company.
--The Motor Boys on the Pacific: Or, The Young Derelict Hunters. Stratemeyer Syndicate. Nuttall, Charles, illus. 20cm. 244p. (The Motor Boys Ser.: Vol. 8). 1909. Cupples & Leon Company.
--The Motor Boys on the Pacific: Or, The Young Derelict Hunters. Stratemeyer Syndicate. Nuttall, Charles, illus. Reissue of 1909 ed. (The Motor Boys Ser.: Vol. 8). 1915. Cupples & Leon.
--The Motor Boys on the Wing: Or, Seeking the Airship Treasure. Stratemeyer Syndicate. Richards, Dick, illus. 20cm. 243p. (The Motor Boys Ser.: Vol. 12). 1912. Cupples & Leon Co.
--The Motor Boys on Thunder Mountain: Or, The Treasure Chest of Blue Rock. Stratemeyer Syndicate. Rogers, Walter S., illus. LC 24-14873. 2 p. l., 248 p. front., plates. 19 1/2 cm. (The Motor Boys Second Ser.: Vol. 22). c.1924. Cupples & Leon Company.
--The Motor Boys: Or, Chums Through Thick and Thin. Stratemeyer Syndicate. Nuttall, Charles, illus. LC 6-24579. vi, 246 p. front., plates. 19 1/2 cm. (The Motor Boys Ser.: Vol. 1). 1906. Cupples & Leon.
--The Motor Boys: Or, Chums Through Thick and Thin. Stratemeyer Syndicate. Nuttall, Charles, illus. Reissue of 1906 ed. (The Motor Boy Ser.: Vol. 1). 1915. Cupples & Leon.
--The Motor Boys Over the Ocean: Or, A Marvelous Rescue in Mid-Air. Stratemeyer Syndicate. Richards, Dick, illus. LC 44-142368. 3 p. l., 241 p. fornt., plates. 19 1/2 cm. (The Motor Boys Ser.: Vol. 11). c.1911. Cupples & Leon Company.
--The Motor Boys Over the Rockies: Or, A Mystery of the Air. Stratemeyer Syndicate. Richards, Dick, illus. 20cm. 248p. (The Motor Boys Ser.: Vol. 10). 1911. Cupples & Leon Company.
--The Motor Boys Overland: Or, A Long Trip for Fun and Adventure. Stratemeyer Syndicate. Nuttall, Charles, illus. Reissue of 1906 ed. (The Motor Boys Ser.: Vol. 2). 1915. Cupples & Leon.
--The Motor Boys Overland: Or, A Long Trip for Fun and Fortune. Stratemeyer Syndicate. Nuttall, Charles, illus. LC 6-28759. vi, 228 p. front., plates. 19 1/2 cm. (The Motor Boys Ser.: Vol. 2). c.1906. Cupples & Leon.
--The Motor Boys Under the Sea: Or, From Airship to Submarine. Stratemeyer Syndicate. Richards, Dick, illus. (The Motor Boys Ser.: Vol. 15). 1914. Cupples & Leon Co.
--Ned, Bob and Jerry at Boxwood Hall: Or, The Motor Boys As Freshmen. Stratemeyer Syndicate. Rogers, Walter S., illus. LC 16-25147. (Also issued as "The Motor Boys at Boxwood Hall; Or, Ned, Bob and Jerry as Freshmen"). 3 p. l., 248 p. front., plates. 19 1/2 cm. (The Motor Boys Second Ser.: Vol. 17). c.1916. Cupples & Leon Company.
--Ned, Bob and Jerry Bound for Home: Or, The Motor Boys on the Wrecked Troopship. Stratemeyer Syndicate. Owen, Robert Emmett (1878-), illus. (Also issued as "The Motor Boys Bound for Home; Or, Ned, Bob and Jerry on the Wrecked Troopship"). (The Motor Boys Second Ser.: Vol. 21). 1920. Cupples & Leon Company.
--Ned, Bob and Jerry in the Army: Or, The Motor Boys as Volunteers. Stratemeyer Syndicate. Owen, Robert Emmett (1878-), illus. (Also issued as "The Motor Boys in the Army; Or, Ned, Bob and Jerry as Volunteers"). (The Motor Boys Second Ser.: Vol. 19). 1918. Cupples & Leon Company.
--Ned, Bob and Jerry on a Ranch: Or, The Motor Boys Among the Cowboys. Stratemeyer Syndicate. Owen, Robert Emmett (1878-), illus. (Also issued as "The Motor Boys on a Ranch; Or, Ned, Bob and Jerry Among the Cowboys"). (The Motor Boys Second Ser.: Vol. 18). 1917. Cupples & Leon Company.
--Ned, Bob and Jerry On the Firing Line: Or, The Motor Boys Fighting for Uncle Sam. Stratemeyer Syndicate. Owen, Robert Emmett (1878-), illus. (Also issued as "The Motor Boys on the Firing Line: Or, Ned, Bob and Jerry Fighting for Uncle Sam"). (The Motor Boys Second Ser.: Vol. 20). 1919. Cupples & Leon Company.
--The Racer Boys at Boarding School: Or, Striving for the Championship. Stratemeyer Syndicate. Rogers, Walter S., illus. LC 12-181142. 2 p. l., 246 p. front., plates. 19 1/2 cm. (The Racer Boys Ser.: Vol. 2). c.1912. Cupples & Leon Company.
--The Racer Boys Forging Ahead: Or, The Rivals of the School League. Stratemeyer Syndicate. Rogers, Walter S., illus. (The Racer Boys Ser.: Vol. 6). 1914. Cupples & Leon.
--The Racer Boys on Guard: Or, The Rebellion at Riverview Hall. Stratemeyer Syndicate. Rogers, Walter S., illus. (The Racer Boys Ser.: Vol. 5). 1913. Cupples & Leon.
--The Racer Boys on the Prairies: Or, The Treasure of Golden Peak. Stratemeyer Syndicate. Rogers, Walter S., illus. LC 13-751942. 2 p. l., 246 p. front., plates. 19 1/2 cm. (The Racer Boys Ser.: Vol. 4). c.1913. Cupples & Leon Company.
--The Racer Boys: Or, The Mystery of the Wreck. Stratemeyer Syndicate. Rogers, Walter S., illus. LC 12-17966. 2 p. l., 244 p. front., plates. 19 1/2 cm. (The Racer Boys Ser.: Vol. 1). c.1912. Cupples & Leon Company.
--The Racer Boys to the Rescue: Or, Stirring Adventures in a Winter Camp. Stratemeyer Syndicate. Rogers, Walter S., illus. (The Racer Boys Ser.: Vol. 3). 1912. Cupples & Leon.

Young, David
--Marooned in Fraggle Rock. McClintock, Barbara, illus. LC 84-6670. (Illus.). 43 p. 23cm. c.1984. (ISBN 0-03-000719-4). Muppet Press : Holt, Rinehart, and Winston.

Young, Dorothea Bennett see Bennett, Dorothea, pseud.

Young, Ed, jt. auth. see Aesopus.

Young, Ed, jt. auth. see Ziner, Feenie.

Young, Ed (1931-)
--High on a Hill: A Book of Chinese Riddles. Young, Ed (1931-), illus. LC 79-24070. (Illus.). 64p. (gr. 3-5). 1980. (ISBN 0-529-05553-8, Philomel). (ISBN 0-529-05554-6). Putnam Pub Group. **Award: (ALA).**
--The Other Bone. Young, Ed (1931-), illus. LC 83-47706. (Illus.). 32p. (gr. k-3). 1984. (ISBN 0-06-026870-0, HarpJ). (ISBN 0-06-026871-9). Har-Row.
--The Rooster's Horns: A Chinese Puppet Play to Make & Perform. Young, Ed (1931-), illus. LC 78-9283. (Unicef Storycraft Bks). (ps-3). 1978. (ISBN 0-529-05446-9). (ISBN 0-529-05447-7). Putnam Pub Group.
--Up a Tree. Young, Ed (1931-), illus. LC 82-47733. p. cm. c.1983. (ISBN 0-06-026813-1). (ISBN 0-06-026814-X). Harper & Row. **Award: (NYT).**

Young, Ed (1931-), illus.
--Tales from the Arabian Nights: Re-Told from the Original Arabic. Dawood, N. J., tr. LC 77-16886. (Illus.). 1978. (ISBN 0-385-12365-5). Doubleday.

Young, Ed (1931-) & Bonnet, Leslie
--The Terrible Nung Gwama: A Chinese Folktale. Young, Ed (1931-), illus. LC 78-18766. (Illus.). 32 p. 22cm. (Series: A Unicef Storycraft Book.). c.1978. (ISBN 0-529-05444-2). (ISBN 0-529-05445-0). Collins.

Young, Egerton Ryerson (1840-1909)
--Duck Lake. (Bks. for Boy Scouts). N.D. Abingdon Press.
--Hector, My Dog: His Autobiography. (Illus.). 332p. N.D. W. A. Wilde Co.
--Just Dogs: Heroes of the North Shore. LC 27-3755. 151 p. col. front., illus. 20 cm. c.1926. The Sunday School Times Company.
--Stories from Indian Wigwams and Northern Camp Fires. (Bks. for Boy Scouts). N.D. Abingdon Press.
--Three Boys in the Wild North Land. Laughlin, J. E., illus. N.D. Methodist Bk Concern.
--Three Boys in the Wild North Land, Summer. Laughlin, J. E., illus. LC 12-40144. 260 p. front., illus., plates. 20 1/2 cm. 1896. Eaton & Mains.
--Three Boys in the Wild Northland. (Bks. for Boy Scouts). N.D. Abingdon Press.
--Winter Adventure of Three Boys in the Great Lone Land. Laughlin, J. E., illus. N.D. Methodist Bk Concern.
--Winter Adventures of Three Boys in the Great Lone Land. N.D. Abingdon Press.
--Winter Adventures of Three Boys in the Great Lone Land. Laughlin, J. E., illus. LC 99-4858. 377 p. incl. front. plates. 20 1/2 cm. c.1899. Eaton & Mains.

Young, Eleanor R. (1918-)
--Fathers, Fathers, Fathers. Young, Eleanor R. (1918-), illus. LC 72-128135. (Illus.). 36 p. 1971. (ISBN 0-513-01108-0). Denison.
--Mothers, Mothers, Mothers. Young, Eleanor R. (1918-), illus. LC 78-99272. (Illus.). 32 p. 1971. (ISBN 0-513-01107-2). Denison.

Young, Elizabeth, jt. auth. see Pardee, Laura.

Young, Ella (1867-1956)
--The Tangle-Coated Horse: And Other Tales, Episodes from the Fionn Saga. Bock, Vera, illus. LC 29-20258. 8 p. l., 186 p. incl. front., illus., plates. 22 1/2 cm. 1929. Longmans, Green and Co. **Award: (JNM).**
--Tangle-Coated Horse & Other Tales: Episodes from the Fionn Saga. Bock, Vera, illus. (Illus.). (gr. 5-9). 1968. (ISBN 0-679-20205-6). McKay.
--The Unicorn with Silver Shoes. Lawson, Robert (1892-1957), illus. LC 32-29194. xiii, 215 p. incl. front., illus., plates. 19 1/2 cm. 1932. Longmans, Green and Co.
--The Unicorn with Silver Shoes. Lawson, Robert (1892-1957), illus. 1960. Mckay.

Young, Ella (1867-1956), retold by.
--Celtic Wonder Tales. new ed. Gonne, Maud, illus. LC 24-26390. vii, 201, 1 p. illus. 20 cm. 1923. E. P. Dutton & Company.
--Wonder Smith & His Son. Artzybasheff, Boris Mikhailovich (1899-1965), illus. (Illus.). (gr. 5-8). 1957. (ISBN 0-679-20256-0). McKay.
--The Wonder Smith and His Son: A Tale from the Golden Childhood of the World. Artzybasheff, Boris Mikhailovich (1899-1965), illus. LC 27-5458. 191 p. incl. plates. 21 cm. 1927. Longmans, Green and Co. **Award: (JNM).**
--The Wonder Smith and His Son: A Tale from the Golden Childhood of the World. Artzybasheff, Boris Mikhailovich (1899-1965), illus. 1927. McKay.

Young, Emily Hilda (1880-)
--Jenny Wren. LC 33-4503. 3 p. l., 3-342 p. 19 1/2 cm. c.1933. Harcourt, Brace and Company.

Young, Epsie, jt. auth. see Sharp, Adda Mai Cummings.

Young, Ernest
--Adventures Among Hunters & Trappers. (The Adventure Library). N.D. J.B. Lippincott.

Young, Ernest & Fairgrieve, James
--Children of Many Lands. N.D. Appleton Century Co.
--Homes Far Away. N.D. Appleton Century Co.

Young, Evelyn Frances (1911-)
--The Tale of Tai. Young, Evelyn Frances (1911-), illus. LC 40-32781. 31 p. col. illus. 17 x 15 1/2 cm. c.1940. Oxford University Press.
--Wu and Lu and Li. Young, Evelyn Frances (1911-), illus. LC 59-7556. unpaged. illus. 18 x 16 cm. 1959, c.1939. H. Z. Walck.
--Wu and Lu and Li. Young, Evelyn Frances (1911-), illus. LC 40-13526. 31 p. col. illus. 17 x 16 cm. c.1939. Oxford University Press.

Young, Faye Early
--Gerald the Third. Lutz, Will, illus. LC 77-85332. (Illus.). 32 p. 28cm. c.1977. (ISBN 0-912500-05-0). La Leche League International.

Young, Frances Y
--The Secret of the Book-Shop: A Mystery Story for Boys and Girls. LC 38-12122. 5 p. l., 15-167, 1 p., 3 l. 1 illus. 20 cm. c.1938. Catholic Library Service.
--Secret of the Dark House: A Mystery Story for Girls. LC 34-5976. 2 p. l., 209 p. front. 20 cm. c.1934. Cupples & Leon Company.
Young, Frederica, jt. auth. see Kohl, Marguerite.
Young, Gerald
--Chuck, Fusky and Snout. (Illus.). (The Little Men Ser.). N.D. A. L. Burt's Pubs.
--Chuck, Fusky, and Snout: A Story of Wild Pigs. (The Rugby Series for Boys and Girls). N.D. A. L. Burt Company.
--The Witch's Kitchen. Pogany, Willy (1882-1955), illus. (Illus.). N.D. Thomas Y. Crowell.
Young, Gloria, pseud., see Seawell, Manon Young McConnell.
Young, Gloria
--Hermit's Hollow. N.D. Wm. B. Eerdmans Publishing Co.
Young, Helen (1938-)
--A Throne for Sesame. Hughes, Shirley (1929-), illus. LC 77-375086. (Illus.). 32 p. 26cm. 1979. (ISBN 0-233-96871-7). Deutsch.
--What Difference Does It Make, Danny?. Blake, Quentin (1932-), illus. LC 80-65665. (Illus.). 96p. (gr. 3-6). 1980. (ISBN 0-233-97248-X). Andre Deutsch.
--What Difference Does It Make Danny?. Blake, Quentin (1932-), illus. (gr. 4-6). 1980. Dutton.
--Wide-Awake Jake. Williams, Jenny (1939-), illus. LC 74-19424. (Illus.). 32 p. 21cm. 1975, c.1974. (ISBN 0-688-22024-X). (ISBN 0-688-22024-X). Morrow.
Young, Isador S
--Carson at Second. LC 66-16537. 191 p. 23 cm. 1966. Follett Pub. Co.
--Carson's Fast Break. LC 69-10599. 192 p. 23cm. 1969. Follett Pub. Co.
--A Hit and a Miss. LC 52-14290. 240 p. 21 cm. N.D. Wilcox and Follett.
--Quarterback Carson. 189 p. 23cm. 1967. Follett.
--The Two-Minute Dribble. LC 64-20350. 192 p. 23 cm. 1964. Follett Pub. Co.
Young, Jan, jt. auth. see Young, Bob.
Young, Janet Randall see Randall, Janet, pseud.
Young, Jim (1930-)
--When yhe Whale Came to My town. Bernstein, Dan, photos by. 1974. Borzoi Books.
Young, John Richard
--Arabian Cow Horse. Bjorklund, Lorence F. (1913-1978), illus. LC 53-10605. 256p. illus. 21cm. 1953. Wilcox and Follett Co.
--Arizona Cutting Horse. LC 56-8410. 207p. 21cm. 1956. Westminster Press.
--Champion of the Cross 5. LC 55-86381. 223p. 21cm. 1955. Westminster Press.
--Olympic Horseman. LC 57-9707. 223 p. 22 cm. 1957. Westminster Press.
Young, Katherine A
--Early Days in the Maple Land: Stories for Children. Heming, Arthur Henry Howard (1870-), illus. (Illus.). 125p. 1910. James Pott & Co.
Young, Lesley (1949-)
--Camembert and the Magic Lamp. LC 79-2256. p. cm. 1979. (ISBN 0-7064-1043-2). Mayflower Books.
--Introducing Camembert. LC 79-2255. p. cm. 1979. (ISBN 0-7064-1040-8). Mayflower Books.
Young, Lillian E
--The Adventures of Tommy Cat the Sailor. Young, Lillian E., illus. LC 28-25567. 165 p. 1 l. incl. col. front. illus., col. plates. 25 cm. c.1928. J. H. Sears & Company, Icn.
--Pussy-Willow's Naughty Kittens. Young, Lillian E., illus. LC 38-12771. 54 p. 1 l., incl. col. front., col. illus., col. plates. 27 1/2 cm. 1924. Funk & Wagnalls Company.
Young, Lois Horton (1911-1981)
--For A Child's Day. Locke, Margo & Locke, Vance, illus. N.D. (ISBN 0-687-13264-9). Abingdon Press.
--The Little Church That Grew. Padgett, Jim, illus. LC 65-14094. 1 v. (unpaged) col. illus. 23 cm. 1965. Abingdon Press.
--No Biscuits at All. Langner, Nola (1930-), illus. (gr. 1-3). 1966. (ISBN 0-377-06701-6). Friend Pr.
--This Is Benjamin. 24p. (ps-3). N.D. (ISBN 0-8170-0473-4). Judson.
--What Can You Decide?. 24p. (ps-3). N.D. (ISBN 0-8170-0476-9). Judson.
--Whatever Happened on Peony Street?. Walker, Jim, illus. (Illus.). 128 p. 21cm. 1968. Friendship Press.
Young, Louise B. (1919-)
--Best Foot Forward. Rivoli, Mario (1943-), illus. (Illus.). 32 p. 1968. Van Nostrand.
Young, Marian C., ed.
--In Your Own Backyard. LC 61-17993. (Illus.). 373 p. 25cm. (Collier's junior classics series). 1962. Crowell-Collier Pub. Co.
Young, Martha see Sheppard, Eli, pseud.
Young, Martha (1868-)
--Behind the Dark Pines. Conde, J. M., illus. LC 72-4641. (Illus.). xiii, 287 p. 22cm. (The Black Heritage Library Collection). 1972. (ISBN 0-8369-9133-8). Books for Libraries Press.
--Behind the Dark Pines. Conde, J. M., illus. LC 12-237157. xiv, 287, 1 p. incl. plates. front. 20 cm. $1.50. 1912. D. Appleton and Company.
--Plantation Bird Legends. Sheppard, Eli, pseud. Conde, J. M., illus. LC 70-152933. (Illus.). 249 p. 23cm. (The Black Heritage Library Collection). 1971, c.1902. (ISBN 0-8369-8778-0). Books for Libraries Press.
--Plantation Bird Legends. Sheppard, Eli, pseud. Conde, J. M., illus. LC 16-25125. 4 p. l., 5-249 p. incl. front., plates. 22 1/2 cm. 1916. D. Appleton and Company.
--Two Little Southern Sisters and Their Garden Plays. N.D. Hinds, Hayden & Eldredge.
--When We Were Wee: Tales of the Ten Grandchildren. Schneider, Sophie, illus. LC 12-216036. vii, 2, 153 p. front., illus. (incl. ports.) 18 cm. (Half-title: Every-child's series). 1912. The Macmillan Company.
Young, Mary
--Singing windows. (Illus.). 1962. Abingdon Press.
Young, Mary Stuart
--Coat of Many Colors. Savage, Steele (1900-), illus. 1940. J. B. Lippincott.
--Young King David. Savage, Steele (1900-), illus. 1948. J. B. Lippincott.
Young, Merwyn
--Adventures of the Cid. N.D. MacMillan.
Young, Michael
--The Imaginary Friend. LC 77-9925. (Illus.). (Moods & Emotions Ser.). (gr. k-3). 1977. (ISBN 0-8172-0960-3). Raintree Pubs.
Young, Mike (1945-)
--The Adventures of SuperTed in Outer Space. Lee, Rob (1948-) & Blake, David (1944-), illus. LC 84-24921. 32p. 1985. (ISBN 0-394-87210-X). Random House.
--SuperTed & the Stolen Rocket Ship. Hutchings, Tony, illus. LC 84-61460. (Illus.). 24p. (SuperTed Mini-Storybooks). (gr. 1-5). 1984. (ISBN 0-394-87154-5, BYR). Random.
--SuperTed and the Train Robbers. Chambless-Rigie, Jane, illus. LC 85-42710. p. cm. (Random House pictureback). c.1985. (ISBN 0-394-87463-3). Random House.
--SuperTed on the Planet Spot. Hutchings, Tony, illus. LC 84-61459. (Illus.). 24p. (SuperTed Mini-Storybooks). (gr. 1-5). 1984. (ISBN 0-394-87153-7, BYR). Random.
Young, Mina Arnold
--Jeannie of the 2-Bar-A. LC 76-21773. p. cm. 1976. (ISBN 0-8024-3443-6). Moody Press.
Young, Miriam Burt (1913-1974)
--A Bear Named George. Berson, Harold (1926-), illus. LC 72-90995. (Illus.). 44 p. 21cm. 1969. Crown Publishers.
--Beware the Polar Bear!. Safety on the Ice. Quackenbush, Robert Mead (1929-), illus. LC 70-116347. (Illus.). 35 p. 24cm. 1970. Lothrop, Lee & Shepard.
--Billy and Milly. Quackenbush, Robert Mead (1929-), illus. (Illus.). 32 p. 26cm. 1968. Lothrop, Lee & Shepard Co.
--Can't You Pretend?. Kellogg, Steven (1941-), illus. LC 71-94861. (Illus.). 31 p. 1970. Putnam.
--Christy and the Cat Jail. Porter, Patricia Grant, illus. LC 72-1083. (Illus.). 92 p. 22cm. 1972. Lothrop, Lee & Shepard.
--The Dollar Horse. Hutchinson, William Miller (1916-), illus. LC 61-10114. (Illus.). 128 p. 22cm. 1961. Harcourt, Brace & World.
--Five Pennies to Spend. Malvern, Corinne (1905-1956), illus. LC 55-14371. unpaged. illus. 21cm. (Little Golden Book, 238). 1955. Simon and Schuster.
--Georgie Finds a Grandpa. Wilkin, Eloise Burns (1904-), illus. LC 55-106773. unpaged. illus. 21cm. (Little Golden Book, 196). 1954. Simon and Schuster.
--If I Drove a Bus. Quackenbush, Robert Mead (1929-), illus. (Illus.). (gr. k-3). 1973. (ISBN 0-685-92927-2). Lothrop.
--If I Drove a Car. Quackenbush, Robert Mead (1929-), illus. LC 70-135297. (Illus.). 32 p. 1971. Lothrop, Lee & Shepard Co.
--If I Drove a Tractor. Quackenbush, Robert Mead (1929-), illus. LC 72-5142. (Illus.). 32p. (gr. k-3). 1973. (ISBN 0-688-41338-2). (ISBN 0-688-51338-7). Lothrop.
--If I Drove a Train. Quackenbush, Robert Mead (1929-), illus. LC 70-177317. (Illus.). 31 p. 1972. Lothrop, Lee & Shepard Co.
--If I Drove a Truck. Quackenbush, Robert Mead (1929-), illus. (Illus.). 31 p. 1967. Lothrop, Lee & Shepard Co.
--If I Flew a Plane. Quackenbush, Robert Mead (1929-), illus. LC 79-101481. (Illus.). 32 p. 1970. Lothrop, Lee & Shephard.
--If I Rode a Dinosaur. Quackenbush, Robert Mead (1929-), illus. LC 74-1186. (Illus.). 32 p. 1974. (ISBN 0-688-41591-1). (ISBN 0-688-41591-1). Lothrop, Lee & Shepard.
--If I Rode a Horse. Quackenbush, Robert Mead (1929-), illus. LC 72-5143. (Illus.). 33 p. 1973. (ISBN 0-688-40042-6). (ISBN 0-688-40042-6). Lothrop, Lee & Shepard Co.
--If I Rode an Elephant. Quackenbush, Robert Mead (1929-), illus. LC 74-732. (Illus.). 32 p. 1974. (ISBN 0-688-41589-X). (ISBN 0-688-41589-X). Lothrop, Lee & Shepard.
--If I Sailed a Boat. Quackenbush, Robert Mead (1929-), illus. LC 72-152841. (Illus.). 32 p. 1971. Lothrop, Lee & Shepard.
--Jellybeans for Breakfast. Komoda, Beverly (1939-), illus. LC 68-21082. (Illus.). 40 p. 1968. Parents' Magazine Press.
--King Basil's Birthday. Chess, Victoria (1939-), illus. LC 73-182288. (Illus.). 40 p. 20cm. 1973. (ISBN 0-531-02594-2). F. Watts.
--Marco's Chance. 1st ed. Sibley, Don (1922-), illus. LC 59-6563. 190 p. illus. 21 cm. 1959. Harcourt, Brace.
--Miss Suzy. Lobel, Arnold Stark (1933-), illus. LC 64-10363. (Illus.). 42 p. 26cm. 1964. Parents' Magazine Press.
--Miss Suzy's Birthday. Lobel, Arnold Stark (1933-), illus. LC 73-22187. (Illus.). 40 p. 26cm. 1974. (ISBN 0-8193-0764-5). (ISBN 0-8193-0764-5). Parents' Magazine Press. **Award: (NYT).**
--Miss Suzy's Christmas. Lobel, Arnold Stark (1933-), illus. LC 72-10211. p. 1973. (ISBN 0-8193-0665-7). (ISBN 0-8193-0666-5). Parents' Magazine Press.
--Miss Suzy's Easter Surprise. Lobel, Arnold Stark (1933-), illus. LC 80-16966. p. cm. 1980, c.1972. (ISBN 0-590-07777-5). Four Winds Press.
--Miss Suzy's Easter Surprise. Lobel, Arnold Stark (1933-), illus. LC 79-174599. (Illus.). 40 p. 26cm. 1972. (ISBN 0-8193-0555-3). (ISBN 0-8193-0556-1). Parents' Magazine Press.
--The Most Beautiful Kitten. Petie, Haris, pseud. (1915-), illus. Petty, Roberta. LC 61-12781. unpaged. illus 23 cm. 1961. Lantern Press.
--No Place for Mitty. LC 75-35606. 123 p. 22cm. c.1976. Four Winds Press.
--Peas in a Pod. Neely, Linda, illus. LC 75-127006. (Illus.). 32 p. 1971. Putnam.
--Please Don't Feed Horace. Graboff, Abner (1919-), illus. LC 61-6485. unpaged, illus. 20 x 26 cm. (A Dial Junior Book). c.1961. Dial.
--Prance, a Carousel Horse. Jones, Amy, illus. LC 50-9443. 116 p. illus. 21 cm. 1950. Crowell.
--The Secret of Stone House Farm. Hutchinson, William Miller (1916-), illus. 192p. N.D. Hartcourt Brace & World Inc.
--Slow As a Snail, Quick As a Bird. Bordigoni, Idelette, illus. LC 70-116339. (Illus.). 40 p. 24cm. 1970. Lothrop, Lee & Shepard Co.
--Something Small. Aloise, Frank E., illus. LC 77-110310. (Illus.). 31 p. 23cm. 1970. Putnam.
--Truth and Consequences. De Groat, Diane (1947-), illus. LC 74-19038. (Illus.). 101 p. 21cm. 1975. (ISBN 0-590-07381-8). Four Winds Press.
--Up and Away!. Savitt, Sam (1917-), illus. LC 60-13705. 191 p. illus. 22 cm. 1960. Harcourt, Brace.
--The Witch Mobile. Chess, Victoria (1939-), illus. LC 73-81923. (Illus.). 48 p. 26cm. 1969. Lothrop, Lee & Shepard Co.
--A Witch's Garden. Robinson, Charles (1931-), illus. LC 72-85922. (Illus.). 156 p. 22cm. 1973. Atheneum.
--A Witch's Garden. Robinson, Charles (1931-), illus. LC 73-9913. (Illus.). 194 p. 25cm. 1973. (ISBN 0-8161-6129-1). G. K. Hall.
Young, Miriam Burt (1913-1974) & Nicklaus, Carol
--So What If It's Raining!. LC 75-19340. (Illus.). 35 p. 26cm. c.1976. (ISBN 0-8193-0803-X). (ISBN 0-8193-0804-8). Parents' Magazine Press.
Young, Murat Bernard Chic see Young, Chic, pseud.
Young, Murat Bernard Chic (1901-1973)
--Blondie and Dagwood's Adventures in Magic: An Original Story About the Bumstead Family. authorized. Young, Murat Bernard Chic (1901-1973), illus. Young, Chic, pseud. LC 45-12225. 3 p. l., 11-248 p. illus. 20 1/2 cm. c.1944. Whitman Publishing Company.
--Blondie and Dagwood's Marvelous Invention: An Original Story About the Bumstead Family. Young, Chic, pseud. authorized. Young, Murat Bernard Chic (1901-1973), illus. Young, Chic, pseud. LC 48-112639. 248 p. illus. 21 cm. 1947. Whitman Pub. Co.
--Blondie and Dagwood's Secret Service: An Original Story About the Bumstead Family. authorized. Young, Murat Bernard Chic (1901-1973), illus. Young, Chic, pseud. LC 42-22262. 3 p. l., 11-248 p. illus. 20 1/2 cm. 1942. Whitman Publishing Company.
--Blondie and Dagwood's Snapshot Clue: An Original Story About the Bumstead Family. Young, Chic, pseud. authorized. Young, Murat Bernard Chic (1901-1973), illus. Young, Chic, pseud. LC 43-227045. 4 p. l., 13-247 p. illus. 20 1/2 cm. 1943. Whitman Publishing Company.
--Blondie from A to Z. LC 43-7518. (Illus.). 27p. 23 x 18cm. 1943. David McKay Company.
--Blondie's Family. Young, Chic, pseud. Young, Murat Bernard Chic (1901-1973), illus. Young, Chic, pseud. N.D (Wonder Books). Grosset & Dunlap.
--Blondie's Family: Cookie, Alexander, and their Dog, Elmer. LC 54-32738. (Illus.). 21cm. (Treasure Bks.). 1954. Treasure Books.
Young, Natalie, jt. auth. see Conger, Marion.
Young, Noela
--Flip, the Flying Possum. Young, Noela, illus. LC 63-14681. unpaged. illus. 19 x 25 cm. 1963. F. Watts.
--Keep Out. Young, Noela, illus. LC 76-43587. (Illus.). 30 p. 27cm. 1977, c.1975. (ISBN 0-529-05334-9). Collins World.
Young-O'Brien, Albert Hayward see O'Brien, Brian, pseud.
Young-O'Brien, Albert Hayward (1898-)
--Ivory, Apes,and Jimibel. O'Brien, Brian, pseud. 1st ed. Grisha, Dotzenko, illus. Grisha, pseud. LC 60-6009. 217 p. illus. 21 cm. 1960. Dutton.
--Windship Boy. O'Brien, Brian, pseud. LC 61-5873. 256 p. illus. 21 cm. 1961. Dutton.
Young, Percy
--Ding Dong Bell: A First Book of Nursery Rhymes. Ardizzone, Edward Jeffrey Irving (1900-1979), illus. LC 69-17097. (Illus.). 36 drawings. index. 143p (Pub. by Denis Dobson, London). (gr. k-4). 1969. (ISBN 0-486-21248-3). Dover.
Young, Randall see Randall, Janet, pseud.
Young, Richard W.
--Nunu the Cricket. Young, Richard W., illus. N.D. Vantage Press.
Young, Robert William see Young, Bob, pseud.
Young, Robert William, jt. auth. see Randall, Janet.
Young, Rodney L., Jr.
--Old Abe: The Eagle Hero. Kaufmann, John (1931-), illus. (Illus.). (gr. k-4). 1972. (ISBN 0-13-633842-9). P-H.
Young, Roger & Caggiano, Rosemary
--The Safari. 48p. (gr. k-8). 1979. (ISBN 0-86704-006-8). Clarus Music.
Young, Scott Alexander (1918-)
--A Boy at the Leaf's Camp. Johnson, Douglas, illus. LC 64-10933. 256 p. illus. 20 cm. c.1963. Little, Brown.
--Boy on Defense. 1st ed. Ponter, James J., illus. LC 53-7331. 246p. illus. 20cm. 1953. (ISBN 0-316-97702-0). Little, Brown.
--The Clue of the Dead Duck. Johnson, Douglas, illus. LC 62-20657. 159 p. illus. 20 cm. (Secret Circle Mysteries, no. 6). 1962. Little, Brown.
--Face-off in Moscow. Shields, Kenneth M., illus. LC 73-4356. (Illus.). 38 p. 23cm. (His Face-Off Ser.). 1973. (ISBN 0-912022-56-6). (ISBN 0-912022-56-6). EMC Corp.
--Learning to Be Captain. Shields, Kenneth M., illus. LC 73-4354. (Illus.). 35 p. 23cm. (His Face-Off Ser.). 1973. (ISBN 0-912022-58-2). (ISBN 0-912022-58-2). EMC Corp.
--The Moscow Challengers. Shields, Kenneth M., illus. LC 73-4355. (Illus.). 38 p. 23cm. (His Face-Off Ser.). 1973. (ISBN 0-912022-57-4). (ISBN 0-912022-55-8). EMC Corp.
--Scrubs on Skates. LC 52-5511. 218 p. illus. 20 cm. 1952. Little, Brown.
--The Silent One Speaks Up. Shields, Kenneth M., illus. LC 73-4353. (Illus.). 34 p. 23cm. (His Face-Off Ser.). 1973. (ISBN 0-912022-59-0). (ISBN 0-912022-52-3). EMC Corp.
Young, Seymour Dilworth (1897-)
--Young Brigham Young. Young, Seymour Dilworth (1897-), illus. LC 62-53434. 169 p. illus. 22 cm. 1962. Bookcraft.
Young, Stanley Preston (1906-1975)
--Mayflower Boy. Shenton, Edward (1895-), illus. LC 44-6540. 6 p. l., 3-272 p. incl. front., illus. 21 cm. 1944. Farrar & Rinehart Inc.
--Tippecanoe and Tyler Too. (Illus.). 1957. Random House Inc.
--Young Hickory: A Story of the Frontier Boyhood and Youth of Andrew Jackson. Fawcett, Robert, illus. LC 40-31387. xii, 271 p. incl. front., illus. 21 cm. c.1940. Farrar & Rinehart, Incorporated.
Young, Virginia Brady (1921-)
--Circle of Thaw. Steffan, Leonard, illus. LC 70-176101. (Illus.). 64p. 1972. (ISBN 0-87929-008-0). Barlenmir.
Young, W. Edward & Hayes, Will
--Norman and the Nursery School. 1949. Platt & Munk Co.
Young, Wesley A. (1898-) & Miklowitz, Gloria D. (1927-)
--The Zoo Was My World. LC 69-13373. (Illus.). 128 p. 24cm. 1969. (ISBN 0-525-43719-3). Dutton.
Young, William P. & Gardner, Horace John (1896-)
--The Year-Round Party Book. 136p. 1957. J B Lippincott Company.

--Things I Like to Look at. Zokeisha, illus. (Illus.). 16p. (A Chubby Board Bk.). (ps-k). 1981. (ISBN 0-671-44451-4, Little Simon). S&S.
--Things I Like to Play with. Zokeisha, illus. (Illus.). 16p. (A Chubby Board Bk.). (ps-k). 1981. (ISBN 0-671-44450-6, Little Simon). S&S.
--Things I Like to Wear. Zokeisha, illus. (Illus.). 16p. (A Chubby Board Bk.). (ps-k). 1981. (ISBN 0-671-44452-2, Little Simon). S&S.
--Three Little Kittens. Zokeisha, illus. (Illus.). 12p. (Puppet Story Board Bks.). (ps-2). 1981. (ISBN 0-671-42641-9, Little Simon). S&S.

Zola, Meguido
--Moving: Blackbirds. Cooper, Victoria, illus. (Illus.). 48p. (Julia Macrae Blackbird Bks). (gr. k-3). N.D. (ISBN 0-531-04605-2). Watts.
--Only the Best. Littlewood, Valerie, illus. LC 80-85291. (Illus.). 32 p. 25cm. 1981. (ISBN 0-531-04066-6). Julia MacRae Books.
--Sharon, Lois & Bram. (gr. 4-6). 1983. (ISBN 0-531-04685-0). Watts.

Zola, Melanie (1952-)
--Peanut Butter Is Forever. MacRae, Jock, illus. LC 85-27739. p. cm. (Schoolhouse novels). 1986, c.1984. (ISBN 0-8086-0314-0). Schoolhouse Press.

Zoline, Pamela (1941-)
--Annika & the Wolves. Zoline, Pamela (1941-), illus. (Illus.). 24p. (Orig.). (gr. 4 up). 1984. (ISBN 0-915124-91-2). Toothpaste.
--Annika and the Wolves: A Fairy Tale. Zoline, Pamela, illus. LC 84-28529. p. cm. 1985. Coffee House Press.

Zoller, Bob (1948-)
--My Sister Is an Only Child. LC 83-9500. p. cm. (Regal galaxy book). c.1983. (ISBN 0-8307-0887-1). Regal Books.
--Night of Fire, Days of Rain. LC 82-7491. (Illus.). 137 p. 21cm. c.1982. (ISBN 0-8307-0844-8). Regal Books.

Zollinger, Gulielma (1856-1917)
--A Boy's Ride. Chambers, Fanny M., illus. LC 9-24698. 339, 1 p. front., 15 pl. 20 cm. 1909. A. C. McClurg & Co.
--Dan Drummond of the Drummonds. LC 7-6656. 315 p. front., plates. 19 1/2 cm. c.1897. The Pilgrim Press.
--Maggie McLanehan. LC 1-256799. 3 p. l., 9-319 p. front., 4 pl. 18 1/2 cm. 1901. A. C. McClurg and Co.
--The Widow O'Callaghan's Boys. new ed., from new plates, with illustrations in color by florence scovel shinn. Shinn, Florence Scovel, illus. LC 5-328571. 317 p. incl. col. front. 19 col. pl. 29 1/2 cm. 1905. A. C. McClurg & Co.

Zolotow, Charlotte Shapiro (1915-)
--All That Sunlight: Poems. Stein, Walter (1924-), illus. (Illus.). 31 p. 22cm. 1967. (ISBN 0-06-026919-7). Harper & Row.
--The Beautiful Christmas Tree. Robbins, Ruth (1917-), illus. 1983. Houghton.
--The Beautiful Christmas Tree. Robbins, Ruth (1917-), illus. LC 70-182950. (Illus.). 32 p. 23cm. 1972. (ISBN 0-87466-004-1). Parnassus Press.
--Big Brother. Chalmers, Mary Eileen (1927-), illus. LC 60-5794. 1960. Harper & Brothers.
--Big Sister and Little Sister. Alexander, Martha G. (1920-), illus. LC 66-8268. (Illus.). 24 p. 27cm. 1966. Harper & Row.
--Bunny Who Found Easter. Peterson, Betty Ferguson (1917-), illus. 1959. (ISBN 0-8382-0132-6, Cadmus Books). E. M. Hale and Company.
--The Bunny Who Found Easter. Peterson, Betty Ferguson (1917-), illus. LC 59-7370. (Illus.). (1 v. unpaged. 19cm. 1959. Parnassus.
--But Not Billy. 1st ed. Chorao, Ann Mckay Sproat (1936-), illus. LC 82-47703. p. cm. c.1983. (ISBN 0-06-026963-4). (ISBN 0-06-026964-2). Harper & Row.
--The City Boy and the Country Horse. Moyers, William (1916-), illus. LC 53-208712. unpaged. illus. 21cm. (Treasure books, 850). 1952. Treasure Books.
--Do You Know What I'll Do?. Williams, Garth Montgomery (1912-), illus. LC 58-7755. unpaged. illus. 28 cm. 1958. Harper. **Award: (ALA).**
--A Father Like That. Shecter, Ben (1935-), illus. LC 70-135778. (Illus.). 32 p. 17cm. 1971. (ISBN 0-06-026950-2). Harper & Row.
--Flocks of Birds. Berg, Joan, pseud. (1942-), illus. Victor, Joan Berg. LC 65-22824. 1v. (unpaged) col. illus. 21cm. 1965. Abelard.
--Flocks of Birds. 1st ed. Bornstein-Lercher, Ruth (1927-), illus. LC 81-43029. (Illus.). 28 p. 21cm. 1981, c.1965. (ISBN 0-690-04112-8). (ISBN 0-690-04113-6). Crowell.
--The Hating Book. Shecter, Ben (1935-), illus. LC 69-14444. (Illus.). 32 p. 1969. Harper & Row.
--Hold My Hand. 1st ed. Di Grazia, Thomas (0000-1983), illus. LC 72-76506. (Illus.). 24 p. 25cm. 1972. (ISBN 0-06-026951-0). (ISBN 0-06-026951-0). Harper & Row.
--I Have a Horse of My Own. Mitsuhashi, Yoko, illus. LC 64-22344. 31 p. col. illus. 19 x 21 cm. 1964. Abelard-Schuman.
--I Have a Horse of My Own. Mitsuhashi, Yoko, illus. LC 79-6196. p. cm. 1980, c.1964. (ISBN 0-690-04046-6). (ISBN 0-690-04047-4). T. Y. Crowell.
--I Know a Lady. Stevenson, James Walker (1929-), illus. LC 83-25361. (Illus.). 24p. (gr. k-3). c.1984. (ISBN 0-688-03837-9). (ISBN 0-688-03838-7). Greenwillow.
--I Want to Be Little. DeLuna, Tony, illus. LC 67-392. (O.s.i.). (Illus.). (Picture Book). (ps-3). 1966. (ISBN 0-200-00028-4). Abelard.
--If It Weren't For You. Shecter, Ben (1935-), illus. 1966. (ISBN 0-8382-1019-8, Cadmus Books). E. M. Hale and Company.
--If It Weren't for You. Shecter, Ben (1935-), illus. LC 66-15682. (Illus.). (gr. k-3). 1966. (ISBN 0-06-026942-1, HarpJ). (ISBN 0-06-026943-X). Har-Row.
--In My Garden. Duvoisin, Roger Antoine (1904-1980), illus. LC 60-12033. unpaged, illus. 26 cm. c.1960. Lothrop, Lee & Shepard.
--Indian Indian. Weisgard, Leonard Joseph (1916-), illus. LC 52-8717. unpaged. illus. 21 cm. (Little golden library, 149). 1952. Simon and Schuster.
--It's Not Fair. 1st ed. Du Bois, William Sherman Pene (1916-), illus. LC 76-3387. p. cm. c.1976. (ISBN 0-06-026934-0). (ISBN 0-06-026935-9). Harper & Row.
--Janey. 1st ed. Himler, Ronald Norbert (1937-), illus. LC 72-9861. (Illus.). 24 p. 22cm. 1973. (ISBN 0-06-026927-8). (ISBN 0-06-026927-8). Harper and Row.
--Little Black Puppy. Obligado, Lilian Isabel (1931-), illus. (Golden Beginning Reader). 1960. Golden Press.
--The Little Black Puppy. Obligado, Lilian Isabel (1931-), illus. (Eager Readers Ser.). (gr. k-3). 1975. (ISBN 0-307-60804-2, Golden Pr). Western Pub.
--The Magic Word. Dart, Eleanor, illus. LC 53-20511. unpaged. illus. 21cm. (Wonder books, 578). 1952. Wonder Books.
--The Man with the Purple Eyes. 1st ed. Lasker, Joseph Leon (1919-), illus. LC 61-7142. (Illus.). 60 p. 22cm. 1961. Abelard-Schuman.
--May I Visit?. 1st ed. Blegvad, Erik (1923-), illus. LC 75-25305. (Illus.). 32 p. 21cm. c.1976. (ISBN 0-06-026932-4). Harper & Row.
--Mister Rabbit & the Lovely Present. Sendak, Maurice Bernard (1928-), illus. (Illus.). (gr. k-2). 1962. (ISBN 0-8382-0538-0). Hale.
--Mister Rabbit & the Lovely Present. Sendak, Maurice Bernard (1928-), illus. LC 62-7590. (Illus.). (gr. k-3). 1962. (ISBN 0-06-026945-6, HarpJ). (ISBN 0-06-026946-4). Har-Row. **Awards: (ALA); (RCM).**
--Mister Rabbit & the Lovely Present. Sendak, Maurice Bernard (1928-), illus. (Illus.). 4-color ils. 32p. (gr. k-3). 1970 (StarLine). Schol Bk Serv.
--Mr. Rabbit and the Lovely Present. Sendak, Maurice Bernard (1928-), illus. (Illus.). 29p. (Harper Trophy Picture Book). 1977, c.1962. (ISBN 0-06-443020-0). Harper & Row.
--My Friend John. Shecter, Ben (1935-), illus. (Illus.). 32 p. 1968. Harper & Row.
--My Grandson Lew. Du Bois, William Sherman Pene (1916-), illus. LC 74-166336. (Illus.). 30 p. 19cm. 1974. (ISBN 0-06-026961-8). Harper & Row.
--The New Friend. 1st ed. McCully, Emily Arnold (1939-), illus. LC 80-67856. (Illus.). 32 p. 21cm. c.1981. (ISBN 0-690-04086-5). (ISBN 0-690-04087-3). Crowell.
--The New Friend. Stewart, Arvis L., illus. LC 68-13237. (Illus.). 31p. 1968. (ISBN 0-200-71580-1). Abelard-Schuman.
--Not A Little Monkey. N.D. E. M.Hale & Co.
--Not a Little Monkey. Duvoisin, Roger Antoine (1904-1980), illus. LC 57-599420. unpaged. illus. 26cm. 1957. Lothrop, Lee & Shepard.
--One Step, Two ... rev ed. Duvoisin, Roger Antoine (1904-1980), illus. LC 55-702751. unpaged. illus. 26cm. c.1955. Lothrop, Lee & Shepard Co.
--One Step, Two ... rev. ed. Wheeler, Cindy (1955-), illus. LC 80-11749. (Illus.). 32 p. 26cm. c.1981. (ISBN 0-688-51971-7). Lothrop, Lee & Shepard Books.
--Over & Over. Williams, Garth Montgomery (1912-), illus. LC 56-8149. (Illus.). (gr. k-2). 1957. (ISBN 0-06-026955-3, HarpJ). (ISBN 0-06-026956-1). Har-Row.
--Park Book. Rey, Hans Augusto (1898-1977), illus. LC 44-9471. (Illus.). (ps-1). 1944. (ISBN 0-06-026970-7, HarpJ). Har-Row.
--Poodle Who Barked at the Wind. Duvoisin, Roger Antoine (1904-1980), illus. (Illus.). (gr. k-3). 1964. (ISBN 0-688-41159-2). Lothrop.
--Quarreling Book. Lobel, Arnold Stark (1933-), illus. 1963. E M Hale.
--The Quarreling Book. Lobel, Arnold Stark (1933-), illus. LC 63-14445. (Illus.). unpaged. 16cm. 1963. Harper & Row.
--The Quiet Mother and the Noisy Little Boy. Werth, Kurt (1896-), illus. LC 53-6731. unpaged. illus. 26cm. 1953. Lothrop, Lee & Shepard Co.
--River Winding. Mizumura, Kazue, illus. LC 77-27670. (Illus.). 40 p. 23cm. 1978. Crowell.
--River Winding. Shekerjian, Regina, illus. LC 70-123519. (Illus.). 32 p. 21cm. 1970. Abelard-Schuman.
--Rose, a Bridge, & a Wild Black Horse. Shulevitz, Uri (1935-), illus. (Illus.). (gr. k-2). 1964. (ISBN 0-8382-0711-1). Hale.
--Rose, a Bridge, & a Wild Black Horse. Shulevitz, Uri (1935-), illus. (Illus.). (gr. k-3). 1964. (ISBN 0-06-026991-X). Har-Row.
--Say It!. Stevenson, James Walker (1929-), illus. LC 79-25115. (Illus.). 25 p. 26cm. c.1980. (ISBN 0-688-80276-1). (ISBN 0-688-84276-3). Greenwillow Books. **Award: (ALA).**
--The Sky Was Blue. 1st ed. Williams, Garth Montgomery (1912-), illus. LC 62-13328. (Illus.). unpaged. 27cm. 1963. Harper & Row.
--Sleepy Book. Bobri, V., pseud. (1898-), illus. Bobritsky, Vladimir. 1958. E M Hale.
--Sleepy Book. Bobri, V., pseud. (1898-), illus. Bobritsky, Vladimir V.. LC 58-10718. (Illus.). (ps-3). 1958. (ISBN 0-688-51178-3). Lothrop.
--Some Things Go Together. Gundersheimer, Karen, illus. LC 82-48694. (Illus.). 26 p. 17cm. 1983, c.1969. (ISBN 0-690-04327-9). (ISBN 0-690-04328-7). Crowell.
--Some Things Go Together. Selig, Sylvie (1942-), illus. (Illus.). 32p. 1969. Abelard-Schuman Press.
--Someday. Lobel, Arnold Stark (1933-), illus. LC 64-16654. (Illus.). 1 v. (unpaged. 1965. Harper & Row.
--Someone New. 1st ed. Blegvad, Erik (1923-), illus. LC 77-11838. (Illus.). 32 p. 24cm. c.1978. (ISBN 0-06-027017-9). (ISBN 0-06-027018-7). Harper & Row.
--The Song. 1st ed. Tafuri, Nancy, illus. LC 81-6357. (Illus.). 24 p. 26cm. c.1982. (ISBN 0-688-00618-3). (ISBN 0-688-00817-8). Greenwillow Books.
--The Storm Book. Graham, Margaret Bloy (1920-), illus. LC 52-7880. (Illus.). (gr. k-3). 1952. (ISBN 0-06-027025-X, HarpJ). (ISBN 0-06-027026-8). Har-Row. **Award: (RCM).**
--Summer Is. Archer, Janet, illus. LC 67-14978. 1 v. (unpaged) col. illus. 19x22cm. 1967. (ISBN 0-200-00033-0). Abelard.
--Summer Is... Bornstein-Lercher, Ruth (1927-), illus. LC 82-45185. (Illus.). 32p. (gr. k-4). 1983. (ISBN 0-690-04303-1, TYC-J). (ISBN 0-690-04304-X). Har-Row.
--The Summer Night. Shecter, Ben (1935-), illus. LC 73-6000. (Illus.). 32 p. 24cm. 1974. (ISBN 0-06-026959-6). (ISBN 0-06-026960-X). Harper & Row.
--Three Funny Friends. Chalmers, Mary Eileen (1927-), illus. LC 61-5779. (Illus.). (ps-1). 1961. (ISBN 0-06-027040-3, HarpJ). Har-Row.
--A Tiger Called Thomas. Werth, Kurt (1896-), illus. LC 63-16777. unpaged. illus. 26 cm. 1963. Lothrop, Lee & Shepard.
--The Unfriendly Book. 1st ed. Du Bois, William Sherman Pene (1916-), illus. LC 74-19581. (Illus.). 32 p. 19cm. 1975. (ISBN 0-06-026929-4). (ISBN 0-06-026931-6). Harper & Row.
--Wake up and Good Night. Weisgard, Leonard Joseph (1916-), illus. LC 75-135187. (Illus.). 29 p. 1971. (ISBN 0-06-027042-X). Harper & Row.
--Week in Yoni's World: Greece. Getsug, Donald, photos by. LC 69-19574. (Illus.). photos. 48p. (Face to Face Bks.). (gr. k-3). 1969. (ISBN 0-02-735850-X, CCPr). (ISBN 0-02-736010-5, CCPr). Macmillan.
--When I Have a Little Girl. Knight, Hilary (1926-), illus. LC 65-24656. 1 v. (unpaged) col. illus. 14 x 16 cm. 1965. Harper & Row.
--When I Have a Son. Knight, Hilary (1926-), illus. LC 67-14072. (Illus.). (gr. k-3). 1967. (ISBN 0-06-027044-6, HarpJ). Har-Row.
--When the Wind Stops. Knotts, Howard Clayton, Jr. (1922-), illus. 1962. E M Hale.
--When the Wind Stops. Knotts, Howard Clayton, Jr. (1922-), illus. LC 74-2635. (Illus.). 30 p. 24cm. c.1975. (ISBN 0-06-026971-5). (ISBN 0-06-026972-3). Harper & Row.
--When the Wind Stops. Lasker, Joseph Leon (1919-), illus. LC 62-17045. unpaged. illus. 26 cm. c.1962. Abelard-Schuman.
--The White Marble. Obligado, Lilian Isabel (1931-), illus. LC 63-16215. 1 v. (unpaged) col. illus. 27 cm. 1963. Abelard-Schuman.
--White Marble. Obligado, Lilian Isabel (1931-), illus. 1963. E M Hale.
--The White Marble. 1st ed. Ray, Deborah (1940-), illus. LC 81-43131. (Illus.). 32 p. 21cm. 1982, c.1963. (ISBN 0-690-04152-7). (ISBN 0-690-04151-9). Crowell.
--William's Doll. Du Bois, William Sherman Pene (1916-), illus. LC 70-183173. (Illus.). 30 p. 19cm. 1972. (ISBN 0-06-027048-9). Harper & Row. **Award: (ALA).**

Zolotow, Charlotte Shapiro (1915-), ed.
--An Overpraised Season: Ten Stories of Youth. LC 73-5499. 176p. (gr. 7 up). 1973. (ISBN 0-06-026953-7, HarpJ). (ISBN 0-06-026954-5). Har-Row.

Zolotow, Charlotte Shapiro (1915-) & Simont, Marc (1915-)
--If You Listen. 1st ed. LC 79-2688. p. cm. c.1980. (ISBN 0-06-027049-7). (ISBN 0-06-027050-0). Harper & Row.

Zook, Ardith
--Captain Gaius Sees a Miracle. 1980. (ISBN 0-570-06133-4, Arch Bk). Concordia.

Zorberg, Rita, illus.
--Quite as a Butterfly. (A Golden Science Reader). N.D. Golden Press.

Zschokke, Heinrich, pseud., see Zschokke, Johann Heinrich Daniel.

Zschokke, Heinrich, et al., pseud. (1771-1848)
--Christmas Stories. Zschokke, Johann Heinrich Daniel. (New Acorn Library). N.D. John C. Winston Co.

Zschokke, Heinrich, pseud. (1771-1848)
--Christmas Stories. Zschokke, Johann Heinrich Daniel. (New International Library). N.D. John C. Winston Co.
--Labor Stands on Gooden Feet. Zschokke, Johann Heinrich Daniel. Yeats, John, tr. N.D. Dodd & Mead.

Zschokke, Johann Heinrich Daniel see Zschokke, Heinrich, pseud.

Zubkoff, Myrtle
--Jackie. Hauptfleisch, Olivia, illus. (Illus.). 1977. (ISBN 0-533-02714-4). Vantage.

Zubkov, Boris
--Tomorrow?...Yesterday?... Yankovskaya, Eleanor & Kabakov, I., trs. from Rus. (Illus.). (ps-3). 1983. (ISBN 0-8285-2430-0, Pub. by Malysh Pubs USSR). Imported Pubns.

Zucca, Mana & Frank, Mabel Livingston
--A Child's Day in Song. Whitelaw, Norah, illus. LC 17-5577. 3 p. l., 3-31 p. col. illus. 30 1/2 cm. c.1916. G. Schirmer.

Zucker, Howard
--The Hamburger with Duck's Feet. Zucker, Howard, illus. (Illus.). 1978. (ISBN 0-89508-019-2). Rainbow Bks.

Zuliani, Vilma
--By George, the Bull. Billa, Jim, illus. (Illus.). (Hermitage Press Bks). (gr. k up). 1977. (ISBN 0-695-80857-5). (ISBN 0-695-40857-7). Follett.
--I Believe in Make Believe. De Claire, Robert, illus. LC 77-74630. (Illus.). 47 p. c.1977. (ISBN 0-89441-001-6). Hermitage Press.
--Randy Robin Finds a Friend. De Claire, Robert, illus. LC 77-74629. (Illus.). 31 p. c.1977. (ISBN 0-89441-002-4). Hermitage Press.
--To Market, to Market to Buy a Fat Fig. Morrissey, K., illus. (Illus.). (Hermitage Press Bks). (gr. k-6). 1977. (ISBN 0-695-80859-1). (ISBN 0-695-40859-3). Follett.

Zulli, Floyd, Jr. (1922-1980), ed. see Poe, Edgar Allan.

Zumwalt, Eva (1936-)
--Sun Dust. Onyshkewych, Zenowij, illus. LC 76-12753. p. cm. c.1976. (ISBN 0-679-20360-5). D. McKay Co.

Zumwalt, Wanda
--In the Listening of My Heart, I Hear the Sleeping Speak. Simons, Susan, ed. LC 77-78604. (Illus.). (gr. 6-12). 1978. (ISBN 0-917188-16-0). Nationwide Pr.

Zuniega, Thelma M.
--The Haunted Cave. (Illus.). (ps-3). 1972. (ISBN 0-686-09535-9). Cellar.
--My Friends. (Illus.). (ps-1). 1972. (ISBN 0-686-09534-0). Cellar.

Zur Muhlen, Herminia
--Fairy Tales for Workers' Children. Gibson, Lydia, illus. Dailes, Ida, tr. from Ger. LC 25-11384. 4 p., l., 3-66 p. illus., col. plates. 29 cm. c.1925. Daily Worker Publishing Co.

Zuromskis, Diane (1943-)
--The Farmer in the Dell. 1st ed. Zuromskis, Diane (1943-), illus. LC 77-17074. (Illus.). 32 p. c.1978. (ISBN 0-316-98889-8). Little, Brown.

Zusman, Evelyn
--The Passover Parrot. Kahn, Katherine Janns, illus. LC 83-22182. (Illus.). 40p. (ps-4). 1984. (ISBN 0-930494-29-6). (ISBN 0-930494-30-X). Kar Ben.

Zwecher, Deborah, ed. see Brandel, Marc.

Zweifel, Frances W. (1931-)
--Bony. Darrow, Whitney, Jr., illus. LC 76-58688. (Illus.). 5 7/8 x 8 1/2. 64p. (18 pt.). (I Can Read Bks.). (gr. k-3). 1977. (ISBN 0-06-027070-5) (ISBN 0-06-027071-3) Har-Row.
--Pickle in the Middle & Other Easy Snacks. Zweifel, Frances W. (1931-), illus. LC 78-19478. (Illus.). 5 7/8 x 8 1/2. 64p. (16 pt.). (I Can Read Bks.). (gr. k-3). 1979. (ISBN 0-06-027072-1) (ISBN 0-06-027073-X) Har-Row.

Zwerin, Anne, tr. from Russian.
--The Magic Pear and Other Legends and Fables from Russia and Other Lands. 1975. (ISBN 0-682-48293-5). Exposition Press.

Zwichel, Alan H., jt. ed. see Kaufman, Bill.
Zwilgmeyer, Dikken, tr. see Poulsson, Anne Emilie.
Zwilgmeyer, Dikken (1859-1913)
--Four Cousins. Heiberg, Astri Welham, illus. Poulsson, Emille (1853-1939), tr. from Norwegian. LC 23-16973. 283 p. col. front., col. plates. 29 cm. c.1923. Lothrop, Lee & Shepard Co.
--Inger Johanne's Lively Doings. Young, Florence Liley, illus. Poulsson, Emilie (1853-1939), tr. from Norwegian. 261 p. incl. col. front. col. plates. 20 cm. c.1926. Lothrop, Lee & Shepard Co.
--Johnny Blossom. Young, Florence Liley, illus. LC 12-22553. ix, 163 p. col. front., col. illus., col. plates. 20 1/2 cm. 1912. The Pilgrim Press.
--What Happened to Inger-Johanne: As Told by Herself. Young, Florence Liley, illus. Poulsson, Emille (1853-1939), tr. from Norwegian. LC 19-15746. 283 p. incl. col. front. col. plates. 20 cm. c.1919. Lothrop, Lee & Shepard Co.
Zwilgmeyer, Dikken (1859-1913) & D'Aulaire, Ingri Mortenson (1904-1980)
--Johnny Blossom. D'Aulaire, Ingri Mortenson (1904-1980) & D'Aulaire, Edgar Parin (1898-), illus. LC 48-8188. vii, 157 p. illus. 23 cm. 1948. Pilgrim Press.
Zylstra, Freida, jt. auth. see Raymond, Margaret Thomsen.

995

Illustrators Index

--*The Looking-Glass for the Mind: Or, Intellectual Mirror; Being an Elegant Collection of the Most Delightful Little Stories, and Interesting Tales, Chiefly Tr.* from That Much Admired Work L'Ami Des Enfans. Berquin, Arnaud (1749-1791). Cooper, Mr., tr. 1807. Printed by McFarlane and Long, No. Broadway. (P.97)

--*The Looking-Glass for the Mind: Or, The Intellectual Mirror; Being an Elegant Collection of the Most Delightful Little Stories, and Interesting Tales, Chiefly Translated from That Much Admired Work L'Ami Des Enfans.* Berquin, Arnaud (1749-1791). Cooper, Mr., tr. 1818. E. Duyckinck. (P.97)

--*Paul and Virginia.* De Saint-Pierre, Jacques Henri Bernardin (1737-1814). Williams, Helen Maria (1762-1827), tr. from Fr. 1850. J. A. & U. P. James. (P.260)

--*Paul & Virginia.* De Saint-Pierre, Jacques Henri Bernardin (1737-1814). Williams, Helen Maria (1762-1827), tr. from Fr. 1805. Published by Evert Duyckinck, No. Pearl-Street. L. Nichols, Printer. (P.260)

--*Pilpay's Fables.* Pilpay. N.D. Houghton Mifflin. (P.726)

--*The Pleasant Journey and Scenes in Town and Country.* Tuttle, George (1804-1872). Teller, Thomas, pseud. 1845. S. Babcock Pref. (P.906)

Anderson, Allen, jt. illus. see Anderson, Harold.

Anderson, Anne

--*Aladdin And The Wonderful Lamp.* Anderson, Anne, ed. N.D. Thomas Nelson & Sons. (P.38)

--*Ali Baba and the Forty Thieves.* Ali Baba. 1928. T. Nelson and Sons. (P.27)

--*The Anne Anderson Fairy-Tale Book.* Anderson, Anne. 1926. T. Nelson and Sons. (P.38)

--*Anne Anderson's Fairy Tales.* Anderson, Anne, ed. c.1935. Whitman Publishing Company. (P.38)

--*The Bitter Green of the Willow: Four Fairy Tales.* Morrison, Peggy, pseud. (0000-1973). Morrison, Margaret Mackie. 1967. Chilton Book Co. (P.665)

--*Grimm's Fairy Stories.* Grimm, Jakob Ludwig Karl (1785-1863) & Grimm, Wilhelm Karl (1786-1859). N.D. Collins. (P.392)

--*Hop O' My Thumb.* Anderson, Anne, ed. N.D. Thomas Nelson & Sons. (P.38)

--*Lie Down Stories.* Joan, Natalie. N.D. Dodge Pub. Co. (P.493)

--*Mr.* Pickles and the Party. Heward, Constance. N.D. Frederick Warne & Co. (P.439)

--*Old English Nursery Songs.* Mansion, Horace, ed. N.D. Brentano's. (P.618)

--*Old Mother Goose.* Anderson, Anne, ed. N.D. Thomas Nelson & Sons. (P.38)

--*Red Shoes.* Anderson, Anne, ed. N.D. Thomas Nelson & Sons. (P.38)

--*The Sleeping Beauty.* Anderson, Anne. 1928. T. Nelson and Sons. (P.38)

--*Snow-Drop and the Seven Dwarfs.* Snow-White and the Seven Dwarfs. 1928. T. Nelson and Sons. (P.839)

--*Snowdrop and the Seven Dwarfs.* Anderson, Anne, ed. 1928. Thomas Nelson & Sons. (P.38)

--*The Water-Babies.* Kingsley, Charles (1819-1875). 1925. T. Nelson & Sons. (P.525)

Anderson, Anne, jt. illus. see Wright, Alan.

Anderson, Anne & Wellman, Mauriete

--*One Hundred Fairy Tales.* Donaldson, Lois (1898-). c.1937. Whitman Publishing Company. (P.280)

Anderson, Bernice Goudy (1894-) & Frank, Sears

--*Indian Sleep Man Tales.* Anderson, Bernice Goudy (1894-). N.D. Caxton Printers. (P.38)

--*Indian Sleep Man Tales.* Anderson, Bernice Goudy (1894-). N.D. Reilly & Lee Co. (P.38)

Anderson, Betty

--*The Big Red Pajama Wagon.* Elting, Mary (1906-). c.1950. Whitman. (P.305)

--*The Flying Sunbeam.* Fairbairn, D. N. 1950. Whitman. (P.316)

Anderson, Carl A., jt. illus. see Merryweather, Jack.

Anderson, Carl (1931-)

--*Just the Two of Them.* Anderson, Mary (1939-). 1974. Atheneum. (P.40)

--*Matilda Investigates.* Anderson, Mary (1939-). 1973. Atheneum. (P.40)

Anderson, Catherine Corley (1909-)

--*Sister Beatrice and the Mission Mystery.* Anderson, Catherine Corley (1909-). 1963. Bruce Pub. Co. (P.38)

--*Sister Beatrice Goes West.* Anderson, Catherine Corley (1909-). 1961. Bruce Pub. Co. (P.38)

Anderson, Clarence William (1891-1971)

--*Another Man O' War.* Anderson, Clarence William (1891-1971). 1966. Macmillan. (P.38)

--*Blaze and the Forest Fire.* Anderson, Clarence William (1891-1971). 1969. Macmillan. (P.38)

--*Blaze and the Gray Spotted Pony.* Anderson, Clarence William (1891-1971). 1974, c.1968. Collier Books. (P.38)

--*Blaze and the Gray Spotted Pony.* Anderson, Clarence William (1891-1971). c.1968. Macmillan. (P.38)

--*Blaze and the Indian Cave.* Anderson, Clarence William (1891-1971). 1964. Macmillan. (P.38)

--*Blaze and the Lost Quarry.* Anderson, Clarence William (1891-1971). 1973, c.1966. Collier Books. (P.38)

--*Blaze and the Lost Quarry.* Anderson, Clarence William (1891-1971). c.1966. Macmillan. (P.38)

--*Blaze Finds Forgotten Roads.* Anderson, Clarence William (1891-1971). 1970. Macmillan. (P.39)

--*Blaze Shows the Way.* Anderson, Clarence William (1891-1971). 1969. Macmillan. (P.39)

--*Bobcat.* Anderson, Clarence William (1891-1971). 1949. Macmillan. (P.39)

--*C.* W. Anderson's Favorite Horse Stories. Anderson, Clarence William (1891-1971), ed. 1967. Dutton. (P.39)

--*Filly for Joan.* Anderson, Clarence William (1891-1971). 1962. Macmillan. (P.39)

--*Honey on a Raft.* Paltenghi, Madeleine (1899-). c.1941. Garden City Publishing Co., Inc. (P.704)

--*Honey, the City Bear.* Paltenghi, Madeleine (1899-). c.1937. Grosset & Dunlap. (P.704)

--*A Horse Named Joe.* 1st ed. Gard, Robert Edward (1910-). c.1956. Duell, Sloan and Pearce. (P.354)

--*The Horse of Hurricane Hill.* Anderson, Clarence William (1891-1971). 1956. Macmillan. (P.39)

--*Horse of Hurricane Hill.* Anderson, Clarence William (1891-1971). 1962. Macmillan. (P.39)

--*Midnight: Rodeo Champion.* Gard, Robert Edward (1910-). 1951. Duell, Sloan and Perce Pub. (P.354)

--*A Pony Called Lightning.* Mason, Miriam Evangeline (1899-1973). 1948. Macmillan Co. (P.628)

--*The Red Roan Pony.* rev. ed. Lippincott, Joseph Wharton (1887-1976). 1951. Lippincott. (P.575)

--*Remus Goes to Town.* Paltenghi, Madeleine (1899-). c.1938. Grosset & Dunlap. (P.704)

--*Rumpus Rabbit.* 1st Ed. ed. Paltenghi, Madeleine (1899-). 1939. London, Harper & Brothers. (P.704)

--*Salute.* Anderson, Clarence William (1891-1971). 1967. Macmillan. (P.39)

--*Salute.* Anderson, Clarence William (1891-1971). 1940. The Macmillan Company. (P.39)

Anderson, Debby

--*Thank You, God.* Anderson, Debby. c.1985. Chariot Books. (P.39)

Anderson, Dennis

--*The Ghost of Padre Island.* Silverthorne, Elizabeth (1930-). 1975. Abingdon Press. (P.824)

Anderson, Douglas (1919-)

--*Acts for Comedy Shows: How to Perform and Write Them.* Howard, Vernon Linwood (1918-). 1964. Sterling Pub. Co. (P.467)

--*Tell Me.* Walpole, Ellen Wales (1907-). 1947. Hinds, Hayden & Eldredge. (P.928)

--*The Toy Show Surprise.* Lindsay, Barbara. 1955. Sterling Pub Co. (P.574)

Anderson, Dr., jt. illus. see Pike, S.

Anderson, Florence Mary

--*The King of Melido.* Peck, Winifred. 1928. Harper & Bros. (P.715)

--*Little Dwarf Nose & The Magic Whistle.* Browne, Edgar Gordon (1871-). 1916. Dodd, Mead & Co. (P.143)

--*The Magic Whistle.* Browne, Edgar Gordon (1871-). 1920. Dodd, Mead & Co. (P.143)

--*Nutcracker & Mouse-King.* Browne, Edgar Gordon (1871-). 1916. Dodd, Mead & Co. (P.143)

Anderson, Fred

--*The Soul of Christmas.* King, Helen Hayes (1936-). 1972. Johnson Pub. Co. (P.523)

Anderson, Frederic A.

--*The Boy Scouts in a Trapper's Camp.* Burgess, Thornton Waldo (1874-1965). 1915. The Penn Publishing Company. (P.153)

--*The Captain.* Pier, Arthur Stanwood (1874-1966). c.1929. The Penn Publishing Company. (P.725)

--*Castaway Island.* Newberry, Perry (1870-). 1917. The Penn Publishing Company. (P.679)

--*The Champion.* Pier, Arthur Stanwood (1874-1966). c.1931. The Penn Publishing Company. (P.725)

--*The Cheer Leader.* Pier, Arthur Stanwood (1874-1966). c.1930. The Penn Publishing Company. (P.725)

--*The Coach.* Pier, Arthur Stanwood (1874-1966). c.1928. The Penn Publishing Company. (P.725)

--*Hilla of Finland.* Malroy, Geneva de. N.D. Thomas Nelson & Sons. (P.616)

--*The Last Cruise of the Panther.* Jenkins, MacGregor (1869-1940). c.1929. The Penn Publishing Company. (P.491)

--*On the Borders with Andrew Jackson.* McIntyre, John Thomas (1871-). 1915. The Penn Publishing Company. (P.604)

--*A Patriot Lad of Old West Point.* Carter, Russell Gordon (1892-1957). c.1936. The Penn Publishing Company. (P.176)

--*The Safety First Club.* Nichols, William Theophilus (1863-). 1916. The Penn Publishing Company. (P.681)

--*The Safety First Club and the Flood.* Nichols, William Theophilus (1863-). 1917. The Penn Publishing Company. (P.681)

--*The Young Journalists.* Jenkins, MacGregor (1869-1940). N.D. Penn Publishing Co. (P.491)

Anderson, Gunnar

--*Oscar Lincoln Busby Stokes.* 1st ed. Sayers, Frances Clarke, Mrs. (1897-1957). 1970. Harcourt, Brace & World. (P.795)

Anderson, Harold

--*Lights off Shore: Or, Sam and the Outlaws of the Bay.* Durell, Charles Pendexter. 1925. Milton Bradley Company. (P.291)

--*Torrance from Texas.* Ames, Joseph Bushnell (1878-1928). 1921. The Century Co. (P.33)

Anderson, Harold N.

--*The Land of Monsters.* Sherman, Harold Morrow (1898-). c.1931. Grosset & Dunlap. (P.819)

Anderson, Harold & Anderson, Allen

--*Pirate of the Pine Lands: Being the Adventures of Young Tom Lansing.* Detzer, Karl William (1891-). c.1929. The Bobbs-Merrill Company. (P.260)

Anderson, Irv

--*The Little Runaway.* Hillert, Margaret (1920-). 1966. Follett Pub. Co. (P.444)

Anderson, J. P., jt. illus. see Kaji, Elsa.

Anderson, Jean

--*A Window for Julie.* Whitney, Phyllis Ayame (1903-). 1943. Houghton Mifflin Company. (P.955)

Anderson, Karl, jt. illus. see Fisher, Harrison.

Anderson, Karl & Brehm, George

--*The Master of Mysteries.* N.D. Bobbs-Merrill Co. (P.39)

Anderson, Kathleen

--*Who Is Victoria?.* 1st ed. Erwin, Betty K. 1973. Little, Brown. (P.309)

Anderson, Laurie

--*Certainly, Carrie, Cut the Cake: Poems A to Z.* Moore, Margaret Rumberger (1903-) & Moore, John Travers (1908-). 1971. Bobbs-Merrill. (P.661)

Anderson, Madge

--*The Cook's Surprise.* Clark, Margery, pseud. Clark, Mary Elizabeth. N.D. Doubleday Page & Co. (P.198)

Anderson, Marvin

--*Pim.* Skerry-Olsen, Eva. 1948. Coslett Publishing Co. (P.828)

Anderson, Peggy Perry (1938-)

--*Blue Bug Goes to the Library.* Poulet, Virginia. c.1979. Children Press. (P.735)

--*Blue Bug's Book of Colors.* Poulet, Virginia. 1981. Childrens Press. (P.735)

Anderson, Peter

--*The Crow and the Snow.* Taines, Gerald. 1963. Artist Pub. Co. (P.876)

Anderson, R. L., Jr.

--*The Abominable Spaceman.* Anderson, R. L., Jr. c.1979. Hobby Horse Pub. (P.40)

Anderson, Robert Lindberg

--*The Fourteenth Dragon.* Seidelman, James Edward & Mintonye, Grace. 1968. H. Quist. (P.808)

--*Hubert, the Caterpillar who Thought he was a Mustache.* Richards, Susan & Stang, Wendy. N.D. Crown Publishers. (P.762)

--*Hubert.* The Caterpillar Who Thought He Was a Moustache. Stang, Wendy & Richards, Susan (1950-). 1973. Dial. (P.848)

--*Hubert.* The Caterpillar Who Thought He Was a Moustache. Stang, Wendy & Richards, Susan (1950-). 1967. H. Quist; Dist. by Crown. **Award: (NYT).** (P.848)

Anderson, Robert Lindberg & Bradford, John Carroll

--*The House That Jack Built, and Other Favorite Jingles.* The, House That Jack Built. 1964. Dell Publ. Col. (P.466)

Anderson, Ronald

--*Hale Merrill's Honey Quest: How One Girl Made the Best of Things.* Harris, Annie Elizabeth. 1918. Lothrop, Lee & Shepard Co. (P.415)

Anderson, Rondi Marie

--*On the Balance Beam.* Robison, Nancy Louise (1934-). 1978. A. Whitman. (P.771)

--*Rivals on Ice.* Van Steenwyk, Elizabeth Ann (1928-). c.1979. A. Whitman. (P.915)

--*Why the Cock Crows Three Times.* Foley, Anna Bernice Williams (1902-). c.1980. Child's World. (P.333)

Anderson, Rus

--*Dangerous Duty.* Small, Sidney Herschel. 1954. Oxford University Press. (P.830)

--*De Tonti of the Iron Hand and the Exploration of the Mississippi.* Heagney, Anne (1901-). 1959. P. J. Kenedy. (P.428)

--*Deep Sea Silver.* Caldero, Gordon. 1958. Little, Brown. (P.162)

--*Flight of the Peacock.* Wibberley, Leonard Patrick O'Connor (1915-). O'Connor, Patrick, pseud. 1954. I. Washburn. (P.955)

--*The Golden Promise.* Blackburn, Edith H. 1956. Abelard-Schuman. (P.104)

--*A Horse of Her Own.* Hudnut, Selma. 1963. Van Nostrand. (P.469)

--*Light in the Early West: Berenice Chouteau.* Schlafly, James J (1919-). 1959. Benziger Bros. (P.799)

--*The Long Hunt.* 1st ed. Simon, Charlie May, Mrs., pseud. (1897-). Fletcher, Charlie May Hogue. 1952. Dutton. (P.824)

--*Maynard, the Nehalem River White Duck & Other Stories.* Mitchell, Kitty. 1974. Exposition. (P.652)

--*Moya and the Flamingoes.* Hallin, Emily Watson. 1969. D. McKay Co. (P.406)

--*Pilgrimage to Freedom.* 1st ed. Cournos, John (1881-1966) & Cournos, Helen Sybil Norton Kestner (1893-). Norton, Sybil, pseud. 1953. Holt. (P.224)

--*Rails Along the Chesapeake.* 1st ed. Tufts, Anne. 1957. Holt. (P.904)

--*The Real Book About Christopher Columbus.* Block, Irvin (1917-). 1953. Garden City Books, by Arrangement with F. Watts New York. (P.109)

--*Rx for Tomorrow.* Nourse, Alan Edward (1928-). N.D. McKay. (P.687)

--*Sky Carnival: A Story of the Barnstorming Days.* Hallstead, William Finn, III (1924-). 1969. D. McKay Co. (P.407)

--*Third Chair Drummer.* King, Martha C. 1970. I. Washburn. (P.524)

--*The Tree-House Watch.* Klyce, Laura Kent. 1955. D. McKay Co. (P.531)

--*Youth, Youth, Youth: An Anthology of Short Stories.* Tibbets, Albert B. (1888-), ed. 1955. Franklin Watts, Inc. (P.891)

Anderson, Scoular

--*Polly at the Window.* Marshall, Sybil Mary Edwards (1913-). 1975. Penguin Books. (P.623)

Anderson, Stephen

--*Too Funny for Words: Gesture Jokes for Children.* Keller, Charles (1942-), compiled by. 1973. Prentice Hall. (P.514)

Anderson, Victor C.

--*David's Star of Bethlehem.* Parmenter, Christine Whiting, Mrs. (1877-). N.D. Thomas Y Crowell Co. (P.707)

--*Tommy Trot's Visit to Santa Claus.* Page, Thomas Nelson (1853-1922). 1908. C. Scribner's Sons. (P.700)

Anderson, Victor (1904-)

--*Christmas Tree Farm.* Gischler, Pearl Clements (1903-) & Hayden, Gwendolyn Lampshire (1904-). 1951. Pacific Press Pub. Association. (P.370)

--*Mystery at Christmas Tree Farm.* Gischler, Pearl Clements (1903-) & Hayden, Gwendolen Lampshire (1904-). 1971. Review and Herald Pub. Association. (P.370)

Anderson, Walter Inglis (1903-1965)

--*Anderson's Alice: Walter Anderson Illustrates Alice's Adventures in Wonderland.* Carroll, Lewis, pseud. (1832-1898). Dodgson, Charles Lutwidge. 1983. University Press of Mississippi. (P.173)

--*Robinson, the Pleasant History of an Unusual Cat.* Anderson, Walter Inglis (1903-1965). c.1982. University Press of Mississippi. (P.40)

Anderson, Wayne (1946-)

--*The Magic Inkstand.* Seidel, Heinrich. Taylor, Elizabeth W., tr. 1982. Merrimack Pub Cir. (P.808)

Anderson, Will

--*Set the Clock.* King, Dorothy N. (1908-). 1942. Harcourt, Brace and Company. (P.523)

Ando, Hiroshige (1797-1858) & Katsushika, Nokusai (1760-1849)

--*The Big Wave.* Buck, Pearl Sydenstricker, Mrs. (1892-1973). 1973, c.1948. J. Day Co. (P.147)

Andrade, Mary F.

--*Marjorie in the Sunny South.* Curtis, Alice Turner, Mrs. (1860-1958). 1912. The Penn Publishing Company. (P.237)

--*A Regular Tomboy.* Mumford, Mary Eno Bassett, Mrs. (1842-). 1913. The Penn Publishing Company. (P.671)

Andrade, Mary F., jt. illus. see Nagel, Eva M.

Andre, Richard

--*The Babes in the Wood: Children in the Wood Ballad.* c.1888. McLoughlin Bros. (P.40)

--*The Blue Bells on the Lea and Ten Other Tales in Verse, 1 of 6 Vols.* Ewing, Juliana Horatia Gatty, Mrs. (1841-1885). 1884. E. & J. B. Young & Co. (P.313)

--*Blue or Red: Or, The Discontented Lobster.* Ewing, Juliana Horatia Gatty, Mrs. (1841-1885). 1883. Young. (P.313)

--*The Brave Little Tailor, and Other Stories from Grimm's Household Tales.* Grimm, Jakob Ludwig Karl (1785-1863) & Grimm, Wilhelm Karl (1786-1859). Boldey, Ella, tr. from Ger. c.1890. McLoughlin Bros. (P.391)

--*Pepperfoot of Thursday Market.* Davis, Robert (1881-). c.1941. Holiday House. (P.247)
--*The Secret Suitcase.* Andrews, Dorothy Westlake & Scott, Louise Binder. 1953. Friendship Press. (P.41)
--*Shark Hole.* Burglon, Nora. 1943. Holiday House. (P.153)
--*The Spy.* Cooper, James Fenimore (1789-1851). N.D. Minton Balch & Co. (P.218)
--*The Turquoise Horse.* Hull, Eleanor Means (1913-). 1955. Friendship Press. (P.472)
--*White Reindeer.* James, Neill. 1940. C. Scribner's Sons. (P.488)

Baldridge, Cyrus LeRoy (1889-) & Quinn, Paul
--*He Went with Marco Polo: A Story of Venice and Cathay.* Kent, Louise Andrews, Mrs. (1886-1969). 1935. Houghton Mifflin Company. (P.519)

Baldwin-Ford, Pamela
--*The Bremen Town Musicians.* Grimm, Jakob Ludwig Karl (1785-1863) & Grimm, Wilhelm Karl (1786-1859). c.1979. Troll Associates. (P.391)
--*The Emperor's New Clothes.* Andersen, Hans Christian (1805-1875). c.1979. Troll Associates. (P.35)
--*The Parsonage Parrot.* Bothwell, Jean (0000-1977). 1969. F. Watts. (P.119)
--*Strange and Eerie Tales.* Denan, Corinne, retold by. c.1980. Troll Associates. (P.256)
--*Tatterhood and Other Tales: Stories of Magic and Adventure.* Phelps, Ethel Johnston (1914-), compiled by. 1978. Feminist Press. (P.723)
--*Witch Tales.* Denan, Corinne, retold by. c.1980. Troll Associates. (P.257)

Baldwin, Jeanne & Baldwin, Victor
--*The Outcast Kitten.* Baldwin, Jeanne & Baldwin, Victor. 1970. Golden Gate Junior Books. (P.65)

Baldwin, Mabel Wilder
--*Sir Knight of the Golden Pathway.* Duryea, Anna S. P. 1896. G. P. Putnam's Sons. (P.292)

Baldwin, Marilyn
--*I'm Glad.* Gale, Elizabeth Wright. 1969. Judson Press. (P.352)

Baldwin, Richard
--*Great Stories About Dogs.* Edwards, Eleanor Middleton, compiled by. c.1965. Hart. (P.297)

Baldwin, Victor, jt. illus. see Baldwin, Jeanne.

Bale, Gary
--*Voyage of the Kon-Tiki.* Engel, Dolores. 1979. Raintree Pubs. (P.307)

Balet, Jan Bernard (1913-)
--*Adding: A Poem.* Rossetti, Christina Georgina (1830-1894). 1964. Holt, Rinehart and Winston. (P.779)
--*Bean Blossom Hill.* King, Martha Bennett. 1958, c.1957. Rand McNally. (P.524)
--*The Fence: A Mexican Tale.* Balet, Jan Bernard (1913-). 1969. Delacorte Press. (P.65)
--*The Five Rollatinis.* Balet, Jan Bernard (1913-). 1959. Lippincott. (P.65)
--*The Gift: A Portuguese Christmas Tale.* Balet, Jan Bernard (1913-). 1967. Delacorte Press. (P.65)
--*Joanjo, a Portuguese Tale.* Balet, Jan Bernard (1913-). 1967. Delacorte. (P.65)
--*Just One Me.* Brothers, Aileen & Holsclaw, Cora. 1967. Follett Pub. Co. (P.137)
--*The King & the Broom Maker.* Balet, Jan Bernard (1913-). 1969. Delacorte. (P.65)
--*The Lazy Lion.* 1st ed. Wing, Helen. 1953. Rand McNally and Container Corp. of America. (P.969)
--*The Mice, the Monks and the Christmas Tree.* Thompson, George Selden (1929-). Selden, George, pseud. 1963. Macmillan. (P.887)
--*The Princess on the Pea and Other Famous Stories.* Andersen, Hans Christian (1805-1875). 1962. Parents' Magazine Press. (P.37)
--*Rosalinda.* Wing, Helen. 1953. Rand McNally & Co. (P.969)
--*Rumpelstiltskin: An Adaptation from Grimms' Fairy Tales.* Grimm, Jakob Ludwig Karl (1785-1863) & Grimm, Wilhelm Karl (1787-1859). Jones, Patricia (1913-), adapted by. c.1954. Rand McNally. **Award: (NYT).** (P.394)

Balian, Lorna (1929-)
--*An Elephant.* Balian, Lorna (1929-). 1964. Abingdon. (P.65)
--*Leprechauns Never Lie.* Balian, Lorna (1929-). c.1980. Abingdon. (P.65)
--*Where in the World Is Henry?.* Balian, Lorna (1929-). 1980, c.1972. Abingdon. (P.66)

Ball, Julia
--*Dildrum, King of the Cats And Other English Folk Stories.* Grice, Frederick (1910-). 1968, c.1967. F. Watts. (P.389)
--*Dildrum, King of the Cats And Other English Folk Stories.* Grice, Frederick (1910-). 1967. Oxford Univ. Pr. (P.389)

Ball, Mary
--*The Twin Umbrellas.* Wilson, Marjorie. 1930. Houghton Mifflin Company. (P.966)

Ball, Robert, jt. illus. see McCurry, Charles.

Ball, Robert (1890-)
--*The Amazing Adventures of Gargantua & His Son Pantagruel: Edited for Boys.* Rabelais, Francois (1495-1553). c.1940. Houghton Mifflin Company. (P.745)
--*Bleak House.* Dickens, Charles John Huffam (1812-1870). N.D. Heritage Press. (P.262)
--*Clara Branton.* Pace, Mildred Mastin (1907-). 1941. Charles Scribner's Sons. (P.699)
--*The Gold-Laced Coat: A Story of Old Niagara.* Orton, Helen Fuller, Mrs. (1872-1955). 1934. Frederick A. Stokes Co. (P.696)
--*The Gold-Laced Coat: A Story of Old Niagra.* Orton, Helen Fuller, Mrs. (1872-1955). 1934. J. B. Lippincott Co. (P.696)
--*Good Housekeeping's Best Book of Animal Stories.* 1st ed. Ball, Robert (1890-), ed. 1957. Good Housekeeping Magazine: Dist. by Prentice-Hall. (P.66)
--*Lad with a Whistle.* Brink, Carol Ryrie, Mrs. (1895-1981). 1941. The Macmillan Company. (P.132)
--*Robinson Crusoe.* Defoe, Daniel (1661-1731). 1948. J. B. Lippincott Co. (P.250)
--*The Secret of the Rosewood Box.* Orton, Helen Fuller, Mrs. (1872-1955). 1937. Frederick A. Stokes Company. (P.696)
--*The Secret of the Rosewood Box.* Orton, Helen Fuller, Mrs. (1872-1955). N.D. J. B. Lippincott. (P.696)
--*Sleepy Tom.* Akers, Dwight. 1939. G. P. Putnam's Sons. (P.16)
--*The Treasure in the Little Trunk.* Orton, Helen Fuller, Mrs. (1872-1955). 1932. Frederick A. Stokes Company. (P.696)
--*The Treasure in the Little Trunk.* Orton, Helen Fuller, Mrs. (1872-1955). 1932. J. B. Lippincott Co. (P.696)
--*The Wind Flower.* Rose, William (1857-). 1918. Henry Holt. (P.777)

Ball, Seymour
--*The Flying V Mystery.* Ames, Joseph Bushnell (1878-1928). c.1928. The Century Co. (P.33)

Ball, Zachary, pseud., see Masters, Kelly Ray.

Ballantine, Bill, pseud., see Ballantine, William Oliver.

Ballantine, Bill, pseud. (1911-)
--*The Man in the Manhole.* Ballantine, William Oliver. Sage, Juniper, pseud. & Brown, Margaret Wise (1910-1952). Hurd, Edith Thacher & Brown, Margaret Wise. 1955. W. R. Scott, Inc. (P.788)
--*The Man in the Manhole and the Fix-It Man.* Ballantine, William Oliver. Sage, Juniper, pseud. & Brown, Margaret Wise (1910-1952). Hurd, Edith Thacher & Brown, Margaret Wise. c.1946. W. R. Scott, Inc. (P.788)

Ballantine, William Oliver see Ballantine, Bill, pseud.

Ballantyne, Robert Michael (1825-1894)
--*The Buffalo Runners: A Tale of the Red River Plains.* Ballantyne, Robert Michael (1825-1894). 1891. Thomas Nelson & Sons. (P.66)
--*Erling the Bold: A Tale of the Norse Sea-Kings.* Ballantyne, Robert Michael (1825-1894). 1874. J. B. Lippincott & Co. (P.66)

Balmer, Clinton
--*Away to Sea.* Meader, Stephen Warren (1892-). c.1931. Harcourt, Brace and Company. (P.637)
--*Blue Pigeons.* Sterne, Emma Gelders, Mrs. (1894-1971). N.D. Dodd Mead & Co. (P.853)
--*Blue Pigeons.* Sterne, Emma Gelders, Mrs. (1894-1971). 1929. Duffield and Company. (P.853)
--*The Glacier Mystery: A Boy's Story of the Tyrolese Alps.* Smith, Sarah Storer (1905-). c.1932. Harcourt, Brace and Company. (P.836)
--*Jerry: The Adventures of an Army Dog.* Meek, Sterner St. Paul (1894-1972). c.1932. The Century Co. (P.638)

Baltermants, Dmitri, photos by.
--*Nikolai Lives in Moscow.* Baltermants, Dmitrii Nikolaevich & Levin, Deana. 1968, c.1966. Hastings House. (P.67)

Baltzer, Hans (1900-)
--*Behind the Circus Tent.* Jacobs, Allan Duane (1934-) & Jacobs, Leland Blair (1907-). 1967. Lerner. (P.486)
--*Black Wolf of the Steppes.* David, Kurt (1924-). 1972, c.1971. Houghton Mifflin. (P.244)
--*Esox: The Story of a Pike.* Zeiske, Wolfgang. 1970. Delacorte Press. (P.992)
--*Gulliver's Travels.* Abridged. Swift, Jonathan (1667-1745). Moss, Elaine, ed. 1963, c.1961. Duell, Sloan and Pearce. (P.874)
--*Jose: A Tale from South America.* Feustel, Gunther. 1968. Delacorte Press. (P.323)
--*Jose: A Tale from South America.* Feustel, Gunther. Humphries, Stella, tr. 1968. Delacorte. (P.323)

Balwin, Michael (1934-)
--*Lark's Castle.* York, Susannah. 1977, c.1976. D. McKay Co. (P.988)

Balzola, Asun
--*A Boy & His Robot.* Garcia Sanchez, Jose Luis & Pacheco, Miguel Angel. 1979. Methuen Inc. (P.354)
--*The Girl with No Name.* Garcia Sanchez, Jose Luis & Pacheco, Miguel Angel. 1979, c.1978. Methuen. (P.354)

Bama, James
--*A Visit to the Hospital.* Chase, Francine. Dunbar, Flanders, intro. by. 1957. Grosset & Dunlap. (P.188)

Banbery, Fred
--*Alfred Hitchcock's Haunted Houseful.* Hitchcock, Alfred Joseph (1899-1980), ed. 1961. Random. (P.446)
--*Alfred Hitchcock's Solve-Them-Yourself Mysteries.* Hitchcock, Alfred Joseph (1899-1980), ed. 1963. Random. (P.446)
--*Haunted Houseful.* Hitchcock, Alfred Joseph (1899-1980), ed. c.1961. Random. (P.447)
--*Paddington at the Circus.* Bond, Thomas Michael (1926-) 1974, c. 1973. Random House (P.114)
--*Paddington at the Seaside.* Bond, Thomas Michael (1926-) 1978, c. 1975 Random House (P.114)
--*Paddington at the Tower.* Bond, Thomas Michael (1926-). 1978, c.1975. Random House. (P.114)
--*Paddington Bear.* Bond, Thomas Michael (1926-). 1973, c.1972. Random House. (P.114)
--*Paddington's Garden.* Bond, Thomas Michael (1926-). 1973, c.1972. Random House. (P.114)
--*Paddington's Lucky Day.* Bond, Thomas Michael (1926-) 1974, c. 1973 Random House (P.114)
--*Solve-Them-Yourself Mysteries.* Hitchcock, Alfred Joseph (1899-1980), ed. 1963. Random House. (P.447)
--*Taller Than Bandai Mountain: The Story of Hideo Noguchi.* D'Amelio, Dan (1927-). 1968. Viking Press. (P.240)

Banek, Yvette
--*A Boy Named Mary Jane, and Other Silly Verse.* Cole, William Rossa (1919-). 1976. Watts. (P.208)

Banfield, V. M.
--*Arabella's New House.* Johnson, Alice Cheney. 1967. Dorrance. (P.493)

Bang, L. & Stine, David L.
--*A Messenger from Santa Claus.* Scribner, Harvey (1850-). 1904. Franklin Printing and Engraving Co. (P.806)

Bang, Molly Garrett see Bang, Garrett,

Bang, Molly Garrett (1943-)
--*The Buried Moon and other Stories.* Bang, Molly Garrett (1943-), ed. 1977. Scribner. (P.68)
--*David's Landing.* Richardson, Judith Benet (1941-). c.1984. Woods Hole Historical Collection. (P.763)
--*The Demons of Rajpur: Five Tales from Bengal.* Bang, Betsy (1912-), tr. 1980. Greenwillow Books. (P.68)
--*The Goblins Giggle, and Other Stories.* Bang, Molly Garrett (1943-), ed. 1973. Scribners. (P.68)
--*The Grey Lady and the Strawberry Snatcher.* Bang, Molly Garrett (1943-). c.1980. Four Winds Press. **Awards: (ALA); (BGH); (RCM).** (P.68)
--*Men from the Village Deep in the Mountains and Other Japanese Folk Tales.* Bang, Molly Garrett. Bang, Garrett, pseud. (1943-), ed. Bang, Molly Garrett. 1973. Macmillan. (P.68)
--*The Old Woman & the Red Pumpkin.* Bang, Betsy (1912-), adapted by. 1975. Macmillan. (P.68)
--*The Old Woman and the Rice Thief.* Bang, Betsy (1912-), tr. c.1978. Greenwillow Books. (P.68)
--*The Paper Crane.* Bang, Molly Garrett (1943-). c.1985. Greenwillow Books. (P.68)
--*Ten, Nine, Eight.* Bang, Molly Garrett (1943-). 1983. Greenwillow. **Awards: (ALA); (RCM).** (P.68)
--*Ten, Nine, Eight.* Bang, Molly Garrett (1943-). 1985, c.1983. Puffin Books. (P.68)
--*Tuntuni, the Tailor Bird.* Bang, Betsy (1912-), tr. c.1978. Greenwillow Books. (P.68)
--*Wiley and the Hairy Man: Adapted from an American Folktale.* Bang, Molly Garrett (1943-), adapted by. c.1976. Macmillan. **Award: (ALA).** (P.68)

Banghart, Jerry
--*The Ominous Dragoon of Dothdura.* Ramtha & Mahr, Douglas J. 1985. Masterworks Inc. (P.747)

Bangurah, Hassan
--*Two African Tales: The Leopard Hunt, and The Devil at Yolahun Bridge.* Nichol, Abioseh. c.1965. Cambridge. (P.681)

Banigan, Kippy & Stearns, Sharon (1912-)
--*So Big Book of Mother Goose.* N.D. Garden City Publishing Co. (P.68)

Banigan, Sharon Church see Stearns, Sharon,

Banish, Roslyn
--*I Want to Tell You About My Baby.* Banish, Roslyn. 1982. Wingbow Press. (P.68)

Bankart, Henry Reginald (1913-)
--*Bolivar.* Bankart, Henry Reginald (1913-). 1941. Smith & Durrell. (P.68)

Banks, Eulalie see Eulalie, pseud.

Banks, Eulalie M. see Eulalie, pseud.

Banks, Joe
--*Land of the Whatsit ... Adventures of Billy and Betty.* Morris, Charles Dexter (1883-). c.1935. The Macaulay Company. (P.664)

Banks, Virginia Mathers
--*Sing Out!.* Dykema, Peter William (1873-), ed. 1946. C. C. Birchard. (P.293)

Banner, Angela, pseud., see Maddison, Angela Mary.

Banner, Angela, pseud. (1923-)
--*Ant & Bee & the Doctor.* Maddison, Angela Mary. Banner, Angela, pseud. (1923-). Maddison, Angela Mary. 1971. Watts. (P.68)
--*Ant and Bee and the Secret.* Maddison, Angela Mary. Banner, Angela, pseud. (1923-). Maddison, Angela Mary. 1970. F. Watts. (P.68)
--*Ant & Bee Go Shopping.* Maddison, Angela Mary. Banner, Angela, pseud. (1923-). Maddison, Angela Mary. 1972. Watts. (P.69)
--*Ant and Bee Time.* Maddison, Angela Mary. Banner, Angela, pseud. (1923-). Maddison, Angela Mary. 1969. F. Watts. (P.69)

Bannerman, Helen Brodie Cowan Watson (1863-1946) & Ver Beck, Frank (1858-1933)
--*The Little Black Sambo Story Book.* Bannerman, Helen Brodie Cowan Watson, Mrs. (1863-1946) & Ver Beck, Frank (1858-). c.1930. Henry Altemus Company. (P.69)
--*The Little Black Sambo Story Book: With the original story.* Bannerman, Helen Brodie Cowan Watson, Mrs. (1863-1946) & Ver Beck, Frank (1858-1933). 1962. Platt & Munk. (P.69)
--*Sambo and the Twins.* Bannerman, Helen Brodie Cowan Watson, Mrs. (1863-1946). 1936. J. B. Lippincott Co. (P.69)
--*Sambo and the Twins, a New Adventure of Little Black Sambo.* Bannerman, Helen Brodie Cowan Watson, Mrs. (1863-1946). N.D. J. P. Lippincott Co. (P.69)
--*Sambo and the Twins Other Tales.* Bannerman, Helen Brodie Cowan Watson, Mrs. (1863-1946). 1936. J. B. Lippincott. (P.69)
--*The Story of Little Black Bobtail.* Bannerman, Helen Brodie Cowan Watson, Mrs. (1863-1946). N.D. J. B. Lippincott Co. (P.69)
--*The Story of Little Black Mingo.* Bannerman, Helen Brodie Cowan Watson, Mrs. (1863-1946). 1902. Frederick A. Stokes Co. (P.69)
--*The Teasing Monkey.* N.D. J. B. Lippincott Co. (P.69)

Bannister, Constance, photos by.
--*Puppy and Me.* Ratzesberger, Anna. c.1955. Rand McNally. (P.750)

Bannon, Laura May, jt. illus. see Gordon, Will.

Bannon, Laura May (0000-1963)
--*Baby Roo.* Bannon, Laura May (0000-1963). 1947. Houghton Mifflin Co. (P.69)
--*The Best House in the World.* Bannon, Laura May (0000-1963). 1952. Houghton Mifflin. (P.69)
--*Big Brother.* Bannon, Laura May (0000-1963). 1950. Whitman. (P.69)
--*Billy and the Bear.* Bannon, Laura May (0000-1963). N.D. Houghton Miffin Co.,. (P.69)
--*Burro Boy and His Big Trouble.* Bannon, Laura May (0000-1963). 1955. Abingdon Press. (P.69)
--*Chang Chee.* Lee, Melicent Humason, Mrs. (1889-1943) & Ho, Jung. 1939. Harper & Brothers. (P.561)
--*The Cousins: Or, Astrid's Happy Summer.* Anderson, Helen Foster (1891-). 1946. Augustana Book Concern. (P.39)
--*The Gift of Hawaii.* Bannon, Laura May (0000-1963). 1961. A. Whitman. (P.69)
--*Gregorio and the White Llama.* Bannon, Laura May (0000-1963). 1944. A. Whitman & Co. (P.69)
--*Hat for a Hero, a Tarascan Boy of Mexico.* Bannon, Laura May (0000-1963). 1954. A. Whitman. (P.69)
--*Hawaiian Coffee Picker.* Bannon, Laura May (0000-1963). 1962. Houghton Mifflin. (P.69)
--*Hop-High, the Goat.* 1st ed. Bannon, Laura May (0000-1963). 1960. Bobbs-Merrill. (P.69)
--*Horse on a Houseboat.* Bannon, Laura May (0000-1963). 1951. Whitman. (P.69)
--*Jo-Jo, the Talking Crow.* Bannon, Laura May (0000-1963). 1958. Houghton Mifflin. (P.69)
--*Katy Comes Next.* Bannon, Laura May (0000-1963). 1959. A. Whitman. (P.69)
--*Little People of the Night.* Bannon, Laura May (0000-1963). c.1963. Houghton Mifflin. (P.69)
--*The Little Sister Doll.* Bannon, Laura May (0000-1963). 1955. A. Whitman. (P.69)
--*The Other Side of the World.* Bannon, Laura May (0000-1963). 1960. Houghton Mifflin. (P.69)
--*Patty Paints a Picture.* Bannon, Laura May (0000-1963). 1946. A. Whitman & Company. (P.69)
--*Pecos Bill.* Bowman, James Cloyd (1880-1961). 1964. A Whitman. (P.122)
--*Red Mittens.* Bannon, Laura May (0000-1963). 1946. Hale. (P.69)
--*Red Mittens.* Bannon, Laura May (0000-1963). 1946. Houghton Mifflin Company. (P.69)

--*Four Dolls*. Godden, Rumer. 1984. Greenwillow. (P.372).

--*From the Fury of the Norsemen and Other Stories from History*. Power, Rhoda Dolores (1890-1957). 1957. Houghton Mifflin. (P.736).

--*A Gift from the Heart: Folk Tales from Bulgaria*. Pridham, Radost (1922-). 1967, c.1966. World Pub. Co. (P.739).

--*Grasshopper & Butterfly*. Piers, Helen. 1975. McGraw. (P.725).

--*The Horse and His Boy*. Lewis, Clive Staples (1898-1963). 1954. Macmillan. **Award: (CMA)**. (P.569).

--*The Horse and His Boy*. Lewis, Clive Staples (1898-1963). 1962. MacMillan Company. (P.569).

--*Horse & His Boy*. Lewis, Clive Staples (1898-1963). 1969. Macmillan. (P.569).

--*The Iron Lion*. Dickinson, Peter (1927-). c.1983. Bedrick-Blackie: Dist. by Harper & Row. (P.265).

--*The Iron Lion*. Dickinson, Peter (1927-). 1984. Harper. (P.265).

--*The Joy of the Court*. De Troyes, Chrestien (1928-). Hieatt, Constance Bartlett (1922-), retold by. 1971. Crowell. (P.260).

--*The Last Battle*. Lewis, Clive Staples (1898-1963). 1956. Macmillan. **Awards: (ALA); (CMA)**. (P.569).

--*The Last Battle*. Lewis, Clive Staples (1898-1963). 1962. MacMillan Company. (P.569).

--*The Lion, the Witch and the Wardrobe*. Lewis, Clive Staples (1898-1963). 1965. MacMillan Company. (P.569).

--*The Lion, the Witch & the Wardrobe*. Lewis, Clive Staples (1898-1963). 1968. Macmillan. (P.569).

--*The Lion, the Witch and the Wardrobe: A Story for Children*. Lewis, Clive Staples (1898-1963). 1950. Macmillan. (P.569).

--*Lorna Doone*. Blackmore, Richard Doddridge (1825-1900). Jones, Olive, ed. 1970. American Education Publications. (P.105).

--*The Magician's Nephew*. Lewis, Clive Staples (1898-1963). 1955. Macmillan. **Award: (ALA)**. (P.569).

--*The Magician's Nephew*. Lewis, Clive Staples (1898-1963). 1970. Macmillan. (P.569).

--*Medieval Tales*. Westwood, Jennifer (1940-), retold by. 1968, c.1967. Coward-McCann. (P.948).

--*Miracle Plays: Seven Medieval Plays for Modern Players*. Malcolmson, Anne Burnett, Mrs. (1910-), ed. 1959. HM. (P.614).

--*The Most Wonderful Animals That Never Were*. 1st ed. Krutch, Joseph Wood (1893-1970). 1969. Houghton Mifflin. (P.541).

--*Prince Caspian*. Lewis, Clive Staples (1898-1963). 1969. Macmillan. (P.569).

--*Prince Caspian: The Return to Narnia*. Lewis, Clive Staples (1898-1963). 1951. Macmillan. (P.569).

--*The Puffin Book of Nursery Rhymes*. Opie, Iona Archibald (1923-) & Opie, Peter (1918-1982), eds. 1963. Penguin Books. (P.695).

--*Saint George and the Dragon: Being the Legend of the Red Cross Knight from the Faerie Queene*. Spenser, Edmund (1552-1599). Warburg, Sandol Stoddard, ed. 1963. Houghton Mifflin. **Award: (ALA)**. (P.843).

--*The Silver Chair*. Lewis, Clive Staples (1898-1963). 1953. Macmillan. (P.569).

--*Silver Chair*. Lewis, Clive Staples (1898-1963). 1967. Macmillan. (P.569).

--*The Silver Chair*. Lewis, Clive Staples (1898-1963). 1969. MacMillan Publishing Company. (P.569).

--*Smith of Wootton Major*. Tolkien, John Ronald Reuel (1892-1973). 1967. Houghton Mifflin. (P.894).

--*Snail and Caterpillar*. Piers, Helen. 1972. American Heritage Press. (P.725).

--*Tales and Legends*. Westwood, Jennifer (1940-), retold by. 1971. Coward, McCann & Geoghegan. (P.948).

--*Tales of Waybeyond*. Hunter, Eileen. 1979. A. Deutsch. (P.474).

--*The Unicorn Window*. Muir, Lynette. 1961. Abelard-Schuman. (P.670).

--*The Upstairs Donkey & Other Stolen Stories*. Morris, James Humphrey (1926-). 1961. Pantheon Books. (P.664).

--*The Voyage of the Dawn Treader*. Lewis, Clive Staples (1898-1963). 1952. Macmillan. (P.569).

--*Voyage of the Dawn Treader*. Lewis, Clive Staples (1898-1963). 1969. Macmillan. (P.569).

Baynton, Martin

--*Big John Turkle*. Hoban, Russell Conwell (1925-). 1984, c.1983. Holt, Rhinehart, and Winston. (P.447).

--*Charlie Meadows*. Hoban, Russell Conwell (1925-). 1984. HR&W. (P.447).

--*Goldilocks & the Three Bears*. 1982. Lothrop. (P.84).

--*Hansel & Gretel*. 1982. Lothrop. (P.84).

--*Jim Frog*. Hoban, Russell Conwell (1925-). 1984, c.1983. HR&W. (P.447).

--*Lavinia Bat*. Hoban, Russell Conwell (1925-). 1984. HR&W. (P.447).

Bayrak, Loba

--*Turkish Fairy Tales*. Ekrem, Selma. 1964. Van Nos Reinhold. (P.300).

Bayzard, P. J. & Burd, Clara Miller

--*Animal Friends Story Book*. Piper, Watty, pseud. (1870-1945), ed. c.1928. The Platt & Munk Co., Inc. (P.727).

Beach, Bettye Rene, jt. illus. see Francis, Philip.

Beach, Bettye Rene

--*Dear Pastor*. Adler, Bill. c.1980. T. Nelson Publishers. (P.11).

--*My Funny Cloud*. 1st ed. Peebles, J. Winston. 1981. Winston-Derek Publishers. (P.715).

Beal, H. Martin

--*The Young Cascarillero: And Colonel Thorndike's Adventures*. Downing, Marlton & French, Henry William. N.D. Lothrop Pub. Co. (P.283).

Bealer, Alex Winkler (1921-1980)

--*The Picture-Skin Story*. Bealer, Alex Winkler, III (1921-1980). 1957. Holiday House. (P.85).

Beales, I. B.

--*An Express of 'Seventy-Six: A Chronicle of the Town of York in the War for Independence*. Hubbard, Lindley Murray. 1906. Little, Brown, and Company. (P.469).

Beales, Joan

--*Snake in the Camp*. Cockett, Mary. 1976, c.1975. Childrens Press. (P.205).

Beals, Dorothy Lee

--*Cowbells for Forget-Me-Not*. Condon, Helen Browne. 1942. T. Nelson and Sons. (P.212).

Beaman, S. G. Hulme

--*The Seven Voyages of Sinbad the Sailor*. Beaman, S. G. Hulme, retold by. 1926. R.M. McBride and Company. (P.85).

Beard, Adelia Belle, jt. illus. see Beard, Lina.

Beard, Alice

--*Elizabeth Bess: A Little Girl of the Sixties*. Scott, Ellen Corrigan, Mrs. (1862-). 1917. The Macmillan Company. (P.804).

--*Honey-Sweet*. Turpin, Edna Henry Lee (1867-). 1911. The Macmillan Company. (P.906).

--*Little Allies: A Story of Four Children*. Hale, Beatrice (1883-). c.1918. Frederick A. Stokes Company. (P.403).

--*The Magic String Book: Being the Thrilling Adventures of the Stringum Family with the String on Which the Thrills Are Strung*. Beard, Alice. c.1916. F.A. Stokes. (P.85).

--*Mary Allen*. Marvin, Eleanor. 1916. Doubleday, Page & Company. (P.627).

--*Peggy of Roundabout Lane*. Turpin, Edna Henry Lee (1867-). 1917. The Macmillan Company. (P.906).

--*Peggy Stewart at School*. Jackson, Gabrielle Emilie Snow, Mrs. (1861-). 1912. The Macmillan Company. (P.484).

--*The Surprise Book*. Beard, Patten. c.1918. The Pilgrim Press. (P.85).

Beard, Daniel Carter, et al. (1859-1941)

--*Old Farm Fairies*. McCook, Henry Christopher (1837-1911). N.D. George W. Jacobs & Co. (P.596).

Beard, Daniel Carter, jt. illus. see Beard, James Carter.

Beard, Daniel Carter (1859-1941)

--*The American Boys' Book of Birds and Brownies of the Woods*. Beard, Daniel Carter (1859-1941). 1923. J. B. Lippincott Company. (P.85).

--*Dan Beard's Animal Book, and Camp-fire Stories*. Beard, Daniel Carter (1859-1941). 1907. Moffat, Yard & Co. (P.85).

Beard, James Carter (1837-)

--*Upon the Tree-Tops*. Miller, Harriet Mann, Mrs. (1831-1918). Miller, Olive Thorne, pseud. N.D. Houghton Mifflin. (P.647).

Beard, James Carter (1837-) & Beard, Daniel Carter (1859-1941)

--*A Frozen Dragon and Other Tales: A Story Book of Natural History for Boys and Girls*. Holder, Charles Frederick (1851-1915). 1888. Dodd, Mead & Company. (P.454).

Beard, Lina (0000-1933) & Beard, Adelia Belle (1857-1920)

--*Mother Nature's Toy Shop*. Beard, Lina & Beard, Adelia Belle (1857-1920). 1918. Charles Scribner's Sons. (P.85).

--*On the Trail*. Beard, Lina & Beard, Adelia Belle (1857-1920). 1915. Charles Scribner's Sons. (P.85).

Beard, Patten

--*Marjorie's Literary Dolls*. Beard, Patten. c.1916. Frederick A. Stokes Company. (P.85).

--*The Toyland Mother Goose*. Mother Goose. Beard, Patten, ed. c.1917. Frederick A. Stokes Company. (P.669).

Bearden, Wanda

--*The Poet*. Nemeth, Doris I. & Kenzie, Peggy, eds. 1982. Fine Arts Soc. (P.678).

--*Poet, Autumn, Nineteen Seventy-Nine*. Nemeth, Doris I., et al., eds. 1979. Fine Arts Soc. (P.678).

Beardsley, Aubrey Vincent (1872-1898)

--*The Story of King Arthur and the Knights of the Table Round*. Brooks, Edward, Dr. (1831-1912). 1900. The Penn Publishing Company. (P.136).

Beardsley, Susan

--*Danny and the Anaconda*. 1st ed. Goody, Phyllis B. c.1975. Exposition Press. (P.376).

--*Julio, the Shoeshine Boy*. Goody, Phyllis B. 1977. Exposition. (P.376).

Bearman, Jane Ruth (1917-)

--*Candle Light Stories*. Freehof, Lillian B. Simon (1906-). 1951. Bloch. (P.343).

--*David*. Bearman, Jane Ruth (1917-). 1965. Jonathan David. (P.85).

--*Shalom!*. Bearman, Jane Ruth (1917-). 1958. Jonathan David Co. (P.85).

Beaton, Monica

--*Our Little Vatican City Cousin*. Farnum, Mabel Adelaide (1887-). c.1934. L. C. Page & Company. (P.318).

Beaton, Ruth

--*Christopher Listens*. Fitzsimons, Ruth Marie Mangan. 1967. Denison. (P.330).

Beatty, Dill

--*Down by the Creek Bank*. Rambo, Dottie. 1979. Impact Tenn. (P.747).

--*Is There Anything I Can Do for You?*. Rambo, Dottie & Huntsinger, Dave. 1979. Impact Tenn. (P.747).

Beatty, Hetty Burlingame (1907-1971)

--*Bronto*. Beatty, Hetty Burlingame (1907-1971). 1952. Doubleday. (P.85).

--*Little Owl Indian*. Beatty, Hetty Burlingame (1907-1971). c.1951. Houghton Mifflin. (P.85).

--*Little Wild Horse*. Beatty, Hetty Burlingame (1907-1971). 1949. Houghton Mifflin Co. (P.85).

--*Moorland Pony*. Beatty, Hetty Burlingame (1907-1971). 1961. Houghton Mifflin. (P.85).

Beaudouin, Frank

--*Clear for Action!*. Meader, Stephen Warren (1892-). c.1940. Harcourt, Brace and Company. (P.637).

--*Flight into Danger*. Mason, Francis Van Wyck (1901-1978). Mason, Frank W., pseud. 1946. J. B. Lippincott Company. (P.628).

--*Ice Patrol: Jim Steele's Adventures with the U. S. Coast Guard*. Bell, Kensil (1907-). U. S. Coast Guard, photos by. 1937. Dodd, Mead & Company. (P.90).

--*Pilots, Man Your Planes!*. Mason, Francis Van Wyck (1901-1978). Mason, Frank W., pseud. 1944. J. B. Lippincott Company. (P.628).

--*Q-Boat*. Rev ed. Mason, Francis Van Wyck (1901-1978). Mason, Frank W., pseud. 1943. J. B. Lippincott Company. (P.628).

Beaudreau, Barbara

--*Indian Canoe-Maker*. Beatty, Patricia Robbins (1922-). c.1960. Idaho, Caxton Printers. (P.86).

--*Indian Canoe- Maker*. Beatty, Patricia Robbins (1922-). N.D. JUV. (P.86).

Beaudry, Jeanne Stauffer

--*The Pelican Tree, and Other Panama Adventures*. Bailey, Jean (1917-) & Lamb, Elizabeth Searle (1917-). 1953. North River Press. (P.60).

Beaujon, Louise

--*Nah le Kah De, He Herds Sheep: The Story of a Navajo Boy*. Harrington, Isis L., Mrs. 1937. E. P. Dutton & Company. (P.414).

Beaumont

--*The Lost Sheep & Other Parables*. Rey, Alfonso. Nevins, Albert J. (1915-), tr. from Sp. 1979. Our Sunday Visitor. (P.758).

--*Poor Lazarus and Other Parables: The Parable of the Sower, the Good Shepherd*. Rey, Alfonso. Nevins, Albert J. (1915-), tr. from Sp. c.1979. Our Sunday Visitor. (P.758).

Beazer, G. Falcon

--*And the Sun God Said: That's Hip*. Gregg, Ernest. 1972. Harper & Row. (P.388).

Bebbe, Robb

--*ABCs for Catholic boys and girls*. 1st ed. Beebe, Catherine (1898-). c.1938. Longmans Green & Co. (P.88).

Becher, Arthur E.

--*The Adventures of Joel Pepper*. Lothrop, Harriet Mulford Stone, Mrs. (1844-1924). Sidney, Margaret, pseud. 1937. Houghton Mifflin Company. (P.586).

--*Ben Pepper*. Lothrop, Harriet Mulford Stone, Mrs. (1844-1924). Sidney, Margaret, pseud. 1937. Houghton Mifflin Company. (P.586).

--*The Boy Captive in Canada*. Smith, Mary Prudence Wells, Mrs. (1840-1930). 1905. Little, Brown, and Company. (P.835).

--*Five Little Peppers Abroad*. Lothrop, Harriet Mulford Stone, Mrs. (1844-1924). Sidney, Margaret, pseud. 1937. Houghton Mifflin Company. (P.586).

--*Five Little Peppers: And Their Friends*. Lothrop, Harriet Mulford Stone, Mrs. (1844-1924). Sidney, Margaret, pseud. 1937. Houghton Mifflin Company. (P.586).

--*Five Little Peppers at School*. Lothrop, Harriet Mulford Stone, Mrs. (1844-1924). Sidney, Margaret, pseud. 1937. Houghton Mifflin Company. (P.586).

--*Five Little Peppers Grown Up*. Lothrop, Harriet Mulford Stone, Mrs. (1844-1924). Sidney, Margaret, pseud. 1937. Houghton Mifflin Company. (P.586).

--*Five Little Peppers in the Little Brown House*. Lothrop, Harriet Mulford Stone, Mrs. (1844-1924). Sidney, Margaret, pseud. 1937. Houghton Mifflin Company. (P.586).

--*Five Little Peppers Midway*. Lothrop, Harriet Mulford Stone, Mrs. (1844-1924). Sidney, Margaret, pseud. 1937. Houghton Mifflin Company. (P.586).

--*The House of the Misty Star*. Little, Frances, pseud. (1863-). Macaulay, Fannie Caldwell. N.D. Century Co. (P.577).

--*In the Days of Young Washington*. Turner, Nancy Byrd (1880-). 1931. Houghton Mifflin Company. (P.906).

--*The Lucky Sixpence*. Knipe, Emilie Benson, Mrs. (1870-1958) & Knipe, Alden Arthur (1870-1950). 1912. The Century Co. (P.532).

--*The Magic Walking-Stick*. Buchan, John (1875-1940). 1932. Houghton Mifflin Company. (P.146).

--*The Mysterious Beacon Light: The Adventures of Four Boys in Labrador*. Walsh, George Ethelbert (1865-1941). 1904. Little, Brown & Co. (P.928).

--*Our Davie Pepper*. Lothrop, Harriet Mulford Stone, Mrs. (1844-1924). Sidney, Margaret, pseud. 1937. Houghton Mifflin Company. (P.586).

--*Phronsie Pepper: The Youngest of the "Five Little Peppers"*. Lothrop, Harriet Mulford Stone, Mrs. (1844-1924). Sidney, Margaret, pseud. 1937. Houghton Mifflin Company. (P.586).

--*The Stories Polly Pepper Told to the Five Little Peppers in the Little Brown House*. Lothrop, Harriet Mulford Stone, Mrs. (1844-1924). Sidney, Margaret, pseud. 1937. Houghton Mifflin Company. (P.586).

Bechtolf, Theodore

--*Ben Stone at Oakdale*. Scott, Morgan. N.D. Hurst & Co. (P.805).

Beck, Charles

--*Buffalo and Beaver*. 1st ed. Meader, Stephen Warren (1892-). 1960. Harcourt, Brace. (P.637).

--*Everglades Adventure*. 1st ed. Meader, Stephen Warren (1892-). 1957. Harcourt, Brace. (P.637).

--*Mr. Sims' Argosy*. Wilcox, Eleanor Reindollar. 1958. Dodd, Mead. (P.958).

--*Mystery of the Marble Zoo*. Clark, Margaret Goff (1913-). 1964. Funk & Wagnalls. (P.198).

--*Mystery of the Piper's Ghost*. Macdonald, Zillah Katherine (1885-). 1972. Schol Bk Serv. (P.600).

--*Robin Hood: The Outlaw of Sherwood Forest*. Prescott, Orville (1908-), ed. 1959. Random House. (P.738).

--*Thinking Machine: Adventures of a Mastermind*. Futrelle, Jacques. 1965. Schol Bk Serv. (P.350).

--*Thinking Machine: Adventures of a Mastermind*. Futrelle, Jacques. 1972. Schol Bk Serv. (P.350).

--*Trail Through Danger*. Steele, William Owen (1917-1979). c.1965. Harcourt. (P.851).

--*Trappers of Venus*. Greene, Joseph Ingham (1897-). c.1961. Golden Press. (P.387).

--*Wild Pony Island*. Meader, Stephen Warren (1892-). 1959. HarBraceJ. (P.637).

--*The Year of the Bloody Sevens*. 1st ed. Steele, William Owen (1917-1979). 1963. Harcourt, Brace & World. **Award: (ALA)**. (P.851).

Beck, Clifford, Jr., jt. illus. see Denetsosie, Hoke.

Beck, Frank Ver

--*Elsie and the Arkansaw Bear: Told in Song and Story*. Paine, Albert Bigelow (1861-1937). c.1909. H. Altemus Company. (P.700).

Beck, Ian

--*Round & Round the Garden*. Williams, Sarah. N.D. Oxford U Pr. (P.964).

Beck, Peggy Paver

--*Black Hawk's Trail*. Bloom, Margaret (1893-). 1931. Laidlaw Brothers. (P.109).

--*The Masked Rider*. Knowles, Mabel Winifred (1875-). Wynne, May, pseud. 1931. Laidlaw Brothers. (P.533).

Becker-Berke, Helmar

--*Keeper of the Wild Bulls*. Sponsel, Heinz. Pauli, Hertha, tr. 1962. Farrar, Straus & Cudahy. (P.845).

Becker, Charlotte, jt. illus. see Richardson, Frederick.

Becker, Charlotte, jt. illus. see Ware, Charlotte.

Becker, Charlotte, jt. illus. see Winter, Milo Kendall.

Becker, Charlotte (1906-)

--*Arabian Nights' Fairy Tales*. N.D. Sears Publishing Co. (P.87).

--*Changeable Charlie*. Blumenthal, Gertrude (1907-1971). 1942. Oxford University Press. (P.110).

--*A Chimp in the Family*. Becker, Charlotte (1906-). 1953. J. Messner. (P.87).

--*Christmas is Coming*. Jones, Manley H. 1939. Houghton Mifflin Co. (P.500).

--*Fairy Tales for Little People: Told for Them*. Catrevas, Christina, ed. c.1927. J. H. Sears & Company, Inc. (P.178).

--*Russian Fairy Tales.* Ponsot, Marie Birmingham, tr. from Fr. 1973. Western Pub. (P.95)
--*Sleeping Beauty and Other Stories.* Goulden, Shirley, retold by. N.D. Grosset & Dunlap. (P.379)
--*The Sleeping Beauty, and Other Tales.* Perrault, Charles (1628-1703). Goulden, Shirley, retold by. 1957. Grosset & Dunlap. (P.719)
--*Tales from the Arabian Nights.* Arabian Nights. Goulden, Shirley, retold by. 1957. Grosset & Dunlap. (P.45)
--*The Three Little Pigs.* Sperber, Ann, tr. from Fr. 1979. Knopf : Distributed by Random House. (P.95)

Berard, Hazel de
--*A Voyage to Treasure Land.* Chandler, Anna Curtis. 1929. Harper & Brothers. (P.183)

Bercher, J. O.
--*The Quest for Fire: A Novel of Prehistoric Times.* Rosny, J. H, pseud. (1856-1940). Boex, J. H.. Talbott, Harold, tr. 1967. Pantheon. (P.778)

Bere, Bagnot de la
--*Don Quixote of La Mancha.* Cervantes Saavedra, Miguel de (1547-1616). N.D. Thomas Y Crowell. (P.180)

Berelson, Howard (1940-)
--*Fairy Rings and Other Mushrooms.* Conklin, Gladys Plemon (1903-). 1973. Holiday House. (P.213)
--*Jellyfishes.* Shepherd, Elizabeth. 1969. Lothrop, Lee & Shepard Co. (P.818)
--*My Friend Andrew.* Collins, Patricia. c.1979. Prentice-Hall. (P.210)
--*On Guard: Living Things Defend Themselves.* Bowman, John Stewart (1931-). 1969. Doubleday. (P.122)

Berenstain, Janice, jt. illus. see Berenstain, Stanley.

Berenstain, Michael (1951-)
--*The Creature Catalog: A Monster Watcher's Guide.* Berenstain, Michael (1951-). 1982. Random. (P.95)
--*King Kong.* Conaway, Judith (1948-) & Lovelace, Delos Wheeler (1894-1967). c.1983. Random House. (P.212)
--*K'tonton on an Island in the Sea: A Hitherto Unreported Episode in the Life of the Jewish Thumbling, K'tonton Ben Baruch Reuben.* Weilerstein, Sadie Rose, Mrs. (1894-). 1976. Jewish Publication Society of America. (P.941)

Berenstain, Stanley (1923-) & Berenstain, Janice (1923-)
--*The Bear Detectives.* Berenstain, Stanley (1923-) & Berenstain, Janice (1923-). 1975. Beginner. (P.95)
--*The Berenstain Bears' Almanac.* Berenstain, Stanley (1923-) & Berenstain, Janice (1923-). 1984. Random. (P.95)
--*The Berenstain Bears & Mama's New Job.* Berenstain, Stanley (1923-) & Berenstain, Janice (1923-). 1984. Random. (P.95)
--*The Berenstain Bears & the Dinosaurs.* Berenstain, Stanley (1923-) & Berenstain, Janice (1923-). 1984. Random. (P.95)
--*The Berenstain Bears & Too Much Junk Food.* Berenstain, Stanley (1923-) & Berenstain, Janice (1923-). 1985. Random. (P.95)
--*The Berenstain Bears' Bath Book.* Berenstain, Stanley (1923-) & Berenstain, Janice (1923-). 1985. Random. (P.95)
--*The Berenstain Bears in the Dark.* Berenstain, Stanley (1923-) & Berenstain, Janice (1923-). 1982. Random House. (P.95)
--*The Berenstain Bears' Olympics.* Berenstain, Stanley (1923-) & Berenstain, Janice (1923-). 1983. Tex Instr Inc. (P.95)
--*The Berenstain Bears on the Moon.* Berenstain, Stanley (1923-) & Berenstain, Janice (1923-). c.1985. Beginner Books. (P.95)

Berenzy, Alix
--*America's Very Own Ghosts.* Cohen, Daniel (1936-). c.1985. Dodd, Mead & Co. (P.206)

Berenzy, Roberta
--*Funny Riddles and Rhymes.* Stromberg, Rose Marie, ed. 1960. Hart Pub. Co. (P.868)
--*A Treasury of Laughs.* Mellon, Robert C, ed. 1960. Hart Pub. Co. (P.640)

Berg, Assaf
--*Adventures in the Galilee.* Biber, Yehoash. Bacon, Josephine, tr. from Hebrew. 1973. Jewish Publication Society of America. (P.101)

Berg, Bjorn (1923-)
--*Emil and Piggy Beast.* Lindgren, Astrid Ericsson (1907-). Heron, Michael, tr. from Fr. 1973. Follett Pub. Co. (P.573)
--*Emil in the Soup Tureen.* Lindgren, Astrid Ericsson (1907-). 1970. Follett. (P.573)
--*Emil's Pranks.* Lindgren, Astrid Ericsson (1907-). 1971. Follett Pub. Co. (P.573)
--*The Goat That Learned to Count.* Proysen, Alf. Ware, Kay & Sutherland, Lucille, eds. c.1961. Webster Pub. Co. (P.741)
--*Little Old Mrs.* Pepperpot. Proysen, Alf. Helweg, Marianne, tr. 1960. Astor-Honor. (P.741)
--*Little Old Mrs.* Pepperpot, and Other Stories. Proysen, Alf. Helweg, Marianne, tr. 1960, c.1959. McDowell, Obolensky. (P.741)
--*Mrs.* Pepperpot Again. Proysen, Alf. Helweg, Marianne, tr. 1961. Astor-Honor. (P.741)
--*Mrs.* Pepperpot Again, and Other Stories. Rev ed. Proysen, Alf. Helweg, Marianne, tr. c.1960. I. Obolensky. (P.741)
--*Mrs.* Pepperpot in the Magic Wood. Proysen, Alf. Helweg, Marianne, tr. 1968. Pantheon. (P.741)
--*Mrs.* Pepperpot to the Rescue. Proysen, Alf. Helweg, Marianne, tr. 1964. Pantheon. (P.741)
--*Mrs.* Pepperpot's Outing. Proysen, Alf. Helweg, Marianne, tr. 1971. Pantheon Books. (P.741)

Berg, Joan, pseud., see Victor, Joan Berg.

Berg, Joan, pseud. (1942-)
Aunt America. Victor, Joan Berg. Bloch, Marie Halun (1910-). 1963. Atheneum. **Award: (ALA).** (P.109)
--*Aunt America.* Victor, Joan Berg. Bloch, Marie Halun (1910-). 1972. Atheneum. (P.109)
--*The First Christmas Gifts.* Victor, Joan Berg. Pauli, Hertha Ernestine (1909-1973). 1965. I. Washburn. (P.711)
--*Flocks of Birds.* Victor, Joan Berg. Zolotow, Charlotte Shapiro (1915-). 1965. Abelard. (P.994)
--*Little Red.* Victor, Joan Berg. Piper, Roberta (1942-). 1963. Scribner. (P.727)
--*Little Two and the Peach Tree.* Victor, Joan Berg. Martin, Patricia Miles (1899-). Miles, Miska, pseud. 1963. Atheneum. (P.625)
--*Oh..* Brother Juniper. Victor, Joan Berg. Benedict, Rex Arthur (1920-). 1963. Pantheon Books. (P.93)
--*The String that Went Up.* Victor, Joan Berg. Burger, Otis Kidwell. 1963. St Martin's Press. (P.151)
--*Tell It Again: Great Tales from Around the World.* Victor, Joan Berg. Hodges, Margaret Moore (1911-), retold by. 1963. Dial Press. (P.449)
--*The Three Princes of Serendip.* Victor, Joan Berg. Armeno, Christoforo. Hodges, Elizabeth Jamison, ed. 1964. Antheneum. (P.47)
--*Three Princes of Serendip.* Victor, Joan Berg. Hodges, Elizabeth Jamison. 1964. Atheneum. (P.448)
--*Winds That Come from Far Away & Other Poems.* Victor, Joan Berg. Minarik, Else Holmelund (1920-). 1964. Har-Row. (P.651)
--*The Wonder of Stones.* Victor, Joan Berg. Gans, Roma (1894-). 1963. Crowell. (P.353)

Berger, Barbara
--*Brothers of the Wind.* Yolen, Jane Hyatt (1939-). c.1981. Philomel Books. (P.986)
--*Grandfather Twilight.* Berger, Barbara. 1984. Putnam Pub Group. (P.96)

Berger, Charles J.
--*The Adventures of Bumpy.* 1st ed. Babbitt, Robert, pseud. (1914-). Bangs, Robert Babbitt. 1974. Exposition Press. (P.58)
--*Mr.* Billiwicket's Burro: Ten Stories. Decker, Margaret S. 1980. Exposition. (P.250)

Berger, David
--*Operation Underground.* Berger, Josef (1903-1971). 1947. Little, Brown and Company. (P.96)
--*Swing Me, Swing Tree: Verse.* 1st ed. Marks, Marcia Bliss. c.1959. Little Brown. (P.620)

Berger, Vivian
--*The Adventures of Oolakuk.* Ruttan, Robert A. 1969. Prentice-Hall. (P.786)
--*Apollo.* Miller, Katherine E. James. 1970. Houghton Mifflin. (P.648)
--*Five Knucklebones.* 1st ed. Fairman, Paul W. 1972. Holt, Rinehart and Winston. (P.316)
--*Holidays in No-End Hollow.* Justus, May (1898-). 1970. Garrard Pub. Co. (P.503)
--*Prince of Judah and Other Stories of a Great Journey.* Goldberg, Israel (1887-). Learsi, Rufus, pseud. 1962. Shengold Publishers. (P.373)

Berger, William Merritt (1872-)
--*The Amazing Adventures of Ali.* Lindsay, Maud McKnight (1874-). c.1931. Lothrop, Lee & Shepard Co. (P.574)
--*Anything Can Happen on the River!.* Brink, Carol Ryrie, Mrs. (1895-1981). 1934. The Macmillan Company. (P.132)
--*Brother Blackfoot.* Sullivan, Alan (1868-). 1927. The Century Co. (P.870)
--*Captain Madeleine.* Du Bois, Mary Constance (1879-). 1928. The Century Co. (P.286)
--*College in Crinoline.* Medary, Marjorie (1890-). 1937. Longmans, Green and Co. (P.638)
--*The Dog That Went to the Doctor and other true stories of Real Animals.* O'Grady, Caroline Geraldine. c.1929. Lothrop, Lee & Shepard Co. (P.691)
--*Giles of the Star: The Boy Who Would Be a Knight.* Rice, Rebecca (1899-). c.1928. Lothrop, Lee & Shepard Co. (P.761)
--*The Joyous Guests.* Lindsay, Maud McKnight (1874-) & Poulsson, Emilie (1853-1939). 1921. Lothrop, Lee & Shepard Co. (P.574)
--*The Joyous Travelers.* Lindsay, Maud McKnight (1874-) & Poulsson, Emilie (1853-1939). c.1919. Lothrop, Lee & Shepard Co. (P.574)
--*Laughing Lad: A Story of Modern France.* Crew, Helen Cecilla Coale, Mrs. (1866-). c.1931. The Century Co. (P.230)
--*Matu, the Iroquois.* Cheyney, Edward Gheen (1878-). 1928. Little, Brown, and Company. (P.190)
--*One Boy Too Many.* Mitchell, Lebbeus (1879-). c.1926. The Century Co. (P.652)
--*Other Arabian Nights.* Katibah, Habeeb Ibrahim. 1928. C. Scribner's Sons. (P.508)
--*A Patriot Maid, and Other Stories.* Knipe, Emilie Benson, Mrs. (1870-1958) & Knipe, Alden Arthur (1870-1950). 1928. The Century Co. (P.532)
--*Raeburn Unafraid.* Bolton, Ivy May (1879-). 1942. Longmans, Green and Co. (P.113)
--*Rhyme Time for Children.* Poulsson, Anne Emilie (1853-1939). c.1929. Lothrop, Lee & Shepard Co. (P.735)
--*The Sea Lord: Francis Drake.* Limpus, Aitken. 1932. The Macmillan Company. (P.572)
--*The Seventh Swordsman.* Hadath, Gunby (1880-1954). c.1932. The Century Co. (P.401)
--*St.* Nicholas Book of Verse. Skinner, Mary Budd, Mrs. & Skinner, Joseph Osmun, eds. 1923. The Century Co. (P.828)
--*Tabitha of Lonely House: A Tale of Old Concord.* Hawthorne, Hildegarde (1871-1952). 1934. D. Appleton-Century Company, Incorporated. (P.423)

Bergere, Richard
--*Jean and Jacqueline: Paris in the Rain.* Bergere, Thea. 1963. McGraw-Hill Book Co. (P.96)
--*Jonathan Visits the White House.* Benchley, Peter Bradford (1940-). 1964. McGraw-Hill. (P.92)
--*When Will My Birthday Be.* Schatz, Letta. 1962. McGraw. (P.798)

Bergeron, Joseph R.
--*Bill's Great Idea.* Colby, Curtis. 1973. EMC Corp. (P.207)
--*The Fight for the Glen.* Colby, Curtis. 1973. EMC Corp. (P.207)
--*Gefahrliche Wege.* De Harven, Emile (1924-). 1975. EMC Corp. (P.251)
--*Goose Rescue.* Colby, Curtis. 1973. EMC Corp. (P.207)
--*The Lightning Round.* St. Sauver, Dennis (1947-). 1973. EMC Corp. (P.789)
--*A Montana Adventure.* St. Sauver, Dennis (1947-). 1973. EMC Corp. (P.789)
--*Night Watch in the Glen.* Colby, Curtis. 1973. EMC Corp. (P.207)
--*Otter in Danger.* Colby, Curtis. 1973. EMC Corp. (P.207)
--*Rescue by Fire.* St. Sauver, Dennis (1947-). 1973. EMC Corp. (P.790)
--*A Ride to Remember.* St. Sauver, Dennis (1947-). 1973. EMC Corp. (P.790)
--*Wilderness Adventure.* Colby, Curtis. 1973. EMC Corp. (P.207)

Berghauer, Meri H.
--*Isadore the Dinosaur.* LaFleur, Tom & Brennan, Gale. 1981. Ideals. (P.543)

Bergmann, Ann (1911-)
--*Blueberry.* 1st ed. Bergmann, Ann (1911-). c.1957. Pageant Press. (P.96)
--*Karl's Wooden Horse.* Donaldson, Lois (1898-). 1970. A. Whitman. (P.280)
--*Karl's Wooden Horse.* Donaldson, Lois (1898-). 1931. Laidlaw Brothers. (P.280)

Bergmann, Franz
--*This Way to the Circus.* Hodel, Emilia. c.1938. Hale, Cushman and Flint. (P.448)

Bergmann, Walter
--*Old and New Bohemian Tales: Original Stories.* Lehman, Anna. c.1926. M. A. Donohue & Company. (P.562)

Bergman Sacksdorff, Astrid, jt. photog. see Sacksdorff, Arne.

Bergman Sucksdorff, Astrid, photos by.
--*The Roe Deer.* Bergman Sucksdorff, Astrid. Tapsell, Alan, tr. from Swedish. 1969. HarBraceJ. (P.96)
--*Tooni, the Elephant Boy.* Bergman Sucksdorff, Astrid. 1971. HarBraceJ. (P.96)

Bering, Claus
--*The Lake People.* Berliner, Franz (1930-). Thygesen-Blecher, Lone, tr. 1973. Putnam. (P.96)

Berkey, Ben B.
--*Hopi Holiday: A Story of the Hopi Indians.* Berkey, Ben B. c.1967. Denison. (P.96)
--*Liberty Hill.* Berkey, Ben B. 1959. Denison. (P.96)
--*Oscar: The Curious Ostrich.* Berkey, Ben B. 1959. T. S. Denison. (P.96)

Berkova, Dagmar
--*Nutcracker.* Hoffmann, Ernst Theodor Amadeus (1776-1822). Petisvka, E., ed. Kuthanova, Olga, tr. 1969. Watts. (P.450)

Berkowitz, Jeannette
--*Adventures of K'tonton.* rev. ed. Weilerstein, Sadie Rose, Mrs. (1894-). 1964. Bloch. (P.941)
--*The Adventures of K'tonton: A Little Jewish Tom Thumb.* Weilerstein, Sadie Rose, Mrs. (1894-). 1935. League Press. (P.941)
--*The Adventures of K'tonton;.* A Little Jewish Tom Thumb. Weilerstein, Sadie Rose, Mrs. (1894-). 1964, c.1935. National Women's League of the United Synagogue. (P.941)
--*Fairy Tales from Baltic Shores: Folk-Lore Stories from Estonia.* Mutt, Eugenie, adapted by. N.D. The Penn Publishing Company. (P.674)
--*Old Swedish Fairy Tales.* Wahlenberg, Anna (1858-1933) & Thomsen, Frede. Patterson, Antoinette De Coursey, Mrs., tr. 1925. The Penn Publishing Company. (P.924)

Berkowitz, Jeannette, jt. illus. see Cramer, Rie.

Berlind, Gary Wayne
--*The Red Rooster Stories.* Goldsmith, Christine. c.1944. House of Field, Inc. (P.374)

Berman, Paul
--*The Make-Believe Empire.* Berman, Paul. 1982. Atheneum. (P.96)

Berman, Sam
--*Shapes.* Poems. Schlein, Miriam (1926-). c.1952. W. R. Scott. (P.799)

Bernadette, pseud., see Watts, Anna Bernadette.

Bernard, C. E. B.
--*Johnny of the 4-H Club.* Lide, Alice Alison, Mrs. (1890-). 1941. Little Brown and Company. (P.571)

Bernard, Debbie
--*Because of a Bone.* Garbar, David & Garbar, Ben. 1978. Rainbow Bks. (P.354)

Bernard, Jiri
--*Simple Stephen & the Magic Fish.* Richter, Konrad. 1983. Faber & Faber. (P.763)
--*Simple Stephen and the Magic Fish: Almost a Fairy Tale.* Richter, Konrad. 1983. Nord-Sud Verlag. (P.763)

Bernard, Lisa
--*Tales for a Child's Heart.* Dravich, Jay. c.1980. Tari Book Publishers. (P.284)

Bernath, Stefen
--*The Family Howl.* Dinneen, Betty (1929-). 1981. Macmillan. (P.266)
--*Spider Jane.* Yolen, Jane Hyatt (1939-). 1978. Coward, McCann & Geoghegan. (P.987)
--*Spider Jane on the Move: Break-of-Day Bk.* Yolen, Jane Hyatt (1939-). 1980. Putnam Pub Group. (P.987)
--*Striped Horses: The Story of a Zebra Family.* Dinneen, Betty (1929-). 1982. Macmillan. (P.266)

Bernbach, Graham, Jr.
--*The Mystery of the King Turtle.* Gregg, Alan. 1943. Doubleday Doran & Co. (P.388)
--*Second Shift.* Crawford, Phyllis (1899-). 1943. H. Holt and Company. (P.229)

Bernheim, Evelyne, jt. illus. see Bernheim, Marc.

Bernheim, Marc (1924-) & Bernheim, Evelyne (1935-)
--*The Drums Speak: The Story of Kofi a Boy of West Africa.* Bernheim, Marc (1924-) & Bernheim, Evelyne (1935-). N.D. Harcourt Brace Jovanovich. (P.97)

Bernstein, Dan, photos by.
--*When yhe Whale Came to My town.* Young, Jim (1930-). 1974. Borzoi Books. (P.990)

Bernstein, Zena
--*Albert the Albert.* Kinsey, Patricia Fuller. 1968. Funk & Wagnalls. (P.527)
--*The Cat, the Horse, and the Miracle.* 1st ed. Lezra, Giggy, pseud. (1934-). Lezra, Grizzella Paull. 1967. Atheneum. (P.571)
--*Down Half the World.* Coatsworth, Elizabeth Jane (1893-). 1968. Macmillan. (P.204)
--*The Good Germ.* Berg, Cherney. 1970. Lion Press. (P.95)
--*The Miracle of the Golden Doors.* Price, Barbara Pradal. 1971. Prentice-Hall. (P.738)
--*Mrs.* Frisby and the Rats of NIMH. 1st ed. O'Brien, Robert C., pseud. (1918-1973). Conly, Robert Leslie. 1971. Atheneum. **Awards: (JNM); (ALA); (BGH).** (P.689)

Beroon, Harold
--*The Silver Button.* Olds, Helen Diehl (1895-1981). 1958. Alfred A Knopf. (P.693)

Berrey, Phoebe
--*Teton Christmas Tales.* Lemon, Betty (1911-1977). c.1979. Teton Bookshop. (P.564)

Berridge, Celia (1943-)
--*Forget-Me-Not.* Rogers, Paul (1950-). 1986, c.1984. Puffin Books. (P.775)
--*Forget-Me-Not.* Rogers, Paul (1950-). 1984. Viking. (P.775)

Berringer, Nick
--*The Super Joke Book.* Brandreth, Gyles Daubeney (1948-). 1983. Sterling Pub. Co. (P.127)

Berry, Anne Scheu
--*Fuzzy Joe Bear.* Horn, Gladys M. c.1954. Whitman Pub. Co. (P.464)
--*Jack and the Beanstalk.* Jack and the Beanstalk. N.D. Rand McNally. (P.483)
--*Peter Rabbit, and Other Stories.* Potter, Helen Beatrix (1866-1943). c.1947. Whitman Pub. Co. (P.734)
--*Tommy and Timmy.* Sankey, Alice Ann-Susan (1910-). 1951. Whitman Pub. Co. (P.793)

Berry, Erick, pseud., see Best, Allena Champlin.

Berry, Erick, pseud., see Kashiwagi, Isami.

--*Pinky Pup: And The Empty Elephant.* Berry, Erick, pseud. Willson, Dixie. c.1928. The P. F. Volland Company. (P.965)

--*The Ranee's Ruby.* Berry, Erick, pseud. Baker, Nina Brown, Mrs. (1888-1957). 1935. Lothrop, Lee and Shepard Company. (P.64)

--*Ranger's ransom: A Story of Ticonderoga.* 1 st. ed. Berry, Erick, pseud. Best, Herbert (1894-). 1953. Aladdin Books. (P.99)

--*Sammy and Silverband: A Tale of the African Jungle.* Berry, Erick, pseud. Miller, Janet. 1931. Houghton Mifflin Company. (P.647)

--*The Secret People: Adventure in Africa.* Berry, Erick, pseud. Holmes, F. Ratcliffe. 1928. Doubleday, Doran & Company, Inc. (P.456)

--*Seven Beaver Skins: A Story of the Dutch in New Amsterdam.* Berry, Erick, pseud. Best, Allena Champlin, Mrs. (1892-1974). Berry, Erick, pseud. 1948. J. C. Winston Co. (P.99)

--*A Shipment for Susannah.* Berry, Erick, pseud. Nolen, Eleanor Weakley, Mrs. 1938. T. Nelson and Sons. (P.684)

--*The Short Sword.* Berry, Erick, pseud. Irwin, Violet Mary (1881-). 1928. The Macmillan Company. (P.482)

--*Son of the Whiteman.* Berry, Erick, pseud. Best, Herbert (1894-). 1931. Doubleday, Doran & Company, Inc. (P.99)

--*Son of the Whiteman.* Berry, Erick, pseud. Best, Herbert (1894-). 1936. Doubleday, Doran & Company, Inc. (P.99)

--*The Spindle Imp and Other Tales of Maya Mith and Folk Lore.* Berry, Erick, pseud. Malkus, Alida Wright Sims, Mrs. (1899-). c.1931. Harcourt, Brace and Company. (P.614)

--*Strings to Adventure.* Berry, Erick, pseud. Best, Allena Champlin, Mrs. (1892-1974). Berry, Erick, pseud. 1935. Lothrop, Lee and Shepard Company. (P.99)

--*Sybil Ludington's Ride.* Berry, Erick, pseud. Best, Allena Champlin, Mrs. (1892-1974). Berry, Erick, pseud. 1952. Viking Press. (P.99)

--*Tal of the Four Tribes.* Berry, Erick, pseud. Best, Herbert (1894-). 1938. Doubleday, Doran & Co., Inc. (P.99)

--*Tea Time Tales.* Berry, Erick, pseud. Fyleman, Rose Amy (1877-1957). 1930. Doubleday, Doran & Company, Inc. (P.350)

--*Those Cartwright Twins.* Berry, Erick, pseud. Garrard, Phillis. 1932. D. Appleton and Company. (P.358)

--*Watergate: A Story of the Irish on the Erie Canal.* 1st ed. Berry, Erick, pseud. Best, Herbert (1894-). 1951. Winston. (P.99)

--*The Wavering Flame: Connecticut, 1776.* Berry, Erick, pseud. Best, Allena Champlin, Mrs. (1892-1974). Berry, Erick, pseud. 1953. Scribner. (P.99)

--*Whistle Round the Bend.* Berry, Erick, pseud. Best, Allena Champlin, Mrs. (1892-1974). Berry, Erick, pseud. c.1941. Oxford University Press. (P.99)

--*White Heron Feather.* Berry, Erick, pseud. Robinson, Gertrude (1876-). c.1930. Harper & Brothers. (P.770)

--*The Winged Girl of Knossos.* Berry, Erick, pseud. Best, Allena Champlin, Mrs. (1892-1974). Berry, Erick, pseud. 1933. D. Appleton-Century Company, Inc. **Award: (JNM).** (P.99)

--*A Year to Grow.* Berry, Erick, pseud. Conway, Helene. 1943. Longmans, Green and Co. (P.214)

Best, Catherine

--*Whys and Otherwise.* Best, Signe Ellison, Mrs. c.1929. The Golden Press. (P.99)

Best-Maugard, Adolfo

--*To and Again.* Brooks, Walter Rollin (1886-1958). 1927. A. A. Knopf. (P.137)

Best, Peggy Worthington

--*The Great Black Robe.* Pitrone, Jean Maddern. c.1965. St. Paul Ed. Dist. Daughters of St. Paul. (P.727)

Best, Roy

--*Little Friends from Many Lands.* Lowe, Edith May Kovar (1905-). Windsor, Mary, pseud. c.1935. Whitman. (P.588)

--*Peter Pan.* Barrie, James Matthew, Sir (1860-1937). N.D. Grosset & Dunlap. (P.76)

--*The Peter Pan Picture Book.* Barrie, James Matthew, Sir (1860-1937). c.1931. Whitman Publishing Company. (P.76)

--*Would You Like to Know Peter.* Lowe, Edith May Kovar (1905-). Windsor, Mary, pseud. c.1935. Whitman. (P.588)

Best, Ruth J.

--*Ella, a Little Schoolgirl of the Sixties: A Book for Children and for Grown-ups Who Remember.* Tappan, Eva March (1854-1930). 1923. Houghton Mifflin Company. (P.878)

Bestall, A. E.

--*The Spanish Goldfish.* Glass, Dudley. N.D. Frederick Warne & Co. (P.370)

--*True Tales of an Old Shellback.* Southwold, Stephen (1887-). 1930. Longmans, Green and Co. (P.841)

Bestor, Don, jt. illus. see Hubbard, Allen.

Besunder, Marvin

--*Memories of Home.* Johnson, Caesar, ed. 1970. C. R. Gibson Co. (P.494)

--*Treasures of Lin Li-Ti.* Cheney, Cora (1916-). 1969. Hawthorn. (P.189)

Beta

--*Enchanted Closet.* Beta. 1967. Lion Bks. (P.99)

Betancourt, A. B.

--*Oliver and the Crying Chip.* Durant, Nancy Miles. 1915. Sherman, French & Company. (P.291)

Bethel, Steve

--*Camp-Out.* Maynard, Joyce (1953-). c.1985. Harcourt Brace Jovanovich. (P.634)

Bethell, Jean (1922-), photos by.

--*Playmates.* Bethell, Jean Frankenberry (1922-). 1981. HR&W. (P.99)

Bethers, Ray (1902-)

--*Islands of Adventure.* Bethers, Ray (1902-). N.D. Hastings House. (P.99)

--*Ports of Adventure.* Bethers, Ray (1902-). 1963. Hastings House. (P.99)

--*Rivers of Adventure.* Bethers, Ray (1902-). N.D. Hastings House. (P.99)

--*Ships of Adventure.* Bethers, Ray (1902-). 1961. Hastings. (P.99)

--*This is Our World.* Bethers, Ray (1902-). 1964. St. Martin's Press. (P.99)

Betta, L.

--*Royal Rogues.* Bancroft, Alberta (1873-). 1901. G.P. Putnam's Sons. (P.68)

Bettina, pseud., see Ehrlich, Bettina Bauer.

Bettina, pseud. (1903-)

--*Favorite Fairy Tales Told in England.* Ehrlich, Bettina Bauer. Haviland, Virginia (1911-) & Jacobs, Joseph (1854-1916), eds. 1959. Little. (P.421)

--*The Magic Christmas Tree.* Ehrlich, Bettina Bauer. Kingman, Lee, pseud. (1919-). Natti, Marylee Kingman. 1956. Ariel Books. (P.524)

--*Sorcerer's Apprentice & Other Stories.* Ehrlich, Bettina Bauer. Hosier, John. 1961. Walck. (P.465)

--*The Swans of Ballycastle.* Ehrlich, Bettina Bauer. Hackett, Walter Anthony (1909-). 1954. Ariel Books. (P.401)

--*The Swans of Ballycastle.* Ehrlich, Bettina Bauer. Hackett, Walter Anthony (1909-). 1968, c.1954. Houghton. (P.401)

Bettini, Lynette

--*Ophelia.* Meeker, Alice MacCutcheon (1904-). 1983. Paulist Pr. (P.639)

Bettoli, Delana

--*Baby's Cradle Book: Beloved Nursery Rhymes.* Namm, Diane, compiled by. 1985. Simon & Schuster. (P.675)

Betts, Anna Whelan

--*Dreamland.* Lippmann, Julie Mathilde (1864-). N.D. Penn Publishing Co. (P.576)

--*Dreamland.* Lippmann, Julie Mathilde (1864-). 1901. The Penn Publishing Company. (P.576)

Betts, Ethel Franklin

--*Babes in Toyland.* MacDonough, Glen (0000-1924) & Chapin, Anna Alice (1880-1930). 1904. Fox, Duffield and Company. (P.600)

--*The Boy Lives on Our Farm.* Riley, James Whitcomb (1849-1916). 1908. Bobbs-Merrill Co. (P.764)

--*The Complete Mother Goose.* Betts, Ethel Franklin. N.D. Frederick A. Stokes Co. (P.100)

--*The Complete Mother Goose.* Mother Goose. 1909. Frederick A. Stokes Company. (P.667)

--*Fairy Tales From Grimm.* Mabie, Hamilton Wright (1846-1916), ed. N.D. Barse & Hopkins. (P.593)

--*Familiar Nursery Jingles.* Betts, Ethel Franklin. N.D. Frederick A. Stokes Co. (P.100)

--*Favorite Nursery Rhymes.* Mother Goose. 1906. F. A. Stokes Company. (P.667)

--*A Host of Children.* Riley, James Whitcomb (1849-1916). 1920. Bobbs-Merrill Co. (P.764)

--*Humpty Dumpty.* N.D. Dodd, Mead & Company. (P.100)

--*If You Don't Watch Out.* Riley, James Whitcomb (1849-1916). 1915. Bobbs-Merrill. (P.764)

--*The Little Grey House.* Taggart, Marion Ames (1866-). 1904. McClure, Phillips & Co. (P.876)

--*The Little Grey House: A Gay Story for Girls.* Taggart, Marion Ames (1866-). 1937. The Sun Dial Press, Inc. (P.876)

--*Little Orphant Annie.* Riley, James Whitcomb (1849-1916). 1915. Bobbs-Merrill. (P.764)

--*A Little Princess.* Burnett, Frances Hodgson, Mrs. (1849-1924). 1905. C. Scribner's Sons. (P.155)

--*A Little Princess.* Burnett, Frances Hodgson, Mrs. (1849-1924). N.D. Charles Scribner's Sons. (P.155)

--*A Little Princess: Being the Whole Story of Sara Crewe Now Told for the First Time.* Burnett, Frances Hodgson, Mrs. (1849-1924). 1974, c.1938. Scribner. (P.155)

--*One Thousand Poems for Children.* Ingpen, Roger, ed. N.D. Macrae Smith. (P.480)

--*One Thousand Poems for Children: A Choice of the Best Verse Old and New.* rev. and enl. ed. Ingpen, Roger, ed. c.1923. G. W. Jacobs and Company. (P.480)

--*The Orphant Annie Book.* Riley, James Whitcomb (1849-1916). 1908. Bobbs-Merrill Co. (P.764)

--*The Raggedy Man.* Riley, James Whitcomb (1849-1916). 1907. Bobbs-Merrill Co. (P.765)

--*Riley Child Verse.* Riley, James Whitcomb (1849-1916). 1908. Bobbs-Merrill Co. (P.765)

--*Riley Child Verse.* Riley, James Whitcomb (1849-1916). 1915. Bobbs-Merrill. (P.765)

--*The Runaway Boy.* Riley, James Whitcomb (1849-1916). 1906. Bobbs-Merrill Co. (P.765)

--*The Runaway Boy: Contains: The Land of Used-to-be, The Boys Candidate, Naughty Claude, Little Mandy's Christmas Tree.* Riley, James Whitcomb (1849-1916). 1915. Bobbs-Merrill. (P.765)

--*The True Story of Humpty Dumpty: How He was Rescued by Three Mortal Children in Make Believe Land.* Chapin, Anna Alice (1880-1920). 1905. Dodd, Mead & Co. (P.184)

--*When the Heart Beats Young.* Riley, James Whitcomb (1849-1916). 1906. Bobbs-Merrill Co. (P.765)

Betts, Harold H.

--*Princess Sayrane: A Romance of the Days of Prester John.* Harrison, Edith Ogden, Mrs. 1910. A. C. McClurg & Co. (P.417)

--*Ruth of the U.S.A.* Balmer, Edwin. N.D. Grosset & Dunlap. (P.67)

Betts, John Henderson

--*Bockers.* Compton, Margaret, pseud. (1852-1903). Harrison, Amelia Williams. N.D. Penn Publishing Co. (P.212)

--*Bockers and His Chum Peggy.* Rev ed. Harrison, Amelia Williams, Mrs. (1852-1903). Compton, Margaret, pseud. 1900. The Penn Publishing Company. (P.417)

--*A Boy in Early Virginia: Or, Adventures with Captain John Smith.* Robins, Edward (1862-). 1901. G. W. Jacobs & Co. (P.769)

--*The Green Door.* Compton, Margaret, pseud. (1852-1903). Harrison, Amelia Williams. 1901. Penn. (P.212)

--*Some Boys' Doings.* Habberton, John (1842-1921). 1901. G. W. Jacobs & Co. (P.401)

--*Tommy's Adventures.* Atwater, Emily Paret (1873-). 1900. G. W. Jacobs & Co. (P.54)

--*The Young Financier.* Rev ed. Stoddard, William Osborn (1835-1925). 1900. The Penn Publishing Company. (P.860)

--*The Young Shipbuilder.* Swett, Sophia Miriam (1858-1912). 1902. Penn. (P.874)

--*The Young Shipbuilder.* Swett, Sophia Miriam (1858-1912). N.D. Penn Publishing Co. (P.874)

Betts, Louis

--*A Child of the Sun.* Banks, Charles Eugene (1852-). 1900. H. S. Stone & Company. (P.68)

Bevans, M. T., jt. illus. see Bevans, T. M.

Bevans, Michael H.

--*Blackie and His Family.* Cook, Mary E. 1949. Brace. (P.215)

Bevans, T. M. & Bevans, M. T.

--*On Our Hill.* Bacon, Josephine Dodge Daskam, Mrs. (1876-1961). 1918. C. Scribner's Sons. (P.58)

Bevans, Tom Torre (1868-1930)

--*Where,oh Where?.* Bevans, Tom Torre (1868-1930). 1939. Viking Press. (P.100)

Beverley, Katherine, jt. illus. see Ellender, Elizabeth.

Beverley, Katherine & Ellender, Elizabeth

--*Mother Goose Songs: First Series.* Haubiel, Charles (1894-) & Mother Goose. 1935. The Composers Press, Inc. (P.420)

Bevins, John, jt. illus. see Bown, Derick.

Bewick, Thomas (1753-1828)

--*Bewick's Select Fables.* N.D. George Routledge & Sons. (P.100)

--*The Fox at the Manger.* 1st ed. Travers, Pamela Lyndon (1906-). 1962. Norton. (P.898)

--*The Vicar of Wakefield.* Goldsmith, Oliver (1728-1774). 1873. G. P. Putnam's Sons. (P.374)

Bewley, Sheila

--*Boy on a White Giraffe.* Catherall, Arthur (1906-). Hallard, Peter J., pseud. 1969. Seabury Press. (P.177)

--*The Guardian Angel.* Ropner, Pamela. 1967, c.1966. Coward-McCann. (P.776)

--*King in a Stable.* Robertson, Jennifer Sinclair (1942-). 1977. Standard Pub. (P.768)

Bewster, Patience

--*Ellsworth and the Cats from Mars.* Brewster, Patience. c.1981. Houghton Mifflin/Clarion Books. (P.130)

Bey, Sarah K., jt. illus. see Pride, Alexis.

Beylon, Catherine M.

--*My Little Pony & the Mystery Chase.* Luke, Melinda (1955-). 1985. Random. (P.590)

--*My Little Pony & The New Friends.* Adams, Edith, pseud. (1932-). Shine, Deborah. 1984. Random. (P.5)

--*My Little Pony, Baby Firefly's Adventure and Other My Little Pony Stories.* Matthews, Maria. 1985. Random House. (P.631)

--*The Runaway Circus.* Long, Ruthanna. 1973. Golden Press. (P.582)

--*Spike and the Magic Shoes.* Luke, Melinda (1955-). c.1985. Random House. (P.590)

Bhang, Dave

--*Charley Yee's New Year.* Anderson, Juanita B. 1970. Follett. (P.39)

Bhusan, Reboti

--*The Donkey on the Bridge.* Jafa, Manorama. 1980. Auromere. (P.488)

--*Stories from Panchatantra, Bk.*II. Shivkumar. 1979. Auromere. (P.821)

Bhushan, Phani

--*Folk Tales from Rajasthan.* Birla, Lakshminiwas L. (1909-). 1964. Asia Pub. House. (P.103)

Bialk, Elisa, pseud., see Krautter, Elisa Bialk.

Bialk, Elisa, pseud. (1912-)

--*Tizz in Texas.* Krautter, Elisa Bialk. Lehmann, Hildegaard. c.1966. Childrens. (P.562)

Bianchi, Martha

--*The Things I Love.* Cecil, Marty. 1968. Exposition Press. (P.179)

Bianco, Pamela (1906-)

--*Away to the Moon.* Symonds, John (1906-). 1956. Lippincott. (P.875)

--*Birthday of the Infanta.* Wilde, Oscar Fingal O'Flahertie Wills (1854-1900). 1929. MacMillan. (P.959)

--*Easter Book of Legends & Stories.* Hazeltine, Alice Isabel (1878-) & Smith, Elva Sophronia (1871-), eds. 1947. Lothrop. (P.427)

--*Land of Dreams.* Blake, William (1757-1827). Bianco, Pamela (1906-), ed. N.D. MacMillan Bks. (P.106)

--*The Little Mermaid.* Andersen, Hans Christian (1805-1875). James, Montague Rhodes (1862-1936), tr. 1935. Holiday House. (P.36)

--*The Little Wooden Doll.* Bianco, Margery Williams, Mrs. (1881-1944). 1925. The Macmillan Company. (P.100)

--*The Little Wooden Doll House.* Bianco, Margery Williams, Mrs. (1881-1944). 1967. MacMillan Publishing Company. (P.100)

--*The Skin Horse.* Bianco, Margery Williams, Mrs. (1881-1944). 1927. Doubleday Doran & Co. (P.100)

--*The Skin Horse.* Bianco, Margery Williams, Mrs. (1881-1944). 1978. Green Tiger Pr. (P.100)

--*The Starlit Journey: A Story.* Bianco, Pamela (1906-). 1933. Macmillan. (P.101)

--*Three Christmas Trees.* Ewing, Juliana Horatia Gatty, Mrs. (1841-1885). 1930. The Macmillan Company. (P.315)

Bias, Joseph A.

--*Juba's Folk Games: A Collection of Afro-American Children's Games.* Allen, Harriette Bias. c.1976. Juba Publications. (P.29)

Bibi & Collin, Hedvig

--*Bibi: A Little Danish Girl.* Michaelis, Karin, pseud. (1872-). Stangeland, Katharina Maria Bech Brondum Michaelis. Hanson, Lida Siboni, tr. 1927. Doubleday, Page & Company. (P.644)

--*Bibi: A Little Danish Girl.* Michaelis, Karin, pseud. (1872-). Stangeland, Katharina Maria Bech Brondum Michaelis. Hanson, Lida Siboni, tr. 1936. Doubleday, Doran & Company, Inc. (P.644)

Bible, Charles (1937-)

--*Black Means ...* Grossman, Barney & Groom, Gladys. 1970. Hill & Wang. (P.396)

--*Brooklyn Story.* 1st ed. Mathis, Sharon Bell (1937-). 1970. Hill and Wang; Distributed by Random House. (P.631)

--*Hamdaani: A Traditional Tale from Zanzibar.* Bible, Charles (1937-). c.1977. Holt, Rinehart and Winston. (P.101)

--*Jennifer's New Chair.* Bible, Charles (1937-). 1978. HR&W. (P.101)

--*Spin a Soft Black Song: Poems for Children.* Giovanni, Nikki (1943-). 1971. Hill and Wang. (P.369)

Bice, Clare (1909-1976)

--*A Dog for Davie's Hill.* Bice, Clare (1909-1976). 1956. Macmillan. (P.101)

--*The Force Carries On.* Longstreth, Thomas Morris (1886-). 1954. Macmillan. (P.583)

--*The Great Canoe.* Leitch, Adelaide (1921-). 1963, c.1962. St. Martin's. (P.563)

--*The Great Island: A Story of Mystery in Newfoundland.* Bice, Clare (1909-1976). 1954. Macmillan. (P.101)

--*Hurricane Treasure.* Bice, Clare (1909-1976). c.1965. Viking. (P.101)

--*Thunder in the Mountains: Legends of Canada.* Hooke, Hilda M. 1947. Oxford U Pr. (P.458)

Bichisecchi, Bini

--*The Park, the Park.* Freschet, Berniece Louise Speck (1927-). 1974. Ginn. (P.345)

Bickford, Nana French

--*America's Daughter.* Halsey, Rena Isabelle (1860-). 1918. Lothrop, Lee & Shepard Co. (P.407)

--*Blue Robin: The Girl Pioneer.* Halsey, Rena Isabelle (1860-). 1917. Lothrop, Lee & Shepard Co. (P.407)

--*In Santa Claus' House.* Irwin, Florence (1869-). 1917. Little, Brown, and Company. (P.482)

--*The Liberty Girl.* Halsey, Rena Isabelle (1860-). c.1919. Lothrop, Lee & Shepard Co. (P.407)

--*Up & Down.* Blair, Mary Robinson (1911-). 1964. Golden Press. (P.105)

Blair, Robert N.

--*Captain and Mate.* Freeman, Ruth Nimmo St. John (1901-) & Freeman, Harrop Arthur (1907-). 1940. A. Whitman. (P.344)

--*Sparks and Little Sparks.* Freeman, Ruth Nimmo St. John (1901-) & Freeman, Harrop Arthur (1907-). 1940. A. Whitman. (P.344)

Blair, Susan B.

--*Little Red-Cap.* Grimm, Jakob Ludwig Karl (1785-1863) & Grimm, Wilhelm Karl (1786-1859). 1964. Holt, Rinehart and Winston. (P.394)

--*The Three Billy-Goats Gruff: A Norwegian Folktale.* Asbjornsen, Peter Christen (1812-1885). 1963. Holt, Rinehart and Winston. (P.51)

Blair, Virginia

--*Ruth Jane Talks with the Animals.* Berry, Claude Perrin (1877-). c.1941. Dorrance and Company. (P.97)

Blair, William

--*Dirt Track Danger.* Bowen, Robert Sidney (1900-1977). 1963. Doubleday. (P.121)

Blaisdell, Albert Franklin (1847-)

--*The Story of the Iliad.* Condensed. Homerus. Church, Alfred John (1829-1912), retold by. c.1886. Clark & Maynard. (P.458)

Blaisdell, E. Warde

--*Dorothys Rabbit Stories.* Calhoun, Mary Elizabeth (1866-). c.1907. T. Y. Crowell & Co. (P.162)

--*Old Man Coyote.* Bayliss, Clara Kern, Mrs. (1848-). 1908. T. Y. Crowell & Co. (P.83)

Blaisdell, Elinore, jt. illus. see Lockridge, Richard.

Blaisdell, Elinore (1904-)

--*Bulfinch's Mytholoy.* Bulfinch, Thomas (1796-1867). N.D. Crowell. (P.148)

--*The Chateau of the Swan.* Holland, Rupert Sargent (1878-1952). c.1939. Farrar & Rinehart, Inc. (P.455)

--*A Child's Life of Jesus.* Oursler, Fulton (1893-1952). N.D. Doubleday & Co. (P.698)

--*Chronicle of the March Family.* Alcott, Louisa May (1832-1888). 1946. Little, Brown & Co. (P.16)

--*The Double Birthday Present.* Hunt, Mabel Leigh (1892-1971). 1948. J. B. Lippincott. (P.474)

--*The Emperor's Nephew: A Story of Charlemagne.* Magoon, Marian Austin Waite, Mrs. (1885-). c.1942. Farrar & Rinehart, Inc. (P.613)

--*Falcon, Fly Back.* Blaisdell, Elinore (1904-). c.1939. J. Messner, Inc. (P.105)

--*Grubby Gets Clean.* Vorse, Mary Ellen (1907-). c.1943. W. R. Scott, Inc. (P.922)

--*A Lad of Old Williamsburg.* Orton, Helen Fuller, Mrs. (1872-1955). 1938. Frederick A. Stokes Company. (P.696)

--*Linda and Dick of Colonial Williamsburg.* Trachsel, Myrtle Jamison, Mrs. 1938. Dodd, Mead and Company. (P.898)

--*Little Men and Jo's Boys.* Alcott, Louisa May (1832-1888). 1946. Little, Brown and Company. (P.17)

--*Little Women.* Alcott, Louisa May (1832-1888). 1946. Little, Brown and Company. (P.17)

--*Matilda's Buttons.* 1st ed. Hunt, Mabel Leigh (1892-1971). 1948. J.B. Lippincott Co. (P.474)

--*The Pastor's Dog.* Heavey, Jean. 1951. Scribner. (P.429)

--*Rhymes and Verses.* De La Mare, Walter John (1873-1956). 1947. Henry Holt & Co. (P.253)

--*The Sixty-Ninety Grandchild.* Hunt, Mabel Leigh (1892-1971). 1951. J. B. Lippincott. (P.474)

--*Stories of King Arthur.* Malory, Thomas, Sir (1410-1471). Cutler, Uriel Waldo (1854-), ed. c.1941. Thomas Y. Crowell Company. (P.615)

--*Theodosia, Daughter of Aaron Burr.* Graff, Polly Anne Colver (1908-). 1941. Farrar & Rinehart. (P.380)

--*Wagon Train West.* Nelson, Rhoda Louise Smith, Mrs. (1891-). 1939. Thomas Y. Crowell Company. (P.678)

--*We Thank Thee.* Emerson, Ralph Waldo (1803-1882). 1955. Whitman Pub. Co. (P.306)

--*With Sword & Song.* Rosenberg, Melrich Vonelm (1905-). 1937. Houghton Mifflin Company. (P.778)

Blaisdell, Elizabeth

--*Tales from Shakespeare.* Lamb, Charles (1775-1834) & Lamb, Mary Ann (1764-1847). 1942. Thomas Y. Crowell. (P.545)

Blaisdell, Paul & Schomburg, Alex

--*The Ant Men: A Science Fantasy Novel.* 1st ed. Cronin, Bernard. North, Eric, pseud. 1955. Winston. (P.232)

Blake, Bud, pseud., see Blake, Julian Watson.

Blake, Bud, pseud. (1918-)

--*The News Time Fun Time Book.* Blake, Julian Watson. Donahue, Elvira, ed. c.1964. Scholastic. (P.280)

Blake, David, jt. illus. see Lee, Rob.

Blake, Julian Watson see Blake, Bud, pseud.

Blake, Marty

--*Pandora: A Raccoon's Journey.* Menino, H. M. 1985. Bradbury Pr. (P.641)

Blake, Pamela

--*Peep-Show: A Book of Rhymes.* Blake, Pamela. 1973. Macmillan. (P.106)

Blake, Quentin see Dr. Seuss, pseud.

Blake, Quentin (1932-)

--*Ace Dragon Ltd.* Hoban, Russell Conwell (1925-). 1981. Merrimack Pub Cir. (P.447)

--*Agaton Sax & Lispington's Grandfather Clock.* Franzen, Nils-Olof (1916-). 1979. Andre Deutsch. (P.342)

--*Agaton Sax & the Big Rig.* Franzen, Nils-Olof (1916-). 1981. Andre Deutsch. (P.342)

--*Agaton Sax and the Diamond Thieves.* Franzen, Nils Olof (1916-). Ramsden, Evelyn, tr. from Swedish. 1980. A. Deutsch. (P.342)

--*Agaton Sax and the Diamond Thieves.* Franzen, Nils Olof (1916-). Ramsden, Evelyn, tr. from Swedish. 1967. Delacorte Press. (P.342)

--*Agaton Sax and the Incredible Max Brothers.* Franzen, Nils Olof (1916-). 1970. Delacorte Press. (P.342)

--*Agaton Sax and the Scotland Yard Mystery.* Franzen, Nils Olof (1916-). 1969. Delacorte Press. (P.342)

--*Albert & the Dragonettes.* Weir, Rosemary Green (1905-). 1977. British Bk Ctr. (P.942)

--*Albert the Dragon.* Weir, Rosemary Green (1905-). 1961. Abelard-Schuman. (P.942)

--*Albert the Dragon and the Centaur.* Weir, Rosemary Green (1905-). 1968. Abelard-Schuman. (P.942)

--*Alphabet Soup.* Yeoman, John (1934-). 1970, c.1969. Follett. (P.986)

--*Arabel and Mortimer.* Aiken, Joan (1924-). 1981. Doubleday. (P.15)

--*Arabel's Raven.* Aiken, Joan (1924-). 1974. Doubleday & Company. (P.15)

--*Aristide.* Tibber, Robert, pseud. (1929-). Friedman, Eve Rosemary Tibber. 1966. Dial Press. (P.891)

--*The Bear's Water Picnic.* Yeoman, John (1934-). 1970. Macmillan. (P.986)

--*The Bear's Winter House.* Yeoman, John (1934-). 1969. World Pub. Co. (P.986)

--*Beatrice and Vanessa.* Yeoman, John (1934-). 1975, c.1974. Macmillan. (P.986)

--*The Bed Book.* Plath, Sylvia (1932-1963). 1976. Faber. (P.728)

--*The BFG.* Dahl, Roald (1916-). 1982. Farrar, Straus, Giroux. (P.238)

--*The BFG.* Dahl, Roald (1916-). 1985, c.1982. Viking Penguin. (P.238)

--*The Boy Who Sprouted Antlers.* Yeoman, John (1934-). 1966, c.1961. Faber & Faber. (P.986)

--*Boy Who Sprouted Antlers.* Yeoman, John (1934-). N.D. Transatlantic. (P.986)

--*A Cat & Mouse Story.* Rosen, Michael (1946-). 1983. Andre Deutsch. (P.777)

--*Custard and Company: Poems.* Nash, Frederic Ogden (1902-1971). Blake, Quentin (1932-), ed. c.1980. Little, Brown. (P.675)

--*Custard and Company: Poems.* Nash, Frederic Ogden (1902-1971). Blake, Quentin (1932-), selected by. 1985, c.1979. Little, Brown. (P.675)

--*Dirty Beasts.* Dahl, Roald (1916-). 1985, c.1983. Puffin Books. (P.238)

--*A Drink of Water, and Other Stories.* Yeoman, John (1934-). 1966, c.1960. Faber & Faber. (P.986)

--*Drink of Water & Other Stories.* Yeoman, John (1934-). N.D. Transatlantic. (P.986)

--*The Enormous Crocodile.* Dahl, Roald (1916-). 1977. Knopf : Distributed by Random House. (P.238)

--*The First Elephant Comes to Ireland.* Zimelman, Nathan (1911-). 1969. Follett Pub. Co. (P.992)

--*Funny Business.* Cunningham, Bronnie, compiled by. 1979. Penguin. (P.235)

--*Further Adventures of Albert the Dragon.* Weir, Rosemary Green (1905-). 1964. Abelard-Schuman. (P.942)

--*The Gentle Knight.* Schickel, Richard Warner (1933-). 1964. Abelard-Schuman. (P.798)

--*George's Marvelous Medicine.* Dahl, Roald (1916-). 1982, c.1981. Knopf : Distributed by Random House. (P.238)

--*Gillygaloos and Gollywhoppers: Tall Tales About Mythical Monsters.* Rees, Ennis Samuel, Jr. (1925-). 1969. Abelard-Schuman. (P.753)

--*Great Day for up!.* Dr. Seuss, pseud. Geisel, Theodor Seuss (1904-). Dr. Seuss, pseud. 1974. Beginner Books. (P.362)

--*Grimble & Grimble at Christmas.* Freud, Clement Raphael (1924-). 1974. Puffin Books. (P.345)

--*Horseshoe Harry and the Whale.* De Leeuw, Adele Louise (1899-). c.1976. Parents' Magazine Press. (P.254)

--*Horseshoe Harry & the Whale.* De Leeuw, Adele Louise (1899-). 1976. Scholastic Inc. (P.254)

--*How the Camel Got His Hump.* Kipling, Joseph Rudyard (1865-1936). 1985. P. Bedrick Books. (P.527)

--*How Tom Beat Captain Najork and His Hired Sportsmen.* Hoban, Russell Conwell (1925-). 1974. Atheneum. (P.447)

--*The Improbable Book of Records.* Blake, Quentin (1932-) & Yeoman, John, eds. 1976. Atheneum. (P.106)

--*Joseph and the Amazing Technicolor Dreamcoat.* Lloyd Webber, Andrew (1948-) & Rice, Tim. c.1982. Holt, Rinehart, and Winston. (P.578)

--*Joseph & the Amazing Technicolor Dreamcoat.* Rice, Tim (1944-) & Webber, Andrew Lloyd (1948-). 1982. HR&W. (P.761)

--*Kibby's Big Feat.* Corddry, Thomas I. 1970. Follett. (P.220)

--*Kidnapped at Christmas: A Play for Children.* Hall, Willis (1929-). 1975. French. (P.406)

--*Listen, and I'll Tell You.* Koren, Edward (1935-). 1964, c.1962. Lippincott. (P.535)

--*Mind Your Own Business.* Rosen, Michael (1946-). 1974. S. G. Phillips. (P.777)

--*Mister Magnolia.* Blake, Quentin (1932-). 1980. Merrimack Pub Cir. **Award: (KGM).** (P.106)

--*Mortimer's Cross.* Aiken, Joan (1924-). 1984, c.1982. HarpJ. (P.15)

--*Mouse Trouble.* Yeoman, John (1934-). 1975, c.1972. Collier Books. (P.986)

--*Mouse Trouble.* Yeoman, John (1934-). 1973, c.1972. Macmillan. (P.986)

--*Mouse Trouble.* Yeoman, John (1934-). 1976. Macmillan. (P.986)

--*Mr. Horrox & the Gratch.* Reeves, James (1909-). 1975. British Bk Ctr. (P.754)

--*My Son-in-law the Hippopotamus.* Ezo. Shelley, Hugh, tr. from Fr. 1962. Abelard-Schumann. (P.315)

--*A Near Thing for Captain Najork.* 1st ed. Hoban, Russell Conwell (1925-). 1976. Atheneum. **Award: (NYT).** (P.447)

--*Of Quarks, Quasars & Other Quirks: Quizzical Poems for the Supersonic Age.* Brewton, Sara Westbrook & Brewton, John Edmund (1898-), eds. 1977. Har-Row. (P.130)

--*Patrick.* Blake, Quentin (1932-). 1969, c.1968. H. Z. Walck. (P.106)

--*Pigeon of Paris.* Carlson, Natalie Savage (1906-). 1975. Schol Bk Serv. (P.169)

--*Pun Fun.* Rees, Ennis Samuel, Jr. (1925-). 1965. Abelard. (P.753)

--*Quentin Blake's Nursery Rhyme Book.* Blake, Quentin (1932-). 1984. Har-Row. (P.106)

--*Quick, Let's Get Out of Here.* Rosen, Michael (1946-). 1984. Andre Deutsch. (P.777)

--*Riddles, Riddles Everywhere.* Rees, Ennis Samuel, Jr. (1925-). 1964. Har-Row. (P.753)

--*Roald Dahl's Revolting Rhymes.* Dahl, Roald (1916-). 1982. Knopf. (P.238)

--*Sixes and Sevens.* Yeoman, John (1934-). 1974, c.1971. Collier Books. (P.986)

--*Snuff.* Blake, Quentin (1932-). 1973. Lippincott. (P.106)

--*The Story of the Dancing Frog.* Blake, Quentin (1932-). 1985. Knopf. (P.106)

--*Tiny Tall Tales.* Rees, Ennis Samuel, Jr. (1925-). 1967. Abelard-Schuman. (P.753)

--*The Twits.* Dahl, Roald (1916-). 1981, c.1980. Knopf ; Distributed by Random House. (P.238)

--*Uncle Cleans Up: More Uncle Stories.* Martin, John Percival (1880-1966). 1967. Coward-McCann. (P.625)

--*Uncle: Stories.* Martin, John Percival (1880-1966). 1966, c.1964. Coward. (P.625)

--*The Whaling Adventure of Bowleg Bill.* De Leeuw, Adele Louise (1899-). c.1976. Parents' Magazine Press. (P.254)

--*What Difference Does It Make, Danny?.* Young, Helen (1938-). 1980. Andre Deutsch. (P.990)

--*What Difference Does It Make Danny?.* Young, Helen (1938-). 1980. Dutton. (P.990)

--*Willie the Squowse.* Allen, Ted. 1978. Hastings House. (P.30)

--*The Witches.* Dahl, Roald (1916-). 1983. FS&G. **Award: (ALA).** (P.238)

--*The Witches.* Dahl, Roald (1916-). 1985, c.1983. Puffin Books. (P.238)

--*The Witch's Cat.* Thompson, Harry Harwood (1894-). 1975, c.1971. Addison-Wesley. (P.887)

--*The Wonderful Button.* Hunter, Evan (1926-). c.1961. Abelard-Schuman. (P.474)

--*Wouldn't You Like to Know.* Rosen, Michael (1946-). 1980. Andre Deutsch. (P.777)

--*You Can't Catch Me!.* Rosen, Michael (1946-). 1981. Andre Deutsch. (P.777)

--*The Young Performing Horse.* Yeoman, John (1934-). 1978, c.1977. Parents' Magazine Press. (P.986)

Blake, Robert

--*The Care Bears & the New Baby.* Kahn, Peggy. 1983. Random. (P.504)

Blake, Vivienne

--*The Alphabet from A to Z.* Gale, Leah. 1942. Simon & Schuster. (P.352)

--*Follow Me Animal Book: Eight Animations.* Swindler, Leona Martha Olsen (1913-). Panlsen, Martha, pseud. c.1945. The Saalfield Publishing Company. (P.875)

--*Little China Pig.* Rawls, Dorothy Dickens. N.D. Rand McNally & Co. (P.750)

--*Little Rabbit's Bath.* Potter, Miriam Clark, Mrs. (1886-1965). c.1948. Rand McNally. (P.735)

--*Little Rabbit's Bath.* Potter, Miriam Clark, Mrs. (1886-1965). 1957, c.1948. Rand McNally. (P.735)

--*Mrs. Duck's Lovely Day.* Blake, Vivienne. c.1955. Rand McNally. (P.106)

--*Peppy, The Lonely Little Puppy.* Friedman, Frieda (1905-). c.1947. Rand, McNally and Co. (P.345)

--*Sleeping Beauty.* Sleeping Beauty. c.1951. Rand McNally. (P.829)

Blake, William (1757-1827)

--*Grain of Sand.* Blake, William (1757-1827). Manning, Rosemary (1911-), ed. N.D. Watts. (P.106)

--*The History of Little Jack.* Day, Thomas (1748-1789). 1977. Garland Pub. (P.248)

--*The History of Little Jack.* Day, Thomas (1748-1789). 1850. W. P. Hazard. (P.248)

--*The Pilgrim's Progress.* Bunyan, John (1628-1688). N.D. Heritage Press. (P.151)

Blaker, Clay

--*The Ghost of Crabtree Hall.* Minshull, Evelyn White (1929-). 1970. Westminster Press. (P.651)

--*The Mystery of the Marmalade Cat.* Howe, Janet Rogers. 1969. Westminister Press. (P.467)

Blampied, Edmund

--*Peter Pan and Wendy.* Barrie, James Matthew, Sir (1860-1937). 1926. Charles Scribner. (P.76)

Blanc, Martine

--*Two Hoots.* Cresswell, Helen. 1978, c.1974. Crown Publishers. (P.230)

--*Two Hoots and the Big Bad Bird.* Cresswell, Helen. 1978, c.1975. Crown Publishers. (P.230)

--*Two Hoots and the King.* Cresswell, Helen. 1978, c.1977. Crown Publishers. (P.230)

--*Two Hoots Go to the Sea.* Cresswell, Helen. 1978, c.1974. Crown Publishers. (P.230)

--*Two Hoots in the Snow.* Cresswell, Helen. 1978, c.1975. Crown Publishers. (P.230)

--*Two Hoots Play Hide-and Seek.* Cresswell, Helen. 1978, c.1977. Crown Publishers. (P.230)

Blanch, Lucile

--*The Winter Nightingale.* Collin Delavaud, Marie Moreal De Brevans (1895-1938). Saunders, Marion, tr. c.1937. Coward-McCann. (P.209)

Blancke, Cecil Trout

--*Verses for Children.* Blancke, Cecil Trout. 1922. The Westminster Press. (P.107)

Blanding, Don (1894-)

--*Fioretta: Or, Cessate De Piagarmi.* Thorpe, Betty (1911-). 1922. Advertiser Publishing Co., Ltd. (P.890)

--*Stowaways in Paradise: Two Boy Adventurers in Hawaii.* Blanding, Don (1894-). 1931. Cosmopolitan Book Corporation. (P.108)

Blankenship, Judy (1944-)

--*Teddy Beddy Bear's Bedtime Songs & Poems.* Blankenship, Judy (1944-). 1984. Random. (P.108)

Blasco, Jesus

--*Ali Baba.* Hayes, Barbara (1944-). c.1984. Rourke Enterprises. (P.425)

--*Donkey Skin.* Hayes, Barbara (1944-). c.1984. Rourke Enterprises. (P.425)

--*The Enchanted Lion.* Hayes, Barbara (1944-). c.1984. Rourke Enterprises. (P.425)

--*Hansel & Gretel.* Hayes, Barbara (1944-). 1984. Rourke Enterprises. (P.425)

--*The Tailor Prince.* Hayes, Barbara (1944-). 1984. Rourke Enterprises. (P.425)

Blashfield, Albert D.

--*The Humming Top: Or, Debit and Credit in the Next World.* Deluxe ed. Gross, Theobald. Teuffel, Blanche Willis Howard Von (1847-1898), tr. c.1903. Frederick A. Stokes Company. (P.396)

--*Tommy-Anne, and the Three Hearts.* Wright, Mabel Osgood, Mrs. (1859-1934). N.D. Grosset & Dunlap. (P.981)

--*Tommy-Anne and the Three Hearts.* Wright, Mabel Osgood, Mrs. (1859-1934). 1896. The Macmillan Company. (P.981)

Blashfield, Edwin Howland

--*Greek Photoplays.* Seachrest, Effie. Seachrest, Effie, photos by. c.1916. Rand, McNally & Company. (P.806)

Blashfield, Edwin Howland & Rogers, W. A.

--*The Clocks of Rondaine and Other Stories.* Stockton, Frank Richard (1834-1902). 1892. C. Scribner's Sons. (P.859)

Blass, Jacqueline

--*Elizabeth Gets Well.* Weber, Alfons (1921-). 1970. Crowell. (P.939)

--*Jacques: The Goatherd.* Cormack, Maribelle B. (1902-) & Alexander, William Prindle (1881-). 1938. D. Appleton-Century Company, Incorporated. (P.221)
--*Madeleine's Court on an Island in Paris.* Criss, Mildred (1890-). 1938. Dodd, Mead & Company. (P.231)
--*The Red Caravan: The Wandering Adventures of Francesca.* Criss, Mildred (1890-). Dimnet, Ernest, frwd. by. 1934. Doubleday Doran & Company, Inc. (P.231)
Brisson, James F.
--*The Door to the Secret City.* Forti, Kathleen J. 1984. Stillpoint. (P.337)
Bristol, Esther Boston (1876-)
--*Funny Fanny and Her Friends.* Reeling, Viola Crouch. c.1939. B. Humphries, Inc. (P.753)
--*Nothing Ever Happens and How It Does: Sixteen True Stories.* Fisher, Dorothea Frances Canfield, Mrs. (1879-1958). 1940. The Beacon Press. (P.328)
Britcher, Phyllis see Gay, Romney, pseud.
Britcher, Phyllis
--*The Capper Cousins.* Carroll, Alice Lee. c.1929. J. H. Sears & Company, Inc. (P.171)
--*The Capper Cousins at the Fair.* Carroll, Alice Lee. c.1930. Sears Publishing Co. (P.171)
--*The Stuffed Parrot.* Fillmore, Parker Hoysted (1878-1944). c.1931. Harcourt, Brace and Company. (P.325)
--*The Two Bobbies.* Baruch, Dorothy Walter, Mrs. (1899-1962). c.1930. The John Day Company. (P.79)
Britt, Stephanie
--*Best Halloween Book.* Whitehead, Patricia. c.1985. Troll Associates. (P.953)
--*The Monster Under My Bed.* Gruber, Suzanne. c.1985. Troll Associates. (P.397)
Britten, W. E. F.
--*The Elf-Errant.* O'Neill, Moira. 1895. Dodd, Mead and Co. (P.694)
Broadhead, Dobson
--*Sandy was a Soldier's Boy: A Fable.* Walker, David Harry (1911-). 1957. Houghton, Mifflin. (P.926)
Broadhead, W. Smithson
--*The Jolliest School of All.* Brazil, Angela (1869-). 1923. Frederick A. Stokes Company. (P.128)
Broadley, G. M.
--*Earthlings: The Story of a Stray and a Waif.* Molesworth, Mary Louisa Stewart, Mrs. (1842-1921). 1892. Young. (P.654)
Brock, C. E., jt. illus. see Brock, Charles Edmond.
Brock, Charles Edmond (1870-1938)
--*The Bell of Santadino.* Townsend, Eric. 1938. David McKay Company. (P.897)
--*California Holiday.* Estcourt, Doris. c.1937. Dodd, Mead & Company. (P.310)
--*A Christmas Carol.* Dickens, Charles John Huffam (1812-1870). N.D. E. P. Dutton & Co. (P.262)
--*A Christmas Carol and The Cricket on the Hearth.* Dickens, Charles John Huffam (1812-1870). 1963. E.P. Dutton & Co. (P.263)
--*The Cricket on The Hearth.* Dickens, Charles John Huffam (1812-1870). N.D. E. P. Dutton & Co. (P.263)
--*The Cuckoo Clock.* Molesworth, Mary Louisa Stewart, Mrs. (1842-1921). 1980. Mayflower Books. (P.654)
--*Emma.* Austen, Jane (1775-1817). 1908. E P Dutton. (P.55)
--*The Heroes of Asgard: Tales from Scandinavian Mythology.* Keary, Annie (1825-1879) & Keary, Eliza, eds. 1976. Core Collection Books. (P.510)
--*The Honourable Mr. Tawnish.* Farnol, John Jeffery (1878-1952). 1913. Little, Brown, and Company. (P.318)
--*The Invisible Playmate and W.V. Her Book.* Canton, William (1845-1926). 1898. Dodd, Mead and Company. (P.166)
--*Little Peter.* Malet, Lucas, pseud. (1852-). Harrison, Mary ST. Leger Kingsley. N.D. George H. Doran. (P.614)
--*Mansfield Park.* Austen, Jane (1775-1817). 1906. E P Dutton. (P.55)
--*Mansfield Park.* Austen, Jane (1775-1817). N.D. Macrae Smith Co. (P.55)
--*Martin Pippin in the Apple Orchard.* Farjeon, Eleanor (1881-1965). 1922. Frederick A. Stokes. (P.317)
--*Northanger Abbey.* Austen, Jane (1775-1817). N.D. E P Dutton. (P.55)
--*Persuasion.* Austen, Jane (1775-1817). N.D. E P Dutton. (P.55)
--*Pride & Prejudice.* Austen, Jane (1775-1817). 1902. E P Dutton. (P.55)
--*Pride and Prejudice.* Austen, Jane (1775-1817). N.D. Macrae Smith Co. (P.55)
--*Railway Children.* Bland, Edith Nesbit, Mrs. (1858-1924). Nesbit, E., pseud. 1961. Penguin. (P.108)
--*The Railway Children.* Bland, Edith Nesbit, Mrs. (1858-1924). 1965. Penguin Books. (P.108)
--*The Railway Children.* Bland, Edith Nesbit, Mrs. (1858-1924). Nesbit, E., pseud. 1906. The Macmillan Company. (P.108)
--*Sense & Sensibility.* Austen, Jane (1775-1817). 1908. E P Dutton. (P.55)
--*Sense and Sensibility.* Austen, Jane (1775-1817). N.D. Macrae Smith Co. (P.55)
--*Tales from the Alhambra.* Irving, Washington (1783-1859). N.D. Houghton Mifflin. (P.482)
--*Travels into Several Remote Nations of the World.* Swift, Jonathan (1667-1745). Craik, Henry, Sir (1846-1927), pref. by. 1923. The Macmillan Company. (P.875)
--*Travels into Several Remote Nations of the World.* Swift, Jonathan (1667-1745). Craik, Henry, Sir (1846-1927), pref. by. 1967. University Microfilms. (P.875)
--*Who was Jane?. A Story for Young People of All Ages.* Sharp, Evelyn (1869-). 1922. Macmillan. (P.816)
--*The Youngest Girl in the School.* Sharp, Evelyn (1869-). 1901. The Macmillan Company. (P.816)
Brock, Charles Edmond (1870-1938) & Brock, Henry Matthew (1875-1960)
--*Emma.* Austen, Jane (1775-1817). 1925. Macrae Smith. (P.55)
--*Favourite Bible Stories.* Tempest, Margaret Mary (1892-1982) & Fryer, Kathleen. N.D. W Collins. (P.881)
Brock, Charles Edmond (1870-1938) & Flint, Russell
--*The Mikado.* Gilbert, William Schwenck, Sir (1836-1911). 1979. Smith Pubs. (P.367)
--*Yeomen of the Guard.* Gilbert, William Schwenck, Sir (1836-1911). 1979. Smith Pubs. (P.367)
Brock, Charles Edmond (1870-1938) & Gardner, Mary Ponton
--*The Pickwick Papers.* Dickens, Charles John Huffam (1812-1870). N.D. Dodd Mead & Co. (P.264)
Brock, Charles Edmond (1870-1938) & Millar, Harold Robert (1869-1939)
--*Oswald Bastable and Others.* Nesbit, E. pseud. (1858-1924). 1960. Coward. (P.678)
--*Oswald Bastable and Others.* Bland, Edith Nesbit, Mrs. (1858-1924). 1960. Coward McCann. (P.108)
--*Oswald Bastable & Others.* Bland, Edith Nesbit, Mrs. (1858-1924). Nesbit, E., pseud. 1960. Dover. (P.108)
--*Oswald Bastable and Others.* Bland, Edith Nesbit, Mrs. (1858-1924). 1960. E. Benn. (P.108)
Brock, Charles Edmund, jt. illus. see Craig, Henry.
Brock, Emma Lillian (1886-1974)
--*Baker's Dozen.* Davis, Mary Gould (1882-). 1930. HarBraceJ. (P.246)
--*Ballet for Mary.* Brock, Emma Lillian (1886-1974). 1954. Knopf. (P.133)
--*Beppo.* Brock, Emma Lillian (1886-1974). 1936. A. Whitman & Co. (P.133)
--*The Birds' Christmas Tree.* Brock, Emma Lillian (1886-1974). 1946. A. A. Knopf. (P.133)
--*Come On-Along, Fish!.* Brock, Emma Lillian (1886-1974). 1957. Alfred A Knopf : distributed by Borzoi Books. (P.133)
--*Drusilla.* Brock, Emma Lillian (1886-1974). 1937. The Macmillan Company. (P.133)
--*The Golden Chick and the Magic Frying Pan.* Chardon, Jeanne. Tubby, Ruth Peckham (1906-) & Chardon, Jeanne, trs. 1935. A. Whitman & Co. (P.186)
--*Granny's Wonderful Chair.* Browne, Frances (1816-1879). 1957. Macmillan. (P.143)
--*Granny's Wonderful Chair.* Browne, Frances (1816-1879). 1924. The Macmillan Company. (P.143)
--*The Greedy Goat.* Brock, Emma Lillian (1886-1974). 1931. A. A. Knopf. (P.133)
--*The Handsome Donkey.* Davis, Mary Gould (1882-). c.1933. Harcourt, Brace and Company. (P.246)
--*Hansi the Stork.* Ludmann, Oscar Henri (1900-). 1932. A. Whitman. (P.590)
--*Heedless Susan Who Sometimes Forgot to Remember.* Brock, Emma Lillian (1886-1974). 1939. A.A. Knopf. (P.133)
--*Here Comes Kristie.* Brock, Emma Lillian (1886-1974). 1942. A. A. Knopf. (P.133)
--*Here Comes Kristie.* Brock, Emma Lillian (1886-1974). 1946. A. A. Knopf. (P.133)
--*High in the Mountains: Robi and Hanni in the Swiss Alps.* Brock, Emma Lillian (1886-1974). 1938. A. Whitman & Co. (P.133)
--*Highdays & Holidays.* Adams, Florence & McCarrick, Elizabeth. 1927. Dutton. (P.5)
--*The Islands of Magic: Legends, Folk and Fairy Tales from the Azores.* Eells, Elsie Spicer, Mrs. (1880-), retold by. c.1922. Harcourt, Brace and Company. (P.298)
--*Johnny Cake.* N.D. G. P. Putnam's Sons. (P.134)
--*Johnny-Cake.* Jacobs, Joseph (1854-1916), ed. 1933. Putnam. (P.487)
--*Kristie and the Colt and the Others.* Brock, Emma Lillian (1886-1974). 1949. A. A. Knopf. (P.133)
--*Kristie Goes to the Fair.* Brock, Emma Lillian (1886-1974). 1953. Knopf. (P.133)
--*Kristie's Buttercup.* Brock, Emma Lillian (1886-1974). 1952. Knopf. (P.133)
--*Little Duchess: Anne of Brittany.* Brock, Emma Lillian (1886-1974). 1948. A. A. Knoff. (P.133)
--*Little Fat Gretchen.* 1st ed. Brock, Emma Lillian (1886-1974). 1934. A.A. Knopf. (P.133)
--*The Little House in Green Valley.* Hunt, Clara Whitehill (1871-). 1932. Houghton Mifflin Company. (P.473)
--*Mary Makes a Cake.* Brock, Emma Lillian (1886-1974). 1964. Knopf. (P.133)
--*Mary on Roller Skates.* Brock, Emma Lillian (1886-1974). 1967. Knopf. (P.133)
--*Mary's Camera.* Brock, Emma Lillian (1886-1974). 1963. Knopf. (P.133)
--*Mary's Secret.* 1st ed. Brock, Emma Lillian (1886-1974). 1962. Knopf. (P.133)
--*Masha: The Little Goose Girl.* Rudolph, Marguerita (1908-). 1939. The Macmillan Company. (P.783)
--*Merrimeg.* Bowen, William (1877-). 1923. The Macmillan Company. (P.121)
--*Mister Wren's House.* Brock, Emma Lillian (1886-1974). 1944. Knopf. (P.133)
--*More Mother Goose Village Stories.* Bigham, Madge Alford (1874-). 1922. Rand McNally & Co. (P.101)
--*Nobody's Mouse.* Brock, Emma Lillian (1886-1974). 1938. A.A. Knopf. (P.133)
--*The Nutcracker and the Mouse-King.* Hoffmann, Ernst Theodor Amadeus (1776-1822). Encking, Louise F., tr. from Ger. c.1930. A. Whitman & Co. (P.450)
--*One Little Indian Boy.* Brock, Emma Lillian (1886-1974). 1932. A.A. Knopf. (P.133)
--*Pancakes and the Merry-Go-Round.* Brock, Emma Lillian (1886-1974). 1960. Alfred A Knopf : distributed by Borzoi Books. (P.133)
--*Pancakes and the Merry-Go-Round.* 1st ed. Brock, Emma Lillian (1886-1974). 1960. Knopf. (P.133)
--*A Pet for Barbie.* Brock, Emma Lillian (1886-1974). 1947. A. A. Knopf. (P.133)
--*Picture Tales from Scandinavia.* Owen, Ruth Bryan, Mrs. (1885-). 1939. Frederick A. Stokes Company, Incorporated. (P.699)
--*Picture Tales from Scandinavia.* Owen, Ruth Bryan, Mrs. (1885-). N.D. J. B. Lippincott. (P.699)
--*Plaid Cow.* Brock, Emma Lillian (1886-1974). 1961. Knopf. (P.133)
--*Plug-Horse Derby.* Brock, Emma Lillian (1886-1974). 1955. Knopf. (P.133)
--*Poogie and Sibella.* Van Housen, Nita. c.1932. A. Whitman & Co. (P.914)
--*The Runaway Sardine.* Brock, Emma Lillian (1886-1974). 1929. A.A. Knopf. (P.133)
--*Sandy's Kingdom.* Davis, Mary Gould (1882-). c.1935. Harcourt, Brace & Company. (P.246)
--*Skipping Island.* Brock, Emma Lillian (1886-1974). 1958. Knopf. (P.133)
--*Surprise Balloon.* Brock, Emma Lillian (1886-1974). 1949. A. A. Knopf. (P.134)
--*Three Golden Oranges and Other Spanish Folk Tales.* Boggs, Ralph Steele (1901-) & Davis, Mary Gould (1882-). 1936. Longmans, Green & Co. (P.112)
--*Three Golden Oranges, and Other Spanish Folk Tales.* Boggs, Ralph Steele (1901-) & Davis, Mary Gould (1882-1956). 1936. McKay. (P.112)
--*Three Ring Circus.* Brock, Emma Lillian (1886-1974). 1950. Knopf. (P.134)
--*Till Potatoes Grow on Trees.* Brock, Emma Lillian (1886-1974). 1938. Knopf. (P.134)
--*To Market to Market.* Brock, Emma Lillian (1886-1974). 1930. Knopf. (P.134)
--*Too Many Turtles.* 1st ed. Brock, Emma Lillian (1886-1974). 1951. Knopf. (P.134)
--*The Topsy-Turvy Family.* Brock, Emma Lillian (1886-1974). 1943. A. A. Knopf. (P.134)
--*Topsy-Turvy Family.* Brock, Emma Lillian (1886-1974). 1962. Knopf. (P.134)
--*The Traveling Gallery.* Schiff, Bessie. 1936. A. Whitman & Co. (P.798)
--*Uncle Bennie Goes Visiting.* Brock, Emma Lillian (1886-1974). 1944. A. A. Knopf. (P.134)
--*The Wise Little Donkey: Memoirs of a Donkey.* Segur, Sophie Rostopchine, Mrs. (1799-1874). Loiseaux, Louis Marie Auguste, tr. c.1931. A. Whitman & Co. (P.808)
Brock, Esther
--*Away with the Circus.* Wise, Winifred Esther (1906-1970). 1936. A. Whitman & Co. (P.972)
Brock, H. M., jt. illus. see Waugh, Ida.
Brock, Henry Matthew, jt. illus. see Brock, Charles Edmond.
Brock, Henry Matthew, jt. illus. see Caldecott, Randolph.
Brock, Henry Matthew, jt. illus. see Dixon, Arthur A.
Brock, Henry Matthew (1875-1960)
--*All About Me: Poems for a Child.* Drinkwater, John (1882-1937), ed. 1928. Houghton Mifflin Company. (P.285)
--*Art Fairy Tales.* Brock, Henry Matthew (1875-1960). N.D. Frederick Warne & Co. (P.134)
--*The Book of Fairy Tales: Contains "Jack and the Beanstalk", "Hop o' My Thumb", "Vale ntine and Orson", and "Jack the Giant Killer".* Valentine and Orson. N.D. Frederick Warne & Co. (P.912)
--*The Book of Nursery Tales.* Mackenzie, Compton Edward Montague, Sir (1883-1972), ed. 1934. F. Warne & Co., Ltd. (P.606)
--*A Christmas Carol.* Dickens, Charles John Huffam (1812-1870). N.D. Dodd, Mead & Co. (P.262)
--*The Dog Crusoe and His Master: A Story of Adventure in the Western Prairies.* Ballantyne, Robert Michael (1825-1894). 1909. C. L. Bowman & Co. (P.66)
--*Fairy Tales and Stories.* Andersen, Hans Christian (1805-1875). 1909. C. L. Bowman. (P.35)
--*The Heroes: Or, Greek Fairy Tales For My Children.* Kingsley, Charles (1819-1875), ed. 1980. Mayflower. (P.525)
--*The Heroes: Or, Greek Fairy Tales for My Children.* Kingsley, Charles (1819-1875). 1928. St Martin. (P.525)
--*Martin Chuzzlewit.* Dickens, Charles John Huffam (1812-1870). N.D. Dodd Mead & Co. (P.263)
--*More About Me: Poems for a Child.* Drinkwater, John (1882-1937). 1930. Houghton Mifflin Company. (P.285)
--*The Old Fairy Tales.* 1916. F. Warne & Co. (P.134)
--*Once on a Time.* Milne, Alan Alexander (1882-1956). 1922. G P Putnam's Sons. (P.650)
--*Pasha the Pom: The Story of a Little Dog.* Frazer, James George, Sir (1854-1941) & Frazer, Lilly Grove, Lady. 1937. David McKay Company. (P.343)
--*Pride & Prejudice.* Austen, Jane (1775-1817). N.D. Macrae Smith. (P.55)
--*Puss in Boots.* Puss in Boots & Perrault, Charles (1628-1703) N.D. F. Warne & Co. (P.742)
--*The Singing Wood.* Frazer, Lilly Grove, Lady. 1931. The Macmillan Company. (P.343)
--*Stories from the Old Testament.* Hislop, James. N.D. Fleming H. Revell Co. (P.446)
--*Tell Me a Bible Story.* Hislop, James. N.D. Fleming H. Revell Co. (P.446)
--*Treasure Island.* Stevenson, Robert Louis (1850-1894). Boas, F., ed. N.D. St. Martin's Press. (P.857)
--*Valentine & Orson.* Valentine and Orson. 1916. F. Warne & Co. (P.912)
Brock, T. A.
--*The World's Wonder Stories.* Whyte, Adam Gowans (1875-). 1917. G. P. Putnam's Sons. (P.955)
Brockman, Ann
--*The House in Hidden Lane: Two Mysteries for Younger Girls.* Seaman, Augusta Huiell, Mrs. (1879-1950). 1931. Doubleday, Doran & Company, Inc. (P.806)
--*We Five.* Whitcomb, Edna Pearle Osborne, Mrs. 1926. Doubleday, Doran & Company, Inc. (P.950)
Brockway, Edith E. (1914-)
--*The Golden Land.* Brockway, Edith E. (1914-). 1968. Herald House. (P.134)
Broderick, Laurence
--*Uncle Matt's Mountain.* Park, Rosina Ruth Lucia (0000-1967). 1962. St. Martin's Press. (P.705)
Broderick, Virginia
--*Paul of St Peter's.* Broderick, Robert C (1913-). 1947. Bruce. Pub. Co. (P.134)
Brodsky, Beverly
--*Gooseberries to Oranges.* 1st ed. Cohen, Barbara (1932-). c.1982. Lothrop, Lee & Shepard. **Award: (ALA).** (P.206)
--*Here Come the Purim Players!.* Cohen, Barbara (1932-). 1984. Lothrop. (P.206)
Brodsky, Harry
--*The Big Parade.* Mockrin, Ida. 1983. Honeycomb Pr. (P.653)
Brody, Marc
--*Puddgin and Twidget: How the Squirrels Got Their Tails.* Acher, Don (1917-). c.1948. Story Book House. (P.4)
Brody, Sheldon
--*Dear Uncle Carlos.* Reit, Seymour (1918-). 1969. McGraw-Hill. (P.757)
--*Jamie Visits the Nurse.* Reit, Seymour (1918-). 1969. McGraw-Hill. (P.757)
Broen, Paul
--*King of the Stallions.* Tracy, Edward B. 1947. Dodd, Mead. (P.898)
Brofsky, Miriam (1929-)
--*All Kinds of Mothers.* Brownstone, Cecily. 1969. D. McKay Co. (P.143)

--*Dorothy Dainty's Visit.* Brooks, Amy (0000-1931). 1914. Lothrop, Lee & Shepard Co. (P.136)
--*Dorothy Dainty's Winter.* Brooks, Amy (0000-1931). 1910. Lothrop, Lee & Shepard. (P.136)
--*Dorothy's Playmates.* Brooks, Amy (0000-1931). 1903. Lee and Shepard. (P.136)
--*The Gingham Bag: The Tale of an Heirloom.* Lothrop, Harriet Mulford Stone, Mrs. (1844-1924). Sidney, Margaret, pseud. c.1896. Lothrop Publishing Company. (P.586)
--*Helen Grant at Aldred House.* Douglas, Amanda Minnie (1837-1916). 1905. Lee and Shepard. (P.281)
--*Helen Grant, Graduate.* Douglas, Amanda Minnie (1837-1916). 1908. Lothrop, Lee & Shepard Co. (P.281)
--*Helen Grant in College.* Douglas, Amanda Minnie (1837-1916). 1906. Lothrop, Lee & Shepard Co. (P.281)
--*Helen Grant, Senior.* Douglas, Amanda Minnie (1837-1916). c.1907. Lothrop, Lee & Shepard Co. (P.282)
--*Helen Grant, Teacher.* Douglas, Amanda Minnie (1837-1916). 1909. Lothrop, Lee and Shepard Co. (P.282)
--*Helen Grant's Decision.* Douglas, Amanda Minnie (1837-1916). 1910. Lothrop,Lee & Shepard. (P.282)
--*Helen Grant's Friends.* Douglas, Amanda Minnie (1837-1916). 1904. Lee and Shepard. (P.282)
--*Helen Grant's Schooldays.* Douglas, Amanda Minnie (1837-1916). 1903. Lee and Shepard. (P.282)
--*Home Songs and Speeches for Boys and Girls.* N.D. Caldwell. (P.136)
--*Home Songs for Little Darlings, 10 vols.* 1905. H M Caldwell Co. (P.136)
--*Jessica's Triumph.* Upham, Grace Le Baron Locke, Mrs. (1845-1916). N.D. Lothrop & Shepard. (P.910)
--*A Jolly Cat Tale.* Brooks, Amy (0000-1931). 1905. Lee and Shepard Company. (P.136)
--*A Jolly Cat Tale.* Brooks, Amy (0000-1931). 1901. Lothrop, Lee & Shepard. (P.136)
--*The Little Lame Prince.* Craik, Dinah Maria Mulock, Mrs. (1826-1887). N.D. L. C. Page & Co. (P.227)
--*Little Sister Prue.* Brooks, Amy (0000-1931). 1908. Lothrop, Lee & Shepard Co. (P.136)
--*Princess Polly.* Brooks, Amy (0000-1931). N.D. A. L. Burt Co. (P.136)
--*Princess Polly.* Brooks, Amy (0000-1931). N.D. Nourse. (P.136)
--*Princess Polly at Cliffmore.* Brooks, Amy (0000-1931). c.1925. A. L. Burt Company. (P.136)
--*Princess Polly at Play.* Brooks, Amy (0000-1931). 1915. A. L. Burt Co. (P.136)
--*Princess Polly at Play.* Brooks, Amy (0000-1931). N.D. Nourse. (P.136)
--*Princess Polly at Play.* Brooks, Amy (0000-1931). c.1915. The Platt & Peck Co. (P.136)
--*Princess Polly at School.* Brooks, Amy (0000-1931). N.D. A. L. Burt Co. (P.136)
--*Princess Polly at School.* Brooks, Amy (0000-1931). N.D. Nourse. (P.136)
--*Princess Polly at School.* Brooks, Amy (0000-1931). c.1912. The Platt & Peck Co. (P.136)
--*Princess Polly by the Sea.* Brooks, Amy (0000-1931). N.D. A. L. Burt Co. (P.136)
--*Princess Polly by the Sea.* Brooks, Amy (0000-1931). N.D. Nourse. (P.136)
--*Princess Polly's Gay Winter.* Brooks, Amy (0000-1931). N.D. A. L. Burt Co. (P.136)
--*Princess Polly's Gay Winter.* Brooks, Amy (0000-1931). N.D. Nourse. (P.136)
--*Princess Polly's Playmates.* Brooks, Amy (0000-1931). N.D. A. L. Burt Co. (P.136)
--*Princess Polly's Playmates.* Brooks, Amy (0000-1931). N.D. Nourse. (P.136)
--*Prue at School.* Brooks, Amy (0000-1931). 1909. Lothrop, Lee & Shepard. (P.136)
--*Prue's Jolly Winter.* Brooks, Amy (0000-1931). 1913. Lothrop, Lee & Shepard Co. (P.136)
--*Prue's Little Friends.* Brooks, Amy (0000-1931). 1912. Lothrop, Lee & Shepard. (P.136)
--*Prue's Merry Times.* Brooks, Amy (0000-1931). 1911. Lothrop Lee & Shepard. (P.136)
--*Prue's Playmates.* Brooks, Amy (0000-1931). 1910. Lothrop, Lee & Shepard Co. (P.136)
--*Randy and Her Friends.* Brooks, Amy (0000-1931). 1902. Lothrop, Lee & Shepard. (P.136)
--*Randy and Prue.* Brooks, Amy (0000-1931). 1903. Lee and Shepard. (P.136)
--*Randy's Good Times.* Brooks, Amy (0000-1931). 1904. Lothrop Lee & Shepard. (P.136)
--*Randy's Loyalty.* Brooks, Amy (0000-1931). 1906. Lothrop, Lee & Shepard Co. (P.136)
--*Randy's Luck.* Brooks, Amy (0000-1931). 1905. Lee and Shepard. (P.136)
--*Randy's Prince.* Brooks, Amy (0000-1931). 1907. Lothrop, Lee & Shepard Co. (P.136)
--*Randy's Summer: A Story for Girls.* Brooks, Amy (0000-1931). 1900. Lee and Shepard. (P.136)
--*Randy's Winter.* Brooks, Amy (0000-1931). 1901. Lothrop, Lee & Shepard. (P.136)
--*Rosalie Dare.* Brooks, Amy (0000-1931). c.1924. Lothrop, Lee & Shepard Co. (P.136)
--*Rosalie Dare's Test.* Brooks, Amy (0000-1931). c.1925. Lothrop, Lee & Shepard Co. (P.136)
--*Told Under the Cherry Trees: A Book for the Young.* Upham, Grace Le Baron Locke, Mrs. (1845-1916). Le Baron, Grace, pseud. 1899. Lee and Shepard. (P.910)

Brooks, Andrea
--*Becky & the Bookworm.* Lexau, Joan M. N.D. Dandelion Pr. (P.570)
--*The Christmas Donkey.* Taylor, T. William. c.1984. Western Pub. Co. (P.881)

Brooks, Andrea, jt. illus. see Spicer-Zerner, Jessie.

Brooks, Dale, photos by.
--*Three Little Bunnies.* Barrows, Ruth Marjorie (1892-1983). Dixon, Ruth, pseud. 1956, c.1950. Rand McNally. (P.77)

Brooks, Kevin
--*A Boy and a Boa.* Israel, Abigail P (1942-). c.1981. Dial Press. (P.483)
--*Window Wishing.* Caines, Jeannette Franklin. c.1980. Harper & Row. (P.161)

Brooks, Mary B.
--*Bobo and the Crocodile.* Rock, Nova. 1961. F. Warne. (P.771)
--*Spotty Finds a Playmate.* Brooks, Mary B. & Carrick, Bruce R. 1963. Golden Press. (P.137)

Brooks, Meredith
--*Around Home: Three Short Stories.* rev. american ed. Cresher, G. R. c.1969. Fearon. (P.230)
--*The Moonstone.* Laklan, Carli (1907-), abridged by. Collins, Wilkie (1824-1889). 1967. Fearon Publishers. (P.210)
--*Over the Rickety Fence.* Battles, Edith, pseud. (1921-). Funk, Thompson. 1967. Fearon Pub. (P.81)

Brooks, Nan
--*The Ball Book.* Hillert, Margaret (1920-). c.1982. Follett Pub. Co. (P.444)
--*Break-in.* Gray, Genevieve Stuck (1920-). 1973. EMC Corp. (P.383)
--*Brian and the Long, Long Scarf.* Hellie, Ann (1925-). 1973. Carolrhoda Books. (P.431)
--*Hot Shot.* Gray, Genevieve Stuck (1920-). 1973. EMC Corp. (P.383)
--*Lost and Found.* Morse, Ann & Morse, Charles. 1973. EMC Corp. (P.666)
--*Max-I-Fish.* Morse, Ann & Morse, Charles. 1973. EMC Corp. (P.666)
--*Stand-off.* Gray, Genevieve Stuck (1920-). 1973. EMC Corp. (P.383)
--*Stray.* Gray, Genevieve Stuck (1920-). 1973. EMC Corp. (P.383)
--*Who Goes to School?.* Hillert, Margaret (1920-). c.1981. Follett. (P.445)

Brooks, Ronald George (1948-)
--*Aranea: A Story about a Spider.* Wagner, Jenny. 1978. Bradbury Pr. (P.923)
--*The Bunyip of Berekley's Creek.* Wagner, Jenny. 1980. Penguin. (P.923)
--*John Brown, Rose, and the Midnight Cat.* Wagner, Jenny. 1978, c.1977. Bradbury Press. **Award: (ALA).** (P.923)
--*Time Sweep.* Weldrick, Valerie. 1978. Lothrop. (P.943)

Brooks, William (1914-)
--*The Black Box.* Carr, Albert B. 1969. Prentice-Hall. (P.170)
--*The Black Box.* Carr, Albert B. 1974. Prentice Hall. (P.170)

Brookshaw, Drake
--*The Monach Light.* Thom, William Albert Strang (1900-). Morrison, J. Strang, pseud. 1961. St. Martin's Press. (P.885)

Broomall, Dorothy Snowden
--*The Country Mouse and the City Mouse.* Broomall, Dorothy Snowden. c.1928. De La Rue Press. (P.137)

Broomfield, Robert (1930-)
--*Dame Wiggins of Lee and Her Seven Wonderful Cats: A Humorous Tale Written Prinicipally by a Lady of Ninety.* Sharpe, Richard Scrafton (0000-1852) & Pearson, Mrs. Ruskin, John (1819-1900), ed. 1963. McGraw-Hill. (P.816)
--*Dame Wiggins of Lee and her Seven Wonderful Cats.* Ruskin, John (1819-1900). 1963. McGraw-Hill Book Co. (P.784)
--*Mister Faksimily and the Tiger.* Hewett, Anita (1918-). 1969, c.1967. Follett. (P.440)
--*Mrs. Mopple's Washing Line.* Hewett, Anita (1918-). 1966. McGraw. (P.440)
--*Mystery of Saint Salgue.* Berna, Paul (1910-). Buchanan-Brown, John, tr. from Fr. 1964. Pantheon. (P.97)
--*The Twelve Days of Christmas: A Picture Book.* Twelve Days of Christmas (English Folk Song). 1965. McGraw-Hill. (P.907)

Brophy, Ruth
--*Danny and the Old Pest.* Holland, Joyce Flint (1921-). c.1966. Denison. (P.455)
--*Denny's Friend Rags.* Talbot, Winifred. 1965. Denison. (P.877)
--*The First Rainbow.* Bergey, Alyce Mae (1934-). N.D. T. S. Denison. (P.96)
--*Happiness Is Smiling.* Gehm, Katherine. c.1966. Denison. (P.362)
--*Harvey Hopper.* Shappel, Bernice Marie (1910-). N.D. Denison. (P.186)
--*Harvey Hopper.* Shappel, Bernice M. c.1966. Denison. (P.815)

Brose, Mabel Rosamond
--*The Motzie stories: True Stories of Children in the Boise Valley During the 1890's.* Brose, Mabel Rosamond. c.1957. Exposition Press. (P.137)

Brostrom, Eileen
--*The Lemonade Lady: An Easy to Read Children's Book.* Weiss, Joan Talmage (1928-). c.1980. Peppertree Pub. (P.942)

Brothers, Betty Miller
--*Ra-Oo and the Porpoise.* Brothers, Betty Miller. 1969, c.1962. Litoky Pub. Co. (P.137)
--*Ra-Oo and the Porpoise: A shipwrecked boy is rescued and cared for by porpoise.* Brothers, Betty Miller. N.D. Wake-Brook House. (P.137)

Brothers, Dalziel, jt. illus. see Emerson, H. H.

Broude, Susan
--*Panchit's Secret.* Wayman, Vivienne. 1976. British Bk Ctr. (P.937)

Brough, Richard
--*Ninety Nine Fables.* March, William, pseud. (1893-1954). Campbell, William Edward March. Going, T William, ed. 1960. University of Alabama Press. (P.619)

Brouwer, Jack
--*Chuffy.* Lawrie, Robert Wheeler. 1959. Fideler Co. (P.556)

Brown, Arthur William
--*Limpy: The Boy Who Felt Neglected.* Johnston, William Andrew (1871-). 1917. Little, Brown, and Company. (P.498)
--*Pidgin Island.* MacGrath, Harold. N.D. Bobbs-Merrill Co. (P.602)
--*Prudence of the Parsonage.* Hueston, Ethel Powelson, Mrs. (1887-). N.D. Bobbs-Merrill Co. (P.470)
--*Redney McGaw: A Story of the Big Show and the Cheerful Spirit.* McFarlane, Arthur Emerson (1876-). 1909. Little,Brown & Co. (P.601)
--*Sunny Slopes.* Hueston, Ethel Powelson, Mrs. (1887-). N.D. Bobbs-Merrill Co. (P.470)

Brown, Arthur William, jt. illus. see Castaigne, Andre.

Brown, Arthur William & Gowing, Louis D.
--*Captain Jack Lorimer: Or, the Young Athletes of Millvale High.* Sawyer, Walter Leon (1862-1915). Standish, Winn, pseud. 1906. L. C. Page & Company. (P.795)

Brown, Barbara Haven
--*A Doll's Day.* Brown, Beatrice Bradshaw. 1931. Little, Brown, and Company. (P.138)
--*A Paris Pair, Their Day's Doings.* Brown, Beatrice Bradshaw. c.1923. E. P. Dutton & Company. (P.138)

Brown, Belmore
--*Sheridan's Twins: A Story of Early Days in Colorado.* Hamp, Sidford Frederick (1855-). 1917. G. P. Putnam's Sons. (P.409)

Brown, Blanche M.
--*What's Keeping You, Santa?.* A Christmas Musical. Pickett, Margaret E. 1983. TP Assocs. (P.725)

Brown, Buck (1936-)
--*ABC Pirate Adventure.* DeLage, Ida (1918-). 1977. Garrard Pub. Co. (P.252)
--*Bug Circus.* Darling, Kathy, pseud. (1943-). Darling, Mary Kathleen. c.1976. Garrard Pub. Co. (P.242)
--*Fritz, the Too-Long Dog.* Lewi, Bee. 1980. Garrard Pub. Co. (P.569)
--*The Jelly Bean Contest.* Darling, Kathy, pseud. (1943-). Darling, Mary Kathleen. 1972. Garrard Pub. Co. (P.242)

Brown, Carol (1937-)
--*A God on Every Mountain Top: Stories of Southwest Indian Sacred Mountains.* Baylor, Byrd (1924-). 1981. Scribner. (P.84)

Brown, Cheryl
--*Herbert the Snail.* Brown, Cheryl. N.D. Van Nostrand Reinhold Co. (P.138)

Brown, Clinton
--*The Hall with Doors.* Zimm, Louise Seymour Hasbrouck (1883-). 1920. The Womans Press. (P.993)

Brown, Cornelia
--*Cardinals in the Pine.* Boyd, Lorenz. Boyd, Loreuz, photos by. 1969. Abingdon Press. (P.122)
--*Elf King Joe.* Parkinson, Ethelyn Minerva (1906-). 1968. Abingdon Press. (P.707)
--*We're off to Catch a Dragon.* Laurence, Ester Hauser (1935-). 1969. Abingdon Press. (P.555)

Brown, Darrell
--*And God Cares for Me.* Breitweiser, Alverta. Breitwetser, Paul, photos by. 1957. Warner Press. (P.129)

Brown, David Scott (1936-)
--*Two Sides of the River.* Crippen, David (1936-). c.1976. Abingdon Press. (P.231)

Brown, David (1926-)
--*Ride the Red Cycle.* Robinet, Harriette Gillem (1931-). 1980. Houghton-Mifflin. (P.769)
--*The Sacrifice.* Vitarelli, Robert, ed. 1973. Xerox Ed Pubns. (P.920)
--*The Sacrifice, and Eight More Short Stories for Girls.* Vitarelli, Robert, ed. 1972. Xerox Education Publications. (P.920)

Brown, Denise
--*One Little Tree.* Almedingen, Martha Edith von (1898-1971). Almedingen, E. M., pseud. N.D. G&D. (P.31)
--*One Little Tree: A Christmas Card of a Finnish Landscape.* Almedingen, Martha Edith von (1898-1971). Almedingen, E. M., pseud. 1968, c.1963. Norton. (P.31)
--*Philip: The Fox, and Other Stories.* Voss-Bark, Doris Lily. 1967, c.1963. Dufour. (P.922)
--*The Young Pavlova.* Almedingen, Martha Edith von (1898-1971). Almedingen, E. M., pseud. 1961. Roy. (P.31)

Brown, Dennis
--*Humphrey's Ride.* Abrahams, Robert David (1905-). 1965, c.1964. Crowell. (P.4)

Brown, Edith
--*The Cheerful Cricket and Others.* Marks, Jeannette Augustus (1875-). 1907. Small, Maynard & Company. (P.620)
--*Folklore Stories and Proverbs.* Wiltse, Sara Eliza (1849-), compiled by. 1900. Ginn & Company. (P.967)
--*John Newsom: A Tale of College Life.* Wilton, William. 1883. Southern Methodist Publishing House. (P.967)
--*Stella's Adventures in Starland.* Rev ed. Sabin, Eldridge Hosmer (1865-1934). 1907. Small, Maynard & Co. (P.787)
--*Wanderfolk in Wonderland.* Guerrier, Edith. N.D. Small, Maynard & Co. (P.398)

Brown, Ethel C.
--*Brothers and Sisters.* Brown, Abbie Farwell (0000-1927). 1906. Houghton, Mifflin and Company. (P.137)
--*Friends and Cousins.* Brown, Abbie Farwell (0000-1927). 1907. Houghton, Mifflin and Company. (P.137)

Brown, Ethel Pennewill
--*Betty Baird.* Weikel, Anna Hamlin. 1906. Little, Brown, and Company. (P.940)
--*Betty Baird's Golden Year.* Weikel, Anna Hamlin. 1909. Little, Brown, and Company. (P.940)
--*Betty Baird's Ventures.* Weikel, Anna Hamlin. 1907. Little, Brown, and Company. (P.940)
--*A Dixie Rose.* Kortrecht, Augusta. 1910. J. B. Lippincott Company. (P.536)
--*Proverb Stories.* Alcott, Louisa May (1832-1888). 1908. Little, Brown, and Company. (P.18)

Brown, Garrett, Jr. & Grant, Louis F.
--*How to Beat the Game.* Brown, Garrett, Jr. 1903. G. W. Dillingham Co. (P.139)

Brown, Gill
--*Songs for Sunshine & Rain: Genesis Project Songbook.* The, Genesis Project, ed. 1981. Genesis Project. (P.363)

Brown, Guy J.
--*Little Brown Bear.* Upham, Elizabeth Norine (1904-). 1947. Child Training Assn. (P.910)

Brown, Howard V.
--*Eskimo Stories.* Smith, Mary Estella (1863-). 1902. Rand, McNally & Company. (P.835)

Brown, Ian
--*Ace the Guard Dog.* Richardson, John (1938-). 1973. Lansdowne. (P.763)
--*Gendarme, the Police Horse.* Richardson, John (1938-). 1971. Lansdowne Press. (P.763)

Brown, James, Jr.
--*Hongry Catch the Foolish Boy.* Graham, Lorenz Bell (1902-). 1973. T Y Crowell. (P.380)

Brown, Joel & Hussett, Milton
--*The Adventures of Coqui & His Friends.* Brown, Joel. Berlitz Institute, tr. from Sp. 1980. New Day NY. (P.139)

Brown, John & Dalziel, Edward (1817-1905)
--*Old Favorite Fairy Tales.* 1882. J B Lippincott. (P.139)

Brown, Judith Gwyn (1933-)
--*ABC Santa Claus.* DeLage, Ida (1918-). c.1978. Garrard Pub. Co. (P.252)
--*Amy Moves In.* 1st ed. Sachs, Marilyn Stickle (1927-). 1964. Doubleday. (P.787)
--*Ben and Annie.* Tate, Joan (1922-). 1974. Doubleday. (P.878)
--*The Best Christmas Pageant Ever.* 1st ed. Robinson, Barbara Webb (1927-). 1972. Harper & Row. (P.769)
--*Brainstormers: Humorous Tales of Ingenious American Boys.* Carlson, Dale Bick (1935-), ed. 1966. Doubleday. (P.169)
--*Butch Elects a Mayor.* Hanff, Helene. 1969. Parents' Magazine Press. (P.410)

--*Jupiter and the Cats.* Goudey, Alice E (1898-). 1953. Scribner. (P.378)

--*The Lost Birthday Present.* Hyndman, Jane Andrews Lee (1912-1978). Wyndham, Lee, pseud. 1957. Dodd, Mead. (P.478)

--*Melody, Mutton Bone, and Sam.* Davis, Lavinia Riker, Mrs. (1909-1961). 1947. Doubleday. (P.246)

--*Merrylegs: The Rocking Pony.* Brown, Paul (1893-1958). c.1946. C. Scribner's Sons. (P.142)

--*Mike of Company D.* Aspden, Don. 1939. C. Scribner's Sons. (P.53)

--*Pamela and the Blue Mare.* 1st ed. O'Connell, Alice Louise (1907-). 1952. Little, Brown. (P.689)

--*Pam's Paradise Ranch: A Story of Hawaii.* Tempski, Armine Von (1899-). 1940. Dodd, Mead. (P.882)

--*Pam's Paradise Ranch: A Story of Hawaii.* Von Tempski, Armine (1899-1943). 1940. Dodd, Mead & Company. (P.921)

--*Plow Penny Mystery.* Davis, Lavinia Riker, Mrs. (1909-1961). 1942. Doubleday, Doran & Company, Inc. (P.246)

--*Puff Ball.* Brown, Paul (1893-1958). 1942. Charles Scribner's Sons. (P.142)

--*Ride 'em, Peggy!.* Bialk, Elisa (1912-). 1950. Houghton Mifflin. (P.100)

--*Riding Rhymes for Young Riders.* Disston, Harry (1899-). 1951. B. Wheelwright Co. (P.273)

--*Riding Rhymes for Young Riders.* Disston, Harry (1899-). 1951. Cumberland Pr. (P.273)

--*Sam Patch: The High, Wide, & Handsome Jumper.* Bontemps, Arna Wendell (1902-1973) & Conroy, Jack, pseud. (1899-). Conroy, John Wesley. 1951. Houghton Mifflin. (P.117)

--*The Seventh's Staghound.* Downey, Fairfax Davis (1893-). 1948. Dodd, Mead. (P.283)

--*Show Pony.* 1st ed. Caffrey, Nancy. 1954. Dutton. (P.161)

--*The Sorrel Stallion.* Grew, David. 1932. C. Scribner's Sons. (P.389)

--*The Sorrel Stallion,.* The Horse That Came Home. Grew, David. 1951. Grosset & Dunlap. (P.389)

--*Sparkie and Puff Ball.* Brown, Paul (1893-1958). c.1954. Scribner. (P.142)

--*The Tall Stallion.* Hoffmann, Eleanor (1895-). 1950. Dodd, Mead. (P.450)

--*War Horse.* Downey, Fairfax Davis (1893-). 1942. Dodd, Mead & Company. (P.283)

--*War Paint.* Brown, Paul (1893-1958). 1936. Scribner. (P.142)

--*Warpath and Cattle Trail.* Collins, Hubert E. Beard, Dan, frwd. by. 1933. William Morrow & Co. (P.210)

--*Warpath and Cattle Trail.* Collins, Hubert E. 1928. William Morrow & Co. (P.210)

--*Wild Horse Island.* Bialk, Elisa (1912-). 1951. Houghton Mifflin. (P.100)

--*The Wild Horse Roundup: A Collection of Stories.* Western Writers of America. Kjelgaard, James Arthur (1910-1959), ed. 1957. Dodd, Mead. (P.948)

--*The Wild Horse Roundup.* Western Writers of America. Kjelgaard, James Arthur (1910-1959), ed. 1974, c.1957. Books for Libraries Press. (P.948)

--*The Wild Stranger.* Burke, Trude. 1953. Holt. (P.154)

--*Your Pony's Trek Around the World.* Brown, Paul (1893-1958). c.1956. Scribner. (P.142)

Brown, Randolph J.

--*The House with Sixty Closets: A Christmas Story for Young Folks and Old Children.* Child, Frank Samuel (1854-). 1899. Lee & Shepard. (P.191)

--*The House with Sixty Closets: A Christmas Story for Young Folks and Old Children.* Child, Frank Samuel (1854-). 1905. Lee and Shepard Company. (P.191)

--*The Little Dreamer's Adventures: A Story of Droll Days and Droll Doings.* Child, Frank Samuel (1854-). 1905. Lee and Shepard Company. (P.191)

Brown, Richard Eric (1946-)

--*Cookie Monster's Book of Cookie Shapes.* Sesame Street. 1979. Western Pub. (P.811)

--*Even the Devil Is Afraid of a Shrew: A Folktale of Lapland.* Stalder, Valerie, retold by. Broekel, Ray, pseud. (1923-), adapted by. Broekel, Rainer Lothar. 1972. Addison-Wesley. (P.848)

--*Frazzle's Fantastic Day: Featuring Jim Henson's Sesame Street Muppets.* Kovacs, Deborah. c.1980. Western Pub. Co. in Conjunction with Children's Television Workshop. (P.536)

--*Gone Fishing.* Long, Earlene R. (1938-). 1984. HM. (P.581)

--*The Great Moon Hoax.* Branley, Franklyn Mansfield (1915-). c.1973. Ginn. (P.127)

--*I Can Do It Myself: Featuring Jim Henson's Sesame Street Muppets.* Kingsley, Emily Perl, et al. (1940-) c.1980. Western Pub. Co. : Children's Televison Workshop. (P.525)

--*I Can Do It Myself.* Kingsley, Emily Perl (1940-). 1981. Western Pub. (P.526)

--*The Marvelous Mud Washing Machine.* Wolcott, Patty (1929-). 1974. Addison-Wesley. (P.973)

--*The Marvelous Mud Washing Machine.* Wolcott, Patty (1929-). 1985, c.1974. Lippincott. (P.973)

--*Mud For Sale.* Nelson, Brenda. 1984. Houghton Mifflin. (P.677)

--*People in Your Neighborhood.* Moss, Jeffrey. 1984. Western Pub. (P.667)

--*Sesame Seasons: Featuring Jim Henson's Sesame Street Muppets.* Hayward, Linda & Henson, Jim, pseud. (1936-). Henson, James Maury. c.1981. Western Pub. Co. (P.426)

--*A Sleepy Story.* Burrowes, Elisabeth. c.1982. Golden Press. (P.156)

--*Special Delivery: Featuring Jim Henson's Sesame Street Muppets.* McLenighan, Valjean (1947-). c.1980. Western Pub. Co. (P.608)

--*What's Mama's Christmas Present?.* Ziefert, Harriet. 1985. Puffin Books. (P.992)

--*When Is Saturday?.* Featuring Jim Henson's Sesame Street Muppets. Kovacs, Deborah & Children's Television Workshop. c.1981. Western Pub. Co. in Conjunction with Children's Television Workshop. (P.536)

--*Where Is My Easter Egg?.* Ziefert, Harriet. 1985. Puffin Books. (P.992)

--*Where's the Halloween Treat?.* Ziefert, Harriet. 1985. Puffin Books. (P.992)

Brown, Ruth

--*A Dark Dark Tale.* Brown, Ruth. 1981. Dial Bks Young. (P.142)

Brown, S. D. & Westmacott, Bernard (1887-)

--*The Cruise of the Gull-Flight.* Corbett, Sidney (1891-). 1937. Longmans, Green and Co. (P.219)

Brown, Theodora

--*Land O' Nod: The Story of Denny's Adventures.* Thomas, Gertrude Ellen Ickler (1895-). 1951. Exposition Press. (P.886)

Brown, Wayne

--*The Sleeping Beauty and Other Tales.* Grimm, Jakob Ludwig Karl (1785-1863) & Grimm, Wilhelm Karl (1786-1859). 1969. Childrens Press. (P.394)

Brown, William Ferdinand (1928-)

--*Dear Folks.* Lowell, Juliet (1901-). 1960. Putnam. (P.588)

Brown & Worcester

--*The Boston, Cries: And the Story of The Little Matchboy.* 1844. J. C. Riker. (P.142)

Browne, Anthony Edward Tudor (1946-)

--*Gorilla.* Browne, Anthony Edward Tudor (1946-). 1984. Watts. **Awards: (KGM); (NYT).** (P.142)

--*Hansel and Gretel.* Grimm, Jakob Ludwig Karl (1785-1863) & Grimm, Wilhelm Karl (1786-1859). 1981. Julia MacRae Books. (P.393)

--*Hansel & Gretel.* Grimm, Jakob Ludwig Karl (1785-1863) & Grimm, Wilhelm Karl (1786-1859). 1982. Watts. (P.393)

--*The Visitors Who Came to Stay.* McAfee, Annalena. 1985, c.1984. Viking Kestrel. (P.593)

--*Willy the Wimp.* Browne, Anthony Edward Tudor (1946-). 1985. Knopf. (P.142)

Browne, Belmore (1880-)

--*The Frozen Barrier: A Story of Adventure on the Coast of Behring Sea.* Browne, Belmore (1880-). 1921. G.P. Putnam's Sons. (P.143)

--*The Quest of the Golden Valley: A Story of Adventure on the Yukon.* Browne, Belmore (1880-). 1916. G.P. Putnam's Sons. (P.143)

--*The White Blanket: The Story of an Alaskan Winter.* Browne, Belmore (1880-). 1917. G.P. Putnam's Sons. (P.143)

Browne, Caroline

--*Why a Donkey Was Chosen.* Gregorowski, Christopher (1940-). c.1975. Doubleday. (P.388)

Browne, Dik (1917-)

--*Most.* Walker, Mort (1923-). 1971. Windmill Books. (P.926)

Browne, Eileen

--*Halloweena Hecatee, and Other Rhymes to Skip to.* Mitchell, Cynthia (1922-). 1979, c.1978. Crowell. (P.652)

Browne, Gordon Frederick, et al. (1858-1932)

--*Dandelion Clocks and Other Tales.* Ewing, Juliana Horatia Gatty, Mrs. (1841-1885). 1887. Young. (P.313)

--*Five Minute Stories.* Molesworth, Mary Louisa Stewart, Mrs. (1839-1921). 1888. E. & J. B. Young & Co. (P.654)

Browne, Gordon Frederick (1858-1932)

--*The Adventures of Robin Hood.* Ritson, Joseph (1752-1803), ed. N.D. George Routledge & Sons. (P.766)

--*Bonnie Prince Charlie: A Tale of Fontenoy and Culloden.* Henty, George Alfred (1832-1902). N.D. A. L. Burt. (P.434)

--*A Book of Discoveries.* Masefield, John Edward (1878-1967). 1910. F. A. Stokes. (P.627)

--*Bound by a Spell: Or, The Haunted Witch of the Forest.* Juv ed. Greene. N.D. Cassell & Co. (P.386)

--*By Sheer Pluck: A Tale of the Ashanti War.* Henty, George Alfred (1832-1902). N.D. The Federal Book Company. (P.435)

--*The Doctor of the "Juliet".* A Story of the Sea. Collingwood, Harry (1851-1920). N.D. Thomas Whittaker. (P.209)

--*Down the Snow Stairs.* Corkran, Alice Abigail (0000-1916). N.D. Dodge Publishing Cp. (P.220)

--*Eric: Or, Little by Little, A Tale of Roslyn School.* 24th ed. Farrar, Frederic William (1831-1903). 1891. A.C. McClurg. (P.318)

--*Fairy Tales.* Aulnoy, Marie Catherine Jumelle de Berneville (1650-1705). Planche, James Robison (1796-1880), tr. N.D. George Routledge & Sons. (P.54)

--*Fairy Tales from Grimm.* Baring-Gould, Sabine, intro. by. N.D. E. & J. B. Young & Co. (P.143)

--*A Flock of Four.* Thorn, Ismay. N.D. Pott & Co. (P.888)

--*The Getting Well of Dorothy.* Clifford, Lucy Lane W. K., Mrs. 1917. E. P. Dutton & Co. (P.202)

--*Godfrey Marten, Schoolboy.* Turley, Charles. 1906. E. P. Dutton & Company. (P.905)

--*The Golden Land: Or, Links from Shore to Shore.* Farjeon, Benjamin Leopold (1833-1903). Evans, Edmund, contrib. by. 1886. Ward, Lock, & Co. (P.316)

--*Gullivers Travels.* Swift, Jonathan (1667-1745). N.D. Charles Scribner's Sons. (P.874)

--*Held Fast for England: A Tale of the Siege of Gibraltar (1779-83).* Henty, George Alfred (1832-1902). 1891. C. Scribner's Sons. (P.435)

--*The Hill that Fell Down.* Sharp, Evelyn (1869-). N.D. Caldwell. (P.816)

--*The History of Don Quixote.* Cervantes Saavedra, Miguel de (1547-1616). Methley, Alice A, ed. 1921. Frederick A. Stokes Company. (P.180)

--*Hop O' My Thumb.* Richards, Laura Elizabeth Howe, Mrs. (1850-1943). N.D. Robert Brothers. (P.762)

--*In Freedom's Cause: A Story of Wallace and Bruce.* Henty, George Alfred (1832-1902). N.D. Blackie & Son, Limited. (P.435)

--*In Freedom's Cause: A Story of Wallace and Bruce.* Henty, George Alfred (1832-1902). N.D. The F. M. Lupton Publishing Company. (P.435)

--*The Lion of St. Mark: A Story of Venice in the Fourteenth Century.* Henty, George Alfred (1832-1902). N.D. M. A. Donohue & Co. (P.436)

--*The Lion of St. Mark: A Story of Venice in the Fourteenth Century.* Henty, George Alfred (1832-1902). N.D. The F. M. Lupton Publishing Company. (P.436)

--*Lost in Samoa: A Tale of Adventure in the Navigator Islands.* Ellis, Edward Sylvester (1840-1916). c.1891. Cassell Publishing Company. (P.303)

--*Maitland Major and Minor.* Turley, Charles. 1906. E. P. Dutton and Company, Plymouth Eng. Printed. (P.905)

--*Margery Redford and Her Friends.* Spielman, M. H. N.D. Frederick A. Stokes. (P.844)

--*Mary's Meadow and Letter from a Little Garden.* Ewing, Juliana Horatia Gatty, Mrs. (1841-1885). Evans, Edmund, contrib. by. 1886. Society for Promoting Christian Knowledge. (P.314)

--*Mary's Meadow and Letters from a Little Garden.* Ewing, Juliana Horatia Gatty, Mrs. (1841-1885). 1886. E. & J. B. Young & Co. (P.314)

--*Master Rockafellar's Voyage.* Russell, William Clark (1844-1911). 1891. T. Whittaker. (P.785)

--*Melchior's Dream, and Other Tales.* Ewing, Juliana Horatia Gatty, Mrs. (1841-1885). N.D. Frederick Stokes. (P.314)

--*My Own Fairy Book.* Lang, Andrew (1844-1912). 1895. Arrowsmith. (P.548)

--*National Rhymes of the Nursery.* Saintsbury, George Edward Bateman (1845-1933), ed. N.D. E. & J B .Young & Co. (P.790)

--*National Rhymes of the Nursery.* Saintsbury, George Edward Bateman (1845-1933), ed. N.D. Frederick A Stokes Co. (P.790)

--*The Peace Egg and a Christmas Mumming Play, 1 of 18 Vols.* Ewing, Juliana Horatia Gatty, Mrs. (1841-1885) & Society for Promoting Christian Knowledge. 1887. Society for Promoting Christian Knowledge. (P.314)

--*Prince Prigio and Prince Ricardo of Pantouflia.* Lang, Andrew (1844-1912), ed. 1976. Garland Pub. (P.549)

--*Prince Ricardo of Pantouflia: Being the Adventures of Prince Prigio's Son.* Lang, Andrew (1844-1912). retold by. 1893. J. W. Arrowsmith Etc. (P.549)

--*The Red Grange.* Molesworth, Mary Louisa Stewart, Mrs. (1842-1921). 1891. Thomas Whittaker. (P.654)

--*Robinson Crusoe.* De foe , D., ed. N.D. Charles Scribner's Sons. (P.260)

--*Siberian Exiles' Children: Or, Thrown on the World, 1 of 20 vols.* Hodder, Edwin (1837-1904). N.D. Methodist Bk Concern. (P.448)

--*Sir Toady Crusoe: The Adventures of Two Boys and a Girl.* Crockett, Samuel Rutherford (1860-1914). 1910. Frederick A. Stokes. (P.231)

--*Snap-Dragons: A Tale of Christmas Eve, and Old Father Christmas, an Old-Fashioned Tale of the Young Days of a Grumpy Old Godfather.* Ewing, Juliana Horatia Gatty, Mrs. (1841-1885). Evans, Edmund, contrib. by. 1888. Society for Promoting Christian Knowledge. (P.314)

--*Snapdragons: A Tale of Christmas Eve, and Old Father Christmas: An Old-Fashioned Tale of the Young Days of a Grumpy Old Godfather.* Ewing, Juliana Horatia Gatty, Mrs. (1841-1885). 1888. Young. (P.314)

--*St. George for England: A Tale of Cressy and Poitiers.* Henty, George Alfred (1832-1902). 1884. Blackie & Son, Limited. (P.436)

--*St. Winifred's: Or, The World of School.* Farrar, Frederic William (1831-1903). 1897. W. L. Allison Co. (P.318)

--*The Story of a Short Life.* N.D. E. & J. B. Young & Co. (P.143)

--*The Story of a Short Life.* Ewing, Juliana Horatia Gatty, Mrs. (1841-1885). 1882. E. & J. B. Young & Co. (P.315)

--*The Story of the Treasure Seekers.* Bland, Edith Nesbit, Mrs. (1858-1924). Nesbit, E., pseud. 1958. Coward. (P.108)

--*Story of the Treasure Seekers.* Bland, Edith Nesbit, Mrs. (1858-1924). Nesbit, E., pseud. 1958. Dover. (P.108)

--*The Surprising Adventures of Sir Toady Lion with Those of General Napoleon Smith: An Improving History for Old Boys, Young Boys, Good Boys, Bad Boys, Little Boys, Cowboys, and Tom-Boys.* Crockett, Samuel Rutherford (1860-1914). c.1897. F. A. Stokes Company. (P.231)

--*The Tales of the Sixty Mandarins.* 2nd ed. Ramasvami Raju, P. V. Morley, Henry (1822-1894), ed. 1886. Cassell & Company, Limited. (P.747)

--*The Tales of the Sixty Mandarins.* Ramasvami Raju, P. V. Morley, Henry (1822-1894), ed. 1943. c.1886. Cassell & Company, Limited. (P.747)

--*The Treasure Seekers.* Bland, Edith Nesbit, Mrs. (1858-1924). Nesbit, E., pseud. N.D. Frederick A. Stokes. (P.108)

--*True to the Old Flag: A Tale of the American War of Independence.* Henty, George Alfred (1832-1902). N.D. Blackie & Son, Limited. (P.436)

--*Under Drake's Flag: A Tale of the Spanish Main.* Henty, George Alfred (1832-1902). 1912. A. L. Burt Company. (P.436)

--*Under Drake's Flag: A Tale of the Spanish Main.* Henty, George Alfred (1832-1902). N.D. A. L. Burt. (P.436)

--*Under Drake's Flag: A Tale of the Spanish Main.* Henty, George Alfred (1832-1902). N.D. Blackie & Son, Limited. (P.436)

--*Under Drake's Flag: A Tale of the Spanish Main.* Henty, George Alfred (1832-1902). 1894. Scribner. (P.436)

--*With Clive in India.* Henty, George Alfred (1832-1902). N.D. Grosset & Dunlap. (P.436)

--*With Clive in India: Or, The Beginnings of an .* Empire. Henty, George Alfred (1832-1902). N.D. A. L. Burt. (P.436)

--*With Clive in India: Or, The Beginnings of an Empire.* Henty, George Alfred (1832-1902). N.D. A. L. Burt Company. (P.436)

--*With Clive in India: Or, The Beginnings of an Empire.* Henty, George Alfred (1832-1902). N.D. A. L. Burt's Pubs. (P.436)

--*With Clive in India: Or, The Beginnings of an Empire.* Henty, George Alfred (1832-1902). 1887. Scribner and Welford. (P.436)

--*With Lee in Virginia: A Story of the American Civil War.* Henty, George Alfred (1832-1902). N.D. A. L. Burt Company. (P.437)

--*With Wolseley to Kumasi: A Tale of the First Ashanti War.* Brereton, Frederick Sadleir (1872-). 1908, c.1907. Blackie and Son, Limited. (P.130)

--*A Young Mutineer.* Meade, L. T., pseud. (1854-1914). Smith, Elizabeth Thomasina Meade. N.D. E. & J. B. Young & Co. (P.637)

--*A Young Mutineer: A Story for Girls.* Smith, Elizabeth Thomasina Meade, Mrs. (1854-1914). Meade, L. T., pseud. N.D. A. L. Burt. (P.832)

--*A Young Mutineer: A Story for Girls.* Smith, Elizabeth Thomasina Meade, Mrs. (1854-1914). Meade, L. T., pseud. 1893. Hurst & Company. (P.832)

Browne, Gordon Frederick (1858-1932) & Baumer, Lewis (1870-)

--*New Treasure Seekers.* Bland, Edith Nesbit, Mrs. (1858-1924). Nesbit, E., pseud. 1962. Dover. (P.107)

Brundage, Frances & Sturges, Lillian Baker
--*The Legend of Sleepy Hollow.* Irving, Washington (1783-1859). c.1926. The Saalfield Publishing Company. (P.481)
Brundage, Frances & Williams, Florence White
--*Story Time: A Collection of Favorite Tales for Girls and Boys.* 1930. The Saalfield Publishing Company. (P.144)
Bruner, Paul
--*The Mathematical Princess, and Other Stories.* Nye, Robert (1939-), ed. 1972, c.1971. Hill & Wang. (P.688)
Brunhoff, Jean De (1899-1937)
--*Babar & Father Christmas.* Brunhoff, Jean de (1899-1937). 1949. Random. (P.144)
--*The Story of Babar, the Little Elephant.* Brunhoff, Jean de (1899-1937). 1933. Random House. (P.144)
--*The Story of Babar, the Little Elephant.* Brunhoff, Jean de (1899-1937). 1937. Random. (P.144)
--*The Story of Babar, the Little Elephant.* Brunhoff, Jean de (1899-1937). c.1960. Random House. (P.144)
--*Travels of Babar.* Brunhoff, Jean de (1899-1937). 1937. Random. (P.144)
Brunhoff, Jean de (1899-1937) & Brunhoff, Laurent de (1925-)
--*Babar's Anniversary Album.* Brunhoff, Jean de (1899-1937) & Brunhoff, Laurent de (1925-). Sendak, Maurice Bernard (1928-), intro. by. 1981. Random. (P.145)
Brunhoff, Laurent de, jt. illus. see Brunhoff, Jean de.
Brunhoff, Laurent de (1925-)
--*Anatole and His Donkey.* Brunhoff, Laurent de (1925-). Howard, Richard, tr. from Fr. 1963. Macmillan. (P.145)
--*Babar & the Ghost.* Brunhoff, Laurent de (1925-). 1981. Random. (P.145)
--*Babar & the Wully-Wully.* Brunhoff, Laurent de (1925-). 1975. Random. (P.145)
--*Babar & the Wully-Wully.* Brunhoff, Laurent de (1925-). N.D. Scholastic Inc. (P.145)
--*Babar Goes on a Picnic.* Brunhoff, Laurent de (1925-). Haas, Merle, tr. 1969. Random House Inc. (P.145)
--*Babar Learns to Cook.* Brunhoff, Laurent de (1925-). 1979. Random. (P.145)
--*Babar Loses His Crown.* Brunhoff, Laurent de (1925-). 1967. Beginner. (P.145)
--*Babar the Magician.* Brunhoff, Laurent de (1925-). 1980. Random. (P.145)
--*Babar Visits Another Planet.* Brunhoff, Laurent de (1925-). Haas, Merle S., tr. 1972. Random House. (P.145)
--*Babar's Bookmobile.* Brunhoff, Laurent de (1925-). 1974. Random. (P.145)
--*Babar's Castle.* Brunhoff, Laurent de (1925-). Haas, Merle S. (1896-1985), tr. 1962. Random. (P.145)
--*Babar's Cousin.* Brunhoff, Laurent de (1925-). Haas, Merle S. (1896-1985), tr. 1952. Random. (P.145)
--*Babar's Cousin: That Rascal Arthur.* Brunhoff, Laurent de (1925-). Haas, Merle, tr. 1952. Random House Inc. (P.145)
--*Babar's Fair Will Be Opened Next Sunday.* Brunhoff, Laurent de (1925-). 1954. Random House. **Award: (NYT).** (P.145)
--*Babar's Games.* Brunhoff, Laurent de (1925-). 1968. Random. (P.145)
--*Babar's Moon Trip.* Brunhoff, Laurent de (1925-). 1969. Random. (P.145)
--*Babar's Mystery.* Brunhoff, Laurent de (1925-). 1978. Random. (P.145)
--*Babar's Picnic.* Brunhoff, Laurent de (1925-). Haas, Merle S. (1896-1985), tr. 1958. Random. (P.145)
--*Babar's Spanish Lessons.* Las Lecciones Espanoles De Babar. Brunhoff, Laurent De (1925-). 1965. Random House. (P.145)
--*Bonhomme.* Brunhoff, Laurent de (1925-). 1965. Pantheon. (P.145)
--*Bonhomme & the Huge Monster.* Brunhoff, Laurent de (1925-). Howard, Richard, tr. from Fr. 1974. Pantheon. (P.145)
--*Captain Serafina.* Brunhoff, Laurent de (1925-). 1963. World Pub. Co. (P.145)
--*The Cats of the Eiffel Tower.* 1st ed. Roselli, Auro (1921-). 1967. Delacorte Press. (P.777)
--*Gregory and Lady Turtle in the Valley of the Music Trees.* Brunhoff, Laurent de (1925-). Howard, Richard, tr. from Fr. 1971. Pantheon Books. (P.145)
--*Gregory & the Turtle.* Brunhoff, Laurent de (1925-). 1971. Pantheon. (P.145)
--*The One Pig with Horns.* Brunhoff, Laurent de (1925-). Howard, Richard (1929-), tr. from Fr. 1979. Pantheon. (P.145)
--*Serafina the Giraffe.* Brunhoff, Laurent de (1925-). 1961. World Pub. Co. (P.145)
--*Serafina's Lucky Find.* 1st ed. Brunhoff, Laurent de (1925-). 1962. World Pub. Co. (P.145)
Brunner, F. Sands
--*The Seminary's Secret.* Hark, Ann. c.1936. J. B. Lippincott Company. (P.413)
Brunner, Klaus
--*Sandy at the Children's Zoo.* Brunner, Klaus & Bolliger, Max. 1967, c.1966. Crowell. (P.145)
--*Sandy at the Children's Zoo.* Bolliger, Max (1929-). Gemming, Elisabeth (1932-), tr. 1967. T Y Crowell. (P.113)
--*Trouble in Brusada.* Brunner, Fritz. Kirkup, James (1927-), tr. 1962. Verry. (P.145)
Brunsman, Jim
--*Leese Webster.* Le Guin, Ursula Kroeber (1929-). 1979. Atheneum. (P.562)
Brunton, Violet
--*Green Magic: A Collection of the World's Best Fairy Tales from All Countries.* O'Brien, Florence Roma Muir Wilson (1891-1930), ed. Wilson, Romer, pseud. c.1928. Harcourt, Brace & Company. (P.689)
--*Silver Magic: A Collection of the World's Best Fairy Tales from All Countries.* O'Brien, Florence Roma Muir Wilson (1891-1930), ed. c.1929. Harcourt, Brace & Company. (P.689)
Brunton, William
--*Moonshine.* Fairy Stories. Brabourne, Edward Hugessen Knatchbull-Hugessen (1829-1893). 1871. Macmillan and Co. (P.123)
Brunton, Winifred, jt. illus. see Geritz, Franz.
Brustlein, Daniel see Alain, pseud.
Brustlein, Daniel, pseud. (1904-)
--*Minette.* Brustlein, Daniel. Alain, pseud. Brustlein, Janice Tworkov. Janice, pseud. c.1959. Whittlesey House. (P.145)
Bruton, W.
--*Johnny Headstrong's trip to Coney Island.* c.1882. McLoughlin Bros. (P.145)
Bryan, Ashley F. (1923-)
--*The Adventures of Aku: Or, How It Came About That We Shall Always See Okra the Cat Lying on a Velvet Cushion, While Okraman the Dog Sleeps Among the Ashes.* Bryan, Ashley F. (1923-). 1976. Atheneum. (P.145)
--*Beat the Story-Drum, Pum-Pum.* Bryan, Ashley F. (1923-). 1980. Atheneum. **Awards: (CSKA); (ALA).** (P.145)
--*The Cat's Purr.* Bryan, Ashley F. (1923-), retold by. 1985. Atheneum. **Award: (ALA).** (P.145)
--*The Dancing Granny.* Bryan, Ashley F. (1923-), ed. 1977. Atheneum. (P.145)
--*I Greet the Dawn: Poem of Paul Laurence Dunbar.* Bryan, Ashley F. (1923-). 1978. Atheneum. (P.145)
--*Jethro and the Jumbie.* Cooper, Susan (1935-). 1979. Atheneum. (P.218)
--*Jim Flying High.* 1st ed. Evans, Mari (1923-). c.1979. Doubleday. (P.311)
--*Moon, for What Do You Wait.* Tagore, Rabindranath, Sir, pseud. (1861-1941). Thakura, Ravindranatha. Lewis, Richard (1935-), ed. 1967. Atheneum. (P.876)
--*The Ox of the Wonderful Horns, and Other African Folktales.* Bryan, Ashley F. (1923-). 1971. Atheneum. (P.145)
--*Walk Together Children.* Bryan, Ashley F. (1923-). N.D. Atheneum. (P.145)
Bryan, Brigitte
--*Alice in Wonderland & Through the Looking Glass.* Carroll, Lewis, pseud. (1832-1898). Dodgson, Charles Lutwidge. 1969. Childrens. (P.172)
--*Alice in Wonderland and Through the Looking-Glass.* complete and unabridged. Dodgson, Charles Lutwidge (1832-1898). Carroll, Lewis, pseud. 1969. Childrens Press. (P.277)
--*Andersen's Fairy Tales.* Andersen, Hans Christian (1805-1875). 1970, c.1969. Childrens Press. (P.34)
--*The Beggar in the Blanket & Other Vietnamese Tales.* Graham, Gail B. 1970. Dial Press. (P.380)
--*The Fox That Wanted Nine Golden Tails.* Knight, Mary (1899-). 1968, c.1969. Macmillan. (P.532)
--*The Keris Emerald.* Johnson, Mary Parke. 1970. Scribner. (P.496)
--*White Horse with Wings.* Davies, Anthea. 1970. Macmillan. (P.244)
--*The Wizard of Oz.* Baum, Lyman Frank (1856-1919). 1969. Childrens Press. (P.82)
Bryan, James
--*The Kitchen Madonna.* Godden, Rumer (1907-). 1967. Viking Press. (P.372)
--*Operation Sippacik.* Godden, Rumer (1907-). 1969. Viking Press. (P.372)
Bryan, Marguerite
--*Happy Tramp.* The Story of a Little Girl and Her Old English Sheep Dog. Denison, Muriel Goggin, Mrs. 1942. Dodd, Mead & Company. (P.257)
--*Sally and Her Kitchens: The Story of Sally Lewis' Career in Home Economics.* Eells, May Worthington. 1939. Dodd, Mead. (P.298)
--*Susannah: A Little Girl with the Mounties.* Denison, Muriel Goggin, Mrs. 1936. Dodd, Mead & Company. (P.257)
--*Susannah at Boarding School.* Denison, Muriel Goggin, Mrs. 1938. Dodd, Mead & Company. (P.257)
--*Susannah of the Yukon.* Denison, Muriel Goggin, Mrs. 1937. Dodd, Mead & Company. (P.257)
--*Susannah Rides Again.* Denison, Muriel Goggin, Mrs. 1940. Dodd, Mead & Company. (P.257)
Bryan, Mary
--*The Little Bee That Couldn't Buzz.* Bryan, Rita. c.1958. Fearon Publishers. (P.145)
Bryans, John Kennedy (1872-)
--*Shadowkids.* Bryans, John Kennedy (1872-). c.1929. The Platt & Munk Co., Inc. (P.145)
--*Shadowkids at Play.* Bryans, John Kennedy (1872-). c.1930. The Platt & Munk Co. Inc. (P.145)
Bryant, David (1938-)
--*The Eagle of Gwernabwy: Tales from Wales.* Llewellyn, Megan. 1970. Pergamon Press. (P.578)
Bryant, Dean
--*See the Bear.* 1953. Rand. (P.146)
--*Teddy Bear of Bumpkin Hollow.* Boucher, Sharon. c.1948. Rand McNally. (P.120)
--*Twilight Tales.* Potter, Miriam Clark, Mrs. (1886-1965). c.1947. Rand, McNally & Company. (P.735)
--*Twilight Tales.* Potter, Miriam Clark, Mrs. (1886-1965). 1962. Rand McNally. (P.735)
Bryant, Samuel Hanks
--*Boy Scouts to the Rescue.* Smith, Leonard K. 1939. Little, Brown and Company. (P.835)
--*The Cruise of the Arctic Star.* O'Dell, Scott (1903-). 1973. HM. (P.690)
--*The King's Fifth.* O'Dell, Scott (1903-). 1966. Houghton. **Awards: (ALA); (JNM).** (P.690)
--*Mister Roberts.* Heggen, Thomas. N.D. Watts. (P.429)
Bryant, William Cullen, jt. illus. see Havell, Herbert Lord.
Bryant, William Cullen (1794-1878)
--*The Family Library of Poetry and Songs.* Bryant, William Cullen (1794-1878). N.D. Fords, Howards & Hulbert. (P.146)
Brychta, Alex (1956-)
--*Eerie, Weird, and Wicked: An Anthology.* Hoke, Helen L., Mrs. (1903-), ed. c.1977. T. Nelson. (P.453)
Brychta, Jan
--*The Little Riddle Book.* Hoke, Helen L., Mrs. (1903-), ed. c.1977. Frank Book Corp. (P.453)
--*Mrs. Discombobulous.* Mahy, Margaret (1936-). 1969. F. Watts. (P.613)
Bryson, Bernarda (1905-1977)
--*Alphabet for Joanna: A Poem.* 1st ed. Gregory, Horace Victor (1898-1982). 1963. Holt, Rinehart and Winston. (P.388)
--*Bright Hunter of the Skies.* Best, Herbert (1894-). c.1961. Macmillan. (P.99)
--*Calendar Moon.* 1st ed. Belting, Natalia Maree (1915-). 1964. Holt, Rinehart and Winston. **Award: (ALA).** (P.91)
--*Gilgamesh: Man's First Story.* Bryson, Bernarda (1905-1977), retold by. 1967. Holt, Rinehart & Winston. **Award: (BGH).** (P.146)
--*The Grindstone of God: A Fable.* 1st ed. Withers, Carl A. (1900-1970), retold by. 1970. Holt, Rinehart and Winston. (P.972)
--*Mr. Chu.* Keating, Norman Connolly. c.1965. Macmillan. (P.510)
--*Pride & Prejudice.* Austen, Jane (1775-1817). 1962. Macmillan. (P.55)
--*The Return of the Twelves.* Clarke, Pauline, pseud. (1921-). Hunter Blair, Pauline Clarke. 1964, c.1962. Coward-McCann. **Awards: (ALA); (CMA).** (P.199)
--*Shephard of the Sun.* Appel, Benjamin (1907-1977). 1961. Astor Books. (P.43)
--*The Storyteller's Pack.* Stockton, Frank Richard (1834-1902). 1968. Trade Publications. (P.860)
--*The Storyteller's Pack: A Frank R.* Stockton Reader. Stockton, Frank Richard (1834-1902). 1968. Scribner. (P.860)
--*The Sun is a Golden Earring.* 1st ed. Belting, Natalia Maree (1915-). 1962. Holt, Rinehart and Winston. **Awards: (ALA); (RCM).** (P.92)
--*The Sun Is a Golden Earring.* Belting, Natalia Maree (1915-). 1973, c.1962. Holt. (P.92)
--*The Twenty Miracles of Saint Nicolas.* Bryson, Bernarda (1905-1977). 1960. Little, Brown and Company. (P.146)
--*The White Falcon.* Ogburn, Charlton, Jr. (1911-). 1955. Houghton Mifflin. (P.691)
--*The Zoo of Zeus: A Handbook of Mythological Beasts and Creatures.* Bryson, Bernarda (1905-1977). 1964. Grossman. (P.146)
Bryson, Charles A.
--*Harriet's Choice.* Abbott, Jane Ludlow Drake, Mrs. (1881-). 1928. J. B. Lippincott Company. (P.3)
Bryson, Marion
--*Little Garden People and What They Do.* Sharp, Ann Pearsall. c.1938. The Saalfield Publishing Company. (P.816)
Brzustowica, Victoria
--*Once-Upon-a-Time Saints: Faith-Tales for Children.* Marbach, Ethel. N.D. St Anthony Mess Pr. (P.619)
Bubley, Esther, photos by.
--*How Puppies Grow.* 1972. Four Winds. (P.146)
Buchanan, Heather S.
--*Emily Mouse Saves the Day.* Buchanan, Heather S. 1985. Dial Books for Young Readers. (P.146)
--*Emily Mouse's First Adventure.* Buchanan, Heather S. 1985. Dial Books for Young Readers. (P.146)
Buchanan, Lilian
--*Cherrys & Company.* Scott, Will. 1966. Verry. (P.805)
--*Cherrys by the Sea.* Scott, Will. 1966. Verry. (P.805)
--*Cherrys of River House.* Scott, Will. 1964. Verry. (P.805)
--*Marlowe Wins a Prize.* Boden, Hilda, pseud. (1901-). Bodenham, Hilda Morris. 1960. David McKay Co. (P.112)
--*Marlows at Castle Cliff.* Boden, Hilda, pseud. (1901-). Bodenham, Hilda Morris. 1961, c.1960. McKay. (P.112)
--*Marlows in Town.* Boden, Hilda, pseud. (1901-). Bodenham, Hilda Morris. 1964. Verry. (P.112)
--*The Mystery of the Missing Man.* Blyton, Enid Mary (1897-1968). 1974. British Bk Ctr. (P.111)
--*The Other Side of the Tunnel.* Kendall, Carol Seeger (1917-). 1957. Abelard- Schuman. (P.517)
--*Starlight.* Hamilton, Esme (1912-). 1960. Barnes. (P.408)
--*Two Lost Emeralds.* Boden, Hilda, pseud. (1901-). Bodenham, Hilda Morris. 1958. Abelard- Schuman. (P.112)
Buchanan, Marian
--*Jesses Dream Skirt.* Mack, Bruce. c.1979. Lollipop Power. (P.604)
Buchanan, Mina
--*Picture Tales from India.* Metzger, Berta. 1942. Frederick A. Stokes Company. (P.643)
--*Tales Told in India.* Metzger, Berta. 1935. H. Milford, Oxford University Press. (P.643)
Buchard, Peter
--*Youngest Shepherd: A Tale of the Nativity.* Borland, Hal Glen (1900-1978). 1962. Lippincott. (P.118)
Buchert, Ilse
--*The Wren and the Bear.* Grimm, Jakob Ludwig Karl (1785-1863) & Grimm, Wilhelm Karl (1786-1859). Nesbitt, Alexander, tr. from Ger. 1971. Third & Elm Press. (P.395)
Buchi, Werner
--*Mau, King of Cats.* Damjan, Mischa. McGovern, Ann, adapted by. 1961. Putnam. (P.240)
Bucholtz-Ross, Linda (1946-)
--*Magnolia's Mixed-up Magic.* Nixon, Joan Lowery (1927-). 1983. Putnam. (P.683)
Buchrig, Rosemary
--*Marcus.* Sankey, Alice Ann-Susan (1910-). 1950. Whitman Pub. Co. (P.793)
Buck, Dorothy
--*Petey.* Jackson, Linda. 1942. Harcourt, Brace and Company. (P.486)
Buck, John
--*Pushball.* Leavey, Thomas. 1980. Rainbow Bks. (P.559)
Buck, Margaret Waring (1910-)
--*Pets from the Pond.* Buck, Margaret Waring (1910-). 1958. Abingdon. (P.147)
Buckels, Alan
--*The Secret of Tarbury Tor.* Vickers, G. C. 1925. D. Appleton and Company. (P.919)
Buckels, Alec
--*Come Hither: A Collection of Rhymes and Poems for the Young of All Ages.* new and rev. ed. De La Mare, Walter John (1873-1956). 1928. Alfred A. Knopf. (P.253)
--*Miss Jemima.* De La Mare, Walter John (1873-1956). 1935. Artist and Writers Guild. (P.253)
--*Tales of the Four Pigs & Brock the Badger.* Uttley, Alison, Mrs., pseud. (1884-1976). Uttley, Alison Jane Taylor. 1939. Merrimack Pub Cir. (P.911)
Buckett, George (1936-)
--*Mitzi's Magic Garden.* Allinson, Beverley Lynn Rouse (1936-). 1971. Garrard Pub. Co. (P.31)
--*Never Talk to Strangers.* Joyce, Irma. 1970. Western Pub. (P.501)
--*Where Did Everybody Go: Funny Rhymes About Place Words.* Smaridge, Norah Antoinette (1903-). 1971. Western Pub. (P.831)
Buckland, Arthur H.
--*The Lost Explorers: A Story of the Trackless Desert.* Macdonald, Alexander (1878-). 1906. Blackie & Son, Limited. (P.598)
Buckland, Arthur H. & Hassall, John (1868-1948)
--*Wouldbegoods.* Bland, Edith Nesbit, Mrs. (1858-1924). Nesbit, E., pseud. 1965. Dover. (P.108)
Buckley, Jim
--*How Really Great to Walk This Way.* Hallinan, Patrick Kenneth (1944-). 1972. Childrens. (P.406)
Buckley, Peter Hays, photos by.
--*Cesare of Italy.* Buckley, Peter Hays. 1954. Franklin Watts, Inc. (P.147)
--*Luis of Spain.* Buckley, Peter Hays. 1955. Franklin Watts, Inc. (P.147)
--*Michel of Switzerland.* Buckley, Peter Hays. 1955. Franklin Watts, Inc. (P.147)
Buckman, Betty Brunner
--*The Perilous Adventures of the Golden Princes.* Maxfield, Mina Rosenthal. 1953. Christopher Pub. House. (P.632)

Burri, Rene
--*Lost Pony.* Mendoza, George (1934-). 1976. SF Bk Co: distribution by Simon and Schuster. (P.641)
Burridge, Marge Opitz
--*The Ugly Duckling.* Andersen, Hans Christian (1805-1875). 1969. Rand McNally. (P.37)
--*Windy The Snow Goose.* Hunt, Robert. 1978. Soc for Visual. (P.474)
Burris, Burmah
--*Barbie's Adventures at Camp.* Memling, Carl (1918-1969). 1964. Random House. (P.640)
--*Gretchen's Hill.* 1st ed. Eyerly, Jeannette Hyde (1908-). 1965. Lippincott. (P.315)
--*The Illustrated Treasury of Poetry for Children.* Ross, David (1896-1975), ed. 1970. Grosset & Dunlap. (P.778)
--*Listen!* and Help Tell the Story. Carlson, Bernice Wells (1910-). 1965. Abingdon Press. (P.168)
Burris, Priscilla
--*Nursery Rhymes & Numbers.* Magos, Eunice & Hornnes, Esther. Sussman, Ellen, ed. 1984. Monkey Sisters. (P.613)
Burroughes, Dorothy Mary Burroughes
--*The Amazing Adventures of Little Brown Bear.* Burroughes, Dorothy Mary Burroughes. 1930. Harper & Brothers Publisher. (P.156)
--*Fifty-One New Nursery Rhymes.* Fyleman, Rose Amy (1877-1957). 1932. Doubleday, Doran and Company, Inc. (P.350)
--*Jack Rabbit, Detective: Or, The Great Pearl Mystery.* Burroughes, Dorothy Mary Burroughes. 1931. Methuen & Co., Ltd. (P.156)
--*The Journeyings of Selina Squirrel and Her Friends.* Burroughes, Dorothy Mary Burroughes. 1931. Harper & Brothers. (P.156)
Burroughs, Gail
--*Moth Manor: A Gothic Tale.* 1st ed. Bacon, Martha Sherman (1917-1981). 1978. Little. (P.58)
Burroughs, John F.
--*Little Black Rabbit.* Duffield, Kenneth Graham. c.1918. Henry Altemus Company. (P.287)
--*The Tale of Two Brothers: "God Is Love", A Brave Coward, Two Mothers.* Murphy, Edward Francis (1892-). c.1921. O'Donovan Brothers. (P.673)
Burrows, Corinne, jt. illus. see Burrows, Ray.
Burrows, Peggy
--*The Gingerbread Man.* Gingerbread Boy. Wadsworth, Wallace Carter (1894-1933), ed. c.1954. Rand McNally. (P.369)
Burrows, Ray & Burrows, Corinne
--*Baboushka.* Scholey, Arthur (1932-). 1983. Good News. (P.800)
Burrows, Tristram Zachary
--*Clowns of the World: A Collection of Clowns and Verses.* Burrows, Cecille Miller. 1980, c.1978. Northwood Institute. (P.157)
Burstein, Chaya M.
--*Hanukkah Cat.* Burstein, Chaya M. 1985. Kar-Ben Copies, Inc. (P.157)
--*No Trouble for Grandpa.* Marron, Carol A. 1983. Raintree Pubs. (P.621)
--*Rifka Bangs the Teakettle.* Burstein, Chaya M. 1970. Harcourt, Brace & World. (P.157)
--*Rifka Grows up.* Burstein, Chaya M. c.1976. Bonim Books. (P.157)
--*Yellow Butter Purple Jelly Red Jam Black Bread.* Hoberman, Mary Ann (1930-). 1981. Viking Pr. (P.448)
Burton, Marilee Robin
--*The Elephant's Nest: Four Wordless Stories.* Burton, Marilee Robin. c.1979. Harper & Row. (P.158)
Burton, Terry
--*Danny's Class.* Swallow, Su. c.1981. Silver Burdett Co. (P.873)
Burton, Virginia Lee (1909-1968)
--*Belinda and the Singing Clock.* Phillips, Ethel Calvert (0000-1947). 1938. HM. (P.723)
--*Calico the Wonder Horse.* Burton, Virginia Lee (1909-1968). 1970. Schol Bk Serv. (P.158)
--*Calico, the Wonder Horse: Or, The Saga of Stewy Slinker;.* Burton, Virginia Lee (1909-1968). 1941. HM (P.158)
--*Calico, the Wonder Horse: Or, The Saga of Stewy Stinker.* Burton, Virginia Lee (1909-1968). 1950. Houghton Mifflin. (P.158)
--*Calico The Wonderful Horse or The Saga of Stewy Stinker.* Burton, Virginia Lee (1909-1968). N.D. E. M. Hale & Co. (P.158)
--*Choo Choo: The Story of the Little Engine Who Ran Away.* Burton, Virginia Lee (1909-1968). 1937. HM. (P.158)
--*Don Coyote.* Peck, Leigh. 1942. Houghton Mifflin Company. (P.714)
--*The Emperor's New Clothes.* Andersen, Hans Christian (1805-1875). 1949. Houghton Mifflin Co. (P.35)
--*The Emperor's New Clothes.* Andersen, Hans Christian (1805-1875). 1962. Houghton. (P.35)
--*Katy and the Big Snow.* Burton, Virginia Lee (1909-1968). 1943. Houghton Mifflin Company. (P.158)
--*Katy and the Big Snow.* Burton, Virginia Lee (1909-1968). 1974, c.1971. Houghton, Mifflin. (P.158)
--*The Little House.* Burton, Virginia Lee (1909-1968). 1942. Houghton Mifflin Co. **Award: (RCM).** (P.158)
--*The Little House.* Burton, Virginia Lee (1909-1968). 1978, c.1942. Houghton Mifflin. (P.158)
--*Maybelle, the Cable Car.* Burton, Virginia Lee (1909-1968). 1952. Houghton Mifflin. (P.158)
--*Mike Mulligan & His Steam Shovel.* Burton, Virginia Lee (1909-1968). 1939. HM. (P.158)
--*Mike Mulligan and His Steam Shovel.* Burton, Virginia Lee (1909-1968). 1977, c.1967. Houghton Mifflin. (P.158)
--*Sad-Faced Boy.* Bontemps, Arna Wendell (1902-1973). 1937. Houghton Miffin Company. (P.117)
--*Song of Robin Hood.* Malcolmson, Anne Burnett, Mrs. (1910-), ed. 1947. HM. **Award: (RCM).** (P.614)
Burton, W. G.
--*When We Were Children.* Green, E. M. N.D. E. P. Dutton & Co. (P.384)
Busby, Jean
--*Gertrude D.* McKelvey's Stories to Grow On: Five Everyday Parables for Boys and Girls. McKelvey, Gertrude Della. 1947. The John C. Winston Company. (P.606)
Busch, Paul
--*The Indian Mummy Mystery.* Nesbit, Troy, pseud. (1907-). Folsom, Franklin Brewster. 1954. Whitman Pub. Co. (P.678)
--*The Merry Adventures of Robin Hood of Great Renown, in Nottinghamshire.* Pyle, Howard (1853-1911). 1955. Whitman Pub. Co. (P.743)
--*Pierre of Kaskaskia: Pioneer Boy of New France.* 1st ed. Belting, Natalia Maree (1915-). 1951. Bobbs-Merrill. (P.91)
--*The Secret of the King's Field: A Story of France in the Eighteenth Century.* 1st ed. Cleven, Cathrine Seward (1906-). 1952. Bobbs-Merrill. (P.202)
--*William Bradford, Pilgrim Boy.* 1st ed. Smith, Bradford (1909-1984). 1953. Bobbs-Merrill. (P.831)
Bush-Brown, Margaret
--*Edna, and Her Brothers.* White, Eliza Orne (1856-1947). 1900. Houghton, Mifflin and Company. (P.951)
Bush, C. G.
--*Daffy Dilly and Her Friends.* N.D. Worthington Company. (P.158)
--*Faith Gartney's Girlhood.* Whitney, Adeline Dutton Train, Mrs. (1824-1906). 1891. Houghton, Mifflin and Company. (P.954)
--*The History of A. B. C. and Other Tales.* N.D. Worthington Company. (P.158)
--*New Nonsense Rhymes.* Beckett, W. H. N.D. G. W. Carleton & Co. (P.87)
--*Rhoda Thornton's Girlhood.* Rev ed. Pratt, Mary Elizabeth Smith. 1901. Lee & Shepard. (P.737)
--*The Wonderful Bag, and What Was In It.* N.D. Worthington Company. (P.158)
Bush, Elizabeth
--*The Twins Who Quarrelled: A Storybook With Pictures to Color.* Bush, Elizabeth. 1982. Vantage. (P.158)
Busoni, Rafaello (1900-1962)
--*The Adventures of Maya the Bee.* Bonsels, Waldemar (1881-). Seltzer, Adele Szold, tr. 1951. Pellegrini & Cudahy. (P.117)
--*Big Tiger & Christian: Their Adventures in Mongolia.* Muhlenweg, Fritz (1898-). McHugh, Isabel & McHugh, Florence, trs. 1952. Pantheon. (P.670)
--*Chancho, a Boy and His Pig in Peru.* Stark, Bernice Sutherland (1915-). 1944. J. Messner, Inc. (P.849)
--*Chooky.* 1st ed. Faulkner, John (1901-1963). 1950. Norton. (P.319)
--*The Christmas Tree Forest.* Alden, Raymond Macdonald (1873-1924). c.1958. Bobbs-Merrill. (P.20)
--*Dick Whittington and His Cat.* Whittington, Richard D. (1423-). 1941. Grosset & Dunlap. (P.955)
--*The Dragon Ship: A Story of the Vikings in America.* Resnick, William S. 1942. Coward-McCann Inc. (P.758)
--*Forward, Commandos!.* Bianco, Margery Williams, Mrs. (1881-1944). 1944. Viking Press. (P.100)
--*A Gift for Genghis Khan.* Alberts, Frances Jacobs (1907-). 1961. Whittlesey House. (P.16)
--*Gregori's Lamb.* Beim, Lorraine Levey (1909-1951) & Beim, Jerrold (1910-1957). c.1948. Saalfield Pub. Co. (P.89)
--*He Was a Child.* Peale, Norman Vincent (1898-). 1957. Prentice Hall. (P.712)
--*Hidden Lights.* Prud'Hommeaux, Rene. 1956. Viking Press. (P.741)
--*The How and Why Wonder Book of Ballet.* Hyndman, Jane Andrews Lee (1912-1978). Wyndham, Lee, pseud. 1961. Grosset & Dunlap. (P.478)
--*Jesus, Son of Mary.* Sheen, Fulton John (1895-1979). 1947. Farrar, Straus and Cudahy, Inc. (P.817)
--*Johnny and His Wonderful Bed.* Townsend, Elisabeth. 1946. S. Daye. (P.897)
--*Knight of Florence.* Evernden, Margery (1916-). 1950. Random House. (P.312)
--*The Lavender Cat.* Lowrey, Janette Sebring (1892-). 1944. Harper & Brothers. (P.589)
--*Mark, Mark, Shut the Door!.* 1st ed. Hawkins, Helena Ann Quail (1905-). 1947. Holiday House. (P.422)
--*Martin's Mice.* Mary Marguerite, Sr. (1895-). N.D. Wilcox & Follett Co. (P.627)
--*Milk Flood.* Corey, Paul Frederick (1903-). 1956. Abelard-Schuman. (P.220)
--*The Missing Brother: A Mystery Story for Older Boys.* Robertson, Keith Carlton (1914-). 1950. Viking Press. (P.768)
--*The Mystery of Burnt Hill.* Robertson, Keith Carlton (1914-). 1952. Viking Press. (P.768)
--*Myths and Legends of the Greeks.* Sissons, Nicola Ann, ed. 1962, c.1960. Hart Pub. Co. (P.827)
--*Page Boy for King Arthur.* Stone, Eugenia (1879-1971). 1949. Wilcox & Follett Co. (P.861)
--*Page Boy of Camelot.* Stone, Eugenia (1879-1971). 1972. Schol Bk Serv. (P.862)
--*Pretty Girls Get There.* Towne, Charles Hanson (1877-). 1941. D. Appleton-Century Company Incorporated. (P.897)
--*The Radio Imp.* 1st ed. Binns, Archie Fred (1899-). 1950. Winston. (P.102)
--*Robin Hood's Arrow.* Stone, Eugenia (1879-1971). 1948. Wilcox & Follett Co. (P.862)
--*Rommany Luck.* Gordon, Patricia (1904-). 1946. The Viking Press. (P.377)
--*Sandalio Goes to Town.* Pollock, Katherine G (1904-). 1942. C. Scribner's Sons. (P.731)
--*Sasha and the Samovar.* Beim, Lorraine Levey (1909-1951) & Beim, Jerrold (1910-1957). 1944. Harocurt, Brace and Company. (P.89)
--*Secret of the Sleeping River.* 1st ed. Binns, Archie Fred (1899-). 1952. Winston. (P.102)
--*Shadow Over Winding Ranch.* Schmidt, Sarah Lindsay (1928-). c.1940. Random House. (P.800)
--*Shipmates Down Under.* Collins, Dale (1897-). 1950. Holiday House. (P.210)
--*Ship's Dog.* Palmer, Robin (1911-). c.1945. Grosset and Dunlap. (P.703)
--*Skookum.* Rev. ed. Evans, Eva Knox, Mrs. (1905-). 1946. Putnam. (P.311)
--*The Spear of Ulysses.* Alessios, Alison Baigrie, Mrs. 1941. Longmans, Green & Co. (P.22)
--*Speed of the Reindeer: A Story of Lapland.* Wilhelmson, Carl. 1954. Viking Press. (P.960)
--*Squire for King Arthur.* Stone, Eugenia (1879-1971). 1955. Follett. (P.862)
--*The Stars Came Down.* Woody, Regina Llewellyn Jones (1894-). 1945. Harcourt, Brace and Company. (P.977)
--*The Sunken Forest.* Prud'Hommeaux, Rene. 1949. Viking Press. (P.741)
--*A Tale of Two Cities.* Dickens, Charles John Huffam (1812-1870). N.D. Grosset & Dunlap. (P.264)
--*Tall Hunter.* Fast, Howard Melvin (1914-). 1942. Har-Row. (P.319)
--*The Tall Hunter.* Reissue ed. Fast, Howard Melvin (1914-). 1966. Harper. (P.319)
--*Third Bible Legend Book.* Freehof, Lillian B. Simon (1906-). N.D. UAHC. (P.343)
--*Tidewater Tales.* Locklin, Anne Littlefield. 1942. The Viking Press. (P.580)
--*Treasury of Christmas Songs & Carols.* Simon, Henry A. 1955. HM. (P.825)
--*Why the Chimes Rang.* Alden, Raymond Macdonald (1873-1924). c.1954. Bobbs-Merrill. (P.20)
--*William Tell.* Schiller, Johann Christoph Friedrich Von (1759-1805). N.D. Heritage Press. (P.799)
--*The Wind and the Fire.* Osborne, Chester Gorham (1915-). 1959. Prentice-Hall. (P.697)
--*The Winds Blow Free: A Story of the American Revolution.* Wilson, Charles George (1906-). 1950. I. Washburn. (P.966)
--*Wings for Nikias: A Story of the Greece of Today.* Blackstock, Josephine. Diamontopoulos, Cimon, frwd. by. 1942. G. P. Putnam's Sons. (P.105)
--*World-Famous Myths and Legends of the Greeks.* Sissons, Nicola Ann, ed. 1960. Hart Pub. Co. (P.827)
--*The Youngest General: A Story of Lafayette.* Gottschalk, Fruma Kasdan (1900-), retold by. 1949. A. A. Knopf. (P.378)
Butcher, Julia
--*The Sheep & the Rowan Tree.* Butcher, Julia. 1984. HR&W. (P.158)
Butel, Lucile
--*Old Gray and the Little White Hen.* Faucher, Paul (1898-). 1966. Golden Press. (P.319)
Butler, Beranice
--*Summer on the Farm.* Sutton, Margaret Beebe, Mrs. (1903-). c.1938. Grosset & Dunlap. (P.873)
Butler, Bonnibel
--*Holland Stories.* Smith, Mary Estella (1863-). 1913. Rand, McNally & Company. (P.835)
--*Holland Stories.* Smith, Mary Estella (1863-). c.1932. Rand, McNally & Company. (P.835)
Butler, C. L.
--*Jenny's Bird-house.* Merriam, Lillie Fuller. 1910. C. M. Clark Publishing Co. (P.642)
Butler, Edith F.
--*Little Friend Lydia.* Phillips, Ethel Calvert (0000-1947). 1920. Houghton Mifflin Company. (P.723)
--*Little Sally Waters.* Phillips, Ethel Calvert (0000-1947). 1926. Houghton Mifflin Company. (P.723)
--*Pretty Polly Perkins.* Phillips, Ethel Calvert (0000-1947). 1925. Houghton Mifflin Company. (P.723)
Butler, Herbert E.
--*Sylvia in Flowerland.* Gardiner, Linda. N.D. E. P. Dutton & Co. (P.354)
Butler, Howard
--*Out to Win: A Baseball Story.* Bonner, Mary Graham (1890-1974). 1947. A. A. Knopf. (P.116)
Butler, John
--*The Fish: The Story of the Stickleback.* Lane, Margaret. 1983. Dial Bks Young. (P.548)
--*The Frog.* Lane, Margaret. 1982. Dial Bks Young. (P.548)
Butler, Stella Mary
--*A Boy Knight.* Scott, Martin Jerome (1865-). 1921. P. J. Kenedy & Sons. (P.805)
Butler-Stoney, T.
--*The Old Woman Who Rode On a Broom.* Butler-Stoney, T. N.D. E. P. Dutton Co. (P.159)
Butler-Stoney, T., jt. illus. see Hassall, John.
Butrick, Lyn M.
--*My Funny Bunny Phone Book.* Harrison, David Lee (1937-). 1980. Western Pub. (P.417)
Butter, C. L.
--*Jenny's Bird House.* Merriam, Lillie Fuller. N.D. L C Page & Co. (P.642)
Buttera, F. J.
--*Natalie and the Brewsters.* Drake, Emily Hopkins. c.1931. Lothrop, Lee & Shepard Co. (P.284)
--*The Secret of Hallam House: A Mystery Story for Girls.* Baker, Nina Brown, Mrs. (1888-1957). c.1931. Lothrop, Lee & Shepard Co. (P.64)
Butterfield, Edwin A., Jr.
--*Dim Thunder.* 1st ed. Gault, William Campbell (1910-). 1958. Dutton. (P.360)
Butterfield, Ned (1917-)
--*Beginner Under the Backboards.* Jackson, Caary Paul (1902-). 1974. Hastings House. (P.484)
--*Bryan's Dog.* Butterworth, William Edmund, III (1929-). Scholefield, Edmund O., pseud. 1967. World Pub. Co. (P.159)
--*Centerman from Quebec: A Hockey Story.* Ilowite, Sheldon A. (1931-). 1972. Hastings House. (P.479)
--*Eric and Dud's Football Bargain.* Jackson, Caary Paul (1902-). 1972. Hastings House. (P.484)
--*Fury on Ice: An American-Canadian Hockey Story.* Ilowite, Sheldon A. (1931-). 1970. Hastings House. (P.479)
--*Hi Packett, Jumping Center.* Zanger, Jack. c.1965. Doubleday. (P.991)
--*Hockey Defenseman.* Ilowite, Sheldon A. (1931-). 1971. Hastings House. (P.479)
--*Lonesome End.* 1st ed. Meader, Stephen Warren (1892-). 1968. Harcourt, Brace & World. (P.637)
--*The Mystery at Monkey Run.* 1st ed. Martin, Fredric, pseud. (1917-). Christopher, Matthew F.. 1966. Little. (P.624)
--*Pass Receiver.* Jackson, Caary Paul (1902-). 1970. Hastings House. (P.484)
--*Penalty Killer: A Hockey Story.* Ilowite, Sheldon A. (1931-). 1973. Hastings House. (P.479)
--*Tom Mosely,.* Midget Leaguer. Jackson, Caary Paul (1902-). 1971. Hastings House. (P.484)
--*Trouble on the Infield.* Napjus, Alice James (1913-). Napjus, James, pseud. 1967. Van Nostrand. (P.675)
Butterworth, Nick
--*B.* B. Blacksheep. 1982. Putnam Pub Group. (P.159)
Butterworth, Pam
--*Quick As a Dodo.* McInerny, Ralph M. c.1978. Vanguard Press. (P.604)
Buttfield, Helen, photos by.
--*Of This World: A Poet's Life in Poetry.* Lewis, Richard (1935-), ed. 1968. Dial. (P.570)
--*The Wind and the Rain: Children's Poems.* Lewis, Richard (1935-), ed. 1968. Simon & Schuster. (P.570)
Button, A. P.
--*The Young Train Dispatcher.* Stevenson, Burton Egbert (1872-1962). 1907. L. C. Page & Company. (P.855)
Button, Albert
--*Blake Redding: A Boy of the Day.* Clark, Natalie Lord Rice, Mrs. (1867-). 1903. Little, Brown, & Co. (P.198)
Butz, Steve
--*Twenty Thousand Leagues Under the Sea.* Verne, Jules (1828-1905). Nordicht, Lillian, adapted by. c.1980. Raintree Publishers. (P.918)

--*Along Laughing Brook.* On the Green Meadows. Burgess, Thornton Waldo (1874-1965). N.D. Little, Brown. (P.152)
--*American Songs for Children.* Palmer, Winthrop Bushnell, Mrs., ed. McCleary, Fione. 1931. The Macmillan Company. (P.595)
--*Animal Stories.* Burgess, Thornton Waldo (1874-1965). c.1942. The Platt & Munk Co., Inc. (P.152)
--*The Animal World of Thornton Burgess.* Burgess, Thornton Waldo (1874-1965). 1961. Platt & Munk. (P.152)
--*Ant Ventures.* Wade, Blanche Elizabeth. c.1924. Rand, McNally & Company. (P.922)
--*At Paddy the Beaver's Pond: A Book of Nature Stories.* 1st ed. Burgess, Thornton Waldo (1874-1965). 1950. Little, Brown. (P.152)
--*At the Smiling-Pool,.* A Book of Nature Stories. Burgess, Thornton Waldo (1874-1965). 1945. Little, Brown and Company. (P.152)
--*Baby Possum's Queer Voyage.* Burgess, Thornton Waldo (1874-1965). 1928. Stoll & Edwards Co. Inc. (P.152)
--*Billy Mink.* Burgess, Thornton Waldo (1874-1965). 1924. Little, Brown, and Company. (P.153)
--*Blacky the Crow.* Burgess, Thornton Waldo (1874-1965). 1922. Little, Brown, and Company. (P.153)
--*Bowser the Hound.* Burgess, Thornton Waldo (1874-1965). 1920. Little, Brown and Company. (P.153)
--*The Burgess Big Book of Green Meadow Stories.* Burgess, Thornton Waldo (1874-1965). 1932. Little, Brown, and Company. (P.153)
--*Buster Bear's Twins.* Burgess, Thornton Waldo (1874-1965). 1923. Little, Brown and Company. (P.153)
--*Caleb Cottontail: His Adventures in Search of the Cotton Plant,.* Cady, Walter Harrison (1877-1970). 1921. Houghton Mifflin Company. (P.161)
--*The Cozy Lion: As Told by Queen Crosspatch.* Burnett, Frances Hodgson, Mrs. (1849-1924). 1907. The Century Co. (P.154)
--*The Crooked Little Path, a Book of Nature Stories.* Burgess, Thornton Waldo (1874-1965). 1946. Little, Brown and Company. (P.153)
--*The Dear Old Briar Patch.* Burgess, Thornton Waldo (1874-1965). 1947. J. B. Lippincott. (P.153)
--*The Dear Old Briar-Patch: A Book of Nature Stories.* Burgess, Thornton Waldo (1874-1965). 1947. Little, Brown. (P.153)
--*Digger the Badger Decides to Stay.* Burgess, Thornton Waldo (1874-1965). 1928. Stoll & Edwards Co. Inc. (P.153)
--*Favorite Tales.* Burgess, Thornton Waldo (1874-1965). 1979. Platt. (P.153)
--*Fifty Favorite Burgess Stories:.* Burgess, Thornton Waldo (1874-1965). 1956. Grosset & Dunlap. (P.153)
--*Garden-Land.* Chambers, Robert William (1865-1933). 1907. D. Appleton and Company. (P.183)
--*Grandfather Frog Gets a Ride.* Burgess, Thornton Waldo (1874-1965). 1928. Stoll & Edwards Co. Inc. (P.153)
--*A Great Joke on Jimmy Skunk.* Burgess, Thornton Waldo (1874-1965). 1928. Stoll & Edwards Co. Inc. (P.153)
--*Happy Jack.* Burgess, Thornton Waldo (1874-1965). 1918. Little, Brown and Company. (P.153)
--*Happy Jack Squirrel Helps Unc' Billy.* Burgess, Thornton Waldo (1874-1965). 1928. Stoll & Edwards Co. Inc. (P.153)
--*The Happychaps.* Wells, Carolyn (1869-1942). 1908. Century Co. (P.944)
--*Jerry Muskrat at Home.* Burgess, Thornton Waldo (1874-1965). 1962, c.1926. Grosset & Dunlap. (P.153)
--*Jerry Muskrat at Home.* Burgess, Thornton Waldo (1874-1965). 1926. Little, Brown, and Company. (P.153)
--*Lightfoot the Deer.* Burgess, Thornton Waldo (1874-1965). 1921. Little, Brown, and Company. (P.153)
--*Little Chuck's Adventure.* Burgess, Thornton Waldo (1874-1965). 1942. McLoughlin Bros., Inc. (P.153)
--*Little Joe Otter.* Burgess, Thornton Waldo (1874-1965). 1925. Little, Brown, and Company. (P.153)
--*Little Pete's Adventure.* Burgess, Thornton Waldo (1874-1965). c.1941. McLoughlin Bros., Inc. (P.153)
--*Little Red's Adventure.* Burgess, Thornton Waldo (1874-1965). c.1942. McLoughlin Bros., Inc. (P.153)
--*Longlegs the Heron.* Burgess, Thornton Waldo (1874-1965). 1962. Grosset & Dunlap. (P.153)
--*Longlegs the Heron.* Burgess, Thornton Waldo (1874-1965). 1927. Little, Brown, and Company. (P.153)
--*Mother West Wind "How" Stories.* Burgess, Thornton Waldo (1874-1965). 1916. Little, Brown and Company. (P.153)
--*Mother West Wind "When" Stories.* Burgess, Thornton Waldo (1874-1965). 1917. Little, Brown, and Company. (P.153)
--*Mother West Wind "Where" Stories.* Burgess, Thornton Waldo (1874-1965). 1918. Little, Brown, and Company. (P.153)
--*Mother West Wind "Why" Stories.* Burgess, Thornton Waldo (1874-1965). 1915. Little, Brown, and Company. (P.153)
--*Mother West Wind's Children.* Burgess, Thornton Waldo (1874-1965). 1962. Little, Brown. (P.153)
--*Mother West Wind's Children.* Burgess, Thornton Waldo (1874-1965). 1985, c.1939. Little, Brown. (P.153)
--*Mother West Wind's Neighbors.* new illustrated. Burgess, Thornton Waldo (1874-1965). Roth, Charles E., frwd. by. 1984. Little, Brown. (P.153)
--*Mrs.* Peter Rabbit. Burgess, Thornton Waldo (1874-1965). 1919. Little, Brown and Company. (P.153)
--*The Neatness of Bobby Coon.* Burgess, Thornton Waldo (1874-1965). 1928. Stoll & Edwards Co. Inc. (P.153)
--*Old Granny Fox.* Burgess, Thornton Waldo (1874-1965). 1920. Little, Brown, and Company. (P.153)
--*Old Mother West Wind.* Golden Anniversary ed. Burgess, Thornton Waldo (1874-1965). 1960. Little, Brown. (P.153)
--*On the Green Meadows: A Book of Nature Stories.* Burgess, Thornton Waldo (1874-1965). 1944. Little Brown and Company. (P.153)
--*Queen Silver-Bell.* Burnett, Frances Hodgson, Mrs. (1849-1924). 1906. Century Co. (P.155)
--*Racketty-Packetty House: As Told by Queen Crosspatch.* Burnett, Frances Hodgson, Mrs. (1849-1924). 1914. The Century Co. (P.155)
--*The Raggedies in Fairyland.* Ripley, George Sherman (1889-). c.1930. Rand, McNally & Company. (P.765)
--*The Raggedy Animal Book.* Ripley, George Sherman (1889-). c.1928. Rand, McNally & Company. (P.765)
--*The Spring Cleaning: As Told by Queen Crosspatch.* Burnett, Frances Hodgson, Mrs. (1849-1924). 1908. The Century Co. (P.155)
--*Tommy and the Wishing-Stone.* Burgess, Thornton Waldo (1874-1965). 1959, c.1921. Grosset & Dunlap. (P.153)
--*Tommy and the Wishing Stone.* Burgess, Thornton Waldo (1874-1965). 1921. Little, Brown. (P.153)
--*Tommy and the Wishing Stone.* Burgess, Thornton Waldo (1874-1965). 1915. The Century Co. (P.153)
--*Tommy's Change of Heart.* Burgess, Thornton Waldo (1874-1965). 1959, c.1921. Grosset & Dunlap. (P.153)
--*Tommy's Change of Heart.* Burgess, Thornton Waldo (1874-1965). 1921. Little, Brown, and Company. (P.153)
--*Tommy's Wishes Come True.* Burgess, Thornton Waldo (1874-1965). 1921. Little, Brown, and Company. (P.153)
--*Whitefoot, the Wood Mouse.* Burgess, Thornton Waldo (1874-1965). 1962, c.1922. Grosset & Dunlap. (P.153)
--*Whitefoot: The Wood Mouse.* Burgess, Thornton Waldo (1874-1965). 1922. Little, Brown and Company. (P.153)
--*The Wishing-Stone Stories.* Burgess, Thornton Waldo (1874-1965). 1935. Little, Brown and Company. (P.153)

Cady, Walter Harrison (1877-1970) & Kerr, George
--*Adventures of Chatterer the Red Squirrel.* Burgess, Thornton Waldo (1874-1965). 1949. Putnam Pub Group. (P.152)
--*Adventures of Mr.* Mocker. Burgess, Thornton Waldo (1874-1965). N.D. G&D. (P.152)
--*Adventures of Old Granny Fox.* Burgess, Thornton Waldo (1874-1965). 1943. Putnam Pub Group. (P.152)
--*Adventures of Reddy Fox.* Burgess, Thornton Waldo (1874-1965). 1950. Putnam Pub Group. (P.152)
--*Adventures of Unc' Billy Possum.* Burgess, Thornton Waldo (1874-1965). 1951. Putnam Pub Group. (P.152)
--*Adventures of Whitefoot the Woodmouse.* Burgess, Thornton Waldo (1874-1965). 1944. Putnam Pub Group. (P.152)
--*Mother West Wind's Children.* Burgess, Thornton Waldo (1874-1965). 1940. Putnam Pub Group. (P.153)
--*Mother West Wind's "How" Stories.* Burgess, Thornton Waldo (1874-1965). 1941. Putnam Pub Group. (P.153)
--*Mother West Wind's "When" Stories.* Burgess, Thornton Waldo (1874-1965). 1941. Putnam Pub Group. (P.153)
--*Mother West Wind's Where Stories.* Burgess, Thornton Waldo (1874-1965). N.D. G&D. (P.153)
--*Mother West Wind's "Why" Stories.* Burgess, Thornton Waldo (1874-1965). 1941. Putnam Pub Group. (P.153)
--*Tommy's Wishes Come True.* Burgess, Thornton Waldo (1874-1965). 1959. G&D. (P.153)

Cady, Walter Harrison (1877-1970) & Smith, Jessie Willcox (1863-1935)
--*Bugs and Wings and Other Things.* Franchot, Annie Wood. c.1918. E. P. Dutton & Company. (P.341)

Cafferty, J. H., jt. illus. see Walcutt, W.

Cagle, Daryl
--*The Dandee Diamond Mystery.* O'Connor, Jane & Milton, Joyce. 1983. Scholastic Inc. (P.690)

Caigoy, Faustino
--*Ying-Ying: Pieces of a Childhood.* Joe, Jeanne. 1982. E-W Pub Co. (P.493)

Cain, Sandra
--*Plays from African Folktales.* Korty, Carol (1937-). 1975. Scribner. (P.536)

Cain, Steven
--*Your Guess Is as Good as Mine.* Ashley, Bernard (1935-). 1984. Watts. (P.52)

Calapai, Letterio (1903-)
--*How God Fix Jonah.* Graham, Lorenz Bell (1902-). 1946. Reynal. (P.380)
--*Tales of Momolu.* Graham, Lorenz Bell (1902-). 1946. Reynal & Hitchcock. (P.381)

Caldecott, Randolph, jt. illus. see Browne, Gordon Frederick.

Caldecott, Randolph (1846-1886)
--*Babes in the Wood.* Caldecott, Randolph (1846-1886). 1879. Warne. (P.161)
--*The Caldecott Aesop: Twenty Fables.* Aesopus. Hearn, Michael Patrick, ed. 1978. Doubleday. (P.13)
--*Caldecott Picture Books: Containing: The Three Jovial Huntsmen, The Queen of Hearts, Sing a Song a Sixpence, The Farmer's Boy.* Caldecott, Randolph (1846-1886). N.D. George Routledge & Sons. (P.161)
--*Caldecott's First Collection.* Caldecott, Randolph (1846-1886). N.D. George Routledge & Sons. (P.161)
--*Caldecott's First Collection: Containing: The Milk Maid, Baby Bunting Hey Diddle Diddle, The Fox Jumped over the Farmer's Gate, The Frog who Would A-Wooing Go.* Caldecott, Randolph (1846-1886). N.D. George Routledge & Sons. (P.161)
--*Caldecott's Picture Books: Containing: "Hey Diddle Diddle" "Baby Bunting" "Ride a Cock Horse" "Where are You Going, My Pretty Maid" "The Frog He Would a-Wooing Go", Book No.* 3. Caldecott, Randolph (1846-1886). N.D. Frederick Warne & Co. (P.161)
--*Caldecott's Picture Books: Containing: The House that Jack Built, John Gilpin, Babes in the Wood, Elegy on a Mad Dog.* Caldecott, Randolph (1846-1886). N.D. George Routledge & Sons. (P.161)
--*Caldecott's Picture Books: Containing:"Come, Lasses and Lads" "The Fox Jumps over the Parson's Gate" "Mrs.* Mary Blaize" "The Great Panjandrum Himself", Book No.4. Caldecott, Randolph (1846-1886). N.D. Frederick Warne & Co. (P.161)
--*Come, Lasses & Lads.* Caldecott, Randolph (1846-1886). 1884. Warne. (P.161)
--*Daddy Darwin's Dovecot.* Ewing, Juliana Horatia Gatty, Mrs. (1841-1885). N.D. E. & J. B. Young & Co. (P.313)
--*Daddy Darwin's Dovecot.* Ewing, Juliana Horatia Gatty, Mrs. (1841-1885). N.D. Robert Brothers. (P.313)
--*Daddy Darwin's Dovecot: A Country Tale.* Ewing, Juliana Horatia Gatty, Mrs. (1841-1885). 1884. E. J. B. Young & Co. (P.313)
--*Diverting History of John Gilpin.* Cowper, William (1731-1800). 1970. Abelard. (P.225)
--*The Diverting History of John Gilpin: Showing How He Went Farther Than He Intended, and Came Safe Home Again.* Cowper, William (1731-1800). 1925. Frederick A. Stokes Company. (P.225)
--*Elegy on a Mad Dog.* Caldecott, Randolph (1846-1886). 1879. Warne. (P.161)
--*Farmer's Boy.* Caldecott, Randolph (1846-1886). 1881. Warne. (P.161)
--*Fox Jumps Over the Parson's Gate.* Caldecott, Randolph (1846-1886). 1883. Warne. (P.161)
--*Frog He Would A-Wooing Go.* Caldecott, Randolph (1846-1886). 1883. Warne. (P.161)
--*House That Jack Built.* Caldecott, Randolph (1846-1886). 1878. Warne. (P.161)
--*The House That Jack Built.* Caldecott, Randolph (1846-1886). 1967. Watts. (P.161)
--*Jackanapes.* Ewing, Juliana Horatia Gatty, Mrs. (1841-1885). 1884. E. and J. B. Young and Co. (P.314)
--*Jackanapes.* Ewing, Juliana Horatia Gatty, Mrs. (1841-1885). N.D. E. S. Gorham. (P.314)
--*Jackanapes.* Ewing, Juliana Horatia Gatty, Mrs. (1841-1885). 1883. J. B. Young. (P.314)
--*Jackanapes.* Ewing, Juliana Horatia Gatty, Mrs. (1841-1885). 1884. Roberts Bros. (P.314)
--*Jackanapes.* Ewing, Juliana Horatia Gatty, Mrs. (1841-1885). Willard, J. H., intro. by. 1903. Henry Altemus Company. (P.314)
--*Jackanapes, Together with Daddy Darwin's Dovecot and Lob Lie-by-the-Fire.* Ewing, Juliana Horatia Gatty, Mrs. (1841-1885). 1966. University Microfilms. (P.314)
--*John Gilpin.* Caldecott, Randolph (1846-1886). 1878. Warne. (P.162)
--*Lob Lie-by-the Fire: Or, The Luck of Lingborough.* Ewing, Juliana Horatia Gatty, Mrs. (1841-1885). Evans, Edmund (1826-1905), contrib. by. 1885. Society for Promoting Christian Knowledge. (P.314)
--*The Owls of Olynn Belfry.* Caldecott, Randolph (1846-1886). 1885. Scribner & Welford. (P.162)
--*The Milkmaid.* Caldecott, Randolph (1846-1886). 1882. Warne. (P.162)
--*Mrs.* Mary Blaize. Caldecott, Randolph (1846-1886). 1885. Warne. (P.162)
--*Queen of Hearts.* Caldecott, Randolph (1846-1886). 1881. Warne. (P.162)
--*R.* Caldecott's Picture Book. Caldecott, Randolph (1846-1886). 1906. F. Warne & Co. (P.162)
--*R.* Caldecott's Picture Book. Caldecott, Randolph (1846-1886). N.D. F. Warne and Co. (P.162)
--*R.* Caldecott's Picture Book: Containing The Diverting History of John Gilpin, The Three Jovial Huntsmen, An Elegy on the Death of a Mad Dog. Caldecott, Randolph (1846-1886) & Goldsmith, Oliver (1728-1774). 1926. F. Warne & Co. Ltd. (P.162)
--*R.* Caldecott's Picture Book: Containing The House That Jack Built, Sing a Song for Sixpence, The Queen of Hearts. Caldecott, Randolph (1846-1886). 1906. F. Warne & Co. (P.162)
--*R.* Caldecott's Picture Book: Containing The House That Jack Built, Sing a Song for Sixpence, The Queen of Hearts. Caldecott, Randolph (1846-1886). 1926. F. Warne & Co. (P.162)
--*R.* Caldecott's Picture Book (No. 2). Containing The Three Jovial Huntsmen, Sing a Song for Sixpence, The Queen of Hearts The Farmer's Boy; All Exhibited in Beautiful Engravings, Many of Which Are Printed in Colours by E. Evans. Caldecott, Randolph (1846-1886). N.D. F. Warne and Co. (P.162)
--*The Randolph Caldecott Picture Book.* Caldecott, Randolph (1846-1886). 1977. Warne. (P.162)
--*Randolph Caldecott's John Gilpin and Other Stories: Containing: The Diverting History of John Gilpin; The House that Jack Built; The Frog He Woulda-Wooing Go; The Milkmaid.* Caldecott, Randolph (1846-1886). 1977. Warne. (P.162)
--*Randolph Caldecott's John Gilpin & Other Stories.* Caldecott, Randolph (1846-1886). 1978. Warne. (P.162)
--*Sing a Song of Sixpence.* Caldecott, Randolph (1846-1886). c.1977. Hart Pub. Co. (P.162)
--*Three Jovial Huntsmen.* Caldecott, Randolph (1846-1886). 1880. Warne. (P.162)
--*Tom Brown's School Days.* Hughes, Thomas (1822-1896). 1888. Porter & Coates. (P.471)
--*Tom Brown's School Days at Rugby.* New ed. Hughes, Thomas (1822-1896). N.D. Porter & Coates. (P.471)
--*What the Blackbird Said: A Story in four Chirps.* Locker, Frederick. N.D. George Routledge. (P.579)

Caldecott, Randolph (1846-1886) & Brock, Henry Matthew (1875-1960)
--*Lob Lie-by-the-Fire: Or, the Luck of Lingborough and the Story of a Short Life.* Ewing, Juliana Horatia Gatty, Mrs. (1841-1885). 1964. E.P. Dutton & Co. (P.314)

Calder, Alexander (1898-1976)
--*Fables of Aesop.* Aesopus. L'Estrange, Roger, Sir (1616-1704), retold by. 1967. Dover. **Award: (NYT).** (P.13)
--*Three Young Rats, and Other Rhymes.* Sweeney, James Johnson (1900-), ed. 1944. C. Valentin. (P.873)
--*Three Young Rats, and Other Rhymes.* 2nd ed. Sweeney, James Johnson (1900-), ed. 1967, c.1946. Mus. of Modern Art. (P.873)

Calder, Carol
--*Fairy Tales from Sweden.* Kaplan, Irma (1900-), retold by. 1967. Follett. (P.508)
--*Swedish Fairy Tales.* Kaplan, Irma, retold by. Hylten-Cavallius, Gunnar Olof (1818-1889). 1967, c.1953. Follett Pub. Co. (P.478)

Calder, Mildred Bussing
--*Dear Mrs.* Bender,. Dictated by Children in a Summer Resort; Illustrated by an Adult in a City. Phillips, Dorothy Waldo, as told to. c.1937. The John C. Winston Company. (P.723)

Calderon, H., jt. illus. see Cope, Charles West.

Calderon, William Frank (1865-1943)
--*The Most Delectable History of Reynard the Fox.* Cole, Henry, Sir (1808-1882). Jacobs, Joseph (1854-1916), ed. 1895. Macmillan and Co. (P.208)
--*The Most Delectable History of Reynard the Fox.* Jacobs, Joseph (1854-1916), ed. Rieff, Phillip, contrib. by. 1967. Schocken. (P.487)

Carroll, Charles Francis (1936-)
--*Me and the Terrible Two.* 1st ed. Conford, Ellen (1942-). 1974. Little, Brown. (P.213)
--*Me and the Terrible Two.* Conford, Ellen (1942-). 1978. Little. (P.213)
Carroll, J. A.
--*How Honey Bear Got His Name.* Hayward, Mildred. 1947. B. Humphries. (P.426)
Carroll, John
--*Silky: An Incredible Tale.* Coatsworth, Elizabeth Jane (1893-). 1953. Pantheon Books Inc. (P.204)
Carroll, Lewis, pseud., see Dodgson, Charles Lutwidge.
Carroll, Lewis, pseud. (1832-1898)
--*Alice's Adventures Underground.* Dodgson, Charles Lutwidge. Carroll, Lewis, pseud. (1832-1898). Dodgson, Charles Lutwidge. 1981. Smith Pubs. (P.173)
--*The Rectory Umbrella and Mischmasch.* Dodgson, Charles Lutwidge. Carroll, Lewis, pseud. (1832-1898). Dodgson, Charles Lutwidge. Milner, Florence, frwd. by. 1932. Dover Books. (P.174)
Carroll, Nancy
--*The Boy Who Ate Flowers.* Sherman, Nancy (1931-). 1960. Platt & Munk Co. (P.819)
Carroll, Ruth Robinson, Mrs. (1899-)
--*The Adventures of Chessie.* Carroll, Ruth Robinson, Mrs. (1899-). N.D. Julian Messner Inc. (P.174)
--*The Animals Came First.* Welch, Jean Louise (1914-). N.D. Henry Z. Walck Inc. (P.943)
--*The Animals Came First.* Welch, Jean Louise, pseud. (1914-). Kempton, Jean Welch. 1948. Oxford University Press. (P.943)
--*Another Singing Time.* Coleman, Satis Narrona Barton, Mrs. (1878-) & Thorn, Alice Green (1890-1942). 1937. John Day Bks. (P.209)
--*Another Singing Time.* Coleman, Satis Narrona Barton, Mrs. (1878-) & Thorn, Alice Green (1890-1942). 1937. Reynal & Hitchcock. (P.209)
--*Beanie.* Carroll, Ruth Robinson, Mrs. (1899-) & Carroll, Archer Latrobe (1894-). 1953. H. Z. Walck. (P.174)
--*Beanie.* Carroll, Ruth Robinson, Mrs. (1899-) & Carroll, Archer Latrobe. 1953. Oxford University Press. (P.174)
--*Bounce and the Bunnies.* Carroll, Ruth Robinson, Mrs. (1899-). N.D. Harcourt Brace & Co. (P.174)
--*Bounce and the Bunnies.* Carroll, Ruth Robinson, Mrs. (1899-). 1934. Reynal & Hitchcock, Inc. (P.174)
--*Bumble Pup.* Carroll, Ruth Robinson, Mrs. (1899-) & Carroll, Archer Latrobe (1894-). 1968. H. Z. Walck. (P.174)
--*Chessie.* Carroll, Ruth Robinson, Mrs. (1899-). N.D. Veritas Press. (P.174)
--*Chessie and Her Kittens.* Carroll, Ruth Robinson, Mrs. (1899-). c.1937. J. Messner, Inc. (P.174)
--*Chessie and Her Kittens.* Carroll, Ruth Robinson, Mrs. (1899-). N.D. Veritas Press. (P.174)
--*Danny & the Poi Pup.* Carroll, Ruth Robinson, Mrs. (1899-) & Carroll, Archer Latrobe (1894-). 1965. Walck. (P.174)
--*Digby, the Only Dog.* Carroll, Ruth Robinson, Mrs. (1899-) & Carroll, Archer Latrobe (1894-). 1959. H. Z. Walck. (P.174)
--*Digby, the Only Dog.* Carroll, Ruth Robinson, Mrs. (1899-) & Carroll, Archer Latrobe (1894-). 1955. Oxford University Press. (P.174)
--*Flight of the Silver Bird.* Carroll, Ruth Robinson, Mrs. (1899-) & Carroll, Archer Latrobe (1894-). c.1939. J. Messner, Inc. (P.174)
--*Hullaballoo: The Elephant Dog.* Carroll, Ruth Robinson, Mrs. (1899-) & Carroll, Archer Latrobe (1894-). 1975. Walck. (P.174)
--*Luck of the Roll and Go.* Carroll, Ruth Robinson, Mrs. (1899-) & Carroll, Archer Latrobe (1894-). 1935. The Macmillan Company. (P.174)
--*The Managing Hen and the Floppy Hound.* Carroll, Ruth Robinson, Mrs. (1899-) & Carroll, Archer Latrobe (1894-). 1972. H. Z. Walck. (P.174)
--*Old Mrs.* Billups and the Black Cats. Carroll, Ruth Robinson, Mrs. (1899-). 1961. H. Z. Walck. (P.174)
--*Peanut.* Carroll, Ruth Robinson, Mrs. (1899-) & Carroll, Archer Latrobe (1894-). 1951. H. Z. Walck. (P.174)
--*Peanut.* Carroll, Ruth Robinson, Mrs. (1899-) & Carroll, Archer Latrobe (1894-). 1951. Oxford University Press. (P.174)
--*Pet Tale.* Carroll, Ruth Robinson, Mrs. (1899-) & Carroll, Archer Latrobe (1894-). 1959, c.1949. H. Z. Walck. (P.174)
--*Pet Tale.* Carroll, Ruth Robinson, Mrs. (1899-) & Carroll, Archer Latrobe (1894-). 1949. Oxford Univ. Press. (P.174)
--*The Picnic Bear.* Carroll, Ruth Robinson, Mrs. (1899-) & Carroll, Archer Latrobe (1894-). c.1966. Walck. (P.174)
--*Picnic Bear.* Carroll, Ruth Robinson, Mrs. (1899-) & Carroll, Archer Latrobe (1894-). 1966. Walck. (P.174)
--*Rolling Down Hill.* Carroll, Ruth Robinson, Mrs. (1899-). 1973. David McKay. (P.174)
--*Rolling Downhill.* Carroll, Ruth Robinson, Mrs. (1899-). 1973. H. Z. Walck. (P.174)
--*Runaway Pony, Runaway Dog.* Carroll, Ruth Robinson, Mrs. (1899-) & Carroll, Archer Latrobe (1894-). 1963. H. Z. Walck. (P.174)
--*Salt and Pepper.* Carroll, Ruth Robinson, Mrs. (1899-) & Carroll, Archer Latrobe (1894-). 1952. H. Z. Walck. (P.174)
--*Salt and Pepper.* Carroll, Ruth Robinson, Mrs. (1899-) & Carroll, Archer Latrobe (1894-). 1952. Oxford University Press. (P.174)
--*School in the Sky.* Carroll, Ruth Robinson, Mrs. (1899-) & Carroll, Archer Latrobe (1894-). 1945. The Macmillan Company. (P.174)
--*Scuffles.* Carroll, Ruth Robinson, Mrs. (1899-) & Carroll, Archer Latrobe (1894-). 1963, c.1943. H. Z. Walck. (P.174)
--*Scuffles.* Carroll, Ruth Robinson, Mrs. (1899-) & Carroll, Archer Latrobe (1894-). 1943. Oxford University Press. (P.174)
--*Though Enough and Easy.* Carroll, Ruth Robinson, Mrs. (1899-) & Carroll, Archer Latrobe (1894-). 1958. H. Z. Walok. (P.174)
--*Tough Enough.* Carroll, Ruth Robinson, Mrs. (1899-) & Carroll, Archer Latrobe (1894-). 1954. H. Z. Walck. (P.174)
--*Tough Enough.* Carroll, Ruth Robinson, Mrs. (1899-) & Carroll, Archer Latrobe (1894-). 1954. Oxford University Press. (P.174)
--*Tough Enough and Sassy.* Carroll, Ruth Robinson, Mrs. (1899-) & Carroll, Archer Latrobe (1894-). 1958. H. Z. Walck. (P.174)
--*Tough Enough's Indians.* Carroll, Ruth Robinson, Mrs. (1899-) & Carroll, Archer Latrobe (1894-). 1960. H. Z. Walck. (P.174)
--*Tough Enough's Pony.* Carroll, Ruth Robinson, Mrs. (1899-) & Carroll, Archer Latrobe (1894-). 1957. H. Z. Walck. (P.174)
--*Tough Enough's Pony.* Carroll, Ruth Robinson, Mrs. (1899-) & Carroll, Archer Latrobe (1894-). 1957. Oxford University Press. (P.174)
--*Tough Enough's Trip.* Carroll, Ruth Robinson, Mrs. (1899-) & Carroll, Archer Latrobe (1894-). 1956. H. Z. Walck. (P.174)
--*Tough Enough's Trip.* Carroll, Ruth Robinson, Mrs. (1899-) & Carroll, Archer Latrobe (1894-). 1956. Oxford University Press. (P.174)
--*Watch the Kitten Grow.* Hall, William Norman (1915-1974). c.1946. Thomas Y. Crowell Company. (P.406)
--*Watch the Puppy Grow.* Hall, William Norman (1915-1974). 1945. T. Y. Crowell Co. (P.406)
--*What Whiskers Did.* Carroll, Ruth Robinson, Mrs. (1899-). 1965. David McKay company. (P.174)
--*What Whiskers Did.* Carroll, Ruth Robinson, Mrs. (1899-). 1965. H. Z. Walck. (P.174)
--*What Whiskers Did: A Story Without Words.* Carroll, Ruth Robinson, Mrs. (1899-). 1932. The Macmillan Company. (P.174)
--*Where's the Bunny.* Carroll, Ruth Robinson, Mrs. (1899-). 1950. David McKay Company. (P.174)
--*Where's the Bunny?.* Carroll, Ruth Robinson, Mrs. (1899-). c.1950. H. Z. Walck. (P.174)
--*Where's the Bunny?.* Carroll, Ruth Robinson, Mrs. (1899-). 1950. Oxford University Press. (P.174)
--*Where's The Kitty.* Carroll, Ruth Robinson, Mrs. (1899-). 1962. David McKay Company. (P.174)
--*Where's the Kitty?.* Carroll, Ruth Robinson, Mrs. (1899-). 1962. H. Z. Walck. (P.174)
--*The Witch Kitten.* Carroll, Ruth Robinson, Mrs. (1899-). 1973. H. Z. Walck. (P.174)
Carroll, Ruth Robinsone (1899-)
--*Chimp & the Clown.* Carroll, Ruth Robinson, Mrs. (1899-). 1968. Walck. (P.174)
Carroll, William
--*Eight Haunted Stories.* Vitarelli, Robert, ed. 1973. Xerox Ed Pubns. (P.920)
Carruth, Jane
--*My Big Book of Farm Animals.* Carruth, Jane. 1973. E.P.Dutton & Co. (P.175)
Carruth, Jane & Embleton, Gerry
--*Little Red Riding Hood.* Embleton, Elisabeth. 1975, c.1973. Collins-World. (P.305)
Carse, Duncan A.
--*Dewdrops from Fairy Land.* Scott, Lucy M. N.D. Frederick Warne & Co. (P.805)
Carsey, Alice
--*The Burro's Moneybag.* Thomas, Margaret Loring, Mrs. 1947. Abingdon-Cokesbury Press. (P.886)
--*The Camp Fire Girls at Lookout Pass.* Sanderson, Margaret Love. c.1917. The Reilly & Britton Co. (P.792)
--*Clover Creek.* Trotler, Grace Violet (1900-). Paschal, Nancy, pseud. 1946. T. Nelson. (P.901)
--*Hans Brinker: Or, The Silver Skates.* Dodge, Mary Elizabeth Mapes, Mrs. (1831-1905). c.1917. Whitman Publishing Co. (P.276)
--*Pinocchio: The Tale of a Puppet.* Lorenzini, Carlo (1826-1890). Collodi, Carlo, pseud. c.1917. Whitman Publishing Co. (P.585)
Carsey, Alice & Foster, Genevieve Stump (1893-1979)
--*The Mason Children.* Armstrong, Edith Mason. c.1932. Rand, McNally & Company. (P.48)
Carson, Charles S.
--*Contrary Mary.* Bailey, Temple. 1914. Penn Pub. Co. (P.60)
Carson, Kelly K. M
--*Noah's and Namah's Ark.* Pomerantz, Charlotte (1930-). c.1981. Holt, Rinehart, and Winston. (P.731)
Carson, Patti & Dellosa, Janet
--*Circus Fun Book.* Carson, Patti & Dellosa, Janet. 1982. Carson-Dellos. (P.175)
--*Spooky Fun Book.* Carson, Patti & Dellosa, Janet. 1981. Carson-Dellos. (P.175)
Carten, Virginia
--*Busy Bodies: The Busy ABCs.* Bowman, Clare. 1959. Rand McNally. (P.122)
--*We Went to the Doctor.* Memling, Carl (1918-1969). 1955. Abelard-Schuman, Inc. (P.640)
--*What's in the Dark?.* Memling, Carl (1918-1969). 1954. Abelard-Schuman. (P.640)
Carter, A. Helene
--*Bemol and Kusum: Children of Bengal.* Wyman, Herbert Elmer (1867-). 1926. World Book Company. (P.983)
--*Two Little Misogynists.* Spitteler, Carl Friedrich George (1845-1924). Roquette-Buisson, Vicomtesse, tr. 1922. H. Holt and Company. (P.845)
Carter, A. Helene, jt. illus. see De Thulstrup, T.
Carter, Barbara (1952-)
--*Deadwood City.* Packard, Edward (1931-). c.1978. Lippincott. (P.699)
--*Journey Under the Sea.* Montgomery, Raymond A., Jr. (1936-). Mountain, Robert, pseud. c.1977. Vermont Crossroads Press. (P.658)
--*Sugarcane Island.* Packard, Edward (1931-). c.1976. Vermont Crossroads Press. (P.699)
--*The Third Planet from Altair.* Packard, Edward (1931-). c.1979. Lippincott. (P.699)
Carter, Betty, jt. illus. see Newton, Ruth E.
Carter, Bruce, pseud., see Hough, Richard Alexander.
Carter, Charlotte Anne
--*The Magic Wishbone.* Lemon, Adele Marie (1901-). 1964. Lawrence Pub. Co. (P.564)
Carter, Debby L.
--*The Buried Treasure.* Bider, Djemma. 1981. Dodd, Mead. (P.101)
--*The Buried Treasure.* Bider, Djemma. 1982. Dodd. (P.101)
--*Smaller Than Most.* Rigby, Shirley Lincoln. c.1985. Harper & Row. (P.764)
Carter, Derek
--*Escape from Velos.* Markham, Marion M. 1981. Childrens Press. (P.620)
Carter, F. A.
--*At the Siege of Quebec.* Kaler, James Otis (1848-1912). 1897. The Penn Publishing Company. (P.504)
--*The Boer Boy of the Transvaal.* Rabb, Kate Milner, Mrs. N.D. Penn Publishing Co. (P.745)
--*The Eve of War.* Foster, Walter Bertram (1869-). 1904. Penn Publishing Co. (P.339)
--*Exiled to Siberia.* Graydon, William Murray (1864-1946). 1900. The Penn Publishing Company. (P.384)
--*The First Cruiser Out.* Stoddard, William Osborn (1835-1925). N.D. Duffield. (P.860)
--*In the Camp of the Creeks.* Pendleton, Louis Beauregard (1861-1939). 1903. The Penn Publishing Company. (P.716)
--*A Moonshiner's Son.* Dromgoole, William Allen, Miss (1860-1934). N.D. Penn Publishing Co. (P.285)
--*A Plebe at West Point.* Malone, Paul Bernard (1872-). 1905. The Penn Publishing Company. (P.615)
--*A Plebe at West Point.* Malone, Paul Bernard (1872-). 1909. The Penn Publishing Company. (P.615)
--*A West Point Cadet.* Malone, Paul Bernard (1872-). 1936. The Penn Publishing Company. (P.615)
--*A West Point Lieutenant.* Malone, Paul Bernard (1872-). 1911. The Penn Publishing Company. (P.615)
--*A West Point Yearling.* Malone, Paul Bernard (1872-). 1907. The Penn Publishing Company. (P.615)
--*A West Point Yearling.* Malone, Paul Bernard (1872-). c.1935. The Penn Publishing Company. (P.615)
--*Winning His Way to West Point.* Malone, Paul Bernard (1872-). 1904. The Penn Publishing Company. (P.615)
--*Winning His Way to West Point.* Malone, Paul Bernard (1872-). 1932. The Penn Publishing Company. (P.615)
--*With Ethan Allen at Ticonderoga.* Foster, Walter Bertram (1869-). 1903. The Penn Publishing Company. (P.339)
--*With Washington at Valley Forge.* Foster, Walter Bertram (1869-). 1902. The Penn Publishing Company. (P.339)
--*The Young Gold Seekers of the Klondike.* Ellis, Edward Sylvester (1840-1916). 1899. The Penn Publishing Company. (P.304)
Carter, Harry
--*The Singing Happy Birthday Book.* Stern, Grace. 1955. J. C. Winston Co. (P.853)
Carter, Helene, jt. illus. see Ransome, Arthur Michell.
Carter, Helene (1887-1960)
--*The Baby Whale, Sharp Ears.* Beaty, John Yocum (1884-). c.1938. J. B. Lippincott Company. (P.86)
--*City Stories Told by City Children As They Go Exploring in New York.* Tchaika, Florence Esther Matthews, Mrs. (1894-) & Coffin, Rebecca Jane, eds. Columbia University. Teachers College. Lincoln School. 1928. The Macmillan Company. (P.881)
--*The Dark Mile.* Broster, Dorothy Kathleen. 1934. Coward-McCann, Inc. (P.137)
--*The Flight of the Heron.* Broster, Dorothy Kathleen. N.D. Coward McCann. (P.137)
--*Grandmother's Doll.* Bouton, Elizabeth Gladwin. 1931. Duffield and Green. (P.120)
--*A Lad of Dundee.* Cuthbert, Gwen & King, Elizabeth Marriot. c.1935. World Book Company. (P.237)
--*Peter Duck.* Ransome, Arthur Michell (1884-1967). c.1933. J. B. Lippincott Company. (P.749)
--*Pierre Keeps Watch.* Gleitsmann, Hertha. Gleit, Maria, pseud. 1944. C. Scribner's Sons. (P.371)
--*Puppet Parade.* Della Chiesa, Carolyn M (1887-). 1932. Longmans, Green and Co. (P.255)
--*Ruth Visits Margot, a Little French Girl.* Keech, Roy A. 1934. A. Whitman & Co. (P.511)
--*Smokey and Pinocchio.* Carter, Helene (1887-1960). 1940. J. B. Lippincott. (P.175)
--*Swallowdale.* Ransome, Arthur Michell (1884-1967). 1932. J. B. Lippincott Company. (P.749)
--*Swallows and Amazons.* Ransome, Arthur Michell (1884-1967). 1931. J. B. Lippincott Company. (P.749)
--*Three of Salu: Around the Year in Northern Italy.* Della Chiesa, Carolyn M (1887-). 1923. World Book Company. (P.255)
--*Water, Water Everywhere.* Walsh, Mary Regina (1889-). N.D. Abingdon Press. (P.928)
--*Winter Holiday.* Ransome, Arthur Michell (1884-1967). c.1934. J. B. Lippincott Company. (P.749)
Carter, Penny
--*Secret of the Old Barn.* Robert, Adrian. 1985. Troll Assocs. (P.767)
Carter, Roberta
--*Fairy Tales.* Grimm, Jakob Ludwig Karl (1785-1863) & Grimm, Wilhelm Karl (1786-1859). Morel, Eve, ed. c.1962. Grosset & Dunlap. (P.391)
--*Grimms' Fairy Tales.* Grimm, Jakob Ludwig Karl (1785-1863) & Grimm, Wilhelm Karl (1786-1859). Morel, Eve, ed. 1962. Putnam Pub Group. (P.392)
Carter, Steve (1947-)
--*The Princess Storybook: Five Favorite Fairy Tales.* Summers, Julia, adapted by. 1976, c.1974. Hallmark. (P.871)
Cartwright, Charles E.
--*Bob Graham at Sea.* Riesenberg, Felix, Jr. (1913-1962). c.1925. Harcourt, Brace and Company. (P.764)
--*Jack Heaton, Oil Propector.* Collins, Archie Frederick (1869-). c.1920. Frederick A. Stokes Company. (P.209)
--*Plow Stories.* Pierson, Clara Dillingham. c.1923. E. P. Dutton & Company. (P.726)
Carty, Leo (1931-)
--*Fifty Thousand Names for Jeff.* Snyder, Anne (1922-). 1973, c.1969. Holt. (P.839)
--*The House on the Mountain.* 1st ed. Clymer, Eleanor Lowenton (1906-). 1971. Dutton. (P.203)
--*I Love Gram.* 1st ed. Sonneborn, Ruth Cantor (1899-1974). 1971. Viking Press. (P.841)
--*Sidewalk Story.* 1st ed. Mathis, Sharon Bell (1937-). 1971. Viking Press. (P.631)
--*A Tree for Tompkins Park.* Thomas, Dawn C. 1971. McGraw-Hill. (P.885)
--*Where Does the Day Go?.* Myers, Walter Dean (1937-). 1969. Parents' Magazine Press. (P.674)
Carver, Marjorie Reineman
--*Grampa Gomez' Garden.* Carver, Marjorie Reineman. Riffel, Maria, tr. from Span. 1977. Margaritas Bks For Brown Eyes. (P.176)
--*The Practically Purple Pumpkin.* Carver, Marjorie Reineman. McKenna, Helen, ed. c.1977. Margarita's Books for Brown Eyes. (P.176)
Cary, pseud., see Cary, Louis Favreau.
Cary, Louis Favreau see Cary, pseud.

--*Two Little Women and Treasure House.* Wells, Carolyn (1869-1942). 1916. Dodd, Mead and Company. (P.944)
--*Two Little Women on a Holiday.* Wells, Carolyn (1869-1942). 1917. Dodd, Mead and Company. (P.944)
--*Under Orders: The Story of Tim and "the Club,".* Latham, Harold Strong (1887-1969). 1918. The Macmillan Company. (P.553)
--*The Waring Girls.* Deland, Ellen Douglas (1860-1922). 1917. D. Appleton and Company. (P.253)
--*Without Valour.* Long, Laura Mooney (1892-1967). 1940. Longmans Green and Co. (P.582)

Caswell, Helen Rayburn (1923-)
--*In Jimmy's Chair.* Sargent, Susan (1951-) & Wirt, Donna Aaron (1951-). 1984. Abingdon. (P.793)
--*A New Song for Christmas.* Caswell, Helen Rayburn (1923-). 1966. Van Nostrand. (P.177)
--*A Wind on the Road.* Caswell, Helen Rayburn (1923-). 1964. Van Nostrand. (P.177)
--*You Are More Wonderful.* Caswell, Helen Rayburn (1923-). N.D. C. R. Gibson Co. (P.177)

Caswell, Leslie & Edwards, Brian (1936-)
--*The Spear Thrower: A Story of Early Man.* Roberts, David (1926-). 1972. Rand McNally. (P.767)

Catania, Tom
--*The Grizzly Bear with the Golden Ears.* George, Jean Craighead (1919-). 1982. Harper. (P.363)

Cate, E. Deane
--*Rip Foster Rides the Gray Planet.* Savage, Blake, pseud. (1914-). Goodwin, Harold Leland. 1952. Whitman Pub. Co. (P.794)

Cate, Patricia
--*By the Sea.* Rev. American ed. Crosher, G. R. c.1969. Fearon Publishers. (P.232)

Caterina, Sr.
--*Little Lord, some thoughts of a Little Red-haired Child.* Caterina, Sr., ed. c.1930. Benziger Brothers. (P.177)

Cather, Carolyn
--*Girl on a Broomstick.* Burt, Katharine Newlin (1882-). 1967. Funk & Wagnalls. (P.157)
--*Gypsy Tales.* Protter, Eric & Protter, Nancy, eds. 1968, c.1967. Lion Press. (P.740)
--*Hear America Singing.* Attaway, William. 1967. Lion. (P.53)
--*October Treasure.* 1st ed. Wuorio, Eva-Lis (1918-). 1966. Holt, Rinehart and Winston. (P.982)
--*One Silver Spur.* Burt, Katharine Newlin (1882-). 1968. Funk & Wagnalls. (P.157)
--*The Shy One.* Nathan, Dorothy Goldeen (0000-1966). 1966. Random House. (P.676)
--*The Trouble on Shake-Rag Creek.* 1st ed. Hubbard, Margaret Ann (1909-). 1967. Doubleday. (P.469)
--*Witch Princess.* Johnson, Dorothy Marie (1905-). 1967. HM. (P.494)

Catherwood, Henry Frederick Ross (1925-)
--*The Jade Amulet.* Linton, Adelin. 1965. Funk & Wagnalls. (P.575)

Catlin, Elizabeth Blanchard
--*Tales of the Open for Little Folks.* Brooks, Virginia Louise. 1921. Printed by George Banta Publishing Co. (P.137)

Cato, Deane
--*Beacon Hill Children: Or, Chronicles of the Corey Family.* Jackson, Elizabeth Rhodes. Dee, as told by. 1947. L. C. Page & Company. (P.484)

Cattaneo, Tony
--*The Walrus & the Carpenter.* Carroll, Lewis, pseud. (1832-1898). Dodgson, Charles Lutwidge. 1975. Warne. (P.174)
--*The Walrus and the Carpenter.* Dodgson, Charles Lutwidge (1832-1898). Carroll, Lewis, pseud. 1974. F. Warne. (P.278)

Caudill-Paye, Judythe (1939-)
--*Just for You.* 1st ed. Schmeltz, Susan Alton. c.1981. Quality Books. (P.800)

Cauldwell, H. T.
--*Pilot Pete.* Villiers, Alan John (1903-). 1954. Scribner. (P.919)

Cauley, Lorinda Bryan (1951-)
--*The Animal Kids.* Cauley, Lorinda Bryan (1951-). c.1979. Putnam. (P.178)
--*Ants Don't Get Sunday Off.* Pollock, Penny (1935-). 1979. Putnam. (P.731)
--*The Bake-off.* Cauley, Lorinda Bryan (1951-). c.1978. Putnam. (P.178)
--*The Beginning of the Armadillos.* Kipling, Joseph Rudyard (1865-1936). c.1985. Harcourt Brace Jovanovich. (P.527)
--*Best of All!.* Hogan, Cecily R. 1979. Western Pub. (P.451)
--*Clancy's Coat.* Bunting, Eve, pseud. (1928-). Bunting, Anne Evelyn. 1984, c.1983. F. Warne. (P.150)
--*The Cock, the Mouse, and the Little Red Hen.* Cauley, Lorinda Bryan (1951-). 1981. Putnam. (P.178)
--*Curley Cat Baby-Sits.* Watson, Pauline (1925-). c.1977. Harcourt Brace Jovanovich. (P.936)
--*The Elephant's Child.* 1st ed. Kipling, Joseph Rudyard (1865-1936). c.1983. Harcourt. (P.527)
--*Goldilocks and the Three Bears.* 1st Peppercorn Paperback ed. The, Three Bears & Cauley, Lorinda Bryan (1951-) 1981. Putnam. (P.890)
--*The Goodnight Circle.* Lesser, Carolyn. 1984. Harcourt. (P.567)
--*The Goose and the Golden Coins.* Cauley, Lorinda Bryan (1951-) & Basile, Giovanni Battista (1575-1632). c.1981. Harcourt Brace Jovanovich. (P.178)
--*The House of the Five Bears.* Jameson, Cynthia. 1978. Putnam Pub Group. (P.489)
--*If You Say So, Claude.* Nixon, Joan Lowery (1927-). 1980. F. Warne. (P.683)
--*Jack and the Beanstalk.* Cauley, Lorinda Bryan (1951-). 1983. G.P. Putnam. (P.178)
--*Joseph Jacobs' the Story of the Three Little Pigs.* 1st ed. Jacobs, Joseph (1854-1916), ed. 1980. Putnam. (P.487)
--*Little Grey Rabbit.* Bowden, Joan Chase (1925-). 1979. Western Pub. (P.120)
--*The New House.* Cauley, Lorinda Bryan (1951-). 1981. HarBraceJ. (P.178)
--*Old Hippo's Easter Egg.* 1st ed. Wahl, Jan (1933-). c.1980. Harcourt Brace Jovanovich. (P.924)
--*The Owl and the Pussycat.* Lear, Edward (1812-1888). 1985. Putnam. (P.558)
--*Rabbits' Search for a Little House.* Kwitz, Mary DeBall. c.1977. Crown Publishers. (P.542)
--*The Slug Who Thought He Was a Snail.* Pollock, Penny (1935-). c.1980. Putnam. (P.731)
--*Small Bear Solves a Mystery.* Holl, Adelaide Hinkle (1910-). c.1979. Garrard Pub. Co. (P.454)
--*The Spitbug Who Couldn't Spit.* Pollock, Penny (1935-). 1980. Putnam. (P.731)
--*The Three Little Kittens.* Cauley, Lorinda Bryan (1951-). c.1982. Putnam. (P.178)
--*The Town Mouse and the Country Mouse.* Cauley, Lorinda Bryan (1951-). c.1984. Putnam Pub Group. (P.178)
--*The Ugly Duckling.* Andersen, Hans Christian (1805-1875). Cauley, Lorinda Bryan (1951-), retold by. c.1979. Harcourt Brace Jovanovich. (P.37)
--*The War Party.* 1st ed. Steele, William Owen (1917-1979). c.1978. Harcourt Brace Jovanovich. (P.851)
--*What Lily Goose Found.* Sumera, Annabelle. 1979. Western Pub. (P.870)
--*Where's Henrietta's Hen?.* Freschet, Berniece Louise Speck (1927-). 1979. Putnam. (P.345)

Caulfield, James
--*Westwind Woods.* Huggler, Thomas E. East, Ben, frwd. by. c.1978. Michigan United Conservation Clubs. (P.470)

Caunan, Manhar
--*Fraggle Rock.* Stevenson, Jocelyn. 1984, c.1983. Holt, Rinehart, and Winston. (P.855)

Cauper, David
--*The Story of the Pilgrims & Their Indian Friends: A Thanksgiving Story for Children.* 3rd ed. Cauper, Eunice. 1984. Branden Pub Co. (P.178)

Causer, Rufus
--*Jean and Tom in Casablanca.* 1st ed. Hargrave, Carrie Guerphan. 1953. Exposition Press. (P.412)

Causey, Lillian
--*Little Red Riding Hood and Other Fairy Tales.* Causey, Lillian. 1918. Penn Pub. Co. (P.178)

Cavaliere, R. J.
--*The Golden Table.* Paine, Ralph Delahaye (1871-1925). 1925. The Penn Publishing Company. (P.700)

Cavallo, John
--*The Weird Witch's Spell: Eight Strange Haunted Tales.* Vitarelli, Robert, ed. 1972. Xerox Education Publications. (P.920)

Cavally, Frederick L., Jr.
--*Mother Goose's Teddy Bears.* Mother Goose. Cavally, Frederick L., Jr., adapted by. 1907. Bobbs-Merrill. (P.669)

Cavanagh, Paul
--*Gleaming Rails.* Dean, Graham M (1904-). 1930. D. Appleton and Company. (P.248)

Caxton, Laura, pseud., see Comins, Elizabeth Barker.

Caxton, Laura, pseud.
--*Marion Berkley, 1 of 3 vols.* Comins, Elizabeth Barker. Caxton, Laura, pseud. Comins, Elizabeth Barker. 1891. Porter & Coates. (P.179)
--*Marion Berkley: A Story for Girls.* Comins, Elizabeth Barker. Caxton, Laura, pseud. Comins, Elizabeth Barker. N.D. Loring. (P.179)

Cayard, Bruce
--*It May Come in Handy Someday.* Tompert, Ann (1918-). 1975. McGraw-Hill. (P.895)

Cazet, Denys (1938-)
--*Big Shoe, Little Shoe.* Cazet, Denys (1938-). 1984. Bradbury Pr. (P.179)
--*Christmas Moon.* Cazet, Denys (1938-). 1984. Bradbury Pr. (P.179)
--*The Duck with Squeaky Feet.* Cazet, Denys (1938-). 1980. Bradbury Press. (P.179)
--*Lucky Me.* Cazet, Denys (1938-). 1981. Bradbury Press. (P.179)
--*Lucky Me.* Cazet, Denys (1938-). 1983. Bradbury Pr. (P.179)
--*Mother Night.* Cazet, Denys (1938-). 1985. Bradbury Press. (P.179)
--*Mud Baths for Everyone.* Cazet, Denys (1938-). 1981. Bradbury Press. (P.179)
--*Saturday.* Cazet, Denys (1938-). 1985. Bradbury Pr. (P.179)
--*You Make the Angels Cry".* Cazet, Denys (1938-). 1982. Bradbury Press. (P.179)
--*You Make the Angels Cry.* Cazet, Denys (1938-). 1983. Bradbury Pr. (P.179)

Cechak, William
--*Hot Springs and Hell.* Randolph, Vance (1892-), ed. 1965. Folklore Associates. (P.748)

Cecil, Hugh
--*The Surprise Bear.* Mirabel, Cecil. 1982. Little. (P.651)

Cellini, Eva
--*I Often Wish: Poems.* Deutsch, Babette (1895-1982). 1966. Funk & Wagnalls. (P.261)
--*Let's Walk Up the Wall.* Johnson, Walter Ryerson (1901-). 1967. Holiday. (P.497)
--*Let's Walk up the Wall.* Johnson, Walter Ryerson (1901-). 1978. Scholastic Inc. (P.497)

Cellini, Joseph, jt. illus. see McCurry, Charles.

Cellini, Joseph (1924-)
--*The Buried Treasure, and Other Picture Tales.* 1st ed. Ross, Eulalie Steinmetz (1910-), ed. 1958. Lippincott. (P.779)
--*Canalboat to Freedom.* Snow, Donald Clifford (1917-). Fall, Thomas, pseud. c.1966. Dial. **Award: (ALA).** (P.838)
--*Davy Jones' Haunted Locker: Great Ghost Stories of the Sea.* Arthur, Robert, pseud. (1909-1969), ed. Feder, Robert Arthur. 1965. Random. (P.50)
--*Dragon Defiant.* Hall, Lynn (1937-) c. 1977. Follett Pub. Co. (P.405)
--*The Ferlie.* McIlwraith, Maureen Mollie Hunter McVeigh (1922-). 1968. Funk & Wagnalls. (P.604)
--*The Great Adventure of Michelangelo.* Abr. and Illus. ed. Stone, Irving (1903-). 1965. Doubleday. (P.862)
--*The Great Dane, Thor.* Farley, Walter Lorimer (1915-). 1966. Random House. (P.317)
--*High Country Adventure.* Rumsey, Marian Barritt (1928-). 1967. W. Morrow. (P.784)
--*His Majesty, the Frog.* Roth, Mary Jane. 1971. Morrow. (P.780)
--*A Horse Called Dragon.* Hall, Lynn (1937-). 1971. Follett. (P.405)
--*Jeremy and the Gorillas.* Gould, Lilian. c.1977. Lothrop, Lee & Shepard. (P.379)
--*Keeping Horse.* Balch, Glenn (1902-). 1966. T Y Crowell. (P.64)
--*The Kelpie's Pearls.* McIlwraith, Maureen Mollie Hunter McVeigh (1922-). 1966, c.1964. Funk & Wagnalls. **Award: (ALA).** (P.604)
--*Lightning Slinger.* Gessner, Lynne (1919-). 1968. Funk & Wagnalls. (P.365)
--*Little Apes.* Conklin, Gladys Plemon (1903-). 1970. Holiday. (P.213)
--*Lynn Hall's Dog Stories.* Hall, Lynn (1937-). 1972. Follett Co. (P.405)
--*Miguel and His Racehorse.* Reid, Barbara (1922-). 1973. Morrow. (P.755)
--*Mustang on the Prairie.* Eberle, Irmengarde (1898-1979). 1968. Doubleday. (P.295)
--*My Daddy Lost His Job.* Stull, Edith Gilbert (1919-). 1967. L. W. Singer Co. (P.869)
--*Mystery on Safari.* Cavanna, Betty (1909-). 1970. Morrow. (P.179)
--*New Day for Dragon.* Hall, Lynn (1937-). 1975. Follett Pub. Co. (P.405)
--*The Red Lion.* Stewart, Neil. 1960. Putnam. (P.858)
--*The Secret of Stonehouse.* Hall, Lynn (1937-). 1968. Follett Pub. Co. (P.405)
--*The Secret Summer of L. E. B.* Wallace, Barbara Brooks (1922-). 1974. Follett. (P.926)
--*Shadows.* Hall, Lynn (1937-). c.1977. Follett Pub. Co. (P.405)
--*Stray.* Hall, Lynn (1937-). 1974. Follett Pub. Co. (P.405)
--*Thomas & the Warlock.* Hunter, Mollie (1922-). 1967. Funk & W. (P.474)
--*To Catch a Tartar.* Hall, Lynn (1937-). 1973. Follett. (P.405)
--*Troublemaker.* Hall, Lynn (1937-). 1974. Follett Pub. Co. (P.405)
--*Walt Disney's Shaggy Dog.* Disney, Walter Elias (1901-1966). Verral, Charles Spain, adapted by. 1959. Golden Press. (P.272)
--*Winter of the Whale: A Novel.* Carse, Robert (1902-1971). 1961. Putnam. (P.175)

Censoni, Robert
--*Cowgirl Kate.* Censoni, Robert. c.1977. Holiday House. (P.180)
--*The Shopping-Bag Lady.* Censoni, Robert. c.1977. Holiday House. (P.180)

Centola, Tom
--*Siren in the Night.* Aylesworth, Jim (1943-). 1983. A. Whitman. (P.57)

Cerna, Dagmar
--*Tale of a Wild Duck.* Moric, Rudo. 1966. Lerner Pubns. (P.663)

Cervantes, Alex
--*Sancho, Pronto, and the Engineer: Sancho, Pronto, y el Ingeniero.* Keats, Mark (1905-). Carrera, Paul, tr. 1976. B. Ethridge-Books. (P.511)
--*Senora Pepino and Her Bad Luck Cats: Senora Pepino y Sus Gatos De Mala Suerte.* Michael Cervantes, Esther De & Cervantes, Alex. Cervantes, Alex, tr. 1976. B. Ethridge-Books. (P.644)

Cesare, Oscar E.
--*The King of Gee-Whiz.* Hough, Emerson (1857-1923). Nesbit, Wilbur Dick (1871-1927), contrib. by. c.1906. The Bobbs-Merrill Company. (P.465)

Cesari, Aura
--*Komo the Shepherd Boy.* Hackman, Martha. 1982. Green Tiger Pr. (P.401)
--*The Old Woman of Trora.* Hackman, Martha. 1982. Green Tiger Pr. (P.401)

Cessna, Dorothy, et al.
--*The Parson's Boys.* Casey, Robert (1856-). 1906. The Parson's Boys Publishing Company. (P.176)

Chacanne, Rose
--*Marjory Fleming: The Youngest Genius.* Van Gelder, Robert. 1940. Dodd, Mead and Company. (P.914)

Chace, Lester M.
--*That's Why Stories.* Dyer, Ruth Omega (1885-). 1916. Lothrop, Lee & Shepard Co. (P.293)

Chace, Lynwood M., photos by.
--*Little Orphan Willie-Mouse: A Story and Actual Photographs of a Real Live Woodmouse.* Chadwick, Evelyn M. 1938. Little, Brown and Company. (P.180)
--*Peter and the Frog's Eye.* King, Julius (1893-). c.1936. The Junior Literary Guild and Grosset & Dunlap. (P.524)

Chad
--*Mighty Mouse.* Sutton, Felix (1910-). 1953. Treasure Books. (P.872)
--*Mighty Mouse and the Sacred Scarecrow.* Sutton, Felix (1910-). 1954. Treasure Books. (P.872)
--*Mighty Mouse: Dinky Learns to Fly.* Sutton, Felix (1910-). 1953. Treasure Books. (P.872)
--*Mighty Mouse, Santa's Helper.* Sutton, Felix (1910-). 1955. Treasure Books. (P.872)
--*Tubby, the Tuba.* Tripp, Paul (1916-). 1954. Treasure Books. (P.900)

Chad, et al.
--*The Terrytoons Playhouse.* Sutton, Felix (1910-) & Jason, Leon. 1958. Grosset & Dunlap. (P.872)

Chadburn, Mabel
--*Mother Goose.* Mother Goose. 1927. J. M. Dent & Sons, Limited. (P.667)

Chadwick, Peter
--*Elephant Boy.* Williams, Susan Margaret. 1964. David McKay Company Inc. (P.964)

Chaffee, Allen
--*Brownie: The Engineer of Beaver Brook.* Bramson, Paul (1855-). N.D. Milton Bradley Co. (P.126)

Chaffin, Donald
--*Fantastic Mr. Fox.* Dahl, Roald (1916-). 1970. Knopf. (P.238)
--*Tortoise Tales.* Manning-Sanders, Ruth (1895-), ed. 1974. T. Nelson. (P.618)

Chagnon, Mary
--*Finist, the Falcon Prince: A Russian Folk Tale.* Platonov, Andrei Platonovich (1899-1951). Regehr, Lydia, tr. c.1973. Carolrhoda Books. (P.728)
--*The Princess and the Unicorn.* Arbore, Lily. 1972. Carolrhoda Books. (P.45)

Chaiko, Ted
--*The Tall Book of Bible Stories.* Gibson, Katharine (1893-). 1980. Har-Row. (P.366)

Chakravarty, Biswaranjan
--*The Story of Ramakrishna.* Smaranananda, Swami. 1976. Vedanta Pr. (P.830)
--*Tales from Ramakrishna.* Ramakrishna, Swami. Ray, Irene R. & Gupta, Mallika C., retold by. 1975. Vedanta Pr. (P.747)

Chakravarty, Pranab
--*Rohanta & Nandriya.* Chaitanya, Krishna. 1979. Auromere. (P.182)

Chakravarty, Purhachandra
--*Ramakrishna for Children.* Vishwashrayananda, Swami. Bagchi, Santosh, tr. from Bengali. 1975. Vedanta Pr. (P.920)

Chakravarty, Saila
--*Dhruva.* Hemalata. 1979. Auromere. (P.432)

Chalkley, Guy Aubrey, photos by.
--*The Desert Pool: A Romance of Wildest Africa.* Chalkley, Guy Aubrey. 1937. Longmans, Green and Co. (P.182)

--*Sandman Christmas Stories.* Walker, Abbie Phillips, Mrs. (1867-). 1918. Harper & Brothers. (P.925)

--*Sandman Tales: Stories for Bedtime.* Walker, Abbie Phillips, Mrs. (1867-). 1917. Harper & Brothers. (P.925)

--*Sandman Twilight Stories.* Walker, Abbie Phillips, Mrs. (1867-). 1918. Harper & Brothers. (P.925)

--*Sandman's Fairy Stoires.* Walker, Abbie Phillips, Mrs. (1867-). c.1922. Harper & Brothers. (P.925)

--*Sandman's Goodnight Stories.* Walker, Abbie Phillips, Mrs. (1867-). c.1921. Harper & Brothers. (P.925)

--*The Sandman's Hour: Stories for Bedtime.* Walker, Abbie Phillips, Mrs. (1867-). 1917. Harper & Brothers. (P.925)

--*Sandman's Might-be-so Stories.* 1st ed. Walker, Abbie Phillips, Mrs. (1867-). 1922. Harper & Brothers. (P.925)

--*Sandman's Stories of Drusilla Doll.* Walker, Abbie Phillips, Mrs. (1867-). 1920. Harper & Brothers. (P.925)

--*The Second Bubble Book, No.* 11. Mayhew, Ralph & Johnson, Burges (1877-1963). 1918. Harper & Brothers. (P.634)

--*Stories East and West.* Peck, Lora B. 1927. Little, Brown, and Company. (P.714)

--*Stories for Good Children.* Peck, Lora B. 1920. Little, Brown, and Company. (P.714)

--*The Third Bubble Book.* Mayhew, Ralph & Johnson, Burges (1877-1963). 1918. Harper & Brothers. (P.634)

--*Tippy-Toe Bubble Book, No.* 11. Mayhew, Ralph & Johnson, Burges (1877-1963). 1920. Harper & Brothers. (P.634)

--*Told by a Dog.* Stephens, Annabel Wiseman. c.1935. Johnson Publishing Company. (P.852)

--*Told by the Sandman: Stories for Bedtime.* Walker, Abbie Phillips, Mrs. (1867-). 1916. Harper & Brothers. (P.925)

--*Wonderdays and Wonderways Through Flowerland: A Summer Adventure of Once Upon a Time.* Tabor, Grace. 1916. R. M. McBride & Company. (P.876)

Chase, Rhoda Campbell & Cugat, Albert

--*Long Legs, Big Mouth, Burning Eyes.* Kovalsky, Olga & Putnam, Brenda. N.D. Milton Bradley Co. (P.536)

Chase, Sidney M.

--*Pleasant Street, Smiling Valley, 10 vols.* Lee, Sarah E. 1905. H M Caldwell Co. (P.561)

Chastain, Madye Lee (1908-)

--*Bright Days.* Chastain, Madye Lee (1908-). 1952. Harcourt, Brace. (P.188)

--*Bright Days, 1 of 50 vols.* Chastain, Madye Lee (1908-). N.D. Lothrop Publishing Co. (P.188)

--*The Cow-Tail Switch & Other West African Stories.* Courlander, Harold (1908-), compiled by. Herzog, George (1901-). 1962. HR&W. (P.439)

--*Dark Treasure.* 1st ed. Chastain, Madye Lee (1908-). 1954. Harcourt, Brace. (P.188)

--*Emmy Keeps a Promise.* Chastain, Madye Lee (1908-). 1956. HarBraceJ. (P.188)

--*Emmy Keeps a Promise.* Chastain, Madye Lee (1908-). 1966. HarBraceJ. (P.188)

--*Fripsey Fun.* 1st ed. Chastain, Madye Lee (1908-). 1955. Harcourt, Brace. (P.188)

--*Fripsey Summer.* 1st ed. Chastain, Madye Lee (1908-). 1953. Harcourt, Brace. (P.188)

--*Jerusha's Ghost.* 1st ed. Chastain, Madye Lee (1908-). 1957. Harcourt, Brace. (P.188)

--*Leave It to the Fripseys.* Chastain, Madye Lee (1908-). 1957. HarBraceJ. (P.188)

--*Let's Play Indian.* Chastain, Madye Lee (1908-). 1950. Grosset & Dunlap. (P.188)

--*Loblolly Farm.* 1st ed. Chastain, Madye Lee (1908-). 1950. Harcourt, Brace. (P.188)

--*Magic Island.* 1st ed. Chastain, Madye Lee (1908-). 1964. Harcourt, Brace & World. (P.188)

--*Nellie.* Chastain, Madye Lee (1908-). 1948. Whitman Pub. Co. (P.188)

--*Plippen's Palace.* 1st ed. Chastain, Madye Lee (1908-). 1961. Harcourt, Brace & Uorld. (P.188)

--*The Sailboat that Ran Away.* Chastain, Madye Lee (1908-). 1950. Whitman. (P.188)

--*Sand in Her Shoes.* 1st ed. Lawrence, Mildred Elwood (1907-). 1949. Harcourt, Brace. (P.556)

--*Steamboat South.* 1st ed. Chastain, Madye Lee (1908-). 1951. Harcourt, Brace. (P.188)

--*Sue Ann's Busy Day.* Scott, Sally. 1948. Harcourt, Brace. (P.805)

--*Summer at Hasty Cove.* 1st ed. Chastain, Madye Lee (1908-). 1959. Harcourt, Brace. (P.188)

Chatalbash, Ron (1959-)

--*Dr.* Blackfoot's Carnival Extraordinaire. 1st ed. Chatalbash, Ron (1959-). 1982. D.R. Godine. (P.188)

--*A Perfect Day for the Movies.* 1st ed. Chatalbash, Ron (1959-). 1983. David R. Godine. (P.188)

Chatel, Ariane

--*Valeriane ...* Grize, Madeleine. c.1960. F. Watts. (P.396)

Chauhan, Manhar

--*Muppet Babies Take a Bath.* Spinner, Stephanie (1943-), ed. N.D. Random. (P.845)

Chauhan, Manhar & Venning, Sue

--*Jim Henson's Muppet Show Pop-Up Book.* Spinner, Stephanie (1943-), ed. Penick, Ib, designed by. 1984. Random. (P.845)

Chauncy, Francis

--*Baseball Spark Plug.* 1st ed. Zanger, Jack. 1963. Doubleday. (P.991)

--*Big Down Gamble.* Etter, Lester Frederick (1904-). 1968. Hastings House. (P.310)

--*Fast Break Forward.* Etter, Lester Frederick (1904-). 1969. Hastings House. (P.310)

--*Golden Gloves Challenger.* Etter, Lester Frederick (1904-). 1967. Hastings House. (P.310)

--*Ollie, the Backward Forward.* Philbrook, Clement E. (1917-). 1970, c.1971. Hastings House. (P.723)

--*Ollie, the Foul Shooter.* Philbrook, Clement E. (1917-). 1984. Hastings. (P.723)

--*Ollie's Team and the Alley Cats.* Philbrook, Clement E. (1917-). 1971. Hastings House. (P.723)

--*Ollie's Team and the Baseball Computer.* Philbrook, Clement E. (1917-). 1967. Hastings. (P.723)

--*Ollie's Team and the Basketball Computer.* Philbrook, Clement E. (1917-). 1969. Hastings House. (P.723)

--*Ollie's Team and the Football Computer.* Philbrook, Clement E. (1917-). 1968. Hastings House. (P.723)

--*Ollie's Team and the Million Dollar Mistake.* Philbrook, Clement E. (1917-). 1973. Hastings House. (P.723)

--*Ollie's Team and the Two Hundred Pound Problem.* Philbrook, Clement E. (1917-). 1972. Hastings House. (P.723)

--*Ollie's Team Plays Biddy Baseball.* Philbrook, Clement E. (1917-). 1970. Hastings House. (P.723)

--*Rookie Catcher with the Atlanta Braves.* Jackson, Caary Paul (1902-). c.1966. Hastings. (P.484)

--*Rookie Running Back.* Hankin, Cliff. 1968. Vanguard Press. (P.410)

--*Soccer Goalie.* Etter, Lester Frederick (1904-). 1969. Hastings House. (P.310)

--*Touchdown for the Enemy.* McCormick, Wilfred F. (1903-). c.1965. Putnam. (P.597)

Chavarria, Luis

--*Stories of Clever Dogs: Old Stories and New.* Lloyd, Ernest, retold by. c.1924. Review and Herald Publishing Assn. (P.578)

Chavez, Edward

--*The Legend of Billy Bluesage.* Lauritzen, Jonreed (1902-). 1961. Little, Brown. **Award: (ALA).** (P.555)

--*Pines for the King's Navy.* 1st ed. Dietz, Lew (1907-). 1955. Little, Brown. (P.266)

Chee, Wendy Kim

--*I Like Poems and Poems Like Me.* Pagliaro, Penny, ed. 1977. Press Pacifica. (P.700)

Cheese, Bernard, jt. illus. see Francis, Frank.

Cheley, Frank Hobart (1889-)

--*Boy Riders of the Rockies: Or, Camping on Top of the World.* Cheley, Frank Hobart (1889-). c.1928. W. A. Wilde Company. (P.189)

--*Buffalo Roost.* Cheley, Frank Hobart (1889-). N.D. Abingdon Press. (P.189)

--*By Ember Glow: Stories Told By a Campfire.* Cheley, Frank Hobart (1889-). c.1937. W. A. Wilde Company. (P.189)

--*The Three Rivers Kids.* Cheley, Frank Hobart (1889-). c.1914. Jennings and Graham. (P.189)

Chen, Tony (1929-)

--*After Dark.* Budney, Blossom. 1975. Lothrop, Lee & Shepard. (P.147)

--*Breakfast with the Birds.* Evans, Doris Portwood. 1972. Putnam. (P.311)

--*The Cozy Book.* Hoberman, Mary Ann (1930-). 1982. Viking. (P.448)

--*Dakota Sons.* Distad, Audree. 1972. Harper & Row. (P.273)

--*Do You Know a Cat?.* Dale, Ruth Bluestone. 1968. L. W. Singer Co. (P.238)

--*The Fisherman's Son.* Ginsburg, Mirra (1919-), adapted by. c.1979. Greenwillow Books. (P.369)

--*Hello, Small Sparrow.* Johnson, Hannah Lyons. 1971. Lothrop, Lee & Shepard Co. (P.495)

--*Hello Small Sparrow.* Johnson, Hannah Lyons. 1970. William Morrow and Company. (P.495)

--*Honschi.* Glasgow, Aline. 1972. Parents' Magazine Press. (P.370)

--*In the City of Paris.* Green, Hannah. c.1985. Doubleday. (P.384)

--*In the Land of Small Dragon.* Clark, Ann Nolan, Mrs. (1896-). 1979. Viking Pr. (P.197)

--*In the Land of Small Dragon: A Vietnamese Folk Tale.* Kha, Dang Manh. Clark, Ann Nolan (1896-), as told to. 1979. Viking Press. (P.521)

--*Little Raccoon.* Noguere, Suzanne (1947-). 1981. HR&W. (P.684)

--*Little Rystu.* Ginsburg, Mirra (1919-). c.1978. Greenwillow Books. (P.369)

--*Once We Went on a Picnic.* Fisher, Aileen Lucia (1906-). 1975. Crowell. (P.328)

--*The Princess and the Admiral.* Pomerantz, Charlotte (1930-). 1974. Addison-Wesley. (P.731)

--*The Riddle of the Drum: A Tale from Tizapan, Mexico.* Aardema, Verna (1911-), retold by. 1979. Scholastic Inc. (P.1)

--*Run, Zebra, Run.* Chen, Tony (1929-). 1972. Lothrop, Lee & Shepard Co. (P.189)

--*Tales from Old China.* Chang, Isabelle Chin (1924-). 1969. Random House. (P.184)

--*There's a Train Going by My Window.* Kesselman, Wendy Ann. 1981. Doubleday. (P.520)

--*There's a Train Going By My Window.* Kesselman, Wendy Ann. 1982. Doubleday. (P.520)

--*To Stand Against the Wind.* Clark, Ann Nolan, Mrs. (1896-). 1978. Viking Press. (P.197)

--*Too Many Crackers.* Buckley, Helen Elizabeth (1918-). 1966. Lothrop, Lee & Shepard Co. (P.147)

--*The White Horse.* Hurd, Edith Thacher, Mrs. (1910-). 1970. Harper & Row. (P.475)

Chen, Tony (1929-) & DeLucia, Carlo

--*The Chocolate Book: A Sampler for Boys and Girls.* Hearn, Michael Patrick, selected by. c.1983. Caedmon. (P.428)

Cheney, Garnett

--*Daisy Dells: Rhymes and Verses.* Denton, Clara Janetta Fort, Mrs. c.1927. A. Whitman & Co. (P.258)

--*Tom Thumb.* Perrault, Charles (1628-1703). N.D. A. Whitman & Co. (P.719)

Cheney, Philip

--*Pearls of Fortune.* Lide, Alice Alison, Mrs. (1890-) & Johansen, Margaret Alison, Mrs. (1896-). 1931. Little, Brown, and Company. (P.571)

--*The Secret Empire: a Boy with La Salle.* Patterson, Henry W. c.1931. Coward-McCann, Inc. (P.710)

--*The Singing Sword: The Story of Sir Ogier the Dane.* Hyde, Mark Powell. 1930. Little, Brown, and Company. (P.478)

Cheng, Hou-Tien (1944-)

--*Six Chinese Brothers: An Ancient Tale.* Cheng, Hou-Tien. c.1979. Holt, Rinehart, and Winston. (P.190)

Cheng, Judith

--*Heaven's Reward: Fairy Tales from China.* Sadler, Catherine Edwards, retold by. 1985. Atheneum. (P.788)

--*Little Women.* Alcott, Louisa May (1832-1888). 1982. Wanderer Books. (P.17)

--*My Little Foster Sister.* Stanek, Muriel Novella (1915-1971). 1981. A. Whitman. (P.848)

--*The Nightingale and the Fool: An Ancient Tale from India.* Chase, Catherine. 1979. Dandelion Press. (P.188)

Cherin, Robin & Reyes, Roger J.

--*My Aunt Otilia's Spirits: Los Espiritus De Mi Tia Otilia.* Bilingual ed. Garcia, Richard (1941-). Guerrero Rea, Jesus, tr. 1978. Children's Book Pr. (P.354)

Chermayeff, Ivan (1932-)

--*Blind Mice and Other Numbers.* Chermayeff, Ivan (1932-). c.1961. Colorcraft. (P.190)

--*Ho for a Hat.* 1st ed. Smith, William Jay (1918-). 1964. Little, Brown and Co. (P.837)

--*Keep It Like a Secret.* 1st ed. Warburg, Sandol Stoddard (1927-). 1961. Little, Brown. (P.930)

--*The New Nutcracker Suite, and Other Innocent Verses.* Nash, Frederic Ogden (1902-1971). 1962. Little, Brown. (P.675)

--*Peter Pumpkin.* 1st ed. Ott, John. Coley, Peter, created by. 1963. Doubleday. (P.697)

--*The Thinking Book.* 1st ed. Warburg, Sandol Stoddard (1927-). 1960. Little, Brown. (P.930)

--*Three Languages.* Grimm, Jakob Ludwig Karl (1785-1863) & Grimm, Wilhelm Karl (1786-1859). 1983. Childrens Bk Co. (P.395)

Cherry, Lynne (1952-)

--*Emir's Education in the Proper Use of Magical Powers.* Roberts, Jane (1929-). 1979. Delacorte. (P.768)

--*Harriet and William and the Terrible Creature.* Carey, Valerie Scho. c.1985. Dutton. (P.167)

--*If I Were in Charge of the World and Other Worries: Poems for Children and Their Parents.* 1st ed. Viorst, Judith. 1981. Atheneum. (P.920)

--*Rabbit Travels.* McCormack, John E. 1984. Dutton. (P.596)

--*The Snail's Spell.* Ryder, Joanne. c.1981. F. Warne. (P.787)

--*When I'm Sleepy.* Howard, Jane R (1935-). c.1985. Dutton. (P.467)

Chesebrough, Thomas W

--*Aesop's Fables.* Aesopus. James, Thomas (1809-1867), ed. 1907. C. W. Bardeen. (P.13)

Chess, Victoria (1939-)

--*The Adventures of Stanley Kane.* Goldberg, Stan J. (1939-) & Chess, Victoria (1939-). 1973. Harcourt Brace Jovanovich. (P.373)

--*Alfred's Alphabet Walk.* Chess, Victoria (1939-). c.1979. Greenwillow Books. (P.190)

--*The Animals' Peace Day.* 1st ed. Wahl, Jan (1933-). 1970. Crown Publishers. (P.924)

--*Bim Dooley Makes His Move.* Schertle, Alice (1941-). 1984. Lothrop. (P.798)

--*Bugs: Poems.* Hoberman, Mary Ann (1930-). 1976. Viking Press. (P.448)

--*Cat and Dog and the ABC's.* Miller, Elizabeth Kubota (1932-) & Cohen, Jane. 1981. Watts. (P.647)

--*Cat and Dog and the Mixed-up Week.* Miller, Elizabeth Kubota (1932-) & Cohen, Jane. 1980. F. Watts. (P.647)

--*Cat and Dog Give a Party.* Miller, Elizabeth Kubota (1932-) & Cohen, Jane. 1980. F. Watts. (P.647)

--*Cat and Dog Have a Contest.* Miller, Elizabeth Kubota (1932-) & Cohen, Jane. 1980. F. Watts. (P.647)

--*Cat and Dog Have a Parade.* Miller, Elizabeth Kubota (1932-) & Cohen, Jane. c.1981. Watts. (P.647)

--*Cat and Dog Raise the Roof.* Miller, Elizabeth Kubota (1932-) & Cohen, Jane. 1980. Watts. (P.647)

--*Cat and Dog Take a Trip.* Miller, Elizabeth Kubota (1932-) & Cohen, Jane. 1980. Watts. (P.647)

--*Fletcher and Zenobia.* Chess, Victoria (1939-) & Gorey, Edward St. John (1925-). 1967. Meredith Press. (P.190)

--*Fletcher and Zenobia Save the Circus.* Gorey, Edward St. John (1925-). 1971. Dodd, Mead. (P.377)

--*The Great Frog Swap.* Roy, Ronald (1940-). c.1981. Pantheon Books. (P.782)

--*King Basil's Birthday.* Young, Miriam Burt (1913-1974). 1973. F. Watts. (P.990)

--*The King Who Could Not Sleep.* Elkin, Benjamin (1911-). 1975. Parents' Magazine Press. (P.301)

--*A Little Touch of Monster.* Lampert, Emily. c.1985. Atlantic Monthly Press. (P.546)

--*Lost in the Store.* Bograd, Larry (1953-). c.1981. Macmillan. (P.112)

--*Millicent the Monster.* Lystad, Mary Hanemann (1928-). 1973. Dial. (P.592)

--*Millicent the Monster.* Lystad, Mary Hanemann (1928-). 1968. H. Quist. (P.592)

--*Once Upon a Time Is Enough.* Stanton, Will (1918-). 1970. Lippincott. (P.849)

--*Peacocks Are Very Special.* Alexander, Sue (1933-). c.1976. Doubleday. (P.23)

--*Poor Esme.* Chess, Victoria (1939-). 1982. Holiday. (P.190)

--*The Queen of Eene.* Prelutsky, Jack. c.1978. Greenwillow Books. **Award: (ALA).** (P.737)

--*Rolling Harvey Down the Hill.* Prelutsky, Jack. c.1980. Greenwillow Books. (P.737)

--*The Sheriff of Rottenshot.* Prelutsky, Jack. 1982. Greenwillow. (P.737)

--*A Ship in a Storm on the Way to Tarshish.* Farber, Norma (1909-1984). c.1977. Greenwillow Books. (P.316)

--*Slugs.* 1st ed. Greenberg, David. c.1983. Little, Brown. (P.386)

--*Taking Care of Melvin.* Sharmat, Marjorie Weinman (1928-). c.1980. Holiday House. (P.815)

--*Tales for the Perfect Child.* Heide, Florence Parry (1919-). 1985. Lothrop, Lee & Shepard Books. (P.430)

--*The Twisted Witch and Other Spooky Riddles.* Adler, David A. (1947-). c.1985. Holiday House. (P.12)

--*Tyrannosaurus Wrecks.* Sterne, Noelle. 1983. Har-Row. (P.854)

--*Tyrannosaurus Wrecks: A Book of Dinosaur Riddles.* Sterne, Noelle. 1979. Har-Row. (P.854)

--*Which Is the Witch?.* Jasner, W. K., pseud. (1915-). Watson, Jane Werner. 1979. Pantheon. (P.490)

--*Which Is the Witch?.* Watson, Jane Werner (1915-). Jasner, W. K., pseud. c.1979. Pantheon Books. (P.936)

--*The Witch Mobile.* Young, Miriam Burt (1913-1974). 1969. Lothrop, Lee & Shepard Co. (P.990)

Chessare, Michele (1921-)

--*The Cardboard Crown.* Bulla, Clyde Robert (1914-). 1984. Har-Row. (P.148)

--*Mothkin Magic.* Tapp, Kathy Kennedy. 1983. Atheneum. (P.878)

--*My Friend the Monster.* Bulla, Clyde Robert (1914-). c.1980. Crowell. (P.149)

--*My Friend the Monster.* Bulla, Clyde Robert (1914-). 1980. Harper. (P.149)

--*The Owlstone Crown.* 1st ed. Kennedy, X. J, pseud. (1929-). Kennedy, Joseph Charles. 1983. Atheneum. (P.518)

--*Prisoner of Vampires.* Garden, Nancy (1938-). 1984. FS&G. (P.354)

--*Who Knew There'd Be Ghosts?.* Brittain, Bill. c.1985. HarpJ. (P.133)

Chesterman, Hugh

--*Mighty Men.* Farjeon, Eleanor (1881-1965). Barnes, C. C., intro. by. c.1926. D. Appleton and Company. (P.317)

Chestnut, Glenn

--*The Bartletts of Box B. Ranch.* Campbell, Camilla B. (1905-). 1949. Whittlesey House. (P.164)

--*Story Without an End.* Carove, Friedrich Wilhelm (1789-1852). Austin, Sarah Taylor, Mrs. (1793-1867), tr. from Ger. N.D. James Miller. (P.170)

Clifford, Judy

--*The Empty Window.* Bunting, Anne Evelyn (1928-). 1980. F. Warne. (P.150)

--*School Mouse & the Hamster.* Harris, Dorothy Joan (1931-). 1979. Warne. (P.415)

Clifford, Sandy

--*The Roquefort Gang.* Clifford, Sandy. 1981. Houghton. (P.202)

--*The Roquefort Gang.* Clifford, Sandy. 1981. Parnassus Press. (P.202)

--*The Smartest Person in the World.* Clifford, Sandy. 1979. Parnassus. (P.202)

Clifton, J. M.

--*Jeanne's House Party.* Colver, Alice Mary Ross, Mrs. (1892-). 1923. The Penn Publishing Company. (P.211)

Clifton, Lee

--*The Scout Who Led an Army.* Ballantyne, Lereine Hoffman, Mrs. (1891-1962). c.1963. St. Martin's. (P.66)

Climo, Lindee

--*Chester's Barn.* Climo, Lindee. 1982. Tundra Bks. **Award: (AFH).** (P.202)

Clinedinst, B. West

--*Chris, the Model Maker: A Story of New York.* Stoddard, William Osborn (1835-1925). 1894. D. Appleton and Company. (P.860)

--*The Half-Back: A Story of School, Football, and Golf.* Barbour, Ralph Henry (1870-1944). 1899. D. Appleton and Company. (P.70)

--*The Red Patriot: A Story of the American Revolution.* Stoddard, William Osborn (1835-1925). 1897. D. Appleton and Company. (P.860)

--*The Spy of Yorktown: A Story of Arnold and Washington in the Last Year of the War of Independence.* Stoddard, William Osborn (1835-1925). 1903. D. Appleton and Company. (P.860)

--*Success Against Odds: Or, How a Boy Made His Way.* Stoddard, William Osborn (1835-1925). 1898. D. Appleton and Company. (P.860)

--*The Windfall.* Stoddard, William Osborn (1835-1925). 1896. D. Appleton and Company. (P.860)

Clinton, Althea L., pseud., see Taylor, Alta Lucretia.

Cloete, Mildred

--*All Those Buckles.* Gaggin, Eva Roe, Mrs. (1879-). 1945. The Viking Press. (P.351)

Cloke, Rene

--*First Book of Hans Christian Andersen Stories.* Andersen, Hans Christian (1805-1875). 1979, c.1975. Derrydale Books. (P.36)

--*Little Folk's Book of Nursery Rhymes.* 1962. Warne. (P.203)

--*Little Folk's Book of Nursery Tales.* 1963. F. Warne. (P.203)

--*Little Folk's Second Book.* Burchell, Kate. 1967, c.1966. F. Warne. (P.151)

--*My First Picture Book of Baby Animals.* Cloke, Rene. c.1980. Derrydale Books. (P.203)

--*My First Picture Book of Fairy Tales.* Cloke, Rene. 1979. Derrydale Books. (P.203)

--*My First Picture Book of Nursery Rhymes.* Cloke, Rene. 1979. Derrydale Books. (P.203)

--*My First Picture Book of Poetry.* Cloke, Rene. c.1980. Derrydale Books. (P.203)

--*My First Picture Book of Telling the Time.* Cloke, Rene. 1979, c.1976. Derrydale Books. (P.203)

--*My First Picture Book of Zoo Animals.* Cloke, Rene. 1980. Derrydale Books. (P.203)

--*My Treasury of Rhymes.* Cloke, Rene. 1979, c.1974. Derrydale Books. (P.203)

--*Sleeping Beauty and Other Tales.* Green, Roger Gilbert Lancelyn (1918-). 1947. British Book Centre Inc. (P.385)

Cloud, Claude Carey (1899-)

--*The Story of Little Black Sambo.* Bannerman, Helen Brodie Cowan Watson, Mrs. (1863-1946). c.1934. Blue Ribbon Press. (P.69)

--*The Tale of Peter Rabbit.* Potter, Helen Beatrix (1866-1943). c.1934. Blue Ribbon Press. (P.734)

--*The Tale of Peter Rabbit.* Potter, Helen Beatrix (1866-1943). N.D. F. Warne. (P.734)

--*The Tale of Peter Rabbit.* Potter, Helen Beatrix (1866-1943). 1951. Frederick Warne & Co. (P.734)

Cloud, Claude Carey (1899-) & Lentz, Harold B.

--*Goldilocks and the Three Bears.* The Illustrated Pop-Up. The, Three Bears. c.1934. Blue Ribbon Press. (P.890)

--*Little Red Riding Hood.* 1934. Blue Ribbon Press. (P.203)

--*Little Red Riding-Hood.* Little Red Riddinghood. c.1934. Blue Ribbon Press. (P.203)

--*Puss in Boots.* Puss in Boots. c.1934. Blue Ribbon Press. (P.742)

Clough, James

--*After Midnight.* Keun, Irmgard (1909-). 1938. A. A. Knopf. (P.521)

Cloven, George & Cloven, Ruth

--*But Not Stanleigh.* Steiner, Barbara Annette (1934-). 1980. Childrens. (P.851)

--*Stanleigh's Wrong-Side-Out Day.* Steiner, Barbara Annette (1934-). c.1982. Childrens Press. (P.851)

Cloven, Ruth, jt. illus. see Cloven, George.

Clowes, Paul

--*The Bunch Quitter.* Patton, Don (1892-). 1935. Macrae Smith Company. (P.710)

Clymer, John F.

--*The Blue-Eyed God.* Rotch, Francis (1885-). 1938. The Caxton Printers, Ltd. (P.780)

Clyne, Barbara

--*Bedtime Stories.* Watts, Mabel Pizzey (1906-). c.1955. Rand McNally. (P.937)

Coalson, Glo (1946-)

--*Abby Takes Over.* La Farge, Phyllis. 1974. Lippincott. (P.543)

--*The Airship Ladyship Adventure.* Gathorne-Hardy, Jonathan G. (1933-). c.1977. Lippincott. (P.360)

--*At the Mouth of the Luckiest River.* Griese, Arnold Alfred (1921-). 1973. Crowell. (P.389)

--*Bright Fawn & Me.* Leech, Jay (1911-) & Spencer, Zane Ann (1935-). 1979. Har-Row. (P.561)

--*By Myself: Poems.* Hopkins, Lee Bennett (1938-), compiled By. 1980. Har-Row. (P.463)

--*Dexter.* Bulla, Clyde Robert (1914-). 1973. Crowell. (P.148)

--*An Eskimo Birthday.* Robinson, Tom D. 1975. Dodd, Mead. (P.770)

--*In a Bottle with a Cork on Top.* Skurzynski, Gloria Joan (1930-). c.1976. Dodd, Mead. (P.828)

--*The Long Hungry Night.* Foster, Elizabeth C. (1881-) & Williams, Slim. 1973. Atheneum. (P.338)

--*Morris and His Brave Lion.* Rogers, Helen Spelman. 1975. McGraw-Hill. (P.775)

--*On Mother's Lap.* Scott, Ann Herbert (1926-). 1972. McGraw-Hill. (P.804)

--*Operation Peeg.* Gathorne-Hardy, Jonathan G. (1933-). 1974. Harper. (P.360)

--*Operation Peeg.* Gathorne-Hardy, Jonathan G. (1933-). 1974, c.1972. Lippincott. (P.360)

--*That's the Way It Is, Amigo.* Colman, Hila. 1975. Crowell. (P.210)

--*Today We Are Brother & Sister.* Adoff, Arnold (1935-). 1981. Lothrop. (P.12)

--*The Wind Is Not a River.* Griese, Arnold Alfred (1921-). c.1978. Crowell. (P.389)

--*Windsong Summer.* Hass, Patricia Cecil. c.1978. Dodd, Mead. (P.419)

Coast, Roger

--*Two Guppies, a Turtle, and Aunt Edna.* Wyse, Lois Helene (1926-). 1966. World Pub. Co. (P.983)

Coates, George, jt. illus. see Lamb, Mildred R.

Coats, Alice Margaret (1905-)

--*The Story of Horace.* Coats, Alice Margaret (1905-). c.1939. Coward McCann, Inc. (P.204)

Cobb, Alma French

--*When I Was a Gay, Wee Child.* Cobb, Alma French. c.1942. The Kaleidograph Press. (P.205)

Cobb, Betty

--*Boy Who Saw an Alligator in His Bathtub.* Winkler, Richard. 1961. Steck-V. (P.969)

--*Buttons and His Sunday Coat.* Pearson, Wanda Lynn. 1959. Steck Co. (P.713)

Cobb, David

--*The Long Arctic Night.* Schmeltzer, Kurt. Brommer, Elizabeth, tr. from Ger. 1952. F. Watts. (P.800)

Cobb, David, jt. illus. see Main, Jean.

Cobb, David & Main, Jean

--*The Log of the Sardis.* 1st American ed. Nicholls, Frederick Francis (1926-). 1963, c.1962. Norton. (P.681)

Cobb, Diane

--*The Way Back.* Cobb, Diane. 1972. Sufism Reoriented. (P.205)

Cobb, Ruth

--*Dollies.* Hunter, Richard. N.D. Frederick A. Stokes Co. (P.475)

Cobbledick, Carol

--*Teen-Age Ghost Stories.* Furman, Abraham Loew (1902-), ed. 1961. Lantern Press. (P.350)

--*Teen-Age Ghost Stories.* Furman, Abraham Loew (1902-), ed. 1967. Lantern Press. (P.350)

Cober, Alan Edwin (1935-)

--*Aaron's Door.* 1st ed. Miles, Miska, pseud. (1899-). Martin, Patricia Miles. c.1977. Little, Brown. (P.645)

--*Beowulf: A New Telling.* Nye, Robert (1939-), ed. 1968. Hill and Wang. (P.688)

--*The Dark is Rising.* Cooper, Susan (1935-). 1973. Atheneum. **Awards: (BGH); (ALA); (JNM); (CMA).** (P.218)

--*Escape.* Hofman, Ota. Backer, Alice, tr. 1970. Knopf. (P.451)

--*Fire Plume: Legends of the American Indians.* Bierhorst, John William (1936-) & Schoolcraft, Henry Rowe (1793-1864), eds. 1969. Dial. (P.101)

--*The Fire Plume: Legends of the American Indians.* Schoolcraft, Henry Rowe (1793-1864) & Bierhorst, John William, eds. 1969. Dial Press. (P.801)

--*Giant Cold.* Dickinson, Peter (1927-). c.1984. Dutton. (P.265)

--*The Gumdrop Necklace.* La Farge, Phyllis. 1967. Knopf. (P.543)

--*Mister Corbett's Ghost.* Garfield, Leon (1921-). 1968. Pantheon Books. **Awards: (NYT).** (P.355)

--*Nothingatall, Nothingatall, Nothingatall.* Smith, Robert Paul (1915-1977). c.1965. Harper. (P.836)

--*Pigeon Man.* Abraham, Jean-Pierre. N.D. Quist. (P.4)

--*Some Things Weird & Wicked: 12 Stories to Chill Your Bones.* Kahn, Joan (1914-), ed. 1976. Pantheon. (P.504)

--*The Tale of a Black Cat.* Withers, Carl A. (1900-1970), adapted by. c.1966. Holt. (P.972)

--*The Tale of a Black Cat.* Withers, Carl A. (1900-1970), adapted by. 1973, c.1966. Holt. (P.972)

--*The Tiger's Bones, and Other Plays for Children.* 1st ed. Hughes, Ted (1930-), ed. 1974. Viking Press. (P.471)

--*Viollet.* Cunningham, Julia Woolfolk (1916-). 1966. Pantheon Books. (P.235)

--*The White Twilight.* 1st ed. Polland, Madeleine Angela Cahill (1918-). 1965, c.1962. Holt, Rinehart and Winston. (P.730)

--*The Wild Ducks and the Goose.* 1st ed. Withers, Carl A. (1900-1970), adapted by. 1968. Holt, Rinehart and Winston. (P.973)

--*Winter's Eve.* Belting, Natalia Maree (1915-). 1969. Holt, Rinehart, and Winston. **Award: (NYT).** (P.92)

Coberly, Elizabeth

--*The Blue Valentine.* newly illustrated. Schultz, Gwendolyn M. 1979, c.1965. Morrow. (P.802)

Coburn, Duncan

--*Come, Jack!.* McCulloch, Robert W. (1868-1946). 1946. Houghton Mifflin Company. (P.597)

--*The Sword Is Drawn.* Norton, Andre, pseud. (1912-). Norton, Alice Mary. Norton, Andre, pseud. 1944. Houghton Mifflin Company. (P.687)

Coburn, Frederick Simpson, et al. (1871-)

--*Boys of Other Countries.* Enl. ed. Taylor, Bayard (1825-1878). 1912. G. P. Putnam's Sons. (P.879)

Cocca-Leffler, Maryann (1958-)

--*Making Friends.* Daly, Kathleen N. c.1984. Parker Bros. (P.240)

--*Oh, So Silly!.* Schmeltz, Susan alton. 1984. Parent's Magazine Press. (P.800)

--*Thanksgiving at the Tappletons'.* Spinelli, Eileen (1942-). 1985, c.1982. Lippincott. (P.844)

Cochran, Bobbye A. (1949-)

--*The Magic Little Ones.* Bedell, Beverly. 1975. Follett. (P.87)

Cochran, Georgia Lee

--*Barnaby Bear and the Black Forest.* Battis, George. 1966. Marlbee Press. (P.80)

Cochran, J. T., jt. illus. see Higgins, Violet Moore.

Cochran, Wallace

--*Eddie Holds on.* Schantz, Daniel. c.1985. Standard Pub. (P.797)

--*Eddie's Impossible Friend.* Schantz, Daniel. c.1985. Standard Pub. (P.797)

--*Upside Down Eddie.* Schantz, Daniel. c.1985. Standard Pub. (P.797)

Cockburn, W. V, jt. illus. see Fitzgerald, William.

Cockerell, Olive

--*The Wind Fairies And Other Stories.* DeMorgan, Mary. N.D. Dutton. (P.256)

Cocks, Myra

--*The Princess with the Pea-Green Nose.* with illustrations by myra cocks. ed. Brabourne, Edward Hugessen Knatchbull-Hugessen (1829-1893). 1927. Harper & Brothers. (P.124)

CoConis, Constantinos see CoConis, Ted, pseud.

CoConis, Ted, pseud., see CoConis, Constantinos.

CoConis, Ted, pseud.

--*Backwards for Luck.* CoConis, Constantinos. Shura, Mary Francis (1923-). 1967. Knopf. (P.822)

--*The Golden God, Apollo.* CoConis, Constantinos. Gates, Doris (1901-). 1983. Penguin Books. (P.359)

--*The Golden God, Apollo.* 1st ed. CoConis, Constantinos. Gates, Doris (1901-). 1973. Viking Press. (P.359)

--*Lulu's Back in Town.* CoConis, Constantinos. Dean, Leigh. 1968. Funk & Wagnalls. (P.248)

--*Pickle.* CoConis, Constantinos. Terris, Susan (1937-). 1973. Four Winds Press. (P.887)

--*The Summer of the Swans.* CoConis, Constantinos. Byars, Betsy Cromer (1928-). c.1981. Puffin Books. (P.160)

--*The Summer of the Swans.* CoConis, Constantinos. Byars, Betsy Cromer (1928-). 1970. Viking Press. **Award: (JNM).** (P.160)

--*Ted and Bobby Look for Something Special.* CoConis, Constantinos. Quigg, Jane. 1969. Funk & Wagnalls. (P.745)

Codd, Michael

--*Chooki and the Ptarmigan.* Codd, Carol. 1976. Walker. (P.206)

--*King Midas.* Storr, Catherine Cole (1913-), retold by. 1985. Raintree Childrens Books. (P.863)

--*King Midas and His Gold.* Storr, Catherine Cole (1913-), retold by. 1986, c.1985. Torstar Books. (P.863)

--*The Trojan Horse.* Storr, Catherine Cole (1913-). c.1985. Raintree Childrens Books. (P.863)

Codd, Mike & Berry, Roland (1951-)

--*The Destruction of Troy.* Wilson, Robert. 1977. Rand. (P.967)

Codorniu, Federico, jt. illus. see Castellon, Federico.

Coe, Lloyd (1899-1976)

--*Boku and the Sound.* Coe, Lloyd (1899-1976). 1950. Thomas Y. Crowell. (P.206)

--*Boku and the Sound.* Coe, Lloyd (1899-1976). 1954. Thomas Y. Crowell Company. (P.206)

--*Charcoal.* Coe, Lloyd (1899-1976). 1946. Thomas Y. Crowell Company. (P.206)

--*Chris Turner, Magican.* Brady, James Thomas (1913-). 1954. Ariel Books. (P.125)

--*Chris Turner, Magician.* Brady, James Thomas (1913-). 1954. Farrar, Straus and Cudahy, Inc. (P.125)

--*Daniel and Drum Rock.* Simister, Florence Parker (1913-). c.1963. Hastings. (P.824)

--*Eric Duffy, American.* 1st ed. Anderson, Bertha Christiana (1887-). 1955. Little, Brown. (P.38)

--*The Fox Hollow Mystery.* Venn, Mary Eleanor (1908-). Adrian, Mary, pseud. 1959. Hastings House. (P.916)

--*The Girl in the Witch House.* Holberg, Ruth Langland, Mrs. (1891-). 1966. Hastings. (P.453)

--*Girl in the Witch House.* Holberg, Ruth Langland, Mrs. (1891-). 1966. Hastings. (P.453)

--*The Grist Mill Secret.* Albrecht, Lillie Vanderveer (1894-). 1962. Hastings House. (P.16)

--*Holding the Fort with Daniel Boone.* Meadowcroft, Enid La Monte, Mrs. (1898-1966). 1958. Crowell. (P.637)

--*Indian Horse Mystery.* Adrian, Mary, pseud. (1908-). Jorgenson, Mary Venn. 1966. Hastings. (P.12)

--*The Indian Horse Mystery.* Venn, Mary Eleanor (1908-). Adrian, Mary, pseud. c.1966. Hastings. (P.917)

--*The Junior Sheriff Mystery.* Venn, Mary Eleanor (1908-). Adrian, Mary, pseud. 1955. Ariel Books. (P.917)

--*Kite Mystery.* Adrian, Mary, pseud. (1908-). Jorgenson, Mary Venn. 1968. Hastings. (P.12)

--*The Kite Mystery.* Venn, Mary Eleanor (1908-). Adrian, Mary, pseud. 1968. Hasting House. (P.917)

--*Mystery of the Dinosaur Bones.* Adrian, Mary, pseud. (1908-). Jorgenson, Mary Venn. 1967. Hastings. (P.12)

--*The Mystery of the Dinosaur Bones.* Venn, Mary Eleanor (1908-). Adrian, Mary, pseud. c.1965. Hastings. (P.917)

--*Mystery of the Night Explorers.* Adrian, Mary, pseud. (1908-). Jorgenson, Mary Venn. 1962. Hastings. (P.12)

--*The Mystery of the Night Explorers.* Venn, Mary Eleanor (1908-). Adrian, Mary, pseud. 1962. Hastings House. (P.917)

--*Nate and the Traveling Store.* Holden, Elisabeth. 1962. Hastings House. (P.453)

--*On Indian Trails with Daniel Boone.* Meadowcroft, Enid La Monte, Mrs. (1898-1966). 1947. Thomas Y. Crowell Company. (P.637)

--*Pewter Plate.* Simister, Florence Parker (1913-). 1957. Hastings. (P.824)

--*Rare Stamp Mystery.* Adrian, Mary, pseud. (1908-). Jorgenson, Mary Venn. 1960. Hastings. (P.12)

--*The Rare Stamp Mystery.* Venn, Mary Eleanor (1908-). 1960. Hastings House. (P.917)

--*Skin Diving Mystery.* Adrian, Mary, pseud. (1908-). Jorgenson, Mary Venn. 1964. Hastings. (P.12)

--*St.* George and the Witches. Dunne, John William (1875-). c.1939. H. Holt and Company. (P.290)

--*Texas Star.* Meadowcroft, Enid La Monte, Mrs. (1898-1966). 1950. Crowell. (P.638)

--*Tinker's Tim and the Witches.* 1st ed. Anderson, Bertha Christiana (1887-). 1953. Little, Brown. (P.38)

--*Tom and the Redcoats.* Spratt, Barnett. 1963. Hastings House. (P.845)

--*Up & Down & Roundabout.* Parsons, Kitty. 1967. Golden Quill. (P.708)

--*Uranium Mystery.* Adrian, Mary, pseud. (1908-). Jorgenson, Mary Venn. 1956. Hastings. (P.12)

--*The Uranium Mystery.* Venn, Mary Eleanor (1908-). Adrian, Mary, pseud. 1956. Hastings House. (P.917)

--*William.* Alexander, Shirley. c.1941. Lothrop, Lee & Shepard Co. (P.23)

--*Fancy Free.* Bryant, Bernice Morgan (1908-). 1949. Bobbs-Merrill Co. (P.146)
--*Gard and Golden Boy.* Phelps, Margaret. 1950. Macrae-Smith. (P.723)
--*Jaro and the Golden Colt.* Phelps, Margaret. 1954. Macrae Smith Co. (P.723)
--*Ketch Dog.* Phelps, Margaret. 1951. Macrae Smith. (P.723)
--*Patricia's Secret.* 1st ed. Leinhauser, Ruth Daggett. 1956. Winston. (P.563)
--*Regular Cowboys.* Phelps, Margaret. 1948. Macrae Smith Co. (P.723)
--*Runaway Teen.* 1st ed. Finlayson, Ann (1925-). 1963. Doubleday. (P.326)
--*The Surprising Adventures of the Magical Monarch of Mo and His People.* Baum, Lyman Frank (1856-1919). 1947. Bobbs-Merrill Co. (P.82)
--*Territory Boy.* Phelps, Margaret. 1953. Macrae Smith. (P.723)
--*Toby on the Sheep Drive.* Phelps, Margaret. 1949. Macrae Smith Co. (P.723)
--*We Were There with Florence Nightingale in the Crimea.* Webb, Robert N. 1958. Grosset & Dunlap. (P.938)
--*Why the Chimes Rang & Other Stories.* Alden, Raymond Macdonald (1873-1924). N.D. Bobbs. (P.20)
--*Why the Chimes Rang: And Other Stories.* Alden, Raymond Macdonald (1873-1924). 1945. The Bobbs-Merrill Company. (P.20)
--*A World of Stories for Children: The Great Fairy, Folk Tales and Legends of the World from the Earliest Times to the Late Nineteenth Century.* Clark, Barrett Harper (1890-) & Jagendorf, Moritz Adolf (1888-1981), eds. 1947. Bobbs-Merrill Co. (P.197)

Copelman, Evelyn & Denslow, William Wallace (1856-1916)
--*The New Wizard of Oz.* Baum, Lyman Frank (1856-1919). 1944. The Bobbs-Merrill Company. (P.82)
--*The Wizard of Oz.* Baum, Lyman Frank (1856-1919). 1956. Grosset & Dunlap. (P.82)

Copley, Heather (1920-)
--*Drums and Trumpets: Poetry for the Youngest.* Clark, Leonard (1906-1981), ed. 1963, c.1962. Dufour. (P.198)
--*Drums & Trumpets: Poetry for the Youngest.* Clark, Leonard (1906-1981), ed. 1979. Merrimack Pub Cir. (P.198)
--*Tales of Ancient Egypt.* Green, Roger Gilbert Lancelyn (1918-), ed. 1972, c.1967. Penguin Bks. in Assn. with Bodley Head. (P.385)

Copley, Heather (1920-) & Chamberlain, Christopher (1918-)
--*Heroes of Greece & Troy.* Green, Roger Gilbert Lancelyn (1918-). 1961. Walck. (P.385)

Copping, Harold (1863-1932)
--*Children's Stories from Dickens.* Dickens, Mary Angela, ed. N.D. David McKay. (P.264)
--*A Madcap.* Smith, Elizabeth Thomasina Meade, Mrs. (1854-1914). 1904. Mershon Co. (P.832)
--*The Pilgrim's Progress.* Bunyan, John (1628-1688). N.D. Fleming H. Revell Co. (P.151)

Coquillot, Jean
--*Heidi Grows up.* Tritten, Charles. Spyri, Johanna Heusser, Mrs. (1827-1901), created by. c.1938. Grosset & Dunlap. (P.901)
--*Heidi Grows up.* Tritten, Charles. Spyri, Johanna Heusser, Mrs. (1827-1901), created by. 1966. Whitman Pub. Co. (P.901)

Corbett, Bertha L.
--*Little Dame Trot.* Byrne, Mary Agnes. 1904. Saalfield Publishing Co. (P.160)
--*The Overall Boys: A First Reader.* Grover, Eulalie Osgood (1873-1958). 1905. Rand, McNally & Company. (P.397)

Corbett, Grahame
--*Guess Who?.* Corbett, Grahame. 1982. Dial Bks Young. (P.219)
--*Who Is Hiding?.* Corbett, Grahame. 1982. Dial Bks Young. (P.219)
--*Who Is Next?.* Corbett, Grahame. 1982. Dial Bks Young. (P.219)
--*Who's Inside?.* Corbett, Grahame. 1982. Dial Bks Young. (P.219)

Corbett, Jennie & Fortnum, Peggy, pseud. (1919-)
--*Swings and Things.* Nuttal-Smith, Margaret Emily Noel. Winn, Alison, pseud. Wharmby, Margot. 1965. Rand McNally. (P.969)

Corbitt, Joan
--*Benji's Riddle Book.* 1982. Antioch Pub Co. (P.219)
--*The Gary Coleman Show: What If Elephants Had Pink Stripes?.* 1983. Antioch Pub Co. (P.219)
--*Is It Saturday Yet?.* Joke & Riddle Book. 1983. Antioch Pub Co. (P.219)

Corbould, jt. illus. see Godwin, James.

Corbould, A. C.
--*Dinglefield: Author of "Girls of the Square".* O'Reilly. N.D. George Routledge & Sons. (P.695)

Corbould, E. H. & Crowquill, Alfred
--*Mother Goose at Home.* N.D. George Routledge & Sons. (P.219)
--*Mother Goose Telling Stories.* N.D. George Routledge & Sons. (P.219)
--*Mother Goose's Fairy Tales: A Collection of all the Old Favorite Nursery Stories in Prose.* N.D. George Routledge & Sons. (P.219)

Corbould, Godwin & Corbould, Harvey
--*Fairy Tales of all Nations.* Planche, James Robinson (1796-1880), tr. N.D. George Routhledge & Sons. (P.219)

Corbould, Harvey, jt. illus. see Corbould, Godwin.

Corbould, Walton
--*Complete Version of the Three Blind Mice.* rev. ed. Ivimey, John William (1868-). 1928. Warne. (P.483)
--*Complete Version of Ye Three Blind Mice.* Ivimey, John William (1868-). 1979. F. Warne. (P.483)

Corcoran, Mark
--*The Brave Little Tailor.* Grimm, Jakob Ludwig Karl (1785-1863) & Grimm, Wilhelm Karl (1786-1859). c.1979. Troll Associates. (P.391)
--*The Mystery of the Rebellious Robot.* Corcoran, Mark. c.1979. Random House. (P.220)
--*Star Wars: The Mystery of the Rebellious Robot.* 1979. Random. (P.220)

Corcos, Loris
--*Patches.* Corcos, Loris. 1941. E. P. Dutton & Company, Inc. (P.220)

Corcos, Lucille (1908-1973)
--*Follow the Sunset.* 1st ed. Schneider, Herman (1905-) & Schneider, Nina (1913-). 1952. Doubleday. (P.800)
--*Joel Gets a Dog.* Corcos, Lucille (1908-1973). 1958. Abelard-Schuman. (P.220)
--*Joel Gets a Haircut.* Corcos, Lucille (1908-1973). 1952. Abelard Press. (P.220)
--*Joel Spends His Money.* Corcos, Lucille (1908-1973). 1954. Abelard-Schuman. (P.220)
--*The Little Lame Prince and The Adventures of a Brownie.* Craik, Dinah Maria Mulock, Mrs. (1826-1887). 1948. Grosset & Dunlap. (P.227)
--*The Little Lame Prince and the Adventures of a Brownie.* popular ed. Craik, Dinah Maria Mulock, Mrs. (1826-1887). N.D. Grosset & Dunlap. (P.227)

Cord, John V.
--*Two Gold Dolphins.* Beresford, Elisabeth. 1964. Bobbs. (P.95)

Cordoso, Rosemary
--*Tom Emperor of the Mountains.* Carja, Ion. 1979. Vantage. (P.168)

Corell, Richard
--*Abilene or Bust!* ... Gulick, Bill, pseud. (1916-) & Rothrock, Thomas. Gulick, Grover C.. 1946. Cupples & Leon Company. (P.399)

Corentin, Philippe
--*Story Number Three: For Children Over Three Years of Age.* Ionesco, Eugene (1912-). Vaughn, Ciba, tr. from Fr. 1971. H. Quist. (P.480)

Corey, Barbara
--*City Fun.* Hillert, Margaret (1920-). c.1981. Follett. (P.444)
--*Run to the Rainbow.* Hillert, Margaret (1920-). c.1981. Follett Pub. Co. (P.444)

Corey, Robert
--*Grandma's Gun.* Martin, Patricia Miles (1899-). 1968. Golden Gate Junior Books. (P.625)
--*Tomasito and the Golden Llamas.* Castellanos, Jane Mollie Robinson (1913-). 1968. Golden Gate Junior Books. (P.177)

Corkery, Glenys
--*Two Bunnykins Out to Sea.* Warrener. 1985. Viking. (P.934)

Cormack, Christopher
--*Carnival.* Menter, Ian. 1983. David & Charles. (P.641)
--*A Turkish Afternoon.* Bennett, Olivia. 1983. David & Charles. (P.94)

Cornwall, W. J., jt. illus. see Howard, M. Maitland.

Correas, Jose
--*The Little Mermaid.* Andersen, Hans Christian (1805-1875). Duffy, Marguerite R., retold by. 1966, c.1963. World Pub. Co. (P.36)
--*Nutcracker.* Latham, Jean Lee (1902-). c.1961. Bobbs-Merrill. (P.553)
--*Pinocchio.* Rouke, Eve, retold by. Lorenzini, Carlo (1826-1890). Collodi, Carlo, pseud. 1965. World Pub. Co. (P.584)
--*Robinson Crusoe.* Rouke, Eve, retold by. 1965. World Pub. Co. (P.780)
--*Snow White.* Grimm, Jakob Ludwig Karl (1785-1863) & Grimm, Wilhelm Karl (1786-1859). Miller, Doris R., pseud., ed. c.1965. World. (P.394)
--*The Timid Dragon: A Folktale from South America.* Selfridge, Barbara, retold by. c.1965. World. (P.809)
--*Tom Thumb.* Perrault, Charles (1628-1703). Miller, Doris R, retold by. c.1965. World. (P.719)
--*The Wolf and the Seven Little Goats.* Grimm, Jakob Ludwig Karl (1785-1863) & Grimm, Wilhelm Karl (1786-1859). Miller, Doris R., pseud., ed. c.1965. World. (P.395)

Correas, Jose, jt. illus. see Ramirez, Pablo.

Correas, Jose & Ramirez, Pablo
--*The Ugly Duckling, Goldilocks and the Three Bears, and The Little Red Hen.* Latham, Jean Lee (1902-), retold by. 1962. Bobbs-Merrill. (P.553)

Correll, Richard
--*Desolation Trail* ... Gulick, Bill, pseud. (1916-) & Rothrock, Thomas. Gulick, Grover C.. 1946. Cupples & Leon Company. (P.399)

Corrigan, Barbara (1922-)
--*Parents Keep Out: Elderly Poems for Youngerly Readers.* 1951. Little, Brown. (P.221)
--*The Story of Nursing.* Dodge, Bertha Sanford (1902-). 1954. Little, Brown. (P.276)
--*The White Elephant Mystery.* Queen, Ellery, Jr., pseud. & Lee, Manfred Bennington (1905-1971). Dannay, Frederic. 1950. Little, Brown. (P.744)
--*The Yellow Cat Mystery.* Queen, Ellery, Jr., pseud. & Lee, Manfred Bennington (1905-1971). Dannay, Frederic. 1952. Little, Brown. (P.744)

Corser, Joan D.
--*The Tales of Mannikin & Bubbikin.* Corser, Joan D. 1984. Vantage. (P.221)

Corsillo, George
--*Stories and Poems You Can Read to Your Grandchildren.* Kotler, Irma M. c.1974. Prince Communications. (P.536)

Corson, C. S.
--*The Boy Scouts in a Trapper's Camp.* Burgess, Thornton Waldo (1874-1965). N.D. Penn Publishilng Co. (P.153)
--*The Boy Scouts of Woodcraft Camp.* Burgess, Thornton Waldo (1874-1965). 1912. The Penn Publishing Company. (P.153)
--*The Boy Scouts on Lost Trail.* Burgess, Thornton Waldo (1874-1965). 1914. The Penn Publishing Company. (P.153)
--*The Boy Scouts on Swift River.* Burgess, Thornton Waldo (1874-1965). 1913. The Penn Publishing Company. (P.153)

Cort, Howard R.
--*Galopoff, the Talking Pony: A Story for Young Folks.* Jenks, Tudor (1857-1922). c.1901. Henry Altemus Company. (P.491)

Cortese, Edward F.
--*Bonny's Boy Returns.* Rechnitzer, Ferdinand Edsted (1894-). 1952. HR&W. (P.752)
--*A Boy for a Man's Job: The Story of the Founding of St. Louis.* 1st ed. Baker, Nina Brown, Mrs. (1888-1957). 1952. Winston. (P.64)
--*Lost Colony: The Mystery of Roanoke Island.* Bothwell, Jean (0000-1977). 1953. Winston. (P.119)
--*To the Shores of Tripoli: A Story of the United States Marines.* Briggs, Berta N. 1955. Winston. (P.131)

Corvus, John
--*Fiddlesticks Joins the Family.* Duncan, Cleo. 1964. United Church Press. (P.289)

Corwin, C. A.
--*The Enchanted Burro.* Lummis, Charles Fletcher (1859-1928). N.D. Doubleday, Page & Co. (P.590)

Corwin, Eleanor
--*The Animals' Train Ride.* Potter, Miriam Clark, Mrs. (1886-1965). c.1953. Rand McNally. (P.735)
--*Benjie Engie.* Devine, Louise Lawrence. 1950. Rand McNally & Co. (P.261)
--*Buddy, the Little Taxi.* Evers, Alf (1905-). N.D. Rand McNally. (P.313)
--*Hoppie the Hopper.* Baller, Albert. 1951. Rand McNally & Co. (P.67)
--*Little Lamb's Hat.* Phillips, Mary Hibbs Geisler, Mrs. (1881-1964). c.1952. Rand McNally. (P.724)
--*Number Nine, the Little Fire Engine.* Wadsworth, Wallace Carter (1894-1933). 1950. Rand McNally. (P.923)
--*Number Nine: The Little Fire Engine.* Wadsworth, Wallace Carter (1894-1933). N.D. Rand McNally. (P.923)
--*Number Nine, the Little Fire Engine.* Wadsworth, Wallace Carter (1894-1933). N.D. Rand McNally. (P.923)

Corwin, Eleanor & Brice, Tony
--*Pop-in, The Bunny.* Baller, Albert. N.D. Rand McNally. (P.67)

Corwin, Judith Hoffman (1946-)
--*Captain Kangaroo's Whole World Catalog.* Krayer, Jim, compiled by. c.1976. Platt & Munk. (P.539)
--*Red Light Says Stop!.* Rinkoff, Barbara Jean Rich (1923-1975). 1974. Lothrop. (P.765)

Corwin, June Atkin (1935-)
--*The Snow Queen.* Andersen, Hans Christian (1805-1875). Keigwin, R. P., tr. 1968, c.1950. Atheneum. (P.37)

Cory, Fanny Young
--*The Babes in the Wood.* Cory, Fanny Young. N.D. Bobbs-Merrill Co. (P.222)
--*The Book of Saints and Friendly Beasts.* Brown, Abbie Farwell (0000-1927). 1976. Core Collection Books. (P.137)
--*The Book of Saints and Friendly Beasts.* Brown, Abbie Farwell (0000-1927). 1900. Houghton, Mifflin and Co. (P.137)
--*The Enchanted Island of Yew: Whereon Prince Marvel Encountered the High Ki of Twi and Other Surprising People.* Baum, Lyman Frank (1856-1919). 1903. The Bobbs-Merrill Companyc. (P.81)
--*The Fairy Changeling.* Spofford, Harriet Elizabeth Prescott, Mrs. (1835-1921). 1911. R. G. Badger. (P.845)
--*The Fanny Cory Mother Goose.* Cory, Fanny Young. N.D. Bobbs-Merrill Co. (P.222)
--*The Fanny Cory Mother Goose: Mother Goose Rhymes and Jingles.* Mother Goose. c.1913. The Bobbs-Merrill Co. (P.667)
--*Five Little Peppers Abroad.* Lothrop, Harriet Mulford Stone, Mrs. (1844-1924). Sidney, Margaret, pseud. 1902. Lothrop Publishing Company. (P.586)
--*Jackieboy in Rainbowland.* Hill, William L. 1911. Rand McNally. (P.444)
--*Josey and the Chipmunk.* Reid, Sydney. 1900. The Century Co. (P.755)
--*Little Boy Blue.* Cory, Fanny Young. N.D. Bobbs-Merrill Co. (P.222)
--*Little Me: In Picture and Verse.* Cory, Fanny Young. c.1936. E. P. Dutton & Co., Inc. (P.222)
--*The Master Key.* Baum, Lyman Frank (1856-1919). N.D. Bobbs-Merrill Co. (P.82)
--*The Master Key.* Baum, Lyman Frank (1856-1919). 1901. Bowen-Merrill Co. (P.82)
--*The Master Key: An Electrical Fairy Tale.* Baum, Lyman Frank (1856-1919). 1976. Dover Publications. (P.82)
--*The Master Key: An Electrical Fairy Tale.* Baum, Lyman Frank (1856-1919). 1974. Hyperion Press. (P.82)
--*Nurse Norah's up-to-date Fairy Tales.* Flower, Elliott (1863-). 1903. J. Pott & Co. (P.333)
--*Our Baby Book.* Cory, Fanny Young. N.D. Bobbs-Merrill Company. (P.222)
--*The Pete & Polly Stories.* Wells, Carolyn (1869-1942). 1902. A. C. McClurg & Company. (P.944)
--*A Pocketful of Posies.* Brown, Abbie Farwell (0000-1927). 1902. Houghton, Mifflin and Company. (P.138)
--*The Queen's Page.* Baker, Cornelia McGhee, Mrs. (1855-). c.1905. The Bobbs-Merrill Company. (P.61)
--*Short Poems for Short People.* Aspinwall, Alicia Stuart, Mrs. c.1929. E. P. Dutton & Co., Inc. (P.53)
--*Sonny Sayings.* Cory, Fanny Young. N.D. E. P. Dutton & Co. (P.222)
--*Sunshine Annie.* Gates, Josephine Scribner, Mrs. (1859-1930). 1910. The Bobbs-Merrill Company. (P.360)
--*The Well in the Wood.* Taylor, Bert Leston (1866-1921). 1904. The Bobbs-Merrill Company. (P.879)
--*Yankee Enchantments.* Loomis, Charles Battell (1861-1911). 1900. McClure, Phillips & Co. (P.583)

Cory, Fanny Young, jt. illus. see Milner, Florence Cushman, Mrs.

Cory, Fanny Young & Varian, George
--*Lucy and Their Majesties, a Comedy in Wax.* Farjeon, Benjamin Leopold (1833-1903). 1904. The Century Co. (P.317)

Cosgrave, John O'Hara, II (1908-1968)
--*Carry on, Mr. Bowditch.* Latham, Jean Lee (1902-). 1955. Houghton Mifflin. **Awards: (JNM); (IBBY); (ALA).** (P.553)
--*The Child's Book of Folklore.* Emrich, Marion Vallat (1910-). Korson, George Gershon (1899-), ed. 1964. Dial Press. (P.307)
--*The Disappearance of Kit Shane.* Wadsworth, Leda A. (1901-). 1942. Rinehart & Co. (P.923)
--*Flashing Harpoons: The/Story Of Whales And Whaling.* Frank, R., Jr., pseud. (1914-). Ross, Frank Xavier. 1958. Thomas Y. Crowell. (P.341)
--*The Gnomobile: A Gnice Gnew Gnarrative with Gnonsense, but Gnothing Gnaughty.* Sinclair, Upton Beall (1878-1968). c.1938. Farrar & Rinehart, Incorporated. (P.826)
--*Picnic Adventures.* Gilman, Elizabeth L., et al., eds. c.1940. Farrar & Rinehart, Inc. (P.368)
--*Tall Ships.* 1st ed. Wilson, Hazel Hutchins, Mrs. (1898-). 1958. Little, Brown. (P.966)
--*Up Anchor!.* Aspden, Don. c.1941. R. M. McBride & Company. (P.53)
--*The Voyage of the Javelin.* 1st ed. Meader, Stephen Warren (1892-). 1959. Harcourt, Brace. (P.637)

Cosgrove, Alice
--*Cappy and the Jet Engine.* Bradley, Duane, pseud. (1914-). Sanborn, Duane. 1957. Lippincott. (P.125)

Cosgrove, Colleen B.
--*Cisco & the Twin Foals.* Field, Arthur W. 1983. Mills Pub Co. (P.324)
--*The Clean-up Crew.* Mills, Dorothy H. 1984. Mills Pub Co. (P.649)

Cosimini, Roland F.
--*Queen Dido's Treasure.* Glanville, Ada H. 1930. Little, Brown, and Company. (P.370)

--*Carcajou.* Montgomery, Rutherford George (1894-). N.D. Reilly & Lee Co. (P.658)
--*Carcajou.* Montgomery, Rutherford George (1894-). 1936. The Caxton Printers, Ltd. (P.658)
--*City Dog.* Raftery, Gerald Bransfield (1905-). 1953. Morrow. (P.747)
--*The Day the Indians Came.* Rydberg, Ernie, pseud. (1901-). Rydberg, Ernest Emil. 1964. D. McKay Co. (P.786)
--*The High Trail.* Koch, Elers. 1953. Caxton Publishers. (P.534)
--*Rockets at Dawn.* Coleman, Earl S (1910-). 1954. Longmans, Green. (P.208)
--*Sandlappers.* Rutherford, Anworth (1877-). 1935. The Caxton Printers, Ltd. (P.786)
--*Sheba, a Grizzly Bear.* Franklin, George Cory (1872-). 1953. Ariel Books. (P.342)
--*Sierra Quest.* 1st ed. Coleman, Earl S (1910-). 1953. Longmans, Green. (P.208)
--*Son of Monte.* Franklin, George Cory (1872-). 1956. Houghton Mifflin. (P.342)
--*Tricky: The Adventures of a Red Fox.* Franklin, George Cory (1872-). 1949. Houghton Mifflin Co. (P.342)
--*Tuffy.* Franklin, George Cory (1872-). 1954. Houghton Mifflin. (P.342)
--*Yellow Eyes.* Montgomery, Rutherford George (1894-). 1932. Caxton Printers. (P.659)
--*Yellow Eyes.* Montgomery, Rutherford George (1894-). 1936. Reilly & Lee Co. (P.659)
--*Zorra: A Fox of the Mountains.* Franklin, George Cory (1872-). 1957. Houghton Mifflin. (P.342)

Cramer, Marie (1887-)
--*The Diamond Princess.* Cramer, Marie (1887-). Hart, John G., tr. c.1931. F. Warne & Co., Inc. (P.228)

Cramer, Rie
--*Favourite French Fairy Tales: Retold from the French of Perrault, Madame D'Aulnoy and Madame Le Prince De Beaumont.* Douglas, Barbara, retold by. Perrault, Charles (1628-1703) & Aulnoy, Marie Catherine Jumelle de Berneville (1650-1705). c.1921. Dodd, Mead & Company. (P.719)
--*Grimm's Fairy Tales.* Grimm, Jakob Ludwig Karl (1785-1863) & Grimm, Wilhelm Karl (1786-1859). Olcott, Frances Jenkins, ed. 1922. The Penn Publishing Company. (P.392)
--*Oriental Fairy Tales.* Arnold, Edwin, Sir (1832-1904), ed. 1923. Duffield & Company. (P.49)
--*The Princess Who Grew.* De Vries, P. J. Cohen. Snitslaar, L., tr. 1927. Frederick A. Stokes Company. (P.261)
--*The Princess Who Grew.* De Vries, P. J. Cohen. Snitzlaar, L., tr. N.D. J. B. Lippincott. (P.261)

Cramer, Rie & Berkowitz, Jeannette
--*Favorite Fairy Tales.* Osborne, Margherita Osborn Cassino, Mrs. (1878-), ed. c.1930. The Penn Publishing Company. (P.697)

Cramer, Vivien Whatmough
--*When I Visit Daddy or Daddy Visits Me.* Gustar, Susan Wakeling (1949-). 1973. S.N. (P.400)

Cramp, Walter Samuel (1867-)
--*He Who Steals (Colui Che Ruba).* A Story for the Young. Baiocco, Alfredo. c.1922. E. P. Dutton & Company. (P.61)

Crampton, Rollin
--*The Alo Man: Stories from the Congo.* Chadwick, Mara Louise Pratt, Mrs. & Lamprey, Louise (1869-1951), eds. 1921. World Book Company. (P.181)

Crandall, C. Leslie
--*The Adventures of Jack & Jill.* Randolph, Clare. 1948. Hollow-Tree House. (P.748)
--*The Bandana Bunny.* McBain, Rhoda. c.1949. Hollow-Tree House. (P.594)
--*Buzzita.* McBain, Rhoda. 1948. Hollow Tree House. (P.594)
--*Nautical Ned.* Randolph, Clare. 1948. Hollow Tree House. (P.748)
--*The Truant Tricycle.* Marion, Francis (1886-1973). c.1948. Hollow Tree House. (P.620)

Crane, Alan H. (1901-)
--*A Carpet of Flowers.* De Trevino, Elizabeth Borton (1904-). 1955. Crowell. (P.260)

Crane, Donn
--*The Adventures of Five Little Scamps: Told.* Crane, Donn. N.D. A. Whitman & Co. (P.228)

Crane, Fisher
--*Grimms' Fairy Tales.* Grimm, Jakob Ludwig Karl (1785-1863) & Grimm, Wilhelm Karl (1786-1859). Crane, Lucy, tr. N.D. D. Lothrop Co. (P.392)

Crane, Lucy (1842-1882)
--*Rumpelstiltskin.* Grimm, Jakob Ludwig Karl (1785-1859) & Grimm, Wilhelm Karl (1785-1863). 1974. Scholastic Inc. (P.394)

Crane, Olive
--*The Flamp: The Ameliorator, and The Schoolboy's Apprentice.* Lucas, Edward Verrall (1868-1938). 1927. Frederick A. Stokes Company. (P.589)

Crane, Stephen (1871-1900) & Shaw, Charles (1941-)
--*The Red Badge of Courage.* Wright, Betty Ren, adapted by. c.1981. Raintree Publishers. (P.980)

Crane, Thomas (1843-) & Houghton, Ellen K. Bolton
--*Abroad.* 1882. M. Ward & Co. (P.228)

Crane, Walter, jt. illus. see Brooke, Leonard Leslie.

Crane, Walter, jt. illus. see DeMorgan, William Frend.

Crane, Walter (1845-1915)
--*The Adventures of Herr Baby.* Molesworth, Mary Louisa Stewart, Mrs. (1842-1921). 1886. Macmillan & Co. (P.653)
--*The Alphabet Bee.* N.D. George Routledge & Sons. (P.229)
--*The Annotated Mother Goose.* Mother Goose. Baring-Gould, William Stuarty (1913-1967) & Baring-Gould, Ceil, annotations by. 1962. Crown. (P.667)
--*The Baby's Opera.* 1981. S&S. (P.229)
--*Beauty and the Beast Picture Book: Containing: Beauty and the Beast, The Frog Prince, The Hind in the Wood.* Crane, Walter (1845-1915). 1911. Dodd Mead & Co. (P.229)
--*The Blue-Beard Picture Book.* N.D. George Routledge & Sons. (P.229)
--*A Book of Christmas Verse.* Beeching, H. C., ed. Crane, Walter, designed by. N.D. Dodd, Mead & Co. (P.88)
--*Bric-a-Brac Stories.* Harrison, Constance Cary Burton, Mrs. (1846-1920). N.D. Charles Scribner's Sons. (P.417)
--*Carrots: Just a Little Boy.* Molesworth, Mary Louisa Stewart, Mrs. (1842-1921). N.D. A. L. Burt Company. (P.653)
--*Carrots: Just a Little Boy.* Molesworth, Mary Louisa Stewart, Mrs. (1842-1921). 1921. Macmillan Co. (P.653)
--*Carrots: Just a Little Boy and A Christmas Child.* Molesworth, Mary Louisa Stewart, Mrs. (1842-1921). 1893. Macmillan and Co. (P.653)
--*Carrots: Just a Little Boy.* Molesworth, Mary Louisa Stewart, Mrs. (1842-1921). 1957. St Martin's Press. (P.653)
--*Chattering Jack Picture Book.* N.D. George Routledge & Sons. (P.229)
--*The Children of the Castle.* Molesworth, Mary Louisa Stewart, Mrs. (1842-1921). 1890. Macmillan. (P.653)
--*The Children's Plutarch: Tales of the Greeks.* Plutarchus & Gould, Frederick James (1855-). 1910. Harper & Brothers. (P.729)
--*The Children's Plutarch: Tales of the Romans.* Gould, Frederick James (1855-). 1910. Harper & Brothers. (P.379)
--*A Christmas Child.* Graham, Ennis, pseud. (1842-). Molesworth, Mary Louisa Stewart. N.D. Macmillian. (P.380)
--*A Christmas Child: A Sketch of a Boy-life.* Molesworth, Mary Louisa Stewart, Mrs. (1842-1921). 1896. Macmillan & Co. (P.653)
--*A Christmas Posy.* Molesworth, Mary Louisa Stewart, Mrs. (1842-1921). 1888. Macmillan. (P.653)
--*Cinderella Picture Book.* 1911. Dodd, Mead & Co. (P.229)
--*The Cuckoo Clock.* Molesworth, Mary Louisa Stewart, Mrs. (1842-1921). N.D. A. L. Burt. (P.654)
--*The Cuckoo Clock.* Molesworth, Mary Louisa Stewart, Mrs. (1842-1921). 1921. Macmillan Company; Etc., Etc. (P.654)
--*The Cuckoo Clock.* Molesworth, Mary Louisa Stewart, Mrs. (1842-1921). N.D. MacMillan & Co. (P.654)
--*The Cuckoo Clock.* Molesworth, Mary Louisa Stewart, Mrs. (1842-1921). N.D. Macmillan. (P.654)
--*The Cuckoo Clock and The Tapestry Room.* Molesworth, Mary Louisa Stewart, Mrs. (1842-1921). Bull, Angela, pref. by. 1976. Garland Pub. (P.654)
--*The Cuckoo Clock and The Tapestry Room.* Molesworth, Mary Louisa Stewart, Mrs. (1842-1921). 1893. Macmillan and Co. (P.654)
--*The Cuckoo Clock and the Tapestry Room.* Molesworth, Mary Louisa Stewart, Mrs. (1842-1921). 1904. The Macmillan Company. (P.654)
--*Don Quixote of the Mancha.* Cervantes Saavedra, Miguel de (1547-1616). Parry, Judge, ed. N.D. Dodd. (P.180)
--*Four Winds Farm.* Molesworth, Mary Louisa Stewart, Mrs. (1842-1921). 1886. Macmillan. (P.654)
--*The Frog Prince: And Other Stories.* Grimm, Jakob Ludwig Karl (1785-1863) & Grimm, Wilhelm Karl (1786-1859). 1981. Smith Pubs. (P.392)
--*Goody Two Shoes Picture Book.* 1911. Dodd, Mead & Co. (P.229)
--*Grandmother Dear.* Molesworth, Mary Louisa Stewart, Mrs. (1842-1921). 1878. MacMillan Bks. (P.654)
--*Grandmother Dear.* Molesworth, Mary Louisa Stewart, Mrs. (1842-1921). N.D. MacMillan & Co. (P.654)
--*Grandmother Dear and Two Little Waifs.* Molesworth, Mary Louisa Stewart, Mrs. (1842-1921). 1893. Macmillan and Co. (P.654)
--*Grimm's Fairy Tales.* Grimm, Jakob Ludwig Karl (1785-1863) & Grimm, Wilhelm Karl (1786-1859). N.D. MacMillan & Co. (P.392)
--*Grimm's Household Stories.* Grimm, Jakob Ludwig Karl (1785-1863) & Grimm, Wilhelm Karl (1786-1859). Crane, Lucy, tr. N.D. Worthington Company. (P.393)
--*The Happy Prince, and Other Tales.* Wilde, Oscar Fingal O'Flahertie Wills (1854-1900). N.D. Robert's Brothers. (P.959)
--*Household Stories.* Grimm, Jakob Ludwig Karl (1785-1863) & Grimm, Wilhelm Karl (1786-1859). Crane, Lucy (1842-1882), tr. 1966. McGraw-Hill. (P.393)
--*Household Stories.* Grimm, Jakob Ludwig Karl (1785-1863) & Grimm, Wilhelm Karl (1786-1859). Crane, Lucy (1842-1882), tr. from Ger. 1923. The Macmillan Company. (P.393)
--*Household Stories.* Grimm, Jakob Ludwig Karl (1785-1863) & Grimm, Wilhelm Karl (1786-1859). N.D. Peter Smith Publisher, Inc. (P.393)
--*Household Stories: From the Collection of the Brothers Grimm.* Grimm, Jakob Ludwig Karl (1785-1863) & Grimm, Wilhelm Karl (1786-1859). Crane, Lucy (1842-1882), tr. 1883. John W. Lovell Company. (P.393)
--*Household Stories from the Collection of the Brothers Grimm.* Grimm, Jakob Ludwig Karl (1785-1863) & Grimm, Wilhelm Karl (1786-1859). Crane, Lucy (1842-1882), tr. N.D. Macmillan. (P.393)
--*Household Stories from the Collection of the Brothers Grimm.* Grimm, Jakob Ludwig Karl (1785-1863) & Grimm, Wilhelm Karl (1786-1859). Crane, Lucy (1842-1862), tr. N.D. T. Y. Crowell & Co. (P.393)
--*Household Stories from the Collection of the Brothers Grimm.* Grimm, Jakob Ludwig Karl (1785-1863) & Grimm, Wilhelm Karl (1786-1859). Crane, Lucy (1842-1882), tr. 1966. University Microfilms. (P.393)
--*Household Stories of the Brothers Grimm.* Grimm, Jakob Ludwig Karl (1785-1863) & Grimm, Wilhelm Karl (1786-1859). Crane, Lucy, tr. 1886. Dover. (P.393)
--*King Luckieboy Picture Book.* N.D. George Routledge & Sons. (P.229)
--*Little Miss Peggy: Only a Nursery Story.* Molesworth, Mary Louisa Stewart, Mrs. (1842-1921). 1887. Macmillan. (P.654)
--*The Magic of Kindness: Or, The Wondrous Story of the Good Huan.* Mayhew, Henry (1812-1887) & Mayhew, Augustus Septimus (1826-1875). 1869. Cassell, Petter, and Galpin. (P.634)
--*Magic of Kindness: Or, The Wondrous Story of the Good Huan.* Mayhew, Henry (1812-1887) & Mayhew, Augustus Septimus (1826-1875). 1882. Harper's. (P.634)
--*The Marquis of Carabas Picture Book.* N.D. George Routledge & Sons. (P.229)
--*Mr.* Michael Mouse Unfolds His Tale. Crane, Walter (1845-1915). 1975. Merrimack. **Award: (NYT).** (P.229)
--*The Musical Cinderella.* Routledge, William. Parker, Louis N., contrib. by. N.D. George Routledge & Sons. (P.781)
--*Old Mother Hubbard Picture Book: Containing: Old Mother Hubbard, The Three Bears, The Absurd ABC.* Crane, Walter (1845-1915). 1911. Dodd Mead & Co. (P.229)
--*The Old Nursery Rhymes: Or, the Merry Heart, 1 of 4 vols.* Crane, Walter (1845-1915). N.D. Cassell, Petter, Galpin. (P.229)
--*The Rectory Children.* Molesworth, Mary Louisa Stewart, Mrs. (1842-1921). 1889. MacMillan Bks. (P.654)
--*Robin Hood.* Henry, Gilbert. N.D. Frederick A. Stokes. (P.433)
--*Rosy.* Molesworth, Mary Louisa Stewart, Mrs. (1842-1921). 1882. MacMillan Bks. (P.654)
--*The Sleeping Beauty Picture Book: Containing: Bluebeard, The Baby's Own Alphabet, The Sleeping Beauty.* Crane, Walter (1845-1915). 1911. Dodd Mead & Co. (P.229)
--*The Song of Sixpence Toy Book.* N.D. George Routledge & Sons. (P.229)
--*Tell Me a Story.* Molesworth, Mary Louisa Stewart, Mrs. (1842-1921). N.D. MacMillan & Co. (P.654)
--*Tell Me a Story and the Adventures of Herr Baby.* Molesworth, Mary Louisa Stewart, Mrs. (1842-1921). 1893. Macmillan and Co. (P.654)
--*Tempest: Temple Shakespeare for Children.* Hoffman, Alice Spencer, retold by. N.D. E P Dutton & Co. (P.450)
--*This Little Pig Picture Book: Containing: This Little Pig, The Fairy Ship, King Luckie Boys Party.* Crane, Walter (1845-1915). 1911. Dodd Mead & Co. (P.229)
--*The Three Bears Picture Book.* N.D. George Routledge & Sons. (P.229)
--*Two Little Waifs.* Molesworth, Mary Louisa Stewart, Mrs. (1942-1921). 1883. MacMillan Bks. (P.654)
--*Walter Crane's Picture Book.* 1903. Cupples & Leon. (P.229)
--*A Wonder Book for Girls & Boys.* Hawthorne, Nathaniel (1804-1864). 1893, c.1892. Houghton, Mifflin. (P.424)
--*Wonder Book for Girls and Boys.* Hawthorne, Nathaniel (1804-1864). 1902. Houghton, Mifflin and Company. (P.424)

Crane, Walter (1845-1921)
--*Us,.* An Old-Fashioned Story. Molesworth, Mary Louisa Stewart, Mrs. (1842-1921). 1885. Harper & Brothers. (P.654)

Crane, Walter (1845-1915) & Brooke, Leonard Leslie (1862-1940)
--*Carrots and A Christmas Child, 1 of 10 Vols.* Molesworth, Mary Louisa Stewart, Mrs. (1842-1921). N.D. Macmillian & Co. (P.653)
--*The Children of the Castle, and Four Winds Farm, 1 of 10 Vols.* Molesworth, Mary Louisa Stewart, Mrs. (1842-1921). N.D. Macmillian & Co. (P.653)
--*Christmas-Tree Land, and A Christmas Posy, 1 of 10 Vols.* Molesworth, Mary Louisa Stewart, Mrs. (1842-1921). 1884. Macmillian & Co. (P.654)
--*Grandmother Dear, and Two Little Waifs, 1 of 10 Vols.* Molesworth, Mary Louisa Stewart, Mrs. (1842-1921). N.D. Macmillian. (P.654)
--*Little Miss Peggy, and Nurse Heather-Dale's Story, 1 of 10 Vols.* Molesworth, Mary Louisa Stewart, Mrs. (1842-1921). N.D. Macmillian & Co. (P.654)
--*Rosy, and The Girls and I, 1 of 10 Vols.* Molesworth, Mary Louisa Stewart, Mrs. (1842-1921). N.D. Macmillian & Co. (P.654)
--*Tell Me a Story, and The Adventures of Herr Baby, 1 of 10 Vols.* Molesworth, Mary Louisa Stewart, Mrs. (1842-1921). N.D. Macmillian & Co. (P.654)
--*Us, and the Rectory Children, 1 of 10 Vols.* Molesworth, Mary Louisa Stewart, Mrs. (1842-1921). N.D. MacMillan & Co. (P.655)

Crane, Walter (1845-1915) & Jacomb-Hood, George Percy (1857-1929)
--*The Happy Prince, and Other Stories.* Wilde, Oscar Fingal O'Flahertie Wills (1854-1900). 1968. Dent. (P.959)
--*The Happy Prince: And Other Tales.* Wilde, Oscar Fingal O'Flahertie Wills (1854-1900). 1967. University Microfilms. (P.959)

Crane, Walter (1845-1915) & Simon, E. M.
--*The Annotated Mother Goose, Nursery Rhymes Old and New.* Mother Goose. Baring-Goould, William Stuart (1913-1967) & Baring-Gould, Ceil, eds. c.1962. C. N. Potter. (P.667)

Crane, Walter (1845-1915) & Wehnert, Edward H.
--*Grimm's Fairy Tales.* Grimm, Jakob Ludwig Karl (1785-1863) & Grimm, Wilhelm Karl (1786-1859). N.D. Donohue, Henneberry & Co. (P.392)

Crank, Bess Bethell & Wuenscher, N. G.
--*Prairie Dogs' Pranks.* Paddock, Anna Georgia. c.1931. The Bethany Press. (P.700)

Cranstoun, Margaret A.
--*Let's Look at the Letters.* Cranstoun, Margaret A. 1967. Holt, Rinehart & Winston. (P.229)

Crapster, Katherine
--*The Gallant Five.* 1st ed. Siksek, Henrietta. 1963. R. B. Luce. (P.823)

Crawford, Bill, pseud., see Crawford, William Hulfish.

Crawford, Bill, pseud. (1913-1982)
--*The Bear & the Beaver.* Crawford, William Hulfish. Frankel, Charles (1917-1979). 1951. Sloane. (P.342)
--*The Bear and the Beaver.* Crawford, William Hulfish. Frankel, Charles (1917-1979). N.D. William Morrow & Co. (P.342)
--*Mickey, the Horse That Volunteered.* Crawford, William Hulfish. Glick, Carl Cannon (1890-1971) & O'Banion, Ansel E., pseud. (1913-1982). Crawford, William Hulfish. 1945. Whittlesey House, McGraw-Hill Book Company, Inc. (P.371)
--*Mickey Wins His Feathers.* Crawford, William Hulfish. Glick, Carl Cannon (1890-1971). 1948. Whittlesey House. (P.371)
--*Valery.* Crawford, William Hulfish. Conger, Elizabeth Mallett. 1944. H. Holt and Company. (P.213)

Crawford, Earl Stetson
--*Freckles.* Porter, Geneva Grace Stratton, Mrs. (1863-1924). 1904. Doubleday. (P.732)
--*Viviette.* Locke, William J. N.D. John Lane. (P.579)

Crawford, Elizabeth D. & Zwerger, Lisbeth
--*Hansel & Gretel.* Grimm, Jakob Ludwig Karl (1785-1863) & Grimm, Wilhelm Karl (1786-1859). 1983. Neugebauer Pr. (P.393)

--*Pong Choolie, You Rascal--!.* 1st ed. Crockett, Lucy Herndon (1914-). 1951. Holt. (P.231)
--*Pong Choolie, You Rascal.* Crockett, Lucy Herndon (1914-). 1966. HR&W. (P.231)
--*Teru: A Tale of Yokohama.* Crockett, Lucy Herndon (1914-). 1950. Holt. (P.231)
--*That Mario.* Crockett, Lucy Herndon (1914-). c.1940. H. Holt and Company. (P.231)
--*Uncle Bouqui of Haiti.* Courlander, Harold (1908-). 1942. W. Morrow. (P.224)

Crockford, J. J.
--*Tony Behind the Scenes: A Story of the Theatre.* Elder, Michael Aiken (1931-). N.D. Transatlantic. (P.300)

Crofut, Susan
--*The Moon on the One Hand: Poetry in Song.* Crofut, William E., III (1934-). Cooper, Kenneth, frwd. by. 1975. Atheneum. **Award: (ALA).** (P.231)

Croll, Carolyn
--*The Bear on the Doorstep.* Flory, Jane Trescott (1917-). 1980. Houghton Mifflin. (P.332)
--*The Big Balloon Race.* Coerr, Eleanor Beatrice (1922-). c.1981. Harper & Row. (P.206)
--*Ramshackle Roost.* Flory, Jane Trescott (1917-). 1972. Houghton Mifflin. (P.332)
--*Too Many Babas.* Croll, Carolyn. 1979. Har-Row. (P.231)
--*The Unexpected Grandchildren.* Flory, Jane Trescott (1917) 1977. Houghton Mifflin (P.332)
--*We'll Have a Friend for Lunch.* Flory, Jane Trescott (1917-). 1974. Houghton Mifflin. (P.332)

Croly, Donald
--*Eye of the Changer: A Northwest Indian Tale.* Ringstad, Muriel E. c.1984. Alaska Northwest Pub. Co. (P.765)

Crombie, Ruth
--*Christopher, the Canary.* Crombie, Ruth. 1935. Whitman Publishing Co. (P.231)

Crombie, Steven
--*The Missing Room & Other Mysteries to Solve.* Lee, Marian (1946-). 1984. Childrens. (P.560)

Crommelynck, Landa
--*Perrault's Fairy Tales.* Perrault, Charles (1628-1703). Moorsom, Sasha, tr. 1972. Doubleday. (P.719)

Crompton, Paul
--*The Good Samaritan.* Storr, Catherine Cole (1913-). 1983. Raintree Pubs. (P.863)

Croome, William H.
--*City Cries: Or, A Peep at Scenes in Town.* An Observer. 1851. G. S. Appleton. (P.34)
--*The Poor Woodcutter and Other Stories.* Arthur, Timothy Shay (1809-1885). 1860. J. B. Lippincott & Co. (P.50)

Crosby, Adelaide Upton, jt. illus. see Clark, Susan H. Mrs., Mrs.

Crosby, Alexander L. (1906-1980)
--*Crazy to Be Alive in Such a Strange World: Poems About People.* Larrick, Nancy (1910-), selected by. 1977. M Evans. (P.552)

Crosby, R. M.
--*Deuces Wild.* MacGrath, Harold. N.D. Bobbs-Merrill Co. (P.602)

Crosby, Sara
--*Helen's Babies.* Holiday ed. Habberton, John (1842-1921). 1905. H M Caldwell Co. (P.401)

Cross, Elizabeth & Congdon, Allen
--*From the Jungle to the Zoo.* Person, Charles. c.1933. Stephen Daye Press. (P.720)

Cross, Genevieve Marion (1910-)
--*Fluff and the Fireman: A Story.* Cross, Genevieve Marion (1910-). c.1947. Cross Publications. (P.232)

Cross, Peter
--*Silly Games.* Lloyd, David (1945-). 1985. Random House. (P.578)
--*The Terrible Thing.* Lloyd, David (1945-). 1985. Random House. (P.578)
--*Trouble for Trumpets.* Cross, Peter. 1985. Random. (P.232)

Cross, Peter, et al.
--*The Sesame Street ABC Storybook: Featuring Jim Henson's Muppets.* Moss, Jeffrey & Stiles, Norman. 1974. Random House. (P.667)

Croswell, Volney
--*How to Hide a Hippopotamus.* Croswell, Volney. 1958. Dodd, Mead & Co. **Award: (NYT).** (P.232)
--*How to Hide a Hippopotamus.* Croswell, Volney. 1958. Hale. (P.232)

Crothers, Rachel
--*Mother Carey's Chicken.* Wiggin, Kate Douglas Smith (1856-1923). 1925. Samuel French. (P.957)

Crouch, Mary Crete
--*Twilight Fairy Tales.* Groves, May Showler. 1914. J. Anderson. (P.397)

Crowder, Phillip, jt. illus. see Chappell, Sean.

Crowe, Jack
--*Hopalong Cassidy and Lucky at Copper Gulch.* Mulford, Clarence Edward (1883-1956), created by. 1950. Garden City Pub. Co. (P.671)
--*Hopalong Cassidy and Lucky at the Double X Ranch.* Mulford, Clarence Edward (1883-1956), created by. 1950. Garden City Pub. Co. (P.671)

Crowe, Jocelyn (1906-)
--*Peacock Pie: A Book of Rhymes.* De La Mare, Walter John (1873-1956). 1936. Henry Holt & Co. (P.253)

Crowell, Elsinore Robinson
--*Behind the Garden Wall.* Wallace, Robert (1932-). c.1913. P. Elder and Company. (P.927)

Crowell, James (1936-)
--*The Fall of the House of Usher.* Poe, Edgar Allan (1809-1849). Cutts, David E., adapted by. 1982. Troll Assocs. (P.729)
--*Ice River.* Green, Phyllis (1932-). 1975. Addison-Wesley. (P.385)

Crowell, Pers (1910-)
--*Big Bad Bear.* Todd, Zula. 1964. Follett. (P.893)
--*Big Red, a Wild Stallion.* Montgomery, Rutherford George (1894-). 1971. Caxton Printers. (P.658)
--*Black Beauty.* Sewell, Anna (1820-1878). 1962. Grosset & Dunlap. (P.812)
--*Cherokee Bill, Oklahoma Pacer.* Bailey, Jean (1917-). 1952. Abingdon-Cokesbury Press. (P.60)
--*Cherokee Bill, Oklahoma Pacer.* Bailey, Jean (1917-). 1970, c.1952. Houghton Mifflin. (P.60)
--*Christmas Horse.* Balch, Glenn (1902-). 1949. Crowell Co. (P.64)
--*The Colt from Horse Heaven Hills.* Brown, Eleanor Frances (1908-). 1956. Messner. (P.138)
--*The First Horseman.* Crowell, Pers (1910-). 1948. Whittlesey House. (P.233)
--*Golden Cloud in Texas.* Silliman, Leland (1906-). 1953. John C. Winston Co. (P.823)
--*Golden Cloud: Palomino of Sunset Hill.* 1st ed. Silliman, Leland (1906-). 1950. Winston. (P.823)
--*Golden Lady.* Brown, Eleanor Frances (1908-). N.D. Lothrop Bks. (P.138)
--*Golden Lady: The Story of an American Show Horse.* Brown, Eleanor Frances (1908-). 1946. Howell, Soskin. (P.138)
--*The Golden Mare.* Corbin, William, pseud. (1916-). McGraw, William Corbin. 1955. Putnam Pub Group. (P.219)
--*Golden Mare.* McGraw, William Corbin (1916-). Corbin, William, pseud. 1955. Coward-McCann. (P.602)
--*Hans and the Winged Horse.* Kellogg, Jean Defrees (1916-1978). 1964. Reilly & Lee. (P.516)
--*A Horse for Peter.* Brown, Eleanor Frances (1908-). 1950. Messner. (P.138)
--*Horse in the Clouds.* Griffiths, Helen (1939-). 1958. Holt. (P.390)
--*Horses are for Warriors.* Sanderson, William Elwood (1903-). 1954. Caxton Printers. (P.792)
--*Horses, Horses, Horses: Palominos and Pintos, Polo Ponies and Plow Horses, Morgans and Mustangs.* Fenner, Phyllis Reid (1899-1982), compiled by. 1949. F. Watts. (P.322)
--*King Moo, the Wordmaker.* Crowell, Pers (1910-). 1976. Caxton Printers. (P.233)
--*Lost Horse.* Balch, Glenn (1902-). 1950. Crowell. (P.64)
--*Lost Horse.* Balch, Glenn (1902-). 1961. Grosset & Dunlap. (P.64)
--*Midnight Colt.* Balch, Glenn (1902-). 1970. Apollo Eds. (P.64)
--*The Midnight Colt.* Balch, Glenn (1902-). 1952. Crowell. (P.64)
--*The Midnight Colt.* Balch, Glenn (1902-). N.D. Peter Smith Publisher, Inc. (P.64)
--*Nez Perce Buffalo Horse.* Sanderson, William Elwood (1903-). 1972. Caxton. (P.792)
--*The Phantom Roan.* 1st ed. Thompson, Harlan H. (1894-). Holt, Stephen, pseud. 1949. Longmans, Green. (P.887)
--*Pitch in His Hair.* 1st ed. Mitchell, Fay Langellier (1884-1964). 1954. Doubleday. (P.652)
--*Pounding Hooves.* Johnston, Dorothy Grunbock (1915-). c.1976. D. C. Cook Pub. Co. (P.497)
--*Rain Cloud, the Wild Mustang.* Kraenzel, Margaret Powell (1899-). 1962. Lothrop, Lee & Shepard. (P.536)
--*The Ranch Beyond the Mountains.* Thompson, Harlan H. (1894-). Holt, Stephen, pseud. 1961. David McKay Company Inc. (P.887)
--*The Ranch Beyond the Mountains.* Thompson, Harlan H. (1894-). Holt, Stephen, pseud. 1961. Longmans, Green. (P.887)
--*Skylark Farm.* Beckman, Joan (1926-). 1950. Whittlesey House. (P.87)
--*Stormy.* 1st ed. Thompson, Harlan H. (1894-). Holt, Stephen, pseud. 1955. Longman, Green. (P.887)
--*The Thought Book.* Crowell, Pers (1910-). 1959. Coward-McCann. (P.233)
--*Wendy Wanted a Pony.* Brown, Eleanor Frances (1908-). 1951. Messner. (P.138)
--*What Can a Horse Do That You Can't Do?.* Crowell, Pers (1910-). c.1954. Whittlesey House. (P.233)
--*The Whistling Stallion.* Thompson, Harlan H. (1894-). Holt, Stephen, pseud. 1951. Longmans, Green. (P.887)
--*Wild Horse.* Balch, Glenn (1902-). 1970, c.1947. Crowell. (P.65)
--*Wild Horse.* Balch, Glenn (1902-). 1947. T. Y. Crowell Co. (P.65)
--*Young Bill Fargo.* 1st ed. Frazier, Neta Lohnes (1890-). 1956. Longmans, Green. (P.343)

Crowle, Pigeon
--*Songs for Michael.* Weatherly, Frederic Edward (1848-1929). 1928. Longmans, Green and Co. (P.938)

Crowninshield, Laura H.
--*Pinafore Poems.* Kennedy, Celia Mary. 1924. G. Wahr. (P.517)

Crowquill, Alfred, pseud., see Forrester, Alfred Henry.

Crowquill, Alfred, jt. illus. see Corbould, E. H.

Crowquill, Alfred, pseud. (1804-1872)
--*Beauty and the Beast.* Forrester, Alfred Henry. Smith, Albert Richard (1816-1860). 1845. Burgess, Stringer, & Co. (P.831)
--*Beauty and the Beast.* Forrester, Alfred Henry. Smith, Albert Richard (1816-1860). N.D. Manhattan Publishing Company. (P.831)
--*Blue Beard.* Forrester, Alfred Henry. Bayley, Frederic William Naylor (1808-1853). 1845. Burgess, Stringer, & Co. (P.83)
--*Fairy Tales, Comprising Patty and Her Pitcher, Tiny and Her Vanity, The Giant and the Dwarf, The Selfish Man, Peter and His Goose, The Giant Hands.* Forrester, Alfred Henry. Forrester, Alfred Henry (1804-1872). 1857. G. Routledge & Co. (P.336)

Crowther, Robert
--*Cockatoo.* Carroll, Gladys Hasty (1904-). 1929. The Macmillan Company. (P.172)
--*David and the Bear Man.* Ashmun, Margaret Eliza. 1929. The Macmillan Company. (P.52)

Croxall, Samuel (0000-1752)
--*Fables of Aesop and Others.* Aesopus. Croxall, Samuel (0000-1752), tr. 1845. T. Cowperthwaite & Co. (P.13)

Cruickshank, Phiz (1815-1882) & Stone, Marcus
--*Christmas Stories.* Dickens, Charles John Huffam (1812-1870). N.D. St Martin's Press. (P.263)
--*David Copperfield.* Dickens, Charles John Huffam (1812-1882). N.D. St Martin's Press. (P.263)
--*Dombey and Son.* Dickens, Charles John Huffam (1812-1870). N.D. St Martin's Press. (P.263)
--*Great Expectation.* Dickens, Charles John Huffam (1812-1870). N.D. St Martin's Press. (P.263)
--*Nicholas Nickelby.* Dickens, Charles John Huffam (1812-1870). N.D. St Martin's Press. (P.263)
--*The Old Curiosity Shop.* Dickens, Charles John Huffam (1812-1870). N.D. St Martin's Press. (P.264)
--*A Tale of Two Cities.* Dickens, Charles John Huffam (1812-1870). N.D. St Martin's Press. (P.264)

Cruikshank, George, jt. illus. see Dore, Louis Christophe Paul Gustave.

Cruikshank, George (1792-1878)
--*The Book of Nonsense.* Lear, Edward (1812-1888). Cruikshank, George (1792-1878), pref. by. Greene, David & Ries, Vera 1977. Garland Pub. (P.558)
--*The Brownies and Other Tales.* Ewing, Juliana Horatia Gatty, Mrs. (1841-1885). N.D. Frederick Stokes. (P.313)
--*The Brownies and Other Tales.* Ewing, Juliana Horatia Gatty, Mrs. (1841-1885). 1901. Hurst. (P.313)
--*Cinderella.* N.D. George Routledge & Sons. (P.233)
--*Cinderella.* Grimm, Jakob Ludwig Karl (1785-1863) & Grimm, Wilhelm Karl (1786-1859). 1969. Hillside Press. (P.391)
--*The Cruikshank Fairy-Book: Four Famous Stories.* Cruikshank, George (1792-1878), ed. 1969. Putnam. (P.233)
--*George Cruikshank's Fairy Library: Including: "Hop-o-My-Thumb", "Jack and the Bean Stalk", "Cinderella", & "Puss in Boots".* N.D. Scribner & Welford. (P.233)
--*Grammer Grethel's Fairy Tales.* Taylor, Edgar (1792-1878), tr. N.D. Dodge Publication Co. (P.233)
--*Grimm's Fairy Tales.* New ed. Grimm, Jakob Ludwig Karl (1785-1863) & Grimm, Wilhelm Karl (1786-1859). N.D. Worthington's. (P.392)
--*Grimm's Goblins.* Grimm, Jakob Ludwig Karl (1785-1863) & Grimm, Wilhelm Karl (1786-1859). 1867. Ticknor & Fields. (P.393)
--*Grimm's Tales.* Grimm, Jakob Ludwig Karl (1785-1863) & Grimm, Wilhelm Karl (1786-1859). Taylor, Edgar, tr. Ruskin, John, ed. Ruskin, John, intro. by. N.D. Estes & Lauriat's. (P.393)
--*Hop O' My Thumb, 1 of 4 Vols.* N.D. George Routledge & Sons. (P.233)
--*Jack and the Bean-Stalk, 1 of 4 Vols.* N.D. George Routledge & Sons. (P.233)
--*Lob Lie-by-the-Fire: Or, The Luck of Lingborough and Other Tales.* Ewing, Juliana Horatia Gatty, Mrs. (1841-1885). 1875. Young. (P.314)
--*Oliver Twist.* Dickens, Charles John Huffam (1812-1870). N.D. Coward-McCann. (P.264)
--*Oliver Twist.* Dickens, Charles John Huffam (1812-1870). N.D. J.B Lippincott. (P.264)
--*Oliver Twist.* Dickens, Charles John Huffam (1812-1870). N.D. Thomas Y. Crowell Co. (P.264)
--*The Pentamerone: The Story of Stories.* New and Rev. ed. Basile, Giovanni Battista (1575-1632). Zimmern, Helen, ed. Taylor, Edward John, tr. N.D. Macmillian & Co. (P.79)
--*The Pilgrim's Progress.* Bunyan, John (1628-1688). N.D. Oxford University Press--American Branch. (P.151)
--*Popular Stories.* Grimm, Jakob Ludwig Karl (1785-1863) & Grimm, Wilhelm Karl (1786-1859). 1937. Oxford University Press. (P.394)
--*Punch and Judy.* N.D. J. S. Ogilvie. (P.233)
--*Puss in Boots, 1 of 4 Vols.* N.D. George Routledge & Sons. (P.233)
--*Yarns of an Old Mariner, 1 of 4 vols.* Clarke, Mary Cowden, Mrs. (1809-1898). 1882. Lee & Shepard. (P.199)

Cruikshank, George (1792-1878) & Wehnert, Edward H.
--*Grimm's Goblins.* Grimm, Jakob Ludwig Karl (1785-1863) & Grimm, Wilhelm Karl (1786-1859). N.D. Worthington Company. (P.393)

Crumling, Roger
--*Billy Between.* Moore, Vardine Russell (1906-) & Conkling, Fleur. 1951. Westminster Press. (P.662)

Crump, Bonnie Lela
--*Bobby Squirrel's Secrets.* Crump, Bonnie Lela. c.1929. R. G. Badger. (P.234)

Crump, Fred H., Jr. (1931-)
--*Clickety Cricket.* Smith, Garry Van Dorin (1933-) & Smith, Vesta Henderson (1933-). 1969. Steck-Vaughn Co. (P.833)
--*Creepy Caterpillar.* Smith, Garry Van Dorin (1933-) & Smith, Vesta Henderson (1933-). 1961. Steck-V. (P.833)
--*Flagon the Dragon.* Smith, Garry Van Dorin (1933-) & Smith, Vesta Henderson (1933-). 1962. Steck-V. (P.833)
--*Florabelle.* Smith, Garry Van Dorin (1933-) & Smith, Vesta Henderson (1933-). 1968. Steck-Vaughn Co. (P.833)
--*Jumping Julius.* Smith, Garry Van Dorin (1933-) & Smith, Vesta Henderson (1933-). 1964. Steck-V. (P.833)
--*Leander Lion.* Smith, Garry Van Dorin (1933-) & Smith, Vesta Henderson (1933-). c.1966. Steck. (P.833)
--*Marigold & the Dragon.* Crump, Fred H., Jr. (1931-). 1964. Steck-V. (P.234)
--*Mitzi.* Smith, Garry Van Dorin (1933-) & Smith, Vesta Henderson (1933-). 1963. Steck-V. (P.833)
--*Poco.* Smith, Garry Van Dorin (1933-) & Smith, Vesta Henderson (1933-). 1975. Ethridge. (P.833)
--*Ringo the Raccoon.* Crump, Fred H., Jr. (1931-). 1982. Ideals. (P.234)
--*The Teeny Weeny Genie.* Crump, Fred H, Jr. (1931-). 1966. Steck-Vaughn. (P.234)

Crump, James Irving (1887-1979)
--*Scouts to the Rescue: Fictionized from the New Universal Chapter Play Starring Jackie Cooper, Illustrated with Scenes from the Motion Picture.* Crump, James Irving (1887-1979). c.1939. Rand, McNally & Company. (P.234)

Crump, Leslie (1894-)
--*Civilizing Cricket: A Story for Girls.* Hooker, Forrestine Cooper, Mrs. (1867-1932). 1927. Doubleday, Page & Company. (P.458)
--*Civilizing Cricket, a Story for Girls.* Hooker, Forrestine Cooper, Mrs. (1867-1932). 1938. The Sun Dial Press. (P.458)
--*Clearport Boys.* Ames, Joseph Bushnell (1878-1928). c.1925. The Century Co. (P.33)
--*The Golden Days of '49: A Tale of the California Diggings.* Munroe, Kirk (1850-1930). 1924. Dodd, Mead & Company. (P.672)
--*Jack Straw in Mexico: How the Engineers Defended the Great Hydro-Electric Plant.* Crump, James Irving (1887-1979). 1914. McBride, Nast & Company. (P.234)
--*Jack Straw, Lighthouse Builder.* Crump, James Irving (1887-1979). 1915. R. M. McBride & Company. (P.234)
--*Left Half Harmon.* Barbour, Ralph Henry (1870-1944). 1921. Dodd, Mead and Company. (P.70)
--*A Princeton Boy in the Revolution.* Tomlinson, Paul Greene (1888-). 1922. Dodd, Mead and Company. (P.895)
--*A Princeton Boy Under the King.* Tomlinson, Paul Greene (1888-). 1921. Dodd, Mead and Company. (P.895)

--*The Man Who Had to Invent a Flying Bicycle.* Willard, Mildred Wilds (1911-). 1967. Stackpole Books. (P.961)
--*Mary's Monster.* Blair, Ruth Van Ness (1912-). 1975. Putnam Pub Group. (P.105)
--*Maypoles & Wood Demons: The Meaning of Trees.* Helfman, Elizabeth Seaver (1911-). 1972. HM. (P.431)
--*Mightiest of Mortals, Heracles.* Gates, Doris (1901-). 1975. Viking Pr. (P.359)
--*Mr.* Charley's Chopsticks. Evans, Doris Portwood. 1972. Coward, McCann & Geoghegan. (P.311)
--*MY Dad Lives in a Downtown Hotel.* Mann, Peggy. 1973. Doubleday and Company. (P.617)
--*My World Is Earth.* Engdahl, Sylvia Louise (1933-). 1979. Atheneum. (P.307)
--*No Boys Allowed.* 1st ed. Terris, Susan (1937-). 1975. Doubleday. (P.882)
--*The Odyssey of Ben O'Neal: A Sequel to Teetoncey and Ben O'Neal and the Third Novel of a Cape Hatteras Trilogy by the Author of "The Cay".* 1st ed. Taylor, Theodore (1922-). c.1977. Doubleday. (P.881)
--*Old Ben.* Stuart, Hilton Jesse (1907-). 1970. McGraw-Hill. (P.869)
--*The Perez Arson Mystery.* Touster, Irwin (1921-) & Curtis, Richard Alan (1937-). 1972. Dial Press. (P.897)
--*The Perilous Gard.* Pope, Elizabeth Marie (1917-). 1976, c.1974. G. K. Hall. (P.732)
--*The Perilous Gard.* Pope, Elizabeth Marie (1917-). 1974. Houghton Mifflin. **Award: (JNM).** (P.732)
--*Ride the Crooked Wind.* Fife, Dale Odile (1910-). 1973. Coward, McCann & Geoghegan. (P.325)
--*Ruffles and Drums.* Cavanna, Betty (1909-). 1975. Morrow. (P.179)
--*The Runaway Bus Mystery.* Touster, Irwin (1921-) & Curtis, Richard Alan (1937-). 1972. Dial Press. (P.897)
--*The Shad Are Running.* St. George, Judith (1931-). 1977. Putnam. (P.789)
--*Small-Boy Chuku.* Wellman, Alice (1900-). 1973. Houghton-Mifflin. (P.943)
--*So, Nothing Is Forever.* Jones, Adrienne (1915-). 1974. Houghton Mifflin. (P.499)
--*Songs and Stories of Afro-Americans.* Glass, Paul, ed. 1971. Grosset & Dunlap. (P.370)
--*Standing in the Magic.* 1st ed. Norris, Gunilla Brodde (1939-). 1974. Dutton. (P.685)
--*The Stones.* Hickman, Janet (1940-). c.1976. Macmillan. (P.441)
--*Summer of the Burning.* Duncombe, Frances Riker (1900-). c.1976. Putnam. (P.289)
--*Teetoncey.* 1st ed. Taylor, Theodore (1922-). 1974. Doubleday. (P.881)
--*Teetoncey and Ben O'Neal.* 1st ed. Taylor, Theodore (1922-). 1975. Doubleday. (P.881)
--*The Testing of Tertius.* Newman, Robert Howard (1909-). 1973. Atheneum. (P.680)
--*Thank You, Jackie Robinson.* Cohen, Barbara (1932-). 1974. Lothrop, Lee & Shepard Co. (P.206)
--*This Is a Recording.* 1st ed. Corcoran, Barbara (1911-). 1971. Atheneum. (P.220)
--*This Star Shall Abide.* 1st ed. Engdahl, Sylvia Louise (1933-). 1972. Atheneum. (P.307)
--*Toliver's Secret.* Brady, Esther Wood (1905-). 1978, c.1976. Crown Publishers. (P.125)
--*The Top Step.* 1st ed. Norris, Gunilla Brodde (1939-). 1970. Atheneum. (P.685)
--*The TV Kid.* Byars, Betsy Cromer (1928-). c.1976. Viking Press. (P.160)
--*Two That Were Tough.* Burch, Robert Joseph (1925-). 1976. Viking Press. (P.151)
--*Universe Ahead: Stories of the Future.* Engdahl, Sylvia Louise (1933-) & Roberson, Rick James (1956-), eds. 1975. Atheneum. (P.307)
--*The Ups and Downs of Marvin.* 1st ed. Hazen, Barbara Shook (1930-). 1976. Atheneum. (P.427)
--*The Walking Zoo of Darwin Dingle.* Hopf, Alice Lightner (1904-). Lightner, A. M., pseud. 1969. Putnam. (P.462)
--*Walking Zoo of Darwin Dingle.* Lightner, A. M., pseud. (1904-). Hopf, Alice Lightner. 1969. Putnam. (P.572)
--*What Happened in Marston.* Garden, Nancy (1938-). 1971. Four Winds Press. (P.354)
--*Who Will Wash the River?.* Orlowsky, Wallace (1939-) & Perera, Thomas Biddle (1938-). 1970. Coward-McCann. (P.696)
--*The Wind in the Willows.* Grahame, Kenneth (1859-1932). 1966. Grosset & Dunlap. (P.381)
--*The Wind in the Willows.* Grahame, Kenneth (1859-1932). 1967. Grosset & Dunlap. (P.381)
--*The Winged Colt of Casa Mia.* Byars, Betsy Cromer (1928-). 1973. Viking Press. (P.160)
--*The Winner.* 1st ed. Smith, Gene (1929-). 1970. Cowles Book Co. (P.833)
--*Winter-Telling Stories.* Marriott, Alice Lee (1910-), ed. 1969. Crowell. (P.621)
--*A Wonder Book.* Hawthorne, Nathaniel (1804-1864). 1967. Grosset & Dunlap. (P.424)
--*The Wonderful Box.* Ames, Mildred (1919-). c.1978. Dutton. (P.33)
--*The Year of the Three-Legged Deer.* Rosenberg, Ethel Clifford (1915-1978). Clifford, Eth, pseud. 1972. Houghton Mifflin. (P.778)
--*Yellow Fur and Little Hawk.* Hays, Wilma Pitchford (1909-). 1978. Coward, McCann & Geoghegan. (P.426)
--*Zenas and the Shaving Mill.* Monjo, Ferdinand Nicolas, III (1924-1978). c.1976. Coward, McCann & Geoghegan. (P.657)

Cugat, Albert, jt. illus. see Chase, Rhoda Campbell.

Cugat, Xavier (1900-)
--*Pepito, the Little Dancing Dog: The Story of Xavier Cugat's Chihuahua.* Evans, Mark. c.1979. Scroll Press. (P.311)

Culfogienis, Angeline
--*Moose, Bruce, and the Goose.* McKinnon, Robert Scott (1937-). 1969. Bobbs-Merrill. (P.607)
--*Wolf in Olga's Kitchen.* Perovskaya, Olga. Glagoleva, Fainna, tr. 1969. Bobbs. (P.718)

Culliford, Pierre see Peyo, pseud.

Culver, Larry
--*Tales from the Wandering Gypsies.* Miller, Joseph (1922-). 1969. Miller Books. (P.648)

Culver, R. K.
--*More About Teddy B.* and Teddy G. The Roosevelt Bears: Being Volume Two Depicting Their Further Travels and Adventures. Eaton, Seymour (1859-1916). 1907. E. Stern & Company, Inc. (P.294)
--*The Roosevelt Bears Abroad.* Eaton, Seymour (1859-1916). 1908. E. Stern & Co., Inc. (P.294)

Cumine, George L.
--*The Red Man's Wonder Book.* Kennedy, Howard Angus (1861-). c.1931. E. P. Dutton & Co., Inc. (P.517)

Cuming, B. L.
--*Awisha's Carpet: The Story of a Little Girl.* Martin, Dahris Butterworth. N.D. Doubleday, Doran. (P.624)
--*Fatma Was a Goose: Tunis Tales.* Martin, Dahris Butterworth. 1929. Doubleday, Doran & Company, Inc. (P.624)

Cumings, Art
--*Astronauts.* Keller, Charles (1942-). c.1984. Prentice-Hall. (P.514)
--*The Cat's Pajamas.* Chittum, Ida (1918-). c.1980. Parents Magazine Press. (P.192)
--*Charlie's Pets.* Ernst, Kathryn Fitzgerald (1942-). c.1978. Crown Publishers. (P.309)
--*A Good Fish Dinner.* Walker, Barbara Kerlin (1921-). 1979, c.1978. Parents' Magazine Press. (P.925)
--*Magic Growing Powder.* Quin-Harkin, Janet (1941-). 1981. Dutton. (P.745)
--*Ohm on the Range: Robot and Computer Jokes.* Keller, Charles (1942-), compiled by. 1982. Prentice Hall. (P.514)
--*One-Minute Bedtime Stories.* 1st ed. Lewis, Shari (1934-) & O'Kun, Lan. c.1982. Doubleday. (P.570)
--*Percy the Parrot Passes the Puck.* Carley, Wayne. 1972. Garrard Pub. Co. (P.168)
--*Percy the Parrot Yelled Quiet!.* Carley, Wayne. 1974. Garrard Pub. Co. (P.168)
--*Please Try to Remember the First of Octember!.* Geisel, Theodor Seuss, pseud. (1904-). Geisel, Theodor Seuss. Sieg, Theo le, pseud. c.1977. Beginner Books. (P.362)
--*Septimus Bean and His Amazing Machine.* Quin-Harkin, Janet (1941-). c.1979. Parent's Magazine Press. (P.745)
--*There's a Monster Eating My House.* Cumings, Art. 1981. Parent Magazine Press. (P.234)
--*Unlucky Day at Camp How-Ja-Do.* Carley, Wayne. 1972. Garrard Pub. Co. (P.168)

Cumings, James
--*George M.* Cohan: Boy Theater Genius. Winders, Gertrude Hecker. 1968. Bobbs-Merrill Co. (P.967)

Cummings, Alison
--*Christmas Is Coming.* Martin, Marcia, pseud. (1918-). Levin, Marcia Obrasky. 1952. Wonder Books. (P.625)
--*In They Go!.* Gerard, Mary Gold (1908-). c.1955. Whitman Pub. Co. (P.364)
--*Johnny Grows up.* Levin, Marcia Lauter Obrasky (1918-). Martin, Marcia, pseud. 1954. Wonder Books. (P.568)
--*Johnny Wants to Be a Policeman.* Granberg, Wilbur John (1906-). 1951. Aladdin Books. (P.381)
--*Just Like Mommy.* Simon, Patty. c.1952. Wonder Books. (P.825)
--*Oklahoma!.* Paper Doll Story Book. Watson, Jane Werner (1915-). 1956. Golden Press. (P.935)
--*Pop-O, the Clown.* Whitteberry, Caroline. 1950. Whitman. (P.955)

Cummings, Alison, jt. illus. see Wilkin, Eloise Burns.

Cummings, Chris
--*The Little Book of Big Bad Jokes.* Meade, Marion (1934-). c.1977. Harvey House. (P.637)
--*Little Book of Daffinitions.* Powers, Thetis. 1977. Harvey. (P.736)
--*The Little Book of Limericks.* Lyfick, Warren, pseud. (1926-), compiled by Reeves, Lawrence F.. c.1978. Harvey House. (P.591)
--*The Punny Pages.* Lyfick, Warren, pseud. (1926-), compiled by Reeves, Lawrence F.. c.1979. Riverhouse Publications : Distributed by Harvey House. (P.591)

Cummings, Pat
--*Fred's First Day.* Warren, Cathy. 1984. Lothrop, Lee & Shepard Books. (P.933)
--*Good News.* Greenfield, Eloise (1929-). 1977. Putnam Pub Group. (P.387)
--*Good News: Formerly "Bubbles".* Greenfield, Eloise (1929-). 1977, c.1972. Coward, McCann & Geoghegan. (P.387)
--*Just Us Women.* Caines, Jeannette Franklin. 1984. Har-Row. (P.161)
--*My Mama Needs Me.* 1st ed. Walter, Mildred Pitts. c.1983. Lothrop, Lee & Shepard Books. **Award: (CSKA).** (P.929)

Cummings, Walter Thies (1933-)
--*The Girl in the White Hat.* Cummings, Walter Thies (1933-). 1959. McGraw. **Award: (NYT).** (P.234)
--*The Kid.* Cummings, Walter Thies (1933-). 1960. McGraw-Hill Book Company. (P.234)
--*Miss Esta Maude's Secret.* Cummings, Walter Thies (1933-). 1961. McGraw-Hill Book Company. (P.234)

Cummings, William Lahey
--*The Giant Book.* De Regniers, Beatrice Schenk Freedman (1914-). c.1966. Atheneum. (P.259)
--*Picture Book Theater: The Mysterious Stranger, the Magic Spell.* De Regniers, Beatrice Schenk Freedman (1914-). c.1982. Clarion Books. (P.259)
--*The Zoo Comes to School: Finger Plays and Action Rhymes.* Colville, M. Josephine. 1973. Teachers Pub. Division, Macmillan. (P.211)

Cummins, James (1914-)
--*The April Fool Mystery.* Nixon, Joan Lowery (1927-). 1980. A. Whitman. (P.683)
--*Ben Hur.* Wallace, Lewis (1827-1905). Kottmeyer, William (1910-), adapted by. 1949. Webster Pub. Co. (P.927)
--*Busy Days with Raggedy Ann & Andy.* Ottum, Bob. 1976. Western Pub. (P.698)
--*The Christmas Eve Mystery.* Nixon, Joan Lowery (1927-). c.1981. A. Whitman. (P.683)
--*The Easter Mystery.* Nixon, Joan Lowery (1927-). 1981. Whitman. (P.683)
--*Flying Feathers: A Slav Folk Tale.* Ericsson, Mary Kentra (1910-). c.1978. Concordia Pub. House. (P.309)
--*The Halloween Mystery.* Nixon, Joan Lowery (1927-). 1979. A. Whitman. (P.683)
--*The Halloween Mystery.* Nixon, Joan Lowery (1927-). 1981, c.1979. Simon & Schuster. (P.683)
--*The Happy Birthday Mystery.* Nixon, Joan Lowery (1927-). 1979. A. Whitman. (P.683)
--*The Happy Birthday Mystery.* Nixon, Joan Lowery (1927-). 1981, c.1979. Little Simon. (P.683)
--*My First Book About Jesus.* Wangerin, Walter, Jr. (1944-). c.1983. Rand McNally. (P.930)
--*The New Year's Mystery.* Nixon, Joan Lowery (1927-). 1979. A. Whitman. (P.683)
--*Semo.* Harrell, Sara Jeanne Gordon (1940-). c.1977. Concordia Pub. House. (P.414)
--*The Thanksgiving Mystery.* Nixon, Joan Lowery (1927-). c.1980. A. Whitman. (P.683)
--*The Thanksgiving Mystery.* Nixon, Joan Lowery (1927-). 1981. Little Simon. (P.683)
--*A Tooth for the Tooth Fairy.* Gunther, Louise. c.1978. Garrard Pub. Co. (P.399)
--*The Valentine Mystery.* Nixon, Joan Lowery (1927-). 1979. A. Whitman. (P.683)
--*The Valentine Mystery.* Nixon, Joan Lowery (1927-). 1981. Little Simon. (P.683)
--*Who Cares.* Brown, Virginia, et al. 1965. McGraw-Hill. (P.142)

Cunette, Lou
--*ABC Halloween Witch.* DeLage, Ida (1918-). c.1977. Garrard Pub. Co. (P.252)
--*April Fool!.* Jacobs, Leland Blair (1907-). 1973. Garrard Pub. Co. (P.487)
--*Bugs Bunny Goes to the Dentist.* Reit, Seymour (1918-). c.1978. Golden Press. (P.757)
--*Come Play Hide and Seek.* Gies, Margaret Brietmaier (1940-). 1975. Garrard Pub. Co. (P.371)
--*The Ghost Said Boo.* McInnes, John (1927-). 1974. Garrard Pub. Co. (P.604)
--*The Grouchy Santa.* Patterson, Lillie G. c.1979. Garrard Pub. Co. (P.710)
--*Tweety and Sylvester: Birds of a Feather.* Reit, Seymour (1918-). c.1977. Golden Press. (P.757)
--*The Witch Who Forgot.* Carley, Wayne. 1974. Garrard Pub. Co. (P.168)

Cunette, Louis
--*Smoke Eater.* Brier, Howard Maxwell (1903-1969). c.1941. Random House. (P.131)
--*XDY and the Soap Box Derby.* Kahmann, Mable Chesley, Mrs. (1901-). c.1941. Random House. (P.504)

Cunningham, Aline
--*An Ark & a Rainbow.* Hancock, Sibyl (1940-). Van Woerkom, Dorothy O'Brien (1924-), ed. 1976. Concordia. (P.410)
--*An Ark and a Rainbow: Noah and the Ark for Beginning Readers : Genesis 6-9 for Children.* Hancock, Sibyl (1940-). c.1976. Concordia Pub. House. (P.410)
--*Climbing up to Nowhere: The Tower of Babel for Beginning Readers : Genesis 10-11: 1-9 for Children.* Hancock, Sibyl (1940-). c.1977. Concordia Pub. House. (P.410)
--*Daniel, Who Dared: Daniel in the Lions' Den for Beginning Readers : Daniel 1: 1-8, 6 for Children.* Christian, Mary Blount (1933-). c.1977. Concordia Pub. House. (P.193)
--*Five Loaves & Two Fishes.* Nixon, Joan Lowery (1927-). Van Woerkom, Dorothy O'Brien (1924-), ed. 1976. Concordia. (P.683)
--*Green Frog.* Cunningham, Aline. N.D. Concordia. (P.235)
--*Jonah, Go to Nineveh!.* Jonah and the Whale for Beginning Readers : the Book of Jonah for Children. Christian, Mary Blount (1933-). c.1976. Concordia Pub. House. (P.193)
--*The Tree & Four Friends.* Cunningham, Aline. N.D. Concordia. (P.235)

Cunningham, Cornelia
--*Spaniards' Mark.* Dwight, Allan, pseud. (1903-1979) & Taylor, Turney Allan. Cole, Lois Dwight. 1933. The Macmillan Company. (P.292)

Cunningham, David (1938-)
--*Benny Uncovers a Mystery.* Warner, Gertrude Chandler (1890-1979). c.1976. A. Whitman. (P.932)
--*Bicycle Mystery.* Warner, Gertrude Chandler (1890-1979). 1970. A. Whitman. (P.932)
--*Bus Station Mystery.* Warner, Gertrude Chandler (1890-1979). 1974. A. Whitman. (P.932)
--*Caboose Mystery.* Warner, Gertrude Chandler (1890-1979). 1966. A. Whitman. (P.932)
--*The Haunting of the Green Bird.* Hall, Lynn (1937-). 1980, c.1981. Follett Pub. Co. (P.405)
--*Houseboat Mystery.* Warner, Gertrude Chandler (1890-1979). 1967. Whitman. (P.932)
--*In the Morning Mist.* Lapp, Eleanor J (1936-). c.1978. A. Whitman. (P.552)
--*Keys for Signe.* Archer, Marion Fuller (1917-). 1965. A. Whitman. (P.46)
--*Lighthouse Mystery.* Warner, Gertrude Chandler (1890-1979). 1963. A Whitman. (P.932)
--*The Mice Came in Early This Year.* Lapp, Eleanor J (1936-). 1976. A. Whitman. (P.552)
--*Mountain Top Mystery.* Warner, Gertrude Chandler (1890-1979). 1964. A. Whitman. (P.932)
--*Mystery Behind the Wall.* Warner, Gertrude Chandler (1890-1979). 1973. A. Whitman. (P.932)
--*Mystery in the Sand.* Warner, Gertrude Chandler (1890-1979). 1971. A Whitman. (P.932)
--*Schoolhouse Mystery.* Warner, Gertrude Chandler (1890-1979). 1965. A. Whitman. (P.932)
--*Snowbound Mystery.* Warner, Gertrude Chandler (1890-1979). 1968. A. Whitman. (P.932)
--*There Is a Happy Land.* Archer, Marion Fuller (1917-). 1963. A Whitman. (P.46)
--*Tree House Mystery.* Warner, Gertrude Chandler (1890-1979). 1969. A. Whitman. (P.932)
--*The Woodshed Mystery.* Warner, Gertrude Chandler (1890-1979). 1962. A. Whitman. (P.932)

Cunningham, Dellwyn
--*Big Treasure Book of Christmas.* N.D. Grosset & Dunlap. (P.235)
--*The Cow in the Silo.* Goodell, Patricia. 1950. Grosset & Dunlap. (P.375)
--*Favorite Christmas Songs & Stories.* Commins, Dorothy Berliner, ed. 1962. Putnam Pub Group. (P.212)
--*Fuzzy Friends in Mother Goose.* Mother Goose. c.1952. Whitman Pub. Co. (P.667)
--*The Goose Who Played the Piano.* Evers, Alf (1905-). 1951. Wonder Books. (P.313)
--*Who Likes Dinner?.* Beyer, Evelyn M. (1907-). c.1953. Wonder Books. (P.100)
--*The Wonder Book of Fun: Poems.* Orleans, Ilo (1897-1962). 1951. Wonder Books. (P.696)
--*The Wonderful Tar-Baby, Told by Uncle Remus: Retold for Little Children.* Harris, Joel Chandler (1848-1908). 1952. Wonder Books. (P.416)

Cunningham, Lois Elizabeth Barstow, Mrs. (1908-) & Bosworth, Elenora (1909-)
--*Rattle: The Story of a Sorrowful Snake.* 1st ed. Cunningham, Lois Elizabeth Barstow, Mrs. (1908-) & Bosworth, Elenora (1909-). 1935. Chapin Press. (P.235)

Cunnings, Edith May
--*Another Story Shop.* Odell, Mary Clemens (1904-). 1947. The Judson Press. (P.690)
--*The Story Shop.* Odell, Margaretta C. (0000-1908). Clemens, Margaret M., intro. by. c.1938. The Judson Press. (P.690)

Dalziel, George, jt. illus. see Houghton, Archibald Boyd.

Dalziel, George, jt. illus. see Speckter, Otto.

Dalziel, George, jt. illus. see Houghton, Archibald Boyd.

Dalziel, George (1815-1902) & Dalziel, Edward (1817-1905)

--*Mother Goose: Or National Nursery Rhymes & Nursery Songs.* Elliott, James William (1833-1915). 1981. Doll Works. (P.302)

--*Mother Goose: or, National Nursery Rhymes & Nursery Songs.* Elliott, James William (1833-1915) 1872. Novello, Ewer, & Co. (P.302)

Dameron, Charles E.

--*Renfrew Rides North.* Erskine, Laurie York (1894-1976). 1931. D. Appleton. (P.309)

Damerow, Abbi

--*Teen-Age Blues.* Verses. Pepper, Nancy. 1948. J. Messner. (P.717)

D'Amico, Oscar

--*Moon Lady.* Assante, Allison. 1968. Distributed by M. W. Lads Pub. Co. (P.53)

Damon, Valerie

--*Daisy Days: Happy Moments of Seeking and Sharing.* Walley, Dean. 1970. Hallmark Cards. (P.927)

Damrosch, Helen, pseud., see Tee-Van, Helen Damrosch.

Damrosch, Helen, pseud. (1893-1976)

--*Sea Monster.* Tee-Van, Helen Damrosch. Knowlton, William (1927-). 1959. Borzoi Books. (P.533)

Dana, Dorathea, pseud., see Dankovszky, Dorathea.

Dana, Dorathea , pseud.

--*The Runaway Shuttle Train.* Dankovszky, Dorathea. Fuller, Muriel (1901-). 1946. David McKay Company. (P.349)

Dana, Mary Pepperell (1914-)

--*Hurry Hurry: A Tale of Calamity and Woe,or: A Lesson in Leisure. Relating the Dire Mishaps Which Befell a Certain Nurse Who Went Too Fast; Together with a Faithful Account of Her Reform: the Whole Comprising a Powerful Lesson.* Hurd, Edith Thacher, Mrs. (1910-). 1938. W.R. Scott. (P.475)

--*The Jingle Book ...* Dana, Mary Pepperell (1914-), compiled by. c.1940. W. R. Scott, Inc. (P.240)

Dance, Robert B.

--*Lone Star Rebel.* Benner, Judith Ann (1942-). 1971. J. F. Blair. (P.93)

Danciger, Leila Nash

--*A. B. C. Bible and Holiday Stories.* Aronoff, Daisy F. N.D. Bloch Publishing Co. (P.49)

D'Andrea, Bernard

--*The Monster Fish.* B. B. 1972. Schol Bk Serv. (P.57)

D'Andrea, Cheslie

--*Christopher Columbus: Sailor and Dreamer.* Bailey, Bernadine Freeman, Mrs. (1901-). 1960. Houghton Mifflin. (P.59)

--*David's Fishing Summer.* Montgomery, Mabel. 1953. Wilcox and Follett Co. (P.658)

--*Juan Ponce De Leon: First in the Land.* Bailey, Bernadine Freeman, Mrs. (1901-). 1958. Houghton Mifflin. (P.59)

--*Magic Word for Elin.* Lide, Alice Alison, Mrs. (1890-) & Johansen, Margaret Alison, Mrs. (1896-). 1958. Abingdon Press. (P.571)

Danforth, Marie L.

--*Short Stories for Short People.* Aspinwall, Alicia Stuart, Mrs. c.1896. E. P. Dutton and Company. (P.53)

Daniel, Alan (1939-)

--*Bunnicula: A Rabbit Tale of Mystery.* Howe, Deborah (1946-1978) & Howe, James (1946-). 1979. Atheneum. **Award: (ALA).** (P.467)

--*Dan Patch And Other Stories of Pioneering in the West.* Bjornson, Magnus F. 1975. Scholastic-Tab Publications. (P.104)

--*The Dog Power Tower.* Allinson, Beverley Lynn Rouse (1936-). 1978, c.1977. Methuen. (P.31)

--*A Horse for Running Buffalo.* Freeman, Madeline A. 1972. Van Nostrand Reinhold. (P.344)

--*I'll Never Love Anything Ever Again.* Delton, Judy (1931-). 1984. A. Whitman. (P.255)

--*Mr.* Peeknuff's Tiny People. Hill, Donna Marie (1921-). 1981. Atheneum. (P.442)

--*The Mystery of Plum Park Pony.* Hall, Lynn (1937-). c.1980. Garrard Pub. Co. (P.405)

--*The Mystery of the Lost and Found Hound.* Hall, Lynn (1937-). c.1979. Garrard Pub. Co. (P.405)

--*This Big Cat, and Other Cats I've Known.* De Regniers, Beatrice Schenk Freedman (1914-). 1985. Crown Books. (P.259)

--*Voyage into Danger: Adventure in the Queen Charlotte Islands.* Ashlee, Ted. 1971. HR&W. (P.52)

--*Wormburners.* Craig, John Ernest (1921-). 1976. Schol Bk Serv. (P.226)

Daniel, Frank

--*Pink Pig and the Nut Tree.* May, Charles Paul (1920-). 1962. A. S. Barnes. (P.632)

Daniels, Julia

--*Me'ow Jones, Belgian Refugee Cat: His Own True Tale As Written Down.* Lyman, Edward Branch. c.1917. George H. Doran Company. (P.591)

Daniels, Neil

--*Ozzie: An Odyssey of Love.* Hudson, Anne & Daniels, Neil. 1983. Kripalu Pubns. (P.469)

Danielson, Barbara

--*Dramatized Ballads.* 1st ed. White, Alice Margaret Geddes & Tobitt, Janet Evelyn. c.1937. E. P. Dutton & Co., Inc. (P.950)

Danish, Barbara (1948-)

--*The Dragon & the Doctor.* Danish, Barbara (1948-). 1971. Feminist Pr. (P.241)

Dankovszky, Dorathea see Dana, Dorathea, pseud.

Dankovszky, Dorathea

--*Good Bye, Bunny Bangs.* Dankovszky, Dorathea. 1956. Abelard Schuman. (P.241)

--*Sugar Bush.* Dana, Dorathea, pseud. Dankovszky, Dorathea. Dana, Dorathea, pseud. 1947. T. Nelson & Sons. (P.241)

Danska, Herbert (1928-)

--*Dark Arrow.* Mulcahy, Lucille Burnett. 1953. Coward-McCann. (P.670)

--*Favorite Fairy Tales Told in Russia.* 1st ed. Haviland, Virginia (1911-), retold by. 1961. Little. (P.421)

--*Francois and the Langouste: A Story of Martinique.* 1st ed. Sadowsky, Ethel S (1927-). 1969. Little, Brown. (P.788)

--*The Other Side of Tomorrow: Original Science Fiction Stories About Young People of the Future.* Elwood, Roger (1943-), ed. 1973. Random House. (P.305)

--*Over the Blue Mountain.* Richter, Conrad Micheal (1890-1968). 1967. Knopf. (P.763)

--*Queen Without Crown.* Polland, Madeleine Angela Cahill (1918-). 1966. HR&W. (P.730)

--*The Real Book of American Tall Tales.* 1st ed. Folsom, Franklin Brewster & Elting, Mary. 1952. Garden City Books, by Arrangement with F. Watts New York. (P.334)

--*Rory, the Red.* Begley, Evelyn M. 1968. Van Nostrand. (P.89)

--*The Story of Lohengrin: The Knight of the Swan.* Orgel, Doris (1929-). 1966. G. P. Putnam's Sons. (P.695)

--*The Story of Our Ancestors.* Edel, May. 1955. Little, Brown. (P.295)

--*The Story of People.* Edel, May. 1953. Little, Brown. (P.296)

--*The Street Kids.* Danska, Herbert (1928-). 1970. Knopf. (P.241)

Darbois, Dominique

--*Achouna, Boy of the Arctic.* Darbois, Dominique. c.1962. Follett Pub. Co. (P.241)

--*Agossou, Boy of Africa.* Darbois, Dominique. c.1962. Follett. (P.241)

--*Aslak, Boy of Lapland.* Darbois, Dominique. Greufebsteub, Sandra, adapted by. Darbois, Dominique 1968. Follett Pub. Co. (P.241)

--*Hassen, Boy Of The Desert.* Darbois, Dominique. 1961. Follett Publishing. (P.241)

--*Kai Ming, Boy Of Hong Kong.* Darbois, Dominique. 1960. Follett Publishing. (P.241)

--*Lakhmi, Girl of India.* Darbois, Dominique. 1964. Follett Pub. Co. (P.241)

--*Noriko, Girl Of Japan.* Darbois, Dominique. 1964. Follett Publishing. (P.241)

--*Parana, Boy of the Amazon.* Maziere, Francis (1924-). 1959. Follett. (P.635)

--*Rikka and Rindji: Children of Bali.* Darbois, Dominique. c.1959. Follett Pub. Co. (P.241)

--*Tacho, Boy of Mexico.* Darbois, Dominique. 1961. Follett. (P.241)

Darby, Elinor

--*Copy Kate.* Hall, Marjory (1908-). 1947. Houghton Mifflin Co. (P.405)

Dargent, Yan (1824-1899)

--*Old Wives' Fables.* Laboulaye, Edouard Rene Lefebvre De (1811-1883). 1884. G. Routledge and Sons. (P.543)

Darien, Elsie

--*A to Z: Alphabet Picture Book.* Lowe, Edith May Kovar (1905-). 1966. Follett Pub. Co. (P.588)

--*Alfie: The Playful Elephant.* Gale, Leah. 1967, c.1966. Follett Pub. Co. (P.352)

--*Mr.* Gallagher's Donkey. Lowe, Edith May Kovar (1905-). Windsor, Mary, pseud. c.1950. Garden City Pub. (P.588)

--*The Story of Willie the Donkey.* Lowe, Edith May Kovar (1905-). Windsor, Mary, pseud. 1950. S. Lowe Co. (P.588)

DaRif, Andrea

--*The Blueberry Cake that Little Fox Baked.* DaRif, Andrea. 1984. Atheneum. (P.242)

--*Puss in Boots.* Perrault, Charles (1628-1703). c.1979. Troll Associates. (P.719)

--*Where Did You Put Your Sleep?.* Newfield, Marcia. 1983. Atheneum. (P.680)

Darley, Felix Octavius Carr, jt. illus. see Cooke, Edna W.

Darley, Felix Octavius Carr, jt. illus. see Nast, Thomas.

Darley, Felix Octavius Carr (1822-1888)

--*Aladdin: Or, The Wonderful Lamp.* Alta ed. 1888. Porter & Coates. (P.242)

--*Calavar: The Knight of the Conquest.* Bird, Dr. N.D. W J Widdleton. (P.102)

--*Children of the Abbey.* Roche, Regina Maria Dalton, Mrs. (1764-1845). N.D. D. Appleton & Co. (P.771)

--*The Clockmaker: The Sayings and Doings of Samuel Slick of Slickville.* Haliburton, Thomas Chandler. N.D. Hurd & Houghton. (P.404)

--*The Cooper Stories: Including: "Stories of the Prarie", "Stories of the Woods" & "Stories of the Sea", 3 vols.* N.D. Houghton, Osgood & Co. (P.242)

--*Irvington Stories.* New, rev. & enlarged. Dodge, Mary Elizabeth Mapes, Mrs. (1831-1905). c.1898. M. A. Donohue. (P.276)

--*Irvington Stories.* New, rev. & enlarged. Dodge, Mary Elizabeth Mapes, Mrs. (1831-1905). 1898. W. L. Allison Co. (P.276)

--*The Lady of the Lake.* Scott, Walter, Sir (1771-1832). N.D. Hurd & Houghton. (P.805)

--*Scottish Chiefs, 1 of 3 Vols.* Porter, Jane (1776-1850). N.D. Porter & Coates. (P.732)

--*Stories of the Woods: Or, Adventures of Leather-Stocking, Selected from the "Leather-Stocking Tales".* Cooper, James Fenimore (1789-1851). 1863. J. G. Gregory. (P.218)

--*Thaddeus of Warsaw.* Porter, Jane (1776-1850). N.D. Porter & Coates. (P.732)

--*Tiny Tim and Dot, and the Fairy Cricket, 1 of 12 Vols.* Dickens, Charles John Huffam (1812-1870). N.D. Clark & Maynard. (P.264)

--*The Two Daughters, 1 of 12 Vols.* Dickens, Charles John Huffam (1812-1870). N.D. Clark & Maynard. (P.264)

--*The Vagabonds.* Trowbridge, John Townsend (1827-1916). N.D. Hurd & Houghton. (P.902)

--*A Visit From Saint Nicholas.* Moore, Clement Clarke (1779-1863). c.1862. J. G. Gregory. (P.660)

--*A Visit from St.* Nicholas. Moore, Clement Clarke (1779-1863). N.D. Estes & Lauriat's. (P.660)

--*A Visit from St.* Nicholas. Moore, Clement Clarke (1779-1863). N.D. Hurd & Houghton. (P.660)

Darley, Felix Octavius Carr (1822-1888) & Nast, Thomas (1840-1902)

--*Boarding-School Days.* Gordon, Clarence (1835-1920). 1873. Hurd and Houghton. (P.376)

Darling, Lois MacIntyre, jt. illus. see Darling, Louis, Jr.

Darling, Lois MacIntyre (1917-)

--*Crocodile Crew.* 1st ed. Watkins, Richard. 1949. Harcourt, Brace. (P.935)

--*Hurricane's Secret.* 1st ed. Watkins, Richard. 1950. Harcourt, Brace. (P.935)

--*Wild Voyageur: Story of a Canada Goose.* 1st ed. Jones, Adrienne (1915-). 1966. Little, Brown. (P.499)

Darling, Louis, Jr. (1916-1970)

--*Beezus and Ramona.* Cleary, Beverly Bunn (1916-). 1955. Morrow. (P.200)

--*Country Garage.* Beim, Jerrold (1910-1957). 1952. Morrow. (P.89)

--*Country School.* Beim, Jerrold (1910-1957). 1955. Morrow. (P.89)

--*Ellen Tebbits.* Cleary, Beverly Bunn (1916-). 1951. Morrow. (P.200)

--*The Enormous Egg.* Butterworth, Oliver (1915-). 1956. Little. (P.159)

--*Eric on the Desert.* Beim, Jerrold (1910-1957). 1953. Morrow. (P.89)

--*Hank and the Kitten.* Dudley, Ruth Hubbell (1905-). 1949. W. Morrow. (P.287)

--*Henry & Beezus.* Cleary, Beverly Bunn (1916-). 1952. Morrow. (P.200)

--*Henry and Ribsy.* Cleary, Beverly Bunn (1916-). 1954. William Morrow & Co. (P.200)

--*Henry and the Clubhouse.* Cleary, Beverly Bunn (1916-). 1962. William Morrow and Company. (P.200)

--*Henry and the Paper Route.* Cleary, Beverly Bunn (1916-). 1957. Morrow. (P.200)

--*Henry Huggins.* Cleary, Beverly Bunn (1916-). 1950. Morrow. (P.200)

--*Hidden Trail.* Kjelgaard, James Arthur (1910-1959). 1962. Holiday House. (P.530)

--*Independent Bluebird.* Gallup, Lucy. 1959. Morrow. (P.353)

--*Islands of the Ocean.* Goetz, Delia (1898-). 1964. Morrow. (P.372)

--*Miss Charity Comes to Stay.* Constant, Alberta Wilson (1908-1981). 1959. Crowell. (P.214)

--*The Mouse and the Motorcycle.* Cleary, Beverly Bunn (1916-). 1965. W. Morrow. **Award: (ALA).** (P.200)

--*Mr.* Bass's Planetoid. Cameron, Eleanor (1912-). 1958. Little. (P.163)

--*Mr.* Peabody's Pesky Ducks. 1st ed. Sharfman, Amalie. 1957. Little, Brown. (P.815)

--*North Winds Blow Free.* Howard, Elizabeth, pseud. (1907-). Mizner, Elizabeth Howard. 1949. W. Morrow. (P.467)

--*Otis Spofford.* Cleary, Beverly Bunn (1916-). 1953. Morrow. (P.200)

--*Peddler's Girl.* Howard, Elizabeth, pseud. (1907-). Mizner, Elizabeth Howard. 1951. Morrow. (P.467)

--*Ramona the Pest.* Cleary, Beverly Bunn (1916-). 1968. W. Morrow. (P.200)

--*Ribsy.* Cleary, Beverly Bunn (1916-). 1964. Morrow. (P.200)

--*Runaway Ralph.* Cleary, Beverly Bunn (1916-). 1970. William Morrow and Company. (P.200)

--*Shag.* McClung, Robert Marshall (1916-). 1960. Morrow. (P.596)

--*Shag, Last of the Plains Buffalo.* McClung, Robert Marshall (1916-). 1960. Morrow. (P.596)

--*Shoeshine Boy.* Beim, Jerrold (1910-1957). 1954. Morrow. (P.89)

--*Stormy.* Kjelgaard, James Arthur (1910-1959). 1959. Holiday House. (P.530)

--*Swimming Hole.* Beim, Jerrold (1910-1957). 1950, c.1951. Morrow. (P.89)

--*Thin Ice.* Beim, Jerrold (1910-1957). 1956. Morrow. (P.89)

--*Time for Gym.* Beim, Jerrold (1910-1957). 1957. Morrow. (P.89)

--*Waggles and the Dog Catcher.* Cook, Marion Belden. 1951. Morrow. (P.215)

--*Watch for a Tall White Sail.* Bell, Margaret Elizabeth (1898-). 1948. Morrow. (P.91)

Darling, Louis, Jr. (1916-1970) & Darling, Lois MacIntyre (1917-)

--*The Sea Serpents Around Us.* Darling, Lois MacIntyre (1917-) & Darling, Louis, Jr. (1916-1970). c.1965. Little. (P.242)

Darnell, Eula K.

--*Sonny & the Mountain.* Darnell, Eula K. 1979. Vantage. (P.242)

Darrel, David

--*Boo Baboon.* Darrel, David. c.1940. C. Scribner's Sons. (P.242)

Darrow, Whitney, Jr.

--*Bony.* Zweifel, Frances W. (1931-). 1977. Har-Row. (P.994)

Darrow, Whitney, Jr. (1909-)

--*The Fireside Book of Fun & Game Songs.* Winn, Marie (1936-), ed. Miller, Allan, contrib. by. 1974. S&S. (P.969)

--*The Four Getsys and What They Forgot.* Prager, Annabelle. c.1982. Pantheon Books. (P.736)

--*Grandma Zoo.* Gordon, Shirley (1921-). c.1978. Harper & Row. (P.377)

--*Kids Sure Rite Funny!.* A Child's Garden of Misinformation. Linkletter, Arthur Gordon (1912-). 1962. B. Geis Associates; Distributed by Random House. (P.574)

--*Shiver, Gobble and Snore: A Story About Why People Need Laws.* Winn, Marie (1936-). 1972. Simon & Schuster. (P.969)

--*The Thief-Catcher: A Story About Why People Pay Taxes.* Winn, Marie (1936-). 1972. Simon and Schuster. (P.969)

--*Unidentified Flying Elephant.* Kraus, Robert (1925-). 1968. S&S. (P.538)

--*Walter, the Homing Pigeon.* Benchley, Nathaniel Goddard (1915-1981). c.1981. Harper & Row. (P.92)

--*What Dr.* Spock didnt tell us. Atkinson, B. M., Jr. 1959. Simon and Schuster. (P.53)

--*Whitney Darrow,Jr.'s*, Unidentified Flying Elephant. Kraus, Robert (1925-). 1968. Windmill Books. (P.538)

Dart, Eleanor

--*Cathy B.* Careful and Billy B. Ware;. A/Child's Book of Safety. Summit, Mildred. 1953. Jolly Books. (P.871)

--*A Hallowe'en Odyssey.* Carol, Lois, pseud. & Winkler, Carol Serra. Winkler, Louis. 1975. Winkler and Winkler. (P.170)

--*Happy Days: What Children Do the Whole Day Through.* Frank, Janet, pseud. (1928-). Dunleavy, Janet Egleson. 1955. Simon and Schuster. (P.341)

--*It's a Date: Boy-Girl Stories for the Teens.* Stowe, Aurelia, ed. 1950. Random House. (P.864)

--*Just Like Daddy.* Simon, Bobby. 1952. Wonder Books. (P.824)

--*King of the Pygmies.* Lahey, Thomas Aquinas (1886-). 1944. St. Anthony Guild Press. (P.544)

--*The Magic Word.* Zolotow, Charlotte Shapiro (1915-). 1952. Wonder Books. (P.994)

--*Romper Room Do Bees: A Book of Manners.* Claster, Nancy. 1956. Simon and Schuster. (P.200)

Da Ru, Peter J.

--*The Adventures of Twinkly Eyes: The Little Black Bear.* Chaffee, Allen. 1919. Milton Bradley Company. (P.181)

--*Chinook: The Cinnamon Cub.* Chaffee, Allen. c.1924. Milton Bradley Company. (P.181)

--*Fuzzy-Wuzz: A Little Brown Bear of the Sierras.* Chaffee, Allen. c.1922. Milton Bradley Company. (P.181)

--*Lost River: Or, The Adventures of Two Boys in the Big Woods.* Chaffee, Allen. 1920. Milton Bradley Company. (P.181)

--*Sitka, the Snow Baby.* Chaffee, Allen. c.1923. Milton Bradley Company. (P.181)

--*Trail and Tree Top.* Chaffee, Allen. 1920. Milton Bradley Co. (P.181)

Daure, Philippe
--*Pim and the Caves of Coscorron.* Loisy, Jeanne (1913-). Emerson, Joyce, tr. from Fr. 1963. Pantheon Books. (P.581)
Davar, Ashok
--*The Wheel of King Asoka.* Davar, Ashok. c.1977. Follett Pub. Co. (P.243)
Davenport, Gilbert Boyd
--*Stories for Creative Acting: Stories Recommended and Used Successfully by Leading Creative Dramatics Directors and Teachers.* Kase, Charles Robert, ed. 1961. French. (P.508)
Davenport, May
--*Dudley Smithwright & the Phantom Voice.* Steinour, Marcus. 1982. Davenport. (P.852)
--*John Hawk: White Man, Black Man, Indian Chief.* Levin, Beatrice. 1982. Davenport. (P.568)
--*Pigalee Pink & Other Stories.* Dorio, Evelyn. Davenport, May, intro. by. 1979. Davenport. (P.281)
Davenport, Roy (1936-), photos by.
--*Sleepy to the Rescue.* McReynolds, Bob (1936-). 1949. Viking Press. (P.611)
Davenport, W. R.
--*Words at Play.* Sutro, Alfred (1869-1933). Smart, Adam, pseud. c.1939. Printed at the Grabhorn Press. (P.872)
David, Brian
--*Robbie of the Kirkhaven Team.* Rowland, Florence Wightman (1900-). c.1973. Ginn. (P.782)
David, Crockett, pseud., see Leisk, David Johnson.
David, Ismar
--*One Hundred Poems About People.* Parker, Elinor Milnor (1906-), compiled by. 1955. T Y Crowell. (P.706)
--*Poems from the German.* Plotz, Helen Ratnoff (1913-), ed. 1967. T Y Crowell. (P.728)
David, Jonathan, pseud., see Ames, Lee Judah.
David, Jonathan, pseud. (1921-)
--*Dugout Mystery.* 1st ed. Ames, Lee Judah. Bonner, Mary Graham (1890-1974). 1953. Knopf. (P.116)
David, Mark
--*Oscar, the Ostrich.* Lawrence, Jerome (1915-). 1940. Random House, Inc. (P.556)
David, Marshall
--*Partners of Powder Hole.* Davis, Robert (1881-). c.1947. Holiday House. (P.247)
Davidow-Goodman, Ann (1932-)
--*Let's Draw Dinosaurs.* Davidow-Goodman, Ann (1932-). 1978. Putnam Pub Group. (P.244)
Davidson, Al
--*The Adventures of Tom Sawyer.* Clemens, Samuel Langhorne (1835-1910). Twain, Mark, pseud. 1970, c.1969. Childrens Press. (P.201)
Davidson, Amanda
--*Teddy's Birthday.* Davidson, Amanda. c.1985. Holt, Rinehart and Winston. (P.244)
Davidson, Bertha G.
--*Almost As Good As a Boy.* Douglas, Amanda Minnie (1837-1916). 1900. Lee and Shepard. (P.281)
--*Almost As Good as a Boy.* Douglas, Amanda Minnie (1837-1916). 1905. Lee and Shepard Company. (P.281)
--*Boy Donald and his Chum.* Shirley, Penn, pseud. (1840-). Clarke, Sarah Jones. 1901. Lee & Shepard. (P.821)
--*Boy Donald and His Hero.* Shirley, Penn, pseud. (1840-). Clarke, Sarah Jones. 1902. Lothrop, Lee & Shepard. (P.821)
--*The Children on the Top Floor.* Rhoades, Nina, pseud. (1863-). Rhoades, Cornelia Harson. 1904. Lee and Shepard. (P.759)
--*Dolly's Double.* Wood, Ethel. 1905. Lothrop Lee & Shepard Co. (P.975)
--*The Double Prince: Or, A Fall Through the Moon.* Bicknell, Frank Martin (1854-). N.D. Caldwell. (P.101)
--*Gipsy Jane.* Cheever, Harriet Anna, Mrs. 1903. Dana Estes & Co. (P.189)
--*Harry's Temptation: Or, Christmas in Canada.* Robinson, Anna, adapted by. 1906. Dana Estes & Co. (P.769)
--*An Honor Girl.* Raymond, Evelyn Hunt, Mrs. (1843-1910). 1904. Lothrop, Lee & Shepard. (P.751)
--*The Little Girl Next Door.* Rhoades, Nina, pseud. (1863-). Rhodes, Cornelia Harson. 1902. Lee and Shepard. (P.760)
--*Little Miss Rosamond.* Rhoades, Nina, pseud. (1863-). Rhoades, Cornelia Harson. 1906. Lothrop, Lee & Shepard Co. (P.760)
--*Lou.* Cheever, Harriet Anna, Mrs. N.D. Dana Estes and Company. (P.189)
--*Marion's Vacation.* Rhoades, Nina, pseud. (1863-). Rhoades , Cornelia Harson. 1907. Lothrop, Lee & Shepard Co. (P.760)
--*Old Lady and Young Laddie: Two Christmas Stories.* Patch, Kate Whiting, Mrs. (1870-). c.1900. J. H. West Company. (P.708)
--*Only Dollie: A Story for Girls.* Rhoades, Nina, pseud. (1863-). Rhoades, Cornelia Harson. 1901. Lothrop, Lee & Shepard. (P.760)
--*Priscilla of the Doll Shop.* Rhoades, Nina, pseud. (1863-). Rhoades, Cornelia Harson. 1907. Lothrop, Lee & Shepard Co. (P.760)
--*The Story of Little Paul.* Knowles, Frederic Lawrence (1869-1905). N.D. Dana Estes and Company. (P.533)
--*Tommy Joyce and Tommy Joy.* Cheever, Harriet Anna, Mrs. 1905. Dana Estes and Company. (P.189)
--*Two Little Street Singers.* Roe, Nora Ardelia Metcalf, Mrs. (1856-1910). 1900. Lee and Shepard. (P.774)
--*Two Little Street Singers.* Roe, Nora Ardelia Metcalf, Mrs. (1856-1910). 1905. Lee and Shepard Company. (P.774)
Davidson, Bertha G., jt. illus. see Keyes, Homer Eaton.
Davidson, Bertha G. & Wheeler, L. J.
--*The Story of Little Peter.* Marryat, Frederick (1792-1848). 1904. D. Estes & Co. (P.621)
Davidson, Clara D.
--*The Golden Palace of Neverland.* Robinson, William Henry (1867-). 1907. E. P. Dutton & Company. (P.770)
--*Happy Days at Hillside.* Morse, Emily Hewitt. c.1911. E. P. Dutton Co. (P.666)
Davidson, Harley F.
--*The Shiny Scoop.* Wing, Camilla. c.1941. Dannie Books. (P.969)
--*The String Bean Horse.* Wing, Camilla. c.1941. Dannie Books. (P.969)
Davidson, Kevin, jt. illus. see Matthews, Patricia Anne.
Davidson, Raymond (1926-)
--*The Genuine, Ingenious, Thrift Shop Genie, Clarrisa Mae Bean & Me.* Keller, Beverly Lou. c.1977. Coward, McCann & Geoghegan. (P.514)
Davidson, Rosalie (1921-)
--*Color My World.* Carley, Wayne. 1974. Garrard Pub. Co. (P.168)
--*Drat the Dragon.* McInnes, John (1927-). 1973. Garrard Pub. Co. (P.604)
--*Who Ever Heard of a Tiger in a Tree.* McInnes, John (1927-). 1971. Garrard Pub. Co. (P.604)
--*Who Is Root Beer?.* Hare, Norma Quarles (1924-). c.1977. Garrard Pub. Co. (P.412)
--*Why Won't the Dragon Roar?.* Rosenbluth, Rosalyn. c.1977. Garrard Pub. Co. (P.778)
Davidson, Ruby & Weihs, Erika (1917-)
--*Alphabet Zoo.* Horowitz, Caroline (1909-). Lansing, Jane K., pseud. 1965. Hart Pub. Co. (P.464)
Davidson, Sandra Calder (1935-)
--*Alligator Smiling in the Sawgrass.* Ironmonger, Ira. 1965. Young Scott Books. (P.481)
--*Sylvester.* Davidson, Sandra Calder (1935-). Calder, Alexander (1898-1976) & Davidson, Jean, trs. from Fr. 1967. Follett Pub. Co. (P.244)
--*Sylvester and the Butterfly Bomb.* Davidson, Sandra Calder (1935-). Kroll, Edite, tr. from Fr. 1972. Doubleday. (P.244)
Davie, Howard
--*The Heroes: Or, Greek Fairy Tales.* Kingsley, Charles (1819-1875). 1927. David McKay Company. (P.524)
--*The Heroes: Or, Greek Fairy Tales.* Kingsley, Charles (1819-1875). N.D. David McKay. (P.524)
Davies, Frank
--*The Mystery of Monster Lake.* Gammon, David J. c.1962. Little, Brown. (P.353)
Davies, J. B.
--*The Mill on the Floss.* Eliot, George, pseud. (1819-1880). Evans, Marian. N.D. Collins. (P.301)
Davies, Sumiko
--*Kittymouse.* Davies, Sumiko. 1979. HarBraceJ. (P.244)
D'Avignon, Sue
--*Fun for Hunkydory.* Justus, May (1898-). 1976. Western Pub. (P.503)
Davina, Frank & Lokvig, Tor
--*Daniel.* Jones, Helen Hinckley (1903-). Ford, Frank, ed. 1970. Word Bks. (P.499)
--*David.* Jones, Helen Hinckley (1903-). Ford, Frank, ed. 1970. Word Bks. (P.499)
--*Esther.* Jones, Helen Hinckley (1903-). Ford, Frank, ed. 1970. Word Bks. (P.499)
--*Joseph.* Jones, Helen Hinckley (1903-). Ford, Frank, ed. 1970. Word Bks. (P.499)
--*Moses.* Jones, Helen Hinckley (1903-). Ford, Frank, ed. 1970. Word Bks. (P.499)
--*Noah.* Jones, Helen Hinckley (1903-). Ford, Frank, ed. 1970. Word Bks. (P.499)
Davine
--*Red Feather.* Fischer, Marjorie, Mrs. 1950. J. Messner. (P.327)
--*Red Feather.* Fischer, Marjorie, Mrs. c.1937. Modern Age Books, Inc. (P.327)
Davis, Allen
--*Displaced Person.* Bloch, Marie Halun (1910-). c.1978. Lothrop, Lee & Shepard. (P.109)
--*Displaced Person.* Bloch, Marie Halun (1910-). 1978. Morrow. (P.109)
--*The Firebug Mystery.* Christian, Mary Blount (1933-). 1981. A. Whitman. (P.193)
--*For Love of Jody.* Branscum, Robbie (1937-). c.1979. Lothrop, Lee & Shepard Books. (P.128)
--*Ghost of the Great River Inn.* Hall, Lynn (1937-). c.1981. Follett Pub. Co. (P.405)
--*I Can Stop Any Time I Want.* Davis, Trivers James. 1974. Prentice Hall. (P.247)
--*I Can Stop Anytime I Want.* Trivers, James. 1974. Prentice-Hall. (P.901)
--*I Love to Laugh.* Nordlicht, Lillian. Silverman, Manuel S., intro. by. c.1980. Raintree Childrens Books. (P.685)
--*An Oak Tree Dies and a Journey Begins.* Norris, Louanne (1930-) & Smith, Howard Everett, Jr. (1927-). c.1979. Crown Publishers. (P.685)
--*The Queen Bee.* Grimm, Jakob Ludwig Karl (1785-1863) & Grimm, Wilhelm Karl (1786-1859). 1983. Childrens Bk Co. (P.394)
--*The Stopping Place.* Dahlstedt, Marden (1921-). c.1976. Putnam. (P.238)
--*A String in the Harp.* Bond, Nancy Barbara (1945-). 1976. Atheneum. **Awards: (IRA); (ALA); (BGH); (JNM).** (P.114)
--*Three Buckets of Daylight.* Branscum, Robbie (1937-). c.1978. Lothrop, Lee & Shepard. (P.128)
Davis, Bette J. (1923-)
--*Freedom Eagle.* Davis, Bette J (1923-). 1972. Lothrop, Lee & Shepard Co. (P.245)
--*Maria Mitchell, Girl Astronomer.* 1st ed. Melin, Grace Hathaway (1892-1973). 1954. Bobbs-Merrill. (P.640)
--*Myths and Legends of the Ages.* rev. ed. Horowitz, Caroline (1909-). French, Marion N., pseud. 1957, c.1956. Hart Pub. Co. (P.464)
--*Narcissa Whitman, Pioneer Girl.* 1st ed. Warner, Ann Spence. 1953. Bobbs-Merrill. (P.931)
Davis, Bill (1949-)
--*The Amazing Mumford Presents the Magic Weather Show: Featuring Jim Henson's Sesame Street Muppets.* Stevenson, Jocelyn. Henson, Jim, pseud. (1936-), created by Henson, James Maury. c.1981. Western Pub. Co. (P.855)
--*A Day in Life of Oscar the Grouch.* Hayward, Linda. 1982. Western Pub. (P.426)
--*A Day in the Life of Oscar the Grouch: Featuring Jim Henson's Sesame Street Muppets.* Hayward, Linda. c.1981. Western Pub. Co. in Conjunction with Children's Television Workshop. (P.426)
Davis, Carl Brandt, jt. illus. see Davis, Dorothy Brandt.
Davis, Daphne
--*The Donald Duck Book.* Davis, Daphne. 1964. Western Pub. (P.245)
Davis, Dimitris (1905-)
--*Aleko's Island.* 1st ed. Fenton, Edward (1917-). 1948. Doubleday. (P.322)
--*Greek Gods and Heroes.* 1st ed. Graves, Robert (1895-). 1960. Doubleday. **Award: (ALA).** (P.382)
--*An Island for a Pelican.* Fenton, Edward (1917-). 1963. Doubleday. (P.322)
--*An Island for a Pelican.* Fenton, Edward (1917-). 1963. E. M. Hale and Company. (P.322)
--*A Present from Petros.* Bishop, Claire Huchet, Mrs. 1961. Viking Press. (P.103)
--*Theras and His Town.* Snedeker, Caroline Dale Parke, Mrs. (1871-1956). 1961. Doubleday. (P.837)
Davis, Dorothy Brandt & Davis, Carl Brandt
--*The Tall Man.* Davis, Dorothy Brandt & Davis, Carl Brandt. 1963. Brethren Press. (P.245)
Davis, Dorothy Brandt & Davis, Sarah Elizabeth
--*The Little Man.* Davis, Dorothy Brandt & Davis, Sarah Elizabeth. 1966. Brethren Pr. (P.245)
Davis, Emma Earlenbaugh
--*Romee Ann, Junior.* Hornibrook, Isabel Katherine (1859-). c.1926. David McKay Company. (P.464)
--*Romee Ann, Sophomore.* Hornibrook, Isabel Katherine (1859-). c.1925. David McKay Company. (P.464)
Davis, Florence, jt. illus. see Armstrong, Tom.
Davis, Francis W.
--*Mac Mallard.* Eschmeyer, Reuben William (1905-). Davis, francis W., designed by. 1953. Fisherman Press. (P.309)
--*Woody Woodcock.* Eschmeyer, Reuben William (1905-). Davis, Francis W., designed by. 1953. Fisherman Press. (P.309)
--*Woody Woodcock.* Eschmeyer, Reuben William (1905-). N.D. Greenberg Publishers. (P.309)
Davis, G. A.
--*The Yellow Dwarf, and Other Stories.* c.1907. McLoughlin Bros. (P.245)
Davis, J. Steeple
--*Deerfoot in the Forest.* Ellis, Edward Sylvester (1840-1916). 1905. The J. C. Winston Co. (P.302)
--*Deerfoot in the Mountains.* Ellis, Edward Sylvester (1840-1916). 1905. John C. Winston. (P.302)
--*Deerfoot on the Prairies.* Ellis, Edward Sylvester (1840-1916). 1905. John C. Winston. (P.302)
--*The Lost Galleon of Doubloon Island.* Foster, Walter Bertram (1869-). 1901. The Penn Publishing Company. (P.339)
--*On Fighting Decks in 1812.* Costello, Frederick Hankerson (1851-1921). c.1899. D. Estes & Company. (P.223)
--*True to His Trust.* Ellis, Edward Sylvester (1840-1916). N.D. Penn Publishing Co. (P.304)
--*True to His Trust.* Ellis, Edward Sylvester (1840-1916). 1897. The Penn Publishing Company. (P.304)
--*Uncrowning a King: A Tale of King Philip's War.* Ellis, Edward Sylvester (1840-1916). N.D. Penn. (P.304)
--*Under the Rattlesnake Flag.* Costello, Frederick Hankerson (1851-1921). c.1898. Estes and Lauriat. (P.223)
Davis, J. Watson
--*Across the Delaware: A Boy's Story of the Battle of Trenton in 1777.* Kaler, James Otis (1848-1912). Otis, James, pseud. 1903. A. L. Burt. (P.504)
--*Adrift on the Pacific: A Boys's Story of the Sea and it's Perils.* Ellis, Edward Sylvester (1840-1916). N.D. A. L. Burt Company. (P.302)
--*Afloat in Freedom's Cause: The Story of Two Boys in the War of 1812.* Kaler, James Otis (1848-1912). Otis, James, pseud. c.1908. A. L. Burt Company. (P.504)
--*Amos Dunkel, Oarsman: A Story of the Whale Boat Navy of 1776.* Kaler, James Otis (1848-1912). Otis, James, pseud. 1901. A. L. Burt. (P.504)
--*At the Siege of Detroit.* Kaler, James Otis (1848-1912). Otis, Kaler, pseud. 1904. A. L. Burt Co. (P.504)
--*Bernard Brook's Adventures: The/Story of a Brave Boy's Trials.* Alger, Horatio, Jr. (1832-1899). 1903. A. L. Burt Company. (P.23)
--*Billy Goat's Story.* Prentice, Amy. c.1906. A. L. Burt Company. (P.737)
--*The Boy Patriot.* Ellis, Edward Sylvester (1840-1916). N.D. A. L. Burt' Pubs. (P.302)
--*The Boy Patriot.* A Story of Jack, the Young Friend of Washington. Ellis, Edward Sylvester (1840-1916). c.1900. A. L. Burt. (P.302)
--*The Boy Pickets.* Chipman, William Pendleton (1848-1912). N.D. A. L. Burt. (P.191)
--*The Boy Truckers: A Story of Florida.* Ely, Wilmer Mateo. c.1905. A. L. Burt Co. (P.305)
--*A Brave Defense.* Chipman, William Pendleton (1848-1912). 1900. A. L. Burt's Pubs. (P.192)
--*Brown Owl's Story.* Prentice, Amy. c.1906. A. L. Burt Company. (P.737)
--*Bunny Rabbit's Story.* Prentice, Amy. c.1906. A. L. Burt Company. (P.737)
--*The Capture of the Laughing Mary: A Story of Three New York Boys in 1776.* Kaler, James Otis (1848-1912). Otis, James, pseud. c.1898. A. L. Burt. (P.505)
--*Commodore Barney's Young Spies: A Boy's Story of the Burning of the City of Washington.* Kaler, James Otis (1848-1912). Otis, James, pseud. c.1907. A. L. Burt Company. (P.505)
--*Corporal Lige's Recruit: A Story of Crown Point and Ticonderoga.* Kaler, James Otis (1848-1912). Otis, James, pseud. 1898. A. L. Burt. (P.505)
--*Corporal 'Lige's Recruit: A Story of Crown Point and Ticonderoga.* Kaler, James Otis (1848-1912). Otis, James, pseud. c.1899. A. L. Burt. (P.505)
--*Croaky Frog's Story.* Prentice, Amy. c.1906. A. L. Burt Company. (P.737)
--*A Cruise with Paul Jones: A Story of Naval Warfare in 1778.* Kaler, James Otis (1848-1912). Otis, James, pseud. 1899. A. L. Burt. (P.505)
--*A Debt of Honor: The Story of Gerald Lane's Success in the Far West.* Alger, Horatio, Jr. (1832-1899). 1900. A. L. Burt. (P.24)
--*The Defense of Fort Henry: A Story of Wheeling Creek in 1777.* Kaler, James Otis (1848-1912). Otis, James, pseud. 1900. A. L. Burt. (P.505)
--*Fighting to Win: The Story of a New York Boy.* Ellis, Edward Sylvester (1840-1916). c.1907. A. L. Burt Company. (P.302)
--*Frisky Squirrel's Story.* Prentice, Amy. c.1906. A. L. Burt Company. (P.737)
--*Gray Goose's Story.* Prentice, Amy. c.1906. A. L. Burt Company. (P.737)
--*Grimm's Fairy Tales.* Grimm, Jakob Ludwig Karl (1785-1863) & Grimm, Wilhelm Karl (1786-1859). Remy, Jean S., retold by. 1901. A. L. Burt Co. (P.392)
--*The History of Tom Thumb.* 1905. A. L. Burt. (P.246)
--*In Defense of Liberty: A Story of the Burning of the British Schooner Gaspee in 1772.* Chipman, William Pendleton (1848-1912). c.1908. A. L. Burt Company. (P.192)
--*In King Philip's War: A Story of Two Boys Captured by the Great Sachem.* Ober, Frederick Albion (1849-1913). c.1907. A. L. Burt Company. (P.689)

De Lanux, Eyre
--*Overheard in a Bubble Chamber & Other Sciencepoems.* Morrison, Lillian (1917-), compiled by. 1981. Lothrop. (P.665)
De Lanux, Jeanne
--*Cease Firing, and Other Stories.* Hulbert, Winifred. 1929. The Macmillan Company. (P.472)
DeLara, George
--*Sports and Games in Verse and Rhyme.* Jacobs, Allan Duane (1934-) & Jacobs, Leland Blair (1907-), eds. 1975. Garrard Pub. Co. (P.486)
DeLara, Phil & Totten, Bob
--*The Road Runner: A Very Scary Lesson.* Schroeder, Russell K. 1979. Western Pub. (P.801)
De La Rosa, Isauro
--*Good Times at the Fair.* Bauer, Helen (1900-). 1957. Melmont Publishers. (P.81)
De'Larrea, Victoria
--*Abracatabby.* Hiller, Catherine (1946-). c.1981. Coward, McCann & Geoghegan. (P.444)
--*Baby Needs Shoes.* Carlson, Dale Bick (1935-). 1974. Atheneum. (P.168)
--*The Blackmail Machine.* Holman, Felice (1919-). 1967, c.1968. Macmillan. (P.456)
--*Candles, Cakes, & Donkey Tails: Birthday Symbols & Celebrations.* Perl, Lila. 1984. HM. (P.718)
--*The Christmas Dolls: A Butterfield Square Story.* York, Carol Beach (1928-). 1967. Watts. (P.988)
--*The Friendly Woods.* House, Charles Albert (1916-). c.1973. Four Winds Press. (P.466)
--*Good Charlotte: A Butterfield Square Story.* York, Carol Beach (1928-). 1969. Watts. (P.988)
--*Good Day Mice: A Butterfield Square Story.* York, Carol Beach (1928-). 1968. Watts. (P.988)
--*The Green Goose.* 1st ed. Koob, Theodora Johanna Foth (1918-). 1967. Lippincott. (P.535)
--*Halloween Treats.* Haywood, Carolyn (1898-). 1981. W. Morrow. (P.427)
--*Herbert's Treasure.* Low, Alice (1926-). 1971. Putnam. (P.588)
--*Juba This and Juba That: Story Hour Stretches for Large or Small Groups.* 1st ed. Tashjian, Virginia A. (1921-), ed. 1969. Little, Brown. (P.878)
--*Jumbo Spencer.* Cresswell, Helen. 1966, c.1963. Lippincott. (P.230)
--*Leprechaun Tales.* 1st ed. Green, Kathleen. 1968. Lippincott. (P.384)
--*Lisa and Lottie.* Kastner, Erich (1899-1974). Brooks, Cyrus, tr. 1969. Knopf. (P.508)
--*Little Is Nice.* 1st ed. Kaufmann, Alicia. 1970. Hawthorn Books. (P.509)
--*Lucy.* Storr, Catherine Cole (1913-). 1968, c.1961. Prentice-Hall. (P.863)
--*Lucy.* Storr, Catherine Cole (1913-). 1974, c.1961. Prentice-Hall. (P.863)
--*Lucy Runs Away.* Storr, Catherine Cole (1913-). 1969. Prentice-Hall. (P.863)
--*Me Is How I Feel: Poems.* Crossen, Stacy Jo. & Covell, Natalie Anne. 1970. Dutton. (P.232)
--*Me Is How I Feel: Poems.* Crossen, Stacy Jo & Covell, Natalie Anne. 1970. McCall Pub. Co. (P.232)
--*Miss Know It All: A Butterfield Square Story.* York, Carol Beach (1928-). c.1966. Watts. (P.988)
--*Miss Know It All Returns: A Butterfield Square Story.* York, Carol Beach (1928-). 1972. Watts. (P.988)
--*No Room for Nicky.* Kaufmann, Alicia. 1969. Hawthorn. (P.509)
--*Orange October.* Inyart, Gene (1927-). 1968. F. Watts. (P.480)
--*The Pheasant on Route Seven.* 1st ed. Starbird, Kaye. 1968. Lippincott. (P.849)
--*Philip and the Pooka.* Green, Kathleen. c.1966. Lippincott. (P.385)
--*Rockabye to Monster Land.* McKee, Frances. 1970. Putnam. (P.605)
--*The Shades.* Brock, Betty (1923-). 1971. Harper & Row. (P.133)
--*The Ten O'Clock Club: A Butterfield Square Story.* York, Carol Beach (1928-). 1970. Watts. (P.988)
--*Waiting for Mama.* De Regniers, Beatrice Schenk Freedman (1914-). 1984. HM. (P.259)
--*Yosemite Tomboy.* Sargent, Shirley (1927-). 1967. Abelard-Schuman. (P.793)
Delattre, Georgette
--*The Black Spaniel Mystery.* Cavanna, Betty (1909-). 1945. The Westminster Press. (P.179)
De Lay, H. S.
--*Billy To-morrow in Camp.* Carr, Sarah Pratt, Mrs. 1910. A. C. McClurg & Co. (P.171)
--*Billy To-Morrow Stands the Test.* Carr, Sarah Pratt, Mrs. 1911. A. C. McClurg & Co. (P.171)
--*The Bob's Hill Braves.* Burton, Charles Pierce (1862-). 1910. H. Holt and Company. (P.157)
--*The Cave of the Bottomless Pool.* Hunting, Henry Gardner (1872-). 1909. H. Holt and Company. (P.475)
--*Chet.* Yates, Katherine Merritte, Mrs. (1865-). 1909. A. C. McClurg & Co. (P.985)
--*The Courier of the Ozarks.* Dunn, Byron Archibald (1842-). 1912. A. C. McClurg & Co. (P.290)
--*The Last Raid.* Dunn, Byron Archibald (1842-). 1914. A. C. McClurg & Co. (P.290)
--*The Scout of Pea Ridge.* Dunn, Byron Archibald (1842-). 1911. A. C. McClurg & Co. (P.290)
--*The Silver Canoe: The Story of the Secret That Had to Be Kept.* Hunting, Henry Gardner (1872-). 1909. A. C. McClurg & Co. (P.475)
--*Storming Vicksburg.* Dunn, Byron Archibald (1842-). 1913. A. C. McClurg & Co. (P.290)
Delcol, Claudia
--*Dr. Moggle's ABC Challenge.* Magel, John. 1985. Rand McNally. (P.613)
De Leeuw, Cateau Wilhelmina (1903-1975)
--*Career for Jennifer.* De Leeuw, Adele Louise (1899-). 1941. The Macmillan Company. (P.254)
--*Island Adventure: A Novel for Girls.* De Leeuw, Adele Louise (1899-). 1934. The Macmillan Company. (P.254)
--*The Patchwork Quilt.* De Leeuw, Adele Louise (1899-). 1943. Little, Brown and Company. (P.254)
--*Place for Herself.* De Leeuw, Adele Louise (1899-). 1937. Macmillan. (P.254)
--*Rika, a Dutch Girl's Vacation in Java.* De Leeuw, Adele Louise (1899-). 1932. The Macmillan Company. (P.254)
--*Year of Promises.* De Leeuw, Adele Louise (1899-). 1936. The Macmillan Company. (P.254)
Delehanty, Frances W.
--*Heralds of the Kin: The Story of the Nativity.* Crownfield, Gertrude (1867-1945). 1931. E. P. Dutton & Co. (P.233)
--*Just Jingles.* Zerbey, Dorthea (1884-). 1935. The Author. (P.992)
--*More Fairy Tale Plays.* Merington, Marguerite. 1917. Duffield & Company. (P.641)
Deler, Sven-Eric & Hallgren, Stig
--*Skrallan and the Pirates.* Lindgren, Astrid Ericsson (1907-). Read, Albert & Sapieha, Christine, trs. 1969, c.1967. Doubleday. (P.573)
Delessert, Etienne, jt. illus. see Holt, Norma.
Delessert, Etienne (1941-)
--*Beauty & the Beast.* Aulnoy, Marie Catherine Jumelle de Berneville (1650-1705). 1983. Childrens Bk Co. (P.54)
--*Being Green.* Raposo, Joseph G. 1973. Western Pub. Co. (P.749)
--*A Christmas Memory.* Capote, Truman (1924-1984). 1983. Childrens Bk Co. (P.166)
--*Just So Stories.* anniversary ed. Kipling, Joseph Rudyard (1865-1936). 1972. Doubleday. **Award: (NYT).** (P.528)
--*The Pony Man.* Lightfoot, Gordon. 1972. Harper's Magazine Press. (P.572)
--*Story Number One: For Children Under Three Years of Age.* Ionesco, Eugene (1912-). Towle, Calvin K., tr. from Fr. 1968. H. Quist; Distributed by Crown Publishers. **Award: (NYT).** (P.480)
--*Story Number Two: For children under Three Years of Age.* Ionesco, Eugene (1912-). N.D. Crown Publishers. (P.480)
--*A Wart Snake in a Fig Tree.* Mendoza, George (1934-). 1976. Dial Bks Young. (P.641)
Delfino, Matte
--*No One Need Ever Know.* Read, Elfreida (1920-). 1971. Ginn. (P.752)
Delhumeau, Annick
--*Jade Tales.* Maurel, Micheline. 1964. Universe. (P.632)
--*Monsieur Bussy, the Celebrated Hamster.* Claude-Lafontaine, Pascale. 1968. McGraw-Hill. (P.200)
DeLipman, M.
--*With Fire and Sword.* N.D. Henry Altemus Co. (P.255)
De Lisle, Gordon, photos by.
--*Andy's Kangaroo; Story.* Nicholson, Joyce Thorpe (1919-). 1965. Lansdowne. (P.681)
--*Kerri and Honey.* Nicholson, Joyce Thorpe (1919-). 1964. Lansdowne. (P.681)
--*Ringtail the Possum.* Nicholson, Joyce Thorpe (1919-). 1966. Lansdowne. (P.681)
Dellenbaugh, Frederic S.
--*Little Smoke: A Tale of the Sioux.* Stoddard, William Osborn (1835-1925). 1891. D. Appleton and Company. (P.860)
Dell'Orco, Pino
--*Za, the Truffle Boy.* 1st ed. Latini, Angela. Colquhoun, Archibald (1912-1964), tr. from Ital. 1961, c.1960. F. Watts. (P.554)
Dellosa, Janet, jt. illus. see Carson, Patti.
De Longpre, Paul (1855-1911)
--*Parables from Nature.* Gatty, Margaret Scott, Mrs. (1809-1873). 1893. G.P. Putnam's Sons. (P.360)
De Lopez, Graciela Carrillo
--*How We Came to the Fifth World: Como Venemos al Quinto Mundo.* Rohmer, Harriet & De Lopez, Graciela Carrillo. N.D. Childrens Book Pr. (P.775)
Del Rossi, Ric
--*What Happened to Hector?.* Teague, Kathleen (1937-). 1974. Garrard Pub. Co. (P.881)
Delstanche, Albert
--*A Boy of Bruges: A Story of Belgian Child Life.* Cammaerts, Emile Leon (1878-1953) & Cammaerts, Tita. c.1918. E. P. Dutton & Company. (P.163)
--*Flemish Legends.* De Coster, Charles T. Taylor, Harold, tr. 1979. Core Collection. (P.250)
De Luca
--*The Bible for Young People.* Daughters of St. Paul. 1969, c.1968. St. Paul Editions. (P.243)
De Luce, Percival
--*Raoul and Iron Hand: Or, Winning the Golden Spurs.* Miller, May Halsey (1865-). N.D. E. P. Dutton & Co. (P.648)
DeLucia, Carlo, jt. illus. see Chen, Tony.
Delulio, John
--*The Day the Animals Left the Zoo.* Delulio, Donata (1941-). 1972. Doubleday. (P.255)
DeLuna, Betty & DeLuna, Tony
--*Starting School.* Stanek, Muriel Novella (1915-1971). c.1981. A. Whitman. (P.848)
De Luna, Tony
--*Don't Forget to Come Back.* Harris, Robie H. c.1978. Knopf : Distributed by Random House. (P.416)
--*First Fairy Tales.* Potter, Grace Elizabeth & Harley, Ruth. 1964. C. E. Merrill Books. (P.733)
--*I Want to Be Little.* Zolotow, Charlotte Shapiro (1915-). 1966. Abelard. (P.994)
--*I Wonder If Herbie's Home Yet.* Kantrowitz, Mildred. 1971. Parents' Magazine Press. (P.507)
--*I'm Not Oscar's Friend Anymore.* 1st ed. Sharmat, Marjorie Weinman (1928-). 1975. Dutton. (P.815)
--*Kenny and His Animal Friends.* Weiss, Joan Talmage (1928-). 1965. Whitman Pub. (P.942)
--*A Monster in the Mailbox.* 1st ed. Gordon, Sheila. c.1978. Dutton. (P.377)
--*Whose Little Red Jacket?.* Green, Mary McBurney (1896-). 1965. F. Watts. (P.385)
DeLuna, Tony, jt. illus. see DeLuna, Betty.
Demarest, Christopher Lynn (1951-)
--*Benedict Finds a Home.* Demarest, Christopher Lynn (1951-). 1982. Lothrop. (P.255)
--*Clemens' Kingdom.* Demarest, Christopher Lynn (1951-). c.1983. Lothrop, Lee & Shepard Books. (P.255)
--*Hedgehog Adventures.* Stanovich, Betty Jo. c.1983. Lothrop, Lee & Shepard Books. (P.849)
--*Hedgehog Surprises.* Stanovich, Betty Jo. 1984. Lothrop. (P.849)
--*Tree House Fun.* Greydanus, Rose. 1980. Troll Assocs. (P.389)
--*World Famous Muriel.* Alexander, Sue (1933-). 1984. Little. (P.23)
--*World Famous Muriel and the Scary Dragon.* Alexander, Sue (1933-). c.1985. Little, Brown. (P.23)
De Martelly, John Stockton (1903-)
--*Wilderness Clearing.* Edmonds, Walter Dumaux (1903-). 1944. Dodd, Mead & Company. (P.297)
De Mejo, Oscar (1911-)
--*The Forty-Niner.* De Mejo, Oscar (1911-). c.1985. Harper & Row. (P.256)
--*The Tiny Visitor.* De Mejo, Oscar (1911-). c.1982. Pantheon Books. **Award: (NYT).** (P.256)
DeMers, Joseph (1910-)
--*Alice in Letterland: ABC.* De Mers, Joseph (1910-). 1946. Mercel Rodd Co. (P.256)
--*Smokey and the Red Fire Engine.* De Mers, Joseph (1910-). 1945. Rogue Press M. Rodd Co., Distributors. (P.256)
--*Sugarfoot and the Merry-Go-Round.* De Mers, Joseph (1910-). 1946. M. Rodd Co. (P.256)
De Meserac, Louis
--*Our Little Brazilian Cousin.* Roulet, Mary F Nixon-, Mrs. 1907. L. C. Page & Company. (P.780)
De Meza, Wilson
--*Children's Thoughts: In Song and Story.* Blake, Louisa Dumaresque. 1883. Cassell & Company, Limited. (P.106)
--*Two Tea Parties.* Vandewater, Rosalie. N.D. Cassell, Petter, Galpin. (P.914)
Demi, pseud., see Hitz, Demi.
Demi, pseud. (1942-)
--*Bong Nam and the Pheasants.* Hitz, Demi. Yoo, Yushin (1940-), retold by. c.1979. Prentice-Hall. (P.988)
--*Dragon Night and Other Lullabies.* 1st ed. Hitz, Demi. Yolen, Jane Hyatt (1939-). c.1980. Methuen. (P.986)
--*Fat Gopal.* Hitz, Demi. Singh, Jacquelin. 1984. HarBraceJ. (P.827)
--*Liang and the Magic Paintbrush.* Hitz, Demi. Demi, pseud. (1942-). Hitz, Demi. c.1980. Holt, Rinehart, and Winston. (P.256)
--*The Nightingale.* Hitz, Demi. Andersen, Hans Christian (1805-1875). Bier, Anna, adapted by. c.1985. Harcourt Brace Jovanovich. **Award: (NYT).** (P.36)
--*Tony's Tunnel.* Hitz, Demi. McGrath, Ann Sperry (1933-). c.1981. Prentice-Hall. (P.602)
--*Watch Harry Grow!.* Hitz, Demi. Demi, pseud. (1942-). Hitz, Demi. 1984. Random. (P.256)
Deming, Edwin Willard, jt. illus. see Mar, Alice.
Deming, Edwin Willard (1860-1942)
--*Children of the River.* Frey, Nina Ames (1902-). 1934. T. Nelson and Sons. (P.345)
--*Cosel with Geronimo on His Last Raid: The Story of an Indian Boy.* Deming, Therese Osterheld, Mrs. (1874-). 1938. F. A. Davis Company. (P.256)
--*The Fur Trail Adventurers.* Wallace, Dillon (1863-1939). 1915. A. C. McClurg & Co. (P.927)
--*In The Fairyland of America: A Tale of the PUkwudiies.* Quick, Herbert. 1901. Frederick A. Stokes. (P.744)
--*Indian Child Life.* Deming, Therese Osterheld, Mrs. (1874-). 1899. F. A. Stokes Company. (P.256)
--*Indian Child Life.* Deming, Therese Osterheld, Mrs. (1874-). c.1927. F. A. Stokes Company. (P.256)
--*Jack Among the Indians.* Grinnell, George Bird (1849-1938). N.D. J. B. Lippincott Co. (P.395)
--*Jack Among the Indians: Or, A Boy's Summer on the Buffalo Plains.* Grinnell, George Bird (1849-1938). 1900. Frederick A. Stokes Company. (P.395)
--*Jack in the Rockies: Or, A Boy's Adventures with a Pack Train.* Grinnell, George Bird (1849-1938). 1904. Frederick A. Stokes Company. (P.395)
--*Jack, The Young Canoeman: An Eastern Boy's Voyage in a Chinook Canoe.* Grinnell, George Bird (1849-1938). 1906. F. A. Stokes Company. (P.395)
--*Jack,the Young Ranchman: Or, A Boy's Adventures in the Rockies.* Grinnell, George Bird (1849-1938). N.D. Frederick A. Strokes. (P.395)
--*Little Brothers of the West.* Deming, Therese Osterheld, Mrs. (1874-). 1902. Frederick A. Stokes Company. (P.256)
--*Many Snows Ago.* Deming, Therese Osterheld, Mrs. (1874-). 1929. Frederick A. Stokes Company. (P.256)
--*Red Folk and Wild Folk.* Deming, Therese (1874-). 1902. Frederick A. Stokes Co. (P.256)
--*Red People of the Wooded Country.* Deming, T.O & Shaw, Thelma. N.D. Albert Whitman & Co. (P.256)
--*Rise of the Lone Star.* Driggs, Howard Roscoe (1873-) & King, Sara S. N.D. J. B. Lippincott Co. (P.285)
--*Wigwam Children.* Deming, Therese Osterheld, Mrs. (1874-). N.D. Frederick A. Stokes. (P.256)
--*Wigwam Evenings: Sioux Folk Tales.* Eastman, Charles Alexander (1858-) & Eastman, Elaine Goodale, Mrs. (1863-). 1909. Little, Brown and Company. (P.294)
Deming, Kathryn O.
--*Original Melodies from Mother Goose.* Mother Goose. Hillegas, Rose T., selected by. c.1938. F. A. Davis Company. (P.669)
De Miskey, Julian (1908-1976)
--*Chucaro, Wild Pony of the Pampa.* 1st ed. Kalnay, Francis (1899-). 1958. Harcourt, Brace. **Awards: (ALA); (JNM).** (P.507)
--*Piccolo.* De Miskey, Julian (1908-1976). 1968. L. W. Singer Co. (P.256)
--*Tim's Mountain.* Montgomery, Rutherford George (1894-). 1959. World Pub. Co. (P.659)
D'Emo, L., jt. illus. see Westmarcott, Bernard.
D'Emo, Leon
--*Dana of the "Sun,".* Fenton, Alfred H. N.D. Farrar & Rinehart. (P.322)
--*New Plays from Old Tales: Arranged for Boys and Girls.* Wright, Harriet Sabra. 1921. The Macmillan Company. (P.981)
--*The North Woods: An Adventure Story for Boys.* Irving, William. 1933. G. P. Putnam's Sons. (P.482)
D'emo, Leon, jt. illus. see Emerson, Caspar.
De Monvel, Boutet R.
--*Girls and Boys.* France, Anatole, pseud. (1844-1924). Thibault, Jacques Anatole Francois. N.D. Duffield. (P.341)
--*Our Children.* France, Anatole, pseud. (1844-1924). Thibault, Jacques Anatole Francois. N.D. Duffield. (P.341)
--*Select Fables From.* La Fontaine, Jean de (1621-1695). Wright, Elizur, Jr., tr. N.D. E. & J. B. Young & Co. (P.544)
Demopoulos, Maria
--*Emily's Rainbow.* Marbach, Ethel. c.1978. Green Tiger Press. (P.619)
De Morgan, William Frend
--*On a Pincushion, and Other Fairy Tales.* DeMorgan, Mary. N.D. E. P. Dutton. (P.256)
DeMorgan, William Frend & Crane, Walter (1845-1915)
--*Complete Fairy Tales.* De Morgan, Mary. N.D. Franklin Watts. (P.256)
Dempster, Al
--*Walt Disney's Cinderella's Friends.* Disney, Walter Elias (1901-1966). Werner, Jane, adapted by. 1957. Golden Press. (P.272)

--*Sally Ann Thunder Ann Whirlwind Crockett.* Cohen, Caron Lee. c.1985. Greenwillow Books. (P.206)

--*Three Friends.* Kraus, Robert (1925-) 1980, c. 1975. Windmill/Wanderer Books (P.538)

--*The Thunder God's Son: A Peruvian Folktale.* Dewey, Ariane (1937-), retold by. c.1981. Greenwillow Books. (P.261)

Dewey, Ariane (1937-) & Aruego, Jose (1932-)

--*Sea Frog, City Frog.* Van Woerkom, Dorothy O'Brien (1924-), retold by. 1975. Macmillan. (P.915)

Dewey, Jennifer

--*The Secret Language of Snow.* Williams, Terry Tempest & Major, Ted, eds. 1984. Sierra Club; Dist. by Pantheon. **Award: (ALA).** (P.964)

Dewey, Katherine

--*Ola and the Runaway Bread.* Himes, Vera Carole. c.1932. Thomas Y. Crowell Co. (P.445)

--*Pepi and the Golden Hawk: A Tale of Old Egypt.* Himes, Vera Carole. c.1932. T. Y. Crowell Company. (P.445)

--*Two Times Two Is Four.* Topelius, Zakarias (1818-1898). Himes, Vera C, adapted by. c.1931. Thomas Y. Crowell Co. (P.896)

Dewey, Kenneth Francis

--*Look with May Ling.* Maxwell, Ruth (1925-). 1974. Ginn. (P.632)

De Wilde, Dick

--*The Little Red Pony.* Bouhuys, Mies & Ridge, Antonia Florence (0000-1981). 1962. Bobbs-Merrill. (P.120)

--*Singing Time: Songs for Nursery & School.* Coleman, Satis Narrona Barton, Mrs. (1878-) & Thorn, Alice Green (1890-1942). c.1929. The John Day Company. (P.209)

--*A Zoo of My Own.* Conyn, Cornelius. 1958. John Day & Co. (P.214)

De Witt, Cornelius Hugh, et al. (1905-)

--*The Golden Treasure Books: Thirty-Four Stories of Fun and Adventure.* Jackson, Kathryn (1907-) & Jackson, Byron (1899-1949). 1951. Simon and Schuster. (P.485)

DeWitt, Cornelius Hugh (1905-)

--*The Golden Book of Words.* Werner, Elsa Jane (1915-). 1949. Simon & Schuster. (P.946)

--*The Golden Encylopedia.* Bennett, Dorothy Agnes (1909-). 1946. Golden Press. (P.93)

--*Horse Stories.* Bechdolt, John Ernest (1884-). 1949. Golden Press. (P.86)

--*Horse Stories.* Bechdolt, John Ernest (1884-). 1950. Simon and Schuster. (P.86)

--*Johnny's Machines.* Palmer, Helen Marion, pseud. (1898-1967). Geisel, Helen. 1949. Simon and Shuster. (P.703)

--*The New Golden Encyclopedia.* Bennett, Dorothy Agnes (1909-). Watson, Jane Werner, rev. by. 1963. Golden Press. (P.93)

--*The Night Before Christmas.* Moore, Clement Clarke (1779-1863). 1946. S&S. (P.660)

--*The Night Before Christmas.* Moore, Clement Clarke (1779-1863). Reed, Mary, ed. 1945. Simon & Schuster. (P.660)

--*Planet Earth.* Ames, Gerald (1906-) & Wyler, Rose. 1963. Golden Press. (P.33)

--*Rob Whitlock, a Pioneer Boy in Old Ohio.* Jackson, Kathryn (1907-) & Jackson, Byron (1899-1949). 1951. Simon and Schuster. (P.485)

--*The Story of Alaska.* Lambert, Clara Breakey, Mrs. c.1940. Harper & Brothers. (P.545)

DeWitt, Elfrieda

--*Santa Mouse.* Brown, Michael (1920-). 1966. Grosset & Dunlap. (P.141)

--*Santa Mouse, Where Are You?.* Brown, Michael (1920-). 1968. Grosset & Dunlap. (P.141)

DeWitt, Elfrieda & De Santis, George

--*A Treasury of Santa Mouse.* Brown, Michael (1920-). 1970. Grosset & Dunlap. (P.141)

DeWitt, Jayne Whistler, jt. illus. see Sorenson, Elizabeth Ann.

DeWitt, Josephine (1907-)

--*Cowboy Ken.* De Witt, Josephine (1907-). 1943. Oxford University Press. (P.262)

--*Felicia: The Curious Cow.* DeWitt, Josephine (1907-). 1940. T. Nelson and Sons. (P.262)

--*The Fisherman and His Cat.* DeWitt, Josephine (1907-). 1937. T. Nelson and Sons. (P.262)

--*Michael Sebastian McKinley Smith.* De Witt, Josephine (1907-). 1942. Thomas Nelson & Co. (P.262)

--*The Milkman's Baby.* DeWitt, Josephine (1907-). 1938. T. Nelson and Sons. (P.262)

--*The Whale and the Ferryboat.* DeWitt, Josephine (1907-). 1939. T. Nelson and Sons. (P.262)

De Wolfe, Henry

--*Johnny Mouse of Corregidor.* Deitrick, Marion Rolfe Johnson (1903-). 1942. The Bobbs-Merrill Company. (P.252)

Dey, Walter

--*The Case of the Stolen Dummy.* Wyatt, George. 1961. Golden Press. (P.982)

--*Journey to Jupiter.* Greene, Joseph Ingham (1897-). 1961. Golden Press. (P.387)

De Yong, Joe

--*Cowboy Hugh: The Oydssey of a Boy.* Nichols, Walter Hammond (1866-). 1927. The Macmillan Company. (P.681)

D. H

--*Murdoch.* Pierce, Hubbell. 1961. Harper. (P.725)

D'Ham, Claude

--*On the Farm.* 1975. Playspaces. (P.262)

D'Harnoncourt, Rene (1901-1968)

--*The Painted Pig.* Morrow, Elizabeth Reeve Cutter, Mrs. (1873-1955). 1942. Borzoi Books. (P.665)

--*The Painted Pig: A Mexican Picture Book.* Morrow, Elizabeth Reeve Cutter, Mrs. (1873-1955). 1930. A. A. Knopf. (P.665)

Dhurandhar, M. V.

--*An Anthology of Indian Tales.* Kincaid, Charles Augustus (1870-1954), ed. 1922. H. Milford, Oxford University Press. (P.523)

--*Deccan Nursery Tales: Or, Fairy Tales from the South.* Kincaid, Charles Augustus (1870-1954), ed. 1971. Grand River Books. (P.523)

Diamond, Donna (1950-)

--*Ann's Spring.* Curley, Daniel (1918-). c.1977. Crowell. (P.235)

--*Are You Sad, Mama?.* 1st ed. Winthrop, Elizabeth, pseud. (1948-). Mahony, Elizabeth Winthrop. c.1979. Harper & Row. (P.970)

--*Beat the Turtle Drum.* Greene, Constance Clarke (1924-). 1976. Viking Press. **Award: (ALA).** (P.386)

--*The Boy Who Sang the Birds.* Weston, John (1932-). c.1976. Scribner. (P.948)

--*Bridge to Terabithia.* Paterson, Katherine Womeldorf (1932-). 1977. Crowell. **Awards: (JNM).** (P.709)

--*Bridge to Terabithia.* Paterson, Katherine Womeldorf (1932-). 1977. Harper. (P.709)

--*The Crystal Child.* Wersba, Barbara (1932-). 1982. Har-Row. (P.946)

--*The Dark Princess.* Kennedy, Jerome Richard (1932-). c.1978. Holiday House. **Award: (ALA).** (P.518)

--*The Enchanted Sticks.* Myers, Steven. 1979. Coward, McCann & Geoghegan. (P.674)

--*A Gift for Mama.* Hautzig, Esther Rudomin (1930-). 1981. Viking Press. **Award: (ALA).** (P.420)

--*Horses of Dreamland.* Duncan, Lois Steinmetz (1934-). c.1985. Little, Brown. (P.289)

--*Keeping it Secret.* Pollock, Penny (1935-). 1982. Putnam. (P.731)

--*Love Poems.* Merriam, Eve (1916-). 1983. A.A. Knopf. (P.642)

--*Mustard.* Graeber, Charlotte Towner. c.1982. Macmillan. (P.380)

--*The Pied Piper of Hamelin.* Diamond, Donna (1950-), retold by. c.1981. Holiday House. (P.262)

--*Red Hart Magic.* Norton, Andre, pseud. (1912-). Norton, Alice Mary. c.1976. Crowell. (P.686)

--*The Remembering Box.* Clifford, Eth, pseud. (1915-). Rosenberg, Ethel Clifford. 1985. Houghton Mifflin. (P.202)

--*Rumpelstiltskin.* Diamond, Donna (1950-), retold by. 1983. Holiday. (P.262)

--*The Seven Ravens.* Diamond, Donna (1950-), retold by. 1979. Viking Pr. (P.262)

--*The Seven Ravens: A Grimm's Fairy Tale.* Grimm, Jakob Ludwig Karl (1785-1863) & Grimm, Wilhelm Karl (1786-1859). Diamond, Donna (1950-), retold by. 1979. Viking Press. (P.394)

--*Swan Lake.* Diamond, Donna (1950-), retold by. c.1979. Holiday House. (P.262)

--*The Transfigured Hart.* Yolen, Jane Hyatt (1939-). 1975. Crowell. (P.987)

Dian, Russell, photos by.

--*The Get-Well Hotel.* Burstein, John (1949-). Durrell, Julie 1980. McGraw-Hill. (P.157)

Dian, Twila

--*A Color & Story Album for Horse Lovers.* Dian, Twila. 1982. Troubador Pr. (P.262)

Di Benedetto, Angelo

--*Pancake Sees the World.* Milwitzy, Selma March. N.D. Comet Press Books. (P.651)

Dicheva, Liljana

--*Rali.* Dichev, Stefan (1920-). 1968, c.1961. Stackpole Books. (P.262)

Dick, Astra Lacis

--*The Biscuit-Tin Family.* Ker Wilson, Barbara (1929-). 1968, c.1967. World Pub. Co. (P.520)

--*The Biscuit-Tin Family.* 1st American ed. Ker Wilson, Barbara (1929-). 1968, c.1967. World Pub. Co. (P.520)

--*Legends of the Gods: Strange and Fascinating Tales from Around the World.* Shelley, Noreen (1920-), retold by. c.1976. Crane Russak. (P.818)

Dick, JoAnn

--*Hope for the Frogs: A Story.* Sparks, Asa Howard (1937-). c.1979. Jalmar Press. (P.842)

--*The Warm Fuzzy Song Book.* Bird, Harriet & Freed, Margaret M. 1980. Jalmar Pr. (P.102)

--*A Warm Fuzzy Tale.* Steiner, Claude (1935-). Freed, Alvyn M. (1913-), intro. by. 1977. Jalmar Pr. (P.852)

Dick, Mike

--*Rick Goes to Little League.* Walker, David G. (1926-). Reese, Pee Wei, intro. by. c.1981. Caroline House. (P.926)

--*Rick Heads for Soccer.* Walker, David G. (1926-). Rote, Kyle, Jr., frwd. by. 1982. Caroline House Publishers. (P.926)

Dickas, Dan

--*The House Biter.* Sheldon, William Denley (1915-). c.1966. Holt, Rinehart and Winston. (P.818)

Dickeman, Mildred R.

--*Little Sister.* Kyle, Margaret. 1927. Harper & Brothers. (P.543)

--*So There!.* Raile, Vilate & Russell, Frank Alden (1908-). 1942. Bookmark Press. (P.747)

Dickens, Frank, pseud., see Huline-Dickens, Frank William.

Dickens, Frank, pseud. (1931-)

--*Albert Herbert Hawkins, the Naughtiest Boy in the World, and the Space Rocket.* Huline-Dickens, Frank William. Dickens, Frank, pseud. (1931-). Huline-Dickens, Frank William. c.1978. Doubleday. (P.264)

Dickens, Jane

--*Undersea Treasure.* Garnett, Richard Duncan Carey (1923-). 1960. Vanguard. (P.358)

Dickerman, Don, jt. illus. see Cooper, Isabel.

Dickey, Robert Livingston (1861-)

--*Black Beauty;.* the Autobiography of a Horse. Sewell, Anna (1820-1878). 1911. Barse & Hopkins. (P.813)

--*Lad.* Terhune, Albert Payson (1872-1942). 1926. E. P. Dutton & Company. (P.882)

Dickinson, Harlyn

--*The Chewing Gum Trees.* Ritchie, Ruth (1900-). Juline, Ruth Bishop, pseud. 1950. Lothrop, Lee & Shepard. (P.766)

Dickinson, Mike

--*My Brother's Silly.* Dickinson, Mike. 1983. Andre Deutsch. (P.265)

Dickson, Ardie

--*Come to the Pond: Vengan Al Estanque.* Dickson, Ardie. c.1976. Mediaworks. (P.265)

Dickson, Charlotte Mason (1895-)

--*Doctor for the Zoo: Verse.* Dickson, Charlotte Mason (1895-). 1948, c.1947. B. Humphries. (P.265)

Dickson, Glenn

--*Who Burned the Hartley House?.* Smith, Carole (1935-). 1985. A. Whitman. (P.831)

Dickson, Mora

--*Tales of an Ashanti Father.* Appiah, Peggy (1921-). 1981. Andre Deutsch. (P.43)

Dickson, Naida (1916-)

--*Big Sister and Tag-Along Teddy.* Dickson, Naida (1916-). 1974. Denison. (P.265)

--*The Happy Moon.* Dickson, Naida (1916-). 1972. T. S. Denison. (P.265)

--*In the Meadow.* Dickson, Naida (1916-). 1971. Denison. (P.265)

--*The Littlest Helper.* Dickson, Naida (1916-). 1971. Denison. (P.265)

Didd, Kay T.

--*Rhymes for Curly Heads.* Akerly, Fredrika G (1898-). c.1949. Decker Press. (P.16)

Didier, Jules

--*French Fairy Tales, 1 of 3 Vols.* Segur, Sophie Rostopchine, Mrs. (1799-1874). Coleman, Mrs., et al., trs. N.D. Porter & Coates. (P.808)

Didier, Jules, jt. illus. see Dore, Louis Christophe Paul Gustave.

Dielmann, Laura Fern, photos by.

--*Just Yesterday.* Martin, Maude Emory. 1944. Hobson Book Press. (P.625)

Dienemann, Debbie

--*The Boy Who Wanted to Be a Missionary.* Ross, Uta V. O. 1984. Abingdon. (P.779)

--*The Good Morning Grump.* Deitz (1947-). c.1982. Abingdon. (P.252)

Dierks, Dennis A.

--*Hans Brinker: Or, the Silver Skates.* Dodge, Mary Elizabeth Mapes, Mrs. (1831-1905). 1969. Childrens. (P.276)

Dietmeier, Mel

--*Potato.* Dietmeier, Mel. 1972. Addison-Wesley. (P.265)

Dietrich, Wilson G. (1916-)

--*Powee in Valentine Land.* Dietrich, Wilson G. (1916-). N.D. Denison. (P.265)

--*Powee's Jack-O-Lantern.* Dietrich, Wilson G. (1916-). 1969. T. S. Denison. (P.265)

Dietz, Birte

--*The Emperor's New Clothes.* Andersen, Hans Christian (1805-1875). 1971. Van Nostrand Reinhold Co. (P.35)

Dietzsch-Capelle, Erika

--*Mumble Bear.* Ruck-Pauquet, Gina. c.1980. Putnam. (P.783)

Diffenderfer, Ed

--*Dream Pirate.* Durish, Jack & Street, Nicki. c.1981. Fearon Education. (P.291)

Diffily, John

--*And the Winds Blew.* Ernest, Bro., pseud. (1897-). Ryan, John D.. 1948. St. Anthony Guild Press. (P.309)

Di Fiori, Lawrence

--*The Alphabet Boat: A Seagoing Alphabet Book.* Mendoza, George (1934-). 1972. American Heritage Press. (P.641)

--*Anna Help Ginger.* Wahl, Jan (1933-). 1971. Putnam. (P.924)

--*Boober Fraggle's Ghosts.* Gikow, Louise. c.1985. Muppet Press : Holt, Rinehart and Winston. (P.366)

--*Cat O' Nine Tales.* Untermeyer, Louis (1885-1977), as told by. 1971. American Heritage Press. (P.910)

--*The Flying Shoes.* Jameson, Cynthia. 1973. Parents' Magazine Press. (P.489)

--*If I Were King of the Universe.* Abelson, Danny (1950-). c.1984. Holt, Rinehart, and Winston. (P.4)

--*Kim's Place And Other Poems.* Hopkins, Lee Bennett (1938-). 1974. Holt, Rinehart and Winston. (P.463)

--*The Man Who Made Everyone Late.* Suhl, Yuri (1908-). 1974. Four Winds Press. (P.870)

--*Palmer Patch.* Wallace, Barbara Brooks (1922-). c.1976. Follett. (P.926)

--*The Radish Day Jubilee.* 1st ed. Bruce, Sheilah B. c.1983. Muppet Press : Holt, Rinehart, and Winston. (P.144)

--*The Strange, but Wonderful, Cosmic Awareness of Duffy Moon.* Robinson, Jean O. (1934-). 1974. Seabury Press. (P.770)

--*The Strawberry Mother Goose.* DiFiori, Lawrence. c.1975. Strawberry Books : Distributed by Larousse. (P.266)

--*Strawberry Mother Goose.* new ed. Hefter, Richard (1942-), ed. 1975. McGraw. (P.429)

--*That's Silly.* 1st ed. Sleator, William Warner, III (1945-). c.1981. Dutton. (P.829)

--*There Really Was a Dodo.* Gordon, Esther Saranga (1935-) & Gordon, Bernard Ludwig (1931-). 1974. Walck. (P.376)

--*A Toad for Tuesday.* Erickson, Russell Everett (1932-). 1974. Lothrop, Lee & Shepard Co. (P.309)

--*Warton and Morton.* Erickson, Russell Everett (1932-). c.1976. Lothrop, Lee & Shepard Co. (P.309)

--*Warton & the Castaways.* Erickson, Russell Everett (1932-). 1982. Lothrop. (P.309)

--*Warton and the King of the Skies.* Erickson, Russell Everett (1932-). c.1978. Lothrop, Lee & Shepard Co. (P.309)

--*Warton and the Traders.* Erickson, Russell Everett (1932-). c.1979. Lothrop, Lee & Shepard Co. (P.309)

--*Warton's Christmas Eve Adventure.* Erickson, Russell Everett (1932-). c.1977. Lothrop, Lee & Shepard Co. (P.309)

--*Where's Goldie?.* DiFiori, Lawrence. 1983. Western Pub. (P.266)

Digby, Desmond

--*Waltzing Matilda.* Paterson, Andrew Barton (1864-1941). 1972, c.1970. Holt, Rinehart and Winston. (P.709)

Di Gemma, Joseph

--*The Diary of Ducky Daddles.* Obenschain, Eunice M. c.1936. Fortuny's. (P.689)

Diggs, Dian & Wilson, Robert Franklin (1937-)

--*Happy Harvest.* 1st ed. Downing, Sybil & Barker, Jane Valentine (1930-). c.1978. Pruett Pub. Co. (P.283)

Di Girolamo, Vittorio

--*Bo & the Sad King.* Di Girolamo, Vittorio (1928-). Eagleson, John & Gray, Rockwell, trs. from Span 1972. Orbis Bks. (P.266)

DiGrazia, Thomas (0000-1983)

--*Amifika.* 1st ed. Clifton, Lucille (1936-). c.1977. Dutton. (P.202)

--*The Blue Butterfly.* 1st ed. O'Gorman, Ned, pseud. (1929-). O'Gorman, Edward Charles. 1971. Harper & Row. (P.691)

--*The Half Sisters.* Carlson, Natalie Savage (1906-). 1970. Harper & Row. (P.169)

--*Hans Christian Andersen's "The Steadfast Tin Soldier".* Andersen, Hans Christian (1805-1875). c.1981. Prentice-Hall. (P.36)

--*Hold My Hand.* 1st ed. Zolotow, Charlotte Shapiro (1915-). 1972. Harper & Row. (P.994)

--*Holiday Tales of Sholom Aleichem.* Rabinovitch, Sholem (1859-1916). Aleichem, Sholem, pseud. Shevrin, Aliza, selected by. Shevrin, Aliza, tr. c.1979. Scribner. (P.745)

--*Lordy, Aunt Hattie.* 1st ed. Thomas, Ianthe (1951-). 1973. Harper & Row. (P.886)

--*The Lost Doll.* Mann, Peggy. 1972. Random House. (P.617)

--*Luvvy and the Girls.* Carlson, Natalie Savage (1906-). 1971. Harper & Row. (P.169)

--*The Merrymaker.* Suhl, Yuri (1908-). 1975. Four Winds Press. (P.870)

--*Miss Maggie.* 1st ed. Rylant, Cynthia. c.1983. Dutton. (P.787)

--*My Friend Jacob.* 1st ed. Clifton, Lucille (1936-). c.1980. Dutton. (P.202)

--*The Orange Scarf.* Geisert, Arthur. 1970. Simon and Schuster. (P.363)

--*Swinging and Swinging.* Manushkin, Frances (1942-). c.1976. Harper & Row. (P.619)

--*Walk Home Tired, Billy Jenkins.* 1st ed. Thomas, Ianthe (1951-). 1974. Harper & Row. (P.886)

Dillon, Corinne Boyd

--*Ban-Joe and Grey Eagle.* McMeekin, Isabel McLennan (1895-). 1951. Watts. (P.609)

--*Buzz Wants a Boat.* Beim, Jerrold (1910-1957). Anderson, Neil, pseud. 1956. Messner. (P.89)

--*A Cap for Mul Chand.* 1st ed. Batchelor, Julie Forsyth. 1950. Harcourt, Brace. (P.79)

--*God's Wonderful World.* Mason, Leckie & Ohanian, Phyllis B. 1954. Random. (P.628)

--*Dumbo*. Disney, Walt, Productions. 1976. Western Pub. (P.267)
--*Dumbo*. Disney, Walt Productions. Sanchez, Rene, tr. 1977. Western Pub. (P.267)
--*Elmer Elephant*. Disney, Walt, Productions. c.1936. David McKay Company. (P.267)
--*The Emperor's New Clothes*. Disney, Walter Elias (1901-1966). 1978. Western Pub. (P.271)
--*Fantasy on Parade*. Disney, Walt, Productions. 1970. Golden Press. (P.267)
--*Fantasyland*. Disney, Walt, Productions. 1965. Golden Press. (P.267)
--*Favorite Nursery Tales*. Disney, Walter Elias (1901-1966). 1977. Western Pub. (P.271)
--*Fun Favorites*. Disney, Walt, Productions. c.1970. Golden Press. (P.267)
--*Gingerbread Man*. Disney, Walt, Studio. 1976. Western Pub. (P.271)
--*Goldilocks & the Three Bears*. Disney, Walter Elias (1901-1966). 1978. Western Pub. (P.271)
--*Goofy Visits the Hospital*. Krauss, Ronnie. 1981. Putnam Pub Group. (P.539)
--*The Grasshopper & the Ants*. Disney, Walter Elias (1901-1966). 1978. Western Pub. (P.271)
--*Great Moments in Fiction*. rev. ed. Disney, Walt, Productions. c.1977. Golden Press. (P.267)
--*Heidi*. Disney, Walt, Studio. 1976. Western Pub. (P.271)
--*Here They Are*. Wavle, Ardra Soule, as told by. c.1940. D. C. Heath and Company. (P.937)
--*How Do You Do?* I'm Winnie the Pooh. Disney, Walt, Productions. 1985. Random. (P.267)
--*If I Met Mickey Mouse*. Disney, Walt, Studio. Duenewald, Doris, ed. 1978. Putnam Pub Group. (P.271)
--*The Jungle Book*. Disney, Walt, Studio. 1979. Western Pub. (P.271)
--*The Jungle Book*. Lewis, Jean (1924-), adapted by. 1967. Golden Press. (P.570)
--*Lady & the Tramp*. Disney, Walter Elias (1901-1966). 1978. Western Pub. (P.271)
--*Lambert the Sheepish Lion*. Disney, Walter Elias (1901-1966). 1978. Western Pub. (P.271)
--*Little Pig's Picnic and Other Stories*. Disney, Walt, Productions & Brown, Margaret Wise (1910-1952) c.1939. D. C. Heath and Company. (P.270)
--*Little Red Hen*. Disney, Walter Elias (1901-1966). 1978. Western Pub. (P.271)
--*Little Red Riding Hood and the Big Bad Wolf*. Disney, Walt, Productions. c.1934. David McKay Company. (P.267)
--*Mad Hatter's Tea Party*. Disney, Walt, Productions. Watson, Jane Werner (1915-) & Kelsey, Richard I., eds. Bedford, Anne North, pseud. 1951. Simon and Schuster. (P.267)
--*Mary Poppins*. Disney, Walter Elias (1901-1966). 1978. Western Pub. (P.271)
--*Mickey Mouse & Goofy: The Big Bear Scare*. Disney, Walter Elias (1901-1966). 1979. Western Pub. (P.271)
--*Mickey Mouse & the Great Lot Plot*. Disney, Walt, Studio. 1976. Western Pub. (P.271)
--*Mickey Mouse & the Mouseketeers: Ghost Town Adventures*. Disney, Walter Elias (1901-1966). 1977. Western Pub. (P.271)
--*Mickey Mouse & the Second Wish*. Disney, Walter Elias (1901-1966). 1973. Western Pub. (P.271)
--*Mickey Mouse & the World's Friendliest Monster*. Disney, Walter Elias (1901-1966). 1976. Western Pub. (P.271)
--*Mickey Mouse: Best Neighbor Contest*. Disney, Walter Elias (1901-1966). 1977. Western Pub. (P.271)
--*The Mickey Mouse Book*. White, Al. 1965. Western Pub. (P.950)
--*Mickey Mouse in Giantland*. Disney, Walt, Productions. c.1934. David McKay Company. (P.267)
--*Mickey Mouse: Missing Mouseketeers*. Disney, Walter Elias (1901-1966). 1977. Western Pub. (P.271)
--*Mickey Mouse Movie Stories*. Disney, Walt, Productions. c.1931. David McKay Company. (P.267)
--*Mickey Mouse Says I Can, Can You?*. Disney, Walt, Studio. Klimo, Kate, ed. 1982. S&S. (P.271)
--*Mickey Mouse: The Kitten Sitters*. Disney, Walter Elias (1901-1966). 1976. Western Pub. (P.271)
--*Mickey Mouse Waddle Book*. Disney, Walt, Productions. c.1934. Blue Ribbon Books, Incorporated. (P.267)
--*Mickey Never Fails*. Palmer, Robin (1911-). c.1939. D. C. Heath and Company. (P.703)
--*Mickey Sees the U.S.A*. Emerson, Caroline Dwight (1891-1973). 1944. D. C. Heath and Company. (P.306)
--*Mickey Visits the Dentist*. Krauss, Ronnie & Disney, Walt, Productions. c.1980. Grosset & Dunlap. (P.539)
--*Mickey's Christmas Carol*. Disney, Walt, Productions. N.D. Western Pub. (P.267)
--*Mickey's Christmas Carol*. Disney, Walt, Studio. N.D. Western Pub. (P.271)
--*More Mother Goose*. Disney, Walter Elias (1901-1966). 1978. Western Pub. (P.271)
--*The Mouseketeer's Train Ride*. Disney, Walter Elias (1901-1966). 1977. Western Pub. (P.271)
--*New Walt Disney Treasury, Ten Favorite Stories*. Disney, Walt, Studio. 1971. Western Pub. (P.271)
--*One Hundred and One Dalmations*. Disney, Walt, Productions. Buettner, Carl, adapted by. McGary, Norman & Mattinson, Sylvia, illus. 1961. Golden Press. (P.267)
--*One Hundred and One Dalmations*. Disney, Walt, Productions. Buettner, Carl, adapted by. Mattinson, Sylvia & Mattinson, Burnett, illus. 1961. Golden Press. (P.267)
--*Peculiar Penguins*. Disney, Walt, Productions. c.1934. David McKay Company. (P.267)
--*The "Pop-up" Silly Symphonies: Containing Babes in the Woods and King Neptune*. Disney, Walt, Productions. c.1933. Blue Ribbon Books, in. (P.267)
--*The Rescuers*. Disney, Walt, Productions. 1977. Western Pub. (P.268)
--*The Robber Kitten*. Disney, Walt Productions. 1935. David McKay Company. (P.268)
--*Robin Hood*. Disney, Walter Elias (1901-1966). 1978. Western Pub. (P.271)
--*The Runaway Lamb at the County Fair*. Disney, Walt, Productions. Svendsen, Julius 1949. Grosset and Dunlap. (P.268)
--*School Days in Disneyville*. Rev. ed. Emerson, Caroline Dwight (1891-1973). 1939. D. C. Heath and Company. (P.306)
--*Snow White and the Seven Dwarfs*. Disney, Walt, Productions. c.1937. David McKay Company. (P.268)
--*Snow White and the Seven Dwarfs*. Disney, Walt, Productions. c.1938. Grosset & Dunlap. (P.268)
--*Snow White & the Seven Dwarfs*. Disney, Walt, Studio. 1976. Western Pub. (P.271)
--*Snow White and the Seven Dwarfs*. Disney, Walt, Studio. c.1938. Whitman. (P.271)
--*Stories from Other Lands*. Disney, Walt, Productions. 1965. Golden Press. (P.268)
--*The Three Orphan Kittens*. Disney, Walt, Productions. c.1935. David McKay Company. (P.268)
--*Tigger & Winnie-the-Pooh*. Disney, Walt, Studio. 1968. Western Pub. (P.271)
--*The Tortoise and the Hare*. Disney, Walt, Productions. c.1935. David McKay Company. (P.268)
--*Treasure Chest*. Disney, Walt, Productions. 1948. Simon and Schuster. (P.268)
--*Uncle Remus Brer Rabbit Stories*. 1977. Western Pub. (P.271)
--*Walt Disney Character Tubby Book*. 1980. S&S. (P.271)
--*The Walt Disney Parade*. Disney, Walt, Productions. c.1940. The Garden City Publishing Co., Inc. (P.268)
--*Walt Disney's Alice in Wonderland Finds the Garden of Live Flowers*. Disney, Walt, Productions. Watson, Jane Werner (1915-) & Grant, Campbell, eds. 1951. Simon and Schuster. (P.268)
--*Walt Disney's Alice in Wonderland*. From the Motion Picture Based on the Story by Lewis Carroll. Disney, Walt, Productions & Carroll, Lewis, pseud. (1832-1898) Dodgson, Charles Lutwidge. Dempster, Al, adapted by. c.1951. Simon and Schuster. (P.270)
--*Walt Disney's Alice in Wonderland Meets the White Rabbit*. Disney, Walt, Productions. Watson, Jane Werner (1915-) & Dempster, Al, eds. 1951. Simon and Schuster. (P.268)
--*Walt Disney's Bambi*. Disney, Walt Productions & Salten, Felix (1860-1945) 1948. Simon and Schuster. (P.270)
--*Walt Disney's "Bambi"*. Disney, Walter Elias (1901-1966). 1949. Golden Press. (P.272)
--*Walt Disney's Bambi*. Disney, Walt Productions. Grant, Bob, adapted by. 1948. Simon and Schuster. (P.268)
--*Walt Disney's Ben and Me*. Authorized. Disney, Walt, Productions. Klein, Earl, adapted by. c.1954. Whitman Pub. Co. (P.268)
--*Walt Disney's Bongo*. Disney, Walt, Productions. Grant, Campbell, adapted by. 1948. Simon and Schuster. (P.268)
--*Walt Disney's Bunny Book*. Werner, Jane (1915-). 1972. Western Pub. (P.946)
--*Walt Disney's Chicken Little*. Disney, Walt, Studio. 1983. Western Pub. (P.271)
--*Walt Disney's Chip 'n' Dale at the Zoo*. Disney, Walt, Productions. Bedford, Annie North, pseud. (1915-) & Bosche, Bill, eds. Watson, Jane Werner. 1954. Simon and Schuster. (P.268)
--*Walt Disney's Cinderella*. Disney, Walt, Studio. 1950. Western Pub. (P.271)
--*Walt Disney's Davy Crockett and Mike Fink*. Disney, Walter Elias (1901-1966). Shapiro, Irwin, adapted by. 1956. Golden Press. (P.272)
--*Walt Disney's Davy Crockett and Mike Fink: The Adventures of the King of the Wild Frontier and the King of the River, on the Ohio and the Mighty Mississippi*. Disney, Walt, Productions. c.1955. Simon and Schuster. (P.269)
--*Walt Disney's Davy Crockett, King of the Wild Frontier*. Disney, Walt, Productions. Shapiro, Irwin (1911-) & Crawford, Mel (1925-), eds. 1955. Simon and Schuster. (P.269)
--*Walt Disney's Davy Crockett's Keelboat Race*. Disney, Walt, Productions. Shapiro, Irwin (1911-) & Crawford, Mel (1925-), eds. 1955. Simon and Schuster. (P.269)
--*Walt Disney's Disneyland on the Air*. Disney, Walt, Productions. Bedford, Annie North, pseud. (1915-) & Armstrong, Samuel, eds. Watson, Jane Werner. 1955. Simon and Schuster. (P.269)
--*Walt Disney's Donald Duck and Chip 'n' Dale*. Authorized. Disney, Walt, Productions. Walsh, Stan & Wolfe, Gene, eds. c.1954. Whitman Pub. Co. (P.269)
--*Walt Disney's Donald Duck and the Hidden Gold*. Disney, Walt, Productions & Watson, Jane Werner (1915-) Taliaferro, Al, adapted by. 1951. Simon and Schuster. (P.269)
--*Walt Disney's Donald Duck and the Mouseketeers: Told by Annie North Bedford; Pseud*. Disney, Walt, Productions. Bedford, Annie North, pseud. (1915-) & Armstrong, Samuel, eds. Watson, Jane Werner. 1956. Simon and Schuster. (P.269)
--*Walt Disney's Donald Duck and the New Birdhouse*. Authorized. Disney, Walt, Productions. Moores, Richard (1909-) & McGary, Norm, eds. c.1956. Whitman Pub. Co. (P.269)
--*Walt Disney's Donald Duck and the Wishing Star*. Authorized. Disney, Walt, Productions. Gonzales, Manuel & MacLaughlin, Don, eds. N.D. Whitman Pub. Co. (P.269)
--*Walt Disney's Donald Duck Goes to Disneyland*. Authorized. Disney, Walt, Productions. Banta, Milt & Boyle, Neil, eds. c.1955. Whitman Pub. Co. (P.269)
--*Walt Disney's Donald Duck Goes to Disneyland*. Authorized. Disney, Walt, Productions. Banta, Milt & Boyle, Neil, illus. 1955. Whitman Pub. Co. (P.269)
--*Walt Disney's Donald Duck in A Bit of a Hit*. Authorized. Disney, Walt, Productions. Strobl, Tony & Boyle, Neil, eds. 1956. Whitman Pub. Co. (P.269)
--*Walt Disney's Donald Duck in Disneyland*. Disney, Walt, Productions. Bedford, Annie North, pseud. (1915-) & Grant, Campbell, eds. Watson, Jane Werner. 1955. Simon and Schuster. (P.269)
--*Walt Disney's Donald Duck in Help Wanted*. Authorized. Disney, Walt, Productions. Wheeler, George, adapted by. c.1955. Whitman Pub. Co. (P.269)
--*Walt Disney's Donald Duck, Prize Diver*. Disney, Walt, Productions. Bedford, Annie North, pseud. (1915-), as told by Watson, Jane Werner. Boyle, Neil 1956. Simon and Schuster. (P.269)
--*Walt Disney's Donald Duck Treasury*. Disney, Walter Elias (1901-1966). Bedford, Annie North, pseud. (1915-), adapted by Watson, Jane Werner. 1957. Golden Press. (P.272)
--*Walt Disney's Donald Duck's Christmas Tree*. Disney, Walt, Productions. Bedford, Annie North, pseud. (1915-) & Moore, Bob, eds. Watson, Jane Werner. 1954. Simon and Schuster. (P.269)
--*Walt Disney's Donald Duck's Safety Book*. Disney, Walt, Productions. Bedford, Annie North, pseud. (1915-) & Gonzales, Manuel, eds. Watson, Jane Werner. 1955, c.1954. Simon and Schuster. (P.269)
--*Walt Disney's Donald Duck's Toy Sailboat*. Disney, Walt, Productions. Bedford, Annie North, pseud. (1915-) & Armstrong, Samuel, eds. Watson, Jane Werner. 1954. Simon and Schuster. (P.269)
--*Walt Disney's Dumbo*. Disney, Walt, Productions. Bedford, Annie North, pseud. (1915-), ed. Watson, Jane Werner. 1947. Simon and Schuster. (P.269)
--*Walt Disney's Dumbo*. Disney, Walt, Productions. Bedford, Annie North, pseud. (1915-), as told by Watson, Jane Werner. Kelsey, Dick, adapted by. 1955. Simon and Schuster. (P.269)
--*Walt Disney's Dumbo*. Bedford, Annie North, pseud. (1915-) & Kelsey, Dick, eds. Watson, Jane Werner. 1972. Western Pub. (P.87)
--*Walt Disney's Dumbo*. Disney, Walter Elias (1901-1966). 1946. Golden Press. (P.272)
--*Walt Disney's Dumbo of the Circus*. Disney, Walt, Productions & Baruch, Dorothy Walter (1899-1962) 1948. D. C. Heath. (P.270)
--*Walt Disney's Goofy and the Tiger Hunt*. Authorized. Disney, Walt, Productions. Moores, Dick & Armstrong, Samuel, eds. c.1954. Whitman Pub. Co. (P.269)
--*Walt Disney's Grandpa Bunny: From the Motion Picture "Funny Little Bunnies"*. Disney, Walt, Studio. Watson, Jane Werner (1915-) & Kelsey, Richard I., eds. 1951. Simon and Schuster. (P.271)
--*Walt Disney's Jiminy Cricket, Fire Fighter*. Disney, Walt, Productions. Bedford, Annie North, pseud. (1915-), as told by Watson, Jane Werner. Armstrong, Samuel 1956. Simon and Schuster. (P.269)
--*Walt Disney's Jiminy Cricket: Fire Fighter*. Told by Annie North Bedford; Pseud. Disney, Walt, Productions & Bedford, Annie North, pseud. (1915-) Watson, Jane Werner. Armstrong, Mel, adapted by. 1956. Simon and Schuster. (P.270)
--*Walt Disney's Johnny Appleseed*. Disney, Walt, Productions. Parmalee, Ted, adapted by. 1949. Simon and Schuster. (P.269)
--*Walt Disney's Lady*. Authorized. Disney, Walt, Productions. Armstrong, Samuel, adapted by. c.1954. Whitman Pub. Co. (P.269)
--*Walt Disney's Lady*. Disney, Walt, Studio. 1976. Western Pub. (P.271)
--*Walt Disney's Lady*. Authorized. Disney, Walt, Productions. Hubbard, Allen & Wolfe, Gene, eds. 1955, c.1954. Whitman Pub. Co. (P.269)
--*Walt Disney's Lady and the Tramp*. Disney, Walt, Productions. Coats, Claude, adapted by. 1955. Simon and Schuster. (P.269)
--*Walt Disney's Lady & the Tramp*. Greene, Ward (1892-). 1972. Western Pub. (P.387)
--*Walt Disney's Lady: From the Motion Picture 'Lady and the Tramp.'*. Disney, Walt, Productions & Greene, Ward Armstrong, Samuel, adapted by. 1955, c.1954. Simon and Schuster. (P.269)
--*Walt Disney's Little Man of Disneyland*. Disney, Walt, Productions. Bedford, Annie North, pseud. (1915-) & Kelsey, Dick, eds. Watson, Jane Werner. 1955. Simon and Schuster. (P.269)
--*The Walt Disney's Littlest Outlaw*. Disney, Walter Elias (1901-1966) & Lindquist, Willis. Greene, Hamilton 1956. Golden Press. (P.272)
--*Walt Disney's Magnificent Mr.* Toad. based on "The Wind in the Willows" by Kenneth Grahame. Disney, Walt, Productions & Grahame, Kenneth (1859-1932) Hench, John, adapted by. 1949. Grosset & Dunlap. (P.270)
--*Walt Disney's Mary Poppins*. Disney, Walt, Studio. Bedford, Anne North, pseud. (1915-), ed. Watson, Jane Werner. 1976. Western Pub. (P.271)
--*Walt Disney's Mickey & His Friends*. 1977. Western Pub. (P.271)
--*Walt Disney's Mickey and the Missing Mouseketeers*. Disney, Walter Elias (1901-1966) & Bedford, Annie North, pseud. (1915-). Watson, Jane Werner. 1956. Golden Press. (P.272)
--*Walt Disney's Mickey Mouse and Pluto Pup*. Disney, Walt, Productions. Beecher, Elizabeth & Grant, Campbell, eds. 1953. Simon and Schuster. (P.269)
--*Walt Disney's Mickey Mouse and the Missing Mouseketeers*. Disney, Walt, Productions. Bedford, Annie North, pseud. (1915-) & Svendson, Julius, eds. Watson, Jane Werner. 1956. Simon and Schuster. (P.269)
--*Walt Disney's Mickey Mouse Birthday Book*. Bedford, Annie North, pseud. (1915-), ed. Watson, Jane Werner. Grant, Campbell 1953. Simon & Schuster. (P.87)
--*Walt Disney's Mickey Mouse Flies the Christmas Mail*. Disney, Walt, Productions. Bedford, Annie North, pseud. (1915-) & Svendson, Julius, eds. Watson, Jane Werner. 1956. Simon and Schuster. (P.269)
--*Walt Disney's Mickey Mouse Goes Christmas Shopping*. Disney, Walt, Productions. Bedford, Annie North, pseud. (1915-) & Moore, Bob, eds. Watson, Jane Werner. 1953. Simon and Schuster. (P.269)
--*Walt Disney's Mickey Mouse in the Wild West*. Disney, Walt, Studio. 1973. Western Pub. (P.271)
--*Walt Disney's Mickey Mouse Picnic*. Disney, Walt, Productions & Werner, Jane (1915-) 1950. Simon and Schuster. (P.270)
--*Walt Disney's Mickey Mouse's Picnic*. Disney, Walter Elias (1901-1966) & Werner, Jane. 1950. Golden Press. (P.273)
--*Walt Disney's Mother Goose*. Dempster, Al, ed. 1952. Western Pub. (P.256)
--*Walt Disney's Mother Goose*. Disney, Walt, Productions. 1949. Simon and Schuster. (P.269)
--*Walt Disney's Mother Goose*. Disney, Walt, Productions. 1970. Western Pub. (P.269)
--*Walt Disney's Mother Goose*. Mother Goose. 1952. Simon and Schuster. (P.669)
--*Walt Disney's Noah's Ark*. Disney, Walt, Productions. Bedford, Annie North, pseud. (1915-) & Grant, Campbell, eds. Watson, Jane Werner. 1952. Simon and Schuster. (P.269)
--*Walt Disney's Nursery Tales*. 1971. Western Pub. (P.271)

--*The Invisible Chimes.* Sutton, Margaret Beebe, Mrs. (1903-). c.1932. Grosset & Dunlap. (P.872)
--*Jonathan Bing and Other Verses.* Curtis Brown, Beatrice (1901-1974). c.1936. Oxford University Press. (P.237)
--*Joy and Pam As Seniors.* Whitehill, Dorothy. c.1932. Grosset & Dunlap. (P.953)
--*Just Like Me.* MacKay, Ruth Clarage (1896-). 1946. Abingdon-Cokesbury Press. (P.605)
--*Little Steps: Children's Poems of Thanks.* Watson, Jane Werner (1915-), ed. Nast, Elsa Ruth, pseud. c.1947. Grosset & Dunlap. (P.936)
--*Littlest Ones.* Doane, Pelagie (1906-1966), ed. 1956. Oxford University Press. (P.275)
--*The Living Portrait.* Sutton, Margaret Beebe, Mrs. (1903-). 1947. Grosset & Dunlap. (P.872)
--*Lollypop: The True Story of a Little Dog.* Sutton, Margaret Beebe, Mrs. (1903-). c.1939. Grosset & Dunlap. (P.872)
--*The Loyal Traitor.* Waite, Helen Elmira (1903-). c.1935. Macrae Smith Company. (P.924)
--*Madcap Jeanie.* Graham, Janette Sargeant. N.D. Dodd, Mead & Co. (P.380)
--*The Magic Makers and the Bramble Bush Man.* Sutton, Margaret Beebe, Mrs. (1903-). c.1936. Grosset & Dunlap. (P.872)
--*The Magic Makers and the Golden Charm.* Sutton, Margaret Beebe, Mrs. (1903-). c.1936. Grosset & Dunlap. (P.872)
--*The Magic Makers in Backwards Land.* Sutton, Margaret Beebe, Mrs. (1903-). c.1936. Grosset & Dunlap. (P.872)
--*The Mark on the Mirror.* Sutton, Margaret Beebe, Mrs. (1903-). 1949. Grosset & Dunlap. (P.872)
--*Mary Paxson: Her Book.* Paxson, Mary Scarborough (1872-). 1931. Doubleday, Doran & Company Inc. (P.712)
--*Mary Paxson: Her Book 1880-1884.* Paxson, Mary Scarborough (1872-). 1936. Doubleday, Doran & Co., Inc. (P.712)
--*The Midnight Visitor.* Sutton, Margaret Beebe, Mrs. (1903-). c.1939. Grosset & Dunlap. (P.872)
--*Molly Whuppie: An Old English Fairy Tale.* Jacobs, Joseph (1854-1916), ed. 1939. Oxford University Press. (P.487)
--*More Silver Pennies.* Thompson, Blanche Jennings (1887-), ed. 1957. Macmillan. (P.886)
--*Morning Light.* 1st ed. Norris, Kathleen Thompson (1880-1966). 1950. Doubleday. (P.685)
--*Mother Goose.* Mother Goose. c.1940. Random House. (P.667)
--*The Mysterious Half Cat.* Sutton, Margaret Beebe, Mrs. (1903-). c.1936. Grosset & Dunlap. (P.872)
--*The Mystic Ball.* Sutton, Margaret Beebe, Mrs. (1903-). c.1934. Grosset & Dunlap. (P.872)
--*The Name on the Bracelet.* Sutton, Margaret Beebe, Mrs. (1903-). c.1940. Grosset & Dunlap. (P.872)
--*The Peacock Farm.* Keyes, Mary Willard. 1934. Longmans, Green and Co. (P.521)
--*Peter's Birthday Party.* Ernest, Edward. 1947. Oxford University Press. (P.309)
--*Poems of Praise.* Doane, Pelagie (1906-1966), selected by. 1955. J. B. Lippincott. (P.275)
--*Polly Peters.* Quigg, Jane. 1942. Oxford University Press. (P.745)
--*The Rainbow Riddle.* Sutton, Margaret Beebe, Mrs. (1903-). 1976, c.1946. Aeonian Press. (P.872)
--*The Rainbow Riddle.* Sutton, Margaret Beebe, Mrs. (1903-). 1946. Grosset & Dunlap. (P.872)
--*The Riddle of the Double Ring.* Sutton, Margaret Beebe, Mrs. (1903-). c.1937. Grosset & Dunlap. (P.872)
--*Sammy Squirrel Goes to Town.* Honness, Elizabeth Hoffman, Mrs. (1904-). 1937. T. Nelson and Sons. (P.458)
--*The Secret of the Barred Window.* Sutton, Margaret Beebe, Mrs. (1903-). 1943. Grosset & Dunlap. (P.872)
--*The Secret of the Musical Tree.* Sutton, Margaret Beebe, Mrs. (1903-). 1948. Grosset & Dunlap. (P.873)
--*Seven Strange Clues.* Sutton, Margaret Beebe, Mrs. (1903-). c.1932. Grossett & Dunlap. (P.873)
--*Singing with Peter and Patsy.* Boesel, Ann Sterling, Mrs. 1944. Oxford University Press. (P.112)
--*A Small Child's Book of Verse.* Doane, Pelagie (1906-1966), compiled by. 1948. Oxford Univ. Press. (P.275)
--*Soldier Sammy.* MacNeil, Marion Gill. c.1942. Oxford University Press. (P.610)
--*The Spirit of Fog Island.* Sutton, Margaret Beebe, Mrs. (1903-). 1951. Grosset & Dunlap. (P.873)
--*Stories to Live By.* McKelvey, Gertrude Della. 1943. John C. Winston. (P.606)
--*Surprise for Susan.* Hitte, Kathryn (1919-). 1950. Abingdon Press. (P.447)
--*The Tail of the Sorry Sorrel Horse.* Honness, Elizabeth Hoffman, Mrs. (1904-). 1936. T. Nelson & Sons. (P.458)
--*Tell Me About the Bible.* Jones, Mary Alice (1898-). 1945. Rand. (P.500)
--*Terror at Moaning Cliff.* Garis, Lillian C. McNamara, Mrs. (1873-1954). c.1935. Grosset & Dunlap. (P.357)
--*This Wonderful Day: Poems of Prayer and Thanksgiving.* Orleans, Ilo (1897-1962). 1958. Union of American Hebrew Congregations. (P.696)
--*Tommy True: A Little Boy Who Was Hungry.* Sutton, Margaret Beebe, Mrs. (1903-). 1942. Oxford University Press. (P.873)
--*Toplofty.* Keyes, Mary Willard. 1931. Longmans, Green and Co. (P.521)
--*The Tower Secret.* Garis, Lillian C. McNamara, Mrs. (1873-1954). c.1933. Grosset & Dunlap. (P.357)
--*Trailer Trio.* Jacobs, Emma Atkins (1885-). 1942. The John C. Winston Company. (P.486)
--*Two Bridgets.* Hathaway, Cynthia. 1941. Doubleday Doran & Co. (P.420)
--*Understanding Kim.* Doane, Pelagie (1906-1966). 1962. Lippincott. (P.275)
--*The Unfinished House.* Sutton, Margaret Beebe, Mrs. (1903-). c.1938. Grosset & Dsnlap. (P.873)
--*The Vanishing Shadow.* Sutton, Margaret Beebe, Mrs. (1903-). 1976, c.1967. Aeonian Press. (P.873)
--*The Vanishing Shadow.* Sutton, Margaret Beebe, Mrs. (1903-). c.1932. Grosset & Dunlap. (P.873)
--*The Vanishing Shadow.* Sutton, Margaret Beebe, Mrs. (1903-). 1964. Grosset & Dunlap. (P.873)
--*The Voice in the Suitcase.* Sutton, Margaret Beebe, Mrs. (1903-). c.1935. Grosset & Dunlap. (P.873)
--*The Wild Warning.* Garis, Lillian C. McNamara, Mrs. (1873-1954). c.1934. Grosset & Dunlap. (P.357)
--*The Yellow Phantom.* Sutton, Margaret Beebe, Mrs. (1903-). c.1933. Grosset & Dunlap. (P.873)

Doares, Robert G.
--*Bible Stories for Boys & Girls.* Engstrom, Theodore Wilhelm (1916-), ed. 1971. Zondervan. (P.307)
--*Prairie Princess.* Epp, Margaret Agnes (1913-). 1967. Moody. (P.308)
--*The Princess and the Pelican.* Epp, Margaret Agnes (1913-). 1968. Moody Press. (P.308)
--*Princess Rides a Panther.* Epp, Margaret Agnes (1913-). 1970. Moody. (P.308)
--*Sarah & the Magic Twenty-Fifth.* Epp, Margaret Agnes (1913-). c.1977. Victor Books. (P.308)
--*Sarah & the Pelican.* Epp, Margaret Agnes (1913-). c.1977. Victor Books. (P.308)
--*Stories for the Children's Hour.* rev. ed. Taylor, Kenneth Nathaniel (1917-), ed. 1968. Moody Press. (P.880)
--*Three Go Searching.* St. John, Patricia Mary (1919-). 1966, c.1965. Moody. (P.789)
--*Windows for Rosemary.* 1st ed. Vance, Marguerite (1889-1965). 1956. Dutton. (P.913)

Dobbins, Dwight
--*What Do You Do with a Drawbridge?.* Dobbins, Dorothy Wyeth (1929-). c.1976. Addison-Wesley. (P.275)

Dobbins, John B., photos by.
--*Art, the Telephone Man.* Dobbins, John B. N.D. Denison. (P.275)
--*Tim Tuttle & the Tomatoes.* Dobbins, Marybelle King (1900-). N.D. Denison. (P.275)

Dobias, Dorothea F.
--*Casey Joins the Circus: A/Story of a Little Tramp Dog and How He "Joined Up" with the Circus.* Dobias, Dorothea F. 1936. Grosset & Dunlap, Inc. (P.275)

Dobias, Frank (1902-)
--*Adventures in Steel.* Davis, Lavinia Riker, Mrs. (1909-1961). c.1938. Modern Age Books, Inc. (P.246)
--*Blackthorn.* Adams, Katharine. 1931. Macmillan Co. (P.5)
--*Boots, the Firemen's Dog.* Christ, Katherine D. c.1936. American Book Company. (P.193)
--*Boys of the Andes.* Desmond, Alice Curtis, Mrs. (1897-) & Malkus, Alida Wright Sims, Mrs. (1899-). c.1941. D. C. Heath and Company. (P.260)
--*Children of the Housetops: A Story of Persia.* Mirza, Youel Benjamin (1886-). 1931. Doubleday, Doran & Company, Inc. (P.651)
--*Clearing Weather.* Meigs, Cornelia Lynde (1884-1973). 1928. Little, Brown, and Company. **Award: (JNM).** (P.639)
--*Danger Zone.* Whitfield, Raoul (1897-1945). 1931. A. A. Knopf. (P.954)
--*David Has His Day.* Borie, Lysbeth Boyd, Mrs. c.1934. J. B. Lippincott Company. (P.118)
--*Five Bears and Miranda.* Sheahan, Henry Beston (1888-1968). Beston, Henry B., pseud. 1939. The Macmillan Company. (P.817)
--*The Gypsy Story Teller.* Morris, Cora, ed. 1931. The Macmillan Company. (P.664)
--*Haunted Airways.* Burtis, Thomson (1896-). 1930. Doubleday, Doran & Company, Inc. (P.157)
--*Highroad to Adventure.* Pease, Clarence Howard (1894-1974). 1939. Doubleday, Doran & Co., Incorporated. (P.718)
--*Little Brown Hen.* Farrow, Dorothy Parmlee Potter, Mrs. (1886-). 1941. The Macmillan Company. (P.318)
--*Lost Squadron.* Cook, Canfield. 1943. Grosset & Dunlap. (P.214)
--*Monty Marine.* MacNeil, Marion Gill. 1943. Oxford University Press. (P.610)
--*New Land: A Novel for Boys and Girls.* Schmidt, Sarah Lindsay (1928-). 1933. R. M. McBride & Company. **Award: (JNM).** (P.800)
--*Once the Hodja.* Kelsey, Alice Geer (1896-). 1943. David McKay Company Inc. (P.517)
--*Once the Hodja.* Kelsey, Alice Geer (1896-). 1943. Longmans, Green and Co. (P.517)
--*Oscar the Trained Seal.* Neikirk, Mabel E. c.1940. Grosset & Dunlap. (P.677)
--*Puss in Boots.* Puss in Boots. 1937. The Macmillan Company. (P.742)
--*Pygmy's Arrow.* Williamson, Thames Ross (1894-). Fleming, Waldo, pseud. 1938. Lothrop, Lee and Shepard Company. (P.965)
--*A Riddle in Fez: A Boys' Story of Morocco.* Williamson, Thames Ross (1894-). Fleming, Waldo, pseud. 1937. Doubleday, Doran & Co., Inc. (P.965)
--*Silver Wings.* Whitfield, Raoul (1897-1945). 1930. A. A. Knopf. (P.954)
--*Sons of the Volsungs.* Morris, William (1834-1896) & Hosford, Dorothy Grant (1900-1952), eds. 1949. Holt. (P.664)
--*Sons of the Volsungs.* Morris, William (1834-1896) & Hosford, Dorothy Grant (1900-1952), eds. 1932. The Macmillan Company. (P.665)
--*Springboard to Tokyo.* Cook, Canfield. 1943. Grosset & Dunlap. (P.214)
--*Straight Shooting: Adventures of a Film Flyer.* Burtis, Thomson (1896-). 1931. Doubleday, Doran & Company, Inc. (P.157)
--*Talking Drums: A Boy's Story of the African Gold Coast.* Williamson, Thames Ross (1894-). Fleming, Waldo, pseud. 1936. Doubleday, Doran & Company, Inc. (P.965)
--*The Thunder Bird.* Evans, Wainwright. 1934. T. Nelson and Sons. (P.312)
--*Trailer Tracks.* Bunn, Harriet F. 1937. The Macmillan Company. (P.149)
--*A Train, a Boat and an Island.* Kuh, Charlotte Greenebaum, Mrs. 1932. The Macmillan Company. (P.541)
--*Twelve Bright Trumpets.* Leighton, Margaret Carver, Mrs. (1896-). 1942. Houghton Mifflin Company. (P.563)
--*Under the Capstone, a Tale of the Channel Islands.* Campbell, Alfred Stuart (1900-). 1940. London, D. Appleton-Century Company, Incorporated. (P.164)
--*The War of the Ghosts: A Flying Adventure Story.* Burtis, Thomson (1896-). 1932. Doubleday, Doran & Company, Inc. (P.157)

Dobias, Frank (1902-) & Goldfield, Robert
--*Gustango Gold.* Parker, Arthur Caswell (1881-1955). 1930. Doubleday, Doran & Company, Inc. (P.706)

Dobias, Frank (1902-) & Haberstock, Robert
--*The Tide's Secret: A Mystery Story.* Fulton, Reed. 1930. Doubleday, Doran & Company, Inc. (P.349)

Dobias, Frank (1902-) & McGuckin, Malcolm, Jr.
--*The Silver Robin.* Marshall, Dean (1900-). 1947. E. P. Dutton & Company, Inc. (P.622)

Dobkin, Alexander (1908-1975)
--*Echoes of Africa in Folk Songs of the Americas.* 2nd rev. ed. Landeck, Beatrice (1904-). 1969. McKay. (P.547)
--*King Arthur & His Knights.* MacLeod, Mary (0000-1914). 1950. World Pub. (P.608)

Dobrin, Arnold (1928-)
--*Benjy's Luck.* Brecht, Edith (1895-1975). 1967. Lippincott. (P.128)
--*El Loro de Juan.* Dobrin, Norma Zane. 1963. Golden Gate Junior Books. (P.276)
--*Going to Moscow, and Other Stories.* Dobrin, Arnold (1928-). 1973. Four Winds Press. (P.275)
--*Irish: The Story of a Girl and Her Horse.* Dobrin, Arnold (1928-). 1976. Walker. (P.275)
--*Jillions of Gerbils.* Dobrin, Arnold (1928-). 1973. Lothrop, Lee & Shepard. (P.275)
--*Josephine's Imagination.* Dobrin, Arnold (1928-). 1973. Schol Bk Serv. (P.275)
--*Josephine's Imagination.* Dobrin, Arnold (1928-). 1975. Scholastic Inc. (P.275)
--*Philip.* Westlake, Donald Edwin (1933-). 1967. Crowell. (P.948)
--*Pink Like the Geranium.* Babbitt, Lorraine. 1974. Childrens Press. (P.57)
--*Scat!.* Dobrin, Arnold (1928-). 1971. Four Winds Press. (P.275)
--*The Snow Fox: A Tale of Canada.* Dobrin, Arnold (1928-). 1968. Coward-McCann. (P.276)
--*Taro and the Sea Turtles: A Tale of Japan.* Dobrin, Arnold (1928-). 1966. Coward. (P.276)
--*To Katmandu: A Story of Nepal.* Dobrin, Arnold (1928-). 1972. Crowell. (P.276)

Docktor, Irv (1918-)
--*Benkei, the Boy Giant.* Fribourg, Marjorie G. (1920-). 1958. Sterling. (P.345)
--*Bimo, Young Hero of Java.* Fribourg, Marjorie G. (1920-). 1958. Sterling Pub. Co. (P.345)
--*Casket & the Sword.* Dale, Norman, pseud. (1901-). Denny, Norman George. 1956. Har-Row. (P.238)
--*The Casket and the Sword.* Denny, Norman George (1901-). Dale, Norman, pseud. 1956. Harper. (P.258)
--*The Illustrated Book of American Folklore: Stories, Legends, Tall Tales, Riddles, and Rhymes.* Botkin, Benjamin Albert (1901-1975) & Withers, Carl A. (1900-1970), eds. 1958. Grosset & Dunlap. (P.119)
--*Li-Ho of the Boat People.* Norcross, Muse A. 1960. F. Watts. (P.685)
--*Mystery at Fearsome Lake.* Govan, Christine Noble, Mrs. (1898-) & West, Emmy, pseud. (1919-). West, Emily Govan. 1960. Sterling Pub. Co. (P.379)
--*Mystery at Plum Nelly.* Govan, Christine Noble, Mrs. (1898-) & West, Emmy, pseud. (1919-). West, Emily Govan. 1959. Sterling Pub. Co. (P.379)
--*Mystery at Rock City.* Govan, Christine Noble, Mrs. (1898-) & West, Emmy, pseud. (1919-). West, Emily Govan. 1960. Sterling Pub. Co. (P.379)
--*The Mystery at the Haunted House.* Govan, Christine Noble, Mrs. (1898-) & West, Emmy, pseud. (1919-). West, Emily Govan. 1959. Sterling Pub. Co. (P.379)
--*Mystery at the Snowed-in Cabin.* Govan, Christine Noble, Mrs. (1898-) & West, Emmy, pseud. (1919-). West, Emily Govan. 1961. Sterling Pub. (P.379)
--*The Mystery of the Vanishing Stamp.* Govan, Christine Noble, Mrs. (1898-) & West, Emily Govan (1919-). 1958. Sterling Publishing Co. (P.379)
--*We Were There at the Battle for Bataan.* Appel, Benjamin (1907-1977). 1957. Grosset & Dunlap. (P.43)
--*We Were There in the Klondike Gold Rush.* Appel, Benjamin (1907-1977). 1956. Grosset & Dunlap. (P.43)

Dr. Seuss, pseud., see Blake, Quentin.

Dr. Seuss, pseud., see Geisel, Theodor Seuss.

Dodd, Edward (1904-)
--*Coyote, the Wonder Wolf.* 1st ed. Lippincott, Joseph Wharton (1887-1976). 1964. Lippincott. (P.575)
--*Flapfoot.* Dodd, Edward (1904-). 1968. L. W. Singer Co. (P.276)

Dodd, Loring Holmes (1879-)
--*The Cocky Cocker Book.* Dodd, Ruth Esleeck (1881-) & Dodd, Loring Holmes (1879-). N.D. Dresser, Chapman & Grimes Inc. (P.276)
--*The Puppy Book: The Story of Wendy, the Puppy Named for Barrie's Famous Heroine.* Dodd, Loring Holmes (1879-) & Dodd, Ruth (1881-). N.D. Lothrop Lee & Shepard Co. (P.276)
--*Wag Tales.* Dodd, Loring Holmes (1879-). 1966. Dresser. (P.276)

Dodd, Lynley Stuart (1941-)
--*My Cat Likes to Hide in Boxes.* Sutton, Evelyn Mary (1906-). 1974, c.1973. Parents' Magazine Press. (P.872)

Dodds, Andrew (1927-)
--*The Big Sea.* Armstrong, Richard (1903-). 1965, c.1964. D. McKay Co. (P.48)

Dodge, Carlota
--*The Teaspoon Tree.* Palmer, Mary Babcock (1916-). 1963. Houghton Mifflin Co. (P.703)

Dodge, Dick (1918-1974)
--*River Circus.* Lathrop, Dorothy West (1892-1974). 1953. Random House. (P.554)
--*Too Many Sisters.* Beim, Jerrold (1910-1957). 1956. Morrow. (P.89)

Dodge, Katharine Sturges
--*Tales of Little Dogs: Verses.* Bond, Carrie Jacobs, Mrs. (1862-1946). 1953, c.1921. P. F. Volland Co. (P.114)

Dodge, Katherine
--*Tongue Dancing.* Swann, Brian. 1984. Rowan Tree. (P.873)

Dodge, Susan
--*Turtle.* Cummings, Betty Sue (1918-). 1981. Atheneum. (P.234)

Dodge, Suzanne C.
--*Escape from the Nuisances.* Chapman, Barbara. 1946. Oxford University Press. (P.186)
--*Salt in Their Hair.* 1st ed. Anderson, Edgar A. 1956. Pageant Press. (P.39)
--*Your Loving Sister, Pat Downing.* Wright, Frances Fitzpatrick (1897-). 1948. Rinehart. (P.981)

Dodgson, Charles Lutwidge see Carroll, Lewis, pseud.

Dodgson, Charles Lutwidge (1832-1898)
--*Alice's Adventures Under Ground: Being a Facsimile of the Original Ms.* Book Afterwards Developed into "Alice's Adventures in Wonderland". Carroll, Lewis, pseud. Dodgson, Charles Lutwidge (1832-1898). Carroll, Lewis, pseud. 1932. The Macmillan Company. (P.278)

--*A Pilgrim Maid: A Story of Plymouth Colony in 1620.* Taggart, Marion Ames (1866-). 1920. Doubleday, Page & Company. (P.876)

Dong-Ho, Choi

--*Two Brothers & Their Magic Gourds.* Adams, Edward B., ed. 1981. C E Tuttle. (P.5)

Donnison, Polly

--*William the Dragon.* Donnison, Polly. 1973. Putnam Pub Group. (P.280)

Donovan, Linford

--*Moses.* Wheeler, Opal (1898-). N.D. Dutton. (P.949)

Donovan, Mary Rose

--*Five Plays and Five Pantomines.* Baldwin, Sidney (1885-). 1922. The Penn Publishing Company. (P.65)

--*Plays for Children in French and English.* Thomason, Caroline Wasson. 1922. The Penn Publishing Company. (P.886)

--*Wee Folks and Mother.* N.D. George W. Jacobs & Co. (P.280)

Dool, Jan

--*The Witch of Pungo, and Other Historical Stories of the Early Colonies.* Kyle, Louisa Venable. 1973. Four O'Clock Farms Pub. Co. (P.543)

Dora

--*Captain Orkle's Treasure.* Micocci, Harriet Palmer. 1961. Astor-Honor. (P.644)

--*Captain Orkle's Treasure.* Micocci, Harriet Palmer. 1961. I. Obolensky. (P.644)

Dorcas, Couri

--*The Circus Train, Verses.* Knittle, Jessie Mahn. c.1948. Whitman Pub. Co. (P.532)

--*Pillow-Time Tales: Fourteen Famous Nursery Stories.* Willard, Annmary, retold by. c.1954. Rand McNally. (P.961)

--*The Truck that Stopped at Village Small.* Knittle, Jessie Mahn. c.1951. Whitman. (P.532)

Dore, Gustave, jt. illus. see Dore, Louis Christophe Paul Gustave.

Dore, Louis Christophe Paul Gustave, jt. illus. see Munro, D. J.

Dore, Louis Christophe Paul Gustave (1832-1883)

--*The Adventures of Baron Munchausen.* Munchausen. c.1936. Three Sirens Press. (P.671)

--*Adventures Of Munchausen.* N.D. Cassell. (P.280)

--*All the French Fairy Tales.* Perrault, Charles (1628-1703). Untermeyer, Louis (1885-1977), retold by. Untermeyer, Louis (1885-1977), frwd. by. 1946. Didier. (P.718)

--*The Children's Book of Poetry.* Coates, Henry Troth (1843-1910), selected by. N.D. Porter & Coates. (P.204)

--*The Children's Book of Poetry: Carefully Selected from the Works of the Best and Most Popular Writers for Children.* Coates, Henry Troth (1843-1910), ed. 1971. Books for Libraries Press. (P.204)

--*Don Quixote.* Cervantes Saavedra, Miguel de (1547-1616). N.D. Modern Library. (P.180)

--*Don Quixote of la Mancha.* Cervantes Saavedra, Miguel de (1547-1616). Starkie, Walter, tr. N.D. St. Martin's Press. (P.180)

--*Dore's Popular Fairy Tales.* N.D. James Miller. (P.280)

--*Droll Stories.* English ed. 1888. R Worthington. (P.280)

--*Fairy Tales Told Again.* N.D. Cassell, Petter & Galpin. (P.280)

--*The Fortress of Fear.* L'Epine, Ernest Louis Victor Jules (1826-1893). Hood, Tom (1835-1974), tr. from French. c.1953. Story Classics. (P.566)

--*French Fairy Tales.* Coleman, Mrs., tr. N.D. Porter & Coates. (P.280)

--*French Fairy Tales.* Perrault, Charles (1628-1703). Untermeyer, Louis (1885-1977), frwd. by. 1945. Didier. (P.719)

--*Geoffrey the Knight: A Tale of Chivalry of the Days of King Arthur.* Jaufre Provencal Romance. 1869. T. Nelson and Sons. (P.490)

--*The Legend of Croquemitaine, and the Chivalric Times of Charlemagne.* L'Epine, Ernest Louis Victor Jules (1826-1893). Hood, Thomas (1835-1874), tr. from Fr. 1866. Cassell, Petter, and Galpin. (P.566)

--*More French Fairy Tales.* Perrault, Charles (1628-1703). Untermeyer, Louis (1885-1977), retold by. 1946. Didier. (P.719)

--*Perrault's Fairy Tales.* Perrault, Charles (1628-1703). Johnson, Alfred Edwin, et al. (1879-), trs. 1969. Dover Publications. (P.719)

--*River Legends.* Brabourne, Edward Hugessen Knatchbull Hugessen (1929-1893). N.D. George Routledge & Sons. (P.124)

--*Singular Travels, Campaigns & Adventures of Baron Munchausen.* Raspe, Rudolf Erich (1737-1794). Carswell, John Patrick (1918-), ed. N.D. Dover. (P.750)

--*Standard Fairy Tales, 1 of 3 Vols.* N.D. Porter & Coates. (P.280)

--*Tales of the Crusades.* Coolidge, Olivia Ensor (1908-). 1970. Houghton Mifflin. (P.216)

Doremus, Hal W.

--*Peter Goes to School.* House, Wanda Rogers. 1953. Wonder Books. (P.466)

Doremus, Robert (1913-)

--*Albert Einstein, Young Thinker.* Hammontree, Marie Gertrude (1913-). 1961. Bobbs-Merrill. (P.409)

--*As the Wheel Turns.* 1st ed. Tufts, Anne. 1952. Holt. (P.904)

--*Beaver Water.* Montgomery, Rutherford George (1894-). c.1956. World Pub. Co. (P.658)

--*Black Beauty.* Sewell, Anna (1820-1878). c.1951. Whitman Pub. Co. (P.812)

--*Blue Dowry.* Updegraff, Florence Maule. 1948. Harcourt, Brace. (P.910)

--*Boy of the Wilderness.* Petty, Emma. 1948. Broadman Press. (P.722)

--*Daniel Boone: Boy Hunter.* Stevenson, Augusta (1869-1976). c.1961. Bobbs-Merrill. (P.854)

--*De Witt Clinton, Boy Builder.* Widdemer, Mabel Cleland (1902-1964). 1961. Bobbs-Merrill. (P.956)

--*Eight Cousins: Or, The Ant-Hill.* Alcott, Louisa May (1832-1888). 1955. Whitman. (P.16)

--*Eight Cousins: Or, The Aunt-Hill.* Alcott, Louisa May (1832-1888). 1955. Whitman Pub. Co. (P.17)

--*Eli Terry: Clockmaker of Connecticut.* Jones, Leslie Allen (1903-). 1942. Farrar & Rinehart, Inc. (P.499)

--*Elizabeth Blackwell, Girl Doctor.* Henry, Joanne Landers (1927-). 1961. Bobbs-Merrill. (P.433)

--*Far West Summer.* Jacobs, Emma Atkins (1885-). 1949. Aladdin Books. (P.486)

--*Favorite Dog Stories.* Bloch, Marguerite. N.D. World Publishing Co. (P.109)

--*Franklin Roosevelt, Boy of the Four Freedoms.* Weil, Ann (1908-). 1962. Bobbs-Merrill. (P.940)

--*George Dewey, Vermont Boy.* Long, Laura Mooney (1892-1967). 1963. Bobbs-Merrill. (P.582)

--*Glenn L.* Martin: Boy Conqueror of the Air. Harley, Ruth W. (1919-). 1967. Bobbs. (P.413)

--*The How and Why Wonder Book of Oceanography.* Scharff, Robert. 1964. Wonder Books. (P.797)

--*Jeb Stuart, Boy in the Saddle.* Winders, Gertrude Hecker. 1959. Bobbs-Merrill. (P.967)

--*Jeb Stuart, Boy in the Saddle.* Winders, Gertrude Hecker. 1959. Bobbs-Merrill. (P.967)

--*Jedediah Smith: Fur Trapper of the Old West.* Burt, Olive Frank Woolley (1894-). 1951. Messner. (P.157)

--*Jim Bridger, Mountain Boy.* 1st ed. Winders, Gertrude Hecker. c.1962. Bobbs-Merrill. (P.967)

--*John Deere, Blacksmith Boy.* Bare, Margaret Ann. 1964. Bobbs-Merrill. (P.71)

--*John Deere, Blacksmith Boy.* Bare, Margaret Ann. 1965, c.1964. Bobbs. (P.71)

--*Juan Ponce De Leon.* 1st ed. Baker, Nina Brown, Mrs. (1888-1957). 1957. Knopf. (P.64)

--*Kit Carson: Boy Trapper.* Stevenson, Augusta (1869-1976). 1962. Bobbs-Merrill. (P.854)

--*Knute Rockne, Young Athlete.* Van Riper, Guernsey, Jr. (1909-). 1959. Bobbs-Merrill. (P.915)

--*Let's Go to a Zoo.* Sootin, Laura. 1959. Putnam. (P.841)

--*The Long Return.* Craig, John Ernest (1921-). 1959. Bobbs-Merrill Co. (P.226)

--*Mystery in the Apple Orchard.* 1st ed. Orton, Helen Fuller, Mrs. (1872-1955). 1954. Lippincott. (P.696)

--*Mystery in the Old Cave.* 1st ed. Orton, Helen Fuller, Mrs. (1872-1955). 1950. Har-Row. (P.696)

--*Mystery in the Old Cave.* 1st ed. Orton, Helen Fuller, Mrs. (1872-1955). 1950. Lippincott. (P.696)

--*Mystery in the Old Red Barn.* 1st ed. Orton, Helen Fuller, Mrs. (1872-1955). 1952. Lippincott. (P.696)

--*Mystery in the Pirate Oak.* 1st ed. Orton, Helen Fuller, Mrs. (1872-1955). 1949. Lippincott Co. (P.696)

--*Mystery of the Hidden Book.* Orton, Helen Fuller, Mrs. (1872-1955). 1953. Lippincott. (P.696)

--*Mystery of the Lost Letter.* Orton, Helen Fuller, Mrs. (1872-1955). 1946. Lippincott. (P.696)

--*Mystery Over the Brick Wall.* Orton, Helen Fuller, Mrs. (1872-1955). 1951. Lippincott. (P.696)

--*Mystery up the Chimney.* Orton, Helen Fuller, Mrs. (1872-1955). 1947. J. B. Lippincott Company. (P.696)

--*Mystery up the Winding Stair.* Orton, Helen Fuller, Mrs. (1872-1955). 1948. J. B. Lippincott Co. (P.696)

--*Osceola: Young Seminole Indian.* Clark, Electa (1910-). c.1965. Bobbs. (P.197)

--*Our Independence and the Constitution.* Fisher, Dorothea Frances Canfield, Mrs. (1879-1958). 1950. Random House. (P.328)

--*Pontiac, Young Ottawa Leader.* Peckham, Howard Henry (1910-). 1963. Bobbs. (P.715)

--*Rachel Jackson, Tennessee Girl.* Govan, Christine Noble, Mrs. (1898-). 1962. Bobbs-Merrill. (P.379)

--*Sacagawea, Bird Girl.* Seymour, Flora Warren Smith (1888-1948). 1959. Bobbs-Merrill. (P.813)

--*Spooks and Spirits and Shadowy Shapes.* 1949. Aladdin Books. (P.280)

--*Spooks & Spirits & Shadowy Shapes.* Brock, Emma Lillian (1886-1974). 1949. Dutton. (P.133)

--*Spooks, and Spirits and Shadowy Shapes.* Brock, Emma Lillian (1886-1974). 1964. E.P. Dutton & Co. (P.134)

--*Squanto: Indian Adventurer.* Graff, S. Stewart (1908-) & Graff, Polly Anne Colver (1908-). c.1965. Garrard. (P.380)

--*Stevie Finds a Way.* Liebers, Ruth (1910-) & Rothenberg, Lillian (1922-). N.D. Abingdon Press. (P.572)

--*Up Goes the House: Adapted from a Story.* Gustavson, Harry (1914-). c.1953. Jolly Books. (P.400)

--*Walt Disney's Old Yeller.* Disney, Walter Elias (1901-1966). Lindquist, Willis, as told by. 1958. Golden Press. (P.272)

--*The Walton Boys and Gold in the Snow.* authorized. Burton, Hal, pseud. (1908-). Burton, Harold Bernard. 1948. Whitman Pub. Co. (P.157)

--*The Walton Boys and Rapids Ahead.* Burton, Hal, pseud. (1908-). Burton, Harold Bernard. 1950. Whitman. (P.157)

--*The Walton Boys in High Country.* Burton, Hal, pseud. (1908-). Burton, Harold Bernard. 1952. Whitman Pub. Co. (P.158)

--*Wilbur and Orville Wright: Boys with Wings.* Stevenson, Augusta (1869-1976). 1959. Bobbs-Merrill. (P.855)

--*William Bradford, Pilgrim Boy.* Smith, William Bradford (1909-). 1963. Bobbs-Merrill. (P.837)

Dorian, Marquerite

--*When the Snow Is Blue.* Dorian, Marguerite. 1960. Lothrop, Lee and Shepard Co. (P.281)

Dorkovszky, Dorathea

--*The Unruly Robin.* Dankovszky, Dorathea. 1953. Abelard Press. (P.241)

Dorman, Michelle

--*Whoever Heard of a Fird?.* Bach, Othello (1941-). c.1984. Caedmon. (P.58)

Dorn, Daniel

--*From Seed to Jack-O-Lantern.* Johnson, Hannah Lyons. 1974. Lothrop. (P.495)

--*Lets Make Jam.* Johnson, Hannah Lyons. 1975. William Morrow and Company. (P.495)

Dornbusch, Margrette Oatway

--*Tony and Toinette in the Tropics.* Harris, Lina Small & Harris, Valeria. 1939. A Whitman & Co. (P.416)

Dorne, Maxwell

--*Mother Goose.* Mother Goose. 1949. Random House. (P.667)

Dorros, Arthur

--*Alligator Shoes.* Dorros, Arthur. 1982. Dutton. (P.281)

--*Charlie's House.* 1st ed. Bulla, Clyde Robert (1914-). c.1983. Crowell. (P.148)

--*Pretzels.* Dorros, Arthur. c.1981. Greenwillow Books. (P.281)

Doseff, Ivan

--*Our Little Bulgarian Cousin.* Winlow, Clara Vostrovsky, Mrs. (1876-). 1913. L. C. Page & Company. (P.969)

Dos Santos, Joyce Audy

--*Be Kind to Your Dog at Christmas.* Costikyan, Barbara. c.1982. Pantheon Books. (P.223)

--*The Day Eli Went Looking for Bear.* Dionetti, Michelle (1947-). c.1980. Addison-Wesley. (P.266)

--*Gus Was a Real Dumb Ghost.* Woolley, Catherine (1904-). Thayer, Jane, pseud. 1982. Morrow. (P.978)

--*Million Dollar Jeans.* 1st ed. Roy, Ronald (1940-). c.1983. Dutton. (P.782)

--*Mrs.* Peloki's Class Play. Oppenheim, Joanne (1934-). 1983. Dodd. (P.695)

--*Mrs.* Peloki's Snake. Oppenheim, Joanne (1934-). 1980. Dodd, Mead. (P.695)

--*Orphan Jeb at the Massacree.* Mooser, Stephen (1941-). 1984. Knopf. (P.662)

--*Piskies, Spriggans, and Other Magical Beings: Tales from the Droll-Teller.* 1st ed. Climo, Shirley (1928-), retold by. 1981. Crowell. (P.202)

--*Sand Dollar, Sand Dollar.* Dos Santos, Joyce Audy. 1980. Harper. (P.281)

Dotterer, Lloyd J.

--*The Built-Upon House.* Heath, Janet Field Curtis (1885-). c.1929. A. Whitman & Co. (P.428)

--*Flappy, the Circus Seal.* Hayes, Gilmore. 1942. The Platt & Munk Co., Inc. (P.425)

--*From Crocus to Snowman.* Bascom, Pearle Boyd. 1948. Abingdon-Cokesbury Press. (P.79)

--*A Little Book of Singing Graces.* Brown, Jeanette Perkins, Mrs. (1887-). N.D. Abingdon-Cokesbury Press. (P.139)

--*Peter Had Courage: A Story for Boys.* Fuess, Claude Moore (1885-). c.1927. Lothrop, Lee & Shepard Co. (P.348)

Dottie

--*Hide-Away Puppy.* Broderick, Jessica Potter. c.1952. Rand McNally. (P.134)

Doty, Roy (1922-)

--*Dede O'Shea.* 1st ed. Goodin, Peggy. 1957. Dutton. (P.375)

--*Dede O'Shea, and Other Stories.* Goodin, Peggy, et al. 1957. Catholic Family Book Club. (P.375)

--*The First Travel Guide to the Moon: What to Pack, How to Go, & What to See When You Get There.* Blumberg, Rhoda (1917-). 1980. Scholastic Inc. (P.110)

--*Girls Can Be Anything.* Klein, Norma (1938-). 1973. Dutton. (P.530)

--*Hamburgers-and Ice Cream for Dessert.* Clymer, Eleanor Lowenton (1906-). 1975. Dutton. (P.203)

--*Take Tarts As Tarts Is Passing.* Clymer, Eleanor Lowenton (1906-). 1974. Dutton. (P.203)

--*Tales of a Fourth Grade Nothing.* Blume, Judy Sussman Kitchens (1938-). 1973. E. P. Dutton & Co. (P.110)

--*Teen Talk.* Glendining, Marion. 1951. Alfred A Knopf : distributed by Borzoi Books. (P.371)

--*Uncle Pockets.* Preston, David R. (1922-). Doty, Roy, created by. N.D. Dodd, Mead. (P.738)

Dotzenko, Grisha

--*African Folk Tales.* Leslau, Charlotte & Leslau, Wolf (1906-), eds. c.1963. Peter Pauper Press. (P.567)

--*Arrow Book of Poetry.* McGovern, Ann. 1965. Scholastic Book Services. (P.602)

--*Christmas Comes Once More.* Luckhardt, Mildred Madeleine Corell (1898-), ed. 1962. Abingdon. (P.590)

Dougherty

--*Tad Sheldon, Boy Scout: Stories of His Patrol.* Wilson, John Fleming (1877-1922). 1913. Sturgis & Walton Company. (P.966)

Dougherty, Charles L.

--*Frontier Priest and Congressman: Father Gabriel Richard, S.S.* Alois, Bro. 1958. Benziger Bros. (P.31)

--*Giant of the Western Trail: Father Peter De Smet.* McHugh, Michael. 1958. Benziger Bros. (P.603)

--*I Know a Dairy Man.* Stanek, Muriel Novella (1915-1971). 1970. Putnam. (P.848)

--*Star of the Mohawk: Kateri Tekakwitha.* MacDonald, Francis. 1958. Benziger Bros. (P.598)

Dougherty, Louis R.

--*Fire, Snow & Water: Or, Life in the Lone Land.* Ellis, Edward Sylvester (1840-1916). c.1908. The J. C. Winston Company. (P.302)

--*The Phantom Auto.* Ellis, Edward Sylvester (1840-1916). c.1908. The J. C. Winston Company. (P.303)

Douglas, Goray

--*Ayo Gurkha!.* Marks, James Macdonald (1921-). 1973. T. Nelson. (P.620)

Douglas, Marian, pseud., see Robinson, Annie Douglas Green.

Douglas, Stephanie

--*Good, Says Jerome.* 1st ed. Clifton, Lucille (1936-). 1973. Dutton. (P.202)

--*Three Wishes.* Clifton, Lucille (1936-). 1976. Viking Press. (P.202)

Douglass, Lucille

--*The Autobiography of a Chinese Dog: Edited by His Missuss.* Ayscough, Florence Wheelock, Mrs. (1878-). 1926. Houghton Mifflin Company. (P.57)

--*Firecracker Land.* Ayscough, Florence Wheelock, Mrs. (1878-). 1932. Houghton Mifflin Co. (P.57)

Douglass, Ralph (1895-)

--*Baby Jack and Jumping Jack Rabbit.* Tireman, Loyd Spencer (1896-). Yrisarri, Evelyn, adapted by. 1943. The University of New Mexico Press. (P.892)

--*Cocky: Stories.* Tireman, Loyd Spencer (1896-). Yrisarri, Evelyn, adapted by. 1946. The University of New Mexico Press. (P.892)

--*Dumbee: Stories.* Tireman, Loyd Spencer (1896-). Yrisarri, Evelyn, adapted by. 1945. The University of New Mexico Press. (P.892)

--*Hop-a-Long: Stories.* Tireman, Loyd Spencer (1896-). Yrisarri, Evelyn, adapted by. 1944. The University of New Mexico Press. (P.892)

Douthwaite, A.

--*Tom-Toms in Kotokro.* Guillot, Rene (1900-1969). 1958. S.G Phillips Inc. (P.399)

--*Tom-Toms in Kotokro.* Guillot, Rene (1900-1969). Rhys, Brian, tr. from Fr. c.1957. Criterion Books. (P.399)

Dove, Arthur Garfield (1880-1946)

--*Jibby Jones: A Story of Mississippi River Adventure for Boys.* Butler, Ellis Parker (1869-1937). 1923. Houghton Mifflin Company. (P.158)

--*Jibby Jones and the Alligator: The Story of the Young Alligator-Hunters of the Upper Mississippi Valley.* Butler, Ellis Parker (1869-1937). 1924. Houghton Mifflin Company. (P.158)

Feiffer, Jules (1929-)
--*The Phantom Tollbooth.* Juster, Norton (1929-). 1961. Epstein & Carroll; Distributed by Random House. (P.503)
--*Phantom Tollbooth.* Juster, Norton (1929-). 1961. Random. (P.503)
Feininger, Lyonel (1871-1956)
--*The Kin-der-Kids: All Thirty-One Strips in Full Color.* Feininger, Lyonel (1871-1956). 1980. Dover. (P.320)
Feldman, Lynne
--*Henry's Tower.* Rosen, David. 1984. Platypus Bks. (P.777)
Feldman, Roper
--*Freeman Earns a Bike.* Brumpton, Karen B. 1984. McVie Pub. (P.144)
Felix, Monique
--*Further Adventures of a Little Mouse Trapped in a Book.* Felix, Monique. 1983. Green Tiger Pr. (P.320)
--*The Further Adventures of the Little Mouse Trapped in a Book.* Felix, Monique. 1984. Green Tiger. (P.320)
--*Hansel & Gretle.* Grimm, Jakob Ludwig Karl (1785-1863) & Grimm, Wilhelm Karl (1786-1859). 1983. Childrens Bk Co. (P.393)
--*If I Were a Sheep.* 1982. Green Tiger Pr. (P.320)
--*Miam, Miam.* N.D. Green Tiger Pr. (P.320)
--*The Peace.* Careme, Maurice (1899-). Neumeyer, Helen, tr. 1982. Green Tiger Pr. (P.166)
--*The Story of a Little Mouse Trapped in a Book.* Felix, Monique. 1980. Green Tiger Pr. (P.320)
Fell, Herbert Granville
--*Stories of Siegfried.* Macgregor, Mary. Chisholm, Louey, ed. 1909. E. P. Dutton & Co. (P.603)
--*A Wonder Book.* Hawthorne, Nathaniel (1804-1864). 1927. J. M. Dent & Sons, Lmited. (P.424)
--*Wonder Stories from Herodotus.* Herodotus. Boden, George Harry & D'Almeida, William Barrington, eds. 1900. Harper & Brothers. (P.438)
Feller, Gene
--*World of Her Own.* library ed. Levinson, Nancy Smiler (1938-). c.1981. Harvey House. (P.568)
Fellin, Peter
--*The Fakir of Jinaika.* Boutelle, Edith W. 1961. Barnes. (P.120)
--*Four Proud Days.* Saxon, Gladys Relyea. 1961. Barnes. (P.795)
--*Niccolo.* Jaeger, Cyril Karel Stuart (1912-). 1961, c.1959. A. S. Barnes & Company, Inc. (P.488)
--*Noah's Shark's Ark.* Friedrich, Priscilla. Friedrich, Otto Alva (1929-), ed. N.D. A . S. Barnes & Co, Inc. (P.346)
--*The Persian Donkey Bead.* Kraenzel, Margaret Powell (1899-). 1960. Barnes. (P.536)
--*The Seven Monkeys.* Frankel, Bernice. 1962. A. S. Barnes. (P.342)
Fellows, Muriel H.
--*The Land of Little Rain: A Story of Hopi Indian Children.* Fellows, Muriel H. 1936. The John C. Winston Company. (P.321)
--*Little Magic Painter: A Story of the Stone Age.* Fellows, Muriel H. c.1938. The John C. Winston Company. (P.321)
Felt, Sue (1924-)
--*Contrary Woodrow.* Felt, Sue (1924-). c.1958. Doubleday. (P.321)
--*Hello-Goodbye.* Felt, Sue (1924-). N.D. Doubleday & Co. (P.321)
--*The Jolly Season.* Stirling, Lilla Mary Elderkin (1902-). 1948. C. Scribner's Sons. (P.859)
--*Melissa.* Forbus, Ina Bell. 1962. Viking Pr. (P.335)
--*Rosa-Too-Little.* Felt, Sue (1924-). 1950. Doubleday. (P.321)
Felten, Major
--*Carol on Broadway.* Boylston, Helen Dore, Mrs. (1895-1984). 1944. Little, Brown and Company. (P.123)
--*Carol on Tour.* Boylston, Helen Dore, Mrs. (1895-1984). 1946. Little, Brown and Company. (P.123)
--*Carol Plays Summer Stock.* Boylston, Helen Dore, Mrs. (1895-1984). 1942. Little, Brown and Company. (P.123)
--*Sue Barton, Staff Nurse.* Boylston, Helen Dore, Mrs. (1895-1984). 1952. Little, Brown & Co. (P.123)
Felton, Major, jt. illus. see Orr, Forrest W.
Felts, Shirley (1934-)
--*Foxglove Tales.* Uttley, Alison, Mrs., pseud. (1884-1976). Uttley, Alice Jane Taylor. Meredith, Lucy, selected by. 1984. Faber & Faber. (P.911)
--*The Giant at the Ford & Other Legends of the Saints.* Synge, Phyllis Ursula (1930-). 1980. Atheneum. (P.875)
--*The Light Beyond the Forest: The Quest for the Holy Grail.* Sutcliff, Rosemary (1920-). 1980, c.1979. Dutton. (P.871)
--*The Magic Umbrella, and Other Stories for Telling.* Colwell, Eileen Hilda (1904-). 1976. Bodley Head. (P.211)
--*The Magic Umbrella and Other Stories for Telling.* Colwell, Eileen Hilda (1904-), ed. 1977. Merrimack. (P.211)
--*The Magic Umbrella, and Other Stories for Telling: With Notes on How to Tell Them.* Colwell, Eileen Hilda (1904-). 1977, c.1976. D. McKay Co. (P.211)
--*The Road to Camlann: The Death of King Arthur.* Sutcliff, Rosemary (1920-). 1982. Dutton. **Award: (ALA).** (P.871)
--*The Secret World of Polly Flint.* Cresswell, Helen. 1984, c.1982. Macmillan. **Award: (ALA).** (P.230)
--*Sun Horse, Moon Horse.* Sutcliff, Rosemary (1920-). 1978, c.1977. Dutton. (P.871)
--*The Sword and the Circle: King Arthur and the Knights of the Round Table.* Sutcliff, Rosemary (1920-) & Malory, Thomas, Sir. 1981. Dutton. (P.871)
Fenn, Harry (1838-1911)
--*Rhymes of the States.* Newkirk, Garrett (1847-1921). 1896. The Century Co. (P.680)
Fennell, Paul J.
--*The Bear Facts.* Culbertson, Mary Haeseler & Culbertson, Polly. 1948. J. C. Winston Co. (P.234)
Fenner, Carol Elizabeth (1929-)
--*Christmas Tree on the Mountain.* Fenner, Carol Elizabeth (1929-). 1966. HarBraceJ. (P.321)
--*Christmas Tree on the Mountain.* 1st. ed. Fenner, Carol Elizabeth (1929-). 1966. Harcourt. (P.321)
--*Lagalag, the Wanderer.* Fenner, Carol Elizabeth (1929-). 1968. Harcourt, Brace & World. (P.321)
--*Tigers in the Cellar.* Fenner, Carol Elizabeth (1929-). 1963. Harcourt, Brace & World. (P.321)
Fennessy, Rena
--*Moses.* Kimenye, Barbara (1940-). 1971. Oxford University Press. (P.522)
--*Moses and Mildred.* Kimenye, Barbara (1940-). 1967. Oxford University Press. (P.522)
--*Moses and the Ghost.* Kimenye, Barbara (1940-). 1971. Oxford University Press. (P.523)
--*Moses and the Kidnappers.* Kimenye, Barbara (1940-). 1968. Oxford University Press. (P.523)
--*Moses in a Muddle.* Kimenye, Barbara (1940-). 1970. Oxford University Press. (P.523)
--*Moses in Trouble.* Kimenye, Barbara (1940-). 1968. Oxford University Press. (P.523)
Fenton, C. L., jt. illus. see Tessin, Louise D.
Fenton, Carroll Lane (1900-1969)
--*Goldie is a Fish.* Fenton, Carroll Lane (1900-1969). 1961. John Day. (P.322)
--*Riches From The Earth.* Fenton, Carroll Lane (1900-1969) & Fenton, Mildred Adams. 1953. John Day & Co. (P.322)
--*Weejack and His Neighbors.* Fenton, Carroll Lane (1900-1969). 1944. The John Day Company. (P.322)
--*Wild Folk at the Pond.* Fenton, Carroll Lane (1900-1969). 1948. John Day Bks. (P.322)
--*Wild Folk at the Seashore.* Fenton, Carroll Lane (1900-1969). 1959. John Day Co. (P.322)
--*Wild Folk in the Desert.* Fenton, Carroll Lane (1900-1969) & Carswell, Evelyn Medicus (1919-). 1958. J. Day Co. (P.322)
--*Wild Folk in the Mountains.* Fenton, Carroll Lane (1900-1969). 1958. John Day & Co. (P.322)
--*Wild Folk In the Woods.* Fenton, Carroll Lane (1900-1969). 1952. John Day & Co. (P.322)
--*Worlds in the Sky.* Fenton, Carroll Lane (1900-1969) & Adams, Mildred. 1963. John Day Co. (P.322)
Fentz, Mike
--*Garfield Goes to a Picnic.* Davis, James Robert (1945-). 1983. Random. (P.246)
--*Garfield, the Knight in Shining Armor.* Davis, James Robert (1945-). c.1982. Random House. (P.246)
Fentz, Mike & Kuhn, Dave
--*Garfield A to Z Zoo.* Davis, James Robert (1945-). Christensen, Anne, ed. 1984. Random. (P.246)
--*Garfield Book of the Seasons.* Davis, James Robert (1945-). Christensen, Anne, ed. 1984. Random. (P.246)
Ferand, Emmy
--*My First Book of Bible Stories.* Walton, Mary Ann. Reed, Mary, ed. 1943. Simon & Schuster. (P.929)
--*My First Book of Bible Stories.* Walton, Mary Ann. 1943. Golden Press. (P.929)
Ferguson, Bruce, photos by.
--*Because I Am Human!.* Buscaglia, Leo F., pseud. (1924-). Buscaglia, Felice Leonardo. c.1972. C. B. Slack. (P.158)
Ferguson, Jack
--*How Rabbit Stole Fire: A Cherokee Legend.* 1st ed. Sterne, Emma Gelders, Mrs. (1894-1971). Broun, Emily, pseud. 1954. Aladdin Books. (P.853)
--*How Rabbit Stole Fire: A Cherokee Legend.* Sterne, Emma Gelders, Mrs. (1894-1971). Broun, Emily, pseud. N.D. E. P. Dutton & Co. (P.853)
--*Revolt in the West: The Story of the Real Rebellion.* McCourt, Edward Alexander (1907-1972). 1958. St. Martin's Press. (P.597)
Ferguson, Walter (1930-)
--*Gray Squirrel.* Venn, Mary Eleanor (1908-). Mary Adrian, pseud. 1955. Holiday House. (P.917)
--*When Animals Change Clothes.* May, Charles Paul (1920-). c.1965. Holiday House. (P.632)
Ferguson, William
--*A Bow for Turtle.* Heiderstadt, Dorothy (1907-). 1960. David Mckay Company Inc. (P.430)
--*The Buckskin Colt.* Grew, David. 1967, c.1962. Grosset & Dunlap. (P.389)
--*Circus Girl Without a Name.* Hays, Wilma Pitchford (1909-). 1970. Washburn. (P.426)
--*Crystal Pie.* Chandler, Edna Walker (1908-1982). 1965. Duell, Sloan and Pearce. (P.183)
--*Flag on the Levee.* Wellman, Manly Wade (1905-). 1955. I. Washburn. (P.943)
--*Frontier Boy: A Story of Oregon.* Arntson, Herbert Edward (1911-). 1967. Washburn. (P.49)
--*River Boy.* Arntson, Herbert Edward (1911-). 1969. Washburn. (P.49)
--*Rookie Fireman.* Crary, Margaret Coleman (1906-). 1967. Washburn. (P.229)
--*The Sword of Ganelon.* Parker, Richard (1915-). c.1958. D. McKay Co. (P.706)
--*Tallmadge's Terry: Action and Espionage in the American Revolution.* Mantel, S. G. c.1965. McKay. (P.618)
--*The Three Pebbles.* Parker, Richard (1915-). 1956. D. McKay Co. (P.706)
--*The Youngest Conquistador.* Mantel, S. G. 1963. D. McKay Co. (P.618)
Feringer, Jo Anne Norling
--*Magic Ring: A Collection of Verse for Children.* Brown, Ruth Archambault (1896-) & Breck, H. Jean. c.1985. American Camping Association. (P.142)
Ferm, Annie S.
--*Changed Lots: Or, Nobody Cares.* Armstrong, Frances. N.D. Brentano's Publications. (P.48)
Fern, Eugene A. (1919-)
--*Birthday Presents.* Fern, Eugene A. (1919-). 1967. Farrar, Straus & Giroux. (P.322)
--*The Library Mice.* Sanders, Anna Pearl Goodman (1935-). 1962. Ariel Books. (P.792)
--*The Little Bear's Mother.* Memling, Carl (1918-1969). 1959. Ariel Books. (P.640)
--*The Most Frightened Hero.* Fern, Eugene A. (1919-). 1961. Coward-McCann. (P.323)
--*The Mud Ponies.* Stoutenburg, Adrien Pearl (1916-). Kendall, Lace, pseud. 1963. Coward-McCann. (P.863)
--*Pepito's Story.* Fern, Eugene A. (1919-). c.1960. Ariel Books. (P.323)
--*What's He Been Up to Now?.* Fern, Eugene A. (1919-). 1961. Dial. (P.323)
Fernald, Anne
--*Fur, Feathers and Fun: A Book for Children.* Cochran, Martha Conney (1870-). 1946, c.1945. Carleton Printing Co. (P.205)
Fernandez, Oscar
--*A Tale of Eternal Life.* Ruth, Eddie. 1981. Am Atheist. (P.786)
Fernando
--*The Treasure of Andor: A Robo Force Adventure.* King, Regina. 1985. Random. (P.524)
Ferns, Ronald George (1925-)
--*Semolina Silkpaws Come to Catstown.* Williams, Gladys. N.D. Lion. (P.963)
--*Semolina Silkpaws Comes to Catstown.* Williams, Gladys. 1967, c.1962. Hart Pub. Co. (P.963)
Ferrandiz
--*The Peaceable Kingdom.* Hazard, David. 1983. Chosen Bks Pub. (P.427)
Ferrero, Elisabetta & Millet, Claude
--*How the Elephant Got Its Trunk, and, Cinderella.* Kipling, Joseph Rudyard (1865-1936). c.1985. Educational Development Corp. (P.528)
Ferris, J. L. G., jt. illus. see Coleman, Ralph Pallen.
Ferro, Walter
--*Cook Inlet Decision.* Pedersen, Elsa Kienitz (1915-). 1963. Atheneum. (P.715)
--*The Heroic Deeds of Beowulf.* Schmitt, Gladys (1909-1972). 1962. Random House. (P.800)
--*West with the White Chiefs.* Harris, Christie Lucy Irwin (1907-). 1965. Atheneum. (P.415)
Ferry, Cay
--*Mr.* Pink and the HOuse on the Roof. Berrien, Edith Heal (1903-). 1941. J. Messner. (P.97)
--*Mr.* Pink and the House on the Roof. Heal, Edith. N.D. Veritas Press. (P.428)
--*Mr.* Pink and the House on the Roof. Heal, Edith (1903-). c.1941. J. Messner, Inc. (P.428)
Fetz, Ingrid (1915-)
--*The Adventure of Walter.* Clymer, Eleanor Lowenton (1906-). 1965. Atheneum. (P.203)
--*The Bear Seeds.* Asendorf, James C. 1969. Little, Brown. (P.51)
--*Benson Boy.* Southall, Ivan Francis (1921-). 1973. Macmillan. (P.841)
--*The Boy Who Lived in the Railroad Depot.* Fife, Dale Odile (1910-). 1968. Coward-McCann. (P.325)
--*Chipmunk in the Forest.* Clymer, Eleanor Lowenton (1906-). 1965. Atheneum. (P.203)
--*Chipmunk in the Forest.* Clymer, Eleanor Lowenton (1906-). 1972. Atheneum. (P.203)
--*Eddie's Menagerie.* Haywood, Carolyn (1898-). 1978. Morrow. (P.427)
--*The Holy Terror.* Mauriac, Francois (1885-1970). 1967. Funk & Wagnalls. (P.632)
--*I Loved Rose Ann.* Hopkins, Lee Bennett (1938-). c.1976. Knopf. (P.463)
--*Kate and the Wild Kittens.* La Farge, Phyllis. 1965. Knopf. (P.543)
--*Last Night I Saw Andromeda.* Anker, Charlotte (1934-). 1975. H. Z. Walck. (P.42)
--*Laughable Limericks.* Brewton, Sara Westbrook & Brewton, John Edmund (1898-), eds. 1965. Har-Row. (P.130)
--*Louly.* Brink, Carol Ryrie, Mrs. (1895-1981). 1974. Macmillan. (P.132)
--*Maurice's Room.* Fox, Paula (1923-). 1966. Macmillan. (P.340)
--*Maurice's Room.* Fox, Paula (1923-). 1985, c.1966. Macmillan. (P.340)
--*Me and Arch and the Pest.* Durham, John (1925-). 1970. Four Winds Press. (P.291)
--*A Monster Too Many.* 1st ed. McNeill, Janet (1907-). 1972. Little, Brown. (P.610)
--*Now That You Are Eight.* Taylor, Sydney Brenner (1904-1978). 1963. Association. (P.880)
--*Now That You Are Seven.* Clymer, Eleanor Lowenton (1906-). 1963. Association.
--*Once I was a Plum Tree.* Hurwitz, Johanna (1937-) c. 1980. Morrow (P.476)
--*Paddy's Preposterous Promises.* Bischoff, Julia Bristol (1909-1970). 1968. Young Scott Books. (P.103)
--*A Pony for the Winter.* Kay, Helen, pseud. (1912-). Goldfrank, Helen Colodny. 1959. Farrar, Straus and Cudahy, Inc. (P.509)
--*Pure Magic.* Coatsworth, Elizabeth Jane (1893-). 1973. Macmillan. (P.204)
--*A Red Carpet for Lafayette.* Foster, Martha Standing. c.1961. Bobbs-Merrill. (P.339)
--*Santiago's Silver Mine.* 1st ed. Clymer, Eleanor Lowenton (1906-). 1973. Atheneum. (P.203)
--*Shoots of Green: Poems for Young Gardeners.* Bramblett, Ella, ed. 1968. T. Y. Crowell Co. (P.126)
--*Sociable Toby.* Clymer, Eleanor Lowenton (1906-). 1956. F. Watts. (P.203)
--*Southern Yankees.* Speicher, Helen Ross Smith (1915-) & Borland, Kathryn Kilby (1916-). 1960. Bobbs-Merrill. (P.843)
--*The Spider, the Cave, and the Pottery Bowl.* 1st ed. Clymer, Eleanor Lowenton (1906-). 1971. Atheneum. (P.203)
--*Tecwyn: The Last of the Welsh Dragons.* Dawson, Mary (1919-). 1967. Parents' Magazine Press. (P.247)
--*The Tiny Little House.* 1st ed. Clymer, Eleanor Lowenton (1906-). 1964. Atheneum. (P.203)
--*The Valentine Box.* Lovelace, Maud Hart, Mrs. (1892-1980). 1966. Crowell. (P.587)
--*Wendy and the Bullies.* Robinson, Nancy Konheim (1942-). c.1980. Hastings House. (P.770)
--*The Were-Fox.* Coatsworth, Elizabeth Jane (1893-). 1975. Collier Books. (P.204)
--*What Goes up Must Come down.* Hurwitz, Johanna (1937-). 1983. Scholastic Inc. (P.476)
--*What's Good for a Six-Year-Old?.* 1st ed. Cole, William Rossa (1919-). 1965. Holt, Rinehart and Winston. (P.208)
--*When Lucy Went Away.* 1st ed. Ross, George Maxim. c.1976. Dutton. (P.779)
--*Where the Good Luck Was.* Molarsky, Osmond (1909-). 1970. H. Z. Walck. (P.653)
Fiammenghi, Gioia (1929-)
--*The Barn: Story.* Roberts, Thomas Sacra (1940-). 1975. McGraw-Hill. (P.768)
--*Belinda's New Spring Hat.* Clymer, Eleanor Lowenton (1906-). 1969. F. Watts. (P.203)
--*Born to Dance Samba.* Cohen, Miriam (1926-). c.1984. Harper & Row. (P.207)
--*Cave Above Delphi.* Corbett, Scott (1913-). 1965. HR&W. (P.219)
--*Chester Jones.* Carleton, Barbee Oliver (1917-). 1963. Holt, Rinehart and Winston. (P.168)
--*Chocolate Fever.* Smith, Robert Kimmel (1930-). 1972. Coward, McCann & Geoghegan. (P.836)
--*The Day Jean-Pierre Joined the Circus.* Gallico, Paul William (1897-1976). 1969. Watts. (P.353)
--*Day Jean-Pierre Went Round the World.* Gallico, Paul William (1897-1976). 1965. Doubleday. (P.353)
--*The Day Jean-Pierre Went Round the World.* Gallico, Paul William (1897-1976). N.D. Doubleday. (P.353)
--*The Day Willie Wasn't.* Corbin, William, pseud. (1916-). McGraw, William Corbin. 1971. Coward. (P.219)
--*The Day Willie Wasn't.* McGraw, William Corbin (1916-). Corbin, William, pseud. 1971. Coward McCann & Geoghegan. (P.602)

--*The Reluctant Dragon.* Nuttall-Smith, Margaret Emily Noel. Grahame, Kenneth (1859-1932). N.D. Dufour. (P.381)
--*Shane Comes to Dublin.* Nutall-Smith, Margaret Emily Noel. Lynch, Patricia Nora (1898-1972). 1958. Criterion Books. (P.592)
--*Shane Comes to Dublin.* Nutall-Smith, Margaret Emily Noel. Lynch, Patricia Nora (1898-1972). 1958. S G Phillips. (P.592)
--*Thursday's Child.* Nuttall-Smith, Margaret Emily Noel. Streatfeild, Noel (1897-). 1971. Random. (P.867)

Fosbery, Ernest
--*David Ransom's Watch.* Alden, Isabella Macdonald (1841-1930). Pansy, pseud. N.D. Lothrop Lee & Shepard Co. (P.19)
--*Doris Farrand's Vocation.* Alden, Isabella Macdonald (1841-1930). Pansy, pseud. 1904. Lothrop Lee & Shepard & Co. (P.19)
--*Ester Ried's Namesake.* Alden, Isabella Macdonald (1841-1930). Pansy, pseud. 1906. Lothrop, Lee & Shepard Co. (P.19)
--*Six Nursery Classics ...* O'Shea, Michael Vincent (1866-1932), ed. 1900. D. C. Health & Co. (P.697)

Foster, Birket
--*Chimes for Childhood: A Collection of Songs for Little Folks.* N.D. Estes and Lauriat's Publications. (P.338)
--*Early Lessons.* Edgeworth, Maria (1767-1849). N.D. George Routledge & Sons. (P.296)
--*Eda Morton and Her Cousins: Or, School-Room Days.* Bell, M. M. N.D. George Routledge & Sons. (P.91)
--*My Father's Garden.* Miller, Thomas. N.D. George Routledge & Sons. (P.649)

Foster, Birket & Leech, Dore
--*Christmas in Song and Story.* N.D. R. Worthington. (P.338)

Foster, Birket & Millais
--*Chimes for Childhood.* N.D. Lee & Shepard. (P.338)

Foster, Brad W.
--*Monica the Computer Mouse.* Bearden, Donna. 1984. SYBEX. (P.85)

Foster, Celeste K.
--*A Bear Can Hibernate-Why Can't I?.* Blair, Ruth Van Ness (1912-). 1972. Denison. (P.105)
--*The Best Color.* Dickson, Naida (1916-). N.D. Denison. (P.265)
--*Casper, the Caterpillar.* Foster, Celeste K. N.D. Denison. (P.338)
--*The Dragon of Cobblestone Castle.* Rose, Nancy Ann (1934-). 1970. T. S. Denison. (P.777)
--*Funny-Talk Freddy.* Rose, Nancy Ann (1934-). 1970. T. S. Denison. (P.777)
--*A Happy Time for Teddy.* Wittman, Harry H. 1971. Denison. (P.973)
--*Jimbo, the Monkey.* Rhodes, Neva E. c.1970. T. S. Denison. (P.760)
--*Jonathan & the Octopus.* Foster, Celeste K. 1958. Denison. (P.338)
--*The Motherless Bug.* Rose, Nancy Ann (1934-). 1971. T. S. Denison. (P.777)
--*Mr. Wiggle's Book.* Craig, Paula M. 1972. Denison. (P.226)
--*My Daddy Abc's.* Kahn, Ruth E. 1969. T. S. Denison. (P.504)
--*Petey, the Discontented Parakeet.* Wittman, Harry H. 1970. T. S. Denison. (P.973)
--*Through My Window.* Becker, Ruby Wirt (1915-). 1969. T. S. Denison. (P.87)
--*Tippy Finds Some Friends.* Salot, Lorraine (1914-). 1971. Denison. (P.790)

Foster, Edith Francis
--*Daddy Joe's Fiddle.* Bickford, Faith. 1903. Dana Estes and Company. (P.101)
--*Grimm's Fairy Tales.* Grimm, Jakob Ludwig Karl (1785-1863) & Grimm, Wilhelm Karl (1786-1859). Pratt, Mara Louise, Mrs., ed. 1892. Educational Publishing Co. (P.392)
--*The Little Owls at Red Gates.* Pratt, Ella Farman, Mrs. (1843-1907). 1903. D. Estes & Company. (P.737)
--*Marigold.* Foster, Edith Francis. c.1906. D. Estes & Company. (P.338)
--*Marigold's Winter.* Foster, Edith Francis. c.1908. D. Estes & Company. (P.338)
--*Mary N' Mary.* Foster, Edith Francis. 1905. Dana Estes & Co. (P.338)
--*Two Children in the Woods.* Richards, Rosalind (1874-). c.1907. D. Estes & Company. (P.762)

Foster, Edith Francis & Johnson, Margaret
--*Picture Stories for Little Folks.* Foster, Edith Francis & Johnson, Margaret. N.D. L. C. Page & Co. (P.338)

Foster, Genevieve Stump, jt. illus. see Carsey, Alice.

Foster, Genevieve Stump (1893-1979)
--*Augustus Caesar's World.* Foster, Genevieve Stump (1893-1979). 1949. Scribner. (P.338)
--*Mary Jane's Friends in Holland.* Judson, Clara Ingram, Mrs. (1879-1960). c.1939. Grosset & Dunlap. (P.502)
--*Pioneer Girl: The Early Life of Frances Willard.* Judson, Clara Ingram, Mrs. (1879-1960). c.1939. Rand McNally & Company. (P.502)
--*The Riddle at Live Oaks: Two Mysteries for Youngest Enthusiasts, Both Boys and Girls.* Seaman, Augusta Huiell, Mrs. (1879-1950). 1934. Doubleday, Doran & Company, Inc. (P.806)
--*The Strange Pettingill Puzzle: Two Mysteries for Boys and Girls.* Seaman, Augusta Huiell, Mrs. (1879-1950). 1936. Doubleday, Doran & Company, Inc. (P.807)

Foster, George
--*Ivanhoe.* Dolch, Edward William (1889-) & Dolch, Marguerite Pierce (1891-). 1961. Garrard. (P.279)
--*Ivanhoe for Pleasure Reading.* Dolch, Edward William (1889-) & Scott, Walter, Sir (1771-1832). 1961. Garrard Press. (P.279)

Foster, Gerald
--*I Have Just Begun to Fight: The Story of John Paul Jones.* Ellsberg, Edward (1891-). 1942. Dodd, Mead, & Company. (P.304)

Foster, Hal, pseud., see Foster, Harold Rudolf.
Foster, Harold Rudolf see Foster, Hal, pseud.
Foster, Harold Rudolf (1892-1982)
--*The Medieval Castle.* Foster, Hal, pseud. Foster, Harold Rudolf (1892-1982). Foster, Hal, pseud. 1957. Hastings House. (P.338)
--*Prince Valiant & the Golden Princess.* Foster, Hal, pseud. Foster, Harold Rudolf (1892-1982). Foster, Hal, pseud. 1968. Hastings. (P.338)
--*Prince Valiant & the Three Challenges.* Foster, Hal, pseud. Foster, Harold Rudolf (1892-1982). Foster, Hal, pseud. 1960. Hastings. (P.338)
--*Prince Valiant Fights Attila the Hun.* Foster, Harold Rudolf (1892-1982). Harold, Hal, pseud. 1952. Hastings House. (P.338)
--*Prince Valiant in the Days of King Arthur.* Foster, Hal, pseud. Foster, Harold Rudolf (1892-1982). Foster, Hal, pseud. 1954. Treasure Books. (P.338)
--*Prince Valiant in the New World.* Foster, Hal, pseud. Foster, Harold Rudolf (1892-1982). Foster, Hal, pseud. 1956. Hastings House. (P.338)
--*Prince Valiant on the Inland Sea.* Foster, Hal, pseud. Foster, Harold Rudolf (1892-1982). Foster, Hal, pseud. 1968. Hastings. (P.338)
--*Prince Valiant on the Inland Sea.* Foster, Hal, pseud. Foster, Harold Rudolf (1892-1982). Foster, Hal, pseud. Trell, Max (1900-), adapted by. 1953. Hastings House. (P.338)
--*Prince Valiant's Perilous Voyage.* Foster, Hal, pseud. Foster, Harold Rudolf (1892-1982). Foster, Hal, pseud. Trell, Max (1900-), adapted by. 1954. Hastings. (P.338)

Foster, Imogene Watson
--*The May Party Mystery And Other Stories.* Baldwin, Dorothy Arno. c.1926. Cokesbury Press. (P.65)

Foster, John M.
--*Air Voyagers of the Arctic: Or, Sky Pilots' Dash Across the Pole.* Langley, John Prentice. c.1929. Barse & Co. (P.550)
--*Alice Ann.* Judson, Clara Ingram, Mrs. (1879-1960). c.1928. Barse & Co. (P.502)
--*Bridging the Seven Seas: Or, On the Air-Lane to Singapore.* Langley, John Prentice. c.1930. Barse & Co. (P.550)
--*The Camp Fire Boys' Canoe Cruise: Or, Stormbound on the Upper Rockaway.* Rathborne, St. George (1854-1928). Clifton, Oliver Lee, pseud. c.1925. Barse & Hopkins. (P.750)
--*Chasing the Setting Sun: Or, A Hop, Skip, and Jump to Australia.* Langley, John Prentice. 1930. Barse & Co. (P.550)
--*The Cliff Island Mystery.* Bartlett, Philip A., pseud. Stratemeyer Syndicate. 1930. Barse & Co. (P.78)
--*The Cliff Island Mystery.* Bartlett, Philip A., pseud. Stratemeyer Syndicate. N.D. Grosset & Dunlap. (P.78)
--*Desert Hawks on the Wing: Or, Headed South, Algiers to Cape Town.* Langley, John Prentice. c.1929. Barse & Co. (P.550)
--*Elizabeth Ann and Doris.* Lawrence, Josephine (1890-1978). c.1928. Barse & Hopkins. (P.556)
--*Elizabeth Ann's Houseboat.* Lawrence, Josephine (1890-1978). c.1929. Barse & Co. (P.556)
--*Feodora: A Story of Camp Kiloleet.* Jewett, Eleanore Myers (1890-1967). c.1927. Barse & Hopkins. (P.492)
--*Joy and Her Chums.* Whitehill, Dorothy. 1928. Barse and Co. (P.953)
--*Joy and Pam a-Sailing.* Whitehill, Dorothy. c.1930. Barse & Co. (P.953)
--*Joy and Pam at Brookside.* Whitehill, Dorothy. c.1929. Barse & Co. (P.953)
--*The Lakeport Bank Mystery.* Bartlett, Philip A., pseud. Stratemeyer Syndicate. 1929. Barse & Co. (P.78)
--*Linda Lane's Big Sister.* Lawrence, Josephine (1890-1978). c.1929. Barse & Co. (P.556)
--*Linda Lane's Problems.* Lawrence, Josephine (1890-1978). 1928. Barse & Co. (P.556)
--*Mary Cinderella Brown.* Whitehill, Dorothy. 1923. D. Appleton and Company. (P.953)
--*Masters of the Air-Lanes: Or, Round the World in Fourteen Days.* Langley, John Prentice. c.1928. Barse & Co. (P.550)
--*The Mystery of the Snowbound Express.* Bartlett, Philip A., pseud. Stratemeyer Syndicate. 1929. Barse & Co. (P.78)
--*The Mystery of the Snowbound Express.* Bartlett, Philip A., pseud. Stratemeyer Syndicate. N.D. Grosset & Dunlap. (P.78)
--*The Mystery of the Circle of Fire.* Bartlett, Philip A., pseud. Stratemeyer Syndicate. 1934. Grosset & Dunlap. (P.78)
--*Nancy Brandon: Idealist.* Garis, Lillian C. McNamara, Mrs. (1873-1954). c.1925. Milton Bradley Company. (P.357)
--*Our Little Lithuanian Cousin.* Winlow, Anna C. c.1926. L. C. Page & Company. (P.969)
--*The Pathfinder's Great Flight: Or, Cloud Chasers Over Amazon Jungles.* Langley, John Prentice. c.1928. Barse & Co. (P.550)
--*Podgy and Sally, Co-Eds.* Weber, Lenora Mattingly, Mrs. (1895-1971). c.1930. Barse & Co. (P.939)
--*Polly's Polly.* Whitehill, Dorothy. c.1925. Barse & Hopkins. (P.953)
--*Polly's Polly at Boarding School.* Whitehill, Dorothy. c.1928. Barse & Co. (P.953)
--*Rex Cole, Junior and the Grinning Ghost.* Chapman, Gordon. c.1931. Barse & Co. (P.186)
--*Ruth Darrow in the Air Derby: Or, Recovering the Silver Trophy.* Wirt, Mildred Augustine (1905-). c.1930. Barse & Co. (P.971)
--*Ruth Darrow in the Fire Patrol: Or, Capturing the Redwood Thieves.* Wirt, Mildred Augustine (1905-). c.1930. Barse & Co. (P.971)
--*Ruth Darrow in Yucatan.* Wirt, Mildred Augustine (1905-). c.1931. Barse & Co. (P.971)
--*The Silver Trapeze.* Starkey, Robert. c.1931. Duffield and Green. (P.849)
--*The Staircase of the Wind: Or, Over the Himalayas to Calcutta.* Langley, John Prentice. c.1931. Barse & Co. (P.550)
--*Sunny Boy and His Big Dog.* White, Ramy Allison, pseud. Stratemeyer Syndicate. 1927. Barse & Hopkins. (P.952)
--*Sunny Boy and His Big Dog.* White, Ramy Allison, pseud. Stratemeyer Syndicate. N.D. Barse & Co. (P.952)
--*Sunny Boy and His Big Dog.* White, Ramy Allison, pseud. Stratemeyer Syndicate. N.D. Grosset & Dunlap. (P.952)
--*Sunny Boy and His Cave.* White, Ramy Allison, pseud. Stratemeyer Syndicate. 1930. Barse & Co. (P.952)
--*Sunny Boy and His Cave.* White, Ramy Allison, pseud. Stratemeyer Syndicate. N.D. Grosset & Dunlap. (P.952)
--*Sunny Boy at Willow Farm.* White, Ramy Allison, pseud. Stratemeyer Syndicate. c.1929. Barse & Co. (P.952)
--*Sunny Boy At Willow Farm.* White, Ramy Allison, pseud. Stratemeyer Syndicate. N.D. Grosset & Dunlap. (P.952)
--*Sunny Boy in the Snow.* White, Ramy Allison, pseud. Stratemeyer Syndicate. c.1928. Barse & Co. (P.952)
--*Sunny Boy In the Snow.* White, Ramy Allison, pseud. Stratemeyer Syndicate. N.D. Grosset & Dunlap. (P.952)
--*That Missing Deed.* Wolverton, Ethel Traugh. c.1931. F. Warne & Co., Inc. (P.975)
--*The Twins a-Visiting.* Whitehill, Dorothy. c.1930. Barse & Co. (P.953)
--*The Twins Abroad.* Whitehill, Dorothy. c.1929. Barse & Co. (P.953)
--*The Twins at Camp.* Whitehill, Dorothy. c.1928. Barse & Co. (P.953)
--*The Two Little Fellows in April.* Lawrence, Josephine (1890-1978). c.1929. Barse & Co. (P.556)
--*The Two Little Fellows' Secret.* Lawrence, Josephine (1890-1978). c.1928. Barse & Co. (P.556)
--*Two Wild Cherries at the Seashore.* Garis, Howard Roger (1873-1962). N.D. Milton Bradley Co. (P.357)
--*Two Wild Cherries in the Country: Or, How Dick and Janet Saved the Mill.* Garis, Howard Roger (1873-1962). 1924. Milton Bradley Company. (P.357)
--*Two Wild Cherries in the Woods: Or, How Dick and Janet Caught the Bear.* Garis, Howard Roger (1873-1962). 1924. Milton Bradley Company. (P.357)
--*Two Wild Cherries: Or, How Dick and Janet Lost Something.* Garis, Howard Roger (1873-1962). 1924. Milton Bradley Company. (P.357)

Foster, John M., jt. illus. see Weber, Sarah Stilwell.

Foster, Laura Louise James (1918-)
--*Keer-Loo, the Life Story of a Young Wood Duck.* Foster, Laura Louise James (1918-). 1965. Naturegraph. (P.339)

Foster, Marcia Lane (1897-)
--*The Baby and the Princess.* Plummer, Gladys. 1969. Warner Press. (P.729)
--*Barbie.* Barne, Kitty, pseud. (1883-1957). Barne, Marion Catherine. 1969. Little, Brown. (P.73)
--*Benjamin's Brother.* Plummer, Gladys. 1969. Warner Pr. (P.729)
--*The Boy Who Gave His Dinner Away.* Plummer, Gladys. 1969. Warner Pr. (P.729)
--*The General and the Slave Girl.* Plummer, Gladys. 1969. Warner Pr. (P.729)
--*In the Den of Lions.* Plummer, Gladys. 1969. Warner Pr. (P.729)
--*Little Sea Dogs And Other Tales of Childhood.* France, Anatole, pseud. (1844-1924). Thibault, Jacques Anatole Francois. May, James Lewis (1873-), tr. 1925. John Lane. (P.341)
--*Noah's Ark.* Plummer, Gladys. 1969. Warner Pr. (P.729)
--*The Secret of the Ambermere Treasure.* Saville, Leonard Malcolm (1901-1982). 1967, c.1953. Criterion Books. (P.794)
--*The Son Who Came Home: Little Folks Bible Stories.* Plummer, Gladys. 1969. Warner Pr. (P.729)
--*The Story of Anna.* Plummer, Gladys. 1969. Warner Pr. (P.729)
--*Underground Alley.* Mayne, William James Carter (1928-). N.D. Dutton. (P.634)
--*Underground Alley.* 1st ed. Mayne, William James Carter (1928-). 1958. Oxford University Press. (P.634)
--*Who Is My Neighbor.* Plummer, Gladys. 1969. Warner Pr. (P.729)
--*The Windmill Family.* Brown, Pamela Beatrice (1924-). 1954. T. Nelson. (P.142)
--*The Windmill Mystery.* Barne, Kitty, pseud. (1883-1957). Barne, Marion Catherine. 1950. Dodd, Mead. (P.73)

Foster, Marian Curtis see Mariana, pseud.

Foster, Marian Curtis (1909-1978)
--*Coco Is Coming.* Mariana, pseud. Peckinpah, Betty. c.1956. Lothrop, Lee & Shepard Co. (P.715)
--*Danny's Pig.* Mariana, pseud. Udry, Janice May (1928-). 1960. Lothrop, Lee, and Shepard Co. (P.908)
--*Doki: The Lonely Papoose.* Mariana, pseud. Foster, Marian Curtis (1909-1978). Mariana, pseud. 1955. Lothrop, Lee & Shepard Co. (P.339)
--*Everybody Has Two Eyes.* Mariana, pseud. Jaszi, Jean Yourd. 1956. Lothrop, Lee & Shepard. (P.490)
--*Journey of Bangwell Putt.* Mariana, pseud. Foster, Marian Curtis (1909-1978). Mariana, pseud. 1965. Lothrop. (P.339)
--*Little Bear Learns to Read the Cookbook.* Mariana, pseud. Brustlein, Janice Tworkov. Janice, pseud. 1969. Lothrop, Lee & Shepard Co. (P.145)
--*Little Bear Marches in the Saint Patrick's Day Parade.* Mariana, pseud. Brustlein, Janice Tworkov. Janice, pseud. N.D. Lothrop. (P.145)
--*Little Bear Marches in the St.* Patricks Day Parade. Mariana, pseud. Brustlein, Janice Tworkov. Janice, pseud. 1969. William Morrow and Company. (P.145)
--*Little Bear's Christmas.* Mariana, pseud. Brustlein, Janice Tworkov. Janice, pseud. 1964. Lothrop. (P.145)
--*Little Bear's New Year's Party.* Mariana, pseud. Brustlein, Janice Tworkov. Janice, pseud. 1973. Lothrop, Lee & Shepard. (P.145)
--*Little Bear's Pancake Party.* Mariana, pseud. Brustlein, Janice Tworkov. Janice, pseud. 1959. Lothrop. (P.145)
--*Little Bear's Sunday Breakfast.* Mariana, pseud. Brustlein, Janice Tworkov. Janice, pseud. 1958. Lothrop, Lee & Shepard Co. (P.145)
--*Little Bear's Thanksgiving.* Mariana, pseud. Brustlein, Janice Tworkov. Janice, pseud. 1967. Lothrop. (P.145)
--*Little Bear's Thanksgiving.* Mariana, pseud. Brustlein, Janice Tworkov. Janice, pseud. 1964. William Morrow and Company. (P.145)
--*The Lonely Little Lady and Her Garden.* Mariana, pseud. Brustlein, Janice Tworkov. Janice, pseud. 1957. Lothrop, Lee & Shepard. (P.145)
--*Miss Flora McFlimsey's Christmas Eve.* Mariana, pseud. Foster, Marian Curtis (1909-1978). Mariana, pseud. 1949. Lothrop. (P.339)
--*Miss Flora McFlimsey's Easter Bonnet.* Mariana, pseud. Foster, Marian Curtis (1909-1978). Mariana, pseud. 1951. Lothrop. (P.339)
--*Miss Flora McFlimsey's May Day.* Mariana, pseud. Foster, Marian Curtis (1909-1978). Mariana, pseud. 1969. Lothrop. (P.339)
--*Miss Flora McFlimsey's Valentine.* Mariana, pseud. Foster, Marian Curtis (1909-1978). Mariana, pseud. 1962. Lothrop, Lee & Shepard Co. (P.339)
--*When You Were a Little Baby.* Mariana, pseud. Berman, Rhoda A. 1954. Lothrop, Lee & Shepard. (P.96)

Foster, Maud C.
--*The Blue Baby and Other Stories.* Molesworth, Mary Louisa Stewart, Mrs. (1842-1921). 1904. Dutton. (P.653)

--*Sky Sabotage.* Dixon, Franklin W, pseud. Stratemeyer Syndicate. 1983, c.1982. Wanderer Books. (P.274)
--*Space Age Terrors!.* Milton, Hilary Herbert (1920-). Schwartz, Betty, ed. 1983. Wanderer Bks. (P.651)
--*Super Sleuths, No. 2.* Keene, Carolyn, pseud. (1894-1982) & Dixon, Franklin W., pseud. Adams, Harriet Stratemeyer. Stratemeyer Syndicate. 1984. Wanderer Bks. (P.513)
--*The Swami's Ring.* Keene, Carolyn, pseud. (1894-1982). Adams, Harriet Stratemeyer. c.1981. Wanderer Books. (P.513)
--*Three for Treasure.* Trask, Margaret Pope (1907-). 1962. Crowell. (P.898)
--*Ticket to Intrigue.* Keene, Carolyn, pseud. (1894-1982) & Dixon, Franklin W, pseud. Adams, Harriet Stratemeyer. Stratemeyer Syndicate. c.1985. Wanderer Books. (P.513)
--*Tiger Rookie.* 1st ed. Scholefield, Edmund O, pseud. (1929-). Butterworth, William Edmund III. 1966. World Pub. Co. (P.800)
--*Too Many Boys.* Tolles, Martha (1921-). c.1965. Nelson. (P.894)
--*Trixie Belden and the Marshland Mystery.* Kenny, Kathryn. 1967. Golden Press. (P.518)
--*The Twin Dilemma.* Keene, Carolyn, pseud. (1894-1982). Adams, Harriet Stratemeyer. 1981. Wanderer Bks. (P.513)
--*Two Girls in New York.* Laklan, Carli (1907-). 1964. Doubleday. (P.544)
--*The Valley Cup.* Green, Anne M. (1922-). 1962. T. Nelson. (P.384)
--*Willie's Whizmobile.* Shapiro, Irwin (1911-). 1973. Garrard Pub. Co. (P.815)
--*The Year at Boggy.* Heck, Bessie Holland (1911-). 1966. World. (P.429)

Frampton, David
--*Joshua in the Promised Land.* Chaikin, Miriam (1928-). 1982. HM. (P.181)
--*King of the Cats, and Other Tales.* Carlson, Natalie Savage (1906-). c.1980. Doubleday. (P.169)
--*The Seventh Day: The Story of the Jewish Sabbath.* Chaikin, Miriam (1928-). 1983, c.1980. Schocken Books. (P.181)

Francis, Frank
--*Grandmother Lucy and Her Hats.* Wood, Joyce (1928-). 1969. Atheneum. (P.976)
--*Grandmother Lucy in Her Garden.* Wood, Joyce (1928-). 1975. Collins-World. (P.976)
--*Natasha's New Doll.* Francis, Frank. 1974, c.1971. Ohara Publications. (P.341)
--*Pelican Park.* Cockett, Mary. 1969. F. Warne. (P.205)
--*Timimoto's Great Adventure.* Francis, Frank. 1969. Holiday House. (P.341)

Francis, Frank & Cheese, Bernard
--*Sing Hey Diddle Diddle: Sixty-Six Nursery Rhymes & Their Traditional Tunes.* Harrop, Beatrice. 1984. Sterling. (P.417)

Francis, Joseph Greene (1849-1930)
--*A Book of Cheerful Cats and Other Animated Animals.* Francis, Joseph Greene (1849-1930). 1903. Century Co. (P.341)
--*The Joyous Aztecs.* Francis, Joseph Greene (1849-1930). N.D. Appleton Century Co. (P.341)

Francis, Joseph Greene (1849-1930) & Shepherd, J. C.
--*Funny Stories About Funny People in Rhymes, Pictures and Jingles.* c.1905. National Publishing Company. (P.341)

Francis, Joyce
--*Operation Panpipes.* Kirk, Stanley Malcolm (1905-). 1949. P. Nevill. (P.529)

Francis, Philip, pseud., see Lockyer, Roger.

Francis, Philip, pseud. (1927-) & Beach, Bettye
--*Lightning in the Bottle.* Lockyer, Roger. Beamer, Charles. c.1981. T. Nelson Publishers. (P.85)

Francis, R. D.
--*The Wooden Bicycle.* Bailey, Janey C. 1965. Vantage Press. (P.60)

Franciscan Sisters
--*Come Listen to a Story.* N.D. Vantage Press. (P.341)

Francois, Andre (1915-)
--*The Adventures of Ulysses.* LeMarchand, Jacques (1908-). Hatt, E. M., tr. 1960. Criterion Books. **Award: (NYT).** (P.564)
--*Arthur, the Dolphin Who Didn't See Venice.* Brinnin, John Malcolm (1906-). N.D. Little, Brown and Company. (P.133)
--*Crocodile Tears.* Francois, Andre (1915-). 1956. R. Delpire. (P.341)
--*Crocodile Tears.* Francois, Andre (1915-). 1956. Universe Books Inc. **Award: (NYT).** (P.341)
--*Crocodile Tears: Larmes De Crocodile.* rev. ed. Francois, Andre (1915-). 1964. Universe. (P.341)
--*Grodge-Cat & the Window Cleaner.* Symonds, John (1906-). 1965. Pantheon. (P.875)
--*An Idea Is Like a Bird: The Story of Herbert-Up-High-in-the-Sky.* Mayer, Peter (1936-). 1962. Orion Press. (P.634)
--*Jack & the Beanstalk.* Aulnoy, Marie Catherine Jumelle de Berneville (1650-1705). 1983. Childrens Bk Co. (P.54)
--*Little Boy Brown.* Harris, Isobel. 1949. J. B. Lippincott Co. (P.415)
--*The Magic Currant Bun.* Symonds, John (1906-). 1952. J. B. Lippincott Co. **Award: (NYT).** (P.875)
--*Roland.* Stephane, Nelly (1921-). 1958. Harcourt, Brace. **Award: (NYT).** (P.852)
--*Story George Told Me.* Symonds, John (1906-). 1964. Pantheon. (P.875)
--*Tom & Tabby.* Symonds, John (1906-). 1964. Universe. (P.875)
--*Travelers Three.* Symonds, John (1906-). 1953. Lippincott. (P.875)
--*You Are Ri-Di-Cu-Lous.* Francois, Andre (1915-). 1970. Pantheon Books. **Award: (NYT).** (P.341)

Francoise, pseud., see Seignobosc, Francoise.

Frandon, Ramona & Hunt, Dave
--*The Story of Superman: Four Little Library Books.* Frandon, Ramona & Hunt, Dave. 1980. Random. (P.341)

Frandsen, Karen G.
--*I Started School Today.* Frandsen, Karen G. 1984. Childrens. (P.341)

Frank, C. D. & Brundage, Frances
--*Billy Whiskers at Home.* Montgomery, Frances Trego. c.1924. The Saalfield Publishing Company. (P.657)

Frank, Jane
--*The Further Adventures of Till Eulenspiegel.* Yoseloff, Thomas (1913-). Stuckey, Lillien, tr. 1957. T. Yoseloff. (P.988)
--*Monica Mink.* Frank, Jane. 1948. Vanguard Press. (P.341)

Frank, Ken
--*The Education of Steven Bell.* Theis, Dan. c.1977. Raintree Editions. (P.884)

Frank, Lola Sharle
--*King Robert, the Resting Ruler.* Pape, Donna Lugg (1930-). 1968. Oddo Publishing. (P.704)
--*Liz Dearly's Silly Glasses.* Pape, Donna Lugg (1930-). 1968. Oddo. (P.704)
--*Professor Fred & the Fid Fuddlephone.* Pape, Donna Lugg (1930-). 1968. Oddo. (P.704)
--*Scientist Sam.* Pape, Donna Lugg (1930-). 1968. Oddo. (P.704)
--*Shoemaker Fooze.* Pape, Donna Lugg (1930-). 1968. Oddo Pub. (P.704)
--*Three Thinkers of Thay-Lee.* Pape, Donna Lugg (1930-). 1968. Oddo. (P.704)

Frank, Mary (1933-)
--*Enchanted: An Incredible Tale.* Coatsworth, Elizabeth Jane (1893-). 1968. Pantheon. (P.204)
--*Son of a Mile-Long Mother.* Gibbs, Alonzo Lawrence (1915-). 1971, c.1970. Bobbs-Merrill. (P.365)

Frank, Robert
--*The Animal Storybook.* Reingold, Beverly, ed. c.1978. Platt & Munk. (P.757)

Frank, Sears, jt. illus. see Anderson, Bernice Goudy.

Franke, Lorraine
--*Pillow Face & Other Stories.* Oana, Robert G. 1978. Northwest Pub. (P.689)

Frankel, Alona
--*The Family of Tiny White Elephants.* Frankel, Alona. 1980, c.1978. Barron's. (P.342)
--*Hello, Clouds.* Renberg, Dalia Hardof. c.1985. Harper & Row. (P.757)

Frankel, Simon
--*All by Myself: France in Story, Song, and Pictures.* Rodax, Yvonne (1921-). c.1954. Winston. (P.773)
--*Boys & Girls & Puppy Dogs.* Frankel, Tamara Wien (1922-). 1948. John Martin's House. (P.342)
--*The Day the Clouds Bumped Noses: Ireland in Story, Song, and Pictures.* Dumas, Edythe. c.1954. Winston. (P.288)
--*Digger Dan.* Watts, Mabel Pizzey (1906-). Lynn, Patricia, pseud. 1953. Whitman Pub. Co. (P.937)
--*Four Puppies Who Wanted a Homee.* Bryan, Dorothy & Bryan, Marguerite. 1950. Wonder Books. (P.145)
--*The Jolly Jumping Man.* Berg, Jean Horton (1913-). 1950. Wonder Books. (P.95)
--*Little Bettina Make Believe: Italy in Story, Song, and Pictures.* Dumas, Edythe. c.1954. Winston. (P.288)
--*Little Old Lady of Cliffside: Norway in Story, Song, and Pictures.* Dumas, Edythe. c.1954. Winston. (P.289)
--*Mr. Moggs' Dogs.* Wright, Betty Ren. c.1954. Whitman Pub. Co. (P.980)
--*The Weeping Pussy Willow.* Frankel, Tamara Wien (1922-). 1947. J. Martin's House. (P.342)

Frankenberg, Robert Clinton (1911-)
--*Adventure in Bangkok.* Hamori, Laszlo Deszo (1911-). MacMillan, Annabelle, pseud. (1922-), tr. Quick, Annabelle. 1966. HarBraceJ. (P.409)
--*All Aboard for Tin Cup.* Reck, Alma Kehoe (1901-). 1962. Scribner. (P.752)
--*American Adventures, 1620-1945.* Coatsworth, Elizabeth Jane (1893-). 1968. Macmillan. (P.204)
--*Big-Enough Boat.* Phillips, Dorothy Evans (1909-). 1956. Follett Pub. Co. (P.723)
--*The Cape May Packet.* 1st ed. Meader, Stephen Warren (1892-). 1969. Harcourt, Brace & World. (P.637)
--*Cherokee Animal Tales.* Mooney, James (1861-1921). Scheer, George Fabian (1917-), ed. 1968. Holiday House. (P.659)
--*Cherokee Animal Tales.* Scheer, George Fabian (1917-), ed. 1968. Holiday. (P.798)
--*Cyclone.* Grant, Bruce (1893-1977). 1959. The World Publishing Company. (P.382)
--*Daddles: The Story of a Plain Hound-Dog.* 1st ed. Sawyer, Ruth Estelle (1880-1970). c.1964. Little, Brown. (P.795)
--*A Dog for Ramon.* Bartosiak, Janet. 1966. Dial Press. (P.78)
--*Dreamboats for Trudy.* 1st ed. Lawrence, Mildred Elwood (1907-). 1954. Harcourt, Brace. (P.556)
--*Escape to Danger.* Hungerford, Edward Buell (1900-). 1949. Wilcox & Follett Co. (P.473)
--*Family Troupe.* Brown, Pamela Beatrice (1924-). 1953. Harcourt, Brace. (P.142)
--*Fiesta Colt.* Farwell, Martha (1901-). 1947. Rinehart & Company, Inc. (P.319)
--*Fire Canoe.* Falk, Elsa (1888-). 1956. Follett Pub. Co. (P.316)
--*Here Comes Parren.* Hildick, Edmund Wallace (1925-). 1972, c.1968. World Pub. (P.442)
--*Indian Fur.* Balch, Glenn (1902-). 1951. Crowell. (P.64)
--*Indian Saddle-up.* Balch, Glenn (1902-). 1953. Crowell. (P.64)
--*Jambo, Sungura!.* Tales from East Africa. Heady, Eleanor Butler (1917-), retold by. c.1965. Norton. (P.428)
--*The King Bear.* Turner, Michael C. 1968. Golden Press. (P.906)
--*The Lady from Black Hawk.* Beatty, Patricia Robbins (1922-). 1967. McGraw-Hill. (P.86)
--*Lion Boy's White Brother.* Stevens, Alden Gifford (1886-). 1951. Lippincott. (P.854)
--*The Lucky Laceys.* 1st ed. Miller, Helen Markley (1899-). 1962. Doubleday. (P.647)
--*Makon and the Dauphin.* Agle, Nan Hayden (1905-). c.1961. Scribners. (P.14)
--*Mark Twain on the Mississippi.* 1st ed. Miers, Earl Schenck (1910-1972). 1957. World Pub. Co. (P.644)
--*McBroom's Ghost.* Fleischman, Albert Sidney (1920-). 1971. Grosset & Dunlap. (P.331)
--*Owls in the Family.* Mowat, Farley McGill (1921-). 1962. Little. (P.670)
--*Sancho of the Long, Long Horns.* 1st ed. Bosworth, Allan Rucker (1901-). 1947. Doubleday. (P.119)
--*The Silver Hills.* Montgomery, Rutherford George (1894-). 1958. World Pub. Co. (P.659)
--*Skookum.* Evans, Eva Knox, Mrs. (1905-). 1966. Houghton Mifflin. (P.311)
--*The Soil That Feeds Us.* Heady, Eleanor Butler (1917-), retold by. 1972. Parents' Magazine Press. (P.428)
--*Tale of Alain.* Ormondroyd, Edward (1925-). 1960. Follett. (P.696)
--*Ten-Cent Island.* 1st ed. Park, Rosina Ruth Lucia (0000-1967). 1968. Doubleday. (P.705)
--*Treasure Island.* Stevenson, Robert Louis (1850-1894). Johnston, Johanna (1914-1982), abridged by. 1960. Doubleday. (P.857)
--*Tree Wagon.* 1st ed. Lampman, Evelyn Sibley (1907-1980). 1953. Doubleday. (P.546)
--*Up-and-Down Inventor.* Woods, Hubert C. 1961. Follett Pub. Co. (P.977)
--*Whaleboat Warriors.* Levy, Mimi Cooper. c.1963. Viking. (P.569)
--*Wild Swans at Suvanto.* Jenkins, Alan Charles (1914-). 1965. Norton. (P.491)
--*Zachary, the Governor's Pig.* Grant, Bruce (1893-1977). 1960. The World Publishing Company. (P.382)
--*Zoo!.* A Book of Poems. Hopkins, Lee Bennett (1938-), ed. 1971. Crown Publishers. (P.463)

Franklin, Harold
--*Boss Cat.* Hunter, Kristin Eggleston (1931-). 1971. Charles Scribner's Sons. (P.474)

Franklin, Jean
--*Blue Jean Days.* Neff, Carolyn & Verett, Dotty. Bachelis, Faren, ed. 1982. Dandy Lion. (P.677)

Franklin, P. J.
--*Dream Keepers: The Young Brontes; a Psycho-Biographical Novella.* Amster, Jane. 1973. William-Frederick Press. (P.33)

Franks, Vanna
--*Th Clubhouse Mystery.* Silsbee, Bill. c.1967. Fearon Pub. (P.823)

Frantz, Estelle V.
--*Peter Rabbit.* Potter, Helen Beatrix (1866-1943). N.D. A. Whitman & Co. (P.733)

Frantz, Kathleen Stowell
--*Mother Goose Fun More Stories in Rhyme.* Byington, Eloise. c.1931. A. Whitman & Co. (P.160)
--*The Wishbone Children.* Byington, Eloise. c.1934. A. Whitman & Co. (P.160)

Frantz, Marie Louise
--*Grandmother's Cooky Jar.* Orton, Helen Fuller, Mrs. (1872-1955). 1930. Frederick A. Stokes Company. (P.696)
--*Grandmother's Cooky Jar.* Orton, Helen Fuller, Mrs. (1872-1955). 1930. J. B. Lippincott Co. (P.696)
--*Snappy, the Puppy-Dog.* Orton, Helen Fuller, Mrs. (1872-1955). 1931. R. M. McBride & Company. (P.696)

Franz, Erik
--*Adventure of Fairy Tinkle Toes.* Elsie-Jean, pseud. (1898-1954). Stern, Elizabeth Gertrude Levin. N.D. A. B. Burt Co. (P.305)
--*Adventures of Fairy Tinkle Toes.* Stern, Elsie Jean (1898-), ed. Elsie-Jean, pseud. 1930. G. Sully & Company. (P.853)

Franz, Jenny
--*See No Evil.* Davis, Emmett A. (1948-). 1983. Raintree Pubs. (P.245)

Franz, Joseph T.
--*When Santa Visits the Moon.* Hyatt, Floyd A. 1977. Vantage. (P.478)

Frascino, Edward
--*Crystal Is My Friend.* Gordon, Shirley (1921-). c.1978. Harper & Row. (P.377)
--*Crystal Is the New Girl.* Gordon, Shirley (1921-). c.1976. Harper & Row. (P.377)
--*Delilah.* Hart, Carole (1943-). 1973. Harper & Row. (P.417)
--*The Dragons of the Queen.* Stolz, Mary Slattery (1920-). 1969. Harper & Row. (P.861)
--*Footsteps in the Fog: Still More Not-So-Scary Stories.* Warren, William E (1941-). c.1985. Prentice-Hall. (P.934)
--*Gladys Told Me to Meet Her Here.* Sharmat, Marjorie Weinman (1928-). 1970. Harper & Row. (P.815)
--*The Graveyard and Other Not-So-Scary Stories.* Warren, William E (1941-). c.1984. Prentice-Hall. (P.934)
--*Happy Birthday, Crystal.* Gordon, Shirley (1921-). c.1981. Harper & Row. (P.377)
--*A Hole, a Box, and a Stick.* Cretan, Gladys Yessayan (1921-). 1972. Lothrop, Lee & Shepard Co. (P.230)
--*Izoo.* 1st ed. Robison, Nancy Louise (1934-). c.1980. Lothrop, Lee & Shepard Books. (P.771)
--*The Little Mermaid.* 1st ed. Andersen, Hans Christian (1805-1875). Le Gallienne, Eva (1899-), tr. 1971. Harper & Row. (P.36)
--*Me and the Bad Guys.* Gordon, Shirley (1921-). c.1980. Harper & Row. (P.377)
--*Oh Brother!.* Keller, Charles (1942-). 1982. Prentice. (P.514)
--*Say Something.* Stolz, Mary Slattery (1920-). 1968. Harper. (P.861)
--*Space Hijack!.* 1st ed. Robison, Nancy Louise (1934-). c.1979. Lothrop, Lee & Shepard Co. (P.771)
--*The Story of a Singular Hen and Her Peculiar Children.* Stolz, Mary Slattery (1920-). 1969. Harper & Row. (P.861)
--*The Thing in the Swamp and More Not-So-Scary Stories.* Warren, William E. (1941-). c.1984. Prentice-Hall. (P.934)
--*The Trumpet of the Swan.* White, Elwyn Brooks (1899-1985). 1970. Harper & Row. **Awards: (IBBY).** (P.951)
--*UFO Kidnap!.* 1st ed. Robison, Nancy Louise (1934-). c.1978. Lothrop, Lee & Shepard Co. (P.771)

Frasconi, Antonio (1919-)
--*Cantilever Rainbow.* Krauss, Ruth Ida (1911-). 1965. Pantheon. (P.539)
--*Crickets and Frogs: A Fable.* Godoy Alcayaga, Lucila (1889-1957). Dana, Doris, tr. from Span. 1972. Atheneum. (P.372)
--*Crickets & Frogs: A Fable in Spanish & English.* Mistral, Gabriela (1919-). Dana, Doris, tr. from Span. 1972. Atheneum. (P.651)
--*The Elephant and His Secret.* 1st ed. Dana, Doris. 1974. Atheneum. (P.240)
--*The Elephant and His Secret.* El Elefante y Su Secreto. 1st ed. Dana, Doris & Godoy Alcayaga, Lucila (1889-1957). 1974. Atheneum. (P.240)
--*Elijah the Slave.* 1st ed. Singer, Isaac Bashevis (1904-), retold by. Singer, Isaac Bashevis (1904-) & Shub, Elizabeth, trs. from Yiddish 1970. Farrar, Straus and Giroux. (P.826)
--*How the Left-Behind Beasts Built Ararat.* Farber, Norma (1909-1984). 1978. Walker. (P.316)
--*The Little Blind Goat.* 1st ed. Wahl, Jan (1933-). c.1981. Stemmer House. (P.924)
--*Monkey Puzzle & Other Poems.* Livingston, Myra Cohn (1926-). 1984. Atheneum. (P.578)
--*One Little Room, an Everywhere: Poems of Love.* Livingston, Myra Cohn (1926-), ed. 1975. Atheneum. (P.578)
--*Overhead the Sun: Lines from Walt Whitman.* 1st ed. Whitman, Walt (1819-1892). 1969. Farrar, Straus and Giroux. **Award: (ALA).** (P.954)
--*See and Say, Guarda E Parla, Mira y Habla, Regarde et Parle: A Picture Book in Four Languages.* 1st ed. Frasconi, Antonio (1919-). 1955. Harcourt, Brace. **Award: (NYT).** (P.342)

--*Hobo Hill.* Philbrook, Elizabeth. 1954. Viking Press. (P.723)
--*Inspector Peckit.* Freeman, Don (1908-1978). 1972. Viking Press. (P.343)
--*Joey's Cat.* Burch, Robert Joseph (1925-). 1969. Viking Pr. (P.151)
--*Joey's Cat.* Burch, Robert Joseph (1925-). 1972. Viking Pr. (P.151)
--*Kid Sister.* Embry, Margaret Jacob (1919-1975). 1958. Holiday House. (P.305)
--*Mike's House.* Sauer, Julia Lina (1891-1985). 1954. Viking Press. (P.794)
--*Monkeys Are Funny That Way.* Koch, Dorothy Clarke (1924-). c.1962. Holiday House. (P.534)
--*Monster Night at Grandma's House.* 1st ed. Peck, Richard (1934-). 1977. Viking Press. (P.714)
--*Mop Top.* Freeman, Don (1908-1978). N.D. E. M. Hale & Co. (P.343)
--*Mop Top.* Freeman, Don (1908-1978). 1978, c.1955. Puffin Books. (P.343)
--*Mop Top.* Freeman, Don (1908-1978). 1955. Viking Press. (P.343)
--*The Night the Lights Went Out.* Freeman, Don (1908-1978). 1958. Viking Press. (P.343)
--*Norman the Doorman.* Freeman, Don (1908-1978). 1978, c.1959. Puffin Books. (P.343)
--*Norman The Doorman.* Freeman, Don (1908-1978). 1959. Viking Press. (P.343)
--*The Paper Party.* Freeman, Don (1908-1978). 1977, c.1974. Puffin Books. (P.343)
--*The Paper Party.* Freeman, Don (1908-1978). 1974. Viking Press. (P.343)
--*Penguins of All People!.* Freeman, Don (1908-1978). 1971. Viking Press. (P.343)
--*A Pocket for Corduroy.* Freeman, Don (1908-1978). 1980. Penguin. (P.343)
--*A Pocket for Corduroy.* Freeman, Don (1908-1978). 1978. Viking Press. (P.343)
--*Quiet!* There's a Canary in the Library. Freeman, Don (1908-1978). 1969. Golden Gate Junior Books. (P.343)
--*A Rainbow of My Own.* Freeman, Don (1908-1978). 1978, c.1966. Puffin Books. (P.343)
--*A Rainbow of My Own.* Freeman, Don (1908-1978). 1966. Viking Press. (P.343)
--*The Seal and the Slick.* Freeman, Don (1908-1978). 1974. Viking Press. (P.343)
--*Seven Days from Sunday.* Galt, Thomas Franklin, Jr. (1908-). 1956. T Y Crowell. (P.353)
--*Seven in a Bed.* Sonneborn, Ruth Cantor (1899-1974). 1968. Viking Press. (P.841)
--*Ski Pup.* Freeman, Don (1908-1978). 1963. Viking Press. (P.343)
--*Space Witch.* Freeman, Don (1908-1978). 1959. Viking Press. (P.343)
--*Space Witch.* Freeman, Don (1908-1978). 1979. Viking. (P.343)
--*Third Monkey.* Clark, Ann Nolan, Mrs. (1896-). c.1956. Viking Press. (P.197)
--*This for That.* Clark, Ann Nolan, Mrs. (1896-). 1965. Childrens. (P.197)
--*Tilly Witch.* Freeman, Don (1908-1978). 1969. Viking Press. (P.343)
--*Tilly Witch.* Freeman, Don (1908-1978). 1975, c.1969. Viking Press. (P.343)
--*The Turtle and the Dove.* Freeman, Don (1908-1978). 1964. Viking Press. (P.343)
--*The Uninvited Donkey.* White, Anne Hitchcock (1902-1970). 1957. Viking Press. (P.951)
--*Voltaire's Micromegas.* Hall, Elizabeth (1929-), adapted by. Voltaire, Francois Marie Arouet De (1694-1778). 1967. Golden Gate Junior Books. (P.921)
--*The Wild Cats of Rome.* Cooper, Elizabeth Keyser (1910-). 1972. Golden Gate Junior Books. (P.217)
--*Will's Quill.* Freeman, Don (1908-1978). 1977, c.1975. Puffin Books. (P.343)
--*Will's Quill.* Freeman, Don (1908-1978). 1975. Viking Press. (P.343)
--*Worst Room in the School.* Muehl, Lois Baker (1920-). 1961. Holiday House. (P.670)

Freeman, Elinor

--*I Wish I Were: Little Verses for Little Children.* Patterson, William H. 1977. Exposition. (P.710)

Freeman, Leila Crocheron

--*Nip and Tuck.* Freeman, Leila Crocheron. c.1926. J. H. Sears & Company, Inc. (P.344)
--*Nip and Tuck in Toyland.* Freeman, Leila Crocheron. c.1927. J. H. Sears & Company, Inc. (P.344)

Freeman, Lydia & Freeman, Don

--*Pet of the Met.* Freeman, Lydia & Freeman, Don (1908-1978). 1953. Viking Press. **Award: (ALA).** (P.344)

Freeman, Margaret (1893-)

--*American Folk & Fairy Tales.* Field, Rachel Lyman (1894-1942), ed. 1929. Scribner. (P.325)
--*At the Inn of the Guardian Angel.* Segur, Sophie Rostopchine, Mrs. (1799-1874). Pendleton, Amena, retold by. 1931. Houghton Mifflin Company. (P.808)
--*Children of Ancient Egypt.* Lamprey, Louise (1869-1951). 1926. Little, Brown and Company. (P.546)
--*The Chimney Cross.* Hadath, Gunby (1880-1954). N.D. J. B. Lipincott. (P.401)
--*Golden-Feather.* Capuana, Luigi (1839-1917). Emmrich, Dorothy, tr. c.1930. E. P. Dutton & Company Inc. (P.166)
--*Long Ago in Egypt.* Lamprey, Louise (1869-1951). 1926. Little, Brown, and Company. (P.547)
--*Long Ago in Gaul.* Lamprey, Louise (1869-1951). 1927. Little, Brown, and Company. (P.547)
--*The Magic City.* Aldis, Dorothy Keeley, Mrs. (1896-1966). N.D. G P Putnam's Sons. (P.21)
--*The Mystery Cross.* Hadath, Gunby (1880-1954). N.D. J. B. Lippincott. (P.401)
--*The Mystery Cross: A Mystery Story for Young People.* Hadath, Gunby (1880-1954). 1931. Frederick A. Stokes Company. (P.401)
--*New German Fairy Tales.* Lebermann, Norbert. Bachmann, Frieda, tr. from Ger. 1930. A. A. Knopf. (P.559)
--*Ragamuffin Marionettes.* Warner, Frances Lester (1888-). 1932. Houghton Mifflin Co. (P.932)
--*Saturday's Children.* Crew, Helen Cicilla Coale, Mrs. (1866-1941). 1927. Little, Brown, and Company. (P.231)
--*Seven to Seven.* Aldis, Dorothy Keeley, Mrs. (1896-1966). 1931. Minton, Balch and Company. (P.21)
--*Squiggles: Or, The Little Red Cape.* Aldis, Dorothy Keeley, Mrs. (1896-1966). 1930. Minton, Balch & Company. (P.21)
--*The Treasure Valley.* Lamprey, Louise (1869-1951). c.1928. W. Morrow & Company. (P.547)

Freeman, Paul K. (1929-1980)

--*Teeny Tiny Duck and the Pretty Money.* Rees, Ennis Samuel, Jr. (1925-). 1967. Prentice. (P.753)

Freeman, Peter

--*Five of Us- and Madeline.* Bland, Edith Nesbit, Mrs. (1858-1924). Nesbit, E., pseud. 1958. Coward. (P.107)
--*Five of Us and Madeline.* Bland, Edith Nesbit, Mrs. (1858-1924). Nesbit, E., pseud. 1960. Coward-McCann Inc. (P.107)

Freeman, Terence Reginald (1909-)

--*The Family at Dowbiggins.* 1st ed. Foulds, Elfrida Vipont Brown (1902-). 1955. Bobbs-Merrill. (P.339)
--*The Guantlet.* Rev. ed. Welch, Ronald, pseud. (1909-). Felton, Ronald Oliver. 1952. Oxford University Press. (P.943)
--*The Lark in the Morn.* Foulds, Elfrida Vipont Brown (1902-). 1948. Oxford University Press. (P.339)

Frees, Harry Whittier, photos by.

--*Animal Land on the Air.* Frees, Harry Whittier. c.1929. Lothrop, Lee & Shepard Co. (P.344)
--*The Animated Mother Goose.* Mother Goose. 1921. Lothrop, Lee & Shepard Co. (P.667)
--*Four Little Bunnies.* Frees, Harry Whittier. c.1935. Rand, McNally & Company. (P.344)
--*Four Little Kittens.* Frees, Harry Whittier. c.1934. Rand, MacNally & Company. (P.344)
--*Four Little Kittens: A Real Live Animal Book.* Barrows, Ruth Marjorie (1892-1983). c.1957. Rand McNally. (P.76)
--*The Four Little Kittens' Christmas.* Frees, Harry Whittier. c.1939. Rand MacNally & Company. (P.344)
--*Four Little Puppies.* Frees, Harry Whittier. c.1935. Rand, MacNally & Company. (P.344)
--*Four Little Puppies: A Real Live Animal Book.* Barrows, Ruth Marjorie (1892-1983). Dixon, Ruth, pseud. c.1957. Rand McNally. (P.76)
--*The Little Folks of Animal Land.* Frees, Harry Whittier. 1915. Lothrop, Lee & Shepard Co. (P.344)
--*The Little Kittens' Mother Goose Rhymes.* Mother Goose. c.1941. Rand McNally & Company. (P.667)
--*More About the Four Little Kittens.* Frees, Harry Whittier. 1938. Rand McNally & Co. (P.344)
--*The Sandman: His Animal Stories.* Frees, Harry Whittier. 1916. The Page Company. (P.344)
--*The Sandman: His Bunny Stories.* Frees, Harry Whittier. 1918. The Page Company. (P.344)
--*The Sandman: His Kittycat Stories.* Frees, Harry Whittier. 1917. The Page Company. (P.344)
--*The Sandman: His Puppy Stories.* Frees, Harry Whittier. 1920. The Page Company. (P.344)
--*Snuggles.* Barrows, Ruth Marjorie (1892-1983). 1935. Rand McNally & Co. (P.77)
--*Snuggles.* Barrows, Ruth Marjorie (1892-1983). Dixon, Ruth, pseud. c.1958. Rand McNally. (P.77)
--*The Story of Bill Bunny.* Frees, Harry Whittier. c.1937. Rand, McNally & Company. (P.344)
--*Whiskers.* Barrows, Ruth Marjorie (1892-1983). 1937. Rand McNally & Co. (P.77)
--*Yip and Yap.* Dixon, Ruth, pseud. (1892-1983). Barrows, Ruth Marjorie. 1936. Rand McNally & Co. (P.275)

Fregosi, Claudia Anne Marie (1946-)

--*Are There Spooks in the Dark?.* Fregosi, Claudia Anne Marie (1946-). c.1976. Four Winds Press. (P.344)

Frei, Doris

--*Slaves of Sultan.* Rogan, James Walkyn (1915-), adapted by. 1951. Mission Press. (P.774)

Freinthal, Katarina

--*The Cave Children.* Tluchor, Alois (1869-1939). Sonnleitner, A. Th., pseud. Bell, Anthea, tr. 1971. S. G. Phillips. (P.893)

Freire, J.

--*Best Book of Sports Stories.* Donnelly, M. A., ed. 1966. Doubleday. (P.280)

Freixas, James

--*Through the Nursery Door.* McKenzie, Isabel. 1914. The Neale Publishing Company. (P.606)

Fremont-Smith, Frances Eliot

--*The House on the Edge of Things.* Eliot, Ethel Cook, Mrs. (1890-). c.1923. Beacon Press. (P.300)

French, Fiona (1944-)

--*Aio, the Rainmaker.* French, Fiona (1944-). 1978. Oxford U Pr. (P.344)
--*The Blue Bird.* French, Fiona (1944-). 1972. H. Z. Walck. (P.344)
--*City of Gold.* French, Fiona (1944-). 1974. H. Z. Walck. (P.344)
--*Going to Squintum's:.* A Foxy Folktale. Westwood, Jennifer (1940-), retold by. 1985. Dial. (P.948)
--*Hunt the Thimble.* French, Fiona (1944-). 1978. Oxford U Pr. (P.344)
--*Jack of Hearts.* French, Fiona (1944-). 1970. Harcourt, Brace & World. (P.344)
--*King Tree.* French, Fiona (1944-). 1973. H. Z. Walck. (P.344)
--*Matteo.* French, Fiona (1944-). 1978. Oxford U Pr. (P.344)
--*The Star Child: A Fairy Tale.* Wilde, Oscar Fingal O'Flahertie Wills (1854-1900). Westwood, Jennifer (1940-), abridged by. c.1979. Four Winds Press. (P.959)

French, Fiona (1944-) & Troughton, Joann

--*Dragons & Other Fabulous Beasts.* Blythe, Richard. 1980. Putnam Pub Group. (P.110)

French, Gillette

--*One to Ten: A Number Book.* 1942. McLoughlin Bros, Inc. (P.344)

French, Henry Willard (1854-)

--*The Young Cascarillero, and Colonel Thorndike's Adventures: A Story of Bark Hunters in the Ecuador Forests, and the Experiences of a Globe Trotter.* Downing, Marlton. 1895. Lothrop Publishing Company. (P.283)

Frenck, Hal

--*Odysseus & the Cyclops.* Homerus. Richardson, I. M., adapted by. 1984. Troll Assocs. (P.457)
--*Odysseus and the Cyclops.* Richardson, I. M, adapted by. c.1984. Troll Associates. (P.762)
--*Odysseus and the Giants.* Richardson, I. M., adapted by. c.1984. Troll Associates. (P.762)
--*Odysseus & the Great Challenge.* Homer. Richardson, I. M., adapted by. 1984. Troll Assocs. (P.457)
--*Odysseus & the Magic of Circe.* Homerus. Richardson, I. M., adapted by. 1984. Troll Assocs. (P.457)
--*Odysseus and the Magic of Circe.* Richardson, I. M, adapted by. c.1984. Troll Associates. (P.762)
--*The Return of Odysseus.* Homerus. Richardson, I. M., adapted by. 1984. Troll Assocs. (P.457)
--*The Return of Odysseus.* Richardson, I. M, adapted by. c.1984. Troll Associates. (P.763)
--*Sparky's Fireman.* Lattin, Anne, pseud. (1903-1979). Cole, Lois Dwight. 1968. Follett. (P.554)
--*Sparky's Fireman.* Lattin, Anne, pseud. (1903-1979). Cole, Lois Dwight. 1968. Follett. (P.554)
--*Tales from the Odyssey.* Richardson, I. M, adapted by. c.1984. Troll Associates. (P.763)
--*The Trouble with Miss Switch.* Wallace, Barbara Brooks (1922-). 1971. Abingdon Press. (P.927)
--*The Voyage of Odysseus.* Richardson, I. M., adapted by. 1984. Troll Assocs. (P.763)
--*When Grandfather Journeys into Winter.* 1st ed. Strete, Craig Kee. c.1979. Greenwillow Books. (P.867)
--*Wild Cat.* Peck, Robert Newton (1928-). 1975. Holiday House. (P.715)
--*The Wooden Horse.* Richardson, I. M., adapted by. 1984. Troll Assocs. (P.763)

Freret, Emily M.

--*The Funny House.* Guyol, Louise Hubert. 1922. B. J. Brimmer Company. (P.400)

Freschet, Gina

--*Bernard and the Catnip Caper.* Freschet, Berniece Louise Speck (1927-). 1981. Scribner's. (P.345)
--*Bernard of Scotland Yard.* Freschet, Berniece Louise Speck (1927-). 1978. Scribner. (P.345)
--*Bernard Sees the World.* Freschet, Berniece Louise Speck (1927-). c.1976. Scribner. (P.345)

Freshman, Shelley

--*Joel Rothman's the Antcyclopedia.* Rothman, Joel (1938-). 1974. Phinmarc Books. (P.780)

Fretz, Frank, jt. illus. see Thompson, Lorin.

Freud, Tom

--*David the Dreamer: His Book of Dreams.* Bergengren, Ralph Wilhelm (1871-). 1922. Atlantic Monthly Press. (P.96)

Freund, Rudolf (1915-1969)

--*The Animals of Farmer Jones.* Gale, Leah. 1942. Simon and Schuster. (P.352)
--*The Animals of Farmer Jones.* Reed, Mary, ed. 1942. Simon & Schuster. (P.753)
--*Danny and Prue.* Tallant, Edith. c.1938. Thomas Y. Crowell Company. (P.877)
--*Iceblink.* Montgomery, Rutherford George (1894-). c.1941. H. Holt and Company. (P.658)
--*The Little Red Hen.* Freund, Rudolf (1915-1969). 1942. Simon and Schuster, Inc. (P.345)

Friday, Theodore

--*Jerry the Jeep.* Hurd, Edith Thacher, Mrs. (1910-). 1945. Lothrop, Lee & Shepard Co. (P.475)

Friedel

--*Yael and the Queen of Goats.* Banai, Margalit (1928-). Reznik, Ruth, tr. 1968. Funk and Wagnalls. (P.67)

Friedman, Arthur (1935-)

--*The Children of Chelm.* Adler, David A (1947-). c.1979. Bonim Books. (P.11)
--*The Hare & the Tortoise.* Aesopus. 1981. Troll Assocs. (P.13)
--*The Hare and the Tortoise.* Aesopus. c.1981. Troll Associates. (P.13)
--*Hershel of Ostropol.* Kimmel, Eric A (1946-). 1981. Jewish Publication Society of America. (P.523)
--*The Three Sillies.* Friedman, Arthur (1935-), ed. c.1981. Troll Associates. (P.345)

Friedman, Irene

--*Away We Go!.* Friedman, Irene. c.1977. Platt & Munk. (P.346)

Friedman, Judith (1935-)

--*The Mystery of Sara Beth.* Putnam, Polly. c.1981. Follett Pub. Co. (P.742)
--*No One Should Have Six Cats!.* Smith, Susan Mathias (1950-). 1982. Follett. (P.837)

Friedman, Marvin (1930-)

--*American Girl Book of Mystery & Suspense Stories.* American Girl Magazine Staff, ed. 1964. Random. (P.33)
--*Annie, Annie.* Cone, Molly Lamken (1918-). 1969. Houghton Mifflin. (P.212)
--*The Bandit of Mok Hill.* 1st ed. Lampman, Evelyn Sibley (1907-1980). 1969. Doubleday. (P.546)
--*Can Do, Missy Charlie.* Wallace, Barbara Brooks (1922-). 1974. Follett Pub. Co. (P.926)
--*Dance Around the Fire.* Cone, Molly Lamken (1918-). 1974. Houghton Mifflin. (P.212)
--*Enoch.* Raymond, Charles. 1969. Houghton Mifflin. (P.751)
--*The Jago Secret.* Shead, Isobel Ann. 1967, c.1966. Follett. (P.817)
--*Next Door.* Harnden, Ruth Peabody. 1970. Houghton Mifflin. (P.414)
--*Pinch.* Callen, Lawrence Willard, Jr. (1927-). 1975. Little, Brown. (P.163)
--*Roar of Engines.* 1st ed. Clarke, John, pseud. Laklan, Carli. 1967. Doubleday. (P.198)
--*Runaway Raft.* Harnden, Ruth Peabody. 1968. Houghton Mifflin. (P.414)
--*Shadow of a Crow.* Pitcher, Marie Elizabeth. 1968. Doubleday. (P.727)
--*Shanta.* Thoger, Marie (1923-). Amos, Eileen, tr. 1968. Follett. (P.885)
--*The Silver Dollar Hoard of Aristotle Gaskin.* 1st ed. Turner, Gerry. 1968. Doubleday. (P.905)
--*Simon.* Cone, Molly Lamken (1918-). 1970. Houghton Mifflin. (P.213)
--*Sorrow's Song.* Callen, Lawrence Willard, Jr. (1927-). c.1979. Little, Brown. (P.163)
--*Those Traver Kids.* Bradbury, Bianca (1908-). 1972. Houghton Mifflin. (P.124)
--*Varnell Roberts, Super-Pigeon.* Gray, Genevieve Stuck (1920-). 1975. Houghton Mifflin. (P.383)
--*You Can't Make Me If I Don't Want to.* Cone, Molly Lamken (1918-). 1971. Houghton Mifflin. (P.213)

Friend, Ellery

--*As Children Do: Poems of Childhood.* Nesbit, Wilbur Dick (1871-1927). c.1929. The P. F. Volland Company. (P.678)

Friend, Esther

--*The Adventures of Pinocchio.* Lorenzini, Carlo (1826-1890). Collodi, Carlo, pseud. c.1939. Rand McNally & Company. (P.584)
--*The Children That Lived in a Shoe.* Pease, Josephine Van Dolzen. 1942. Rand McNally & Company. (P.714)
--*The Five Little Kids.* Buchanan, Gladys. c.1941. Rand McNally & Company. (P.146)
--*The Great Big Noise.* Weir, Ruth Cromer (1912-). c.1948. Wilcox & Follett Co. (P.942)
--*Little Red Riding Hood.* 1950. Rand McNally. (P.346)
--*Mother Goose.* Mother Goose. c.1947. Rand McNally & Company. (P.667)
--*My Toys.* Goldin, Augusta R. (1906-). c.1955. Rand McNally. (P.373)

--*Cinderella's Mouse, and Other Fairy Tales.* 1st ed. Fry, Rosalie Kingsmill (1911-). 1953. Dutton. (P.348)
--*Deep in the Forest.* Fry, Rosalie Kingsmill (1911-). N.D. Dodd, Mead & Co. (P.348)
--*The Echo Song.* Fry, Rosalie Kingsmill (1911-). 1962. E. P. Dutton & Co. (P.348)
--*Fly Home, Colombina.* Fry, Rosalie Kingsmill (1911-). 1960. E. P. Dutton & Co. (P.348)
--*A Ghost, a Witch, & Goblin.* Fry, Rosalie Kingsmill (1911-). 1971. Schol Bk Serv. (P.348)
--*Ladybug!* Ladybug!. Fry, Rosalie Kingsmill (1911-). 1940. E. P. Dutton & Co., Inc. (P.348)
--*The Land of Lost Handkerchiefs.* 1st ed. Knight, Marjorie. 1954. Dutton. (P.532)
--*Matelot, Little Salior of Brittany.* Fry, Rosalie Kingsmill (1911-). 1958. E. P. Dutton & Co. (P.348)
--*Mountain Door.* Fry, Rosalie Kingsmill (1911-). 1961. Dutton. (P.348)
--*Pipkin Sees the World.* Fry, Rosalie Kingsmill (1911-). 1951. Dutton. (P.348)
--*Riddle of the Figurehead.* Fry, Rosalie Kingsmill (1911-). 1963. Dutton. (P.348)
--*Secret of the Ron Mor Skerry.* Fry, Rosalie Kingsmill (1911-). 1959. E. P. Dutton & Co. (P.348)
--*The Water-Babies: A Fairy Tale for a Land-Baby.* Kingsley, Charles (1819-1875). 1957. Dent. (P.525)
--*The Water Babies: A Fairy Tale for a Land Baby.* Kingsley, Charles (1819-1875). 1957. E.P. Dutton & Co. (P.525)
--*The Wind Call.* Fry, Rosalie Kingsmill (1911-). 1955. Dent. (P.348)
--*The Wind Call.* Fry, Rosalie Kingsmill (1911-). N.D. E. P. Dutton & Co. (P.348)

Fry, Rosalind
--*In Praise of Babies.* Adler, James B., ed. 1968. Doubleday. (P.12)
--*Is This My Dinner?.* Black, Irma Simonton, Mrs. (1906-1972). 1972. A. Whitman. (P.104)
--*Lost at the Fair.* 1st ed. Sharp, Margery (1905-). 1965. Little, Brown. (P.816)
--*Monster!* Monster!. Harrison, David Lee (1937-). 1975. Western Pub. (P.417)
--*One to Teeter-Totter.* Battles, Edith, pseud. (1921-). Funk, Thompson. 1973. A. Whitman. (P.81)
--*Three Giant Stories.* Conger, Lesley, pseud. (1922-). Suttles, Shirley Smith. 1968. Four Winds Press. (P.213)
--*Three Giant Stories.* Conger, Lesley, pseud. (1922-). Suttles, shirley Smith. 1968. Scholastic Book Services. (P.213)
--*Tree for Rent.* Shaw, Richard (1923-), ed. 1971. A. Whitman. (P.816)

Fry, Rowena
--*Miss Quinn's Secret.* Aldis, Dorothy Keeley, Mrs. (1896-1966). 1949. G. P. Putnam's Sons. (P.21)

Fry, W. H.
--*Billy Whiskers' Kids: Or, Day and Night.* Montgomery, Frances Trego. 1971. Dover Publications. (P.658)
--*Billy Whiskers' Kids: Or, Day and Night.* Montgomery, Frances Trego. 1903. The Saalfield Publishing Co. (P.658)
--*Billy Whiskers: The Autobiography of a Goat.* Montgomery, Frances Trego. 1969. Dover Publications. (P.658)
--*Billy Whiskers: The Autobiography of a Goat.* Montgomery, Frances Trego. 1903. The Saalfield Publishing Co. (P.658)
--*The Boy Land Boomer: Or, Dick Arbuckle's adventures in Oklahoma.* Bonehill, Captain Ralph, pseud. (1862-1930). Stratemeyer, Edward L.. 1902. Saalfield Publishing Co. (P.114)
--*Far Past the Frontier: Or, Two Boy Pioneers.* Braden, James Andrew (1872-). 1902. The Saalfield Publishing Co. (P.124)
--*His Mother's Letter: Or, The Boy Wails Search.* Merrill, J. M. 1902. The Saalfield Pub. Co. (P.642)
--*Jewel Story Book.* Evans, Florence Adele (1879-). 1903. The Saalfield Pub. Company. (P.311)
--*Larry Barlow's Ambition: Or, The Adventures of a Young Fireman.* Winfield, Arthur M., pseud. (1862-1930). Stratemeyer, Edward L.. 1902. Saalfield Publishing. (P.967)
--*Mr.* Bunny, his book. Sutton, Adah Louise (1865-). 1900. Saalfield Publishing Co. (P.872)
--*Ralph Granger's Fortunes.* Brown, William Perry. 1902. Saalfield Publishing Co. (P.142)
--*A Struggle for a Fortune.* Fosdick, Charles Austin (1842-1915). Castlemon, Harry, pseud. 1902. The Saalfield Publishing Co. (P.338)

Frye, Mary Hamilton
--*Fairy Tales Every Child Should Know.* Mabie, Hamilton Wright (1846-1916), ed. 1915. Doubleday, Page & Company. (P.593)
--*Fairy Tales Every Child Should Know.* Mabie, Hamilton Wright (1846-1916), ed. N.D. Garden City Publishing Co., Inc. (P.593)
--*Myths Every Child Should Know.* Mabie, Hamilton Wright (1846-1916), ed. 1914. Doubleday, Page & Company. (P.593)
--*Tilly-Tod.* Vining, Elizabeth Gray (1902-). 1929. Doubleday, Doran & Company, Inc. (P.920)
--*The Wonderful Adventures of Nils.* Lagerlof, Selma Ottiliana Lovisa (1858-1940). Howard, Velma Swanston, Mrs. (1868-), ed. Howard, Velma Swanston, Mrs. (1868-), tr. from Swedish. 1913. Doubleday, Page & Company. (P.544)

Frye, Mary Hamilton & Federer, C. A.
--*Myths Every Child Should Know.* Mabie, Hamilton Wright (1846-1916), ed. N.D. Garden City Publishing Co., Inc. (P.593)

Frye, Pearl (1917-)
--*Alberta for Short.* 1st ed. Frye, Pearl (1917-). 1953. Little, Brown. (P.348)

Fuchs, Erich (1916-)
--*Journey to the Moon.* Fuchs, Erich (1916-). 1970. Delacorte. (P.348)

Fuchs, Gertraut, jt. illus. see Wolf, Ingrid.

Fuchshuber, Annegert
--*A Christmas Star.* Fuchshuber, Annegert. N.D. Merry Thoughts. (P.348)
--*The Wishing Hat.* Fuchshuber, Annegert. Crawford, Elizabeth D., tr. from Ger. 1977. Morrow. (P.348)

Fudala, Rose Mary
--*Magic Monsters Count to Ten.* Moncure, Jane Belk (1926-). c.1979. Distributed by Childrens Press. (P.655)
--*The Parade of Shapes.* Tester, Sylvia Root (1939-). c.1976. Child's World. (P.883)

Fudge, Sybil & Hawkins, Jody
--*Little Brown Koko at Work and Play.* Hunt, Blanche Seale, Mrs. c.1959. C. E. I. Pub. Co. (P.473)
--*Little Brown Koko's Pets and Playmates.* Hunt, Blanche Seale, Mrs. c.1959. C. E. L. Pub. Co. (P.473)

Fufuka, Mahiri
--*My Daddy Is a Cool Dude, and Other Poems.* Fufuka, Karama, pseud. (1951-). Morgan, Sharon Antonia. 1975. Dial Press. (P.348)
--*Poochie.* Pontiflet, Ted (1932-). c.1978. Dial Press. (P.731)

Fuhrman, James
--*Poems for Young Children.* Roes, Mimi. 1979. Teacher Update. (P.774)

Fujii, Kingo
--*The Three Treasures: Myths of Old Japan.* Cox, Miriam Stewart. c.1964. Harper. (P.225)

Fujikawa, Gyo
--*Betty Bear's Birthday.* Fujikawa, Gyo. c.1977. Grosset & Dunlap. (P.349)
--*Betty Bear's Birthday.* Fujikawa, Gyo. 1977. Putnam Pub Group. (P.349)
--*A Child's Book of Poems.* Fujikawa, Gyo, compiled by. 1969. Grosset & Dunlap. (P.349)
--*A Child's Garden of Verses.* Stevenson, Robert Louis (1850-1894). c.1957. Grosset & Dunlap. (P.856)
--*A Child's Garden of Verses.* Stevenson, Robert Louis (1850-1894). 1964. Grosset & Dunlap. (P.856)
--*A Child's Garden of Verses.* Stevenson, Robert Louis (1850-1894). 1957. Putnam. (P.856)
--*Fairy Tales.* Fujikawa, Gyo, ed. 1980. Platt. (P.349)
--*Fairy Tales.* Fujikawa, Gyo, selected by. 1970. Putnam Pub Group. (P.349)
--*Fairy Tales & Fables.* Fujikawa, Gyo, compiled by. 1970. Putnam Pub Group. (P.349)
--*Fairy Tales and Fables.* Morel, Eve, compiled by. 1970. Grosset & Dunlap. (P.662)
--*The Flyaway Kite.* Fujikawa, Gyo. 1981. Putnam Pub Group. (P.349)
--*Fraidy Cat.* Fujikawa, Gyo. c.1982. Grosset & Dunlap. (P.349)
--*Gyo Fujikawa's Oh, What a Busy Day!.* Fujikawa, Gyo. c.1976. Grosset & Dunlap. (P.349)
--*Here I Am.* Fujikawa, Gyo. 1981. Putnam Pub Group. (P.349)
--*Jenny and Jupie.* Fujikawa, Gyo. c.1981. Grosset & Dunlap. (P.349)
--*Jenny & Jupie to the Rescue.* Fujikawa, Gyo. 1982. Putnam Pub Group. (P.349)
--*Jenny Learns a Lesson.* Fujikawa, Gyo. c.1980. Grosset & Dunlap. (P.349)
--*The Magic Show.* Fujikawa, Gyo. c.1981. Grosset & Dunlap. (P.349)
--*Me Too!.* Fujikawa, Gyo. c.1982. Grosset & Dunlap. (P.349)
--*Millie's Secret.* Fujikawa, Gyo. Duenewald, Doris, ed. 1978. Putnam Pub Group. (P.349)
--*Mother Goose.* Mother Goose. 1968. Grosset & Dunlap. (P.667)
--*My Animal Friend.* Fujikawa, Gyo. 1981. Putnam Pub Group. (P.349)
--*My Favorite Thing.* Fujikawa, Gyo. c.1978. Grosset & Dunlap. (P.349)
--*The Night Before Christmas.* 1980. Platt. (P.349)
--*The Night Before Christmas.* 1980. Putnam Pub Group. (P.349)
--*The Night Before Christmas.* Moore, Clement Clarke (1779-1863). 1961. Grosset & Dunlap. (P.660)
--*Oh, What a Busy Day.* Fujikawa, Gyo. 1976. Putnam Pub Group. (P.349)
--*Our Best Friends.* Fujikawa, Gyo. c.1977. Grosset & Dunlap. (P.349)
--*Our Best Friends.* Fujikawa, Gyo. 1977. Putnam Pub Group. (P.349)
--*Poems for Children.* Fujikawa, Gyo, compiled by. 1980. Platt. (P.349)
--*Poems for Children.* Fujikawa, Gyo, compiled by. N.D. Putnam Pub Group. (P.349)
--*Puppies, Pussy Cats, and Other Friends.* Fujikawa, Gyo. c.1975. Grosset & Dunlap. (P.349)
--*Sam's All-Wrong Day.* Fujikawa, Gyo. c.1982. Grosset & Dunlap. (P.349)
--*Shags Finds a Kitten.* Fujikawa, Gyo. c.1983. Grosset & Dunlap. (P.349)
--*Shags Has a Dream.* Fujikawa, Gyo. 1981. Putnam Pub Group. (P.349)
--*The Singing Mother Goose Book.* Mother Goose. 1955. J. C. Winston Co. (P.669)
--*Sleepy Time.* Fujikawa, Gyo. c.1975. Grosset & Dunlap. (P.349)
--*Surprise!* Surprise!. Fujikawa, Gyo. c.1978. Grosset & Dunlap. (P.349)
--*That's Not Fair.* Fujikawa, Gyo. c.1983. Grosset & Dunlap. (P.349)
--*That's Not Fair!.* Fujikawa, Gyo. 1983. Grosset. (P.349)
--*Welcome Is a Wonderful Word.* Fujikawa, Gyo. N.D. Putnam Pub Group. (P.349)
--*Year in, Year Out.* Fujikawa, Gyo. 1981. Putnam Pub Group. (P.349)

Fujishiro, Seiji
--*Japanese Children's Songs.* Tsugawa, Shuichi, ed. Niwa, Tamako (1922-) & Terry, Maranell, trs. 1963, c.1959. Fuji Pub. Co., Dist. Rutland, Vt., Japan Pubns. (P.902)

Fujita, Miho
--*Things I Like to Do.* Archibald, Leon. c.1985. Simon & Schuster. (P.46)

Fujiwara, Michiko see Saito, Michiko, pseud.

Fukuda, Shosuke
--*The Ogre and His Bride.* Kishi, Nami (1913-). 1971. Parents Magazine Press. (P.529)

Fulda, Elizabeth
--*The Shoemaker of the Stars, and Other Poems.* De Witt, Samuel Aaron (1891-). 1941, c.1940. Parnassus Press. (P.262)

Fulkerson, Helen
--*Mister Zip & U.* S. Mail. Barr, Jene (1900-). 1964. A Whitman. (P.75)

Fullen, Harriet Louise
--*My Shadow Self.* Fullen, Harriet Louise. 1931. Spanish American Institute Press. (P.349)

Fuller, Arthur
--*The Biscuit Eater.* Street, James Howell (1903-1954). 1941. The Dial Press. (P.867)
--*Jim Hunter: Sportsman.* Holland, Raymond Prunty, Jr. (1910-). 1937. Houghton Mifflin Company. (P.455)

Fuller, Caroline Macomber, photos by.
--*The Alley Cat's Kitten.* Fuller, Caroline Macomber. 1904. Little, Brown, and Company. (P.349)
--*The Flight of Puss Pandora.* Fuller, Caroline Macomber. 1906. Little, Brown, and Company. (P.349)

Fuller, Eunice
--*The Book of Friendly Giants.* Fuller, Eunice. 1914. The Century Company. (P.349)

Fuller, Harvey K.
--*A Dog of Flanders.* De La Ramee, Marie Louise (1839-1908). Ouida, pseud. c.1927. A. Whitman Company. (P.253)
--*Manuel Goes to Sea.* Fuller, Harvey K. 1948. Whittlesey House. (P.349)

Fuller, Nancy Lee
--*Fuffie's Problem.* Fuller, Nancy Lee. 1969. T. W. Denison. (P.349)
--*Saturday Cat.* Fuller, Nancy Lee. 1969. T. S. Denison. (P.349)
--*Willie Can Fly.* Dean, Anabel (1915-). c.1970. Denison. (P.248)
--*Willie Can Not Squirm.* Dean, Anabel (1915-). 1970. T. S. Denison. (P.248)
--*Willie Can Ride.* Dean, Anabel (1915-). 1970. T. S. Denison. (P.248)

Fuller, Ralph B.
--*The Lost Monkey.* Rice, Lucia Webster. c.1923. Newson & Company. (P.761)

Fuller, Roseanne
--*Six Horses and a Caravan.* 1st ed. Stewart, Christine & Yager, Julie. 1965, c.1964. U. Smith. (P.858)

Fullerton, Len
--*Zoo-Man Stories.* Gillespie, Thomas Haining. 1960. Taplinger Pub. Co. (P.368)

Fullerton, Pam
--*Blue Colt.* 1st ed. Bourne, Eulalia. 1979. Northland. (P.120)

Fulleylove, John
--*Bible Stories for Young People.* Dawes, Sarah Elizabeth, Mrs. (1832-). N.D. Thomas Y. Crowell Co. (P.247)

Fulton, Geoffrey P., photos by.
--*No, No, Natalie.* Moremen, Grace. 1973. Childrens Press. (P.663)

Fulton, George
--*The Eagles Have Flown.* 1st ed. Williamson, Joanne Small (1926-). 1957. Knopf. (P.964)
--*Henry Hudson.* 1st ed. Baker, Nina Brown, Mrs. (1888-1957). 1958. Knopf. (P.64)
--*Holiday in Washington.* Carpenter, Frances Aretta (1890-1972). 1958. Alfred A Knopf : distributed by Borzoi Books. (P.170)
--*Little Maverick Cow.* Coates, Belle (1896-). 1957. Scribner. (P.203)
--*Nelly Bly.* Baker, Nina Brown, Mrs. (1888-1957). 1956. Holt, Rineheart and Winston. (P.64)

Fulton, Ginger A.
--*My Jesus Pocketbook of God's Fruit.* Phillips, Cheryl M. & Harvey, Bonnie C., eds. 1983. Stirrup Assoc. (P.723)
--*My Jesus Pocketbook of Noah & the Floating Zoo.* Stirrup Associates, Inc. Harvey, Bonnie C. & Phillips, Cheryl M., eds. 1984. Stirrup Assoc. (P.859)
--*My Jesus Pocketbook of the Lord's Prayer.* Phillips, Cheryl M. & Harvey, Bonnie C., eds. 1983. Stirrup Assoc. (P.723)

Fulton, Gwen
--*Did You Ever?.* Traditional Verse. Fulton, Gwen. 1981. Merrimack Pub Cir. (P.349)
--*The Owl and the Pussycat.* Lear, Edward (1812-1888). 1977. Atheneum. (P.558)

Fulton, John, pseud., see Short, John Fulton.

Fulton, John
--*Champion Caddy.* Renick, Marion Lewis (1905-). 1943. C. Scribner's Sons. (P.758)

Fulwider, Edwin
--*Tommy Trout.* Eschmeyer, Reuben William (1905-). Fulwider, Edwin, designed by. 1951. Fisherman Press. (P.309)

Fumagalli, Barbara Juster
--*Swing Around the Sun: Poems.* Esbensen, Barbara Juster. 1965. Lerner Publications Co. (P.309)

Funai, Mamoru R. (1932-)
--*Big Fight.* Buck, Pearl Sydenstricker, Mrs. (1892-1973). 1965. Har-Row. (P.147)
--*The Burning Rice Fields.* Bryant, Sara Cone (1873-). 1963. Holt, Rinehart and Winston. (P.146)
--*Cartoons for Kids.* Funai, Mamoru R. (1932-). 1977. P-H. (P.349)
--*Dinosaur Funny Bones: Poems.* Polhamus, Jean Burt. 1974. Prentice-Hall. (P.730)
--*The Dolls' Day for Yoshiko.* Ishii, Momoko (1907-). Mizuta, Yone, tr. 1966. Follett Pub. Co. (P.483)
--*Dolphin.* Morris, Robert A. 1975. Har-Row. (P.664)
--*The First Book of Short Verse.* Howard, Coralie, pseud. (1930-), ed. Cogswell, Coralie Norris. 1964. Watts. (P.466)
--*The Flying Lesson of Gerald Pelican.* Benchley, Nathaniel Goddard (1915-1981). 1970. Harper & Row. (P.92)
--*Folk Songs of China, Japan, Korea.* Dietz, Betty Warner, pseud. (1908-) & Park, Thomas C., eds. Dietz, Elizabeth H.. 1964. John Day. (P.265)
--*The House that Guilda Drew.* Parker, Richard (1915-). 1964. Bobbs-Merrill. (P.706)
--*How a Rock Came to Be in a Fence on a Road Near a Town.* Ruchlis, Hyman (1913-). Selsam, Millicent Ellis (1912-), ed. 1973. Walker & Co. (P.783)
--*Kim Walk-in-My-Shoes.* Price, Olive M. (1903-). 1968. Coward-McCann. (P.739)
--*The Last Little Dragon.* Price, Roger (1921-). 1969. Harper & Row. (P.739)
--*The Little Red Train.* Weelen, Guy. 1966. Lee and Shepard. (P.940)
--*The Little Red Train.* Weelen, Guy. c.1966. Lothrop. (P.940)
--*Little Red Train.* Wheelen, Guy. 1966. Lothrop. (P.949)
--*Little Sponge Fisherman.* Rowland, Florence Wightman (1900-). 1969. Putnam. (P.782)
--*The Man Who Cooked for Himself.* Krasilovsky, Phyllis (1926-). c.1981. Parents Magazine Press. (P.537)
--*Matthew, Mark, Luke, and John.* Buck, Pearl Sydenstricker, Mrs. (1892-1973). 1967, c.1966. John Day Co. (P.147)
--*Mister Turtle's Magic Glasses.* Thayer, Jane, pseud. (1904-). Woolley, Catherine. 1971. Morrow. (P.884)
--*Moke & Poki in the Rain Forest.* Funai, Mamoru R. (1932-). 1972. Har-Row. (P.349)
--*Moke and Poki in the Rain Forest.* Funai, Mamoru R. (1932-). 1972. Harper & Row. (P.349)
--*Moon of the Big-Dog.* 1st ed. Leech, Jay (1911-) & Spencer, Zane Ann (1935-). c.1980. Crowell. (P.561)
--*Mr.* Turtle's Magic Glasses. Woolley, Catherine (1904-). 1971. Morrow. (P.978)
--*My Turtle Died Today.* Stull, Edith Gilbert (1919-). 1964. Holt, Rinehart, and Winston. (P.869)
--*The New Schoolmaster.* Naylor, Phyllis Reynolds (1933-). 1967. Silver Burdett Co. (P.676)
--*Ninji's Magic.* MacIntyre, Elisabeth (1916-). 1966. Knopf. (P.604)
--*Nufu & the Turkeyfish.* Beaty, Janice Janowski (1930-). 1969. Pantheon. (P.86)

--*Teen-Age Science Fiction Stories.* Elam, Richard Mace, Jr. (1920-). Leyson, Burr W. 1952. Lantern Press. (P.300)
--*That Summer with Lexy.* McKim, Audrey Margaret (1909-). N.D. Abingdon. (P.607)
--*Thunder in His Moccasins.* Place, Marian Templeton (1910-). White, Dale, pseud. 1962. Viking Press. (P.728)
--*Timothy & the Snakes.* Gee, Maurine H. 1960. Morrow. (P.361)
--*Too Many Fathers.* 1st ed. Paradis, Marjorie Bartholomew (1886-1970). 1963. Atheneum. (P.705)
--*The Trouble with Toby.* Cone, Molly Lamken (1918-). 1961. Houghton Mifflin. (P.213)
--*Tundra, Arctic Sled Dog.* Marsh, Roy Simpson. 1968. Macrae Smith Co. (P.622)
--*The Twins at Thatchem Quickett.* Robinson, Martha. 1962. Washburn. (P.770)
--*We Were There with Lincoln in the White House.* Miers, Earl Schenck (1910-1972). 1963. Grosset & Dunlap. (P.644)
--*Wee Little Man.* Berg, Jean Horton (1913-). 1963. Follett. (P.96)
--*Where Speed Is King: Stories of Racing Adventure.* Fenner, Phyllis Reid (1899-1982), selected by. 1972. Morrow. (P.322)
--*Whistle for a Wind: Maine 1820.* Ogilvie, Elisabeth May (1917-). 1954. Scribner. (P.691)
--*Wild Geese Flying.* Meigs, Cornelia Lynde (1884-1973). 1957. Macmillan. (P.639)
--*The Winner.* Carse, Robert (1902-1971). 1955. Scribner. (P.175)
--*Wolf Dog Valley.* Gilbert, Kenneth (1889-). 1956. Holt. (P.367)
--*Young Buckskin Spy.* Loring, Selden M. 1954. Lantern Press. (P.585)
--*Young Circus Detective.* Coombs, Charles Ira (1914-). 1954. Lantern Press. (P.216)
--*Young Crow Raider.* Kroll, Francis Lynde (1904-1973). c.1954. Grosset & Dunlap. (P.540)
--*Young Crow Raider.* Kroll, Francis Lynde (1904-1973). 1954. Lantern Press. (P.540)
--*Young Deputy Smith.* Place, Marian Templeton (1910-). Hite, Dale, pseud. 1961. Viking Press. (P.728)
--*Young Hero of the Range.* Payne, Stephen. 1954. Lantern Press. (P.712)
--*Young Infield Rookie.* Coombs, Charles Ira (1914-). 1954. Lantern Press. (P.216)
--*Young Medicine Man.* Kroll, Francis Lynde (1904-1973). 1956. Lantern Press. (P.540)
--*Young Pony Express Rider.* Coombs, Charles Ira (1914-). 1953. Lantern Press. (P.216)
--*Young Readers Baseball Mystery.* Coombs, Charles Ira (1914-). 1959. Grosset & Dunlap. (P.216)
--*Young Readers Basketball Stories.* Coombs, Charles Ira (1914-). 1954, c.1951. Grosset & Dunlap. (P.216)
--*Young Readers Basketball Stories.* Coombs, Charles Ira (1914-). 1951. Lantern Press. (P.216)
--*Young Readers Circus Mystery.* Coombs, Charles Ira (1914-). N.D. Grosset & Dunlap. (P.216)
--*Young Readers Cowboy Stories.* Regli, Adolph Casper (1896-1952). 1953, c.1951. Grossett & Dunlap. (P.754)
--*Young Readers Detective Stories.* Coombs, Charles Ira (1914-). 1961, c.1951. Grosset & Dunlap. (P.216)
--*Young Readers Detective Stories.* Coombs, Charles Ira (1914-). 1951. Lantern Press. (P.216)
--*Young Readers Horse Stories.* Furman, Abraham Loew (1902-), ed. 1951. Lantern Press. (P.350)
--*Young Readers Indian Stories.* Furman, Abraham Loew (1902-), ed. 1951. Lantern Press. (P.350)
--*Young Readers Indoor Sports Stories.* Coombs, Charles Ira (1914-). 1961, c.1952. Grosset & Dunlap. (P.216)
--*Young Readers Indoor Sports Stories.* Coombs, Charles Ira (1914-). 1952. Lantern Press. (P.216)
--*Young Readers Mystery Stories.* Coombs, Charles Ira (1914-). 1953, c.1951. Grosset & Dunlap. (P.216)
--*Young Readers Mystery Stories.* Coombs, Charles Ira (1914-). 1951. Lantern Press. (P.216)
--*Young Readers Outdoor Sports Stories.* Furman, Abraham Loew (1902-), ed. 1951. Lantern Press. (P.350)
--*Young Readers Pioneer Stories.* Furman, Abraham Loew (1902-), ed. 1951. Lantern Press. (P.350)
--*Young Readers Railroad Stories.* Coombs, Charles Ira (1914-). 1961, c.1953. Grosset & Dunlap. (P.216)
--*Young Readers Railroad Stories.* Coombs, Charles Ira (1914-). 1953. Lantern Press. (P.216)
--*Young Readers Sports Treasury.* Coombs, Charles Ira (1914-). 1952. Lantern Press. (P.216)
--*Young Readers Stories of the Diamond.* Coombs, Charles Ira (1914-). 1961, c.1951. Grosset & Dunlap. (P.216)
--*Young Readers Stories of the Diamond.* Coombs, Charles Ira (1914-). 1951. Lantern Press. (P.216)
--*Young Readers Stories of the West.* Payne, Stephen. 1951. Lantern Press. (P.712)
--*Young Readers Water Sports Stories.* Coombs, Charles Ira (1914-). c.1952. Grosset & Dunlap. (P.216)
--*Young Readers Water Sports Stories.* Coombs, Charles Ira (1914-). 1952. Lantern Press. (P.216)
--*Young Readers Wild Life Stories.* Furman, Abraham Loew (1902-), ed. N.D. Lantern Press. (P.350)
--*Young Sand Hills Cowboy.* Kroll, Francis Lynde (1904-1973). N.D. Grosset & Dunlap. (P.540)
--*Young Sand Hills Cowboy.* Kroll, Francis Lynde (1904-1973). 1953. Lantern Press. (P.540)
--*Young Sioux Warrior.* Kroll, Francis Lynde (1904-1973). N.D. Grosset & Dunlap. (P.540)
--*Young Sioux Warrior.* Kroll, Francis Lynde (1904-1973). 1952. Lantern Press. (P.540)
--*Young Visitor to Mars.* Elam, Richard Mace, Jr. (1920-). 1953. Lantern Press. (P.300)

Geer, Charles Hand (1922-) & Tate, Sally
--*Joyful Poems for Children.* Riley, James Whitcomb (1849-1916). 1960. Bobbs-Merrill. (P.764)

Geer, Garrett
--*The Turnabout Twins.* Daringer, Helen Fern (1892-). 1960. Harcourt, Brace. (P.242)

Geer, Terrence
--*Coral Reef Castaway.* Catherall, Arthur (1906-). 1960. Criterion Books. (P.177)

Gehm, Charles C.
--*A Dream for Addie.* Rock, Gail. 1975. Knopf ; Distributed by Random House. (P.771)
--*The House Without a Christmas Tree.* Rock, Gail. 1974. Knopf. (P.771)
--*Soup.* Peck, Robert Newton (1928-). 1979, c.1974. Dell Pub. Co. (P.715)
--*Soup.* Peck, Robert Newton (1928-). 1974. Knopf. (P.715)
--*Soup's Drum.* Peck, Robert Newton (1928-). 1980. Knopf. (P.715)
--*The Thanksgiving Treasure.* Rock, Gail. 1974. Knopf; Distributed by Random House. (P.771)

Gehr, Mary
--*The Angel Who Guarded the Toys, and Other Stories.* Burton, Doris. 1955. H. Regnery Co. (P.157)
--*Big Store, Funny Door.* Russell, Betty. 1955. A. Whitman. (P.785)
--*Fluffy and Bluffy.* Dalton, Alene. 1951. Childrens Press Inc. (P.239)
--*Fluffy and Bluffy.* Dalton, Alene. N.D. Grosset & Dunlap. (P.239)
--*Funny Boots.* Russell, Betty. 1951. A. Whitman. (P.785)
--*Happy Gingerbread Boy: A Modern Version.* Mallon, Caroline H. 1946. The Children's Company. (P.615)
--*Little Tweet.* Holloway, Charles W. 1952. Whitman. (P.456)
--*Mary Jane Ellen McCling.* Small, William J. 1956. A. Whitman. (P.830)
--*My First Mother Goose.* Mother Goose. Watkins, Sylvestre C. (1911-), ed. 1946. Wilcox & Follett Co. (P.669)
--*Run Sheep, Run.* Russell, Betty. 1952. A. Whitman. (P.785)
--*Snoopy Gets a Name.* Dryer, Marion M. 1946. The Children's Company. (P.285)
--*The Story of the Man in the Moon.* Mallon, Caroline H. 1946. The Children's Company. (P.615)
--*Surprise Island.* Warner, Gertrude Chandler (1890-1979). 1949. Scott, Foresman. (P.932)
--*Three Sides and the Round One.* Friskey, Margaret Richards (1901-). 1973. Childrens Press. (P.347)
--*The True Book of Little People.* Copeland, Donald McKillop. 1953. Childrens Press. (P.218)
--*We're Going to Town.* 1st ed. Aldis, Dorothy Keeley, Mrs. (1896-1966). 1952. Bobbs-Merrill. (P.21)
--*What Is the Color of the Wide, Wide World?.* Friskey, Margaret Richards (1901-). 1973. Childrens Press. (P.347)
--*The Yellow House Mystery.* Warner, Gertrude Chandler (1890-1979). 1953. A. Whitman. (P.932)

Gehring, Jack
--*Do You Know?.* Odor, Ruth Shannon (1926-). 1977. Standard Pub. (P.690)

Geiger, Paul
--*The Mystery of the Diamond in the Wood.* Kherdian, David (1931-). c.1983. Knopf. (P.521)
--*Spring & the Shadow Man.* Johnson, Emily Rhoads. 1984. Dodd. (P.495)

Geisel, Theodor Seuss see Dr. Seuss, pseud.
Geisel, Theodor Seuss see Lesieg, Theo, pseud.

Geisel, Theodor Seuss (1904-)
--*And to Think That I Saw It on Mulberry Street.* Dr. Seuss, pseud. Geisel, Theodor Seuss (1904-). Dr. Seuss, pseud. 1937. Hale. (P.362)
--*And to Think That I Saw It on Mulberry Street.* Dr. Seuss, pseud. Geisel, Theodor Seuss (1904-). Dr. Seuss, pseud. 1937. Th Vanguard Press. (P.362)
--*Bartholomew & the Oobleck.* Dr. Seuss, pseud. Geisel, Theodor Seuss (1904-). Dr. Seuss, pseud. 1949. Random. **Award: (RCM).** (P.362)
--*The Butter Battle Book.* Dr. Seuss, pseud. Geisel, Theodor Seuss (1904-). Dr. Seuss, pseud. 1984. Random. (P.362)
--*Cat in the Hat.* Dr. Seuss, pseud. Geisel, Theodor Seuss (1904-). Dr. Seuss, pseud. 1957. Beginner. (P.362)
--*The Cat in the Hat.* Dr. Seuss, pseud. Geisel, Theodor Seuss (1904-). Dr. Seuss, pseud. 1957. Houghton Mifflin. (P.362)
--*The Cat in the Hat.* Dr. Seuss, pseud. Geisel, Theodor Seuss (1904-). Dr. Seuss, pseud. 1957. Random House. (P.362)
--*Cat in the Hat Comes Back.* Dr. Seuss, pseud. Geisel, Theodor Seuss (1904-). Dr. Seuss, pseud. 1958. Beginner. (P.362)
--*The Cat in the Hat Comes Back.* Dr. Seuss, pseud. Geisel, Theodor Seuss (1904-). Dr. Seuss, pseud. 1958. Random House. (P.362)
--*The Cat in the Hat in English & Spanish.* Dr. Seuss, pseud. Geisel, Theodor Seuss (1904-). Dr. Seuss, pseud. Rivera, Carlos, tr. 1967. Beginner. (P.362)
--*Cat in the Hat Songbook.* Dr. Seuss, pseud. Geisel, Theodor Seuss (1904-). Dr. Seuss, pseud. 1967. Beginner. (P.362)
--*Did I Ever Tell You How Lucky You Are?.* Dr. Seuss, pseud. Geisel, Theodor Seuss (1904-). Dr. Seuss, pseud. 1973. Random House. (P.362)
--*Dr.* Seuss Storytime. Dr. Seuss, pseud. Geisel, Theodor Seuss (1904-). Dr. Seuss, pseud. 1974. Random House. (P.362)
--*Dr.* Seuss's ABC. Dr. Seuss, pseud. Geisel, Theodor Seuss (1904-). Dr. Seuss, pseud. 1963. Beginner. (P.362)
--*Dr.* Seuss's ABC. Dr. Seuss, pseud. Geisel, Theodor Seuss (1904-). Dr. Seuss, pseud. 1963. Beginner Books. (P.362)
--*Dr.* Seuss's Sleep Book. Dr. Seuss, pseud. Geisel, Theodor Seuss (1904-). Dr. Seuss, pseud. 1962. Random. (P.362)
--*Five Hundred Hats of Bartholomew Cubbins.* Dr. Seuss, pseud. Geisel, Theodor Seuss (1904-). Dr. Seuss, pseud. 1938. Hale. (P.362)
--*Five Hundred Hats of Bartholomew Cubbins.* Dr. Seuss, pseud. Geisel, Theodor Seuss (1904-). Seuss, Dr., pseud. 1938. Vanguard. (P.362)
--*The Foot Book.* Dr. Seuss, pseud. Geisel, Theodor Seuss (1904-). Dr. Seuss, pseud. 1968. Random House. (P.362)
--*Fox in Socks.* Dr. Seuss, pseud. Geisel, Theodor Seuss (1904-). Dr. Seuss, pseud. 1965. Beginner. (P.362)
--*Green Eggs & Ham.* Dr. Seuss, pseud. Geisel, Theodor Seuss (1904-). Dr. Seuss, pseud. 1960. Beginner. (P.362)
--*Happy Birthday to You.* Dr. Seuss, pseud. Geisel, Theodor Seuss (1904-). Dr. Seuss, pseud. 1959. Random. (P.362)
--*Hop on Pop.* Dr. Seuss, pseud. Geisel, Theodor Seuss (1904-). Dr. Seuss, pseud. 1963. Beginner. (P.362)
--*Horton Hatches the Egg.* Dr. Seuss, pseud. Geisel, Theodor Seuss (1904-). Dr. Seuss, pseud. 1940. Random. (P.362)
--*Horton Hears a Who.* Dr. Seuss, pseud. Geisel, Theodor Seuss (1904-). Dr. Seuss, pseud. 1954. Random. (P.362)
--*How the Grinch Stole Christmas.* Dr. Seuss, pseud. Geisel, Theodor Seuss (1904-). Dr. Seuss, pseud. 1957. Random. (P.362)
--*Hunches in Bunches.* Dr. Seuss, pseud. Geisel, Theodor Seuss, pseud. (1904-). Geisel, Theodor Seuss. Dr. Seuss, pseud. 1982. Random. (P.362)
--*I Can Lick Thirty Tigers Today & Other Stories.* Dr. Seuss, pseud. Geisel, Theodor Seuss (1904-). Dr. Seuss, pseud. 1969. Random. (P.362)
--*I Can Read with My Eyes Shut.* Dr. Seuss, pseud. Geisel, Theodor Seuss (1904-). Dr. Seuss, pseud. 1978. Beginner Books. (P.362)
--*I Had Trouble in Getting to Solla Sollew.* Dr. Seuss, pseud. Geisel, Theodor Seuss (1904-). 1965. Random. (P.362)
--*If I Ran the Circus.* Dr. Seuss, pseud. Geisel, Theodor Seuss (1904-). Dr. Seuss, pseud. 1956. Random. (P.362)
--*If I Ran the Zoo.* Dr. Seuss, pseud. Geisel, Theodor Seuss (1904-). Dr. Seuss, pseud. 1950. Random. **Award: (RCM).** (P.362)
--*King's Stilts.* Dr. Seuss, pseud. Geisel, Theodor Seuss (1904-). Dr. Seuss, pseud. 1939. Random. (P.362)
--*Lorax.* Dr. Seuss, pseud. Geisel, Theodor Seuss (1904-). Dr. Seuss, pseud. 1971. Random. (P.362)
--*McElligot's Pool.* Dr. Seuss, pseud. Geisel, Theodor Seuss (1904-). Dr. Seuss, pseud. N.D. E. M. Hale & Co. (P.362)
--*McElligot's Pool.* Dr. Seuss, pseud. Geisel, Theodor Seuss (1904-). Dr. Seuss, pseud. 1947. Random House. **Award: (RCM).** (P.362)
--*Mister Brown Can Moo, Can You.* Dr. Seuss, pseud. Geisel, Theodor Seuss (1904-). Dr. Seuss, pseud. 1970. Random. (P.362)
--*Oh, Say Can You Say?.* Dr. Seuss, pseud. Geisel, Theodor Seuss (1904-). Dr. Seuss, pseud. 1979. Beginner. (P.362)
--*On Beyond Zebra.* Dr. Seuss, pseud. Geisel, Theodor Seuss (1904-). Dr. Seuss, pseud. 1955. Hale. (P.362)
--*On Beyond Zebra.* Dr. Seuss, pseud. Geisel, Theodor Seuss (1904-). Dr. Seuss, pseud. 1955. Random. (P.362)
--*On Beyond Zebra.* Dr. Seuss, pseud. Geisel, Theodor Seuss (1904-). Dr. Seuss, pseud. 1955. Random. (P.362)
--*One Fish Two Fish Red Fish Blue Fish.* Dr. Seuss, pseud. Geisel, Theodor Seuss (1904-). Dr. Seuss, pseud. 1960. Beginner. (P.362)
--*A Prayer For a Child.* Dr. Seuss, pseud. Geisel, Theodor Seuss (1904-). Dr. Seuss, pseud. 1958. Random House Inc. (P.362)
--*Scrambled Eggs Super.* Dr. Seuss, pseud. Geisel, Theodor Seuss (1904-). Dr. Seuss, pseud. 1953. Random. (P.362)
--*The Shape of Me and Other Stuff.* Dr. Seuss, pseud. Geisel, Theodor Seuss (1904-). Dr. Seuss, pseud. 1973. Beginner Books. (P.362)
--*Sneetches & Other Stories.* Dr. Seuss, pseud. Geisel, Theodor Seuss (1904-). Dr. Seuss, pseud. 1961. Random. (P.363)
--*Ten Apples up on Top!.* Lesieg, Theo, pseud. Geisel, Theodor Seuss (1904-). Lesieg, Theo, pseud. 1961. Beginner Books. (P.363)
--*There's a Wocket in My Pocket!.* Geisel, Theodor Seuss (1904-). Dr. Seuss, pseud. 1974. Beginner Books. (P.363)
--*Thidwick: The Big-Hearted Moose.* Dr. Seuss, pseud. Geisel, Theodor Seuss (1904-). Dr. Seuss, pseud. 1948. Random. (P.363)
--*Tribune.* Dr. Seuss, pseud. Geisel, Theodor Seuss (1904-). Dr. Seuss, pseud. N.D. The Vanguard Press. (P.363)
--*Yertle the Turtle & Other Stories.* Dr. Seuss, pseud. Geisel, Theodor Seuss (1904-). Dr. Seuss, pseud. 1958. Random. (P.363)

Geisel, Theodor Seuss (1904-) & Vallier, Jean
--*Cat in the Hat in English and French.* Dr. Seuss, pseud. Geisel, Theodor Seuss (1904-). 1967. Beginner. (P.362)

Geisert, Arthur
--*Pa's Balloon & Other Pig Tales.* Geisert, Arthur. 1984. HM. (P.363)
--*Prisoners of the Scrambling Dragon.* Monjo, Ferdinand Nicolas, III (1924-1978). c.1980. Holt, Rinehart and Winston. (P.657)

Geissler, Rudolph
--*Our Country Home.* N.D. Pott, Young, & Co. (P.363)

Geiszel, Margaret Malpass
--*King Arthur and His Knights of the Round Table.* Williams, Henry Meade (1899-). c.1928. J. H. Sears & Company, Inc. (P.963)
--*Robin Hood.* Williams, Henry Meade (1899-). Malcolm, Arthur, pseud. c.1927. J. H. Sears & Company, Inc. (P.963)

Gekiere, Madeleine, jt. illus. see Sewell, Helen Moore.

Gekiere, Madeleine (1919-)
--*The Fisherman and His Wife.* Grimm, Jakob Ludwig Karl (1785-1863) & Grimm, Wilhelm Karl (1786-1859). c.1957. Pantheon Books. **Award: (NYT).** (P.391)
--*The Frilly Lily and The Princess.* Gekiere, Madeleine (1919-). 1960. J. B. Lippincott. (P.363)
--*Gwendolyn.* Helm, Ruth H. (1918-). 1952. Oxford University Press. (P.431)
--*John J.* Plenty and Fiddler Dan: A New Fable of the Grasshopper and the Ant. Ciardi, John Anthony (1916-). 1963. Lippincott. **Awards: (NYT); (ALA).** (P.196)
--*Mr.* Putterbee's Jungle. Helm, Ruth H. (1918-). 1953. Oxford University Press. (P.431)
--*Peterli and the Mountain.* Engelhard, Georgia. 1954. Lippincott. (P.307)
--*The Reason for the Pelican.* Ciardi, John Anthony (1916-). 1959. Lippincott. **Award: (NYT).** (P.196)
--*Switch on the Night.* Bradbury, Ray Douglas (1920-). c.1955. Pantheon Books. **Awards: (NYT); (ALA).** (P.124)

Gelb, Philip
--*The Merry Gentlemen of Japan: A Children's Story.* Reiter, Herman William (1911-) & Chartoc, Shepard (1910-), eds. Gilbert, William Schwenck, Sir (1836-1911) & Sullivan, Arthur Seymour, Sir (1842-1900). 1935. The Bass Publishers. (P.367)

Geldart, Bill
--*The Fox at Drummers' Darkness.* Stranger, Joyce, pseud. Wilson, Joyce Muriel Judson. 1977, c.1976. Farrar, Straus and Giroux. (P.864)

--*The Singing Weaver and Other Stories: Hero Tales of the Reformation.* Seebach, Julius Frederick (1869-) & Seebach, Margaret Rebecca Himes (1875-). 1917. The Lutheran Publication Society. (P.807)
--*The Story of Little Goody Two-Shoes: Who from a State of Rags and Care, and Having Shoes but Half a Pair, Their Fortune and Their Fame Would Fix, and Gallop in a Coach and Six.* Goody Two Shoes. 1944. Grosset & Dunlap. (P.376)

Gillette, Guy, photos by.
--*Simpson.* Jones, Lee. 1960. Holt, Rinehart and Winston. (P.499)

Gillette, Henry Sampson (1915-)
--*Adam Gray: Stowaway: A Story of the China Trade.* Arntson, Herbert Edward (1911-). 1961. F. Watts. (P.49)
--*The Green Cockade.* Allen, Merritt Parmelee (1892-1954). 1942. Longmans, Green & Co. (P.30)
--*Mark Twain: Boy of Old Missouri.* Mason, Miriam Evangeline (1899-1973). 1962. Bobbs. (P.628)
--*Old Wolf: The Story of Israel Putnam.* Dean, Leon W. (1889-). 1942. Farrar & Rinehart, Inc. (P.248)
--*Stark of the North Country.* Dean, Leon W (1889-). c.1941. Farrar & Rinehart. (P.248)
--*Two Guns in Old Oregon.* Arntson, Herbert Edward (1911-). 1964. F. Watts. (P.49)

Gilliam, Stan
--*Katie and the Computer.* D'Ignazio, Frederick (1949-). 1980. Creative Computing. (P.266)

Gillies, Margaret & Smith, Richard S.
--*Memoirs of a London Doll.* new ed. Horne, Richard Henry (1803-1884). Fisher, Margery Tuner (1913-), ed. 1968. Macmillan. (P.464)

Gillin, Denver
--*Swiss Family Robinson.* Wyss, Johann David Von (1743-1818). Memling, Carl (1918-1969), adapted by. 1961. Golden Press. (P.984)

Gillis, Paul
--*Goldie.* Gillis, Everett A. 1982. Pisces Pr TX. (P.368)

Gilman, Esther (1925-)
--*Little Boat Lighter than a Cork.* Krauss, Ruth Ida (1911-). 1975. J. Philip O'Hara Inc. (P.539)
--*Little Boat Lighter Than a Cork.* Krauss, Ruth Ida (1911-). c.1976. Magic Circle Press. (P.539)
--*The Little Girl and Her Mother.* De Regniers, Beatrice Schenk Freedman (1914-). c.1963. Vanguard Press. (P.259)
--*Nothing but a Dog.* 1st ed. Katz, Bobbi (1933-). 1972. Feminist Press. (P.509)

Gilmore, H. H.
--*Pitching for Pawling.* Temple, Willard Henry (1912-). c.1940. Farrar & Rinehart, Inc. (P.881)

Gilmour, Janet L.
--*Stories from Chinese History.* Roe, Nora Ardelia Metcalf, Mrs. (1856-1910). 1917. Frederick A. Stokes Company. (P.774)

Gilmour, Marie E.
--*Naughty Frisky.* Beimes, Charlotte Reger. c.1937. H. A. Beimes. (P.89)

Gimenez, Juan
--*Journey to Nazgar's Fortress: A Robo Force Adventure.* Chatham, Bill. 1985. Random. (P.188)

Gincano, John
--*Bimbo and His Jacket.* Hunter, Kay. 1935. Gabriel Sons & Co. (P.474)
--*Blockade Runner: A Tale of Adventure Aboard the Robert E. Lee.* Heagney, Harold Jerome (1890-). 1939. Longmans, Green and Co. (P.428)
--*Prairie Anchorage.* Medary, Marjorie (1890-). 1933. Longmans, Green and Co. (P.638)
--*Preacher's Kid.* Haystead, Ladd (1903-). 1942. G. P. Putnam's Sons. (P.426)
--*Riders of the Royal Road: A Tale of the Camino Real.* Hawthorne, Hildegarde (1871-1952). 1932. D. Appleton & Comapny. (P.423)
--*The Will to Win and Other Stories.* Meader, Stephen Warren (1892-). c.1936. Harcourt, Brace and Company. (P.637)

Gindraux, Jim
--*A Walk in the Neighborhood.* Behrens, June York (1925-). 1968. Elk Grove Press. (P.89)

Ginnings, Harriet Wilcoxen (1905-)
--*Animal ABC.* Ginnings, Harriett Wilcoxen (1905-). c.1949. Whitman Pub. Co. (P.369)

Ginnings, Harriett Wilcoxen see Harriett, pseud.

Ginther, Mary Pemberton
--*Beth Anne Goes to School.* Ginther, Mary Pemberton. 1919. The Penn Publishing Company. (P.369)
--*Beth Anne Herself.* Ginther, Mary Pemberton. 1915. The Penn Publishing Company. (P.369)
--*Beth Anne: Really-for-Truly.* Ginther, Mary Pemberton. 1916. The Penn Publishing Company. (P.369)
--*Beth Anne's New Cousin.* Ginther, Mary Pemberton. 1917. The Penn Publishing Company. (P.369)
--*Betsy Hale.* Ginther, Mary Pemberton. c.1923. The John C. Winston Company. (P.369)
--*Betsy Hale Succeeds.* Ginther, Mary Pemberton. c.1923. The John C. Winston Company. (P.369)
--*Betsy Hale Tries.* Ginther, Mary Pemberton. c.1923. The John C. Winston Company. (P.369)
--*Hilda of Grey Cot.* Ginther, Mary Pemberton. 1923. The Penn Publishing Co. (P.369)
--*Hilda of Laudis and Company.* Ginther, Mary Pemberton. 1924. The Penn Publishing Company. (P.369)
--*Hilda of the Green Smock.* Ginther, Mary Pemberton. 1925. The Penn Publishing Company. (P.369)
--*Hilda of the Three Star Ranch.* Ginther, Mary Pemberton. 1926. The Penn Publishing Company. (P.369)
--*Nancy Lee.* Dunton, Edith Kellogg (1875-). Warde, Margaret, pseud. N.D. Penn Publishing Co. (P.291)
--*Nancy Lee's Lookout.* Dunton, Edith Kellogg (1875-). Warde, Margaret, pseud. N.D. Penn Publishing Co. (P.291)
--*Nancy Lee's Namesake.* Dunton, Edith Kellogg (1875-). Warde, Margaret, pseud. 1918. The Penn Publishing Company. (P.291)
--*Nancy Lee's Spring Term.* Dunton, Edith Kellogg (1875-). Warde, Margaret, pseud. N.D. Penn Publilshing Co. (P.291)
--*Nancy Lee's Spring Term.* Dunton, Edith Kellogg (1875-). Warde, Margaret, pseud. 1913. The Penn Publishing Company. (P.291)
--*The Ranch Girls in Europe.* Vandercook, Margaret O'Bannon Womack, Mrs. (1876-). c.1914. The John C. Winston Company. (P.913)
--*The Secret Stair.* Ginther, Mary Pemberton. c.1928. Macrae Smith Company. (P.369)

Giordano, Dick & Andru, Ross
--*Wonder Woman.* Penick, Ib, designed by. c.1980. Random House. (P.369)

Giordano, Joe
--*Children's Bible Stories from the Old Testament.* Hannon, Ruth. 1978. Western Pub. (P.411)
--*My Very First Story Book.* Klugmann, Judith. 1962. Doubleday. (P.531)
--*The Owl Who Loved Sunshine.* Cary, Mary. 1977. Western Pub. (P.176)

Giordano, Richard
--*The Trail of Danger.* Wallerstein, James S. 1972. Aurelon. (P.927)

Giovannetti, Pericle
--*Hamid of Apeppo.* King, David Clive (1924-). 1958. Macmillan. (P.523)
--*Max.* Giovannetti, Pericle. 1977. Atheneum. (P.369)

Giovanopoulos, Paul Arthur (1939-)
--*Free As a Frog.* Hodges, Elizabeth Jamison. 1969. A-W. **Award: (NYT).** (P.448)
--*George and Red.* Coatsworth, Elizabeth Jane (1893-). 1969. Macmillan. (P.204)
--*How Many Miles to Babylon?.* Fox, Paula (1923-). 1980. Bradbury Pr. (P.340)
--*How Many Miles to Babylon.* Fox, Paula (1923-). 1967. D White. (P.340)
--*The Long Black Schooner: The Voyage of the Amistad.* Sterne, Emma Gelders, Mrs. (1894-1971). 1968. Follett Pub. Co. (P.853)
--*The Looking Down Game.* Dean, Leigh. 1968. Funk & Wagnalls. (P.248)
--*Real Tin Flower: Poems about the World at Nine.* Barnstone, Aliki (1956-). 1968. Macmillan. **Award: (NYT).** (P.74)
--*Rufus Gideon Grant.* Dean, Leigh. 1970. Scribner. (P.248)
--*A Time for Watching.* Norris, Gunilla Brodde (1939-). 1969. Knopf. (P.685)
--*Toto and the Aardvark.* Linde, Freda. Berends, Polly Berrien (1939-) & Berends, Jan, trs. from Afrikaans 1969. Doubleday. (P.573)

Giovetti
--*My Book of Goldilocks and the Three Bears.* 1962. Maxton Pub. Corp. (P.369)

Girard, Marv
--*A Giant Walked Among Them: Half-Tall Tales of Paul Bunyan and His Loggers.* Girard, Hazel B. c.1977. M. Jones Co. (P.370)

Gironi, Tiziana
--*The Ugly Duckling.* Andersen, Hans Christian (1805-1875). Alex, Marlee, tr. 1985. Barron's. (P.37)

Gist, Linda
--*Better Never Than Late: A Tale Without a Moral.* Hoss, Phoebe Wilson. 1971. Collins-World. (P.465)

Gittleman, Len
--*Is It Hard?* Is It Easy. Green, Mary McBurney (1896-). c.1960. W. R. Scott. (P.385)

Givens-Duzak
--*Linda Just Right.* Miller, Jane (1919-). 1946. The Vanguard Press, Inc. (P.647)

Givens, Gogo, photos by.
--*Jimmy Jumparound.* Miller, Jane (1919-). 1947. Vanguard Press. (P.647)

Giventer, Abbi
--*Susan Sometimes.* Krasilovsky, Phyllis (1926-). 1962. Macmillan. (P.537)
--*What Happened to Jenny.* Berrien, Edith Heal (1903-). 1962. Atheneum. (P.97)

Glackens, Louis M.
--*Andy's Adventures on Noah's Ark.* Doty, Douglas Zabriskie. 1902. J. F. Taylor & Co. (P.281)
--*The Last Tenet Imposed Upon the Khan of Tomathoz.* Roe, William James. Genone, Hudor, pseud. 1892. C. H. Kerr and Company. (P.774)
--*Monsieur and Madame.* Dimock, Edwin. 1924. Harper & Bros. (P.266)
--*Tell 'em Again Tales.* Day, Marguerite. 1924. Duffield & Company. (P.248)
--*Yesterday's Children.* Tanner, Edwin Platt (1874-). c.1927. Rand, McNally & Company. (P.877)

Glackens, W.
--*Santa Claus's Partner.* Page, Thomas Nelson (1853-1922). 1899. C. Scribner's Sons. (P.700)

Glanckoff, Samuel (1894-)
--*The Romance of Antar.* Tietjens, Eunice Hammond, Mrs. (1884-1944). 1929. Coward-McCann, Inc. (P.891)
--*Senor Zero.* Smith, Henry Justin (1875-). c.1931. Harcourt, Brace and Co. (P.834)
--*The Wonder Stick.* Coblentz, Stanton Arthur (1896-). 1929. Cosmopolitan Book Corporations. (P.205)

Glannon, Edward John (1911-)
--*Everybody Eats.* Green, Mary McBurney (1896-). 1946. W. R. Scott. (P.385)
--*Guess What's in the Grass.* Mitchell, Lucy Sprague, Mrs. (1878-). c.1945. W. R. Scott, Inc. (P.652)

Glanzman, Louis S. (1922-)
--*The Adventures of Hercules.* Fadiman, Clifton Paul (1904-). c.1960. Random House. (P.315)
--*Adventures of the Range Rider.* Sutton, Felix (1910-). 1955, c.1956. Wonder Books. (P.872)
--*The Bear's House.* Sachs, Marilyn Stickle (1927-). Ellen, Fran, created by. 1971. Doubleday and Company. (P.787)
--*Ben Hur.* Wallace, Lewis (1827-1905). 1959. Grosset & Dunlap. (P.927)
--*Big Music Or, Twenty Merry Tales to Tell.* Bleecker, Mary Noel, ed. 1946. The Viking Press. (P.109)
--*Bill Bergson, Master Detective.* Lindgren, Astrid Ericsson (1907-). Antoine, Herbert, tr. from Swedish. 1952. Viking Pr. (P.573)
--*Bill Bergson, Master Detective.* Lindgren, Astrid Ericsson (1907-). 1968. Viking Pr. (P.573)
--*The Haunted Hound.* 1st ed. White, Robb (1909-). 1950. Doubleday. (P.953)
--*It's America for Me: A Freedom Book.* Martin, William Ivan, Jr. (1916-). 1970. Bowmar. (P.626)
--*Juan.* Stolz, Mary Slattery (1920-). 1970. Harper & Row. (P.861)
--*Kidnapped.* Stevenson, Robert Louis (1850-1894). Sutton, Felix (1910-), abridged by. 1960. Grosset & Dunlap. (P.857)
--*The Lost Treasure Box.* 1st ed. Rushmore, Helen (1898-). 1949. Harcourt, Brace. (P.784)
--*Marv.* 1st ed. Sachs, Marilyn Stickle (1927-). 1970. Doubleday. (P.787)
--*The Mule Skinners.* Richardson, Myra Reed. 1945. The Viking Press. (P.763)
--*My Brother, Angel.* Beckett, Hilary. 1971. Dodd, Mead. (P.87)
--*The Noonday Friends.* Stolz, Mary Slattery (1920-). 1965. Harper. **Awards: (ALA); (JNM).** (P.861)
--*Papeek.* Van Loon, Dirk. 1970. Lippincott. (P.915)
--*Peter and Veronica.* 1st ed. Sachs, Marilyn Stickle (1927-). 1969. Doubleday. (P.787)
--*Pippi Goes on Board.* Lindgren, Astrid Ericsson (1907-). Lamborn, Florence, tr. from Swedish. 1957. Viking Press. (P.573)
--*Pippi Goes on Board.* Lindgren, Astrid Ericsson (1907-). 1977, c.1957. Puffin Books. (P.573)
--*Pippi in the South Seas.* Lindgren, Astrid Ericsson (1907-). Bothmer, Gerry, tr. 1959. Viking Press. (P.573)
--*Pippi in the South Seas.* Lindgren, Astrid Ericsson (1907-). 1977. Puffin Books. (P.573)
--*Pippi Longstocking.* Lindgren, Astrid Ericsson (1907-). Lamborn, Florence (1922-), tr. from Swedish. 1950. Viking Press. (P.573)
--*Pippi Longstocking.* Lindgren, Astrid Ericsson (1907-). 1977. Puffin Books. (P.573)
--*The Sword of King Arthur.* Williams, Jay (1914-1978), adapted by. 1968. Crowell. (P.963)
--*Toby Tyler.* Kaler, James Otis (1848-1912). Otis, James, pseud. 1947. World Pub. (P.506)
--*Toby Tyler: Or, Ten Weeks With a Circus.* Kaler, James Otis (1848-1912). Otis, James, pseud. Becker, May Lamberton (1873-1958), intro. by. 1947. World Pub. Co. (P.506)
--*Treasure Was Their Quest.* Bunce, William Harvey (1903-). 1947. Harcourt, Brace. (P.149)
--*The Truth About Mary Rose.* 1st ed. Sachs, Marilyn Stickle (1927-). 1973. Doubleday. (P.788)
--*Veronica Ganz.* 1st ed. Sachs, Marilyn Stickle (1927-). 1968. Doubleday. **Award: (ALA).** (P.788)
--*The Wish-Tree.* Ciardi, John Anthony (1916-). 1962. Crowell-Collier Press. (P.196)
--*A Wonderful, Terrible Time.* Stolz, Mary Slattery (1920-). 1967. Harper & Row. (P.861)

Glasbergen, Randy
--*Ickle McNoo.* Danforth, Wendy. 1974. Allied Publications. (P.240)

Glaser, Byron
--*The Gift of the Magi.* Henry, O., pseud. (1862-1910). Porter, William Sidney. c.1980. Creative Education. (P.434)
--*The Ransom of Red Chief.* Henry, O., pseud. (1862-1910). Porter, William Sidney. c.1980. Creative Education. (P.434)
--*To Build a Fire.* London, Jack (1876-1916). c.1980. Creative Education. (P.581)

Glaser, Byron, jt. illus. see Neumeier, Marty.

Glaser, Marvin
--*Amber Wellington, Daredevil.* Glaser, Dianne Elizabeth (1937-). 1975. Walker. (P.370)
--*Amber Wellington, Witch Watcher.* Glaser, Dianne Elizabeth (1937-). 1976. Walker. (P.370)

Glaser, Michael
--*Does Anyone Know Where a Hermit Crab Goes?.* Glaser, Michael. 1983. Knickerbocker. (P.370)

Glaser, Milton (1929-)
--*Cats and Bats and Things with Wings: Poems.* Aiken, Conrad Potter (1889-1973). 1965. Atheneum. **Award: (ALA).** (P.15)
--*Fierce and Gentle Warriors: Three Stories.* 1st ed. Sholokhov, Mikhail Aleksandrovich (1905-1984). Morton, Miriam (1918-), tr. 1967. Doubleday. (P.821)
--*Fish in the Sky.* 1st ed. Mendoza, George (1934-). 1971. Doubleday. (P.641)
--*Help, Help, the Globolinks.* Menotti, Gian-Carlo (1911-). Dean, Leigh, adapted by. 1970. McGraw. **Award: (NYT).** (P.641)
--*If Apples Had Teeth.* Glaser, Milton (1929-) & Glaser, Shirley. 1960. Alfred A Knopf : distributed by Borzoi Books. (P.370)
--*The Smallest Elephant in the World.* Tresselt, Alvin R. (1916-). 1959. Knopf. (P.900)

Glass, Andrew
--*Banjo.* Peck, Robert Newton (1928-). 1982. Knopf. (P.714)
--*Devil's Donkey.* Brittain, Bill. 1981. Harper & Row. **Award: (ALA).** (P.133)
--*The Fido Frame-Up.* Singer, Marilyn (1948-). 1983. Warne. (P.827)
--*The Ghost in the Lagoon.* Carlson, Natalie Savage (1906-). 1984. Lothrop. (P.169)
--*The Gift.* Nixon, Joan Lowery (1927-). 1983, c.1982. Macmillan. (P.683)
--*The Glass Ring.* Kennedy, Mary. N.D. Dandelion Pr. (P.518)
--*Graven Images: Three Stories.* 1st ed. Fleischman, Paul. 1982. Har-Row. **Awards: (ALA); (JNM).** (P.331)
--*Jackson Makes His Move: Story and Pictures.* Glass, Andrew. c.1982. F. Warne. (P.370)
--*My Brother Tries to Make Me Laugh.* Glass, Andrew. 1984. LOthrop. (P.370)
--*A Nose for Trouble.* Singer, Marilyn (1948-). c.1985. Holt, Rinehart, and Winston. (P.827)
--*Spooky and the Ghost Cat.* 1st ed. Carlson, Natalie Savage (1906-). c.1985. Lothrop, Lee & Shepard Books. (P.169)
--*Spooky Night.* Carlson, Natalie Savage (1906-). c.1982. Lothrop, Lee & Shepard. (P.169)
--*Terrible Tyrannosaurus.* 1st ed. Charlton, Elizabeth (1937-). c.1981. Elsevier/Nelson Books. (P.187)
--*The Wish Giver: Three Tales of Coven Tree.* Brittain, Bill. 1983. Har-Row. **Awards: (ALA); (JNM).** (P.133)

Glass, Marvin
--*Ghostly Fun.* McGovern, Ann. 1971. Scholastic Inc. (P.602)
--*Ghosts Who Went to School.* Spearing, Judith Mary Harlow (1922-). c.1966. Atheneum. (P.842)
--*The Museum House Ghosts.* 1st ed. Spearing, Judith Mary Harlow (1922-). 1960. Atheneum. (P.842)

Glass, Wilma Baker
--*Little Toy Dog, and Other Poems.* Steele, Rose Yarbrough (1898-). 1948. Story Book Press. (P.850)

Glasser, Judith
--*The Case of the Cackling Car: A Sam and Dave Mystery Story.* Singer, Marilyn (1948-). c.1985. Harper & Row. (P.827)
--*The Case of the Sabotaged School Play.* Singer, Marilyn (1948-). 1984. Har-Row. (P.827)
--*A Clue in Code.* Singer, Marilyn (1948-). 1985. HarpJ. (P.827)
--*Leroy Is Missing.* Singer, Marilyn (1948-). 1984. Har-Row. (P.827)
--*Mr.* Radagast Makes an Unexpected Journey. 1st ed. Nastick, Sharon. c.1981. Crowell. (P.676)
--*The Problem with Pulcifer.* 1st ed. Heide, Florence Parry (1919-). c.1982. Lippincott. (P.430)

--*Raggedy Ann and the Hoppy Toad.* Gruelle, John Barton (1880-1938). c.1940. McLoughlin Bros., Inc. (P.397)
--*Raggedy Ann and the Hoppy Toad.* Gruelle, John Barton (1880-1938). c.1943. McLoughlin Bros., Inc. (P.397)
--*Raggedy Ann and the Laughing Brook.* Gruelle, John Barton (1880-1938). c.1940. McLoughlin Bros., Inc. (P.397)
--*Raggedy Ann and the Laughing Brook.* Gruelle, John Barton (1880-1938). c.1943. McLoughlin Bros., Inc. (P.397)
--*Raggedy Ann and the Left Handed Safety Pin.* Gruelle, John Barton (1880-1938). c.1935. Whitman Publishing Company. (P.397)
--*Raggedy Ann Helps Grandpa Hoppergrass.* Gruelle, John Barton (1880-1938). c.1940. McLoughlin Bros., Inc. (P.397)
--*Raggedy Ann Helps Grandpa Hoppergrass.* Gruelle, John Barton (1880-1938). c.1943. McLoughlin Bros., Inc. (P.397)
--*Raggedy Ann in Cookie Land.* Gruelle, John Barton (1880-1938). N.D. Bobbs. (P.398)
--*Raggedy Ann in Cookie Land.* Gruelle, John Barton (1880-1938). N.D. Johnny Gruelle Co. (P.398)
--*Raggedy Ann in the Deep Deep Woods.* Gruelle, John Barton (1880-1938). 1930. Bobbs-Merrill. (P.398)
--*Raggedy Ann in the Deep, Deep Woods.* Gruelle, John Barton (1880-1938). c.1930. The P. F. Volland Company. (P.398)
--*Raggedy Ann in the Garden.* Gruelle, John Barton (1880-1938). c.1940. McLoughlin Bros., Inc. (P.398)
--*Raggedy Ann in the Garden.* Gruelle, John Barton (1880-1938). c.1943. McLoughlin Bros., Inc. (P.398)
--*Raggedy Ann in the Golden Meadow.* Gruelle, John Barton (1880-1938). c.1935. Whitman Publishing Company. (P.398)
--*Raggedy Ann in the Magic Book.* Gruelle, John Barton (1880-1938). 1939. Bobbs-Merill. (P.398)
--*Raggedy Ann in the Magic Book.* Gruelle, John Barton (1880-1938). c.1939. Johnny Gruelle Company. (P.398)
--*Raggedy Ann in the Snow White Castle.* Gruelle, John Barton (1880-1938). 1946. Bobbs-Merrill. (P.398)
--*Raggedy Ann in the Snow White Castle.* Gruelle, John Barton (1880-1938). 1946. The Johnny Gruelle Company. (P.398)
--*Raggedy Ann Stories.* Gruelle, John Barton (1880-1938). 1918. Bobbs-Merrill. (P.398)
--*Raggedy Ann Stories.* Gruelle, John Barton (1880-1938). 1947. Johnny Gruelle Co. (P.398)
--*Raggedy Ann Stories.* Gruelle, John Barton (1880-1938). c.1918. P. F. Volland Company. (P.398)
--*Raggedy Ann's Alphabet Book.* Gruelle, John Barton (1880-1938). 1925. The P. F. Volland Company. (P.398)
--*Raggedy Ann's Lucky Pennies.* Gruelle, John Barton (1880-1938). 1932. Bobbs-Merrill. (P.398)
--*Raggedy Ann's Lucky Pennies.* Gruelle, John Barton (1880-1938). c.1932. The P. F. Volland Company. (P.398)
--*Raggedy Ann's Magical Wishes.* Gruelle, John Barton (1880-1938). 1928. Bobbs-Merrill. (P.398)
--*Raggedy Ann's Magical Wishes.* Gruelle, John Barton (1880-1938). c.1928. P. F. Volland Company. (P.398)
--*Raggedy Ann's Wishing Pebble.* Gruelle, John Barton (1880-1938). N.D. Bobbs. (P.398)
--*Raggedy Ann's Wishing Pebble.* Gruelle, John Barton (1880-1938). N.D. P. F. Volland Co. (P.398)
--*Rhymes for Kindly Children.* Fairmont, Ethel. N.D. A. L. Burt Co. (P.316)
--*Rhymes for Kindly Children: Modern Mother Goose Jingles.* Fairmont, Ethel. c.1937. The Wise-Parslow Company. (P.316)
--*Rhymes for Kindly Children: Modern Mother Goose Jingles.* Snyder, Fairmont. c.1916. P. F. Volland & Co. (P.839)
--*Wooden Willie.* Gruelle, John Barton (1880-1938). c.1927. The P. F. Volland Company. (P.398)

Gruelle, John Barton (1880-1938) & Coussens, Penrhyn W (1873-)
--*Grimm's Fairy Tales.* New & Complete ed. Grimm, Jakob Ludwig Karl (1785-1863) & Grimm, Wilhelm Karl (1786-1859). Hunt, Margaret Raine (1831-1912), tr. from German. 1915. Cupples & Leon. (P.392)

Gruelle, John Barton (1880-1938) & Gooch, Thelma
--*The All About Story Book.* 1929. Cupples & Leon Co. (P.398)

Gruelle, John Barton (1880-1938) & Gruelle, Worth
--*Raggedy Granny Stories.* Salzberg, Doris Thorner. 1977. Bobbs-Merrill. (P.790)
--*Raggedy Ann and Andy and The Nice Fat Policeman.* Gruelle, John Barton (1880-1938). N.D. The Johnny Gruelle Co. (P.397)

Gruelle, Justin C.
--*A Mother Goose Parade.* Gruelle, Justin C. c.1929. The P. F. Vollani Co. (P.398)
--*Nannette.* Fox, Frances Margaret (1870-). c.1929. The P. F. Volland Company. (P.340)
--*Once Round the Sun.* Titchenell, Elsa Brita (1915-). 1950. Theosophical University Press. (P.892)
--*Once Round the Sun.* Titchenell, Elsa Brita (1915-). 1981. Theosophical University Press. (P.892)

Gruelle, Worth, jt. illus. see Gruelle, John Barton.

Gruen, Chuck
--*The Doll House Mystery.* Jacobs, Flora Gill (1918-). 1958. Coward-McCann. (P.486)
--*Little Chief Mischief.* Salter-Mathieson, Nigel Cedric Stephen (1932-). 1962. Astor-Honor. (P.790)

Gruger, F. R.
--*Real Boys.* Shute, Henry Augustus (1856-1943). 1905. G W Dillingham. (P.822)
--*Real Boys.* Being the Doings of Plupy, Beany, Pewt, Puzzy, Whack, Bug, Skinny, Chick, Pop, Pile, and Some of the Girls. Shute, Henry Augustus (1856-1943). 1905. M. A. Donohue & Company. (P.822)

Gruger, J. W.
--*Plucky Dick.* Ellis, Edward Sylvester (1840-1916). c.1907. The J. C. Winston Company. (P.303)
--*Tam, or, Holding the Fort.* Ellis, Edward Sylvester (1840-1916). c.1907. The J. C. Winston Company. (P.303)

Gruger, Johannes
--*Lia and the Red Carnations.* Steinmann-Brunner, Elsa (1901-). Winston, Richard (1917-1979) & Winston, Clara, trs. from Ger. 1960. Pantheon Books. (P.852)
--*The Sing Song Picture Book.* Gruger, Heribert (1900-). Gram-Swing, Betty, tr. 1931. J. B. Lippincott Company. (P.398)

Grumbine, E. Evalyn
--*Child Life Adventure and Mystery Stories: A Collection of Favorite Stories for Boys and Girls.* Child Life. c.1940. Rand McNally & Company. (P.191)

Grunwald, Ch.
--*Boys and Girls of Seventy-Seven.* Smith, Mary Prudence Wells, Mrs. (1840-1930). 1909. Little, Brown, and Company. (P.835)
--*Boys of the Border.* Smith, Mary Prudence Wells, Mrs. (1840-1930). 1907. Little, Brown, and Company. (P.835)
--*Pelham and His Friend Tim.* French, Allen (1870-1946). 1906. Little, Brown, and Company. (P.344)

Gruter, Arnold
--*One Unicorn: A Counting Book.* Tester, Sylvia Root (1939-). c.1977. Child's World. (P.883)

Gruttner, Roswitha
--*The Rabbit and the Turnip: A Chinese Fable.* Sadler, Richard, tr. from Ger. 1968. Doubleday. (P.398)

Gschwind, William
--*Plush.* Derman, Sarah Audrey (1915-). 1952. Follett. (P.260)

Guarcello, Giovanni
--*Lion for Niccolby Sacher.* Philipson, Susan S. 1963. Pantheon. (P.723)

Guard, Gretchen (1937-)
--*Dierdre: A Celtic Legend.* Guard, David (1934-). 1981, c.1977. Celestial Arts. (P.398)

Guarducci, Iris
--*The Three Candles of Little Veronica.* 2nd ed. Kyber, Manfred (1880-1933). Reinhardt, Rosamond, tr. from Ger. 1975. Waldorf Pr. (P.542)
--*The Three Candles of Little Veronica: The Story of a Child's Soul in This World & the Other.* Kyber, Manfred (1880-1933). Reinhardt, Rosamund, tr. from Ger. Reinhardt, Rosamond, intro. by. 1972. Waldorf Pr. (P.542)

Guarino, Joseph
--*Davy Crockett, Indian Fighter.* Hazen, Barbara Shook (1930-) & Disney, Walt, Productions. 1975. Pyramid Communications. (P.427)
--*Mustangs!.* Daly, Kathleen N. 1975. Pyramid Communications. (P.240)
--*The Sky's the Limit.* Crume, Vic. 1975. Pyramid Communications. (P.233)
--*The Whiz Kid & the Carnival Caper.* Crume, Vic. 1975. BJ Pub Group. (P.233)
--*The Whiz Kid and the Carnival Caper.* Crume, Vic. 1975. Pyramid Communications. (P.233)

Gubin, Mark
--*I'll Get Even.* Conaway, Judith (1948-). c.1977. Raintree Editions. (P.212)
--*New Wheels.* McLenighan, Valjean (1947-). c.1978. Childrens Press. (P.608)

Guerin, Penny
--*Rainy Day Rhymes: A Collection of Chants, Forecasts & Tales.* Palmer, Michele, ed. 1984. Rocking Horse. (P.703)

Guerin, Theodore
--*Let's Go.* Crawford, Phyllis (1899-). 1949. H. Holt. (P.229)

Guerra, Aldo, jt. illus. see Baraldi, Severino.

Guerriero, Salvatore, Jr.
--*The Adventures of Tom & Fiore.* Puma, Thomas. 1983. Vantage. (P.741)

Guertik, Helene
--*Animals I Like.* Louv's. c.1935. Artists and Writers Guild, Inc. (P.587)
--*The Every Day Book, for Youth.* Lida (1793-1860). Raymond, Louise (1907-), tr. 1834. Carter, Hendee and Co. (P.571)

Guertik, Helene, jt. illus. see Raymond, Louise.

Guggenheim, Hans (1924-)
--*Augustine Came to Kent.* Willard, Barbara Mary (1909-). 1963. Doubleday. (P.961)
--*The Elephant's Bathtub.* Carpenter, Frances Aretta (1890-1972). 1962. E. M. Hale and Company. (P.170)
--*The Elephant's Bathtub: Wonder Tales from the Far East.* 1st ed. Carpenter, Frances Aretta (1890-1972). 1962. Doubleday. (P.170)
--*What Then, Raman?.* Arora, Shirley Lease (1930-). 1960. Follett Pub. Co. (P.49)

Gugler, Janine
--*Zoup Soup.* Palmer, Michele. c.1978. Rocking Horse Press. (P.703)

Guida, Lisa Chauncy
--*Mattie's Money Tree.* German, Don (1931-). 1984. Westminster. (P.364)

Guidice, Rick
--*King of the Stars.* Kelley, Leo Patrick (1928-). c.1979. Fearon Pitman Publishers. (P.515)
--*Vacation in Space.* Kelley, Leo Patrick (1928-). 1980, c.1979. Fearon Pitman Publishers. (P.515)

Guie, Heister Dean
--*Coyote Stories.* Mourning Dove (1888-). Guie, Heister Dean, ed. McWhorter, L. V., notes by. 1933. The Caxton Printers, Ltd. (P.670)

Guignebault, Paul
--*The Story of Pierre Pons.* De Miomandre, Francis (1880-). Rich, Edwin Gile (1879-), tr. c.1929. E. P. Dutton & Co., Inc. (P.256)

Guilbeau, Honore Cooke (1907-)
--*The Birthday Tree.* Collier, Ethel (1903-). 1961. W. R. Scott. (P.209)
--*A Connecticut Yankee in King Arthur's Court.* Clemens, Samuel Langhorne (1835-1910). Twain, Mark, pseud. N.D. Heritage Press. (P.201)
--*Hundreds and Hundreds of Strawberries.* Collier, Ethel (1903-). 1969. Young Scott Books. (P.209)
--*Mrs.* Magpie's Invention. Guilbeau, Honore Cooke (1907-). 1971. Young Scott Books. (P.398)
--*Who Goes There in My Garden?.* Collier, Ethel (1903-). c.1963. Young Scott Books. (P.209)

Guild, Marion
--*Rudolph the Red-Nosed Reindeer & Rudolph Shines Again.* May, Robert Lewis (1905-1976). 1964. Follett. (P.633)
--*Rudolph, the Red-Nosed Reindeer, Shines Again.* May, Robert Lewis (1905-1976). c.1954. Maxton. (P.633)
--*Winking Willie.* May, Robert Lewis (1905-1976). c.1948. Maxton Publishers. (P.633)

Guillot, Rene (1900-1969)
--*The Wind of Chance.* Guillot, Rene (1900-1969). 1958. S.G. Phillips Inc. (P.399)

Guirma, Frederic
--*Tales of Mogho: African Stories from Upper Volta.* Guirma, Frederic. Skinner, E., pref. by. 1971. Macmillan. (P.399)

Guitar, Jeremy, jt. illus. see McQueen, Lucinda.

Guitierez, Domy
--*The House of the Seven Gables.* Hawthorne, Nathaniel (1804-1864) & Trinidad, Angel. Farr, Naunerle, ed. c.1977. Pendulum Press. (P.424)

Gullerud, Randi
--*The Children & the Flowers.* Denver, John, pseud. (1944-). Deutschendorf, Henry John Jr.. 1979. Green Tiger Pr. (P.258)

Gullikson, Karen
--*Dreams of Cloud Dancing.* 1st ed. Dravich, Jay. c.1982. Tari Book Publishers. (P.284)

Gulloch, June
--*Poems for Playtime.* Gilmore, Mary Cameron (1865-1962) & Pender, Lydia Podger (1907-). 1969. Hamlyn. (P.369)

Gully, Jim, photos by.
--*Friends Learn Ballet.* u.s. ed. Brian, Janeen. 1985. G. Stevens Pub. (P.130)
--*Grandpa Loves Us.* north american ed. Ridyard, David. c.1985. Gareth Stevens Pub. (P.764)
--*Sometimes I Have to.* north american ed. Ridyard, David. 1985. Gareth Stevens Pub. (P.764)

Guminski, Marsha
--*Mr.* Privacy. 1st ed. Trott, Susan (1937-). 1972. Little, Brown. (P.901)

Gumpertz, Robert (1925-)
--*Professor Twill's Travels.* Gumpertz, Robert (1925-). 1968. Houghton Mifflin. (P.399)

Gundelfinger, John
--*False Start.* Rabin, Gil. 1969. Harper & Row. (P.745)
--*Take My Waking Slow.* 1st ed. Norris, Gunilla Brodde (1939-). 1970. Atheneum. (P.685)
--*White Witch of Kynance.* Calhoun, Mary, pseud. (1926-). Wilkins, Mary Huiskamp. 1970. Har-Row. (P.162)
--*White Witch of Kynance.* Calhoun, Mary, pseud. (1926-). Wilkins, Mary Huiskamp. 1971. Har-Row. (P.162)

Gundersheimer, Karen
--*Beany.* Feder, Jane (1940-). c.1979. Pantheon Books. **Award: (ALA).** (P.320)
--*Nightdances.* Skofield, James. c.1981. Harper & Row. (P.828)
--*Some Things Go Together.* Zolotow, Charlotte Shapiro (1915-). 1983, c.1969. Crowell. (P.994)
--*A Special Trade.* Wittman, Sally Anne Christianson (1941-). c.1978. Harper & Row. **Award: (ALA).** (P.973)
--*The Tomorrow Book.* Schwerin, Doris Halpern (1922-). c.1984. Pantheon Books. (P.804)
--*The Witch Who Was Afraid of Witches.* Low, Alice (1926-). c.1978. Pantheon Books. (P.588)

Gunn, Archie
--*Deeds of Daring Done by Girls.* Moore, Hannah Woodbridge Hudson, Mrs. (1857-1927). 1906. Frederick A. Stokes Company. (P.661)

Gunn, Donald
--*Freddie.* Reilly, Frank A. N.D. Farrar & Rinehart. (P.756)

Gunn, Gwennet W.
--*Topsy-Turvey.* N.D. Frederick Warne & Co. (P.399)

Gunn, M. G.
--*The Stolen Aeroplane: Or, How Bud Wilson Made Good.* Lamar, Ashton, pseud. (1863-). Sayler, Harry Lincoln. N.D. Reilly & Britton Co. (P.544)

Gunn, W. L., jt. illus. see Riesenberg, S. H.

Gunnison, Nina Ann
--*Alex Makes New Friends.* Gunnison, Nina Ann. 1972. Strode Publishers. (P.399)

Gunston, William Tudor (1927-)
--*The Little Old Portrait.* Molesworth, Mary Louisa Stewart, Mrs. (1842-1921). 1884. E. & J. B. Young & Co. (P.654)

Gupta, M. L. Dutta
--*Krishna & Sudama.* Shivkumar. 1979. Auromere. (P.821)

Gurbutt, Barry
--*Richard's Wheel.* Lingstrom, Freda. 1963, c.1961. Roy Publishers. (P.574)

Gurney, J. Eric (1910-)
--*The Digging-Est Dog.* Perkins, Albert Rogers (1904-1975). 1967. Beginner Books. (P.717)
--*Eric Gurney's Pop-up Book of Dogs.* Gurney, T. Eric (1910-). 1973. Random House. (P.400)
--*Hand, Hand, Fingers, Thumb.* Perkins, Albert Rogers (1904-1975). 1969. Random House. (P.718)
--*Someone Is Eating the Sun.* Sonneborn, Ruth Cantor (1899-1974). 1974. Random House. (P.841)
--*The Strange Dreams of Rover Jones.* Armour, Richard Willard (1906-). 1973. McGraw-Hill. (P.48)

Gurney, John
--*The Temptation of Wilfred Malachey.* Buckley, William Frank, Jr. (1925-). 1985. Ariel Books : Workman. (P.147)

Gurney, Nancy Bankart
--*Pink Furniture: A Tale for Lovely Children with Noble Natures.* Coppard, Alfred Edgar (1878-1951). c.1930. J. Cape & H. Smith. (P.219)

Gurvin, Abe
--*Star Stories.* Foley, Anna Bernice Williams (1902-). 1970. Dutton. (P.333)
--*Star Stories.* Foley, Anna Bernice Williams (1902-). 1970. McCall Publishing Company. (P.333)

Gusman, Annie
--*Blanquette.* Farber, Norma (1909-1984). 1980, c.1979. Addison-Wesley. (P.316)
--*Bonzo Beaver.* Crowley, Arthur McBlair (1945-). 1980. Houghton Mifflin. (P.233)
--*The Boogey Man.* Crowley, Arthur McBlair (1945-). 1978. Houghton Mifflin. (P.233)
--*Jokes to Read in the Dark.* Corbett, Scott (1913-). c.1980. Dutton. (P.219)
--*Jokes to Tell to Your Worst Enemy.* Corbett, Scott (1913-). 1984. Dutton. (P.219)
--*Look at Me.* Ricks, Charlotte Hall & Gusman, Annie. 1979. Houghton Mifflin. (P.763)
--*Rat Stew.* Silvis, Craig. 1979. Houghton Mifflin. (P.824)
--*Small Cloud.* Dewey, Ariane (1937-). 1984. Dutton. (P.261)
--*The Ugly Book.* Crowley, Arthur McBlair (1945-). 1982. Houghton Mifflin. (P.233)
--*Up the Down Elevator.* Farber, Norma (1909-1984). 1979. Addison-Wesley. (P.316)
--*The Wagon Man.* Crowley, Arthur McBlair (1945-). 1981. Houghton Mifflin. (P.233)

--*The Desert Home: Or, the Adventures of a Lost Family in the Wilderness.* Reid, Thomas Mayne (1818-1883). 1864. Ticknor and Fields. (P.755)
--*The Desert Home: Or, the Adventures of a Lost Family in the Wilderness.* New ed. Reid, Thomas Mayne (1818-1883). Stoddard, Richard Henry (1825-1903), memoir by. 1885. T. R. Knox & Co. (P.755)
--*Gay's Fables.* Owen, O. F., ed. N.D. R. Worthington. (P.699)
--*Lane's Arabian Nights: The Thousand and One Nights Commonly Called the Arabian Nights' Entertainment, 3 Vols.* Lane, Edward William (1801-1876), tr. from Arabic. N.D. Estes & Lauriat's. (P.418)
--*Tales from the Thousand and One Nights.* Dawood, Nessim Joseph (1927-), tr. 1973. Penguin Books. (P.418)
--*The Young Voyageurs: Or, The Boy Hunters in the North.* Reid, Thomas Mayne (1818-1883). 1857. Ticknor and Fields. (P.756)
--*The Young Voyageurs: Or, The Boy Hunters in the North.* New ed. Reid, Thomas Mayne (1818-1883). Stoddard, Richard Henry (1825-1903), memoir by. 1885. T. R. Knox & Co. (P.756)
--*The Young Yagers: Or, A Narrative of Hunting Adventures in Southern Africa.* New ed. Reid, Thomas Mayne (1818-1883). Stoddard, Richard Henry (1825-1903), memoir by. 1885. T. R. Knox & Co. (P.756)

Harwood, John
--*Aladdin and His Wonderful Lamp: From the Arabian Nights' Entertainment.* Aladdin. 1947. Penguin Books. (P.16)
--*The Old Woman and Her Pig.* Old Woman and Her Pig. 1944. Penguin Books, Limited. (P.692)
--*Puffin Rhymes.* 1944. Penguin Books, Limited. (P.418)

Hasenfus, Richard C.
--*Marie Visits the Zoo.* 1st ed. Hasenfus, Nathaniel John (1900-). 1953. Sagadahoc Pub. Co. (P.419)

Haskett, Edythe Rance (1915-)
--*Some Gold, a Little Ivory: Country Tales from Ghana and the Ivory Coast.* Haskett, Edythe Rance (1915-), ed. 1971. John Day Co. (P.419)

Haskett, Merelaine
--*Grandpa Haskett Presents: Original New Christmas Stories for the Young & Young-at-Heart.* Haskett, William P. Haskett, M. R., ed. Haskett, M. R., intro. by. 1982. Haskett Spec. (P.419)

Haslam, John
--*Follow This Line.* O'Leary, Michael. 1967. Abelard-Schuman. (P.693)

Haslewood, Constance
--*Little Folks' Fairy tales.* N.D. Frederick Warne & Co. (P.419)
--*Old Mother Goose's Nursery Songs.* N.D. Frederick Warne & Co. (P.419)
--*Songs from Nursery Land.* N.D. Frederick Warne & Co. (P.419)

Hass, E. A.
--*Incognito Mosquito, Private Insective.* Hass, E. A. 1982. Lothrop. (P.419)

Hassall, Joan (1906-)
--*All Day Long: An Anthology of Poetry for Children.* Whitlock, Pamela, ed. 1954. Oxford University Press. (P.954)
--*Oxford Nursery Rhyme Book.* Opie, Iona Archibald (1923-) & Opie, Peter (1918-1982), eds. 1955. Oxford U Pr. (P.695)
--*Quiet As Moss.* Young, Andrew (1885-1971). 1962. Dufour Editions. (P.988)

Hassall, John, jt. illus. see Buckland, Arthur H.
Hassall, John, jt. illus. see Aldin, Cecil Charles Windsor.

Hassall, John (1868-1948)
--*Friday and Saturday: The Adventures of Two Little Pickles.* Byron, May Clarissa Gillington (0000-1936). N.D. George H Doran. (P.161)
--*Little Robin Hood.* Byron, May Clarissa Gillington (0000-1936). N.D. George H Doran. (P.161)
--*Mother Goose's Nursery Rhymes.* Mother Goose. Jerold, Walter Copeland, ed. N.D. Dodge Publishing Company. (P.669)

Hassall, John (1868-1948) & Aldin, Cecil Charles Windsor (1870-1935)
--*Two Well-Worn Shoes Stories.* N.D. E. P. Dutton and Co. (P.419)

Hassall, John (1868-1948) & Butler-Stoney, T.
--*The Princess and the Dragon.* Hamer, Sam Hield (1869-). N.D. Dana Estes & Co. (P.407)

Hassam, F. Childe (1859-1935)
--*Bye O Baby Ballads.* Pratt, Charles Stuart (1854-). c.1887. D. Lothrop & Co. (P.737)
--*Dilly and the Captain, 1 of 3 vols.* Lothrop, Harriet Mulford Stone, Mrs. (1844-1924). Sidney, Margaret, pseud. c.1887. D. Lothrop Company. (P.586)
--*Doll Rosy's days.* Bates, Clara Doty, Mrs. (1838-1895), ed. c.1884. D. Lothrop & Co. (P.80)
--*A New Departure for Girls.* Lothrop, Harriet Mulford Stone, Mrs. (1844-1924). Sidney, Margaret, pseud. c.1886. D. Lothrop and Company. (P.586)
--*Who Told It to Me.* Lothrop, Harriet Mulford Stone, Mrs. Sidney, Margaret, pseud. N.D. Lothrop Publishing Co. (P.586)

Hasselriis, Else
--*The Nutcracker of Nuremberg.* Dumas, Alexandre (1802-1870). Gingras, Grace, ed. 1930. R. M. McBride & Company. (P.288)
--*Riddle of the Sands.* Childers, Erskine. 1970. Dutton. (P.191)
--*Shen of the Sea: A Book for Children.* Chrisman, Arthur Bowie (1889-1953). 1926. Dutton. **Award: (JNM).** (P.193)
--*Shen of the Sea: Chinese Stories for Children.* Chrisman, Arthur Bowie (1889-1953). 1968, c.1953. Dutton. (P.193)
--*The Wind That Wouldn't Blow: Stories of the Merry Middle Kingdom for Children, and Myself.* Chrisman, Arthur Bowie (1889-1953). 1927. Dutton. (P.193)

Hasselriis, Malthe M. (1888-1970)
--*Favorite Poems.* Field, Eugene (1850-1895). c.1940. Grosset & Dunlap. (P.324)
--*Tales of a Chinese Grandmother.* Carpenter, Frances Aretta (1890-1972). 1973. C. E. Tuttle Co. (P.170)
--*Tales of a Chinese Grandmother.* Carpenter, Frances Aretta (1890-1972). 1937. Doubleday, Doran & Company, Inc. (P.170)
--*Tales of a Korean Grandmother.* Carpenter, Frances Aretta (1890-1972). 1973. C. E. Tuttle Co. (P.170)

Haste, Laurence B.
--*Yonder the Golden Gate: A Story of Old San Francisco.* Darby, Ada Claire (1883-). 1939. Frederick A. Stokes Company. (P.242)

Hastings, David, jt. illus. see Kushe, Kathy.

Hastings, Howard Livingston (1887-)
--*The Aircraft Boys And the Phantom Airplane.* Hoover, Latharo. c.1932. Henry Altemus Company. (P.459)
--*Animal Life in the Wilderness.* Hastings, Howard Livingston (1887-). c.1936. Cupples & Leon Company. (P.419)
--*Around the World in Ten Days.* Fraser, Chelsea Curtis (1876-). c.1922. Thomas Y. Crowell Company. (P.342)
--*Ben Oakman, Stroke.* Patten, Gilbert (1866-1945). Standish, Burt L., pseud. c.1925. Barse & Hopkins. (P.709)
--*Billie Bradley at Three-Towers Hall: Or, Leading a Needed Rebellion.* Wheeler, Janet D., pseud. Stratemeyer Syndicate. 1920. George Sully & Co. (P.949)
--*Bomba the Jungle Boy Among the Slaves: Or, Daring Adventures in the Valley of Skulls.* Rockwood, Roy, pseud. Stratemeyer Syndicate. c.1929. Cupples & Leon Company. (P.772)
--*Bomba the Jungle Boy Among the Slaves.* Rockwood, Roy, pseud. Stratemeyer Syndicate. N.D. McLoughlin Brothers - Clover Books. (P.772)
--*Bomba the Jungle Boy and the Cannibals: Or, Winning Against Native Dangers.* Rockwood, Roy, pseud. Stratemeyer Syndicate. c.1932. Cupples & Leon Company. (P.772)
--*Bomba the Jungle Boy and the Hostile Chieftain: Or, A Hazardous Trek to the Sea.* Rockwood, Roy, pseud. Stratemeyer Syndicate. c.1934. Cupples & Leon Company. (P.772)
--*Bomba the Jungle Boy and the Lost Explorers: Or, A Wonderful Revelation.* Rockwood, Roy, pseud. Stratemeyer Syndicate. c.1930. Cupples & Leon Company. (P.772)
--*Bomba the Jungle Boy and the Lost Explorers.* Rockwood, Roy, pseud. Stratemeyer Syndicate. 1953. Grosset & Dunlap. (P.772)
--*Bomba the Jungle Boy and the Painted Hunters: Or, A Long Search Rewarded.* Rockwood, Roy, pseud. Stratemeyer Syndicate. c.1932. Cupples & Leon Company. (P.772)
--*Bomba the Jungle Boy and the River Demons: Or, Outwitting the Savage Medicine Man.* Rockwood, Roy, pseud. Stratemeyer Syndicate. c.1933. Cupples & Leon Company. (P.772)
--*Bomba the Jungle Boy in a Strange Land: Or, Facing the Unknown.* Rockwood, Roy, pseud. Stratemeyer Syndicate. c.1931. Cupples & Leon Company. (P.772)
--*Bomba the Jungle Boy in the Land of Burning Lava: Or, Outwitting Superstitious Natives.* Rockwood, Roy, pseud. Stratemeyer Syndicate. c.1936. Cupples & Leon Company. (P.772)
--*Bomba the Jungle Boy in the Perilous Kingdom: Or, Braving Strange Hazards.* Rockwood, Roy, pseud. Stratemeyer Syndicate. c.1937. Cupples & Leon Company. (P.772)
--*Bomba the Jungle Boy in the Steaming Grotto: Or, Victorious Through Flame and Fury.* Rockwood, Roy, pseud. Stratemeyer Syndicate. c.1938. Cupples & Leon Company. (P.772)
--*Bomba the Jungle Boy in the Swamp of Death: Or, The Sacred Alligators of Abarago.* Rockwood, Roy, pseud. Stratemeyer Syndicate. c.1929. Cupples & Leon Company. (P.773)
--*Bomba the Jungle Boy on the Underground River: Or, The Cave of Bottomless Pits.* Rockwood, Roy, pseud. Stratemeyer Syndicate. c.1930. Cupples & Leon Company. (P.773)
--*Bomba the Jungle Boy Trapped by the Cyclone: Or, Shipwrecked on the Swirling Seas.* Rockwood, Roy, pseud. Stratemeyer Syndicate. c.1935. Cupples & Leon Company. (P.773)
--*The Bronze Turkey.* Willis, Elizabeth Powers, Mrs. c.1928. Thomas Y. Crowell Company. (P.965)
--*Bushy-Boy and the Fox Hounds.* Campbell, Ruth, Mrs. c.1931. Sears Publishing Company, Inc. (P.165)
--*California: A Romantic Story for Young People.* McSpadden, Joseph Walker (1874-). 1926. J. H. Sears & Co. (P.611)
--*The Carcajou: A Mystery of the Northwest.* Snell, LeRoy W. c.1931. Cupples & Leon Company. (P.838)
--*The Comeback: The Story of the Heart of a Day.* Mills, Joe. c.1926. J. H. Sears & Company, Inc. (P.649)
--*The Corner House Girls Facing the World: Why They Had To, How They Did It, and What Came of It.* Hill, Grace Brooks, pseud. Stratemeyer Syndicate. 1926. Barse & Hopkins. (P.443)
--*The Grateful Fairy.* Sappington, Thomas Lambert (1870-). c.1922. Barse & Hopkins. (P.793)
--*Hit by Pitcher.* Sherman, Harold Morrow (1898-). c.1928. Grosset & Dunlap. (P.819)
--*Hot-Dog Partners.* Heyliger, William (1884-1955). c.1931. Grosset & Dunlap. (P.440)
--*Jack Sutherland: A Tale of Bloody Marsh.* Oertel, Theodore Eugene (1864-). 1974, c.1926. Reprint Co. (P.690)
--*Jack Sutherland: A Tale of Bloody Marsh.* Oertel, Theodore Eugene (1864-). c.1926. Thomas Y. Crowell Company. (P.690)
--*Kipling's Stories for Boys.* Kipling, Joseph Rudyard (1865-1936). c.1931. Cupples & Leon Company. (P.528)
--*Lego Lamb, Southpaw.* Patten, Gilbert (1866-1945). Standish, Burt L., pseud. c.1923. Barse & Hopkins. (P.710)
--*Mark Gilmore, Scout of the Air.* Fitzhugh, Percy Keese (1876-). c.1930. Grosset & Dunlap. (P.329)
--*Mark Gilmore, Speed Flyer.* Fitzhugh, Percy Keese (1876-). c.1931. Grosset & Dunlap. (P.329)
--*Mark Gilmore's Lucky Landing.* Fitzhugh, Percy Keese (1876-). c.1931. Grosset & Dunlap. (P.329)
--*Randy Starr Above Stormy Seas: Or, The Sky Flyers on a Perilous Journey.* Martin, Eugene, pseud. Stratemeyer Syndicate. 1931. Henry Altemus Co. (P.624)
--*Randy Starr After an Air Prize: Or, The Sky Flyers in a Dash Down the States.* Martin, Eugene, pseud. Stratemeyer Syndicate. 1931. Henry Altemus Co. (P.624)
--*Randy Starr Leading the Air Circus: Or, The Sky Flyers in a Daring Stunt.* Martin, Eugene, pseud. Stratemeyer Syndicate. 1932. Henry Altemus Co. (P.624)
--*Simon Kenton, the Scout: A Tale of Frontier Life During the Revolution.* Corby, Jane Irenita (1899-). c.1925. Thomas Y. Crowell Company. (P.219)
--*Skinny McCord.* Fitzhugh, Percy Keese (1876-). c.1928. Grosset & Dunlap. (P.330)
--*Sons of Old Eli.* Patten, Gilbert (1866-1945). Standish, Burt L., pseud. c.1923. Barse & Hopkins. (P.710)
--*Spiffy Henshaw.* Fitzhugh, Percy Keese (1876-). c.1929. Grosset & Dunlap. (P.330)
--*The Story of Terrible Terry.* Fitzhugh, Percy Keese (1876-). c.1930. Grosset & Dunlap. (P.330)
--*Sunny Boy and His Games.* White, Ramy Allison, pseud. Stratemeyer Syndicate. c.1923. Barse & Hopkins. (P.952)
--*Sunny Boy and His Games.* White, Ramy Allison, pseud. Stratemeyer Syndicate. N.D. Barse & Co. (P.952)
--*Sunny Boy and His Games.* White, Ramy Allison, pseud. Stratemeyer Syndicate. N.D. Grosset & Dunlap. (P.952)
--*Sunny Boy and His Playmates.* White, Ramy Allison, pseud. Stratemeyer Syndicate. 1922. Barse & Hopkins. (P.952)
--*Sunny Boy and His Playmates.* White, Ramy Allison, pseud. Stratemeyer Syndicate. N.D. Barse & Co. (P.952)
--*Sunny Boy and His Playmates.* White, Ramy Allison, pseud. Stratemeyer Syndicate. N.D. Grosset & Dunlap. (P.952)
--*Sunny Boy in School and Out.* White, Ramy Allison, pseud. Stratemeyer Syndicate. 1921. Barse & Hopkins. (P.952)
--*Sunny Boy In School and Out.* White, Ramy Allison, pseud. Stratemeyer Syndicate. N.D. Barse & Co. (P.952)
--*Sunny Boy In School and Out.* White, Ramy Allison, pseud. Stratemeyer Syndicate. N.D. Grosset & Dunlap. (P.952)
--*Sunny Boy in the Far West.* White, Ramy Allison, pseud. Stratemeyer Syndicate. c.1924. Barse & Hopkins. (P.952)
--*Sunny Boy in the Far West.* White, Ramy Allison, pseud. Stratemeyer Syndicate. N.D. Barse & Co. (P.952)
--*Sunny Boy In the Far West.* White, Ramy Allison, pseud. Stratemeyer Syndicate. N.D. Grosset & Dunlap. (P.952)
--*Sunny Boy on the Ocean.* White, Ramy Allison, pseud. Stratemeyer Syndicate. c.1925. Barse & Hopkins. (P.952)
--*Sunny Boy on the Ocean.* White, Ramy Allison, pseud. Stratemeyer Syndicate. N.D. Barse & Co. (P.952)
--*Sunny Boy On the Ocean.* White, Ramy Allison, pseud. Stratemeyer Syndicate. N.D. Grosset & Dunlap. (P.952)
--*Sunny Boy with the Circus.* White, Ramy Allison, pseud. Stratemeyer Syndicate. c.1926. Barse & Hopkins. (P.952)
--*Sunny Boy with the Circus.* White, Ramy Allison, pseud. Stratemeyer Syndicate. N.D. Barse & Co. (P.953)
--*Sunny Boy With the Circus.* White, Ramy Allison, pseud. Stratemeyer Syndicate. N.D. Grosset & Dunlap. (P.953)
--*Tom Martin the Breaker Boy.* Phelps, R. P. c.1926. Cupples & Leon Company. (P.723)
--*Tom Slade at Bear Mountain.* Fitzhugh, Percy Keese (1876-). c.1925. Grosset & Dunlap. (P.330)
--*Tom Slade at Shadow Isle.* Fitzhugh, Percy Keese (1876-). c.1928. Grosset & Dunlap. (P.330)
--*Tom Slade in the Haunted Cavern.* Fitzhugh, Percy Keese (1876-). c.1929. Grosset & Dunlap. (P.330)
--*Tom Slade on Overlook Mountain.* Fitzhugh, Percy Keese (1876-). c.1923. Grosset & Dunlap. (P.330)
--*Top Horse of Crescent Ranch.* Hastings, Howard Livingston (1887-). 1942. Cupples & Leon Company. (P.419)
--*Watch, Shepherd of the Range.* Hastings, Howard Livingston (1887-). c.1939. Cupples & Leon Company. (P.419)
--*Westy Martin in the Land of the Purple Sage.* Fitzhugh, Percy Keese (1876-). c.1929. Grosset & Dunlap. (P.330)
--*Westy Martin on the Mississippi.* Fitzhugh, Percy Keese (1876-). c.1930. Grosset & Dunlap. (P.330)
--*Westy Martin on the Old Indian Trail.* Fitzhugh, Percy Keese (1876-). c.1928. Grosset & Dunlap. (P.330)
--*The Whipper-Snapper.* Parker, Charles E. 1926. Frederick A. Stokes Company. (P.706)
--*Wigwag Weigand.* Fitzhugh, Percy Keese (1876-). c.1929. Grosset & Dunlap. (P.330)
--*The Witness Tree.* Wire, Harold Channing. c.1930. Thomas Y. Crowell Company. (P.971)
--*Yank Brown, Miler.* Stone, David. c.1923. Barse & Hopkins. (P.861)
--*Yank Brown, Pitcher.* Stone, David. 1924. Barse & Hopkins. (P.861)

Hastings, Ian (1912-)
--*Dragons & Stuff.* Morgan, Lenore H. (1908-1976). 1970. Oddo. (P.663)
--*Rufus and Christopher and the Box of Laughter.* Hastings, Ian (1912-). 1972. Oddo Pub. (P.419)
--*Rufus and Christopher and the Magic Bubble.* Hastings, Eileen. c.1974. Oddo Pub. (P.419)
--*Rufus and Christopher in the Land of Lies.* Hastings, Ian (1912-). 1972. Oddo Pub. (P.419)

Hatch, W. M.
--*The Further Adventures of Puss in Boots.* Gray, Nicholas Stuart (1922-1981). 1971. Faber & Faber. (P.383)

Hatherell, William
--*The Next-Door House.* Molesworth, Mary Louisa Stewart, Mrs. (1842-1921). 1892. Cassell Publishing Company. (P.654)
--*The Prince and the Pauper.* Clemens, Samuel Langhorne (1835-1910). Twain, Mark, pseud. 1909. Harper. (P.201)
--*Sentimental Tommy.* N.D. Charles Scribner's Sons. (P.420)

Hatheway, Katherine Butler
--*Mr.* Muffet's Cat and Her Trip to Paris. Hathaway, Katharine Butler. 1934. Harper & Brothers. (P.420)

Hatsuyama, Shigeru
--*Swan Lake.* Kishida, Eriko (1929-). Herring, Ann K., tr. 1970. Japan Pubns. (P.529)

--*Dance, Dance, Amy-Chan!.* Hawkinson, Lucy Ozone (1924-1971). 1964. A. Whitman. (P.422)
--*Days I Like.* Hawkinson, Lucy Ozone (1924-1971). 1965. A. Whitman. (P.422)
--*Just One More Block.* Mayers, Patrick. 1970. A. Whitman. (P.634)
--*Left, Right, Left, Right!.* Stanek, Muriel Novella (1915-1971). 1969. A. Whitman. (P.848)
--*The New River Train.* Hawkinson, Lucy Ozone (1924-1971). 1970. A.Whitman. (P.422)
--*Pockets.* Hawkinson, Lucy Ozone (1924-1971). c.1955. Whitman Pub. Co. (P.422)
--*Surprise!.* Hawkinson, Lucy Ozone (1924-1971). c.1956. Rand McNally. (P.422)
--*Tall Tina.* Stanek, Muriel Novella (1915-1971). 1970. A. Whitman. (P.848)

Hawkinson, Lucy Ozone (1924-1971) & Hawkinson, John Samuel (1912-)
--*Good Morning, Teacher.* Barr, Jene (1900-). 1957. A. Whitman. (P.75)
--*I Want to Be a Fisherman.* Greene, Carla (1916-). c.1957. Childrens Press. (P.386)
--*Up the Big Mountain.* Koch, Dorothy Clarke (1924-). 1964. Holiday House. (P.534)

Hawley, Carl Tracey
--*The Age of Fable.* Bulfinch, Thomas (1796-1867) & Lee, Edgar. c.1905. The Saalfield Publishing Company. (P.148)

Hawthorne, Paul
--*Billy Whiskers Adventures.* rev. ed. Montgomery, Frances Trego. 1920. Saalfield Pub. CO. (P.657)
--*Billy Whiskers Adventures.* Montgomery, Frances Trego. 1922. Saalfield. (P.657)
--*Billy Whiskers Frolics.* Montgomery, Frances Trego. 1923. Saalfield. (P.657)
--*Billy Whiskers in the Movies.* Montgomery, Frances Trego. c.1921. The Saalfield Publishing Company. (P.658)

Haxton, Elaine
--*Parrot in a Flame Tree.* Haxton, Elaine. 1971. St Martin. (P.424)
--*A Parrot in a Flame Tree: Adapted from a Medieval Christmas Carol.* Haxton, Elaine. 1968. F. W. Cheshire. (P.424)

Hay, Dean
--*Tisi and the Pageant.* Dutton, Geoffrey Piers Henry (1922-). 1968. Rigby. (P.292)

Hay, Dean, photos by.
--*Now I Can Count.* Hay, Dean. 1968. Lion Press. (P.424)

Hay, Stuart
--*Eileen's Adventures in Wordland: The Life Story of Our Word Friends.* Rev ed. Macdonald, Zillah Katherine (1885-). 1920. Frederick A. Stokes Company. (P.600)

Hayashi, Yoshio
--*Japanese Children's Stories.* 2nd ed. Sakade, Florence, ed. 1959. C. E. Tuttle Co. (P.790)
--*Kintaro's Adventures & Other Stories.* Sakade, Florence. 1958. C E Tuttle. (P.790)

Hayden, Chuck
--*Orange Oliver, the Kitten Who Wore Glasses.* Lasson, Robert (1922-). Hayden, Chuck, designed by. c.1957. D. McKay Co. (P.553)

Hayden, Emily, photos by.
--*My Animals and Me.* Agle, Nan Hayden (1905-). 1970. Seabury. (P.14)

Haydon, Harold (1909-)
--*The Village That Learned to Read.* Tarshis, Elizabeth Kent, Mrs. (1913-). 1941. Houghton Mifflin Company. (P.878)

Hayes, Geoffrey (1947-)
--*The Alligator & His Uncle Tooth.* Hayes, Geoffrey (1947-). 1977. Har-Row. (P.425)
--*Bear by Himself.* Hayes, Geoffrey (1947-). c.1976. Harper & Row. (P.425)
--*Beyond the Troll Bridge: A Fairy Tale.* Hayes, Geoffrey (1947-). 1979. Harper & Row. (P.425)
--*Christmas in Puttyville.* Hayes, Geoffrey (1947-). c.1985. Random House. (P.425)
--*Elroy & the Witch's Child.* Hayes, Geoffrey (1947-). 1982. Har-Row. (P.425)
--*Hocus & Pocus at the Circus.* Manushkin, Frances (1942-). 1983. Har-Row. (P.618)
--*Moon Dragon.* Manushkin, Frances (1942-). c.1982. Macmillan. (P.618)
--*Muffie Mouse and the Busy Birthday.* Nixon, Joan Lowery (1927-). c.1978. Seabury Press. (P.683)
--*The Mystery of the Pirate Ghost: An Otto & Uncle Tooth Adventure.* Hayes, Geoffrey (1947-). 1985. Random. (P.425)
--*Patrick and Ted.* Hayes, Geoffrey (1947-). 1984. Four Winds Press. (P.425)
--*Patrick Buys a Coat.* Hayes, Geoffrey (1947-). c.1985. Knopf : Distributed by Random House. (P.425)
--*Patrick Comes to Puttyville, and Other Stories.* Hayes, Geoffrey (1947-). c.1978. Harper & Row. (P.425)
--*Patrick Eats His Dinner.* Hayes, Geoffrey (1947-). c.1985. Knopf : Distributed by Random House. (P.425)
--*Patrick Goes to Bed.* Hayes, Geoffrey (1947-). c.1985. Knopf. (P.425)
--*Patrick Takes a Bath.* Hayes, Geoffrey (1947-). c.1985. Knopf : Distributed by Random Press. (P.425)
--*The Secret Inside.* Hayes, Geoffrey (1947-). c.1980. Harper & Row. (P.425)
--*When the Wind Blew.* Brown, Margaret Wise (1910-1952). 1977, c.1937. Harper & Row. **Award: (NYT).** (P.141)

Hayes, Hobart Vance
--*The Adventure.* Hayes, Hobart Vance. 1965. Westminster Press. (P.425)

Hayes, Katharine W.
--*Dicket: A Story of Friendships.* Abbott, Jane Ludlow Drake, Mrs. (1881-). 1933. J. B. Lippincott Company. (P.3)
--*Pirates and Pigeons: Famous Stories of Boyhood Years.* Sechrist, Elizabeth Hough, Mrs. (1903-), ed. c.1933. J. B. Lippincott. (P.807)

Hayes, Stephen
--*Fast Draw Freddie.* Hamsa, Bobbie (1944-) & Hillerich, Robert L. (1927-). c.1984. Childrens Press. (P.409)
--*Pancakes, Crackers, and Pizza: A Book About Shapes.* Eberts, Marjorie & Gisler, Margaret. c.1984. Childrens Press. (P.295)

Hayes, William Dimitt (1913-)
--*How the True Facts Started in Simpsonville, and Other Tales of the West.* 1st ed. Hayes, William Dimitt (1913-). 1972. Atheneum. (P.426)
--*Hunter's Hill.* Wallace, May Nickerson (1902-). 1955. D. McKay Co. (P.927)
--*The Important Pockets of Paul.* Moore, Lilian. 1954. D. McKay Co. (P.661)
--*Let's Dance a Story.* Mace, Katherine Keeler (1921-). 1955. Abelard-Schuman. (P.600)
--*The Monkey Tree.* Hayes, William Dimitt (1913-). c.1963. Putnam. (P.426)
--*Only the Strong.* 1st ed. Du Soe, Robert C. 1955. Longmans, Green. (P.292)
--*Penguins Are Penguins.* Longstreth, Joseph (1920-). 1955. Abelard-Schuman. (P.583)
--*Project, Genius.* 1st ed. Hayes, William Dimitt (1913-). 1962. Atheneum. (P.426)
--*Project Scoop.* 1st ed. Hayes, William Dimitt (1913-). 1966. Atheneum. (P.426)
--*Project, Scoop.* Hayes, William Dimitt (1913-). 1972. Atheneum. (P.426)
--*Remarkable History of Tony Beaver.* Cober, Mary E. 1968. McKay. (P.205)
--*Sebastian and The Dragon.* Kumin, Maxine Winokur (1925-). 1960. E. M. Hale & Co. (P.541)
--*Sebastian and the Dragon.* Kumin, Maxine Winokur (1925-). 1960. Putnam. (P.541)
--*Tiger Tizzy.* Longstreth, Joseph (1920-). Hayes, William Dimitt, designed by. 1954. Abelard Press. (P.583)
--*Wonder Tales of Horses and Heroes.* Carpenter, Frances Aretta (1890-1972). 1952. Doubleday. (P.170)
--*Young-Scientist Takes a Ride: Guide to Outdoor Observations from a Car Window.* Barr, George (1907-). 1960. Whittlesay House. (P.75)

Hayes, William Dimitt (1913-), photos by.
--*The Cub Scout Book of Cowboys and Indians.* Andreas, Evelyn, retold by. 1954. Wonder Books. (P.40)

Haygood, Preston
--*Nebraska and His Granny.* Love, Rose Leary. 1936. Tuskegee Institute Press. (P.587)

Haynes, Avril
--*Norah to the Rescue.* Swindells, Robert Edward (1939-). N.D. Putnam Pub Group. (P.875)

Haynes, Bob
--*Mister Mergatroid.* Ward, Nanda Weedon (1932-). 1960. Hastings House. (P.931)
--*Mr. Meadowlark.* Ward, Nanda Weedon (1932-). N.D. Hasting House Publishers Inc. (P.931)
--*Wellington and the Witch.* Ward, Nanda Weedon (1932-). 1959. Hastings House. (P.931)

Haynes, Lee
--*Little Indian.* Cory, David Magie (1872-1966). c.1922. The Saalfield Publishing Company. (P.221)
--*Star Boy.* Cory, David Magie (1872-1966). c.1922. The Saalfield Publishing Company. (P.222)
--*White Feather.* Cory, David Magie (1872-1966). c.1922. The Saalfield Publishing Company. (P.222)

Hays, Ethel
--*The Cat That Would Be King.* Woods, Ruth Maurine. 1952. Saalfield Pub. Co. (P.977)
--*The Goody-Good Book of Stories.* Swindler, Leona Martha Olsen (1913-). Paulsen, Martha, pseud. c.1943. The Saalfield Publishing Company. (P.875)
--*My Favorite Story Book.* c.1942. The Saalfield Publishing Company. (P.426)
--*Poco and the Parrot.* Chinn, Laurene Chambers (1902-1978). 1947. O. Saalfield Pub. Co. (P.191)
--*Raggedy Ann and the Slippery Slide.* Gruelle, John Barton (1880-1938). 1947. Saalfield Pub. Co. (P.397)
--*Raggedy Ann at the End of the Rainbow.* Gruelle, John Barton (1880-1938). 1947. Saalfield Pub. Co. (P.397)
--*Raggedy Ann's Adventure.* Gruelle, John Barton (1880-1938). 1947. Saalfield Pub. Co. (P.398)
--*Raggedy Ann's Mystery.* Gruelle, John Barton (1880-1938). 1947. Saalfield Pub. Co. (P.398)

Hays, Ethel, jt. illus. see Lohman, Fred D.

Hays, Ethel & Turner, Dolly
--*Famous Romances.* Shankland, Frank North. c.1943. R. Speller. (P.814)

Hayton, Hilary & McCallum, Graham (1943-)
--*Mr. Egbert Nosh.* Groves, Paul (1930-). 1972, c.1970. Childrens Press. (P.397)

Hayward, Walter
--*A Picnic for Bunnykins.* Warrener. 1984. Viking Kestrel. (P.934)
--*Picnic for Bunnykins.* Warrener. 1985. Viking. (P.934)
--*Two Bunnykins Out to Tea.* Warrener. 1984. Viking Kestrel. (P.934)

Haywood, Carolyn (1898-)
--*Annie Pat & Eddie.* Haywood, Carolyn (1898-). 1960. Morrow. (P.427)
--*Away Went the Balloons.* Haywood, Carolyn (1898-). 1973. Morrow. (P.427)
--*B Is for Betsy.* Haywood, Carolyn (1898-). c.1939. Harcourt, Brace and Company. (P.427)
--*Back to School with Betsy.* Haywood, Carolyn (1898-). 1943. Harcourt, Brace and Company. (P.427)
--*Betsy and Billy.* Haywood, Carolyn (1898-). c.1941. Harcourt, Brace and Company. (P.427)
--*Betsy and Billy.* 1st ed. Haywood, Carolyn (1898-). 1979, c.1941. Harcourt Brace Jovanovich. (P.427)
--*Betsy and Mr. Kilpatrick.* Haywood, Carolyn (1898-). 1967. W. Morrow. (P.427)
--*Betsy and the Boys.* Haywood, Carolyn (1898-). 1945. Harcourt, Brace and Company. (P.427)
--*Betsy and the Boys.* Haywood, Carolyn (1898-). 1978, c.1973. Harcourt Brace Jovanovich. (P.427)
--*Betsy & the Circus.* Haywood, Carolyn (1898-). 1954. Morrow. (P.427)
--*Betsy's Busy Summer.* Haywood, Carolyn (1898-). 1956. Morrow. (P.427)
--*Betsy's Little Star.* Haywood, Carolyn (1898-). 1950. Morrow. (P.427)
--*Betsy's Winterhouse.* Haywood, Carolyn (1898-). 1958. Morrow. (P.427)
--*C" Is for Cupcake.* Haywood, Carolyn (1898-). 1974. Morrow. (P.427)
--*Dot for Short.* Friedman, Frieda (1905-). 1947. W. Morrow and Company. (P.345)
--*Eddie & Gardenia.* Haywood, Carolyn (1898-). 1951. Morrow. (P.427)
--*Eddie and His Big Deals.* Haywood, Carolyn (1898-). 1955. Morrow. (P.427)
--*Eddie and Louella.* Haywood, Carolyn (1898-). 1959. Morrow. (P.427)
--*Eddie and the Fire Engine.* Haywood, Carolyn (1898-). 1949. W. Morrow. (P.427)
--*Eddie Makes Music.* Haywood, Carolyn (1898-). 1957. Morrow. (P.427)
--*Eddie the Dog Holder.* Haywood, Carolyn (1898-). 1966. Morrow. (P.427)
--*Eddie's Green Thumb.* Haywood, Carolyn (1898-). 1964. W. Morrow. (P.427)
--*Eddie's Happenings.* Haywood, Carolyn (1898-). 1971. Morrow. (P.427)
--*Eddie's Pay Dirt.* Haywood, Carolyn (1898-). 1953. Morrow. (P.427)
--*Eddie's Valuable Property.* Haywood, Carolyn (1898-). 1975. Morrow. (P.427)
--*Ever-Ready Eddie.* Haywood, Carolyn (1898-). 1968. W. Morrow. (P.427)
--*Here Comes the Bus!.* Haywood, Carolyn (1898-). 1963. Morrow. (P.427)
--*Here's a Penny.* Haywood, Carolyn (1898-). 1944. Harcourt, Brace and Company. (P.427)
--*Little Eddie.* Haywood, Carolyn (1898-). 1947. W. Morrow. (P.427)
--*Merry Christmas from Betsy.* Haywood, Carolyn (1898-). 1970. W. Morrow. (P.427)
--*The Mixed-up Twins.* Haywood, Carolyn (1898-). 1952. Morrow. (P.427)
--*Penny and Peter.* Haywood, Carolyn (1898-). 1946. Harcourt, Brace and Company. (P.427)
--*Penny Goes to Camp.* Haywood, Carolyn (1898-). 1948. W. Morrow. (P.427)
--*The Pine Barrens Mystery.* Seaman, Augusta Huiell, Mrs. (1879-1950). 1937. Doubleday, Doran & Company, Incorporated. (P.806)
--*Primrose Day.* Haywood, Carolyn (1898-). 1942. Harcourt, Brace and Company. (P.427)
--*Robert Rows the River.* Haywood, Carolyn (1898-). 1965. Morrow. (P.427)
--*Snowbound With Besty.* Haywood, Carolyn (1898-). 1962. William Morrow and Company. (P.427)
--*A Sundae with Judy.* Friedman, Frieda (1905-). 1949. W. Morrow. (P.345)
--*Taffy & Melissa Molasess.* 1st ed. Haywood, Carolyn (1898-). 1969. Morrow. (P.427)
--*Two and Two Are Four.* Haywood, Carolyn (1898-). c.1940. Harcourt, Brace and Company. (P.427)

Haywood, Carolyn (1898-) & Smith, Jessie Willcox (1863-1935)
--*Bobs, King of the Fortunate Isle.* Franchot, Annie Wood. c.1928. E. P. Dutton & Co., Inc. (P.341)

Haywood, Helen
--*The Mouse That Ran.* Haywood, Helen. N.D. Frederick Warne & Co. (P.427)

Hazard, Eleanor Lanahan
--*How to Travel with Grownups.* Bridgman, Elizabeth P (1921-). c.1980. Crowell. (P.130)
--*Monkey.* N.D. Green Tiger Pr. (P.427)
--*Somebody Spilled the Sky.* 1st ed. Krauss, Ruth Ida (1911-). c.1979. Greenwillow Books. (P.539)

Hazelden, John
--*Little Stories of Our Country.* Hazelden, John. N.D. The Reilly & Britton Co. (P.427)

Hazelrigg, Paul, jt. illus. see Merryweather, Jack.

Hazelton, Isaac Brewster
--*The Admiral's Aid: A Story of Life in the New Navy.* Clark, Henry Howard (1845-). 1902. Lothrop,Lee & Shepard. (P.197)
--*Barclay Back.* Barbour, Ralph Henry (1870-1944). 1942. D. Appleton-Century Company, Incorporated. (P.70)
--*Blue Jeans.* Beim, Lorraine Levey (1909-1951) & Beim, Jerrold (1910-1957). 1941. Harcourt, Brace and Company. (P.89)
--*Chula: Son of the Mound Builders.* Bunce, William Harvey (1903-). 1942. E. P. Dutton and Company, Inc. (P.149)
--*Dave Porter in the South Seas: Or, The Strange Cruise of the Stormy Petrel.* Stratemeyer, Edward L. (1862-1930). 1906. Lothrop, Lee & Shepard. (P.865)
--*Defending the Bank.* Van Zile, Edward Sims (1863-1931). 1903. Lothrop Publishing Company. (P.915)
--*Fox Island.* Pinkerton, Kathrene Sutherland Gedney, Mrs. (1887-1967). 1942. Harcourt, Brace and Company. (P.726)
--*Hunting the Sky Spies: Or, Testing the Invisible Plane.* Dixon, Franklin W., pseud. Stratemeyer Syndicate. c.1941. Grosset & Dunlap. (P.273)
--*Jemima, Daughter of Daniel Boone.* Sutton, Margaret Beebe, Mrs. (1903-). 1942. C. Scribner's Sons. (P.872)
--*Long Bridge Boys: A Story of 1861.* Stoddard, William Osborn (1835-1925). 1904. Lothrop Publishing Company. (P.860)
--*The Mutineers.* Williams, Eustace Leroy. 1903. Lothrop Lee & Shepard Co. (P.962)
--*Nimble-Legs: A Story for Boys.* Capauna, Luigi (1839-1917). Cooper, Frederic Taber (1834-1897), tr. 1927. Longmans, Green and Co. (P.166)
--*The Pursuit Patrol: Or, Chasing the Platinum Pirates.* Dixon, Franklin W., pseud. Stratemeyer Syndicate. 1943. Grosset & Dunlap. (P.274)
--*War Belts of Pontiac.* Bunce, William Harvey (1903-). 1943. E. P. Dutton and Company. (P.149)

Hazen, Nancy
--*Grownups Cry Too: Los Adultos Tambien Lloran.* 2d ed. Hazen, Nancy. Cotera, Martha P., tr. c.1978. Lollipop Power. (P.427)

Hazleton & Willoughby
--*Fat Albert & the Cosby Kids: Getting It Together.* French, Laura (1949-). 1975. Western Pub. (P.344)

Hazlewood, Charlotte
--*The Discontented Clam: And Other Stories.* Hazlewood, Francis Tomlinson (1839-1908). 1911. Sherman, French & Company. (P.428)

Headland, Isaac Taylor (1859-1942)
--*The Chinese Boy and Girl.* Headland, Isaac Taylor (1859-1942), ed. Headland, Isaac Taylor (1859-1942), tr. 1901. Fleming H. Revell Company. (P.428)
--*Chinese Mother Goose Rhymes.* Headland, Isaac Taylor (1859-1942), tr. c.1900. Fleming H. Revell Company. (P.428)

Headley, Adriane Moulton
--*The Mystery of the Pink Waterfall.* Moulton, R. Dwayne. 1980. Pandora's Treasures. (P.670)

Healey, Katherine G.
--*Chico: The Story of a Homing Pigeon.* Blanchard, Lucy Mansfield Blanchard, Mrs. (1870-). c.1922. Houghton Mifflin Company. (P.107)
--*A Little-Singing Bird.* Blanchard, Lucy Mansfield Blanchard, Mrs. (1870-). c.1923. Houghton Mifflin Company. (P.107)

Healy, Daty
--*Cat Tales from Many Lands.* Healy, Daty, selected by. 1932. C. Scribner's Sons. (P.428)
--*Funny Friends.* Healy, Daty. 1932. Charles Scribner's Sons. (P.428)

Hearlin, C.
--*The Flying Squad.* Bishop, William Avery (1894-) & Stuart-Wortley, Rothesay (1892-1926). 1938. The Sun Dial Press, Inc. (P.104)

Hearn, Diane Dawson
--*The Doozer Disaster.* Muntean, Michaela. 1984. HR&W. (P.672)

--*Robert and the Rainbow and Other Stories.* Jones, Mary Alice (1898-). c.1926. Cokesbury Press. (P.500)
Henderson, Marion, jt. illus. see Henderson, Doris.
Henderson, Richard (1924-)
--*First Sail for Skipper.* Henderson, Richard (1924-). c.1960. Reilly & Lee. (P.433)
Henderson, William P
--*Adams Dream, and Two Other Miracle Plays for Children.* Corbin, Alice. N.D. Charles Scribner's Sons. (P.219)
--*Andersen's Best Fairy Tales.* Andersen, Hans Christian (1805-1875). Henderson, Alice Corbin, tr. 1911. Rand, McNally & Co. (P.34)
Hendrick, Joseph (1934-)
--*The Wonderful Wings of Harold Harrabescu.* McHargue, Georgess (1941-). 1971. Delacorte Press. (P.603)
Hendricks, Donald (1932-)
--*Day of the Earthlings.* Bunting, Anne Evelyn (1928-). c.1978. Creative Education. (P.150)
--*The Followers.* Bunting, Anne Evelyn (1928-). c.1978. Creative Education. (P.150)
--*The Island of One.* Bunting, Anne Evelyn (1928-). c.1978. Creative Education. (P.150)
--*The Mask.* Bunting, Anne Evelyn (1928-). c.1978. Creative Education. (P.150)
--*The Mirror Planet.* Bunting, Anne Evelyn (1928-). c.1978. Creative Education. (P.150)
--*My Dad's a Smokejumper.* Hill, Mary L. 1978. Childrens. (P.444)
--*The Robot People.* Bunting, Anne Evelyn (1928-). c.1978. Creative Education. (P.150)
--*The Space People.* Bunting, Anne Evelyn (1928-). c.1978. Creative Education. (P.150)
--*The Undersea People.* Bunting, Anne Evelyn (1928-). c.1978. Creative Education. (P.150)
Hendrickson, David (1896-)
--*At the End of Nowhere.* Means, Florence Crannell, Mrs. (1891-1980) & Riggs, Frances. 1940. Houghton Mifflin Company. (P.638)
--*Off to Philadelphia!.* Allee, Marjorie Hill, Mrs. (1890-1945). 1936. Houghton Mifflin Company. (P.28)
--*A Plantation Christmas.* Peterkin, Julia Mood (1880-1961). N.D. Ayer Co. (P.720)
--*Runaway Linda.* Allee, Marjorie Hill, Mrs. (1890-1945). 1939. Houghton Mifflin. (P.28)
--*The Story of Andrew Jackson.* Meadowcroft, Enid La Monte, Mrs. (1898-1966). 1953. Grosset & Dunlap. (P.637)
--*The Story of Christopher Columbus.* Baker, Nina Brown, Mrs. (1888-1957). 1952. Grosset & Dunlap. (P.64)
--*Swords of Steel: The Story of a Gettysburg Boy.* Singmaster, Elsie (1879-1958). 1933. Houghton Mifflin Company. **Award: (JNM).** (P.827)
Hendrickson, June
--*Bantie and Her Chicks.* Graeber, Jean Boreman (1909-). 1959. Melmont Publishers. (P.380)
Henkes, Kevin
--*Clean Enough.* Henkes, Kevin. c.1982. Greenwillow Books. (P.433)
--*Margaret & Taylor.* 1st ed. Henkes, Kevin. c.1983. Greenwillow. (P.433)
--*Return to Sender.* Henkes, Kevin. 1984. Greenwillow. (P.433)
Henn, Shirley
--*Adventures of Hooty Owl and His Friends.* Henn, Shirley. 1955. Exposition Press. (P.433)
Henneberger, Robert G. (1921-)
--*Andy Finds a Way.* Stuart, Hilton Jesse (1907-). 1961. Whittlesey House. (P.869)
--*Barn Cat.* Coates, Belle (1896-). 1955. Scribner. (P.203)
--*Baseball Pals.* Christopher, Matthew F. (1917-). 1956. Little. (P.194)
--*Basketball Clown.* Jackson, Caary Paul (1902-). Jackson, O. B., pseud. 1956. Whittlesey House. (P.484)
--*The Beatinest Boy.* Stuart, Hilton Jesse (1907-). 1953. Whittlesey House. (P.869)
--*Chaplain in Gray, Abram Ryan: Poet-Priest of the Confederacy.* Heagney, Harold Jerome (1890-). 1958. Kenedy. (P.428)
--*Children of the Great Smoky Mountains.* 1st ed. Justus, May (1898-). 1952. Dutton. (P.503)
--*Cub Scout at Last!.* Felsen, Henry Gregor (1916-). 1952. Scribner. (P.321)
--*Cub Scout at Last.* Felsen, Henry Gregor (1916-). 1952. Trade Publications. (P.321)
--*Dogs in the Family.* Musgrave, Florence (1902-). 1952. Houghton Mifflin. (P.674)
--*Freshman Forward.* Jackson, Caary Paul (1902-). Jackson, O. B., pseud. 1959. Whittlesey House. (P.484)
--*Hamlet and Brownswiggle.* Reynolds, Barbara Leonard. 1954. Scribner. (P.759)
--*High School Backstop.* Jackson, Caary Paul (1902-). Jackson, O. B., pseud. 1963. Whittlesey House. (P.484)
--*The Highly Trained Dogs of Professor Petit.* Brink, Carol Ryrie, Mrs. (1895-1981). 1953. Macmillan. (P.132)
--*His Indian Brother.* Wilson, Hazel Hutchins, Mrs. (1898-). 1955. Abingdon Press. (P.966)
--*His Indian Brother.* Wilson, Hazel Hutchins, Mrs. (1898-). 1970, c.1955. Houghton Mifflin. (P.966)
--*Julie's Secret Sloth.* Jackson, Jacqueline (1928-). 1953. Little, Brown. (P.485)
--*Jumping Johnny and Skedaddle.* Justus, May (1898-). 1958. Row, Peterson. (P.503)
--*A Lion in the Woods.* 1st ed. Dolbier, Maurice Wyman (1912-). c.1955. Little, Brown. (P.278)
--*Little Dog Sniff and the Twins.* 1st ed. Smith, Geraldine Foster. 1955. Dutton. (P.833)
--*The Lucky Baseball Bat.* 1st ed. Christopher, Matthew F (1917-). 1954. Little, Brown. (P.194)
--*Mickey the Monkey.* De Leeuw, Adele Louise (1899-). 1952. Little, Brown. (P.254)
--*Molly and the Golden Wedding.* 1st ed. Sheehy, Emma Dickson. 1956. Holt. (P.817)
--*Pelican Prill.* 1st ed. Forsyth, Gloria. 1956. Dutton. (P.336)
--*Penny's Worth of Character.* Stuart, Hilton Jesse (1907-). 1964. McGraw. (P.869)
--*A Penny's Worth of Character.* Stuart, Hilton Jesse (1907-). 1954. Whittlesey House. (P.869)
--*Prairie Star.* Morgan, Nina Hermanna. 1955. Viking Press. (P.663)
--*Puck Grabber.* Jackson, Caary Paul (1902-). 1957. Whittlesey House. (P.484)
--*Red Mule.* Stuart, Hilton Jesse (1907-). 1955. Whittlesey House. (P.869)
--*A Ride with Huey, the Engineer.* Stuart, Hilton Jesse (1907-). 1966. McGraw. (P.869)
--*The Rightful Owner.* Stuart, Hilton Jesse (1907-). 1960. Whittlesey House. (P.869)
Short Guard. Jackson, Caary Paul (1902-) Jackson, O. B., pseud. 1961. McGraw. (P.484)
--*The Short guard.* Jackson, Caary Paul (1902-) & Jackson, O. B. 1961. Whittlesey House. (P.484)
--*Star Kicker.* Jackson, Caary Paul (1902-). Jackson, O. B., pseud. 1955. Whittlesey House. (P.484)
--*Stowaway to the Mushroom Planet.* 1st ed. Cameron, Eleanor (1912-). 1956. Little, Brown. (P.163)
--*The Surprise of Their Lives.* 1st ed. Wilson, Hazel Hutchins, Mrs. (1898-). 1957. Little, Brown. (P.966)
--*Torten's Christmas Secret.* Dolbier, Maurice Wyman (1912-). 1951. Little. (P.278)
--*White Sails to China.* Bulla, Clyde Robert (1914-). 1955. Crowell. (P.149)
--*The Wonderful Flight to the Mushroom Planet.* 1st ed. Cameron, Eleanor (1912-). 1954. Little, Brown. (P.163)
--*The Year of the Mintie May.* Sanders, Margaret Webb. 1954. Putnam. (P.792)
--*The Young Islanders.* Ogilvie, Elisabeth May (1917-). 1960. Whittlesey House. (P.691)
Hennessy, W. J.
--*An Enchanted Garden: Fairy Stories.* Molesworth, Mary Louisa Stewart, Mrs. (1842-1921). 1892. Cassell. (P.654)
Henning, Albin
--*Alder Gulch Gold.* Schultz, James Willard (1859-1947). 1931. Houghton Mifflin Company. (P.802)
--*Sun-Up on the Range.* Litten, Frederic Nelson (1885-1951). 1930. D. Appleton and Company. (P.576)
Henning, Amy
--*King Beetle-Tamer, and Other Lighthearted Wonder Tales.* Wyatt, Isabel. c.1979. Dawne-Leigh Publications. (P.982)
Henning, Frederick
--*Sudden Voyage.* 1st ed. Amrein, Vera R. 1954. Harcourt, Brace. (P.33)
Henning, Paul, photos by.
--*First Things: A Picture Book in Natural Color Photos.* Adams, George A. 1947. Platt & Munk Co. (P.5)
Henriksen, Harold
--*Almost a Champion.* Deegan, Paul Joseph (1937-). 1975. Amecus Street; Distributed by Childrens Press, Chicago. (P.250)
--*Close but Not Quite.* Deegan, Paul Joseph (1937-). 1975. Amecus Street; Distributed by Childrens Press, Chicago. (P.250)
--*Dan Moves up.* Deegan, Paul Joseph (1937-). 1975. Amecus Street; Distributed by Childrens Press, Chicago. (P.250)
--*Important Decision.* Deegan, Paul Joseph (1937-). 1975. Amecus Street; Distributed by Childrens Press, Chicago. (P.250)
Henriksen, Harold, jt. illus. see Nelson, John.
Henriquez, Elsa
--*The Magic Orange Tree, and Other Haitian Folk Tales.* Wolkstein, Diane (1942-). c.1978. Knopf : Distributed by Random House. **Award: (ALA).** (P.974)
--*The Magic Orange Tree, and Other Haitian Folktales.* Wolkstein, Diane (1942-). 1980, c.1978. Schocken Books. (P.974)
Henry, Darin
--*Tawache & the Legend of Sacred Mountain.* James, William. Tittle, Sharon, ed. 1984. James Pub Inc. (P.489)
Henry, J.
--*The Village Pest: A Story of David.* Rollins, Montgomery (1867-1918). 1917. Lothrop, Lee & Shepard Co. (P.775)
Henry, Marie H.
--*Bunnies All Day Long.* Ehrlich, Amy (1942-). 1985. Dial Books for Young Readers. (P.299)
--*Bunnies and Their Grandma.* Ehrlich, Amy (1942-). 1985. Dial Books for Young Readers. (P.299)
Henry, Steve
--*There Was an Old Lady.* Pettigrew, Shirley. c.1974. Coward, McCann & Geoghegan. (P.722)
Henry, William
--*Peter Pelican-Pedro Pelicano.* Roa, Annia. 1974. Island Pr. (P.766)
Henschen, Helga
--*Pigge Lunke.* Knutsson, Gosta Lars August (1908-). Berzins, Helga, tr. 1961. Bobbs-Merrill. (P.534)
Henson Associates
--*Muppet Madness.* Henson Associates. 1980. Random. (P.434)
Henson, Tex
--*On Halloween.* Ward, Elaine M. 1982. Argus Comm. (P.930)
--*Sean the Bunny: An Easter Story.* Ward, Elaine M. 1982. Argus Comm. (P.930)
--*The Thanksgiving Feast.* Ward, Elaine M. 1982. Argus Comm. (P.930)
Henstra, Friso (1928-)
--*Forgetful Fred.* Williams, Jay (1914-1978). 1974. Parents' Magazine Press. (P.963)
--*The Little Spotted Fish.* Yolen, Jane Hyatt (1939-). 1975. Seabury Press. (P.986)
--*Mighty Mizzling Mouse.* 1st ed. Henstra, Friso (1928-). c.1983. Lippincott. (P.434)
--*Mighty Mizzling Mouse & the Red Cabbage House.* Henstra, Friso (1928-). 1984. Little. (P.434)
--*Petronella.* Williams, Jay (1914-1978). 1973. Parents' Magazine Press. (P.963)
--*The Practical Princess.* Williams, Jay (1914-1978). 1969. Parents' Magazine Press. (P.963)
--*The Round Sultan and the Straight Answer.* Walker, Barbara Kerlin (1921-). 1970. Parents' Magazine Press. (P.926)
--*School for Sillies.* Williams, Jay (1914-1978). 1969. Parents' Magazine Press. (P.963)
--*Seven at One Blow.* Williams, Jay (1914-1978), retold by. 1972. Parents' Magazine Press. (P.963)
--*The Silver Whistle.* Williams, Jay (1914-1978). 1971. Parents' Magazine Press. (P.963)
--*Space Cats.* Kroll, Steven (1941-). c.1979. Holiday House. (P.540)
--*Stupid Marco.* Williams, Jay (1914-1978). 1970. Parents' Magazine Press. (P.963)
--*The Terrible Tales of Happy Days School.* 1st ed. Duncan, Lois Steinmetz (1934-). c.1983. Little, Brown. (P.289)
--*Wait and See.* Henstra, Friso (1928-). c.1978. Addison-Wesley Pub. Co. (P.434)
--*The Wicked Tricks of Tyl Uilenspiegel.* Williams, Jay (1914-1978), retold by. Eulenspiegel, Till. c.1978. Four Winds Press. (P.311)
--*The Youngest Captain.* Williams, Jay (1914-1978). 1972. Parents' Magazine Press. (P.963)
Hentschel, Harriet L. (1922-)
--*The Flip Flap Book.* Lowe, Edith May Kovar (1905-). Windsor, Mary, pseud. c.1950. Garden City Pub. Co. (P.588)
--*Near the Friendly Meadows.* 1950. John Martin's House. (P.434)
Herb Halpern Productions
--*The Day God Made It Rain: I Kings 17-18 for Children.* Kolbrek, Loyal (1914-). c.1976. Concordia Publishing House. (P.535)
Herbert, Helen
--*Cats.* Graham-Cameron, Mike. 1978. Merrimack Pub Cir. (P.380)
--*Cycling on Dizzy Duncan.* Siddons, Suzy. 1980. Merrimack Pub Cir. (P.823)
Herbert, Robert Gaston
--*The Adventures of Chicchi.* Lombroso-Carrara, Paola. Curtis, Mary Ellen Wood & Aspinwall, Marguerite, trs. 1927. G. P. Putnam's Sons. (P.581)
--*Air Service Boys Flying for France: Or, The Young Heroes of the Lafayette Escadrille.* Beach, Charles Amory, pseud. Stratemeyer Syndicate. 1918. George Sully & Co. (P.84)
--*Air Service Boys Flying for France: Or, The Young Heroes of the Lafayette Escadrille.* Beach, Charles Amory, pseud. Stratemeyer Syndicate. N.D. World Syndicate Publishing Co. (P.84)
--*Air Service Boys Over the Enemy's Lines: Or, The German Spy's Secret.* Beach, Charles Amory, pseud. Stratemeyer Syndicate. 1918. George Sully & Co. (P.84)
--*Air Service Boys Over the Enemy's Lines: Or, The German Spy's Secret.* Beach, Charles Amory, pseud. Stratemeyer Syndicate. N.D. World Syndicate Publishing Co. (P.84)
--*Air Service Boys Over the Rhine: Or, Fighting Above the Clouds.* Beach, Charles Amory, pseud. Stratemeyer Syndicate. 1918. George Sully & Co. (P.84)
--*Air Service Boys Over the Rhine: Or, Fighting Above the Clouds.* Beach, Charles Amory, pseud. Stratemeyer Syndicate. N.D. World Syndicate Publishing Co. (P.84)
--*Army Boys in France: Or, From Training Camp to Trenches.* Randall, Homer. c.1918. G. Sully & Company. (P.748)
--*Army Boys in the French Trenches: Or, Hand to Hand Fighting with the Enemy.* Randall, Homer. c.1918. G. Sully & Company. (P.748)
--*Four Little Blossoms and their Winter Fun.* Hawley, Mabel C., pseud. Stratemeyer Syndicate. N.D. Cupples & Leon Co. (P.422)
--*Four Little Blossoms and Their Winter Fun.* Hawley, Mabel C., pseud. Stratemeyer Syndicate. 1920. George Sully & Co. (P.422)
--*Four Little Blossoms at Brookside Farm.* Hawley, Mabel C., pseud. Stratemeyer Syndicate. N.D. Cupples & Leon Co. (P.422)
--*Four Little Blossoms at Brookside Farm.* Hawley, Mabel C., pseud. Stratemeyer Syndicate. 1920. George Sully & Co. (P.422)
--*Four Little Blossoms at Brookside Farm.* Hawley, Mabel C., pseud. Stratemeyer Syndicate. 1938. Saalfield Publishing Co. (P.422)
--*Four Little Blossoms at Oak Hill School.* Hawley, Mabel C., pseud. Stratemeyer Syndicate. N.D. Cupples & Leon Co. (P.422)
--*Four Little Blossoms at Oak Hill School.* Hawley, Mabel C., pseud. Stratemeyer Syndicate. 1920. George Sully & Co. (P.422)
--*Four Little Blossoms at Oak Hill School.* Hawley, Mabel C., pseud. Stratemeyer Syndicate. 1938. Saalfield Publishing Co. (P.422)
--*Jerry on Safari: Seven Thousand Mile Journey from Cairo to the Cape.* Von Hoffman, Carl (1889-). c.1936. J. B. Lippincott Company. (P.921)
--*The Little Gingerbread Man.* Putnam, George Haven. 1910. G. P. Putnam's Sons. (P.742)
--*Navy Boys After the Submarines: Or, Protecting the Giant Convoy.* Davidson, Halsey. c.1918. G. Sully & Company. (P.244)
--*Navy Boys Chasing a Sea Raider: Or, Landing a Million Dollar Prize.* Davidson, Halsey. 1918. G. Sully & Company. (P.244)
Herbert, Tom
--*I Like School.* Kingsley, Emily Perl (1940-). 1981. Western Pub. (P.526)
--*I Like School: Featuring Jim Henson's Sesame Street Muppets.* Muntean, Michaela & Children's Television Workshop. Henson, James Maury (1936-), created by. c.1980. Western Pub. Co. (P.672)
Herbst, Valerie
--*Great Day in Ghana: Kwasi Goes to Town.* Kaye, Geraldine Hughesdon (1925-). 1962. Abelard-Schuman. (P.510)
Herbster, Mary L.
--*Look What I Found.* Case, Marshal Taylor (1941-). Case, Marshal T., photos by. 1971. Chatham Pr. (P.176)
Herd, Constance
--*Remi.* Malot, Hector Henri (1830-1907). 1970. Hawthorn. (P.615)
Herford, Oliver, jt. illus. see Little, Edward R.
Herford, Oliver (1863-1935)
--*Aaron in the Wildwoods.* Harris, Joel Chandler (1848-1908). 1897. Houghton Mifflin. (P.415)
--*The Adventures of Luisa in Mexico.* James, Winifred Lewellin. c.1930. E. P. Dutton & Co., Inc. (P.489)
--*Alice's Adventures in Wonderland.* Dodgson, Charles Lutwidge (1832-1898). Carroll, Lewis, pseud. Long, William Joseph (1867-), ed. c.1917. Ginn and Company. (P.277)
--*The Astonishing Tale of a Pen and Ink Puppet.* Herford, Oliver (1863-1935). N.D. Charles Scribner's Sons. (P.437)
--*The Bashful Earthquake and Other Fables and Verses.* Herford, Oliver (1863-1935). 1898. Charles Scribner's Sons. (P.437)
--*Behind Time.* Lathrop, George Parsons (1851-1898). 1886. Cassell & Company, Limited. (P.554)
--*Behind Time.* Lathrop, George Parsons (1851-1898). 1895. The Cassell Publishing Co. (P.554)
--*The Bird-Nest Boarding House.* Reed, Verbena. c.1922. E. P. Dutton & Company. (P.753)
--*The Fairy Godmother-in-Law.* Herford, Oliver (1863-1935). 1905. Charles Scribner's Sons. (P.437)
--*The Herford Aesop: Fifty Fables in Verse.* Aesopus. Herford, Oliver (1863-1935), ed. c.1921. Ginn and Company. (P.14)
--*A Kitten's Garden of Verses.* Herford, Oliver (1863-1935). 1911. Charles Scribner's Sons. (P.437)

--*A Little Book of Bores.* Herford, Oliver (1863-1935). 1906. Charles Scribner's Sons. (P.437)
--*Little Mr.* Thimblefinger and His Queer County: What the Children Saw and Heard There. Harris, Joel Chandler (1848-1908). 1894. Houghton, Mifflin and Company. (P.415)
--*Little Mr.* Thimblefinger & His Queer Country: What the Children Saw & Heard There, 1 of 4 vols. Harris, Joel Chandler (1848-1908). 1900. Houghton Mifflin & Co. (P.415)
--*More Animals.* Herford, Oliver (1863-1935). 1901. Charles Scribner's Sons. (P.437)
--*The Mouse-Colored Road.* Thompson, Vance (1863-1925). 1913. D. Appleton and Company. (P.888)
--*Mr.* Rabbit at Home: A Sequel to Little Mr. Thimblefinger and His Queer Country. Harris, Joel Chandler (1848-1908). 1895. Houghton, Mifflin and Company. (P.415)
--*The Mythological Zoo.* Herford, Oliver (1863-1935). 1912. Charles Scribner's Sons. (P.437)
--*Overheard in a Garden.* Herford, Oliver (1863-1935). 1900. Charles Scribner's Sons. (P.437)
--*The Rubaiyat of a Persian Kitten.* Herford, Oliver (1863-1935). 1904. Charles Scribner's Sons. (P.437)
--*The Story of Aaron.* Harris, Joel Chandler (1848-1908). N.D. Grosset & Dunlap. (P.415)
--*The Story of Aaron(So Named), the Son of Ben Ali: Told By His Friends and Aquaintances.* Harris, Joel Chandler (1848-1908). 1896. Houghton Mifflin. (P.415)
--*Timothy's Quest.* Wiggin, Kate Douglas Smith (1856-1923). 1890. Houghton Mifflin. (P.958)
--*Two In a Zoo.* Dunham, Curtis. 1904. Bobbs-Merrill Co. (P.289)

Herge, pseud., see Remi, Georges.

Herge, pseud. (1907-1983)
--*Cigars of the Pharaoh: The Adventures of Tintin.* Remi, Georges. Herge, pseud. (1907-1983). Remi, Georges. 1975. Little Brown and Company. (P.437)
--*Destination Moon.* Remi, Georges. Herge, pseud. (1907-1983). Remi, Georges. N.D. French & Eur. (P.437)
--*Destination Moon.* Remi, Georges. Herge, pseud. (1907-1983). Remi, Georges. 1960. Golden Press. (P.437)
--*Destination Moon.* Remi, Georges. Herge, pseud. (1907-1983). Remi, Georges. Lonsdale-Cooper, Leslie & Turner, Michael, trs. c.1976. Little, Brown. (P.437)
--*Flight Seven Fourteen: The Adventure of Tintin.* Remi, Georges. Herge, pseud. (1907-1983). Remi, Georges. 1975. Little Brown and Company. (P.437)
--*Land of the Black Gold: The Adventure of Tintin.* Remi, Georges. Herge, pseud. (1907-1983). Remi, Georges. 1974. Little Brown and Company. (P.437)
--*Prisoners of the Sun: The Adventure Tintin.* Remi, Georges. Herge, pseud. (1907-1983). Remi, Georges. 1975. Little Brown and Company. (P.438)
--*The Seven Crystal Balls: The Adventures of Tintin.* Remi, Georges. Herge, pseud. (1907-1983). Remi, Georges. 1975. Little Brown and Company. (P.438)

Herget, H. M.
--*Tupak of the Incas.* Means, Philip Ainsworth (1892-). Dalgliesh, Alice (1893-), ed. 1942. C. Scribner's Sons. (P.638)

Herkimer, Lawrence Russell (1925-)
--*Go!* Fight! Win!. Phillips, Betty L. Shepherd, Francis, photos by. 1981. Delacorte. (P.723)

Herman, Pat
--*The Touchlings.* Fox, Michael Wilson (1937-). c.1981. Acropolis Books. (P.340)

Herman, R. C
--*Eagle Trap.* Bliss, Ronald Gene (1942-). Davenport, May, intro. by. 1982. Davenport. (P.109)

Herman, Toni
--*The Big Cereal Gyp.* Herman, Charlotte (1937-). 1975. J. Philip O'Hara Inc. (P.438)

Herman, Victor J. (1919-)
--*Juanito's Railroad in the Sky.* Herman, Victor J (1919-). c.1976. Golden Press. (P.438)
--*My Days Are Made of Butterflies.* Martin, William Ivan, Jr. (1916-), adapted by. Galea'i Fa'apouli, Sano M. c.1970. Holt, Rinehart and Winston. (P.353)

Hermann, Reinhard
--*Joseph in Egypt.* Wiemer, Rudolf Otto (1905-). 1968. Augsburg. (P.956)

Hermanson, Dennis Everett (1947-)
--*Lands End.* Stolz, Mary Slattery (1920-). 1973. Harper & Row. (P.861)
--*Lands End.* 1st ed. Stolz, Mary Slattery (1920-). 1976, c.1973. Harper and Row. (P.861)

Herndon, Betty Boulton (1908-)
--*Adventures in Cactus Land.* Herndon, Betty Boulton (1908-). 1950. Caxton Publishers. (P.438)
--*Bill and the Clown Bird.* Herndon, Betty Boulton (1908-). 1957. Caxton Printers. (P.438)

Herndon, Nancy
--*Teddy Beddy Bear's Bedtime Book.* Slier, Debby. c.1985. Random House. (P.829)

Heron, Michal
--*Bird Seed & Lightning.* Borisoff, Norman. 1972. Creative Educational Society. (P.118)
--*Don't Give up.* Borisoff, Norman. 1972. Creative Educational Society. (P.118)
--*Unknown Avenues.* Borisoff, Norman. 1972. Creative Educational Society. (P.118)
--*Walkie-Talkie Patrol.* Borisoff, Norman. 1972. Creative Educational Society. (P.118)
--*Who's There.* Borisoff, Norman. 1972. Creative Educational Society. (P.118)

Heron, Michal, photos by.
--*Robby on Ice.* Swinburne, Laurence (1924-). 1972. Creative Educational Society. (P.875)

Herr, Laetitia
--*Everyday Susan: A Story for Girls.* Leonard, Mary Finley (1862-). c.1912. Thomas Y. Crowell Company. (P.566)

Herrera, Julio, jt. illus. see Lisman, Sharon.

Herrera, Velino (1902-)
--*In My Mother's House.* Clark, Ann Nolan, Mrs. (1896-). 1941. The Viking Press. **Award: (RCM).** (P.197)
--*People of the Crimson Evening.* Underhill, Ruth Murray (1884-). 1951. U. S. Indian Service. (P.909)

Herrero, Lowell
--*What Can I Do with a Paper Bag?.* Ambrose, Mary N. 1969. L. W. Singer Co. (P.32)

Herric, Pru
--*Bats & Gloves of Glory.* Renick, Marion Lewis (1905-). 1956. Scribner. (P.758)
--*The Hollyberrys.* Dalgliesh, Alice (1893-1979) & Bennett, Cleo. c.1939. C. Scribner's Sons. (P.239)
--*House on the Corner.* Cooper, Mattie Lula (1914-). 1963. Friendship Press. (P.218)
--*Jimmy's Own Basketball.* Renick, Marion Lewis (1905-). 1952. Charles Scribner's Sons. (P.758)
--*John's Back Yard Camp.* Renick, Marion Lewis (1905-). 1954. Scribner. (P.758)
--*Land of Silence.* Wright, Anna Maria Rose, Mrs. (1890-1968). 1962. Friendship Press. (P.980)
--*The Little Theatre.* Kenney, Pegeen. 1950. Garden City Pub. (P.518)
--*Pete's Home Run.* Renick, Marion Lewis (1905-). 1952. Scribner. (P.758)
--*Steve Marches with the General.* Renick, Marion Lewis (1905-). 1962. Scribner. (P.758)
--*Tiger Tail Village.* Millen, Nina. 1962. Friendship Press. (P.645)
--*Todd's Snow Patrol.* Renick, Marion Lewis (1905-). 1955. Scribner. (P.758)
--*Tune-in Again: Uncle Mal's Second Story Book.* Claire, Malcolm (1898-). Bailey, Bernadine Freeman, Mrs., ed. c.1940. Grosset & Dunlap. (P.196)
--*Tune-in Tales: Uncle Mal's Own Story Book.* Claire, Malcolm (1898-). Bailey, Bernadine Freeman, Mrs., ed. c.1939. Grosset & Dunlap. (P.196)

Herric, Pru & Wetmore, Mildred
--*The Story Book of Whitie and Pinkie.* Scott, Lydia. c.1940. McLoughlin Bross., Inc. (P.805)

Herrick, Arthur R.
--*Castle Secrets.* Seivwright, Jean. 1931. Little, Brown, and Company. (P.809)

Herrick, H. W.
--*John Gay: Work for Boys, 4.* Abbott, Jacob (1803-1879). N.D. Hurd & Houghton. (P.2)
--*Mary Gay: Work for Girls, 4.* Abbott, Jacob (1803-1879). N.D. HUrd & HOughton. (P.2)
--*Undine, and Other Tales.* Fouque, Friedrich De la Motte (1777-1843). N.D. Hurd & Houghton. (P.339)
--*William Gay: Play for Boys, 6 Vols.* Abbott, Jacob (1803-1879). N.D. Hurd & Houghton. (P.3)

Herrick, Henry H.
--*The Hero of the Hills.* Browne, George Waldo (1851-1930). N.D. L. C. Page. (P.143)

Herrick, Herb
--*Mars.* Asimov, Isaac (1920-). 1967. Follett Pub. Co. (P.52)

Herring, Ann
--*Jack & the Beanstalk.* Watanabe, Ryuhei. N.D. Japan Pubns. (P.934)

Herring, Lee
--*Milton and His Magic Motorcycle: A Drug Abuse Prevention Program.* Swenson, Mary. c.1972. Printed by Tane Press. (P.874)

Herrington, Roger
--*About a Bicycle for Linda.* Baker, Eugene H. 1968. Melmont Publishers. (P.62)
--*Bone People.* Bamman, Henry A., et al. (1918-) 1970. Benefic Press. (P.67)
--*Cowboy Marshal.* Russell, Donald Bert (1899-). 1970. Benefic Press. (P.785)
--*Cowboy Matt and Belleza.* Haynes, Doris McGee. 1973. Benefic Press. (P.426)
--*Inviso Man.* Bamman, Henry A., et al. (1918-) 1970. Benefic Press. (P.67)
--*Milky Way.* Bamman, Henry A., et al. (1918-) 1970. Benefic Press. (P.67)
--*Mystery Adventure at Longcliff Inn.* Bamman, Henry A. (1918-) & Kennedy, Leonard. 1969. Benefic Press. (P.67)
--*No Turning Back.* Lunemann, Evelyn. 1969. Benefic Press. (P.591)
--*Space Pirate.* Bamman, Henry A., et al. (1918-) 1970. Benefic Press. (P.67)
--*Ten Feet Tall.* Lunemann, Evelyn. 1969. Benefic Press. (P.591)
--*Toby on the Move.* Podendorf, Illa (1903-1983). 1970. Childrens Press. (P.729)

Herrington, Roger & Rohrer, George
--*Mystery Adventure.* Bamman, Henry A., et al. (1918-) 1969. Benefic Press. (P.67)

Herriot, Alan B.
--*Fireside Tales of the Traveller Children: Twelve Scottish Stories.* Milliamson, Duncan. 1985. Crown. (P.649)

Herriott, Ruth Elizabeth
--*The Jungle Jingle Book.* Herriott, Hallie Irene. 1910. Carnation Press. (P.438)

Herrman, Carl T.
--*Doubloons.* Chapman, Maristan, pseud. (1891-1972) & Chapman, Mary Ilsley. Chapman, John Stanton Higham. 1960. Barnes. (P.186)

Herrmann, Reinhard
--*Christmas Story.* Wiemer, Rudolf Otto (1905-). 1968. Augsburg. (P.956)
--*Come Unto Me.* Wiemer, Rudolf Otto (1905-). 1968. Augsburg. (P.956)
--*Joseph & His Brothers.* Wiemer, Rudolf Otto (1905-). 1968. Augsburg. (P.956)
--*Noah & His Ark.* Applebee, C. J. N.D. Merry Thoughts. (P.43)
--*Noah's Ark.* Wiemer, Rudolf Otto (1905-). Martinsen, Paul T., tr. 1967. Augsburg Pub. House. (P.956)
--*The Prodigal Son.* Wiemer, Rudolf Otto (1905-). Martinsen, Paul T., tr. c.1967. Augsburg. (P.956)
--*Prodigal Son.* Wiemer, Rudolf Otto (1905-). 1968. Augsburg. (P.956)
--*Wise Men from the East.* Bouhuys, Mies. 1968. Augsburg. (P.120)

Herrmann, Reinhard & Martinsen, Paul T.
--*Jonah and the Big Fish.* Wiemer, Rudolf Otto (1905-). c.1967. Augsburg. (P.956)

Herrmanns, Ralph (1933-)
--*The Car Named Julia.* Herrmanns, Ralph (1933-). MacMillan, Annabelle, pseud. (1922-), tr. from Swedish. Quick, Annabelle. 1964, c.1963. Harcourt. (P.438)

Hershenson, Roberta
--*Ramon's Adventures in the Library.* Vreeken, Elizabeth. 1967. Oceana. (P.922)

Hershon, M.
--*Little Red Wagon Painted Blue.* Hershon, Robert Richard (1914-). N.D. Unicorn Press. (P.438)

Herter, Albert (1871-)
--*Tales of the Enchanted Islands of the Atlantic.* Higginson, Thomas Wentworth (1823-1911), ed. 1976. Core Collection Books. (P.441)
--*Tales of the Enchanted Islands of the Atlantic.* Higginson, Thomas Wentworth (1823-1911), ed. 1898. The Macmillan Company; Etc., Etc. (P.441)
--*Tales of the Enchanted Islands of the Atlantic.* Higginson, Thomas Wentworth (1823-1911), ed. 1923. The Macmillan Company. (P.441)

Hertz, Ole
--*Tobias Catches Trout.* Hertz, Ole. Tobias, Tobi (1938-), tr. from Danish. 1984. Carolrhoda Bks. (P.438)
--*Tobias Goes Ice Fishing.* Hertz, Ole. Tobias, Tobi (1938-), tr. from Danish. 1984. Carolrhoda Bks. (P.438)
--*Tobias Has a Birthday.* Hertz, Ole. Tobias, Tobi (1938-), tr. from Danish. 1984. Carolrhoda Bks. (P.438)

Hervert, Fuka
--*James Steel Smith's City Song.* Smith, James Steel. c.1970. Holt, Rinehart & Winston. (P.834)

Herwig, Mary, jt. illus. see Herwig, William.

Herwig, William & Herwig, Mary
--*The Quest of the Golden Star.* Cross, Elsa, Mrs. 1925. The Printshop Company, Ltd. (P.232)

Herzog, Charles, 3rd
--*Eliot's Ark.* Eliot, Sonny, pseud. (1926-). Eliot, Marvin. 1972. Wayne St U Pr. (P.301)

Hesik, Blue
--*The Magic King.* Hillig, Chuck. 1984. Stillpoint. (P.445)

Heslop, Michael
--*The Grey King.* 1st ed. Cooper, Susan (1935-). 1975. Atheneum. **Awards: (JNM); (ALA); (CMA).** (P.218)
--*Silver on the Tree.* Cooper, Susan (1935-). 1977. Atheneum. (P.218)

Hess, Erwin L.
--*Eight Cousins: Or, The Aunt-Hill.* Alcott, Louisa May (1832-1888). c.1940. Whitman Publishing Company. (P.17)
--*Gene Autry and the Redwood Pirates: An Original Story Featuring Gene Autry, Famous Motion Picture Star, As the Hero.* authorized. Hamilton, Bob (1931-). 1946. Whitman Publishing Company. (P.408)
--*Grimm's Fairy Tales.* Grimm, Jakob Ludwig Karl (1785-1863) & Grimm, Wilhelm Karl (1786-1859). c.1941. Whitman Publishing Company. (P.392)
--*Gulliver's Travels: Including A Voyage to Lilliput, A Voyage to Brobdingnag, A Voyage to Laputa, A Voyage to the Country of the Houyhnhnms.* Swift, Jonathan (1667-1745). c.1940. Whitman Publishing Company. (P.874)
--*Joe Strong and His Box of Mystery: Or, The Ten Thousand Dollar Prize Trick.* Barnum, Vance, pseud. Stratemeyer Syndicate. N.D. Whitman Publishing Co. (P.74)
--*Joe Strong and His Wings of Steel: Or, A Young Acrobat in the Clouds.* Barnum, Vance, pseud. Stratemeyer Syndicate. N.D. Whitman Publishing Co. (P.74)
--*Joe Strong on the High Wire: Or, Motorcycle Perils of the Air.* Barnum, Vance, pseud. Stratemeyer Syndicate. N.D. Whitman Publishing Co. (P.74)
--*Joe Strong on the Trapeze: Or, The Daring Feats of a Young Circus Performer.* Barnum, Vance, pseud. Stratemeyer Syndicate. N.D. Whitman Publishing Co. (P.74)
--*Joe Strong, the Boy Fire-Eater: Or, The Most Dangerous Performance on Record.* Barnum, Vance, pseud. Stratemeyer Syndicate. N.D. Whitman Publishing Co. (P.74)
--*Joe Strong, the Boy Fish: Or, Marvelous Doings in a Big Tank.* Barnum, Vance, pseud. Stratemeyer Syndicate. N.D. Whitman Publishing Co. (P.74)
--*Joe Strong, the Boy Wizard: Or, The Mysteries of Magic Exposed.* Barnum, Vance, pseud. Stratemeyer Syndicate. N.D. Whitman Publishing Co. (P.74)
--*Little Men.* Alcott, Louisa May (1832-1888). c.1940. Whitman Publishing Company. (P.17)
--*The Merry Adventures of Robin Hood of Great Renown, in Nottinghamshire.* Pyle, Howard (1853-1911). c.1940. Whitman Publishing Company. (P.743)
--*Roy Rogers and the Gopher Creek Gunman: An Original Story Featuring Roy Rogers, Famous Motion Picture Star, As the Hero.* authorized. Middleton, Don. 1945. Whitman Publishing Company. (P.644)

Hess, Franklin
--*Polo Pals.* Thompson, May Hall. 1945. Caxton Printers. (P.887)

Hess, Harold W.
--*Tales of a Grandmother.* Sand, George, pseud. (1804-1876). Dudevant, Amandine Lucile Aurore Dupin. Bloom, Margaret (1893-), tr. 1930. J. B. Lippincott Company. (P.791)

Hess, Lilo (1916-), photos by.
--*A Cat's Nine Lives.* Hess, Lilo (1916-). 1984. Scribner. (P.439)
--*Diary of a Rabbit.* Hess, Lilo (1916-). 1982. Scribner. (P.439)
--*Easter in November.* Hess, Lilo (1916-). c.1964. Crowell. (P.439)
--*Fawn in the Woods.* Eberle, Irmengarde (1898-1979). 1962. Crowell. (P.295)
--*Foxes in the Woodshed.* Hess, Lilo (1916-). 1966. Charles Scribner's Sons. (P.439)
--*The Good Luck Dog.* Hess, Lilo (1916-). c.1985. Scribner's. (P.439)
--*Listen to Your Kitten Purr.* Hess, Lilo (1916-). c.1980. Scribner. (P.439)
--*Monkeys & Apes Without Trees.* Hess, Lilo (1916-). 1973. Scribner. (P.439)
--*Mouse & Company.* Hess, Lilo (1916-). 1972. Scribner. (P.439)
--*Pigeons Everywhere.* Hess, Lilo (1916-). 1967. Scribners. (P.439)
--*The Praying Mantis, Insect Cannibal.* Hess, Lilo (1916-). 1971. Scribner. (P.439)
--*A Puppy for You.* Hess, Lilo (1916-). 1976. Scribner. (P.439)
--*Rabbits in the Meadow.* Hess, Lilo (1916-). 1963. T Y Crowell. (P.439)
--*The Remarkable Chameleon.* Hess, Lilo (1916-). 1968. Charles Scribner's Sons. (P.439)
--*Sea Horses.* Hess, Lilo (1916-). 1966. Charles Scribner's Sons. (P.439)
--*Shetland Ponies.* Hess, Lilo (1916-). 1964. Crowell. (P.439)
--*A Snail's Pace.* Hess, Lilo (1916-). 1974. Scribner. (P.439)

Hess, Lowell
--*Aladdin and His Magic Lamp.* Daly, Kathleen N., as told by. 1959. Golden Press. (P.240)
--*Ali Baba and the Forty Thieves.* 1958. Golden Press. (P.439)
--*Fairy Tales.* Andersen, Hans Christian (1805-1875). White, Anne Terry (1906-), ed. c.1958. Simon and Schuster. (P.35)

--*The Second Mate of the Myradale.* Lesterman, John. c.1929. Harcourt, Brace and Company. (P.567)
Hilder, Rowland (1905-) & Southern, Richard
--*A Sailor of Napoleon: A Tale of the Sea.* Lesterman, John. c.1927. Harcourt, Brace and Company. (P.567)
Hilgerdt, Erik
--*I, Tut: The Boy Who Became Pharaoh.* Schlein, Miriam (1926-). 1978. Four Winds. (P.799)
Hill, Adrian Keith Graham (1895-1977)
--*Adrift in the Arctic.* Thom, William Albert Strang (1900-). Morrison, J. Strang, pseud. 1930. Oxford University Press, H. Milford. (P.885)
Hill, Donna Marie (1921-)
--*Not One More Day.* Hill, Donna Marie (1921-). 1957. Viking Press. (P.442)
--*The Sea Cart.* Konkle, Janet Everest (1917-). 1961. Abingdon Press. (P.535)
Hill, Dorothy (1924-)
--*The House Without a Home.* Brown, Beth (1909-). 1970. Lion Press. (P.138)
--*Mom!* I Need Glasses!. Wolff, Angelika. 1970. Lion Press. (P.974)
Hill, Eric
--*Baby Bear's Bedtime.* Hill, Eric. Schulman, Janet, ed. 1984. Random. (P.442)
--*Donde Esta Spot?.* Hill, Eric. 1983. Putnam Pub Group. (P.442)
--*The Fourth Adventure of the S.* S. Happiness Crew: Visit to a Magic Mountain. Dutton, June. c.1983. Determined Productions. (P.292)
--*Good Morning, Baby Bear.* Hill, Eric. Schulman, Janet, ed. 1984. Random. (P.442)
--*Here's Spot!.* Hill, Eric. 1983. Putnam Pub Group. (P.442)
--*Hoke's Jokes, Cartoons & Funny Things.* Hoke, Helen L., Mrs. (1903-), ed. 1974, c.1973. Watts. (P.453)
--*El Primer Paseo de Spot.* Hill, Eric. 1983. Putnam Pub Group. (P.443)
--*La Primera Navidad de Spot.* Hill, Eric. 1983. Putnam Pub Group. (P.443)
--*Spot Goes to School.* Hill, Eric. 1984. Putnam Pub Group. (P.443)
--*Spot Learns to Count.* Hill, Eric. 1983. Putnam Pub Group. (P.443)
--*Spot Tells the Time.* Hill, Eric. 1983. Putnam Pub Group. (P.443)
--*Spot's Alphabet.* Hill, Eric. 1983. Putnam Pub Group. (P.443)
--*Spot's Busy Year.* Hill, Eric. 1983. Putnam Pub Group. (P.443)
--*Spot's First Christmas.* Hill, Eric. 1983. Putnam Pub Group. (P.443)
--*Spot's Toys.* Hill, Eric. 1984. Putnam Pub Group. (P.443)
Hill, Florence
--*Deborah Sampson Goes to War.* Bryna, Stevens. 1984. Carolrhoda Bks. (P.146)
Hill, Gregory
--*Trouble, Trouble, Trouble.* Sandberg, Karl C., adapted by. c.1976. Carolrhoda Books. (P.791)
Hill, Helen, jt. illus. see Maxwell, Violet.
Hill, Helen & Maxwell, Violet
--*The Adventures of Galley Jack: Ship's Cat to the Susan P.* Meservey. Maxwell, Violet & Hill, Helen. 1929. Harper & Brothers. (P.632)
--*The Astonishing Letter.* Hill, Helen & Maxwell, Violet. 1938. Harper & Brothers. (P.443)
--*Charlie and His Coast Guards.* Hill, Helen & Maxwell, Violet. 1925. The Macmillan Company. (P.443)
--*Charlie and His Friends.* Hill, Helen & Maxwell, Violet. 1927. The Macmillan Company. (P.443)
--*Charlie & His Kitten Topsy.* Hill, Helen & Maxwell, Violet. N.D. Macmillan. (P.443)
--*Charlie & His Puppy Bingo.* Hill, Helen & Maxwell, Violet. N.D. Macmillan. (P.443)
--*Charlie and His Puppy Bingo.* Hill, Helen & Maxwell, Violet. 1923. The Macmillan Company. (P.443)
--*Charlie and the Surprise House.* Hill, Helen & Maxwell, Violet. 1926. The Macmillan Company. (P.443)
--*Galley Jack Crosses the Line.* Maxwell, Violet & Hill, Helen. 1930. Harper & Brothers. (P.632)
--*The Golden Goat.* Hill, Helen & Maxwell, Violet. 1929. The Macmillan Company. (P.443)
--*The Little Lost Shepherd.* Hill, Helen & Maxwell, Violet. 1931. The Macmillan Company. (P.443)
--*Little Tonino.* Hill, Helen & Maxwell, Violet. 1928. The Macmillan Company. (P.443)
--*Napoleon's Story Book.* Hill, Helen & Maxwell, Violet. 1930. The Macmillan Company. (P.443)
--*Rudi of the Toll Gate.* Hill, Helen & Maxwell, Violet. 1932. The Macmillan Company. (P.443)
--*The Saintons Go to Bethlehem.* Hill, Helen & Maxwell, Violet. 1935. The Macmillan Company. (P.443)
--*When Marius Was Ten.* Hill, Helen & Maxwell, Violet. 1937. The Macmillan Company. (P.443)
Hill, Homer
--*The Little Bus that Liked Home Best.* Scheidlinger, Lucy Prince. 1955. J. C. Winston Co. (P.798)
Hill, James (1914-)
--*The Pied Piper, and Other Fairy Tales.* Jacobs, Joseph (1854-1916), ed. 1963. Macmillan. (P.487)
--*Pied Piper & Other Fairy Tales.* Jacobs, Joseph (1854-1916), ed. 1968. Macmillan. (P.487)
--*The Pied Piper and other Tales.* Jacobs, Joseph (1854-1916), ed. 1963. MacMillan Co. (P.487)
Hill, Leonard Erskine (1866-)
--*The Jolly Tinker: And Other Tales.* Hill, Leonard Erskine (1866-). 1929. J. B. Lippincott Company. (P.443)
Hill, Mabel Betsy, jt. illus. see Brownscombe, J.
Hill, Mabel Betsy (1877-)
--*Along Comes Judy Jo.* Hill, Mabel Betsy (1877-). 1943. Frederick A. Stokes Company. (P.443)
--*Along Comes Judy Jo.* Hill, Mabel Betsy (1877-). N.D. J. B. LIppincott Co. (P.443)
--*The Big Brewster Family: A Story of Plymouth in 1623.* Lucas, Jannette May (1885-). 1946. J. B. Lippincott Company. (P.589)
--*Big, Little, Smaller and Least.* Hill, Mabel Betsy (1877-). 1936. Frederick A. Stokes Company. (P.443)
--*Big, Little, Smaller and Least.* Hill, Mabel Betsy (1877-). N.D. J. B. LIppincott. (P.443)
--*Danny's Country Store.* Orton, Helen Fuller, Mrs. (1872-1955). 1935. Frederick A. Stokes Company. (P.696)
--*Danny's Country Store.* Orton, Helen Fuller, Mrs. (1872-1955). 1935. J. B. Lippincott Co. (P.696)
--*A Day With Mopsy.* Hill, Mabel Betsy (1877-). N.D. J. P. LIppincott. (P.443)
--*Dilly Was Different: The Story of a Little Pilgraim.* Maynard, Lorraine. c.1932. S. Gabriel Son & Company. (P.634)
--*The Enchanted Playhouse.* 1st ed. Hill, Mabel Betsy (1877-). 1950. Lippincott. (P.443)
--*The Extra-Special Room.* Hill, Margaret Ohler (1915-). 1962. Little, Brown. (P.444)
--*Jack O'Lantern for Judy Jo.* Hill, Mabel Betsy (1877-). N.D. J. B. Lippincott. (P.443)
--*Jack O'lantern for Judy Jo: An Apple Market Street Story.* Hill, Mabel Betsy (1877-). c.1940. Frederick A. Stokes Company, Inc. (P.443)
--*Judy Jo's Magic Island.* Hill, Mabel Betsy (1877-). 1953. Lippincott. (P.443)
--*Lamp-light Tales.* Bouve, Pauline Carrington Rust, Mrs. 1922. Grosset & Dunlap. (P.120)
--*The Old House at Duck Light Cove.* Hill, Mabel Betsy (1877-). 1946. J. B. Lippincott Company. (P.443)
--*The Red and White Secret.* Peple, Florence Selden. 1931. Garrett & Massie. (P.717)
--*The Snowed-in Family: A Judy Jo Story.* Hill, Mabel Betsy (1877-). 1951. Lippincott. (P.443)
--*Summer Comes to Apple Market Street.* Hill, Mabel Betsy (1877-). 1937. Frederick A. Stokes Company. (P.443)
--*Summer Comes to Apple Market Street.* Hill, Mabel Betsy (1877-). 1937. J. B. Lippincott Co. (P.443)
--*Surprise for Judy Jo.* Hill, Mabel Betsy (1877-). 1939. J. B. Lippincott Co. (P.443)
--*Surprise for Judy Jo: An Apple Market Street Story.* Hill, Mabel Betsy (1877-). 1939. Frederick A. Stokes Company, Inc. (P.444)
--*Welcome House.* Moore, Jessie Eleanor (1886-). c.1939. Friendship Press. (P.661)
Hill, Marjorie
--*Eemi: The Story of a Clown.* Duncombe, Frances Riker (1900-). 1946. H. Holt and Company. (P.289)
--*The Little Red Ferry Boat: Story.* Potter, Russell (1897-). 1947. H. Holt. (P.735)
Hill, Mildred Lowry
--*Hoppity Bunny's Hop.* DeHuff, Elizabeth Willis, Mrs. (1892-). 1939. The Caxton Printers, Ltd. (P.251)
Hill, Mimi Clare & Draper, Kayren
--*The Storyland Tree.* Lindsay, Maud McKnight (1874-). c.1933. Lothrop, Lee & Shepard Co. (P.574)
Hill, Patricia
--*We Sing and Read.* Kuhmerker, Lisa & Newbern, Kenneth. 1972. John Day Co.; Distributed by Steck-Vaughn Co., Austin, Tex. (P.541)
Hill, Roger
--*The Old Man of Mow.* Garner, Alan (1935-). 1970, c.1967. Doubleday. (P.358)
Hill, Sandra
--*Abecedarian.* Coffey, Brian. 1974. Advent Books. (P.206)
Hill, Tom (1922-)
--*Tom Turtle.* Hill, Christopher (1950-). 1974. Ginn. (P.442)
Hiller, Lejaren A.
--*The Elm-Tree Fairy Book: Favorite Fairy Tales.* Johnson, Clifton (1865-1940), ed. 1908. Little, Brown, & Company. (P.494)
Hillerich, Robert L. & Sharp, Gene (1923-)
--*Where Is It?.* Lillegard, Dee. c.1984. Childrens Press. (P.572)
Hilliam, B. C.
--*Chuckles, This Idiocy.* Alden, John Carver. 1920. Marshall Jones. (P.20)
Hillinger, Edith
--*The Horse in Striped Pajamas.* Berg, Cherney. c.1969. Lancelot Press. (P.95)
--*The Pet Show.* Johnson, Audrey Pike (1915-). 1972. Ginn. (P.494)
Hillman, Priscilla (1940-)
--*A Merry-Mouse Book of Nursery Rhymes.* 1st ed. Hillman, Priscilla (1940-). c.1981. Doubleday. (P.445)
--*Minnikin, Midgie, and Moppet: A Mouse Story.* Holl, Adelaide Hinkle (1910-). c.1977. Golden Press. (P.454)
Hills, Gillian
--*Digby: The Biggest Dog in the World.* Bear, Carolyn D. 1974. Har-Row. (P.85)
Hills, Laura C.
--*Flower Folk.* Pratt, Anna M. 1890. Frederick A. Stokes. (P.736)
--*Friends from My Garden.* Pratt, Anna M. 1890. Frederick A. Stokes Company. (P.736)
--*John Halifax, Gentleman.* New ed. Craik, Dinah Maria Mulock, Mrs. (1826-1887). N.D. Joseph Knight & Co. (P.227)
Hills, Robert
--*Loggerhead.* Stark, Jack (1914-). 1973. E A Seemann. (P.849)
--*The Sponge Pirates & Other Stories.* rev. ed. Stark, Jack (1914-). 1973. E A Seemann. (P.849)
Him, jt. illus. see Lewitt.
Him, George (1900-1982)
--*The Day with the Duke.* Thwaite, Ann Barbara Harrop (1932-). 1969. World Pub. Co. (P.891)
--*Folk Tales for Reading and Telling.* Berg, Leila Rita (1917-). 1966. World Pub. Co. (P.96)
--*The Giant, Alexander.* Herrmann, Frank (1927-). 1965, c.1964. Whittlesey-McGraw. (P.438)
--*The Giant Alexander and Hannibal the Elephant.* Herrmann, Frank (1927-). 1972. McGraw-Hill. (P.438)
--*Giant Alexander & the Circus.* Herrmann, Frank (1927-). 1966. McGraw. (P.438)
--*The Giant Alexander in America.* Herrmann, Frank (1927-). 1968. McGraw-Hill. (P.438)
--*Squawky.* Potter, Stephen (1900-1969). 1964. Hale. (P.735)
--*Squawky: The Adventures of a Clasperchoice.* Potter, Stephen (1900-1969). 1964. Lippincott. (P.735)
Himler, Ronald Norbert (1937-)
--*After the Goat Man.* Byars, Betsy Cromer (1928-). 1982, c.1974. Puffin. (P.160)
--*After the Goat Man.* Byars, Betsy Cromer (1928-). 1974. The Viking Press. (P.160)
--*Allison's Grandfather.* Peavy, Linda (1943-). 1981. Scribner. (P.714)
--*Baby.* Manushkin, Frances (1942-). 1972. Harper & Row. (P.618)
--*Bedtime Mother Goose.* Stone, Evelyn (1879-1971), ed. 1980. Western Pub. (P.862)
--*The Best Town in the World.* Baylor, Byrd (1924-). 1983. Scribner. (P.84)
--*The Blue Stone.* Kennedy, Jerome Richard (1932-). c.1976. Holiday House. **Award: (ALA).** (P.517)
--*Bruno.* Broger, Achim (1944-). 1975. Morrow. (P.134)
--*Bubblebath!.* 1st ed. Manushkin, Frances (1942-). 1974. Harper & Row. (P.618)
--*Bunk Beds.* 1st ed. Winthrop, Elizabeth, pseud. (1948-). Mahony, Elizabeth Winthrop. 1972. Harper & Row. (P.970)
--*Bus Ride.* Jewell, Nancy (1940-). c.1978. Harper & Row. (P.492)
--*Conquista!.* Bulla, Clyde Robert (1914-) & Syson, Michael. c.1978. Crowell. (P.149)
--*Curly and the Wild Boar.* 1st ed. Gipson, Frederick Benjamin (1908-1973). c.1979. Harper & Row. (P.369)
--*Daddy.* Caines, Jeannette Franklin. c.1977. Harper & Row. (P.161)
--*Dakota Dugout.* Turner, Ann Warren (1945-). c.1985. Macmillan. (P.905)
--*Eye Winker, Tom Tinker, Chin Chopper.* Glazer, Tom (1914-), ed. 1978. Doubleday. (P.370)
--*Glad Day and Other Classical Poems for Children.* Himler, Ronald Norbert (1937-). 1972. Putnam. (P.445)
--*Good Wife, Good Wife.* Dickerson, Louise. 1977. McGraw-Hill. (P.264)
--*The House on Deer Track Trail.* Kelly, Marty, pseud. (1914-). Kelly, Martha Rose. c.1976. McGraw-Hill. (P.516)
--*Hut School and the Wartime Home-Front Heroes.* Burch, Robert Joseph (1925-). 1974. Viking Press. (P.151)
--*I Am Going Nowhere: Nonsense Rhymes.* Brower, Millicent. 1972. Putnam. (P.137)
--*I Am the Running Girl.* Adoff, Arnold (1935-). c.1979. Harper & Row. (P.12)
--*Inside My Feet: The Story of a Giant.* Kennedy, Jerome Richard (1932-). c.1979. Harper & Row. (P.518)
--*Janey.* 1st ed. Zolotow, Charlotte Shapiro (1915-). 1973. Harper and Row. (P.994)
--*Jem's Island.* Lasky, Kathryn (1944-). 1982. Scribner. (P.553)
--*Kon-Tiki.* Norby, Lisa. 1984. Random. (P.685)
--*The Lion's Tail.* Davis, Douglas Fredell (1935-). 1980. Atheneum. (P.245)
--*Little Arliss.* Gipson, Frederick Benjamin (1908-1973). 1980, c.1978. Harper & Row. (P.369)
--*Make a Circle, Keep Us in: Poems for a Good Day.* Adoff, Arnold (1935-). 1975. Delacorte Press. (P.12)
--*Moon Song.* Baylor, Byrd (1924-). c.1982. Scribner. (P.84)
--*Morris Brookside, a Dog.* Sharmat, Marjorie Weinman (1928-). 1973. Holiday. (P.815)
--*Morris Brookside Is Missing.* Sharmat, Marjorie Weinman (1928-). 1974. Holiday House. (P.815)
--*Pea Patch Island.* Curren, Polly (1917-). 1975. Golden Press. (P.236)
--*Tornado!* Poems. Adoff, Arnold (1935-). c.1977. Delacorte Press. (P.12)
--*Trouble for Lucy.* Stevens, Carla McBride (1928-). c.1979. Seabury Press. (P.854)
--*Under the Early Morning Trees: Poems.* Adoff, Arnold (1935-). c.1978. Dutton. (P.12)
--*The Upside-Down Cat.* Parsons, Elizabeth (1937-). 1981. Atheneum. (P.708)
--*Wind Rose.* Dragonwagon, Crescent (1952-). 1976. Har-Row. (P.284)
Himmelman, John
--*Amanda and the Witch Switch: Story and Pictures.* Himmelman, John. 1985. Viking Kestrel. (P.445)
--*Charlotte Cheetham, Master of Disaster.* Holmes, Barbara Ware. c.1985. Harper & Row. (P.456)
--*Talester the Lizard.* Himmelman, John. c.1982. Dial Press. (P.445)
Himmelsbach, Paula B.
--*Faith Palmer in New York.* Woolley, Lazelle Thayer, Mrs. (1872-). 1914. The Penn Publishing Company. (P.978)
--*Faith Palmer in Washington.* Woolley, Lazelle Thayer, Mrs. (1872-). 1915. The Penn Publishing Company. (P.978)
--*A Freshman Co-Ed.* Lee, Alice Louise (1868-). 1910. The Penn Publishing Company. (P.559)
--*A Freshman Co-Ed.* Lee, Alice Louise (1868-). c.1938. The Penn Publishing Company. (P.559)
--*A Junior Co-Ed.* Lee, Alice Louise (1868-). 1912. The Penn Publishing Company. (P.559)
--*A Senior Co-Ed.* Lee, Alice Louise (1868-). 1913. The Penn Publishing Company. (P.559)
--*A Sophomore Co-Ed.* Lee, Alice Louise (1868-). 1911. The Penn Publishing Company. (P.559)
Hindley, G. A.
--*In the Heart of the Rockies: A Story of Adventure in Colorado.* Henty, George Alfred (1832-1902). 1894. C. Scribner's Sons. (P.435)
Hinds, Helen Marie
--*Long Look House.* Abbott, Edward. N.D. Noyes, Snow and Company. (P.1)
--*Mabel on Midsummer Day: A Story of the Olden Time.* Howitt, Mary Botham, Mrs. (1799-1888). 1881. J. R. Osgood and Company. (P.468)
--*Out Doors at Long Look.* Abbott, Edward. N.D. Noyes, Snow and Company. (P.1)
Hinds, Robert William
--*Ride the Far Wind.* 1st ed. Jones, Adrienne (1915-). 1964. Little, Brown. (P.499)
Hine, H. G.
--*The House that Jack Built.* N.D. Green Tiger Pr. (P.445)
Hines, Anna Grossnickle
--*All by Myself.* Hines, Anna Grossnickle. c.1985. Clarion Books. (P.445)
--*Bethany for Real.* Hines, Anna Grossnickle. c.1985. Greenwillow Books. (P.445)
--*Come to the Meadow.* Hines, Anna Grossnickle. 1984. Hm. (P.445)
--*Don't Worry, I'll Find You.* Hines, Anna Grossnickle. 1986, c.1985. Dutton. (P.445)
--*Maybe a Band-Aid Will Help.* Hines, Anna Grossnickle. 1984. Dutton. (P.445)
--*Taste the Raindrops.* Hines, Anna Grossnickle. c.1983. Greenwillow Books. (P.445)
Hines, Lee
--*The Flamingo Feather.* Munroe, Kirk (1850-1930). Kottmeyer, William (1910-), adapted by. 1949. Webster Pub. Co. (P.672)
Hines, Robert W.
--*Honker: The Story of a Wild Goose.* McClung, Robert Marshall (1916-). 1965. Morrow. (P.595)
--*Samson, Last of the California Grizzlies.* McClung, Robert Marshall (1916-). 1973. Morrow. (P.596)

Holland, Marion (1908-)
--*A Big Ball of String.* Holland, Marion (1908-). 1958. Beginner Books; Distributed by Random House. (P.455)
--*Billy Had a System.* 1st ed. Holland, Marion (1908-). 1952. Knopf. (P.455)
--*Billy's Clubhouse.* Holland, Marion (1908-). 1955. Knopf. (P.455)
--*No Children, No Pets.* Holland, Marion (1908-). 1956. Knopf. (P.455)
--*The Secret Horse.* Holland, Marion (1908-). 1959. Little, Brown. (P.455)
--*Teddy's Camp-Out.* Holland, Marion (1908-). 1963. Knopf. (P.455)
--*A Tree for Teddy.* 1st ed. Holland, Marion (1908-). 1957. Knopf. (P.455)
--*You Never Can Tell.* Ritter, Elizabeth Hart, Mrs. (1897-). 1947. Grosset & Dunlap. (P.766)
Holland, Marion (1908-) & Holland, Rebecca
--*Casey Jones Rides Vanity.* Holland, Marion (1908-). N.D. Little, Brown. (P.455)
Holland, Rebecca, jt. illus. see Holland, Marion.
Holland, Sylvia
--*The Magic Key.* Johnstone, Muriel. 1952. Avon Pub. Co. (P.498)
Hollander, Carl
--*Fairy Tales of Denmark.* Spink, Reginald William (1905-), retold by. 1961. Dutton. (P.845)
--*Legacy of Magic.* Kooiker, Leonie., pseud. (1927-). Kooyker-Romijn, Johanna Maria. 1981. Morrow. (P.535)
--*The Magic Stone.* Kooiker, Leonie, pseud. (1927-). Kooyker-Romijn, Johanna Maria. Winston, Richard & Winston, Clara, trs. from Dutch 1978. Morrow. **Award: (IBBY).** (P.535)
Hollander, Edward S., photos by.
--*Follow Me, Everybody.* Bettinger, Craig. 1968. Doubleday. (P.100)
Hollander, Nicole
--*The Bee & the Rose.* Derosa, Peter Clement (1932-). 1975. Argus Comm. (P.260)
Holle, Erich
--*Archibald, the Traveling Poodle.* Kumin, Maxine Winokur (1925-). 1963, c.1960. Putnam. (P.541)
--*Click and the Toyshop.* Schnack, Friedrich (1888-). Rapoport, Eileen, tr. from Ger. 1967. Abelard. (P.800)
--*The Thousand and One Days.* Fehse, Willi Richard (1906-) & Petis De la Croix, Francois (1653-1713). Bell, Anthea, tr. from Fr. 1971. Abelard-Schuman. (P.320)
Hollerbach, Serge
--*Gunnar Scores a Goal.* Thorvall, Kerstin (1925-). Parker, Anne, tr. from Swedish. 1968. Harcourt, Brace & World. (P.890)
--*Westaway.* 1st ed. Philbrick, Charles Horace, II (1922-1971). 1968. Harcourt, Brace & World. (P.723)
Holley, Lee
--*The Amazing Adventures of Dennis the Menace.* Memling, Carl (1918-1969). Memling, Carl (1918-1969), adapted by. 1961. Random House. (P.640)
--*The Dennis the Menace Storybook.* Memling, Carl (1918-1969) & Ketcham, Hank, pseud. (1920-), eds. Ketcham, Henry King. Denice the Menace, Television Program. 1960. Random House. (P.640)
Holley, Lee, jt. illus. see Pratt, Hawley.
Holling, Holling Clancy, jt. illus. see Cooney, Barbara.
Holling, Holling Clancy, jt. illus. see Holling, Lucille Webster, Mrs.
Holling, Holling Clancy (1900-1973)
--*Claws of the Thunderbird: A Tale of Three Lost Indians.* Holling, Holling Clancy (1900-1973). c.1928. The P. F. Volland Company. (P.455)
--*Little Big-Bye-and-Bye.* Holling, Holling Clancy (1900-1973). c.1926. The P. F. Volland Company. (P.455)
--*Minn of the Mississippi.* Holling, Holling Clancy (1900-1973). 1951. E M Hale. (P.455)
--*Minn of the Mississippi.* Holling, Holling Clancy (1900-1973). 1951. Houghton Mifflin. **Award: (JNM).** (P.455)
--*Paddle-to-the-Sea.* Holling, Holling Clancy (1900-1973). 1941. Houghton Mifflin Company. **Award: (RCM).** (P.455)
--*Rocky Billy: The Story of the Bounding Career of a Rocky Mountain Goat.* Holling, Holling Clancy (1900-1973). 1928. The Macmillan Company. (P.455)
--*Rum-Tum-Tummy: The Elephant Who Ate.* Holling, Holling Clancy (1900-1973). 1928. Saalfield. (P.455)
--*Seabird.* Holling, Holling Clancy (1900-1973). 1948. Houghton, Mifflin Co. **Award: (JNM).** (P.455)
--*Tree in the Trail.* Holling, Holling Clancy (1900-1973). 1942. Houghton Mifflin Company. (P.455)
--*The Twins Who Flew Around the World.* Holling, Holling Clancy (1900-1973). c.1931. The Platt and Munk Co. Inc. (P.455)
Holling, Holling Clancy (1900-1973) & Cooney, Barbara
--*The Blot: Little City Cat.* Crawford, Phyllis (1899-). 1946. H. Holt & Company. (P.229)
Holling, Holling Clancy (1900-1973) & Holling, Lucille Webster
--*Pagoo.* Holling, Holling Clancy (1900-1973). 1957. E M Hale. (P.455)
--*Pagoo.* Holling, Holling Clancy (1900-1973). 1957. Houghton Mifflin. (P.455)
--*Three Little Indians.* Leavitt, Ann H. c.1937. Rand, McNally & Company. (P.559)
Holling, Lucille Webster, Mrs., jt. illus. see Holling, Holling Clancy.
Holling, Lucille Webster, Mrs. (1900-)
--*Around a Toadstool Table: A Child's Book of Verse.* Bennett, Rowena Bastin, Mrs. (1896-). 1920. Thomas S. Rockwell Company. (P.94)
--*Choo-Me-Choo.* Holling, Holling Clancy (1900-1973). 1928. Buzza. (P.455)
--*Kimo.* Bailey, Alice Cooper (1890-). c.1928. The P. F. Volland Company. (P.59)
--*Little Buffalo Boy.* Holling, Holling Clancy (1900-1973). c.1939. Garden City Publishing Company, Inc. (P.455)
--*Songs from around a Toadstool Table: A Child's Book of Verse.* Bennett, Rowena Bastin, Mrs. (1896-). 1937. Follett Pub. Co. (P.94)
Holling, Lucille Webster, Mrs. (1900-) & Holling, Holling Clancy (1900-1973)
--*Children of Other Lands.* Piper, Watty, pseud. (1870-1945), ed. Bragg, Mabel Caroline. c.1933. The Platt & Munk Co., Inc. (P.727)
--*The Road in Storyland.* Piper, Watty, pseud. (1870-1945), ed. Bragg, Mabel Caroline. 1952. Platt & Munk. (P.727)
--*The Road in Storyland.* Piper, Watty, pseud. (1870-1945), ed. Bragg, Mabel Caroline. c.1932. The Platt & Munk Co., Inc. (P.727)
Hollinger, Deanne
--*Andrew and the Alchemist.* 1st ed. Byfield, Barbara Ninde (1930-). c.1977. Doubleday. (P.160)
--*The Burglar Next Door.* Williams, Jay (1914-1978). c.1976. Four Winds Press. (P.963)
--*Good-by to Stony Crick.* Borland, Kathryn Kilby (1916-) & Speicher, Helen Ross Smith (1915-). 1974, c.1975. McGraw-Hill. (P.118)
--*The Man Who Made Gold.* Byfield, Barbara NInde (1930-). 1981. Scholastic Inc. (P.160)
--*Touchmark.* Lawrence, Mildred Elwood (1907-). 1975. Harcourt Brace Jovanovich. (P.556)
Hollingsworth, Alvin C.
--*Black Out Loud.* Adoff, Arnold (1935-), ed. 1970. Macmillan. (P.12)
--*I'd Like the Goo-Gen-Heim.* Hollingsworth, Alvin C. 1970. Reilly & Lee Books. (P.455)
Hollingsworth, Will
--*Boy of the Desert.* Tietjens, Eunice Hammond, Mrs. (1884-1944). 1928. Coward-McCann, Inc. (P.891)
Hollis, Marcia
--*The Witch of Shakerag Hollow, and Other Sewanee Ghosts.* Hollis, Marcia. 1973. University Press. (P.456)
Holloway, Edward Stratton, jt. illus. see Underwood, Clarence F.
Holloway, Jim
--*Isle of Illusion.* Simon, Madeleine. c.1983. TSR. (P.825)
--*Raid on Nightmare Castle.* McGuire, Catherine. c.1983. TSR, Inc. (P.603)
Holloway, W. Herbert
--*Fairy Tales from South Africa.* Bourhill, E. J, Mrs. & Drake, J. B., Mrs. 1972. Books for Libraries Press. (P.120)
Hollowood, Jane
--*Bonjour Philippine.* Paullin, Ellen (1915-). 1968. Reilly & Lee. (P.711)
--*Maggie & the Birthday Surprise.* Hollowood, Jane. N.D. Merry Thoughts. (P.456)
--*Maggie & the Chickens.* Hollowood, Jane. N.D. Merry Thoughts. (P.456)
--*Maggie in the Snow.* Hollowood, Jane. N.D. Merry Thoughts. (P.456)
Hollreiser, Lenny
--*Pounditout.* Camerer, Devid M (1915-). 1954. Barnes. (P.163)
Holm, John R.
--*C Minus.* Holm, John R. 1972. Schol Bk Serv. (P.456)
Holman, Nance
--*Crate Train.* Seymour, Dorothy Jane Zander (1928-). 1969. Wonder. (P.813)
--*Tent.* Seymour, Dorothy Jane Zander (1928-). 1965. Wonder. (P.813)
Holmberg, Lisbeth
--*Augusta Can Do Anything!.* Sundh, Kerstin (1912-). 1973. Putnam. (P.871)
Holmboe, Othar
--*Lisbeth Longfrock.* Aanrud, Hans (1863-). Poulsson, Laura Elizabeth (1851-), tr. 1907. Ginn & Company. (P.1)
Holmer, Edvin K.
--*Happy Days.* Thor, Mabel Nelson. 1949. Augustana Book Concern. (P.888)
--*A Purple Pig for Pedro.* Bjork, Elizabeth C. 1943. The Wartburg Press. (P.104)
Holmes, Bea
--*Crazy Mary.* Cone, Molly Lamken (1918-). c.1966. Houghton. (P.212)
--*The Maid of Artemis.* Coolidge, Olivia Ensor (1908-). 1969. Houghton Mifflin. (P.216)
--*Phoebe Snow.* Hall, Elizabeth (1929-). 1968. Houghton Mifflin. (P.404)
--*The Real Dream.* Cone, Molly Lamken (1918-). 1964. Houghton Mifflin. (P.213)
--*Search for the Crescent Moon.* Rosenberg, Ethel Clifford (1915-1978). Clifford, Eth, pseud. 1973. Houghton Mifflin. (P.778)
--*Sue Ellen.* Hunter, Edith Fisher (1919-). 1969. Houghton Mifflin. (P.474)
--*The Tamarack Tree.* Underwood, Mary Betty (1921-). 1971. Houghton Mifflin. (P.909)
Holmes, Blanche Fisher, jt. illus. see Holmes, Thomas W.
Holmes, Gerald L.
--*Alkali County Tales.* Erickson, John R. 1984. Maverick Bks. (P.308)
--*Cowboys are Partly Human.* Erickson, John R. 1983. Maverick Bks. (P.308)
--*The Further Adventures of Hank the Cowdog.* Erickson, John R. 1983. Maverick Bks. (P.308)
Holmes, Lenard
--*The Henneker Diamonds: Based Upon an Episode in Captain Marryat's Famous Story--The Little Savage.* Marryat, Frederick (1792-1848). Bernard, Joseph, ed. 1930. Thomas S. Rockwell Company. (P.621)
Holmes, Louis F.
--*Color Me Brown.* rev. ed. Giles, Lucille. 1974. Johnson Chi. (P.367)
Holmes, Mildred Helen
--*Bible Babies: How Some of These Grew.* Thompson, Elizabeth Ann. 1938. Polzin Press. (P.887)
Holmes, Robin (1940-)
--*Makah: Indian Whale hunters.* McReavy, John Morgan. 1973. Naturegraph Publishers. (P.611)
Holmes, Rosinda & Westover, Ned
--*Robin Deer.* rev. ed. Cossi, Olga (1921-). Brown, Vinson, ed. 1968. Naturegraph. (P.223)
Holmes, Thomas W. & Holmes, Blanche Fisher
--*The Real Book of Nursery Tales.* Storeis of the Three Little Pigs, Henny Penny, the Three Bears, Little Red Ridinghood and the Three Little Kittens. 1950. Garden City Pub. Co. (P.456)
Holmgren, George Ellen, pseud., see Holmgren, Helen Jean.
Holmgren, George Ellen, Sr., pseud. (1930-)
--*The Aeneid: A Retelling for Young People.* Holmgren, Helen Jean. Vergilius Maro, Publius (1919-). Gerdes, Florence Marie, retold by. 1969. St. Martin's Press. (P.917)
Holmgren, Helen Jean see Holmgren, George Ellen, pseud.
Holmgren, John
--*The Twins and Trusty.* McDevitt, Jean. 1958. Row, Peterson. (P.598)
Holsopple, Theobald
--*Little Daughter of Mexico.* Stoker, Catharine Ulmer. c.1937. Dealey and Lowe. (P.861)
Holt, Eunice M.
--*Happy Feet, a Book of Verse for Children.* Booth, Clarice Foster. 1951. Exposition Press. (P.117)
Holt, Norma
--*Angelita.* Kesselman, Wendy Ann. 1970. Hill and Wang. (P.520)
--*The Blue Rose.* 1st ed. Klein, Gerda Weissman (1924-). 1974. L. Hill. (P.530)
--*Joey.* Kesselman, Wendy Ann. 1972. L. Hill. (P.520)
Holt, Norma & Delessert, Etienne (1941-)
--*The Secret Seller.* Lifton, Betty Jean (1926-). 1968. W. W. Norton. (P.572)
Holt, Norma & Schmid, Eleonore
--*Franz Tovey and the Rare Animals.* Kesselman, Wendy Ann. 1968. H. Quist. (P.520)
Holtan, Gene
--*Black and Blue Magic.* Snyder, Zilpha Keatley (1927-). 1966. Atheneum. (P.839)
--*Old Blue: You Good Dog You.* Taylor, Mark (1927-). 1970. Childrens. (P.880)
--*Sheriff Stonehead and the Teen-Age Termites.* Beatty, Jerome, Jr. (1918-). 1970. Young Scott Books. (P.86)
--*Silly Billy's Alphabet.* Libbey, Ruth Everding & Libbin, Richard. 1964. Golden Gate Junior Books. (P.571)
Holzing, Herbert
--*The Stolen Fire.* Baumann, Hans (1914-). Humphries, Stella, tr. 1974, c.1972. Pantheon Books. (P.83)
--*The Stolen Fire: Legends of Heroes & Rebels from Around the World.* Baumann, Hans (1914-). 1973. Pantheon. (P.83)
Hom, Nancy
--*The Little Weaver of Thai-Yen Village: Co Beth-det Lang Thai-Yen.* Tran Khanh Tuyet. Jenkins, Christopher N. H. & Tran Khanh Tuyet, trs. c.1977. Childrens Book Pr. (P.898)
Homar, Lorenzo (1913-)
--*The Three Wishes.* Alegria, Ricardo E. (1921-), ed. 1968. H B J. (P.21)
--*The Three Wishes: A Collection of Puerto Rican Folktales.* Alegria, Ricardo E (1921-), ed. 1969. Harcourt, Brace & World. (P.21)
Homer, Caroline
--*The Mystery of Pelican Cove.* Radford, Ruby Lorraine (1891-1971). c.1934. The Penn Publishing Company. (P.746)
Honigman, Marian
--*Nicky's Football Team.* Renick, Marion Lewis (1905-). 1951. Scribner. (P.758)
--*Three Boys & a Helicopter.* Agle, Nan Hayden (1905-) & Wilson, Ellen Janet Cameron (0000-1976). 1958. Scribner. (P.14)
--*Three Boys and a Lighthouse.* Agle, Nan Hayden (1905-) & Wilson, Ellen Janet Cameron (0000-1976). 1951. Scribner. (P.14)
--*Three Boys and a Mine.* Agle, Nan Hayden (1905-) & Wilson, Ellen Janet Cameron (0000-1976). 1954. Scribner. (P.14)
--*Three Boys and a Train.* Agle, Nan Hayden (1905-) & Wilson, Ellen Janet Cameron (0000-1976). 1956. Scribner. (P.14)
--*Three Boys and a Tugboat.* Agle, Nan Hayden (1905-) & Wilson, Ellen Janet Cameron (0000-1976). 1953. Scribner. (P.14)
--*Three Boys and H20.* Agle, Nan Hayden (1905-) & Wilson, Ellen Janet Cameron (0000-1976). 1968. Scribner. (P.14)
--*Three Boys and Space.* Agle, Nan Hayden (1905-) & Wilson, Ellen Janet Cameron (0000-1976). 1962. Scribner. (P.14)
--*Three Boys and the Remarkable Cow.* Agle, Nan Hayden (1905-) & Wilson, Ellen Janet Cameron (0000-1976). 1952. Scribner. (P.14)
Honore, Paul (1885-)
--*Bushrangers.* Finger, Charles Joseph (1871-1941). N.D. Robert M. McBride &. (P.325)
--*Highwaymen.* Finger, Charles Joseph (1871-1941). N.D. Robert M. McBride &. (P.325)
--*Tales Worth Telling.* Finger, Charles Joseph (1871-1941). c.1927. The Century Co. (P.325)
--*Winged Horse Anthology.* Auslander, Joseph & Hill, Frank Ernest (1888-1916), eds. 1949. Doubleday. (P.55)
Hood, Egon
--*Billy Bunny.* Rowland, Jasper M (1910-). c.1945. The American Crayon Company. (P.782)
--*Chipper.* Rowland, Jasper M (1910-). c.1946. The American Crayon Company. (P.782)
--*Garibaldi: Knight of Liberty.* Burton, Jean. 1945. Alfred A. Knopf. (P.158)
Hood, G. P., jt. illus. see Ford, Henry Justice.
Hood, Garry R.
--*A Cry in the Wind.* Carper, L. Dean (1931-). 1973. Herald Pub. House. (P.170)
Hood, George W.
--*The Brazilian Fairy Book.* Eells, Elsie Spicer, Mrs. (1880-). 1926. Frederick A. Stokes Company. (P.298)
--*The Chinese Fairy Book.* Wilhelm, Richard (1873-1930). Martens, Frederick Herman (1874-1932), tr. c.1921. Frederick A. Stokes Company. (P.960)
--*The Danish Fairy Book.* Stroebe, Klara (1887-), ed. Martens, Frederick Herman (1874-1932), tr. c.1922. Frederick A. Stokes Company. (P.868)
--*Dick Judson: Boy Scout Ranger.* Park, George Frederick (1872-1931). 1916. R. M. McBride & Company. (P.705)
--*Fairy Tales from the Orient.* Martens, Frederick Herman (1874-1932). 1923. R. M. McBride & Company. (P.623)
--*Fairy Tales of Eastern Europe.* Curtin, Jeremiah (1840-1906). 1914. McBride, Nast & Company. (P.236)
--*The Jewish Fairy Book.* Friedlander, Gerald (1871-), ed. c.1920. Frederick A. Stokes Company. (P.345)
--*The Norwegian Fairy Book.* Stroebe, Klara (1887-), ed. Martens, Frederick Herman (1874-1932), tr. c.1922. Frederick A. Stokes Company. (P.868)
--*Rumpty-Dudget's Tower: A Fairy Tale.* Hawthorne, Julian (1846-1934). 1924. Frederick A. Stokes Company. (P.423)
--*The Swedish Fairy Book.* Stroebe, Klara (1887-), ed. Martens, Frederick Herman (1874-1932), tr. c.1921. Frederick A. Stokes Company. (P.868)
--*Tales of Washington Irving's Alhambra.* Irving, Washington (1783-1859). Cheney, Leila H., ed. c.1917. J. B. Lippincott Company. (P.482)
--*With Taro and Hana in Japan.* Sugimoto, Etsu Inagaki & Austen, Nancy Virginia. 1926. Frederick A. Stokes Company. (P.870)
Hood, Susan
--*First Crop.* Bell, Gertrude Wood (1911-). 1973. Independence Press. (P.90)

Hunt, Lionel A.
--*Aurie's Wooden Leg.* Hunt, Lionel A. N.D. Moody Press. (P.473)
Hunt, Lynn Bogue
--*Bill, The Broadbill Swordfish.* Farrington, Selwyn Kip, Jr. (1904-). N.D. Coward-McCann. (P.318)
--*Black Wings: The Unbeatable Crow.* 1st ed. Lippincott, Joseph Wharton (1887-1976). 1947. J. B. Lippincott Co. (P.575)
--*Broken Fang.* Montgomery, Rutherford George (1894-). N.D. Caxton Printers. (P.658)
--*Broken Fang.* Montgomery, Rutherford George (1894-). c.1935. M. A. Donohue & Company. (P.658)
--*Fur Sign.* Evarts, Hal George (1887-). 1922. Little, Brown, and Company. (P.312)
--*Prince Jan, St.* Bernard. Hooker, Forrestine Cooper, Mrs. (1867-1932). 1946. Doubleday & Co., Inc. (P.458)
--*Prince Jan.*, St. Bernard: How a Dog from the Land of Snow Made Good in the Land of No Snow. Hooker, Forrestine Cooper, Mrs. (1867-1932). 1921. And Toronto, Doubleday, Page & Company. (P.459)
--*The Red Roan Pony.* Lippincott, Joseph Wharton (1887-1976). c.1934. The Penn Publishing Company. (P.575)
--*Son of the Walrus King.* McCracken, Harold (1894-). 1944. J. B. Lippincott Company. (P.597)
Hunt, Peter (1922-)
--*Paintbox Summer.* Cavanna, Betty (1909-). 1949. Westminster. (P.179)
Hunt, Regina Victoria
--*A Candle for Our Lady.* Hunt, Regina Victoria. 1955. Bruce Pub. Co. (P.474)
Hunt, William Holman (1827-1910)
--*Parables from Nature.* Gatty, Margaret Scott, Mrs. (1809-1873). Johnson, Diane, pref. by. 1976. Garland Pub. (P.360)
Hunter, Cecilia Bull & Ogden, Caroline
--*Childhood.* Johnson, Burges (1877-1963), ed. 1912. Thomas Y. Crowell Company. (P.494)
Hunter, Cora Work
--*The Little Strawman.* Hunter, Cora Work. c.1914. Rand, McNally & Company. (P.474)
Hunter, Eleanor Augusta
--*Some Friends of Mine.* Hunter, Eleanor Augusta (1855-). 1889. Hunt & Eaton. (P.474)
--*Some Friends of Mine.* Hunter, Eleanor Augusta (1855-). N.D. Methodist Bk Concern. (P.474)
Hunter, Frances Tipton
--*Boo, Who Used to Be Scared of the Dark.* Leaf, Wilbur Munro (1905-1976). c.1948. Random House. (P.558)
--*The Frances Tipton Hunter Picture Book.* Barrows, Ruth Marjorie (1892-1983). c.1935. Whitman Publishing Company. (P.76)
Hunter, Hiram
--*Which One Are You?.* A Conscience Book for Little Folks. Hunter, Hiram. 1918. Little Folks Pub. Co. (P.474)
Hunter, James Hogg (1890-)
--*Uncle Jim's Stories from Nature's Wonderland.* Hunter, James Hogg (1890-). 1953. Zondervan Pub. House. (P.474)
Hunter, John (1891-)
--*The White Phantom.* Hunter, John (1891-). 1935. H. Smith and R. Haas. (P.474)
Hunter, Mark, jt. illus. see Hunter, Ted.
Hunter, Mel (1927-)
--*The Donkey with Diamond Ears: A Salute to Little Donkeys at Work in the Jewel Mines of Brazil.* Price, Olive M. (1903-). 1962. Coward-McCann. (P.739)
--*Friction.* Victor, Edward (1914-). 1961. Follett Pub. Co. (P.919)
--*Good Housekeeping's Best Book of Nature Stories.* 1st ed. Evans, Pauline Rush, ed. 1957. Good Housekeeping Magazine Distributed by Prentice-Hall, Englewood Cliffs, N.J. (P.312)
--*The Phantom Reindeer.* Price, Olive M. (1903-). 1961. Coward-McCann. (P.739)
--*Second Satellite.* Richardson, Robert Shirley (1902-). 1956. Whittlesey House. (P.763)
--*Snowy: The Story of an Egret.* Bancroft, Griffing (1907-). 1970. Dutton. (P.68)
--*Snowy: The Story of an Egret.* Bancroft, Griffing (1907-). 1970. McCall. (P.68)
Hunter, Susan
--*The Sword in the Stone.* Storr, Catherine Cole (1913-). 1985. Raintree Childrens Books. (P.863)
Hunter, Ted & Hunter, Mark
--*The Remarkable Harry.* Hunter, Evan (1926-). 1961. Abelard-Schuman. (P.474)
Hunter, Virginia
--*Our Animal Friends: A Real Live Animal Book.* Hunter, Virginia. c.1956. Rand McNally. (P.475)
Hunter, Warren
--*The Amazing Land of Wew.* Kaufer, John G (1905-). 1954. Steck Co. (P.509)
--*Stories of Christmas and the Bowie Knife.* Dobie, James Frank (1888-1964). 1953. Steck Co. (P.275)
--*Tales of the Western World: Folk Tales of the Americas.* Suddeth, Ruth Elgin & Morenus, Constance Gay. 1953. Steck Co. (P.870)
--*Twelve Legendary Stories of Texas.* Chapman, Iva. 1940. The Naylor Company. (P.186)
--*Two Silly Kings.* Phillips, Loretta (1893-) & Phillips, Prentice (1894-). 1964. Steck-V. (P.724)
Hunter, William (1942-)
--*Adventures of Ulysses.* Evslin, Bernard (1922-). 1970. Schol Bk Serv. (P.313)
--*The Balloon Farm.* Slicer, Margaret O (1920-). 1968. Abingdon Press. (P.829)
Huntington, Will
--*A Little Old Man.* Norton, Natalie. 1959. Rand McNally. (P.687)
Huppi, Vernon
--*Adventuring with David.* Boyle, Emily Joyce (1901-). c.1961. Abingdon Press. (P.123)
Hurd, Clement (1908-)
--*The Annie Moran.* Hurd, Edith Thacher, Mrs. (1910-). c.1942. Lothrop, Lee & Shepard Co. (P.475)
--*The Bad Little Duckhunter.* Brown, Margaret Wise (1910-1952). 1947. W. R. Scott. (P.140)
--*Benny the Bulldozer.* Hurd, Edith Thacher, Mrs. (1910-). c.1947. Lothrop, Lee & Shepard Co. (P.475)
--*The Blue Heron Tree.* Hurd, Edith Thacher, Mrs. (1910-). 1968. Viking Press. (P.475)
--*Bumble Bugs and Elephants.* Brown, Margaret Wise (1910-1952). 1938. Scott. (P.140)
--*Bumble Bugs and Elephants: A Big and Little Book.* Hurd, Clement (1908-). Brown, Margaret Wise (1910-1952), contrib. by. 1938. W. R. Scott. (P.475)
--*Caboose.* Hurd, Edith Thacher, Mrs. (1910-). 1950. Lothrop Bks. (P.475)
--*The Cat From Telegraph Hill.* Hurd, Edith Thacher, Mrs. (1910-). N.D. E. M. Hale & Co. (P.475)
--*Catfish.* 1st ed. Hurd, Edith Thacher, Mrs. (1910-). 1970. Viking Press. (P.475)
--*Catfish and the Kidnapped Cat.* 1st ed. Hurd, Edith Thacher, Mrs. (1910-). 1974. Harper & Row. (P.475)
--*Christmas Eve.* Hurd, Edith Thacher, Mrs. (1910-). 1962. Harper & Row. (P.475)
--*Come and Have Fun.* Hurd, Edith Thacher, Mrs. (1910-). 1962. Har-Row. (P.475)
--*Day the Sun Danced.* Hurd, Edith Thacher, Mrs. (1910-). 1966. Har-Row. (P.475)
--*The Devil's Tail: Adventures of a Printer's Apprentice in Early Williamsburg.* 1st ed. Hurd, Edith Thacher, Mrs. (1910-). c.1954. Doubleday. (P.475)
--*Diggers.* Brown, Margaret Wise (1910-1952). 1960. Har-Row. (P.140)
--*Engine, Engine, No.* 9. Hurd, Edith Thacher, Mrs. (1910-). c.1940. Lothrop, Lee & Shepard Co. (P.475)
--*The Faraway Christmas: A Story of the Farallon Islands.* Hurd, Edith Thacher, Mrs. (1910-). c.1958. Lothrop, Lee and Shepard. (P.475)
--*Follow Tomas.* Hurd, Edith Thacher, Mrs. (1910-). 1963. Dial Press. (P.475)
--*Follow Tomas.* Hurd, Edith Thacher, Mrs. (1910-). 1963. E. M. Hale and Company. (P.475)
--*Fox in a Box.* 1st ed. Hurd, Edith Thacher, Mrs. (1910-). c.1957. Doubleday. (P.475)
--*The Galleon from Manila.* Hurd, Edith Thacher, Mrs. (1910-). 1949. Oxford Univ. Press. (P.475)
--*Goodnight Moon.* Brown, Margaret Wise (1910-1952). 1947. Har-Row. (P.140)
--*Goodnight Moon.* Brown, Margaret Wise (1910-1952). 1977. Har-Row. (P.140)
--*Hello Peter.* Gipson, Morrell (1920-). 1948. Doubleday. (P.370)
--*Hurry Hurry.* Hurd, Edith Thacher, Mrs. (1910-). 1960. Harper. (P.475)
--*It's Snowing.* Hurd, Edith Thacher, Mrs. (1910-). 1957. Sterling Pub. Co. (P.475)
--*Johnny Lion's Bad Day.* Hurd, Edith Thacher, Mrs. (1910-). 1970. Har-Row. (P.475)
--*Johnny Lion's Book.* Hurd, Edith Thacher, Mrs. (1910-). 1965. Har-Row. (P.475)
--*Johnny Lion's Rubber Boots.* 1st ed. Hurd, Edith Thacher, Mrs. (1910-). 1972. Harper & Row. (P.475)
--*Last One Home Is a Green Pig.* Hurd, Edith Thacher, Mrs. (1910-). 1959. Har-Row. (P.475)
--*The Lion on Scott Street.* Siepmann, Jane. N.D. Oxford University Press. (P.823)
--*The Lion on Scott Street.* Siepmann, Jane. 1952. Walck. (P.823)
--*The Little Brass Band.* Brown, Margaret Wise (1910-1952). 1955. Harper. (P.141)
--*Little Dog, Dreaming.* Hurd, Edith Thacher, Mrs. (1910-) & Hurd, Thacher (1949-). 1967. Harper & Row. (P.476)
--*Look for a Bird.* Hurd, Edith Thacher, Mrs. (1910-). 1977. Har-Row. (P.475)
--*Mary's Scary House.* Hurd, Edith Thacher, Mrs. (1910-). 1956. Sterling Pub. Co. (P.475)
--*The Merry Chase.* Hurd, Clement (1908-). N.D. Random House. (P.475)
--*Mister Charlie, the Fireman's Friend.* Hurd, Edith Thacher, Mrs. (1910-). 1958. Hale. (P.475)
--*Monkey in the Jungle.* Preston, Edna Mitchell. 1968. Viking Press. **Award: (BGH).** (P.738)
--*The Mother Beaver.* 1st ed. Hurd, Edith Thacher, Mrs. (1910-). 1971. Little, Brown. (P.475)
--*The Mother Deer.* Hurd, Edith Thacher, Mrs. (1910-). 1972. Little. (P.475)
--*The Mother Owl.* Hurd, Edith Thacher, Mrs. (1910-). 1974. Little Brown and Company. (P.475)
--*The Mother Whale.* Hurd, Edith Thacher, Mrs. (1910-). N.D. Little Brown and Company. (P.475)
--*Mr.* Charlie's Camping Trip. Hurd, Edith Thacher, Mrs. (1910-). N.D. E. M. Hale & Co. (P.475)
--*Mr.* Charlie's Farm. Hurd, Edith Thacher, Mrs. (1910-). 1960. Lippincott. (P.475)
--*Mr.* Charlie's Gas Station. Hurd, Edith Thacher, Mrs. (1910-). c.1956. Lippincott. (P.475)
--*Mr.* Charlie's Pet Shop. Hurd, Edith Thacher, Mrs. (1910-). N.D. E. M. Hale & Co. (P.475)
--*My World.* Brown, Margaret Wise (1910-1952). c.1949. Harper. (P.141)
--*Nicholas.* Cowles, Ginny (1924-). 1975. Seabury Press. (P.224)
--*Nino & His Fish.* Hurd, Edith Thacher, Mrs. (1910-). N.D. E. M. Hale & Co. (P.475)
--*No Funny Business.* Hurd, Edith Thacher, Mrs. (1910-). 1962. Har-Row. (P.475)
--*Old Silversides.* Hurd, Edith Thacher, Mrs. (1910-). 1951. Hale. (P.475)
--*Old Silversides.* Hurd, Edith Thacher, Mrs. (1910-). N.D. Lothrop, Lee & Shepard. (P.475)
--*The Peppermint Family.* Brown, Margaret Wise (1910-1952). 1950. Harper & Bros. (P.141)
--*The Race.* Hurd, Clement (1908-). N.D. Random House. (P.475)
--*The Race Between the Monkey and the Duck.* Hurd, Clement (1908-). 1946. Wonder Books. (P.475)
--*Rain and the Valley.* Hurd, Edith Thacher, Mrs. (1910-). 1968. Coward-McCann. (P.475)
--*Run, Run, Run.* Hurd, Clement (1908-). 1951. Harper. (P.475)
--*The Runaway Bunny.* Brown, Margaret Wise (1910-1952). 1942. Harper & Brothers. (P.141)
--*The Runaway Bunny.* Revised. Brown, Margaret Wise (1910-1952). 1962. Harper. (P.141)
--*The Runaway Bunny.* Brown, Margaret Wise (1910-1952). 1972, c.1942. Harper & Row. (P.141)
--*Seraphine Went Walking.* Serrage, Jane. c.1944. E. P. Dutton and Company, Inc. (P.810)
--*The So-So Cat.* Hurd, Edith Thacher, Mrs. (1910-). 1965. Harper & Row. (P.475)
--*Speedy, the Hook & Ladder Truck.* Hurd, Edith Thacher, Mrs. (1910-). c.1942. Lothrup, Lee & Shepard Co. (P.475)
--*St.* George's Day in Williamsburg. Hurd, Edith Thacher, Mrs. (1910-). c.1952. Colonial Williamsburg. (P.475)
--*Stop Stop.* Hurd, Edith Thacher, Mrs. (1910-). 1961. Har-Row. (P.475)
--*Stop, Stop.* Hurd, Edith Thacher, Mrs. (1910-). 1961. Harper. (P.475)
--*Toughy and His Trailer Truck.* Hurd, Edith Thacher, Mrs. (1910-). c.1948. Lothrop, Lee & Shepard Co. (P.475)
--*Under the Lemon Tree.* 1st ed. Hurd, Edith Thacher, Mrs. (1910-). c.1980. Little, Brown. (P.475)
--*What Whale, Where.* Hurd, Edith Thacher, Mrs. (1910-). 1966. Har-Row. (P.475)
--*Wildfire.* 1st ed. Valens, Evans G. (1920-). 1963. World Pub. Co. (P.912)
--*Willy's Farm.* Hurd, Edith Thacher, Mrs. (1910-). 1949. Lothrop, Lee and Shepard. (P.475)
--*Wilson's World.* 1st ed. Hurd, Edith Thacher, Mrs. (1910-). 1971. Harper & Row. (P.475)
--*Windy & The Willow Whistle.* Hurd, Edith Thacher, Mrs. (1910-). N.D. E. M. Hale & Co. (P.475)
--*Windy and the Willow Whistle.* Hurd, Edith Thacher, Mrs. (1910-). 1956. Sterling Pub. Co. (P.475)
--*Wingfin and Topple.* Valens, Evans G., Jr. (1920-). 1962. World Publ Co. **Award: (ALA).** (P.912)
--*Winter's Birds.* Garelick, May (1910-). 1965. Young Scott Books. (P.355)
--*The World ... Is Round.* Stein, Gertrude (1874-1946). c.1939. W. R. Scott, Inc. (P.851)
--*The World Is Round.* Stein, Gertrude (1874-1946). 1966, c.1939. Young Scott Books. (P.851)
Hurd, Peter, jt. illus. see Wyeth, Newell Convers.
Hurd, Peter (1904-1984)
--*A Book of the Great Old Stories.* Hoppin, Frederick Street, retold by. c.1931. David McKay Company. (P.463)
--*Deep Silver: A Story of the Cod Banks.* Burglon, Nora. 1938. Houghton Mifflin Company. (P.153)
--*Gone Haywire.* Rollins, Philip Ashton (1869-). N.D. Charles Scribner's Sons. (P.775)
--*Great Adventures in History and Legend.* Hoppin, Frederick Street. c.1940. David McKay Company. (P.463)
--*Great Stories of the Sea & Ships.* Wyeth, Newell Convers (1882-1945). c.1940. David McKay Company. (P.983)
--*Heroes of the Olden Time.* Baldwin, James (1841-1925). N.D. Charles Scribner's Sons. (P.65)
--*Injuns Comin'!.* Pearson, Molly Winston, Mrs. (1876-) & Bullis, Franklin Howard (1860-). 1935. C. Scribner's Sons. (P.713)
--*Marauders of the Sea.* Wyeth, Newell Convers (1882-1945), ed. N.D. G P Putnam's Sons. (P.983)
--*The P-Zoo.* Hamilton, Elizabeth (1945-). Gag, Flavia, contrib. by. N.D. Coward-McCann. (P.408)
--*The Story of Roland.* Baldwin, James (1841-1925). c.1930. C. Scribner's Sons. (P.65)
--*The Story of Siegfried.* Baldwin, James (1841-1925). c.1931. C. Scribner's Sons. (P.65)
--*Swift Rivers.* Meigs, Cornelia Lynde (1884-1973). 1937. Little, Brown and Company. (P.639)
Hurd, Thacher (1949-)
--*Axle the Freeway Cat.* Hurd, Thacher (1949-). c.1981. Harper & Row. (P.476)
--*Hobo Dog.* Hurd, Thacher (1949-). 1981. Scholastic Inc. (P.476)
--*Mama Don't Allow.* Hurd, Thacher (1949-). 1984. HarpJ. **Award: (BGH).** (P.476)
--*Mystery on the Docks.* 1st ed. Hurd, Thacher (1949-). c.1983. Harper & Row. (P.476)
--*The Old Chair.* Hurd, Thacher (1949-). c.1978. Greenwillow Books. (P.476)
--*The Quiet Evening.* Hurd, Thacher (1949-). c.1978. Greenwillow Books. (P.476)
Hurford, Miriam Story
--*Daniel Boone.* Shapiro, Irwin (1911-). 1956. Simon and Schuster. (P.814)
Hurlimann, Ruth (1939-)
--*The Mouse with the Daisy Hat.* Hurlimann, Ruth (1939-). 1971. D. White. (P.476)
--*The Proud White Cat.* Hurlimann, Ruth (1939-), retold by. Bell, Anthea, tr. 1977. Morrow. (P.476)
Hurst, Earl Oliver
--*Playmates in Print, Verses and Stories for Children.* Whiteman, Edna. c.1926. T. Nelson & Sons. (P.954)
Hurst, Fannie (1889-1968)
--*Anitra's Dance.* Hurst, Fannie (1889-1968). 1934. Harper & Brothers. (P.476)
Hurst, Hal
--*Through the Sikh War: A Tale of the Conquest of the Punjaub.* Henty, George Alfred (1832-1902). 1893. C. Scribner's Sons. (P.436)
Hurst, Irene
--*One, Two, Three, Four and Many More: Stories.* Hurst, Irene. 1957. Comet Press Books. (P.476)
Hurwitz, Claudine see Claudine, pseud.
Hurwitz, Claudine
--*Rabash.* Claudine, pseud. Hurwitz, Claudine. Claudine, pseud. c.1965. Macmillan. (P.476)
Hurwitz, Harriet
--*Casey's Sore-Throat Day.* Brown, Myra Berry (1918-). 1964. F. Watts. (P.142)
Hurwitz, Johanna (1937-)
--*Nora and Mrs.* Mind-Your-Own-Business. Jeschke, Susan (1942-). 1977. Morrow. (P.492)
--*Superduper Teddy.* Jeschke, Susan (1942-). 1980. Morrow. (P.492)
Hurwitz, Johanna (1937-) & Johnson, Pamela
--*The Rabbi's Girls.* 1982. Morrow. **Award: (ALA).** (P.476)
Husch, Mary Louise
--*Cougar Pass.* Wood, Elizabeth Lambert, Mrs. N.D. Binfords & Mort. (P.975)
--*Silver House of Klone Chuck.* Wood, Elizabeth Lambert, Mrs. N.D. Binfords & Mort. (P.975)
Hussett, Milton, jt. illus. see Brown, Joel.
Husted, Mary Irving
--*Cunning-Cunning and His Merry Comrades.* Husted, Mary Irving. N.D. Lothrop Lee & Shepard Co. (P.476)
Huston, Ed
--*This Bus Is Stuffed to the Brim!.* Marshall, George. 1976. Mediaworks. (P.623)
Hutaf, August W.
--*Mrs. Goose, her book.* Switzer, Maurice. 1907. Moffat, Yard & Co. (P.875)
Hutchens, Paul (1902-1977)
--*The Sugar Creek Gang & Blue Cow.* Hutchens, Paul (1902-1977). 1971. Moody. (P.476)
--*The Sugar Creek Gang & the Watermelon Mystery.* Hutchens, Paul (1902-1977). 1971. Moody. (P.477)
Hutcheson, James
--*A Magic Book of Birds.* Haddon, Tessa. 1976. Canongate. (P.401)
Hutchings
--*The Gingerbread Man.* Cork, Denise. 1972. Rand. (P.220)

--*The Ghost Next Door.* 1st ed. St. John, Wylly Folk (1908-). 1971. Harper & Row. (P.789)
--*Greedy Mariani: And Other Folktales of the Antilles.* Carter, Dorothy Sharp (1921-), ed. 1974. Atheneum. (P.175)
--*Greta the Strong.* Sobol, Donald J. (1924-). 1970. Follett Pub. Co. (P.840)
--*The Half-Time Gypsy.* 1st ed. Varney, Joyce. 1968. Bobbs-Merrill. (P.916)
--*A Hidden Magic.* Vande Velde, Vivian. c.1985. Crown. (P.913)
--*Home.* 1st ed. Hearne, Betsy Gould. 1979. Atheneum. (P.428)
--*How Does it Feel to Be Old?.* Farber, Norma (1909-1984). 1979. Dutton. (P.316)
--*How I Went Shopping and What I Got.* 1st ed. Clymer, Eleanor Lowenton (1906-). 1972. Holt, Rinehart and Winston. (P.203)
--*How Six Found Christmas.* 1st ed. Hyman, Trina Schart (1939-). 1969. Little, Brown. (P.478)
--*Jane, Wishing.* Tobias, Tobi (1938-). c.1977. Viking Press. (P.893)
--*Joanna Runs Away.* 1st ed. La Farge, Phyllis. 1973. Holt, Rinehart and Winston. (P.543)
--*Joy to the World: Christmas Legends.* Sawyer, Ruth Estelle (1880-1970). 1966. Little. **Award: (ALA).** (P.795)
--*King Stork.* 1st ed. Pyle, Howard (1853-1911). 1973. Little, Brown. **Award: (BGH).** (P.742)
--*Let's Steal the Moon: Jewish Tales, Ancient and Recent.* 1st ed. Serwer, Blanche Luria (1910-). 1970. Little, Brown. (P.811)
--*Listen, Children, Listen: An Anthology of Poems for the Very Young.* Livingston, Myra Cohn (1926-), ed. 1972. Harcourt Brace Jovanovich. (P.578)
--*The Little Red Flower.* Tripp, Paul (1916-). 1968. Doubleday. (P.900)
--*Little Red Riding Hood.* Hyman, Trina Schart (1939-), retold by. 1982. Holiday. **Awards: (ALA); (RCM).** (P.478)
--*Magic Heart.* Wahl, Jan (1933-). 1972. Seabury Press. (P.924)
--*Magic in the Mist.* Kimmel, Margaret Mary. 1975. Atheneum. (P.523)
--*The Magic Maker.* 1st ed. Varney, Joyce. 1967, c.1966. Bobbs-Merrill. (P.916)
--*Magical Melons.* Brink, Carol Ryrie, Mrs. (1895-1981). 1944. Macmillan. (P.132)
--*The Man Who Loved Books.* Fritz, Jean Guttery (1915-). 1981. Putnam Pub Group. (P.347)
--*The Marrow of the World.* 1st ed. Nichols, Johanna Ruth (1948-). 1972. Atheneum. **Award: (CLA).** (P.681)
--*The Mechanical Doll.* Stearns, Pamela Fujimoto (1935-). 1979. Houghton Mifflin. (P.850)
--*Meet Guguze.* Vangeli, Spiridon (1932-). Morton, Miriam (1918-), tr. c.1977. Addison Wesley. (P.914)
--*Moon Eyes.* Poole, Josephine (1933-). 1967. Little, Brown. (P.731)
--*The Moon Singer.* Bulla, Clyde Robert (1914-). 1969. Crowell. (P.149)
--*The Night Journey.* Lasky, Kathryn (1944-). 1981. F. Warne. **Award: (ALA).** (P.553)
--*On to Widecombe Fair.* Gauch, Patricia Lee (1934-). c.1978. Putnam. **Award: (BGH).** (P.360)
--*Peter Pan.* Barrie, James Matthew, Sir (1860-1937). 1980. Scribner. (P.76)
--*The Popular Girls Club.* Krasilovsky, Phyllis (1926-). 1972. Simon and Schuster. (P.537)
--*Princess Rosetta & the Popcorn Man.* Wilkins, Mary Eleanor (1852-1930). Greene, Ellin, retold by. 1971. Lothrop. (P.961)
--*Princess Rosetta and the Popcorn Man, from The Pot of Gold.* Greene, Ellin, Mrs. (1918-), ed. Freeman, Mary Eleanor Wilkins (1852-1930). 1971. Lothrop, Lee & Shepard Co. (P.344)
--*The Pumpkin Giant.* Greene, Ellin (1918-) & Freeman, Mary Eleanor Wilkins (1852-1930). 1970. Lothrop, Lee & Shepard Co. (P.387)
--*The Quitting Deal.* 1st ed. Tobias, Tobi (1938-). 1975. Viking Press. (P.893)
--*Rapunzel.* Grimm, Jakob Ludwig Karl (1785-1863) & Grimm, Wilhelm Karl (1786-1859). Rogasky, Barbara, retold by. 1982. Holiday. **Award: (ALA).** (P.394)
--*Riddles, Riddles from A to Z.* Memling, Carl (1918-1969). 1962. Western Pub. (P.640)
--*A Room Made of Windows.* Cameron, Eleanor (1912-). 1971. Little, Brown. **Awards: (BGH); (ALA).** (P.163)
--*Saint George and the Dragon: A Golden Legend.* 1st ed. Hodges, Margaret Moore (1911-), adapted by. c.1984. Little, Brown. **Awards: (NYT); (RCM); (ALA).** (P.449)
--*Sarah and Katie.* 1st ed. White, Dori (1919-). 1972. Harper & Row. (P.951)
--*The Shy Little Girl.* Krasilovsky, Phyllis (1926-). 1970. Houghton Mifflin. (P.537)
--*Sir Machinery.* McGowen, Tom, pseud. (1927-). McGowen, Thomas. 1971. Follett. (P.602)
--*The Sleeping Beauty.* 1st ed. Grimm, Jakob Ludwig Karl (1785-1863) & Grimm, Wilhelm Karl (1786-1859). Hyman, Trina Schart (1939-), adapted by. 1977, c.1976. Little, Brown. (P.394)
--*Snow White.* 1st ed. Grimm, Jakob Ludwig Karl (1785-1863) & Grimm, Wilhelm Karl (1786-1859). Heins, Paul (1909-), tr. from Ger. 1974. Little, Brown. (P.394)
--*South Star.* 1st ed. Hearne, Betsy Gould. 1977. Atheneum. (P.428)
--*Star Mother's Youngest Child.* Moeri, Louise (1924-). 1975. Houghton Mifflin. (P.653)
--*Stuck with Luck.* 1st ed. Johnson, Elizabeth (1911-). 1967. Little, Brown. (P.495)
--*Take It or Leave It.* Molarsky, Osmond (1909-). 1971. H. Z. Walck. (P.653)
--*Tight Times.* Hazen, Barbara Shook (1930-). 1983. Puffin Books. (P.427)
--*Tight Times.* Hazen, Barbara Shook (1930-). 1979. Viking Press. (P.427)
--*Two Queens of Heaven, Aphrodite and Demeter.* Gates, Doris (1901-). 1983. Puffin Books. (P.359)
--*Two Queens of Heaven, Aphrodite, Demeter.* Gates, Doris (1901-). 1974. Viking Press. (P.359)
--*The Ugly Duckling & Two Other Stories.* Andersen, Hans Christian (1805-1875). Moore, Lilian, ed. 1973. Schol Bk Serv. (P.38)
--*The Vi-Daylin Book of Minnie the Mump, and Other Stories.* Tripp, Paul (1916-). 1970. Ross Laboratories. (P.900)
--*A Walk Out of the World.* Nichols, Johanna Ruth (1948-). 1969. Harcourt, Brace & World. **Award: (ALA).** (P.681)
--*The Walking Stones: A Story of Suspense.* McIlwraith, Maureen Mollie Hunter McVeigh (1922-). 1973, c.1970. Harper. (P.604)
--*The Wanderers.* Coatsworth, Elizabeth Jane (1893-). 1972. Four Winds Press. (P.204)
--*Who Says So?.* Hendrich, Paula Griffith (1928-). 1973, c.1972. G. K. Hall. (P.433)
--*Who Says So.* Hendrich, Paula Griffith (1928-). 1972. William Morrow and Company. (P.433)
--*Witch Poems.* Wallace, Daisy. c.1976. Holiday House. (P.927)
--*A Wreath of Carols.* Owen, Betty Meek (1913-) & Macewen, Mary E., eds. 1967. Four Winds Press. (P.698)
--*Wreath of Carols.* Owen, Betty Meek (1913-) & MacEwen, Mary E., eds. 1968. Schol Bk Serv. (P.698)
--*You've come a Long Way Sybil Macintosh.* Herman, Charlotte (1937-). 1974. J. Philip O'Hara Inc. (P.438)

Hyman, Trina Schart (1939-) & Knight, Hilary
--*The Cat Walked Through the Casserole: And Other Poems for Children.* Espeland, Pamela Lee (1951-) & Waniek, Marilyn Nelson (1946-). c.1984. Carolrhoda Bks. (P.310)

Iannelli, Margaret
--*My Viking Book.* Harshaw, Ruth Hetzel, Mrs. (1890-1968). Washburne, Carleton Wolsey (1889-), ed. c.1934. Rand, McNally & Company. (P.417)
--*Reindeer of the Waves.* Harshaw, Ruth Hetzel, Mrs. (1890-1968). Washburne, Carleton Wolsey (1889-), ed. c.1934. Rand, McNally & Company. (P.417)

Ibrahim, Abdullah
--*A Time of Darkness.* Frazer, Shamus. 1975. Oxford U Pr. (P.343)

Ichikawa, Satomi (1939-)
--*Friends.* Ichikawa, Satomi (1939-). 1977, c.1976. Parents' Magazine Press. (P.479)
--*From Morn to Midnight.* Ichikawa, Satomi (1939-). Moss, Elaine Dora (1924-), selected by. 1977. Har-Row. (P.479)
--*Keep Running, Allen!.* Bulla, Clyde Robert (1914-). c.1978. Crowell. (P.149)
--*Merry Christmas: Children at Christmastime Around the World.* Wilson, Robina Beckles (1930-). 1983. Philomel Books. (P.967)
--*Playtime.* Mitchell, Cynthia (1922-). 1979, c.1978. Collins. (P.652)
--*Sun Through Small Leaves: Poems of Spring.* Ichikawa, Satomi (1939-). c.1980. Collins. (P.479)
--*Suzanne & Nicholas at the Market.* Ichikawa, Satomi (1939-). 1978. Watts. (P.479)
--*Suzette & Nicholas & the Seasons Clock.* Mangin, Marie F. 1982. Putnam Pub Group. (P.616)
--*Suzette and Nicholas and the Sunijudi Circus.* Lochak, Michele (1936-). 1980, c.1979. Philomel Books. (P.579)
--*Suzette & Nicholas & the Sunijudi Circus.* Lochak, Michele (1936-) & Mangin, Marie-France. 1981. Putnam Pub Group. (P.579)
--*Under the Cherry Tree.* Mitchell, Cynthia (1922-). 1979. Putnam Pub Group. (P.652)

Ickes, Paul
--*The Indian Nugget.* King, Julius (1893-). c.1931. W. J. Black, Inc. (P.523)

Icove, David B.
--*Bobby's Diary.* Roche, Ruth A. 1944. Action Play-Books Inc. (P.771)
--*Indian Legends.* Roche, Ruth A. N.D. Action Play-Books. (P.771)
--*Peter Pupp.* Roche, Ruth A. 1944. Action Play-Books Inc. (P.771)

Ideals Staff
--*Deluxe Story of Christmas for Children.* Ideals Staff. 1984. Ideals. (P.479)

Iessel, Manon
--*The Mink and the Fairy.* 1st English language ed. Robitaillie, Henriette. Beaman, Sallie Louise, tr. from Fr. 1954. Exposition Press. (P.771)

Iguchi, Bunshu
--*The Old Man Who Made the Trees Bloom.* Shibano, Tamizo. Ooka, D. T., tr. from Japanese. 1985. Heian Intl. (P.820)

Ihms, Jimmie
--*Mystery of Superstition Mountain.* Arnold, Oren (1900-). 1972. Harvey House. (P.49)

Ihrig, Robert
--*Strange Summer in Stratford.* 1st ed. Perez, Norah A. 1968. Little, Brown. (P.717)

Iizawa, Tadasu (1909-) & Hijikata, Shigemi (1915-)
--*Baby's Santa Mouse.* Brown, Michael (1920-). 1969. Grosset & Dunlap. (P.141)
--*Bedtime Stories.* 1970. G&D. (P.479)
--*Child's Garden of Verses.* 1970. G&D. (P.479)
--*The Elves and the Shoemaker.* Grimm, Jakob Ludwig Karl (1785-1863) & Grimm, Wilhelm Karl (1786-1859). 1971. Grosset & Dunlap. (P.391)
--*Goldilocks and the Three Bears.* 1971. Grosset & Dunlap. (P.479)
--*The Grosset Treasury of Nursery Rhymes and Stories.* 1971. Grosset & Dunlap. (P.479)
--*Hansel & Gretel.* 1981. Putnam Pub Group. (P.479)
--*Little Nursery Rhymes.* 1970. G&D. (P.479)
--*The Little Red Hen.* 1981. Putnam Pub Group. (P.479)
--*Little Red Riding Hood.* 1971. Grosset & Dunlap. (P.479)
--*Peter Rabbit.* 1981. Putnam Pub Group. (P.479)
--*Pinocchio.* 1970. G&D. (P.479)
--*Pinocchio.* Lorenzini, Carlo (1826-1890). Collodi, Carlo, pseud. 1971. Grosset & Dunlap. (P.584)
--*A Puppet Treasure Book of Fairy Tales.* 1981. Putnam Pub Group. (P.479)
--*A Puppet Treasure Book of Nursery Rhymes.* 1981. Putnam Pub Group. (P.479)
--*The Real Princess.* Andersen, Hans Christian (1805-1875). 1971. Grosset & Dunlap. (P.37)
--*Rumpelstiltskin.* 1971. Grosset & Dunlap. (P.479)
--*Sleeping Beauty.* Grimm, Jakob Ludwig Karl (1785-1863) & Grimm, Wilhelm Karl (1786-1859). 1971. Grosset & Dunlap. (P.394)
--*Sleeping Beauty.* 1972. Putnam Pub Group. (P.479)
--*Snow White & the Seven Dwarfs.* 1981. Putnam Pub Group. (P.479)
--*Three Little Pigs.* 1970. G&D. (P.479)
--*The Three Little Pigs.* 1971. Grosset & Dunlap. (P.479)
--*Tom Thumb.* 1971. Grosset & Dunlap. (P.479)
--*The Ugly Duckling.* Andersen, Hans Christian (1805-1875). 1971. Grosset & Dunlap. (P.37)
--*What Time Is It?.* 1981. Putnam Pub Group. (P.479)

Iizawa, Tadasu (1909-) & Kawamoto, Kihachiro
--*Christmas Songs and Verse.* 1971. Grosset & Dunlap. (P.479)

Ike, Jane Hori
--*The Doll Book.* Draper, Delores. 1977. Western Pub. (P.284)
--*A Japanese Fairy Tale.* Ike, Jane Hori & Zimmerman, Baruch. c.1982. F. Warne. (P.479)

Illingworth, L. G.
--*The King's Mule.* Akers, Dwight. c.1933. Minton, Balch & Company. (P.16)

Illman, Marjorie Kincaid
--*Hermie's Trailer House.* Guberlet, Muriel Lewin. N.D. Jaques Cattell Press. (P.398)

Ilona, pseud., see Segner, Ellen.

Ilona, pseud.
--*Jimmy Wins a Prize.* Segner, Ellen. Gale, Helen Mary (1912-). 1946. John Martin's House, Inc. (P.352)

Ilsley, Velma Elizabeth (1918-)
--*Brownies--Hurry.* Adshead, Gladys Lucy (1896-). 1959. Walck. (P.12)
--*Brownies its Christmas.* Abel, Ruth. 1955. Henry Z. Walck, Inc. (P.3)
--*Brownies Its Christmas.* Adshead, Gladys Lucy (1896-). 1955. Henry Z. Walck, Inc., Publishers. (P.12)
--*The Cat Across the Way.* Huston, Anne. 1968. Seabury Press. (P.476)
--*Cristy at Skippinghills.* 1st ed. Hunt, Mabel Leigh (1892-1971). 1958. Lippincott. (P.474)
--*Enchanted Sixteen.* 1st ed. Conrad, Sybil (1921-). 1957. Holt. (P.214)
--*For Each a Dream.* 1st ed. Jacobs, Emma Atkins (1885-). 1958. Holt. (P.486)
--*The Giving Gift.* Power-Waters, Alma Shelley (1896-). 1962. Farrar, Straus & Cudahy. (P.736)
--*The Heart of Camp Whippoorwill.* Miller, Alice Patricia McCarthy. 1960. Lippincott. (P.646)
--*Joe Bean.* Agle, Nan Hayden (1905-). c.1967. Seabury. (P.14)
--*Kate and the Apple Tree.* Agle, Nan Hayden (1905-). c.1965. Seabury. (P.14)
--*Miss Jellytot's Visit.* 1st ed. Hunt, Mabel Leigh (1892-1971). 1955. Lippincott. (P.474)
--*Mungo.* Fry, Rosalie Kingsmill (1911-). 1972. Farrar, Straus & Giroux. (P.348)
--*Mystery at the Doll Hospital.* 1st ed. Honness, Elizabeth Hoffman, Mrs. (1904-). 1955. Lippincott. (P.458)
--*Mystery at the Shoals.* Bradley, Duane, pseud. (1914-). Sanborn, Duane. 1962. Lippincott. (P.125)
--*Mystery of Hurricane Castle.* Nixon, Joan Lowery (1927-). 1964. Criterion Books. (P.683)
--*Mystery of the Black Sheep.* Weir, Rosemary Green (1905-). 1964, c.1963. Criterion Books. (P.942)
--*Only Jane.* Cone, Molly Lamken (1918-). 1960. T. Nelson. (P.213)
--*Our New Baby's ABC.* Lord, Beman (1924-). 1964. David McKay Company. (P.584)
--*Our New Baby's ABC.* Lord, Beman (1924-). 1964. H. Z. Walck. (P.584)
--*Princess Hynchatti and Some Other Surprises.* Lee, Tanith (1947-). 1973, c.1972. Farrar, Straus and Giroux. (P.561)
--*She and the Dubious Three.* Crayder, Dorothy. 1974. Atheneum. (P.230)
--*She, the Adventuress.* Crayder, Dorothy. 1973. Atheneum. (P.230)
--*She, the Adventuress.* Crayder, Dorothy. 1979. Atheneum. (P.230)
--*Sing Out, Charley!.* Hodges, Margaret Moore (1911-). 1968. Farrar, Straus & Giroux. (P.449)
--*Smallest Brownie's Fearful Adventure.* Adshead, Gladys Lucy (1896-). 1961. Walck. (P.12)
--*Stars for Cristy.* 1st ed. Hunt, Mabel Leigh (1892-1971). 1956. Lippincott. (P.474)
--*Stormy Summer.* Harrington, Lyn Davis (1911-). 1956. Abelard-Schuman. (P.414)
--*Time for Lissa.* Caudill, Rebecca (1899-). 1959. Hale. (P.178)
--*Time for Lissa.* Caudill, Rebecca (1899-). 1959. T. Nelson. (P.178)
--*To Live a Lie.* Alexander, Anne Barbara Cooke (1913-). 1975. Atheneum. (P.22)
--*What's a Cousin?.* Olds, Helen Diehl (1895-1981). 1962. Knopf. (P.693)

Iltis, Julia
--*Behind the Magic Line.* 1st ed. Erwin, Betty K. 1969. Little, Brown. (P.309)

Ilyin, Gleb
--*A Child's Garden: A Fantasy.* Barnett, Maybelle Fuller, Mrs. 1941. Margent Press. (P.73)

Imhoff, Howard
--*Other People's Children.* Peckham, Betty Clock (1906-). 1943. T. Nelson and Sons. (P.715)

Imsand, Marcel & Marshall, Rita
--*The Fir Tree.* american ed. Andersen, Hans Christian (1805-1875). c.1983. Creative Education. (P.35)

Incisa, Monica
--*The Forgetful Wishing Well: Poems for Young People.* Kennedy, X. J., pseud. (1929-). Kennedy, Joseph Charles. 1985. Atheneum. **Award: (ALA).** (P.518)
--*Whiff, Sniff, Nibble, & Chew: The Gingerbread Boy Retold.* Pomerantz, Charlotte (1930-). 1984. Greenwillow. (P.731)

Inckel, A. E.
--*They're Drowning Our Village.* Rutgers van der Loeff-Basenau, Anna Maria Margarethe (1910-). Edwards, Roy, tr. from Dutch. 1960, c.1959. F. Watts. (P.786)

Inderieden, Nancy
--*Alaska Woman.* Gray, Genevieve Stuck (1920-). 1977. EMC Corp. (P.383)
--*All Along the Way.* Moore, John Travers (1908-). 1973. Carolrhoda Bks. (P.661)
--*A Better Bit and Bridle.* Dubrovin, Vivian (1931-). 1975. EMC Corp. (P.286)
--*The Bridge to Blue Hill.* Tenpas, Margaret Susan Lyon (1923-). 1972. Carolrhoda Books. (P.882)
--*The Cats of Kilkenny.* Zimelman, Nathan (1911-). 1972. Carolrhoda Books. (P.992)
--*A Chance to Win.* Dubrovin, Vivian (1931-). 1975. EMC Corp. (P.286)
--*The Dark Side of Nowhere.* Gray, Genevieve Stuck (1920-). 1977. EMC Corp. (P.383)
--*The Dirty Boy.* Kavet, Robert (1924-). 1971. Carolrhoda Books. (P.509)
--*Has Anyone Seen Buddy Bascom?.* Gray, Genevieve Stuck (1920-). 1977. EMC Corp. (P.383)
--*My Sister.* Hirsch, Karen (1941-). 1977. Carolrhoda Bks. (P.446)

--*Grampa-Lop.* Cosgrove, Stephen Edward (1945-). 1984, c.1981. Rourke Enterprises. (P.222)
--*Hucklebug.* Cosgrove, Stephen Edward (1945-). 1978, c.1975. Creative Education. (P.222)
--*Hucklebug.* Cosgrove, Stephen Edward (1945-). c.1975. Serendipity Press. (P.222)
--*In Search of the Saveopotomas.* Cosgrove, Stephen Edward (1945-). 1979. Creative Education. (P.222)
--*In Search of the Saveopotomas.* Cosgrove, Stephen Edward (1945-). c.1974. Serendipity Press. (P.222)
--*Jake O'Shawnasey.* Cosgrove, Stephen Edward (1945-). 1975. Price Stern. (P.222)
--*Jake O'Shawnasey.* Cosgrove, Stephen Edward (1945-). c.1975. Serendipity Press. (P.222)
--*Jingle Bear.* Cosgrove, Stephen Edward (1945-). 1985. Rourke Enterprises. (P.222)
--*Kartusch.* Cosgrove, Stephen Edward (1945-). c.1978. Creative Education. (P.222)
--*Kiyomi.* Cosgrove, Stephen Edward (1945-). 1984. Price Stern. (P.222)
--*Kiyomi.* Cosgrove, Stephen Edward (1945-). 1985. Rourke Enterprises. (P.222)
--*Leo the Lop.* Cosgrove, Stephen Edward (1945-). 1979. Creative Education. (P.222)
--*Leo the Lop.* Cosgrove, Stephen Edward (1945-). c.1977. Serendipity Press. (P.222)
--*Leo the Lop - Tail Three.* Cosgrove, Stephen Edward (1945-). 1980. Price Stern. (P.222)
--*Leo the Lop, Tail Three, Bk.* 1. Cosgrove, Stephen Edward (1945-). 1981. Creative Ed. (P.222)
--*Leo the Lop (Tail Two).* Cosgrove, Stephen Edward (1945-). 1979. Price Stern. (P.222)
--*Little Mouse on the Prairie.* Cosgrove, Stephen Edward (1945-). c.1978. Creative Education. (P.222)
--*Maui-Maui.* Cosgrove, Stephen Edward (1945-). 1979. Price Stern. (P.222)
--*Ming Ling.* Cosgrove, Stephen Edward (1945-). 1983. Price Stern. (P.222)
--*Ming Ling.* Cosgrove, Stephen Edward (1945-). c.1984. Rourke Enterprises. (P.223)
--*Minikin.* Cosgrove, Stephen Edward (1945-). 1984. Price Stern. (P.223)
--*Minikin.* Cosgrove, Stephen Edward (1945-). 1985. Rourke Enterprises. (P.223)
--*Morgan and Me.* Cosgrove, Stephen Edward (1945-). c.1975. Serendipity Press. (P.223)
--*Morgan & Yew.* Cosgrove, Stephen Edward (1945-). 1984. Price Stern. (P.223)
--*Morgan and Yew.* Cosgrove, Stephen Edward (1945-). c.1984. Rourke Enterprises. (P.223)
--*Morgan Mine.* Cosgrove, Stephen Edward (1945-). 1984, c.1982. Rourke Enterprises. (P.223)
--*Morgan Morning.* Cosgrove, Stephen Edward (1945-). 1984, c.1982. Rourke Enterprises. (P.223)
--*The Muffin Muncher.* Cosgrove, Stephen Edward (1945-). 1979. Creative Education. (P.223)
--*The Muffin Muncher.* Cosgrove, Stephen Edward (1945-). c.1974. Serendipity Press. (P.223)
--*Raz-Ma-Taz.* Cosgrove, Stephen Edward (1945-). c.1984. Rourke Enterprises. (P.223)
--*Serendipity.* Cosgrove, Stephen Edward (1945-). 1979. Creative Education. (P.223)
--*Serendipity.* Cosgrove, Stephen Edward (1945-). c.1974. Serendipity Press. (P.223)
--*Serendipity Box Set, No.* 4. Cosgrove, Stephen Edward (1945-). 1980. Price Stern. (P.223)
--*Shimmeree.* Cosgrove, Stephen Edward (1945-). 1981. Creative Ed. (P.223)
--*Shimmeree.* Cosgrove, Stephen Edward (1945-). 1980. Price Stern. (P.223)
--*Snaffles, Bk.* 3. Cosgrove, Stephen Edward (1945-). 1981. Creative Ed. (P.223)
--*Snaffles.* Cosgrove, Stephen Edward (1945-). 1980. Price Stern. (P.223)
--*Squeakers.* Cosgrove, Stephen Edward (1945-). 1985. Rourke Enterprises. (P.223)
--*Tee-Tee.* Cosgrove, Stephen Edward (1945-). 1983. Price Stern. (P.223)
--*Tee-Tee.* Cosgrove, Stephen Edward (1945-). c.1984. Rourke Enterprises. (P.223)
--*Trafalgar True.* Cosgrove, Stephen Edward (1945-). 1981. Creative Ed. (P.223)
--*Trapper.* Cosgrove, Stephen Edward (1945-). 1982. Price Stern. (P.223)
--*Trapper.* Cosgrove, Stephen Edward (1945-). c.1984. Rourke Enterprises. (P.223)
--*Wheedle on the Needle.* Cosgrove, Stephen Edward (1945-). 1978. Creative Education. (P.223)
--*Wheedle on the Needle.* Cosgrove, Stephen Edward (1945-). c.1974. Serendipity Press. (P.223)

James, Ron, jt. photog. see James, Toni.

James, Sandra

--*Abigail Adams: A Girl of Colonial Days.* 1st ed. Wagoner, Jean Brown (1896-). 1949. Bobbs-Merrill Co. (P.923)
--*Betsy Ross, Girl of Old Philadelphia.* 1st ed. Weil, Ann Yezner, Mrs. (1908-1969). 1954. Bobbs-Merrill. (P.940)
--*Dolly Madison, Quaker Girl.* 1st ed. Monsell, Helen Albee (1895-1971). 1944. Bobbs-Merrill. (P.657)
--*Dolly Madison, Quaker Girl.* Monsell, Helen Albee (1895-1971). 1953. Bobbs-Merrill. (P.657)
--*Ethan Allen, Green Mountain Boy.* 1st ed. Winders, Gertrude Hecker. 1954. Bobbs-Merrill. (P.967)
--*Her Star in Sight: Mary Carstens in Medical School.* Meese, Mildred Foulke, Mrs. 1942. The Bobbs-Merrill Company. (P.639)
--*Jane Addams: Little Lame Girl.* Wagoner, Jean Brown (1896-). 1944. The Bobbs-Merrill Company. (P.924)
--*John Sevier: A Pioneer Boy.* 1st ed. Steele, William Owen (1917-1979). 1953. Bobbs-Merrill. (P.850)
--*Jon of the Albany Belle.* 1st ed. Langdale, Hazel Louise Raybold, Mrs. (1889-). 1943. E. P. Dutton and Company, Inc. (P.550)
--*The Lark in the Morn.* Foulds, Elfrida Vipont Brown (1902-). 1951. Bobbs-Merrill. (P.339)
--*The Lark on the Wing.* Foulds, Elfrida Vipont Brown (1902-). 1951. Bobbs-Merrill. **Award: (CMA).** (P.339)
--*A Little Maid of Boston.* Curtis, Alice Turner, Mrs. (1860-1958). 1954. Knopf. (P.236)
--*A Little Maid of Bunker Hill.* Curtis, Alice Turner, Mrs. (1860-1958). 1952. Knopf. (P.236)
--*A Little Maid of Fort Pitt.* Curtis, Alice Turner, Mrs. (1860-1958). 1953. Knopf. (P.236)
--*A Little Maid of Lexington.* Curtis, Alice Turner, Mrs. (1860-1958). 1955. Knopf. (P.236)
--*A Little Maid of Maryland.* Curtis, Alice Turner, Mrs. (1860-1958). 1952. Knopf. (P.236)
--*A Little Maid of Massachusetts Colony.* Curtis, Alice Turner, Mrs. (1860-1958). 1951. Knopf. (P.236)
--*A Little Maid of Mohawk Valley.* Curtis, Alice Turner, Mrs. (1860-1958). 1952. Knopf. (P.236)
--*A Little Maid of Monmouth.* Curtis, Alice Turner, Mrs. (1860-1958). 1953. Knopf. (P.236)
--*A Little Maid of Nantucket.* Curtis, Alice Turner, Mrs. (1860-1958). 1950. Knopf. (P.236)
--*A Little Maid of Narragansett Bay.* Curtis, Alice Turner, Mrs. (1860-1958). 1954. Knopf. (P.236)
--*A Little Maid of New Hampshire.* Curtis, Alice Turner, Mrs. (1860-1958). 1954. Knopf. (P.236)
--*A Little Maid of New Orleans.* Curtis, Alice Turner, Mrs. (1860-1958). 1949. A. A. Knopf. (P.236)
--*A Little Maid of Newport.* 1st Borzoi ed. Curtis, Alice Turner, Mrs. (1860-1958). 1955. Knopf. (P.236)
--*A Little Maid of Old Connecticut.* Curtis, Alice Turner, Mrs. (1860-1958). 1953. Knopf. (P.236)
--*A Little Maid of Old Maine.* Curtis, Alice Turner, Mrs. (1860-1958). 1953. Knopf. (P.236)
--*A Little Maid of Old New York.* Curtis, Alice Turner, Mrs. (1860-1958). 1951. Knopf. (P.236)
--*A Little Maid of Old Philadelphia.* Curtis, Alice Turner, Mrs. (1860-1958). 1955. Knopf. (P.236)
--*A Little Maid of Province Town.* Curtis, Alice Turner, Mrs. (1860-1958). 1954. Knopf. (P.236)
--*A Little Maid of Quebec.* 1st Borzoi ed. Curtis, Alice Turner, Mrs. (1860-1958). 1955. Knopf. (P.236)
--*A Little Maid of South Carolina.* Curtis, Alice Turner, Mrs. (1860-1958). 1952. Knopf. (P.236)
--*A Little Maid of Ticonderoga.* Curtis, Alice Turner, Mrs. (1860-1958). 1954. Knopf. (P.236)
--*A Little Maid of Valley Forge.* 1st Borzoi ed. Curtis, Alice Turner, Mrs. (1860-1958). 1951. Knopf. (P.236)
--*A Little Maid of Vermont.* Curtis, Alice Turner, Mrs. (1860-1958). 1948. A. A. Knopf. (P.236)
--*A Little Maid of Virginia.* 1st Borzoi Ed. ed. Curtis, Alice Turner, Mrs. (1860-1958). 1951. Knopf. (P.237)
--*Louisa Alcott, Girl of Old Boston.* 1st ed. Wagoner, Jean Brown (1896-). 1943. The Bobbs-Merrill Company. (P.924)
--*Lucretia Mott, Girl of Old Nantucket.* 1st ed. Burnett, Constance Buel (1893-). 1951. Bobbs-Merrill. (P.154)
--*Mark of Seneca Basin.* 1st ed. Langdale, Hazel Louise Raybold, Mrs. (1889-). 1942. E. P. Dutton and Company, Inc. (P.550)
--*Martha Washington: Girl of Old Virginia.* 1st ed. Wagoner, Jean Brown (1896-). 1947. Bobbs-Merrill Co. (P.924)
--*Martha Washington of Old Virginia.* Wagoner, Jean Brown (1896-). 1953. Bobbs-Merrill. (P.924)
--*Mary Carstens, M.D.;.* Her Interne Year at Victory Hospital. Meese, Mildred Foulke, Mrs. 1943. The Bobbs-Merrill Company. (P.639)
--*Michael and the Captain.* Holberg, Ruth Langland, Mrs. (1891-). 1944. Thomas Y. Crowell Company. (P.453)
--*Molly Pitcher, Girl Patriot.* Stevenson, Augusta (1869-1976). 1952. Bobbs-Merrill. (P.855)
--*Mount Delightful: The Story of Ellen Evans and Her Dog Taffy.* Youmans, Eleanor Williams, Mrs. 1944. The Bobbs-Merrill Company. (P.988)
--*Mystery at the Old Place.* Orton, Helen Fuller, Mrs. (1872-1955). 1943. Frederick A. Stokes Company. (P.696)
--*Mystery of the Secret Drawer.* Orton, Helen Fuller, Mrs. (1872-1955). 1945. J. B. Lippincott Company. (P.696)
--*Over the Hills to Nugget.* Fisher, Aileen Lucia (1906-). 1949. Aladdin Books. (P.328)
--*Peter Pigeon.* Gibke, Carl H. & Bower, Mary Ruth. 1941. Grosset & Dunlop. (P.366)
--*Rachel Jackson, Tennessee Girl.* 1st ed. Govan, Christine Noble, Mrs. (1898-). 1955. Bobbs-Merrill. (P.379)
--*The School Bell Rings.* Sickels, Evelyn Ray (1895-). 1942. C. Scribner's Sons. (P.823)
--*The Secret of the Closed Gate.* Leighton, Margaret Carver, Mrs. (1896-). 1944. The John C. Winston Company. (P.563)
--*Silver for General Washington: A Story of Valley Forge.* Meadowcroft, Enid La Monte, Mrs. (1898-1966). 1944. Thomas Y. Crowell Company. (P.637)
--*Star-Spangled Summer.* Lambert, Janet (1895-1973). 1941. E. P. Dutton & Company, Inc. (P.546)
--*Teddy Roosevelt, All-Round Boy.* 1st ed. Parks, Edd Winfield (1906-1968). 1953. Bobbs-Merrill. (P.707)
--*Treasure Cave Trail: An Adventure of the Young Billings.* Merrill, Marion. 1943. W. Morrow and Company. (P.642)
--*The Young Billings of Buckhorn.* Merrill, Marion. 1942. W. Morrow and Company. (P.642)
--*Young Mr.* Meeker and His Exciting Journey to Oregon. Mason, Miriam Evangeline (1899-1973). 1952. Bobbs-Merrill. (P.628)

James, Toni & James, Ron (1938-), photos by

--*Norton and Gus.* Rector, Margaret Hayden. c.1976. Grossmont Press. (P.752)

James, William

--*Peter and the Rocket Ship.* Corson, Hazel W (1906-). 1955. Beckley-Cardy Co. (P.221)
--*Peter and the Two-Hour Moon.* Corson, Hazel W (1906-). 1956. Beckley-Cardy Co. (P.221)

James, William Roderick (1892-1942)

--*All in the Day's Riding.* James, William Roderick (1892-1942). 1933. Charles Scribner's Sons. (P.489)
--*All in the Day's Riding.* James, William Roderick (1892-1942). N.D. World Publishing Co. (P.489)
--*Big-Enough.* James, William Roderick (1892-1942). 1931. C. Scribner's Sons. (P.489)
--*Big-Enough.* James, William Roderick (1892-1942). N.D. World Publishing Co. (P.489)
--*Cow Country: Stories.* James, William Roderick (1892-1942). 1973, c.1927. Univ. of Nebraska Pr. (P.489)
--*Cowboy in the Making.* James, William Roderick (1892-1942). 1937. Charles Scribner's Sons. (P.489)
--*The Dark Horse.* James, William Roderick (1892-1942). 1939. C. Scribner's Sons. (P.489)
--*Home Ranch.* James, William Roderick (1892-1942). 1935. Charles Scribner's Sons. (P.489)
--*In the Saddle with Uncle Bill.* James, William Roderick (1892-1942). 1935. C. Scribner's Sons. (P.489)
--*Look-See with Uncle Bill.* James, William Roderick (1892-1942). 1938. C. Scribner's Sons. (P.489)
--*My First Horse.* James, William Roderick (1892-1942). 1940. C. Scribner's Sons. (P.489)
--*Sand.* James, William Roderick (1892-1942). 1929. C. Scribner's Sons. (P.489)
--*Scorpion: A Good Bad Horse.* James, William Roderick (1892-1942). 1936. Charles Scribner's Sons. (P.489)
--*Smoky, the Cowhorse.* James, William Roderick (1892-1942). 1926. Scribner. **Award: (JNM).** (P.489)
--*Smoky: The Story of a Cow-Pony.* James, William Roderick (1892-1942). N.D. Charles Scribner's Sons'. (P.489)
--*Sun Up: Tales of the Cow Camps.* James, William Roderick (1892-1942). 1931. Charles Scribner's Sons. (P.489)
--*The Three Mustangeers.* James, William Roderick (1892-1942). 1933. World Publishing Co. (P.489)
--*Uncle Bill: A Tale of Two Kids and a Cowboy.* James, William Roderick (1892-1942). 1932. C. Scribner's Sons. (P.489)
--*Will James Book of Cowboy Stories.* James, William Roderick (1892-1942). 1935. Scribner. (P.489)
--*Young Cowboy.* James, William Roderick (1892-1942). 1935. C. Scribner's Sons. (P.489)

Jameson, Arthur

--*Heidi.* Spyri, Johanna Heusser (1827-1901). c.1944. Whitman Publishing Co. (P.846)
--*On Shining Rails: Stories About Trains.* Troxell, Eleanor & Dudley, Dessalee Ryan, Mrs. c.1939. C. Scribner's Sons. (P.902)
--*The Three Musketeers.* Dumas, Alexandre (1802-1870). c.1945. Whitman Publishing Company. (P.288)

Jameson, Helen D. & Flack, Marjorie (1897-1958)

--*All Together: A Child's Treasury of Verse, Including Selections from Everything and Anything, Here, There, and Everywhere, Hop, Skip, and Jump, Before Things Happen, with Poems Previously Unpublished in Book Form.* Aldis, Dorothy Keeley, Mrs. (1896-1966). 1952. Putnam. (P.21)
--*All Together: A Child's Treasury of Verse.* Aldis, Dorothy Keeley, Mrs. (1896-1966). 1952. Putnam Pub Group. (P.21)

Jamieson, Lindsey, jt. illus. see Meade, Javier.

Jamison, Doug

--*Mice Are Rather Nice: Poems About Mice.* Moore, Vardine Russell (1906-). 1981. Atheneum. (P.662)

Jandolo, Rina de Felici

--*The Little Swiss Guard.* Dick, Mary. 1955. Bruce Publishing Co. (P.262)

Janecek, Ota

--*A Garland of Children's Verse.* Bradford, Barbara Taylor (1933-) & Halas, Frantisek (1901-1949). 1968. Lion Press. (P.124)

Janecke, Sue

--*Cubby Ball's Narrow Escapes.* Charnock, Richard W. N.D. Vantage. (P.187)

Janeway, Hestermary

--*Rufie Had a Monkey!.* Sechrist, Elizabeth Hough, Mrs. (1903-). c.1939. David McKay Company. (P.807)

Janjic, Penelope

--*Wake up!* It's Night. Odell, Carol. 1967, c.1966. Angus & Robertson. (P.690)

Janosch, pseud., see Eckert, Horst.

Janosch, pseud. (1931-)

--*Bollerbam.* Eckert, Horst. Janosch, pseud. (1931-). Eckert, Horst. 1969. Walck. (P.489)
--*A Boy Called Spoons.* Eckert, Horst. Heckmann, Herbert (1931-). 1975. British Bk Ctr. (P.429)
--*Crocodile Who Wouldn't Be King.* Eckert, Horst. Janosch, pseud. (1931-). Eckert, Horst. 1971. Putnam. (P.489)
--*Hey Presto!* You're a Bear!. Eckert, Horst. Janosch, pseud. (1931-). Eckert, Horst. Flugge, Klauss, tr. 1980, c.1977. Little, Brown. (P.489)
--*How Does a Czar Eat Potatoes?.* Eckert, Horst. Rose, Anne K. 1973. Lothrop, Lee & Shepard Co. (P.777)
--*Joshua & the Magic Fiddle.* Eckert, Horst. Janosch, pseud. (1931-). Eckert, Horst. 1968. Collins-World. (P.489)
--*Lazy Blackbird & Other Verses.* Eckert, Horst. Prelutsky, Jack. 1969. Macmillan. (P.737)
--*Leo the Magic Flea: Or, the Lion Hunt in Upper Fimmel.* Eckert, Horst. Janosch, pseud. (1931-). Eckert, Horst. 1975. British Bk Ctr. (P.489)
--*Magic Automobile.* Eckert, Horst. Janosch, pseud. (1931-). Eckert, Horst. 1971. Crown. (P.489)
--*Tales of the Lying Nutcracker.* Eckert, Horst. Janosch, pseud. (1931-). Eckert, Horst. 1975. British Bk Ctr. (P.489)
--*Thieves & the Raven.* Eckert, Horst. Janosch, pseud. (1931-). Eckert, Horst. Shub, Elizabeth, tr. 1970. Macmillan. (P.489)

Jansons, Inese

--*Gabby Gaffer.* Justus, May (1898-). 1975. Dillon Press. (P.503)
--*The Sea Wedding and Other Stories from Estonia.* Hoffmann, Margaret Jones (1910-) & Maas, Selve. 1975. Dillon Press. (P.451)

Jansson, A. L.

--*The Hobby Hoss Fair.* Jansson, A. L. 1905. H M Caldwell Co. (P.489)

Jansson, Arthur August (1890-)

--*Bare Hands: Being the Story of the Extraordinary Steam Boat That Was Built on Devil's Island off the Coast of Alaska by Four Shipwrecked Men.* Daniel, Hawthorne (1890-). 1929. Coward-McCann, Inc. (P.241)
--*Pantaloons: Adventures of a Baby Elephant.* Johnson, Osa Helen Leighty (1894-1953). c.1941. Random House. (P.496)
--*Snowball: Adventures of a Young Gorilla.* Johnson, Osa Helen Leighty (1894-1953). 1942. Random House. (P.496)
--*Tarnish,.* The/True Story of a Lion Cub. Johnson, Osa Helen Leighty (1894-1953). 1944. Wilcox & Follett Co. (P.496)

Jansson, Tove (1914-)

--*Alice's Adventures in Wonderland.* Carroll, Lewis, pseud. (1832-1898). Dodgson, Charles Lutwidge. 1977. Delacorte. (P.173)

--*Kelpie: A Shetland Pony.* Johnson, Margaret Sweet (1893-1964). 1962. Morrow. (P.496)

--*Lance of Oak Valley.* Johnson, Margaret Sweet (1893-1964). 1963. Morrow. (P.496)

--*Larry of Snowy Ridge.* Johnson, Margaret Sweet (1893-1964). 1956. Morrow. (P.496)

--*Megan,.* A Welsh Corgi. Johnson, Margaret Sweet (1893-1964). 1957. Morrow. (P.496)

--*Miss Kelly.* Holding, Elisabeth Sanxay (1889-). 1947. W. Morrow. (P.454)

--*Randy and the Queen of Sheba.* Johnson, Margaret Sweet (1893-1964). 1951. Morrow. (P.496)

--*Red Joker.* Johnson, Margaret Sweet (1893-1964). 1950. Morrow. (P.496)

--*Sam and the Inkspot.* Johnson, Margaret Sweet (1893-1964). 1953. Morrow. (P.496)

--*Silver Dawn.* Johnson, Margaret Sweet (1893-1964). 1958. W. Morrow. (P.496)

--*Snowshoe Paws.* Johnson, Margaret Sweet (1893-1964). 1949. W. Morrow. (P.496)

--*Stowaway Cat.* Johnson, Margaret Sweet (1893-1964). 1955. W. Morrow. (P.496)

--*Tally-Ho.* Johnson, Margaret Sweet (1893-1964) & Johnson, Helen Lossing, Mrs. (1865-1946). c.1936. Harcourt, Brace and Company. (P.496)

--*Wilderness Pup.* Johnson, Margaret Sweet (1893-1964). 1954. Wm. Morrow. (P.496)

Johnson, Margaret Sweet (1893-1964) & Johnson, Helen Lossing, Mrs. (1865-1946)
--*Carlo,.* The/Hound Who Thought He Was a Calf. Johnson, Margaret Sweet (1893-1964) & Johnson, Helen Lossing, Mrs. (1865-1946). c.1941. Harcourt, Brace and Company. (P.496)

--*Derry: The Wolfhound.* Johnson, Margaret Sweet (1893-1964) & Johnson, Helen Lossing, Mrs. (1865-1946). 1943. Harcourt, Brace and Company. (P.496)

--*Dixie Dobie: A Sable Island Pony.* Johnson, Margaret Sweet (1893-1964) & Johnson, Helen Lossing, Mrs. (1865-1946). 1945. Harcourt, Brace and Company. (P.496)

--*Sir Lancelot and Scamp.* Johnson, Margaret Sweet (1893-1964) & Johnson, Helen Lossing, Mrs. (1865-1946). 1945. Harcourt, Brace and Company. (P.496)

--*The Smallest Puppy.* Johnson, Margaret Sweet (1893-1964) & Johnson, Helen Lossing, Mrs. (1865-1946). c.1940. Harcourt, Brace and Company. (P.496)

--*A Spaniel of Old Plymouth.* Johnson, Margaret Sweet (1893-1964) & Johnson, Helen Lossing, Mrs. (1865-1946). c.1937. Harcourt, Brace and Company. (P.496)

--*Stablemates: The Story of Dick and Daisy.* Johnson, Margaret Sweet (1893-1964) & Johnson, Helen Lossing, Mrs. (1865-1946). 1942. Harcourt, Brace and Company. (P.496)

--*The Story of Rickey.* Johnson, Margaret Sweet (1893-1964) & Johnson, Helen Lossing, Mrs. (1865-1946). c.1939. Harcourt, Brace and Company. (P.496)

--*Tim: A Dog of the Mountains.* Johnson, Margaret Sweet (1893-1964) & Johnson, Helen Lossing, Mrs. (1865-1946). c.1940. Harcourt, Brace and Company. (P.496)

--*Vicki: A Guide Dog.* Johnson, Margaret Sweet (1893-1964) & Johnson, Helen Lossing (1865-1946). 1946. Harcourt, Brace and Company. (P.496)

Johnson, Margaret (1860-)
--*Polly.* Lothrop, Harriet Mulford Stone, Mrs. (1844-1924). Sidney, Margaret, pseud. N.D. D. Lothrop Co. (P.586)

--*What O'Clock Jingles.* Johnson, Margaret (1860-). 1887. D. Lothrop Co. (P.496)

--*Where Was the Little White Dog.* Johnson, Margaret (1860-). N.D. Dana Estes and Company. (P.496)

Johnson, Marilue Carol see **Marilue, pseud.**
Johnson, Marilue Carolyn see **Marilue, pseud.**
Johnson, Marilue Carolyn (1931-)
--*Bobby Bear Goes Fishing.* Helmrath, Marilyn Olear & Bartlett, Janet La Spiza. 1968. Oddo Publishing Inc. (P.432)

Johnson, Merle
--*A Bad Boy's Diary: As Related by Himself.* Gray, Walter T., pseud. (1831-1853). Victor, Metta Victoria Fuller. 1911. J. S. Ogilvie Publishing Company. (P.384)

--*The Remarkable Adventures of Little Boy Pip ...* Francis, Philip W. c.1907. P. Elder & Company. (P.341)

Johnson, Merrily
--*Book of Me.* Walley, Dean. 1971. Hallmark. (P.927)

--*Jonathan Small and Elizabeth Blue: A Friendship Story.* Walley, Dean. 1970. Hallmark Children's Editions. (P.927)

Johnson, Milton (1932-)
--*The Black Pearl.* O'Dell, Scott (1903-). 1967. Houghton Mifflin. **Award: (JNM).** (P.690)

--*Come by Here.* Coolidge, Olivia Ensor (1908-). 1970. Houghton Mifflin. **Award: (BGH).** (P.216)

--*The Dark Canoe.* O'Dell, Scott (1903-). 1968. Houghton Mifflin. (P.690)

--*Follow the Golden Goose.* Veglahn, Nancy Crary (1937-). 1970. Addison-Wesley. (P.916)

--*The Little Fishes.* Haugaard, Erik Christian (1923-). 1967. Houghton Mifflin. **Award: (BGH).** (P.420)

--*Men of Athens.* Coolidge, Olivia Ensor (1908-). 1962. Houghton Mifflin. (P.216)

--*Orphans of the Wind.* Haugaard, Erik Christian (1923-). 1966. HM. (P.420)

Johnson, Neil
--*The Haunted House.* Klimo, Kate, ed. 1982. S&S. (P.531)

Johnson, P. D.
--*The Game and the Candle.* Ingram, Eleanor M. N.D. Bobbs-Merrill Co. (P.480)

Johnson, Pamela
--*Hello- Wrong Number.* Sachs, Marilyn Stickle (1927-). c.1981. Dutton. (P.787)

--*Nothing Rhymes with April.* 1st ed. Karp, Naomi J (1926-). 1974. HarBrace J. (P.508)

--*Positively No Pets Allowed.* 1st ed. Zimelman, Nathan (1911-) & Johnson, Pamela. c.1980. Dutton. (P.993)

--*Quentin Corn.* Stolz, Mary Slattery (1920-). 1985. Godine. (P.861)

--*The Rabbi's Girls.* Hurwitz, Johanna (1937-) c. 1982. Morrow. (P.476)

--*Rattlesnake Cave.* 1st ed. Lampman, Evelyn Sibley (1907-1980). 1974. Atheneum. (P.546)

--*The Talking Parcel.* Durrell, Gerald Malcolm (1925-). 1975. Harper. (P.291)

--*The Talking Parcel.* Durrell, Gerald Malcolm (1925-). 1975. Lippincott. (P.291)

--*Trig.* 1st ed. Peck, Robert Newton (1928-). c.1977. Little, Brown. (P.715)

--*Trig Goes Ape.* 1st ed. Peck, Robert Newton (1928-). c.1980. Little, Brown. (P.715)

--*Trig or Treat.* 1st ed. Peck, Robert Newton (1928-). c.1982. Little, Brown. (P.715)

--*Trig Sees Red.* 1st ed. Peck, Robert Newton (1928-). c.1978. Little, Brown. (P.715)

Johnson, Pamela, jt. illus. see Hurwitz, Johanna.
Johnson, Priscilla M.
--*Oliver.* Wickstrom, Lois (1948-). 1978. Spring. (P.956)

Johnson, Priscilla M., jt. illus. see Mion, Francie.
Johnson, Ray (1900-)
--*Scanlon of the Sub Service.* 1st ed. Senseney, Dan. 1963. Doubleday. (P.810)

--*A Summer to Remember.* 1st ed. Finlayson, Ann (1925-). 1964. Doubleday. (P.326)

--*Tom Swift and His Cosmotron Express.* Appleton, Victor, II, pseud. (1894-1982). Adams, Harriet Stratemeyer.1970. G & D. (P.45)

--*Tom Swift and His Dyna-4 Capsule.* Appleton, Victor, II, pseud. (1894-1982). Adams, Harriet Stratemeyer. 1969. Grosset and Dunlap. (P.45)

--*Tom Swift and His G-Force Inverter.* Appleton, Victor, II, pseud. (1894-1982). Adams, Harriet Stratemeyer. 1968. Grosset and Dunlap. (P.45)

--*Tom Swift and the Captive Planetoid.* Appleton, Victor, II, pseud. (1894-1982). Adams, Harriet Stratemeyer. 1967. Grosset & Dunlap. (P.45)

--*Tom Swift and the Mystery Comet.* Appleton, Victor, II, pseud. (1894-1982). Adams, Harriet Stratemeyer. 1966. Grosset and Dunlap. (P.45)

Johnson, Richard (1953-)
--*The Peanut Butter Hamster, and Other Animal Tails.* Fox, Grace. c.1979. Victor Books. (P.340)

Johnson, Robert Ward
--*A Wonder Book.* Hawthorne, Nathaniel (1804-1864). Thorndike, Edward Lee (1874-), ed. c.1935. D. Appleton-Century Company, Incorporated. (P.424)

Johnson, Scott
--*The Golden Book of Zoo Animals.* Bridges, William Andrew (1901-). 1962. Golden Press. (P.130)

Johnson, Sheila
--*The King and the Mangoes.* Davis, Grania (1943-), adapted by. Gellek, Nazli. c.1975. Dharma Pub. (P.363)

Johnson, Townley
--*The Bushman Speaks.* Phillips, Mary. 1961. H. Timmins. (P.724)

Johnson, V. C.
--*Bride Comes To Yellow Sky.* Crane, Stephen Townley (1871-1900). 1982. Creative Ed. (P.228)

--*The Open Boat.* Crane, Stephen Townley (1871-1900). 1982. Creative Ed. (P.228)

Johnson, Vie
--*I Want to Be a Teacher.* Greene, Carla (1916-). 1957. Childrens Press. (P.386)

Johnson, W. Branch (1893-)
--*Folk Tales of Brittany.* Johnson, W. Branch (1893-). N.D. Frederick A. Stokes. (P.497)

--*Folk Tales of Provence.* Johnson, W. Branch (1893-). N.D. Frederick A. Stokes Co. (P.497)

Johnson, W. Cameron
--*Return of the Indian Spirit.* Brown, Vinson (1912-) & Johnson, Phyllis. 1982, c.1981. Celestial Arts. (P.142)

Johnson, William R.
--*How Many Angels in the Sky.* Werner, Pat. 1965. Augsburg Pub. House. (P.946)

Johnston, Arnold Banniza (1895-)
--*May I Keep Dogs!.* Barne, Kitty, pseud. (1883-1957). Barne, Marion Catherine. 1942. Dodd, Mead & Company. (P.73)

Johnston, Arnrid
--*The Little Black Calf.* Foyle, Kathleen. 1952. F. Warne. (P.340)

Johnston, Clifford
--*Eyes for Eric, and Other Stories: For Children from Four to Eight Years of Age.* Moore, Jessie Eleanor (1886-), ed. 1963. Published for the Cooperative Publication Association by Abingdon Press. (P.661)

--*Isaiah, Messenger for God.* Heifner, Fred. c.1978. Broadman Press. (P.430)

--*Joshua Poole and Sunrise.* Collins, David Raymond (1940-). c.1980. Broadman Press. (P.210)

--*Joshua Poole and the Special Flowers.* Collins, David Raymond (1940-). c.1981. Broadman Press. (P.210)

--*Joshua Poole Hated School.* Collins, David Raymond (1940-). 1977, c.1976. Broadman Press. (P.210)

--*Judges and Kings: God's Chosen Leaders.* McElrath, William N. (1932-). c.1979. Broadman Press. (P.600)

Johnston, Joe
--*The Adventures of Teebo: A Tale of Magic & Suspense.* Johnston, Joe. 1984. Random. (P.498)

Johnston, Johanna (1914-1982)
--*All Kinds of Kings in Fact and Legend, from Hammurabi to Louis XIV.* 1st ed. Karmiller, Murry. 1970. Norton. (P.508)

Johnston, Lyn Beverly, jt. illus. see Johnston, Richard.
Johnston, Lynn Beverley (1947-)
--*Is This "One of Those Days," Daddy?.* Johnston, Lynn Beverley (1947-). 1982. Andrews & McMeel. (P.498)

Johnston, M. D.
--*The Little Discoverers.* Le Feuvre, Amy (0000-1929). 1924. H. Milford. (P.562)

Johnston, Mary G. & Sacker, Amy M.
--*Ole Mammy's Torment.* Johnston, Annie Fellows, Mrs. (1863-1931). 1897. L. C. Page and Company. (P.497)

Johnston, Moira
--*Confessions of a Toe Hanger.* Harris, Christie Lucy Irwin (1907-). 1967. Atheneum. (P.415)

--*You Have to Draw the Line Somewhere.* Harris, Christie Lucy Irwin (1907-). 1964. Atheneum. (P.415)

Johnston, Richard & Johnston, Lyn Beverly (1947-)
--*An Alphabet of Christmas.* Wells, Lorraine. 1971. Judson. (P.945)

Johnstone, Anne Grahame, jt. illus. see Johnstone, Janet Grahame.
Johnstone, Anne Grahame & Johnstone, Janet Grahame
--*Gondoliers.* Gilbert, William Schwenck, Sir (1836-1911) & Sullivan, Arthur Seymour, Sir (1842-1900). N.D. Watts. (P.367)

--*H M S Pinafore.* Mearns, Martha. N.D. Watts. (P.638)

--*Mikado.* Gilbert, William Schwenck, Sir (1836-1911) & Sullivan, Arthur Seymour, Sir (1842-1900). Mearns, Martha, ed. 1967. Watts. (P.367)

--*Pirates of Penzance.* Gilbert, William Schwenck, Sir (1836-1911) & Sullivan, Arthur Seymour, Sir (1842-1900). N.D. Watts. (P.367)

--*Yeomen of the Guard.* Gilbert, William Schwenck, Sir (1836-1911) & Sullivan, Arthur Seymour, Sir (1842-1900). Mearns, Martha, ed. 1967. Watts. (P.367)

Johnstone, Janet Grahame, jt. illus. see Johnstone, Anne Grahame.
Johnstone, Janet Grahame & Johnstone, Anne Grahame
--*Book of Fairy Tales.* N.D. Merry Thoughts. (P.498)

--*Folk Tales of the World.* Green, Roger Gilbert Lancelyn (1918-). 1966. Ginn. (P.385)

--*Gift Book of Fairy Tales.* N.D. Merry Thoughts. (P.498)

--*Gift Book of Nursery Rhymes.* N.D. Merry Thoughts. (P.498)

--*New Gift Book of Nursery Rhymes.* N.D. Borden. (P.498)

--*New Gift Book of Nursery Rhymes.* N.D. Merry Thoughts. (P.498)

--*Puppy Dog Rhymes.* Johnstone, Janet Grahame & Johnstone, Anne Grahame. N.D. Merry Thoughts. (P.498)

--*Pussy Cat Rhymes.* Johnstone, Janet Grahame & Johnstone, Anne Grahame. N.D. Merry Thoughts. (P.498)

--*Stories from Hans Christian Andersen.* Andersen, Hans Christian (1805-1875). Broadley, Mae, retold by. 1971. Platt. (P.37)

Johnstone, Sally
--*Sam & Company.* Johnstone, Sally, ed. 1982. IWP Pub. (P.498)

Jolly, Cheryl
--*Jackie.* 1st ed. Lewis, Luevester. 1970. Third World Press. (P.570)

Jonas, Ann (1919-)
--*Holes & Peeks.* Jonas, Ann (1919-). 1984. Greenwillow. **Award: (ALA).** (P.498)

--*The Quilt.* Jonas, Ann (1919-). 1984. Greenwillow. **Award: (ALA).** (P.498)

--*Round Trip.* 1st ed. Jonas, Ann (1919-). c.1983. Greenwillow Books. **Awards: (NYT); (ALA).** (P.498)

--*The Trek.* Jonas, Ann (1919-). 1985. Greenwillow. (P.498)

--*Two Bear Cubs.* Jonas, Ann (1919-). c.1982. Greenwillow Books. (P.498)

Jones, A. Garth, jt. illus. see Nelson, Harold.
Jones, A. Robert
--*Cherry stones garden swings.* Eastwick, Ivy Ethel Olive. N.D. Abingdon Press. (P.294)

Jones, Adele W.
--*Hester's Counterpart: A Story of Boarding School Life.* Baird, Jean Katherine (1872-). 1910. Lothrop, Lee & Shepard. (P.61)

Jones, Aletha
--*God Loves to Talk to Boys While They're Fishin.* Gaither, Bill & Gaither, Gloria. 1975. Impact Tenn. (P.352)

--*I'm a Promise.* Gaither, Bill & Gaither, Gloria. 1977. Impact Tenn. (P.352)

--*Jesus, I Heard You Had a Big House, Vol. 7.* Gaither, Bill & Gaither, Gloria. 1977. Impact Tenn. (P.352)

--*This Is the Day That the Lord Hath Made.* Gaither, Bill & Gaither, Gloria. 1977. Impact Tenn. (P.352)

--*This Little Light of Mine.* Gaither, Bill & Gaither, Gloria. 1975. Impact Tenn. (P.352)

Jones, Aletha & Lerner, Sheralyn
--*God Can.* Gaither, Bill & Gaither, Gloria. 1977. Impact Tenn. (P.352)

--*Let All the Little Children Praise the Lord.* Gaither, Bill & Gaither, Gloria. 1977. Impact Tenn. (P.352)

--*That's Him.* MacKenzie, Joy. 1977. Impact Tenn. (P.606)

Jones, Amy
--*Prance, a Carousel Horse.* Young, Miriam Burt (1913-1974). 1950. Crowell. (P.990)

Jones, Bayard
--*A Cadet of Belgium: An American Boy in the Great War.* Smith, Arthur Douglas Howden (1887-). c.1915. George H. Doran Company. (P.831)

--*In Defence of Paris: An American Boy in the Trenches.* Smith, Arthur Douglas Howden (1887-). c.1915. George H. Doran Company. (P.831)

Jones, Bayard F., jt. illus. see Jacobs, W. L.
Jones, Beryl Bailey
--*The Queen Who Longed for Snow.* Hackett, Walter Anthony (1909-). 1954. Houghton Mifflin Co. (P.401)

Jones, Bob (1926-)
--*Jelly Belly.* Smith, Robert Kimmel (1930-). c.1981. Delacorte Press. (P.836)

Jones, Brent
--*I Know You Cheated.* McLenighan, Valjean (1947-). c.1977. Raintree Editions. (P.608)

Jones, Carol
--*The Day Tuk Became a Hunter & Other Eskimo Stories.* Melzack, Ronald (1929-). 1967. Dodd, Mead. (P.640)

--*The Hornstranders.* Boucher, Alan Estcourt (1918-). 1969, c.1966. Meredith Press. (P.119)

Jones, Catherine O.
--*Three Little Clouds.* Scanlon, Marion Stephany. 1959. T. S. Denison. (P.796)

Jones, Ceri
--*I Thought I Saw.* 1974. Playspaces. (P.499)

Jones, Ceri, jt. illus. see Adams, Pam.
Jones, Chuck
--*A Cricket in Times Square.* Jones, Chuck. 1984. Ideals. (P.499)

Jones, Dan (1948-)
--*The Hocus-Pocus Dilemma.* Kibbe, Pat. c.1979. Knopf : Distributed by Random House. (P.522)

--*The Secret Life of the Underwear Champ.* Miles, Betty (1928-). c.1981. Knopf. (P.645)

Jones, Dennis
--*Cheerful Chad and Other Children of God.* Truitt, Gloria A. (1939-). c.1985. Concordia Pub. House. (P.902)

Jones, Dick
--*Plantonio, the Pride of the Plain.* Jones, Dick, ed. N.D. Harcourt Brace & Co. (P.499)

Jones, Elizabeth Ivins
--*The Little Wilful Princess.* Cory, David Magie (1872-1966). 1918. Moffat, Yard and Company. (P.222)

Kedwards, E. J.
--*The Wanderings of Ulysses.* Harrison, George Bagshawe (1894-), ed. 1937. T. Nelson and Sons, Ltd. (P.417)
Keegan, Marcia (1943-)
--*Only the Moon & Me.* Margolis, Richard Jules (1929-). 1969. Lippincott. (P.619)
Keegan, Marcia (1943-), photos by.
--*Moonsong Lullaby.* Highwater, Jamake Mamake (1942-). c.1981. Lothrop, Lee & Shepard Books. **Award: (ALA).** (P.441)
Keele, Norman
--*I'm a Lucky Dog: Jill, the Airedale.* Hamilton, Elaine (1937-). 1937. David McKay Co. (P.408)
Keeler, Katherine Southwick (1887-)
--*The Kitten Stand.* Coatsworth, Elizabeth Jane (1893-). 1945. Grosset & Dunlap. (P.204)
Keeler, Louise
--*Elfin Songs of Sunland.* 3rd ed. Keeler, Charles Augustus (1871-). 1914. G. P. Putnam's Sons. (P.511)
--*Elfin Songs of Sunland.* 4th ed. Keeler, Charles Augustus (1871-). c.1920. Live Oak Publishing Company. (P.511)
Keely, John
--*Dream Dancer.* Bolton, Evelyn, pseud. (1928-). Bunting, Anne Evelyn. 1974. Creative Education; Distributed by Childrens Press, Chicago. (P.113)
--*Goodbye, Charlie.* Bolton, Evelyn, pseud. (1928-). Bunting, Anne Evelyn. 1974. Creative Education; Distributed by Childrens Press, Chicago. (P.113)
--*Lady's Girl.* Bolton, Evelyn, pseud. (1928-). Bunting, Anne Evelyn. 1974. Creative Education; Distributed by Childrens Press, Chicago. (P.113)
--*The Loud-Noisy, Dirty-Grimy, Bad & Naughty Twins: Synonyms.* Tester, Sylvia Root (1939-). 1977. Childrens. (P.883)
--*Never Monkey with a Monkey: Homographic Homophones.* Tester, Sylvia Root (1939-). 1977. Childrens. (P.883)
--*Ride When You're Ready.* Bolton, Evelyn, pseud. (1928-). Bunting, Anne Evelyn. 1974. Creative Education; Distributed by Childrens Press, Chicago. (P.113)
--*Stable of Fear.* Bolton, Evelyn, pseud. (1928-). Bunting, Anne Evelyn. 1974. Creative Education; Distributed by Childrens Press, Chicago. (P.113)
--*The Team Manager.* Deegan, Paul Joseph (1937-). 1974. Creative Education. (P.250)
--*The Tournaments.* Deegan, Paul Joseph (1937-). 1974. Creative Education. (P.250)
--*The Wild Horses.* Bunting, Anne Evelyn (1928-). 1974. Creative Education; Distributed by Childrens Press, Chicago. (P.150)
--*You Dance Like an Ostrich!.* Similes. Tester, Sylvia Root (1939-). 1978. Childrens. (P.883)
Keen, E.
--*Larry Hudson's Ambition.* Kaler, James Otis (1848-1912). Otis, James, pseud. 1901. L. C. Page & Co. (P.505)
Keenan, Elaine Faris
--*The Secret World of Teddy Bears: A Rare and Privileged Glimpse into the Lives They Lead When You're Not There.* Prince, Pamela. 1983. Harmony Books. (P.740)
Keenan, Elaine Faris & Sansone, Ken
--*Teddy Bears' Christmas.* Prince, Pamela. 1985. Crown Publishers. (P.740)
--*Teddy Bears' Christmas: Holiday Greetings from the Secret World of Teddy Bears.* Prince, Pamela. c.1985. Harmony Books. (P.740)
Keene, Charles S.
--*The Boy Tar: Or, A Voyage in the Dark.* new ed. Reid, Thomas Mayne (1818-1883). Stoddard, Richard Henry (1825-1903), memoir by. 1885. T. R. Knox & Co. (P.755)
Keene, Ray
--*Sidonie.* 1st ed. Seibert, Elizabeth G. 1962. Bobbs-Merrill. (P.808)
Keep, Virginia
--*The April Fool Doll.* Gates, Josephine Scribner, Mrs. (1859-1930). 1908. Bobbs-Merrill Co. (P.360)
--*Little Girl Blue.* Gates, Josephine Scribner, Mrs. (1859-1930). N.D. Houghton Miffliln Co. (P.360)
--*Little Girl Blue Lives in the Woods till She Learns to Say Please.* Gates, Josephine Scribner, Mrs. (1859-1950). 1910. Houghton Mifflin Co. (P.360)
--*Little Red, White and Blue.* Gates, Josephine Scribner, Mrs. (1859-1930). 1906. The Bobbs-Merrill Company. (P.360)
--*Little Saint Sunshine.* Goss, Charles Frederick. N.D. Bobbs-Merrill Co. (P.378)
--*The Live Dolls' Busy Days.* Gates, Josephine Scribner, Mrs. (1859-1930). 1985, c.1907. Doll Works. (P.360)
--*The Live Dolls' Busy Days.* Gates, Josephine Scribner, Mrs. (1859-1930). 1907. The Bobbs-Merrill Company. (P.360)
--*The Live Doll's House Party.* Gates, Josephine Scribner, Mrs. (1859-1930). 1984, c.1906. Doll Works. (P.360)
--*The Live Dolls' House Party.* Gates, Josephine Scribner, Mrs. (1859-1930). 1906. The Bobbs-Merrill Company. (P.360)
--*The Live Dolls in Fairyland.* Gates, Josephine Scribner, Mrs. (1859-1930). 1911. The Bobbs-Merrill Company. (P.360)
--*The Live Doll's Party Days.* Gates, Josephine Scribner, Mrs. (1859-1930). 1910. Bobbs-Merrill Co. (P.360)
--*The Live Doll's Party Days.* Gates, Josephine Scribner, Mrs. (1859-1930). 1981. Doll Works. (P.360)
--*The Live Dolls: Play Days.* Gates, Josephine Scribner, Mrs. (1859-1930). 1908. The Bobbs-Merrill Company. (P.360)
--*Martha-Jane: Nursery Nonsense.* Krag, Martha Ann & Reynolds, Florence Krag. 1905. Bobbs-Merrill Co. (P.536)
--*More About Live Dolls.* Gates, Josephine Scribner, Mrs. (1859-1930). 1903. The Franklin Printing & Engraving Company. (P.360)
--*More About the Live Dolls.* Gates, Josephine Scribner, Mrs. (1859-1930). N.D. Bobbs-Merrill. (P.360)
--*The Story of Live Dolls.* Gates, Josephine Scribner, Mrs. (1859-1930). 1981. Doll Works. (P.360)
--*The Story of Live Dolls.* Gates, Josephine Scribner, Mrs. (1859-1930). 1901. The Bobbs-Merrill Company. (P.360)
--*The Story of the Lost Doll.* Gates, Josephine Scribner, Mrs. (1859-1930). 1905. The Bobbs-Merrill Company. (P.360)
--*The Story of the Three Dolls.* Gates, Josephine Scribner, Mrs. (1859-1930). c.1905. The Bobbs-Merrill Company. (P.360)
--*Two Prisoners.* Page, Thomas Nelson (1853-1922). 1903. R. H. Russell. (P.700)
Keep, Virginia, jt. illus. see Christy, Howard Chandler.
Keeping, Charles William James, jt. illus. see Kennedy, Richard.
Keeping, Charles William James (1924-)
--*About the Sleeping Beauty.* Travers, Pamela Lyndon (1906-). 1975. McGraw-Hill. (P.898)
--*Alfie and the Ferryboat.* Keeping, Charles William James (1924-). 1968. Oxford Univ. Press. (P.513)
--*Alfie Finds the Other Side of the World.* Keeping, Charles William James (1924-). 1968. F. Watts. (P.513)
--*The Apple Stone.* Gray, Nicholas Stuart (1922-1981). 1969. Meredith Press. (P.383)
--*The Beginning of the Armadilloes: A Just So Story.* Kipling, Joseph Rudyard (1865-1936). 1983. P Bedrick Bks. (P.527)
--*Bent Is the Bow.* Trease, Robert Geoffrey (1909-). 1967, c.1965. Nelson. (P.898)
--*Beowulf.* Crossley-Holland, Kevin, ed. Crossley-Holland, Kevin, tr. 1984. Merrimack. (P.232)
--*Beowulf.* Sutcliff, Rosemary (1920-), ed. 1962. Dutton. (P.871)
--*Beowulf.* Sutcliff, Rosemary (1920-), ed. 1984. Peter Smith. (P.871)
--*Blood Feud.* Sutcliff, Rosemary (1920-). 1976. Oxford University Press. (P.871)
--*A Boy and His Bike.* Potts, Richard (1938-). 1976. D. Dobson. (P.735)
--*Break in the Sun: A Novel.* Ashley, Bernard (1935-). 1980. S. G. Phillips. (P.52)
--*The Castle & the Harp.* Rush, Philip (1908-). 1964. McGraw. (P.784)
--*Celtic Folk and Fairy Tales.* 1st ed. Protter, Eric & Protter, Nancy, eds. Donohue, H. E. F., intro. by. 1966. Duell, Sloan and Pearce. (P.740)
--*Charley, Charlotte, and the Golden Canary.* Keeping, Charles William James (1924-). 1967. F. Watts. **Award: (KGM).** (P.513)
--*The Christmas Story.* Keeping, Charles William James (1924-), retold by. 1969. Watts. (P.513)
--*The Cold Flame.* Reeves, James (1909-), retold by. Grimm, Jakob Ludwig Karl (1785-1863) & Grimm, Wilhelm Karl (1786-1858). 1969, c.1967. Meredith Press. (P.391)
--*Dawn Wind.* Sutcliff, Rosemary (1920-). 1973, c.1961. H. Z. Walck. (P.871)
--*Dawn Wind.* Sutcliff, Rosemary (1920-). 1962, c.1961. Walck. (P.871)
--*The Dream Time.* Treece, Henry (1911-1966). 1968. Meredith Press. (P.899)
--*Elidor.* Garner, Alan (1935-). 1978. Collins. (P.358)
--*Elidor.* Garner, Alan (1935-). 1967, c.1965. H. Z. Walck. (P.358)
--*Five Fables from France.* Cooper, Lee Pelham (1926-). 1970. Abelard-Schuman. (P.218)
--*Flood Warning.* Berna, Paul (1910-). Buchanan-Brown, John (1929-), tr. from Fr. 1963. Pantheon Books. (P.96)
--*The Golden Shadow.* Garfield, Leon (1921-) & Blishen, Edward (1920-). 1973. Longman Young Books. (P.355)
--*The Golden Shadow.* Garfield, Leon (1921-) & Blishen, Edward (1920-). 1973. Pantheon Books. (P.355)
--*Grimbold's Other World.* Gray, Nicholas Stuart (1922-1981). 1968, c.1963. Meredith Press. (P.383)
--*Haunts, Haunts, Haunts.* Hoke, Helen L., Mrs. (1903-), ed. 1977. F. Watts. (P.453)
--*Horned Helmet.* Treece, Henry (1911-1966). c.1963. Criterion Books. (P.899)
--*The Invaders: Three Stories.* Treece, Henry (1911-1966). 1972. Crowell. (P.899)
--*Island of the Great Yellow Ox.* Macken, Walter (1915-1967). c.1966. Macmillan. (P.606)
--*Joseph's Yard.* Keeping, Charles William James (1924-). 1969. F. Watts. (P.513)
--*A Kind of Wild Justice: A Novel.* Ashley, Bernard (1935-). 1979, c.1978. S. G. Phillips. (P.52)
--*King Horn.* Crossley-Holland, Kevin (1941-). 1966, c.1965. Dutton. (P.232)
--*The King's Contest, and Other North African Tales.* Holding, James Clark Carlisle, Jr. (1907-). 1964. Abelard-Schuman. (P.454)
--*Knights, Beasts, and Wonders: Tales and Legends from Mediaeval Britain.* Miller, Margaret J., pseud. (1911-). Dale, Margaret Jessy Miller. 1969. D. White. (P.648)
--*Knight's Fee.* Sutcliff, Rosemary (1920-). 1960. H. Z. Walck. **Award: (ALA).** (P.871)
--*The Knights of the Golden Table.* Almedingen, Martha Edith von (1898-1971). Almedingen, E. M., pseud. 1964, c.1963. Lippincott. (P.31)
--*The Lantern Bearers.* Sutcliff, Rosemary (1920-). 1959. H. Z. Walck. **Award: (CMA).** (P.871)
--*The Last Viking.* Treece, Henry (1911-1966). 1966, c.1964. Pantheon Books. (P.899)
--*Lost John: A Young Outlaw in the Forest of Arden.* Picard, Barbara Leonie (1917-). 1963, c.1962. Criterion Books. (P.724)
--*The Magic Horns: Folk Tales from Africa.* Stuart, Forbes (1924-). 1976, c.1974. Addison-Wesley Pub. Co. (P.869)
--*Mainly in Moonlight: Ten Stories of Sorcery and the Supernatural.* Gray, Nicholas Stuart (1922-1981). 1967, c.1965. Meredith Press. (P.383)
--*Miss Emily & the Bird of Make-Believe.* Keeping, Charles William James (1924-). 1981. State Mutual Bk. (P.513)
--*Molly O' the Moors: The Story of a Pony.* Keeping, Charles William James (1924-). c.1966. World Pub. Co. (P.513)
--*Monsters, Monsters, Monsters.* Hoke, Helen L., Mrs. (1903-), ed. 1974. F. Watts. (P.453)
--*Monsters, Monsters, Monsters.* Hoke, Helen L., Mrs. (1903-), ed. 1975. Watts. (P.453)
--*The Nanny Goat and the Fierce Dog.* Keeping, Charles William James (1924-). 1974, c.1973. S. G. Phillips. (P.513)
--*Poet's Tales: A New Book of Story Poems.* rev. ed. Cole, William Rossa (1919-), ed. 1971. World Pub. (P.208)
--*Poko and the Golden Demon.* Holding, James Clark Carlisle, Jr. (1907-). 1968. Abelard-Schuman. (P.454)
--*The Queen of Trent.* Dawson, Mitchell. 1961. Abelard-Schuman. (P.247)
--*The Red Towers of Granada.* Trease, Robert Geoffrey (1909-). 1967, c.1966. Vanguard Press. (P.899)
--*Shaun and the Cart-Horse.* Keeping, Charles William James (1924-). 1966. F. Watts. (P.513)
--*The Silver Branch.* Sutcliff, Rosemary (1920-). 1959. H. Z. Walck. **Award: (CMA).** (P.871)
--*The Sky-Eater and Other South Sea Tales.* Holding, James Clark Carlisle, Jr. (1907-). 1965. Abelard-Schuman. (P.454)
--*The Smartest Man in Ireland.* Hunter, Mollie (1922-). 1965, c.1963. Funk & Wagnalls. (P.474)
--*Spectres, Spooks and Shuddery Shades.* Hoke, Helen L., Mrs. (1903-), ed. 1977. F. Watts. (P.453)
--*The Spider's Web.* Keeping, Charles William James (1924-). 1972. Oxford University Press. (P.513)
--*Splintered Sword.* Treece, Henry (1911-1966). 1966, c.1965. Duell Dist. Meredith. (P.899)
--*Swords from the North.* Treece, Henry (1911-1966). 1967. Pantheon. (P.899)
--*Tale of Ancient Israel.* Green, Roger Gilbert Lancelyn (1918-), ed. 1969. Dutton. (P.385)
--*Terry on the Fence.* Ashley, Bernard (1935-). 1977, c.1975. S. G. Phillips. (P.52)
--*Through the Window.* Keeping, Charles William James (1924-). 1970. F. Watts. (P.513)
--*Tinker Tailor and Other Folk Song Tales: Folk Song Tales.* Keeping, Charles William James (1924-), compiled by. 1968. World Pub. (P.513)
--*The Treasure of Siegfried.* Almedingen, Martha Edith von (1898-1971) & Nibelungenlied. Almedingen, E. M., pseud. 1965, c.1964. Lippincott. (P.31)
--*The Twelve Labors of Hercules.* Newman, Robert Howard (1909-). 1972. Crowell. (P.680)
--*The Valley of the Frost Giants.* Shura, Mary Francis (1923-). 1971. Lothrop, Lee & Shepard. (P.822)
--*Warrior Scarlet.* Sutcliff, Rosemary (1920-). 1958. H. Z. Walck. **Awards: (ALA); (CMA).** (P.871)
--*Warrior Scarlet.* Rev. ed. Sutcliff, Rosemary (1920-). 1966, c.1958. Walck. (P.871)
--*Weirdies, Weirdies, Weirdies.* Hoke, Helen L., Mrs. (1903-), ed. 1975. Watts. (P.453)
--*Weland, Smith of the Gods.* Synge, Phyllis Ursula (1930-). 1973. S. G. Phillips. (P.875)
--*Willie's Fire-Engine.* Keeping, Charles William James (1924-). 1980. Oxford University Press. (P.513)
--*With Books on Her Head.* 1st ed. Chandler, Edna Walker (1908-1982). 1967. Meredith Press. (P.184)
--*Wizards & Wampum: Legends of the Iroquois.* Squire, Roger, retold by. 1972. Abelard. (P.847)
Keepling, William James (1924-)
--*A Kind of Wild Justice.* Ashley, Bernard (1935-). 1979, c.1978. Oxford University Press. **Award: (CMA).** (P.52)
Keer, Anne Judith (1923-)
--*The Tiger Who Came to Tea.* Kerr, Anne-Judith (1923-). 1968. Coward-McCann. (P.520)
Kehlmann, Lilly
--*The Heart of a Boy: Translated from the Italian, Cuore, and Abridged.* Amicis, Edmondo De (1846-1908). Jewett, Sophie, tr. 1960. F. Ungar Pub. Co. (P.33)
Keith, Bros
--*The House of Dies Drear.* Hamilton, Virginia (1936-). 1984, c.1968. Collier Books. (P.408)
Keith, Dora Wheeler
--*Doubledarling and the Dream Spinner.* Wheeler, Candace, Mrs. N.D. Duffield & Co. (P.949)
Keith, Dora Wheeler & Nugent, Meredith
--*Sunbeam Stories and Others.* Flint, Annie Austin (1866-). 1897. Bonnell, Silver & Company. (P.332)
Keith, Eros
--*Anchor's Aweigh: The Story of David Glasgow Farragut.* Latham, Jean Lee (1902-). 1968. Harper & Row. (P.553)
--*Bedita's Bad Day.* Keith, Eros. 1971. Bradbury Pr. (P.514)
--*The Biggest Noise.* Keith, Eros. N.D. Har-Row. (P.514)
--*The Donkey Prince.* Carter, Angela (1940-). 1970. Simon and Schuster. (P.175)
--*The Faithless Lollybird.* Aiken, Joan (1924-). 1978. Doubleday. (P.15)
--*From New Bedford to Siberia: A Yankee Whaleman in the Frozen North.* 1st ed. Beatty, Jerome, Jr. (1918-). c.1977. Doubleday. (P.85)
--*The House of Dies Drear.* Hamilton, Virginia (1936-). 1968. Macmillan. **Award: (ALA).** (P.408)
--*I Need a Friend.* Kafka, Sherry (1937-). 1971. Putnam. (P.504)
--*In a Blue Velvet Dress.* 1st ed. Sefton, Catherine. 1973. Harper & Row. (P.808)
--*Ivanov Seven.* Janeway, Elizabeth (1913-). 1967. Harper & Row. (P.489)
--*Kevin.* Moery, Robert. 1970. Bradbury Press. (P.653)
--*The King's Falcon.* Fox, Paula (1923-). 1969. Bradbury Press. (P.340)
--*The MacLeod Place.* Armstrong, William Howard (1914-). 1972. Coward, McCann & Geoghegan. (P.48)
--*Mama's Ghosts.* Lorenzo, Carol Lee (1939-). 1974. Harper & Row. (P.585)
--*Mama's Ghosts.* 1st ed. Lorenzo, Carol Lee (1939-). 1978. Harper and Row. (P.585)
--*Miss Z, the Dark Young Lady.* Carter, Angela (1940-). 1970. Simon and Schuster. (P.175)
--*The Moon Is Like a Silver Sickle: A Celebration of Poetry by Russian Children.* Morton, Miriam (1918-), ed. 1972. Simon and Schuster. (P.666)
--*A Namesake for Nathan: Being an Account of Captain Nathan Hale by His Twelve-Year-Old Sister, Joanna.* Monjo, Ferdinand Nicolas, III (1924-1978). c.1977. Coward, McCann & Geoghegan. (P.656)
--*The Other World: Myths of the Celts.* Hodges, Margaret Moore (1911-), retold by. 1973. Farrar, Straus and Giroux. (P.449)
--*The Slave Dancer.* Fox, Paula (1923-). 1973. Bradbury Pr. **Awards: (JNM); (ALA).** (P.340)
--*Small Lot.* Keith, Eros. 1968. Bradbury Pr. (P.514)
--*A Song About You.* 1st ed. Froman, Robert Winslow (1917-). 1975. Doubleday. (P.347)
--*Undine.* Fouque, Friedrich De la Motte (1777-1843). Schwebell, Gertrude Clorius, ed. 1957. S&S. (P.339)
Keith, Ward
--*Timothy Tiger.* Barrows, Ruth Marjorie (1892-1983). 1943. Rand McNally & Co. (P.77)

--*The Little Duck Said Quack, Quack, Quack.* Barnett, Grace Treleven (1899-) & Barnett, Olive Elizabeth (1911-). 1955. Wonder Books. (P.73)

--*Mystery Mansion.* Griffin, Velma. 1958. Westminster Press. (P.390)

--*Mystery of the Bells.* Moore, Vardine Russell (1906-). 1955. Westminster Press. (P.662)

Kendrick, Charles

--*Around the House.* Willett, Edward (1923-). c.1882. R. Worthington. (P.962)

--*Cats Cradle: Rhymes for Children.* New. ed. Willett, Edward (1923-). 1881. Worthington's Sons. (P.962)

Kendrick, Dennis

--*The Fox with Cold Feet.* Singer, Bill. 1980. Parents Magazine Press. (P.826)

--*Monster Birthday.* Kroll, Steven (1941-). c.1980. Holiday House. (P.540)

--*The Sand Lot.* Christian, Mary Blount (1933-). c.1978. Harvey House. (P.194)

--*Scarlet Monster Lives Here.* 1st ed. Sharmat, Marjorie Weinman (1928-). c.1979. Harper & Row. (P.815)

--*Silly Animal Jokes and Riddles.* Simon, Seymour (1931-). c.1980. McGraw-Hill. (P.825)

--*The Three Billy Goats Gruff.* random house student book program ed. Kendrick, Dennis, retold by. c.1979. Random House. (P.517)

Kendrick, John & May, Warren

--*A Guide to the Use of Street-Folk-Musical Games in the Classroom: Vol. II, Chanting Games.* Hillery, Mable & Hall, Patricia. Freeman, Harold, Jr., intro. by. 1981. ILM. (P.445)

Kenelski, Maurice

--*The Little Green Man.* Damjan, Mischa. 1972, c.1971. Parents' Magazine Press. (P.240)

Kennaway, Adrienne (1945-)

--*Greedy Zebra.* Mwenye Hadithi. c.1984. Little, Brown. (P.674)

Kenne, Alex

--*Tag-Along.* Frankel, Bernice. 1962. Parents' Magazine Press. (P.342)

Kennedy, A. E.

--*Adventures of Tim Rabbit.* Uttley, Alison, Mrs., pseud. (1884-1976). Uttley, Alice Jane Taylor. 1945. Faber & Faber. (P.911)

--*Mother Nature's Secrets.* Tralle, Bertha Baldwin, Mrs. c.1930. S. Gabriel Sons & Company. (P.898)

--*Sam Pig Goes to the Seaside.* Uttley, Alison, Mrs., pseud. (1884-1976). Uttley, Alice Jane Taylor. N.D. Transatlantic Arts. (P.911)

--*Tim Rabbit and Company.* Uttley, Alison, Mrs., pseud. (1884-1976). Uttley, Alice Jane Taylor. 1959. Transatlantic Arts. (P.911)

Kennedy, A. E. & Paflin, Roberta

--*The Little Chick That Would Not Go to Bed.* Deihl, Edna Groff, Mrs. (1881-1935). 1942. S. Gabriel Sons & Company. (P.251)

--*The Little Pig That Would Not Get up.* Deihl, Edna Groff, Mrs. (1881-1935). 1944. S. Gabriel Sons and Company. (P.251)

--*The Little Rabbit That Would Not Eat.* Deihl, Edna Groff, Mrs. (1881-1935). 1942. S. Gabriel Sons & Company. (P.251)

Kennedy, Anna Margaret

--*Lill By-Golly.* Boardman, Laurel. 1943. Rockwell-Darmay Publications. (P.111)

Kennedy, Emilie (1951-)

--*A Sky for Henry.* Strodder, Chris (1956-). c.1985. Red Hen Press. (P.868)

Kennedy, Harry Otis

--*The Airship Boys in the Great War: Or, The Rescue of Bob Russell.* Cass, De Lysle F. 1915. The Reilly & Britton Co. (P.177)

--*The Army Alphabet.* Baum, Lyman Frank (1856-1919). 1900. George M. Hill. (P.81)

Kennedy, Harry Otis & Chard

--*Old Mother Hubbard: The Old Rhymes and Jingles with New Pictures.* Martin, Sarah Catherine (1768-1826). 1902. Jamieson-Higgins Co. (P.625)

Kennedy, Harry Otis & Costello, Charles Jerome

--*The Navy Alphabet: Verse.* Baum, Lyman Frank (1856-1919). 1900. G. M. Hill Company. (P.82)

Kennedy, Helen McCormick

--*Billy's Princess.* Haskell, Helen Eggleston, Mrs. (1871-). 1907. L. C. Page & Company. (P.419)

Kennedy, J. W. Ferguson

--*American Patty: A Story of Eighteen-Twelve.* Thompson, Adele Eugenia (1849-). 1909. Lothrop, Lee & Shepard Co. (P.886)

--*The Armed Ship America: Or, When We Sailed from Salem, 1 of 3 vols.* Kaler, James Otis (1848-1912). Otis, James, pseud. 1900. Dana Estes & Co. (P.504)

--*Bessie among the Mountain, 1 of 6 vols.* Mathews, Joanna Hooe (1849-1901). N.D. H. M. Caldwell Co. (P.629)

--*Bessie and Her Friends, 1 of 6 vols.* Mathews, Joanna Hooe (1849-1901). N.D. H. M. Caldwell Co. (P.629)

--*Bessie at School, 1 of 6 vols.* Mathews, Joanna Hooe (1849-1901). N.D. H. M. Caldwell. (P.630)

--*Bessie at the Seaside, 1 of 6 vols.* Mathews, Joanna Hooe (1849-1901). N.D. H. M. Caldwell Co. (P.630)

--*Bessie in the City, 1 of 6 vols.* Mathews, Joanna Hooe (1849-1901). N.D. H. M. Caldwell Co. (P.630)

--*Bessie on Her Travels, 1 of 6 vols.* Mathews, Joanna Hooe (1849-1901). N.D. H. M. Caldwell Co. (P.630)

--*The Boy Duck Hunters.* Kellogg, Frank Eugene (1854-). 1900. Dana Estes & Co. (P.516)

--*The Boys of Pigeon Camp: Their Luck and Fun.* Doyle, Martha Claire Macgowan, Mrs. (1869-). James, Martha, pseud. 1907. Lothrop, Lee & Shepard Co. (P.284)

--*Captain Tom, the Privateersman, 1 of 3 vols.* Kaler, James Otis (1848-1912). Otis, James, pseud. N.D. Dana Estes & Co. (P.505)

--*Captain Tom: The Privateersman of the Armed Brig Chasseur.* Kaler, James Otis (1848-1912). Otis, James, pseud. 1899. D. Estes & Company. (P.505)

--*The Crooked Trail.* Miller, Lewis Bennett (1861-). N.D. Dana Estes & Co. (P.648)

--*The Cruise of the Comet, 1 of 3 vols.* Kaler, James Otis (1848-1912). Otis, James, pseud. N.D. Dana Estes & Co. (P.505)

--*The Cruise of the Phoebe: A Story of Lobster Buying on the Eastern Coast.* Kaler, James Otis (1848-1912). Otis, James, pseud. c.1908. D. Estes and Company. (P.505)

--*The Cruise of the Phoebe: Or, Lobster Buying on the Eastern Coast.* Kaler, James Otis (1848-1912). Otis, James, pseud. N.D. Page Co. (P.505)

--*Dan Monroe, a Story of Bunker Hill.* Stoddard, William Osborn (1835-1925). N.D. Lothrop Pub. Co. (P.860)

--*Dorcaster Days.* Plympton, Almira George (1852-1939). 1907. Little, Brown, and Company. (P.729)

--*Elizabeth, Betsy, and Bess.* Blanchard, Amy Ella (1856-1926). c.1913. W. A. Wilde Co. (P.106)

--*From Low to High Gear.* Ellis, Edward Sylvester (1840-1916). c.1906. D. Estes & Company. (P.302)

--*The Gold Bug.* Poe, Edgar Allan (1809-1849). N.D. Dana Estes & Co. (P.729)

--*The Hero of Pigeon Camp; or How Lucci Made Good.* Doyle, Martha Claire Macgowan, Mrs. (1869-). James, Martha, pseud. 1908. Lothrop, Lee & Shepard Co. (P.284)

--*An Island Secret.* McAllister, Earle Cabot. c.1909. D. Estes & Company. (P.593)

--*Judy.* Bailey, Temple. 1907. Little, Brown, and Company. (P.60)

--*A Lassie of the Isles.* Thompson, Adele Eugenia (1849-). 1903. Lee and Shepard. (P.886)

--*The Little Heroine at School.* Curtis, Alice Turner, Mrs. (1860-1958). 1909. Lothrop, Lee & Shepard Co. (P.236)

--*The Lost Dragon.* Ellis, Edward Sylvester (1840-1916). c.1907. D. Estes & Co. (P.303)

--*Lucky Ned.* Ellis, Edward Sylvester (1840-1916). 1902. Dana Estes and Co. (P.303)

--*The Minute Boys of Bunker Hill, 1 of 2 vols.* Stratemeyer, Edward L. (1862-1930). 1899. Dana Estes & Co. (P.865)

--*The Minute Boys of Bunker Hill.* Stratemeyer, Edward L. (1862-1930). N.D. L. C. Page & Co. (P.865)

--*The Minute Boys of South Carolina: A Story of "How We Boys Aided Marion, the Swamp Fox".* Kaler, James Otis (1848-1912). Otis, James, pseud. c.1907. D. Estes & Company. (P.506)

--*The Old Monday Farm.* Baker, Louise Regina (1868-). N.D. Dana Estes and Company. (P.63)

--*On the Trail of the Sioux: Or, The Adventures of Two Boy Scouts on the Minnesota Frontier.* Lange, Dietrich (1863-). 1912. Lothrop, Lee & Shepard Co. (P.550)

--*On Tower Island.* McAllister, Earle Cabot. c.1907. D. Estes & Company. (P.593)

--*Our Jim: Or, The Power of Example.* Ellis, Edward Sylvester (1840-1916). c.1901. D. Estes & Company. (P.303)

--*The P. Q. & G. Or, "As the Twig Is Bent the Tree's Inclined,".* Ellis, Edward Sylvester (1840-1916). c.1908. D. Estes & Company. (P.303)

--*Patriot and Tory.* Ellis, Edward Sylvester (1840-1916). 1904. Dana Estes and Company. (P.303)

--*Plucky Jo.* Ellis, Edward Sylvester (1840-1916). 1905. Dana Estes and Company. (P.303)

--*Saddles and Lariats.* Miller, Lewis Bennett (1861-). N.D. L. C. Page & Co. (P.648)

--*The Sarah Jane, Dicky Dalton, Captain: A Story of Tugboating in Portland Harbor.* Kaler, James Otis (1848-1912). Otis, James, pseud. c.1909. D. Estes & Company. (P.506)

--*The Sarah Jane: Dicky Dalton, Captain (A Story of Tugboating in Portland Harbour).* Kaler, James Otis (1848-1912). Otis, James, pseud. N.D. L. C. Page & Co. (P.506)

--*A Sheaf of Stories.* Woolsey, Sarah Chauncey (1835-1905). Coolidge, Susan, pseud. 1906. Little, Brown, and Company. (P.979)

--*Silver Pitchers, and Independence, a Centennial Love.* Alcott, Louisa May (1832-1888). 1908. Little. Brown. (P.18)

--*The Story-Book House.* Walsh, Honor. 1903. D. Estes & Company. (P.928)

--*The Story of the Cid for Young People.* Wilson, Calvin Dill (1857-). retold by. 1901. Lee and Shepard. (P.965)

--*The Story of the Cid: For Young People.* Wilson, Calvin Dill (1857-), retold by. 1905. Lee and Shepard Company. (P.965)

--*Tim and Roy in Camp.* Pendleton, Frank. 1910. Lothrop, Lee & Shepard Co. (P.716)

--*Trail and Trading Post: Or, The Young Hunters of the Ohio.* Stratemeyer, Edward L. (1862-1930). 1906. Lothrop, Lee & Shepard Co. (P.866)

--*True Blue: A Story of Luck and Pluck.* Ellis, Edward Sylvester (1840-1916). 1903. Dana Estes and Company. (P.304)

--*Two Cadets with Washington.* Stoddard, William Osborn (1835-1925). 1906. Lothrop, Lee & Shepard Co. (P.860)

--*Unlucky Tib.* Ellis, Edward Sylvester (1840-1916). N.D. Dana Estes & Co. (P.304)

--*The Voyage of the Charlemagne.* Stoddard, William Osborn (1835-1925). N.D. Dana Estes & Co. (P.860)

--*The White River Raft.* Miller, Lewis Bennett (1861-). N.D. Dana Estes & Co. (P.648)

--*With Taylor on the Rio Grande.* Bonehill, Captain Ralph, pseud. (1862-1930). Stratemeyer, Edward L. 1901. Dana Estes & Co. (P.115)

--*With Taylor on the Rio Grande.* Stratemeyer, Edward L. (1862-1930). c.1909. Lothrop, Lee & Shepard Co. (P.866)

--*With Taylor on the Rio Grande.* Stratemeyer, Edward L. (1862-1930). 1917. Lothrop, Lee & Shepard Co. (P.866)

--*With Taylor on the Rio Grande.* Stratemeyer, Edward L. (1862-1930). 1930. Lothrop, Lee & Shepard. (P.866)

--*The Young Express Agent.* Kellogg, Frank Eugene (1854-). c.1906. D. Estes & Company. (P.516)

Kennedy, Janet

--*The Things I Can Do.* Kennedy, Janet. c.1952. Saalfield Pub. Co. (P.517)

Kennedy, John T.

--*Gallant Old Engine.* Awdry, Wilbert Vere (1911-). 1966, c.1962. Edward Ward. (P.57)

Kennedy, Paul Edward (1929-)

--*The Adventures of Ricky and Chub.* Shay, Myrtle. c.1965. Lantern. (P.817)

--*Aggie, Maggie, and Tish.* 1st ed. Erwin, Betty K. 1965. Little, Brown. (P.309)

--*At the Butt End of a Rainbow.* Livesey, Claire Warner (1927-). 1970. Harvey. (P.577)

--*Cousin Tryg.* Baker, Laura Nelson (1911-). 1966. Lippincott. (P.63)

--*Dahlbe Family Horse.* Baker, Laura Nelson (1911-). 1964. Dial. (P.63)

--*Dolly Moses: The Cat and the Clam Chowder.* Chase, Mary Ellen (1887-1973). 1964. W. W. Norton. (P.188)

--*The Forest House.* Allen, Elizabeth (1914-). 1967. Dutton. (P.29)

--*Grandma's Holidays.* Adelberg, Doris, pseud. (1929-). Orgel, Doris. 1963. Dial. (P.11)

--*Hannah Elizabeth.* Rich, Elaine Summers (1926-). 1964. Har-Row. (P.761)

--*Hibernian Nights.* MacManus, Seumas (1869-1960). 1963. Macmillan. **Award: (ALA).** (P.609)

--*If Wishes Were Horses.* 1st ed. Robertson, Keith Carlton (1914-). 1958. Harper. (P.768)

--*Legends & Folk Tales of Holland.* De Leeuw, Adele Louise (1899-). 1963. T. Nelson. (P.254)

--*The Magic Jacket.* De La Mare, Walter John (1873-1956). 1962. Knopf. **Award: (ALA).** (P.253)

--*Mountain Magic for Rosy.* Ormsby, Virginia Haire. 1969. Crown Publishers. (P.696)

--*My Horse Says.* Schroeder, Mary N. (1903-). 1965, c.1963. Coward. (P.801)

--*Penny a Day.* De La Mare, Walter John (1873-1956). 1960. Knopf. (P.253)

--*Persian Folk and Fairy Tales.* Mehdevi, Anne Marie Sinclair, retold by. 1965. Knopf. **Award: (ALA).** (P.639)

--*Richard Mansfield: The Prince of Donkeys.* Chase, Mary Ellen (1887-1973). 1964. Norton. (P.188)

--*The Seal of Jai.* Booz, Elizabeth Benson. 1968. Macmillan. (P.117)

--*The Secret of Solitary Cove.* Evatt, Harriet, Mrs. (1895-). 1964. Bobbs-Merrill. (P.312)

--*Skeleton in Armor.* Longfellow, Henry Wadsworth (1807-1882). 1967. P-H. (P.582)

--*The Skeleton in Armor.* Longfellow, Henry Wadsworth (1807-1882). 1963. Prentice-Hall. (P.582)

--*The Summer Sleigh Ride.* 1st ed. Erwin, Betty K. 1966. Little. (P.309)

--*Twelve People Are Not a Dozen.* Mikura, Vera Ferra (1923-). Hutter, Catherine, tr. from Ger. 1965. Bobbs. (P.644)

--*Victoria: A Pig in a Pram.* Chase, Mary Ellen (1887-1973). 1963. Norton. (P.188)

--*Where's Aggie.* 1st ed. Erwin, Betty K. 1967. Little. (P.309)

Kennedy, Richard (1910-)

--*Apple Acre.* rev ed. Bell, Adrian Hanbury (1901-1980). 1964. Verry. (P.90)

--*Ballet Dance for Two.* Ure, Jean. 1960. Franklin Watts, Inc. (P.910)

--*Barney the Donkey.* Casserley, Anne Thomasine. 1961. A. S. Barnes. (P.177)

--*Barney the Donkey.* Casserley, Anne Thomasine. 1938. Harper & Brothers. (P.177)

--*The Beginning Was a Dutchman.* Mitchell, Isla. 1946. Dodd, Mead & Company. (P.652)

--*The Black Pigeon.* Pullen, Alan & Rapstoff, Cyril. N.D. Merry Thoughts. (P.741)

--*Black Pigeon.* Pullen, Alan & Rapstoff, Cyril. 1965. Verry. (P.741)

--*Blue Veil and Black Gold.* Maine, Trevor. 1965, c.1961. Roy. (P.613)

--*Border Riding.* Tranter, Nigel Godwin (1909-). 1959. Verry. (P.898)

--*Castaway Christmas.* Baker, Margaret Joyce (1918-). 1964. FS&G. (P.63)

--*The Children of the Marshes.* Baudouy, Michel Aime (1909-). Hopkins, Gerard, tr. 1959. NPatheon. (P.81)

--*The Company at the Mill.* Hooper, Muriel. 1964, c.1963. Faber and Faber. (P.459)

--*The Cruise of the Santa Maria.* Dillon, Eilis (1920-). 1967. Funk & Wagnalls. (P.266)

--*Devil's Dump.* Pullen, Alan & Rapstoff, Cyril. N.D. Merry Thoughts. (P.741)

--*The Fantastic Brother.* Guillot, Rene (1900-1969). Hampton, Christopher (1929-), tr. from Fr. 1963. Rand McNally. (P.399)

--*Finn the Wolfhound.* Dawson, Alec John (1872-1951). 1962. Brockhampton Press. (P.247)

--*The Forbidden Island.* Dixon, Marjorie Mack (1887-). 1960. Criterion Books. (P.275)

--*Giant of the Bush.* Kiddell, John (1922-). 1963. Bobbs. (P.522)

--*God and Mr. Sourpuss.* Judah, Aaron (1923-). 1960, c.1959. Barnes. (P.501)

--*The Green Coated boy.* Dixon, Marjorie Mack (1887-). 1959. A. S. Barnes & Company, Inc. (P.275)

--*Head in the Clouds.* Southall, Ivan Francis (1921-). 1973, c.1972. Macmillan. (P.841)

--*A Head on her shoulders.* Bond, Gladys Baker (1912-). 1963. Obelard-Schumann. (P.114)

--*A Herd of Deer.* Dillon, Eilis (1920-). 1970, c.1969. Funk & Wagnalls. (P.266)

--*Hogboon of Hell & Other Strange Orkney Tales.* Cutt, Margaret Nancy & Cutt, William Towrie (1898-). 1979. Andre Deutsch. (P.238)

--*The Horse on Ben Ave.* Wayne, Mel. 1962, c.1961. Duell, Sloan and Pearce. (P.937)

--*The Horse Without a Head.* Berna, Paul (1910-). Buchanan-Brown, John (1929-), tr. from Fr. 1959, c.1958. Pantheon Books. **Award: (ALA).** (P.96)

--*The Island of Horses.* Dillon, Eilis (1920-). 1957, c.1956. Funk & Wagnalls. (P.266)

--*Jan Son of Finn.* Dawson, Alec John (1872-1951). 1963. Lawrence Verry Inc. (P.247)

--*The Key and the Chest.* Monckton, Ella (1899-). 1957. Warne. (P.655)

--*The Last Straw.* Pullen, Alan & Rapstoff, Cyril. N.D. Merry Thoughts. (P.741)

--*Lee Nationi: Young Navajo.* Acker, Helen. 1958. Abelard- Schuman. (P.4)

--*The Lion Cub.* Dillon, Eilis (1920-). 1967, c.1966. Duell, Sloan and Pearce. (P.266)

--*The Lost Island.* Dillon, Eilis (1920-). 1954. Funk & Wagnalls. (P.266)

--*The Man in the Train.* Pullen, Alan & Rapstoff, Cyril. N.D. Merry Thoughts. (P.741)

--*Man in the Train.* Pullen, Alan & Rapstoff, Cyril. 1965. Verry. (P.741)

--*Martin Pippin in the Apple Orchard.* Farjeon, Eleanor (1881-1965). 1961. Lippincott. (P.317)

--*Michael and His Friends.* Casserley, Anne Thomasine. 1961. A. S. Barnes. (P.177)

--*Middle Island Mystery.* Chandler, Ruth Forbes (1894-1978). 1961. Abelard-Schuman. (P.184)

--*A Night in Town.* Pullen, Alan & Rapstoff, Cyril. N.D. Merry Thoughts. (P.741)

--*Night in Town.* Pullen, Alan & Rapstoff, Cyril. 1966. Verry. (P.741)

--*No Boats on Bannermere.* Trease, Robert Geoffrey (1909-). 1965. Norton. (P.899)

--*The Old House.* Pullen, Alan & Rapstoff, Cyril. N.D. Merry Thoughts. (P.741)

--*Old House.* Pullen, Alan & Rapstoff, Cyril. 1965. Verry. (P.741)

--*On the Hook.* Pullen, Alan & Rapstoff, Cyril. N.D. Merry Thoughts. (P.741)

--*On the Hook.* Pullen, Alan & Rapstoff, Cyril. 1966. Verry. (P.741)

--*Outcast.* Sutcliff, Rosemary (1920-). 1955. Oxford University Press. (P.871)

--*Outcast.* Sutcliff, Rosemary (1920-). 1955. Walck. (P.871)

--*The Big Mile Race.* 1st ed. Kessler, Leonard P. (1921-). c.1983. Greenwillow Books. (P.520)
--*Big Red Bus.* Kessler, Ethel (1921-) & Kessler, Leonard P. (1921-). c.1957. Doubleday. **Award: (NYT).** (P.520)
--*Big Tracks, Little Tracks.* Branley, Franklyn Mansfield (1915-). 1960. Crowell. (P.127)
--*Binky Brothers and the Fearless Four.* Lawrence, James Duncan (1918-). 1970. Harper & Row. (P.556)
--*Binky Brothers, Detectives.* Lawrence, James Duncan (1918-). 1968. Harper & Row. (P.556)
--*Binky Brothers, Detectives.* Lawrence, James Duncan (1918-). 1978, c.1968. Harper & Row. (P.556)
--*A Book of Astronauts for You.* Branley, Franklyn Mansfield (1915-). 1963. Crowell. (P.127)
--*The Boy Who Could Make Things.* 1st ed. Preston, Edna Mitchell. 1970. Viking Press. (P.738)
--*Brave Daniel: The Story of a Brave Boy.* Klein, Leonore Glotzer (1916-). c.1958. Scott. (P.530)
--*Choo-Choo Train.* Pennington, Lillian Boyer. N.D. G&D. (P.716)
--*Church, Crunch.* Kessler, Ethel (1921-) & Kessler, Leonard P. (1921-). c.1955. Doubleday. (P.520)
--*Colors, Colors All Around.* Scott, Rochelle. 1965. Grossett & Dunlap. (P.805)
--*Cowboys: What Do They Do?.* Greene, Carla (1916-). 1972. Har-Row. (P.386)
--*The Day Daddy Stayed Home.* Kessler, Ethel (1921-) & Kessler, Leonard P. (1921-). c.1959. Doubleday. (P.520)
--*Deer in the Snow.* Schlein, Miriam (1926-). 1956. Abelard-Schuman. (P.799)
--*Did You Ever Hear a Klunk Say Please?.* Kessler, Leonard P. (1921-). 1967. Dodd, Mead. (P.521)
--*Do Baby Bears Sit in Chairs?.* What Animals Do. 1st ed. Kessler, Ethel (1921-) & Kessler, Leonard P. (1921-). 1961. Doubleday. (P.520)
--*Doctors and Nurses, What Do They Do?.* Greene, Carla (1916-). 1963. Harper & Row. (P.386)
--*Duck on a Truck.* Kessler, Leonard P. (1921-). 1961. Wonder. (P.521)
--*The Elephant in the Barn.* Wood, James Playsted (1905-). 1961. Harper. (P.975)
--*The Family Under the Moon.* Jewell, Nancy (1940-). c.1976. Harper & Row. (P.492)
--*Fast Is Not a Ladybug.* Schlein, Miriam (1926-). 1953. A-W. (P.799)
--*Fast Is Not a Ladybug: A Book About Fast and Slow Things.* Schlein, Miriam (1926-). 1953. W. R. Scott. (P.799)
--*The Forgetful Pirate.* Kessler, Leonard P. (1921-). 1974. Garrard Pub. Co. (P.521)
--*Grandpa Witch and the Magic Doobelator.* Kessler, Ethel (1921-) & Kessler, Leonard P. (1921-). c.1981. Macmillan. (P.520)
--*Heavy Is a Hippopotamus.* Schlein, Miriam (1926-). c.1954. W. R. Scott. **Award: (NYT).** (P.799)
--*Hello, Aurora.* Vestly, Anne Catharina (1920-). Fairfax, Jane, ed. Amos, Eileen, tr. 1974. T. Y. Crowell. (P.919)
--*Here Comes the Strikeout.* Kessler, Leonard P. (1921-). 1965. Har-Row. (P.521)
--*Hey Diddle Diddle.* Kessler, Leonard P. (1921-). c.1980. Garrard Pub. Co. (P.521)
--*Homer and the Ghost.* Margolis, Richard Jules (1929-). 1975, c.1972. Collier Books. (P.619)
--*Homer & the Ghost.* Margolis, Richard Jules (1929-). 1976. Macmillan. (P.619)
--*Homer the Hunter.* Margolis, Richard Jules (1929-). 1972. Macmillan. (P.619)
--*Hooray for Chocolate, and Other Easy-to-Read Jingles.* Hymes, Lucia Manley (1907-) & Hymes, James L. (1913-). 1960. W. R. Scott. (P.478)
--*A Horse in the House.* Crowell, Maryalicia. c.1957. Young Scott Books. (P.233)
--*How Old Is Old?.* Kessler, Leonard P. (1921-). 1967. Harvey House. (P.521)
--*How Old is Old?.* Klein, Leonore Glotzer (1916-). 1967. Harvey House. (P.530)
--*I Go Out.* Rukeyser, Muriel (1913-1980). c.1961. Harper. (P.783)
--*I Was Thinking: Poems.* Littledale, Freya Lota (1929-). c.1979. Greenwillow Books. (P.577)
--*Indian Big and Indian Little.* Russell, Solveig Paulson (1904-). 1964. Bobbs-Merrill. (P.785)
--*It's About Time.* Schlein, Miriam (1926-). 1955. W. R. Scott. (P.799)
--*Kick, Pass, and Run.* Kessler, Leonard P. (1921-). 1966. Harper & Row. (P.521)
--*Kim and Me.* Kessler, Ethel (1921-) & Kessler, Leonard P. (1921-). c.1960. Doubleday, Junior Books. (P.520)
--*Last One in Is a Rotten Egg.* Kessler, Leonard P. (1921-). 1969. Harper & Row. (P.521)
--*Lost Race of Mars.* 1st ed. Silverberg, Robert (1935-), ed. 1960. Winston. (P.823)
--*Mixed-up Mother Goose.* Dawson, Diane. 1980. Garrard Pub. Co. (P.247)
--*Mister Pine's Mixed-up Signs.* Kessler, Leonard P. (1921-). N.D. Wonder. (P.521)
--*Mr. Pine's Mixed-up Signs.* Kessler, Leonard P (1921-). 1961. Grosset & Dunlap. (P.521)
--*Mr. Pine's Purple House.* Kessler, Leonard P. (1921-). 1965. Grosset. (P.521)
--*Mr. Pine's Storybook.* Kessler, Leonard P. (1921-). c.1982. Grosset & Dunlap. (P.521)
--*Mrs. Pine Takes a Trip.* Kessler, Leonard P (1921-). 1966. Grosset & Dunlap. (P.521)
--*My Hideout.* Whisman, Molly. 1969. Harper & Row. (P.950)
--*Night Story.* Kessler, Ethel (1921-) & Kessler, Leonard P. (1921-). c.1981. Macmillan. (P.520)
--*Old Turtle's Baseball Stories.* Kessler, Leonard P. (1921-). c.1982. Greenwillow Books. (P.521)
--*Old Turtle's Riddle & Joke Book.* Kessler, Leonard P. (1921-). 1986. Greenwillow. (P.521)
--*Old Turtle's Winter Games.* Kessler, Leonard P. (1921-). 1983. Greenwillow Books. (P.521)
--*On Your Mark, Get Set, Go!.* The First All-Animal Olympics. Kessler, Leonard P. (1921-). 1972. Harper & Row. (P.521)
--*Oodles of Noodles.* Hymes, James L., Jr. & Hymes, Lucia Manley (1907-). 1964. A-W. (P.478)
--*Our Tooth Story: A Tale of Twenty Teeth.* Kessler, Ethel (1921-) & Kessler, Leonard P. (1921-). 1972. Dodd, Mead. (P.520)
--*Peek-a-Boo.* Kessler, Ethel (1921-) & Kessler, Leonard P. (1921-). c.1956. Doubleday. (P.520)
--*Pesah Is Coming.* Chanover, Hyman (1920-) & Chanover, Alice. c.1956. United Synagogue. (P.184)
--*Pesah Is Here.* Chanover, Hyman (1920-) & Chanover, Alice. c.1956. United Synagogue. (P.184)
--*Pig's New Hat.* Kessler, Ethel (1921-) & Kessler, Leonard P. (1921-). c.1981. Garrard Pub. Co. (P.520)
--*Pig's Orange House.* Kessler, Ethel (1921-) & Kessler, Leonard P. (1921-). c.1981. Garrard Pub. Co. (P.520)
--*The Pirates' Adventure on Spooky Island.* Kessler, Leonard P. (1921-). c.1979. Garrard Pub. Co. (P.521)
--*Plink, Plink!.* Goes the Water in My Sink. Kessler, Ethel (1921-) & Kessler, Leonard P. (1921-). c.1954. Doubleday. (P.520)
--*Policemen and Firemen: What Do They Do?.* Greene, Carla (1916-). 1962. Harper. (P.386)
--*Riddles That Rhyme for Halloween Time.* Kessler, Leonard P. (1921-). c.1978. Garrard Pub. Co. (P.521)
--*The Sad Tale of the Careless Klunks.* Kessler, Leonard P. (1921-). c.1965. Dodd. (P.521)
--*Slush, Slush!.* Kessler, Ethel (1921-) & Kessler, Leonard P. (1921-). 1973. Parents' Magazine Press. (P.520)
--*Soldiers and Sailors: What Do They Do?.* Greene, Carla (1916-). 1963. Harper & Row. (P.386)
--*Soup for the King: A Fable.* Kessler, Leonard P. (1921-). 1969. Grosset & Dunlap. (P.521)
--*Splish Splash.* Kessler, Ethel (1921-) & Kessler, Leonard P. (1921-). 1973. Parents' Magazine Press. (P.520)
--*The Sukkah & the Big Wind.* Edelman, Lily Judith (1915-1981). 1956. United Syn Bk. (P.296)
--*Super Bowl.* Kessler, Leonard P. (1921-). c.1980. Greenwillow Books. (P.521)
--*The Sweeneys from 9D.* Kessler, Ethel (1921-) & Kessler, Leonard P. (1921-). c.1985. Macmillan. (P.520)
--*A Tale of Two Bicycles: Safety on Your Bike.* Kessler, Leonard P. (1921-). 1971. Lothrop, Lee & Shepard Co. (P.521)
--*Teddy and the Ice Cream Man.* Fiedler, Jeanette Feldman. 1957. Ableard-Schuman. (P.324)
--*Time to Play, Time to Sleep.* Kessler, Ethel (1921-) & Kessler, Leonard P. (1921-). 1981. Garrard. (P.520)
--*Tommy Learns to Drive a Tractor.* Lewellen, John Bryan (1910-). 1958. Crowell. (P.569)
--*Tommy Learns to Fly.* Lewellen, John Bryan (1910-). 1956. Crowell. (P.569)
--*Too Many Rabbits.* Parish, Peggy (1927-). 1974. Macmillan. (P.705)
--*Truck Drivers: What Do They Do?.* Greene, Carla (1916-). 1967. Har-Row. (P.386)
--*What Do You Play on a Summer Day?.* Kessler, Ethel (1921-) & Kessler, Leonard P. (1921-). 1977. Parents' Magazine Press. (P.520)
--*What Have I Got.* McClintock, Mike, pseud. (1906-1967). McClintock, Marshall. 1961. Har-Row. (P.595)
--*What's Inside the Box?.* Kessler, Ethel (1921-) & Kessler, Leonard P. (1921-). c.1976. Dodd, Mead. (P.520)
--*What's up, Doc?.* Doctor & Dentist Jokes. Keller, Charles (1942-). 1984. P-H. (P.514)
--*The Worst Team Ever.* Kessler, Leonard P. (1921-). c.1985. Greenwillow Books. (P.521)

Kesteven, Peter
--*Magic and Gold: Tales from Northern Europe.* 1st ed. Cockett, Mary. 1970. Pergamon Press. (P.205)
--*Red Gaskell's Gold.* Bowood, Richard, pseud. (1906-). Daniell, David Scott. 1966. St. Martin's Press. (P.122)
--*Rough Passage.* Bateman, Robert Moyes Carruthers (1922-1973). 1966, c.1965. Duell, Sloan and Pearce. (P.80)

Ketcham, Hank, pseud., see Ketcham, Henry King.

Ketcham, Hank, pseud.
--*Dennis the Menace Camps Out.* Ketcham, Henry King. Toole, Fred. 1958. Rand, McNally. (P.896)

Ketcham, Henry King see Ketcham, Hank, pseud.

Kettelkamp, Larry Dale (1933-)
--*Some Are Small.* Dolch, Edward William (1889-) & Dolch, Marguerite Pierce, Mrs. (1891-). c.1959. Garrard Pub. Co. (P.279)

Kettelwell, John
--*The Story of Aladdin and the Wonderful Lamp.* Aladdin. Kettelwell, John, ed. Walpole, Hugh, pref. by. 1928. A. A. Knopf. (P.16)

Kettlewell, Doritie
--*The Marlows & the Traitor.* Forest, Antonia. 1953. Faber & Faber. (P.335)
--*The Wolf Who Was Sorry.* Ainsworth, Ruth (1908-). 1968, c.1964. Roy Publishers. (P.15)

Keussen, Gudrun
--*This Is How We Live in the Country.* Keussen, Gudrun & Ars Edition Staff. 1983. Ars Edition. (P.521)
--*This Is How We Live in the Town.* Keussen, Gudrun & Ars Edition Staff. 1983. Ars Edition. (P.521)

Key, A., jt. illus. see West, D.

Key, Alexander Hill (1904-1979)
--*Belle River Friends in Wings and Feathers.* Clark, Bertha. c.1928. Lyons and Carnahan. (P.197)
--*Belle River Friends in Wings and Feathers.* Clark, Bertha. c.1938. Lyons and Carnahan. (P.197)
--*Belle River Friends in Wings and Feathers.* Clark, Bertha. 1952. Lyons and Carnahan. (P.197)
--*Blunder's Mystery Companions.* Pettee, Florence Mae (1888-). Harper, Wilhelmina, intro. by. c.1929. A. Whitman & Co. (P.722)
--*Bolts, a Robot Dog.* Key, Alexander Hill (1904-1979). c.1966. Westminster. (P.521)
--*The Book of Dragons.* Fuller, Muriel (1901-), ed. 1931. R. M. McBride & Company. (P.349)
--*Deep Treasure: A Story of the Greek Sponge Fishers of Florida.* Blackford, Charles Minor, III (1898-). 1954. Winston. (P.105)
--*Ladd of the Big Swamp: A Story of the Okefenokee Settlement.* 1st ed. Matschat, Cecile Hulse. 1954. Winston. (P.631)
--*Liberty or Death: The Narrative of William Dunbar, Partisan.* 1st ed. Key, Alexander Hill (1904-1979). 1936. Harper Brothers. (P.521)
--*Loony Coon: Antics of a Rollicking Raccoon.* 1st ed. Campbell, Samuel Arthur (1895-). 1954. Bobbs-Merrill Co. (P.165)
--*Lorna Doone.* Blackmore, Richard Doddridge (1825-1899). N.D. Scott Foresman & Co. (P.105)
--*Marko, the King's Son, Hero of the Serbs.* Manning, Clarence Augustus (1893-1972) & Fuller, O. Muiriel. 1932. R. M. McBride & Company. (P.617)
--*The Red Eagle: Being the Adventurous Tale of Two Young Flyers.* Key, Alexander Hill (1904-1979). 1935. A. L. Burt Co. (P.521)
--*Rivets & Sprockets.* large type ed. Key, Alexander Hill (1904-1979). 1964. Westminster. (P.521)
--*Six Great Stories.* Moderow, Gertrude, et al., eds. c.1937. Scott, Foresman and Company. (P.653)
--*Sprockets: A Little Robot.* large type ed. Key, Alexander Hill (1904-1979). 1963. Westminster. (P.521)
--*Stories of Belle River.* Clark, Bertha. 1942. Lyons and Carnahan. (P.197)
--*Stormy, The Brave Sponge Diver.* Prichard, Lillian. 1955. The Dietz Press. (P.739)
--*When Washington Danced: A Tale of the American Revolution.* Stratton, Clarence (1880-). Moderow, Gertrude, adapted by. c.1938. Scott, Foresman and Company. (P.867)
--*Work and Play on Belle River Farm.* Clark, Bertha. c.1928. Lyons and Carnahan. (P.197)
--*The Young Douglas.* Nolan, Jeannette Covert, Mrs. (1896-1974). 1934. R. M. McBride & Company. (P.684)

Key, Alexander Hill (1904-1979) & Milhous, Katherine (1894-1977)
--*Story Parade: A Collection of Modern Stories for Boys and Girls.* Hawthorne, Hildegarde (1871-1952), ed. c.1940. The John C. Winston Company. (P.423)

Key, Theodore (1912-)
--*The Biggest Dog in the World.* 1st ed. Key, Theodore (1912-). 1960. Dutton. (P.521)
--*Diz and Liz.* Key, Theodore (1912-). N.D. G&D. (P.521)
--*Hazel Power.* Key, Theodore (1912-). 1971. Curtis. (P.521)
--*Ms Hazel.* Key, Theodore (1912-). 1972. Curtis. (P.521)
--*Right on Hazel.* Key, Theodore (1912-). 1972. Curtis. (P.521)
--*Ted Key's Diz and Liz.* Key, Theodore (1912-). 1966. Wonder Books. (P.521)

Keyes, Homer Eaton & Davidson, Bertha G.
--*Kitty-Cat Tales.* Carrick, Alice Van Leer (1875-). 1907. Lothrop, Lee & Shepard Co. (P.171)
--*Kitty-Cat Tales.* Carrick, Alice Van Leer (1875-). c.1932. Lothrop, Lee & Shepard Co. (P.171)

Keys, Robert
--*Big City ABC.* Staats, Sara Rader. 1968. Follett Pub. Co. (P.847)

Keyser, Corinne
--*Georgie's Capital.* Coon, Martha Sutherland (1884-). 1967. Harvey House. (P.216)
--*Someone I Know.* Adorjan, Carol Madden (1934-). 1968. Random House. (P.12)

Keysher, Elizabeth
--*Noll and the Fairies.* White, Hervey (1866-1944). N.D. Duffield & Co. (P.952)

Khemraj, P.
--*Tales for All Times.* Rungachary, Santha. 1979. Auromere. (P.784)

Kiakshuk, jt. illus. see Pudlo.

Kibbee, Gordon
--*Once There Was and Twice There Wasn't.* Walker, Barbara Kerlin (1921-), ed. 1968. Follett. (P.926)

Kicevac-Popovic, Bosiljka
--*Milan and His Runaway Uncle.* Kriskovic, Josip. Heppell, Muriel, tr. 1970. Stackpole Books. (P.540)

Kiddell-Monroe, Joan (1908-)
--*The Adventures of Odysseus.* Lang, Andrew (1844-1912), retold by. 1962. Dent. (P.548)
--*The Adventures of Odysseus.* Lang, Andrew (1844-1912), retold by. 1962. Dutton. (P.548)
--*The Aeneid of Virgil.* Taylor, Norman Burke (1885-), retold by. Virgilius Maro, Publius (1919-). 1961. H. Z. Walck. (P.920)
--*Aesop's Fables.* Warrington, John, tr. 1961. Dutton. (P.522)
--*African Myths & Legends.* Arnott, Kathleen (1914-), ed. 1963. Walck. (P.49)
--*Ambaril.* Forbes-Watson, R. 1963. Roy Publishers. (P.335)
--*Book of Myths.* Green, Roger Gilbert Lancelyn (1918-), ed. N.D. Dutton. (P.385)
--*A Book of Myths.* Green, Roger Gilbert Lancelyn (1918-), ed. 1965. J. M. Dent. (P.385)
--*Chinese Myths and Fantasies.* Birch, Cyril (1925-). 1961. H. Z. Walck. (P.102)
--*Crazy Castle.* Severn, David, pseud. (1918-). Unwin, David Storr. 1952. Macmillan. (P.812)
--*The Curse of Cain: Bible Stories.* Southall, Ivan Francis (1921-). 1968. St Martin. (P.841)
--*English Fables and Fairy Stories.* Reeves, James (1909-), retold by. 1954. Henry Z. Walck Inc. **Award: (CMA).** (P.754)
--*French Legends, Tales, and Fairy Stories.* 1st Ed. ed. Picard, Barbara Leonie (1917-), retold by. 1955. H. Z. Walck. (P.725)
--*French Legends Tales and Fairy Stories.* Picard, Barbara Leonie (1917-), retold by. 1955. Oxford University Press. (P.725)
--*Fury, Son of the Wilds.* Peel, Hazel Mary (1930-). 1959. F. Watts. (P.715)
--*German Hero-Sagas & Folk-Tales.* Picard, Barbara Leonie (1917-), retold by. 1958. Walck. (P.725)
--*The Great Barrier Reef.* Patchett, Mary Osborne Elwyn (1897-). 1958. Bobbs-Merril. (P.708)
--*The Great Gale.* Burton, Hester Wood-Hill (1913-). 1963, c.1960. Oxford University Press. (P.158)
--*Grishka and the Bear.* Guillot, Rene (1900-1969). Marsh, Gwen, tr. from Fr. 1960, c.1959. Criterion Books. **Award: (ALA).** (P.399)
--*The Heroes.* Kingsley, Charles (1819-1875). 1963. E.P. Dutton & Co. (P.524)
--*The Iliad of Homer.* Homerus. Picard, Barbara Leonie (1917-), ed. 1960. H. Z. Walck. **Award: (ALA).** (P.457)
--*India's Tales & Legends.* Gray, John E., retold by. 1961. Walck. (P.383)

--*The Nip and Tuck War.* Mian, Mary Lawrence Shipman. 1964. Houghton-Mifflin. (P.644)

--*Perihan's Promise, Turkish Relatives, and the Dirty Old Imam.* Chetin, Helen (1922-). 1973. Houghton Mifflin. (P.190)

--*Petey.* Cavanna, Betty (1909-). 1973. Westminster Press. (P.179)

--*The Pig at Thirty-Seven Pinecrest Drive.* 1st ed. Fleming, Susan (1932-). c.1981. Westminster Press. (P.331)

--*Poor Stainless: A New Story About the Borrowers.* Norton, Mary, Mrs. (1903-). 1971, c.1966. Harcourt Brace Jovanovich. (P.687)

--*Poor Stainless: A New Story About the Borrowers.* Norton, Mary, Mrs. (1903-). 1985, c.1966. Harcourt Brace Jovanovich. (P.687)

--*Ride a Wild Horse.* Carlsen, Ruth Christoffer (1918-). 1970. Houghton Mifflin. (P.168)

--*Rookfleas in the Cellar.* 1st ed. Pierik, Robert (1921-). c.1979. Westminster Press. (P.725)

--*The Secret of the Crazy Quilt.* Hightower, Florence Cole (1916-1981). 1972. Houghton Mifflin. (P.441)

--*The Small Circus.* Lansing, Elisabeth Carleton Hubbard (1911-). 1957. Crowell. (P.551)

--*A Snake Named Sam.* Warren, Mary Phraner (1929-). 1969. Westminster Press. (P.933)

--*Sore Loser.* Gray, Genevieve Stuck (1920-). 1974. Houghton Mifflin. (P.383)

--*A Spell is Cast.* Cameron, Eleanor (1912-). 1964. Little Brown. (P.163)

--*Spring Comes Riding.* Cavanna, Betty (1909-). 1950. Westminster Press. (P.179)

--*Stand up, Lucy.* Hall, Elizabeth (1929-). 1971. Houghton Mifflin. (P.404)

--*Summer of the White Reindeer.* large type ed. Pohlmann, Lillian Grenfell (1902-). 1965. Westminster. (P.730)

--*The Swapping Boy.* 1st ed. Langstaff, John Meredith (1920-). 1960. Harcourt, Brace. (P.551)

--*The Terrible Churnadryne.* Cameron, Eleanor (1912-). 1959. Little. (P.163)

--*This Stranger, My Son.* Baker, Elizabeth Gillette (1923-). 1971. Houghton Mifflin. (P.61)

--*To Make a Wee Moon.* Naylor, Phyllis Reynolds (1933-). 1969. Follett Pub. Co. (P.676)

Krush, Joe, jt. illus. see Krush, Beth.

Krush, Joe (1918-)

--*Big Caesar.* Ogburn, Charlton, Jr. (1911-). 1958. Houghton Mifflin. (P.691)

--*Black Magic at Brillstone.* Heide, Florence Parry (1919-) & Heide, Roxanne. 1981. A. Whitman. (P.430)

--*Body in the Brillstone Garage.* Heide, Florence Parry (1919-) & Heide, Roxanne. 1979. A. Whitman. (P.430)

--*The Body in the Brillstone Garage.* Heide, Florence Parry (1919-) & Heide, Roxanne. 1980. Whitman. (P.430)

--*Boy Heroes of Chapultepec: A Story of the Mexican War.* 1st ed. Chambers, Maria Cristina Mena. 1953. Winston. (P.182)

--*Brillstone Break-in.* Heide, Florence Parry (1919-) & Heide, Roxanne. c.1977. A. Whitman. (P.430)

--*Chica.* 1st ed. Scott, Sally. 1954. Harcourt, Brace. (P.805)

--*Cress Delahanty.* West, Jessamyn (1907-). 1954. HarBraceJ. (P.947)

--*The Face at the Brillstone Window.* Heide, Florence Parry (1919-) & Heide, Roxanne. 1978. A. Whitman. (P.430)

--*Fear at Brillstone.* Heide, Florence Parry (1919-) & Heide, Roxanne. c.1978. A. Whitman. (P.430)

--*Huon of the Horn: Being a Tale of That Duke of Bordeaux Who Came to Sorrow at the Hands of Charlemagne and Yet Won the Favor of Oberon, the Elf King, to His Lasting Fame and Great Glory.* 1st ed. Norton, Alice Mary (1912-). Norton, Andre, pseud. 1951. Harcourt, Brace. (P.686)

--*Magic Elizabeth.* Kassirer, Norma. 1966. Viking Press. (P.508)

--*The Minstrel Knight.* Rush, Philip (1908-). 1956. Bobbs Merrill. (P.784)

--*Ol' Dan Tucker.* Langstaff, John Meredith (1920-). 1963. Harcourt, Brace & World. (P.551)

--*The Ponder Heart.* 1st ed. Welty, Eudora (1909-). c.1954. Harcourt, Brace. (P.945)

--*The Secret Fiord.* Trease, Robert Geoffrey (1909-). 1950. Harcourt, Brace. (P.899)

--*Shadow of the Hawk.* Trease, Robert Geoffrey (1909-). 1949. Harcourt, Brace. (P.899)

--*Trumpets in the West.* Trease, Robert Geoffrey (1909-). 1947. Harcourt, Brace. (P.899)

Krush, Joe (1918-) & Krush, Beth (1918-)

--*The Beast with the Magical Horn.* 1st ed. Cameron, Eleanor (1912-). 1963. Little, Brown. (P.163)

--*Emily's Runaway Imagination.* Cleary, Beverly Bunn (1916-). 1961. Morrow. (P.200)

--*Fifteen.* Cleary, Beverly Bunn (1916-). 1956. Morrow. (P.200)

--*Gone-Away Lake.* 1st ed. Enright, Elizabeth (1909-1968). 1957. Harcourt, Brace. **Awards: (ALA); (JNM).** (P.308)

--*Miracles on Maple Hill.* 1st ed. Sorensen, Virginia Eggertsen (1912-). 1956. Harcourt, Brace. **Awards: (JNM); (ALA).** (P.841)

--*The Mysterious Christmas Shell.* 1st ed. Cameron, Eleanor (1912-). 1961. Little, Brown. (P.163)

--*Mystery of the Pirate's Ghost.* 1st ed. Honness, Elizabeth Hoffman, Mrs. (1904-). 1966. Lippincott. (P.458)

--*Mystery of the Secret Message.* Honness, Elizabeth Hoffman, Mrs. (1904-). 1961. Lippincott. (P.458)

--*Return to Gone-Away.* Enright, Elizabeth (1909-1968). 1973, c.1961. Harcourt. (P.308)

--*River School Detectives.* Warren, Mary Phraner (1929-). 1974. Westminster Press. (P.933)

--*Sister of the Bride.* Cleary, Beverly Bunn (1916-). 1963. Morrow. (P.201)

--*The Stagecoach Robbery.* Archer, Peter. 1949. Simon and Schuster. (P.46)

--*Storybook.* Kramer, Nora (1896-1984), ed. 1955. Gilbert Press; Distributed by J. Messner. (P.537)

--*Storybook: The 2d Nora Kramer Storybook.* Kramer, Nora (1896-1984), ed. 1956. Gilbert Press; Distributed by J. Messner. (P.537)

--*Those Miller Girls.* Constant, Alberta Wilson (1908-1981). c.1965. Crowell. **Award: (ALA).** (P.214)

Krusz, Arthur

--*A Visit to the Dentist.* Garn, Bernard J., Dr. N.D. Grosset & Dunlap. (P.358)

--*Visit to the Dentist.* Garn, Bernard J., Dr. 1959. Wonder. (P.358)

Krynski, Sheila

--*Four & Twenty Blackbirds.* Brabazon, Francis. 1975. Sheriar Pr. (P.123)

Krysher, Elizabeth

--*Noll and the Fairies.* White, Hervey (1866-1944). 1903. H. S. Stone and Company. (P.952)

Kubasts, Voljtech

--*Once Upon a Time.* Green, Roger Gilbert Lancelyn (1918-). 1963. Golden Press. (P.385)

Kubiak, Faith

--*Mind How the Sun Goes: A Folktale of the Maine Islands.* Churchill, Eton F. 1974. Courier-Gazette, Inc. (P.195)

Kubinyi, Laszlo (1937-)

--*The Adventures of Yoo-Lah-Teen: A Legend of the Salish Coastal Indians.* Pugh, Ellen Tiffany (1920-). 1975. Dial Press. (P.741)

--*And Tomorrow the Stars: A Fictionized Biography Story of John Cabot.* Hill, Kay, pseud. (1917-). Hill, Kathleen Louise. 1968. Dodd. **Award: (CLA).** (P.443)

--*The Boy Who Made Dragonfly: A Zuni Myth.* Hillerman, Tony (1925-). 1972. Harper & Row. (P.444)

--*The Cat and the Flying Machine.* Kubinyi, Laszlo (1937-). 1970. Simon and Schuster. (P.541)

--*The Dagger & the Bird.* Greaves, Margaret (1914-). 1975. Har-Row. (P.384)

--*The Dagger and the Bird: A Story of Suspense.* Greaves, Margaret (1914-). 1975. Harper & Row. (P.384)

--*The Fox, the Dog, and the Griffin.* Anderson, Poul William (1926-), ed. Molbech, Christian (1783-1857). c.1966. Doubleday. (P.653)

--*Haran's Journey.* Stoutenburg, Adrien Pearl (1916-). 1971. Dial Press. (P.863)

--*The Haunted Mountain.* Hunter, Mollie (1922-). 1972. Har-Row. **Award: (ALA).** (P.474)

--*The Haunted Mountain.* Hunter, Mollie (1922-). 1973. Har-Row. (P.474)

--*The Haunted Mountain.* McIlwraith, Maureen Mollie Hunter McVeigh (1922-). 1972. Harper & Row. **Award: (ALA).** (P.604)

--*I Hear You Smiling.* Holman, Felice (1919-). 1973. Scribner. (P.456)

--*I Hear You Smiling, and Other Poems.* Holman, Felice (1919-). 1973. Scribner. (P.456)

--*The Last of the Really Great Whangdoodles.* Andrews, Julie (1935-). 1974. Har-Row. (P.41)

--*Our Fathers Had Powerful Songs.* Belting, Natalia Maree (1915-), compiled by. 1974. Dutton. (P.92)

--*Patsy Jefferson's Diary.* Bourne, Miriam Anne (1931-). c.1976. Coward, McCann & Geoghegan. (P.120)

--*Poltergeists: Hauntings & the Haunted.* Knight, David Carpenter (1925-). 1972. Lippincott. (P.532)

--*The Silver Crane.* Lifton, Betty Jean (1926-). 1971. Seabury Press. (P.572)

--*Slater's Mill.* Monjo, Ferdinand Nicolas, III (1924-1978). 1972. Simon and Schuster. (P.657)

--*The Town Cats and Other Tales.* Alexander, Lloyd Chudley (1924-). 1977. Dutton. (P.22)

--*Winter Tales from Poland.* 1st ed. Wojciechowska, Maia Teresa (1927-). 1973. Doubleday. (P.973)

--*Witches, Wit, and a Werewolf.* Hardendorff, Jeanne B., retold by. 1971. Lippincott. (P.411)

--*The Wizard in the Tree.* Alexander, Lloyd Chudley (1924-). 1975. Dutton. (P.22)

--*Zeki and the Talking Cat Shukru.* Kubinyi, Laszlo (1937-). 1970. Simon and Schuster. (P.541)

Kubler, Arthur

--*Peter and the Rabbits.* Kubler, Arthur, retold by. Hoover, Roseanna, tr. 1969. Atheneum. (P.541)

--*Tomaya.* Kubler, Arthur. Hoover, Roseanna, tr. 1971. Atheneum. (P.541)

Kubler, Susanne

--*The Three Friends.* Kubler, Susanne. 1985, c.1984. Macmillan. (P.541)

Kuchera, John

--*The I-Dont-Want-To-Go-To-Bed Book for Girls.* Wyse, Lois Helene (1926-). 1963. Macmillan Company. (P.983)

--*The I-Dont-Want-To-Go-To-Bed Books for Boys.* Wyse, Lois Helene (1926-). 1963. Macmillan Company. (P.983)

Kuckei, Helge

--*The Three Times Lost Dog.* Hocker, Karla (1901-). Aubry, Lynn, tr. from Ger. 1967. Atheneum. (P.448)

Kudlacek, Jan (1928-)

--*Julian in the Autumn Woods.* Lukesova, Milena. c.1977. Holt/Rinehart/Winston. (P.590)

--*The Little Girl and the Rain.* Lukesova, Milena. c.1978. Holt, Rinehart and Winston. (P.590)

--*Petrushka.* 1971. Watts. (P.541)

--*Petrushka.* Hejna, Olga (1928-), ed. Gissing, Vera, tr. 1971. Watts. (P.431)

Kueker, Don

--*My Bible Story Book: Bible Stories for Small Children.* Fletcher, Sarah. 1974. Concordia Pub. House. (P.331)

--*My Stories About God's People.* Fletcher, Sarah. 1974. Concordia. (P.331)

--*My Stories About Jesus.* Fletcher, Sarah. 1974. Concordia. (P.331)

Kueskin, Sam

--*Kent Barstow, Special Agent.* Montgomery, Rutherford George (1894-). 1958. Duell, Sloan ,Pearce. (P.658)

--*Tom Pittman, U. S. A. F.* Montgomery, Rutherford George (1894-). 1957. Duell, Sloan, Pearce. (P.659)

Kuhn, Bob

--*Beau, from Both Ends of His Leash.* Wolters, Richard A. (1920-). c.1966. Dutton. (P.975)

--*Big Red.* Kjelgaard, James Arthur (1910-1959). 1945. Holiday House. (P.529)

--*Big Red: The Story of a Champion Irish Setter and a Trapper's Son Who Grew up Together, Roaming the Wilderness.* New ed. Kjelgaard, James Arthur (1910-1959). 1956, c.1945. Holiday House. (P.529)

--*Brushland Bill.* Huzarski, Richard C. 1943. Thomas Y. Crowell Co. (P.478)

--*Children of the Covered Wagon.* rev. ed. Carr, Mary Jane (1899-). 1957. Har-Row. (P.171)

--*Children of the Covered Wagon: A Story of the Old Oregon Trail.* Carr, Mary Jane (1899-). 1944. Thomas Y. Crowell Company. (P.171)

--*Kalak of the Ice.* Kjelgaard, James Arthur (1910-1959). 1949. Holiday House. (P.530)

--*Marty Markham.* Watkin, Lawrence Edward (1901-). 1942. H. Holt and Company. (P.934)

Kuhn, Dave, jt. illus. see Fentz, Mike.

Kukenthal, Fritz

--*The Toy Maker: How a Tree Became a Toy Village.* Thelen, Gerda. Encking, Louise Franziska (1879-), retold by. 1935. A. Whitman & Co. (P.885)

--*The Toymaker.* Encking, Louise F. N.D. Albert Whitman & Co. (P.307)

Kuklin, Susan, photos by.

--*Nightmares from Space.* DeWeese, Gene (1934-). 1981. Watts. (P.261)

Kumlien, Bertil

--*Spiro of the Sponge Fleet.* Chapin, Henry (1893-1983) & Throckmorton, Peter. 1964. Little, Brown. (P.184)

Kumme, Walter

--*Checkers.* Loeb, Marjorie. c.1946. K. Miles. (P.580)

Kunhardt, Dorothy Meserve, Mrs. (1901-1979)

--*Brave Mr. Buckingham.* Kunhardt, Dorothy Meserve, Mrs. (1901-1979). 1935. Harcourt, Brace. (P.541)

--*David's Birthday Party.* Kunhardt, Dorothy Meserve, Mrs. (1901-1979). c.1940. Rand McNally & Company. (P.541)

--*Junket Is Nice.* Kunhardt, Dorothy Meserve, Mrs. (1901-1979). c.1933. Harcourt, Brace and Company. (P.542)

--*Lucky Mrs. Ticklefeather and Other Funny Stories: The Best of Dorothy Kunhardt.* Kunhardt, Dorothy Meserve, Mrs. (1901-1979). 1973. Golden Press. (P.542)

--*More Please.* Kunhardt, Dorothy Meserve, Mrs. (1901-1979). 1946. Simon and Shuster. (P.542)

--*Now Open the Box.* Kunhardt, Dorothy Meserve, Mrs. (1901-1979). c.1934. Harcourt, Brace and Company. (P.542)

--*Pat the Bunny.* Kunhardt, Dorothy Meserve, Mrs. (1901-1979). 1940. Simon and Shuster. (P.542)

--*Pat the Bunny.* Kunhardt, Dorothy Meserve, Mrs. (1901-1979). 1962. Western Pub. (P.542)

--*Pudding Is Nice.* Kunhardt, Dorothy Meserve, Mrs. (1901-1979). 1975. Bookstore Pr. (P.542)

--*Rennet Dessert Is Nice.* Kunhardt, Dorothy Meserve, Mrs. (1901-1979). c.1947. Forbes Lithograph Mfg. Co. (P.542)

--*The Telephone Book.* Kunhardt, Dorothy Meserve, Mrs. (1901-1979). 1942. Simon and Shuster. (P.542)

--*Tickle the Pig.* Kunhardt, Dorothy Meserve, Mrs. (1901-1979). 1965. Golden Press. (P.542)

--*Wise Old Aard-Vark.* Kunhardt, Dorothy Meserve, Mrs. (1901-1979). 1936. The Viking Press. (P.542)

Kunnas, Mauri

--*The Best Sports Book in theWhole Wide World.* Hunnas, Mauri. Steffa, Tim, tr. from Finnish. c.1984. Crown. (P.473)

--*The Nighttime Book.* Kunnas, Mauri. 1985. Crown Pub. (P.542)

Kunnas, Mauri, jt. illus. see Kunnas, Tarja.

Kunnas, Mauri & Kunnas, Tarja

--*Santa Claus and His Elves.* Kunnas, Mauri & Kunnas, Tarja. 1985. Crown Publishers. (P.542)

Kunnas, Tarja, jt. illus. see Kunnas, Mauri.

Kunnas, Tarja & Kunnas, Mauri

--*Santa Claus and His Elves.* Kunnas, Mauri. c.1982. Harmony Books. (P.542)

Kunstler, Morton (1927-)

--*Bob, Son of Battle.* Ollivant, Alfred (1874-1927). Price, Olive M. (1903-), ed. 1960. Grosset & Dunlap. (P.693)

--*Furious Moose of the Wilderness.* Kjelgaard, James Arthur (1910-1959). c.1965. Dodd. (P.530)

--*King of the Grizzlies.* Seton, Ernest Evan Thompson (1860-1946). 1970. Scholastic Inc. (P.811)

--*King of the Grizzlies.* Seton, Ernest Evan Thompson (1860-1946). 1973. Schol Bk Serv. (P.811)

Kunz, Anita (1956-)

--*The Lady of the Strawberries.* Chetin, Helen (1922-). 1984. Vanguard Press. (P.190)

Kunz, Edith

--*The Pied Piper of Hamelin: A Child's Story.* Browning, Robert (1812-1889). N.D. Rand McNally Co. (P.143)

Kuo, Anna

--*A Fairy Tale for Kelly.* Galuski, Dawn. 1977. Vantage. (P.353)

--*Mr. Inchworm's Lost Family.* Surprenant, Mary L. 1977. Vantage. (P.871)

Kurek, Sarah C.

--*For Patriot Dream.* Cathon, Laura Elizabeth (1908-) & Schmidt, Thusnelda, eds. N.D. Abingdon Press. (P.178)

--*I Learn About Sharing.* Roorbach, Harriet A. N.D. Abingdon Press. (P.776)

--*Mystery of Scorpion Creek.* Lee, Wayne C. (1917-). c.1966. Abingdon. (P.561)

--*What Makes Siggy Smart?.* Balzano, Jeanne Koppel (1912-). 1967. Abingdon Press. (P.67)

--*What Makes Siggy Smart.* Bell, Gina, pseud. (1912-). Balzano, Jeanne Koppel. 1967. Abingdon. (P.90)

Kurelek, William (1927-1977)

--*Fox Mykyta.* Franko, Ivan (1856-1916). Melnyk, Bohdan (1914-), tr. c.1978. Tundra Books. (P.342)

--*Lumberjack.* Kurelek, William (1927-1977). 1974. HM. **Award: (NYT).** (P.542)

--*A Prairie Boy's Summer.* Kurelek, William (1927-1977). 1975. HM. (P.542)

--*A Prairie Boy's Winter.* Kurelek, William (1927-1977). 1973. HM. **Awards: (NYT); (BGH).** (P.542)

Kuriloff, Ron

--*Old Wattles.* 1st ed. Catlin, Wynelle (1930-). 1975. Doubleday. (P.178)

Kuroi, Ken

--*Little Bunny's Christmas Present.* Yazaki, Setsuo. Ooka, D. T., tr. from Japanese. 1983. Heian Intl. (P.985)

Kurosaki, Yoshisuke

--*Japanese Children's Favorite Stories.* 2d ed. rev. Sakade, Florence, ed. 1958. C. E. Tuttle Co. (P.790)

--*Peach Boy & Other Stories.* Sakade, Florence. 1958. C E Tuttle. (P.790)

Kurtycz, Marcos

--*Tigers & Opossums: Animal legends.* Kurtycz, Marcos & Garcia Kobeh, Ana, eds. Hall, Felicia M., tr. 1984. Little. (P.542)

Kushe, Kathy & Hastings, David

--*It Must Have Been McNutt.* Leech, Bryan Jeffery (1931-) & Sadler, Glenn Edward (1935-). 1974. G/L Regal Books. (P.561)

Kusho, Ralla

--*Tibetan Folk Tales.* Hyde-Chambers, Fredrick & Hyde-Chambers, Audrey. 1981. Shambhala. (P.478)

Kuskin, Karla Seidman see Charles, Nicholas, pseud.

Kuskin, Karla Seidman (1932-)

--*ABCDEFGHIJKLMNOPQRSTUVWXYZ.* Kuskin, Karla Seidman (1932-). 1963. Harper & Row. (P.542)

--*Nobody's Perfect, Not Even My Mother.* Simon, Norma Feldstein (1927-). c.1981. A. Whitman. (P.825)
--*Oh, That Cat!.* Simon, Norma Feldstein (1927-). 1985. A. Whitman. (P.825)
--*One More Thing, Dad.* Thompson, Susan L. c.1980. A. Whitman. (P.888)
--*Rozy Dozy.* Russell, Solveig Paulson (1904-). 1975. Abingdon Press. (P.785)
--*Shhhh!.* Kline, Suzy. 1984. A. Whitman. (P.531)
--*That's Just Fine, and Who-O-O Did It.* Lexau, Joan M, retold by. 1971. Garrard Pub. Co. (P.571)
--*Where Does My Cat Sleep?.* Simon, Norma Feldstein (1927-). 1982. A. Whitman. (P.825)
--*Will Dad Ever Move Back Home?.* Hogan, Paula Z. Muir, Martha F., intro. by. c.1980. Raintree Childrens Books. (P.452)

Lederer, Charlotte Bacskay, Mrs. (1872-)
--*The Children of the Rising Sun.* Craine, Edith Janice (1881-). c.1931. The World Syndicate Publishing Company. (P.228)
--*D: Stephen the Valiant.* Daru, Juliska, pseud. (1881-). Craine, Edith Janice. N.D. E. P. Dutton & Co. (P.242)
--*Ginevra: A Romance.* Watson, Virginia Cruse (1872-). c.1929. E. P. Dutton & Co., Inc. (P.936)
--*Malou, a Little Swiss Girl.* Criss, Mildred (1890-). 1929. Doubleday, Doran & Company, Inc. (P.231)
--*Peter.* Craine, Edith Janice (1881-). Daru, Juliska, pseud. c.1931. E. P. Dutton & Co., Inc. (P.228)
--*Peter.* Daru, Juliska, pseud. (1881-). Craine, Edith Janice. 1931. E. P. Dutton & Co. (P.242)
--*Stephen the Valiant.* Craine, Edith Janice (1881-). Daru, Juliska, pseud. c.1930. E. P. Dutton & Co., Inc. (P.228)
--*Tales from the Crescent Moon.* McNeer, May Yonge (1902-). c.1930. Farrar & Rinehart Incorporated. (P.610)
--*Tinka, Minka and Linka.* McNeer, May Yonge (1902-). 1931. A. A. Knopf. (P.610)
--*Yanko in America.* Lederer, Charlotte Balskay (1872-). 1943. Thomas Y. Crowell Company. (P.559)

Lederman, Janet (1930-)
--*Tom Tooth Runs Away.* Lederman, Janet (1930-) & Hines, Marie (1901-). 1953, c.1952. Visual Press. (P.559)

Le Duc, G.
--*Kent Fielding's Ventures.* Thurston, Ida Treadwell, Mrs. (1848-1918). 1897. A. I. Bradley & Co. (P.891)

Ledyard, Addie
--*Bed-Time Stories.* Moulton, Louise Chandler, Mrs. (1835-1908). 1899. Little, Brown, and Company. (P.669)
--*Jolly Times: Or, Child Life on a Farm.* Thorne, P., pseud. (1840-). Smith, Mary Prudence Wells. N.D. Messrs. Roberts Brothers. (P.889)
--*Letters from a Cat.* N.D. Messrs. Roberts Brothers. (P.559)
--*Letters from a Cat: Pub. by Her Mistress for the Benefit of All Cats and the Amusement of Little Children.* Jackson, Helen Maria Fiske Hunt, Mrs. (1831-1885). 1879. Roberts Brothers. (P.485)
--*Letters from a Cat: Published by Her Mistress for the Benefit of All Cats and the Amusement of Little Children.* Jackson, Helen Maria Fiske Hunt, Mrs. (1831-1885). 1906. Little, Brown, and Company. (P.485)
--*Mammy Titleback and Her Family.* N.D. Messrs. Roberts Brothers. (P.559)
--*Mammy Tittleback and Her Family: A True Story of Seventeen Cats.* Jackson, Helen Maria Fiske Hunt, Mrs. (1831-1885). 1881. Roberts Brothers. (P.485)
--*Mischief's Thanksgiving, and Other Stories.* Woolsey, Sarah Chauncey (1835-1905). Coolidge, Susan, pseud. 1874. Roberts Brothers. (P.979)
--*More Bed-Time Stories.* Moulton, Louise Chandler, Mrs. (1835-1908). 1901. Little, Brown, and Company. (P.669)
--*More Bed-Time Stories.* Moulton, Louise Chandler, Mrs. (1835-1908). 1875. Roberts Brothers. (P.670)
--*New Bed-Time Stories.* Moulton, Louise Chandler, Mrs. (1835-1908). 1880. Roberts Brothers. (P.670)
--*The New-Year's Bargain.* Woolsey, Sarah Chauncey (1835-1905). Coolidge, Susan, pseud. 1898. Little, Brown and Company. (P.979)
--*The New-Year's Bargain.* Woolsey, Sarah Chauncey (1835-1905). Coolidge, Susan, pseud. 1898. Little Brown & Co. (P.979)
--*The New-Year's Bargain.* Woolsey, Sarah Chauncey (1835-1905). Coolidge, Susan, pseud. 1872. Roberts Brothers. (P.979)
--*The New-Year's Bargain: A Christmas Story For Children.* Woolsey, Sarah Chauncey (1835-1905). Coolidge, Susan, pseud. N.D. Messrs. Roberts Brothers. (P.979)
--*What Katy Did.* Woolsey, Sarah Chauncey (1835-1905). Coolidge, Susan, pseud. 1976, c.1872. Garland Pub. (P.979)
--*What Katy Did.* A Story. Woolsey, Sarah Chauncey (1835-1905). Coolidge, Susan, pseud. 1900. Little, Brown, and Company. (P.979)
--*What Katy Did: A Story.* Woolsey, Sarah Chauncey (1835-1905). Coolidge, Susan, pseud. 1873. Roberts Brothers. (P.979)

Ledyard, Addie, et al.
--*Little-Folk Songs.* White, Alexina B. N.D. Estes & Lauriat's. (P.950)

Ledyard, Addie, jt. illus. see Eytinge, Sol.

Ledyard, Addie, jt. illus. see Greenaway, Kate.

Ledyard, Addie & Greenaway, Kate (1846-1901)
--*Five Mice in a Mouse Trap.* Richards, Laura Elizabeth Howe, Mrs. (1850-1943). N.D. Estes & Lauriat's. (P.761)

Ledyard, Addie & Shepherd, Jesse C.
--*Christmas Rhymes and New Year's Chimes.* Brine, Mary Dow Northam, Mrs. N.D. Worthington Company. (P.132)

Lee, Alan
--*The Golden Book of the Mysterious.* Watson, Jane Werner (1915-) & Chaneles, Sol. 1976. Western Pub. (P.936)
--*Puppet Show.* Peters, Sharon. 1980. Troll Assocs. (P.720)

Lee, Alison
--*The Ladder Mystery.* Lee, Alison. 1942. Lothrop, Lee & Shepard Company. (P.559)

Lee, Carol
--*Porkadot, the City-Bred Pig.* Steinberg, Phillip Orso (1921-). 1959. T. S. Denison. (P.851)

Lee, Carvel Bigham (1910-)
--*Bessie, the Messy Penguin.* Holland, Joyce Flint (1921-). 1960. T. S. Denison. (P.455)
--*George: The Discontented Giraffe.* Steinberg, Phillip Orso (1921-). 1957. T. S. Denison Co. (P.851)
--*Johnny Hop's Adventure.* Roberts, Mary E. 1960. T. S. Denison. (P.768)

Lee, Charles (1926-)
--*The Shoe Game: A Navajo Legend.* Cathey, Wallace & Aragon, Claude. 1971. Dept. of Research and Publications, Independent District No. (P.178)

Lee, Doris Emrick (1905-1983)
--*Gone Is My Goose.* Koch, Dorothy Clarke (1924-). c.1956. Holiday House. (P.534)
--*The Great Quillow.* Thurber, James Grover (1894-1961). 1944. Harcourt, Brace and Company. (P.890)
--*The Great Quillow.* Thurber, James Grover (1894-1961). 1975, c.1944. Harcourt Brace Jovanovich. (P.890)
--*The Hired Man's Elephant.* Stong, Philip Duffield (1899-1957). 1939. Dodd, Mead and Company. (P.862)
--*Mr. Benedict's Lion.* Edmonds, Walter Dumaux (1903-). 1950. Dodd, Mead. (P.297)
--*Touch Blue.* Morrison, Lillian (1917-), compiled by. 1958. T. Crowell. (P.665)

Lee, Dudley, photos by.
--*Tommy Tomato Saves the Garden.* Lansburgh, Jane & Wilson, Scott. 1937. Oquaga Press, Inc. (P.551)

Lee, Eileen Littlefield
--*Henrietta.* Self, Margaret Cabell (1902-). 1966. Vanguard Press. (P.809)

Lee, Eleanor
--*My Blue Book: Adventures for Young Children.* Read, Helen S. Hill, Patty Smith & Reed, Mary Maud (1880-1960), eds. N.D. Charles Scribner's Sons. (P.752)

Lee, Ella Dolbear
--*Dandie: The Tale of a Yellow Cat.* Hungerford, Florence. c.1924. Rand, McNally & Company. (P.473)
--*The Ella Dolbear Lee Mother Goose.* Mother Goose. c.1918. M. A. Donohue & Company. (P.667)
--*Fifty Famous Fairy Tales.* McGovern, Mary Harriet (1881-). c.1917. Whitman Publishing Co. (P.602)
--*Little Sisters to the Camp Fire Girls: Or, The Blue Birds of Grassy Bank.* Hyde, E A Watson. N.D. Rand McNally. (P.478)
--*Loraine and the Little People of Spring.* Gordon, Elizabeth (1866-1922). c.1918. Rand, McNally & Company. (P.376)
--*Where Pussies Grow.* Grove, Harriet Lee. N.D. Methodist Book Concern. (P.396)

Lee, G. E. & Jacobs, Helen M.
--*The Old Willow-Tree and Other Stories.* Ewald, Carl (1856-1908). Teixeira De Mattos, Alexander Louis (1865-1921), tr. 1923. Frederick A. Stokes Company. (P.313)

Lee, Harry H.
--*Jim Bridger, Mountain Boy.* 1955. Bobbs-Merrill. (P.560)

Lee, Jan
--*Angel Island Prisoner.* Chetin, Helen (1922-). Harvey, Catherine, tr. 1982. New Seed. (P.190)

Lee, Jared D.
--*Dynamite's Funny Book of the Sad Facts of Life.* Stine, Jovial Bob, pseud. (1943-). Stine, Robert Lawrence. 1980. Scholastic Inc. (P.858)
--*One Day at School.* Luttrell, Ida (1934-). 1983. Harcourt Brace Jovanovich. (P.591)
--*Roger' Upside-Down Day.* Wright, Betty Ren. 1980. Western Pub. (P.980)
--*You Can Go Jump.* McLenighan, Valjean (1947-). c.1977. Follett. (P.608)

Lee, Jeanne M.
--*Legend of the Li River: An Ancient Chinese Tale.* Lee, Jeanne M, retold by. c.1983. Holt, Rinehart, and Winston. (P.560)
--*Legend of the Milky Way.* 1st ed. Lee, Jeanne M., retold by. c.1982. Holt, Rinehart, and Winston. (P.560)
--*Toad Is the Uncle of Heaven: A Vietnamese Folk Tale.* Lee, Jeanne M., retold by. c.1985. Holt, Rinehart and Winston. (P.560)

Lee, Jim
--*Tai-Lee's Precious Seed.* Beck, Mary I. 1948. Friendship Press. (P.87)

Lee, Jody
--*Anne of Green Gables Picture Book.* Montgomery, Lucy Maud (1874-1942). 1983. G&D. (P.658)

Lee, Lake W.
--*My House is the Nicest Place.* White, Florence Meiman (1910-). 1963. Golden, Gate Junior Books. (P.951)

Lee, Leslie W.
--*At the Jungle's Edge: A Boy and Girl of Costa Rica.* Lee, Melicent Humason, Mrs. (1889-1943). c.1938. Thomas Y. Crowell Company. (P.561)
--*Children of Banana Land.* Lee, Melicent Humason, Mrs. (1889-1943). c.1936. Thomas Y. Crowell Company. (P.561)
--*Indians of the Oaks.* new ed. Lee, Melicent Humason, Mrs. (1889-1943). 1978. Acoma Books. (P.561)
--*Indians of the Oaks.* new ed. Lee, Melicent Humason, Mrs. (1889-1943). c.1937. Ginn and Company. (P.561)
--*Our Little Guatemalan Cousin.* 1st ed. Lee, Melicent Humason, Mrs. (1889-1943). c.1937. L.C. Page & Company. (P.561)
--*Pablo and Petra, a Boy and Girl of Mexico.* Lee, Melicent Humason, Mrs. (1889-1943). c.1934. Thomas Y. Crowell Company. (P.561)
--*Pi-Yuck of the West Coast, Salt Water Boy.* Lee, Melicent Humason, Mrs. (1889-1943). 1941. The Caxton Printers, Ltd. (P.561)
--*Volcanoes in the Sun: A Boy and Girl of Guatemala.* Lee, Melicent Humason, Mrs. (1889-1943). c.1937. Thomas Y. Crowell Company. (P.561)

Lee, Manfred Bennington (1905-1971)
--*The Red Chipmunk Mystery.* Queen, Ellery, Jr., pseud. Dannay, Frederic. 1946. J. B. Lippincott Company. (P.744)
--*The Siamese Twin Mystery.* Queen, Ellery, Jr., pseud. Dannay, Frederic. N.D. World Publishing. (P.744)

Lee, Manning De Villeneuve, jt. illus. see Barnhart, Nancy.

Lee, Manning De Villeneuve, jt. illus. see Cooper, Marjorie.

Lee, Manning de Villeneuve, jt. illus. see D'Aulaire, Edgar Parin.

Lee, Manning De Villeneuve (1894-1980)
--*Ace of the Airways.* Powell, Ardon Van Buren (1886-). c.1933. The Penn Publishing Company. (P.735)
--*Adventure Isle.* England, George Allan (1877-). c.1926. The Century Co. (P.307)
--*Adventure North.* Emery, Russell Guy (1908-). 1947. Macrae-Smith-Company. (P.307)
--*All Hands Stand By!.* Barbour, Ralph Henry (1870-1944). 1942. D. Appleton-Century Company, Incorporated. (P.70)
--*Aunt Flora.* Coatsworth, Elizabeth Jane (1893-). 1953. Macmillan. (P.204)
--*The Bascom Chest: A Story for Boys.* Loomis, Alfred Fullerton (1890-). c.1926. The Century Co. (P.583)
--*The Beckoning Road.* Snedeker, Caroline Dale Parke, Mrs. (1871-1956). 1929. Doubleday, Doran & Company, Inc. (P.837)
--*Bible Stories for Little Children.* Jones, Mary Alice (1898-). N.D. Rand McNally. (P.500)
--*The Black Arrowhead: Legends of Long Island.* Snedeker, Caroline Dale Parke, Mrs. (1871-1956). 1929. Doubleday, Doran & Company, Inc. (P.837)
--*The Blue Fairy Book.* Lang, Andrew (1844-1912), ed. 1926. Macrae Smith Company. (P.548)
--*Boston Belles.* Coatsworth, Elizabeth Jane (1893-). 1952. Macmillan. (P.204)
--*The Boys and Sally Down on a Plantation.* Knox, Rose Bell (1879-). 1930. Doubleday, Doran & Company, Inc. (P.533)
--*The Brass Keys of Kenwick.* Seaman, Augusta Huiell, Mrs. (1879-1950). c.1931. Doubleday, Doran & Company, Inc. (P.806)
--*Buffalo Trace.* Eifert, Virginia S. 1955. Dodd. **Award: (ALA).** (P.299)
--*Bugie: A Puppy in Old Yorktown.* Andrews, Mary Evans. 1958. Rand McNally. (P.41)
--*The Burro Tamer.* Hayes, Florence Sooy (1895-). 1946. Random House. (P.425)
--*Cadmus Henry.* Edmonds, Walter Dumaux (1903-). 1949. Dodd. (P.297)
--*The Call of the Clouds.* Powell, Ardon Van Buren (1886-). c.1932. The Penn Publishing Company. (P.735)
--*Caravans to Santa Fe.* McDonough, Marian McIntyre. c.1940. The Penn Publishing Company. (P.600)
--*The Case of the Calico Crab.* Seaman, Augusta Huiell, Mrs. (1879-1950). 1942. D. Appleton-Century Company, Incorporated. (P.806)
--*The Charlemonte Crest: A Mystery of Modern Haiti.* Seaman, Augusta Huiell, Mrs. (1879-1950). 1930. Doubleday, Doran & Company, Inc. (P.806)
--*Chatt Roland: A Story of American Fish Pirates.* Righter, Linwood Layton (1881-). N.D. Doubleday, Doran & Company, Inc. (P.764)
--*Cherry Ann and the Dragon Horse.* Coatsworth, Elizabeth Jane (1893-). 1955. Macmillan. (P.204)
--*City of Adventure.* Carter, Russell Gordon (1892-1957). c.1934. The Penn Publishing Company. (P.176)
--*Coin and Crossbones.* Longstreth, Thomas Morris (1886-). c.1925. The Century Co. (P.583)
--*Colt of Destiny: A Story of the California Missions.* Malkus, Alida Wright Sims, Mrs. (1899-). 1950. Winston. (P.614)
--*Corporal Bess: The Story of a Boy and a Dog.* Edmonds, Walter Dumaux (1903-). 1952. Dodd, Mead. (P.297)
--*Cousins' Luck in the Louisiana Bayou Country.* Knox, Rose Bell (1879-). 1940. The Macmillan Company. (P.533)
--*Cowboys, Cowboys, Cowboys: Stories of Roundups & Rodeos, Branding & Bronco-Busting;.* Fenner, Phyllis Reid (1899-1982), compiled by. 1950. F. Watts. (P.322)
--*The Crimson Road.* Playfair, Robert Smith. 1938. Houghton Mifflin Company. (P.728)
--*The Curious Affair at Heron Shoals.* Seaman, Augusta Huiell, Mrs. (1879-1950). 1940. D. Appleton-Century Company Incorporated. (P.806)
--*Dangerous Island.* Mindlin, Helen Mather-Smith. 1956. Dodd, Mead. (P.651)
--*Davy Jone's Locker: An Adventure Story of the Astorian Expedition.* Fulton, Reed. 1928. Doubleday, Doran & Company, Inc. (P.349)
--*Drumbeats in Williamsburg: A Story of Washington, Lafayette and Yorktown.* Lawrence, Isabelle Wentworth. 1965. Rand McNally. (P.556)
--*Dusky Day: A College Story.* Means, Florence Crannell, Mrs. (1891-1980) & Riggs, Frances. 1933. Houghton Mifflin Company. (P.638)
--*Dusty of the Double Seven.* Dean, Graham M. (1904-). 1948. Viking Press. (P.248)
--*Elves & the Shoemaker.* Grimm, Jakob Ludwig Karl (1785-1863) & Grimm, Wilhelm Karl. 1964. Hale. (P.391)
--*English Oak and Spanish Gold.* Mawhinney, Thomas A. H. 1943. David McKay Co. (P.632)
--*English Oak and Spanish Gold.* Mawhinney, Thomas A. H. 1926. The Penn Publishing Company. (P.632)
--*Fighting Yankee.* Pike, Robert Everding (1905-). 1955. Abelard-Schuman. (P.726)
--*From Star to Star: A Story of Krakow in 1493.* Kelly, Eric Philbrook (1884-1960). 1944. J. B. Lippincott Company. (P.516)
--*The Front Page Mystery.* Dean, Graham M (1904-). 1931. D. Appleton and Co. (P.248)
--*Fuller at Harvard.* Playfair, Robert Smith. 1939. Houghton Mifflin Company. (P.728)
--*Ghosts, Ghosts, Ghosts.* Fenner, Phyllis Reid (1899-1982), compiled by. 1952. Watts.(P.322)
--*Ghosts, Ghosts, Ghosts: An Anthology of Short Stories.* Fenner, Phyllis Reid (1899-1982), ed. 1955. Franklin Watts, Inc. (P.322)
--*Ghosts, Ghosts, Ghosts: Stories of Spooks and Spirits, Haunts and Hobgoblins, Werewolves and Will-O'-the-Wisps.* Rev. ed. Fenner, Phyllis Reid (1899-1982), compiled by. 1952. F. Watts. (P.322)
--*Ghosts of the Scarlet Fleet.* Mountevans, Edward Ratcliffe Garth Russell Evans (1880-1957). 1932. Farrar & Rinehart, Incorporated. (P.670)
--*The Golden Imp.* Chase, Josephine (0000-1931). c.1933. The Penn Publishing Co. (P.188)
--*Gray Caps.* Knox, Rose Bell (1879-). 1932. Doubleday, Doran & Company, Inc. (P.533)

--*Eric & the Mad Inventor.* Sheridan, John. 1979. Bobbs. (P.819)
--*Eric the Wild Car.* Sheridan, John. 1979. Bobbs. (P.819)

Livraghi, Virginio
--*Brer Rabbit.* Hayes, Barbara (1944-). c.1984. Rourke Enterprises. (P.425)

Livsey, Carmon V.
--*Cuddle Bear of Piney Forest.* Halladay, Anne M, Mrs. c.1930. The Bethany Press. (P.406)

Llewellyn, Bill
--*Starship Through Space.* Stine, George Harry (1928-). Correy, Lee, pseud. 1954. Holt. (P.858)

Llimona, Mercedes
--*The Adventures of Strawberry Shortcake and Her Friends.* Wallner, Alexandra (1946-). c.1980. Random House. (P.928)
--*The Seasons with Strawberry Shortcake.* Llimona, Mercedes. c.1980. Random House. (P.578)
--*Strawberry Shortcake's Favorite Mother Goose Rhymes.* Llimona, Mercedes. 1983. Random House. (P.578)

Lloyd, Errol (1943-)
--*Doctor Shawn.* Breinburg, Petronella (1927-). 1975, c.1974. Crowell. (P.129)
--*Shawn Goes to School.* Breinburg, Petronella (1927-). 1974, c.1973. Crowell. (P.129)
--*Shawn Goes to School.* Breinburg, Petronella (1927-). 1974. Harper. (P.129)
--*Shawn's Red Bike.* Breinburg, Petronella (1927-). 1976, c.1975. Crowell. (P.129)

Lloyd, Katharine C.
--*King of the Tinkers.* Lynch, Patricia Nora (1898-1972). 1938. E. P. Dutton & Company, Inc. (P.592)

Lloyd, Megan
--*All Those Mothers at the Manger.* Farber, Norma (1909-1984). 1985, c.1979. Harper & Row. (P.316)
--*Chicken Tricks.* 1st ed. Lloyd, Megan. c.1983. Harper & Row. (P.578)
--*Lonesome Lester.* Luttrell, Ida (1934-). 1984. Harper & Row. (P.591)
--*Surprises.* Hopkins, Lee Bennett (1938-). 1984. Harper. **Award: (ALA).** (P.463)
--*There Goes the Ghost.* Sherrow, Victoria. c.1985. HarpJ. (P.820)

Lloyd, Pamela
--*Ikerchat and Sarah.* Lloyd, Pamela. 1960. Reily & Lee and Company. (P.578)
--*Samuel, the Ambitious Flea.* Lloyd, Pamela. 1961. Reilly & Lee. (P.578)

Lloyd, R. J.
--*What Is the Truth?.* A Farmyard Fable for the Young. Hughes, Ted (1930-). 1984. Faber. (P.471)

Lloyd, Stanley
--*Bonny the Pony.* Clarke, Ruth. 1948. Frederick Warne & Co. (P.200)
--*The Chestnut Filly.* Cumming, Primrose Amy (1915-). 1940. M. S. Mill Co., Inc. (P.234)
--*Riding Days.* Oliver, Marjorie Mary (1890-). 1948. Westminster Press. (P.693)
--*Silver Snaffles: A Story of a Shetland Pony.* Cumming, Primrose Amy (1915-). 1937. M. S. Mill Co., Inc. (P.234)
--*The Wednesday Pony.* Cumming, Primrose Amy (1915-). 1939. M. S. Mill Co., Inc. (P.234)

Lloyd, T. Ivestor (1905-)
--*Runaway Mike.* Helme, Eleanor Edith. 1937. C. Scribner's Sons. (P.431)

Lo-An
--*House in the Bend of Bourbon Street.* Flettrich, Terry. 1974. Pelican. (P.332)

Lobe, Mira
--*Pig in a Muddle.* Opgenoorth, Winifred. 1984. Merrimack Pub Cir. (P.695)
--*Valerie and the Good-Night Swing.* Opgenoorth, Winfred & Carter, Peter. 1983. Merrimack Pub Cir. (P.695)

Lobel, Adrianne
--*Danby and George.* Baker, Betty Lou (1928-). c.1981. Greenwillow Books. (P.61)

Lobel, Anita Kempler (1934-)
--*Ants Are Fun.* Myrick, Mildred. 1968. Har-Row. (P.675)
--*A Birthday for the Princess.* Lobel, Anita Kempler (1934-). 1973. Harper & Row. (P.579)
--*Clever Kate.* Shub, Elizabeth, adapted by. Grimm, Jakob Ludwig Karl (1785-1863) & Grimm, Wilhelm Karl (1786-1859). 1973. Macmillan. (P.391)
--*Cock-A-Doodle Doo, Cock-A-Doodle Dandy.* Kapp, Paul. 1965. Har-Row. (P.508)
--*Cock-a-Doodle-Doo, Cock-a-Doodle-Dandy.* Kapp, Paul. c.1966. Harper. (P.508)
--*Dinosaur Time.* Parish, Peggy (1927-). 1974. Har-Row. (P.705)
--*Fanny's Sister.* Lively, Penelope (1933-). 1980. Dutton. (P.577)
--*How the Rooster Saved the Day.* Lobel, Arnold Stark (1933-). c.1977. Greenwillow Books. (P.579)
--*How the Rooster Saved the Day.* Lobel, Arnold Stark (1933-). 1979, c.1977. Puffin Books. (P.579)
--*How the Tsar Drinks Tea.* Elkin, Benjamin (1911-). 1971. Parents' Magazine Press. (P.301)
--*Indian Summer.* Monjo, Ferdinand Nicolas, III (1924-1978). 1968. Har-Row. (P.656)
--*King Rooster, Queen Hen.* Lobel, Anita Kempler (1934-). 1975. Greenwillow Books. **Award: (ALA).** (P.579)
--*King Rooster, Queen Hen.* Lobel, Anita Kempler (1934-). 1975. Macmillan. (P.579)
--*Little John.* 1st ed. Orgel, Doris (1929-), retold by. 1972. Farrar, Straus, Giroux. (P.695)
--*Little John.* Orgel, Doris (1929-), ed. 1974. FS&G. (P.695)
--*The Little Wooden Farmer.* new ed. Dalgliesh, Alice (1893-1979). 1968, c.1930. Macmillan. (P.239)
--*The Night Before Christmas.* Moore, Clement Clarke (1779-1863). 1984. Knopf. (P.660)
--*On Market Street.* Lobel, Arnold Stark (1933-). c.1981. Greenwillow Books. **Awards: (NYT); (ALA); (BGH); (RCM).** (P.579)
--*One for the Price of Two.* Jameson, Cynthia. 1972. Parents' Magazine Press. (P.489)
--*The Pancake.* Lobel, Anita Kempler (1934-). c.1978. Greenwillow Books. (P.579)
--*Peter Penny's Dance.* Quin-Harkin, Janet (1941-). c.1976. Dial Press. (P.745)
--*Peter Penny's Dance.* Quin-Harkin, Janet (1941-). 1979. Dial Bks Young. (P.745)
--*Potatoes, Potatoes.* Lobel, Anita Kempler (1934-). 1967. Harper & Row. (P.579)
--*Puppy Summer.* DeJong, Meindert (1906-). 1965. Har-Row. (P.252)
--*The Rose in My Garden.* Lobel, Arnold Stark (1933-). 1984. Greenwillow. (P.579)
--*The Seamstress of Salzburg.* Lobel, Anita Kempler (1934-). 1970. Harper & Row. (P.579)
--*Singing Bee!.* A Collection of Favorite Children's Songs. Hart, Jane, compiled by. 1982. Lothrop. (P.418)
--*Soldier, Soldier, Won't You Marry Me?.* 1st ed. Langstaff, John Meredith (1920-), ed. 1972. Doubleday. (P.551)
--*Someone Small.* Borack, Barbara (1942-). 1969. Harper & Row. (P.117)
--*The Straw Maid.* Lobel, Anita Kempler (1934-). 1983. Greenwillow. (P.579)
--*Sven's Bridge.* Lobel, Anita Kempler (1934-). 1965. Harper & Row. **Award: (NYT).** (P.579)
--*Three Rolls and One Doughnut.* Ginsburg, Mirra (1919-), retold by. 1970. Dial Press. (P.369)
--*The Troll Music.* Lobel, Anita Kempler (1934-). 1966. Har-Row. (P.579)
--*Under a Mushroom.* Lobel, Anita Kempler (1934-). 1970. Harper & Row. (P.579)
--*The Uproar.* Orgel, Doris (1929-). 1970. McGraw-Hill. (P.695)
--*The Wisest Man in the World: A Legend of Ancient Israel.* Elkin, Benjamin (1911-). 1968. Parents' Magazine Press. (P.301)
--*The Wishing Penny, and Other Stories.* Lobel, Anita Kempler (1934-). 1967. Parents' Magazine Press. (P.579)

Lobel, Arnold Stark (1933-)
--*As I Was Crossing Boston Common.* Farber, Norma (1909-1984). 1975, c.1973. E. P. Dutton. **Award: (ALA).** (P.316)
--*As Right As Right Can Be.* Rose, Anne K. c.1976. Dial Press. **Award: (NYT).** (P.777)
--*The Bears of the Air.* Lobel, Arnold Stark (1933-). 1965. Harper & Row. (P.579)
--*Benny's Animals, and How He Put Them in Order.* Selsam, Millicent Ellis (1912-). 1966. Harper & Row. (P.809)
--*The Book of Pigericks.* 1st ed. Lobel, Arnold Stark (1933-). c.1983. Harper & Row. **Award: (ALA).** (P.579)
--*Circus.* Prelutsky, Jack. 1978, c.1974. Collier Books. (P.737)
--*Circus.* Prelutsky, Jack. 1974. Macmillan. (P.737)
--*The Clay Pot Boy.* Jameson, Cynthia. 1973. Coward, McCann & Geoghegan. (P.489)
--*The Comic Adventures of Old Mother Hubbard & Her Dog.* Mother Goose. Martin, Sarah Catherine (1768-1826), ed. 1968. Bradbury Pr. (P.667)
--*Comic Adventures of Old Mother Hubbard & Her Dog.* Martin, Sarah Catherine (1768-1826). 1968. P-H. (P.625)
--*Days with Frog and Toad.* Lobel, Arnold Stark (1933-). c.1979. Harper & Row. **Award: (ALA).** (P.579)
--*Dudley Pippin.* Ressner, Philip (1922-). 1965. Harper. (P.758)
--*Fables.* Lobel, Arnold Stark (1933-). c.1980. Harper & Row. **Awards: (RCM); (ALA).** (P.579)
--*The Four Little Children Who Went Around the World.* Lear, Edward (1812-1888). 1968. Macmillan. (P.558)
--*Frog & Toad All Year.* Lobel, Arnold Stark (1933-). 1976. Har-Row. (P.579)
--*Frog and Toad All Year.* Lobel, Arnold Stark (1933-). c.1976. Harper & Row. **Award: (ALA).** (P.579)
--*Frog and Toad Are Friends.* Lobel, Arnold Stark (1933-). 1970. Harper & Row. **Award: (RCM).** (P.579)
--*Frog and Toad are Friends.* Lobel, Arnold Stark (1933-). 1979. Harper & Row. (P.579)
--*The Frog & Toad Coloring Book.* Lobel, Arnold Stark (1933-). 1981. Har-Row. (P.579)
--*Frog and Toad Together.* Lobel, Arnold Stark (1933-). 1972. Harper & Row. **Awards: (ALA); (JNM).** (P.579)
--*Giant John.* Lobel, Arnold Stark (1933-). 1964. E. M. Hale and Company. (P.579)
--*Giant John.* Lobel, Arnold Stark (1933-). 1964. Harper & Row. (P.579)
--*Good Ethan.* Fox, Paula (1923-). 1973. Bradbury Press. (P.340)
--*The Great Blueness and Other Predicaments.* Lobel, Arnold Stark (1933-). 1968. Harper & Row. (P.579)
--*Gregory Griggs and Other Nursery Rhyme People.* Lobel, Arnold Stark (1933-). c.1978. Greenwillow Books. **Award: (ALA).** (P.579)
--*Greg's Microscope.* Selsam, Millicent Ellis (1912-). 1963. Harper & Row. (P.810)
--*Hansel & Gretel.* Grimm, Jakob Ludwig Karl (1785-1863) & Grimm, Wilhelm Karl (1786-1859). 1971. Delacorte. (P.393)
--*The Headless Horseman Rides Tonight: More Poems to Trouble Your Sleep.* 1st ed. Prelutsky, Jack. 1980. Greenwillow. **Awards: (NYT).** (P.737)
--*Hildilid's Night.* Ryan, Cheli Duran. 1971. Macmillan. **Awards: (ALA); (RCM).** (P.786)
--*Hildilid's Night.* Ryan, Cheli Duran. 1974. Macmillan. (P.786)
--*A Holiday for Mister Muster.* Lobel, Arnold Stark (1933-). 1963. Harper & Row. **Award: (NYT).** (P.579)
--*A Holiday for Mr. Muster.* Lobel, Arnold Stark (1933-). 1980. Scholastic Inc. (P.579)
--*The Ice-Cream Cone Coot, and Other Rare Birds.* Lobel, Arnold Stark (1933-). 1980, c.1971. Four Winds Press. (P.579)
--*The Ice-Cream Cone Coot, and Other Rare Birds.* Lobel, Arnold Stark (1933-). 1971. Parents' Magazine Press. (P.579)
--*I'll Fix Anthony.* Viorst, Judith. 1969. Harper & Row. (P.920)
--*Junk Day on Juniper Street & Other Easy to Read Stories.* Moore, Lilian. 1968. Parents. (P.661)
--*Let's Get Turtles.* Selsam, Millicent Ellis (1912-). 1965. Har-Row. (P.810)
--*Little Runner of the Longhouse.* Baker, Betty Lou (1928-). 1962. Har-Row. (P.61)
--*Lucille.* Lobel, Arnold Stark (1933-). 1964. Harper & Row. (P.579)
--*The Magic Spectacles.* Moore, Lilian. 1966, c.1965. Parents' Magazine Press. (P.661)
--*The Man Who Took the Indoors Out.* Lobel, Arnold Stark (1933-). 1974. Harper & Row. **Award: (NYT).** (P.579)
--*Martha, the Movie Mouse.* Lobel, Arnold Stark (1933-). 1966. Harper & Row. (P.579)
--*The Master of Miracle: A New Novel of the Golem.* Ish-Kishor, Sulamith (1896-1977). 1971. Harper & Row. **Award: (ALA).** (P.483)
--*The Mean Old Mean Hyena.* Prelutsky, Jack. c.1978. Greenwillow Books. (P.737)
--*Merry Merry Fibruary.* Orgel, Doris (1929-). c.1977. Parents' Magazine Press. **Award: (NYT).** (P.695)
--*Ming Lo Moves the Mountain.* Lobel, Arnold Stark (1933-). c.1982. Greenwillow Books. **Award: (ALA).** (P.579)
--*Miss Suzy.* Young, Miriam Burt (1913-1974). 1964. Parents' Magazine Press. (P.990)
--*Miss Suzy's Birthday.* Young, Miriam Burt (1913-1974). 1974. Parents' Magazine Press. **Award: (NYT).** (P.990)
--*Miss Suzy's Christmas.* Young, Miriam Burt (1913-1974). 1973. Parents' Magazine Press. (P.990)
--*Miss Suzy's Easter Surprise.* Young, Miriam Burt (1913-1974). 1980, c.1972. Four Winds Press. (P.990)
--*Miss Suzy's Easter Surprise.* Young, Miriam Burt (1913-1974). 1972. Parents' Magazine Press. (P.990)
--*More Tales of Oliver Pig.* Van Leeuwen, Jean (1937-). c.1981. Dial Press. **Award: (ALA).** (P.914)
--*Mouse Soup.* Lobel, Arnold Stark (1933-). 1977. Har-Row. (P.579)
--*Mouse Tales.* Lobel, Arnold Stark (1933-). 1972. Harper & Row. (P.579)
--*The New Vestments.* Lear, Edward (1812-1888). 1970. Bradbury Press. (P.558)
--*Nightmares: Poems to Trouble Your Sleep.* Prelutsky, Jack. c.1976. Greenwillow Books. **Award: (ALA).** (P.737)
--*On the Day Peter Stuyvesant Sailed into Town.* Lobel, Arnold Stark (1933-). 1971. Harper & Row. **Award: (ALA).** (P.579)
--*Oscar Otter.* Benchley, Nathaniel Goddard (1915-1981). 1966. Har-Row. (P.92)
--*Oscar Otter.* Benchley, Nathaniel Goddard (1915-1981). 1980. Har-Row. (P.92)
--*Owl at Home.* Lobel, Arnold Stark (1933-). c.1975. Harper & Row. **Award: (ALA).** (P.579)
--*Prince Bertram the Bad.* Lobel, Arnold Stark (1933-). 1963. Harper & Row. (P.579)
--*Quarreling Book.* Zolotow, Charlotte Shapiro (1915-). 1963. E M Hale. (P.994)
--*The Quarreling Book.* Zolotow, Charlotte Shapiro (1915-). 1963. Harper & Row. (P.994)
--*The Random House Book of Poetry for Children.* Prelutsky, Jack, compiled by. 1983. Random House. **Award: (ALA).** (P.737)
--*Red Fox & His Canoe.* Benchley, Nathaniel Goddard (1915-1981). 1964. Har-Row. (P.92)
--*Red Tag Comes Back.* Phleger, Fred B. (1909-). 1961. Har-Row. (P.724)
--*Sam the Minuteman.* Benchley, Nathaniel Goddard (1915-1981). 1969. Har-Row. (P.92)
--*The Secret Three.* Myrick, Mildred. 1963. Har-Row. (P.675)
--*Small Pig.* Lobel, Arnold Stark (1933-). 1969. Har-Row. (P.579)
--*Someday.* Zolotow, Charlotte Shapiro (1915-). 1965. Harper & Row. (P.994)
--*Something Old, Something New.* Rhinehart, Susan Oneacre (1938-). 1961. Har-Row. (P.759)
--*The Star Thief.* DiNoto, Andrea. 1967. Macmillan. (P.266)
--*The Strange Disappearance of Arthur Cluck.* Benchley, Nathaniel. 1967. Har-Row. (P.92)
--*The Tale of Meshka the Kvetch.* Chapman, Carol. c.1980. Dutton. (P.186)
--*Tales of Oliver Pig.* Van Leeuwen, Jean (1937-). c.1979. Dial Press. (P.914)
--*The Terrible Tiger.* Prelutsky, Jack. 1969, c.1970. Collier Books. (P.737)
--*Terry and the Caterpillars.* Selsam, Millicent Ellis (1912-). 1962. Harper & Row. (P.810)
--*A Three Hat Day.* Geringer, Laura (1948-). c.1985. Harper & Row. **Award: (ALA).** (P.364)
--*Tot Botut & His Little Flute.* Cathon, Laura Elizabeth (1908-). 1970. Macmillan. (P.178)
--*Uncle Elephant.* Lobel, Arnold Stark (1933-). 1982. Har-Row. (P.579)
--*Uncle Elephant.* Lobel, Arnold Stark (1933-). c.1981. Harper & Row. **Award: (ALA).** (P.579)
--*Whiskers and Rhymes.* Lobel, Arnold Stark (1933-). c.1984. Greenwillow Books. (P.579)
--*Wishing Penny & Other Fantasy Stories.* Tresselt, Alvin R. (1916-), ed. 1967. Parents. (P.900)
--*The Witch on the Corner.* 1st ed. Holman, Felice (1919-). 1966. Norton. (P.456)
--*A Zoo for Mister Muster.* Lobel, Arnold Stark (1933-). 1962. Harper. (P.579)

Lobingier, Elizabeth Erwin Miller, Mrs. (1889-)
--*Ship East--Ship West.* Lobingier, Elizabeth Erwin Miller, Mrs. (1889-). c.1937. Friendship Press. (P.579)

Lobue, Elisa
--*Big Foot, Little Foot.* Kimball, Kathleen. c.1979. West Village Pub. Co. (P.522)

Loccisano, Karen
--*Ballet Magic.* Robison, Nancy Louise (1934-). 1981. A. Whitman. (P.771)
--*When the Dolls Woke.* Stover, Marjorie Filley (1914-). 1985. A. Whitman. (P.864)

Locke, Margo
--*Birthday Present.* Martin, Patricia Miles (1899-). 1963. Abingdon. (P.625)
--*The Broomtail Bronc.* Martin, Patricia Miles (1899-). c.1964. Abingdon. (P.625)
--*Chandler Chipmunk's Flying Lesson, and Other Stories.* Martin, Patricia Miles (1899-). 1960. Abingdon Press. (P.625)
--*Cubby's World: Story of a Baby Bear.* Trent, Robbie (1894-). 1966. Abingdon. (P.899)
--*I Can See What God Does.* Wolcott, Carolyn Muller. 1969. Abingdon Press. (P.973)
--*Impatient Jonathan.* Smaridge, Norah Antoinette (1903-). 1964. Abingdon Press. (P.830)
--*Smart Bear.* Tichenor, Tom (1923-). 1970. Abingdon Press. (P.891)
--*Twelve Years, Twelve Animals.* Samuel, Yoshiko. 1972. Abingdon Press. (P.791)

Locke, Margo & Locke, Vance
--*For A Child's Day.* Young, Lois Horton (1911-1981). N.D. Abingdon Press. (P.990)

Locke, Vance
--*Annie Oakley, Little Sure Shot.* Wilson, Ellen Janet Cameron (0000-1976). 1962. Bobbs-Merrill. (P.966)
--*The Biggest Family in the Town.* Hoke, Helen L., Mrs. (1903-). Sterling, Helen, pseud. c.1947. D. McKay. (P.453)
--*The Biggest Family in Town.* Sterling, Helen, pseud. (1903-). Hoke, Helen L.. N.D. David McKay Co. (P.853)

--*Steamboat Bill and the Captain's Top Hat.* Shapiro, Irwin (1911-). 1943. J. Messner Inc. (P.815)

--*The Stone-Faced Boy.* Fox, Paula (1923-). 1968. Bradbury Press. **Award: (ALA).** (P.340)

--*Story of Mark Twain.* Howard, Joan. N.D. G&D. (P.467)

--*The Story of Mark Twain.* Gordon, Patricia (1904-). Howard, Joan, pseud. Meadowcroft, Enid La Monte, Mrs. (1898-1966), ed. 1953. Grosset & Dunlap. (P.377)

--*Summer Growing Time.* 1st ed. Jolly, Erin. Kelley, Sally, pseud. 1971. Viking Press. (P.498)

--*A Tale of Two Houses.* Dyer, Caroline. 1944. Whittlesey House. (P.293)

--*The Three Famous Ugly Sisters.* Dyer, Caroline. 1946. Whittlesey House, McGraw-Hill Book Company Inc. (P.293)

McKay, Donald A. (1895-) & Daugherty, James Henry (1889-1974)

--*Heroes in American Folklore.* Shapiro, Irwin (1911-). 1962. Messner. (P.815)

McKay, Donald A. (1895-) & Polseno, Jo

--*The Adventures of Huckleberry Finn.* Twain, Mark, pseud. (1835-1910). Clemens, Samuel Langhorne. N.D. Putnam Pub Group. (P.906)

McKean, Else

--*Wee Robin's Christmas Song: Adapted from an Old Tale, with Songs.* Stern, Elsie Jean (1898-), ed. 1945. T. Nelson & Sons. (P.853)

McKean, Else, photos by.

--*David's Bad Day.* McKean, Else. 1949. Shady Hill Press. (P.605)

--*David's Bad Day.* McKean, Else. N.D. Vanguard Press. (P.605)

MacKean, Emma C.

--*Alice in Wonderland.* Dodgson, Charles Lutwidge (1832-1898). Carroll, Lewis, pseud. c.1943. McLoughlin Bros., Inc. (P.277)

--*Alice's Adventures in Wonderland.* Dodgson, Charles Lutwidge (1832-1898). Carroll, Lewis, pseud. c.1932. McLoughlin Brothers, Inc. (P.277)

--*Cinderella.* Cinderella. c.1943. McLoughlin Bros., Inc. (P.196)

--*Goldilocks and the Three Bears.* 1943. McLoughlin Bros., Inc. (P.605)

--*Little Red Riding Hood.* 1943. McLoughlin Bros. Inc. (P.605)

--*Little Red Riding Hood.* Little Red Riding Hood. c.1943. McLoughlin Bros., Inc. (P.577)

McKean, Lloyd

--*The Postman.* Marshak, Samuil Iakovlevich (1887-1964). 1948. Shady Hill Press. (P.622)

McKeating, Eileen

--*Gopher, Tanker & the Admiral.* Climo, Shirley (1928-). 1984. Har-Row. (P.202)

McKee, David (1935-)

--*A Book of Elephants.* Wales, Katie, compiled by. 1977. Parent's Magazine Press. (P.925)

--*The Day the Tide Went Out ... and Out ... and Out ... and Out ... and Out ... and Out.* McKee, David (1935-). 1976, c.1975. Abelard-Schuman. (P.605)

--*The Day the Tide Went Out- and Out-.* McKee, David (1935-). c.1985. P. Bedrick Books. (P.605)

--*Elmer: The Story of a Patchwork Elephant.* McKee, David (1935-). 1968. McGraw-Hill. (P.605)

--*Game Songs with Prof. Dogg's Troupe: Forty-four Songs and Games with Activities.* Powell, Harriett. 1984. Sterling. (P.736)

--*Hans in Luck.* McKee, David (1935-), retold by. 1967. Abelard. (P.605)

--*I Hate My Teddy Bear.* McKee, David (1935-). 1984. HM. (P.605)

--*Joseph, the Border Guard.* Baumann, Kurt (1909-). 1972, c.1971. Parents' Magazine Press. (P.83)

--*Joseph, the Border Guard.* Baumann, Kurt (1909-). 1972. Scholastic Inc. (P.83)

--*Lord Rex, the Lion Who Wished.* McKee, David (1935-). 1973. Abelard-Schuman. (P.605)

--*The Magician and the Petnapping.* McKee, David (1935-). 1976. Abelard-Schuman. (P.605)

--*The Magician and the Petnapping.* McKee, David (1935-). 1976. Houghton Mifflin. (P.605)

--*The Magician and the Sorcerer.* McKee, David (1935-). 1974. Parents' Magazine Press. (P.605)

--*The Magician Who Lost His Magic.* McKee, David (1935-). 1970. Abelard-Schuman. (P.605)

--*The Man Who Was Going to Mind the House.* Asbjornsen, Peter Christen (1812-1885). McKee, David (1935-), retold by. 1973, c.1972. Abelard-Schumann. (P.51)

--*Mark and the Monocycle.* McKee, David (1935-). 1968. Abelard-Schuman. (P.605)

--*Mr. Benn: Red Knight.* McKee, David (1935-). 1968. McGraw-Hill. (P.605)

--*Mr.* Drackle and His Dragons. Froman, Elizabeth Hull (1920-1975). 1971. Watts. (P.347)

--*Not Now, Bernard.* McKee, David (1935-). c.1980. Methuen. (P.605)

--*One, Two, Three, Four, Five, Six, Seven, Eight, Nine Benn.* McKee, David (1935-). 1970. McGraw-Hill. (P.605)

--*Paddington and the Knickerbocker Rainbow.* Bond, Thomas Michael (1926-). 1984. Putnam. (P.114)

--*Paddington at the Fair.* Bond, Thomas Michael (1926-). 1986, c.1985. Putnam. (P.114)

--*Paddington at the Zoo.* Bond, Thomas Michael (1926-). N.D. Putnam. (P.114)

--*Paddington's Art Exhibition.* Bond, Thomas Michael (1926-). 1986, c.1985. Putnam. (P.114)

--*Tusk Tusk.* McKee, David (1935-). 1979. Barron. (P.605)

--*Two Admirals.* McKee, David (1935-). c.1977. Houghton Mifflin. (P.605)

--*Two Can Toucan.* McKee, David (1935-). 1965, c.1964. Abelard. (P.605)

--*Two Can Toucan.* McKee, David (1935-). 1964. Hale. (P.605)

--*Two Monsters.* McKee, David (1935-). 1986, c.1985. Bradbury Press. (P.605)

McKee, John Dukes

--*American Riddles in Rhyme.* Murphy, Ruby Bradford. 1955. Abingdon. (P.673)

--*Big and Little Brothers.* Geijerstam, Gustaf Af (1858-1909). Lifschultz, Burton Benjamin, tr. 1930. Thomas S. Rockwell Company. (P.362)

--*The Big Show.* Baskerville, Mary. c.1932. Rand McNally & Co. (P.79)

--*Circus Babies.* Gale, Mary Elizabeth. N.D. Rand McNally & Co. (P.352)

--*Lucky Year.* Aldis, Dorothy Keeley, Mrs. (1896-1966). 1951. Rand McNally. (P.21)

--*The Magic Umbrella.* Barrows, Ruth Marjorie (1892-1983). c.1937. Follett Publishing Co. (P.76)

--*The Magic Umbrella Abroad.* Barrows, Ruth Marjorie (1892-1983). 1930. Thomas S. Rockwell Co. (P.76)

McKee, Robinson

--*Animal Stories.* Scott, Theresa Ann (1904-), ed. Robinson, pseud. 1947. Wonder Books; Distributed by Random House. (P.805)

McKeehan, Murray

--*Valuable Kindling.* Moore, Jessie Eleanor (1886-), ed. c.1963. Pub. for the Cooperative Pubn. Assn. by Abingdon. (P.661)

Mckell, James C.

--*Eagle Cliff.* Chapman, Maristan, pseud. (1891-1972) & Chapman, Mary Ilsley. Chapman, John Stanton Higham. 1934. D. Appleton-Century Company, Incorported. (P.186)

--*Flood in Glen Hazard.* Chapman, Maristan, pseud. (1891-1972) & Chapman, Mary Ilsley. Chapman, John Stanton Higham. 1939. D. Appleton-Century Company, Incorporated. (P.186)

--*The Gallant Crosby, a Baseball Story.* Heyliger, William (1884-1955). 1933. D. Appleton and Company. (P.440)

--*Glen Hazard Cowboys.* Chapman, Maristan, pseud. (1891-1972) & Chapman, Mary Ilsley. Chapman, John Stanton Higham. 1940. D. Appleton-Century Company, Incorporated. (P.186)

--*Gulf Coast Treasure.* Chapman, Maristan, pseud. (1891-1972) & Chapman, Mary Ilsley. Chapman, John Stanton Higham. 1941. D. Appleton-Century Company, Incorporated. (P.186)

--*Marsh Island Mystery.* Chapman, Maristan, pseud. (1891-1972) & Chapman, Mary Ilsley. Chapman, John Stanton Higham. 1936. D. Appleton-Century Company, Incorporated. (P.186)

--*Mystery of the Broken Key.* Chapman, Maristan, pseud. (1891-1972) & Chapman, Mary Ilsley. Chapman, John Stanton Higham. 1938. D. Appleton-Century Company, Incorporated. (P.186)

--*Mystery on the Mississippi.* Chapman, Maristan, pseud. (1891-1972) & Chapman, Mary Ilsley. Chapman, John Stanton Higham. 1942. D. Appleton-Century Company, Incorporated. (P.186)

--*Rogues on Red Hill.* Chapman, Maristan, pseud. (1891-1972) & Chapman, Mary Ilsley. Chapman, John Stanton Higham. 1937. D. Appleton-Century Company, Incorporated. (P.186)

--*Secret of Wild Cat Cave.* Chapman, Maristan, pseud. (1891-1972) & Chapman, Mary Ilsley. Chapman, John Stanton Higham. 1944. D. Appleton-Century Company, Incorporated. (P.186)

--*The Timber Trail.* Chapman, Maristan, pseud. (1891-1972) & Chapman, Mary Ilsley. Chapman, John Stanton Higham. 1933. D. Appleton-Century Company, Incorporated. (P.186)

--*Wild Cat Ridge.* Chapman, Maristan, pseud. (1891-1972) & Chapman, Mary Ilsley. Chapman, John Stanton Higham. 1932. D. Appleton and Company. (P.186)

McKenna, John F., jt. illus. see Petie, Haris.

McKenna, Paul

--*The Adventures of Rattlesnake Ralph.* Reynolds, Alfred Christopher (1911-). 1973. Scribner. (P.759)

McKenna, Terry (1949-)

--*The Fox & the Circus Bear.* McKenna, Terry (1949-). 1982. David & Charles. (P.606)

Mackensie, Rene

--*Fairy Tales of India.* Ker Wilson, Barbara (1929-), retold by. 1960. E. P. Dutton & Co. (P.520)

MacKenzie, Garry (1921-)

--*The Adventures of Walter M.* Duffle Duff. Kelley, Sam. 1952. Lothrop, Lee & Shepard. (P.515)

--*April Showers: Poems.* Love, Katherine Isabel (1907-), ed. 1948. T. Y. Crowell Co. (P.587)

--*Flickertail.* Bailey, Carolyn Sherwin (1875-1961). 1962. H. Z. Walck. (P.60)

--*Freddie the Owl.* Andros, Guy. 1947. Oxford University Press. (P.41)

--*The Garden Under the Sea.* Thompson, George Selden (1929-). Selden, George, pseud. 1957. Viking Press. (P.887)

--*The Heir to Christmas.* Gordon, Patricia (1904-). 1953. Viking Press. (P.377)

--*Here Come the Bears.* Goudey, Alice E. (1898-). 1954. Scribner. (P.378)

--*Here Come the Beavers!.* Goudey, Alice E. (1898-). 1957. Scribner. (P.378)

--*Here Come the Cottontails!.* Goudey, Alice E. (1898-). N.D. Scribners. (P.378)

--*Here Come the Deer.* Goudey, Alice E. (1898-). 1955. Scribner. (P.378)

--*Here Come the Elephants!.* Goudey, Alice E (1898-). 1955. Scribner. (P.378)

--*Here Come the Lions!.* Goudey, Alice E (1898-). 1956. Scribner. (P.378)

--*Here Come the Seals!.* Goudey, Alice E (1898-). 1957. Scribner. (P.378)

--*Here Come the Whales!.* Goudey, Alice E (1898-). 1956. Scribner. (P.378)

--*Here Come the Wild Dogs.* Goudey, Alice E. (1898-). 1958. Scribner. (P.378)

--*Homer Sees the Queen.* Baker, Margaret Joyce (1918-). 1953. McGraw Hill. (P.63)

--*Homer Sees the Queen.* Baker, Margaret Joyce (1918-). 1953. Whittlesey House. (P.63)

--*McGonnigle's Lake.* Montgomery, Rutherford George (1894-). 1953. Doubleday. (P.658)

--*Miss Brimble's Happy Birthday.* Quigg, Jane. 1955. Oxford University Press. (P.744)

--*Mother Goose.* Mother Goose. 1949. Crowell Co. (P.667)

--*Mr.* Flip Flop. Garrett, Helen (1895-). 1948. Viking Press. (P.358)

--*The Oldest Secret.* Gordon, Patricia (1904-). 1953. Viking Press. (P.377)

--*Quillenback for Fire Chief.* Howard, Joan. 1951. Henry Z. Walck, Inc. (P.467)

--*Quillenback for Fire Chief.* Howard, Joan. 1951. Oxford University Press. (P.467)

--*Read to Me Again.* Child Study Association of America, compiled by. 1961. Crowell. (P.191)

--*Small Fry.* Merriam, Eve (1916-). 1965. Knopf. (P.642)

--*The Taming of Giants.* Gordon, Patricia (1904-). Howard, Joan, pseud. 1950. Viking Press. (P.377)

--*Timothy Tattercoat.* Chaney, Maryel & Chaney, Ronald. 1958. Houghton Mifflin. (P.184)

--*Treasury of Games, Riddles, Stunts, Tricks, Tongue-Twisters, Rhymes, Chanting, Singing.* Withers, Carl A. (1900-1970), ed. 1969. G&D. (P.973)

--*Two for a walk.* Kravetz, Nathan (1921-). 1954. Henry Z. Walck, Inx. (P.539)

--*Two for a Walk.* Kravetz, Nathan (1921-). 1954. Oxford University Press. (P.539)

--*Uncle Sylvester.* Gordon, Patricia (1904-). Howard, Joan, pseud. 1950. Oxford University Press. (P.377)

--*Up and Over the Hill.* Simon, Norma Feldstein (1927-). c.1957. Lippincott. (P.825)

--*The Wind and Peter.* Tresselt, Alvin R. (1916-). 1948. Oxford University Press. (P.900)

MacKenzie, T. Blakeley

--*Aladdin: or, The wonderful Lamp & Ali Baba and the Forty Thieves.* N.D. A. Whitman & Co. (P.607)

McKeown, Anne Cordts

--*Children of the Cruces Trail.* Core, Susie Pearl. c.1946. North River Press. (P.220)

--*Christmas on the Isthmus.* Core, Susie Pearl. c.1936. Clermont Press. (P.220)

--*An Odyssey of the Spanish Main.* Core, Susie Pearl. c.1937. Clermont Press. (P.220)

--*Panama's Jungle Book.* Core, Susie Pearl. c.1936. Clermont Press. (P.220)

McKernan, Frank

--*The Boy Electrician: Or, The Secret Society of the Jolly Philosophers.* Houston, Edwin James (1847-1914). 1907. J. B. Lippincott Company. (P.466)

--*The Boy Electricians As Detectives.* Houston, Edwin James (1847-1914). 1912. J. B. Lippincott Company. (P.466)

--*David Crockett Scout.* Allen, Charles F. N.D. J. B. Lippincott Co. (P.29)

--*In the Wyoming Valley: A Story of the Massacre in the Time of the Revolution.* Tomlinson, Everett Titsworth (1859-1931). 1901. The Griffith & Rowland Press. (P.895)

McKesson, Malcolm F

--*Flashbacks: Poems for Children.* limited 1st. Rhodes, Irma G & Peschel, Enid Rhodes (1943-). c.1978. Dragon's Teeth Press. (P.760)

Mackey, John

--*Alexander's Horses.* 1st ed. Powers, Alfred. 1959. Longmans, Green. (P.736)

--*Alexander's Horses.* Powers, Alfred. 1959. McKay. (P.736)

--*The Rise of the Thunderer.* Galt, Thomas Franklin, Jr. (1908-). 1954. Crowell. (P.353)

McKibbin, Bill

--*Samantha's Secret Room.* Cook, Lyn, pseud. (1918-). Waddell, Evelyn Margaret. 1964. St. Martin's Press. (P.215)

--*Three Hundred Sixty-Five Bedtime Stories.* Gilbertson, Mildred Geiger (1908-). 1970. Western Pub. Co. (P.367)

Mackie, Frederick J, Jr.

--*The Outer Darkness.* Wallerstein, James S. 1977, c.1976. Aurelon Tales. (P.927)

McKie, Roy

--*Bennett Cerf's Book of Animal Riddles.* Cerf, Bennett Alfred (1898-1971). 1964. Beginner. (P.180)

--*Bennett Cerf's Book of Riddles.* Cerf, Bennett Alfred (1898-1971). 1960. Beginner. (P.180)

--*Color and Colors with George, Josie, and Me.* Hirschfeld, Phyllis. 1968. Random House. (P.446)

--*A Day of Your Own: Your Birthday.* Boys'Edition ed. Low, Alice (1926-). 1964. Random House. (P.588)

--*The Eye Book.* Geisel, Theodor Seuss (1904-). LeSieg, Theo, pseud. 1968. Random House. (P.362)

--*Guess a Rhyme: Poems to Complete!* Riddles to Solve!. Weinberg, Larry. 1982. Random. (P.941)

--*In a People House.* Geisel, Theodor Seuss (1904-). Dr. Seuss, pseud. 1972. Random House. (P.362)

--*The Joey Story.* Warren, Rosanna Phelps. 1964. Random House. (P.934)

--*The Many Mice of Mr. Brice.* Geisel, Theodor Seuss (1904-). Sieg, Theo Le, pseud. N.D. Random House. (P.362)

--*My Book About Me, by Me Myself.* I Wrote It! I Drew It!. Geisel, Theodor Seuss (1904-). Dr. Seuss, pseud. 1969. Beginner Books. (P.362)

--*The Night Before Christmas.* Moore, Clement Clarke (1779-1863). 1963. Random House. (P.660)

--*Noah's Ark.* O'Connor, Jane & Risom, Ole, eds. 1984. Random. (P.690)

--*The Nose Book.* Perkins, Albert Rogers (1904-1975). 1970. Random House. (P.718)

--*Sense and Senses with George, Josie, and Me.* Hirschfeld, Phyllis. 1968. Random House. (P.446)

--*Summer.* Low, Alice (1926-). 1963. Beginner Books. (P.588)

--*Would You Rather Be a Bullfrog?.* Le S eg, Theo, pseud. (1904-). Geisel, Theodor Seuss. 1975. Random. (P.567)

Mackie, Sheila

--*Adventure in Glide's Garden.* Legere, Terri (1953-). 1978. Oriel Press. (P.562)

--*Adventure in Glide's Garden.* Legere, Terri (1953-). N.D. Routledge & Kegan. (P.562)

McKillip, Kathy

--*The Night Gift.* 1st ed. McKillip, Patricia Anne (1948-). 1976. Atheneum. (P.607)

McKim, Sam

--*Walt Disney's Toby Tyler.* Disney, Walter Elias (1901-1966). Memling, Carl (1918-1969), adapted by. 1960. Golden Press. (P.272)

McKimson, Thomas, jt. illus. see Anderson, Al.

McKimson, Thomas, jt. illus. see Kelsey, Richmond I.

McKimson, Tom, jt. illus. see Totten, Bob.

Mackin, Bernice Roberts

--*How Tommy Was Cured of Crying And Other Rhymes for the Little Ones.* Waite, Gertrude R. Mitchell. c.1900. The Abbey Press. (P.924)

McKinley, Clare

--*Amos Learns to Talk: The Story of a Little Duck.* Bradbury, Bianca (1908-). c.1951. Rand McNally. (P.124)

--*Chester: The Little Pony.* Gunder, Eman. 1956, c.1951. Rand McNally. (P.399)

--*Chester, the Little Pony.* Gunder, Eman. N.D. Rand McNally. (P.399)

--*The Jolly Jingle Book.* Jackson, Leroy Freeman (1881-). 1951. Rand McNally. (P.486)

--*Little Red Wagon.* Cederborg, Hazel P. N.D. Rand McNally & Co. (P.180)

--*Misty, the Wonder Pony.* Henry, Marguerite (1902-). 1961, c.1956. Rand McNally. (P.433)

--*Misty, the Wonder Pony: By Misty, Herself.* Henry, Marguerite (1902-). c.1956. Rand McNally. (P.433)

--*Mr.* Bear's House. Rothe, Fenella. c.1953. Rand McNally. (P.780)

--*Mr.* Bear's House. Rothe, Fenella. 1958, c.1953. Rand McNally. (P.780)

--*Christmas Miniature.* Buck, Pearl Sydenstricker, Mrs. (1892-1973). 1957. John Day. (P.147)
--*Five Little Peppers.* Lothrop, Harriet Mulford Stone, Mrs. (1844-1924). Sidney, Margaret, pseud. Fadiman, Clifton (1904-), afterword by. 1962. Macmillan. (P.586)
--*Ginny Harris on Stage.* 1st ed. Fiore, Evelyn L. (1918-). 1965. Doubleday. (P.327)
--*Little Men.* Alcott, Louisa May (1832-1888). 1963. Grosset & Dunlap. (P.17)
--*Little Women.* Alcott, Louisa May (1832-1888). 1963. Grosset & Dunlap. (P.17)
--*Read Me a Poem: Children's Favorite Poetry.* Buell, Ellen Lewis, ed. c.1965. Grosset. (P.148)
--*Wendy's Private Life.* 1st ed. Holberg, Ruth Langland, Mrs. (1891-). 1959. Doubleday. (P.453)
--*The Wizard of Oz.* Baum, Lyman Frank (1856-1919). 1963. Grosset & Dunlap. (P.82)

Magennis, Bev
--*Martin's Father.* 2d ed. Eichler, Margrit (1942-). c.1977. Lollipop Power. (P.299)

Mager, Gus
--*Gewallopus: The Story of a Playful Horse.* Goldsmith, Elsie Helen Borg, Mrs. (1885-). 1926. A. & C. Boni. (P.374)

Maggard, John
--*Beyond the Mountain, Beyond the Forest.* Fradin, Dennis Brindell (1945-). c.1978. Childrens Press. (P.340)
--*Cave Painter.* Fradin, Dennis Brindell (1945-). 1978. Childrens Press. (P.340)
--*Shell Hunter.* Geren, Carl. c.1977. Childrens Press. (P.364)

Maggio, Michael I.
--*The City Without Color.* Maggio, Michael I. c.1980. Newridge Pub. Co. (P.613)

Magine, John (1921-)
--*Birthday Surprise.* Sabin, Louis (1930-). 1981. Troll Assocs. (P.787)
--*Christmas Surprise.* Gordon, Sharon. 1980. Troll Assocs. (P.377)
--*Friendly Snowman.* Gordon, Sharon. 1980. Troll Assocs. (P.377)
--*Magic Monsters Learn About Safety.* Tester, Sylvia Root (1939-). 1979. Childs World. (P.883)
--*Sing Me a Song.* Johnston, Mary Anne (1936-). c.1977. Child's World. (P.498)

Magine, Sharon
--*Easter Bunny's Lost Egg.* Gordon, Sharon. 1980. Troll Assocs. (P.377)

Magleby, McRay
--*In the Strange, Strange Wood.* Bell, Gail Winther (1936-). 1972. Brigham Young University Publications. (P.90)

Magnani, Rudolph
--*Runaway.* Neigoff, Mike (1920-). 1974. Benefic Press. (P.677)
--*Tennis Champ.* Lunemann, Evelyn. 1972. Benefic Press. (P.591)

Magner, Adelaide
--*Tales of a Terrier.* Allen, Anne Story. 1903. Abbey Press. (P.29)

Magner, Helen
--*When the World Is New.* Fuller, Lois Compton, Mrs. c.1934. Dorrance & Co., Inc. (P.349)

Magnie, Bernice
--*Black Beauty.* Sewell, Anna (1820-1878). Claire, Malcolm, as told by. Uncle Mal, pseud. 1946. Prang Company. (P.812)
--*Sondo, a Liberian Boy.* Joseph, Alfred Ward. c.1936. A. Whitman & Co. (P.501)

Magnus, Erica
--*Old Lars.* Magnus, Erica. c.1984. Carolrhoda. (P.613)

Magnusen, Robert
--*Cougar.* Montgomery, Rutherford George (1894-). 1961. Golden Press. (P.658)
--*The Mystery of the Merry Magician.* Queen, Ellery, Jr., pseud. & Lee, Manfred Bennington (1905-1971). Dannay, Frederic. 1961. Golden Press. (P.744)
--*The Mystery of the Vanished Victim.* Queen, Ellery, Jr., pseud. & Lee, Manfred Bennington (1905-1971). Dannay, Frederic. 1962. Golden Press. (P.744)

Magnuson, Diana
--*The Gazelle & the Hunter.* Foley, Anna Bernice Williams (1902-). 1980. Childrens. (P.333)
--*The Gazelle and the Hunter: A Persian Folk Tale.* Foley, Anna Bernice Williams (1902-). 1980. Child's World. (P.333)
--*Jeanies Valentines.* Rarick, Carrie. 1982. Modern Curr. (P.749)
--*Jokes & More Jokes.* Ziegler, Sandra K. (1938-). 1983. Childrens. (P.992)
--*Knock-Knocks, Limericks, & Other Silly Sayings.* Ziegler, Sandra K. (1938-). 1983. Childrens. (P.992)
--*Magic Monsters Look for Colors.* Moncure, Jane Belk (1926-). c.1979. Child's World. (P.655)
--*Magic Monsters Look for Shapes.* Moncure, Jane Belk (1926-). c.1979. Child's World. (P.655)
--*Not I, Not I.* Hillert, Margaret (1920-). c.1981. Follett Pub. Co. (P.444)
--*Riddles and More Riddles.* Shannon, J. Michael. c.1983. Children's Press. (P.814)
--*Rudolph Shines Again.* May, Robert Lewis (1905-1976). 1981, c.1954. Follett. (P.633)
--*Rudolph the Red-Nosed Reindeer.* May, Robert Lewis (1905-1976). 1980, c.1939. Follett Pub. Co. (P.633)
--*We Visit the Zoo.* Wannamaker, Bruce, pseud. (1926-). Moncure, Jane Belk. 1976. Childs World. (P.930)
--*What Do the Animals Do in the Zoo?.* Moncure, Jane Belk (1926-). c.1976. Child's World. (P.656)

Magrath, W.
--*Fred, and Maria, and Me.* Rev ed. Prentiss, Elizabeth Payson, Mrs. (1818-1878). 1868. C. Scribner & Company. (P.738)

Maguire, Emma M.
--*Sixteen Little Indian Stories.* Maguire, Emma M. 1922. A. Flanagan Company. (P.613)
--*Two Little Indians.* Maguire, Emma M. c.1908. A. Flanagan Company. (P.613)

Mahacek, Lou
--*Child's Treasure Book of Fireside Tales.* Anderson, Kenneth (1917-). 1950. Zondervan. (P.39)

Mahan, Benton
--*Goldilocks and the Three Bears.* c.1981. Troll Associates. (P.613)
--*Little Red Riding Hood.* Grimm, Jakob Ludwig Karl (1785-1863) & Grimm, Wilhelm Karl (1786-1859). 1981. Troll Assocs. (P.394)
--*Little Red Riding Hood.* Little Red Riding Hood. c.1981. Troll Associates. (P.577)
--*Pink Pink.* DeLage, Ida (1918-). 1973. Garrard Pub. Co. (P.252)
--*Who Lives Here?.* Latham, Jean Lee (1902-). 1974. Garrard Pub. Co. (P.553)

Mahan, Joan
--*Art, the Altogether Aged Aardvark.* Mahan, Joan. 1975. Aurora Publishers. (P.613)

Mahmoudi, Massood & Shearer, Tony
--*The Story As Told.* Mahmoudi, Jalil. 1973. Naturegraph Publishers. (P.613)

Mahon, Ty
--*Stories of the First American Animals.* Langford, George (1876-). c.1923. Boni and Liveright. (P.550)

Mahoney, Marion L., jt. illus. see Perkins, Lucy Fitch, Mrs.

Mahony, Felix
--*Won in the Ninth.* Mathewson, Christopher (1880-1925). Mathewson, Christy, pseud. Aulick, Will Wroth (1873-), ed. 1910. R. J. Bodmer Company. (P.630)
--*Won in the Ninth.* Mathewson, Christopher (1880-1925). Aulick, Will Wroth (1873-), ed. c.1916. The New York Book Company. (P.630)

Mahood, Kenneth (1930-)
--*The Bus Under the Leaves.* Mahy, Margaret (1936-). 1975. Biblio Dist. (P.613)
--*Fifty Million Sausages.* Benedictus, Roger. 1975. A. Deutsch. (P.93)
--*The Laughing Dragon.* Mahood, Kenneth (1930-). c.1970. Scribner. (P.613)
--*Losing Willy.* Mahood, Kenneth (1930-). c.1977. Prentice-Hall. (P.613)
--*Why Are There More Questions Than Answers, Grandad?.* Mahood, Kenneth (1930-). 1974. Bradbury Press. (P.613)
--*The Wizard of Gauze.* Keller, Charles (1942-), compiled by. c.1979. Prentice-Hall. (P.514)

Mai, jt. illus. see Robin.

Mai, Vo-Dinh
--*The Land I Lost: Adventures of a Boy in Vietnam.* Huynh, Quang Nhuong (1946-). 1982. Harper & Row. (P.478)

Maidoff, Jules
--*A Fiesta of Folk Songs from Spain and Latin America.* Yurchenco, Henrietta (1916-), ed. 1967. G. P. Putnam's Sons. (P.991)
--*The Potter's Four Sons.* Gold, Sharlya. 1969. Doubleday. (P.373)
--*The Potter's Four Sons: A Fable.* Gold, Sharlya. 1970. Doubleday. (P.373)

Maier-Furstenfeld, Emil
--*Jesus and the Fisherman.* Maier-Furstenfeld, Emil. Spiegil, Magdalena, contrib. by. 1983. Abingdon. (P.613)
--*Jesus Befriends Zacchaeus.* Maier-Furstenfeld, Emil. Spiegel, Magdalena, contrib. by. 1983. Abingdon Press. (P.613)
--*The Loving Father.* Maier-Furstenfeld, Emil. Spiegel, Magdalena, contrib. by. 1983. Abingdon Press. (P.613)

Maik, Henri, pseud., see Hecht, Henri Joseph.

Maik, Henri, pseud. (1922-)
--*The Flying Lion.* Hecht, Henri Joseph. Maik, Henri, pseud. (1922-). Hecht, Henri Joseph. 1971, c.1970. Putnam. (P.613)
--*The Foolish Bird.* Hecht, Henri Joseph. Maik, Henri, pseud. (1922-). Hecht, Henri Joseph. 1968. R. B. Luce. (P.613)

Maillard, Katharina
--*Circus Magic: Verses.* Banigan, Sharon Stearns (1912-). 1959, c.1958. Dutton. (P.68)

Main, Jean, jt. illus. see Cobb, David.

Main, Jean & Cobb, David
--*And Not to Yield: A Story of the Outward Bound School of Adventure.* Villiers, Alan John (1903-). 1953. Scribner. (P.919)

Main, Mildred Miles (1898-)
--*Polly, Patsy, and Pat.* Main, Mildred Miles (1898-). N.D. Wilcox & Follett Co. (P.613)

Maitin, Samuel
--*Gentle, Gentle Thursday.* Shepherd, Gene D & Martin, William Ivan, Jr. (1916-). 1970. Bowmar. (P.818)
--*Spooky Sounds.* Noodles, pseud. Hahn, Frank G.. c.1979. Holt, Rinehart, and Winston. (P.684)

Maitland, Antony Jasper (1935-)
--*Aidan Chambers' Book of Ghosts and Hauntings.* Chambers, Aidan (1934-). 1973. Longman Young Books. (P.182)
--*Aidan Chambers' Book of Ghosts and Hauntings.* Chambers, Aidan (1934-). 1973. Puffin Books. (P.182)
--*The Bear Who Liked Hugging People, and Other Stories.* Ainsworth, Ruth (1908-). 1978, c.1976. C. Russak. (P.15)
--*Ben Goes to the City.* Maitland, Antony Jasper (1935-). 1967, c.1964. Delacorte Press. (P.614)
--*Black Jack.* Garfield, Leon (1921-). 1968. Longmans. **Award: (CMA).** (P.355)
--*Black Jack.* Garfield, Leon (1921-). 1969, c.1968. Pantheon Books. (P.355)
--*Captain Sintar.* Robinson, Richard Gavin. 1969, c.1967. Dutton. (P.770)
--*Devil in the Fog.* Garfield, Leon (1921-). 1966. Pantheon Books. (P.355)
--*Dick Whittington: A Story from England.* Causley, Charles Stanley (1917-). 1979. Penguin. (P.178)
--*The Drummer Boy.* Garfield, Leon (1921-). 1970. Pantheon. **Award: (CMA).** (P.355)
--*The Ghost Downstairs.* Garfield, Leon (1921-). 1972. Pantheon Books. **Award: (ALA).** (P.355)
--*The Ghost of Thomas Kempe.* Lively, Penelope (1933-). 1973. Dutton. **Award: (CMA).** (P.577)
--*Green Fairy Book.* Lang, Andrew (1844-1912) & Alderson, Brian W., eds. 1978. Kestrel Books. (P.549)
--*The Happy Planet.* Clarke, Joan B (1921-). 1965. Lothrop, Lee & Shepard. (P.198)
--*Idle Jack.* Maitland, Antony Jasper (1935-). 1979. Farrar, Straus and Giroux. (P.614)
--*Jack Holborn.* Garfield, Leon (1921-). 1964. Constable Young Books. (P.355)
--*Jack Holborn.* Garfield, Leon (1921-). 1965. Pantheon Books. (P.355)
--*James & the Roman Silver.* Maitland, Antony Jasper (1935-). 1965. Verry. (P.614)
--*More Tales of Shellover.* Ainsworth, Ruth (1908-). 1968. Roy Publishers. (P.15)
--*Mrs. Cockle's Cat.* Pearce, Ann Philippa (1920-). 1962. Lippincott. **Award: (KGM).** (P.712)
--*Out of Hand.* Smith, Emma (1923-). 1964, c.1963. Harcourt, Brace. (P.833)
--*The Phantom Cyclist, and Other Ghost Stories.* Ainsworth, Ruth (1908-). 1974, c.1971. Follett Pub. Co. (P.15)
--*A Proper Place for Chip.* Molloy, Anne Stearns Baker (1907-). 1963. Hastings. (P.655)
--*The Quest.* 1st ed. Stephan, Hanna (1902-). Goodall, Daphne Machin, tr. 1968, c.1967. Little, Brown. (P.852)
--*The Runaway Settlers: An Historical Novel.* 1st ed. Locke, Elsie (1912-). 1966. Dutton. (P.579)
--*The Secret of the Shed.* Maitland, Antony Jasper (1935-). 1963. Duell Sloan & Pearce. (P.614)
--*Smith.* Garfield, Leon (1921-). 1967. Pantheon Books. **Awards: (BGH); (CMA).** (P.355)
--*The Ten Tales of Shellover.* Ainsworth, Ruth (1908-). 1968, c.1963. Roy Publishers. (P.15)
--*To London!* To London!. Willard, Barbara Mary (1909-). 1968. Weybright and Talley. (P.961)
--*The Usurping Ghost and Other Encounters and Experiences.* Dickinson, Susan (1931-). 1971, c.1970. E. P. Dutton. (P.265)
--*The Wonder-Dog: The Collected Children's Stories of Richard Hughes.* Hughes, Richard Arthur Warren (1900-1976). c.1977. Greenwillow Books. (P.470)

Majewska, Maria
--*A Place to Hide.* Gillham, Bill, pseud. Gillham, William Edward Charles. 1983. Andre Deutsch. (P.368)

Majewski, Mary Agnes
--*Master Mozart: A Story of Wolfgang Amadeus Mozart.* Schmid, Evan (1920-). 1954. Dujarie Press. (P.800)

Majima, Setsuko
--*Song of the Sour Plum.* Majima, Setsuko. 1968. Walker & Co. (P.614)
--*Songs of the Sour Plum.* Hirawa, Jasuko. 1968. Weatherhill. (P.446)

Major, Clare Tree
--*Playing Theatro: Six Plays for Children.* Major, Clare Tree. c.1930. Oxford University Press. (P.614)

Makower, Sylvia
--*Samson's Breakfast.* Makower, Sylvia. 1967. Mulberry Pr. (P.614)

Makowski, Julius
--*Make Me a Farm.* Pokorska, Christina. N.D. Roy. (P.730)

Malcher, Lucretia
--*The Umbrella Bird, and Other Verses.* Johnson, Emillie Louise Dickey (1892-). Johnson, Emilie Fendall, 1939. Falmouth Book House. (P.495)

Maley, Thomas
--*Across the Bridge.* 1st ed. Beim, Jerrold (1910-1957). 1951. Harcourt, Brace. (P.89)
--*Stories to Begin on.* Bacmeister, Rhoda Warner, Mrs. (1893-). 1940. E. P. Dutton & Co., Inc. (P.58)

Malik, George A.
--*Ladd of the Lone Star.* 1st ed. Bosworth, Allan Rucker (1901-). 1952. Aladdin Books. (P.119)
--*Quadrus and Goliath.* Ben-Moring, Alvin Lester (1931-). c.1976. Westminster Press. (P.92)

Malish, Miro
--*A Spider Danced a Cosy Jig.* Layton, Irving (1912-). Cameron, Elspeth (1943-), ed. 1984. Stoddart. (P.557)

Malkus, Alida Wright Sims, Mrs. (1899-)
--*Along the Inca Highway.* Malkus, Alida Wright Sims, Mrs. (1899-). c.1941. D. C. Health and Company. (P.614)
--*Chula of the Magic Islands.* Malkus, Alida Wright Sims, Mrs. (1899-). 1948. Saalfield Co. (P.614)
--*Constancia Lona.* 1st ed. Malkus, Alida Wright Sims, Mrs. (1899-). 1947. Doubleday. (P.614)
--*The Silver Llama.* Malkus, Alida Wright Sims, Mrs. (1899-). c.1939. The John C. Winston Company. (P.614)
--*Through the Wall: A Boy's Struggle for Freedom.* Malkus, Alida Wright Sims, Mrs. (1899-). 1962. Grosset & Dunlap. (P.614)

Mallett, Anne (1913-)
--*The Secret Kitten.* Mallett, Anne (1913-). 1972. Parents' Magazine Press. (P.614)

Mallison, Clare
--*The Wooster-Poosters.* Mallison, Clare. c.1931. Frederick A. Stokes Co. (P.615)

Mallon, Grace
--*Anahita and Her Dancing Bear.* Butler, Nina. 1945. W. Hebberd. (P.159)
--*Lota of the Little Trees.* Prior, Beatrix, Mrs. 1936. Suttonhouse, Ltd. (P.740)
--*Near-Side-and-Far.* Justus, May (1898-). c.1936. Suttonhouse, Ltd. (P.503)

Mallory, Edgar
--*Hand-Me- Down House.* Norfleet, Mary Crockett (1919-). 1962. John Knox Press. (P.685)

Malman
--*Carol's Side of the Street.* Beim, Lorraine Levey (1909-1951). 1951. HarBraceJ. (P.89)

Malmberg, Hans
--*The Wonderful Adventures of Nils.* Lagerlof, Selma Ottiliana Lovisa (1858-1940). Aurell, Tage & Aurell, Kathrine, eds. Oldenburg, Richard E., tr. 1967. Doubleday. (P.544)

Malmeda, Joseph W.
--*Reuben's Portion.* Edwards, Josephine Cunnington (1904-). 1957. Southern Pub. Association. (P.297)
--*Tales from Africa.* Edwards, Josephine Cunnington (1904-). 1956. Southern Pub. Association. (P.297)

Malnate, Edmond V.
--*Tuffy.* Malnate, Edmond V. 1946. R. Speller. (P.615)

Malone, Joe
--*Bungry, the Dog of the Rockies.* Jones, Juanita Nuttall (1912-). c.1940. Manfred, Van Nort & Co. (P.499)

Maloney, David
--*To Yellowstone, the Journey Home.* McKinnon, Robert Scott (1937-). 1975. Holt, Rinehart and Winston. (P.607)

Maloney, Katie, photos by.
--*I Dare You!.* Conaway, Judith (1948-). 1977. Raintree Pubs. (P.212)
--*A Long Trip to Work: A Turkish Worker Travels to Germany.* Conaway, Judith (1948-). 1977. Soc for Visual. (P.212)
--*The New City People: A Guatemalan Family Makes the Big Move.* Conaway, Judith (1948-). 1977. Soc for Visual. (P.212)
--*Was My Face Red.* Conaway, Judith (1948-). N.D. Raintree Pubs. (P.212)

Maloney, Mary P., jt. illus. see Fleming, Stanley.

--*In Blue and White: The Adventure and Misadventures of Humphrey Vandyne, Trooper in Washington's Lifeguard.* Brooks, Elbridge Streeter (1846-1902). 1899. Lothrop Publishing Company. (P.136)
--*In Camp at Fort Brady.* Theiss, Lewis Edwin (1878-1963). c.1914. W. A. Wilde Company. (P.885)
--*In Camp with the Muskoday Camp Fire Girls.* Blanchard, Amy Ella (1856-1926). c.1917. W. A. Wilde Company. (P.106)
--*In Kings' House: A Romance of the Days of Queen Anne.* Dorr, Julia C. R. N.D. L. C. Page. (P.281)
--*In Kings' Houses: A Romance of the Days of Queen Anne.* Dorr, Julia C. R. N.D. Page Co. (P.281)
--*In the Days of Jefferson: Or, The Six Golden Horseshoes, a Tale of Republican Simplicity.* Butterworth, Hezekiah (1839-1905). 1900. D. Appleton and Company. (P.159)
--*Isla Heron.* 5th thousand. ed. Richards, Laura Elizabeth Howe, Mrs. (1850-1943). c.1896. Estes and Lauriat. (P.762)
--*Isla Heron.* Richards, Laura Elizabeth Howe, Mrs. (1850-1943). N.D. Page Co. (P.762)
--*Jack in the Bush: Or, A Summer on a Salmon River.* Grant, Robert (1852-). 1893. C. Scribner's Sons. (P.382)
--*Jim of Hellas: Or, In Durance Vile.* Richards, Laura Elizabeth Howe, Mrs. (1850-1943). N.D. Page Co. (P.762)
--*Joe's Signal Code.* Hesser, Reiff W. 1905. Lee and Shepard Company. (P.439)
--*Joey at the Fair.* Kaler, James Otis (1848-1912). Otis, James, pseud. 1906. T. Y. Crowell & Co. (P.505)
--*Johnny Appleseed.* Atkinson, Eleanor Stackhouse, Mrs. (1863-). 1915. Harper & Bros. (P.53)
--*Joy Bells: A Quinnebasset story.* Clarke, Rebecca Sophia (1833-1906). May, Sophie, pseud. 1903. Lee and Shepard. (P.199)
--*Kibboo Ganey: Or, The Lost Chief of the Copper Mountain.* A Story of Travel and Adventure in the Heart of Africa. Wentworth, Walter. 1889. Roberts Brothers. (P.946)
--*The Kingdom of Coins and the Queer People Who Lived There.* Gilman, Bradley (1857-1932). 1894. Roberts Brothers. (P.368)
--*A Lass of Dorchester.* Barnes, Annie Maria (1857-). 1904. Lee and Shepard. (P.73)
--*Last of the Mohicans.* Cooper, James Fenimore (1789-1851). 1915. Thomas Y Crowell. (P.217)
--*The Lead-Hunters of the Ozarks.* Winbo. ne Hardy Lathan (1877-). 1927. Lothrop, Lee & Shepard Co. (P.967)
--*Lieutenant Ralph Osborn Aboard a Torpedo Boat Destroyer: Being the Story of How Ralph Osborn Became a Lieutenant and of His Cruises in an American Torpedo Boat Destroyer in West Indian Waters.* Beach, Edward Latimer (1918-). c.1912. W. A. Wilde Company. (P.84)
--*The Lion-Tamer's Little Girl.* Swett, Sophia Miriam (1858-1912). 1903. S. E. Cassino. (P.874)
--*Little Betty Blew.* Barnes, Annie Maria (1857-). N.D. Lothrop, Lee & Shepard. (P.73)
--*A Little Maid of Boston Town.* Lothrop, Harriet Mulford Stone, Mrs. (1844-1924). Sidney, Margaret, pseud. N.D. Lothrop, Lee & Shepard. (P.586)
--*A Little Maid of Concord Town: A Romance of the American Revolution.* Lothrop, Harriet Mulford Stone, Mrs. (1844-1924). Sidney, Margaret, pseud. c.1900. Lothrop Publishing Company. (P.586)
--*A Little Maid of Picardy.* Blanchard, Amy Ella (1856-1926). c.1919. W. A. Wilde Company. (P.107)
--*The Little Queen.* Madden, Eva Annie (1863-). 1910. W. A. Wilde Co. (P.612)
--*Little Tom and Maggie.* Eliot, George, pseud. (1819-1880). Evans, Marian. N.D. Dana Estes and Company. (P.300)
--*Little Women: Or, Meg, Jo, Beth and Amy.* Alcott, Louisa May (1832-1888). Garrett, Edmund H., photos by. 1908. Little, Brown, and Company. (P.18)
--*Lonely O'Malley: A Story of Boy Life.* Stringer, Arthur John Arbuthnott (1874-). 1905. Houghton, Mifflin and Company. (P.868)
--*Lonely O'Malley: A Story of Boy Life.* Stringer, Arthur John Arbuthnott (1874-). c.1924. The Bobbs-Merrill Company. (P.868)
--*Long Knives: The Story of How They Won the West.* Eggleston, George Cary (1839-1911). 1907. Lothrop, Lee & Shepard Co. (P.298)
--*Long Tom and How They Got Him,.* Swett, Sophia Miriam (1858-1912). 1903. S. E. Casino. (P.874)
--*A Lost Hero.* Ward, Elizabeth Stuart Phelps, Mrs. (1844-1911). N.D. Robert Brothers. (P.930)
--*Love Me, Love My Dog.* Verhoeff, Carolyn. 1922. The Page Company. (P.917)
--*A Loyal Lass: A Story of the Niagara Campaign of 1814.* Blanchard, Amy Ella (1856-1926). 1902. W. A. Wilde Company. (P.107)
--*Lucky Penny of Thistle Troop: A Girl Scout Story.* Blanchard, Amy Ella (1856-1926). c.1920. W. A. Wilde Company. (P.107)
--*Lumberjack Bob: A Story of a Lumber Camp in the Alleghanies.* Theiss, Lewis Edwin (1878-1963). c.1916. W. A. Wilde Company. (P.885)
--*A Maid of Salem Towne.* Madison, Lucy Foster, Mrs. (1865-). 1934. The Penn Publishing Company. (P.612)
--*Marie.* Richards, Laura Elizabeth Howe, Mrs. (1850-1943). N.D. Page Co. (P.762)
--*Mary Ware in Texas.* Johnston, Annie Fellows, Mrs. (1863-1931). 1910. L. C. Page. (P.497)
--*Melody.* Holiday ed. Richards, Laura Elizabeth Howe, Mrs. (1850-1943). N.D. Estes & Lauriat's. (P.762)
--*Melody.* Richards, Laura Elizabeth Howe, Mrs. (1850-1943). N.D. Page Co. (P.762)
--*The Merrymakers in Chicago and Their Adventures in That Great City.* Williams, Wilbur Herschel (1874-). 1920. The Page Company. (P.964)
--*Midshipman Ralph Osborn at Sea: A Story of the U.S. Navy.* Beach, Edward Latimer (1918-). N.D. W. A. Wilde. (P.84)
--*The Mills of Tuxbury.* Townsend, Virginia Frances (1836-1920). c.1871. Loring. (P.897)
--*The Mohawk Ranger.* Lange, Dietrich (1863-). c.1922. Lothrop, Lee & Shepard Co. (P.550)
--*My Friend Jim: A/Story of Real Boys and for them.* Doyle, Martha Claire MacGowan, Mrs. (1869-). James, Martha, pseud. 1901. Lothrop,Lee & Shepard. (P.284)
--*The Mystery of Chimney Rock: Being a Story of the Search for Gold in the Land of the Ute Indians in "the Days of '49".* Cheley, Frank Hobart (1889-). c.1924. W. A. Wilde Company. (P.189)
--*Nautilus.* Richards, Laura Elizabeth Howe, Mrs. (1850-1943). N.D. Page Co. (P.762)
--*On Land & Sea with Caesar.* Wells, Reuben Field (1880-). 1926. Biblo. (P.945)
--*On Land and Sea with Caesar: Or, Following the Eagles.* Wells, Reuben Field (1880-). 1959. Biblo and Tannen. (P.945)
--*On Land and Sea with Caesar: Or, Following the Eagles.* Wells, Reuben Field (1880-). c.1926. Lothrop, Lee & Shepard Co. (P.945)
--*The Orcutt Girls: Or, One Term at the Academy.* Vaile, Charlotte Marion White, Mrs. (1852-1902). 1896. W. A. Wilde & Company. (P.911)
--*Our Little Florentine Cousin of Long Ago, Being the Story of Filippo, a Boy of Renaissance Florence.* Winlow, Anna C. c.1929. L. C. Page & Company. (P.969)
--*A Pair of Madcaps.* Trowbridge, John Townsend (1827-1916). 1909. Lothrop, Lee & Shepard Co. (P.901)
--*Peanut-Cub Reporter.* Eaton, Walter Prichard (1878-). N.D. W. A. Wilde. (P.295)
--*Peaseblossom's Lion.* Swett, Sophia Miriam (1858-1912). 1903. S. E. Cassino. (P.874)
--*Peggy Raymond's Way: Or, Blossom Time at Friendly-Terrace.* Smith, Harriet Lummis, Mrs. 1922. The Page Company. (P.834)
--*Penelope's Problems.* Castelhun, Dorothea. 1922. The Page Company. (P.177)
--*The Penhallow Family: A Story.* Jamison, Cecilia Viets Dakin, Mrs. (1844-1909). 1905. W. A. Wilde Company. (P.489)
--*Phebe, Her Profession.* Ray, Anna Chapin (1865-1945). 1900. Little, Brown, and Company. (P.751)
--*The Pioneer Boys of Kansas: Or, A Prairie Home in Buffalo Land.* Adams, Harrison, pseud. (1854-1928). Rathborne, St. George. 1928. L. C. Page & Company. (P.5)
--*The Pioneer Boys of the Colorado: Or, Braving the Perils of the Grand Canyon Country.* Adams, Harrison, pseud. (1854-1928). Rathborne, St. George. c.1926. L. C. Page & Company. (P.5)
--*The Pleasant Street Partnership: A Neighborhood Story.* Leonard, Mary Finley (1862-). 1903. W. A. Wilde Company. (P.566)
--*Princess Wisla.* Swett, Sophia Miriam (1858-1912). 1908. Little, Brown, and Company. (P.874)
--*Prisoners of the Pirates.* N.D. The Page Co. (P.642)
--*The Pursuit of Happiness: A Story of New York Young People in the Time of the Revolution.* Ashton, Leonora Sill. c.1932. Lothrop, Lea & Shepard Co. (P.52)
--*The Rainbow Bridge: A Story.* Fox, Frances Margaret (1870-). c.1905. W. A. Wilde Company. (P.340)
--*Ralph Osborn--Midshipman at Annapolis: A Story of Life at the U.S. Naval Academy.* Beach, Edward Latimer (1918-). c.1909. W. A. Wilde Company. (P.84)
--*The Red Pirogue: A Tale of Adventure in the Canadian Wilds.* Goodridge Roberts, George Edward Theodore (1877-1953). 1924. L. C. Page and Company (Incorporated). (P.375)
--*Reels and Spindles: A Story of Mill Life.* Raymond, Evelyn Hunt, Mrs. (1843-1910). c.1900. W. A. Wilde Company. (P.751)
--*Rocky Fork, 1 of 4 vols.* Catherwood, Mary Hartwell, Mrs. (1847-1902). 1882. D Lothrop. (P.178)
--*Rocky Fork.* new ed. Catherwood, Mary Hartwell, Mrs. (1847-1902). c.1911. Lothrop, Lee & Shepard Co. (P.178)
--*Roger Paulding: Apprentice Seaman.* Beach, Edward Latimer (1918-). 1911. The Penn Publishing Company. (P.84)
--*Roger Paulding, Ensign.* Beach, Edward Latimer (1918-). 1914. Penn Publishing Co. (P.84)
--*Roger Paulding, Gunner.* Beach, Edward Latimer (1918-). 1913. The Penn Publishing Company. (P.84)
--*Roger Paulding, Gunner's Mate.* Beach, Edward Latimer (1918-). 1912. The Penn Publishing Company. (P.84)
--*Romulus and Remus: A Dog Story.* Talbot, Charles Remington (1851-1891). 1888. D. Lothrop Company. (P.877)
--*Rosin the Beau.* Richards, Laura Elizabeth Howe, Mrs. (1850-1943). N.D. Page Co. (P.762)
--*Sailing Under Sealed Orders: A Story of the Navigator of the "Greenville".* Parker, Thomas Drayton (1871-). c.1921. W. A. Wilde Company. (P.707)
--*The Sea Captain's Children.* Foot, Katherine B. 1905. S. E. Cassino & Son. (P.334)
--*The Secret Wireless: Or, the Spy Hunt of the Camp Brady Patrol.* Theiss, Lewis Edwin (1878-1963). c.1918. W. A. Wilde Company. (P.885)
--*Seraph the Little Violiniste.* Jamison, Cecilia Viets Dakin, Mrs. (1844-1909). c.1896. W. A. Wilde & Company. (P.489)
--*The Sioux Runner.* Lange, Dietrich (1863-). c.1924. Lothrop, Lee & Shepard Co. (P.550)
--*Six Boys.* Champney, Elizabeth Williams, Mrs. (1850-1922). c.1893. Estes and Lauriat. (P.183)
--*Six Boys.* Champney, Elizabeth Williams, Mrs. (1850-1922). N.D. L. C. Page & Co. (P.183)
--*The Six Little Pennypackers: Or, From Little Bear Lighthouse to London.* Swett, Sophia Miriam (1858-1912). 1911. Dana Estes & Co. (P.874)
--*The Slave Prince: A Tale of Ancient Greece and of the Siege of Troy.* Mackaye, Arthur Loring (1890-). c.1926. L. C. Page & Company. (P.605)
--*Snow-White: Or, The House in the Wood.* Richards, Laura Elizabeth Howe, Mrs. (1850-1943). N.D. Dana Estes & Co. (P.762)
--*Snow-White: Or, The House in the Wood.* Richards, Laura Elizabeth Howe, Mrs. (1850-1943). N.D. Page Co. (P.762)
--*The Soldiers of the Duke.* Madden, Eva Annie (1863-). c.1904. W. A. Wilde Company. (P.612)
--*Some Say, and a Companion Story, "Neighbors in Cyrus".* Richards, Laura Elizabeth Howe, Mrs. (1850-1943). N.D. Page Co. (P.762)
--*A Son of Old Ironsides: The Story of a boy on the United States Frigate Constitution during the War of 1812.* Barrows, John Stewart. c.1931. Lothrop Lee & Shephard. (P.76)
--*A Son of the Revolution: Being the Story of Young Tom Edwards, Adventurer ...* in the Days of Burr's Conspiracy. Brooks, Elbridge Streeter (1846-1902). c.1898. W. A. Wilde & Company. (P.136)
--*The Spectacle Man: A Story of the Missing Bridge.* Leonard, Mary Finley (1862-). c.1901. W. A. Wilde Company. (P.566)
--*Star Bright.* Richards, Laura Elizabeth Howe, Mrs. (1850-1943). c.1927. L. C. Page & Company. (P.762)
--*The Story of Magellan and the Discovery of the Philippines.* Butterworth, Hezekiah (1839-1905). 1899. D. Appleton and Company. (P.159)
--*Sue Orcutt: A Sequel to "The Orcutt Girls".* Vaile, Charlotte Marion White, Mrs. (1852-1902). 1897. W. A. Wilde & Company. (P.911)
--*Suwanee River Tales.* McDowell, Katherine Sherwood Bonner, Mrs. (1849-1883). Kirk, Sophia, ed. 1972, c.1884. Books for Libraries Press. (P.600)
--*Suwanee River Tales.* McDowell, Katherine Sherwood Bonner, Mrs. (1849-1884). Kirk, Sophia, ed. 1884. Roberts Brothers. (P.600)
--*Three Little Daughters of the Revolution.* Perry, Nora (1831-1896). N.D. Houghton & Mifflin. (P.720)
--*The Wireless Patrol at Camp Brady.* Theiss, Lewis Edwin (1878-1963). c.1917. W. A. Wilde Company. (P.885)
--*With Caesar's Legions: The Adventures of Two Roman Youths in the Conquest of Gaul.* Wells, Reuben Field (1880-). 1960, c.1951. Biblioand Tannen. (P.945)
--*With Caesar's Legions: The Adventures of Two Roman Youths in the Conquest of Gaul.* Wells, Reuben Field (1880-). c.1923. Lothrop, Lee & Shepard Co. (P.945)
--*The Yellow-Capped Monkey.* Swett, Sophia Miriam (1858-1912). 1903. S. E. Cassino. (P.874)
--*The Young Crusader, How Richard of Devon Served Richard the Lion-Hearted.* Story, Walter Scott. c.1923. Lothrop, Lee & Shepard Co. (P.863)
--*The Young Moose Hunters: A Backwoods-Boy's Story.* Stephens, Charles Asbury (1845-1931). 1874. H. L. Shepard & Co. (P.852)
--*The Young Telephone Inventor: Or, Winning with the Wire.* Weir, Hugh Cosgro (1884-1934). c.1917. W. A. Wilde Company. (P.941)
--*The Young Wheat Scout.* Weir, Hugh Cosgro (1884-1934). 1915. W. A. Wilde Company. (P.941)
--*The Young Wireless Operator--As a Fire Patrol: Or, the Story of a Young Wireless Amateur Who Made Good As a Fire Patrol.* Theiss, Lewis Edwin (1878-1963). c.1921. W. A. Wilde Company. (P.885)
--*The Young Wireless Operator--with the Oyster Fleet: How Alec Cunningham Won His Way to the Top in the Oyster Business.* Theiss, Lewis Edwin (1878-1963). c.1922. W. A. Wilde Company. (P.885)
--*The Young Wireless Operator--with the U.S.* Secret Service: Winning His Way in the Secret Service. Theiss, Lewis Edwin (1878-1963). c.1923. W. A. Wilde Company. (P.885)

Merrill, Frank Thayer (1848-) & Bridgman, Lewis Jesse (1857-1931)
--*The Parson's Miracle: Christmas in America.* Butterworth, Hezekiah (1839-1905). N.D. Estes & Lauriat's. (P.159)

Merrill, Frank Thayer (1848-) & Garrett, Edmund Henry (1853-1929)
--*On the Tree-Top: Children's Favorite Stories, Versified.* by clara doty bates and others. illustrations by frank t. merrill, edmund h. garrett, and other well known artists. Bates, Clara Doty, Mrs. (1838-1895), ed. c.1891. D. Lothrop Company. (P.80)

Merrill, Frank Thayer (1848-) & Lewis, Robert
--*From the Hudson to the Neva.* Ker, David (1842-1914). 1883. D. Lothrop and Company. (P.519)

Merrill, Katherine
--*Edda and the Oak.* Peattie, Elia Wilkinson, Mrs. (1862-). c.1911. Rand, McNally and Co. (P.714)

Merrill, Marion
--*The Animated Pinocchio.* Lorenzini, Carlo (1826-1890). Collodi, Carlo, pseud. 1945. Cima Pub. Co. (P.584)
--*Captain Peggy of the Mamie L.* Reynolds, Helen Mary Greenwood Campbell Dickson (1884-1969). 1943. T. Nelson and Sons. (P.759)
--*Syd of Tar-Paper Shack.* Merrill, Marion. 1947. Wilcox & Follett Co. (P.642)

Merriman, Anne
--*The Fairy Book.* Oswell, Kate Forrest. 1912. Macmillan Co. (P.697)

Merrit, Dora W.
--*The Story of Four Little Sabots.* Merrit, Dora W. N.D. Frederick Warne & Co. (P.642)

Merritt, Edna
--*Treasure Things.* Wynne, Annette (1885-), ed. c.1922. P. F. Volland Company. (P.983)

Merritt, Hale
--*The Adventures of Snooki and Snak.* Roy, Lillian Elizabeth Becker, Mrs. (1868-1932). c.1928. Grosset & Dunlap. (P.782)
--*The Adventures of Sonny and Sue.* Roy, Lillian Elizabeth Becker, Mrs. (1868-1932). c.1928. Grosset & Dunlap. (P.782)

Merritt, Muriel (1905-)
--*Give Them Wings: Poems for Children.* 1st ed. Merritt, Muriel (1905-). c.1973. H Stewart. (P.642)

Merritt, Warren Chase
--*Long Rifle Vanguard.* Staffelbach, Elmer Hubert (1893-). 1953. H. Wagner Pub. Co. (P.847)
--*The Secret of Lonesome Valley a Story of Adventure: A Story of Adventure and Life in the Range Country, Ranch and the Cattle I ndustry.* Toles, Elsie (1888-) & Toles, Myriam Sarah (1894-). 1949. Harr Wagner Pub. Co. (P.893)
--*The Secret of Lonesome Valley: And Life in the Range Country.* Toles, Elsie (1888-) & Toles, Myriam Sarah (1894-). 1955. H. Wagner Pub. Co. (P.893)

Merryweather, Jack
--*Alec Majors.* Anderson, Anita Melva (1906-) & Regli, Adolph Casper. Betts, Emmett A., ed. 1953. Wheeler Pub. Co. (P.38)
--*Cattle Cars.* Chandler, Edna Walker (1908-1982). 1970. Benefic Press. (P.183)
--*Cattle Drive.* Chandler, Edna Walker (1908-1982). 1966. Benefic Press. (P.183)
--*Chief Black Hawk.* rev. ed. Beals, Frank Lee (1881-1972). 1960. Wheeler Pub. Co. (P.85)
--*Circus Train.* Chandler, Edna Walker (1908-1982). 1971. Benefic Press. (P.183)
--*Cowboy Sam.* Chandler, Edna Walker (1908-1982). 1951. Beckley-Cardy Co. (P.183)
--*Cowboy Sam.* Chandler, Edna Walker (1908-1982). 1951. Benefic Press. (P.183)

--*Little Long Rifle.* 1st ed. Parks, Edd Winfield (1906-1968). 1949. Bobbs-Merrill Co. (P.707)
--*Moose Country: A Boy Naturalist in an Ancient Forest.* 1st ed. Campbell, Samuel Arthur (1895-). 1950. Bobbs-Merrill. (P.165)
--*The Mysterious Caboose.* Bonner, Mary Graham (1890-1974). 1949. A. A. Knopf. (P.116)
--*Winning Dive, a Camp Story.* 1st ed. Bonner, Mary Graham (1890-1974). 1950. Knopf. (P.116)

Meylan, Paul J.
--*The Children Who Ran Away.* Sharp, Evelyn (1869-). 1903. Macmillan Co. (P.816)
--*Miss Selina Lue and The Soap-Box Babies.* Daviess, Maria Thompson (1872-1924). N.D. Bobbs-Merrill Company. (P.245)

Meynelle, Louis
--*The Boys' Browning, 1 of 25 vols.* Browning, Robert (1812-1889). N.D. Dana Estes & Co. (P.143)
--*For His Country, and Grandmother and the Crow.* Saunders, Margaret Marshall (1861-1947). 1900. L. C. Page & Company. (P.794)
--*For the Liberty of Texas.* Bonehill, Captain Ralph, pseud. (1862-1930). Stratemeyer, Edward L.. 1900. Dana Estes & Co. (P.114)
--*For the Liberty of Texas.* Stratemeyer, Edward L. (1862-1930). 1909. Lothrop, Lee & Shepard Co. (P.865)
--*For the Liberty of Texas.* Stratemeyer, Edward L. (1862-1930). 1917. Lothrop, Lee & Shepard Co. (P.865)
--*For the Liberty of Texas.* Stratemeyer, Edward L. (1862-1930). 1930. Lothrop, Lee & Shepard Co. (P.865)
--*Harum-Scarum Joe.* Dromgoole, William Allen, Miss (1860-1934). 1899. D. Estes & Company. (P.285)
--*The Little Colonel's House Party.* Johnston, Annie Fellows, Mrs. (1863-1931). 1901. L. C. Page and Company. (P.497)
--*The Little Colonel's House Party.* Johnston, Annie Fellows, Mrs. (1863-1931). 1919. The Page Company. (P.497)
--*Two American Boys in Hawaii.* Browne, George Waldo (1851-1930). N.D. D. Estes & Company. (P.143)
--*The Young Folks' Browning.* Browning, Robert (1812-1889). Tapper, Thomas, annotations by. N.D. L. C. Page & Co. (P.143)
--*The Young Gunbearer: A Tale of the Neutral Ground, Acadia and the Siege of Louisburg.* Browne, George Waldo (1851-1930). 1900. L.C. Page & Company. (P.143)

MGM Cartoons
--*M G M's Tom and Jerry's Merry Christmas.* Archer, Peter & Loew's Incorporated. Eisenberg, Harvey & Armstrong, Samuel, eds. 1954. Simon and Schuster. (P.46)

Miake, L. K.
--*Arturo, Bernardo, Carlotta.* Freeman, Dorothy Rhodes. 1969. Elk Grove Press. (P.343)

Miao Ti
--*Snowflakes.* Yang Shuo. 1979. China Bks. (P.985)

Miatta, Musu
--*Grains of Pepper: Folktales from Liberia.* Haskett, Edythe Rance (1915-), ed. 1967. John Day Co. (P.419)

Micale, Albert (1913-)
--*The Best Summer.* Wildes, Newlin B. 1965. Rand McNally. (P.960)
--*Blazing Mountain.* Weddle, Ferris (1922-). 1961. Watts. (P.940)
--*The Capture of West Wind.* Montgomery, Rutherford George (1894-). 1962. Duell, Sloan and Pearce. (P.658)
--*Climb to the Top.* 1st ed. Kostka, Matthew. 1962. Doubleday. (P.536)
--*Hackamore.* 1st ed. Lynch, Helen. 1961. Duell, Sloan and Pearce. (P.591)
--*High School Drop Out.* 1st ed. Clarke, John, pseud. Laklan, Carli. 1964. Doubleday. (P.198)
--*The Horse That Had Everything.* Wildes, Newlin B. 1966. Rand McNally. (P.960)
--*Let's Go to the Moon.* rev. ed. Chester, Michael Arthur (1928-). 1974. Putnam. (P.190)
--*The Sign of the Open Hand.* Coates, Belle (1896-). 1962. Scribner. (P.203)
--*Trouble at Paintrock: A Penny of Paintrock Story.* Annixter, Jane, pseud. (1903-) & Annixter, Paul, pseud. (1894-). Sturtzel, Jane Levington Comfort. Sturtzel, Howard Allison. 1962. Golden Press. (P.42)

Michael, Arthur C.
--*A Christmas Carol.* Dickens, Charles John Huffam (1812-1870). N.D. George H. Doran. (P.263)
--*My Book of Beautiful Legends.* Chaundler, Christine (1887-1972) & Wood, Eric. 1916. Funk and Wagnalls Company. (P.189)
--*My Book of Stories from the Poets: Told in Prose.* Chaundler, Christine (1887-1972). 1920. Funk and Wagnalls Company. (P.189)

Michael-Dansac, Monique (1806-1854)
--*Peronnique: A Celtic Folk Tale from Brittany.* Souvestre, Emile. 1970, c.1969. Atheneum. (P.841)

Michaels, Elizabeth Sykes
--*Patty Reed's Doll.* Laurgaard, Rachel Kelley. 1956. Caxton Printers. (P.555)

Michaels, Robert (1926-)
--*Murgatroyd & Mabel.* Court, Wesli (1940-). 1978. Mathom. (P.224)
--*Murgatroyd and Mabel.* Turco, Lewis. Court, Wesli, pseud. c.1978. Mathom Pub. Co. (P.905)

Michal, Marie
--*What Hides Inside?.* Elwart, Joan Potter (1927-). 1972. Rand McNally. (P.305)

Micheal, F. H.
--*Princess Fairstar: A Story of the Days of Charles I.* Everett-Green, Evelyn (1856-1932). 1902. Dutton. (P.312)

Michel, Guy
--*The Birthday Cow.* Merriam, Eve (1916-). c.1978. Knopf. (P.641)

Michelini, Carlo A.
--*Round in a Circle.* Hooker, Yvonne. 1983. Putnam Pub Group. (P.459)

Michelini, Carlo A. & Vanetti, Giorgio
--*Jungle Noises.* Suben, Eric. 1984. Western Pub. (P.870)

Michell, Gladys Turley
--*Farm ABC.* Lynn, Patricia, pseud. (1906-). Watts, Mabel Pizzey. c.1954. Whitman Pub. Co. (P.592)
--*Farm ABC.* Watts, Mabel Pizzey (1906-). Lynn, Patricia, pseud. 1954. Whitman Pub. Co. (P.937)
--*When We Grow Up.* Michell, Gladys Turley. 1943. A. Whitman & Co. (P.644)

Michini, Albert
--*Adventure in Deepmore Cave.* Casewit, Curtis Werner (1922-). 1965. Doubleday. (P.176)
--*The Case of the Iceland Dogs.* Cheney, Cora (1916-). c.1977. Dodd, Mead. (P.189)
--*Flash Flood at Hollow Creek.* Paradis, Marjorie Bartholomew (1886-1970). 1963. Westminster Press. (P.704)
--*The Golden Stallion & the Mysterious Feud.* Montgomery, Rutherford George (1894-). 1967. Little. (P.658)
--*Kennaquhair.* Hooker, Ruth (1920-). c.1976. Abingdon. (P.459)
--*Thirteen Ghostly Yarns.* Rev. ed. Sechrist, Elizabeth Hough, Mrs. (1903-), ed. 1963. Macrae Smith. (P.807)
--*Wufu: The Story of a Little Brown Bat.* Freschet, Berniece Louise Speck (1927-). c.1975. Putnam. (P.345)

Michl, Reinhard
--*The Foundling Fox.* Korschunow, Irina. Skofield, James, tr. from Ger. 1984. HarpJ. (P.536)
--*Mischa & His Brothers.* Baumann, Hans (1914-). Neumeyer, Peter, tr. from Ger. 1985. Green Tiger Pr. (P.83)

Mickelson, Melva
--*God's Wonderful World.* Moore, John Travers (1908-). 1964. Augsburg. (P.661)
--*Little Star.* Hanson, Eugene Kenneth (1930-). 1960. Augsburg Pub. House. (P.411)
--*The Music Box Maker.* Doederlein, Gertrude. 1957. Augsburg Pub. (P.278)
--*Torarin: A Historical Novel of 12th Century Norway.* Borch, Anka. Herberg, Ruth M., tr. 1968. Augsburg Pub. House. (P.117)

Mickish, Verle L.
--*Corn for the Palace.* Crary, Margaret Coleman (1906-) & Voss, Carroll. 1963. Prentice-Hall. (P.229)

Micklewright, Robert (1923-)
--*Anna.* Almedingen, Martha Edith von (1898-1971). Almedingen, E. M., pseud. 1972. Oxford University Press. (P.31)
--*The Drugged Cornet and Other Mystery Stories.* Dickinson, Susan (1931-), ed. 1973, c.1972. Dutton. (P.265)

Miclat, Alex
--*Poky Little Puppy Follows His Nose Home.* Holl, Adelaide Hinkle (1910-). 1977. Western Pub. (P.454)

Midderigh-Bokhorst, B.
--*Marian and Marion.* Selleger-Elout, J M & Van Stockum, Hilda Gerarda (1908-). 1949. Viking Press. (P.809)

Middlebrook, Georgia
--*Timothy's Twelve Months.* Boyle, Emily Joyce (1901-). 1952. Abingdon-Cokesbury Press. (P.123)

Middlebrooks, Janilee, jt. illus. see McLaughlin, Jean.

Mieke, Anne
--*The Fastest Gun Alive & Other Night Adventures.* Wilson, David H. 1981. Merrimack Pub Cir. (P.966)
--*The Mystical Beast.* Farthing, Alison. 1978, c.1976. Hastings House Publishers. (P.319)

Mier, Richard John
--*Baby Blue Eyes, and Other Stories.* Phelps, Norris McDonald. 1941. W. G. Clark. (P.723)

Mihel, Merrily
--*All About You.* Mahan, Gail. 1967. Hallmark Editions. (P.613)
--*All About You.* Peterson, Gail Mahan. 1967. Hallmark Editions. (P.721)

Mikolaycak, Charles, jt. illus. see Dabcovich, Lydia.

Mikolaycak, Charles (1937-)
--*Baboushak: An Old Russian Tale.* Mikolaycak, Charles (1937-), retold by. 1984. Holiday House. **Award: (NYT).** (P.644)
--*Banner Over Me.* Greenleaf, Margery. 1968. Follett. (P.387)
--*The Binding of Isaac.* Cohen, Barbara (1932-). c.1978. Lothrop Lee & Shepard. (P.206)
--*The Boy Who Tried to Cheat Death.* 1st ed. Mikolaycak, Charles (1937-) & Kismaric, Carole (1942-), eds. Asbjornsen, Peter Christen (1812-1885) & Moe, Jorgen Engebretsen (1813-1882). 1971. Doubleday. (P.51)
--*Captain Grey.* Avi, pseud. (1937-). Wortis, Avi. c.1977. Pantheon Books. (P.56)
--*The Changing Maze.* Snyder, Zilpha Keatley (1927-). c.1985. Macmillan. (P.839)
--*A Child Is Born: The Christmas Story.* Winthrop, Elizabeth, pseud. (1948-), adapted by Mahony, Elizabeth Winthrop. 1983. Holiday. (P.970)
--*The Christmas Spider: A Puppet Play from Poland & Other Traditional Games, Crafts & Activities.* Holz, Loretta Marie (1943-). 1980. Putnam Pub Group. (P.457)
--*The Cobbler's Reward.* Reid, Barbara (1922-) & Reid, Ewa Malewicz. c.1978. Macmillan. (P.755)
--*A Fair Wind for Troy.* Gates, Doris (1901-). 1976. Viking Press. (P.359)
--*A Fair Wind for Troy.* Gates, Doris (1901-). 1984. Viking Press. (P.359)
--*The Feast Day.* Fadiman, Edwin, Jr. (1925-). 1973. Little. (P.315)
--*The Feral Child.* Sundell, Eric. 1971. Abelard-Schuman. (P.871)
--*The Gorgon's Head: A Myth from the Isles of Greece.* 1st ed. Hodges, Margaret Moore (1911-), retold by. 1972. Little, Brown. (P.449)
--*The Great Wolf and the Good Woodsman.* Hoover, Helen Drusilla Blackburn (1910-1984). 1967. Parents' Magazine Press. (P.459)
--*Grimm's Golden Goose.* Grimm, Jakob Ludwig Karl (1785-1863). 1969. Random. (P.391)
--*The Highwayman.* Noyes, Alfred (1880-1958). 1983. Lothrop. (P.688)
--*The Highwayman.* Noyes, Alfred (1880-1958). 1982. Merrimack Pub Cir. (P.688)
--*How the Hare Told the Truth About His Horse.* Walker, Barbara Kerlin (1921-). 1972. Parents' Magazine Press. (P.925)
--*How Wilka Went to Sea, and Other Tales from West of the Urals.* Ginsburg, Mirra (1919-), ed. 1975. Crown Publishers. **Award: (ALA).** (P.369)
--*I Am Joseph.* Cohen, Barbara (1932-). 1980. Lothrop. **Award: (ALA).** (P.206)
--*In the Morning of Time.* King, Cynthia (1925-). 1973. Scholastic Inc. (P.523)
--*In the Morning of Time: The Story of the Norse God Balder.* King, Cynthia (1925-). 1970. Schol Bk Serv. (P.523)
--*Johnny's Egg.* Long, Earlene R. (1938-) & Slavin, Neal. c.1980. Addison-Wesley. (P.581)
--*Journey to the Bright Kingdom.* Winthrop, Elizabeth, pseud. (1948-). Mahony, Elizabeth Winthrop. c.1979. Holiday House. (P.970)
--*Little Red Riding-Hood.* 1968. C. R. Gibson Co. (P.644)
--*Little Red Riding-Hood.* Grimm, Jakob Ludwig Karl (1785-1863) & Grimm, Wilhelm Karl (1786-1859). 1968. C. R. Gibson. (P.394)
--*Little Red Riding Hood.* Hoff, Sydney (1912-). 1968. C. R. Gibson Company. (P.449)
--*The Man Who Could Call Down Owls.* Bunting, Eve, pseud. (1928-). Bunting, Anne Evelyn. 1984. Macmillan. (P.150)
--*Mourka, the Mighty Cat.* Hyndman, Jane Andrews Lee (1912-1978). Wyndham, Lee, pseud. 1969. Parents. (P.478)
--*Nine Crying Dolls: A Story from Poland.* Pellowski, Anne (1933-) & United States Committee for UNICEF. c.1980. Philomel Books in Cooperation with the U.S. Committee for UNICEF. (P.716)
--*Perfect Crane.* Laurin, Anne, pseud. (1953-). McLaurin, Anne. 1981. Harper & Row. (P.555)
--*Peter and the Wolf.* 1st ed. Prokofiev, Sergei Sergeevich (1891-1953). Carlson, Maria, tr. 1982. Viking Press. (P.740)
--*The Pretzel Hero: A Story of Old Vienna.* Rinkoff, Barbara Jean Rich (1923-1975). 1970. Parents' Magazine Press. (P.765)
--*Russian Tales of Fabulous Beasts and Marvels.* Hyndman, Jane Andrews Lee (1912-1978). Wyndham, Lee, pseud. 1969. Parents' Magazine Press. (P.478)
--*Russian Tales of Fabulous Beasts & Marvels.* Hyndman, Jane Andrews Lee (1912-1978). Wyndham, Lee, pseud. 1969. Scholastic Inc. (P.478)
--*Shipwreck.* Cumberlege, Vera G (1908-). 1974. Follett Pub. Co. (P.234)
--*Signs and Wonders.* Evslin, Bernard (1922-). c.1981. Four Winds Press. (P.313)
--*Signs & Wonders: Tales from the Old Testament.* Evslin, Bernard (1922-). 1982. Scholastic Inc. (P.313)
--*Sister of the Birds, and Other Gypsy Tales.* Ficowski, Jerzy. Borski, Lucia Merecka, tr. c.1976. Abingdon. (P.323)
--*The Surprising Things Maui Did.* Williams, Jay (1914-1978). c.1979. Four Winds Press. (P.963)
--*The Tale of Tawny and Dingo.* Armstrong, William Howard (1914-). c.1979. Harper & Row. (P.48)
--*Three Wanderers from Wapping.* Farber, Norma (1909-1984). c.1978. Addison-Wesley. (P.316)
--*Tiger Watch.* 1st ed. Wahl, Jan (1933-). c.1982. Harcourt Brace Jovanovich. (P.924)
--*The Twelve Clever Brothers and Other Fools.* Ginsburg, Mirra (1919-), ed. 1979. Harper. (P.369)
--*The Twelve Clever Brothers and Other Fools: Russian Folk Tales.* Ginsburg, Mirra (1919-), ed. c.1979. Lippincott. (P.369)

Mikulova, Milada
--*Coppelia.* 1971. Watts. (P.644)
--*Coppelia.* Borska, Ilona & Hoffmann, Ernst Theodor Amadeus (1776-1822). Sebestiakov, Yvonne, tr. 1971. Watts. (P.118)

Miles, Cyril (1918-)
--*A Carpet of Flowers: Una Alfombra de Flores.* De Trevino, Elizabeth Borton (1904-). 1975. Ethridge. (P.260)

Miles, E. B., jt. illus. see Mudge, E. Lynn.

Miles, Elizabeth
--*Mokey's Birthday Present.* Weiss, Ellen. c.1985. Holt, Rinehart, and Winston. (P.942)
--*Santa's Christmas Journey.* Brooke, Roger. 1984. Raintree Pubs. (P.135)

Miles, Harold W.
--*Girls in the High Sierras: A Tale of the Sierra Nevada with Himalayan Echoes.* Barrett, Katharine Ruth Ellis, Mrs. (1879-). 1924. Doubleday, Page & Company. (P.75)

Miles, Helen
--*The Little Christian's Pilgrimage.* Bunyan, John (1628-1688). N.D. E & J B Young. (P.150)

Milhous, Katherine, jt. illus. see Key, Alexander Hill.

Milhous, Katherine (1894-1977)
--*Along Janet's Road.* Dalgliesh, Alice (1893-1979). 1946. C. Scribner's Sons. (P.238)
--*Appolonia's Valentine.* Milhous, Katherine (1894-1977). 1954. Scribner. (P.645)
--*Billy Button's Butter'd Biscuit.* Hunt, Mabel Leigh (1892-1971). 1941. Frederick A. Stokes Company. (P.473)
--*Billy Button's Butter'd Biscuit.* Hunt, Mabel Leigh (1892-1971). N.D. J. B. Lippincott. (P.473)
--*A Book for Jennifer: A Story of London Children in the Eighteenth Century and of Mr. Newbery's Juvenile Library.* Dalgliesh, Alice (1893-1979). 1940. C. Scribner's Sons. (P.238)
--*The Brownies.* Ewing, Juliana Horatia Gatty, Mrs. (1841-1885). 1946. Charles Scribner's Sons. (P.313)
--*Corporal Keeperupper.* Milhous, Katherine (1894-1977). 1943. C. Scribner's Sons. (P.645)
--*The Egg Tree.* Milhous, Katherine (1894-1977). 1950. Scribner. **Award: (RCM).** (P.645)
--*The First Christmas Crib.* Milhous, Katherine (1894-1977). 1944. C. Scribner's Sons. (P.645)
--*Happily Ever After.* Dalgliesh, Alice (1893-1979). Wheelock, John Hall (1886-1978), tr. c.1939. C. Scribner's Sons. (P.239)
--*Herodia, the Lovely Puppet.* Milhous, Katherine (1894-1977). 1942. C. Scribner's Sons. (P.645)
--*The Little Angel: A Story of Old Rio.* Dalgliesh, Alice (1893-1979). 1943. C. Scribner's Sons. (P.239)
--*Once on a Time.* Dalgliesh, Alice (1893-1979). c.1938. C. Scribner's Sons. (P.239)
--*Patrick and the Golden Slippers.* Milhous, Katherine (1894-1977). c.1951. Scribner. (P.645)
--*Peter Piper's Pickled Peppers.* Hunt, Mabel Leigh (1892-1971). 1942. Frederick A. Stokes Company. (P.474)
--*Peter Piper's Pickled Peppers.* Milhous, Katherine (1894-1977). N.D. J. B. LIppincott. (P.645)
--*The Silver Pencil.* 1894- ed. Dalgliesh, Alice (1893-1979). 1944. C. Scribner's Sons. **Award: (JNM).** (P.239)
--*Snow over Bethlehem.* Milhous, Katherine (1894-1977). 1945. Charles Scribner's Sons. (P.645)
--*With Bells on.* Milhous, Katherine (1894-1977). 1955. Scribner. (P.645)

Milius, Winifred
--*Here Comes Daddy.* Milius, Winifred. 1944. William R. Scott Inc. (P.645)

Mill, Eleanor
--*Book of Hugh Flower.* Beers, Lorna Doone (1897-). 1952. Har-Row. (P.88)
--*The Book of Hugh Flower.* 1st ed. Beers, Lorna Doone (1897-). 1952. Harper. (P.88)

Nast & Stevens
--*Cross and Crescent: Or, Young America in Turkey and Greece, 1 of 12 vols.* Adams, William Taylor (1822-1897). 1882. Lee & Shepard. (P.7)
--*Dikes and Ditches: Or, Young America in Holland and Belgium, 1 of 12 vols.* Adams, William Taylor (1822-1897). 1882. Lee & Shepard. (P.7)
--*Down the Rhine: Or, Young America in Germany, 1 of 12 vols.* Adams, William Taylor (1822-1897). 1882. Lee & Shepard. (P.7)
--*Isles of the Sea: Or, Young America Homeward Bound, 1 of 12 vols.* Adams, William Taylor (1822-1897). 1882. Lee & Shepard. (P.8)
--*Northern Lands: Or, Young America in Russia and Prussia, 1 of 12 vols.* Adams, William Taylor (1822-1897). 1882. Lee & Shepard. (P.8)
--*Palace and Cottage: Or, Young America in France and Switzerland, 1 of 12 vols.* Adams, William Taylor (1822-1897). 1882. Lee & Shepard. (P.9)
--*Red Cross: Or, Young America in England and Wales, 1 of 12 vols.* Adams, William Taylor (1822-1897). 1882. Lee & Shepard. (P.9)
--*Shamrock and Thistle: Or, Young America in Ireland and Scotland, 1 of 11 vols.* Adams, William Taylor (1822-1897). 1868. Lee & Shepard. (P.9)
--*Sunny Shores: Or, Young America in Italy and Austria, 1 of 12 vols.* Adams, William Taylor (1822-1897). 1882. Lee & Shepard. (P.10)
--*Up the Baltic: Or, Young America in Norway, Sweden, and Denmark, 1 of 12 vols.* Adams, William Taylor (1822-1897). 1882. Lee & Shepard. (P.10)
--*Vine and Olive: Or, Young America in Spain and Portugal, 1 of 12 vols.* Adams, William Taylor (1822-1897). 1882. Lee & Shepard. (P.10)
--*Young America Abroad Series, 12 vols.* Adams, William Taylor (1822-1897). 1882. Lee & Shepard. (P.10)
Nathan, Robert Gruntal (1894-)
--*Tina Mina.* Mayer, Dorothy. 1930. Houghton Mifflin Co. (P.633)
Native Artists
--*Our Little Chinese Cousin.* Headland, Isaac Taylor (1859-1942). 1903. L. C. Page & Co. (P.428)
Natti, Susanna (1948-)
--*The Acorn Quest.* Yolen, Jane Hyatt (1939-). c.1981. Crowell. (P.986)
--*The Almost Awful Play.* Giff, Patricia Reilly (1935-). 1985. Puffin Books. (P.366)
--*The Almost Awful Play.* Giff, Patricia Reilly (1935-). 1984. Viking. (P.366)
--*Cam Jansen & Mystery Carnival Prize.* Adler, David A. (1947-). 1984. Viking. (P.11)
--*Cam Jansen and the Mystery at the Monkey House.* Adler, David A. (1947-). 1985. Viking Kestrel. (P.11)
--*Cam Jansen & the Mystery Monster Movie.* Adler, David A. (1947-). 1984. Viking. (P.11)
--*Cam Jansen & the Mystery of the Babe Ruth Baseball.* Adler, David A. (1947-). 1982. Viking Pr. (P.11)
--*Cam Jansen and the Mystery of the Circus Clown.* Adler, David A (1947-). 1983. Viking Press. (P.11)
--*Cam Jansen and the Mystery of the Dinosaur Bones.* Adler, David A (1947-). 1981. Viking Press. (P.11)
--*Cam Jansen and the Mystery of the Gold Coins.* Adler, David A (1947-). 1982. Viking Press. (P.11)
--*Cam Jansen and the Mystery of the Stolen Diamonds.* Adler, David A (1947-). 1980. Viking Press. (P.11)
--*Cam Jansen and the Mystery of the Television Dog.* Adler, David A (1947-). 1981. Viking. (P.11)
--*Cam Jansen and the Mystery of the U.F.O.* Adler, David A (1947-). 1980. Viking Press. (P.11)
--*Dinosaurs & Beasts of Yore.* Cole, William Rossa (1919-), ed. 1979. Putnam Pub Group. (P.208)
--*Dinosaurs and Beasts of Yore: Poems.* Cole, William Rossa (1919-), selected by. 1979. Collins. (P.208)
--*The Downtown Fairy Godmother.* Pomerantz, Charlotte (1930-). c.1978. Addison-Wesley. (P.731)
--*Frederick's Alligator.* Peterson, Esther Allen (1934-). 1979. Crown. (P.721)
--*Frederick's Alligator.* Peterson, Esther Allen (1934-). 1981. Scholastic Inc. (P.721)
--*Harold Thinks Big.* Murphy, Jim (1947-). c.1980. Crown Publishers. (P.673)
--*Helpful Hattie.* 1st ed. Quin-Harkin, Janet (1941-). c.1983. Harcourt Brace Jovanovich. (P.745)
--*I Am Three.* Fitzhugh, Louise (1928-1974). 1982. Delacorte. (P.329)
--*Midnight Moon.* Watson, Clyde (1947-). 1979. Collins. (P.935)
--*The Mystery on Bleeker Street.* Hooks, William H. (1921-). 1980. Knopf. (P.459)
--*Penelope Gets Wheels.* Peterson, Esther Allen (1934-). c.1982. Crown. (P.721)
--*Today Was a Terrible Day.* Giff, Patricia Reilly (1935-). 1984, c.1980. Penguin Books. (P.366)
--*Today Was a Terrible Day.* Giff, Patricia Reilly (1935-). 1980. Viking Press. (P.366)
--*Watch Out, Ronald Morgan!.* Giff, Patricia Reilly (1935-). 1985. Viking Kestrel. (P.366)
Nav, Carol
--*Pueblo Playmates.* Brown, Marjorie Webber. 1938. A. Whitman & Co. (P.141)
Nay, Carol, photos by.
--*Timmy Rides the China Clipper.* Nay, Carol. 1939. A. Whitman & Co. (P.676)
Naylor, Penelope (1941-)
--*A Tree Called Moses.* Baker, Laura Nelson (1911-). 1966. Antheneum Publishers. (P.63)
Naylor, Raymon
--*Alaska Bush Pilot.* Coombs, Charles Ira (1914-). 1963. Harper & Row. (P.216)
--*The Fire Dragon: A Story of the Great Chicago Fire.* Smith, Fredrika Shumway (1877-1968). 1956. Rand McNally. (P.833)
--*Frank Luke, Balloon Buster.* Coombs, Charles Ira (1914-). Betts, Emmett A., ed. 1967. Harper & Row. (P.216)
--*Rocket Pioneer.* Coombs, Charles Ira (1914-). Betts, Emmett Albert (1903-), ed. c.1965. Harper. (P.216)
Neale, Marguerite B.
--*The Bogie Man.* Dimmick, Ruth Crosby. 1906. John C. Winston. (P.266)
Neale, Sidnee
--*Basketball Bones.* Francis, Helen Dannefer (1915-). 1962. Hastings House. (P.341)
--*Billy Joe and the Rangers.* Harris, Harry M. 1966, c.1965. Hastings. (P.415)
--*Bold Beginning.* Carr, Harriett Helen (1899-). 1964. Hastings House. (P.171)
--*First Party.* Gilbert, Miriam, pseud. (1919-1978). Presberg, Miriam Goldstein. 1966. Hastings. (P.367)
--*Two Dates for Mike.* Musgrave, Florence (1902-). 1973, c.1964. G. K. Hall. (P.674)
--*Two Dates for Mike.* Musgrave, Florence (1902-). 1964. Hastings House. (P.674)
Neals, Otto
--*The Adventures of Tony, David & Marc: Reading from A-Z.* De Vane, Lenchen Coleman. 1976. Exposition. (P.261)
Nealy, Sid H.
--*In the Trail of the Pack-Mule.* Nealy, Sid H. c.1902. F. T. Neely. (P.676)
Neary, Donna J.
--*An Occurence at Owl Creek Bridge.* Bierce, Ambrose (1842-1914). c.1980. Creative Education. (P.101)
Nebel, Gustave E.
--*The Good Tiger.* Bowen, Elizabeth (1899-1973). c.1965. Knopf. (P.121)
--*The Happy Pair and Otjher Love Stories.* Chaikin, Miriam (1928-). 1972. Putnam. (P.181)
--*Little Foreign Devil.* Alexander, Anne Barbara Cooke (1913-). 1970. Atheneum. (P.22)
--*The Moon Guitar.* Niemeyer, Marie. 1969. F. Watts. (P.682)
--*My Village, My World.* Sanford, David E. 1969. Crown Publishers. (P.792)
--*Mystery at Dark Wood.* York, Carol Beach (1928-). 1972. Watts. (P.988)
--*New Song.* Hanley, Eve. 1967. Weybright. (P.410)
--*The Old Witch Goes to the Ball.* DeLage, Ida (1918-). 1969. Garrard Pub. Co. (P.252)
--*The Sandy Shoes Mystery.* Mooney, Elizabeth Comstock (1918-). 1970. Lippincott. (P.659)
--*Secret of the Jade Pavilion.* Sherry, Dulcie Sylvia (1932-). 1967, c.1966. Lippincott. (P.820)
--*The Secret Spenders.* Hildick, Edmund Wallace (1925-). 1971. Crown Publishers. (P.442)
--*The Secret Winners.* Hildick, Edmund Wallace (1925-). 1970. Crown Publishers. (P.442)
--*Teacher's Pest.* 1st ed. Smaridge, Norah Antoinette (1903-). 1968. Hawthorn Books. (P.831)
Nechamkin, Sarah
--*Heroes & Monsters.* Reeves, James (1909-), retold by. 1978. Hippocrene Bks. (P.754)
--*Russian Fairy Tales.* Budberg, Moura & Williams-Ellis, Amabel (1894-), eds. Budberg, Moura & Williams-Ellis, Amabel, trs. 1967, c.1965. F. Warne. (P.147)
--*Russian Fairy Tales.* Williams-Ellis, Amabel, Mrs. (1894-) & Budberg, Moura, eds. 1967. Warne. (P.962)
Neden, Vivienne Dugdale
--*The Princess and the Enchanted Wood: And Other Fairy Tales.* Ashe, Marjorie Dugdale. 1951. Exposition Press. (P.51)
Neebe, William
--*Muggsy: The Make Believe Puppy.* Lieberthal, Jules M. c.1956. Rand McNally. (P.572)
--*Nine Make a Team.* Neigoff, Mike (1920-). 1963. A. Whitman. (P.677)
--*North Star.* Fradin, Dennis Brindell (1945-). 1978. Children's Press. (P.340)
--*Sergeant Preston and Rex.* Striker, Francis Hamilton (1903-1962). c.1956. Rand McNally. (P.868)
--*Slowpoke: The Lazy Little Puppy.* Lieberthal, Jules M. c.1957. Rand McNally. (P.572)
--*Snoopy, the Nosey Little Puppy.* Lieberthal, Jules M. c.1955. Rand McNally. (P.572)
--*The Three Billy Goats Gruff.* Asbjornsen, Peter Christen (1812-1885). O'Grady, Alice & Throop, Frances (1868-), trs. c.1957. Rand McNally. (P.51)
Neebe, William, jt. illus. see Endres, Helen.
Neebe, William, jt. illus. see Endres, Helen Elise.
Needler, Jerry
--*The Blue Caboose.* Hamilton, Dorothy Drumm (1906-1983). 1973. Herald Press. (P.408)
Neely, Jan & Alvarado, Peter
--*New Friends for the Saggy Baggy Elephant.* Holl, Adelaide Hinkle (1910-). 1976. Western Pub. (P.454)
Neely, Keith R. (1943-)
--*The Ainslee Stories.* Campbell, Helen Stuart, Mrs. (1839-1918). Weeks, Helen C., pseud. 1868. Hurd and Houghton Etc. (P.164)
--*The Christmas Duck.* Gire, Ken, Jr. 1983. Mott Media. (P.370)
--*Don't Bite the Dinosaur.* Campion, Mike (1941-) & Campion, Kathy (1943-). c.1982. Moody Press. (P.165)
--*The Ghost in the Gym.* Van Steenwyk, Elizabeth Ann (1928-). 1983. Childrens. (P.915)
--*Jesus Makes Me Well.* Kohler, Christine (1953-). c.1985. Concordia Pub. House. (P.534)
--*My Friend Is Moving.* Kohler, Christine (1953-). c.1985. Concordia Pub. House. (P.534)
--*The Perfect Hiding Place.* Campion, Mike (1941-) & Campion, Kathy (1943-). c.1982. Moody Press. (P.165)
--*The Secret of the Spotted Horse.* Van Steenwyk, Elizabeth Ann (1928-). 1983. Childrens. (P.915)
--*The Southpaw from Sonora Mystery.* Van Steenwyk, Elizabeth Ann (1928-). 1983. Childrens. (P.915)
--*Terror on the Rebound.* Van Steenwyk, Elizabeth Ann (1928-). 1983. Childrens. (P.915)
--*The Very Special Stone.* Campion, Mike (1941-) & Campion, Kathy (1943-). c.1982. Moody Press. (P.165)
Neely, Linda
--*The Adventures of Little White Possum.* Wayne, Donald, pseud. (1930-). Dodd, Wayne Donald. 1970. Putnam. (P.937)
--*Peas in a Pod.* Young, Miriam Burt (1913-1974). 1971. Putnam. (P.990)
Neese, Marcia A.
--*Everyone Is Special.* Neese, Marcia A. Oelerich, Marjorie L. & Cranfill, John, eds. 1984. Baker St Prod. (P.677)
--*Have You Ever Tried.* Neese, Marcia A. Oelerich, Marjorie L. & Cranfill, John, eds. 1984. Baker St Prod. (P.677)
--*Homesick.* Neese, Marcia A. Oelerich, Marjorie L. & Cranfill, John, eds. 1984. Baker St Prod. (P.677)
--*I'm Afraid of the Dark.* Neese, Marcia A. Oelerich, Marjorie, ed. 1984. Baker St Prod. (P.677)
--*Not a Thing to Wear.* Neese, Marcia A. Oelerich, Marjorie L. & Cranfill, John, eds. 1984. Baker St Prod. (P.677)
--*To Be a Friend.* Neese, Marcia A. Oelerich, Marjorie L. & Cranfill, John, eds. 1984. Baker St Prod. (P.677)
Negreiros, Almada, jt. illus. see Levine, David.
Negri, Rocco (1932-)
--*Androcles and the Lion: Retold from Apion.* Hawkins, Helena Ann Quail (1905-) & Apion. 1970. Coward-McCann. (P.422)
--*Bantu Tales.* 1st ed. Holladay, Virginia. Crane, Louise, ed. 1970. Viking Press. (P.454)
--*Casa Means Home.* Campion, Nardi Reeder (1917-). 1970. Holt, Rinehart and Winston. (P.165)
--*Charlie Dick.* 1st ed. Fisher, Laura Harrison (1934-). 1972. Holt, Rinehart and Winston. (P.328)
--*Coplas:.* Folk Poems in Spanish and English. Talbot, Toby (1928-), ed. 1972. Four Winds Press. (P.877)
--*The Dancing Monkey.* Garfield, Nancy. 1970. Putnam. (P.355)
--*Fee, Fi, Fo, Fum: Friendly and Funny Giants.* Stoutenburg, Adrien Pearl (1916-). 1969. Viking Press. (P.863)
--*The Giant Under the Snow: A Story of Suspense.* Gordon, John William (1925-). 1970. Harper & Row. (P.377)
--*The Giant Under the Snow: A Story of Suspense.* Gordon, John William (1925-). 1975, c.1970. Harper & Row. (P.377)
--*The Great Fire.* Dickens, Monica Enid (1915-). 1973, c.1970. Doubleday. (P.264)
--*Heracles the Strong.* Serraillier, Ian Lucien (1912-). 1970. H. Z. Walck. (P.810)
--*The Indians & the Strangers.* Johnston, Johanna (1914-1982). 1972. Dodd. (P.498)
--*Journey Outside.* Steele, Mary Quintard Govan (1922-). 1969. Viking Press. **Awards: (ALA); (JNM).** (P.850)
--*The Legs of the Moon.* Jacobs, Francine (1935-). 1971. Coward, McCann & Geoghegan. (P.486)
--*The Magic Pumpkin.* Skurzynski, Gloria (1930-). 1971. Four Winds Press. (P.828)
--*Maildun the Voyager.* Reeves, James (1909-), retold by. 1972, c.1971. H. Z. Walck. (P.754)
--*On the Banks of the Hudson: A View of Its History & Folklore.* Lord, Beman (1924-). 1971. Walck. (P.584)
--*The One Bad Thing About Father.* Monjo, Ferdinand Nicolas, III (1924-1978). 1970. Harper & Row. (P.656)
--*Pampalche of the Silver Teeth.* Ginsburg, Mirra (1919-), ed. Ginsburg, Mirra, tr. c.1976. Crown. (P.369)
--*Renfroe's Christmas.* Burch, Robert Joseph (1925-). 1968. Viking Press. (P.151)
--*The Son of the Leopard.* 1st ed. Courlander, Harold (1908-). 1974. Crown Publishers. (P.223)
--*Tales from Count Lucanor.* Manuel, Don Juan (1282-1347). Talbot, Toby (1928-), tr. from Span. 1970. Dial. (P.618)
--*Toto.* Moskin, Marietta Dunston (1928-). 1971. Coward, McCann & Geoghegan. (P.666)
--*Trouble River.* Byars, Betsy Cromer (1928-). 1969. Viking Press. (P.160)
--*Where I Begin.* Abbott, Sarah. 1970. Coward-McCann. (P.3)
Negron, Bill
--*The Cardinal's Snuffbox.* Roseman, Kenneth David (1939-). c.1982. Union of American Hebrew Congregations. (P.777)
--*Enrique: A Challenge Book.* Figueroa, Pablo (1938-). 1970. Hill & Wang. (P.325)
--*The Mark of Conte.* 1st ed. Levitin, Sonia (1934-). 1976. Atheneum. (P.568)
--*Tejanos.* Foster, Ed. Santos, Richard G., intro. by. 1970. Hill and Wang; Distributed by Random House. (P.338)
Negulesco, Dusty
--*Dear Matilda: Letters from Mike to Matilda.* 1st ed. Saunders, Violette. 1957. Exposition Press. (P.794)
Neher, Julie & Redding, Jane
--*Say Hello to the Care Bear Cousin.* Polter, David. 1985. Random. (P.731)
Neibart, Wally
--*Isaac Asimov's Limericks for Children.* Asimov, Isaac (1920-). 1984. Caedmon. (P.52)
Neide, Peter
--*The Yellow Boat.* Bufalari, Giuseppe (1927-). Marci, Alfeo, tr. 1969. Knopf. (P.148)
Neidigh, Sherry
--*Huckleberry Finn.* Twain, Mark, pseud. (1835-1910). Clemens, Samuel Langhorne. Edwards, June, adapted by. 1980. Raintree Pubs. (P.907)
--*Huckleberry Finn.* Twain, Mark, pseud. (1835-1910). Clemens, Samuel Langhorne. Stewart, Diana, adapted by. 1983. Raintree Pubs. (P.907)
Neigher, Hy
--*Rhyme-Land.* Scharfstein, Edythe (1922-) & Scharfstein, Sol. 1952, c.1951. Ktav Pub. House. (P.797)
Neill, Eileen Mueller
--*Out the Door.* Matthias, Catherine (1945-). 1982. Childrens Press. (P.631)
Neill, John Rea, jt. illus. see Denslow, William Wallace.
Neill, John Rea, jt. illus. see Gringhuis, Richard H.
Neill, John Rea, jt. illus. see Salg, Bert N.
Neill, John Rea, jt. illus. see Schaeffer, Mead.
Neill, John Rea (1878-1943)
--*The Adventures of a Brownie, 2 in 1.* N.D. Reilly & Britton Co. (P.677)
--*Alice's Adventures in Wonderland and Through The Looking Glass, 2 Vols.* in 1. N.D. Reilly & Britton Co. (P.677)
--*Andersen's Fairy Tales, 2 Vols.* in 1. N.D. Reilly & Britton Co. (P.677)
--*Baum's Own Book.* N.D. The Reilly & Britton Co. (P.677)
--*Black Beauty and The Little Lame Prince, 2 Vols.* in 1. N.D. Reilly & Britton Co. (P.677)
--*Bob Thorpe: Sky Fighter in Italy.* Bishop, Austin. 1920. Harcourt, Brace and Howe. (P.103)
--*Bob Thorpe: Sky Fighter in the Lafayette Flying Corps.* Bishop, Austin. 1919. Harcourt, Brace and Howe. (P.103)
--*Captain Salt in Oz.* Thompson, Ruth Plumly (1893-1976). Baum, Lyman Frank (1856-1919), created by. c.1936. The Reilly & Lee Co. (P.888)
--*Children's Poems That Never Grow Old: For Little Folks from Six to Twelve Years Old.* Benoit, Clement F. (1833-1937), ed. c.1922. The Reilly & Lee Co. (P.94)

Nelson, Harold & Jones, A. Garth
--*A Real Queen's Fairy Tales.* Elisabeth, Queen Consort Of Charles I King Of Rumania, pseud. (1843-1916). Bengescu, Carmen Sylva. Hopkirk, Edith, tr. Davis, George T. B., intro. by. 1901. Davis and Company. (P.301)
--*A Real Queen's Fairy Tales.* Elizabeth Queen Consort of Charles I (1843-1916). Hopkirk, Edith, Miss, tr. N.D. Frederick A. Stokes. (P.301)

Nelson, Jane E.
--*God Cares When I Do Something Stupid.* Murphy, Elspeth Campbell. c.1984. Chariot Books. (P.673)
--*God Cares When I Don't Know What to Do.* Murphy, Elspeth Campbell. c.1984. Chariot Books. (P.673)
--*God Cares When I Don't Know What to Do.* Murphy, Elspeth Campbell. 1985, c.1984. Cook. (P.673)
--*God Cares When I Need to Talk to Somebody.* Murphy, Elspeth Campbell. c.1984. Chariot Books. (P.673)
--*God Cares When I'm All Tired Out.* Murphy, Elspeth Campbell. c.1983. Chariot Books. (P.673)
--*God Cares When I'm Disappointed.* Murphy, Elspeth Campbell. c.1983. Chariot Books. (P.673)
--*God Cares When I'm Feeling Mean.* Murphy, Elspeth Campbell. 1985. Cook. (P.673)
--*God Cares When I'm Sorry.* Murphy, Elspeth Campbell. c.1983. Chariot Books. (P.673)
--*God Cares When I'm Wondering.* Murphy, Elspeth Campbell. c.1984. Chariot Books. (P.673)
--*God Cares When I'm Wondering.* Murphy, Elspeth Campbell. 1985. Cook. (P.673)
--*God Cares When Somebody Hurts Me.* Murphy, Elspeth Campbell. 1984. Chariot Books. (P.673)
--*Sarah Jane.* Archer, Marion Fuller (1917-). 1971. A Whitman. (P.46)

Nelson, John (1928-)
--*I'm Glad I'm Little.* Wulf, Kathleen (1941-). c.1976. Child's World. (P.982)

Nelson, John (1928-) & Henriksen, Harold
--*Squanto: The Indian Who Saved the Pilgrims.* Grant, Matthew G, pseud. (1931-). May, Julian. 1974. Creative Education; Distributed by Childrens Press, Chicago. (P.382)

Nelson, Mary Elizabeth & Nelson, Rhoda Louise Smith, Mrs. (1891-)
--*This Is Freedom.* Nelson, Rhoda Louise Smith, Mrs. (1891-). 1940. Dodd, Mead & Company. (P.678)

Nelson, Ralph Lewis
--*The Mysterious Little Girl.* Stockwell, Grace. c.1924. The Century Co. (P.860)
--*Paddles: The Story of a Sea Lion.* Tracy, Edward B. 1942. G. P. Putnam's Sons. (P.898)

Nelson, Rhoda Louise Smith, Mrs., jt. illus. see Nelson, Mary Elizabeth.

Nelson, Rick
--*The Adventures of Davy & Bartholomew.* Wright, Joseph Lord. 1979. Delanie Way. (P.981)

Nelson, Rosalie
--*Linda's El Dorado: A Mystery Adventure Story of Washington Territory in 1852.* Chaffee, Allen. c.1928. The Century Co. (P.181)

Nemo
--*Wild Animals.* Andrews, Martin & Pucci, Mario. 1970. Platt & Munk. (P.41)

Nena
--*Smarty Pants.* Painter, Barbara. 1950. House-Warven. (P.701)

Nendick, Buckton
--*Let's Pretend: A Book of Children's Plays.* Barbee, Lindsey (1876-). c.1917. T.S. Denison & Company. (P.70)

Nenninger, Jerome D.
--*Pekan the Shadow.* Montgomery, Rutherford George (1894-). 1970. Caxton Printers. (P.658)
--*Phantom Killer of the Flying M.* Wood, David, Jr. (1901-). 1971. Caxton Printers. (P.975)
--*Rufus.* Montgomery, Rutherford George (1894-). 1973. Caxton Printers. (P.659)

Nerlinger, Joe
--*Jerry Finds Ants.* Darby, Gene Kegley (1921-). 1964. Steck-V. (P.242)
--*Jerry Finds Bees.* Darby, Gene Kegley (1921-). 1967. Steck- Vaughan. (P.242)
--*Jerry Finds Spiders.* Darby, Gene Kegley (1921-). 1969. Steck-Vaughn Co. (P.242)
--*Leonard Discovers America.* Darby, Gene Kegley (1921-). N.D. Addison-Wesley. (P.242)
--*Leonard Visits Dinosaur Land.* Darby, Gene Kegley (1921-). N.D. Addison-Wesley. (P.242)

Nerlove, Evelyn
--*Who Is David?. A Story of an Adopted Adolescent and His Friends.* Nerlove, Evelyn. c.1985. Child Welfare League of America. (P.678)

Nerman, Einar (1888-)
--*Fairy Tales from the North.* Nerman, Einar (1888-), retold by. 1946. A. A. Knopf. (P.678)

--*The Goose Girl, and Other Tales from Brothers Grimm.* Grimm, Jakob Ludwig Karl (1785-1863) & Grimm, Wilhelm Karl (1786-1859). 1929. The Macmillan Company. (P.392)

Nesbitt, Esta (1918-)
--*Audun and His Bear.* 1st ed. Schiller, Barbara Heyman (1928-). 1968. Holt, Rinehart, and Winston. (P.799)
--*The Earth Is on a Fish's Back: Tales of Beginnings.* Belting, Natalia Maree (1915-). c.1965. Holt. (P.91)
--*Jon the Unlucky.* 1st ed. Coatsworth, Elizabeth Jane (1893-). 1964. Holt, Rinehart and Winston. (P.204)
--*Scarlet Sails.* Green, Alexander. Whitney, Thomas Porter (1917-), tr. 1967. Scribner. (P.384)
--*The Stars are Silver Reindeers.* 1st ed. Belting, Natalia Maree (1915-). 1966. Holt, Rinehart and Winston. (P.91)
--*Town Across the Water.* Polland, Madeleine Angela Cahill (1918-). 1963. HR&W. (P.730)

Nesbitt, Jan
--*Legends of the Sun and Moon.* Hadley, Eric & Hadley, Tessa. 1983. Cambridge University Press. (P.402)

Nesbitt, Philip
--*Bears, Pirates and Silver Lace: Stories of Old California.* Fisher, Anne Benson (1898-). 1944. Binfords & Mort. (P.328)
--*Trum Peter's Tea Party.* Nesbitt, Philip. 1931. Coward-McCann, Inc. (P.678)

Neset, Malvin
--*Great Day in Norway: The Seventeenth of May.* Hopp, Zinken (1905-). Ramholt, Toni, tr. 1962. Abelard-Schuman. (P.463)
--*The Magic Chalk.* Hopp, Zinken (1905-). Bergendahl, Suzanne H., tr. 1959. D. McKay Co. (P.463)

Ness, Evaline Michelow, Mrs. (1911-)
--*Across from Indian Shore.* Robinson, Barbara Webb (1927-). 1962. Lothrop, Lee and Shepard. (P.769)
--*All in the Morning Early.* Nic Leodhas, Sorche, pseud. (1898-1969). Alger, Leclaire Gowans. 1963. HR&W. Awards: (ALA); (RCM). (P.681)
--*Amelia Mixed the Mustard and Other Poems.* Ness, Evaline Michelow, Mrs. (1911-), selected by. 1975. Scribner. Award: (ALA). (P.678)
--*The Brave & the Fair.* Ferris, Helen Josephine (1890-1969), ed. 1960. HR&W. (P.323)
--*The Bridge.* Ogburn, Charlton, Jr. (1911-). 1957. Houghton Mifflin. (P.691)
--*Candle Tales.* Cunningham, Julia Woolfolk (1916-). 1964. Pantheon Books. (P.235)
--*Coll and His White Pig.* Alexander, Lloyd Chudley (1924-). 1965. Holt, Rinehart and Winston. (P.22)
--*The Devil's Bridge: A Legend.* Scribner, Charles, Jr. (1921-), retold by. 1978. Scribner. (P.806)
--*Do You Have the Time, Lydia?.* 1st ed. Ness, Evaline Michelow, Mrs. (1911-). 1971. E. P. Dutton. (P.678)
--*Don't You Remember?.* 1st ed. Clifton, Lucille (1936-). 1973. Dutton. (P.202)
--*Everett Anderson's Christmas Coming.* 1st ed. Clifton, Lucille (1936-). 1971. Holt, Rinehart and Winston. (P.202)
--*Exactly Alike.* Ness, Evaline Michelow, Mrs. (1911-). 1964. Scribner. Award: (NYT). (P.678)
--*Favorite Fairy Tales Told in Italy.* Haviland, Virginia (1911-), retold by. 1965. Little. (P.421)
--*Fierce the Lion.* Ness, Evaline Michelow, Mrs. (1911-). c.1980. Holiday House. (P.678)
--*Funny Town.* Merriam, Eve (1916-). 1963. Crowell Collier Press. (P.642)
--*A Gift for Sula Sula.* Ness, Evaline Michelow, Mrs. (1911-). 1963. Scribner. (P.678)
--*The Girl and the Goatherd: Or, This and That and Thus and So.* 1st ed. Ness, Evaline Michelow, Mrs. (1911-). 1970. E. P. Dutton. (P.678)
--*The Hand-Me-Down Doll.* 1st ed. Kroll, Steven (1941-). 1983. Holiday. (P.540)
--*Joey and the Birthday Present.* Kumin, Maxine Winokur (1925-) & Sexton, Anne Harvey, Mrs. (1928-1974). 1971. McGraw-Hill. (P.541)
--*Josefina February.* Ness, Evaline Michelow, Mrs. (1911-). 1963. Scribner. Award: (ALA). (P.678)
--*Josie and the Snow.* Buckley, Helen Elizabeth (1918-). 1964. Lothrop, Lee & Shepard Co. (P.147)
--*Josie's Buttercup.* Buckley, Helen Elizabeth (1918-). 1967. Lothrop, Lee & Shepard. (P.147)
--*Kellyburn Braes.* Nic Leodhas, Sorche, pseud. (1898-1969). Alger, Leclaire Gowans. 1968. HR&W. Award: (ALA). (P.681)
--*Listen-- the Birds: Poems.* Miller, Mary Britton (1883-1975). 1961. Pantheon. Award: (NYT). (P.648)

--*Lonely Maria.* Coatsworth, Elizabeth Jane (1893-). 1960. Pantheon Books. (P.204)
--*Long, Broad & Quickeye.* Ness, Evaline Michelow, Mrs. (1911-), adapted by. 1969. Scribner. (P.678)
--*Macaroon.* Cunningham, Julia Woolfolk (1916-). 1962. Pantheon Books. (P.235)
--*Marcella's Guardian Angel.* Ness, Evaline Michelow, Mrs. (1911-). c.1979. Holiday House. (P.678)
--*Mr. Miacca: An English Folk Tale.* 1st ed. Ness, Evaline Michelow, Mrs. (1911-). 1967. Holt, Rinehart and Winston. (P.678)
--*Old Mother Hubbard & Her Dog.* Mother Goose. 1972. HR&W. Award: (ALA). (P.669)
--*Ondine: The Story of a Bird Who Was Different.* Osborne, Maurice Machado (1924-). 1960. Houghton Mifflin. (P.697)
--*Pavo & the Princess.* Ness, Evaline Michelow, Mrs. (1911-). 1964. Scribner. (P.678)
--*Pierino and the Bell.* Cassedy, Sylvia (1930-). c.1966. Doubleday. (P.177)
--*A Pocketful of Cricket.* 1st ed. Caudill, Rebecca (1899-). 1964. Holt, Rinehart and Winston. Awards: (ALA); (RCM). (P.178)
--*The Princess and the Lion.* Coatsworth, Elizabeth Jane (1893-). 1963. Pantheon. Award: (ALA). (P.204)
--*Sam, Bangs & Moonshine.* Ness, Evaline Michelow, Mrs. (1911-). 1966. HR&W. Awards: (RCM); (ALA). (P.678)
--*Scottish Songbook.* Nic Leodhas, Sorche, pseud. (1898-1969). Alger, Leclaire Gowans. 1969. HR&W. (P.682)
--*A Shaker Paper House.* Ness, Evaline Michelow, Mrs. (1911-). 1979. Scribner. (P.678)
--*The Sherwood Ring.* Pope, Elizabeth Marie (1917-). 1958. Houghton Mifflin. Award: (ALA). (P.732)
--*Some Cheese for Charles.* Buckley, Helen Elizabeth (1918-). 1963. Lothrop, Lee & Shepard Co. (P.147)
--*Some of the Days of Everett Anderson.* 1st ed. Clifton, Lucille (1936-). 1970. Holt, Rinehart and Winston. (P.202)
--*The Steamroller: A Fantasy.* Brown, Margaret Wise (1910-1952). 1974. Walker. (P.141)
--*The Story of Ophelia.* 1st ed. Gibbons, Mary Le Duc (1907-). c.1954. Doubleday. (P.365)
--*Thistle and Thyme: Tales and Legends from Scotland.* 1st ed. Nic Leodhas, Sorche, pseud. (1898-1969), ed. Alger, Leclaire Gowans. 1962. Holt, Rinehart and Winston. Awards: (ALA); (JNM). (P.682)
--*Tom Tit Tot: An English Folk Tale.* Jacobs, Joseph (1854-1916), ed. c.1965. Scribners. Awards: (ALA); (RCM). (P.487)
--*The Truthful Harp.* Alexander, Lloyd Chudley (1924-). 1967. Holt, Rinehart and Winston. (P.22)
--*The Warmint.* Ness, Evaline Michelow, Mrs. (1911-). 1976. Scribner. (P.678)
--*What Color Is Caesar?.* Kumin, Maxine Winokur (1925-).c.1978. McGraw-Hill. (P.541)
--*Where Did Josie Go?.* Buckley, Helen Elizabeth (1918-). 1962. Lothrop, Lee & Shepard. (P.147)
--*The Wizard's Tears.* Kumin, Maxine Winokur (1925-) & Sexton, Anne Harvey (1928-1974). 1975. McGraw-Hill. (P.541)
--*The Woman of the Wood: A Tale from Old Russia.* Black, Algernon David (1900-). 1973. Holt, Rinehart and Winston. (P.104)
--*Yeck Eck.* 1st ed. Ness, Evaline Michelow, Mrs. (1911-). 1974. Dutton. (P.678)

Ness, Eveline Michelow, Mrs. (1911-)
--*The Warmint: A Poem.* De La Mare, Walter John (1873-1956). c.1976. Scribner. (P.253)

Nesslage, Kent
--*Three Pals on the Desert.* Adams, Lawrence Stowell (1875-). Miles, Sande, pseud. 1946. R. M. McBride & Company. (P.6)

Nestor, H., photos by.
--*Equal Start: A New School, a New Chance.* Hadsell, Virginia T. & Newcom, Grethel C. Sullivan, N. V., intro. by. 1968. Glide. (P.402)
--*On the Go.* Hadsell, Virginia T. N.D. Glide. (P.402)

Netherwood, Anne (1940-)
--*Modern Ballads & Story Poems.* Causley, Charles Stanley (1917-), ed. 1965. Watts. (P.178)

Neuhart, Marilyn
--*Nabob and the Geranium.* Miller, Judith Ransom. 1967. Golden Gate Junior Books. (P.648)

Neuhaus, David
--*His Finest Hour.* Neuhaus, David. 1984. Viking. (P.678)

Neuman, Daisy
--*Timothy Travels.* Neumann, Daisy. N.D. Coward McCann. (P.678)

Neumann, Erwin R. F.
--*In the Days of the Han.* Jagendorf, Moritz Adolf (1888-1981). 1936. Sutton-House, Ltd. (P.488)

Neumeier, Marty
--*An Occurrence at Owl Creek Bridge.* Bierce, Ambrose (1842-1914). 1980. Creative Ed. (P.101)

Neumeier, Marty & Glaser, Byron
--*Action Alphabet.* Neumeier, Marty & Glaser, Byron. 1985. Greenwillow. (P.678)

Neuner, Lilian
--*Pam Pam.* Osgood, Harriett Keeney (1905-). 1943. Oxford University Press. (P.697)
--*Presents from Pam Pam.* Osgood, Harriett Keeney (1905-). 1945. Oxford University Press. (P.697)
--*Yukon River Children.* Rev ed. Osgood, Harriett Keeney (1905-). 1944. Oxford University Press. (P.697)

Nevell, Peter S.
--*Tommy Toddles.* Lee, Albert (1868-). 1896. Harper & Brothers. (P.559)

Nevil, Susan R.
--*The Biblical Zoo.* Nevil, Susan R. N.D. David McKay Co. (P.678)

Neville, Ray
--*A Bird in the Hand.* Lomask, Milton Nachman (1909-). 1964. Bruce Pub. Co. (P.581)

Neville, Vera (1900-1978)
--*Betsy and Joe: A Betsy-Tracy High School Story.* Lovelace, Maud Hart, Mrs. (1892-1980). 1948. Har-Row. (P.587)
--*Betsy and the Great World.* Lovelace, Maud Hart, Mrs. (1892-1980). 1952. Thomas T. Crowell. (P.587)
--*Betsy in Spite of Herself.* Lovelace, Maud Hart, Mrs. (1892-1980). 1946. Thomas Y. Crowell Company. (P.587)
--*Betsy Was a Junior: A Betsy-Tacy High School Story.* Lovelace, Maud Hart, Mrs. (1892-1980). 1947. Har-Row. (P.587)
--*Betsy Was a Junior: A Betsy-Tacy High School Story.* Lovelace, Maud Hart, Mrs. (1892-1980). 1947. T. Y. Crowell Co. (P.587)
--*Betsy's Wedding.* Lovelace, Maud Hart, Mrs. (1892-1980). 1955. Har-Row. (P.587)
--*Bright Summer.* 1st ed. Rydberg, Ernie, pseud. (1901-). Rydberg, Ernest Emil. 1953. Longmans, Green. (P.786)
--*Brownie of the Circus and Other Stories of Today.* Harper, Wilhelmina (1884-1973), ed. c.1941. David McKay Company. (P.414)
--*Carney's House Party: A Deep Valley Story.* Lovelace, Maud Hart, Mrs. (1892-1980). 1949. T. Y. Crowell Co. (P.587)
--*The Cherry Street House.* Nolen, Eleanor Weakley, Mrs. 1939. T. Nelson and Sons. (P.684)
--*Easter Surprise.* Rathbun, Helen Kelleher (1918-). 1947. Thomas Y. Crowell Company. (P.750)
--*Emily of Deep Valley.* Lovelace, Maud Hart, Mrs. (1892-1980). 1950. Crowell. (P.587)
--*Five Go Adventuring Again.* Blyton, Enid Mary (1897-1968). 1951. Crowell. (P.110)
--*Five on a Treasure Island.* Blyton, Enid Mary (1897-1968). 1950. Crowell. (P.110)
--*Georgie's Pets.* Conger, Marion (1915-). N.D. Abingdon Press. (P.213)
--*Heaven to Betsy.* Lovelace, Maud Hart, Mrs. (1892-1980). 1980, c.1979. Harper & Row. (P.587)
--*Heaven to Betsy: A Betsy-Tacy High School Story.* Lovelace, Maud Hart, Mrs. (1892-1980). 1945. Thomas Y. Crowell Company. (P.587)
--*Highway Past Her Door.* Thompson, Mary Wolfe, Mrs. (1886-). 1938. Longmans, Green and Co. (P.887)
--*Ingrid's Holidays.* Lindegren, Signe, Mrs. Schleef, Caroline, tr. 1932. The Macmillan Company. (P.573)
--*Keepsakes: Stories.* Blondell, Richard, ed. 1936. T. Nelson and Sons. (P.109)
--*Lazy Liza Lizard.* Rains, Marie Curtis. c.1938. The John C. Winston Company. (P.747)
--*Lazy Liza Lizard's Tricks.* 1st ed. Rains, Marie Curtis. 1953. Winston. (P.747)
--*A Lion for Patsy.* Mason, Miriam Evangeline (1899-1973). 1947. D. McKay Co. (P.628)
--*Little Bo.* Neville, Vera (1900-1978). 1940. T. Nelson and Sons. (P.679)
--*The Lonely Little Pig and Other Animal Tales.* Harper, Wilhelmina (1884-1973), ed. c.1938. David McKay Company. (P.414)
--*Muddy Paws.* Smith, Dorothy Johnson (1898-). 1948. T. Y. Crowell Co. (P.832)
--*Peter Painter.* Webber, Frank Martin. 1940. David McKay Co. (P.938)
--*Peter Painter and the Holidays.* Webber, Frank Martin. c.1942. David McKay Company. (P.938)
--*Peter Painter's Merry-Go-Round.* Webber, Frank Martin. 1946. David McKay Company. (P.938)
--*Pigtail Pioneer.* 1st ed. McDonald, Lucile Saunders, Mrs. (1898-) & Ross, Zola Helen (1912-). 1956. Winston. (P.600)
--*Safety for Sandy.* Neville, Vera (1900-1978). 1940. T. Nelson and Sons. (P.679)
--*Two Hundred Pennies.* Woolley, Catherine (1904-). 1947. W. Morrow. (P.978)
--*Winona's Pony Cart.* Lovelace, Maud Hart, Mrs. (1892-1980). 1953. Crowell. (P.587)

--*Velveteen Rabbit: Or, How Toys Become Real.* Bianco, Margery Williams, Mrs. (1881-1944). 1958. Doubleday. (P.100)

Nicklaus, Carol

--*Alph & Ralph.* Ingle, Annie. 1980. Dutton. (P.480)
--*Aurora Presents Don Bluth Productions' The Secret of Nimh: Mrs.* Brisby and the Magic Stone. Ingoglia, Gina, adapted by. c.1982. Golden Press. (P.480)
--*Big Bird Gets Lost.* Thackray, Patricia. c.1978. Western Pub. Co. (P.883)
--*The Bionic Banana.* Churchill, Elmer Richard (1937-) & Churchill, Linda R. (1938-). 1979. F. Watts. (P.195)
--*Elephant in the Kitchen.* Smith, Winsome. 1983. Scholastic Inc. (P.837)
--*Footprints in the Refrigerator.* Boyd, Selma & Boyd, Pauline. 1982. F. Watts. (P.122)
--*Harry the Hider.* Nicklaus, Carol. 1979. F. Watts. (P.681)
--*Hey, Kid!.* Gelman, Rita Golden (1937-). 1977. F. Watts. (P.363)
--*Hosea Globe and the Fantastical Peg-Legged Chu.* 1st ed. Beeks, Graydon (1919-). 1975. Atheneum. (P.88)
--*Hugh and Fitzhugh.* Goodspeed, Peter (1944-). 1974. Platt & Munk. (P.376)
--*I Can Dress Myself.* Dickson, Anna H. 1983. Western Pub. Co. (P.265)
--*If I Lived Alone: Featuring Jim Henson's Sesame Street Muppets.* Muntean, Michaela & Children's Television Workshop. Henson, James Maury (1936-), created by. c.1980. Western Pub. Co. (P.672)
--*Ivan the Great.* Cusack, Isabel Langis. c.1978. Crowell. (P.237)
--*Katy Rose Is Mad.* Nicklaus, Carol. c.1975. Platt & Munk. (P.681)
--*Konrad.* Nostlinger, Christine. Bell, Anthea, tr. from Ger. 1977. F. Watts. **Award: (MLB).** (P.687)
--*Look!* Look!. A Story Book. Heide, Florence Parry (1919-). 1971. E.P. Dutton & Co. (P.429)
--*Look!* Look! A Story Book. Heide, Florence Parry (1919-). 1971. McCall Pub. Co. (P.430)
--*Loosen Your Ears.* Farley, Carol J. (1936-). 1977. Atheneum. (P.317)
--*Mabel and the Rainbow.* Nicklaus, Carol. c.1975. Platt & Munk. (P.681)
--*Madge's Magic Show.* Thaler, Mike (1936-). 1978. F. Watts. (P.883)
--*Raggedy Ann and Andy and How Raggedy Ann Was Born.* Spinner, Stephanie (1943-), adapted by. c.1982. Bobbs-Merrill. (P.845)
--*Raggedy Ann's Sweet & Dandy, Sugar Candy.* Thackray, Patricia. 1977. Western Pub. (P.883)
--*Shadow, the Cigar-Smoking Cat.* 1st ed. Potter, Bronson & Ashworth, Rala. 1972. Atheneum. (P.733)
--*The Sick of Being Sick Book.* Stine, Jovial Bob, pseud. (1943-) & Stine, Jane. Stine, Robert Lawrence. Durrell, Ann, ed. 1982. Scholastic Inc. (P.858)
--*The Sick of Being Sick Book.* Stine, Jovial Bob, pseud. (1943-) & Stine, Jane. Stine, Robert Lawrence. 1980. Dutton. (P.858)
--*The Six-Million-Dollar Cucumber: Riddles and Fun for Children.* Churchill, Elmer Richard (1937-) & Churchill, Eric. 1976. F. Watts. (P.195)
--*Taffy Finds a Halloween Witch.* Pape, Donna Lugg (1930-). 1975. Garrard Pub. Co. (P.704)
--*That's Not Chester!.* Nicklaus, Carol. c.1975. Platt & Munk. (P.681)
--*What's That Noise?.* Nicklaus, Carol. c.1975. Platt & Munk. (P.681)

Nickless, Betty, photos by.

--*Skipper Coon's Security.* Nickless, Betty. 1966. Review and Herald Pub. Association. (P.681)

Nickless, Will (1902-)

--*The Book of Fables: Including Fables by La Fontaine, John Gay, Robert Dodsley, Christian Gellert, Gotthold Lessing, Claris De Florian, Ivan Kriloff, and Others.* La Fontaine, Jean De (1621-1695) & Gay, John. 1963, c.1962. Warne. (P.544)
--*The Further Adventures of Robinson Crusoe.* Treece, Henry (1911-1966). Defoe, Daniel (1660-1731), created by. 1958. Criterion Books. (P.899)
--*Owlglass.* Nickless, Will (1902-). 1964. John Day. (P.681)
--*Owlglass.* 1st ed. Nickless, Will (1902-). 1966, c.1964. John Day. (P.681)
--*Stories of Famous Sea Adventures.* Knight, Frank, pseud. (1905-). Knight, Francis Edgar. 1967. Westminster. (P.532)
--*Stories of Famous Ships.* Knight, Frank, pseud. (1905-). Knight, Francis Edgar. 1966. Westminster. (P.532)
--*The Ugly Duckling.* Andersen, Hans Christian (1805-1875). N.D. Penguin Books. (P.37)

Nicks, Anna S.

--*Then Marched the Brave.* Comstock, Harriet Theresa Smith, Mrs. (1860-). 1904. H. Altemus Company. (P.212)

Niclas, Yolla (1900-), photos by.

--*The Flower of Vassiliki: A Story of Greece.* Niclas, Yolla (1900-). 1968. Seabury Press. (P.681)

Nicolas, pseud., see Mordvinoff, Nicolas.

Nicolas, pseud. (1911-1973)

--*Alphonse, That Bearded One.* 1st ed. Mordvinoff, Nicolas. Carlson, Natalie Savage (1906-). 1954. Harcourt, Brace. **Award: (ALA).** (P.169)
--*Big Steve, the Double Quick Tunnelman.* Mordvinoff, Nicolas. Bloch, Marie Halun (1910-). 1952. Coward-McCann. (P.109)
--*Daniel Boone's Echo.* 1st ed. Mordvinoff, Nicolas. Steele, William Owen (1917-1979). 1957. Harcourt, Brace. (P.850)
--*Davy Crockett's Earthquake.* 1st ed. Mordvinoff, Nicolas. Steele, William Owen (1917-1979). 1956. Harcourt, Brace. (P.850)
--*Evangeline, Pigeon of Paris.* Mordvinoff, Nicolas. Carlson, Natalie Savage (1906-). 1960. Harcourt, Brace. (P.169)
--*Panchito.* Mordvinoff, Nicolas. Good, Loren D. 1956, c.1955. Coward-McCann. (P.375)
--*Russet & the Two Reds.* Mordvinoff, Nicolas. Nicolas, pseud. (1911-1973) & Will, pseud. (1904-1974). Mordvinoff, Nicolas. Lipkind, William. 1962. Hale. (P.682)

Nicoll, Bee

--*Wadleigh.* Carling, James L. 1980. Dutton. (P.168)

Nicollet

--*Poor Little Stephen Girard.* Twain, Mark, pseud. (1835-1910). Clemens, Samuel Langhorne. 1981. Schocken Books. (P.907)

Niefert, Bessie Potter

--*A Basket of Verses.* Chew, Nathaniel Durbin. c.1941. Dorrance and Company. (P.190)

Nielsen, Billie

--*Big Meeting Day and Other Festival Tales.* N.D. Aladdin Bks. (P.682)

Nielsen, Jon (1912-)

--*Adventures of Tom Sawyer.* Clemens, Samuel Langhorne (1835-1910). Twain, Mark, pseud. Sutton, Felix (1910-), adapted by. 1955. Wonder Books. (P.201)
--*Bamboo Key.* Wadsworth, Leda A. (1901-). 1948. Rinehart & Co. (P.923)
--*Boy on the Mayflower.* Vinton, Iris. 1965, c.1957. Four Winds Press Dist Scholastic. (P.920)
--*Cyrus McCormick: Farmer Boy.* Dobler, Lavinia G. (1910-). c.1961. Bobbs. (P.275)
--*Holiday in Alaska.* Savage, Alma Helen (1900-). c.1944. D. C. Heath and Company. (P.794)
--*Journey into Danger.* 1st ed. Faulkner, Nancy, pseud. (1906-). Faulkner, Anne Irvin. 1966. Doubleday. (P.319)
--*Little Giant.* De Quincey, A. 1946. Howell, Soskin. (P.259)
--*Little Lame Prince.* new ed. Craik, Dinah Maria Mulock, Mrs. (1826-1887). 1975. Collins Pubs. (P.227)
--*The Little Lame Prince.* Mulock, Dinah Maria, pseud. (1826-1887). Craik, Dinah Maria Mulock. 1948. World Pub. (P.671)
--*Pilgrim Neighbors: More True Pilgrim Stories.* Hall, Elvajean (1910-). 1964. Rand McNally. (P.404)
--*Pilgrim Stories: From Margaret Pumphrey's Pilgrim Stories.* Rev ed. Hall, Elvajean (1910-), ed. 1968, c.1962. Houghton. (P.405)
--*Pilgrim Stories: From Margaret Pumphrey's Pilgrim Stories.* Rev ed. Hall, Elvajean (1910-), ed. c.1962. Rand McNally. (P.405)
--*Puzzle of the Talking Monkey.* Wadsworth, Leda A. (1901-). 1947. Rinehart. (P.923)
--*The Undergrounders.* Bradbury, Bianca (1908-). c.1966. Washburn. (P.124)
--*Wild Bill Hickok.* Sutton, Felix (1910-). 1957, c.1956. Wonder Books. (P.872)
--*Wish on an Apple.* Garst, Doris Shannon (1899-). 1948. Abingdon-Cokesbury Press. (P.359)
--*The Wishing Pearl, and Other Tales of Vietnam.* Nielsen, Kay (1923-) & Nielsen, Jon (1912-). Lam Chan Quan, tr. 1969. Harvey House. (P.682)

Nielsen, Kay Rasmus (1886-1957)

--*East of the Sun & West of the Moon.* Asbjornsen, Peter Christen (1812-1885) & Moe, Jorgen Engebretsen (1813-1882). 1977. Doubleday. (P.51)
--*East of the Sun and West of the Moon: Old Tales from the North.* Asbjornsen, Peter Christen (1812-1885) & Moe, Jorgen Engebretsen (1813-1882). 1977. Doubleday. (P.51)
--*East of the Sun and West of the Moon: Old Tales from the North.* Asbjornsen, Peter Christen (1812-1885) & Moe, Jorgen Engebretsen (1813-1882). Dasent, George Webbe, Sir (1817-1896), tr. 1922. G. H. Doran Company. (P.51)
--*East of the Sun and West of the Moon: Old Tales from the North.* Asbjornsen, Peter Christen (1812-1885). Dasent, George Webbe, Sir (1817-1896), tr. N.D. Garden City Publishing Company, Inc. (P.51)
--*East of the Sun and West of the Moon: Old Tales from the North.* Asbjornsen, Peter Christen (1812-1885) & Moe, Jorgen Engebretsen (1813-1882). Dasent, George Webbe, Sir (1817-1896), tr. N.D. George H. Doran Company. (P.51)
--*Fairy Tales.* Andersen, Hans Christian (1805-1875). 1932. Garden City Publishing Company, Inc. (P.35)
--*Fairy Tales of Hans Christian Andersen.* Holme, Bryan (1913-), ed. 1981. Viking Pr. (P.456)
--*Fairy Tales of the Brothers Grimm.* Grimm, Jakob Ludwig Karl (1785-1863) & Grimm, Wilhelm Karl (1786-1859). Holme, Bayan, intro. by. 1979. Metropolitan Museum of Art. (P.391)
--*Fairy Tales of the Brothers Grimm.* Grimm, Jakob Ludwig Karl (1785-1863) & Grimm, Wilhelm Karl (1786-1859). Holme, Bryan (1913-), ed. 1979. Viking Pr. (P.391)
--*Fairytales.* Andersen, Hans Christian (1805-1875). 1981. Museum of Modern Art - Viking. (P.35)
--*Red Magic: A Collection of the World's Best Fairy Tales from All Countries.* O'Brien, Florence Roma Muir Wilson (1891-1930), ed. Wilson, Romer, pseud. c.1931. Harcourt, Brace & Company. (P.689)
--*Three Princesses in the Blue Mountains.* 1975. Seattle Bk. (P.682)
--*Three Princesses of Whiteland.* 1975. Seattle Bk. (P.682)
--*The Twelve Dancing Princesses and Other Fairy Tales.* Quiller-Couch, Arthur Thomas, Sir (1863-1944), retold by. 1930. Doubleday, Doran & Company, Inc. (P.745)
--*The Twelve Dancing Princesses and Other Fairy Tales.* Quiller-Couch, Arthur Thomas, Sir (1863-1944), retold by. 1923. George H. Doran Company. (P.745)

Niemann, Gail

--*Rabbits, Rabbits.* 1st ed. Fisher, Aileen Lucia (1906-). c.1983. Harper & Row. (P.328)

Nightingale, Paula

--*Katya and the Crocodile.* Gernet, Nina Vladimirovna (1904-) & Jagdfeld, G. Corrin, Stephen, tr. from Russian. 1968. Gerrards Cross, Smythe. (P.364)
--*Katya & the Crocodile.* Gernet, Nina Vladimirovna (1904-) & Jagdfeld, G. Corrin, Stephen, tr. 1969. Transatlantic. (P.364)

Nightingale, Sandy Ann

--*Hansel and Gretel.* Grimm, Jakob Ludwig Karl (1785-1863) & Grimm, Wilhelm Karl (1786-1859). c.1985. Random House. (P.393)
--*Rumpelstiltskin.* Daniels, Patricia, adapted by. 1980. Raintree Childrens Books. (P.241)

Nigognossian, Christine Willis

--*Thumbelina.* Andersen, Hans Christian (1805-1875). c.1979. Troll Associates. (P.37)

Nigro, Joanne

--*Look!* Look!. A/Clown Book. Reit, Seymour (1918-). 1962. Golden Press. (P.757)

Niizaka, Kazuo (1943-)

--*Clouds.* Bradford, Henry. 1975. Addison-Wesley. (P.124)
--*Clouds.* Niizaka, Kazuo (1943-). 1975. A-W. (P.682)

Nikolaki, Z. P.

--*Sylvia's Experiment: The Story of an Unrelated Family.* Chalmers, Margaret Rebecca Piper, Mrs. (1879-). Piper, Margaret Rebecca, pseud. 1914. The Page Company. (P.182)

Nikolsky, G.

--*Plutonia.* 1st ed. Obruchev, Vladimir Afanasevich. Solasko, Fainna, tr. from Russian. 1961. Criterion Books. (P.689)

Niland, Deborah, jt. illus. see Niland, Kilmeny.

Niland, Deborah (1951-)

--*Stuff & Nonsense.* Dugan, Michael Gray (1947-), ed. 1977, c.1974. Collins World. (P.287)
--*The Sugar-Plum Christmas Book: A Book For Christmas and All the Days of the Year.* Chapman, Jean. 1982. Children's Press. (P.186)
--*Velvet Paws & Whiskers.* Chapman, Jean. 1982. Childrens. (P.186)
--*When the Wind Changed.* Park, Rosina Ruth Lucia (0000-1967). 1981. Coward, McCann & Geoghegan. (P.705)

Niland, Kilmeny

--*Pancakes and Painted Eggs: A Book for Easter and All the Days of the Year.* Chapman, Jean. 1982. Children's Press. (P.186)

Niland, Kilmeny & Niland, Deborah (1951-)

--*The Gigantic Balloon.* Park, Rosina Ruth Lucia (0000-1967). 1976. Parents' Magazine Press. (P.705)
--*Mulga Bill's Bicycle.* Paterson, Andrew Barton (1864-1941). 1975. Scholastic Inc. (P.709)
--*Mulga Bill's Bicycle: Poem.* Paterson, Andrew Barton (1864-1941). 1975, c.1973. Parents' Magazine Press. (P.709)

Niles, Helen J.

--*The Doll that was Lost and Found.* Gates, Josephine Scribner, Mrs. (1859-1930). 1903. The Franklin Printing and Engraving Co. (P.360)

Nilsson, Lennart & Szasz, Suzanne Shorr

--*The Secret World of the Baby.* Day, Beth Feagles (1924-) & Liley, Helen Margaret Irwin (1928-). 1968. Random House. (P.248)

Nims, W. C.

--*Midnight Moon.* Lyons, Dorothy Marawee (1907-). c.1941. Harcourt, Brace and Company. (P.592)
--*Mr. Nip & Mr. Tuck in the Air.* Emerson, Caroline Dwight (1891-1973). 1946. E. P. Dutton and Company, Inc. (P.306)
--*Wild Palomino.* Thompson, Harlan H. (1894-). Holt, Stephen, pseud. N.D. Grosset & Dunlap. (P.887)
--*Wild Palomino.* Thompson, Harlan H. (1894-). Holt, Stephen, pseud. 1946. Longmans, Green and Co. (P.887)

Nino, Alex

--*Moby Dick.* new ed. Melville, Herman (1819-1891). Shapiro, Irwin (1911-), ed. 1973. Pendulum Pr. (P.640)
--*The Time Machine.* new ed. Wells, Herbert George (1866-1946). Binder, Otto, ed. 1973. Pendulum Pr. (P.945)

Ninon, pseud., see MacKnight, Ninon.

Ninon, pseud. (1908-)

--*ABC of Cars and Trucks.* 1st ed. MacKnight, Ninon. Alexander, Anne Barbara Cooke (1913-). c.1956. Doubleday. (P.22)
--*Songs for a Child.* MacKnight, Ninon. Weigl, Vally. c.1962. Westminster. (P.940)

Nipp, Susan

--*Wee Sing Campfire Songs.* Beall, Pamela. 1982. Price Stern. (P.85)
--*Wee Sing Silly Songs.* Beall, Pamela. 1982. Price Stern. (P.85)
--*Wee Sing Silly Songs Book & Cassette.* Beall, Pamela. 1983. Price Stern. (P.85)

Ni Rinn, Brid

--*Fionn and His Companions.* O'Grady, Standish James (1846-1928). 1970. Talbot Press. (P.691)

Nisbet, Noel Laura (1887-)

--*Cossack Fairy Tales and Folk Tales.* Bain, Robert Nisbet (1854-1909), ed. 1975. Kraus Reprint Co. (P.60)
--*The Enchanted Lochan: Stories of Celtic Mythology.* Brunton, F Carmichael. 1917. Thomas Y. Crowell Company. (P.145)

Nishimaki, Kayako

--*The Land of Lost Buttons.* Nishimaki, Kayako & Nakamura, Shigeo. Tresselt, Alvin R. (1916-), tr. 1970. Parents' Magazine Press. (P.683)

Nishino, Masahiko

--*Legends of Japan.* Naito, Hiroshi (1925-), retold by. 1972. Charles E. Tuttle. (P.675)

Nisson, Ken

--*Rattlesnake Run.* Lazarus, Keo Felker (1913-). 1968. Follett Pub. Co. (P.557)

Nister, Ernest

--*Animal Tales.* Nister, Ernest. N.D. Putnam Pub Group. (P.683)
--*Little Tales from Long Ago.* Nister, Ernest. 1979. Delacorte. (P.683)

Niswonger, Newall A.

--*Daisy.* Brasier, Inez. 1951. Southern Pub. Association. (P.128)

Nivola, Claire

--*Disobedient Eels.* Cimino, Maria. 1971. Pantheon. (P.196)
--*The Messy Rabbit.* Nivola, Ruth. 1978. Pantheon Books. (P.683)

Nix, Robert

--*Great Day in Holland: The Skating Race.* Rutgers van der Loeff-Basenau, Anna Maria Margaretha (1910-). Anthony, Henrietta, tr. from Dutch. c.1965. Abelard. (P.786)

Nixon, Gloria, jt. illus. see Armacost, Arlene.

Nixon, K., pseud., see Nixon, Kathleen Irene Blundell.

Nixon, Kathleen Irene Blundell see Nixon, K., pseud.

Nixon, Kathleen Irene Blundell

--*Animal Legends.* Nixon, Kathleen Irene Blundell, retold by. 1966. Warne. (P.683)
--*Animals and Birds in Folklore.* Nixon, K., pseud. Nixon, Kathleen Irene Blundell, retold by. Nixon, K., pseud. 1969. F. Warne. (P.683)
--*Animals & Birds in Folklore.* Nixon, Kathleen Irene Blundell. 1970. Warne. (P.683)
--*Pindi Poo.* Nixon, Kathleen Irene Blundell. Nixon, K., pseud. 1957. F. Warne. (P.683)
--*Pindi Poo.* Nixon, K., pseud. Nixon, Kathleen Irene Blundell. Nixon, K., pseud. 1959. Warne. (P.683)
--*Poo Pushti.* Nixon, Kathleen Irene Blundell. Nixon, K., pseud. c.1959. F. Warne. (P.683)
--*Puck's Broom: The Wonderful Adventures of George Henry & His Dog Alexander Who Went to Seek Their Fortunes in the Once Upon a Time Land.* Browne, Edgar Gordon (1871-). 1923. Moffat, Yard & Company. (P.143)
--*Pushti.* Nixon, Kathleen Irene Blundell. 1956. F. Warne. (P.683)
--*Strange Animal Friendships.* Nixon, K., pseud. Nixon, Kathleen Irene Blundell. Nixon, K., pseud. c.1967. Warne. (P.683)

--*Little Wolf and the Upstairs Bear: A Counting Story.* Obligado, Lilian Isabel (1931-). 1979. Viking Press. (P.689)
--*Lop Ear and Little Gray.* Friend, Morton. 1968. L. W. Singer Co. (P.346)
--*Magdalena.* 1st ed. Shotwell, Louisa Rossiter (1902-). 1971. Viking Press. (P.821)
--*Masie & the Persian Pink Petunias.* Olsen, Aileen. 1970. Abelard. (P.694)
--*Mr.* Toast and the Woolly Mammoth. Brent, Stuart. c.1966. Viking. (P.129)
--*My Friend.* Fulton, Mary J. 1973. Golden Press. (P.349)
--*The Mystery Gatepost.* Bothwell, Jean (0000-1977). 1964. Dial Press. (P.119)
--*The New Puppy.* Daly, Kathleen N. 1959. Golden Press. (P.240)
--*Nursery Rhymes.* c.1980. Golden Press. (P.689)
--*One Terrific Thanksgiving.* Sharmat, Marjorie Weinman (1928-). 1985. Holiday House. (P.815)
--*One to Make Ready.* Bragdon, Elspeth MacDuffle (1897-). 1959. Viking Press. (P.125)
--*Papa's Secret Chocolate Dessert.* Sharfman, Amalie. 1972. Lothrop, Lee & Shepard Co. (P.815)
--*Pickles and Jake.* 1st ed. Chenery, Janet Dai (1923-). 1977, c.1975. Puffin Books. (P.189)
--*Pickles and Jake.* Chenery, Janet Dai (1923-). 1975. Viking Press. (P.189)
--*The Pig That Ate Truffles.* MacIntyre, Carlyle Ferren (1890-). 1963. Golden Press. (P.604)
--*The Pig that Ate Truffles.* MacIntyre, C. F. 1963. Golden Press. (P.608)
--*Pinky in Persia.* Boyle, Kay (1903-). 1968. Crowell-Collier. (P.123)
--*Pinky in Persia.* Boyle, Kay (1903-). 1968. Macmillan Company. (P.123)
--*Pinky: The Cat Who Liked to Sleep.* Boyle, Kay (1903-). N.D. Crowell-Collier. (P.123)
--*Pinky, the Cat Who Liked to Sleep.* Boyle, Kay (1903-). 1968. Macmillan. (P.123)
--*Pussycat Tiger.* Bacon, Joan. 1972. Western Pub. (P.58)
--*Sad Day, Glad Day.* Thompson, Vivian Laubach (1911-). c.1962. Holiday House. (P.888)
--*The Secret Elephants.* Marsden, Catharine. c.1966. Dutton. (P.621)
--*The Story of the Three Bears.* 1980. Western Pub. (P.689)
--*The Taste of Spruce Gum.* 1st ed. Jackson, Jacqueline (1928-). 1966. Little Brown. **Award: (ALA).** (P.485)
--*There Is a Tide.* Bragdon, Elspeth MacDuffle (1897-). 1964. Viking Press. (P.125)
--*The Three Billy Goats Gruff.* Asbjornsen, Peter Christen (1812-1885) & Moe, Jorgen Engebretsen (1813-1882). Rudin, Ellen (1812-1885), retold by. c.1982. Golden Press. (P.51)
--*Three Little Kittens.* 1974. Random House. (P.689)
--*Trixie and the Tiger.* Cabassa, Victoria (1912-). 1967. Abelard-Schuman. (P.161)
--*Trixie and the Tiger.* Cabassa, Victoria (1912-). 1968. Abelard. (P.161)
--*The Wait-for-Me Kitten.* Scarry, Patricia Murphy (1924-). 1962. Western Pub. (P.796)
--*The White Marble.* Zolotow, Charlotte Shapiro (1915-). 1963. Abelard-Schuman. (P.994)
--*White Marble.* Zolotow, Charlotte Shapiro (1915-). 1963. E M Hale. (P.994)
--*Who's That in the Mirror?.* Berends, Polly Berrien, Mrs. (1939-). 1969, c.1968. Random House. (P.95)
--*Wise Dog.* 1st ed. Wright, Josephine Lord. c.1966. Dutton. (P.981)
--*The Wolf and the Seven Kids.* Grimm, Jakob Ludwig Karl (1785-1863) & Grimm, Wilhelm Karl (1786-1859). c.1978. Random House. (P.395)

Obrant, Susan (1946-)
--*Mother O'pearl: Three Tales.* Fletcher, David, pseud. (1940-). Barber, Dulan F.. 1970. Pantheon Books. (P.331)

O'Brian, William
--*All About Oscar, the Trained Seal.* Neikirk, Mabel E. 1943. The John C. Winston Company. (P.677)
--*The Ear Book.* Perkins, Albert Rogers (1904-1975). 1968. Random House. (P.718)
--*Hawk of Hawk Clan.* Johansen, Margaret Alison, Mrs. 1941. Longmans, Green and Co. (P.493)
--*Messenger to the Pharaoh: A/Story of Ancient Egypt.* 1st ed. Williamson, Thames Ross (1894-). De Wolfe, Morgan, pseud. 1937. Longmans, Green and Co. (P.965)

O'Brien, Harriet
--*Blue Treasure: The Mystery of Tamarind Court.* Girvan, Helen Masterman, Mrs. (1891-). c.1937. Farrar & Rinehart, Inc. (P.370)
--*The Friendly-Terrace Quartette: How Peggy and Priscilla and Amy and Ruth Did Their Share on the Farm and in the Shop.* Smith, Harriet Lummis, Mrs. 1920. The Page Company. (P.834)
--*Marjory the Circus Girl.* Allen, Alice E. 1918. The Page Company. (P.29)
--*Nancy Porter's Opportunity.* Taggart, Marion Ames (1866-). 1912. L. C. Page and Company. (P.876)
--*Our Little Finnish Cousin.* Winlow, Clara Vostrovsky, Mrs. (1876-). 1918. The Page Company. (P.969)
--*Our Little Polish Cousin.* Mendel, Florence Emma Voigt, Mrs. (1874-). 1912. L. C. Page & Company. (P.640)

O'Brien, John (1953-)
--*Circus!* Circus!. Poems. Hopkins, Lee Bennett (1938-), ed. c.1982. Knopf. (P.463)
--*Favorite Tales of Monsters and Trolls.* Jonsen, George, retold by. c.1977. Random House. (P.500)
--*Flapdoodle: Pure Nonsense from American Folklore.* Schwartz, Alvin (1927-), compiled by. 1980. Harper. (P.803)
--*Flapdoodle: Pure Nonsense from American Folklore.* 1st ed. Schwartz, Alvin (1927-), compiled by. c.1980. Lippincott. (P.803)
--*Macmillan Fairy Tale Alphabet Book.* Hall, Nancy Christensen. 1983. Macmillan. (P.406)
--*One Big Wish.* Williams, Jay (1914-1978). c.1980. Macmillan. (P.963)

O'Brien, Ken & Dempster, Al
--*Walt Disney's Snow White and the Seven Dwarfs.* Disney, Walter Elias (1901-1966). 1957. Golden Press. (P.272)

O'Brien, Thomas M.
--*You Can Find a Snail.* Miller, Patricia K & Seligman, Iran L. 1963. Holt, Rinehart and Winston. (P.649)

O'Brien, Warren S.
--*Adventures Along the Cumberland.* N.D. Vantage Press. (P.689)

Obrist, Jurg
--*Fluffy, the Story of a Cat.* Obrist, Jurg. 1979. Atheneum. (P.689)
--*The Lonely Prince.* Bolliger, Max (1929-). 1982, c.1981. Antheneum. (P.113)
--*The Miser Who Wanted the Sun.* Obrist, Jurg. 1984. Atheneum. (P.689)
--*The Perils of Putney.* 1st ed. Krensky, Stephen Alan (1953-). 1978. Atheneum. (P.539)
--*The Robot & Rebecca: The Mystery of the Code-Carrying Kids.* Yolen, Jane Hyatt (1939-). 1980. Knopf. (P.987)

Obschleger, Gail
--*Robert Benjamin and the Disappearing Act.* 1st ed. Grise, Jeannette, pseud. (1935-). Thomas, Jeannette Grise. c.1980. Westminster Press. (P.395)

O'Clery, Ann
--*The Mystery of Black Sod Point.* O'Clery, Helen Gallagher (1910-). 1959. Watts. (P.689)

O'Connell, Terence
--*The Test of Courage & All Things Come of Age.* O'Flaherty, Liam (1896-). 1984. Irish Bks Media. (P.691)

O'Connor, Barbara
--*Manny's Whale.* Starbuck, Deborah. 1985. Gemstone Books. (P.849)
--*The Menehune & the Nene.* Yamashita, Susan. 1984. Pr Pacifica. (P.985)

O'Connor, David & Sibbick, John
--*Gods and Pharaohs from Egyptian Mythology.* Harris, Geraldine. 1983. Schocken. (P.415)

O'Connor, John
--*Wood Is Sweet.* Clare, John. Powell, David, ed. 1968. Watts. (P.197)

O'Connor, John, jt. illus. see McPhail, Michael David.

O'Connor, Tim
--*Clown Book.* Slevin, Jeri S. 1980. Western Pub. (P.829)

O'D, Pat
--*Diddle Daddle Duckling.* Bennett, Grace Irene. 1934. Whitman Publishing Co. (P.93)

O'Donnell, Leo
--*The King's Spurs.* Carter, Russell Gordon (1892-1957). 1930. Little, Brown, and Company. (P.176)

O'Dwyer, Chung S. & Fwhang, Duk S.
--*Mi Jun's Difficult Decision.* Burkholder, Ruth C. 1984. Friend Pr. (P.154)

Oechsli, Kelly (1918-)
--*ABC Pigs Go to Market.* DeLage, Ida (1918-). c.1977. Garrard Pub. Co. (P.252)
--*Alphonse-the-Swordfish and Willie-the-Wisp.* 1st ed. Small, Richard Loring. 1963. Bobbs-Merrill. (P.830)
--*Arithmetic in Verse and Rhyme.* Jacobs, Allan Duane (1934-) & Jacobs, Leland Blair (1907-), eds. 1971. Garrard Pub. Co. (P.486)
--*Bear Before Breakfast.* Clifford, Eth, pseud. (1915-). Rosenberg, Ethel Clifford. 1962. Putnam. (P.202)
--*A Bear Before Breakfast.* Rosenberg, Ethel Clifford (1915-1978). Clifford, Eth, pseud. 1962. Putnam. (P.778)
--*The Birthday Car.* Hillert, Margaret (1920-). 1966. Follett Pub. Co. (P.444)
--*Boober Fraggle's Celery Souffle.* Gikow, Louise. 1984. HR&W. (P.366)
--*Boober Fraggle's Recipe.* Gikow, Louise. c.1984. Holt, Rhinehart, and Winston. (P.366)
--*The Bug Man.* Ward, Martha Eads (1921-). 1972. Abingdon Press. (P.931)
--*Christmas Trick or Treat.* Patterson, Lillie G. 1979. Garrard Pub. Co. (P.710)
--*Dear Dolphin.* Kenny, Herbert Andrew (1912-). 1967. Random House. (P.518)
--*The Dog Who Insisted He Wasn't.* 1st ed. Singer, Marilyn (1948-). c.1976. Dutton. (P.827)
--*The Dragon in the Clock Box.* Craig, M. Jean. 1962. W. W. Norton. **Award: (ALA).** (P.226)
--*The Dragon's Handbook.* Rinkoff, Barbara Jean Rich (1923-1975). c.1966. Nelson. (P.765)
--*The Easter Bunny's Secret.* Darling, Kathy, pseud. (1943-). Darling, Mary Kathleen. c.1978. Garrard Pub. Co. (P.242)
--*Eleven and Three Are Poetry.* Nohelty, Sally, ed. 1964. Holt. (P.684)
--*Everything Changes.* Philipson, Morris H. (1926-). 1972. Pantheon Books. (P.723)
--*Family for Sarah Ann.* Curren, Polly (1917-). 1962. Bobbs. (P.235)
--*Green Is Like a Meadow of Grass: An Anthology of Children's Pleasure in Poetry.* Larrick, Nancy (1910-), selected by. Lehigh University,Bethlehem, Pa. School of Education. 1968. Garrard Pub. Co. (P.552)
--*Hello, Pleasant Places!.* Jacobs, Leland Blair (1907-), ed. 1972. Garrard Pub. Co. (P.487)
--*Herbie's Troubles.* Chapman, Carol. c.1981. Dutton. (P.186)
--*Hidalgo and the Gringo Train.* 1st ed. Griffith, Fay. 1958. Dutton. (P.390)
--*House for Little Red.* Hillert, Margaret (1920-). 1970. Modern Curr. (P.444)
--*Humpty Dumpty's Bedtime Stories.* 1971. Parents' Magazine Press. (P.690)
--*Humpty Dumpty's Bedtime Stories.* Tresselt, Alvin R. (1916-), ed. 1971. Scholastic Inc. (P.900)
--*Humpty Dumpty's Holiday Stories.* 1973. Parents' Magazine Press. (P.690)
--*Humpty Dumpty's Holiday Stories.* 1973. Parent's Magazine Press. (P.690)
--*Humpty Dumpty's Holiday Stories.* Tresselt, Alvin R. (1916-), ed. 1973. Scholastic Inc. (P.900)
--*Hunting of the Snark.* Carroll, Lewis, pseud. (1832-1898). Dodgson, Charles Lutwidge. 1966. Pantheon. (P.173)
--*If I Could, I Would.* Collins, David Raymond (1940-). c.1979. Garrard Pub. Co. (P.210)
--*It's Schooltime.* Oechsli, Kelly (1918-). 1967. Holt, Rinehart and Winston. (P.690)
--*Jack Frost and the Magic Paint Brush.* Darling, Kathy, pseud. (1943-). Darling, Mary Kathleen. c.1977. Garrard Pub. Co. (P.242)
--*Joy Money.* Bartlett, Margaret Farrington (1896-). N.D. Duell. (P.78)
--*Monkey & the Bee.* Jacobs, Leland Blair (1907-). 1969. Western Pub. (P.487)
--*More of the Songs We Sing.* Coopersmith, Harry (1903-), ed. 1970. United Syn Bk. (P.218)
--*Oh, Tony: A Story About Sizes.* Daly, Eileen. 1971. Western Pub. (P.239)
--*Old Stormalong: Hero of the Seven Seas.* DeLeeuw, Adele Louise (1899-). 1967. Garrard. (P.254)
--*Old Stormalong: Hero of the Seven Seas.* DeLeeuw, Adele Louise (1899-). c.1967. Garrard Pub. Co. (P.254)
--*Peter Bull: An Old Danish Tale.* 1st ed. Oechsli, Helen, retold by. 1971. Viking Press. (P.690)
--*Piper, Pipe That Song Again!.* Poems for Boys and Girls. Larrick, Nancy (1910-). 1965. Random House. (P.552)
--*The Plaid Peacock.* Alan, Sandy (1909-). 1965. Pantheon Books. (P.16)
--*Playtime in the City.* Jacobs, Leland Blair (1907-), ed. 1971. Garrard Pub. Co. (P.487)
--*Poetry for Holidays.* Larrick, Nancy (1910-). c.1966. Garrard. (P.552)
--*Poetry for Spring.* Patterson, Lillie G. 1973. Garrard Pub. Co. (P.710)
--*Poetry for Winter.* Jacobs, Leland Blair (1907-), ed. 1970. Garrard Pub. Co. (P.487)
--*Red and the Pumpkins.* 1st ed. Stevenson, Jocelyn. Henson, Jim, pseud. (1936-), created by Henson, James Maury. c.1983. Muppet Press : Holt, Rinehart, and Winston. (P.855)
--*Sam on the Jolly Blue.* Nissen, Betty B. 1968. Random House. (P.683)
--*Seeds of Time: Selections from Shakespeare.* Shakespeare, William (1564-1616). Grohskopf, Bernice, compiled by. 1963. Atheneum. (P.814)
--*Story of Johnny Appleseed.* Anderson, LaVere Francis Shoenfelt (1907-). 1974. Garrard. (P.39)
--*Surprise!* Surprise! Guess What's Inside. Oechsli, Kelly (1918-). 1967. Holt, Rinehart and Winston. (P.690)
--*Ten Pennies for Candy.* Wing, Henry Ritchet. 1963. Holt, Rinehart and Winston. (P.969)
--*Up and Down the Escalator.* Martin, William Ivan, Jr. (1916-). 1970. Holt, Rinehart and Winston. (P.626)
--*Upside Down Day.* Scheer, Julian Weisel (1926-). 1968. Holiday House. (P.798)
--*Walter the Wolf.* Sharmat, Marjorie Weinman (1928-). 1975. Holiday House. (P.815)
--*Weeny Witch.* DeLage, Ida (1918-). 1968. Garrard Pub. Co. (P.252)

Oehler, Bernice
--*Chico the Circus Cherub.* May, Stella Burke, Mrs. 1928. D. Appleton & Company. (P.633)

Oehler, Bernice Olivia, jt. illus. see Norcross, Grace.

Oehler, Bernice Olivia (1881-)
--*The Boat with a Red Sail.* Peat, Emily May Caskill. c.1948. Saalfield Pub. Co. (P.714)
--*Bob Vincent: Veterinarian.* 1st ed. Evans, Edna Hoffman (1913-). 1949. E. P. Dutton. (P.311)
--*Chico's Three Ring School.* May, Stella Burke, Mrs. 1929. D. Appleton & Company. (P.633)
--*Song Wings.* Finn, William Joseph (1881-) & Scholastica, Mary (1893-), eds. c.1940. C. C. Birchard & Company. (P.326)

Oertel, et al.
--*Adventures in Fairy Land.* Stoddard, Richard Henry (1825-1903). N.D. Thomas R. Knox & Co. (P.860)

Offen, Hilda
--*A Treasury of Animal Stories.* Yeatman, Linda, ed. c.1982. Little Simon. (P.986)
--*A Treasury of Bedtime Stories.* Yeatman, Linda, ed. c.1981. Little Simon. (P.986)

Ogawa, Heidi
--*The Magnificent Pumpkin.* Plasmati, Valdine. 1959. Viking Press. (P.728)

Ogawa, Sanchi
--*Japanese Fairy Tales.* Williston, Teresa Peirce, retold by. 1904. Rand, McNally & Co. (P.965)
--*Japanese Fairy Tales.* Williston, Teresa Peirce, retold by. c.1911. Rand McNally & Co. (P.965)
--*Japanese Fairy Tales.* Williston, Teresa Peirce, retold by. 1932. Rand, McNally. (P.965)

Ogden, Caroline, jt. illus. see Hunter, Cecilia Bull.

Ogden, H. A.
--*A Boy of the First Empire.* Brooks, Elbridge Streeter (1846-1902). 1895. The Century Co. (P.136)
--*A Little Queen of Hearts: An International Story.* Ide, Frances Otis Ogden, Mrs. (1853-1927). c.1893. Frederick A. Stokes Company. (P.479)
--*A Loyal Little Red-Coat: A Story of Child-Life in New York a Hundred Years Ago.* Ide, Frances Otis Ogden, Mrs. (1853-1927). 1890. Frederick A. Stokes Company. (P.479)

Ogden, Ray
--*Thirteen Uncanny Tales.* Green, Roger Gilbert Lancelyn (1918-), compiled by. 1970. Dutton. (P.385)

Ogden, William
--*The Dog That Called the Signals.* Christopher, Matthew F. (1917-). c.1982. Little, Brown and Co. (P.194)
--*The Dog That Stole Football Plays.* Christopher, Matthew F (1917-). c.1980. Little, Brown. (P.194)
--*The Great McGoniggle Rides Shotgun.* 1st ed. Corbett, Scott (1913-). c.1977. Little, Brown. (P.219)
--*The Great McGoniggle Switches Pitches.* 1st ed. Corbett, Scott (1913-). c.1980. Little, Brown. (P.219)
--*The Great McGoniggle's Gray Ghost.* 1st ed. Corbett, Scott (1913-). 1975. Little, Brown. (P.219)
--*The Great McGoniggle's Key Play.* 1st ed. Corbett, Scott (1913-). c.1976. Little, Brown. (P.219)

Ogg, Oscar John (1908-1971)
--*Down the Ohio with Clark.* Lender, Charles Franklin. c.1937. Thomas Y. Crowell Company. (P.564)
--*The Green One.* Brodersen, Lelia. 1936. B. Mussey. (P.134)
--*The Knights at Bay.* Lindsay, Philip (1906-). c.1935. Loring & Mussey. (P.574)
--*Prairie Chautauqua.* Fargo, Lucille Foster (1880-). 1943. Dodd, Mead & Company. (P.316)

Ogilvie, Marta
--*George and Robert.* Ogilvie, Marta. c.1978. Flyingfish Press. (P.691)
--*Sailing on Firefly.* Ogilvie, Marta. c.1978. Flyingfish Press. (P.691)

Ogle, Richard B.
--*Claudius the Bee.* Leeming, John Fishwick (1895-). 1937. The Viking Press. (P.561)
--*He Sailed With Dampier.* Rush, Philip (1908-). 1947. Boardman. (P.784)
--*Thanks to Claudius.* Leeming, John Fishwick (1895-). 1939. The Viking Press. (P.561)

Ohanian, Nancy
--*Time Explorers, Inc.* Hildick, Edmund Wallace (1925-). c.1976. Doubleday. (P.442)

O'Hara, John
--*Guns for the Saratoga.* 1st ed. Meader, Stephen Warren (1892-). 1955. Harcourt, Brace. (P.637)

O'Hara, Marie
--*Animal Pets from Near and Far: A Book of True Stories.* Sloane, Anna Bogenholm. c.1927. Beckley-Cardy Company. (P.829)

--The Kewpies and Dotty Darling: Verse and Pictures. O'Neill, Rose Cecil (1874-). c.1912. George H. Doran Company. (P.694)
--The Kewpies and the Runaway Baby: Story and Pictures. O'Neill, Rose Cecil (1874-). 1928. Doubleday, Doran & Company, Inc. (P.695)
--A Little Question in Ladies' Rights. Fillmore, Parker Hoysted (1878-1944). 1916. John Lane Company. (P.325)
--Tomorrow's House: The Tiny Angel. O'Neil, George. 1930. E. P. Dutton & Co. (P.694)

O'Neill, Steve
--Doctor Dinosaur. Polhamus, Jean Burt. 1975. P-H. (P.730)

Onfroy De Breville, Jacques Marie Gaston (1858-)
--The Story of Naughty Kildeen. Maria Queen Consort of Ferdinand King of Rumania (1875-1938). 1922. H. Milford, Oxford University Press. (P.619)
--The Story of Naughty Kildeen. Maria Queen Consort of Ferdinand King of Rumania (1875-1938). 1927. Harcourt, Brace and Company. (P.619)

Ono, Chiyo (1941-)
--The Boy & the Bird. Fujita, Tamao (1905-). Tucker, Kiyoto, tr. from Japanese. 1972. John Day Co. (P.349)
--Which Way, Geta?. Ono, Chiyo (1941-). 1969. Nelson. (P.695)

Ono, Kaoru (1930-)
--Five Little Fingers. Ono, Kaoru (1930-). 1969. C. E. Tuttle Co. (P.695)

Onslow, Lola
--Oh! Dear, Dear!. Frankau, Ronald. N.D. Frederick Warne & Co. (P.341)

Onyshkewych, Zenowij
--Jenny's Corner. Bell, Frederic. 1974. Random House. (P.90)
--Sun Dust. Zumwalt, Eva (1936-). c.1976. D. McKay Co. (P.994)

Oonark
--I Breathe a New Song: Poems of the Eskimo. Lewis, Richard (1935-), ed. 1971. Simon. (P.570)

Oosterhous, Lucille J.
--Oops, Here Goes Perry. Oosterhous, Lucille J. N.D. Vantage Press. (P.695)

Operti, Albert, jt. illus. see Peary, Robert Edwin.

Opgenoorth, Winifried
--The Snowman Who Went for a Walk. Lobe, Mira. 1984. Morrow. (P.579)

Opitz, Marge
--Feathered Friends. Watts, Mabel Pizzey (1906-). 1957. Rand McNally. (P.937)
--Little Bear. Hunter, Virginia. c.1956. Rand McNally. (P.475)
--Little Deer. Zimmerman, Naoma (1914-). c.1956. Rand McNally. (P.993)
--Miss Frances Story Book of Pets for the Very Young. Horwich, Frances Rappaport (1908-), ed. 1956. Rand McNally. (P.465)
--Tim Trains His Terrier. Berrien, Edith Heal (1903-). 1952. A. Whitman. (P.97)
--What Happened to George!. Engebretson, Betty. 1958. Rand McNally. (P.307)

Oppenheimer, Amy V.
--Us Kids. Oppenheimer, Amy V. c.1932. S. Gabriel Sons & Company. (P.695)

Opper, Frederick Burr (1857-1937)
--Aesop's Fables. Aesopus. 1916. J. B. Lippincott Company. (P.13)
--Aesop's Fables. 2d ed. Aesopus. 1917. J. B. Lippincott Company. (P.13)
--Aesop's Fables. Aesopus. N.D. J. B. Lippincott. (P.13)
--Mother Goose's Nursery Rhymes. Mother Goose. 1900. J. B. Lippincott Company. (P.669)
--Mother Goose's Nursery Rhymes. Mother Goose. c.1916. J. B. Lippincott Company. (P.669)
--Slate-and-pencil People. Opper, Emma A. c.1885. White Stokes & Allan. (P.695)
--The Story of Happy Hooligan. Kinnaird, Marion. c.1932. McLoughlin Bros. (P.527)

Opper, John
--Roberta E. Lee. Davis, Burke (1913-). 1956. J. F. Blair. (P.245)

Oppermann-Dimov, Christina
--My Old Grandad. Harranth, Wolf. Carter, Peter, tr. 1984. Merrimack Pub Cir. (P.414)

Oram, Peter
--What's Happened to Auntie Jean?. White, Paul. 1976. Regal. (P.952)

Orbaan, Albert F. (1913-)
--The Bamboo School in Bali. Last, Jef, pseud. (1898-) & Tisna, Udayana Pandji. Last, Josephus Carel Franciscus. Moskin, Marietta (1928-), tr. from Dutch. 1969. J. Day. (P.553)
--Bamboo School in Bali. Tisna, Udayana Pandji & Last, Jef, pseud. (1898-1972). Last, Josephus Carel Franciscus. Moskin, Marietta Dunston (1928-), tr. 1969. John Day. (P.892)
--Blast-off!. Cassiday, Bruce Bingham (1920-). 1964. Doubleday. (P.177)
--Cappy and the River. Avery, Lynn, pseud. (1903-1979). Cole, Lois Dwight. 1960. Duell, Sloan and Pearce Pub. (P.56)
--Civil War Sailor. Werstein, Irving (1914-1971). c.1962. Doubleday. (P.946)
--Cliff Dwellers of Walnut Canyan. Fenton, Carroll Lane (1900-1969) & Alice, Epstein. 1960. John Day & Co. (P.322)
--Cross Among the Tomahawks. 1st ed. Lomask, Milton Nachman (1909-). c.1961. Doubleday. (P.581)
--Danny & the Great Ape Komba. Gardner, Richard A. (1931-). 1962. John Day. (P.355)
--The Dark Keep. Alter, Robert Edmond (1925-1965). 1962. Putnam. (P.31)
--The Day of the Arkansas. Alter, Robert Edmond (1925-1965). c.1965. Putnam. (P.31)
--Desperate Voyage. 1st ed. Armstrong, Rodolfo L (1918-). 1953. Dutton. (P.48)
--A Farm for Juliana. 1st ed. Dilliard, Maud Esther (1916-). 1951. Dutton. (P.266)
--The Gold Penny. Blanton, Catherine (1907-). 1957. J. Day Co. (P.108)
--The Golden Glory. 1st ed. McMeekin, Isabel McLennan (1895-). 1963. Duell, Sloan and Pearce. (P.609)
--Gunpowder Girl. Savage, Josephine. 1958. J. Day Co. (P.794)
--Hidden Pond. 1st ed. Girvan, Helen Masterman, Mrs. (1891-). 1951. Dutton. (P.370)
--The Hidey Hole: The Mystery of the Old Winslow Homestead. Clinard, Dorothy Long (1909-) & Newby, Dorothy D. (1909-). 1960. Duell, Sloan and Pearce. (P.203)
--High Spy. Alter, Robert Edmond (1925-1965). 1967. Putnam. (P.31)
--Jack Wade, Fighter for Liberty. 1st ed. Werstein, Irving (1914-1971). 1963. Doubleday. (P.946)
--Jayhawker Johnny. Burt, Olive Frank Woolley (1894-). 1966. John Day. (P.157)
--John Charles Fremont: Trail Marker of the Old West (January 21, 1813-July 13, 1890). Burt, Olive Frank Woolley (1894-). 1955. J. Messner. (P.157)
--Kent Barstow, Space Man. Montgomery, Rutherford George (1894-). 1961. Duell, Sloan Pearce. (P.658)
--Keys to Fortune. 1st ed. McGuire, Frances Lynch (1869-1947). 1954. Dutton. (P.603)
--The Laughing Falcon. Whitehouse, Arthur George Joseph (1895-1979). Whitehouse, Arch, pseud. 1969. Putnam. (P.953)
--A Long Ago Christmas. Martin, Patricia Miles (1899-). 1968. Putnam. (P.625)
--The Lost Wagon. Kjelgaard, James Arthur (1910-1959). 1955. Dodd Mead. (P.530)
--Lucky Four. Graff, Polly Anne Colver (1908-). 1960. Duell, Sloan and Pearce. (P.380)
--Mike Mars and the Mystery Satellite. 1st ed. Wollheim, Donald Allen (1914-). 1963. Doubleday. (P.974)
--Mike Mars Around the Moon. Wollheim, Donald Allen (1914-). 1964. Doubleday. (P.974)
--Mike Mars, Astronaut. 1st ed. Wollheim, Donald Allen (1914-). 1961. Doubleday. (P.974)
--Mike Mars at Cape Canaveral. 1st ed. Wollheim, Donald Allen (1914-). 1961. Doubleday. (P.974)
--Mike Mars Flies the Dyna-Soar. 1st ed. Wollheim, Donald Allen (1914-). 1962. Doubleday. (P.974)
--Mike Mars Flies the X-15. 1st ed. Wollheim, Donald Allen (1914-). 1961. Doubleday. (P.974)
--Mike Mars, South Pole Spaceman. 1st ed. Wollheim, Donald Allen (1914-). 1962. Doubleday. (P.974)
--Morgan's Long Rifles. Taylor, Allan (1897-). 1965. Putnam. (P.879)
--Murphy Higheagle, Paratrooper. Chamberlain, William Edwin (1903-). 1966. John Day. (P.182)
--No Room for a Dog. Holland, Marion (1908-). 1959. Random House. (P.455)
--Oh, Susanna!. Williams, Dorothy Jeanne (1930-). Williams, J. R., pseud. 1963. Putnam. (P.962)
--Pennywink Carnival. 1st ed. Clark, Electa (1910-). 1950. Bobbs-Merrill. (P.197)
--The Pennywinks. 1st ed. Clark, Electa (1910-). 1949. Bobbs-Merrill Co. (P.197)
--Putt-Putt Skipper. Wriston, Hildreth Tyler. 1958. Ariel Books. (P.982)
--Rabble on a Hill. Alter, Robert Edmond (1925-1965). 1964. Putnam. (P.31)
--The Rattlesnake God. Holden, John. 1959. John Day Co. (P.453)
--Rough Water. Pertwee, Roland (1885-1963). 1957. Bobbs-Merrill Co. (P.720)
--Scarlet Streamers. Whitehouse, Arthur George Joseph (1895-1979). Whitehouse, Arch, pseud. 1967. Putnam. (P.953)
--The Secret of Barnegat Light. McGuire, Frances lynch (1869-1947). N.D. Dutton. (P.603)
--The Shadow of Robbers' Roost. 1st ed. Rushmore, Helen (1898-). 1960. World Pub. Co. (P.784)
--Spies with Wings. Whitehouse, Arthur George Joseph (1895-1979). Whitehouse, Arch, pseud. 1967, c.1966. Putnam. (P.953)
--Thunder Rolling: The Story of Chief Joseph. Miller, Helen Markley (1899-). 1959. Putnam's Sons. (P.647)
--Time Machine to the Rescue. Keith, Donald, pseud. (1917-). Monroe, Keith. 1967. Putnam. (P.513)
--To Race Again. Green, Anne M. (1922-). 1961. T. Nelson. (P.384)
--The Twins of Old Flatbush. 1st. ed. Dilliard, Maud Esther (1916-). 1952. Dutton. (P.266)
--Two Sieges of the Alamo. Alter, Robert Edmond (1925-1965). c.1965. Putnam. (P.32)
--Warrior's Moon. Capon, Paul (1912-1969). 1964. Putnam. (P.166)
--We Were There on the Santa Fe Trail. Taylor, Ross McLaury (1909-1977). Webb, Walter Prescott (1913-), ed. 1960. Grosset & Dunlap. (P.880)
--Wishing Boy of New Netherland. 1st ed. Dilliard, Maud Esther (1916-). 1950. Dutton. (P.266)
--Wishing Boy of New Netherland. Dilliard, Maud Esther (1916-). N.D. E. P. Dutton & Co. (P.266)

Orbaau, Albert F. (1913-)
--The Sound of Axes. Smith, Fredrika Shumway (1877-1968). c.1965. Rand McNally. (P.833)

Orbach, Ruth Gary (1941-)
--Acorns and Stew. Orbach, Ruth Gary (1941-). c.1975. Collins. (P.695)
--Apple Pigs. Orbach, Ruth Gary (1941-). 1977, c.1976. Collins. (P.695)
--Please Send a Panda. Orbach, Ruth Gary (1941-). 1978. Collins. (P.695)

Orban, Paul
--Cave of Danger. Walton, Bryce (1918-). 1967. Crowell. (P.929)
--Father of the American Navy, John Barry. Anderson, Floyd (1906-). 1959. Benziger Bros. (P.39)

Orczy, Emma Magdelena Rosalia Maria Josefa Barbara, jt. illus. see Barstow, Montagu.

Ordell, Dorothy Fuller
--Red Shoes: Thoughts by Carlisle Ellis. Barrett, Katharine Ruth Ellis, Mrs. (1879-). 1930. The Woman Press. (P.75)

Ordway, Jerry
--Four Golden Everything Workbooks: Featuring Marvel Superheroes. Gregg, Leslie. 1980. Western Pub. (P.388)

Oreb, Tom
--Walt Disney's Once upon a Wintertime. Disney, Walter Elias (1901-1966). Oreb, Tom, ed. Disney Walt, Studio 1950. Golden Press. (P.272)

Orehek, Don
--Gag Galaxy: Outer Space Jokes and Riddles. tempo library ed. Poole, Gary Thomas (1931-). c.1980. Tempo Books. (P.731)

O'Reilly, E. Dorothy
--A Child's Garden of Verses. Stevenson, Robert Louis (1850-1894). c.1908. A. Flanagan Co. (P.856)
--A Child's Garden of Verses. Stevenson, Robert Louis (1850-1894). 1923. A. Flanagan Co. (P.856)
--Escape at Bedtime and Other Poems. Stevenson, Robert Louis (1850-1894). 1922. A. Flanagan Company. (P.857)
--My Shadow, and other Poems. Stevenson, Robert Louis (1850-1894). 1922. Flanagan Co. (P.857)
--My Ship and I, and other Poems. Stevenson, Robert Louis (1850-1894). 1922. Flanagan Co. (P.857)
--My Treasure, and other Poems. Stevenson, Robert Louis (1850-1894). 1922. A. Flanagan Co. (P.857)

O'Reilly, Susan
--Arkansas Stories. 1st ed. Simon, Charlie May, Mrs., pseud. (1897-). Fletcher, Charlie May Hogue. Hagen, Lyman B, ed. 1981. August House. (P.824)
--Christmas Every Friday, and Other Christmas Stories. Simon, Charlie May, Mrs., pseud. (1897-). Fletcher, Charlie May Hogue. Hagen, Lyman B., ed. 1981. August House. (P.824)

Orellana, Ramon F.
--Grandmother Orphan. Green, Phyllis (1932-). 1975. J. Philip O'Hara Inc. (P.385)
--I Wished I Lived at the Playground: Yo Quisiera Vivir En un Parque De Juegos. Nims, Bonnie. Orellana, Ramon S., tr. 1972. O'Hara. (P.683)

Oreshnik, A. F., pseud., see Nussbaum, Albert F..

Oreshnik, A. F., pseud. (1934-)
--The Demeter Star. Nussbaum, Albert F.. Oreshnik, A. F., pseud. (1934-). Nussbaum, Albert F.. 1978. Childrens. (P.695)
--The Demeter Star. Nussbaum, Albert F.. Oreshnik, A. F, pseud. (1934-). Nussbaum, Albert F.. c.1977. Fearon-Pitman Publishers. (P.695)

Orfe, Joan
--From Sea to Shining Sea. Hein, Lucille Eleanor (1915-). c.1975. Judson Press. (P.430)
--Happy Birthday. Kerr, Pearl. 1969. Judson. (P.520)
--My Very Special Friend. Hein, Lucille Eleanor (1915-). 1974. Judson Press. (P.430)
--A Tree I Can Call My Own. Hein, Lucille Eleanor (1915-). 1974. Judson Press. (P.430)
--Walking in God's World. Hein, Lucille Eleanor (1915-). 1972. Judson Press. (P.430)

Orlando, Joe, jt. illus. see Andru, Ross.

Orlando, Rosalie
--I Didn't Want to Be Nice. Jones, Penelope (1938-). c.1977. Bradbury Press. (P.500)

Orloff, Denis
--Game Plan for Disaster. Dixon, Franklin W, pseud. Stratemeyer Syndicate. c.1982. Wanderer Books. (P.273)
--Trapped at Sea. Dixon, Franklin W, pseud. Stratemeyer Syndicate. c.1982. Wanderer Books. (P.274)

Orloff, Gregory
--Adventures Fishing. Egan, Evelyn & Hurlbert, Delpha. 1959. Benefic Press. (P.298)
--Adventures with Animals. Sandrus, Mary Yost. 1958. Scott, Foresman. (P.792)
--Heroes All: Tales of Real Dogs. Pease, Eleanor Fairchild, Mrs. 1940. A. Whitman. (P.714)
--In Reindeer Land. Thorsmark, Thora. 1942. Row, Peterson and Company. (P.890)
--The Luck of the House: The Story of a Family and a Sword. Bedford-Atkins, Gladys. 1938. A. Whitman & Co. (P.88)

Orlowski, Dennis
--I Have a Stepfamily... But. Kirkland, Dianna C. 1981. Aid-U Pub. (P.529)
--Last Year I Failed...But. Kirkland, Dianna C. 1981. Aid-U Pub. (P.529)
--My Dad Is Unemployed... but. Morris-Vann, Artie M. 1981. Aid-U Pub. (P.664)

Ormai, Stella
--Bizzy Bones and Uncle Ezra. Martin, Jacqueline Briggs. 1984. Lothrop. (P.624)
--Creatures: Poems. Hopkins, Lee Bennett (1938-). c.1985. Harcourt Brace Jovanovich. (P.463)
--Creatures: Poetry. Hopkins, Lee Bennett (1938-), ed. 1985. Farrar Strauss. (P.463)
--Mystery at Mouse House. Hare, Norma Quarles (1924-). c.1980. Garrard Pub. Co. (P.412)
--Shadow Magic. Simon, Seymour (1931-). 1985. Lothrop. (P.825)

Ormerod, Jan
--Dad's Back. Ormerod, Jan. 1985. Lothrop, Lee & Shepard Books. **Award: (ALA).** (P.696)
--Moonlight. Ormerod, Jan. c.1982. Lothrop, Lee & Shepard Books. **Award: (ALA).** (P.696)
--One-Hundred-One Things to Do With a Baby. Ormerod, Jan. 1984. Lothrop. (P.696)

Ormsbee, J. & Ryland, R. K.
--Ben, the Battle Horse: A Story of the Great War. Dyer, Walter Alden (1878-1943). 1919. H. Holt and Company. (P.293)

Ormsby, Virginia Haire
--The Big Banyan Tree. Ormsby, Virginia Haire. 1964. Lippincott. (P.696)
--Cunning Is Better Than Strong. 1st ed. Ormsby, Virginia Haire. 1960. Lippincott. (P.696)
--Here We Go. Ormsby, Virginia Haire. 1955. Lippincott. (P.696)
--It's Saturday. Ormsby, Virginia Haire. 1956. Lippincott. (P.696)
--The Little Country Schoolhouse. Ormsby, Virginia Haire. 1958. Lippincott. (P.696)
--Long, Lonesome Train Whistle. 1st ed. Ormsby, Virginia Haire. 1961. Lippincott. (P.696)
--Right-Handed Horse. Ormsby, Virginia Haire. 1963. Lippincott. (P.696)
--Twenty-One Children. Ormsby, Virginia Haire. 1957. Lippincott. (P.696)
--Twenty-One Children Plus Ten. Ormsby, Virginia Haire. 1971. Lippincott. (P.696)
--What's Wrong with Julio?. Ormsby, Virginia Haire. 1965. Lippincott. (P.696)

O'Rosson, Shawn, jt. illus. see Nyce, Helen Von Strecker.

Orpen, Mary-Amy
--Mr. Hobbs Can Fix It. Pickard, Vera E. 1948. Abingdon-Cokesbury Press. (P.725)
--Mr. Hobbs Can Fix it. Pickard, Vera E. 1948. Abingdon. (P.725)

Orr, Charles & White, Martin
--A Second Poetry Book. Foster, John Lawrence (1930-), ed. 1982. Merrimack Pub Cir. (P.338)

Orr, Chris (1943-) & White, Martin
--A First Poetry Book. Foster, John Lawrence (1930-), compiled by. 1982. Merrimack Pub Cir. (P.338)
--A First Poetry Book. Foster, John Lawrence (1930-), ed. 1979. Oxford University Press. (P.338)

Orr, Forrest
--The Red Dory. Wilson, Hazel Hutchins, Mrs. (1898-). 1939. Little, Brown and Company. (P.966)

Orr, Forrest W.
--Cynthia of Bee Tree Hollow. Fox, Genevieve May. 1948. Little, Brown. (P.340)
--The Dawn Hill Brand: A Story of Australia. Ross, Margaret Isabel (1897-). 1939. Houghton Mifflin Company. (P.779)
--Green Treasure. Fox, Genevieve May. 1941. Little, Brown and Company. (P.340)
--High-Water Cargo. Dorian, Edith Mc Ewen (1900-). 1965. Rutgers. (P.280)

--*Dressing.* Oxenbury, Helen (1938-). 1981. Simon & Schuster. (P.699)
--*Eating Out.* Oxenbury, Helen (1938-). c.1983. Dial Press. (P.699)
--*Elephant Girl.* Cutler, Ivor (1923-). 1976, c.1975. Morrow. (P.237)
--*First Day of School.* Oxenbury, Helen (1938-). 1983. Dutton. (P.699)
--*Good Night, Good Morning.* Oxenbury, Helen (1938-). 1982. Dial Press. (P.699)
--*Grandma and Grandpa.* Oxenbury, Helen (1938-). 1984. Dial Books for Young Readers. (P.699)
--*The Great Big Enormous Turnip.* Tolstoy, Aleksei Nikolaevich (1882-1945). 1968. F. Watts. (P.894)
--*The Great Big Enormous Turnip.* Tolstoy, Aleksei Nikolaevich (1882-1945). 1969. Watts. (P.894)
--*The Helen Oxenbury Nursery Story Book.* Oxenbury, Helen (1938-). c.1985. Knopf : Distributed by Random House. (P.699)
--*Hunting of the Snark.* Carroll, Lewis, pseud. (1832-1898). Dodgson, Charles Lutwidge. 1971. Watts. (P.173)
--*The Important Visitor.* Oxenbury, Helen (1938-). 1984. Dial Bks Young. (P.699)
--*Letters of Thanks.* Kempadoo, Manghanita. 1969. Simon & Schuster. (P.517)
--*Meal One.* Cutler, Ivor (1923-). 1971. F. Watts. (P.237)
--*Monkey See, Monkey Do.* Oxenbury, Helen (1938-). c.1982. Dial Press. (P.699)
--*Mother's Helper.* Oxenbury, Helen (1938-). c.1982. Dial Press. (P.699)
--*Numbers of Things.* Oxenbury, Helen (1938-). 1968. F. Watts. (P.699)
--*Our Dog.* Oxenbury, Helen (1938-). 1984. Dial Bks for Young Readers. (P.699)
--*Pig Tale.* Oxenbury, Helen (1938-). 1973. Morrow. (P.699)
--*Playing.* Oxenbury, Helen (1938-). 1981. Simon & Schuster. (P.699)
--*The Quangle Wangle's Hat.* Lear, Edward (1812-1888). 1970. Watts. **Award: (KGM).** (P.558)
--*The Queen and Rosie Randall.* Oxenbury, Helen (1938-). 1979. Morrow. (P.699)
--*Shopping Trip.* Oxenbury, Helen (1938-). c.1982. Dial Press. (P.699)
--*Tiny Tim.* Oxenbury, Helen (1938-) & Bennett, Jill (1947-), eds. N.D. Delacorte. (P.699)
--*Tiny Tim: Verses for Children.* Bennett, Jill (1947-), selected by. 1982. Delacorte. (P.94)
--*Working.* Oxenbury, Helen (1938-). 1981. Simon & Schuster. (P.699)

Oxenham, J.
--*Mystery Stories for Girls.* Oxenham, J., ed. 1969. Western Pub. (P.699)

Ozone, Lucy
--*Little Duckling.* Wing, Helen. c.1956. Rand McNally. (P.969)

Paamoni, Zev
--*Aaron, the High Priest.* Paamoni, Zev. 1970. Shulsinger Sales. (P.699)
--*The Adventures of Jacob.* Paamoni, Zev. 1970. Shulsinger Sales. (P.699)
--*Benjamin, the Littlest Brother.* Paamoni, Zev. 1970. Shulsinger Sales. (P.699)
--*Yitzchak, Son of Abraham.* Paamoni, Zev. 1970. Shulsinger Sales. (P.699)

Pache, Jocelyne
--*The Fantastic Story of King Brioche, the First.* Jenny, Anne. 1973, c.1970. Lothrop, Lee & Shepard Co. (P.492)

Pack, Elizabeth, jt. illus. see Ayer, Margaret.

Packard, H. W.
--*Our Little Saxon Cousin of Long Ago: Being the Story of Turgar, a Boy of Anglo-Saxons, in the Time of Alfred the Great.* Cowles, Julia Darrow, Mrs. (1862-1919). 1916. The Page Company. (P.225)
--*Our Little Viking Cousin of Long Ago, Being the Story of Biarne Herjulfson, a Boy of Norway.* Johnston, Charles Haven Ladd (1877-1943). 1916. The Page Company. (P.497)

Padersen, V., jt. illus. see Weir, Harrison William.

Padgett, Jim
--*Ahmed, Boy of Jerusalem.* Barstad, Glenna & Thomsen, Halvard J. c.1965. Southern Pub. (P.77)
--*A Boy Hears Stories From the Old Testament.* Fraser, Edith Emily Rose Oram (1903-). 1967. Abingdon. (P.342)
--*Butterfly Blue.* Wilhelm, Kathryn Stephenson (1915-). 1966. Southern Pub. Association. (P.960)
--*Children of the Four Winds.* Sparks, Enid. 1969. Southern Pub. Association. (P.842)
--*Come Meet My Friends Who Work at Church.* Caton, Dorothy Webber. 1964. Abingdon Press. (P.178)
--*Come, Walk with Me.* Perkins, Barbara C. 1968. Broadman. (P.718)
--*Donkey Tales.* Pelaez, Jill (1924-). 1971. Abingdon Press. (P.716)
--*The Eagle that Went to War and Other Stories.* Paddock, Charles Lee (1891-). 1962. Southern Pub, Association. (P.700)
--*The Hot Brick, and Other Stories.* Wilhelm, Kathryn Stephenson (1915-). 1966. Southern Pub. Association. (P.960)
--*John the Baptist: Forerunner of Jesus.* Human, Johnnie. 1978. Broadman. (P.472)
--*Kamwendo.* Edwards, Josephine Cunnington (1904-). 1966. Southern Pub. Assn. (P.297)
--*The Little Church That Grew.* Young, Lois Horton (1911-1981). 1965. Abingdon Press. (P.990)
--*Louisiana Stories for Boys and Girls.* Bougere, Marguerite Bondy, ed. 1966. Louisiana State University Press. (P.120)
--*Margie Asks Why.* Winn, Laura Rocke (1902-). 1963. Southern Pub. Assn. (P.969)
--*Montana Meadow Star.* Bartlett, Alice Wiles. 1965. Southern Pub. Association. (P.77)
--*Once Upon a Summer.* Parker, Lois Mary (1912-). 1970. Southern Pub. Association. (P.706)
--*Peewee.* Crow, Bertha. c.1963. Southern Pub. Association. (P.233)
--*Pony Boy.* Peden, Pearle. 1963. Southern Pub. Association. (P.715)
--*Rupert Piper & the Boy Who Could Knit.* Parkinson, Ethelyn Minerva (1906-). c.1979. Abingdon. (P.707)
--*The Secret of Big Skookum.* Schumann, Elizabeth Creighton (1907-). 1963. Abingdon. (P.803)
--*Through the Week with Jesus.* Sparks, Enid. 1968. Southern Pub. Association. (P.842)
--*To Find Jesus.* Peterson, Barbara N. & Peterson, Edward C. 1967. Abingdon. (P.721)
--*The Walking River: And Other Stories.* Branch, Mary (1910-). 1969. Southern Pub. Association. (P.126)

Padgett, Jim & Gretzer, John
--*Our Happy Family.* Elkins, Ella Ruth (1929-). 1967. Southern Pub. Association. (P.301)

Padilla, Stan (1945-)
--*Song of the Seven Herbs.* Walking Night Bear, pseud. Binder, Henryk. 1983. Gold Circle Productions. (P.926)

Paek, Min
--*Aekyung's Dream.* Paek, Min. 1979. Childrens Book Pr. (P.700)

Paflin, Roberta, pseud., see Petty, Roberta Harris Pfafflin.

Paflin, Roberta, jt. illus. see Kennedy, A. E.

Paflin, Roberta, jt. illus. see Russell, Mary La Fetra.

Paflin, Roberta, pseud. (1903-)
--*Ann Porter, Nurse: A Career Story for Older Girls.* Petty, Roberta Harris Pfaflin. Anderson, Betty Baxter. 1942. Cupples & Leon Co. (P.38)
--*Baxter Beaver.* Petty, Roberta Harris Pfafflin. Chaffee, Letitia. 1942. David McKay Company. (P.181)
--*Connie Benton, Reporter: A Career Story for Older Girls.* Petty, Roberta Harris Pfafflin. Anderson, Betty Baxter. c.1941. Cupples & Leon Company. (P.38)
--*Counting Rhymes.* Petty, Roberta Harris Pfafflin. Reed, Mary Maud (1880-1960), ed. 1942. Simon & Schuster. (P.753)
--*Five Little Peppers and How They Grew.* Petty, Roberta Harris Pfafflin. Lothrop, Harriet Mulford Stone, Mrs. (1844-1924). Sidney, Margaret, pseud. 1951. Whitman Pub. Co. (P.586)
--*The Gingerbread House.* Petty, Roberta Harris Pfafflin. Andrews, Frank Emerson (1902-1978). 1943. Oxford University Press. (P.41)
--*Good Night.* Petty, Roberta Harris Pfafflin. Burrowes, Elisabeth. c.1954. Whitman Pub. Co. (P.156)
--*Julia Brent of the WAAC: A Career Story for Older Girls.* Petty, Roberta Harris Pfafflin. Anderson, Betty Baxter. 1943. Cupples & Leon Company. (P.38)
--*Just Jenifer.* Petty, Roberta Harris Pfaflin. Lambert, Janet (1895-1973). 1945. E. P. Dutton & Company, Inc. (P.546)
--*The Little Dog That Would Not Wag His Tail.* Petty, Roberta Harris Pfafflin. Deihl, Edna Groff, Mrs. (1881-1935). c.1941. S. Gabriel Sons & Company. (P.251)
--*The Little Kitten That Would Not Wash Its Face.* Petty, Roberta Harris Pfafflin. Deihl, Edna Groff, Mrs. (1881-1935). c.1941. S. Gabriel Sons & Company. (P.251)
--*Little Thunder.* Petty, Roberta Harris Pfafflin. Burrowes, Elisabeth. 1945. E. P. Dutton & Co., Inc. (P.156)
--*Miss Canary, If You Please.* Petty, Roberta Harris Pfafflin. Chaffee, Letitia. 1942. Cupples and Leon Company. (P.181)
--*Mother Goose Tells Time.* Petty, Roberta Harris Pfafflin. Mother Goose. Schneider, Alice, ed. 1945. The Citadel Press. (P.668)
--*Nancy Blake, Copywriter: A Career Story for Older Girls.* Petty, Roberta Harris Pfafflin. Anderson, Betty Baxter. 1942. Cupples & Leon Company. (P.38)
--*The Night Before Christmas.* Petty, Roberta Harris Pfafflin. Moore, Clement Clarke (1779-1863). 1944. E. P. Dutton & Co. (P.660)
--*Peek a Boo.* Petty, Roberta Harris Pfafflin. Chaffee, Letitia. c.1942. Cupples & Leon Company. (P.181)
--*Peggy Wayne, Sky Girl: A Career Story for Older Girls.* Petty, Roberta Harris Pfafflin. Anderson, Betty Baxter. c.1941. Cupples & Leon Company. (P.38)
--*Sky Service.* Petty, Roberta Harris Pfafflin. Lansing, Elisabeth Carleton Hubbard (1911-). 1939. Thomas Y. Crowell Company. (P.551)
--*Susie Cucumber: She Writes Letters.* Petty, Roberta Harris Pfaflin. Richardson, Cynthia B. 1944. S. Gabriel Sons & Company. (P.762)
--*Tales from Andersen.* Petty, Roberta Harris Pfafflin. Andersen, Hans Christian (1805-1875). Wright, Sarah K, ed. 1946. E. P. Dutton & Co., Inc. (P.37)
--*Tales from Grimm.* Petty, Roberta Harris Pfafflin. Wright, Sarah K., ed. N.D. E. P. Dutton & Co. (P.981)
--*This Little Piggy and Other Counting Rhymes.* Petty, Roberta Harris Pfafflin. Fraser, Phyllis Maurine (1915-), ed. 1942. Simon and Schuster, Inc. (P.342)
--*Up and Down South America.* Petty, Roberta Harris Pfafflin. Halladay, Anne M, Mrs. 1942. Friendship Press. (P.406)
--*What's Coming.* Petty, Roberta Harris Pfaflin. Ridgway, Marion V. 1944. Howell Soskin. (P.764)
--*Young Tom Jefferson's Adventure Chest.* Petty, Roberta Harris Pfafflin. Davis, Betty Elise. 1942. M. S. Mill Co., Inc. (P.245)

Page, Don (1946-)
--*Drip Drop.* Gordon, Sharon. c.1981. Troll Associates. (P.377)
--*Play Ball, Kate!.* Gordon, Sharon. c.1981. Troll Associates. (P.377)
--*Tick Tock Clock.* Gordon, Sharon. c.1982. Troll Associates. (P.377)
--*Trouble in Space.* Greydanus, Rose. c.1981. Troll Associates. (P.389)
--*Valentine's Day Grump.* Greydanus, Rose. c.1981. Troll Associates. (P.389)
--*What a Funny Bunny.* Whitehead, Patricia. c.1985. Troll Associates. (P.953)

Page, Gilbert
--*Barn Yard Ditties.* Duane, Mary Morris. c.1937. Chapman & Grimes. (P.285)

Page, Helen
--*The Gingham Dog and the Calico Cat.* Field, Eugene (1850-1895). c.1956. Follett Pub. Co. (P.324)
--*Winnie-the-Pooh.* Milne, Alan Alexander (1882-1956). 1946. John Martin's House, Inc. (P.650)
--*Wynken, Blynken, and Nod.* Field, Eugene (1850-1895). c.1956. Follett Pub. Co. (P.324)
--*Wynken, Blynken, & Nod.* Field, Eugene (1850-1895) & Lowe Corporation. N.D. New Century. (P.324)
--*Wynken, Blynken, and Nod and The Gingham Dog and The Calico Cat.* Field, Eugene (1850-1895). c.1956. Wilcox & Follett Co. (P.324)

Page, Joseph
--*The Mystery of Grandfather's Coat.* 1st ed. Monsell, Helen Albee (1895-1971). 1948. Bobbs-Merrill Co. (P.657)

Paget-Fredericks, Joseph E. P. Rous-Marten (1903-1963)
--*Edna St.*Vincent Millay's Poems Selected for Young People. Millay, Edna St. Vincent (1892-1950). 1929. Har-Row. (P.645)
--*Edna St.*Vincent Millay's Poems Selected for Young People. Millay, Edna St. Vincent (1892-1950). 1962. Harper & Bros. (P.645)
--*A Gift for Merimond.* Anderson, Mildred Napier. 1953. Oxford University Press. (P.40)
--*Green Pipes: Poems and Pictures.* Paget-Fredericks, Joseph E. P. Rous-Marten (1903-1963). 1929. Macmillan. (P.700)
--*The Macaroni Tree: A Medley of Fancies and Fairies from the Land of Make Believe.* Amsden, Dora, Mrs. (1858-). 1927. W. Hebberd. (P.33)
--*Miss Pert's Christmas Tree.* Paget-Fredericks, Joseph E. P. Rous-Marten (1903-1963). 1929. Macmillan. (P.700)
--*Sandra and the Right Prince.* Anderson, Mildred Napier. 1951. Oxford University Press. (P.40)

Paget, H. M.
--*Captain Bayley's Heir: A Tale of the Gold Fileds of California, 1 of 5 vols.* Henty, George Alfred (1832-1902). N.D. A. L. Burt's Pubs. (P.435)

Paget, Sidney
--*Sherlock Holmes Investigates.* Doyle, Arthur Conan, Sir (1859-1930). 1966. Lothrop. (P.283)

Paget, Walter
--*The Arabian Nights.* Rouse, William Henry Denham (1863-), intro. by. 1907. E. Nister. (P.781)
--*At Agincourt: A Tale of the White Hoods of Paris.* Henty, George Alfred (1832-1902). 1896. C. Scribner's Sons. (P.434)
--*At the Point of the Bayonet: A Tale of the Mahratta War.* Henty, George Alfred (1832-1902). 1901. C. Scribner's Sons. (P.434)
--*Condemned as a Nihilist: A Story of Escape from Siberia.* Henty, George Alfred (1832-1902). 1892. Charles Scribner's Sons'. (P.435)
--*Through Three Campaigns: A Story of Chitral, Tirah, and Ashanti.* Henty, George Alfred (1832-1902). 1903. C. Scribner's Sons. (P.436)
--*Through Three Campaigns: A Story of Chitral, Tirah and Ashanti.* Henty, George Alfred (1832-1902). N.D. Grosset & Dunlap. (P.436)
--*Treasure Island.* N.D. Charles Scribner's Sons. (P.700)
--*Treasure Island.* a limited. Stevenson, Robert Louis (1850-1894). 1978. Franklin Library. (P.857)
--*Treasure Island.* Stevenson, Robert Louis (1850-1894). West, Michael, ed. 1937. Longmans, Green. (P.857)
--*The Treasure of the Incas: A Tale of Adventure in Peru.* Henty, George Alfred (1832-1902). 1902. C. Scribner's Sons. (P.436)
--*The Treasure of the Incas: A Tale of Adventures in Peru.* Henty, George Alfred (1832-1902). N.D. Grosset & Dunlap. (P.436)
--*Under Wellington's Command: A Tale of the Peninsular War.* Henty, George Alfred (1832-1902). 1898. C. Scribner's Sons. (P.436)
--*Under Wellington's Command: A Tale of the Peninsular War.* Henty, George Alfred (1832-1902). 1903. C. Scribner's Sons. (P.436)
--*With Frederick the Great: A Story of the Seven Years' War.* Henty, George Alfred (1832-1902). 1897. C. Scribner's Sons. (P.436)
--*With Moore at Corunna.* Henty, George Alfred (1832-1902). 1897. C. Scribner's Sons. (P.437)
--*With the Allies to Pekin: A Tale of the Relief of the Legations.* Henty, George Alfred (1832-1902). 1903. C. Scribner's Sons. (P.437)
--*With the Allies to Pekin: A Tale of the Relief of the Legations.* Henty, George Alfred (1832-1902). N.D. Grosset & Dunlap. (P.437)
--*With the British Legion: A Story of the Carlist Wars.* Henty, George Alfred (1832-1902). 1902. C. Scribner's Sons. (P.437)
--*Won by the Sword: A Tale of the Thirty Years' War.* Henty, George Alfred (1832-1902). 1899. C. Scribner's Sons. (P.437)

Pagram, Edward
--*Famous Stories of the Sea and Ships.* Gribble, Leonard Reginald (1908-), ed. c.1964. Hill & Wang. (P.389)
--*Famous Tales of the Fantastic.* Van Thal, Herbert Maurice (1904-), ed. 1965. Hill & Wang. (P.915)
--*The Golden Lure: Stories of Famous Lost Treasures.* Burke, James Wakefield. 1964. Hill & Wang. (P.154)
--*Great Ghost Stories.* Van Thal, Herbert Maurice (1904-), ed. 1960. Hill & Wang. (P.915)
--*Great Tales of Mystery.* Bull, Randolph Cecil, ed. 1960. Hill and Wang. (P.148)

Pahz, Anne Cheryl Suzanne (1949-)
--*Robin Sees a Song.* Pahz, James Alon (1943-) & Pahz, Anne Cheryl Suzanne (1949-). c.1977. National Association of the Deaf. (P.700)

Paige, John
--*Crocodile's Eggs for Supper & Other Animal Tales from Northern Uganda.* Bere, Rennie Montague (1907-). 1979. Andre Deutsch. (P.95)

Pailthorpe, Doris & Robinson, Thomas Heath (1869-1950)
--*The Adventures of Ulysses.* Lamb, Charles (1775-1834), adapted by. 1926. Frederick A. Stokes Company. (P.545)

Pailthorpe, Frederic W.
--*Great Expectations.* Dickens, Charles John Huffam (1812-1870). N.D. Dodd, Mead & Co. (P.263)

Paine, A. L.
--*Outside of things: A sky book.* Bailey, Alice Ward, Mrs. (1857-). 1899. E. P. Dutton & Co. (P.59)

Painter-Duhring, M.
--*For Freedom and for Gaul.* Anderson, Paul Lewis (1880-1956). 1957, c.1931. Biblo and Tannen. (P.40)
--*For Freedom and Gaul.* Anderson, Paul Lewis (1880-1956). 1931. D. Appleton and Company. (P.40)
--*The Knights of St.* John. Anderson, Paul Lewis (1880-1956). 1932. D. Appleton and Company. (P.40)

Pairpoint, Nellie M.
--*Jacinth and Her Fairy Friends.* Pairpoint, Nellie M. c.1922. W. A. Wilde Company. (P.701)
--*Noel and the Little People of the Woods.* Pairpoint, Nellie M. c.1921. W. A. Wilde Company. (P.701)

Paiss, Jana
--*Joshua's Dream.* Segal, Sheila F. c.1985. Union of American Hebrew Congregations. (P.808)

Parry, Anna W.
--*The Girls of Bonnie Castle ...* Forrester, Izola Louise (1878-). 1900. G. W. Jacobs & Co. (P.336)

Parry, David
--*The Roan Colt.* Ottley, Reginald Leslie. 1967. Harcourt, Brace & World. (P.698)

Parry, Ivor
--*King of the Mountain.* Martin, William Ivan, Jr. (1916-). 1970. Holt, Rinehart and Winston. (P.626)

Parry, Marian (1924-)
--*The Ballad of the Long-Tailed Rat.* Pomerantz, Charlotte (1930-). 1975. Macmillan. (P.731)
--*The Birds of Basel.* Parry, Marian (1924-), adapted by. 1969. Knopf. (P.707)
--*City Mouse, Country Mouse & Two More Mouse Tales from Aesop.* Parry, Marian (1924-), adapted by. 1971. Scholastic Inc. (P.707)
--*City Mouse, Country Mouse & Two More Mouse Tales from Aesop.* Parry, Marian (1924-), adapted by. 1973. Schol Bk Serv. (P.707)
--*I Am a Big Help.* Parry, Marian (1924-), adapted by. c.1980. Greenwillow Books. (P.707)
--*King of the Fish.* Parry, Marian (1924-), adapted by. 1977. Macmillan. (P.707)
--*The Lazies: Tales of the Peoples of Russia.* Ginsburg, Mirra (1919-), ed. 1973. Macmillan. (P.369)
--*Roger and the Devil.* Parry, Marian (1924-), adapted by. 1972. Knopf. (P.707)
--*The Space Child's Mother Goose.* Winsor, Frederick. 1963. Simon and Schuster. (P.970)
--*The Zoo Conspiracy.* Levin, Betty (1927-). 1973. Hastings House. (P.568)

Parske, Edward A., jt. illus. see Fyson, Dorothy R.

Parsons, Priscilla B.
--*The Claim-Jumpers.* Hoyt, Charles A. c.1927. The Century Co. (P.468)
--*Cornelia's Customers.* Winters, Jane. c.1928. The Century Co. (P.970)
--*The Girl Reporter.* Claudy, Carl Harry (1879-). 1930. Litle, Brown & Co. (P.200)
--*Tony and the Big Top.* Chaffee, Allen. c.1925. The Century Co. (P.181)

Parsons, Rita
--*Foxy.* Montgomery, John (1916-). 1960, c.1959. F. Watts. (P.658)
--*Lions & Karen.* Dinneen, Betty (1929-). 1964. Verry. (P.266)
--*My Friend Foxy.* Montgomery, John (1916-). 1962, c.1961. F. Watts. (P.658)

Parsons, Virginia
--*Animal Parade.* 1st ed. Parsons, Virginia. Parsons, Virginia, selected by. 1970. Doubleday. (P.708)
--*A Christmas Panorama.* Parsons, Virginia. 1977. Doubleday. (P.708)
--*Christmas Panorama.* Parsons, Virginia. N.D. Doubleday. (P.708)
--*First Things.* 1982. Western Pub. (P.708)
--*The Fourteen Bears, Summer and Winter.* Scott, Evelyn D., Mrs. (1893-1963). 1973. Golden Press. (P.804)
--*The Giant Happy Nursery Book.* Parsons, Virginia. 1970. Doubleday. (P.708)
--*Homes.* Parsons, Virginia. N.D. Doubleday. (P.708)
--*Homes.* 1st ed. Parsons, Virginia. 1958. Garden City Books. (P.708)
--*Let's Read a Story: Modern, Gay Stories for Boys and Girls.* 1st ed. Gruenberg, Sidonie Matsner (1881-1974), ed. 1957. Garden City Books. (P.398)
--*Lots and Lots of Bedtime Stories.* Parsons, Virginia. 1971. American Heritage Press. (P.708)
--*Loud.* 1st ed. Parsons, Virginia. 1967. World Pub. Co. (P.708)
--*Night.* 1st ed. Parsons, Virginia. 1958. Garden City Books. (P.708)
--*Pinocchio and Geppetto.* Parsons, Virginia, ed. 1979. McGraw-Hill. (P.708)
--*Pinocchio and the Money Tree.* Parsons, Virginia, ed. 1979. McGraw-Hill. (P.708)
--*Pinocchio Goes on the Stage.* Parsons, Virginia, ed. 1979. McGraw-Hill. (P.708)
--*Pinocchio Plays Truant.* Parsons, Virginia, ed. 1979. McGraw-Hill. (P.708)
--*Play.* 1st ed. Parsons, Virginia. 1963. Doubleday. (P.708)
--*Quiet.* 1st ed. Parsons, Virginia. 1967. World Pub. Co. (P.708)
--*Rain.* 1st ed. Parsons, Virginia. 1961. Doubleday. (P.708)
--*Rides.* 1st ed. Parsons, Virginia. 1964. Doubleday. (P.708)
--*Ring for Liberty.* Parsons, Virginia. 1975. Golden Press. (P.708)
--*Snow.* Parsons, Virginia. 1962. Doubleday. (P.708)
--*Whatever Happens to Baby Animals.* Hall, Bill. 1973. Western Pub. (P.404)

--*Whatever Happens to Baby Horses?.* Hall, Bill. 1965. Golden Press. (P.404)
--*Whatever Happens to Bear Cubs?.* Hall, Bill. 1968. Golden Press. (P.404)
--*Whatever Happens to Kittens?.* Hall, Bill. 1967. Golden Press. (P.404)
--*Whatever Happens to Puppies?.* Hall, Bill. 1966, c.1965. Golden Press. (P.404)

Parsons, Virginia & Waters, Sheila
--*The Friendly Beasts & A Partridge in a Pear Tree: A Christmas Panorama.* 1966. Doubleday. (P.708)

Partch, Virgil Franklin see Vip, pseud.

Partch, Virgil Franklin, II (1916-)
--*Christmas Cookie Sprinkle Snitcher.* Vip, pseud. Partch, Virgil Franklin, II (1916-) & Kraus, Robert (1925-). Vip, pseud. 1969. S&S. (P.708)
--*Ludwig the Dog Who Snored Symphonies.* Vip, pseud. Kraus, Robert (1925-). 1973. E.P. Dutton & Co. (P.538)
--*Ludwig the Dog Who Snored Symphonies.* Vip, pseud. Kraus, Robert (1925-). 1981. Windmill Books. (P.538)
--*Ludwig: the Dog Who Snored Symphonies.* Vip, pseud. Partch, Virgil Franklin, II (1916-) & Kraus, Robert (1925-). Vip, pseud. 1971. Windmill Books. (P.708)
--*Shaggy Fur Face.* Vip, pseud. Kraus, Robert (1925-). 1973. Dutton. (P.538)
--*Shaggy Fur Face.* Vip, pseud. Kraus, Robert (1925-). 1971. Windmill Bks. (P.538)
--*Shaggy Fur Face.* Vip, pseud. Kraus, Robert (1925-). 1980, c.1971. Windmill Bks. (P.538)
--*Shaggy Fur Face.* Vip, pseud. Partch, Virgil Franklin, II (1916-) & Kraus, Robert (1925-). Vip, pseud. 1980, c.1971. Windmill Books. (P.708)
--*Vip's Mistake Book.* Vip, pseud. Kraus, Robert (1925-). 1970. Windmill Bks. (P.538)

Partridge, B.
--*Clementina.* Mason, Alfred Edward Woodley. 1901. F. A. Stokes Co. (P.628)

Partridge, Chuck
--*Mile High Surprise.* Partridge, Chuck. 1980. Xerox Ed Pubns. (P.708)

Partridge, Jenny Lilian (1947-)
--*Colonel Grunt.* Partridge, Jenny Lilian (1947-). 1982, c.1980. Holt, Rinehart and Winston. (P.708)
--*Dominic Sly.* Partridge, Jenny Lilian (1947-). 1983, c.1981. Holt, Rinehart, and Winston. (P.708)
--*Grandma Snuffles.* 1st ed. Partridge, Jenny Lilian (1947-). 1983, c.1981. Holt, Rinehart, and Winston. (P.708)
--*Harriet Plume.* Partridge, Jenny Lilian (1947-). 1983. HR&W. (P.708)
--*Hopfellow.* Partridge, Jenny Lilian (1947-). 1982, c.1980. Holt, Rinehart and Winston. (P.708)
--*Lop-Ear.* Partridge, Jenny Lilian (1947-). 1983, c.1981. Holt, Rinehart, and Winston. (P.708)
--*Mr. Squint.* Partridge, Jenny Lilian (1947-). 1982, c.1980. Holt, Rinehart and Winston. (P.708)
--*Peterkin Pollensnuff.* Partridge, Jenny Lilian (1947-). 1982, c.1980. Holt, Rinehart, and Winston. (P.708)

Partridge, Pat (1945-)
--*Betsey's Bee Tree.* Knox, Margaret (1924-). c.1980. Shoal Creek Publishers. (P.533)

Parzen, Trude
--*The Magic Kite-Tail, and Other Stories.* Strauss, Ludwig (1892-1953). Wallower, Arthur, tr. 1967. Van Nostrand. (P.867)

Pascal, David (1918-)
--*Fifteen Fables of Krylov.* Krylov, Ivan Andreevich (1768-1844). Daniels, Guy (1919-), tr. 1965. Macmillan. (P.541)
--*The Silly Knight.* Pascal, David (1918-). 1967. Funk & Wagnalls. (P.708)

Pascal, Theo
--*Johnny Groundhog's Shadow.* Payne, Emmy, pseud. (1919-). West, Emily Govan. 1948. Houghton Mifflin Co. (P.712)

Paschal, Mary
--*Afiong: A Story of West Africa.* Rev ed. Eleanor, Mary, Mother (1903-). 1959. Bruce Pub. Co. (P.300)

Paschal, Rose
--*Mother Goose.* Mother Goose. c.1951. Whitman Pub. (P.667)

Pasquier, J. A.
--*Clarissa: or, the Mervyn Inheritance.* Bowman, Anne. N.D. George Routledge & Sons. (P.122)

Pasquier, J. A. & Wolf, J.
--*Mrs. Overtheway's Remembrances.* Ewing, Juliana Horatia Gatty, Mrs. (1841-1885). 1881. Roberts. (P.314)
--*Mrs. Overtheway's Remembrances.* Ewing, Juliana Horatia Gatty, Mrs. (1841-1885). 1887. Roberts Brothers. (P.314)
--*Mrs. Overtheway's Remembrances.* Ewing, Juliana Horatia Gatty, Mrs. (1841-1885). 1889. Roberts Brothers. (P.314)

Pastic, George
--*The Violin.* Allen, Robert Thomas. 1977. McGraw. (P.30)

Pastor, Rosita
--*Horace.* 1st ed. Urquhart, Elizabeth. 1951. Dutton. (P.911)

Pasutanavin, Supee
--*Tales from Thailand.* Toth, Marian Davies, as told by. 1971. Tuttle. (P.896)

Patch, Lila
--*The Alphabet Tree.* Auerbach, Stevanne (1938-). c.1985. Windswept House. (P.54)

Pate, Rodney
--*An Apartment's No Place for a Kid.* Knox-Wagner, Elaine. 1985. A. Whitman. (P.533)
--*My Dad Is Really Something.* Osborn, Lois. 1983. A. Whitman. (P.697)

Pateman, May
--*Babo: A South Seas Boy.* Pateman, May. c.1931. Friendship Press. (P.709)

Patersham, Miska, jt. illus. see Petersham, Maud Sylvia Fuller, Mrs.

Paterson, A. S.
--*New Zealand Beckons.* MacPherson, Ma Lean. 1952. Dodd, Mead. (P.611)

Paterson, Brian, jt. illus. see Paterson, Cynthia.

Paterson, C.
--*Bunch of Berries, and the Diversions.* Scott, L. N.D. Publication of E. P. Dutton & Co. (P.805)

Paterson, Cora E. M.
--*Joyous Stories from Music's Wonderland: Music Talks to the Children.* Jones, George Kirkham (1876-). 1955. Macmillan. (P.499)

Paterson, Cynthia & Paterson, Brian
--*The Foxwood Treasure.* Paterson, Cynthia & Paterson, Brian. 1985. Barron's. (P.709)
--*Robbery at Foxwood.* Paterson, Cynthia & Paterson, Brian. 1985. Barron's. (P.709)

Paterson, Diane R. Cole (1946-)
--*The Bathtub Ocean.* Paterson, Diane R. Cole (1946-). c.1979. Dial Press. (P.709)
--*The Bee Sneeze.* Keller, Beverly Lou. 1982. Coward, McCann & Geoghegan. (P.514)
--*The Biggest Bubble in the World.* Lorimer, Janet. 1982. F. Watts. (P.585)
--*The Biggest Snowstorm Ever.* Paterson, Diane R. Cole (1946-). 1974. Dial Press. (P.709)
--*The Bravest Babysitter.* Greenberg, Barbara (1940-). c.1977. Dial Press. (P.386)
--*Coyote for a Day.* Caras, Roger Andrew (1928-). 1977. Dutton. (P.166)
--*Eat!.* Paterson, Diane R. Cole (1946-). 1975. Dial Press. (P.709)
--*Eat!.* Paterson, Diane R. Cole (1946-). 1977, c.1975. Dial Press. (P.709)
--*Everybody Knows That!.* Pearson, Susan (1946-). c.1978. Dial Press. (P.713)
--*Fiona's Bee.* Keller, Beverly Lou. 1975. Putnam Pub Group. (P.514)
--*Fiona's Flea.* Keller, Beverly Lou. c.1981. Coward, McCann & Geoghegan. (P.514)
--*The Golden Goose.* Grimm, Jakob Ludwig Karl (1785-1863) & Grimm, Wilhelm Karl (1786-1859). c.1981. Troll Associates. (P.392)
--*I Hate Kisses.* Harris, Robie H. & Paterson, Diane (1946-). c.1980. Knopf. (P.416)
--*If I Were a Toad.* Paterson, Diane R. Cole (1946-). c.1977. Dial Press. (P.709)
--*Kittens for Nothing.* 1st ed. Kraus, Robert (1925-). c.1976. Windmill Books. (P.538)
--*Monnie Hates Lydia.* Pearson, Susan (1946-). 1975. Dial Press. (P.713)
--*Pinocchio & the Great Whale.* Lorenzini, Carlo (1826-1890). Collodi, Carlo, pseud. Cutts, David E., adapted by. 1982. Troll Assocs. (P.585)
--*Pinocchio & the Puppet Show.* Lorenzini, Carlo (1826-1890). Collodi, Carlo, pseud. Cutts, David E., adapted by. 1982. Troll Assocs. (P.585)
--*Pinocchio Goes to School.* Lorenzini, Carlo (1826-1890). Collodi, Carlo, pseud. Cutts, David E., adapted by. 1982. Troll Assocs. (P.585)
--*Pinocchio Meets the Cat & Fox.* Lorenzini, Carlo (1826-1890). Collodi, Carlo, pseud. Cutts, David E., adapted by. 1982. Troll Assocs. (P.585)
--*Smile for Auntie.* Paterson, Diane R. Cole (1946-). c.1976. Dial Press. (P.709)
--*Soap and Suds.* Paterson, Diane R. Cole (1946-). 1984. Knopf. (P.709)
--*Stone Soup.* Paterson, Diane R. Cole (1946-). c.1981. Troll Associates. (P.709)
--*Too Many Books!.* Bauer, Caroline Feller (1935-). c.1984. F. Warne. (P.81)
--*Wretched Rachel.* Paterson, Diane R. Cole (1946-). c.1978. Dial Press. (P.709)

Paterson, Elizabeth
--*Verses for Children.* Taylor, Joye. 1939. Whitcombe & Tombs, Limited. (P.880)

Patina, Maureen
--*Goodness Gracious: The Story of a Very Special Whale.* 1st ed. Levitt, Harry. 1980. Ranger Associates. (P.568)

Paton, C. Marion
--*Muskoka Holiday.* Boyle, Emily Joyce (1901-). 1959. St Martin's Press. (P.123)

Paton, Jane Elizabeth (1934-)
--*The Amazing Mr. Prothero.* Arundel, Honor (1919-1973). 1972. T. Nelson. (P.50)

--*Anna of the Bears.* Rongen, Bjorn (1906-). Ramsden, Evelyn, tr. 1967, c.1965. Farrar, Straus & Giroux. (P.776)
--*Anna of the Bears.* Rongen, Bjorn (1906-). 1965. Methuen. (P.776)
--*Around the Seasons: Poems by Eleanor Farjeon.* Farjeon, Eleanor (1881-1965). 1969. Walck. (P.317)
--*Beware of This Animal.* Moray Williams, Ursula (1911-). 1965. Dial Press. (P.662)
--*Bonfire in the Wind and the Faraway Princess.* Oliver, Jane, pseud. (1903-1970). Rees, Helen Christina Easson Evans. 1962. St Martin's Press. (P.693)
--*A Dog and a Half.* Willard, Barbara Mary (1909-). 1971. T. Nelson. (P.961)
--*Faraway Princess.* Oliver, Jane, pseud. (1903-1970). Rees, Helen Christina Easson Evans. 1962. St. Martin's Press. (P.693)
--*Hello, I'm Karen.* Sutherland, Margaret (1941-). 1976, c.1974. Coward, McCann & Geoghegan. (P.872)
--*I Didn't Invite You to My Party.* McNeill, Janet (1907-). 1967. Hamish Hamilton. (P.610)
--*The Mfums.* Grove, Elizabeth. 1967. World Pub. Co. (P.396)
--*Moonball.* Moray Williams, Ursula (1911-). 1967. Hawthorn. (P.662)
--*The Moonball.* Moray Williams, Ursula (1911-). 1967, c.1965. Meredith. (P.662)
--*The Moonball.* Moray Williams, Ursula (1911-). 1972. Schol Bk Serv. (P.662)
--*Mr. Garden.* Farjeon, Eleanor (1881-1965). 1966, c.1965. Walck. (P.317)
--*Ragged Robin.* Reeves, James (1909-). 1961. Dutton. **Award:** (CMA). (P.754)
--*Surprise Island.* Willard, Barbara Mary (1909-). 1981, c.1969. Elsevier-Dutton Pub. Co. (P.961)
--*Surprise Island.* Willard, Barbara Mary (1909-). 1969. Meredith Press. (P.961)
--*Three Girls and a Secret.* Guillot, Rene (1900-1969). Selby-Lowndes, Joan, tr. from Fr. 1963. F. Watts. (P.399)
--*The Twins of Ceylon.* Williams, Harry (1903-). Power, Rhoda, intro. by. 1965. Dufour. (P.963)

Paton, Joseph Noel, Sir (1821-1901)
--*The Story of Wandering Willie.* Yonge, Charlotte Mary (1823-1901). N.D. Macmillan & Co. (P.988)
--*The Water-Babies: A Fairy Tale for a Land-Baby.* Kingsley, Charles (1819-1875). 1881. Macmillan and Co. (P.525)

Paton, Joseph Noel, Sir (1821-1901) & Skelton, P.
--*The Water Babies: A Fairy Tale for a Land Baby.* Kingsley, Charles (1819-1875). 1885. Macmillan Co. (P.525)
--*The Water Babies: A Fairy Tale for a Land Baby, Vol. IX.* Kingsley, Charles (1819-1875). N.D. Macmillan & Co. (P.525)

Patri, Angelo (1876-)
--*Moments of Enchantment.* Junior High School Principals Association of New York City. 1941. Duenewald Printing Corporation. (P.503)

Patric
--*The Cry of the Conch.* Roop, Peter. 1984. Pr Pacifica. (P.776)

Pattee, Elsie Dodge
--*The Animal Book.* Butler, William Allen (1825-1902). 1914. Frederick A. Stokes. (P.159)

Patten, Toni
--*Monty of Montego.* Durstine, Virginia Gardiner. 1963. Bobbs-Merrill. (P.292)
--*The Path of the Raven.* Boucher, Alan Estcourt (1918-). 1960. Hastings House. (P.120)

Patterson, Diane R. Cole (1946-)
--*Hey, Cowboy!.* Paterson, Diane R. Cole (1946-). c.1983. Knopf. (P.709)
--*If I Were Strong Enough.* Zimelman, Nathan (1911-). c.1982. Abingdon. (P.992)

Patterson, Dorothea
--*The Flying Cat.* Bell, Vicars Walker (1904-). 1965, c.1964. Roy Publishers. (P.91)

Patterson, Frances
--*The Children of Hill Crest.* Weber, Mary Bond. 1951. Exposition Press. (P.939)

Patterson, Geoffrey (1943-)
--*Chestnut Farm.* Patterson, Geoffrey (1943-). 1980. Deutsch. (P.710)
--*A Pig's Tale.* Patterson, Geoffrey (1943-). 1984. Dutton. (P.710)

Patterson, Malcolm
--*The Red Light.* Weigall, Constance E. C. N.D. Cassell & Co. (P.940)

Patterson, Nancy-Lou & Long, James
--*Cartoon Catechism.* Patterson, Nancy-Lou & Long, James. N.D. Morehouse-Barlow. (P.710)

Patterson, Robert (1899-)
--*Anne of Green Gables.* Montgomery, Lucy Maud (1874-1942). Cushing, Mary W. & Williams, D. C., eds. 1961. Grosset & Dunlap. (P.658)
--*Barbie and the Ghost Town Mystery.* Woolvin, Eleanor K. 1965. Random House. (P.979)
--*Barbie in Television.* Duest, Marianne. c.1964. Random House. (P.287)

--*Tyltyl: Being the Story of Maurice Maeterlinck's Play, "The Bethrothal".* Maeterlinck, Maurice (1862-1949). Teixeira De Mattos, Alexander Louis (1865-1921), tr. 1920. Dodd, Mead and Company. (P.612)

Pavey, Peter

--*I'm Taggarty Toad.* Pavey, Peter. 1980. Bradbury Press. (P.712)

--*One Dragon's Dream.* Pavey, Peter. 1979, c.1978. Bradbury Press. (P.712)

Pavia, Cathy J.

--*Cathy and Company and Bumper the Bully.* Schertle, Alice (1941-). N.D. Childrens Press. (P.798)

--*Cathy and Company & Hank, the Horse.* Schertle, Alice (1941-). c.1980. Childrens Press. (P.798)

--*Cathy and Company, and Mean Mr.* Meeker. Schertle, Alice (1941-). c.1980. Childrens Press. (P.798)

--*Cathy and Company and the Double Dare.* Schertle, Alice (1941-). c.1980. Childrens Press. (P.798)

--*Cathy and Company and the Green Ghost.* Schertle, Alice (1941-). c.1980. Childrens Press. (P.798)

--*Cathy and Company and the Nosy Neighbor.* Schertle, Alice (1941-). c.1980. Childrens Press. (P.798)

Pavlishin, Gennadii

--*Folk Tales of the Amur: Russian Stories from the Far East.* Nagishkin, Dmitrii. Lehrman, Emily, tr. 1980. Harry N. Abrams. (P.675)

Paxson, Diana L.

--*Folk Tales from Persia.* Feinstein, Alan Shawn (1931-). 1971. A. S. Barnes. (P.320)

--*Folk Tales from Portugal.* Feinstein, Alan Shawn (1931-). 1972. A. S. Barnes. (P.320)

Payne, A. B.

--*Pip, Squeak, and Wilfred: Their "Luvly" Adventures.* Lamb, Bertram John (1887-). Uncle Dick, pseud. c.1921. E. P. Dutton & Company. (P.544)

Payne, Anthony

--*Crafty the Cat: And Five More Tales for Animal Lovers.* Williams, Gladys. 1973. Rand. (P.963)

Payne, Joan Balfour (1923-1973)

--*Ambrose.* Payne, Joan Balfour (1923-1973). 1956. Hastings House. (P.712)

--*Charlie from Yonder.* Payne, Joan Balfour (1923-1973). 1962. Hastings House. (P.712)

--*The Desperate Dragons.* Lloyd, Mary Norris (1908-). 1960. Hastings House. (P.578)

--*General Billycock's Pigs.* Payne, Joan Balfour (1923-1973). 1961. Hastings House. (P.712)

--*The Journey of Josiah talltatters.* Payne, Josephine Balfour. N.D. E . M. Hale and Co. (P.712)

--*The Journey of Josiah Taltatters.* Payne, Josephine Balfour. c.1953. Ariel Books. (P.712)

--*Kate and the Devil.* Holberg, Ruth Langland, Mrs. (1891-). 1968. Hastings House. (P.453)

--*The Last Giant.* Payne, Josephine Balfour. 1947. G. P. Putnam's Sons. (P.712)

--*The Leprechaun of Bayou Luce.* Payne, Joan Balfour (1923-1973). 1957. Hastings House. (P.712)

--*Leprechaun of Bayou Luce.* Payne, Joan Balfour (1923-1973). 1969. Hastings. (P.712)

--*Lester and His Hound Pup.* Justus, May (1898-). 1960. Hastings House. (P.503)

--*The Little Green Island.* Payne, Josephine Balfour. 1942. G. P. Putnam's Sons. (P.712)

--*Magnificent Milo.* Payne, Joan Balfour (1923-1973). 1958. Hastings House. (P.712)

--*Miss Betty of Bonnet Rock School: 1864-1865.* Spratt, Barnett. c.1965. Hastings. (P.845)

--*A New Home for Billy.* Justus, May (1898-). 1966. Hastings. (P.503)

--*Once There was Olga.* Payne, Josephine Balfour. 1944. G. P. Putnam's Sons. (P.712)

--*Pangur Ban.* Payne, Joan Balfour (1923-1973). 1966. Hastings. (P.712)

--*The Piebald Princess.* Payne, Joan Balfour (1923-1973). 1954. Ariel Books. (P.712)

--*The Piebald Princess.* Payne, Joan Balfour (1923-1973). N.D. E. M. Hale and Co. (P.712)

--*The Raven, and Other Fairy Tales.* Payne, Joan Balfour (1923-1973), retold by. 1969. Hastings House. (P.712)

--*The Sable that Stayed.* Payne, Josephine Balfour. N.D. E. M. Hale & Co. (P.712)

--*Spinning Wheel Secret.* Albrecht, Lillie Vanderveer (1894-). 1965. Hastings. (P.16)

--*The Stable that Stayed.* Payne, Josephine Balfour. 1952. Ariel Books. (P.712)

--*Tea Meeting Winner.* Palmer, Edith. 1964. Hastings. (P.703)

--*Then Came Mister Billy Barker.* Justus, May (1898-). 1959. Hastings. (P.503)

Payne, Roger

--*Doctor with Wings.* Aldous, Allan. 1961, c.1960. Criterion Books. (P.21)

--*The Dog Who Came to Visit.* Eberle, Irmengarde (1898-1979). 1967. Abelard-Schuman. (P.295)

--*Dog Who Came to Visit.* Irmengarde, Eberle. 1967. Abelard. (P.481)

--*End of the Outlaws.* Patchett, Mary Osborne Elwyn (1897-). 1961. Bobbs. (P.708)

--*The Golden Wolf.* Patchett, Mary Osborne Elwyn (1897-). 1965, c.1962. Bobbs. (P.708)

--*Night of the Black Frost.* Catherall, Arthur (1906-). 1968. Lothrop, Lee & Shepard. (P.177)

--*Pepe's Island.* Morgan, Bryan Stanford & Morgan, Joan. c.1966. Criterion. (P.663)

--*The Secret Sea.* Armstrong, Richard (1903-). 1966. D. McKay Co. (P.48)

--*The Smugglers.* Kimenye, Barbara (1940-). 1966. Nelson. (P.523)

--*Summer on Wild Horse Island.* Patchett, Mary Osborne Elwyn (1897-). 1967, c.1965. Meredith Press. (P.709)

--*Tiger in the Dark.* Patchett, Mary Osborne Elwyn (1897-). 1966, c.1964. Duell. (P.709)

--*Tiger in the Dark.* Patchett, Mary Osborne Elwyn (1897-). 1966. Hawthorn. (P.709)

--*War Dog.* Treece, Henry (1911-1966). 1963, c.1962. Criterion. (P.899)

--*Warrimoo.* 1st ed. Patchett, Mary Osborne Elwyn (1897-). 1963. Bobbs-Merrill. (P.709)

Payne, Sally

--*The Little Neighbor.* Kelly, Jim (1943-). 1975. MacMillan Publishing company. (P.516)

--*Neighbors.* Kelly, Jim (1943-). 1972. Scarecrow Publications. (P.516)

--*Neighbors: Small Star Stories.* Kelly, Jim (1943-). 1975. MacMillan Publishing Company. (P.516)

--*The Secret Hole.* Kelly, Jim (1943-). 1975. MacMillan Publishing Company. (P.516)

--*Star Flowers: Small Star Stories.* Kelly, Jim (1943-). 1975. MacMillan Publishing Company. (P.516)

--*Wads and Gina's Songbook.* Kelly, Jim (1943-). 1975. MacMillan Publishing Company. (P.516)

Payne, Wyndham

--*Meddlesome Matty and Other Poems for Infant Minds.* Taylor, Jane, et al. (1783-1824) Sitwell, Edith, Dame (1887-1964), intro. by. 1926. The Viking Press. (P.880)

--*The Mysterious Toyshop: A Fairy Tale.* Beaumont, Cyril William (1891-1976). 1985. Metropolitan Museum of Art and Holt, Rinehart and Winston. (P.86)

Paynter, Grace M. & Von Bernuth, Lecian

--*Little Miss April.* Robinson, Anne Mathilde. c.1931. Oglethorpe University Press. (P.769)

Payson, Dale (1943-)

--*Almost Twins.* Payson, Dale (1943-). 1974. Prentice-Hall. (P.712)

--*Amish Boy.* Rowland, Florence Wightman (1900-). 1970. Putnam. (P.782)

--*Amish Wedding.* Rowland, Florence Wightman (1900-). 1971. Putnam. (P.782)

--*Ann Aurelia and Dorothy.* Carlson, Natalie Savage (1906-). 1968. Harper. (P.169)

--*The Crackajack Pony.* Burgwyn, Mebane Holoman (1914-). 1969. Lippincott. (P.154)

--*The Friendship Hedge.* 1st ed. Norris, Gunilla Brodde (1939-). 1973. Dutton. (P.685)

--*If You Listen.* 1st ed. Norris, Gunilla Brodde (1939-). 1971. Atheneum. (P.685)

--*The Lucky Stone.* Clifton, Lucille (1936-). c.1979. Delacorte Press. (P.202)

--*The Magic Castle Fairytale Book.* Farris, Stella. 1978. Random. (P.318)

--*The Magic of the Little People.* Cohen, Daniel (1936-). 1974. Messner. (P.206)

--*The Mulberry Music.* 1st ed. Orgel, Doris (1929-). 1971. Harper & Row. (P.695)

--*My Turn, Your Turn.* Watson, Pauline (1925-). c.1978. Prentice-Hall. (P.936)

--*The Mystery of the Spider Doll.* York, Carol Beach (1928-). 1973. F. Watts. (P.988)

--*Next Door to Xanadu: A Novel.* Orgel, Doris (1929-). 1969. Harper & Row. (P.695)

--*Puffy P. Pushycat, Problem Solver.* Fisher, Lois I (1948-). 1983. Dodd, Mead. (P.328)

--*A Question of Time.* Anastasio, Dina (1941-). c.1978. Dutton. (P.34)

--*The Seven Stone.* Shura, Mary Francis (1923-). 1972. Holiday House. (P.822)

--*The Silver Crown.* O'Brien, Robert C, pseud. (1918-1973). Conly, Robert Leslie. 1973, c.1968. Atheneum. (P.689)

--*The Sleepy Time Treasury.* Payson, Dale (1943-) & Wyatt, Karen, eds. 1975. Prentice-Hall. (P.712)

--*Tatu and the Honey Bird.* Wellman, Alice (1900-). 1972. Putnam. (P.943)

--*The Youngest.* Thayer, Marjorie. c.1982. Dodd, Mead. (P.884)

Payzant, Charles

--*And Juan.* Shannon, Terry, pseud. Mercer, Jessie. 1961. A. Whitman. (P.814)

--*Around the World with Gogo.* Shannon, Terry, pseud. Mercer, Jessie. c.1964. Golden Gate. (P.814)

--*A Dog Team for Ongluk.* Shannon, Terry, pseud. Mercer, Jessie. 1962. Melmont Publishers. (P.814)

--*Indians of the Past and Present.* Shannon, Terry, pseud. Mercer, Jessie. N.D. Albert Whitman & Company. (P.814)

--*Kidlik's Kayak.* Shannon, Terry, pseud. Mercer, Jessie. 1959. A. Whitman. (P.814)

--*Little Wolf, the Rain Dancer.* Shannon, Terry, pseud. Mercer, Jessie. N.D. Albert Whitman & Co. (P.814)

--*A Playmate for Puna.* Shannon, Terry, pseud. Mercer, Jessie. 1963. Melmont. (P.814)

--*Red is for Luck.* Shannon, Terry, pseud. Mercer, Jessie. 1963. Golden Gate Junior Books. (P.814)

--*Ride the Ice Down!.* Shannon, Terry, pseud. Mercer, Jessie. 1970. Childrens Press. (P.814)

--*Running Fox, the Eagle Hunter.* Shannon, Terry, pseud. Mercer, Jessie. 1957. Whitman. (P.814)

--*Today Is Story Day: A Tale for Every Day of the Week.* Shannon, Terry, pseud. & Payzant, Charles. Mercer, Jessie. 1954. Aladdin Books. (P.814)

--*Tyee's Totem Pole.* Shannon, Terry, pseud. Mercer, Jessie. 1955. A Whitman. (P.814)

--*Wakapoo and the Flying Arrows.* Shannon, Terry, pseud. Mercer, Jessie. c.1963. A. Whitman. (P.814)

--*The Yellow Shoes.* Graydon, William R. 1963. Golden Gate Junior Books. (P.384)

Paz, Henry

--*The Painted Arrow.* Gaither, Frances Ormond Jones, Mrs. (1889-). 1931. The Macmillan Company. (P.352)

Peabody, Marion L.

--*The Fairy Spinning Wheel and the Tales it Spun.* Mendes, Catulle (1841-1909). Vivian, Thomas Jondrie (1855-), tr. from Fr. 1898. G. Badger & Co. (P.640)

--*The Family Spinning Wheel and the Tales it Spun.* Mendes, Catulle (1841-1909). Vivian, Thomas Jondrie (1855-), tr. from French. 1898. R. G. Badger & Co. (P.640)

--*The History of Little Goody Two Shoes: Otherwise Called Mrs.* Margery Two Shoes ... Welsh, Charles (1850-1914), ed. 1901. D. C. Heath & Co. (P.945)

Peace, Bessie Collins

--*From Sioux to Susan.* Daulton, Agnes Warner McClelland, Mrs. (1867-). 1909. The Century Co. (P.243)

Peacock, Ralph

--*Both Sides the Border: A Tale of Hotspur and Glendower.* Henty, George Alfred (1832-1902). 1898. C. Scribner's Sons. (P.435)

--*A Knight of the White Cross: A Tale of the Siege of Rhodes.* Henty, George Alfred (1832-1902). 1895. C. Scribner's Sons. (P.436)

--*Wulf the Saxon: A Story of the Norman Conquest.* Henty, George Alfred (1832-1902). 1908. C. Scribner's Sons. (P.437)

Peake, Channing, jt. illus. see Grant, Campbell.

Peake, Katy

--*Wings of the Morning.* Cunningham, Julia Woolfolk (1916-). 1971. Golden Gate Junior Books. (P.235)

Peake, Mervyn Lawrence (1911-1968)

--*The Book of Lyonne.* Drake, Burgess. N.D. British Book Centre. (P.284)

--*Captain Slaughterboard Drops Anchor.* Peake, Mervyn Lawrence (1911-1968). 1967, c.1939. Macmillan. (P.712)

--*Captain Slaughterboard Drops Anchor.* Peake, Mervyn Lawrence (1911-1968). N.D. Transatlantic Arts, Inc. (P.712)

--*The Hunting of the Snark.* Carroll, Lewis, pseud. (1832-1898). Dodgson, Charles Lutwidge. 1970. Merrimack. (P.173)

--*The Hunting of the Snark: An Agony in Eight Fits.* Carroll, Lewis, pseud. (1832-1898). Dodgson, Charles Lutwidge. 1978. Merrimack Pub Cir. (P.173)

--*The Pot of Gold,.* Judah, Aaron (1923-). 1960, c.1959. Barnes. (P.501)

--*Ride a Cock-Horse and other Nursey Rhymes.* 1979. Merrimack Pub Cir. (P.712)

Pear, Jeannie

--*A Good & Perfect Gift.* Bacigalupa, Andrea (1923-). c.1978. Our Sunday Visitor. (P.58)

--*The Song of Guadalupana.* Bacigalupa, Drew (1923-). c.1979. Our Sunday Visitor. (P.58)

Pearce, Jessie H.

--*Aunt Reesie and the Triplets.* 1st ed. 1954. Exposition Press. (P.713)

Pearce, Leighton

--*Poppyland.* Stacpoole, Henry De Vere (1865-). 1914. John Lane. (P.847)

Pearce, William Houghton Sprague (1864-)

--*Toot!* Toot! Puff! Puff! Ding! Dong!. Pearce, William Houghton Sprague (1864-). 1934. Stoll & Einson Games Inc. (P.713)

Pearlman, Mal

--*The Scrambled Circus.* Malkan, Pauline Darling (1889-) & De Vora, Anna. Malkan, Peedie, pseud. c.1939. Dorrance and Company. (P.614)

Pears, Charles (1873-1958)

--*The Pedlar's Pack.* Baldwin, Alfred, Mrs. N.D. W. & R. Chambers, Limited. (P.65)

--*Salt-Water Poems & Ballads.* Masefield, John Edward (1878-1967). 1953. Macmillan. (P.627)

--*Salt-Water Poems and Ballads.* Masefield, John Edward (1878-1967). 1960. Macmillan. (P.627)

Pears, Charles (1873-1958) & Robinson, Thomas Heath (1869-1950)

--*Alice in Wonderland.* Carroll, Lewis, pseud. (1832-1898). Dodgson, Charles Lutwidge. N.D. Collins. (P.172)

Pearse, Alfred (1856-)

--*By England's Aid: Or, the Freeing of the Netherlands (1585-1604).* Henty, George Alfred (1832-1902). N.D. A. L. Burt. (P.435)

--*By England's Aid: Or, the Freeing of the Netherlands (1585-1604).* Henty, George Alfred (1832-1902). N.D. A. L. Burt. (P.435)

--*By England's Aid: Or, The Freeing of the Netherlands (1585-1604).* Henty, George Alfred (1832-1902). 1890. Blackie & Son, Limited. (P.435)

--*By England's Aid: Or, The Freeing of the Netherlands (1585-1604).* Henty, George Alfred (1832-1902). 1894. C. Scribner's Sons. (P.435)

--*By England's Aid: or, The Freeing of the Netherlands (1585-1604).* Henty, George Alfred (1832-1902). N.D. Donohue Brothers. (P.435)

--*Maori and Settler: A Story of the New Zealand War.* Henty, George Alfred (1832-1902). N.D. M. A. Donohue & Co. (P.436)

--*Redskin and Cow-Boy: A Tale of the Western Plains.* Henty, George Alfred (1832-1902). 1891. C. Scribner's Sons. (P.436)

--*Redskin and Cowboy.* Henty, George Alfred (1832-1902). N.D. Grosset & Dunlap. (P.436)

--*The Thirsty Sword: A Story of the Norse Invasion of Scotland (1262-1263).* Leighton, Robert (1859-). N.D. Grosset & Dunlap. (P.563)

Pearse, Susan Beatrice

--*Ameliar Anne and the Green Umbrella.* Heward, Constance. c.1920. G. W. Jacobs & Company. (P.439)

--*Ameliar Anne & The Green Umbrella.* Heward, Constance. N.D. Macrae Smith. (P.439)

--*Ameliaranne and the Big Treasure.* Joan, Natalie. 1932. David McKay Company. (P.493)

--*Ameliaranne and the Green Umbrella.* Heward, Constance. N.D. British Book Centre. (P.439)

--*Ameliaranne and the Magic Ring.* Farjeon, Eleanor (1881-1965). 1933. David McKay Company. (P.317)

--*Ameliaranne and the Monkey.* Heward, Constance. c.1929. David McKay Company. (P.439)

--*Ameliaranne at the Circus.* Gilmour, Margaret. c.1931. David McKay Company. (P.369)

--*Ameliaranne at the Farm.* Heward, Constance. 1937. David McKay Company. (P.439)

--*Ameliaranne at the Seaside.* Farjeon, Eleanor (1881-1965). N.D. David McKay Co. (P.317)

--*Ameliaranne Camps Out.* Heward, Constance. 1939. David McKay Company. (P.439)

--*Ameliaranne Gives a Christmas Party.* Heward, Constance. 1938. David McKay Company. (P.439)

--*Ameliaranne in Town.* Joan, Natalie. c.1930. David McKay Company. (P.493)

--*Ameliaranne Keeps School.* Heward, Constance. 1940. David McKay Company. (P.439)

--*Ameliaranne Keeps Shop.* Heward, Constance. c.1928. David McKay Company. (P.439)

--*Ameliaranne's Washing-Day.* Farjeon, Eleanor (1881-1965). 1934. David McKay Company. (P.317)

--*Captain Boldheart and Other Stories in A Holiday Romance.* Dickens, Charles John Huffam (1812-1870). 1927. The Macmillan Company. (P.262)

--*Honey for Tea.* Strong, Patience. 1950. Dutton. (P.868)

--*The Twins and Tabiffa.* Heward, Constance. c.1923. G. W. Jacobs & Co. (P.439)

--*The Twins & Tabiffa.* Heward, Constance. N.D. Macrae Smith. (P.439)

Pearson, Charles, jt. illus. see Pearson, Jeanne.

Pearson, Charles E.

--*Ride the Red-Eyed Wind.* Pearson, M. Jeanne. c.1978. Dillon Press. (P.713)

Pearson, Charles E. & Pearson, Jeanne

--*A Pony in the Yard.* Pearson, M. Jeanne. 1971. T. S. Denison. (P.713)

Pearson, Clyde

--*Boy Alone.* Ottley, Reginald Leslie. 1966, c.1965. Harcourt. **Award: (ALA).** (P.698)

--*Holy Man's Secret: A Story of India.* Bothwell, Jean (0000-1977). 1967. Abelard. (P.119)

--*The Holy Man's Secret: A Story of India.* Bothwell, Jean (0000-1977). 1968, c.1967. Abelard-Schuman. (P.119)

--*The River Kings.* Fatchen, Max (1920-). 1968, c.1966. St Martin's Press. (P.319)

Pearson, Jeanne

--*Little Indians' ABC.* Lucero, Faustina H. 1974. Oddo. (P.589)

Pearson, Jeanne, jt. illus. see Pearson, Charles E.

Pearson, Jeanne & Pearson, Charles

--*Dips 'n' Doodles.* Symons, Catherine & Westcott, Alvin M. 1970. Oddo Pub. (P.875)

--*Cyrus the Unsinkable Sea Serpent.* Peet, William Bartlett. Peet, Bill, pseud. (1915-). Peet, William Bartlett. 1975. Houghton Mifflin. (P.715)

--*Eli.* Peet, William Bartlett. Peet, Bill, pseud. (1915-). Peet, William Bartlett. 1978. Houghton Mifflin. (P.715)

--*Ella.* Peet, William Bartlett. Peet, Bill, pseud. (1915-). Peet, William Bartlett. 1964. Houghton Mifflin. (P.715)

--*Encore for Eleanor.* Peet, William Bartlett. Peet, Bill, pseud. (1915-). Peet, William Bartlett. 1981. Houghton Mifflin. (P.715)

--*Farewell to Shady Glade.* Peet, William Bartlett. Peet, Bill, pseud. (1915-). Peet, William Bartlett. 1966. Houghton Mifflin. (P.715)

--*Fly, Homer, Fly.* Peet, William Bartlett. Peet, Bill, pseud. (1915-). Peet, William Bartlett. 1969. Houghton Mifflin. (P.715)

--*The Gnats of Knotty Pine.* Peet, William Bartlett. Peet, Bill, pseud. (1915-). Peet, William Bartlett. 1975. Houghton Mifflin. (P.715)

--*How Droofus the Dragon Lost His Head.* Peet, William Bartlett. Peet, Bill, pseud. (1915-). Peet, William Bartlett. 1971. Houghton Mifflin Co. (P.715)

--*Hubert's Hair-Raising Adventure.* Peet, William Bartlett. Peet, Bill, pseud. (1915-). Peet, William Bartlett. 1979. HM. (P.715)

--*Hubert's Hair-Raising Adventure.* Peet, William Bartlett. Peet, Bill, pseud. (1915-). Peet, William Bartlett. 1959. Houghton Mifflin. (P.715)

--*Huge Harold.* Peet, William Bartlett. Peet, Bill, pseud. (1915-). Peet, William Bartlett. 1961. HM. (P.715)

--*Huge Harold.* Peet, William Bartlett. Peet, Bill, pseud. (1915-). Peet, William Bartlett. 1982. HM. (P.715)

--*Jennifer and Josephine.* Peet, William Bartlett. Peet, Bill, pseud. (1915-). Peet, William Bartlett. 1967. Houghton Mifflin. (P.715)

--*Kermit The Hermit.* Peet, William Bartlett. Peet, Bill (1915-). 1958. E. M. Hale And Company. (P.715)

--*Kermit the Hermit.* Peet, William Bartlett. Peet, Bill, pseud. (1915-). Peet, William Bartlett. 1965. Houghton Mifflin. (P.715)

--*The Kweeks of Kookatumdee.* Peet, William Bartlett. Peet, Bill, pseud. (1915-). Peet, William Bartlett. 1985. Houghton Mifflin. (P.715)

--*The Luckiest One of All.* Peet, William Bartlett. Peet, Bill, pseud. (1915-). Peet, William Bartlett. 1982. Houghton Mifflin. (P.715)

--*Merle the High Flying Squirrel.* Peet, William Bartlett. Peet, Bill, pseud. (1915-). Peet, William Bartlett. 1974. Houghton Mifflin. (P.715)

--*No Such Things.* Peet, William Bartlett. Peet, Bill, pseud. (1915-). Peet, William Bartlett. 1983. Houghton Mifflin. (P.715)

--*The Pinkish, Purplish, Bluish Egg.* Peet, William Bartlett. Peet, Bill, pseud. (1915-). Peet, William Bartlett. 1963. Houghton Mifflin. (P.715)

--*Randy's Dandy Lions.* Peet, William Bartlett. Peet, Bill, pseud. (1915-). Peet, William Bartlett. 1964. Houghton Mifflin. (P.715)

--*Smokey.* Peet, William Bartlett. Peet, Bill, pseud. (1915-). Peet, William Bartlett. 1962. Houghton Mifflin. (P.715)

--*The Spooky Tail of Prewitt Peacock.* Peet, William Bartlett. Peet, Bill, pseud. (1915-). Peet, William Bartlett. 1972, c.1973. Houghton Mifflin. (P.715)

--*Walt Disney's Goliath II.* Peet, William Bartlett. Disney, Walter Elias (1901-1966) & Peet, Bill (1915-). 1959. Golden Press. (P.272)

--*Walt Disney's So Dear to My Heart.* Peet, William Bartlett. Disney, Walter Elias (1901-1966). Palmer, Helen, adapted by. 1949. Golden Press. (P.272)

--*The Whingdingdilly.* Peet, William Bartlett. Peet, Bill, pseud. (1915-). Peet, William Bartlett. 1970. Houghton Mifflin. (P.715)

--*The Wump World.* Peet, William Bartlett. Peet, Bill, pseud. (1915-). Peet, William Bartlett. 1970. Houghton-Mifflin. (P.715)

Peet, Creighton Byrd (1899-1977), photos by.

--*Captain Teddy and Sailor Chips.* Peet, Creighton Byrd (1899-1977). c.1935. Loring & Mussey. (P.715)

--*Dude Ranch: The Story of a Modern Cowboy.* Peet, Creighton Byrd (1899-1977). 1939. A. Whitman & Co. (P.715)

--*Mike the Cat.* Peet, Creighton Byrd (1899-1977). c.1939. H. Holt. and Company. (P.716)

--*Mike the Cat.* Peet, Creighton Byrd (1899-1977). 1934. Loring & Mussey. (P.716)

--*The Runaway Train.* Peet, Creighton Byrd (1899-1977). 1943. H. Holt and Company. (P.716)

Peet, William Bartlett see Peet, Bill, pseud.

Peg, Gianni

--*Alex, the Amazing Juggler.* Peg, Gianni & Ferraro, Renato. 1981. Holt, Rinehart and Winston. (P.716)

Peilong, Liang

--*Hedgehog's New House.* Yuzher, Ding. N.D. China Bks. (P.991)

Peirce, Gerry see Stutters, Percival, pseud.

Peirce, Gerry

--*How Percival Caught the Python.* Stutters, Percival, pseud. Peirce, Gerry. Stutters, Percival, pseud. c.1937. Holiday House. (P.716)

--*How Percival Caught the Tiger.* Stutters, Percival, pseud. Peirce, Gerry. Stutters, Percival, pseud. c.1936. Holiday House. (P.716)

Peirce, H. Winthrop

--*The Patriot Schoolmaster: Or, The Adventures of the Two Boston Cannon, the "Adams" and "Hancock". A Tale of the Minute Men and the Sons of Liberty.* Butterworth, Hezekiah (1839-1905). 1894. D. Appleton and Company. (P.159)

--*The Wampum Belt: Or, "The Fairest Page of History"; a Tale of William Penn's Treaty with the Indians.* Butterworth, Hezekiah (1839-1905). 1896. D. Appleton and Company. (P.159)

Peirce, Waldo (1884-1970)

--*The Careless Clock: Poems About Children in the Family.* Van Doren, Mark Albert (1894-1972). 1947. W. Sloane Associates. (P.914)

--*The Children's Hour.* 1944. The Hyperion Press, Distributed by Duell, Sloan and Pearce. (P.716)

--*The Magic Bed-Knob: How to Become a Witch in Ten Easy Lessons.* Norton, Mary, Mrs. (1903-). c.1943. The Hyperion Press, Distributed by G. O. Putnam's Sons. (P.687)

--*Squawky and Bawky.* Lofting, Lynne. c.1939. C. Scribner's Sons. (P.580)

Peirson, Katharine

--*Uncle Sam's Family.* McConnell, Dorothy F. c.1924. Coucil of Women for Home Missions and Missionary Education Movement. (P.596)

Pekarsky, Mel

--*The Animal Hat Shop.* Murphey, Sara. 1964. Follett Pub. Co. (P.673)

--*The Curious Cow.* Meeks, Esther K. (1909-). 1960. Follett. (P.639)

--*The Curious Cow.* Meeks, Esther K. (1909-). 1973. Schol Bk Serv. (P.639)

--*Little Quack.* Woods, Ruth Maurine. 1961. Follett Pub. Co. (P.977)

--*The Little Red Hen.* Berg, Jean Horton (1913-), ed. 1963. Follett Pub. Co. (P.96)

--*The Magic Beans.* Hillert, Margaret (1920-). 1966. Follett Pub. Co. (P.444)

--*The Three Goats.* Hillert, Margaret (1920-). 1963. Follett Pub. Co. (P.445)

--*Three Goats.* Hillert, Margaret (1920-). 1963. Modern Curr. (P.445)

Pelavin, Cheryl (1946-)

--*Dumb Joey.* 1st ed. Gelman, Rita Golden (1937-). 1973. Holt, Rinehart and Winston. (P.363)

--*The Little Brown Bear.* Pelavin, Cheryl (1946-). 1972. Putnam. (P.716)

--*The Marshmallow Caper.* Miklowitz, Gloria D (1927-). 1971. Putnam. (P.644)

--*Ruby's Revenge.* Pelavin, Cheryl (1946-). 1972. Putnam. (P.716)

--*The Scary Woods.* Keller, Victor. 1971. Four Winds Press. (P.514)

--*There Once Was a Cat.* Pelavin, Cheryl (1946-). 1969. Dial Press. (P.716)

Pelch, Adalbert

--*Viva Mexico.* Bruckner, Karl (1906-). N.D. Roy. (P.144)

Pelikan, Judy

--*If We Could Make Wishes.* Holl, Adelaide Hinkle (1910-). c.1977. Garrard Pub. Co. (P.454)

Pelkey, Sofia

--*Holidays of Legend: From New Year's to Christmas.* Arthur, Mildred H. 1971. Harvey. (P.49)

Pell, Roy

--*The Crisscross Shadow.* Dixon, Franklin W, pseud. Stratemeyer Syndicate. 1953. Grosset & Dunlap. (P.273)

--*The Secret of Wildcat Swamp.* Dixon, Franklin W, pseud. Stratemeyer Syndicate. 1952. Grosset & Dunlap. (P.274)

Pell, William B.

--*Daddy's Good Night Stories.* Smith, George Henry (1873-). 1914. McDevitt-Wilson's. (P.833)

Pellei, Ida

--*Cat & the Fiddle & Other Stories.* Clare, Helen, pseud. (1921-). Hunter Blair, Pauline Clarke. 1968. P-H. (P.196)

--*The Cat and the Fiddle, and Other Stories.* Clare, Helen, pseud. (1921-). Hunter Blair, Pauline Clarke. 1968. Prentice-Hall. (P.196)

Peller, Jackie

--*Animal Jingles.* Georgiana. 1950. Whitman. (P.364)

--*Lucky Four Leaf Clover.* Antonie, Rosalind Lane. 1949. Whitman Pub. Co. (P.43)

--*The Three Little Pigs.* Three Little Pigs. c.1954. Wonder Books. (P.890)

Peller, Jackie, jt. illus. see Tamburine, Jean.

Peller, Jackie & Tamburine, Jean (1930-)

--*Little Red Riding Hood and The Three Little Pigs.* N.D. Grosset & Dunlap. (P.716)

--*Little Red Riding Hood and The Three Little Pigs.* N.D. Wonder Books. (P.716)

Pellicer, Joseph Luis

--*The Geese That Sang.* Trento, Florence. 1960. Morrow. (P.899)

--*John Marshall, Boy of Young America.* Monsell, Helen Albee (1895-1971). 1962. Bobbs-Merrill. (P.657)

--*Peter Stuyvesant, Boy with Wooden Shoes.* Widdemer, Mabel Cleland (1902-1964). 1950. Bobbs-Merrill. (P.956)

--*Song for a Lute.* 1st ed. Vance, Marguerite (1889-1965). 1958. Dutton. (P.913)

Pels, Winslow (1947-)

--*Spectacles.* Beattie, Ann (1947-). 1985. Ariel Books : Workman. (P.85)

Peltier, Pam

--*My "A" Book.* special rev. ed. Moncure, Jane Belk (1926-). c.1984. Child's World. (P.655)

--*My "A" Sound Box.* Moncure, Jane Belk (1926-). c.1984. Child's World. (P.655)

--*My First Halloween Book.* Reece, Colleen L & Child's World (Firm). c.1984. Childrens Press. (P.753)

--*My First Valentine's Day Book.* Bennett, Marian. c.1985. Childrens Press. (P.94)

--*My "U" Book.* special rev. ed. Moncure, Jane Belk (1926-). c.1984. Child's World. (P.656)

--*My "U" Sound Box.* Moncure, Jane Belk (1926-). c.1984. Child's World. (P.656)

Peltzer, Remi

--*The Redcomb and the Fox.* Coen, Fabio. c.1979. Knopf. (P.206)

Pena, Narciso

--*Kikiriki: Stories & Poems in English & Spanish for Children.* Pena, Sylvia Cavazos, ed. 1981. Arte Publico. (P.716)

Penalva

--*Robo Force & the Giant Robot.* McEvoy, Seth. 1985. Random. (P.601)

Pendergrass, Mark

--*In the Land of the Music Machine.* Weber, Ane. 1984. Cook. (P.939)

--*Return to the Land of the Music Machine.* Weber, Ane. 1984. Cook. (P.939)

Pendle, Alexy

--*The Children of Hermitage.* Crompton, Frances Eliza. 1971. St. Martins Press. (P.232)

--*Great Dragon Competition & Other Stories.* Cunliffe, John Arthur (1933-). 1980. Andre Deutsch. (P.235)

--*Miss Rivers and Miss Bridges.* Symons, Dorothy Geraldine (1909-). 1972, c.1971. Macmillan. (P.875)

--*Riddles & Rhymes & Rigmaroles.* Cunliffe, John Arthur (1933-). 1982. Andre Deutsch. (P.235)

--*The Workhouse Child.* Symons, Dorothy Geraldine (1909-). 1971, c.1969. Macmillan. (P.875)

Pendleton, Cora Landrum

--*Children of the King.* Pendleton, Cora Landrum. 1955. Review and Herald Association. (P.716)

--*Richard and Judy.* Pendleton, Cora Landrum. 1954. Printed by the Review and Herald Pub. Association. (P.716)

Penfield, George W.

--*Officer Bear of the Alder Bottom: And Other Stories About the Alder Bottom Folks.* Hugo, Frederick. c.1933. Smith Publicity Co. (P.472)

Penick, Ib, jt. illus. see Baker, Darrell.

Penney, Janice

--*Add-A-Rhyme.* Cunningham, Virginia (1909-). c.1941. Garden City Pub. Co. (P.235)

--*His Name is Jesus.* Wilder, John Watson. N.D. Reilly & Lee. (P.959)

Penney, Lizzie, Miss

--*Brave Boys and Girls, 1 of 6 Vols.* Penney, Lizzie, Miss, ed. N.D. National Temperance Society. (P.716)

--*Bright Stories for Young Readers, 1 of 6 Vols.* Penney, Lizzie, Miss, ed. N.D. National Temperance Society. (P.716)

--*Buttercups and Daisies.* Penney, Lizzie, Miss. N.D. DeWolfe, Fiske & Co. (P.716)

--*Buttercups and Daisies.* Penney, Lizzie, Miss. N.D. Dodd, Mead & Co. (P.716)

--*Buttercups and Daisies.* Penney, Lizzie, Miss. N.D. George H. Doran. (P.716)

--*Dainty Bits, 1 of 6 Vols.* Penney, Lizzie, Miss, ed. N.D. National Temperance Society. (P.716)

--*Fire-Side Stories.* Penney, Lizzie, Miss, ed. N.D. National Temperance Society's Publications. (P.716)

--*Gems for Bands of Hope.* Penney, Lizzie, Miss, ed. N.D. National Temperance Society's Publications. (P.716)

--*Home Stories for Little Folks.* Penney, Lizzie, Miss. 1898. J. B. Dunn. (P.716)

--*Little Dew-Drops, 1 of 6 Vols.* Penney, Lizzie, Miss, ed. N.D. National Temperance Society. (P.716)

--*Little People's Favorite, 1 of 6 Vols.* Penney, Lizzie, Miss, ed. N.D. National Temperance Society. (P.716)

--*Little Stories for Little People.* Penney, Lizzie, Miss, ed. N.D. National Temperance Society's Publications. (P.716)

--*Our Pets.* Penney, Lizzie, Miss, ed. N.D. National Temperance Society's Publications. (P.716)

--*Pebbles and Pearls, 1 of 6 Vols.* Penney, Lizzie, Miss, ed. N.D. National Temperance Society. (P.716)

--*Pebbles from the Brook.* Penney, Lizzie, Miss, ed. N.D. National Temperance Society's Publications. (P.716)

--*Stories of Little Heroes.* Penney, Lizzie, Miss. 1898. J. B. Dunn. (P.716)

--*Wee Girls and Boys.* Penney, Lizzie, Miss. 1898. J. B. Dunn. (P.716)

Pennington, Eunice (1923-)

--*Perry, the Pet Pig.* Pennington, Eunice (1923-). 1966. Pennington. (P.716)

Pennington, Harper

--*When the Heart Is Young.* Whitelock, William Wallace (1869-). 1902. E. P. Dutton & Company. (P.954)

Pennington, Pat

--*Melinda's Doll House.* Edmundson, Bess. c.1963. Dorrance. (P.297)

Pennock, Anne

--*The Second Froggy Fairy Book.* Biddle, Anthony Joseph Drexel (1874-). 1898. D. Biddle. (P.101)

Peper, Niel

--*Patsy's Best Summer.* Menius, Opal. 1959. A-W. (P.641)

--*Patsy's Best Summer: A Story.* Menius, Opal. 1959. Scott. (P.641)

Peppe, Rodney Darrell (1934-)

--*The Alphabet Book.* Peppe, Rodney Darrell (1934-). 1968. Four Winds Press. (P.717)

--*Cat & Mouse.* Peppe, Rodney Darrell (1934-). 1980. Penguin. (P.717)

--*Cat & Mouse: A Book of Rhymes.* Peppe, Rodney Darrell (1934-). N.D. HR&W. (P.717)

--*Hey, Riddle Diddle.* Peppe, Rodney Darrell (1934-), ed. 1979. Penguin. (P.717)

--*Hey Riddle Diddle: A Book of Traditional Riddles.* 1971. Holt, Rinehart and Winston. (P.717)

--*The House That Jack Built.* 1970. Delacorte Press. (P.717)

--*Humpty Dumpty.* Peppe, Rodney Darrell (1934-). 1976, c.1975. Viking Press. (P.717)

--*The Kettleship Pirates.* Peppe, Rodney Darrell (1934-). 1983. Lothrop. (P.717)

--*The Little Painter.* Marchant, Ralph & Marchant, Jill. 1971. Carolrhoda Books. (P.619)

--*The Mice and the Flying Basket.* Peppe, Rodney Darrell (1934-). c.1985. Lothrop, Lee & Shepard Books. (P.717)

--*The Mice Who Lived in a Shoe.* Peppe, Rodney Darrell (1934-). 1982, c.1981. Lothrop, Lee & Shepard Books. (P.717)

--*Odd One Out.* 1st American ed. Peppe, Rodney Darrell (1934-). 1974. Viking Press. (P.717)

--*Run Rabbit, Run.* Peppe, Rodney Darrell (1934-). 1982. Delacorte. (P.717)

--*Simple Simon.* 1973, c.1972. Holt, Rinehart and Winston. (P.717)

--*Three Little Pigs.* Peppe, Rodney Darrell (1934-) & Jacobs, Joseph (1854-1916). c.1979. Lothrop, Lee & Shepard Books. (P.717)

Pepper, Dennis

--*The Elephant Book.* Pepper, Dennis. 1984. Merrimack Pub Cir. (P.717)

Perard, Victor Semon (1870-1957)

--*The Bob's Cave Boys: A Sequel to "The Boys of Bob's Hill", Being More About the Doings of the "Band", As Told by the "Secretary".* Burton, Charles Pierce (1862-). 1909. H. Holt and Company. (P.157)

--*Felicia and the Sandman.* Fezandie, Hector. c.1935. The Somerset Press. (P.323)

--*In African Forest and Jungle.* Du Chaillu, Paul Belloni (1831-1903). 1903. C. Scribner's Sons. (P.286)

--*King Mombo.* Du Chaillu, Paul Belloni (1831-1903). 1902. C. Scribner's Sons. (P.286)

--*The Land of Lost Dolls: Or, Really-Truly and Otherwise.* Fezandie, Hector. 1937. T. F. Kyle. (P.323)

--*Lost Covers.* Turpin, Edna Henry Lee (1867-). c.1937. Random House. (P.906)

--*Pete Cow-Puncher: A Story of the Texas Plains.* Ames, Joseph Bushnell (1878-1928). 1908. H. Holt and Company. (P.33)

--*The Quietness of Dick.* Vernede, Robert Ernest (1875-1917). 1911. H. Holt and Company. (P.918)

--*Rip Van Winkle.* Irving, Washington (1783-1859). N.D. Frederick A. Stokes. (P.482)

--*Rip Van Winkle.* Irving, Washington (1783-1859). N.D. J. B. Lippincott. (P.482)

--*The Secret of Old Thunder-Head.* Irwin, Louise Godfrey. 1909. H. Holt and Company. (P.482)

--*Through Swamp and Glade: A Tale of the Seminole War.* Munroe, Kirk (1850-1930). 1896. C. Scribner's Sons. (P.672)

--*A Patriot Lad of Old Philadelphia.* Carter, Russell Gordon (1892-1957). 1924. The Penn Publishing Company. (P.176)
--*A Patriot Lad of Old Salem.* Carter, Russell Gordon (1892-1957). 1925. The Penn Publishing Company. (P.176)
--*Peter and the Wanderlust.* Moray Williams, Ursula (1911-). c.1940. J. B. Lippincott Company. (P.662)
--*A Prairie Rose.* Bush, Bertha Evangeline (1866-). 1925. Little, Brown and Company. (P.158)
--*Princesses & Peasant Boys: Tales of Enchantment.* Fenner, Phyllis Reid (1899-1982), selected by. 1944. A. A. Knopf. (P.322)
--*Pugnax the Gladiator.* Anderson, Paul Lewis (1880-1956). 1959, c.1939. Biblo and Tannen. (P.40)
--*Pugnax the Gladiator.* Anderson, Paul Lewis (1880-1956). 1939. D. Appleton-Century Company, Incorporated. (P.40)
--*Quest of the Sages' Stone.* Reinherz, Nathan (1910-). 1951. Crowell. (P.757)
--*Razzberry Jamboree.* Kohler, Julilly House (1908-1976). 1957. Crowell. (P.534)
--*The Red Prior's Legacy: The Story of the Adventures of an American Boy in the French Revolution.* Bill, Alfred Hoyt (1879-1964). 1929. Longmans, Green & Co. (P.102)
--*River of the West: The Story of the Boston Men.* 1st ed. Sperry, Armstrong W. (1897-1976). 1952. Winston. (P.843)
--*Robert the Roundhead.* Stratton, Clarence (1880-). 1930. Oxford University Press. (P.866)
--*Robinson Crusoe.* Defoe, Daniel (1661-1731) & Thorndike, Edward Lee (1874-). c.1936. D. Appleton-Century Company, Incorporated. (P.251)
--*The Royal Road.* 1st ed. Simon, Charlie May, Mrs., pseud. (1897-). Fletcher, Charlie May Hogue. 1948. E. P. Dutton. (P.825)
--*Sacramento Sam.* Moore, David William (1895-1954). 1951. Crowell. (P.660)
--*The Scarlet Jib.* Moore, David William (1895-1954). 1950. Crowell. (P.660)
--*Shadow of the Crown: A Story of Malta.* 1st ed. Bolton, Ivy May (1879-). 1931. Longmans, Green and Co. (P.113)
--*The Shoo-Fly Pie.* Jordan, Mildred Anne (1901-). 1944. A. A. Knopf. (P.501)
--*The Spanish Cave.* Household, Geoffrey Edward West (1900-). 1936. Little, Brown, and Company. (P.466)
--*Sprigs of Hemlock: A Tale of the Shays Rebellion.* Dyer, Walter Alden (1878-1943). c.1931. The Century Co. (P.293)
--*The Story of Beowulf: Retold from the Ancient Epic.* Riggs, Strafford, ed. c.1933. D. Appleton-Century Company, Incorporated. (P.764)
--*The Story of Rolf and the Viking's Bow.* French, Allen (1870-1946). 1924. Little, Brown, and Company. (P.344)
--*Tales of the Gauchos.* Hudson, William Henry (1841-1922). Coatsworth, Elizabeth Jane (1893-), ed. 1946. A. A. Knopf. (P.469)
--*Tales of True Knights.* Krapp, George Philip (1872-1934). 1921. The Century Co. (P.537)
--*Tangle-Britches.* Peckham, Betty Clock (1906-). N.D. E. P. Dutton & Co. (P.715)
--*Tangle-Britches, a Pennsylvania Dutch Story.* 1st ed. Peckham, Betty Clock (1906-). 1954. Aladdin Books. (P.715)
--*There Was a Horse: Folktales from Many Lands.* Fenner, Phyllis Reid (1899-1982), selected by. 1941. A. A. Knopf. (P.322)
--*Time to Laugh: Funny Tales from Here and There.* Fenner, Phyllis Reid (1899-1982), selected by. 1942. A. A. Knopf. (P.322)
--*The Trade Wind.* Meigs, Cornelia Lynde (1884-1973). 1927. Little, Brown, and Company. (P.639)
--*Trading East.* Smith, Edith Freelove. 1930. Little, Brown, and Company. (P.832)
--*Treason at the Point.* Nolan, Jeannette Covert, Mrs. (1896-1974). 1944. J. Messner, Inc. (P.684)
--*Under Two Eagles.* Crew, Helen Cecilla Coale, Mrs. (1866-1941). 1929. Little, Brown, and Company. (P.231)
--*Valley of Rebellion: A Story of America's First Armed Revolt Against British Authority.* 1st ed. Cooke, Donald Ewin (1916-). 1955. Winston. (P.215)
--*The Vikings.* Janeway, Elizabeth (1913-). 1951. Random House. (P.489)
--*The Vikings.* Janeway, Elizabeth (1913-). 1981. Random. (P.489)
--*Washington Adventure.* Banks, Stockton Voorhees (1908-1980). 1950. Whittlesey House. (P.68)
--*When Guns Thundered at Tripoli.* Finger, Charles Joseph (1871-1941). c.1937. H. Holt and Company. (P.325)
--*White Birds Island.* Skrebitskii, Georgii Alekseevich (1903-). Voynow, Zina, tr. from Russian. 1948. Knopf. (P.828)
--*The Widow Woman and Her Goat.* Walsh, Mary Regina (1889-). 1949. A. A. Knopf. (P.928)
--*Wild Boy.* 1st ed. Snow, Donald Clifford (1917-). Fall, Thomas, pseud. 1965. Dial Press. (P.838)
--*Winter on the Johnny Smoker.* Comfort, Mildred Houghton (1886-). 1943. W. Morrow & Comapny. (P.212)
--*With La Salle, the Explorer.* Watson, Virginia Cruse (1872-). 1922. H. Holt & Company. (P.936)
--*With Might and Main: Stories of Skill and Wit.* 1st ed. Fenner, Phyllis Reid (1899-1982), selected by. 1948. A. A. Knopf. (P.322)
--*The Yankee Captain in Patagonia.* Finger, Charles Joseph (1871-1941). c.1941. Grosset & Dunlap. (P.325)
--*You Fight for Treasure.* Stackpole, Edoward Alexander (1903-). N.D. William Morrow & Co. (P.847)
--*You Shall Have a Carriage.* Coatsworth, Elizabeth Jane (1893-). 1941. The Macmillan Company. (P.204)

Pitzenberger, Lawrence J. & Govern, Elaine R. (1939-), photos by
--*Ice Cream Next Summer.* Govern, Elaine R. (1939-). 1973. A. Whitman. (P.379)

Piussi-Campbell, Judy
--*Big Red Hen.* 1st ed. O'Neill, Mary Le Duc (1908-). 1971. Doubleday. (P.694)
--*Poor Merlo.* 1st ed. O'Neill, Mary Le Duc (1908-). 1967. Atheneum. (P.694)
--*The Talking Crocodile.* Dostoevsky, Fyodor Mikhailovich (1821-1881). Campbell, M. Rudolph, adapted by. 1968. Atheneum. (P.281)
--*Talking Crocodile.* Dostoevsky, Fyodor Mikhailovich (1821-1881). Campbell, M. Rudolph, adapted by. 1968. Atheneum. (P.281)
--*Words, Words, Words.* 1st ed. O'Neill, Mary Le Duc (1908-). 1966. Doubleday. (P.694)

Pizer, Ellen
--*The Lie.* Helena, Ann. c.1977. Raintree Editions. (P.431)

Plaisted, Florence
--*Catharine's Proxy.* Hamlin, Myra Louisa Sawyer, Mrs. (1856-). 1902. Little, Brown, and Company. (P.409)

Plasencia, Peter P.
--*In the Deep Blue Sea.* Morgan, Elizabeth. 1962. Prentice-Hall. (P.663)
--*Space Alphabet.* Zacks, Irene. 1964. Prentice-Hall. (P.991)
--*Windwagon Smith.* Rees, Ennis Samuel, Jr. (1925-). 1966. Prentice. (P.753)

Platt, Margaret
--*Bright Morning.* Bianco, Margery Williams, Mrs. (1881-1944). 1942. Viking Press. (P.100)
--*The House Between.* Parton, Ethel (1862-1944). 1943. Viking Press. (P.708)
--*The Lost Locket: The Newburyport of 1830.* Parton, Ethel (1862-1944). 1940. The Viking Press. (P.708)
--*Tabitha Mary: A Little Girl of 1810.* Parton, Ethel (1862-1944). 1933. The Viking Press. (P.708)
--*The Year Without a Summer: A Story of 1816.* Parton, Ethel (1862-1944). 1945. The Viking Press. (P.708)

Pletsch, Oscar, et al. (1830-1888)
--*Nursery Carols.* Monsell, John Samuel Bowley (1811-1875). N.D. Pott, Young & Co. (P.657)

Pletsch, Oscar (1830-1888)
--*Baby Ballads.* Baker, George Melville (1832-1890). 1877. Lee and Shepard. (P.62)
--*Buttercups and Daisies.* 1875. George Routledge & Sons. (P.728)
--*Chimes and Rhymes for Youthful Times.* N.D. George Routledge & Sons. (P.728)
--*The Golden Harp.* Dulcken, Henry William, Dr. (1832-1894). N.D. George Routledge & Sons. (P.288)
--*One by One.* Dulcken, Henry William, Dr. (1832-1894). N.D. George Routledge & Sons. (P.288)
--*One by One: A Child's Book of Fables and Tales.* Dulcken, Henry William, Dr. (1832-1894). N.D. George Routledge & Sons. (P.288)
--*Rhyme and Reason.* Dulcken, Henry William, Dr. (1832-1894). N.D. George Routledge & Sons. (P.288)
--*Rhyme and Reason: A Picture boook of Verses for Little Folks.* Dulcken, Henry William, Dr. (1832-1894). N.D. George Routledge & Sons. (P.288)

Ploss, Douglas A.
--*The Tweens at Deep Lake: An Original American Fantasy.* Ploss, Douglas A. 1979. D A Ploss. (P.728)

Plume, Ilse
--*The Bremen Town Musicians.* 1st ed. Plume, Ilse. c.1980. Doubleday. **Awards: (ALA); (RCM).** (P.729)
--*The Hedgehog Boy: A Latvian Folktale.* Langton, Jane Gillson (1922-). c.1985. Harper & Row. (P.551)
--*The Velveteen Rabbit: Or, How Toys Become Real.* Bianco, Margery Williams, Mrs. (1881-1944). 1983. Godine. (P.100)

Plummer, Nancy
--*Try Again Tommy.* Boyle, Emily Joyce (1901-). c.1956. Abingdon Press. (P.123)

Plummer, William Kirtman
--*Aesop's Fables.* Aesopus. 1963. Grosset & Dunlap. (P.13)
--*Assignment in Alaska.* James, Josephine, pseud. (1894-) & Lindsay, Barbara. Sterne, Emma Gelders. c.1961. Golden Press. (P.488)
--*Courage in Crisis.* James, Josephine, pseud. (1894-) & Lindsay, Barbara. Sterne, Emma Gelders. 1964. Golden Press. (P.488)
--*Cruising to Danger.* Allan, Mabel Esther (1915-). Hagon, Priscilla, pseud. c.1966. World. (P.28)
--*Henry Wadsworth Longfellow, Gifted Young Poet.* Melin, Grace Hathaway (1892-1973). 1968. Bobbs-Merril Co. (P.640)
--*Junior Nurse.* James, Josephine, pseud. (1894-) & Lindsay, Barbara. Sterne, Emma Gelders. 1960. Golden Press. (P.488)
--*Morning, Noon, Night.* Wilson, Dorothy (1920-). 1963. Grosset & Dunlop. (P.966)
--*Mystery at Saint-Hilaire.* Allan, Mabel Esther (1915-). Hagon, Priscilla, pseud. 1968. World Pub. Co. (P.28)
--*Mystery at the Villa Bianca.* Allan, Mabel Esther (1915-). Hagon, Priscilla, pseud. 1969. World Pub. Co. (P.28)
--*Off-Duty Nurse.* James, Josephine, pseud. (1894-) & Lindsay, Barbara. Sterne, Emma Gelders. 1964. Golden Press. (P.488)
--*The Patient in Two-Zero-Two.* James, Josephine, pseud. (1894-) & Lindsay, Barbara. Sterne, Emma Gelders. 1961. Golden Press. (P.488)
--*Private Nurse.* James, Josephine, pseud. (1894-) & Lindsay, Barbara. Sterne, Emma Gelders. 1962. Golden Press. (P.488)
--*Search for an Island.* James, Josephine, pseud. (1894-) & Lindsay, Barbara. Sterne, Emma Gelders. 1963. Golden Press. (P.488)
--*Senior Nurse.* James, Josephine, pseud. (1894-) & Lindsay, Barbara. Sterne, Emma Gelders. 1960. Golden Press. (P.488)
--*Ship's Boy with Magellan.* 1st ed. Lomask, Milton Nachman (1909-). c.1960. Doubleday. (P.581)
--*Sierra Adventure.* James, Josephine, pseud. (1894-) & Lindsay, Barbara. Sterne, Emma Gelders. 1964. Golden Press. (P.488)
--*We Were There at the Driving of the Golden Spike.* Shepherd, David Gwynne (1924-). 1960. Grosset & Dunlap. (P.818)
--*Where Valor Lies.* DeLeeuw, Cateau Wilhelmina (1903-1975). 1959. Doubleday. (P.255)

Plump, Nikolaus
--*Plum Blossom and Kai Lin.* Weiss-Sonnenburg, Hedwig. 1960. Franklin Watts, Inc. (P.943)

Plunkett, Barbara
--*Lovely Lana, the Hula Champion.* Carver, Marjorie Reineman. 1978. Margaritas Bks for Brown Eyes. (P.176)
--*Sam Diego, a Coloring Adventure in San Diego, California.* Plunkett, Barbara. 1977. Rand-Tofua. (P.729)

Plympton, Almira George (1852-1939)
--*Betty, a Butterfly.* Plympton, Almira George (1852-1939). 1891. Roberts Brothers. (P.729)
--*The Black Dog and Other Stories.* Plympton, Almira George (1852-1939). 1896. Roberts Brothers. (P.729)
--*Bonnie, Little Bonibel" and Her "Day off,".* A Story. Brine, Mary Dow Northam, Mrs. 1890. E. P. Dutton and Company. (P.132)
--*Dear Daughter Dorothy.* Plympton, Almira George (1852-1939). N.D. Little, Brown. (P.729)
--*Dear Daughter Dorothy.* Plympton, Almira George (1852-1939). 1890. Roberts Brothers. (P.729)
--*Flipwing, the Spy.* A Fable for Children. Wesselhoeft, Elizabeth Foster Pope, Mrs. (1840-1919). Wesselhoeft, Lily F., pseud. 1889. Roberts Brothers. (P.946)
--*A Flower of the Wilderness.* Rev ed. Plympton, Almira George (1852-1939). 1899. Little, Brown, and Company. (P.729)
--*Little Olive the Heiress.* Plympton, Almira George (1852-1939). c.1899. Little, Brown, and Company. (P.729)
--*The Little Sister of Wilifred.* Plympton, Almira George (1852-1939). 1892. Roberts Brothers. (P.729)
--*The Mary Jane Papers.* Plympton, Almira George (1852-1939). 1906. F. A. Stokes Company. (P.729)
--*The Mary Jane Papers: A Book for Girls.* Plympton, Almira George (1852-1939). 1884. White, Stokes, & Allen. (P.729)
--*Penelope Prig and Other Stories.* Plympton, Almira George (1852-1939). 1894. Roberts Brothers. (P.729)
--*Rags and Velvet Gowns.* Plympton, Almira George (1852-1939). 1894. Roberts Brothers. (P.729)
--*Robin Recruit.* Plympton, Almira George (1852-1939). 1893. Roberts Brothers. (P.729)
--*Two Dogs and a Donkey.* Plympton, Almira George (1852-1939). 1900. Little, Brown and Company. (P.729)
--*Wanolasset, The-Little-One-Who-Laughs.* Plympton, Almira George (1852-1939). 1897. Roberts Brothers. (P.729)

Pocock, Guy Noel (1880-)
--*Fairy Tales.* Grimm, Jakob Ludwig Karl (1785-1863) & Grimm, Wilhelm Karl (1786-1859). N.D. George H Doran. (P.391)
--*Grimm's Fairy Tales.* Grimm, Jakob Ludwig Karl (1785-1863) & Grimm, Wilhelm Karl (1786-1859). 1930. Garden City Publishing Company, Inc. (P.392)
--*The Life and Strange Surprising Adventures of Robinson Crusoe, of York, Mariner: As Related by Himself.* Defoe, Daniel (1661-1731). 1931. Garden City Publishing Company, Inc. (P.250)
--*Robinson Crusoe.* Defoe, Daniel (1661-1731). N.D. George H Doran. (P.251)

Poe, Lucy Arnold
--*Mid-Summer Day: A Tale of the Olden Time.* Howitt, Mary Botham, Mrs. (1799-1888). c.1931. R. G. Badger. (P.468)

Poehlmann, Joanna
--*Just-Alike Princes.* Meek, Pauline Palmer (1917-). c.1966. Whitman Pub. Co. (P.638)
--*The Poky Little Puppy.* 1981. Western Pub. (P.730)

Pogany, Elaine Cox, Mrs. & Pogany, Willy (1882-1955)
--*Peterkin.* Pogany, Elaine Cox, Mrs. & Pogany, Willy (1882-1955). c.1940. David McKay Company. (P.730)

Pogany, Willy
--*The Hungarian Fairy Book.* Pogany, Nandor, ed. 1913. Frederick A. Stokes. (P.730)

Pogany, Willy, jt. illus. see Pogany, Elaine Cox, Mrs.

Pogany, Willy (1882-)
--*Golden Cockerel.* Pushkin, Alexander Sergeyevich (1799-1837). Pogany, Elaine Cox, Mrs., ed. 1938. T. Nelson and sons. (P.742)

Pogany, Willy (1882-1955)
--*The Adventures of Haroun Er Raschid: And Other Tales from the Arabian Nights.* Olcott, Frances Jenkins (1872-1963), ed. 1923. H. Holt & Company. (P.692)
--*The Adventures of Odysseus and the Tale of Troy: The Children's Homer.* Colum, Padraic (1881-1972). 1962. Macmillan. (P.211)
--*ALice in Wonderland.* Carroll, Lewis, pseud. (1832-1898). Dodgson, Charles Lutwidge. N.D. E. P. Dutton & Co. (P.172)
--*Alice's Adventures in Wonderland.* Dodgson, Charles Lutwidge (1832-1898). Carroll, Lewis, pseud. c.1929. E. P. Dutton and Company. (P.277)
--*The Children of Odin.* Colum, Padraic (1881-1972). c.1920. The Macmillan Company. (P.211)
--*The Children of Odin: The Book of Northern Myths.* Colum, Padraic (1881-1972). 1984, c.1920. Collier Books. (P.211)
--*The Children of Odin: The Book of Northern Myths.* Colum, Padraic (1881-1972). 1962, c.1920. Macmillan. (P.211)
--*Children's Homer The Adventures of Odysseus and the Tale of Troy.* Colum, Padraic (1881-1972). 1918. Macmillan. (P.211)
--*The Children's Homer: The Adventures of Odysseus and the Tale of Troy.* Colum, Padraic (1881-1972) & Homerus. 1962, c.1946. Macmillan. (P.211)
--*Children's Plays.* Skinner, Eleanor Louise (1872-) & Skinner, Ada Maria (1878-), eds. 1919. D. Appleton and Company. (P.828)
--*Fairy Flowers: Nature Legends of Facts & Fantasy.* Newman, Isidora. c.1926. H. Holt and Company. (P.680)
--*Fairy Flowers: Nature Legends of Facts & Fantasy.* Newman, Isidora. 1926. H. Milford, Oxford University Press. (P.680)
--*Folks Tales from Many Lands.* Gask, Lilian (1865-). N.D. Thomas Y. Crowell Co. (P.359)
--*Forty-four Turkish Fairy Tales.* Kunos, Ignacz (1862-1945), compiled by. Kunos, Ignacz (1882-), tr. 1914. T. Y. Crowell Co. (P.542)
--*The Frenzied Prince: Being Heroic Stories of Ancient Ireland.* Colum, Padraic (1881-1972). 1943. David McKay Company. (P.211)
--*The Golden Cockerel.* Pogany, Elaine Cox, Mrs. N.D. Thomas Nelson & Co. (P.730)
--*The Golden Fleece and the Heroes Who Lived Before Achilles.* Colum, Padraic (1881-1972). 1962. Macmillan. (P.211)
--*The Golden Fleece and the Heroes Who Lived Before Achilles.* Colum, Padraic (1881-1972). 1983, c.1921. Macmillan. (P.211)
--*The Golden Fleece and the Heroes Who Lived Before Achilles.* Colum, Padraic (1881-1972). c.1921. The Macmillan Company. **Award: (JNM).** (P.211)

Prouty, Esther
--*Crazy Quilt Circus.* Dettinger, Alma. c.1933. R. H. Cunningham. (P.260)

Provensen, Alice, jt. illus. see Provensen, Martin.

Provensen, Alice (1918-) & Provensen, Martin (1916-)
--*Aesop's Fables.* Aesopus. Untermeyer, Louis (1885-1977), ed. c.1965. Golden. (P.13)
--*The Animal Farm.* Provensen, Alice (1918-) & Provensen, Martin (1916-). 1952. Simon and Schuster. **Award: (NYT).** (P.741)
--*Birds, Beasts, and the Third Thing: Poems.* Lawrence, David Herbert (1885-1930). Provensen, Alice (1918-) & Provensen, Martin (1916-), eds. Hall, Donald, intro. by. c.1982. Viking Press. **Award: (ALA).** (P.556)
--*A Child's Garden of Verses.* Stevenson, Robert Louis (1850-1894). 1964, c.1951. Golden Press. (P.856)
--*A Child's Garden of Verses.* Stevenson, Robert Louis (1850-1894). 1973, c.1957. Grosset & Dunlap. (P.856)
--*A Child's Garden of Verses.* Stevenson, Robert Louis (1850-1894). 1951. Simon and Schuster. (P.856)
--*A Child's Garden of Verses: Selections from Robert L.* Stevenson. Stevenson, Robert Louis (1850-1894). 1975. Western Pub. (P.856)
--*The Color Kittens.* Brown, Margaret Wise (1910-1952). c.1949. Simon and Schuster. (P.140)
--*The Color Kittens: A Child's First Book About Colors.* Brown, Margaret Wise (1910-1952). c.1958. Golden Press. (P.140)
--*Fireside Book of Folk Songs.* Boni, Margaret Bradford (1893-1974) & Lloyd, Norman (1909-1980). 1966. S&S. (P.116)
--*Fireside Book of Folk Songs.* Boni, Margaret Bradford (1893-1974) & Lloyd, Norman (1909-1980). 1947. Simon & Schuster. (P.116)
--*The First Noel.* 1959. Golden Press. (P.741)
--*Funny Bunny.* Learnard, Rachel. 1950. Simon and Schuster. (P.559)
--*The Fuzzy Duckling.* Watson, Jane Werner (1915-). 1963, c.1949. Golden Press. (P.935)
--*The Fuzzy Duckling.* Werner, Jane, pseud. (1915-). Watson, Jane Werner. 1949. Simon and Schuster. (P.946)
--*The Fuzzy Duckling.* Watson, Jane Werner (1915-). 1949. Simon and Schuster. (P.935)
--*Giant Golden Mother Goose.* Werner, Jane (1915-). 1948. Western Pub. (P.946)
--*The Golden Book of Fun and Nonsense.* Untermeyer, Louis (1885-1977), compiled by. 1970. Golden Press. (P.910)
--*The Golden Circus.* Jackson, Kathryn (1907-). 1950. Simon and Schuster. (P.485)
--*The Golden Mother Goose.* Bennett, Dorothy Agnes (1909-), ed. 1976. Western Pub. (P.93)
--*The Golden Mother Goose: 367 Childhood Favorites.* Watson, Jane Werner (1915-), ed. 1948. Simon and Schuster. (P.936)
--*The Golden Serpent.* Myers, Walter Dean (1937-). 1980. Viking Press. (P.674)
--*Golden Treasury of Myths & Legends.* White, Anne Terry (1896-), ed. 1959. Western Pub. (P.951)
--*A Horse and a Hound, a Goat and a Gander.* Provensen, Alice (1918-) & Provensen, Martin (1916-). 1980. Atheneum. (P.741)
--*The Ilaid the Odyssey.* Homerus. Watson, Jane Werner (1915-), ed. 1964. Western Pub. (P.457)
--*The Iliad and the Odyssey: The Heroic Story of the Trojan War, the Fabulous Adventures of Odysseus.* Watson, Jane Werner (1915-), adapted by. Homer. 1964, c.1956. Golden Press. (P.457)
--*The Iliad and the Odyssey: The Heroic Story of the Trojan War and the Fabulous Adventures of Odysseus.* Watson, Jane Werner (1915-), adapted by. 1956. Simon and Schuster. (P.936)
--*Karen's Curiosity.* Provensen, Alice (1918-) & Provensen, Martin (1916-). 1963. Golden Press. **Award: (NYT).** (P.741)
--*Karen's Opposites.* Provensen, Alice (1918-) & Provensen, Martin (1916-). 1963. Golden Press. (P.741)
--*Katie the Kitten.* Jackson, Kathryn (1907-) & Jackson, Byron (1899-1949). 1949. Simon and Schuster. (P.485)
--*Legendary Animals.* Untermeyer, Bryna Ivens (1909-) & Untermeyer, Louis (1885-1977), eds. 1963. Golden Press. (P.909)
--*The Little Fat Policeman.* Brown, Margaret Wise (1910-1952) & Hurd, Edith Thacher, Mrs. (1910-). 1950. Simon & Schuster. (P.141)
--*Mother Goose.* Mother Goose. Provensen, Alice (1918-) & Provensen, Martin (1916-), eds. 1976. Random House. **Award: (NYT).** (P.667)
--*Mr.* Noah and His Family. Werner, Jane (1915-). 1948. Simon and Schuster. (P.946)
--*Mr.* Noah and His Family. Watson, Jane Werner (1915-). 1948. Simon and Schuster. (P.935)
--*My Little Hen.* Provensen, Alice (1918-) & Provensen, Martin (1916-). 1973. Random House. (P.741)
--*No Bath Tonight.* Yolen, Jane Hyatt (1939-). 1978. Viking. (P.987)
--*Old Mother Hubbard.* 1982. Random. (P.741)
--*Our Animal Friends at Maple Hill Farm.* Provensen, Alice (1918-) & Provensen, Martin (1916-). 1974. Random House. (P.741)
--*An Owl and Three Pussycats.* Provensen, Alice (1918-) & Provensen, Martin (1916-). 1981. Atheneum. (P.741)
--*A Peaceable Kingdom: The Shaker Abecedarius.* Provensen, Alice (1918-) & Provensen, Martin (1916-). 1981, c.1978. Puffin Books. (P.741)
--*A Peaceable Kingdom: The Shaker Abecedarius.* Provensen, Alice (1918-) & Provensen, Martin (1916-). 1978. Viking Press. **Awards: (NYT); (ALA).** (P.741)
--*The Provensen Book of Fairy Tales.* Provensen, Alice (1918-) & Provensen, Martin (1916-), eds. 1971. Random House. (P.741)
--*Roses Are Red.* Are Violets Blue? A First Book About Color. Provensen, Alice (1918-) & Provensen, Martin (1916-). 1973. Random House. (P.741)
--*Tales from the Ballet.* Untermeyer, Louis (1885-1977). 1968. Western Pub. (P.910)
--*A Visit to William Blake's Inn: Poems for Innocent & Experienced Travelers.* Willard, Nancy (1936-). 1981. HarBraceJ. **Awards: (JNM); (ALA); (RCM).** (P.961)
--*What Is a Color?.* Provensen, Alice (1918-) & Provensen, Martin (1916-). 1967. Golden Press. (P.741)
--*Who's in the Egg.* Provensen, Alice (1918-) & Provensen, Martin (1916-). 1970. Golden Press. (P.741)

Provensen, Martin, jt. illus. see Provensen, Alice.

Provensen, Martin (1916-) & Provensen, Alice (1918-)
--*Herbert's Zoo and Other Lively Tales.* Bianco, Margery Williams, Mrs. (1881-1944) & Burgess, Thornton Waldo (1874-1965). N.D. Simon and Schuster. (P.101)
--*The Year at Maple Hill Farm.* Provensen, Alice (1918-) & Provensen, Martin (1916-). 1978. Atheneum. (P.741)

Provest, Jon
--*Duck in the Park, Duck in the Dark.* Begley, Evelyn M. 1974. Ginn. (P.89)
--*Said the Little Raccoon to the Moon.* Morton, Miriam (1918-), ed. 1974. Ginn. (P.666)

Provonsha, Clyde N.
--*Growing Pains in Nature Study.* Steele, Edwin E. 1956. Southern Pub. Association. (P.850)
--*Ringtail, and Other Stories.* Haughey, Paul S. 1955. Southern Pub. Association. (P.420)

Provost, Charles Hope
--*Timothy and His Friends.* Ireland, Mary Eliza Haines, Mrs. (1834-1927). 1902. The Saalfield Publishing Co. (P.481)

Pruett, Rose Marie
--*Michael the Magnificent.* Simpson, Phyllis. 1967. Steck-Vaughn Co. (P.826)

Pruszynska, Aniela (1888-)
--*The Blacksmith of Vilno.* Kelly, Eric Philbrook (1884-1960). N.D. MacMillan. (P.516)
--*The Girl Who Ruled a Kingdom.* Kellogg, Charlotte Hoffman, Mrs. 1938. D. Appleton-Century Company, Incorporated. (P.515)
--*Golden Star of Halich.* Kelly, Eric Philbrook (1884-1960). N.D. MacMillan. (P.516)
--*The Trumpeter of Krakow.* Kelly, Eric Philbrook (1884-1960). 1928. MacMillan Bks. **Award: (JNM).** (P.516)
--*The Trumpeter of Krakow.* Kelly, Eric Philbrook (1884-1960). 1973, c.1956. MacMillan. (P.516)

Pryse, Gerald Spencer, jt. illus. see Millar, Harold Robert.

Przondak, Catherine
--*Tales from Ransom Valley: Animal Adventures for Little Folk.* 1st ed. Rhodes, Gerald P (1904-). 1953. Exposition Press. (P.760)

Publisher's Photo Service, photos by.
--*In the Air.* MacCarthy, Josephine. 1935. Whitman Publishing. (P.595)

Pucci, Albert John (1920-)
--*Across Five Aprils.* Hunt, Irene (1907-). 1964. Follett Pub. Co. **Awards: (ALA); (JNM).** (P.473)
--*Four to Get Ready!.* Laughlin, Florence Young (1910-). 1968. Western Pub. Co. (P.555)
--*Home in Flames.* Winn, Janet Bruce (1928-). 1972. Follett. (P.969)
--*Jonathan.* Vance, Eleanor Graham (1908-). c.1966. Follett. (P.912)
--*The Riddle Walk.* Moore, Lilian. 1971. Garrard Pub. Co. (P.661)
--*Tail Twisters.* Fisher, Aileen Lucia (1906-). 1973. Bowmar. (P.328)

Pucci, Albert John (1920-) & Barber, Ray
--*A Spooky Story.* Martin, William Ivan, Jr. (1916-). c.1970. Holt, Rinehart and Winston. (P.626)

Pudlo & Kiakshuk
--*Eskimo Songs and Stories.* Field, Edward (1924-) & Rasmussen, Knud Johan Victor (1879-1933). Field, Edward (1924-), tr. 1973. Delacorte Press/S. Lawrence. (P.324)

Puente, H., jt. illus. see Bridges, M. B.

Puett, Judith Flippo
--*Trigo-Kit.* Puett, Judith Flippo. 1970. Naylor Co. (P.741)

Pugh, Clifton
--*Death of a Wombat.* Smith, Ivan. 1973. Scribner. (P.834)

Pugh, Mabel (1891-)
--*Blackbeard's Treasure: A Tale of the Famous Pirate, Captain Teach.* Oertel, Theodore Eugene (1864-). c.1927. Thomas Y. Crowell Company. (P.690)
--*Little Carolina Blue Bonnet.* Pugh, Mabel (1891-). c.1933. Thomas Y. Crowell Co. (P.741)
--*The Other Side of the Mountain.* Justus, May (1898-). 1931. Doubleday, Doran & Company, Inc. (P.503)
--*Peter Pocket: A Little Boy of the Cumberland Mountains.* Justus, May (1898-). 1927. Doubleday, Page, & Company. (P.503)
--*Peter Pocket's Books: Including Peter Pocket and Peter Pocket's Luck.* Justus, May (1898-). 1934. Doubleday, Doran & Company, Inc. (P.503)
--*Peter Pocket's Luck.* 1st ed. Justus, May (1898-). 1930. Doubleday, Doran & Company, Inc. (P.503)
--*Remember and Forget.* Davis, Julia (1900-). c.1932. E. P. Dutton & Company, Inc. (P.246)

Pulido, Shirley
--*Aha and the Jewel of Mystery.* Boshinski, Blanche (1922-). 1968. Parents' Magazine Press. (P.118)

Pullinger, Herbert
--*The Boy Geologist at School and in Camp.* Houston, Edwin James (1847-1914). c.1907. H. Altemus Company. (P.466)
--*The Boy Scouts of Birch-Bank Island.* Holland, Rupert Sargent (1878-1952). 1911. J. B. Lippincott Company. (P.455)
--*Longshore Boys.* Stoddard, William Osborn, Jr. (1873-). 1909. J. B. Lippincott Company. (P.860)
--*Pewee" Clinton, Plebe: A Story of Annapolis.* Stevens, William Oliver (1878-1955). 1912. J. B. Lippincott Company. (P.854)

Purcell, Darryle
--*Calling Earth.* Land, Charles. c.1978. Creative Education. (P.547)

Purdy, Susan Gold (1939-)
--*Suddenly-a Witch!.* Bowen, Irene. 1970. Lippincott. (P.121)

Puricelli, Luigi, jt. illus. see Cristini, Ermanno.

Purtscher, Alfons
--*Rosina Copper, the Mystery Mare.* Barne, Kitty, pseud. (1883-1957). Barne, Marion Catherine. 1956. Dutton. (P.73)

Purvis, Kenny
--*Mrs.* Purvis Visits the SEASHORE. Purvis, Mary E. 1983. Childrens Ctr. (P.742)

Purvis, Mary
--*Animal Alphabet: Wild Animals.* Purvis, Mary E. 1984. Childrens Ctr. (P.742)

Purvis, Susan, jt. photog. see Strauss, Stan.

Puskas, James
--*Purro and the Prattleberries.* Newton, Suzanne (1936-). 1970, c.1971. Westminster Press. (P.681)

Putnam, Claude George
--*Dickey Wickey, the Flying Frog: Desert Fairy Tales.* Putnam, Claude George. c.1933. Suttonhouse. (P.742)

Putney, Effie Florence
--*Doris Marjorie and Her Tales of Fairy Land.* McDaniels, M Alberta. 1930. Educator Supply Company. (P.598)

Puttcamp, Rita
--*Operation Bro-Kee.* Puttcamp, Rita & Willman, Gordon. c.1978. Concordia Pub. House. (P.742)

Pyk, Jan (1934-)
--*The Hammer of Thunder.* Pyk, Ann Phillips (1937-), retold by. Edda, Samundar. 1972. Putnam. (P.742)
--*Karlsson-on-the-Roof.* Lindgren, Astrid Ericsson (1907-). Turner, Marianne, tr. 1971. Viking Press. (P.573)
--*Luap.* Brindel, June Rachuy (1919-). 1971. Bobbs-Merrill. (P.132)
--*Nessie the Monster.* Hughes, Ted (1930-). 1974, c.1964. Bobbs-Merrill. (P.471)
--*The Owl Who Was Afraid of the Dark.* Tomlinson, Jill (1931-1976). 1971, c.1968. Bobbs-Merrill. (P.895)
--*Your Ant is a Which: Fun With Homophones.* 1st ed. Hunt, Bernice Kohn (1920-). c.1976. Harcourt Brace Jovanovich. (P.473)

Pyke, Eliza
--*The Admiral and Others.* Temple, Peggy (1913-). Adcock, St. John, frwd. by. c.1927. E. P. Dutton & Company. (P.881)

Pyle, Howard (1853-1911)
--*The Garden Behind the Moon: A Real Story of the Moon Angel.* Pyle, Howard (1853-1911). 1895. C. Scribner's Sons. (P.742)
--*Howard Pyle's Book of Pirates: Fiction, Fact and Fancy Concerning the Buccaneers of the Spanish Main.* Pyle, Howard (1853-1911). Johnson, Merle De Vore (1874-1935), ed. 1921. Har-Row. (P.742)
--*King Arthur and His Knights.* Malory, Thomas, Sir (1410-1471). MacLeod, Mary (0000-1914), retold by. 1966, c.1964. Parents' Magazine's Cultural Institute. (P.615)
--*The Merry Adventures of Robin Hood.* Pyle, Howard (1853-1911). N.D. Charles Scribner's Sons. (P.743)
--*The Merry Adventures of Robin Hood.* Pyle, Howard (1853-1911). N.D. Peter Smith Publisher, Inc. (P.743)
--*The Merry Adventures of Robin Hood of Great Renown, in Nottinghamshire.* Pyle, Howard (1853-1911). 1883. C. Scribner's Sons. (P.743)
--*The Merry Adventures of Robin Hood of Great Renown, in Nottinghamshire.* Pyle, Howard (1853-1911). 1933. C. Scribner's Sons. (P.743)
--*The Merry Adventures of Robin Hood of Great Renown in Nottinghamshire.* Pyle, Howard (1853-1911). 1946. C. Scribner's Sons. (P.743)
--*The Merry Adventures of Robin Hood: Of Great Renown in Nottinghamshire.* Pyle, Howard (1853-1911). 1968. Dover Publications. (P.743)
--*The Merry Adventures of Robin Hood of Great Renown in Nottinghamshire.* Pyle, Howard (1853-1911). 1966. Junior Deluxe Editions. (P.743)
--*The Merry Adventures of Robin Hood of Great Renown, in Nottinghamshire.* Pyle, Howard (1853-1911). 1966. University Microfilms. (P.743)
--*Otto of the Silver Hand.* Pyle, Howard (1853-1911). 1888. C. Scribner's Sons. (P.743)
--*Otto of the Silver Hand.* Pyle, Howard (1853-1911). 1903. C. Scribner's Sons. (P.743)
--*Otto of the Silver Hand.* Pyle, Howard (1853-1911). 1967. Dover Publications. (P.743)
--*Otto of the Silver Hand.* Pyle, Howard (1853-1911). 1960. Looking Glass Library; Distributed by Random House. (P.743)
--*Otto of the Silver Hand.* Pyle, Howard (1853-1911). 1901. Scribner. (P.743)
--*Otto of the Silver Hand.* Pyle, Howard (1853-1911). 1957. Scribner. (P.743)
--*Otto of the Solver Hand.* Pyle, Howard (1853-1911). 1916. Dover. (P.743)
--*Pepper and Salt.* Pyle, Howard (1853-1911). 1941. Harper. (P.743)
--*Pepper & Salt, or Seasoning for Young Folk: Or, Seasoning for Young Folk.* Pyle, Howard (1853-1911). N.D. Dover. (P.743)
--*Pepper & Salt: Or Seasoning for Young Folks.* Pyle, Howard (1853-1911). N.D. Har-Row. (P.743)
--*Robin Hood.* Gilbert, Henry (1868-). 1964. Parents' Magazine Press. (P.367)
--*Some Merry Adventures of Robin Hood.* Pyle, Howard (1853-1911). 1967. Watts. (P.743)
--*Some Merry Adventures of Robin Hood of Great Renown in Nottinghamshire.* Pyle, Howard (1853-1911). 1902. C. Scribner's Sons. (P.743)
--*Some Merry Adventures of Robin Hood of Great Renown in Nottinghamshire.* Pyle, Howard (1853-1911). c.1935. C. Scribner's Sons. (P.743)
--*Some Merry Adventures of Robin Hood of Great Renown in Nottinghamshire.* Pyle, Howard (1853-1911). 1954. Scribner. (P.743)
--*Storied Holidays.* Brooks, Elbridge Streeter (1846-1902). N.D. Lothrop Lee & Shepard Co. (P.136)
--*The Story of King Arthur and His Knights.* Pyle, Howard (1853-1911), ed. 1903. C. Scribner's Sons. (P.743)
--*The Story of King Arthur and His Knights.* Pyle, Howard (1853-1911). 1965. Dover. (P.743)
--*The Story of King Arthur and His Knights.* Pyle, Howard (1853-1911). 1965. Grosset & Dunlap. (P.743)
--*The Story of King Arthur and His Knights.* Pyle, Howard (1853-1911). 1966. P. Smith. (P.743)
--*The Story of Siegfried.* Baldwin, James (1841-1925). 1882. C. Scribner's Sons. (P.65)
--*The Story of Siegfried.* Baldwin, James (1841-1925). 1888. C. Scribner's Sons. (P.65)
--*The Story of Siegfried.* Baldwin, James (1841-1925). 1904. C. Scribner's Sons. (P.65)
--*The Story of Sir Launcelot and His Companions.* Pyle, Howard (1853-1911). 1907. C. Scribner's Sons. (P.743)
--*The Story of Sir Launcelot and His Companions.* Pyle, Howard (1853-1911). 1933. C. Scribner's Sons. (P.743)
--*The Story of the Champions of the Round Table.* Pyle, Howard (1853-1911). 1905. C. Scribner's Sons. (P.743)
--*The Story of the Champions of the Round Table.* Pyle, Howard (1853-1911). 1933. C. Scribner's Sons. (P.743)
--*The Story of the Champions of the Round Table.* Pyle, Howard (1853-1911). N.D. C. Scribner's Sons. (P.743)
--*The Story of the Champions of the Round Table.* Pyle, Howard (1853-1911). 1968. Dover Publications. (P.743)

--*Piet Potter to the Rescue.* Quackenbush, Robert Mead (1929-). c.1981. McGraw-Hill. (P.744)
--*Piet Potter's First Case.* Quackenbush, Robert Mead (1929-). 1980. McGraw-Hill. (P.744)
--*Piet Potter's Hot Clue.* Quackenbush, Robert Mead (1929-). c.1982. McGraw-Hill. (P.744)
--*Poems for Counting.* Quackenbush, Robert Mead (1929-), compiled by. 1963. Holt. (P.744)
--*Poems for Galloping.* Quackenbush, Robert Mead (1929-), compiled by. 1963. Holt. (P.744)
--*Pop!* Goes the Weasel and Yankee Doodle: New York in 1776 and Today. Quackenbush, Robert Mead (1929-). c.1976. Lippincott. (P.744)
--*Rakoto and the Drongo Bird.* McKown, Robin (0000-1976). c.1966. Lothrop. (P.607)
--*Rickshaw to Horror: A Miss Mallard Mystery.* Quackenbush, Robert Mead (1929-). 1984. P-H. (P.744)
--*The Scribbler.* Mendoza, George (1934-). 1971. Holt, Rinehart & Winston. (P.641)
--*Seal Harbor.* Waters, John Frederick (1930-). 1973. Warne. (P.934)
--*The Selfish Giant.* Wilde, Oscar Fingal O'Flahertie Wills (1854-1900). 1965. Holt, Rinehart and Winston. (P.959)
--*She'll Be Comin' 'round the Mountain.* Quackenbush, Robert Mead (1929-). 1973. Lippincott. (P.744)
--*Sheriff Sally Gopher and the Haunted Dance Hall.* Quackenbush, Robert Mead (1929-). c.1977. Lothrop, Lee & Shepard Co. (P.744)
--*Sheriff Sally Gopher and the Thanksgiving Caper.* Quackenbush, Robert Mead (1929-). c.1982. Lothrop, Lee & Shepard. (P.744)
--*Six Silver Spoons.* Lowrey, Janette Sebring (1892-). 1971. Har-Row. (P.589)
--*Skip to My Lou.* Quackenbush, Robert Mead (1929-). 1975. Lippincott. (P.744)
--*Stairway to Doom: A Miss Mallard Mystery.* Quackenbush, Robert Mead (1929-). c.1983. Prentice-Hall. (P.744)
--*A Sunday in Autumn.* Rowley, Anthony (1920-). c.1967. L. W. Singer Co. (P.782)
--*Taxi to Intrigue.* Quackenbush, Robert Mead (1929-). 1984. P-H. (P.744)
--*There'll Be a Hot Time in the Old Town Tonight.* Quackenbush, Robert Mead (1929-). 1974. Lippincott. (P.744)
--*Too Many Lollipops.* Quackenbush, Robert Mead (1929-). 1975. Parents' Magazine Press. (P.744)
--*The Two Worlds of Damyan.* Bloch, Marie Halun (1910-). 1966. Atheneum. (P.109)
--*When the Monkeys Wore Sombreros.* Prieto, Mariana Beeching (1912-). 1969. Harvey House. (P.740)
--*The Wizard Islands.* Yolen, Jane Hyatt (1939-). 1973. Crowell. (P.987)

Quade, Lester
--*Rajah, the Story of a Bird.* Rawson, Elsie Lewis. 1949. Review and Herald Pub. Association. (P.750)

Quail, David
--*The Little Lion.* Quail, David. N.D. Farrar, Straus & Cudahy. (P.744)

Quarterman, Leonora
--*Mr.* Simmie: Or, The Square Dance in the Clearing. Reddy, Marie E. c.1940. The Christopher Publishing House. (P.752)

Quenell, Midge
--*Going Places.* Fisher, Aileen Lucia (1906-). 1973. Bowmar. (P.327)

Quennell, Marjorie Courtney (1884-1972)
--*Disappearing Island.* Kyle, Elisabeth, pseud. (0000-1982). Dunlop, Agnes Mary Robertson. 1944. Houghton Mifflin Company. (P.543)

Quest, Dan
--*Look, Hiroshi!.* Zimelman, Nathan (1911-). 1973, c.1972. Aurora Publishers. (P.992)

Quigley, E. B.
--*Wild Horse Tamer.* Balch, Glenn (1902-). 1955. Crowell. (P.65)

Quigley, Ray
--*Ben Franklin, Boy Printer.* Stevenson, Augusta (1869-1976). 1962. Bobbs. (P.854)
--*Lightning on Ice.* 1st ed. Phillips, Maurice Jack (1914-1976). 1963. Doubleday. (P.724)

Quinn, Dave
--*The Tooth of Time: A Philmont Adventure.* Sterling, Gray. 1955. M. Jones Co. (P.853)

Quinn, Jeri
--*Bubbles.* Rukeyser, Muriel (1913-1980). 1967. Harcourt, Brace & World. (P.783)

Quinn, Margrit Fiddle
--*Rackety, That Very Special Rabbit.* Friskey, Margaret Richards (1901-). 1975. Childrens Press. (P.347)

Quinn, Paul
--*The Boy Who Lived on London Bridge.* Holland, Rupert Sargent (1878-1952). 1938. Macrae Smith Company. (P.455)
--*Boy's Club.* Siegel, Max (1904-1972). 1939. Houghton Mifflin Company. (P.823)
--*He Went with Magellan.* Kent, Louise Andrews, Mrs. (1886-1969). 1943. Houghton Mifflin Company. (P.519)
--*The Little American Girl.* Allee, Marjorie Hill, Mrs. (1890-1945). 1938. Houghton Mifflin Company. (P.28)
--*Penny for Luck: A Story of the Rockies.* Revised. Means, Florence Crannell, Mrs. (1891-1980) & Riggs, Frances. 1935. Houghton Mifflin Company. (P.638)
--*Redcoats at Castine.* Patterson, Arthur Willis (1888-). 1938. Stephen Daye Press. (P.710)
--*Riding West on the Pony Express.* Skelton, Charles L. 1955. Macmillan. (P.827)
--*Riding West on the Pony Express.* Skelton, Charles L. 1937. The Macmillan Company. (P.827)
--*Roll Out the Tanks.* McGaughey, William Howard (1912-). 1942. Macrae-Smith-Company. (P.601)
--*Son of the Iroquois.* Bunce, William Harvey (1903-). 1936. MacRae Smith Co. (P.149)
--*Tiger Bridge: A Story of Railroad Building in Indo-China.* Miller, Warren Hastings (1876-). c.1937. L. C. Page & Company. (P.649)
--*White Wind: An Account of the Oates Land Party of the Biggers' Antarctic Expedition of 193- to 193-.* Ross, Margaret Isabel (1897-). 1937. Harper & Brothers. (P.779)
--*Wreckers Reef.* Holland, Rupert Sargent (1878-1952). c.1941. Macrae Smith Company. (P.455)

Quinn, Paul, jt. illus. see Baldridge, Cyrus LeRoy.

Quinn, Sidney
--*The Fork in the Trail.* 1st ed. Gendron, Val. 1952. Longmans, Green. (P.363)
--*Gil's Discovery in the Mine.* 1st ed. Lee, Rector Lawrence. 1957. Little, Brown. (P.561)
--*The Greatest Adventure: A Story of Jack London.* 1st ed. Lane, Frederick A. 1954. Aladdin Books. (P.548)
--*Mystery Mine.* Sinclair, Kenneth L (1910-). 1951. Winston. (P.826)
--*Randy Visits the Doctor.* Lakritz, Esther Himmelman (1928-). c.1962. Broadman Press. (P.544)
--*Rod's Dog.* Bailey, Jean (1917-). 1954. Abingdon Press. (P.60)
--*Sara's Trek.* Schloneger, Florence E. 1982. Faith & Life. (P.799)
--*Sunken Timbers.* Hoppenstedt, Elbert M (1917-). c.1938. David McKay Co. (P.463)

Quinn, Tom
--*Time for Gym.* Beim, Jerrold (1910-1957). 1968, c.1957. Houghton. (P.89)

Quint, Frances H.
--*Stories Round the Year: From Rosh Hashanah to Shavuot.* 2d rev. ed. Marenof, Martha, ed. 1969. Dot Publications. (P.619)

Quintanilla, Luis (1900-)
--*The Four Little Foxes.* Schlein, Miriam (1926-). c.1953. W.R. Scott. (P.799)

Quiram, Harold, jt. illus. see Quiram, Marjorie.

Quiram, Marjorie & Quiram, Harold
--*Sammy: The Christmas Adventure.* St. John, Elizabeth, pseud. (1907-). John, Elizabeth Beaman. Handel, Joanna, ed. 1976. Handel & Sons Publishing. (P.789)
--*Sammy, the White House Mouse.* St. John, Elizabeth, pseud. (1907-). John, Elizabeth Beaman. Handel, Joanna, ed. 1976. Handel. (P.789)

Quirk, Thomas
--*The Ghost Garden.* 1st ed. Feil, Hila (1942-). 1975, c.1976. Atheneum. (P.320)

Rabens, Neil W.
--*Bunker Bear.* Rabens, Neil W. Bennett, Marian, ed. 1978. Standard Pub. (P.745)
--*One Happy Little Songbird.* Rabens, Neil W. 1979. Standard Pub. (P.745)

Rabinowitz, Sandy (1954-)
--*A Colt Named Mischief.* Rabinowitz, Sandy (1954-). c.1979. Doubleday. (P.745)
--*How I Trained My Cat.* Rabinowitz, Sandy (1954-). 1981. Doubleday. (P.745)
--*The Red Horse and the Bluebird.* Rabinowitz, Sandy (1954-). 1975. Harper & Row. (P.745)
--*The Something-Special Horse.* Hall, Lynn (1937-). c.1985. Scribner. (P.405)

Rache, Elmer
--*Uncle Wiggily and the Littletails.* Garis, Howard Roger (1873-1962). 1942. The Platt & Munk Co., Inc. (P.357)
--*Uncle Wiggily in the Country.* Garis, Howard Roger (1873-1962). c.1940. The Platt & Munk Co., Inc. (P.357)
--*Uncle Wiggily on the Farm.* Garis, Howard Roger (1873-1962). c.1939. The Platt & Munk Co., Inc. (P.357)
--*Uncle Wiggily's Adventures.* Garis, Howard Roger (1873-1962). c.1940. The Platt & Munk Co. Inc. (P.357)
--*Uncle Wiggily's Auto Sled.* Garis, Howard Roger (1873-1962). 1936. Platt & Munk co. (P.357)
--*Uncle Wiggily's Automobile.* Garis, Howard Roger (1873-1962). c.1939. The Platt & Munk Co., Inc. (P.357)
--*Uncle Wiggily's Fortune.* Garis, Howard Roger (1873-1962). 1942. The Platt & Munk Co., Inc. (P.357)
--*Uncle Wiggily's Happy Days.* Garis, Howard Roger (1873-1962). 1947. The Platt & Munk Co., Inc. (P.357)
--*Uncle Wiggily's Travels.* Garis, Howard Roger (1873-1962). c.1939. The Platt & Munk Co., Inc. (P.357)

Rachel
--*Cradle Rhymes.* Horn, Gladys M. 1949. Whitman Pub. Co. (P.464)

Rackham, Arthur, jt. illus. see Ford, Julia Lauren.

Rackham, Arthur, jt. illus. see Greenaway, Kate.

Rackham, Arthur (1867-1939)
--*Aesop's Fables.* 1967. Franklin Watts Single Titles. (P.745)
--*Aesop's Fables.* Aesopus. N.D. Doubleday Page & Co. (P.13)
--*Aesop's Fables.* Aesopus. Vernon Jones, Vernon Stanley, tr. Chesterton, Gilbert Keith (1874-1936), intro. by. 1968. F. Watts. (P.13)
--*Aesop's Fables.* Aesopus. Vernon Jones, Vernon Stanley, tr. Chesterton, Gilbert Keith (1874-1936), intro. by. c.1939. Garden City Publishing Co., Inc. (P.13)
--*AEsop's Fables: A New Translation.* Aesopus. Chesterton, Gilbert Keith, intro. by. Jones Vernon, Vernon Stanley (1874-1936), adapted by. 1912. Doubleday, Page & Co. (P.13)
--*Alice in Wonderland.* Carroll, Lewis, pseud. (1832-1898). Dodgson, Charles Lutwidge. N.D. Doubleday, Page & Co. (P.172)
--*Alice's Adventures in Wonderland.* Carroll, Lewis, pseud. (1832-1898). Dodgson, Charles Lutwidge. Dobson, Austin, pref. by. 1975. Viking Pr. (P.173)
--*Alice's Adventures in Wonderland.* Carroll, Lewis, pseud. (1832-1898). Dodgson, Charles Lutwidge. Dobson, Austin, pref. by. 1966. Watts. (P.173)
--*Alice's Adventures in Wonderland.* Dodgson, Charles Lutwidge (1832-1898). Carroll, Lewis, pseud. 1975. Viking Press. (P.277)
--*Alice's Adventures in Wonderland.* Dodgson, Charles Lutwidge (1832-1898). Carroll, Lewis, pseud. 1907. W. Heinemann. (P.277)
--*The Allies Fairy Book.* N.D. J.B Lippincott. (P.745)
--*Andersen's Fairy Tales.* Andersen, Hans Christian (1805-1875). N.D. David McKay Co. (P.34)
--*The Arthur Rackham Fairy Book.* 1933. J. B. Lippincott Co. (P.745)
--*The Arthur Rackham Fairy Book.* Rackham, Arthur (1867-1939), ed. 1950. Har-Row. (P.745)
--*The Book of Betty Barber.* Browne, Maggie, pseud. Andrew, Margaret Hamer. 1914. R. G. Badger. (P.143)
--*Carroll's Alice's Adventures in Wonderland.* Carroll, Lewis, pseud. (1832-1898). Dodgson, Charles Lutwidge. N.D. Doubleday Page & Co. (P.173)
--*A Christmas Carol.* Dickens, Charles John Huffam (1812-1870). 1952. J. B. Lippincott Co. (P.263)
--*Cinderella.* N.D. J.B. Lippincott. (P.745)
--*Cinderella.* Evans, Charles Seddon (1883-1944). 1919. J. B. Lippincott. (P.311)
--*Cinderella.* Evans, Charles Seddon (1883-1944). 1978. Penguin Books. (P.311)
--*Cinderella.* Evans, Charles Seddon (1883-1944). 1972. Viking Press. (P.311)
--*Cinderella.* Rackham, Arthur (1867-1939), retold by. 1978. Penguin. (P.745)
--*English Fairy Tales.* Steel, Flora Annie Webster, Mrs. (1847-1929), retold by. Fadiman, Clifton, afterword by. 1962. Macmillan. (P.850)
--*English Fairy Tales.* Steel, Flora Annie Webster, Mrs. (1847-1929), retold by. 1918. The Macmillan Company. (P.850)
--*English Fairy Tales.* Steel, Flora Annie Webster, Mrs. (1847-1929), retold by. 1923. The Macmillan Company. (P.850)
--*Fairy Tales.* Andersen, Hans Christian (1805-1875). 1932. David McKay Company. (P.35)
--*Fairy Tales from Many Lands.* 1974. Viking Press. (P.745)
--*Fairy Tales from Many Lands.* Rackham, Arthur (1867-1939), ed. 1978. Penguin Books. (P.745)
--*Fairy Tales of the Brothers Grimm.* Grimm, Jakob Ludwig Karl (1785-1863) & Grimm, Wilhelm Karl (1786-1859). Lucas, Alice, tr from Ger. 1902. J. B. Lippincott Co.; Etc., Etc. (P.391)
--*Goblin Market.* Rossetti, Christina Georgina (1830-1894). 1969. F. Watts. (P.779)
--*Goblin Market.* Rossetti, Christina Georgina (1830-1894). N.D. J. B. Lippincott. (P.779)
--*Greek Heroes by Lechner.* Niebuhr, Barthold George (1776-1831). N.D. Longmans,Green & Co. (P.682)
--*Grimm's Fairy Tales.* Grimm, Jakob Ludwig Karl (1785-1863) & Grimm, Wilhelm Karl (1786-1859). N.D. Doubleday, Page, & Co. (P.392)
--*Grimm's Fairy Tales.* Grimm, Jakob Ludwig Karl (1785-1863) & Grimm, Wilhelm Karl (1786-1859). Lucas, Edgar, Mrs., tr. N.D. J.B. Lippincott. (P.392)
--*Grimm's Fairy Tales.* Grimm, Jakob Ludwig Karl (1785-1863) & Grimm, Wilhelm Karl (1786-1859). Lucas, Edgar, Mrs., tr. 1966, c.1964. Parents' Magazine's Cultural Institute. (P.392)
--*Grimm's Fairy Tales: Twenty Stories.* Grimm, Jakob Ludwig Karl (1785-1863) & Grimm, Wilhelm Karl (1786-1859). 1978. Penguin Books. (P.393)
--*Grimm's Fairy Tales: Twenty Stories.* Grimm, Jakob Ludwig Karl (1785-1863) & Grimm, Wilhelm Karl (1786-1859). 1973. Viking Press. (P.393)
--*Gulliver's Travels.* Swift, Jonathan (1667-1745). N.D. David McKay Co. (P.874)
--*Gulliver's Travels.* Swift, Jonathan (1667-1745). N.D. E. P. Dutton & Co. (P.874)
--*Hansel and Gretel.* Grimm, Jakob Ludwig Karl (1785-1863) & Grimm, Wilhelm Karl (1786-1859). N.D. E P Dutton. (P.393)
--*Hansel & Grethel & Other Tales.* Grimm, Jakob Ludwig Karl (1785-1863) & Grimm, Wilhelm Karl (1786-1859). Lucas, Alice, tr. from Ger. 1920. E. P. Dutton & Company. (P.393)
--*Ingoldsby Legends: Or, Mirth or Marvels.* Ingoldsby, Thomas (1788-1845). 1898. E P Dutton. (P.480)
--*Irish Fairy Tales.* Stephens, James (1882-1950). 1968, c.1920. Macmillan. (P.853)
--*Irish Fairy Tales.* Stephens, James (1882-1950). 1923. The Macmillan Company. (P.853)
--*J.* M. Barrie's Peter Pan in Kensington Gardens. Barrie, James Matthew, Sir (1860-1937). Byron, May Clarissa Gillington, Mrs., ed. 1930. C. Scribner's Sons. (P.76)
--*The King of the Golden River.* Ruskin, John (1819-1900). 1932. J. B. Lippincott Co. (P.784)
--*The Land of Enchantment.* Rackham, Arthur (1867-1939), ed. N.D. Cassell & Co. (P.745)
--*The Large Type Mother Goose.* N.D. Franklin Watts. (P.745)
--*Little Brother and Little Sister and Other Tales by the Brothers Grimm.* Grimm, Jakob Ludwig Karl (1785-1863) & Grimm, Wilhelm Karl (1786-1859). 1917. Dodd Mead. (P.393)
--*The Lonesomest Doll.* Brown, Abbie Farwell (0000-1927). c.1928. Houghton Mifflin Co. (P.138)
--*A Midsummer Night's Dream.* Shakespeare, William (1564-1616). N.D. Doubleday Page & Co. (P.814)
--*Mother Goose.* 1969. Watts. (P.745)
--*Mother Goose.* Mother Goose. N.D. Century Co. (P.668)
--*Mother Goose Nursery Rhymes.* Mother Goose. 1969. F. Watts. (P.668)
--*Mother Goose Nursery Rhymes.* Reprint ed. Mother Goose. Rackham, Arthur (1867-1939), selected by. 1975. Viking Press. (P.668)
--*Mother Goose: The Old Nursery Rhymes.* 1978. S J Durst. (P.746)
--*Mother Goose: The Old Nursery Rhymes.* Mother Goose. 1913. The Century Co. (P.668)
--*The Night Before Christmas.* Moore, Clement Clarke (1779-1863). 1977. Doubleday. (P.660)
--*The Night Before Christmas.* Moore, Clement Clarke (1779-1863). N.D. Lippincott. (P.660)
--*The Night Before Christmas.* Moore, Clement Clarke (1779-1863). c.1976. Weathervane Books : Distributed by Crown Publishers. (P.660)
--*Once Upon a Time: The Fairy Tale World of Arthur Rackham.* Darrell, Margery. 1972. Viking Press. (P.242)
--*Peter Pan and Wendy for Boys and Girls.* Barrie, James Matthew, Sir (1860-1937). Byron, May, retold by. N.D. Charles Scribner's Sons. (P.76)
--*Peter Pan and Wendy for Little People.* Barrie, James Matthew, Sir (1860-1937). Bryon, May, retold by. N.D. Charles Scribner's Sons. (P.76)
--*Peter Pan in Kensington gardens.* Barrie, James Matthew, Sir (1860-1937). Byron, May Clarissa Gillington, Mrs., ed. 1930. Charles Scribner's Sons. (P.76)
--*Peter Pan in Kensington Gardens.* Barrie, James Matthew, Sir (1860-1937). Byron, May Clarissa Gillington, Mrs., ed. 1957. Scribner. (P.76)
--*The Pied Piper of Hamelin.* Browning, Robert (1812-1889). 1934. J. B. Lippincott Co. (P.143)
--*Poe's Tales, 8.* Poe, Edgar Allan (1809-1849). N.D. J. P. Lippincott. (P.729)
--*Poor Cecco: The Wonderful Story of a Wonderful Wooden Dog Who Was the Jolliest Toy in the House Until He Went Out to Explore the World.* Bianco, Margery Williams, Mrs. (1881-1944). c.1925. George H. Doran Company. (P.100)
--*Puck of Pook's Hill.* Kipling, Joseph Rudyard (1865-1936). 1968. Dover. (P.528)
--*The Rainbow Book.* Spielmann, M. H. 1910. Frederick Warne & Co. (P.844)
--*Rip Van Winkle.* Irving, Washington (1783-1859). 1910. Doubleday, Page & Co. (P.482)
--*Rip Van Winkle.* Irving, Washington (1783-1859). 1967. Lippincott. (P.482)

--*The Musicians of Bremen.* Grimm, Jakob Ludwig Karl (1785-1863) & Grimm, Wilhelm Karl (1786-1859). Rouke, Eve, ed. 1966. World Pub. Co. (P.394)

--*The Old Goose Woman.* Grimm, Jakob Ludwig Karl (1785-1863) & Grimm, Wilhelm Karl (1786-1859). 1966. World Pub. Co. (P.394)

--*Puss in Boots.* Latham, Jean Lee (1902-), retold by. c.1961. Bobbs-Merrill. (P.553)

--*Puss in Boots.* Puss in Boots. Miller, Doris R, pseud., retold by Mosesson, Gloria Rubin. 1966. World. (P.742)

--*The Selfish Giant.* Rouke, Eve, ed. Wilde, Oscar Fingal O'Flahertie Wills (1854-1900). c.1965. World. (P.959)

--*The Three Bears.* The, Three Bears & Winokur, Joan Gelman (1935-) 1966. World Pub. Co. (P.890)

--*The Three Bears.* The, Three Bears. Winokur, Joan Gelman (1935-), retold by. 1966. World. (P.890)

--*Three Little Pigs.* Three Little Pigs. Winokur, Joan Gelman (1935-), retold by. 1966. World. (P.890)

--*Thumbelina.* Andersen, Hans Christian (1805-1875). Duffy, Marguerite R., ed. c.1965. World. (P.37)

--*Wa O'Ka.* Latham, Jean Lee (1902-), retold by. c.1961. Bobbs-Merrill. (P.553)

--*Wa O'Ka.* Latham, Jean Lee (1902-). N.D. Bobbs. (P.553)

Ramirez, Pablo, jt. illus. see Correas, Jose.

Ramirez, Pablo & Correas, Jose

--*The Brave Little Tailor, Hansel and Gretel and Jack and the Beanstalk.* Latham, Jean Lee (1902-), retold by. 1962. Bobbs-Merrill. (P.553)

Ramon, Estelle

--*Smooth As Silk.* 2nd ed. Philipps, Myra. 1979. Basin Pub. (P.723)

Ramsay, Marjorie B.

--*Nyra.* Ramsay, Marjorie B. 1979. Triumph Pub. (P.747)

Ramsden, Evelyn, jt. illus. see Pinto, Ralph.

Ramsey, Ted

--*Katie Did.* Galbraith, Kathryn Osebold. 1982. Atheneum. (P.352)

Ramstad, Josie Winship

--*Ferocious Sarah.* Ramstad, Josie Winship & Benson, Ethel Mitchell. c.1979. Talespinner Publications. (P.747)

Ramstad, Ralph

--*The Flying Rangers.* Reiner, William Buck (1910-1975). 1954. J. Messner. (P.757)

--*Oliver Becomes a Weatherman.* Bechdolt, John Ernest (1884-). 1953. J. Messner. (P.86)

--*Oliver Sounds off!.* Bechdolt, John Ernest (1884-). 1953. J. Messner. (P.86)

Ramus, Michael

--*Andy Jackson's Water Well.* Steele, William Owen (1917-1979). 1959. Harcourt, Brace. (P.850)

Rand, Amy Carol

--*The Doctor's Little Girl.* Taggart, Marion Ames (1866-). 1907. L. C. Page and Company. (P.876)

Rand, Paul (1914-)

--*I Know a Lot of Things.* 1 st ed. Rand, Ann Binkley. 1956. Harcourt, Brace. **Award: (NYT).** (P.747)

--*I Know a Lot of Things.* Rand, Ann Binkley. 1973. c.1956. Harcourt. (P.747)

Rand, Ted

--*America, I Know You: A Freedom Book.* Martin, William Ivan, Jr. (1916-). 1970. Published by the Bill Martin Corp. for Bowmar. (P.626)

--*The Ghost-Eye Tree.* Martin, William Ivan, Jr. (1916-) & Archambault, John. c.1985. Holt, Rinehart and Winston. (P.626)

--*The Phantom Athlete: A Diary of Great Events in My Life.* Noodles, pseud. Hahn, Frank G.. c.1979. Holt, Rinehart, and Winston. (P.684)

Randall, Christine

--*Laugh Lines.* Keller, Charles (1942-). 1974. Prentice-Hall. (P.514)

Randall, George Archibald (1887-)

--*Saddle up.* Randall, George Archibald (1887-). 1941. E. P. Dutton & Company, Inc. (P.748)

Randolph, David

--*An Air Express Holdup: Or, How Pilot George Selkirk Carried Through.* Wright, Philip Lee. c.1930. Barse & Co. (P.981)

--*Bob Chase after Grizzly Bears.* Warner, Frank A., pseud. Stratemeyer Syndicate. 1929. Barse & Co. (P.932)

--*Bob Chase After Grizzly Bears.* Warner, Frank A., pseud. Stratemeyer Syndicate. N.D. Grosset & Dunlap. (P.932)

--*Bob Chase in the Tiger's Lair.* Warner, Frank A., pseud. Stratemeyer Syndicate. c.1929. Barse & Co. (P.932)

--*Bob Chase in the Tiger's Lair.* Warner, Frank A., pseud. Stratemeyer Syndicate. N.D. Grosset & Dunlap. (P.932)

--*Bob Chase with the Big Moose Hunters.* Warner, Frank A., pseud. Stratemeyer Syndicate. c.1929. Barse & Co. (P.932)

--*Bob Chase with the Big Moose Hunters.* Warner, Frank A., pseud. Stratemeyer Syndicate. N.D. Grosset & Dunlap. (P.932)

--*Bob Chase with the Lion Hunters.* Warner, Frank A., pseud. Stratemeyer Syndicate. c.1930. Barse & Co. (P.932)

--*Bob Chase with the Lion Hunters.* Warner, Frank A., pseud. Stratemeyer Syndicate. N.D. Grosset & Dunlap. (P.932)

--*The East Bound Air Mail: Or, Fighting Fog, Storm and Hard Luck.* Wright, Philip Lee. c.1930. Barse & Co. (P.981)

--*Lanky Lawson and His Trained Zebra: How He Happened to Get the Beast, How the Cantankerous Animal Performed and What Happened at the County Fair.* Roe, Harry Mason, pseud. Stratemeyer Syndicate. 1930. Barse & Co. (P.774)

--*Lanky Lawson, the Boy from Nowhere: How He Arrived at Beanville, What Beanville Did to Him, and What He Did to Beanville.* Roe, Harry Mason, pseud. Stratemeyer Syndicate. 1929. Barse & Co. (P.774)

--*Lanky Lawson with the One-Ring Circus: How He Joined the Show, What He Did to the Wild Animals, What Happened When the Circus Collapsed.* Roe, Harry Mason, pseud. Stratemeyer Syndicate. 1929. Barse & Co. (P.774)

Randolph, Grace F., jt. illus. see Mitchell, Edith.

Rands, Audrey

--*Punki, Her Story of the Island of Java.* Rands, Minnie Frost (1889-). 1947. Island Press. (P.748)

Rands, William Brighty (1823-1882) & Millais, J. E.

--*Lilliput Levee: A Book of Rhymes for Children.* N.D. George Routledge & Sons. (P.748)

Ranft, Max

--*Adam Bradford, Cowboy.* Russell, Donald Bert (1899-). 1970. Benefic Press. (P.785)

--*Cowboy on the Trail.* Russell, Donald Bert (1899-). 1970. Benefic Press. (P.785)

--*Cowboy Soldier.* Russell, Donald Bert (1899-). 1970. Benefic Press. (P.785)

--*Fairway Danger.* Lunemann, Evelyn. 1969. Benefic Press. (P.591)

--*The Witch Book.* Ranft, Max. c.1976. Rand McNally. (P.748)

Rankin, Hugh

--*Johnny Goes a-Hunting.* Hooper, Cyrus Lauron. c.1925. Rand, McNally & Company. (P.459)

Rankins, James F.

--*Strangers in the Desert.* Russell, Alice Dyar. 1938. Harper & Brothers. (P.785)

Rannells, Will (1892-)

--*The Great Adventures of Jack, Jock and Funny.* Youmans, Eleanor Williams, Mrs. c.1938. The Bobbs-Merrill Company. (P.988)

--*Timmy: The Dog That Was Different.* Youmans, Eleanor Williams, Mrs. c.1941. The Bobbs-Merrill Company. (P.988)

--*Waif: The Story of Spe.* Youmans, Eleanor Williams, Mrs. & Rannells, Will (1892-). c.1937. The Bobbs-Merrill Company. (P.988)

Ransley, H. Hallowell

--*June's Quest: Her Adventures on the Highway.* Kerigan, Florence (1896-). c.1931. Lothrop, Lee & Shepard Co. (P.519)

--*Steadfast Macrea.* Vincent, Wallace Dunbar. 1928. The Union Press. (P.920)

Ransome, Arthur Michell (1884-1967)

--*The Big Six.* Ransome, Arthur Michell (1884-1967). 1980. Merrimack. (P.749)

--*The Big Six.* Ransome, Arthur Michell (1884-1967). 1941. The Macmillan Company. (P.749)

--*Coot Club.* Ransome, Arthur Michell (1884-1967). 1980. Merrimack. (P.749)

--*Great Northern.* Ransome, Arthur Michell (1884-1967). 1980. Merrimack. (P.749)

--*Missee Lee.* Ransome, Arthur Michell (1884-1967). 1980. Merrimack. (P.749)

--*My Big Book of Nursery Tales.* 1979, c.1975. Derrydale Books. (P.749)

--*Peter Duck.* Ransome, Arthur Michell (1884-1967). 1980. Merrimack. (P.749)

--*The Picts & the Martyrs: Or, Not Welcome at All.* Ransome, Arthur Michell (1884-1967). 1980. Merrimack Pub Cir. (P.749)

--*Pigeon Post.* Ransome, Arthur Michell (1884-1967). 1980. Merrimack. (P.749)

--*Secret Walter.* Ransome, Arthur Michell (1884-1967). 1980. Merrimack. (P.749)

--*Swallowdale.* Ransome, Arthur Michell (1884-1967). 1980. Merrimack. (P.749)

--*Swallows and Amazons.* Ransome, Arthur Michell (1884-1967). 1980. Merrimack. (P.749)

--*We Didn't Mean to Go to Sea.* Ransome, Arthur Michell (1884-1967). 1938. The Macmillan Company. (P.749)

--*Winter Holiday.* Ransome, Arthur Michell (1884-1967). 1980. Merrimack. (P.749)

Ransome, Arthur Michell (1884-1967) & Carter, Helene (1887-1960)

--*Coot Club.* Ransome, Arthur Michell (1884-1967). c.1935. J. B. Lippincott Company. (P.749)

Rao, Anthony

--*The Bloodhound Gang in the Case of the Cackling Ghost.* Fleischman, Albert Sidney (1920-). c.1981. Random House/Children's Television Workshop. (P.331)

--*Children's Own Stories.* Myers, Caroline Elizabeth Clark (1887-1980), ed. 1970. Highlights. (P.674)

--*Christmas Wishes.* Myers, Garry Cleveland (1884-1971). c.1972. Highlights for Children. (P.674)

--*The Cow in the Kitchen: A Folk Tale.* Johnson, Evelyne (1932-), retold by. c.1983. Little Simon. (P.495)

--*The Highlights Book of Nursery Rhymes.* Highlights for Children Inc. 1974. Highlights for Children, Inc. (P.749)

--*Let's Go All Around the Neighborhood.* Thomas, Patty. c.1982. Golden Press. (P.886)

--*Shirlick Holmes and the Case of the Wandering Wardrobe.* Yolen, Jane Hyatt (1939-). 1981. Coward, McCann & Geoghegan. (P.987)

--*The Three Investigator's Book of Mystery Puzzles.* McCall, Barbara. 1982. Random. (P.594)

--*Yellow Fur and Little Hawk.* Hays, Wilma Pitchford (1909-). 1980. Putnam. (P.426)

Rapaport, Stella Fread

--*The Bear, Ship of Many Lives.* Rapaport, Stella Fread. 1962. Dodd, Mead. (P.749)

--*Binkley's Bottleneck.* Rapaport, Stella Fread. 1956. Putnam. (P.749)

--*Horse Chestnut Hideaway.* Rapaport, Stella Fread. 1956. Putnam. (P.749)

--*Reindeer Rescue.* Rapaport, Stella Fread. 1955. Putnam. (P.749)

--*A Whittle Too Much.* Rapaport, Stella Fread. 1955. G. P. Putnam's Sons. (P.749)

Raphael, Elaine, pseud., see Bolognese, Elaine Raphael Chionchio.

Raphael, Elaine, jt. illus. see Bolognese, Donald Alan.

Raphael, Elaine, pseud. (1933-)

--*Benny, the Misfit.* Bolognese, Elaine Raphael Chionchio. Colman, Hila. 1973. Crowell. (P.210)

--*Circus Fun.* Bolognese, Elaine Raphael Chionchio. Hillert, Margaret (1920-). 1969. Follett Pub. Co. (P.444)

--*Havelok the Dane.* Bolognese, Elaine Raphael Chionchio. Serraillier, Ian Lucien (1912-), retold by. 1967. H. Z. Walck. (P.811)

--*Poems from Italy.* Bolognese, Elaine Raphael Chionchio. Smith, William Jay (1918-), ed. 1972. Crowell. (P.837)

--*Tales of Ancient Egypt.* Bolognese, Elaine Raphael Chionchio. Green, Roger Gilbert Lancelyn (1918-), ed. 1968. Penguin. (P.385)

Rapin, William (1949-)

--*A Penguin in New York.* Rapin, William (1949-). c.1984. Coffee House Press. (P.749)

Rapp, Rita

--*Journey to the End of the Earth.* Skjonsberg, Gunnar. Ware, Kay (1916-) & Sutherland, Lucille, eds. 1963, c.1961. Webster Pub. Co. (P.828)

--*The Little Woman Who Forgot Everything.* Beattie, Janet. Ware, Kay & Sutherland, Lucille, eds. c.1961. Webster Pub. Co. (P.85)

Raskin, Ellen (1928-1984)

--*A & The: Or, Willian T. E. C.umgarten Comes to Town.* Raskin, Ellen (1928-1984). 1970. Atheneum. (P.749)

--*And It Rained.* Raskin, Ellen (1928-1984). 1969. Atheneum. **Award: (ALA).** (P.749)

--*Come Along!.* Caudill, Rebecca (1899-). 1969. Holt, Rinehart and Winston. (P.178)

--*Ellen Grae.* 1st ed. Cleaver, Vera & Cleaver, Bill. 1967. Lippincott. (P.201)

--*Figgs & Phantoms.* Raskin, Ellen (1928-1984). 1974. E. P. Dutton. **Award: (JNM).** (P.749)

--*Franklin Stein.* Raskin, Ellen (1928-1984). 1972. Atheneum. (P.749)

--*Franklin Stein.* Raskin, Ellen (1928-1984). 1972. Atheneum. (P.749)

--*Ghost in a Four-Room Apartment.* Raskin, Ellen (1928-1984). 1969. Atheneum. (P.749)

--*Goblin Market.* Rossetti, Christina Georgina (1830-1894). 1970. E. P. Dutton. (P.779)

--*Happy Christmas: Tales for Boys & Girls.* Bishop, Claire Huchet, Mrs., ed. 1956. Ungar. (P.103)

--*Inatuk's Friend.* 1st ed. Morrow, Suzanne Stark. 1968. Little, Brown. (P.666)

--*The King of Men.* Coolidge, Olivia Ensor (1908-). 1966. Houghton. **Award: (ALA).** (P.216)

--*Lady Ellen Grae.* 1st ed. Cleaver, Vera & Cleaver, Bill (1920-1981). 1968. Lippincott. (P.201)

--*Mama, I Wish I Was Snow: Child, You'd Be Very Cold.* 1st ed. Krauss, Ruth Ida (1911-). 1962. Atheneum. (P.539)

--*Moe Q. McGlutch, He Smoked Too Much.* Raskin, Ellen (1928-1984). 1973. Parents' Magazine Press. (P.749)

--*Moose, Goose, and Little Nobody.* Raskin, Ellen (1928-1984). 1980, c.1974. Four Winds Press. (P.749)

--*Moose, Goose, and Little Nobody.* Raskin, Ellen (1928-1984). 1974. Parents' Magazine Press. (P.749)

--*The Mysterious Disappearance of Leon (I Mean Noel).* 1st ed. Raskin, Ellen (1928-1984). 1971. Dutton. **Award: (ALA).** (P.749)

--*The Mysterious Disappearance of Leon (I Mean Noel).* Raskin, Ellen (1928-1984). 1980. Dutton. (P.749)

--*The Mysterious Disappearance of Leon (I Mean Noel).* Raskin, Ellen (1928-1984). 1973, c.1971. E. P. Dutton & Co. (P.749)

--*Nothing Ever Happens on My Block.* Raskin, Ellen (1928-1984). 1966. Atheneum. **Awards: (NYT); (ALA).** (P.749)

--*A Paper Zoo: A Collection of Animal Poems by Modern American Poets.* Weiss, Renee Karol (1923-), ed. 1968. Macmillan. (P.943)

--*Paths of Poetry: Twenty-Five Poets & Their Poems.* Untermeyer, Louis (1885-1977), ed. 1966. Delacorte. (P.910)

--*Piping Down the Valleys Wild: Poetry for the Young of All Ages.* Larrick, Nancy (1910-), selected by. 1968. Delacorte. (P.552)

--*Piping Down the Valleys Wild: Poetry for the Young of All Ages.* Larrick, Nancy (1910-), selected by. 1985, c.1968. Delacorte Press. (P.552)

--*Poems of Edgar Allan Poe.* Poe, Edgar Allan (1809-1849). Macdonald, Dwight (1906-1982), ed. 1965. Har-Row. (P.729)

--*Shrieks at Midnight: Macabre Poems, Eerie & Humorous.* Brewton, Sara Westbrook & Brewton, John Edmund (1898-), eds. 1969. Har-Row. **Award: (ALA).** (P.130)

--*Silly Songs and Sad.* Raskin, Ellen (1928-1984). 1967. Crowell. (P.749)

--*Songs of Innocence.* 1st ed. Raskin, Ellen (1928-1984). Weissman, Dick, contrib. by. 1966. Doubleday. (P.749)

--*Spectacles.* Raskin, Ellen (1928-1984). 1968. Atheneum. **Awards: (NYT); (ALA).** (P.749)

--*The Tattooed Potato and Other Clues.* Raskin, Ellen (1928-1984). 1975. Dutton. **Award: (ALA).** (P.749)

--*Twenty-Two, Twenty-Three.* Raskin, Ellen (1928-1984). 1976. Atheneum. **Award: (ALA).** (P.749)

--*We Alcotts: The Story of Louisa M. Alcott's Family As Seen Through the Eyes of "Marmee," Mother of Little Women.* Fisher, Aileen Lucia (1906-) & Rabe, Olive Hanson (0000-1968). 1968. Atheneum. (P.328)

--*We Dickinsons: The Life of Emily Dickinson As Seen Through the Eyes of Her Brother Austin.* Fisher, Aileen Lucia (1906-) & Rabe, Olive Hanson (0000-1968). 1965. Atheneum. (P.328)

--*Who, Said Sue, Said Whoo?.* Raskin, Ellen (1928-1984). 1973. Atheneum. **Awards: (ALA); (BGH).** (P.749)

--*The World's Greatest Freak Show.* Raskin, Ellen (1928-1984). 1971. Atheneum. (P.749)

Ratcliff, Ernest

--*Near East Adventure.* Charlton, Lionel Evelyn Oswald (1879-). 1934. T. Nelson and Sons Ltd. (P.187)

Raubsteiner, Oscar W., Jr.

--*Mother, Read Us a Poem.* Woellwarth, Mary Elise. c.1938. The Queen's Work. (P.973)

Rauch, Roberta

--*The Fish with the Deep Sea Smile.* Brown, Margaret Wise (1910-1952). c.1938. E.P. Dutton & Co., Inc. (P.140)

Rauh, Herb

--*Double-Rhyme-Our Brat Cat.* Punnett, Richard Douglas (1924-). c.1985. Child's World. (P.742)

Rausch, Jane

--*Ruth Ann and Polly; a Story for Children.* 1st ed. Petry, Mercedes Mills. 1956. Exposition Press. (P.722)

Ravelle, M., jt. photog. see Taber, Ralph Graham.

Raven, Gertrude

--*Eric.* Bloom, Patti A. 1980. Vantage. (P.109)

Raverat, Gwendolen Mary (1885-1957)

--*The Cambridge Book of Poetry for Children.* New. ed. Grahame, Kenneth (1859-1932), ed. c.1933. G. P. Putnam's Sons. (P.381)

--*The Cambridge Book of Poetry for Children.* New. ed. Grahame, Kenneth (1859-1932), ed. 1932. The University Press. (P.381)

--*Countess Kate.* Yonge, Charlotte Mary (1823-1901). 1960. Looking Glass Library; Distributed by Random House. (P.987)

--*Four Tales from Hans Anderson: A New Version of the First Four.* Andersen, Hans Christian (1805-1875). Keigwin, R. P., ed. 1935. The University Press. (P.36)

--*Over the Garden Wall.* Farjeon, Eleanor (1881-1965). 1933. Frederick A. Stokes Company. (P.317)

--*Over the Garden Wall.* Farjeon, Eleanor (1881-1965). N.D. J. B. Lippincott. (P.317)

Ravielli, Louis

--*Brownie Makes the Headlines.* Wear, Ted, pseud. (1902-). Wear, Theodore Graham. 1953. J. Messner. (P.937)

Reed, Barbara

--*The Peanut Elephant.* Gardner, Grace H. 1957. William-Frederick Press. (P.355)

Reed, Charles W.

--*Jason's Quest.* Lowell, Daniel Ozro Smith (1851-). 1893. Leach, Shewell & Sanborn. (P.588)

--*Jason's Quest.* Lowell, Daniel Ozro Smith (1851-). 1905. Lee and Shepard Company. (P.588)

--*Return of the Fairies.* Bellamy, Charles Joseph (1852-1910). 1899. Little Folks Publishing Company. (P.91)

Reed, Earl Howell (1863-1931)

--*The Silver Arrow and Other Indian Romances of the Dune Country.* Reed, Earl Howell (1863-1931). Nicolson, John Urban (1885-), contrib. by. 1926. Reilly & Lee. (P.753)

Reed, Edward Tennyson (1860-1933)

--*Beasts.* Derrydale, Reginald. c.1977. Hart Pub. Co. (P.260)

Reed, Ethel

--*The Arabella and Araminta Stories.* 5th ed. Smith, Gertrude (1860-1917). Wilkins, Mary E., intro. by. 1902. Small, Maynard & Company. (P.833)

--*In Childhood's Country.* Moulton, Louise Chandler, Mrs. (1835-1908). 1896. Copeland & Day. (P.669)

--*In Childhood's Country.* Moulton, Louise Chandler, Mrs. (1835-1908). N.D. Small, Maynard & Co. (P.669)

Reed, Mabel

--*In the Land of the Grasshopper Song.* Arnold, Mary Ellicott. N.D. Vantage Press. (P.49)

Reed, Philip G. (1908-)

--*A Christmas Carol.* Dickens, Charles John Huffam (1812-1870). 1940. Holiday House. (P.263)

--*Many Moons.* Thurber, James Grover (1894-1961). 1958. A.M. & R.W. Roe. (P.890)

--*Many Moons.* Thurber, James Grover (1894-1961). 1958. Printed by A. M. & R. W. Roe. (P.890)

--*Mother Goose and Nursery Rhymes.* 1979, c.1963. Regnery Gateway. (P.753)

--*Mother Goose and Nursery Rhymes.* 1st ed. Mother Goose. 1963. Atheneum. **Awards: (ALA); (RCM).** (P.668)

--*The Seven Voyages of Sindbad the Sailor.* Sindbad the Sailor. 1962. Atheneum. (P.826)

--*The Seven Voyages of Sindbad the Sailor from the Arabian Nights Entertainment.* Sindbad the Sailor. 1939. Printed by the Broadside Press for Holiday House of New York City. (P.826)

--*Sinbad the Sailor.* N.D. Holiday House. (P.753)

Reed, Susan

--*The Easter Rainbow.* Blair, Perry. 1981. Blair Pub. (P.105)

Reed, Tom (1947-)

--*Melissa on Parade.* Reed, Tom (1947-). c.1979. Bradbury Press. (P.753)

Reed, Veronica, pseud., see Sherman, Theresa.

Reed, Veronica, pseud. (1916-)

--*Auction Today.* 1st ed. Sherman, Theresa. Hilles, Helen Train, Mrs. c.1956. Lippincott. (P.445)

--*Bertie and Eddie.* Sherman, Theresa. Hall, Rosalys Haskell (1914-). 1956. Henry Z. Walck, Inc., Publishers. (P.406)

--*Bertie and Eddie.* Sherman, Theresa. Hall, Rosalys Haskell (1914-). 1956. Oxford University Press. (P.406)

--*A Dance for Duley.* Sherman, Theresa. Williams, Henry Lionel (1895-1974). 1957. Arco Pub. Co. (P.963)

--*Dorinda's Diamonds.* Sherman, Theresa. Shutter, Lilly. 1955. T. Nelson. (P.822)

--*Dorothy Gordon's Treasure Bag of Game Songs.* Sherman, Theresa. Gordon, Dorothy Lerner (1893-1970), ed. Buchman, Adele c.1939. E. P. Dutton & Co., Inc. (P.376)

--*Kappy Oliver.* 1st ed. Sherman, Theresa. Walker, Nona. 1956. Holt. (P.926)

--*Miracle for Mingo.* 1st ed. Sherman, Theresa. Forsee, Frances Aylesa. 1956. Lippincott. (P.336)

--*The New Tuba.* Sherman, Theresa. Tripp, Edward. 1955. Henry Z. Walck, Inc., Publishers. (P.900)

--*The New Tuba.* Sherman, Theresa. Tripp, Edward. 1955. Oxford University Press. (P.900)

--*A Room for Cathy.* Sherman, Theresa. Woolley, Catherine (1904-). Thayer, Jane, pseud. 1956. Morrow. (P.978)

--*The Singing Glasses.* Sherman, Theresa. Williams, Henry Lionel (1895-1974). 1957. Arco Pub. Co. (P.963)

--*Smoky.* Sherman, Theresa. Elting, Mary (1906-). c.1947. Whitman Pub. Co. (P.305)

--*Those Cats!.* Sherman, Theresa. Cunningham, Virginia (1909-). c.1947. Whitman Pub. Co. (P.235)

--*Tor and Azor.* Sherman, Theresa. Crowley, Maude. 1955. Oxford University Press. (P.233)

--*Tor and Azor.* Sherman, Theresa. Crowley, Maude. 1955. Walck. (P.233)

--*The Trail of the Hunter's Horn.* Sherman, Theresa. Clark, Billy Curtis (1928-). 1957. Putnam. (P.197)

Reed, Walt

--*Cherokee Strip: The Race for Land.* 1st ed. Fisher, Aileen Lucia (1906-). 1956. Aladdin Books. (P.327)

--*Samuel Morse: Inquisitive Boy.* Snow, Dorothea Johnston (1909-). 1960. Bobbs-Merrill. (P.839)

Reedstrom, Ernest Lisle (1928-)

--*Cowboy on the Mountain.* Simonson, Mary Jane, pseud. Wheeler, Mary Jane. 1970. Benefic Press. (P.826)

--*Cowboy Without a Horse.* Simonson, Mary Jane, pseud. Wheeler, Mary Jane. 1970. Benefic Press. (P.826)

Reedy, Carol

--*Lonka Belle's Vacation.* Booker, Barbara A. 1977. Vantage. (P.117)

Rees, Gary & Thomas, Mark

--*The Demon Headmaster.* Cross, Gillian Clare (1945-). 1983. Merrimack Pub Cir. (P.232)

Rees-Hansen, Gloria

--*Desi & Gooie's Desert Tails.* Rees-Hansen, Gloria. 1984. Vantage. (P.754)

Rees, Helen Christina Easson Evans see Oliver, Jane, pseud.

Reese, Bob

--*Arbor Day.* Reese, Bob. Jordan, Alton, ed. 1977. ARO Pub. (P.754)

--*Calico Jack and the Desert Critters.* Reese, Bob. c.1983. Childrens Press. (P.754)

--*Coral Reef.* Reese, Bob. 1983. Childrens. (P.754)

--*Crab Apple.* Reese, Bob. Wasserman, Dan, ed. 1979. ARO Pub. (P.754)

--*Crazy Cat.* Reese, Ron. Jordan, Alton, ed. 1974. ARO Pub. (P.754)

--*The Critter Race.* Reese, Bob. 1981. Childrens Press. (P.754)

--*Dale the Whale.* Reese, Bob. c.1983. Children's Press. (P.754)

--*Fire Drill.* Cox, Mike, et al. Wasserman, Dan, ed. 1979. ARO Pub. (P.225)

--*Flowers.* Cox, Mike & Cox, Kris. Wasserman, Dan, ed. 1979. ARO Pub. (P.225)

--*Freddie Freighliner to the Rescue.* George, David L. 1983. Childrens. (P.363)

--*Funny Bunny.* Schoder, Judith. Wasserman, Dan, ed. 1979. ARO Pub. (P.800)

--*Groundhog Day.* Shebar, Sharon Sigmond (1945-) & Schoder, Judy. Jordan, Alton, ed. 1977. ARO Pub. (P.817)

--*Halloween.* Reese, Ron. Jordan, Alton, ed. 1977. ARO Pub. (P.754)

--*The Hero.* Stoddard, Darrell. Jordan, Alton, ed. 1974. ARO Pub. (P.860)

--*Huzzard Buzzard.* Reese, Bob. 1981. Childrens Press. (P.754)

--*I Can Eat an Elephant.* Reese, Nancy. Jordan, Alton, ed. 1975. ARO Pub. (P.754)

--*Lactus Cactus.* Reese, Bob. 1981. Childrens Press. (P.754)

--*Little Dinosaur.* Reese, Bob. Wasserman, Dan, ed. 1979. ARO Pub. (P.754)

--*The Little Mouse.* Willoughby, Alana. Jordan, Alton, ed. 1974. ARO Pub. (P.965)

--*Mosquito.* Reese, Ron. Jordan, Alton, ed. 1975. ARO Pub. (P.754)

--*My Dolly.* Willoughby, Alana. Wasserman, Dan, ed. 1979. ARO Pub. (P.965)

--*Night Monsters.* Shebar, Sharon Sigmond (1945-). Wasserman, Dan, ed. 1979. ARO Pub. (P.817)

--*Ocean Fish School.* Reese, Bob. 1983. Childrens. (P.754)

--*Ollie Owl.* Burke, Suzanne. Jordan, Alton, ed. 1975. ARO Pub. (P.154)

--*Oola Oyster.* Reese, Bob. 1983. Childrens. (P.754)

--*The Pamba and the Bink.* Reese, Bob. c.1984. Aro Pub. (P.754)

--*Purple Bear.* Reese, Nancy. Jordan, Alton, ed. 1975. ARO Pub. (P.754)

--*Rapid Robert and Hiss the Snake.* Reese, Bob. c.1983. Childrens Press. (P.754)

--*Rapid Robert Roadrunner.* Reese, Bob. 1981. Childrens Press. (P.754)

--*Sammy Skunk.* Reese, Ron. Jordan, Alton, ed. 1974. ARO Pub. (P.754)

--*Scary Larry Meets Big Willie.* Reese, Bob. 1983. Childrens Press. (P.754)

--*Scary Larry the Very Very Hairy Tarantula.* Reese, Bob. 1981. Childrens. (P.754)

--*Smiley Snake.* Reese, Nancy. Jordan, Alton, ed. 1974. ARO Pub. (P.754)

--*Spongee Sponge.* Reese, Bob. 1983. Childrens. (P.754)

--*Sunshine.* Reese, Bob. Wasserman, Dan, ed. 1979. ARO Pub. (P.754)

--*Tweedle-De-Dee Tumbleweed.* Reese, Bob. 1981. Childrens Press. (P.754)

--*Wellington Pelican.* Reese, Bob. 1983. Childrens. (P.754)

--*Who's New at the Zoo.* Winder, Jack. Wasserman, Dan, ed. 1979. Aro Pub. (P.967)

Reese, Claudia

--*Hardwood Hero.* Bottom, Raymond (1927-) & Robertson, O. J. 1971. Abingdon Press. (P.119)

Reese, Ralph

--*The Race Forever.* Montgomery, Raymond A., Jr. (1936-). 1983. Random. (P.658)

Reetz, Wilhelm

--*A Doll, Two Children and Three Storks.* Ubertis-Gray, Corinna Teresa (1877-). Teresah, pseud. Emmrich, Dorothy, tr. from Ital. c.1931. E. P. Dutton & Co., Inc. (P.908)

Reeves, Norman

--*Happy Times in Norway.* Undset, Sigrid (1882-1949). 1942. A. A. Knopf. (P.909)

--*Into the Wind.* Mallette, Gertrude Ethel (1887-). 1941. Doubleday, Doran & Co., Inc. (P.615)

--*Lupe and the Senorita.* Kahmann, Mable Chesley, Mrs. (1901-). c.1938. Random House. (P.504)

--*Single Stones.* Mallette, Gertrude Ethel (1887-). 1940. Doubleday, Doran & Co., Inc. (P.615)

Reeves, Richard S.

--*Horse Named Kelso.* Johnson, Pat & Osborne, Walter. DuPont, R. C., Mrs., intro. by. 1970. Funk & W. (P.496)

Reeves, Ruth

--*Tal: His Marvelous Adventures with Noom-Zor-Noom.* Cooper, Paul Fenimore. c.1929. W. Morrow & Co. (P.218)

Reeves, William

--*The Pirates of the Deep Green Sea.* Linklater, Eric Robert Russell (1899-1974). 1949. Macmillan. (P.574)

--*Three Finger Jack's Treasure.* Sherlock, Philip Manderson, Sir (1902-). 1962, c.1961. Macmillan. (P.819)

--*Three Finger Jack's Treasure.* Sherlock, Philip Manderson, Sir (1902-). 1961. St Martin's Press. (P.819)

--*The Witch's Cat.* Nye, A. A. N.D. St. Martin's Press. (P.688)

Regier, Robert

--*The Sun & the Wind.* Lehn, Cornelia (1920-). 1983. Faith & Life. (P.562)

Regina

--*A Dog of Flanders.* De La Ramee, Marie Louise (1839-1908). Ouida, pseud. c.1930. Beckley-Cardy Company. (P.254)

Regina, jt. illus. see Ludwig.

Regina & Ludwig

--*Pursuit of the Flying Baby: A Faithful Account of the Strange Happenings to William Thompson After His Mother Told Him to Mind the Baby.* Eastman, Fred (1886-). c.1928. Willett, Clark & Colby. (P.294)

--*The Twins in Fruitland.* Jay, Gladys (1902-). 1929. Beckley-Cardy Company. (P.490)

Reich, Karoly

--*Hide-&-Seek.* Szecsi, Katalin. N.D. Newbury Bks. (P.876)

--*It All Started with the Big Green Fish.* Kormos, Istvan. Ribianszky, Alexandra, tr. from Hungarian. 1979. Intl Pubns Serv. (P.536)

--*It All Started with the Big Green Fish.* Kormos, Istvan. Ribianszky, Alexandra, tr. N.D. Newbury Bks Inc. (P.536)

Reichman, Edith

--*The Busy Children.* 1949. John Martin's House. (P.755)

--*The Story of Cooky.* Kennedy, Marian. 1944. Rand McNally & Company. (P.518)

Reid, Ace

--*Cowpokes Cookbook & Cartoons.* 12th ed. Reid, Ace. N.D. Reid Ent. (P.755)

--*Cowpokes Cow Country Cartoons.* 14th ed. Reid, Ace. Barker, S. Omar, intro. by. N.D. Reid Ent. (P.755)

--*Cowpokes Rarin' to Go.* 2nd ed. Reid, Ace. N.D. Reid Ent. (P.755)

--*Cowpokes Tales & Cartoons.* 2nd ed. Reid, Ace. Pickens, Slim, intro. by. N.D. Reid Ent. (P.755)

--*Cowpokes Wanted.* 12th ed. Reid, Ace. Gipson, Fred, intro. by. N.D. Reid Ent. (P.755)

--*Draggin' S Ranch Cowpokes.* 14th ed. Reid, Ace. N.D. Reid Ent. (P.755)

--*More Cowpokes.* 14th ed. Reid, Ace. Robertson, Frank C., intro. by. N.D. Reid Ent. (P.755)

Reid, Albert T.

--*Tom McNeal's Fables.* McNeal, Thomas Allen (1853-). 1905. Crane & Co. (P.610)

Reid, Bill

--*Raven's Cry.* 1st ed. Harris, Christie Lucy Irwin (1907-). 1966. Atheneum. **Awards: (ALA); (CLA).** (P.415)

Reid, James (1907-)

--*The Cave Mystery: A Boys' Story of the Spanish Pyrenees.* Williamson, Thames Ross (1894-). Smith, S. S., pseud. c.1935. Harcourt, Barce and Company. (P.964)

--*The Falcon Mystery: A Boys' Story of the Hungarian Plain.* Williamson, Thames Ross (1894-). Smith, S. S., pseud. c.1936. Harcourt, Brace and Company. (P.964)

--*Five Little Indians.* Henderson, Rose. 1931. R. M. McBride & Company. (P.433)

--*The Gypsy and the Bear and Other Fairy Tales.* Borski, Lucia Merecka, Mrs. & Miller, Kate B., trs. from Pol. Kelly, Eric P., frwd. by. 1933. Longmans, Green and Co. (P.755)

--*Hannibal's Elephants.* Powers, Alfred. 1944. Longmans, Green & Co. (P.736)

--*Hannibal's Elephants.* Powers, Alfred. 1944. McKay. (P.736)

--*Hurricane Sands.* Barbour, Ralph Henry (1870-1944). 1940. D. Appleton-Century Company, Incorporated. (P.70)

--*Kitchen Magic.* Cassady, Constance. N.D. Farrar & Rinehart. (P.177)

--*The Lapp Mystery: A Boy's Story of Finnish Lapland.* Williamson, Thames Ross (1894-). Smith, S. S., pseud. c.1934. Harcourt, Brace and Company. (P.965)

--*Lost Island.* Burglon, Nora. c.1939. The John C. Winston Company. (P.153)

--*Memorial to George.* Champneys, Adelaide, ed. 1929. The Books-Merrill Company. (P.183)

--*Not Really!.* Eleven Jolly Stories. Frost, Lesley (1899-1983). Untermeyer, Louis (1885-1977), intro. by. c.1939. Coward-McCann, Inc. (P.348)

--*Peter, Peter, Pumpkin Eater.* Reid, James (1907-). 1970. Fortress Press. (P.755)

--*Pogo: The Circus Horse.* Berger, Josef (1903-1971). c.1934. Coward, McCann, Inc. (P.96)

--*Ralestone Luck.* Norton, Andre, pseud. (1912-). Norton, Alice Mary. 1938. D. Appleton-Century Company, Incorporated. (P.686)

--*Ringtail.* Gall, Alice Crew, Mrs. (1878-1949) & Crew, Fleming H. (1882-). c.1933. Oxford University Press. (P.353)

--*Sailing for Gold.* Johnson, Clifton (1865-1940). c.1938. G. P. Putnam's Sons. (P.494)

--*The Spy Mystery: A Boys' Story of Soviet Russia.* Williamson, Thames Ross (1894-). Smith, S. S., pseud. c.1937. Harcourt, Brace and Company. (P.965)

--*This Wooden Pig Went with Dora.* Lindsay, Walter (1870-). 1930. R. M. McBride & Company. (P.574)

Reid, Mary M.

--*Fuzzy Four-Footed Folks.* Krecker, Ada May. 1902. Jamieson-Higgins Co. (P.539)

Reid, Stephen (1873-1934)

--*The Boy's Cuchulain.* Hull, Eleanor Means (1913-). 1910. Thomas Y. Crowell Co. (P.472)

--*The Boys' Cuchulain: Heroic Legends of Ireland.* Cuchulain. Hull, Eleanor (1860-1935), ed. 1910. Thomas Y. Crowell Co. (P.234)

--*Frank Brown: Sea Apprentice.* Bullen, Frank Thomas (1857-1915). 1926. D. McKay. (P.149)

--*Jim Davis.* Masefield, John Edward (1878-1967). 1924. D. McKay. (P.627)

--*Jim Davis.* Masefield, John Edward (1878-1967). 1942. D. McKay Company. (P.627)

--*The Magic Casement: An Anthology of Fairy Poetry.* Noyes, Alfred (1880-1958), ed. 1909. E. P. Dutton & Co. (P.688)

--*Treasure Island.* Stevenson, Robert Louis (1850-1894). N.D. Thomas Y. Crowell Co. (P.857)

--*A Wonder-Book and Tanglewood Tales.* Hawthorne, Nathaniel (1804-1864). 1934. D. McKay. (P.424)

Reid, Terry

--*Brother Jerome & the Lion.* Reid, Terry, retold by. 1966. Abelard. (P.755)

--*Nikos and the Ikon.* Reid, Terry. 1970, c.1969. Abelard-Schuman. (P.755)

Reidel, Marlene

--*Albert and His Adventures.* Stearns, Monroe Mather (1913-). 1961. Bobbs-Merrill. (P.850)

--*Eric's Journey.* Stearns, Monroe Mather (1913-). 1960. Lippincott. (P.850)

--*Gabriel & His Magic Wand.* Stearns, Monroe Mather (1913-). 1962. Lippincott. (P.850)

--*Kasimir's Journey.* Stearns, Monroe Mather (1913-). 1959. Lippincott. **Award: (NYT).** (P.850)

--*Kasimir's Journey: Verse.* Stearns, Monroe Mather (1913-). 1957. Lippincott. (P.850)

Reidy, Kathleen

--*Alphabet Sheep.* Mendoza, George (1934-). c.1982. Grosset & Dunlap. (P.641)

--*Counting Sheep.* Mendoza, George (1934-). c.1982. Grosset & Dunlap. (P.641)

--*The Sheepish Book of Opposites.* Mendoza, George (1934-). c.1982. Grosset & Dunlap. (P.641)

--*Silly Sheep & Other Sheepish Rhymes.* Mendoza, George (1934-). 1982. Putnam Pub Group. (P.641)

Reifsnyder, Marylou

--*The Turquoise Horse: Prose & Poetry of the American Indian.* Hood, Flora Mae (1898-), ed. 1972. Putnam. (P.458)

Reig, June (1933-)

--*The Diary of the Boy King, Tut Ankh Amen.* Reig, June (1933-). 1979. Scribner. (P.756)

Reilly, Jack

--*You Are What You Are.* McLenighan, Valjean (1947-). c.1977. Follet Pub. Co. (P.608)

Reilly, Veronica

--*Always Alvin.* Van Allen, Diane. 1984. Pohl Assoc. (P.912)

--*Show and Tell.* Fletcher, Helen Jill (1910-). 1968. Platt & Munk. (P.331)
--*Soft As a Bunny.* Lowery, Lawrence F. 1969. Western Pub. (P.589)
Renkis, Rosemarie
--*Cat Royal.* Brady, Charles Andrew (1912-). 1947. Sheed and Ward. (P.125)
Renner, Hans Peter
--*The World of the Pharaohs.* Baumann, Hans (1914-). Winston, Richard & Winston, Clara, trs. Burges, Albert, photos by. 1960. Pantheon Books. (P.83)
Reppy, Nell
--*Come Play with Us.* Carlile, Bess Howell. 1947. Rand McNally. (P.168)
--*A Penny for Candy.* Devine, Louise Lawrence. N.D. Rand McNally & Co. (P.261)
Reschofsky, Jean
--*Crin-Blanc.* Guillot, Rene (1900-1969). 1963. Franklin Watts. (P.399)
--*The Wild White Stallion.* Guillot, Rene (1900-1969). Marsh, Gwen, tr. from Fr. 1961. F. Watts. (P.399)
Resko, John
--*The Snowplow that Tried to Go South.* Walters, George. N.D. Aladdin Bks. (P.929)
--*The Snowplow that Tried to Go South.* Walters, George. N.D. E. P. Dutton & Co. (P.929)
Ressler, William
--*Terry and the Mysterious Monkey.* 1st ed. Coryell, Hugh (1913-). 1952. Winston. (P.222)
Rethi, Lili (1894-)
--*Big Bridge to Brooklyn: The Roebling Story.* 1st ed. Browin, Frances Williams (1898-). 1956. Aladdin Books. (P.137)
--*The Double Quest.* Sobol, Donald J (1924-). 1957. F. Watts. (P.839)
--*Favorite Tales of Long Ago.* Baldwin, James (1841-1925). 1955. Aladdin Books. (P.65)
--*Favorite Tales of Long Ago.* Baldwin, James (1841-1925). N.D. E. P. Dutton & Co. (P.65)
--*Is This My Love?.* Finney, Gertrude Elva Bridgeman (1892-). 1956. Longmans, Green. (P.327)
--*Legends of the Saints.* Turnbull, E. Lucia, retold by. 1959. Lippincott. (P.905)
--*Man and Grasses.* Froman, Robert Winslow (1917-). 1963. J B Lippincott Company. (P.347)
--*Mother Goose goes to War.* Lin, Beth. 1962. Exposition Press. (P.573)
--*St.* Elizabeth's Three Crowns. Thompson, Blanche Jennings (1887-). 1958. Vision Books. (P.886)
--*St.* Thomas More of London. Ince, Elizabeth M. 1957. Vision Books. (P.479)
--*Temple of the Sun: A Boy Fights for Montezuma.* 1st ed. Lampman, Evelyn Sibley (1907-1980). 1964. Doubleday. (P.546)
--*The Turn in the Road.* DeLeeuw, Cateau Wilhelmina (1903-1975). 1961. Nelson. (P.255)
Rettich, Rolf
--*The Castle of the Red Gorillas.* Ecke, Wolfgang (1927-). c.1983. Prentice-Hall. (P.295)
--*Engine Fourteen-Fourteen.* Rosenfeld, Friedrich (1902-). Feld, Friedrich, pseud. Koenig, Marion, tr. 1965. A. Whitman. (P.778)
--*The Face at the Window.* Ecke, Wolfgang (1927-). 1983. P-H. (P.295)
--*The Face at the Window.* Ecke, Wolfgang (1927-). Humphries, Stella, tr. from Ger. 1979. P-H. (P.295)
--*The Invisible Witness.* Ecke, Wolfgang (1927-). 1981. P-H. (P.295)
--*The Silver Touch and Other Family Christmas Stories.* Rettich, Margret. Crawford, Elizabeth D., tr. from Ger. 1978. W. Morrow. (P.758)
--*The Tightwad's Curse and Other Pleasantly Chilling Stories.* Rettich, Margret. Crawford, Elizabeth D., tr. from Ger. 1979. Morrow. (P.758)
Rettich, Rolf & Langenfass, Hansjorg
--*The Bank Holdup.* Ecke, Wolfgang (1927-). 1982. Prentice-Hall. (P.295)
--*The Midnight Chess Game.* Ecke, Wolfgang (1927-). 1985, c.1983. Prentice-Hall. (P.295)
Rettig, Anne
--*Andro, Star of Bethlehem.* Claire, Anne. Mahany, Patricia, ed. 1983. Standard Pub. (P.196)
--*Andro, the Star of Bethlehem.* Claire, Anne. 1981. Standard Pub. (P.196)
Reusswig, William
--*A Fox Story.* Sollers, Allan A. c.1963. Holt Rinehart and Winston. (P.840)
--*The Story of Crazy Horse.* Meadowcroft, Enid La Monte, Mrs. (1898-1966). 1954. Grosset & Dunlap. (P.638)
--*We Were There with the California Rancheros.* Thompson, Harlan H. (1894-). Holt, Stephen, pseud. Lewis, Oscar, ed. 1960. Grosset & Dunlap. (P.887)
Reuter-Pacyna, John
--*Zero Makes Me Hungry: A Collection of Poems for Today.* Lueders, Edward George (1923-) & St. John, Primus, eds. 1976. Lothrop. **Award: (ALA).** (P.590)
Reuterdahl, H., jt. illus. see Aylward, William James.
Revitt, Peter
--*Ballet & the Dance.* Woodward, Ian. 1978. Merrimack Bk Serv. (P.977)
Rey, Hans Augusto (1898-1977)
--*Billy's Picture.* Rey, Hans Augusto (1898-1977) & Rey, Margret Elisabeth Waldstein (1906-). 1948. Harper. (P.758)
--*Cecily G.* & the Nine Monkeys. Rey, Hans Augusto (1898-1977). 1977. HM. (P.758)
--*Cecily G.* and the Nine Monkeys. Rey, Hans Augusto (1898-1977) & Rey, Margret Elisabeth Waldstein (1906-). 1942. Houghton Mifflin Company. (P.758)
--*Curious George.* Rey, Hans Augusto (1898-1977) & Rey, Margret Elisabeth Waldstein (1906-). 1941. Houghton Mifflin Company. (P.758)
--*Curious George.* Rey, Hans Augusto (1898-1977) & Rey, Margret Elisabeth Waldstein (1906-). 1973, c.1941. Houghton Mifflin. (P.758)
--*Curious George Flies a Kite.* Rey, Margret Elisabeth Waldstein (1906-) & Rey, Hans Augusto (1898-1977). 1977. HM. (P.759)
--*Curious George Gets a Medal.* Rey, Hans Augusto (1898-1977) & Rey, Margret Elisabeth Waldstein (1906-). 1957. Houghton Mifflin. **Award: (NYT).** (P.758)
--*Curious George Goes to the Hospital.* Rey, Hans Augusto (1898-1977) & Rey, Margret Elisabeth Waldstein (1906-). 1966. HM. (P.758)
--*Curious George Goes to the Hospital.* Rey, Hans Augusto (1898-1977) & Rey, Margret Elisabeth Waldstein (1906-). 1970. Schol Bk Serv. (P.758)
--*Curious George Learns the Alphabet.* Rey, Hans Augusto (1898-1977) & Rey, Margret Elisabeth Waldstein (1906-). 1973. HM. (P.758)
--*Curious George Rides a Bike.* Rey, Hans Augusto (1898-1977) & Rey, Margret Elisabeth Waldstein (1906-). 1973, c.1952. Houghton Mifflin. (P.758)
--*Curious George Takes a Job.* Rey, Hans Augusto (1898-1977) & Rey, Margret Elisabeth Waldstein (1906-). 1947. Houghton Mifflin Co. (P.758)
--*Curious George Takes a Job.* Rey, Hans Augusto (1898-1977) & Rey, Margret Elisabeth Waldstein (1906-). 1974, c.1947. Houghton, Mifflin. (P.758)
--*Don't Frighten the Lion!.* Brown, Margaret Wise (1910-1952). N.D. Harper & Bros. (P.140)
--*Egbert.* Gilbert, Paul Thomas (1876-). N.D. Harper & Bros. (P.367)
--*Egbert and His Marvelous Adventures.* Gilbert, Paul Thomas (1876-). 1944. Harper & Brothers. (P.367)
--*Elizabite: The Adventures of a Carnivorous Plant.* Rey, Hans Augusto (1898-1977). 1962. Har-Row. (P.758)
--*Elizabite: The Adventures of a Carnivorous Plant.* Rey, Hans Augusto (1898-1977) & Rey, Margret Elisabeth Waldstein (1906-). 1942. Harper & Brothers. (P.758)
--*Feed the Animals.* Rey, Hans Augusto (1898-1977) & Rey, Margret Elisabeth Waldstein (1906-). c.1944. Houghton Mifflin Company. (P.759)
--*How Do You Get There?.* Rey, Hans Augusto (1898-1977) & Rey, Margret Elisabeth Waldstein (1906-). c.1941. Houghton Mifflin Company. (P.759)
--*Humpty Dumpty and Other Mother Goose Songs.* Rey, Hans Augusto (1898-1977). 1943. Harper & Brothers. (P.758)
--*Katy No-Pocket.* Payne, Emmy, pseud. (1919-). West, Emily Govan. 1944. Houghton Mifflin Company. (P.712)
--*Park Book.* Zolotow, Charlotte Shapiro (1915-). 1944. Har-Row. (P.994)
--*The Polite Penguin.* Brown, Margaret Wise (1910-1952). c.1941. Harper & Brothers. (P.141)
--*Pretzel.* 1st ed. Rey, Margret Elisabeth Waldstein (1906-). 1944. Harper & Brothers. (P.759)
--*Pretzel and the Puppies.* Rey, Margret Elisabeth Waldstein (1906-). 1946. Harper & Brothers. (P.759)
--*See the Circus.* Rey, Hans Augusto (1898-1977) & Rey, Margret Elisabeth Waldstein (1906-). 1956. Houghton Mifflin. (P.759)
--*Tit for Tat.* Rey, Hans Augusto (1898-1977) & Rey, Margret Elisabeth Waldstein (1906-). 1942. Harper & Brothers. (P.759)
--*Where's My Baby?.* Rey, Hans Augusto (1898-1977) & Rey, Margret Elisabeth Waldstein (1906-). c.1943. Houghton Mifflin Company. (P.759)
Reyes, Roger I
--*The Little Horse of Seven Colors: El Caballito De Siete Colores.* Rohmer, Harriet & Anchondo, Mary, eds. c.1976. Children's Book Press. (P.775)
--*Skyworld Woman: La Mujer Del Mundo-Cielo.* Rohmer, Harriet & Anchondo, Mary, eds. c.1975. Children's Book Press. (P.775)
Reyes, Roger J., jt. illus. see Cherin, Robin.
Reynolds, Al
--*The Football Dragon.* Reynolds, Jamie. 1981. Bozo Pr. (P.759)
Reynolds, Alfred Christopher (1911-)
--*The Pond on My Windowsill.* Reynolds, Alfred Christopher (1911-). 1970. Pantheon Books. (P.759)
Reynolds, Cuyler (1866-)
--*The Rosamond Tales: Sixteen Short Stories Intended for Children.* Reynolds, Cuyler (1866-). 1901. L. C. Page & Co. (P.759)
Reynolds, Doris
--*Beth and Seth.* Varble, Rachel Margaret McBrayer, Mrs. 1959. Doubleday. (P.916)
--*Child of the Arctic.* Woods, Hubert C. 1962. Follett Pub. Co. (P.977)
--*That Jones Girl.* Friermood, Elisabeth Hamilton (1903-). 1956. Doubleday. (P.346)
Reynolds, E. Evan
--*The White Cheyenne.* Terrett, Courtenay (1901-). 1949. Dodd, Mead. (P.882)
Reynolds, Jessie & Royt, Mary
--*John Martin's Stories for Children.* Shepard, Morgan (1865-). Martin, John, pseud. c.1936. Whitman Publishing Company. (P.818)
Reynolds, Julie
--*The Woman Who Knocked out Sugar Ray.* Dranow, Ralph. Darlington, Sandy & Reynolds, Julie, eds. 1982. Arrowhead Pr. (P.284)
Reynolds, Lynn Hutchinson (1940-)
--*The Gift.* Walcott, Cynthia K. c.1976. Baha'i Pub. Trust. (P.925)
Reynolds, Warwick, jt. illus. see Bransom, Paul.
Reynolds, Warwick (1880-)
--*Dwellers in the Jungle.* Casserly, Gordon. 1927. Frederick A. Stokes Company. (P.177)
Rhead, Frederick Alfred, jt. illus. see Rhead, Louis John.
Rhead, Louis John (1857-1926)
--*Aesop's Fables.* Aesopus. c.1927. Harper & Brothers. (P.13)
--*The Arabian Nights' Entertainments.* 1916. Harper & Brothers. (P.759)
--*Easter Joys.* Longfellow, Henry Wadsworth (1807-1882). N.D. Dodge. (P.582)
--*The Fairy Book: The Best Popular Stories.* Craik, Dinah Maria Mulock, Mrs. (1826-1887). c.1922. Harper and Brothers. (P.227)
--*Grimm's Fairy Tales: Stories and Tales of Elves, Goblins and Fairies.* Grimm, Jakob Ludwig Karl (1785-1863) & Grimm, Wilhelm Karl (1786-1859). 1917. Harper & Brothers. (P.393)
--*Hans Andersen's Fairy Tales and Wonder Stories.* Andersen, Hans Christian (1805-1875). Howells, W. D., intro. by. 1914. Harper & Brother. (P.36)
--*Hans Brinker: Or, The Silver Skates.* Dodge, Mary Elizabeth Mapes, Mrs. (1831-1905). c.1924. Harper and Brothers. (P.276)
--*Heidi.* Spyri, Johanna Heusser (1827-1901). c.1925. Harper & Brothers. (P.846)
--*Pets.* Haines, Alice Calhoun. 1904. Frederick A. Stokes Co. (P.402)
--*The Pilgrim's Progress.* Bunyan, John (1628-1688). Potter, Henry C., intro. by. N.D. Century Co. (P.151)
--*The Swiss Family Robinson: Or, The Adventures of a Shipwrecked Family on an Uninhabited Isle Near New Guinea.* Wyss, Johann David Von (1743-1818). N.D. Harper & Brothers. (P.984)
--*The Swiss Family Robinson: Or, The Adventures of a Shipwrecked Family on an Uninhabited Isle Near New Guinea.* Wyss, Johann David Von (1743-1818). Wyss, Johann Rudolf (1781-1830), rev. by. Paull, Henry H. B., Mrs., tr. 1909. Harper & Brothers. (P.984)
Rhead, Louis John (1857-1926) & Rhead, Frederick Alfred (1855-)
--*Robinson Crusoe.* Defoe, Daniel (1661-1731). 1966. University Microfilms. (P.251)
Rhead, Louis John (1857-1926) & Schoonover, Frank Earle (1877-1972)
--*Hans Brinker.* Dodge, Mary Elizabeth Mapes, Mrs. (1831-1905). N.D. Harper & Bros. (P.276)
--*Kidnapped.* Stevenson, Robert Louis (1850-1894). N.D. Harper & Bros. (P.857)
--*King Arthur and His Knights.* Knowles, James, Sir, compiled by. N.D. Harper & Bros. (P.533)
--*Tales from Shakespeare.* Lamb, Charles (1775-1834) & Lamb, Mary Ann (1764-1847). N.D. Harper & Bros. (P.545)
--*Tom Brown's School-Days.* Hughes, Thomas (1822-1896). c.1911. Harper & Brothers. (P.471)
--*Treasure Island.* Stevenson, Robert Louis (1850-1894). N.D. Harper & Bros. (P.857)
Rhie, Schi-Zhin (1936-), photos by.
--*Soon-Hee in America.* Rhie, Schi-Zhin (1936-). 1977. Hollym Intl. (P.759)
Rhoades, Elizabeth
--*Dorothy Brown: A Story for Girls.* Rhoades, Nina, pseud. (1863-). Rhoades, Cornelia Harson. 1909. Lothrop, Lee & Shepard. (P.759)
Rhoads, Marie P.
--*Paul, the Hunchback.* Rhoads, Marie P. N.D. IEM-HOTEP. (P.760)
Rhodes, Priscilla
--*The Deadly Duke Football Mystery.* Longmeyer, Carole Marsh. N.D. Gallopade Pub Group. (P.583)
--*The Great Clemson Football Mystery.* Longmeyer, Carole Marsh. 1983. Gallopade Pub Group. (P.583)
--*The Lost Colony Storybook.* Longmeyer, Carole Marsh. 1983. Gallopade Pub Group. (P.583)
--*The Mad Maryland Football Mystery.* Longmeyer, Carole Marsh. N.D. Gallopade Pub Group. (P.583)
--*The Strange NC State Football Mystery.* Longmeyer, Carole Marsh. N.D. Gallopade Pub Group. (P.583)
--*The Terrifying Georgia Tech Football Mystery.* Longmeyer, Carole Marsh. 1983. Gallopade Pub Group. (P.583)
--*Those Whose Names Were Terrible.* Longmeyer, Carole Marsh. 1983. Gallopade Pub Group. (P.583)
--*The Very Scary Virginia Football Mystery.* Longmeyer, Carole Marsh. N.D. Gallopade Pub Group. (P.583)
--*The Wild Wake Forest Football Mystery.* Longmeyer, Carole Marsh. N.D. Gallopade Pub Group. (P.583)
Rhys, Megan, jt. illus. see Tarrant, Margaret Winifred.
Ribas, Marta
--*Rednose the Elf.* Giuliano, William. 1966. Marand Pub Co. (P.370)
Ribbons, Ian (1924-)
--*Bowman of Crecy.* Welch, Ronald, pseud. (1909-). Felton, Ronald Oliver. 1967, c.1966. Criterion. (P.943)
--*Bowman of Crecy.* Welch, Ronald, pseud. (1909-). Felton, Ronald Oliver. 1966. Oxford U.P. (P.943)
--*Fanny.* Almedingen, Martha Edith Von (1898-1971). Almedingen, E. M., pseud. 1970. FS&G. (P.31)
--*The Fox Hole.* Southall, Ivan Francis (1921-). 1967. St. Martin's Press. (P.841)
--*High Courage.* Weir, Rosemary Green (1905-). 1967. Farrar, Straus & Giroux. (P.942)
--*Let the Balloon Go.* Southall, Ivan Francis (1921-). 1968. St. Martin's Press. (P.841)
--*Linnets and Valerians.* Goudge, Elizabeth (1900-1984). 1964. Coward-McCann. **Award: (ALA).** (P.378)
--*Monday, Twenty-One October Eighteen-Five: The Day of Trafalgar.* Ribbons, Ian (1924-). 1968. Oxford University Press. (P.760)
--*Sea Gull.* Farmer, Penelope Jane (1939-). c.1966. Harcourt. (P.318)
--*Ten Tales of Detection.* Green, Roger Gilbert Lancelyn (1918-), ed. 1967. Dutton. (P.385)
Rice, Alma
--*Hansel and Grethel: Adapted from the Story by Brothers Grimm.* Grimm, Jakob Ludwig Karl (1785-1863) & Grimm, Wilhelm Karl (1786-1859). 1943. McLoughlin Brothers, Inc. (P.393)
Rice, Betty
--*Fire and Water, and Other Hawaiian Legends.* Lyons, Barbara Baldwin (1912-), retold by. 1973. C. E. Tuttle Co. (P.592)
Rice, Dorothy
--*The Gypsy Laddie.* Rice, Dorothy. 1972. Atheneum. (P.760)
Rice, Elizabeth (1913-)
--*The Bear Who Lost His Hair.* Bruce, Mary (1927-). 1968. Steck-Vaughn Co. (P.144)
--*Benje, the Squirrel Who Lost His Tail.* Rice, Elizabeth (1913-). 1969. Childrens Press. (P.760)
--*Chichi's Magic.* Sharp, Adda Mai Cummings & Young, Epsie. 1954. Steck-V. (P.815)
--*Chippy Chipmunk's Vacation.* Sharp, Adda Mai Cummings & Young, Epsie. 1965. Steck-V. (P.815)
--*Daffy.* Sharp, Adda Mai Cummings. 1950. Steck Co. (P.815)
--*Did You Ever.* Sharp, Adda Mai Cummings & Young, Epsie. 1957. Steck-V. (P.816)
--*Downy Duck Grows Up.* Sharp, Adda Mai Cummings & Young, Epsie. 1965. Steck-V. (P.816)
--*Every Day a Surprise.* Sharp, Adda Mai Cummings & Young, Epsie. 1957. Steck-V. (P.816)
--*Fun for Ozzie.* Tompert, Ann (1918-). 1971. Stack-Vaughn Co. (P.895)
--*Gee Whillikins.* Sharp, Adda Mai Cummings. 1950. Steck-V. (P.815)
--*Gordo & the Hidden Treasure.* Sharp, Adda Mai Cummings & Young, Epsie. 1955. Steck-V. (P.816)
--*Gordo and the Hidden Treasures.* Sharp, Adda Mai Cummings & Young, Epsie. N.D. World Publishing Co. (P.816)
--*Heart of the Wild.* Sharp, Adda Mai Cummings & Young, Epsie. 1955. Steck-V. (P.816)
--*Henry and Benjamin.* Rice, Elizabeth (1913-). 1970. Steck-Vaughn. (P.760)

--*The Jack Rabbit.* DeVault, Marion Vere (1922-). 1959. Stock Co. (P.261)
--*Just for Manuel.* Hampton, Doris. 1971. Steck-Vaughn Co. (P.409)
--*The League of Unusual Animals.* Friedrich, Priscilla & Friedrich, Otto Alva (1929-). c.1965. Steck. (P.346)
--*Little Pup.* Weir, LaVada. 1969. Steck-Vaughn Co. (P.942)
--*The Little Shell Hunter.* Sorrells, Dorothy C. 1961. Simon and Schuster. (P.841)
--*The Little Shell Hunter.* Sorrells, Dorothy C. 1961. Steck Co. (P.841)
--*Log Fort Adventures.* McCall, Edith Sansom (1911-). 1958. Childrens Press. (P.594)
--*Men on Iron Horses.* McCall, Edith Sansom (1911-). 1960. Childrens Press. (P.594)
--*Once When I Was Five.* Zimelman, Nathan (1911-). 1967. Steck-Vaughn Co. (P.993)
--*Over the Mormon Trail.* Jones, Helen Hinckley (1903-). 1963. Childrens Press. (P.499)
--*Pioneer Show Folk.* McCall, Edith Sansom (1911-). 1963. Childrens. (P.594)
--*Pioneering on the Plains.* McCall, Edith Sansom (1911-). 1962. Childrens Press. (P.594)
--*Pioneering on the Plains.* McCall, Edith Sansom (1911-). 1980. Childrens. (P.594)
--*Pioneers on Early Waterways: Davy Crockett to Mark Twain.* McCall, Edith Sansom (1911-). 1961. Childrens Press. (P.594)
--*Road Runner.* Munch, Theodore William (1919-) & De Vault, M. Vere. 1958. Steck-V. (P.671)
--*Settlers on a Strange Shore.* McCall, Edith Sansom (1911-). c.1960. Childrens Press. (P.594)
--*Settlers on a Strange Shore.* McCall, Edith Sansom (1911-). 1980. Childrens. (P.594)
--*Wagons Over the Mountains.* McCall, Edith Sansom (1911-). 1961. Childrens Press. (P.594)
--*Wagons Over the Mountains.* McCall, Edith Sansom (1911-). 1980. Childrens. (P.594)

Rogers, Cecilia, jt. illus. see Munson, Harold W.

Rogers, Cedric (1915-)
--*Rags, Bottles, and Bones.* Paul's Amazing Collection. Rogers, Cedric (1915-). 1962. D. McKay Co. (P.774)
--*A Triumph for Flavius.* Snedeker, Caroline Dale Parke, Mrs. (1871-1956). 1955. Lothrop. (P.838)
--*Tweeney.* Foreman, Harvey. 1959. Lothrop, Lee & Shepard. (P.335)

Rogers, Frances (1888-1974)
--*Big Miss Liberty.* Rogers, Frances (1888-1974). 1938. Frederick A. Stokes Company. (P.774)
--*Big Miss Liberty.* Rogers, Frances (1888-1974). N.D. J. B. Lippincott. (P.774)
--*Chico: The Story of a Homing Pigeon.* New ed. Blanchard, Lucy Mansfield Blanchard, Mrs. (1870-). c.1929. Houghton Mifflin Company. (P.107)
--*Doris of Dobbs Ferry.* Wells, Carolyn (1869-1942). c.1917. George H. Doran Company. (P.943)
--*Fire Engine Boy.* Rogers, Frances (1888-1974). 1953. Lippincott. (P.774)
--*Hollyhock House: A Story for Girls.* Taggart, Marion Ames (1866-). 1916. Doubleday, Page & Company. (P.876)
--*Indigo Treasure.* Rogers, Frances (1888-1974). c.1941. Frederick A. Stokes Company. (P.774)
--*Jeremy Pepper.* Rogers, Frances (1888-1974) & Beard, Alice. 1946. J. B. Lippincott Company. (P.774)
--*Little Miss Fales.* Knipe, Emilie Benson, Mrs. (1870-1958) & Knipe, Alden Arthur (1870-1950). 1910. Harper & Brothers. (P.532)
--*Paul Revere: Patriot on Horseback.* Rogers, Frances (1888-1974) & Beard, Alice. 1943. Frederick A. Stokes Company. (P.774)

Rogers, Franke
--*The Robin Family Keeps Christmas.* Rogers, Franke. 1953. Lothrop, Lee & Shepard Co. (P.774)

Rogers, Hubert
--*The Flood-Fighters: A Boy's Adventures with the Raging Missisippi.* Williamson, Thames Ross (1894-). 1931. Houghton Mifflin Company. (P.964)
--*Nicho of the River.* Richardson, Tracy. 1958. Stephen Greene Press. (P.763)
--*Opening Davy Jone's Locker: A Boy Explores the Bottom of the Sea.* Williamson, Thames Ross (1894-). 1930. Houghton Mifflin Company. (P.965)
--*Spanish Ingots.* Ellsberg, Edward (1891-). 1937. Dodd, Mead & Company. (P.304)
--*Submarine Treasure.* Ellsberg, Edward (1891-). 1953, c.1936. Dodd, Mead. (P.304)

Rogers, Jackie
--*Cosmic Kidnappers.* Randall, E. T. 1985. Troll Assocs. (P.748)
--*Goblin Tales.* Denan, Corinne, retold by. c.1980. Troll Associates. (P.256)
--*The Marathon Race Mystery.* McNear, Robert (1930-). 1985. Troll Assocs. (P.610)
--*The Missing Rock Star Caper.* McVey, R. Parker. 1985. Troll Assocs. (P.611)
--*Mystery at the Ball Game.* McVey, R. Parker. c.1985. Troll Associates. (P.612)
--*Mystery at the Bike Race.* Topper, Frank. 1985. Troll Assocs. (P.896)
--*Target: Earth.* Randall, E. T. 1985. Troll Assocs. (P.748)
--*Thieves from Space.* Randall, E. T. 1985. Troll Assocs. (P.748)
--*Town in Terror.* Randall, E. T. c.1985. Troll Associates. (P.748)

Rogers, Joe
--*Dairyman Don.* Chapin, Cynthia. 1964. A Whitman. (P.184)
--*Fire Snorkel Number 7.* Barr, Jene (1900-). c.1965. A. Whitman. (P.75)
--*Fun Days.* Hillert, Margaret (1920-). c.1982. Follett Pub. Co. (P.444)
--*The House That Jack Built.* 1968, c.1967. Lothrop, Lee & Shephard Co. (P.775)
--*One Is the Engine: A Counting Book.* Meeks, Esther K. (1909-). 1972. Follett Pub. Co. (P.639)

Rogers, Joe, jt. illus. see Everds, John.

Rogers, Julia
--*Planet X.* Kiefer, Mildred S. 1953. J. Messner. (P.522)
--*Planet X.* Kiefer, Mildred S. 1965, c.1953. Melmont. (P.522)
--*Planet X.* New ed. Kiefer, Mildred S. Wyler, Rose (1909-), ed. 1965, c.1953. Melmont. (P.522)

Rogers , Lou
--*The Rise of the Red Alders.* Rogers, Lou. 1928. Harper & Brothers. (P.775)
--*Ska-Denge: Beaver for Revenge.* Rogers, Lou. 1929. Harper & Brothers. (P.775)

Rogers, Mabel & DeFrehn, Sarah E.
--*The Book of Live Dolls: An Omnibus for Children.* Gates, Josephine Scribner, Mrs. (1859-1930). 1945. The Bobbs-Merrill Company. (P.360)

Rogers, Mary (1931-)
--*Freaky Friday.* 1st ed. Rodgers, Mary (1931-). 1977, c.1972. Harper & Row. (P.774)

Rogers, Richard
--*McBride's Latest Dialogues: A Collection of Dialogues, Parlor Dramas, Colloquies, and Amateur Plays Designed for the Use of Young People in Schools.* McBride, H. Elliott. c.1889. J. S. Ogilvie. (P.594)
--*The Vengeance of Fu Chang.* c.1932. Oxford University Press. (P.775)

Rogers, Terrance
--*Mommies & Daddies Work.* Dayton, Laura. N.D. Dandelion Pr. (P.248)

Rogers, W. A.
--*The Boy Settlers: A Story of Early Times in Kansas.* Brooks, Noah (1830-1903). 1891. C. Scribner's Sons. (P.137)
--*The Boy Settlers: A Story of Early Times in Kansas.* Brooks, Noah (1830-1903). 1906. C. Scribner's Sons. (P.137)
--*The Copper Princess: A Story of Lake Superior Mines.* Munroe, Kirk (1850-1930). 1898. Harper & Brothers. (P.672)
--*Jenny Wren's Boarding House: A Story of a Newsboy life in New York.* Kaler, James Otis (1848-1912). Otis, James, pseud. N.D. Estes & Lauriat's. (P.505)
--*Jenny Wren's Boarding-House: A Story of Newsboy Life in New York.* Kaler, James Otis (1848-1912). Otis, James, pseud. c.1893. Estes and Lauriat. (P.505)
--*Jenny Wren's Boarding House: Stories of Newsboy Life in New York.* Kaler, James Otis (1848-1912). Otis, James, pseud. N.D. Dana Estes & Co. (P.505)
--*Mr.* Stubbs's Brother. Kaler, James Otis (1848-1912). Otis, James, pseud. 1883. Harper & Brothers. (P.506)
--*Mr.* Stubbs's Brother. Kaler, James Otis (1848-1912). Otis, James, pseud. 1903. Harper & Brothers. (P.506)
--*The Ready Rangers: A Story of Boys, Boats, and Bicycles, Fire-Buckets and Fun.* Munroe, Kirk (1850-1930). c.1897. Lothrop Pub. (P.672)
--*Rick Dale: A Story of the Northwest Coast.* Munroe, Kirk (1850-1930). 1896. Harper (P.672)
--*Secrets of Roseladies.* Catherwood, Mary Hartwell, Mrs. (1847-1902). 1888. Lothrop. (P.178)
--*Teddy and Carrots: Or, Two Merchants of Newspaper Row.* Kaler, James Otis (1848-1912). Otis, James, pseud. N.D. Dana Estes and Company. (P.506)
--*Teddy and Carrots: Two Merchants of Newspaper Now.* Kaler, James Otis (1848-1912). Otis, James, pseud. c.1896. Estes and Lauriat. (P.506)
--*Tim and Tip: Or, The Adventures of a Boy and a Dog.* Kaler, James Otis (1848-1912). Otis, James, pseud. 1883. Harper & Bros. (P.506)
--*Toby Tyler: Or, Ten Weeks with a Circus.* Kaler, James Otis (1848-1912). Otis, James, pseud. 1881. Harper & Brothers. (P.506)
--*Toby Tyler: Or, Ten Weeks with a Circus.* Kaler, James Otis (1848-1912). Otis, James, pseud. 1902. Harper & Brothers. (P.506)
--*Toby Tyler: Or Ten Weeks with a Circus.* Kaler, James Otis (1848-1912). Otis, James, pseud. c.1920. Harper & Brothers. (P.506)

Rogers, W. A., jt. illus. see Blashfield, Edwin Howland.

Rogers, Walter S.
--*The X Bar X Boys at Grizzly Pass.* Rev. ed. Ferris, James Cody, pseud. Stratemeyer Syndicate. 1929. Grosset & Dunlap. (P.323)
--*The X Bar X Boys at Nugget Camp.* Ferris, James Cody, pseud. Stratemeyer Syndicate. 1928. Grosset & Dunlap. (P.323)
--*The X Bar X Boys at Rustlers' Gap.* Ferris, James Cody, pseud. Stratemeyer Syndicate. 1929. Grosset & Dunlap. (P.323)
--*The X Bar X Boys at the Round-Up.* Ferris, James Cody, pseud. Stratemeyer Syndicate. 1927. Grosset & Dunlap. (P.323)
--*The X Bar X Boys in Thunder Canyon.* Ferris, James Cody, pseud. Stratemeyer Syndicate. 1926. Grosset & Dunlap. (P.323)
--*The X Bar X Boys Lost in the Rockies.* Ferris, James Cody, pseud. Stratemeyer Syndicate. 1930. Grosset & Dunlap. (P.323)
--*The X Bar X Boys on Big Bison Trail.* Ferris, James Cody, pseud. Stratemeyer Syndicate. 1927. Grosset & Dunlap. (P.323)
--*The X Bar X Boys on the Ranch.* Ferris, James Cody, pseud. Stratemeyer Syndicate. 1926. Grosset & Dunlap. (P.323)
--*The X Bar X Boys on Whirlpool River.* Ferris, James Cody, pseud. Stratemeyer Syndicate. 1926. Grosset & Dunlap. (P.323)
--*The X Bar X Boys Riding for Life.* Ferris, James Cody, pseud. Stratemeyer Syndicate. 1931. Grosset & Dunlap. (P.323)
--*Across the Pacific: Or, Ted Scott's Hop to Australia.* Dixon, Franklin W., pseud. Stratemeyer Syndicate. c.1928. Grosset & Dunlap. (P.273)
--*Air Service Boys Flying for Victory: Or, Bombing the Last German Stronghold.* Beach, Charles Amory, pseud. Stratemeyer Syndicate. 1919. George Sully & Co. (P.84)
--*Air Service Boys Flying for Victory: Or, Bombing the Last German Stronghold.* Beach, Charles Amory, pseud. Stratemeyer Syndicate. N.D. World Syndicate Publishing Co. (P.84)
--*The Barbarian: Or, Will Bradford's School Days at St. Jo's.* Corcoran, Brewer (1877-). 1917. The Page Company. (P.220)
--*Baseball Joe at Yale: Or, Pitching for the College Championship.* Chadwick, Lester, pseud. Stratemeyer Syndicate. 1913. Cupples & Leon Co. (P.181)
--*Baseball Joe in the Big League: Or, A Young Pitcher's Hardest Struggles.* Chadwick, Lester, pseud. Stratemeyer Syndicate. 1915. Cupples & Leon Co. (P.181)
--*Baseball Joe in the Central League: Or, Making Good as a Professional Pitcher.* Chadwick, Lester, pseud. Stratemeyer Syndicate. 1914. Cupples & Leon Co. (P.181)
--*Baseball Joe of the Silver Stars: Or, The Rivals of Riverside.* Chadwick, Lester, pseud. Stratemeyer Syndicate. 1912. Cupples & Leon Co. (P.181)
--*Baseball Joe on the School Nine: Or, Pitching for the Blue Banner.* Chadwick, Lester, pseud. Stratemeyer Syndicate. 1912. Cupples & Leon Co. (P.181)
--*Ben Hardy's Flying Machine: Or, Making a Record for Himself.* Webster, Frank V., pseud. Stratemeyer Syndicate. N.D. Cupples & Leon. (P.939)
--*Betty Gordon and Her School Chums: Or, Bringing the Rebels to Terms.* Emerson, Alice B., pseud. Stratemeyer Syndicate. 1924. Cupples & Leon Co. (P.306)
--*Between the Lines in Belgium: A Boys' Story of the Great European War.* Ames, Franklin T. c.1915. Dodd, Mead and Company. (P.33)
--*Between the Lines in France: A Boys' Story of the Great European War.* Ames, Franklin T. c.1915. Dodd, Mead and Company. (P.33)
--*Billie Bradley at Twin Lakes: Or, Jolly Schoolgirls Afloat and Ashore.* Wheeler, Janet D., pseud. Stratemeyer Syndicate. 1922. George Sully & Co. (P.949)
--*Blackie, a Lost Cat: Her Many Adventures.* Barnum, Richard, pseud. Stratemeyer Syndicate. 1916. Barse & Hopkins. (P.74)
--*The Bobbsey Twins and Baby May.* Hope, Laura Lee, pseud. Stratemeyer Syndicate. 1924. Grosset & Dunlap. (P.460)
--*The Bobbsey Twins at Cedar Camp.* Hope, Laura Lee, pseud. Stratemeyer Syndicate. 1921. Grosset & Dunlap. (P.460)
--*The Bobbsey Twins at Home.* Hope, Laura Lee, pseud. Stratemeyer Syndicate. 1916. Grosset & Dunlap. (P.460)
--*The Bobbsey Twins at Spruce Lake.* Hope, Laura Lee, pseud. Stratemeyer Syndicate. c.1930. Grosset & Dunlap. (P.460)
--*The Bobbsey Twins at the County Fair.* Hope, Laura Lee, pseud. Stratemeyer Syndicate. 1922. Grosset & Dunlap. (P.460)
--*The Bobbsey Twins in a Great City.* Hope, Laura Lee, pseud. Stratemeyer Syndicate. 1917. Grosset & Dunlap. (P.460)
--*The Bobbsey Twins in the Great West.* Hope, Laura Lee, pseud. Stratemeyer Syndicate. 1920. Grosset & Dunlap. (P.460)
--*The Bobbsey Twins in Washington.* Hope, Laura Lee, pseud. Stratemeyer Syndicate. 1919. Grosset & Dunlap. (P.460)
--*The Bobbsey Twins on Blueberry Island.* Hope, Laura Lee, pseud. Stratemeyer Syndicate. 1917. Grosset & Dunlap. (P.461)
--*The Bobbsey Twins on the Deep Blue Sea.* Hope, Laura Lee, pseud. Stratemeyer Syndicate. 1918. Grosset & Dunlap. (P.461)
--*The Bobbsey Twins: Or, Merry Days Indoors and Out.* rev. & enl. ed. Hope, Laura Lee, pseud. Stratemeyer Syndicate. 1928. G&D (P.461)
--*The Bobbsey Twins Treasure Hunting.* Hope, Laura Lee, pseud. Stratemeyer Syndicate. c.1929. Grosset & Dunlap. (P.461)
--*The Bobbsey Twins' Wonderful Secret.* Hope, Laura Lee, pseud. Stratemeyer Syndicate. c.1931. Grosset & Dunlap. (P.461)
--*Bobby Blake in the Frozen North: Or, The Old Eskimo's Last Message.* Warner, Frank A., pseud. Stratemeyer Syndicate. c.1923. Barse (P.932)
--*Bobby Blake in the Frozen North: Or, The Old Eskimo's Last Message.* Warner, Frank A., pseud. Stratemeyer Syndicate. N.D. Barse & Co. (P.932)
--*Bobby Blake in the Frozen North: Or, The Old Eskimo's Last Message.* Warner, Frank A., pseud. Stratemeyer Syndicate. N.D. G & D (P.932)
--*Bobby Blake on a Plantation: Or, Lost in the Great Swamp.* Warner, Frank A., pseud. Stratemeyer Syndicate. c.1922. Barse. (P.932)
--*Bobby Blake on a Plantation: Or, Lost in the Great Swamp.* Warner, Frank A., pseud. Stratemeyer Syndicate. N.D. Barse. (P.932)
--*Bobby Blake on a Plantation: Or, Lost in the Great Swamp.* Warner, Frank A., pseud. Stratemeyer Syndicate. N.D. G& D. (P.932)
--*Bomba the Jungle Boy.* Rockwood, Roy, pseud. Stratemeyer Syndicate. 1953. G & D. (P.772)
--*Bomba the Jungle Boy.* Rockwood, Roy, pseud. Stratemeyer Syndicate. c.1978. G & D. (P.772)
--*Bomba the Jungle Boy.* Rockwood, Roy, pseud. Stratemeyer Syndicate. N.D. McLoughlin Brothers - Clover Books. (P.772)
--*Bomba the Jungle Boy at the Giant Cataract: Or, Chief Nascanora and His Captives.* Rockwood, Roy, pseud. Stratemeyer Syndicate. 1926. Cupples & Leon Co. (P.772)
--*Bomba the Jungle Boy at the Giant Cataract.* Rockwood, Roy, pseud. Stratemeyer Syndicate. 1953. Grosset & Dunlap. (P.772)
--*Bomba the Jungle Boy at the Giant Cataract.* Rockwood, Roy, pseud. Stratemeyer Syndicate. N.D. McLoughlin Brothers - Clover Books. (P.772)
--*Bomba the Jungle Boy at the Moving Mountain: Or, the Mystery of the Caves of Fire.* Rockwood, Roy, pseud. Stratemeyer Syndicate. 1926. Cupples & Leon Co. (P.772)
--*Bomba the Jungle Boy at the Moving Mountain.* Rockwood, Roy, pseud. Stratemeyer Syndicate. 1953. Grosset & Dunlap. (P.772)
--*Bomba the Jungle Boy at the Moving Mountain.* Rockwood, Roy, pseud. Stratemeyer Syndicate. N.D. McLoughlin Brothers - Clover Books. (P.772)
--*Bomba the Jungle Boy in the Abandoned City: Or, A Treasure Ten Thousand Years Old.* Rockwood, Roy, pseud. Stratemeyer Syndicate. 1927. Cupples & Leon Co. (P.772)
--*Bomba the Jungle Boy in the Abandoned City.* Rockwood, Roy, pseud. Stratemeyer Syndicate. 1953. Grosset & Dunlap. (P.772)
--*Bomba the Jungle Boy in the Abandoned City.* Rockwood, Roy, pseud. Stratemeyer Syndicate. N.D. McLoughlin Brothers - Clover Books. (P.772)
--*Bomba the Jungle Boy on Jaguar Island.* Rockwood, Roy, pseud. Stratemeyer Syndicate. N.D. McLoughlin Brothers - Clover Books. (P.773)
--*Bomba the Jungle Boy on Jaguar Island.* Rockwood, Roy, pseud. Stratemeyer Syndicate. 1953. Grosset & Dunlap. (P.773)
--*Bomba the Jungle Boy on Jaguar Island: Or, Adrift on the River of Mystery.* Rockwood, Roy, pseud. Stratemeyer Syndicate. 1927. Cupples & Leon Co. (P.773)
--*Bomba the Jungle Boy on Terror Trail.* Rockwood, Roy, pseud. Stratemeyer Syndicate. 1953. Grosset & Dunlap. (P.773)
--*Bomba the Jungle Boy on Terror Trail.* Rockwood, Roy, pseud. Stratemeyer Syndicate. N.D. McLoughlin Brothers - Clover Books. (P.773)
--*Bomba the Jungle Boy on Terror Trail: Or, The Mysterious Men from the Sky.* Rockwood, Roy, pseud. Stratemeyer Syndicate. c.1928. Cupples & Leon Company. (P.773)
--*Bomba the Jungle Boy: Or, The Old Naturalist's Secret.* Rockwood, Roy, pseud. Stratemeyer Syndicate. 1926. Cupples & Leon Co. (P.773)
--*Bomba the Jungle Boy: The Moving Mountain.* Rockwood, Roy, pseud. Stratemeyer Syndicate. c.1978. Grosset & Dunlap. (P.773)

--*The Boy Scouts of Lenox: Or, The Hike Over Big Bear Mountain.* Webster, Frank V., pseud. Stratemeyer Syndicate. 1915. Cupples & Leon Company. (P.939)

--*The Boys of Columbia High in Camp: Or, The Rivalry of the Old School League.* Forbes, Graham B., pseud. Stratemeyer Syndicate. 1920. Grosset & Dunlap. (P.334)

--*The Boys of Columbia High in Track Athletics: Or, A Long Run that Won.* Forbes, Graham B., pseud. Stratemeyer Syndicate. 1913. Grosset & Dunlap. (P.334)

--*The Boys of Columbia High in Winter Sports: Or, Stirring Doings on Skates and Iceboats.* Forbes, Graham B., pseud. Stratemeyer Syndicate. 1915. Grosset & Dunlap. (P.334)

--*The Boys of Columbia High on the Diamond: Or, Winning Out by Pluck.* Forbes, Graham B., pseud. Stratemeyer Syndicate. 1912, c.1911. Grosset & Dunlap. (P.334)

--*The Boys of Columbia High on the Gridiron: Or, The Struggle for the Silver Cup.* Forbes, Graham B., pseud. Stratemeyer Syndicate. 1912, c.1911. Grosset & Dunlap. (P.334)

--*The Boys of Columbia High on the Ice: Or, Out for the Hockey Championship.* Forbes, Graham B., pseud. Stratemeyer Syndicate. 1912, c.1911. Grosset & Dunlap. (P.334)

--*The Boys of Columbia High on the River: Or, The Boat Race Plot that Failed.* Forbes, Graham B., pseud. Stratemeyer Syndicate. 1912, c.1911. Grosset & Dunlap. (P.334)

--*The Boys of Columbia High: Or, The All Around Rivals of the School.* Forbes, Graham B., pseud. Stratemeyer Syndicate. 1912, c.1911. Grosset & Dunlap. (P.334)

--*The Boys of the Wireless: Or, A Stirring Rescue from the Deep.* Webster, Frank V., pseud. Stratemeyer Syndicate. c.1912. Cupples & Leon Company. (P.939)

--*Buck's Home Run Drive: Or, The Chester Boys Winning Against Odds.* Dawson, Elmer A, pseud. Stratemeyer Syndicate. 1931. Grosset & Dunlap. (P.247)

--*Buck's Winning Hit: Or, The Chester Boys Making a Record.* Dawson, Elmer A, pseud. Stratemeyer Syndicate. 1930. Grosset & Dunlap. (P.247)

--*Bunny Brown and His Sister Sue and Their Trick Dog.* Hope, Laura Lee, pseud. Stratemeyer Syndicate. 1923. Grosset & Dunlap. (P.461)

--*Bunny Brown and His Sister Sue at a Sugar Camp.* Hope, Laura Lee, pseud. Stratemeyer Syndicate. 1924. Grosset & Dunlap. (P.461)

--*Bunny Brown and His Sister Sue at Berry Hill.* Hope, Laura Lee, pseud. Stratemeyer Syndicate. c.1929. Grosset & Dunlap. (P.461)

--*Bunny Brown and His Sister Sue at Christmas Tree Cove.* Hope, Laura Lee, pseud. Stratemeyer Syndicate. 1920. Grosset & Dunlap. (P.461)

--*Bunny Brown and His Sister Sue at Shore Acres.* Hope, Laura Lee, pseud. Stratemeyer Syndicate. c.1928. Grosset & Dunlap. (P.461)

--*Bunny Brown and His Sister Sue at Sky Top.* Hope, Laura Lee, pseud. Stratemeyer Syndicate. c.1930. Grosset & Dunlap. (P.461)

--*Bunny Brown and His Sister Sue at the Summer Carnival.* Hope, Laura Lee, pseud. Stratemeyer Syndicate. c.1931. Grosset & Dunlap. (P.461)

--*Bunny Brown and His Sister Sue Giving a Show.* Hope, Laura Lee, pseud. Stratemeyer Syndicate. 1919. Grosset & Dunlap. (P.461)

--*Bunny Brown and His Sister Sue in the Sunny South.* Hope, Laura Lee, pseud. Stratemeyer Syndicate. 1921. Grosset & Dunlap. (P.461)

--*Bunny Brown and His Sister Sue Keeping Store.* Hope, Laura Lee, pseud. Stratemeyer Syndicate. 1922. Grosset & Dunlap. (P.461)

--*Bunny Brown and His Sister Sue on Jack Frost Island.* Hope, Laura Lee, pseud. Stratemeyer Syndicate. 1927. Grosset & Dunlap. (P.461)

--*Bunny Brown and His Sister Sue on the Rolling Ocean.* Hope, Laura Lee, pseud. Stratemeyer Syndicate. 1925. Grosset & Dunlap. (P.461)

--*Buz and Fury.* Dawson, Francis Warrington (1878-). 1923. The Honest Truth Publishing Co. (P.247)

--*Cowboy Dave: Or, The Round Up at Rolling River.* Webster, Frank V., pseud. Stratemeyer Syndicate. 1915. Cupples & Leon Company. (P.939)

--*Danger Trails of the Sky: Or, Ted Scott's Great Mountain Climb.* Dixon, Franklin W, pseud. Stratemeyer Syndicate. c.1931. Grosset & Dunlap. (P.273)

--*Dave Porter and His Double: Or, The Disappearance of the Basswood Fortune.* Stratemeyer, Edward L. (1862-1930). 1916. Lothrop, Lee & Shepard Co. (P.865)

--*Dave Porter at Bear Camp: Or, The Wild Man of Mirror Lake.* Stratemeyer, Edward L. (1862-1930). 1915. Lothrop, Lee & Shepard Co. (P.865)

--*Dave Porter in the Gold Fields: Or, The Search for the Landslide Mine.* Stratemeyer, Edward L. (1862-1930). 1914. Lothrop, Lee & Shepard Co. (P.865)

--*Dave Porter's Great Search: Or, The Perils of a Young Civil Engineer.* Stratemeyer, Edward L. (1862-1930). 1917. Lothrop, Lee & Shepard Co. (P.865)

--*Don Sturdy Across the North Pole: Or, Cast Away in the Land of Ice.* Appleton, Victor, pseud. Stratemeyer Syndicate. c.1925. Grosset & Dunlap. (P.43)

--*Don Sturdy Among the Gorillas: Or, Adrift in the Great Jungle.* Appleton, Victor, pseud. Stratemeyer Syndicate. 1927. Grosset & Dunlap. (P.43)

--*Don Sturdy Captured by Head Hunters: Or, Adrift in the Wilds of Borneo.* Appleton, Victor, pseud. Stratemeyer Syndicate. c.1928. Grosset & Dunlap. (P.43)

--*Don Sturdy in Lion Land: Or, The Strange Clearing in the Jungle.* Appleton, Victor, pseud. Stratemeyer Syndicate. c.1929. Grosset & Dunlap. (P.43)

--*Don Sturdy in the Land of Giants: Or, Captives of the Savage Patagonians.* Appleton, Victor, pseud. Stratemeyer Syndicate. c.1930. Grosset & Dunlap. (P.43)

--*Don Sturdy in the Land of Volcanoes: Or, The Trail of the Ten Thousand Smokes.* Appleton, Victor, pseud. Stratemeyer Syndicate. c.1925. Grosset & Dunlap. (P.43)

--*Don Sturdy In the Port of Lost Ships: Or, Adrift in the Sargasso Sea.* Appleton, Victor, pseud. Stratemeyer Syndicate. 1926. Grosset & Dunlap. (P.43)

--*Don Sturdy in the Tombs of Gold: Or, The Old Egyptian's Great Secret.* Appleton, Victor, pseud. Stratemeyer Syndicate. c.1925. Grosset & Dunlap. (P.43)

--*Don Sturdy on the Desert of Mystery: Or, Autoing in the Land of Caravans.* Appleton, Victor, pseud. Stratemeyer Syndicate. c.1925. Grosset & Dunlap. (P.43)

--*Don Sturdy on the Ocean Bottom: Or, The Strange Cruise of the Phantom.* Appleton, Victor, pseud. Stratemeyer Syndicate. c.1931. Grosset & Dunlap. (P.43)

--*Don Sturdy with the Big Snake Hunters: Or, Lost in the Jungles of the Amazon.* Appleton, Victor, pseud. Stratemeyer Syndicate. c.1925. Grosset & Dunlap. (P.43)

--*Dorothy Dale in the West.* Penrose, Margaret, pseud. Stratemeyer Syndicate. c.1915. Cupples & Leon Company. (P.717)

--*Dorothy Dale's Promise.* Penrose, Margaret, pseud. Stratemeyer Syndicate. c.1914. Cupples & Leon Company. (P.717)

--*First Stop Honolulu: Or, Ted Scott Over the Pacific.* Dixon, Franklin W., pseud. Stratemeyer Syndicate. c.1927. Grosset & Dunlap. (P.273)

--*Flop Ear, the Funny Rabbit.* Barnum, Richard, pseud. Stratemeyer Syndicate. 1916. Barse & Hopkins. (P.74)

--*The Flyaways and Cinderella.* Hardy, Alice Dale, pseud. Stratemeyer Syndicate. 1925. Grosset & Dunlap. (P.412)

--*The Flyaways and Goldilocks.* Hardy, Alice Dale, pseud. Stratemeyer Syndicate. 1925. Grosset & Dunlap. (P.412)

--*The Flyaways and Little Red Riding Hood.* Hardy, Alice Dale, pseud. Stratemeyer Syndicate. 1925. Grosset & Dunlap. (P.412)

--*Flying Against Time: Or, Ted Scott Breaking the Ocean to Ocean Record.* Dixon, Franklin W., pseud. Stratemeyer Syndicate. c.1929. Grosset & Dunlap. (P.273)

--*Flying to the Rescue: Or, Ted Scott and the Big Dirigible.* Dixon, Franklin W., pseud. Stratemeyer Syndicate. c.1930. Grosset & Dunlap. (P.273)

--*Four Little Blossoms on Apple Tree Island.* Hawley, Mabel C., pseud. Stratemeyer Syndicate. N.D. Cupples & Leon Co. (P.422)

--*Four Little Blossoms on Apple Tree Island.* Hawley, Mabel C., pseud. Stratemeyer Syndicate. 1921. George Sully & Co. (P.422)

--*Fred Fenton in the Line: Or, The Football Boys of Riverport School.* Chapman, Allen, pseud. Stratemeyer Syndicate. 1913. Cupples & Leon Co. (P.185)

--*Fred Fenton Marathon Runner: Or, The Great Race at Riverport School.* Chapman, Allen, pseud. Stratemeyer Syndicate. N.D. Cupples & Leon Co. (P.185)

--*Fred Fenton on the Crew: Or, The Young Oarsmen of Riverport School.* Chapman, Allen, pseud. Stratemeyer Syndicate. 1913. Cupples & Leon Co. (P.185)

--*Fred Fenton on the Track: Or, The Athletes of Riverport School.* Chapman, Allen, pseud. Stratemeyer Syndicate. 1913. Cupples & Leon Co. (P.185)

--*Fred Fenton the Pitcher: Or, The Rivals of Riverport School.* Chapman, Allen, pseud. Stratemeyer Syndicate. 1913. Cupples & Leon Co. (P.185)

--*Garry Grayson at Lenox High: Or, the Champions of the Football League.* Dawson, Elmer A., pseud. Stratemeyer Syndicate. 1926. Grosset & Dunlap. (P.247)

--*Garry Grayson at Stanley Prep: Or, The Football Rivals of Riverview.* Dawson, Elmer A., pseud. Stratemeyer Syndicate. 1927. Grosset & Dunlap. (P.247)

--*Garry Grayson Hitting the Line: Or, Stanley Prep on a New Gridiron.* Dawson, Elmer A, pseud. Stratemeyer Syndicate. 1929. Grosset & Dunlap. (P.247)

--*Garry Grayson Showing His Speed: Or, a Daring Run on the Gridiron.* Dawson, Elmer A., pseud. Stratemeyer Syndicate. 1927. Grosset & Dunlap. (P.247)

--*Garry Grayson's Double Signals: Or, Vanquishing the Football Plotters.* Dawson, Elmer A, pseud. Stratemeyer Syndicate. 1931. Grosset & Dunlap. (P.247)

--*Garry Grayson's Double Signals: Or, Vanquishing the Football Plotters.* Dawson, Elmer A., pseud. Stratemeyer Syndicate. N.D. Whitman Publishing Co. (P.247)

--*Garry Grayson's Football Rivals: Or, the Secret of the Stolen Signals.* Dawson, Elmer A., pseud. Stratemeyer Syndicate. 1926. Grosset & Dunlap. (P.247)

--*Garry Grayson's Hill Street Eleven: Or, The Football Boys of Lenox.* Dawson, Elmer A., pseud. Stratemeyer Syndicate. 1926. Grosset & Dunlap. (P.247)

--*Garry Grayson's Winning Kick: Or, Battling for Honor.* Dawson, Elmer A, pseud. Stratemeyer Syndicate. 1928. Grosset & Dunlap. (P.247)

--*Garry Grayson's Winning Touchdown: Or, Putting Passmore Tech on the Map.* Dawson, Elmer A, pseud. Stratemeyer Syndicate. 1930. Grosset & Dunlap. (P.247)

--*Garry Grayson's Winning Touchdown: Or, Putting Passmore Tech on the Map.* Dawson, Elmer A., pseud. Stratemeyer Syndicate. N.D. Whitman Publishing Co. (P.247)

--*The Girls of Central High in Camp: Or, The Old Professor's Secret.* Morrison, Gertrude W., pseud. Stratemeyer Syndicate. 1915. Grosset & Dunlap. (P.665)

--*The Girls of Central High in Camp: Or, The Old Professor's Secret.* Morrison, Gertrude W., pseud. Stratemeyer Syndicate. N.D. Saalfield Publishing Co. (P.665)

--*The Girls of Central High in Camp: Or, The Old Professor's Secret.* Morrison, Gertrude W., pseud. Stratemeyer Syndicate. N.D. World Syndicate Publishing Co. (P.665)

--*The Girls of Hillcrest Farm: Or, The Secret of the Rocks.* Marlowe, Amy Bell, pseud. Stratemeyer Syndicate. 1914. Grosset & Dunlap. (P.621)

--*The Girls of Rivercliff School: Or, Beth Baldwin's Resolve.* Marlowe, Amy Bell, pseud. Stratemeyer Syndicate. 1916. Grosset & Dunlap. (P.621)

--*The Great Airport Mystery.* Dixon, Franklin W, pseud. Stratemeyer Syndicate. c.1930. Grosset & Dunlap. (P.273)

--*Harry Watson's High School Days: Or, The Rivals of Rivertown.* Webster, Frank V., pseud. Stratemeyer Syndicate. 1912. Cupples & Leon Company. (P.939)

--*Honey Bunch, Her First Auto Tour.* Thorndyke, Helen Louise, pseud. Stratemeyer Syndicate. 1926. Grosset & Dunlap. (P.889)

--*Honey Bunch, Her First Days in Camp.* Thorndyke, Helen Louise, pseud. Stratemeyer Syndicate. 1925. Grosset & Dunlap. (P.889)

--*Honey Bunch, Her First Days on the Farm.* Thorndyke, Helen Louise, pseud. Stratemeyer Syndicate. 1923. Grosset & Dunlap. (P.889)

--*Honey Bunch, Her First Little Garden.* Thorndyke, Helen Louise, pseud. Stratemeyer Syndicate. 1924. Grosset & Dunlap. (P.889)

--*Honey Bunch, Her First Summer on an Island.* Thorndyke, Helen Louise, pseud. Stratemeyer Syndicate. c.1929. Grosset & Dunlap. (P.889)

--*Honey Bunch, Her First Summer on an Island.* Thorndyke, Helen Louise, pseud. Stratemeyer Syndicate. N.D. McLoughlin Brothers - Clover Books. (P.889)

--*Honey Bunch, Her First Trip in an Airplane.* Thorndyke, Helen Louise, pseud. Stratemeyer Syndicate. c.1931. Grosset & Dunlap. (P.889)

--*Honey Bunch, Her First Trip in an Airplane.* Thorndyke, Helen Louise, pseud. Stratemeyer Syndicate. N.D. McLoughlin Brothers - Clover Books. (P.889)

--*Honey Bunch, Her First Trip on the Great Lakes.* Thorndyke, Helen Louise, pseud. Stratemeyer Syndicate. c.1930. Grosset & Dunlap. (P.889)

--*Honey Bunch, Her First Trip on the Ocean.* Thorndyke, Helen Louise, pseud. Stratemeyer Syndicate. 1927. Grosset & Dunlap. (P.889)

--*Honey Bunch, Her First Trip West.* Thorndyke, Helen Louise, pseud. Stratemeyer Syndicate. c.1928. Grosset & Dunlap. (P.889)

--*Honey Bunch, Her First Trip West.* Thorndyke, Helen Louise, pseud. Stratemeyer Syndicate. N.D. McLoughlin Brothers - Clover Books. (P.889)

--*Honey Bunch, Her First Visit to the City.* Thorndyke, Helen Louise, pseud. Stratemeyer Syndicate. 1923. Grosset & Dunlap. (P.889)

--*Honey Bunch, Her First Visit to the Seashore.* Thorndyke, Helen Louise, pseud. Stratemeyer Syndicate. 1924. Grosset & Dunlap. (P.889)

--*Honey Bunch, Just a Little Girl.* Thorndyke, Helen Louise, pseud. Stratemeyer Syndicate. 1923. Grosset & Dunlap. (P.889)

--*The House on the Cliff.* Dixon, Franklin W., pseud. Stratemeyer Syndicate. 1927. Grosset & Dunlap. (P.273)

--*Hunting for Hidden Gold.* Dixon, Franklin W., pseud. Stratemeyer Syndicate. c.1928. Grossett & Dunlap. (P.273)

--*Jack of the Pony Express: Or, The Young Rider of the Mountain Trails.* Webster, Frank V., pseud. Stratemeyer Syndicate. 1915. Cupples & Leon Company. (P.939)

--*Janice Day at Poketown.* Long, Helen Beecher, pseud. Stratemeyer Syndicate. 1914. Sully & Kleinteich. (P.581)

--*Janice Day at Poketown.* Long, Helen Beecher, pseud. Stratemeyer Syndicate. N.D. The Christian Herald. (P.581)

--*Joe Strong and His Box of Mystery: Or, The Ten Thousand Dollar Prize Trick.* Barnum, Vance, pseud. Stratemeyer Syndicate. 1916. George Sully & Co. (P.74)

--*Joe Strong and His Wings of Steel: Or, A Young Acrobat in the Clouds.* Barnum, Vance, pseud. Stratemeyer Syndicate. 1916. George Sully & Co. (P.74)

--*Joe Strong on the High Wire: Or, Motorcycle Perils of the Air.* Barnum, Vance, pseud. Stratemeyer Syndicate. 1916. George Sully & Co. (P.74)

--*Joe Strong on the Trapeze: Or, The Daring Feats of a Young Circus Performer.* Barnum, Vance, pseud. Stratemeyer Syndicate. 1916. George Sully & Co. (P.74)

--*Joe Strong, the Boy Fire-Eater: Or, The Most Dangerous Performance on Record.* Barnum, Vance, pseud. Stratemeyer Syndicate. 1916. George Sully & Co. (P.74)

--*Joe Strong, the Boy Fish: Or, Marvellous Doings in a Big Tank.* Barnum, Vance, pseud. Stratemeyer Syndicate. 1916. George Sully & Co. (P.74)

--*Joe Strong, the Boy Wizard: Or, The Mysteries of Magic Exposed.* Barnum, Vance, pseud. Stratemeyer Syndicate. 1916. George Sully & Co. (P.74)

--*Larry's Fadeaway: Or, The Chester Boys Saving the Nine.* Dawson, Elmer A, pseud. Stratemeyer Syndicate. 1930. Grosset & Dunlap. (P.247)

--*Light Foot, the Leaping Goat: His Many Adventures.* Barnum, Richard, pseud. Stratemeyer Syndicate. 1917. Barse & Hopkins. (P.74)

--*A Little Miss Nobody: Or, With the Girls of Pinewood Hall.* Marlowe, Amy Bell, pseud. Stratemeyer Syndicate. 1914. Grosset & Dunlap. (P.621)

--*Little Woodcrafters' Fun on the Farm.* Roy, Lillian Elizabeth Becker, Mrs. (1868-1932). c.1928. Grosset & Dunlap. (P.782)

--*The Lone Eagle of the Border: Or, Ted Scott and the Diamond Smugglers.* Dixon, Franklin W., pseud. Stratemeyer Syndicate. c.1929. Grosset & Dunlap. (P.274)

--*Lost at the South Pole: Or, Ted Scott in Blizzard Land.* Dixon, Franklin W., pseud. Stratemeyer Syndicate. c.1930. Grosset & Dunlap. (P.274)

--*The Missing Chums.* Dixon, Franklin W., pseud. Stratemeyer Syndicate. c.1928. Grosset & Dunlap. (P.274)

--*The Motion Picture Chums at the Fair: Or, The Greatest Film Ever Exhibited.* Appleton, Victor, pseud. Stratemeyer Syndicate. 1915. Grosset & Dunlap. (P.43)

--*The Motion Picture Chums' New Idea: Or, The First Educational Photo Playhouse.* Appleton, Victor, pseud. Stratemeyer Syndicate. 1914. Grosset & Dunlap. (P.43)

--*The Motion Picture Chums' Outdoor Exhibition: Or, The Film That Solved a Mystery.* Appleton, Victor, pseud. Stratemeyer Syndicate. 1914. Grosset & Dunlap. (P.43)

--*The Motion Picture Chums' War Spectacle: Or, The Film That Won the Prize.* Appleton, Victor, pseud. Stratemeyer Syndicate. 1916. Grosset & Dunlap. (P.43)

--*The Motor Boys on Road and River: Or, Racing to Save a Life.* Young, Clarence, pseud. Stratemeyer Syndicate. c.1915. Cupples & Leon Company. (P.989)

--*The Motor Boys on Thunder Mountain: Or, The Treasure Chest of Blue Rock.* Young, Clarence, pseud. Stratemeyer Syndicate. c.1924. Cupples & Leon Company. (P.989)

--*The Motor Girls at Camp Surprise: Or, The Cave in the Mountains.* Penrose, Margaret, pseud. Stratemeyer Syndicate. 1916. Cupples & Leon Company. (P.717)

--*The Motor Girls on Crystal Bay: Or, The Secret of the Red Oar.* Penrose, Margaret, pseud. Stratemeyer Syndicate. 1914. Cupples & Leon Company. (P.717)

--*The Motor Girls on Waters Blue: Or, The Strange Cruise of the Tartar.* Penrose, Margaret, pseud. Stratemeyer Syndicate. 1915. Cupples & Leon Company. (P.717)

--*The Moving Picture Boys and the Flood: Or, Perilous Days on the Mississippi.* Appleton, Victor, pseud. Stratemeyer Syndicate. 1914. Grosset & Dunlap. (P.44)

--*The Moving Picture Boys at Panama: Or, Stirring Adventures Along the Great Canal.* Appleton, Victor, pseud. Stratemeyer Syndicate. 1915. Grosset & Dunlap. (P.44)

--*The Moving Picture Boys in Earthquake Land: Or, Working Amid Many Perils.* Appleton, Victor, pseud. Stratemeyer Syndicate. 1913. Grosset & Dunlap. (P.44)

--*The Moving Picture Boys in the Jungle: Or, Stirring Times Among the Wild Animals.* Appleton, Victor, pseud. Stratemeyer Syndicate. 1913. Grosset & Dunlap. (P.44)

--*The Moving Picture Boys in the West: Or, Taking Scenes Among the Cowboys and Indians.* Appleton, Victor, pseud. Stratemeyer Syndicate. 1913. Grosset & Dunlap. (P.44)

--*The Moving Picture Boys' New Idea.* Appleton, Victor, pseud. Stratemeyer Syndicate. 1922. Grosset & Dunlap. (P.44)

--*The Moving Picture Boys on the Coast: Or, Showing the Perils of the Deep.* Appleton, Victor, pseud. Stratemeyer Syndicate. 1913. Grosset & Dunlap. (P.44)

--*The Moving Picture Boys: Or, The Perils of a Great City Depicted.* Appleton, Victor, pseud. Stratemeyer Syndicate. 1913. Grosset & Dunlap. (P.44)

--*The Moving Picture Boys' Outdoor Exhibition: Or, The Film That Solved a Mystery.* Appleton, Victor, pseud. Stratemeyer Syndicate. 1922. Grosset & Dunlap. (P.44)

--*The Moving Picture Boys Under the Sea: Or, The Treasure of the Lost Ship.* Appleton, Victor, pseud. Stratemeyer Syndicate. 1916. Grosset & Dunlap. (P.44)

--*The Moving Picture Girls at Oak Farm: Or, Queer Happenings While Taking Rural Plays.* Hope, Laura Lee, pseud. Stratemeyer Syndicate. 1914. Grosset & Dunlap. (P.461)

--*The Moving Picture Girls at Oak Farm: Or, Queer Happenings While Taking Rural Plays.* Hope, Laura Lee, pseud. Stratemeyer Syndicate. N.D. World Syndicate Publishing Co. (P.461)

--*The Moving Picture Girls at Rocky Ranch: Or, Great Days Among the Cowboys.* Hope, Laura Lee, pseud. Stratemeyer Syndicate. 1914. Grosset & Dunlap. (P.461)

--*The Moving Picture Girls at Rocky Ranch: Or, Great Days Among the Cowboys.* Hope, Laura Lee, pseud. Stratemeyer Syndicate. N.D. World Syndicate Publishing Co. (P.461)

--*The Moving Picture Girls at Sea: Or, A Pictured Shipwreck That Became Real.* Hope, Laura Lee, pseud. Stratemeyer Syndicate. 1915. Grosset & Dunlap. (P.461)

--*The Moving Picture Girls at Sea: Or, A Pictured Shipwreck that Became Real.* Hope, Laura Lee, pseud. Stratemeyer Syndicate. N.D. World Syndicate Publishing Co. (P.461)

--*The Moving Picture Girls in War Plays: Or, The Sham Battles at Oak Farm.* Hope, Laura Lee, pseud. Stratemeyer Syndicate. 1916. Grosset & Dunlap. (P.461)

--*The Moving Picture Girls in War Plays: Or, The Sham Battles at Oak Farm.* Hope, Laura Lee, pseud. Stratemeyer Syndicate. N.D. World Syndicate Publishing Co. (P.461)

--*The Moving Picture Girls: Or, First Appearances in Photo Dramas.* Hope, Laura Lee, pseud. Stratemeyer Syndicate. 1914. Grosset & Dunlap. (P.461)

--*The Moving Picture Girls: Or, First Appearances in Photo Dramas.* Hope, Laura Lee, pseud. Stratemeyer Syndicate. N.D. World Syndicate Publishing Co. (P.461)

--*The Moving Picture Girls Snowbound: Or, The Proof on the Film.* Hope, Laura Lee, pseud. Stratemeyer Syndicate. 1914. Grosset & Dunlap. (P.461)

--*The Moving Picture Girls Snowbound: Or, The Proof on the Film.* Hope, Laura Lee, pseud. Stratemeyer Syndicate. N.D. World Syndicate Publishing Co. (P.461)

--*The Moving Picture Girls Under the Palms: Or, Lost in the Wilds of Florida.* Hope, Laura Lee, pseud. Stratemeyer Syndicate. 1914. Grosset & Dunlap. (P.461)

--*The Moving Picture Girls Under the Palms: Or, Lost in the Wilds of Florida.* Hope, Laura Lee, pseud. Stratemeyer Syndicate. N.D. World Syndicate Publishing Co. (P.461)

--*The Mystery of Cabin Island.* Dixon, Franklin W., pseud. Stratemeyer Syndicate. c.1929. Grosset & Dunlap. (P.274)

--*Ned, Bob and Jerry at Boxwood Hall: Or, The Motor Boys As Freshmen.* Young, Clarence, pseud. Stratemeyer Syndicate. c.1916. Cupples & Leon Company. (P.989)

--*Nell Grayson's Ranching Days: Or, A City Girl in the Great West.* Barton, May Hollis, pseud. Stratemeyer Syndicate. 1926. Cupples & Leon Co. (P.78)

--*The Oldest of Four: Or, Natalie's Way Out.* Marlowe, Amy Bell, pseud. Stratemeyer Syndicate. 1914. Grosset & Dunlap. (P.621)

--*Oriole's Adventures.* Marlowe, Amy Bell, pseud. Stratemeyer Syndicate. 1933. Grosset & Dunlap. (P.621)

--*Our Little Cossack Cousin in Siberia.* Postnikov, Fedor Alexis (1872-). 1916. The Page Company. (P.733)

--*The Outdoor Chums at Cabin Point: Or, The Golden Cup Mystery.* Allen, Captain Quincy, pseud. Stratemeyer Syndicate. 1916. Grosset & Dunlap. (P.29)

--*The Outdoor Chums in the Big Woods: Or, The Rival Hunters of Lumber Run.* Allen, Captain Quincy, pseud. Stratemeyer Syndicate. 1915. Grosset & Dunlap. (P.29)

--*The Outdoor Girls Along the Coast: Or, The Cruise of the Motor Boat Liberty.* Hope, Laura Lee, pseud. Stratemeyer Syndicate. 1926. Grosset & Dunlap. (P.461)

--*The Outdoor Girls Around the Campfire: Or, The Old Maid of the Mountains.* Hope, Laura Lee, pseud. Stratemeyer Syndicate. 1923. Grosset & Dunlap. (P.462)

--*The Outdoor Girls at Bluff Point: Or, A Wreck and a Rescue.* Hope, Laura Lee, pseud. Stratemeyer Syndicate. N.D. Grosset & Dunlap. (P.462)

--*The Outdoor Girls at Cedar Ridge: Or, The Mystery of the Old Windmill.* Hope, Laura Lee, pseud. Stratemeyer Syndicate. c.1931. Grosset & Dunlap. (P.462)

--*The Outdoor Girls at Foaming Falls: Or, Robina of Red Kennels.* Hope, Laura Lee, pseud. Stratemeyer Syndicate. c.1925. Grosset & Dunlap. (P.462)

--*The Outdoor Girls at New Moon Ranch: Or, Riding with the Cowboys.* Hope, Laura Lee, pseud. Stratemeyer Syndicate. c.1928. Grosset & Dunlap. (P.462)

--*The Outdoor Girls at Ocean View: Or, The Box that was Found in the Sand.* Hope, Laura Lee, pseud. Stratemeyer Syndicate. 1915. Grosset & Dunlap. (P.462)

--*The Outdoor Girls at Spring Hill Farm: Or, The Ghost of the Old Milk House.* Hope, Laura Lee, pseud. Stratemeyer Syndicate. 1927. Grosset & Dunlap. (P.462)

--*The Outdoor Girls at Wild Rose Lodge: Or, The Hermit of Moonlight Falls.* Hope, Laura Lee, pseud. Stratemeyer Syndicate. 1921. Grosset & Dunlap. (P.462)

--*The Outdoor Girls in Army Service: Or, Doing Their Bit for the Soldier Boys.* Hope, Laura Lee, pseud. Stratemeyer Syndicate. 1918. Grosset & Dunlap. (P.462)

--*The Outdoor Girls in the Saddle: Or, The Girl Miner of Gold Run.* Hope, Laura Lee, pseud. Stratemeyer Syndicate. 1922. Grosset & Dunlap. (P.462)

--*The Outdoor Girls on a Canoe Trip: Or, The Secret of the Brown Mill.* Hope, Laura Lee, pseud. Stratemeyer Syndicate. c.1930. Grosset & Dunlap. (P.462)

--*The Outdoor Girls on a Hike: Or, The Mystery of the Deserted Airplane.* Hope, Laura Lee, pseud. Stratemeyer Syndicate. c.1929. Grosset & Dunlap. (P.462)

--*The Outdoor Girls on Cape Cod: Or, Sally Ann of Lighthouse Rock.* Hope, Laura Lee, pseud. Stratemeyer Syndicate. 1924. Grosset & Dunlap. (P.462)

--*The Outdoor Girls on Pine Island: Or, A Cave and What it Contained.* Hope, Laura Lee, pseud. Stratemeyer Syndicate. 1916. Grosset & Dunlap. (P.462)

--*Over the Jungle Trails: Or, Ted Scott and the Missing Explorers.* Dixon, Franklin W., pseud. Stratemeyer Syndicate. c.1929. Grosset & Dunlap. (P.274)

--*Over the Ocean to Paris: Or, Ted Scott's Daring Long Distance Flight.* Dixon, Franklin W., pseud. Stratemeyer Syndicate. c.1927. Grosset & Dunlap. (P.274)

--*Over the Rockies with the Air Mail: Or, Ted Scott Lost in the Wilderness.* Dixon, Franklin W., pseud. Stratemeyer Syndicate. c.1927. Grosset & Dunlap. (P.274)

--*The Pick-up Nine: Or, The Chester Boys on the Diamond.* Dawson, Elmer A, pseud. Stratemeyer Syndicate. 1930. Grosset & Dunlap. (P.247)

--*The Pioneer Boys of the Columbia: Or, In the Wilderness of the Great Northwest.* Adams, Harrison, pseud. (1854-1928). Rathborne, St. George. 1916. L. C. Page & Company. (P.5)

--*The Pioneer Boys of the Missouri: Or, In the Country of the Sioux.* Adams, Harrison, pseud. (1854-1928). Rathborne, St. George. 1914. L. C. Page & Company. (P.5)

--*The Pioneer Boys of the Yellowstone: Or, Lost in the Land of Wonders.* Adams, Harrison, pseud. (1854-1928). Rathborne, St. George. 1915. L. C. Page & Company. (P.5)

--*The Racer Boys at Boarding School: Or, Striving for the Championship.* Young, Clarence, pseud. Stratemeyer Syndicate. c.1912. Cupples & Leon Company. (P.989)

--*The Racer Boys Forging Ahead: Or, The Rivals of the School League.* Young, Clarence, pseud. Stratemeyer Syndicate. 1914. Cupples & Leon. (P.989)

--*The Racer Boys on Guard: Or, The Rebellion at Riverview Hall.* Young, Clarence, pseud. Stratemeyer Syndicate. 1913. Cupples & Leon. (P.989)

--*The Racer Boys on the Prairies: Or, The Treasure of Golden Peak.* Young, Clarence, pseud. Stratemeyer Syndicate. c.1913. Cupples & Leon Company. (P.989)

--*The Racer Boys: Or, The Mystery of the Wreck.* Young, Clarence, pseud. Stratemeyer Syndicate. c.1912. Cupples & Leon Company. (P.989)

--*The Racer Boys to the Rescue: Or, Stirring Adventures in a Winter Camp.* Young, Clarence, pseud. Stratemeyer Syndicate. 1912. Cupples & Leon. (P.989)

--*The Radio Boys Aiding the Snow Bound: Or, Starvation Days at Lumber Run.* Chapman, Allen, pseud. Stratemeyer Syndicate. Binns, Jack, frwd. by. c.1928. Grosset & Dunlap. (P.185)

--*The Radio Boys at Mountain Pass: Or, The Midnight Call for Assistance.* Chapman, Allen, pseud. Stratemeyer Syndicate. Binns, Jack, frwd. by. 1922. Grosset & Dunlap. (P.185)

--*The Radio Boys at Ocean Point: Or, The Message that Saved the Ship.* Chapman, Allen, pseud. Stratemeyer Syndicate. Binns, Jack, frwd. by. 1922. Grosset & Dunlap. (P.185)

--*The Radio Boys at the Sending Station: Or, Making Good in the Wireless Room.* Chapman, Allen, pseud. Stratemeyer Syndicate. Binns, Jack, frwd. by. 1922. Grosset & Dunlap. (P.185)

--*The Radio Boys' First Wireless: Or, Winning the Ferberton Prize.* Chapman, Allen, pseud. Stratemeyer Syndicate. Binns, Jack, frwd. by. 1922. Grosset & Dunlap. (P.185)

--*The Radio Boys In Gold Valley: Or, The Mystery of the Deserted Mining Camp.* Chapman, Allen, pseud. Stratemeyer Syndicate. Binns, Jack, frwd. by. 1926. Grosset & Dunlap. (P.185)

--*The Radio Boys on Signal Island: Or, Watching for the Ships of Mystery.* Chapman, Allen, pseud. Stratemeyer Syndicate. Binns, Jack, frwd. by. 1926. Grosset & Dunlap. (P.185)

--*The Radio Boys on the Pacific: Or, Shipwrecked on an Unknown Island.* Chapman, Allen, pseud. Stratemeyer Syndicate. Binns, Jack, frwd. by. c.1929. Grosset & Dunlap. (P.185)

--*The Radio Boys to the Rescue: Or, The Search for the Barmore Twins.* Chapman, Allen, pseud. Stratemeyer Syndicate. Binns, Jack, frwd. by. c.1930. Grosset & Dunlap. (P.185)

--*The Radio Boys Trailing a Voice: Or, Solving a Wireless Mystery.* Chapman, Allen, pseud. Stratemeyer Syndicate. Binns, Jack, frwd. by. 1922. Grosset & Dunlap. (P.185)

--*The Radio Boys with the Flood Fighters: Or, Saving the City in the Valley.* Chapman, Allen, pseud. Stratemeyer Syndicate. Binns, Jack, frwd. by. c.1925. Grosset & Dunlap. (P.185)

--*The Radio Boys with the Iceberg Patrol: Or, Making Safe the Ocean Lanes.* Chapman, Allen, pseud. Stratemeyer Syndicate. Binns, Jack, frwd. by. 1924. Grosset & Dunlap. (P.185)

--*Ralph and the Missing Mail Pouch: Or, The Stolen Government Bonds.* Chapman, Allen, pseud. Stratemeyer Syndicate. 1924. Grosset & Dunlap. (P.185)

--*Ralph and the Train Wreckers: Or, The Secret of the Blue Freight Cars.* Chapman, Allen, pseud. Stratemeyer Syndicate. c.1928. Grosset & Dunlap. (P.185)

--*Ralph on the Midnight Flyer: Or, The Wreck at Shadow Valley.* Chapman, Allen, pseud. Stratemeyer Syndicate. c.1923. Grosset & Dunlap. (P.185)

--*Ralph on the Mountain Division: Or, Fighting both Flames and Flood.* Chapman, Allen, pseud. Stratemeyer Syndicate. 1927. Grosset & Dunlap. (P.185)

--*Rescued in the Clouds: Or, Ted Scott, Hero of the Air.* Dixon, Franklin W., pseud. Stratemeyer Syndicate. c.1927. Grosset & Dunlap. (P.274)

--*The Riddle Club at Home: How the Club was Formed, What Riddles were Asked and How the Members Solved a Mystery.* Hardy, Alice Dale, pseud. Stratemeyer Syndicate. 1924. Grosset & Dunlap. (P.412)

--*The Riddle Club at Rocky Falls: How They Went up the River, What Adventures They Had in the Woods, and How They Solved the Mystery of the Deserted Hotel.* Hardy, Alice Dale, pseud. Stratemeyer Syndicate. 1929. Grosset & Dunlap. (P.412)

--*The Riddle Club at Shadybrook: Why They Went There, What Happened on the Way and What Occurred during Their Absence from Home.* Hardy, Alice Dale, pseud. Stratemeyer Syndicate. 1926. Grosset & Dunlap. (P.412)

--*The Riddle Club at Sunrise Beach: How They Toured to the Shore, What Happened on the Sand and How They Solved the Mystery of Rattlesnake Island.* Hardy, Alice Dale, pseud. Stratemeyer Syndicate. 1925. Grosset & Dunlap. (P.412)

--*The Riddle Club in Camp: How They Journeyed to the Lake, What Happened around the Campfire and How a Forgotten Name was Recalled.* Hardy, Alice Dale, pseud. Stratemeyer Syndicate. 1924. Grosset & Dunlap. (P.412)

--*The Riddle Club Through the Holidays: The Club and Its Doings, How the Riddles were Solved and What the Snowman Revealed.* Hardy, Alice Dale, pseud. Stratemeyer Syndicate. 1924. Grosset & Dunlap. (P.412)

--*The Rover Boys at Big Bear Lake: Or, The Camps of the Rival Cadets.* Winfield, Arthur M., pseud. (1862-1930). Stratemeyer, Edward L.. 1923. Grosset & Dunlap. (P.968)

--*The Rover Boys at Big Horn Ranch: Or, The Cowboys' Double Round-up.* Winfield, Arthur M., pseud. (1862-1930). Stratemeyer, Edward L.. 1922. Grosset & Dunlap. (P.968)

--*The Rover Boys at Colby Hall: Or, The Struggles of the Young Cadets.* Winfield, Arthur M., pseud. (1862-1930). Stratemeyer, Edward L.. c.1917. Grosset & Dunlap. (P.968)

--*The Rover Boys Down East: Or, The Struggle for the Stanhope Fortune.* Winfield, Arthur M., pseud. (1862-1930). Stratemeyer, Edward L.. c.1911. Grosset & Dunlap. (P.968)

--*The Rover Boys in Business: Or, the Search for the Missing Bonds.* Winfield, Arthur M., pseud. (1862-1930). Stratemeyer, Edward L.. c.1915. Grosset & Dunlap. (P.968)

--*The Rover Boys in New York: Or, Saving Their Father's Honor.* Winfield, Arthur M., pseud. (1862-1930). Stratemeyer, Edward L.. c.1913. Grosset & Dunlap. (P.968)

--*The Rover Boys in the Air: Or, From College Campus to Clouds.* Winfield, Arthur M., pseud. (1862-1930). Stratemeyer, Edward L.. c.1912. Grosset & Dunlap. (P.968)

--*The Rover Boys in the Land of Luck: Or, Stirring Adventures in the Oil Fields.* Winfield, Arthur M., pseud. (1862-1930). Stratemeyer, Edward L.. 1921. Grosset & Dunlap. (P.968)

--*The Rover Boys on a Hunt: Or, The Mysterious House in the Woods.* Winfield, Arthur M., pseud. (1862-1930). Stratemeyer, Edward L.. 1920. Grosset & Dunlap. (P.968)

--*The Rover Boys on a Tour: Or, Last Days at Brill College.* Winfield, Arthur M., pseud. (1862-1930). Stratemeyer, Edward L.. 1916. Grosset & Dunlap. (P.968)

--*The Rover Boys on Snowshoe Island: Or, The Old Lumberman's Treasure Box.* Winfield, Arthur M., pseud. (1862-1930). Stratemeyer, Edward L.. 1918. Grosset & Dunlap. (P.968)

--*The Rover Boys on Sunset Trail: Or, The Old Miner's Mysterious Message.* Winfield, Arthur M., pseud. (1862-1930). Stratemeyer, Edward L.. c.1925. Grosset & Dunlap. (P.968)

--*The Rover Boys Shipwrecked: Or, A Thrilling Hunt for Pirates' Gold.* Winfield, Arthur M., pseud. (1862-1930). Stratemeyer, Edward L.. 1924. Grosset & Dunlap. (P.969)

--*The Rover Boys Under Canvas: Or, The Mystery of the Wrecked Submarine.* Winfield, Arthur M., pseud. (1862-1930). Stratemeyer, Edward L.. c.1919. Grosset & Dunlap. (P.969)

--*The Rover Boys Winning a Fortune: Or, Strenuous Days Afloat and Ashore.* Winfield, Arthur M., pseud. (1862-1930). Stratemeyer, Edward L.. 1926. Grosset & Dunlap. (P.969)

--*The Rushton Boys at Rally Hall: Or, Great Days in School and Out.* Davenport, Spencer, pseud. Stratemeyer Syndicate. 1918. George Sully & Co. (P.243)

--*The Rushton Boys at Rally Hall: Or, Great Days in School and Out.* Davenport, Spencer, pseud. Stratemeyer Syndicate. 1916. Hearst's International Library. (P.243)

--*The Rushton Boys at Rally Hall: Or, Great Days in School and Out.* Davenport, Spencer, pseud. Stratemeyer Syndicate. N.D. Whitman Publishing Co. (P.244)

--*The Rushton Boys at Treasure Cove: Or, The Missing Chest of Gold.* Davenport, Spencer, pseud. Stratemeyer Syndicate. 1918. George Sully & Co. (P.244)

--*The Rushton Boys at Treasure Cove: Or, The Missing Oaken Chest.* Davenport, Spencer, pseud. Stratemeyer Syndicate. 1916. Hearst's International Library. (P.244)

--*The Rushton Boys at Treasure Cove: Or, The Missing Oaken Chest.* Davenport, Spencer, pseud. Stratemeyer Syndicate. N.D. Whitman Publishing Co. (P.244)

Ross, Marvin
--*The Jackal at Jericho.* N.D. Beta Bk. (P.779)
--*The Lion in the Den.* N.D. Beta Bk. (P.779)
Ross, Michael
--*All Alone in the World.* Spyri, Johanna Heusser (1827-1901). Calthrop, M. E., tr. 1959. E. P. Dutton & Co. (P.845)
--*The Pet Lamb, and Other Swiss Stories.* Spyri, Johanna Heusser (1827-1901). Clathrop, M. E. & Popper, E. M., trs. from Ger. 1956. E. P. Dutton. (P.846)
Ross, Santee (1889-1965)
--*Rusty, a Cowboy of the Old West.* Santee, Ross (1889-1965). 1950. Scribner. (P.793)
Ross, Tom
--*Haunted Places.* Hoffman, Betsy. 1982. Messner. (P.450)
Ross, Tony (1938-)
--*The Boy Who Cried Wolf.* Ross, Tony (1938-). 1985. Dial Books for Young Readers. (P.779)
--*The Charge of the Mouse Brigade.* Stone, Bernard & Low, Alice (1926-). 1979. Pantheon Books. (P.861)
--*The Enchanted Pig: An Old Rumanian Tale.* Ross, Tony (1938-), retold by. 1983. Peter Bedrick Books. (P.779)
--*The Greedy Little Cobbler.* Ross, Tony (1938-). 1980, c.1979. Barron's. (P.779)
--*Hugo & Oddsock.* Ross, Tony (1938-). 1978. Follett. (P.779)
--*Hugo and the Man Who Stole Colors.* Ross, Tony (1938-). c.1977. Follett Pub. Co. (P.779)
--*Hugo & the Wicked Winter.* Ross, Tony (1938-). N.D. Beekman Pubs. (P.779)
--*I'm Coming to Get You.* Ross, Tony (1938-). 1984. Dial Bks for Young Readers. (P.779)
--*Invasion from Below the Earth.* Curtis, Philip Delacourt (1920-). 1981, c.1980. Knopf : Distributed by Random House. (P.237)
--*Invasion of the Brain Sharpeners.* Curtis, Philip Delacourt (1920-). 1980, c.1979. Knopf. (P.237)
--*Invasion of the Comet People: A Capers Book.* Curtis, Philip Delacourt (1920-). 1983. Knopf. (P.237)
--*Jack and the Beanstalk.* Ross, Tony (1938-). 1981, c.1980. Delacorte Press. (P.779)
--*Naughty Nicky.* Ross, Tony (1938-). 1983, c.1982. Holt, Rinehart, and Winston. (P.779)
--*The Pied Piper of Hamelin.* Ross, Tony (1938-), retold by. 1978, c.1977. Lothrop, Lee & Shepard Co. (P.779)
--*Puss in Boots: The Story of a Sneaky Cat.* Ross, Tony (1938-). 1981. Delacorte Press. (P.779)
--*The Tale of Admiral Mouse.* Stone, Bernard. 1982, c.1981. Holt, Rinehart, and Winston. (P.861)
--*The Three Pigs.* Ross, Tony (1938-). 1983. Pantheon Books. (P.779)
--*Towser & Sadie's Birthday.* Ross, Tony (1938-). 1984. Pantheon. (P.779)
--*Towser & the Terrible Thing.* Ross, Tony (1938-). 1984. Pantheon. (P.779)
--*Towser and the Water Rats.* Ross, Tony (1938-). 1984. Pantheon. (P.779)
Rosse, Allianora
--*The Best Day for Every Little Girl.* Murray, Kathryn Kohnfelder (1906-). 1960. Simon and Schuster. (P.673)
--*Michael Hendee.* Butler, Cynthia. 1976, c.1975. Regional Center for Educational Training. (P.158)
Rosse, Herman
--*Katrina and Jan.* Bailey, Alice Cooper (1890-). N.D. A. L. Burt Co. (P.59)
--*Katrina and Jan.* Bailey, Alice Cooper (1890-). c.1923. P. F. Volland Company. (P.59)
--*More Really So Stories.* Gordon, Elizabeth (1866-1922). N.D A. L. Burt Co. (P.376)
--*Wonder Tales from Pirate Isles: Chiefly Translated from the Dutch.* Olcott, Frances Jenkins (1872-1963), ed. 1927. Longmans, Green and Co. (P.692)
--*Wonder Tales from Windmill Lands: From the Dutch and Other Sources.* Olcott, Frances Jenkins (1872-1963), ed. 1926. Longmans, Green and Co. (P.692)
Rosselli, Colette (1916-)
--*I Went to the Animal Fair.* Cole, William Rossa (1919-), ed. N.D. Putnam Pub Group. (P.208)
--*I Went to the Animal Fair.* Cole, William Rossa (1919-), ed. 1958. World Pub. **Award: (ALA).** (P.208)
--*I Went to the Animal Fair: A Book of Animal Poems.* 1st ed. Cole, William Rossa (1919-), ed. 1975, c.1958. Collins. (P.208)
Rossi, Kendall
--*Dennie's Way.* Malone, Mary. 1964. Dodd, Mead & Co. (P.615)
--*Hi Jolly.* Kjelgaard, James Arthur (1910-1959). 1959. Dodd, Mead. (P.530)
--*Sixteen, and Other Stories.* McGivern, Maureen Daly (1921-). 1961. Dodd, Mead. (P.602)
--*Ulysses and His Woodland Zoo.* Kjelgaard, James Arthur (1910-1959). 1960. Dodd, Mead. (P.530)
Rossit, Harry
--*Star Magicians.* Martin, Anna. c.1978. Leswing Press. (P.624)

--*Star Peril.* Martin, Anna. c.1978. Leswing Press. (P.624)
Ross-Moore, Sharon, jt. illus. see Paris, Pat.
Rossner, Ruth
--*A Walk on a Snowy Night.* Delton, Judy (1931-). 1982. Harper. (P.255)
Rotan, Thurman, Mrs. (1873-1958), photos by.
--*Five Cats from Siam.* Becker, May Lamberton, Mrs. (1873-1958). N.D. Robert M. McBride Co. (P.87)
Roth, Arnold (1929-)
--*Go on Wheels.* Schwartz, Julius (1907-). 1966. McGraw-Hill. (P.803)
--*Grimm's Fairy Tales.* Grimm, Jakob Ludwig Karl (1785-1863) & Grimm, Wilhelm Karl (1786-1859). 1963. Macmillan. (P.392)
--*The Inchworm War and the Butterfly Peace.* Brower, Brock Hendrickson (1931-). 1970. Doubleday. (P.137)
--*Isabel's Noel.* Yolen, Jane Hyatt (1939-). 1967. Funk & Wagnalls. (P.986)
--*Wally the Wordworm.* Fadiman, Clifton Paul (1904-). 1964. Macmillan. (P.315)
--*The Witch Who Wasn't.* Yolen, Jane Hyatt (1939-). 1964. Macmillan. (P.987)
Roth, Arnold (1929-) & Kelly, Walter Crawford (1913-1973)
--*Houseful of Laughter.* Cerf, Bennett Alfred (1898-1971). c.1963. Random. (P.180)
Roth, Carmel, jt. photog. see Lindauer, Gloria Kitt.
Roth, Carmel & Kitt, Gloria, photos by
--*A Different Kind of Birthday.* Rosenbaum, Eileen (1936-). 1968, c.1969. Doubleday. (P.777)
Roth, George (1932-)
--*Middl'un.* Burleson, Elizabeth. 1968. Follett Pub. Co. (P.154)
--*Ride a Wild Dream.* Hall, Lynn (1937-). 1969. Follett Pub. Co. (P.405)
--*Skyrockets for the President.* Laughlin, Florence Young (1910-). 1973. Rand. (P.555)
Roth, Harold
--*Paul David Silverman Is a Father.* 1st ed. Cone, Molly Lamken (1918-). c.1983. Dutton. (P.213)
Roth, Henry
--*Polly of the Pines: A Patriot Girl of the Carolinas.* Thompson, Adele Eugenia (1849-). 1906. Lothrop, Lee & Shepard Co. (P.886)
Roth, Judith Shuman
--*Alfred.* 1st ed. Udry, Janice May (1928-). c.1960. A. Whitman. (P.908)
--*Hannah the Helper.* Orbach, Ruth Gary (1941-). 1961. A. Whitman. (P.695)
--*Pat, the Playground Leader.* Garber, Elizabeth Mason. 1961. A. Whitman. (P.354)
Roth, Lazlo
--*The Hill That Grew.* Meeks, Esther K. (1909-). 1959. Follett Pub. Co. (P.639)
Roth, Naema see Ylval, pseud.
Roth, Naema (1869-)
--*Luz Star-Eye's Dream Journey to the Isles of the Southern Sea: A Story for Children.* Ylval, pseud. Roth, Naema (1869-). Ylval, pseud. c.1912. The Aryan Theosophical Press. (P.780)
Roth, Susan L.
--*Patchwork Tales.* Phang, Ruth & Roth, Susan L. 1984. Atheneum. (P.723)
Rothfuchs, Heiner
--*Illampu.* Radau, Hanns (1901-). 1962. Abelard-Schuman. (P.746)
--*The Last Chief, Alaskan Trapper.* Radau, Hanns (1901-). Long, Dorothy, tr. from Ger. 1965. Abelard-Schuman. (P.746)
--*Little Fox, Alaskan Trapper.* Radau, Hanns (1901-). Long, Dorothy, tr. 1963. Abelard-Schuman. (P.746)
--*Shooting Star.* Wolfel, Ursula. Bell, Anthea, tr. 1981. State Mutual Bk. (P.974)
--*Sons of the Steppe.* Baumann, Hans (1914-). McHugh, Isabel & McHugh, Florence, trs. 1958. Walck. **Award: (ALA).** (P.83)
Rott, Nick
--*Po Fananga: Folk Tales of Tonga.* Posesi Fanual, Tupou. 1975. Rand-Tofua. (P.733)
Roughsey, Dick (1921-)
--*The Giant Devil Dingo.* Roughsey, Dick (1921-). 1975, c.1973. Macmillan. (P.780)
Round, Graham
--*Elijah & the Great Drought.* 1982. Winston Pr. (P.780)
--*The Kind Stranger.* Doney, Meryl. 1982. Winston Pr. (P.280)
--*Te Lost Sheep.* Doney, Meryl. 1982. Winston Pr. (P.280)
--*The Loving Father.* Doney, Meryl. 1982. Winston Pr. (P.280)
--*Miriam & the Princess of Egypt.* 1982. Winston Pr. (P.780)
--*Naaman & the Little Servant Girl.* 1982. Winston Pr. (P.780)
--*The Two Houses.* Doney, Meryl. 1982. Winston Pr. (P.280)
Rounds, Glen Harold (1906-)
--*Aesop's Fables.* Aesopus. James, Thomas & Townsend, George Fyler (1815-1900), trs. 1949. J.B. Lippincott Co. (P.13)

--*Aesop's Fables.* Aesopus. Townsend, George Fyler (1815-1900) & James, Thomas, trs. 1949. J. B. Lippincott Co. (P.13)
--*Beaver Business.* Rounds, Glen Harold (1906-). 1960. E. M. Hale and Company. (P.780)
--*Big Blue Island.* 1st ed. Gage, Wilson, pseud. (1922-). Steele, Mary Quintard Govan. 1964. Collins Pubs. **Award: (ALA).** (P.351)
--*Billy Boy.* Chase, Richard (1904-), compiled by. c.1966. Golden Gate. **Award: (ALA).** (P.188)
--*The Blind Colt.* Rounds, Glen Harold (1906-). N.D. E . M . Hale and co. (P.780)
--*The Blind Colt.* Rounds, Glen Harold (1906-). c.1941. Holiday House. (P.780)
--*The Blind Colt.* Rounds, Glen Harold (1906-). 1960. Holiday House. (P.780)
--*Blind Outlaw.* Rounds, Glen Harold (1906-). c.1980. Holiday House. (P.780)
--*The Boll Weevil.* Rounds, Glen Harold (1906-). 1967. Golden Gate Junior Books. (P.780)
--*Buffalo Harvest.* Rounds, Glen Harold (1906-). 1952. Holiday House. (P.780)
--*Casey Jones: The Story of a Brave Engineer.* Rounds, Glen Harold (1906-). 1968. Childrens. (P.780)
--*Contrary Jenkins.* Caudill, Rebecca (1899-) & Ayars, James Sterling (1898-). 1969. Holt, Rinehart and Winston. (P.178)
--*The Crocodile's Mouth: Folk-Song Stories.* Stoutenburg, Adrien Pearl (1916-). 1966. Viking. (P.863)
--*Dan & the Miranda.* Gage, Wilson, pseud. (1922-). Steele, Mary Quintard Govan. 1962. World Pub. (P.351)
--*The Day the Circus Came to Lone Tree.* Rounds, Glen Harold (1906-). 1973. Holiday House. (P.780)
--*Down in the Boondocks.* Gage, Wilson, pseud. (1922-). Steele, Mary Quintard Govan. 1977. Greenwillow. (P.351)
--*Down in the Boondocks.* Gage, Wilson, pseud. (1922-). Steele, Mary Quintard Govan. 1977. Morrow. (P.351)
--*Elephant & Friends.* Freschet, Berniece Louise Speck (1927-). c.1977. Scribner. (P.345)
--*Farmer Hoo and the Baboons.* Chittum, Ida (1918-). 1971. Delacorte Press. (P.192)
--*The Farmer's Friends.* Rounds, Glen Harold (1906-). N.D. Holiday House. (P.780)
--*Flipper: A Sea-Lion.* Black, Irma Simonton, Mrs. (1906-1972). c.1940. Holiday House. (P.104)
--*Go Find Hanka!.* Crosby, Alexander L. (1906-1980). 1970. Golden Gate Junior Books. (P.232)
--*Halfway Up the Mountain.* Gilchrist, Theo E. 1978. Harper. (P.367)
--*Halfway up the Mountain.* Gilchrist, Theo E. c.1978. Lippincott. (P.367)
--*The Happy Dromedary.* Freschet, Berniece Louise Speck (1927-). 1977. Scribner. (P.345)
--*Haunt Fox.* Kjelgaard, James Arthur (1910-1959). 1954. Holiday House. (P.530)
--*How the People Sang the Mountains Up: How and Why Stories.* Leach, Maria (1892-1977). 1967. Viking Press. (P.557)
--*Hunted Horses.* Rounds, Glen Harold (1906-). 1951. Holiday House. (P.780)
--*Hush up!.* Aylesworth, Jim (1943-). c.1980. Holt, Rinehart and Winston. (P.57)
--*I'm Going on a Bear Hunt.* 1st ed. Sivulich, Sandra Jeanne Stroner (1941-). 1973. Dutton. (P.827)
--*Jennie Jenkins.* 1st ed. Taylor, Mark (1927-). 1975. Little, Brown. (P.880)
--*Kickle Snifters and Other Fearsome Critters Collected from American Folklore.* Schwartz, Alvin (1927-), ed. 1976. Harper. (P.803)
--*Kickle Snifters and Other Fearsome Critters.* Schwartz, Alvin (1927-), retold by. c.1976. Lippincott. (P.803)
--*Little Black Bear Goes for a Walk.* Freschet, Berniece Louise Speck (1927-). 1977. Scribner. (P.345)
--*Lizard Lying in the Sun.* Freschet, Berniece Louise Speck (1927-). 1975. Scribner. (P.345)
--*Lone Muskrat.* Rounds, Glen Harold (1906-). 1953. Holiday. (P.781)
--*Lucky Ladybugs.* Conklin, Gladys Plemon (1903-). 1968. Holiday House. (P.213)
--*The Lucky Man.* Christian, Mary Blount (1933-). c.1979. Macmillan. (P.193)
--*Lumbercamp.* Rounds, Glen Harold (1906-). N.D. Holiday House. (P.781)
--*Mike's Toads.* Gage, Wilson, pseud. (1922-). Steele, Mary Quintard Govan. 1970. World. (P.351)
--*The Morning the Sun Refused to Rise: An Original Paul Bunyan Tale.* Rounds, Glen Harold (1906-). 1984. Holiday. (P.781)
--*Mr. Yowder and the Giant Bull Snake.* Rounds, Glen Harold (1906-). c.1978. Holiday House. **Award: (ALA).** (P.781)
--*Mr. Yowder and the Lion Roar Capsules.* Rounds, Glen Harold (1906-). c.1976. Holiday House. (P.781)
--*Mr. Yowder and the Steamboat.* Rounds, Glen Harold (1906-). 1976. Holiday House. (P.781)
--*Mr. Yowder and the Train Robbers.* Rounds, Glen Harold (1906-). c.1981. Holiday House. **Award: (ALA).** (P.781)

--*Mr. Yowder and the Windwagon.* Rounds, Glen Harold (1906-). c.1983. Holiday House. (P.781)
--*Mr. Yowder, the Peripatetic Sign Painter: Three Tall Tales.* Rounds, Glen Harold (1906-). c.1980. Holiday House. (P.781)
--*Ol' Paul, the Mighty Logger.* Rounds, Glen Harold (1906-). 1949. Holiday. (P.781)
--*Ol' Paul, the Mighty Logger: Being a True Account of the Seemingly Incredible exploits and Inventions of the Great Paul Bunyan.* Rounds, Glen Harold (1906-). 1936. Holiday House. (P.781)
--*Ol' Paul, the Mighty Logger: Being a True Account of the Seemingly Incredible Exploits and Inventions of the Great Paul Bunyan.* 40th anniversary ed. Rounds, Glen Harold (1906-). 1976. Holiday House. (P.781)
--*Once We Had a Horse.* Rounds, Glen Harold (1906-). 1971. Holiday House. (P.781)
--*Pay Dirt.* Rounds, Glen Harold (1906-). 1938. Holiday House. (P.781)
--*Rodeo.* Rounds, Glen Harold (1906-). N.D. Holiday House. (P.781)
--*The Saving of P. S. Branscum.* Robbie (1937-). c.1977. Doubleday. (P.128)
--*The Snake Tree.* Rounds, Glen Harold (1906-). 1966. World Pub. Co. (P.781)
--*Squash Pie.* Gage, Wilson, pseud. (1922-). Steele, Mary Quintard Govan. 1976. Greenwillow. (P.351)
--*Squash Pie.* Gage, Wilson, pseud. (1922-). Steele, Mary Quintard Govan. 1976. Greenwillow. **Award: (ALA).** (P.351)
--*Stolen Pony.* Rounds, Glen Harold (1906-). 1948. E M Hale. (P.781)
--*Stolen Pony.* Rounds, Glen Harold (1906-). 1948. Holiday House. (P.781)
--*Stolen Pony.* Rounds, Glen Harold (1906-). 1969. Holiday House. (P.781)
--*The Strawberry Roan.* Rounds, Glen Harold (1906-). 1970. Golden Gate Junior Books. (P.781)
--*Sweet Betsy from Pike.* Rounds, Glen Harold (1906-). 1973. Children's Press. (P.781)
--*Tall Tale America.* Blair, Walter (1900-). 1944. Putnam Pub Group. (P.105)
--*Three Fools and a Horse.* Baker, Betty Lou (1928-). c.1975. Macmillan. (P.61)
--*Toby, Granny, and George.* Branscum, Robbie (1937-). c.1976. Doubleday. (P.128)
--*Tomfoolery: Trickery and Foolery with Words.* Schwartz, Alvin (1927-). ed. 1973. Harper. (P.803)
--*Tomfoolery: Trickery and Foolery with Words.* Schwartz, Alvin (1927-), retold by. 1973. Lippincott. (P.803)
--*A Twister of Twists, a Tangler of Tongues.* Schwartz, Alvin (1927-), compiled by. 1972. Harper. (P.803)
--*A Twister of Twists, a Tangler of Tongues: Tongue Twisters.* Schwartz, Alvin (1927-), ed. 1972. Lippincott. (P.803)
--*Uncle Lemon's Spring.* 1st ed. Yolen, Jane Hyatt (1939-). c.1981. Dutton. (P.987)
--*Uncle Swithin's Inventions.* Webb, Wheaton Phillips (1911-). 1947. Holiday House. (P.938)
--*Washday on Noah's Ark: A Story of Noah's Ark According to Glen Rounds.* Rounds, Glen Harold (1906-). c.1985. Holiday House. (P.781)
--*The Whistle Punk of Camp Fifteen: Being the Life and Good Times of the New Whistle Punk of Camp Fifteen up Horse Crick Way.* Rounds, Glen Harold (1906-). 1959. Holiday House. (P.781)
--*Whitey and Jinglebob.* Rounds, Glen Harold (1906-). 1946. Grosset and Dunlap. (P.781)
--*Whitey and the Blizzard.* Rounds, Glen Harold (1906-). 1952. Holiday House. (P.781)
--*Whitey and the Colt-Killer.* Rounds, Glen Harold (1906-). 1982, c.1962. Avon Books. (P.781)
--*Whitey & the Colt-Killer.* Rounds, Glen Harold (1906-). 1962. Holiday House. (P.781)
--*Whitey and the Rustlers.* Rounds, Glen Harold (1906-). 1951. Holiday House. (P.781)
--*Whitey & the Wild Horse.* Rounds, Glen Harold (1906-). 1958. Holiday House. (P.781)
--*Whitey Looks for a Job.* Rounds, Glen Harold (1906-). 1944. Grosset and Dunlap. (P.781)
--*Whitey Ropes & Rides.* Rounds, Glen Harold (1906-). N.D. E. M. Hale & Co. (P.781)
--*Whitey Ropes & Rides.* Rounds, Glen Harold (1906-). 1956. Holiday House. (P.781)
--*Whitey Takes a Trip.* Rounds, Glen Harold (1906-). 1954. Holiday House. (P.781)
--*Whitey's First Round-Up.* Rounds, Glen Harold (1906-). 1942. Grosset & Dunlap. (P.781)
--*Whitey's First Roundup.* Rounds, Glen Harold (1906-). 1982, c.1960. Avon Books. (P.781)
--*Whitey's First Roundup.* Rounds, Glen Harold (1906-). 1960. Holiday House. (P.781)
--*Whitey's New Saddle.* Rounds, Glen Harold (1906-). 1982, c.1963. Avon Books. (P.781)
--*Whitey's New Saddle.* Rounds, Glen Harold (1906-). 1963. Holiday House. (P.781)
--*Whitey's Sunday Horse.* Rounds, Glen Harold (1906-). c.1943. Grosset & Dunlap. (P.781)

--*Thuvia, Maid of Mars.* Burroughs, Edgar Rice (1875-1950). 1921. A. C. McClurg. (P.156)
--*The Warlord of Mars.* Burroughs, Edgar Rice (1875-1950). 1919. A. C. McClurg. (P.156)
--*With the Army of the Potomac.* Dunn, Byron Archibald (1842-). 1917. A. C. McClurg & Co. (P.290)
--*The Young Arctic Traders: Further Adventures of the Arctic Stowaways.* Wallace, Dillon (1863-1939). 1921. A. C. McClurg & Co. (P.927)

St. John, J. Allen & Enright, Walter J.
--*King Arthur and His Knights.* Warren, Maude Lavinia Radford, Mrs. (1875-1934). c.1916. Rand, McNally & Company. (P.933)

St. John, James Allen (1872-1957)
--*The Face in the Pool: A/Faerie Tale.* St. John, James Allen (1872-1957). 1905. A. C. McClurg. (P.789)

St. John, Mimi
--*Amanda and Heather, and Company.* Abercrombie, Barbara. 1979. Dandelion Press. (P.4)
--*Good Night!.* Grimes, Frances H. N.D. Dandelion Pr. (P.391)

St. Tamara, pseud., see Kolba, St. Tamara.

St. Tamara, pseud.
--*Save That Raccoon!.* Kolba, St. Tamara. Miklowitz, Gloria D (1927-). c.1978. Harcourt Brace Jovanovich. (P.644)

Sainte-Croix
--*Bill Bunny's Surprise.* 1972. Western Pub. (P.790)

Sainte-Croix, Gaston De, jt. illus. see Dimpre, Henri.

Saintsbury, Dana
--*The Doll's House.* Godden, Rumer (1907-). N.D. Viking Press. (P.372)
--*The Mousewife.* Godden, Rumer (1907-). 1951. Viking Press. (P.372)

Saito, Manabu C.
--*Boy Who Drew Cats & Other Tales.* Hearn, Lafcadio (1850-1904). 1963. Macmillan. (P.428)

Saito, Michiko, pseud., see Fujiwara, Michiko.

Saito, Michiko, pseud. (1946-)
--*Jenny's Journey.* Fujiwara, Michiko. Saito, Michiko (1946-). 1974. McGraw-Hill. (P.790)

Sakai, Sanryo
--*Kappa's Tug-of-War with Big Brown Horse: The Story of a Japanese Water Imp.* 1st ed. Baruch, Dorothy Walter, Mrs. (1899-1962). 1962. C. E. Tuttle. **Award: (ALA).** (P.79)

Sakakura, Yoshinobu & Mitsui, Eiichi
--*Old Tales of Japan.* Yasuda, Yuri, ed. N.D. Charles E. Tuttle Co. (P.985)

Saks, Sylvia
--*Let's Go Home.* Millikin, Virginia Greene, Mrs. N.D. Lothrop, Lee & Shepard. (P.649)
--*Wait till September.* Whiteley, Mary (1913-). 1954. Lee & Shepard. (P.954)

Salander, Carol
--*Gary & Larry Gopher & Their Friends: Adventures in the Wilderness.* Salander, Eric L. 1982. Delgren Bks. (P.790)
--*Gary & Larry Gopher & Their Friends: The Legend of Sir Swen Squirrel.* Salander, Eric L. 1982. Delgren Bks. (P.790)

Salcedo, Maggie
--*Fortune's Caravan.* Javal, Lily Leon-Levy. Field, Rachel Lyman (1894-1942), adapted by. Saunders, Marion, tr. 1933. W. Morrow & Company. (P.490)
--*Long Ago in Rouen.* Withers, Ida M. 1937. Oxford University Press. (P.973)

Saldutti, Denise
--*I Think He Likes Me.* Winthrop, Elizabeth, pseud. (1948-). Mahony, Elizabeth Winthrop. 1979. Harper. (P.970)
--*I Think He Likes Me.* Winthrop, Elizabeth, pseud. (1948-). Mahony, Elizabeth Winthrop. c.1980. Harper & Row. (P.970)
--*The Moon.* Stevenson, Robert Louis (1850-1894). 1984. Harper. (P.857)
--*My Brother Ange.* 1st ed. McCaffrey, Mary. c.1982. Crowell. (P.594)
--*My Brother Ange.* McCaffrey, Mary. 1982. Harper & Row. (P.594)

Sale, Isabel & Sale, John Morton
--*The Yellow Cat.* Grigs, Mary. 1937. H. Milford, Oxford University Press. (P.390)

Sale, John Morton, jt. illus. see Sale, Isabel.

Salem, Mary Miller
--*Playland Pony.* Meeks, Esther K. (1909-). 1950. Follett. (P.639)

Salg, Bert N.
--*Andy Blake.* Lee, Edward Edson (1884-1944). Edwards, Leo, pseud. 1928. Grosset & Dunlap. (P.560)
--*Andy Blake and the Pot of Gold.* Lee, Edward Edson (1884-1944). Edwards, Leo, pseud. 1930. Grosset & Dunlap. (P.560)
--*Andy Blake in Advertising.* Lee, Edward Edson (1884-1944). Edwards, Leo, pseud. 1922. D. Appleton and Company. (P.560)
--*Andy Blake's Comet Coaster.* Lee, Edward Edson (1884-1944). Edwards, Leo, pseud. c.1928. Grosset & Dunlap. (P.560)
--*Andy Blake's Secret Service.* Lee, Edward Edson (1884-1944). Edwards, Leo, pseud. 1929. Grossett & Dunlap. (P.560)
--*Bean Ball Bill And Other Stories.* Heyliger, William (1884-1955). c.1930. Grosset & Dunlap. (P.440)
--*The Big Leaguer.* Heyliger, William (1884-1955). c.1936. The Goldsmith Publishing Company. (P.440)
--*Bill Darrow's Victory.* Heyliger, William (1884-1955). c.1930. Grosset & Dunlap. (P.440)
--*The Clue at Skeleton Rocks.* Lloyd, Hugh. c.1931. Grosset & Dunlap. (P.578)
--*The Copperhead Trail Mystery.* Lloyd, Hugh. c.1931. Grosset & Dunlap. (P.578)
--*Dill Darrow's Victory.* Heyliger, William (1884-1955). c.1930. Grosset & Dunlap. (P.440)
--*The Doom of Stark House.* Lloyd, Hugh. c.1933. Grosset & Dunlap. (P.578)
--*The Hermit of Gordon's Creek.* Lloyd, Hugh. c.1931. Grosset & Dunlap. (P.578)
--*Jerry Hicks and His Gang.* Heyliger, William (1884-1955). c.1929. Grosset & Dunlap. (P.440)
--*Jerry Hicks, Explorer.* Heyliger, William (1884-1955). c.1930. Grosset & Dunlap. (P.440)
--*Jerry Hicks, Ghost Hunter.* Heyliger, William (1884-1955). c.1929. Grosset & Dunlap. (P.440)
--*Jerry Todd and the Bob-Tailed Elephant.* Lee, Edward Edson (1884-1944). Edwards, Leo, pseud. 1929. Grosset & Dunlap. (P.560)
--*Jerry Todd and the Buffalo Bill Bathtub.* Lee, Edward Edson (1884-1944). Edwards, Leo, pseud. 1936. Grosset & Dunlap. (P.560)
--*Jerry Todd and the Flying Flapdoodle.* Lee, Edward Edson (1884-1944). Edwards, Leo, pseud. 1934. Grosset & Dunlap. (P.560)
--*Jerry Todd and the Whispering Mummy.* Lee, Edward Edson (1884-1944). Edwards, Leo, pseud. c.1924. Grosset & Dunlap. (P.560)
--*Jerry Todd, Caveman.* Lee, Edward Edson (1884-1944). Edwards, Leo, pseud. 1932. Grosset & Dunlap. (P.560)
--*Jerry Todd, Editor-in-Grief.* Lee, Edward Edson (1884-1944). Edwards, Leo, pseud. c.1930. Grosset & Dunlap. (P.560)
--*Jerry Todd, Pirate.* Lee, Edward Edson (1884-1944). Edwards, Leo, pseud. 1928. Grosset & Dunlap. (P.560)
--*Jim Spurling, Millman.* Tolman, Albert Walter (1866-). c.1921. Harper & Brothers. (P.894)
--*Kidnapped in the Jungle.* Lloyd, Hugh. c.1931. Grosset & Dunlap. (P.578)
--*The King of the Trail.* Blake, Emma Turner. 1928. I. Washburn. (P.106)
--*The Lonesome Swamp Mystery.* Lloyd, Hugh. c.1932. Grosset & Dunlap. (P.578)
--*The Lost Mine of the Amazon.* Lloyd, Hugh. c.1933. Grosset & Dunlap. (P.578)
--*The Mysterious Arab.* Lloyd, Hugh. c.1931. Grosset & Dunlap. (P.578)
--*Poppy Ott & Co. Inferior Decorators.* Lee, Edward Edson (1884-1944). Edwards, Leo, pseud. 1937. Grosset & Dunlap. (P.560)
--*Poppy Ott and the Freckled Goldfish.* Lee, Edward Edson (1884-1944). Edwards, Leo, pseud. 1828. Grosset & Dunlap. (P.560)
--*Poppy Ott and the Prancing Pancake.* Lee, Edward Edson (1884-1944). Edwards, Leo, pseud. c.1930. Grosset & Dunlap. (P.560)
--*Poppy Ott and the Tittering Totem.* Lee, Edward Edson (1884-1944). Edwards, Leo, pseud. 1929. Grosset & Dunlap. (P.560)
--*Poppy Ott Hits the Trial.* Lee, Edward Edson (1884-1944). Edwards, Leo, pseud. 1933. Grosset & Dunlap. (P.560)
--*The Smugglers' Secret.* Lloyd, Hugh. c.1931. Grosset & Dunlap. (P.578)
--*Trigger Berg and His Seven Hundred Mouse Traps.* Lee, Edward Edson (1884-1944). Edwards, Leo, pseud. 1930. Grosset & Dunlap. (P.560)
--*Trigger Berg and the Cockeyed Ghost.* Lee, Edward Edson (1884-1944). Edwards, Leo, pseud. 1933. Grosset & Dunlap. (P.560)
--*Trigger Berg and the Sacred Pig.* Lee, Edward Edson (1884-1944). Edwards, Leo, pseud. 1931. Grosset & Dunlap. (P.560)
--*Trigger Berg and the Treasure Tree.* Lee, Edward Edson (1884-1944). Edwards, Leo, pseud. 1930. Grosset & Dunlap. (P.560)
--*Tuffy Bean and the Lost Fortune.* Lee, Edward Edson (1884-1944). Edwards, Leo, pseud. 1932. Grosset & Dunlap. (P.560)
--*Tuffy Bean at Funny-Bone Farm.* Lee, Edward Edson (1884-1944). Edwards, Leo, pseud. 1931. Grosset & Dunlap. (P.560)
--*Tuffy Bean's One-Ring Circus.* Lee, Edward Edson (1884-1944). Edwards, Leo, pseud. 1931. Grosset & Dunlap. (P.560)
--*Tuffy Bean's Puppy Days.* Lee, Edward Edson (1884-1944). Edwards, Leo, pseud. 1931. Grosset & Dunlap. (P.560)
--*Yours Truly, Jerry Hicks.* Heyliger, William (1884-1955). c.1929. Grosset & Dunlap. (P.440)

Salg, Bert N. & Neill, John Rea (1878-1943)
--*What's the Joke?.* Stories Boys Like. Rigney, Francis Joseph (1882-), ed. c.1932. D. Appleton and Company. (P.764)

Salih, Metin
--*Daisy's Discovery.* Kelley, Anne. 1985. Barron's. (P.515)

Salisbury, Kent & Zanazanian, Adrina
--*The Headstart Book of Be Nimble & Be Quick.* Lewis, Shari (1934-) & Reinach, Jacquelyn. 1968. McGraw-Hill. (P.570)

Sallak, Albert
--*The Fat of the Cat, and Other Stories.* Keller, Gottfried (1819-1890). Untermeyer, Louis (1885-1977), tr. c.1925. Harcourt, Brace and Company. (P.514)

Sallis, Helen
--*The Long Walk.* Mattingley, Christobel Rosemary (1931-). 1976. Thomas Nelson (Australia). (P.631)

Salls, Anne Chipman
--*My Animal Friends.* Chidsey, Alan Lake. 1967. Chidsey-Kevan Enterprises. (P.191)

Salmon, Balliol
--*The Head Girl at the Gables.* Brazil, Angela (1869-). c.1920. Frederick A. Stokes Company. (P.128)
--*The Luckiest Girl in the School.* Brazil, Angela (1869-). 1922. Frederick A. Stokes Company. (P.128)
--*The Madcap of the School.* Brazil, Angela (1869-). 1922. Frederick A. Stokes Company. (P.128)
--*A Popular Schoolgirl.* Brazil, Angela (1869-). 1921. Frederick A. Stokes Company. (P.128)

Salsbury, Donald
--*Whitie.* Cross, Marguerite S. 1977. Vantage. (P.232)

Salter, Florence
--*Sally's Lost Shoe and Other Stories.* Laughlin, Florence Young (1910-). 1944. Rand McNally & Company. (P.555)

Salter, George
--*Do Not Disturb: The Adventures of M'm and Teddy.* Luling, Elizabeth & Thompson, Sylvia Elizabeth Afiola (1902-). c.1937. Oxford University Press. (P.590)

Saltzberg, Barney
--*The Yawn.* Saltzberg, Barney. 1985. Atheneum. (P.790)

Salzman, Frederic
--*Growing up in Alaska: A Story for Children About Today's Eskimos.* Bunn, Iola Finch. 1965. Exposition Press. (P.149)

Salzman, Yuri
--*Chameleons' Rainbow.* Walton, Marilyn Jeffers. 1985. Raintree Publishers. (P.929)
--*The Fox's Lair.* McMahan, Ian. c.1983. Macmillan. (P.608)
--*The Great Gradepoint Mystery.* Bartholomew, Barbara (1941-). 1983. Macmillan. (P.77)
--*Guess Who's Coming to My Tea Party.* Williams, Barbara M. (1925-). c.1978. Holt, Rinehart and Winston. (P.962)
--*The Little Hen & the Giant.* Polushkin, Maria. 1977. Har-Row. (P.731)
--*The Little Hen & the Giant.* Polushkin, Maria. 1979. Scholastic Inc. (P.731)
--*The Man Who Entered a Contest.* 1st ed. Krasilovsky, Phyllis (1926-). c.1980. Doubleday. (P.537)
--*The Night Before Christmas.* Moore, Clement Clarke (1779-1863). c.1979. Random House. (P.660)
--*The Tickle Tree.* Manushkin, Frances (1942-). c.1982. Clarion Books. (P.619)
--*Two Homes for Lynn.* Noble, June (1979-). c.1979. Holt, Rinehart and Winston. (P.684)
--*Where Do I Fit in?.* Noble, June (1979-). c.1981. Holt, Rinehart, and Winston. (P.684)

Sambin, Michele
--*Caught in the Rain.* 1st ed. Ferro, Beatriz. c.1980. Doubleday. (P.323)
--*Francie's Paper Puppy.* Broger, Achim (1944-). 1984. Picture Bk Studio USA. (P.134)

Sambourne, Linley
--*Fairy Tales.* Andersen, Hans Christian (1805-1875). Lucas, Edgar, Mrs., tr. N.D. Macmillian & Co. (P.35)
--*The Water-Babies.* Kingsley, Charles (1819-1875). 1966. University Microfilms. (P.525)
--*The Water-Babies: A Fairy Tale for a Land-Baby.* New ed. Kingsley, Charles (1819-1875). 1889. Macmillan and Co. (P.525)
--*The Water-Babies: A Fairy Tale for a Land-Baby.* New ed. Kingsley, Charles (1819-1875). 1901. The Macmillan Company; Etc., Etc. (P.525)

Sample, Anna Eliza
--*Fluffy Cat's Tail.* Sample, Anna Eliza. c.1931. A. Whitman & Co. (P.791)
--*My Cut-a-Picture Book.* Sample, Anna Eliza. 1926. Silver, Burdett. (P.791)

Sampson, Barbara
--*Teddy Bears' Picnic.* Kennedy, Jimmy (1903-1984). 1978. Merrimack Pub Cir. (P.518)

Sampson, Florence
--*Famous Fables from AEsop: Cut Paper Silhouettes.* Aesopus. c.1933. The Harter Publishing Company. (P.13)
--*My Caravan: A Book of Poems for Boys and Girls in Search of Adventure.* Grover, Eulalie Osgood (1873-1958), ed. 1931. Laidlow Brothers. (P.397)

Sampson, Katherine
--*Doctor Dan at the Circus.* Wilkins, Pauline. 1960. Golden Press. (P.961)
--*Narcissa Whitman, Pioneer Girl.* Warner, Ann Spence. 1959. Bobbs-Merrill. (P.931)
--*Richard Byrd, Boy of the South Pole.* Van Riper, Guernsey (1909-). 1962. Bobbs-Merrill. (P.915)
--*Sam Houston: Boy Chieftain.* Stevenson, Augusta (1869-1976). 1962. Bobbs-Merrill. (P.855)

Sampson, Pamela
--*The Incredible Invention of Alexander Woodmouse.* Sampson, Pamela. c.1982. Rand McNally. (P.791)
--*A Mouse Family Album.* Sampson, Pamela. c.1980. Rand McNally. (P.791)

Samsa, Ermanno
--*The Lazy Beaver.* Gallo, Giovanni. 1983. Philomel Books. (P.353)

Samson, Anne Stringer (1933-)
--*Draw Me An Elephant.* Samson, Anne Stringer (1933-). 1967. Doubleday. (P.791)
--*How Carla Saw the Shalako God.* Young, Biloine W. (1926-) & Wilson, Mary (1926-). c.1972. Printed by Independence Press. (P.988)
--*Jennie Redbird Finds Her Friends.* Young, Biloine W. (1926-) & Wilson, Mary (1926-). 1973, c.1972. Independence Press. (P.988)
--*Lines, Spines, and Porcupines.* 1st ed. Samson, Anne Stringer (1933-). 1969. Doubleday. (P.791)
--*The Medicine Man Who Went to School.* Young, Biloine W. (1926-) & Wilson, Mary (1926-). 1973, c.1972. Independence Press. (P.988)

Samuel, A. Nupo
--*Iyabo of Nigeria.* Johnston, Rhod O. 1973. Alpha Iota. (P.498)

Samuel, Cordelle
--*A Saddle at Bontharambo.* Samuel, Helen Jo (1909-). 1950. Longmans, Green. (P.791)

Samuel, D. T.
--*English Poems for All Peoples.* Mattam, Donald (1909-), ed. 1966. Pergamon. (P.631)

Samuel, Genevieve Fush
--*Holiday-Time Stories.* Deihl, Edna Groff, Mrs. (1881-1935). c.1930. A. Whitman & Co. (P.251)

Samuels, Barbara
--*The Bananas Move to the Ceiling.* Manes, Esther & Manes, Stephen (1949-). 1983. F. Watts. (P.616)
--*Faye & Dolores.* Samuels, Barbara. 1985. Bradbury Pr. (P.791)
--*Faye and Dolores.* Samuels, Barbara. c.1985. Bradbury Press. (P.791)

Samuels, George H., jt. illus. see Fletcher, Sydney E.

Samuelson, Val
--*Listen, My Children: Poems for Boys and Girls.* Harrison, Gertude, Mrs. c.1940. H. Harrison. (P.417)

Sanborn, F. C. & Railton, Fanny, Mrs.
--*More Mother Stories.* Lindsay, Maud McKnight (1874-). 1905. Milton Bradley Company. (P.574)

Sancha, Sheila (1924-)
--*The Castle Story.* Sancha, Sheila (1924-). 1984. Har-Row. (P.791)
--*Knight After Knight.* Sancha, Sheila (1924-). 1975. Collins-World. (P.791)

Sanchez, Carlos M. (1908-)
--*Aztec Drums.* Lide, Alice Alison, Mrs. (1890-). 1938. Longmans, Green and Co. (P.571)
--*Filippo the Joggleur: A Romance of Franciscan Times.* Downes, Harriet Street. 1932. Longmans, Green and Co. (P.283)
--*Mystery of World's End.* Bamberger, Helen R., Mrs. (1888-). 1930. Longmans, Green and Co. (P.67)
--*Perez & Martina.* rev. ed. Belpre, Pura (1899-1982). 1961. Warne. (P.91)
--*Picture Tales from Spain.* Sawyer, Ruth Estelle (1880-1970). 1936. Frederick A. Stokes Company. (P.795)
--*Picture Tales from Spain.* Sawyer, Ruth Estelle (1880-1970). 1936. J. B. Lippincott Co. (P.795)
--*Princess of Yucatan.* Lide, Alice Alison, Mrs. (1890-). 1939. Longmans, Green and Co. (P.571)
--*The Scarlet Fringe.* Fernald, Helen Clark (1888-) & Slocombe, Edwin M. 1931. Longmans, Green and Co. (P.323)
--*Swain's Saga.* Smith, Arthur Douglas Howden (1887-). 1931. The Macmillan Company. (P.831)

Sanchez, Fred
--*Captive of the Delawares.* Nevin, Evelyn Cook (1910-). 1952. Abingdon-Cokesbury Press. (P.679)
Sand, Beverly V.
--*A Little Book of Poems.* Sand, Gertrude M. 1972. Blackstock Press. (P.791)
Sanden, Howard A.
--*The Wise Men's Camel Boy.* Stein, Hazel. 1965. Augsburg Pub. House. (P.851)
Sanders, Beryl
--*Brogeen and the Little Wind: A Brogeen Story.* Lynch, Patricia Nora (1898-1972). 1963, c.1962. Roy Publishers. (P.592)
--*Happy Christmas.* Seymour, William Kean (1887-) & Smith, John (1924-), eds. 1968. Westminster Press. (P.813)
--*The Princess in the Tower.* Forman, Joan. 1978. Faber & Faber. (P.336)
--*Thursday Rides Again.* Bond, Thomas Michael (1926-). 1969, c.1968. Lothrop, Lee & Shepard Co. (P.114)
Sanders, Krister H.
--*Arnis, the Little Star That Couldn't Shine: A Space Tale.* Sanders, D. Johnson De Santa. 1972. Exposition. (P.792)
Sanders, Malika
--*The Story of Noah.* Hajj 'Abd al-Hayy al-Amin. 1980. Iqra. (P.403)
Sanderson, Ivan Terence (1911-1973)
--*Mystery Schooner.* Roberts, Terence, pseud. (1911-1973). Sanderson, Ivan Terence. 1944. The Viking Press. (P.768)
--*Treks Across the Veldt.* Waldeck, Theodore J. (1894-). N.D. Viking Press. (P.925)
Sanderson, Ruth
--*The Animal, the Vegetable, and John D Jones.* Byars, Betsy Cromer (1928-). c.1982. Delacorte Press. (P.160)
--*The Beast of Lor.* Bulla, Clyde Robert (1914-). 1977. Crowell. (P.148)
--*Buck, Wild.* Balch, Glenn (1902-). c.1976. Crowell. (P.64)
--*Buck, Wild.* Balch, Glenn (1902-). 1976. Har-Row. (P.64)
--*Caught in the Turtle.* Gorog, Judith. 1983. Philomel Books. (P.377)
--*A Different Kind of Gold.* 1st ed. Stern, Cecily. c.1981. Harper & Row. (P.853)
--*Don't Hurt Laurie!.* 1st ed. Roberts, Willo Davis (1928-). 1977. Atheneum. (P.768)
--*The Dune Buggy Mystery.* Hope, Laura Lee, pseud. Stratemeyer Syndicate. c.1981. Wanderer Books. (P.461)
--*First Serve.* Towne, Mary, pseud. (1934-). Spelman, Mary. 1976. Atheneum. (P.897)
--*The Flying Saucer Mystery.* Keene, Carolyn, pseud. (1894-1982). Adams, Harriet Stratemeyer. c.1980. Wanderer Books. (P.511)
--*Good Dog Poems.* Cole, William Rossa (1919-). 1980. Scribner. (P.208)
--*Grandma's Beach Surprise.* List, Ilka Katherine (1935-). c.1975. Putnam. (P.576)
--*The Greek Symbol Mystery.* Keene, Carolyn, pseud. (1894-1982). Adams, Harriet Stratemeyer. c.1981. Wanderer Books. (P.511)
--*Heidi.* Spyri, Johanna Heusser (1827-1901). 1984. Knopf. (P.846)
--*The Hideaway Summer.* 1st ed. Renner, Beverly Hollett (1929-). c.1978. Harper & Row. (P.758)
--*Into the Dream.* 1st ed. Sleator, William Warner, III (1945-). c.1979. Dutton. (P.829)
--*The Kachina Doll Mystery.* Keene, Carolyn, pseud. (1894-1982). Adams, Harriet Stratemeyer. c.1981. Wanderer Books. (P.512)
--*The Little Engine That Could.* Piper, Watty, pseud. (1870-1945), retold by Bragg, Mabel Caroline. 1954. Platt & Munk Co. (P.727)
--*The Missing Pony Mystery.* Hope, Laura Lee, pseud. Stratemeyer Syndicate. c.1981. Wanderer Books. (P.461)
--*The Mysterious Moortown Bridge.* Hall, Lynn (1937-). 1980, c.1981. Follett Pub. Co. (P.405)
--*The Mystery of Pony Hollow.* Hall, Lynn (1937-). c.1978. Garrard Pub. Co. (P.405)
--*The Mystery of the Caramel Cat.* Hall, Lynn (1937-). 1981. Garrard Pub. Co. (P.405)
--*The Mystery of the Missing Pony.* Chittenden, Margaret (1935-). c.1980. Garrard Pub. Co. (P.192)
--*One of the Family.* Archer, Peggy. 1983. Western Pub. (P.46)
--*One of Us.* Amdur, Nikki. 1981. Dial Press. (P.32)
--*Poochie & the Four Seasons Fair.* Webb, Joan. 1983. Western Pub. (P.938)
--*The Pudgy Bunny Book.* 1984. Putnam Pub Group. (P.792)
--*Robert Louis Stevenson's A Child's Garden of Verses.* Stevenson, Robert Louis (1850-1894). c.1977. Platt and Munk. (P.857)
--*The Rose Parade Mystery.* Hope, Laura Lee, pseud. Stratemeyer Syndicate. c.1981. Wanderer Books. (P.462)
--*Samantha on Stage.* Farrar, Susan Clement (1917-). c.1979. Dial Press. (P.318)
--*The Sara Summer.* Hahn, Mary Downing. c.1979. Houghton Mifflin/Clarion Books. (P.402)
--*The Season of Silence.* 1st ed. Shura, Mary Francis (1923-). 1976. Atheneum. (P.822)
--*The Secret in the Old Lace.* Keene, Carolyn, pseud. (1894-1982). Adams, Harriet Stratemeyer. c.1980. Wanderer Books. (P.512)
--*The Secret in the Pirate's Cave.* Hope, Laura Lee, pseud. Stratemeyer Syndicate. c.1980. Wanderer Books. (P.462)
--*The Store-Bought Doll.* Meyer, Lois. 1983. Western Pub. (P.643)
--*The Triple Hoax.* Keene, Carolyn, pseud. (1894-1982). Adams, Harriet Stratemeyer. 1979. Wanderer Books. (P.513)
--*We Remember Philip.* Simon, Norma Feldstein (1927-). c.1979. A. Whitman. (P.825)
--*When You Were a Baby.* Hayward, Linda. c.1982. Golden Press. (P.426)
Sanderson, Ruth & Lenski, Lois (1893-1974)
--*The Little Engine That Could.* Piper, Watty, pseud. (1870-1945), ed. Bragg, Mabel Caroline. c.1976. Platt & Munk. (P.727)
Sanderson, William
--*The Black Dog Mystery.* Queen, Ellery, Jr., pseud. & Lee, Manfred Bennington (1905-1971). Dannay, Frederic. 1941. Frederick A. Stokes Company. (P.744)
--*The Cold Stone Heart.* Hauff, Wilhelm (1802-1827). Schalit, Michael, tr. c.1965. M. Schalit, Dover St. (P.420)
--*Fafan in China.* Lederer, Joe (1907-). Rounds, Margaret, tr. c.1939. Holiday House. (P.559)
Sandford, John
--*Good Show.* Adams, Phylliss & Hartson, Eleanore. 1982. Modern Curr. (P.6)
--*The Gum on the Drum: Grades K-2.* Gregorich, Barbara. Hoffman, Joan, ed. 1984. Sch Zone Pub Co. (P.388)
--*Jump In!* Now!. Adams, Phylliss & Hartson, Eleanore. 1982. Modern Curr. (P.6)
--*Nine Men Chase a Hen: Grades K-2.* Gregorich, Barbara. Hoffman, Joan, ed. 1984. Sch Zone Pub Co. (P.388)
--*Stop the Bed.* Adams, Phylliss, et al. 1982. Modern Curr. (P.6)
--*This Way Down.* Adams, Phylliss & Hartson, Eleanore. 1982. Modern Curr. (P.6)
--*Time Out!.* Adams, Phylliss & Hartson, Eleanore. 1982. Modern Curr. (P.6)
--*Where Is Here?.* Adams, Phylliss & Hartson, Eleanore. 1982. Modern Curr. (P.6)
Sandford, Lloyd
--*Black Jack, Last of the Big Alligators.* McClung, Robert Marshall (1916-). 1967. Morrow. (P.595)
--*The Duck That Flew Backwards.* Tracy, Donald Fiske (1905-1976). 1950. Dial Press. (P.898)
--*Orphan Otter.* Catherall, Arthur (1906-). 1963. Harcourt, Brace & World. (P.178)
--*Otus: The Story of a Screech Owl.* McClung, Robert Marshall (1916-). 1959. Morrow. (P.596)
--*Screamer, Last of the Eastern Panthers.* McClung, Robert Marshall (1916-). 1964. W. Morrow. (P.596)
--*Vulcan: The Story of a Bald Eagle.* McClung, Robert Marshall (1916-). 1955. Morrow. (P.596)
--*Whooping Crane.* McClung, Robert Marshall (1916-). 1959. Morrow. (P.596)
Sandford, Lloyd & McClung, Robert Marshall (1916-)
--*Scoop, Last of the Brown Pelicans.* McClung, Robert Marshall (1916-). 1972. Morrow.(P.596)
Sandham, Henry
--*Boy Tramps: Or, Across Canada.* Oxley, James MacDonald (1855-). 1896. Thomas Y. Crowell. (P.699)
--*Editha's Burglar, 1 of 25 vols.* Burnett, Frances Hodgson, Mrs. (1849-1924). N.D. Dana Estes & Co. (P.155)
--*Editha's Burglar.* Burnett, Frances Hodgson, Mrs. (1849-1924). N.D. H. M. Caldwell Co. (P.155)
--*Editha's Burglar.* Burnett, Frances Hodgson, Mrs. (1849-1924). N.D. L. C. Page & Co. (P.155)
--*Juan and Juanita.* Barnum, Frances Courtenay Baylor, Mrs. (1848-1920). 1888. Ticknor and Company. (P.74)
Sandheim, May
--*Nursery Song Book.* Moore, H. Keatley, ed. N.D. Dutton. (P.661)
Sandin, Joan (1942-)
--*The Bell Ringer & the Pirates.* Coerr, Eleanor Beatrice (1922-). 1983. Har-Row. (P.206)
--*Bird.* Skorpen, Liesel Moak (1935-). c.1976. Harper & Row. (P.828)
--*The Blue Umbrella.* York, Carol Beach (1928-). 1968. F. Watts. (P.988)
--*A Boy Called Fish.* Morgan, Alison Mary (1930-). 1973. Harper & Row. (P.663)
--*But What About Me?.* 1st ed. Love, Sandra Weller (1940-). c.1976. Harcourt Brace Jovanovich. (P.587)
--*Clipper Ship.* Lewis, Thomas Parker (1936-). c.1978. Harper & Row. (P.570)
--*Crocodile and Hen.* Lexau, Joan M, retold by. 1969. Harper & Row. (P.571)
--*Daniel's Duck.* Bulla, Clyde Robert (1914-). c.1978. Harper & Row. **Award: (ALA).** (P.148)
--*Daniel's Duck.* Bulla, Clyde Robert (1914-). 1979. Har-Row. (P.148)
--*The December Dog.* 1st ed. Robinson, Jan M. (1933-). 1969. Lippincott. (P.770)
--*From Anna.* Little, Flora Jean (1932-). 1972. Harper & Row. (P.576)
--*Grandpa's Maria.* Hellberg, Hans-Eric (1927-). Crampton, Patricia, tr. from Swedish. 1974. Morrow. (P.431)
--*Hey, What's Wrong with This One?.* Wojciechowska, Maia Teresa (1927-). 1969. Harper & Row. (P.973)
--*Hill of Fire.* Lewis, Thomas Parker (1936-). 1971. Harper & Row. (P.570)
--*Ickle Bickle Robin.* Preston, Edna Mitchell. 1973. F. Watts. (P.738)
--*It all Began with a Drip, Drip, Drip.* Lexau, Joan M. 1970. E.P. Dutton & Co. (P.571)
--*It All Began with a Drip, Drip, Drip.* Lexau, Joan M, retold by. 1970. McCall Pub. Co. (P.571)
--*The Lemming Condition.* Arkin, Alan Wolf (1934-). c.1976. Harper & Row. (P.47)
--*The Little Fox.* Brecht, Edith (1895-1975). 1968. Lippincott. (P.128)
--*The Long Way to a New Land.* Sandin, Joan (1942-). c.1981. Harper & Row. **Award: (ALA).** (P.792)
--*Look Through My Window.* Little, Flora Jean (1932-). 1970. Harper & Row. (P.577)
--*Michael.* Skorpen, Liesel Moak (1935-). c.1975. Harper & Row. (P.828)
--*Midnite: The Story of a Wild Colonial Boy.* Stow, Randolph (1935-). 1968. Prentice-Hall. (P.864)
--*The Mysterious Red Tape Gang.* Nixon, Joan Lowery (1927-). 1974. Putnam. (P.683)
--*A Private Matter.* 1st ed. Ewing, Kathryn (1921-). 1975. Harcourt Brace Jovanovich. (P.315)
--*Rani, Queen of the Jungle.* Georgiou, Constantine (1927-). 1970. Prentice-Hall. (P.364)
--*Rani, Queen of the Jungle.* Georgiou, Constantine (1927-). 1974, c.1970. Prentice Hall. (P.364)
--*The Secret Box.* Cole, Joanna. 1971. Morrow. (P.208)
--*Small Wolf.* Benchley, Nathaniel Goddard (1915-1981). 1972. Har-Row. (P.92)
--*Tales from the Welsh Hills.* Pugh, Ellen Tiffany (1920-). 1968. Dodd, Mead. (P.741)
--*Time for Uncle Joe.* Jewell, Nancy (1940-). c.1981. Harper & Row. (P.492)
--*A Trainful of Strangers.* 1st ed. Hull, Eleanor Means (1913-). 1968. Atheneum. (P.472)
--*True Tall Tales of Stormalong: Sailor of the Seven Seas.* Felton, Harold William (1902-). 1968. Prentice-Hall. (P.321)
--*Woodchuck.* McNulty, Faith (1918-). 1974. Har-Row. (P.610)
--*A Year in the Life of Rosie Bernard.* Brenner, Barbara Johnes (1925-). 1971. Harper & Row. (P.129)
Sandland, Reg
--*The Moonpath, and Other Tales of the Bizarre.* Swindells, Robert Edward (1939-). 1983, c.1979. Carolrhoda Books. (P.875)
--*The Story of Cadmus.* Espeland, Pamela Lee (1951-). c.1980. Carolrhoda Books. (P.310)
--*Theseus and the Road to Athens.* Espeland, Pamela Lee (1951-). c.1981. Carolrhoda Books. (P.310)
Sandoz, Edouard Marcel (1918-)
--*Greek Myths.* Coolidge, Olivia Ensor (1908-). 1949. Houghton Mifflin Co. (P.216)
--*Legends of the North.* Coolidge, Olivia Ensor (1908-). 1951. HM. (P.216)
--*The Sword and the Scythe.* Williams, Jay (1914-1978). 1946. Oxford University Press. (P.963)
--*Trojan War.* Coolidge, Olivia Ensor (1908-). 1952. HM. (P.216)
--*Twice Besieged.* Sandoz, Edouard Marcel (1881-). 1947. Oxford Univ. Press. (P.792)
Sandra, James
--*Dolly Madison, Quaker Girl.* Monsell, Helen Albee (1895-1971). 1944. The Bobbs-Merrill Company. (P.657)
Sanford, Jim
--*The Animals.* Rice, Earle, Jr. c.1979. Fearon Pitman Publishers. (P.760)
Sanford, Margaret Landers
--*The Teddy Bear A-B-C.* Johnson, Laura Rinkle. 1907. Caldwell. (P.495)
Sanford, Ted
--*A Pasture for Peterkin.* 1st ed. Sanford, Agnes Mary White (1897-). 1956. Macalester Park Pub. Co. (P.792)
Sansone, Ken, jt. illus. see Keenan, Elaine Faris.
San Souci, Daniel
--*The Bedtime Book.* San Souci, Robert D. (1946-). c.1985. Little Simon. (P.793)
--*The Brave Little Tailor.* Grimm, Jakob Ludwig Karl (1785-1863) & Grimm, Wilhelm Karl (1786-1859). San Souci, Robert D. (1946-), adapted by. c.1982. Doubleday. (P.391)
--*Hidden Places.* Root, Phyllis. 1983. Raintree Pubs. (P.776)
--*The Legend of Scarface: A Blackfoot Indian Tale.* 1st ed. San Souci, Robert D. (1946-), adapted by. c.1978. Doubleday. **Award: (NYT).** (P.793)
--*Rip Van Winkle.* Gipson, Morrell (1920-), retold by. 1984. Doubleday. (P.370)
--*Song of Sedna: Sea-Goddess of the North.* San Souci, Robert D. (1946-). c.1981. Doubleday. (P.793)
--*Trapped in the Slickrock Canyon.* Skurzynski, Gloria Joan (1930-). c.1984. Lothrop, Lee & Shepard. (P.828)
Santa, Monica
--*The Golden Goose.* Hillert, Margaret (1920-), adapted by. c.1978. Follett Pub. Co. (P.445)
Santee, Ross, jt. illus. see Dennis, Wesley.
Santee, Ross (1889-1965)
--*Mountain Pony.* Larom, Henry V. (1903-1975). N.D. G&D. (P.552)
--*Mountain Pony and the Elkhorn Mystery.* Larom, Henry V (1903-1975). 1950. Whittlesey House. (P.552)
--*Mountain Pony and the Pinto Colt.* Larom, Henry V (1903-1975). 1947. Whittlesey House. (P.552)
--*Mountain Pony and the Rodeo Mystery.* Larom, Henry V (1903-1975). 1949. Whittlesey House. (P.552)
--*The Pooch.* Santee, Ross (1889-1965). 1931. The Cosmopolitan Book Corporation. (P.793)
--*Sleepy Black,.* the Story of a Horse. Santee, Ross (1889-1965). c.1933. Farrar & Rinehart, Incorporated. (P.793)
--*Stirrup High.* Coburn, Walt (1889-). Gipson, Frederick Benjamin (1908-1973), intro. by. 1957. J. Messner. (P.205)
Santiago, Nilo
--*Return to Ramos.* Cardenas, Leo. 1970. Hill & Wang. (P.166)
--*Viva la Patria.* Campbell, Camilla B. (1905-). 1970. Hill and Wang; Distributed by Random House. (P.164)
Santin, Federico
--*Little Red Riding Hood.* Santin, Federico, retold by. c.1961. Duell, Sloan and Pearce. (P.793)
--*Scandanavian Fairy Tales.* Pitt, Giordano. King, Leon, tr. 1962. Golden Press. (P.727)
--*Scandinavian Fairy Tales.* King, Leon, tr. 1962. Golden Press. (P.793)
--*Three Little Pigs.* Santin, Federico, retold by. c.1962. Des Moines. (P.793)
Santoro, Christopher
--*A Garden for Miss Mouse.* Muntean, Michaela. 1982. Parents. (P.672)
--*Here Comes Santa Claus.* Hover, M. 1982. Western Pub. (P.466)
--*Panda Bear's Paintbox.* Muntean, Michaela. 1981. Western Pub. (P.672)
--*Panda Bear's Secret.* Muntean, Michaela. 1983. Western Pub. (P.672)
Santos, Duarte
--*The Master of Song.* Santos, Elsie S. 1984. Shawme Ent. (P.793)
--*The Mystery at Shawme Pond.* Santos, Elsie S. Alvaro, Albert M., ed. 1983. Shawme Ent. (P.793)
Santos, George
--*Black Beauty.* Sewell, Anna (1820-1878). Levin, Marcia Lauter Obrasky (1918-), retold by. Martin, Marcia, pseud. 1952. Wonder Books. (P.812)
--*Black Beauty.* Sewell, Anna (1820-1878). Levin, Marcia Lauter Obrasky (1918-), retold by. 1952. Wonder Books. (P.812)
--*Black Beauty.* Martin, Marcia, pseud. (1918-), retold by Levin, Marcia Obrasky. 1952. Wonder Books. (P.625)
Sanz, Juan C.
--*The Adventures of the Jackson Kids.* Jackson, George. 1983. G D Jackson. (P.485)
--*Jonny Lincoln & His Three Dogs.* Carver, Joyce S. 1982. Exposition. (P.176)
Saphore, Athena & Leary, Judith M.
--*Strawberry Shortcake's Sunny Day Poems: A Happy Collection of Classic Children's Verses.* c.1981. Random House. (P.793)
Sapieha, Christine
--*The Island of Cats.* Fremantle, Anne Jackson (1910-). 1964. I. Obolensky. (P.344)
Sarabasha, Susan
--*Prune.* Ross, Ramon Royal. 1984. Atheneum. (P.779)
Sardella, Lou
--*Sandman Tales.* Newhouse, Wilfred John (1894-). c.1954. Sandman Press. (P.680)
--*Six Stories about Mollie the Bell Cow.* Newhouse, Wilfred John (1894-). 1957. Sandman Press. (P.680)
--*Six Stories about Prim the Kitten and Curly the Collie.* Newhouse, Wilfred John (1894-). 1957. Sandman Press. (P.680)
Sarg, Anthony Frederick see Sarg, Tony, pseud.
Sarg, Tony, pseud., see Sarg, Anthony Frederick.

--*A Farm in the Family.* Ross, Margaret Isabel (1897-). 1943. Harper & Brothers. (P.779)
--*The Fish Hawk's Nest.* 1st ed. Meader, Stephen Warren (1892-). 1952. Harcourt, Brace. (P.637)
--*Freedom River.* Douglas, Marjory Stoneman (1890-). 1953. Scribner. (P.282)
--*Freedom River: Florida, 1845;.* Douglas, Marjory Stoneman (1890-). 1953. Scribner. (P.282)
--*The Gray Dog from Galtymore.* Chipperfield, Joseph Eugene (1912-1980). 1962. McKay. (P.192)
--*Jill's Victory.* 1st ed. Bialk, Elisa (1912-). 1952. World Pub. Co. (P.100)
--*Jonathan Goes West.* Meader, Stephen Warren (1892-). 1946. Harcourt, Brace and Company. (P.637)
--*Jumper, the Life of a Siberian Horse.* Kalashnikoff, Nicholas (1888-1961). 1944. C. Scribner's Sons. (P.504)
--*The Last Fort.* Coatsworth, Elizabeth Jane (1893-). 1953. Holt, Rinehart and Winston. (P.204)
--*Last Fort.* Coatsworth, Elizabeth Jane (1893-). 1952. HR&W. (P.204)
--*The Little Stray Dog.* De Jong, Meindert (1906-). 1943. Harper & Brothers. (P.252)
--*The Long Trains Roll.* Meader, Stephen Warren (1892-). 1944. Harcourt, Brace and Company. (P.637)
--*Longshanks.* Meader, Stephen Warren (1892-). N.D. Harcourt, Brace and Co., Inc. (P.637)
--*Mark of a Champion.* Scott, Thurman Thomas. 1960. Longmans, Green. (P.805)
--*Mayflower Boy.* Young, Stanley Preston (1906-1975). 1944. Farrar & Rinehart Inc. (P.990)
--*Mill Creek Mystery.* Chapman, Maristan, pseud. (1891-1972) & Chapman, Mary Ilsley. Chapman, John Stanton Higham. 1940. D. Appleton-Century Company, Incorporated. (P.186)
--*Mountain Mystery.* Chapman, Maristan, pseud. (1891-1972) & Chapman, Mary Ilsley. Chapman, John Stanton Higham. 1941. D. Appleton-Century Company, Incorporated. (P.186)
--*Northend Wildcats.* Davis, Clyde Brion (1894-1962). c.1938. Farrar & Rinehart, Inc. (P.245)
--*On Stage, Mr.* Jefferson!. 1st ed. Latham, Jean Lee (1902-). 1958. Harper. (P.553)
--*On to Oregon.* The Story of a Pioneer Boy. Morrow, Honore McCue Willsie, Mrs. (1880-1940). 1946. W. Morrow and Company. (P.666)
--*Rescue Dog of the High Pass.* Kjelgaard, James Arthur (1910-1959). 1958. Dodd, Mead. (P.530)
--*River of the Wolves.* Meader, Stephen Warren (1892-). 1948. Harcourt, Brace. (P.637)
--*Road to Down Under.* Cormack, Maribelle B. (1902-). 1944. D. Appleton-Century Company, Incorporated. (P.221)
--*Sailor in the Sun.* White, Robb (1909-). c.1941. Harper & Brothers. (P.953)
--*Saint George & the Dragon.* Johnson, Richard (1573-1659) & Kingston, William Henry Giles (1814-1880). 1949. Limited Editions Club. (P.496)
--*The Sea Snake.* Meader, Stephen Warren (1892-). 1943. Harcourt, Brace and Company. (P.637)
--*The Secret Motorcar.* Denny, Norman George (1901-). Dale, Norman, pseud. 1957, c.1954. Harper. (P.258)
--*Seek the Dark Gold.* Lundy, Jo Evalin. Best, Allena Champlin, Mrs. (1892-1974), ed. Berry, Erick, pseud. N.D. John C. Winston Co. (P.590)
--*Shadow in the Pines.* Rev ed. Meader, Stephen Warren (1892-). 1942. Harcourt, Brace and Company. (P.637)
--*Spinney and Spike and the B-29.* Davis, Lavinia Riker, Mrs. (1909-1961). 1944. C. Scribner's Sons. (P.246)
--*Swamp Cat.* Kjelgaard, James Arthur (1910-1959). 1957. Dodd, Mead. (P.530)
--*T-Model Tommy.* Rev ed. Meader, Stephen Warren (1892-). c.1938. Harcourt, Brace and Company. (P.637)
--*T-Model Tommy.* Meader, Stephen Warren (1892-). c.1940. Harcourt, Brace and Company. (P.637)
--*Thunder.* 1st ed. Cooper, Page (1891-). 1954. World Pub. Co. (P.218)
--*Thunder.* 1st ed. Cooper, Page (1891-). c.1954. World Pub. Co. (P.218)
--*Victory at Bear Cove: A Story of Alaska.* Pedersen, Elsa Kienitz (1915-). 1959. Abingdon Press. (P.715)
--*Whaler Round the Horn.* 1st ed. Meader, Stephen Warren (1892-). 1950. Harcourt, Brace. (P.637)
--*Wolf Dog of Ambush Canyon: A Montana Mystery Story.* 1st ed. Sykes, Jo. 1959. Winston. (P.875)
--*The Year of Jubilo.* Sawyer, Ruth Estelle (1880-1970). 1940. The Viking Press. (P.795)
--*The Yearling.* Rawlings, Marjorie Kinnan (1896-1953). 1938. Scribner. (P.750)

Shenton, Edward (1895-), photos by.
--*Song Dog: The Story of a Coyote.* Hoyt, Vance Joseph (1889-). c.1939. The John C. Winston Company. (P.468)

Shenton, Edward (1895-) & Meader, Stephen Warren
--*The Black Buccaneer.* Rev ed. Meader, Stephen Warren (1892-). 1942. Harcourt, Brace and Company. (P.637)

Shenton, Ken
--*Little Gumdrop: Story.* Race, Elizabeth. c.1952. McKnight & McKnight. (P.745)

Shepard, Ernest Howard (1879-1976)
--*At the Back of the North Wind.* Macdonald, George (1824-1905). 1957. Dent. (P.598)
--*At the Back of the North Wind.* MacDonald, George (1824-1905). 1956. E. P. Dutton & Co. (P.599)
--*Ben and Brock.* Shepard, Ernest Howard (1879-1976). 1966. Doubleday. (P.818)
--*Bertie's Escapade.* Grahame, Kenneth (1859-1932). 1949. J. B. Lippincott Co. (P.381)
--*Betsy and Joe.* 1st ed. Shepard, Ernest Howard (1879-1976). 1967, c.1966. Dutton. (P.818)
--*Bevis: The/Story of a Boy.* Jefferies, Richard (1848-1887). Jackson, Brian (1933-1983), ed. 1974. Puffin Books. (P.491)
--*Bevis: The Story of a Boy.* Jefferies, Richard (1848-1887). N.D. British Book Centre. (P.491)
--*Bevis,.* The Story of a Boy. Jefferies, Richard (1848-1887). N.D. Peter Smith. (P.491)
--*The Brownies, and Other Stories.* Ewing, Juliana Horatia Gatty, Mrs. (1841-1885). 1954. Dent. (P.313)
--*Brownies & Other Stories.* Ewing, Juliana Horatia Gatty, Mrs. (1841-1885). 1954. Dutton. (P.313)
--*The Christopher Robin Book of Verse.* 1st. ed. Milne, Alan Alexander (1882-1956). 1967. Dutton. (P.650)
--*The Christopher Robin Verses.* Milne, Alan Alexander (1882-1956). 1932. E. P. Dutton & Co. (P.650)
--*Crystal Mountain.* Rugh, Belle Dorman (1908-). 1955. Houghton Mifflin. **Award: (ALA).** (P.783)
--*The Cuckoo Clock.* Molesworth, Mary Louisa Stewart, Mrs. (1842-1921). N.D. E. P. Dutton & Co. (P.654)
--*The Flattered Flying Fish and Other Poems.* 1st ed. Rieu, Emile Victor (1887-). 1962. Dutton. (P.764)
--*Frogmorton.* Colling, Susan. 1956, c.1955. Knopf. (P.209)
--*Frogmorton.* Collins, Susan. 1956. Alfred A Knopf : distributed by Borzoi Books. (P.210)
--*The Glass Slipper.* Farjeon, Eleanor (1881-1965). 1955. Oxford University Press. (P.317)
--*The Glass Slipper.* Farjeon, Eleanor (1881-1965). 1956, c.1955. Viking Press. (P.317)
--*Hans Andersen's Fairy Tales.* Andersen, Hans Christian (1805-1875). N.D. Henry Z. Walck Inc. (P.36)
--*The Holly Tree and Other Christmas Stories.* Dickens, Charles John Huffam (1812-1870). N.D. Charles Scribner's Sons. (P.263)
--*The House at Pooh Corner.* Milne, Alan Alexander (1882-1956). 1961, c.1928. Dutton. (P.650)
--*The House at Pooh Corner.* Milne, Alan Alexander (1882-1956). c.1928. E. P. Dutton & Co., Inc. (P.650)
--*Introducing Winnie-the-Pooh, and Other Selections.* Milne, Alan Alexander (1882-1956). 1947. E. P. Dutton. (P.650)
--*The Islanders.* Pertwee, Roland (1885-1963). 1956. Bobbs- Merrill. (P.720)
--*The King's Breakfast, and Other Selections.* Milne, Alan Alexander (1882-1956). c.1947. E. P. Dutton. (P.650)
--*Let's Pretend: Poems.* Agnew, Georgette. 1927. G. P. Putnam's Sons. (P.14)
--*Modern Fairy Stories.* Green, Roger Gilbert Lancelyn (1918-), ed. 1955. Dent. (P.385)
--*Modern Fairy Stories.* Green, Roger Gilbert Lancelyn (1918-), ed. 1956. Dutton. (P.385)
--*Mother Goose.* Mother Goose. Milne, Alan Alexander (1882-1956), adapted by. N.D. E. P. Dutton & Co. (P.667)
--*Now We Are Six.* Milne, Alan Alexander (1882-1956). 1961, c.1927. Dutton. (P.650)
--*Old Greek Fairy Tales.* Green, Roger Gilbert Lancelyn (1918-), ed. 1969, c.1958. Roy Publishers. (P.385)
--*The Old Sailor, and Other Selections.* Milne, Alan Alexander (1882-1956). 1947. E. P. Dutton. (P.650)
--*Playtime & Company: A Book for Children.* Lucas, Edward Verrall (1868-1938). c.1925. George H. Doran Company. (P.589)
--*Pooh Song Book.* Milne, Alan Alexander (1882-1956). 1961. Dutton. (P.650)
--*The Pooh Story Book.* Milne, Alan Alexander (1882-1956). 1965. Dutton. (P.650)
--*Pooh's Alphabet Book.* Milne, Alan Alexander (1882-1956). 1975. Dutton. (P.650)
--*Pooh's Bedtime Book.* 1st ed. Milne, Alan Alexander (1882-1956). c.1980. Dutton. (P.650)
--*Pooh's Birthday Book.* 1st ed. Milne, Alan Alexander (1882-1956). 1963. Dutton. (P.650)
--*Pooh's Counting Book.* Milne, Alan Alexander (1882-1956). c.1982. Dutton. (P.650)
--*Pooh's Pot O'honey.* Milne, Alan Alexander (1882-1956). 1968. Dutton. (P.650)
--*Pooh's Quiz Book.* 1st ed. Milne, Alan Alexander (1882-1956). c.1977. Dutton. (P.650)
--*The Reluctant Dragon.* Grahame, Kenneth (1859-1932). 1953. Holiday House. (P.381)
--*The Silver Curlew.* Farjeon, Eleanor (1881-1965). 1953. Oxford University Press. **Award: (ALA).** (P.317)
--*The Silver Curlew.* Farjeon, Eleanor (1881-1965). 1954, c.1953. Viking Press. (P.317)
--*Sneezles, and Other Selections.* Milne, Alan Alexander (1882-1956). 1947. E. P. Dutton. (P.650)
--*The Very Young Calendar, 1930.* Milne, Alan Alexander (1882-1956). 1929. E. P. Dutton & Co., Inc. (P.650)
--*When We Were Very Young.* Milne, Alan Alexander (1882-1956). 1961, c.1924. Dutton. (P.650)
--*When We Were Very Young.* Milne, Alan Alexander (1882-1956). 1924. E. P. Dutton & Co. (P.650)
--*When We Were Very Young.* Milne, Alan Alexander (1882-1956). 1966. E.P. Dutton & Co. (P.650)
--*The Wind in the Willows.* Grahame, Kenneth (1859-1932). Dillenbeck, Marsden V. & Brooks, Ellen W., intro. by. 1967. Scribners. (P.381)
--*The Wind in the Willows.* Grahame, Kenneth (1859-1932). 1933. C. Scribner's Sons. (P.381)
--*The Wind in the Willows.* Grahame, Kenneth (1859-1932). c.1935. C. Scribner's Sons. (P.381)
--*The Wind in the Willows.* Grahame, Kenneth (1859-1932). 1953. Scribner. (P.381)
--*The Wind in the Willows.* Grahame, Kenneth (1859-1932). 1960. Scribner. (P.381)
--*The Wind in the Willows.* Grahame, Kenneth (1859-1932). 1964. Scribner. (P.381)
--*The Wind in the Willows.* Grahame, Kenneth (1859-1932). 1983, c.1981. Scribner. (P.381)
--*Winnie-Ille-Pu: A Latin Version of A.* A. Milne's Winnie-the-Pooh. Milne, Alan Alexander (1882-1956). Lenard, Alexander, tr. 1984. Dutton. (P.650)
--*Winnie-the-Pooh.* Milne, Alan Alexander (1882-1956). 1954, c.1926. Dutton. (P.650)
--*Winnie-the-Pooh.* Milne, Alan Alexander (1882-1956). 1961, c.1954. Dutton. (P.650)
--*Winnie-the-Pooh.* Milne, Alan Alexander (1882-1956). 1961, c.1926. Dutton. (P.650)
--*Winnie-the-Pooh.* Milne, Alan Alexander (1882-1956). 1974, c.1926. Dutton. (P.650)
--*Winnie-the-Pooh.* Milne, Alan Alexander (1882-1956). 1926. E. P. Dutton & Co. (P.650)
--*Winnie-the-Pooh and Eeyore's Tail.* Milne, Alan Alexander (1882-1956). 1952. Dutton. (P.650)
--*Winnie the Pooh & His Friends.* N.D. Platt. (P.818)
--*Winnie-the-Pooh and the Bees.* Milne, Alan Alexander (1882-1956). 1952. Dutton. (P.650)
--*The World of Christopher Robin: The Complete When We Were Very Young and Now We Are Six.* Milne, Alan Alexander (1882-1956). 1958. Dutton. (P.650)
--*The World of Pooh: The Complete Winnie-the-Pooh and The House at Pooh Corner.* Milne, Alan Alexander (1882-1956). 1957. Dutton. (P.650)

Shepard, Ernest Howard (1879-1976) & Scott, Hilda
--*Winnie-the-Pooh.* 1st ed. Milne, Alan Alexander (1882-1956). 1974, c.1926. Dutton. (P.650)

Shepard, Mac
--*Big Bug, Little Bug.* Berg, Jean Horton (1913-). N.D. Follett. (P.95)
--*The Moon of the Bears.* George, Jean Craighead (1919-). 1967. Thomas Y. Crowell. (P.363)

Shepard, Mary Eleanor (1909-)
--*Adventure May Be Anywhere.* Manning-Sanders, Ruth (1895-). 1939. Frederick A. Stokes Company. (P.617)
--*Adventure May Be Anywhere.* Manning-Sanders, Ruth (1895-). N.D. J. B. Lippincott. (P.617)
--*Happy Ever After.* Travers, Pamela Lyndon (1906-). 1940. Reynal & Hitchcock. (P.898)
--*Mary Poppins.* Travers, Pamela Lyndon (1906-). 1934. Harcourt. (P.898)
--*Mary Poppins.* Travers, Pamela Lyndon (1906-). c.1962. Harcourt, Brace & World. (P.898)
--*Mary Poppins.* rev. ed. Travers, Pamela Lyndon (1906-). c.1981. Harcourt Brace Jovanovich. (P.898)
--*Mary Poppins.* Travers, Pamela Lyndon (1906-). 1985, c.1934. Harcourt Brace Jovanovich. (P.898)
--*Mary Poppins.* Travers, Pamela Lyndon (1906-). c.1934. Reynal & Hitchcock. (P.898)
--*Mary Poppins and Mary Poppins Comes Back.* Travers, Pamela Lyndon (1906-). 1955. Harcourt Brace Jovanovich. (P.898)
--*Mary Poppins Comes Back.* Travers, Pamela Lyndon (1906-). 1962, c.1935. Harcourt, Brace & World. (P.898)
--*Mary Poppins Comes Back.* Travers, Pamela Lyndon (1906-). 1975, c.1963. Harcourt Brace Jovanovich. (P.898)
--*Mary Poppins Comes Back.* Travers, Pamela Lyndon (1906-). c.1935. Reynal & Hitchcock. (P.898)
--*Mary Poppins from A to Z.* 1st ed. Travers, Pamela Lyndon (1906-). 1962. Harcourt, Brace & World. (P.898)
--*Mary Poppins in Cherry Tree Lane.* Travers, Pamela Lyndon (1906-). 1982. Delacorte Press. (P.898)
--*Mary Poppins in the Kitchen.* Rev ed. Travers, Pamela Lyndon (1906-) & Moore-Betty, Maurice. 1978. HarBraceJ. (P.898)
--*Mary Poppins in the Kitchen: A Cookery Book with a Story.* Travers, Pamela Lyndon (1906-) & Moore-Betty, Maurice. 1975. HarBraceJ. (P.898)
--*Mary Poppins in the Park.* Travers, Pamela Lyndon (1906-). 1952. Harcourt, Brace. (P.898)
--*Mary Poppins in the Park.* Travers, Pamela Lyndon (1906-). 1962, c.1952. Harcourt, Brace & World. (P.898)
--*Mary Poppins in the Park.* Travers, Pamela Lyndon (1906-). 1976, c.1952. Harcourt Brace Jovanovich. (P.898)
--*Mary Poppins Opens the Door.* Travers, Pamela Lyndon (1906-). 1962, c.1943. Harcourt, Brace & World. (P.898)
--*Pigeon Post.* Ransome, Arthur Michell (1884-1967). c.1937. J. B. Lippincott Company. (P.749)
--*Prince Rabbit, and the Princess Who Could Not Laugh.* 1st ed. Milne, Alan Alexander (1882-1956). 1966. Dutton. (P.650)

Shepard, Mary Eleanor (1909-) & Sims, Agnes
--*The Complete Mary Poppins, 4 vols.* Travers, Pamela Lyndon (1906-). 1976. HarBraceJ. (P.898)
--*Mary Poppins; and Mary Poppins Comes Back.* Travers, Pamela Lyndon (1906-). 1964, c.1963. Harcourt, Brace & World. (P.898)
--*Mary Poppins and Mary Poppins Comes Back.* Travers, Pamela Lyndon (1906-). 1937. Reynal & Hitchcock. (P.898)
--*Mary Poppins Opens the Door.* Travers, Pamela Lyndon (1906-). 1976, c.1943. Harcourt Brace Jovanovich. (P.898)
--*Mary Poppins Opens the Door.* Travers, Pamela Lyndon (1906-). 1943. Reynal & Hitchcock. (P.898)

Shepard, Richard
--*Attack of the Space Creatures.* Rattiner, Dan. N.D. Permanent Press. (P.750)

Sheperd, J. Clinton
--*Boy Hunters in Demerara.* Hartley, George Inness (1887-). 1921. The Century Co. (P.418)

Shephard, Mary

Shepherd
--*Christmas Elves: Or, the Tales of the Day Fairies.* Sage, Agnes Carolyn (1854-). 1888. R Worthington. (P.788)

Shepherd, Dorothy W.
--*Boxes Are Wishes.* Shepherd, Dorothy W. 1959. Steck-V. (P.818)

Shepherd, Irana
--*Jack & the Beanstalk.* N.D. Price Stern. (P.818)

Shepherd, J. A.
--*The Story of Chanticleer.* Rostand, Edmond Eugene Alexis (1868-1918). Hann, Florence Yates, adapted by. 1913. Frederick A. Stokes Company. (P.780)
--*A Thorough-Bred Mongrel: The Tale of a Dog, Told by a Dog to Lovers of Dogs.* Townesend, Stephen Chapman Tyler (1860-1914). Burnett, Frances Hodgson, Mrs. (1849-1924), pref. by. c.1901. Frederick A. Stokes Company. (P.897)
--*Three Jovial Puppies.* Cuming, Edward William Dirom (1862-). N.D. Caldwell. (P.234)
--*Wonders in Monsterland.* Cuming, Edward William Dirom (1862-). N.D. Longmans, Green and Co. (P.234)

Shepherd, J. C., jt. illus. see Francis, Joseph Greene.

Shepherd, J. Clinton
--*Flamingo Prince.* Hall, Rubylea Ray (1910-). 1954. Duell, Sloan and Pearce. (P.406)
--*The Hill of Adventure.* Adair, Aldon, pseud. (1884-1973). Meigs, Cornelia Lynde. 1922. The Century Co. (P.4)
--*Old Ruddy and Other Forest People.* Willenborg, Lee. c.1935. Rand, McNally & Company. (P.961)

Shepherd, Jesse C., jt. illus. see Ledyard, Addie.

--*Bruno the Pretzel Man.* Davis, Edward E. 1984. HarpJ. (P.245)
--*The Castle in the Silver Wood and Other Scandinavian Fairy Tales.* Owen, Ruth Bryan, Mrs. (1885-), tr. 1939. Dodd, Mead and Company. (P.826)
--*Chasing After Annie.* 1st ed. Sharmat, Marjorie Weinman (1928-). c.1981. Harper & Row. (P.815)
--*The Contests at Cowlick.* Kennedy, Jerome Richard (1932-). 1975. Little, Brown. (P.518)
--*Danger in Dinosaur Valley.* Nixon, Joan Lowery (1927-). c.1978. Putnam. (P.683)
--*Deer Mountain Hideaway.* Lansing, Elisabeth Carleton Hubbard (1911-). 1953. Thomas Y. Crowell. (P.551)
--*Deer River Raft.* Lansing, Elisabeth Carleton Hubbard (1911-). 1955. Crowell. (P.551)
--*Dougal's Wish.* Nic Leodhas, Sorche, pseud. (1898-1969). Alger, Leclaire Gowans. 1942. Harper & Brothers. (P.681)
--*The Duck-Footed Hound.* Kjelgaard, James Arthur (1910-1959). 1960. Crowell. (P.530)
--*The Elephant Who Couldn't Forget.* McNulty, Faith (1918-). 1980. Har-Row. (P.610)
--*The Elephant Who Couldn't Forget.* McNulty, Faith (1918-). c.1980. Harper & Row. (P.610)
--*Every Time I Climb a Tree.* 1st ed. McCord, David Thompson Watson (1897-). 1967. Little, Brown. (P.596)
--*First Christmas.* Trent, Robbie (1894-). 1948. Har-Row. (P.899)
--*The First Story.* Brown, Margaret Wise (1910-1952). 1947. Harper. (P.140)
--*Fish Head.* Fritz, Jean Guttery (1915-). 1954. Coward-McCann. (P.347)
--*Flying Ebony.* Vinton, Iris. 1947. Dodd, Mead & Company. (P.920)
--*Glenda.* Udry, Janice May (1928-). 1969. Harper & Row. (P.908)
--*Good Luck Duck.* DeJong, Meindert (1906-). 1950. Har-Row. (P.252)
--*A Good Man and His Good Wife.* Krauss, Ruth Ida (1911-). 1962. Harper & Row. (P.539)
--*The Happy Day.* Krauss, Ruth Ida (1911-). 1949. Har-Row. **Award: (RCM).** (P.539)
--*The Happy Day.* Krauss, Ruth Ida (1911-). 1980. Har-Row. (P.539)
--*How Come Elephants.* Simont, Marc (1915-). 1965. Har-Row. (P.826)
--*I Know a Magic House.* Schwartz, Julius (1907-). 1956. McGraw. (P.803)
--*I Know a Magic House.* Schwartz, Julius (1907-). 1956. Whittlesey House. (P.803)
--*In the Year of the Boar and Jackie Robinson.* 1st ed. Lord, Bette Bao (1938-). c.1984. Harper & Row. **Award: (ALA).** (P.584)
--*Isabella, Young Queen of Spain.* Criss, Mildred (1890-). 1941. Dodd, Mead & Company. (P.231)
--*Jareb.* Powell, Miriam. Morgan, Mary, pseud. 1952. Crowell. (P.736)
--*The Knight of the Golden Plain.* 1st ed. Hunter, Mollie (1922-). c.1983. Harper & Row. (P.474)
--*Lieutenant Colonel & the Gypsy.* Garcia Lorca, Federico (1898-1936). Simont, Marc (1915-), tr. 1971. Doubleday. (P.354)
--*Martin's Hats.* Blos, Joan Winsor (1928-). 1984. Morrow. (P.110)
--*Mimi Picture and Story.* Simont, Marc (1915-). 1954. Harper & Brothers. (P.826)
--*Mouse and Tim.* McNulty, Faith (1918-). c.1978. Harper & Row. (P.610)
--*My Father's Collie.* Kjelgaard, James Arthur (1910-1959). 1960. Dodd Mead. (P.530)
--*My Uncle Nikos.* Delton, Julie (1959-). c.1983. Crowell. (P.255)
--*Nate the Great.* Sharmat, Marjorie Weinman (1928-). 1972. Coward, McCann & Geoghegan. (P.815)
--*Nate the Great and the Fishy Prize.* Sharmat, Marjorie Weinman (1928-). c.1985. Coward-McCann. (P.815)
--*Nate the Great and the Lost List.* Sharmat, Marjorie Weinman (1928-). c.1975. Coward, McCann & Geoghegan. (P.815)
--*Nate the Great and the Missing Key.* Sharmat, Marjorie Weinman (1928-). c.1981. Coward, McCann & Geoghegan. (P.815)
--*Nate the Great and the Phony Clue.* Sharmat, Marjorie Weinman (1928-). c.1977. Coward, McCann & Geoghegan. (P.815)
--*Nate the Great and the Snowy Trail.* Sharmat, Marjorie Weinman (1928-). c.1982. Coward, McCann & Geoghegan. (P.815)
--*Nate the Great and the Sticky Case.* Sharmat, Marjorie Weinman (1928-). c.1978. Coward, McCann & Geoghegan. (P.815)
--*Nate the Great Goes Undercover.* Sharmat, Marjorie Weinman (1928-). 1974. Coward, McCann & Geoghegan. (P.815)
--*Nellie and Her Flying Crocodile.* Walsh, Chad (1914-). 1956. Harper. (P.928)
--*Nellie and Her Flying Crocodile.* Walsh, Chad (1914-). 1979, c.1956. Harper & Row. (P.928)
--*No More Monsters for Me!.* Parish, Peggy (1927-). 1982. Har-Row. (P.705)
--*No More Monsters for Me!.* Parish, Peggy (1927-). 1981. Harper & Row. (P.705)
--*The Philharmonic Gets Dressed.* 1st ed. Kuskin, Karla Seidman (1932-). c.1982. Harper & Row. **Award: (ALA).** (P.542)
--*Pigeon, Fly Home!.* Liggett, Thomas (1918-). 1956. Holiday House. (P.572)
--*The Pirate of Chatham Square: A Story of Old New York.* Sterne, Emma Gelders, Mrs. (1894-1971). 1939. Dodd, Mead & Company. (P.853)
--*Pocahontas, Young American Princess.* Criss, Mildred (1890-). 1943. Dodd, Mead & Company. (P.231)
--*Rainbow Book of American Folk Tales & Legends.* Leach, Maria (1892-1977). 1958. World Pub. (P.557)
--*Red Fairy Book.* new ed. Lang, Andrew (1844-1912), ed. 1948. Longmans, Green. (P.549)
--*Reddy Rattler and Pictures Easy Eagle.* Sharmat, Mitchell (1927-). c.1979. Doubleday. (P.815)
--*Sarah Deborah's Day.* Jackson, Charlotte E Cobden, Mrs. (1902-). 1941. Dodd, Mead & Company. (P.484)
--*The Seal That Couldn't Swim.* 1st ed. Ladas, Alexis. 1959. Little, Brown. (P.543)
--*Speak Up: More Rhymes of the Never Was and Always Is.* 1st ed. McCord, David Thompson Watson (1897-). c.1980. Little, Brown. (P.596)
--*The Star in the Pail.* McCord, David Thompson Watson (1897-). 1975. Little. (P.596)
--*The Star in the Pail: Poems.* 1st ed. McCord, David Thompson Watson (1897-). 1975. Little, Brown. (P.596)
--*Ten Copycats in a Boat & Other Riddles.* Schwartz, Alvin (1927-), retold by. 1980. Har-Row. (P.803)
--*The Thirteen Clocks.* Thurber, James Grover (1894-1961). 1950. Simon and Schuster. (P.890)
--*The Three-Day Enchantment.* Hunter, Mollie (1922-). c.1985. Harper & Row. (P.474)
--*Timmy and the Tiger.* Paradis, Marjorie Bartholomew (1886-1970). 1952. Harper. (P.705)
--*The Trail-Driving Rooster.* Gipson, Frederick Benjamin (1908-1973). 1955. Harper. (P.369)
--*Tree Is Nice.* Udry, Janice May (1928-). 1956. Har-Row. **Awards: (RCM); (ALA).** (P.908)
--*The Welcome.* Deutsch, Babette (1895-1982). 1942. Harper & Brothers. (P.261)
--*Wilderness Clearing.* Edmonds, Walter Dumaux (1903-). 1958. Dodd. (P.297)
--*Wolfie.* Chenery, Janet Dai (1923-). 1969. Harper & Row. (P.189)
--*The Wonderful O.* Thurber, James Grover (1894-1961). 1957. Simon and Schuster. (P.890)
--*The Wonderful O.* Thurber, James Grover (1894-1961). 1976, c.1957. Simon and Schuster. (P.890)

Simpson, Florence
--*My Caravan.* Grover, Eulalie Osgood (1873-1958), ed. 1976. Granger Bk. (P.397)

Simpson, Jean
--*The Humpty Dumpty Book.* Mother Goose. 1964. Golden Press. (P.667)
--*Train.* Fritz, Jean Guttery (1915-). 1969. G&D. (P.347)
--*What's in Mommy's Pocketbook.* McHargue, Georgess (1941-). 1971. Western Pub. (P.603)

Sims, Agnes, jt. illus. see Shepard, Mary Eleanor.

Sims, Blanche
--*December Secrets.* Giff, Patricia Reilly (1935-). 1986, c.1984. Delacorte Press. (P.366)
--*Eddie, Incorporated.* Naylor, Phyllis Reynolds (1933-). 1980. Atheneum. (P.676)
--*Jelly and the Spaceboat.* Parenteau, Shirley Laurolyn (1935-). 1981. Coward, McCann & Geoghegan. (P.705)
--*Me and Katie (the Pest).* Martin, Ann Matthews (1955-). c.1985. Holiday House. (P.624)
--*Miss Plunkett to the Rescue.* Flory, Jane Trescott (1917-). 1983. Houghton Mifflin. (P.332)
--*Mrs.* Minetta's Carpool. Spurr, Elizabeth. 1985. Atheneum. (P.845)
--*Mystery of the Disappearing Dogs.* Brenner, Barbara Johnes (1925-). c.1982. Knopf. (P.129)
--*Mystery of the Plumed Serpent.* Brenner, Barbara Johnes (1925-). 1981, c.1972. Knopf : Distributed by Random House. (P.129)
--*Nutty for President.* 1st ed. Hughes, Dean (1943-). 1981. Atheneum. (P.470)
--*Oliver and the Lucky Duck.* McBrier, Page. c.1985. Troll Associates. (P.594)
--*Oliver's Lucky Day.* McBrier, Page. c.1985. Troll Associates. (P.594)
--*Purple Climbing Days.* Giff, Patricia Reilly (1935-). 1986, c.1985. Delacorte Press. (P.366)
--*Say "Cheese".* Giff, Patricia Reilly (1935-). 1986, c.1985. Delacorte Press. (P.366)
--*Secret of the Magic Potion.* Bolton, Elizabeth. c.1985. Troll Associates. (P.113)
--*Sometimes I Wish I Were Mindy.* Levine, Abby & Levine, Sarah. 1986. A. Whitman & Co. (P.568)
--*The Spook Birds.* Bunting, Anne Evelyn (1928-). c.1981. A. Whitman. (P.150)
--*Stage Fright.* Martin, Ann Matthews (1955-). 1984. Holiday. (P.624)
--*The Valentine Star.* Giff, Patricia Reilly (1935-). 1986, c.1985. Delacorte Press. (P.366)

Sims, Deborah
--*Harold and the Dinosaur Mystery.* Frost, Erica, pseud. (1930-). Supraner, Robyn. c.1979. Troll Associates. (P.348)
--*Mike's New Bike.* Greydanus, Rose. 1980. Troll Assocs. (P.389)
--*Mud Pies.* Grey, Judith. c.1981. Troll Associates. (P.389)
--*Three Little Witches.* Gordon, Sharon. 1980. Troll Assocs. (P.377)
--*The Tooth Fairy.* Peters, Sharon. c.1981. Troll Associates. (P.720)
--*What a Dog.* Gordon, Sharon. 1980. Troll Assocs. (P.377)

Sims, Lynda
--*Old Friends, New Friends.* North, Emily. 1980. Childrens Press. (P.686)

Simunek, Kate
--*Tabletop Theatres.* Cochrane, Louise Morley (1918-). 1974, c.1973. Plays, Inc. (P.205)

Sinclair, Cecilia
--*West African Folk-Tales.* Barker, William Henry (1882-1929) & Sinclair, Cecilia. Roberts, Hermese, frwd. by. 1972. Metro Books. (P.72)

Sinclair, McDonald
--*More Stories from the Arabian Nights.* Burton, Richard, Sir (1821-1890), tr. from Arabic. Franklyn, Julian (1899-1970), ed. 1957. Associated Booksellers. (P.342)

Singer, Gloria (1949-)
--*At the Beach.* Tobias, Tobi (1938-). c.1978. D. McKay. (P.893)
--*The Blue Poodle Mystery.* Hope, Laura Lee, pseud. Stratemeyer Syndicate. c.1980. Wanderer Books. (P.459)
--*Summer of the Stallion.* Hanson, June Andrea (1941-). c.1979. Macmillan. (P.411)

Singer, Mel
--*The Black Stallion Mystery.* Farley, Walter Lorimer (1915-). 1957. Random House. (P.317)

Sinnickson, Tom
--*Cowman's Kingdom.* 1st ed. Collier, Edmund. 1952. Aladdin Books. (P.209)
--*Raggedy Andy's Surprise.* Gruelle, John Barton (1880-1938). 1953. Wonder Books. (P.397)
--*Raggedy Ann and Marcella's First Day at School.* Gruelle, John Barton (1880-1938). 1952. Wonder Books. (P.397)
--*Raggedy Ann's Merriest Christmas.* Gruelle, John Barton (1880-1938). 1952. Wonder Books. (P.398)

Sirdofsky, Sam
--*Katie and the Catastrophe.* Lloyd, Mary Norris (1908-). 1968. Reilly & Lee. (P.578)

Sis, Peter
--*Bean Boy.* Shannon, George William Bones (1952-). 1984. Greenwillow. (P.814)
--*Jed and the Space Bandits.* Marzollo, Jean & Marzollo, Claudio. 1985. Dial Books for Young Readers. (P.627)
--*Stories to Solve: Folktales from Around the World.* Shannon, George William Bones (1952-). c.1985. Greenwillow Books. (P.814)

Skaar, Grace Marion Brown, jt. illus. see Bloch, Lucienne.

Skaar, Grace Marion Brown (1903-)
--*A Boy and His Horse.* Skaar, Grace Marion Brown (1903-). 1958. Scott. (P.827)
--*The Little Red House.* Skaar, Grace Marion Brown (1903-). 1955. W. R. Scott, Inc. (P.827)
--*Nothing but Cats and All About Dogs: Two Very Young Stories, 2 vols.* in 1. Skaar, Grace Marion Brown (1903-). 1966, c.1949. Wm. R. Scott. (P.827)
--*The Very Little Dog.* Skaar, Grace Marion Brown (1903-). c.1949. W. R. Scott. (P.827)
--*What Do the Animals Say?.* Skaar, Grace Marion Brown (1903-). 1968. Young Scott Books. (P.827)

Skaff, Lamese M.
--*Tim and the Green-Eyed Monster.* Reinecke, Esther E. 1959. T. S. Denison. (P.757)
--*Tim & The Green-Eyed Monster.* Reinecke, Esther E. N.D. T. S. Denison & Co. (P.757)
--*Tim Listens and Learns.* Reinecke, Esther E. 1960. Denison. (P.757)

Skar, Cynthia S.
--*Bobbi Saves Christmas!.* Sharp, Mary. 1981. Bobbi Ent. (P.816)

Skardinski, Stanley
--*The Beggars' Christmas.* Aurelio, John. c.1979. Paulist Press. (P.55)
--*The Boy Who Stole the Christmas Star.* Aurelio, John. 1981. Crossroad. (P.55)
--*The Drought on Ziax II.* Morressy, John (1930-). 1978. Walker. (P.664)
--*The Humans of Ziax II.* Morressy, John (1930-). 1974. Walker. (P.664)
--*Trudel's Siege.* Alcott, Louisa May (1832-1888). 1976. McGraw-Hill. (P.18)

Skargon, Yvonne
--*Plant Facts and Fancies.* Woods, Sylvia. 1985. Faber and Faber. (P.977)

Skauge, Sven
--*The Tale of Tiny Tutak.* Wiig, Hanna. 1957. Lippincott. (P.958)

Skeaping, John Rattenbury (1901-1980)
--*A Squirrel Called Rufus.* Church, Richard Thomas (1893-1972). 1946. The John C. Winston Company. (P.195)

Skeen, John R.
--*The Froggy Fairy Book.* 2d ed. Biddle, Anthony Joseph Drexel (1874-). 1897. D. Biddle. (P.101)
--*The Froggy Fairy Book.* 3d ed. Biddle, Anthony Joseph Drexel (1874-). 1897. D. Biddle. (P.101)
--*The Froggy Fairy Book.* Biddle, Anthony Joseph Drexel (1874-). 1896. Drexel-Biddle & Bradley Publishing Company. (P.101)

Skelton, J. R.
--*Stories of Beowulf: Told to the Children.* Marshall, Henrietta Elizabeth (1876-). Chiholm, Louey, ed. 1908. T. C. & E. C. Jack. (P.623)

Skelton, P., jt. illus. see Paton, Joseph Noel, Sir.

Skillen, Peggy Owens
--*Songs the Sandman Sings.* Reed, Gwendolyn Elizabeth (1932-), compiled by. 1969. Atheneum. (P.753)

Skilleter, Andrew, et al.
--*Galactic Adventures.* Baker, Fred, et al. 1980. Rand. (P.62)

Skimore, T. D., jt. illus. see Wood, Franklin T.

Skinner, T.
--*Tommy with the Big Tents.* Root, Harvey Woods (1876-). c.1924. Harper & Brothers. (P.776)

Skoog, Paul R.
--*A Trip to the Moon: A/Story in Rhyme for Children.* 1st ed. Tyner, Frederick D. 1939. The Author. (P.907)

Skoog, Roberta
--*A Merry Christmas to You ... and a Happy Chanukah, Too!.* Boonin, Harriet. 1972. Schmitt, Hall & McCreary. (P.117)

Skotting, Aase
--*Forest and Fiords.* Bailey, Bernadine Freeman, Mrs. (1901-). 1952. Beckley-Cardy. (P.59)

Skrenda, Alfred
--*Lefty Leighton.* Fitzhugh, Percy Keese (1876-). c.1930. Grosset & Dunlap. (P.329)

Skrocki, Edward A.
--*The Adventures of Starbeem and Re-Koil.* Donovan, D. J. 1967. House of Ideas. (P.280)
--*Now Mildred.* Donovan, D. J. 1968. House of Ideas. (P.280)

Skurzynski, Gloria Joan (1930-)
--*Swept in the Wave of Terror.* Skurzynski, Gloria Joan (1930-). c.1985. Lothrop, Lee & Shepard Books. (P.828)

Slackman, Charles B. (1934-)
--*Angry Kate.* Janeway, Elizabeth (1913-). 1963. Harper & Row. (P.489)
--*Famous Sally.* Jackson, Shirley (1919-1965). 1966. Harlin Quist; Distributed by Crown Publishers. (P.486)
--*I Hate to Take a Bath.* Barrett, Judith (1941-). 1975. Atheneum Publishers. (P.75)
--*I Hate to Take a Bath.* Barrett, Judith (1941-). 1975. Four Winds Press. (P.75)

Slade, C. Arnold
--*Bible for Children.* Hill, Margaret Livingston. N.D. David McKay Co. (P.444)

Slagboom, Teco
--*Spiders are Spinners.* Rosen, Ellsworth. 1968. Houghton Mifflin. (P.777)

Slater, Cher
--*Magic-Go-Round.* Bell, Elizabeth Rose (1912-). 1974. Childrens Press. (P.90)
--*The Spooky Hand Mystery.* Lyles, Vina Honish (1935-). 1973. Childrens Press. (P.591)

Slater, Christopher
--*Big Snowy.* Slater, Jim (1929-). 1981. Random. (P.829)
--*Bignose.* Slater, Jim (1929-). c.1979. Random House. (P.829)
--*The Great Gulper.* Slater, Jim (1929-). 1981, c.1979. Random House. (P.829)
--*The Tricky Troggle.* Slater, Jim (1929-). 1981. Random. (P.829)

Slattery, Sarah J.
--*The Happiest One.* Ilich, John (1933-). c.1981. Bengal Press. (P.479)

Sleight, Katy
--*I Can.* Tarsky, Sue. 1985. Random House. (P.878)
--*Who Goes Splash?.* Tarsky, Sue. 1985. Random House. (P.878)

Sloan, Donna
--*Fat Cat Coloring & Limerick Bk.* Whyte, Malcolm Kenneth, Jr. (1933-). 1967. Troubador Pr. (P.955)
--*Love Bug Coloring & Limerick Bk.* Whyte, Malcolm Kenneth, Jr. (1933-). 1968. Troubador Pr. (P.955)

Sloan, Ellen
--*ABC Easter Bunny.* DeLage, Ida (1918-). c.1979. Garrard Pub. Co. (P.252)
--*ABC Fire Dogs.* DeLage, Ida (1918-). 1977. Garrard Pub. Co. (P.252)
--*Frannie's Flower.* DeLage, Ida (1918-). c.1979. Garrard Pub. Co. (P.252)

--*Nuts to You & Nuts to Me: An Alphabet of Poems.* Solbert, Romaine G.. Hoberman, Mary Ann (1930-). 1974. Knopf; Distributed by Random House. (P.448)
--*Poems Make Pictures: Pictures Make Poems.* Solbert, Romaine G.. Rimanelli, Giose (1926-) & Pimsleur, Paul (1927-1976). 1972. Pantheon Books. (P.765)
--*The Pushcart War.* Solbert, Romaine G.. Merrill, Jean. 1985, c.1964. Harper & Row. (P.642)
--*The Pushcart War.* Solbert, Romaine G.. Merrill, Jean Fairbanks (1923-). 1964. Children's Press. (P.642)
--*Pushcart War.* Solbert, Romaine G.. Merrill, Jean Fairbanks (1923-). 1964. E M Hale. (P.642)
--*The Pushcart War.* Solbert, Romaine G.. Merrill, Jean Fairbanks (1923-). N.D. Grosset & Dunlap. (P.642)
--*The Pushcart War.* Solbert, Romaine G.. Merrill, Jean Fairbanks (1923-). 1964. W. R. Scott. **Award: (ALA).** (P.642)
--*Red Riding.* Solbert, Romaine G.. Merrill, Jean Fairbanks (1923-). 1968. Pantheon. (P.642)
--*Red Riding: A Story of How Katy Tells Tony a Story Because It Is Raining.* Solbert, Romaine G.. Merrill, Jean Fairbanks (1923-). 1968. Pantheon Books. (P.642)
--*Shan's Lucky Knife.* Solbert, Romaine G.. Merrill, Jean Fairbanks (1923-). 1960. W. R. Scott. (P.642)
--*Snug in the Snow.* Solbert, Romaine G.. Low, Elizabeth Hammond (1898-). 1963. Little. (P.588)
--*A Song for Gar.* Solbert, Romaine G.. Merrill, Jean Fairbanks (1923-). 1957. Whittlesey House. (P.642)
--*The Superlative Horse.* Solbert, Romaine G.. Merrill, Jean Fairbanks (1923-). 1961. W. R. Scott. **Award: (ALA).** (P.642)
--*Thirty Two Feet of Insides.* Solbert, Romaine G.. Solbert, Ronni, pseud. (1925-). Solbert, Romaine G.. 1970. Pantheon. (P.840)
--*The Travels of Marco.* Solbert, Romaine G.. Merrill, Jean Fairbanks (1923-). 1956. Knopf. (P.642)
--*Travels of Marco.* Solbert, Romaine G.. Merrill, Jean Fairbanks (1923-). 1965. Knopf. (P.642)
--*The Tree House of Jimmy Domino.* Solbert, Romaine G.. Merrill, Jean Fairbanks (1923-). 1954. Coward-McCann, Inc. (P.642)
--*The Tree House of Jimmy Domino.* Solbert, Romaine G.. Merrill, Jean Fairbanks (1923-). 1955. Oxford University Press. (P.642)
--*The Tree House of Jimmy Domino.* Solbert, Romaine G.. Merrill, Jean Fairbanks (1923-). 1955. Walck. (P.642)
--*The Two Runaways.* Solbert, Romaine G.. Havard, Aline (1889-). 1959. Lothrop, Lee & Shepard Co. (P.421)
--*The Very Nice Things.* Solbert, Romaine G.. Merrill, Jean Fairbanks (1923-). 1959. Harper. (P.642)
--*White Monkey King: A Chinese Fable.* Solbert, Romaine G.. Wriggins, Sally Hovey (1922-), retold by. Wu, Ch'eng-En, adapted by. c.1977. Pantheon Books. (P.980)
--*Woody and Me.* Solbert, Romaine G.. Neville, Mary (1915-). 1966. Pantheon Books. (P.679)
--*The Woover.* Solbert, Romaine G.. Merrill, Jean Fairbanks (1923-). 1952. Coward-McCann. (P.642)
--*Youngest Camel.* Solbert, Romaine G.. Boyle, Kay (1903-). 1959. Har-Row. (P.123)
--*The Youngest Camel: Reconsidered and Rewritten.* Solbert, Romaine G.. Boyle, Kay (1903-). 1967, c.1959. Harper. (P.123)

Sole, Vendrell Carme (1944-)
--*The Child Who Cried in the Night.* Garcia Sanchez, Jose Luis & Pacheco, Miguel Angel. 1979. Methuen Inc. (P.354)
--*Elephants Never Jump: Story.* Easton, Violet. c.1985. Atlantic Monthly Press. (P.294)
--*The Giant Child.* Garcia Sanchez, Jose Luis & Pacheco, Miguel Angel. 1979, c.1978. Methuen. (P.354)
--*Jon's Moon.* Sole-Vendrell, Carme (1944-). 1982. Schocken. (P.840)
--*What's Behind That Tree?.* Williams, Leslie (1941-). 1984. Bedrick/Blackie. (P.964)

Solem, Dan
--*The Little House on Wheels.* Benedict, Steve (1899-). N.D. C. (P.93)

Solenewitsch, George
--*Our Sun and the Worlds Around It: Planets, Moons, Comets, and Other Wonders of the Solar System.* Lyon, Jene. c.1957. Simon and Schuster. (P.592)

Soles, William
--*The Sword with the Golden Hilt.* Evernden, Margery (1916-). 1950. Caxton Printers. (P.312)

Solonovich, George
--*Do You Know About Stars?.* Freeman, Mae Blacker (1907-). 1970. Random House. (P.344)

Solum, Suzanne
--*Such a Fuss with a Hippopotamus.* Reed, Betty Jane (1921-). 1974. T. S. Denison. (P.753)

Somerfield, Thomas (1870-)
--*The Rajah of Gungra.* Marsh, D. E. (1900-). 1937. David McKay Company. (P.621)

Somerfield, Thomas (1870-) & Mills, Reginald
--*The Raid of the Terribore: A Modern Adventure Story.* Mackworth, John Dolben (1887-). c.1937. J. B. Lippincott Company. (P.607)
--*The Secret Aeroplane.* Marsh, D. E. (1900-). 1937. David McKay Company. (P.621)

Sommer, Edwin G.
--*The Golden Bird and Other Stories.* Gibson, Katharine (1893-). Walker, Caroline Burnite, intro. by. 1927. The Macmillan Company. (P.366)
--*The Golden Bird and Other Stories.* Gibson, Katharine (1893-). Walker, Caroline Burnite, intro. by. 1935. The Macmillan Company. (P.366)
--*Jane and Jerry.* Whiteman, Edna. 1929. T. Nelson & Sons. (P.954)

Sommers, Linda
--*Billy's Basketball.* Tester, Sylvia Root (1939-). c.1976: Child's World. (P.883)
--*Carla-Too-Little.* Tester, Sylvia Root (1939-). c.1976. Child's World. (P.883)
--*Jill Wins a Friend.* Rivers, Kay McClanahan (1944-). c.1976. Child's World. (P.766)
--*The Little Lost Lamb.* Odor, Ruth Shannon (1926-). 1979. Childs World. (P.690)
--*The Shoemaker and the Christmas Elves: A Folk Tale from Germany.* Grimm, Jakob Ludwig Karl (1785-1863) & Grimm, Wilhelm Karl (1786-1859). Moncure, Jane Belk (1926-), retold by. c.1980. Child's World. (P.394)

Sommerschield, Rose
--*Dogs Don't Belong on Beds.* Bloome, Enid P. (1925-). 1971. Doubleday. (P.110)
--*London Villains Falling Down.* Caufield, Donald E & Caufield, Lora Joan. 1969. Doubleday. (P.178)

Somppi, Lilly
--*Little Lamb.* Martin, Dahris Butterworth. 1938. Harper & Brothers. (P.624)
--*The Runaway Deer.* Fleury, Barbara Frances (1907-). 1938. The Macmillan Co. (P.332)

Sondern, Ferd A.
--*Adventures with the Buttonwoods.* Beiler, Edna (1923-). 1960. Herald Pr. (P.89)
--*Finnerty Flynn and the Singing City.* Gesner, Clark (1938-). 1969. Lancelot Press. (P.365)
--*Mitsy Buttonwood.* Beiler, Edna (1923-). c.1963. Herald Press. (P.89)

Sono, Kazuhiko
--*Origami Storybook: Japanese Paper-Folding Play.* Sakade, Florence. N.D. C E Tuttle. (P.790)

Sookikian, Charles J.
--*Stranded!.* Bodie, Idella Fallow (1925-). 1984. Sandlapper Pub Co. (P.112)

Soper, Eileen Alice (1905-)
--*Five Go to Smuggler's Top: Another Adventure of the Four Children And Timmy the Dog.* Blyton, Enid Mary (1897-1968). 1960. Reilly & Lee. (P.110)
--*Five on the Track of a Spook Train.* Blyton, Enid Mary (1897-1968). 1972. Atheneum. (P.110)
--*Five Run Away Together: The Third Story of the Adventures of the Four Children and Their Dog.* Blyton, Enid Mary (1897-1968). 1960. Reilly & Lee Co. (P.111)
--*The Song of Lambert.* De La Roche, Mazo (1885-1961). 1956, c.1955. Little, Brown. (P.254)

Soper, George (1870-)
--*The Water Babies: A Fairy Tale for a Land Baby.* Kingsley, Charles (1819-1875). N.D. Baker & Taylor Co. (P.525)

Sopher, Aaron (1905-)
--*Princess Mary of Maryland.* Agle, Nan Hayden (1905-). N.D. Gale Reprints. (P.14)
--*Princess Mary of Maryland.* Agle, Nan Hayden (1905-). 1956. Scribner. (P.14)
--*Princess Mary of Maryland.* Agle, Nan Hayden (1905-). 1967, c.1956. Tradition Press. (P.14)

Sopko, Eugen
--*The Miller, His Son, and Their Donkey: A Fable from Aesop.* Aesopus. 1985. North-South Books : Distributed in the U.S. by Holt, Rinehart, and Winston. (P.14)
--*Townsfolk and Countryfolk.* Sopko, Eugen. 1982. Faber and Faber. (P.841)

Sorel, Edward (1929-)
--*The Duck in the Gun.* Cowley, Cassia Joy (1936-). 1969. Doubleday. (P.225)
--*The Goings on at Little Wishful.* Miller, Warren. 1959. Little, Brown. (P.649)
--*Gwendolyn and the Weathercock.* Sherman, Nancy (1931-). 1963. Golden Press. **Award: (NYT).** (P.819)
--*Gwendolyn, the Miracle Hen.* Sherman, Nancy (1931-). c.1961. Golden Press. (P.819)
--*King Carlo of Capri.* Freely Adapted from Riquet with the Tuft of Hair by Charles Perrault. 1st ed. Miller, Warren, ed. Perrault, Charles (1628-1703). 1958. Harcourt, Brace. (P.719)
--*Magical Storybook.* Williams, Jay (1914-1978). 1972. American Heritage Press. (P.963)
--*Pablo Paints a Picture.* 1st ed. Miler, Warren. 1959. Little, Brown. **Award: (NYT).** (P.644)
--*The Pirates of Penzance.* Gilbert, William Schwenck, Sir (1836-1911) & Sullivan, Arthur Seymour, Sir (1842-1900). Botsford, Ward, adapted by. 1981. Random. (P.367)
--*The Pirates of Penzance.* Botsford, Ward & Gilbert, William Schwenck, Sir (1836-1911). 1981. Random House. (P.119)
--*What's Good for a Five-Year-Old?.* 1st ed. Cole, William Rossa (1919-). 1969. Holt, Rinehart & Winston. (P.208)

Sorenson, Elizabeth Ann & DeWitt, Jayne Whistler
--*Good Neighbors.* McCurry, Bertha B. Moore (1890-). 1950, c.1949. Moody Press. (P.597)

Sorine, Daniel S., photos by.
--*Our Ballet Class.* Sorine, Stephanie Riva (1954-). 1981. Knopf. (P.841)

Sorotzkim, Bracha
--*Avi Names His Price.* Weinbach, Sheindel. 1976. Feldheim. (P.941)

Sorrentino, Santo
--*The Mystery of Rawhide Gap.* Scott, Dan, pseud. Stratemeyer Syndicate. 1960. Grosset & Dunlap. (P.804)

Sotomayor, Antonio (1902-)
--*The Best Birthday.* 1st ed. Hawkins, Helena Ann Quail (1905-). 1954. Doubleday. (P.422)
--*Indian Tales from Guatemala.* Jessup, Marie Hendrick & Simpson, Lesley Byrd. 1936. Charles Scribner's Sons. (P.492)
--*Khasa Goes to the Fiesta.* Sotomayor, Antonio (1902-). 1967. Doubleday. (P.841)
--*Treasure of the Tortoise Islands.* Von Hagen, Victor Wolfgang (1908-) & Hawkins, Quail. c.1940. Harcourt, Brace and Company. (P.921)

Soucheck, Margaret A.
--*What is Pink?.* A Poem. Rossetti, Christina Georgina (1830-1894). 1963. Holt, Rinehart and Winston. (P.779)

Souder, Jim
--*The Diary of an Acorn.* Burdette, Myron (1909-). 1974. Dorrance. (P.151)

Southall, Joseph E.
--*The Story of Blue Beard.* Perrault, Charles (1628-1703). 1895. Lawrence and Bullen. (P.719)

Southard, Frank R. (1882-)
--*The Flying Boat.* McLean, Robert Norris (1882-). c.1935. Friendship Press. (P.608)

Southby, Logi
--*The Hostages and Other Stories for Boys and Girls.* Mitchison, Naomi Margaret Haldane, Mrs. (1897-). c.1931. Harcourt, Brace and Company. (P.652)

Southern, Richard, jt. illus. see Hilder, Rowland.

Souza, Paul
--*Andy and the Wild Wood Ducks.* Shott, Mayo. 1959. Melmont Pub. (P.821)
--*Roy Rogers and Dale Evans in Big Toppers.* c.1956. Whitman Pub. (P.842)
--*Roy Rogers and the Desert Treasure.* Sankey, Alice Ann-Susan (1910-). c.1954. Whitman Pub. Co. (P.793)
--*Walt Disney's Stormy.* Disney, Walt, Productions. c.1954. Whitman Pub. Co. (P.270)

Sovek, Charles
--*Amazing Adventures.* Verdick, Mary Peyton (1923-), ed. 1972. Xerox Ed Pubns. (P.917)
--*The Ghost Ship.* Verdick, Mary Peyton (1923-), ed. 1976. Xerox Ed Pubns. (P.917)
--*Old Yellow Eyes.* Mooney, Thomas J. (1927-), ed. 1976. Xerox Ed Pubns. (P.659)
--*The Third Arm.* Otfinoski, Steven. Verdick, Mary Peyton (1923-), ed. N.D. Xerox Ed Pubns. (P.697)
--*Varoom.* Mooney, Thomas J. (1927-), ed. 1973. Xerox Ed Pubns. (P.659)
--*Varoom!.* Eight Short Stories of Wheels and Speed. Mooney, Thomas J. (1927-), ed. 1972. Xerox Education Publications. (P.659)

Sowell, Floyd (1929-)
--*Adam in Blunderland.* 1st ed. Teague, Bob, pseud. (1929-). Teague, Robert. 1971. Doubleday. (P.881)
--*Dogs of Fear: A Story of Modern Africa.* Nagenda, Musa, pseud. (1928-). Howard, Moses Leon. 1972. Holt, Rinehart and Winston. (P.675)
--*A Kite for Bennie.* Gray, Genevieve Stuck (1920-). 1972. McGraw-Hill. (P.383)
--*The Treasure of the Muleteer, and Other Spanish Tales.* Jimenez-Landi, Antonio. Blackburn, Paul, tr. 1974. Doubleday. (P.493)
--*Walk Together: Five Plays on Human Rights.* Henderson, Nancy Wallace (1916-). 1972. Messner. (P.433)

Sowell, William R., jt. illus. see Vosburgh, Leonard W.

Sowerby, J. G. & Emmerson, H. H.
--*Afternoon Tea.* Yonge, Charlotte Mary (1823-1901). N.D. R Worthington. (P.987)

Sowerby, Millicent
--*Alice in Wonderland.* Carroll, Lewis, pseud. (1832-1898). Dodgson, Charles Lutwidge. N.D. Duffield. (P.172)
--*Bumbletoes.* Sowerby, Katherine Githa. N.D. Duffield & Co. (P.842)
--*A Child's Garden of Verses.* Stevenson, Robert Louis (1850-1894). 1908. C. Scribner's Sons. (P.856)
--*Cinderella.* Sowerby, Katherine Githa. N.D. George H Doran. (P.842)
--*The Dainty Book.* Sowerby, Katherine Githa. N.D. George H Doran & Co. (P.842)
--*The Gay Book.* Sowerby, Katherine Githa & Joan, Natalie. 1935. Artists and Writers Guild. (P.842)
--*The Glad Book.* authorized. Joan, Natalie & Sowerby, Githa. c.1935. Artists and Writers Guild, Inc. (P.493)
--*Grimm's Fairy Tales.* Grimm, Jakob Ludwig Karl (1785-1863) & Grimm, Wilhelm Karl (1786-1859). Sowerby, Katherine Githa, retold by. 1910. Frederick A. Stokes. (P.392)
--*Little Plays for Little People.* Sowerby, Katherine Githa. N.D. George H Doran. (P.842)
--*Little Plays for Little People.* Sowerby, Katherine Githa. N.D. Hodder & Stoughton. (P.842)
--*Little Stories for Little People.* Sowerby, Katherine Githa. N.D. George H Doran & Co. (P.842)
--*The Merry Book: A Dainty Little Book of Verse and Pictures.* Sowerby, Katherine Githa. N.D. George H Doran. (P.842)
--*My Birthday: The Fortune of the Day in Picture and Rhyme.* Sowerby, Katherine Githa. N.D. George H Doran. (P.842)
--*Poems of Childhood.* Sowerby, Katherine Githa. N.D. George H Doran. (P.842)
--*The Pretty Book.* Sowerby, Katherine Githa. N.D. George H Doran. (P.842)
--*The Quaint Book.* Sowerby, Katherine Githa. N.D. George H Doran. (P.842)

Sowter, Nita
--*Apple Pie.* Wellington, Anne. 1978. Prentice-Hall. (P.943)

Soyer, Rebecca S.
--*The Adventures of Yemima, and Other Stories.* 1st ed. Soyer, Abraham (1867-1940). Beagle, Rebecca S., tr. Beagle, Peter Soyer (1939-) Soyer, Raphael (1899-) 1979. Viking Press. (P.842)

Spades, Jean
--*Maggie in Fashion:.* Advertising, Display, Promotion. Pennoyer, Sara Waller (1900-). 1961. Dodd, Mead. (P.716)

Spaenkuch, August
--*A Freshman Scout at College: A Story of Life at Columbia at the Time of the Abolition of Football.* Jenkins, Marshall. 1914. D. Appleton and Company. (P.491)

Spalding, Frank
--*Yea, Sheriton!.* Pierrot, George Francis (1898-1980). 1925. Doubleday, Page & Company. (P.725)

Spalding, Tony
--*Snow White and the Seven Dwarfs.* Daniels, Patricia, ed. c.1980. Raintree Childrens Books. (P.241)

Spaliviero, Franco, jt. illus. see Scarato, Giorgio.

Spandorf, Lily
--*Arthur, the White House Mouse.* 1st ed. Blair, Anne Denton. c.1975. Media/America. (P.105)

Spanfeller, James John (1930-)
--*The Blue Fairy Book: Selected Tales from the Collection.* Lang, Andrew (1844-1912), ed. 1969. Junior Deluxe Editions. (P.548)
--*The Boy Who Wasn't Lonely.* Parker, Richard (1915-). c.1965. Bobbs. (P.706)
--*A Crazy Flight, and Other Poems.* Livingston, Myra Cohn (1926-). 1969. Harcourt, Brace & World. (P.578)
--*Doug Meets the Nutcracker.* Hooks, William H. (1921-). c.1977. F. Warne. (P.459)
--*Drop Dead.* Cunningham, Julia Woolfolk (1916-). 1965. Pantheon. (P.235)
--*Emma in Winter.* Farmer, Penelope Jane (1939-). 1966. Harcourt, Brace & World. (P.318)
--*Four Way Stop, and Other Poems.* Livingston, Myra Cohn (1926-). 1976. Atheneum. (P.578)
--*God Loves You: Our Family's Favorite Stories & Prayers.* Marshall, Sarah Catherine Wood (1914-1983). 1967. McGraw. (P.623)
--*Indian Hill.* Bulla, Clyde Robert (1914-). 1963. Crowell. (P.148)
--*Jo's Boys.* Alcott, Louisa May (1832-1888). 1962. Collier Books. (P.17)
--*Little Men: Life at Plumfield with Jo's Boys.* Alcott, Louisa May (1832-1888). 1962. Collier Books. (P.17)
--*Macaroon.* Cunningham, Julia Woolfolk (1916-). 1965. Pantheon Books. (P.235)
--*The Malibu and Other Poems.* Livingston, Myra Cohn (1926-). 1972. Atheneum. (P.578)

--*Porter, the Pouting Pigeon.* Holland, Joyce Flint (1921-). 1960. T. S. Denison. (P.455)
--*Pudgy, the Porpoise.* Sandberg, Harold William (1902-). 1960. T. S. Denison. (P.791)
--*Randy Raindrop Takes a Trip.* Shigley, Forest Dwight (1930-). 1960. Denison. (P.820)
--*Rocky: The Rocket Mouse.* Bergey, Alyce Mae (1934-). 1961. T. S. Denison. (P.96)
--*The Round Robin.* Holland, Joyce Flint (1921-). 1960. T. S. Denison. (P.455)
--*Snowshoe.* Anderson, Edna A. 1961. T. S. Denison. (P.39)
--*A Special Day.* Bomar, Frances M. N.D. Denison. (P.113)
--*Timmy the Timid Turtle.* Holland, Joyce Flint (1921-). 1960. T. S. Denison. (P.455)

Spiegle, Dan
--*The Trap.* DuBay, W. 1983. Western Pub. (P.286)

Spier, Jo
--*Black Within & Red Without: A Book of Riddles.* Morrison, Lillian (1917-), compiled by. 1953. Har-Row. (P.665)
--*The Musical Night Before Christmas.* Moore, Clement Clarke (1779-1863). 1955. J. C. Winston Co. (P.660)
--*The Squirrel and the Harp.* DeJong, David Cornel (1905-1967). 1966. Macmillan. (P.252)
--*The Story of Louis Pasteur.* Malkus, Alida Wright Sims, Mrs. (1899-). 1952. Grosset & Dunlap. (P.614)

Spier, Peter Edward (1927-)
--*And So My Garden Grows.* Spier, Peter Edward (1927-). 1969. Doubleday. (P.844)
--*The Book of Jonah.* Spier, Peter Edward (1927-), retold by. 1985. Doubleday. (P.844)
--*Bored-Nothing to Do!.* Spier, Peter Edward (1927-). c.1978. Doubleday. (P.844)
--*Boss Chombale.* Hubbard, Margaret Carson. c.1957. Crowell. (P.469)
--*Boy Overboard!.* Grant, Captain George Hook (1896-). 1961. Little, Brown and Company. (P.382)
--*A Cabin for the Mary Christmas.* 1st ed. Amrein, Vera R. 1955. Harcourt, Brace. (P.33)
--*Cargo for Jennifer.* 1st ed. Vetter, Marjorie Meyn. 1954. Longmans, Green. (P.919)
--*Cocoa.* 1st ed. Otto, Margaret Glover (1909-1976). 1953. Holt. (P.698)
--*The Cow Who Fell in the Canal.* 1st ed. Krasilovsky, Phyllis (1926-). c.1957. Doubleday. (P.537)
--*The Erie Canal.* Spier, Peter Edward (1927-). 1973, c.1970. Doubleday. (P.844)
--*Esmeralda Ahoy!.* 1st ed. Fairholme, Elizabeth (1910-) & Powell, Pamela. 1959. Doubleday. (P.316)
--*The Fox Went Out on a Chilly Night.* Spier, Peter Edward (1927-). 1961. Doubleday. **Awards: (ALA); (RCM).** (P.844)
--*Hans Brinker: Or The Silver Skates.* Dodge, Mary Elizabeth Mapes, Mrs. (1831-1905). 1958. Scribner. (P.276)
--*Hector, The Stowaway Dog.* Dobson, Kenneth. 1958. Little, Brown. (P.276)
--*Here & There: One Hundred Poems About Places.* Parker, Elinor Milnor (1906-), compiled by. 1967. T Y Crowell. (P.706)
--*Hippolyte: Crab King.* Anderson, Joy Conrad (1928-). 1956. Hale. (P.39)
--*Hippolyte: Crab King.* Anderson, Joy Conrad (1928-). 1956. Harcourt, Brace. (P.39)
--*Hurrah, We're Outward Bound!.* 1st ed. Spier, Peter Edward (1927-). 1968. Doubleday. (P.844)
--*Island City: Adventures in Old New York.* Davis, Lavinia Riker, Mrs. (1909-1961). c.1961. Doubleday. (P.246)
--*Last Hurdle.* Franklin, Freida Kenyon (1921-). Brown, F. K., pseud. 1970. Apollo Eds. (P.342)
--*Last Hurdle.* Franklin, Frieda Kenyon (1921-). 1953. Crowell. (P.342)
--*Little Lord Fauntleroy.* Burnett, Frances Hodgson, Mrs. (1849-1924). 1954. Junior Deluxe Editions. (P.155)
--*The Little Riders.* Shemin, Margaretha Hoeneveld (1928-). 1963. Coward-McCann. (P.818)
--*London Bridge Is Falling Down!.* Spier, Peter Edward (1927-). 1967. Doubleday. **Award: (BGH).** (P.844)
--*The Mystery of Mont Saint-Michel.* 1st ed. Rouze, Michel. 1955. Holt. (P.781)
--*The Mystery of Willet.* Watkins, Richard. 1959. T. Nelson. (P.935)
--*Noah's Ark.* 1st ed. Revius, Jacobus (1586-1658). Spier, Peter Edward (1927-), tr. from Dutch. c.1977. Doubleday. **Awards: (NYT); (IBBY); (RCM).** (P.758)
--*Noah's Ark.* Spier, Peter Edward (1927-). 1981. Doubleday. **Award: (ABA).** (P.844)
--*Oh, Were They Ever Happy!.* Spier, Peter Edward (1927-). c.1978. Doubleday. **Award: (ALA).** (P.844)
--*One Hundred More Story Poems.* Parker, Elinor Milnor (1906-), compiled by. 1960. Crowell. (P.706)
--*Peter Spier's Christmas!.* Spier, Peter Edward (1927-). 1983. Doubleday. (P.844)
--*Peter Spier's Little Bible Storybooks.* Seymour, Peter. 1983. Doubleday. (P.813)
--*Peter Spier's Little Ducks.* Spier, Peter Edward (1927-). 1984. Doubleday. (P.844)
--*Peter Spier's Little Rabbits.* Spier, Peter Edward (1927-). 1984. Doubleday. (P.844)
--*Peter Spier's Rain.* Spier, Peter Edward (1927-). c.1982. Doubleday. **Award: (ALA).** (P.844)
--*Sea Broke Through.* Flakkeberg, Ardo. 1960. Knopf. (P.330)
--*The Star-Spangled Banner.* 1st ed. Key, Francis Scott (1779-1843). 1973. Doubleday. (P.521)
--*Tam Morgan: The Liveliest Girl in Salem.* 1st ed. Holberg, Ruth Langland, Mrs. (1891-). 1953. Doubleday. (P.453)
--*Tin Lizzie.* Spier, Peter Edward (1927-). c.1975. Doubleday. (P.844)
--*To Market!* To Market!. Spier, Peter Edward (1927-). 1967. Doubleday. (P.844)
--*To Market!* To Market!. Spier, Peter Edward (1927-). 1973, c.1967. Doubleday. (P.844)
--*Wonder Tales of Seas and Ships.* 1st ed. Carpenter, Frances Aretta (1890-1972). 1959. Doubleday. (P.170)

Spilka, Arnold (1917-)
--*Aloha from Bobby.* Spilka, Arnold (1917-). 1962. Walck. (P.844)
--*Bats and Balls.* Lord, Beman (1924-). 1962. H. Z. Walck. (P.584)
--*Best Little House.* Fisher, Aileen Lucia (1906-). 1966. T Y Crowell. (P.327)
--*Careful Carlos.* Sage, Michael. 1967. Holiday. (P.788)
--*Deep in a Haystack.* Sage, Michael. 1966. Viking. (P.788)
--*Dippy Dos & Don'ts.* Sage, Michael. 1967. Viking Press. (P.788)
--*Guards for Matt.* Lord, Beman (1924-). 1961. H. Z. Walck. (P.584)
--*A Home for Penny.* Hark, Mildred (1908-) & McQueen, Noel. 1959. Watts. (P.413)
--*If You Talked to a Boar.* Sage, Michael. 1960. J. B. Lippincott. (P.788)
--*A Lion I Can Do Without.* Spilka, Arnold (1917-). 1964. Walck. (P.844)
--*Mystery Guest at Left End.* Lord, Beman (1924-). 1964. H. Z. Walck. (P.584)
--*The Mystery of Barrowmead Hill.* Edwards, Bertram, pseud. (1912-). Edwards, Herbert Charles. 1959. David McKay Co. (P.297)
--*Mystery Player at Left End.* Lord, Beman (1924-). 1969. Schol Bk Serv. (P.584)
--*A New Star in the Big Cage.* 1st ed. Lang, Don & Sage, Michael. 1963. Lippincott. (P.550)
--*Penny in Hawaii.* Charlton, Ella Mae. 1964. Abingdon. (P.187)
--*The Perfect Pitch.* Lord, Beman (1924-). 1981, c.1965. Gregg Press. (P.584)
--*Quarter backs Aim.* Lord, Beman (1924-). 1968. David McKay Company. (P.584)
--*Quarterback's Aim.* Lord, Beman (1924-). 1960. H. Z. Walck. (P.584)
--*Robin Hood of Sherwood Forest.* McGovern, Ann. 1968. Crowell. (P.602)
--*Rock Hounds.* Lampman, Evelyn Sibley (1907-1980). 1958. Doubleday. (P.546)
--*Rough Ice.* Lord, Beman (1924-). 1963. H. Z. Walck. (P.584)
--*The Salty Skinners.* De Leeuw, Adele Louise (1899-) & De Leeuw, Cateau Wilhelmina (1903-1975). 1964. Little, Brown. (P.254)
--*The Tree and Me.* Sage, Michael. 1970. H. Z. Walck. (P.788)
--*The Trouble with Francis.* Lord, Beman (1924-). 1958. H. Z. Walck. (P.584)
--*Whom Shall I Marry?.* Spilka, Arnold (1917-). 1960. Holiday House. (P.844)
--*You Better Come Home with Me.* Lawson, John Shults. c.1966. Crowell. (P.557)

Spina, Paul
--*Alfred Hitchcock's Sinister Spies.* Hitchcock, Alfred Joseph (1899-1980), ed. 1966. Random House. (P.446)
--*The Red-Headed League and The Adventure of the Speckled Band.* Doyle, Arthur Conan, Sir (1859-1930). 1968. F. Watts. (P.283)
--*Rogues Gallery: A Variety of Mystery Stories.* Gibson, Walter, ed. 1969. Doubleday. (P.366)
--*A Tree Grew and Birds Flew.* Spina, Paul. 1967. H. Quist; Distributed by Crown Publishers. (P.844)

Spivak, I. Howard
--*I Have Feelings.* Berger, Terry (1933-). 1971. Behavioral Publications. (P.96)

Spivey, Elvera
--*The Little Computer.* Tom, Mr. 1978. Oddo. (P.894)
--*Queen Fussy.* Tom, Mr. 1973. Ten Publications. (P.894)

Spofford, Barbara
--*The Friendly Shepherdess.* Spofford, Barbara. 1933. Little, Brown & Co. (P.845)

Spohn, Cliff
--*So Wild a Dream.* Florentz, Christopher. 1979. Childrens Press. (P.332)

Spollen, Christopher J. (1952-)
--*Mishka, Pishka, & Fishka, and Other Galician Tales.* Kimmel, Eric A (1946-). c.1976. Coward, McCann & Geoghegan. (P.523)
--*Tales from the Steppes.* Jameson, Cynthia. c.1975. Coward, McCann & Geoghegan. (P.489)

Spooner, M. Dibdin
--*The Golden Staircase: Poems and Verses for Children.* Chisholm, Louey, ed. 1907. G. P. Putnam's Sons. (P.192)

Spooner, Malcolm
--*It Doesn't Always Have to Rhyme.* Merriam, Eve (1916-). 1964. Atheneum. (P.642)

Spoor, Mary L., jt. illus. see Wright, Blanche Fisher.

Spoors, Lorraine
--*Mac, the Fire Fighter.* Anderson, Edna A. 1959. T. S. Denison. (P.39)

Sporn, Michael
--*Gudgekin, the Thistle Girl, & Other Tales.* Gardner, John Champlin, Jr. (1933-1982). c.1976. Knopf. (P.355)
--*The King of the Hummingbirds and Other Tales.* Gardner, John Champlin, Jr. (1933-1982). 1977. Knopf. (P.355)

Sprackling, Nelson
--*The Tinmaker Man of New Amsterdam.* Best, Allena Champlin, Mrs. (1892-1974). Berry, Erick, pseud. c.1941. The John C. Winston Company. (P.99)

Spradling, Frank
--*The Boy Explorers in Darkest New Guinea.* Miller, Warren Hastings (1876-). c.1921. Harper & Brothers. (P.649)

Sprague, Rose Mueller
--*Old Stories in New Attire.* Sprague, Rose Mueller. c.1888. L. Prang & Co. (P.845)
--*The Shepherd's Dream.* Grimm, Jakob Ludwig Karl (1785-1863) & Grimm, Wilhelm Karl (1786-1859). Sprague, Mary A., tr. from Ger. 1893. L. Prang & Company. (P.394)

Sprattler, Rob
--*Killer, the Outrageous Hawk.* Robison, Bonnie (1924-). Zillmer, Rolf, designed by. 1974. Childrens Press. (P.770)
--*Springboard to Summer.* Bunting, Anne Evelyn (1928-). 1975. Childrens Press. (P.150)

Spreen, Meta, jt. illus. see Brauer, Katherine.

Spring, Grace J.
--*The Furry Wind.* 1st ed. Boyd, Patricia Ryerson (1935-). c.1982. Andrew Mountain Press. (P.122)

Spring, Ira L. (1918-)
--*Lars Olav: A Boy of Norway.* Edwards, Harvey (1929-) & Spring, Ira (1918-). 1969. HarBraceJ. (P.297)
--*Sigemi: A Japanese Village Girl.* Kirk, Ruth (1918-). N.D. Harcourt Brace Jovanovich. (P.529)

Springer, Mark
--*Penny, the Medicine Maker: The Story of Penicillin.* Epstein, Sherrie S. 1960. Medical Books for Children. (P.308)

Springsteel, Bernard
--*The Coat of Many Colors: The Story of Joseph.* Boruch, Behn. c.1959. Hebrew Pub. Co. (P.118)

Spruance, Benton
--*Hill Doctor.* 1st ed. Skidmore, Hubert Standish (1911-). 1940. Doubleday, Doran & Company, Inc. (P.828)
--*River Rising!.* Skidmore, Hubert Standish (1911-). 1939. Doubleday, Doran & Company, Inc. (P.828)

SPS Studios
--*Dreamie Jeannie of Krumpetville.* Krumpet, Susie & Krumpet, Stevie. 1979. Character Imprints. (P.541)
--*Happy Zappy of Krumpetville.* Krumpet, Susie & Krumpet, Stevie. 1979. Character Imprints. (P.541)
--*Messie Bessie of Krumpetville.* Krumpet, Susie & Krumpet, Stevie. N.D. Character Imprints. (P.541)

Spurrier, Arnrid
--*We'll Meet in England.* Barne, Kitty, pseud. (1883-1957). Barne, Marion Catherine. N.D. Dodd Mead & Co. (P.73)

Spurrier, Steven
--*Nicholas Nickleby.* Dickens, Charles John Huffam (1812-1870). N.D. Heritage Press. (P.264)
--*Tumbledown Dick: All People and No Plot.* Spring, Howard (1889-1965). 1940. The Viking Press. (P.845)

Spyer, Helen
--*Not Enough Beds for the Babies.* Hoberman, Mary Ann (1930-). c.1965. Little. (P.448)

Squire, Maud Hunt, jt. illus. see Mars, Ethel.

Squire, Maud Hunt (1873-)
--*Fairy Tales from Folk Lore.* Williams, Wilbur Herschel (1874-). 1908. Moffat, Yard & Company. (P.964)
--*Hindu Stories.* Williston, Teresa Peirce, retold by. c.1925. New York, Rand, McNally & Company. (P.965)
--*Hindu Tales.* Williston, Teresa Peirce, retold by. c.1917. New York, Rand, McNally & Company. (P.965)
--*Ted in Mythland.* Schwed, Hermine. 1907. Moffat, Yard & Co. (P.804)
--*When I was Little.* Kelley, Ethel M. 1915. Rand McNally. (P.515)

Squire, Maud Hunt (1873-) & Mars, Ethel (1876-)
--*The Adventures of Ulysses.* Lamb, Charles (1775-1834), adapted by. 1902. R. H. Russell. (P.545)
--*A Child's Garden of Verse.* Stevenson, Robert Louis (1850-1894). N.D. R. H. Russell. (P.856)
--*The Heroes: Or, Greek Fairy Tales for My Children.* Kingsley, Charles (1819-1875). 1970. Schocken Books. (P.525)
--*The Roggie and Reggie Stories.* Smith, Gertrude (1860-1917). 1900. Harper & Brothers. (P.834)
--*The Stories of Peter and Ellen.* Smith, Gertrude (1860-1917). 1903. Harper & Brothers. (P.834)

Squires, C. Clyde
--*The Boarded-up House.* Seaman, Augusta Huiell, Mrs. (1879-1950). 1915. The Century Co. (P.806)
--*Cinderella's Granddaughter.* Gilchrist, Beth Bradford (1879-1957). 1918. The Century Co. (P.367)

Staake, Frieda
--*Pet Parade.* Walley, Dean. 1970. Hallmark. (P.927)
--*Zoo Parade.* Walley, Dean & Cunningham, Ed. 1970. Hallmark. (P.928)

Stabilis, Vincent
--*Children Playing School.* Stabilis, Vincent (1884-). c.1941. House of Field, Inc. (P.847)

Stacey, W. S.
--*The Baymen of Belize and How They Wrested British Honduras from the Spaniards: Told by One of Them.* Forbes, Steven (1766-). Williams, E. W., ed. N.D. Society for Promoting Christian Knowledge. (P.335)
--*The Burges Letters: A Record of Child Life in the Sixties.* Bayly, Ada Ellen (1857-1903). Lyall, Edna, pseud. 1902. Longmans, Green, and Co. (P.84)
--*Follow My Leader: Or, The Boys of Templeton, 8 vols.* Reed, Talbot Baines. 1905. Cassell & Co. (P.753)
--*Frank's Life Battle: Or, The Three Friends, 1 vol.* Juv ed. Redford, Christian. N.D. Cassell & Co. (P.752)
--*In Greek Waters: A Story of the Grecian War of Independence (1821-1827).* Henty, George Alfred (1832-1902). 1892. C. Scribner's Sons. (P.435)
--*Merry Girls of England.* Smith, Elizabeth Thomasina Meade, Mrs. (1854-1914). Meade, L. T., pseud. 1897. A. I. Bradley & Co. (P.832)
--*Robin's Ride.* Adams, Ellinor Davenport. N.D. Cassell & Co.'s Pubs. (P.5)
--*Under the Lone Star: A Story of Revolution in Nicaragua.* Hayens, Herbert (1861-). N.D. Thomas Nelson & Sons. (P.425)
--*The White Conquerors: A Tale of Toltec and Aztec.* Munroe, Kirk (1850-1930). 1893. C. Scribner's Sons. (P.672)

Stackpool, Walter (1917-)
--*Nonsense Places: An Absurd Australian Alphabet.* Dugan, Michael Gray (1947-). 1976. Collins. (P.287)
--*A Secret to Sell: A Story of the First Settlement in Western Australia.* Lear, Melva Gwendoline Bartlett. 1966, c.1965. Roy. (P.559)

Stackpool, Will
--*The Tambai Treasure.* Porteous, S. R. 1958. Tri-Ocean Books. (P.732)

Stadler, John
--*Animal Cafe.* Stadler, John. 1980. Bradbury Press. (P.847)
--*Cat at Bat.* Stadler, John. c.1979. Dutton. (P.847)
--*Gorman and the Treasure Chest.* Stadler, John. 1982. Bradbury Press. (P.847)
--*Gorman & the Treasure Chest.* Stadler, John. 1984. Bradbury Pr. (P.847)
--*Hector, the Accordion-Nosed Dog.* Stadler, John. 1983. Bradbury Pr. (P.847)
--*Monster Rolling Skull and Other Native American Tales.* Gustafson, Anita, retold by. c.1980. Crowell. (P.400)
--*Rodney & Lucinda's Amazing Race.* Stadler, John. 1981. Bradbury Pr. (P.847)

Stage, Ruth
--*Ten of a Kind.* Beiler, Edna (1923-). 1953. Herald Press. (P.89)

Stahl, Benjamin
--*Almost a Hero.* Bulla, Clyde Robert (1914-). c.1981. Dutton. (P.148)
--*Blackbeard's Ghost.* Stahl, Benjamin (1910-). 1965. Houghton Mifflin. (P.847)
--*Byrd's Dogs, Sledging at the South Pole.* O'Brien, John Sherman (1898-1938). 1931. Thomas S. Rockwell. (P.689)
--*The Cave: What Lives There.* Bronin, Andrew (1947-). 1972. Putnam Pub Group. (P.134)

--*Polly Perkins' Adventures.* New ed. Liddell, Eva Louise Barnes. 1905. Henry Altemus Co. (P.571)

Strelett, E., jt. illus. see Marks, J.

Strellett, E. & Marks, J.
--*Jewish Fairy Tales and Fables.* Landa, Gertrude. Aunt Naomi, pseud. 1908. Bloch Publishing Co. (P.547)

Stren, Patti
--*Eating Ice Cream with a Werewolf.* Green, Phyllis (1932-). 1983. Harper & Row. (P.385)

--*My First Day at School.* Sellers, Ronnie (1948-). 1985. Caedmon. (P.809)

--*Wings.* Kennedy, Mary. 1980. Scholastic Inc. (P.518)

Stretton, Hesba (1832-1911)
--*Mother Goose and Other Stories.* Mother Goose. N.D. John C. Winston & Co. (P.668)

Strezki, Frances
--*Peter the Great.* Farrell, Maria Owens. c.1932. Marya Press. (P.318)

Strimban, Jack, jt. illus. see Strimban, Robert.

Strimban, Robert & Strimban, Jack
--*Adventures with a Ball.* Milgrom, Harry (1912-). 1965. Dutton. (P.645)

--*Five Is 5.* Fehr, Howard Franklin (1901-1982). c.1963. Holt, Rinehart and Winston. (P.320)

--*I've Got Your Number, John.* Berg, Olive S. c.1965. Holt, Rinehart and Winston. (P.96)

Strimple, Helen
--*Lindy Lou and the Green Umbrella.* Strimple, Helen. 1946. Broadman Press. (P.868)

--*Use-Over Nursery Rhymes.* Peacock, Margaret. Langworthy, Emma, ed. c.1940. Hand-Craft Industries. (P.712)

Strindberg, Gert
--*Norwegian Fairy Tales.* Strindberg, Gert, ed. 1968. Follett Pub. Co. (P.868)

Stringer, Agnes & Andrewes, D.
--*The Little Maid Who Danced to Every Mood, and the Knight Who Wanted the Best of Everything.* Nyblom, Helena Augusta Roed (1843-1926). James, A. W., tr. from Swedish. N.D. Dana Estes & Co. (P.688)

Stringer, Michael
--*Baron Battleaxe and the Magic Carpet.* Henwood, Kay (1924-). 1976. Dent. (P.437)

Strobel, Tom
--*Crash in the Wilderness.* Black, Susan Adams (1953-). c.1980. Raintree Pub. (P.104)

Strobel & Mattinson
--*Donald Duck on Tom Sawyer's Island.* Snow, Dorothea Johnston (1909-). 1978. Western Pub. (P.839)

Strobl, Anthony, jt. illus. see Anderson, Al.

Strobl, Anthony & Totten, Bob
--*Bugs Bunny's Carrot Machine.* Carlisle, Clark, pseud. (1907-). Holding, James Clark Carlisle Jr.. 1976. Western Pub. (P.168)

Strobl, Tony, jt. illus. see MacLaughlin, Don.

Strobridge, Robert
--*Generous Vinegrower.* Pottebaum, Gerald A. (1934-). 1965. Pflaum-Standard. (P.733)

Stroeyer, Poul (1923-)
--*The Cantankerous Crow.* Hellsing, Lennart (1919-). 1962. Astor Books. (P.431)

--*The Cantankerous Crow.* Hellsing, Lennart (1919-). Maze, Nancy, adapted by. 1959. McDowell, Obolensky. (P.431)

--*The Pirate Book.* Hellsing, Lennart (1919-). Smith, William J., tr. from Swedish. 1972. Delacorte. (P.431)

Strok, Susan
--*A New Adventure.* Hoffman, Mary Ann (1949-) & Sitler, Filomena (1949-). c.1981. Naval Institute Press. (P.450)

--*A Special Family.* Hoffman, Mary Ann (1949-) & Sitler, Filomena (1949-). c.1981. Naval Institute Press. (P.450)

Strong, Arline
--*A Crack in the Pavement.* 1st ed. Howell, Ruth Rea. 1970. Atheneum. (P.468)

--*Glowing in the Dark.* Strong, Arline. 1975. Atheneum. (P.868)

--*Lions in the Grass: The Story of the Dandelion.* Busch, Phyllis S. (1909-). 1968. World Pub. (P.158)

--*Once There Was a Tree: The Story of the Tree, a Changing Home for Plants and Animals.* Busch, Phyllis S (1909-). 1968. World Pub. Co. (P.158)

--*Puddles and Ponds: Living Things in Watery Places.* Busch, Phyllis S (1909-). 1969. World Pub. Co. (P.158)

Strong, William
--*The Pilgrim's Progress.* Bunyan, John (1628-1688). N.D. E P Dutton. (P.151)

Strother, Elsie Francis Warmouth Weitzel (1912-) & Strothmann, F.
--*Lions 'n' Things.* Strother, Elsie Francis Warmouth Weitzel (1912-). 1968. Vantage. (P.868)

Strother, Sanford
--*Guardians of the Sea.* Theiss, Lewis Edwin (1878-1963). 1936. T. Nelson and Sons. (P.885)

Strothmann, F., jt. illus. see Strother, Elsie Francis Warmouth Weitzel.

Strothmann, F.
--*Bristles.* Bird, Theodocia Walton. 1930. Little, Brown, and Company. (P.102)

--*The Jumping Frog.* Twain, Mark, pseud. (1835-1910). Clemens, Samuel Langhorne. 1903. Dover Books. (P.907)

--*Over the Nonsense Road.* Gulliver, Lucile. 1910. D. Appleton and Company. (P.399)

--*Wish in the Dark.* Weber, Lenora Mattingly, Mrs. (1895-1971). 1931. Little, Brown, and Company. (P.939)

--*The Wonderful Voyages of Cap'n Pen.* Shumway, Harry Irving (1883-). 1929. Little, Brown, and Company. (P.822)

Strothmann, W.
--*In the Reign of Queen Dick.* Wells, Carolyn (1869-1942). 1904. D. Appleton and Company. (P.944)

Strouth, Mike
--*The Adventures of Super Pickle.* Walley, Dean. 1972. Hallmark. (P.927)

Stroyer, Poul (1923-)
--*It's a Deal.* Stroyer, Poul (1923-). 1960. Astor Books. (P.868)

--*It's A Deal.* Stroyer, Poul (1923-). 1960. McDowell, Obolensky. (P.868)

--*Second Treasure Chest of Tales.* Stroyer, Poul (1923-). 1960. Astor-Honor. (P.868)

--*Treasure Chest of Tales.* Stroyer, Poul (1923-). 1959. Astor-Honor. (P.868)

Struges, Lillian
--*Fairy Tale Princes and Princesses: The Stories Children Like Best.* c.1926. The Saalfield Publishing Company. (P.868)

Strugnell, Alison
--*Fairy Tales.* Strugnell, Alison. 1975. Faber & Faber. (P.868)

Strugnell, Ann
--*The Bongleweed.* Cresswell, Helen. 1973. Macmillan. (P.230)

--*The Faber Book of Modern Fairy Tales.* Corrin, Sara & Corrin, Stephen, eds. c.1981. Faber and Faber. (P.221)

--*The Fool and the Dancing Bear.* 1st ed. Stearns, Pamela Fujimoto (1935-). c.1979. Little, Brown. (P.850)

--*Into the Painted Bear Lair.* Stearns, Pamela Fujimoto (1935-). 1976. Houghton Mifflin. (P.850)

--*More Stories Julian Tells.* Cameron, Ann (1943-). 1985. Knopf. (P.163)

--*Mr. McFadden's Hallowe'en.* Godden, Rumer (1907-). 1975. Viking Press. (P.372)

--*North American Legends.* Haviland, Virginia (1911-), retold by. 1979. Collins. (P.421)

--*Sara and the Door.* Jensen, Virginia Allen (1927-). c.1977. Addison-Wesley. (P.492)

--*Sara and the Door.* Jensen, Virginia Allen (1927-). 1977. Children's Press. (P.492)

--*Sara and the Door.* Jensen, Virginia Allen (1927-). 1985. c.1977. Lippincott. (P.492)

--*The Stories Julian Tells.* 1st ed. Cameron, Ann (1943-). c.1981. Pantheon Books. **Award: (ALA).** (P.163)

Struwer, Ardy
--*Grandfather's Straw Hat.* Ware, Kay & Sutherland, Lucille, eds. 1964. McGraw-Hill. (P.931)

Struyck, Hanneke
--*Bobby Bear.* Struyck, Hanneke. 1984. Barron's. (P.869)

--*Emily Elephant.* Struyck, Hanneke. 1984. Barron's. (P.869)

--*Helen Hare.* Struyck, Hanneke. 1984. Barron's Educational Series, Inc. (P.869)

--*Mark Mouse.* Struyck, Hanneke. 1984. Barron's Educational Series. (P.869)

Stuart, Bertha
--*One Day in Betty's Life.* Gates, Josephine Scribner, Mrs. (1859-1930) & Salter, Mary Turner. N.D. Bobbs-Merrill Co. (P.360)

Stuart, Bertha, jt. illus. see Christy, Howard Chandler.

Stuart, Carl
--*Shirleybird.* Manushkin, Frances (1942-). 1975. Harper & Row. (P.618)

Stuart, Liza
--*The Lion is Busy.* Cleveland, Patience. c.1963. Atlantis Books. (P.202)

Stuart, Ruth McEnery
--*Gobolinks, for Young and Old.* Paine, Albert Bigelow (1861-1937). N.D. The Century Co. (P.700)

Stubblefield, Hord
--*Little Burma.* McClung, Robert Marshall (1916-). 1958. Morrow. (P.595)

Stubbs, Joanna
--*Banger.* Figes, Eva (1932-). 1968. Lion. (P.325)

--*The Family at Ditlabeng.* Mitchison, Naomi Margaret Haldane, Mrs. (1897-). 1970. c.1969. Farrar, Straus & Giroux. (P.652)

--*Journey into War.* Donaldson, Margaret C (1926-). 1979. A. Deutsch. (P.280)

--*Koto and the Lagoon.* Kaye, Geraldine Hughesdon (1925-). 1969. c.1967. Funk & Wagnalls. (P.510)

--*Lame Duck.* Morgan, Geoffrey (1916-). 1977. British Bk Ctr. (P.663)

--*The Moon's on Fire.* Donaldson, Margaret C (1926-). 1980. A. Deutsch. (P.280)

--*Scribble Sam.* Figes, Eva (1932-). 1971. McKay. (P.325)

--*The Talking Rock.* Ainsworth, Ruth (1908-). 1979. Deutsch. (P.15)

Stubenberg, Stanley
--*Young Folk's Hawaiian Time.* rev ed. Pitchford, Gene. 1965. Borden. (P.727)

Stubenhaus, Joanne
--*Chummy Chipmunk's First Family.* Barton, Amsel. 1976. Exposition. (P.78)

Stubis, Talivaldis (1926-)
--*Don't Tell the Scarecrow & Other Japanese Poems.* Issa, et al. 1970. Schol Bk Serv. (P.483)

--*Don't Tell the Scarecrow & Other Japanese Poems.* Issa, et al. 1974. Schol Bk Serv. (P.483)

--*Funny Magic.* Wyler, Rose (1909-) & Ames, Gerald (1906-). 1975. Scholastic Inc. (P.983)

--*Little Lamb's Curls.* MacMillan, Polly Miller. c.1962. Lothrop, Lee & Shepard. (P.609)

--*Magic Secrets.* Wyler, Rose (1909-) & Ames, Gerald (1906-). 1967. Har-Row. (P.983)

--*Me!. A Book of Poems.* Hopkins, Lee Bennett (1938-), ed. 1970. Seabury Press. (P.463)

--*Patrick Michael Kevin.* Peckinpah, Betty. c.1961. Lothrop, Lee & Shepard Co. (P.715)

--*Prove It!.* Wyler, Rose & Ames, Gerald. 1963. Har-Row. (P.983)

--*Real Science Riddles.* Wyler, Rose (1909-). 1972. Hastings House. (P.983)

--*Sam's Place: Poems from the Country.* Moore, Lilian. 1973. Atheneum. (P.661)

--*Spooky Tricks.* Wyler, Rose & Ames, Gerald. 1968. Har-Row. (P.983)

Stubley, Trevor Hugh (1932-)
--*Angry River.* Bond, Ruskin (1924-). 1974, c.1972. Penguin. (P.114)

--*At Willie Tucker's Place.* Morgan, Alison Mary (1930-). 1976, c.1975. Elsevier-Nelson. (P.663)

--*Bisha of Burundi.* Clifford, Mary Louise Beneway (1926-). 1973. Crowell. (P.202)

--*Dog!.* Andrew, Prudence Hastings (1924-). 1973. T. Nelson. (P.40)

--*Flying Free.* Cate, Richard Edward Nelson (1932-). 1977, c.1975. T. Nelson. (P.177)

--*The Incline.* Mayne, William James Carter (1928-). 1972. Dutton. (P.634)

--*Kulumi the Brave: A Zulu Tale.* Seed, Jenny, pseud. (1930-). Seed, Cecile Eugenie. 1970. World Pub. Co. (P.807)

--*Mother Goose Abroad.* Tucker, Nicholas (1936-), ed. 1973. Crowell. (P.904)

--*Mother Goose Abroad: Nursery Rhymes.* Tucker, Nicholas (1936-), ed. 1975. Har-Row. (P.904)

--*Mother Goose Lost: Nursery Rhymes.* Tucker, Nicholas (1936-), ed. 1971. Crowell. (P.904)

--*Never Is a Long, Long Time.* Cate, Richard Edward Nelson (1932-). c.1976. Nelson. (P.177)

--*A Nice Day Out?.* Cate, Richard Edward Nelson (1932-). 1980. c.1981. Elsevier/Nelson Books. (P.177)

--*Old Dog, New Tricks.* Cate, Richard Edward Nelson (1932-). 1981. c.1978. Elsevier/Nelson Books. (P.177)

--*Salt & Gold: Tales from Czechoslovakia.* Burg, Marie. 1976. Blackie. (P.151)

--*Vengeance of the Zulu King.* Seed, Jenny, pseud. (1930-). Seed, Cecile Eugenie. 1971. Pantheon. (P.808)

--*The Yellow Airplane.* Mayne, William James Carter (1928-). 1974. T. Nelson. (P.634)

Stuckenschneider, Placid
--*Behind the Pine Curtain: Portraits of Peter Prep.* Thole, Simeon (1935-). 1979. Liturgical Press. (P.885)

Students of the Art Department, U. S. Indian School
--*Feast Day in Nambe.* U. S. Bureau of Indian Affairs & Tubbs, Rhoda Brandt, Rose Katherine (1877-), ed. 1941. Haskell Institute. (P.909)

Studio Brambilla, Milan
--*Snowy: The Little White Horse.* Reynolds, Suzanne (1951-1962). 1965. Golden Press. (P.759)

Stuecklin, Karl W.
--*Golden Shore: Great Short Stories Selected for Young Readers.* Peden, William Harwood (1913-). 1967. Platt. (P.715)

--*Olaf and the Frump.* Nielsen, Harry A. 1969. Doubleday. (P.682)

--*The Stupid Lion, and Other Stories.* Jacobs, Leland Blair (1907-), ed. 1969. L. W. Singer Co. (P.487)

Stuker, Chris
--*Rooney Crooney's Second Chance.* Miller, E. Lorraine. 1978. Miller Ent. (P.646)

Stull, Betty
--*Five Cent, Five Cent (Liberia).* Chandler, Edna Walker (1908-1982). 1967. A Whitman. (P.183)

Stupica, Marlenka
--*The Magic Ring: A Picture Story from Yugoslavia.* Valjavac, Matija Kracmanov (1831-1897) & Vipotnik, Cene. 1968, c.1957. World Pub. Co. (P.912)

Sturges, Katharine
--*Beatrice the Brave.* Varble, Rachel Margaret McBrayer, Mrs. 1934. Little, Brown and Company. (P.916)

--*For Children Only.* Underhill, Andrew Findlay (1859-). c.1939. McLaughlin Bros., Inc. (P.909)

--*The Rhymes of Goocy Goggles and His Pollywog Named "Woggles".* Underhill, Andrew Findlay (1859-). c.1926. McLaughlin Bros., Inc. (P.909)

--*Sister Anne.* Potter, Helen Beatrix (1866-1943). c.1932. David McKay Company. (P.734)

--*Why the Chimes Rang: And Other Stories.* Alden, Raymond Macdonald (1873-1924). c.1924. The Bobbs-Merrill Company. (P.20)

Sturges, Lillian Baker, jt. illus. see Brundage, Frances.

Sturgill, Susan
--*Animal Fair: Poems.* Danforth, Amy. c.1983. Cricket Publications. (P.240)

Sturgis, Katharine
--*Omar, the Discontented Cat.* 3rd ed. Chamberlin, Ethel Clere. 1925. The P.F. Volland Company. (P.182)

Sturtevant, Harriet
--*Nancy and Jane.* Alexander, Florence Bibo. 1945. Howell, Soskin. (P.22)

--*Training Pants.* Ellison, Virginia Howell (1910-). 1946. Howell, Soskin. (P.304)

Sturtevant, Helena
--*John Whopper, The Newsboy.* New ed. Clark, Thomas March (1812-1903). Potter, Henry C., intro. by. 1905. The Page Company. (P.198)

Sturtevant, Wallis H.
--*Days of the Leaders.* Lamprey, Louise (1869-1951). 1925. Frederick A. Stokes Company. (P.547)

Stutters, Percival, pseud., see Peirce, Gerry.

Suares, Jean-Claude
--*Crash Helmet.* Allard, Harry. c.1977. Prentice-Hall. (P.28)

--*The King's Trousers.* Kraus, Robert (1925-). 1979. Windmill Books. (P.538)

Suba, Susanne (1913-)
--*Ann of Bar Ton Ranch.* Stevens, Elizabeth Welty. 1938. A. A. Knopf. (P.854)

--*The Coat-Hanger Christmas Tree.* 1st ed. Estes, Eleanor (1906-1979). 1973. Atheneum. (P.310)

--*Dancing to Danger.* Allan, Mabel Esther (1915-). Hogon, Priscilla, pseud. 1967. World Pub. Co. (P.28)

--*The Drugstore Cat.* Petry, Ann Lane (1911-). 1949. T. Y. Crowell Co. (P.722)

--*Eddie Elephant Has a Party.* Harbaugh, Rose Oller. 1947. Rand McNally. (P.411)

--*The Elegant Elephant.* McCracken, Russell. 1944. Rand McNally & Company. (P.597)

--*Favorite Fairy Tales Told in Germany.* 1st ed. Grimm, Jakob Ludwig Karl (1785-1863) & Grimm, Wilhelm Karl (1786-1859). Haviland, Virginia (1911-), retold by. 1959. Little, Brown. (P.391)

--*The First Christmas.* Glover, Florida. N.D. E. P. Dutton & Co. (P.371)

--*Five True Dog Stories.* Davidson, Mickie, pseud. (1936-). Davidson, Margaret. 1977. Scholastic Inc. (P.244)

--*A Flower From Dinah.* Vance, Marguerite (1889-1965). 1962. E. P. Dutton & Co. (P.912)

--*The Gentle Giraffe.* McCracken, Russell. c.1945. Rand McNally & Company. (P.597)

--*The Hobo Hound.* Edwards, May. 1947. Rand, McNally. (P.298)

--*The Homemade Year.* 1st ed. Lawrence, Mildred Elwood (1907-). 1950. Harcourt, Brace. (P.556)

--*The Hunting Trip.* Burch, Robert Joseph (1925-). 1971. Scribner. (P.151)

--*Jaime and His Hen Pollita.* Butterfield, Marguerite Antoinette (1900-). 1957. Scribner. (P.159)

--*The Little Cat That Could Not Sleep.* Fox, Frances Margaret (1870-). 1941. E. P. Dutton & Co., Inc. (P.340)

--*Little Coquette: The Story of a French Girlhood.* McCormick, Renee De Fontarce (1899-). McCormick, Leander James (1888-), tr. 1944. Houghton Mifflin Company. (P.596)

--*Lottie's Valentine.* Eyre, Katherine Wigmore (1901-1970). c.1941. Oxford University Press. (P.315)

--*The Man with the Bushy Beard & Other Tales.* Suba, Susanne (1913-). 1969. Viking Press. (P.870)

--*Marya of Clark Avenue.* Bloch, Marie Halun (1910-). 1957. Coward-McCann. (P.109)

--*The Monkeys & the Pedlar.* 1st ed. Suba, Susanne (1913-). 1970. Viking Press. (P.870)

Svendson, Julius (1919-) & Satterfield, C. W.
--*Walt Disney's Sleeping Beauty and the Good Faries.* Disney, Walter Elias (1901-1966) & Strebe, Dorothy. Satterfield, C. W., adapted by. 1958. Golden Press. (P.273)
Svenonius, Arthur, photos by.
--*A Horse Astray in Stockholm.* Lengstrand, Rolf. Seidler, Lotte, tr. 1965. Lerner Publications Co. (P.564)
--*The Long Pony Race.* Lengstrand, Rolf & Rolen, Pierre L. Turner, Marianne, tr. 1966. Knopf. (P.564)
Svensson, Borje
--*Baby Jesus.* Bennett, Marian. 1979. Standard Pub. (P.94)
--*Daniel in the Lions Den.* Bennett, Marian. 1978. Standard Pub. (P.94)
--*David & Goliath.* Bennett, Marian. 1978. Standard Pub. (P.94)
--*The Good Samaritan.* Bennett, Marian. 1978. Standard Pub. (P.94)
--*Little Lamb.* Bennett, Marian. 1979. Standard Pub. (P.94)
--*The Littlest Angel.* Tazewell, Charles (1900-1972). Dudley, Dick, designed by. 1985, c.1964. Ideals Pub. Corp. (P.881)
--*Pop-up David & Goliath.* Miller, Albert Griffith (1905-1982), ed. 1970. Random. (P.646)
--*The Story of Moses.* Bennett, Marian. 1979. Standard Pub. (P.94)
--*The Story of Noah.* Bennett, Marian. 1979. Standard Pub. (P.94)
Svensson, Kamma
--*Yougga Finds Mother Teresa: The Adventures of a Beggar Boy in India.* Bang, Kirsten. 1983. Seabury Press. (P.68)
Swain, Su Zan
--*The Rocky Mountains.* Zim, herbert Spencer (1909-). 1964. Golden Press. (P.992)
Swan, Curt, jt. illus. see Serpe, Jerry.
Swan, Kay
--*The Tick Tock Clock Book.* Swan, Kay. c.1929. Stoll & Edwards Co., Inc. (P.873)
Swan, Peter Charles (1921-)
--*The Sloth and the Gnu.* Flanders, Michael Henry (1922-1975). 1974. F. Warne. (P.330)
Swan, Susan Elizabeth (1944-)
--*The Case of the Horrible Swamp Monster.* Stevenson, Drew (1947-). 1984. Dodd. (P.855)
--*Chester.* Shura, Mary Francis (1923-). c.1980. Dodd, Mead. (P.822)
--*Dinosaur Mysteries.* Elting, Mary (1906-) & Goodman, Ann Davidow (1932-). 1980. Platt. (P.305)
--*Dinosaur Mysteries.* Elting, Mary (1906-) & Goodman, Ann Davidow (1932-). 1980. Putnam Pub Group. (P.305)
--*Eleanor.* Shura, Mary Francis (1923-). 1983. Dodd, Mead. (P.822)
--*I Don't Believe in Elves.* Woolley, Catherine (1904-). 1975. Morrow. (P.978)
--*Jefferson.* Shura, Mary Francis, pseud. (1923-). Craig, Mary Francis. 1984. Dodd. (P.822)
--*Plays Children Love: A Treasury of Contemporary and Classic Plays for Children.* Harris, Aurand (1915-) & Jennings, Coleman A. (1933-), eds. Martin, Mary, frwd. by. 1981. Doubleday. (P.415)
--*The Twelve Days of Christmas.* c.1981. Troll Associates. (P.873)
Swanberg, Nancie
--*Lillan.* 1st ed. Norris, Gunilla Brodde (1939-). 1968. Atheneum. (P.685)
Swann, Louisa le Teller
--*The Adventure Hour.* Swann, Louisa le Teller, ed. 1936. F. Warne & Co., Ltd. (P.873)
--*The Leisure Hour.* Swann, Louisa le Teller, ed. c.1936. F. Warne & Co., Ltd. (P.873)
--*The Treasure Hour.* Swann, Louisa le Teller, ed. 1935. F. Warne & Co., Ltd. (P.873)
Swanson, Dick, photos by.
--*Six Days to Saturday: Joe Paterno and Penn State.* NewCombe, Jack. 1974. Farrar, Straus and Giroux. (P.679)
Swanson, J. M.
--*A Promise to Keep.* Smart, James Dick (1906-1982). 1949. Westminster. (P.831)
Swanson, J. N.
--*Rodeo Days.* Clemons, Elizabeth. 1960. J. B. Lippincott. (P.201)
--*Rodeo Days.* Clemons, Elizabeth, pseud. Nowell, Elizabeth Cameron. 1960. Lane Book Co. (P.201)
Swanson, Jean D.
--*Butterscotch and the Happy Barnyard.* Wilson, Charles Morrow (1905-1977). N.D. Caxton Printers. (P.966)
Swanson, Judy
--*Lord, I'm Back Again: Story Devotions for Girls.* Warren, Mary Phraner (1929-). c.1981. Augsburg Pub. House. (P.933)
--*The Purple Sea Horse, and Other Stories.* King, Loretta (1913-). 1980, c.1979. Woodland Pub. Co. (P.524)
Swanson, Maggie
--*All Around the Farm.* Low, Alice (1926-). c.1984. Random House. (P.588)
--*Big & Little Stories.* Muntean, Michaela. 1982. Western Pub. (P.672)
--*The Case of the Missing Duckie.* Hayward, Linda & Henson, Jim, pseud. (1936-). Henson, James Maury. c.1981. Western Pub. Co. in Conjunction with Children's Television Workshop. (P.426)
--*The Curious Little Kitten.* Hayward, Linda. c.1982. Golden Press. (P.426)
--*The Curious Little Kitten on the Farm.* 1982. Western Pub. (P.873)
--*The Curious Little Kitten: Sniff Sniff Book.* Hayward, Linda. 1983. Western Pub. (P.426)
--*The Curious Little Kitten's First Christmas.* Hayward, Linda. c.1984. Western Pub. Co. (P.426)
--*Farley Goes to the Doctor: Featuring Jim Henson's Sesame Street Muppets.* Kingsley, Emily Perl (1940-). c.1980. Western Pub. Co. (P.525)
--*Grover Sleeps Over.* Winthrop, Elizabeth, pseud. (1948-). Mahony, Elizabeth Winthrop. c.1984. Published by Western Pub. Co. in Conjunction with Children's Television Workshop. (P.970)
--*The Rabbit's Adventure.* Wright, Betty Ren. 1979. Western Pub. (P.980)
--*Sweet Dreams on Sesame Street: Featuring Jim Henson's Sesame Street Muppets.* Sesame Street. Schulman, Janet (1933-), ed. 1983. Random House CTW. (P.873)
--*Up & Down Book Starring Ernie & Bert.* Sesame Street. N.D. Western Pub. (P.811)
Swanson, Robert
--*The Prisoner of Vega.* 1977. Random. (P.873)
--*The Prisoner of Vega.* Lerner, Sharon Ruth (1938-1982) & Cerf, Christopher Bennett (1941-). c.1977. Random House. (P.566)
Swanson, Wallace & Kropa, Susan
--*It's a Special Day.* Lipson, Greta. 1978. Good Apple. (P.576)
Swart, Gerry
--*Hi, Teddy!.* 1973. Western Pub. (P.873)
--*Let's Go to the Park.* 1975. Western Pub. (P.873)
Swartz, Maude Kierce
--*Backyard Playmates: A Book of Verse for Children.* Swartz, Maude Kierce. 1952. Exposition Press. (P.873)
Swartz, Walter
--*Going to the Hospital.* Clark, Bettina & Coleman, Lester L. 1971. Random. (P.197)
Swayne, Samuel F. (1907-) & Swayne, Zoa Lourana Shaw (1905-)
--*Great-Grandfather in the Honey Tree.* Swayne, Samuel F (1907-) & Swayne, Zoa Lourana Shaw (1905-). 1949. Viking Press. (P.873)
Swayne, Zoa Lourana Shaw, jt. illus. see Swayne, Samuel F.
Sweat, Lynn
--*Amelia Bedelia and the Baby.* Parish, Peggy (1927-). c.1981. Greenwillow Books. (P.705)
--*Amelia Bedelia Goes Camping.* Parish, Peggy (1927-). c.1985. Greenwillow Books. (P.705)
--*Amelia Bedelia Helps Out.* Parish, Peggy (1927-). c.1979. Greenwillow Books. (P.705)
--*The Cats' Burglar.* Parish, Peggy (1927-). c.1983. Greenwillow Books. (P.705)
--*Cluck, the Captain's Chicken.* Sweat, Lynn. 1966. Macmillan. (P.873)
--*Dragons of Peking: A Chinese Folk Legend.* Porter, Wesley. 1979. F. Watts. (P.733)
--*First Winter, First Summer: An American Indian Folk Legend.* Porter, Wesley. 1979. F. Watts. (P.733)
--*The Garden Is Doing Fine.* 1st ed. Farley, Carol J (1936-). 1975. Atheneum. (P.317)
--*Good Work, Amelia Bedelia.* Parish, Peggy (1927-). c.1976. Greenwillow Books. (P.705)
--*Granny, the Baby, and the Big Gray Thing.* Parish, Peggy (1927-). 1972. Macmillan. (P.705)
--*The Lever and the Pulley.* Hellman, Harold (1927-). 1971. M. Evans; Distributed in Association with Lippincott, Philadelphia. (P.431)
--*The Magic Kettle: A Japanese Folk Legend.* Porter, Wesley. 1979. Watts. (P.733)
--*Teach Us, Amelia Bedelia.* Parish, Peggy (1927-). c.1977. Greenwillow Books. (P.705)
--*Wizard Tales.* Denan, Corinne, retold by. c.1980. Troll Associates. (P.257)
--*The Wonderful Hunting Dog.* Sweat, Lynn. 1973. Macmillan. (P.873)
Sweeney
--*Mother Goose.* Mother Goose. N.D. D. Lothrop Co. (P.668)
--*Mother Goose Jingles.* Mother Goose. N.D. D. Lothrop & Co. (P.668)
Sweeney, Dan
--*Eastward Sweeps the Current.* Malkus, Alida Wright Sims, Mrs. (1899-). N.D. John C. Winston. (P.614)
--*Jenny's Secret Island: A Story of Bermuda.* Garrard, Phillis. 1943. The John C. Winston Company. (P.358)
Sweeney, Morgan J. see Boz, pseud.
Sweeney, Morgan J.
--*Chronicles of the Stimpcett Family and Others.* Boz, pseud. Diaz, Abby Morton, Mrs. (1821-1904). 1882. D. Lothrop and Company. (P.262)
--*Polly Cologne.* Boz, pseud. Diaz, Abby Morton, Mrs. (1821-1904) & Mahony, Bertha E. 1930. Lothrop, Lee & Shepard Co. (P.262)
--*Rainy-Day Plays.* Humphrey, Frances A., Mrs. c.1884. D. Lothrop and Company. (P.473)
Sweeney, Nora
--*Anne Thornton.* Anthony, Lotta Rowe. 1925. The Penn Publishing Company. (P.43)
--*Louie Maude and the Mary Ann.* Griffith, Helen Sherman, Mrs. (1873-). 1927. The Penn Publishing Company. (P.390)
--*The Mystery of the Bradley Pearls.* Radford, Ruby Lorraine (1891-1971). c.1930. The Penn Publishing Company. (P.746)
--*A Yankee Girl at Hampton Roads.* Curtis, Alice Turner, Mrs. (1860-1958). 1927. The Penn Publishing Company. (P.237)
Sweeney, Nora & Smith, Wuanita (1866-)
--*Why, Virginia!.* Griffith, Helen Sherman, Mrs. (1873-). 1924. The Penn Publishing Company. (P.390)
Sweeny, William K., jt. illus. see Wrightman, Francis P.
Sweet, Edward
--*Just Like Nancy.* Cumming, Marian. 1953. Harcourt, Brace. (P.234)
Sweet, Ozzie, photos by.
--*Alligator.* Scott, Jack D. 1984. Putnam Pub Group. (P.804)
Sweet, Valerie
--*The Silver Secret.* Tennyson, Margaret. 1959. F. Warne. (P.882)
Sweetland, Robert
--*Fit for a King.* Sheldon, Aure (1917-1976). c.1974. Carolrhoda Books. (P.818)
--*Yelly Kelly.* Rose, Nancy Ann (1934-). 1970. T. S. Denison. (P.777)
Sweetman, Daniel
--*The Cuckoo Clock Adventure.* Lam, Roger. Gibb, George, ed. 1983. Six Pr. (P.544)
Sweney, Fredric
--*The Frightened Hare.* Russell, Franklin Alexander (1926-). 1966. HR&W. (P.785)
Swenson, Seri
--*You Can Depend on Me.* Reuter, Margaret. 1980. Childrens Press. (P.758)
Swiderska, Barbara
--*The Apple of Youth, and Other Russian Folk Stories.* Yeoman, John (1934-). 1968, c.1967. F. Watts. (P.986)
--*Apple of Youth & Other Russian Folk Stories.* Yeoman, John (1934-). 1969. Watts. (P.986)
--*The Clever Mouse.* Reeves, James (1909-). 1976. Chatto and Windus. (P.754)
--*The Fisherman's Bride.* Swiderska, Barbara. 1971. Scroll Press. (P.874)
--*Puffin Book of Magic Verse.* Causley, Charles Stanley (1917-), ed. 1974. Penguin. (P.178)
Swift, Don
--*Jingle Pennies.* Aratari, Anthony. 1978. Ave Maria. (P.45)
Swift, Edd, pseud., see Swift, Edward.
Swift, Edd, pseud. (1943-)
--*Ted and Priscilla.* Swift, Edward. Swift, Edd, pseud. (1943-). Swift, Edward. 1971. Hawthorn Books. (P.874)
Swift, Edward see Swift, Edd, pseud.
Swigart, Mary Ruth
--*Johnny Bushytail.* 1st ed. Haskin, Janet. 1957. Vantage Press. (P.419)
Swiller, Al
--*I Got a Camel for Christmas.* Swiller, Al. 1963. Grosset & Dunlap. (P.875)
--*Party at the Zoo.* Roethke, Theodore Huebner (1908-1963). 1963. Crowell-Collier Press. (P.774)
Swindells, Robert Edward (1939-)
--*A Candle in the Night.* Swindells, Robert Edward (1939-). 1975. David & Charles. (P.875)
--*When Darkness Comes.* Swindells, Robert Edward (1939-). 1975, c.1973. Morrow. (P.875)
Swinnertop, James
--*The Little Boy Who Lived On the Hill.* New ed. Laurie, Annie. N.D. Desmond Fitzgerald Inc. Distributed by Warne & Co. (P.555)
--*The Little Boy Who Lived on the Hill.* Laurie, Annie. N.D. Doxey's Pubs. (P.555)
Swisher, Paul D.
--*Bob Hanson, Eagle Scout.* Carter, Russell Gordon (1892-1957). 1923. The Penn Publishing Company. (P.176)
Switton, Florence Weinstock (1886-)
--*In Picture Land: Children's Favorite Masterpieces, with Little Stories in Verse.* Switton, Florence Weinstock (1886-). 1917. Daughaday and Company. (P.875)
Swofford, Jeanette
--*The Blueberry Troll.* Springstubb, Tricia (1950-). c.1981. Carolrhoda Books. (P.845)
--*The Dawdlewalk.* Tobias, Tobi (1938-). c.1983. Carolrhoda Books. (P.893)
Swope, Martha, photos by.
--*A Midsummer Night's Dream: The Story of the New York City Ballet's Production.* Lassalle, Nancy. c.1977. Dodd, Mead. (P.553)
--*The Nutcracker: The Story of the New York City Ballet's Production Told in Pictures.* c.1975. Dodd, Mead. (P.875)
Sydlik, Danilea & Campbell, Elisa L.
--*Sunshine, Rainbows & Friends.* Beyl, Judith. 1980. West Village. (P.100)
Sydney, Margaret, pseud., see Lothrop, Harriet Mulford Stone.
Syfret, Anne
--*Mot, Ybbat and Little Pharaoh.* Syfret, Anne. 1976. McGraw-Hill. (P.875)
Sylvester, Margo
--*Little Peter's Task.* Bigot, Marie Healy (1843-). Magurie, Hortenmse G., tr. c.1931. Heath & Co. (P.102)
Sylvester, Natalie Gabry (1922-)
--*Summer on Cleo's Island.* Sylvester, Natalie Gabry (1922-). c.1977. Farrar, Straus and Giroux. (P.875)
Symington, J. A.
--*The Adventures of Robinson Crusoe on His Island.* Defoe, Daniel (1661-1731). Tilney, Frederick Colin, ed. N.D. E. P. Dutton & Co. (P.250)
Syrett, Nellie
--*The Other Side of the Sun: Fairy Tales.* Sharp, Evelyn (1869-). 1900. John Lane. (P.816)
Syversen, S. Storm
--*Tales of Norway for Children.* 1st ed. Christianson, Nora D. 1955. Vantage Press. (P.194)
Syverson, Henry
--*Aesop's Fables.* Coblentz, Stanton Arthur (1896-). 1968. C. R. Gibson Co. (P.205)
Szafranski, Kurt
--*Admiral Bobby.* Froschel, George (1891-). Naumburg, Elsa H., tr. from Ger. 1931. Harper & Brothers. (P.347)
Szalay, Lajos
--*The Gypsy Tree.* Collier, Ethel (1903-). 1966. A-W. (P.209)
Szasz, Frank
--*Animal Stories.* Denison, Carol. 1963, c.1957. Golden Press. (P.257)
--*The Golden Storytime Book of Animal Stories.* Szasz, Frank. 1957. Golden Press. (P.876)
Szasz, Suzanne Shorr, jt. illus. see Nilsson, Lennart.
Szasz, Suzanne Shorr (1919-), photos by.
--*Now I Have a Daddy Haircut.* Appell, Clara & Appell, Morey. 1960. Dodd, Mead. (P.43)
Szeghy, Joe
--*The Dancing Bear, and Other Stories.* Greene, Carol (1906-). 1973. Concordia Pub. House. (P.386)
Szekeres, Cyndy (1933-)
--*Argentaybee and the Boonie.* Hiller, Catherine (1946-). c.1979. Coward, McCann & Geoghegan. (P.444)
--*Baby Bear's Surprise.* Szekeres, Cyndy (1933-). c.1984. Golden Book. (P.876)
--*Bedtime for Bears.* Holl, Adelaide Hinkle (1910-). 1973. Garrard Pub. Co. (P.454)
--*A Birthday ABC.* McGill, Marci. c.1982. Golden Press. (P.601)
--*Brian's Secret Errand.* 1st ed. Lonergan, Joy. 1969. Doubleday. (P.581)
--*Brimhall Comes to Stay.* 1st ed. Delton, Judy (1931-). c.1978. Lothrop, Lee & Shepard. (P.255)
--*A Child's First Book of Nursery Tales.* Lanes, Selma Gordon (1929-), ed. 1983. Western Pub. (P.548)
--*A Child's First Book of Poems.* c.1981. Golden Press. (P.876)
--*The Clumpets Go Sailing.* Wahl, Jan (1933-). 1975. Parents' Magazine Press. (P.924)
--*Doctor Rabbit's Foundling.* Wahl, Jan (1933-). c.1977. Pantheon Books. (P.924)
--*Doctor Rabbit's Lost Scout.* Wahl, Jan (1933-). c.1979. Pantheon Books. (P.924)
--*Edgemont.* Sharmat, Marjorie Weinman (1928-). c.1976. Coward, McCann & Geoghegan. (P.815)
--*The Fattest Bear in the First Grade.* Robinson, Barbara Webb (1927-). 1969. Random House. (P.769)
--*Five Little Foxes in the Snow.* Johnston, Susan T. (1942-). Johnston, Tony, pseud. 1977. Putnam. (P.498)
--*Four-Ring Three.* Bourne, Miriam Anne (1931-). 1973. Coward, McCann & Geoghegan. (P.120)
--*The Girl Who Was a Cowboy.* 1st ed. Krasilovsky, Phyllis (1926-). 1965. Doubleday. (P.537)
--*Good Night, Orange Monster.* 1st ed. Lifton, Betty Jean (1926-). 1972. Atheneum. (P.572)
--*Goodbye, Hello.* Welber, Robert. 1974. Pantheon Books. (P.943)
--*Great-Grandmother Cat Tales.* Wahl, Jan (1933-). c.1976. Pantheon Books. (P.924)
--*Gus and Buster Work Things Out.* Bronin, Andrew (1947-). 1975. Coward, McCann & Geoghegan. (P.134)
--*Halloween Parade.* Lystad, Mary Hanemann (1928-). 1973. Putnam. (P.592)

--*Fish Story.* Tallon, Robert (1935-). c.1977. Holt, Rinehart and Winston. (P.877)
--*Flea Story.* Tallon, Robert (1935-). c.1977. Holt, Rinehart and Winston. (P.877)
--*Hurry! Dinner Is at Six!.* 1st ed. Smith, Ruth Leslie (1902-). 1969. Bobbs-Merrill. (P.836)
--*Latouse My Moose.* Tallon, Robert (1935-). 1983. Knopf. (P.877)
--*Little Cloud.* Tallon, Robert (1935-). c.1978. Parents' Magazine Press. (P.877)
--*Mooseberry and the Fuzzo Makers.* Tallon, Robert (1935-). 1984. Knopf. (P.877)
--*Rhoda's Restaurant.* Tallon, Robert (1935-). 1973. Bobbs-Merrill. (P.877)
--*Rotten Kidphabets.* Tallon, Robert (1935-). 1975. Holt, Rinehart and Winston. (P.877)
--*Sam Sunday and the Strange Disappearance of Chester Cats.* Supraner, Robyn (1930-). c.1978. Parents' Magazine Press. (P.871)
--*The Things in Dolores' Piano.* Tallon, Robert (1935-). 1970. Bobbs-Merrill. (P.877)
--*Worm Story.* Tallon, Robert (1935-). c.1978. Holt, Rinehart and Winston. (P.877)
--*ZAG: A Search Through the Alphabet.* Tallon, Robert (1935-). c.1976. Holt, Rinehart and Winston. (P.877)
--*Zoophabets.* Tallon, Robert (1935-). 1971. Bobbs-Merrill. (P.877)

Taloac, Gerry
--*Ivanhoe.* Farr, Naunerle C., adapted by. 1979, c.1978. Pendulum Press. (P.318)

Taloac, Gerry & Redondo, N.
--*The Best of Poe.* new & abr. ed. Poe, Edgar Allan (1809-1849). Farr, Naunerle, ed. 1977. Pendulum Pr. (P.729)

Tamburine, Jean, jt. illus. see Peller, Jackie.

Tamburine, Jean (1930-)
--*Almost Big Enough.* Tamburine, Jean (1930-). 1963. Abingdon. (P.877)
--*Almost Big Enough.* Tamburine, Jean (1930-). 1963. Hale. (P.877)
--*Barney, Bring Your Banjo.* 1st ed. Justus, May (1898-). 1959. Holt. (P.503)
--*Big Log Mountain.* 1st ed. Justus, May (1898-). 1958. Holt. (P.503)
--*Billy Whiskers' Twins.* Wing, Helen. c.1956. Rand McNally. (P.969)
--*The Complete Peddler's Pack: Games, Songs, Rhymes, and Riddles from Mountain Folklore.* Justus, May (1898-). 1967. University of Tennessee Press. (P.503)
--*The Five Little Bears.* North, Sterling (1906-1974). c.1955. Rand McNally. (P.686)
--*The Goat That Went to School.* Francis, Sally R. 1953, c.1952. Rand McNally. (P.341)
--*Help Mr. Willy Nilly: A Story-Book Game.* Fritz, Jean Guttery (1915-). 1954. Treasure Books. (P.347)
--*How Now Brown Cow.* Tamburine, Jean (1930-). 1967. Abingdon Press. (P.877)
--*I Think I Will Go to the Hospital.* Tamburine, Jean (1930-). 1965. Abingdon Press. (P.877)
--*It's Nice to Be Little.* Stanley, John (1914-). c.1965. Rand McNally. (P.849)
--*Little Red Riding Hood.* Little Red Riding Hood. 1954. Wonder Books. (P.577)
--*Moving Day.* 1st ed. Hilles, Helen Train, Mrs. 1954. Lippincott. (P.445)
--*Peddler's Park.* 1st ed. Justus, May (1898-). 1957. Holt. (P.503)
--*Peter Pocket and His Pickle Pup.* Justus, May (1898-). 1953. Holt. (P.503)
--*Pillowtime Tales.* De Groot, Marion K. c.1956. Rand McNally. (P.251)
--*Pudgy the Little Bear.* Barrows, Ruth Marjorie (1892-1983). 1972. Rand. (P.76)
--*The Right House for Rowdy.* Justus, May (1898-). 1960. Holt, Rinehart and Winston. (P.503)
--*Scamper.* Barrows, Ruth Marjorie (1892-1983). c.1959. Rand McNally. (P.77)
--*See Me Grow.* White, Mary Sue. c.1966. Abingdon. (P.952)
--*Smoky Mountain Sampler: Stories.* Justus, May (1898-). 1962. Abingdon. (P.503)
--*Something Was Missing.* Guittard, Helen. 1969. Follett Pub. Co. (P.399)
--*Surprise for Peter Pocket.* Justus, May (1898-). 1955. HR&W. (P.503)
--*Use Your Head, Hildy.* Justus, May (1898-). 1956. HR&W. (P.503)
--*Who Wants Willy Wells?.* Balzano, Jeanne Koppel (1912-). 1965. Abingdon Press. (P.67)
--*Who Wants Willy Wells.* Bell, Gina, pseud. (1912-). Balzano, Jeanne Koppel. N.D. Abingdon. (P.90)
--*Winds A'Blowing.* Justus, May (1898-). 1961. Abingdon Press. (P.503)

Tamburine, Jean (1930-) & Peller, Jackie
--*The Three Little Pigs and Little Red Riding Hood: Two Complete Stories.* Three Little Pigs. c.1954. Grosset & Dunlap. (P.890)

Tamer, Salem
--*Blades of Grass.* 1st ed. Miller, Helen Markley (1899-). 1963. Doubleday. (P.647)
--*Bobbie, a Great Collie.* rev. ed. Alexander, Charles (1897-1962). 1966. Dodd. (P.22)
--*Cuff, a Baby Bear.* Voight, Virginia Frances (1909-). 1969. Putnam. (P.921)
--*Mystery of the Chinatown Pearls.* Antoncich, Betty Kennedy (1913-). 1965. McKay. (P.43)
--*Riddle of Raven Hollow.* Shura, Mary Francis (1923-). 1976. Scholastic Inc. (P.822)
--*The Riddle of Raven's Gulch.* Shura, Mary Francis (1923-). 1975. Dodd, Mead. (P.822)
--*Secret of the Sea Legacy.* Raimondi, Emily. 1974. Vanguard Press. (P.747)
--*Silver Stories and Golden Verse: An Anthology for Children About the Catholic Way of Life.* Cuneo, Mary Louise Hector & Cuneo, Paul, eds. c.1965. Dodd. (P.235)

Tanaka, Beatrice
--*The Tortoise and the Sword: A Vietnamese Legend.* Tanaka, Beatrice, retold by. 1972. Lothrop, Lee & Shepard Co. (P.877)

Tanaka, Hideyuki
--*The Happy Dog.* Tanaka, Hideyuki. 1983, c.1981. Atheneum. (P.877)

Tandy, Russell H.
--*Betty Gordon and the Hale Twins: Or, An Exciting Vacation.* Emerson, Alice B., pseud. Stratemeyer Syndicate. 1929. Cupples & Leon Co. (P.306)
--*Betty Gordon at Mystery Farm: Or, Strange Doings at Rocky Ridge.* Emerson, Alice B., pseud. Stratemeyer Syndicate. 1930. Cupples & Leon Co. (P.306)
--*The Bungalow Mystery.* Keene, Carolyn, pseud. (1894-1982). Adams, Harriet Stratemeyer. c.1930. Grosset & Dunlap. (P.511)
--*Cast Away in the Land of Snow: Or, Jerry Ford Among the Polar Bears.* Moore, Fenworth, pseud. Stratemeyer Syndicate. 1931. Cupples & Leon Co. (P.660)
--*Charlotte Cross and Aunt Deb: Or, The Queerest Trip on Record.* Barton, May Hollis, pseud. Stratemeyer Syndicate. 1931. Cupples & Leon Co. (P.78)
--*The Clue in the Crumbling Wall.* Keene, Carolyn, pseud. (1894-1982). Adams, Harriet Stratemeyer. 1945. Grosset & Dunlap. (P.511)
--*The Clue in the Diary.* Keene, Carolyn, pseud. (1894-1982). Adams, Harriet Stratemeyer. c.1932. Grosset & Dunlap. (P.511)
--*The Clue in the Jewel Box.* Keene, Carolyn, pseud. (1894-1982). Adams, Harriet Stratemeyer. 1943. Grosset & Dunlap. (P.511)
--*The Clue of the Broken Locket.* Keene, Carolyn, pseud. (1894-1982). Adams, Harriet Stratemeyer. c.1934. Grosset & Dunlap. (P.511)
--*The Clue of the Tapping Heels.* Keene, Carolyn, pseud. (1894-1982). Adams, Harriet Stratemeyer. c.1939. Grosset & Dunlap. (P.511)
--*The Haunted Bridge.* Keene, Carolyn, pseud. (1894-1982). Adams, Harriet Stratemeyer. c.1937. Grosset & Dunlap. (P.512)
--*The Hidden Staircase.* Keene, Carolyn, pseud. (1894-1982). Adams, Harriet Stratemeyer. c.1930. Grosset & Dunlap. (P.512)
--*Hold That Line!.* Sherman, Harold Morrow (1898-). c.1930. Grosset & Dunlap. (P.819)
--*Joyous Peggy.* Copp, Lillian Grace. 1931. Cupples & Leon Company. (P.218)
--*Kate Martin's Problem: Or, Facing the Wide World.* Barton, May Hollis, pseud. Stratemeyer Syndicate. 1929. Cupples & Leon Co. (P.78)
--*Lost in the Caves of Gold: Or, Jerry Ford Among the Mountains of Mystery.* Moore, Fenworth, pseud. Stratemeyer Syndicate. 1931. Cupples & Leon Co. (P.660)
--*The Message in the Hollow Oak.* Keene, Carolyn, pseud. (1894-1982). Adams, Harriet Stratemeyer. c.1935. Grosset & Dunlap. (P.512)
--*The Mystery at Lilac Inn.* Keene, Carolyn, pseud. (1894-1982). Adams, Harriet Stratemeyer. c.1930. Grosset & Dunlap. (P.512)
--*The Mystery at the Moss-Covered Mansion.* Keene, Carolyn, pseud. (1894-1982). Adams, Harriet Stratemeyer. c.1941. Grosset & Dunlap. (P.512)
--*The Mystery of the Brass Bound Trunk.* Keene, Carolyn, pseud. (1894-1982). Adams, Harriet Stratemeyer. c.1940. Grosset & Dunlap. (P.512)
--*The Mystery of the Ivory Charm.* Keene, Carolyn, pseud. (1894-1982). Adams, Harriet Stratemeyer. c.1936. Grosset & Dunlap. (P.512)
--*The Mystery of the Tolling Bell.* Keene, Carolyn, pseud. (1894-1982). Adams, Harriet Stratemeyer. 1946. Grosset & Dunlap. (P.512)
--*Nancy's Mysterious Letter.* Keene, Carolyn, pseud. (1894-1982). Adams, Harriet Stratemeyer. c.1932. Grosset & Dunlap. (P.512)
--*The Password to Larkspur Lane.* Keene, Carolyn, pseud. (1894-1982). Adams, Harriet Stratemeyer. c.1933. Grosset & Dunlap. (P.512)
--*The Phantom Freighter.* Dixon, Franklin W, pseud. Stratemeyer Syndicate. 1947. Grosset & Dunlap. (P.274)
--*Polly and Carola at Ravenswood.* Roy, Lillian Elizabeth Becker, Mrs. (1868-1932). c.1931. Grosset & Dunlap. (P.782)
--*Polly Learns to Fly.* Roy, Lillian Elizabeth Becker, Mrs. (1868-1932). c.1932. Grosset & Dunlap. (P.782)
--*Prisoners on the Pirate Ship: Or, Jerry Ford and the Yellow Men.* Moore, Fenworth, pseud. Stratemeyer Syndicate. 1932. Cupples & Leon Co. (P.660)
--*The Quest of the Missing Map.* Keene, Carolyn, pseud. (1894-1982). Adams, Harriet Stratemeyer. c.1942. Grosset & Dunlap. (P.512)
--*Roy Blakeley up in the Air.* Fitzhugh, Percy Keese (1876-). c.1931. Grosset & Dunlap. (P.329)
--*Ruth Fielding and Her Crowning Victory: Or, Winning Honors Abroad.* Emerson, Alice B., pseud. Stratemeyer Syndicate. 1934. Cupples & Leon Co. (P.306)
--*Ruth Fielding and Her Double.* Emerson, Alice B., pseud. Stratemeyer Syndicate. 1932. Cupples & Leon Co. (P.306)
--*Ruth Fielding and Her Greatest Triumph: Or, Saving Her Company from Disaster.* Emerson, Alice B., pseud. Stratemeyer Syndicate. 1933. Cupples & Leon Co. (P.306)
--*Sallie's Test of Skill: Or, Winning the Trophy.* Barton, May Hollis, pseud. Stratemeyer Syndicate. 1931. Cupples & Leon Co. (P.78)
--*The Search for Peggy Ann: Or, A Mystery of the Flood.* Barton, May Hollis, pseud. Stratemeyer Syndicate. 1930. Cupples & Leon Co. (P.78)
--*The Secret at Shadow Ranch.* Keene, Carolyn, pseud. (1894-1982). Adams, Harriet Stratemeyer. c.1931. Grosset & Dunlap. (P.512)
--*The Secret in the Old Attic.* Keene, Carolyn, pseud. (1894-1982). Adams, Harriet Stratemeyer. 1944. Grosset & Dunlap. (P.512)
--*The Secret in the Old Well.* Keene, Carolyn, pseud. (1894-1982). Adams, Harriet Stratemeyer. 1944. Grosset & Dunlap. (P.512)
--*The Secret of Red Gate Farm.* Keene, Carolyn, pseud. (1894-1982). Adams, Harriet Stratemeyer. c.1931. Grosset & Dunlap. (P.512)
--*The Secret of Skull Mountain.* Dixon, Franklin W, pseud. Stratemeyer Syndicate. 1948. Grosset & Dunlap. (P.274)
--*The Secret of the Lost Tunnel.* Dixon, Franklin W, pseud. Stratemeyer Syndicate. 1950. Grosset & Dunlap. (P.274)
--*The Secret of the Old Clock.* Keene, Carolyn, pseud. (1894-1982). Adams, Harriet Stratemeyer. c.1930. Grosset & Dunlap. (P.513)
--*The Secret Panel.* Dixon, Franklin W., pseud. Stratemeyer Syndicate. 1946. Grosset & Dunlap. (P.274)
--*The Short-Wave Mystery.* Dixon, Franklin W., pseud. Stratemeyer Syndicate. 1945. Grosset & Dunlap. (P.274)
--*The Sign of the Crooked Arrow.* Dixon, Franklin W, pseud. Stratemeyer Syndicate. 1949. Grosset & Dunlap. (P.274)
--*The Sign of the Twisted Candles.* Keene, Carolyn, pseud. (1894-1982). Adams, Harriet Stratemeyer. c.1933. Grosset & Dunlap. (P.513)
--*The Wailing Siren Mystery.* Dixon, Franklin W, pseud. Stratemeyer Syndicate. 1951. Grosset & Dunlap. (P.274)
--*The Whispering Statue.* Keene, Carolyn, pseud. (1894-1982). Adams, Harriet Stratemeyer. c.1937. Grosset & Dunlap. (P.513)
--*Who Closed the Door: Or, Perry Pierce and the Old Storehouse Mystery.* Locke, Clinton W., pseud. Stratemeyer Syndicate. 1931. Henry Altemus Co. (P.579)
--*Who Hid the Key: Or, Perry Pierce Tracing Counterfeit Money.* Locke, Clinton W., pseud. Stratemeyer Syndicate. 1932. Henry Altemus Co. (P.579)
--*Who Opened the Safe: Or, Perry Pierce and the Secret Cipher Mystery.* Locke, Clinton W., pseud. Stratemeyer Syndicate. 1931. Henry Altemus Co. (P.579)
--*Wind's in the West.* Lawrence, Josephine (1890-1978). c.1931. Cupples & Leon Company. (P.556)
--*Wrecked on Cannibal Island: Or, Jerry Ford's Adventures Among Savages.* Moore, Fenworth, pseud. Stratemeyer Syndicate. 1931. Cupples & Leon Co. (P.661)

Tang, You-Shah
--*Pie-Biter.* McCunn, Ruthanne L. 1983. Design Ent SF. (P.597)

Taniguchi, Kazuko (1946-)
--*Monster Mary, Mischief Maker.* Taniguchi, Kazuko (1946-). c.1976. McGraw-Hill. (P.877)

Tanis, William
--*Heroes of the Western Outposts.* McCall, Edith Sansom (1911-). c.1960. Childrens Press. (P.594)
--*Heroes of Western Outposts.* McCall, Edith Sansom (1911-). 1980. Childrens. (P.594)

Taniuchi, Kota (1947-)
--*The North Star Man.* Taniuchi, Kota (1947-). Fujita, Tamao (1905-), tr. 1970, c.1969. Watts. (P.877)
--*Trolley.* Taniuchi, Kota (1947-). 1971, c.1969. F. Watts. (P.877)
--*Up on a Hilltop.* Taniuchi, Kota (1947-). 1971, c.1969. F. Watts. (P.877)
--*Who's Calling Me?.* Taniuchi, Kota (1947-). 1973. H. Z. Walck. (P.877)

Taniuchi, Rokur O.
--*Winds and Wildcat Places.* 1st ed. Miyazawa, Kenji (1896-1933). 1967. Kodansha International. (P.652)

Tanner, Dorothy
--*Legends from the Red Man's Forest.* Tanner, Dorothy. c.1895. A. Flanagan. (P.877)

Tanner, Suzy-Jane
--*Critter Chronicles: Fables for Here and Now.* Barnetson, John. 1982. Celestial Arts. (P.73)
--*Follow the Star.* Powers, Mala (1931-). c.1980. Dawne-Leigh Publications. (P.736)
--*Grow up, Mom.* Tanner, Suzy-Jane. 1985. Roundtable Pub. (P.878)
--*My Uncle Lancelot.* Tanner, Suzy-Jane. 1985. Roundtable Pub. (P.878)

Tanobe, Miyuki (1937-)
--*Children of Quebec.* Tanobe, Miyuki (1937-). N.D. Tundra Bks. (P.878)

Tansley, Eric
--*Ajax, Golden Dog of the Australian Bush.* Patchett, Mary Osborne Elwyn (1897-). 1954, c.1953. Bobbs-Merrill. (P.708)
--*Uncle Whiskers.* Brown, Philip. 1975. Little. (P.142)

Tarbell, Harlan
--*Cinderella and Five Other Fairy Plays.* Barbee, Lindsey (1876-). c.1922. T.S. Denison & Company. (P.70)

Tardi, Jacques
--*The Enchanted Pig: Rumanian Fairy Tale.* american ed. c.1984. Creative Education. (P.878)

Tarkington, Kate
--*Rex Goes to the Rodeo.* Tarkington, Kate. c.1955. Naylor Co. (P.878)

Tarrant, Carol
--*Sleeping Beauty.* Daniels, Patricia, adapted by. c.1980. Raintree Childrens Books. (P.241)

Tarrant, Margaret Winifred (1888-)
--*The Book of the Clock.* Golding, Harry. N.D. George Sully & Co. (P.373)
--*Joan in Flowerland.* Tarrant, Margaret Winifred (1888-) & Dutton, Lewis. 1935. F. Warne & Co., Ltd. (P.878)
--*Johann the Woodcarver.* Wood, Gilmore. N.D. Frederick Warne & Co. (P.975)
--*The Little White Gate.* Hoatson, Florence. 1925. Thomas Y. Crowell Company. (P.447)
--*The Littlest One.* Webb, Marion St. John Adcock, Mrs. (1840-1930). N.D. Frederick A. Stokes Co. (P.938)
--*Lucy Mary.* Herbertson, Agnes Grozier. N.D. Dodge Publishing Co. (P.437)
--*The Margaret Tarrant Christmas Book.* Tarrant, Margaret Winifred (1888-). N.D. Hale Cushman & Flint. (P.878)
--*The Margaret Tarrant Nursery Rhyme Book.* Tarrant, Margaret Winifred (1888-). N.D. E. P. Dutton & Co. (P.878)
--*Margaret Tarrant's Fairy Tales.* Tarrant, Margaret Winifred (1888-). 1978. Har-Row. (P.878)
--*Margaret Tarrant's Nursery Rhymes.* Tarrant, Margaret Winifred (1888-). 1978. Har-Row. (P.878)
--*Mother Goose Nursery Tales.* Tarrant, Margaret Winifred (1888-), ed. N.D. Frederick A. Stokes. (P.878)
--*The Pied Piper of Hamelin.* Browning, Robert (1812-1889). N.D. E P Dutton. (P.143)
--*Rhymes of Old Times.* N.D. Hale Cushman & Flint. (P.878)
--*Rhymes of Old Times.* Medici Society. Tarrant, Margaret Winifred (1888-) 1925. The Medici Society. (P.878)
--*Songs with Music: From 'A Child's Garden of Verses'.* Stevenson, Robert Louis (1850-1894). Crawford, Thomas (1860-), contrib. by. 1936. T. Nelson & Sons. (P.857)
--*Three Chums, Peggy, Prince, and Bobby.* Leighton, Mary (1866-). c.1939. Chapman & Grimes. (P.563)
--*The Water Babies.* Kingsley, Charles (1819-1875). N.D. E P Dutton. (P.525)
--*The Water Babies.* Kingsley, Charles (1819-1875). 1914. J. M. Dent & Sons, Ltd. (P.525)

Tarrant, Margaret Winifred (1888-) & Rhys, Megan
--*In Wheelabout and Cockalone.* Rhys, Grace Little, Mrs. (1865-1929), ed. 1918. Frederick A. Stokes. (P.760)

Tarrant, Percy
--*Comrades Ever!.* Lynn, Escott, pseud. (1866-1950). Lawrence, Christopher George Holman. 1921. J. B. Lippincott Company. (P.592)
--*Gay.* Whitaker, Evelyn. 1903. Little Brown & Co. (P.950)

Tenniel, John, Sir (1820-1914) & Stanley, Diana (1909-)
--*Alice's Adventures in Wonderland and Through the Looking-Glass.* Carroll, Lewis, pseud. (1832-1898). Dodgson, Charles Lutwidge. 1964. Dent. (P.173)
--*Alice's Adventures in Wonderland and Through the Looking Glass.* Carroll, Lewis, pseud. (1832-1898). Dodgson, Charles Lutwidge. 1954. E.P.Dutton & Co. (P.173)
Tenniel, John, Sir (1820-1914) & Stevens, Beatrice (1876-)
--*Alice's Adventures in Wonderland, and Through the Looking-glass.* Carroll, Lewis, pseud. (1832-1898). Dodgson, Charles Lutwidge. Farwell, Abbie, intro. by. 1903. P. F. Collier & Son. (P.173)
Tenniel, John, Sir (1820-1914) & Thomson, Emily Gertrude
--*The Nursery "Alice".* Dodgson, Charles Lutwidge (1832-1898). Carroll, Lewis, pseud. Gardner, Martin (1914-), intro. by. 1966. McGraw-Hill. (P.278)
Tennyson, Noel
--*Christmas Carols: A Treasury of Holiday Favorites with Words & Pictures.* 1983. Random. (P.882)
--*Santa Is Coming.* 1981. Random. (P.882)
Teppich, John
--*The Seven Little Pifflesniffs.* Richardson, Margaret Stimson. 1952. Abingdon-Cokesbury Press. (P.763)
--*Which Witch.* Lasson, Robert (1922-). N.D. E. M. Hale & Co. (P.553)
Terlesky, Vitalie Z.
--*To a Little Child.* Sutton, Edith Gideon, Mrs. c.1931. B. Humphries, Inc. (P.872)
Ternei, Dora
--*Myeko's Gift.* Haugaard, Kay. 1967, c.1966. Abelard. (P.420)
Terrel, Mary Field, Mrs.
--*Big Family.* Kelsey, Alice Geer (1896-). 1950. Westminster Press. (P.517)
--*Bird-House to Let.* Terrel, Mary Field, Mrs. 1931. Frederick A. Stokes Company. (P.882)
Tesa, Rudi
--*Clappity Clap!.* A Book about Sharing. Ziefert, Harriet. 1984. Viking. (P.992)
--*Diggety Dig: A Book About Playing.* Ziefert, Harriet. N.D. Viking Press. (P.992)
--*Munchety Munch!.* A Book about Eating. Ziefert, Harriet. 1984. Viking. (P.992)
--*Zippety Zip: A Book About Dressing.* Ziefert, Harriet. 1984. Viking Press. (P.992)
Tessin, Louise D.
--*Bunny Bearskin.* Winfrey, Guy. N.D. Milton Bradley Co. (P.969)
--*Pussy Purr-Mew the Diary of a Kitten.* Winfrey, Guy. c.1927. Milton Bradley Company. (P.969)
Tessin, Louise D. & Fenton, C. L.
--*Western Wild Life.* Chaffee, Allen. N.D. Caxton Printers. (P.181)
Tessin, Marion Von
--*The Long-haired Elephant Child.* Tessin, Marion Von. 1958. Pantheon. (P.883)
Tessmann, Kurt
--*Foxy and the Badgers.* Montgomery, John (1916-). 1969, c.1968. Schocken Books. (P.658)
Testa, Fulvio
--*The Butterfly Collector.* Lewis, Naomi. 1979, c.1978. Prentice-Hall. (P.570)
--*If You Seek Adventure.* Testa, Fulvio. 1984. Dial Bks for Young Readers. (P.883)
--*If You Take a Paint Brush.* Testa, Fulvio. 1983. Dial Press. (P.883)
--*If You Take a Pencil.* Testa, Fulvio. c.1982. Dial Press. (P.883)
--*The Land Where the Ice Cream Grows.* Testa, Fulvio. Burgess, Anthony, pseud. (1917-), as told by Wilson, John Anthony Burgess. 1979. Doubleday. (P.883)
--*Leaves.* Testa, Fulvio. 1983, c.1980. Bedrick Books: Dist. by Harper & Row. (P.883)
--*A Long Trip to Tea Time.* Burgess, Anthony, pseud. (1917-). Wilson, John Anthony Burgess. 1976. Stonehill Pub Co. (P.152)
--*Never Satisfied.* Testa, Fulvio. 1980. Faber and Faber in Association with Nord-Sud Verlag. (P.883)
--*Never Satisfied.* Testa, Fulvio. 1982. Faber. (P.883)
--*The Nightingale.* Andersen, Hans Christian (1805-1875). Pelgrave, E. J. (1805-1875), adapted by. 1974. Abelard-Schuman. (P.36)
--*The Paper Airplane.* Testa, Fulvio & Baumann, Kurt. c.1981. Little, Brown. (P.883)
--*A Short Step.* Testa, Fulvio. 1979. Mayflower Books. (P.883)
Testa, Vivien
--*The Story of Sam Coho.* Humphreville, Frances Tibbets (1909-). 1947. House of Field-Doubleday. (P.472)
Tetlow, George (1934-)
--*Come Back, Peter.* Woodberry, Joan Merle (1921-). 1972, c.1968. Crowell. (P.976)
--*Come Back Peter.* Woodberry, Joan Merle (1921-). 1968. Tri-Ocean Books. (P.976)
Tetlow, John (1842-1911)
--*The Heroes: Or, Greek Fairy Tales for My Children.* ed. Kingsley, Charles (1819-1875). 1885. Ginn, Heath, & Co. (P.525)
Thackeray, William Makepeace, et al. (1811-1863)
--*The Rose & the Ring With the Magic Fish-bone: Or, the History of Prince Giglio and Prince Bulbo with the Magic Fish-bone.* Thackeray, William Makepeace (1811-1863) & Dickens, Charles John Huffam (1812-1870). 1959. Dent. (P.883)
Thackeray, William Makepeace, jt. illus. see Falls, Charles Buckles.
Thackeray, William Makepeace, jt. illus. see Hogarth, Paul.
Thackeray, William Makepeace (1811-1863)
--*The Awful History of Bluebeard.* Perrault, Charles (1628-1703). 1924. J. Kern. (P.718)
--*Maudie's Mush Pots.* Woods, Joan Le Suer (1932-). 1963. Abingdon Press. (P.977)
--*The Rose & the Ring.* Thackeray, William Makepeace (1811-1863). Preston, Phyllis, ed. 1926. J. M. Dent & Sons, Ltd. (P.883)
--*The Rose and the Ring.* Thackeray, William Makepeace (1811-1863). N.D. Brentano's. (P.883)
--*The Rose and the Ring.* Thackeray, William Makepeace (1811-1863). N.D. Frederick A. Stokes Co. (P.883)
--*The Rose and the Ring.* Thackeray, William Makepeace (1811-1863). N.D. MacMillan Bks. (P.883)
--*The Rose and the ring.* Thackeray, William Makepeace (1811-1863). N.D. St Martin's Press. (P.883)
--*The Rose and the Ring: Or, The History of Prince Giglio and Prince Bulbo.* A Fireside Pantomime for Great and Small Children. Thackeray, William Makepeace (1811-1863). N.D. Caldwell. (P.883)
--*The Rose and the Ring: Or, The History of Prince Giglio and Prince Bulbo.* A Fireside Pantomime for Great and Small Children. Thackeray, William Makepeace (1811-1863). N.D. Estes & Lauriat's. (P.883)
--*Rose and the Ring: Or, The History of Prince Giglio and Prince Bulbo/A Fireside Pantomime for Great and Small Children.* Thackeray, William Makepeace (1811-1863). N.D. H. M. Caldwell Co. (P.883)
--*The Rose and the Ring: Or, The History of Prince Giglio and Prince Bulbo.* A Fireside Pantomime for Great and Small Children. Thackeray, William Makepeace (1811-1863). N.D. Putman. (P.883)
--*The Rose and the Ring: Or, the History of Prince Giglio and Prince Bulbo; a Fire-Side Pantomime for Great and Small Children.* Thackeray, William Makepeace (1811-1863). 1967. University Microfilms. (P.883)

Thackeray, William Makepeace (1811-1863) & Gilbert, John

--*The Rose and the Ring: Or, Prince Giglio and Prince Bulo.* Thackeray, William Makepeace (1811-1863). 1959. Dutton. (P.883)

Thakura, Ravindranathu see Tagore, Rbanindranath, pseud.

Thal, Samuel (1903-)
--*Okinpochee Bird Family.* Thal, Samuel (1903-). N.D. Branden. (P.883)
Thaler, Mike (1936-)
--*Clown's Smile.* Thaler, Mike (1936-). 1962. Har-Row. (P.883)
--*Funny Bones: Cartoon Monster Riddles.* Thaler, Mike (1936-). 1976. F. Watts. (P.883)
--*Give Up?.* Cole, William Rossa (1919-). 1978. Watts. (P.208)
--*The King's Flower.* Thaler, Mike (1936-). 1963. Orion Press. (P.883)
--*Knock Knocks, the Most Ever.* Cole, William Rossa (1919-). 1976. F. Watts. (P.208)
--*Knock Knocks You've Never Heard Before.* Cole, William Rossa (1919-). 1977. F. Watts. (P.208)
--*Magic Boy.* Thaler, Mike (1936-). 1961. Har-Row. (P.883)
--*Magic Letter Riddles.* Thaler, Mike (1936-). 1974. Schol Bk Serv. (P.883)
--*Moonboy.* Thaler, Mike (1936-). 1964. Harper & Row. (P.883)
--*Never Tickle a Turtle: Cartoons, Riddles & Funny Stories.* Thaler, Mike (1936-). 1977. Watts. (P.884)
--*Penny Pencil: The Story of a Pencil.* Thaler, Mike (1936-). c.1963. Harper & Row. (P.884)
--*Riddle Riot.* Thaler, Mike (1936-). 1976. Scholastic Inc. (P.884)
--*Soup with Quackers: Funny Cartoon Riddles.* Thaler, Mike (1936-). 1976. Watts. (P.884)
--*What's up Duck.* Thaler, Mike (1936-). 1978. Watts. (P.884)
--*Wuzzles.* Thaler, Mike (1936-). 1976. Scholastic Inc. (P.884)
--*The Yellow Brick Toad: Funny Frog Cartoons, Riddles, and Silly Stories.* Thaler, Mike (1936-). 1978. Doubleday. (P.884)
Thamer, Katie
--*The Black Horse.* Mayer, Marianna (1945-). 1984. Dial Bks Young Readers. (P.633)
--*The Little Mermaid.* Andersen, Hans Christian (1805-1875). c.1984. D.R. Godine. (P.36)
--*The Red Shoes.* Andersen, Hans Christian (1805-1875). 1982. Green Tiger Pr. (P.37)
--*The Song of Songs: King James Version.* McClasky, Stephen 1982. Green Tiger Pr. (P.884)
Tharlet, Eve
--*Dizzy from Fools.* Miller, M. L. c.1985. Picture Book Studio USA. (P.648)
Thatcher, Frances
--*Percival's Party.* Hynard, Julia. 1983, c.1981. Childrens Press. (P.478)
--*Sam Cat.* Humphries, Gillian M. 1984, c.1983. Childrens Press International. (P.473)
--*Snowy the Rabbit.* Hynard, Stephen. 1983, c.1980. Childrens Press. (P.478)
--*Snuffles' House.* Faunce-Brown, Daphne. 1983, c.1980. Childrens Press. (P.319)
Thaxton, Daniel Earl
--*You Can Fly, Why Can't I?.* Kullberg, Mary E. 1969. Houghton Mifflin. (P.541)
Thayer, Bert Clark
--*Jinny: The Story of a Filly.* Thayer, Bert Clark. N.D. Farrar & Rinehart. (P.884)
Thayer, Emma Redington Lee (1874-1973)
--*The Magic Garden.* Porter, Geneva Grace Stratton, Mrs. (1863-1924). 1927. Doubleday, Page & Company. (P.732)
--*Princess Rags and Tatters.* Comstock, Harriet Theresa Smith, Mrs. (1860-). 1912. Doubleday, Page & Company. (P.212)
Thayer, Harriet Maxon
--*The Genial Sultan the Princess Who Could Not See, Late for the Coronation.* Thayer, Harriet Maxon. c.1923. Dorrance. (P.884)
Thayer, Wildie
--*Flower Fancies from Fairyland.* Thayer, Wildie. c.1911. The C. M. Clark Publishing Co. (P.884)
Theaker, Harry G.
--*Children's Stories from Japanese Fairy Tales and Legends.* Kato, N. Vredenburg, Deric Walcott (1860-), ed. N.D. R. Tuck & Sons, Ltd. (P.508)
--*Children's Stories from the Arabian Nights.* Woolf, Rose Yeatman. N.D. David McKay. (P.977)
Theakston, Margaret
--*The Red Racing Car.* Swallow, Su. Steele, Philip, ed. 1980. Silver Burdett Co. (P.873)
Theesfeld, Nola
--*Silver Linings.* Theesfeld, Nola. c.1929. Augustana Book Concern. (P.884)
Theibert, Philip Richard
--*General Jim.* Davis, Hazel H. 1958. Bethany Pr. (P.246)
Thelen, Mary
--*The Hospital Scares Me.* Hogan, Paula Z & Hogan, Kirk. Wilson, Jerriann Myers, intro. by. c.1980. Raintree Childrens Books. (P.452)
Thelwell, Norman (1923-)
--*Away went Galloper.* Baker, Margaret (1890-). 1964. Atheneum. (P.63)
--*Thelwell's Brat Race.* Thelwell, Norman (1923-). 1977. Scribner. (P.885)
Themerson, Franciszka
--*Mr.* Rouse Builds His House. Themerson, Stefan (1910-) & Wright, Barbara. c.1951. Lothrop, Lee & Shepard Co. (P.885)
Theobalds, Prue

--*Chike and the River.* Achebe, Chinua (1930-). 1966. University Press. (P.4)
--*The Golden Cockerel: Three Stories of Magic and Witchcraft from Russian Opera.* Gibson, Enid. 1963. H. Z. Walck. (P.366)
--*Marvella's Hobby.* Cushman, Jerome. 1962. Abelard-Schuman. (P.237)
--*Rocket Mouse.* Priestley, Lee Shore (1904-). 1961. Abelard-Schuman. (P.739)
--*Stop the Typewriters.* Sargent, Shirley (1927-). 1963. Abelard-Schuman. (P.793)
Theurer, Marilyn C.
--*The Kingdom of Wundle.* Siegel, Robert Harold (1939-). 1982. Good News. (P.823)
Thewlis, Diana
--*Johnny Castleseed.* Ormondroyd, Edward (1925-). 1985. Houghton Mifflin. (P.696)
Thiele, Leo P.
--*Colonists & Caravans: Return to Santa Fe and The Name Day of Dona Clara.* Kelly, Bernadine Creswell. 1950. University Pub. Co. (P.516)
--*Lujan Returns.* Kelly, Bernadine Creswell. 1950. University Pub. Co. (P.516)
--*Tales for a Tenderfoot.* Kelly, Bernadine Creswell. 1950. University Pub. Co. (P.516)
--*Trail Riders.* Kelly, Bernadine Creswell. 1950. University Pub. Co. (P.516)
Thiele, Reinhold
--*After School: Books of Adventure For Boys.* Overton, Robert. N.D. Frederick A Stokes Co. (P.698)
--*Light Out.* Overton, Robert. N.D. Dana Estes & Co. (P.698)
--*Lights Out: Book Of Adventure For Boys.* Overton, Robert. N.D. Frederick A. Stokes Co. (P.698)
Thielmann, Joseph Charles, photos by.
--*Suzy Goes to Mexico.* Thielmann, Mary Carney. 1942. A. Whitman and Company. (P.885)
Thieme, A.
--*Fighting Blood: A Tale of Kitchener's Campaign in the Soudan.* Haines, Donal Hamilton (1886-). 1927. Houghton Mifflin Company. (P.402)
Thieme, Channing
--*There's a Caterpillar in My Lemonade.* Gregory, Diana Jean (1933-). c.1980. Addison-Wesley Pub. Co. (P.388)
Thiess, Anne
--*Tobi.* Wilson, Joyce Lancaster. 1968. Funk & Wagnalls. (P.966)
Thiess, Anne & Thiess, Walter
--*Hannibal.* Thiess, Anne & Thiess, Walter. 1968. Funk & Wagnalls. (P.885)
Thiess, Walter, jt. illus. see Thiess, Anne.
Thiselton-Dyer, Thomas Firminger (1848-)
--*Folk-Lore of Women.* 1968. Singing Tree Press. (P.885)
Thistlethwaite, Miles (1945-)
--*Storm & Other Old English Riddles.* Crossley-Holland, Kevin (1941-), ed. Crossley-Holland, Kevin, tr. 1970. FS&G. (P.232)
Thoburn, Jean
--*Away in a Manger: Christmas Verses.* Thoburn, Jean, selected by. 1942. Oxford University Press. (P.885)
Thoele, Lillian
--*Cactus.* Struble, Virginia (1900-). 1958. Bethany Press. (P.868)
Thole, Dorothy
--*Tatum's Favorite Shape.* Thole, Dorothy. 1978. Scholastic Inc. (P.885)
Thollander, Earl Gustave (1922-)
--*Aukele the Fearless: A Legend of Old Hawaii.* Thompson, Vivian Laubach (1911-). 1972. Golden Gate Junior Books. (P.888)
--*Bug Haiku.* Hackett, James W. 1968. Japan Pubns. (P.401)
--*The Cuckoo's Reward: A Folk Tale from Mexico in Spanish and English Cuento Popular De Mexico En Espanol E Ingles.* 1st ed. Kouzel, Daisy, adapted by. c.1977. Doubleday. (P.536)
--*The Dog and the Boat Boy.* Martin, Patricia Miles (1899-). 1969. Putnam. (P.625)
--*Going up.* Paddock, Charles Lee (1891-). 1953. Pacific Press Pub. Association. (P.700)
--*The Hullabaloo ABC.* Cleary, Beverly Bunn (1916-). c.1960. Parnassus Press. (P.200)
--*Jump Frog Jump.* Martin, Patricia Miles (1899-). c.1965. Putnam. (P.625)
--*Kala and the Sea Bird.* Mullins, Vera Annie Cooper (1903-). c.1966. Golden Gate. (P.671)
--*Keola's Hawaiian Donkey.* Thompson, Vivian Laubach (1911-). 1966. Golden Gate Junior Books. (P.888)
--*Little Brown Bat.* Voight, Virginia Frances (1909-). 1969. G P Putnum's Sons. (P.921)
--*Maui-Full-of-Tricks: A Legend of Old Hawaii.* Thompson, Vivian Laubach (1911-). 1970. Golden Gate Junior Books. (P.888)
--*Mrs.* Crumble & Fire Engine No. 7. Martin, Patricia Miles (1899-). 1966. Putnam Sons. (P.625)
--*No NO Risina.* Martin, Patricia Miles (1899-). 1964. G P Putnum's Sons. (P.625)
--*Ramon Makes a Trade.* Ritchie, Barbara Gibbons. 1959. Parnassus. (P.766)
--*Sad Song, Happy Song.* Miklowitz, Gloria D. (1927-). 1973. Putnam. (P.644)
--*School for Julio: A See and Read Storybook.* Rowland, Florence Wightman (1900-). 1968. Putnam. (P.782)
--*The Singing Leaf.* Rowland, Florence Wightman (1900-). c.1965. Putnam. (P.782)
--*To Catch a Mongoose.* Ritchie, Barbara Gibbons. 1964. Parnassus. (P.766)
--*Where's Jeremy?.* Brown, Myra Berry (1918-). 1968. Golden Gate Junior Books. (P.142)
Thom, William Albert Strang see Morrison, J. Strang, pseud.
Thom, William Albert Strang (1900-)
--*Wind Force Seven.* Morrison, J. Strang, pseud. Thom, William Albert Strang (1900-). Morrison, J. Strang, pseud. 1958. Macmillan. (P.885)
Thomas, Albertine
--*Tales from Herodotus.* 1 st. ed. Thomas, Albertine, retold by. 1966. Pageant. (P.885)
Thomas, Allan (1901-)
--*The Beautiful Ship: A Story of the Great Lakes.* Prescott, John Brewster (1919-). 1952. Longmans, Green. (P.738)
--*Behind the Zuni Masks.* Gendron, Val. 1958. Longmans, Green. (P.363)
--*The Half-Pint Jinni and Other Stories.* Dolbier, Maurice Wyman (1912-). 1948. Random House. (P.278)
--*Hillhaven.* Thompson, Mary Wolfe, Mrs. (1886-). 1949. Longmans, Green. (P.887)

Uzilevsky, Marcus
--*Old Testament Color & Story.* Uzilevsky, Marcus. 1974. Troubador Pr. (P.911)
Vaccarello, Paul (1945-)
--*After the End.* Asimov, Isaac, et al. (1920-), eds. c.1981. Raintree. (P.52)
Vachula, Monica
--*The Crest and the Hide, and Other African Stories of Heroes, Chiefs, Bards, Hunters, Sorcerers, and Common People.* Courlander, Harold (1908-), compiled by. c.1982. Coward, McCann & Geoghegan. **Award: (ALA).** (P.224)
--*In Bikole: Modern Stories of Life in a West African Village.* Gilroy, Thomas Laurence (1951-). 1978. Knopf: Distributed by Random House. (P.369)
Vaes, Alain
--*The Porcelain Pepper Pot.* Vaes, Alain. 1982. Little. (P.911)
--*The Steadfast Tin Soldier.* Andersen, Hans Christian (1805-1875). 1983. Little. (P.37)
Vaeth, Susan
--*Ishkabibble!.* Crayder, Dorothy & Vaeth, Susan. 1976. Atheneum. (P.230)
--*Soonie and the Dragon.* Murphy, Shirley Rousseau (1928-). 1979. Atheneum. (P.673)
Vail, Claudine Cook
--*Stories I Like.* Pulliam, Roy Avron (1902-) & Darby, Oscar Nolan, eds. 1949. Steck Co. (P.741)
Valens, Evans G., Jr. (1920-)
--*Me and Frumpet: An Adventure with Size and Science.* 1st ed. Valens, Evans G., Jr. (1920-). Teller, Edward (1908-), frwd. by. 1958. Dutton. (P.912)
Valenti, Angelo
--*St.* Valentine's Day. Bulla, Clyde Robert (1914-). 1965. Harper. (P.149)
Valentine
--*Count of Monte Cristo.* Dumas, Alexandre (1802-1870). N.D. George Routledge & Sons. (P.288)
Valentine, A. C.
--*The Blue Grotto Terror.* Claudy, Carl Harry (1879-). c.1934. Grosset & Dunlap. (P.200)
--*The Land of No Shadow.* Claudy, Carl Harry (1879-). c.1933. Grosset & Dunlap. (P.200)
--*The Mystery Men of Mars.* Claudy, Carl Harry (1879-). c.1933. Grosset & Dunlap. (P.200)
--*A Thousand Years a Minute.* Claudy, Carl Harry (1879-). c.1933. Grosset & Dunlap. (P.200)
Valentine, Donald Graham (1929-)
--*By Jiminy.* Daniell, David Scott, pseud. (1906-1965). Daniell, Albert Scott. 1962. Verry. (P.241)
--*Found In the Forest.* Elliott, Lydia S. 1958. F. Warne. (P.302)
--*Horseshoe Reef.* Armstrong, Richard (1903-). 1961. Duell sloan & Pearce. (P.48)
--*Trial Trip.* Armstrong, Richard (1903-). 1963, c.1962. Criterion Books. (P.48)
Valentine, Louis Chapin (1889-)
--*The Lonely Fisherman.* Valentine, Louis Chapin (1889-). c.1933. Thomas Y. Crowell Company. (P.912)
--*Turquoise Boy and White Shell Girl.* Walton, Eda Lou. c.1933. Thomas Y. Crowell Company. (P.929)
Valentino, Paul
--*Amerigo Vespucci.* 1st ed. Baker, Nina Brown, Mrs. (1888-1957). 1956. Knopf. (P.64)
--*Lucky Potato Harvest.* Rev. ed. Olds, Helen Diehl (1895-1981). 1964. Melmont Publishers. (P.693)
--*Sara's Lucky Harvest.* Olds, Helen Diehl (1895-1981). 1953. J. Messner. (P.693)
--*Squaw Boy.* Balch, Glenn (1902-). 1952. Crowell. (P.64)
Valintcourt, Honore
--*The City Under the Back Steps.* 1st ed. Lampman, Evelyn Sibley (1907-1980). 1960. Doubleday. (P.546)
Valla, Victor
--*Juan, Carmela & the Pirates.* Bennett, Gertrude. 1978. Vantage. (P.93)
Vallario, Jean
--*Echoes of the Sea: Poems.* Parker, Elinor Milnor (1906-), compiled by. c.1977. Scribner. (P.706)
Vallejo, Boris
--*Boris.* Vallejo, Boris. 1979. Western Pub. (P.912)
--*The Boy Who Saved the Stars.* Vallejo, Boris. c.1978. O'Quinn Studios. (P.912)
Vallejo, Kay
--*Ulysses and the Cyclops: A Tale from Homer's Odyssey.* 1st ed. Cullen, James J & Homerus. 1956. Microclassics Press. (P.234)
Vallely, Henry E.
--*The Adventures of Tom Sawyer.* Clemens, Samuel Langhorne (1835-1910). Twain, Mark, pseud. c.1944. Whitman Publishing Co. (P.201)
--*Ann Rutherford and the Key to Nightmare Hall: An Original Story Featuring Ann Rutherford, Famous Motion-Picture Player, As the Heroine.* authorized. Heisenfelt, Kathryn. 1942. Whitman Publishing Company. (P.430)
--*Ann Sheridan and the Sign of the Sphinx: An Original Story Featuring Ann Sheridan, Famous Motion Picture Star, As the Heroine.* authorized. Heisenfelt, Kathryn. 1943. Whitman Publishing Company. (P.430)
--*Betty Grable and the House with the Iron Shutters: An Original Story Featuring Betty Grable, Famous Motion Picture Star, As the Heroine.* authorized. Heisenfelt, Kathryn. 1943. Whitman Publishing Company. (P.430)
--*Bonita Granville and the Mystery of Star Island: An Original Story Featuring Bonita Granville, Famous Motion-Picture Player, As the Heroine.* authorized. Heisenfelt, Kathryn. 1942. Whitman Publishing Company. (P.431)
--*A Boy Fighter with Andrew Jackson.* Thomas, Harlan C, pseud. (1903-1966). Keating, Lawrence A.. 1946. Whitman Publishing Company. (P.886)
--*A Boy Sailor with John Paul Jones.* Thomas, Harlan C, pseud. (1903-1966). Keating, Lawrence A.. 1946. Whitman Publishing Company. (P.886)
--*Dorothy Lamour and the Haunted Lighthouse: An Original Story Featuring Dorothy Lamour As the Heroine.* authorized. Radford, Ruby Lorraine (1891-1971). Bailey, Matilda, pseud. 1947. Whitman Pub. Co. (P.746)
--*Gene Tierney and the Invisible Wedding Gift: An Original Story Featuring Gene Tierney, Famous Motion Picture Star, As the Heroine.* authorized. Heisenfelt, Kathryn. 1947. Whitman Pub. Co. (P.431)
--*Ginger Rogers and the Riddle of the Scarlet Cloak: An Original Story Featuring Ginger Rogers, Famous Motion-Picture Star, As the Heroine.* authorized. Rogers, Lela Emogene Owens. c.1942. Whitman Publishing Company. (P.775)
--*Gregory Peck and the Red Box Enigma: An Original Story Featuring Gregory Peck, Famous Motion Picture Star, As the Hero.* authorized. Heisenfelt, Kathryn. 1947. Whitman Pub. Co. (P.431)
--*Jane Withers and the Hidden Room: An Original Story Featuring Jane Withers, Famous Motion-Picture Star, As the Heroine.* authorized. Packer, Eleanor Lewis. 1942. Whitman Publishing Company. (P.700)
--*Jane Withers and the Phantom Violin.* authorized. Snell, Roy Judson (1878-). 1943. Whitman Publishing Company. (P.838)
--*Jane Withers and the Swamp Wizard: An Original Story Featuring Jane Withers, Famous Motion Picture Star, As the Heroine.* authorized ed. illustrated by henry e. vallely. Heisenfelt, Kathryn. 1944. Whitman Publishing Company. (P.431)
--*John Payne and the Menace at Hawk's Nest.* authorized. Heisenfelt, Kathryn. 1943. Whitman Publishing Company. (P.431)
--*Kitty Carter, Canteen Girl.* Radford, Ruby Lorraine (1891-1971). 1944. Whitman Publishing Company. (P.746)
--*Laura Lee Hope's The Bobbsey Twins.* rev. ed. Hope, Laura Lee, pseud. Stratemeyer Syndicate. Kline, Bennett, retold by. c.1940. Whitman Publishing Company. (P.461)
--*The Lone Wolf and the Hidden Empire.* authorized. Smith, Carl W. Vance, Louis Joseph, created by. 1947. Whitman Pub. Co. (P.831)
--*The Long Rider and the Treasure of Vanished Men.* Du Bois, Gaylord. 1946. Whitman Publishing Company. (P.286)
--*March Anson and Scoot Bailey of the U.S.* Navy. Duncan, Gregory, pseud. (1906-1967). McClintock, Marshall. 1944. Whitman Publishing Company. (P.289)
--*Nancy Dale Army Nurse.* Radford, Ruby Lorraine (1891-1971). 1944. Whitman Publishing Company. (P.746)
--*Patty O'Neal on the Airways.* Radford, Ruby Lorraine (1891-1971). 1946. Whitman Publishing Company. (P.746)
--*Shirley Temple and the Spirit of Dragonwood: An Original Story Featuring Shirley Temple, Famous Motion Picture Star, As the Heroine.* authorized. Heisenfelt, Kathryn. 1945. Whitman Publishing Company. (P.431)
--*Tom Harmon and the Great Gridiron Plot: An Original Story Featuring Tom Harmon, Famous Football Star, As the Hero.* authorized. Dender, Jay, pseud. (1922-1983). Deindorfer, Robert Greene. 1946. Whitman Publishing Co. (P.257)
Vallentine, J. Manson
--*Legends from the Living Sea.* Salmon, Douglas. 1974. Island Pr. (P.790)
Vallier, Jean, jt. illus. see Geisel, Theodor Seuss.
Valpy, Judith
--*Letters from Foxy.* Ross, David (1935-). 1968, c.1966. Pantheon. (P.778)
--*Running to Paradise.* Yeats, William Butler (1865-1939). Crossley-Holland, Kevin, ed. 1968. Macmillan. (P.986)
--*The Vanishing Garden.* Beresford, Elisabeth. 1967, c.1965. Funk & Wagnalls. (P.95)
Van, Doren Margaret, jt. illus. see Richards, George Mather.
Van Abbe, Salaman (1883-1955)
--*Good Wives.* Alcott, Louisa May (1832-1888). 1953. Dutton. (P.17)
--*Little Women.* Alcott, Louisa May (1832-1888). 1948. Dutton. (P.17)
--*Little Women.* Alcott, Louisa May (1832-1888). 1964. Dutton. (P.17)
--*Little Women.* Alcott, Louisa May (1832-1888). 1951. E.P. Dutton & Co. (P.17)
--*Robin Hood.* Oman, Carola Mary Anima (1897-1978). 1949. E. P. Dutton & Co. (P.694)
--*Tom Brown's Schooldays.* Hughes, Thomas (1822-1896). 1951. Dent. (P.471)
--*Tom Brown's Schooldays.* Hughes, Thomas (1822-1896). 1949. Dutton. (P.471)
--*Tom Brown's SchoolDays.* Hughes, Thomas (1822-1896). 1951. E.P. Dutton & Co. (P.471)
--*Treasure Island.* Stevenson, Robert Louis (1850-1894). N.D. E. P. Dutton & Co. (P.857)
--*A Wonder Book.* Hawthorne, Nathaniel (1804-1864). 1949. Dutton. (P.424)
Van Allsburg, Chris
--*Ben's Dream.* Van Allsburg, Chris. 1982. Houghton Mifflin. **Award: (NYT).** (P.912)
--*The Garden of Abdul Gasazi.* Van Allsburg, Chris. 1979. Houghton Mifflin. **Awards: (BGH); (ALA); (NYT); (RCM).** (P.912)
--*Jumanji.* Van Allsburg, Chris. 1981. Houghton Mifflin Co. **Awards: (RCM); (NYT); (ALA); (BGH).** (P.912)
--*The Mysteries of Harris Burdick.* Van Allsburg, Chris. 1984. Houghton Mifflin. **Awards: (BGH); (ALA).** (P.912)
--*The Polar Express.* Van Allsburg, Chris. 1985. Houghton Mifflin. **Awards: (NYT); (ALA); (RCM).** (P.912)
--*The Wreck of the Zephyr.* Van Allsburg, Chris. 1983. HM. **Awards: (NYT); (ALA).** (P.912)
Van Arnam, Margaret Newton
--*The Hidden Treasure.* Bothwell, Jean (0000-1977). 1954. Friendship Press. (P.119)
Van Aver, Philip
--*Mother Goose: Twenty Nursery Rhymes.* Van Aver, Philip, ed. 1970. Grabhorn-Hoyem. (P.912)
Van Beek, Elly
--*Corso the Donkey.* Pothast-Gimberg, C. E. Van Stockum, Hilda Gerarda, tr. 1963. Dutton. (P.733)
Vance, Charles
--*Theatre for Children.* rev. ed. Ward, Winifred Louise (1884-). 1950. Childrens Theatre. (P.931)
--*Theatre for Children.* 3d ed., rev. Ward, Winifred Louise (1884-). 1958. Childrens Theatre. (P.931)
Van De Bovenkamp, Valli
--*The Flight of the Kite Merriweather.* 1st ed. Teal, Mildred. 1968. Atheneum. (P.881)
Van De Hulst, Willem Gerrit (1879-)
--*The Big Read-to-Me Story Book.* Van De Hulst, Willem Gerrit (1879-). Schooland, Marian, tr. c.1963. Zondervan Pub. House. (P.913)
Van Demark, Paul
--*Cricket.* Hamilton, Dorothy Drumm (1906-1983). 1975. Herald Press. (P.408)
--*Sissy Kid Brother.* Mueller, Amelia (1911-). 1975. Herald Press. (P.670)
--*Straight Mark.* Hamilton, Dorothy Drumm (1906-1983). 1976. Herald Press. (P.408)
Vandenberg, Gerard, photos by.
--*Sebastian and the Sausages.* Burstall, Tim. 1965. Lansdowne, Stamped on P. : Dist. by Sportshelf. (P.157)
Van Der Beek, Harmsen
--*Be Brave, Little Noddy!.* Blyton, Enid Mary (1897-1968). 1974. British Bk Ctr. (P.110)
--*Cheer up, Little Noddy!.* Blyton, Enid Mary (1897-1968). 1974. British Bk Ctr. (P.110)
--*Do Look Out, Noddy!.* Blyton, Enid Mary (1897-1968). 1974. British Bk Ctr. (P.110)
--*Here Comes Noddy Again.* Blyton, Enid Mary (1897-1968). 1974. British Bk Ctr. (P.111)
--*Hurrah for Little Noddy.* Blyton, Enid Mary (1897-1968). 1974. British Bk Ctr. (P.111)
--*Mr. Plod & Little Noddy.* Blyton, Enid Mary (1897-1968). 1974. British Bk Ctr. (P.111)
--*Noddy & His Car.* Blyton, Enid Mary (1897-1968). 1974. British Bk Ctr. (P.111)
--*Noddy & Tessie Bear.* Blyton, Enid Mary (1897-1968). 1974. British Bk Ctr. (P.111)
--*Noddy & the Aeroplane.* Blyton, Enid Mary (1897-1968). 1974. British Bk Ctr. (P.111)
--*Noddy & the Bumpy Dog.* Blyton, Enid Mary (1897-1968). 1974. British Bk Ctr. (P.111)
--*Noddy & the Bunkey.* Blyton, Enid Mary (1897-1968). 1974. British Bk Ctr. (P.111)
--*Noddy & the Magic Rubber.* Blyton, Enid Mary (1897-1968). 1974. British Bk Ctr. (P.111)
--*Noddy & the Tootles.* Blyton, Enid Mary (1897-1968). 1974. British Bk Ctr. (P.111)
--*Noddy at the Seaside.* Blyton, Enid Mary (1897-1968). 1974. British Bk Ctr. (P.111)
--*Noddy Gets into Trouble.* Blyton, Enid Mary (1897-1968). 1974. British Bk Ctr. (P.111)
--*Noddy Goes to School.* Blyton, Enid Mary (1897-1968). 1974. British Bk Ctr. (P.111)
--*Noddy Goes to Sea.* Blyton, Enid Mary (1897-1968). 1974. British Bk Ctr. (P.111)
--*Noddy Goes to the Fair.* Blyton, Enid Mary (1897-1968). 1974. British Bk Ctr. (P.111)
--*Noddy Goes to Toyland.* Blyton, Enid Mary (1897-1968). 1974. British Bk Ctr. (P.111)
--*Noddy Has an Adventure.* Blyton, Enid Mary (1897-1968). 1974. British Bk Ctr. (P.111)
--*Noddy Meets Father Christmas.* Blyton, Enid Mary (1897-1968). 1974. British Bk Ctr. (P.111)
--*Well Done Noddy!.* Blyton, Enid Mary (1897-1968). 1974. British Bk Ctr. (P.111)
--*You Funny Little Noddy.* Blyton, Enid Mary (1897-1968). 1974. British Bk Ctr. (P.111)
--*You're a Good Friend, Noddy!.* Blyton, Enid Mary (1897-1968). 1974. British Bk Ctr. (P.111)
Vanderlaan, Si
--*Brave Eagle.* Verral, Charles Spain (1904-). 1957. Golden Press. (P.918)
Van der Meer, Atie
--*Monster Island.* Van der Meer, Ron (1945-). c.1981. Holt, Rinehart, and Winston. (P.913)
Van der Meer, Madge E.
--*The Miracle Pond.* Van der Meer, Wybe J. 1979. Vermeer Arts. (P.913)
--*The Miracle Pond.* 2nd ed. Van Der Meer, Wybe J. 1980. Vermeer Arts. (P.913)
Van der Meer, Ron
--*Roaring Lion Tales.* Presencer, Alain. 1984. P Bedrick Bks. (P.738)
Vandevort, C. S.
--*Memoirs of Simple Simon.* Keeler, David Burr. 1901. R. H. Russell. (P.511)
Vandivert, William, photos by.
--*Barnaby.* Vandivert, Rita Andre (1905-). 1963. Dodd, Mead. (P.914)
--*The Porcupine Known As J.* R. Vandivert, Rita Andre (1905-). 1959. Dodd, Mead. (P.914)
Van Doren, Margaret (1917-)
--*The Black Pup.* Brooks, Anne. 1938. The Viking Press. (P.136)
--*Fala: A President's Dog.* Mussey, Virginia Howell (1910-). c.1941. Howell, Soskin. (P.674)
--*One Summer: A Story.* Klaw, Barbara Van Doren (1920-). Gale, Martin, pseud. 1936. The Viking Press. (P.530)
--*One Winter.* Klaw, Barbara Van Doren (1920-). Gale, Martin, pseud. 1938. Viking Press. (P.530)
--*A Pony Named Nubbin: A Story.* Klaw, Barbara Van Doren (1920-). Gale, Martin, pseud. 1939. The Viking Press. (P.530)
--*Thomas Retires.* Van Doren, Margaret (1917-). 1939. Viking Press. (P.914)
--*The Transparent Tree.* Van Doren, Mark Albert (1894-1972). c.1940. H. Holt and Company. (P.914)
Van Dresser, William
--*Paul and Rhoda.* Kilbourne, Fannie. 1921. Dodd, Mead and Company. (P.522)
--*Pep: The Story of a Brave Dog.* Hawkes, Clarence (1869-). c.1922. Milton Bradley Company. (P.421)
--*Unexplored!.* Chaffee, Allen. 1922. Milton Bradley Company. (P.181)
Van Dun, Anke
--*My Busy Day.* N.D. Platt. (P.914)
Van Dyck
--*The Pied Piper of Hamelin.* Browning, Robert (1812-1889). N.D. Frederick Warne & Co. (P.143)
Vanecek, Kueta
--*Cats' Opera.* Dillon, Eilis (1920-). 1963. Bobbs. (P.266)
Van Eersel, Otto
--*I Heard, Said the Bird.* Berends, Polly Berrien, Mrs. (1939-). 1969. L. W. Singer Co. (P.95)
Vanetti, Giorgio, jt. illus. see Conte, Patrizia.
Vanetti, Giorgio, jt. illus. see Michelini, Carlo A.
Van Everen, Jay
--*Big Fellow, the Story of a Road-Making Machine.* Baruch, Dorothy Walter, Mrs. (1899-1962). 1929. Harper & Brothers. (P.78)
--*Fillmore Folk Tales: Selected for Young Folks from "Mighty Mikko" and "The Laughing Prince".* Fillmore, Parker Hoysted (1878-1944). Harper, Wilhelmina (1884-1973), selected by. 1926. Harcourt, Brace and Company. (P.325)
--*The Fossil Fountain.* Mason, Arthur (1876-) & Frank, Mary. 1928. Doubleday, Doran & Company, Inc. (P.628)
--*Laughing Prince.* Fillmore, Parker Hoysted (1878-1944). 1921. HarBraceJ. (P.325)
--*Mighty Mikko: A Book of Finnish Fairy Tales and Folk Tales.* Fillmore, Parker Hoysted (1878-1944). c.1922. Harcourt, Brace and Company. (P.325)
--*Red Caps and Lilies.* Adams, Katharine. 1924. The Macmillan Company. (P.6)
--*Story Telling New & Old.* Colum, Padraic (1881-1972). 1968. Macmillan. (P.211)
--*The Truce of the Wolf and Other Tales of Old Italy.* Davis, Mary Gould (1882-), ed. c.1931. Harcourt, Brace and Company. **Award: (JNM).** (P.246)

Vasnetsov, Y.
--*The Three Bears.* The, Three Bears & Tolstoy, Leo Nikolaevich (1828-1910) 1976. Imported Pubns. (P.890)
Vassos, John (1898-), photos by.
--*Rex and Lobo.* Vassos, John (1898-). 1946. E. P. Dutton & Co., Inc. (P.916)
Vaughan, Anne, jt. illus. see Lownsbery, Eloise.
Vaughan, Anne (1913-)
--*Appleseed Farm.* Douglas, Emily Taft (1899-). 1948. Abingdon-Cokesbury Press. (P.282)
--*The Firehouse Mystery.* Venn, Mary Eleanor (1908-). Adrian, Mary, pseud. 1950. Houghton, Mifflin. (P.916)
--*Gift of the Forest.* Singh, Reginald Lal & Lownsbery, Eloise (1888-). 1942. Longmans, Green and Co. (P.827)
--*Jungle Boy.* Cunningham, Grace F. Carveth, Lysle, pseud. 1945. Longmans, Green and Co., Inc. (P.235)
--*Kodru, the Monkey.* Smith, Eugene Cadwallader (1877-). 1941. A. A. Knopf. (P.833)
--*Kongo the Elephant ...* Smith, Eugene Cadwallader (1877-). 1939. A. A. Knopf. (P.833)
--*Moro Boy.* Cunningham, Grace F. Carveth, Lysle, pseud. N.D. Longmans, Green. (P.235)
--*Nobody's Doll.* De Leeuw, Adele Louise (1899-). 1946. Little, Brown and Company. (P.254)
--*Olive Fairy Book.* New ed. Lang, Andrew (1844-1912), ed. Davis, Mary Gould, et al. 1949. Longmans, Green. (P.549)
--*On Hampton Street.* 1st ed. Williams, Alice Marietta (1901-). 1947. Longmans, Green. (P.962)
--*Susan and the Butterbees.* Bergengren, Ralph Wilhelm (1871-). 1947. Longmans, Green and Co. (P.96)
--*Vagabonds All.* Seth-Smith, Elsie K (1883-). 1946. Houghton Mifflin Company. (P.811)
Vaughan, Eileen Fox
--*Benny the Bus.* Horn, Gladys M. 1950. Whitman. (P.464)
--*Mother Goose.* Mother Goose. c.1950. Whitman Pub. Co. (P.668)
--*Mother Goose.* Mother Goose. c.1953. Whitman Pub. Co. (P.668)
--*Whoopee, Hunkydory-.* Justus, May (1898-). 1953, c.1952. Whitman Pub. Co. (P.503)
Vaughan-Jackson, Genevieve (1913-)
--*American Alligator.* Adrian, Mary, pseud. (1908-). Jorgenson, Mary Venn. N.D. Hastings. (P.12)
--*Carramore.* Vaughan-Jackson, Genevieve. 1968. Hastings. (P.916)
--*The Grass Was That High.* Pitkin, Dorothy Horton (1899-1972). 1959. Pantheon Books. (P.727)
--*A Handful of Flowers: Poems.* Miller, Mary Britton (1883-1975). 1959. Pantheon. (P.648)
--*Hide and Seek.* Coatsworth, Elizabeth Jane (1893-). 1956. Pantheon. (P.204)
--*The Little Dancer.* Hill, Lorna (1902-). 1957. T. Nelson. (P.443)
--*Mouse Chorus.* Coatsworth, Elizabeth Jane (1893-). 1955. Pantheon. (P.204)
--*Skip.* Fisher, Aileen Lucia (1906-). 1958. Nelson. (P.328)
--*The Stranger.* Weaver, Stella. 1956. Pantheon Books. (P.938)
--*Trailer Tribe.* Musgrave, Florence (1902-). 1955. Ariel Books. (P.674)
Vaughn, Frank E.
--*All Horses Go to Heaven.* Brown, Beth (1909-). 1963. G&D. (P.138)
--*The Magnificent House of Man Alone: An Osage Indian Story.* Rushmore, Helen (1898-). 1968. Garrard. (P.784)
--*Teen-Age Humorous Stories.* Furman, Abraham Loew (1902-), ed. Allen, Merritt Parmelee, et al. (1892-1954) 1957. Lantern Press. (P.30)
--*Teen-Age Small Boat Stories.* Strong, Paschal Neilson, et al. (1901-) Furman, Abraham Loew (1902-), ed. 1959. Lantern Press. (P.868)
--*Teen-Age Super Science Stories.* Elam, Richard Mace, Jr. (1920-). 1961, c.1957. Grosset & Dunlap. (P.300)
--*Teen-Age Super Science Stories.* Elam, Richard Mace, Jr. (1920-). 1957. Lantern Press. (P.300)
--*Tom Corbett's Wonder Book of Space.* Levin, Marcia Lauter Obrasky (1918-). Martin, Marcia, pseud. 1953. Wonder Books. (P.568)
--*Tom Corbett's Wonder Book of Space.* Martin, Marcia, pseud. (1918-). Levin, Marcia Obrasky. 1953. Wonder Books. (P.625)
--*We Were There at Pearl Harbor.* Sutton, Felix (1910-). Kitts, Willard A., ed. 1957. Grosset & Dunlap. (P.872)
--*We Were there on the Nautilus.* Webb, Robert N. 1961. Grosset & Dunlap. (P.938)
--*We Were There with the Pony Express.* Steele, William Owen (1917-1979). 1956. Grosset & Dunlap. (P.851)
--*The Wonder Book of Cowboys.* Peters, Lisa. 1955, c.1956. Wonder Books. (P.720)
Vavra, Robert James (1935-)
--*Anna & Dula.* Vavra, Robert James (1935-). 1966. HarBraceJ. (P.916)
--*Felipe the Bullfighter.* 1st ed. Vavra, Robert James (1935-). N.D. HarBraceJ. (P.916)
--*The Story of Taou.* Vavra, Robert James (1935-). 1969. Dial Press. (P.916)
Vawter, Will
--*The Adventures of a Brownie As Told to My Child.* Craik, Dinah Maria Mulock, Mrs. (1826-1887). Washburne, Marion Foster, Mrs. (1863-), ed. c.1911. Rand, McNally & Company. (P.227)
--*The Ballads of Bourbonnais.* Amsbary, Wallace Bruce. N.D. Bobbs-Merrill Co. (P.33)
--*Book of Joyous Children.* Riley, James Whitcomb (1849-1916). 1902. Bobbs-Merrill Co. (P.764)
--*The Book of Joyous Children.* Riley, James Whitcomb (1849-1916). 1969. Books for Libraries Press. (P.764)
--*The Boys of the Old Glee Club.* Riley, James Whitcomb (1849-1916). Booth, Franklin, designed by. N.D. Bobbs-Merrill Co. (P.764)
--*Gray Moon Tales.* Mitchell, Minnie Belle Alexander, Mrs. (1860-). c.1926. The Bobbs-Merrill Company. (P.652)
--*The Rabbit's Ransom.* Vawter, Clara. c.1902. The Bobbs-Merrill Company. (P.916)
--*Riley Child-Rhymes.* Riley, James Whitcomb (1849-1916). 1915. Bobbs-Merrill. (P.765)
--*Riley Child-Rhymes.* Riley, James Whitcomb (1849-1916). 1970. Books for Libraries Press. (P.765)
--*Riley Child-Rhymes.* Riley, James Whitcomb (1849-1916). 1899. The Bowen-Merrill Company. (P.765)
--*Riley Child-Rhymes.* Riley, James Whitcomb (1849-1916). c.1920. The Bobbs-Merrill Company. (P.765)
--*Riley Child-Rhymes: Collection of the Favorites of Mr.* Riley's Popular Poems of Childhood. Riley, James Whitcomb (1849-1916). 1905. Bobbs-Merrill. (P.765)
--*Riley Child-Rhymes: With Hoosier Pictures.* Riley, James Whitcomb (1849-1916). N.D. Bowen-Merrill Pub. (P.765)
--*Riley Fairy Tales.* Riley, James Whitcomb (1849-1916). 1923. Bobbs-Merrill Co. (P.765)
--*Riley Farm-Rhymes.* Riley, James Whitcomb (1849-1916). 1915. Bobbs-Merrill. (P.765)
--*Riley Farm Rhymes.* Riley, James Whitcomb (1849-1916). 1901. Bowen-Merrill Co. (P.765)
--*Riley Songs of Home.* Riley, James Whitcomb (1849-1916). 1915. Bobbs-Merrill. (P.765)
--*Riley Songs of Summer.* Riley, James Whitcomb (1849-1916). 1908. Bobbs-Merrill. (P.765)
--*Riley's Farm-Rhymes.* Riley, James Whitcomb (1849-1916). 1905. Bobbs-Merrill Co. (P.765)
--*Riley's Songs of Friendship.* Riley, James Whitcomb (1849-1916). 1915. Bobbs-Merrill Co. (P.765)
--*Tales of Kankakee Land.* Bartlett, Charles Henry (1853-). 1904. Charles Scribner's Sons. (P.77)
--*When the Frost is on the Punkin, and other poems.* Riley, James Whitcomb (1849-1916). 1911. Bobbs-Merrill Co. (P.765)
Vawter, Will, jt. illus. see Relyea, Charles M.
Vawter, Will & Clay, John Cecil
--*His Pa's Romance.* Riley, James Whitcomb (1849-1916). 1903. Bobbs-Merrill Co. (P.764)
Vawter, Will & Relyea, Charles M.
--*A Defective Santa Claus.* Riley, James Whitcomb (1849-1916). 1915. Bobbs-Merill. (P.764)
--*A Defective Santa Claus: A Christmas Poem.* Riley, James Whitcomb (1849-1916). 1905. Bobbs-Merrill Co. (P.764)
Vayssieres, Jean J.
--*Gulliver's Stories.* Dolch, Edward William (1889-) & Dolch, Marguerite Pierce. 1976. Scholastic Inc. (P.279)
Veale, Tony
--*Hippo, Potta & Muss.* Softly, Barbara Frewin (1924-). 1969. Harvey. (P.840)
--*A Lemon-Yellow Elephant Called Trunk.* Softly, Barbara Frewin (1924-). 1971, c.1970. Harvey House. (P.840)
Vebell, Ed.
--*Alfred Hitchcock and the Three Investigators in The Mystery of the Singing Serpent.* Carey, Mary Virginia (1925-) & Arthur, Robert, pseud. (1909-1969). Feder, Robert Arthur. 1972. Random House. (P.167)
--*The American Girl: The American Girl Book of Sports Stories.* American Girl Magazine Staff, ed. N.D. Random. (P.33)
Vedder, S. H.
--*Bully, Fag, and Hero.* Mansford, Charles J. N.D. L. C. Page & Co. (P.618)
Veen, Mary
--*Merideth Was Afraid.* Veen, Mary. 1969. Childrens Press. (P.916)
Vegh, Steven, Jr.
--*Papi.* Hull, Eleanor Means (1913-). 1953. Friendship Press. (P.472)
--*The Round-up at Bar-C Ranch.* 1st ed. Cross, Genevieve Marion (1910-). 1950. Cross Publications. (P.232)
--*Tommy and the Indians.* Cross, Genevieve Marion (1910-). 1950. Cross Publications. (P.232)
Veise, Inger
--*Jimmy Flies.* Heiderstadt, Dorothy (1907-). 1930. Frederick A. Stokes Company. (P.430)
Velde, Robert
--*The Happy Hippopotami.* Martin, William Ivan, Jr. (1916-). 1970. Holt, Rinehart and Winston. (P.626)
--*The Pecan Tree.* Robinson, Matthew (1937-). 1971. Random House. (P.770)
Velez, Walter
--*How The Ewoks Saved the Trees: An Old Ewok Legend.* Howe, James (1946-). 1984. Random. (P.467)
Vella, Ed
--*A Day with Tupi: An Authentic Story of an Indian Boy in California's Mountains.* Hubbard, Fran (1924-). 1966. Ginn. (P.469)
Velthuijs, Max (1923-)
--*The Little Boy and the Big Fish.* Velthuijs, Max (1923-). 1969. Platt & Munk. (P.916)
--*The Poor Woodcutter and the Dove.* Velthuijs, Max (1923-). 1971. Delacorte Press. (P.916)
--*The Wolf and the Kid.* Damjan, Mischa. 1968, c.1967. McGraw-Hill. (P.240)
Venable, Jim
--*Glue Fingers.* 1st ed. Christopher, Matthew F (1917-). 1975. Little, Brown. (P.194)
Vendrell, Carme Sole (1944-)
--*A Bear in the Air.* Williams, Leslie (1941-). 1980, c.1979. Stemmer House Publishers. (P.964)
Venezia, Mike
--*The I Don't Want to Go to School Book.* Gross, Alan (1947-). c.1982. Childrens Press. (P.396)
--*Ask a Silly Question.* Wakefield, Joyce. 1979. Childrens Press. (P.925)
--*What If the Teacher Calls on Me?.* Gross, Alan (1947-). c.1979. Childrens Press. (P.396)
Venning, Sue
--*Best Friends.* 1st ed. Stevenson, Jocelyn. c.1984. Muppet Press : Holt, Rinehart, and Winston. (P.855)
--*Jim Henson's Muppet Show Bill.* 1982. Random. (P.917)
--*Kermit and Cleopigtra: Starring Jim Henson's Muppets.* Williams, Gregory (1952-). 1981. Random House/Muppet Press. (P.963)
--*The Muppet Babies' ABC.* Spinner, Stephanie (1943-), ed. 1984. Random. (P.845)
--*Two for the Show.* Calhoun, Horace B. 1982. Random. (P.162)
--*What Do Doozers Do?.* Muntean, Michaela. 1984. HR&W. (P.672)
Venning, Sue, jt. illus. see Chauhan, Manhar.
Veno, Joseph
--*The Best Invention of All.* Slepian, Janice B & Seidler, Ann G. (1925-). 1967. Crowell-Collier Press. (P.829)
--*The Count's Number Parade.* Stiles, Norman. 1977. Western Pub. (P.858)
--*The Day That Monday Run Away.* Heit, Robert. 1969. Lion Press. (P.431)
--*Have You Seen My Puppy.* Holl, Adelaide Hinkle (1910-). 1968. Random. (P.454)
--*Horace the Friendly Octopus.* Drdek, Richard E. 1965. Allyn and Bacon. (P.284)
Ventura, Piero Luigi (1937-)
--*Ten Brothers with Camels.* Cretan, Gladys Yessayan (1921-). 1975. Golden Press. (P.230)
--*Vanuk Vanuk.* 1st ed. Sperandio, Guido. Murgo, Jane, tr. 1973. Doubleday. (P.843)
Ver Beck, Frank, jt. illus. see Bannerman, Helen Brodie Cowan Watson.
VerBeck, Frank (1858-1933)
--*The Arkansaw Bear.* Paine, Albert Bigelow (1861-1937). 1925. Harper. (P.700)
--*The Arkansaw Bear: A Tale of Fanciful Adventure told in Song and Story.* New ed. Paine, Albert Bigelow (1861-1937). 1902. Henry Altemus Co. (P.700)
--*The Arkansaw Bear: A Tale of Fanciful Adventure; Told in Song and Story.* Paine, Albert Bigelow (1861-1937). 1898. R. H. Russell; Etc., Etc. (P.700)
--*The Arkansaw Bear: Complete, Being "The Arkansaw Bear" and "The Arkansaw Bear and Elsie"*...Told in Song and Story. Paine, Albert Bigelow (1861-1937). c.1929. H. Altemus Company. (P.700)
--*Bobbylinkapoo.* Marburg, Theodore (1862-). c.1937. Dorrance and Company. (P.619)
--*Donegal Fairy Stories.* MacManus, Seumas (1869-1960). 1968. Dover Publications. (P.609)
--*Little Black Sambo and the Monkey People.* VerBeck, Frank (1858-1933). c.1928. Henry Altemus Company. (P.917)
--*Little Black Sambo in the Bears' Den.* VerBeck, Frank (1858-1933). c.1930. Henry Altemus Company. (P.917)
--*The Little Boy Book.* Whitney, Helen Hay, Mrs. 1900. R. H. Russell. (P.954)
--*The Magical Monarch of Mo.* Baum, Lyman Frank (1856-1919). 1905. Bobbs-Merrill Co. (P.81)
--*A New Wonderland.* Baum, Lyman Frank (1856-1919). 1900. R. H. Russell. (P.82)
--*The Surprising Adventures of the Magical Monarch of Mo and His People.* Baum, Lyman Frank (1856-1919). 1968. Dover Publications. (P.82)
--*Ver Beck's Bears in Mother Goose Land.* Mother Goose & Rion, Hanna. N.D. George H Doran & Co. (P.669)
VerBeck, Frank (1858-1933) & Johnson, Charles Howard
--*Half-Hours with Jimmieboy.* Bangs, John Kendrick (1862-1922). N.D. De Witt Publishing House. (P.68)
Ver Beck, William Francis (1858-)
--*Little Black Sambo and the Crocodiles.* Ver Beck, William Francis (1858-). 1930. Henry Altemus Company. (P.917)
Verbeek, Gustave
--*The Little Boy and the Elephant.* Frankenstein, Gustavus. 1904. C. Altemus Company. (P.342)
--*Nigger Baby and Nine Beasts.* Porter, Alma Florence. 1901. Ess Ess Publishing Company. (P.732)
--*Rataplan, a Rogue Elephant, and Other Stories.* Velvin, Ellen. 1902. H. Altemus Company. (P.916)
Vereck, Frank, jt. illus. see Frost, Arthur Burdett.
Verity, Esme
--*Dancing Peel.* Hill, Lorna (1902-). 1954. T. Nelson. (P.443)
Verling, John
--*The Mine of Lost Days.* Brandel, Marc, pseud. (1919-). Beresford, Marcus. 1974. Lippincott. (P.127)
Vernam, Roger
--*Mark of the Leopard.* 1st ed. Stevens, Alden Gifford (1886-) & Kendall, Patricia. 1947. J. B. Lippincott Co. (P.854)
--*The White Buffalo.* Nicholson, John D. c.1965. Platt & Munk. (P.681)
Verney, John, Sir (1913-)
--*The Elephant War.* Avery, Gillian Elise (1926-). 1971, c.1960. Holt, Rinehart and Winston. (P.56)
--*Friday's Tunnel.* Verney, John (1913-). 1966, c.1959. Holt. **Award: (CMA).** (P.918)
--*The Italian Spring.* Avery, Gillian Elise (1926-). 1972, c.1964. Holt, Rinehart and Winston. (P.56)
--*Our Friend Jennings.* Buckeridge, Anthony Malcolm (1912-). 1967, c.1958. Penguin Books. (P.147)
--*To Tame a Sister.* Avery, Gillian Elise (1926-). 1964, c.1961. Van Nostrand. (P.56)
--*To Tame a Sister.* Avery, Gillian Elise (1926-). 1973, c.1961. Viking Press. (P.56)
Vernon, David Thomas
--*The Unknown Indian.* Browne, Gertrude Bell, Mrs. N.D. A. Whitman & Co. (P.143)
Vernon, Ethel S.
--*The Big Goose and the Little Hen.* Woodruff, Jacob Lyon (1868-). c.1932. A. Whitman & Co. (P.977)
--*The Story of Heidi.* Spyri, Johanna Heusser (1827-1901). c.1934. Whitman Publishing Company. (P.846)
Verpilleux, Emile Antoine (1888-)
--*Martine and Michel: A Story of the French Jura Mountains.* Criss, Mildred (1890-). 1936. Doubleday, Doran & Company, Inc. (P.231)
--*The Picture Book of Robinson Crusoe.* Moore, Elizabeth C, Mrs., adapted by. Defoe, Daniel (1661-1731). 1931. The Macmillan Company. (P.250)
--*The Shadow of the Sword.* Daniel, Hawthorne (1890-). 1930. The Macmillan Company. (P.241)
Verrier, Suzanne
--*Blockade.* Beatty, Jerome, Jr. (1918-). 1971. Doubleday. (P.85)
--*The Button Boat.* 1st ed. Swarthout, Glendon Fred (1918-) & Swarthout, Kathryn (1919-). 1969. N.Y., Doubleday. (P.873)
--*I Am a Man: Ode to Martin Luther King, Jr.* Merriam, Eve (1916-). 1971. Doubleday. (P.642)
--*Maestro Spinetti's Music Shop.* 1st ed. Hull, Anne A. 1971. Doubleday. (P.472)
--*Titus Tidewater.* Verrier, Suzanne. 1970. Doubleday. (P.918)
--*The Tooth and My Father.* 1st ed. Saroyan, William (1908-1981). 1974. Doubleday. (P.793)
Verrill, Alpheus Hyatt (1871-)
--*The Boy Adventurers in the Forbidden Land.* Verrill, Alpheus Hyatt (1871-). 1922. G. P. Putnam's Sons. (P.919)
--*The Boy Adventurers in the Land of El Dorado.* Verrill, Alpheus Hyatt (1871-). 1923. G. P. Putnam's Sons. (P.919)
--*The Boy Adventurers in the Land of the Monkey Men.* Verrill, Alpheus Hyatt (1871-). 1923. G. P. Putnam's Sons. (P.919)
--*The Boy Adventurers in the Unknown Land.* Verrill, Alpheus Hyatt (1871-). 1924. G. P. Putnam's Sons. (P.919)
--*The Treasure of Bloody Gut.* Verrill, Alpheus Hyatt (1871-). c.1937. G. P. Putnam's Sons. (P.919)

--*The Brocaded Slipper and Other Vietnamese Tales.* Vuong, Lynette Dyer (1938-). c.1982. Addison-Wesley. (P.922)
--*The Brocaded Slipper and Other Vietnamese Tales.* Vuong, Lynette Dyer (1938-). 1985, c.1982. Lippincott. (P.922)
--*First Snow.* Coutant, Helen H. (1909-). 1974. Knopf; Distributed by Random House. (P.224)
--*The Gift.* Coutant, Helen H. (1909-). c.1983. Knopf. (P.224)
--*The Happy Funeral.* Bunting, Anne Evelyn (1928-). c.1982. Harper & Row. (P.150)
--*The Magic Drum.* Kirkup, James (1927-). 1973. Knopf; Distributed by Random House. (P.529)
--*A Thousand Pails of Water.* Roy, Ronald (1940-). c.1978. Pantheon. (P.782)
--*Toad Is the Emperor's Uncle.* Vo-Dinh, Mai (1933-). 1970. Doubleday. (P.920)

Voake, Charlotte
--*Over the Moon: A Book of Nursery Rhymes.* Voake, Charlotte. Lloyd, Davide, intro. by. 1985. C.N. Potter : Distributed by Crown. (P.920)
--*The Way to Sattin Shore.* Pearce, Ann Philippa (1920-). c.1983. Greenwillow Books. **Award: (ALA).** (P.713)
--*The Way to Sattin Shore.* Pearce, Ann Philippa (1920-). 1985, c.1983. Puffin Books. (P.713)

Vogel, Herman
--*Fairy Tale Procession.* N.D. Green Tiger Pr. (P.921)
--*Hermine's Triumphs.* Colomb, Josephine Blanche Bouchet (1833-1892). 1892. D. Appleton and Company. (P.210)

Vogel, Ilse-Margret (1918-)
--*Bear in the Boat.* Vogel, Ilse-Margret (1918-). 1979. Western Pub. (P.921)
--*City Cats, Country Cats.* Hazen, Barbara Shook (1930-). 1969. Western Pub. (P.427)
--*Come on!* Play Ball!. Vogel, Ilse-Margret (1918-). 1969. Western Pub. (P.921)
--*Daisy Dog's Wake-Up Book.* Vogel, Ilse-Margret (1918-). 1979. Western Pub. (P.921)
--*Dodo Every Day.* Vogel, Ilse-Margret (1918-). c.1977. Harper & Row. (P.921)
--*Farewell, Aunt Isabelle.* Vogel, Ilse-Margret (1918-). 1979. Har-Row. (P.921)
--*Hello, Henry.* Vogel, Ilse Margret (1918-). c.1965. Parents' Mag. (P.921)
--*Little Plays for Little People.* Humpty Dumpty's Magazine Editors. Martin, Judith, intro. by. c.1965. Parents' Mag. (P.473)
--*My Little Dinosaur.* Vogel, Ilse-Margret (1918-). 1971. Western Pub. (P.921)
--*My Summer Brother.* 1st ed. Vogel, Ilse-Margret (1918-). c.1981. Harper & Row. (P.921)
--*My Twin Sister Erika.* Vogel, Ilse Margret (1918-). c.1976. Harper & Row. (P.921)
--*One Is No Fun, but Twenty Is Plenty!.* Vogel, Ilse-Margret (1918-). c.1965. Atheneum. (P.921)
--*One Is No Fun but Twenty Is Plenty.* Vogel, Ilse-Margret (1918-). 1972. Atheneum. (P.921)
--*One Is No Fun but Twenty Is Plenty.* Vogel, Ilse-Margret (1918-). 1965. Hale. (P.921)
--*Peek-A-Boo.* Vogel, Ilse-Margret (1918-). 1970. Western Pub. (P.921)
--*The Rainbow Dress, and Other Tollush Tales.* Vogel, Ilse Margret (1918-). c.1975. Harper & Row. (P.921)
--*Tikhon.* Vogel, Ilse-Margret (1918-). 1984. Har-Row. (P.921)
--*Willy, Willy, Don't Be Silly.* Vogel, Ilse-Margret (1918-). 1965. Atheneum. (P.921)

Vogele & Zefers
--*The Gobbly Wobblyn.* Wittmaak, Harold S. c.1924. The Gobbly Wobblyn Publishing Co. (P.973)

Vogt, Marie Bollinger (1921-)
--*Jill and the Nutcracker Ballet.* Vogt, Marie Bollinger (1921-). 1974. J. F. Blair. (P.921)

Vojtech, Anna
--*The Star Husband.* 1st ed. Mobley, Jane. c.1979. Doubleday. (P.652)

Vollmar, Clyde R.
--*Clarabelle Hatches Ten: An Educational and Entertaining True Story.* Marlowe, Helena. c.1962. Bobbs. (P.621)

Volwell, Ed
--*American Girl Book of Sports Stories.* American Girl Magazine Staff, ed. 1965. Random. (P.33)

Von
--*Macbeth.* folio ed. Shakespeare, William (1564-1616). c.1982. Workman. (P.814)

Von Bernuth, Lecian, jt. illus. see Paynter, Grace M.

Vondersmith, David
--*Arabella, the Fighting Cow: A Story in Verse.* 1st ed. Vondersmith, David. 1955. Exposition Press. (P.921)

Von Dombrowski, Katharina
--*Little Jungle Village.* Waldeck, JoBesse McElveen, Mrs. 1940. The Viking Press. (P.925)

Von Hippel, Ursula
--*The Craziest Halloween.* Von Hippel, Ursula. 1957. Coward-McCann. (P.921)
--*The Craziest Halloween.* Von Hippel, Ursula. 1957. Putnam Pub Group. (P.921)

Von Hofsten, Hugo
--*Billy Whiskers' Grandchildren of the Ojibways.* Montgomery, Frances Trego. c.1909. Brewer, Barse & Co. (P.657)
--*Cats and Kitts.* Montgomery, Frances Trego. N.D. Barse & Hopkins. (P.658)
--*Chickens and Chicks.* Montgomery, Frances Trego. N.D. Barse & Hopkins. (P.658)
--*Dogs and Puppies.* Montgomery, Frances Trego. N.D. Barse & Hopkins. (P.658)
--*Mother Goose Jungle Book.* Mother Goose. 1903. The Madison Book Co. (P.668)
--*Pigs and Piggies.* Montgomery, Frances Trego. N.D. Barse & Hopkins. (P.658)

Von Ilg, Gary (1938-)
--*When the Corn Is Red.* Shor, Pekay (1926-), retold by. 1973. Abingdon Press. (P.821)

Von Landau, Helena, jt. illus. see Meister, Charles E.

Von Lewinski, Anneliese
--*When Star Children Play.* Klett, Gertrud Ingeborg (1871-). 1930. Longmans, Green and Co. (P.531)

Von Rapp, Frederic J.
--*A Maid in Arcady.* Barbour, Ralph Henry (1870-1944). 1906. J. B. Lippincott Company. (P.71)

Von Saltza, Phillip
--*Ben Bidwell: A Tale of the Old Frontier.* Krapp, George Philip (1872-1934). c.1927. Rand, McNally & Company. (P.537)
--*Fanton Farm: A Story of Country Life.* Krapp, George Philip (1872-1934). c.1927. Rand, McNally & Company. (P.537)
--*Inland Oceans: A Tale of the Great Lakes.* Krapp, George Philip (1872-1934). c.1927. Rand, McNally & Company. (P.537)
--*Kipwillie: A Story of City Life.* Krapp, George Philip (1872-1934). c.1927. Rand, McNally & Company. (P.537)
--*Sixty Years Ago: A Tale of the Civil War.* Krapp, George Philip (1872-1934). c.1927. Rand, McNally & Company. (P.537)
--*Tongo: A Tale of the Great Plains.* Krapp, George Philip (1872-1934). c.1927. Rand McNally & Company. (P.537)

Von Schmidt, Eric (1931-)
--*The Ballad of Bad Ben Bilge.* Von Schmidt, Eric (1931-). c.1965. Houghton. (P.921)
--*By the Great Horn Spoon!.* Fleischman, Albert Sidney (1920-). 1963. Little, Brown. (P.331)
--*Chauncy & the Grand Rascal.* Fleischman, Albert Sidney (1920-). 1966. Little. (P.331)
--*Come for to Sing.* Von Schmidt, Eric (1931-). 1963. HM. (P.921)
--*The Ghost on Saturday Night.* 1st ed. Fleischman, Albert Sidney (1920-). 1974. Little, Brown. (P.331)
--*The Glitter- Eyed Wouser.* 1st ed. Lauritzen, Jonreed (1902-). 1960. Brown. (P.555)
--*The Gnu and the Guru Go Behind the Beyond: A Cautionary Tale.* Clifford, Peggy, pseud. (1929-). Clifford, Margaret Cort. 1970. Houghton Mifflin. **Award: (NYT).** (P.202)
--*The Haunting of America: Ghost Stories from Our Past.* Anderson, Jean (1913-). 1973. Houghton Mifflin. (P.39)
--*Hee Haw.* McGovern, Ann. 1969. Houghton Mifflin. (P.602)
--*Humbug Mountain.* 1st ed. Fleischman, Albert Sidney (1920-). c.1978. Little, Brown. **Award: (BGH).** (P.331)
--*Jim Bridger's Alarm Clock, and Other Tall Tales.* Fleischman, Albert Sidney (1920-). c.1978. E. P. Dutton. (P.331)
--*Jingo Django.* 1st ed. Fleischman, Albert Sidney (1920-). 1971. Little, Brown. **Award: (ALA).** (P.331)
--*The Last Trip of the Juno.* Ervin, Janet Halliday (1923-). 1970. Follett Pub. Co. (P.309)
--*Me and the Man on the Moon-Eyed Horse.* 1st ed. Fleischman, Albert Sidney (1920-). c.1977. Little, Brown. (P.331)
--*Mr.* Chris and the Instant Animals. Von Schmidt, Eric (1931-). 1967. Houghton Mifflin. (P.921)
--*Mr. Mysterious & Company.* 1st ed. Fleischman, Albert Sidney (1920-). 1962. Little, Brown. (P.331)
--*Mr.* Mysterious's Secrets of Magic. Fleischman, Albert Sidney (1920-). 1975. Little. (P.331)
--*Take Three Witches.* Mian, Mary Lawrence Shipman. 1971. Houghton Mifflin. (P.644)
--*Tales of a Common Pigeon.* Weeks, Sara. 1960. Houghton Mifflin. (P.940)
--*Treasure of the High Country.* 1st ed. Lauritzen, Jonreed (1902-). 1959. Little, Brown. (P.555)
--*The Two Giants.* Bunting, Anne Evelyn (1928-). 1971, c.1972. Ginn. (P.150)
--*Valley of the Bear: A Novel of the North Plains Sioux.* Allen, Henry Wilson (1912-). 1964. Houghton Mifflin. (P.29)
--*Young Man Who Wouldn't Hoe Corn.* Von Schmidt, Eric (1931-). 1964. HM. (P.921)

Von Schmidt, Harold (1896-1982)
--*Homespun.* Best, Allena Champlin (1892-1974). Berry, Erick, pseud. 1937. Lothrop Lee & Shepard. (P.99)
--*Indian Gold.* Mack, Orin. 1933. A. A. Knopf. (P.604)
--*Queer Person.* Hubbard, Ralph. 1930. Doubleday, Doran & Company, Inc. **Award: (JNM).** (P.469)
--*Queer Person.* Hubbard, Ralph. 1978. Theodore Roosevelt Nature and History Association. (P.469)

Von Storp, Eitel
--*I'll Build My Friend a Mountain.* Katz, Bobbi (1933-). 1973. Schol Bk Serv. (P.509)

Von Zitzewitz, Hoot
--*Easter Chimes: Stories for Easter & the Spring.* New Rev.Ed. ed. Harper, Wilhelmina (1884-1973), ed. 1967. Dutton. (P.414)
--*Easter Chimes: Stories for Easter and the Spring Season.* New Rev. Ed. ed. Harper, Wilhelmina (1884-1973), ed. 1965. Dutton. (P.414)

Voorhies, Stephen J.
--*Adventure North.* Pinkerton, Kathrene Sutherland Gedney, Mrs. (1887-1967). c.1940. Carrick & Evans, Inc. (P.726)
--*Adventure North.* Pinkerton, Kathrene Sutherland Gedney, Mrs. (1887-1967). 1940. Harcourt. (P.726)
--*Deep Wood.* Trevor, Elleston, pseud. (1920-). Dudley-Smith, Trevor. 1947. Longmans, Green. (P.900)
--*The General's Boots.* Frazier, Neta Lohnes (1890-). 1965. D. McKay Co. (P.343)
--*Hail, Nathan Hale!.* Main, Mildred Miles (1898-). c.1965. Abingdon. (P.613)
--*Heather Hill.* 1st ed. Trevor, Elleston, pseud. (1920-). Dudley-Smith, Trevor. 1948. Longmans, Green. (P.900)
--*The Mudhen.* Allen, Merritt Parmelee (1892-1954). 1945. Longmans, Green and Co., Inc. (P.30)
--*The Mudhen Acts Naturally.* 1st ed. Allen, Merritt Parmelee (1892-1954). 1955. Longmans, Green. (P.30)
--*The Mudhen and the Walrus.* 1st ed. Allen, Merritt Parmelee (1892-1954). 1950. Longmans, Green. (P.30)
--*The Mystery in the Jeep.* 1st ed. Rydberg, Ernie, pseud. (1901-). Rydberg, Ernest Emil. 1959. Longmans, Green. (P.786)
--*The Spell of the White Sturgeon.* Kjelgaard, James Arthur (1910-1959). 1953. Dodd, Mead. (P.530)
--*Wheels of Empire.* Banning, George Hugh. 1935. T. Nelson and Sons. (P.69)
--*The White Man Comes.* Spoerer, George Richard. 1934. T. Nelson & Sons. (P.845)
--*Windmill Pilot.* Archibald, Joseph Stopford (1898-). 1963. D. McKay Co. (P.46)

Vorhand, Rachel
--*Oh, Zalmy!.* Or, Tales of Two Esthers, Bk. 3. Kleinbard, Gitel. 1979. Mah Tov Pubns. (P.531)

Vosburgh, Leonard W. (1912-)
--*Andy Jackson: Long Journey to the White House.* 1st ed. Angell, Polly. 1956. Aladdin Books. (P.41)
--*Benjy Brant: Dragooning with the Swamp Fox.* Koob, Theodora Johanna Foth (1918-). 1965. Lippincott. (P.535)
--*The Boy with Wings.* DeLeeuw, Adele Louise (1899-). 1971. Nautilus Books. (P.254)
--*Calico Row.* Budd, Lillian Peterson (1897-). 1965. A. Whitman. (P.147)
--*Chingo Smith of the Erie Canal.* Adams, Samuel Hopkins (1871-). 1958. Random Houe. (P.6)
--*Courageous Comrades.* Smith, Fredrika Shumway (1877-1968). 1960. Rand McNally. (P.833)
--*Crown Point: The Destiny Road.* Wilson, Charles Morrow (1905-1977). 1965. McKay. (P.966)
--*Davy Crockett.* Ford, Anne. 1961. Putnam Pub Group. (P.335)
--*Family Album of Favorite Poems.* Ernest, P. Edward, ed. 1959. Putnam Pub Group. (P.309)
--*Fear in the Forest.* De Leeuw, Cateau Wilhelmina (1903-1975). 1960. Nelson. (P.255)
--*The Fighting Quaker: The Southern Campaigns of General Nathanael Greene.* 1st ed. Latham, Frank Brown (1910-). 1953. Aladdin Books. (P.553)
--*A Flag for Lafitte: Story of the Battle of New Orleans.* 1st ed. Lane, Frederick A. 1954. Aladdin Books. (P.547)
--*Galleys East!.* Gladd, Arthur Anthony (1913-). c.1961. Dodd, Mead. (P.370)
--*The Great Turkey Drive.* Wilson, Charles Morrow (1905-1977). 1964. McKay. (P.966)
--*Guns for General Washington.* Downey, Fairfax Davis (1893-). c.1961. Nelson. (P.283)
--*Larry.* Budd, Lillian Peterson (1897-). 1966. D. McKay Co. (P.147)
--*The Law or the Gun: The Mormons at Far West.* 1st ed. Latham, Frank Brown (1910-). 1955. Aladdin Books. (P.553)
--*The Longest Day of the Year.* 1st ed. Marquis, Helen. 1969. Meredith Press. (P.621)
--*My Cousin Abe.* Fisher, Aileen Lucia (1906-). c.1962. Nelson. **Award: (ALA).** (P.328)
--*Navy Style.* Orlob, Helen (1908-). c.1962. Nelson. (P.696)
--*Never Go Anywhere with Digby.* Parkinson, Ethelyn Minerva (1906-). 1971. Abingdon Press. (P.707)
--*On Lennox Moor.* Kyle, Elisabeth, pseud. (0000-1982). Dunlop, Agnes Mary Robertson. 1954. Thomas Nelson & Sons. (P.543)
--*Outlaw Voyage.* 1st ed. Gendron, Val. 1955. World Pub. Co. (P.363)
--*Pirates in Petticoats.* Yolen, Jane Hyatt (1939-). 1963. D. McKay Co. (P.987)
--*The Proving Years.* De Leeuw, Cateau Wilhelmina (1903-1975). c.1962. Nelson. (P.255)
--*The Saracen Steed.* Gladd, Arthur Anthony (1913-). 1960. Dodd, Mead & Co. (P.370)
--*The Story of Franklin D.* Roosevelt. Hickok, Lorena A (1892-1968). 1956. Grosset & Dunlap. (P.441)
--*Summer on the Salt Fork.* Voils, Jessie Wiley. 1969. Meredith Press. (P.921)
--*This Land Is Mine: An Anthology of American Verse.* Hine, Alfred Blakelee (1915-), ed. 1965. Lippincott. (P.445)
--*To the Walls of Cartagena.* Dwight, Allan, pseud. (1903-1979) & Taylor, Turney Allan. Cole, Lois Dwight. 1967. Colonial Williamsburg; Distributed by Holt, Rinehart, and Winston, New York. (P.292)
--*Toppy and the Circuit Rider.* Spratt, Barnett. 1957. Abingdon Press. (P.845)
--*We Were There at the Battle of Gettysburg.* Malkus, Alida Wright Sims, Mrs. (1899-). Miers, Earl S., ed. 1955. Grosset & Dunlap. (P.614)
--*We Were There When Grant Met Lee at Appomattox.* Miers, Earl Schenck (1910-1972). Catton, Bruce (1899-1978), ed. 1960. Grosset & Dunlap. (P.644)
--*We Were There with Richard the Lionhearted in the Crusades.* Webb, Robert N. 1957. Grosset & Dunlap. (P.938)
--*Wilderness Teacher.* Ball, Zachary, pseud. (1897-) & Fowler, Myra. Masters, Kelly Ray. 1956. Rand McNally. (P.66)
--*Yankee Privateer.* 1st ed. Norton, Alice Mary (1912-). Norton, Andre, pseud. 1955. World Pub. Co. (P.686)

Vosburgh, Leonard W. (1912-) & Sowell, William R.
--*Along Our Way.* Rickard, John Allison (1892-) & Martin, Clyde Inez. 1958. W. S. Benson. (P.763)

Vosburgh, R. G.
--*Elizabeth Hobart at Exeter Hall.* Baird, Jean Katherine (1872-). c.1907. The Saalfield Publishing Company. (P.61)
--*The Honor Girl.* Baird, Jean Katherine (1872-). c.1907. The Saalfield Publishing Company. (P.61)
--*Little Rhody.* Baird, Jean Katherine (1872-). c.1907. The Saalfield Publishing Company. (P.61)
--*The Trail of the Seneca.* Braden, James Andrew (1872-). c.1907. The Saalfield Publishing Company. (P.124)

Voter, Thomas W.
--*Broken Dykes: A Story of the Siege of Leyden.* Daniel, Hawthorne (1890-). 1934. The Macmillan Company. (P.241)
--*Rocket Ship Galileo.* Heinlein, Robert Anson (1907-). 1947. C. Scribner's Sons. (P.430)
--*Shuttle and Sword: The Adventures of a Weaver's Son in Old Flanders.* Daniel, Hawthorne (1890-). 1932. The Macmillan Company. (P.241)

Voute, Kathleen (1892-)
--*Caroline and Her Kettle Named Maud.* Mason, Miriam Evangeline (1899-1973). 1951. Macmillan. (P.628)
--*Caroline and Her Kettle Named Maud.* Mason, Miriam Evangeline (1899-1973). 1967. MacMillan Publishing Company. (P.628)
--*Coon Holler.* 1st ed. Cook, Olive Rambo (1892-). 1958. Longmans, Green. (P.215)
--*Don's Great Discovery.* Roberts, Mary Duffy (1925-). 1959. I. Washburn. (P.768)
--*The Hidden Garden.* Bennett, Mabel R. 1955. J. Day. (P.94)
--*The House of the Swan.* Coatsworth, Elizabeth Jane (1893-). 1948. Macmillan Co. (P.204)
--*In Bible Days.* Hartman, Gertrude (1876-1955). 1948. Macmillan. (P.418)
--*Let's Go to Candy Factory.* Buchheimer, Naomi Barnett (1927-). 1957. Putnam. (P.146)
--*The Magic Ball from Mars.* Biemiller, Carl Ludwig (1912-1979). 1953. Morrow. (P.101)
--*The Magic Ring.* Frazier, Neta Lohnes (1890-). 1959. Longmans, Green. (P.343)
--*The Mysterious Trunk.* Johnson, Elizabeth Harrover. 1960. Washburn. (P.494)

--*The Snow Book.* Evans, Eva Knox, Mrs. (1905-). c.1965. Little. (P.311)
--*Sugar on Snow.* Watson, Nancy Dingman. 1964. Viking Press. (P.936)
--*Tatty Mae & Catty Mae.* Martin, William Ivan, Jr. (1916-). 1970. Holt, Rinehart and Winston. (P.626)
--*They Were Made of Rawhide.* Peck, Leigh. 1954. Houghton Mifflin. (P.714)
--*Thor's Visit to the Land of the Giants.* Ross, Nancy Wilson (1905-). 1959. Random House. (P.779)
--*Three Against the Sea.* White, Robb (1909-). c.1940. Harper & Brothers. (P.953)
--*Toby and Doll.* 1st ed. Watson, Nancy Dingman. 1955. Bobbs-Merrill. (P.936)
--*Tommy's Mommy's Fish.* 1st ed. Watson, Nancy Dingman. 1971. Viking Press. (P.936)
--*Uncle Wiggily and the Runaway Cheese.* Garis, Howard Roger (1873-1962). c.1977. Platt & Munk. (P.357)
--*Uncle Wiggily & the Sugar Cookie.* Garis, Howard Roger (1873-1962). 1977. Platt. (P.357)
--*Uncle Wiggily's Happy Days.* Garis, Howard Roger (1873-1962). c.1976. Platt & Munk. (P.357)
--*A Visit from Saint Nicholas.* Moore, Clement Clarke (1779-1863). 1945. The Peter Pauper Press. (P.660)
--*What Does A Begin with?.* Watson, Nancy Dingman. 1956. Knopf. (P.936)
--*Wheels Over the Bridge.* De Jong, Meindert (1906-). c.1941. Harper & Brothers. (P.252)
--*When Is Tomorrow?.* Watson, Nancy Dingman. 1955. Knopf. (P.936)
--*Where the Brook Begins.* Bartlett, Margaret Farrington (1896-). 1961. Crowell. (P.78)
--*Whose Birthday Is It?.* Watson, Nancy Dingman. 1954. Knopf. (P.936)
--*Willie & the Wildcat Well.* Constant, Alberta Wilson (1908-1981). 1962. T Y Crowell. **Award: (ALA).** (P.214)
--*The Wonder Cat.* Martin, Dahris Butterworth. 1942. Thomas Y. Crowell Company. (P.624)

Watson, Bessie Crawford, Mrs., photos by.
--*The Singing Dog, and a Whole Gallery of Barnyard Friends.* Carter, Russell Gordon (1892-1957). c.1931. The Penn Publishing Company. (P.176)

Watson, Carol Stuart
--*Flower Fables.* Gary, Charles L. 1978. EPM Publications. (P.359)
--*Hey-Ey-Ey, Lock!.* Fradin, Morris. 1974. See-and-Know Press. (P.341)
--*Hurrah for Arthur!.* A Mount Vernon Birthday Party. 1st ed. Blair, Anne Denton. c.1982. Seven Locks Press. (P.105)
--*Where's Rachel?.* Another Adventure of Arthur, the White House Mouse. Blair, Anne Denton. 1978. Acropolis Books. (P.105)

Watson, Clyde (1947-)
--*How Does It Feel to Be a Tree?.* Morse, Flo (1921-). c.1976. Parents' Magazine Press. (P.666)

Watson, Elizabeth E.
--*God Didn't Put Elephants in Trees.* Watson, Elizabeth E. 1981. Broadman. (P.935)
--*Pigs Oink, Yes, They Do.* Watson, Elizabeth E. 1984. Broadman. (P.935)

Watson, Ernest W.
--*Soldier of the Sun: A Story of Peru in the Days of the Incas.* Desmond, Alice Curtis, Mrs. (1897-). 1939. Dodd, Mead and Company. (P.260)

Watson, Eva Auld
--*Children of South Africa.* 1st ed. Stinetorf, Louise Allender (1900-). 1945. J. B. Lippincott. (P.859)
--*Chuck Martinez.* Holton, Priscilla. 1940. Longmans, Green and Co. (P.457)
--*Coat for a Soldier.* Updegraff, Florence Maule. c.1941. Harcourt, Brace and Company. (P.910)
--*The Green Turtle Mystery.* Queen, Ellery, Jr., pseud. & Lee, Manfred Bennington (1905-1971). Dannay, Frederic. 1944. J. B. Lippincott Company. (P.744)
--*Lion Boy: A Story of East Africa.* Stevens, Alden Gifford (1886-). 1938. Frederick A. Stokes Company. (P.854)
--*Traveler's Candle.* Updegraff, Florence Maule. 1942. Harcourt, Brace and Company. (P.910)

Watson, Harry S.
--*Grimm's Fairy Tales.* Grimm, Jakob Ludwig Karl (1785-1863) & Grimm, Wilhelm Karl (1786-1859). 1894. The Cassell Publishing Co. (P.392)

Watson, Henry S.
--*The Adventures of Arnold Adair, American Ace.* Driggs, Laurence La Tourette (1876-). 1918. Little Brown & Co. (P.285)
--*Arnold Adair with the English Aces: Being the Further Flying Adventures of an American Aviator.* Driggs, Laurence La Tourette (1876-). 1922. Little, Brown, and Company. (P.285)
--*The Fourth Down.* Quirk, Leslie W (1882-). 1912. Little, Brown, and Company. (P.745)
--*Freshman Dorn, Pitcher.* Quirk, Leslie W (1882-). 1911. The Century Co. (P.745)
--*The Freshman Eight.* Quirk, Leslie W (1882-). 1913. Little, Brown, and Company. (P.745)
--*Ice-Boat Number One.* Quirk, Leslie W (1882-). 1916. Little, Brown, and Company. (P.745)
--*The Third Strike.* Quirk, Leslie W (1882-). 1914. Little, Brown, and Company. (P.745)
--*The Wilderness Castaways.* Wallace, Dillon (1863-1939). N.D. A. C. McClurg & Co. (P.927)

Watson, Howard N.
--*Garbage Can Cat.* Sharoff, Victor. 1969. Westminster Press. (P.815)

Watson, J. D., jt. illus. see Gilbert, John Clitherae.

Watson, J. D., jt. illus. see Wehnert, Edward H.

Watson, J. Davis
--*Heidi: A Story for Girls.* Spyri, Johanna Heusser (1827-1901). Melcon, H. A., tr. from Ger. c.1901. A. L. Burt. (P.846)
--*The Pilgrim's Progress.* N.D. George Routledge & Sons. (P.935)
--*Robinson Crusoe.* N.D. George Routledge & Sons. (P.935)

Watson, Joseph, Mrs.
--*Pets.* Lowe, Edith May Kovar (1905-). Windsor, Mary, pseud. 1935. Whitman. (P.588)

Watson, Marquerite
--*Cottontail Capers.* Watson, Marquerite Lee. 1944. Pelican Publishing Company. (P.936)

Watson, Wendy McLeod (1942-)
--*Applebet: An ABC.* Watson, Clyde (1947-). 1982. Farrar, Straus, Giroux. (P.935)
--*Belinda's Hurricane.* Winthrop, Elizabeth, pseud. (1948-). Mahony, Elizabeth Winthrop. 1984. Dutton. (P.970)
--*Betsy's Up-and-Down Year.* Pellowski, Anne (1933-). 1983. Philomel Books. (P.716)
--*The Biggest, Meanest, Ugliest Dog in the Whole Wide World.* Jones, Rebecca Castaldi (1947-). c.1982. Macmillan. (P.500)
--*The Birthday Goat.* Watson, Nancy Dingman. 1974. Crowell. (P.936)
--*The Bunnies' Christmas Eve.* Watson, Wendy Mcleod (1942-). c.1983. Philomel Books. (P.936)
--*Button Eye's Orange.* Wahl, Jan (1933-). 1980. F. Warne. (P.924)
--*Catch Me & Kiss Me & Say It Again.* Watson, Clyde (1947-). c.1978. Collins. (P.935)
--*Catch Me and Kiss Me and Say it Again.* Watson, Clyde (1947-). 1983. Putnam. (P.935)
--*The Country Mouse and the Town Mouse.* Aesopus. 1967. Stinehour Press. (P.13)
--*The Cruise of the Aardvark.* Nash, Frederic Ogden (1902-1971). 1967. M. Evans; Distributed in Association with Lippincott, Philadelphia. (P.675)
--*Daughter of Liberty.* Boutwell, Edna (1894-). 1975, c.1967. Collins & World. (P.120)
--*Father Fox's Feast of Songs.* Watson, Clyde (1947-). 1983. Putnam Pub Group. (P.935)
--*Father Fox's Penny-Rhymes.* Watson, Clyde (1947-). 1971. Harper. (P.935)
--*Father Fox's Pennyrhymes.* Watson, Clyde (1947-). 1971. Crowell. **Award: (ALA).** (P.935)
--*First Farm in the Valley: Anna's Story.* Pellowski, Anne (1933-). 1982. Philomel Books. (P.716)
--*Fisherman Lullabies.* Watson, Wendy McLeod (1942-) & Watson, Clyde (1947-). 1968. World Pub. (P.936)
--*Happy Birthday from Carolyn Haywood.* Haywood, Carolyn (1898-). 1984. Morrow. (P.427)
--*Has Winter Come?.* Watson, Wendy McLeod (1942-). c.1978. Collins. (P.936)
--*The Hedgehog and the Hare.* Watson, Wendy McLeod (1942-) & Grimm, Jakob Ludwig Karl (1785-1863). 1969. World Pub. Co. (P.936)
--*Hickory Stick Rag.* Watson, Clyde (1947-). c.1976. Crowell. (P.935)
--*How Brown Mouse Kept Christmas.* Watson, Clyde (1947-). 1980. Farrar, Straus, Giroux. (P.935)
--*I Love My Baby Sister (Most of the Time).* Edelman, Elaine. c.1984. Lothrop, Lee & Shepard. (P.296)
--*I Love My Baby Sister (Most of the Time).* Edelman, Elaine. 1985, c.1984. Puffin Books. (P.296)
--*Jamie's Story.* Watson, Wendy McLeod (1942-). c.1981. Putnam. (P.936)
--*Jenny's Cat.* 1st ed. Miles, Miska, pseud. (1899-). Martin, Patricia Miles. c.1979. Dutton. (P.625)
--*Lizzie, the Lost Toys Witch.* Harmer, Mabel (1894-). 1970. Macrae Smith. (P.413)
--*Lollipop.* Watson, Wendy McLeod (1942-). 1976. Crowell. (P.936)
--*Lollipop.* Watson, Wendy McLeod (1942-). 1978, c.1976. Puffin Books. (P.936)
--*Magic in the Alley.* Calhoun, Mary, pseud. (1926-). Wilkins, Mary Huiskamp. 1970. Atheneum. (P.162)
--*Moving.* Watson, Wendy McLeod (1942-). c.1978. Crowell. (P.936)
--*Muncus Agruncus, a Bad Little Mouse.* 1st ed. Watson, Nancy Dingman. c.1976. Golden Press. (P.936)
--*Open the Door and See All the People.* Bulla, Clyde Robert (1914-). 1972. Crowell. (P.149)
--*Quips and Quirks.* Watson, Clyde (1947-). 1975. Harper. (P.935)
--*Rosabel's Secret.* Christgau, Alice Erickson (1902-). 1967. Young Scott Books. (P.193)
--*The Spider Plant.* Speevack, Yetta. 1965. Atheneum. (P.843)
--*Stairstep Farm: Anna Rose's Story.* Pellowski, Anne (1933-). 1981. Philomel Books. (P.716)
--*The Strawman Who Smiled by Mistake.* 1st ed. Tripp, Paul (1916-). 1967. Doubleday. (P.900)
--*Tom Fox and the Apple Pie.* Watson, Clyde (1947-). 1972. Crowell. (P.935)
--*Tom Fox and the Apple Pie.* Watson, Clyde (1947-). 1972. Harper. (P.935)
--*Uncle Fonzo's Ford.* 1st ed. Martin, Patricia Miles (1899-). Miles, Miska, pseud. 1968. Little, Brown. (P.625)
--*Uncle Fonzo's Ford.* Miles, Miska, pseud. (1899-). Martin, Patricia Miles. 1968. Little, Brown. (P.645)
--*Upside Down and Inside Out: Poems for All Your Pockets.* Katz, Bobbi (1933-). 1973. F. Watts. (P.509)
--*Very Important Cat.* Watson, Wendy McLeod (1942-). 1958. Dodd, Mead. (P.936)
--*When Noodlehead Went to The Fair.* Hitte, Kathryn. 1968. Parents' Magazine Press. (P.420)
--*When Noodlehead Went to the Fair.* Hitte, Kathryn (1919-). 1968. Parents' Magazine Press. (P.447)
--*Willow Wind Farm: Betsy's Story.* Pellowski, Anne (1933-). 1981. Putnam Pub Group. (P.716)
--*Winding Valley Farm: Annie's Story.* Pellowski, Anne (1933-). 1982. Philomel Books. (P.716)
--*Winter Night.* Watson, Wendy Mcleod (1942-). 1977. Crowell. (P.936)

Watson, William R.
--*A Trip on a Ship.* Greene, Carla (1916-). 1958. Lantern Press. (P.386)

Watt, Linnie, jt. illus. see Wilson, Ernest.

Watters, Patricia
--*Tahko, the Indian Boy, "Namameha and Watomilka" and Father Rene's Last Journey: Three Stories of Valor.* Rogan, James Watkyn (1915-), adapted by. 1951. Mission Press. (P.774)

Watts, Anna Bernadette see Bernadette, pseud.

Watts, Anna Bernadette (1942-)
--*Animal Folk Tales Around the World.* Arnott, Kathleen (1914-), ed. 1971, c.1970. H. Z. Walck. (P.49)
--*The Big Book of Stories from Many Lands.* Power, Rhoda Dolores (1890-1957). 1970, c.1969. Watts. (P.736)
--*Brigitte & Ferdinand: A Love Story.* Bernadette, pseud. Watts, Anna Bernadette (1942-). Bernadette, pseud. 1976. P-H. (P.937)
--*The Clock in the Tower.* Ehrhardt, Von Reinhold (1900-). N.D. Scroll Pr. (P.299)
--*David's Waiting Day.* Bernadette, pseud. Watts, Anna Bernadette (1942-). Bernadette, pseud. 1978. P-H. (P.937)
--*Goldilocks and the Three Bears.* The, Three Bears. Watts, Anna Bernadette (1942-), retold by. 1985. North-South Books : Distributed in the U.S. by Holt, Rinehart, and Winston. (P.890)
--*Green is Beautiful.* Rogers, Margaret (1942-). N.D. State Mutual Bk. (P.775)
--*Hans the Miller Man.* Bernadette, pseud. Watts, Anna Bernadette (1942-). Bernadette, pseud. 1969. McGraw. (P.937)
--*Jorinda and Joringel.* Grimm, Jakob Ludwig Karl (1785-1863) & Grimm, Wilhelm Karl (1786-1859). 1970. World Pub. Co. (P.393)
--*Kikeri: Or, The Proud Red Rooster.* Ehrhardt, Von Reinhold (1900-). 1969. World Pub. Co. (P.299)
--*Kikeri: Or, The Proud Red Rooster.* Ehrhardt, Von Reinhold (1900-). 1970. World Pub. (P.299)
--*The Lady of Shalott.* Tennyson, Alfred Lord (1809-1892). 1968. F. Watts. (P.882)
--*Little Red Riding Hood.* Grimm, Jakob Ludwig Karl (1785-1863) & Grimm, Wilhelm Karl (1786-1859). 1972. Scholastic Inc. (P.394)
--*Little Red Riding Hood.* Grimm, Jakob Ludwig Karl (1785-1863) & Grimm, Wilhelm Karl (1786-1859). 1969. World Pub. Co. (P.394)
--*Look, Do, and Listen.* Ainsworth, Ruth (1908-). 1969. F. Watts. (P.15)
--*One's None: Old Rhymes for New Tongues.* Reeves, James (1909-), ed. 1969. F. Watts. (P.754)
--*Rapunzel.* Grimm, Jakob Ludwig Karl (1785-1863) & Grimm, Wilhelm Karl (1786-1859). Watts, Anna Bernadette (1942-), retold by. 1975. Crowell. (P.394)
--*Snow White.* Grimm, Jakob Ludwig Karl (1785-1863) & Grimm, Wilhelm Karl (1786-1859). 1983. Faber and Faber. (P.394)
--*Three Grimms' Fairy Tales: The Fox & the Geese, The Magic Porridge Pot, The Silver Pennies, 3 bks.* Grimm, Jakob Ludwig Karl (1785-1859) & Grimm, Wilhelm Karl. 1981. Little. (P.395)
--*Three Tales.* Grimm, Jakob Ludwig Karl (1785-1863) & Grimm, Wilhelm Karl (1786-1859). Watts, Anna Bernadette (1942-), retold by. 1980. Little, Brown. (P.395)
--*Varenka.* Bernadette, pseud. Watts, Anna Bernadette (1942-). Bernadette, pseud. 1972, c.1971. Putnam. (P.937)

Watts, charles Edwin (1929-)
--*Alexander Fiddlewhistle.* Watts, Charles Edwin (1929-). 1960. Helicon Press. (P.937)
--*Taumac.* Gribbin, Raymond William. 1960. Helicon Press. (P.389)

Watts, Ethel Franklin
--*Fairy Tales from Grimm.* Mabie, Hamilton Wright (1846-1916), ed. N.D. Edward Stern & Co. (P.593)

Watts, James (1955-)
--*The Trouble on Janus.* Slote, Alfred (1926-). c.1985. Lippincott. (P.830)

Watts, John Francis (1926-)
--*When Sea and Sky Are Blue.* Parr, Letitia Evelyn (1906-). 1971, c.1970. Scroll Press. (P.707)

Watts, Marjorie-Ann
--*The Adventures of Polly and the Wolf.* Storr, Catherine Cole (1913-). 1970, c.1957. M. Smith Co. (P.863)
--*The Adventures of Polly and the Wolf.* Storr, Catherine Cole (1913-). N.D. Transatlantic Arts, Inc. (P.863)
--*Bettina's Secret.* Hallqvist, Britt G. (1914-). Parker, Anne, tr. from Swedish. 1967. Harcourt, Brace & World. (P.407)
--*Clever Polly & the Stupid Wolf.* Storr, Catherine Cole (1913-). 1968. Penguin. (P.863)
--*Crocodile Medicine.* Watts, Marjorie-Ann. 1978, c.1977. F. Warne. (P.937)
--*Crocodile Plaster.* Watts, Marjorie-Ann. N.D. Dutton. (P.937)
--*The Dragon Clock.* Watts, Marjorie-Ann. 1975. David & Charles. (P.937)
--*The Magic Drawing Pencil.* Storr, Catherine Cole (1913-). 1960. Barnes. (P.863)
--*Marianne & Mark.* Storr, Catherine Cole (1913-). 1979. Faber & Faber. (P.863)
--*Marianne Dreams.* rev. ed. Storr, Catherine Cole (1913-). 1964. Penguin Books. (P.863)
--*Marianne Dreams.* Storr, Catherine Cole (1913-). N.D. Transatlantic Arts. (P.863)
--*Mulroy's Magic.* Watts, Marjorie-Ann. 1975. Puffin Books. (P.937)
--*Zebra Goes to School.* Watts, Marjorie-Ann. 1981. Andre Deutsch. (P.937)

Waudby, Roberta F. C., jt. illus. see Wood, Elsie Anna.

Waugh, Dorothy (1896-)
--*Muriel Saves String.* Waugh, Dorothy (1896-). 1956. D. McKay Co. (P.937)

Waugh, Gwenyth
--*Gray Wolf Stories: Indian Mystery Tales of Coyote, Animals and Men.* Sexton, Bernard. Gray Wolf, Peter, pseud. 1921. The Macmillan Company. (P.813)
--*Gray Wolf Stories: Indian Mystery Tales of Coyote, Animals and Men.* Sexton, Bernard. Gray Wolf, Peter, pseud. 1941. The Caxton Printers, Ltd. (P.813)

Waugh, Ida
--*An Odd Little Lass.* Wright, Jessie E., Mrs., pseud. Whitcomb, Jessie Wright. N.D. Penn Publishing Co. (P.981)
--*Baby Blossom.* Blanchard, Amy Ella (1856-1926). 1888. R Worthington. (P.106)
--*Bonnie Bairns.* Blanchard, Amy Ella (1856-1926). 1888. R Worthington. (P.106)
--*A Daughter of Freedom: A Story of the Latter Period of the War for Independence.* Blanchard, Amy Ella (1856-1926). 1900. W. A. Wilde Company. (P.106)
--*A Daughter of the Forest.* Raymond, Evelyn Hunt, Mrs. (1843-1910). 1902. The Penn Publishing Company. (P.751)
--*Dimple Dallas.* Blanchard, Amy Ella (1856-1926). 1900. G. W. Jacobs & Co. (P.106)
--*Dorothy Day.* Lippmann, Julie Mathilde (1864-). N.D. Penn Publishing Co. (P.576)
--*Dorothy Day: A Story for Girls.* Lippmann, Julie Mathilde (1864-). 1898. The Penn Publishing Company. (P.576)
--*Earning Her Way: A Story for Girls.* Johnson, Clarke, Mrs. N.D. Penn Publishing Co. (P.494)
--*Earning Her Way to College: A Story for Girls.* Johnson, Clarke, Mrs. 1900. The Penn Publishing Company. (P.494)
--*An Every-Day Heroine.* Denison, Mary Andrews, Mrs. (1826-1911). N.D. Penn Publishing Co. (P.257)
--*An Everyday Heroine: A Story for Girls.* Denison, Mary Andrews, Mrs. (1826-1911). 1896. Penn. (P.257)
--*The Ferry Maid of the Chattahoochee.* Barnes, Annie Maria (1857-). 1899. Penn Publishing Co. (P.73)
--*The Ferry Maid of the Chattahoochee: A Story for Girls.* Barnes, Annie Maria (1857-). 1899. The Penn. Pub. Co. (P.73)

ILLUSTRATOR INDEX WEISGARD, LEONARD

--*The Fantastic Toy Shop: La Boutique Fantasque.* Weil, Lisl (1910-), retold by. Respighi, Ottorino (1879-1936). c.1966. Abelard-Schuman. (P.758)
--*Fat Ernest.* Weil, Lisl (1910-). 1973. Parents' Magazine Press. (P.941)
--*Fifty-One Sycamore Lane.* Sharmat, Marjorie Weinman (1928-). 1971. Macmillan. (P.815)
--*The Foolish King.* Weil, Lisl (1910-), retold by. c.1982. Macmillan. (P.941)
--*The Funny Old Bag.* Weil, Lisl (1910-). 1974. Parents' Magazine Press. (P.941)
--*Gertie and Gus.* Weil, Lisl (1910-). c.1977. Parents' Magazine Press. (P.941)
--*Gertie and Gus.* Weil, Lisl (1910-). 1978, c.1977. Parents' Magazine Press. (P.941)
--*Gillie and the Flattering Fox.* Weil, Lisl (1910-), adapted by. 1978. Atheneum. (P.941)
--*The Golden Spinning Wheel: An Old Bohemian Folk Tale.* Weil, Lisl (1910-), adapted by. 1969. Macmillan Co. (P.941)
--*The Great Rabbit Rip-off.* Hildick, Edmund Wallace (1925-). 1977, c.1976. Macmillan. (P.442)
--*Happy Birthday in Barcelona.* Weil, Lisl (1910-). c.1965. Houghton. (P.941)
--*The Hopping Knapsack.* Weil, Lisl (1910-). 1970. Macmillan. (P.941)
--*House for Henrietta.* Lansing, Elisabeth Carleton Hubbard (1911-). 1958. T Y Crowell. (P.551)
--*I Wish: I Wish.* Weil, Lisl (1910-). N.D. E. M. Hale & Co. (P.941)
--*I Wish, I Wish.* Weil, Lisl (1910-). 1957. Houghton Mifflin. (P.941)
--*I Wish, I Wish.* Weil, Lisl (1910-). 1972, c.1957. Houghton. (P.941)
--*I Wonder Why?* Thought the Owl: An Old World Tale Retold. Bevans, Margaret Van Doren (1917-), ed. 1965. Putnam. (P.100)
--*If Eggs Had Legs: Nonsense & Some Sense.* Weil, Lisl (1910-). 1976. Doubleday. (P.941)
--*Jacoble Tells the Truth.* Weil, Lisl (1910-). 1946. Houghton Mifflin Co. (P.941)
--*Katie & Those Boys.* Tolles, Martha (1921-). 1976. Scholastic Inc. (P.894)
--*King Midas' Secret & Other Follies.* Weil, Lisl (1910-). 1969. McGraw. (P.941)
--*The Lancelot Closes at Five.* Sharmat, Marjorie Weinman (1928-). c.1976. Macmillan. (P.815)
--*The Lionhearted One.* Weil, Lisl (1910-). 1962. HM. (P.941)
--*Little Chestnut Tree Story.* Weil, Lisl (1910-). 1973. Schol Bk Serv. (P.941)
--*The Little Store on the Corner.* Miller, Alice Patricia McCarthy. 1974. Scholastic Inc. (P.646)
--*The Long Christmas Eve.* Duryea, Elizabeth. 1954. Houghton Mifflin Co. (P.292)
--*Master of All Masters: A Folktale.* Weil, Lisl (1910-). 1973. Scholastic Magazines. (P.941)
--*Mat and Mandy and the Big Dog, Bigger.* Simon, Ruth Corabel Shimer (1918-). 1954. Crowell. (P.825)
--*Mat and Mandy and the Little Old Car.* Simon, Ruth Corabel Shimer (1918-). 1952. Thomas Y. Crowell. (P.825)
--*McGurk Gets Good and Mad.* Hildick, Edmund Wallace (1925-). c.1982. Macmillan. (P.442)
--*Melissa.* Weil, Lisl (1910-). c.1966. Macmillan. (P.941)
--*Melissa's Friend Fabrizzio.* Weil, Lisl (1910-). 1967. Macmillan. (P.941)
--*Mimi.* Weil, Lisl (1910-). 1961. HM. (P.941)
--*Mindy.* Shiefman, Vicky (1942-). 1974. Macmillan. (P.820)
--*Mister Bear Goes to Boston.* French, Marion Flood (1920-). 1955. Follett. (P.344)
--*Mother Goose Picture Riddles: A Book of Rebuses.* Weil, Lisl (1910-), adapted by. c.1981. Holiday House. (P.941)
--*Of Wicked Monsters and Wondrous Creatures.* Weil, Lisl (1910-). 1985. Atheneum. (P.941)
--*Our World to You With Love.* Weil, Lisl (1910-). 1983. Atheneum. (P.941)
--*Out & In.* Hulbert, Elizabeth McKey. 1972. Schol Bk Serv. (P.472)
--*Owl and Other Scrambles.* Weil, Lisl (1910-). McLeod, Emilie Warren, ed. c.1980. Dutton. (P.941)
--*Pudding's Wonderful Bone.* Weil, Lisl (1910-). 1956. Crowell. (P.941)
--*Ralphi Rhino.* Weil, Lisl (1910-). 1974. Walker. (P.941)
--*The Riddle Monster.* Weil, Lisl (1910-). 1981, c.1980. Clarion Books. (P.941)
--*Sheep Ahoy.* Kingman, Lee, pseud. (1919-). Natti, Marylee Kingman. 1963. Houghton Mifflin. (P.524)
--*Shivers and the Case of the Secret Hamburgers.* Weil, Lisl (1910-). 1967. Houghton Mifflin. (P.941)
--*The Sorcerer's Apprentice.* Weil, Lisl (1910-), adapted by. 1962. Little. (P.941)
--*The Spy in the Neighborhood.* Sharmat, Marjorie Weinman (1928-). 1974, c.1971. Collier Books. (P.815)
--*Step on It, Andrew.* Hazen, Barbara Shook (1930-). 1980. Atheneum. (P.427)
--*Stories from the Peterkin Papers.* Hale, Lucretia Peabody (1820-1900). 1972. Schol Bk Serv. (P.404)
--*The Story of the Wise Men & the Child.* Weil, Lisl (1910-). 1981. Atheneum. (P.941)
--*The Super-Duper Car.* Govan, Christine Noble, Mrs. (1898-). 1952. Houghton Mifflin. (P.379)
--*The Thirsty Lion.* Forbes, Katherine Russell. 1950. Crowell. (P.335)
--*Three Birthday Wishes.* Holberg, Ruth Langland, Mrs. (1891-). 1953. Crowell. (P.453)
--*To Sail a Ship of Treasures.* Weil, Lisl (1910-). 1984. Atheneum. (P.941)
--*Told Under the City Umbrella.* Association for Childhood Education International, ed. 1972. Macmillan. (P.53)
--*Tony for Keeps: A Story of a House on Wheels.* 1st ed. Clark, Electa (1910-). 1955. Winston. (P.197)
--*The Very First Story Ever Told.* Weil, Lisl (1910-). 1976. Atheneum. (P.941)
--*A Visit with Rosalind.* Sharmat, Marjorie Weinman (1928-). 1971, c.1972. Macmillan. (P.815)
--*Walt and Pepper.* Weil, Lisl (1910-). 1974. Parents' Magazine Press. (P.941)
--*What Will I Wear?.* Olds, Helen Diehl (1895-1981). 1961. Knopf. (P.693)
--*When Animals Had Fire.* Weil, Lisl (1910-). 1982. Atheneum. (P.941)
--*The Wiggler.* Weil, Lisl (1910-). 1971. Houghton Mifflin. (P.941)
--*The Windmill Family.* Brown, Pamela Beatrice (1924-). c.1954. T. Y. Crowell Co. (P.142)

Weiler, Mary
--*The Whale People.* Haig-Brown, Roderick Langmere (1908-1976). 1963. Morrow. **Award: (CLA).** (P.402)

Wein, Charlotte Epstein
--*Maybe Tomorrow I'll Have a Good Time.* Soderstrom, Mary (1942-). 1981. Human Sciences Press. (P.840)

Weinbaum, Sonia see Wyntree, Sonia, pseud.

Weinbaum, Sonia (1919-)
--*Lisbeth and the Clam.* 1st ed. Wyntree, Sonia, pseud. Weinbaum, Sonia (1919-). Wyntree, Sonia, pseud. 1947. Rockport Press. (P.941)

Weinberg, Kay
--*The Horrible Terrible Dragon: A Folktale.* Weinberg, Michael A. 1949. Weinberg. (P.941)

Weiner, Beth Lee
--*The After School Book.* Calmenson, Stephanie (1952-). c.1984. Grosset & Dunlap. (P.163)
--*Archer Armadillo's Secret Room.* Singer, Marilyn (1948-). c.1985. Macmillan. (P.827)
--*The Kindergarten Book.* Calmenson, Stephanie (1952-). 1983. Putnam Pub Group. (P.163)
--*Mr.* Sniff and the Motel Mystery. Lewis, Thomas Parker (1936-). c.1984. Harper & Row. (P.570)

Weiner, Sandra (1922-), photos by.
--*It's Wings That Make Birds Fly: The Story of a Boy.* Weiner, Sandra (1922-). 1968. Pantheon Books. (P.941)
--*They Call Me Jack: The Story of a Boy from Puerto Rico.* Weiner, Sandra (1922-). 1973. Pantheon. (P.941)

Weinhaus, Karen Ann
--*All of Our Noses Are Here and Other Noodle Tales.* Schwartz, Alvin (1927-), retold by. c.1985. HarpJ. (P.803)
--*Carnival and Kopeck and More About Hannah.* Skolsky, Mindy Warshaw. c.1979. Harper & Row. (P.828)
--*Chicken at the Window.* Weinhaus, Karen Ann. 1981. Har-Row. (P.941)
--*Hannah and the Best Father on Route Nine-W.* Skolsky, Mindy Warshaw. c.1982. Harper & Row. (P.828)
--*Hannah Is a Palindrome.* 1st ed. Skolsky, Mindy Warshaw. c.1980. Harper & Row. (P.828)
--*Knock at a Star: A Child's Introduction to Poetry.* 1st ed. Kennedy, X. J., pseud. (1929-) & Kennedy, Dorothy Mintzlaff, eds. Kennedy, Joseph Charles. c.1982. Little, Brown. (P.518)
--*Margie and Me.* Wirth, Beverly. c.1983. Four Winds Press. (P.971)
--*Papa and Mama Biederbeck.* Mantinband, Gerda. 1983. Houghton Mifflin. (P.618)
--*The Perfect Christmas Picture.* Manushkin, Frances (1942-). 1980. Har-Row. (P.618)
--*The Perfect Christmas Picture.* Manushkin, Frances (1942-). c.1980. Harper & Row. (P.618)
--*Poem Stew.* Cole, William Rossa (1919-), selected by. 1981. Harper. (P.208)
--*Poem Stew.* 1st ed. Cole, William Rossa (1919-), selected by. c.1981. J.B. Lippincott. (P.208)
--*Samson Svenson's Baby.* 1st ed. Moore, Sheila. c.1983. Harper & Row. (P.662)
--*There Is a Carrot in My Ear, and Other Noodle Tales.* Schwartz, Alvin (1927-), retold by. c.1982. Harper & Row. (P.803)
--*Tickle a Pickle.* Turner, Ann Warren (1945-). 1984. Four Winds Press. (P.905)
--*The Whistling Teakettle and Other Stories About Hannah.* 1st ed. Skolsky, Mindy Warshaw. c.1977. Harper & Row. (P.828)

Weinhaus, Karen T.
--*Music for Ones & Twos: Songs & Games for the Very Young Child.* Glazer, Tom (1914-), ed. 1983. Doubleday. (P.370)

Weinheimer, George
--*The Dreaming Zoo.* Unterecker, John Eugene (1922-). c.1965. Walck. (P.909)

Weiniger, Egon
--*We Four Together.* Weissenstein, Helen (1900-). 1947. D. McKay Co. (P.943)

Weinman, Fred
--*Good Morning, Farm.* Wright, Betty Ren. 1964. Whitman Pub. Co. (P.980)

Weir, Harrison, jt. illus. see Linson, Corwin Knapp.

Weir, Harrison William, jt. illus. see Absolon, John.

Weir, Harrison William, jt. illus. see Gilbert, John Clitherae.

Weir, Harrison William (1824-1906)
--*Aesop's Fables.* Aesopus, et al. N.D. Belford, Clarke. (P.14)
--*Aesop's Fables.* Aesopus. N.D. George Routledge & Sons. (P.13)
--*Aesop's Fables.* Townsend, George Fyler (1815-1900), tr. N.D. George Routledge & Sons. (P.941)
--*Aesops Fables.* Aesopus. Townsend, George Fyler (1814-1900), tr. N.D. George Routledge (P.13)
--*Animal Sagacity.* Hall, S. C. N.D. George Routledge & Sons. (P.406)
--*Aunt Louisa's Home Favorite, 1 of 19 Vols.* N.D. Scribner & Welford. (P.941)
--*The Australian Crusoes.* Lee, R., Mrs. N.D. Lee & Shepard. (P.561)
--*The Castaways: or, The Adventures of a Family in the Wilds of Africa.* Bowman, Anne. N.D. George Routledge & Sons; Dist. by E. P. Dutton. (P.122)
--*Chatterbox Circus.* Francis, Laurence H., ed. N.D. Dana Estes and Company. (P.341)
--*Chatterbox Menagerie.* Francis, Laurence H., ed. N.D. Dana Estes and Company. (P.341)
--*The Chatterbox of Wild Animals.* Chatterbox. Robinson, Anna, ed. c.1909. D. Estes and Company. (P.188)
--*Chatterbox Picture Book.* Francis, Laurence H., ed. N.D. Dana Estes and Company. (P.341)
--*Chatterbox Wild West.* Francis, Laurence H., ed. N.D. Dana Estes and Company. (P.341)
--*Chatterbox Zoo.* Francis, Laurence H., ed. N.D. Dana Estes and Company. (P.341)
--*Children's Picture Fable-Book.* N.D. George Routledge & Sons. (P.941)
--*The Courtship and Wedding of Cock Robin and Jenny Wren.* Cock Robin. 1951. Sheldon Blakeman. (P.205)
--*Digby Heathcote: Or, The Early Days of a Country Gentleman's Son and Heir.* Kingston, William Henry Giles (1814-1880). N.D. George Routledge & Sons. (P.526)
--*The Dove and Other Stories, 1 of 6 Vols.* N.D. Sheldon & Co. (P.941)
--*Every Inch a King: Or, The Adventures of Rex and His Friends.* N.D. E P Dutton. (P.941)
--*Favourite Fables in Prose and Verse.* 1870. L. Nelson and Sons. (P.941)
--*Frank Wildman's Adventures on Sea and Land.* Gerstacker, Friedrich William Christian (1816-1872). N.D. George Routledge & Sons. (P.365)
--*Hardy and Hunter: A Boy's own Story.* Ward, Elizabeth Stuart Phelps, Mrs. (1844-1911). N.D. George Routledge & Sons. (P.930)
--*Little Lilla, 1 of 6 Vols.* N.D. Sheldon & Co. (P.941)
--*Stories of Animal Sagacity.* Kingston, William Henry Giles (1814-1880). N.D. Thomas Nelson & Sons. (P.527)
--*The African Crusoes.* Lee, R., Mrs. N.D. Lee & Shepard. (P.561)
--*White Elephant: The Hunters of Ava and the King of the Golden Foot.* Dalton, William (1821-). N.D. Pott, Young & Co. (P.239)
--*The Young Whaler: Or, the Adventures of Charles Holberg.* Gerstacker, Friedrich William Christian (1816-1872). N.D. George Routledge & Sons. (P.365)

Weir, Harrison William (1824-1906) & Absolon
--*Popular Nursery Tales and Rhymes.* N.D. George Routledge & Sons. (P.941)

Weir, Harrison William (1824-1906) & Greenaway, J.
--*Aesop's Fables.* Aesopus. Townesend, George Fyler (1814-1900), tr. 1964. Parents' Magazine Press. (P.13)
--*Aesop's Fables.* Aesopus. Townsend, George Fyler (1814-1900), tr. 1968. International Collectors' Library. (P.13)

Weir, Harrison William (1824-1906) & Padersen, V.
--*Fairy Tales.* Andersen, Hans Christian (1805-1875) & Bayes, A. W. N.D. Henry T. Coates & Co. (P.28)

Weisbecker, Philippe, photos by.
--*Slash: An Aligator's Story.* Kesselman, Wendy Ann. 1971. H. Quist. (P.520)

Weiseman, Bernard (1922-)
--*Morris Is a Cowboy: A Policeman, and a Baby Sitter.* Wiseman, Bernard (1922-). 1960. Harper. (P.972)

Weisgard, Leonard Joseph, jt. illus. see Smith, Kay Lovelace.

Weisgard, Leonard Joseph (1916-)
--*Abner's Cabin.* Evers, Alf (1905-). c.1957. F. Watts. (P.312)
--*Adam and the Golden Cock.* Dalgliesh, Alice (1893-1979). 1959. Scribner. (P.238)
--*Alice's Adventures in Wonderland, And Through the Looking Glass.* Dodgson, Charles Lutwidge (1832-1898). Carroll, Lewis, pseud. 1949. Harper. (P.277)
--*Americans Every One.* Davis, Lavinia Riker, Mrs. (1909-1961). 1942. Doubleday, Doran & Co., Inc. (P.246)
--*And It Came to Pass.* Slaughter, Jean (1929-). 1971. Macmillan. (P.829)
--*And It Came to Pass.* Slaughter, Jean (1929-). 1973. Macmillan. (P.829)
--*Andersen's Fairy Tales.* Andersen, Hans Christian (1805-1875). N.D. Doubleday. (P.34)
--*Baby Elephant & the Secret Wishes.* Joslin, Sesyle (1929-). 1962. HarBraceJ. (P.501)
--*Baby Elephant Goes to China.* Joslin, Sesyle (1929-). 1963. Harcourt, Brace & World. (P.501)
--*Baby Elephant's Baby Book.* Joslin, Sesyle (1929-). 1964. HarBraceJ. (P.501)
--*Baby Elephant's Trunk.* Joslin, Sesyle (1929-). 1961. Harcourt, Brace & World. **Award: (ALA).** (P.501)
--*The Beach Before Breakfast.* Kumin, Maxine Winokur (1925-). 1964. Putnam Pub Group. (P.541)
--*The Beloved Friend.* Vance, Marguerite (1889-1965). 1963. Colonial Williamsburg; Distributed by Holt, Rinehart and Winston, New York. (P.912)
--*Big Book of Nursery Tales.* Brown, Margaret Wise (1910-1952). N.D. Grosset & Dunlap. (P.140)
--*Big Book of Nursery Tales.* Weisgard, Leonard Joseph (1916-). 1962. Putnam Pub Group. (P.942)
--*The Big Book of Train Stories.* Weisgard, Leonard Joseph (1916-). c.1955. Grosset & Dunlap. (P.942)
--*Big Dog, Little Dog.* MacDonald, Golden, pseud. (1910-1952). Brown, Margaret Wise. 1943. Doubleday, Doran & Company, Inc. (P.599)
--*The Big Treasure Book of Nursery Tales.* Andreas, Evelyn, retold by. c.1954. Grosset & Dunlap. (P.40)
--*The Big Treasure Book of Nursery Tales.* Weisgard, Leonard Joseph (1916-). N.D. Grosset & Dunlap. (P.942)
--*The Boat That Mooed.* Fry, Christopher (1907-). 1965. Macmillan. (P.348)
--*Brave Baby Elephant.* Joslin, Sesyle (1929-). 1960. HarBraceJ. (P.501)
--*Bucky Bear, Who Would Not Take His Nap.* Wayne, Elaine. 1944. Lothrop, Lee & Shepard Co. (P.937)
--*Calf, Goodnight.* 1st ed. Jewell, Nancy (1940-). 1973. Harper & Row. (P.492)
--*Cinderella.* Weisgard, Leonard Joseph (1916-), retold by. c.1938. Garden City Publishing Co., Inc. (P.942)
--*City Country ABC.* Gipson, Morrell (1920-). c.1946. Garden City Pub. Co. (P.369)
--*The City Noisy Book.* Brown, Margaret Wise (1910-1952). 1976. Har-Row. (P.140)
--*The Clean Pig.* Weisgard, Leonard Joseph (1916-). 1952. Scribner. (P.942)
--*Country Noisy Book.* Brown, Margaret Wise (1910-1952). 1940. Har-Row. (P.140)
--*The Country Noisy Book.* Brown, Margaret Wise (1910-1952). N.D. William R. Scott Inc. (P.140)
--*The Courage of Sarah Noble.* Dalgliesh, Alice (1893-1979). 1954. Scribner. **Awards: (ALA); (JNM).** (P.239)
--*The Cozy Hour Storybook.* Kramer, Nora (1896-1984), ed. 1960. Random House. (P.537)
--*Cynthia and the Unicorn.* Freeman, Jean Todd (1929-). 1967. Norton. (P.344)
--*The Dark Wood of the Golden Birds.* Brown, Margaret Wise (1910-1952). 1950. Harper. (P.140)
--*Do You Want to Hear a Secret.* Redman, Sylvia Berger. 1960. Lothrop, Lee and Shepard Co. (P.753)
--*Doctor Proctor and Mrs.* Merriwether. Black, Irma Simonton, Mrs. (1906-1972). 1971. A. Whitman. (P.104)
--*Dorinda.* Howard, Elizabeth, pseud. (1907-). Mizner, Elizabeth Howard. 1944. Lothrop, Lee & Shepard Co. (P.467)

Whitehead, Samuel B
--*The Mystery of Robin Hood: Fact or Fantasy?*. Lisker, Tom (1928-). c.1979. C.P.I. (P.576)

Whitehorse, Roland
--*Winter-Telling Stories*. Marriott, Alice Lee (1910-). N.D. William Sloane Associates. (P.621)

Whitelaw, Norah
--*A Child's Day in Song*. Zucca, Mana & Frank, Mabel Livingston. c.1916. G. Schirmer. (P.994)

Whitelock, Louise Clarkson (1865-1928)
--*Little Stay-at-Home, and Her Friends*. Whitelock, Louise Clarkson, Mrs. (1865-1928). 1879. F. W. Robinson & Co. (P.954)

Whitemore, Constance
--*A Visit from St. Nicholas*. Moore, Clement Clarke (1779-1863). 1925. The Macmillan Company. (P.660)

Whitemore, Lee
--*C. J. Dennis' Slippery-Dip: Fun for Kids*. Dennis, Clarence James (1876-1938) & Whitmore, Lee. 1976. Angus and Robertson. (P.257)

Whiteside, Karen
--*Brother Mouky and the Falling Sun*. Whiteside, Karen. c.1980. Harper & Row. (P.954)

Whiting, John Downes (1884-)
--*Meetinghouse Bay*. Patterson, Henry W. c.1941. Coward-McCann, Inc. (P.710)
--*Moby Dick*. New ed. Melville, Herman (1819-1891). N.D. Sears Publishing Co. (P.640)
--*Mystery Island*. Barbour, Ralph Henry (1870-1944). c.1931. The Century Co. (P.71)
--*The Raid of the Ottawa*. Lange, Dietrich (1863-). 1921. Lothrop, Lee & Shepard Co. (P.550)
--*River Gold*. Paxton, Mary. c.1928. The Bobbs-Merrill Company. (P.712)
--*South of Zero: The Journal of John Hale Meredith While with the Clark-Jamison Antarctic Expedition of 191- to 191-*. Ross, Margaret Isabel (1897-). 1931. Harper & Brothers. (P.779)
--*The Strange Inventor: A Curious Adventure Sory*. Hyde, Mark Powell. 1927. Doubleday, Page & Company. (P.478)
--*The Trail of Fire: A Story of the Famous Alabama*. Whiting, John Downes (1884-). c.1930. The Bobbs-Merrill Company. (P.954)

Whitlock, Pamela (1921-1982)
--*Escape to Persia*. Hull, Katharine (1921-1977) & Whitlock, Pamela (1921-1982). 1968. J. Cape. (P.472)
--*Oxus in Summer*. Hull, Katharine (1921-1977) & Whitlock, Pamela (1921-1982). 1969. J. Cape. (P.472)
--*Oxus in Summer*. Hull, Katharine (1921-1977) & Whitlock, Pamela (1921-1982). 1940. The Macmillan Company. (P.472)

Whitman, Franklin J., Jr.
--*The Small One*. Tazewell, Charles (1900-1972). 1947. Holt Rinehart & Winston. (P.881)
--*The Small One*. Tazewell, Charles (1900-1972). 1947. John C. Winston Co. (P.881)

Whitman, Maurice
--*The After-Harvest Festival: The Story of a Girl of the Old Kankakee*. Arbuckle, Dorothy Fry (1910-1982). 1955. Dodd, Mead. (P.45)

Whitmore, Carol
--*Berry Ripe Moon*. Whitmore, Carol & Day, Michael E. c.1977. Tide Grass Press. (P.954)

Whitney, Alexandra (1922-)
--*Stiff Ears; Animal Folktales of the North American Indian*. Whitney, Alexandra (1922-). 1974. H. Z. Walck. (P.954)

Whitney, E. J.
--*Walter in Athens, 1 of 6*. Eddy, Daniel Clarke (1823-1896). N.D. Sheldon & Co. (P.295)
--*Walter in Constantinople, 1 of 6*. Eddy, Daniel Clarke (1823-1896). N.D. Sheldon & Co. (P.295)
--*Walter in Damascus*. Eddy, Daniel Clarke (1823-1896). N.D. Sheldon & Co. (P.295)
--*Walter in Egypt, 1 of 6*. Eddy, Daniel Clarke (1823-1896). N.D. Sheldon & Co. (P.295)
--*Walter in Jerusalem, 1 of 6*. Eddy, Daniel Clarke (1823-1896). N.D. Sheldon & Co. (P.295)
--*Walter in Samaria, 1 of 6*. Eddy, Daniel Clarke (1823-1896). N.D. Sheldon & Co. (P.295)

Whitney, Elinor (1889-)
--*Tyke-y, His Book and His Mark*. Whitney, Elinor (1889-). 1925. The Macmillan Company. (P.954)

Whitney, George Gillett
--*Enchanting Jenny Lind*. Benet, Laura (1884-1979). N.D. Dodd Mead & Co. (P.93)
--*Penn*. Gray, Elizabeth Janet (1902-). N.D. Viking Press. (P.383)
--*When Grandfather Was a Boy*. Bailey, Carolyn Sherwin (1875-1961). c.1928. Ginn and Company. (P.60)
--*When Master Thomas Was a Boy*. Brown, Thomas Kite (1851-1929). c.1929. The John C. Winston Company. (P.142)

--*Winter's Mischief*. Allee, Marjorie Hill, Mrs. (1890-1945). 1942. Houghton Mifflin Company. (P.29)

Whitney, H.
--*The Biggle De Boo and the Big Boo Hoo*. Godfrey, Maude Corey. 1931. Printed by A. R. F. Brandes. (P.372)

Whitney, H. & Whitney, I.
--*Castle Blair: A Story of Youthful Days*. Lugard, Flora Louisa Shaw, Lady (1852-1929). 1902. D. C. Heath & Co. (P.590)

Whitney, I., jt. illus. see Whitney, H.

Whitson, Elizabeth
--*The Casual Observatory*. Whitson, Elizabeth. 1975. C. R. Gibson Co. (P.955)

Whitson, Jack
--*Rudolph the Rooster*. Chappel, Bernice Marie (1910-). 1969. Bethany Press. (P.186)

Whittam, Geoffrey William (1916-)
--*All Because of Dawks*. Reid, Meta Mayne. 1955. Macmillan. (P.755)
--*The Baffling Bluejays*. Anderson, Bertha Christiana (1887-). 1958. Obelard-Schumann. (P.38)
--*China Sea Jigsaw*. Catherall, Arthur (1906-). 1962. Roy. (P.177)
--*Dangerous Cargo*. Catherall, Arthur (1906-). 1961, c.1960. Roy Publishers. (P.177)
--*Dawks Does It Again*. Reid, Meta Mayne. 1956. Macmillan. (P.755)
--*Dawks on Robbers' Mountain*. Reid, Meta Mayne. 1957. St Martin's Press. (P.755)
--*Death of an Oil Rig*. Catherall, Arthur (1906-). 1969. S. G. Phillips. (P.177)
--*Dolphin Summer*. Edwards, Monica Le Doux Newton (1912-). 1971, c.1963. Hawthorn Books. (P.298)
--*Family on the Tide*. Knight, Frank, pseud. (1905-). Knight, Francis Edgar. 1956. St Martin's Press. (P.532)
--*Family on the Tide: A Junior Novel for Girls*. Knight, Frank, pseud. (1905-). Knight, Francis Edgar. 1956. Macmillan. (P.532)
--*Hornblower Goes to Sea*. Forester, Cecil Scott (1899-1966). Griggs, G. P., ed. 1965, c.1948. Little. (P.335)
--*Hornblower in Captivity*. Forester, Cecil Scott (1899-1966). 1965. Little. (P.335)
--*Hornblower Takes Command*. Forester, Cecil Scott (1899-1966). Griggs, G. P., selected by. 1965, c.1937. Little. (P.336)
--*Hornblower's Triumph*. Forester, Cecil Scott (1899-1966). Griggs, G. P., ed. 1965, c.1945. Little. (P.336)
--*Jackie Won a Pony*. Berrisford, Judith Mary, pseud. (1921-). Lewis, Judith Mary. 1958. Verry. (P.97)
--*Jackie's Pony Patrol*. Berrisford, Judith Mary, pseud. (1921-). Lewis, Judith Mary. 1961. Verry. (P.97)
--*Lucky Lure at Arrow Point*. Daem, Mary, pseud. (1914-). Daem, Thelma Mary Bannerman. 1959. Abelard-Schuman. (P.238)
--*Muskoka Holiday*. Boyle, Emily Joyce (1901-). N.D. Macmillan. (P.123)
--*The Mystery of the Dolls House*. Moir, Kathleen. 1962. F. Warne. (P.653)
--*The Ponies Next Door*. Berrisford, Judith Mary, pseud. (1921-). Lewis, Judith Mary. 1955, c.1954. Dodd, Mead. (P.97)
--*Sea Wolves*. Catherall, Arthur (1906-). 1959. Roy. (P.178)
--*Sealskin for Silk*. Chessman, Evelyn. 1956. Abelard-Schuman. (P.190)
--*Storm on Kildoney*. Reid, Meta Mayne. 1961. St Martin's Press. (P.755)
--*Summer of Decision*. Allan, Mabel Esther (1915-). 1957. Abelard-Schuman. (P.28)
--*Tanker Trap*. Catherall, Arthur (1906-). 1966, c.1965. Roy. (P.178)
--*Ten Fathoms Deep*. Catherall, Arthur (1906-). 1967, c.1968. Criterion Books. (P.178)
--*Tortoise the Trickster, and Other Folktales from Cameroon*. Todd, Loreto (1942-). 1978. Routledge & Kegan Paul. (P.893)
--*Tortoise the Trickster and Other Folktales from Cameroon*. Todd, Loreto (1942-). 1979. Schocken. (P.893)
--*The Whistling Mountain*. Daem, Mary, pseud. (1914-). Daem, Thelma Mary Bannerman. 1960. Abelard-Schuman. (P.238)

Whittemore, Constance
--*Adventures in France: The Story of Jean and Fanchon*. Olcott, Virginia. 1953. Grosset & Dunlap. (P.692)
--*Adventures in Holland: The Story of Klass and Jansje*. Olcott, Virginia. 1953. Grosset & Dunlap. (P.692)
--*Adventures in Italy: The Story of Beppo and Lucia*. Olcott, Virginia. 1953. Grosset & Dunlap. (P.692)
--*Adventures in Norway: The Story of Olaf and Ane*. Olcott, Virginia. 1953. Grosset &Dunlap. (P.692)
--*Adventures in Sweden: The Story of Erik and Britta*. Olcott, Virginia. 1953. Grosset & Dunlap. (P.692)
--*Adventures in Switzerland: The Story of Anton and Trini*. Olcott, Virginia. 1953. Grosset & Dunlap. (P.692)

--*Anton and Trini, Children of the Alpland*. Olcott, Virginia. c.1930. Silver, Burdett and Company. (P.692)
--*The Batter and Spoon Fairies*. Teall, Edna A. W., Mrs. 1929. Harper & Brothers. (P.881)
--*Beppo and Lucia, Children of Sunny Italy*. Olcott, Virginia. c.1934. Silver, Burdett and Company. (P.692)
--*Diana's Rosebush*. White, Eliza Orne (1856-1947). 1927. Houghton Mifflin Company. (P.951)
--*Erik and Britta, Children of Flowery Sweden*. Olcott, Virginia. c.1937. Silver Burdett Company. (P.692)
--*Heidi*. Spyri, Johanna Heusser (1827-1901). c.1927. Thomas Y. Crowell Company. (P.846)
--*Jean and Fanchon, Children of Fair France*. Olcott, Virginia. c.1931. Silver, Burdett and Company. (P.692)
--*Karl and Gretel, Children of the Fatherland*. Olcott, Virginia. c.1932. Silver, Burdett and Company. (P.692)
--*Klaas and Jansje, Children of the Dikes*. Olcott, Virginia. c.1933. Silver, Burdett and Company. (P.692)
--*Market Day and Holiday: Stories of the World's Children*. Olcott, Virginia. c.1941. Silver Burdett Company. (P.692)
--*Mary Redding Takes Charge*. Almond, Linda Stevens. c.1926. Thomas Y. Crowell Company. (P.31)
--*Olof and Ane, Children of the Northland*. Olcott, Virginia. c.1938. Silver Burdett Company. (P.692)
--*The Trail of the Comet*. Allen, Gladys. 1929. Doubleday, Doran & Company, Inc. (P.29)
--*Wonder Tales from Fairy Isles: England, Cornwall, Wales, Scotland, Man, and Ireland*. Olcott, Frances Jenkins (1872-1963), ed. 1929. Longmans, Green and Co. (P.692)

Whittemore, Ed
--*By Air Express to Venus: Or, Captives of a Strange People*. Rockwood, Roy, pseud. Stratemeyer Syndicate. c.1929. Cupples & Leon Company. (P.773)
--*By Air Express to Venus: Or, Captives of a Strange People*. Rockwood, Roy, pseud. Stratemeyer Syndicate. N.D. Whitman Publishing Co. (P.773)

Whittingham, William
--*The Trail of the Deadly Image*. 1st ed. Johnson, Walter Ryerson (1901-). 1963. Collier Books. (P.497)
--*The Trail of the Golden Feather*. 1st ed. Johnson, Walter Ryerson (1901-). 1963. Collier Books. (P.497)
--*The Trail of the Moaning Ghost*. 1st ed. Johnson, Walter Ryerson (1901-). 1963. Collier Books. (P.497)
--*The Trail of the Witchwood Treasure*. Johnson, Walter Ryerson (1901-). 1963. Collier Books. (P.497)

Whitwell, T. M. R.
--*Psmith in the City*. Wodehouse, Pelham Grenville (1881-1975). N.D. MacMillan Bks. (P.973)

Whydale, E. Herbert
--*The Old Nurse's Stocking-Basket*. Farjeon, Eleanor (1881-1965). 1931. Frederick A. Stokes Company. (P.317)

Whymper, Edward
--*Sam Franklin's Savings Bank*. new engravings. ed. Stretton, Hesba (1832-1911). N.D. Fleming H Revell. (P.867)

Wiberg, Harald Albin (1908-)
--*The Bears of Big Stream Valley*. Burman, Edor (1913-). Bothmer, Gerry, tr. 1968. Delacorte Press. (P.154)
--*The Big Snowstorm*. Peterson, Hans (1922-). Bibb, Eric, tr. 1975. Coward, McCann & Geoghegan. (P.721)
--*Christmas at the Tomten's Farm*. Wiberg, Harald Albin (1908-). 1968. Coward-McCann. (P.956)
--*Christmas in the Stable*. Lindgren, Astrid Ericsson (1907-). 1962. Coward-McCann. (P.573)
--*Christmas in the Stable*. new ed. Lindgren, Astrid Ericsson (1907-). 1979. Putnam Pub Group. (P.573)
--*The Christmas Tomten*. Rydberg, Viktor. Jennings, Linda M, adapted by. Blecher, Lone Thygesen & Blecher, George, trs. from Swedish c.1981. Coward, McCann & Geoghegan. (P.787)
--*Three Wolverines of Rushing Valley*. Burman, Edor (1913-). Macmillan, Annabelle, pseud. (1922-), tr. from Swedish. Quick, Annabelle. 1966. Dutton. (P.154)
--*The Tomten: Adapted by Astrid Lingren from a poem by Viktor Rydberg*. Lindgren, Astrid Ericsson (1907-). 1961. Coward-McCann. (P.573)
--*The Tomten and the Fox*. Forsslund, Karl Erik (1872-1941). Lindgren, Astrid Ericsson (1907-), adapted by. 1965, c.1966. Coward-McCann. **Award: (ALA)**. (P.336)
--*When Peter Was Lost in the Forest*. Peterson, Hans (1922-). 1970. Coward-McCann. (P.721)

Wiberg, Harold Albin (1908-)
--*Benjamin Has a Birthday*. Ware, Kay (1916-) & Sutherland, Lucille, eds. 1964. Webster Division, McGraw-Hill. (P.931)

Wicasta, Sanyan T.
--*Ceremony-In the Circle of Life*. White Deer of Autumn. 1982. Carnival Pr. (P.953)

Wickart, Terry L.
--*The Night Light*. Smith, Susan Mathias (1950-). c.1981. Follett Pub. Co. (P.837)

Wickham, W. H.
--*Horseman's Island*. Oliver, Marjorie Mary (1890-). 1950. Westminster Press. (P.693)
--*Sentinel in the Saddle*. Jones, Lloid (1908-) & Jones, Juanita Nuttall (1912-). 1951. Westminster Press. (P.499)

Wickham, Wilmer
--*Scouting for Washington*. Donaldson, Lois (1898-). 1951. Whitman. (P.280)

Wiedenbeck, Emilie Agnes see Mabie, Peter, pseud.

Wiedenbeck, Emilie Agnes (1896-)
--*Chicken Little*. Mabie, Peter, pseud. Wiedenbeck, Emilie Agnes (1896-). Mabie, Peter, pseud. c.1931. Whitman Publishing Company. (P.956)
--*A Child's Garden of Verses*. Mabie, Peter, pseud. Stevenson, Robert Louis (1850-1894). 1946. James & Jonathan Co. (P.856)
--*Gingerbread Stories*. Mabie, Peter, pseud. Wiedenbeck, Emilie Agnes (1896-). Mabie, Peter, pseud. c.1931. Whitman Publishing Company. (P.956)
--*The Little Duck Who Loved the Rain*. Mabie, Peter, pseud. Wiedenbeck, Emilie Agnes (1896-). Mabie, Peter, pseud. 1946. Wilcox & Follett Co. (P.956)
--*Old Friends of Ours, Story and Pictures*. Mabie, Peter, pseud. Wiedenbeck, Emilie Agnes (1896-). Mabie, Peter, pseud. c.1931. Whitman Publishing Company. (P.956)
--*The Splendid Zoo*. Mabie, Peter, pseud. Wiedenbeck, Emilie Agnes (1896-). Mabie, Peter, pseud. c.1936. Whitman Publishing Company. (P.956)

Wiederseim, Grace G.
--*Kiddie Land*. Hays, Margaret G. N.D. George W. Jacobs & Co. (P.426)
--*Kiddie Rhymes*. Hays, Margaret G. N.D. George W. Jacobs & Co. (P.426)
--*Mollie and the Unwiseman Abroad*. Bangs, John Kendrick (1862-1922). 1910. J. B. Lippincott Company. (P.68)
--*Nursery Rhymes from Mother Goose*. Wiederseim, Grace G. N.D. Charles Scribner's Sons. (P.956)
--*The Turr'ble Tales of Kaptin Kiddo*. Hays, Margaret G. N.D. Edward Stern & Co. (P.426)

Wiegman, Lies, photos by.
--*My Kangaroo Phoebe*. Limmer, Hans (1926-). 1970. Hill & Wang. (P.572)

Wier, Don
--*The Victors*. Craine, Edith Janice (1881-). c.1933. Duffield and Green. (P.228)

Wierman, Eugenie
--*The Proud Roxana*. Dow, Ethel Constance (1890-). N.D. Edward Stern & Co. (P.282)

Wiese, Kurt, jt. illus. see Tyng, Griswold.

Wiese, Kurt, jt. illus. see Wessell, Wellington.

Wiese, Kurt (1887-1974)
--*Abraham, the Itinerant Mouse*. Hutter, Donald (1932-). 1947. Dodd, Mead. (P.477)
--*Adventure in Black and White*. Gatti, Attilio (1896-). 1943. C. Scribner's Sons. (P.360)
--*The Adventures of Duc of Indochina*. Nevins, Albert J. (1915-). 1955. Dodd, Mead (P.679)
--*The Adventures of Kenji of Japan*. Nevins, Albert J. (1915-). 1952. Dodd, Mead. (P.679)
--*The Adventures of Mario*. Bonsels, Waldemar (1881-). Chambers, Whittaker (1901-1961), tr. 1930. A. & C. Boni. (P.117)
--*The Adventures of Monkey: Adapted from the Translation Made from the Chinese of Wu Cheng-En*. Waley, Arthur. 1944. The John Day Company. (P.925)
--*The Adventures of Pancho of Peru*. Nevins, Albert J (1915-). 1953. Dodd, Mead. (P.679)
--*The Adventures of Ramon of Bolivia*. Nevins, Albert J (1915-). 1954. Dodd, Mead. (P.679)
--*The Adventures of Wu Han of Korea*. Nevins, Albert J. (1915-). 1951. Dodd, Mead. (P.679)
--*Alaskan Hunter*. Hayes, Florence Sooy (1895-). 1959. Houghton Mifflin. (P.425)
--*Alexander: The Tale of a Monkey*. Brown, Marion Marsh (1908-) & Brown, Edith (1887-1974). c.1934. The Bobbs-Merrill Company. (P.141)
--*Alice-Albert Elephant*. Hayes, Marjorie. 1938. Little, Brown and Company. (P.425)
--*All the Mowgli Stories*. Kipling, Joseph Rudyard (1865-1936). 1936. Doubleday. (P.527)

--*Moo-Wee, the Musk-Ox.* Rev ed. McConnell, Jane Tompkins (1898-). 1938. F. A. Stokes Co. (P.596)
--*Moo-Wee The Musk- Ox.* Tompkins, Jane. N.D. J. B. Lippincott. (P.895)
--*More Favorite Storie Old and New for Boys and Girls.* Rev. and enl. ed. Gruenberg, Sidonie Matsner (1881-1974), ed. 1960, c.1948. Doubleday. (P.398)
--*More to and Again.* Brooks, Walter Rollin (1886-1958). 1930. A. A. Knopf. (P.137)
--*The Most Beautiful House and Other Stories.* Pauli, Hertha Ernestine (1909-1973). 1949. A. A. Knopf. (P.711)
--*The Motorman.* Rev ed. Kuh, Charlotte Greenebaum, Mrs. 1929. The Macmillan Company. (P.541)
--*Mpengo of the Congo.* McGavran, Grace Winifred. 1945. Friendship Press. (P.601)
--*Mr. Piper's Bus.* Clymer, Eleanor Lowenton (1906-). 1961. Dodd, Mead. (P.203)
--*Mr.* Red Squirrel. 1st ed. Robinson, Thomas Pendleton (1878-). 1943. The Viking Press. (P.770)
--*Mr.* Two of Everything. Klutch, M. S. 1946. Coward-McCann, Inc. (P.531)
--*Mrs Piggle-Wiggle's Magic.* 1st ed. MacDonald, Betty Bard. 1949. Lippincott. (P.598)
--*Muffy: The Tale of a Muskrat.* Bird, Zenobia, pseud. Le Fevre, Laura Zenobia. 1941. A. Whitman & Company. (P.102)
--*Mulberry Village: A Story of Country Life in China.* Hollister, Mary Brewster, Mrs. (1891-). 1933. Dodd, Mead & Company. (P.456)
--*Muskox: Little Tooktoo's Friend.* Rev ed. Stafford, Marie Peary (1893-). 1931. W. Morrow & Co. (P.847)
--*The Mystery Dogs of Glen Hazard.* Chapman, Maristan, pseud. (1891-1972) & Chapman, Mary Ilsley. Chapman, John Stanton Higham. c.1941. Grosset & Dunlap. (P.186)
--*Nibby.* Meyer, Ann. 1952. Coward-McCann, Inc. (P.643)
--*Nibs: The Orphan Deer of the Adirondacks.* Lang, Don. 1942. Grosset & Dunlap. (P.550)
--*Ning's Pony.* Hawkes, Hester (1900-). 1953. Coward-McCann. (P.422)
--*No-Sitch, the Hound.* Stong, Philip Duffield (1899-1957). 1936. Dodd, Mead & Company. (P.862)
--*O-Go the Beaver.* Kelly, Raymond Ransome (1882-). 1934. A. Whitman & Co. (P.516)
--*Odie Seeks a Friend.* King, Julius (1893-). c.1934. Coward-McCann, Inc. (P.524)
--*Ootah and His Puppy.* Peary, Marie Ahnighito (1893-1978). c.1942. D.C. Heath and Company. (P.713)
--*The Other Twins.* 1st ed. McConnell, Jane Tompkins (1898-). 1955. Lippincott. (P.596)
--*Paddy's Christmas.* Monsell, Helen Albee (1895-1971). 1942. A. A. Knopf. (P.657)
--*Pal: The Story of an Airedale.* Jenkins, Alexander C. 1930. D. Appleton and Company. (P.491)
--*Panther Magic.* Baker, Olaf. 1928. Dodd, Mead & Company. (P.64)
--*The Parrot Dealer.* Wiese, Kurt (1887-1974). N.D. Coward-McCann. (P.957)
--*The Parrot Dealer.* Wiese, Kurt (1887-1974). N.D. Grosset & Dunlap. (P.957)
--*Pecos Bill and Lightning.* Peck, Leigh. 1940. Houghton Mifflin Company. (P.714)
--*Peetie: The Story of a Real Cat.* 1st ed. Jones, Inis Weed. c.1935. R. M. McBride & Co. (P.499)
--*The Penguin Twins.* Tompkins, Jane. 1939. Frederick A. Stokes Company. (P.896)
--*The Penguin Twins.* Tompkins, Jane. N.D. J. B. Lippincott. (P.896)
--*Phil Stong's Big Book: Farm Boy, High Water and No-Sitch, the Hound.* Stong, Philip Duffield (1899-1957). 1961. Dodd, Mead. (P.862)
--*Pierre of the Big Top: The Story of a Circus Poodle.* Meek, Sterner St. Paul (1894-1972). 1956. Dodd, Mead. (P.638)
--*Pika and the Roses.* Coatsworth, Elizabeth Jane (1893-). c.1959. Pantheon. (P.204)
--*Pinocchio.* Lorenzini, Carlo (1826-1890). Collodi, Carlo, pseud. Murray, Mary Alice, tr. 1928. T. Nelson and Sons. (P.585)
--*The Poetic Parrot.* Mackay, Margaret Mackprang (1907-). 1951. J. Day Co. (P.605)
--*The Polar Bear Twins.* Tompkins, Jane. 1937. Frederick A. Stokes Company. (P.896)
--*The Polar Bear Twins.* Tompkins, Jane. N.D. J. B. Lippincott. (P.896)
--*The Policeman.* Kuh, Charlotte Greenebaum, Mrs. 1929. The Macmillan Company. (P.541)
--*Poodle-Oodle of Doodle Farm.* Mackall, Lawton (1888-) & Mackall, Ruth. 1929. Frederick A. Stokes Company. (P.605)
--*Poole-Doodle of Doodle Farm.* MacGowan, Alice (1858-). N.D. J. B. Lippincott. (P.602)
--*The Porcupine Twins.* 1st ed. McConnell, Jane Tompkins (1898-). 1954. Lippincott. (P.596)
--*Positive Pete!.* Stong, Philip Duffield (1899-1957). 1947. Dodd, Mead. (P.862)
--*The Postman.* Kuh, Charlotte Greenebaum, Mrs. 1929. The Macmillan Company. (P.541)
--*The Prince and the Porker.* Stong, Philip Duffield (1899-1957). 1950. Dodd, Mead. (P.862)
--*A Puppy for Keeps.* Hawkins, Helena Ann Quail (1905-). 1943. Holiday House. (P.422)
--*Quest in the Desert.* Andrews, Roy C. 1950. Viking Pr. (P.41)
--*Quest of the Snow Leopard.* Andrews, Roy C. 1955. Viking Pr. (P.41)
--*Rabbit Bros.* Circus: One Night Only. Wiese, Kurt (1887-1974). 1963. Viking Press. (P.957)
--*The Rabbits' Revenge.* Wiese, Kurt (1887-1974). c.1940. Coward-McCann, Inc. (P.957)
--*The Raccoon Twins.* Tompkins, Jane. 1942. Frederick A. Stokes Company. (P.896)
--*The Raccoon Twins.* Tompkins, Jane. N.D. J. B. Lippincott. (P.896)
--*The Race for Land.* Prout, Vera Julia. 1954. Dodd, Mead. (P.741)
--*Ranger: Sea Dog of the Royal Mounted.* Strong, Charles Stanley (1906-). 1948. J. C. Winston Co. (P.868)
--*Ranger, Seadog of the Royal Mounted.* Strong, Charles Stanley (1906-). 1948. Holt Rinehart & Winston. (P.868)
--*Ranger's Arctic Patrol.* Strong, Charles Stanley (1906-). 1952. Winston. (P.868)
--*The Red Rajah.* Kent, Louise Andrews, Mrs. (1886-1969). 1933. Houghton Mifflin Company. (P.519)
--*The Red Squirrel Twins.* 1st ed. McConnell, Jane Tompkins (1898-). 1950. Lippincott. (P.596)
--*The Reindeer Twins.* 1st ed. McConnell, Jane Tompkins (1898-). 1956. Lippincott. (P.596)
--*The Return of Silver Chief.* O'Brien, John Sherman (1898-1938). 1946. Holt, Rinehart and Winston. (P.689)
--*The Return of Silver Chief.* O'Brien, John Sherman (1898-1938). 1943. The John C. Winston Company. (P.689)
--*River Children: A Story of Boat Life in China.* Hollister, Mary Brewster, Mrs. (1891-). 1935. Dodd, Mead & Company. (P.456)
--*Rivers to the Sea: A Novel.* 1st ed. Strommen, Irene Hugsen. 1955. Augsburg Pub. House. (P.868)
--*Rocco Came in.* Beecroft, John William Richard (1902-1966). 1959. Dodd, Mead. (P.88)
--*Roger and the Fishes.* Jackson, Charlotte E. Cobden, Mrs. (1902-). 1943. Dodd, Mead & Company. (P.484)
--*Rolling Show.* Voight, Virginia Frances (1909-). 1956. Holiday House. (P.921)
--*Rosie, the Rhino.* Conger, Marion (1915-). 1948. Abingdon-Cokesbury Press. (P.213)
--*The Round Meadow.* Oldrin, John (1901-). 1951. Viking Press. (P.693)
--*The Roundhouse Cat, and Other Railroad Animals.* Hubbard, Freeman Henry (1894-). 1951. Whittlesey House. (P.469)
--*Royal Red.* 1st ed. O'Brien, John Sherman (1898-1938). 1951. Winston. (P.689)
--*Sandy: The Tin Soldier of the A.E.F.* Connor, John Hal. 1931. Laidlaw Brothers. (P.214)
--*Saranga, the Pygmy.* Gatti, Attilio (1896-). 1939. C. Scribner's Sons. (P.360)
--*The Search for the Gold Fishhook.* Hoffmann, Eleanor (1895-). 1951. Dodd, Mead. (P.450)
--*Silk and Satin Lane.* Wood, Esther, pseud. (1905-). Brady, Esther Wood. 1939. Longmans, Green and Co. (P.975)
--*Silk and Satin Lane.* Wood, Esther, pseud. (1905-). Brady, Esther Wood. 1939. McKay. (P.975)
--*Silver Chief: Dog of the North.* O'Brien, John Sherman (1898-1938). 1933. Holt, Rinehart and Winston. (P.689)
--*Silver Chief: Dog of the North.* O'Brien, John Sherman (1898-1938). c.1933. The John C. Winston Company. (P.689)
--*Silver Chief to the Rescue.* O'Brien, John Sherman (1898-1938). c.1937. The John C. Winston Company. (P.689)
--*Silver Chief's Big Game Trail.* Miller, Albert Griffith (1905-1982). 1962, c.1961. Grosset & Dunlap. (P.646)
--*Silver Chief's Big Game Trail.* 1st ed. Miller, Albert Griffith (1905-1982). 1961. Holt, Rinehart and Winston. (P.646)
--*Silver Chief's Revenge.* 1st ed. O'Brien, John Sherman (1898-1938). 1954. Winston. (P.689)
--*Silver from the Sea.* rev. ed. Tooze, Ruth Anderson (1892-1972). 1962. Viking Pr. (P.896)
--*Skeeter,.* The Story of an Arabian Gazelle. Shaffer, Robert. 1952. Dodd, Mead. (P.814)
--*Sly Mongoose.* Pollock, Katherine G (1904-). 1943. C. Scribner's Sons. (P.731)
--*Snow for Christmas, Story.* Bowen, Vernon. c.1953. D. McKay Co. (P.121)
--*The Snowshoe Twins.* Tompkins, Jane. c.1941. Frederick A. Stokes Company. (P.896)
--*The Snowshoe Twins.* Tompkins, Jane. N.D. J. B. Lippincott. (P.896)
--*Snowy for Luck.* Goode, Arthur Russell (1889-). Russell, Arthur, pseud. 1934. A. Whitman & Co. (P.375)
--*Spike of Swift River.* O'Brien, John Sherman (1898-1938). 1942. The John C. Winston Company. (P.689)
--*Stories of Jesus.* Smither, Ethel Lisle (1887-1974). N.D. Abingdon Press. (P.837)
--*The Story About Ping.* Flack, Marjorie (1897-1958). 1977, c.1933. Puffin Books. (P.330)
--*The Story About Ping.* Flack, Marjorie (1897-1958). c.1933. The Viking Press. (P.330)
--*The Story of Freginald.* Brooks, Walter Rollin (1886-1958). 1936. A. A. Knopf. (P.137)
--*The Streamlined Pig.* Brown, Margaret Wise (1910-1952). 1938. Harper & Brothers. (P.141)
--*Su-Mei's Golden Year.* Bro, Marguerite Harmon (1894-1977). N.D. Doubleday. (P.133)
--*Su-Mei's Golden Years.* 1st ed. Bro, Margueritte Harmon (1894-1977). 1950. Doubleday. (P.133)
--*The Tale of Two Horses.* Tschiffely, Aime Felix (1895-). Graham, Robert Bontine Cunninghame (1852-1936), pref. by. 1935. Simon and Schuster. (P.902)
--*Tents in the Wilderness.* Lips, Julius Ernst (1895-). N.D. J. B. Lippincott. (P.576)
--*Tents in the Wilderness: The Story of a Labrador Indian Boy.* Lips, Julius Ernst (1895-). 1942. Frederick A. Stokes Company. (P.576)
--*The Thief in the Attic.* Wiese, Kurt (1887-1974). c.1965. Viking. (P.957)
--*The Three Little Kittens, with New Pictures.* Wiese, Kurt (1887-1974). 1928. Macmillan Co. (P.957)
--*Three Seeds.* Hawkes, Hester (1900-). 1956. Coward-McCann. (P.422)
--*Tito, the Pig of Guatemala.* Jackson, Charlotte E. Cobden, Mrs. (1902-). 1940. Dodd, Mead and Co. (P.484)
--*Toco Toucan.* Bridges, William Andrew (1901-). c.1940. Harper & Brothers. (P.130)
--*Tommy's Wonderful Airplane.* Clymer, Eleanor Lowenton (1906-). 1951. Dodd, Mead. (P.203)
--*Too Many Dogs.* Hawkins, Helena Ann Quail (1905-). 1946. Holiday House. (P.422)
--*The Tooseys.* La Rue, Mabel Guinnip, Mrs. 1938. T. Nelson and Sons. (P.553)
--*The Trail of the Buffalo.* Montgomery, Rutherford George (1894-). 1939. Houghton Mifflin Company. (P.659)
--*The Train That Never Came Back, and Other Railroad Stories.* Hubbard, Freeman Henry (1894-). 1952. Whittlesey House. (P.469)
--*Tramp, the Sheep Dog.* Lang, Don. c.1943. Grosset & Dunlap. (P.550)
--*The Truffle Pig.* Bishop, Claire Huchet, Mrs. 1971. Coward, McCann & Geoghegan. (P.103)
--*Twenty-Two Bears.* Bishop, Claire Huchet, Mrs. 1964. Viking Press. (P.103)
--*Valiant: Dog of the Timberline.* O'Brien, John Sherman (1898-1938). N.D. G&D. (P.689)
--*Valiant: Dog of the Timberline.* O'Brien, John Sherman (1898-1938). c.1935. The John C. Winston Company. (P.689)
--*Wagtail.* Gall, Alice Crew, Mrs. (1878-1949) & Crew, Fleming H. (1882-). c.1932. Oxford University Press. (P.353)
--*Wagtail.* Gall, Alice Crew, Mrs. (1878-1949) & Crew, Fleming H. (1882-). N.D. Walck. (P.353)
--*Walking Hat.* 1st ed. Hall, William Norman (1915-1974). N.D. Knopf. (P.406)
--*Wallie, the Walrus.* Wiese, Kurt (1887-1974). 1930. Coward-McCann, Inc. (P.957)
--*Way Down Cellar.* Stong, Philip Duffield (1899-1957). 1942. Dodd, Mead & Company. (P.862)
--*Way Down Cellar.* Stong, Philip Duffield (1899-1957). 1942. E M Hale. (P.862)
--*Whampoa.* Daniel, Hawthorne (1890-). 1941. Thomas Y. Crowell Company. (P.241)
--*What Every Young Rabbit Should Know.* Denison, Carol. 1948. Dodd, Mead. (P.257)
--*What?,Another Cat!.* Beecroft, John William Richard (1902-1966). 1960. Dodd, Mead. (P.88)
--*When the Typhoon Blows.* Lewis, Elizabeth Foreman, Mrs. (1892-1958). 1942. The John C. Winston Company. (P.569)
--*Where Any Young Cat Might Be.* Denison, Carol & Cummin, Jane. 1956. Dodd, Mead. (P.257)
--*The White Leopard: A Tale of the African Bush.* Rev ed. Fletcher, Inglis Clark, Mrs. (1888-). c.1931. The Bobbs-Merrill Company. (P.331)
--*The White Panther.* Waldeck, Theodore J. (1894-). 1941. The Viking Press. (P.925)
--*White Stars of Freedom.* Isasi, Mirim Erena & Denny, Melcena Burns. 1942. A. Whitman & Company. (P.482)
--*Wiggins for President.* Brooks, Walter Rollin (1886-1958). 1939. A. A. Knopf. (P.137)
--*William Colgate, Yeoman of Kent.* rev ed. Carver, Saxon Rowe (1905-). 1957. Broadman Press. (P.176)
--*Wind on the Prairie.* Weber, Lenora Mattingly, Mrs. (1895-1971). 1929. Little, Brown, and Company. (P.939)
--*The Wizard and His Magic Powder:.* Tales of the Channel Island. Campbell, Alfred Stuart (1900-). 1945. A. A. Knopf. (P.164)
--*The Wolf-Tracker.* Grey, Zane (1872-1939). 1930. Harper & Brothers. (P.389)
--*The Wonderful Adventures of Ting Ling.* Bowen, Vernon. c.1952. D. McKay Co. (P.121)
--*World Song.* Clark, Ann Nolan, Mrs. (1896-). 1960. Viking Press. (P.197)
--*Yen-Foh, a Chinese Boy.* Eldridge, Ethel J., Mrs., adapted by. 1935. A. Whitman & Co. (P.300)
--*Yinka-Tu the Yak.* Lide, Alice Alison, Mrs. (1890-). 1938. The Viking Press. (P.571)
--*Young Fu of the Upper Yangtze.* Lewis, Elizabeth Foreman, Mrs. (1892-1958). 1963, c.1932. Holt, Rinehart and Winston. (P.569)
--*Young Fu of the Upper Yangtze.* Lewis, Elizabeth Foreman, Mrs. (1892-1958). c.1932. The John C. Winston Company. **Award: (JNM).** (P.569)
--*Young Settler.* Stong, Philip Duffield (1899-1957). 1938. Dodd, Mead & Company. (P.862)

Wiese, Kurt (1887-1974) & Gleeson, J. M.
--*Kipling Stories and Poems Every Child Should Know.* Kipling, Joseph Rudyard (1865-1936). 1938. Garden City Publishing Co., Inc. (P.528)

Wiesenberg, Louis
--*Peter Hale.* Davis, Julia (1900-). 1939. E. P. Dutton & Co., Inc. (P.246)

Wiesner, David
--*The Boy Who Spoke Chimp.* Yolen, Jane Hyatt (1939-). c.1981. Knopf : Distributed by Random House. (P.986)
--*The Dark Green Tunnel.* Eckert, Allan W. (1931-). 1984. Little. (P.295)
--*Honest Andrew.* 1st ed. Skurzynski, Gloria Joan (1930-). c.1980. Harcourt Brace Jovanovich. (P.828)
--*Neptune Rising: Songs and Tales of the Undersea Folk.* Yolen, Jane Hyatt (1939-). 1982. Philomel Books. (P.987)
--*The One Bad Thing About Birthdays.* 1st ed. Collins, David Raymond (1940-). c.1981. Harcourt Brace Jovanovich. (P.210)
--*Owly.* Thaler, Mike (1936-). c.1982. Harper & Row. (P.884)
--*The Ugly Princess.* Luenn, Nancy. c.1981. Little, Brown. (P.590)
--*The Wand: The Return to Mesmeria.* Eckert, Allan W. (1931-). c.1985. Little, Brown. (P.295)

Wiesner, William (1899-)
--*Al and the Magic Lamp.* Elkin, Benjamin (1911-). 1963. E. M. Hale and Company. (P.301)
--*Al and the Magic Lamp.* 1st ed. Elkin, Benjamin (1911-). 1963. Harper & Row. (P.301)
--*Blunderbus.* McGinley, Phyllis (1905-1978). 1951. Lippincott. (P.601)
--*The Constant Little Mouse.* Wiesner, William (1899-). 1971. Four Winds Press. (P.957)
--*Funny Questions and Funny Answers.* Wiesner, William (1899-). 1970. Follett. (P.957)
--*Ghosts & Goblins.* New Rev. Ed. ed. Harper, Wilhelmina (1884-1973), ed. 1965. Dutton. (P.414)
--*Grabbit the Rascal.* Wiesner, William (1899-). 1969. Viking Press. (P.957)
--*Green Noses.* Wiesner, William (1899-). 1969. Four Winds Press. (P.957)
--*The Gunniwolf.* Harper, Wilhelmina (1884-1973), retold by. 1967, c.1918. Dutton. (P.414)
--*Hansel & Gretel.* Wiesner, William (1899-), ed. 1971. HM. (P.957)
--*Hansel and Gretel: A Shadow Puppet Picture Book.* Wiesner, William (1899-). 1971. Seabury Press. (P.957)
--*Happy-Go-Lucky.* Wiesner, William (1899-). 1970. Seabury Press. (P.957)
--*Hobnob.* Wilson, Christopher Bernard. 1968. Viking Press. (P.966)
--*How Silly Can You Be?.* A Book of Jokes. Wiesner, William (1899-). 1974. Seabury Press. (P.957)
--*How Silly Can You Be?.* A/Book of Jokes. Wiesner, William (1899-), compiled by. 1974. Seabury Press. (P.957)
--*Jack & the Beanstalk.* Wiesner, William (1899-), ed. 1973. Schol Bk Serv. (P.957)
--*Jack & the Beanstalk.* Wiesner, William (1899-), ed. N.D. Scholastic Inc. (P.957)
--*Joco and the Fishbone: An Arabian Nights Tale.* Wiesner, William (1899-). 1966. Viking. (P.957)
--*Little Sarah and Her Johnny Cake.* Wiesner, William (1899-). 1974. Walck. (P.957)
--*The Little Wooden Pony.* Woods, Ruth Maurine. 1946. The Saalfield Publishing Company. (P.977)
--*The Magic Slippers.* 1st ed. Wiesner, William (1899-). 1967. Norton. (P.957)
--*Magic Tales and Magic Tricks.* Wiesner, William (1899-). 1974. Charles Scribner's Sons. (P.957)
--*Moon Stories.* Wiesner, William (1899-). 1973. Seabury Press. (P.957)

--*Brian Wildsmith's "The Twelve Days of Christmas".* Wildsmith, Brian Lawrence (1930-). 1979. Watts. (P.960)
--*Cat on the Mat.* Wildsmith, Brian Lawrence (1930-). 1983. Merrimack Pub Cir. (P.960)
--*A Child's Garden of Verses.* Stevenson, Robert Louis (1850-1894). 1966. Oxford U.P. (P.856)
--*A Child's Garden of Verses.* Stevenson, Robert Louis (1850-1894). 1966. Watts. **Award: (ALA).** (P.856)
--*The Daffodil Bird.* Tomalin, Ruth. 1960, c.1959. Barnes. (P.894)
--*Daisy.* Wildsmith, Brian Lawrence (1930-). 1984. Pantheon Books. (P.960)
--*Fifer for the Union.* Allen, Lorenzo. 1964. Morrow. (P.30)
--*Give a Dog a Bone.* Wildsmith, Brian Lawrence (1930-). c.1985. Pantheon Books. (P.960)
--*The Hare and the Tortoise.* Wildsmith, Brian Lawrence (1930-), ed. 1967, c.1966. F. Watts. (P.960)
--*Havelok the Dane.* Crossley-Holland, Kevin (1941-). 1965. Dutton. (P.232)
--*High Sang the Sword.* 1st ed. O'Faolain, Eileen, Mrs. 1959. Oxford University Press. (P.691)
--*Hunt for the Yule Log.* Morgan, Carol McAfee. 1957. Abelard-Schuman. (P.663)
--*Hunter and His Dog.* Wildsmith, Brian Lawrence (1930-). 1979. Oxford University Press. (P.960)
--*The Iron Charm.* 1st ed. Williamson, Joanne Small (1926-). 1964. Knopf. (P.964)
--*The Knights of King Midas.* Berna, Paul (1910-). 1961. Pantheon Books. **Award: (ALA).** (P.97)
--*The Lazy Bear.* Wildsmith, Brian Lawrence (1930-). 1973. Oxford University Pr. (P.960)
--*The Lazy Bear.* Wildsmith, Brian Lawrence (1930-). 1974, c.1973. Watts. (P.960)
--*The Lion & the Rat: A Fable.* De La Fontaine, Jean. 1963. Merrimack Pub Cir. **Award: (KGM).** (P.252)
--*The Lion and the Rat: A Fable.* La Fontaine, Jean De (1621-1695). 1963. F. Watts. **Award: (ALA).** (P.544)
--*The Lion & the Rat: A Fable by La Fontaine.* Wildsmith, Brian Lawrence (1930-). N.D. Merrimack Pub Cir. (P.960)
--*The Little Wood Duck.* Wildsmith, Brian Lawrence (1930-). 1973, c.1972. F. Watts. (P.960)
--*The Little Wood Duck.* Wildsmith, Brian Lawrence (1930-). 1972. Oxford University Press. (P.960)
--*Maurice Maeterlinck's Blue Bird.* Wildsmith, Brian Lawrence (1930-), ed. 1976. Watts. (P.960)
--*The Miller, the Boy, and the Donkey.* La Fontaine, Jean de (1621-1695). N.D. Oxford. (P.544)
--*The Miller, the Boy, and the Donkey.* Wildsmith, Brian Lawrence (1930-), ed. 1969. F. Watts. (P.960)
--*The Miller, the Boy & the Donkey.* Wildsmith, Brian Lawrence (1930-), ed. 1984. Merrimack Pub Cir. (P.960)
--*Mother Goose.* Mother Goose. Wildsmith, Brain Lawrence (1930-), retold by. 1982. Merrimack Pub Cir. (P.668)
--*Myths of the Norsemen.* Green, Roger Gilbert Lancelyn (1918-), ed. 1964. Dufour. (P.385)
--*Myths of the Norsemen.* Green, Roger Gilbert Lancelyn (1918-). 1970. Penguin. (P.385)
--*The North Wind & the Sun.* La Fontaine, Jean De (1621-1695). 1964. Watts. **Award: (ALA).** (P.544)
--*The Owl and the Woodpecker.* Wildsmith, Brian Lawrence (1930-). 1972, c.1971. F. Watts. (P.960)
--*The Owl and the Woodpecker.* Wildsmith, Brian Lawrence (1930-). 1971. Oxford University Press. (P.960)
--*Oxford Book of Poetry for Children.* Blishen, Edward (1920-), ed. 1964, c.1963. F. Watts. **Award: (ALA).** (P.109)
--*Oxford Book of Poetry for Children.* Blishen, Edward (1920-), ed. 1984. P. Bedrick Books. (P.109)
--*Oxford Book of Poetry for Children.* Wildsmith, Brian Lawrence (1930-). N.D. Merrimack Pub Cir. (P.960)
--*Pelican.* Wildsmith, Brian Lawrence (1930-). 1983. Pantheon Books. (P.960)
--*Prince of the Jungle.* Guillot, Rene (1900-1969). Rhys, Brian, tr. from Fr. 1959. Criterion Books. (P.399)
--*Prince of the Jungle.* Guillot, Rene (1900-1969). Rhys, Brian, tr. 1959. S G Phillips. (P.399)
--*Professor Noah's Spaceship.* Wildsmith, Brian Lawrence (1930-). 1980. Oxford University Press. (P.960)
--*Python's Party.* Wildsmith, Brian Lawrence (1930-). 1975. Franklin Watts. (P.960)
--*Python's Party.* Wildsmith, Brian Lawrence (1930-). 1974. Oxford University Press. (P.960)
--*The Rich Man and the Shoe-Maker: A Fable.* La Fontaine, Jean De (1621-1695). 1979. Oxford University Press. (P.544)
--*The Rich Man and the Shoe-Maker: A Fable.* La Fontaine, Jean De (1621-1695). 1966, c.1965. Watts. **Award: (ALA).** (P.544)
--*The Secret Friends.* Chauncy, Nancen Beryl Masterman (1900-1970). 1962. Franklin Watts. (P.189)
--*Tales from the Arabian Nights.* Lorimer, E. O. 1962. Walck. (P.585)
--*Tangara:.* 'Let's Set off Again'. 1st ed. Chauncy, Nancen Beryl Masterman (1900-1970). 1960. Oxford University Press. (P.189)
--*The True Cross.* Wildsmith, Brian Lawrence (1930-). 1978. Watts. (P.960)
--*The Trunk.* Wildsmith, Brian Lawrence (1930-). 1983. Merrimack Pub Cir. (P.960)
--*What the Moon Saw.* Wildsmith, Brian Lawrence (1930-). 1978. Oxford U Pr. (P.960)

Wiles, Frank
--*The Princess of the School.* Brazil, Angela (1869-). 1921. Frederick A. Stokes Company. (P.128)

Wiles, Julian
--*The Tradd Street Follies.* Wiles, Julian. c.1978. Tradd Street Press. (P.960)

Wiley, Hugh
--*For Texas and Freedom.* Staffelbach, Elmer Hubert (1893-). 1953. Harr Wagner Pub. Co. (P.847)
--*For Texas and Freedom.* Staffelbach, Elmer Hubert (1893-). 1948. Macrae, Smith Co. (P.847)

Wilhelm, Hans (1945-)
--*Bunny Trouble.* Wilhelm, Hans (1945-). c.1985. Scholastic Inc. (P.960)
--*Don't Give Up, Josephine!.* Wilhelm, Hans (1945-). 1985. Random. (P.960)
--*The Funniest Riddle Book Ever!.* Rosenbloom, Joseph (1928-). c.1985. Sterling Pub. Co. (P.778)
--*I'll Always Love You.* Wilhelm, Hans (1945-). c.1985. Crown. (P.960)
--*A New Home, a New Friend.* Wilhelm, Hans (1945-). c.1985. Random House. (P.960)
--*Our Christmas, 1985.* c.1985. Grolier Enterprises. (P.960)
--*Pancake Pie.* Nordqvist, Sven. 1985. Morrow. (P.685)
--*Pat Boone's Favorite Bible Stories for the Very Young.* Boone, Pat (1934-). 1984. Random. (P.117)

Wilhelmina
--*The Story of Berta and Beth.* Feehan, Mary Edward, Sr. (1878-), as told by. Clementia, pseud. c.1924. Matre & Company. (P.320)

Wilhoite, Mariel
--*Rime, Rhythm and Song for the Child of Today.* Martin, Florence Marie (1913-) & Burnett, Elizabeth. 1942. Hall & McCreary Company. (P.624)

Wilin, Eloise
--*A Baby is Born.* Levine, Milton I. & Seligmann, Jean H. 1962. Golden Press. (P.568)

Wilke, William
--*Wild Animals of Africa.* Northey, Neil Wayne. 1948. Pacific Press Pub. (P.686)

Wilkey, Elmira
--*Sugar Gets the Skunk.* Moran, Martha Manker. 1977. Exposition. (P.662)

Wilkin, Eloise Burns (1904-)
--*Apple Tree Cottage.* Voight, Virginia Frances (1909-). 1949. Holiday House. (P.921)
--*Baby Listens.* Wilkin, Eloise Burns (1904-). 1960. Golden Press. (P.960)
--*Baby's First Christmas.* Wilkin, Eloise Burns (1904-). 1959. Golden Press. (P.960)
--*Baby's First Christmas.* Wilkin, Eloise Burns (1904-). 1980. Random. (P.960)
--*Baby's Mother Goose.* Mother Goose. 1975. Western Pub. (P.667)
--*Baby's Mother Goose.* Wilkin, Eloise Burns (1904-). 1958. Golden Press. (P.960)
--*The Birthday Story.* Buntain, Ruth Jaeger. 1953. Holiday House. (P.150)
--*The Boy with a Drum.* Harrison, David Lee (1937-). 1971. Golden Press. (P.417)
--*The Busy ABC.* c.1950. Whitman. (P.961)
--*Busy Timmy.* Jackson, Kathryn (1907-) & Jackson, Byron (1899-1949). 1948. Simon and Schuster. (P.485)
--*A Child's Garden of Verses.* Stevenson, Robert Louis (1850-1894). Wilkin, Eloise Burns (1904-), selected by. 1957. Simon and Schuster. (P.856)
--*A Child's Garden Verses.* Stevenson, Robert Louis (1850-1894). 1957. Golden Pr.(P.856)
--*The Choosing Book.* Dalgliesh, Alice (1893-1979). 1932. The Macmillan Co.(P.239)
--*The Christmas Story.* Werner, Jane (1915-), adapted by. 1952. Golden Press. (P.946)
--*Come Play House.* Osswald, Edith. 1948. Simon and Schuster. (P.697)
--*Company for Susie.* Crawford, John. Gregg, John, pseud. 1947. Howell, Soskin. (P.229)
--*A Day at the Playground.* Schlein, Miriam (1926-). 1951. Simon and Schuster. (P.799)
--*Eloise Wilkin Four Baby's First Golden Books, 4 bks.* Wilkin, Eloise Burns (1904-). 1981. Western Pub. (P.960)
--*First Bible Stories.* Watson, Jane Werner (1915-). 1954. Simon and Schuster. (P.935)
--*First BIble Stories.* Werner, Jane (1915-). 1954. Golden Press. (P.946)
--*Fix It, Please!.* Mitchell, Lucy Sprague, Mrs. (1878-). 1947. Simon and Schuster. (P.652)
--*Georgie Finds a Grandpa.* Young, Miriam Burt (1913-1974). 1954. Simon and Schuster. (P.990)
--*A Giant Little Golden Book of Birds.* Watson, Jane Werner (1915-). 1958. Simon and Schuster. (P.935)
--*Going-on-Nine.* Stone, Amy Wentworth. c.1939. Lothrop, Lee and Shepard Company. (P.861)
--*A Good House for a Mouse.* Eberle, Irmengarde (1898-1979). c.1940. J. Messner Inc. (P.295)
--*Good Morning and Good Night.* Werner, Jane (1915-). 1949, c.1948. Simon and Schuster. (P.946)
--*The Great Gold Piece Mystery.* Honness, Elizabeth Hoffman, Mrs. (1904-). 1960, c.1944. Lippincott. (P.458)
--*The Great Gold Piece Mystery.* Honness, Elizabeth Hoffman, Mrs. (1904-). 1944. Oxford University Press. (P.458)
--*Hansel and Gretel.* Grimm, Jakob Ludwig Karl (1785-1863) & Grimm, Wilhelm Karl (1786-1859). 1954. Simon and Schuster. (P.393)
--*Hansel & Gretel.* Grimm, Jakob Ludwig Karl (1785-1863) & Grimm, Wilhelm Karl (1786-1859). 1976. Western Pub. (P.393)
--*Hi Ho!* Three in a Row. Woodcock, Louise Phinney (1892-). 1954. Simon and Schuster. (P.976)
--*How Big Is Baby?.* Wilkin, Eloise Burns (1904-). 1980. Western Pub. (P.960)
--*I Hear: Sounds in a Child's World.* Ogle, Lucille & Thoburn, Tina. 1971. American Heritage Press. (P.691)
--*Jenny Jones and Skid.* Quigg, Jane. 1947. Oxford Univ. Press. (P.744)
--*Kitty Come Down.* Bacon, Frances Elizabeth Atchinson (1903-). 1944. Oxford University Press. (P.58)
--*Ladybug, Ladybug, and Other Nursery Rhymes.* Wilkin, Eloise Burns (1904-). c.1979. Random House. (P.960)
--*Linda and Her Little Sister.* Wilkin, Eloise Burns (1904-). 1955, c.1954. Simon and Schuster. (P.960)
--*The Little Book.* Wilkin, Eloise Burns (1904-). 1981. Western Pub. (P.960)
--*The Little Golden Holiday Book.* Conger, Marion (1915-). 1951. Simon and Schuster. (P.213)
--*The Make-Believe Parade.* Margo, Jan. 1949. Wonder Books. (P.619)
--*Mrs.* Peregrine and the Yak. Burns, Esther. c.1938. Ph. Holt and Company. (P.156)
--*Mrs.* Peregrine at the Fair. Burns, Esther. c.1939. J. Messner, Inc. (P.156)
--*My Baby Brother.* Scarry, Patricia Murphy (1924-). c.1956. Simon And Schuster. (P.796)
--*My Good Morning Book.* Wilkin, Eloise Burns (1904-). c.1983. Golden Press. (P.960)
--*My Goodnight Book.* Wilkin, Eloise Burns (1904-). 1981. Western Pub. (P.960)
--*My Kitten.* Scarry, Patricia Murphy (1924-). 1953. Simon and Schuster. (P.796)
--*My Pets.* Scarry, Patricia Murphy (1924-). 1959. Golden Press. (P.796)
--*My Puppy.* Scarry, Patricia Murphy (1924-). 1955. Simon and Schuster. (P.796)
--*My Snuggly Bunny.* Scarry, Patricia Murphy (1924-). 1956. Simon and Schuster. (P.796)
--*My Teddy Bear.* Scarry, Patricia Murphy (1924-). 1954. Golden Press. (P.796)
--*My Teddy Bear.* Scarry, Patricia Murphy (1924-). 1953. Simon and Schuster. (P.796)
--*My Toy Box.* Jackson, Kathryn (1907-) & Jackson, Byron (1899-1949). 1952. Simon and Schuster. (P.485)
--*The New Baby.* Shane, Ruth & Shane, Harold Gray (1914-). 1979, c.1948. Golden Press. (P.814)
--*The New House in the Forest.* Mitchell, Lucy Sprague, Mrs. (1878-). 1946. Simon and Schuster. (P.652)
--*The New House in the Forest.* Mitchell, Lucy Sprague, Mrs. (1878-). Reed, Mary, ed. 1945. Simon & Schuster. (P.652)
--*The Night Before Christmas.* Moore, Clement Clarke (1779-1863). 1955. Golden Press. (P.660)
--*The Night Before Christmas.* Moore, Clement Clarke (1779-1863). 1956. Golden Press. (P.660)
--*The Night Before Christmas.* Moore, Clement Clarke (1779-1863). 1955. Simon and Schuster. (P.660)
--*The Night Before Christmas.* Moore, Clement Clarke (1779-1863). 1956. Simon and Schuster. (P.660)
--*Noises and Mr.* Flibberty-Jib. Crampton, Gertrude (1909-). 1947. Simon and Schuster. (P.228)
--*Nursery Rhymes.* Wilkin, Eloise Burns (1904-). c.1979. Random House. (P.960)
--*The Once-Upon-a-Time Scratch and Sniff Book: Stories.* Long, Ruthanna, adapted by. Grimm, Jakob Ludwig Karl (1785-1863) & Grimm, Jakob Ludwig Karl (1785-1863). c.1978. Golden Press. (P.391)
--*Poems to Read to the Very Young.* Frank, Josette (1893-), ed. c.1982. Random House. (P.341)
--*Rainbow for Me.* Kiser, Martha Gwinn. 1948. Random House. (P.529)
--*Robin and Angus.* Robinson, Mabel Louise (1874-1962). 1931. The Macmillan Company. (P.770)
--*Robin and Tito.* Robinson, Mabel Louise (1874-1962). 1930. The Macmillan Company. (P.770)
--*Rock-a-Bye Baby.* Wilkin, Eloise Burns (1904-). 1984. Random. (P.960)
--*Rock-A-Bye, Baby: Nursery Songs & Cradle Games.* Wilkin, Eloise Burns (1904-). 1981. Random. (P.960)
--*Seatmates.* Reely, Mary Katharine (1881-). 1949. F. Watts. (P.753)
--*Sheep Wagon Family.* Richardson, Myra Reed. N.D. Dodd Mead & Co. (P.763)
--*Sheep Wagon Family.* Richardson, Myra Reed. 1941. R. M. McBride & Company. (P.763)
--*Sunshine for Merrily.* Kiser, Martha Gwinn. 1949. Random House. (P.529)
--*The Thank You Book.* Zens, Patricia Martin (1926-). 1967. Golden Press. (P.992)
--*The Tune Is In the Tree.* Lovelace, Maud Hart, Mrs. (1892-1980). 1950. Thomas Y. Crowell Co. (P.587)
--*The Twins: The Story of Two Little Girls Who Look Alike.* Shane, Ruth & Shane, Harold Gray (1914-). 1955. Simon and Schuster. (P.814)
--*The Visit.* Esley, Joan. c.1980. Rand McNally. (P.310)
--*We Help Mommy.* Cushman, Jean (1904-). 1959. Golden Press. (P.237)
--*Wiggles.* Woodcock, Louise Phinney (1892-). 1953. Simon and Schuster. (P.976)
--*The Wonders of the Seasons.* Parker, Bertha Morris (1890-1980). 1967, c.1966. Golden Press. (P.706)

Wilkin, Eloise Burns (1904-) & Cummings, Alison
--*Singing and Rhyming.* Pitts, Lilla Belle. 1950. Ginn. (P.728)

Wilkins, Hugo
--*Monica Goes to Madagascar.* Mezger, Max (1876-). Darnton, Maida Castelhun, Mrs., tr. c.1936. Coward, McCann, Inc. (P.644)

Wilkins, Mary Huiskamp see Calhoun, Mary, pseud.

Wilkins, Sarah & Mennella, Roxanna
--*Dolls.* Wilkins, Sarah & Mennella, Roxanna. Fisher, Barbara, ed. 1984. Ten Penny. (P.961)

Wilkinson, Barry
--*Agib and the Honey Cakes.* Lines, Kathleen, retold by. 1972. H. Z. Walck. (P.574)
--*Diverting Adventures of Tom Thumb.* Wilkinson, Barry. 1969. HarBraceJ. (P.961)
--*Lazy Jack.* Jacobs, Joseph (1854-1916), ed. 1970. Collins-World. (P.487)
--*Lazy Jack: A Picture Book.* Jacobs, Joseph (1854-1916), ed. 1970, c.1969. World Pub. Co. (P.487)
--*The Mouse Who Wanted to Be a Man.* Howell, Margaret. 1973. Longman Young Books. (P.468)
--*Pascal and the Lioness.* Guillot, Rene (1900-1969). Holyoak, Christine, ed. Holyoak, Christine, tr. from Fr. 1965. McGraw-Hill. (P.399)
--*Puss in Boots or the Master Cat.* Perrault, Charles (1628-1703). 1969. Collins-World. (P.719)
--*The Secret of the Missing Boat.* Berna, Paul (1910-). Buchanan-Brown, John (1929-), tr. from Fr. 1967, c.1966. Pantheon. (P.97)
--*Story of Aladdin.* Lewis, Naomi, retold by. 1970. Walck. (P.570)
--*Sun and Moon.* Mitchison, Naomi Margaret Haldane, Mrs. (1897-). 1973. T. Nelson. (P.652)

Wilkinson, Barry, jt. illus. see Sumiko.

Wilkinson, Gerald
--*Dawn and Dusk: Poems of Our Time.* Causley, Charles Stanley (1917-). 1963. Watts. (P.178)

Wilkinson, H. B.
--*Son of Robin Hood in Nottingham.* Castleton, Paul A. 1942. Cupples & Leon Company. (P.177)

Wilkon, Jozef (1930-)
--*Bonko.* Schnell, Robert Wolfgang. 1970, c.1969. Scroll Press. (P.800)
--*The Crane with One Leg.* Schaaf, Paul (1897-). 1965, c.1964. Warne. (P.797)
--*Herr Minkepatt and His Friends.* Valentin, Ursula. Roget, Elizabeth, tr. 1965. Braziller. (P.912)
--*The Shaggy Little Dog.* Maksimovic, Desanka (1898-). 1983. Faber and Faber. (P.614)

--*My Bedtime Book.* Williams, Garth Montgomery (1912-). 1964, c.1963. Golden Press. (P.963)

--*My Big Golden Counting Book.* Moore, Lilian. c.1957. Simon and Schuster. (P.661)

--*My First Counting Book.* Moore, Lilian. 1956. Simon and Schuster. (P.661)

--*On the Banks of Plum Creek.* newly illustrated, uniform. Wilder, Laura Ingalls, Mrs. (1867-1957). 1953. Harper. (P.959)

--*Over & Over.* Zolotow, Charlotte Shapiro (1915-). 1957. Har-Row. (P.994)

--*Push Kitty.* Wahl, Jan (1933-). 1968. Harper & Row. (P.924)

--*The Rabbits' Wedding.* Williams, Garth Montgomery (1912-). 1958. Harper. (P.963)

--*The Rescuers.* 1st ed. Sharp, Margery (1905-). 1959. Little, Brown. (P.816)

--*Ride a Purple Pelican.* Prelutsky, Jack. c.1985. Greenwillow Books. (P.737)

--*Robin Hood.* Gilbert, Henry (1868-). 1948. J. B. Lippincott Co. (P.367)

--*The Sailor Dog.* Brown, Margaret Wise (1910-1952). 1953. Simon and Schuster. (P.141)

--*Silly Mysteries.* Petersen, John. 1976. Scholastic Inc. (P.720)

--*The Sky Was Blue.* 1st ed. Zolotow, Charlotte Shapiro (1915-). 1963. Harper & Row. (P.994)

--*Stuart Little.* White, Elwyn Brooks (1899-1985). 1945. Harper & Brothers. (P.951)

--*Stuart Little.* White, Elwyn Brooks (1899-1985). 1973, c.1945. Harper & Row. (P.951)

--*A Tale of Tails.* MacPherson, Elizabeth H. 1962. Golden Press. (P.611)

--*Tale of Tails.* MacPherson, Elizabeth H. 1971. Western Pub. (P.611)

--*The Tall Book of Make-Believe.* Watson, Jane Werner (1915-), compiled by. 1950. Harper. (P.936)

--*The Tall Book of Make-Believe.* Werner, Jane (1915-). 1980. Har-Row. (P.946)

--*Tall Book of Make-Believe.* Williams, Garth Montgomery (1912-). 1950. Har-Row. (P.963)

--*The Tall Book of Make Believe.* Williams, Garth Montgomery (1912-). 1950. Harper & Brothers. (P.963)

--*These Happy Golden Years.* newly illustrated, uniform. Wilder, Laura Ingalls, Mrs. (1867-1957). 1953. Harper. (P.959)

--*Three Bedtime Stories.* Williams, Garth Montgomery (1912-). 1958. Western Pub. (P.963)

--*Three Bedtime Stories.* Williams, Garth Montgomery (1912-). 1983. Western Pub. (P.963)

--*Three Little Animals.* Brown, Margaret Wise (1910-1952). 1956. Harper. (P.141)

--*Tiny Animal Stories.* Kunhardt, Dorothy Meserve, Mrs. (1901-1979). 1948. Simon and Schuster. (P.542)

--*Tiny Golden Library.* Kunhardt, Dorothy Meserve, Mrs. (1901-1979). 1968. Western Pub. (P.542)

--*Tiny Golden Library: A Dozen Animal Nonsense Tales.* Kunhardt, Dorothy Meserve, Mrs. (1901-1979). 1980. Western Pub. (P.542)

--*Tiny Nonsense Stories.* Kunhardt, Dorothy Meserve, Mrs. (1901-1979). 1949. S & S. (P.542)

--*Tucker's Countryside.* Thompson, George Selden (1929-). Selden, George, pseud. 1969. FS&G. (P.887)

--*The Turret.* Sharp, Margery (1905-). 1963. Little Brown and Co. (P.816)

--*Wait till the Moon Is Full.* Brown, Margaret Wise (1910-1952). 1948. Harper. (P.141)

Williams, Garth Montgomery (1912-) & Miller, John Parr

--*Lucky Mrs. Ticklefeather and Other Funny Stories.* Kunhardt, Dorothy Meserve, Mrs. (1901-1979). 1973. Western Pub. (P.542)

Williams, George Alfred (1875-)

--*Boys and Girls from Thackeray.* Sweetser, Kate Dickinson (0000-1939). 1907. Harper & Brothers. (P.874)

--*The Boy's Book of Pirates.* Williams, George Alfred (1875-). c.1913. Frederick A. Stokes Co. (P.963)

--*The Boys of Bob's Hill: Adventures of Tom Chapin and the "Band", As Told by the "Secretary".* Burton, Charles Pierce (1862-). 1905. H. Holt and Company. (P.157)

--*The Magic Book: Adventures of Jack and Betty.* Williams, Clara Andrews, Mrs. (1882-). c.1912. Frederick A. Stokes Company. (P.962)

--*Micky of the Alley.* Sweeter, Kate Dickinson (0000-1939). 1903. D. Appleton & Co. (P.874)

--*Micky of the Alley and Other Youngsters.* Sweetser, Kate Dickinson (0000-1939). 1903. D. Appleton & Co. (P.874)

--*Midshipman in the Pacific: His Adventures on Whaler, Trader and Frigate,.* Brady, Cyrus Townsend (1861-1920). 1904. Scribner. (P.125)

--*The Most beautiful thing in the world.* Swift, Fletcher Harper (1876-). 1914. American Tract Society. (P.874)

--*The Most Beautiful Thing in the World.* Swift, Fletcher Harper (1876-). 1905. E. P. Dutton. (P.874)

--*Teddy Baird's Luck.* Sweetser, Kate Dickinson (0000-1939). 1904. D. Appleton & Co. (P.874)

Williams, Herb

--*The Little Red Hen.* La Pequena Gallina Roja. Williams, Letty. 1969. Prentice-Hall. (P.964)

--*The Tiger!.* El Tigre!. Williams, Letty. Chaves, Doris, et al., trs. 1970. Prentice-Hall. (P.964)

Williams, Herbert Deland

--*Good Times in the Woods.* Lange, Dietrich (1863-). c.1923. Newson & Company. (P.550)

Williams, Hubert

--*The Smallest Tortoise of All.* Whipple, Dorothy (1893-). 1964. Warne. (P.950)

--*Smallest Tortoise of All.* Whipple, Dorothy (1893-). 1965. Warne. (P.950)

--*The Tale of a Very Little Tortoise.* Whipple, Dorothy (1893-). 1962. F. Warne. (P.950)

--*The Window Tulip.* Hill, Elizabeth Starr (1925-). c.1964. F. Warne. (P.442)

Williams, J. L. S.

--*The Story of Rustem, and Other Persian Hero Tales from Firdusi.* Renninger, Elizabeth D. & Firdausi. 1909. C. Scribner's Sons. (P.758)

Williams, J. Scott

--*High Benton.* Heyliger, William (1884-1955). 1919. D. Appleton and Company. (P.440)

Williams, Jenny (1939-)

--*The Boy with Two Shadows.* Mahy, Margaret (1936-). 1971. F. Watts. (P.613)

--*Dragon and Monster Tales.* Denan, Corinne, retold by. c.1980. Troll Associates. (P.256)

--*Fixing Fences.* Moncure, Jane Belk (1926-). Wannamaker, Bruce, pseud. c.1984. Dandelion House. (P.655)

--*Hugging.* Dellinger, Annetta E. c.1985. Child's World. (P.255)

--*Leaf Magic.* Mahy, Margaret (1936-). 1977, c.1976. Parents' Magazine Press. (P.613)

--*A Lion in the Meadow.* Mahy, Margaret (1936-). 1969. Watts. (P.613)

--*My Brother Is Afraid of Just About Everything.* Osborn, Lois. 1982. A. Whitman. (P.697)

--*Pray in This Way.* Richards, Dorothy Fay (1915-). c.1983. Dandelion House. (P.761)

--*Rooms for Rent.* Mahy, Margaret (1936-). 1974. F. Watts. (P.613)

--*Scandinavian Stories.* Sperry, Margaret (1905-), adapted by. 1971. F. Watts. (P.844)

--*The Silver Wood.* Kirby, Douglas J (1929-). 1967, c.1966. Four Winds Press. (P.528)

--*The Ugly Duckling.* Andersen, Hans Christian (1805-1875). c.1979. Troll Associates. (P.37)

--*Uncle Bumble.* Williams, Jenny (1939-). 1970. American Heritage Press. (P.964)

--*A Wet Monday.* Edwards, Dorothy (1914-1982). 1976. Morrow. (P.297)

--*Wide-Awake Jake.* Young, Helen (1938-). 1975, c.1974. Morrow. (P.990)

--*The Witch in the Cherry Tree.* Mahy, Margaret (1936-). 1974, c.1973. Parents' Magazine Press. (P.613)

Williams, Jim

--*More Tales from Norway.* 1st ed. Christianson, Nora D. 1956. Vantage Press. (P.194)

Williams, Kathleen M.

--*The Hounds of Black Maggy.* Crowder, Dorothy Elizabeth. 1967. Roy. (P.233)

--*The House of the Bittern.* Ropner, Pamela. 1967, c.1965. Coward-McCann. (P.776)

Williams, Keith Shaw

--*Kutkos, Chinook Tyee.* Colbert, Mildred. c.1942. D.C. Heath and Company. (P.207)

Williams, Lee

--*Cowboy on Ice.* Maxwell, R. H. 1975. Childrens Press. (P.632)

Williams, Louise C.

--*Boy Donald.* Shirley, Penn, pseud. (1840-). Clarke, Sarah Jones. 1900. Lee & Shepard. (P.821)

Williams-McKenna, Barbara

--*According to Amos.* Benson, Ginny, pseud. (1923-). Benson, Virginia. c.1981. A & P Books. (P.94)

Williams, Morris Meredith

--*The Scottish Fairy Book.* Grierson, Elizabeth Wilson. 1910. Frederick A. Stokes Co. (P.389)

Williams, Oriet

--*Bobby Blake on Mystery Mountain.* Warner, Frank A., pseud. Stratemeyer Syndicate. 1926. Barse & Hopkins. (P.932)

--*Bobby Blake on Mystery Mountain.* Warner, Frank A., pseud. Stratemeyer Syndicate. N.D. Barse & Co. (P.932)

--*Bobby Blake on Mystery Mountain.* Warner, Frank A., pseud. Stratemeyer Syndicate. N.D. Grosset & Dunlap. (P.932)

--*Welcome Barbara.* Cooney, Kathleen. c.1926. Barse & Co. (P.217)

Williams, Patrick

--*The Sanguman: A Dirk Rogers Adventure.* Crisp, Frank Robson (1915-). 1966, c.1965. C. McCutcheon. (P.231)

Williams, Richard

--*The Exploits of the Incomparable Mulla Nasrudin.* Nasreddin, Hoca (1924-), compiled by. Shah, Idries Sayed (1924-). 1967, c.1966. Simon and Schuster. (P.814)

--*The Exploits of the Incomparable Mulla Nasrudin.* Shah, Idries Sayed (1924-). 1972, c.1966. Dutton. (P.814)

Williams, Richard (1950-)

--*Herbie Jones.* Kline, Suzy. c.1985. G.P. Putnam's Sons. (P.531)

Williams, Robert J., Jr. (1895-)

--*The Forgotten Birthday.* Saul, George Brandon (1901-). 1971. Walton Press. (P.794)

--*King Noggin.* Saul, George Brandon (1901-). 1971. Walton Press. (P.794)

Williams, Ted C. (1930-), photos by.

--*Big Bad Ernie.* Shea, George (1940-). c.1978. Creative Education. (P.817)

Williams, Terry, photos by.

--*Magic Lights & Streets of Shining Jet.* Saunders, Dennis, ed. 1977, c.1974. Greenwillow Books. (P.794)

Williams, True

--*Peck's Bad Boy and His Pa.* Complete Ed. ed. Peck, George Wilbur (1840-1916). Bleiler, E. F., intro. by. 1958. Dover Publications. (P.714)

--*Pecks Bad Boy and His Pa.* Peck, George Wilbur (1840-1916). 1900. George M Hill Co. (P.714)

--*Peck's Bad Boy and His Pa.* Peck, George Wilbur (1840-1916). N.D. Thompson & Thomas. (P.714)

--*Peck's Bad Boy and His Pa.* Peck, George Wilbur (1840-1916). c.1893. W. B. Conkey Company. (P.714)

Williams, Urasula Moray, jt. illus. see Williams, Barbara Moray.

Williams, Vera B.

--*A Chair for My Mother.* 1st ed. Williams, Vera B. c.1982. Greenwillow Books. **Awards: (BGH); (ALA); (RCM).** (P.964)

--*The Great Watermelon Birthday.* 1st ed. Williams, Vera B. c.1980. Greenwillow Books. (P.964)

--*Music, Music for Everyone.* Williams, Vera B. 1984. Greenwillow. **Award: (ALA).** (P.964)

--*Something Special for Me.* 1st ed. Williams, Vera B. c.1983. Greenwillow Books. **Award: (ALA).** (P.964)

--*Three Days on a River in a Red Canoe.* Williams, Vera B. c.1981. Greenwillow Books. (P.964)

Williams, Violet M.

--*Twenty-Six ABC Stories.* Williams, Violet M. N.D. Merry Thoughts. (P.964)

Williamson, Ada Clendenin

--*Blue Heron Cove.* McKinney, Fanny Lee. 1918. H. Holt and Company. (P.607)

--*The Castaways of Pete's Patch.* Rankin, Carroll Watson, Mrs. (1870-). 1911. H. Holt and Company. (P.748)

--*The Christmas Makers' Club.* Sawyer, Edith Augusta (1869-). 1908. L. C. Page & Company. (P.795)

--*The Cinder Pond.* Rankin, Carroll Watson, Mrs. (1870-). 1915. Henry Holt. (P.748)

--*Glenloch Girls.* Remick, Grace May. 1909. The Penn Publishing Company. (P.757)

--*Glenloch Girls.* Remick, Grace May. c.1937. The Penn Publishing Company. (P.757)

--*Glenloch Girls Abroad.* Remick, Grace May. 1910. The Penn Publishing Company. (P.757)

--*Glenloch Girls Abroad.* Remick, Grace May. c.1938. The Penn Publishing Company. (P.757)

--*Glenloch Girls at Camp West.* Remick, Grace May. 1912. The Penn Publishing Company. (P.757)

--*Glenloch Girl's Club.* Remick, Grace May. N.D. Penn Publishing Co. (P.757)

--*The Glory of Peggy Harrison.* Powel, Harford Willing Hare, Jr. (1887-) & Carter, Russell Gordon. 1927. The Penn Publising Company. (P.735)

--*Helen and the Fifth Cousins: The Adventure with Judith, the Hermit, and Some Other People.* Gilchrist, Beth Bradford (1879-1957). 1915. The Penn Publishing Company. (P.367)

--*Helen and the Find-Out Club: The Adventure with the Girl Across the Street.* Gilchrist, Beth Bradford (1879-1957). 1914. The Penn Publishing Company. (P.367)

--*Helen and the Uninvited Guests: The Adventure with the Yellow-Goggles Lady.* Gilchrist, Beth Bradford (1879-1957). 1913. The Penn Publishing Company. (P.367)

--*Helen Over the Wall: The Adventure with the Fairy Godmother.* Gilchrist, Beth Bradford (1879-1957). 1912. The Penn Publishing Company. (P.367)

--*Jane Stuart at Rivercroft.* Remick, Grace May. 1915. Penn Publishing Co. (P.757)

--*Jane Stuart, Comrade.* Remick, Grace May. 1916. The Penn Publishing Company. (P.757)

--*Jane Stuart, Twin.* Remick, Grace May. 1913. The Penn Publishing Company. (P.757)

--*Jane Stuart's Chum.* Remick, Grace May. 1914. Penn Publishing Co. (P.757)

--*A Little Princess of the Patio.* Giggins, Aileen Cleveland (1882-). N.D. Penn Publishing Co. (P.366)

--*A Little Princess of the Patio.* Higgins, Aileen Cleveland (1882-). 1911. The Penn Publishing Company. (P.441)

--*A Little Princess of the Pines.* Higgins, Aileen Cleveland (1882-). 1910. The Penn Publishing Company. (P.441)

--*A Little Princess of the Ranch.* Giggins, Aileen Cleveland (1882-). N.D. Penn Publishing Co. (P.366)

--*A Little Princess of the Ranch.* Higgins, Aileen Cleveland (1882-). 1914. The Penn Publishing Company. (P.441)

--*A Little Princess of the Stars and Stripes.* Higgins, Aileen Cleveland (1882-). 1915. The Penn Publishing Company. (P.441)

--*A Little Princess of Tonopah.* Higgins, Aileen Cleveland (1882-). 1909. The Penn Publishing Company. (P.441)

--*Margery Morris.* Gray, Violet Gordon. 1917. The Penn Publishing Company. (P.384)

--*Margery Morris--Mascot.* Gray, Violet Gordon. 1919. The Penn Publishing Company. (P.384)

--*Margery Morris and Plain Jane.* Gray, Violet Gordon. 1920. The Penn Publishing Company. (P.384)

--*Margery Morris in the Pine Woods.* Gray, Violet Gordon. N.D. Penn. (P.384)

--*On Parole.* Siviter, Anna Pierpont, Mrs. (1859-) & Siviter, Frances Pierpont. 1916. H. Holt and Company. (P.827)

--*The Pearl Ring.* Bradley, Mary Emily Neely, Mrs. (1835-1898). c.1906. H. Altemus Company. (P.125)

--*Ruthie.* Duganne, Phyllis. 1921. Harcourt, Brace and Company. (P.287)

--*The Sandman: His Farm Stories.* Hopkins, William John (1863-). 1903. L. C. Page & Company. (P.463)

--*The Sandman: More Farm Stories.* Hopkins, William John (1863-). 1904. L. C. Page & Company. (P.463)

--*The Silver Tarn.* Adams, Katharine. 1924. The Macmillan Company. (P.6)

--*Understood Betsy.* Fisher, Dorothea Frances Canfield, Mrs. (1879-1958). 1917. H. Holt and Company. (P.328)

--*When Jean and I Were Sophomores.* Schwartz, Julia Augusta (1873-). 1918. The Penn Publishing Company. (P.803)

Williamson, Audrey

--*I Want to Be a Baker.* Greene, Carla (1916-). 1956. Childrens Press. (P.386)

--*I Want to Be a Coal Miner.* Greene, Carla (1916-). 1957. Childrens Press. (P.386)

--*I Want to Be an Orange Grower.* Greene, Carla (1916-). 1956. Childrens Press. (P.386)

Williamson, Dorie

--*Wonder Tales of Ancient Wales.* Henderson, Bernard Lionel Kingston & Jones, Stephen. N.D. Small,Maynard & Co. (P.432)

Williamson, Franklin, jt. photog. see Faulkner, Douglas.

Williamson, Gertrude M.

--*Pierre of the Island.* Stack, Nicolette Meredith McGuire (1896-). 1954. Bruce Pub. Co. (P.847)

--*Two to Get Ready.* Stack, Nicolette Meredith McGuire (1896-). 1953. Caxton Printers. (P.847)

--*Wagon to a Star.* McGuire, Frances Lynch (1869-1947). 1951. Caxton Printers. (P.603)

Williamson, Irene

--*The Mary Plain Omnibus.* Rae, Gwynedd (1892-). 1976. Routledge and Kegan Paul. (P.746)

Williamson, J.

--*Girls New and Old.* Smith, Elizabeth Thomasina Meade, Mrs. (1854-1914). Meade, L. T., pseud. c.1895. The Cassell Publishing Co. (P.832)

Williamson, Jane

--*The Trouble with Alaric.* 1st ed. Williamson, Jane Burnett. 1975. Farrar, Straus and Giroux. (P.964)

Williamson, John

--*Robinson Crusoe.* Defoe, Daniel (1661-1731). N.D. J.B. Lippincott. (P.251)

Williamson, Richard L.

--*Dick Burgess of Bosham.* Vignoles, Keith H. 1976. Ian Harrap. (P.919)

Williford, Hollis

--*Adventure on the Wind.* Piccard, Joan Russell. 1971. Nash Pub. (P.725)

Williges, Mel

--*I Am a Thief.* 1st ed. Roy, Ronald (1940-). c.1982. E.P. Dutton. (P.782)

Willis, Bess Goe

--*Betty Gordon and the Lost Pearls: Or, A Mystery of the Seaside.* Emerson, Alice B., pseud. Stratemeyer Syndicate. 1927. Cupples & Leon Co. (P.306)

--*Hail, Virginia!.* Griffith, Helen Sherman, Mrs. (1873-). c.1930. The Penn Publishing Company. (P.390)

--*Joanna Gray.* White, Nelia Gardner (1894-). 1928. The Penn Publishing Company. (P.952)

--*Kristin.* White, Nelia Gardner (1894-). c.1929. The Penn Publishing Company. (P.952)

--*Little Miss Duck.* A. E. H. c.1930. Henry Altemus Company. (P.1)

--*The Little Mouse.* Davis, Harriet Ide Eager (1892-1974) & Eager, John Howard (1848-). c.1928. Henry Altemus Company. (P.246)

--*Tom Fairfield's School Days: Or, The Chums of Elmwood Hall.* Chapman, Allen, pseud. Stratemeyer Syndicate. N.D. Cupples & Leon Co. (P.185)
--*Toodle and Noodle Flattail.* Garis, Howard Roger (1873-1962). 1919. A. L. Burt Co. (P.357)
--*Uncle Wiggily and Baby Bunty.* Garis, Howard Roger (1873-1962). 1920. A. L. Burt Company. (P.357)
--*Uncle Wiggily and Baby Bunty.* Garis, Howard Roger (1873-1962). 1920. A. L. Burt. (P.357)
--*Uncle Wiggily's Adventures.* Garis, Howard Roger (1873-1962). c.1912. R. F. Fenno & Company. (P.357)
--*Uncle Wiggily's Airship.* Garis, Howard Roger (1873-1962). N.D. A. L. Burt Company. (P.357)
--*Uncle Wiggily's Airship.* Garis, Howard Roger (1873-1962). c.1939. The Platt & Munk Co., Inc. (P.357)
--*Uncle Wiggily's Travels.* Garis, Howard Roger (1873-1962). N.D. A. L. Burt Company. (P.357)
--*Uncle Wiggily's Travels.* Garis, Howard Roger (1873-1962). N.D. A. L. Burt Company. (P.357)

Wisdom, Leon B.
--*Escape to Witch Mountain.* Key, Alexander Hill (1904-1979). 1968. Westminster Press. (P.521)

Wise, Daniel
--*Elber's Return: Foxy at Home Again, 1 of 6 V0ls.* Forrester, Francis (1813-1898). N.D. Methodist Book Concern. (P.336)
--*Florence Baldwin's Picnic: And What a Game of It, 1 of 6 Vols.* Forrester, Francis (1813-1898). N.D. Methodist Book Concern. (P.336)

Wise, Joyce M.
--*Jay's Fat Cat.* Wise, Francis H. & Wise, Joyce M. 1974. Wise Pub. (P.972)
--*Park the Car.* Wise, Francis H. & Wise, Joyce M. 1975. Wise Pub. (P.972)

Wise, Lu Celia
--*Alli Gator Gets a Bump on His Nose.* Searcy, Margaret Zehmer (1926-). c.1978. Portals Press. (P.807)
--*The Race of Flitty Hummingbird and Flappy Crane: An Indian Legend.* Searcy, Margaret Zehmer (1926-), retold by. c.1980. Portals Press. (P.807)
--*Tiny Bat and the Ball Game.* Swanton, John Reed (1873-1958). Searcy, Margaret Zehmer (1926-), retold by. c.1978. Portals Press. (P.873)

Wise, Patrick, jt. illus. see Steward, Jan.

Wiseman, Bernard (1922-)
--*Billy Learns Karate.* Wiseman, Bernard (1922-). c.1976. Holt, Rinehart and Winston. (P.972)
--*Bobby and Boo, the Little Spaceman.* Wiseman, Bernard (1922-). c.1978. Holt, Rinehart and Winston. (P.972)
--*Cats! Cats! Cats!.* Wiseman, Bernard (1922-). 1984. Parents. (P.972)
--*Christmas with Morris and Boris.* 1st ed. Wiseman, Bernard (1922-). c.1983. Little, Brown. (P.972)
--*The Clowns Nose.* Wiseman, Bernard (1922-). 1981. Garrard Pub. Co. (P.972)
--*Detective Dog.* Wiseman, Bernard (1922-). 1971. Platt & Munk. (P.972)
--*Doctor Duck & Nurse Swan.* Wiseman, Bernard (1922-). 1984. Dutton. (P.972)
--*Don't Make Fun!.* Wiseman, Bernard (1922-). 1982. Houghton Mifflin. (P.972)
--*Elmer's Egg.* Wiseman, Bernard (1922-). 1983. Scholastic Inc. (P.972)
--*George's Store.* Asch, Frank (1946-). c.1983. Parents Magazine Press. (P.51)
--*Halloween with Morris and Boris.* Wiseman, Bernard (1922-). 1975. Dodd, Mead. (P.972)
--*The Hat That Grew.* Wiseman, Bernard (1922-). 1967. Hale. (P.972)
--*Hats and Coats, Cows and Goats.* Wiseman, Bernard (1922-). 1971. Platt & Munk. (P.972)
--*Iglook's Seal.* Wiseman, Bernard (1922-). 1977. Dodd, Mead. (P.972)
--*Log & Admiral Frog.* Wiseman, Bernard (1922-). 1961. Har-Row. (P.972)
--*The Lucky Runner.* Wiseman, Bernard (1922-). c.1979. Garrard Pub. Co. (P.972)
--*Morris and Boris: Three Stories.* Wiseman, Bernard (1922-). 1974. Dodd, Mead. (P.972)
--*Morris Goes to School.* Wiseman, Bernard (1922-). 1970. Harper & Row. (P.972)
--*Morris Has a Birthday Party!.* 1st ed. Wiseman, Bernard (1922-). c.1983. Little, Brown. (P.972)
--*Morris Has a Cold.* Wiseman, Bernard (1922-). c.1978. Dodd, Mead. (P.972)
--*Morris Is a Cowboy: A Policeman and Baby Sitter.* Wiseman, Bernard (1922-). 1960. Har-Row. (P.972)
--*Morris Tells Boris Mother Moose Stories and Rhymes.* Wiseman, Bernard (1922-). c.1979. Dodd, Mead. (P.972)
--*Morris Tells Boris Mother Moose Stories & Rhymes.* Wiseman, Bernard (1922-). 1980. Scholastic Inc. (P.972)
--*Morris the Moose.* Wiseman, Bernard (1922-). 1959. Harper. (P.972)
--*Morris the Moose Goes to School.* Wiseman, Bernard (1922-). 1972. Scholastic Inc. (P.972)
--*My Googoo.* Wiseman, Bernard (1922-). 1979. Holt, Rinehart and Winston. (P.972)
--*The Nutty Nature Book.* Wiseman, Bernard (1922-). 1971. Platt & Munk. (P.972)
--*Oscar Is a Mama!.* Wiseman, Bernard (1922-). c.1980. Garrard Pub. Co. (P.972)
--*Penny's Poodle Puppy, Pickle.* Wiseman, Bernard (1922-). c.1980. Garrard Pub. Co. (P.972)
--*Quick Quackers.* Wiseman, Bernard (1922-). c.1979. Garrard Pub. Co. (P.972)
--*Tails Are Not for Painting.* Wiseman, Bernard (1922-). c.1980. Garrard Pub. Co. (P.972)
--*Three Stories About Morris & Boris.* Wiseman, Bernard (1922-). 1976. Scholastic Inc. (P.972)
--*The Very Bumpy Bus Ride.* Muntean, Michaela. c.1981. Parents Magazine Press. (P.672)

Wiser, Guy Brown (1895-)
--*Peter Penguin.* Davis, Alice Vaught. 1939. G. P. Putnam, Inc. (P.245)
--*Timothy Turtle.* Davis, Alice Vaught. 1940. HarBraceJ. (P.245)
--*Timothy Turtle.* Davis, Alice Vaught. 1972. HarBraceJ. (P.245)

Wishnefsky, Philip
--*The Island of Dark Wood.* Whitney, Phyllis Ayame (1903-). 1951. Westminster Press. (P.955)

Wiskur, Darrell D.
--*Annie Lee and the Wooden Skates.* rev. ed. Friskey, Margaret Richards (1901-). 1969. Childrens Press. (P.346)
--*Butternut Bill and His Friends.* McCall, Edith Sansom (1911-). 1968. Benefic Press. (P.594)
--*Butternut Bill and the Train.* McCall, Edith Sansom (1911-). 1969. Benefic Press. (P.594)
--*Cat-Cat.* Gibson, Gertrude Hevener (1906-). 1970. Childrens Press. (P.366)
--*Hard Luck Horse.* Brown, Fern G. (1918-). 1975. A. Whitman. (P.139)
--*I Want to Be a Forester.* Baker, Eugene H. 1969. Childrens Press. (P.62)
--*I Want to Be a Weatherman.* Baker, Eugene H. 1972. Childrens Press. (P.62)
--*Jockey-or Else!.* Brown, Fern G. (1918-). 1978. A. Whitman. (P.139)
--*John Alden and the Pilgrim Cow.* Friskey, Margaret Richards (1901-). 1972. Childrens Press. (P.346)
--*Lucky: A Lead of Book.* Berger, Terry (1933-). 1974. J. Philip O'Hara Inc. (P.96)
--*Popcorn Patch.* Chandler, Edna Walker (1908-1982). 1969. A. Whitman. (P.184)
--*Silver Dollar City's ABC Words & Rhymes.* Wiskur, Darrell D. Silver Dollar City, Inc., ed. 1977. Silver Dollar. (P.972)
--*Steel Driving Man: The Legend of John Henry.* Stein, Richard Conrad (1937-). 1969. Childrens Press. (P.851)
--*Tad Lincoln and the Green Umbrella.* rev. ed. Friskey, Margaret Richards (1901-). 1969. Childrens Press. (P.347)
--*Three Children and a Firehorse.* Kenoyer, Natlee Peoples (1907-). 1969. Bethany Press. (P.518)

Withington, Elizabeth R.
--*The Adventures of Joan.* Rhoades, Nina, pseud. (1863-). Rhoades, Cornelia Harson. c.1924. Lothrop, Lee & Shepard Co. (P.759)
--*Anne of Green Gables.* Montgomery, Lucy Maud (1874-1942). 1908. Page Co. (P.658)
--*Barbara Winthrop Abroad.* Broughall, Helen Katherine. 1929. L. C. Page & Company. (P.137)
--*Barbara Winthrop at Boarding School.* Broughall, Helen Katherine. c.1925. L. C. Page & Company, Incorporated. (P.137)
--*Barbara Winthrop at Camp.* Broughall, Helen Katherine. c.1926. L. C. Page & Company Incorporated. (P.137)
--*Barbara Winthrop Graduate.* Broughall, Helen Katherine. 1927. L. C. Page & Company Incorporated. (P.137)
--*Blue Bonnet: Debutante.* Richards, Lela Horn, Mrs. (1870-). 1917. The Page Company. (P.762)
--*Blue Bonnet: Debutante.* Richards, Lela Horn, Mrs. (1870-). 1921. The Page Company. (P.762)
--*Denise of the Three Pines.* Sawyer, Edith Augusta (1869-). 1922. Page Co. (P.795)
--*The Girl from Arizona.* Rhoades, Nina, pseud. (1863-). Rhoades, Cornelia Harson. 1913. Lothrop, Lee & Shepard Co. (P.760)
--*Hester's Wage-Earning.* Baird, Jean Katherine (1872-). 1912. Lothrop, Lea & Shepard Co. (P.61)
--*Honor Bright's New Adventure.* Richards, Laura Elizabeth Howe, Mrs. (1850-1943). c.1925. L. C. Page & Company. (P.762)
--*The House on the Hill.* Chalmers, Margaret Rebecca Piper, Mrs. (1879-). 1917. The Page Company. (P.182)
--*The "Icicle" Melts: A Story for Girls.* Waite, Helen Elmira (1903-). c.1929. Lothrop, Lee & Shepard Co. (P.924)
--*The Independence of Nan.* Rhoades, Nina, pseud. (1863-). Rhoades, Cornelia Harson. 1916. Lothrop, Lee & Shepard Co. (P.760)
--*Laddie, the Master of the House.* Wesselhoeft, Elizabeth Foster Pope, Mrs. (1840-1919). Wesselhoeft, Lily F., pseud. 1913. Little, Brown, and Company. (P.946)
--*Little Glad Heart.* Almond, Linda Stevens. 1922. The Page Company. (P.31)
--*Little Queen Esther.* Rhoades, Nina, pseud. (1863-). Rhoades, Cornelia Harson. 1912. Lothrop, Lee & Shepard Co. (P.760)
--*Maisie's Merry Christmas.* Rhoades, Nina, pseud. (1863-). Rhoades, Cornelia Harson. 1911. Lothrop, Lee & Shepard Co. (P.760)
--*Making Mary Lizzie Happy.* Rhoades, Nina, pseud. (1863-). Rhoades, Cornelia Harson. 1914. Lothrop, Lee & Shepard Co. (P.760)
--*Marjory's Discovery: How the Rosemary Twins Guarded the Pearl Necklaces.* Allen, Alice E. 1923. L.C. Page & Company. (P.29)
--*Marjory's House Party.* Allen, Alice E. 1921. The Page Company. (P.29)
--*Mother Tucker's Seven.* Wray, Angelina W. N.D. Lothrop, Lee & Shepard. (P.980)
--*The Other Sylvia.* Rhoades, Nina, pseud. (1863-). Rhoades, Cornelia Harson. 1910. Lothrop,Lee & Shepard. (P.760)
--*Our Little Ukrainian Cousin.* Winlow, Clara Vostrovsky, Mrs. (1876-) & Winlow, Anna C. c.1925. L. C. Page & Company. (P.969)
--*Our Little West Indian Cousin.* Taylor, Emily Goddard. 1922. The Page Company. (P.879)
--*Patricia and the Other Girls.* Murphy, Marguerite. c.1926. Lothrop, Lee & Shepard Co. (P.673)
--*Patricia from New York.* Murphy, Marguerite. c.1925. Lothrop, Lee & Shepard Co. (P.673)
--*Patricia's Problem.* Murphy, Marguerite. c.1927. Lothrop, Lee & Shepard Co. (P.673)
--*Penelope in California.* Castelhun, Dorothea. c.1926. L. C. Page & Company (Incorporated. (P.177)
--*Puzzling Pepita.* Rhoades, Nina, pseud. (1863-). Rhoades, Cornelia Harson. c.1923. Lothrop, Lee & Shepard Co. (P.760)
--*A Real Cinderella.* Rhoades, Nina, pseud. (1863-). Rhoades, Cornelia Harson. 1915. Lothrop, Lee & Shepard Co. (P.760)
--*Those Thornton Girls.* Oliver, Mary Ethel. c.1930. Lothrop, Lee & Shepard Co. (P.693)
--*Victorine's Book.* Rhoades, Nina, pseud. (1863-). Rhoades, Cornelia Harson. 1911. Lothrop, Lee & Shepard Co. (P.760)
--*When Gretel Was Fifteen.* Rhoades, Nina, pseud. (1863-). Rhoades, Cornelia Harson. 1921. Lothrop, Lee & Shepard Co. (P.760)
--*You're Young But Once.* Clancy, Louise Marks Breitenbach, Mrs. N.D. Page Co. (P.196)

Withington, Elizabeth R. & Martin, Gertrude E.
--*Nan's Christmas Boarder.* Fox, Frances Margaret (1870-). 1924. L. C. Page. (P.340)

Witney, Frederic C.
--*The English Fairy Books.* Rhys, Ernest (1859-1946), ed. 1916. F. A. Stokes. (P.760)

Witry, Aline
--*Prince Harold.* Brown, Levant Frederick. 1902. L. C. Page & Co. (P.140)

Witt, Edith
--*My Happy Dreamland Book.* Sussmann, Christel. Carr, Rowen, adapted by. 1970. Platt. (P.871)
--*Our Favorite Things.* Kruss, James (1926-). Carr, Rowen, ed. 1970, c.1969. Platt. (P.541)
--*The Tailor and the Giant.* Cleve, Valerie & Kruss, James (1926-). 1972. Platt. (P.201)
--*This Is Yellow & This Is Red.* Allen, Robert. 1969. Platt. (P.30)
--*This Is Yellow and This Is Red.* Garfinkel, Bernard Max (1929-). Allen, Robert, pseud. N.D. Platt & Munk. (P.355)

Witten, Bunty
--*Rip Darcy, Adventurer.* O'Brien, John Sherman (1898-1938). Witten, George & Schindler, Raymond C., intro. by. c.1938. The John C. Winston Company. (P.689)

Witter, Barbara (1920-)
--*The Christmas Lamb.* Witter, Barbara (1920-). 1977. Hunter Bks. (P.973)
--*Duncan, the Donkey's Colt.* Witter, Barbara (1920-). 1977. Hunter Bks. (P.973)
--*The Fallen Sparrow.* Witter, Barbara (1920-). 1977. Hunter Bks. (P.973)

Wittert, Elaine
--*Conrad the Clock.* Barr, Jene (1900-). 1944. Wilcox & Follett. (P.75)

Wittmack, Edgar Franklin
--*Joe Below Zero: A Story of Mystery and Adventure in the North Woods.* Ostergaard, V. 1943. David McKay Company. (P.697)
--*The Mystery of the Dark Mountains.* Wells, Lee E. 1946. David McKay Company. (P.945)
--*Rough Riders Ho!.* Montgomery, Rutherford George (1894-). 1946. David McKay Company. (P.659)
--*Sea Raiders Ho!.* Montgomery, Rutherford George (1894-). 1945. David McKay Company. (P.659)
--*Thumbs Up!.* Montgomery, Rutherford George (1894-). 1942. David McKay Company. (P.659)

Wittman, Sally Anne Christianson (1941-)
--*Pelly and Peak.* Wittman, Sally Anne Christianson (1941-). c.1978. Harper & Row. (P.973)
--*Plenty of Pelly & Peak.* Wittman, Sally Anne Christianson (1941-). 1980. Har-Row. (P.973)

Wittner, Erma Jane
--*Suzie: A Shy Little Mouse.* Wittner, Ruth W. c.1934. The Harter Publishing Company. (P.973)

Woehr, Lois
--*Susanna's Candlestick.* Albrecht, Lillie Vanderveer (1894-). 1970. Hastings House. (P.16)

Woerner, K. S.
--*Ann Thorne comes to America.* Bertram, Rosamund. 1941. William Morrow & Co. (P.98)

Wohlberg, Ben
--*The Deer at Our House.* Caldwell, Erskine (1903-). c.1966. Collier. (P.162)

Wohlberg, Meg (1905-)
--*The Adventures of Mabel.* Peck, Harry Thurston (1856-1914). 1963. New York Graphic Society. (P.714)
--*Andy & His Fine Friends.* Thayer, Jane, pseud. (1904-). Woolley, Catherine. 1960. Morrow. (P.884)
--*Andy & Mister Cunningham.* Thayer, Jane, pseud. (1904-). Woolley, Catherine. 1969. Morrow. (P.884)
--*Andy and Mr. Cunningham.* Woolley, Catherine (1904-). 1969. Morrow. (P.978)
--*Andy & the Runaway Horse.* Thayer, Jane, pseud. (1904-). Woolley, Catherine. 1963. Morrow. (P.884)
--*Andy and the Runaway Horse.* Woolley, Catherine (1904-). 1963. Morrow. (P.978)
--*Andy Wouldn't Talk.* Woolley, Catherine (1904-). Thayer, Jane, pseud. 1958. W. Morrow. (P.978)
--*Andy's Square Blue Animal.* Woolley, Catherine (1904-). Thayer, Jane, pseud. 1962. Morrow. (P.978)
--*Baby in the Schoolroom.* Hendrich, Paula Griffith (1928-). 1962. Lothrop, Lee & Shepard. (P.433)
--*The Bear Who Couldn't Sleep.* Pomerantz, Charlotte (1930-). 1965. Morrow. (P.731)
--*Billie.* Slobodkina, Esphyr (1908-). 1959. Lothrop, Lee and Shepard. (P.830)
--*Bounce: The Story of a Kitten.* Horn, Gladys M. c.1941. The John C. Winston Company. (P.464)
--*A Contrary Little Quail.* Thayer, Jane, pseud. (1904-). Woolley, Catherine. 1968. Morrow. (P.884)
--*Demi, the Baby Sitter.* Van Den Honert, Dorry. 1961. Morrow. (P.913)
--*Donny: The Boy Who Made a Home for Animals.* De Leeuw, Adele Louise (1899-). 1957. Little, Brown. (P.254)
--*Elijah the Fishbite.* Turnbull, Agnes Sligh, Mrs. (1888-1982). 1940. The Macmillan Company. (P.905)
--*Five Cents to See the Monkey.* Cook, Marion Belden. 1956. Knopf. (P.215)
--*The Fuzzy Kitten.* Hoke, Helen L., Mrs. (1903-) & Teichner, Miriam. c.1941. J. Messner, Inc. (P.453)
--*God Gave Us Seasons.* Wolcott, Carolyn Muller. c.1958. Abingdon Press. (P.973)
--*God Made Me to Grow.* Wolcott, Carolyn Muller. c.1960. Abingdon Press. (P.973)
--*Jody's Wonderful Day.* N.D. Lothrop Lee & Shepard. (P.973)
--*Little Bimbo and the Lion.* Wohlberg, Meg (1905-). 1942. The John C. Winston Company. (P.973)
--*Lunch for Lennie.* Woolley, Catherine (1904-). 1952. William Morrow & Co. (P.978)
--*Matilda and Her Family.* Mason, Miriam Evangeline (1899-1973). 1942. The Macmillan Company. (P.628)
--*Next Door to Laura Linda.* Udry, Janice May (1928-). c.1965. A. Whitman. (P.908)
--*The Night Before Christmas.* Moore, Clement Clarke (1779-1863). c.1944. Crown Publishers. (P.660)
--*The Night Before Christmas, in Texas, That Is.* Harris, Leon A., Jr. (1926-). N.D. Lothrop, Lee & Shepard. (P.416)
--*Night Before Christmas-in Texas, That Is.* Harris, Leon A., Jr. (1926-). 1977. Pelican. (P.416)
--*Puppy in the Pet Shop Window.* Schrank, Joseph (1900-1984). 1961. Lothrop. (P.801)
--*The Real Santa Claus.* Walters, Marguerite. 1950. Lothrop, Lee & Shepard. (P.929)

--*Virginia Lee.* Judson, Clara Ingram, Mrs. (1879-1960). N.D. Barse & Hopkins. (P.502)
--*With Pershing at the Front: America's Soldiers in the Trenches.* Kay, Ross. c.1918. Barse & Hopkins. (P.510)
--*Yank Brown, Honor Man.* Stone, David. c.1925. Barse & Hopkins. (P.861)

Wrenn, Thomas N.
--*Air Scout: An American Boy's Adventures When the Big War in Europe Began.* Kay, Ross. c.1914. Barse & Hopkins. (P.510)
--*Joy and Pam.* Whitehill, Dorothy. N.D. Grosset & Dunlap. (P.953)
--*Tell-Me-Why Stories About Animals.* Claudy, Carl Harry (1879-). 1914. McBride, Nast & Company. (P.200)
--*Tell-Me-Why Stories About Color and Sound.* Claudy, Carl Harry (1879-). 1915. R. M. McBride & Company. (P.200)
--*Tell-Me-Why Stories About Great Discoveries.* Claudy, Carl Harry (1879-). 1916. R. M. McBride & Company. (P.200)

Wright, Alan & Anderson, Anne
--*Cuddly Kitty and Busy Bunny.* Dennis, Clara G. 1927. T. Nelson & Sons. (P.257)
--*Podgy Puppy and Naughty Neddy.* Dennis, Clara G. 1927. T. Nelson & Sons. (P.257)

Wright, Annette
--*The Day the Mountains Played.* Wright, Judith Arundell (1915-). 1960. Tri-Ocean Book.(P.981)

Wright, Barton
--*Little Cloud and the Great Plains Hunters: Fifteen Thousand Years Ago.* Stevens, Mary Ellen & Sayles, Edwin Booth (1892-). 1962. Reilly & Lee. (P.854)
--*Throw Stone, the First American Boy: Twenty-Five Thousand Years Ago.* Sayles, Edwin Booth (1892-) & Stevens, Mary Ellen. 1960. Reilly Lee,. (P.796)

Wright, Blanche Fisher (1878-)
--*Little Brothers to the Scouts.* Hyde, E A Watson. N.D. Rand McNally. (P.478)
--*Nursery Tales from Many Lands.* Skinner, Eleanor Louise (1872-), ed. c.1917. C. Scribner's Sons. (P.828)
--*Nursery Tales from Many Lands.* Skinner, Eleanor Louise (1872-), ed. c.1935. C. Scribner's Sons. (P.828)
--*The Peter Patter Book: Rimes for Children.* Jackson, Leroy Freeman (1881-). c.1918. Rand, McNally & Co. (P.486)
--*The Peter Patter Book: Rimes for Children.* Jackson, Leroy Freeman (1881-). c.1925. Rand, McNally & Company. (P.486)
--*Real Mother Goose.* 1944. Hale. (P.980)
--*The Real Mother Goose.* 1916. Rand. (P.980)
--*The Real Mother Goose.* 1941. Rand McNally & Co. (P.980)
--*The Real Mother Goose.* Special anniversary ed. Arbuthnot, May Hill, intro. by. 1965, c.1916. Rand MacNally. (P.980)
--*The Real Mother Goose.* Mother Goose. N.D. Rand McNally Publication. (P.669)

Wright, Blanche Fisher (1878-) & Spoor, Mary L.
--*The Sunny-Sulky Book.* Rippey, Sarah Cory. c.1915. Rand, McNally & Company. (P.765)

Wright, Cameron
--*The Boy Who Had No Birthday.* Hunt, Mabel Leigh (1892-1971). 1935. Frederick A. Stokes Company. (P.474)
--*The Boy Who Had No Birthday.* Hunt, Mabel Leigh (1892-1971). 1935. J. B. Lippincott. (P.474)
--*Bugles at Midnight.* Reynolds, John Murray (1901-). 1931. D. Appleton and Company. (P.759)
--*Look Away, Dixie Land!".* Darby, Ada Claire (1883-). c.1941. Frederick A. Stokes Company. (P.242)
--*Look Away, Dixie Land!.* Darby, Ada Claire (1883-). N.D. J. B. Lippincott Co. (P.242)
--*Lucinda: A Little Girl of Eighteen-Sixty.* Hunt, Mabel Leigh (1892-1971). 1934. Frederick A. Stokes Company. (P.474)
--*Lucinda: A Little Girl of Eighteen-Sixty.* Hunt, Mabel Leigh (1892-1971). 1934. J. B. Lippincott. (P.474)
--*Riding the Tom-Tom Trail: A Pioneer Boy Among the Indians.* Erskine, Gladys Shaw, Mrs. (1895-). 1941. W. Marrow & Co. (P.309)
--*Swift Walker: A True Story of the American Fur Trade.* Wise, Winifred Esther (1906-1970). c.1937. Harcourt, Brace and Company. (P.972)

Wright, Cheri
--*Inside Me, Outside Me: Songs to Sing, Games, Rhymes, Puzzles, and Think Poems.* Lamb, Elizabeth Searle (1917-). 1974. Unity Books. (P.545)

Wright, Christine
--*Stories and Rhymes for a Child.* Bailey, Carolyn Sherwin (1875-1961). 1909. M. Bradley Company. (P.60)

Wright, Curt, photos by.
--*Changing Bodies, Changing Goals & Other Youth Soccer Stories.* Russman, Penny & Wright, Sheila. Woog, Dan, ed. 1984. Ascot Pr. (P.785)

Wright, Dare, photos by.
--*The Doll and the Kitten.* Wright, Dare (1926-). 1960. Doubleday. (P.980)
--*The Little One.* Wright, Dare (1926-). 1959. Doubleday. (P.980)
--*The Lonely Doll.* Wright, Dare (1926-). 1957. Doubleday. (P.980)

Wright, Dare (1926-)
--*Look at a Calf.* Wright, Dare (1926-). 1974. Random. (P.980)

Wright, Freire
--*Winter's Tales.* 1st ed. Foreman, Michael (1938-). c.1979. Doubleday. (P.335)

Wright, Freire, jt. illus. see Foreman, Michael.

Wright, Freire & Foreman, Michael (1938-)
--*Borrowed Feathers, and Other Fables.* Stevens, Bryna, ed. c.1977. Random House. (P.854)

Wright-Frierson, Virginia
--*Big Boy, Little Boy.* Stanovich, Betty Jo. c.1984. Lothrop, Lee & Shepard Books. (P.849)
--*When the Tide Is Low.* 1st ed. Cole, Sheila Rotenberg (1939-). 1985. Lothrop. (P.208)

Wright, G.
--*The Water Babies.* Kingsley, Charles (1819-1875). 1900. A. Wessels Co. (P.525)

Wright, G. E. & Heustis, Louise
--*The Beacon Prize Medals, and other stories.* Paine, Albert Bigelow (1861-1937). 1899. Baker & Taylor Co. (P.700)

Wright, George
--*A Country Child.* Showerman, Grant (1870-). 1917. The Century Co. (P.821)
--*Judith.* Alexander, Grace. N.D. Bobbs-Merrill Co. (P.22)
--*Judith's Garden.* Bassett, Mary E. Stone, Mrs. 1902. Lothrop, Lee & Shepard. (P.79)
--*Norse Stories.* Edda Snorra Sturlusonar. Mabie, Hamilton Wright (1846-1916), retold by. 1901. Dodd, Mead and Company. (P.295)
--*Norse Stories.* Edda Snorra Sturlusonar. Mabie, Hamilton Wright (1846-1916) & Bates, Katharine Lee (1850-1929), eds. 1902. Rand, McNally & Company. (P.295)
--*Rose O'the River.* Wiggin, Kate Douglas Smith (1856-1923). 1905. Houghton Mifflin. (P.957)
--*The Southerners.* Townsend, Cyrus. N.D. Charles Scribner's Sons. (P.897)
--*The Way of a Man.* Hough, Emerson (1857-1923). N.D. Bobbs-Merrill Co. (P.465)

Wright, Gilbert S.
--*The Children's Dickens: Stories Selected from the Various Tales by Charles Dickens.* Dickens, Charles John Huffam (1812-1870). N.D. George H. Doran. (P.262)

Wright, Joe
--*The Archery Contest.* Saddler, Allen, pseud. (1923-). Richards, Ronald Charles William. 1983. Merrimack Pub Cir. (P.788)
--*The Fishing Competition.* Saddler, Allen, pseud. (1923-). Richards, Ronald Charles William. 1983. Oxford U Pr. (P.788)
--*The King & the Invisible Dwarf.* Saddler, Allen, pseud. (1923-). Richards, Ronald Charles William. 1983. Oxford U Pr. (P.788)
--*The King Gets Fit.* Saddler, Allen, pseud. (1923-). Richards, Ronald Charles William. 1983. Merrimack Pub Cir. (P.788)
--*Mrs. Plug the Plumber.* Ahlberg, Allan. 1982, c.1980. Golden Press. (P.14)

Wright, John
--*I Had a Little.* Levarie, Norma. 1961. Random House. (P.567)

Wright, Joseph
--*What-a-Mess.* Muir, Frank (1920-). c.1977. Doubleday. (P.670)
--*What-a-Mess, the Good.* Muir, Frank (1920-). c.1978. Doubleday. (P.670)

Wright, Kathleen Mary
--*A Candle, a Feather, a Wooden Spoon.* Jacobs, Linda C. (1943-). 1974. EMC Corp. (P.487)
--*Checkmate Julie.* Jacobs, Linda C. (1943-). 1974. EMC Corp. (P.487)
--*Everyone's Watching Tammy.* Jacobs, Linda C. (1943-). 1974. EMC Corp. (P.487)
--*Will the Real Jeannie Murphy Please Stand Up.* Jacobs, Linda C. (1943-). 1974. EMC Corp. (P.487)

Wright, Mabel Osgood, Mrs.
--*Dogtown: Being Some Chapters from the Annals of the Waddles Family, Set Down in the Language of Housepeople.* Wright, Mabel Osgood, Mrs. (1859-1934). 1902. The Macmillan Company. (P.981)

Wright, Mary Sherwood
--*All by Ourselves.* Robinson, Mabel Louise (1874-1962). c.1924. E. P. Dutton & Company. (P.770)
--*Tales That Nimko Told.* Pulver, Mary Brecht. c.1925. The Century Co. (P.741)

Wright, Matvyn
--*Andy Pandy & the Gingerbread Man.* Bird, Maria. 1973. O'Hara. (P.102)
--*Andy Pandy & the Hedgehog.* Bird, Maria. 1973. O'Hara. (P.102)
--*Andy Pandy Paints His House.* Bird, Maria. 1972. O'Hara. (P.102)
--*Andy Pandy's Kite.* Bird, Maria. 1972. O'Hara. (P.102)
--*Andy Pandy's New Pet.* Bird, Maria. 1973. O'Hara. (P.102)
--*Andy Pandy's Puppy.* Bird, Maria. 1972. O'Hara. (P.102)
--*Andy Pandy's Shop.* Bird, Maria. 1972. O'Hara. (P.102)
--*Andy Pandy's Weather House.* Bird, Maria. 1973. O'Hara. (P.102)
--*Sherpa Adventure.* Styles, Frank Showell (1908-). c.1960. Vanguard Press. (P.869)

Wright, Meg
--*Three Stories from India.* 1984. BCM Inc. (P.981)

Wright, Morris
--*Kenji and the Lost Kite.* Martin, Anne Crittendon (1922-). c.1962. Convention Press. (P.624)

Wright, Pauline, Miss
--*Keep-Well Stories for Little Folks.* Jones, May Farinholt (1868-). 1916. J. B. Lippincott Company. (P.500)

Wright, Spencer
--*The Menehunes.* Day, Emily Foster. N.D. Paul Elder & Company Catalogue. (P.248)

Wright, T.
--*King Arthur and the Knights of the Round Table.* Malory, Thomas, Sir (1410-1471). N.D. Distributed by Charles Scribner's Sons. (P.615)

Wright, Walter
--*The Maverick Moon.* Wright, Walter (1937-). c.1979. Random House. (P.982)

Wright, Wayne
--*Cheepers in Special Times to Share.* Wolf, Jill. 1984. Antioch Pub Co. (P.974)

Wright, Wynna
--*Goose Towne Tales.* Lawton, Alice. c.1927. Thomas Y. Crowell Company. (P.557)

Wrightman, Francis P. & Sweeny, William K.
--*Teddy-B & Teddy-G: The Bear Detectives.* Eaton, Seymour (1859-1916). 1909. E. Stern & Co., Inc. (P.294)

Wrigley, Denis
--*Fives, Sixes & Sevens.* Stephenson, Marjorie. 1969. Warne. (P.853)
--*The Little Giant James.* Wrigley, Denis. 1978. Merrimack Pub Cir. (P.982)
--*One, Two, Three, Four: Number Rhymes and Finger Games.* Grice, Mary, ed. 1971, c.1970. F. Warne. (P.389)
--*People of the Bible.* Northcott, William Cecil (1902-). 1967. Westminster Press. (P.686)
--*Round About Eight: Poems for Today.* Palmer, Geoffrey & Lloyd, Noel, eds. 1973, c.1972. F. Warne. (P.703)
--*Round About Six.* Rawlins, Margaret G., compiled by. 1973. F. Warne. (P.750)

Wrigley, Elsie
--*Fleas.* Cole, Joanna. 1973. Morrow. (P.208)

Wronker, Lili Cassel see Cassel, Lili, pseud.

Wronker, Lili Cassel (1924-)
--*The Children of the Old House.* Borchard, Ruth Berendsohn (1910-). 1963. Doubleday. (P.117)

Wronker, Lili Cassell (1925-)
--*Tell About the Cowbarn, Daddy.* Merrill, Jean Fairbanks (1923-). 1963. Young Scott Books. (P.642)

Wuenscher, N. G., jt. illus. see Crank, Bess Bethell.

Wuerfel, Lillian B.
--*The Children's Treasury.* Barrows, Ruth Marjorie (1892-1983), ed. N.D. Consolidated Book Publishers. (P.77)
--*Towpath Andy.* Taylor, Florance Walton, Mrs. 1938. A. Whitman & Co. (P.879)

Wuerfel, Lillian B., jt. illus. see Papadopoulos, Electra.

Wurmfeld, Hope
--*Black Is Beautiful.* McGovern, Ann. 1969. Four Winds Press. (P.602)
--*Feeling Mad-Feeling Sad-Feeling Bad-Feeling Glad.* McGovern, Ann. 1978. Magic Circle Pr. (P.602)

Wurtz, Adam
--*The Giant from the Little Island.* Kreye, Walter. 1971, c.1970. Crowell. (P.539)

Wurzer, Karl
--*The Ski Trail Mystery.* McDonnell, Virginia Bleecker (1917-). c.1966. Macrae. (P.600)

Wu Tai-Sheng, jt. illus. see Chiang Cheng-An.

Wu Wen-Yuan
--*The Magic Gourd.* Chang Tien-Yi. Yang, Gladys, tr. from Chinese. 1979. China Bks. (P.184)

Wyatt, Stanley
--*The Bells on Finland Street.* Cook, Lyn, pseud. (1918-). Waddell, Evelyn Margaret. 1950. Macmillan. (P.215)
--*Wagons West.* Craig, John Ernest (1921-). 1956, c.1955. Dodd, Mead. (P.226)

Wyeth, Andrew Newell, jt. illus. see Wyeth, Newell Convers.

Wyeth, Andrew Newell (1917-)
--*The Lost Baron: A Story of England in the Year 1200.* French, Allen (1870-1946). 1940. Houghton Mifflin Company. (P.344)
--*The Nub.* White, Robb (1909-). 1935. Little, Brown, and Company. (P.953)
--*The Sea Bird Islands.* Foote, Agnes Cope. 1939. Little, Brown and Company. (P.334)
--*The Smuggler's Sloop.* White, Robb (1909-). 1947. Doubleday. (P.953)
--*The Smuggler's Sloop.* White, Robb (1909-). 1937. Little, Brown and Company. (P.953)

Wyeth, Newell Convers, jt. illus. see Stephens, Alice Barber.

Wyeth, Newell Convers (1882-1945)
--*The Adventures of Tom Sawyer.* Twain, Mark, pseud. (1835-1910). Clemens, Samuel Langhorne. N.D. John C. Winston. (P.907)
--*Anthology of Children's Literature.* 5th ed. Johnson, Edna, ed. c.1977. Houghton Mifflin. (P.494)
--*The Black Arrow.* Stevenson, Robert Louis (1850-1894). 1955. Charles Scribner's Sons. (P.856)
--*Blackfeet Indian Stories.* Grinnell, George Bird (1849-1938). N.D. Charles Scribner's Sons. (P.395)
--*The Boy's King Arthur.* Malory, Thomas, Sir (1410-1471). Lanier, Sidney (1842-1881), ed. 1917. C. Scribner's Sons. (P.615)
--*The Boy's King Arthur.* Lanier, Sidney (1842-1881), ed. 1952. Scribner. (P.551)
--*The Boy's King Arthur.* Malory, Thomas, Sir (1410-1471). Lanier, Sidney (1842-1881), ed. N.D. Scribner. (P.615)
--*The Courtship of Myles Standish.* Longfellow, Henry Wadsworth (1807-1882). N.D. Houghton Mifflin Co. (P.582)
--*The Deerslayer.* Cooper, James Fenimore (1789-1851). N.D. Charles Scribner's Sons. (P.217)
--*Deerslayer: Or, The First War-Path.* Cooper, James Fenimore (1789-1851). 1929. Scribner. (P.217)
--*Drums.* Boyd, James (1888-1944). 1928. Charles Scribner's Sons. (P.122)
--*Kidnapped.* Stevenson, Robert Louis (1850-1894). 1941. Scribner. (P.857)
--*Kidnapped.* Stevenson, Robert Louis (1850-1894). 1973, c.1913. Scribner. (P.857)
--*The Last of the Mohicans.* Cooper, James Fenimore (1789-1851). 1919. Charles Scribner's Sons. (P.217)
--*Legends of Charlemagne.* Bulfinch, Thomas (1796-1867). N.D. Cosmopolitan Book Co. (P.148)
--*Little Shepherd of Kingdom Come.* Fox, John William, Jr. (1862-1919). 1931. Scribner. (P.340)
--*Michael Strogoff.* Verne, Jules (1828-1905). 1927. Scribner. (P.918)
--*Micheal Strogoff; a Courier of the Czar.* Verne, Jules (1828-1905). 1955. Scribner. (P.918)
--*Mysterious Island.* Verne, Jules (1828-1905). 1920. Charles Scribner's Sons. (P.918)
--*Ramona.* New ed. Jackson, Helen Maria Fiske Hunt, Mrs. (1831-1885). 1939. Little. (P.485)
--*Rip Van Winkle.* Irving, Washington (1783-1859). 1921. David McKay Co. (P.482)
--*Robin Hood.* Creswick, Paul (1866-1947). 1917. Charles Scribner's Sons. (P.230)
--*Robin Hood.* Creswick, Paul (1866-1947). 1917. D. McKay. (P.230)
--*Robin Hood.* Creswick, Paul (1866-1947). 1921. David McKay. (P.230)
--*Robin Hood.* Creswick, Paul (1866-1947). 1957. Scribner. (P.230)
--*Robin Hood.* Creswick, Paul (1866-1947). 1984. Scribners. (P.230)
--*Robinson Crusoe.* Defoe, Daniel (1661-1731). 1920. Charles Scribner's Sons. (P.251)
--*Robinson Crusoe.* DeFoe, Daniel (1661-1731). N.D. David McKay Co. (P.251)
--*Robinson Crusoe.* Defoe, Daniel (1661-1731). 1957. Scribner. (P.251)
--*Robinson Crusoe.* Defoe, Daniel (1661-1731). 1983. Scribner. (P.251)
--*Robinson Crusoe.* Defoe, Daniel (1661-1731). Wyeth, Newell Convers (1882-1945), pref. by. N.D. Cosmopolitan Publications. (P.251)
--*The Sampo: A Wonder Tale of the Old North.* Baldwin, James (1841-1925). 1917. C. Scribner's Sons. (P.65)
--*The Sampo: Hero Adventures from the Finnish Kalevala.* Baldwin, James (1841-1925). 1912. C. Scribner's Sons. (P.65)
--*The Scottish Chiefs.* Porter, Jane (1776-1850). 1956. Scribner. (P.732)
--*The Scottish Chiefs.* Porter, Jane (1776-1850). Wiggin, Kate Douglas Smith (1856-1923) & Smith, Nora Archibald, eds. 1921. Charles Scribner's Sons. (P.732)
--*Treasure Island.* Stevenson, Robert Louis (1850-1894). 1939. Scribner. (P.857)
--*Treasure Island.* Anniversary ed. Stevenson, Robert Louis (1850-1894). 1981. Scribner. (P.857)
--*Treasure Island.* Stevenson, Robert Louis (1850-1894). N.D. Scribner. (P.857)
--*Westward Ho.* Kingsley, Charles (1819-1875). N.D. Scribner. (P.525)
--*White Company.* Doyle, Arthur Conan, Sir (1859-1930). N.D. McKay. (P.284)